YEARBOOK OF INTERNATIONAL ORGANIZATIONS 2023 - 2024

Publication history

1905 – 1907
Institut International de la Paix, Monaco
– *Annuaire de la Vie internationale*: 1905–1906–1907 (1ère série).

1908 – 1911
Union of International Associations / Central Office of International Associations
– *Annuaire de la Vie internationale* (with the collaboration of the Institut International de Bibliographie and the Institut International de la Paix) 1908–1909 (2ème série)
– *Annuaire de la Vie internationale* (with the support of the Carnegie Endowment for International Peace) 1910–1911 (2ème série)

1921 – 1939
Continuation by the League of Nations (Geneva) of the initiative of the Union of International Associations
– *Répertoire des Organisations internationales*: 1925, 1936 (French ed.)
– *Handbook of International Organizations*: 1926, 1929, 1938 (English ed.)
– *Répertoire des Organisations internationales / Handbook of International Organizations*: 1921, 1923 (bi-lingual ed.)

1948 (1st ed.) – 1950 (3rd ed.)
Editions de l'Annuaire des Organisations Internationales S.A. (Geneva)
– *Annuaire des Organisations Internationales / Yearbook of International Organizations.* 1948 (1st ed.), 1949 (2nd ed.), 1950 (3rd ed.) (with the collaboration of the Union of International Associations)

1951 (4th ed.) – 1980 (18th ed.)
Union of International Associations (Brussels) based on an agreement with the United Nations resulting from a resolution of the Economic and Social Council
– *Yearbook of International Organizations*, 1951/52 (4th ed.), 1954/55 (5th ed.)
– *Annuaire des Organisations Internationales*, 1956/57 (6th ed.)
– *Yearbook of International Organizations*, 1958/59 (7th ed.)
– *Annuaire des Organisations Internationales*, 1960/61 (8th ed.)
– *Yearbook of International Organizations*, 1962/63 (9th ed.), 1964/65 (10th ed.), 1966/67 (11th ed.), 1968/69 (12th ed.), 1970/71 (13th ed.), 1972/73 (14th ed.)
– *Yearbook of International Organizations / Annuaire des Organisations Internationales*, 1974 (15th ed.)
– *Yearbook of International Organizations*, 1976/77 (16th ed.), 1978/79 (17th ed.)
– *Annuaire des Organisations Internationales*, 1980 (16/18th ed.)

1981 (19th ed.)
Edited by the Union of International Associations (Brussels). Published jointly with the International Chamber of Commerce (Paris)
– *Yearbook of International Organizations*, 1981 (19th ed.)

1983 (20th ed.) – 2010 (47th ed.)
Edited by the Union of International Associations (Brussels). Published, with four supplementary volumes, by K.G. Saur Verlag (Munich)
– *Yearbook of International Organizations*
  – Volume 1: Organization descriptions, from 1983 (20th ed.) to 1998 (35th ed.) and in 2 parts (1A and 1B) since 1999 (36th ed.)
  – Volume 2: Geographic Volume: International Organization Participation; Country directory of secretariats and membership, since 1983 (1st ed.)
  – Volume 3: Subject volume: Global Action Networks; Classified directory by subject and region, since 1983 (1st ed.)
  – Volume 4: Bibliographic volume: International Organization Bibliography and Resources, since 1996 (1st ed.)
  – Volume 5: Statistics, Visualizations and Patterns, since 2001 (1st ed.)
  – Volume 6: Who's Who in International Organizations, since 2007 (1st ed.)
  – CD-ROM version: Yearbook / Annuaire Plus, 1995 (1st ed.) – 2008 (15th ed.)

2011 (48th ed.) – 2017 (54th ed.)
Edited by the Union of International Associations (Brussels). Published by Brill / Martinus Nijhoff Publishers (Leiden/Boston)
– *Yearbook of International Organizations: Guide to Global Civil Society Networks*
  – Volume 1: Organization Descriptions and Cross-references, in 2 parts (1A and 1B)
  – Volume 2: Geographical Index: country directory of secretariats and memberships
  – Volume 3: Global Action Networks: subject directory and index
  – Volume 4: International Organization Bibliography and Resources
  – Volume 5: Statistics, Visualizations and Patterns
  – Volume 6: Who's Who in International Organizations

2018 (55th ed.) –
Edited by the Union of International Associations (Brussels). Published by Brill / Martinus Nijhoff Publishers (Leiden/Boston)
– *Yearbook of International Organizations: Guide to Global Civil Society Networks*
  – Volume 1: Organization Descriptions and Cross-references, in 2 parts (1A and 1B)
  – Volume 2: Geographical Index: country directory of secretariats and memberships
  – Volume 3: Global Action Networks: subject directory and index
  – Volume 4: International Organization Bibliography and Resources
  – Volume 5: Statistics, Visualizations and Patterns
  – Volume 6: Global Civil Society and the United Nations Sustainable Development Goals

The *Yearbook of International Organizations* is also available online. See https://uia.org/

The editors

Union of International Associations (UIA)
Rue Washington 40, B-1050 Brussels, Belgium
Tel: (32 2) 640 18 08
E-mail: uia@uia.org
Website: https://uia.org/

EDITED BY THE UNION OF INTERNATIONAL ASSOCIATIONS

YEARBOOK OF INTERNATIONAL ORGANIZATIONS 2023 - 2024

GUIDE TO GLOBAL CIVIL SOCIETY NETWORKS

EDITION 60

VOLUME 1B (*INT* TO Z)
ORGANIZATION DESCRIPTIONS AND CROSS-REFERENCES

UIA

TUTA SUB AEGIDE PALLAS · 1683 ·

BRILL

The following people contributed to this edition:

Carine Faveere
Carol Williams
Chloé Houyoux
Christelle Behets
Clara Fernández López
Frédéric Magin
João Andrade
Joel Fischer
Judy Wickens
Kimberly Trathen
Leslie Selvais
Liesbeth Van Hulle *(Editor-in-Chief)*
Nordine Bittich
Rachele Dahle
Ryan Brubaker
Jacques de Mévius
Sylvie Hosselet
Yolande Vlaminck

Special thanks to:

Alessandro Cortese
Brigitte Motte
Cyril Ritchie
Danièle Vranken
Dianne Dillon-Ridgley
Dragana Avramov
Esperanza Duran
Jacqueline Staniforth
Jacques de Mévius
Judy Wickens
Marc Bontemps
Marilyn Mehlmann
Marisha Wojciechowska-Shibuya
Rolf Reinhardt
Seya Immonen
Sheila Bordier
Simone Van Beek
Tim Casswell
Yves Moreau

The Editors dedicate this edition to

Régine Toussaint, editor from 1981 to 2021

and

Nancy Carfrae, editor from 1984 to 2021

Thank you, ladies!

Information researched and edited by
Union of International Associations
Rue Washington 40
B-1050 Brussels, Belgium

Koninklijke Brill NV, Leiden, The Netherlands.
Koninklijke Brill NV incorporates the imprints Brill, Brill Nijhoff, Brill Hotei, Brill Schöningh, Brill Fink, Brill mentis, Vandenhoeck & Ruprecht, Böhlau, V&R unipress and Wageningen Academic.

Typeset by
bsix information exchange GmbH
Sophienstraße 40
D-38118 Braunschweig, Germany

Printed on acid free paper.

Library of Congress Card Number: 49-22132
ISSN: 2211-3010
ISBN: Yearbook Volume 1 (A and B): 978-90-04-54680-6
Yearbook Volumes 1-6 Set: 978-90-04-54794-0
UIA Publication Number: 501

Contents

This Volume

Organization descriptions

Appearing in alphabetical order of title, with index of abbreviations, other language titles, previous and alternative titles and abbreviations, subsidiary titles and abbreviations all inserted in the same alphabetical sequence.

Part 1A

Part 1B

Other Volumes

Further information can be found at https://uia.org

Table des matières

Ce volume

Descriptions des organisations

Classées par ordre alphabétique du nom en anglais, ou du sigle, si celui-ci est plus connu, dans une séquence unique qui contient également: les sigles, les noms dans d'autres langues que l'anglais, les noms et abréviations alternatifs et du passé, les noms et abréviations secondaires.

Partie 1A

Partie 1B

Autres volumes

Informations complémentaires sur le web https://uia.org

The YEARBOOK series

All these publications are also available online. For further information please see https://uia.org/

VOLUME 1 (Parts 1A and 1B): ORGANIZATION DESCRIPTIONS AND CROSS-REFERENCES
Descriptions of intergovernmental and non-governmental organizations, covering every field of human activity. Listed in alphabetic order of title.
Contents of descriptions: Descriptions, varying in length from several lines to several pages, include: organization names in all relevant languages; principal and secondary addresses; main activities and programmes; personnel and finances; technical and regional commissions; history, goals, structure; inter-organizational links; languages used; membership by country.
Cross-references: Integrated into the alphabetic sequence of descriptions are cross-references to related organizations. Access is possible via organization names in English, French and other working languages and via all initials or abbreviations in various languages.

VOLUME 2: GEOGRAPHICAL INDEX: COUNTRY DIRECTORY OF SECRETARIATS AND MEMBERSHIPS
– Organizations classified by country of secretariat(s)
– Organizations classified by countries of location of membership
– Statistics by country and city
Can be used to locate international organizations by country of secretariat or membership. Each organization is listed with its complete address under the country or countries in which it has established a main secretariat.

VOLUME 3: GLOBAL ACTION NETWORKS: SUBJECT DIRECTORY AND INDEX
– Organizations classified by subject concerns
– Organizations classified by regional concerns
– Organizations classified by type
– Statistics by subject
– Index (with introductory comments):
  – subject keywords in all available languages
  – keywords from organization names in English and French
Groups organizations into general and detailed subject categories. Can be used as an index to descriptions in Volume 1. Each organization is listed with its complete address.

VOLUME 4: INTERNATIONAL ORGANIZATION BIBLIOGRAPHY AND RESOURCES
– Bibliography of studies on international non-profit organizations
– Organization publications
– Indexes
Includes major and periodical publications of international organizations, together with bibliographic information on research on NGOs.

VOLUME 5: STATISTICS, VISUALIZATIONS AND PATTERNS
- Detailed statistical tables of information in Volumes 1, 2, 3, 4 and 6.
- Historical statistical summaries and analyses
- Visual representations of statistical data and networks
- Statistical data on the meetings of international organizations

VOLUME 6: GLOBAL CIVIL SOCIETY AND THE UNITED NATIONS SUSTAINABLE DEVELOPMENT GOALS
In 2015 the United Nations adopted a set of seventeen goals “to end poverty, protect the planet and ensure prosperity for all”, with specific targets for each goal to be achieved by 2030. These are the Sustainable Development Goals [SDGs] of the United Nations, or "Transforming our World: the 2030 Agenda for Sustainable Development". The UN calls on governments, the private sector, individuals and civil society bodies to join together to achieve these goals.
This volume groups international organizations by the seventeen UN Sustainable Development Goals, indicating which organizations are – or could be – concerned with which SDGs. It can also be used as an index to descriptions in Volume 1. Each organization is listed with its complete address.

INTERNATIONAL CONGRESS CALENDAR
Lists future international meetings with details of place, date, subject and organizer, including complete address, and cross-referencing the Yearbook where possible. Geographical and chronological listings. Index by subject.

HISTORICAL INTERNATIONAL ORGANIZATION DOCUMENTS
– *Annuaire de la Vie Internationale.* Editions 1905, 1906, 1907, 1908-9, 1910-11, totalling 4,741 pages
– *Code des Voeux Internationaux* (Classification of resolutions of international organizations) Edition 1923, 940 pages

La série YEARBOOK

Tous ces publications sont également disponible en ligne. Pour plus d'informations, veuillez consulter https://uia.org/

VOLUME 1 (Parties 1A et 1B): DESCRIPTIONS DES ORGANISATIONS ET LEURS LIENS
Descriptions des organisations intergouvernementales et non-gouvernementales qui couvrent tous les domaines d'activités. Présentation par ordre alphabétique des titres.
Contenu des descriptions: titres de l'organisation; adresses principale et secondaires; activités et programmes; personnel et finances; commissions; historique, buts, structure; liens avec d'autres organisations; langues utilisées; membrariat par pays.
Références croisées: Des références croisées à des organisations apparentées sont intégrées dans la séquence alphabétique des descriptions. L'accès à ces organisations est possible via les titres et les abréviations en toutes langues de travail.

VOLUME 2: INDEX GEOGRAPHIQUE : REPERTOIRE DES SECRETARIATS ET MEMBRARIATS PAR PAYS
– Organisations classées selon le pays siège de leur secrétariat
– Organisations classées selon les pays de leurs membres
– Statistiques par pays et par ville
Peut-être utilisé pour localiser des organisations internationales par pays de secrétariat ou de membrariat. Chaque organisation est reprise avec son adresse complète.

VOLUME 3: RESEAUX D'ACTION GLOBALE : REPERTOIRE THEMATIQUE ET INDEX
– Organisations classées par sujet, par région, et par catégorie
– Statistiques par sujet.
– Index des mots clés
Regroupe les organisations internationales en catégories de sujets. Ces catégories, générales ou spécifiques, peuvent être utilisées comme index aux notices du Volume 1. Chaque organisation est reprise avec son adresse complète.

VOLUME 4: BIBLIOGRAPHIE ET RESSOURCES DES ORGANISATIONS INTERNATIONALES
– Bibliographie des études sur les organisations internationales sans but lucratif
– Publications des organisations
– Indexes
Regroupe les publications principales et périodiques des organisations internationales, de même qu'une information bibliographique sur des études réalisées sur les ONG.

VOLUME 5: STATISTIQUES, VISUALIZATIONS ET REPRESENTATIONS
- Tableaux statistiques détaillés des informations incorporés dans les volumes 1, 2, 3, 4 et 6.
- Résumés statistiques historiques et analyses
- Présentation visuelle des données statistiques et des réseaux.
- Données statistiques sur les réunions des organisations.

VOLUME 6: LA SOCIÉTÉ CIVILE MONDIALE ET LES OBJECTIFS DES NATIONS UNIES POUR LE DÉVELOPPEMENT DURABLE
En 2015, les Nations Unies ont adopté un ensemble de dix-sept objectifs «pour mettre fin à la pauvreté, protéger la planète et assurer la prospérité pour tous», avec des cibles spécifiques pour chaque objectif à atteindre d'ici 2030. Ce sont les objectifs de développement durable (ODD) des Nations Unies, ou «Transformer notre monde: l'Agenda 2030 pour le développement durable. L'ONU appelle les gouvernements, le secteur privé, les individus et les organismes de la société civile à se regrouper pour atteindre ces objectifs.
Ce volume regroupe les organisations internationales selon les dix-sept objectifs de développement durable des Nations Unies, indiquant quelles organisations sont - ou pourraient être - concernées par les ODD. Il peut également être utilisé comme répertoire pour les descriptions du Volume 1. Chaque organisation y figure avec son adresse complète.

INTERNATIONAL CONGRESS CALENDAR
Recense les futures réunions internationales, mentionnant le lieu, la date, le sujet, l'organisateur, l'adresse complète et, dans la mesure du possible, le renvoi à l'Annuaire. Listes géographique et chronologique. Index thématique.

HISTORICAL INTERNATIONAL ORGANIZATION DOCUMENTS
– *Annuaire de la Vie Internationale.* Editions 1905, 1906, 1907, 1908-9, 1910-11, totalling 4,741 pages
– *Code des Voeux Internationaux* (Classification of resolutions of international organizations) Edition 1923, 940 page

This alphabetical listing is continued from Volume 1A.

La séquence alphabétique dans ce volume est la suite de celle contenue dans le Volume1A.

DISCLAIMER. The organizations described in this Yearbook are invited annually to update their profiles. By updating or approving a profile, the organization gives its fully informed permission to the Union of International Associations (UIA) to collect, save and use the data the organization thus submits, in order to execute UIA's core activities as set out in https://uia.org/core-activities. At any time an organization described in this Yearbook may ask UIA to remove, free of charge, its contact details by writing to uia@uia.org. UIA is responsible for processing the data it receives in accordance with the *General Data Protection Regulation* of the European Union. UIA will take all reasonable measures to ensure the protection of the data it holds. Those who submit data acknowledge and agree that the transmission of data is never without risk and therefore potential damage due to the unlawful use of information by third parties cannot be claimed from UIA. For more information, please see https://uia.org/privacypolicy

♦ IntACT – International Association of Computed Tomography (unconfirmed)
♦ **INTAF** International Task Force for the Rural Poor (#15656)
♦ **iNTA** International Network of Tropical Architecture (#14336)
♦ **INTA** International Trademark Association (#15706)
♦ INTA / see International Urban Development Association (#15832)
♦ **INTA** International Urban Development Association (#15832)
♦ **INTAL** Instituto para la Integración de América Latina y el Caribe (#11271)
♦ INTAL – International Action for Liberation (internationally oriented national body)
♦ INTAMIC – International Association for Microcircuit Cards (inactive)
♦ INTAP – International Conference on Intelligent Technologies and Applications (meeting series)
♦ INTAPUC / see International Solid Waste Association (#15567)
♦ INTAR – International Arts Relations (internationally oriented national body)
♦ INTASCALE / see Worldscale Association (#21765)
♦ **INTBAU** International Network for Traditional Building, Architecture and Urbanism (#14334)
♦ **INTDS** International Nuclear Target Development Society (#14383)
♦ Intealth / see Foundation for the Advancement of International Medical Education and Research
♦ INTEC – Fundación Europea para la Innovación y Desarrollo de la Tecnología (unconfirmed)
♦ **INTECOL** International Association for Ecology (#11856)
♦ INTECOM – International Council for Technical Communication (inactive)
♦ Integrability in Gauge and String Theory (meeting series)
♦ Integra Foundation (internationally oriented national body)

♦ Integral 11364

CEO c/o Myers Clark, Egale 1, 76-80 St Albans Road, Watford, WD17 1DL, UK. E-mail: enquiries@integralalliance.org.
URL: http://www.integralalliance.org/

History 2004, UK. Former names and other names: *Integral Alliance* – former. Registration: Charity Commission, No/ID: 1112515, England and Wales; Companies House, No/ID: 5442605, England and Wales. **Aims** As a global alliance of *Christian relief* and *development* agencies, work together to maximize the holistic impact of Christian response to the *poor* worldwide. **Structure** Board; Executive Committee; Groups (4); Secretariat. **Staff** 2.50 FTE, paid. **Publications** *Integral News*.
Members Agencies (20) in 13 countries and territories:
Australia, Belgium, Canada, Denmark, France, Hong Kong, Netherlands, New Zealand, Norway, Slovakia, Switzerland, UK, USA.
Included in the above, 16 organizations listed in this Yearbook:
CEDAR Fund; *European Academy of Occupational Health Psychology (EA-OHP, #05805)*; *Integra Foundation*; *MAP International (#16569)*; *Mission East*; *Norwegian Mission Alliance*; *Service d'entraide et de liaison (SEL)*; *Strømme Foundation (SF)*; *Tear*; *TEAR Australia*; *TEAR Fund*; *Tearfund Canada*; *TearFund, Schweiz*; *Tearfund, UK*; *World Relief*; *World Renew*. [2022/XJ3266/y/**C**]

♦ Integral Alliance / see Integral (#11364)

♦ Integral Europe (IE) 11365

Contact c/o Integral Impulzus Kft, Lövőház u 24, Budapest 1024, Hungary. E-mail: info@integraleuropeanconference.com.
URL: http://integraleurope.org/

History 2012. **Aims** Embody, represent, teach, develop and give voice to integral consciousness and its resulting practical applications on a European basis. **Structure** Board. **Events** *Integral European Conference* Siófok (Hungary) 2023, *Integral European Conference* Siófok (Hungary) 2022, *Conference* Siófok (Hungary) 2021, *Conference* 2020, *Online Conference* 2020. [2020/XJ9673/**F**]

♦ Integralistic Movement (inactive)
♦ Integral Yoga Academy of Australasia (internationally oriented national body)

♦ Integrated Assessment Modeling Consortium (IAMC) 11366

Contact c/o CMCC, Via delle Libertà 12, 30175 Venice VE, Italy. E-mail: iamc@iamconsortium.org.
URL: http://iamconsortium.org/

History 2007. Created in response to a call from *Intergovernmental Panel on Climate Change (IPCC, #11499)*. More formal structure adopted 2009. **Aims** Facilitate and foster development of integrated assessment models (IAMs), peer interaction and vetting of research associated with IAMs, and the conduct of research employing IAMs, including model diagnosis, intercomparison, and coordinated studies; promote, facilitate and help coordinate interactions between IAMC members and members of other research communities studying *climate change*; provide a point of contact with other institutions and organizations. **Structure** Scientific Steering Committee; Scientific Working Groups; Advisory Council. **Languages** English. **Activities** Awards/prizes/competitions; events/meetings; networking/liaising. **Events** *Annual Meeting* 2021, *Annual Meeting* 2020, *Scenarios Forum for Climate and Societal Futures* Denver, CO (USA) 2019, *Annual Meeting* Tsukuba (Japan) 2019, *Annual Meeting* Seville (Spain) 2018.
Members Full in 17 countries:
Austria, Brazil, Canada, China, Finland, France, Germany, Greece, India, Italy, Japan, Korea Rep, Netherlands, Norway, Spain, Sweden, Switzerland, Thailand, UK, USA.
Included in the above, 9 organizations listed in this Yearbook:
Centre for International Climate and Environmental Research, Oslo (CICERO); *Centro Euro-Mediterraneo per i Cambiamenti Climatici (CMCC)*; *International Bank for Reconstruction and Development (IBRD, #12317)* (World Bank); *International Institute for Applied Systems Analysis (IIASA, #13861)*; *International Research Centre on Environment and Development (CIRED)*; *Joint Research Centre (JRC, #16147)*; *Potsdam Institute for Climate Impact Research (PIK)*; *Research Institute of Innovative Technology for the Earth (RITE)*; *Tyndall Centre for Climate Change Research*. [2021.09.02/XM8582/y/**C**]

♦ Integrated Assessment Society, The (TIAS) 11367

Hon Pres c/o Inst of Environmental Systems Research, Barbarastrasse 12, Osnabrück University, 49069 Osnabrück, Germany. E-mail: info@tias-web.info.
URL: http://www.tias-web.info/

History 31 Oct 2003, Osnabrück (Germany). **Aims** Promote a community of inter-disciplinary and disciplinary scientists, analysts and practitioners who develop and use integrated assessment; encourage development and application of integrated assessment. **Structure** General Meeting (annual); Board. **Languages** English. **Staff** 0.10 FTE, paid. **Finance** Sources: members' dues. **Activities** Events/meetings; networking/liaising; training/education. **Publications** *TIAS Newsletter* (4 a year). *TIAS Report Series*.
Members Members in 27 countries:
Australia, Austria, Belgium, Brazil, Canada, Chile, China, Denmark, Finland, France, Germany, Hungary, Ireland, Italy, Japan, Kenya, Netherlands, Norway, Pakistan, Portugal, South Africa, Spain, Sweden, Switzerland, UK, United Arab Emirates, USA.
NGO Relations Also links with national institutions and universities. [2023.02.15/XM2832/**F**]

♦ Integrated Carbon Observation System (ICOS) 11368

Dir Gen Erik Palménin aukio 1, FI-00560 Helsinki, Finland. T. +358503523299. E-mail: info@icos-ri.eu – icos-comms@icos-ri.eu.
URL: https://www.icos-cp.eu/

History 2008. Also known as *Integration Carbon Observation System Infrastructure Committee (ICOS-RI)*. Awarded the status of *European Research Infrastructure Consortium (ERIC)* 2015, a legal status designed to facilitate the joint establishment and operation of research infrastructures of European interest, and since then also known as *ICOS ERIC*. Registration: EU Transparency Register, No/ID: 486249932803-02, Start date: 8 Oct 2018. **Aims** Produce standardized data on *greenhouse gas* concentrations in the atmosphere, as well as on carbon fluxes between the atmosphere, the earth and oceans. **Structure** General Assembly; Scientific Advisory Body; Ethical Advisor Board; Research Infrastructure Committee; Monitoring Station Assemblies; Carbon Portal; National Networks; Central Facilities; Head Office, headed by Director General. **Finance** Members' dues. **Activities** Knowledge management/information dissemination; events/meetings. **Events** *ICOS Science Conference* 2024, *ICOS Science Conference* Utrecht (Netherlands) 2022, *Nordic Symposium* Helsinki (Finland) 2021, *Science Conference on Greenhouse Gases and Biogeochemical Cycles* Utrecht (Netherlands) 2020, *ENVRIplus Project Final Meeting* Brussels (Belgium) 2019. **Publications** *ICOS Impact Assessment Report 2018*; *ICOS Progress Report 2015-2017*.
Members Scientists (over 500) and scientific organizations (over 70) in 12 countries:
Belgium, Czechia, Denmark, Finland, France, Germany, Italy, Netherlands, Norway, Sweden, Switzerland, UK.
IGO Relations *European Commission (EC, #06633)*. Partner of: *Group on Earth Observations (GEO, #10735)*. **NGO Relations** Cooperates with (1): *FLUXNET (#09803)*. [2022/XM5202/**F**]

♦ Integrated Marketing Communications Council of Europe (IMCC) . . 11369

Project Manager c/o EACA, Bd Brand Whitlock 152, 1200 Brussels, Belgium. T. +3227400710 – +3227400711. Fax +3227400717.
URL: http://www.imcceurope.com/

History 1980. Is a part of *European Association of Communications Agencies (EACA, #05983)*. Former names and other names: *European Federation of Sales Promotion (EFSP)* – former (1980); *Fédération européenne pour la promotion de vente (FEPV)* – former (1980); *Promotional Marketing Council of Europe (PMC)* – former (2007). **Aims** Advocate industry standards for honest, effective Integrated Marketing Communications campaigns, high professional standards and awareness of its contribution in a free market economy; provide a forum for discussion and establish opportunities for cross-border research and promotion to improve results through the entire Integrated Marketing Communications process. **Structure** General Assembly (annual); Council. **Languages** English. **Finance** Sources: members' dues. **Activities** Awards/prizes/competitions; certification/accreditation; training/education.
Members National associations in 7 countries:
Austria, Czechia, Germany, Greece, Ireland, Italy, Spain. [2021.09.07/XD6009/**E**]

♦ Integrated Spatial Potential Initiative for Renewables in Europe (INSPIRE) 11370

Coordinator INSPIRE Secretariat, Ricardo Energy and Environment, The Gemini Bldg, Fermi Avenue, Harwell Intl Business Centr, Didcot, OX11 0QR, UK. T. +441235753088. Fax +441235753001.

Aims Link renewable *energy* resource-mapping with economic and life cycle analysis modelling; develop tools for *biomass*-to-energy systems, linking financial analysis with resource mapping; extend this approach to include *environmental* costs and develop a partial life-cycle analysis capability; assess the applicability of methodology to wind, bio-waste and micro-hydro energy resources; harness results of other *EU* funded projects. **Activities** Research and development.
Members National partners in 10 countries:
Austria, Denmark, Finland, France, Greece, Ireland, Netherlands, Portugal, Sweden, UK.
Regional members (2), listed in this Yearbook:
Joint Research Centre (JRC, #16147); *Scandinavian Simulation Society (SIMS, #19100)*.
IGO Relations Partners: *European Commission (EC, #06633)*; Joint Research Centre (JRC); *Statistical Office of the European Union (Eurostat, #19974)*. **NGO Relations** *European Spatial Data Research (EuroSDR, #08806)*. [2018.01.24/XF6882/y/**F**]

♦ Integrating Content and Language in Higher Education (ICLHE) . . . 11371

Chair Van Wachtendonckplein 4, 6321 BG Wijlre, Netherlands. T. +31621243991. E-mail: info@iclhe.org.
URL: https://iclhe.org/

History 1 Jan 2010. Founded, originating from conferences organized since 1990s. **Aims** Promote exchange of opinions, experiences, initiatives and research concerning the interface between content and language in higher education. **Structure** Annual General Meetings; Board. **Languages** English. **Finance** Sources: meeting proceeds; members' dues. **Activities** Events/meetings. **Events** *Symposium* Vienna (Austria) 2023, *EMI and Englishization – Reflecting on the Changing University* Maastricht (Netherlands) 2022, *Conference* Maastricht (Netherlands) 2021, *The Englishization of Higher Education – A Phenomenon of Glocalization* Maastricht (Netherlands) 2021, *Transdisciplinary Collaboration in ICLHE and EMI* Mons (Belgium) 2020. **Publications** *ICLHE Newsletter*. *Integrating Content and Language in Higher Education: Perspectives on Professional Practice* (2017); *Integrating Content and Language in Higher Education: From Theory to Practice* (2015). Conference proceedings; books.
Members Individuals in 27 countries:
Australia, Austria, Belgium, Canada, Croatia, Denmark, Finland, France, Germany, Ireland, Israel, Italy, Japan, Korea Rep, Mexico, Netherlands, New Zealand, Norway, Poland, South Africa, Spain, Sweden, Switzerland, UK, United Arab Emirates, USA, Vietnam. [2022/XJ6152/v/**D**]

♦ Integrating Healthcare Enterprise International (IHE International) . 11372

Sec c/o RSNA, 820 Jorie Blvd, Oak Brook IL 60523-2251, USA.
URL: http://www.ihe.net/

History USA. Registration: USA, Illinois. **Aims** Improve the ability of computer systems in healthcare to share information so that all information relevant to a patient's care is available to the patients and the care provider when required. **Structure** International Board. Committees (3): Testing and Tools; Marketing and Communication; Domain Coordination. Domain Committees; Advisory Panel; National and Regional Deployment Committees; Liaison Organizations. Secretariat. IHE Deployment Committees Worldwide (5): Europe; North America; South America; Asia Pacific; Middle East. **Activities** Training/education; events/meetings. **Events** *Annual Connectathon Meeting* Daegu (Korea Rep) 2018, *Connectathon Meeting* The Hague (Netherlands) 2018, *Annual Connectathon Meeting* Daegu (Korea Rep) 2017, *Connectathon Meeting* Vienna (Austria) 2014.
Members Organizations (over 200): governmental and non-profit; Health IT and consulting companies; Healthcare provider organizations; Standards development organizations. Included in the above, 8 organizations listed in this Yearbook:
European Association of Hospital Managers (EAHM, #06073); *European Association of Hospital Pharmacists (EAHP, #06074)*; *European Society of Radiology (ESR, #08720)*; *International Clinical Cytometry Society (ICCS)*; *International Council of Nurses (ICN, #13054)*; *International Society for Advancement of Cytometry (ISAC, #14900)*; *Royal Australasian College of Surgeons (RACS)*; *Royal Australian and New Zealand College of Radiologists (RANZCR)*. [2022/XJ6000/y/**F**]

♦ Integration Carbon Observation System Infrastructure Committee / see Integrated Carbon Observation System (#11368)
♦ Integrity Action (internationally oriented national body)
♦ INTELEC – International Telecommunications Energy Conference (meeting series)
♦ Intellectbase International Consortium (internationally oriented national body)

♦ Intelligent Autonomous Systems Society (IAS) 11373

Secretariat c/o DEI, Via Gradenigo 6/a, 35131 Padua PD, Italy. E-mail: secretary@ias-society.org.
URL: http://www.ias-society.org/

History 14 Jul 1994. Founded by Prof Louis Hertzberger, Prof Takeo Kanade and Prof Hirochika Inoue, following apparent interest for establishing the Society after the first three IAS Conferences. **Aims** Organize the International Conference on Intelligent Autonomous Systems (IAS), thereby strengthening the community. **Structure** Governing Board; Executive Committee; Honorary Board. **Finance** Members' dues. **Activities** Events/meetings. **Events** *International Conference on Intelligent Autonomous Systems* Suwon (Korea Rep) 2023, *International Conference on Intelligent Autonomous Systems (IAS)* Zagreb (Croatia) 2022, *International Conference on Intelligent Autonomous Systems (IAS)* Singapore (Singapore) 2021, *International Conference on Intelligent Autonomous Systems (IAS)* Singapore (Singapore) 2020, *International Conference on Intelligent Autonomous Systems (IAS)* Baden Baden (Germany) 2018. **Publications** *Robotics and Autonomous Systems* – affiliated journal, and includes a news page from the Society. **Members** Membership can be acquired either by participating at an IAS Conference, that allows to apply freely for IAS membership for the two subsequent years, or by subscribing to the journal. Membership countries not specified. [2021/XF4973/**F**]

♦ Intelligent Building Group (IBG) 11374

Admin Office Riverside Building, County Hall, London, SE1 7PB, UK. T. +442079289150. Fax +448453307267. E-mail: info@ibgroup.org.uk.
URL: http://www.ibgroup.org.uk/

History 1992, as *European Intelligent Building Group (EIBG)*. **Aims** Communicate and deliver the benefits of intelligent buildings to all stakeholders, whether they be involved in the development, design, construction, use or safety. **Structure** General Assembly (annual). Management Board, comprising President, Chairman, Vice-Chairman, Treasurer, Administrator, 9 members and 3 co-opted members. **Languages** English. **Staff** 2.00 FTE, paid; 2.00 FTE, voluntary. **Finance** Members' dues (annual): pounds300 – pounds900 depending on size of organization; corporate rate of pounds2,000 (annually) for multiple membership. Other sources: subscription fees; sales of publications; events. **Activities** Operates as an independent, open network for research, learning, collaboration and action; assists members in learning about new and better methods of building that are more efficient in terms of how they are built, what they are built of, energy consumption both in their building materials and in their operating costs and how they are managed; creates direct channels between market decision makers, consultants, researchers, intelligent building suppliers and those involved in the supply chain and through these channels, produces and disseminates independent authoritative information on the market for intelligent buildings both nationally and internationally; links end user experiences and demands to products and services available from suppliers; develops and funds research and education projects. Organizes: Members' Meetings (monthly); seminars; conferences; site visits; missions. **Events** *International conference on intelligent buildings / Conference* Watford (UK) 1998. **Publications** *EIBG Newsletter*. *EIBG Directory of Intelligent Buildings*. Conference, seminars and meeting papers.

Members Standard; Corporate; Affiliate; End User companies, organizations, universities in 19 countries:
Austria, Belgium, Canada, Cyprus, Denmark, France, Germany, Greece, Israel, Malaysia, Netherlands, Norway, Poland, Russia, Singapore, Sweden, Switzerland, UK, USA.

Included in the above, 1 organization listed in this Yearbook:
European Bank for Reconstruction and Development (EBRD, #06315). [2013/XD6934/y/**D**]

♦ Intelligent Manufacturing Systems (IMS) 11375

Managing Dir IMS International, 4601 N Fairfax Drive, Suite 1200, Arlington VA 22203, USA.
URL: http://www.ims.org/

History 1995, in order to provide a framework for cooperative R and D to share costs, risks, and expertise leading to improved manufacturing operations, enhanced international competitiveness, and technology breakthroughs via industrially driven R and D and innovation. Phase I: 1995-2005. Phase II as from 2005. **Aims** As an industry-led research and development programme: facilitate research in advanced manufacturing through international cooperation; develop the next generation of manufacturing and processing technologies. **Structure** Steering Committee, headed by Chairman. Regional Secretariats; Inter-Regional Secretariat. Chairmanship rotates on a regular basis. **Languages** English. **Activities** *'Coaching Services'* – Support services to SME's and MNEs for project formation offered through Manufacturing Technology Programme (MTP), launched in spring of 2010. Project facilitators (coaches) and are available in every IMS region. Coaches may also introduce existing project opportunities to potential partners, and thread running projects together in order to increase efficiency and expertise. Coaches work in partnership with IMS Regional Secretariats in identifying opportunities to provide personalized one-on-one service and activities, and to raise awareness of programmes and activities to industry, industry associations, funding agencies and research institutions. *'Workshops'* – Conducts project workshops (2 a year). Workshops aim to promote formation of new projects, review ongoing research, and disseminate results of research conducted. *'Forums'* – Conducts annual forum which include the above workshop objectives with a wider scope to include other research-related topics. **Events** *Meeting* Busan (Korea Rep) 2007, *International conference on changeable, agile, reconfigurable and virtual production* Toronto, ON (Canada) 2007. **Publications** Annual Report; other publications.

Members Full; Associate. Companies and institutions in 31 countries (other countries pending):
Austria, Belgium, Bulgaria, Cyprus, Czechia, Denmark, Estonia, Finland, France, Germany, Greece, Hungary, Ireland, Italy, Korea Rep, Latvia, Lithuania, Luxembourg, Malta, Mexico, Netherlands, Poland, Portugal, Romania, Slovakia, Slovenia, Spain, Sweden, Switzerland, UK, USA.

Regional organization (1):
European Commission (EC, #06633).

IGO Relations *European Commission (EC, #06633)* chairs the organization. [2020/XM3135/**F**]

♦ INTELSAT / see International Telecommunications Satellite Organization (#15670)
♦ IntEnt – Internationalizing Entrepreneurship Education and Training – Conference (meeting series)

♦ InterAcademy Partnership (IAP) 11376

Acting Exec Dir Nat'l Acs Sciences, Engineering & Medicine, 500 Fifth St NW, Washington DC 20001, USA. E-mail: secretariat@iapartnership.org.
Coordinator c/o TWAS, Strada Costiera 11, 34151 Trieste TS, Italy. E-mail: iap@twas.org.
URL: http://www.interacademies.org/

History Mar 2016. Launched on merger of *IAP – The Global Network of Science Academies (inactive)*, *InterAcademy Medical Panel (IAMP, inactive)* and *InterAcademy Council (IAC, inactive)*. Registration: Non-profit 501(c)(3), No/ID: 81-2774070, Start date: 2018, USA, Washington DC. **Structure** Steering Committee; Board; Secretariat. IAP for Science (IAP-S); IAP for Health (IAP-H); IAP for Research (IAP-R). Regional Networks (4): *Association of Academies and Societies of Sciences in Asia (AASSA, #02341)*; *European Academies' Science Advisory Council (EASAC, #05778)*; *InterAmerican Network of Academies of Science (IANAS, #11441)*; *Network of African Science Academies (NASAC, #16987)*. **Activities** Training/education; advocacy/lobbying/activism. **Events** *Conference and General Assembly* Incheon (Korea Rep) 2019. **Publications** *InterAcademy News Bulletin* (2-3 a year) – electronic.

Members Academies of science, medicine and engineering (138) in 104 countries and territories:
Afghanistan, Albania, Argentina, Armenia, Australia, Austria, Bangladesh, Belarus, Belgium, Benin, Bolivia, Bosnia-Herzegovina, Brazil, Bulgaria, Burkina Faso, Cameroon, Canada, Chile, China, Colombia, Croatia, Cuba, Czechia, Denmark, Dominican Rep, Ecuador, Egypt, Estonia, Ethiopia, Finland, France, Georgia, Germany, Ghana, Greece, Guatemala, Holy See, Honduras, Hungary, India, Indonesia, Iran Islamic Rep, Ireland, Israel, Italy, Japan, Jordan, Kazakhstan, Kenya, Korea Rep, Kosovo, Kyrgyzstan, Latvia, Lebanon, Lithuania, Madagascar, Malaysia, Mauritius, Mexico, Moldova, Mongolia, Montenegro, Morocco, Mozambique, Nepal, Netherlands, New Zealand, Nicaragua, Nigeria, North Macedonia, Norway, Pakistan, Palestine, Peru, Philippines, Poland, Portugal, Romania, Russia, Senegal, Serbia, Singapore, Slovakia, Slovenia, South Africa, Spain, Sri Lanka, Sudan, Sweden, Switzerland, Tajikistan, Tanzania UR, Thailand, Trinidad-Tobago, Türkiye, Uganda, UK, Ukraine, Uruguay, USA, Uzbekistan, Venezuela, Zambia, Zimbabwe.

Included in the above, 17 organizations listed in this Yearbook:
Academia de Ciencias de América Latina (ACAL, #00010); *African Academy of Sciences (AAS, #00193)*; *Association of Academies and Societies of Sciences in Asia (AASSA, #02341)*; *Caribbean Academy of Sciences (CAS)*; *Caribbean Scientific Union (#03553)*; *Euro-Mediterranean Academic Network (EMAN, #05716)*; *European Academies' Science Advisory Council (EASAC, #05778)*; *European Academy of Sciences and Arts (EASA, #05814)*; *Federation of European Academies of Medicine (FEAM, #09490)*; *Global Young Academy (GYA, #10662)*; *InterAmerican Network of Academies of Science (IANAS, #11441)*; *Islamic World Academy of Sciences (IAS, #16057)*; *Network of Academies of Sciences in Countries of Organization of Islamic Conference (NASIC, #16981)*; *Network of African Science Academies (NASAC, #16987)*; *TWAS (#20270)*; *World Academy of Art and Science (WAAS, #21065)*.

Observers and other partners (21):
- *African Development Bank (ADB, #00283)*;
- *Asian Development Bank (ADB, #01422)*;
- *Environmental Defense Fund (EDF)*;
- *European Bank for Reconstruction and Development (EBRD, #06315)*;
- *European Union (EU, #08967)*;
- *FAO (#09260)*;
- *Inter-American Development Bank (IDB, #11427)*;
- *International Bank for Reconstruction and Development (IBRD, #12317)*;
- *International Centre for Genetic Engineering and Biotechnology (ICGEB, #12494)*;
- *International Council of Academies of Engineering and Technological Sciences (CAETS, #12982)*;
- *International Science Council (ISC, #14796)*;
- *Organization for Women in Science for the Developing World (OWSD, #17890)*;
- *RAND Europe*;
- *Science Council of Asia (SCA, #19137)*;
- *Statistical, Economic and Social Research and Training Centre for Islamic Countries (SESRIC, #19971)*;
- *UNDP (#20292)*;
- *UNEP (#20299)*;
- *UNESCO (#20322)*;
- *United Nations (UN, #20515)*;
- *Wellcome Trust*;
- *WHO (#20950)*. [2020/XM6996/y/**F**]

♦ **INTERACT4C** International Association Connecting Technologies for Citizens (#11809)
♦ **INTERACT** INTERACT – International Network for Terrestrial Research and Monitoring in the Arctic (#11377)

♦ INTERACT – International Network for Terrestrial Research and Monitoring in the Arctic (INTERACT) 11377

Coordinator Dept of Physical Geography and Ecosystem Science, Lund University, Sölvegatan 12, SE-223 62 Lund, Sweden. T. +46462224480.
Scientific Coordinator Dept of Plant and Animal Sciences, Univ of Sheffield, Western Bank, Sheffield, S10 2TN, UK. T. +441457763003. Fax +441452682521.
URL: http://www.eu-interact.org/

History An infrastructure project under the auspices of SCANNET, which gathers over 80 terrestrial bases in the Arctic. Also serves as a network of *International Arctic Science Committee (IASC, #11668)*. **Aims** Build capacity for circumarctic research and monitoring. **Structure** Coordinating Office; Station Managers Forum; Transnational Access Coordination Office. **Languages** English. **Finance** Through EU Framework grants. **Activities** Monitoring/evaluation; research/documentation; knowledge management/information dissemination; events/meetings; capacity building. **Events** *Station Managers Forum* Bressanone (Italy) 2018, *Station Managers Forum* Hvalsø (Denmark) 2015, *Station Managers Forum* Finland 2014, *Station Managers Forum* Abisko (Sweden) 2013, *Station Managers Forum* Nuuk (Greenland) 2013. **Publications** *INTERACT Management Planning for Arctic and Northern Alpine Research Stations* (2015); *INTERACT Research and Monitoring* (2015); *INTERACT Station Catalogue* (2015); *INTERACT Stories of Arctic Science* (2015); *INTERACT Station Catalogue* (2012). **IGO Relations** Cooperates with: *Arctic Monitoring and Assessment Programme (AMAP, #01100)*. **NGO Relations** Partners include: *Arctic Institute of North America (AINA, #01099)*; *Circumpolar Biodiversity Monitoring Program (CBMP, #03941)*; *World Wide Fund for Nature (WWF, #21922)*. [2019/XJ9347/**F**]

♦ InterAction – American Council for Voluntary International Action (internationally oriented national body)

♦ InterAction Council (IAC) 11378

SG 100 King St W, Suite 5700, Toronto ON M5X 1C7, Canada. T. +19056599797. E-mail: info@interactioncouncil.org.
URL: http://www.interactioncouncil.org/

History Mar 1983, Vienna (Austria). Founded with the initial sponsorship of *Global Committee of Parliamentarians on Population and Development (GCPPD, inactive)* and *UNDP (#20292)*. Former names and other names: *InterAction Council of Former Heads of State and Government (InterAction Council)* – full title. **Aims** Mobilize the experience and international contacts of a group of statesmen; provide former heads of government with a forum through which they may inspire greater public understanding of, and stimulate effective policy action by their successors on, fundamental issues vital to the future of humanity. **Structure** Council of former heads of state or government (meets annually); Executive Committee. **Languages** English. **Staff** 7.00 FTE, voluntary. **Finance** Sources: government support; private foundations. Supported by: private corporations; individuals. Annual budget: 800,000 USD. **Activities** Advocacy/lobbying/activism; events/meetings. **Events** *Annual Plenary Meeting* Valletta (Malta) 2021, *Annual Plenary Meeting* Cartagena de Indias (Colombia) 2019, *Annual Plenary Meeting* Beijing (China) 2018, *Annual Plenary Meeting* Dublin (Ireland) 2017, *Annual Plenary Session* Baku (Azerbaijan) 2016. **Publications** *The Dublin Charter for One Health* (2017); *Ethics in Decision Making* (2014); *Global Agenda 2013: Water, Energy, and the Arab Awakening* (2014); *The Global Water Crisis: Addressing an Urgent Security Issue* (2012); *Hiroshima Declaration* (2010); *Bridging the Divide* (2008); *Universal Declaration of Human Responsibilities* (1997).

Members Former heads of state and government from 39 countries and territories:
Austria, Brazil, Canada, Colombia, Costa Rica, Croatia, Cyprus, Czechia, Finland, France, Germany, Greece, Guinea, Hong Kong, Hungary, Iceland, India, Indonesia, Iran Islamic Rep, Ireland, Italy, Jamaica, Korea Rep, Latvia, Malaysia, Malta, Mexico, New Zealand, Nigeria, Norway, Poland, Russia, Saudi Arabia, Singapore, Slovenia, Timor-Leste, UK, Ukraine, USA. [2023.02.14/XF9305/v/**F**]

♦ InterAction Council of Former Heads of State and Government / see InterAction Council (#11378)
♦ InterAction Council / see InterAction Council (#11378)

♦ Interaction Design Association (IxDA) 11379

Exec Dir address not obtained. E-mail: info@ixda.org.
URL: http://ixda.org/

History 2003. Incorporated 2005. **Aims** Advance the practice of Interaction Design. **Structure** Board of Directors. **Languages** English. **Staff** 1.00 FTE, paid. **Activities** Awards/prizes/competitions; events/meetings; networking/liaising. **Events** *Conference* Zurich (Switzerland) 2023, *Conference* 2022, *Conference* Montréal, QC (Canada) 2021, *Conference* Milan (Italy) 2020, *Conference* Seattle, WA (USA) 2019. **Publications** *IxDA Newsletter*. **Members** Individuals. Membership countries not specified. **NGO Relations** Partner of (1): Design Declaration. [2021.06.15/XM7378/v/**C**]

♦ Interaction terre-océan dans les zones côtières / see Future Earth Coasts (#10049)
♦ Interactive Advertising Bureau / see IAB Global Network (#11003)
♦ Interactive Advertising Bureau Europe / see IAB Europe (#11002)
♦ Interactive Health Network (internationally oriented national body)
♦ Interactive Multimedia and Collaborative Communications Alliance (internationally oriented national body)

♦ Interactive Software Federation of Europe (ISFE) 11380

Fédération européenne des logiciels de loisirs – Europäischer Verband der Unterhaltungssoftware

SG Rue Guimard 15, 1040 Brussels, Belgium. T. +3226121777. E-mail: info@isfe.eu.
Office Manager address not obtained.
URL: http://www.isfe.eu/

History Oct 1997. Registration: Banque-Carrefour des Entreprises, No/ID: 0478.918.395, Start date: 5 Dec 2002, Belgium; EU Transparency Register, No/ID: 20586492362-11, Start date: 28 Sep 2009. **Aims** Ensure the voice of a responsible games ecosystem is heard and understood, that its creative and economic potential is supported and celebrated, and that players around the world continue to enjoy great video game playing experiences. **Structure** Board of Directors. **Languages** Dutch, English, French, German. **Staff** 7.00 FTE, paid. **Activities** Awareness raising; events/meetings.

Members Founding members in 5 countries:
France, Germany, Italy, Netherlands, UK.

National Trade Associations in countries:
Austria, France, Germany, Italy, Netherlands, Poland, Portugal, Switzerland, UK.
Association for the Nordic Game Industry (ANGI, #02829).

Consultative Status Consultative status granted from: *World Intellectual Property Organization (WIPO, #21593)* (Permanent Observer Status). **NGO Relations** Member of (1): *European Internet Forum (EIF, #07591)* (Associate). [2022.05.10/XD7588/y/**D**]

♦ INTERACT Research Centre / see Centre for Pentecostal and Charismatic Studies

♦ Inter-Africa Group – Centre for Dialogue on Humanitarian, Peace and Development Issues in the Horn of Africa (IAG) 11381

Exec Dir PO Box 1631, Addis Ababa, Ethiopia. T. +2511518790. Fax +2511517554.

History 1989, Nairobi (Kenya). **Aims** Advance humanitarian principles, peace and development in the Horn of Africa through a programme combining research, dialogue, public education and advocacy; undertake anticipatory and current studies and analysis of strategic and critical problems and policies relating to the region's peace, including economic and social development issues and environmental concerns; disseminate the findings of the studies and research activities for educational and policy changes; enhance peace efforts by establishing common political *commitment* among leaders of the region for observance of humanitarian principles, especially during situation of armed conflict. **Structure** Executive Board, consisting of 7 members. **Finance** Grants from: *Canadian International Development Agency (CIDA, inactive)*; *Christian Aid*; *Ford Foundation (#09858)*; *Heinrich Böll Foundation*; *International Bank for Reconstruction and Development (IBRD, #12317)*; *Oxfam Novib*; *Swedish International Development Cooperation Agency (Sida)*; *United States Agency for International Development (USAID)*; governments of Denmark, Germany, Norway, Netherlands,

UK. **Activities** Serves as a forum for debate and reflection on issues of peace and development; assists policy-makers and donor institutions in improving provisions of humanitarian assistance in times of crisis; encourages cooperation among governments, political entities, donors communities, United Nations and other concerned parties in the Horn region to ensure prompt and adequate response to humanitarian and economic needs of the region; through expert consultations, brainstorming sessions and efforts to sensitize public opinion, promotes greater awareness and understanding for victims of disaster and armed conflict and assists in developing national and international consensus in coherent and timely response; works towards peaceful resolution of conflicts in the region and lobbies for strict observance of international humanitarian principles, protection of civilians and observance of human rights principles. Areas of activity: Humanitarianism and Peace Building Program; Governance and Democratic Development; Economic Reform and Poverty Alleviation; NGO Networking Services. Conferences, symposia, publications, networking. Reference library. **Events** *Conference on human rights in the transition in Sudan* Kampala (Uganda) 1999. **Publications** *Issues Note* (occasional); *NGO Networking Service Monthly Update*; *NNS Notes*; *The Update*. Symposium papers.
Members Covers 7 countries:
Djibouti, Eritrea, Ethiopia, Kenya, Somalia, Sudan, Uganda.
IGO Relations *Intergovernmental Authority on Development (IGAD, #11472)*; *UNICEF (#20332)*; *United Nations Economic Commission for Africa (ECA, #20554)*; *UNHCR (#20327)*. **NGO Relations** Member of: *CIVICUS: World Alliance for Citizen Participation (#03962)*; *Global Partnership for the Prevention of Armed Conflict (GPPAC, #10538)*; *FEWER – Forum on Early Warning and Early Response (inactive)*. [2014/XE2038/**E**]

♦ Interafricaine socialiste et démocratique (inactive)
♦ Inter-African Bureau for Animal Health / see Interafrican Bureau for Animal Resources (#11382)

♦ Interafrican Bureau for Animal Resources (AU-IBAR) 11382

Bureau interafricain des ressources animales (UA-BIRA)
Dir Kenindia Business Park Bldg – Museum Hill, Westlands Road, PO Box 30786, Nairobi, 00100, Kenya. T. +254203674000. Fax +254203674341. E-mail: ibar.office@au-ibar.org.
URL: http://www.au-ibar.org/
History 1951, as *Inter-African Bureau for Epizootic Diseases (IBED)* within the framework of *Commission for Technical Cooperation in Africa South of the Sahara (CTCA, inactive)*. Subsequently became *Inter-African Bureau for Animal Health (IBAH)*. Present name adopted in Feb 1970. Previously also known under the acronym *IBAR – BIRA*. Functions as a specialized technical office falling within the framework of the Department of Rural Economy and Agriculture (DREA) of *African Union (AU, #00488)*. **Aims** Support and coordinate utilization of animals (livestock, fisheries and wildlife) as a resource for human wellbeing in Member States of the African Union, and contribute to economic development. **Structure** Headed by Director; Units (6); Advisory Committee; Editorial Board. Secretariat of: *International Scientific Council for Trypanosomiasis Research and Control (ISCTRC, #14809)*; Secretariat for Animal Health Standards. **Languages** Arabic, English, French, Portuguese. **Staff** 100.00 FTE, paid. **Finance** Core budget from African Union Commission; additional budget funding through projects with partners, including: *African Development Bank (ADB, #00283)*; *Bill and Melinda Gates Foundation (BMGF)*; *DANIDA*; *Department for International Development (DFID, inactive)*; *Deutsche Gesellschaft für Internationale Zusammenarbeit (GIZ)*; *European Commission (EC, #06633)*; *Global Environment Facility (GEF, #10346)*; *International Bank for Reconstruction and Development (IBRD, #12317)*; Spanish Government; *United States Agency for International Development (USAID)*. Annual budget: about US$ 36 million. **Activities** Guidance/assistance/consulting; capacity building; standards/guidelines; networking/liaising; knowledge management/information dissemination. **Events** *African Great Lakes Conference* Entebbe (Uganda) 2017, *Tenure and Fishing Rights Global Forum on Rights-Based Approaches for Fisheries* Siem Reap (Cambodia) 2015, *International conference on avian influenza* Bamako (Mali) 2006, *Seminar on the implementation of animal health standards* Cairo (Egypt) 2004, *Biennial Meeting* Nairobi (Kenya) 1989. **Publications** *Bulletin of Animal Health and Production in Africa* (4 a year); *Pan African Animal Health Year Book* in English, French. *PAAT Technical and Scientific Series*.
Members Governments of 55 countries:
Algeria, Angola, Benin, Botswana, Burkina Faso, Burundi, Cameroon, Cape Verde, Central African Rep, Chad, Comoros, Congo Brazzaville, Congo DR, Côte d'Ivoire, Djibouti, Egypt, Equatorial Guinea, Eritrea, Eswatini, Ethiopia, Gabon, Gambia, Ghana, Guinea, Guinea-Bissau, Kenya, Lesotho, Liberia, Libya, Madagascar, Malawi, Mali, Mauritania, Mauritius, Morocco, Mozambique, Namibia, Niger, Nigeria, Rwanda, Sahara West, Sao Tomé-Principe, Senegal, Seychelles, Sierra Leone, Somalia, South Africa, South Sudan, Sudan, Tanzania UR, Togo, Tunisia, Uganda, Zambia, Zimbabwe.
NGO Relations Observer to: *GALVmed (#10066)*. [2017.06.01/XE3867/**E***]

♦ Inter-African Bureau for Development and Cooperation (inactive)
♦ Inter-African Bureau for Epizootic Diseases / see Interafrican Bureau for Animal Resources (#11382)
♦ Inter-African Bureau of Epizootic Diseases (inactive)

♦ Inter-African Coffee Organization (IACO) 11383

Organisation interafricaine du café (OIAC)
SG BP V 210, Abidjan, Côte d'Ivoire. T. +22520216131 – +22520216185. Fax +22520216212. E-mail: sg@iaco-oiac.org.
Assistant to the SG address not obtained.
Street Address 3rd floor, Immeuble CAISTAB, Plateau, Abidjan, Côte d'Ivoire.
URL: http://www.iaco-oiac.org/
History 7 Dec 1960, Antananarivo (Madagascar). Founded on signature of an agreement by founder member States, following recommendations of Inter-African Conference of Coffee Producers, Sep 1959, Brussels (Belgium). Agreement amended: 1971; 1979; 1985: 1998. **Aims** Study common problems concerning African coffee, including production, processing and marketing, in order to ensure the smooth disposal of production and the optimum level of selling prices. **Structure** General Assembly (annual); Board of Directors. Promotion and Sales Coordination Committee; Consultative Group; Production Committee; Finance Committee. **Languages** English, French. **Staff** 10.00 FTE, paid. **Finance** Sources: members' dues. **Activities** Promotes stabilization of coffee prices on the international market; coordinates, as far as possible, trade policies of member States; studies marketing problems and market trends, making recommendations for, and implementing, International Coffee Agreement (1962, 1976, 1983, 1994, 1998); creation of a Cup Tasting Centre in Abidjan (Côte d'Ivoire) and Coffee Information Centres in consumer countries. Coordinates *African Coffee Research Network (ACRN, #00253)*. **Events** *General Assembly* Accra (Ghana) 2020, *Annual General Assembly* Nairobi (Kenya) 2019, *Annual General Assembly* Libreville (Gabon) 2018, *Annual General Assembly* Lomé (Togo) 2013, *Annual General Assembly* Abidjan (Côte d'Ivoire) 2011. **Publications** *African Coffee* (4 a year) in English, French.
Members African coffee producing countries (23):
Angola, Benin, Burundi, Cameroon, Central African Rep, Congo Brazzaville, Congo DR, Côte d'Ivoire, Equatorial Guinea, Ethiopia, Gabon, Ghana, Guinea, Kenya, Liberia, Madagascar, Nigeria, Rwanda, Sierra Leone, Togo, Uganda, Zambia, Zimbabwe.
IGO Relations Observer status with (2): *African Development Bank (ADB, #00283)*; *United Nations Economic Commission for Africa (ECA, #20554)*. Sister organization to: *International Coffee Organization (ICO, #12630)*; *Organisation africaine et malgache du café (OAMCAF, no recent information)*. Formal cooperation arrangement with: *African Development Bank Group (ADB Group, #00284)*. Participates in the activities of: *FAO (#09260)*; *UNCTAD (#20285)*. [2021/XD1040/**D***]

♦ Inter African Committee / see Inter-African Committee on Traditional Practices Affecting the Health of Women and Children (#11384)
♦ Inter-African Committee on African Medicinal Plants and Traditional Medicine (inactive)
♦ Inter-African Committee for Hydraulic Studies (inactive)
♦ Inter-African Committee on Oceanography, Sea and Inland Fisheries (no recent information)
♦ Inter-African Committee on Statistics (inactive)
♦ Inter-African Committee on Traditional Practices / see Inter-African Committee on Traditional Practices Affecting the Health of Women and Children (#11384)

♦ Inter-African Committee on Traditional Practices Affecting the Health of Women and Children (IAC) 11384

Comité Inter-Africain sur les pratiques traditionnelles ayant effet sur la santé des femmes et des enfants (CI-AF)
Exec Dir c/o ECA/IAC, PO Box 3001, Addis Ababa, Ethiopia. T. +251115515793. Fax +251115515793. E-mail: interafricanc@gmail.com.
Liaison Office Chemin de Balexert 9, 1219 Geneva, Switzerland. T. +41227971680. Fax +41227971682.
URL: http://www.iac-ciaf.net/
History Founded to continue the work of the international Seminar on Traditional Practices Affecting the Health of Women and Children in Africa, 6-10 Feb 1984, Dakar. Former names and other names: *Inter African Committee* – former; *Inter-African Committee on Traditional Practices* – former; *IAC* – former. **Aims** Promote *gender* equality and justice by eliminating harmful traditional practices, so as to enable African women to fully participate in the social, cultural and political development of their continent; reduce the rate of *morbidity* and *mortality* of women and children through the eradication of *female genital mutilation* and other harmful traditional practices; promote traditional practices that benefit health and *well-being* of women and children. **Structure** General Assembly; Executive Board; Headquarters in Addis Ababa (Ethiopia); Liaison Office in Geneva (Switzerland). **Languages** English, French. **Staff** 15.00 FTE, paid. **Finance** Sources: donations; government support; grants; international organizations. **Activities** Advocacy/lobbying/activism; awareness raising; events/meetings; financial and/or material support; projects/programmes; training/education. **Events** *Triennial General Assembly / Regional Conference and General Assembly* Ouagadougou (Burkina Faso) 2014, *Regional Conference and General Assembly* Abidjan (Côte d'Ivoire) 2011, *Geneva Summit for Human Rights, Tolerance and Democracy* Geneva (Switzerland) 2010, *Geneva Summit for Human Rights, Tolerance and Democracy* Geneva (Switzerland) 2009, *Triennial general assembly / Regional Conference and General Assembly* Cairo (Egypt) 2008. **Publications** *IAC Newsletter* (2 a year) in English, French. *Book on the Use of Indicators in the Campaign Against Female Genitale Mutilation* (2nd ed 2003). Journals; bulletins; brochures; posters; reports; surveys; films; documentaries; manuals.
Members National Committees in 29 countries:
Angola, Benin, Burkina Faso, Cameroon, Central African Rep, Chad, Congo Brazzaville, Congo DR, Côte d'Ivoire, Djibouti, Egypt, Ethiopia, Gambia, Ghana, Guinea, Guinea-Bissau, Kenya, Liberia, Mali, Mauritania, Niger, Nigeria, Senegal, Sierra Leone, Somalia, Sudan, Tanzania UR, Togo, Uganda.
Affiliates in 15 countries :
Belgium, Canada, France, Germany, India, Italy, Japan, Netherlands, New Zealand, Norway, Spain, Sweden, Switzerland, UK, USA.
Consultative Status Consultative status granted from: *ECOSOC (#05331)* (Special); *United Nations Population Fund (UNFPA, #20612)*. **IGO Relations** Observer status with (1): *African Union (AU, #00488)*. **NGO Relations** Member of (7): *Alliance for Health Promotion (A4HP, #00687)*; Comic Relief (UK); *Committee of NGOs on Human Rights, Geneva (#04275)*; *Conference of Non-Governmental Organizations in Consultative Relationship with the United Nations (CONGO, #04635)*; *NGO Committee on the Status of Women, Geneva (#17117)*; *The Girl Generation*; *Unis pour l'Equite et la Fin du Racisme (UFER, #20490)*. Cooperates with (5): *Foundation for Women's Health Research and Development (FORWARD)*; *Italian Association for Women in Development ONLUS (AIDOS)*; *NGO Committee on the Status of Women, New York NY (see: #04635)*; *No Peace Without Justice (NPWJ, #17155)*; *Rädda Barnen – Save the Children Sweden*. [2021.06.02/XE4064/**E**]

♦ Inter-African Conference on Insurance Markets 11385

Conférence interafricaine des marchés d'assurances (CIMA)
SG Centre ville, Av de Kerelle, BP 2750, Libreville, Gabon. T. +24111724318. Fax +24111724319. E-mail: cima@cima-afrique.org.
URL: http://www.cima-afrique.org/
History 10 Jul 1992, Yaoundé (Cameroon). Established on signature of a Treaty by 14 African governments instituting an integrated organization of the insurance industry. Replaces *Conférence internationale des contrôles d'assurance des Etats africains (CICA, inactive)*. **Aims** Reinforce and consolidate close cooperation in the field of insurance so that markets are capable of guaranteed coverage better adapted to African realities and taking account of contributing possibilities and risks of the agricultural and rural sector, as well as links to foreign trade where technically feasible; encourage, in view of augmenting retention at the national and regional level, installation of facilities allowing insurance and/or reinsurance organizations to bring about business exchanges using adequate techniques; make appropriate technical and mathematical provisions generated by operations of insurance and reinsurance, subject to technical requirements relative to insurance risks and the type of reinsurance coverage provided, as well as safety, liquidity, profitability and diversity, in order to allow local investment under the best conditions to profit the economy of member countries or the region; pursue training policy of management and technicians in the field fulfilling the needs of businesses and administrations in member countries; rationalize their human resources management through specialized and continuing education; create common structures, implementation definitions of policy guidelines and decisions in the above mentioned fields; harmonize and unify legislative and legal policy relating to technical operations of insurance/reinsurance with applicable controls of insurance/reinsurance organizations practised in their territory, as well as all other objectives likely to contribute to the industry, to development of management instruments and to methods of risk prevention in member states. **Structure** *Conseil des ministres des assurances (CMA, see: #11385)*; *Commission régionale de contrôle des assurances dans les Etats africains (CRCA, see: #11385)*; General Secretariat. Specialized autonomous institutions set up under CICA and maintained under CIMA: *Compagnie commune de réassurance des Etats membres de la CICA (CICA-RE, no recent information)*; *Institut international des assurances, Yaoundé (IIA, #11309)*. **Languages** French. **Staff** 26 contractual; 11 non-contractual. **Finance** Sources: members' dues. **Activities** Carries out regular on-sight controls of insurance companies operating in member countries through the Regional Commission of Insurance Control; evaluates financial situation of companies and, where necessary, takes measures of rectification or sanctions. Treaty sets out a 'Single Code' for insurance. Organizes: meetings; Expert Committee meetings; round tables; CIMA Days. **Publications** *CRCA Activity Report* (2 a year); *CIMA Activity Rreport* (annual); *CIMA Insurance Markets Report* (annual). Official bulletins.
Members Open to all African governments. Currently signed and ratified by governments of 14 countries:
Benin, Burkina Faso, Cameroon, Central African Rep, Chad, Congo Brazzaville, Côte d'Ivoire, Gabon, Guinea, Guinea-Bissau, Mali, Niger, Senegal, Togo.
Observer government of 1 country:
France.
IGO Relations Partner of (8): *African Reinsurance Corporation (AFRICA RE, #00438)*; *Banque centrale des Etats de l'Afrique de l'Ouest (BCEAO, #03167)*; *Banque des Etats de l'Afrique centrale (BEAC, #03169)*; *Communauté économique et monétaire d'Afrique centrale (CEMAC, #04374)*; *Economic and Statistical Observatory for Sub-Saharan Africa (AFRISTAT, #05321)*; *Economic Community of West African States (ECOWAS, #05312)*; *Organisation pour l'Harmonisation en Afrique du Droit des Affaires (OHADA, #17806)*; *Zone franc (#22037)*. Participates in the activities of: *UNCTAD (#20285)*. **NGO Relations** Member of (1): *International Association of Insurance Supervisors (IAIS, #11966)*. Partner of (3): *African Insurance Organization (AIO, #00343)*; *Conférence interafricaine de la prévoyance sociale (CIPRES, #04610)*; *Federation of African National Insurance Companies (#09408)*. [2022/XD4487/**D***]

♦ Inter-African Council for Philosophy (no recent information)
♦ Inter-African Forest Industries Association (inactive)
♦ Inter-African Labour Institute (inactive)
♦ Inter-African Network for Women, Media, Gender and Development (inactive)
♦ Inter-African Organization for the Quality of Life (inactive)
♦ Inter-African Pedological Service (inactive)
♦ Inter-African Phyto-Sanitary Council / see Inter-African Phytosanitary Council (#11386)

♦ Inter-African Phytosanitary Council (AU-IAPSC) 11386

Conseil phytosanitaire interafricain (CPI)
Dir PO Box 4170, Yaoundé, Cameroon. T. +2372211969. Fax +2372211967. E-mail: au-cpi@au-appo.org.
URL: https://auiapsc.org/
History 1954, London (UK). Established following recommendations, 1951, of FAO; the secretariat was supported by the then *'Commonwealth Agricultural Bureaux (CAB)'*, currently CAB International. In 1960, became part of the then *Commission for Technical Cooperation in Africa South of the Sahara (CTCA, inactive)*, which was transformed in 1965 into the *African Union Scientific Technical Research Commission (AU STRC, #00493)*. IAPSC was thus legally part of *Organization of African Unity (OAU, inactive)*. Currently part of *African Union (AU, #00488)*. Secretariat transferred to Yaoundé (Cameroon) in 1967. Former names and other names: *Commission phytosanitaire interafricaine* – former; *OAU-STRC-IAPSC* – former; *Inter-African Phyto-Sanitary Council* – alias. **Aims** Advise member states on technical, administrative and legislative

measures necessary to prevent the introduction of *diseases*, *pests* and other *plant* enemies in all regions of Africa; improve *agricultural* production in Africa; train staff involved in agricultural activities in AU member states; initiate and encourage crop pest and disease research; serve as phytosanitary information centre for Africa and as scientific and technical liaison for national, regional and international services. **Structure** General Assembly; Executive Committee; Group of Scientific Consultants; Scientific Secretariat in Yaoundé (Cameroon). **Languages** Arabic, English, French, Portuguese. **Finance** Sources: contributions of member/participating states. Annual budget depends on the assignments to be carried out that year. **Activities** Projects/programmes. **Events** *Regional Plant Protection Organizations (RPPOs) Annual Technical Consultation* London (UK) 2022, *Regional Plant Protection Organizations (RPPOs) Annual Technical Consultation* Rome (Italy) 2021, *Regional Plant Protection Organizations (RPPOs) Annual Technical Consultation* Rome (Italy) 2020, *Regional Plant Protection Organizations (RPPOs) Annual Technical Consultation* Abuja (Nigeria) 2019, *Regional Plant Protection Organizations (RPPOs) Annual Technical Consultation* Lima (Peru) 2018. **Publications** *IAPSC News* (12 a year); *Bulletin d'informations phytosanitaires* (4 a year); *African Journal of Plant Protection* (2 a year); *Réglementation phytosanitaire coordonnée pour l'Afrique. Carte de distribution des principles maladies et ennemis animaux des plantes* – map. Annual report; indexes; catalogues; legislative texts; sectoral reports. Information Services: The Centre includes a documentation department, library, scientific information and publications departments. **Information Services** *Centre de documentation et de ressources de l'information (CDRI)* – publishes research results, collects, collates and disseminates information, carries out information surveys on major databases. The Centre includes a documentation department, library, scientific information and publications departments.
Members Governments of 53 countries:
Algeria, Angola, Benin, Botswana, Burkina Faso, Burundi, Cameroon, Cape Verde, Central African Rep, Chad, Comoros, Congo Brazzaville, Congo DR, Côte d'Ivoire, Djibouti, Egypt, Equatorial Guinea, Eritrea, Eswatini, Ethiopia, Gabon, Gambia, Ghana, Guinea, Guinea-Bissau, Kenya, Lesotho, Liberia, Libya, Madagascar, Malawi, Mali, Mauritania, Mauritius, Mozambique, Namibia, Niger, Nigeria, Rwanda, Sahara West, Sao Tomé-Principe, Senegal, Seychelles, Sierra Leone, Somalia, South Africa, Sudan, Tanzania UR, Togo, Tunisia, Uganda, Zambia, Zimbabwe.
IGO Relations Serves as one of 10 Regional Plant Protection Organizations (RPPOs) of *International Plant Protection Convention, 1951 (IPPC, 1951)*. Technical cooperation with: *CABI (#03393)*; *Centre de coopération internationale en recherche agronomique pour le développement (CIRAD, #03733)*; *Comité permanent inter-Etats de lutte contre la sécheresse dans le Sahel (CILSS, #04195)*; *Deutsche Gesellschaft für Technische Zusammenarbeit (GTZ, inactive)*; *European and Mediterranean Plant Protection Organization (EPPO, #07773)*; *FAO (#09260)*; *Institut de recherche pour le développement (IRD)*; *International Rice Research Institute (IRRI, #14754)*; *North American Plant Protection Organization (NAPPO, #17567)*; *Organisation internationale de la Francophonie (OIF, #17809)*; *Organismo Internacional Regional de Sanidad Agropecuaria (OIRSA, #17830)*. **NGO Relations** Cooperates with: *International Centre for Tropical Agriculture (#12527)*. Instrumental in setting up: *African Network of Research on Storage Insects (ANERSI, #00394)*. [2020/XE3869/**E***]

♦ Inter-African Public Administration Seminar / see African Association for Public Administration and Management (#00215)
♦ Inter-African Union of Human Rights (inactive)
♦ Inter-African Union of Lawyers (inactive)
♦ Inter-African Union of Professional Pastoral Organizations (no recent information)
♦ Interagency Coalition on AIDS and Development (internationally oriented national body)
♦ Inter-Agency Committee on Women and Gender Equality / see Inter-Agency Network on Women and Gender Equality (#11388)
♦ Inter-Agency Coordination Panel on Juvenile Justice / see Interagency Panel on Juvenile Justice (#11390)

♦ Inter-agency Network for Education in Emergencies (INEE) 11387

Réseau inter-agences pour l'éducation en situations d'urgence – Red Interagencial para Educación en Situaciones de Emergencias – Rede Interinstitucional para a Educação em Situações de Emergência

Secretariat c/o Intl Rescue Committee, 122 East 42nd St, 14th floor, New York NY 10168, USA. E-mail: network@inee.org.
Main Website: http://inee.org

History 10 Nov 2000, Geneva (Switzerland). Founded following a Strategy Session on Education Emergencies of *World Education Forum (#21371)*, 2000, Dakar (Senegal). **Aims** Ensure the right to a quality, safe and relevant education for all who live in emergency and crisis contexts through prevention, preparedness, response and recovery. **Structure** Steering Group; Working Groups; Reference Groups; Language Communities; Community of Practice; Secretariat. **Languages** Arabic, English, French, Portuguese, Spanish. **Staff** 25.00 FTE, paid. **Finance** Funded by contributions from multi- and bi-lateral donors, UN agencies, private foundations and NGOs. **Activities** Advocacy/lobbying/activism; events/meetings; knowledge management/information dissemination; networking/liaising; politics/policy/regulatory; standards/guidelines; training/education. Active in all member countries. **Events** *Round Table* Nairobi (Kenya) 2018, *Collective consultation on minimum standards* Amman (Jordan) 2004, *Meeting on minimum standards for education in emergencies* Kathmandu (Nepal) 2004. **Publications** *INEE Bi-Weekly Bulletin* (bi-weekly); *Language Newsletters* (12 a year) in Arabic, French, Portuguese, Spanish; *Journal on Education in Emergencies* (irregular). Guidance notes; advocacy briefs; thematic papers; background papers; handbooks; framing papers; good practice guides. **Information Services** *Distance Education Database*; *EiE Glossary*; *INEE Help Desk*; *INEE Resource Database*; *INEE website* in Arabic, English, French, Portuguese, Spanish; *Measurement Library*.
Members Over 19,000 individual members affiliated with over 4,000 organizations and institutions in 190 countries. Membership countries not specified.
Institutional partners (66):
– *ACDI/VOCA*;
– *Action Against Hunger (#00086)*;
– *ActionAid (#00087)*;
– *Advancing Girls' Education in Africa (AGE Africa)*;
– *Adventist Development and Relief Agency International (ADRA, #00131)*;
– *Africa Educational Trust*;
– *Africa Network Campaign on Education for All (ANCEFA, #00302)*;
– *Aga Khan Foundation (AKF, #00545)*;
– *Agency for Technical Cooperation and Development (ACTED)*;
– *Aide et action France*;
– *Association for the Development of Education in Africa (ADEA, #02471)*;
– *AVSI Foundation*;
– *CARE International (CI, #03429)*;
– *Caritas Internationalis (CI, #03580)*;
– *Catholic Relief Services (CRS, #03608)*;
– *ChildFund International (#03869)*;
– *Children in Crisis*;
– *Comic Relief*;
– *Concern Worldwide*;
– *Department for International Development (DFID, inactive)*;
– *Deutsche Gesellschaft für Internationale Zusammenarbeit (GIZ)*;
– *Education Above All (EAA)*;
– *Education Development Center (EDC)*;
– *Education Development Trust*;
– *Education International (EI, #05371)*;
– *Enabling Education Network (EENET, #05450)*;
– *European Commission (EC, #06633)* (EuropeAid);
– *FHI 360*;
– *Finn Church Aid (FCA)*;
– *Global Campaign for Education (GCE, #10264)*;
– *Global Coalition to Protect Education from Attack (GCPEA, #10295)*;
– *Global Partnership for Education (GPE, #10531)*;
– *ILO (#11123)*;
– *International Bank for Reconstruction and Development (IBRD, #12317)*;
– *International Federation of Red Cross and Red Crescent Societies (#13526)*;
– *International Forum for Capacity Building (IFCB, no recent information)*;
– *International Organization for Migration (IOM, #14454)*;
– *International Rescue Committee (IRC, #14717)*;
– *INTERSOS*;
– *Mercy Corps International (MCI)*;
– *Mission Aviation Fellowship (MAF, #16829)*;
– *Norwegian Agency for Development Cooperation (Norad)*;
– *Norwegian Refugee Council (NRC)*;
– *Organisation internationale de la Francophonie (OIF, #17809)*;
– *Oxfam International (#17922)*;
– *Plan International (#18386)*;
– *Reach Out to Asia (ROTA)*;
– *RedR International (#18729)*;
– *Relief International*;
– *Right to Education Initiative (RTE, #18942)*;
– *Right to Play International (#18945)*;
– *Save the Children International (#19058)*;
– *SIL International (#19278)*;
– *Swisspeace*;
– *UNDP (#20292)*;
– *UNESCO (#20322)*;
– *UNHCR (#20327)*;
– *UNICEF (#20332)*;
– *United Nations Office for the Coordination of Humanitarian Affairs (OCHA, #20593)*;
– *United Nations Relief and Works Agency for Palestine Refugees in the Near East (UNRWA, #20622)*;
– *United States Agency for International Development (USAID)*;
– *United States Institute of Peace (USIP)*;
– *War Child International (#20817)*;
– *Women's Refugee Commission (WRC)*;
– *World Food Programme (WFP, #21510)*;
– *World Vision International (WVI, #21904)*.

IGO Relations Affiliated with (3): *UNESCO (#20322)*; *UNHCR (#20327)*; *UNICEF (#20332)*. **NGO Relations** Secretariat housed by: *International Rescue Committee (IRC, #14717)*. Member of: *Global Coalition to Protect Education from Attack (GCPEA, #10295)*; *New World Hope Organization (NWHO)*. Participates in: *Global Partnership on Children with Disabilities (GPcwd, #10529)*. [2022.05.03/XF7183/y/**F**]

♦ Inter-Agency Network on Women and Gender Equality (IANWGE) . . 11388

Réseau interinstitutions pour les femmes et l'égalité des sexes – Red Interinstitucional sobre la Mujer y la Igualdad entre los Géneros

Sec c/o UN Women, UN System Coordination Division, 405 East 42nd St, New York NY 10017, USA. T. +16467814400. Fax +1646781444. E-mail: ianwge@un.org.
URL: http://www.un.org/womenwatch/ianwge

History as *Inter-Agency Committee on Women and Gender Equality (IACWGE)*, within the framework of *United Nations (UN, #20515)*, responding to *United Nations System Chief Executives Board for Coordination (CEB, #20636)*. **Events** *Session* New York, NY (USA) 2014, *Session* New York, NY (USA) 2013, *Session* New York, NY (USA) 2012, *Session* New York, NY (USA) 2011, *Session* New York, NY (USA) 2010. **IGO Relations** Instrumental in setting up: *WomenWatch (#21040)*. *OECD Development Assistance Committee (DAC, see: #17693)*. [2018/XE3863/**E***]

♦ Interagency Operations Advisory Group (IOAG) 11389

Exec Secretariat NASA Headquarters, 300 E St SW, Washington DC 20546-0001, USA. T. +12023581912. Fax +12023582830.
Chairman ESA-ESOC, Robert-Bosch Str 5, 64293 Darmstadt, Germany. T. +496151902012.
URL: http://www.ioag.org/

History 1999. Formally established by *Interoperability Plenary (IOP)*, Jun 1999. **Aims** Oversee the development of collaborative, interoperable *space communications* and *navigation* services for the benefit of all members' spaceflight missions; understand issues related to interagency interoperability and other space communications matters; identify solutions complying with IOP policies; recommend resolutions to the IOP for specific actions by the IOP. **Structure** Governing Body: Interoperability Plenary (IOP); Chairman; Agency Lead and Delegates; Subgroups; Permanent Executive Secretariat. **Languages** English. **Staff** None. **Finance** Hosting agency funds meetings; member and observer agencies provide funding for participation of representatives; Secretariat and website funded by one of the member agencies. **Activities** Research/documentation; events/meetings. **Publications** Service Catalogues; Mission Models; Communication Assets Datasheets. **Information Services** *GNSS User Missions Database*.
Members National agencies (6) in 6 countries:
Canada, France, Germany, Italy, Japan, USA.
Intergovernmental agency:
European Space Agency (ESA, #08798).
Observer agencies (6):
China, Korea Rep, Russia, South Africa, UK, United Arab Emirates.
IGO Relations Observer status with: *International Committee on Global Navigation Satellite Systems (ICG, #12775)*. **NGO Relations** Cooperates with: *Consultative Committee for Space Data Systems (CCSDS, #04764)*; *Space Frequency Coordination Group (SFCG, #19897)*. [2019.12.17/XJ7428/**E***]

♦ Interagency Panel on Juvenile Justice (IPJJ) 11390

Contact Rue de Varembé 1, PO Box 88, 1211 Geneva 20, Switzerland. T. +41227340558. Fax +41227401145. E-mail: contact@ipjj.org.
URL: http://www.ipjj.org

History as *Inter-Agency Coordination Panel on Juvenile Justice*, by *ECOSOC (#05331)* Resolution 1997/30. **Aims** Facilitate and enhance country and global level coordination in juvenile justice in accordance with the Convention on the Rights of the Child and other relevant international norms and standards; function as a platform for exchange of information and expertise at national, regional and international levels. **Languages** English, French. **Publications** *Ten-Point Plan for Fair and Effective Criminal Justice for Children* (2012) in English, French, Russian, Spanish; *Criteria for the Design and Evaluation of Juvenile Justice Reform Programmes* (2011) in English, French, Russian, Spanish; *Protecting the Rights of Children in Conflict with the Law* (2006) in Arabic, English, French, Russian, Spanish. Manuals; toolkits.
Members Organizations (currently 13):
Child Rights International Network (CRIN, #03885); *Committee on the Rights of the Child (#04283)*; *Defence for Children International (DCI, #05025)*; *International Association of Youth and Family Judges and Magistrates (IAYFJM, #12283)*; *International Juvenile Justice Observatory (IJJO)*; *Office of the United Nations High Commissioner for Human Rights (OHCHR, #17697)*; *Penal Reform International (PRI, #18290)*; *Terre des hommes Foundation (Tdh Foundation, #20132)*; *UNDP (#20292)*; *UNICEF (#20332)*; United Nations Department of Peacekeeping Organizations (DPKO); *United Nations Office on Drugs and Crime (UNODC, #20596)*; *World Organisation Against Torture (OMCT, #21685)*. [2012.10.25/XM1572/y/**E***]

♦ Inter-Agency Regional Analysts Network / see Inter-Agency Research and Analysis Network (#11391)

♦ Inter-Agency Research and Analysis Network (IARAN) 11391

Dir 14b Walterton Road, London, W93PN, UK.
Dir address not obtained.
URL: https://www.iaran.org/

History 2012. Originated in *Institut de relations internationales et stratégiques (IRIS)*. Entered a test phase in *Save the Children International (#19058)*, 2013. From 2014, partnered with futures-oriented organizations. Moved to pilot phase at *Action Against Hunger (#00086)*, 2015. From 2016, a legal consortium of multiple agencies and universities. 2019 became an independent consultancy company. Former names and other names: *Inter-Agency Regional Analysts Network* – former. **Aims** Through analysis and scenario building, enable aid organizations to plan into the future, pre-empt change, build adaptable and impactful strategies, and ultimately save time, money and lives. **Structure** Two Directors. **Languages** English, French. **Staff** 2.00 FTE, paid. **Finance** Sources: private foundations; revenue from activities/projects. **Activities** Events/meetings; research/documentation. **Publications** Reports; infographics; videos; executive summaries. [2023/XM5989/**F**]

♦ Inter-Agency Space Debris Coordination Committee (IADC) 11392

Address not obtained.
URL: http://www.iadc-online.org/

History 1993. **Aims** Exchange information on space debris research, facilitate opportunities for cooperation in space debris research, review the progress of ongoing cooperative activities; identify debris mitigation options. **Structure** Steering Group; Working Groups (4). **Activities** Working Groups (4): Environment and Database; Measurements; Mitigation; Protection. **Events** *Meeting* Tsukuba (Japan) 2018, *Meeting* Darmstadt (Germany) 1999, *Meeting* Toulouse (France) 1998.
Members National space agencies in 10 countries:
China, France, Germany, India, Italy, Japan, Russia, UK, Ukraine, USA.
International organization (1):
European Space Agency (ESA, #08798). [2011/XE4381/**E**]

♦ Inter-Agency Standing Committee (IASC) 11393

Comité Permanent Inter-Organisations

Chief Av de la Paix 8-14, 1211 Geneva 10, Switzerland. T. +41229171438. E-mail: iasccorrespondence@un.org.
New York Secretariat 1 United Nations Plaza, New York NY 10017, USA. T. +12129635582.
URL: https://interagencystandingcommittee.org/

History Established Jun 1992, by *United Nations (UN, #20515)* General Assembly resolution 46/182. **Aims** Ensure coherence of preparedness and response efforts, formulate policy, and agree on priorities for strengthened humanitarian action. **Structure** Principles Meeting (meets twice a year); Working Group (IASC-WG); Principals Steering Group; Emergency Directors Group (EDG). Task Teams (TTs); Reference Groups (RGs); Senior Transformative Agenda Implementation Team (STAIT); Global Cluster Coordinators (GCC). Secretariat located within *United Nations Office for the Coordination of Humanitarian Affairs (OCHA, #20593).* Clusters include: *Emergency Telecommunications Cluster (ETC, #05438); Global Camp Coordination and Camp Management Cluster (CCCM Cluster, #10268); Global Cluster for Early Recovery (GCER, inactive); Global Shelter Cluster (GSC, #10594); Global WASH Cluster (GWC, #10651).* **Activities** Politics/policy/regulatory; events/meetings; training/education. **Events** *Meeting* Geneva (Switzerland) 2009. **Publications** Guidelines.
Members International organizations (9 Full and 9 Standing Invitees). Full members:
FAO (#09260); UNDP (#20292); UNHCR (#20327); UNICEF (#20332); United Nations Human Settlements Programme (UN-Habitat, #20572); United Nations Office for the Coordination of Humanitarian Affairs (OCHA, #20593); United Nations Population Fund (UNFPA, #20612); WHO (#20950); World Food Programme (WFP, #21510).
Standing Invitees:
American Council for Voluntary International Action (InterAction); International Bank for Reconstruction and Development (IBRD, #12317) (World Bank); *International Committee of the Red Cross (ICRC, #12799); International Council of Voluntary Agencies (ICVA, #13092); International Federation of Red Cross and Red Crescent Societies (#13526); International Organization for Migration (IOM, #14454); Office of the United Nations High Commissioner for Human Rights (OHCHR, #17697);* SR on the Human Rights IDPs; *Steering Committee for Humanitarian Response (SCHR, #19978).*
NGO Relations NGOs represented by 3 consortia: *American Council for Voluntary International Action (InterAction); International Council of Voluntary Agencies (ICVA, #13092); Steering Committee for Humanitarian Response (SCHR, #19978).* [2019.12.11/XE4201/y/**E***]

♦ Inter-Agency Task Force on Employment and Sustainable Livelihoods for All (inactive)
♦ Inter-Agency Task Force on Enabling Environment for Economic and Social Development (inactive)
♦ Inter-Agency Task Force on Forests / see Collaborative Partnership on Forests (#04100)

♦ Inter-Agency Task Team on Children affected by AIDS (IATT) 11394

Contact address not obtained. E-mail: iattcaba@unicef.org.
URL: http://www.iattcaba.org/

History 2001, by *Joint United Nations Programme on HIV/AIDS (UNAIDS, #16149)* Committee of Cosponsoring Organizations. Original title: *Inter-Agency Task Team on Orphans and other Vulnerable Children.* Changed title to *Inter-Agency Task Team on Children and HIV and AIDS*, 2004. Also known as *IATT-CABA.* **Structure** Global Partners Forum (GPF). Steering Committee. Thematic Working Groups. **Events** *Global Partners Forum* New York, NY (USA) 2011, *Global Partners Forum* Dublin (Ireland) 2008.
Members Organizations (26):
- *Department for International Development (DFID, inactive);*
- *Firelight Foundation;*
- *Global Fund to Fight AIDS, Tuberculosis and Malaria (Global Fund, #10383);*
- *Grow Up Free from Poverty Coalition;*
- *HelpAge International (#10904);*
- *ILO (#11123);*
- *International Bank for Reconstruction and Development (IBRD, #12317)* (World Bank);
- *International Food Policy Research Institute (IFPRI, #13622);*
- *Joint United Nations Programme on HIV/AIDS (UNAIDS, #16149);*
- *Kreditanstalt für Wiederaufbau (KfW);*
- MACRO International;
- *Population Council (#18458);*
- *REPSSI (#18848);*
- *Save the Children Federation (SCF);*
- *SOS-Kinderdorf International (#19693);*
- South African Human Sciences Research Council;
- *UNICEF (#20332);*
- *United States Agency for International Development (USAID);*
- University College London;
- US Health Resources and Services Administration;
- US President's Emergency Plan for AIDS Relief;
- *Voluntary Service Overseas (VSO);*
- *World Food Programme (WFP, #21510);*
- *World Vision International (WVI, #21904);*
- World Vision UK.

NGO Relations Member of: *Regional Inter-Agency Task Team on Children and AIDS in Eastern and Southern Africa (RIATT-ESA, #18791).* [2013/XJ7263/y/**E**]

♦ Inter-Agency Task Team on Children and HIV and AIDS / see Inter-Agency Task Team on Children affected by AIDS (#11394)
♦ Inter-Agency Task Team on Orphans and other Vulnerable Children / see Inter-Agency Task Team on Children affected by AIDS (#11394)
♦ Inter Agency Working Group / see United Nations Evaluation Group (#20560)
♦ Inter-Agency Working Group on Desertification (inactive)
♦ Inter aide (internationally oriented national body)
♦ Inter-Aid and Fraternity / see Entraide et fraternité
♦ Interallied Confederation of Medical Reserve Officers (#04555)
♦ Interallied Confederation of Reserve Non Commissioned Officers (#04556)
♦ Interallied Confederation of Reserve Officers (#04557)
♦ Inter-Allied Council for Sport / see Conseil international du sport militaire (#04695)
♦ Interallied Federation of Escapists in War (inactive)
♦ Inter-Allied Federation of Ex-Servicemen (inactive)
♦ Inter-Allied Reparations Agency (inactive)

♦ Inter-American Accounting Association (IAA) 11395

Association interaméricaine de comptabilité – Asociación Interamericana de Contabilidad (AIC) – Associação Interamericana de Contabilidade

Pres address not obtained.
URL: http://www.contadores-aic.org/

History 5 May 1949, San Juan (Puerto Rico), as *Inter-American Accounting Conference.* Current name adopted 1974. **Aims** Foster greater communication among sponsoring bodies; increase the level of skill and expertise of the accountant in the Americas. **Structure** Board of Directors (meets at biennial Conference and the Congress Summit of the Americas), consisting of one representative of each member organization or sponsoring body. Executive Committee, comprising President, Vice-President and 5 members. Honour Committee of 5 members. Technical Inter-American Commissions (9): Accounting Investigation; Audit; Governmental Sector; Education; Administration and Finance; Ethics and the Exercise of Professional Activity; Economical and Fiscal Integration; SME; Technology Systems. **Languages** English, Portuguese, Spanish. **Staff** 5.00 FTE, paid. **Finance** Members' dues: US$ 50. **Activities** Organizes conferences, congresses, seminars and courses. **Events** *Biennial Conference* Dominican Rep 2015, *Biennial Conference* Santa Cruz (Bolivia) 2007, *Interamerican regional seminar on accounting* Arequipa (Peru) 2005, *Biennial Conference* Bahia (Brazil) 2005, *Biennial Conference* Salvador (Brazil) 2005. **Publications** *Interamerican Bulletin* (4 a year) in English, Spanish; *Interamerican Magazine* (4 a year). Directory of associate members (every 3 years); conference reports.
Members Adhering Individual; Adhering Institutional. Member organizations or sponsoring bodies (2,000) in 23 countries:
Argentina, Bolivia, Brazil, Canada, Chile, Colombia, Costa Rica, Cuba, Dominican Rep, Ecuador, El Salvador, Guatemala, Haiti, Honduras, Mexico, Nicaragua, Panama, Paraguay, Peru, Puerto Rico, Uruguay, USA, Venezuela.
IGO Relations *Intergovernmental Working Group of Experts on International Standards of Accounting and Reporting (ISAR, #11503).* **NGO Relations** Recognized as regional organization by: *International Federation of Accountants (IFAC, #13335).* [2015/XD6610/**D**]

♦ Inter-American Accounting Conference / see Inter-American Accounting Association (#11395)

♦ Inter-American Accreditation Cooperation (IAAC) 11396

Foro de Organismos de Acreditación de América

Exec Sec Entidad Mexicana de Acreditación, Manuel Maria Contreras 133, piso 2, Col Cuauhtémoc DR, 06597 Mexico City CDMX, Mexico. T. +525591484300ext4358. Fax +525555910529. E-mail: secretariat@iaac.org.mx.
URL: http://www.iaac.org.mx/

History 22 Nov 1996, Montevideo (Uruguay), by delegates from 17 American governmental organizations concerned with standardization of technical specifications, tests and procedures. **Aims** Promote international recognition of the accreditations granted by participating accreditation bodies and the acceptance of certificates of *conformity* and *tests* results issued by conformity assessment organizations and laboratory accredited by them; facilitate *trade* among American countries by promoting cooperation among accreditation bodies and other interested organizations. **Structure** Plenary Committee; Executive Committee. Working Groups (5). **Languages** English, Portuguese, Spanish. **Activities** Working Groups (5): Guidance and General Documentation; Conformity Assessment, Technical Assistance and Training; Multilateral Recognition Agreement; Public Relations and Promotion; Calibration and Testing Activities. **Events** *Annual General Assembly* Port-of-Spain (Trinidad-Tobago) 2013, *Annual General Assembly* Cartagena de Indias (Colombia) 2012, *Annual General Assembly* Quito (Ecuador) 2011, *Annual General Assembly* Antigua (Guatemala) 2003, *Annual Plenary Meeting* San José (Costa Rica) 1999. **Publications** *IAAC Bulletin* in English, Spanish.
Members Accreditation bodies of certification, inspection bodies, testing and calibration laboratories and other interested parties. Full members (15) in 14 countries:
Argentina, Bolivia, Brazil, Chile, Colombia, Costa Rica, El Salvador, Guatemala, Mexico, Paraguay, Peru, Uruguay, USA (2), Venezuela.
Associated members (7), of which 2 included in this Yearbook:
Andean Community (#00817); Pan American Standards Commission (#18133).
NGO Relations Cooperates with: *Inter-American Foundation (IAF, #11431); International Accreditation Forum (IAF, #11584); International Laboratory Accreditation Cooperation (ILAC, #13995); Latin American Association of Design (ALADI, #16238).* Member of: *Pan American Standards Commission (#18133).* Memorandum of Understanding with: *Asia Pacific Accreditation Cooperation (APAC, #01816).* [2008/XF4519/y/**F**]

♦ Inter-American Agency for Cooperation and Development (IACD) .. 11397

Agencia Interamericana para la Cooperación y el Desarrollo (AICD)

Gen Dir c/o SEDI, 1889 F St NW – 7th Floor, Washington DC 20024, USA. E-mail: kosborne@oas.org.
Chair address not obtained.
URL: http://www.oas.org/en/sedi/

History Nov 1999. Set up at special session of General Assembly of *OAS (#17629)*, following proposal, 1998, by USA. A subsidiary body of *Inter-American Council for Integral Development (#11423).* **Aims** Promote, coordinate, manage and facilitate the planning and execution of programs, projects and activities within the scope of the OAS charter and, in particular, the framework of the Strategic Plan for Partnership for Development of CIDI. **Structure** Management Board; Executive Secretariat for Integral Development (SEDI). **Finance** "Seed money" from USA funding to strengthen OAS development programs is used to attract matching funds for new projects and establish a capital fund for scholarships. **Activities** Provides non-refundable technical cooperation to OAS member states wanting to finance projects and activities within 8 priority areas of hemispheric development: economic diversification and integration, trade liberalization and market access; education; sustainable development; social development / creation of productive employment; democracy; scientific development / exchange and transfer of technology; sustainable development of tourism; culture. **IGO Relations** *US-Central American Free Trade Agreement (CAFTA, 2004).* [2022/XE4189/**E***]

♦ Inter-American Air Forces Academy (internationally oriented national body)
♦ Inter-American Air Transport Confederation (inactive)
♦ Inter-American Amateur Radio Service Convention (1987 treaty)
♦ Inter-American Arrangement Concerning Radiocommunications, 1937 (1937 treaty)
♦ Inter-American Association of Agricultural Librarians, Documentalists and Information Specialists (no recent information)
♦ Inter-American Association of Broadcasters / see International Association of Broadcasting (#11738)
♦ Inter-American Association of Choral Directors (inactive)
♦ Inter-American Association for Democracy and Freedom (inactive)

♦ Interamerican Association for Environmental Defense 11398

Asociación Interamericana para la Defensa del Ambiente (AIDA)

Co-Exec Dir c/o Earthjustice, 50 California St – Ste 500, San Francisco CA 94111, USA. T. +14152172053. Fax +14152172040. E-mail: aida@aida-americas.org.
Co-Exec Dir c/o CEMDA, Atlixco 138, Colonia Condesa, 06140 Mexico City CDMX, Mexico. T. +525552120141. E-mail: aida@aida-americas.org.
URL: http://www.aida-americas.org/

History Founded in 1998, as a non-profit environmental law organization. **Aims** Work across international borders to defend threatened *ecosystems* and the human communities that depend on them; defend the individual and collective right to a healthy environment through development, implementation and enforcement of international law. **Structure** Board of Directors. **Languages** English, Portuguese, Spanish. **Staff** 14.00 FTE, paid. **Activities** Networking/liaising; awareness raising; knowledge management/information dissemination. **Publications** *A Human Crisis: Climate Change and Human Rights in Latin America* (2011); *Environmental Defense Guide: Building Strategies for Litigating Cases before the Inter-American System of Human Rights* (2010).
Members AIDA Partners (9) with participating organizations in 8 countries:
Argentina, Canada, Chile, Costa Rica, Ecuador, Mexico, Peru, USA.
Included in the above, 2 organizations listed in this Yearbook:
Center for Human Rights and Environment (CEDHA); Earthjustice.
Consultative Status Consultative status granted from: *ECOSOC (#05331)* (Special). **IGO Relations** Accredited by: *Green Climate Fund (GCF, #10714).* **NGO Relations** Cooperates with: *Global Call for Climate Action (GCCA, inactive).* Member of: *Global Coral Reef Monitoring Network (GCRMN, #10306).* [2017.06.01/XJ2242/y/**D**]

♦ Inter-American Association of Gastroenterology / see Organización Panamericana de Gastroenterologia (#17847)

♦ Inter-American Association of Industrial Property / see Asociación Interamericana de la Propiedad Intelectual (#02161)
♦ Interamerican Association of Intellectual Property (#02161)
♦ Inter-American Association of Juvenile Magistrates (inactive)

♦ Interamerican Association of Pediatric Otorhinolaryngology (IAPO) 11399

Asociación Interamericana de Otorrinolaringología Pediátrica

Sec Rua Mato Grosso, 306 cj 1511, Sao Paulo SP, 01239-040, Brazil. T. +551121146510. E-mail: primavera@iapo.org.br.
Pres Edificio Omega, Oficina 3 – piso 7, calle 1, Ave 14 y 16, San José, San José, San José, Costa Rica. T. +5062572121. E-mail: fedemuri@yahoo.com.
URL: http://www.iapo.org.br/

History Nov 1995, Argentina. **Aims** Disseminate knowledge of oto-rhino-laryngology in children worldwide. **Structure** Board of Directors, including President, Past President, President Elect, General Secretary and Treasurer. **Languages** English, Portuguese, Spanish. **Staff** None. **Finance** Members' dues. **Events** *Symposium of Pediatric Otorhynolaringology* Sao Paulo (Brazil) 2020, *Symposium of Pediatric Otorhynolaringology* Sao Paulo (Brazil) 2018, *International symposium on pediatric ear, nose and throat* Sao Paulo (Brazil) 2011, *International symposium on pediatric infections diseases in ear, nose and throat* Sao Paulo (Brazil) 2007, *Conference* Cartagena de Indias (Colombia) 2006. **Publications** Manuals.
Members Individuals in 60 countries and territories:
Algeria, Angola, Argentina, Australia, Bahamas, Belarus, Belgium, Bolivia, Brazil, Burkina Faso, Canada, Chile, China, Colombia, Costa Rica, Côte d'Ivoire, Cuba, Czechia, Denmark, Dominican Rep, Ecuador, Egypt, El Salvador, Estonia, Finland, France, Guatemala, Honduras, Hong Kong, Hungary, India, Iraq, Italy, Jordan, Mexico, Mozambique, Netherlands, New Zealand, Nicaragua, Nigeria, Norway, Panama, Paraguay, Peru, Poland, Portugal, Russia, Saudi Arabia, Serbia, Slovakia, Slovenia, South Africa, Spain, St Kitts-Nevis, Thailand, Türkiye, UK, Uruguay, USA, Venezuela.
NGO Relations *European Society of Pediatric Otorhinolaryngology (ESPO, #08692)*; national societies.
[2022/XM0311/**D**]

♦ Inter-American Association of Private International Law Professors (inactive)
♦ Inter-American Association of Professors of Sanitary and Environmental Engineering (no recent information)
♦ Inter-American Association of Public Prosecution / see Asociación Iberoamericana de Ministerios Públicos (#02149)
♦ Inter-American Association of Sanitary Engineering / see Inter-American Association of Sanitary and Environmental Engineering (#11400)
♦ Inter-American Association of Sanitary Engineering and Environmental Sciences / see Inter-American Association of Sanitary and Environmental Engineering (#11400)

♦ Inter-American Association of Sanitary and Environmental Engineering 11400

Association interaméricaine de génie sanitaire et des sciences de l'environnement – Asociación Interamericana de Ingenieria Sanitaria y Ambiental (AIDIS) – Associação Interamericana de Engenharia Sanitaria e Ambiental

Main Office Av Angélica 2355 A13 Conj 132, Consolação, Sao Paulo SP, 01227-200, Brazil. T. +551138124080. Fax +551138142441. E-mail: aidis@aidisnet.org.
URL: http://www.aidisnet.org/

History 14 Apr 1948, Santiago (Chile), as *Inter-American Association of Sanitary Engineering – Asociación Interamericana de Ingenieria Sanitaria*. Previously also referred to as *Inter-American Association of Sanitary Engineering and Environmental Sciences (IAASEES)*. Constitution amended Jun 1976, Buenos Aires (Argentina); current constitution approved Oct 1992, Buenos Aires. Legally registered in Caracas (Venezuela) and in Sao Paulo (Brazil). Since 1999, a regional group of: *International Water Association (IWA, #15865)*. **Aims** Promote development of sanitary engineering and environmental sciences in the Americas; promote scientific and technological contributions toward public health and environmental sanitation. **Structure** General Assembly (every 2 years). Executive Committee, consisting of President, Past-President, International Vice-President, President Elect, Technical Vice-President, Vice-Presidents of Regions I, II, III and IV, Financial Vice-President, Development Vice-President, General Treasurer, Executive Director and General Secretary. Fiscal Council. Technical Committee. Consultative Council. **Languages** English, French, Portuguese, Spanish. **Staff** 2.00 FTE, paid; 23.00 FTE, voluntary. **Finance** Members' dues. Grant from PAHO. **Activities** National Sections develop national and regional programmes. Information and service to members, promotion of scientific interchanges, collaboration with national and international institutions in every matter related to sanitary engineering. **Events** *Biennial Congress* Tegucigalpa (Honduras) 2013, *Biennial Congress* Salvador (Brazil) 2012, *Biennial Congress* Punta Cana (Dominican Rep) 2010, *Biennial Congress* Santiago (Chile) 2008, *Biennial Congress* Punta del Este (Uruguay) 2006. **Publications** *Desafio* (4 a year) – newsletter; *A and S-Ambiente y Saneamiento* (2 a year) – magazine; *Ingenieria Sanitaria* (2 a year) – magazine; *Cuadernos Técnicos* – jointly with PAHO.
Members National; Collective or Individual; Collective or Individual Contributing; Founding; Honorary; Distinguished Membership. National sections in 24 countries:
Argentina, Bolivia, Brazil, Canada, Chile, Colombia, Costa Rica, Cuba, Dominican Rep, Ecuador, El Salvador, Guatemala, Haiti, Honduras, Mexico, Nicaragua, Panama, Paraguay, Peru, Puerto Rico, Trinidad-Tobago, Uruguay, USA, Venezuela.
IGO Relations Official relations with: *Pan American Health Organization (PAHO, #18108)*. Cooperation with: *OAS (#17629)*. **NGO Relations** Member of: *Global Water Operators' Partnerships Alliance (GWOPA, #10652)*; *World Water Council (WWC, #21908)*.
[2018/XD1049/**D**]

♦ Inter-American Association of Securities Commissions (inactive)
♦ Inter-American Association for Training in Tourism and Hotel Management (inactive)
♦ Inter-American Association of Translators (inactive)
♦ Inter-American Bank (inactive)

♦ Inter-American Bar Association (IABA) 11401

Fédération interaméricaine des avocats – Federación Interamericana de Abogados (FIA) – Federação Interamericana de Advogados

Pres 1889 F St NW, 3rd Floor, Ste 355, Washington DC 20006, USA. T. +12024665944. Fax +12024665946. E-mail: president@iaba.org – iaba@iaba.org.
URL: http://www.iaba.org/

History 16 May 1940, Washington DC (USA), at 8th American Scientific Congress, by representatives of 44 professional organizations distributed among 17 nations of the Western Hemisphere; 1st Congress, 1941, Havana (Cuba). Constitution amended, 1956, Dallas TX (USA), at 9th Conference, to provide for individuals as members. **Aims** Provide a permanent forum for exchange of professional views and information for lawyers to promote the rule of law and protect democratic institutions in the Americas; establish and maintain relations among national and local organizations of lawyers in the region; advance the science of jurisprudence, particularly the study of comparative law; promote uniformity of laws; promote the rule of law and the administration of justice, encouraging establishment and maintenance of independent judicial systems in all countries of the Americas; preserve and defend human rights and liberties; guarantee to the peoples of the hemisphere the free exercise of their civil and political rights under democratic principles; uphold the honour of the legal profession; encourage cordial intercourse and fellowship among lawyers of the Americas. **Structure** Council; Executive Committee; Sections (2); Permanent Committees (20). Affiliated organizations: *Inter-American Academy of Comparative Law (no recent information)*; *Inter-American Bar Foundation (see: #11401)*; *Inter-American Copyright Institute (ICI, #11421)*. **Languages** English, French, Portuguese, Spanish. **Staff** 4.00 FTE, paid. **Finance** Members' dues. **Activities** Events/meetings. **Events** *Annual Conference* Nassau (Bahamas) 2009, *Annual Conference* Lima (Peru) 2008, *Annual Conference* Mexico City (Mexico) 2007, *Seminar on challenges of environmental law in the new millenium* Lima (Peru) 2006, *Annual Conference* San Salvador (El Salvador) 2006. **Publications** *IABA Newsletter* (2-3 a year) in English, Spanish. Conference proceedings.
Members Individuals in 37 countries and territories:
Antigua-Barbuda, Argentina, Bahamas, Barbados, Belize, Bolivia, Brazil, Cayman Is, Chile, Colombia, Costa Rica, Ecuador, El Salvador, France, Germany, Guatemala, Guyana, Honduras, Hong Kong, India, Italy, Jamaica, Mexico, Panama, Paraguay, Peru, Puerto Rico, Spain, Suriname, Switzerland, Trinidad-Tobago, UK, Uruguay, USA, Venezuela, Virgin Is UK, Virgin Is USA.
National and constituent regional associations (51) in 24 countries and territories:
Argentina, Aruba, Bahamas, Bolivia, Brazil, Canada, Chile, Costa Rica, Cuba, Dominican Rep, Ecuador, El Salvador, Guatemala, Haiti, Honduras, Mexico, Nicaragua, Panama, Paraguay, Peru, Puerto Rico, Uruguay, USA, Venezuela.
Included in the above, 2 organizations listed in this Yearbook:
Customs and International Trade Bar Association (CITBA); *Phi Delta Phi International Legal Fraternity*.
Consultative Status Consultative status granted from: *OAS (#17629)*. **NGO Relations** Member of: *International Criminal Bar (ICB, #13107)*; *International Legal Assistance Consortium (ILAC, #14025)*. Instrumental in setting up *International Federation of Women Lawyers (FIDA, #13578)*.
[2020.03.04/XD1050/y/**D**]

♦ Inter-American Bar Foundation (see: #11401)
♦ Inter-American Bibliographical and Library Association (inactive)

♦ Inter-American Biodiversity Information Network (IABIN) 11402

Red Interamericana de Información sobre Biodiversidad – Rede Interamericana de Informação a Biodiversidad

Contact address not obtained. T. +5073170111. Fax +5073173799.
URL: http://www.oas.org/en/sedi/dsd/iabin/

History 1999, officially set up. Mandated in Initiative 31 of the 'Action Plan' prepared at the 'Summit of the Americas on Sustainable Development', Dec 1996, Santa Cruz (Bolivia). Previously also referred to as *Réseau d'information sur la biodiversité inter-américaine – Red de Información Interamericana sobre Diversidad Biológica – Rede de Informações Interamericana sobre a Biodiversidade*. **Aims** Promote compatible means of production, collection, organization, communication and exchange of biodiversity information relevant to the advancement of science, improvement of decision-making and support of education. **Structure** Council (meets annually), composed of Focal Points. Executive Committee. Technical Working Groups. **Finance** Funded through services rendered by participating countries. Additional project money received from: Brazilian Ministry of Environment; *'Organization of American States' – OAS (#17629)*; *United States Agency for International Development (USAID)*; United States Department of State; US Geological Survey. **Activities** Development of an invasive species information system; survey of New World holdings in European collections; harmonization of metadata initiatives; training. **Events** *Council Meeting* Panama 2005, *Meeting* Panama (Panama) 2005, *Joint Latin America and Caribbean regional meeting / Council Meeting* Cancún (Mexico) 2003, *Meeting* Cancún (Mexico) 2003, *Meeting* 2002. **Publications** Reports; technical and institutional issues.
Members Full in 34 countries:
Antigua-Barbuda, Argentina, Bahamas, Barbados, Belize, Bolivia, Brazil, Canada, Chile, Colombia, Costa Rica, Dominica, Dominican Rep, Ecuador, El Salvador, Grenada, Guatemala, Guyana, Haiti, Honduras, Jamaica, Mexico, Nicaragua, Panama, Paraguay, Peru, St Kitts-Nevis, St Lucia, St Vincent-Grenadines, Suriname, Trinidad-Tobago, Uruguay, USA, Venezuela.
IGO Relations Memorandum of Understanding with: *Global Biodiversity Information Facility (GBIF, #10250)*.
[2009/XF4945/**F**]

♦ Inter-American Board of Agriculture (see: #11434)
♦ Inter-American Broadcasters Association / see International Association of Broadcasting (#11738)
♦ Inter-American Capital Markets Institute (inactive)
♦ Inter-American Caribbean Union (inactive)

♦ Inter-American Catholic Education Association (ICCE) 11403

Confédération interaméricaine de l'enseignement catholique – Confederación Interamericana de Educación Católica (CIEC) – Confederação Interamericana de Educação Católica

SG Calle 78 No 12-16 – Ofc 101, Bogota, Bogota DC, Colombia. T. +5713003380. Fax +5713003380. E-mail: secretariageneral@ciec.edu.co – asistente@ciec.edu.co.
URL: http://www.ciec.edu.co/

History Founded 7 Jun 1945, Bogota, during 1st inter-American conference of catholic education. Statutes modified: 1957; 1958; 1970; 1975; 2005. Also referred to in English as *Inter-American Confederation of Catholic Education (IACCE)*. Registered in accordance with Colombian law, May 1946. **Aims** Defend the principles of Catholic education; promote the perfecting of teaching; contribute to improving the relations between the American peoples with the aim of reinforcing mutual understanding and peace; stimulate the creation and development of educational associations. **Structure** General Assembly (annual), consisting of Presidents of national federations. Council, consisting of representatives of 5 American countries. **Languages** English, Spanish. **Staff** 2.00 FTE, paid. **Finance** Members' dues. Donations. **Activities** Coordinates Catholic education in the Americas. Regional secretariat for the Americas of *Catholic International Education Office (#03604)* and permanent member of the latter's Council. Educative projet (general level and for each federation separately). Programme of education for peace. Organizes seminars and congresses. **Events** *Congress / Triennial Congress* Panama (Panama) 2013, *Congress / Triennial Congress* Santo Domingo (Dominican Rep) 2010, *Congress / Triennial Congress* Buenos Aires (Argentina) 2007, *Congress / Triennial Congress* Santiago (Chile) 2004, *Triennial Congress* Mexico City (Mexico) 2001. **Publications** *Revista Educación Hoy* (4 a year). *Perspectivas Latinoamericanas*. Collection of booklets and books in Spanish.
Members National federations in 23 countries:
Argentina, Bolivia, Brazil, Canada, Chile, Colombia, Costa Rica, Curaçao, Dominican Rep, Ecuador, El Salvador, Guatemala, Haiti, Honduras, Mexico, Nicaragua, Panama, Paraguay, Peru, Puerto Rico, Uruguay, USA, Venezuela.
Consultative Status Consultative status granted from: *OAS (#17629)*. **IGO Relations** *Organization of Ibero-American States for Education, Science and Culture (#17871)*.
[2013.10.31/XD5047/**D**]

♦ Inter-American Catholic Social Action Confederation (inactive)
♦ Inter-American Cement Federation (#09330)
♦ Inter-American Center for Crafts and Popular Arts (#03801)
♦ Inter-American Center for the Development of Archives (inactive)
♦ Inter-American Center for Development and Environmental and Territorial Research (internationally oriented national body)
♦ Inter-American Center of High Studies in Public Relations and Public Opinion (internationally oriented national body)
♦ Inter-American Center for the Integral Development of Water and Land Resources / see Centro Interamericano de Desarrollo e Investigación Ambiental y Territorial
♦ Inter-American Center for Research and Studies in Educational Planning (no recent information)
♦ Inter-American Center for Social Security Studies (#03803)
♦ Inter-American Centre for Conservation and Restoration of Books, Documents and Photographic Material (no recent information)
♦ Interamerican Centre for Cooperation and Capacity Building (internationally oriented national body)
♦ Inter-American Centre for Knowledge Development in Vocational Training (#03802)

♦ Inter-American Centre for Studies on Water Resources 11404

Centro Interamericano de Recursos del Agua (CIRA)

Coordinator Carretera Toluca Atlacomulco, Km 14-5, Unidad San Cayetano, CP 50200 Toluca MEX, Mexico. T. +52722965550 – +52722965551. E-mail: ciramex@uaemex.mx.
URL: http://cira.uaemex.mx/

History Apr 1989, Mexico City (Mexico), within the framework of *Inter-American Organization for Higher Education (IOHE, #11442)*, following series of annual workshops, since 1986, organized by Université Laval, Québec (Canada), in collaboration with Mexican universities and with the participation of experts and students from 15 Latin American countries. **Aims** Train experts in the field of water resource management with appropriate modern techniques, focusing especially on protection, preservation and recuperation of water resources. **Activities** Series of intensive 2-12 week courses for professors, postgraduate students and professionals; support for masters' degree and doctoral theses; assistance for multidisciplinary projects in the field of hydrology; support in setting up a computer centre interconnected with existing centres; support in creating a scientific library and diffusing research work. **Events** *International seminar* Havana (Cuba) 1998.
[2013.08.12/XE1438/**E**]

♦ Inter-American Centre for Tax Administrations 11405

Centre interaméricain des administrations fiscales – Centro Interamericano de Administraciones Tributarias (CIAT) – Centro Interamericano de Administrações Tributarias

Exec Sec Ava Ramon Arias, PO Box 0834-02129, Panama, Panamá, Panama PANAMá, Panama. T. +5072652766 – +5073072428 – +5072231044. Fax +5072644926. E-mail: ciat@ciat.org.

URL: http://www.ciat.org/
History Founded 1 May 1967, Panama, as *Inter-American Centre for Tax Administrators – Centre interaméricain des administrateurs fiscaux – Centro Interamericano de Administradores Tributarios – Centro Interamericano de Administradores Tributarios*, at the Constitutive General Assembly, when Bylaws were adopted. Bylaws partially amended at subsequent assemblies: 1970, Montevideo (Uruguay); 1972, Asunción (Paraguay); 1975, Ottawa (Canada); 1987, Ottawa; 1989, Montevideo; 1991, Washington DC (USA); 1993, Santiago (Chile); 1997, Buenos Aires (Argentina); 2000, Washington DC; 2001, Santiago; 2003, Cancún (Mexico); 2004, Cochabamba (Bolivia); 2005 Buenos Aires. Registered in accordance with the law of Panama, 30 Jan 1969. **Aims** Promote an environment of mutual cooperation; provide a forum for the exchange of experiences among its members, assisting them in improving their tax administrations based upon their needs. **Structure** General Assembly (annual); Executive Council; Executive Secretariat; national representatives (directors of tax administrations); Body of Correspondents. **Languages** English, French, Portuguese, Spanish. **Staff** 38.00 FTE, paid. **Finance** Members' dues, determined according to GNP. Other sources: fees for technical cooperation services; funding from associate member countries and international organizations maintaining agreements with CIAT. **Activities** Main programs: *'International Meetings'* – organizes: General Assembly; technical conferences; seminars; working groups; annual courses on tax institutions and techniques, on customs for Latin American countries and on tax management and administration (for countries of the Caribbean). *'Tax Studies'* – annual essay contest (sponsored by Institute of Fiscal Studies, Spain); research works. *'Technical Cooperation'* – specific technical cooperation projects in tax administrations, supported by IDB, World Bank and IMF and with assistance from tax administrations of associate members; apprenticeship programme for officials from one country to gain experience of tax administration in another country. *'Internal Administration'* – including finance and staff management. *'Training – CIAT Courses'*. *'Taxation Program'* – training program for Spanish-speaking officials. Online shop. Instrumental in setting up: *Council of Executive Secretaries of Tax Organizations (CESTO, inactive)*. **Events** *International Tax Dialogue Global Conference* Paris (France) 2015, *General Assembly* Rio de Janeiro (Brazil) 2014, *General Assembly* Buenos Aires (Argentina) 2013, *Technical Conference* Amsterdam (Netherlands) 2012, *General Assembly* Santiago (Chile) 2012. **Publications** *CIAT Newsletter*; *My CIAT Executive Newsletter*; *Tax Administration Review CIAT/AEAT/IEF*. *CIAT Thematic Tax Series*. *CIAT Internal Audit Manual*; *CIAT Model Code of Conduct*; *CIAT Model Tax Code*; *CIAT Thematic Tax Bibliographic*; *Examinations Handbook*; *Handbook for Tax Administrations*; *Human Resources Handbook*; *Manual CIAT on Tax Intelligence*. Proceedings of general assemblies and technical conferences. Information Services: Maintains an online specialized library. **Information Services** *CIAT Taxation Data Base*; *Information and Enquiries*.
Members Tax administrations, generally represented by their respective Tax Directors. Members in 34 countries and territories:
Argentina, Aruba, Barbados, Bermuda, Bolivia, Brazil, Canada, Chile, Colombia, Costa Rica, Cuba, Dominican Rep, Ecuador, El Salvador, France, Guatemala, Haiti, Honduras, Italy, Jamaica, Mexico, Netherlands, Nicaragua, Panama, Paraguay, Peru, Portugal, Spain, Suriname, Trinidad-Tobago, Uruguay, USA, Venezuela.
Associate members in 4 countries:
Czechia, India, Kenya, South Africa.
IGO Relations Observer with: *Global Forum on Transparency and Exchange of Information for Tax Purposes (#10379)*. [2014/XE1698/**D**]

♦ Inter-American Centre for Tax Administrators / see Inter-American Centre for Tax Administrations (#11405)
♦ Inter-American Chamber of Shipping Agent National Associations (#03400)

♦ Inter-American Children's Institute (IACI) 11406

Institut interaméricain de l'enfant – Instituto Interamericano del Niño, la Niña y Adolescentes (IIN) – Instituto Interamericano da Criança

Dir Gen Av 8 de Octubre 2904, PO Box 16212, 11600 Montevideo, Uruguay. T. +59824872150. E-mail: direcciongral@iinoea.org – comunicacion@iinoea.org.
URL: http://www.iin.oea.org/

History 9 Jun 1927, as *American International Institute for the Protection of Childhood – Instituto Internacional Americano de Protección a la Infancia*, in accordance with resolution of 4th Pan-American Child Congress, 1924. Current title adopted, 1957. In Spanish previously also known as *Instituto Interamericano del Niño*. Statutes modified: 1946; 1949; 1955; 1957; 1962; 1977; 1988. Statutes most recently amended in 1998. Recognized as a specialized agency of *OAS (#17629)*, 1949, on signature of an agreement by IACI Directing Council and the Council of OAS; new agreement concluded between OAS and IACI, 1975, sets out the legal basis of the Institute and its relations with OAS and with the other Inter-American specialized organizations. **Aims** Stimulate and promote the development of an alert awareness of all problems related to children, *adolescents*, *motherhood*, the *family* and the community of the *Americas*; awaken or increase a sense of social *responsibility* towards these problems; channel this sense of responsibility into carrying out activities to solve such problems. **Structure** Pan-American Child Congress (every 4 years). Directing Council (meets at least once a year), consisting of one representative from each OAS member country. Central Office, headed by Director-General. **Languages** English, French, Portuguese, Spanish. **Staff** 24.00 FTE, paid. **Finance** OAS regular funds; special funds. **Events** *Meeting* Mexico City (Mexico) 2004, *Pan-American child congress* Mexico City (Mexico) 2004, *Meeting* Santiago (Chile) 2003, *Meeting / Directing Council Meeting* Canada 2000, *Pan American Child Congress / Directing Council Meeting* Buenos Aires (Argentina) 1999. **Publications** *Bibliographical Journal on Children and Family* (2 a year); *IIN Boletin* (2 a year). Information Services: *Programa Interamericano de Información sobre Niñez y Familia (PIINFA)* – comprises 8 projects, including *'Proyecto de Información Documental (PID)'*. **Information Services** *Centro de Información Computerizada (CIC)* – implements PIINFA's 'Proyecto de Información Documental (PID)'; *Inter-American Child Information Network (RIIN)* – links 16 countries through a network of 56 information centers and is also referred to as Children's Information Network of the Americas; *Inter-American Disability Data System (SINDI)*; *Proyecto de Información Documental (PID)*.
Members Governments of the 35 OAS member countries (" – the Government of Cuba has been suspended from participation in the Inter-American System since 1962):
Antigua-Barbuda, Argentina, Bahamas, Barbados, Belize, Bolivia, Brazil, Canada, Chile, Colombia, Costa Rica, Cuba (*), Dominica, Dominican Rep, Ecuador, El Salvador, Grenada, Guatemala, Guyana, Haiti, Honduras, Jamaica, Mexico, Nicaragua, Panama, Paraguay, Peru, St Kitts-Nevis, St Lucia, St Vincent-Grenadines, Suriname, Trinidad-Tobago, Uruguay, USA, Venezuela.
Permanent Observers (45 countries):
Algeria, Angola, Austria, Belgium, Bosnia-Herzegovina, Bulgaria, Croatia, Cyprus, Czechia, Egypt, Equatorial Guinea, Finland, France, Germany, Ghana, Greece, Holy See, Hungary, India, Israel, Italy, Japan, Kazakhstan, Korea Rep, Latvia, Lebanon, Morocco, Netherlands, Pakistan, Philippines, Poland, Portugal, Romania, Russia, Saudi Arabia, Spain, Sri Lanka, Sweden, Switzerland, Thailand, Tunisia, Türkiye, UK, Ukraine, Yemen.
International Permanent Observer (1):
European Union (EU, #08967).
IGO Relations Among others, links with: *Comisión Interamericana de Mujeres (CIM, #04137)*; *The Hague Conference on Private International Law (HCCH, #10850)*; *Instituto Latinoamericano de las Naciones Unidas para la Prevención del Delito y Tratamiento del Delincuente (ILANUD, #11347)*; *Inter-American Commission on Human Rights (IACHR, #11411)*; *Inter-American Council for Integral Development (#11423)*; *Inter-American Drug Abuse Control Commission (#11429)*; *Inter-American Indian Institute (IAII, inactive)*; *Inter-American Institute for Cooperation on Agriculture (IICA, #11434)*; *International Development Research Centre (IDRC, #13162)*; *Pan American Health Organization (PAHO, #18108)*; *UNESCO (#20322)*; *UNICEF (#20332)*.
NGO Relations Member of: *Childwatch International Research Network (#03887)*; *End Corporal Punishment (#05457)*; *Ibero-American Group on Communication and Disability (no recent information)*; *Movimiento Mundial por la Infancia de Latinoamérica y El Caribe (MMI-LAC, #16873)*. Links with a number of national organizations and the following international bodies:
- *Centro para la Investigación y el Desarrollo Económico y Social de Amazonas (CIDESAM, no recent information)*;
- *Defence for Children International (DCI, #05025)*;
- *Fundación de Estudios e Investigaciones Latinoamericanas (FEILAT, no recent information)*;
- *Instituto Interamericano de Derechos Humanos (IIDH, #11334)*;
- *International Catholic Child Bureau (#12450)*;
- *International Play Association (IPA, #14604)*;
- *International Social Service (ISS, #14886)*;
- *International Union of Notaries (#15795)*;
- *Latin American Association for Human Rights (#16243)*;
- *Rädda Barnen – Save the Children Sweden*;
- *World Family Organization (WFO, #21399)*. [2018/XE1054/j/**E***]

♦ Inter-American Citrus Network (IACNET) 11407

Red Interamericana de Citricos (RIAC)

Coordinator INCA, Carretera a Tapaste km 3-5, San José de las Lajas, Havana, Cuba. Fax +53478835086. E-mail: mcperez@inca.edu.cu – riac@iift.cu – horacio@imporvg.cu.
URL: http://www.riacnet.net/

History Established 18 Apr 1991, Santiago (Chile), resulting from a joint effort of *FAO Regional Office for Latin America and the Caribbean (FAO/RLC, #09268)* and Plant Production and Protection Division and Commodities and Trade Division of *FAO (#09260)*, developed within the framework of the *Intergovernmental Group on Citrus Fruit (#11487)*. Originated from a proposal made by FAO at 8th Session of the Intergovernmental Group, Sep 1989, Montevideo (Uruguay). Also referred to as: *Technical Cooperation Network on Citrus Production, Improvement and Trade Development in Latin America and the Caribbean*; *Inter-American Network on Citrus Production Improvement and Trade Development*; *Intergovernmental Network on the Improvement of Production and Development of Trade of Citrus Fruit*. **Aims** Promote technical and economic cooperation actions among the citrus growing countries of the American continent. **Structure** Coordinators (3); Working Groups (6). **Languages** English, Spanish. **Staff** 37.00 FTE, voluntary. **Finance** Eventual financing from *FAO (#09260)*. Projects may be financed by *Common Fund for Commodities (CFC, #04293)*. National institutions frequently contribute with specific activities organized by IACNET in their countries. **Activities** Events/meetings; certification/accreditation; research/documentation; guidance/assistance/consulting; knowledge management/information dissemination; monitoring/evaluation. **Events** *International workshop on postharvest technologies* Havana (Cuba) 2000, *Regional workshop on citrus bioclimatology* Havana (Cuba) 2000. **Publications** *Inter-American Citrus Network Newsletter* (3 a year); *Citrus in the Americas* – journal.
Members Institutions and farmers organizations in 28 countries:
Antigua-Barbuda, Argentina, Bahamas, Belize, Brazil, Chile, Colombia, Costa Rica, Cuba, Dominican Rep, Ecuador, El Salvador, French Antilles, Guatemala, Guyana, Haiti, Honduras, Jamaica, Mexico, Nicaragua, Panama, Paraguay, Peru, Suriname, Trinidad-Tobago, Uruguay, USA, Venezuela.
IGO Relations Cooperative with: *Caribbean Agricultural Science and Technology Networking System (PROCICARIBE, no recent information)*; *Technical Cooperation Network on Agricultural Biotechnology in Latin America and the Caribbean (no recent information)*. [2017.02.01/XF1457/**F***]

♦ Inter-American Coffee Agreement (1940 treaty)
♦ Inter-American Coffee Board (inactive)

♦ Inter-American College of Physicians and Surgeons (ICPS) 11408

Collège interaméricain de médecins et de chirurgiens – Colegio Interamericano de Médicos y Cirujanos

Address not obtained.
URL: http://www.icps.org/

History 1979. **Events** *Hispanic medical congress* San Antonio, TX (USA) 1995. **Publications** *Médico Interamericano* (12 a year); *Inter-American Medical Directory* (every 2 years). **Members** Physicians and surgeons in the Americas. Membership countries not specified. **NGO Relations** *Pan American Development Foundation (PADF, #18094)*. [2009/XF0154/**F**]

♦ Inter-American College of Radiology (IACR) 11409

Colegio Interamericano de Radiologia (CIR)

Exec Dir Barranca del Muerto 520 Col Alpes, CP 01010 Mexico City CDMX, Mexico. E-mail: cir.admin@servimed.com.mx.
URL: http://www.webcir.org/

History 1943, Buenos Aires (Argentina). Registered in accordance with Mexican law. **Aims** Associate radiologists of the American continent, Spain and Portugal through their respective national societies; guard and protect radiology standards and ethics in their respective countries; encourage and assist in the formation of national societies of diagnostic radiology in countries presently lacking such societies. **Structure** Council. **Languages** English, Portuguese, Spanish. **Activities** Networking/liaising; publishing activities; events/meetings. **Events** *Biennial Congress* Punta Cana (Dominican Rep) 2018, *Biennial Congress* Lima (Peru) 2016, *Biennial Congress* Cartagena de Indias (Colombia) 2014, *Biennial Congress* El Salvador 2012, *Biennial Congress* Santiago (Chile) 2010. **Publications** *NOTiCIR* (12 a year) – newsletter; *Organo Informativo Mensual del Colegio Interamericano de Radiologia* (12 a year) in Spanish – with English and Portuguese summaries.
Members National Societies; Individuals. Members in 25 countries:
Argentina, Belize, Bolivia, Brazil, Canada, Chile, Colombia, Costa Rica, Cuba, Dominican Rep, Ecuador, El Salvador, Guatemala, Honduras, Mexico, Nicaragua, Panama, Paraguay, Peru, Portugal, Puerto Rico, Spain, Uruguay, USA, Venezuela.
Consultative Status Consultative status granted from: *OAS (#17629)*. **IGO Relations** Official relations with: *Pan American Health Organization (PAHO, #18108)*. **NGO Relations** *International Commission on Radiation Units and Measurements (ICRU, #12722)*; *International Society of Radiology (ISR, #15412)*; *Latin American Federation of Societies of Ultrasound in Medicine and Biology (#16333)*; *Sociedad Iberoamericana de Imagen Mamaria (SIBIM, #19371)*. [2019.02.11/XF5008/**F**]

♦ Inter-American Commercial Arbitration Commission (IACAC) 11410

Commission interaméricaine d'arbitrage commercial – Comisión Interamericana de Arbitraje Comercial – Comissão Interamericana de Arbitragem Comercial

Address not obtained.
URL: http://www.ciac-iacac.org/

History 25 Apr 1934, Montevideo (Uruguay), by *'American Arbitration Association'* and *'Council of Inter-American Relations'*, following Resolution XLI of the 7th International Conference of American States, Dec 1933, Montevideo. Rules of Procedure last amended I Nov 1996. **Aims** Establish, maintain and administer throughout the Western Hemisphere a system for *settlement*, by arbitration or *conciliation*, of international *commercial disputes*. **Structure** Commission (meets at least every 2 years), consisting of a Delegate and an Alternate Delegate from each National Section. Executive Committee, consisting of President, Vice President, Director General, Secretary, Assistant Director General, Treasurer and other members. National Sections or Representatives in almost all countries in the Western Hemisphere; where none as yet exists, the Commission performs all activities that would otherwise be performed by a National Section. **Languages** English, French, Portuguese, Spanish. **Finance** Case fees; contributions from National Sections, organizations and institutions. **Activities** More than 2,000 cases have been solved by adjustment or by arbitration awards. Coordinates activities of National Sections; working in cooperation with National Sections, provides service to parties who request conciliation or arbitration in accordance with the rules of the Commission; serves as an appointing authority for arbitrators; authorizes establishment of commercial arbitration tribunals; arranges for the conduct of arbitrations; recommends enactment or amendment of arbitration laws. Promulgation, at termination of 1st Specialized Inter-American Conference on Private International Law, 30 Jan 1975, Panama, of *Inter-American Convention on International Commercial Arbitration (1975)*, establishing a legal framework in the Western Hemisphere for effective recognition and enforcement of arbitral clauses and awards. The Convention has been ratified by: Argentina, Brazil, Chile, Colombia, Costa Rica, Ecuador, El Salvador, Guatemala (Guatemala), Honduras, Mexico, Panama, Paraguay, Peru, USA, Uruguay and Venezuela. Assisted in setting up of *Institute for Transnational Arbitration (ITA)*. **Events** *Conferencia* Tegucigalpa (Honduras) 2009, *Conference* Santo Domingo (Dominican Rep) 2006, *Conference* Santiago (Chile) 2003, *Conference* Seville (Spain) 2003, *Conference* Guadalajara (Mexico) 2002. **Publications** *IACAC Newsletter* (4 a year). *IACAC Rules of Procedure*.
Members National sections in 18 countries:
Argentina, Bolivia, Brazil, Canada, Chile, Colombia, Costa Rica, Dominican Rep, Ecuador, Guatemala, Mexico, Panama, Paraguay, Peru, Spain, Uruguay, USA, Venezuela.
IGO Relations Provides from time to time reports to: *OAS (#17629)*. **NGO Relations** *International Federation of Commercial Arbitration Institutions (IFCAI)*. [2013/XE1056/**E**]

♦ Inter-American Commission on Education (#04136)

♦ Inter-American Commission on Human Rights (IACHR) 11411

Commission interaméricaine des droits de l'homme – Comisión Interamericana de Derechos Humanos (CIDH) – Comissão Interamericana de Direitos Humanos

Pres c/o OAS, 1889 F St NW, Washington DC 20006, USA. T. +12023709000. Fax +12024583992 – +12024586215. E-mail: cidhdenuncias@oas.org.
URL: http://www.cidh.oas.org/

History Established 8 Aug 1959, Santiago (Chile), at 5th Meeting of Consultation of Ministers of Foreign Affairs, to carry out provisions of the *American Declaration of the Rights and Duties of Man*, signed 1948, Bogota. Statute approved 25 May 1960, by *OAS (#17629)*; amended 1965, Rio de Janeiro (Brazil). New Statute approved by OAS General Assembly, Oct 1979, following coming into effect of *Inter-American Convention on Human Rights (Pact of San José de Costa Rica, 1969)*, 18 Jul 1978. New regulations: adopted Apr 1980; modified 29 Jun 1987. *Inter-American Declaration of Principles on Freedom of Expression* approved at 108th regular session, Oct 2000. **Aims** Promote observance and protection of human rights in the Americas; serve as a consultative body to the OAS in these matters. **Structure** Comprises 7 members, elected in their individual capacity by the General Assembly of the OAS and representing all OAS member states. Board, comprising President, First Vice-President and Second Vice-President. **Languages** English, French, Portuguese, Spanish. **Finance** Contributions of member states (budget of OAS); contributions from other entities. Annual budget: US$ 9 million. **Activities** The American Convention on Human Rights, currently ratified by 25 OAS member states: sets forth the structure, competence and procedure of the Commission; establishes the obligations of states party to the Convention to respect the rights and freedoms recognized in the Convention and to adopt internal measures to give them effect. The Commission exercises jurisdiction over the remaining member states through OAS Charter and its prior practice and applies the American Declaration of the Rights and Duties of Man. It: investigates complaints of individuals and institutions alleging violations of human rights in OAS member countries; prepares studies and reports and distributes them to interested bodies; organizes lectures, seminars and exchange of information to promote interest in the study of human rights at academic and professional levels. Current concerns: codification and progressive development of international human rights law in the Inter-American system; human rights of indigenous groups; human rights, political rights and representative democracy in the Inter-American system. **Events** *Regular Session* 2019, *Regular Session* 2019, *Regular Session* Cochabamba (Bolivia) 2019, *Regular Session* Ecuador 2019, *Regular Session* Washington, DC (USA) 2018. **Publications** *Inter-American Yearbook on Human Rights*. Annual report; reports on the situation of human rights in member states. Library specializing in Human Rights Law (8,000 volumes). **Members** Commission comprises 7 members. States having ratified the Convention, currently 25 (not specified). **IGO Relations** Close cooperation with: *Corte Interamericana de Derechos Humanos (Corte IDH, #04851)*. **NGO Relations** Supports: *Instituto Interamericano de Derechos Humanos (IIDH, #11334)*. Informal contacts with: *International Institute of Humanitarian Law (IIHL, #13885)*. Member of *Inter-Agency Consultation on Race in Latin America (IAC, no recent information)*. Cooperates with: *Asociación Interamericana de Defensorias Públicas (AIDEF, #02159)*. [2017.07.18/XE7981/E*]

♦ Inter-American Commission for Territorial Administration (inactive)
♦ Inter-American Commission of Women (#04137)

♦ Inter-American Committee Against Terrorism 11412

Comité Interamericano Contra el Terrorismo (CICTE)

Exec Sec c/o OAS, 1889 F St NW, GSB-120 A, Washington DC 20006, USA. T. +12024584973. Fax +12024583857.
URL: http://www.cicte.oas.org/

History Jun 1999, Guatemala (Guatemala), within the framework of *OAS (#17629)*, at regular session of OAS General Assembly. Set up following adoption of an anti-terrorism action plan by OAS member countries at 1st *Inter-American Specialized Conference on Terrorism*, 1996, Lima (Peru), and creation of the Committee framework at follow-up conference, Nov 1998, Mar del Plata (Argentina). First meeting: Oct 1999. **Aims** Allow the region's governments to: share expertise and information on the activities of individuals, groups and movements linked to international terrorism; cooperate in tracking their methods of operation and sources of financing; to develop anti-terrorism training programs. **Structure** Committee (meets at least annually). **Events** *Preventing Violent Extremism – Good Practices for Engaging Youth through Sports Programs* 2020, *Workshop on Port Cooperation and Maritime Security* Belize City (Belize) 2017, *Workshop on Advanced Port Security Drills and Exercises* Lima (Peru) 2015, *Session* Montevideo (Uruguay) 2004, *Counter-terrorism convention implementation seminar* Nassau (Bahamas) 2004. **IGO Relations** Observer status: *Financial Action Task Force (FATF, #09765)*. [2016/XK2187/E*]

♦ Inter-American Committee on Avian Health (#04170)
♦ Inter-American Committee for Crop Protection (inactive)
♦ Inter-American Committee for the Dairy Industries (inactive)

♦ Inter-American Committee of Mathematics Education (IACME) 11413

Comité interaméricain d'éducation mathématique – Comité Interamericano de Educación Matematica (CIAEM) – Comitê Inter-Americano de Educação Matematica

Pres Paseo de la Reforma 383, 7o Piso, Colonia Cuauhtémoc, Delegació Cuauhtémoc, 06500 Mexico City CDMX, Mexico. E-mail: ciaem.iacme@gmail.com.
URL: http://www.ciaem-iacme.org/

History 1961, Bogota (Colombia). **Aims** Promote teaching and learning of mathematics in the Americas. **Structure** General Assembly; Advisory Council; Executive Committee; National Representatives. **Languages** English, French, Portuguese, Spanish. **Staff** None paid. **Finance** Sources: donations; meeting proceeds. **Activities** Awards/prizes/competitions; awareness raising; events/meetings; networking/liaising; publishing activities. **Events** *Inter-American Conference on Mathematics Education* Lima (Peru) 2023, *Inter-American Conference on Mathematics Education* Medellin (Colombia) 2019, *Inter-American Conference on Mathematics Education* Tuxtla Gutiérrez (Mexico) 2015, *Inter-American Conference on Mathematics Education* Recife (Brazil) 2011, *Inter-American Conference on Mathematics Education* Santiago de Querétaro (Mexico) 2007. **Publications** Conference proceedings.
Members Full in 28 countries and territories:
Argentina, Bolivia, Brazil, Canada, Chile, Colombia, Costa Rica, Cuba, Dominican Rep, Ecuador, El Salvador, France, Guatemala, Haiti, Honduras, Jamaica, Mexico, Nicaragua, Panama, Paraguay, Peru, Portugal, Puerto Rico, Spain, Suriname, Uruguay, USA, Venezuela.
NGO Relations Regional affiliate of: *International Commission on Mathematical Instruction (ICMI, #12700)*. [2022.05.04/XF0815/E]

♦ Inter-American Committee on Natural Disaster Reduction (IACNDR) 11414

Comité Interamericano para la Reducción de Desastres Naturales

Contact c/o OAS, 1889 F St NW, Washington DC , 20006, USA. T. +12024583000.

History 1999, by *OAS (#17629)*. **Aims** Promote dialogue, reflection and the development of priorities and policy proposals regarding sustainable disaster management and reduction among member states of the Organization of American States. **Activities** Working Groups (3): Emergency Preparedness and Response; Financing and Natural Disaster Reduction; Vulnerability Assessment and Indexing. **IGO Relations** Organizations involved: *Inter-American Council for Integral Development (#11423)*; *Inter-American Development Bank (IDB, #11427)*; *Inter-American Institute for Cooperation on Agriculture (IICA, #11434)*; *Pan American Health Organization (PAHO, #18108)*; *Pan American Institute of Geography and History (PAIGH, #18113)*. [2014/XE4660/E*]

♦ Inter-American Committee on Peaceful Settlement (inactive)

♦ Inter-American Committee on Ports 11415

Comisión Interamericana de Puertos (CIP)

Exec Sec 1889 F St NW, Suite 695, Washington DC 20006, USA. T. +12024586286. Fax +12024583571. E-mail: cip@oas.org.
URL: http://www.portalcip.org/

History 1956, by *OAS (#17629)*, as *Inter-American Port Conference*. Transformed into a permanent forum of OAS by General Assembly, under current title, 1998. **Aims** Bring together the National Port Authorities of all OAS Member States to facilitate competitive, sustainable, secure and inclusive port development in collaboration with the private sector. **Structure** Executive Board (CECIP); Technical Advisory Groups (TAGs) (6); Secretariat. **Languages** English, French, Portuguese, Spanish. **Staff** 4.00 FTE, paid. **Events** *Biennial Meeting* Washington, DC (USA) 2014, *Biennial Meeting* Cartagena de Indias (Colombia) 2013, *Biennial Meeting* Lima (Peru) 2012, *Biennial meeting / Meeting* Panama (Panama) 2010, *Conference on coasts, marine structures and breakwaters* Edinburgh (UK) 2009. **Publications** *CIP Magazine*; *Inter-American Committee on Ports Newsletter Highlights*.
Members Port authorities of 34 countries:
Antigua-Barbuda, Argentina, Bahamas, Barbados, Belize, Bolivia, Brazil, Canada, Chile, Colombia, Costa Rica, Dominica, Dominican Rep, Ecuador, El Salvador, Grenada, Guatemala, Guyana, Haiti, Honduras, Jamaica, Mexico, Nicaragua, Panama, Paraguay, Peru, St Kitts-Nevis, St Lucia, St Vincent-Grenadines, Suriname, Trinidad-Tobago, Uruguay, USA, Venezuela. [2019.02.12/XE3917/E*]

♦ Inter-American Committee on Social Development (#04135)
♦ Inter-American Committee of Societies for Electron Microscopy – Comité Interamericano das Sociedades de Microscopia (#04171)

♦ Inter-American Competitiveness Network 11416

Red Interamericana de Competitividad (RIAC)

Contact address not obtained. E-mail: riac@oas.org.
URL: http://riacnet.org/

History 29 Sep 2009, Santiago (Chile). **Structure** Steering Committee. **Events** *Annual Americas Competitiveness Forum* Mexico 2016, *Annual Americas Competitiveness Forum / Annual Meeting Americas Competitiveness Forum* Guatemala (Guatemala) 2015, *Annual Americas Competitiveness Forum / Annual Meeting Americas Competitiveness Forum* Port-of-Spain (Trinidad-Tobago) 2014, *Annual Americas Competitiveness Forum / Annual Meeting Americas Competitiveness Forum* Panama (Panama) 2013, *Annual Americas Competitiveness Forum / Annual Meeting Americas Competitiveness Forum* Cali (Colombia) 2012.
Members Countries – public, private and/or public-private institutions responsible for promoting competitiveness; Supporting institutions – multilateral/academic institutions; Partners. Country members (34):
Antigua-Barbuda, Argentina, Bahamas, Barbados, Belize, Bolivia, Brazil, Canada, Chile, Colombia, Costa Rica, Dominica, Dominican Rep, Ecuador, El Salvador, Grenada, Guatemala, Guyana, Haiti, Honduras, Jamaica, Mexico, Nicaragua, Panama, Paraguay, Peru, St Kitts-Nevis, St Lucia, St Vincent-Grenadines, Suriname, Trinidad-Tobago, Uruguay, USA, Venezuela.
Supporting institutions (10):
Central American Bank for Economic Integration (CABEI, #03658); *Compete Caribbean (#04415)*; *Development Bank of Latin America (CAF, #05055)*; *Global Federation of Competitiveness Councils (GFCC, #10355)*; *Inter-American Development Bank (IDB, #11427)*; Monterrey Institute of Technology and Higher Education; *OAS (#17629)*; *Secretaría Permanente del Tratado General de Integración Económica Centroamericana (SIECA, #19195)*; *United Nations Economic Commission for Latin America and the Caribbean (ECLAC, #20556)*; *United Nations Institute for Training and Research (UNITAR, #20576)* (CIFAL Global Network).
Partners in 6 countries:
Argentina, Colombia, Guatemala, Peru, Spain, Uruguay. [2015/XJ9106/F]

♦ Inter-American Confederation of Catholic Education / see Inter-American Catholic Education Association (#11403)
♦ Inter-American Confederation of Cattlemen (no recent information)

♦ Inter-American Confederation of Chemical Engineering (IACChE) .. 11417

Confédération Interaméricaine de Génie Chimique – Confederación Interamericana de Ingenieria Quimica (CIIQ) – Confederação Interamericana de Engenharia Quimica

Pres c/o CSCHE-CIC, 222 Queen St, Suite 400, Ottawa ON K1P 5V9, Canada.
SG address not obtained.
URL: http://www.ciiq.org/

History 1961, Puerto Rico. **Events** *Interamerican Congress of Chemical Engineering* Buenos Aires (Argentina) 2023, *Interamerican Congress of Chemical Engineering* Buenos Aires (Argentina) 2022, *Interamerican Congress of Chemical Engineering* Buenos Aires (Argentina) 2021, *Interamerican Congress of Chemical Engineering* Toronto, ON (Canada) 2018, *Interamerican Congress of Chemical Engineering* Cusco (Peru) 2016.
Members In 18 countries and territories:
Argentina, Bolivia, Brazil, Canada, Chile, Colombia, Dominican Rep, Ecuador, El Salvador, Guatemala, Mexico, Nicaragua, Panama, Peru, Puerto Rico, Uruguay, USA, Venezuela.
NGO Relations Member of: *World Chemical Engineering Council (WCEC, #21271)*. [2021/XD5226/D]

♦ Inter-American Confederation for Continental Defense against Communism (inactive)

♦ Inter-American Confederation of Public Relations 11418

Confédération interaméricaine de relations publiques – Confederación Interamericana de Relaciones Públicas (CONFIARP) – Confederação Interamericana de Relações Públicas

SG Avenida Sur 3, Esquina de Pinto, Edificio IUDERP, Santa Rosalia, Caracas 1010 DF, Venezuela.
Pres address not obtained.

History 27 Sep 1961, Caracas (Venezuela). 27-30 Sep 1961, Caracas (Venezuela), as *Inter-American Federation of Public Relations Associations (IFPRA) – Fédération interaméricaine des associations de relations publiques – Federación Interamericana de Asociaciones de Relaciones Públicas (FIARP) – Federação Interamericana de Associações de Relações Públicas*, during 2nd Inter-American Public Relations Conference, first steps having been taken 26 Sep 1960, Mexico City (Mexico). Statutes revised 22 Sep 1974. *Confederação Interamericana de Relações Públicas (CONFIARP, #04436)*, is a group of 5 member countries that separated and has been operating under the same name since 2003. **Aims** Seek to standardize public relations practices, ethics and standards; serve as an instrument for the exchange of ideas and the advancement of harmony, mutual respect and collaboration among the peoples of the Western Hemisphere. **Structure** Board of Directors (meeting annually); Board of Counsellors; Inter-American Congress (every 2 years). **Languages** Portuguese, Spanish. **Finance** Members' dues. **Events** *Forum* Montevideo (Uruguay) 2013, *Biennial Congress* Acapulco (Mexico) 2012, *Forum* Ecuador 2006, *Congress* Caracas (Venezuela) 2005, *Forum* San Juan (Puerto Rico) 2003. **Publications** *Revista FIARP*.
Members National associations in 8 countries:
Brazil, Chile, Colombia, Costa Rica, Cuba, Puerto Rico, Uruguay, Venezuela.
Consultative Status Consultative status granted from: *OAS (#17629)*. **NGO Relations** Instrumental in setting up: *Inter-American Center of High Studies in Public Relations and Public Opinion (CIESURP)*. [2013/XD1075/D]

♦ Interamerican Confederation of Public Relations (#04436)
♦ Inter-American Conference of Ministers of Labor (no recent information)
♦ Inter-American Conference on Plant Health (inactive)

♦ Inter-American Conference on Social Security (ICSS) 11419

Conferencia Interamericana de Seguridad Social (CISS)

SG San Ramón s/n., Colonia San Jerónimo Lídice, Alcaldía Magdalena Contreras, 10100 Mexico City CDMX, Mexico. T. +525553774700. E-mail: secretaria.general@ciss-bienestar.org – ciss@ciss-bienestar.org.
URL: https://ciss-bienestar.org/

History 16 Sep 1942, Santiago (Chile). Founded following the work of *Comité Interamericano de Iniciativas en Materia de Seguridad Social – Inter-American Committee for Initiatives in Matters of Social Security*, set up 10-12 Dec 1940, Lima (Peru). Present Statute approved at 1st General Extraordinary Assembly, 1988, Mexico City (Mexico); bylaws also include modifications approved by 16th General Assembly, 1992, Acapulco (Mexico). Former names and other names: *Conferência Interamericana de Seguridade Social (CESI)* – former; *Conférence interaméricaine de sécurité sociale (CISS)* – former. **Aims** Contribute to social security development in countries of America; cooperate with social security institutions and administrations; issue statements, pass resolutions and make recommendations regarding social security and promote their diffusion so they can be included in policies and planning programs; encourage cooperation and exchange of experience among social security institutions and administrations, and with institutions and organizations of a similar nature; encourage and guide human resources training in the field. **Structure** General Assembly. *Comité Permanente Interamericano de Seguridad Social (CPISS, see: #11419)* (executive and governing body). Secretariat General. *'American Commissions of Social Security (CASS)'* (6): 1. American Actuary and Finance Commission (CAAF); 2. American Commission for Older Adults (CADAM); 3. American Legal Social Commission (CAJS); 4. American Medical Social Commission (CAMS); 5. American Commission on Organization and Administrative Systems (CAOSA); 6. American Working Risk Prevention Commission (CAPRT). Sub-regions: I – Andean; II – Central America; III – South Cone; IV – North America and the English Speaking Caribbean; V – Mexico and the Latin Caribbean. *Centro Interamericano de Estudios de Seguridad Social (CIESS, #03803)*. **Languages** English, Spanish. **Staff** 46.00 FTE, paid. **Finance** Sources: members' dues. **Activities** Events/meetings. Organizes: annual assembly; annual meetings; international technical meetings; regional

seminars. **Events** *Annual General Assembly* San Salvador (El Salvador) 2013, *Internatinal conference on social determinants of health* Mexico City (Mexico) 2011, *Annual General Assembly* Panama (Panama) 2010, *Annual General Assembly* Guatemala (Guatemala) 2009, *Annual General Assembly* Salvador (Brazil) 2008. **Publications** *Well-Being and Social Policy Magazine* (6 a year) in English, Spanish; *Americas Social Security Report* (annual) in English, Portuguese, Spanish; *Bulletin of the Sub-Region V – Mexico and the Latin Caribbean* in Spanish; *Revista CIESS* in English, Spanish. Study series; monograph series; working papers.
Members Health care and social security institutions (83) in 35 countries and territories:
Anguilla, Antigua-Barbuda, Argentina, Aruba, Bahamas, Barbados, Belize, Bolivia, Brazil, Canada, Chile, Colombia, Costa Rica, Cuba, Dominica, Dominican Rep, Ecuador, El Salvador, Grenada, Guatemala, Haiti, Honduras, Jamaica, Mexico, Nicaragua, Panama, Paraguay, Peru, St Kitts-Nevis, St Lucia, St Vincent-Grenadines, Trinidad-Tobago, Turks-Caicos, Uruguay, Virgin Is UK.
[2022.11.29/XD1066/**F***]

♦ Inter-American Congress of Ministers and High-Level Authorities of Tourism (see: #11423)
♦ Inter-American Convention Against Corruption (1996 treaty)
♦ Inter-American Convention Against the Illicit Manufacturing of and Trafficking in Firearms, Ammunition, Explosives and other Related Materials (1997 treaty)
♦ Inter-American Convention Against Racism and all Forms of Discrimination and Intolerance (unconfirmed)
♦ Inter-American Convention Against Terrorism (2002 treaty)
♦ Inter-American convention to combat money laundering (unconfirmed)
♦ Inter-American Convention on Conflict of Laws Concerning the Adoption of Minors (1984 treaty)
♦ Inter-American Convention on Conflict of Laws Concerning Bills of Exchange, Promissory Notes and Invoices (1975 treaty)
♦ Inter-American Convention on Conflict of Laws Concerning Checks, 1975 (1975 treaty)
♦ Inter-American Convention on Conflicts of Laws Concerning Checks, 1979 (1979 treaty)
♦ Inter-American Convention on Conflicts of Laws Concerning Commercial Companies (1979 treaty)
♦ Inter-American Convention on Contracts for the International Carriage of Goods by Road (1989 treaty)
♦ Inter-American Convention on Domicile of Natural Persons in Private International Law (1979 treaty)
♦ Inter-American Convention on Electrical Communications (1924 treaty)
♦ Inter-American Convention on the Elimination of all Forms of Discrimination Against Persons with Disabilities (1999 treaty)
♦ Inter-American Convention on Execution of Preventive Measures (1979 treaty)
♦ Inter-American Convention on Extradition (1981 treaty)
♦ Inter-American Convention on Extraterritorial Validity of Foreign Judgments and Arbitral Awards (1979 treaty)
♦ Inter-American Convention to Facilitate Disaster Assistance (1991 treaty)
♦ Inter-American Convention on Facilitation of International Waterborne Transportation (1963 treaty)
♦ Inter-American Convention on Forced Disappearance of Persons (1994 treaty)
♦ Inter-American Convention on General Rules of Private International Law (1979 treaty)
♦ Inter-American Convention on the Granting of Civil Rights to Women (1948 treaty)
♦ Inter-American Convention on the Granting of Political Rights to Women (1948 treaty)
♦ Inter-American Convention on Human Rights (1969 treaty)
♦ Inter-American Convention on the International Amateur Radio Permit (1995 treaty)
♦ Inter-American Convention on International Commercial Arbitration (1975 treaty)
♦ Inter-American Convention on the International Return of Children (1989 treaty)
♦ Inter-American Convention on International Traffic in Minors (1994 treaty)
♦ Inter-American Convention on Jurisdiction in the International Sphere for the Extraterritorial Validity of Foreign Judgments (1984 treaty)
♦ Inter-American Convention on the Law Applicable to International Contracts (1994 treaty)
♦ Inter-American Convention on the Legal Regime of Powers of Attorney to be Used Abroad (1975 treaty)
♦ Inter-American Convention on Letters Rogatory (1975 treaty)
♦ Inter-American Convention on Mutual Assistance in Criminal Matters (1992 treaty)
♦ Inter-American Convention on Personality and Capacity of Juridical Persons in Private International Law (1984 treaty)
♦ Inter-American Convention on the Prevention, Punishment and Eradication of Violence Against Women (1994 treaty)
♦ Inter-American Convention to Prevent and Punish Torture (1985 treaty)
♦ Inter-American Convention on Proof of and Information on Foreign Law (1979 treaty)
♦ Inter-American Convention for the Protection and Conservation of Sea Turtles (1996 treaty)
♦ Inter-American Convention on the Rights of the Author in Literary, Scientific, and Artistic Works (1946 treaty)
♦ Inter-American Convention on Serving Criminal Sentences Abroad (1993 treaty)
♦ Inter-American Convention on Support Obligations (1989 treaty)
♦ Inter-American Convention on the Taking of Evidence Abroad (1975 treaty)
♦ Inter-American Convention on Transparency in Conventional Weapons Acquisitions (1999 treaty)

♦ Inter-American Cooperative Institute (ICI) 11420

Institut coopératif interaméricain – Instituto Cooperativo Interamericano
Contact Ave La Pulida, Pueblo Nuevo, Apartado T, 9A, Panama, Panamá, Panama PANAMá, Panama. T. +5072246019 – +5072240527. Fax +5072215385. E-mail: icipan@cwpanama.net – ici@sinfo.net.
URL: http://www.icipanama.org/
History Founded Jul 1963, Panama. Panamanian staff and membership. **Aims** Prepare young men and women as leaders to work in *Latin America* in promoting *social justice*. **Activities** Organizes two 100-day courses each year and a variety of shorter courses for students who undertake to work in Latin America (an average of 16 countries participate in these events). **Publications** *Boletin Latinoamericano* (2 a year). Letters; pamphlets. **IGO Relations** *Conferencia de Autoridades Cinematograficas de Iberoamérica (CACI, no recent information); Centro Interamericano para el Desarrollo del Conocimiento en la Formación Profesional (OIT/Cinterfor, #03802); Italian-Latin American Institute (ILAI, #16071).* **NGO Relations** *Asociación Latinoamericana de Centros de Educación Cooperativa (ALCECOOP, no recent information); Centro Interuniversitario de Desarrollo (CINDA, #03809); Consejo de Educación de Adultos de América Latina (CEAAL, #04707); Instituto Intercultural para la Autogestión y la Acción Comunal (INAUCO, #11335); Organization of the Cooperatives of America (OCA, inactive); The Reality Of Aid (ROA, #18626).* Member of: *Intercontinental Network for the Promotion of the Social Solidarity Economy (INPSSE, #11463).* [2014/XE4385/j/**E**]

♦ Inter-American Copyright Institute (ICI) 11421

Institut interaméricain de droit d'auteur (IIDA) – Instituto Interamericano de Derecho de Autor (IIDA) – Instituto Interamericano de Direito de Autor (IIDA)
SG Pico 2052, 3 piso 14, C1429EFH Buenos Aires, Argentina. T. +541147015600.
Pres Av Las Heras 4025, 17° D, C1425ATE Buenos Aires, Argentina. T. +5448045532.
URL: http://www.iidautor.org/
History 1973, Rio de Janeiro (Brazil). Founded during XVIII Conference of *Inter-American Bar Association (IABA, #11401).* Legally recognized Apr 1974. Constitution registered in Sao Paulo (Brazil). **Aims** Promote the study and progress of effective *protection* of rights of *intellectual property* in *America*, coordinating the efforts of specialists, as well as those of entities wishing to contribute to the broadest defence of such rights. **Structure** Executive Council, consisting of President, not less than 12 and not more than 16 Vice Presidents, Secretary General, Assistant Secretary General. Committees (5): Legislation; Communication; Publications; Related Rights; Governmental Agencies – Relations. **Languages** English, French, Portuguese, Spanish. **Events** *Regional conference* Buenos Aires (Argentina) 1990, *Regional conference* Sao Paulo (Brazil) 1989, *Regional conference* Lima (Peru) 1988, *Regional conference* Sao Paulo (Brazil) 1988, *Regional Conference* Mexico City (Mexico) 1986. **Publications** *Inter-American Review of Intellectual Property Law* (4 a year) in English, French, Portuguese, Spanish.
Members National copyright institutes; Individuals. Members in 17 countries:
Argentina, Bolivia, Brazil, Chile, Colombia, Costa Rica, Ecuador, El Salvador, Haiti, Mexico, Panama, Paraguay, Peru, Puerto Rico, Uruguay, USA, Venezuela.
Consultative Status Consultative status granted from: *World Intellectual Property Organization (WIPO, #21593)* (Permanent Observer Status). **IGO Relations** Observer status with (1): *Union for the International Registration of Audiovisual Works (#20444).* Cooperates with (1): *OAS (#17629).* [2023.02.13/XE4588/j/**E**]

♦ Inter-American Council of Commerce and Production (no recent information)

♦ Inter-American Council on Indigenous Spirituality 11422

Consejo Interamericano Sobre la Espiritualidad Indigena (CISEI)
Argentinian Chapter Jufré 705, Buenos Aires, Argentina. T. +5491165141650. E-mail: ciseiargentina@gmail.com.
URL: http://ciseiweb.wordpress.com/
History Founded 28 Jun 1996, Morelia (Mexico), during the first 'International Forum of Indigenous Spirituality of the Americas'. **Aims** Defend the rights to preserve culture and spirituality of all native-indigenous people of the Americas. **Structure** Council. **Languages** English, Spanish. **Staff** 3.00 FTE, voluntary. Other voluntary as needed. **Finance** Members' dues. Grants and funding from international organizations and foundations. **Activities** Events/meetings. **Events** *Forum* Buenos Aires (Argentina) 2012, *Forum* Guayana (Venezuela) 2010, *Forum* Santiago Atitlan (Guatemala) 2007, *Forum* Mexico City (Mexico) 2004, *Forum* Morelia (Mexico) 2004. **Publications** *CISEI Bulletin. Espiritualidad de los Pueblos Indigenas de América* (2000) by Marina Villalobos Diaz and Raquel Gutiérrez Najera.
Members Individuals (38) in 14 countries:
Argentina, Brazil, Canada, Chile, Ecuador, France, Germany, Guatemala, Israel, Mexico, Peru, Uruguay, USA, Venezuela.
[2018.09.11/XD7789/**D**]

♦ Inter-American Council for Integral Development 11423

Conseil interaméricain pour le développement intégré – Consejo Interamericano para el Desarrollo Integral (CIDI)
Sec OAS, 1889 F St NW, 7th Floor, Washington DC 20006, USA. T. +12024583574. Fax +120245835263.
URL: http://www.sedi.oas.org/
History 29 Jan 1996, as a primary instrument of cooperation of *OAS (#17629)*, following a proposal 8 Jun 1993, Managua (Nicaragua), at 19th Special Session of OAS General Assembly, when *'Protocol of Managua'* was approved. Replaces *Inter-American Economic and Social Council (IA-ECOSOC, inactive)* and *Inter-American Council for Education, Science and Culture (inactive).* **Aims** Give new impetus and approach to the promotion of cooperation in the Americas to achieve integral development and help eliminate extreme *poverty* in the Hemisphere; serve as a high level intergovernmental political forum to promote inter-American dialogue on subjects relevant to the Inter-American agenda regarding integral and *sustainable development*; operate as a catalyst to promote new types of cooperation among OAS member state institutions and between them and other institutions of the inter-American system, by giving preference to multilateral projects; meet new goals identified by the OAS in the field of development cooperation; foster partnerships with institutions and actors interested in associating with the OAS for cooperation in the Hemisphere. **Structure** Council, comprising ministerial-level representatives of governments of OAS member states, reports directly to OAS General Assembly and has decision-making capacity in matters of partnership for development. *Permanent Executive Committee of the Inter-American Council for Integral Development (CEPCIDI)*, set up 1996, is a permanent commission with executive authority which ensures coordinated execution of the Council's decisions, approves cooperation activities and makes recommendations for planning, programming, budgeting, management control, follow-up and evaluation of cooperation projects and activities. *Executive Secretariat for Integral Development (SEDI)* is responsible for planning, programming, coordinating, evaluating, monitoring and advising on activities within the framework of CIDI policies and priorities. Also within the framework of CIDI: SEDI's *Inter-American Horizontal Cooperation System (SICH); Inter-American Agency for Cooperation and Development (IACD, #11397); Inter-American Congress of Ministers and High-Level Authorities of Tourism (IATC, see: #11423).* Committees (4): *Inter-American Committee on Culture (no recent information); 'Inter-American Committee on Social Development'; 'Inter-American Committee on Sustainable Development and Environment'; 'Inter-American Committee on Science and Technology'.* OAS General Secretariat supports CIDI activities. **Languages** English, French, Portuguese, Spanish. **Finance** Cooperation activities financed through Special Multilateral Fund (550 projects to the value of US$ 70 million since 1996); technical exchange programs financed through government support; leverage resources for innovative initiatives through *The Trust for the Americas (#20252).* **Activities** Formulates *'Strategic Plan for Partnership for Development'*, which establishes objectives, lines of action and basic responsibilities for different sectors of cooperative action within the framework of policies and priorities established by OAS General Assembly. Current Strategic Plan (2002-2005) covers development cooperation through concentrated efforts in 8 areas: Social development and creation of productive employment; Education; Economic diversification and integration, trade liberalization and market access; Scientific development and exchange, and transfer of technology; Strengthening of democratic institutions; Sustainable development of tourism; Sustainable development and the environment; Culture. **Events** *Americas Competitiveness Forum* Port-of-Spain (Trinidad-Tobago) 2014, *Meeting of ministers of education* Quito (Ecuador) 2009, *Meeting of ministers of education* Cartagena de Indias (Colombia) 2007, *Meeting of ministers of education* Scarborough (Trinidad-Tobago) 2005, *Meeting of ministers and high level authorities of science and technology* Lima (Peru) 2004. **Publications** *Inter-American Review of Bibliography* – journal; *La Educación* – journal. *INTERAMER Collection* – series. *Cultura y Desarrollo en América Latina y el Caribe: Las Perspectivas Futuras para el Próximo Milenio; Perceptions of Sustainability: A Framework for the 21st Century; Sustainable Development in Latin America; Technical Cooperation Needs for Hemispheric Trade Negotiations; Toward International Cooperation in Education for the Integration of the Americas; Towards a More Sustainable and Competitive Caribbean Tourism Sector.* Annual Report. **Members** OAS member states (34). **IGO Relations** Cooperative relations and partnerships with: *Caribbean Tourism Organization (CTO, #03561); Comisión Interamericana de Mujeres (CIM, #04137); Comisión Interamericana de Telecomunicaciones (CITEL, #04138); Common Market of Scientific and Technological Knowledge (MERCOCYT Program, no recent information); Inter-American Children's Institute (IACI, #11406); Inter-American Committee on Natural Disaster Reduction (IACNDR, #11414); Inter-American Development Bank (IDB, #11427); Inter-American Institute for Cooperation on Agriculture (IICA, #11434); International Bank for Reconstruction and Development (IBRD, #12317); Pan American Health Organization (PAHO, #18108); UNEP (#20299); UNDP (#20292); UNICEF (#20332); United Nations Economic Commission for Latin America and the Caribbean (ECLAC, #20556).* **NGO Relations** Cooperative relations and partnerships with: *Hemisphere Wide Inter-University Scientific and Technological Information Network (RedHUCyT, no recent information); Inter-American Water Resources Network (IWRN, no recent information).*
[2014/XE2432/**E***]

♦ Inter-American Council of Jurists (inactive)

♦ Inter-American Council on Physics Education 11424

Consejo Interamericana sobre Educación en Fisica
Pres Univ Nacional de Tucuman, Av Independencia 1800, 4000 San Miguel de Tucuman, Argentina. T. +543814364093. E-mail: cyt-facet@herrera.unt.edu.ar.
URL: http://www.physics.ohio-state.edu/~aubrecht/IACPE.html
History 1963, Brazil. Also known as *Council of the Inter-American Conference on Physics Education – Consejo para las Conferencias Interamericanas sobre Educación en Fisica.* **Aims** Unite physics educators of the Americas; stimulate networking and exchanging of instructional resources and research findings. **Structure** Meeting (every 3 years, at Conference). Executive Committee (meets sporadically), composed of President, Vice-President and Executive Secretary. Countries with physics teaching organizations may become members; after inactivity, they must rejoin. Smaller countries have one member on Council; largest countries (Brazil, USA) have 3 members. **Staff** Voluntary. **Finance** No budget. Meetings depend on funding organizations such as *UNESCO (#20322)* and *International Union of Pure and Applied Physics (IUPAP, #15810)*, on local hemispheric sources of funding and on funding from the host country. **Events** *Triennial inter-American conference* Guayaquil (Ecuador) 2012, *Triennial Inter-American Conference* Cartagena de Indias (Colombia) 2009, *Triennial Inter-American Conference* Medellin (Colombia) 2009, *Triennial inter-American conference on physics education / Triennial Inter-American Conference* San José (Costa Rica) 2006, *Triennial inter-American conference on physics education / Triennial Inter-American Conference* Havana (Cuba) 2003. **Publications** Conference proceedings.
Members Members in 14 countries:
Argentina, Brazil, Canada, Chile, Colombia, Costa Rica, Cuba, Ecuador, Jamaica, Mexico, Panama, Uruguay, USA, Venezuela.
[2011.06.01/XD4990/**F**]

♦ Inter-American Court of Human Rights (#04851)

♦ Inter-American Court of International Justice (unconfirmed)
♦ Inter-American Culture and Development Foundation (internationally oriented national body)

♦ Inter-American Defense Board (IADB) 11425

Organisation interaméricaine de défense (OID) – Junta Interamericana de Defensa (JID)

Contact 2600 NW 16th St, Washington DC 20441, USA. T. +12029396041. E-mail: jid@jid.org.
URL: http://www.jid.org/

History 30 Mar 1942, Washington DC (USA), by decision of 3rd Meeting of Consultation of Ministers of Foreign Affairs of the American Republics, Jan 1942, Rio de Janeiro (Brazil). Regulation went into effect, 1 Sep 1948. Regulations revised: 1949; 1964; 2007. The new Regulation, 14 Jun 2007, constitutes the Guidelines and Procedures to follow by the Member States and Components of IADB as an Entity of the *OAS (#17629)*, as established in the new Statute approved at the XXXII General Extraordinary Assembly, 15 March 2006, Washington DC. The Regulation marks the legal incorporation of the IADB into the bosom of the OAS, a process that was initiated in 1948 after its first 6 years of existence and that culminates 64 years after its creation, allowing it to share the same objectives under the same institutional roof under the basic principles of civilian oversight and the democratic formation of its authorities. **Aims** Provide the OAS and its Member States with technical and educational advice and consultancy services on matters related to *military* and defence issues in the Hemisphere in order to contribute to the fulfillment of the OAS Charter. **Structure** Council of Delegates, composed of national delegations of Member States along with Chair and Vice-Chair. Secretariat, headed by Director-General, composed of Sub-Secretariat for Advisory Services (SAS) and Sub-Secretariat for Administrative and Conference Services (SACS). It provides advisory, administrative, financial and logistics support. Educational component: *Inter-American Defense College (IADC, #11426)*. **Languages** English, Portuguese, Spanish. **Staff** Within the organs of the IADB there are 3 distinct categories of positions: Representational Positions – within the Council of Delegates, which are composed of the national representatives of Member States; Elected Positions – 10, within the Board; Advisory and Support Positions – constitute majority of positions, representing both military and civilian personnel. **Finance** Annual contribution under the annual programme-budget approved by the OAS General Assembly. **Publications** *White Paper on Security and National Defense for the Sustainable Economic and Social Development of Haiti*.
Members Of the 35 OAS member nations, the following 28 countries are members of the IADB:
Antigua-Barbuda, Argentina, Barbados, Belize, Brazil, Canada, Chile, Colombia, Dominican Rep, Ecuador, El Salvador, Grenada, Guatemala, Guyana, Haiti, Honduras, Jamaica, Mexico, Nicaragua, Panama, Paraguay, Peru, St Kitts-Nevis, Suriname, Trinidad-Tobago, Uruguay, USA, Venezuela.
Observers in 8 countries:
China, Denmark, France, Italy, Netherlands, Portugal, Spain, UK. [2019.12.19/XE1068/**E***]

♦ Inter-American Defense College (IADC) 11426

Collège interaméricain de défense – Colegio Interamericano de Defensa

Main Office 210 B St SW, Bldg 52 Fort McNair, Washington DC 20319-5008, USA. T. +12026461333. Fax +12026461340.
Contact c/o Inter-American Defense Board, 2600 NW 16th St, Washington DC 20441, USA. T. +12029396041. Fax +12023872880.
URL: http://www.colegio-id.org/

History Formally opened 9 Oct 1962. **Structure** Educational institution of *Inter-American Defense Board (IADB, #11425)*. Responsible to the General Assembly of: *OAS (#17629)*. **Languages** English, French, Portuguese, Spanish. **Activities** Training/education. Offers executive level instruction to selected defence, and security leaders from OAS member countries. [2015.11.12/XF6532/**E***]

♦ Inter-American Democracy Network (#18692)

♦ Inter-American Development Bank (IDB) 11427

Banque interaméricaine de développement (BID) – Banco Interamericano de Desarrollo (BID) – Banco Interamericano de Desenvolvimento (BID)

Pres IDB Headquarters, 1300 New York Avenue, Washington DC 20577, USA. T. +12026231000. Fax +12026233096. E-mail: pic@iadb.org.
Country Representative in Europe Carlos Jarque, IDB Special Office in Europe, 66 avenue d'Iéna, 75116 Paris, France. T. +33140693100. Fax +33140693120.
Office in Japan Fukoku Seimei Building, 16F 2-2-2 Uchisaiwaicho, Chiyoda-ku, Tokyo, 100 Japan. T. +81335910461.
URL: http://www.iadb.org/

History 8 Apr 1959, Washington DC (USA), on signature by delegates of the then 21 members of *OAS (#17629)* of an Agreement which entered into effect 30 Dec 1959. Started operations 1 Oct 1960. Agreement modified: 1 Jun 1976; 28 Apr 1977; 31 Dec 1987. Previously also referred to by English initials *IDB*. **Aims** Help accelerate economic and social development in Latin America and the Caribbean; use its own capital, funds raised in financial markets and other resources, for financing the development of borrowing member countries; supplement private investment when private capital is not available on reasonable terms and conditions; provide technical assistance for the preparation, financing and implementation of development plans and projects; prioritize: Poverty reduction; Sustainable Energy and climate change; Water and other infrastructure; Education and innovation; Opportunities for the majority; Regional integration; Private sector development; Regional integration. **Structure** Board of Governors (meeting annually), consisting of representatives of each member country, usually ministers of finance, presidents of central banks of officers of comparable rank. Board of Executive Directors of 14 members. Headquarters in Washington DC (USA); Country offices in each member country, plus in Paris (France) and Tokyo (Japan). Office of Institutional Integrity. Representatives for Europe and for the Institute for the Integration of Latin America and the Caribbean, an administrative unit of the Bank. **Staff** Disputes dealt with through *Inter-American Development Bank Administrative Tribunal (no recent information)*.
Finance Owned by member countries, who subscribe capital and contributions; Charter ensures that regional developing country members are majority shareholder as a group. Borrows under favourable conditions on financial markets in Japan, USA, Europe, Latin America and the Caribbean. For 2010: total assets – US$ 87,217 million.
Funds entrusted to IDB by member and non-member countries: US$ 525 million Social Progress Trust Fund, administered for the USA; 2 funds totalling Can $ 79 million, administered for Canada; an pounds8 million fund administered for the United Kingdom; a Swiss Fr 45 million fund administered for Switzerland; 2 funds totalling US$ 14 million, administered for Sweden; a US$ 2 million fund administered for Norway; a US$ 23 million fund administered for Argentina; 2 funds totalling euro 4 million, administered for the European Community; 2 funds totalling Yen 13,853 million administered for Japan; a euro 490 million fund administered for Spain; a euro 6.5 million fund administered for Belgium; 3 funds totalling euro 4,000 million administered for Italy; a US$ 500,000 fund administered for Portugal; a US$ 1 million fund administered for Austria; a euro 150,000 administered for Germany; and a US$ 100,000 fund administered for Israel.
Activities Finances projects whose specific goal is to improve lives of the people of Latin America and the Caribbean, such as road-building, installing power lines, opening health clinics, providing safe drinking water and promoting small business; it also provides technical cooperation to strengthen development institutions in the region and help identify and carry out investment projects. Current emphasis: targeting low-income groups principally through social programmes; state modernization to support consolidation of democracy by strengthening fiscal administration, judicial systems, legislatures and the role of civil society organizations; complementing ongoing public sector and economic reform through infrastructure projects for modernizing energy, transport and communications systems, especially strengthening private sector participation. In addition:*Inter-American Investment Corporation (IIC, #11438)* encourages the establishment, expansion and modernization of private – preferably small or medium-scale – enterprises;*Multilateral Investment Fund (MIF, #16887)* emphasizes start-ups, innovations and activities with demonstration value; Asset and new liability policy approved, Jul 2010, by IDB Board of Executive Directors. Lending instruments from ordinary capital (5): sovereign obligation loans (single currency facility loans); LIBOR-based or fixed-rate loans (US dollars only) which carry a government guarantee and are lent on to private sector borrowers; loans to finance private sector operations, not carrying a government guarantee; sovereign local currency loans; sovereign obligation emergency loans. Loans from the Fund for Special Operations are made under easier amortization and interest terms. Loans from funds under administration are extended under terms and conditions as agreed to between the Bank and the countries providing the funds. The Bank approved an offer to convert outstanding and undisbursed loan balanced to US$ LIBOR-based or fixed-base cost rate, Jan 2009.*Institute for the Integration of Latin America and the Caribbean (#11271)* conducts research on institutional, legal, social, political and economic aspects of the process of integration and provides an advisory service to the Bank, to private institutions and to governments.*Inter-American Institute for Economic and Social Development (INDES, #11436)* trains senior officials in modern techniques of social policy management.*Latin American and Caribbean Research Network (#16284)* provides grant funding to leading research centers in the region to conduct studies on economic and social problems selected by IDB in consultation with the development policy community. In 1995, the Bank also set up a *'Task Force on Women'*.*Inter-American Initiative on Social Capital, Ethics and Development (see: #11427)* strengthens ethical values and social capital in the countries of the region.
/Disbursements/ Sectoral distribution for 1999: *'Productive Sectors'* – Agriculture and fisheries – US$ 100 million Industry, mining and tourism – US$ 1,211 million (12.8%); Science and technology – US$ 251 million (2.6%). *'Physical Infrastructure'* – Energy – US$ 367 million (3.9%); Transportation and communications – US$ 690 million (7.3%); *'Social Sectors'* – Sanitation – US$ 492 million (5.2%); Urban development – US$ 233 million (2.5%); Education – US$ 400 million (4.2%); Social investment – US$ 2,484 million (26.2%); Health – US$ 475 million (5%) Environment – US$ 82 million (0.9%); Microenterprise – US$ 100 million (1.1%). *'Others'* – Reform and modernization of the state – US$ 2,344 million (24.7%); Export financing – US$ 18 million (0.3%); Others – US$ 240 million (2.5%).
Cumulative lending and technical cooperation as at end 1999 was over US$ 104,000 million for projects whose total cost was US$ 254,000 million.
Events *Annual Meeting* Guayaquil (Ecuador) 2019, *Global Conference on Jobs and Inclusive Growth* Montego Bay (Jamaica) 2019, *Conference on Commodities, Volatility and Risk Management* Paris (France) 2019, *Digitalization of Tax Administration Forum* Seoul (Korea Rep) 2019, *Korea-LAC Business Summit* Seoul (Korea Rep) 2019. **Publications** *The IDB* (12 a year) – newsletter; *IDB Projects* (10 a year) – journal; *Pocket profiles* (annual) – brochure, social and economic indicators. *Economic and Social Progress in Latin America Report* – (every 2 years) series. *Financial Risk Management: A Practical Approach for Emerging Markets* (2000); *Wanted: World Financial Stability* (2000); *Social Protection for Equity and Growth* (2000); *Safe Money: Building Effective Credit Unions in Latin America* (2000); *Too Close to Home: Domestic Violence in the Americas* (1999); *Forest Resource Policy in Latin America* (1999); *Old Cities, New Assets: Preserving Latin America's Urban Heritage* (1999) by Eduardo Rojas; *Can Privatization Deliver ? Infrastructure for Latin America* (1999); *Microfinance and Poverty: Questioning the Conventional Wisdom* (1999) by Hege Gulli; *Progress, Poverty and Exclusion: An Economic History of Latin America in the 20th Century* (1998) by Rosemary Thorp; *Pathways to Growth: Comparing East Asia and Latin America* (1997); *Opportunity Foregone: Education in Brazil* (1996); *Reforming the Labour Market in a Liberalized Economy* (1996); *Human Resources in Latin America and the Caribbean* (1996) by Jere R Behrman; *Reforma, recuperación y crecimiento: América Latina y Medio Oriente* (1996); *Foreign Direct Investment in Latin America* (1996); *Expanding Access to Financial Services in Latin America* (1996); *Volatile Capital Flows: Taming their Impact on Latin America* (1996); *Choices and Change: Reflections on the Caribbean* (1996); *Benefits and Beneficiaries: An Introduction to Estimating Distributional Effects in Cost-Benefit Analysis* (1996) by Elio Londero; *Banking Crises in Latin America* (1996); *Banking Crises in Latin America* (1996); *Women in the Americas: Bridging the Gender Gap* (1995); *Latin America in Graphs: Demographic, Economic and Social Trends 1974-1995* (1995); *Fiscal Decentralization in Latin America* (1995); *Public Finances, Stabilization and Structural Reform in Latin America* (1994); *Politicas de ajuste y pobreza: falsos dilemas, verdaderos problemas* (1994); *Art of Latin America 1900-1980* (1994) by Marta Traba; *Human Resources and the Adjustment Process* (1994); *Foreign Capital in Latin America* (1994); *Social Security Systems in Latin America* (1994); *Social Service Delivery Systems: An Agenda for Reform* (1994); *En Route to Modern Growth: Latin America in the 1990s* (1994); *Community Organizations in Latin America* (1994); *Agenda 21 and Latin America: The Challenge of Implementing Environmental Law and Policy* (1994). Annual report; proceedings of annual meetings; conference proceedings; sector brochure series; occasional paper series; various occasional publications; loan announcements; statistical tables; brochures; videos. Most publications in English, Spanish.
Members Regional members in the Western hemisphere; nonregional members in Europe, Asia and the Middle East. Governments of 48 countries:
Argentina, Austria, Bahamas, Barbados, Belgium, Belize, Bolivia, Brazil, Canada, Chile, China, Colombia, Costa Rica, Croatia, Denmark, Dominican Rep, Ecuador, El Salvador, Finland, France, Germany, Guatemala, Guyana, Haiti, Honduras, Israel, Italy, Jamaica, Japan, Korea Rep, Mexico, Netherlands, Nicaragua, Norway, Panama, Paraguay, Peru, Portugal, Slovenia, Spain, Suriname, Sweden, Switzerland, Trinidad-Tobago, UK, Uruguay, USA, Venezuela.
IGO Relations Permanent Observer to: *ECOSOC (#05331)*. Observer status with: *International Organization for Migration (IOM, #14454)*; *Sistema Económico Latinoamericano (SELA, #19294)*; *World Trade Organization (WTO, #21864)*. Observer to General Assembly of: *United Nations (UN, #20515)*. Observer to: *International Fund for Agricultural Development (IFAD, #13692)*. Formal agreement with: *UNESCO (#20322)*. Partnership agreement with: *OECD (#17693)*. Cooperation agreement with: *International Institute for Democracy and Electoral Assistance (International IDEA, #13872)*. Participates in the activities of: *UNCTAD (#20285)*. Close cooperation with: *Caribbean Development Bank (CDB, #03492)* – resolution of 1974, came into effect 1977, allows IDB to lend through CDB to all CDB member countries whether or not members of IDB; *United Nations Economic Commission for Latin America and the Caribbean (ECLAC, #20556)*. Memorandum of Understanding signed with: *World Customs Organization (WCO, #21350)*. Member of: *Committee of International Development Institutions on the Environment (CIDIE, no recent information)*; *Global Bioenergy Partnership (GBEP, #10251)*; *International Rice Research Institute (IRRI, #14754)*; *Organization of the Petroleum Exporting Countries (OPEC, #17881)*. Cooperates with governments and international agencies in: *Consultative Group to Assist the Poor (CGAP, #04768)*. Accredited by: *United Nations Framework Convention on Climate Change – Secretariat (UNFCCC, #20564)*. Invited to sessions of Intergovernmental Council of: *International Programme for the Development of Communication (IPDC, #14651)*. Supports: *Caribbean Regional Technical Assistance Centre (CARTAC, #03550)*. Instrumental in setting up: *Bank of the South*; *Partnership for Democratic Governance (PDG, inactive)*; *Fondo Regional de Tecnologia Agropecuaria (FONTAGRO, #09834)*; *Global Environment Facility (GEF, #10346)*. **NGO Relations** Member of: *Better Than Cash Alliance (#03220)*; *Inter-Agency Consultation on Race in Latin America (IAC, no recent information)*; *International Consortium on Governmental Financial Management (ICGFM, #12915)*; *International Institute of Administrative Sciences (IIAS, #13859)*; *International Land Coalition (ILC, #13999)*; *International Network for Environmental Compliance and Enforcement (INECE, #14261)*; *International Society of Tropical Foresters (ISTF, #15522)*. Associate member of: *Inter-American Savings and Loan Bank (inactive)*; *Asociación Latinoamericana de Instituciones Financieras para el Desarrollo (ALIDE, #02233)*; *Latin American Industrialists Association (#16341)*. Member of: *Global Road Safety Partnership (GRSP, #10581)*. Supports: *Academy for Educational Development (AED, inactive)*; *Environmental Management Secretariat for Latin America and the Caribbean (EMS, no recent information)*; *Helen Kellogg Institute for International Studies*; *HelpAge International (#10904)*; *Latin American Art Resource Project (LAARP)*. Instrumental in setting up: *Digital Diaspora Network – Latin American and Caribbean (no recent information)*; *Euro-Latin Study Network on Integration and Trade (ELSNIT, #05701)*; *Inter-American Culture and Development Foundation (IACDF)*; *Latin America-Caribbean and Asia-Pacific Economics and Business Association (LAEBA, no recent information)*. [2015/XF1069/**F***]

♦ Inter-American Development Commission (inactive)
♦ Inter-American Dialogue (internationally oriented national body)

♦ Inter-American Distance Education Consortium 11428

Consortium-réseau d'éducation à distance – Consorcio-Red de Educación a Distancia (CREAD) – Consórcio-Rede de Educação à Distância

Exec Dir PO Box 4374, Hallandale Beach FL 33008-4374, USA. T. +19542954336.
URL: http://www.cread.org/

History 6 Nov 1990, Caracas (Venezuela). Founded at 15th World Conference of ICDE, as a self-managed programme of *Inter-American Organization for Higher Education (IOHE, #11442)*. Became, Oct 1993, an independent distance education network. **Aims** Promote exchange of *human resources* through the development of a technical assistance roster (database) among members; foster inter-institutional cooperation among the *Americas*; identify, update and catalogue existing resources; develop new distance education projects; have member institutions analyse their human, financial and technical resources, and finished distance education materials; maximize resources; promote the use of a common satellite for educational purposes throughout the hemisphere. **Structure** Board of Directors. Regions (9): Andean; Anglophone Canada; Brazil; Caribbean; Central American; Francophone Canada; Mexico; Southern Cone; United States of America. **Activities** Training/education; networking/liaising; knowledge management/information dissemination; events/

meetings; guidance/assistance/consulting. **Events** *Mercosur y sul conference* Buenos Aires (Argentina) 2007, *Conference on workforce and employment* Guadalajara (Mexico) 2007, *International distance education conference* Guadalajara (Mexico) 2007, *Assises européennes du paysage* Paris (France) 2007, *Virtual Educa : international conference on education, training and new technologies* São José dos Campos (Brazil) 2007. **Publications** *CREAD Electronic Newsletter* (4 a year) in English, Portuguese, Spanish.
Members Institutional; Individual. Members in 22 countries:
Argentina, Barbados, Brazil, Canada, Chile, Colombia, Costa Rica, Cuba, Dominican Rep, Ecuador, Guatemala, Haiti, Honduras, Mexico, Panama, Peru, Philippines, Portugal, Puerto Rico, Spain, USA, Venezuela.
Included in the above, 8 organizations listed in this Yearbook:
Canadian International Development Agency (CIDA, inactive); Florida International University (FIU); Instituto Latinoamericano de la Comunicación Educativa (ILCE, #11343); Inter-American Organization for Higher Education; *International University Consortium (IUC, no recent information);* National Autonomous University of Mexico (UNAM); *OAS (#17629); Universidad Intercontinental (no recent information).* [2018/XF1694/y/**F**]

♦ Inter-American Drug Abuse Control Commission 11429

Commission interaméricaine de lutte contre l'abus des drogues – Comisión Interamericana para el Control del Abuso de Drogas (CICAD) – Comissão Interamericana para o Controle do Abuso de Drogas

Secretariat c/o OAS, 1889 F St NW, Washington DC 20006, USA. T. +12023705069. Fax +12024583658.
URL: http://www.cicad.oas.org/

History Established Nov 1986, Washington DC (USA), by General Assembly of the *OAS (#17629)* through resolution AG/RES 813 (XVI-0/86). A technically autonomous agency of OAS working within the framework of 'Inter-American Program of Action of Rio de Janeiro (Brazil) Against the Illicit Use and Production of Narcotic Drugs and Psychotropic Substances and Traffic Therein', the Anti-Drug Strategy in the Hemisphere (1996) and the mandates of the OAS General Assembly. **Aims** Alleviate the immediate and substantial threat to political stability, democratic institutions and the economic growth and wellbeing of the peoples of the *Americas* by: reducing *illicit* drug production, supply, *trafficking* and use/abuse and its detrimental societal effects; controlling illicit trafficking in and use/abuse of legal drugs. Promote and strengthen inter-American cooperation to attack the complex transnational chain of operations that makes up illicit drug trafficking – including production, manufacture, distribution, marketing, use/abuse – and its effects, such as *money laundering* and arms trafficking. **Structure** Plenary Session of the Commission (twice a year). Secretary General of OAS appoints Executive Secretary, Assistant Executive Secretary and professional and administrative staff. Chairman and Vice-Chairman elected yearly. **Languages** English, French, Portuguese, Spanish. **Staff** 38.00 FTE, paid. **Finance** OAS budget covers half staff costs and some overheads. Programme activities financed from: OAS budget; voluntary contributions of OAS member governments and other interested governments; contributions from public and private international, regional and national organizations. **Activities** Operations concentrated in the following areas: Legal Development; Money Laundering Control; Demand Reduction; Supply Reduction; Alternative Development; Arms Control; Strengthening of National Drug Commissions (Institution Building); Statistics, Information and Research – created *Inter-American Observatory on Drugs (OID, see: #11429)* in 2000; Multilateral Evaluation Mechanism. Western Hemisphere Heads of State and Government, drew up a mandate at 2nd Summit of the Americas, Apr 1998, Santiago de Chile, committing CICAD member states to developing a singular and objective process of multilateral governmental evaluation in order to monitor the progress of their individual and collective efforts to deal with the diverse manifestations of the drug problem in the hemisphere. *'Multilateral Evaluation Mechanism (MEM)'*, created in 1999 in response to that mandate, is a peer review process in which countries assess each others' efforts. **Events** *European Conference on Addictive Behaviours and Dependencies* Lisbon (Portugal) 2015, *Regular session* Washington, DC (USA) 2010, *Regular session* Miami, FL (USA) 2009, *Regular session* Washington, DC (USA) 2009, *Regular session* Santiago (Chile) 2008. **Publications** *Directory of Governmental Organizations and Institutions Charged with the Fight Against the Illicit Production, Trafficking, Use and Abuse of Narcotic Drugs and Psychotropic Substances* (2004) in English, Spanish; *Comparative Study of Drug Use in the Americas* (2004) in Spanish; *Statistical Summary on Drugs* (2004) in English, Spanish; *Comparative Study of Drug Use in the Caribbean: Barbados, Belize and Guyana* (2003) in English; *The Multilateral Evaluation Mechanism's Evaluation of Progress in Drug Control 2001-2002* (2003); *Drug Addiction and its Treatment* (2000) in Spanish; *Directory of Experts and Agencies Responsible for Alternative Development Programs and Initiatives in the Hemisphere* (1998) in English, Spanish; *Directory of Authorities Responsible for the Control of Precursors and Chemical Products Used in the Production of Illicit Drugs* (1997) in English, Spanish; *Comprehensive Education to Prevent Drug Abuse: New Challenges in Central America, Panama and the Dominican Republic* (1996) in English, Spanish; *Communications against Drugs: Evaluation of Campaigns in the Americas* (1992) in English, Spanish; *The Chance to Grow: Education for Drug Abuse Prevention* (1990) in English, Spanish. Action programs; declarations; model regulations; statistical summaries; hempispheric reports.
Members Governments of 34 countries:
Antigua-Barbuda, Argentina, Bahamas, Barbados, Belize, Bolivia, Brazil, Canada, Chile, Colombia, Costa Rica, Dominica, Dominican Rep, Ecuador, El Salvador, Grenada, Guatemala, Guyana, Haiti, Honduras, Jamaica, Mexico, Nicaragua, Panama, Paraguay, Peru, St Kitts-Nevis, St Lucia, St Vincent-Grenadines, Suriname, Trinidad-Tobago, Uruguay, USA, Venezuela.
IGO Relations
- *Bioversity International (#03262);*
- *Caribbean Community (CARICOM, #03476);*
- *Caribbean Customs Law Enforcement Council (CCLEC, #03487);*
- *Caribbean Financial Action Task Force (CFATF, #03505)*
- *Comisión Interamericana de Mujeres (CIM, #04137);*
- *European Commission (EC, #06633);*
- *European Monitoring Centre for Drugs and Drug Addiction (EMCDDA, #07820);*
- *Financial Action Task Force (FATF, #09765);*
- *Grupo de Acción Financiera de Latinoamérica (GAFILAT, #10799);*
- *Heads of National Drug Law Enforcement Agencies (HONLEA);*
- *Inter-American Children's Institute (IACI, #11406);*
- *Inter-American Defense Board (IADB, #11425);*
- *Inter-American Development Bank (IDB, #11427);*
- *Inter-American Institute for Cooperation on Agriculture (IICA, #11434);*
- *International Criminal Police Organization – INTERPOL (ICPO-INTERPOL, #13110);*
- *International Maritime Organization (IMO, #14102);*
- *International Narcotics Control Board (INCB, #14212);*
- *Pan American Health Organization (PAHO, #18108);*
- *United Nations Commission on Narcotic Drugs (CND, #20532);*
- *United Nations Office on Drugs and Crime (UNODC, #20596);*
- *United Nations Regional Centre for Peace, Disarmament and Development in Latin America and the Caribbean (UNLIREC, #20618);*
- *World Customs Organization (WCO, #21350).*

NGO Relations Links with a large number of national and international organizations (not specified). [2019/XE0985/**E***]

- ♦ Inter-American Education Association (inactive)
- ♦ Inter-American Electrical Communication Commission / see Comisión Interamericana de Telecomunicaciones (#04138)
- ♦ Inter-American Escadrille (inactive)
- ♦ Inter-American Export Promotion Centre (inactive)
- ♦ Inter-American Federation for Adult Education (inactive)
- ♦ Inter-American Federation of Automobile Clubs / see Federación Internacional del Automóvil Region IV (#09337)
- ♦ Inter-American Federation of Construction Consortia (inactive)
- ♦ Inter-American Federation of the Construction Industry (#09333)
- ♦ Inter-American Federation of Entertainment Workers (inactive)
- ♦ Interamerican Federation of Human Resource Management / see Federación Interamericana de Asociaciones de Gestión Humana (#09329)
- ♦ Inter-American Federation of Information Technology, Telecommunications and Electronics Chambers (no recent information)
- ♦ Inter-American Federation of Insurance Companies (#09331)
- ♦ Inter-American Federation of Municipal Credit and Assistance Institutions (inactive)
- ♦ Inter-American Federation of Personnel Administration / see Federación Interamericana de Asociaciones de Gestión Humana (#09329)
- ♦ Inter-American Federation of Personnel Management / see Federación Interamericana de Asociaciones de Gestión Humana (#09329)
- ♦ Inter-American Federation of Public Relations Associations / see Inter-American Confederation of Public Relations (#11418)

♦ Inter-American Federation of Secretaries 11430

Fédération interaméricaine des secrétaires – Federación Interamericana de Asociaciones de Secretarias (FIAS)

Sec Col Nstra Sra Del Pilar 12, Zaragoza, La Libertad, El Salvador. E-mail: sunshine.vilma@gmail.com.
URL: http://fiasfederacion.com/

History 26 Apr 1970, Buenos Aires (Argentina), on the occasion of 1st Interamerican Congress of Secretaries. **Aims** Work toward the technical, moral, cultural and social betterment of the secretary. **Structure** General Assembly (every 2 years); Executive Board, consisting of President, Secretary and Treasurer (all from the same country). Three regions, each with own Vice-President. Permanent Secretariat, headed by Permanent Secretary. **Languages** Dutch, English, French, Portuguese, Spanish. **Staff** Voluntary. **Finance** Members' dues. Budget (annual): US$ 20,000. **Activities** Creation of secretariat schools at university level. **Events** *Biennial Congress* San José (Costa Rica) 2012, *Biennial Congress* Florianópolis (Brazil) 2010, *Biennial Congress* Panama (Panama) 2008, *Biennial congress* Willemstad (Aruba) 1990, *Biennial Congress* Willemstad (Curaçao) 1990. **Publications** *FIAS Bulletin* (4 a year).
Members Associations of secretaries in 21 countries and territories:
Argentina, Aruba, Bolivia, Bonaire Is, Brazil, Chile, Colombia, Costa Rica, Curaçao, Dominican Rep, Ecuador, El Salvador, Guatemala, Haiti, Honduras, Mexico, Nicaragua, Panama, Paraguay, Peru, Venezuela.
Observers in 2 countries:
Portugal, Spain.
Consultative Status Consultative status granted from: *OAS (#17629).* [2014/XD4003/**D**]

- ♦ Inter-American Federation of Societies of Authors and Composers (inactive)
- ♦ Inter-American Federation of Touring and Automobile Clubs / see Federación Internacional del Automóvil Region IV (#09337)
- ♦ Inter-American Federation of Working Newspapermen's Organizations (inactive)
- ♦ Inter-American Financial and Economic Advisory Committee (inactive)
- ♦ Inter-American Food Laboratory Network / see Red Interamericana de Laboratorios de Analisis de Alimentos (#18694)

♦ Inter-American Foundation (IAF) 11431

Fondation inter-américaine – Fundación Interamericana

Pres/CEO 1331 Pennsylvania Ave NW, Ste 1200, Washington DC 20004, USA. T. +12023604530. E-mail: inquiries@iaf.gov.
URL: http://www.iaf.gov/

History Founded 1970, following decision of USA Congress, 1969. **Aims** Support community, regional and national level *nongovernmental* organizations in strengthening bonds of friendship and understanding among peoples of the Western hemisphere; support *self-help* efforts to enlarge opportunity for individual development in *Latin America* and the *Caribbean* by making grants to local private organizations so as to support poor people's initiatives; encourage establishment and growth of private and governmental democratic institutions appropriate to the needs of individual sovereign nations of the region. **Structure** Board; Advisory Council to the Board of Directors. Offices (7): President; General Counsel; Evaluation and Audit; Networks and Strategic Initiatives; Grantmaking and Portfolio Management; Operations; External and Government Affairs. **Languages** English, Portuguese, Spanish. **Staff** 38.00 FTE, paid. **Finance** Sources: US Congressional appropriations; Social Progress Trust Fund, administered by *Inter-American Development Bank (IDB, #11427).* Budget (annual): US$ 25 million. **Activities** Financial and/or material support; knowledge management/information dissemination; events/meetings. **Events** *Building democracy from the grassroots* Washington, DC (USA) 2001. **Publications** *Grassroots Development* in English, Spanish. Annual Report; books; monographs; Special Papers. **NGO Relations** Member of: *Red Interamericana de Fundaciones y Acciones Empresariales para el Desarrollo de Base (RedEAmérica, #18693); Worldwide Initiatives for Grantmaker Support (WINGS, #21926).* [2014.12.05/XF1369/f/**F**]

- ♦ Inter-American Foundation for Tropical Research, Guatemala (internationally oriented national body)
- ♦ Inter-American Group of Coordination in Vegetal Health (no recent information)
- ♦ Inter-American Heart Foundation / see InterAmerican Heart Foundation (#11432)

♦ InterAmerican Heart Foundation (IAHF) 11432

Fundación InterAmericana del Corazón (FIC) – Fundação InterAmericana do Coração

Exec Dir 7272 Greenville Ave, Dallas TX 75231-4596, USA. T. +12147061354. E-mail: iahf@interamericanheart.org.
URL: http://interamericanheart.org/

History Sep 1992, under the auspices of *World Heart Federation (WHF, #21562),* and with the support of *Inter-American Society of Cardiology (ISC, #11448),* the American Heart Association, and other regional associations. Statement of Intent signed 17 Apr 1994, Mexico City (Mexico), by representatives of 12 countries. Approved 9 Sept 1994, Berlin (Germany), by WHF as its American continental federation. Previously also referred to as *Inter-American Heart Foundation (IAHF) – Fundación Interamericana del Corazón (FIC).* **Aims** Promote an environment throughout the Americas that is conducive to the prevention of heart disease and stroke. **Structure** Board of Directors; Executive Director. **Languages** English, Portuguese, Spanish. **Finance** Members' dues. Other sources: corporate donations and in-kind support; foundation grants; royalties; fees for services. **Activities** Advocacy/lobbying/activism; awards/prizes/competitions; training/education; events/meetings; knowledge management/information dissemination; healthcare. **Events** *Latin American and Caribbean Conference on Tobacco or Health* Montevideo (Uruguay) 2017, *Meeting* Dallas, TX (USA) 1998, *Meeting* Rio de Janeiro (Brazil) 1998, *Forum* Buenos Aires (Argentina) 1996, *Forum and delegate assembly* New Orleans, LA (USA) 1996. **Publications** *Hearts of the Americas* (3 a year) in English, Spanish; *InterAmerican Cardiovascular Emergencies* – newsletter. *ECC International Guidelines* – series. Information Services: maintains electronic forums for Coalición Latinoamérica Saludable (CLAS).
Members Organizations (36) and individuals in 19 countries:
Argentina, Barbados, Brazil, Canada, Chile, Colombia, Costa Rica, Dominican Rep, Ecuador, Jamaica, Mexico, Panama, Paraguay, Peru, Puerto Rico, Trinidad-Tobago, Uruguay, USA, Venezuela.
IGO Relations Official relations with: *Pan American Health Organization (PAHO, #18108).* **NGO Relations** Member of: *Framework Convention Alliance (FCA, #09981); Healthy Caribbean Coalition (HCC, #10893); International Liaison Committee on Resuscitation (ILCOR, #14036); The NCD Alliance (NCDA, #16963). Caribbean Cardiac Society (CCS, #03467)* is a member. [2020/XF3098/f/**F**]

- ♦ Inter-American Hospital Association (inactive)
- ♦ Inter-American Hotel Association (no recent information)

♦ Inter-American Housing Union 11433

Unión Interamericana para la Vivienda (UNIAPRAVI) – União Interamericana para a Habitação

Pres Bajada Balta no 169, 4 piso, Casilla Postal 18-1366, 18, Lima, Peru. T. +5114446611 – +5114446605 – +5114446975. Fax +5114446600. E-mail: consultas@uniapravi.org – uniapravi@uniapravi.org.
URL: http://www.uniapravi.org/

History 12 Nov 1964, Caracas (Venezuela), as *Inter-American Union of Savings and Loan for Housing,* pursuant to the resolution and agreement of 2nd Interamerican Savings and Loan Conference, 23 Jan 1964, Santiago (Chile). Previously also referred to in English as *Inter-American Save and Loan for Housing Union.* By-Laws modified and current name adopted, 9 May 1985, allowing enlargement of membership by incorporating financial institutions which, although not savings and loan associations, make a significant contribution to housing in their countries. **Aims** Promote and provide advice for the definition of instruments and mechanisms in the generation of public policies and best practices for development and sustainable housing finance, through studies, services, transfer of best practices and creating spaces for exchange between public and private actors in an inclusive way. **Structure** General Assembly (annual). Board of Directors, comprising President, Past-President, 2 Vice-Presidents, Titular Director and Deputy Director for each country, and former Presidents. Executive Committee, consisting of President, Past President, 2 Vice-Presidents, Regional Directors and elected former Presidents. Central Office. **Languages** English, Portuguese, Spanish. **Staff** 3.00 FTE, paid. **Finance** Members' dues. Other sources: sale of publications; services. **Activities** Conducts studies, seminars and technical assistance; organizes international meetings, conferences, fora and conventions; offers training opportunities; produces and distributes technical and institutional publications. **Events** *Annual Conference* Cancún (Mexico) 2016, *Annual Inter-American Housing Conference* Mexico City (Mexico) 2012, *Interamerican forum on housing finance* Lima (Peru) 2010, *Seminar on mortgage banks* Panama (Panama) 2010, *International seminar on housing finance* Mexico City (Mexico) 2009. **Publications** *Boletin UNIAPRAVI* (4 a year); *Cuadernos* (4 a year). Books; conference proceedings.

Members Active; Associate; Honorary. Institutions (about 100) in 22 countries:
Argentina, Bolivia, Brazil, Canada, Chile, Colombia, Costa Rica, Dominican Rep, Ecuador, El Salvador, Guatemala, Honduras, Jamaica, Mexico, Nicaragua, Panama, Paraguay, Peru, Spain, UK, USA, Venezuela.

Consultative Status Consultative status granted from: *ECOSOC (#05331)* (Special). **IGO Relations** Cooperates with: *OAS (#17629)*. Associated with Department of Global Communications of the United Nations. **NGO Relations** Regional affiliate of: *International Union for Housing Finance (IUHF, #15780)*. Joint activities with: *Inter-American Savings and Loan Bank (inactive)*. [2016/XD1108/**D**]

♦ Inter-American and Iberian Public Budget Association / see Public Budget International Association (#18564)
♦ Inter-American Initiative on Social Capital, Ethics and Development (see: #11427)
♦ Inter-American Institute of Administrative Sciences / see Fundación Internacional y para Iberoamérica de Administración y Politicas Públicas (#10030)
♦ Inter-American Institute of Agricultural Sciences / see Inter-American Institute for Cooperation on Agriculture (#11434)

♦ Inter-American Institute for Cooperation on Agriculture (IICA) 11434

Institut interaméricain de coopération pour l'agriculture (IICA) – Instituto Interamericano de Cooperación para la Agricultura (IICA) – Instituto Interamericano de Cooperação para a Agricultura (IICA)

Dir Gen Apartado Postal 55, San José, Coronado, 2200, Costa Rica. T. +5062160222. Fax +5062160233. E-mail: iica.cr@iica.int – iicahq@iica.int.
Washington Office IICA, 1889 K St – Suite 306, Washington DC 20006, USA. T. +12024583767 – +12024583768. Fax +12024586335. E-mail: iica.us@iica.int.
URL: http://www.iica.int/

History 7 Oct 1942, as *Inter-American Institute of Agricultural Sciences (IAIAS) – Institut interaméricain des sciences agricoles (IISA) – Instituto Interamericano de Ciencias Agrícolas (IICA)*, on the basis of a multilateral Convention, opened for signature by member countries of the then *'Pan American Union (PAU)'*, currently *OAS (#17629)*. By virtue of that Convention, contracting states recognized the permanent status of the institution and its status as a legal entity in accordance with their own legislation. Executive Headquarters were originally established at PAU, with field operations in Turrialba (Costa Rica), but were transferred to Turrialba in 1946 and to San José (Costa Rica) in 1960. A convention for adoption of the present title opened for signature, 6 Mar 1979, and was adopted 8 Dec 1980, when two-thirds of the states party to the 1944 Convention had deposited their instruments of ratification. IICA is a specialized agency of the Inter-American System. Statutes registered in *'UNTS 1/19557'*. **Aims** Support efforts of Member States to achieve progress and prosperity in the hemisphere through the modernization of the *rural* sector, the promotion of *food security* and the development of an agricultural sector that is competitive, technologically prepared, *environmentally* managed and socially equitable for the peoples of the Americas. **Structure** Governing bodies: *Inter-American Board of Agriculture (IABA, see: #11434)* (meets every 2 years), comprises the 34 member countries. *'Executive Committee'* (meets annually), comprises 12 Member States, elected on the basis of a system of partial rotation and equitable geographic distribution. *'General Directorate'* as Executive Organ, comprising technical and administrative units. *'Technical Secretariat'*. Provides secretariat for: *Central American Agricultural Council (#03657)*; *Consejo Regional de Cooperación Agrícola de Centroamérica, México y la República Dominicana (CORECA, no recent information)*. Set up: *Distance Learning Center (CECADI, see: #11434)*. **Languages** English, French, Portuguese, Spanish. **Staff** 655.00 FTE, paid. **Finance** Annual quotas of member countries. Other sources: agreements; contracts; contributions and grants signed with national and international organizations.

Activities *'Technical Secretariat'* supported by 6 specialized thematic areas:
– *'Trade Policy and Negotiations'* – supports countries' efforts to increase their capabilities to analyse, define, implement and reach agreement at the regional level on public policies and agricultural trade negotiations;
– *'Agribusiness Development'* – helps countries identify and take advantage of market opportunities; strengthens public and private institutions dedicated to developing and promoting agribusiness; integrates IICA activities related to agribusiness development;
– *'Technology and Innovation'* – contributes to rural poverty alleviation, improved competitiveness and efficient use of natural resources by supporting countries' efforts to transform institutional structures for technological innovation and modernize science and technology policies;
– *'Agricultural Health and Food Safety'* – assists Member States in strengthening animal health, plant health and food safety capabilities so as to compete successfully in national and international markets and contribute to safeguarding consumer health;
– *'Sustainable Rural Development'* – supports Member States' efforts and strengthens their institutional capabilities in reducing rural poverty, increasing rural prosperity and improving capacities of rural people, so as to accelerate development through sustainable use of natural resources;
– *'Education and Training'* – supports Member States in developing and upgrading human capital and talent for sustainable development of agriculture and improvement of rural life, through training in strategic subject areas, modernization of educational programs and dialogue on agricultural and rural education in the Americas.

Regional programmes include: *Programa Cooperativo de Investigación y Transferencia de Tecnología Agropecuaria para la Subregión Andina (PROCIANDINO, no recent information)*; *Programa Cooperative de Investigación, Desarrollo e Innovación Agrícolo para los Trópicos Suramericanos (PROCITROPICOS, #18521)*; *Programa Cooperativo para el Desarrollo Tecnológico Agroalimentario y Agroindustrial del Cono Sur (PROCISUR, #18522)*; *Regional Cooperative Program for the Technological Development and Modernization of Coffee Cultivation in Central America, Panama, Dominican Rep and Jamaica (#18775)*.*Fondo Regional de Tecnologia Agropecuaria (FONTAGRO, #09834)*, set up with IDB, promotes competitiveness in the sector. Sponsors: *Caribbean Agricultural Science and Technology Networking System (PROCICARIBE, no recent information)*. Also includes: *Red de Bolsas Agropecuarias de las Américas (INTERBOLSAS, see: #11434)*.

Events *IPPC Regional Workshop for Caribbean* Bridgetown (Barbados) 2017, *IPPC Regional Workshop for Latin America* Cusco (Peru) 2017, *IPPC Regional Workshop for Caribbean* Christ Church (Barbados) 2016, *IPPC Regional Workshop for Latin America* Panama (Panama) 2016, *Meeting of Ministers of Agriculture of Americas* Cancún (Mexico) 2015. **Publications** *IICA Technical Series*. *IICA Technical Monographs*. Annual Report; magazines; technical bulletins; books; manuals. **Information Services** *ISAPLAC* – animal production; *PRODAR* – agroindustry; *Servicio Especializado de Documentación, Información e Informatica* – access to statistical and bibliographic information on agriculture in the hemisphere; facilitates access to modern information systems so as to improve flow of data among members; *SIDALC*.

Members Governments of 34 countries:
Antigua-Barbuda, Argentina, Bahamas, Barbados, Belize, Bolivia, Brazil, Canada, Chile, Colombia, Costa Rica, Dominica, Dominican Rep, Ecuador, El Salvador, Grenada, Guatemala, Guyana, Haiti, Honduras, Jamaica, Mexico, Nicaragua, Panama, Paraguay, Peru, St Kitts-Nevis, St Lucia, St Vincent-Grenadines, Suriname, Trinidad-Tobago, Uruguay, USA, Venezuela.
Permanent observers in 17 countries:
Austria, Belgium, Czechia, Egypt, France, Germany, Hungary, Israel, Italy, Japan, Korea Rep, Netherlands, Poland, Portugal, Romania, Russia, Spain.
Regional permanent observer, listed in this Yearbook:
European Union (EU, #08967).

IGO Relations *World Trade Organization (WTO, #21864)* (Observer Status). Participates as observer in the activities of: *Codex Alimentarius Commission (CAC, #04081)*. Accredited to the Conference of the Parties of: *Secretariat of the United Nations Convention to Combat Desertification (Secretariat of the UNCCD, #19208)*. Cooperation with the councils of ministers of agriculture in the Southern, Andean and Caribbean regions. Also cooperation with agencies of the Inter-American System, regional and subregional agencies, agencies of the United Nations System, other international agencies and institutions of permanent observers and donor countries, including the following listed in this Yearbook:
– *Bioversity International (#03262)*;
– *Central American Bank for Economic Integration (CABEI, #03658)*;
– *Centre de coopération internationale en recherche agronomique pour le développement (CIRAD, #03733)*;
– *Centre technique de coopération agricole et rurale (CTA, inactive)*;
– European Community;
– *FAO (#09260)*;
– *Inter-American Development Bank (IDB, #11427)*;
– *International Bank for Reconstruction and Development (IBRD, #12317)*;
– *International Development Research Centre (IDRC, #13162)*;
– *International Fund for Agricultural Development (IFAD, #13692)*;
– *International Organization for Migration (IOM, #14454)*;
– *Japan International Cooperation Agency (JICA)*;
– *Swiss Agency for Development and Cooperation (SDC)*;
– *Tropical Agriculture Research and Higher Education Center (#20246)*;
– *UNDP (#20292)*;
– *UNESCO (#20322)*;
– *United States Agency for International Development (USAID)*;
– *World Food Programme (WFP, #21510)*.

Party to: *Agreement Concluded between the Governments of El Salvador, Honduras and Guatemala, the Inter-American Institute for Cooperation on Agriculture and the OAS General Secretariat Relative to an Extension for the Technical Cooperation for Execution of the Integral Development Plan for the Border Region Shared by the Three Countries (Trifinio plan, 1994)*.

NGO Relations Member of: *Climate and Clean Air Coalition (CCAC, #04010)*; *Global Alliance for Climate-Smart Agriculture (GACSA, #10189)*; *Global Development Learning Network (GDLN, #10317)*; *Global Open Data for Agriculture and Nutrition (GODAN, #10514)*; *World Water Council (WWC, #21908)*. Instrumental in setting up: *e-Agriculture (#00575)*. Cooperation with: *Caribbean – Central American Action (CCAA, inactive)*; *Caribbean Council of Higher Education in Agriculture (CACHE, #03484)*; *Confederación de Cooperativas del Caribe, Centro y Suramérica (CCC-CA, #04445)*; *Earth Council Alliance (ECA, inactive)*; *International Centre for Tropical Agriculture (#12527)*; *International Food Policy Research Institute (IFPRI, #13622)*; *International Maize and Wheat Improvement Center (#14077)*; *W K Kellogg Foundation (WKKF)*. [2013/XE1083/j/**E***]

♦ Inter-American Institute on Disability / see Inter-American Institute on Disability and Inclusive Development (#11435)

♦ Inter-American Institute on Disability and Inclusive Development (IIDI) 11435

Instituto Interamericano sobre Discapacidad – Instituto Inter-Americano sobre Deficiência

Exec Dir Senior Adviser, Children with Disabilities, UNICEF House, 3 UN Plaza Room 452, New York NY 10017, USA. T. +12128246067. Fax +12127354420. E-mail: iidienred@gmail.com.
URL: http://www.iidi.org/

History 14 Jan 1999, Washington, DC (USA). Former names and other names: *Inter-American Institute on Disability (IID)* – former; *Instituto Interamericano sobre Discapacidad* – former; *Instituto Inter-Americano sobre Deficiência* – former. **Aims** Act as a catalyst and information center, subsidizing and influencing the development of public policies in the disability field that will effectively contribute to social inclusion leading to the full exercise of citizenship; provide technical assistance to both public and private sectors, as well as to advocacy organizations of people with disabilities, professionals in the field, universities and technological research centers; contribute to improved public education in disability related subjects; contribute to the empowerment of the vast social sector comprised of persons with disabilities. **Structure** Executive Committee, comprising Board of Directors, Council of National representatives, Advisory Committee and International Support Network. Divisions (5): Public Policies; Research and Studies; Media and Information; Projects and Development; Training and Capacity Building. **Activities** Organizes *'Inter-American Conference on Disability and Development'*. [2011/XE3422/j/**E**]

♦ Inter-American Institute for Economic and Social Development (INDES) 11436

Instituto Interamericano para el Desarrollo Económico y Social

Dir c/o IDB Headquarters, 1300 New York Avenue NW, Washington DC 20577, USA. T. +12026231000. Fax +12026233096.
URL: https://indesvirtual.iadb.org/

History within the framework of *Inter-American Development Bank (IDB, #11427)*, as *Inter-American Institute for Social Development – Instituto Interamericano para el Desarrollo Social*. **Aims** Contribute to improve the effectiveness of development policies, programs and projects; connect knowledge, ideas and practices of IADB and other development partners to key clients, counterparts and the development community in the region, enhancing access to learning opportunities on topics related to social and economic development through the use of state-of-the-art platforms and technologies. **Languages** English, French, Portuguese, Spanish. **Staff** 35.00 FTE, paid. **Finance** Financed by administrative budget, agreements with national or local governments, and technical cooperation funds. **Activities** Major areas: social policy design; management of social programs and projects; strategic planning in the social sectors; targeting; intergovernmental management and negotiation; audit and evaluation techniques. Conducts training programmes at headquarters plus regional and country-specific programmes in the countries concerned. Workshops, seminars and courses, face to face, e-learning and blended. **Events** *Workshop on development effectiveness and management for results in Asia, Latin America and the Caribbean* Tokyo (Japan) 2007. **Publications** Educational and library materials. **Members** Not a membership organization. [2018/XE2773/j/**E***]

♦ Inter-American Institute for Global Change Research (IAI) 11437

Instituto Interamericano para la Investigación del Cambio Global

Exec Dir Av Italia 6201, Ed Los Tilos 102, 11500 Montevideo, Uruguay. T. +59826039558. E-mail: soledad@dir.iai.int.
URL: http://www.iai.int/

History 13 May 1992, Montevideo (Uruguay), when 12 governments of Latin America and North America signed the Agreement Establishing the Institute. The Agreement entered into force 11 Mar 1994 with the formal ratification of the Agreement by 6 countries. **Aims** Promote regional cooperation for *interdisciplinary* research on aspects of global change related to the sciences of earth, ocean, atmosphere and environment and to social sciences, with particular attention to impacts on *ecosystems* and *biodiversity*, to socio-economic impacts and technologies and economic aspects associated with the mitigation of and adaptation to global change; improve public awareness and provide scientific information to governments for the development of public policy relevant to global change. **Structure** Conference of the Parties (annual); Executive Council; Scientific Advisory Committee; Institute Research Centres; Affiliated Research Institutions; Directorate, composed of Director and staff. **Languages** English, French, Portuguese, Spanish. **Staff** 13.00 FTE, paid. **Finance** Voluntary contributions pledged annually for a 3-year period by the Parties. **Activities** Research/documentation; projects/programmes; capacity building; training/education; events. **Events** *Conference of the Parties* Montevideo (Uruguay) 2021, *Conference of the Parties* Asunción (Paraguay) 2020, *Conference of the Parties* Brasilia (Brazil) 2019, *Meeting* Colombia 2017, *Conference of the Parties* Santiago (Chile) 2016. **Publications** *IAI Newsletter* in English, Spanish. Annual Report. Research and Planning Activities. Workshop reports.

Members Governments of 19 countries:
Argentina, Bolivia, Brazil, Canada, Chile, Colombia, Costa Rica, Cuba, Dominican Rep, Ecuador, Guatemala, Jamaica, Mexico, Panama, Paraguay, Peru, Uruguay, USA, Venezuela.

IGO Relations Accredited by: *United Nations Framework Convention on Climate Change – Secretariat (UNFCCC, #20564)*. [2019.12.05/XE1921/j/**E***]

♦ Inter-American Institute of Human Rights (#11334)
♦ Inter-American Institute of International Legal Studies (inactive)
♦ Inter-American Institute for Labour Studies (inactive)
♦ Inter-American Institute of Municipal and Institutional History (inactive)
♦ Inter-American Institute of Music (inactive)
♦ Inter-American Institute for Social Development / see Inter-American Institute for Economic and Social Development (#11436)

♦ Inter-American Investment Corporation (IIC) 11438

Société interaméricaine d'investissement (SII) – Corporación Interamericana de Inversiones (CII) – Corporação Interamericana de Investimentos (CII)

Communications Officer 1350 New York Ave NW, Washington DC 20577, USA. T. +12026233900. Fax +12026233815.
URL: https://idbinvest.org

History 23 Mar 1986. Established on signature of an Agreement, as a multilateral investment corporation affiliated with *Inter-American Development Bank (IDB, #11427)*. Implementation of operational phases started in Sep 1988; full operations began 1989. Agreement amended by resolution effective 3 Oct 1995. Mandate expanded and rebranded in 2017. Former names and other names: *IDB Invest* – legal name (3 Nov 2017). **Aims** Promote economic development of Latin American and Caribbean member countries by providing financing for small and medium-sized private enterprises. **Structure** Board of Directors; Board of Executive Directors; Chief Executive Officer. **Languages** English, French, Portuguese, Spanish. **Finance** Initial capital – Replenishment for an additional US$ 500 million was approved in 1999 to be paid in between 2000 and 2007. As of March 2008, repaid capital is US$658 million. **Activities** Financial and/or material support. **Events** *Annual Meeting* Guayaquil (Ecuador) 2019, *Annual Meeting* Mendoza (Argentina) 2018, *Annual Meeting* Asunción (Paraguay) 2017, *Annual Meeting* Nassau (Bahamas) 2016, *Annual Meeting* Busan (Korea Rep) 2015. **Publications** Annual Report; pamphlets.

Members Governments of 45 countries:
Argentina, Austria, Bahamas, Barbados, Belgium, Belize, Bolivia, Brazil, Canada, Chile, China, Colombia, Costa Rica, Denmark, Dominican Rep, Ecuador, El Salvador, Finland, France, Germany, Guatemala, Guyana, Haiti, Honduras, Israel, Italy, Jamaica, Japan, Korea Rep, Mexico, Netherlands, Nicaragua, Norway, Panama, Paraguay, Peru, Portugal, Spain, Suriname, Sweden, Switzerland, Trinidad-Tobago, Uruguay, USA, Venezuela.

NGO Relations Partner of: *Global Forum on Law, Justice and Development (GFLJD, #10373)*. Member of: *International Network for Small and Medium Sized Enterprises (INSME, #14325)*; *SME Finance Forum (#19323)*. [2021/XF0291/e/**F***]

♦ Inter-American Juridical Committee (see: #17629)

♦ Inter-American Legal Services Association (ILSA) 11439

Institut interaméricain des services juridiques alternatifs – Instituto Latinoamericano de Servicios Legales

Dir Apartado Aéreo 077844, Calle 38, No 16-45, Bogota, Bogota DC, Colombia. T. +5712884772. Fax +5712884854. E-mail: jestrada@ilsa.org.co.
Pres address not obtained.
URL: http://www.ilsa.org.co/

History 1979. Also referred to as *Asociación Interamericana de Servicios Legales Alternativos*. **Aims** Promote alternative legal services, community self organization and critical transformation of the legal profession; work on reconversion of the human rights struggle. **Structure** International Board of Directors; Executive Director. **Languages** English, French, Portuguese, Spanish. **Staff** 20.00 FTE, paid; 3.00 FTE, voluntary. **Finance** Sources: donations; sale of publications; consultations. **Activities** Runs mobile school on alternative legal services. Carries out critical research on legal practices. Organizes human rights seminars. Studies: legal pluralism and alternative law; legal change and community self-organization. **Events** *Conference on sex tourism, sex work and Caribbean development paradigms* Kingston (Jamaica) 1998. **Publications** *Portavoz* (6 a year) – bulletin; *Beyond Law* (3 a year) – journal; *El Otro Derecho* (3 a year) – journal. *Derechos Humanos y Servicios Legales en el Campo* (1988); *Los Abogados y la Democracia en América Latina* (1986) by J Falcao et al. Information Services: Documentation centre. **IGO Relations** Partner of: *UNHCR (#20327)*. **NGO Relations** Member of: *EarthAction (EA, #05159)*; *Ford Foundation (#09858)*; *Inter-American Bar Association (IABA, #11401)*; *International Federation for Human Rights (#13452)*. Cooperates with: *Centre for Research on Latin America and the Caribbean (CERLAC)*. [2014/XD1240/**D**]

♦ Inter-American Metrology System 11440

Sistema Inter-Americano de Metrologia (SIM)

Secretariat Avda Italia 6201, 11500 Montevideo, Uruguay. T. +59898602386. E-mail: secretariat.sim.org@gmail.com.
Main Website: https://sim-metrologia.org/

History 1979. Established within *OAS (#17629)*. Reorganized Jan 1995. Current statutes adopted 2016. Registration: Start date: 2016, Uruguay. **Aims** Promote international, regional and, particularly, Inter-American cooperation in metrology issues. **Structure** General Assembly; Council; Secretariat. **Events** *General Assembly* Quito (Ecuador) 1999, *General Assembly* Heredia (Costa Rica) 1998, *General Assembly* Querétaro (Mexico) 1997, *General Assembly* Rio de Janeiro (Brazil) 1995, *General Assembly* Buenos Aires (Argentina) 1992. **Publications** *De Acuerdo*; *INFOSIM Magazine*. Technical publications. **Members** National metrology institutes in 30 countries. Membership countries not specified. **IGO Relations** Cooperates with (3): *Bureau international des poids et mesures (BIPM, #03367)*; *International Organization of Legal Metrology (#14451)*; *Intra-Africa Metrology System (AFRIMETS, #15992)*. **NGO Relations** Cooperates with (4): *Asia Pacific Metrology Programme (APMP, #01957)*; *European Association of National Metrology Institutes (EURAMET, #06129)*; *Inter-American Accreditation Cooperation (IAAC, #11396)*; *Pan American Standards Commission (#18133)*. [2020.04.30/XF5765/**F**]

♦ Inter-American Mine Workers Federation (inactive)
♦ Inter-American Music Council (no recent information)

♦ InterAmerican Network of Academies of Science (IANAS) 11441

Red Interamericana de Academias de Ciencias

Secretariat Academia Mexicana de Ciencias, Calle Cipreses s/n, Km 23/5 Carretera Federal México-Cuernavaca, 14400 Tlalpan CDMX, Mexico. T. +525555736501 – +525558495522. Fax +525558495112. E-mail: ianas2011@hotmail.com.
USA Office The Beckman Center, Office No 12, 100 Academy Way, Irvine CA 92617, USA. T. +19497212200.
URL: http://www.ianas.org/

History May 2004. A regional branch of *IAP – The Global Network of Science Academies (inactive)*. **Aims** Support cooperation towards the strengthening of science and technology as a tool for advancing research and development, prosperity and equity in the Americas. **Structure** Executive Committee, comprising 2 Co-Chairs and 7 members. **Languages** English. **Staff** Part-time from Science Academies. **Finance** Core funding from *IAP – The Global Network of Science Academies (inactive)*. Member academies provide financial support for activities organized in their countries. **Activities** Meeting activities. **Events** *General Assembly* Ottawa, ON (Canada) 2010.

Members Academies in 17 countries:
Argentina, Bolivia, Brazil, Canada, Chile, Colombia, Costa Rica, Cuba, Dominican Rep, Guatemala, Mexico, Peru, USA, Venezuela.

Included in the above, 3 organizations listed in this Yearbook:
Academia de Ciencias de América Latina (ACAL, #00010); *Caribbean Academy of Sciences (CAS)*; *Caribbean Scientific Union (#03553)*.

IGO Relations Recognized by Permanent Council of *OAS (#17629)*. **NGO Relations** Supports: *Red Latinoamericana de Ciencias Biológicas (RELAB, #18706)*. Regional network of: *InterAcademy Partnership (IAP, #11376)*. [2012.09.11/XJ8268/y/**D**]

♦ Inter-American Network on Citrus Production Improvement and Trade Development / see Inter-American Citrus Network (#11407)
♦ Inter-American Network for Environmental Protection (no recent information)
♦ Inter-American Network of Food Analysis Laboratories (#18694)
♦ Interamerican Network for Healthful Housing (#18695)
♦ Inter-American Network of Women's Shelters (unconfirmed)
♦ Inter-American Nuclear Energy Commission (inactive)
♦ Inter-American Observatory on Drugs (see: #11429)
♦ Inter-American Open University (internationally oriented national body)

♦ Inter-American Organization for Higher Education (IOHE) 11442

Organisation universitaire interaméricaine (OUI) – Organización Universitaria Interamericana (OUI) – Organização Universitária Interamericana (OUI)

Pres/Founder 3744 Jean-Brillant, Suite 592, Montréal QC H3T 1P1, Canada. T. +15143436980. E-mail: info@oui-iohe.org.
URL: http://www.oui-iohe.org/

History 1979. Founded as a response to the lack of collaborative linkages between universities in the Americas. Statutes adopted 11 Oct 1999, Québec QC (Canada). Registration: Costa Rica. **Aims** Build common spaces in higher education in the Americas to promote cooperation among members institutions; foster development of the quality of higher education across the hemisphere; encourage pooling of resources to improve quality of higher education; serve as a network of partners supporting inter-American university cooperation; provide a vision of the Americas based on solidarity and mutual assistance. **Structure** General Assembly (annual); Board of Directors; Regional Councils. Regions (9): Canada; USA; Mexico; Central America; Caribbean; Andean countries; Colombia; Brazil; Southern Cone. **Languages** English, French, Portuguese, Spanish. **Staff** 4.00 FTE, paid. **Finance** Members' dues based on number of students. Other sources: special contributions by universities; Government of Canada, and especially *Canadian International Development Agency (CIDA, inactive)*; *Inter-American Development Bank (IDB, #11427)*; *International Development Research Centre (IDRC, #13162)*; Government of Québec (Canada); foundations, associations, and regional, national, and international organizations; contributions from members of financial, material, and human resources towards the realization of special activities. **Activities** Events/meetings; knowledge management/information dissemination; networking/liaising; projects/programmes. **Events** *Conference of the Americas on International Education / Congrès des Amériques sur l'éducation internationale / Congreso de las Américas sobre Educación Internacional* Las Vegas, NV (USA) 2023, *Conference of the Americas on International Education / Congrès des Amériques sur l'éducation internationale / Congreso de las Américas sobre Educación Internacional* Santiago (Chile) 2021, *Conference of the Americas on International Education* Bogota (Colombia) 2019, *Conference of the Americas on International Education* Montréal, QC (Canada) 2017, *Conference of the Americas on International Education* Quito (Ecuador) 2015.

Members Higher education institutions and associations (over 120), in 25 countries:
Argentina, Bolivia, Brazil, Canada, Chile, Colombia, Costa Rica, Cuba, Dominican Rep, Ecuador, El Salvador, Guatemala, Guyana, Haiti, Honduras, Jamaica, Mexico, Nicaragua, Panama, Paraguay, Peru, Trinidad-Tobago, Uruguay, USA, Venezuela.

Member university associations (33) and other organizations in 14 countries:
Bolivia, Brazil, Canada, Chile, Colombia, Costa Rica, Dominican Rep, Ecuador, Guatemala, Jamaica, Mexico, Peru, USA, Venezuela.

Included in the above, 6 organizations listed in this Yearbook:
Asociación de Universidades de América Latina y el Caribe para la Integración (AUALCPI, #02305); *Centro Interuniversitario de Desarrollo (CINDA, #03809)*; *Confederación Universitaria Centroamericana (CSUCA, #04497)*; *Consortium for North American Higher Education Collaboration (CONAHEC, #04756)*; *Inter-American Distance Education Consortium (#11428)*; *Universities Caribbean (#20694)*.

Consultative Status Consultative status granted from: *UNESCO (#20322)* (Consultative Status). **IGO Relations** *Inter-American Development Bank (IDB, #11427)*; *OAS (#17629)*; *Pan American Health Organization (PAHO, #18108)*; *Confederación Parlamentaria de las Américas (COPA, #04479)*; *UNESCO International Institute for Higher Education in Latin America and the Caribbean (#20309)*; *UNESCO Regional Bureau for Education in Latin America and the Caribbean (#20318)*. **NGO Relations** *Agence universitaire de la Francophonie (AUF, #00548)*; *Association of Universities of Latin America and the Caribbean (#02970)*; *College of the Americas (COLAM, #04104)*; *Consortium for North American Higher Education Collaboration (CONAHEC, #04756)*; *Cooperación Latino Americana de Redes Avanzadas (RedCLARA, #04790)*; *European University Association (EUA, #09027)*; *Hispanic Association of Colleges and Universities (HACU)*; *Institute of University Management and Leadership (IGLU-Leaders, #11298)*; *Instituto Latinoamericano y del Caribe de Calidad en Educación Superior a Distancia (CALED, #11342)* *Inter-American Centre for Studies on Water Resources (#11404)*; *Inter-American Distance Education Consortium (#11428)*; *International Association of Universities (IAU, #12246)*; *Latin American and Caribbean Consortium of Engineering Institutions (LACCEI, #16270)*; *Latin American Council of Business Schools (#16308)*; *Red Interamericana para el Mejoramiento de la Calidad Ambiental (RICA, no recent information)*; *Virtual Educa (#20787)*. [2023.02.15/XD0169/y/**D**]

♦ Inter-American Organization on Inter-Municipal Cooperation / see Organización Iberoamericana de Cooperación Intermunicipal (#17839)
♦ Inter-American Parents' Union (inactive)
♦ Inter-American Peace Committee (inactive)
♦ Inter-American Peace Force (inactive)
♦ Inter American Philatelic Federation (#09332)

♦ Inter-American Photochemical Society (I-APS) 11443

Sec Chemistry Dept, Wake Forest University, Salem Hall, Box 7486, Winston-Salem NC 27109, USA.
URL: http://www.i-aps.org/

History 1982. **Activities** Awards: I-APS Award in Photochemistry; I-APS Young Investigator Award; Gerhard Closs Student Award. **Events** *Winter Conference* Sarasota, FL (USA) 2014, *Meeting* St Petersburg, FL (USA) 2007, *Meeting* USA 2007, *Meeting* Salvador (Brazil) 2006, *Meeting* Clearwater, FL (USA) 2005. **Publications** *I-APS Newsletter* (2 a year). **Members** Individuals (over 400). Membership countries not specified. [2014/XD6888/**D**]

♦ Inter-American Planning Society (inactive)
♦ Inter-American Police Academy (inactive)
♦ Inter-American Port Conference / see Inter-American Committee on Ports (#11415)

♦ Inter American Press Association (IAPA) 11444

Association interaméricaine de la presse – Sociedad Interamericana de Prensa (SIP) – Sociedade Interamericana de Imprensa

Exec Dir 3511 NW 91st Avenue, Doral FL 33172, USA. T. +13056342465 – +13059873363. Fax +13056352272. E-mail: info@sipiapa.org.
URL: http://www.sipiapa.org/

History 1942, Mexico City (Mexico), a first *'Pan American Congress of Journalists'* having been held 1926, Washington DC (USA). Reorganized at 6th Inter-American Press Conference, 1950, New York NY (USA), when Constitution was adopted. **Aims** Protect freedom of the press in the Americas and defend and promote the right of the American peoples to be fully and freely informed through an independent press; foster and protect press freedom by publishing facts of any action or attempt to restrict that freedom in the Western Hemisphere; foster general and specific press interests; promote and maintain the dignity, rights and responsibilities of the profession of *journalism*; encourage uniform standards of professional and business conduct; promote greater exchange among American peoples in support of basic principles of a free society and individual liberty. **Structure** General Assembly (annual). Board of Directors (meets annually), consisting of 60 members. Executive Committee, comprising 20 members. Advisory Council, composed of 33 members. Committees (13): Awards; Chapultepec; Finance; Freedom of the Press; Foundations; Future Sites; Impunity; International Affairs; Legal; Membership; Nominations; Program; Internet. **Languages** English, Portuguese, Spanish. **Staff** 12.00 FTE, paid. **Finance** Members' dues. Other sources: contributions; grants; convention and seminar fees. **Activities** Maintains: *Inter-American Press Association Press Institute (see: #11444)*, which organizes seminars and produces publications; *IAPA Scholarship Fund (no recent information)*, set up 1954. Set up: *Office of Certified Circulation (OCC)*, started 1954, which subsequently became autonomous and was then replaced by national and regional organizations which continue helping to increase advertising income and thus financial independence. **Events** *Annual General Assembly* Madrid (Spain) 2021, *Midyear Meeting* Saltillo (Mexico) 2021, *Annual General Assembly* Doral, FL (USA) 2020, *Midyear Meeting* Saltillo (Mexico) 2020, *Annual General Assembly* Coral Gables, FL (USA) 2019. **Publications** *IAPA News* (12 a year) in English, Spanish; *Hora de Cierre* (4 a year) in Spanish – print and online. Periodic reports on state of the press in each country; proceedings of annual meetings.

Members Active (newspapers and magazines published 6 or more times a year); Associate; Life, totalling 1,421 individual members, in 35 countries and territories:
Antigua-Barbuda, Argentina, Aruba, Bahamas, Barbados, Belize, Bermuda, Bolivia, Brazil, Canada, Chile, Colombia, Costa Rica, Cuba, Curaçao, Dominican Rep, Ecuador, El Salvador, Grenada, Guatemala, Guyana, Haiti, Honduras, Jamaica, Mexico, Nicaragua, Panama, Paraguay, Peru, Puerto Rico, Suriname, Trinidad-Tobago, Uruguay, USA, Venezuela.

Consultative Status Consultative status granted from: *ECOSOC (#05331)* (Special); *UNESCO (#20322)* (Associate Status). **IGO Relations** Close cooperation with: *OAS (#17629)*. Associated with Department of Global Communications of the United Nations. Invited to sessions of Intergovernmental Council of: *International Programme for the Development of Communication (IPDC, #14651)*. **NGO Relations** Member of: *IFEX (#11100)*. [2020.03.03/XD1094/**D**]

- ♦ Inter-American Press Association Press Institute (see: #11444)
- ♦ Inter-American Program for Education (no recent information)
- ♦ Inter-American Public Budget Association / see Public Budget International Association (#18564)
- ♦ Inter-American Publishers Group (#10805)
- ♦ Inter-American Radio Agreement, 1940 (1940 treaty)
- ♦ Inter-American Radio Agreement, 1949 (1949 treaty)
- ♦ Inter-American Radiocommunications Convention, 1937 (1937 treaty)
- ♦ Inter-American Radio Office (inactive)
- ♦ Inter-American Regional Organization of the International Federation of Commercial, Clerical, Professional and Technical Employees / see UNI Global Union – Americas Regional Office (#20340)
- ♦ Inter-American Rural Housing Association (inactive)
- ♦ Inter-American Safety Council (no recent information)
- ♦ Inter-American Save and Loan for Housing Union / see Inter-American Housing Union (#11433)

♦ Inter-American Scout Committee (ISC) 11445

Comité interaméricain de scoutisme – Comité Scout Interamericano (CSI)

Panama Office City of Knowledge – building 172, Panama, Panamá, Panama PANAMá, Panama. T. +5073171158 – +5073171808. E-mail: interamerica@scout.org.
URL: http://www.scout.org/

History 1946, Bogota (Colombia). Founded at first Inter-American Scout Conference, inspired by Resolution 'L' of the Inter-American Conference for the Consolidation of Peace, 1936, Buenos Aires (Argentina). Former names and other names: *Consejo Interamericano de Escultismo (CIE)* – alias. **Aims** Provide technical assistance to national Scout associations in the region, in the fields of: programme, training, *professional* Scout service, community development; improve Scouting at all levels. **Structure** Committee, consisting of 10 members elected by *Inter-American Scout Conference*, meets at least once a year. *Inter-American Scout Office – Oficina Scout Interamericana*, an integral part of *World Organization of the Scout Movement (WOSM, #21693)*, acts as regional secretariat. Regional Executive Commissioners. **Languages** English, Spanish. **Staff** 9.00 FTE, paid; 80.00 FTE, voluntary. **Finance** Regional fees. Donations; grants; interest from *Interamerican Scout Foundation (ISF, #11446)*. Budget (annual): US$ 290,000. **Activities** Carries out courses, seminars, workshops. **Events** *Triennial Inter-American Scout Conference* Argentina 2013, *Inter-American Jamboree* Bogota (Colombia) 2013, *Triennial inter-American scout conference* Panama (Panama) 2010, *Pan-American jamboree* Toluca (Mexico) 2010, *Pan-American moot* Cochabamba (Bolivia) 2008. **Publications** *SIS Bulletin* (12 a year). Scout manuals and literature; poster and leaflets.
Members Scout associations, representing over 4,500,000 individuals, in 35 countries and territories:
Anguilla, Antigua-Barbuda, Argentina, Bahamas, Barbados, Belize, Bolivia, Brazil, Canada, Chile, Colombia, Costa Rica, Dominica, Dominican Rep, Ecuador, El Salvador, Grenada, Guatemala, Guyana, Haiti, Honduras, Jamaica, Mexico, Nicaragua, Panama, Paraguay, Peru, St Kitts-Nevis, St Lucia, St Vincent-Grenadines, Suriname, Trinidad-Tobago, Uruguay, USA, Venezuela.
IGO Relations Advisory body to Committee on Youth Affairs of: *OAS (#17629)*. Contacts with: *UNDP (#20292)*; *UNEP (#20299)*; *UNICEF (#20332)*. [2014.02.26/XD1638/**D**]

♦ Interamerican Scout Foundation (ISF) 11446

Contact 1325 W Walnut Hill Ln, PO Box 152079, Irving TX 75015-2079, USA. E-mail: intnldiv@netbsa.org.
URL: http://www.interamfoundation.org/

History 1980, Santiago (Chile), at XII Inter-American Scout Conference, within the framework of *Inter-American Scout Committee (ISC, #11445)*, as *Inter-American Scout Fund (ISF)*. 1994, became a separate legal entity, registered in Texas (USA). **Aims** Support Scout associations in countries of the American continent so that greater numbers of *young* people may benefit from the Scout programme and ensure continuity of the movement. **Finance** Pledged gifts giving status of gold, silver or bronze medal of the Order of the Condor. [2008/XK0424/f/**F**]

- ♦ Inter-American Scout Fund / see Interamerican Scout Foundation (#11446)

♦ Inter-American Social Protection Network (IASPN) 11447

Red Interamericana de Protección Social (RIPSO)

Contact c/o OAS, 1889 F St NW 7th Floor, Washington DC 20006, USA.
URL: https://socialprotection.org/connect/stakeholders/inter-american-social-protection-network-iaspn

Aims Promote the exchange and transfer of experiences and knowledge on social protection. **IGO Relations** *OAS (#17629)*. [2021/XJ7192/**F**]

- ♦ Inter-American Social Welfare Conference (inactive)
- ♦ Inter-American Society of Anthropology and Geography (inactive)

♦ Inter-American Society of Cardiology (ISC) 11448

Société interaméricaine de cardiologie – Sociedad Interamericana de Cardiologia (SIAC) – Sociedade Interamericana de Cardiologia (SIAC)

Permanent Address c/o INC Ignacio Chavez, Juan Badiano 1, Col Sección XVI, Tlalpan, 14080 Mexico City CDMX, Mexico. T. +525555135177. E-mail: siac@siacardio.org.
URL: http://www.siacardio.com/

History 1944, Mexico City (Mexico). Founded at inaugural ceremony, on the initiative of Dr Ignacio Chávez. Statutes revised 1968, Lima (Peru). **Aims** Promote optical cardiovascular health and healthcare for all people of the Americas through education and continuing professional development; encourage research and training; facilitate professional development; promote visiting fellowship exchanges. **Structure** General Assembly (at least every 2 years, at Inter-American Congress), consisting of one representative from each Latin American country and 2 representatives each from Canada and USA. Executive Board. Congress rotates among countries in South America, Central America and the Caribbean and North America. Secretariat in Mexico. **Languages** English, Portuguese, Spanish. **Staff** 1.50 FTE, paid. **Finance** Members' dues. Other sources: solicited support (unrestricted educational grants); Congress revenues. **Activities** Organizes: Inter-American Congress of Cardiology (IACC) every 2 years; other conferences and internet educational opportunities. Facilitates postgraduate scholarship exchanges. Developing standardized training criteria and fellowship certification. **Events** *Virtual Congress* 2021, *Congreso Interamericano de Cardiologia / Inter-American Congress of Cardiology (IACC)* Punta Cana (Dominican Rep) 2019, *Congress* Panama (Panama) 2017, *Congress* Santiago (Chile) 2015, *Congress* Buenos Aires (Argentina) 2013. **Publications** *IASC Bulletin* (2 a year); *IASC Newsletter* – online. Information leaflets.
Members National associations, comprising about 22,000 individuals, in 23 countries:
Argentina, Bolivia, Brazil, Canada, Chile, Colombia, Costa Rica, Cuba, Dominican Rep, Ecuador, El Salvador, Guatemala, Honduras, Mexico, Nicaragua, Panama, Paraguay, Peru, Puerto Rico, Uruguay, USA, Venezuela.
Also members in Caribbean. Membership countries not specified.
NGO Relations Member of: *The NCD Alliance (NCDA, #16963)*; *World Heart Federation (WHF, #21562)*. [2021/XD1100/**D**]

- ♦ Inter-American Society for Chemotherapy (no recent information)
- ♦ Inter-American Society for Cooperative Finance Development (inactive)
- ♦ Interamerican Society of Digestive Endoscopy (#19384)
- ♦ Inter-American Society for Educational Administration (inactive)
- ♦ Inter-American Society for the Freedom of Commercial Speech (no recent information)

♦ Inter-American Society of Hypertension (IASH) 11449

Sociedad Interamericana de Hipertensión – Sociedade Interamericana de Hipertensão

Pres Inst Mexicano de Salud Cardiovascular, Tuxpan 16, 06760 Mexico City CDMX, Mexico. T. +5215554040801.
URL: http://iashonline.org/

History Founded May 1980, when incorporated in the state of Ohio (USA), a *Pan American Symposium on Vasoactive Peptides and Hypertension* having first met as a formal meeting, Aug 1974, Mendoza (Argentina). **Aims** Understand, prevent and control hypertension and *vascular diseases* with emphasis on bridging basic, translational and clinical research across the Americas. **Structure** Board of Trustees; Executive Committee. **Languages** English, Portuguese, Spanish. **Staff** Voluntary. **Finance** No members' dues. Annual budget: US$ 50,000. **Activities** Events/meetings; projects/programmes; training/education; awards/prizes/competitions; financial and/or material support. **Events** *Scientific Meeting* Guayaquil (Ecuador) 2018, *Triennial Scientific Meeting* Mendoza (Argentina) 2017, *Triennial Scientific Meeting* Salvador (Brazil) 2014, *Triennial Scientific Meeting* Orlando, FL (USA) 2011, *Biennial scientific meeting* Belo Horizonte (Brazil) 2009. **Publications** Meeting proceedings (every 2 years).
Members Scientists and physicians and persons interested in the field of hypertension and vascular disease in 38 countries and territories:
Argentina, Australia, Austria, Brazil, Bulgaria, Canada, Chile, China, Colombia, Costa Rica, Cuba, Dominican Rep, Ecuador, El Salvador, Germany, Greece, Guatemala, Haiti, Honduras, India, Israel, Italy, Japan, Mexico, Neth Antilles, Nicaragua, Pakistan, Panama, Peru, Puerto Rico, Russia, Slovenia, Spain, Switzerland, Taiwan, Uruguay, USA, Venezuela.
NGO Relations Member of: *World Hypertension League (WHL, #21574)*. [2019.12.13/XD1455/**D**]

- ♦ Inter-American Society of Philosophy (#19385)

♦ Inter-American Society of Psychology (ISP) 11450

Société interaméricaine de psychologie – Sociedad Interamericana de Psicologia (SIP) – Sociedade Interamericana de Psicologia (SIP)

Gen Sec Universidad de Puerto Rico, 1187 Calle Flamboyan, San Juan PR PR-00926-1117, USA. E-mail: b.ortiz@upr.edu – sip.oficinacentral@upr.edu.
URL: http://www.sipsych.org/

History 17 Dec 1951, Mexico City (Mexico). Constitution adopted at 2nd Congress, Dec 1954, Mexico City. Constitution revised: Dec 1955, Austin TX (USA); 1967, Mexico City. Previously also known under the acronym *IASP*. **Aims** Foster scientific and professional relationships among persons concerned with psychology and related fields in the countries of North America, Central America, the Caribbean and South America and promote the development of the behavioural sciences in the Western Hemisphere; help further research, scholarly dialogue and interaction throughout the Americas; strive to contribute to international understanding by fostering learning about cultural differences and encouraging psychologists to interact across national boundaries. **Structure** Board of Governors. Officers: President; President-Elect; Past-President; 3 Regional Vice-Presidents; Treasurer; Secretary General; 3 Executive Secretaries. **Languages** English, French, Portuguese, Spanish. **Staff** 1.00 FTE, voluntary. **Finance** Members' dues. **Activities** Promotes exchange of students and research in psychology in North, Central and South America; facilitates exchange of published works; assists visitors in centres of training and research; organizes seminars and biennial congresses; awards biennial Student Prize. Central Office acts as focal point for information exchange – research, publications, training opportunities. **Events** *Biennial Congress* Asunción (Paraguay) 2023, *Biennial Congress* 2021, *Biennial Congress* Havana (Cuba) 2019, *Biennial Congress* Mérida (Mexico) 2017, *Biennial Congress* Lima (Peru) 2015. **Publications** *Interamerican Psychologist* (2 a year) – newsletter; *Revista Interamericana de Psicologia – Interamerican Journal of Psychology* (2 a year). *Latin American Psychology – A Bibliography* (1976); *Avances en Psicologia Contemporanea*. Proceedings of Congresses.
Members Individuals (over 1,000) in 38 countries and territories:
Argentina, Australia, Austria, Bolivia, Brazil, Canada, Chile, Colombia, Costa Rica, Cuba, Dominican Rep, Ecuador, El Salvador, France, Germany, Guatemala, Honduras, Italy, Jamaica, Mexico, Netherlands, Nicaragua, Norway, Panama, Paraguay, Peru, Portugal, Puerto Rico, Spain, Sweden, Switzerland, Trinidad-Tobago, Ukraine, Uruguay, USA, Venezuela.
IGO Relations *UNESCO (#20322)*. **NGO Relations** Associate of: *International Union of Psychological Science (IUPsyS, #15807)*. [2020/XD1101/v/**D**]

♦ InterAmerican Society of Tropical Horticulture (ISTH) 11451

Sociedad InterAmericana de Horticultura Tropical – Sociedade InterAmericana de Horticultura Tropical

Exec Dir Embrapa Tropical Agroindustry, Rua Dra Sara Mesquita 2270, Pici 60 511-110, Fortaleza CE, Brazil. T. +558533917204. Fax +558533917222.
URL: https://iasth.org/

History 1951, USA. Current title adopted when group was separated from ASHS. Former names and other names: *Caribbean Group of the American Society for Horticultar Science (ASHS)* – former (1951 to 1966); *American Society for Horticultural Science – Tropical Region* – former (1966 to 1986). **Aims** Foster the study, appreciation and economic viability of horticultural crops in the tropics. **Structure** Officers: President; Vice-President; Executive Director; Treasurer; Secretary; 6 Committee Members; Country Representatives; 9 Editorial Committee Chairs; 2 Journal Editors; 2 Newsletter Editors; Electronic Media Editor. **Languages** English, Portuguese, Spanish. **Staff** 11.00 FTE, voluntary. **Finance** Members' dues: Student – US$ 20 – 40; Professional – US$ 60; Institutional – US$ 90; Contributor – minimum US$ 120. **Events** *Annual Meeting* 2018, *Annual Meeting* Porto Seguro (Brazil) 2017, *Annual Meeting* Añasco (Puerto Rico) 2016, *Annual Meeting* Manaus (Brazil) 2015, *Annual Meeting* Medellin (Colombia) 2014. **Publications** *Journal of the ISTH* (annual); *ISTH Newsletter* (at least annual).
Members Categories Undergraduate Student; Graduate Student; Professional; Institutional; Contributor. Members in 35 countries and territories:
Argentina, Australia, Belgium, Bermuda, Bolivia, Brazil, Canada, Cayman Is, Chile, Colombia, Costa Rica, Cuba, Dominican Rep, Ecuador, El Salvador, France, Guatemala, Honduras, Israel, Italy, Jamaica, Japan, Mexico, Netherlands, New Zealand, Peru, Portugal, Puerto Rico, South Africa, Spain, Trinidad-Tobago, UK, USA, Venezuela, Virgin Is USA.
NGO Relations In partnership with: *International Society for Horticultural Science (ISHS, #15180)*. [2019/XD7619/**D**]

- ♦ Inter-American Specialized Conference on Private International Law (meeting series)

♦ Inter-American Statistical Institute (IASI) 11452

Institut interaméricain de statistique – Instituto Interamericano de Estadistica

Exec Dir PO Box 0832-01855, Panama, Panamá, Panama PANAMá, Panama. T. +50766746279. E-mail: fabpan@cwpanama.net.
URL: https://www.inec.gob.pa/iasi/

History 12 May 1940, Washington, DC (USA). Statutes revised: 1948; 1950; 1960; 1967; 1983; 1987; 1999; 2008; 2013. **Aims** Promote statistical development in the American region. **Structure** Executive Committee; Permanent Office; Editorial Office; Advisory Board; Sections; Working Groups. **Languages** English, French, Portuguese, Spanish. **Staff** 3.50 FTE, paid. **Finance** Sources: government support; grants; international organizations; members' dues. Annual budget: 30,000 USD (2021). **Activities** Events/meetings; knowledge management/information dissemination; networking/liaising; projects/programmes; publishing activities; research/documentation. **Events** *Meeting on Public Statistics* Lima (Peru) 2014, *Meeting on Public Statistics* Rio de Janeiro (Brazil) 2012, *Meeting on Public Statistics* Asunción (Paraguay) 2010, *Seminar on Applied Statistics* Medellin (Colombia) 2010, *Meeting* Lima (Peru) 2009. **Publications** *Boletin Informativo* – newsletter; *Estadistica* – journal.
Members Individual (240); Institutional – Affiliated and Sponsoring – (49) in 36 countries:
Antigua-Barbuda, Argentina, Bahamas, Barbados, Belize, Bolivia, Brazil, Canada, Chile, Colombia, Costa Rica, Dominica, Dominican Rep, Ecuador, El Salvador, Grenada, Guatemala, Guyana, Haiti, Honduras, Jamaica, Malta, Mexico, Nicaragua, Panama, Paraguay, Peru, Spain, St Kitts-Nevis, St Lucia, St Vincent-Grenadines, Suriname, Trinidad-Tobago, Uruguay, USA, Venezuela.
Consultative Status Consultative status granted from: *ECOSOC (#05331)* (Special). **IGO Relations** Associated with Department of Global Communications of the United Nations. **NGO Relations** Member of (1): *International Statistical Institute (ISI, #15603)*. [2022.05.05/XE1102/j/**E**]

- ♦ Inter-American Statistical Training Centre (no recent information)
- ♦ Inter-American Telecommunication Commission (#04138)
- ♦ Inter-American Telecommunications Convention, 1945 (1945 treaty)

♦ Inter-American Theosophical Federation (IATF) 11453

Federación Teosófica Interamericana (FTI)

Contact 1501 S Spaulding Ave, Los Angeles CA 9019, USA.
Pres address not obtained. T. +50622963572. Fax +50622965758.

Sec address not obtained.
History Founded around 1970. Incorporated in the USA, 2002. **Aims** Form a nucleus of universal brotherhood of humanity, without distinction of race, creed, sex, caste or colour; encourage comparative study of religions, philosophy and science; investigate unexplained laws of nature and the powers latent in humanity. **Structure** A federation of *Theosophical Society (TS, #20141)*. President; Vice-President; Secretary; Treasurer; 2 Auditors. **Languages** English, Spanish. **Staff** 5.00 FTE, voluntary. **Finance** Voluntary members' contributions. **Activities** Organizes conferences and seminars. **Events** *Congress* Wheaton, IL (USA) 2008, *Congress* San José (Costa Rica) 2005. **Publications** Books; pamphlet.
Members Individuals in 17 countries and territories:
Argentina, Bolivia, Brazil, Canada, Chile, Colombia, Costa Rica, Cuba, Dominican Rep, El Salvador, Guatemala, Mexico, Nicaragua, Peru, Puerto Rico, Uruguay, USA.
Honorary member in one country:
Spain. [2020/XD7321/**D**]

♦ Inter-American Trade Mark Bureau (inactive)
♦ Interamerican Transportation Chamber / see International Chamber of the Transport Industry (#12536)
♦ Inter-American Transport Chamber / see International Chamber of the Transport Industry (#12536)
♦ Inter-American Treaty on Good Offices and Mediation (1936 treaty)
♦ Inter-American Treaty of Reciprocal Assistance (1947 treaty)

♦ Inter-American Tropical Tuna Commission (IATTC) 11454

Comisión Interamericana del Atún Tropical (CIAT)
Dir 8901 La Jolla Shores Drive, La Jolla CA 92037-1509, USA. T. +18585467100. Fax +18585467133.
Senior Policy Advisor address not obtained.
URL: http://www.iattc.org/
History Established 31 May 1949, Washington DC (USA), on signature of Convention between USA and Costa Rica. Convention entered into force in 1950. Jun 2003, Antigua (Guatemala), adoption of the *Convention for the Strengthening of the Inter-American Tropical Tuna Commission Established by the 1949 Convention Between the United States of America and the Republic of Costa Rica (Antigua Convention)*, replacing previous Convention. Opening for signature, 14 Nov 2003, Washington DC (USA); entry into force, 27 Aug 2010. **Aims** Ensure long-term *conservation* and *sustainable* use of stocks of tunas and tuna-like species and other species of fish taken by vessels fishing for tunas and tuna-like species in the Convention Area, in accordance with relevant rules of international law. **Structure** Commission; Committees (3); Working Groups. **Languages** English, Spanish. **Staff** 74.00 FTE, paid. **Finance** Members' dues. Other sources: funds with voluntary contributions. **Activities** Awareness raising; capacity building; events/meetings; financial and/or material support; knowledge management/information dissemination; monitoring/evaluation; politics/policy/regulatory; projects/programmes; publishing activities; research and development; research/documentation; standards/guidelines; management of treaties and agreements. **Events** *Meeting* Bilbao (Spain) 2019, *Meeting* San Diego, CA (USA) 2018, *Meeting* La Jolla, CA (USA) 2017, *Meeting* Mexico City (Mexico) 2017, *Resumed session* La Jolla, CA (USA) 2016. **Publications** *IATTC Bulletin* in English, Spanish. Annual report in English, Spanish; Fishery Status Reports in English/Spanish; Special Reports in English, Spanish or English/Spanish; Stock Assessment Reports in English, Spanish.
Members Parties to the Antigua Convention (14):
Belize, Canada, China, Costa Rica, El Salvador, France, Guatemala, Japan, Kiribati, Korea Rep, Mexico, Nicaragua, Panama, USA.
Regional entity party to the Convention:
European Union (EU, #08967).
Written communication of commitment by one government:
Taiwan.
Parties to the 1949 Convention (5):
Colombia, Ecuador, Peru, Vanuatu, Venezuela.
Cooperating non-members (5):
Bolivia, Chile, Honduras, Indonesia, Liberia.
IGO Relations Relationship agreement with: *Comisión Permanente del Pacífico Sur (CPPS, #04141)*; *FAO (#09260)*; *Indian Ocean Tuna Commission (IOTC, #11162)*; *International Commission for the Conservation of Atlantic Tunas (ICCAT, #12675)*; *International Scientific Committee for Tuna and Tuna-like Species in the North Pacific Ocean (ISC, #14807)*; *Western and Central Pacific Fisheries Commission (WCPFC, #20912)*. Observer member of: *Commission for the Conservation of Southern Bluefin Tuna (CCSBT, #04207)*. **NGO Relations** NGOs having observer status include: *BirdLife International (#03266)*; *Conservation International (CI)*; *Greenpeace International (#10727)*; *Humane Society International (HSI, #10966)*; *International Seafood Sustainability Foundation (ISSF)*; *Marine Stewardship Council (MSC, #16580)*; *Ocean Conservancy*; *Organization for the Promotion of Responsible Tuna Fisheries (OPRT, #17886)*; *Pew Charitable Trusts*; *Whale and Dolphin Conservation (WDC)*; *World Wide Fund for Nature (WWF, #21922)* (World Wildlife Fund). [2020.03.04/XD1107/**D***]

♦ Inter-American Union of Electoral Organizations (#20413)
♦ Inter-American Union of Savings and Loan for Housing / see Inter-American Housing Union (#11433)
♦ Inter-American University (inactive)
♦ Inter-American University Council for Economic and Social Development (no recent information)
♦ Inter-American University of Puerto Rico (internationally oriented national body)

♦ Interarab Cambist Association (ICA) 11455

Association cambiste interarabe
Secretariat Central District, Atrium Building, 1st floor, Beirut, Lebanon. T. +9611970833. Fax +9611970834. E-mail: relhage@ica-arab.com.
URL: http://www.ica-arab.com/
History 1972, Beirut (Lebanon). Founded following agreement by foreign exchange dealers representing 13 Arab countries. Former names and other names: *Forex Club Interarab* – former. **Aims** Foster understanding and cooperation between *dealers* in *Arab banks*; promote friendship amongst members. **Languages** Arabic, English. **Staff** 1.00 FTE, paid. 5 temporary. **Finance** Conference proceeds. **Activities** Organizes: annual Congress with trade show; regular trainings; workshops. **Events** *Annual Congress* Dubai (United Arab Emirates) 2021, *World Congress* Dubai (United Arab Emirates) 2021, *World Congress* Dubai (United Arab Emirates) 2020, *Annual Congress* Manama (Bahrain) 2019, *Annual Congress* Cairo (Egypt) 2018.
Members Dealers in 13 countries:
Algeria, Bahrain, Egypt, Jordan, Kuwait, Lebanon, Morocco, Oman, Palestine, Qatar, Saudi Arabia, Tunisia, United Arab Emirates.
NGO Relations Cooperates with (1): *Financial Markets Association (FMA, #09767)*. [2020/XD5353/**D**]

♦ Inter-Arab Investment Guarantee Corporation / see Arab Investment and Export Credit Guarantee Corporation (#00997)
♦ Inter-Arab Union of Hotels and Tourism (inactive)
♦ INTERARTS Foundation (internationally oriented national body)

♦ Inter-Asia Cultural Studies Society (IACS Society) 11456

Gen Sec Inst for East Asian Studies, Sungkonghoe Uni, Hang-dong 1-1, Guro-gu, Seoul 08368, Korea Rep. E-mail: interasiaculturalstudies@gmail.com – iacssc@gmail.com.
URL: http://culturalstudies.asia/
History 2004. Formed as a response to Inter-Asia Cultural Studies project, which started in the late 1990s. Developed into a more institutionalized international society, 2011. Registration: Hong Kong. **Aims** Create and encourage a trans-border academic programme between Asian academic institutions. **Structure** Board; Executive Committee. Includes Inter-Asia Cultural Studies Institutions Consortium. **Activities** Events/meetings; training/education. **Events** *Conference* Singapore (Singapore) 2021, *Inter-Asia Cultural Studies Society Conference* Dumaguete City (Philippines) 2019, *Beyond the Cultural Industry Conference* Singapore (Singapore) 2013, *IACS Graduate Conference* Singapore (Singapore) 2013. [2021/AA1847/**D**]

♦ INTERASMA 11457

Exec Dir Univ Hosp San Martino, Largo R Benzi 10, 16132 Genoa GE, Italy.
SG address not obtained.
URL: http://www.interasma.org/
History 9 Dec 1954, Milan (Italy). Founding meeting, 25 May 1955, Utrecht (Netherlands). Constitution amended: 23 May 1966; 7 Oct 1975. Former names and other names: *International Association of Asthmology (INTERASMA)* – former; *Association internationale d'asthmologie* – former; *Asociación Internacional de Asmologia* – former; *Internationale Gesellschaft für Astmologie* – former; *GAA INTERASMA Global Asthma Association* – full title. Registration: Start date: 1954, Italy, Milan. **Aims** Develop theoretical and practical knowledge of the *immunopathology* of bronchial asthma and related diseases with special consideration of *prophylaxis* and *rehabilitation*. **Structure** General Assembly (every 3 years) elects Executive Committee, composed of President, First Vice-President, Second Vice-President, Secretary General, Treasurer and 8 members-at-large. Consultative Committee, consisting of Executive Committee plus Chairmen of 'Chapters' (12), representing: East Europe; West Europe; South Africa; Central Africa; North Africa; South Asia; Central Asia; North Asia; South America; Central America; North America; Australia. **Languages** English, French, German, Russian, Spanish. **Staff** 0.50 FTE, paid. **Finance** Sources: members' dues. **Activities** Events/meetings. **Events** *World Congress of Asthma* Avignon (France) 2021, *World Congress* Stresa (Italy) 2020, *Congress* Toyoake (Japan) 2019, *World Congress* Tokyo (Japan) 2018, *World Congress* Madrid (Spain) 2016. **Publications** *Allergy and Clinical Immunology International* – journal; *Journal of Investigational Allergy and Clinicla Immunology*.
Members Ordinary, Founding, Honorary and Corporate. National sections, totalling 1,100 individuals, in 86 countries and territories:
Algeria, Argentina, Australia, Austria, Azerbaijan, Belgium, Bosnia-Herzegovina, Brazil, Bulgaria, Burkina Faso, Cameroon, Canada, Central African Rep, Chile, China, Colombia, Comoros, Congo Brazzaville, Côte d'Ivoire, Croatia, Cuba, Cyprus, Czechia, Denmark, Dominican Rep, Egypt, Estonia, Finland, France, Georgia, Germany, Greece, Haiti, Hong Kong, Hungary, Iceland, India, Indonesia, Ireland, Israel, Italy, Japan, Kazakhstan, Korea DPR, Korea Rep, Lebanon, Lithuania, Luxembourg, Madagascar, Malaysia, Mexico, Morocco, Netherlands, New Zealand, Nicaragua, Nigeria, North Macedonia, Norway, Pakistan, Panama, Peru, Philippines, Poland, Portugal, Romania, Russia, Saudi Arabia, Serbia, Singapore, Slovakia, Slovenia, South Africa, Spain, Sri Lanka, Sweden, Switzerland, Syrian AR, Taiwan, Tunisia, Türkiye, UK, Ukraine, United Arab Emirates, Uruguay, USA, Uzbekistan.
NGO Relations Member of (2): *Global Alliance Against Chronic Respiratory Diseases (GARD, #10182)*; *World Allergy Organization – IAACI (WAO, #21077)*. [2021/XB1256/**B**]

♦ INTER-ASSO – Asociatiei Internationale a Fostilor Detinuti Politici si Victimelor Communismului (no recent information)
♦ **InterAutoGlass** International Automotive Glass Federation (#12300)

♦ Interbalkan Environment Center (i-BEC) 11458

Scientific Coordinator 18 Louton Str, 572 00 Lagadas, Greece. T. +302394023485. Fax +302394023485. E-mail: info@i-bec.org.
URL: http://www.i-bec.org/
History 30 Jul 2007, by Regional Development Fund of Central Macedonia, Research Committee of Aristotle University of Thessaloniki and Municipality of Lagadas (Greece) in the framework of the project "Establishment of Balkan Environment Center", through funds from *INTERREG V (#15966)* (then III). **Aims** Promote a collaborative approach to sustainable management and protection of natural resources fostering harmonious socio-economic development in Greece, the broader Balkan region and beyond. **Structure** International Board Departments (4): Administration; Products, Services and Infrastructure; Initiatives and Projects; Networking and Capacity Building. **Publications** *I-BEC Newsletter*. **IGO Relations** Partner of: *EuroGEOSS (#05685)*; *Global Alliances for Water and Climate (GAfWaC, #10230)*; *Group on Earth Observations (GEO, #10735)*. [2018.01.29/XM5938/**E**]

♦ Inter Band / see InterBand
♦ InterBand (internationally oriented national body)
♦ Inter-Bank Online System / see IBOS Association (#11038)
♦ INTERBOLSAS – Red de Bolsas Agropecuarias de las Américas (see: #11434)
♦ INTERBOR (inactive)
♦ **INTERBULL** International Bull Evaluation Service (#12410)
♦ **INTERCABLE** International Association of Cable Product and Machinery Manufactures (#11752)
♦ Intercambio Internacional Cristiano de Jóvenes / see International Cultural Youth Exchange (#13122)
♦ Intercambio Internacional Cultural Juvenil (#13122)
♦ Intercambios Culturales en el Mediterraneo (#05281)
♦ Intercamhs – International Alliance for Child and Adolescent Mental Health and Schools (inactive)
♦ Intercapsula Europa (meeting series)
♦ **INTERCARGO** International Association of Dry Cargo Shipowners (#11853)
♦ INTERCHIME – Conférence internationale des industries de procédés (meeting series)
♦ Interchim – International Organization for Cooperation in Small Volume Chemicals Production (inactive)
♦ Interchurch Action for Latin America / see SOLIDARIDAD Network (#19681)
♦ Inter-Church Coordination Committee for Development Projects / see ICCO – Interchurch Organization for Development Cooperation
♦ Interchurch Medical Assistance / see IMA World Health
♦ Interchurch Peace Council of the Netherlands / see PAX

♦ Interciencia Association (IA) 11459

Association Interciencia – Asociación Interciencia – Associação Interciencia
Exec Dir c/o APANAC, Apartado 0824-00172, Panama, Panamá, Panama PANAMá, Panama. T. +5075236311. Fax +5072640789.
Pres c/o Asociación Argentina para el Progreso de la Ciencia, Avda Alvear 1711, 4th Floor, Buenos Aires, Argentina. T. +541167727968. Fax +541167727886.
URL: http://www.interciencia.org/
History Founded 10 Jul 1974, Recife (Brazil), following initiatives at Intercontinental Scientific Meeting, 1973, Mexico City (Mexico). Statutes adopted 31 Jan 1975, New York NY (USA); amended 14 Oct 1979, San José (Costa Rica), 4 Dec 1992 Miami FL (USA), 4 Jan 1993 Puerto Rico, 25 Aug 1995, Puerto Rico, 13 Jul 2001, Salvador da Bahia (Brazil). Registered in accordance with Venezuelan law, 1975. **Aims** Unite the *scientific* community of the *Americas* in order to better serve development of the nations and the well-being of their peoples; promote in a cooperative manner the use of *science* and technology to benefit the people of the continent; stimulate formation of associations for advancement of science where they do not as yet exist. **Structure** Annual Meeting; Coordinating Committee; Executive Committee; Leonard Rieser Endowment Fund Committee. **Languages** English, French, Portuguese, Spanish. **Staff** 5.00 FTE, voluntary. **Finance** Annual quotas. Support from: national organizations; Leonard Reiser Endowment Fund. **Activities** Events/meetings; publishing activities; training/education; networking/liaising. **Events** *Symposium on Cities of Science/Knowledge in the Americas* Santa Cruz (Bolivia) 2015. **Publications** *Interciencia* (12 a year) in English, Portuguese, Spanish – open access journal. Symposium proceedings.
Members Associations for the advancement of science, totalling over 200,000 individuals, in 11 countries:
Argentina, Bolivia, Brazil, Canada, Chile, Colombia, Costa Rica, Mexico, Panama, USA, Venezuela. [2019.02.13/XD4312/**D**]

♦ **Intercoiffure Mondial** Internationale des coiffeurs de dames (#13218)
♦ **INTERCO** International Council on Jewish Social and Welfare Services (#13035)
♦ INTERCOKE – Association internationale des cokes (inactive)
♦ **INTERCOLOR** Commission internationale pour la couleur dans la mode et le textile (#04218)
♦ INTERCOM – ICOM International Committee for Museum Management (see: #13051)
♦ Intercomité de secours aux réfugiés de l'Europe centrale (inactive)
♦ INTERCON / see Intercontinental Church Society (#11460)
♦ Intercontainer-Interfrigo – International Company for the Development of Combined Transport and of Controlled-Temperature Transport (inactive)
♦ Intercontinental Association of Experts for INDustrial EXplosion Protection (unconfirmed)
♦ Intercontinental Centre of Biological Research (inactive)
♦ Intercontinental Christian Fraternity of People with Disabilities (religious order)

♦ Intercontinental Church Society (ICS) 11460

Communications Coordinator Unit 11 Ensign Business Centre, Westwood Way, Westwood Business Park, Coventry, CV4 8JA, UK. T. +442476463940. E-mail: enquiries@ics-uk.org.
URL: http://www.ics-uk.org/

History 30 Jun 1823. Founded as 'Newfoundland School Society'. Became: 15 May 1838, 'Colonial Church Society'; 1 Jan 1851, 'Colonial Church and School Society'. Former names and other names: *Colonial and Continental Church Society* – former (1 Jan 1861 to 1 Jul 1958); *Commonwealth and Continental Church Society* – former (1 Jul 1958 to 11 Jun 1979); *INTERCON* – former. Registration: Companies House, No/ID: 03630342, Start date: 11 Sep 1998, England and Wales; Charity Commission, No/ID: 1072584, Start date: 25 Nov 1998, England and Wales. **Aims** Advance the *Christian* Gospel by evangelical mission and ministry in English for everyone. **Structure** General Meeting (annual); Council; Main Office in Coventry (UK). **Languages** English. **Staff** 4.00 FTE, paid. **Finance** Sources: subscriptions; donations; legacies. **Activities** Religious activities. **Events** *Chaplains and Families Conference* Beatenberg (Switzerland) 2021, *Chaplains and Families Conference* Hoddesdon (UK) 2020, *Annual General Meeting* Warwick (UK) 2019, *Chaplains and Families Conference* Hoddesdon (UK) 2018, *Chaplains and Families Conference* Battle (UK) 2016. **Publications** *ICS News and Prayer Update* (12 a year); *ICS News and Prayer Diary* (3 a year). Occasional publications.
Members Chaplaincies in 5 countries and territories:
Belgium, France, Netherlands, Spain, Switzerland.
Associate chaplains in 13 countries and territories:
Algeria, Belgium, Brazil, Chile, Czechia, Egypt, Falklands/Malvinas, France, Germany, Netherlands, Switzerland, Tunisia, Türkiye.
Holiday chaplaincies in 2 countries:
Greece, Switzerland.
NGO Relations Member of (1): *Global Connections.* [2023/XD4732/**D**]

- ♦ Intercontinental Community Organizations Front (no recent information)
- ♦ Intercontinental Federation of Behavioural Optometry (inactive)

♦ Intercontinental Group of Department Stores (IGDS) 11461

Groupe intercontinental des grands magasins
Secretariat Birmensdorferstr 55, 8004 Zurich ZH, Switzerland. T. +41442953080. Fax +41442915000. E-mail: info@igds.org.
URL: https://www.igds.org/
History Founded Jun 1946, Lugano (Switzerland). **Aims** Provide exclusive support to its department store members and keep them abreast of trends, developments and innovation in retailing. **Structure** General Assembly; Secretariat. **Finance** Sources: members' dues. **Activities** Awards/prizes/competitions; events/meetings; networking/liaising; research/documentation. **Events** *World Department Store Forum* Tokyo (Japan) 2019.
Members Leading Department stores (43) in 36 countries and territories:
Australia, Austria, Canada, Chile, China, Cyprus, Czechia, Denmark, Estonia, France, Germany, Greece, Hong Kong, India, Indonesia, Ireland, Italy, Japan, Korea Rep, Malaysia, Mexico, Netherlands, New Zealand, Philippines, Qatar, Russia, Singapore, South Africa, Sri Lanka, Switzerland, Taiwan, Thailand, Türkiye, UK, United Arab Emirates, USA. [2022/XU1739/**C**]

♦ Intercontinental Grouping of Accountants and Lawyers (IGAL) 11462

Administration 2 rue Marie Laurencin, 78200 Buchelay, France. T. +33183492314. Fax +33183492314.
Registered Office 37 Warren Str, London, W1T 6AD, UK.
URL: http://www.igal-network.com/
History Oct 2004, through merger of *International Grouping of Lawyers (IGL)* and InterContinental Consultants (ICC). UK Company Limited by Guarantee. **Aims** Generate business opportunities for members and their clients; provide international legal, auditing and accountancy services of the highest standards; provide a global forum for the professional exchange of ideas, firm management and social interaction. **Structure** Annual General Meetings. **Languages** English. **Staff** 1.00 FTE, paid; 9.00 FTE, voluntary. **Finance** Members' dues. **Activities** Knowledge management/information dissemination; networking/liaising; events/meetings. **Events** *Annual General Meeting* Singapore (Singapore) 2018, *Spring Meeting* Munich (Germany) 2017, *Annual General Meeting* Toronto, ON (Canada) 2017, *Annual General Meeting* Amsterdam (Netherlands) 2016, *Spring Meeting* Paris (France) 2016. **Publications** *IGAL Newsletter* (4 a year). [2015.08.26/XJ2965/e/**F**]

♦ Intercontinental Network for the Promotion of the Social Solidarity Economy (INPSSE) 11463

Réseau intercontinental de promotion de l'économie sociale et solidaire (RIPESS) – Red Intercontinental de Promoción de la Economia Social y Solidaria
Exec Coordinator address not obtained. E-mail: prevencionraul@yahoo.es – info@ripess.org.
Exec Sec address not obtained. E-mail: laure.jongejans@ripess.org.
URL: http://www.ripess.org/
History Dec 2002, Dakar (Senegal), following 2nd International Meeting on the Globalization of Solidarity, 2001, Québec QC (Canada). **Aims** Build and promote the social solidarity economy (SSE), which takes into account the social and ethical dimension in all its economic activities. **Structure** Board of Directors; Coordinator; Vice-Coordinator. **Languages** English, French, Spanish. **Staff** 1.00 FTE, paid. **Finance** Main contributions from *Fondation Charles Léopold Mayer pour le progrès de l'homme (FPH, #09815).* **Activities** Networking/liaising; guidance/assistance/consulting; advocacy/lobbying/activism; awareness raising; projects/programmes. **Events** *International Meeting on the Globalization of Solidarity* Quezon City (Philippines) 2013, *International Meeting on the Globalization of Solidarity* Luxembourg (Luxembourg) 2009, *International Meeting on the Globalization of Solidarity* Dakar (Senegal) 2005, *International Meeting on the Globabilization of Solidarity* Québec, QC (Canada) 2001, *International Meeting on the Globalization of Solidarity* Lima (Peru) 1997. **Publications** Newsletter (6 a year).
Members Continental networks (6):
African Network for Integrated Development (ANID, #00390); Asian Solidarity Economy Coalition (ASEC, #01754); Jobs Australia – for Oceania; *RIPESS Europe – Economy Solidarity Europe (RIPESS Europe, #18952);* RIPESS LAC (Latin America and Caribbean); RIPESS North America.
Networks within the continental federations represent 60 countries:
Algeria, Argentina, Australia, Austria, Bangladesh, Belgium, Benin, Bhutan, Bolivia, Brazil, Burkina Faso, Cambodia, Cameroon, Canada, Chile, China, Colombia, Congo DR, Côte d'Ivoire, Cuba, Ecuador, France, Gabon, Hong Kong, India, Indonesia, Italy, Japan, Korea Rep, Laos, Luxembourg, Malaysia, Mali, Mauritius, Mexico, Mongolia, Morocco, Myanmar, Nepal, Niger, Pakistan, Panama, Peru, Philippines, Portugal, Romania, Senegal, Singapore, Spain, Sri Lanka, Switzerland, Taiwan, Thailand, Timor-Leste, Togo, Tunisia, Uruguay, USA, Venezuela, Vietnam.
Included in the above, 10 organizations listed in this Yearbook:
Centro de Investigaciones de la Economia Mundial, Habana (CIEM); Global Citizens for Sustainable Developm-ent (GCSD); Global Social Economy Forum (GSEF, #10603); Inter-American Cooperative Institute (ICI, #11420); International Association of Investors in the Social Economy (INAISE, #11971); International Network URGENCI (#14339); Latin American and Caribbean Network of Small Fairtrade Producers (#16282); Latin American Coordination Table for Fair Trade (#16307); Pacific Asia Resource Centre (PARC); Red Latinoamericana de Socio-Economia Solidaria (Red LASES, #18720).
Consultative Status Consultative status granted from: *ECOSOC (#05331)* (Special); *UNCTAD (#20285)* (General). **NGO Relations** Cooperates with (1): *Economy for the Common Good (ECG, #05323).* [2019.02.14/XM1897/y/**F**]

- ♦ Intercontinental Union of Women Working in the Home (#20378)

♦ Intercoop Europe (ICE) 11464

Sec c/o fenaco Cooperative, Erlachstrasse 5, 3001 Bern, Switzerland. E-mail: info@fenaco.com.
History 1 Jul 1990. Founded by merger of *International Agricultural Cooperative Society (inactive)* and the Division for cooperative economic activities of *European Confederation of Agriculture (CEA, inactive).* Former names and other names: *International Society of European Agricultural Cooperatives (INTERCOOP EUROPE)* – former. **Aims** Build a European network of cooperative and cooperative-minded farm input suppliers so as to support the economic interests of their core activities in agriculture, garden retailing and related activities. **Activities** Events/meetings. **Events** *General Assembly* Bern (Switzerland) 2019, *Joint meeting* Québec, QC (Canada) 1999.
Members Full (16); Associate (2). Members in 12 countries:
Austria, Belgium, Denmark, Finland, France, Germany, Ireland, Luxembourg, Netherlands, Norway, Sweden, Switzerland. [2019/XD2288/**D**]

- ♦ INTERCOOP EUROPE / see Intercoop Europe (#11464)
- ♦ Intercult (internationally oriented national body)
- ♦ Intercultural Association / see Inter-Cultural Association (#11465)

♦ Inter-Cultural Association (ICA) 11465

Association fraternelle internationale (AFI)
SG Bd Lambermont 392, 1030 Brussels, Belgium. T. +3226487401. E-mail: assfrain@afi-ica.org.
URL: http://www.afi-ica.org/
History 1937, Verviers (Belgium), on the initiative of André Boland and Yvonne Poncelet, as *Auxiliaires Laïques des Mission (ALM).* Name changed: 1952, to *Auxiliaires féminines internationales (AFI-ICA)*; 1973, to *Intercultural Association – Association interculturelle (AI).* Current title adopted 1981. Previously also referred to as *ALM International.* Registered in accordance with Belgian law. Registration: Banque-Carrefour des Entreprises, No/ID: 0471.079.807, Start date: 23 Oct 2000. **Aims** Promote dialogue, cooperation and solidarity among men and women, in a *Christian* perspective and beyond the borders dividing human beings. **Structure** General Assembly; Administrative Council; International Secretariat, located in Brussels (Belgium). **Languages** English, French. **Staff** 2.00 FTE, paid. Several voluntary. **Finance** Members' dues. **Activities** Training/education; knowledge management/information dissemination; guidance/assistance/consulting. **Events** *Meeting* Brussels (Belgium) 1992, *Meeting* Hofheim (Germany) 1992, *Meeting* Seoul (Korea Rep) 1992. **Publications** *Intercom* (6 a year).
Members Individuals (230) in 25 countries and territories:
Argentina, Austria, Belgium, Bolivia, Brazil, Burkina Faso, Cambodia, Canada, Congo DR, Egypt, France, Germany, Haiti, Italy, Japan, Jordan, Korea Rep, Lebanon, Palestine, Peru, Rwanda, Switzerland, Syrian AR, USA, Vietnam.
NGO Relations Member of: *Federation of European and International Associations Established in Belgium (FAIB, #09508); World Organisation Against Torture (OMCT, #21685).* Founder member of: *Unis pour l'Equite et la Fin du Racisme (UFER, #20490).* [2019/XF1111/**F**]

- ♦ Intercultural Development Research Association (internationally oriented national body)
- ♦ Intercultural Institute for Self-Management and Community Action (#11335)
- ♦ Intercultural Institute Timisoara (internationally oriented national body)

♦ Intercultural Open University Foundation (IOU) 11466

Contact 2401 Woodland Lane, Arden, Wilmington DE 19810, USA. T. +13023521733.
Spain Office Seco de Lucena 11, 18009 Granada, Spain.
URL: http://www.ioufoundation.org/
History 1981. Also known under the acronym *IOUF.* Registered in accordance with Dutch and US laws. **Aims** Prove innovative, socially relevant educational programmes to diverse adult populations; actively seek to identify and reach those underserved by higher education. **Structure** Board of Governors. **Activities** Offers degrees. **NGO Relations** Instrumental in setting up: *European Foundation for Quality in eLearning (EFQUEL, inactive).* Member of: *EDEN Digital Learning Europe (EDEN, #05356); International Association of Educators for World Peace (IAEWP); International Council for Innovation in Higher Education (ICIE); International Mentoring Association (IMA).* [2011/XJ4654/t/**F**]

- ♦ **interdiac** International Academy for Diaconia and Social Action, Central & Eastern Europe (#11545)
- ♦ Interdisciplinary Commission on Bioindicators / see International Commission on Bioindicators (#12667)
- ♦ Interdisciplinary European Conference on Entrepreneurship Research (meeting series)
- ♦ Interdisciplinary Social Sciences Knowledge Community / see Interdisciplinary Social Sciences Research Network (#11467)

♦ Interdisciplinary Social Sciences Research Network 11467

Contact address not obtained. E-mail: support@cgnetworks.org.
URL: http://thesocialsciences.com/
History 2006. Founded at first International Conference on Interdisciplinary Social Sciences. Former names and other names: *Interdisciplinary Social Sciences Knowledge Community* – former. **Aims** Provide a forum to meet others in the field, share ideas, and publish work. **Structure** Advisory Board. **Activities** Events/meetings; knowledge management/information dissemination; networking/liaising; publishing activities. **Events** *International Conference on Interdisciplinary Social Sciences* Hiroshima (Japan) 2017, *International Conference on Interdisciplinary Social Sciences* London (UK) 2016, *International Conference on Interdisciplinary Social Sciences* Split (Croatia) 2015, *International Conference on Interdisciplinary Social Sciences* Vancouver, BC (Canada) 2014, *International Conference on Interdisciplinary Social Sciences* Prague (Czech Rep) 2013. **Publications** *Interdisciplinary Social Sciences* (4 a year) – electronic newsletter; *Interdisciplinary Social Sciences Journal Collection* – consisting of 9 journals and an annual review. *Interdisciplinary Social Sciences Book Imprint.* [2022.02.08/XM5207/**F**]

- ♦ Interdisciplinary World Congress on Low Back and Pelvic Girdle Pain (meeting series)
- ♦ Interdisciplines (internationally oriented national body)
- ♦ **INTEREG** Internationales Institut für Nationalitätenrecht und Regionalismus (#13300)
- ♦ Interelektro – International Organization for Economic and Scientific Technical Cooperation for Electrical Engineering (inactive)
- ♦ Interelektronika (inactive)
- ♦ Interessengemeinschaft der Führenden Holzbe- und Verarbeitungsmaschinen-Grosshändler Europas / see Combois (#04122)
- ♦ Interest Community of Resisters in Countries Occupied by Fascists (inactive)

♦ Interest Group on Algorithmic Foundations of Information Technology (IGAFIT) 11468

Contact address not obtained.
URL: https://igafit.mimuw.edu.pl/
History 2014. **Aims** Integrate the European algorithms community; identify key researcyh challenges and themes. **Activities** Events/meetings. **Events** *Highlights of Algorithms Conference* Prague (Czechia) 2023, *Highlights of Algorithms Conference* London (UK) 2022, *Highlights of Algorithms Conference* London (UK) 2021, *Highlights of Algorithms Conference* Zurich (Switzerland) 2020, *Highlights of Algorithms Conference* Copenhagen (Denmark) 2019.
Members Individuals (about 60) in 16 countries:
Austria, Denmark, Finland, France, Germany, Iceland, Israel, Italy, Netherlands, Norway, Poland, Slovenia, Sweden, Switzerland, UK, USA. [2022/AA2380/v/**F**]

- ♦ Intereurop / see International Travel Insurance Alliance e.V. (#15728)

♦ Intereuropean Commission on Church and School (ICCS) 11469

Commission intereuropéenne Eglise et école
Sec Comenius Inst, Schreiberstrasse 12, 48149 Münster, Germany. T. +492519810125. Fax +492519810150. E-mail: iccs@comenius.de.
Pres address not obtained.
URL: https://iccs.icu/
History Founded 1958, to provide a framework for cooperation in monitoring and developing the place of religious education in European schools and of other issues in church/school relationship. A simple form of statute adopted in 1966. Statutes revised 1982, Utrecht (Netherlands). **Aims** Provide a forum in which developments in church/school relationship – and in *religious education* in particular – can be discussed, and solutions to common problems can be jointly sought. **Structure** Conference (every 3 years); Board. **Languages** English, French, German. **Staff** 0.50 FTE, paid. **Finance** Secretariat costs supported by Norwegian Ministry of Education, and subvention of participants from poorer countries or churches. Additional funds from churches and member organizations; support from charities for certain activities or publications. Expenses for Board members and participants of conferences and working groups covered by their own organizations. **Activities** Events/meetings; publishing activities. **Events** *Conference* Klingenthal (France) 2014, *Triennial Conference* Prague (Czech Rep) 2011, *Conference on diversity shaping Europe's future / Triennial Conference / Meeting* Berlin (Germany) 2008, *Triennial Conference* Otepää (Estonia) 2006, *Triennial Conference* Budapest (Hungary) 2003. **Publications** *ICCS Newsletter* (2 a year). *Education for Democratic Citizenship* (2014); *Religious Education in Europe: Situation and current trends in Schools* (2007). *Education for Religion and Democracy in the Context of Intercultural Dialogue* (2008) – CD-ROM. Conference proceedings; working group reports.

Members Membership open to Churches, organizations and individuals. Correspondents (not more than 2 representatives per country) in 26 countries:
Austria, Belgium, Bulgaria, Czechia, Denmark, Estonia, Finland, France, Georgia, Germany, Greece, Hungary, Ireland, Italy, Latvia, Luxembourg, Netherlands, Norway, Poland, Romania, Russia, Slovakia, Spain, Sweden, Switzerland, UK.
Consultative Status Consultative status granted from: *Council of Europe (CE, #04881)* (Participatory Status). **NGO Relations** Member of: *Coordinating Group for Religion in Education (CoGREE, #04823).*
[2022/XE0745/**E**]

- ♦ Inter-European Parliamentary Forum on Population and Development / see European Parliamentary Forum for Sexual & Reproductive Rights (#08149)
- ♦ InterExchange (internationally oriented national body)
- ♦ INTEREXPO (inactive)
- ♦ INTERFAIS – International Food Aid Information System (inactive)
- ♦ Interfaith Center on Corporate Responsibility (internationally oriented national body)
- ♦ Interfaith Center for Peace and Justice, Gettysburg PA (internationally oriented national body)
- ♦ Interfaith Fellowship – World Congress of Faiths / see World Congress of Faiths (#21304)
- ♦ Interfaith International (internationally oriented national body)
- ♦ Interfaith Peace-Builders / see Eyewitness Palestine

♦ INTERFERRY 11470

CEO PO Box 53532, RPO Broadmead, Victoria BC V8X 5K2, Canada. T. +12067784289. E-mail: ceo@interferry.com.
Director address not obtained.
Europe Office Rue Ducale 67/B2, 1000 Brussels, Belgium.
URL: http://www.interferry.com/

History 1976, New York, NY (USA). Former names and other names: *International Marine Transit Association (IMTA)* – former (1976 to 2001). **Aims** As an association of the worldwide *ferry* industry, represent owners, operators and associated *marine* industries and organizations. **Structure** Board of Directors; CEO. **Languages** English. **Staff** 5.00 FTE, paid. **Finance** Sources: meeting proceeds; members' dues. **Activities** Advocacy/lobbying/activism; events/meetings; knowledge management/information dissemination. **Events** *Annual Interferry Conference* Seattle, WA (USA) 2022, *Annual Interferry Conference* Santander (Spain) 2021, *Annual Conference* London (UK) 2019, *Annual Conference* Cancún (Mexico) 2018, *Annual Conference* Split (Croatia) 2017. **Publications** *Interferry News* – e-mail newsletter. Conference proceedings.
Members Ferry owners and operators, shipyards, naval architects, marine engineers, manufacturers, suppliers, consultants, shipbrokers, government agencies and academics. Members in 34 countries:
Australia, Bahamas, Brazil, Canada, China, Denmark, Egypt, Finland, France, Germany, Greece, Ireland, Italy, Kuwait, Malta, Mexico, Morocco, Netherlands, New Zealand, North Macedonia, Norway, Oman, Philippines, Portugal, Saudi Arabia, Singapore, Spain, Sweden, Switzerland, Thailand, Türkiye, UK, United Arab Emirates, USA.
Consultative Status Consultative status granted from: *ECOSOC (#05331)* (Ros C); *International Maritime Organization (IMO, #14102).* **NGO Relations** Cooperates with (1): *Worldwide Ferry Safety Association (WFSA, #21921).* Cooperates with: national organizations. [2022/XD5124/**D**]

- ♦ **INTERFILM** International Interchurch Film Organization (#13943)
- ♦ INTERFINISH / see International Union for Surface Finishing (#15821)
- ♦ INTER-FOLK – Internasjonalt Folkehøgskole-Engasjement i Den Tredje Verda (internationally oriented national body)
- ♦ Intergeotechnika (inactive)
- ♦ Intergormash (inactive)

♦ Intergovernmental Action Group against Money Laundering in West Africa 11471

Groupe Intergouvernemental d'Action contre le Blanchiment d'Argent en Afrique de l'Ouest (GIABA) – Grupo InterGovernamental de Acção contra o Branqueamento de Dinheiro em Africa Ocidental

Dir Gen Complexe SICAP Point E, Avenue Cheikh Anta Diop x Canal IV, 1er Etage – Immeuble A, BP 32400 Ponty, Dakar, Senegal. T. +221338591818. Fax +221338241745.
URL: http://www.giaba.org/

History Established Dec 1999, Lomé (Togo), at Summit of *Economic Community of West African States (ECOWAS, #05312)*, by the Heads of State and Governments. Original title: *Intergovernmental Task Force Against Money Laundering in Africa (ITFMLA).* Statutes adopted Dec 2000, Bamako (Mali); revised Jan 2006 to take on the Board Countering the Financing of Terrorism. Recognized as a *Financial Action Task Force (FATF, #09765)* – style Regional Body, Jun 2006, and admitted into the FATF as an observer. Became associate member of FATF, Jun 2010. **Aims** Facilitate adoption and implementation of Anti-Money Laundering (AML) and Counter-Financing of Terrorism (CFT) in West Africa. **Structure** GIABA Ministerial Committee (GMC); Technical Commission; Secretariat in Dakar (Senegal). **Languages** English, French, Portuguese. **Staff** 60.00 FTE, paid. **Finance** ECOWAS Community Levy Fund (main source); partnership funded projects. **Activities** Monitoring/evaluation; guidance/assistance/consulting; capacity building; research/documentation; advocacy/lobbying/activism; events/meetings. Active in ECOWAS member states. **Events** *Plenary Meeting* Sierra Leone 2009, *Plenary Meeting* Accra (Ghana) 2008, *Plenary Meeting* Gambia 2007. **Publications** *GIABA M and E Report* (annual). *Typologies Report* – series. Annual Report; mutual evaluation reports.
Members Countries (17):
Benin, Burkina Faso, Cape Verde, Comoros, Côte d'Ivoire, Gambia, Ghana, Guinea, Guinea-Bissau, Liberia, Mali, Niger, Nigeria, Sao Tomé-Principe, Senegal, Sierra Leone, Togo.
IGO Relations Observer status with: *African Development Bank (ADB, #00283); Commonwealth Secretariat (#04362); Economic Community of West African States (ECOWAS, #05312); UNCTAD (#20285); West African Monetary Agency (WAMA, #20887); West African Monetary Institute (WAMI, #20888); West African Institute for Financial and Economic Management (WAIFEM, #20883).* Member of: *Asia/Pacific Group on Money Laundering (APG, #01921).* [2019.12.11/XJ4048/**F***]

- ♦ Intergovernmental Agency for the French-Speaking Community (inactive)
- ♦ Intergovernmental Agreement on Dry Ports (2013 treaty)
- ♦ Intergovernmental Agreement on the Establishment of an Inter-African Motor Vehicle Third Party Liability Insurance Card (1978 treaty)

♦ Intergovernmental Authority on Development (IGAD) 11472

Autorité intergouvernementale pour le développement

Exec Sec Avenue Georges Clemenceau, PO Box 2653, Djibouti, Djibouti. T. +25321354050. Fax +25321356994. E-mail: info@igad.int.
URL: http://igad.int/

History 21 Mar 1996, Nairobi (Kenya). Established on signature of an amended agreement by Assembly of Heads of State and Government, arising from decision in "Declaration of IGADD Heads of State and Government on the Revitalization of IGADD and on Expanded Cooperation Among Member States", signed 18 Apr 1995, Addis Ababa (Ethiopia). Set up to revitalize and expand cooperation among member states of *Inter-Governmental Authority on Drought and Development (IGADD, inactive)*, established Jan 1986. **Aims** Promote joint development strategies and gradually harmonize macro-*economic* policies and programmes in social, technological and scientific fields; harmonize policies with regard to trade, customs, transport, communications, agriculture and natural resources and promote free movement of goods, services and people and establishment of residence; create an enabling environment for foreign, cross-border and domestic *trade* and *investment*; achieve sub-regional *food security* and encourage and assist efforts of member states to collectively combat drought and other natural and man-made disasters and their consequences; initiate and promote programmes and projects for sustainable development of natural resources and environment protection; develop and improve a coordinated and complementary infrastructure, particularly in the areas of transport and energy; promote peace and stability in the sub-region and create mechanisms within the sub-region for inter and intra-state conflict prevention, management and resolution through dialogue; mobilize resources for the implementation of emergency, short, medium and long-term programmes within the framework of sub-regional cooperation; promote and realize the objectives of COMESA and the *African* Economic Community; facilitate, promote and strengthen cooperation in research, development and application in the fields of science and technology. **Structure** Assembly of Heads of State and Government (annual). Council of Ministers (meets twice a year), comprising Minister of Foreign Affairs and one other focal minister from each state. Committee of Ambassadors, comprising ambassadors or plenipotentiaries of member states accredited to the country of Headquarters, namely Djibouti (Djibouti). Secretariat, headed by Executive Secretary and comprising: /Office of the Executive Secretary/ including Internal Auditor and 3 sections: Administration and Finance; Information and Documentation; Fund Mobilization. /Division of Economic Cooperation/ including 3 sections: Trade, Industry and Tourism; Transport, Communication and Telecommunication; Telecommunications; Women Desk. /Division of Agriculture and Environment/ including 3 sections: Agricultural Development and Food Security; Natural Resources Development and Energy; Environment Protection. /Division of Political and Humanitarian Affairs/ including 4 sections: Conflict Prevention, Management and Resolution; Disaster Management; Telecommunications; Women Desk. **Languages** English, French. **Finance** Secretariat financed by assessed contributions from member states. Sub-regional projects and programmes financed by grants and donations from the international community, including the United Nations system, regional and international financial institutions. Annual budget: 1,500,000 USD. **Activities** Capacity building. Coordinates sub-regional programmes within 3 broad priority areas of cooperation: food security and environment; infrastructure development; conflict prevention, management and resolution and humanitarian affairs. **Events** *Conference on Migration and Institution Building in the Horn of Africa* Djibouti (Djibouti) 2014, *Meeting on operationalizing the Ouagadougou Action Plan to Combat Trafficking In Human Beings Especially Women and Children* Arusha (Tanzania UR) 2011, *Korea-Africa Symposium on Coping with Climate Change* Seoul (Korea Rep) 2011, *Terrorism* Khartoum (Sudan) 2002, *Assembly of heads of state and government / Summit of Heads of State and Government* Khartoum (Sudan) 2000. **Publications** *EWFIS Newsletter*; *Food Situation Bulletin*; *IGAD News*. *IGAD Forges Regional Cooperation in the Horn of Africa*. Annual Report. Summit Proceedings. Information Services: Databases: IGAD Experts; IGAD Institutions; IGAD Library. **Information Services** *Environment Information System/Network*; *Information Network on Natural Resources Management*; *Marketing Information System*; *Regional Integrated Information System* – integrating 'Early Warning Food Information System for Food Security'.
Members Governments of 7 countries:
Djibouti, Eritrea, Ethiopia, Kenya, Somalia, Sudan, Uganda.
IGO Relations Observer status with (3): *Codex Alimentarius Commission (CAC, #04081)*; *International Fund for Agricultural Development (IFAD, #13692)*; *United Nations (UN, #20515)* (General Assembly). Accredited to the Conference of the Parties of: *Secretariat of the United Nations Convention to Combat Desertification (Secretariat of the UNCCD, #19208).* Regional Economic Community of: *African Union (AU, #00488).* Member of: *Africa Partnership Forum (APF, #00510). Intergovernmental Organizations Conference (IGO Conference, #11498).* Adheres to: *Global Partnership for Effective Development Co-operation (GPEDC, #10532).* **NGO Relations** Memorandum of Understanding with: *African Research and Resource Forum (ARRF, #00441); Nile Basin Discourse (NBD, #17139).* Member of: *Réseau de prévention des crises alimentaires (RPCA, #18905).* Partner of: *Global Resilience Partnership (GRP, #10577).* [2020/XF4199/**F***]

- ♦ Inter-Governmental Authority on Drought and Development (inactive)
- ♦ Intergovernmental Aviation Committee / see Interstate Aviation Committee (#15977)
- ♦ Intergovernmental Bureau for Informatics (inactive)
- ♦ Intergovernmental Collaborative Action Fund for Excellence (internationally oriented national body)
- ♦ Intergovernmental Commission for Chagas' Disease (no recent information)
- ♦ Intergovernmental Commission for Cooperation of Socialist Countries in the Field of Computer Technology (inactive)
- ♦ Intergovernmental Committee for the Application of the International Convention on the Recognition of Studies, Diplomas and Degrees in Higher Education in the Arab and European States bordering on the Mediterranean (inactive)
- ♦ Intergovernmental Committee to Combat Desertification in the Sudano-Sahelian Region / see Comité permanent inter-Etats de lutte contre la sécheresse dans le Sahel (#04195)
- ♦ Intergovernmental Committee for European Migration / see International Organization for Migration (#14454)

♦ Intergovernmental Committee for the Global Ocean Observing System (I-GOOS) 11473

Address not obtained.
URL: http://www.ioc-goos.org/

History 1992, Paris (France), as the *IOC Committee for GOOS* (resolution EX-XXV 3), by IOC Executive Council during the 25th Session, in order to replace, inter alia, the Committee on Ocean Processes and Climate. Serves as the recognized forum for discussion of *Global Ocean Observing System (GOOS, #10511)* among governments. Has been referred to as *Joint IOC-WMO-UNEP Committee for the Global Ocean Observing System – Comité COI-OMM-PNUE pour le Système mondial d'observation de l'océan.* Ceased to exist 31 Dec 2011, by Resolution XXVI-8 of IOC Assembly. **Aims** Promote, coordinate, implement and manage the Global Ocean Observing System (GOOS). **Structure** Committee comprises representatives designated by OIC member states. Executive Board carries out intersessional work, and includes Chairperson (elected), 4 regional Vice-Chairpersons and (all ex-officio) the GOOS Scientific Steering Committee Chairperson, GOOS Regional Council Chairperson and Director of the Secretariat. **Languages** English, French, Russian, Spanish. **Staff** 5.00 FTE, paid. **Finance** Regular budget (annual) of about US$ 250,000 provided by *NATO Hawk Production and Logistics Organization (NHPLO, no recent information)* of UNESCO. Augmented by an additional US$ 500,000 from extrabudgetary contributions provided primarily by member states, but also other intergovernmental and nongovernmental sponsors including: *UNEP (#20299); World Meteorological Organization (WMO, #21649); International Council for Science (ICSU, inactive).* The observing system itself, GOOS, is funded entirely by participating member states. **Activities** Identifies resources needed for GOOS and the means for obtaining them; develops and updates plans for, initiates implementation stages and monitors the progress of GOOS; develops such plans on the advice of the GOOS Technical and Scientific Advisory Panel and other scientific and technical groups as appropriate; maintains liaison with related research projects as input to the design of GOOS and helps GOOS respond to research needs; is responsible for the representation of GOOS at meetings of other bodies. Committee initially met annually in alternating Plenary and Planning Session, until 1997; currently meets in Plenary Session every 2 years (always in Paris); Planning Session has been subsumed with GOOS Steering Committee. **Events** *Plenary Session* Paris (France) 2011, *Session / Plenary Session* Paris (France) 2009, *Session / Plenary Session* Paris (France) 2007, *Session / Plenary Session* Paris (France) 2005, *Session / Plenary Session* Paris (France) 2003. [2011.08.24/XE3162/**E***]

♦ Intergovernmental Committee of the International Convention of Rome for the Protection of Performers, Producers of Phonograms and Broadcasting Organizations 11474

Comité intergouvernemental de la Convention internationale de Rome sur la protection des artistes interprètes ou exécutants, des producteurs de phonogrammes et des organismes de radiodiffusion

Address not obtained.
URL: http://www.wipo.int/treaties/en/ip/rome/

History 26 Oct 1961, Rome (Italy), by virtue of Article 32 of *International Convention for the Protection of Performers, Producers of Phonograms and Broadcasting Organizations (Rome Convention, 1961)*, under the auspices of *ILO (#11123), UNESCO (#20322)* and *World Intellectual Property Organization (WIPO, #21593).* Also referred to as *Intergovernmental Committee of the Rome Convention.* **Aims** Secure protection in *performances* of performers, phonograms of producers of phonograms and broadcasting organizations. **Structure** Committee, elected by the Contracting States, elects own Chairman and Officers and studies questions concerning the application and operation of the Convention and collects proposals and prepare documentation for possible revision of the Convention. Joint Secretariat with *International Union for the Protection of Literary and Artistic Works (Bern Union, #15806)*, provided by Directors-General of ILO, UNESCO and WIPO. **Finance** Expenses of members are borne by their respective Governments. **Events** *Ordinary session* Geneva (Switzerland) 2009, *Ordinary session* Paris (France) 2005, *Ordinary session* Geneva (Switzerland) 2001, *Ordinary session* Geneva (Switzerland) 1999, *Ordinary session* Paris (France) 1997.
Members Open to States party to the Rome Convention or to the Universal Copyright Convention. States members of the Intergovernmental Committee set up by the Rome Convention (12):

Colombia, El Salvador, Finland, France, Greece, Hungary, Japan, Poland, Romania, Togo, Türkiye, UK.
IGO Relations Organizations admitted as observers: *Council of Europe (CE, #04881); European Commission (EC, #06633); International Institute for the Unification of Private Law (UNIDROIT, #13934); League of Arab States (LAS, #16420); OAS (#17629); United Nations (UN, #20515).*
NGO Relations Organizations admitted as observers:
- *African Union of Broadcasting (AUB, #00490);*
- *Asia-Pacific Broadcasting Union (ABU, #01863);*
- *GIGAEurope AISBL (#10151);*
- *Confédération internationale des travailleurs intellectuels (CITI, #04564);*
- *European Broadcasting Union (EBU, #06404);*
- *Independent Film Producers International Association (IFPIA, no recent information);*
- *International Association of Broadcasting (IAB, #11738);*
- *International Bureau of the Societies Administering the Rights of Mechanical Recording and Reproduction (#12416);*
- *International Federation of Actors (#13337);*
- *International Federation of Film Distributors Associations (#13428);*
- *International Federation of Film Producers' Associations (#13429);*
- *International Federation of Musicians (#13486);*
- *International Hotel and Restaurant Association (IH&RA, #13813)*, replacing *International Organization of Hotel and Restaurant Associations (International HO-RE-CA, inactive);*
- *International Institute of Communications (IIC, #13870);*
- *International Law Association (ILA, #14003);*
- *International Literary and Artistic Association (#14058);*
- *International Publishers Association (IPA, #14675);*
- *International Secretariat for Arts, Mass Media and Entertainment Trade Unions (ISETU, inactive);*
- *International Theatre Institute (ITI, #15683);*
- *International Union of Cinemas (#15763);*
- *International Writers Guild (IWG, inactive);*
- *Internationale Gesellschaft für Urheberrecht (INTERGU, no recent information);*
- *Organización de Telecomunicaciones de Iberoamérica (OTI, #17851).* [2018/XE1113/**E***]

♦ Intergovernmental Committee for Migration / see International Organization for Migration (#14454)

♦ Intergovernmental Committee for Physical Education and Sport . . . 11475

Comité intergouvernemental pour l'éducation physique et le sport (CIGEPS) – Comité Intergubernamental para la Educación Física y el Deporte

Contact Youth and Sport Section, Social and Human Sciences Sector, 1 rue Miollis, 75015 Paris, France. T. +33145683852.
URL: https://www.unesco.org/en/sport-and-anti-doping/cigeps

History 1978. Established within the framework of *UNESCO (#20322).* **Aims** Develop physical education and sport throughout the world; supervise related UNESCO activities; promote an International Charter of physical education and sport. **Structure** Committee of 18 member states elected by UNESCO General Conference. Permanent Consultative Council, comprising representatives of: (a) WHO and UNDP; (b) other regional and interregional intergovernmental organizations; (c) International Olympic Committee; (d) international non-governmental organizations designated by the Committee which maintain official relations with UNESCO, including ICSSPE and WFSGI. Bureau. Under revised statutes, 1990, assumed control of *International Fund for the Development of Physical Education and Sport (FIDEPS, no recent information).* **Events** *Plenary Session* Paris (France) 2022, *Plenary Session* Paris (France) 2014, *Plenary Session* Paris (France) 2010, *Plenary Session* Paris (France) 2009, *Plenary Session* Paris (France) 2008.
Members UNESCO member states (18) serving on the Committee:
Argentina, Azerbaijan, Bahrain, Colombia, Finland, Gambia, Germany, Japan, Madagascar, Malaysia, Mexico, Russia, South Africa, Tunisia, Türkiye, Turkmenistan, Ukraine, United Arab Emirates.
NGO Relations Member of Permanent Consultative Council (PCC): *WomenSport International (WSI, #21033).* [2019/XE9702/**E***]

♦ Intergovernmental Committee for Promoting the Return of Cultural Property to its Countries of Origin or its Restitution in case of Illicit Appropriation 11476

Comité intergouvernemental pour la promotion du retour de biens culturels à leur pays d'origine ou de leur restitution en cas d'appropriation illégale – Comité Intergubernamental para la Promoción del Retorno de Bienes Culturales hacia sus Paises de Origen o su Restitución en Caso de Apropiación Ilicita

Contact Dir Culture/Emergencies – Sec 1970 Conv, CLT/HER/MHM, 7 place de Fontenoy, 75352 Paris 07, France. T. +33145681840. E-mail: convention1970@unesco.org.
URL: https://en.unesco.org/fighttrafficking/icprcp

History Nov 1978, Paris (France). Established by resolution 4/7.6/5 of 20th General Conference of *UNESCO (#20322).* Former names and other names: *Comité Intergubernamental para Fomentar el Retorno de los Bienes Culturales a sus Paises de Origen o su Restitución en caso de Apropiación Ilicita* – alias; *"Return & Restitution" Intergovernmental Committee* – alias. **Aims** Seek ways and means of facilitating bilateral negotiations for the restitution or return of cultural property to its countries of origin and promote multilateral and bilateral cooperation around this issue; encourage the necessary research and studies for the establishment of coherent programmes for the constitution of representative collections in countries whose cultural heritage has been dispersed; foster a public information campaign on the real nature, scale and scope of the problem of restitution or return; guide the planning and implementation of UNESCO's programme of activities with regard to restitution or return; encourage the establishment or reinforcement of museums or other institutions for the conservation of cultural property and the training of the necessary scientific and technical personnel; promote exchanges of cultural property; provide mediation and conciliation for Member States; report on its activities in accordance with the Recommendation to the General Conference of UNESCO at each of its ordinary sessions. **Structure** Committee of 22 Member States of UNESCO (meeting in regular plenary session at least once and not more than twice every 2 years), elected by its General Conference at its ordinary sessions, taking into account the need to ensure equitable geographical distribution and appropriate rotation, as well as the representative character of those States in respect of the contribution they are able to make to the restitution or return of cultural property to its countries of origin. Bureau, consisting of Chairman, 4 Vice-Chairmen and Rapporteur. Secretariat provided by the Director-General of UNESCO. Ad hoc subcommittees. **Languages** Arabic, English, French, Russian, Spanish. **Staff** 2.00 FTE, paid. **Finance** Each Member State and Associate Member State of UNESCO bears the expense of participation of its representatives in sessions of the Commission and of subsidiary organs, its Bureau and its ad hoc subcommittees. **Activities** Promotion of bilateral negotiations; international cooperation. Measures taken to combat the illicit traffic of cultural property. Public information; good offices. **Events** *Session* Paris (France) 2014, *Session* Paris (France) 2012, *Session* Paris (France) 2011, *Session* Paris (France) 2010, *Session* Paris (France) 2009.
Members 22 Member States (with office expiry dates listed behind each country):
Argentina (2019), Armenia (2019), Austria (2019), Benin (2021), China (2019), Ecuador (2021), Egypt (2019), Guatemala (2021), Hungary (2019), Iraq (2021), Italy (2019), Japan (2019), Korea DPR (2021), Korea Rep (2021), Mali (2021), Mexico (2021), Pakistan (2021), Romania (2019), Saudi Arabia (2019), Tanzania UR (2019), Türkiye (2019), Zambia (2019).
IGO Relations Organizations invited to the sessions of the Committee: *Arab League Educational, Cultural and Scientific Organization (ALECSO, #01003); Council of Europe (CE, #04881); European Commission (EC, #06633); International Centre for the Study of the Preservation and Restoration of Cultural Property (ICCROM, #12521); International Criminal Police Organization – INTERPOL (ICPO-INTERPOL, #13110); International Development Law Organization (IDLO, #13161); International Institute for the Unification of Private Law (UNIDROIT, #13934); Organisation internationale de la Francophonie (OIF, #17809); World Customs Organization (WCO, #21350).* **NGO Relations** Organizations invited to the sessions of the Committee: *Association internationale des critiques d'art (AICA, #02680); International Association of Dealers in Ancient Art (IADAA, #11835); International Bar Association (IBA, #12320); International Confederation of Art Dealers (#12848); International Council on Monuments and Sites (ICOMOS, #13049); International Council of Museums (ICOM, #13051); International Foundation for Art Research (IFAR); Organization of Museums, Monuments and Sites of Africa (OMMSA, no recent information); World Federation of Friends of Museums (WFFM, #21435).* [2019/XE5009/**E***]

♦ Intergovernmental Committee for the Protection of the Cultural and Natural Heritage of Outstanding Universal Value / see World Heritage Committee (#21567)

♦ Intergovernmental Committee for the Protection of the World Cultural and Natural Heritage / see World Heritage Committee (#21567)
♦ Intergovernmental Committee on Refugees (inactive)
♦ Intergovernmental Committee of the River Plate Basin Countries (#04172)
♦ Intergovernmental Committee of the Rome Convention / see Intergovernmental Committee of the International Convention of Rome for the Protection of Performers, Producers of Phonograms and Broadcasting Organizations (#11474)

♦ Intergovernmental Committee for the Safeguarding of the Intangible Cultural Heritage 11477

Comité intergouvernemental de sauvegarde du patrimoine culturel immatériel – Comité Intergubernamental para la Salvaguardia del Patrimonio Cultural Inmaterial

Secretariat UNESCO, Living Heritage Entity (CLT/LHE), 7 place de Fontenoy, 75352 Paris 07, France. T. +33145684395. E-mail: ich@unesco.org.
URL: http://ich.unesco.org/

History 2003, within *UNESCO (#20322)*, upon the entering into force of the *Convention for the Safeguarding of Intangible Cultural Heritage (2003).* **Aims** Promote the objectives of the Convention and encourage and monitor the implementation thereof; provide guidance on best practices and make recommendations on measures for the safeguarding of intangible cultural heritage; inscribe elements of intangible cultural heritage on the Lists of the Convention. **Structure** Bureau. **Events** *Session* Bogota (Colombia) 2019, *Session* Paris (France) 2018, *Session* Port Louis (Mauritius) 2018, *Session* Jeju (Korea Rep) 2017, *Session* Addis Ababa (Ethiopia) 2016.
Members States Members of the Committee (24):
Armenia, Austria, Azerbaijan, Cameroon, China, Colombia, Cuba, Cyprus, Djibouti, Guatemala, Jamaica, Japan, Kazakhstan, Kuwait, Lebanon, Mauritius, Netherlands, Palestine, Philippines, Poland, Senegal, Sri Lanka, Togo, Zambia. [2021/XM0735/**E***]

♦ Intergovernmental Committee of the Universal Copyright Convention (IGC) 11478

Comité intergouvernemental de la convention universelle sur le droit d'auteur – Comité Intergubernamental de la Convención Universal sobre Derecho de Autor

Legal Officer c/o UNESCO, Div of Arts and Cultural Enterprise, 7 place de Fontenoy, 75700 Paris, France. T. +33145683740. Fax +33145685589.
URL: http://www.unesco.org/

History 10 Jul 1974, Paris (France), on coming into force of *Universal Copyright Convention, 1971 (1971)*, which had been signed 24 Jul 1971, Paris, revising and replacing *Universal Copyright Convention, 1952 (1952)*, adopted 6 Sep 1952, Geneva (Switzerland). On coming into force of the new Convention, the Intergovernmental Committee established under the 1952 Convention decided to adjourn its meetings sine die and transfer its functions to the Committee of the 1971 Convention; to date, 99 countries have adhered to 1952 convention and 64 to the 1971 convention. **Aims** Study problems concerning application and operation of both 1952 and 1971 texts of the Universal Copyright Convention; make preparation for periodic revisions thereof; study any other problems concerning international *protection* of copyright in cooperation with interested international organizations. **Structure** Committee of 18 member states meets at the request of a third of its members; at the end of each ordinary session, it partially renews the composition of the Committee and elects a Chairman and 2 Vice-Chairmen from among delegates. The Committee may establish subsidiary bodies for the study of particular problems or performance of particular tasks. Unless decided otherwise, meetings are closed. **Languages** Arabic, English, French, Russian, Spanish. **Staff** Secretariat provided by UNESCO. **Finance** Funded by UNESCO's ordinary budget. **Activities** At its 14th Session, Jun 2010, the Committee examined, inter alia: state of ratification or adherence to the Universal Copyright Convention; legal and technical assistance to states to develop national legislation and infrastructure in the field of copyright; state of ratification or adherence to the *International Convention for the Protection of Performers, Producers of Phonograms and Broadcasting Organizations (Rome Convention, 1961)*; application of *Convention for the Protection of Producers of Phonograms Against Unauthorized Duplication of Their Phonograms (Geneva Convention, 1971)*; the *Convention Relating to the Distribution of Programme-carrying Signals Transmitted by Satellite (Brussels Convention, 1974)*; the *Multilateral Convention for the Avoidance of Double Taxation of Copyright Royalties and Additional Protocol (Madrid Multilateral Convention, 1979)*; challenges of striking the right balance between copyright protection and access to knowledge, information and culture, piracy problem as well as the issue concerning future sessions of the Committee. **Events** *Biennial ordinary session* Paris (France) 2005, *Biennial ordinary session* Paris (France) 2001, *Biennial ordinary session* Paris (France) 1997, *Biennial ordinary session* Paris (France) 1995, *Biennial ordinary session* Paris (France) 1993. **Publications** *Copyright Laws and Treaties of the World* (every 1-2 years) in English, French, Spanish – loose-leaf binder; *Copyright Bulletin* in Arabic, Chinese, English, French, Russian, Spanish – online. Information Services: Database on copyright laws and treaties.
Members States represented on 2010 Committee (18):
Algeria, Austria, Brazil, Cameroon, Croatia, Cuba, Czechia, Greece, Guatemala, India, Israel, Japan, Morocco, Peru, Portugal, Russia, Ukraine, USA.
IGO Relations The following (or their representatives) may attend meetings in an advisory capacity: Director-General of *UNESCO (#20322)*; Director General of *World Intellectual Property Organization (WIPO, #21593)*; Secretary-General of *OAS (#17629)*; Secretary-General of *Council of Europe (CE, #04881)*; Director-General of *Arab League Educational, Cultural and Scientific Organization (ALECSO, #01003).* Interested intergovernmental organizations may be invited by the Committee or may them selves apply to the Committee to be allowed to be represented at sessions by observers. **NGO Relations** Interested international or national non-governmental organizations may be invited by the Committee to be represented as observers at all or particular sessions, or a specific meeting of a session. [2010.08.25/XC1115/**E***]

♦ Inter-Governmental Consultations on Asylum, Refugee and Migration Policies in Europe, North America and Australia / see Inter-Governmental Consultations on Migration, Asylum and Refugees (#11479)

♦ Inter-Governmental Consultations on Migration, Asylum and Refugees (IGC) 11479

Secretariat 37-39 rue de Vermont, 1202 Geneva 10, Switzerland. T. +41229196600. E-mail: admin@igc.ch.
URL: http://www.igc.ch/

History Established as an informal, non-decision making forum for intergovernmental information exchange, within the framework of *UNHCR (#20327). 'Consultations'* initiated in 1985; independent Secretariat, set up Jun 1991. Former names and other names: *Inter-Governmental Consultations on Asylum, Refugee and Migration Policies in Europe, North America and Australia (IGC)* – former. **Aims** Act as a forum for information exchange and policy concertation among participating governments; through inter-governmental meetings in the framework of informal 'consultations' (senior official and expert levels), seek innovative solutions and strategies to the rapidly changing asylum, refugee and migration situation worldwide. **Structure** Annual senior officials' meeting.' Independent Secretariat, located in Geneva (Switzerland), while reporting to participating states and being under their full supervision, enjoys diplomatic status with technical backup from IOM by way of a special administrative agreement. **Languages** English. **Staff** 5 professionals, government-seconded officers, consultants, interns, technical and administrative support staff. **Finance** Sources: members' dues. Annual budget: 2,160,000 USD. **Activities** Events/meetings; knowledge management/information dissemination; politics/policy/regulatory. **Publications** *Report on Asylum Procedures* (2009, 2012, 2015). *In a Constructive, Informal and Pragmatic Spirit – Thirty Years of the IGC* Publication date: 2018
Members Participating states (18):
Australia, Belgium, Canada, Denmark, Finland, Germany, Greece, Ireland, Netherlands, New Zealand, Norway, Poland, Portugal, Spain, Sweden, Switzerland, UK, USA.
Regional participants (3):
European Union (EU, #08967); International Organization for Migration (IOM, #14454); UNHCR (#20327).
IGO Relations Cooperates with (9): *Council of Europe (CE, #04881); European Union Agency for Asylum (EUAA, #08968); European Union (EU, #08967); Frontex, the European Border and Coast Guard Agency (#10005); International Organization for Migration (IOM, #14454); OECD (#17693); UNHCR (#20327); United Nations Economic Commission for Europe (UNECE, #20555); United Nations Office on Drugs and Crime (UNODC, #20596).* [2022.10.11/XK1474/y/**E***]

♦ Intergovernmental Coordination Group for the Indian Ocean Tsunami Warning and Mitigation System (ICG IOTWS) 11480

Secretariat IOC, 1 rue Miollis, 75352 Paris CEDEX 15, France. T. +33145683983. Fax +33145685810 – +33145685812. E-mail: ioc.secretariat@unesco.org.
URL: http://ioc.unesco.org/indotsunami/
History 30 Jun 2005. Subsidiary body of *Intergovernmental Oceanographic Commission (IOC, #11496)*. **Events** *Session* Jakarta (Indonesia) 2012, *Session* Melbourne, VIC (Australia) 2011, *Session* Banda Aceh (Indonesia) 2010, *Session* Hyderabad (India) 2009, *Session* Athens (Greece) 2008. [2009/XM0419/**E***]

♦ Intergovernmental Coordination Group for the Pacific Tsunami Warning and Mitigation System (ICG/PTWS) 11481

Exec Sec IOC Assistant DG UNESCO, 1 rue Miollis, 75732 Paris CEDEX 15, France. T. +33145683983. Fax +33145685812.
Technical Sec address not obtained.
ITIC Dir UNESCO/IOC-NOAA ITIC, 1845 Wasp Blvd – Bldg 176, Honolulu HI 96818, USA. T. +18087256050. Fax +18087256055. E-mail: itic.tsunami@noaa.gov.
URL: http://www.ioc-tsunami.org/
History Established 1965, Honolulu HI (USA), as *International Coordination Group for the Tsunami Warning System in the Pacific (ITSU)*, a subsidiary body of *Intergovernmental Oceanographic Commission (IOC, #11496)*. First session: Mar 1968, Honolulu HI (USA). **Aims** Coordinate international tsunami warnings and mitigation activities. **Structure** Tsunami Unit in IOC Paris Headquarters serves as Secretariat; *International Tsunami Information Center (ITIC, #15740)* serves as technical and capacity building resource to Member States; *Pacific Tsunami Warning Center (PTWC)* serves as operation headquarters; sub-regional centres in Japan and Alaska (USA). Counterparts in the Caribbean, Mediterranean and Indian Ocean. **Activities** Events/meetings; advocacy/lobbying/activism. **Events** *Biennial Session* Sendai (Japan) 2021, *Biennial Session* Vladivostok (Russia) 2013, *Biennial Session* Valparaiso (Chile) 2005, *Biennial Session* Wellington (New Zealand) 2003, *Biennial Session* Cartagena de Indias (Colombia) 2001. **Publications** *Tsunami Newsletter*. Brochures.
Members Member States (46):
Australia, Brunei Darussalam, Cambodia, Canada, Chile, China, Colombia, Cook Is, Costa Rica, Ecuador, El Salvador, Fiji, France, Guatemala, Honduras, Hong Kong, Indonesia, Japan, Kiribati, Korea DPR, Korea Rep, Macau, Malaysia, Marshall Is, Mexico, Micronesia FS, Nauru, New Zealand, Nicaragua, Palau, Panama, Papua New Guinea, Peru, Philippines, Russia, Samoa, Singapore, Solomon Is, Thailand, Timor-Leste, Tokelau, Tonga, Tuvalu, USA, Vanuatu, Vietnam. [2019/XE0888/**E***]

♦ Intergovernmental Coordination Group for the Tsunami Early Warning and Mitigation System in the North-eastern Atlantic, the Mediterranean and Connected Seas (ICG/NEAMTWS) 11482

Secretariat c/o IOC/UNESCO, 1 rue Miollis, 75732 Paris CEDEX 15, France. E-mail: f.santoro@unesco.org.
URL: http://www.ioc-tsunami.org/
History Jun 2005, when formally established through Resolution IOC-XXIII-14 of *Intergovernmental Oceanographic Commission (IOC, #11496)*. **Aims** Coordinate the establishment of a tsunami early warning system for *Europe* and the Mediterranean. **Structure** Chairperson; 2 Vice-Chairpersons. Working Groups and Task Teams. **Activities** Working Groups (4): Hazard Assessment and Modelling; Seismic and Geophysical Measurements; Sea Level Data Collection and Exchange, Including Offshore Tsunami Detection and Instruments; Public Awareness, Preparedness and Mitigation. Task Team on Communication Test and Tsunami Exercises. **Events** *Session* Southampton (UK) 2012. [2012/XJ5638/**E***]

♦ Intergovernmental Coordination Group for Tsunami and Other Coastal Hazards Warning System for the Caribbean and Adjacent Regions (ICG/CARIBE EWS) 11483

Secretariat IOC, Q4 avenue Sir Guy Forget, BP 7, Quatre-Bornes, Mauritius. T. +2304259564 – +2304251652. Fax +2304252709. E-mail: secretariat@coi-ioc.org.
URL: http://www.ioc-tsunami.org/
History Established 2005, as a subsidiary body of *Intergovernmental Oceanographic Commission (IOC, #11496)* and *UNESCO (#20322)*. **Aims** Provide efficient assistance on tsunami risk reduction to Member States in the Caribbean region. [2008/XM0420/**E***]

♦ Intergovernmental Council of Copper Exporting Countries (inactive)
♦ Intergovernmental Council for Oil and Gas (no recent information)
♦ Intergovernmental Council on Standardization, Metrology and Certification / see EuroAsian Interstate Council for Standardization, Metrology and Certification (#05639)
♦ Intergovernmental Follow-up and Coordination Committee of the Group of 77 on Economic Cooperation among Developing Countries (see: #10732)
♦ Intergovernmental Forum on Chemical Safety (inactive)

♦ Intergovernmental Forum on Mining, Minerals, Metals and Sustainable Development (IGF) 11484

Dir c/o IISD, 220 Laurier Avenue West, Ste 1100, Ottawa ON K1P 5Z9, Canada. T. +16137788767. E-mail: secretariat@igfmining.org.
URL: https://www.igfmining.org/
History 2005, Geneva (Switzerland). Emerged from the 2002 World Summit on Sustainable Development, Johannesburg (South Africa). Functions as a voluntary initiative. **Aims** Provide opportunities for national governments with an interest in mining to work collectively to advance the priorities identified in the Johannesburg Plan of Implementation and more recently the UN's Sustainable Development Goals (SDGs) and Agenda 2030. **Structure** Annual General Meeting; Executive Committee; Secretariat. **Finance** Funded by Government of Canada. **Activities** Capacity building; events/meetings; research/documentation; training/education. **Events** *Annual General Meeting* Geneva (Switzerland) 2022, *Annual General Meeting* 2021, *Annual General Meeting* 2020, *Annual General Meeting* Geneva (Switzerland) 2019, *Annual General Meeting* Geneva (Switzerland) 2018. **Publications** *IGF News*.
Members Governments (79):
Afghanistan, Argentina, Armenia, Bhutan, Bolivia, Botswana, Brazil, Burkina Faso, Burundi, Cambodia, Cameroon, Canada, Chad, Colombia, Congo Brazzaville, Costa Rica, Dominican Rep, Ecuador, Egypt, El Salvador, Eswatini, Ethiopia, Fiji, France, Gabon, Georgia, Germany, Ghana, Guatemala, Guinea, Guyana, Honduras, India, Iran Islamic Rep, Ireland, Jamaica, Kazakhstan, Kenya, Kyrgyzstan, Laos, Lesotho, Liberia, Madagascar, Malawi, Mali, Mauritania, Mexico, Mongolia, Morocco, Mozambique, Myanmar, Namibia, Netherlands, Niger, Nigeria, Panama, Papua New Guinea, Paraguay, Peru, Philippines, Romania, Russia, Rwanda, Saudi Arabia, Senegal, Sierra Leone, Somalia, South Africa, South Sudan, Sudan, Suriname, Sweden, Tanzania UR, Thailand, Uganda, UK, Uruguay, USA, Zambia.
NGO Relations Secretariat provided by: *International Institute for Sustainable Development (IISD, #13930)*. [2022/XM5522/**F***]

♦ Intergovernmental Foundation for Educational, Scientific and Cultural Cooperation (IFESCCO) 11485

Contact 1st Spasonalivskovsky per – d 4, Moscow MOSKVA, Russia, 119049. T. +74954116128. Fax +74992380676.
URL: http://www.mfgs-sng.org/eng/
History 25 May 2006, Dushanbe (Tajikistan), under agreement signed at meeting of Council of the Heads of Government of *Commonwealth of Independent States (CIS, #04341)*. **Aims** Contribute to the further development of humanitarian cooperation and intercultural communication in the Commonwealth of Independent States in the area of education, science, culture, mass communications, information, archives, sport, tourism and youth matters. **Structure** Management Board.
Members Signatory States (8):
Armenia, Azerbaijan, Belarus, Kazakhstan, Kyrgyzstan, Russia, Tajikistan, Uzbekistan.
IGO Relations Memorandum of Understanding with: *Commonwealth of Independent States (CIS, #04341)*; *Eurasian Economic Community (EurAseC, inactive)*; *International Organization of Turkic Culture (TURKSOY, #14482)*; *UNESCO (#20322)*. [2011/XJ2639/f/**F***]

♦ Intergovernmental Group on Bananas and on Tropical Fruits 11486

Groupe intergouvernemental sur la banane et les fruits tropicaux
Address not obtained.
URL: http://www.fao.org/economic/est/est-commodities/en/
History within the framework of *FAO (#09260)* and as a designated International Commodity Body of *Common Fund for Commodities (CFC, #04293)*. First session 4-8 May 1999, Gold Coast, (Australia). **Structure** Includes 2 sub-groups: *Intergovernmental Sub-Group on Bananas*, deriving from *Intergovernmental Group on Bananas (inactive)*, set up in 1965. **Events** *Session* Puerto de la Cruz (Spain) 2004, *Session* San José (Costa Rica) 2001, *Session* Gold Coast, QLD (Australia) 1999.
Members Governments of 24 countries:
Australia, Bangladesh, Belgium, Cameroon, Costa Rica, Côte d'Ivoire, Ecuador, Fiji, Finland, France, Germany, Greece, Guatemala, Guinea, Honduras, Indonesia, Ireland, Malaysia, Netherlands, Panama, Philippines, Spain, Thailand, UK.
Intergovernmental community:
European Union (EU, #08967).
IGO Relations *CGIAR System Organization (CGIAR, #03843)*. Observers: *Organisation of African, Caribbean and Pacific States (OACPS, #17796)*; *International Bank for Reconstruction and Development (IBRD, #12317)*; *International Trade Centre (ITC, #15703)*. **NGO Relations** Observers: *International Centre of Insect Physiology and Ecology (ICIPE, #12499)*. [2011/XE4198/**E***]

♦ Intergovernmental Group on Citrus Fruit 11487

Groupe Intergouvernemental sur les Agrumes – Grupo Intergubernamental de la FAO sobre Frutos Citricos
Address not obtained.
URL: http://www.fao.org/
History 1959, by the Committee on Commodity Problems (CCP) of *FAO (#09260)*, for 2 years. Following an extension, its period was indefinitely extended by the CCP, 1965. First session May 1960. Revised rules adopted at 2nd session, 1961, and at 7th session, 1986. An Intergovernmental Group (IGG) with Technical Secretariat the responsibility of FAO. **Aims** Study problems affecting the long-term equilibrium of *production* and *consumption* of citrus products and *economic* aspects of problems arising from the *perishable* nature of citrus fruit; consider how best to deal with any special difficulties that may exist or may be expected to arise. **Structure** Steering Sub-Group. **Languages** English, French, Spanish. **Activities** Monitors and reviews prospects for production, consumption, trade and prices, providing an authoritative assessment for governments and market operators. Encourages: trade liberalization; market-oriented production policies; rationalization of the production base through inter-country cooperation. Acts as International Commodity Body (ICB) to develop projects to submit to the Common Fund for Commodities. **Events** *Session* Havana (Cuba) 2003, *Session* Valencia (Spain) 1998, *Session* Rome (Italy) 1996, *Session* Albufeira (Portugal) 1993, *Session* Portugal 1993.
Members Open to all FAO Member Nations and Associate Members substantially interested in production or consumption of, and trade in, citrus fruits and citrus products. Interested non-Member Nations that are Members of the United Nations, any of its specialized agencies or the International Atomic Energy Agency may be admitted to membership by the FAO Council. Member Nations having attended the 9th and 10th Sessions, governments of 33 countries:
Angola, Argentina, Belgium, Belize, Brazil, Canada, Chile, Costa Rica, Cuba, Cyprus, Ecuador, Egypt, El Salvador, France, Germany, Greece, Haiti, Iran Islamic Rep, Israel, Italy, Jamaica, Japan, Mexico, Morocco, Netherlands, Portugal, Spain, Thailand, Tunisia, Türkiye, UK, Uruguay, USA.
International organization (1):
European Union (EU, #08967).
IGO Relations Designed International Commodity Body of: *Common Fund for Commodities (CFC, #04293)*. Instrumental in setting up: *Inter-American Citrus Network (IACNET, #11407)*. [2012/XE3038/**E***]

♦ Intergovernmental Group on Coconut and Coconut Products / see Intergovernmental Group on Oilseeds, Oils and Fats (#11492)

♦ Intergovernmental Group on Grains 11488

Groupe intergouvernemental sur les céréales – Grupo Intergubernamental sobre Cereales
Sec c/o FAO Trade and Markets Div, Viale delle Terme di Caracalla, 00153 Rome RM, Italy. T. +39657051. Fax +39657053152.
URL: http://www.fao.org/
History Established 1957, by the Committee on Commodity Problems of *FAO (#09260)*; first session May 1957. Revised rules adopted at 21st Session. An Intergovernmental Group (IGG) with Technical Secretariat the responsibility of FAO. A Sub-Committee of the Committee on Commodity Problems. **Aims** Consider matters related to all grains, other than rice, including review of national grain policies and their international effects; study *production*, *consumption* and stocks of, and *trade* in, grains; consider how best to deal with any special difficulties which may exist, or may be expected to arise; give special emphasis to problems relating to coarse grains, grains as *animal feed* and to *developing countries*. **Structure** Session every 2 years. **Languages** English, French, Spanish. **Activities** Reviews world supply, demand and trade situation and outlook for wheat and coarse grains; analyses selected major issues of the world grain economy; assists *Committee on World Food Security*, including evaluation of world cereal stock situation; considering effects of trade liberalization. **Events** *Extraordinary Intersessional Meeting* Rome (Italy) 2010, *Meeting* Santiago (Chile) 2009, *Meeting* Istanbul (Turkey) 2007, *Meeting* Rome (Italy) 2004, *Session* Rome (Italy) 2004.
Members Open to all FAO member nations and associate members substantially interested in production or consumption of, and trade in, grains. Interested non-member nations that are members of the United Nations, any of its specialized agencies or the International Atomic Energy Agency may be admitted to membership by the FAO Council. Attending the 26th Session, governments of 62 countries:
Algeria, Angola, Argentina, Austria, Bangladesh, Belgium, Brazil, Burkina Faso, Cameroon, Canada, Chad, China, Cyprus, Czechia, Denmark, Ecuador, Egypt, Ethiopia, France, Germany, Ghana, Guinea, Haiti, Hungary, India, Iran Islamic Rep, Iraq, Italy, Japan, Kenya, Korea Rep, Lesotho, Libya, Lithuania, Madagascar, Malaysia, Mexico, Morocco, Myanmar, Netherlands, Niger, Nigeria, Pakistan, Panama, Peru, Philippines, Poland, Saudi Arabia, Senegal, Slovakia, South Africa, Spain, Sudan, Sweden, Tanzania UR, Thailand, Tunisia, Uganda, UK, Uruguay, USA, Zimbabwe.
International organization attending 26th session (1):
European Union (EU, #08967).
International organizations (4):
Common Fund for Commodities (CFC, #04293); *OECD (#17693)*; *United Nations Economic Commission for Europe (UNECE, #20555)*; *World Food Programme (WFP, #21510)*. [2013.11.28/XE3056/y/**E***]

♦ Intergovernmental Group on Hard Fibres (IGG on Hard Fibres) 11489

Groupe intergouvernemental sur les fibres dures – Grupo Intergubernamenal sobre Fibras Duras
Contact c/o FAO Trade and Markets Div, Viale delle Terme di Caracalla, 00153 Rome RM, Italy.
URL: http://www.fao.org/
History Established 1966, by the Committee on Commodity Problems of *FAO (#09260)*; first session Sep 1966; 26th session 1992. Rules of procedure adopted at first session. An Intergovernmental Group (IGG) with Technical Secretariat the responsibility of FAO. Acts as International Commodity Body in relation to the Common Fund for Commodities. **Aims** Provide a forum for consultation on and studies of *economic* aspects of *production*, local *processing*, *marketing*, *trade* and *consumption* of *abaca*, *sisal*, *henequen*, more recently *coir*, and other hard fibres, individually and as a group; study marketing practices and their improvement; consider causes of disequilibrium between production and consumption, including *competition* with *synthetics* and the development of new uses; consider, implement and monitor measures to deal with special difficulties which may exist or may be expected to arise. **Structure** Advisory Working Party on Hard Fibre Research; Sub-Group of Sisal and Henequen Producing Countries. **Languages** English, French, Spanish. **Staff** 3.00 FTE, paid. **Activities** Guidance/assistance/consulting. **Events** *Session* Bogota (Colombia) 2014, *Session* Negombo (Sri Lanka) 2013, *Session* Salvador (Brazil) 2011, *Session* Manila (Philippines) 2009, *Session* Rome (Italy) 2007.
Members Open to all FAO Member Nations and Associate Members substantially interested in production or consumption of, and trade in, hard fibres. Interested non-Member Nations that are Members of the United Nations, any of its specialized agencies or the International Atomic Energy Agency may be admitted to membership by the FAO Council. Member Nations, governments of 56 countries:

Algeria, Angola, Argentina, Australia, Austria, Belgium, Brazil, Canada, Chile, China, Colombia, Cuba, Denmark, Dominican Rep, Ecuador, Egypt, El Salvador, Ethiopia, Finland, France, Germany, Ghana, Greece, Haiti, Hungary, India, Ireland, Italy, Japan, Kenya, Korea DPR, Korea Rep, Madagascar, Malaysia, Mexico, Mozambique, Netherlands, New Zealand, Nigeria, Norway, Peru, Philippines, Poland, Portugal, Serbia, Spain, Sri Lanka, Sudan, Sweden, Tanzania UR, Thailand, Türkiye, Uganda, UK, USA, Venezuela.
International organization:
Common Fund for Commodities (CFC, #04293). [2017/XE3073/y/**E***]

♦ Intergovernmental Group on Jute, Kenaf and Allied Fibres (IGG on Jute, Kenal and Allied Fibres) 11490

Groupe intergouvernemental sur le jute, le kenaf et les fibres apparentees

Secretariat c/o FAO, Viale delle Terme di Caracalla, 00153 Rome RM, Italy. T. +39652251. Fax +39652253152 – +39652255155. E-mail: martina.guerra@fao.org.
URL: http://www.fao.org/

History Established 1963, by the Committee on Commodity Problems of *FAO (#09260)*; first session Sep 1964. Revised rules adopted at 17th Session, Dec 1981. An Intergovernmental Group (IGG) with Technical Secretariat the responsibility of FAO. **Aims** Provide a forum for consultation on and studies of the *economic* aspects of *production, marketing, trade* and *consumption* of jute, kenaf and allied fibres; study marketing practices and their improvement; consider causes of disequilibrium between production and consumption; develop suitable measures to deal with special difficulties which may exist or may be expected to arise. **Structure** Sessions twice a year to 1976, then normally annually. **Languages** English, French, Spanish. **Activities** Monitors market developments; assesses longer term outlook; makes indicative price recommendations. Current concerns: implications of packaging legislation on jute packaging; comparative advantages of jute against synthetic bags for longer-term storage of agricultural products. **Events** *Session* Negombo (Sri Lanka) 2013, *Session* Salvador (Brazil) 2011, *Session* Manila (Philippines) 2009, *Session* Rome (Italy) 2007, *Session* Rome (Italy) 2004.
Members Open to all FAO Member Nations and Associate Members interested in production or consumption of, and trade in, jute, kenaf and allied fibres. Interested non-Member Nations that are Members of the United Nations, any of its specialized agencies or the International Atomic Energy Agency may be admitted to membership by the FAO Council. Member Nations having attended the 30th Session, governments of 26 countries:
Bangladesh, Belgium, Brazil, China, Congo Brazzaville, Egypt, France, Germany, India, Indonesia, Iran Islamic Rep, Italy, Kenya, Lithuania, Madagascar, Malaysia, Mexico, Netherlands, Nigeria, Pakistan, Peru, Spain, Sudan, Thailand, Türkiye, USA.
Observer (1):
Ukraine.
Regional integration body (1):
European Union (EU, #08967).
IGO Relations *International Jute Organization (IJO, inactive).* **NGO Relations** *European Cooperative Research Network on Flax and other Bast Plants (see: #08871).* [2019/XE3046/**E***]

♦ Intergovernmental Group on Meat / see Intergovernmental Group on Meat and Dairy Products (#11491)

♦ Intergovernmental Group on Meat and Dairy Products 11491

Groupe intergouvernemental sur la viande et les produits laitiers – Grupo Intergubernamental sobre la Carne y los Productos Lacteos

Contact address not obtained. E-mail: upali.galketiaratchilage@fao.org.
URL: http://www.fao.org/

History 1970, by the Committee on Commodity Problems of *FAO (#09260)*, as *Study Group on Meat*. 1st session: Jun 1971. Rules of procedure adopted at 1st session, revised at 10th session, 1983. An Intergovernmental Group (IGG) with Technical Secretariat the responsibility of FAO. Also referred to as *Intergovernmental Group on Meat*. **Aims** Provide a forum for consultation on and studies of international *trade*, *production* and and *consumption* of meat, with emphasis on problems involved in *livestock* development and meat *marketing*; analyse programmes related to expansion of meat production and their influence on trade; analyse short-, medium- and long-term production, consumption and market prospects for meat and *meat products*; exchange information on up-to-date techniques to improve *productivity* of the livestock sector in *developing countries*, while adhering to strict meat *hygiene* and *veterinary* and *sanitary* regulations; identify problem areas in world trade and inform competent bodies of their scope and magnitude. **Structure** Session (every 2 years). Includes *Intergovernmental Sub-Group on Hides and Skins (#11502)*. **Languages** English, French, Spanish. **Events** *Session* Winnipeg, MB (Canada) 2004, *Session* Rome (Italy) 2002, *Session* Rome (Italy) 2001, *Session* Rome (Italy) 2000, *Session* Bologna (Italy) 1996.
Members Open to all FAO Member Nations and Associate Members substantially interested in production or consumption of, and trade in, meat and meat products. Interested non-Member Nations that are Members of the United Nations, any of its specialized agencies or the International Atomic Energy Agency may be admitted to membership by the FAO Council. Member Nations having attended the 15th Session, governments of 55 countries:
Afghanistan, Algeria, Angola, Argentina, Australia, Austria, Belgium, Brazil, Cameroon, Chad, Costa Rica, Côte d'Ivoire, Croatia, Cyprus, Czechia, Denmark, Dominican Rep, Egypt, Eswatini, Ethiopia, Finland, France, Germany, Hungary, Ireland, Italy, Japan, Kenya, Libya, Lithuania, Madagascar, Malaysia, Mexico, Netherlands, New Zealand, Niger, Nigeria, Pakistan, Peru, Portugal, Romania, Saudi Arabia, Slovakia, South Africa, Spain, Sudan, Sweden, Tanzania UR, Thailand, Tunisia, Uganda, UK, Uruguay, USA, Zimbabwe.
Regional integration body (1):
European Union (EU, #08967).
Observers in 1 country:
Russia.
International organizations as observers (5):
Common Fund for Commodities (CFC, #04293); General Agreement on Tariffs and Trade (GATT, inactive); International Trade Centre (ITC, #15703); OECD (#17693); United Nations Economic Commission for Europe (UNECE, #20555). [2020/XE3014/y/**E***]

♦ Intergovernmental Group on Oilseeds, Oils and Fats 11492

Groupe intergouvernemental sur les graines oléagineuses et les matières grasses – Grupo Intergubernamental sobre Semillas Oleaginosas, Aceites y Grasas

Sec FAO Commodities / Trade Division, Via Terme Caracalla, 00153 Rome RM, Italy. T. +39657053498. Fax +39657054495.
URL: http://www.fao.org/economic/est/en/

History 1965, by the Committee on Commodity Problems of *FAO (#09260)*, as *Intergovernmental Group on Coconut and Coconut Products*; terms of reference expanded to cover all oilseeds, oils and fats. First session Sep 1966. Revised rules adopted at 16th session, Mar 1982. An Intergovernmental Group (IGG) with Technical Secretariat the responsibility of FAO. **Aims** Provide a forum for study and consultation on *economic* aspects of *production, processing, consumption, trade* and *marketing* of oilseeds, oils, fats, *oilcakes* and meals, with particular attention to problems of *developing countries*; identify specific problems calling for short-term action and consider all measures which could contribute to solution of medium- and long-term problems; submit practical proposals for intergovernmental arrangements. **Structure** Session (irregular). Membership open to all FAO Member Nations and appointed observers from intergovernmental, non-governmental, academic and private sector organizations interested in production or consumption of, and trade in, oilseeds, ils and fats and their products. Interested-non-Member Nations that are Members of the United Nations, any of its specialized agencies or the International Atomic Energy Agency may be admitted to membership by the FAO Council. **Languages** English, French, Spanish. **Finance** Regular programme funds. **Activities** Politics/policy/regulatory; monitoring/assessment; research and development. **Events** *Biennial Session* Rome (Italy) 2009, *Session* Rome (Italy) 2007, *Session* Rome (Italy) 2005, *Biennial Session* Rome (Italy) 2001, *Session* Rome (Italy) 2001. **Publications** *Oilseeds, Oils and Meals – Monthly Price and Policy Update* (10 a year); *Oilcrops, Oils and Meals – Global Market Assessment* (2 a year).
Members Delegates from 48 member countries having attended the 28th Session (10-12 Dec 1997, Rome):
Angola, Argentina, Bangladesh, Belgium, Bolivia, Brazil, Canada, China, Costa Rica, Cyprus, Czechia, Ecuador, Egypt, Finland, France, Germany, Ghana, Guatemala, Honduras, Hungary, India, Indonesia, Italy, Japan, Kenya, Libya, Lithuania, Madagascar, Malaysia, Mexico, Morocco, Netherlands, Pakistan, Panama, Philippines, Senegal, Slovakia, South Africa, Spain, Sri Lanka, Sudan, Sweden, Tanzania UR, Thailand, Türkiye, Uganda, UK, USA.
Regional integration EU entity (a member) which also attended the 28th Session:
European Union (EU, #08967).
Representatives of 4 international and regional organizations having attended the 28th Session (10-12 Dec 1997, Rome):
Bureau for the Development of Research on Tropical Perennial Oil Crops (no recent information); Common Fund for Commodities (CFC, #04293); International Coconut Community (ICC, #12628); OECD (#17693).
IGO Relations Designated International Commodity Body of: *Common Fund for Commodities (CFC, #04293).* [2016.06.20/XE3031/y/**E***]

♦ Intergovernmental Group on Rice 11493

Groupe intergouvernemental sur le riz – Grupo Intergubernamental sobre Arroz

Officer c/o FAO, Commodities and Trade Div, Viale delle Terme di Caracalla, 00100 Rome RM, Italy. T. +39657054136. Fax +39657054495. E-mail: fao@fao.org – rice-network@fao.org.
URL: http://www.fao.org/economic/est/commodity-markets-monitoring-and-outlo ok/rice/rice-meetings/en/

History 1955, as *Consultative Sub-Committee on the Economic Aspects of Rice*, by Committee on Commodity Problems of *FAO (#09260)*. Subsequently referred to as *Study Group on Rice*. First session Nov 1956. Rules of procedure adopted at 25th Session, Apr 1982. An Intergovernmental Group (IGG) with Technical Secretariat under the responsibility of FAO. **Aims** Provide a forum for consultation on and studies of the *economic* aspects of rice, paying particular attention to any special difficulties that exist or are likely to arise in international *trade* of rice; discuss changes in international environment, including the international trade negotiations, but also dealing with structural changes of markets. **Structure** Session (when required). **Languages** English, French, Spanish. **Finance** Biennial Budget from FAO. **Activities** Knowledge management/information dissemination; research/documentation. **Events** *Session* Rome (Italy) 2010, *Session* Santiago (Chile) 2009, *Session* Istanbul (Turkey) 2007, *Session* Rome (Italy) 2004, *Session* Rome (Italy) 2004. **Publications** *Rice Market Monitor* (4 a year). *National Rice Policy Studies* – series. *Comparison of the Cost of Producing Rice in Selected Countries; Demand for Rice and Other Foodgrains in Selected Asian Countries; Directory of Governmental and Quasi-Governmental Rice Trading Agencies.* Reports; papers.
Members Open to all FAO Member Nations and Associate Members substantially interested in the production or consumption of, and trade in, rice. Interested non-Member Nations that are Members of the United Nations, any of its specialized agencies or the International Atomic Energy Agency may be admitted to membership by FAO Council. Member Nations having attended 38th Session (35):
Australia, Belgium, China, Colombia, Côte d'Ivoire, Egypt, France, Germany, Greece, Guinea, Guyana, Hungary, Indonesia, Iran Islamic Rep, Italy, Japan, Kenya, Korea Rep, Malaysia, Mexico, Morocco, Netherlands, Nigeria, Pakistan, Philippines, Portugal, Senegal, Spain, Suriname, Switzerland, Syrian AR, Thailand, UK, Uruguay, USA.
Regional integration EU body (1):
European Union (EU, #08967).
Observer (1):
Russia.
IGO Relations International Commodity Body for: *Common Fund for Commodities (CFC, #04293).* Sessions held jointly with: *Intergovernmental Group on Grains (#11488).* [2014.11.11/XE3066/**E***]

♦ Intergovernmental Group on Tea 11494

Groupe intergouvernemental sur le thé – Grupo Intergubernamental sobre el Té

Contact FAO Trade and Markets Div, Viale delle Terme di Caracalla, 00153 Rome RM, Italy.
URL: http://www.fao.org/

History Established 1969, as 'Consultative Committee on Tea', by the Committee on Commodity Problems of *FAO (#09260)*; first session Dec 1969; 21st session 2014. Present name adopted, 1971. An Intergovernmental Group (IGG) with Technical Secretariat the responsibility of FAO. **Aims** Provide a forum for consultation on and studies of all problems connected with tea; in particular, conduct a continuing review of short- and long-term developments in tea *production, consumption, trade* and *prices*, study *market* structure and promotion of tea consumption, and consider international action and prepare proposals for submission to governments. **Structure** Working Groups (WGs): Maximum Residue Levels (MRLs); MRLs in the Brew; Tea Trade and Quality; Organic Tea; Climate Change; Smallholders. Task Force on Statistics. **Languages** English, French, Spanish. **Activities** Monitoring/evaluation. **Events** *Session* Bandung (Indonesia) 2014, *Session* Colombo (Sri Lanka) 2012, *Session* Bali (Indonesia) 2005, *Session* Colombo (Sri Lanka) 2003, *Session* Delhi (India) 2001.
Members Open to all FAO Member Nations and Associate Members substantially interested in production or consumption of, and trade in, tea. interested non-Member Nations that are Members of the United Nations, any of its specialized agencies or the International Atomic Energy Agency may be admitted to membership by the FAO Council. Membership countries not specified. Regional integration body (1):
Regional integration body (1):
European Union (EU, #08967). [2018/XE3069/**E***]

♦ Intergovernmental Group of Twenty-Four on International Monetary Affairs (Group of Twenty-Four) 11495

Groupe intergouvernemental des vingt-quatre pour les questions monétaires internationales (Groupe des vingt-quatre)

Dir 700 19th St NW, HQ1 Mailstop 12-012, Washington DC 20431, USA. T. +12026236101. Fax +12026236000. E-mail: g24@g24.org.
URL: http://www.g24.org/

History Jan 1972, Lima (Peru). Founded following a Ministerial Meeting of the *Group of 77 (G-77, #10732)*, 7 Nov 1971, Lima. First Meeting of Deputies, 3-5 Apr 1972, Caracas (Venezuela). First Meeting of Ministers: 6-7 Apr 1972, Caracas. Former names and other names: *Group of 24* – alias; *G-24* – alias. **Aims** Coordinate the position of developing countries on monetary and development issues in the deliberations and decisions of the Bretton Woods Institutions (BWIs). **Structure** Group comprises representative countries from 3 regions: Africa; Asia; Latin America and Caribbean. Meeting of Ministers and Meeting of Deputies, both twice a year before spring and fall sessions of *International Monetary and Financial Committee (IMFC, #14179)* and *Joint Ministerial Committee of the Boards of Governors of the Bank and the Fund on the Transfer of Real Resources to Developing Countries (Development Committee, #16141).* Ad-hoc Task Forces and Working Groups. **Languages** Arabic, English, French, Spanish. **Staff** 4.00 FTE, paid. **Finance** Sources: members' dues. **Activities** Advises IMF and World Bank. Instrumental in setting up, 26 Jul 1972, the *'Committee on Reform of the International Monetary System and Related Issues'*, subsequently known as *'Committee of 20'* or *'Committee of Twenty'*, which was superseded by IMF Interim Committee. Reports and makes recommendations to IMF Interim Committee and to the World Bank Development Committee. Study programme provides coordinated research and technical support to developing countries through formulation of a common strategy on international macro-economic relations, helping them explore possible solutions to collective problems and enabling them to present these more cogently and persuasively at global level. Active Research Program provides technical support for developing country policy positions. **Events** *Deputies Meeting* Washington, DC (USA) 2021, *Deputies Meeting* Washington, DC (USA) 2021, *Ministers and Governors Meeting* Washington, DC (USA) 2021, *Ministers and Governors Meeting* Washington, DC (USA) 2021, *Ministers and Governors Meeting* Washington, DC (USA) 2020. **Publications** *G-24 Discussion Paper Series; Working Paper Series on Infrastructure Financing in the Developing World. Reforming the Governance ofthe IMF and the World Bank* (2005); *The IMF and the World Bank at Sixty* (2004); *Challenges to the IMF and The World Bank, Developing Country Views* (2003); *The Role of the IMF in Adjustment with Growth* (1987); *The Functioning and Improvement of the International Monetary System* (1985); *A Revised Program of Action Towards Reform of the International Monetary and Financial System* (1984). Research papers, available on website.
Members Member Countries (28):
Algeria, Argentina, Brazil, Colombia, Congo DR, Côte d'Ivoire, Ecuador, Egypt, Ethiopia, Gabon, Ghana, Guatemala, Haiti, India, Iran Islamic Rep, Kenya, Lebanon, Mexico, Morocco, Nigeria, Pakistan, Peru, Philippines, South Africa, Sri Lanka, Syrian AR, Trinidad-Tobago, Venezuela.
Special Observer:
China.
Observers in 4 countries:
Angola, Indonesia, Saudi Arabia, United Arab Emirates. [2022.02.15/XF5980/**F***]

♦ Intergovernmental Group on Wine and Vine Products (inactive)

♦ Inter-Governmental Maritime Consultative Organization / see International Maritime Organization (#14102)

♦ Intergovernmental Negotiating Committee for a Legally Binding Agreement on Forests in Europe (inactive)
♦ Intergovernmental Network on the Improvement of Production and Development of Trade of Citrus Fruit / see Inter-American Citrus Network (#11407)

♦ Intergovernmental Oceanographic Commission (IOC) 11496

Commission océanographique intergouvernementale (COI) – Comisión Oceanografica Intergubernamental (COI) – Mezpravitelstvennaja Okeanograficeskaja Komissija (MOK)

Exec Sec 7 Place de Fontenoy, 75352 Paris CEDEX 17, France. T. +33145682411.
Chairman Oceanography Dept, Navy Hydrographic Service, Av Montes de Oca 2124, C1270ABV, Buenos Aires, Argentina.
URL: http://ioc.unesco.org

History 1960, Paris (France). Established as a body with functional autonomy within *UNESCO (#20322)*, in accordance with a resolution of Intergovernmental Conference on Oceanographic Research, Jul 1960, Copenhagen (Denmark), by decision of 11th General Conference of UNESCO, Nov 1960. The only competent organization for marine science within the UN System. First met at UNESCO Headquarters, 19-27 Oct 1961. Initially 40 states became members. Statutes modified: 1970; 1987; 1999 by General Conference of UNESCO at its 30th session. Former names and other names: *Intergovernmental Oceanographic Commission (IOC) of the United Nations Educational, Scientific and Cultural Organization (UNESCO)* – full title. **Aims** Promote international cooperation and coordinate programmes in research, services and capacity-building, in order to learn more about the nature and resources of the ocean and coastal areas, and apply that knowledge for the improvement of management, sustainable development, the protection of the marine environment, and the decision-making processes of Member States.
Structure Assembly (every 2 years) in Paris (France); Executive Council (meeting annually). Technical and regional subsidiary bodies, including joint bodies with other organizations:
- *IOC Sub-Commission for the Caribbean and Adjacent Regions (IOCARIBE, #16003)*;
- *IOC Sub-Commission for the Western Pacific (WESTPAC, see: #11496)*;
- *IOC Sub-Commission for Africa and the Adjacent Island States (IOCAFRICA, see: #11496)*;
- *IOC Regional Committee for the Central Indian Ocean (IOCINDIO, see: #11496)*;
- *Black Sea Regional Committee (BSRC)*;
- *Intergovernmental Coordination Group for the Pacific Tsunami Warning and Mitigation System (ICG/PTWS, #11481)*;
- *Intergovernmental Coordination Group for the Indian Ocean Tsunami Warning and Mitigation System (ICG IOTWS, #11480)*;
- *Intergovernmental Coordination Group for Tsunami and Other Coastal Hazards Warning System for the Caribbean and Adjacent Regions (ICG/CARIBE EWS, #11483)*;
- *Intergovernmental Coordination Group for the Tsunami Early Warning and Mitigation System in the North-eastern Atlantic, the Mediterranean and Connected Seas (ICG/NEAMTWS, #11482)*;
- IOC Committee on *International Oceanographic Data and Information Exchange (IODE, #14396)*;
- *Global Ocean Observing System (GOOS, #10511)* Steering Committee;
- *IOC Intergovernmental Panel on Harmful Blooms (IPHAB, #16002)*;
- *IOC Group of Experts on the Global Sea-Level Observing System (GLOSS, see: #11496)*;
- *OIC Working Group on Tsunamis and Other Hazards Related to Sea-Level Warning and Mitigation Systems (TOWS-WG)*;
- *Advisory Body of Experts on the Law of the Sea (ABE-LOS)*.

Other joint groups: *Joint Group of Experts on the Scientific Aspects of Marine Environmental Protection (GESAMP, #16131)*; *Joint IOC/IHO Guiding Committee for the General Bathymetric Chart of the Oceans (GEBCO, #16137)*; *Joint WMO-IOC Technical Commission for Oceanography and Marine Meteorology (JCOMM, #16151)*; *World Climate Research Programme (WCRP, #21279)*. Together with IHO, provides joint committees for: *International Bathymetric Chart of the Caribbean Sea and the Gulf of Mexico (IBCCA)*; *International Bathymetric Chart of the Central Eastern Atlantic (IBCEA)*; *International Bathymetric Chart of the Mediterranean (IBCM)*; *International Bathymetric Chart of the Western Indian Ocean (IBCWIO)*. Contributes to: *United Nations Framework Convention on Climate Change (UNFCCC, 1992)*.
Languages English, French, Russian, Spanish. **Staff** 47.00 FTE, paid. **Finance** Multi-agency Secretariat (UN, UNESCO, WMO, FAO, IMO and seconded professionals by Member States); Services provided by UNESCO; operational funds (UNESCO); contributions from IOC Member States (Trust Fund); support in kind from UN, FAO, WMO, IMO. Annual budget: 2,000,000 USD. **Activities** Guidance/assistance/consulting; knowledge management/information dissemination; monitoring/evaluation; research and development; research/documentation; standards/guidelines; training/education. **Events** *International Ocean Data Conference* Sopot (Poland) 2022, *Joint Meeting on the Role of Oceran Literacy and Responsible Research and Innovation in Supporting Effective Ocean Governance* Brussels (Belgium) 2019, *Workshop on a Framework for Cooperative Studies in the Western Pacific Marginal Seas* Seoul (Korea Rep) 2019, *Regional Planning Workshop for the North Pacific and Western Pacific Marginal Seas towards the UN Decade of Ocean Science for Sustainable Development* Tokyo (Japan) 2019, *Annual Meeting* Weymouth (UK) 2019. **Publications** *HAN: Harmful Algae News* – electronic newsletter; *IOCNews* – electronic newsletter; *JCOMM Newsletter*. *Oceanographic Methodology*. IOC Policy Briefs; IOC Manuals and Guides; IOC Workshop Reports; Summary Reports of the Assembly and Executive Council sessions; Reports of Expert Groups and similar bodies; brochures.
Information Services *Directory of European Aquatic Science Libraries and Information Centres (EURASLIC)*; *Global Directory of Marine and Freshwater Professionals (GLODIR)*; *IOC Electronic Library (UNESDOC)*; *IOC/UNESCO Acronyms*; *Marine Information Centre (MIC)* – documentation centre with UNESCO; *MEDI Database*; *Oceans Activities and Meetings List*.
Members Governments of 150 States:
Afghanistan, Albania, Algeria, Angola, Argentina, Australia, Austria, Azerbaijan, Bahamas, Bangladesh, Barbados, Belgium, Belize, Benin, Brazil, Bulgaria, Cameroon, Canada, Cape Verde, Chile, China, Colombia, Comoros, Congo Brazzaville, Congo DR, Cook Is, Costa Rica, Côte d'Ivoire, Croatia, Cuba, Cyprus, Czechia, Denmark, Djibouti, Dominica, Dominican Rep, Ecuador, Egypt, El Salvador, Equatorial Guinea, Eritrea, Estonia, Ethiopia, Fiji, Finland, France, Gabon, Gambia, Georgia, Germany, Ghana, Greece, Grenada, Guatemala, Guinea, Guinea-Bissau, Guyana, Haiti, Honduras, Iceland, India, Indonesia, Iran Islamic Rep, Iraq, Ireland, Israel, Italy, Jamaica, Japan, Jordan, Kazakhstan, Kenya, Kiribati, Korea DPR, Korea Rep, Kuwait, Lebanon, Libya, Madagascar, Malaysia, Maldives, Malta, Mauritania, Mauritius, Mexico, Monaco, Montenegro, Morocco, Mozambique, Myanmar, Namibia, Nauru, Netherlands, New Zealand, Nicaragua, Nigeria, Niue, Norway, Oman, Pakistan, Palau, Panama, Papua New Guinea, Peru, Philippines, Poland, Portugal, Qatar, Romania, Russia, Samoa, Saudi Arabia, Senegal, Serbia, Seychelles, Sierra Leone, Singapore, Slovenia, Solomon Is, Somalia, South Africa, Spain, Sri Lanka, St Kitts-Nevis, St Lucia, St Vincent-Grenadines, Sudan, Suriname, Sweden, Switzerland, Syrian AR, Tanzania UR, Thailand, Timor-Leste, Togo, Tonga, Trinidad-Tobago, Tunisia, Türkiye, Turkmenistan, Tuvalu, UK, Ukraine, United Arab Emirates, Uruguay, USA, Vanuatu, Venezuela, Vietnam, Yemen.
IGO Relations UN members of ICSPRO: *FAO (#09260)*; *International Maritime Organization (IMO, #14102)*; United Nations Division for Ocean Affairs and the Law of the Sea (DOALOS); *World Meteorological Organization (WMO, #21649)*. Agreement with: *Caribbean Regional Fisheries Mechanism (CRFM, #03547)*; *Comisión Permanente del Pacífico Sur (CPPS, #04141)*; *Coordinating Committee for Geoscience Programmes in East and Southeast Asia (CCOP, #04816)*; *International Atomic Energy Agency (IAEA, #12294)*; *International Council for the Exploration of the Sea (ICES, #13021)*; *International Hydrographic Organization (IHO, #13825)*; *The Mediterranean Science Commission (CIESM, #16674)*; *UNEP (#20299)*. Member of: *Coordination Group for Meteorological Satellites (CGMS, #04827)*; *UN-OCEANS (#20711)*. Cooperates with: *Caribbean Action Plan (CAR, #03432)*; *Caribbean Environment Programme (CEP, #03497)*; *Group on Earth Observations (GEO, #10735)*; *Inter-Islamic Science and Technology Network on Oceanography (#11514)*; *West and Central African Action Plan (WACAF, no recent information)*. Observer status with: *Baltic Marine Environment Protection Commission – Helsinki Commission (HELCOM, #03126)*; *Hydrographic Commission on Antarctica (HCA, see: #13825)*. Recognized as the competent international organization in the fields of Marine Scientific Research (Part XIII) and Transfer of Marine Technology (Part XIV) through *United Nations Convention on the Law of the Sea (UNCLOS, 1982)*. Instrumental in setting up: *Indian Ocean Marine Affairs Cooperation (IOMAC, no recent information)*; *Inter-American Institute for Global Change Research (IAI, #11437)*.
- *Coordinating Committee for Geoscience Programmes in East and Southeast Asia (CCOP, #04816)*;
- *South-West Atlantic Action Plan (no recent information)*;
- UN Global Environmental Facility's Programme for Environmental Management and Protection of the Black Sea;
- *UNDP (#20292)*;
- *UNESCO Asia-Pacific Regional Bureau for Communication and Information (#20300)*;
- *UNESCO Environment and Development in Coastal Regions and Small Islands (UNESCO CSI Programme, see: #20322)*;
- *UNESCO Office, Cairo – Regional Bureau for Sciences in the Arab States (ROSTAS, #20312)*;
- *UNESCO Office, Montevideo – Regional Bureau for Sciences in Latin America and the Caribbean (#20314)*;
- *UNESCO Office, Nairobi – Regional Bureau for Sciences in Africa (ROSTA, inactive)*;
- *UNESCO Office in Venice – UNESCO Regional Bureau for Science and Culture in Europe (BRESCE, #20316)*;
- *UNIDO (#20336)*;
- *United Nations Economic Commission for Africa (ECA, #20554)*;
- *United Nations Economic Commission for Europe (UNECE, #20555)*;
- *United Nations Economic Commission for Latin America and the Caribbean (ECLAC, #20556)*;
- *United Nations Economic and Social Commission for Asia and the Pacific (ESCAP, #20557)*;
- *United Nations Framework Convention on Climate Change – Secretariat (UNFCCC, #20564)*;
- *United Nations University (UNU, #20642)*;
- *World Weather Watch (WWW, #21910)*.

NGO Relations Member of: *Advisory Committee on Protection of the Sea (ACOPS, #00139)*; *Partnership for Observation of the Global Oceans (POGO, #18239)*; *Ocean Observations Panel for Climate (OOPC, #17683)*. Advisory body: Advisory Committee on Marine Resources Research. Instrumental in setting up: *GOOS Regional Alliance for the South East Pacific (GRASP, #10682)*; *IOC Science and Communication Centre on Harmful Algae (see: #11496)*; *International Ocean Colour Coordinating Group (IOCCG, #14392)*.
Cooperates with:
- *Comité International Radio-Maritime (CIRM, #04186)*;
- *Commission for the Geological Map of the World (CGMW, #04216)*;
- *Commission mondiale d'éthique des connaissances scientifiques et des technologies de l'UNESCO (COMEST, #04235)*;
- *Floating University (FU, #09796)*;
- *Global Forum on Oceans, Coasts and Islands (GOF, #10377)*;
- *Institute of Marine Engineering, Science and Technology (IMarEST, #11280)*;
- *International Association of Biological Oceanography (IABO, #11726)*;
- *International Association for the Physical Sciences of the Oceans (IAPSO, #12082)*;
- *International Geographical Union (IGU, #13713)*;
- *International Ocean Institute (IOI, #14394)*;
- *International Society of Limnology (#15232)*;
- *International Union of Biological Sciences (IUBS, #15760)*;
- *International Union for Conservation of Nature and Natural Resources (IUCN, #15766)*;
- *International Union of Geodesy and Geophysics (IUGG, #15776)*;
- *International Water Resources Association (IWRA, #15871)*;
- *Pacific Science Association (PSA, #18003)*;
- *Permanent Service for Mean Sea Level (PSMSL, #18333)*;
- *Scientific Committee on Problems of the Environment (SCOPE, #19150)*. [2022.02.02/XE1118/**E***]

♦ Intergovernmental Oceanographic Commission (IOC) of the United Nations Educational, Scientific and Cultural Organization (UNESCO) / see Intergovernmental Oceanographic Commission (#11496)
♦ Intergovernmental Organisation for International Carriage by Rail (#17807)

♦ Intergovernmental Organization for Marketing Information and Technical Advisory Services for Fishery Products in the Asia and Pacific Region (INFOFISH) 11497

Organisation intergouvernementale de renseignements et de conseils techniques pour la commercialisation des produits de la pêche en Asie et dans le Pacifique

Dir Wisma LKIM, Jalan Desaria, Jalan Pulau Meranti, 47120 Puchong, Selangor, Malaysia. T. +60380668112. Fax +60380603697. E-mail: info@infofish.org – director@infofish.org.
URL: http://www.infofish.org/

History 1981, Kuala Lumpur (Malaysia). Established as a regional project of *FAO (#09260)*. Since 1987, an inter-governmental organization. **Aims** Provide marketing support for fish producers and exporters in the Asia-Pacific region; enable the fisheries of the Contracting Parties to develop in accordance with current and future market demand and take full advantage of the potential offered by their fishery resources; contribute to the upgrading and modernization of fisheries of the Contracting Parties; contribute to more balanced supplies of fishery products to the Contracting Parties; make the best use of export opportunities within and outside Asia and Pacific region; promote technical and economic cooperation among Contracting Parties in this sector. **Structure** Governing Council. **Languages** English. **Staff** 20.00 FTE, paid. **Activities** Events/meetings; guidance/assistance/consulting; training/education. **Events** *Tuna Trade Conference* Bangkok (Thailand) 2022, *Tuna Trade Conference* 2021, *Tuna Trade Conference* Bangkok (Thailand) 2020, *Tuna Trade Conference* Bangkok (Thailand) 2018, *Tuna Trade Conference* Bangkok (Thailand) 2016. **Publications** *INFOFISH International* (6 a year) in English – with summaries in Arabic/Chinese/French/Spanish – jointly with other network mebmers; *Information Digest on Fishing Technology, Fishing Gear and Methods, Vessels and Equipment* (4 a year) in English – newsletter – mainly related to Asia/Padific region; *The Fish Inspector* (4 a year) – newsletter; *INFOFISH Trade News* (2 a month) in English. Specific bibliographies.
Members Representatives of 12 countries (membership at government level):
Bangladesh, Cambodia, Fiji, Iran Islamic Rep, Malaysia, Maldives, Pakistan, Papua New Guinea, Philippines, Solomon Is, Sri Lanka, Thailand. [2023.02.15/XE4083/**F***]

♦ Intergovernmental Organizations Conference (IGO Conference) 11498

SG Via Bonomelli 1, 28100 Novara NO, Italy. T. +3932130340. Fax +39321681732. E-mail: secretariat@igo-conference.org.
URL: http://www.igo-conference.org/en/index/

History 15 Sep 2006, upon entering into force of the *'Treaty establishing the IGO Conference'*. In Jun 2006 at the Nairobi Conference, the following inter-governmental organizations approved the text of the Treaty and began its formal undertaking: *Intergovernmental University Institute of Co-operation (IUIC)*; *International Centre for Food Micro-Algae Against Malnutrition (ICFAM)*; *Intergovernmental Council for Food Micro-algae (ICOFAM)*. **Aims** Serve as a forum for dialogue, mutual knowledge and cooperation among intergovernmental organizations (IGOs). **Structure** General Council (legislative body). Permanent Secretariat (executive body). Departments (4): Conference Affairs; Institutional Relations; Management; Budget.
Members Governments of 50 countries:
Albania, Argentina, Armenia, Azerbaijan, Bahamas, Bahrain, Belgium, Bulgaria, Cape Verde, China, Congo DR, Cyprus, Djibouti, Egypt, Estonia, Ethiopia, Fiji, Finland, Georgia, Ghana, Guatemala, Haiti, Iceland, Jamaica, Japan, Kenya, Korea Rep, Latvia, Lithuania, Malaysia, Malta, Mauritius, Moldova, Nicaragua, North Macedonia, Peru, Philippines, Romania, Saudi Arabia, Senegal, Spain, St Lucia, St Vincent-Grenadines, Suriname, Tanzania UR, Tonga, Trinidad-Tobago, Tunisia, Turkmenistan, Vanuatu.
Organizations (41), listed in this Yearbook:
- *Abdus Salam International Centre for Theoretical Physics (ICTP, #00005)*;
- *African Intellectual Property Organization (#00344)*;
- *African Regional Centre of Technology (ARCT, #00432)*;
- *African Regional Intellectual Property Organization (ARIPO, #00434)*;
- *African Union (AU, #00488)*;
- *Africa Rice Center (AfricaRice, #00518)*;
- *Andean Parliament (#00820)*;
- *Asian-African Legal Consultative Organization (AALCO, #01303)*;
- *Association of Caribbean States (ACS, #02411)*;
- *Benelux Office for Intellectual Property (BOIP, #03202)*;
- *Caribbean Community (CARICOM, #03476)*;
- *Central American Integration System (#03671)*;
- *Collaborative Intergovernmental Scientific Research Institute (CISRI, #04098)*;
- *Commission de l'Océan Indien (COI, #04236)*;
- *Commonwealth of Independent States (CIS, #04341)*;
- *Comunidade dos Países de Língua Portuguesa (CPLP, #04430)*;
- *Contadora Parliament (#04776)*;
- *Council of Arab Economic Unity (CAEU, #04859)*;
- *Eurasian Economic Community (EurAseC, inactive)*;
- *FAO (#09260)*;
- *Intergovernmental Authority on Development (IGAD, #11472)*;
- *Intergovernmental University Institute of Co-operation (IUIC)*;
- *International Centre for Food Micro-Algae Against Malnutrition (ICFAM)*;
- *International Centre for Promotion of Enterprises (ICPE, #12509)*;
- *International Civil Aviation Organization (ICAO, #12581)*;
- *International Criminal Police Organization – INTERPOL (ICPO-INTERPOL, #13110)*;
- *International Maize and Wheat Improvement Center (#14077)*;
- *International Narcotics Control Board (INCB, #14212)*;
- *International Olive Council (IOC, #14405)*;
- *International Sericultural Commission (ISC, #14837)*;
- *Inter-State School of Hydraulic and Rural Engineering for Senior Technicians (#15981)*;
- *Islamic Centre for Development of Trade (ICDT, #16035)*;
- *Organisation of Islamic Cooperation (OIC, #17813)*;

- *Organisation pour la mise en valeur du fleuve Sénégal (OMVS, #17815)*;
- *Organization for Democracy and Economic Development (GUAM, #17861)*;
- *Partners in Population and Development (PPD, #18247)*;
- *Sistema Económico Latinoamericano (SELA, #19294)*;
- *South Asia Cooperative Environment Programme (SACEP, #19714)*;
- *Trade and Development Bank (TDB, #20181)*;
- *World Food Programme (WFP, #21510)*. [2019.03.03/XJ0805/E*]

♦ Intergovernmental Panel on Climate Change (IPCC) 11499

Groupe d'experts intergouvernemental sur l'évolution du climat (GIEC)

Sec c/o WMO, Case Postale 2300, Av de la Paix 7 bis, 1211 Geneva 2, Switzerland. T. +41227308208 – +41227308254 – +41227308284. Fax +41227308025 – +41227308013. E-mail: ipcc-sec@wmo.int.
URL: http://www.ipcc.ch/

History 1988. Established by *World Meteorological Organization (WMO, #21649)* and *UNEP (#20299)*. Nobel Peace Prize Winner, 2007. **Aims** As a scientific and intergovernmental body, review and assess the most recent scientific, technical and socio-economic information produced worldwide relevant to the understanding of climate change for decision-makers. **Structure** Plenary session (1-2 a year); Bureau; Working Groups (3); Task Force Bureau on National Greenhouse Gas Inventories; Technical Support Unit; Secretariat. **Languages** Arabic, Chinese, English, French, Russian, Spanish. **Staff** 13.00 FTE, paid. **Finance** Main sources: direct contributions to IPCC Trust Fund by WMO and UNEP; voluntary contributions to IPCC Trust Fund by member states of UN and WMO and by *United Nations Framework Convention on Climate Change – Secretariat (UNFCCC, #20564)*. Governments of France (Working Group I), Germany (Working Group II), UK (Working Group III) and Japan (Task Force Inventories) host the respective Technical Support Units. WMO covers personnel costs of IPCC Secretary and housing of the Secretariat; UNEP covers expenses of the Deputy Secretary. Annual budget: 10,000,000 CHF. **Activities** Monitoring/evaluation; research/documentation; guidance/assistance/consulting. Main activity is production of periodical assessment reports with Fifth Assessment Report (AR5) finalized in 2014. Working Group I (Physical Science Basis) assesses the physical scientific aspects of the climate system and climate change; Working Group II (Impacts, Adaptation and Vulnerability) assesses vulnerability of socio-economic and natural systems to climate change, negative and positive consequences of climate change, and options for adapting to it; Working Group III (Mitigation): assesses options for mitigating climate change through limiting or preventing greenhouse gas emissions and enhancing activities that remove them from the atmosphere. **Events** *Plenary Session* Geneva (Switzerland) 2022, *Plenary Session* Geneva (Switzerland) 2022, *Plenary Session* Geneva (Switzerland) 2022, *Plenary Session* Geneva (Switzerland) 2021, *Plenary Session* Geneva (Switzerland) 2020. **Publications** *Special Report on Global Warming of 1.5degreesC* (2018). Assessment reports; methodology reports; special reports; technical papers; workshop proceedings.
Members Membership open to all Member States of the United Nations and the WMO. Members in 192 countries and territories:
Afghanistan, Albania, Algeria, Andorra, Angola, Antigua-Barbuda, Argentina, Armenia, Australia, Austria, Azerbaijan, Bahamas, Bahrain, Bangladesh, Barbados, Belarus, Belgium, Belize, Benin, Bhutan, Bolivia, Bosnia-Herzegovina, Botswana, Brazil, Brunei Darussalam, Bulgaria, Burkina Faso, Burundi, Cambodia, Cameroon, Canada, Cape Verde, Central African Rep, Chad, Chile, China, Colombia, Comoros, Congo Brazzaville, Congo DR, Cook Is, Costa Rica, Côte d'Ivoire, Croatia, Cuba, Cyprus, Czechia, Denmark, Ecuador, Egypt, El Salvador, Equatorial Guinea, Eritrea, Estonia, Eswatini, Ethiopia, Fiji, Finland, France, Gabon, Gambia, Georgia, Germany, Ghana, Greece, Grenada, Guatemala, Guinea, Guinea-Bissau, Guyana, Haiti, Honduras, Hungary, Iceland, India, Indonesia, Iran Islamic Rep, Iraq, Ireland, Israel, Italy, Jamaica, Japan, Jordan, Kazakhstan, Kenya, Kiribati, Korea DPR, Korea Rep, Kuwait, Kyrgyzstan, Laos, Latvia, Lebanon, Lesotho, Liberia, Libya, Liechtenstein, Lithuania, Luxembourg, Madagascar, Malawi, Malaysia, Maldives, Mali, Malta, Marshall Is, Mauritania, Mauritius, Mexico, Micronesia FS, Moldova, Monaco, Mongolia, Montenegro, Morocco, Mozambique, Myanmar, Namibia, Nauru, Nepal, Netherlands, New Zealand, Nicaragua, Niger, Nigeria, Niue, North Macedonia, Norway, Oman, Pakistan, Palau, Panama, Papua New Guinea, Paraguay, Peru, Philippines, Poland, Portugal, Qatar, Romania, Russia, Rwanda, Samoa, San Marino, Sao Tomé-Principe, Saudi Arabia, Senegal, Serbia, Seychelles, Sierra Leone, Singapore, Slovakia, Slovenia, Solomon Is, Somalia, South Africa, South Sudan, Spain, Sri Lanka, St Kitts-Nevis, St Lucia, St Vincent-Grenadines, Sudan, Suriname, Sweden, Switzerland, Syrian AR, Tajikistan, Tanzania UR, Thailand, Timor-Leste, Togo, Tonga, Trinidad-Tobago, Tunisia, Türkiye, Turkmenistan, Tuvalu, Uganda, UK, Ukraine, United Arab Emirates, Uruguay, USA, Uzbekistan, Vanuatu, Venezuela, Vietnam, Yemen, Zambia, Zimbabwe.
IGO Relations 30 UN Bodies and Organizations as Participating Organizations; 25 IGOs as Observer Organizations, including: *Convention on Biological Diversity (Biodiversity convention, 1992)*; *United Nations Convention to Combat Desertification (UNCCD, 1994)*; *United Nations Framework Convention on Climate Change (UNFCCC, 1992)*; *Vienna Convention for the Protection of the Ozone Layer (Ozone treaty, 1985)* and its *Montreal Protocol on Substances that Deplete the Ozone Layer (1987)*. **NGO Relations** 105 accredited NGOs as Observers. [2021/XF1308/E*]

♦ Intergovernmental Renewable Energy Organization (inactive)

♦ Intergovernmental Science-Policy Platform on Biodiversity and Ecosystem Services (IPBES) 11500

Secretariat 10th floor, Platz der VN 1, 53113 Bonn, Germany. E-mail: secretariat@ipbes.net.
URL: http://www.ipbes.net/

History 21 Apr 2012, Panama (Panama). Proposed 2007, 3 intergovernmental and multi-stakeholder meetings in 2008, 2009, 2010. Officially set up by over 90 governments, 2012, with Bonn (Germany) hosting Secretariat. **Aims** Strengthen the science-policy interface for biodiversity and ecosystem services for the conservation and sustainable use of biodiversity, long-term human well-being and sustainable development. **Events** *Plenary Session* Bonn (Germany) 2022, *Plenary Session* Paris (France) 2019, *Plenary Session* Medellín (Colombia) 2018, *Plenary Session* Bonn (Germany) 2017, *Plenary Session* Kuala Lumpur (Malaysia) 2016. [2022.10.25/XM3233/E*]

♦ Inter-Governmental Standing Committee on Shipping (ISCOS) 11501

Secretariat PO Box 89112-80100, Mombasa, Kenya. T. +254202332670 – +254202533490. E-mail: info@iscosafricashipping.org.
Street Address Links Road Near AAR Nyali, Mombasa, Kenya.
URL: http://www.iscosafricashipping.org/

History 1967. Permanent Secretariat set up 1974, Mombasa (Kenya). Establishment agreement signed in 1987 and amended by Protocol, 27 Apr 2006. **Aims** Conduct negotiations with shipping conferences, *shipowners*, operators of shipping lines and other related bodies concerning *freight rates* and conditions of *maritime transport*; undertake research and compile statistical data with a view to advising governments on the level and structure of freight rates, *port* operating costs, conditions of marine carriage and other factors related to sea transportation; advise governments on the best means of containing increases in freight rates and transport costs or other adverse changes within the shipping industry; carry out studies on request of any member government. **Structure** Council of Ministers; Committee of Representatives; Secretariat, headed by Secretary General. **Staff** 8.00 FTE, paid. **Finance** Member Governments' contributions. **Activities** ISCOS concentrates its activities on specific areas: shipping; ports; multimodal transport.
Members Governments of 4 countries:
Kenya, Tanzania UR, Uganda, Zambia.
IGO Relations Cooperation agreement with: *International Maritime Organization (IMO, #14102)*. Participates in the activities of: *UNCTAD (#20285)*. Represented in subsectoral working group of: *United Nations Transport and Communications Decade in Africa (UNTACDA, inactive)*. [2017.03.08/XE0007/D*]

♦ Intergovernmental Sub-Group on Hides and Skins 11502

Sous-Groupe intergouvernemental sur des cuirs et peaux – Subgrupo Intergubernamental sobre los Cueros y Pieles

Address not obtained.
URL: http://www.fao.org/economic/est/est-commodities/hides-skins/

History within the framework of *FAO (#09260)*, a Sub-Group of *Intergovernmental Group on Meat and Dairy Products (#11491)*. An Intergovernmental Group (IGG) with Technical Secretariat the responsibility of FAO. **Languages** English, French, Spanish. **Events** *Session* Arusha (Tanzania UR) 2006, *Session* Rome (Italy) 2003, *Session* Rome (Italy) 2003, *Session* Rome (Italy) 2001, *Session* Rome (Italy) 2001.
Members All FAO member countries which produce hides and skins. Representatives in 24 countries:
Algeria, Angola, Brazil, Bulgaria, Ecuador, Ethiopia, Finland, Germany, Greece, Guatemala, Iran Islamic Rep, Kenya, Libya, Malaysia, Mali, Mexico, Nicaragua, Niger, Nigeria, Philippines, Spain, Sudan, Tanzania UR, UK.
Also regional integration EU entity:
European Union (EU, #08967).
IGO Relations A designated International Commodity Body of: *Common Fund for Commodities (CFC, #04293)*. Observers at the 8th Session: *International Trade Centre (ITC, #15703)*; *UNIDO (#20336)*. **NGO Relations** Observers at the 8th Session: *Confédération des associations nationales de tanneurs et mégissiers de la Communauté européenne (COTANCE, #04515)*; *Eastern and Southern Africa Leather Industries Association (ESALIA, no recent information)*. [2013.06.06/XE2268/E*]

♦ Intergovernmental Task Force Against Money Laundering in Africa / see Intergovernmental Action Group against Money Laundering in West Africa (#11471)
♦ Intergovernmental Technical Working Group on Animal Genetic Resources for Food and Agriculture (see: #09260)
♦ Intergovernmental TV and Radio Corporation (no recent information)
♦ Intergovernmental University Institute of Co-operation (internationally oriented national body)

♦ Intergovernmental Working Group of Experts on International Standards of Accounting and Reporting (ISAR) 11503

Groupe intergouvernemental d'experts des normes internationales de comptabilité et de publication – Grupo Intergubernamental de Trabajo de Expertos en Normas Internacionales de Contabilidad y Presentación de Informes

Contact Accounting and Corporate Governance Section, Div on Investment and Enterprise – UNCTAD, Palais des Nations, Avenue de la Paix 8-14, 1211 Geneva, Switzerland. T. +41229170122. E-mail: isar@unctad.org.
URL: https://isar.unctad.org/

History 27 Oct 1982, New York, NY (USA). Part of the institutional machinery of *UNCTAD (#20285)*. Set up by resolution 1982/67 of *ECOSOC (#05331)*, originally as part of *United Nations Commission on Transnational Corporations (inactive)*. Until 2008, came within UNCTAD's *Commission on Investment, Technology and Related Financial Issues (inactive)*, which was set up in 1996 and derived from the United Nations Commission. Serviced by UNCTAD through Division of Investment and Enterprise. **Aims** Promote international *harmonization* of corporate accounting and reporting practices; serve as an international body for the consideration of issues of accounting and reporting falling within the scope of the work of the Commission on Investment, Technology and Related Financial issues, in order to improve the availability and comparability of information disclosed by *transnational corporations*; review developments in this field, including the work of standard-setting bodies; concentrate on establishing priorities, taking into account the needs of home and host countries, particularly those of developing countries; assist *developing countries* and *countries in transition* via technical assistance in accounting reform and retraining. **Languages** Arabic, Chinese, English, French, Russian, Spanish. **Activities** Research/documentation. **Events** *Session* Geneva (Switzerland) 2020, *Session* Geneva (Switzerland) 2019, *Session* Geneva (Switzerland) 2018, *Session* Geneva (Switzerland) 2017, *Session* Geneva (Switzerland) 2016. **Publications** *International Accounting and Reporting Review* (annual). *A Banker's View of Commercial Bank Disclosures: Report of a Forum* (1997); *Responsibilities and Liabilities of Accountants and Auditors: Proceedings of a Forum* (1996); *Accounting for Sustainable Forestry Management: A Case Study* (1994); *Conclusions on Accounting and Reporting by Transnational Corporations* (1994); *Accounting, Valuation and Privatization* (1993); *Environmental Accounting: Current Issues, Abstracts, Bibliography* (1992); *Accounting for East-West Joint Ventures* (1991); *Curricula for Accounting Education for East-West Joint Ventures in Centrally Planned Economies* (1990); *Joint Ventures in Accounting in the USSR: Direction for Change* (1990); *Objectives and Concepts Underlying Financial Statements* (1989).
Members Experts from 34 countries – currently 10 are vacant:
Albania, Belarus, Brazil, Cambodia, Cameroon, China, Colombia, Côte d'Ivoire, Egypt, Gambia, Germany, Guatemala, Italy, Kazakhstan, Kenya, Kyrgyzstan, Morocco, Netherlands, Nigeria, Philippines, Russia, Saudi Arabia, UK, USA.
IGO Relations *European Commission (EC, #06633)*; *International Bank for Reconstruction and Development (IBRD, #12317)*; *International Monetary Fund (IMF, #14180)*; *OECD (#17693)*. [2021/XE0197/E*]

♦ Intergovernment Institution for the use of Micro-Algae Spirulina against Malnutrition (IIMSAM) 11504

SG 884 47st Second Ave, Dag Hammarskjold UN Ctr PO Box 20075, New York NY 10017, USA. T. +16455687806. Fax +16455687807. E-mail: frontdesk@iimsam.org.
URL: http://www.iimsam.org/

History 2001, USA. **Aims** Raise the level of nutrition and improve public health through Spirulina; disseminate Spirulina to eradicate malnutrition, achieve food security and bridge the health divide, prioritizing developing countries, small island developing states and least developed countries; promote the use of Spirulina against severe malnutrition and related illnesses. **Structure** Council; Executive Plenipotentiary; Extraordinariare Secretariat. **Languages** Arabic, English, Spanish. **Staff** 5.00 FTE, paid; 135.00 FTE, voluntary. **Finance** Private ex-gratia contributions; other sources. **Activities** Active in: Burundi, China, Egypt, Haiti, Iraq, Jordan, Kenya, Mexico, Niger, Nigeria, Palestine, Saudi Arabia, United Arab Emirates. **Publications** *IIMSAM Newsletter* (weekly).
Members Governments of 8 countries:
Dominican Rep, Equatorial Guinea, Guinea, Guinea-Bissau, Haiti, Kenya, Sao Tomé-Principe, Senegal.
IGO Relations Observer to: *ECOSOC (#05331)*. **NGO Relations** NGOs related in the field of acute malnutrition; strategic partners, not specified. [2020/XM1861/j/E*]

♦ Intergraf 11505

SG Av Louise 130A – box 2, 1050 Brussels, Belgium. T. +3222308646. E-mail: office@intergraf.eu.
Main Website: http://www.intergraf.eu/

History Jan 1930, Berlin (Germany). Conceived in June 1923, Gothenburg (Sweden), following 1st International Congress of Master Printers. Incorporate *Group of Federations of Graphics Industries in the European Communities (EUROGRAF, inactive)*, since 1983. Former names and other names: *International Bureau of the Federations of Master Printers* – former (1930 to 1946); *International Master Printers Association (IMPA)* – former (1946 to 1984); *International Confederation for Printing and Allied Industries (INTERGRAF)* – former (1984 to 2012); *European Federation for Print and Digital Communication (INTERGRAF)* – former (2012 to 2019). Registration: Banque-Carrefour des Entreprises, No/ID: 0425.751.311, Start date: 30 May 1984, Belgium; EU Transparency Register, No/ID: 15519132837-45, Start date: 18 Dec 2009. **Aims** Promote and protect the interests of the graphic industry at European level. **Structure** General Assembly (annual); Board; Steering Committee. **Languages** English, French, German, Greek, Hungarian, Romanian. **Staff** 7.50 FTE, paid. **Finance** Sources: members' dues; revenue from activities/projects; sale of products; sale of publications. **Activities** Advocacy/lobbying/activism; events/meetings; knowledge management/information dissemination; networking/liaising. **Events** *Annual Print Matters for the Future Conference* Stockholm (Sweden) 2022, *General Assembly* Stockholm (Sweden) 2022, *General Assembly* 2021, *Intergraf Currency + Identity Online Conference* 2021, *General Assembly* 2020. **Publications** *Intergraf Annual Economic Report* (annual). Studies; research reports.
Members National federations (21) in 20 countries:
Austria, Belgium, Bulgaria, Denmark, Estonia, Finland, France, Germany, Hungary, Iceland, Italy, Latvia, Lithuania, Luxembourg, Netherlands, Norway, Portugal, Sweden, Switzerland (x2), UK.
11 Associate members (11) in 8 countries:
Austria, Belgium, Germany, Italy, Poland, Spain, Switzerland, UK.
IGO Relations Links with European institutions. **NGO Relations** Cooperates with (10): *BUSINESSEUROPE (#03381)*; *European Paper Recycling Council (EPRC, #08139)*; *European Platform for Chemicals Using Manufacturing Industries (CheMI, #08223)*; *European Rotogravure Association (ERA, #08404)*; *FESPA (#09739)*; *FTA Europe (#10012)*; *Industry4Europe (#11181)*; *International Currency Association (ICA, #13123)*; *Search and Information Industry Association (Siinda, #19188)*; *World Print and Communication Forum (WPCF, #21737)*. Instrumental in setting up (1): *European Mail Industry Platform (EMIP, inactive)*. Cooperates with: European Solvents VOC Coordination Group (ES-VOC-CG) and other European publishers, paper and related associations, printing-related associations. [2022.10.19/XC1437/y/D]

♦ INTERGRAF / see Intergraf (#11505)
♦ INTERGU – Internationale Gesellschaft für Urheberrecht (no recent information)
♦ Inter-Hemispheric Education Resource Center / see International Relations Center
♦ Interhemispheric Resource Center / see International Relations Center

♦ Interim Agreement on International Civil Aviation (1944 treaty)
♦ Interimausschuss für das Gemeinschaftspatent (inactive)
♦ Interim Baltic Marine Environment Protection Commission / see Baltic Marine Environment Protection Commission – Helsinki Commission (#03126)
♦ Interim Board of Veterinary Specialization / see European Board of Veterinary Specialisation (#06375)
♦ Interim Committee of the Board of Governors of the International Monetary Fund on the International Monetary System / see International Monetary and Financial Committee (#14179)
♦ Interim Committee of the Consultative Non-Governmental Organizations (inactive)
♦ Interim Committee for Coordination of Investigations of the Lower Mekong Basin (inactive)
♦ Interim Committee / see International Monetary and Financial Committee (#14179)
♦ Interim Convention on Conservation of North Pacific Fur Seals (1957 treaty)
♦ Interim Coordinating Committee for International Commodity Arrangements (inactive)
♦ Interim Emergency Multinational Force in Bunia / see United Nations Organization Stabilization Mission in the Democratic Republic of Congo (#20605)
♦ Interim Mekong Committee – Interim Committee for Coordination of Investigations of the Lower Mekong Basin (inactive)
♦ Interim Multilateral Fund / see Multilateral Fund for the Implementation of the Montreal Protocol (#16885)
♦ Interim North American Regional Broadcasting Agreement (1946 treaty)
♦ Interim Scientific Committee for Tuna and Tuna-like Species in the North Pacific Ocean / see International Scientific Committee for Tuna and Tuna-like Species in the North Pacific Ocean (#14807)

♦ Inter-Islamic Network on Biosaline Agriculture (INBA) 11506

Réseau inter-islamique d'agriculture biosaline

Contact ICBA, PO Box 14660, Dubai, United Arab Emirates. T. +97143361100. Fax +97143361155. E-mail: inba@biosaline.org.ae – s.ismail@biosaline.org.ae.
URL: http://www.biosaline.org/Default.aspx?pid=240

History Feb 2002, Islamabad (Pakistan), under the auspices of *OIC Ministerial Standing Committee on Scientific and Technological Cooperation (COMSTECH, #17702)*, within *Organisation of Islamic Cooperation (OIC, #17813)*. **Aims** Promote research and information sharing on biosaline agriculture in the region. **Structure** Steering Committee; Executive Council, including President (ICBA Director General) and Executive Director. **Finance** Members' dues. **Activities** Organizes seminars, workshops and training courses. **Events** *Workshop* Dubai (United Arab Emirates) 2007, *International workshop on technological advances in seawater desalination and its impact on the coastal environment* Dubai (United Arab Emirates) 2003. **Publications** *Biosalinity News* (3 a year). *Marine Pollution and the Impacts of Seawater Desalination Plants on Coastal Environment*; *Who-is-Who in Biosaline Agriculture*. Directory.
Members Full in 4 countries:
Oman, Pakistan, Saudi Arabia, United Arab Emirates.
IGO Relations Contacts with: *Inter-Islamic Network on Genetic Engineering and Biotechnology (INOGE, #11507)*; *Inter-Islamic Network on Tropical Medicine (INTROM, #11512)*; *Inter-Islamic Network on Water Resources Development and Management (INWRDAM, #11513)*. [2008/XF6773/F*]

♦ Inter-Islamic Network on Genetic Engineering and Biotechnology (INOGE) 11507

Réseau inter-islamique de génie génétique et de la biotechnologie

Exec Dir Gen c/o ASRT, 101 Qasr El Aini Street, PO Box 43/11516, Cairo, 11516, Egypt. T. +2027021326. Fax +2027021270. E-mail: asrt@asrt.sci.eg.

History 28 Oct 1987, Cairo (Egypt). 28-29 Oct 1987, Cairo (Egypt), as an independent, autonomous and self-governing institution under the umbrella of *OIC Ministerial Standing Committee on Scientific and Technological Cooperation (COMSTECH, #17702)* of *Organisation of Islamic Cooperation (OIC, #17813)*. Originally planned as *Islamic Centre for Genetic Engineering and Biotechnology*. **Aims** Cooperate in research areas of common interest with a view to mutual assistance in building capability in the field; exchange information and maintain continuing dialogue on developments in the field for mutual benefit and use; initiate joint projects of research and development of common interest to member countries; assist in training of quality *manpower* in the field for *Muslim* countries. **Structure** General Assembly, consisting of representatives of member states. Executive Committee, composed of President, Vice-President and 2 elected members. Secretariat, headed by Executive Director. **Languages** Arabic, English, French. **Finance** Member states' contributions. Other sources: COMSTECH, ASRT and other OIC agencies; international agencies; private donations. **Activities** Training courses; research programme; meetings. **Events** *Regional workshop on bioethics and biosafety measures in biotechnology research and development in OIC member countries* Borg el-Arab (Egypt) 2002, *Emergency : international conference for disaster management* Cairo (Egypt) 1990, *International meeting on road safety and accidents* Cairo (Egypt) 1990, *Meeting* Cairo (Egypt) 1987. **Publications** *INOGE Newsletter*. *Bio-Organic Farming Systems for Sustainable Agriculture*. Brochures. Information Services: Databank on developments in the field, for use of member states and other Muslim countries.
Members Full in 20 countries:
Algeria, Bangladesh, Egypt, Gambia, Indonesia, Iran Islamic Rep, Iraq, Kuwait, Malaysia, Morocco, Niger, Nigeria, Pakistan, Saudi Arabia, Senegal, Sudan, Syrian AR, Tunisia, Türkiye, Yemen. [2009/XF0807/F*]

♦ Inter Islamic Network on Information Technology (INIT) 11508

Réseau inter-islamique de la technologie informatique

Exec Dir 4th Floor – Fac Block I, COMSATS Inst of Information Technology, Park Road – Chak Shahzad, Islamabad, Pakistan. T. +925190495100. Fax +92519247006.
Manager Ovvice 002, CUBATOR1NE, COMSATS Inst of Information Technology, Park Road – Chak Shahzad, Islamabad, Pakistan. T. +925190419581. Fax +92519247006.
URL: http://www.init.org.pk/

History Established 28 Jul 2005, Islamabad (Pakistan). Proposal to set up the Network approved by the 10th General Assembly of *OIC Ministerial Standing Committee on Scientific and Technological Cooperation (COMSTECH, #17702)* of *Organisation of Islamic Cooperation (OIC, #17813)*, held 16-18 Feb 2002, Islamabad. COMSATS Institut of Information Technology (CIIT), Islamabad, is the host institution and the Government of Pakistan is the host government. **Aims** Comply with the desires of the Muslim community for utilizing, directing and encouraging the use of Information Technologies and associated systems to promote collaboration and cooperation in building human resources and institutional capacity. **Structure** General Body (meets every 2 years), including President and Executive Director/Secretary. Permanent secretariat at CIIT. **Languages** Arabic, English, French. **Staff** 11.00 FTE, paid. **Finance** Members' dues. Government funded. **Activities** Knowledge management/information dissemination; guidance/assistance/consulting; training/education; networking/liaising; events/meetings. **Events** *International Workshop on Applications of ICTs in Education, Healthcare and Agriculture* Amman (Jordan) 2016, *Workshop on ICTs for Development* Islamabad (Pakistan) 2016, *International Workshop on Applications of ICTs in Education, Healthcare and Agriculture* Rabat (Morocco) 2015, *Inaugural meeting* Abu Dhabi (United Arab Emirates) 2005, *International conference* Abu Dhabi (United Arab Emirates) 2005. **Publications** *FOCUS INIT* – newsletter. **IGO Relations** *Commission on Science and Technology for Sustainable Development in the South (COMSATS, #04239)*; *FAO (#09260)*; *International Telecommunication Union (ITU, #15673)*; *Islamic World Educational, Scientific and Cultural Organization (ICESCO, #16058)*; *OIC Ministerial Standing Committee on Scientific and Technological Cooperation (COMSTECH, #17702)*; *Organisation of Islamic Cooperation (OIC, #17813)*; *UNESCO (#20322)*. **NGO Relations** Universities and research organizations from OIC Member States. [2018/XM0312/F*]

♦ Inter-Islamic Network of Nanotechnology (INN) 11509

CEO PO Box 14155-4777, Teheran, Iran Islamic Rep. T. +982188771626 – +982188771627. Fax +982188773351. E-mail: inn@comstech-nanonet.org.
Contact Materials and Energy Research Center (MERC), Imam Khomeini Blvd, Meshkindasht, Karaj ALBORZ, 31787-316, Iran Islamic Rep. T. +982636280050 – +982636280051. Fax +982636201888.
URL: http://www.comstech-nanonet.org/

History Approved under Article 25 of Resolution, Apr 2008, Islamabad (Pakistan), at 13th General Assembly of *OIC Ministerial Standing Committee on Scientific and Technological Cooperation (COMSTECH, #17702)*. Within the framework of *Organisation of Islamic Cooperation (OIC, #17813)*. Founded 8 Jan 2012, Teheran (Iran Islamic Rep). **Aims** Foster closer cooperation among Muslim countries in development and management of nanotechnology resources. **Structure** General Assembly; Executive Committee; Secretariat. **Languages** Arabic, English, French. **Activities** Projects/programmes; knowledge management/information dissemination; events/meetings. **Events** *Conference on Nanotechnology and Nanomedicine* Karaj (Iran Islamic Rep) 2017.
Members Governments of 21 countries and territories:
Afghanistan, Algeria, Bangladesh, India, Iran Islamic Rep, Iraq, Jordan, Kazakhstan, Kenya, Kyrgyzstan, Lebanon, Malaysia, Netherlands, Oman, Pakistan, Palestine, Somalia, South Africa, Tajikistan, Tunisia, United Arab Emirates.
[2019.12.29/XJ7814/F*]

♦ Inter-Islamic Network on Oceanography / see Inter-Islamic Science and Technology Network on Oceanography (#11514)

♦ Inter-Islamic Network on Renewable Energy Sources (INRES) 11510

Réseau inter-islamique pour l'energie renouvelable

Address not obtained.

History Oct 1987, Islamabad (Pakistan), within the framework of the Plan of Action of *OIC Ministerial Standing Committee on Scientific and Technological Cooperation (COMSTECH, #17702)*, at the instigation of *Islamic Foundation for Science, Technology and Development (IFSTAD, inactive)*, then a specialized agency of *Organisation of Islamic Cooperation (OIC, #17813)*. Previously also referred to as *International Network on Renewable Energy Sources*. Currently suspended (2013). **Aims** Cooperate in research areas of common interest with a view mutual assistance in building capability in the field; exchange information and maintain continuing dialogue on developments in the field for mutual benefit and use; initiate joint research and development projects of common interest to member countries; assist in training of quality manpower for *Muslim* countries in the field. **Structure** General Body, consisting of the focal institutions of the Network plus a representative of IFSTAD. Executive Committee (meeting at least once a year). **Languages** Arabic, English, French. **Finance** Member states' contributions. Other sources: IFSTAD and other OIC agencies; international agencies; private donations; income from donations and services. **Activities** Organizes symposia and workshops. Develops a 'Solar Park'. Engages in joint research projects and studies. **Events** *Meeting* Islamabad (Pakistan) 1987. **Publications** Information Services: Databank for use by members of the Network and other Muslim countries.
Members Governments of 8 countries:
Indonesia, Iraq, Jordan, Morocco, Niger, Pakistan, Saudi Arabia, Türkiye.
Governments, willing to join, of 11 countries:
Algeria, Cameroon, Egypt, Gambia, Iran Islamic Rep, Mali, Mauritania, Qatar, Senegal, Sudan, Syrian AR. [2010/XF2128/F*]

♦ Inter-Islamic Network on Space Sciences and Technology (ISNET) . 11511

Secretariat SUPARCO Headquarters, Suparco Road, PO Box 8402, Karachi 75270, Pakistan. T. +922134694939 – +92213469076579 ext 2012. Fax +922134644941 – +922134644928. E-mail: admin@isnet.org.pk – isnetsectt@gmail.com.
URL: http://www.isnet.org.pk/

History 30 Sep 1987, Karachi (Pakistan). Founded 30 Sep – 1 Oct 1987, Karachi (Pakistan), as an independent, autonomous and self-governing institution under the umbrella of *OIC Ministerial Standing Committee on Scientific and Technological Cooperation (COMSTECH, #17702)* of the *Organisation of Islamic Cooperation (OIC, #17813)* as one of 6 inter-Islamic networks in various fields of modern science and technology. Decision to set up these networks taken at 3rd Meeting of the COMSTECH, 19-22 Nov 1986, Islamabad (Pakistan). Originally planned as *Islamic Institute of Space Science Research*. **Aims** Promote space sciences, space technology and their applications for peaceful purposes in OIC member countries. **Structure** Governing Body; Executive Council; Secretariat, managed by Executive Director. **Languages** Arabic, English, French. **Staff** 3.00 FTE, paid. **Finance** Contributions from member states. Other sources: COMSTECH and other OIC agencies; *Islamic Development Bank (IsDB, #16044)*; international agencies; income from services. **Activities** Knowledge management/information dissemination; assistance/advice/consulting; research and development; training/education; events/meetings. **Events** *International Conference on the Use of Space Technology for Water Management* Islamabad (Pakistan) 2018, *United Nations/Morocco International Conference on the Use of Space Technology for Water Management* Rabat (Morocco) 2014, *International Workshop on Integrated Use of Space Technologies for Food and Water Security* Islamabad (Pakistan) 2013, *Workshop on Space Applications for Disaster Risk Reduction and Management* Teheran (Iran Islamic Rep) 2013, *International seminar on remote sensing for water resources management* Damascus (Syrian AR) 2007. **Publications** *ISNET Newsletter*. Biennial Activity Report. Workshop proceedings; introductory literature.
Members Governments of 16 countries (" Founding member countries):
Azerbaijan, Bangladesh (*), Egypt, Indonesia (*), Iran Islamic Rep, Iraq (*), Jordan, Morocco (*), Niger (*), Pakistan (*), Saudi Arabia (*), Senegal, Sudan, Syrian AR, Tunisia (*), Türkiye (*).
IGO Relations Permanent observer of: *Committee on the Peaceful Uses of Outer Space (COPUOS, #04277)*. Observer of: *Group on Earth Observations (GEO, #10735)*. [2022/XF2091/F*]

♦ Inter-Islamic Network on Tropical Medicine (INTROM) 11512

Exec Dir Natl Inst of Health Malaysia, Jalan Setia Murni U13/52, Seksyen U13 Setia Alam, 40170 Shah Alam, Selangor, Malaysia. T. +60333628900. E-mail: tahir.a@moh.gov.my – dirpa@imr.gov.my.
URL: http://www.imr.gov.my/collaborations.html

History 19 Oct 1987, Kuala Lumpur (Malaysia). Established at the instigation of *Islamic Foundation for Science, Technology and Development (IFSTAD, inactive)*, as an independent, autonomous, self-governing institution under the umbrella of *OIC Ministerial Standing Committee on Scientific and Technological Cooperation (COMSTECH, #17702)* of the *Organisation of Islamic Cooperation (OIC, #17813)*. Former names and other names: *Islamic Institute of Tropical Medicine* – former. **Aims** Strengthen the individual and collective capacity of OIC countries in science and technology through cooperation, collaboration, and networking resources for socioeconomic development and rapid industrialization in member countries. **Languages** English. **Finance** Sources: government support; grants; international organizations. Supported by: *Islamic Development Bank (IsDB, #16044)*; Ministry of Health of Malaysia; *OIC Ministerial Standing Committee on Scientific and Technological Cooperation (COMSTECH, #17702)*. **Activities** Events/meetings; projects/programmes; research and development; training/education. **Members** Membership countries not specified.
IGO Relations Secretariat provided by: *SEAMEO TROPMED Regional Centre for Microbiology, Parasitology and Entomology (#19185)*. [2023.02.16/XF0806/F*]

♦ Inter-Islamic Network on Veterinary Science Research, Khartoum (unconfirmed)

♦ Inter-Islamic Network on Water Resources Development and Management (INWRDAM) 11513

Réseau islamique de développement et de gestion des ressources hydrauliques

Exec Dir PO Box 1460, PC 11941 Jubieha, Amman, Jordan. T. +96265332993. Fax +96265332969. E-mail: inwrdam@nic.net.jo.
URL: http://www.inwrdam.org.jo/

History 8 Jul 1987, Amman (Jordan), under the umbrella of *OIC Ministerial Standing Committee on Scientific and Technological Cooperation (COMSTECH, #17702)* and at the instigation of *Islamic Foundation for Science, Technology and Development (IFSTAD, inactive)*, then a subsidiary organ of the *Organisation of Islamic Cooperation (OIC, #17813)*. Originally planned as *Islamic Institute of Water Resources Management*. Also referred to as *Islamic Network of Water Resources Development and Management*. **Aims** Promote scientific and technological cooperation and facilitate transfer of know-how; ensure proper planning of water resources development, effective management, sufficient utilization and *conservation* of water resources as required for future *economic growth*. **Structure** Governing Body, consisting of representatives of Member States, a representative of COMSTECH and a representative of OIC General Secretariat. Executive Council, comprising President of the Network (ex-officio Chairman) and representatives of 3 Member States, together with Executive Director as Secretary. Secretariat, headed by Executive Director. **Languages** Arabic, English, French. **Staff** 4.00 FTE, paid. **Finance** Contributions of Member States. Other financial resources: funds from COMSTECH; funds from the Higher Council for Science and Technology (HCST) – Jordan; grants from OIC and its organs and institutions; donations and subsidies from other organizations; income generated through publications, consultancies, services. **Activities** Knowledge management/information dissemination; research/documentation; training/education; events/meetings; projects/programmes. **Events** *Arab water forum* Cairo (Egypt) 2011, *Regional Training Workshop* Aqaba (Jordan) 2009, *Regional Training Workshop* Istanbul (Turkey) 2009, *Regional Training Workshop* Tunis (Tunisia) 2009, *Regional Training Workshop* Damascus (Syrian AR) 2008. **Publications** Proceedings of training workshops; books; monographs.

Members Governments of 19 countries:
Bahrain, Bangladesh, Egypt, Iraq, Jordan, Lebanon, Malaysia, Mali, Niger, Oman, Pakistan, Saudi Arabia, Sudan, Syrian AR, Tajikistan, Tunisia, Türkiye, Uzbekistan, Yemen.
IGO Relations Memorandum of Understanding with: *Regional Centre on Agrarian Reform and Rural Development for the Near East (#18755)*. Cooperates with: *Islamic World Educational, Scientific and Cultural Organization (ICESCO, #16058)*. [2019.12.15/XF2127/**F***]

♦ Inter-Islamic Science and Technology Network on Oceanography . . 11514

Réseau inter-islamique de science et technologie de l'océanographie – Islam Ülkeleri Osinografi Bilim ve Teknoloji Agi

Exec Dir DEU/DBTE, Baku Bulvari no 100, Inciralti, 35340 Izmir/Izmir, Türkiye. T. +902322791522 – +902322786525. Fax +902322785082. E-mail: inoc@inoctr.org.
Pres address not obtained.
URL: http://www.inoctr.org/

History 10 Nov 1987, Izmir (Türkiye). Founded 10-12 Nov 1987, Izmir (Turkey), under the name *Inter-Islamic Network on Oceanography (INOC)*, as an independent, autonomous and self-governing institution under the umbrella of *OIC Ministerial Standing Committee on Scientific and Technological Cooperation (COMSTECH, #17702)* of *Organisation of Islamic Cooperation (OIC, #17813)*. Originally planned as *Islamic Institute of Oceanography*. **Aims** Cooperate in research areas of common interest with a view to mutual assistance in building capability in the field of oceanography; exchange information; initiate joint research activities; develop projects; assist in training of students and quality manpower. **Structure** Executive Committee; Steering Committee. **Languages** English, French. **Staff** 2.50 FTE, voluntary. **Finance** Members' dues. Other sources: assistance from COMSTECH, OIC and international agencies; private donations. **Activities** Events/meetings. Setting up an Oceanographic Information and Data Centre for Islamic countries. **Events** *International Congress on Estuaries and Coastal Protected Areas* Izmir (Turkey) 2014, *International Conference on Oceanography and Sustainable Marine Production* Kuantan (Malaysia) 2013, *International Conference on Land-Sea Interactions in the Coastal Zone* Byblos (Lebanon) 2012, *Meeting* Jounieh (Lebanon) 2012, *International symposium on marine ecosystems, natural products and their bioactive metabolites / Meeting* Bogor (Indonesia) 2011. **Publications** *INOC News* (4 a year) – newsletter. Reports; proceedings.
Members Institutions in 20 countries and territories:
Algeria, Bangladesh, Egypt, Indonesia, Iran Islamic Rep, Iraq, Jordan, Kuwait, Lebanon, Libya, Malaysia, Morocco, Northern Cyprus, Oman, Pakistan, Qatar, Senegal, Tunisia, Türkiye, United Arab Emirates. [2022/XF0809/**F***]

♦ Inter-Island Tourism Policy Forum (ITOP Forum) 11515

Secretariat 2F Tourism Research Ctr, Jeju Welcome Center, 23 Seondeok-ro, Jeju 63122, Korea Rep. E-mail: itop@ijto.or.kr.
URL: http://www.itop-forum.org/

History 1997, Jeju (Korea Rep). **Aims** Explore the world tourism market jointly by bring together islands that have cultural sympathy and similar tourism structure and policy. **Languages** English. **Events** *Global Policy Seminar* Jeju (Korea Rep) 2020, *Global Policy Seminar* Jeju (Korea Rep) 2020, *Forum* Okinawa (Japan) 2019, *Forum* Jeju (Korea Rep) 2018, *Global Policy Seminar* Jeju (Korea Rep) 2017. **Publications** *ITOP Newsletter*.
Members Full in 11 countries:
China, Indonesia, Japan, Korea Rep, Malaysia, Philippines, Spain, Sri Lanka, Tanzania UR, Thailand, USA. [2019/XJ9665/**F**]

- ♦ INTERJUV – International Youth Confederation (inactive)
- ♦ Interkabel (inactive)
- ♦ Interkerkelijke Aktie voor Latijns Amerika / see SOLIDARIDAD Network (#19681)
- ♦ Interkerkelijke Coördinatie Commissie Ontwikkelingsprojekten / see ICCO – Interchurch Organization for Development Cooperation
- ♦ Interkerkelijk Vredesberaad / see PAX
- ♦ Inter-Knowing Foundation (internationally oriented national body)
- ♦ INTERKOM – Internationale Kommunikation und Kultur (internationally oriented national body)
- ♦ Interkomitee voor Hulp aan de Vluchtelingen uit Midden Europa (inactive)

♦ INTERKULTUR 11516

Main Office Ruhberg 1, 35463 Fernwald, Germany. T. +49640446974925.
URL: http://www.interkultur.com/

History 14 Mar 1990. Former names and other names: *INTERKULTUR Foundation* – former; *Förderverein Interkultur* – former. Registration: Start date: 25 Apr 1990, Germany. **Aims** Promote *art* and *culture*. **Structure** General Assembly; Managing Committee; World Choir Council. **Finance** Members' dues. **Activities** Events/meetings; awards/prizes/competitions. **Events** *World Choir Games* Auckland (New Zealand) 2024, *World Choir Games* Gangneung (Korea Rep) 2022, *World Choir Games* Antwerp (Belgium) / Ghent (Belgium) 2021, *World Choir Games* Antwerp (Belgium) 2020, *World Choir Games* Riga (Latvia) 2014. [2018.01.26/XJ5851/**F**]

- ♦ INTERKULTUR Foundation / see INTERKULTUR (#11516)
- ♦ **Interlaw** International Association of Independent Law Firms (#11958)

♦ Interlegal 11517

Sec c/o Spieker and Jaeger, Kronenburgallee 5, 44139 Dortmund, Germany. T. +492319585875. Fax +49231958584975.
Pres c/o Orbis Legal Advisory Ltd, 153/3 – 4th floor, Goldenland Bldg, Soi Mahardlekluang 1, Rajdamri Rd, Bangkok, 10330, Thailand. T. +6626841212. Fax +6626845990. E-mail: president@interlegal.net.
URL: http://www.interlegal.net/

History 1987, Lisbon (Portugal). Founded as an organization of the type *European Economic Interest Grouping (EEIG, #06960)*. Originally incorporated with the law of Luxembourg. Former names and other names: *Eurojurist* – former; *Eurojust Network* – former (1994 to 1996). Registration: Switzerland. **Aims** Provide clients with ready access to high quality legal advice from firms with local knowledge to help them in their international and cross border transactions; provide members with the opportunity to meet and develop professional expertise and close personal working relationships. **Structure** General Assembly (twice a year); Executive Committee; Marketing Committee; Specialist Groups. **Languages** English, French, German, Portuguese, Russian, Spanish. **Staff** 1.00 FTE, paid; 5.00 FTE, voluntary. **Finance** Sources: members' dues. **Activities** Events/meetings; networking/liaising. **Events** *Half-Yearly Meeting* Istanbul (Turkey) 2020, *Half-Yearly Meeting* Delhi (India) 2019, *Half-Yearly Meeting* Thessaloniki (Greece) 2019, *Half-Yearly Meeting* Luxembourg (Luxembourg) 2018, *Half-Yearly Meeting* Moscow (Russia) 2018. **Publications** *Members News Updates* (bi-weekly).
Members Full (48) in 46 countries and territories:
Argentina, Australia, Austria, Belgium, Brazil, Canada, Chile, China, Côte d'Ivoire, Croatia, Cyprus, Czechia, Denmark, Egypt, France, Germany, Greece, Hungary, India, Italy, Japan, Lebanon, Liechtenstein, Luxembourg, Malta, Mexico, Monaco, Netherlands, Norway, Poland, Portugal, Russia, Serbia, Singapore, Slovakia, Spain, Sweden, Switzerland, Thailand, Tunisia, Türkiye, UK, Ukraine, Uruguay, USA, Virgin Is USA.
NGO Relations Cooperates with: *EuraAudit International (#05594)*. [2020.05.15/XM3737/**F**]

- ♦ Interlegal Foundation / see International Public Foundation (#14667)
- ♦ **INTERLEGAL** International Public Foundation (#14667)

♦ Interlex Group 11518

Pres 200 W Madison, Suite 3000, Chicago IL 60606, USA. T. +13122241214.
Dir Administration address not obtained. T. +13122242515.
URL: https://www.interlexgroup.com/

History Founded 1973. Full title: *THE INTERLEX Group – International Law Firm Network*. **Aims** Provide a complete range of international legal and business services to clients.
Members Firms (49) in 63 countries and territories:
Albania, Angola, Argentina, Australia, Austria, Belarus, Belgium, Bosnia-Herzegovina, Brazil, Bulgaria, Canada, Chile, China, Colombia, Costa Rica, Croatia, Czechia, Denmark, El Salvador, Estonia, Finland, France, Germany, Greece, Guatemala, Honduras, Hong Kong, Hungary, India, Indonesia, Ireland, Israel, Italy, Japan, Korea Rep, Latvia, Lithuania, Luxembourg, Malaysia, Mexico, Netherlands, New Zealand, Nicaragua, Norway, Peru, Philippines, Poland, Portugal, Romania, Russia, Serbia, Singapore, Slovakia, Slovenia, South Africa, Spain, Sweden, Switzerland, Taiwan, Türkiye, UK, Ukraine, Uruguay, USA.
NGO Relations Member of: *Association of International Law Firm Networks (AILFN, #02753)*. Affiliated with: *LEX Africa (#16449)*. [2020/XM8856/**F**]

- ♦ Interlighter – International Shipping Company / see Asociación Panamericana y Caribeña de Hipnosis Terapéutica (#02286)
- ♦ Interline ULD User Group / see ULD CARE (#20278)
- ♦ Interlingue-Union (inactive)

♦ INTERMAG 11519

Contact Coordinating Centre, Rue Jacques de Lalaing 28, 1040 Brussels, Belgium. T. +3222825114.

History Founded 1963. **Aims** Increase international cooperation among *TV* programmes under public control through programme exchange. **Structure** General Assembly. **Languages** English. **Finance** Members' dues. **Activities** Networking/liaising; events/meetings. **Events** *General Assembly* Stockholm (Sweden) 2015.
Members Full in 7 countries:
Czechia, Finland, Germany, Italy, Norway, Sweden, Switzerland. [2016.12.14/XD4830/**F**]

♦ InterManager 11520

SG 12 Brisbane St, Douglas, IM1 3JJ, UK. T. +447624498266.
Registered Office Demetriades Law Office, 284 Arch Markarios III Ave, Fortuna Court Block B, PO Box 50132, CY-3601 Limassol, Cyprus.
URL: http://www.intermanager.org/

History Apr 1991, London (UK). Former names and other names: *International Ship Managers' Association (ISMA)* – former (Apr 1991 to 2005); *InterManager – International Ship Managers' Association* – full title (2005). Registration: Cyprus. **Aims** Federate and serve the needs of the *shipping management* industry; improve standards in ship management and achieve a safer, environmentally more protective, more reliable and more controllable industry; address and propose solutions to the sector's current issues; speak in public fora on behalf of the industry; work with international regulators on the creation of standards and rules that protect the sector's interests; get involved in industry-wide projects, so as to create KPI standards for the shipping industry and review certain issues involving criminalization of crews in cases of marine incidents. **Structure** General Meeting (annual). Executive Committee. Code Committee. Committees (4): Manning and Training; IMO-EU; Communications; New Products. **Languages** English. **Staff** 1.00 FTE, paid. **Finance** Members' dues: US$ 1,500 – US$ 23,000, depending on size of company. **Activities** Organizes: seafarers' and shore training courses; ship-management related conferences; seminars. Contributes to international studies. **Events** *Annual General Meeting* London (UK) 2009, *Annual General Meeting* Singapore (Singapore) 2008, *Annual General Meeting* Limassol (Cyprus) 2006, *Annual General Meeting* Cyprus 1994. **Members** Full Shipowners, ship managers and crew managers worldwide. Associate Companies involved in the provision of goods or services. membership countries not specified. **Consultative Status** Consultative status granted from: *ECOSOC (#05331)* (Ros C); *International Maritime Organization (IMO, #14102)*. **IGO Relations** *European Commission (EC, #06633)*. **NGO Relations** Affiliate member of: *International Salvage Union (ISU, #14779)*. Member of: *Maritime Piracy Humanitarian Response Programme (MPHRP, #16583)*. [2021/XD9045/**D**]

- ♦ InterManager – International Ship Managers' Association / see InterManager (#11520)
- ♦ Intermarc Software Group / see European Library Automation Group (#07692)
- ♦ Intermed / see Dooley Foundation Intermed International
- ♦ Intermediate Technology Development Group / see Practical Action (#18475)

♦ Intermediterranean Commission (IMC) 11521

Commission interméditerranéenne (CIM) – Comisión Intermediterranea – Inter-Mittelmeer-Kommission – Comissão Intermediterranica – Commissione Intermediterranea – Endomesogiaki Epitropi

Exec Sec c/o CPMR, 6 rue Saint-Martin, 35700 Rennes, France. T. +33299354060. Fax +33299302451.
URL: http://medregions.com/

History 1990, Seville (Spain), at first meeting. Comes within the framework of *Conference of Peripheral Maritime Regions of Europe (CPMR, #04638)*. **Aims** Promote increased *solidarity* among European regions around the Mediterranean basin; ensure that the regions' specific problems are taken into consideration and that better coordination is achieved between European, regional and national policies. **Structure** General Assembly (annual); Political Bureau; Working Groups. **Finance** Members' dues. Contributions from the regions. Budget (annual): euro 2.5 million. **Events** *General Assembly* Venice (Italy) 2016, *Plenary Assembly* Naples (Italy) 2008, *Plenary Assembly* Granada (Spain) 2007, *Plenary Assembly* Arles (France) 2006, *Plenary Assembly* Valencia (Spain) 2005.
Members Regions (40) in 9 countries:
Albania, Cyprus, France, Greece, Italy, Malta, Morocco, Spain, Tunisia.
IGO Relations *Council of Europe (CE, #04881)*; *European Commission (EC, #06633)*; *Union for the Mediterranean (UfM, #20457)*. [2016/XK0534/**E**]

- ♦ Inter-Mediterranean Linguistics Association (inactive)
- ♦ Intermensa / see Mensa International (#16714)
- ♦ **INTERMEPA** International Marine Environment Protection Association (#14092)
- ♦ INTERMETALL – Organization for Cooperation in Iron and Steel Industry (inactive)
- ♦ INTERMET – International Association for Metropolitan Research and Development (inactive)
- ♦ Intermetro (inactive)
- ♦ Inter-Mittelmeer-Kommission (#11521)
- ♦ Intermón / see INTERMON OXFAM
- ♦ INTERMON OXFAM (internationally oriented national body)
- ♦ INTERMON OXFAM Foundation / see INTERMON OXFAM
- ♦ Intermorgeo (inactive)
- ♦ InterNACHI – International Association of Certified Home Inspectors (internationally oriented national body)
- ♦ Internacia Agrikultura Esperanto-Asocio (no recent information)
- ♦ Internacia Asocio de Bankistoj Esperantistaj (inactive)
- ♦ Internacia Asocio de Bibliistoj kaj Orientalistoj (inactive)
- ♦ Internacia Asocio de la Esperantistaj Fervojistoj (inactive)
- ♦ Internacia Asocio de Esperantistaj Matematikistoj (no recent information)
- ♦ Internacia Asocio de Liberpenso (#11906)
- ♦ Internacia Asocio de Postmark-Kolektantoj (inactive)
- ♦ Internacia Centro de la Neutrala Esperanto Movado (inactive)
- ♦ Internacia Centro pri Kulturo kaj Turismo en Bydgoszcz (no recent information)
- ♦ Internacia Esperanto-Asocio de Juristoj (inactive)
- ♦ Internacia Esperanto-Instituto (#13302)
- ♦ Internacia Esperanto-Ligo (inactive)
- ♦ Internacia Fervojista Esperanto Federacio (#13415)
- ♦ Internacia Geografa Asocio (inactive)
- ♦ Internacia Katolika Unuigo Esperantista (#12455)

♦ Internacia Komerca kaj Ekonomia Fakgrupo (IKEF) 11522

Contact Marie Popelinplantsoen 3 – bus 0402, 8000 Bruges, Belgium.
URL: http://www.ikef.org/

History Founded 6 Aug 1985, Augsburg (Germany FR), during the annual congress of *Universal Esperanto Association (UEA, #20676)*. **Aims** Stimulate the use of *Esperanto* in international *commerce*. **Languages** Esperanto. **Staff** 0.50 FTE, voluntary. **Finance** Members' dues. Other sources: donations; commissions. **Activities** Publishing activities; events/meetings. **Events** *Annual Meeting* Nitra (Slovakia) 2016, *Annual Meeting* Lille (France) 2015, *Annual Meeting* Reykjavik (Iceland) 2013, *Regional Meeting* Suzhou (China) 2013, *Regional Meeting* Changsha (China) 2012.
Members Individuals (about 100) in 33 countries:
Albania, Angola, Austria, Belgium, Brazil, Bulgaria, China, Croatia, Czechia, Denmark, Estonia, France, Germany, Ghana, Hungary, India, Israel, Italy, Japan, Korea Rep, Latvia, Lithuania, Netherlands, Nigeria, Norway, Poland, Portugal, Senegal, Spain, Sweden, UK, Ukraine, USA.
NGO Relations Affiliated member of UEA. [2016.10.19/XE4087/**v/E**]

♦ Internacia Komitato por Etnaj Liberecoj (IKEL) 11523

Pres Damo de Vi, 171 allée du Quart d'Amo, 74140 Chens-sur-Léman, France.
URL: http://ikel.stel.net/index.html

History 1978, Barcelona (Spain). Also referred to by other language titles as *International Committee for Ethnic Freedoms – Comité international pour les libertés ethniques – Comité Internacional para las Libertades Etnicas – Internationales Komitee für Ethnische Freiheiten*. **Aims** Collect and distribute information on the situation and development of *ethnic* groups and *minorities* and their *freedoms*; intercede with authorities. **Languages** Esperanto. **Staff** 8.00 FTE, voluntary. **Activities** Holds meetings (annually) in conjunction with UEA World Congress. **Events** *Seminar* Copenhagen (Denmark) 2011, *Seminar* Havana (Cuba) 2010, *Seminar* Bialystok (Poland) 2009, *Seminar* Rotterdam (Netherlands) 2008, *Seminar* Yokohama (Japan) 2007. **Publications** *Etnismo* (3 a year) – magazine.
Members Ethnic groups (46) and persons without defining their ethnic groups (34) in 30 countries:
Austria, Belgium, Canada, Chile, Congo DR, Finland, France, Georgia, Germany, Hungary, Iceland, Ireland, Israel, Italy, Japan, Kazakhstan, Lithuania, Luxembourg, Netherlands, Norway, Poland, Portugal, Romania, Serbia, Slovenia, Spain, Sweden, Switzerland, UK, USA.
NGO Relations Member of: *Universal Esperanto Association (UEA, #20676).* [2012.06.01/XD1398/**F**]

- ♦ Internacia Komunista Esperantista Kolektivo (#12819)
- ♦ Internacia Kultura Servo (internationally oriented national body)
- ♦ Internacia Laboristo Asocio (#15906)
- ♦ Internacia Ligo / see Universal Esperanto Association (#20676)
- ♦ Internacia Ligo de Agrikulturaj Specialistoj-Esperantistoj (inactive)
- ♦ Internacia Ligo de Esperantistaj Instruistoj / see ESPERANTO + EDUKADO (#05544)

♦ Internacia Ligo de Esperantistaj Radio-Amatoroj (ILERA) 11524

Ligue internationale des radio-amateurs espérantistes – International League of Esperantist Radio Amateurs

Contact c/o Chile Esperanto Assoc, Rodriguez 424, 3349001 Curicó, Maule, Chile. T. +56752318543. E-mail: informaciones@esperanto.cl.
Pres Minami Karasuyama 2-8, 1-1104 Setaguaya-ku, Tokyo, 157-0062 Japan. E-mail: ja1fxz@yahoo.co.jp.
URL: http://www.facebook.com/esperanto.ilera/

History 4 Aug 1970, Vienna (Austria). **Aims** Link radio amateurs who use or wish to learn Esperanto; set up network of ILERA stations to demonstrate usefulness of Esperanto in radio communication; deal with technical problems involved in this area; set up an amateur radio station at every Esperanto Congress. **Structure** General Assembly (annual, in conjunction with UEA World Congress). Officers: President; Vice-President; General Secretary. Sectional representatives. **Languages** Esperanto. **Staff** Voluntary. **Finance** Sources: members' dues. **Events** *Annual General Assembly* Helsinki (Finland) 2013, *Annual General Assembly* Hanoi (Vietnam) 2012, *Annual General Assembly* Copenhagen (Denmark) 2011, *Annual General Assembly* Havana (Cuba) 2010, *Annual world congress / Annual General Assembly* Bialystok (Poland) 2009. **Publications** *ILERA-Bulteno.*
Members Individuals and affiliated national sections. Members in 36 countries:
Argentina, Australia, Austria, Bosnia-Herzegovina, Brazil, Bulgaria, Canada, Chile, China, Croatia, Cuba, Czechia, Estonia, France, Germany, Honduras, Hungary, Israel, Italy, Japan, Korea Rep, Latvia, Lithuania, Mexico, New Zealand, Norway, Poland, Portugal, Romania, Russia, Serbia, Spain, Sweden, UK, Ukraine, USA.
NGO Relations Member of: *Universal Esperanto Association (UEA, #20676).* [2017/XC4004/**C**]

- ♦ Internacia Naturista Organizo Esperantista (#14220)
- ♦ Internacia Porpac-Gazetaroficejo (inactive)
- ♦ Internacia Registrolibro de la Civitanoj del Mondo / see Registre des Citoyens du Monde (#18822)
- ♦ Internacia Reto por Senfumigi Hospitalojn / see Anti-Smoking International Alliance (#00861)
- ♦ Internacia Scienca Akademio Comenius (#14795)
- ♦ Internacia Scienca Asocio Esperantlingva (#13301)

♦ Internacia Scienca Instituto Ivo Lapenna (ISIIL) 11525

Ivo Lapenna International Scientific Institute

Pres c/o Univ degli Studi di Padova, Dipto Di Matematica Pura Ed Appliccata, Via Alberto Cavalletto 6, 35122 Padua PD, Italy. T. +39498275906.
URL: http://www.ivolapenna.org/

History 23 Aug 1997, Vienna (Austria). Previously also referred to in English as *International Institute of Science Ivo Lapenna.* **Aims** Make known the ideas and work of Ivo Lapenna. **Structure** President; Councillors (9). **Languages** Esperanto. **Staff** 2.00 FTE, voluntary. **Finance** Budget administered by Ivo Lapenna Foundation. **Activities** Events/meetings. **Events** *General Conference* Reykjavik (Iceland) 2013, *General Conference* Copenhagen (Denmark) 2012, *General Conference* Hanoi (Vietnam) 2012, *General Conference* Copenhagen (Denmark) 2011. **Publications** *Ivo Lapenna: Elektitaj tekstoj pri internacia juro* (2017); *Ivo Lapenna: Esploro kaj dokumentado* (2014).
Members Full in 6 countries:
Austria, Denmark, France, Germany, Italy, Sweden.
NGO Relations Associated with: *Universal Esperanto Association (UEA, #20676).* [2019.10.29/XE4524/j/**E**]

- ♦ Internacia Scienca Kolegio (see: #00617)
- ♦ Internacia Societo de Amikeco kaj Bonvolo (#15132)
- ♦ Internacia Societo de Arkitektoj kaj Konstruistoj Esperantistoj (inactive)
- ♦ Internacia Unuigo de Esperantistaj Vegetaranoj / see World Esperantist Vegetarian Association (#21389)
- ♦ Internacia Unuîgo de la Esperantistoj-Filologoj (inactive)
- ♦ Internacia Vegetara Unuigxo (#15842)
- ♦ Internacio Ligo (inactive)
- ♦ Internacio de Militgerezistantoj (#20818)
- ♦ Internacionala Koku Pludinataju Asociacija (#15691)
- ♦ Internacional Demócrata de Centro (#03792)
- ♦ Internacional Demócrata Cristiana / see Centrist Democrat International (#03792)
- ♦ Internacional de la Educación (#05371)
- ♦ Internacional Femenina Demócrata Cristiana (inactive)
- ♦ Internacional de los Foros del Campo Lacaniano / see Internationale des Forums – Ecole de Psychanalyse des Forum du Champ Lacanien (#13234)
- ♦ Internacional de los Foros – Escuela de Psicoanalisis de los Foros del Campo Lacaniano (#13234)
- ♦ Internacional dos Fóruns – Escuela de Psicanalise dos Fóruns do Campo Lacaniano (#13234)
- ♦ Internacional Liberal (#16454)
- ♦ Internacional Liberal y Progresista / see Liberal International (#16454)
- ♦ Internacionalna Liga Humanista za Mir i Toleranciju (#14019)
- ♦ Internacional de Productores de Seguros y Reaseguros / see BIPAR – European Federation of Insurance Intermediaries (#03263)
- ♦ Internacional de la Puerta Abierta, para la Emanicipación Económica de la Trabajadora (no recent information)
- ♦ Internacional de Resistentes a la Guerra (#20818)
- ♦ Internacional de Servicios Públicos (#18572)
- ♦ Internacional Socialista (#19340)
- ♦ Internacional Socialista de Mujeres (#19341)
- ♦ Internacional de Trabajadores de la Construcción y la Madera (#03355)
- ♦ Internal Agreement on the Financing and Administration of Community Aid (1979 treaty)
- ♦ Internal Agreement on the Measures and Procedures Required for Implementation of the Second ACP-EEC Convention of Lomé (1979 treaty)

♦ Internal Displacement Monitoring Centre (IDMC) 11526

Dir La Voie-Creuse 16, 1202 Geneva, Switzerland. T. +41225523600. E-mail: info@idmc.ch.
Special Adviser to the Director address not obtained.
URL: http://www.internal-displacement.org/

History 1998. Set up as part of *Norwegian Refugee Council (NRC).* **Aims** Provide high-quality data, analysis and expertise on internal displacement with the aim of informing policy and operational decisions that can reduce the risk of future displacement and improve the lives of internally displaced people (IDP) worldwide. **Structure** Director's Office. Departments (2): Programmes; External Relations. **Languages** English. **Staff** 34.00 FTE, paid. **Finance** Norway's Ministry of Foreign Affairs; US Department of State's Bureau of Population, Refugees, and Migration; Australia's Department of Foreign Affairs and Trade; Switzerland's Federal Department of Foreign Assistance; Liechtenstein's Ministry of Foreign Affairs; Federal Foreign Office of Germany. Supported by: *European Union (EU, #08967); International Organization for Migration (IOM, #14454); Swedish International Development Cooperation Agency (Sida); United States Agency for International Development (USAID).* **Activities** Guidance/assistance/consulting; knowledge management/ information dissemination; monitoring/evaluation; research/documentation. **Publications** *Global Report on Internal Displacement (GRID)* (annual). **NGO Relations** Partners with peer NGOs and agencies. [2023.02.15/XM7216/**E**]

- ♦ Internasionale Vereniging van Afrikaanse Jeugdiges (unconfirmed)
- ♦ Det Internasjonale Edvard Grieg Selskap (#13232)
- ♦ Internasjonale Forum for Person Sentrert Tilnaerming (meeting series)
- ♦ Internasjonale fråregna om menneskerettane (1948 treaty)
- ♦ Internasjonale Tommerflotteroranisasjonen (#15691)
- ♦ Internasjonal Forening for Otto Gross Studier (#12060)
- ♦ Internasjonalt Folkehøgskole-Engasjement i Den Tredje Verda (internationally oriented national body)
- ♦ Internasjonalt Nettverk for Steder hvor det er godt å leve / see Cittaslow (#03958)

♦ Internatioanl Betting Integrity Association (IBIA) 11527

SG Rond Point Schuman 11, 1040 Brussels, Belgium. T. +3222567565. E-mail: info@ibia.bet.
URL: https://ibia.bet/

History 2005. Former names and other names: *European Sport Security Association* – former; *ESSA – Sport Betting Integrity (ESSA)* – former. Registration: Banque-Carrefour des Entreprises, No/ID: 0899.815.946, Start date: 19 May 2008, Belgium; EU Transparency Register, No/ID: 17258866933-24, Start date: 13 Oct 2011. **Aims** Protect betting corruption to protect the integrity of sport and of their businesses. **Structure** Board of Directors. **Activities** Monitoring/evaluation; politics/policy/regulatory; standards/guidelines. **NGO Relations** *International Olympic Committee (IOC, #14408); International Federation of Association Football (#13360).* [2022/XM5649/**D**]

- ♦ Internationaal Belasting Documentatie Bureau / see International Bureau of Fiscal Documentation (#12415)
- ♦ Internationaal Bodemkundig Museum / see ISRIC – World Soil Information (#16068)
- ♦ Internationaal Bureau voor de Bekendmaking der Toltarieven (#13124)
- ♦ Internationaal Bureau van de Betonwarenindustrie (#03363)
- ♦ Internationaal Centrum voor Bodem-referentie en -informatie / see ISRIC – World Soil Information (#16068)
- ♦ Internationaal Centrum voor Onderzoek van Steenmerken (#03763)
- ♦ Internationaal Christelijk Steunfonds / see ICS
- ♦ Internationaal Comité voor Europese Veiligheid en Samenwerking (inactive)
- ♦ Internationaal Comité ter Bescherming van de Bretonse Taal (#12761)
- ♦ Internationaal Comité van Wapen- en Militair-Historische Musea en Verzamelingen (#12790)
- ♦ Internationaal Congres voor de Nieuwe Evangelisatie (meeting series)
- ♦ Internationaal Gerechtshof (#13098)
- ♦ Internationaal Hulpbetoon van Caritas Catholica / see International Relief Service of Caritas Catholica, Belgium
- ♦ Internationaal Instituut Kanunnik Triest (#13866)
- ♦ Internationaal Instituut voor Kulturele Zaken (#11251)
- ♦ Internationaal Instituut voor Sociale Geschiedenis (internationally oriented national body)
- ♦ Internationaal Instituut voor Waterbouwkunde en Milieubeheer / see IHE Delft Institute for Water Education (#11110)
- ♦ Internationaal Kolpingwerk / see KOLPING INTERNATIONAL (#16203)
- ♦ Internationaal Olympisch Komitee (#14408)
- ♦ Internationaal Register van Wereldburgers / see Registre des Citoyens du Monde (#18822)
- ♦ Internationaal Samenwerkingsverband van Waterleidingbedrijven in het Rijnstroomgebied (#13215)
- ♦ Internationaal Standaard Boeknummer / see International ISBN Agency (#13955)
- ♦ Internationaal Statistisch Instituut (#15603)
- ♦ Internationaal Studiecomité Betreffende de Ommegangsreuzen (inactive)
- ♦ Internationaal Studie-instituut voor de Middenstand (inactive)
- ♦ Internationaal Symposium over Fytofarmacie en Fytiatrie (meeting series)
- ♦ Internationaal Verband van Organisaties voor Christelijke Opvoeding en Onderwijs (#11770)
- ♦ Internationaal Verbindingscomité voor de Broderie, Gordijnen en Kant (inactive)
- ♦ Internationaal Verbond der Federaties van Melkkleinhandelsorganisaties (inactive)
- ♦ Internationaal Verbond voor Geloofsvrijheid (#12130)
- ♦ Internationaal Verbond van de Groothandel in Bloemkwekerijprodukten / see UNION FLEURS (#20408)
- ♦ Internationaal Wol Secretariaat (inactive)
- ♦ International 11 Metre One-Design Class Association (see: #21760)
- ♦ International 12 Metre Class Association (see: #21760)
- ♦ International 14 Class Association (see: #21760)

♦ International 210 Association 11528

Pres address not obtained. E-mail: admin@210class.com.
URL: http://www.210class.com/

History 1946. **Aims** Organize *sailing* events. [2019/XN2315/**E**]

- ♦ International 2,4 Metre Class Association (see: #21760)
- ♦ International 29er Class Association (see: #21760)
- ♦ International 420 Class Association (see: #21760)
- ♦ International 470 Class Association (see: #21760)
- ♦ International 49er Class Association (see: #21760)
- ♦ International 505 Yacht Racing Association (see: #21760)
- ♦ International 5,5 Metre Class Association (see: #21760)
- ♦ International 8 Metre Association (see: #21760)

♦ International Abalone Society (IAS) 11529

Pres Investigaciones Oceanológicas, Univ Autónoma de Baja California, PO Box 453, 22870 Enseñada BC, Mexico.
Sec College of Ocean and Earth Sciences, Xiamen Univ, Xiang'an Campus, Xiamen, 361102 Fujian, China. E-mail: mail@internationalabalonesociety.org.
URL: http://internationalabalonesociety.net/

History 1997. **Aims** Promote research on abalone; facilitate distribution of information on abalone; promote cooperation between abalone researchers and members of the abalone industry. **Structure** Executive Committee. **Languages** English. **Staff** Voluntary. **Finance** Sources: meeting proceeds; members' dues. **Activities** Awards/prizes/competitions; events/meetings. **Events** *International Abalone Symposium* Auckland (New Zealand) 2023, *International Abalone Symposium* Auckland (New Zealand) 2021, *International Abalone Symposium* Xiamen (China) 2018, *International Abalone Symposium* Yeosu (Korea Rep) 2015, *International Abalone Symposium* Hobart, TAS (Australia) 2012. **Publications** *Journal of Shellfish Research.* **Members** Ordinary; Student; Retired; Honorary. Members in 15 countries. Membership countries not specified. [2022.11.03/XM4309/**C**]

♦ International Abilympic Federation (IAF) 11530

Exec Committee Member PO Box 358, Mirrabooka, Perth WA 6941, Australia. T. +61892488828. E-mail: abily@iinet.net.au.
Pres address not obtained.
URL: https://abilympics-france.fr/en/international-abilympics-federation-iaf/

History Oct 1985, Bogota (Colombia), during 3rd International Abilympics, at suggestion of Prof Harry Fang. Fundamental principles and guidelines for implementing Abilympics adopted 1991, Hong Kong, at 3rd International Abilympics. **Aims** Improve skills and develop potential ability of *disabled* people; stimulate desire of disabled persons to participate in economic activities of society; increase public awareness of capabilities of disabled persons; promote international friendship and exchange of knowledge and information; ensure involvement of governments and states in issues concerning disabled citizens. **Structure** General Assembly; Executive Committee, meeting annually at Assembly of Rehabilitation International (RI). **Languages** English. **Activities** Guidance/assistance/consulting; knowledge management/information dissemination. **Events** *International Abilympics* Seoul (Korea Rep) 2011, *International abilympics conference, meeting and symposium / International Abilympics* Shizuoka (Japan) 2007, *Meeting* Shizuoka (Japan) 2007, *International abilympics conference, meeting and symposium* Delhi (India) 2003, *Meeting / International Abilympics* Delhi (India) 2003. **Publications** *IAF Newsletter* (annual).
Members Organizations (35) in 24 countries and territories:
Australia, Austria, Bangladesh, Brunei Darussalam, China, Colombia, Czechia, France, Ghana, Hong Kong, India, Indonesia, Japan, Korea Rep, Liberia, Pakistan, Philippines, Poland, Slovakia, Sri Lanka, Taiwan, Thailand, USA, Zimbabwe.
[2012.08.03/XD3700/**C**]

- ♦ International Abolitionist Federation (inactive)
- ♦ International Abstaining Motorists' Association (inactive)
- ♦ International ACAC – International Association for College Admissions Counseling (internationally oriented national body)
- ♦ International Academic Association for the Advancement of Learning-centred Higher Education – Learning in Higher Education / see Learning in Higher Education (#16429)

♦ International Academic Association on Planning, Law and Property Rights (PLPR) 11531

SG August-Schmidt-Str 10, 44221 Dortmund, Germany. E-mail: secretary@plpr-association.org – info@plpr-association.org.
URL: http://www.plpr-association.org/

History Proposed during the 1998 conference of *Association of European Schools of Planning (AESOP, #02542)*. Formally set up 2007, Amsterdam (Netherlands) with the temporary title *International Academic Group on Planning, Law and Property Rights*. Statutes approved 13 Feb 2008, Ålborg (Denmark); adjusted 28 May 2011, Edmonton AB (Canada). **Aims** Foster international academic knowledge exchange on the themes of planning, law, and property rights. **Structure** General Assembly (at annual Congress); Executive Committee. **Languages** English. **Staff** Voluntary. **Finance** Sources: meeting proceeds; sponsorship. **Activities** Events/meetings. **Events** *Conference* Usti nad Labem (Czechia) 2020, *Conference* College Station, TX (USA) 2019, *Conference* Novi Sad (Serbia) 2018, *Conference* Hong Kong (Hong Kong) 2017, *Conference* Bern (Switzerland) 2016. **Publications** *PLPR Newsletter*.
Members Full in 52 countries:
Albania, Argentina, Australia, Austria, Belgium, Brazil, Bulgaria, Canada, Chile, China, Czechia, Denmark, Estonia, Fiji, Finland, France, Georgia, Germany, Greece, India, Iran Islamic Rep, Ireland, Israel, Italy, Japan, Kenya, Korea Rep, Lithuania, Malaysia, Mexico, Netherlands, New Zealand, Nigeria, Norway, Poland, Portugal, Romania, Russia, Serbia, Singapore, Slovenia, South Africa, Spain, Sri Lanka, Sweden, Switzerland, Türkiye, Uganda, UK, Ukraine, Uruguay, USA.
NGO Relations Cooperates with: *Association of European Schools of Planning (AESOP, #02542)*; national societies. [2018.10.10/XJ7651/**C**]

♦ International Academic Consortium for Sustainable Cities (IACSC) . 11532

Secretariat Global Cooperation Inst for Sustainable Cities, Yokohama City Univ, 22-2 Seto, Kanazawa-ku, Yokohama KANAGAWA, 236-0027 Japan. E-mail: kokusai@yokohama-cu.ac.jp.
URL: https://www-user.yokohama-cu.ac.jp/~english/index.php/global/gci/iacsc/

History Sep 2009, Japan. **Aims** Establish and strengthen the linkage between *universities* and the cities where they belong towards capacity building for a sustainable society. **Structure** General Assembly. **Activities** Events/meetings. **Events** *Symposium* Yokohama (Japan) 2021, *Symposium* Ho Chi Minh City (Vietnam) 2020, *Symposium* Makassar (Indonesia) 2019, *Symposium* Manila (Philippines) 2018, *Symposium* Bangkok (Thailand) 2017.
Members Universities in 7 countries:
Indonesia, Japan, Korea Rep, Malaysia, Philippines, Thailand, Vietnam.
IGO Relations Partnership with: *Asian Development Bank (ADB, #01422)*; *Japan International Cooperation Agency (JICA)*. **NGO Relations** Partnership with: *Regional Network of Local Authorities for the Management of Human Settlements (CITYNET, #18799)*; *Institute for Global Environmental Strategies (IGES, #11266)*.
[2020.03.12/XM4692/**D**]

♦ International Academic Forum (IAFOR) 11533

Main Office Sakae 1-16-26 201, Naka Ward, Nagoya AICHI, 460-0008 Japan. E-mail: kmana@iafor.org.
URL: http://iafor.org/

History 2009, Nagoya (Japan). In the USA registered as *IAFOR Research Foundation*. Registration: Japan. **Aims** Provide and promote meaningful dialogue irrespective of international borders. **Structure** Executive Council; International Advisory Board. **Activities** Events/meetings; research/documentation; networking/liaising; awards/prizes/competitions. **Events** *Asian Conference on Aging & Gerontology (Agen)* Tokyo (Japan) 2023, *Asian Conference on Arts & Humanities (ACAH)* Tokyo (Japan) 2023, *Asian Conference on Asian Studies (ACAS)* Tokyo (Japan) 2023, *Asian Conference on Psychology and the Behavioral Sciences (ACP)* Tokyo (Japan) 2023, *Asian Conference on Social Sciences (ACSS)* Tokyo (Japan) 2023. **Publications** *IAFOR Journal*.
Members Leaders and opinion formers worldwide. [2020/XJ5572/**F**]

- ♦ International Academic Forum, Bonn / see Internationales Wissenschaftsforum Bonn
- ♦ International Academic Group on Planning, Law and Property Rights / see International Academic Association on Planning, Law and Property Rights (#11531)
- ♦ International Academic Research and Technology Center (internationally oriented national body)
- ♦ International Academic Union / see Union académique internationale (#20345)
- ♦ International Academies of Emergency Dispatch (internationally oriented national body)
- ♦ International Academy (inactive)

♦ International Academy for Adhesive Dentistry (IAAD) 11534

SG address not obtained.
URL: https://adhesivedentistry.org/

History 14 Jun 2013, USA. Registration: Switzerland. **Aims** Foster the benefits of adhesive and minimally invasive dentistry among researchers, dentists, dental students, the dental industry, and patients. **Structure** General Assembly; Executive Committee. **Finance** Sources: members' dues. **Activities** Events/meetings; training/education. **Events** *Meeting* Seattle, WA (USA) 2025, *Meeting* Zurich (Switzerland) 2023, *Meeting* Piracicaba (Brazil) 2021, *Meeting* Bologna (Italy) 2019, *Meeting* Philadelphia, PA (USA) 2017. **Publications** *The Journal of Adhesive Dentistry* (6 a year).
Members Individuals in 15 countries and territories:
Brazil, France, Germany, Hong Kong, India, Ireland, Israel, Italy, Japan, Portugal, Russia, Saudi Arabia, Switzerland, United Arab Emirates, USA. [2021/AA2284/v/**C**]

♦ International Academy of Architecture (IAA) 11535

Académie internationale d'architecture – Academia Internacional de Arquitectura – Mezdunarodnaja Akademija Arhitektury

Gen Sec Maria Luisa Blvd 40, 1202 Sofia, Bulgaria. T. +35929434950. E-mail: iaarch@yahoo.com.
Pres address not obtained.
URL: http://iaa-ngo.com/

History 21 Sep 1987. **Aims** Stimulate development of architecture, urban planning and architectural theory. **Structure** General Assembly (plenary session every 2 years); Academic Council. **Languages** English. **Staff** 3.00 FTE, paid. **Finance** Sources: members' dues; revenue from activities/projects; subscriptions. **Activities** Awards/prizes/competitions; events/meetings; guidance/assistance/consulting; training/education. **Events** *INTERARCH: Forum* Sofia (Bulgaria) 2020, *INTERARCH: Triennial Forum* Sofia (Bulgaria) 2018, *INTERARCH – Triennial World Forum* Sofia (Bulgaria) 2015, *INTERARCH : triennial world forum* Sofia (Bulgaria) 2012, *International meeting* Kusadasi (Turkey) 2011. **Publications** Books; programmes.
Members Academicians (67) and Professors (106) in 36 countries:
Austria, Belarus, Belgium, Brazil, Bulgaria, Canada, Chile, China, Denmark, Finland, France, Georgia, Germany, Greece, India, Italy, Japan, Jordan, Kazakhstan, Malaysia, Malta, Mexico, Netherlands, Poland, Portugal, Russia, Serbia, Slovakia, Spain, Sweden, Switzerland, Türkiye, UK, Ukraine, USA, Uzbekistan.
Consultative Status Consultative status granted from: *ECOSOC (#05331)* (Special); *UNICEF (#20332)*; *UNIDO (#20336)*. **IGO Relations** Accredited by: *United Nations Office at Vienna (UNOV, #20604)*. Agreement with: *United Nations Human Settlements Programme (UN-Habitat, #20572)*. Memorandum of understanding with: *United Nations Development and Technical Cooperation Programme (inactive)*. Associated with Department of Global Communications of the United Nations. **NGO Relations** Agreements with: *Pan American Federation of Architects' Associations (#18098)*; *Union internationale des architectes (UIA, #20419)*. [2022/XF1991/v/**F**]

♦ International Academy of Astronautics (IAA) 11536

Académie internationale d'astronautique – Academia Internacional de Astronautica – Internationale Astronautische Akademie

SG PO Box 1268-16, 75766 Paris CEDEX 16, France. T. +33147238215. Fax +33147238216.
Street Address 6 rue Galilée, 75016 Paris, France.
URL: http://www.iaaweb.org/

History 16 Aug 1960, Stockholm (Sweden), during 11th International Astronautical Congress by Theodore Von Karman. Statutes most recently revised: 1998. **Aims** Foster development of astronautics for *peaceful* purposes; recognize individuals who have distinguished themselves in a related branch of science or technology; provide a programme through which members may contribute to international endeavours and cooperation in the advancement of *aerospace science*; cooperate with national academies of sciences or engineering. **Structure** General Meeting (every 2 years). Board of Trustees (meets twice a year), consisting of President Past-President 4 Vice-Presidents, and 28 Trustees, 7 from each of 4 Sections: Basic Sciences, Engineering Sciences; Life Sciences; Social Sciences. **Languages** English, French, German, Russian. **Staff** 4.00 FTE, paid; 10.00 FTE, voluntary. **Finance** Sources: grants; donations; income from publications. Budget (annual): about US$ 200,000. **Activities** Events/meetings; research/documentation; awards/prizes/competitions. **Events** *Planetary Defense Conferencce* Vienna (Austria) 2021, *Humans in Space Symposium* Dubai (United Arab Emirates) 2019, *Planetary Defense Conference* Washington, DC (USA) 2019, *Humans in Space Symposium* Shenzhen (China) 2017, *Planetary Defense Conference* Tokyo (Japan) 2017. **Publications** *Acta Astronautica* (12 a year) in English; *IAA Newsletter* (4 a year). Dictionaries in English, French, Spanish, Russian, German, Arabic, Bulgarian, Chinese, Czech, Dutch, Greek, Hindi, Hungarian, Italian, Japanese, Polish, Portuguese, Swedish, Turkish. Proceedings of symposia; technical reports; cosmic planning studies. **Information Services** *Terminology Database* – multilingual.
Members Individuals (1,162) in 68 countries and territories:
Algeria, Argentina, Armenia, Australia, Austria, Bahrain, Belgium, Bolivia, Brazil, Bulgaria, Burkina Faso, Canada, Chile, China, Colombia, Congo DR, Côte d'Ivoire, Croatia, Cuba, Czechia, Denmark, Egypt, Ethiopia, Finland, France, Germany, Greece, Hungary, India, Indonesia, Ireland, Israel, Italy, Japan, Korea Rep, Kuwait, Malaysia, Mexico, Mongolia, Morocco, Netherlands, Nigeria, North Macedonia, Norway, Pakistan, Poland, Romania, Russia, Saudi Arabia, Senegal, Serbia, Singapore, Slovakia, Slovenia, Spain, Sri Lanka, Sweden, Switzerland, Syrian AR, Taiwan, Thailand, Tunisia, Türkiye, UK, Ukraine, Uruguay, USA, Venezuela.
IGO Relations Observer status with: *Committee on the Peaceful Uses of Outer Space (COPUOS, #04277)*. **NGO Relations** In liaison with technical committees of: *International Organization for Standardization (ISO, #14473)*. Close links and joint activities with: *Committee on Space Research (COSPAR, #04287)*; *International Astronautical Federation (IAF, #12286)*; *International Institute of Space Law (IISL, #13926)*; *University Space Engineering Consortium (UNISEC-Global, #20704)*; national academies of science throughout the world.
[2015/XC1125/v/**F**]

♦ International Academy of Aviation and Space Medicine (IAASM) .. 11537

Académie internationale de médecine aéronautique et spatiale (AIMAS) – Academia Internacional de Medicina Aeronautica y Espacial

Pres address not obtained. E-mail: president@iaasm.org – secretary-general@iaasm.org.
URL: http://www.iaasm.org/

History 27 Apr 1959, Los Angeles, CA (USA). Founded as successor body to *International Board of Aviation Medicine (inactive)*, set up 29 Apr 1955, Marion (USA). Registration: Start date: 1994, New Zealand; Start date: 1976, End date: 1994, Canada; Start date: 29 Dec 1971, End date: 1976, France; Start date: 18 Nov 1959, End date: 1971, Belgium. **Aims** Provide information, leadership and mentorship; advance knowledge and understanding of aviation and space medicine through worldwide initiatives in education, training, research and practice. **Structure** General Assembly (at least twice a year); Council; Rotating Secretariat changes about every 5 years. **Languages** English, French. **Staff** 1.00 FTE, voluntary. **Finance** Sources: meeting proceeds; members' dues. Annual budget: 25,000 USD. **Activities** Events/meetings; financial and/or material support; networking/liaising; training/education. **Events** *Annual Congress* Paris (France) 2022, *Annual Congress* Paris (France) 2021, *Annual Congress* Paris (France) 2020, *Annual Congress* Debrecen (Hungary) 2019, *Annual Congress* Bangkok (Thailand) 2018. **Publications** Monographs.
Members Individuals (235) in 48 countries:
Argentina, Australia, Austria, Belgium, Brazil, Bulgaria, Canada, China, Colombia, Congo DR, Côte d'Ivoire, Croatia, Cyprus, Denmark, Finland, France, Germany, Guatemala, Hungary, India, Iran Islamic Rep, Ireland, Israel, Japan, Jordan, Malta, Mexico, Moldova, Namibia, Netherlands, New Zealand, Norway, Pakistan, Panama, Peru, Poland, Portugal, Romania, Singapore, Slovenia, South Africa, Spain, Sweden, Switzerland, Thailand, UK, United Arab Emirates, USA.
Consultative Status Consultative status granted from: *ECOSOC (#05331)* (Ros C). [2021.06.15/XC1126/v/**C**]

- ♦ International Academy of Ayurveda (internationally oriented national body)
- ♦ International Academy of Broadcasting (internationally oriented national body)

♦ International Academy of Business and Economics (IABE) 11538

Contact 10940 Trinity Pkwy STE C-185, Stockton CA 95219, USA. E-mail: admin@iabe.org.
URL: http://www.iabe.eu/

History 2001, USA. **Aims** Promote international exchange of state-of-the-art knowledge and ideas in research, teaching, and managerial best practices to help improve nations' productivity and competitiveness. **Structure** Editorial Board. **Languages** English. **Activities** Publishing activities; events/meetings. **Events** *Conference* Florence (Italy) / Pisa (Italy) 2016, *Conference* Las Vegas, NV (USA) 2015, *Conference* Orlando, FL (USA) 2015, *Conference* Rome (Italy) 2015, *Conference* San Francisco, CA (USA) 2015. **Publications** *California Business Review (CBR)*; *European Journal of Business Research (EJBR)*; *European Journal of Management (EJM)*; *International Journal of Business Research (IJBR)*; *International Journal of Business Strategy (IJBS)*; *International Journal of E-Business (IJEB)*; *International Journal of Strategic Management (IJSM)*; *Journal of Academy of Business and Economics (JABE)*; *Journal of International Business and Economics (JIBE)*; *Journal of International Finance and Economics (JIFE)*; *Journal of International Finance Studies (JIFS)*; *Journal of International Management Studies (JIMS)*; *Review of Business Research (RBR)*. Proceedings.
Members Full in 13 countries:
Australia, Austria, Brazil, Canada, Croatia, Egypt, Germany, India, Italy, Nigeria, Romania, Thailand, USA.
[2015.05.04/XJ8975/**D**]

- ♦ International Academy of Business and Public Disciplines (internationally oriented national body)
- ♦ International Academy of Cardiology (internationally oriented national body)

♦ International Academy of Cardiovascular Sciences (IACS) 11539

Exec Dir IACS, c/o St Boniface General Hospital, Research Centre, 351 Tache Ave, R4020, Winnipeg MB R2H 2A6, Canada. T. +12042353417. E-mail: iacs@sbrc.ca.
URL: http://www.heartacademy.org/

History Founded 1996, by renowned cardiovascular scientists, surgeons and cardiologists. **Aims** Promote cardiovascular *education* of professionals and lay people; recognize major cardiovascular achievement throughout the world. **Structure** IACS Sections (6): Japan; India; South America; Europe; North America; China. **Activities** Awards/prizes/competitions; events/meetings; knowledge management/information dissemination; training/education. **Events** *Meeting* Budapest (Hungary) 2022, *Meeting* Belgrade (Serbia) 2015, *ICCAD : International Congress on Coronary Artery Disease* Florence (Italy) 2015, *Meeting* Budapest (Hungary) 2014, *Scientific forum* Salvador (Brazil) 2011. **Publications** *CV NETWORK* (4 a year) – official bulletin. Journals; books; symposia proceedings.
Members Categories Full; Fellows; Corporate; Patrons and Supporters. Fellows in 43 countries and territories:
Antigua, Argentina, Australia, Belgium, Brazil, Canada, Chile, China, Cuba, Czechia, Denmark, Egypt, Estonia, France, Germany, Hong Kong, Hungary, Iceland, India, Indonesia, Iran Islamic Rep, Israel, Italy, Jamaica, Japan, Kuwait, Mexico, Mongolia, Netherlands, Pakistan, Poland, Puerto Rico, Romania, Russia, Slovakia, South Africa, Sweden, Switzerland, Thailand, Türkiye, UK, Uruguay, USA.
NGO Relations *Heartbeat International Foundation (#10896); International Society for Cardiovascular Translational Research (ISCTR, #14997); The NCD Alliance (NCDA, #16963); World Heart Federation (WHF, #21562)*; national organizations. [2020/XJ1930/**C**]

♦ International Academy of Ceramics (IAC) 11540

Académie Internationale de la Céramique (AIC) – Academia Internacional de la Ceramica
Coordinator c/o Musée Ariana, Ave de la Paix 10, 1202 Geneva, Switzerland. T. +41224185476. Fax +41224185451. E-mail: contacts@aic-iac.org – info@aic-iac.org.
URL: http://www.aic-iac.org/
History 1952, Geneva (Switzerland). Registration: Switzerland. **Aims** Encourage cultural cooperation among ceramists throughout the world; facilitate communication between ceramists and museum curators, experts, connoisseurs, amateurs, cultural institutions and associations; stimulate interest in and promotion of ceramic art; support the work of living ceramist *artists*. **Structure** General Assembly (every 2 years). Council (annual) of 15 to 18 members. Bureau, consisting of President, Vice-Presidents, Secretary-General and Treasurer. Committees. Congresses open. **Languages** English, French. **Staff** Voluntary. **Finance** Sources: members' dues. **Activities** Organizes exhibitions, symposia and cultural exchanges. **Events** *Biennial General Assembly* Rovaniemi (Finland) / Posio (Finland) 2021, *Biennial General Assembly* Rovaniemi (Finland) / Posio (Finland) 2020, *Biennial General Assembly* New Taipei City (Taiwan) 2018, *Biennial General Assembly* Barcelona (Spain) 2016, *Biennial General Assembly* Dublin (Ireland) 2014. **Publications** *Céramique*. Reports of meetings (available for members only). Information Services: Documentation centre, set up 1973, Geneva (Switzerland), at the Ariana Museum, where AIC is located.
Members Individual, Collective and Honorary. Members (475) in 54 countries and territories:
Argentina, Australia, Austria, Belgium, Bosnia-Herzegovina, Brazil, Cambodia, Canada, China, Croatia, Czechia, Denmark, Estonia, Finland, France, Germany, Greece, Hungary, Iceland, Ireland, Israel, Italy, Jamaica, Japan, Kenya, Korea Rep, Kyrgyzstan, Latvia, Lithuania, Luxembourg, Martinique, Mexico, Netherlands, New Zealand, Nicaragua, Niger, North Macedonia, Norway, Pakistan, Paraguay, Poland, Portugal, Puerto Rico, Romania, Russia, Serbia, Slovakia, South Africa, Spain, Sweden, Switzerland, Taiwan, Tunisia, Türkiye, UK, USA, Venezuela.
Consultative Status Consultative status granted from: *UNESCO (#20322)* (Consultative Status). **NGO Relations** Member of: *Fédération des Institutions Internationales établies à Genève (FIIG, #09599)*. [2022/XC1127/**C**]

♦ International Academy of Chefs / see World Master Chefs Society (#21639)
♦ International Academy for Clinical Hematology (unconfirmed)

♦ International Academy of Collaborative Professionals (IACP) 11541

Admin Assistant address not obtained. E-mail: info@collaborativepractice.com.
Dir address not obtained.
URL: https://www.collaborativepractice.com/
History 1999, USA. Former names and other names: *American Institute of Collaborative Professionals (AICP)* – former (2001). Registration: 501(c)(3), Start date: 1999, USA. **Aims** Transform the way families resolve conflict by building a global community of Collaborative Practice and consensual dispute resolution professionals. **Structure** Board of Directors. Committees. **Activities** Events/meetings; training/education. [2022/AA2226/**C**]

♦ International Academy of Comparative Law (#00027)
♦ International Academy of Computerized Dentistry / see International Society of Computerized Dentistry
♦ International Academy of Conscientiology / see International Academy of Consciousness
♦ International Academy of Consciousness (internationally oriented national body)

♦ International Academy of Cosmetic Dermatology (IACD) 11542

SG 1508 Creswood Rd, Philadelphia PA 19115, USA. E-mail: iacdworld@yahoo.com.
Pres 1845 Walnut St, Suite 1650, Philadelphia PA 19103, USA.
URL: https://iacdworld.org/
History 1995. **Aims** Provide educational opportunities of an international nature covering advances in cosmeceuticals, cosmetic surgery, pharmaceuticals and dermatology. **Languages** English. **Staff** 1.00 FTE, paid. **Finance** Sources: members' dues. **Activities** Events/meetings. **Events** *World Congress* St Julian's (Malta) 2022, *World Congress* Dresden (Germany) 2021, *World Congress* Lima (Peru) 2019, *World Congress* Dubrovnik (Croatia) 2018, *World Congress* Bangalore (India) 2017. **Publications** *Clinics in Dermatology; Journal of Cosmetic Dermatology; SKINmed*. [2022/XD8611/**D**]

♦ International Academy of Cosmetic Surgery (IACS) 11543

Address not obtained.
URL: http://www.ijcs.org/
History Founded 1970. **Events** *Abu Dhabi International Conference on Dermatology and Aesthetics* Abu Dhabi (United Arab Emirates) 2022, *Abu Dhabi International Conference on Dermatology and Aesthetics* Abu Dhabi (United Arab Emirates) 2020, *Abu Dhabi International Conference on Dermatology and Aesthetics* Abu Dhabi (United Arab Emirates) 2019, *Abu Dhabi International Conference on Dermatology and Aesthetics* Abu Dhabi (United Arab Emirates) 2018, *Abu Dhabi International Conference on Dermatology and Aesthetics* Abu Dhabi (United Arab Emirates) 2017. **Publications** *International Journal of Aesthetic Cosmetic Beauty Surgery* (periodical).
Members Full in 28 countries and territories:
Argentina, Australia, Austria, Bahrain, Belgium, Brazil, Canada, France, Germany, Greece, Indonesia, Israel, Italy, Kuwait, Lebanon, Malaysia, Netherlands, Pakistan, Philippines, Portugal, Saudi Arabia, Singapore, Sweden, Taiwan, Thailand, Türkiye, United Arab Emirates, USA.
Divisions (9):
American Association of Cosmetic Maxillo-Facial Surgeons; *Asian Pacific Academy of Cosmetic Surgery (APACS, no recent information); Balkan Academy of Cosmetic Surgery (BACS, #03064); International Society of Lipo-Suction Surgery (no recent information); International Society of Oculo-Facial Cosmetic Surgeons (no recent information); Mesoamerican Academy of Cosmetic Surgery (MSAACS)*; Saigon Academy of Cosmetic Surgery; *South American Academy of Cosmetic Surgery (SAACS, #19700); World Hair Society (WHS, no recent information)*. [2016/XD0152/y/**D**]

♦ International Academy of Cytology (IAC) 11544

Académie internationale de cytologie – Academia Internacional de Citologia – Internationale Akademie für Zytologie
Sec-Treas PO Box 1347, 79103 Freiburg, Germany. T. +497612923801. Fax +497612923802. E-mail: centraloffice@cytology-iac.org.
URL: http://www.cytology-iac.org/
History 13 Jul 1957, Brussels (Belgium). Absorbed, 2 Sep 1961, *International Academy of Gynecological Cytology (IAGC, inactive)*. Registration: Banque Carrefour des Entreprises, No/ID: VZW BE0.534.418.926, Start date: 2017, Belgium, Antwerp; Swiss Civil Code, End date: 2017, Switzerland. **Aims** Encourage cooperation among persons actively engaged in the practice of *clinical* cytology; foster and facilitate international exchange of knowledge and information on specialized problems in the field; standardize terminology; stimulate development of all phases of clinical cytology; encourage research. **Structure** Congress (every 3 years); Executive Council; Committees (18). **Languages** English. **Finance** Sources: grants; meeting proceeds; members' dues; sale of publications. **Events** *International Congress of Cytology* Florence (Italy) 2025, *International Congress of Cytology* Baltimore, MD (USA) 2022, *International Congress of Cytology* Sydney, NSW (Australia) 2019, *International Congress of Cytology* Yokohama (Japan) 2016, *International Congress of Cytology* Paris (France) 2013. **Publications** *Acta Cytologica* (6 a year) in English.
Members Fellows; Members; Honorary Fellows; Members of Affiliated Societies; Cytotechnologist Members; Cytotechnologist Fellows; Professional Non-medical Members; Members Emeritus; Fellows Emeritus. Individuals in 83 countries and territories (including West Indies – membership countries not specified):
Argentina, Australia, Austria, Bahamas, Bahrain, Bangladesh, Barbados, Belgium, Bhutan, Bolivia, Bosnia-Herzegovina, Brazil, Brunei Darussalam, Canada, Cayman Is, Chile, China, Colombia, Croatia, Cyprus, Czechia, Denmark, Egypt, Estonia, Finland, France, Germany, Greece, Hong Kong, Hungary, Iceland, India, Indonesia, Iran Islamic Rep, Ireland, Israel, Italy, Jamaica, Japan, Jordan, Kazakhstan, Korea Rep, Kuwait, Luxembourg, Macau, Malaysia, Malta, Mexico, Nepal, Netherlands, New Zealand, Nigeria, Norway, Oman, Pakistan, Paraguay, Peru, Philippines, Poland, Portugal, Puerto Rico, Qatar, Romania, Russia, Saudi Arabia, Singapore, Slovakia, Slovenia, South Africa, Spain, Sri Lanka, Sweden, Switzerland, Taiwan, Thailand, Türkiye, UK, United Arab Emirates, Uruguay, USA, Vietnam.
Affiliated societies (over 52) in 47 countries and territories:
Argentina, Australia, Austria, Belgium, Bolivia, Brazil, Canada, Chile, China, Colombia, Croatia, Czechia, Denmark, Finland, France, Germany, Greece, Hong Kong, Hungary, India, Iran Islamic Rep, Ireland, Israel, Italy, Japan, Kazakhstan, Korea Rep, Mexico, Netherlands, New Zealand, Norway, Paraguay, Peru, Poland, Portugal, Romania, Russia, Slovakia, Slovenia, South Africa, Spain, Sweden, Switzerland, Taiwan, Türkiye, UK, Uruguay.
Included in the above affiliated societies, 2 organizations listed in this Yearbook:
European Federation of Cytology Societies (EFCS, #07097); Sociedad Latinoamericana de Citopatología (SLAC, #19398). [2022.10.11/XB1128/v/**B**]

♦ International Academy for Diaconia and Social Action, Central & Eastern Europe (interdiac) 11545

Dir Dukelská 264/5, 737 01 Cesky Tesin, Czechia. T. +420731401449. E-mail: office@interdiac.eu.
URL: https://interdiac.eu/
History 2008. Registration: Czech Rep. **Structure** Executive Board; Advisory Board; Honorary Council. **Activities** Networking/liaising; research/documentation; training/education. **NGO Relations** Partner of (3): *European Federation for Diaconia (Eurodiaconia, #07099); International Society for the Research and Study of Diaconia and Christian Social Practice (ReDi, #15424); The Lutheran World Federation (LWF, #16532)*. [2021/AA1822/j/**F**]

♦ International Academy of Dialogue Among Cultures and Civilizations (internationally oriented national body)

♦ International Academy for Digital Dental Medicine (IADDM) 11546

Pres Splügenstrasse 10, 8002 Zurich ZH, Switzerland. T. +41445004220. Fax +41445004223. E-mail: contact@iaddm.com.
URL: http://iaddm.com/
History Current constitution adopted Jul 2014, Freiburg (Switzerland). Registered in accordance with Swiss Civil Code. **Aims** Promote advancement of digital dental medicine; foster convergence towards the highest standards in all facets of of digital dental medicine throughout the dental community worldwide; disseminate knowledge and understanding in the field. **Structure** Executive Committee. **Activities** Events/meetings; knowledge management/information dissemination; research/documentation; training/education. **Events** *Annual Meeting* Turin (Italy) 2021, *Annual Meeting* Nara (Japan) 2019, *Annual Meeting* Shanghai (China) 2018, *Annual Meeting* Berlin (Germany) 2017, *Plenary Meeting* Busan (Korea Rep) 2016. **Publications** *IADDM Newsletter*. [2018/XM5820/**C**]

♦ International Academy of Ecology and Life Protection Sciences (internationally oriented national body)
♦ International Academy of Emergency Dispatch / see International Academies of Emergency Dispatch
♦ International Academy of Environmental Safety (internationally oriented national body)
♦ International Academy of Environmental Sanitation and Public Health (internationally oriented national body)

♦ International Academy of Equilibrium Researchers (Barany Society) 11547

Secretariat ORL Dept Surgical Sciences, Akademiska Sjukhuset, SE-751 85 Uppsala, Sweden. T. +46186115365. Fax +4618558231.
URL: http://baranysociety.nl/
History 1960, in memory of Robert Barany (1876-1936), professor of otorhinolaryngology, University of Uppsala (Sweden). **Aims** Increase contact among scientists engaged in *vestibular* research; stimulate *otoneurological* research. **Events** *Congress* Madrid (Spain) 2020, *Congress* Uppsala (Sweden) 2018, *Symposium* Incheon (Korea Rep) 2016, *Congress* Seoul (Korea Rep) 2016, *Congress* Buenos Aires (Argentina) 2014.
Members Full in 40 countries and territories:
Argentina, Australia, Austria, Belgium, Brazil, Canada, Chile, Croatia, Czechia, Denmark, Finland, France, Germany, Greece, Hungary, Iceland, India, Ireland, Israel, Italy, Japan, Korea Rep, Mexico, Netherlands, Norway, Poland, Portugal, Russia, Slovakia, Slovenia, Spain, Sweden, Switzerland, Taiwan, Thailand, Türkiye, UK, Uruguay, USA, Venezuela. [2016.06.01/XE4231/**E**]

♦ International Academy of Family Lawyers (IAFL) 11548

Exec Dir address not obtained.
Registered Office One North Lexington Ave, White Plains NY 10601, USA.
URL: http://www.iafl.com/
History 1986. Former names and other names: *International Academy of Matrimonial Lawyers (IAML)* – former (1986 to 2015). Registration: USA. **Aims** Improve the practice of law and administration of justice in the area of divorce and family law throughout the world. **Structure** Executive Committee; Board of Governors. Chapters USA; European Canadian; Asia Pacific. Committees and Subcommittees. **Events** *Annual General Meeting* 2021, *Asia Pacific Chapter Meeting* 2021, *European Chapter Meeting* 2021, *USA Chapter Meeting* 2021, *European Chapter Meeting* 2020. **IGO Relations** *The Hague Conference on Private International Law (HCCH, #10850)*. [2022/XG6354/**C**]

♦ International Academy of Forensic Medicine and Social Medicine / see International Academy of Legal Medicine (#11555)
♦ International Academy for Freedom of Religion and Belief (internationally oriented national body)
♦ International Academy of Gastronomy (unconfirmed)
♦ International Academy of Genealogy (#00028)
♦ International Academy of Gnathology (internationally oriented national body)
♦ International Academy of Gynecological Cytology (inactive)
♦ International Academy of Health / see International Health Academy

♦ International Academy of Heraldry 11549

Académie internationale d'héraldique (AIH)
SG Tesdorpfsvej 59, 2000 Frederiksberg, Denmark.
Pres address not obtained.
URL: http://www.aih-1949.com/
History 9 Feb 1949, Paris (France). Statutes adopted Feb 1949, and revised: 6 Nov 1965; 5 Sep 1976; 28 Aug 1980; 28 Aug 2013; 18 Aug 2022. Registration: Swiss Civil Code, Switzerland. **Aims** Unite officers in charge of State heraldic services and the principal specialists in heraldry and allied sciences. **Structure** General Assembly (annual); Executive Committee; Bureau; Specialized Commissions (3). **Languages** English, French. **Staff** 11.00 FTE, paid. **Finance** Sources: members' dues. **Activities** Awards/prizes/competitions; events/meetings; publishing activities; research/documentation. **Events** *Colloquiumn* Lund (Sweden) 2023, *Colloquium* Antwerp (Belgium) 2019, *Colloquium* Copenhagen (Denmark) 2017, *International Colloquium on Genealogy* Madrid (Spain) 2015, *Colloquium* Saint-Jean-du-Gard (France) 2015. **Publications** Conference proceedings.
Members Full: Academicians (71); Associate (68). Full in 22 countries:
Australia, Austria, Belgium, Canada, Denmark, Finland, France, Germany, Hungary, Ireland, Italy, Lithuania, Netherlands, Norway, Portugal, Romania, Russia, Slovakia, Spain, Sweden, Switzerland, UK.
Associate in 31 countries:
Austria, Belgium, Brazil, Bulgaria, Canada, Chile, Croatia, Czechia, Finland, France, Georgia, Germany, Italy, Luxembourg, Mexico, Moldova, Netherlands, New Zealand, North Macedonia, Norway, Portugal, Romania, Russia, San Marino, Slovenia, Spain, Sweden, Switzerland, UK, Ukraine, USA. [2023.02.14/XC1129/v/**C**]

♦ International Academy of the History of Medicine (inactive)
♦ International Academy of the History of Pharmacy (no recent information)

♦ International Academy of History of Science 11550
Académie internationale d'histoire des sciences

Permanent Sec c/o NHRF, 48 Vassileos Constantinou Ave, 116 35 Athens, Greece. T. +302107273516. Fax +302107246618.
Pres address not obtained.
URL: http://www.aihs-iahs.org/

History 17 Aug 1928, Oslo (Norway), as *International Committee of the History of Science – Comité international d'histoire des sciences.* Statutes most recently updated 2001. **Structure** Council, comprising former Presidents (ex officio), President, 3 Vice-Presidents, Permanent Secretary-Treasurer and Archivist. **Finance** Sources: gifts and legacies; contributions of members. **Events** *Quadrennial General Assembly* Manchester (UK) 2013, *Quadrennial General Assembly* Budapest (Hungary) 2010, *Quadrennial General Assembly* Beijing (China) 2005, *Quadrennial General Assembly* Mexico City (Mexico) 2001, *Quadrennial General Assembly* Liège (Belgium) 1997. **Publications** *Archives internationales d'histoire des sciences* (2 a year). *De Diversis Artibus* – 3-6 vol annually.

Members Individual Effective (161); Corresponding (237); Honorary. Members in 41 countries:
Armenia, Australia, Austria, Belarus, Belgium, Bosnia-Herzegovina, Brazil, Bulgaria, Canada, China, Croatia, Czechia, Denmark, Finland, France, Georgia, Germany, Hungary, India, Ireland, Israel, Italy, Japan, Lithuania, Mexico, Mozambique, Netherlands, Norway, Poland, Romania, Russia, Singapore, Spain, Sweden, Switzerland, Tunisia, Türkiye, UK, Uruguay, USA, Uzbekistan.

NGO Relations Associate member of: *Union académique internationale (UAI, #20345).* Associated with the Division of History of Science of: *International Union of History and Philosophy of Science and Technology (IUHPST, #15779).* [2019/XF4153/v/F]

♦ International Academy of Humanism (internationally oriented national body)

♦ International Academy of Human Reproduction (IAHR) 11551
Associazione Accademia Internazionale per la Riproduzione Umana

Gen Sec Dept of Gynecology and Obstetrics, Kiel University, Christian-Albrechts-Platz 4, 24118 Kiel, Germany. E-mail: info@humanrep.org – secretariat@humanrepacademy.org.
Pres Dept of Obstetrics and Gynocology, Hebrew Univ of Jerusalem, Ein-Kerem Campus, POB 91120, Jerusalem, Israel.
URL: http://www.humanrepacademy.org/

History 1974. Former names and other names: *International Association on Human Reproduction* – alias; *Association internationale de la reproduction humaine* – alias. Registration: Switzerland. **Aims** Extend knowledge in all aspects of human reproduction, fertility and infertility, family planning, and population affairs; encourage exchange of clinical experience and promote scientific thought and investigation; consider the ethical and social implications of the current practice of human reproduction and reproductive biology. **Structure** General Assembly; Executive Committee. **Activities** Events/meetings; publishing activities; training/education. **Events** *World Congress* Venice (Italy) 2023, *World Congress* Jerusalem (Israel) 2021, *World Congress* Dublin (Ireland) 2019, *World Congress* Rome (Italy) 2017, *World Congress* Berlin (Germany) 2015. **Publications** *Reproductive Medicine for Clinicians* – book series.

Members Ordinary; Honorary. Individuals in 16 countries:
Australia, Austria, Canada, Chile, Croatia, Germany, Greece, Israel, Italy, Poland, Romania, Russia, Spain, Switzerland, UK, USA. [2019.02.27/XD6210/v/D]

♦ International Academy IMOS – Interallied Military Organization 'Sphinx' (internationally oriented national body)
♦ International Academy for Innovative Pedagogy, Psychology and Economics, Free University of Berlin (internationally oriented national body)
♦ International Academy of Integrated Dentistry (#00014)
♦ International Academy of Interdisciplinary Dentistry / see International Conference of Occlusion Medicine (#12884)

♦ International Academy of International Sexology 11552
Academia Internacional de Sexologia Médica (AISM)

Pres CIPPSV, Avenida Paramaconi, Torre Bianco, Urb San Bernardino, Caracas DF, Venezuela.
Facebook: https://www.facebook.com/AcademiaAISM

Structure Executive Committee, comprising President, Secretary General, Treasurer and 5 members. **Languages** English, Portuguese, Spanish. **Events** *Annual Meeting* Medellin (Colombia) 2012. **NGO Relations** Cooperates with (1): *Latin American Federation of Sexology and Sexual Education Societies (#16331).* [2021/XJ5584/D]

♦ International Academy of Investigative Psychology (inactive)

♦ International Academy of Laser Medicine and Surgery (IALMS) 11553

Pres Univ of Siena, General Surgery Spec School, Inst Laser Medicine, Borgo Pinti 57, 50121 Florence FI, Italy. T. +39552342330. Fax +395539069632. E-mail: secretary@ialms.international.
URL: http://ialms.international/

History 19 Oct 2000, Florence (Italy). Registration: Italy. **Aims** Foster high quality teaching and research related to the use of light and lasers in science. **Structure** General Assembly (annual). Executive Committee of up to 9 members, including President and Secretary. Board of Auditors. **Languages** English. **Staff** 2.50 FTE, voluntary. **Finance** Members' dues. Donations. **Activities** Organizes congresses and courses. Organizes annual Laser Florence Conference and the special version of the conference Laser Florence Youth, both always in Florence (Italy). **Events** *LASER FLORENCE : International Congress on Laser Medicine and Surgery* Florence (Italy) 2019, *LASER FLORENCE : International Congress on Laser Medicine and Surgery* Florence (Italy) 2017, *LASER FLORENCE : International Congress on Laser Medicine and Surgery* Florence (Italy) 2015, *LASER FLORENCE : International Congress on Laser Medicine* Florence (Italy) 2013, *LASER FLORENCE : International Congress on Laser Medicine* Florence (Italy) 2012. **Publications** *Lasers in Medical Sciences.* Congress proceedings.

Members in 61 countries and territories:
Argentina, Australia, Austria, Bahrain, Belarus, Belgium, Bosnia-Herzegovina, Brazil, Cameroon, Canada, China, Colombia, Croatia, Czechia, Denmark, Ecuador, Egypt, Estonia, Finland, France, Germany, Greece, Hong Kong, Hungary, India, Iran Islamic Rep, Ireland, Israel, Italy, Japan, Kuwait, Latvia, Libya, Lithuania, Malaysia, Mauritius, Mexico, Moldova, Montenegro, Morocco, Netherlands, New Zealand, Nigeria, Norway, Pakistan, Poland, Portugal, Romania, Russia, Serbia, Singapore, Slovenia, South Africa, Spain, Sweden, Switzerland, UK, United Arab Emirates, Uruguay, USA, Venezuela. [2019/XE4272/E]

♦ International Academy of Law and Mental Health (IALMH) 11554
Académie internationale de droit et de santé mentale

Exec Dir Fac de médecine Univ de Montréal, CP 6128, Succ Centre-Ville, Montréal QC H3C 3J7, Canada. T. +15143435938. Fax +15143432452. E-mail: admin@ialmh.org.
URL: http://www.ialmh.org/

History 1981. **Structure** Board of Directors, President, Honorary President, 2 Vice-Presidents, Immediate Past President, Vice-President of Research and Policy, Secretary General, Treasurer and 24 members. **Activities** Organizes: biennial Congress on Law and Mental Health; regional meetings. **Events** *International Congress* Lyon (France) 2022, *International Congress* Lyon (France) 2021, *International Congress* Rome (Italy) 2019, *International Congress* Prague (Czechia) 2017, *International Congress* Vienna (Austria) 2015. **Publications** *International Journal of Law and Psychiatry* (6 a year) – affiliated publication. [2014/XF6168/F]

♦ International Academy of Legal Medicine (IALM) 11555
Académie internationale de médecine légale

Pres Univ of Padova, via Falloppio 50, 35121 Padua PD, Italy.
URL: http://www.ialm.info/

History Founded 1938, Bonn (Germany), at 1st International Congress on Legal Medicine, as *International Academy of Legal Medicine and Social Medicine – Académie internationale de médecine légale et de médecine sociale.* Statutes revised: 1947, Brussels/Liège; 1973, Rome (Italy); 2009; 2015. Also referred to as *International Academy of Forensic Medicine and Social Medicine.* **Aims** Further scientific progress in the field of legal medicine, including medico-legal *psychiatry*, social medicine, industrial medicine, *criminology*, *toxicology* and medical *ethics*. **Structure** Presidium. **Languages** English. **Staff** 5.00 FTE, paid. **Finance** Sources: members' dues. **Activities** Awareness raising; events/meetings; knowledge management/information dissemination; networking/liaising; publishing activities; standards/guidelines. **Events** *Triennial Congress* Geneva (Switzerland) 2021, *Triennial Congress* Fukuoka (Japan) 2018, *IALM Intersocietal Symposium* Venice (Italy) 2016, *Triennial Congress* Dubai (United Arab Emirates) 2015, *Triennial Congress* Istanbul (Turkey) 2012. **Publications** *Bulletin of International Academy of Legal Medicine* (4 a year) – also special issues; *Newsletter of International Academy of Legal Medicine* (3 a year); *International Journal of Legal Medicine.* **Members** Titular and Emeritus in all continents and 64 countries. Membership countries not specified. [2018.09.19/XC1130/v/C]

♦ International Academy of Legal Medicine and Social Medicine / see International Academy of Legal Medicine (#11555)

♦ International Academy of Linguistic Law (IALL) 11556
Académie internationale de droit linguistique (AIDL)

SG/Pres Suite J-4, 6000 chemin Deacon, Montréal QC H3S 2T9, Canada. T. +15143450718. Fax +15143450860. E-mail: aca.inter@bell.net.
URL: http://www.iall-aidl.org/

History Sep 1984. Founded by 100 Founding Members. Former names and other names: *International Institute of Comparative Linguistic Law* – former; *Institut international de droit linguistique comparé (IIDLC)* – former. Registration: Registraire des Entreprises du Québec, Canada, Québec. **Aims** Bring together jurists, linguists, social scientists and all those worldwide who are interested, scientifically or professionally, in issues pertaining to linguistic diversity as well as to law and language, especially to comparative linguistic law. **Structure** General Assembly (at biennial conference). Decisions taken on consensus basis. **Languages** English, French. **Staff** 2.50 FTE, voluntary. **Finance** Conferences financed by universities, governments and corporations. **Activities** Events/meetings; guidance/assistance/consulting; networking/liaising. **Events** *Biennial Conference* Tizi Ouzou (Algeria) 2022, *Biennial Conference* Poznań (Poland) 2019, *Biennial Conference* Hangzhou (China) 2017, *Biennial Conference* Teramo (Italy) 2015, *Biennial Conference* Chiang Mai (Thailand) 2012. **Publications** *Special Issue of the International Academy of Linguistic Law* (2020) by Prof Dr Joseph-G. Turi; *Law, Language and Justice* (2017); *Représentations sociales des langues et politiques linguistiques* (2016); *Law, Language and the Multilingual State* (2013); *Law, Language and Linguistic Diversity* (2006); *Language, Law and Equality* (1993); *Language and Law – Langue et Droit* (1989).

Members Jurists; linguists; social scientists; Chapters. Individuals (over 500) in 77 countries and territories:
Algeria, Argentina, Armenia, Australia, Austria, Belarus, Belgium, Bosnia-Herzegovina, Brazil, Cameroon, Canada, China, Colombia, Côte d'Ivoire, Croatia, Cuba, Cyprus, Czechia, Denmark, Egypt, Estonia, Eswatini, Fiji, Finland, France, Germany, Greece, Haiti, Hong Kong, Hungary, Iceland, India, Indonesia, Ireland, Israel, Italy, Japan, Latvia, Libya, Lithuania, Madagascar, Malaysia, Malta, Mexico, Moldova, Montenegro, Morocco, Nepal, Netherlands, New Zealand, Nigeria, Norway, Palestine, Panama, Papua New Guinea, Philippines, Poland, Portugal, Puerto Rico, Romania, Russia, Senegal, Serbia, Singapore, Slovakia, Slovenia, South Africa, Spain, Sweden, Switzerland, Taiwan, Tunisia, Türkiye, UK, Ukraine, USA, Vietnam. [2021.10.01/XE4750/v/E]

♦ International Academy of Management (internationally oriented national body)
♦ International Academy of Mantemach (inactive)

♦ International Academy of Manual/Musculoskeletal Medicine (IAMMM) 11557

Contact address not obtained. E-mail: info@iammm.net.
URL: http://www.iammm.net/

History Set up 1997, as a Scientific Committee of *Fédération internationale de médecine manuelle (FIMM, #09642).* Transformed into *FIMM International Academy of Manual/Musculoskeletal Medicine*, 2004. Since 2008 independent of FIMM. **Aims** Make manual/musculoskeletal medicine a scientifically based discipline. **Structure** General Assembly; Executive Board; Science Board. **Finance** Members' dues. **Events** *Conference* Liverpool (UK) 2019, *Conference* Zurich (Switzerland) 2018, *Conference* Brussels (Belgium) 2015, *Conference* Berlin (Germany) 2014, *Conference* Bordeaux (France) 2013. **Publications** *International Musculoskeletal Medicine* – journal. [2015/XM4144/E]

♦ International Academy of Matrimonial Lawyers / see International Academy of Family Lawyers (#11548)
♦ International Academy of Mediators (internationally oriented national body)
♦ International Academy of Modern Art (internationally oriented national body)

♦ International Academy of Molecular Quantum Sciences (IAQMS) 11558
Académie internationale des sciences moléculaires quantiques

Pres Univ de Montpellier, 163 rue Auguste Broussonnet, 34090 Montpellier, France.
URL: http://www.iaqms.org/

History 1967, Menton (France). **Structure** Bureau, comprising President, Vice-President, General Secretary, Treasurer and 1 further member. **Events** *Triennial International Congress of Quantum Chemistry* Bratislava (Slovakia) 2021, *Triennial International Congress of Quantum Chemistry* Menton (France) 2018, *Triennial International Congress of Quantum Chemistry* Beijing (China) 2015, *Symposium* Kobe (Japan) 2015, *Triennial International Congress of Quantum Chemistry* Boulder, CO (USA) 2012. [2019/XN3572/E]

♦ International Academy of Nurse Editors / see International Academy of Nursing Editors (#11559)

♦ International Academy of Nursing Editors (INANE) 11559

Address not obtained.
URL: https://nursingeditors.com/

History 1982. An informal and volunteer-only grouping. Former names and other names: *International Academy of Nurse Editors* – alias. **Structure** Secretariat rotates. **Events** *Annual Conference* Padua (Italy) 2026, *Annual Conference* Minneapolis, MN (USA) 2025, *Annual Conference* Asheville, NC (USA) 2024, *Annual Conference* Dublin (Ireland) 2023, *Annual Conference* Nashville, TN (USA) 2022. [2022/XE4549/E]

♦ International Academy on Nutrition and Aging (IANA) 11560

General Secretariat 43 Chemin Del Prat, 31320 Auzeville-Tolosane, France.
URL: http://www.iana-congress.eu/

History 1999. **Aims** Contribute to the development of the knowledge about problems concerning nutrition and aging. **Activities** Organizes annual scientific meeting, alternately in Albuquerque (USA) and Europe; organizes workshops. **Events** *Congress* Barcelona (Spain) 2015, *Nutrition and aging – from cells to body systems and populations* Albuquerque, NM (USA) 2014, *Nutrition and physical and cognitive frailty including sarcopenia* Seoul (Korea Rep) 2013, *Congress / Conference* Albuquerque, NM (USA) 2012, *Congress* Bologna (Italy) 2011. **Publications** *Journal of Nutrition, Health and Aging.* [2014/XE4157/E]

♦ International Academy of Olympic Chiropractic Officers (IAOCO) 11561

Pres 546 Broad Ave, Englewood NJ 07631, USA. T. +12015691444. Fax +12015691445.
URL: http://iaoco.org/

History 9 Jan 1998, USA, following unofficial activities begun in 1987, as an honorary society for chiropractic physicians who have served as 'Official Team Doctors' in the Olympic movement. No recent information. [2015/XE3685/E]

♦ International Academy of Ophthalmology (#00017)

♦ International Academy of Oral Medicine (IAOM) 11562

Contact c/o Univ of London, Eastman Dental Inst for Oral Health Care Sciences, 256 Gray's Inn Road, London, WC1X 8LD, UK. T. +442079151038. Fax +442079151039.

History May 2001, Montréal, QC (Canada). Former names and other names: *International Federation of Oral Medicine (IFOM)* – former (May 2001). **Aims** Promote collaboration, education and research in oral medicine; promote continuing education in oral medicine in the dental profession; promote interest of research in oral medicine at other institutions, professional associations and industries; inform governments and other official institutions of the significance of oral medicine for oral health and prevention of oral diseases. **Structure** Chair; Secretary; Meeting Organizer. **Languages** English. **Staff** 1.00 FTE, paid. **Finance** Sources: meeting proceeds. **Activities** Events/meetings. **Events** *International dental days* Montréal, QC (Canada) 2001. [2011.10.20/XD8474/D]

♦ International Academy of Oral Medicine and Toxicology (internationally oriented national body)

♦ International Academy of Oral Oncology (IAOO) 11563

Pres Princess Margaret Cancer Centre – UHN, 200 Elisabeth Street, Toronto ON M5G 2 C4, Canada.
URL: http://www.iaoo.pro/

History 2005. Registered in accordance with UK law. **Aims** Raise standards in cancer care; foster and advance education, research and clinical management in all matters related to oral oncology. **Structure** General Meeting; Council. Officers: President; Vice-President; Secretary-General; Treasurer; Programme Chairman. **Languages** English. **Staff** 1.00 FTE, paid. **Finance** Members' dues. **Events** *World Congress* Rome (Italy) 2019, *World Congress* Bangalore (India) 2017, *World Congress* Sao Paulo (Brazil) 2015, *World congress* Rhodes Is (Greece) 2013, *World congress* Singapore (Singapore) 2011. **Publications** *Oral Oncology* – journal.
Members Individuals in 27 countries:
Argentina, Australia, Austria, Brazil, Canada, Czechia, Denmark, Finland, France, Germany, Greece, Hungary, India, Israel, Italy, Japan, Jordan, Korea Rep, Malaysia, Netherlands, Norway, Portugal, Sweden, Switzerland, Türkiye, UK, USA.
IGO Relations *WHO (#20950).* [2018/XM2294/v/**E**]

♦ International Academy of Orthodontics / see International Association for Orthodontics (#12058)

♦ International Academy of Orthokeratology (IAO) 11564

Address not obtained.
URL: https://www.myopiamanagement.info/

History Apr 2010. Former names and other names: *International Academy of Orthokeratology and Myopia Control (IAOMC)* – former. **Aims** Promote the art of Orthokeratology throughout the world. **Structure** Board of Directors. European section: *European Academy of Orthokeratology and Myopia Control (EurOK).* [2020/AA2055/**C**]

♦ International Academy of Orthokeratology and Myopia Control / see International Academy of Orthokeratology (#11564)

♦ International Academy of Orthopedic Medicine (IAOMED) 11565

IAOM Europe Sprangerweg 3, 37075 Göttingen, Germany. T. +495513838588. Fax +495513838599. E-mail: info@iaom.de – info@iaom.eu.
IAOM US PO Box 65179, Tucson AZ 85728-5179, USA. T. +15203184266. Fax +18666984832. E-mail: info@iaom-us.com.
URL: https://www.iaom.eu/

History 1978, Delft (Netherlands). Former names and other names: *International Association of Academies of Orthopedic Medicine (IAAOM)* – former (1978 to 1991). **Aims** Provide continuing education opportunities for physicians and physical therapists seeking expertise in orthopedic medicine and manual therapy. [2022/XE4652/**E**]

♦ International Academy of Osteopathic Medicine (inactive)

♦ International Academy of Osteopathy (IAO) 11566

Contact Bollebergen 2B, 9052 Ghent, Belgium. T. +3292330403. E-mail: info@osteopathy.eu.
URL: http://www.osteopathie.eu/

History 1987. **Aims** Train students to be safe, competent and independent osteopaths. **Activities** Training/education.
Members Full in 3 countries:
Belgium, Germany, Netherlands.
NGO Relations Partner member of: *Osteopathic International Alliance (OIA, #17910).* [2022.03.08/XN7574/**D**]

♦ International Academy of Pathology (IAP) 11567

Académie internationale de pathologie – Academia Internacional de Patologia

Sec Univ of Manchester, School of Medical Sciences, Oxford Rd, Manchester, M13 9PL, UK.
URL: http://www.iapcentral.org/

History 15 May 1906, Montréal, QC (Canada). New Constitution and Bylaws adopted 1969. Statutes amended 17 Oct 1976, Washington DC (USA). Former names and other names: *International Association of Medical Museums* – former (15 May 1906 to 1955); *Association internationale des musées médicaux* – former (15 May 1906 to 1955). Registration: USA, Washington DC. **Aims** Advance pathology through educational exchanges worldwide; provide access to valid, currently authenticated and trusted knowledge; provide a forum for the presentation and discussion of advances in the understanding of pathologic processes and for the presentation and critical evaluation of scientific, technological and methodological advances. **Structure** Scientific Session (every 2 years). International Council, composed of Executive Committee (President, President-elect, Secretary, Treasurer, Regional Vice-Presidents and Past President), Councillors and Editor of 'International Pathology'. **Languages** English. **Staff** 1.00 FTE, paid. **Finance** Members' dues (annual): US$ 6. **Activities** Coordinates biennial International Congress. Organizes: divisional meetings (at least once a year); feature training courses; biennial regional meetings. Divisions include *United States and Canadian Academy of Pathology (USCAP).* Currently establishing additional divisions in developing countries. Instrumental in setting up *International Paediatric Pathology Association (IPPA, #14498),* Oct 1976, Washington DC (USA). **Events** *International Congress (IAP2026)* Fukuoka (Japan) 2026, *International Congress* Cancún (Mexico) 2024, *International Congress* Sydney, NSW (Australia) 2022, *Asia Pacific Meeting* Okayama (Japan) 2021, *Biennial International Congress* Manchester (UK) 2020. **Publications** *International Pathology* (4 a year).
Members National and Regional Divisions (45 in 2012); Individuals (about 17,500), mostly members of Divisions Regular, Junior, Associate, Sustaining, Emeritus, Honorary. Members in 99 countries and territories:
Algeria, Argentina, Australia, Austria, Belgium, Benin, Bolivia, Brazil, Burkina Faso, Burundi, Cameroon, Canada, Chile, China, Comoros, Congo Brazzaville, Congo DR, Costa Rica, Côte d'Ivoire, Cuba, Czechia, Denmark, Djibouti, Egypt, Estonia, Finland, France, Gabon, Gambia, Georgia, Germany, Ghana, Greece, Guinea, Hong Kong, Hungary, India, Indonesia, Iraq, Ireland, Israel, Italy, Japan, Jordan, Kenya, Korea Rep, Kuwait, Latvia, Lebanon, Liberia, Libya, Lithuania, Mali, Mauritania, Mexico, Morocco, Netherlands, New Zealand, Nicaragua, Niger, Nigeria, Norway, Oman, Pakistan, Palestine, Panama, Papua New Guinea, Philippines, Poland, Portugal, Puerto Rico, Qatar, Romania, Russia, Rwanda, Saudi Arabia, Senegal, Sierra Leone, Slovakia, Somalia, South Africa, Spain, Sudan, Sweden, Switzerland, Syrian AR, Taiwan, Tanzania UR, Thailand, Togo, Tunisia, Türkiye, Uganda, UK, Ukraine, United Arab Emirates, Uruguay, USA, Yemen.
Consultative Status Consultative status granted from: *ECOSOC (#05331)* (Ros C). **IGO Relations** Accredited by: *United Nations Office at Vienna (UNOV, #20604).* [2020/XB1132/**C**]

♦ International Academy of Perinatal Medicine (IAPM) 11568

SG address not obtained.
URL: https://iaperinatalmedicine.org/

History 2005. Created with the agreement of the Presidents of: *World Association of Perinatal Medicine (WAPM, #21170); European Association of Perinatal Medicine (EAPM, #06148); International Society – The Fetus as a Patient (#15118).* **Aims** Promote the study of scientific principles and practical applications in the area of Perinatal Medicine. **Structure** Plenary Meeting; International Council; Board of Directors. **Activities** Events/meetings; projects/programmes. **Events** *Annual Meeting* Marrakech (Morocco) 2021, *Annual Meeting* Marrakech (Morocco) 2020, *Annual meeting* Dubrovnik (Croatia) 2009. [2021/AA1908/**E**]

♦ International Academy of Periodontology 11569

Académie internationale de parodontologie

Executive Officer The Forsyth Institute, 245 First St, 17th Flr Rm 1755, Cambridge MA 02142, USA. T. +16178928536. Fax +16172628021.
Sec Guarulhos Univ, Praca Tereza Cristina 88, Sao Paulo SP, Brazil. E-mail: mferes@ung.br.
URL: http://www.perioiap.org/

History 1985. **Aims** Improve knowledge and disseminate information about periodontics worldwide to those having an interest in prevention and treatment of diseases of the periodontium by: advancing international cooperation on a personal basis and in cooperation with national or international periodontal societies and research groups and appropriate health organizations; ensuring adequate representation of the specialty to medical and dental professions; advising in creation and coordination of undergraduate and postgraduate educational programs, especially in countries with limited resources; disseminating amongst members and others advancements in theory and practice of periodontology; promoting international exchange and communications between individuals of all nations, in pursuance of these objects so as to promote periodontal health worldwide. **Structure** Officers: President, President Elect, Immediate Past President, Vice-President, Secretary Treasurer, Executive Director, Editor. Board includes 2 regional representatives for each of 4 regions: Europe; Asia/Pacific; Africa/Middle East; North/South America. **Events** *Biennial Congress* Bangkok (Thailand) 2019, *Biennial Congress* Sibiu (Romania) 2017, *Biennial Congress* Santiago (Chile) 2015, *Biennial Congress* Shenzhen (China) 2013, *Biennial Congress* Lviv (Ukraine) 2011. **Publications** *Journal of the International Academy of Periodontology (JIAP)* (4 a year). **Members** Membership countries not specified. **NGO Relations** Affiliate member association of: *FDI – World Dental Federation (#09281).* [2015/XE1958/**E**]

♦ International Academy of Philosophy of Sciences (IAPS) 11570

Académie internationale de philosophie des sciences (AIPS)

Secretariat Rue Marie de Bourgogne 8, 1050 Brussels, Belgium. T. +3225121549. Fax +3225121884. E-mail: academies@skynet.be.
Pres Dépt de Philosophie, Univ de Lorraine, 34 Cours Léopold, 54000 Nancy, France.
URL: http://www.lesacademies.net/

History Founded 1947, Brussels (Belgium). One of two academies constituting *International Institute for Theoretical Sciences.* **Aims** Promote collaboration among philosophers and scientists for development of an intellectual synthesis capable of bringing the contributions of philosophy and science to unity for a better understanding of our present civilization. **Structure** General Assembly (every 3 years); Academic Council. **Languages** English, French. **Staff** 1.00 FTE, voluntary. **Finance** General secretariat expenses covered by Secretariat General of the Institute. **Events** *Annual International Meeting* Amsterdam (Netherlands) 2018, *Annual International Meeting* Lisbon (Portugal) 2017, *Congress on Scientific Realism* Ferrol (Spain) 2015, *Annual International Meeting* Varese (Italy) 2015, *Annual International Meeting* Pont-à-Mousson (France) 2014. **Publications** Meeting proceedings; books.
Members Individuals in 21 countries:
Austria, Belgium, Canada, Chile, Croatia, Denmark, Finland, France, Germany, Hungary, Italy, Japan, Netherlands, Norway, Peru, Russia, Spain, Sweden, Switzerland, UK, USA.
NGO Relations Member of: *International Federation of Philosophical Societies (FISP, #13507).* [2016.10.19/XD9279/v/**E**]

♦ International Academy of Physician Associate Educators (IAPAE) . . 11571

Address not obtained.
URL: https://iapae.com/

History 2008. **Aims** Maximize the contribution of physician associate professionals to global health care. **Structure** Board. **Activities** Events/meetings; training/education. **Events** *Conference* 2020, *Conference* Winterthur (Switzerland) 2019, *Conference* Lusaka (Zambia) 2018, *Conference* Lexington, KY (USA) 2017, *Conference* Birmingham (UK) 2016. [2021/AA1882/**C**]

♦ International Academy of Positive and Cross-Cultural Psychotherapy (internationally oriented national body)

♦ International Academy of Practical Theology 11572

Sec Fac of Theology and Religious Studies, KU Leuven, St-Michielsstr 6 – box 3101, 3000 Leuven, Belgium.
URL: http://www.ia-practicaltheology.org/

History Founded 1991, Princeton NJ (USA). Current by-laws adopted 26 Apr 1997; revised 11 Apr 2001, 4 Apr 2007 and 24 Apr 2017. **Aims** Stimulate study of and critical reflection on practical theological thought and action. **Structure** Executive Committee. Working Groups. **Languages** English. **Finance** Sources: members' dues. **Activities** Events/meetings; training/education. **Events** *Conference* Seoul (Korea Rep) 2023, *Conference* Leuven (Belgium) 2021, *(De)coloniality and religious practices – liberating hope* São Leopoldo (Brazil) 2019, *Conference* Oslo (Norway) 2017, *Conference* Gyeongju (Korea Rep) 1997. **Publications** *International Journal of Practical Theology.* Conference papers.
Members Active; Retired; Associate. Individuals in 19 countries:
Australia, Austria, Belgium, Brazil, Canada, Croatia, Finland, Germany, India, Italy, Korea Rep, Netherlands, Norway, South Africa, Spain, Sweden, Switzerland, UK, USA. [2022/XN7407/**C**]

♦ International Academy for Quality (IAQ) 11573

Contact c/o ASQ, 600 N Plankinton Ave, PO Box 3005, Milwaukee WI 53203, USA. T. +14142742241. Fax +14147658670.
Chairman address not obtained.
URL: https://iaquality.org/

History Founded Jun 1966, New York NY (USA), as *International Association for Quality.* Current Constitution and Rules of Procedure approved Jul 1974, revised 1990. Headquarters moved to Milwaukee WI (USA), 1999. **Aims** Advance quality worldwide for the benefit of humanity; pursue excellence through professionalism based on fundamental *values* of: respect for the individual; *integrity* in thought and action; *compassion* for all living beings. **Structure** General Assembly; Executive Committee; Board of Directors; Nomination Committee for Election of Academicians. **Languages** English. **Staff** 0.50 FTE, paid. **Finance** Sources: meeting proceeds; members' dues; sale of publications. **Activities** Awards/prizes/competitions; events/meetings; publishing activities; research and development. **Events** *World Quality Forum* Shanghai (China) 2019, *World Quality Forum* Bled (Slovenia) 2017, *World Quality Forum* Budapest (Hungary) 2015, *International Conference on Quality* Tokyo (Japan) 2014, *Triennial Conference* Astana (Kazakhstan) 2013.
Members Academicians (70) in 28 countries and territories:
Argentina, Australia, Austria, Belgium, Brazil, Canada, China, Denmark, Finland, France, Germany, Hungary, Ireland, Israel, Italy, Japan, Liechtenstein, Norway, Philippines, Portugal, Singapore, South Africa, Spain, Sweden, Switzerland, Taiwan, UK, USA.
NGO Relations Participant pf: *United Nations Global Compact (#20567).* [2017.10.11/XC4332/v/**C**]

♦ International Academy of Rapprochement between Islamic Madhahib (internationally oriented national body)
♦ International Academy of Religious Sciences (#00031)

♦ International Academy for Research in Learning Disabilities (IARLD) 11574

Pres Harvard Medical School, 21 Autumn St, Brookline MA 02215, USA. E-mail: iarld@primedu.uoa.gr.
URL: http://www.iarld.com/

History 1976, by Dr William Cruickshank and Dr Jacob Valk. **Aims** Provide a forum for the exchange of information and the advancement of knowledge regarding learning disabilities. **Structure** Executive Board; Standing Committees (3). **Languages** English. **Finance** Sources: members' dues. **Activities** Awards/prizes/competitions; events/meetings. **Events** *Annual Conference* Crete (Greece) 2019, *Annual Conference* Ghent (Belgium) 2018, *Annual Conference* Brisbane, QLD (Australia) 2017, *Annual Conference* Austin, TX (USA) 2016, *Conference* Vancouver, BC (Canada) 2015. **Publications** *IARLD Updates* (periodical); *International Journal for Research in Learning Disabilities (IJRLD)* (periodical).
Members Individuals in 30 countries and territories:
Australia, Belgium, Brazil, Canada, Czechia, Denmark, Finland, Germany, Greece, Hong Kong, India, Israel, Italy, Japan, Jordan, Kuwait, Lithuania, Mexico, Netherlands, New Zealand, Norway, Poland, Portugal, Slovenia, Spain, Switzerland, Taiwan, Türkiye, UK, USA. [2020.03.10/XG5419/v/**C**]

♦ International Academy of Rural Advisors (#13212)
♦ International Academy of Sciences, San Marino (#00617)

♦ International Academy of Sex Research (IASR) 11575

Sec-Treas c/o NYMC, 40 Sunshine Cottage Rd, Valhalla NY 10595, USA.
URL: http://www.iasrsite.org/

History 1974. **Aims** Promote high standards of research and scholarship in the field of sexual behaviour by fostering communication and cooperation among scholars engaged in such research. **Finance** Members' dues: US$ 110. **Events** *Meeting / Virtual Conference* 2021, *Meeting* 2020, *Meeting* Mexico City (Mexico) 2019, *Meeting* Madrid (Spain) 2018, *Meeting* Charleston, SC (USA) 2017. **Publications** *Archives of Sexual Behaviour.*
Members Full; Associate. Individuals (328, of whom 192 in USA) in 28 countries and territories:
Australia, Belgium, Brazil, Canada, China, Colombia, Croatia, Czechia, Denmark, Finland, France, Germany, Hungary, India, Israel, Italy, Korea Rep, Netherlands, Northern Ireland, Norway, Poland, Russia, Slovakia, Spain, Sweden, Switzerland, UK, USA. [2021/XD3521/v/**D**]

♦ International Academy of Singing (inactive)

♦ International Academy of Social Sciences (unconfirmed)
♦ International Academy of Sport Science and Technology (internationally oriented national body)

♦ International Academy for the Study of Tourism 11576

Académie internationale pour les études du tourisme

Secretariat Dir c/o School of Hotel and Tourism Management, Hong Kong Polytechnic Univ, 17 Science Museum Road, Tsim Sha Tsui East, Kowloon, Hong Kong. T. +85234002211. Fax +85223626422.

Founding Pres Univ of Wisconsin-Stout, Menomonie WI 54751, USA. T. +17152322339. Fax +17152323200.

URL: http://www.tourismscholars.org/

History 1988, Santander (Spain). Previously known under the acronym *IAST*. **Aims** Further scholarly research and professional investigation of tourism; encourage application of findings and advance international diffusion and exchange of tourism knowledge. **Structure** Executive Committee. **Languages** English. **Staff** 1.00 FTE, paid. **Finance** Members' dues. **Activities** Knowledge management/information dissemination; events/meetings; publishing activities. **Events** *Biennial Symposium* Bali (Indonesia) 2019, *Biennial Symposium* Guangzhou (China) 2017, *Biennial Symposium* Rhodes Is (Greece) 2015, *Biennial Symposium* Faro (Portugal) 2013, *Biennial Symposium* Chiayi City (Taiwan) 2011. **Publications** Newsletter (3 a year). Books.

Members Individuals who have made outstanding contributions to the advancement of research and scholarship in the field of tourism and who are active in this area. Members in 22 countries:

Argentina, Australia, Austria, Belgium, Canada, China, Croatia, Denmark, France, India, Israel, Japan, Korea Rep, New Zealand, Slovenia, Spain, Switzerland, Thailand, Türkiye, UK, USA, Vietnam. [2020.01.09/XE1309/v/E]

♦ International Academy of Suicide Research (IASR) 11577

Pres Sackler Fac of Medicine, Tel Aviv Univ, 6997801 Ramat Aviv, Israel.

Sec address not obtained.

URL: https://suicide-research.org/

History Current constitution revised Nov 2019. Registration: Canada. **Aims** Promote the highest quality suicide research. **Structure** Board. **Finance** Sources: members' dues. **Activities** Awards/prizes/competitions; events/meetings; knowledge management/information dissemination; training/education. **Events** *International Summit on Suicide Research* Barcelona (Spain) 2023, *International Summit on Suicide Research* 2021, *International Summit on Suicide Research* Miami Beach, FL (USA) 2019, *International Summit on Suicide Research* Henderson, NV (USA) 2017, *International Summit on Suicide Research* New York, NY (USA) 2015. **Publications** *Archives of Suicide Research*; *IASR Newsletter*. [2021/AA1751/C]

♦ International Academy for Systems and Cybernetic Sciences (IASCYS) 11578

SG Maison Bouet, 9 route de Saint Armou, LasClaveries, 64450 Thèze, France.

URL: http://www.iascys.org/

History Founded by *International Federation for Systems Research (IFSR, #13564)*. Constitution approved 7 Apr 2010, Vienna (Austria). Registered under French law 14 Jul 2016. **Aims** Honour distinguished researchers; develop innovative research topics and promote establishment of collaborative research networks in systemics and cybernetics; support young researchers in the field; promote international networks for post-graduate education on systems thinking and cybernetics; strengthen links between all actors involved. **Structure** General Assembly; Executive Committee. **Languages** English, French, German, Mandarin Chinese, Russian, Spanish. **Staff** 70.00 FTE, voluntary. **Finance** No budget. **Activities** Events/meetings. **Events** *General Assembly* Vienna (Austria) 2014, *General Assembly* Chengdu (China) 2010. **Publications** Irregular editions of proceedings, books, online papers and presentations, and reports.

Members Academics in 27 countries:

Argentina, Australia, Austria, Belgium, Canada, Chile, China, Denmark, France, Germany, Hungary, Ireland, Italy, Japan, Montenegro, Netherlands, North Macedonia, Poland, Portugal, Romania, Russia, Slovenia, Spain, Sweden, Switzerland, UK, USA. [2019.12.11/XJ5273/E]

♦ International Academy of Telepathology (IAT) 11579

Contact Institute of Pathology, Univ of Freiburg, Breisacherstr 64, 9106 Freiburg, Germany.

History 5 Apr 2002. **Structure** Board. **Events** *European Congress* Venice (Italy) 2012, *International Congress on Virtual Microscopy* Venice (Italy) 2012, *European congress* Vilnius (Lithuania) 2010, *International congress on virtual microscopy* Vilnius (Lithuania) 2010, *International congress on virtual microscopy* Toledo (Spain) 2008. **Publications** *Diagnostic Pathology* – journal.

Members Individuals in 5 countries:

Austria, Croatia, Germany, Italy, Poland. [2012/XJ0655/D]

♦ International Academy of Television Arts and Sciences (internationally oriented national body)
♦ International Academy of Tourism (inactive)

♦ International Academy of Tumor Marker Oncology (IATMO) 11580

SG NADH Handels GmbH, Schwarzspanierstrasse 15, 1090 Vienna, Austria. T. +43136169961. Fax +431361699611.

History 20 Feb 1984. Registered as a non profit organization for charitable purposes in New York State (USA). **Aims** Promote and review study in the field through research and development of tumour markers by: (a) facilitating and encouraging the assembling, acquaintance and association of scientists engaged in the field and in other related disciplines; (b) disseminating, discussing and publishing results of research and related matters of interest in the field, including organization of meetings. **Structure** Scientific Advisory Council, usually consisting of 2 advisors form each country. Officers: President, Vice-President and Secretary General. **Finance** No membership fees. Main source: financial outcome of annual meetings. **Events** *International conference on human tumor markers / Conference* Trieste (Italy) 2007, *International conference on human tumor markers / Conference* Varese (Italy) 2005, *International conference on human tumor markers / Conference* Xian (China) 2004, *International conference on human tumor markers* Karlovy Vary (Czech Rep) 2002, *Conference* Siena (Italy) 2002.

Members Individuals in 13 countries:

Austria, Brazil, Canada, China, France, Germany, Italy, Japan, Russia, Sweden, Switzerland, Türkiye, USA. [2013.06.01/XE4092/v/E]

♦ International Academy of Wood Science (IAWS) 11581

Académie internationale des sciences du bois – Internationale Akademie der Wissenschaft vom Holz

Sec SilviScan Pty, 8 Dobell Place, Doncaster East, Melbourne VIC 3109, Australia. T. +61407922274.

URL: http://www.iaws-web.org/

History 2 Jun 1966, Paris (France). **Aims** Promote the highest standards of research in the science and technology of wood; seek to recognize outstanding accomplishments of wood scientists throughout the world. **Structure** Plenary Meeting. Academy Board, consisting of 18 Fellows, including Officers (President, Vice-President, Secretary and Treasurer). **Finance** Voluntary contributions from Fellows; contributions from supporting members. **Events** *Annual Plenary Meeting* Graz (Austria) 2019, *Annual Plenary Meeting* Guadalajara (Mexico) 2018, *Annual Plenary Meeting* Bali (Indonesia) 2017, *Annual Plenary Meeting* Paris (France) 2016, *Annual Plenary Meeting* Québec, QC (Canada) 2015. **Publications** *IAWS Bulletin* (2 a year); *Wood Science and Technology* – journal.

Members Fellows; Supporting Members organizations and individuals. Fellows in 35 countries and territories:

Australia, Austria, Brazil, Canada, Chile, China, Czechia, Denmark, Egypt, Finland, France, Germany, Greece, Hungary, India, Israel, Italy, Japan, Korea Rep, Latvia, Mexico, Netherlands, New Zealand, Norway, Philippines, Poland, Romania, Russia, South Africa, Spain, Sweden, Switzerland, Taiwan, UK, USA. [2016/XF0126/F]

♦ International A-Catamaran Association (see: #21760)
♦ International Access 23 Class Association / see International Hansa Class Association (#13773)
♦ International Accountability Project / see African Private Equity and Venture Capital Association (#00425)
♦ International Accountability Project (internationally oriented national body)
♦ International Accountancy Association (inactive)
♦ International Accounting Academy (inactive)

♦ International Accounting Education Standards Board (IAESB) 11582

Dir c/o IFAC, 529 5th Ave, New York NY 10017, USA.

URL: http://www.iaesb.org/

History Set up by *International Federation of Accountants (IFAC, #13335)* to function as an independent standard-setting body under the auspices of IFAC. **Aims** Develop guidance to improve the standards of accountancy education worldwide. **Structure** Work is overseen by the Public Interest Oversight Board. Consultative Advisory Group. Board members are nominated by IFAC member bodies, the Transnational Auditors Committee; public members may be nominated by member bodies, the TAC, other organizations and the general public. **Languages** English. **Activities** Develops and issues standards, practice statements, information papers and other information documents; pronouncements are based on input from the Consultative Advisory Group, IFAC member bodies and their members, and the general public. Promotes adoption and implementation of the International Education Standards; develops education benchmarks for measuring the implementation of the International Education Standards; advances international debate on emerging issues relating to the education, development and assessment of professional accountants; acts as a catalyst in bringing together developed and developing nations, as well as countries in transition, to assist in advancement of accountancy education programmes worldwide. **Events** *Meeting* Singapore (Singapore) 2010. **Publications** *International Education Information Papers for Professional Accountants*; *International Education Practice Statements for Professional Accountants (IEPSs)*; *International Education Standards for Professional Accountants (IESs)*. [2020/XJ1895/E]

♦ International Accounting Standards Board (IASB) 11583

Conseil international des normes comptables

Main Office Columbus Building, 7 Westferry Circus, Canary Wharf, London, E14 4HD, UK. T. +442072466410. E-mail: info@ifrs.org.

URL: http://www.ifrs.org/

History 29 Jun 1973, London (UK). Founded on signature of an agreement by professional accountancy bodies of 9 countries. Agreement amended 10 Oct 1977, Munich (Germany FR). Reconstituted under current title, 6 Feb 2001, London, under the auspices of the not-for-profit *International Financial Reporting Standards Foundation (IFRS Foundation, #13603)*. Operations based in London. Former names and other names: *International Accounting Standards Committee (IASC)* – former; *International Accounting Standards Committee Foundation (IASC Foundation')* – former. Registration: USA, Delaware. **Aims** In the public interest, develop a single set of high quality, understandable and enforceable global accounting standards requiring transparent and comparable information in general purpose *financial statements*; cooperate with national accounting standard setters to achieve worldwide convergence in accounting standards. **Structure** Monitoring Board; Trustees. **Languages** English. **Staff** 150.00 FTE, paid. **Finance** Source: IFRS Foundation. **Activities** Standards/guidelines; events/meetings. **Events** *Research Forum* London (UK) 2021, *Research Forum* Oxford (UK) 2020, *Research Forum* Short Hills, NJ (USA) 2019, *Meeting* London (UK) 2018, *Research Forum* Sydney, NSW (Australia) 2018. **Publications** *IASB Update* (11 a year); *IFRIC Update*; *IFRS for SMEs Update*; *Translations Update*; *XBRL Update*. **Members** Not a membership organization. [2022/XB4328/E]

♦ International Accounting Standards Committee / see International Accounting Standards Board (#11583)
♦ International Accounting Standards Committee Foundation / see International Accounting Standards Board (#11583)
♦ International Accounting Standards Committee Foundation / see International Financial Reporting Standards Foundation (#13603)

♦ International Accreditation Forum (IAF) 11584

Sec PO Box 1811, Chelsea QC J9B 1A1, Canada. T. +16134548159. E-mail: secretary@iaf.nu – iaf@iaf.nu.

URL: http://www.iaf.nu/

History Apr 1993, Geneva (Switzerland). Registration: Start date: Sep 1998, USA, State of Delaware. **Aims** Develop a world wide programme of conformity assessment which will promote elimination of non-*tariff* barriers to *trade* through the Multilateral Recognition Arrangement (MLA). **Structure** General Assembly; Board of Directors; Executive Committee; Committees (7). **Languages** English. **Staff** 4.00 FTE, paid. **Finance** Sources: meeting proceeds; members' dues. Annual budget: 606,200 USD (2020). **Activities** Certification/accreditation; guidance/assistance/consulting; projects/programmes. **Events** *Joint Midterm Meeting* Montréal, QC (Canada) 2022, *Joint Midterm Meeting* Rhodes, NSW (Australia) 2021, *Joint Midterm Meeting* Beijing (China) 2020, *Annual Plenary Meeting* Chelsea, QC (Canada) 2020, *Joint Midterm Meeting* Montréal, QC (Canada) 2020. **Publications** *IAF Outlook* (3 a year). Series of documents; communiques.

Members Accreditation bodies (94) in 108 countries and territories:

Albania, Algeria, Angola, Argentina, Australia, Austria, Bahrain, Belarus, Belgium, Benin, Botswana, Brazil, Bulgaria, Burkina Faso, Canada, Chile, China, Colombia, Comoros, Congo DR, Costa Rica, Côte d'Ivoire, Cyprus, Czechia, Denmark, Ecuador, Egypt, Eswatini, Ethiopia, Finland, France, Georgia, Germany, Ghana, Greece, Guinea-Bissau, Hong Kong, Hungary, India, Indonesia, Iran Islamic Rep, Ireland, Italy, Japan, Jordan, Kazakhstan, Kenya, Korea Rep, Kosovo, Kuwait, Latvia, Lesotho, Lithuania, Luxembourg, Madagascar, Malawi, Malaysia, Mali, Mauritius, Mexico, Moldova, Mongolia, Morocco, Mozambique, Namibia, Netherlands, New Zealand, Niger, Nigeria, North Macedonia, Norway, Oman, Pakistan, Peru, Philippines, Poland, Portugal, Qatar, Romania, Russia, Saudi Arabia, Senegal, Serbia, Seychelles, Singapore, Slovakia, Slovenia, South Africa, Spain, Sri Lanka, Sweden, Switzerland, Taiwan, Tanzania UR, Thailand, Togo, Tunisia, Türkiye, UK, Ukraine, United Arab Emirates, Uruguay, USA, Uzbekistan, Vietnam, Yemen, Zambia, Zimbabwe.

Regional Accreditation Groups (6):

African Accreditation Cooperation (AFRAC, #00196); *Arab Accreditation Cooperation (ARAC, #00892)*; *Asia Pacific Accreditation Cooperation (APAC, #01816)*; *European Cooperation for Accreditation (EA, #06782)*; *Inter-American Accreditation Cooperation (IAAC, #11396)*; *Southern African Development Community (SADC, #19843)* (Cooperation in Accreditation SADCA).

Associations (28) in 10 countries::

Australia, Brazil, France, Germany, India, Italy, Japan, Switzerland, UK, USA.

Included in the above, 14 organizations listed in this Yearbook:

Dental Trade Alliance (DTA); *European Federation of Associations of Certification Bodies (EFAC, #07049)*; *European Organization for Quality (EOQ, #08112)*; *FAMI-QS (#09256)*; *GLOBALG.A.P (#10386)*; *Independent International Organization for Certification (IIOC, #11149)*; *International Aerospace Quality Group (IAQG, #11594)*; *International Certification Network (IQNet, #12532)*; *International Personnel Certification Association (IPC, #14560)*; *IOAS (#16001)*; *PEFC Council (#18288)*; *Telecommunications Industry Association (TIA)*; *The Consumer Goods Forum (CGF, #04772)*; *TIC Council (#20160)*. [2022.10.27/XC0095/y/C]

♦ International Accreditation for Learning Institutions / see EDU (#05363)
♦ International Accreditation and Recognition Council / see International Approval and Registration Centre (#11660)
♦ International Act Concerning Intellectual Cooperation (1938 treaty)
♦ International Action Center, New York (internationally oriented national body)
♦ International Action Centre for Pollution Incidents Response in the North-East Atlantic (#03757)
♦ International Action for Liberation (internationally oriented national body)
♦ International Action Network for Gender Equity and Law (internationally oriented national body)

♦ International Action Network on Small Arms (IANSA) 11585

Chair address not obtained. E-mail: communication@iansa.org.

Co-Chair address not obtained.

URL: http://www.iansa.org/

History 1998. Launched May 1999, The Hague (Netherlands), at conference organized by *Hague Appeal for Peace (HAP, #10848)*. Also referred to in French as *Réseau d'action international sur les armes légères (RAIAL)*. **Aims** As the global movement against *gun* violence, stop the proliferation and misuse of small arms and light weapons; make people safer by reducing demand for such weapons, improving *firearm* regulation and strengthening controls on arms transfers; promote local, national, regional and global measures to strengthen human *security*. **Structure** Board. International Advisory Council. Secretariat located in London (UK). Liaison Offices (2): Johannesburg (South Africa); New York NY (USA). **Languages** English, French, Spanish. **Staff** Secretariat: 5, supported by interns; Johannesburg (South Africa): 1; New York NY (USA): 1. **Finance** Current donors: Governments of Belgium, Germany, Norway; *Australian Aid (inactive)*; *Joseph Rowntree Charitable Trust*; *Oxfam Novib*. **Activities** Awareness raising; networking/liaising. **Publications** *IANSA Update* (weekly); *Africa Bulletin* (4 a year); *UN Bulletin* (4 a year); *Women's Network* (4 a year) – bulletin. *Survivors – Women Affected By Gun Violence Speak Out* (2nd ed 2011).

Members Full; Supporters; Information Contacts; Honorary. Full: civil society organizations (over 250) in 95 countries:
Afghanistan, Algeria, Angola, Antigua-Barbuda, Argentina, Austria, Azerbaijan, Bahrain, Bangladesh, Belarus, Belgium, Benin, Brazil, Burkina Faso, Burundi, Cameroon, Canada, Central African Rep, Chad, Chile, Colombia, Congo Brazzaville, Congo DR, Costa Rica, Côte d'Ivoire, Djibouti, Dominican Rep, Ecuador, Egypt, El Salvador, Equatorial Guinea, Fiji, Finland, France, Gabon, Gambia, Georgia, Germany, Ghana, Guatemala, Guyana, India, Iraq, Israel, Jamaica, Japan, Jordan, Kenya, Kosovo, Lebanon, Lesotho, Liberia, Malawi, Mali, Mexico, Mozambique, Namibia, Nepal, Netherlands, New Zealand, Nicaragua, Niger, Nigeria, North Macedonia, Norway, Pakistan, Paraguay, Peru, Philippines, Portugal, Rwanda, Sao Tomé-Principe, Senegal, Serbia, Sierra Leone, Somalia, South Africa, South Sudan, Spain, Sri Lanka, Sudan, Sweden, Switzerland, Tanzania UR, Thailand, Togo, Trinidad-Tobago, Tunisia, Türkiye, Uganda, UK, Uruguay, USA, Venezuela, Yemen.
Included in the above, 33 organizations listed in this Yearbook:
- *Acronym Institute for Disarmament Diplomacy*;
- *Africa-Europe Faith and Justice Network (AEFJN, #00171)*;
- *Africa Peace Forum (APFO)*;
- *Amnesty International (AI, #00801)*;
- *Asian Youth Centre (AYC, #01787)*;
- *Defend International (DI, #05027)*;
- *Eastern Africa Action Network on Small Arms (EAANSA, #05217)*;
- *Fellowship of Christian Councils and Churches in the Great Lakes and Horn of Africa (FECCLAHA, #09723)*;
- *Foundation for Security and Development in Africa (FOSDA)*;
- *Fundación Comunidad Esperanza y Justicia Internacional (FUNCEJI)*;
- *Groupe de recherche et d'information sur la paix et la sécurité (GRIP)*;
- *Indian Institute for Peace, Disarmament and Environmental Protection (IIPDEP)*;
- *Instituto Caribeño para el Estado de Derecho (ICED)*;
- *Instituto Latinoamericano de Seguridad y Democracia (ILSED, no recent information)*;
- *International Centre on Conflict and Negotiation (ICCN)*;
- *International Institute for Human Rights, Environment and Development (INHURED International, #13886)*;
- *International Peace Bureau (IPB, #14535)*;
- *International Physicians for the Prevention of Nuclear War (IPPNW, #14578)*;
- *Latin American Circle for International Studies (LACIS)*;
- *Maryknoll Office for Global Concern (MOGC)*;
- *Oxfam International (#17922)*;
- *Pax Christi – International Catholic Peace Movement (#18266)*;
- *People for Peace in Africa (PPA)*;
- *Permanent Peace Movement (PPM)*;
- *Quaker United Nations Office (QUNO, #18588)*;
- *Religions for Peace (RfP, #18831)*;
- *Réseau interafricain des habitants (RIAH, no recent information)*;
- *Saferworld*;
- *The Eastern African Sub-Regional Support Initiative for the Advancement of Women (EASSI, #05225)*;
- *Umut Foundation*;
- *Vision GRAM-International*;
- *West Africa Action Network on Small Arms (WAANSA, #20863)*;
- *Women's International League for Peace and Freedom (WILPF, #21024)*.

Consultative Status Consultative status granted from: *ECOSOC (#05331)* (Special). **IGO Relations** Signed memorandum of understanding with UN Office for Disarmament Affairs. **NGO Relations** Member of: *Control Arms (#04782)*. [2017/XF5678/y/**F**]

♦ International Actuarial Association (IAA) 11586

Association actuarielle internationale (AAI) – Asociación Internacional de Actuarios – Internationale Aktuarvereinigung

Exec Dir 99 Metcalfe St, Ste 1203, Ottawa ON K1P 6L7, Canada. T. +16132360886 ext 123. Fax +16132361386. E-mail: secretariat@actuaries.org.
URL: https://www.actuaries.org//iaa

History 1895, Brussels (Belgium). New constitution adopted June 8, 1998. Revised April 18, 1999; December 11, 1999; November 21, 2000; October 7, 2001; March 16, 2002, May 17, 2003; November 25, 2003; November 13, 2004; November 19, 2005; May 28, 2006; April 18, 2007; June 14, 2008; March 6, 2010, September 10, 2012, March 25, 2013, February 1, 2014, February 17, 2017; October 7, 2018; November 21, 2019. Former names and other names: *Permanent Committee of International Congresses of Actuaries* – former (1895 to 1968); *Comité permanent des congrès internationaux des actuaires* – former (1895 to 1968); *Comité Permanent des Congrès d'Actuaires* – former (1895 to 1968). Registration: Switzerland. **Aims** Inform and influence global stakeholders; assure the reputation of the profession; advance the competency of the profession. **Structure** Congress (every 4 years); Council; Executive Committee. Sections (7): *'Actuarial Approach for Financial Risks (AFIR)'*, *'Actuarial Studies in Non-Life Insurance (ASTIN)'*, *International Association of Consulting Actuaries (IACA, #11813)*, *'IAA Health Section (IAAHS)'*, *'Pensions, Benefits and Social Security (PBSS)'*, *'IAA Life Section (IAALS)'*; Statutory Committees (3); Other Committees (13). **Languages** English, French. **Staff** 11.00 FTE, paid. **Finance** Sources: contributions; members' dues; sale of publications. **Activities** Advocacy/lobbying/activism; events/meetings; financial and/or material support; standards/guidelines. **Events** *International Congress of Actuaries* Tokyo (Japan) 2026, *Meeting* Seoul (Korea Rep) 2024, *International Congress of Actuaries* Sydney, NSW (Australia) 2023, *Meeting* Sydney, NSW (Australia) 2023, *Meeting* Brussels (Belgium) 2022. **Publications** *ASTIN Bulletin – The Journal of the IAA* (3 a year); *IAA Newsletter* (6 regular issues a year and 2 special is); *News Release* (about 12 a year). *Risk Adjustments for Insurance Contracts under IFRS 17* (2018); *Discount Rates in Financial Reporting: A Practical Guide* (2013); *Stochastic Modeling – Theory and Reality from an Actuarial Perspective* (2010). Annual Report; congress and section colloquium proceedings; papers; reports; memoranda.
Members Full; Associate; Partner; Observer; Patron. Members in 65 countries and territories:
Argentina, Australia, Austria, Belgium, Bosnia-Herzegovina, Brazil, Bulgaria, Canada, China, Colombia, Côte d'Ivoire, Croatia, Cyprus, Czechia, Denmark, Egypt, Estonia, Finland, France, Germany, Ghana, Greece, Hong Kong, Hungary, Iceland, India, Indonesia, Ireland, Israel, Italy, Japan, Kazakhstan, Kenya, Korea Rep, Latvia, Lebanon, Lithuania, Malaysia, Mexico, Morocco, Netherlands, New Zealand, Nigeria, North Macedonia, Norway, Pakistan, Philippines, Poland, Portugal, Romania, Russia, Serbia, Singapore, Slovakia, Slovenia, South Africa, Spain, Sri Lanka, Sweden, Switzerland, Taiwan, Thailand, Türkiye, UK, USA.
Also members in the Caribbean and Central America (countries not specified).
Associate in 29 countries and territories:
Albania, Argentina, Armenia, Azerbaijan, Bangladesh, Benin, Bosnia-Herzegovina, Channel Is, Chile, Ecuador, Georgia, Iran Islamic Rep, Luxembourg, Mexico, Moldova, Mongolia, Montenegro, Mozambique, Namibia, Panama, Russia, Senegal, Tanzania UR, Togo, Tunisia, Uganda, Ukraine, Zambia, Zimbabwe.
Partners (5):
International Accounting Standards Board (IASB, #11583); *International Association of Insurance Supervisors (IAIS, #11966)*; *International Organisation of Pension Supervisors (IOPS, #14432)*; *International Social Security Association (ISSA, #14885)*; *OECD (#17693)*.
Consultative Status Consultative status granted from: *ILO (#11123)* (Special List); *UNCTAD (#20285)* (General Category). **NGO Relations** Member of (2): *International Organisation of Pension Supervisors (IOPS, #14432)*; *Microinsurance Network (#16747)*. [2023/XB1138/y/**B**]

♦ International Acupuncture Association of Physical Therapists (IAAPT) 11587

Sec AUT, 55 Wellesley St E, Auckland 1010, New Zealand. E-mail: contact@iaapt.physio.
Chairman address not obtained. E-mail: chair@iaapt.wcpt.org.
URL: https://iaapt.physio/

History 1991, London (UK). Official subgroup of *World Confederation for Physical Therapy (WCPT, #21293)* since 1999. **Aims** Promote the use of acupuncture, dry needling and related techniques by physiotherapists globally. **Structure** Executive Committee; International Committee. **Languages** English. **Staff** Voluntary. **Finance** Members' dues. **Activities** Training/education; events/meetings. **Events** *Annual General Meeting* Cape Town (South Africa) 2017, *Annual General Meeting* Singapore (Singapore) 2015, *Annual general meeting / General Meeting* Amsterdam (Netherlands) 2011, *Conference* Chesham (UK) 2001. **Publications** *Meridian Worldwide* (2 a year) – newsletter.
Members Organizations in 10 countries and territories:
Argentina, Australia, Canada, Cyprus, Denmark, Greece, Hong Kong, Ireland, New Zealand, UK.
NGO Relations Member of (1): *World Confederation for Physical Therapy (WCPT, #21293)*. [2023/XE4136/**E**]

♦ International Acupuncture Institute (internationally oriented national body)
♦ International Acupuncture Society (internationally oriented national body)
♦ International Adam Smith Society (internationally oriented national body)
♦ International Adkins Chiti: Women in Music Foundation (internationally oriented national body)
♦ International Administrative Science Association (internationally oriented national body)

♦ International Adsorption Society (IAS) 11588

Sec-Treas School of Chemical and Biomolecular Engineering, Georgia Inst of Technology, 311 Ferst Dr NW, Atlanta GA 30332-0100, USA. T. +14048945254.
Former Pres ETH Swiss Federal Inst of Technology – Zurich, Inst of Process Engineering, Sonneggstrasse 3, 8092 Zurich ZH, Switzerland. T. +41446322456. Fax +41446321141.
URL: http://ias.vub.ac.be/

History May 1989, Sonthofen (Germany FR). **Aims** Serve people, firms and organizations who seek to advance the art, science, and technology of adsorption and related subjects; sponsor scientific research in the field of adsorption. **Structure** General Meeting (every 3 years). Board of Directors; Officers (3). **Languages** English. **Staff** 1.00 FTE, paid; 3.00 FTE, voluntary. **Finance** Members' dues. **Activities** Organizes: triennial conference; meetings; seminars. **Events** *Triennial Conference* Baltimore, MD (USA) 2013, *Triennial Conference* Awaji (Japan) 2010, *Triennial Conference* Japan 2010, *Pacific basin conference on adsorption science and technology* Singapore (Singapore) 2009, *Triennial Conference* Italy 2007. **Publications** *Adsorption* (6 a year). Research reports. **Members** Membership countries not specified. [2015/XD2888/**D**]

♦ International Advanced Robotics Programme (IARP) 11589

Sec RURobots, PO Box 248, Manchester, M28 1WF, UK. T. +441617993898. Fax +441617033745.
Pres c/o NSF, 24 Stone Pine Court, Baltimore MD 21208, USA. Fax +14105165553.
URL: http://iarp.isir.upmc.fr/

History 1982, Versailles, during Economic Summit of *Group of Eight (G-8, #10745)* (formerly referred to as Group of Seven – G-8). **Aims** Foster international cooperation aiming to develop robot systems able to dispense with human exposure to difficult activities in harsh, demanding or dangerous conditions or environments. **Structure** Annual Joint Coordinating Forum (JCF), organized on a rotating basis by member countries, is the governing body. Executive Committee, comprising President, Vice-President, General Secretary and 2 JCF Chairs (current and incoming). Working Groups; Secretariat. **Languages** English. **Staff** 2.00 FTE, paid. **Finance** No overall budget; members cover expenses entailed by initiatives and activities; secretariat expenses covered by government of France. **Activities** Research/documentation; events/meetings. **Events** *Annual Joint Coordination Forum* Beijing (China) 2009, *Annual Joint Coordination Forum* Baden Baden (Germany) 2008, *Annual Joint Coordination Forum* San Diego, CA (USA) 2007, *Workshop on micro and nano robotics* Paris (France) 2006, *Workshop on robot dependability in human environments* Rome (Italy) 2006. **Publications** Annual Report; technical field reports.
Members Full governments of 17 countries:
Australia, Austria, Belgium, Brazil, Canada, China, France, Germany, Hungary, Italy, Japan, Korea Rep, Poland, Russia, Spain, UK, USA.
Observers government of 1 country:
New Zealand.
Regional organization (1), listed in this Yearbook:
European Union (EU, #08967). [2016/XF7144/**F***]

♦ International Advertising Association (IAA) 11590

Association internationale de publicité – Asociación Internacional de Publicidad

Main Office 511 Ave of Americas, Ste 4017, New York NY 10011, USA. E-mail: iaa@iaaglobal.org.
URL: http://www.iaaglobal.org/

History 1938. World Service Center located in New York NY (USA). Former names and other names: *Export Advertising Association* – former (1938 to 1953). **Aims** Promote the critical role and value of advertising as the driving force behind healthy economies and the foundation of diverse, independent *media* and an open society; defend and advance *freedom* of commercial speech, *consumer* choice and the right of consumers to receive full information about products and services legal on the market place; encourage greater practice and acceptance of advertising *self-regulation*; provide a forum to debate emerging professional marketing communications issues and their consequences in the fast changing world environment; take the lead in state-of-the-art professional development through education and training for the marketing communications industry of the future. **Structure** Board of Directors, led by Chairman, World President, Senior Vice-President, Secretary, Treasurer and 5 Vice-Presidents/Area Directors. Local chapters. Committees. **Languages** English. **Staff** 2.00 FTE, paid. **Finance** Sources: members' dues. Other sources: advertising; conferences. **Activities** Main areas: Professional Development Programme; Internships; Education; Public Service Advertising; Value of Advertising Campaigns; Economic Impact Studies; Consumer Attitude Studies. Organizes: world congresses (every 2 years); international symposia. Local chapters organize frequent conferences, seminars and workshops on selected topics. **Events** *World Congress* Malaysia 2023, *IAA World Congress* St Petersburg (Russia) 2021, *Biennial Congress* St Petersburg (Russia) 2020, *IAA World Congress* Kochi (India) 2019, *Global Conference* Bucharest (Romania) 2017. **Publications** *IAA Network News* – electronic newsletter. Annual Report.
Members Local chapters; Corporate members; organizational members; individual members (over 4,000); Accredited institutes (57). Chapters in 35 countries and territories:
Australia, Austria, Bahrain, Bulgaria, China, Denmark, Egypt, Ghana, Hungary, India, Indonesia, Italy, Japan, Jordan, Korea Rep, Kuwait, Lebanon, Malaysia, Malta, Netherlands, Pakistan, Poland, Romania, Russia, Serbia, Singapore, Spain, Sri Lanka, Sweden, Switzerland, Taiwan, Türkiye, UK, United Arab Emirates, USA.
Corporate members in 70 countries:
Bahrain, Japan, Russia, Saudi Arabia, UK, United Arab Emirates, USA.
Organizational in 12 countries:
Australia, Belgium, El Salvador, France, India, Japan, Malaysia, Russia, Switzerland, Thailand, UK, USA.
Included in the above, 5 organizations listed in this Yearbook:
Asian Federation of Advertising Associations (AFAA, #01452); *European Advertising Standards Alliance (EASA, #05829)*; *FIPP (#09776)*; *World Federation of Advertisers (WFA, #21407)*; *World Out of Home Organization (WOO, #21702)*.
Consultative Status Consultative status granted from: *ECOSOC (#05331)* (Ros A); *UNESCO (#20322)* (Consultative Status); *World Intellectual Property Organization (WIPO, #21593)* (Permanent Observer Status). **IGO Relations** Accredited by (1): *United Nations Office at Vienna (UNOV, #20604)*. Associated with Department of Global Communications of the United Nations. Invited to sessions of Intergovernmental Council of: *International Programme for the Development of Communication (IPDC, #14651)*. **NGO Relations** Member of: *New York NGO Committee on Drugs (NYNGOC, #17097)*. Industry member of: *European Advertising Standards Alliance (EASA, #05829)*; *International Council for Advertising Self-Regulation (ICAS, #12984)*. [2021/XB1139/y/**B**]

♦ International Advisory Commission on the Principle of Precaution (IACPP) 11591

Commission internationale consultative principe de précaution (CICPP)

Address not obtained.

History Founded in France, by Philippe Jean Coulomb and Marcel Piquemal. **NGO Relations** *Observatoire des missions publiques en Europe (OMIPE, no recent information)*. [2014/XM1436/**E**]

♦ International Advisory Committee / see Africa Transport Policy Program (#00527)
♦ International Advisory Council for Homosexual Men and Women in Alcoholics Anonymous / see Gays and Lesbians in Alcoholics Anonymous
♦ International Advisory Council of the International Teletraffic Congress (see: #15674)
♦ International Advocacy and Resource Centre on the Human Rights of Migrant Workers (internationally oriented national body)

♦ International Advocate for Glycoprotein Storage Diseases (ISMRD) . 11592

Main Office 20880 Canyon View Dr, Saratoga CA 95070, USA. E-mail: info@ismrd.org.
URL: http://www.ismrd.org/

History Mar 1999, USA. Founded on the initiative of Paul Murphy and Debora Murphy. Former names and other names: *International Society for Mannosidosis and Related Diseases (ISMRD)* – former. Registration: Section 501(c)(3), No/ID: 52-2164838, USA, State of Maryland. **Aims** Advocate for families and patients affected by one of the following disorders: Alpha-Mannosidosis; Aspartylglucosaminuria; Beta-Mannosidosis; Fucosidosis; Galactosialidosis; Sialidosis (Mucolipidosis I); Mucolipidosis II, II/III, III alpha/beta; Mucolipidosis

Ill Gamma; Schindler Disease. **Structure** Board of Directors. **Languages** Arabic, French, Portuguese, Slovene. **Activities** Advocacy/lobbying/activism; events/meetings; healthcare. **Events** *International Conference* Atlanta, GA (USA) 2019, *International Conference* Rome (Italy) 2017, *International Conference* St Louis, MO (USA) 2015, *International Conference* Charleston, SC (USA) 2012, *International Conference* Ann Arbor, MI (USA) 2007. **Publications** *Pathways* (4 a year).
Members Members in 23 countries and territories:
Australia, Austria, Brazil, Denmark, France, Greece, India, Ireland, Italy, Jordan, Malaysia, Morocco, Netherlands, New Zealand, Northern Ireland, Norway, Pakistan, Russia, Saudi Arabia, Slovenia, Sweden, UK, USA.
NGO Relations Member of (3): *Global Genes* (RARE Foundation Alliance); NORD; Rare Voices Australia.
[2022.10.11/XD9344/**C**]

♦ International Aerobatic Club (internationally oriented national body)
♦ International Aerosol Association (inactive)

♦ International Aerosol Research Assembly (IARA) 11593

Sec Environmental Processes Lab, PO Box 2208, 700 13 Heraklion, Greece. E-mail: mihalo@chemistry.uoc.gr.
Pres KAPAR, SNU Office 1508, 1 Gwanak-ro, Gwanak-gu, Seoul 151-742, Korea Rep.
URL: http://www.iara.org/
History 1986, Berlin West (Germany FR), at 2nd International Aerosol Conference, following planning meeting at 1st Conference, 1984, Minneapolis MN (USA). **Aims** Organize International Aerosol Conferences (every 4 years); promote scientific understanding and provide international collaboration in the field of aerosol research. **Structure** Assembly of delegates appointed by representative organizations. Officers: President, Vice-President and Secretary. Vice-President prepares conference and is usually from host country; he or she becomes President for the next term. **Languages** English. **Activities** Events/meetings. **Events** *Quadrennial International Aerosol Conference* Athens (Greece) 2022, *Quadrennial International Aerosol Conference* St Louis, MO (USA) 2018, *Quadrennial International Aerosol Conference* Busan (Korea Rep) 2014, *Quadrennial international aerosol conference* Helsinki (Finland) 2010, *Quadrennial international aerosol conference* St Paul, MN (USA) 2006.
Members Aerosol organizations in 32 countries:
Australia, Austria, Belgium, Brazil, Canada, China, Czechia, Denmark, Finland, France, Germany, Greece, Hungary, India, Ireland, Israel, Italy, Korea Rep, Mexico, Netherlands, New Zealand, Norway, Poland, Portugal, Romania, Russia, Spain, Sweden, Switzerland, Taiwan, UK, USA.
Regional organization (2):
Gesellschaft für Aerosolforschung (GAeF, #10140); Nordic Society for Aerosol Research (NOSA, #17410).
[2017/XF1249/**F**]

♦ International Aerospace Quality Group (IAQG) 11594

Pres Rue Montoyer 10, 1000 Brussels, Belgium.
Operations Manager address not obtained.
URL: http://www.sae.org/iaqg/
History Founded 1998, as a dedicated Working Group of *SAE International*. Became independent association, registered in accordance with Belgian law, 15 Dec 2013. **Aims** Implement initiatives that make significant improvements in quality and reductions in cost throughout the value stream of products and services by establishing and maintaining dynamic cooperation, based on trust, between international aerospace and defense companies. **Structure** General Assembly. Regions (3): *Americas Aerospace Quality Group (AAQG); Asia Pacific Aerospace Quality Group (APAQG, #01820); European Aerospace Quality Group (EAQG, #05838).* **Languages** English. **Staff** None. Working contribution made by IAQG Company Members and IAQG contractors. **Finance** 91xx certification fees. Annual budget: about US$ 2,000,000. **Activities** Standards/guidelines; certification/accreditation. Active worldwide. **Events** *General Assembly* Brussels (Belgium) 2021, *General Assembly* San Diego, CA (USA) 2020, *General Assembly* Berlin (Germany) 2019, *General Assembly* Busan (Korea Rep) 2018, *General Assembly* Stockholm (Sweden) 2017. **Publications** Standards; handbook.
Members Private aerospace industry companies (67) in 22 countries and territories:
Austria, Belgium, Brazil, Canada, China, France, Germany, Indonesia, Israel, Italy, Japan, Korea Rep, Netherlands, Russia, Saudi Arabia, Singapore, Spain, Sweden, Taiwan, UK, Ukraine, USA.
NGO Relations Member of: *International Accreditation Forum (IAF, #11584).* [2015.06.01/XM1819/**F**]

♦ International Affairs Centre / see Ralph J Bunche International Affairs Center
♦ International Affairs Institute, Rome (internationally oriented national body)
♦ International Affairs Network (inactive)
♦ International Affiliate of the Academy of Nutrition and Dietetics (internationally oriented national body)
♦ International Affiliation of Tongue-tie Professionals (internationally oriented national body)

♦ International Affiliation of Writers' Guilds (IAWG) 11595

Address not obtained.
URL: http://iawg.org/
History 1986, Toronto ON (Canada), replacing *International Writers Guild (IWG, inactive).* **Aims** Procure adequate international laws or treaties; improve relations among nations in copyright, labour relations and taxation; promote freedom of expression and of communication and to oppose censorship in whatever form it may take; promote fair dealings and to cultivate harmony, cordial relationship and understanding among the members of affiliated Guilds; procure better working conditions for members of the affiliated Guilds; disseminate information on members' rights and interests; enforce standard minimum contracts established by any of the affiliated Guilds in radio, television and motion pictures. **Structure** Affiliation Conference. Officers: Chairman, Secretary. **Languages** English. **Staff** One part-time, paid. **Events** *World Conference* Copenhagen (Denmark) 2021, *World Conference* Copenhagen (Denmark) 2020, *World Conference* Berlin (Germany) 2018, *Meeting* Athens (Greece) 2009, *World Conference* Athens (Greece) 2009.
Members Writers' Guilds (10) in 8 countries:
Australia, Canada, France, Ireland, Mexico, New Zealand, UK, USA.
Consultative Status Consultative status granted from: *World Intellectual Property Organization (WIPO, #21593)* (Permanent Observer Status). [2020/XF1797/**F**]

♦ International African Institute (IAI) 11596

Institut Africain International
Administrative Officer c/o School of Oriental and African Studies, University of London, Thornhaugh Street, Russell Square, London, WC1H 0XG, UK. T. +442078984435. Fax +442078984419. E-mail: am131@soas.ac.uk – iai@soas.ac.uk.
Hon Dir address not obtained.
URL: https://www.internationalafricaninstitute.org/
History 1926, London (UK). Former names and other names: *International Institute of African Languages and Cultures* – former; *Institut international des langues et civilisations africaines* – former. Registration: Companies House, No/ID: 04133841, Start date: 29 Dec 2000, England and Wales; Charity Commission, No/ID: 1084798, Start date: 30 Jan 2001, England and Wales. **Aims** Facilitate communication between scholars within the continent and Africanists throughout the world; promote international research and publication; promote African studies. **Structure** Council (meets every 2 years); Publications Committee; Board of Trustees. **Languages** English, French. **Staff** 2.00 FTE, paid. **Finance** Sources: grants; investments; sale of publications. **Activities** Events/meetings; publishing activities. **Events** *Seminar* Nairobi (Kenya) 2004, *General members meeting* London (UK) 1995, *Migration and development* Tunis (Tunisia) 1995, *Conference on arts and society in Africa* UK 1995, *Pre-seminar workshop* Rome (Italy) 1993. **Publications** *Africa* (4 a year); *Journal of African Cultural Studies* (3 a year); *Africa Bibliography* (annual). *African Arguments; Classics in African Anthropology; International African Library Series; International African Seminar Series; Readings in African Studies.* Monographs on African ethnography, history, sociology and linguistics. **NGO Relations** Instrumental in setting up: Committee of the Centre of African Studies, University of London; Council of the African Studies Association of the UK (ASAUK); *West African Museums Programme (WAMP, #20890).* [2022/XF1142/j/**F**]

♦ International African Law Association (inactive)
♦ International African Migratory Locust Organisation (inactive)
♦ International Agency of the Association of Netherlands Municipalities (internationally oriented national body)
♦ International Agency for Crime Prevention, Criminal Law and Jurisdiction (internationally oriented national body)
♦ International Agency for Economic Development (internationally oriented national body)

♦ International Agency for the Prevention of Blindness (IAPB) 11597

Organisation mondiale contre la cécité
CEO c/o WeWork, 1 St Katharine's Way, London Intl House 6th Floor, London, E1W 1UN, UK. T. +442039508778. E-mail: communications@iapb.org.
URL: http://www.iapb.org/
History 1975. Took over and expanded activities of *Association internationale de prophylaxie de la cécité (AIPC, inactive)*, founded 14 Sep 1929, The Hague (Netherlands), within the framework of *International Council of Ophthalmology (ICO, #13057).* Registration: Charity Commission, No/ID: 1100559, England and Wales; Companies House, No/ID: 04620869, Start date: 18 Dec 2002, England. **Aims** Eliminate the main causes of avoidable blindness and *visual impairment* by bringing together governments and non-governmental agencies to facilitate planning, development and implementation of sustainable national eye care programmes. **Structure** Council of Members (meets annually); Board of Trustees; Honorary Affiliates (2). **Languages** Chinese, English, French, German, Spanish. **Staff** 20.00 FTE, paid. **Finance** Sources: donations; grants; members' dues. **Activities** Events/meetings; knowledge management/information dissemination; networking/liaising; research and development. **Events** *2030 IN SIGHT LIVE Meeting* Dubai (United Arab Emirates) 2022, *Quadrennial General Assembly* Singapore (Singapore) 2021, *Quadrennial General Assembly* Singapore (Singapore) 2020, *Quadrennial General Assembly* Durban (South Africa) 2016, *Quadrennial general assembly* Hyderabad (India) 2012. **Publications** Proceedings of General Assemblies; case studies; reports. **Members** NGOs; Associations; societies; institutions; hospitals; corporations; foundations. Individual: Honorary members and ophthalmologists. **Consultative Status** Consultative status granted from: *ECOSOC (#05331)* (Ros C); *UNICEF (#20332); WHO (#20950)* (Official Relations). **IGO Relations** Accredited by: *United Nations Office at Vienna (UNOV, #20604).* Links with the WHO Programme for the Prevention of Blindness. Associated with Department of Global Communications of the United Nations. **NGO Relations** Member of (8): *British Overseas NGO's for Development (BOND); European Coalition for Vision (ECV); Global Health Council (GHC, #10402); International Coalition for Trachoma Control (ICTC, #12624); Neglected Tropical Diseased NGO Network (NNN, #16969); NGO Committee on UNICEF (#17120); Partnership Committee to the WHO Programme for the Prevention of Blindness (Partnership Committee, no recent information); World Blind Union (WBU, #21234).* Joint congresses with: *International Organization Against Trachoma (IOAT, #14436).* Latin American Regional Committee acts as Prevention of Blindness committee of: *Latin American Blind Union (#16256).* Founding member of: *Vision Alliance (#20796).* Joint initiative with: *VISION 2020 – The Right to Sight (inactive).*
[2022.05.13/XC1224/y/**D**]

♦ International Agency for the Prevention of Deafness / see Hearing International (#10895)

♦ International Agency for Research on Cancer (IARC) 11598

Centre international de Recherche sur le Cancer (CIRC)
Communications Officer 150 cours Albert Thomas, 69372 Lyon CEDEX 08, France. T. +33472738478. E-mail: com@iarc.fr.
URL: http://www.iarc.who.int/
History Established by the World Health Assembly, pursuant to Article 18 of the Constitution, in Resolution WHA18.44, within the framework of *WHO (#20950).* Following the decision of the Governing Council, the seat of the Agency is in Lyon (France). **Aims** Promote international collaboration in cancer research; serve as a means through which Participating States and WHO, in liaison with the UICC and other interested international organizations, may cooperate in stimulation and support of research related to the causes and prevention of cancer. **Structure** Governing Council, composed of one representative of each Participating State and Director-General of WHO. Scientific Council, consisting of scientists selected on the basis of their technical competence in cancer research and allied fields. Secretariat, consisting of technical and administrative personnel and of IARC Director (who is selected by the Governing Council and appointed by Director-General of WHO). All other staff members are appointed in accordance with an agreement between the Director-General of WHO and the Director of IARC. Research Groups. **Languages** English, French. **Staff** 233.00 FTE, paid. Personnel negotiations through *IARC Staff Association (#11006).* **Finance** Sources: contributions of member/participating states. **Activities** Awards/prizes/competitions; events/meetings; knowledge management/information dissemination; research and development; training/education. **Events** *Meeting on Emerging Issues in Oncogenic Virus Research* Bevagna (Italy) 2022, *Mutant P53 Workshop* Lyon (France) 2019, *Workshop on Emerging Issues in Oncogenic Virus Research* Bevagna (Italy) 2018, *P53 Workshop* Singapore (Singapore) 2017, *Global cancer, occurence, causes, and avenues to prevention* Lyon (France) 2016. **Publications** *IARC Biennial Report* (every 2 years). *IARC Monographs on the Identification of Carcinogenic Hazards to Humans* (2020) – vol 124; *IARC Handbooks of Cancer Prevention* (2019) – vol 17; *Cancer Incidence in Five Continents* – 11 vols published to date. *WHO Classification of Tumours* (5th ed); *World Cancer Report.* Scientific publications; technical publications; working group reports.
Members Participating States: Member States of WHO considered by 2/3 majority of IARC Governing Council to be able to contribute effectively to the scientific and technical work of the Agency. Governments of 27 countries:
Australia, Austria, Belgium, Brazil, Canada, China, Denmark, Finland, France, Germany, Hungary, India, Iran Islamic Rep, Ireland, Italy, Japan, Korea Rep, Morocco, Netherlands, Norway, Qatar, Russia, Spain, Sweden, Switzerland, UK, USA.
IGO Relations Compiles statistics and carries out collaborative research contracts for the: *European Commission (EC, #06633).* Observer to: *Biobanking and BioMolecular resources Research Infrastructure (BBMRI-ERIC, #03237).* **NGO Relations** Member of (2): *Alliance for Cervical Cancer Prevention (ACCP, #00663)* (Founding); *Global Alliance for Genomics and Health (GA4GH, #10199).* Cooperates with (1): *Union for International Cancer Control (UICC, #20415).* [2022.02.07/XE3549/**E***]

♦ International Agency for Rural Industrialization (no recent information)
♦ International Agrarian Bureau (inactive)
♦ International Agrarian Institute (inactive)
♦ International Agreement Concerning the Conveyance of Corpses (1937 treaty)
♦ International Agreement on Jute and Jute Products, 1982 (1982 treaty)
♦ International Agreement on Jute and Jute Products, 1989 (1989 treaty)
♦ International Agreement on Natural Rubber, 1987 (1987 treaty)
♦ International Agreement on Olive Oil and Table Olives, 2005 (2005 treaty)
♦ International Agreement on Olive Oil and Table Olives, 2015 (2015 treaty)
♦ International Agreement on Olive Oil and Tables Olives, 1986 (1986 treaty)
♦ International Agreement on the Procedure for the Establishment of Tariffs for Intra-European Scheduled Air Services (1987 treaty)
♦ International Agreement on the Procedure for the Establishment of Tariffs for Scheduled Air Services (1967 treaty)
♦ International Agreement Regarding the Maintenance of Certain Lights in the Red Sea (1962 treaty)
♦ International Agreement for the Regulation of Whaling (1937 treaty)
♦ International Agreement Relating to the Exportation of Bones (1929 treaty)
♦ International Agreement Relating to the Exportation of Hides and Skins (1928 treaty)
♦ International Agreement Relating to Statistics of Causes of Death (1934 treaty)
♦ International Agreement on the Sharing of Capacity on Intra-European Scheduled Air Services (1987 treaty)
♦ International Agreement for the Suppression of the Circulation of Obscene Publications, 1910 (1910 treaty)
♦ International Agreement for the Suppression of the White Slave Traffic (1904 treaty)
♦ International Agribusiness Management Association / see International Food and Agribusiness Management Association (#13619)
♦ International Agrichar Initiative / see International Biochar Initiative (#12342)
♦ International Agricultural College, Deventer / see Van Hall Larenstein University of Applied Sciences
♦ International Agricultural Cooperative Society (inactive)
♦ International Agricultural Credit Conference / see Confédération internationale du crédit agricole (#04560)

- ♦ International Agricultural Exchange Association (inactive)
- ♦ International Agricultural Students Association of the Americas (inactive)
- ♦ International Agricultural Trade Research Consortium (internationally oriented national body)
- ♦ International Agricultural Training Programme (internationally oriented national body)
- ♦ International Agricultural Union for Fixing the Price of Cereals (inactive)

♦ International Agri-Food Network (IAFN) 11599

Secretariat address not obtained.
Chair c/o International Seed Federation, Rte du Reposoir 7, 1260 Nyon VD, Switzerland.
URL: http://www.agrifood.net/

History Nov 1996, Rome (Italy). Founded during first World Food Summit, as an informal network. **Aims** Foster cooperation and understanding among the international agri-food sector; coordinate activities. **Structure** Annual General Meeting and quarterly calls. **Languages** English. **Finance** Sources: members' dues. **Activities** Advocacy/lobbying/activism; events/meetings; knowledge management/information dissemination; networking/liaising. **Publications** Position papers.
Members Organizations (22):
- Canada Grains Council;
- Canadian Canola Growers Association (CCGA);
- *CropLife International (#04966)*;
- Ecuadorian Cluster Bananero;
- *Global Dairy Platform (GDP, #10314)*;
- *Global Farmer Network (GFN, #10354)*;
- *Global Pulse Confederation (GPC, #10562)*;
- *Grain and Feed Trade Association (GAFTA, #10692)*;
- *Health for Animals (#10870)*;
- Himalayan Apple Growers Society (HAGS);
- Indonesian Farmers Society Organization;
- *Institute of Food Technologists (IFT)*;
- *International Chamber of Commerce (ICC, #12534)*;
- *International Dairy Federation (IDF, #13128)*;
- *International Fertilizer Association (IFA, #13589)*;
- *International Food and Beverage Alliance (IFBA, #13620)*;
- *International Seed Federation (ISF, #14828)*;
- *Nuffield International – Nuffield Farming Scholarships Trust (#17624)*;
- Nuffield Ireland;
- Solutions from the Land;
- US Grains Council;
- US Soybean Export Council (USSEC).

NGO Relations Supports (1): *Farming First*. [2022.06.16/XF4819/y/**F**]

- ♦ International Aid (internationally oriented national body)
- ♦ International Aid for Refugees (inactive)

♦ International AIDS Economics Network (IAEN) 11600

Contact 16320 E Crystal Point Dr, Fountain Hills AZ 85268, USA.
URL: http://www.iaen.org/

History Founded 1993. **Aims** Provide data, tools and analysis on the economics of *HIV*/AIDS prevention and treatment in developing countries, for compassionate, cost-effective responses to the global epidemic. **Structure** Board. **Staff** 2.00 FTE, paid; 1.00 FTE, voluntary. **Finance** Supported by: *Bill and Melinda Gates Foundation (BMGF)*. **Activities** Research/documentation; knowledge management/information dissemination; meeting activities. **Events** *Conference* Melbourne, VIC (Australia) 2014, *Conference* Washington, DC (USA) 2012, *Conference* Vienna (Austria) 2010, *Conference* Mexico City (Mexico) 2008, *Annual conference / Conference* Washington, DC (USA) 2003. **Publications** *IAEN Newsletter*.
Members Economists (about 4,900), mainly in 5 countries:
Ethiopia, Kenya, Nigeria, South Africa, USA.
IGO Relations Cooperates with: Centers for Disease Control and Prevention (CDC); *Joint United Nations Programme on HIV/AIDS (UNAIDS, #16149)*; *United States Agency for International Development (USAID)*. **NGO Relations** Cooperates with: *Bill and Melinda Gates Foundation (BMGF)*; Rush Foundation.
[2014.06.01/XF6410/**F**]

- ♦ International AIDS Empowerment (internationally oriented national body)
- ♦ International Aid Services (internationally oriented national body)

♦ International AIDS Society (IAS) 11601

Société international du SIDA
Exec Dir Av de France 23, 1202 Geneva, Switzerland. T. +41227100800. Fax +41227100899. E-mail: info@iasociety.org.
Contact address not obtained.
URL: http://www.iasociety.org/

History 1988. Reorganized 1994, in connection with the Yokohama International AIDS Conference, when the Society became registered and Bylaws were written. Registration: Swiss Civil Code, No/ID: CH-660.1.312.004-6, Start date: 16 Jun 2004, Switzerland, Geneva. **Aims** Lead collective action on every front of the global HIV response through membership base, scientific authority and convening power. **Structure** Governing Council; Geographical Regions (5): USA and Canada; Europe; Africa; Latin America and Caribbean; Asia and the Pacific Islands. **Languages** English. **Staff** 59.40 FTE, paid. **Activities** Advocacy/lobbying/activism; capacity building; events/meetings; knowledge management/information dissemination; monitoring/evaluation; projects/programmes; publishing activities; training/education. **Events** *International AIDS Conference* Montréal, QC (Canada) 2022, *IAS Conference on HIV Science* Berlin (Germany) 2021, *HIV Research for Prevention Conference (HIVR4P//Virtual)* Geneva (Switzerland) 2021, *International AIDS Conference* 2020, *IAS Conference on HIV Science* Mexico City (Mexico) 2019. **Publications** *Journal of the International AIDS Society (JIAS)*. **Members** Individuals (over 15,000) in over 170 countries. Membership countries not specified. **Consultative Status** Consultative status granted from: *ECOSOC (#05331)* (Special). **NGO Relations** Member of (1): *Associations and Conference Forum (AC Forum, #02909)*.
[2022.10.18/XE1939/**B**]

- ♦ International AIDS Trust (internationally oriented national body)

♦ International AIDS Vaccine Initiative (IAVI) 11602

Headquarters 125 Broad St, 9th Fl, New York NY 10004, USA. T. +12128471111. Fax +12128471112. E-mail: info@iavi.org.
Europe Office Van Diemenstraat 48, 1013 NH Amsterdam, Netherlands.
URL: http://www.iavi.org/

History Jan 1996, USA, on the initiative of Dr Seth Berkley. Registration: 501(c)(3) non-profit, USA; EU Transparency Register, No/ID: 685996941523-19, Start date: 1 Mar 2021. **Aims** Ensure the development of safe, effective, accessible, preventive *HIV* vaccines for use throughout the world. **Structure** Board of Directors; Scientific Advisory Committee; Political Advisory Committee. Regional offices (4): Europe; Eastern Africa; Souther Africa; India. **Finance** Financial and in-kind supporters: governments of Canada, Denmark, Ireland, Netherlands, Norway, Spain, Sweden, UK, USA, Basque Autonomous Government and *European Commission (EC, #06633)*; multilateral organizations such as *International Bank for Reconstruction and Development (IBRD, #12317)* (World Bank); national foundations, including *Bill and Melinda Gates Foundation (BMGF)*, *The William and Flora Hewlett Foundation* and *The Rockefeller Foundation (#18966)*; corporate donors; charities; private donors and individuals. **Activities** Financial and/or material supports; networking/liaising; advocacy/lobbying/activism. **Events** *HIVR4P : HIV Research for Prevention International Conference* Chicago, IL (USA) 2016, *Meeting* Amsterdam (Netherlands) 2014, *Regional consultation on HIV vaccine research and development in Africa* Addis Ababa (Ethiopia) 2006, *Inter-country parliamentarian workshop on HIV/AIDS* Bangkok (Thailand) 2003, *International policy-makers conference* Delhi (India) 2002. **Publications** *VAX* (12 a year) – bulletin; *IAVI Report* (6 a year) – newsletter; *Scientific Blueprint* (every 2 years). *Policy Briefs*; *Policy Discussion Papers*; *Policy Working Papers*. **IGO Relations** Collaborating Centre of *Joint United Nations Programme on HIV/AIDS (UNAIDS, #16149)*. **NGO Relations** Member of: *Commonwealth HIV and AIDS Action Group (Para55, no recent information)*; *Global Health Council (GHC, #10402)*; *Global Health Technologies Coalition (GHTC)*; *Extractive Industries Transparency Initiative (EITI, #09229)*; *NonProfit Organizations Knowledge Initiative (NPOKI)*; *TB Europe Coalition (TBEC, #20104)*; *UK Consortium on AIDS and International Development*. Stakeholder in: *Global HIV Vaccine Enterprise (#10410)*. [2020/XF3902/**F**]

- ♦ International Aid Sweden / see International Aid Services

♦ International AIDS Women's Caucus (IAWC) 11603

Contact Parana 135, fl 3, dpt 13, Buenos Aires, Argentina. T. +541143722763. Fax +541143722763.
URL: https://aidswomencaucus.wordpress.com/

History 1992, Amsterdam (Netherlands), during VIII International Conference on AIDS. Initially a caucus of *International AIDS Society (IAS, #11601)*. **Aims** Promote the human *rights* of women affected and infected by *HIV*/AIDS. **Structure** Steering Committee.
Members National organizations (3) in 3 countries:
Argentina, India, USA.
International organizations (10):
ActionAid (#00087) (Zimbabwe); *Asian-Pacific Resource and Research Centre for Women (ARROW, #01629)*; *ASTRA – Central and Eastern European Women's Network for Sexual and Reproductive Health and Rights (ASTRA Network, #02996)*; *Center for Health and Gender Equity (CHANGE)*; *Center for Women's Global Leadership (CWGL)*; *Ford Foundation (#09858)*; *International Planned Parenthood Federation (IPPF, #14589)* (Western Hemisphere); *International Women's Health Coalition (IWHC)*; *Latin American and Caribbean Council of AIDS Service Organizations (LACCASO, #16272)*; *World Young Women's Christian Association (World YWCA, #21947)*.
NGO Relations Partner of: *Global Coalition on Women and AIDS (GCWA, #10297)*. Member of: *ATHENA Network (ATHENA, #03004)*. [2013/XM3426/y/**F**]

♦ International Aid Transparency Initiative (IATI) 11604

Initiative internationale pour la transparence de l'aide
Contact address not obtained. E-mail: info@iatistandard.org.
URL: https://iatistandard.org/

History 2008. Founded following the Accra High Level Forum on Aid Effectiveness. **Aims** Improve transparency of aid in order to increase its effectiveness in tackling *poverty*; bring together donor and developing countries, civil society organizations and other experts in aid information. **Structure** Technical Advisory Group (TAG); Steering Committee, comprising representatives from bilateral and multilateral donors, partner countries, civil society organizations and experts in aid information, including: *Development Gateway (#05056)* and *Transparency International (TI, #20223)*; Secretariat hosted by consortium of *UNDP (#20292)*, *United Nations Office for Project Services (UNOPS, #20602)*, Sweden, Ghana and Development Initiatives for Poverty Reduction. **Events** *Meeting* Montréal, QC (Canada) 2014.
Members Open to all donor organizations (bilateral, multilateral, foundations, CSOs). Members must agree to sign the IATI Accra Statement and endorse the Framework for Implementation. Donors/Signatories (37):
- *Adaptation Fund (AF, #00109)*;
- *African Development Bank (ADB, #00283)*;
- *Asian Development Bank (ADB, #01422)*;
- *Australian Aid (inactive)*;
- *Canadian International Development Agency (CIDA, inactive)*;
- CDC;
- *Department for International Development (DFID, inactive)*;
- Dutch Ministry of Foreign Affairs – Development Cooperation;
- *European Commission (EC, #06633)*;
- Federal Ministry for Economic Cooperation and Development of Germany;
- *Gavi – The Vaccine Alliance (Gavi, #10077)*;
- *Global Environment Facility (GEF, #10346)*;
- *Global Fund to Fight AIDS, Tuberculosis and Malaria (Global Fund, #10383)*;
- Government of Belgium;
- Government of the USA;
- *ILO (#11123)*;
- *Inter-American Development Bank (IDB, #11427)*;
- *International Bank for Reconstruction and Development (IBRD, #12317)* (World Bank);
- *International Fund for Agricultural Development (IFAD, #13692)*;
- *Irish Aid*;
- Ministry of Foreign Affairs of Denmark;
- Ministry of Foreign Affairs of Finland;
- *New Zealand Ministry of Foreign Affairs and Trade – New Zealand Aid Programme*;
- *Norwegian Agency for Development Cooperation (Norad)*;
- Spanish Ministry of Foreign Affairs and Cooperation;
- *Swedish International Development Cooperation Agency (Sida)*;
- *Swiss Agency for Development and Cooperation (SDC)*;
- *The William and Flora Hewlett Foundation*;
- *UNDP (#20292)*;
- *UNICEF (#20332)*;
- *United Nations Capital Development Fund (UNCDF, #20524)*;
- *United Nations Human Settlements Programme (UN-Habitat, #20572)*;
- *United Nations Office for Project Services (UNOPS, #20602)*;
- *United Nations Office for the Coordination of Humanitarian Affairs (OCHA, #20593)*;
- *United Nations Population Fund (UNFPA, #20612)*;
- *UN Women (#20724)*;
- *World Food Programme (WFP, #21510)*.

Also open to partner countries that endorse the initiative. Countries that have endorsed IATI (22):
Bangladesh, Burkina Faso, Colombia, Congo Brazzaville, Congo DR, Dominican Rep, Ghana, Honduras, Indonesia, Lebanon, Liberia, Madagascar, Malawi, Moldova, Montenegro, Nepal, Papua New Guinea, Rwanda, Sierra Leone, Syrian AR, Tanzania UR, Vietnam. [2022/XJ2493/y/**F**]

- ♦ **International AIED Society** International Artificial Intelligence in Education Society (#11672)

♦ International Aikido Federation (IAF) 11605

Fédération internationale d'aikido (FIA)
Chairman 4327 51st St, Boulder CO 80301, USA. E-mail: general.secretary@aikido-international.org.
URL: http://www.aikido-international.org/

History 1975. **Aims** Support and nurture the practise of Aikido; provide for international spread of Aikido as the practise of a moral, spiritual and physical discipline created by the founder, Morihei Ueshiba; promote the practise of Aikido and its instruction, in accordance with guidelines laid down by the Hombu. **Structure** General Assembly (every 4 years, during Congress); Senior Council; Directing Committee. **Languages** English, French, Japanese. **Staff** 15.00 FTE, voluntary. **Finance** Sources: members' dues. **Activities** Events/meetings. **Events** *General Assembly* Boulder, CO (USA) 2021, *Congress and General Assembly* Takasaki (Japan) 2016, *Congress and General Assembly* Tokyo (Japan) 2012, *Congress and general assembly* Tanabe (Japan) 2008, *Congress and general assembly / Congress* Tokyo (Japan) 2004.
Members National organizations (56) which have recognition from the Aikikai Hombu, in 56 countries and territories:
Argentina, Australia, Belgium, Brazil, Bulgaria, Chile, Colombia, Croatia, Czechia, Denmark, Egypt, England, Estonia, Finland, France, Germany, Greece, Hong Kong, Hungary, Indonesia, Ireland, Italy, Japan, Korea Rep, Kyrgyzstan, Lebanon, Lithuania, Luxembourg, Macau, Malaysia, Mexico, Monaco, Morocco, Netherlands, New Zealand, Norway, Paraguay, Philippines, Poland, Portugal, Romania, Russia, Scotland, Singapore, Slovakia, Slovenia, South Africa, Spain, Sweden, Switzerland, Taiwan, Thailand, Ukraine, Uruguay, USA, Venezuela.
NGO Relations Member of (3): *Alliance of Independent recognised Members of Sport (AIMS, #00690)*; *International World Games Association (IWGA, #15914)*; *Olympic Movement (#17719)*. Cooperates with (1): *International Testing Agency (ITA, #15678)*. Recognized by: *International Olympic Committee (IOC, #14408)*.
[2020.03.04/XD1536/**C**]

♦ International Airborne Geophysics Safety Association (IAGSA) 11606

Main Office 144 Harry MacKay Rd, Woodlawn, Ottawa ON K0A 3M0, Canada. T. +16138321646.
URL: http://www.iagsa.ca/

History Nov 1995. **Aims** Promote and enhance safety in the airborne geophysics *survey industry*. **Structure** Executive Committee; Technical Committee. [2016/XF3839/**F**]

♦ International Air Cadet Exchange Association (IACEA) 11607

SG 11210 Wascana Meadows, Regina SK S4V 2V5, Canada.
URL: http://www.iacea.com/

History Mid-1950s. Developed from proposal on exchanges at meeting, 11 Apr 1946, Montréal QC (Canada), of UK Air Training Corps (ATC) with Air Cadet League of Canada (ACLC). Plan extended to include Civil Air Patrol (CAP), USA, at ACLC Annual Meeting, Feb 1948, following contacts in 1947; subsequent exchanges included Sweden, then Norway, Netherlands and Denmark, and then up to 19 countries including some in South America. Former names and other names: *IACE* – alias. **Aims** Foster international understanding, goodwill and friendship among *young people* who have an interest in *aviation*. **Structure** Planning Conference (annual); Standing Committee. **Languages** English. **Staff** 4.00 FTE, voluntary. **Finance** Sources: members' dues. **Activities** Events/meetings. **Events** *Annual Planning Conference* USA 2023, *Annual Planning Conference* UK 2022, *Annual Planning Conference* USA 2021, *Annual Planning Conference* Bruges (Belgium) 2020, *Annual Planning Conference* Jiaozhou (China) / Rizhao (China) / Yantai (China) / Qingdao (China) 2019. **Publications** *IACEA Handbook* (annual).
Members National air cadet or aviation/aeronautical organizations in 16 countries and territories:
Australia, Belgium, Canada, China, France, Germany, Hong Kong, Japan, Korea Rep, Netherlands, New Zealand, Philippines, Switzerland, Türkiye, UK, USA. [2022.02.03/XD7287/**C**]

♦ The International Air Cargo Association (TIACA) 11608

Dir-Gen PO Box 661510, Miami FL 33266-1510, USA. T. +17862657011. Fax +17862657012. E-mail: secretariat@tiaca.org – secgen@tiaca.org.
URL: https://tiaca.org/

History 1990. Former names and other names: *International Air Cargo Forum Association* – former. Registration: Start date: 1994, Cayman Is; Start date: 2004, USA. **Aims** Act as the voice of the air logistics industry; advance its role in world trade; improve industry cooperation and innovation; provide leadership in expanding global commerce through distribution by air; share knowledge and enhance quality and efficiency; develop vehicles for education and trade. **Structure** Board of Directors. Committees. **Languages** English. **Staff** 6.00 FTE, paid. **Finance** Sources: meeting proceeds; members' dues. **Activities** Events/meetings; politics/policy/regulatory; training/education. **Events** *International Air Cargo Forum* Miami, FL (USA) 2022, *International Air Cargo Forum* Miami, FL (USA) 2020, *International Air Cargo Forum* Toronto, ON (Canada) 2018, *International Air Cargo Forum* Paris (France) 2016, *Biennial Forum / ACF* Seoul (Korea Rep) 2014. **Publications** *TIACA Times* – newsletter; *TIACA Weekly Regulatory Update*.
Members All major segments of the air cargo and logistics industry air and surface carriers, freight forwarders, integrators, shippers, vendors, manufacturers, airports, countries, financial institutions, consultants and associations, mainly in the USA. Trustees; Corporate; Affiliate, in 52 countries and territories:
Armenia, Australia, Austria, Azerbaijan, Bangladesh, Belgium, Canada, China, Czechia, Denmark, Egypt, Finland, France, Germany, Greece, Hong Kong, Hungary, Iceland, India, Ireland, Italy, Jordan, Kazakhstan, Kenya, Korea DPR, Korea Rep, Kuwait, Luxembourg, Malaysia, Mexico, Nepal, Netherlands, Norway, Pakistan, Russia, Saudi Arabia, South Africa, Spain, Sri Lanka, Sweden, Switzerland, Taiwan, Thailand, Trinidad-Tobago, Türkiye, UK, Ukraine, United Arab Emirates, USA, Uzbekistan, Yemen, Zimbabwe.
Organizations in 12 countries and territories:
Australia, Canada, Hong Kong, Malaysia, Netherlands, Norway, Spain, Switzerland, Thailand, UK, United Arab Emirates, USA.
Consultative Status Consultative status granted from: *UNCTAD (#20285)* (Special Category). **IGO Relations** Memorandum of Understanding with (1): *World Customs Organization (WCO, #21350)*. [2022/XD5384/**C**]

♦ International Air Cargo Forum Association / see The International Air Cargo Association (#11608)
♦ International Air Carrier Association / see Airlines International Representation in Europe (#00608)
♦ International Airline Navigators Council (inactive)

♦ International Airline Passengers Association (IAPA) 11609

UK Office PO Box 816, Haywards Heath, RH16 9LS, UK. T. +442088653272. Fax +442086810234. E-mail: info.london@iapa.com.
Registered Address Cutlers Exchange, 123 Houndsditch, London, EC3A 7BU, UK.
URL: http://www.iapa.com/

History 1960, New York NY (USA), as Airways Club. European office founded in 1977; Hong Kong office in 1982, when current title was adopted. Registered in accordance to UK law: 2577549. **Aims** Represent the interests of frequent air travelers by providing them with special discounts on items such as hotel accommodation, car rental and insurance, in addition to protecting and promoting their rights as airline passengers. **Structure** Offices: London (UK); Dallas TX (USA); Hong Kong. **Languages** Arabic, Dutch, English, Finnish, French, German, Italian, Norwegian, Spanish, Swedish. **Finance** Members' dues. **Activities** Negotiates reduced rates with hotels and car rental companies. Offers passenger insurance. Luggage retrieval service. Specialist team advises on aspects of safety, service and pricing. **Publications** *IAPA World* (4 a year) – newsletter. Directory of hotels. **Members** Individual members (over 400,000). Membership countries not specified. **NGO Relations** Member of: *World-Wide Business Centres Network (no recent information)*. [2017/XD6960/**E**]

♦ International Airlines Technical Pool (IATP) 11610

Headquarters 17 rue Jean Pierre Sauvage, L-2514 Luxembourg, Luxembourg. T. +352226684184. Fax +352226684185. E-mail: info@iatp.com.
URL: https://www.iatp.com/

History 1948. Established on an informal basis. Organized as the 'Consolidated Pool', 1960. Merged with *North American Airlines Technical Pool (NAATP)*, 1977. **Aims** Provide excellent technical performance in aircraft operations. **Structure** Management Committee. **Activities** Events/meetings; knowledge management/information dissemination; networking/liaising. **Events** *Conference* Copenhagen (Denmark) 2021, *Conference* Luxembourg (Luxembourg) 2021, *Conference* Luxembourg (Luxembourg) 2020, *Conference* Nashville, TN (USA) 2020, *Conference* Rome (Italy) 2019. **Members** Full: airlines; Associate: service providers, spare providers, manufacturers and MROs. Membership countries not specified. [2020.10.13/XF3846/**F**]

♦ International Airlines Travel Agent Network (internationally oriented national body)

♦ International Airline Training Fund (IATF) 11611

Secretariat Route de l'Aéroport 33, PO Box 416, 1215 Geneva 15, Switzerland. T. +41227702525. Fax +41227983553. E-mail: iatf@iata.org.
Montréal Office PO Box 113, Montréal QC H4Z 1M1, Canada. T. +15148740202. Fax +15148749632.
URL: http://www.iata.org/about/Pages/iatf.aspx

History 1984, as two separate not-for-profit organizations, one in Switzerland, and the other in the State of Maryland (USA), the concept of establishing IATF having been approved, Nov 1982, by a resolution of 38th Annual General Meeting of *International Air Transport Association (IATA, #11614)*. IATF started operations in 1985. **Aims** Provide *scholarships* to staff of developing nations airlines to enable them to attend training courses run by IATA or at well established airline training centres. **Structure** Council (Switzerland), consisting of President, Vice-President, 5 members, Secretary and Treasurer. Board of Directors (USA), comprising President, Vice-President, 5 members, Secretary and Treasurer. **Finance** Financed by cash and in-kind donations from companies, organizations and individuals directly or indirectly connected with commercial aviation. Scholarship Expenditure Budget (annual): US$ 212,130. **Activities** During the last 10 years IATA has granted 900 scholarships both cash and in-kind worth US$ 1.4 million. **Events** *Biennial international waters conference* Dubrovnik (Croatia) 2011.
Members Individuals in 7 countries:
Canada, France, India, Ireland, South Africa, Switzerland, USA. [2018/XF2235/fv/**F**]

♦ International Airport Watch Association (unconfirmed)

♦ International Air Rail Organization (IARO) 11612

Admin Dir Ste 3 – Charter House, 26 Claremont Road, Surbiton, KT6 4QZ, UK. T. +442083900000. Fax +448707620434.
URL: http://www.iaro.com/

History Feb 1997. Registration: Charity Commission, England and Wales; EU Transparency Register, No/ID: 81881203322-94. **Aims** Promote quality practice and encourage innovative ideas. **Structure** General Meeting (annual). Board. **Languages** English. **Staff** 2.50 FTE, paid. **Finance** Members' subscriptions. **Activities** Organizes workshops and seminars. Produces research and research reports. Task Forces (4): Airport gateway hubs; Integrated interface planning; Pictograms, signage and intermodal information; Through ticketing. **Events** *Rail links to airport cities* Manchester (UK) 2015, *Extending rail links at a growing airport* Milan (Italy) 2015, *Effect of EU on air-rail links* Brussels (Belgium) 2014, *Air-rail links in the planning stage* London (UK) 2014, *Which air-rail service – metro, express or commuter?* Stockholm (Sweden) 2014. **Publications** *Air Rail Links* – guide; *IARO Express*. Reports.
Members Organizations in 15 countries and territories:
Belgium, Canada, France, Germany, Hong Kong, Italy, Malaysia, Netherlands, Norway, Russia, Spain, Sweden, Switzerland, UK, USA. [2021/XD7061/**D**]

♦ International Air Safety Association (inactive)
♦ International Air Services Transit Agreement (1944 treaty)

♦ International Air and Shipping Association (IASA) 11613

Gen Manager Badgemore Place, Badgemore House, Henley-on-Thames, RG9 4NR, UK. T. +441491412708.
URL: http://www.iasa.net/

Structure General Assembly. Member Directors (5). **Languages** English. **Staff** 1.00 FTE, paid. **Finance** Finances held at Companies House UK (non-profit). **Events** *General Assembly* Baku (Azerbaijan) 2019, *General Assembly* Shanghai (China) 2018, *General Assembly* Madrid (Spain) 2017, *General Assembly* Bali (Indonesia) 2016, *General Assembly* Dubai (United Arab Emirates) 2015. **Publications** *Subscript to ACN*. **Members** Freight forwarders in countries worldwide. Membership countries not specified. [2017/XF4190/**F**]

♦ International Air Transport Agreement (1944 treaty)

♦ International Air Transport Association (IATA) 11614

Association du transport aérien international – Asociación de Transporte Aéreo Internacional
Dir-Gen IATA Executive Office – IATA Centre, 33 Route de l'Aéroport, PO Box 416 – 15 Airport, 1215 Geneva, Switzerland. T. +41227702525. Fax +41227983553. E-mail: corpcomms@iata.org.
Head Office 800 Place Victoria, PO Box 113, Montréal QC H4Z 1M1, Canada. T. +15148740202. Fax +15148749632.
URL: http://www.iata.org/

History 19 Apr 1945, Havana (Cuba). Founded following preliminary meetings of airline operators attached to national delegations at International Civil Aviation Conference, 1944, Chicago IL (USA).
Successor in function to *International Air Traffic Association – Association internationale du trafic aérien*, set up 28 Aug 1919, The Hague (Netherlands).
Legal status by Act of Canadian Parliament, first session, 20th Parliament, 9 Sep 1945, with Royal Assent, 18 Dec 1945.
Certain functions, notably those exercised by IATA Traffic Conferences, are stipulated in bilateral air transport agreements between many states.
Originally, any airline which became an Active Member automatically took part in Traffic Conferences, which met regularly to coordinate international tariffs and establish related conditions and procedures. From 1978, the system was restructured to provide increased flexibility for members, such that all members are involved in trade association (non-tariff) activities but participation in coordination of international fares and rates (tariff coordination) is optional. Registration: EU Transparency Register, No/ID: 1805107590-28; Canada.
Aims Represent, lead and serve the *airline industry*; working together to shape the future growth of a safe, secure and sustainable air transport industry that connects and enriches our world; assist the industry to achieve adequate levels of profitability; provide high quality, value for money, industry-required products and services that meet the needs of the customer; develop cost-effective, environmentally-friendly standards and procedures to facilitate operation of international air transport; identify and articulate common industry positions and support the resolution of key industry issues; provide a working environment which attracts, retains and develops committed employees. **Structure** Annual General Meeting; Board of Governors; Chair Committee acts as Steering Group; Strategy and Policy COmmission (SPC); Nominating Committee; Advisory Councils; Secretariat, headed by Director General; 5 Regional Offices. **Languages** English, French, Spanish. **Staff** 1400.00 FTE, paid. **Finance** Expenses covered by member companies' dues (within certain limits, based on proportion of international scheduled traffic carried), account for about 20% of budget, the remainder deriving from charges for services rendered.
Activities Services 4 groups interested in smooth operation of the world transport system:
- *'Airlines'* – Exploits opportunities and solves problems in joint ways beyond the resources of a single company. Individual networks are linked into a worldwide system, despite differences in languages, currencies, laws and national customs.
- *'Governments'* – Provides experience and expertise in developing industry working standards, allowing governments to dispense with the effort and expense involved in bilateral negotiations.
- *'Third Parties'* – Serves as a collective link between third parties (such as travel and cargo agents and equipment and systems suppliers) and the airlines: provides neutrally applied agency service standards and professional skills for passenger and cargo agents to make representations to the industry; enables equipment manufacturers and others to join airline meetings which define the way air transport is conducted.
- *'General Public'* – By simplifying the travel and shipping process, contributes to cheaper tickets and shipping costs by helping control airline costs and enables individual passengers to reserve a complex journey involving several countries and airlines through one transaction.

'Industry Viability and Recognition':
- /Taxation/ – publishes worldwide taxes on aviation, makes representations to governments where necessary and also fights some taxes in the courts.
- /User charges/ – aims to ensure that airlines are charged only for the services they require and use and that charges are cost-related.
- /Fuel trade/ – directs efforts at monitoring jet fuel prices worldwide and securing reductions.
- /Currency/ – organizes representations or missions to countries in which funds are blocked.

'Safety and Security' – Through technical offices.
- /Flight operations/ – Shares the experience of individual airlines with the whole industry. Works on aircraft minimum separation standards, collision avoidance, precision landing aids and ground obstacle avoidance. Emphasizes human factors in aviation through annual conferences and data dissemination.
- /Avionics/ – Fosters developments leading to enhanced safety and reduced costs, aiming to achieve worldwide implementation of ICAO's *Future Air Navigation System (FANS)*, an automated concept of communications, navigation, surveillance/air traffic management (CNS/ATM) using already existing geostationary satellites and airborne avionics packages.
- /Security/ – Security staff provide industry input to national and international governmental security standards and their implementation. Makes airport security surveys on request.

'Industry Support':
- /Infrastructure/ – Works through the technical department, through membership of the Air Transport Action Group and in close consultation with Eurocontrol and the European Civil Aviation Conference, to avoid congestion due to inadequacies in airport terminals, taxi-ways, runways, access roads, Air Traffic Control (ATC) systems and trained personnel. In the long-term, aims to provide adequate ATC supply worldwide through FANS. Current emphasis is on the Asia/Pacific region.
- /Environment/ – Provides a clearinghouse for related legislation, monitors international debate and promotes common industry positions, including support for coordinated phasing out of old aircraft types and noise-compatible land-use planning.
- /Legal support/ – Working with member airlines to provide a radically reformed system of compensation for passenger death or injury within the framework of the Warsaw Convention.
- /Consumer dialogue/ – Maintains contact with international consumer groups on such questions as safety, security, taxation, denied boarding and air transport congestion.

'Standards and Procedures':
- /Traffic services/ – *Multilateral Interline Traffic Agreements (MITA)*, signed by nearly 300 airlines, are the basis for airlines' interline network, in which each other's tickets and waybills are accepted on a reciprocal basis in association with SITA and ARINC.
- /Passenger and cargo services conference resolutions/ – These prescribe a variety of standard formats and technical specifications for tickets and waybills.
- /Passenger Services/ – IATA Partnership Programmes and Registered Suppliers and Industry Associates Programme aim to automate systems so as to speed up the process at airport terminals and onto flights at lower cost, while maintaining security and border formality requirements. Other concerns include standards for carrying disabled passengers, live animals and dangerous goods, and the handling of checked baggage – the latter including development with SITA of the 'BAHAMAS' baggage tracing system.
- /Scheduling/ – Offers a forum allowing voluntary agreement on allocation of worldwide airport capacity.
- /Facilitation/ – Works to reduce 'red tape' in movement of goods and people through airports.
- /Fraud prevention/ – Trains ticket processors to recognize invalid travel documents; identifies black-listed tickets through 'TICKETS' joint automated service with *Aeronautical Radio Inc (ARINC)*.

'Products and Services':
- /IATA Currency Clearance Service (ICCS)/ – Offsets equal and opposite currency flows. *Interline Data Exchange Centre (IDEC)* – Allows airlines to exchange ticket and waybill data.
- /Revenue Accounting/ – Training courses.
- /IATA Procuration Service (IPS)/ – Allocates revenue to individual carriers providing part of a transport service.
- /Insurance services/ – Uses cooperative insurance schemes to minimize cost to the airline industry.
- /IATA Yield Management Service (IYMS)/ – Affords access to state-of-the-art revenue management technology.
- /Tariff coordination/ – Since 1946, acts as a forum for tariff negotiation among governments.

– /Agency programmes/ – Accreditation of travel and cargo agents, awarding of diplomas following IATA/UFTAA (passenger) or IATA/FIATA (cargo) training course.
– /Billing and Settlement Plans/ and /Cargo Account Settlement Systems/ – Transfer of revenue to appropriate individual agents.
– /Travel Industry Designator Service (TIDS)/ – Unique numeric coding for reservation and commission tracking. Other services include: Travel Agent card; computer-based training; human resource development through training programme for staff from less developed nations; management information service; market and economic analysis, traffic and airport forecasting, data collection development; seminars and symposia; consultancy services.

Events *Slot Conference* 2023, *Slot Conference* 2023, *IATA Safety Conference* Dubai (United Arab Emirates) 2022, *IATA World Passenger Symposium (WPS)* Manama (Bahrain) 2022, *Slot Conference* Melbourne, VIC (Australia) 2022. **Publications** *Airlines* (6 a year); *World Air Transport Statistics* (annual). *Dangerous Goods Regulations*. Annual Review; airline operating statistics; airport and en route charges; worldwide taxes on aviation; resolutions. Information Services: Producing an environmental databank.

Members Open to any operating company licensed to provide scheduled air service by a government eligible for membership of ICAO. All members are involved in Trade Association (non-tariff) activities, with optional participation in coordination of international fares and rates. Active: airlines engaged directly in international operations (trade association and tariff coordination); airlines (about 290) in 124 countries and territories.
Albania, Algeria, Angola, Antigua-Barbuda, Argentina, Armenia, Australia, Austria, Azerbaijan, Bahamas, Bahrain, Bangladesh, Belarus, Belgium, Bolivia, Botswana, Brazil, Brunei Darussalam, Bulgaria, Burkina Faso, Cambodia, Cameroon, Canada, Cape Verde, Cayman Is, Chile, China, Colombia, Congo DR, Costa Rica, Croatia, Cuba, Cyprus, Czechia, Ecuador, Egypt, El Salvador, Ethiopia, Faeroe Is, Fiji, Finland, France, Georgia, Germany, Ghana, Greece, Guadeloupe, Hong Kong, Iceland, India, Indonesia, Iran Islamic Rep, Ireland, Israel, Italy, Japan, Jordan, Kazakhstan, Kenya, Korea DPR, Kuwait, Laos, Latvia, Lebanon, Luxembourg, Macau, Madagascar, Malaysia, Malta, Mauritania, Mexico, Moldova, Mongolia, Montenegro, Morocco, Mozambique, Myanmar, Namibia, Netherlands, New Caledonia, New Zealand, Nigeria, Norway, Oman, Pakistan, Panama, Papua New Guinea, Paraguay, Peru, Philippines, Poland, Polynesia Fr, Portugal, Qatar, Réunion, Romania, Russia, Rwanda, Saudi Arabia, Serbia, Seychelles, Singapore, Solomon Is, South Africa, Spain, Sri Lanka, Suriname, Sweden, Switzerland, Syrian AR, Taiwan, Tajikistan, Tanzania UR, Thailand, Trinidad-Tobago, Tunisia, Türkiye, UK, Ukraine, United Arab Emirates, USA, Uzbekistan, Vanuatu, Vietnam.
Included in the above, 4 airlines listed in this Yearbook:
Air Baltic Corporation (#00600); *Gulf Air (#10821)*; *Scandinavian Airlines System (SAS, #19069)*; *Trans Mediterranean Airways (TMA, no recent information)*.
Associate: domestic airlines (15) in 14 countries and territories:
Algeria, Argentina, Australia, Brazil, China, Germany, Italy, Mexico, Nigeria, Polynesia Fr, Portugal, South Africa, USA, Zambia.

Consultative Status Consultative status granted from: *UNCTAD (#20285)* (Special Category); *WHO (#20950)* (Official Relations); *International Atomic Energy Agency (IAEA, #12294)*; *World Intellectual Property Organization (WIPO, #21593)* (Permanent Observer Status). **IGO Relations** Working relations with: *International Telecommunication Union (ITU, #15673)*. Affiliate member of: *World Tourism Organization (UNWTO, #21861)*. Memorandum of Understanding signed with: *World Customs Organization (WCO, #21350)*. Accredited by: *United Nations Framework Convention on Climate Change – Secretariat (UNFCCC, #20564)*; *United Nations Office at Vienna (UNOV, #20604)*. Observer Status granted by: *Committee on the Peaceful Uses of Outer Space (COPUOS, #04277)*. **NGO Relations** Member of: *Bureau international des containers et du transport intermodal (BIC, #03364)*. In liaison with technical committees of: *International Organization for Standardization (ISO, #14473)*. Close cooperation with: *Fédération internationale des associations de transitaires et assimilés (FIATA, #09610)*; *United Federation of Travel Agents' Associations (UFTAA, #20509)*. Instrumental in setting up: *International Industry Working Group (IIWG, #13841)*. [2022.02.03/XB1149/y/**B**]

♦ International Airway Management Society (unconfirmed)

♦ International Alert 11615

CEO Offley Works, 1 Pickle Mews, Oval, London, SW9 0FJ, UK. T. +442076276800. Fax +442076276900. E-mail: info@international-alert.org.
URL: http://www.international-alert.org/

History 1986. Founded as a development and human rights group. Took over activities of *Peaceworkers UK (inactive)*, 1 Sep 2006. Registration: Charity Commission, No/ID: 327553, England and Wales; EU Transparency Register, No/ID: 135314647826-36, Start date: 5 Oct 2022. **Aims** Work with people directly affected by conflict to find peaceful solutions; shape policies and practices to support peace; collaborate with those striving for peace to strengthen impact. **Structure** Board of Trustees; Senior Management Team. **Languages** Arabic, English, French, Russian. **Staff** 200.00 FTE, paid. **Finance** Sources: donations; government support; international organizations; private foundations. **Activities** Events/meetings. Active in: Transcaucasia. **Events** *Latin American regional conference* 1995, *Seminar on conflict in the post-soviet republics* London (UK) 1995, *Seminar on European NGOs interested in conflict prevention* Oslo (Norway) 1995, *Vers un consortium européen pour la prévention des conflits* Oslo (Norway) 1995, *Martin Ennals Memorial symposium on self-determination* Saskatoon, SK (Canada) 1993. **Publications** Research reports; position papers; policy briefs; background papers. **Members** Not a membership organization. **Consultative Status** Consultative status granted from: *African Commission on Human and Peoples' Rights (ACHPR, #00255)* (Observer); *ECOSOC (#05331)* (Special). **NGO Relations** Member of (1): *Environmental Peacebuilding Association (EnPAx, #05509)*. [2022/XF1978/**F**]

♦ International Alexander Lernet-Holenia Society 11616

Internationale Alexander Lernet-Holenia Gesellschaft
Contact c/o Österreichische Gesellschaft für Literatur, Herrengasse 5, 1010 Vienna, Austria. T. +4315338159. E-mail: office@ogl.at.
Contact Dept of Languages and Cultures – Univ of Colorado, Colorado Springs CO 80933, USA. T. +17192553562. E-mail: belvederefilm@yahoo.com.
URL: http://www.lernet-holenia.com/

History 1998, Vienna (Austria). **Aims** Promote and study of the work of Austrian *author* Alexander Lernet-Holenia. **Structure** Executive Board, comprising President, 2 Vice-Presidents and 3 members. International Advisory Board. **Languages** English, French, German, Spanish. **Finance** Members' dues. **Activities** Sponsors and cosponsors international conferences, dramatic research and literary symposia, and texts dealing with the author and his/her work. **Events** *Meeting on literature of the postwar era* Dortmund (Germany) 2003.
Members Full in 9 countries:
Austria, France, Germany, Italy, Poland, Romania, Russia, UK, USA. [2018/XE4142/**E**]

♦ International Alfred Schutz Circle for Phenomenology and Interpretive Social Science (Schutz Circle) 11617

Contact Uni Konstanz, Postfach 35, 78475 Konstanz, Germany. E-mail: schutzcircle@uni-konstanz.de.
URL: http://www.schutzcircle.org/

History 2011, New York, NY (USA). Proposed Oct 2011; founding meeting held May 2012, New York NY (USA). Current constitution adopted May 2016, Tokyo (Japan). **Aims** Promote a fruitful and free exchange of ideas and research topics within the thematic and theoretical horizon of the Schutzian paradigm; encourage convergent tendencies with this school of thought. **Structure** General Assembly; Executive Committee. **Languages** English. **Staff** 5.00 FTE, voluntary. **Finance** Members' dues. **Activities** Events/meetings; awards/prizes/competitions. **Events** *Conference* St Louis, MO (USA) 2021, *Conference* St Louis, MO (USA) 2020, *Knowledge, nescience and the (new) media* Konstanz (Germany) 2018, *The symbolic construction of reality* Tokyo (Japan) 2016, *Conference* Buenos Aires (Argentina) 2014. **Publications** *Schutzian Research* – journal.
Members Full in 13 countries:
Argentina, Austria, Brazil, Czechia, Finland, France, Germany, Hungary, Italy, Japan, Mexico, Switzerland, USA. [2019.03.01/XM7514/**E**]

♦ International Allelopathy Society (IAS) 11618

Pres c/o IMBE, Aix-Marseille Univ, 421 av Escadrille Normandie Niémen, 13397 Marseille, France. E-mail: mreigosa@uvigo.es.
URL: http://allelopathy-society.osupytheas.fr/

History 5 Sep 1994, Delhi (India). **Aims** Provide a scientific organization for scientists working in allelopathy and related disciplines worldwide, strengthen the bonds between them and promote exchange of ideas, knowledge and experience related to allelopathic science; help apply allelopathic research in practice to increase crop productivity, develop sustainable agriculture by natural or *organic* farming and reduce environmental pollution; encourage basic/fundamental research in understanding the mechanisms of allelopathy with *ecological* relevance; encourage national and international research projects and research teams and facilitate exchange of scientists between countries. **Structure** General Meeting (every 3 years). Executive Council (meets at least every 3 years) comprising President, Immediate Past President, President-Elect, Vice-Presidents (6, one each from Africa, Asia, Australia, Europe, North America, South America), Programme Vice-President, Secretary, Treasurer and Editor. Country Coordinators. **Languages** English. **Staff** None. **Finance** Sources: donations; grants; members' dues; sale of publications. **Activities** Conducts research on mechanisms involving plant-plant, plant-microorganism, plant-virus, plant-insect and plant-soil-plant interactions. Research areas include study of biological functions of secondary metabolizes, their significance in biological control of growth individually or synergistically, their importance at all levels of biological organization, their evolutionary origin and their application to needs of the international community of allelopathic scientists, agricultural scientists, plant physiologists, weed scientists, ecologists, environmentalists, microbiologists, plant pathologists, entomologists, natural products chemists/biochemists/biologists, workers in other disciplines and farmers. Offers awards; provides financial grants to university students for projects on allelopathy, especially in developing countries. Organizes: International Congress on Allelopathy; European Allelopathy Symposium; other congresses; workshops. **Events** *World Congress* Canberra, ACT (Australia) 2021, *World Congress* Canberra, ACT (Australia) 2020, *World Congress* Marseille (France) 2017, *World Congress* Vigo (Spain) 2014, *World congress* Guangzhou (China) 2011. **Publications** *IAS Newsletter* (4 a year); *International Allelopathy Journal*; *Triennial Directory of Members*. Books; bulletins; monographs.
Members Regular; Life; Emeritus; Student; Honorary; Society; Corporate. Members in 51 countries and territories:
Algeria, Argentina, Australia, Austria, Bolivia, Brazil, Bulgaria, Canada, Chile, China, Colombia, Costa Rica, Cuba, Czechia, Egypt, Finland, France, Germany, Ghana, Hungary, India, Iran Islamic Rep, Ireland, Israel, Japan, Jordan, Kenya, Korea Rep, Lesotho, Malaysia, Mauritius, Mexico, Moldova, Nepal, Pakistan, Philippines, Poland, Puerto Rico, Russia, South Africa, Spain, Taiwan, Thailand, Trinidad-Tobago, Tunisia, Türkiye, UK, Ukraine, Uruguay, USA, Uzbekistan. [2020/XC0089/**C**]

♦ International Alliance of Academies of Childhood Disability (IAACD) 11619

Contact EACD, c/o Neuropediatrics, Astrid Lindgren's Hosp, SE-171 76 Stockholm, Sweden. T. +46708730830.
Contact AACPDM, c/o Kluge Children's Rehabilitation Center, 2270 Ivy Road (250 West), Charlottesville VA 22903, USA. T. +14349240245. E-mail: rds8z@virginia.edu.
URL: https://www.ausacpdm.org.au/about/iaacd/

History Set up when Memorandum of Understanding was signed by American Academy of Cerebral Palsy and Developmental Medicine (AACPDM), *Australasian Academy of Cerebral Palsy and Developmental Medicine (AusACPDM)* and *European Academy of Childhood Disability (EACD, #05783)*. Memorandum effective Dec 2016. **Aims** Improve the health and well-being of children and youth with disabilities around the globe; enhance local multidisciplinary professional capacity and expertise through international collaboration of academies of childhood disability. **Structure** Steering Group. **Activities** Events/meetings; financial and/or material support; networking/liaising; standards/guidelines. **Events** *Meeting* Melbourne, VIC (Australia) 2022, *Meeting* Anaheim, CA (USA) 2019, *Meeting* Stockholm (Sweden) 2016.
Members Institutions (3):
American Academy of Cerebral Palsy and Development Medicine (AACPDM); *Australasian Academy of Cerebral Palsy and Developmental Medicine (AusACPDM)*; *European Academy of Childhood Disability (EACD, #05783)*. [2018/XM4234/y/**C**]

♦ International Alliance Against Cancers of the Skin 11620

Pres c/o Skin Cancer Foundation, 149 Madison Avenue, Ste 901, New York NY 10016, USA. E-mail: info@skincancer.org.
URL: http://www.skincancer.org/international/international-alliance

Aims Urge public health officials throughout the world to place skin cancer education high on the agenda; be a catalyst for skin cancer education partnerships with the media, public health organizations and educators. **Activities** Events/meetings.
Members Full in 26 countries:
Argentina, Austria, Belgium, Brazil, Canada, Colombia, Costa Rica, Ecuador, France, Germany, Greece, Ireland, Israel, Italy, Jordan, Kuwait, Mexico, Netherlands, Philippines, Portugal, Romania, Spain, Switzerland, Thailand, UK, USA. [2016.06.01/XM4277/**C**]

♦ International Alliance of ALS/MND Associations 11621

Exec Dir c/o ALS Association, 1275 K St NW, Washington DC 20005, USA. E-mail: alliance@als-mnd.org.
Registered Address 10-15 Notre Dame Mews, Northampton, NN1 2BG, UK. T. +441604611821. Fax +441604624726.
URL: http://www.alsmndalliance.org/

History Founded Nov 1992, following the 3rd annual Research Symposium, Solihull (UK). Registration: Charity Commission, No/ID: 1079504, Start date: 23 Feb 2000, England and Wales. **Aims** Increase awareness of Amyotrophic Lateral Sclerosis (ALS)/Moto Neuron Disease (MND) worldwide; exchange and disseminate information; improve the quality of care; stimulate and support research; provide an international identity. **Structure** Board of Directors; Secretariat. **Languages** English. **Staff** 1.00 FTE, paid. **Finance** Members' dues, based on income. Other sources: sponsorship funds for annual events; designated donor funds; fundraising; donations. **Activities** Awards and grants: Forbes Norris Award; Humanitarian Award; Alliance Support Grant. Programmes: Partnership Programme; recognition of Global ALS/MND Day; Patient's Rights Campaign; March of Faces. Organizes Annual Alliance Meeting, Allied Professionals Forum and Ask the Experts events (in conjunction with Symposium). **Events** *International Symposium on ALS/MND* Basel (Switzerland) 2023, *International Symposium on ALS/MND* Washington, DC (USA) 2022, *International Symposium on ALS/MND* Washington, DC (USA) 2021, *International Symposium on ALS/MND* Montréal, QC (Canada) 2020, *International Symposium on ALS/MND* Perth, WA (Australia) 2019. **Publications** *Information Update* (4 a year); *Directory of Associations for People with ALS/MND* (regular). Policy documents and resources.
Members National organizations (40) in 29 countries:
Australia, Belgium, Brazil, Canada, Colombia, Croatia, Denmark, Finland, France, Germany, Iceland, Ireland, Israel, Italy, Japan, Mexico, Moldova, Netherlands, New Zealand, Poland, Serbia, Slovenia, South Africa, Spain, Switzerland, Taiwan, Türkiye, UK, USA.
Associated members in 6 countries and territories:
Australia, Brazil, Japan, Netherlands, Sweden, USA. [2022/XC0046/**C**]

♦ International Alliance of Assistive Technology Organizations / see Global Alliance of Assistive Technology Organizations (#10185)
♦ The International Alliance: An Association of Executive and Professional Women / see The International Alliance for Women (#11640)
♦ International Alliance – Association of Former Students of the Cité internationale universitaire de Paris (#00693)
♦ International Alliance of Associations and Movements 5 a day / see Global Alliance to Promote Fruits and Vegetable Consumption "5 a day" (#10221)

♦ International Alliance for Biological Standardization (IABS) 11622

Main Office Rue Mina-Audemars 3, 1204 Geneva, Switzerland. E-mail: iabs@iabs.org.
Dir 15 rue de la Balme, 69003 Lyon, France. T. +33426021810. Fax +33688071824.
URL: http://www.iabs.org/

History 1955, Lyon (France). Founded by a group of independent experts in biologicals, as a commission of *International Union of Microbiological Societies (IUMS, #15794)*. A joint committee of *IUMS Division of Bacteriology and Applied Microbiology (BAM, see: #15794)* and *IUMS Division of Virology (see: #15794)*. Originally also a committee of *IUMS Division of Mycology (see: #15794)*. Former names and other names: *International Association for Biologicals (IABS)* – former (1955); *International Association of Biological Standardization (IABS)* – former; *Association internationale de standardization biologique (AISB)* – former. Registration: No/ID: 080.018.022, Switzerland. **Aims** Promote scientific and medical advancement of biologicals through partnership with those involved in research, development, production and regulation of human and veterinary biological *products*; provide a forum to reach consensus on topics important to medical scientists and other *health care* professionals; create a dynamic interface among leaders in clinical and basic research, biological product development, public health, manufacturing and regulation; educate health care professionals on relevant topics; promote these aims among workers on scientific issues in the *biopharmaceutical* industry,

public health organizations, regulatory bodies, academic medicine and research; ensure approval of new biological products which are safe and effective. **Structure** General Assembly (every 2 years). Board of 15 members. Officers: President; Vice-President; Secretary; Scientific Committee Chairman; Editorial Committee Chairman; Treasurer. **Languages** English. **Staff** 2.00 FTE, paid. **Finance** Members' dues: Swiss Fr 188 (including publication subscription) or Swiss Fr 50 (without publication). **Activities** Events/meetings. **Events** *Conference* Munich (Germany) 2021, *Conference* Ottawa, ON (Canada) 2021, *Statistics Workshop* Geneva (Switzerland) 2020, *Meeting* Lyon (France) 2020, *Cell Therapy Conference* Tokyo (Japan) 2020. **Publications** *Biologicals* (6 a year); *Developments in Biologicals*; *IABS Newsletter*.
Members Individual; collective (institutes, laboratories or other organizations). Members (about 450) in 37 countries and territories:
Algeria, Argentina, Australia, Austria, Belgium, Brazil, Canada, China, Croatia, Cuba, Czechia, Denmark, Finland, France, Germany, Hungary, India, Indonesia, Iran Islamic Rep, Italy, Japan, Netherlands, New Zealand, Nigeria, Norway, Peru, Romania, Russia, Singapore, South Africa, Spain, Sweden, Switzerland, Taiwan, Tanzania UR, UK, USA.
Consultative Status Consultative status granted from: *WHO (#20950)* (Official Relations). **NGO Relations** Member of: *Developing Countries Vaccine Manufacturers Network (DCVMN, #05052)*. [2022/XC4498/C]

♦ International Alliance of Carer Organizations (IACO) 11623
Exec Advisor c/o Natl Alliance for Caregiving, 4720 Montgomery Lane, Ste 205, Bethesda MD 20814, USA. T. +13017188444.
URL: http://www.internationalcarers.org/
History 2012. Inaugural meeting, London (UK). **Aims** Investigate and address issues of international family caregiving so as to increase public awareness of the needs of the *family* caregiver on a global scale; provide research, awareness and education regarding family carers on a global scale. **Structure** General Assembly; Governing Board; Special Advisors; Active Committees. **Languages** English. **Staff** 6.00 FTE, paid. **Finance** Sources: grants; members' dues. **Activities** Awareness raising; events/meetings; research/documentation; training/education. **Publications** Guides; studies.
Members Full in 15 countries and territories:
Australia, Canada, Denmark, Finland, France, India, Ireland, Israel, Japan, Netherlands, New Zealand, Sweden, Taiwan, UK, USA.
Included in the above, 1 organization listed in this Yearbook:
Associate members in 3 countries and territories:
England, Mexico, Sweden.
Regional Associate member:
Consultative Status Consultative status granted from: *ECOSOC (#05331)* (Special). [2018.03.09/XM6198/y/C]

♦ International Alliance of Catholic Development Agencies / see CIDSE (#03926)

♦ International Alliance of Catholic Knights (IACK) 11624
SG 34 Kingswood View, Kingswood Heights, Dublin, CO. DUBLIN, Ireland. E-mail: secretarygeneral@iack.org.
URL: http://www.iack.org/
History Founded 1979, Glasgow (UK). 1981, approved by the Holy See as a Catholic international organization. **Aims** Bring the message of *Christ* to all people; support the Pope and bishops, priests and religious throughout the world; nurture the faith of members and of Catholics; foster unity of members through prayer; promote establishment of Orders of Catholic Knights. **Structure** An umbrella organization. **Languages** English. **Staff** Voluntary. **Finance** Members' dues. **Activities** Networking/liaising; projects/programmes. **Events** *Conference* Glasgow (UK) 2019, *Conference* Washington, DC (USA) 2017, *Conference* Perth, WA (Australia) 2015, *Conference* Banjul (Gambia) 2013, *Conference* New Orleans, LA (USA) 2009. **Publications** *IACK Newsletter*.
Members Orders in 16 countries:
Australia, Austria, Belgium, Canada, Gambia, Ghana, Ireland, Liberia, Mauritius, New Zealand, Nigeria, Pakistan, South Africa, Togo, UK, USA.
Including 1 organization listed in this Yearbook:
Knights of Columbus (K of C). [2021/XN4484/y/E]

♦ International Alliance for Child and Adolescent Mental Health and Schools (inactive)

♦ International Alliance for the Control of Scabies (IACS) 11625
Contact address not obtained. E-mail: info@controlscabies.org.
URL: http://controlscabies.org/
History 2012. **Aims** Control human scabies; promote health and wellbeing of all those living in affected communities. **Structure** Steering Committee. **Events** *Annual Meeting* Washington, DC (USA) 2013. **NGO Relations** Member of (1): *Neglected Tropical Diseased NGO Network (NNN, #16969)*. [2020/XJ7175/C]

♦ International Alliance for Cooperation among Schools (inactive)
♦ International Alliance for defending Rights and Freedom (internationally oriented national body)

♦ International Alliance of Dermatology Patient Organizations (IAPDO) 11626
CEO 43 Florence Street, Ottawa ON K2P 0W6, Canada. T. +16137018385. E-mail: info@globalskin.org.
URL: https://globalskin.org/
History Jun 2015, Vancouver, BC (Canada). Founded at 1st *International Dermatology Patient Organizations Conference*. Former names and other names: *GlobalSkin* – alias. **Aims** Improve the lives of dermatology patients worldwide. **Structure** Annual General Meeting; Board of Directors; Management Team. **Activities** Advocacy/lobbying/activism; events/meetings; guidance/assistance/consulting; research/documentation. **Events** *GlobalSkin Conference ELEVATE 2023* Brussels (Belgium) 2023, *GlobalSkin Virtual Conference – Thrive 2021* 2021, *Meeting* Madrid (Spain) 2019, *GlobalSkin Conference* Milan (Italy) 2019. **Publications** *GlobalSkin Newsletter*. **Members** Patient associations (over 160) subdivided into 3 categories: Full; Associate; Affiliate. Membership countries not specified. **NGO Relations** Member of (3): *European Patients' Forum (EPF, #08172)*; *Rare Diseases International (RDI, #18621)* (Associate); *World Patients Alliance (WPA)*. Cooperates with (2): *European Academy of Dermatology and Venereology (EADV, #05788)*; *International Federation of Psoriasis Associations (IFPA, #13520)*. [2022/AA0548/C]

♦ International Alliance of Dietary Food Supplement Associations (IADSA) 11627
Secretariat Gridiron Building, One Pancras Square, London, N1C 4AG, UK. T. +447903731078. E-mail: iadsa@iadsa.org.
URL: http://www.iadsa.org/
History 1998. Registered in accordance with Belgian law. **Aims** Promote the dietary supplementary industry worldwide. **Structure** Executive Council, of which *Food Supplements Europe (#09852)* is member. **Finance** Members' dues. **Activities** Represents the dietary supplementary industry to global policy making bodies; provides regulatory and policy information on dietary supplements, ensuring that there is an awareness and understanding of new developments; coordinates strategy and action on global regulatory issues, particularly in relation to Codex Alimentarius initiatives on vitamin and mineral supplements, additives and health claims; helps establishment of new dietary supplement associations and supports existing national associations; organizes conferences and workshops. **Events** *Meeting* Copenhagen (Denmark) 2020, *Annual Meeting* Sydney, NSW (Australia) 2019, *Annual Meeting* London (UK) 2018, *Annual Meeting* Seoul (Korea Rep) 2017, *Scientific Forum* Jakarta (Indonesia) 2013. **Publications** *E-Newsletter*, *IADSA Newsflash*.
Members Associations (55) in 42 countries and territories:
Argentina, Australia, Belgium, Brazil, Bulgaria, Canada, Czechia, Denmark, Finland, France, Germany, Hong Kong, Hungary, India, Indonesia, Ireland, Italy, Japan, Kenya, Korea Rep, Malaysia, Mexico, Netherlands, Norway, Peru, Poland, Portugal, Romania, Russia, Singapore, Slovakia, Slovenia, South Africa, Spain, Sweden, Thailand, Türkiye, Uganda, UK, Uruguay, USA, Vietnam.
IGO Relations Participates as observer in the activities of: *Codex Alimentarius Commission (CAC, #04081)*. [2016/XF6366/F]

♦ International Alliance for Distribution by Cable / see GIGAEurope AISBL (#10151)
♦ International Alliance to End Genocide / see Alliance Against Genocide (#00655)

♦ International Alliance of Equestrian Journalists (IAEJ) 11628
Pres PO Box 670, Aurora ON L4G 4J9, Canada. T. +19057270107. Fax +19058411530.
URL: http://www.equijournalists.com/
History 1966. **Aims** Promote and maintain contacts among equestrian journalists worldwide. **Structure** Bureau, comprising President, 2 Vice-Presidents, Secretary and 5 further members. **Activities** Organizes annual meeting. **Publications** *IAEJ News*.
Members Individuals (350) in 22 countries.
Argentina, Australia, Belgium, Brazil, Canada, Croatia, Czechia, Finland, France, Germany, Ireland, Italy, Mexico, Netherlands, Poland, Portugal, Romania, Spain, Sweden, Switzerland, UK, USA. [2010/XF1674/F]

♦ International Alliance of Healthcare Educators (internationally oriented national body)
♦ International Alliance of Independent Publishers (internationally oriented national body)

♦ International Alliance of the Indigenous Tribal Peoples of the Tropical Forests (IAITPTF) 11629
Alliance internationale des peuples autochtones-tribaux des forêts tropicales – Alianza Mundial de los Pueblos Indigenas y Tribales de los Bosques Tropicales
Exec Sec 6/1 Moo 1, Suthep Rd, Suthep Sub-district, Muang District, Chiang Mai, 50200, Thailand. T. +6653904037. Fax +6653277645.
URL: http://www.international-alliance.org/
History 15 Feb 1992, Penang (Malaysia), on resolution of *'Conference of Indigenous-Tribal Peoples of Tropical Forests'* and drawing up of Charter. In French also referred to as *Alliance internationale des peuples indigènes des forêts tropicales*. **Aims** Secure respect for indigenous rights, territories, institutions and processes; promote an indigenous model of socially and environmentally sensitive *development* and *conservation* in tropical forest regions. **Structure** International Conference (supreme decision-making body). International Coordinating Committee, comprising coordinators of the 9 autonomous regions: South Asia; South East Asia; Bahasa; Pacific; East Africa; Central Africa; West Africa; Meso America; South America. International Technical Secretariat; Regional secretariats. **Languages** English, French, Spanish. **Staff** 5.00 FTE, paid. **Finance** Core budget provided by: *Oxfam Novib*. Contribution from various organizations, including the following bodies listed in this Yearbook: *DANIDA*; *Department for International Development Cooperation*; *European Commission (EC, #06633)*; *Ford Foundation (#09858)*; *German Catholic Bishops' Organisation for Development Cooperation (MISEREOR)*; *Global Environment Facility (GEF, #10346)*; *ICCO – Interchurch Organization for Development Cooperation*; *Norwegian Agency for Development Cooperation (Norad)*; *Swiss Agency for Development and Cooperation (SDC)*; *UNDP (#20292)*. **Activities** Capacity building; training/education; knowledge management/information dissemination. **Events** *Conference* Bangkok (Thailand) 2009, *Conference* Nairobi (Kenya) 2002, *Conference* Accra (Ghana) 2000, *Joint workshop* Geneva (Switzerland) 1999, *Affirming our rights to land, water, forest and identity* Nagpur (India) 1997. **Publications** *Voices of the Rainforest* – bulletin. *Our Knowledge for Our Survival*.
Members Indigenous and Tribal organizations in 58 countries and territories:
Argentina, Bangladesh, Belize, Benin, Bhutan, Bolivia, Brazil, Burundi, Cambodia, Cameroon, Central African Rep, Colombia, Congo Brazzaville, Congo DR, Costa Rica, Ecuador, El Salvador, Ethiopia, Fiji, Gabon, Gambia, Guatemala, Guiana Fr, Guyana, Honduras, India, Indonesia, Kenya, Laos, Liberia, Malaysia, Mexico, Myanmar, Nepal, New Caledonia, Nicaragua, Niger, Nigeria, Panama, Papua New Guinea, Paraguay, Peru, Philippines, Rwanda, Senegal, Sierra Leone, Solomon Is, Somalia, Sri Lanka, Sudan, Suriname, Tanzania UR, Thailand, Togo, Uganda, Vanuatu, Venezuela, Vietnam.
Included in the above, one organization listed in this Yearbook:
Coordinadora de las Organizaciones Indígenas de la Cuenca Amazónica (COICA, #04811).
Consultative Status Consultative status granted from: *UNEP (#20299)*. **IGO Relations** Accredited by: *United Nations Framework Convention on Climate Change – Secretariat (UNFCCC, #20564)*. **NGO Relations** Founding member of: *Global Forest Coalition (GFC, #10368)*. Member of: *Forest Peoples Programme (FPP, #09865)*; *International Indigenous Forum on Biodiversity (IIFB, #13837)*. Links with a large number of international bodies, including: *Climate Alliance (#04005)*; *Fern (#09736)*; *Indigenous Peoples' International Centre for Policy Research and Education (Tebtebba Foundation)*; *Minority Rights Group International (MRG, #16820)*; *Saami Council (#19012)*; *Survival International (#20047)*; *World Rainforest Movement (WRM, #21745)*. [2015/XF2640/y/F]

♦ International Alliance of Inhabitants (unconfirmed)
♦ International Alliance for Interoperability / see buildingSMART International (#03353)
♦ International Alliance of Iranian Students (internationally oriented national body)
♦ International Alliance of Journalists (internationally oriented national body)
♦ International Alliance of Journalists and Writers in the Latin Languages (inactive)
♦ International Alliance on Land Tenure and Administration (internationally oriented national body)
♦ International Alliance of Leading Education Institutes / see International Network of Education Institutes (#14256)

♦ International Alliance of Marine-Related Institutions (IAMRI) 11630
SG College Environmental and Marine Sciences and Technology, Pukyong National Univ, Daeyeon Campus 599-1, Busan 608-737, Korea Rep. E-mail: secretarygeneral@iamri.org.
Secretariat Ocean Univ of China, 238 Songling Road, Qingdao, 266100 Shandong, China. T. +8653266786553. Fax +8653266782805. E-mail: secretariat@iamri.org.
URL: www.iamri.org/
Aims Promote and advance education and scientific and technological development in all aspects of marine sciences; provide a forum for discussion and dissemination of information. **Structure** General Conference; Board; Secretariat. **Activities** Organizes seminars, workshops and meetings. **Events** *Annual Meeting* Busan (Korea Rep) 2016, *Symposium on Scientific Challenges in Ocean and Coastal Systems* Busan (Korea Rep) 2016, *Meeting* Busan (Korea Rep) 2007.
Members Universities (9) in 9 countries:
Australia, Canada, China, France, Germany, Japan, Korea Rep, UK, USA. [2018/XM3608/D]

♦ International Alliance of Messianic Congregations and Synagogues (IAMCS) 11631
Chairman PO Box 1570, Havertown PA 19083, USA. T. +12154525590. E-mail: office@iamcs.org.
URL: http://iamcs.org/
History 1986. **Finance** Donations. **Events** *Annual Messianic rabbis conference / Annual Messianic Rabbis' Conference* Philadelphia, PA (USA) 1993, *Annual messianic rabbis conference* Philadelphia, PA (USA) 1991. **Publications** *Spirit of Messiah*.
Members Sections in 7 countries:
Australia, Belgium, Canada, France, Mexico, UK, USA. [2015/XF1394/F]

♦ International Alliance of Mountain Film 11632
Coordinator c/o Area Documentazione Museomontagna, Salita al Cal Torino 12, Monte dei Cappucini, 10131 Turin TO, Italy. T. +39116604104. Fax +39116604622. E-mail: posta@museomontagna.org.
URL: http://www.mountainfilmalliance.org/
History Feb 2000, Turin (Italy). **Aims** Promote, enhance and conserve mountain cinematography through communal projects that would flank or be incorporated into the regular institutional activities of member bodies.
Members Festivals (19) and a museum in 16 countries:
Argentina, Austria, Bulgaria, Canada, Czechia, France, Germany, Italy, Nepal, Poland, Russia, Slovakia, Slovenia, Spain, Switzerland, UK.
NGO Relations Member of: *Mountain Partnership (MP, #16862)*. [2012/XF6729/F]

♦ International Alliance of Patients' Organizations (IAPO) 11633
Alliance internationale des organisations de patients – Alianza International de Organizaciones de Patientes – Internationale Allianz von Patienten-Organisationen
CEO 49-51 East Road, London, N1 6AH, UK. T. +442072508277 – +442072508280. Fax +442072508285. E-mail: info@iapo.org.uk.
URL: http://www.iapo.org.uk/

History 1999. Registration: Charity, No/ID: 1155577, England and Wales; EU Transparency Register, No/ID: 345908340255-48, Start date: 9 Nov 2020. **Aims** Work at international, regional, national and local levels to represent and support patients, their families and carers. **Structure** Governing Board. **Languages** English. **Staff** 7.00 FTE, paid. 0.5 – 1 FTE, voluntary. **Finance** Sources: donations; grants; members' dues; sale of publications. **Activities** Advocacy/lobbying/activism; awards/prizes/competitions; capacity building; events/meetings; networking/liaising. **Events** *Latin American Patients Congress* London (UK) 2022, *Global Patients Congress* 2020, *Global Patients Congress* Miami, FL (USA) 2018, *Global Forum on Incontinence* Rome (Italy) 2018, *Global Patients Congress* Croydon (UK) 2016. **Publications** *IAPO Newsletter* (12 a year). Research results.

Members Full (174); Associate (30). Patients' organizations – international; regional; national; local. Full National members in 49 countries and territories:
Argentina, Australia, Brazil, Bulgaria, Canada, China, Croatia, Cyprus, Czechia, Denmark, Estonia, Finland, Germany, Ghana, Greece, Guatemala, Hungary, Ireland, Israel, Italy, Japan, Liberia, Lithuania, Malawi, Mexico, Morocco, Netherlands, New Zealand, Nigeria, Pakistan, Peru, Philippines, Poland, Portugal, Romania, Russia, Slovakia, Slovenia, South Africa, Spain, Sri Lanka, Taiwan, Türkiye, Uganda, UK, Ukraine, USA, Venezuela, Zambia.
Full international and regional organizations (27):
- *Africa Psoriasis Organization (APSO, #00515)*;
- Alagille Syndrome Alliance;
- *Alzheimer's Disease International (ADI, #00762)*;
- *Association of European Coeliac Societies (AOECS, #02504)*;
- *Community Health and Information Network (CHAIN, #04400)*;
- *Confederation of Meningitis Organisations (CoMO, #04568)*;
- Easter Seals;
- *European AIDS Treatment Group (EATG, #05850)*;
- *European Federation of Crohn's and Ulcerative Colitis Associations (EFCCA, #07095)*;
- *EURORDIS – Rare Diseases Europe (#09175)*;
- *Global Alliance of Mental Illness Advocacy Networks – Europe (GAMIAN Europe, #10211)*;
- *Global Colon Cancer Association (GCCA, #10300)*;
- *Iatrogenic Europe Unite – Alliance (IEU, #11010)*;
- *International Consumer Support for Infertility Community (iCSi, #12932)*;
- *International Diabetes Federation (IDF, #13164)*;
- *International Dupuytren Society (#13210)*;
- *International Federation of Psoriasis Associations (IFPA, #13520)*;
- *International Genetic Alliance (IGA, #13709)*;
- *International Patient Organization for Primary Immunodeficiencies (IPOPI, #14533)*;
- Livestrong;
- *LUPUS EUROPE (#16524)*;
- *Multiple Sclerosis International Federation (MSIF, #16899)*;
- *New World Hope Organization (NWHO)*;
- *Thalassaemia International Federation (#20139)*;
- *World Federation for Incontinence and Pelvic Problems (WFIPP, #21440)*;
- *World Federation of Hemophilia (WFH, #21437)*;
- *World Headache Alliance (WHA, #21555)*.

Associate national organizations in 53 countries and territories:
Afghanistan, Argentina, Australia, Bosnia-Herzegovina, Brazil, Bulgaria, Cameroon, Canada, Chile, China, Colombia, Croatia, Cyprus, Czechia, Egypt, El Salvador, Georgia, Germany, Ghana, Guatemala, India, Israel, Italy, Japan, Kenya, Korea Rep, Liberia, Malawi, Mexico, Morocco, New Zealand, Nigeria, North Macedonia, Pakistan, Peru, Philippines, Poland, Portugal, Romania, Russia, Slovakia, South Africa, Spain, Sri Lanka, Taiwan, Thailand, Türkiye, Uganda, UK, Ukraine, USA, Venezuela, Zambia.
Associate international and regional organizations (5):
Cochrane Consumer Network; *European Lung Foundation (ELF, #07718)*; *Healthcare Compliance Packaging Council Europe (HCPC Europe, #10874)*; *International Painful Bladder Foundation (IPBF, #14499)*; Thrombosis Research Institute.

Consultative Status Consultative status granted from: *ECOSOC (#05331)* (Special); *WHO (#20950)* (Official Relations). **NGO Relations** Member of (1): *Health First Europe (HFE, #10881)*. Observer of: *Alliance for Safe Online Pharmacy – EU (ASOP EU, #00720)*. Collaborates with: *World Medical Association (WMA, #21646)*.
[2022/XF6021/y/F]

♦ International Alliance for Phytobiomes Research 11634

Exec Dir 4620 Village Terrace Ct, Eau Claire WI 54701, USA. T. +13016189543.
URL: http://www.phytobiomesalliance.org/

History 2016. Former names and other names: *Phytobiomes Alliance* – alias. Registration: Section 501(c)(3), USA. **Aims** Establish a science and technology foundation for site-specific, phytobiome-based enhancement of the sustainable production of food, feed, and fiber. **Structure** Board of Directors; Scientific Coordinating Committee; Working Groups. **Languages** English. **Staff** 3.00 FTE, paid. **Finance** Sources: contributions; sponsorship. Annual budget: 180,000 USD. **Activities** Events/meetings; knowledge management/information dissemination; projects/programmes. **Events** *International Phytobiomes Conference* Denver, CO (USA) 2022, *International Phytobiomes Conference* Denver, CO (USA) 2020, *International Phytobiomes Conference* Montpellier (France) 2018, *International Phytobiomes Conference* Santa Fe, NM (USA) 2016.

Members Organizations in 25 countries:
Australia, Austria, Belgium, Brazil, Canada, China, Colombia, Denmark, Finland, France, Germany, India, Indonesia, Israel, Italy, Netherlands, Pakistan, Portugal, Serbia, South Africa, Spain, Switzerland, Tunisia, UK, USA. [2021.06.23/XM8836/C]

♦ International Alliance for the Protection of Heritage in Conflict Areas (ALIPH) 11635

Alliance internationale pour la protection du patrimoine dans les zones en conflit

Exec Dir Chemin de Balexert 7-9, 1219 Châtelaine, Switzerland. T. +41227951800. E-mail: contact@aliph-foundation.org.
URL: https://www.aliph-foundation.org/

History Mar 2017. Founded on the initiative of France and the United Arab Emirates. Registration: Swiss Civil Code, Switzerland; EU Transparency Register, No/ID: 558292944369-93, Start date: 19 Oct 2021. **Aims** Act in favour of cultural heritage in conflict areas. **Structure** Board; Scientific Committee; Secretariat. **Activities** Financial and/or material support; projects/programmes. Active in: Afghanistan, Bangladesh, Cambodia, Congo DR, Côte d'Ivoire, Eritrea, Georgia, Iraq, Lebanon, Libya, Mali, Mauritania, Niger, Palestine, Somalia, Sudan, Syrian AR, Türkiye, Yemen. [2020/AA1216/F]

♦ International Alliance of Research Library Associations (IARLA) ... 11636

Address not obtained.
URL: https://iarla.org/

History 2016. **Aims** Advance and promote a shared understanding of the major challenges and opportunities faced by modern research libraries. **Structure** Informal structure. **Activities** Events/meetings; networking/liaising; research/documentation.

Members Founding academic and research library associations (5) in 4 countries:
Australia, Canada, UK, USA.
Association of European Research Libraries (#02540). [2020/AA1125/y/F]

♦ International Alliance of Research Universities (IARU) 11637

Contact Univ of Cambridge, The Old Schools, Trinity Lane, Cambridge, CB2 1TN, UK. E-mail: iaru@admin.cam.ac.uk.
URL: http://www.iaruni.org/

History 2006. Founded as a collaboration between 10 research-intensive universities, namely: Australian National University; ETH Zurich; National University of Singapore; Peking University; University of California, Berkeley; University of Cambridge; University of Copenhagen; University of Oxford; University of Tokyo; Yale University. Membership extended to include University of Cape Town, 2016. **Aims** Address challenges facing humanity, specifically those related to climate change, aging, longevity and health. **Structure** Chair and Secretariat serve 2 year terms. Presidents, Senior Officers and Working Groups Meetings. **Languages** English. **Staff** 2.00 FTE, paid. **Finance** Sources: members' dues. **Activities** Events/meetings; networking/liaising; research/documentation; training/education. **Events** *Presidents' Meeting* Zurich (Switzerland) 2023, *Presidents' Meeting* Cambridge (UK) 2022, *Senior Officers' Meeting* Oxford (UK) 2022, *Senior Officers' Meeting* Cambridge (UK) 2021, *Senior Officers' Meeting* Oxford (UK) 2016. **Publications** *Global Priorities, Educated Solutions: the role of academia in advaning the Sustainable Development Goals*; *Green Guide for Universities*; *How to Make a Green Campus*.

Members Universities (11) in 9 countries:
Australia, China, Denmark, Japan, Singapore, South Africa, Switzerland, UK, USA. [2022.06.22/XJ2440/C]

♦ International Alliance for Responsible Drinking (IARD) 11638

CEO The Jefferson Bldg, 1225 19th St NW, Ste 500, Washington DC 20036, USA. T. +12029861159. Fax +12029862080. E-mail: info@iard.org.
URL: http://www.iard.org/

History Launched 2015, resulting from merger of *International Center for Alcohol Policies (ICAP, inactive)* with *Global Alcohol Producers Group (GAPG, inactive)*. **Aims** Contribute to the reduction of harmful drinking; promote responsible drinking worldwide. **Structure** Board of Directors; CEO Group. **Members** Beer, wine and spirits producers. Membership countries not specified. **Consultative Status** Consultative status granted from: *ECOSOC (#05331)* (Special). [2017/XM4153/C]

♦ International Alliance for School Accreditation (internationally oriented national body)
♦ International Alliance of Socialist Democrats (inactive)
♦ International Alliance for Sustainable Agriculture / see Alliance for Sustainability
♦ International Alliance of Theatrical Stage Employees and Moving Picture Machine Operators of the United States and Canada / see International Alliance of Theatrical Stage Employees, Moving Picture Technicians, Artists and Allied Crafts of the United States, its Territories and Canada
♦ International Alliance of Theatrical Stage Employees, Moving Picture Technicians, Artists and Allied Crafts of the United States and Canada / see International Alliance of Theatrical Stage Employees, Moving Picture Technicians, Artists and Allied Crafts of the United States, its Territories and Canada
♦ International Alliance of Theatrical Stage Employees, Moving Picture Technicians, Artists and Allied Crafts of the United States, its Territories and Canada (internationally oriented national body)

♦ International Alliance of Women (IAW) 11639

Alliance internationale des femmes (AIF) – Alianza Internacional de Mujeres – Internationaler Frauen-Verband

Acting SG Av Louis Casaï 81, 1216 Cointrin GE, Switzerland. E-mail: iawsecgen@womenalliance.org.
URL: http://www.womenalliance.org/

History Feb 1902, Washington DC (USA), under the inspiration of Susan Anthony, Elisabeth Stanton and Carrie Chapmann Cat, as *International Alliance of Women for Suffrage and Legal Citizenship – Alliance internationale pour le suffrage et l'action civique et politique des femmes*. At 2nd meeting, 3-4 Jun 1904, Berlin (Germany), formally constituted under the name *International Woman Suffrage Alliance – Alliance internationale pour le suffrage des femmes*, also known as *International Suffrage Alliance*. Congress of 1926, Paris (France), changed name to *International Alliance of Women for Suffrage and Equal Citizenship*. Present name adopted 1946, with the sub-title *Equal Rights – Equal Responsibilities – Droits égaux – responsabilités égales*. Individual members meeting in congress, 28 Apr 1915, The Hague (Netherlands), were instrumental in setting up *'International Women's Committee for a Durable Peace'*, which became *Women's International League for Peace and Freedom (WILPF, #21024)*, 1919, Zurich (Switzerland). Current *'Action Programme'* adopted Oct 2017, at 37th Congress, Nicosia (Cyprus). **Aims** Promote human rights and empowerment of women in all spheres of life; ensure that the status of every individual without distinction on grounds of sex, sexual orientation, age, race, religious or political persuasion or any other ground shall be based on respect for the person; promote social justice; work for peace and good understanding among peoples. **Structure** Congress (every 3 years); Executive Board (annual); International Committee Meeting. Regional Vice-Presidents (6): Anglophone Africa; Francophone Africa; North America; Arab Region; Asia; Europe. Regional Coordinator (1): Pacific. Commissions (7). Ad-hoc Committees (7). **Languages** English, French. **Staff** Voluntary. **Finance** Sources: donations; gifts, legacies; members' dues. Other sources: affiliation and association fees. **Activities** Advocacy/lobbying/activism; events/meetings; networking/liaising. **Events** *Congress* 2022, *Triennial Congress* Lagos (Nigeria) 2020, *International Meeting* Lahore (Pakistan) 2019, *Triennial Congress* Nicosia (Cyprus) 2017, *Meeting* Victoria Falls (Zimbabwe) 2016. **Publications** *IAW Newsletter* (12 a year) – electronic newsletter; *International Women's News* (3 a year) in English, French; *President's Newsletter* (intermittent) – electronic. *Equal Rights – Equal Responsibilties Centenary Celebration* (2007) in English, French; *Just Sufragii Centenary Edition* (2004); *The International Woman Suffrage Alliance: Its History from 1904 to 1929* (1929); *Women's Rights are Human Rights*. Books; monographs; brochures; reports of Congresses and Seminars.

Members Affiliated societies (29); Associated societies (21); Individuals (about 300). Membership countries not specified. Affiliated societies in 26 countries:
Affiliated societies in 26 countries:
Australia, Bangladesh, Canada, Cyprus, Denmark, Egypt, Finland, France, Germany, Greece, Iceland, India, Israel, Kuwait, Lithuania, Mauritius, Netherlands, Norway, Pakistan, Philippines, Sri Lanka, Sweden, Switzerland, USA, Zambia, Zimbabwe.
Associate societies in 16 countries:
Australia, Bangladesh, Benin, Burkina Faso, Cameroon, Congo Brazzaville, France, Germany, India, Nepal, Serbia, South Africa, Togo, Uganda, UK, Zimbabwe.

Consultative Status Consultative status granted from: *ECOSOC (#05331)* (General); *UNESCO (#20322)* (Consultative Status); *ILO (#11123)* (Special List); *FAO (#09260)* (Liaison Status); *UNCTAD (#20285)* (General Category); *WHO (#20950)* (Official Relations); *UNEP (#20299)*; *UNICEF (#20332)*; *UNIDO (#20336)*; *Council of Europe (CE, #04881)* (Participatory Status). **IGO Relations** Maintains relations with: *United Nations Population Fund (UNFPA, #20612)*. Close cooperation with: *United Nations Commission on the Status of Women (CSW, #20536)*. Accredited by: *United Nations Office at Vienna (UNOV, #20604)*. Associated with Department of Global Communications of the United Nations. **NGO Relations** Board member of: *European Women's Lobby (EWL, #09102)*. Member of: *Committee of NGOs on Human Rights, Geneva (#04275)*; *Conference of Non-Governmental Organizations in Consultative Relationship with the United Nations (CONGO, #04635)*; *Framework Convention Alliance (FCA, #09981)*; *Global Gender and Climate Alliance (GGCA, no recent information)*; *International Action Network on Small Arms (IANSA, #11585)*; *NGO Committee on the Status of Women, Geneva (#17117)*; *UNCAC Coalition (#20283)*; *Vienna NGO Committee on the Status of Women (#20775)*. [2022/XB1152/B]

♦ The International Alliance for Women (TIAW) 11640

Pres 167 Todd Pl NE, Washington DC 20002, USA. E-mail: admin@tiaw.org.
URL: http://www.tiaw.org/

History 1980, Baltimore, MD (USA). Founded as US National Alliance of Professional and Executive Women's Networks. Former names and other names: *The International Alliance: An Association of Executive and Professional Women (TIA)* – former (1986 to 2002). **Aims** Provide mentoring and other support services to women entrepreneurs to ensure their businesses are sustainable. **Structure** Board. **Activities** Awards/prizes/competitions; capacity building; events/meetings; financial and/or material support; projects/programmes. **Events** *Global Forum* Sydney, NSW (Australia) 2019, *Global Forum* Washington, DC (USA) 2012, *Global partnership forum* Washington, DC (USA) 2003, *Annual conference* Toronto, ON (Canada) 2001, *Annual conference* Sarasota, FL (USA) 1992. **Publications** *TIAW Connections*. [2020.04.30/XF5841/F]

♦ International Alliance for Women in Music (IAWM) 11641

Pres M319 Scales Fine Arts Center, 7345 Reynolda Station, Winston-Salem NC 27109-7345, USA. E-mail: president@iawm.org.
URL: http://www.iawm.org/

History Founded 1 Jan 1995, by merger of American Women Composers, *International Congress on Women in Music (ICWM, inactive)* and *International League of Women Composers (ILWC, inactive)*. Registered in accordance with the laws of the USA. **Aims** Increase and enhance musical activities and opportunities; promote all aspects of the music of women. **Structure** Board. Committees (9): Administrative; Advocacy; Awards (including Annual Concert); Communication; Congress; Development; Finance; Membership; Nominations/Elections. **Languages** English. **Staff** 17.50 FTE, voluntary. **Finance** Members' dues. Other sources: Contributions; grants. Budget (annual): US$ 30,000. **Activities** Knowledge management/information dissemination; advocacy/lobbying/activism; events/meetings. **Events** *Congress / International Congress on Women in Music* Flagstaff, AZ (USA) 2011, *Congress* Tempe, AZ (USA) 2010, *Congress / International Congress on Women in Music* Beijing (China) 2008, *Congress / International Congress on Women in Music* Miami, FL (USA) 2006, *International Congress on Women in Music* London (UK) 1999. **Publications** *IAWM Journal* (2 a year).

Members Affiliate – music organizations in 31 countries and territories:

Argentina, Australia, Austria, Belgium, Brazil, Canada, China, Cuba, Denmark, France, Germany, Greece, Hong Kong, Ireland, Israel, Italy, Japan, Korea Rep, Kosovo, Latvia, Luxembourg, Mexico, Netherlands, Romania, Spain, Sri Lanka, Sweden, Switzerland, Taiwan, UK, USA.
Publishers, journals and other organizations that are not membership-based, in 5 countries:
Australia, Ireland, Sweden, UK, USA. [2014.06.01/XF4014/F]

♦ International Alliance of Women for Suffrage and Equal Citizenship / see International Alliance of Women (#11639)
♦ International Alliance of Women for Suffrage and Legal Citizenship / see International Alliance of Women (#11639)

♦ International Alliance of Youth Writing Centers 11642

Address not obtained.
URL: https://www.youthwriting.org/
History 2018, Amsterdam (Netherlands). Centres are not formally connected. **Aims** Join hands so as to provide young people places where they can write and be heard. **Publications** *Illustoria.*
Members Centres in 15 countries:
Argentina, Australia, Austria, Canada, Chile, Denmark, Iceland, Ireland, Italy, Netherlands, Pakistan, Spain, Sweden, UK, USA. [2022/AA2924/F]

♦ International Aluminium Institute (IAI) 11643

Institut international d'aluminium
SG Level 3, 2 Duke Street, London, SW1Y 6BN, UK. T. +442079300528.
URL: http://www.world-aluminium.org/
History 28 Apr 1972, London (UK). Articles amended: 11 May 1974; 14 May 1976; 15 Apr 1977; 11 May 1982; 13 May 1983. New articles adopted 12 May 1986; amended May 1988, May 1992, May 2009, May 2014. Former names and other names: *International Primary Aluminium Institute (IPAI)* – former (Apr 1972); *Institut international d'aluminium primaire* – former (Apr 1972). Registration: Companies House, England and Wales. **Aims** Promote understanding of the worlds's aluminium industry and broader use of its products. **Structure** General Meeting (annual); Board of Directors; Chairmen; Committees (6). Meetings closed. **Languages** English. **Staff** 4.00 FTE, paid. **Finance** Sources: members' dues. **Activities** Events/meetings; financial and/or material support; networking/liaising; publishing activities; research/documentation. **Events** *World Aluminium Conference* London (UK) 2023, *Annual General Meeting* Hong Kong (Hong Kong) 2014, *Annual General Meeting* London (UK) 2013, *Annual General Meeting* Dubai (United Arab Emirates) 2012, *International Conference on Environment Health and Safety Aspects Related to the Production of Aluminium* Montréal, QC (Canada) 2012. **Publications** *Statistical Survey Forms: Anode Effect*; *Statistical Survey Forms: Capacity*; *Statistical Survey Forms: Energy*; *Statistical Survey Forms: Production*; *Statistical Survey Forms: Safety.* Congress proceedings; survey reports; updates; various reports. **Members** Companies (27) responsible for over 60% of global bauxite, alumina and aluminium production. Represents every continent except Antarctica. Membership countries not specified. **Consultative Status** Consultative status granted from: *UNCTAD (#20285)* (Special Category). **IGO Relations** Observer status with: *Codex Alimentarius Commission (CAC, #04081).* **NGO Relations** Cooperates with: *Business and Industry Advisory Committee to the OECD (BIAC, #03385)*; *International Organization for Standardization (ISO, #14473)*; *World Business Council for Sustainable Development (WBCSD, #21254).* Member of: *International Council on Mining and Metals (ICMM, #13048).* [2020/XC4528/j/C]

♦ International Amalgamation of Unions of Automobile and Farm Machinery Workers (IAUAFMW) 11644

Pres 42 Leninsky Prospekt, Moscow MOSKVA, Russia, 119119. T. +74959388413. Fax +74959388615. E-mail: afw@fnpr.ru.
URL: http://en.vkp.ru/
Members Trade unions in the CIS region (membership countries not specified). **IGO Relations** *Commonwealth of Independent States (CIS, #04341).* **NGO Relations** Affiliated with: *General Confederation of Trade Unions (GCTU, #10108).* [2020/XM2454/D]

♦ International Amateur Athletic Federation / see World Athletics (#21209)
♦ International Amateur Baseball Federation (inactive)
♦ International Amateur Basketball Federation / see Fédération internationale de basketball (#09614)
♦ International Amateur Bowling Association (inactive)
♦ International Amateur Boxing Association / see International Boxing Association (#12385)
♦ International Amateur Handball Federation (inactive)
♦ International Amateur Karate Federation / see International Traditional Federation of Karate (#15711)
♦ International Amateur Kickboxing Sport Association (inactive)

♦ International Amateur-Professional Photoelectric Photometry (IAPPP) 11645

Pres A J Dyer Observatory, 1000 Oman Drive, Brentwood TN 37027, USA. T. +16153734897. Fax +16153713904.
History Founded Jun 1980. **Aims** Facilitate collaborative *astronomical* research between amateur, student and professional astronomers by providing a medium for the exchange of practical information. **Structure** Committees; regional "Wings" (currently in 23 countries). **Staff** 1.50 FTE, voluntary. **Finance** Members' dues. Budget (annual): about. US$ 15,000. **Activities** Financial and/or material support; knowledge management/information dissemination. **Events** *Symposium* Nashville, TN (USA) 2000, *Astronomical photoelectric photometry, amateur and professional collaboration* Nashville, TN (USA) 1999, *Astronomical photoelectric photometry* Nashville, TN (USA) 1998. **Publications** *IAPPP Communications* (4 a year) – journal.
Members Individuals (more than 1,200) in 56 countries and territories:
Argentina, Armenia, Australia, Austria, Azerbaijan, Bermuda, Bosnia-Herzegovina, Bulgaria, Canada, Chile, China, Czechia, Denmark, Estonia, Finland, France, Georgia, Germany, Greece, Hong Kong, Hungary, India, Indonesia, Ireland, Italy, Japan, Kazakhstan, Korea Rep, Latvia, Lithuania, Malaysia, Mexico, Netherlands, New Zealand, Norway, Poland, Portugal, Puerto Rico, Romania, Russia, Saudi Arabia, Slovenia, South Africa, Spain, Sweden, Switzerland, Taiwan, Tajikistan, Thailand, Türkiye, UK, Ukraine, Uruguay, USA, Uzbekistan, Venezuela. [2016/XD5797/tv/F]

♦ International Amateur Racquetball Federation / see International Racquetball Federation (#14683)
♦ International Amateur Radio Club (internationally oriented national body)

♦ International Amateur Radio Union (IARU) 11646

Union internationale des radio-amateurs – Unión Internacional de Radioaficionados
Sec PO Box 310905, Newington CT 06131-0905, USA. T. +18605940200. Fax +18605940259. E-mail: secretary@iaru.org – iaru@iaru.org.
URL: https://www.iaru.org/
History 18 Apr 1925, Paris (France). Former names and other names: *Union internationale des amateurs de télégraphes sans fil* – former. **Aims** Promote and coordinate two-way amateur radio *communication*; encourage agreements between national amateur radio societies on matters of common interest and welfare; advance radio art; represent two-way amateur radio communication interests at and between international *telecommunication* conferences; encourage international friendship. **Structure** Officers: President; Vice-President; Secretary. Regional organizations: Regions 1, 2 and 3, as those of International Telecommunication Union (ITU), meet every 3 years. **Languages** English, Spanish. **Staff** Supplied by American Radio Relay League. **Finance** Expenses met by International Secretariat (ARRL) together with contributions from regional organizations. **Activities** Networking/liaising. **Events** *Europe, Africa, Middle East and Northern Asia regional conference* Novi Sad (Serbia) 2020, *Asia Pacific Regional Conference* Seoul (Korea Rep) 2018, *Europe, Africa, Middle East and Northern Asia regional conference* Landshut (Germany) 2017, *Meeting* Vienna (Austria) 2016, *Asia Pacific Regional Conference* Bali (Indonesia) 2015. **Publications** *Region 1 News* – electronic; *Region 2 News* – electronic; *Region 3 News* – electronic. *Calendar* – internal.
Members National societies in 167 countries and territories:
Albania, Algeria, Andorra, Anguilla, Antigua-Barbuda, Argentina, Armenia, Aruba, Australia, Austria, Azerbaijan, Bahamas, Bahrain, Bangladesh, Barbados, Belarus, Belgium, Belize, Bermuda, Bolivia, Bosnia-Herzegovina, Botswana, Brazil, Brunei Darussalam, Bulgaria, Burkina Faso, Cameroon, Canada, Cayman Is, Chile, China, Colombia, Congo Brazzaville, Congo DR, Costa Rica, Côte d'Ivoire, Croatia, Cuba, Curaçao, Cyprus, Czechia, Denmark, Djibouti, Dominica, Dominican Rep, Ecuador, Egypt, El Salvador, Estonia, Eswatini, Ethiopia, Faeroe Is, Fiji, Finland, France, Gabon, Gambia, Georgia, Germany, Ghana, Gibraltar, Greece, Grenada, Guatemala, Guinea, Guyana, Haiti, Honduras, Hong Kong, Hungary, Iceland, India, Indonesia, Iraq, Ireland, Israel, Italy, Jamaica, Japan, Jordan, Kazakhstan, Kenya, Korea Rep, Kosovo, Kuwait, Latvia, Lebanon, Lesotho, Liberia, Liechtenstein, Lithuania, Luxembourg, Macau, Malaysia, Mali, Malta, Mauritius, Mexico, Moldova, Monaco, Mongolia, Montenegro, Montserrat, Morocco, Mozambique, Namibia, Netherlands, New Caledonia, New Zealand, Nicaragua, Nigeria, Norway, Oman, Pakistan, Panama, Paraguay, Peru, Philippines, Pitcairn, Poland, Polynesia Fr, Portugal, Qatar, Romania, Russia, Samoa, San Marino, Saudi Arabia, Senegal, Serbia, Seychelles, Sierra Leone, Singapore, Slovakia, Slovenia, Solomon Is, South Africa, Spain, Sri Lanka, St Kitts-Nevis, St Vincent-Grenadines, Suriname, Sweden, Switzerland, Syrian AR, Taiwan, Tajikistan, Tanzania UR, Thailand, Tonga, Trinidad-Tobago, Tunisia, Türkiye, Turkmenistan, Turks-Caicos, Uganda, UK, Ukraine, United Arab Emirates, Uruguay, USA, Vanuatu, Venezuela, Vietnam, Virgin Is UK, Zambia, Zimbabwe.
Consultative Status Consultative status granted from: *ECOSOC (#05331)* (Ros C). **IGO Relations** Memorandum of Understanding with: *International Telecommunication Union (ITU, #15673)* and member of its Radiocommunication and Telecommunication Development Sectors. Operational agreement with *United Nations Office for the Coordination of Humanitarian Affairs (OCHA, #20593).* **NGO Relations** Memorandum of Understanding with: *International Federation of Red Cross and Red Crescent Societies (#13526).* Technical Liaison Partner with: *European Committee for Electrotechnical Standardization (CENELEC, #06647).* [2021.11.01/XB1159/B]

♦ International Amateur Rugby Federation / see Rugby Europe (#18998)
♦ International Amateur Sambo Federation / see Fédération internationale de SAMBO (#09655)
♦ International Amateur Swimming Federation / see World Aquatics (#21100)

♦ International Amateur Theatre Association (AITA/IATA) 11647

Association internationale du théâtre amateur (AITA/IATA) – Asociación Internacional del Teatro de Arte (AITA/IATA)
Secretariat MAI Rue Washington 40, 1050 Brussels, Belgium. E-mail: secretariat@aitaiata.net.
URL: http://www.aitaiata.net/
History 20 Jan 1952, Brussels (Belgium). Founded when statutes were adopted, as an organization for understanding and education through the theatre. Current constitution adopted, 1969, Monaco; amended: 1975 Oklahoma City OH (USA); 1977, Monaco; 1979, Blagoevgrad (Bulgaria), 1991, Halden (Norway); 1993, Monaco; 1995, Ankara (Turkey); 2001, Monaco; 2003, Canada; 2005, Monaco; 2007, Korea Rep; 2009, Monaco; 2011, Norway; 2013, Monaco; 2015, Belgium (Flanders); 2017, Monaco (constitution updated); 2018, Lingen (Germany); 2019, Saint John NB (Canada); 2020, by Zoom; 2021, Monaco (constitution updated); 2022, by Zoom. Former names and other names: *Internationale Amateur-Theater-Vereinigung* – former. Registration: Banque-Carrefour des Entreprises, No/ID: 0863.683.050, Start date: 26 Feb 2004, Belgium. **Aims** Promote understanding and education through theatre. **Structure** General Assembly; Council; Regional/Cultural Groupings (7) include *Comité international des fédérations théâtrales d'amateurs de culture latine (CIFTA, #04176)* and *North European Amateur Theatre Alliance (NEATA, #17597)*; Working Groups; General Secretariat based in London (UK). **Languages** English, French, Spanish. **Staff** 0.50 FTE, paid. **Finance** Sources: subscriptions. **Activities** Events/meetings; networking/liaising; training/education. **Events** *General Assembly* Brussels (Belgium) 2022, *General Assembly* Monaco (Monaco) 2021, *General Assembly* Brussels (Belgium) 2020, *General Assembly* Saint John, NB (Canada) 2019, *Drama in Education Congress* Wagna (Austria) 2019. **Publications** *50th Anniversary of AITA/IATA* (2002). Biennial Review (2015). Congress reports; guidelines.
Members National Centre members in 31 countries and territories:
Austria, Bangladesh, Belgium, Czechia, Denmark, Estonia, Faeroe Is, Finland, Flanders, France, Germany, Great Britain, Hungary, Iceland, Israel, Italy, Japan, Korea Rep, Latvia, Lithuania, Monaco, North Macedonia, Russia, Slovakia, Slovenia, South Tyrol, Spain, Sweden, Uganda, USA, Zimbabwe.
Membes also in Catalonia.
Associate members: bodies pursuing amateur and/or educational drama theatre in 38 countries and territories:
Argentina, Armenia, Australia, Austria, Belarus, Belgium, Bulgaria, Canada, Central African Rep, Colombia, Côte d'Ivoire, Denmark, Finland, Flanders, France, Germany, Great Britain, Greece, India, Indonesia, Ireland, Italy, Japan, Korea Rep, Malaysia, Mexico, Netherlands, New Zealand, Norway, Paraguay, Portugal, Qatar, Russia, Singapore, Slovenia, South Tyrol, Spain, USA.
Consultative Status Consultative status granted from: *UNESCO (#20322)* (Consultative Status). **NGO Relations** Member of (1): *Federation of European and International Associations Established in Belgium (FAIB, #09508).* [2022.10.21/XC1162/B]

♦ International Amateur Wrestling Federation / see United World Wrestling (#20665)

♦ International American Studies Association (IASA) 11648

Pres address not obtained.
Past Pres Dipto di Studi Europei/Americani/Interculturali, Univ "Sapienza", Piazzale Aldo Moro 5, 00185 Rome RM, Italy.
URL: https://iasa-world.org/
History 1 Jun 2000, Bellagio (Italy). Registration: Netherlands. **Aims** Further the exchange of ideas and information among scholars from all nations and various disciplines who study and teach American studies. **Structure** General Assembly; Executive Council. **Languages** English. **Staff** 4.00 FTE, paid. **Finance** Sources: donations; meeting proceeds; members' dues. **Events** *Biennial World Congress* New Delhi (India) 2022, *Biennial World Congress* Madrid (Spain) 2019, *Biennial World Congress* Seoul (Korea Rep) 2015, *Biennial World Congress* Szczecin (Poland) 2013, *Biennial world congress* Rio de Janeiro (Brazil) 2011. **Publications** *Review of International American Studies (RIAS)* (2 a year) – online. Books.
Members Individuals in 51 countries and territories:
Algeria, Argentina, Australia, Austria, Belgium, Bosnia-Herzegovina, Brazil, Bulgaria, Canada, Chile, China, Croatia, Cyprus, Czechia, Denmark, Estonia, Finland, France, Germany, Ghana, Greece, Hong Kong, Hungary, India, Indonesia, Ireland, Israel, Italy, Japan, Mexico, Netherlands, New Zealand, Norway, Palestine, Peru, Philippines, Poland, Portugal, Romania, Russia, Serbia, South Africa, Spain, Sweden, Taiwan, Thailand, Tunisia, Türkiye, UK, USA. [2022.06.19/XD8925/D]

♦ International Ammunition Association (internationally oriented national body)

♦ International Anal Neoplasia Society (IANS) 11649

Pres PO Box 2023, Montgomery Village MD 20886, USA. Fax +13013305028. E-mail: iansociety@gmail.com.
URL: http://ians.memberlodge.org/
Aims Provide a forum for individuals with a broad spectrum of background, viewpoints and geographic origin, an exchange of ideas and dissemination of knowledge regarding the pathogenesis, diagnosis, treatment and prevention of anal neoplasia. **Activities** Training/education. **Events** *Scientific Meeting* Amsterdam (Netherlands) 2019, *Scientific Meeting* Montréal, QC (Canada) 2018, *Scientific Meeting* Atlanta, GA (USA) 2015. [2015/XJ9142/C]

♦ International Analog Forestry Network (IAFN) 11650

Réseau International de Foresterie Analogue (RIFA) – Red Internacional de Foresteria Analoga
Pres PO Box 512, Montes de Oca, San José, San José, San José, 2050, Costa Rica. T. +50622484500. E-mail: isabel@analogforestry.org – info@analogforestry.org.
Chair address not obtained. T. +50684885260.
URL: http://www.analogforestry.org/
History Founded 1996, Ecuador. Secretariat relocated to Costa Rica, 2006. **Aims** Promote application and appreciation of analog forestry techniques as a critical component of a new *rural development* paradigm. **Structure** Board; Secretariat. **Languages** English, French, Spanish. **Staff** 2.00 FTE, paid. **Finance** Institutional funding from partners. Annual budget: about US$ 110,000. **Activities** Certification/accreditation; capacity building; knowledge management/information dissemination. **Publications** *Analog Forests* (12 a year) in English, French, Spanish – newsletter. Guides.
Members Full in 20 countries:
Australia, Belgium, Benin, Bolivia, Cameroon, Canada, Costa Rica, Cuba, Dominican Rep, Ecuador, France, Honduras, India, Mexico, Netherlands, Peru, Spain, Sri Lanka, Togo, USA. [2017.10.24/XJ7821/F]

♦ International Anaplastology Association 11651

Exec Dir PO Box 8685, Delray Beach FL 33482, USA. T. +12026422053. E-mail: executivedirector@anaplastology.org.
URL: http://www.anaplastology.org/

History 1980, Palo Alto CA (USA), as *American Anaplastology Association.* Current title adopted 2008. Incorporated in the State of California (USA). **Aims** Promote quality patient care by supporting the development of best practices in anaplastology through educational conferences, networking, publication, and advocacy opportunities. **Structure** Board, comprising President, President-Elect, Vice-President-Elect, Immediate Past-President, Secretary, Treasurer, 2 Directors and Committee Chairs. Committees (6): Newsletter; Public Relations; Future Sites; Education; Web Site; Membership. Administrative Office, headed by Executive Director. **Events** *Annual Conference* Delray Beach, FL (USA) 2022, *Annual Conference* Delray Beach, FL (USA) 2021, *Annual Conference* Lima (Peru) 2020, *Annual Conference* Scottsdale, AZ (USA) 2019, *Annual Conference* Québec, QC (Canada) 2018. **Publications** *International Journal of Anaplastology.*
Members Individuals in 17 countries and territories:
Australia, Belgium, Canada, Czechia, France, Germany, Hong Kong, India, Italy, Japan, Netherlands, Saudi Arabia, Spain, Sweden, Switzerland, UK, USA. [2015/XW0282/v/**C**]

- ♦ International Anatomical Sciences and Cell Biology Conference (meeting series)
- ♦ International Andalusian Horse Association / see International Andalusian and Lusitano Horse Association (#11652)

♦ International Andalusian and Lusitano Horse Association (IALHA) . 11652

Pres 101 Carnoustie North, Box 200, Birmingham AL 35242, USA. T. +12059958900. Fax +12059958966. E-mail: president@ialha.org – infoshare@ialha.com.
URL: http://www.ialha.org/

History 1977, as *International Andalusian Horse Association.* **Publications** *The Andalusian* (6 a year).
Members in 8 countries:
Australia, Canada, Costa Rica, France, Japan, Mexico, UK, USA. [2015/XE2621/**E**]

- ♦ International Andrology Society / see International Society of Andrology (#14918)
- ♦ International Anesthesia Research Society (internationally oriented national body)
- ♦ International Anglican Family Network (see: #00827)
- ♦ International Anglican Fellowship (see: #20193)
- ♦ International Anglican Women's Network (see: #00827)
- ♦ International Angling Confederation (#04562)
- ♦ International Animal Rescue (internationally oriented national body)
- ♦ International Animated Film Association (#02698)
- ♦ International ANSWER (internationally oriented national body)

♦ International Antarctic Institute 11653

Secretariat Inst of Low Temp Sci, Hokkaido University Kita 19 Nishi 8, Kita-ku, Sapporo HOKKAIDO, 060-0819 Japan.
URL: https://www.ees.hokudai.ac.jp/IAI/english/index_en.html

History 8 Jul 2006, following 2004 planning meeting held in Hobart (Australia). **Aims** Facilitate cooperation and collaboration between members in Antarctic multidisciplinary education; develop multi-disciplinary and multi institute degrees conferred by Members in Antarctic education. **Structure** Council, comprising one representative of each of the members. Secretariat, headed by Director.
Members Institutions in 13 countries:
Australia, Brazil, Chile, France, Germany, Italy, Japan, Malaysia, New Zealand, Norway, Spain, UK, USA.
Associate (7), include the following 2 listed in this Yearbook:
Cousteau Society; *International Polar Foundation (IPF).*
NGO Relations Memorandum of Understanding with: *Association of Polar Early Career Scientists (APECS, #02864).* [2019/XM4588/jy/**E**]

- ♦ International Anti-Communist Union (inactive)

♦ International Anti-Corruption Academy (IACA) 11654

Académie internationale de lutte contre la corruption

Contact Muenchendorfer Str 2, 2361 Laxenburg, Austria. T. +432236710718100. Fax +432236710718311. E-mail: mail@iaca.int.
URL: http://www.iaca.int/

History 8 Mar 2011. The *United Nations Office on Drugs and Crime (UNODC, #20596)*, the guardian of the United Nations Convention against Corruption (UNCAC), the *European Anti-Fraud Office (#05906)*, *International Criminal Police Organization – INTERPOL (ICPO-INTERPOL, #13110)*, the Republic of Austria and other stakeholders were the driving forces behind the Academy's establishment. Official launch during Inaugural Conference, Sep 2010, Vienna (Austria). **Aims** Overcome current shortcomings in knowledge and practice in the field of anti-corruption; empower professionals for the challenges of tomorrow; deliver and facilitate anti-corruption training for professionals and practitioners from all sectors of society; advance the goals of the United Nations Convention against Corruption; provide support and technical assistance to a wide variety of stakeholders. **Structure** Assembly of the Parties; Board of Governors; Dean; International Senior Advisory Board; International Academic Advisory Board. **Languages** English. **Staff** Staff includes personnel seconded by Parties. **Finance** Voluntary contributions from Parties, the private sector and other donors; tuition fees; service revenues. **Activities** Training/education; networking/liaising; knowledge management/information dissemination; events/meetings. **Events** *From vision to reality – a new and holistic approach to fighting corruption* Vienna (Austria) 2010. **Publications** *Alumni Magazine*; *IACA Newsletter*. *International Anti-Corruption Summer Academy* – series. Annual Report; bulletins; programme brochures; research papers; master theses.
Members Signatory states/Parties (47):
Afghanistan, Albania, Australia, Austria, Azerbaijan, Bolivia, Bosnia-Herzegovina, Brazil, Bulgaria, Burkina Faso, Chile, Croatia, Cyprus, Czechia, Egypt, Hungary, India, Indonesia, Iraq, Israel, Jordan, Korea Rep, Latvia, Liechtenstein, Lithuania, Luxembourg, Malaysia, Maldives, Mexico, Moldova, Mongolia, Montenegro, Nigeria, North Macedonia, Pakistan, Panama, Philippines, Romania, Russia, Saudi Arabia, Serbia, Slovakia, Slovenia, Spain, Syrian AR, Thailand, Türkiye.
Signatory organizations/Parties (4):
EUCLID; *European Public Law Organization (EPLO, #08299)*; *International Centre for Migration Policy Development (ICMPD, #12503)*; *International Organization for Migration (IOM, #14454).*
Signatories apart from Parties (17):
Argentina, Benin, Cape Verde, Congo DR, Greece, Kenya, Libya, Mali, Mozambique, Peru, Portugal, Senegal, Togo, Uganda, UK, Yemen, Zambia.
IGO Relations Observer status with (4): *ECOSOC (#05331)*; *Group of States Against Corruption (#10789)*; *International Organization for Migration (IOM, #14454)*; *United Nations (UN, #20515)* (General Assembly). Partnership relations with: *European Contact-point Network against Corruption (EACN, #06776)*; *European Partners against Corruption (EPAC, #08153)*; *International Bank for Reconstruction and Development (IBRD, #12317)* (World Bank); *International Association of Anti-Corruption Authorities (IAACA, #11703)*; *International Development Law Organization (IDLO, #13161)*; *OAS (#17629)*; *OECD (#17693)*; *Organization for Security and Cooperation in Europe (OSCE, #17887).* **NGO Relations** Partnership relations with: *Basel Institute on Governance*; *Global Organization of Parliamentarians Against Corruption (GOPAC, #10518)*; *International Association of Prosecutors (IAP, #12111)*; *International Ombudsman Institute (IOI, #14411)*; *International Organization of Supreme Audit Institutions (INTOSAI, #14478)*; *Transparency International (TI, #20223)*; *World Economic Forum (WEF, #21367).* [2019.06.21/XJ2625/y/**E***]

- ♦ International Anti-Corruption Conference (meeting series)

♦ International Anti-Corruption Conference Council (IACC Council) . . 11655

Contact c/o Transparency Int, Alt-Moabit 96, 10559 Berlin, Germany. T. +49303438200. Fax +493034703912. E-mail: iacc@transparency.org.
URL: https://iaccseries.org/

History Sep 1996. Founded as the body responsible for convening *International Anti-Corruption Conference (IACC).* **Aims** Organize the International Anti-Corruption Conference; raise awareness of the problems of corruption and its consequences in both the public and private sectors; examine trends in relation to corruption in different parts of the world; discuss and formulate strategies for combating corruption in both public and private sectors; analyse and consider various strategies that have been applied in combating corruption, their outcomes and their utility in different cultural, geographic and political contexts; provide a space for innovation and cutting edge solutions to the problems corruption poses. **Structure** Council; Programme Committee; Secretariat provided by *Transparency International (TI, #20223).* **Languages** Arabic, Chinese, English, French, Russian, Spanish. **Staff** Varying. **Finance** Funding of conferences: host country and donors. **Activities** Events/meetings. **Events** *Biennial International Anticorruption Conference* 2020, *Biennial International Anticorruption Conference* Copenhagen (Denmark) 2018, *Biennial International Anticorruption Conference* Panama (Panama) 2016, *Biennial International Anticorruption Conference* Putrajaya (Malaysia) 2015, *Biennial International Anticorruption Conference* Brasilia (Brazil) 2012. **Members** Not a membership organization. Delegates attending conferences come from all over the world. **NGO Relations** Links with NGOs throughout the world (not specified). [2021/XE4212/**E**]

- ♦ International Anti-Counterfeiting Coalition / see International Anticounterfeiting Coalition (#11656)

♦ International Anticounterfeiting Coalition (IACC) 11656

Coalition internationale anti-contrefaçon

Pres 727 15th St NW, 9th Floor, Washington DC 20005, USA. T. +12022236667. Fax +12022236668. E-mail: iacc@iacc.org.
URL: http://www.iacc.org/

History 1978. Previously also written as *International Anti-Counterfeiting Coalition.* EU Transparency Register: 25801888507-71. **Aims** Combat counterfeiting of brand name merchandise and patent and copyright piracy, by promoting laws, regulations, and directives designed to render theft of intellectual property undesirable and unprofitable. **Structure** Board of Directors, comprising Chairman, President, Treasurer, Secretary and 20 Directors. **Staff** 3.00 FTE, paid. **Finance** Members' dues. **Activities** Provides training to law enforcement officials, the counterfeit product identification and product security methods. Campaigns. **Events** *Anti-Counterfeiting* Nur-Sultan (Kazakhstan) 2021, *Annual Spring Meeting* Boston, MA (USA) 2019, *Annual Spring Meeting* Seattle, WA (USA) 2018, *Annual Spring Meeting* Barcelona (Spain) 2017, *Annual Fall Meeting* Scottsdale, AZ (USA) 2016. **Publications** *IACC Update* (12 a year).
Members Corporations product security companies, law firms and investigators (150) in Americas, Europe, Asia, Africa and Australasia. Members in 21 countries:
Australia, Belgium, Canada, Colombia, France, Germany, Hong Kong, Japan, Mexico, Netherlands, New Zealand, Pakistan, Panama, South Africa, Spain, Sweden, Switzerland, Taiwan, UK, USA, Venezuela.
Consultative Status Consultative status granted from: *World Intellectual Property Organization (WIPO, #21593)* (Permanent Observer Status). **IGO Relations** *International Criminal Police Organization – INTERPOL (ICPO-INTERPOL, #13110)*; *United Nations Economic Commission for Europe (UNECE, #20555)*; *World Customs Organization (WCO, #21350).* [2018/XF1042/**F**]

- ♦ International Antifascist Solidarity (inactive)
- ♦ International Anti-Hunting Committee (internationally oriented national body)
- ♦ International Antimilitarist Bureau Against War and Reaction (inactive)
- ♦ International Antimilitarist Union (inactive)

♦ International Antimony Association (i2a) 11657

Main Office Avenue de Broqueville 12, 1150 Brussels, Belgium. T. +3227623093.
URL: http://www.antimony.com/

History 2000, as *International Antimony Oxide Industry Association (IAOIA).* Includes activities of (US) Antimony Oxide Industry Association, founded 1978. Current title adopted, Jan 2008. Registered in accordance with Belgian law. **Aims** Serve interests of producers, users and other stakeholders worldwide concerning environmental, health and safety regulatory affairs of antimony substances and their uses. **Structure** General Assembly (2 a year). Board of Directors (meets twice a year), comprising 2 representatives for each region, including Chairman, Vice-Chairman, Secretary General and Treasurer. Technical Group. **Languages** English. **Staff** Employees of one of the members provide staff, except Secretary-General. **Finance** Members' dues. Budget (annual) depends on yearly costs: over euro 600,000. **Activities** Research/documentation; knowledge management/information dissemination. **Publications** *i2a Newsletter.*
Members Full – antimony oxide producers; Associate – companies that do not produce antimony oxide but are stakeholders ith a commercial interest in antimony oxide, such as producers of related products, distributors or consumers. Members in 6 countries:
Belgium, China, France, Japan, Spain, USA.
NGO Relations Member of (2): *Association européenne des métaux (EUROMETAUX, #02578)*; *International Council on Mining and Metals (ICMM, #13048).* Full member of: *Critical Raw Materials Alliance (CRM Alliance, #04959).* Partner of: *Conseil européen de l'industrie chimique (CEFIC, #04687).* [2018/XD9129/**D**]

- ♦ International Antimony Oxide Industry Association / see International Antimony Association (#11657)
- ♦ International Anti-Nuclear Movement 'Nevada-Semey / see International Antinuclear Movement 'Nevada-Semipalatinsk'
- ♦ International Antinuclear Movement 'Nevada-Semipalatinsk' (internationally oriented national body)
- ♦ International Anti-Opium Association (inactive)

♦ International Anti-Poaching Foundation (IAPF) 11658

Contact Stanley and Livingstone Private Game Reserve, PO Box 44, Victoria Falls, Matabeleland North, Victoria Falls MATABELELAND NORTH, Zimbabwe. E-mail: info@iapf.org.
URL: http://www.iapf.org/

History 2009. Registered in accordance with the laws of: Australia – 57142987782; South Africa – 930045174; Zimbabwe; USA – 32-0408734. **Aims** Promote *wildlife* conservation through direct action. **Structure** Steering Committee. Each IAPF entity is governed by Board of Directors or Trustees. Advisory Committee. [2016/XM5142/f/**F**]

- ♦ International Antiterrorism Unity (internationally oriented national body)
- ♦ International Anti-Vaccination League (inactive)
- ♦ International Antiviral Therapy Evaluation Center (internationally oriented national body)
- ♦ International Antivivisection League (inactive)
- ♦ International Anti-War Medical Association (inactive)
- ♦ International ANTOR Committee (inactive)
- ♦ International Aphasia Rehabilitation Conference (meeting series)
- ♦ International Apostolic Movement of the Independent Social Categories / see Mouvement international d'apostolat des milieux sociaux indépendants (#16864)

♦ International Apparel Federation (IAF) 11659

Fédération internationale de l'industrie de l'habillement – Internationaler Verband der Bekleidungsindustrie

SG PO Box 762, 3700 AT Zeist, Netherlands. T. +31302320908. Fax +31302320999. E-mail: info@iafnet.com.
Street address Arnhemse Bovenweg 100, 3708 AG Zeist, Netherlands.
URL: https://www.iafnet.com/

History Founded 2 Jun 1977, by *European Clothing Association (ECLA, inactive)* and national organizations of Japan and USA, following *'Williamsburg Resolution'*, Jun 1976, Stockholm (Sweden). Incorporated, London (UK). Registration: Netherlands. **Aims** Unite all stakeholders of the fashion and apparel industry, including brands, retailers, manufacturers, suppliers and country associations to enable and promote smarter, stronger and more sustainable supply chains. **Structure** General Assembly (annual); Board of Directors; Executive Committee; Committees (3). **Languages** English. **Staff** 6.00 FTE, paid. **Finance** by subscription. **Activities** Awards/prizes/competitions; events/meetings; knowledge management/information dissemination. **Events** *World Fashion Convention* Dhaka (Bangladesh) 2022, *World Fashion Convention* Antwerp (Belgium) 2021, *Digital Pre-Convention Meeting* Antwerp (Belgium) 2020, *World Fashion Convention* Antwerp (Belgium) 2020, *World Fashion Convention* Lahore (Pakistan) 2019. **Publications** Members' newsletter (12 a year). Press releases. Information Services: Online apparel documentation and information system.
Members Associations in 27 countries and territories:
Bangladesh, Belgium, Brazil, China, Colombia, Denmark, France, Germany, Greece, Hong Kong, India, Italy, Japan, Korea Rep, Madagascar, Mauritius, Mexico, Morocco, Netherlands, Pakistan, Portugal, South Africa, Sweden, Taiwan, Türkiye, UK, USA.
Individuals in 17 countries and territories:
Argentina, Australia, Brazil, Canada, Chile, China, Colombia, Cyprus, Czechia, Hong Kong, Hungary, India, Ireland, Malaysia, Pakistan, Singapore, South Africa.
European national organizations represented by European regional body:

EURATEX – The European Apparel and Textile Confederation (EURATEX, #05616).
Associate members (72); corporate members (26). Membership countries not specified.
NGO Relations Cooperates with: *Groupement International de l'Etiquetage pour l'Entretien des Textiles (GINETEX, #10761).* [2021/XD5144/t/C]

♦ International Approval and Registration Centre (IARC) 11660

Sec PO Box 2092, Nerang MDC, Gold Coast QLD 4211, Australia. T. +61755621088. Fax +61755621099. E-mail: admin@iarcedu.com.
UK Office PO Box 4171, Stourbridge, DY8 2WZ, UK.
URL: http://www.iarcedu.com/

History 1999, as *International Accreditation and Recognition Council (IARC).* Registered in accordance with Australian law: ABN 13 383 495 140. **Aims** Provide a simple system, for distinguishing quality, post secondary education including vocational education, distance education, and adult and continuing education. **Structure** Executive Committee Board; Regional Committee Board. **Activities** Networking/liaising; awards/prizes/competitions; monitoring/evaluation.
Members Full in 14 countries:
Australia, Bahamas, Bangladesh, Ireland, Israel, Italy, Kenya, Mauritius, New Zealand, Panama, Spain, UK, United Arab Emirates, USA.
Included in the above, 1 organization listed in this Yearbook:
International Culture University (ICU). [2021/XJ7377/D]

♦ International Aquarium Network (IAN) 11661

Chairman Nausicaa, Boulevard Sainte Beuve, BP 187, 62203 Boulogne-sur-Mer, France. E-mail: communication@nausicaa.fr.
URL: http://www.intaquaforum.org/

History Dec 2004, Monterey, CA (USA). Founded during 6th International Aquarium Congress, and confirmed at 2008 IAC, Shanghai (China). **Aims** Improve worldwide communication among public aquarium professionals in order to: strengthen capacity building; promote sustainable practices; conserve global aquatic ecosystems. **Structure** Board of Directors. **Languages** English. **Staff** None. **Finance** None. **Activities** Capacity building; events/meetings; knowledge management/information dissemination. **Events** *International Aquarium Congress* Boulogne-sur-Mer (France) 2022, *International Aquarium Congress* Boulogne-sur-Mer (France) 2021, *Biennial Congress* Fukushima (Japan) 2018, *International Aquarium Congress* Vancouver, BC (Canada) 2016, *International Aquarium Congress* Cape Town (South Africa) 2012. **Publications** Congress proceedings. **NGO Relations** Partners: *European Union of Aquarium Curators (EUAC, #08975); World Ocean Network (WON, #21681);* national organizations. [2018.06.22/XM1352/c/F]

♦ International Aquathlon Association (IAA) 11662

Address not obtained.

History 30 Mar 1996, Moscow (Russia). **Aims** Develop the *water sport wrestling*, aquathlon. **Structure** Directing Committee, comprising President, Vice-President, General Secretary, Treasurer and 9 Directors. **Languages** English, Russian. **Staff** 2.50 FTE, paid. **Finance** Income from courses and sponsors. Budget (annual): US$ 100,000. **Activities** Organizes World and European championships and competitions; trains and certifies aquathlon instructors and coaches. **Events** *Congress* Sochi (Russia) 2009, *Congress* Tarhankut (Ukraine) 2008. **Publications** Books, articles.
Members in 10 countries:
Belarus, Germany, India, Israel, Lithuania, Moldova, Russia, Spain, Ukraine, USA.
NGO Relations Member of: *International Association of Traditional Wrestling Sports (IATWS, no recent information).* [2008.09.24/XM2368/D]

♦ International Aquatic Board / see Internationale Akademie für Bäder-, Sport-, und Freizeitbauten (#13211)

♦ International Aquatic Plants Group (IAPG) 11663

Chair address not obtained.

Structure An informal group. International Scientific Committee. **Activities** Events/meetings. [2020/AA0317/v/F]

♦ International Arab Aluminium Conference (meeting series)

♦ International Arabidopsis Informatics Consortium (IAIC) 11664

Contact address not obtained. E-mail: arabidopsisinformatics@gmail.com.
URL: http://www.arabidopsisinformatics.org/

Structure Steering Committee; Scientific Advisory Board; Scientific Advisory Panel. Working Groups. **Activities** Knowledge management/information dissemination. **NGO Relations** *Multinational Arabidopsis Steering Committee (MASC, #16894).* [2016/XM4607/D]

♦ International Arab Society of Certified Accountants (IASCA) 11665

Exec Dir PO Box 921100, Amman 11192, Jordan. T. +96265100900. Fax +96265100901. E-mail: info@iascasociety.org.
URL: http://www.iascasociety.org/

History 12 Jan 1984, London (UK). Former names and other names: *The Arab Society of Certified Accountants (ASCA)* – legal name. Registration: Start date: 24 Feb 1994, Jordan. **Aims** Advance the profession of accountancy, auditing and other related fields throughout the Arab world. **Structure** General Meeting (annual); Board of Directors; Executive Committee. **Languages** Arabic, English. **Staff** 9.00 FTE, paid. **Finance** Sources: fees for services; members' dues; sale of publications. **Activities** Certification/accreditation; events/meetings; guidance/assistance/consulting; publishing activities; standards/guidelines; training/education. **Events** *International Professional Conference* Manama (Bahrain) 2018, *Conference to develop accounting education in the Arab countries and the GCC* Kuwait 2006, *Arab international accounting conference* Abu Dhabi (United Arab Emirates) 2000, *Seminar on accounting for environment in the Middle East* Bahrain 1999, *Seminar on accounting for environment in the Middle East* Alexandria (Egypt) 1998. **Publications** *IASCA Monthly Newsletter.* Standards; handbooks; guides.
Members Individuals with acceptable level of competence in accounting and practical experience in 18 countries and territories:
Algeria, Bahrain, Egypt, Iraq, Jordan, Kuwait, Lebanon, Libya, Morocco, Oman, Palestine, Qatar, Saudi Arabia, Sudan, Syrian AR, Tunisia, United Arab Emirates, Yemen.
Consultative Status Consultative status granted from: *ECOSOC (#05331)* (Ros A). **IGO Relations** Accredited by (1): *United Nations Office at Vienna (UNOV, #20604).* Associated with Department of Global Communications of the United Nations. **NGO Relations** Board member of: *International Auditing and Assurance Standards Board (IAASB, #12296).* Member of: *International Federation of Accountants (IFAC, #13335).* [2023.02.15/XD2068/v/D]

♦ International Aral Sea Rehabilitation Fund / see International Fund for Saving the Aral Sea (#13694)
♦ International Arbitration League (inactive)
♦ International Archaeology and Historical Linguistics Society (unconfirmed)
♦ International Archery Federation / see World Archery (#21105)
♦ International Architects, Designers, Planners for the Prevention of Nuclear War / see International Architects, Designers, Planners for Social Responsibility (#11666)

♦ International Architects, Designers, Planners for Social Responsibility (ARC-PEACE) 11666

Sec/Chief Admin Officer School of Architecture and the Built Environment, KTH, SE-100 44 Stockholm, Sweden. T. +4687908522. E-mail: dickurba@gmail.com.
URL: http://arcpeace.org/web/

History Founded 15 Jul 1987, Brighton (UK), as *International Architects, Designers, Planners for the Prevention of Nuclear War (IADPNW).* Present name adopted at IUA Congress, 1990, Montréal QC (Canada). Charter revised, 18 Jun 1993, Chicago IL (USA) and 17 Apr 2008, Barcelona (Spain). Registered in accordance with Swedish law. **Aims** Pursue actively the reduction and subsequent elimination of nuclear, biological, chemical weapons and other means of mass annihilation, both on earth and in space, and support avenues for non-violent resolution of conflicts; exercise professional expertise in helping to protect the natural environment from further destruction and to design, improve and preserve a socially responsible built environment, including disaster risk management and human safety; support diversion of funds from weaponry to the above needs and to other critical obligations of society; promote enabling housing strategies, methods and techniques to enhance capability of people, particularly the poor, to build their own housing and living environment and also improve the same. **Structure** General Assembly (every 2 years). Board of up to 20 members, including Executive Committee, comprising 2 Co-Chairs, Secretary and Treasurer. **Languages** English. **Staff** None. **Finance** Members' dues. Other sources: contributions; donations. **Events** *Meeting* Copenhagen (Denmark) 2012, *Meeting* Stockholm (Sweden) 2010, *Meeting* Khartoum (Sudan) 2009, *Meeting* Barcelona (Spain) 2008, *Meeting* Vancouver, BC (Canada) 2006. **Publications** *ARC PEACE Newsletter* (4 a year).
Members Organizations or individual architects, designers, planners or students. Organizations in 8 countries:
Australia, Cuba, India, Peru, Sudan, Thailand, UK, USA.
Included in the above, 1 organization listed in this Yearbook:
Scientists for Global Responsibility (SGR).
Individuals in 31 countries:
Australia, Bahrain, Bangladesh, Canada, Colombia, Croatia, Cuba, France, Germany, India, Indonesia, Japan, Kenya, Malaysia, Nepal, New Zealand, North Macedonia, Norway, Peru, Poland, Russia, Serbia, Spain, Sri Lanka, Sudan, Sweden, Thailand, Tunisia, Uganda, UK, USA.
Consultative Status Consultative status granted from: *ECOSOC (#05331)* (Special). [2013.06.12/XF2151/F]

♦ International Archives Congress (meeting series)
♦ International Archive of Women in Architecture (internationally oriented national body)

♦ International Arctic Buoy Programme (IABP) 11667

Coordinator Polar Sci Cntr Appl Physics Lab, Univ of Washington, 1013 NE 40th St, Seattle WA 98105-6698, USA. T. +12066852571. Fax +12066163142.
Chair 1-26 Earth Sciences Building, Office Tory 2-105C, University of Alberta, Edmonton AB T6G 2E3, Canada.
URL: https://iabp.apl.uw.edu/

Events *Annual Meeting* Incheon (Korea Rep) 2016, *Annual Meeting* Oslo (Norway) 2010, *Annual meeting* Washington, DC (USA) 2007, *Annual meeting* Bremerhaven (Germany) 2006, *Annual meeting* Seattle, WA (USA) 2005.
Members Full in 10 countries:
Canada, China, Finland, France, Germany, Japan, Norway, Russia, UK, USA. [2019/XE3928/E]

♦ International Arctic Forum (meeting series)

♦ International Arctic Science Committee (IASC) 11668

Contact Borgir, Nordurslód, 600 Akureyri, Iceland. T. +3545155824. E-mail: info@iasc.info.
URL: http://www.iasc.info/

History 28 Aug 1990. Began operations in 1991. **Aims** Encourage, facilitate and promote leading-edge multi-disciplinary research to foster a greater scientific understanding of the Arctic region and its role in the Earth system. **Structure** Council (meets annually, during the Arctic Science Summit Week); Executive Committee; Working Groups (5); Action Groups (temporary); Secretariat, headed by Executive Secretary. Advisory Group: *International Science Initiative in the Russian Arctic (ISIRA).* **Languages** English. **Staff** 3.00 FTE, paid. **Finance** Sources: contributions; members' dues. Financing of secretariat provided by Iceland. **Activities** Capacity building; knowledge management/information dissemination; research/documentation. **Events** *Biennial Arctic Observing Summit* Tromsø (Norway) 2022, *Annual Arctic Science Summit* Lisbon (Portugal) 2021, *Annual Arctic Science Summit* Akureyri (Iceland) 2020, *Biennial Arctic Observing Summit* Akureyri (Iceland) 2020, *Annual Arctic Science Summit* Arkhangelsk (Russia) 2019. **Publications** *IASC Progress* (12 a year); *IASC Bulletin* (annual). *The Arctic Meeting Calendar* – jointly with Arctic Research Consortium of the United States, as a service to the Arctic community.
Members National scientific organizations covering all fields of Arctic research. Members in 23 countries:
Austria, Canada, China, Czechia, Denmark, Finland, France, Germany, Iceland, India, Italy, Japan, Korea Rep, Netherlands, Norway, Poland, Portugal, Russia, Spain, Sweden, Switzerland, UK, USA.
IGO Relations Observer to: *Arctic Council (#01097).* **NGO Relations** Member of: *International Science Council (ISC, #14796).* Connections to numerous international Arctic organizations, including: Asian Forum for Polar Sciences (AFoPS); *Association of Polar Early Career Scientists (APECS, #02864); Circumpolar Health Research Network (CirchNet, #03942); European Polar Board (EPB, #08238); Forum of Arctic Research Operators (FARO, #09898); International Arctic Social Sciences Association (IASSA, #11669); International Association of Cryospheric Sciences (IACS, #11829); International Permafrost Association (IPA, #14558); Pacific Arctic Group (PAG, #17926); University of the Arctic (UArctic, #20696); World Climate Research Programme (WCRP, #21279)* Climate and Cryosphere (CliC). [2020.09.21/XD1606/C]

♦ International Arctic Social Sciences Association (IASSA) 11669

Sec ARCTICentern, 348 ITTC, 1227 27th St, Cedar Falls IA 50614-0406, USA. T. +13192733778. Fax +13192737103.
URL: http://www.iassa.org/

History 1990, Fairbanks AK (USA), following proposal at *'Conference on Coordination of Research in the Arctic'*, Leningrad (USSR), 1988. **Aims** Promote and stimulate international cooperation and increase participation of social scientists in national and international Arctic research. **Structure** General Assembly; Council; Secretariat. **Languages** English. **Staff** 1.00 FTE, paid. **Finance** Members' dues. **Activities** Research/documentation; awards/prizes/competitions. **Events** *International Congress of Arctic Social Sciences (ICASS)* Bodø (Norway) 2024, *International Congress of Arctic Social Sciences (ICASS)* Arkhangelsk (Russia) 2021, *International Congress of Arctic Social Sciences (ICASS)* Umeå (Sweden) 2017, *Annual Arctic Science Summit* Toyama City (Japan) 2015, *International Congress of Arctic Social Sciences (ICASS)* Prince George, BC (Canada) 2014. **Publications** *IASSA Newsletter* (2 a year). *Topics in Arctic Social Sciences* – series.
Members Full in 26 countries and territories:
Australia, Austria, Brazil, Bulgaria, Canada, China, Denmark, Estonia, Finland, France, Germany, Greenland, Iceland, Italy, Japan, Netherlands, New Zealand, Nigeria, Norway, Poland, Russia, Spain, Sweden, Switzerland, UK, USA.
IGO Relations Observer of: *Arctic Council (#01097).* **NGO Relations** Memorandum of Understanding with: *Association of Polar Early Career Scientists (APECS, #02864).* Member of: *International Science Council (ISC, #14796).* [2019.02.28/XD5135/D]

♦ International Arctic Workshop (meeting series)
♦ International Arid Lands Consortium (internationally oriented national body)

♦ International Aroid Society (IAS) 11670

Contact PO Box 43-1853, Miami FL 33143, USA. E-mail: huntington@aroid.org.
URL: http://www.aroid.org/

History Aug 1977, Miami FL (USA). **Aims** Support education, research and *horticulture* through publications, awards and events. **Structure** Board of Directors. **Languages** English. **Staff** 0.50 FTE, voluntary. **Finance** Members' dues. Proceeds from events. **Activities** Events/meetings; publishing activities; awards/prizes/competitions. **Events** *Symposium / International Aroid Symposium* Hanoi (Vietnam) 2013, *Symposium / International Aroid Symposium* Nancy (France) 2009, *Annual members meeting* Miami, FL (USA) 2005, *Symposium / International Aroid Symposium* Kuching (Malaysia) 2004, *Symposium* St Louis, MO (USA) 1999. **Publications** *IAS Newsletter* (4 a year); *Aroideana* (annual) – journal.
Members Individuals in 51 countries:
Australia, Austria, Bahamas, Bangladesh, Belgium, Belize, Bermuda, Brazil, Canada, China, Colombia, Costa Rica, Croatia, Cuba, Czechia, Dominica, Ecuador, France, Germany, Guiana Fr, India, Indonesia, Ireland, Israel, Italy, Japan, Korea Rep, Malaysia, Mexico, Netherlands, New Zealand, Norway, Peru, Philippines, Poland, Portugal, Russia, Saudi Arabia, Singapore, Slovakia, South Africa, Spain, Sweden, Switzerland, Taiwan, Thailand, Türkiye, UK, Ukraine, USA, Vietnam. [2015.08.29/XN2853/v/F]

♦ International Art Cinemas Confederation / see International Confederation of Art Cinemas (#12847)
♦ International Arthroscopy Association (inactive)

♦ International Arthurian Society (IAS) 11671

Société internationale arthurienne (SIA) – Internationale Artusgesellschaft

Pres c/o Univ of Western Australia, 35 Stirling Highway, Perth WA 6009, Australia. T. +61864882185. Fax +61864881030.

URL: http://www.internationalarthuriansociety.com/
History 2 Sep 1948, Quimper (France). Founded 2-7 Sep 1948, Quimper (France), during 2nd Arthurian Congress. **Aims** Study Arthurian works and *legends* of the *Round Table* – in *mediaeval* and post-mediaeval *literature* of all countries, and the problems arising therefrom. **Structure** General Assembly (every 3 years); Central Committee (meets every 3 years), consisting of International Officers and national Presidents. **Languages** English, French, German. **Staff** None. **Finance** Each National Section is responsible for deciding the rate of annual dues. **Activities** Knowledge management/information dissemination; events/meetings. **Events** *Triennial Congress* Catania (Italy) 2021, *Triennial Congress* Catania (Italy) 2020, *Triennial Congress* Würzburg (Germany) 2017, *Triennial Congress* Bucharest (Romania) 2014, *International Conference* Oslo (Norway) 2013. **Publications** *Bibliography of the International Arthurian Society* (annual); *Journal of the International Arthurian Society* (annual).
Members Individuals (over 1,500) in 38 countries and territories:
Argentina, Australia, Austria, Belgium, Brazil, Bulgaria, Canada, Congo Brazzaville, Congo DR, Côte d'Ivoire, Denmark, Finland, France, Germany, Greece, Hungary, Ireland, Israel, Italy, Japan, Korea Rep, Luxembourg, Morocco, Netherlands, New Zealand, Nigeria, Norway, Poland, Portugal, Puerto Rico, Romania, South Africa, Spain, Sweden, Switzerland, Türkiye, UK, USA.
[2020.01.10/XE3853/v/**E**]

♦ International Article Numbering Association / see GS1 (#10809)

♦ International Artificial Intelligence in Education Society (International AIED Society) 11672

Main Office c/o ICCS/HCRC, School of Informatics, 10 Crichton St, Edinburgh, EH8 9AB, UK. E-mail: press@iaied.org.
URL: http://iaied.org/
History 1997. **Aims** Advance knowledge and promote research and development in the field of artificial intelligence in education. **Structure** Management Board; Executive Committee; Advisory Board. **Languages** English. **Finance** Members' dues. Annual budget: about pounds7,500. **Events** *International Conference on Artificial Intelligence in Education* Utrecht (Netherlands) 2021, *International Conference on Artificial Intelligence in Education* Ifrane (Morocco) 2020, *International Conference on Artificial Intelligence in Education* Chicago, IL (USA) 2019, *International Conference on Artificial Intelligence in Education* London (UK) 2018, *International Conferenece on Artificial Intelligence in Education* Madrid (Spain) 2015. **Publications** *International Journal of Artificial Intelligence in Education.* Recommendations.
Members Individuals (240) in 33 countries and territories:
Argentina, Australia, Austria, Bahrain, Belgium, Brazil, Canada, Egypt, Finland, France, Germany, Greece, Hong Kong, Israel, Italy, Japan, Korea Rep, Malaysia, Mexico, Netherlands, New Zealand, Norway, Portugal, Russia, Serbia, Singapore, Spain, Sweden, Switzerland, Taiwan, UK, Ukraine, USA.
[2021/XD6616/v/**D**]

♦ International Artist Managers' Association (IAMA) 11673

Chief Exec West Wing, Somerset House, Strand, London, WC2R 1LA, UK. T. +442073797336. E-mail: om@iamaworld.com – info@iamaworld.com.
Main: https://www.iamaworld.com/
History 1954. Former names and other names: *British Association of Concert Agents* – former (1954 to 1996). Registration: Companies House, No/ID: 02427894, Start date: 25 Sep 1989, England and Wales. **Aims** Bring good business practice to the sector so that confidence is inspired and a measure of security lent to those working within the *classical music* sector. **Structure** Executive Board. **Languages** English, German. **Staff** 3.00 FTE, paid. **Finance** Sources: members' dues; revenue from activities/projects; sale of publications. **Activities** Advocacy/lobbying/activism; events/meetings; knowledge management/information dissemination. **Events** *International Conference* Vienna (Austria) 2023, *International Conference* Zurich (Switzerland) 2022, *International Conference* Copenhagen (Denmark) 2021, *International Conference* Barcelona (Spain) 2020, *International Conference* Düsseldorf (Germany) 2019. **Publications** *IAMA e-bulletin.* Directory of artist listings and their management.
Members Full; Full Non-Profit; Affiliate; Group. Members include 4 organizations listed in this Yearbook:
Association Européenne des Agents Artistiques (AEAA, #02554); Association of Asia Pacific Performing Arts Centres (AAPPAC, #02387); International Society for the Performing Arts Foundation (ISPA, #15350); World Federation of International Music Competitions (WFIMC, #21445). [2022.06.15/XG6396/y/**C**]

♦ The International Art Market Studies Association (TIAMSA) 11674

Address not obtained.
URL: https://www.artmarketstudies.org/
History 31 May 2016. Launched July 2016. Current constitution approved July 2017. **Aims** Support the understanding and study of art markets of all periods and geographic areas. **Structure** Annual General Meeting; Board. **Finance** Sources: members' dues. **Events** *Annual Conference* Edinburgh (UK) 2021, *Conference* Lisbon (Portugal) 2019, *Conference* Edinburgh (UK) 2018, *Conference* London (UK) 2017. **Members** Individuals; Corporate. Members (over 300). Membership countries not specified. [2020/AA0359/**D**]

♦ International Art Medal Federation 11675

Fédération Internationale de la Médaille d'Art (FIDEM)
SG Uilenkamp 18, 3972 XR Driebergen, Netherlands. E-mail: secretary-general@fidem-medals.org.
Treas Imprensa Nacional-Casa da Moeda, PT-SA, 1000-042 Lisbon, Portugal.
URL: http://www.fidem-medals.org/
History 1937, France. Former names and other names: *International Federation of Medal Producers* – former (1937 to 1963); *Fédération internationale des éditeurs de médailles* – former (1937 to 1963); *International Federation of Medals* – former (1963 to 2007); *Fédération internationale de la médaille* – former (1963 to 2007). **Aims** Promote and diffuse the art of medals at international level, make the art known and guarantee recognition of its place among other arts by increasing awareness of the art, history and technology of art medals. **Structure** General Assembly; Delegates' Meeting; Consultative Committee; Executive Committee. **Languages** English, French. **Staff** Voluntary. **Finance** Sources: members' dues. **Activities** Awards/prizes/competitions; events/meetings; knowledge management/information dissemination; research/documentation. **Events** *Congress* Florence (Italy) 2023, *Congress* Tokyo (Japan) 2021, *Congress* Tokyo (Japan) 2020, *Congress* Ottawa, ON (Canada) 2018, *Congress* Namur (Belgium) / Ghent (Belgium) 2016. **Publications** *Médailles* (2 a year) – magazine; *The Medal* (2 a year). Congress proceedings. **Information Services** *Modern Art Medal Database.*
Members Organizations and individuals in 45 countries and territories:
Argentina, Armenia, Australia, Austria, Belarus, Belgium, Bulgaria, Canada, Chile, China, Congo DR, Croatia, Czechia, Denmark, Finland, France, Germany, Great Britain, Greece, Hungary, Iran Islamic Rep, Ireland, Israel, Italy, Japan, Latvia, Lithuania, Luxembourg, Mexico, Netherlands, New Zealand, Norway, Philippines, Poland, Portugal, Romania, Russia, Slovakia, Slovenia, South Africa, Spain, Sweden, Switzerland, Ukraine, USA. [2022.05.11/XD1955/**D**]

♦ International Arts Association (no recent information)

♦ International Arts and Entertainment Alliance (IAEA) 11676

Sec c/o FIM, 21 bis rue Victor Massé, 75009 Paris, France. T. +33145263123. Fax +33145263157.
URL: http://www.iaea-globalunion.org/
History Statutes adopted, 1 Aug 2001, Brussels (Belgium). **Structure** General Conference. Board, consisting of 2 representatives of each member, and including President and Secretary. Regional organizations: *European Arts and Entertainment Alliance (EAEA, #05918)*; Coordinadora Regional del Espectaculo de las Americas (CREA).
Members Organizations (3):
International Federation of Actors (#13337); International Federation of Musicians (#13486); Media and Entertainment (MEI) Section of.
NGO Relations Member of: *Global Union Federations (GUF, #10638).* [2021/XM1581/y/**C**]

♦ International Arts-Medicine Association (inactive)
♦ International Arts Relations (internationally oriented national body)
♦ International Asbestos Information Committee / see International Chrysotile Association (#12570)
♦ International Ascent / see Vie montante internationale (#20769)
♦ International Asian Folklore Society (unconfirmed)

♦ International Assembly of Capitals and Cities (IACC) 11677

Contact address not obtained. T. +7952901590 – +7952911290. Fax +7959560052. E-mail: mag_oo@rambler.ru.
URL: http://www.e-gorod.ru/
History 2 Sep 1998. **Aims** Create conditions for the sustainable development of urban economies in CIS member states; increase living standards; share experience and implement joint projects. **Events** *Session* Minsk (Belarus) 2006, *European-Pacific congress* Vladivostok (Russia) 2003. [2014/XF6975/**F**]

♦ International Assembly of French-Speaking Parliamentarians / see Assemblée parlementaire de la Francophonie (#02312)
♦ International Assembly of National Organizations of Sport (inactive)
♦ International Assembly of NGOs concerned with the Environment (inactive)
♦ International Assembly of Winter Sports Federations / see Association of the International Olympic Winter Sports Federations (#02757)
♦ International Assets Valuation Standards Committee / see International Valuation Standards Council (#15840)
♦ International Assistance Foundation (internationally oriented national body)
♦ International Association of Abattoirs for Farmyard Animals (inactive)

♦ International Association of Academicians (IAASSE) 11678

Coordinator 657 S 6th Ave, Suite 203, City of Industry CA 91746-3026, USA. E-mail: info@iaasse.org.
URL: http://www.iaasse.org/
History 2012, India. Former names and other names: *International Association of Academicians, Scholars, Scientists and Engineers (IAASSE)* – former. Registration: USA. **Aims** Serve scholars, students, scientists and engineers to share resources, inspire research and address the challenges of the latest technological development and knowledge. **Structure** Executive Board; Headquarters, headed by Executive Director. **Languages** English. **Staff** 3.00 FTE, paid; 30.00 FTE, voluntary. **Finance** Sources: donations; meeting proceeds; members' dues. Annual budget: 5,000 USD. **Activities** Events/meetings; knowledge management/information dissemination; networking/liaising; publishing activities; training/education. **Events** *International Conference on Computers and Management* Jaipur (India) 2015, *International Conference on Cyber Security* Redlands, CA (USA) 2015. **Publications** *International Journal of Advanced Studies in Computer Science and Engineering (IJASCSE); International Journal of Advanced Studies of Scientific Research (IJASSR); International Journal of Big Data and Cloud Computing (IJBDCC); International Journal of Computational Intelligence and IoT (IJCIIoT); International Journal of Deep Learning, AI and Robotics (IJDLAIR); International Journal of Information Systems and Management Science (IJISMS).*
Members Full (over 5,000) in 13 countries:
Bangladesh, China, Ethiopia, Germany, India, Iran Islamic Rep, Iraq, Malaysia, Malta, Nigeria, UK, United Arab Emirates, USA.
[2023.02.15/XJ8629/s/**C**]

♦ International Association of Academicians, Scholars, Scientists and Engineers / see International Association of Academicians (#11678)
♦ International Association of Academies (inactive)
♦ International Association of Academies of Orthopedic Medicine / see International Academy of Orthopedic Medicine (#11565)

♦ International Association of Academies of Sciences (IAAS) 11679

Pres 54 Volodymyrska St, Kiev, 01601, Ukraine. T. +38442396711. Fax +38442343243. E-mail: sknd@nas.gov.ua.
URL: http://www.iaas.nas.gov.ua/
History 23 Sep 1993, Kiev (Ukraine). **Aims** Coordinate scholarship, research policies, use of facilities and cooperation in fundamental research of member academies of science; assist in integration of science and education and in ensuring free exchange of information resources among members; provide a constructive dialogue with the authorities of CIS countries in order to support science and international scientific cooperation; promote a common scientific space for CIS countries. **Structure** Council (meeting once or twice a year) comprises Presidents of member academies or their delegates. Officers: President; Vice-President. Scientific Councils. **Languages** English, Russian. **Finance** Members finance activities carried out within their own territory. **Activities** Prepares international research programmes, in particular on environmental protection and powder metallurgy; sponsors subregional cooperation of Academies of Ukraine, Belarus and Moldova; organizes common use of unique scientific equipment and installations; organizes international conferences and seminars; awards medal "For the Promotion of the Development of Science". **Events** *Symposium* Kiev (Ukraine) 2013, *Symposium* Alushta (Ukraine) 2009, *Symposium* Kiev (Ukraine) 2008, *Symposium* Minsk (Belarus) 2008, *Symposium* Kiev (Ukraine) 2007. **Publications** *Society and Economy* (12 a year) in Russian; *IAAS Bulletin* in Russian.
Members Full academies of sciences; Observer; Associate. Full in 13 countries:
Armenia, Azerbaijan, Belarus, Georgia, Kazakhstan, Kyrgyzstan, Moldova, Russia, Tajikistan, Turkmenistan, Ukraine, Uzbekistan, Vietnam.
Observer in 1 country:
Slovakia.
Associate (7) in 2 countries:
Belarus, Russia.
Included in the above, 1 organization listed in this Yearbook:
Joint Institute for Nuclear Research (JINR, #16134).
Consultative Status Consultative status granted from: *UNESCO (#20322)* (Consultative Status). **NGO Relations** Joint meetings with: *Euroasian Universities Association (EUA, #05641).* [2013/XD7131/**D**]

♦ International Association of Accessibility Professionals (IAAP) 11680

Managing Dir 6300 Powers Ferry R, Ste 600-300, Atlanta GA 30339, USA. T. +19412541797. E-mail: info@accessibilityassociation.org.
URL: http://www.accessibilityassociation.org/
History Since Jul 2016, a division of *Global Initiative for Inclusive Information and Communication Technologies (G3ict, #10425).* **Aims** Define, promote and improve the accessibility profession globally through networking, education and certification in order to enable the creation of accessible products, content and services. **Structure** Global Leadership Council. **Activities** Certification/accreditation; training/education. **Events** *European Accessibility Summit* Brussels (Belgium) 2022. **Publications** *Accessibility Now News.*
Members Full (over 1700), including 123 organizational members, in 42 countries. Membership countries not specified. [2019/XM7615/t/**E**]

♦ International Association for Accident and Traffic Medicine / see International Traffic Medicine Association (#15713)

♦ International Association of Accountants, Auditors and Tax Consultants (IECnet) 11681

Contact Espace Descartes, 16 rue Albert Einstein, 77420 Champs-sur-Marne, France. T. +33164617453. E-mail: info@iecnet.net.
URL: http://iecnet.net/
History 1987, France. **Structure** Board; Executive Committee. Tax Team; Committee on Auditing; PR/BD Committee. **Events** *EMEA Meeting* Amsterdam (Netherlands) 2022, *Annual General Meeting* Hammamet (Tunisia) 2022, *Staff Seminar* Lisbon (Portugal) 2022, *America Regional Meeting* Mexico City (Mexico) 2022, *Europe Middle East and Africa Meeting* Barcelona (Spain) 2016.
Members Companies (over 80) in 68 countries and territories:
Argentina, Australia, Austria, Belgium, Benin, Bolivia, Brazil, Burkina Faso, Canada, Chile, China, Colombia, Congo Brazzaville, Côte d'Ivoire, Cyprus, Denmark, Djibouti, Ecuador, Egypt, El Salvador, Finland, France, Georgia, Germany, Hong Kong, India, Indonesia, Ireland, Israel, Italy, Japan, Jordan, Kazakhstan, Korea Rep, Kuwait, Lebanon, Luxembourg, Malaysia, Malta, Mauritius, Mexico, Morocco, Netherlands, Nigeria, Pakistan, Panama, Paraguay, Peru, Poland, Portugal, Qatar, Russia, Saudi Arabia, Senegal, Seychelles, Singapore, Spain, Sri Lanka, Switzerland, Togo, Tunisia, Türkiye, UK, United Arab Emirates, Uruguay, USA, Vietnam, Yemen. [2022.10.17/XM5218/**C**]

♦ International Association for Accounting Education and Research (IAAER) 11682

Dir Research Univ of Dayton, School Business Admin, 300 College Park, Dayton OH 45469-2242, USA.
Pres Swinburne Univ, PO Box 218, Hawthorn VIC 3122, Australia.
URL: http://www.iaaer.org/

History 1984, Toronto (Canada). **Aims** Promote excellence in accounting education and research on a worldwide basis; maximize the contribution of accounting academics to the development and maintenance of high quality, globally recognized standards of accounting practice. **Structure** General Meeting (at least annual); Executive Committee; Advisory Board. Office at DePaul University, Chicago IL (USA). **Languages** English. **Finance** Sources: contributions; members' dues. **Activities** Events/meetings; research and development; standards/guidelines. **Events** *World Congress of Accounting Educators and Researchers* Paris (France) 2022, *World Congress of Accounting Educators* Sydney, NSW (Australia) 2018, *World Congress of Accounting Educators* Florence (Italy) 2014, *World Congress of Accounting Educators* Singapore (Singapore) 2010, *International Research Conference* Sydney, NSW (Australia) 2008. **Publications** *Accounting Education: An international journal*; *Journal of International Financial Management and Accounting.*
Members Student; Individual Faculty; University; Institution. Institutions (14) in 12 countries and territories:
Azerbaijan, Belgium, India, Jamaica, Japan, Mexico, Nigeria, Romania, Taiwan, Trinidad-Tobago, Uruguay, USA.
Universities (23) in 12 countries and territories:
Germany, Japan, Nigeria, Poland, Romania, Singapore, Switzerland, Taiwan, UK, United Arab Emirates, Uruguay, USA.
[2019.10.17/XC0099/**C**]

♦ International Association of Administrative Professionals (internationally oriented national body)

♦ International Association for Adolescent Health (IAAH) 11683

Admin Dir c/o School of Nursing UMN, 5-140 Weaver-Densford Hall, 308 Harvard St SE, Minneapolis MN 55455, USA.
URL: http://www.iaah.org/

History 25 Mar 1987, Sydney, NSW (Australia). Founded on signature of a Charter by participants at 4th International Symposium on Adolescent Health. Registration: Canada. **Aims** Foster deeper understanding of the importance of youth health; encourage cooperation and collaboration between youth and adults and between professionals and organizations focused on youth health issues; promote and support development of national associations dedicated to youth health; advocate for improved youth health services, training, research, and policy development. **Structure** General Meeting (every 4 years, at Congress); Council; Executive Committee. **Languages** English. **Staff** 0.50 FTE, paid. **Finance** Sources: meeting proceeds; members' dues. Other sources: Donations through 'Friends of IAAH' fund. **Activities** Advocacy/lobbying/activism; networking/liaising. **Events** *World Congress on Adolescent Health* 2024, *European Regional Conference* Athens (Greece) 2022, *World Congress on Adolescent Health* Lima (Peru) 2021, *World Congress on Adolescent Health* Lima (Peru) 2020, *Annual European Meeting* Chisinau (Moldova) 2018. **Publications** Occasional special publications; educational materials. Information Services: Registry of members' interests and expertise.
Members Organizations (") and individuals (over 300) in 50 countries and territories:
Argentina (*), Australia (*), Bangladesh, Bermuda, Brazil, Cameroon, Canada (*), Chile, China, Colombia, Congo DR, Costa Rica, Ecuador, Finland, France, Ghana, Hong Kong, India (*), Israel (*), Italy, Jamaica, Japan, Jordan, Kenya, Malta, Mexico (*), Namibia, Netherlands, New Zealand (*), Nigeria, Norway, Pakistan, Peru, Philippines, Portugal, Puerto Rico, Saudi Arabia, Senegal, Sierra Leone, Spain (*), Sweden, Switzerland (*), Thailand, Tonga, Trinidad-Tobago, Uganda, UK, Uruguay, USA (*), Venezuela.
NGO Relations Member of: *End Corporal Punishment (#05457).* [2022/XD0912/**C**]

♦ International Association of Advanced Materials (IAAM) 11684

SG Gammalkilsvägen 18, SE-590 53 Ulrika, Sweden. T. +4613132424. E-mail: contact@iaamonline.org – secretarygeneral@iaamonline.org.
Pres address not obtained.
URL: https://www.iaamonline.org/

History 20 Jan 2010. Registration: No/ID: 802503-6784, Sweden. **Aims** Provide a forum for the expanding field of advanced materials from across the world. **Structure** Executive Board. **Languages** English. **Activities** Awards/prizes/competitions; events/meetings; knowledge management/information dissemination; publishing activities. **Events** *European Advanced Materials Congress* Stockholm (Sweden) 2021, *European Advanced Materials Congress* Stockholm (Sweden) 2019, *Advanced Materials World Congress* Singapore (Singapore) 2018, *International Conference on Smart Energy Technologies* Singapore (Singapore) 2017, *European Advanced Materials Congress* Stockholm (Sweden) 2017. **Publications** *Advanced Materials Letters* (4 a year) in English – Journal; *Advanced Materials Proceedings* (annual) in English – Journal; *Video Proceedings of Advanced Materials* (annual) in English – Journal. **Members** Individuals (about 60,000) in 140 countries. Membership countries not specified. [2022.06.14/XJ9636/**C**]

♦ International Association for the Advancement of Curriculum Studies (IAACS) 11685

Contact address not obtained. E-mail: iaacs.ca@gmail.com.
URL: http://www.iaacs.ca/

History Current constitution ratified Apr 2001. **Aims** Support a worldwide – but not uniform – field of curriculum studies. **Structure** General Assembly. Executive/Coordinating Council, comprising President, Vice-President, Treasurer and Secretary. Committees (6): Conferences; Affiliated Societies; Membership; Technology; Publications; Nominations. **Events** *World Curriculum Studies Conference* Braga (Portugal) 2022, *World Curriculum Studies Conference* Melbourne, VIC (Australia) 2018, *World Curriculum Studies Conference* Ottawa, ON (Canada) 2015, *World Curriculum Studies Conference* Rio de Janeiro (Brazil) 2012, *World Curriculum Studies Conference* Stellenbosch (South Africa) 2009. **Publications** *Transnational Curriculum Inquiry (TCI)* – online journal.
Members Full in 33 countries:
Argentina, Armenia, Australia, Bangladesh, Brazil, Bulgaria, Canada, China, Cyprus, Denmark, El Salvador, Estonia, Ethiopia, Finland, India, Iran Islamic Rep, Israel, Italy, Japan, Korea Rep, Mexico, Nigeria, Philippines, Poland, Portugal, Russia, Singapore, Spain, Sweden, Switzerland, Türkiye, USA, Zimbabwe.
NGO Relations *European Association of Curriculum Studies (Euro-ACS, #06001).* [2019/XJ6755/**B**]

♦ International Association for the Advancement of Educational Research / see Association mondiale des sciences de l'éducation (#02811)
♦ International Association for the Advancement of Gestalt Therapy (internationally oriented national body)
♦ International Association for the Advancement of Hegelian Studies (#13247)

♦ International Association for the Advancement of High Pressure Science and Technology (AIRAPT) 11686

Association internationale pour l'avancement de la recherche et de la technologie aux hautes pressions

Pres Physics Dept, Washington Univ, St Louis MO 63130, USA. E-mail: president@airapt.org.
URL: http://www.airapt.org/

History Aug 1965, Le Creusot (France). 29 Oct 1969, Brussels (Belgium), where Association was originally located. Statutes revised 1970. Former names and other names: *International Organization for the Advancement of High Pressure Research* – former (1965 to 1970). Registration: Start date: Sep 2019, End date: Aug 2023, USA. **Aims** Advance high pressure science and technology by: promoting contacts among scientists and organizations of different countries with interest in the science and technology of high pressure and related fields; organizing conferences and meetings; collection and dissemination of information; promotion of cooperative research and development. **Structure** General Assembly (every 2 years, at International Conference); Executive Committee; Administrative Office. **Languages** English. **Finance** Sources: members' dues. **Activities** Awards/prizes/competitions; events/meetings; training/education. **Events** *International Conference* Edinburgh (UK) 2023, *International Conference* Edinburgh (UK) 2021, *International Conference* Rio de Janeiro (Brazil) 2019, *International Conference* Beijing (China) 2017, *International Conference* Madrid (Spain) 2015.
Members Regular; Honorary; Ex-Officio; Industrial. Members in 20 countries:
Argentina, Belgium, Brazil, Canada, China, France, Germany, Hungary, Israel, Italy, Japan, Korea Rep, Poland, Qatar, Russia, Slovakia, South Africa, Sweden, UK, USA.
NGO Relations Affiliated with (1): *Committee on Data for Science and Technology (CODATA, #04247).*
[2023.02.14/XD2316/**D**]

♦ International Association for the Advancement of Innovative Approaches to Global Challenges (IAAI) 11687

International Vereinigung zur Förderung innovativer Ansätze der Auseinandersetzung mit global Herausforderungen – Mednarodno zdruzenje za pospesevanje inovantivnih pristopov k resevanju globalnih izzivov

Exec Dir Neuer Platz 10/I, 9020 Klagenfurt am Wörthersee, Austria. E-mail: office@glocha.info.
URL: http://www.glocha.info/

History 2 Mar 2007, Bled (Slovenia). Registration: No/ID: 918790591, Austria. **Aims** Set up an ecosystem – the Global Challenges Action Network (GloCha) and corresponding intellectual, technologiccal and institutional infrastructure for all of society engagement in the implementation of global goals. **Structure** General Assembly; Management Team; Scientific Advisory Board. **Languages** English, German, Slovene. **Staff** 1.00 FTE, paid. **Finance** Members' contributions; support from local and sub-national public authorities; crowdfunding; large scale support from signatories of the Giving Pledge. **Activities** Advocacy/lobbying/activism; events/meetings; knowledge management/information dissemination; research and development; research/documentation. **Events** *Workshop on Youth Empowerment for Agenda 2030 Action through Social Entrepreneurship and Digital Social Currencies* Vienna (Austria) 2017, *General Assembly* New York, NY (USA) 2016, *Conference on Sustainable Development, Innovation and Youth* Klagenfurt am Wörthersee (Austria) 2014, *General Assembly* Bled (Slovenia) 2010. **Publications** *Innovation for Sustainable Development* (2012) – Informal Rio+20 Issues Brief on Innovation; *Systemic Innovation in Resource Mobilization for Sustainable Development Engaging Local Actors in Provision of Global Public Goods*; *The Rio+20 Global Youth Music Contest Journey Towards the Future We Want* – photo documentary. Posters; brochures. **Members** (100) in 20 countries (not specified). **Consultative Status** Consultative status granted from: *ECOSOC (#05331)* (Special). **IGO Relations** Accredited as Observer to: *Green Climate Fund (GCF, #10714)*; *United Nations Framework Convention on Climate Change – Secretariat (UNFCCC, #20564)*. GloCha partners include: *UNESCO (#20322)* – UNESCO Management of Social Transformations Program; *United Nations Human Settlements Programme (UN-Habitat, #20572)* – Urban Economy and Youth Unit. Associated with Department of Global Communications of the United Nations. **NGO Relations** Member of (3): *Climate Chain Coalition (CCC, #04008)*; *European Association for Local Democracy (ALDA, #06110)*; *United Nations Academic Impact (UNAI, #20516).* Partner of (1): *Citizens' Climate Engagement Network (CCEN, #03955).* Other partners: civil society networks, national and sub-national public authorities, and youth organizations from Europe, USA, China and Africa.
[2021/XJ8367/**D**]

♦ International Association for the Advancement of Methods for System Analysis and Design (no recent information)

♦ International Association for the Advancement of Modelling and Simulation Techniques in Enterprises (AMSE) 11688

Gen Sec 16 av de Grange Blanche, 69160 Tassin-la-Demi-Lune, France. E-mail: cbv@univ-lyon1.fr.
Pres Av da Diagonal 690, 08021 Barcelona, Spain.
URL: http://www.amse-modeling.com/

History Founded 1980. Registered in accordance with French law. **Aims** Strengthen contacts among developers and users of modelling and simulation methods. **Structure** General Assembly; Governing Board; Executive Committee. **Languages** English. **Finance** Members' dues. **Activities** Meeting activities; training / education; research / dissemination; research / development. **Events** *International Conference on Economics and Management / General Assembly* Castellón de la Plana (Spain) 2013, *International Conference / General Assembly* Chania (Greece) 2013, *International Conference / General Assembly* Minsk (Belarus) 2012, *International Conference in Modeling and Simulation on Engineering, Economics and Management / General Assembly* New York, NY (USA) 2012, *International Conference on Modeling and Simulation in Engineering, Economics and Management for Sustainable Development / General Assembly* Rio de Janeiro (Brazil) 2012. **Publications** *Advances in Modelling* – (1-2 a year) series; *Modelling, Measurement and Simulation* – (1-2 a year) series. *Best-of Book* – selected conference papers.
Members Individuals; Institutions, in 43 countries and territories:
Algeria, Argentina, Australia, Bahrain, Belarus, Brazil, Canada, Chile, China, Cuba, Czechia, Egypt, France, Germany, Greece, Hong Kong, India, Iraq, Italy, Kazakhstan, Libya, Montenegro, Morocco, Nigeria, Poland, Portugal, Qatar, Romania, Russia, Saudi Arabia, Serbia, Singapore, South Africa, Spain, Taiwan, Tunisia, Türkiye, UK, Ukraine, United Arab Emirates, USA, Venezuela, Yemen. [2016.12.14/XF0755/**F**]

♦ International Association for the Advancement of Space Safety (IAASS) 11689

Exec Dir Kapteynstraat 1, 2201 BB Noordwijk, Netherlands. T. +31712020023. Fax +31643552918. E-mail: secretariat@iaass.org – iaass.secretariat@gmail.com – spacesafety@iaass.org.
URL: http://iaass.space-safety.org/

History 16 Apr 2004, Netherlands. **Aims** Further international cooperation and scientific advancement in the field of space systems safety. **Structure** General Assembly; Board; Management Team; Standing Committee; Technical Committees. Committee: President, Executive Director, Technical Director, Secretary, Treasurer and Chairs of Standing Committees. Standing Committees (6): Training Program; Safety Awards; Membership; Information and Communications; Conference Planning; Academic. Technical Committees. **Languages** English. **Staff** 0.50 FTE, paid. Voluntary. **Finance** Members' dues. Other sources: course fees; book publications; revenues from conferences; sponsor donations. Budget (annual): euro 60,000. **Activities** Guidance/assistance/consulting; training/education; events/meetings. **Events** *Conference on Making Space Travel Safer* Osaka (Japan) 2023, *Managing Risk in Space* Rotterdam (Netherlands) 2021, *Making Safety Happen* El Segundo, CA (USA) 2019, *Manfred Lachs International Conference* Montréal, QC (Canada) 2017, *Know safety, no pain* Toulouse (France) 2017. **Publications** *Space Safety Magazine. Safety Design for Space Systems*; *Space Safety Regulations and Standards.*
Members in 13 countries:
Belgium, Brazil, Canada, Finland, France, Germany, Italy, Japan, Netherlands, Russia, Singapore, UK, USA.
Consultative Status Consultative status granted from: *ECOSOC (#05331)* (Special). **IGO Relations** Observer status with: *Committee on the Peaceful Uses of Outer Space (COPUOS, #04277).* **NGO Relations** Member of: *International Astronautical Federation (IAF, #12286).* [2017/XJ0137/**D**]

♦ International Association for the Advancement of Special Education / see International Association for Special Education (#12174)

♦ International Association for the Advancement of Teaching and Research in Intellectual Property (ATRIP) 11690

Association internationale pour la promotion de l'enseignement et de la recherche en propriété intellectuelle – Asociación Internacional para el Progreso de la Enseñanza y de la Investigación de la Propiedad Intelectual

Pres Max Planck Inst for Intellectual Property Competition and Tax Law, Marstallplatz 1, 80539 Munich, Germany. T. +488924246404. Fax +488924246501.
URL: http://www.atrip.org/

History 14 Jul 1981. Also known as *International Association of Teachers and Researchers in Intellectual Property* and *International Association of Intellectual Property Professors.* **Aims** Contribute to the advancement of teaching and research in the field of intellectual property *law.* **Structure** Executive Committee, consisting of President, President-Elect, Treasurer and 6 other members. **Events** *Annual Congress* Copenhagen (Denmark) 2022, *Annual Congress* Copenhagen (Denmark) 2021, *Annual Congress* Seoul (Korea Rep) 2020, *Annual Congress* Nashville, TN (USA) 2019, *Annual Congress* Helsinki (Finland) 2018. **Members** Full in 60 countries (membership countries not specified). **Consultative Status** Consultative status granted from: *World Intellectual Property Organization (WIPO, #21593)* (Permanent Observer Status). [2020/XD4031/**D**]

♦ International Association for Aerobiology (IAA) 11691

Association internationale d'aérobiologie

SG address not obtained.
URL: https://sites.google.com/site/aerobiologyinternational/

History 11 Sep 1974, The Hague (Netherlands). Founded during 1st International Congress of Ecology, as a commission of *International Union of Biological Sciences (IUBS, #15760)*. **Aims** Develop aerobiology as a scientific discipline; promote the practical application of pollen concentration monitoring in different fields; promote educational activity within the aerobiological network interests; cooperate with aerobiological networks and societies of common interest. **Structure** Council of up to 40 members; Executive Committee, consisting of President, Vice President, Secretary-General, Treasurer, Past President, Newsletter Editor, Webmaster and 3 members. **Languages** English. **Finance** Sources: members' dues. **Activities** Awards/prizes/competitions; training/education. **Events** *Congress* Worcester (UK) 2023, *Congress* Worcester (UK) 2022, *Quadrennial Congress* Parma (Italy) 2018, *Quadrennial Congress* Sydney, NSW (Australia) 2014, *Quadrennial congress* Buenos Aires (Argentina) 2010. **Publications** *International Aerobiology Newsletter* (2 a year) – paper and electronic.
Members Individuals (429) in 42 countries and territories:
Argentina, Australia, Austria, Barbados, Belgium, Canada, China, Colombia, Croatia, Denmark, Dominican Rep, Estonia, Finland, France, Greece, Hungary, Iceland, India, Israel, Italy, Kuwait, Lithuania, Madagascar, Mexico, Netherlands, New Zealand, Norway, Pakistan, Poland, Portugal, Russia, Saudi Arabia, Serbia, Slovenia, Spain, Sweden, Switzerland, Taiwan, Türkiye, UK, Uruguay, USA.
National (6) and international (2) associated organizations, including 2 organizations listed in this Yearbook:
Nordisk Aerobiologisk Förening (NAF, #17481); *Pan American Aerobiology Association (PAAA, #18078)*.
NGO Relations Affiliated with (1): *International Federation of Palynological Societies (IFPS, #13498)*. Scientific member of: *International Union of Biological Sciences (IUBS, #15760)*. [2023.02.15/XE0869/y/**E**]

♦ International Association for Aesthetics (IAA) 11692

Association internationale d'esthétique (AIE) – Internationale Vereinigung für Ästhetik
Contact Erasmus Univ Rotterdam, Fac of Philosophy, Room H5-17, PO 1738, 3000 DR Rotterdam, Netherlands. T. +31134088965.
URL: http://www.iaaesthetics.org/
History 1984, Montréal QC (Canada). Took over activities of *International Committee for Aesthetics (inactive)*. **Aims** Give institutional recognition, world-wide, to aesthetics as a field of humanistic knowledge; encourage and promote inquiry in aesthetics; disseminate findings; expedite exchange between national societies of aesthetics; promote creation of national societies in countries where none are in existence; provide a forum for aestheticians who are not members of any national society. **Structure** Executive Committee, comprising President, 1st and 2nd Vice-Presidents, Secretary General, Assistant Secretary General, 26 Delegates, 5 Delegates-at-Large, 1 ex-officio member, 4 Honorary Life Members, Newsletter Editor, Website Editor and Guardian of the Yearbook. **Finance** Members' dues (3 years): Regular, US$ 20; Student, US$ 10. **Activities** Organizes international congress. **Events** *Possible worlds of contemporary aesthetics – aesthetics between history, geography and media* Belgrade (Serbia) 2019, *Aesthetics and mass culture* Seoul (Korea Rep) 2016, *Congress* Krakow (Poland) 2013, *Congress* Beijing (China) 2010, *Aesthetics bridging cultures* Ankara (Turkey) 2007. **Publications** *International Newsletter for Aesthetics* (2 a year); *International Yearbook of Aesthetics*.
Members National societies (28); scholars (over 600) interested in philosophical or other kinds of aesthetics and in related areas such as art history, comparative literature, musicology, visual arts and cultural studies.
Societies in 27 countries:
Argentina, Australia (includes New Zealand), Brazil, Canada, Chile, China, Croatia, Finland, France, Germany, Greece, Israel, Italy, Japan, Korea Rep, Latvia, Lithuania, Mexico, Netherlands, Poland, Russia, Serbia, Slovenia, Tunisia, Türkiye, UK, USA.
Included in the above, 1 regional organization:
The Nordic Society for Aesthetics (#17411).
NGO Relations Member of: *International Council for Philosophy and Human Sciences (CIPSH, #13061)*; *International Federation of Philosophical Societies (FISP, #13507)*. [2013/XF3334/y/**F**]

- ♦ International Association of African Writers (inactive)
- ♦ International Association of African Youths (unconfirmed)

♦ International Association against Drug Trafficking and Drug Abuse (IADTDA) 11693

Exec Dir 3 Fr Nansen Blvd, 1000 Sofia, Bulgaria. T. +35929863024. Fax +35929814967. E-mail: iadtda@abv.bg – info@iadtda.org.
Representative to United Nations 258-03 Kensington Place, Great Neck NY 11020, USA. T. +15164664063. Fax +17753836294.
URL: http://www.iadtda.org/
History 1991, Moscow (USSR). Previously also known under the acronym *IAADADT*. **Aims** Halt the spreading of drug addiction in Russia and other states; assist in uniting forces to coordinate activities in the fight against illegal turn of drugs and drug trafficking; research and implement of projects and programs directed to the reduction of drug demand; participate in the establishment of a network of special medical centers for drug addicts and their social rehabilitation. **Structure** Conference; Observer Committee; Board, including President; Departments. **Finance** Members' dues. Charitable assistance. **Activities** Organizes: Annual symposium; meetings, conferences, symposia and other events. **Events** *General Meeting* Sofia (Bulgaria) 2008, *World anti-drugs congress* Moscow (Russia) 1999, *International meeting on the organization of narcological care under insurance medicare* Moscow (Russia) 1993, *International colloquium* Moscow (Russia) 1992, *International symposium on women and the world against drugs* Moscow (Russia) 1992. **Publications** Articles; books.
Members Representatives (1,137) from 29 countries:
Armenia, Austria, Azerbaijan, Belarus, Belgium, Bolivia, Bulgaria, China, Cyprus, Estonia, France, Georgia, Germany, Greece, India, Italy, Japan, Kazakhstan, Kyrgyzstan, Latvia, Malaysia, Russia, Serbia, Spain, Tajikistan, Ukraine, United Arab Emirates, USA, Uzbekistan.
IGO Relations Observer status in Committee at General Secretariat of: *International Criminal Police Organization – INTERPOL (ICPO-INTERPOL, #13110)*. Associated with Department of Global Communications of the United Nations. [2015/XF4168/**F**]

- ♦ International Association Against Experiments on the Human Foetus (inactive)

♦ International Association Against Painful Experiments on Animals (IAAPEA) 11694

Association internationale contre les expériences douloureuses sur les animaux – Asociación Internacional contra los Experimentos Dolorosos en Animales – Internationale Vereinigung gegen Qualvolle Tierversuche
Contact PO Box 14, Hayling Island, PO11 9BF, UK. T. +442392463738 – +442392463738. E-mail: iaapea@hotmail.com.
History 24 Apr 1969, London (UK). **Aims** Promote cooperation among all opposed to experiments causing pain and/or suffering to animals, including processes carried out for scientific, medical, cosmetic, industrial, agricultural or any other purpose; awaken the conscience of mankind to the iniquity of such experiments and obtain legislation totally prohibiting them; encourage the development and adoption of humane, alternative methods of research and treatment. **Structure** General Assembly (every 2 years); Board of Management; Executive Committee of 5 members, including President, Secretary-General and Honorary Treasurer; Consultant on Alternative Programmes; Honorary Scientific Consultants (5); Honorary Scientific Vice-Presidents (8). **Languages** English, French, German. **Staff** Voluntary. **Finance** Members' dues: Full pounds250; Associate on a scale up to pounds250. Voluntary contributions and donations by 'Friends of the IAAPEA'. **Activities** Supports and lobbies internationally for development and adoption of non-animal replacement programmes; seeks ways of arousing public opinion; assists and coordinates actions of member societies; assists new and small societies, and those in countries where there is little support for animal defence, to find out where and how research animals are being used in their respective countries and how to set up programmes to raise consciousness and bring alternatives into use; established 24 April as *World Day for Laboratory Animals*; promotes *'International Charter for Health and Humane Research'*; cooperates with other organizations, for example in securing a ban on export of monkeys from India for experimentation; organizes specialized conferences and seminars. Current concerns: *Convention on International Trade in Endangered Species of Wild Fauna and Flora (CITES, 1973)*; religion and responsibility towards animals; lobbying UNESCO on setting up an independent commission to assess validity of animal-based research and potential of other techniques. **Events** *Biennial General Assembly* Helsingborg (Sweden) 1996, *Biennial General Assembly* Athens (Greece) 1994, *World congress against vivisection / Biennial General Assembly* Athens (Greece) 1994, *Biennial General Assembly* Milan (Italy) 1992, *Biennial General Assembly* Philadelphia, PA (USA) 1989. **Publications** *IAAPEA Newsletter*; *International Animal Action* – bulletin. *Fatal Mistakes* – monograph series. *Animal Sacrifices* by Tom Regan; *Entering the Gates of Hell: Laboratory Cruelty You Were Not Meant to See*; *International Charter for Health and Humane Research* in English, Portuguese, Spanish; *Science on Trial* by Robert Sharpe; *The Cruel Deception* by Robert Sharpe. *Creatures of God* in Arabic, English – video; *The Parliament of the Doomed* in English, Italian, Norwegian – video. Newsletters; documentary films.
Members Constituent societies (over 60) in 33 countries and territories:
Argentina, Australia, Brazil, Canada, Chile, Colombia, Croatia, Denmark, France, Germany, Greece, Hong Kong, Hungary, India, Ireland, Israel, Italy, Mexico, Netherlands, New Zealand, Norway, Peru, Poland, Portugal, Russia, Serbia, South Africa, Spain, Sweden, Taiwan, UK, USA, Venezuela.
Consultative Status Consultative status granted from: *ECOSOC (#05331)* (Special). **IGO Relations** Accredited by: *United Nations Office at Vienna (UNOV, #20604)*. Associated with Department of Global Communications of the United Nations. **NGO Relations** Cooperates with: *World Animal Protection (#21092)*. [2020/XC4082/**C**]

- ♦ International Association Against Torture (no recent information)
- ♦ International Association Against Tuberculosis / see International Union Against Tuberculosis and Lung Disease (#15752)
- ♦ International Association of Agricultural College Workers (no recent information)

♦ International Association of Agricultural Economists (IAAE) 11695

Association internationale des économistes agronomiques (AIEA) – Asociación Internacional de Economistas Agricolas
Pres 411 Richmond Street East, Suite 200, Toronto ON M5A 3S5, Canada. E-mail: info@iaae-agecon.org.
URL: http://www.iaae-agecon.org/
History 1929, Dartington Hall (UK). Founded by representatives of 11 countries. **Aims** Foster the application of agricultural economics to improve *rural* economic and social conditions; advance knowledge of agriculture's economic organization; facilitate communication and information exchange among those concerned with rural welfare. **Structure** Conference (every 3 years); Board. **Languages** English. **Staff** Voluntary. **Finance** Sources: members' dues. **Activities** Events/meetings. **Events** *Triennial Conference* New Delhi (India) 2024, *Triennial Conference* 2021, *Triennial Conference* Vancouver, BC (Canada) 2018, *Triennial Conference* Milan (Italy) 2015, *Workshop* Leuven (Belgium) 2013. **Publications** *Agricultural Economics: The Journal of the International Association of Agricultural Economists* (6 a year); *IAAE Newsletter* (2 a year). Conference proceedings.
Members Professional agricultural economists and those involved with agribusiness organizations in 100 countries and territories:
Argentina, Armenia, Australia, Austria, Bahrain, Bangladesh, Belgium, Benin, Botswana, Brazil, Bulgaria, Cameroon, Canada, Chile, China, Colombia, Costa Rica, Czechia, Denmark, Dominican Rep, Ecuador, Egypt, Estonia, Eswatini, Ethiopia, Fiji, Finland, France, Georgia, Germany, Ghana, Greece, Honduras, Hungary, India, Indonesia, Iran Islamic Rep, Ireland, Israel, Italy, Japan, Kazakhstan, Kenya, Korea Rep, Laos, Latvia, Lesotho, Lithuania, Madagascar, Malawi, Malaysia, Mali, Mexico, Mongolia, Morocco, Mozambique, Namibia, Nepal, Netherlands, New Zealand, Nicaragua, Nigeria, Norway, Oman, Pakistan, Panama, Peru, Philippines, Poland, Portugal, Romania, Russia, Rwanda, Saudi Arabia, Senegal, Serbia, Sierra Leone, Slovakia, Slovenia, South Africa, Spain, Sri Lanka, Sudan, Sweden, Switzerland, Syrian AR, Taiwan, Tanzania UR, Thailand, Togo, Trinidad-Tobago, Türkiye, Uganda, UK, Ukraine, Uruguay, USA, Vietnam, Zambia, Zimbabwe.
Consultative Status Consultative status granted from: *ECOSOC (#05331)* (Ros C); *FAO (#09260)* (Special Status); *UNCTAD (#20285)* (General Category). [2021.09.14/XB1246/**B**]

- ♦ International Association of Agricultural Information Specialists (inactive)
- ♦ International Association of Agriculturalists (inactive)
- ♦ International Association of Agricultural Medicine / see International Association of Rural Health and Medicine (#12140)
- ♦ International Association of Agricultural Medicine and Rural Health / see International Association of Rural Health and Medicine (#12140)
- ♦ International Association of Agricultural Missions / see Agricultural Missions
- ♦ International Association of Agricultural Museums (#02720)
- ♦ International Association of Agricultural Production Insurers (#02671)
- ♦ International Association of Agricultural Students / see International Association of Students in Agricultural and Related Sciences (#12191)
- ♦ International Association for Agricultural Sustainability (unconfirmed)
- ♦ International Association of Aircraft Brokers and Agents (inactive)
- ♦ International Association of Aircraft Industry Workers' Unions (no recent information)

♦ International Association of Airline Internal Auditors (IAAIA) 11696

Treas Internal Audit Dept – Emirates Airline, PO Box 686, Dubai, United Arab Emirates. T. +97147082882.
URL: http://www.iaaia.com/
History 1991. **Aims** Exchange information on challenges and best practices experienced within Internal Audit departments. **Structure** Executive Committee. **Finance** Sources: members' dues. **Events** *Annual Conference* Berlin (Germany) 2015, *Annual Conference* Chicago, IL (USA) 2013, *Annual Conference* Muscat (Oman) 2012, *Annual Conference* London (UK) 2011. **Publications** *IAAIA News*. **Members** Airlines (over 70). Membership countries not specified. [2014.06.19/XJ6466/**C**]

- ♦ International Association of Airport Duty Free Stores (internationally oriented national body)

♦ International Association of Airport Executives (IAAE) 11697

Chair Lee County Port Authority, 11000 Terminal Access Rd, Fort Myers FL 33913, USA.
Vice-Chair IAAE Head Office, Barclay Bldg, 601 Madison St, Alexandria VA 22314, USA. T. +17038240500. Fax +17038201395.
URL: http://www.iaae.org/
History Founded 1992. Registered in the State of Illinois (USA). **Aims** Advanced airport management education and professional development worldwide. **Events** *The Role of Airports in the European Union and Transatlantic Trade and Investment Partnership Conference* Sofia (Bulgaria) 2016, *Annual North America/Central Europe Airport Issues Conference* St Julian's (Malta) 2016, *Annual North America/Central Europe Airport Issues Conference* Dubrovnik (Croatia) 2015, *Annual Central Europe/US airport issues conference* Munich (Germany) 2007, *Central Europe/US regional development conference* Wroclaw (Poland) 2007. **Publications** *International Airport Report* (12 a year) – newsletter. **Members** Affiliate; Associate; Corporate. Membership countries not specified. **NGO Relations** Affiliated with: American Association of Airport Executives (AAAE). [2018/XD5408/**D**]

- ♦ International Association of Airport and Seaport Police / see InterPortPolice (#15963)
- ♦ International Association of Allergists / see World Allergy Organization – IAACI (#21077)
- ♦ International Association of Allergology / see World Allergy Organization – IAACI (#21077)
- ♦ International Association of Allergology and Clinical Immunology / see World Allergy Organization – IAACI (#21077)
- ♦ International Association of Altrusa Clubs / see Altrusa International (#00757)

♦ International Association for Ambulatory Surgery (IAAS) 11698

Association internationale pour la chirurgie ambulatoire – Internationale Vereinigung für Ambulante Chirurgie
Hon Sec Amsterdam, 1011 AA Amsterdam, Netherlands. E-mail: president@theiaas.net.
Pres address not obtained.
URL: https://www.theiaas.net
History 17 Mar 1995, Brussels (Belgium). Original bylaws adopted Brussels, 21 May 1996; revised Geneva (Switzerland), 22 Apr 2001. Registration: Banque-Carrefour des Entreprises, No/ID: 0458.707.654, Start date: 12 Sep 1996, Belgium. **Aims** Serve as an international multidisciplinary forum for exchange of information on and advancement of ambulatory surgery; encourage its high quality development and expansion; promote education and research in the field and disseminate research results; establish guidelines and act as advisory body for development and maintenance of high standards of patient care; establish close relations with relevant organizations and stimulate development of national societies in the field. **Structure** General Assembly; Executive Committee. **Languages** English. **Finance** Sources: members' dues; sponsorship. **Activities** Events/meetings. **Events** *International Congress of Ambulatory Surgery* Oslo (Norway) 2024, *International Congress on Ambulatory Surgery* Bruges (Belgium) 2022, *International Congress on Ambulatory Surgery* Bruges (Belgium) 2021, *Congress* Budaörs (Hungary) 2020, *European Congress* Madrid (Spain) 2020. **Publications** *Ambulatory Surgery* (4 a year).

Members Full; Associate; Honorary; Founding. National associations in 19 countries:
Australia, Belgium, Brazil, China, Croatia, Denmark, Finland, France, Germany, Hungary, India, Italy, Netherlands, Norway, Poland, Portugal, Spain, UK, USA. [2022.12.12/XD4987/D]

♦ International Association of Amusement Parks / see International Association of Amusement Parks and Attractions (#11699)

♦ International Association of Amusement Parks and Attractions (IAAPA) 11699

Association internationale des parcs d'amusement et de distraction

Headquarters 4155 West Taft Vineland Rd, Orlando FL 32837, USA. T. +13213197600. Fax +13213197690. E-mail: iaapa@iaapa.org.

Membership Manager Sint-Lazaruslaan 4, WeWork, Sint-Joost-ten-Noode, 1210 Brussels, Belgium. T. +3227906018. E-mail: emea@iaapa.org.

URL: http://www.iaapa.org/

History 1918. Founded as (US) National Association of Amusement Parks. *International Association for the Leisure and Entertainment Industry (IALEI, inactive)* merged into IAAPA, Oct 2009. Former names and other names: *International Association of Amusement Parks (IAAP)* – former (1962 to 1972); *National Outdoor Showmen's Association (NOSA)* – former (1918 to 1920); *National Association of Amusement Parks (NAAP)* – former (1920 to 1934); *National Association of Amusement Parks, Pools, and Beaches (NAAPB)* – former (1934 to 1962). **Aims** Serve members by promoting safe operations, global development, professional growth and commercial success of the amusement parks and attractions *industry*. **Structure** Board of Directors; Committees; Main Office in Alexandria VA (USA). Offices (4): Asia Pacific; European; Latin America; North American. **Activities** Certification/accreditation; events/meetings. **Events** *IAAPA Expo Europe & Conference* London (UK) 2022, *IAAPA Expo Europe & Conference* Barcelona (Spain) 2021, *Latin American Summit* Foz do Iguaçu (Brazil) 2021, *Annual Convention* Orlando, FL (USA) 2021, *Annual Convention* Orlando, FL (USA) 2020. **Publications** *Funworld* (12 a year); *International Directory and Buyer's Guide* (annual).

Members Amusement parks and attractions (5,500) in 72 countries and territories:
Argentina, Aruba, Australia, Austria, Bahrain, Bangladesh, Belgium, Bermuda, Brazil, Bulgaria, Canada, Chile, China, Colombia, Costa Rica, Czechia, Denmark, Dominican Rep, Ecuador, Egypt, El Salvador, Finland, France, Germany, Ghana, Guatemala, Hungary, India, Indonesia, Iran Islamic Rep, Ireland, Israel, Italy, Japan, Korea Rep, Kuwait, Lebanon, Luxembourg, Malaysia, Malta, Mexico, Morocco, Netherlands, New Zealand, Nigeria, Norway, Oman, Pakistan, Panama, Paraguay, Peru, Philippines, Poland, Portugal, Qatar, Russia, Saudi Arabia, Singapore, Slovenia, South Africa, Spain, Sri Lanka, Sweden, Switzerland, Taiwan, Thailand, Türkiye, UK, United Arab Emirates, USA, Venezuela.

IGO Relations Agreement with: *Council of Europe (CE, #04881)*. **NGO Relations** Member of (2): *European Tourism Manifesto (#08921)*; *Network for the European Private Sector in Tourism (NET, #17027)*. Partner of (1): *International Institute for Peace through Tourism (IIPT)*. [2021.08.31/XF5483/F]

♦ International Association for Analogue Computation / see International Association for Mathematics and Computers in Simulation (#12019)

♦ International Association for Analytical Psychology (IAAP) 11700

Association internationale de psychologie analytique (AIPA) – Asociación Internacional de Psicologia Analitica – Internationale Gesellschaft für Analytische Psychologie (IGFAP) – Associazione Internazionale di Psicologia Analitica

Secretariat Postfach 6, 8042 Zurich ZH, Switzerland. Fax +41442729606. E-mail: iaapsecretary@iaap.org.

URL: http://www.iaap.org/

History 1955, Zurich (Switzerland). Statutes adopted 31 Aug 1962; amended 1 Sep 1971, 6 Sep 1977, 22 Mar 1983, Sep 1986, Aug 1992, Aug 1995, Aug 2001, Cambridge (UK); Aug 2004, Barcelona (Spain); Aug 2007, Cape Town (South Africa). **Aims** Promote study and disseminate knowledge of analytical psychology; encourage maintenance of high standards of training and practice. **Structure** Meeting of Delegates (every 3 years, at Congress), groups being represented by delegates according to membership; Executive Committee, comprising President (who acts as Chairperson), President Elect, 2 Vice-Presidents, Secretary and 9 members. **Languages** English, French, German, Italian, Spanish. **Staff** 1.00 FTE, paid. **Finance** Sources: members' dues. **Activities** Organizes international and regional congresses. **Events** *International Congress for Analytical Psychology* Buenos Aires (Argentina) 2022, *International Congress for Analytical Psychology* Vienna (Austria) 2019, *Triennial International Congress* Kyoto (Japan) 2016, *Triennial International Congress* Copenhagen (Denmark) 2013, *Latin American Conference* Florianópolis (Brazil) 2012. **Publications** *International Association for Analytical Psychology Newsletter* (annual). Congress proceedings.

Members Groups (55); individuals (63) where no group exists. Members in 38 countries:
Argentina, Australia, Austria, Belgium, Brazil, Bulgaria, Canada, Chile, China, Czechia, Denmark, Estonia, Finland, France, Germany, Hong Kong, Ireland, Israel, Italy, Japan, Korea Rep, Lithuania, Mexico, Netherlands, New Zealand, Norway, Poland, Russia, Serbia, South Africa, Spain, Sweden, Switzerland, UK, Ukraine, Uruguay, USA, Venezuela. [2018/XD5539/C]

♦ International Association for Animal Hospice and Palliative Care (internationally oriented national body)

♦ International Association for Anselm Studies (IAAS) 11701

Sec Blackfriars Hall, St Giles, Oxford, OX1 3LY, UK. E-mail: secretary@anselmstudies.org.

URL: https://www.anselmstudies.org/

History 2015, Boston, MA (USA). Successor organization to International Anselm Committee, which had organized conferences and meetings from 1959 to the early 2000s. **Aims** Promote the study of: the life and thought of Saint Anselm of Canterbury (also known as Anselm of Aosta and Anselm of Bec); the influences on the life and thought of Saint Anselm; the reception of the work of Saint Anselm during his life and following his death to the present day. **Structure** General Meeting; Committee. **Activities** Events/meetings; knowledge management/information dissemination. **Events** *Conference* Durham (UK) 2019. [2021/AA1945/D]

♦ International Association of Antarctica Tour Operators (IAATO) 11702

Exec Dir 50 South County Commons Way, Unit E-5B, Kingston RI SOUTH 02879, USA. T. +14018419700. Fax +14018419704. E-mail: iaato@iaato.org.

Admin Officer address not obtained.

URL: http://www.iaato.org/

History 1991. **Aims** Advocate, promote and practise safe and environmentally responsible *travel* to Antarctica. **Structure** Executive Committee; Secretariat. **Languages** English. **Staff** 1.00 FTE, paid. **Finance** Members' dues. **Events** *General Assembly* Newport, RI (USA) 2018, *General Assembly* Rotterdam (Netherlands) 2015, *Annual general meeting / Annual Meeting* Uruguay 2008, *Annual general meeting / Annual Meeting* Hobart, TAS (Australia) 2007, *Annual general meeting / Annual Meeting* Washington, DC (USA) 2006.

Members Full; Provisional; Probational; Associate. Companies (over 100) in 15 countries:
Argentina, Australia, Belgium, Canada, Chile, France, Germany, Italy, Japan, Netherlands, New Zealand, Norway, Sweden, UK, USA.

IGO Relations Member of: *Hydrographic Commission on Antarctica (HCA, see: #13825)*. [2018/XD7383/D]

♦ International Association of Anthroposophic Pharmacists (internationally oriented national body)
♦ International Association of Anthroposophic Physicians / see Internationale Vereinigung Anthroposophischer Ärztegesellschaften (#13314)

♦ International Association of Anti-Corruption Authorities (IAACA) .. 11703

Contact Units 1801-1802, 18/F, The FOYER, 625 King's Road, Quarry Bay, Hong Kong, Central and Western, Hong Kong. T. +85228263361. E-mail: info@iaaca.net.

URL: https://www.iaaca.net/

History Initiated following adoption by General Assembly of *United Nations Convention Against Corruption (UNCAC, 2003)*, 31 Oct 2003, and its signature, Dec 2003, Mérida (Mexico). Established Oct 2006, Beijing (China), during first annual conference and general meeting, with the support of *United Nations Office on Drugs and Crime (UNODC, #20596)* and the Supreme People's Procuratorate of the People's Republic of China. Registration: 2006, China, Beijing.

Aims Promote the effective implementation of the UNCAC; assist anti-corruption authorities internationally in the prevention of and fight against corruption and for that purpose:
- promote international cooperation in the prevention, investigation and adjudication of corruption offences, including through law enforcement cooperation, mutual legal assistance and extradition as well as in tracing, seizure, freezing, confiscation and return of the proceeds of corruption offences;
- promote measures for the prevention of corruption in both the public and private sectors;
- promote networking, informal and formal relationships, cooperation and coordination between anti-corruption authorities and between anti-corruption authorities and other competent authorities, including law enforcement, judicial and administrative authorities both domestically and internationally;
- facilitate the exchange and dissemination of expertise and experience among anti-corruption authorities;
- promote examination of comparative criminal law and procedure and best practices and to assist anti-corruption authorities engaged in reform programmes and related activities;
- promote examination and dissemination of preventive measures;
- cooperate with international organisations in furtherance of the foregoing objectives;
- promote a culture of independence, professionalism, transparency, integrity and accountability of anti-corruption authorities.

Structure General Meeting; Executive Committee. **Languages** English. **Finance** Currently, no membership fee is required from members. **Activities** Events/meetings. **Events** *Annual Conference and General Meeting* 2022, *Executive Committee Meeting* Hong Kong (Hong Kong) 2022, *Executive Committee Meeting* Hong Kong (Hong Kong) 2022, *Executive Committee Meeting* Hong Kong (Hong Kong) 2022, *Annual Conference and General Meeting* Doha (Qatar) 2021. **Members** Authorities (as defined in the United Nations Convention against Corruption, articles 6 and 36) established under the laws of a State Party to the UNCAC, a country or a jurisdictional area shall be eligible for organizational membership in the Association. Member Organizations are categorized under five regional groups with reference to the United Nations Regional Groups of Member States: Africa States, Asia-Pacific States, Eastern European States, Latin American and Caribbean States, Western European and other States. More details on https://www.iaaca.net/about-us **IGO Relations** Close working partners include: *European Contact-point Network against Corruption (EACN, #06776)*; *European Partners against Corruption (EPAC, #08153)*; *International Anti-Corruption Academy (IACA, #11654)*; Network of Corruption Prevention Authorities (NCPA); *United Nations Office on Drugs and Crime (UNODC, #20596)*. [2022.12.19/XM3806/y/E*]

♦ International Association for Applied Econometrics (IAAE) 11704

Contact Univ of Cambridge, Fac of Economics, Austin Robinson Bldg, Sidgwick Avenue, Cambridge, CB3 9DD, UK. E-mail: enquiries@appliedeconometrics.org.

URL: http://appliedeconometrics.org/

Aims Advance the education of the public in the subject of econometrics and its applications to a variety of fields in economics. **Structure** Directors. **Finance** Sources: members' dues. **Activities** Awards/prizes/competitions; events/meetings; knowledge management/information dissemination; research/documentation. **Events** *Annual Conference* Oslo (Norway) 2023, *Annual Conference* London (UK) 2022, *Annual Conference* Rotterdam (Netherlands) 2021, *Annual Conference* London (UK) 2020, *Annual Conference* Nicosia (Cyprus) 2019. **Members** Individual; Institutional. Membership countries not specified. [2018/XM6560/C]

♦ International Association of Applied Linguistics (#02713)
♦ International Association for Applied Mathematics and Mechanics (internationally oriented national body)

♦ International Association of Applied Psychology (IAAP) 11705

Association internationale de psychologie appliquée (AIPA)

SG 8365 Keystone Crossing, Suite 107, Indianapolis IN 46240, USA. T. +13172059480. Fax +13172059481. E-mail: secretarygeneral@iaapsy.org.

Pres address not obtained.

URL: http://www.iaapsy.org/

History Sep 1920, Geneva (Switzerland). Former names and other names: *International Association of Psychotechnics* – former; *Association internationale de psychotechnique (AIP)* – former. Registration: Start date: 7 Nov 2017, USA; French Ministerial Decree, Start date: 12 May 1952, France. **Aims** Promote the science and practice of applied psychology; facilitate interaction and communication among applied psychologists around the world. **Structure** Board of Directors; Executive Committee. Membership open; congresses open. **Languages** English, French. **Staff** 5.00 FTE, paid. Several voluntary. **Finance** Sources: members' dues; sale of publications. **Activities** Events/meetings; knowledge management/information dissemination; networking/liaising; publishing activities. **Events** *International Congress of Applied Psychology* Beijing (China) 2023, *International Congress of Applied Psychology* Beijing (China) 2022, *International Congress of Applied Psychology* Montréal, QC (Canada) 2018, *International Congress of Applied Psychology* Paris (France) 2014, *Eastern Africa Regional Conference of Psychology* Kampala (Uganda) 2013. **Publications** *IAAP E-News* (12 a year); *Applied Psychology: An International Review* (4 a year); *Applied Psychology: Health and Well-Being* (4 a year); *Applied Psychology Around the World* (3 a year).

Members Full; Fellow; Student; Honorary; Alliance. Members in 96 countries and territories:
Albania, Algeria, Angola, Argentina, Armenia, Australia, Austria, Barbados, Belgium, Brazil, Bulgaria, Burundi, Cameroon, Canada, Canaries, Chile, China, Colombia, Congo Brazzaville, Congo DR, Costa Rica, Croatia, Cuba, Cyprus, Czechia, Denmark, Dominican Rep, Ecuador, Egypt, El Salvador, Estonia, Finland, France, Georgia, Germany, Greece, Guatemala, Haiti, Honduras, Hong Kong, Hungary, Iceland, India, Indonesia, Iran Islamic Rep, Ireland, Israel, Italy, Jamaica, Japan, Kenya, Korea DPR, Korea Rep, Latvia, Lithuania, Luxembourg, Malaysia, Mali, Mexico, Morocco, Namibia, Netherlands, New Zealand, Nicaragua, Nigeria, Norway, Paraguay, Peru, Philippines, Poland, Portugal, Puerto Rico, Romania, Russia, Saudi Arabia, Singapore, Slovakia, Slovenia, South Africa, Spain, Suriname, Sweden, Switzerland, Taiwan, Tanzania UR, Thailand, Trinidad-Tobago, Türkiye, Uganda, UK, Ukraine, Uruguay, USA, Venezuela, Vietnam, Zimbabwe.

Consultative Status Consultative status granted from: *ECOSOC (#05331)* (Special). **NGO Relations** Member of: *Conference of Non-Governmental Organizations in Consultative Relationship with the United Nations (CONGO, #04635)*; *International Science Council (ISC, #14796)*; *Vienna NGO Committee on Drugs (VNGOC, #20773)*. Division of Psychology and National Development cooperates with: *International Network of Psychology and the Developing World (INPDW, see: #15807)*; *International Test Commission (ITC, #15677)*. [2023.01.11/XB1253/v/B]

♦ International Association of Aquaculture Economics and Management (IAAEM) 11706

Pres Inst for Sustainable Food Systems, School of Forest Resources and Conservation, Univ of Florida, PO Box 110180, Gainesville FL 32611-0180, USA.

URL: http://www.iaaem.org/

History Founded 17 Dec 1993, Keelung (Taiwan), during International Symposium of Socio-economics and Aquaculture. Also referred to as *International Association of Aquaculture Economists and Management*. **Aims** Promote socio-economic research and information exchange in the field. **Structure** Executive Committee; Secretariat. **Languages** English. **Staff** 2.00 FTE, paid. **Finance** Sources: members' dues. **Activities** Events/meetings; networking/liaising. **Events** *Biennial Meeting* Las Vegas, NV (USA) 2016, *Biennial Meeting* Prague (Czech Rep) 2012, *Biennial Meeting* San Diego, CA (USA) 2010, *Biennial Meeting* Veracruz, CHIS (Mexico) 2008, *Biennial Meeting* Las Vegas, NV (USA) 2006. **Publications** *Aquaculture Economics and Management* (4 a year) – official journal; *IAAEM Newsletter*.

Members Institutions and individuals in 38 countries and territories:
Australia, Brazil, Canada, Chile, China, Costa Rica, Côte d'Ivoire, Denmark, Egypt, France, Germany, Ghana, Hong Kong, Hungary, India, Indonesia, Iran Islamic Rep, Israel, Italy, Japan, Kenya, Korea Rep, Malaysia, Mexico, Namibia, Netherlands, Nigeria, Norway, Philippines, Portugal, Saudi Arabia, Spain, Sri Lanka, Taiwan, Tanzania UR, Thailand, UK, USA. [2017.10.26/XD3830/C]

♦ International Association of Aquaculture Economists and Management / see International Association of Aquaculture Economics and Management (#11706)
♦ International Association for Aquatic Animal Medicine (internationally oriented national body)

♦ International Association of Aquatic and Marine Science Libraries and Information Centers (IAMSLIC) 11707

Contact Janet Webster, Hatfield Marine Science Center, Oregon State Univ, 2030 S Marine Science Drive, Newport OR 97365, USA. E-mail: janet.webster@oregonstate.edu.

URL: http://www.iamslic.org/

History 1975, Woods Hole MA (USA), as *International Association of Marine Science Libraries and Information Centers*. **Aims** Promote cooperation and sharing of resources among libraries and information centers which specialize in any aspect of marine or aquatic sciences. **Structure** Officers: President; President-Elect; Secretary; Treasurer; Past President. Standing Committees (6). Includes: *European Association of Aquatic Sciences Libraries and Information Centres (EURASLIC, #05939)*. **Languages** English. **Activities** Knowledge management/information dissemination. **Events** *Annual Conference* Port Aransas, TX (USA) 2019, *Annual Conference* Entebbe (Uganda) 2018, *Annual Conference* Honolulu, HI (USA) 2017, *Annual Conference* Mérida (Mexico) 2016, *Annual Conference* Rome (Italy) 2015. **Publications** *International Directory of Marine Science Libraries and Information Centers* (1987). Conference proceedings.

Members Individuals; Organizations. Members in 59 countries and territories:
Argentina, Australia, Belgium, Belize, Bermuda, Brazil, Bulgaria, Cameroon, Canada, Chile, China, Colombia, Côte d'Ivoire, Cuba, Denmark, Ecuador, Egypt, Fiji, France, Germany, Ghana, Greece, Guinea, Hong Kong, Iceland, Ireland, Israel, Italy, Japan, Kenya, Kuwait, Malawi, Malta, Mauritius, Mexico, Morocco, Mozambique, Namibia, New Zealand, Panama, Peru, Poland, Portugal, Puerto Rico, Russia, Senegal, Seychelles, Solomon Is, South Africa, Switzerland, Tanzania UR, Thailand, Uganda, UK, Ukraine, United Arab Emirates, USA, Venezuela, Vietnam.
IGO Relations Partnership with: *FAO (#09260)*; *International Oceanographic Data and Information Exchange (IODE, #14396)*; *North Pacific Marine Science Organization (PICES, #17602)*. [2017/XD0633/**C**]

♦ International Association of Arabic Dialectology (#02683)
♦ International Association of Arab Pharmacy Colleges (inactive)

♦ International Association for Archaeological Research in Western & Central Asia (ARWA) 11708

Sec address not obtained.
Pres address not obtained.
URL: https://arwa-international.org/
History 2020, Belgium. Registration: Start date: 2020, Belgium. **Aims** Establish a worldwide link between scholars, to defend the archaeological discipline and its scientists. **Structure** Executive Board; Communication Unit. **Languages** English. **Finance** Sources: members' dues. **Activities** Events/meetings; training/education. **Events** *Congress* Bern (Switzerland) 2024, *Congress* Bern (Switzerland) 2022. **Publications** *ARWA Journal*. **Members** Affiliated members (over 470) in 47 countries. Membership countries not specified. [2021.02.09/AA1065/**D**]

♦ International Association of Architects and Surveyors (inactive)

♦ International Association of Armenian Studies 11709

Association internationale des études arméniennes (AIEA)
Pres Centre de Recherches Arménologiques, Univ of Geneva, 22 blvd des Philosophes, 1211 Geneva 4, Switzerland. T. +41223797210. Fax +41223797124.
Sec Univ of Vienna, Inst für Geschichte, Universitätsring 1, 1010 Vienna, Austria.
URL: http://sites.uclouvain.be/aiea/en/aiea/
History 1982. Registration: No/ID: KVK 40447057, Netherlands. **Aims** Promote Armenian studies. **Structure** General Assembly (annual); Committee. **Languages** Armenian, English, French, German, Italian. **Staff** 7.00 FTE, paid. **Finance** Sources: members' dues. **Activities** Events/meetings. **Events** *General Conference* Halle (Saale) (Germany) 2021, *General Conference* Halle (Saale) (Germany) 2020, *General Conference* Oxford (UK) 2017, *General Conference* Yerevan (Armenia) 2014, *General Conference* Budapest (Hungary) 2011. **Publications** *AIEA Newsletter* (annual); *Handbook of Oriental Studies/Handbuch der Orientalistik* in English, German. Books.
Members Full; Associate. Members in 30 countries:
Argentina, Armenia, Australia, Austria, Belarus, Belgium, Bulgaria, Canada, Cyprus, Denmark, Egypt, France, Germany, Holy See, Hungary, Ireland, Israel, Italy, Latvia, Netherlands, Poland, Romania, Russia, Spain, Sweden, Switzerland, Türkiye, UK, Ukraine, USA.
NGO Relations Member of (1): *International Union for Oriental and Asian Studies (IUOAS, inactive)*. [2021/XE4046/v/**E**]

♦ International Association of Arson Investigators (internationally oriented national body)

♦ International Association of Art (IAA) 11710

Association internationale des arts plastiques (AIAP) – Asociación Internacional de Artes Plasticas – Internationale Gesellschaft der Bildenden Künste
Exec Sec UNESCO, 1 rue Miollis, 75015 Paris, France. T. +33145684454. E-mail: iaa.aiap@gmail.com.
Pres Macka Demokrasi Parki, Sanatchi Islikleri, 34398 Istanbul/Istanbul, Türkiye. T. +902122973120. E-mail: iaa.aiapworldpresident@yahoo.com.
URL: http://www.aiap-iaa.org/
History Sep 1952, Venice (Italy), at International Conference of Artists, held under auspices of UNESCO. Aims declared at 1st General Assembly, 1954, Venice. Also referred to in English as *International Association of Art – Painting, Sculpture, Print-making* and as *International Association of the Plastic Arts*. **Aims** Stimulate international cooperation among artists of all countries, nations or peoples; improve the economic and social position of artists at national and international levels and defend their material and moral rights. **Structure** General Assembly (every 4 years); Executive Committee; Executive Secretary. Regional networks include: *International Association of Art – Europe (IAA Europe, #11711)*. **Languages** English, French. **Staff** 3.00 FTE, paid. **Activities** Events/meetings. **Events** *General Assembly* Pilsen (Czech Rep) 2015, *General Assembly* Guadalajara (Mexico) 2011, *General Assembly* Beijing (China) 2005, *General Assembly* Athens (Greece) 2002, *General Assembly* Tlaxcala (Mexico) 1995. **Publications** *IAA Newsletter* (4 a year) in English, French.
Members National committees for the visual arts organized by professional painters, sculptors and engravers. Members in 65 countries:
Algeria, Argentina, Armenia, Austria, Azerbaijan, Belarus, Belgium, Bolivia, Bosnia-Herzegovina, Brazil, Bulgaria, Canada, Chile, China, Costa Rica, Croatia, Cyprus, Czechia, Denmark, Dominican Rep, Estonia, Finland, France, Germany, Ghana, Greece, Honduras, Hungary, Iceland, Ireland, Israel, Italy, Japan, Korea Rep, Latvia, Lithuania, Luxembourg, Madagascar, Mauritius, Mexico, Moldova, Monaco, Mongolia, Montenegro, Morocco, Netherlands, Nicaragua, North Macedonia, Norway, Panama, Peru, Poland, Puerto Rico, Russia, San Marino, Slovakia, South Africa, Spain, Sweden, Switzerland, Tanzania UR, Tunisia, Türkiye, Ukraine, Venezuela.
Included in the above, 1 organization listed in this Yearbook:
Internationale Gesellschaft der Bildende Künste (IGBK).
Consultative Status Consultative status granted from: *ECOSOC (#05331)* (Ros C); *UNESCO (#20322)* (Consultative Status); *World Intellectual Property Organization (WIPO, #21593)* (Permanent Observer Status). **NGO Relations** Member of: *International Conference of NGOs (#12883)*; *International Federation of Interior Architects / Designers (IFI, #13460)*. [2019.09.26/XB1254/**B**]

♦ International Association of Art Critics (#02680)
♦ International Association Artes Renascentes (#02670)

♦ International Association of Art – Europe (IAA Europe) 11711

Sec Slovak Union of Visual Arts, Dostojevského rad 2, 811 09 Bratislava, Slovakia. T. +421252962402. E-mail: office@svu.sk.
Pres PO Box 22436, CY-1521 Nicosia, Cyprus. T. +35722466426. Fax +35722466424. E-mail: ekatek@cytanet.com.cy.
URL: http://www.iaa-europe.eu/
History as one of the 5 cultural regions *International Association of Art (IAA, #11710)*. **Aims** Promote exchanges among artists and organizations engaged in art and culture within Europe and beyond; promote discussion and elaboration of artistic matters within Europe; promote information flow regarding eg working conditions, social security systems, authors' rights and free flow of artworks; make artists' interests known to European political institutions and their representatives. **Structure** General Assembly. Executive Committee, comprising President, Vice-President, Treasurer, Secretary, Coordinator and 3 members. **Events** *General Assembly* Helsinki (Finland) 2022, *General Assembly* Bratislava (Slovakia) 2019, *General Assembly* Brussels (Belgium) 2018, *General Assembly* Dublin (Ireland) 2017, *General Assembly* Berlin (Germany) 2016.
Members National Committees in 43 countries:
Armenia, Austria, Azerbaijan, Belarus, Belgium, Bosnia-Herzegovina, Bulgaria, Cyprus, Czechia, Denmark, Estonia, Finland, France, Georgia, Germany, Greece, Hungary, Iceland, Ireland, Israel, Italy, Kazakhstan, Latvia, Liechtenstein, Lithuania, Moldova, Monaco, Montenegro, Netherlands, Norway, Poland, Romania, Russia, San Marino, Serbia, Slovakia, Slovenia, Spain, Sweden, Switzerland, Türkiye, Ukraine, Uzbekistan.
NGO Relations Cooperates with: *Culture Action Europe (CAE, #04981)*; *European Council of Artists (ECA, #06805)*. [2011/XJ3813/**E**]

♦ International Association of Art-Exhibition-Directors / see IKT International Association of Curators of Contemporary Art (#11116)

♦ International Association for Artificial Intelligence and Law (IAAIL) 11712

Pres ITTIG-CNR, Via dei Barucci 20, 50127 Florence FI, Italy. E-mail: secretary@iaail.org.
Sec-Treas address not obtained.
URL: http://www.iaail.org/
History 1982. **Aims** Support, develop and promote artificial intelligence and law at the international level. **Structure** Executive Board. **Languages** English. **Finance** Conference registration fees; sponsorships. **Events** *Biennial Conference* Sao Paulo (Brazil) 2021, *Biennial Conference* Montréal, QC (Canada) 2019, *Biennial Conference* London (UK) 2017, *Biennial Conference* San Diego, CA (USA) 2015, *Biennial Conference* Rome (Italy) 2013. **Publications** *Artificial Intelligence and Law* – journal. Conference proceedings.
Members Individuals in 67 countries and territories:
Albania, Argentina, Australia, Austria, Bangladesh, Barbados, Belgium, Brazil, Canada, China, Colombia, Costa Rica, Croatia, Cyprus, Denmark, Ecuador, Egypt, Estonia, Finland, France, Germany, Greece, Hong Kong, Hungary, India, Indonesia, Iran Islamic Rep, Iraq, Ireland, Israel, Italy, Japan, Jordan, Korea Rep, Lesotho, Lithuania, Luxembourg, Malta, Mauritius, Mexico, Morocco, Netherlands, New Zealand, Nigeria, Norway, Oman, Pakistan, Peru, Philippines, Poland, Portugal, Romania, Russia, Serbia, Slovenia, South Africa, Spain, Sri Lanka, Sweden, Switzerland, Taiwan, Thailand, Trinidad-Tobago, Türkiye, UK, Ukraine, USA. [2021/XD6625/v/**D**]

♦ International Association of Art – Painting, Sculpture, Print-making / see International Association of Art (#11710)
♦ International Association for Arts and Audiovisual Media (inactive)
♦ International Association of Arts and Cultural Management (#02716)

♦ International Association for the Arts, the Media and Creativity by and with Disabled People (EUCREA International) 11713

Association européenne pour la créativité des personnes handicapées
Contact c/o Cemaforre, 3 villa Saint-Fargeau, 75020 Paris, France. T. +33672802362.
Registered Office 32 Square Ambiorix, Bte 47, 1040 Brussels, Belgium.
History 1988, Brussels (Belgium). Founded as *European Association for Creativity by Disabled People – Association européenne pour la créativité des personnes handicapées*, with the assistance of *European Commission (EC, #06633)*. Also previously referred to as *EUCREA Europe (Europe créativité)*. Present name adopted, 2000. Registration: Banque-Carrefour des Entreprises, No/ID: 0434.149.729, Start date: 5 May 1988, Belgium. **Aims** Promote and support networking and initiatives that extend the potential for people in the European Union with disabilities to be involved with arts and culture. **Structure** General Assembly (at Colloquium); Board of Directors; Executive Board, comprising President, Treasurer and Secretary. National committees. **Activities** International exchange. **Events** *Congress on disability and art / European Colloquium* Paris (France) 2003, *Colloquium / European Colloquium* Maastricht (Netherlands) 1992, *European colloquium* Dublin (Ireland) 1991.
Members National Committees in 15 countries:
Austria, Belgium, Denmark, Finland, France, Germany, Greece, Ireland, Italy, Luxembourg, Netherlands, Portugal, Spain, Sweden, UK. [2021/XF1516/**F**]

♦ International Association for Asia Pacific Studies (IAAPS) 11714

SG Research Office, Ritsumeikan Asia Pacific Univ, 1-1 Jumonjibaru, Beppu-City, Oita, 874-8577 Japan. T. +81977781134. Fax +81977771135. E-mail: rcaps@apu.ac.jp – iaaps@apu.ac.jp.
URL: http://www.apu.ac.jp/iaaps/
History Set up 2010. **Aims** Shape and promote Asia Pacific Studies; contribute to the further development of the region through the accumulation and publication of research in particular disciplines and on subregions of the Asia Pacific. **Structure** General Meeting (annual); Board of Directors; Advisory Board. **Languages** English. **Staff** 5.00 FTE, paid. **Finance** Members' dues. **Activities** Events/meetings; research/documentation. **Events** *Annual Conference* Incheon (Korea Rep) 2014, *Annual Conference* Manila (Philippines) 2013, *Annual Conference* Hong Kong (Hong Kong) 2012, *Annual Conference* Oita (Japan) 2011, *Annual Conference* Oita (Japan) 2010. **Publications** *Asia Pacific World* – journal. **IGO Relations** *United Nations Economic and Social Commission for Asia and the Pacific (ESCAP, #20557)*. [2018/XJ9560/**D**]

♦ International Association for Asphalt in Building Construction (inactive)

♦ International Association of Assay Offices (IAAO) 11715

Contact c/o Assay Office London, Goldsmiths' Hall, Foster Lane, London, EC2V 6BN, UK. T. +442076068971. E-mail: info@assayofficelondon.co.uk.
URL: http://www.theiaao.org/
History 1992, London (UK), as *Association of European Assay Offices (AEAO) – Association des bureaux de garantie européens*. Current title adopted, 2008. **Aims** Act as a forum for exchange of information and promotion of technical cooperation between authorized state assay offices with a view to provide a representative liaison body for communication with appropriate organizations. **Structure** Chairman; 2 Deputy Chairmen; Secretary-Treasurer. **Languages** English. **Staff** None. **Finance** Members' dues. Administration paid by the London (UK) Assay Office. **Activities** Knowledge management/information dissemination; networking/liaising. **Events** *Meeting* Riga (Latvia) 2019, *Meeting* Riga (Latvia) 2018, *Meeting* Porto (Portugal) 2017, *Meeting* Geneva (Switzerland) 2012, *Meeting* Warsaw (Poland) 2011.
Members Full in 36 countries:
Austria, Bosnia-Herzegovina, China, Croatia, Cyprus, Czechia, Denmark, Estonia, Finland, France, Germany, Hungary, Ireland, Israel, Italy, Japan, Latvia, Lithuania, Mauritius, Moldova, Netherlands, North Macedonia, Norway, Poland, Portugal, Romania, Serbia, Singapore, Slovakia, Slovenia, Spain, Sweden, Switzerland, UK, Ukraine.
IGO Relations *Convention on the Control and Marking of Articles of Precious Metals (Hallmarking convention, 1972)*; *European Commission (EC, #06633)*. **NGO Relations** Member of: *International Laboratory Accreditation Cooperation (ILAC, #13995)*. In liaison with technical committees of: *International Organization for Standardization (ISO, #14473)*. [2018.10.31/XD4091/**D**]

♦ International Association of Assembly Managers / see International Association of Venue Managers
♦ International Association of Assessing Officers (internationally oriented national body)
♦ International Association of Assistance Dog Partners (internationally oriented national body)
♦ International Association of Association Management Companies / see AMC Institute

♦ International Association for Assyriology 11716

Main Office PO Box 9515, 2300 RA Leiden, Netherlands. T. +31715272034. Fax +31715273310. E-mail: office@iaassyriology.com.
URL: https://iaassyriology.com/
History Jul 2003, London (UK). Founded during *International Congress of Assyriology and Near Eastern Archaeology (RAI)*. Registration: Netherlands. **Aims** Promote Cuneiform and Near Eastern *archaeology* studies. **Structure** General Meeting (annual); Board; Honorary Council. **Activities** Awards/prizes/competitions; events/meetings. **Events** *Rencontre Assyriologique Internationale (RAI)* Prague (Czechia) 2025, *Rencontre Assyriologique Internationale (RAI)* Helsinki (Finland) 2024, *Rencontre Assyriologique Internationale (RAI)* Leiden (Netherlands) 2023, *Rencontre Assyriologique Internationale (RAI)* Mainz (Germany) / Frankfurt-Main (Germany) 2022, *Rencontre Assyriologique Internationale (RAI)* Turin (Italy) 2021. **Members** Individuals and organizations. Membership countries not specified. [2021.02.16/XM4512/**D**]

♦ International Association of Astacology (IAA) 11717

Association internationale d'astacologie
Sec Auburn Univ, School of Fisheries, Aquaculture, and Aquatic Sciences, 203 Swingle Hall, Auburn AL 36849, USA. T. +13348449249.
URL: https://www.astacology.org/
History Sep 1972, Hinterthal (Austria), at First International Crayfish Symposium. **Aims** Encourage international scientific study of freshwater *crayfish*, their conservation and wise utilization; apply research results to freshwater aquaculture of various species; provide for dissemination of research findings and discussion of relevant problems. **Structure** Business Meeting (every 2-3 years). Executive Board, composed of Officers (President, President-Elect, Secretary-Treasurer and Immediate Past President) and up to 11 members appointed by the President. **Languages** English. **Staff** Voluntary. **Finance** Members' dues (intersymposium period): Student US$ 20; regular US$ 40; business/institutional US$ 80. **Activities** Organizes symposia (every 2 or 3 years); co-sponsors regional, national and international meetings. **Events** *Biennial Symposium* Hluboka nad Vltavou (Czechia) 2022, *Biennial Symposium* Hluboka nad Vltavou (Czechia) 2020, *Biennial Symposium* Pittsburgh, PA (USA) 2018, *Biennial Symposium* Madrid (Spain) 2016, *Joint Meeting* Sydney, NSW (Australia) 2015. **Publications** *IAA Newsletter* (4 a year); *IAA Directory* (every 2 years) – online; *Crayfish News*; *Freshwater Crayfish: A Journal of Astacology* – symposium proceedings.

Members Regular; Student; Honorary; Business/Institutional, in 44 countries and territories:
Argentina, Australia, Austria, Belarus, Belgium, Brazil, Bulgaria, Canada, Chile, China, Croatia, Cyprus, Czechia, Denmark, Ecuador, Egypt, Estonia, Finland, France, Germany, Hungary, Ireland, Israel, Italy, Japan, Kenya, Lebanon, Luxembourg, Mexico, Netherlands, New Zealand, Norway, Peru, Philippines, Portugal, Russia, South Africa, Spain, Sweden, Switzerland, Türkiye, UK, USA, Zambia. [2020/XC4451/**C**]

- ♦ International Association of Asthmology / see INTERASMA (#11457)

♦ International Association of Astronomical Artists (IAAA) 11718

Pres address not obtained. E-mail: iaaa-president@iaaa.org – iaaa-treasurer@iaaa.org.
URL: http://iaaa.org/

History 1982. **Aims** Implement and participate in astronomical and space art projects; promote education on astronomical art; foster international cooperation in artistic work inspired by exploration of the universe. **Activities** annual workshop held worldwide. **Publications** *PULSAR* (2 a year) – newsletter.
Members Individuals in 12 countries:
Argentina, Canada, France, Germany, Greece, Iceland, Italy, Japan, Spain, Switzerland, UK, USA. [2021/XD8872/**D**]

- ♦ International Association of Asylum Seekers and Refugees (unconfirmed)
- ♦ International Association of Athletes Against Drugs (no recent information)
- ♦ International Association of Athletic Administrators and Coaches (unconfirmed)
- ♦ International Association of Athletics Federations / see World Athletics (#21209)
- ♦ International Association for Audio-Visual Media in Historical Research and Education / see International Association for Media and History (#12023)
- ♦ International Association of Audiovisual Writers and Directors (no recent information)
- ♦ International Association of Auditorium Managers / see International Association of Venue Managers
- ♦ International Association of Authors of Comics and Cartoons (inactive)
- ♦ International Association of Authors, Composers and Writers (inactive)
- ♦ International Association Autism – Europe / see Autism-Europe (#03040)
- ♦ International Association for Automation of Analytical Chemistry (inactive)

♦ International Association for Automation and Robotics in Construction (IAARC) 11719

Gen Sec Univ of Oulu, Fac of Technology, PO Box 4200, FI-90014 Oulu, Finland. E-mail: secretariat@iaarc.org.
URL: http://www.iaarc.org/

History 1990. Founded following foundation of construction robotics lab in 1989. **Aims** Promote automation and robotics in construction for prefabrication, on site, and facility management, robot oriented design. **Structure** Board of Directors; Academy in Munich (Germany). **Languages** English. **Staff** 1.50 FTE, paid. **Finance** Members' dues. Budget: euro 12,000. **Activities** Training/education. **Events** *International Symposium on Automation and Robotics in Construction (ISARC)* Chennai (India) 2023, *International Symposium on Automation and Robotics in Construction (ISARC)* Bogota (Colombia) 2022, *International Symposium on Automation and Robotics in Construction (ISARC)* Dubai (United Arab Emirates) 2021, *Symposium* Kitakyushu (Japan) 2020, *Symposium* Banff, AB (Canada) 2019. **Publications** *Automation in Construction* – journal; *Catalogue of Robots and Automated Machines in Construction*. Proceedings.
Members Individuals and organizations. Members in 17 countries and territories:
Canada, Finland, France, Germany, India, Israel, Italy, Japan, Korea Rep, Netherlands, Poland, Russia, Slovakia, Sweden, Taiwan, UK, USA. [2022/XD8114/**D**]

♦ International Association of Auto Theft Investigators (IAATI) 11720

Exec Dir PO Box 223, Clinton NY 13323-0223, USA. T. +13158531913. Fax +13158331310.
URL: http://www.iaati.org/

History May 1953, Oklahoma City OK (USA), when Constitution and By-Laws were adopted. Chartered in accordance with the laws of the State of Oklahoma (USA). **Aims** Improve communication and coordination among professional auto theft investigators. **Structure** Executive Board; Committee Chairs; Chapters and Branches (7). **Events** *Seminar* Orlando, FL (USA) 2010, *Annual conference* Auckland (New Zealand) 2009, *Seminar* Denver, CO (USA) 2009, *Annual seminar* Vernon (France) 2009, *Annual Conference* Westminster, CO (USA) 2009. **Publications** *The APB* (4 a year).
Members Individuals (3,500) (mainly in USA) in 45 countries and territories:
Australia, Austria, Belgium, Bolivia, Botswana, Canada, Colombia, Congo DR, Costa Rica, Czechia, Denmark, Dominican Rep, Ecuador, El Salvador, Estonia, Finland, France, Germany, Guatemala, Honduras, Hong Kong, Hungary, Ireland, Israel, Italy, Jamaica, Kenya, Latvia, Mexico, Netherlands, New Zealand, Norway, Panama, Poland, Slovenia, South Africa, Spain, Sweden, Switzerland, Tanzania UR, Thailand, UK, USA, Zambia, Zimbabwe. [2018.06.25/XF2942/v/**F**]

- ♦ International Association of Average Adjusters (#02809)
- ♦ International Association of Avian Trainers and Educators (internationally oriented national body)

♦ International Association of Aviation Personnel Schools (IAAPS) . . 11721

Sec/Treas De duiker 65, 3461 JE Linschoten, Netherlands. T. +31651580901. E-mail: secretary@iaaps.info.
URL: https://www.iaaps.info/

History Oct 1995. Former names and other names: *European Association of Aviation Personnel Schools (EAAPS)* – former. Registration: Chamber of Commerce, No/ID: 40048968, Netherlands. **Aims** Contribute to high quality training of aviation personnel. **Structure** Executive Committee. **Languages** English. **Staff** 0.10 FTE, paid; 5.00 FTE, voluntary. **Finance** Sources: members' dues. Annual budget: 20,000 EUR. **Activities** Advocacy/lobbying/activism; events/meetings. **Events** *Annual General Assembly* Berlin (Germany) 2021.
Members Full in 16 countries:
Austria, Denmark, Finland, France, Germany, Greece, Ireland, Netherlands, Norway, Spain, Sweden, Switzerland, Tunisia, Türkiye, UK, USA. [2023.02.14/XM6859/**D**]

- ♦ International Association of Baby Boxes (unconfirmed)
- ♦ International Association of the Bald-Heads (no recent information)
- ♦ International Association of Bass Hotels and Resorts / see IHG Owners Association (#11112)

♦ International Association for Bear Research and Management (IBA) 11722

Pres 15542 County Rd 72, Warba MN 55793, USA.
URL: http://www.bearbiology.com/

History 1968. Also known as *International Bear Association*. **Aims** Foster communication and cooperation in research, care and management of bears and their habitat. **Structure** Council. Officers, comprising President, 2 Vice-Presidents, Secretary and Treasurer. **Languages** English. **Staff** Voluntary. **Finance** Members' dues. Other sources: conference profits; private donations. **Activities** Events/meetings. **Events** *Conference* Kalispell, MT (USA) 2021, *Conference* Ljubljana (Slovenia) 2018, *Conference* Quito (Ecuador) 2017, *Conference* Thessaloniki (Greece) 2014, *Conference* Provo, UT (USA) 2013. **Publications** *International Bear News* (4 a year); *Ursus* (annual) – journal.
Members Organizations in 19 countries:
Bulgaria, Canada, Colombia, France, Indonesia, Italy, Japan, Latvia, Netherlands, Norway, Peru, Romania, Slovenia, Spain, Sweden, Switzerland, UK, Ukraine, USA.
Individuals (680) in 46 countries and territories:
Albania, Australia, Austria, Bosnia-Herzegovina, Canada, China, Czechia, Denmark, Ecuador, Estonia, Finland, France, Georgia, Germany, Greece, Hong Kong, Hungary, India, Indonesia, Israel, Italy, Japan, Kazakhstan, Korea Rep, Laos, Latvia, Mexico, Mongolia, Netherlands, North Macedonia, Norway, Pakistan, Poland, Romania, Russia, Slovenia, South Africa, Spain, Sweden, Switzerland, Taiwan, Türkiye, UK, Ukraine, USA, Venezuela.
NGO Relations Provides two co-chairs for: *International Union for Conservation of Nature and Natural Resources (IUCN, #15766)* – SSC Bear Specialist Group. [2014/XD6364/**D**]

- ♦ International Association Bible and Computers (inactive)
- ♦ International Association of Bible Leagues / see Bible League International (#03225)
- ♦ International Association of Biblicists and Orientalists (inactive)
- ♦ International Association of Bibliology (inactive)
- ♦ International Association of Bibliophiles (#02673)

♦ International Association of Bicentenary Family Companies (The Henokiens) 11723

Association Internationale d'Entreprises Familiales and Bicentenaires (Les Hénokiens)

Contact address not obtained. E-mail: info@henokiens.com.
URL: http://www.henokiens.com/

History 1981. Registration: Start date: 24 Feb 1981, France. **Aims** Develop membership worldwide based on the value of the concept of family businesses; demonstrate that this type of enterprise can serve as a model for tomorrow's economy; encourage transmission of the cultural and traditional values of family businesses, ensuring their sustainability. **Activities** Awards/prizes/competitions; events/meetings; knowledge management/information dissemination; networking/liaising; projects/programmes. **Events** *Annual Congress* Lyon (France) 2020, *Annual Congress* London (UK) 2019, *Annual Congress* Vienna (Austria) 2017. **Publications** Case studies. **Members** Families and companies (51) in Europe and Japan. Membership countries not specified.
NGO Relations Member of (1): *European Family Businesses (EFB, #07028)*. [2022.10.17/XM6027/**C**]

♦ International Association for the Biennial of Young Artists from Europe and the Mediterranean 11724

Association internationale pour la Biennale des jeunes créateurs de l'Europe et de la Méditerranée (BJCEM)

Exec Dir Cortile del Maglio, via Andreis 18 int 18/c, 10152 Turin TO, Italy. T. +391119504733. Fax +39110433406. E-mail: communication@bjcem.org – adm.bjcem@gmail.com.
Registered Office Fidelium, Bd Saint Michel 65, 1040 Brussels, Belgium.
URL: http://www.bjcem.org/

History Jul 2001, Sarajevo (Bosnia-Herzegovina). Founded during 10th Biennial. Registration: Banque-Carrefour des Entreprises, Belgium. **Aims** Create opportunities for young creators of training, mobility, exchange, mutual understanding, intercultural dialogue and collaboration. **Structure** General Assembly (2 or 3 a year); Board of Directors; National Committees. **Languages** Arabic, English, French, Italian. **Staff** 1.50 FTE, paid. External collaboration: 1. **Finance** Sources: members' dues; revenue from activities/projects. **Activities** Events/meetings. **Events** *Biennial for Young Artists from Europe and the Mediterranean* Skopje (Macedonia) 2009, *Biennial meeting / Biennial for Young Artists from Europe and the Mediterranean* Naples (Italy) 2005, *Biennial meeting / Biennial for Young Artists from Europe and the Mediterranean* Athens (Greece) 2003, *Biennial for Young Artists from Europe and the Mediterranean* Sarajevo (Bosnia-Herzegovina) 2001, *Biennial for Young Artists from Europe and the Mediterranean* Rome (Italy) 1999.
Members Members (47) in 16 countries:
Albania, Bosnia-Herzegovina, Cyprus, France, Greece, Italy, Lebanon, Malta, Montenegro, Norway, San Marino, Serbia, Slovenia, Spain, Türkiye, UK.
NGO Relations Member of (2): *Culture Action Europe (CAE, #04981)*; *European Association of Creative Writing Programmes (EACWP, #05996)*. [2021.02.17/XD8448/**D**]

- ♦ International Association for Binocular Vision (#13315)

♦ International Association of Bioethics (IAB) 11725

Association internationale de bioéthique

Secretariat 7101 Av du Parc, Montréal QC H3N 1X7, Canada. E-mail: iabioethics.contact@gmail.com.
Pres School of Public Health, University of Montreal, 7101 Av du Parc, 3rd floor, Montréal QC H3N 1X9, Canada.
URL: http://iab-website.iab-secretariat.org/

History 7 Oct 1992, Amsterdam (Netherlands). **Aims** Facilitate contacts and exchange of information between those working in bioethics in different parts of the world; organize international conferences on bioethics; encourage the development of research and teaching in bioethics; uphold the value of free, open and reasoned discussion of issues in bioethics. **Structure** Board of Directors, consisting of President, Vice-President, Secretary, Treasurer and 17 other members. **Languages** English. **Staff** 0.50 FTE, paid. **Finance** Sources: members' dues. **Activities** Networks on specific issues (16): Feminist approaches to bioethics; Research within human subjects; Corruption and honesty in health care systems; Informed consent; Genetics; Allocation of health care resources; Termination of treatment: Euthanasia; Hospital ethics committees; Reproductive rights; Psychiatric ethics; Bioethics education network; Islamic bioethics; Nursing ethics; Ethics and intellectual disability; Environmental bioethics; Definition of death. **Events** *Solidarity and Autonomy – Bridging the Tensions* Philadelphia, PA (USA) 2020, *World Congress* Karnataka (India) 2018, *World Congress* Edinburgh (UK) 2016, *World Congress* Mexico City (Mexico) 2014, *World Congress* Rotterdam (Netherlands) 2012. **Publications** *IAB News* (irregular); *Bioethics* – official journal.
Members Institutions (54) in 20 countries:
Argentina, Australia, Brazil, Canada, China, Colombia, Denmark, Egypt, Greece, Italy, Japan, Netherlands, New Zealand, Norway, Puerto Rico, Spain, Sweden, Switzerland, UK, USA.
Individuals (540) in 40 countries and territories:
Argentina, Australia, Bangladesh, Belgium, Brazil, Bulgaria, Cameroon, Canada, Chile, China, Colombia, Croatia, Cuba, Denmark, Finland, France, Germany, Hong Kong, Hungary, Indonesia, Israel, Italy, Japan, Korea Rep, Malaysia, Mexico, Netherlands, New Zealand, Norway, Philippines, Puerto Rico, Russia, Singapore, Slovenia, Spain, Sweden, Switzerland, UK, Uruguay, USA. [2020/XD3186/**C**]

- ♦ International Association for Biography and Autobiography / see International Auto/Biography Association (#12299)
- ♦ International Association for Biologically Closed Electric Circuits in Biomedicine (inactive)

♦ International Association of Biological Oceanography (IABO) 11726

Association internationale d'océanographie biologique (AIOB)

Pres Inst for Marine Remote Sensing – College of Marine Science, Knight Oceanographic Research Ctr, St Petersburg FL 33701, USA.
Sec Chulalongkorn Univ, CEMB – Fac of Science, Bangkok, 10330, Thailand. T. +6622185394.
URL: http://www.iabo.org/

History Jun 1966, Moscow (Russia). Founded at 2nd International Congress of Oceanography. **Aims** Advance knowledge of the biology of the sea by providing opportunities for communication among *marine* biologists. **Structure** General Assembly; Executive Committee. Division of Environmental Biology of *International Union of Biological Sciences (IUBS, #15760)*. **Languages** English. **Staff** None. **Finance** Subventions from IUBS. **Activities** Events/meetings; networking/liaising. **Events** *World Conference on Marine Biodiversity* Ghent (Belgium) 2026, *General Assembly* Penang (Malaysia) 2023, *World Conference on Marine Biodiversity* Penang (Malaysia) 2023, *General Assembly* Auckland (New Zealand) 2020, *World Conference on Marine Biodiversity* St Petersburg, FL (USA) 2020.
Members National correspondents in 33 countries and territories:
Argentina, Australia, Austria, Belgium, Brazil, Canada, Chile, China, Denmark, Egypt, Finland, France, Germany, Greece, India, Ireland, Italy, Japan, Malaysia, Mexico, Monaco, Netherlands, New Zealand, Norway, Poland, Portugal, Saudi Arabia, South Africa, Spain, Sweden, Taiwan, UK, USA.
IGO Relations Observer status with: *International Council for the Exploration of the Sea (ICES, #13021)*. **NGO Relations** Cooperates with (1): *Marine Biodiversity Observation Network (MBON)*. Represented in: *Scientific Committee on Oceanic Research (SCOR, #19149)*. [2023/XC1257/**C**]

- ♦ International Association for Biologicals / see International Alliance for Biological Standardization (#11622)
- ♦ International Association of Biological Standardization / see International Alliance for Biological Standardization (#11622)
- ♦ International Association of Biologists Technicians (#02747)
- ♦ International Association for Biology of Senescence Research (inactive)
- ♦ International Association of Biomedical Gerontology (no recent information)
- ♦ International Association of Black Professional Fire Fighters (internationally oriented national body)
- ♦ International Association for Blended Learning (unconfirmed)
- ♦ International Association for Blind Students (inactive)

♦ International Association of the Body and Trailer Building Industry (CLCCR) 11727

Association internationale de la construction de carrosseries et de remorques – Internationaler Verband der Aufbauten- und Anhängerindustrie

SG BluePoint Brussels, Bd Auguste Reyers 80, Schaerbeek, 1030 Brussels, Belgium.
URL: http://www.clccr.eu/
History 1961, Frankfurt-Main (Germany FR), as *Liaison Committee of Coachwork and Trailer Builders – Comité de liaison de la construction de carrosseries et de remorques (CLCCR) – Verbindungsausschuss der Aufbauten- und Anhängerindustrie – Comitato di Collegamento della Costruzione di Carrozzerie e Rimorchi – Verbindingscomité voor de Carrosserie- en Aanhangwagenbouw*. New title adopted, 8 Sep 2008, when registered as an international association. Still known under the abbreviation *CLCCR*. Registered in accordance with Belgian law. EU Transparency Register: 452292722494-55. **Aims** Defend the material and intellectual interests of auto body and trailer manufacturers. **Structure** General Assembly (annual); Council; Committees; Working Groups. **Activities** Networking/liaising; knowledge management/information dissemination; projects/programmes.
Members Full; Associate; Honorary. National organizations in 15 countries:
Austria, Belgium, Finland, France, Germany, Greece, Italy, Netherlands, Norway, Poland, Portugal, Spain, Sweden, Türkiye, UK.
IGO Relations Recognized by: *European Commission (EC, #06633).* [2019.07.03/XD2923/t/**D**]

♦ International Association of Bodywork Repairers (#02741)

♦ International Association of Bookkeepers (IAB) 11728

Chief Exec 110 Bishopsgate, London, EC2N 4AY, UK. T. +442081878888. E-mail: mail@iab.org.uk.
URL: http://www.iab.org.uk/
History 1973, London (UK). Registration: Companies house, No/ID: 1119378, Start date: 21 Jun 1973, England and Wales. **Aims** Support and promote *professional* bookkeepers, office managers, payroll managers, etc; represent their interests to external bodies; foster competence, *integrity* and public confidence; conduct examinations and award *qualifications* which are recognized and respected worldwide. **Structure** General Meeting (annual); Council; Executive; International Representative Offices. **Languages** English, Estonian, Latvian, Russian. **Staff** 13.00 FTE, paid. **Finance** Members' dues. Revenue from registration for qualifications/ examinations. **Activities** Training/education; certification/accreditation; awards/prizes/competitions; events/ meetings. **Events** *Annual Convention* London (UK) 2014, *Annual Convention* London (UK) 2013, *Convention / Annual Convention* York (UK) 1999, *Convention* York (UK) 1999, *Convention / Annual Convention* Eastbourne (UK) 1998. **Publications** *IAB Newsletter* (12 a year); *The Bookkeeper* – magazine.
Members Fellow; Member; Registered Student. Individuals (over 10,000) mostly in UK but in a total of 63 countries and territories:
Algeria, Australia, Azerbaijan, Bahrain, Barbados, Belarus, Belgium, Belize, Bermuda, Brunei Darussalam, Canada, Cayman Is, Channel Is, China, Cyprus, Dominican Rep, Estonia, France, Gambia, Germany, Ghana, Gibraltar, Guyana, Hong Kong, Hungary, Iraq, Ireland, Isle of Man, Kazakhstan, Latvia, Lebanon, Lithuania, Malawi, Malaysia, Maldives, Malta, Mauritius, Netherlands, New Zealand, Nigeria, Oman, Pakistan, Papua New Guinea, Poland, Qatar, Russia, Saudi Arabia, Singapore, South Africa, Spain, Sri Lanka, Switzerland, Taiwan, Tanzania UR, Trinidad-Tobago, Uganda, UK, Ukraine, United Arab Emirates, USA, Yemen, Zambia, Zimbabwe. [2021/XF5501/ev/**F**]

♦ International Association of Book and Paper Conservators 11729

Internationale Arbeitsgemeinschaft der Archiv-, Bibliotheks- und Graphikrestauratoren (IADA)
Pres Folger Shakespeare Library, 201 East Capitol St SE, Washington DC 20003, USA. T. +12026750332. Fax +12025650317.
Vice Pres Universitätsbibliothek, Papendiek 14, 37073 Göttingen, Germany. T. +49551395202. Fax +49551395288. E-mail: restaurierung@mail.sub.uni-goettingen.de.
URL: http://www.iada-home.org/
History 28 Feb 1957, as *Arbeitsgemeinschaft der Archivrestauratoren (AdA)*. Current title adopted, 1967. Previously referred to as *International Association for Conservation of Books, Paper and Archival Material – Association internationale pour la conservation des livres, du papier et du matériel d'archives*. Registered charity. **Aims** At international level: work towards the improvement of the professional education of conservators/restorers; promote information exchange. **Structure** General Assembly (every 4 years). Executive Board, comprising President, Vice-President, Treasurer, Editor, Secretary and 5 members. **Languages** English, German. **Staff** Voluntary. **Finance** Members' dues. **Events** *Symposium* 2022, *Quadrennial Congress* Warsaw (Poland) 2019, *Quadrennial Congress* Berlin (Germany) 2015, *Symposium* Amsterdam (Netherlands) 2014, *Quadrennial Congress* Bern (Switzerland) 2011. **Publications** *Journal of Paper Conservation* (4 a year) – magazine; *IADA Reports – Mitteilungen der IADA.*
Members Full in 26 countries:
Austria, Belgium, Canada, Croatia, Czechia, Denmark, Finland, France, Germany, Greece, Hungary, Ireland, Italy, Japan, Liechtenstein, Netherlands, Norway, Poland, Romania, Slovenia, Spain, Sweden, Switzerland, UK, United Arab Emirates, USA.
NGO Relations Member of: *European Confederation of Conservator-Restorers' Organisations (ECCO, #06701).* [2013/XD1266/**D**]

♦ International Association of Botanical and Mycological Societies (IABMS) 11730

Association internationale des sociétés de botanique et de mycologie
Sec c/o Paleontology Dept, Natural History Museum, Cirkusová 1740, 193 00 Prague 9, Czechia.
Chairperson address not obtained.
URL: https://www.iaptglobal.org/iabms
History 1981, Sydney, NSW (Australia). Founded during 13th *International Botanical Congress (IBC)*, to replace the former Division of Botany and Mycology within the *International Union of Biological Sciences (IUBS, #15760)*. Currently functions as "Botany General" Commission of IUBS. Current Constitution adopted by the Board of IABMS meeting, 2 Sep 1993, Yokohama (Japan). Acts as the body charged with the responsibility of ensuring the ongoing continuance of International Botanical Congresses (IBC). **Aims** Promote exchange of information among adhering organizations, coordinate and further their aims and efforts; encourage international scientific bodies with an interest in plant sciences, not already members of IUBS, to apply for scientific membership so as to be able to adhere to IABMS.
Structure General Assembly (every 6 years, at the closing of International Botanical Congress); Board. Sections (7): General Botany; *International Association for Plant Taxonomy (IAPT, #12092); International Mycological Association (IMA, #14203); International Organization of Palaeobotany (IOP, #14459); International Plant Growth Substances Association (IPGSA, #14591); International Society for Horticultural Science (ISHS, #15180); International Society for Plant Pathology (ISPP, #15371).*
Commissions (11):
- General Committee on Botanical Nomenclature;
- *International Association of Botanic Gardens (IABG, #11731);*
- *International Commission for the Nomenclature of Cultivated Plants (ICNCP, see: #15760);*
- *International Commission for Plant-Pollinator Relationships (ICPPR, #12716);*
- *International Organization for Succulent Plant Study (IOS, #14477);*
- *International Phycological Society (IPS, #14576);*
- Standing Committee for *International Plant Protection Congresses (IPPC);*
- *International Seed Testing Association (ISTA, #14829);*
- *International Society for Mushroom Science (ISMS, #15286);*
- *Organization for the Phyto-Taxonomic Investigation of the Mediterranean Area (OPTIMA, #17884).*

Languages English. **Staff** 2.00 FTE, voluntary. **Finance** None. **Activities** Events/meetings; knowledge management/information dissemination. **Events** *International Botanical Congress* 2029, *International Botanical Congress* Madrid (Spain) 2024, *Six-Yearly International Botanical Congress* Madrid (Spain) 2024, *International Botanical Congress* Rio de Janeiro (Brazil) 2023, *International Botanical Congress* Shenzhen (China) 2017.
Members Adhering Organizations in 49 countries and territories:
Argentina, Australia, Austria, Belgium, Brazil, Bulgaria, Canada, Chile, China, Czechia, Denmark, Egypt, Finland, France, Germany, Ghana, Greece, Hong Kong, Hungary, India, Iraq, Ireland, Israel, Italy, Japan, Jordan, Korea Rep, Mexico, Monaco, Netherlands, New Zealand, Norway, Philippines, Poland, Portugal, Romania, Russia, Saudi Arabia, Serbia, Singapore, South Africa, Spain, Sweden, Switzerland, Taiwan, Thailand, UK, USA, Venezuela.
Included in the above, 3 organizations listed in this Yearbook:
Australasian Mycological Society (AMS); International Society for Mushroom Science (ISMS, #15286); Southern African Society for Plant Pathology (SASPP, #19863). [2022/XD8030/y/**B**]

♦ International Association of Botanic Gardens (IABG) 11731

Association internationale des jardins botaniques
SG SCIB-CAS, Xingke Road 723, Guangzhou, Tianhe District, 510650 Guangdong, China.
Pres Univ of Reading – Biology, Whiteknights, PO Box 217, Reading, RG6 6AH, UK.
URL: http://www.bgci.org/global/iabg/
History 1954, Paris (France), at 8th International Botanical Congress. Statutes adopted in 1965; revised 1987. In 1981 became a separate section of *International Union of Biological Sciences (IUBS, #15760)*. Currently exists as regional chapters. **Aims** Promote: international cooperation, and documentation and exchange of information, plants and specimens of mutual interest, among botanic gardens, arboreta and other similar institutes maintaining scientific collections of living plants; study of taxonomy of cultivated plants. Promote and foster conservation and preservation of rare and/or endangered plants, through their cultivation and by other means, within botanic gardens, arboreta and other similar institutes. **Structure** Assembly (at least every 3 years). Council, consisting of the Executive Committee – comprising President, Vice-Presidents (2), the immediate past-President and Secretary and 10 further Councillors. Regional Chapters (4): Asia; European-Mediterranean; Eastern Europe and former USSR; Latin America. **Languages** English. **Activities** Holds meetings: every 6 years during *International Botanical Congress (IBC)*, simultaneous with *International Association for Plant Taxonomy (IAPT, #12092)*; and every 4 years at *International Horticultural Congress*. **Events** *International Meeting* Guangzhou (China) 2012, *International Meeting* Córdoba (Spain) 2001, *General meeting and conference* Nanjing (China) 1993, *Conference* Tokyo (Japan) 1991, *Joint symposium* Paris (France) 1988. **Publications** *International Directory of Botanical Gardens.* **Members** Currently no individual membership. Regional chapters have their own members. **NGO Relations** Member of: *International Association of Botanical and Mycological Societies (IABMS, #11730).* [2013/XC1258/**F**]

♦ International Association of Botanists (inactive)

♦ International Association for Boundary Element Methods (IABEM) . 11732

Pres Graduate School of Informatics, Kyoto Univ, Kyoto, 606-8501 Japan. E-mail: nchml@i.kyoto-u.ac.jp.
URL: http://www.iabem.org/
History Founded 1988, on the initiative of Thomas A Cruse, Luigi Morino and Shoichi Kobayashi. **Aims** Advance research and development of the boundary integral equation (BIE) and boundary element method (BEM); promote applications of the BEM in industries. **Structure** Executive Council; Scientific Advisory Committee. **Languages** English. **Activities** Events/meetings. **Events** *Symposium* Shenzhen (China) 2020, *Symposium* Paris (France) 2018, *Symposium* Golden, CO (USA) 2016, *Symposium* Zhengzhou (China) 2014, *Symposium* Santiago (Chile) 2013.
Members Individuals in 27 countries:
Australia, Austria, Brazil, Bulgaria, Canada, Chile, China, France, Germany, Greece, India, Iran Islamic Rep, Italy, Japan, Korea Rep, Netherlands, New Zealand, Poland, Portugal, Romania, Russia, Serbia, Slovenia, Spain, UK, Ukraine, USA.
NGO Relations Affiliated organization of: *International Union of Theoretical and Applied Mechanics (IUTAM, #15823).* [2018.10.30/XD3818/v/**C**]

♦ International Association of the Bread Industry / see Association internationale de la boulangerie industrielle (#02674)

♦ International Association for Breast Cancer Research (IABCR) 11733

SG Univ of Cambridge, Dept of Pathology, Tennis Court Road, Cambridge, CB2 1QP, UK. T. +441223333725. E-mail: cjw53@cam.ac.uk.
Chairman Dept of Medicine and Biochemistry, McGill Univ Health Centre, Royal Victoria Hosp, 687 Pine Ave, Montréal QC H3A 1A1, Canada.
URL: http://www.mcrc.manchester.ac.uk/conference/
History 1983, Denver CO (USA), following a series of symposia and conferences on breast cancer in man and experimental animals started in 1955. **Aims** Advance progress of research directed toward effective control of breast cancer by stimulating basic and clinical breast cancer research. **Structure** Board of Governors, elects Chairman and Secretary General; President is last Congress Organizer. **Languages** English. **Staff** All voluntary; hosting institutions provide some secretarial support. **Finance** None. **Activities** Events/meetings; networking/ liaising; knowledge management/information dissemination. **Events** *Congress* Quintana Roo (Mexico) 2023, *Congress* Egmond aan Zee (Netherlands) 2019, *Congress* Portland, OR (USA) 2016, *Congress* Sydney, NSW (Australia) 2014, *Congress* Manchester (UK) 2012. **Members** Individuals clinicians or researchers in the field of breast cancer. Membership countries not specified. **NGO Relations** *Council for International Organizations of Medical Sciences (CIOMS, #04905).* [2015.11.02/XD4369/**D**]

♦ International Association for Breath Research (IABR) 11734

Address not obtained.
URL: http://iabr.voc-research.at/
History May 2005, Vienna (Austria). **Aims** Promote scientific research and development in the field of breath analysis. **Structure** Scientific Board. **Events** *Breath Summit* Pisa (Italy) 2022, *Breath Summit* Loughborough (UK) 2019, *Breath Summit* Maastricht (Netherlands) 2018, *Breath Summit* Zurich (Switzerland) 2016, *Conference* Vienna (Austria) 2015. **Publications** *Journal of Breath Research.* [2015/XM3866/**C**]

♦ International Association of Breeders and Distributors of Ornamental Plant Varieties (FLEUROSELECT) 11735

SG Jacoba van Bejerenweg 97-1A, 2215 KW Voorhout, Netherlands. T. +31713649101. Fax +31713649102. E-mail: info@fleuroselect.com.
URL: http://www.fleuroselect.com/
History 29 May 1970, Frankfurt-Main (Germany). Founded as *European Organization for Testing New Flowerseeds*. Subsequently changed to: *Association of Breeders and European Distributors of Flower Seed Varieties*. Registration: No/ID: KVK 40409594, Netherlands. **Aims** Test, promote and protect new ornamental plant varieties from seeds and cuttings; offer an international platform for the industry. **Structure** Board of Directors; Entries and Evaluation Committee; Secretariat. **Languages** Dutch, English, French, German, Italian, Spanish. **Staff** 3.00 FTE, paid. **Finance** Members' dues. Other sources: entrance fees; assessment fees; convention and other participation fees. **Activities** Research and development; events/meetings. **Events** *Annual Convention* Amsterdam (Netherlands) 2020, *Annual Convention* Kassel (Germany) 2019, *Annual Convention* Barcelona (Spain) 2018, *Annual Convention* Budapest (Hungary) 2017, *Home Garden Conference* Paris (France) 2017.
Members International ornamental plant breeders and merchants. Members in 19 countries and territories:
Austria, Belgium, Chile, Denmark, France, Germany, Hungary, Israel, Italy, Japan, Netherlands, Poland, Russia, Spain, Sweden, Switzerland, Taiwan, UK, USA. [2021/XD0313/**D**]

♦ International Association for Bridge Maintenance and Safety (IABMAS) 11736

SG Technical Univ of Catalonia, School of Civil Engineering, c/Jordi Girona 1-3 Campus Nord, Modul C1, 08034 Barcelona, Spain. T. +3434016513. Fax +3434054135.
Pres Civl Eng – Lehigh Univ, 117 ATLSS Dr, Imbt Labs, Bethlehem PA 18015-4729, USA. T. +16107586103. Fax +16107584115.
URL: http://www.iabmas.org/
History Founded 1999. **Aims** Promote international cooperation in the fields of bridge maintenance, safety and management. **Structure** Executive Committee. **Languages** English. **Staff** None. **Finance** No budget. **Activities** Events/meetings; training/education. **Events** *International Conference on Bridge Maintenance, Safety and Management* Copenhagen (Denmark) 2024, *International Conference on Bridge Maintenance, Safety and Management* Barcelona (Spain) 2022, *International Conference on Bridge Maintenance, Safety and Management* Sapporo (Japan) 2021, *International Conference on Bridge Maintenance, Safety and Management* Sapporo (Japan) 2020, *International Conference on Bridge Maintenance, Safety and Management* Melbourne, VIC (Australia) 2018. **Publications** *Journal of Structure and Infrastructure Engineering.*
Members Collective (103) and individuals (1,410) in 57 countries:
Argentina, Australia, Austria, Bangladesh, Belgium, Brazil, Canada, Chile, China, Colombia, Costa Rica, Croatia, Czechia, Denmark, Dominican Rep, Egypt, Finland, France, Germany, Greece, India, Indonesia, Iran Islamic Rep, Ireland, Israel, Italy, Japan, Jordan, Korea Rep, Kuwait, Lebanon, Mexico, Mozambique, Netherlands, New Zealand, Nigeria, North Macedonia, Norway, Peru, Poland, Portugal, Puerto Rico, Romania, Russia, Saudi Arabia, Singapore, Slovenia, South Africa, Spain, Sri Lanka, Sweden, Switzerland, Türkiye, UK, Uruguay, USA, Venezuela. [2020/XD8401/**D**]

♦ International Association for Bridge and Structural Engineering (IABSE) 11737

Association internationale des ponts et charpentes (AIPC) – Internationale Vereinigung für Brückenbau und Hochbau (IVBH)

Exec Dir Junghozstrasse 28, 8050 Zurich ZH, Switzerland. T. +41434439765. E-mail: secretariat@iabse.org.

URL: http://www.iabse.org/

History 29 Oct 1929, Zurich (Switzerland). **Aims** Promote international cooperation among engineers and researchers, and particularly representatives of science, industry and public authorities; encourage awareness and responsibility of members towards the needs of society; promote exchange of technical and scientific knowledge. **Structure** Permanent Committee (meeting once a year); Executive and Technical Committee. **Languages** English. **Staff** 5.00 FTE, paid. **Finance** Sources: meeting proceeds; members' dues; sale of publications. Annual budget: 1,000,000 CHF. **Activities** Awards/prizes/competitions; events/meetings; knowledge management/information dissemination; networking/liaising; publishing activities; training/education. **Events** *IABSE Spring Symposium* Manchester (UK) 2024, *IABSE Spring Symposium* Istanbul (Türkiye) 2023, *Congress* New Delhi (India) 2023, *Congress* Nanjing (China) 2022, *IABSE Spring Symposium* Prague (Czechia) 2022. **Publications** *Structural Engineering International (SEI)* (4 a year). *Structural Engineering Document (SED).* Conference proceedings; documents; case studies; guidelines. **Members** Individual (3,000) and Collective (governments and local authorities, universities, scientific institutes, associations and firms) in over 100 countries. Membership countries not specified. **Consultative Status** Consultative status granted from: *ECOSOC (#05331)* (Ros A). **IGO Relations** Accredited by (1): *United Nations Office at Vienna (UNOV, #20604).* Recognized by (1): *European Commission (EC, #06633).* Associated with Department of Global Communications of the United Nations. **NGO Relations** In liaison with technical committees of: *International Organization for Standardization (ISO, #14473).* Founding member of: *Liaison Committee of International Associations of Civil Engineering (#16453)* and member of its *Joint Committee on Structural Safety (JCSS, #16126)*, together with *European Convention for Constructional Steelwork (ECCS, #06779)*; *International Association for Shell and Spatial Structures (IASS, #12162)*; *International Council for Research and Innovation in Building and Construction (CIB, #13069)*; *Réunion internationale des laboratoires d'essais et de recherches sur les matériaux et les constructions (RILEM, #18930).* [2023.02.27/XB1177/**B**]

- ♦ International Association of Bridge and Structural Iron Workers of America / see International Association of Bridge, Structural, Ornamental and Reinforcing Iron Workers
- ♦ International Association of Bridge, Structural and Ornamental Iron Workers / see International Association of Bridge, Structural, Ornamental and Reinforcing Iron Workers
- ♦ International Association of Bridge, Structural, Ornamental and Reinforcing Iron Workers (internationally oriented national body)

♦ International Association of Broadcasting (IAB) 11738

Association internationale de radiodiffusion (AIR) – Asociación Internacional de Radiodifusión (AIR)

Gen Dir IAB Central Office, Carlos Quijano 1264, 11100 Montevideo, Uruguay. T. +59829011319 – +59829031879. Fax +59829080458. E-mail: mail@airiab.com.

URL: http://www.airiab.com/

History 1946, Mexico City (Mexico), as *Inter-American Association of Broadcasters (IAAB) – Association interaméricaine de radiodiffusion – Asociación Interamericana de Radiodifusión (AIR) – Associação Interamericana de Radiodifusão.* Was also sometimes referred to as *Inter-American Broadcasters Association.* Present name adopted 1985. **Aims** Defend broadcasting, whether *radio* or *television*, as a free means of expression of thought; work for freedom of social communication media; promote cooperation of broadcasters in activities of public interest and social services and the effective representation of broadcasting interests in official or private national and international organizations; sponsor world and regional conferences of a technical, legal or educational nature. **Structure** General Assembly (annual); Board of Directors (meeting twice a year); Executive Group. **Languages** English, French, Spanish. **Finance** Members' dues. **Activities** Standing Committees: Legal; Technical; On Copyright; On Freedom of Expression. **Events** *Annual General Assembly* Lima (Peru) 2011, *Annual General Assembly* Madrid (Spain) 2000, *Annual General Assembly* Colombia 1995, *Annual General Assembly* Porlamar (Venezuela) 1994, *Annual General Assembly* Venezuela 1994. **Publications** *La Gaceta de AIR* (4 a year).

Members Institutional; Individual; Supporting; Honorary. National associations or private broadcasters and radio and television enterprises, acting individually or collectively. Members in 24 countries:

Argentina, Austria, Bolivia, Brazil, Canada, Chile, Colombia, Costa Rica, Dominican Rep, Ecuador, El Salvador, Estonia, Guatemala, Honduras, Italy, Mexico, Nicaragua, Panama, Paraguay, Peru, Spain, Uruguay, USA, Venezuela.

Consultative Status Consultative status granted from: *ECOSOC (#05331)* (Ros); *UNESCO (#20322)* (Associate Status); *World Intellectual Property Organization (WIPO, #21593)* (Permanent Observer Status); *OAS (#17629).* **IGO Relations** Working relations with: *International Telecommunication Union (ITU, #15673)*, especially its Radiocommunication Observer to: *Intergovernmental Committee of the International Convention of Rome for the Protection of Performers, Producers of Phonograms and Broadcasting Organizations (#11474)*; *Union for the International Registration of Audiovisual Works (#20444).* Accredited by: *United Nations Office at Vienna (UNOV, #20604).* Associated with Department of Global Communications of the United Nations. Related union: *Arab States Broadcasting Union (ASBU, #01050).* **NGO Relations** Organizes: *World Conference of Broadcasting Unions*, together with related unions *Asia-Pacific Broadcasting Union (ABU, #01863)*; *Caribbean Broadcasting Union (CBU, #03465)*; *European Broadcasting Union (EBU, #06404)*; *Organización de Telecomunicaciones de Iberoamérica (OTI, #17851)*; *North American Broadcasters Association (NABA, #17561)*; *African Union of Broadcasting (AUB, #00490).* Member of: *World Broadcasting Unions (WBU, #21247).* Participates in: *Encuentro Latinoamericano de Informatica e Industrias de Información (ELAII).* [2012/XD1046/**D**]

♦ International Association of Broadcasting Manufacturers (IABM) 11739

Main Office Basepoint Business Centre, Oakfield Close, Tewkesbury, GL20 8SD, UK. E-mail: info@theiabm.org.

Business Intelligence Unit 21 Rue Glesener, L-1631 Luxembourg, Luxembourg.

URL: http://www.theiabm.org/

History Sep 1976, London (UK). Registration: Companies House, No/ID: 5262009, England and Wales. **Aims** Represent manufacturers and suppliers of products and services to the broadcasting and electronic media industries; identify and promote members' interests; provide benefits and services which enhance their business performance. **Structure** Members Board; Secretariat. Sub-Committees (2): Marketing; Technical. **Languages** English. **Staff** Paid. **Finance** Members' dues (annual). **Activities** Representation on bodies concerned with broadcasting and equipment. Cooperation with official bodies in the setting-up of technical standards for broadcasting equipment. Represented on IBC Management Committee and IBC Partner. *Peter Wayne Award for Design and Innovation.* Market Research. Awarding of Student and Training Bursaries. Training and Educational Liaison. Organizes Annual Conference in London (UK) since 2007. **Events** *Annual Conference* Heathrow (UK) 2014, *International Braodcasting Convention* Amsterdam (Netherlands) 2013, *Annual Conference* UK 2010, *Annual Conference* London (UK) 2009, *Annual Conference* London (UK) 2007. **Publications** *E-Newsletter* (12 a year) – electronic; *IABM Journal* (4 a year) – newsletter; *Broadcast and Media Technology Industry Guide* (annual).

Members Broadcasting equipment manufacturers (over 300) in 24 countries:

Austria, Belgium, Canada, China, Czechia, Denmark, Finland, France, Germany, Greece, India, Ireland, Israel, Italy, Japan, Korea Rep, Netherlands, Norway, Russia, Singapore, Sweden, Switzerland, UK, USA.

IGO Relations *International Telecommunication Union (ITU, #15673)* (Radiocommunication Sector). **NGO Relations** *Asia-Pacific Broadcasting Union (ABU, #01863)*; *Audio Engineering Society (AES, #03014)*; *European Broadcasting Union (EBU, #06404)*; *IBC (#11011)*; *Institute of Electrical and Electronics Engineers (IEEE, #11259)*; *International Electrotechnical Commission (IEC, #13255)*; *Society of Motion Picture and Television Engineers (SMPTE).* [2022/XD9744/**D**]

♦ International Association of Broadcast Meteorology (IABM) 11740

Sec 2 Larkshill Close, New Milton, BH25 5RN, UK. T. +441425610383. E-mail: secretary@iabm.org.

URL: http://www.iabm.org/

History Nov 1994, Spain. Nov 1994, Gran Canaria (Spain). Formally set up 9 Mar 1995. Registered in accordance with Irish law. Registered as a private company limited by guarantee. **Aims** Promote networking and contact between *weather* broadcasters internationally; act as a representative voice for the profession in communication with other agencies. **Structure** Board of Directors. **Languages** English. **Staff** None. **Finance** Sources: members' dues. **Events** *Annual General Meeting* Budapest (Hungary) 2018, *Annual General Meeting* Trieste (Italy) 2016, *Annual General Meeting* New Milton (UK) 2015, *Annual General Meeting* New Milton (UK) 2014, *Annual General Meeting* Reading, PA (USA) 2013. **Publications** *UP FRONT* (4 a year) – magazine. **IGO Relations** Consultative Status with: *World Meteorological Organization (WMO, #21649).* **NGO Relations** Member of: *International Forum of Meteorological Societies (IFMS, #13644).* [2018/XN8771/**C**]

♦ International Association of Bryologists (IAB) 11741

Sec-Treas c/o Field Museum, 1400 South Lake Shore Dr, Chicago IL 60605, USA. E-mail: iab@fieldmuseum.org.

Pres c/o College of Liberal Arts and Sciences, UCONN, 75 N Eagleville Rd, Unit 3043, Storrs CT 06269-3043, USA.

URL: http://www.bryology.org/

History 1969, Seattle, WA (USA). Founded during the XI International Botanical Congress. **Aims** Promote international cooperation and communication among bryologists, whether amateur or professional. **Structure** Council, comprising President, 1st, 2nd and 3rd Vice-Presidents, Secretary-Treasurer and 11 members. **Languages** English. **Finance** Sources: members' dues. **Events** *Biennial Conference* Madrid (Spain) 2019, *Biennial Conference* Shenzhen (China) 2017, *Biennial Conference* Puerto Williams (Chile) 2015, *Biennial Conference* London (UK) 2013, *Biennial conference / Biennial General Meeting* Melbourne, VIC (Australia) 2011. **Publications** *Bryological Times* (4 a year); *Bulletin of Bryology* (2 a year). Proceedings.

Members Individuals in 41 countries and territories:

Argentina, Australia, Austria, Belgium, Bolivia, Brazil, Canada, Chile, China, Colombia, Costa Rica, Czechia, Denmark, Finland, France, Germany, Hungary, India, Israel, Italy, Japan, Luxembourg, Malaysia, Mexico, Netherlands, New Zealand, Nigeria, Norway, Panama, Poland, Portugal, Serbia, Singapore, South Africa, Spain, Sweden, Switzerland, Taiwan, Tanzania UR, Türkiye, UK. [2020/XD1676/v/**B**]

- ♦ International Association for Bucco-Dental Health (inactive)

♦ International Association of Buddhist Culture (IABC) 11742

Chair 302 Namba Royal Heights, 112 Nakaicho, Kyoto, 600-8219 Japan. E-mail: iabc@office.email.ne.jp.

URL: http://www.ne.jp/asahi/iabc/homepage/

History 1980. **Aims** Promote Buddhism throughout the world, especially the *'other power'* teaching of Shinran or *Shin* Buddhism. **Structure** President, Honorary President, Chairman and 10 directors. **Activities** Sponsors conferences, lectures, seminars; offers subsidies to Buddhist groups and scholarships to well-motivated students of Buddhist philosophy and culture. **Events** *Biennial European Shin conference* Southampton (UK) 2018, *Korea-China-Japan Buddhist Goodwill Conference* Seoul (Korea Rep) 2017, *Biennial European Shin conference* Antwerp (Belgium) 2004, *Biennial European Shin conference / European Shin Conference* Lausanne (Switzerland) 2002, *Biennial European Shin conference / European Shin Conference* Düsseldorf (Germany) 2000. **Publications** *International Journal of Buddhist Culture*; *Shin Buddhist – Journal of Shin Buddhists. Encounter with the Nembuts Way* (2002) – Collection of Interviews – European Nembuts Friends; *Jodo Shinshu and Christianity* (1990) by A Peel – Japanese translation; *Myokonin O-Karu and Her Poems of Shinjen* (1990) by H Ishida; *European Myokonin* (1989) by Rev Harry Pipper – Japanese translation; *The Nembutsu Way* (1987) by Shoken Yamasaki in English, Japanese; *Bamboo Rain* (1986) by L Rosenthal in English; *From the Cross to the Pundarika* by Jean Eracle – Japanese translation. Translations of the Tannisho into French, German, Esperanto; other translations; pamphlet series.

Members Individuals in 12 countries:

Australia, Austria, Belgium, Brazil, Canada, Germany, Japan, Kenya, Poland, Switzerland, UK, USA.

NGO Relations Closely connected – and joint conference – with: *Jôdo Shin Buddhist Community – Europe (no recent information).* [2014/XD0370/v/**E**]

♦ International Association of Buddhist Studies (IABS) 11743

Association internationale d'études bouddhiques

Treas SLAS Dept, Univ of Lausanne-Anthropole, 1015 Lausanne VD, Switzerland. T. +41216923010. Fax +41793561766 – +41796923045. E-mail: iabs.treasurer@unil.ch.

Pres address not obtained.

URL: http://www.iabsinfo.net/

History Aug 1976, Madison WI (USA). Incorporated in 1977. **Aims** Promote and support scholarship in Buddhist studies in a spirit of non-sectarian tolerance and with scientific research and communication. **Structure** Board of Directors (meets at the time of Conferences), consisting of President, Treasurer, Editor, General Secretary, 4 Regional Secretaries and members-at-large. **Languages** English. **Staff** 3.00 FTE, voluntary. **Finance** Sources: donations; members' dues. Other sources: Fonds Elisabet de Boer; publications revenue. **Events** *Conference* Seoul (Korea Rep) 2022, *Conference* Seoul (Korea Rep) 2021, *Conference* Seoul (Korea Rep) 2020, *Conference* Toronto, ON (Canada) 2017, *Conference* Vienna (Austria) 2014. **Publications** *Journal of the IABS* (annual).

Members Individual; Life; Student; Institutional; Honorary; Founder. Scholars from various disciplines and promoters of Buddhist studies in 46 countries and territories:

Argentina, Australia, Austria, Bangladesh, Belgium, Brazil, Cambodia, Canada, China, Croatia, Czechia, Denmark, Estonia, Finland, France, Germany, Hong Kong, Hungary, India, Ireland, Israel, Italy, Japan, Korea Rep, Lithuania, Luxembourg, Macau, Malta, Mexico, Myanmar, Nepal, Netherlands, New Zealand, Norway, Philippines, Poland, Russia, Singapore, Spain, Sri Lanka, Sweden, Switzerland, Taiwan, Thailand, UK, USA.

NGO Relations Affiliated with: *International Union for Oriental and Asian Studies (IUOAS, inactive).* Cooperates in related fields of interest with: *International Congress of Asian and North African Studies (ICANAS, #12891).* [2018/XC8977/v/**C**]

♦ International Association of Buddhist Universities (IABU) 11744

Chairman Mahachulalongkornrajavidyalaya Univ, Ayutthaya, 79 M 1, Phahon Yothin Road, Kilometer 55, Lam Sai, Wang Noi, Phra Nakhon, Phra Nakhon Si Ayutthaya, Ayutthaya, Thailand. T. +663524800. Fax +6635248006. E-mail: rector@mcu.ac.th.

URL: http://www.iabu.org

History Founded 28 May 2007, Bangkok (Thailand). **Aims** As an international forum for institutes of Buddhist higher education, network, understand, and benefit from the richness and variety of the multinational Buddhist tradition; propagate the Buddha-Dharma through collaborative academic channels; raise academic standards throughout the Buddhist world; maximize academic potentials and abilities. **Structure** Executive Council of 18 members; International Secretariat. **Languages** English, Thai. **Finance** Members' dues. Funded by the Royal Government of the Kingdom of Thailand their sponsorship of the United Nations Day of Vesak (UNDV). **Activities** Events/meetings. **Events** *Conference* Bangkok (Thailand) 2017, *Conference* Bangkok (Thailand) 2011. **Publications** *JIABU* – journal. Academic Conference papers.

Members Universities and institutes (about 100) in 17 countries and territories:

Cambodia, China, Hungary, India, Indonesia, Japan, Korea Rep, Laos, Malaysia, Mongolia, Myanmar, Singapore, Sri Lanka, Taiwan, Thailand, USA, Vietnam.

NGO Relations *International Council for the Day of VESAK (ICDV, #13012).* [2020/XJ2784/**D**]

♦ International Association of Building Companions 11745

Association internationale des compagnons-bâtisseurs – Internationaler Bauorden (IBO) – Internationale Bouworde (IBO)

Pres Schützenstr 1, 67061 Ludwigshafen, Germany. T. +4962163554946. Fax +4962163554947. E-mail: info@bauorden.de.

URL: https://bauorden.eu/

History 1953, Belgium. Statutes adopted 22 Jan 1962; modified 25 Sep 1975. New statutes: 5 Apr 1986; 4 Dec 1988. Former names and other names: *International Builders' Order* – alias. Registration: Belgium. **Aims** Develop concrete action in support of *underprivileged* individuals, groups and peoples in all parts of the world, particularly *housing* work projects and *community* development; encourage *volunteers* to have a world attitude and increased consciousness of social and human problems, arising from interaction between practical work and thought; contribute to awakening group and community awareness. **Structure** General Assembly (every 2 years); Consultative Council, comprising representatives of national secretariats. **Languages** Dutch,

English, French, German, Italian, Portuguese, Spanish. **Staff** Part time, volunteers. **Finance** Members' dues, as determined by General Assembly. **Activities** Organizes: work camps and community development projects in Europe, Africa, Latin America and Asia, working with local organizations to build, renovate and upgrade accommodation for needy people; international youth workcamps in Europe all year round and particularly during the holiday periods. **Events** *General Assembly* Graz (Austria) 2002, *General Assembly* France 2000, *General Assembly* Switzerland 1998, *General Assembly* Belgium 1992, *General Assembly* Belgium 1990. **Publications** *Wir Helfen Bauen* (5 a year); *IBO-Aktivitäten* (annual).
Members National associations (9); Long-term workers' group (SIBO, marked "). Members in 9 countries:
Austria, Belgium (*), Congo DR, France (*), Germany, Hungary, Italy, Netherlands, Switzerland.
'Sympathizers' in 4 territories:
Czechia, Poland, Portugal.
IGO Relations *European Youth Foundation (EYF, #09141).* [2022/XC1260/**F**]

♦ International Association of Building Contractors / see Fédération internationale des entreprises de nettoyage (#09628)

♦ International Association of Building Physics (IABP) 11746

Address not obtained.
URL: https://www.iabp.info/

History Founded 2000, Eindhoven (Netherlands), at first International Building Physics Conference (IBPC). **Aims** Further advance building physics, the body of knowledge that underpins most building engineering applications and provides design tools for achieving adequate building performance. **Structure** No formal structure. International Building Physics Conference (every 3 years). **Languages** English. **Staff** None. **Activities** Events/meetings; training/education; networking/liaising; knowledge management/information dissemination. **Events** *International Buildings Physics Conference* Toronto, ON (Canada) 2024, *International Buildings Physics Conference* Copenhagen (Denmark) 2021, *Triennial Conference* Syracuse, NY (USA) 2018, *Triennial Conference* Turin (Italy) 2015, *Central European Symposium on Building Physics* Vienna (Austria) 2013. **Publications** *International Journal of Building Physics.* Conference proceedings. **Members** Triennium 2015-2018 individuals (659) in 44 countries. Membership countries not specified. **IGO Relations** None. **NGO Relations** None. [2021/XM2513/**D**]

♦ International Association of Building Service Contractors (#09628)

♦ International Association of Business Communicators (IABC) 11747

Main Office 330 N Wabash Ave, Ste 2000, Chicago IL 60611, USA. E-mail: member_relations@iabc.com.
URL: http://www.iabc.com/

History 1970. Founded by merger of *'American Association of Industrial Editors'* and *International Council of Industrial Editors* (set up in 1941 under a different name). **Aims** Provide learning opportunities that give members the tools and information they need in their chosen disciplines; share among members global communication practices, ideas and experiences that will enable them to develop highly ethical and effective performance standards; shape the future of the *profession* through ground-breaking research; lead the way in the use of advanced information technology in the profession; unite the communication profession worldwide in one diverse, multi-faceted organization. **Structure** Executive Board. Districts/regions (12): USA (7); Canada (2); Central and South America; Asia/Pacific Region; Europe/Africa Region. **Activities** Events/meetings; awards/prizes/competitions; certification/accreditation; research/documentation. **Events** *World Conference* Toronto, ON (Canada) 2023, *World Conference* New York, NY (USA) 2022, *World Conference* Chicago, IL (USA) 2021, *World Conference* Chicago, IL (USA) 2020, *World Conference* Vancouver, BC (Canada) 2019. **Publications** *Communication World* (9 a year). *Communicators Guide to Marketing.* Handbooks. **Information Services** *Speakers Bureau* – computerized database.
Members Chapters (109), in 12 districts, grouping over 13,000 members, in 51 countries and territories:
Argentina, Australia, Austria, Belgium, Botswana, Brazil, Canada, Cayman Is, Chile, China, Colombia, Denmark, England, Finland, France, Germany, Ghana, Hong Kong, Iceland, India, Indonesia, Ireland, Italy, Japan, Korea Rep, Macau, Malaysia, Mexico, Namibia, Netherlands, New Zealand, Nigeria, Norway, Pakistan, Philippines, Portugal, Saudi Arabia, Scotland, Singapore, Slovenia, South Africa, Spain, Sweden, Switzerland, Taiwan, Tanzania UR, Thailand, Türkiye, United Arab Emirates, USA, Venezuela. [2020/XF2935/v/**F**]

♦ International Association of Business and Parliament (inactive)

♦ International Association for Business and Society (IABS) 11748

Exec Dir c/o BYU Romney Inst, 770 Tanner Bldg, Provo UT 84602, USA. E-mail: iabs@iabs.net.
URL: http://www.iabs.net/

History 1990. **Aims** Promote research and teaching about the relationships between business, government and society. **Structure** Council, including President, Past-President, President-Elect, Conference Chair and Conference Chair Elect. **Events** *Annual Conference* Brussels (Belgium) 2021, *Annual Conference* Lisbon (Portugal) 2020, *Annual Conference* San Diego, CA (USA) 2019, *Annual Conference* Hong Kong (Hong Kong) 2018, *Annual Conference* Amsterdam (Netherlands) 2017. **Publications** *Business and Society* (4 a year). Conference proceedings. **Members** Scholars (300) in 20 countries. Membership countries not specified. [2020/XN6862/**D**]

♦ International Association of Butterfly Exhibitions / see International Association of Butterfly Exhibitors and Suppliers (#11749)

♦ International Association of Butterfly Exhibitors and Suppliers (IABES) 11749

Contact c/o Museum of Life & Science, 433 Murray Ave, Durham NC 37704, USA. E-mail: info@iabes.org.
URL: http://iabes.org/

History 2001. Former names and other names: *International Association of Butterfly Exhibitions (IABE)* – former (2001 to 2008). **Aims** Protect wild butterflies and their habitats by promoting sustainable butterfly exhibits and their suppliers; support conservation, research, and public education. **Structure** Board of Directors. Committees. **Activities** Advocacy/lobbying/activism; events/meetings. **Events** *International Conference of Butterfly Exhibitors and Suppliers* Stratford-upon-Avon (UK) 2020, *International Conference of Butterfly Exhibitors and Suppliers* Orlando, FL (USA) 2019, *International Conference of Butterfly Exhibitors and Suppliers* Malindi (Kenya) 2018, *International Conference of Butterfly Exhibitors and Suppliers* Rotterdam (Netherlands) 2017, *International Conference of Butterfly Exhibitors and Suppliers* Tucson, AZ (USA) 2016.
Members Individuals in 14 countries:
Belgium, Canada, Costa Rica, Czechia, Ecuador, Germany, Israel, Italy, Kenya, Netherlands, Spain, Switzerland, UK, USA. [2020/AA1873/v/**C**]

♦ International Association of Buying and Marketing Groups (inactive)

♦ International Association of Byron Societies (IABS) 11750

Joint International Pres Samuel Alexander Bldg W1-08, School of Arts, Univ of Manchester, Manchester, M13 9PL, UK.
URL: http://www.internationalassociationofbyronsocieties.org/

History 22 Jan 1876. Statutes revised 1971. Former names and other names: *International Byron Society* – former (1876). **Structure** General Meeting; Board; Advisory Board. **Finance** Members' dues. **Activities** Events/meetings; awards/prizes/competitions. **Events** *International Byron Conference* Russia 2022, *International Byron Conference* Thessaloniki (Greece) 2021, *International Byron Conference* Thessaloniki (Greece) 2020, *International Byron Conference* Vechta (Germany) 2019, *International Conference* Paris (France) 2016. **Publications** *The Byron Journal.* [2021/XN1637/**E**]

♦ International Association for Byzantine Studies 11751

Association internationale des études byzantines (AIEB)

Sec address not obtained.
Pres address not obtained.
URL: http://www.aiebnet.gr/

History 1948. Founded in Paris (France) and Brussels (Belgium) (simultaneously), during 6th and 7th International Congresses of Byzantine Studies. **Aims** Promote Byzantine studies in all member countries. **Structure** General Assembly; International Committee; Bureau; Commissions (8). **Languages** English, French, German, Greek, Italian, Russian. **Staff** 1.00 FTE, voluntary. **Finance** Sources: members' dues. **Events** *International Congress of Byzantine Studies* Venice (Italy) / Padua (Italy) 2022, *International Congress of Byzantine Studies* Istanbul (Turkey) 2021, *International Congress of Byzantine Studies* Belgrade (Serbia) 2016, *Meeting* Athens (Greece) 2013, *International Congress of Byzantine Studies* Sofia (Bulgaria) 2011.
Members National Committees in 39 countries:
Albania, Argentina, Armenia, Australia, Austria, Belgium, Bulgaria, Canada, Chile, China, Croatia, Cyprus, Czechia, Denmark, Estonia, Finland, France, Georgia, Germany, Greece, Holy See, Hungary, Ireland, Israel, Italy, Japan, Netherlands, North Macedonia, Norway, Poland, Romania, Russia, Serbia, Slovakia, Spain, Sweden, Türkiye, UK, USA.
NGO Relations Member of (1): *Fédération internationale des associations d'études classiques (FIEC, #09607).* Cooperates with (1): *International Committee of Historical Sciences (ICHS, #12777).* [2023.02.17/XD1178/**C**]

♦ International Association of Cable Product and Machinery Manufactures (INTERCABLE) 11752

Vice-Pres sh Entuziasrov 5, Moscow MOSKVA, Russia, 111024. T. +74959118330. Fax +74953626042.
URL: http://www.interkabel.com/

Aims Provide assistance in technical and commercial activities. **Structure** Board; Executive Director. **Finance** Members' dues. **Events** *General Meeting* Samara (Russia) 2021, *General Meeting* Helsinki (Finland) 2016, *General Meeting* Baku (Azerbaijan) 2013, *General Meeting* Prague (Czech Rep) 2013, *General Meeting* Hévíz (Hungary) 2012.
Members Full in 22 countries:
Austria, Azerbaijan, Belarus, Belgium, Canada, Czechia, Finland, France, Germany, Greece, Hungary, Italy, Netherlands, Poland, Russia, Serbia, Slovakia, Spain, Switzerland, Ukraine, USA, Uzbekistan. [2020/XJ6512/**D**]

♦ International Association of Cancer Registries (IACR) 11753

Association internationale des registres du cancer – Asociación Internacional de Registros del Cancer

Exec Sec c/o IARC, 150 Cours Albert-Thomas, 69372 Lyon CEDEX 08, France. T. +33472738056. Fax +33472738696. E-mail: iacr@iarc.fr.
URL: http://www.iacr.com.fr/

History 1966, Tokyo (Japan). **Aims** Foster exchange of information between cancer registries internationally; improve quality of data and comparability between registries by *standardizing* methods of registration, definition and coding; disseminate information on the multiple uses of cancer registry data in the planning and evaluation of cancer prevention and therapy, and in epidemiological research into the causes of cancer. **Structure** Executive Board, comprising President, Immediate Past President, General Secretary, Executive Secretary, Treasurer and 9 Regional Representatives. Regions (6): Africa; Europe; North America; Central and South America; Asia; Oceania. **Languages** English. **Finance** Sources: members' dues. **Events** *Annual Scientific Conference* Lyon (France) 2022, *Annual Scientific Conference* Lyon (France) 2021, *Annual Scientific Conference* Nouméa (New Caledonia) 2020, *Annual Scientific Conference* Vancouver, BC (Canada) 2019, *Annual Scientific Conference* Arequipa (Peru) 2018. **Publications** *Asia Pacific Journal of Cancer Prevention*; *European Journal of Cancer Prevention*; *IACR Newsletter*. *Cancer Incidence in Five Continents* – in association with IARC; *International Incidence of Childhood Cancer* – in association with IARC. Monographs on cancer registration; cancer registration software.
Members Voting; Associate. Organizations and individuals in 120 countries and territories:
Albania, Algeria, Argentina, Australia, Austria, Bahrain, Bangladesh, Belarus, Belgium, Bermuda, Bolivia, Bosnia-Herzegovina, Brazil, Bulgaria, Burkina Faso, Canada, Chile, China, Colombia, Congo Brazzaville, Costa Rica, Côte d'Ivoire, Croatia, Cuba, Cyprus, Czechia, Denmark, Ecuador, Egypt, Estonia, Eswatini, Fiji, Finland, France, Gambia, Georgia, Germany, Gibraltar, Greece, Guadeloupe, Guatemala, Guinea, Honduras, Hungary, Iceland, India, Indonesia, Iran Islamic Rep, Ireland, Israel, Italy, Jamaica, Japan, Jordan, Kenya, Korea Rep, Kuwait, Kyrgyzstan, Latvia, Lithuania, Luxembourg, Malawi, Malaysia, Mali, Malta, Martinique, Mauritius, Mexico, Montenegro, Morocco, Myanmar, Netherlands, New Caledonia, New Zealand, Nicaragua, Niger, Nigeria, Norway, Oman, Pakistan, Palestine, Panama, Paraguay, Peru, Philippines, Poland, Portugal, Puerto Rico, Réunion, Romania, Russia, Rwanda, San Marino, Saudi Arabia, Serbia, Singapore, Slovakia, Slovenia, South Africa, Spain, Sudan, Suriname, Sweden, Switzerland, Taiwan, Tanzania UR, Thailand, Trinidad-Tobago, Tunisia, Türkiye, Uganda, UK, Ukraine, Uruguay, USA, Vanuatu, Venezuela, Vietnam, Zimbabwe.
Consultative Status Consultative status granted from: *ECOSOC (#05331)* (Ros C); *WHO (#20950)* (Official Relations). **NGO Relations** Joint publication with: *Asian Pacific Organization for Cancer Prevention (APOCP).* [2021/XC6440/**B**]

♦ International Association for Cannabinoid Medicines (IACM) 11754

Association Internationale pour les Cannabinoïdes en Médecine – Asociación Internacional por los Medicamentos Cannabinoides – Internationale Arbeitsgemeinschaft für Cannabinoidmedikamente – Internationale Associatie voor Cannabinoïden als Medicijn

Exec Dir Bahnhofsallee 9, 32839 Steinheim, Germany. T. +4952339539213. Fax +4952339537095. E-mail: info@cannabis-med.org.
URL: http://www.cannabis-med.org/

History Mar 2000. Former names and other names: *International Association for Cannabis as Medicine (IACM)* – former (Mar 2000); *Association internationale pour le cannabis médicale* – former (Mar 2000); *Asociación Internacional por el Cannabis como Medicamento* – former (Mar 2000); *Internationale Arbeitsgemeinschaft Cannabis als Medizin* – former (Mar 2000); *Associação Internacional para o Uso Medicinal da Cannabis* – former (Mar 2000); *Associazione Internazionale per la Cannabis come Medicina* – former (Mar 2000); *Internationale Associatie voor Cannabis als Medicijn* – former (Mar 2000); *Medunarodno Udruzenje za Cannabis kao Lijek* – former. **Aims** Advance knowledge on cannabis, cannabinoides, the endocannabinoid system and related topics, especially with regard to their therapeutic potential. **Structure** General Meeting (annual); Board of Directors; Patient Representative. **Languages** English, French, German. **Finance** Sources: donations; members' dues. **Activities** Events/meetings; knowledge management/information dissemination; networking/liaising; research/documentation. **Events** *Conference on Cannabinoids in Medicine* Basel (Switzerland) 2022, *Conference* Basel (Switzerland) 2021, *Conference* Mexico City (Mexico) 2020, *Conference* Berlin (Germany) 2019, *Conference* Cologne (Germany) 2017. **Publications** *IACM Bulletin* (bi-weekly) in Dutch, English, French, German, Italian, Spanish; *CANNABINOIDS* – online journal. **Members** Regular – individuals who completed a degree in medicine or pharmacy, cannabis and cannabinoid researchers; other individuals with special knowledge on annabis/cannabinoids; students of medicine or pharmacology; medicinal institutions and organizations; Associate. Membership countries not specified. [2022/XM2742/**D**]

♦ International Association for Cannabis as Medicine / see International Association for Cannabinoid Medicines (#11754)

♦ International Association of Cape Horners 11755

Association internationale des capitaines au long cours 'cap-horniers' (AICH)

Address not obtained.
URL: http://www.capehorners.org/

History 1937, Saint-Malo (France), as *Amicale internationale des capitaines au long cours Cap Horniers.* In English previously referred to as *International Circle of Sea Captains who have rounded the Cape Horn.* **Aims** Promote and strengthen friendship between those who have sailed round Cape Horn in a commercial sailing vessel; keep alive memories of the sailors of stout ships that used to sail round Cape Horn. **Events** *Congress* Mariehamn (Finland) 2000, *World Congress* Nyborg (Denmark) 1993, *World congress* Nyborg (Denmark) 1993, *Congress* Mariehamn (Finland) 1992, *World Congress* Turku (Finland) 1989. **Publications** *The Cape Horner* (2 a year). **Members** Individuals. Membership countries not specified. [2016/XE3098/**E**]

♦ International Association of Cardio HIIT Sports / see International Federation of Cardio HIIT BodyWeight Exercise

♦ International Association for Caribbean Archaeology (IACA) 11756

Association internationale d'archéologie de la Caraïbe (AIAC) – Asociación Internacional de Arqueologia del Caribe (AIAC)

Organizing Committee Chair address not obtained. T. +3402774072.
URL: http://iaca2017stcroix.org/

History 1962, as *International Association for the Study of Pre-Columbian Cultures of the Lesser Antilles*. Current title adopted 1985. **Aims** Promote good management of Caribbean archaeology at both the local and regional levels. **Structure** Officers: President; 2 Vice-Presidents; Treasurer; Secretary; 2 Directors; 2 Congress Chairmen; Past President; Co-opted member. **Finance** Members' dues. **Events** *Biennial Congress* San Juan (Puerto Rico) 2013, *Biennial Congress* Schoelcher (Martinique) 2011, *Biennial Congress* Havana (Cuba) 2009, *Biennial Congress* Havana (Cuba) 2009, *Biennial Congress* Jamaica 2007. **Publications** *IACA Newsletter*. **Members** Membership countries not specified. **NGO Relations** *Museums Association of the Caribbean (MAC, #16909)*. [2017/XD3065/D]

♦ International Association of Catalysis Societies (IACS) 11757

Pres Univ degli Studi di Messina, Piazza Pugliatti 1, 98122 Messina ME, Italy.
Sec Catalytic Reaction Chemistry, State key Lab of Catalysis, Dalian Inst of Chemic Physics, 457 Zhongshan Road, Dalian, 116023 Liaoning, China.
Treas School of Chemistry, Cardiff Univ, PO Box 912, Cardiff, CF10 3TB, UK.
URL: http://www.iacs-catalysis.org/

History 1956, as *International Congress on Catalysis*. Present name adopted 1996. Current version of constitution adopted, 11 Jul 2004, Paris (France). **Aims** Promote scientific and technological progress in the field of catalytic *chemistry*; provide a forum for formal and informal discussions amongst scientists and engineers. **Structure** Council of 28 members (every 4 years). Executive Committee, comprising President, Vice-President, Treasurer, Secretary and Officer. **Languages** English. **Staff** None. **Finance** Registration fees. **Activities** Sponsors the *'International Catalysis Award'*. **Events** *2020 vision for catalysis* San Diego, CA (USA) 2020, *Congress* Beijing (China) 2016, *Congress* Munich (Germany) 2012, *Quadrennial congress / Congress* Seoul (Korea Rep) 2008, *Quadrennial congress / Congress* Paris (France) 2004. **Publications** *IACS Newsletter*. **Members** Full in 30 countries:
Argentina, Australia, Austria, Belgium, Brazil, Bulgaria, Canada, Chile, China, Czechia, Finland, France, Germany, Hungary, India, Italy, Japan, Korea Rep, Mexico, Netherlands, Norway, Poland, Portugal, Russia, Slovakia, South Africa, Spain, UK, USA, Venezuela.
NGO Relations Associated organization of: *International Union of Pure and Applied Chemistry (IUPAC, #15809)*. [2018/XD7242/B]

♦ International Association of Catholic Bioethicists (IACB) 11758

Contact 1247 Kilborn Pl, Ottawa ON K1H 6K9, Canada. E-mail: administration@iacb.ca.
URL: http://iacb.ca/

History 2003, during first colloquium. Secretariat established, 2004. Statutes and by-laws approved by national presidents of *Sovereign Military Hospitaller Order of St John of Jerusalem, of Rhodes and of Malta (SMOM)*. **Aims** Promote in-depth and free discussion, research, professional development and publications in bioethics from Catholic and religious perspectives; foster communication, collaboration and cooperation among bioethicists and bioethics institutes; provide consultation to the associations and works of SMOM on bioethical issues. **Structure** Governing Council; Associates; Secretariat. **Languages** English. **Finance** Sources: members' dues. **Activities** Events/meetings; publishing activities; research/documentation; training/education. **Events** *Colloquium* Rome (Italy) 2022, *Colloquium* Québec, QC (Canada) 2019, *Colloquium* Rome (Italy) 2017, *Colloquium* Montréal, QC (Canada) 2015, *Colloquium* Rome (Italy) 2013. **Members** Full; Associate. Membership countries not specified. [2015.07.20/XM8249/C]

♦ International Association of Catholic Health Care Institutions (no recent information)

♦ International Association of Catholic Medical Schools (IACMS) 11759

Association internationale des facultés de médecine catholiques (AIFMC)

Pres Fac de Medicina, Univ Cat de Valencia "San Vicente Martir", C/ Guillem de Castro 94, 46003 Valencia, Spain.
SG Escuela de Medicina, Univ Anahuac, Avenida Lomas de Anahuac s/n, Anahuac, Mexico City CDMX, Mexico. T. +525556270210ext7212. Fax +525552515163.

History Sectorial group of *International Federation of Catholic Universities (IFCU, #13381)*. **Events** *International Congress* Valencia (Spain) 2015. [2014/XD7961/D]

♦ International Association of Catholic Missiologists (IACM) 11760

Association internationale des missiologues catholiques – Asociación internacional de misionólogos católicos – Associazione internazionale dei missiologi cattolici

Contact Inst für Weltkirche und Mission, Offenbacher Landstr 224, 60559 Frankfurt-Main, Germany. E-mail: office@iacm-catholic.org.
URL: https://www.iacm-catholic.org/

History 21 Oct 2000, Rome (Italy). **Aims** Promote missiological research, studies and educational activities; encourage collaboration among Catholic missiologists. **Structure** General Assembly (every 4 years); Executive Board; Continental Area Representatives. **Languages** English. **Staff** Voluntary. **Finance** Members' dues. **Activities** Events/meetings. **Events** *International Conference* Rome (Italy) 2021, *General Assembly* Pattaya (Thailand) 2017, *International Conference* Pattaya (Thailand) 2017, *General Assembly* Nairobi (Kenya) 2013, *International Conference* Nairobi (Kenya) 2013. **Publications** *Christian Witness in a Multi-religious World* (2018) by Viviano Rocco – Asian Study Centre, Osaka. Monumenta Missionalia 6; *Sharing Diversity in Missiological Research and Education* (2006) by Juan F Gorski and L Stanislaus – Indian Society for Promoting Christian Knowledge and Ishvani Kendra. Delhi; *Compartir la diversidad en la misionologia cuestiones de lenguaje teológico* (2004) by Tomichá Charupá and Roberto Gorski et al – Editorial Verbo Divino. Cochabamba; *Cristologia e Missione oggi* (1st ed 2001) by Colzani and Gianfrancesco et al – Urbaniana University Press. Rome. **Members** Individual; Corporate; Honorary. Membership countries not specified. [2020.03.16/XD7771/D]

♦ International Association of Catholics for the Progress of Science (inactive)
♦ International Association of CDS/ISIS Systems and New Information Technologies Users and Developers / see International Association of Users and Developers of Electronic Libraries and New Information Technologies (#12252)
♦ International Association for Cell Culture (inactive)

♦ International Association of Centers for Federal Studies (IACFS) ... 11761

Pres Inst for Comparative Federalism, Eurac Research, Viale Druso 1, 39100 Bolzano, Italy. T. +39471055200.
Sec/Treas Dullah Omar Inst, Univ of Western Cape, Robert Sobukwe Road, Bellville, 7525, South Africa. T. +270219592951. Fax +27219592912. E-mail: doi@uwc.ac.za.
URL: http://www.iacfs.org/

History 1977. **Aims** Promote and develop knowledge and understanding of, and research on, the use of federal principles in all parts of the world. **Structure** Board of Directors; Executive Committee. **Languages** English. **Staff** None. **Finance** Sources: members' dues. **Activities** Events/meetings; knowledge management/information dissemination; publishing activities; research/documentation. **Events** *Annual Conference* Cape Town (South Africa) 2020, *Annual Conference* Speyer (Germany) 2019, *Annual Conference* Canberra, ACT (Australia) 2018, *Annual Conference* Fribourg (Switzerland) 2017, *Annual Conference* Delhi (India) 2016. **Publications** *Intergovernmental Relations in Federal Systems: Comparative Structures and Dynamics* (2015); *Political Parties and Civil Society in Federal Countries* (2015). Conference proceedings. **Members** Institutes (31) in 18 countries:
Argentina, Australia, Austria, Belgium, Canada, Ethiopia, France, Germany, India, Italy, Mexico, Nigeria, Russia, South Africa, Spain, Switzerland, UK, USA.
Included in the above, 2 institutes listed in this Yearbook:
Centre international de formation européenne (CIFE, #03755); *Europäisches Zentrum für Föderalismus-Forschung (EZFF)*. [2021.06.08/XD5839/y/D]

♦ International Association Centre (internationally oriented national body)

♦ International Association of Centrers for Peirce Studies (IACPS) ... 11762

Sec Dept of Intl Business Communication Studies, Copenhagen Business School, Dalgas Have 15, 2000 Frederiksberg, Denmark. T. +4538153132.
Pres 1367 Northview Ave, Atlanta GA 30306, USA. T. +14043130202.

History 1 Jan 2008. **Aims** Develop an applied Peircean (Bio) *Semiotics* that encompasses and integrates modern *cybernetics*, system theory and information theory/science and embodies *cognitive* science and *linguistics* in a new *cybersemiotic* framework. Refers to the work of Charles Sanders Peirce (1839-1914). **Languages** Danish, English. **Staff** 5.00 FTE, voluntary. **Finance** None. **Events** *Meeting* Denver, CO (USA) 2003. **Publications** *Cybernetics and Human Knowing* – journal. Books. **NGO Relations** Member of: *International Federation of Philosophical Societies (FISP, #13507)*. [2016.06.01/XM2990/E]

♦ International Association for Cereal Chemistry / see ICC – International Association for Cereal Science and Technology (#11048)
♦ International Association of Certified Home Inspectors (internationally oriented national body)
♦ International Association of Certified Indoor Air Consultants (internationally oriented national body)
♦ International Association of Certified Thermographers (internationally oriented national body)
♦ International Association of Certified Valuation Specialists (internationally oriented national body)
♦ International Association of Chain Stores / see The Consumer Goods Forum (#04772)
♦ International Association of Charities (#02675)
♦ International Association of Charities of St Vincent de Paul / see Association Internationale des Charités (#02675)

♦ International Association of Chemical and Allied Industries Workers' Trade Unions 11763

Pres 42 Leninsky Prospekt, Moscow MOSKVA, Russia, 119119. T. +74959388360. Fax +74959309918. E-mail: priem@chemprof.ru – orgotdel@chemprof.ru.

History Former names and other names: *International Association of Chemical and Allied Workers' Unions* – former. **Members** Trade unions in the CIS region. Membership countries not specified. **NGO Relations** Member of (1): *General Confederation of Trade Unions (GCTU, #10108)*. [2021.09.01/XM2477/D]

♦ International Association of Chemical and Allied Workers' Unions / see International Association of Chemical and Allied Industries Workers' Trade Unions (#11763)
♦ International Association of Chemical Expertise (inactive)

♦ International Association on Chemical Thermodynamics (IACT) ... 11764

Sec Thermodynamics Research Unit, Research Office, Univ of KwaZulu-Natal, Govan Mbeki Centre, Westvill Campus, Durban, 4000, South Africa. E-mail: ramjuger@ukzn.ac.za.
URL: http://www.iactweb.org/

History Aug 2002, Rostock (Germany), by former members of IUPAC Commission on Thermodynamics, during 17th IUPAC Conference on Chemical Thermodynamics. **Aims** Establish the highest standards in thermodynamic research and routine thermodynamic property measurement; promote critical compilation, dissemination and application of thermodynamic data; develop theoretical understanding of such properties; advance understanding, teaching and use of thermodynamic principles, procedures and data. **Structure** Board of Directors, comprising Chair, Immediate Past-Chair, Chair-Elect, Secretary, Treasurer, 6 Directors and 5 Counsellors. Committees. Task Groups (13). **Languages** English. **Staff** Voluntary. **Finance** Subscriptions; sponsors; awards. Budget (annual): about pounds2000. **Activities** Presents: Rossini Lectureship Award, at biennial International Conference on Chemical Thermodynamics, in recognition of a significant contribution to the field of thermodynamics; Junior Awards and Poster Prizes, at other thermodynamics conferences. **Events** *Biennial International Conference on Chemical Thermodynamics* Osaka (Japan) 2023, *Biennial International Conference on Chemical Thermodynamics* Durban (South Africa) 2014, *Biennial international conference on chemical thermodynamics / Biennial Conference on Chemical Thermodynamics* Armação de Búzios (Brazil) 2012, *Biennial Conference on Chemical Thermodynamics* Tokyo (Japan) 2010, *Biennial international conference on chemical thermodynamics* Tsukuba (Japan) 2010. **Publications** Rossini Lecture; lectures from conferences.
Members in 25 countries:
Austria, Belarus, Belgium, Brazil, Canada, China, Colombia, Czechia, Finland, France, Germany, Iran Islamic Rep, Italy, Japan, Netherlands, New Zealand, Poland, Portugal, Romania, Russia, South Africa, Spain, Sweden, UK, USA.
NGO Relations Associate Member of: *International Union of Pure and Applied Chemistry (IUPAC, #15809)*. [2015/XM0055/D]

♦ International Association of Chemistry Societies (inactive)
♦ International Association of Chess Press (inactive)

♦ International Association of Chiefs of Police (IACP) 11765

Association internationale des chefs de police (IACP) – Asociación Internacional de Jefes de Policia

Contact 44 Canal Center Plaza, Ste 200, Alexandria VA 22314, USA. T. +17038366767.
URL: http://www.theiacp.org/

History 1893, Chicago, IL (USA). Registration: 501(c)(3) not-for-profit, USA, Viriginia. **Aims** Foster police cooperation and exchange of information and experience among police administrators throughout the world; bring about recruitment and training of qualified persons; encourage adherence of all police officers to high *professional* standards of performance and conduct. **Structure** Executive Committee; Board of Officers. President. Standing committees. **Activities** Events/meetings; guidance/assistance/consulting; research and development; training/education. Instrumental in setting up *International Policy Academy, Washington DC (no recent information)* and *IACP Center for the Study of International Criminality*, 1982. **Events** *Annual Conference* Denver, CO (USA) 2025, *Annual Conference* Boston, MA (USA) 2024, *Annual Conference* San Diego, CA (USA) 2023, *Annual Conference* Dallas, TX (USA) 2022, *Annual Conference* New Orleans, LA (USA) 2021. **Publications** *The Police Chief* (12 a year).
Members Administrative level police officers (31,000) in public law enforcement agencies. Active, Associate, Sustaining and Life Members in 94 countries:
Albania, Argentina, Australia, Austria, Bahamas, Bahrain, Bangladesh, Barbados, Belgium, Benin, Bosnia-Herzegovina, Botswana, Brazil, Bulgaria, Canada, Chile, China, Colombia, Costa Rica, Czechia, Denmark, Djibouti, Dominican Rep, Egypt, El Salvador, Estonia, Eswatini, Ethiopia, Finland, France, Germany, Ghana, Grenada, Haiti, Hungary, Iceland, India, Indonesia, Ireland, Israel, Italy, Jamaica, Japan, Korea Rep, Kuwait, Latvia, Lebanon, Lesotho, Liberia, Lithuania, Luxembourg, Malaysia, Malta, Mauritius, Mexico, Micronesia FS, Monaco, Namibia, Nepal, Netherlands, New Zealand, Niger, Nigeria, Norway, Oman, Pakistan, Panama, Philippines, Portugal, Romania, Russia, Rwanda, Saudi Arabia, Serbia, Singapore, Slovenia, South Africa, Spain, St Kitts-Nevis, St Lucia, Sweden, Switzerland, Taiwan, Tanzania UR, Thailand, Trinidad-Tobago, Türkiye, UK, United Arab Emirates, Uruguay, USA, Uzbekistan, Venezuela, Yemen.
Consultative Status Consultative status granted from: *ECOSOC (#05331)* (Ros A). **IGO Relations** Accredited by: *United Nations Office at Vienna (UNOV, #20604)*. **NGO Relations** Member of: *Alliance of NGOs on Crime Prevention and Criminal Justice (#00709)*; *Association of Caribbean Commissioners of Police (ACCP, #02403)*; *European Network of Policewomen (ENP, #07970)*; *Police Chiefs Spouses Worldwide (no recent information)*. [2021/XF0111/v/C]

♦ International Association for Child and Adolescent Psychiatry and Allied Professions (IACAPAP) 11766

Association Internationale de Psychiatrie de l'Enfant, de l'Adolescent, et des Professions Associees – Asociación Internacional de Psiquiatria Infantil y Profesiones Afines – Associação Internacional de Psiquiatria da Infância e Adolescência e Profissões Afins

SG c/o MLL Meyerlustenberger Lachenal Froriep Ltd, Rue du Rhône 65, PO Box 3199, 1211 Geneva, Switzerland. E-mail: info@iacapap.org.
URL: https://iacapap.org

History 1937, Paris (France). Founded at 1st International Congress of Child Psychiatry. Previously registered under USA law in the State of Massachusettes, 1954. Former names and other names: *International Association for Child Psychiatry (IACP)* – former (1948); *Comité international de psychiatrie infantile* – former; *International Committee for Child Psychiatry* – former (1937); *International Association for Child Psychiatry and Allied Professions (IACP&AP)* – former (1958 to 1978). Registration: Switzerland Commercial Register, Switzerland. **Aims** Promote child and adolescent psychiatry and the mental health and development of children and adolescents through policy, practice, training and research. **Structure** General Assembly (every 4 years); Executive Committee; Bureau. **Languages** English, French. **Staff** 1.00 FTE, paid. **Finance** Sources: donations; fundraising; grants; members' dues. **Activities** Advocacy/lobbying/activism; events/meetings; projects/programmes; publishing activities; training/education. **Events** *World Congress* Rio de Janeiro (Brazil)

2024, *World Congress* Dubai (United Arab Emirates) 2022, *World Congress* Singapore (Singapore) 2020, *World Congress* Prague (Czechia) 2018, *Conference on Systems of Care for Autism Spectrum Disorder* Dubai (United Arab Emirates) 2017. **Publications** *IACAPAP E-Bulletin* (4 a year); *IACAPAP CAMPH Journal. IACAPAP E-Textbook.* Declarations; guidelines.
Members Full Members (62); Affiliate Members (8); Individual. Members in 88 countries and territories:
Afghanistan, Albania, Algeria, Argentina, Australia, Austria, Bangladesh, Belgium, Bosnia-Herzegovina, Brazil, Bulgaria, Burundi, Cameroon, Canada, Chile, China, Colombia, Czechia, Denmark, Dominican Rep, Ecuador, Egypt, Estonia, Ethiopia, Finland, France, Georgia, Germany, Ghana, Greece, Haiti, Hong Kong, Hungary, Iceland, India, Indonesia, Iran Islamic Rep, Iraq, Ireland, Israel, Italy, Japan, Jordan, Kenya, Korea Rep, Kosovo, Latvia, Lebanon, Liberia, Lithuania, Malaysia, Mexico, Nepal, Netherlands, New Zealand, Nigeria, North Macedonia, Norway, Oman, Pakistan, Paraguay, Philippines, Poland, Portugal, Romania, Russia, Saudi Arabia, Serbia, Singapore, Slovakia, Slovenia, South Africa, Spain, Sri Lanka, St Lucia, Sudan, Sweden, Switzerland, Taiwan, Tunisia, Türkiye, Uganda, UK, Ukraine, United Arab Emirates, Uruguay, USA, Vietnam.
Consultative Status Consultative status granted from: *WHO (#20950)* (Official Relations). **NGO Relations** Memorandum of Understanding with (1): *World Association for Infant Mental Health (WAIMH, #21146).*
[2023.03.04/XC1180/**C**]

♦ International Association for Child Psychiatry / see International Association for Child and Adolescent Psychiatry and Allied Professions (#11766)
♦ International Association for Child Psychiatry and Allied Professions / see International Association for Child and Adolescent Psychiatry and Allied Professions (#11766)
♦ International Association for Children's Social and Economics Education / see International Association for Citizenship, Social and Economics Education (#11773)

♦ International Association for Children's Spirituality (IACS) 11767

Chair c/o UPSem, 3401 Brook Rd, Richmond VA 23227, USA.
Communications Officer address not obtained.
URL: http://www.childrenspirituality.org/
History 2006. Founded at 7th International Conference on Children's Spirituality, following the success of the conference series and journal. **Aims** Promote research and practice in relation to children's spirituality; promote effective communication and information distribution between those involved in the development of research and practice which focuses on children's spirituality; promote children's spirituality as an important educational focus within wider contexts. **Structure** Executive Committee. **Finance** Sources: members' dues. **Activities** Events/meetings. **Events** *Annual General Meeting* 2020, *Symposium* Liverpool (UK) 2020, *Conference* Québec, QC (Canada) 2018, *Conference* Lincoln (UK) 2016, *Conference* Puerto Ordaz (Venezuela) 2014. **Publications** *International Journal of Children's Spirituality.* [2020/XM5908/**C**]

♦ International Association for the Child's Right to Play / see International Play Association (#14604)

♦ International Association of Chinese Linguistics (IACL) 11768

Vice Exec Sec Dept Linguistica and Translation, City Univ of Hong Kong, 83 Tat Chee Avenue, Kowloon, Hong Kong.
Exec Sec Inst of Linguistics, Chinese Ac Social Sciences, No 5, Jian Guo Men Nei Da Jie, 100732 Beijing, China. T. +861085195392.
URL: http://www.iacling.org/
History Statutes adopted 25 Jun 1992, Singapore (Singapore). Amended Jun 1993. Registered in the State of California (USA). **Aims** Promote scientific research on Chinese *languages* and their dialects. **Structure** Business Meeting (annual, at Conference); Executive Committee (meets annually); Programme Committee. **Languages** Chinese, English. **Finance** Members' dues. **Activities** Awards/prizes/competitions; events/meetings. **Events** *Annual Conference* Hong Kong (Hong Kong) 2022, *Annual Conference* Kobe (Japan) 2019, *Annual Conference* Madison, WI (USA) 2018, *Annual Conference* Budapest (Hungary) 2017, *Annual Conference* Beijing (China) 2016. **Publications** *IACL Newsletter* (3 a year).
Members Regular; Student; Life individuals in 28 countries and territories:
Australia, Belgium, Bulgaria, Canada, China, Czechia, France, Germany, Hong Kong, India, Israel, Italy, Japan, Korea Rep, Malaysia, Mongolia, Netherlands, New Zealand, Norway, Poland, Russia, Singapore, Sweden, Switzerland, Taiwan, Thailand, UK, USA. [2017.03.08/XD7567/v/**D**]

♦ International Association of Chinese Professionals in Geographic Information Sciences (internationally oriented national body)

♦ International Association of Chinese Professionals in Global Positioning Systems (CPGPS) 11769

Dir CPGPS Headquarters, Dept of Geomatics Engineering, Univ of Calgary, 2500 University Drive NW, Calgary AB T2N 1N4, Canada. T. +14032208150. Fax +14032841980.
URL: http://www.cpgps.org/
Aims Promote the exchange of ideas among professionals in the field of satellite navigation and positioning on information, knowledge, scientific research and applications of satellite positioning systems; promote professional development of the members; increase understanding and cooperation between members and other professionals. **Structure** Executive Committee; Board of Directors. Officers: President; Vice-President; Secretary General; Treasurer. Regional offices (11), headed by Director. Committees (10). **Events** *International Conference* Shanghai (China) 2016, *International Symposium on Mobile Mapping Technology* Sydney, NSW (Australia) 2015, *International Conference on Geoinformatics* Toronto, ON (Canada) 2005. **Publications** *CPGPS Newsletter*; *Journal of Global Positioning Systems.* **NGO Relations** *International Association of Chinese Professionals in Geographic Information Sciences (CPGIS).* [2011/XM0163/t/**D**]

♦ International Association for Christian Education 11770

Fédération internationale protestante de l'enseignement – Internationaler Verband für Christliche Erziehung und Bildung (IV) – Internationaal Verband van Organisaties voor Christelijke Opvoeding en Onderwijs
Sec Kalkumer Schloßallee 28, 40489 Düsseldorf, Germany. T. +491716279504.
Pres Pr Beatrixlaan 4, 2404 XS Alphen aan den Rijn, Netherlands.
URL: http://www.int-v.org/
History Founded 1927. Previous title in German: *Internationaler Verband Evangelischer Erzieher (IV).* **Aims** Support and improve cooperation among organizations with a Christian orientation active in the field of education, training and development; act as spokesman for Christian schools and teaching to churches in Europe and to European institutions. **Structure** General Assembly (annual); Board. **Languages** English, German. **Staff** Voluntary. **Finance** Members' dues. Gifts. **Activities** Events/meetings. **Events** *General Assembly* Riga (Latvia) 2022, *General Assembly* Vienna (Austria) 2019, *General Assembly* Tallinn (Estonia) 2018, *A pedagogy of hope in a changing Europe – approaches, perspectives and challenges for schools* Bad Wildbad (Germany) 2017, *General Assembly* Dublin (Ireland) 2017. **Publications** *Education for Democratic Citizenship in the Context of Europe* (2013).
Members Organizations in 11 countries:
Austria, Estonia, France, Germany, Hungary, Ireland, Netherlands, Poland, Slovakia, Switzerland, UK.
NGO Relations Member of: *Coordinating Group for Religion in Education (CoGREE, #04823); Réseau International de l'Enseignement Protestant (RIEP).* [2022/XD2062/**D**]

♦ International Association of Chronometry (inactive)
♦ International Association: the Cinema Against War (inactive)

♦ International Association of Cinema, Audiovisual and Media Schools 11771

Centre international de liaison des écoles de cinéma et de télévision (CILECT)
Exec Dir 108a Rakovsky Str, 1000 Sofia, Bulgaria. T. +359887646370. E-mail: executive.director@cilect.org.
URL: http://www.cilect.org/
History 8 May 1955, Cannes (France), at 2nd international meeting of film and television schools. Structure modified: 18 May 1958, Cannes (France); 31 May 1960, Lódz (Poland); 1963, Vienna (Austria); 1972, Moscow (USSR); 1990, Blois (France); 2010, Barcelona (Spain), 2016, Brisbane (Australia). Former names and other names: *International Association of Film and Television Schools* – alias; *Association Internationale des Écoles de Cinéma et de Télévision* – alias; *Asociación Internacional de Escuelas de Cine y Televisión* – alias; *International Liaison Centre for Film and Television Schools* – former. **Aims** Develop and promote the highest standards of education, research and training for film, television and related media. **Structure** General Assembly (annual); Executive Council, including President and Chairs of Regional Bodies: *CILECT Africa Regional Association (CARA, see: #11771)*; *CILECT Asia-Pacific Association (CAPA, see: #11771)*; *European Grouping of Film and Television Schools (GEECT, see: #11771)*; *CILECT Ibero América (CIBA, see: #11771)*; CILECT North America (CNA). Executive Director. **Languages** English. **Finance** Sources: donations; gifts, legacies; members' dues. **Activities** Events/meetings; guidance/assistance/consulting; knowledge management/information dissemination; networking/liaising; research/documentation. **Events** *Biennial International Congress* Los Angeles, CA (USA) 2014, *Biennial Congress and General Assembly* Newport Beach, CA (USA) 2014, *The impact of the digital age in the CILECT schools' teaching curricula* Buenos Aires (Argentina) 2013, *Biennial International Congress* Cape Town (South Africa) 2012, *Biennial congress and general assembly / Biennial International Congress* Barcelona (Spain) 2010. **Publications** Proceedings of conferences and general assemblies; information on film education curricula; news of member institutions.
Members Institutional – Full, Candidate and Partner (schools); Honorary (individuals); Corresponding (teachers); Sustaining (business and non-profit agencies). Institutional members (180) in 64 countries and territories:
Albania, Argentina, Australia, Austria, Belgium, Benin, Brazil, Bulgaria, Burkina Faso, Cameroon, Canada, China, Colombia, Costa Rica, Croatia, Cuba, Czechia, Denmark, Ecuador, Estonia, Finland, France, Georgia, Germany, Ghana, Greece, Hong Kong, Hungary, Iceland, India, Indonesia, Ireland, Israel, Italy, Japan, Kenya, Korea Rep, Latvia, Lebanon, Lithuania, Mexico, Morocco, Netherlands, New Zealand, Norway, Philippines, Poland, Portugal, Romania, Russia, Serbia, Singapore, Slovakia, Slovenia, South Africa, Spain, Sweden, Switzerland, Taiwan, Türkiye, UK, Uruguay, USA, Vietnam.
Included in the above, 6 organizations listed in this Yearbook:
American Film Institute (AFI); European Film College (EFC); ifs internationale filmschule köln (ifs); Institut international de l'image et du son (IIIS); International Cinema and Television School (#12572); Universidad Iberoamericana, México (UIA).
Honorary (7) in 7 countries:
Brazil, Croatia, Denmark, Germany, Italy, Philippines, USA.
Corresponding (14) in 8 countries:
Australia, Czechia, Hungary, Israel, Singapore, South Africa, UK, USA.
Consultative Status Consultative status granted from: *UNESCO (#20322)* (Consultative Status). **NGO Relations** Member of (1): *International Council for Film, Television and Audiovisual Communication (IFTC, #13022).* [2023.02.19/XC2227/y/**C**]

♦ International Association of CIP Professionals (IACIPP) 11772

Dir address not obtained. E-mail: info@cip-association.org.
URL: http://cip-association.org/
History Former names and other names: *International Association of Critical Infrastructure Protection Professionals* – full title. **Aims** Share ideas, information, experiences, technology and best practice; develop a strategic qualification programme. **Structure** Executive Board; Regional Directors. **Languages** English. **Activities** Events/meetings. **Events** *Critical Infrastructure Protection and Resilience Europe Conference* Bucharest (Romania) 2022, *Critical Infrastructure Protection and Resilience Europe Conference* Bucharest (Romania) 2021, *Critical Infrastructure Protection and Resilience Americas Conference* New Orleans, LA (USA) 2021, *Critical Infrastructure Protection and Resilience Europe Conference* Bucharest (Romania) 2020, *Critical Infrastructure Protection and Resilience Americas Conference* New Orleans, LA (USA) 2020. **Publications** *IACIPP Newsletter* (12 a year); *World Security Report* (4 a year). [2021.09.01/XM6258/t/**C**]

♦ International Association of Circumpolar Health Publishers (inactive)
♦ International Association of CIS Exchanges / see International Association of Exchanges of the Commonwealth of Independent States Countries (#11884)
♦ International Association of the Cities Against Drugs (inactive)
♦ International Association Cities and Ports / see Association internationale villes et ports – réseau mondial des villes portuaires (#02751)

♦ International Association for Citizenship, Social and Economics Education (IACSEE) 11773

Chair Dept of Educational Studies, Univ of Glasgow, 11 Eldon Street, Glasgow, G3 6NH, UK. T. +441413303011.
URL: http://www.iacsee.org/
History Founded Jan 1994, as *International Association for Children's Social and Economics Education.* Name changed, Jul 2001. **Aims** Advance theoretical and practical knowledge about children in the areas of their social and economics understanding and learning. **Languages** English. **Staff** 4.00 FTE, voluntary. **Finance** Members' dues. Business sponsorship. **Events** *Conference* Bath (UK) 2011, *Conference* Kelowna, BC (Canada) 2009, *Conference* Tartu (Estonia) 2007, *Conference* Chicago, IL (USA) 2005, *Global challenges – local responses* Egmond aan Zee (Netherlands) 2003. **Publications** *Citizenship, Social Economics Education* (3 a year) – journal; *IACSEE Newsletter* (2 a year). Conference proceedings.
Members National corresponding organizations and individuals. Organizations in 2 countries:
Denmark, UK.
Individuals in 15 countries:
Australia, Brazil, Canada, Czechia, Germany, Japan, Mexico, Netherlands, New Zealand, Norway, Russia, Spain, Sweden, UK, USA. [2016/XD4376/**D**]

♦ International Association of City Museums (no recent information)

♦ International Association of Civil Aviation Chaplains (IACAC) 11774

Association internationale d'aumôniers de l'aviation civile
Sec Melbourne Airport, Departure Dr, Melbourne VIC 3045, Australia. E-mail: meh@iinet.net.au.
Pres Charles de Gaulle Airport, 95700 Roissy, France. E-mail: president@iacac.aero.
URL: http://www.iacac.aero/
History 21 Sep 1967, Brussels (Belgium). Constitution accepted and approved 10 Oct 1986, Melbourne (Australia); amended and approved Johannesburg (South Africa), 2000, Paris (France), 2002, Lusaka (Zambia), 2009, Aberdeen (UK) 2011, New York NY (USA) 2015, Charlotte NC (USA) 2018. **Aims** Enhance communication among *airport* chaplains and chapels throughout the world; develop policies and procedures on the world level; establish an airport chapel and chaplaincy in every international airport. **Structure** General Meeting (annual); Board. **Languages** English, French. **Staff** Voluntary. **Finance** Sources: members' dues. Annual budget: 7,000 USD. **Activities** Events/meetings. **Events** *Annual Meeting* London (UK) 2022, *Annual Meeting* Nairobi (Kenya) 2021, *Annual Meeting* 2020, *Annual Meeting* Melbourne, VIC (Australia) 2019, *Annual Meeting* Charlotte, NC (USA) 2018. **Publications** *IACAC Newsletter* (12 a year).
Members Active; Associate; Honorary; Retired. Chaplaincies in 34 countries and territories:
Australia, Austria, Belgium, Brazil, Canada, Channel Is, Colombia, Congo DR, Costa Rica, France, Germany, Ghana, Hong Kong, Hungary, Ireland, Italy, Kenya, Latvia, Malta, Netherlands, Nigeria, Norway, Philippines, Poland, Portugal, Puerto Rico, South Africa, Spain, Sweden, Switzerland, Türkiye, UK, USA, Zambia. [2021.09.02/XD5505/v/**C**]

♦ International Association of Civil Aviation Workers' Unions 11775

Pres 19 Islam Safarli, AZ 1005 Baku, Azerbaijan.
URL: http://en.vkp.ru/
Publications *Inform-Contact* (4 a year). **Members** Trade unions in the CIS region (membership countries not specified). **NGO Relations** Member of (1): *General Confederation of Trade Unions (GCTU, #10108).* [2020/XM2452/**D**]

♦ International Association of Civil Engineering Students (IACES) ... 11776

SG c/o Coordination Center LC Porto, Rua Roberto Frias, s/n Edificio G, Sala G117, 4200-465 Porto, Portugal. T. +351932100470. E-mail: iaces@fe.up.pt – iacesboard@gmail.com.
Registered Office Stevinweg 1, kl 62, 2628 CN Delft, Netherlands.
Facebook: https://www.facebook.com/iacesofficial
History 1989, Delft (Netherlands). **Aims** Develop contacts between civil engineering students; provide mutual information and support concerning civil engineering studies; inform governments, trade and industry, universities and institutions of students' points of view on international issues which concern them; promote international understanding and goodwill. **Structure** General Assembly of Representatives (annual). General Board from at least 4 countries, comprising President, 2 Vice Presidents, Secretary and Treasurer. Coordination Centre. Local Committees at each university. Alumni Club. International Working Groups. **Languages** English. **Staff** 5.00 FTE, voluntary. **Finance** Members' dues. Other sources: donations;

sponsorship. **Activities** Through local committees: (i) Organizes: Academic Congress of Civil Engineering Students (ACCESS); Midterm Meeting (MTM); spring, summer and winter courses; study visits and exchanges; practical work abroad. (ii) Collects and presents information on civil engineering faculties through *'LINK Report'*. **Events** *ACCESS Congress* Istanbul (Turkey) 2015, *ACCESS Congress* Istanbul (Turkey) 2013, *ACCESS Congress* Karlsruhe (Germany) 2012, *ACCESS Congress* Skopje (Macedonia) / Ohrid (Macedonia) 2011, *ACCESS congress* Wuppertal (Germany) 2010. **Publications** *IACES Newsletter* (24 a year). *IACES Yearbook*; *LINK Reports*. Course reports.
Members Committees (25) and individuals (32) in 33 countries and territories:
Australia, Bosnia-Herzegovina, Bulgaria, Croatia, Czechia, Egypt, Finland, Germany, Ghana, Greece, Indonesia, Iran Islamic Rep, Italy, Kosovo (UNMIK), Netherlands, Nigeria, North Macedonia, Norway, Philippines, Poland, Portugal, Romania, Serbia, Slovakia, Slovenia, Spain, Sri Lanka, Sudan, Sweden, Türkiye, UK, United Arab Emirates, USA.
NGO Relations Informal links with: *Board of European Students of Technology (BEST, #03294)*; *The European Law Students' Association (ELSA, #07660)*; *International Association for the Exchange of Students for Technical Experience (IAESTE, #11885)*. [2022/XD4781/**D**]

♦ International Association for Civilian Oversight of Law Enforcement (inactive)
♦ International Association of Civil Servants (no recent information)

♦ International Association of Claim Professionals (IACP) 11777

Main Office PO Box 564, Palisades NY 10964, USA. E-mail: execdirector@iaclpro.org.
URL: http://www.iaclpro.com/
History 1970, USA, as *Excess/Surplus Lines Claims Association (SLCA)*. 2009, present name adopted. **Structure** Board of Directors, comprising President, Vice-President, Secretary, Treasurer, Assistant Treasurer, Immediate Past President and 7 members. **Events** *Annual Conference* Greensboro, GA (USA) 2023, *Annual Conference* Phoenix, AZ (USA) 2022, *European Conference* St Andrews (UK) 2022, *European Conference* Madrid (Spain) 2017, *Annual Conference* Marana, AZ (USA) 2013. [2019/XJ2470/t/**C**]

♦ International Association for Classical Archaeology (#02988)

♦ International Association of Classification Societies (IACS) 11778

Association internationale des sociétés de classification
SG 4 Matthew Parker Street, London, SW1H 9NP, UK. T. +442079760660. E-mail: permsec@iacs.org.uk.
URL: http://www.iacs.org.uk/
History 11 Sep 1968, Hamburg (Germany). Founded with 10 member societies, Classification Societies having previously held the following Conferences: 1939, Rome (Italy); 1955, Paris (France); 1959, London (UK); 1965 New York NY (USA); 1968 Oslo (Norway). Set up 'IACS Permanent Office', Apr 1992, in London. Registration: EU Transparency Register, No/ID: 80305287660-27. **Aims** Promote improvements of standards of safety at sea and prevention of pollution of marine environment; consult and cooperate with relevant international and maritime organizations; cooperate closely with the world's maritime industries; establish standards, guidelines and rules for design, construction and survey of ships and other marine structures. **Structure** Council (meets twice a year); General Policy Group; Quality Committee Working Groups; Permanent Secretariat in London (UK). Meetings closed. **Languages** English. **Staff** 19.00 FTE, paid. **Finance** Sources: members' dues. **Activities** Monitoring/evaluation; research/documentation; standards/guidelines. **Events** *Round Table* Singapore (Singapore) 2019, *Round Table* London (UK) 2017, *Machinery Panel Meeting* Busan (Korea Rep) 2016, *Machinery Panel Meeting* Busan (Korea Rep) 2016, *Machinery Panel Meeting* Busan (Korea Rep) 2015. **Publications** *IACS Annual Review* (annual) in English. *IACS Rapid Reference Manuals*. Technical resolutions and statements; basic information.
Members Full: classification societies in 12 countries:
China, Croatia, France, Germany, India, Italy, Japan, Korea Rep, Norway, Poland, UK, USA.
Consultative Status Consultative status granted from: *ECOSOC (#05331)* (Ros); *International Maritime Organization (IMO, #14102)* (since 1969, permanent representative since 1976); *UNCTAD (#20285)* (Special Category). **NGO Relations** Consultative member of: *Comité maritime international (CMI, #04192)*. Cooperates with: *International Organization for Standardization (ISO, #14473)*. [2022.05.26/XD6997/**D**]

♦ International Association of Cleaning Companies / see Fédération internationale des entreprises de nettoyage (#09628)
♦ International Association for Clean Technology (inactive)
♦ International Association of Clerks, Recorders, Election Officials and Treasurers (internationally oriented national body)
♦ International Association of Clinical Biochemists / see International Federation of Clinical Chemistry and Laboratory Medicine (#13392)

♦ International Association of Clinical Forensic Medicine (IACFM) . . . 11779

Pres address not obtained.
Main Website: http://iacfm.org/
History 1984. Founded prior to First World Meeting of Police Surgeons or Police Examiners, Aug 1987, Wichita KS (USA). Former names and other names: *World Police Medical Officers (WPMO)* – former (1984 to 24 Aug 2017). **Aims** Encourage international collaboration in clinical forensic medicine, particularly for forensic physicians working with law enforcement agencies from around the world. **Structure** President elected every three years; Board of past Presidents. **Languages** English. **Staff** 1.00 FTE, voluntary. **Activities** Healthcare. **Events** *Triennial Congress* Sydney, NSW (Australia) 2023, *Triennial Conference* Sydney, NSW (Australia) 2020, *Triennial Conference* Toronto, ON (Canada) 2017, *Triennial Conference* Seoul (Korea Rep) 2014, *Triennial Conference* Funchal (Portugal) 2011. **Members** Membership countries not specified. **NGO Relations** As of 2008 meeting now co-meeting with *International Association of Forensic Sciences (IAFS, #11900)*. [2021.02.17/XD5498/**D**]

♦ International Association of Clinical Laser Acupuncturists (no recent information)

♦ International Association of Coaching Institutes (ICI) 11780

Pres NLP and Coaching Inst Berlin, Winterfeldstr 97, 10777 Berlin, Germany. T. +493021478174. E-mail: president@coaching-institutes.net.
URL: http://www.coaching-institutes.net/
History 2006, having existed since 2001 as part of *International Association of NLP Institutes (IN, #12050)*. **Aims** Develop the highest ethics and quality standards in coaching; bridge effective practical application of coaching with academic education, theory and research. **Structure** Board of Directors; Presidents; Ambassadors. Standards Commissions; Developmental Commissions. **Activities** Events/meetings; standards/guidelines; training/education. **Events** *NLP and Coaching World Congress* Hammamet (Tunisia) 2019, *NLP and Coaching World Congress* Paris (France) 2017.
Members Individuals in 53 countries and territories:
Afghanistan, Argentina, Australia, Austria, Belgium, Bosnia-Herzegovina, Brazil, Canada, Chile, China, Colombia, Costa Rica, Croatia, Denmark, Egypt, France, Germany, Guadeloupe, India, Iran Islamic Rep, Israel, Italy, Japan, Kenya, Liechtenstein, Luxembourg, Malaysia, Mauritius, Mexico, Montenegro, Netherlands, New Zealand, Nicaragua, Norway, Panama, Peru, Poland, Portugal, Romania, Russia, Saudi Arabia, Serbia, Singapore, Spain, Sweden, Switzerland, Thailand, Tunisia, Türkiye, UK, Uruguay, USA, Venezuela.
NGO Relations *European Coaching Association (ECA)*; *World Hypnosis Organization (WHO, #21575)*. [2018/XM6481/v/**C**]

♦ International Association of Cognitive Behavioral Therapy (IACBT) . 11781

Pres c/o Harbor UCLA MC, 1000 W Carson St, Box 498, Torrance CA 90509, USA.
URL: https://i-acbt.com/
History 1990. Former names and other names: *International Association for Cognitive Psychotherapy (IACP)* – former (1990 to 2021). **Aims** Alleviate human suffering by facilitating worldwide development, utilization and growth of cognitive psychotherapy as a scientific discipline and professional activity. **Structure** General Meeting; Board of Directors of 10 members. **Languages** English. **Staff** 1.00 FTE, paid. **Finance** Members' dues. Conference fees. **Activities** Events/meetings; research and development. **Events** *International Congress of Cognitive Psychotherapy* St Petersburg (Russia) 2024, *International Congress of Cognitive Psychotherapy* Rome (Italy) 2021, *International Congress of Cognitive Psychotherapy* Rome (Italy) 2020, *International Congress of Cognitive Psychotherapy* Cluj-Napoca (Romania) 2017, *International Congress of Cognitive Psychotherapy* Hong Kong (Hong Kong) 2014. **Publications** *Advances in Cognitive Therapy* – newsletter; *International Clinical Referral Directory* – online; *International Journal of Cognitive Therapy*. Membership directory.
Members (209) in 39 countries and territories:
Argentina, Australia, Brazil, Canada, Colombia, Croatia, Cyprus, Denmark, Egypt, Finland, France, Germany, Greece, Hong Kong, Iran Islamic Rep, Ireland, Israel, Italy, Japan, Korea Rep, Kuwait, Lebanon, Mexico, Netherlands, New Zealand, Norway, Peru, Philippines, Portugal, Romania, Russia, Saudi Arabia, South Africa, Spain, Sweden, Switzerland, Türkiye, UK, USA.
NGO Relations Member of (1): *World Confederation of Cognitive and Behavioural Therapies (WCCBT, #21292)*. [2021/XD6827/**D**]

♦ International Association for Cognitive Education / see International Association for Cognitive Education and Psychology (#11782)

♦ International Association for Cognitive Education and Psychology (IACEP) 11782

Pres School of Education, Fac of Social Sciences, Building 905 – Room 409, Bar-Ilan University, 5290002 Ramat Gan, Israel. E-mail: president@iacep-coged.org.
URL: http://www.iacep-coged.org/
History Founded Nov 1988, Lake Louise AB (Canada), as *International Association for Cognitive Education (IACE) – Association internationale pour l'éducation cognitive – Asociación Internacional para Educación Cognoscitiva – Internationale Vereinigung für Kognitives Lernen – Internationale Organisatie voor Cognitieve Educatie*. **Aims** Advance cognitive education; promote, stimulate and disseminate applications of knowledge on the development, acquisition and application of logical thought. **Structure** Executive Committee; Standing Committees. **Languages** English. **Staff** None. **Finance** Members' dues. Journal subscriptions. **Activities** Events/meetings. **Events** *Biennial Conference* Athens (Greece) 2015, *Biennial Conference* Leiden (Netherlands) 2013, *Biennial Conference* Boston, MA (USA) 2011, *Biennial Conference* Osnabrück (Germany) 2009, *Biennial conference* Knoxville, TN (USA) 2007. **Publications** *Cognitive Education/Education Cognitive/ Educación Cognoscitiva* – newsletter; *Journal of Cognitive Education and Psychology*.
Members Full in 29 countries and territories:
Australia, Austria, Bolivia, Brazil, Canada, Cuba, Cyprus, Dominican Rep, Finland, France, Germany, Hong Kong, Ireland, Israel, Italy, Mexico, Micronesia FS, Netherlands, Norway, Portugal, Puerto Rico, Romania, Russia, Singapore, South Africa, Sweden, Switzerland, UK, USA. [2015.06.24/XD3763/**D**]

♦ International Association for Cognitive Psychotherapy / see International Association of Cognitive Behavioral Therapy (#11781)

♦ International Association for Cognitive Science (IACS) 11783

Sec Gen Hankuk Univ of Foreign Studies, 81 Oedae-ro, Mohyeon, Yongin GYEONGGI 17035, Korea Rep.
URL: http://www.cogsci.org.cn/iacs/
History Current statutes effective as of 1 Jan 2009. **Aims** Provide a forum for the development of cognitive science in the Asia-Pacific and other regions. **Structure** General Assembly; Steering Committee; Consultation Board; Secretariat Bureau. **Languages** English. **Staff** All voluntary. **Finance** Conference revenue. **Activities** Events/meetings. **Events** *ICCS : International Conference on Cognitive Science* Seoul (Korea Rep) 2019, *ICCS : International Conference on Cognitive Science* Taipei (Taiwan) 2017, *ICCS : International Conference on Cognitive Science* Turin (Italy) 2015, *ICCS : International Conference on Cognitive Science* Kuching (Malaysia) 2013, *ICCS : International Conference on Cognitive Science / ICCS Conference* Sapporo (Japan) 2012. **Publications** *Journal of Cognitive Science* (3 a year). Conference proceedings.
Members in 11 countries and territories:
Australia, Canada, China, Indonesia, Italy, Japan, Korea Rep, Malaysia, Philippines, Taiwan, USA.
IGO Relations None. [2015.09.16/XJ4867/**D**]

♦ International Association for the Cognitive Science of Religion (IACSR) 11784

SG Univ of Otago, Room 106, Dept of Theology and Religion, PO Box 56, Dunedin, New Zealand.
Pres Univ of Connecticut – Anthropology, 354 Mansfield Road Unit 1176, Storrs CT 06269, USA.
URL: http://www.iacsr.com/
History 2006. Registered in the State of Georgia (USA). **Aims** Promote the cognitive science of religion through international collaboration of all scholars whose research has a bearing on the subject. **Structure** General Assembly; Executive Committee. **Languages** English. **Staff** Voluntary. **Finance** Sources: members' dues. **Activities** Events/meetings; knowledge management/information dissemination; research/documentation. **Events** *Biennial Meeting* Dunedin (New Zealand) 2020, *Biennial Meeting* Boston, MA (USA) 2018, *Biennial Meeting* Vancouver, BC (Canada) 2016, *Biennial Meeting* Brno (Czech Rep) 2014, *Biennial Meeting* Aarhus (Denmark) 2012. **Publications** *Journal for the Cognitive Science of Religion*.
Members Full in 20 countries:
Australia, Belgium, Canada, Cuba, Czechia, Denmark, France, Germany, Greece, Korea Rep, Netherlands, New Zealand, Norway, Poland, Portugal, Saudi Arabia, Spain, Sweden, UK, USA.
NGO Relations Affiliate member of: American Academy of Religion; *International Association for the History of Religions (IAHR, #11936)*. [2018.09.06/XM6372/**C**]

♦ International Association for Cognitive Semiotics (IACS) 11785

Sec address not obtained.
URL: http://iacs.dk/
History 2013, Aarhus (Denmark). Founded in connection with the 8th Conference of *Nordic Association for Semiotic Studies (NASS, #17205)*. **Aims** Promote research and higher education in the transdisciplinary field of cognitive semiotics, encouraging cooperation among researchers with background in semiotics, linguistics, and cognitive science, as well as other related fields. **Structure** General Assembly; Governing Board. **Languages** English. **Finance** Sources: members' dues. **Activities** Events/meetings; networking/liaising; research and development. **Events** *Conference* Aachen (Germany) 2020, *Conference* Toronto, ON (Canada) 2018, *Conference* Lublin (Poland) 2016, *Conference* Lund (Sweden) 2014. [2020/AA0982/**C**]

♦ International Association of Cold Regions Development Studies (IACORDS) 11786

Secretariat c/o Div of Engineering and Policy for Cold Regional Development, Hokkaido Univ, Graduate School of Engineering, North 13 West 8, Sapporo HOKKAIDO, 060-8628 Japan. Fax +81117066216. E-mail: iscord@eng.hokudai.ac.jp.
URL: http://www.eng.hokudai.ac.jp/labo/tra/iscord/
History 1994. Online Forum *International Society of Cold Regions Development (ISCORD-AQ)*, founded 2000. **Languages** English. **Activities** Events/meetings. **Events** *ISCORD Triennial Symposium* Oulu (Finland) 2019, *ISCORD Triennial Symposium* Incheon (Korea Rep) 2016, *ISCORD Triennial Symposium / Symposium* Anchorage, AK (USA) 2013, *ISCORD Triennial Symposium / Symposium* Yakutsk (Russia) 2010, *ISCORD Triennial Symposium / Symposium* Tampere (Finland) 2007. [2016.11.18/XD7811/**D**]

♦ International Association for Cold Storage Construction / see Controlled Environment Building Association (#04783)
♦ International Association of Cold Storage Contractors / see Controlled Environment Building Association (#04783)
♦ International Association of Collectors of Slag Minerals (inactive)
♦ International Association for College Admissions Counseling (internationally oriented national body)

♦ International Association of Colleges of Laboratory Animal Medicine (IACLAM) 11787

Sec address not obtained.
URL: http://www.iaclam.org/
History 2005, St Louis MO (USA). **Aims** Provide a common platform at the global level for communication by, and representation of, diplomates of member colleges; promote the welfare and responsible use of laboratory animals. **Structure** Board.
Members National and regional colleges (4). National members in 3 countries:
Japan, Korea Rep, USA.
Regional member:
European College of Laboratory Animal Medicine (ECLAM, #06611).
NGO Relations Associate member of: *World Veterinary Association (WVA, #21901)*. [2019/XJ1055/y/**C**]

♦ International Association of Colleges of Physical Education / see Association internationale des écoles supérieures d'éducation physique (#02685)

♦ International Association of Colloid and Interface Scientists (IACIS) 11788

Hon Sec/Treas School of Chemistry, Univ of Bristol, Cantock's Close, Bristol, BS8 1TS, UK. E-mail: secretary@iacis.net.
URL: https://www.iacis.net/

History Aug 1979, Stockholm (Sweden). Founded during 3rd Conference on Surface and Colloid Science (ICSCS), as the first international organization in the field of colloid and interface science. **Aims** Promote international cooperation among colloid and interface scientists; encourage advancement in the field of colloid and interface science; promote the stature and understanding of colloid and interface science, both theoretical and applied. **Structure** Council; Standing Committee. **Languages** English. **Staff** Voluntary. **Finance** Sources: members' dues. **Activities** Awards/prizes/competitions; events/meetings; financial and/or material support. **Events** *Conference* Brisbane, QLD (Australia) 2022, *Triennial International Conference on Surface and Colloid Science* Rotterdam (Netherlands) 2018, *Triennial International Conference on Surface and Colloid Science / International Conference on Surface and Colloid Science* Mainz (Germany) 2015, *International Conference on Surface and Colloid Science* Sendai (Japan) 2012, *World congress on emulsions* Lyon (France) 2010. **Publications** *IACIS Newsletter* (4-5 a year).
Members Individual; Chapter; Corporate (available at the discretion of Council). Members in 44 countries and territories:
Argentina, Australia, Belgium, Brazil, Bulgaria, Canada, China, Croatia, Ecuador, Finland, France, Georgia, Germany, Greece, Hungary, India, Iran Islamic Rep, Ireland, Israel, Italy, Japan, Kazakhstan, Korea Rep, Kuwait, Malaysia, Mexico, Netherlands, Nigeria, Norway, Pakistan, Poland, Portugal, Romania, Russia, Serbia, Singapore, Spain, Sweden, Switzerland, Taiwan, Tanzania UR, Türkiye, UK, USA. [2022.02.02/XF5721/**C**]

♦ International Association of Colon Hydrotherapy (internationally oriented national body)
♦ International Association of Colon Therapy / see International Association of Colon Hydrotherapy
♦ International Association of Color Manufacturers (internationally oriented national body)
♦ International Association of Colour Consultants/Designers (unconfirmed)

♦ International Association of Combative Sports (IACS) 11789

Contact Fitworld 45 SF, Pari Chowk, Near Ansal Plaza, Noida, Uttar Pradesh GREATER 201310, Noida UTTAR PRADESH GREATER 201310, India. E-mail: combativesports@hotmail.com.
URL: http://www.combativesports.org/

Structure General Assembly; Executive Council. **Activities** Sporting activities; training/education.
Members National members in 8 countries:
Afghanistan, Bangladesh, India, Iran Islamic Rep, Nepal, Pakistan, South Africa, Sri Lanka.
NGO Relations Member of (1): *International Sport Network Organization (ISNO, #15592).* Partner of (2): *General Association of Asia Pacific Sports Federations (GAAPSF, #10106); International Federation of Mallyuddha (IFM). International Federation of Armsports (IFA).* [2020/XM6673/**C**]

♦ International Association for Commerce and Management (inactive)

♦ International Association for Commodity Science and Technology . 11790

Association internationale de la science de la marchandise et de la technologie de base – Internationale Gesellschaft für Warenwissenschaften und Technologie (IGWT)

Contact Dept Socioeconomics, WU Vienna Univ of Economics and Business, Welthandelsplatz 1, 1020 Vienna, Austria. T. +431313364806.
URL: http://www.wu.ac.at/itnp/igwt/

History 8 Oct 1976, Salzburg (Austria) and Vienna (Austria) (simultaneously). Previously also known under the English acronym *IACST*. Registered in accordance with Austrian law, Oct 1978. **Aims** Contribute to knowledge of commodities at every level of education, in the economy, in every branch of public administration and with the consumer, on environment protection and on sustainable development. **Structure** General Assembly (every 2 years); Executive Board; National Committees (8). **Languages** English, German. **Staff** 1.00 FTE, voluntary. **Finance** Sources: donations; members' dues. **Events** *Biennial Symposium* Bratislava (Slovakia) 2021, *Biennial Symposium* Bratislava (Slovakia) 2020, *Biennial Symposium* Rome (Italy) / Gaeta (Italy) 2018, *Biennial Symposium* Varna (Bulgaria) 2016, *Biennial Symposium* Krakow (Poland) 2014. **Publications** *Forum Ware*; *Forum Ware International*. Circulare.
Members Associations and individuals in 28 countries and territories:
Austria, Belgium, Bosnia-Herzegovina, Bulgaria, China, Croatia, Czechia, Finland, France, Germany, Hungary, Israel, Italy, Japan, Korea Rep, Lithuania, Montenegro, Netherlands, Poland, Russia, Serbia, Slovakia, Slovenia, Switzerland, Taiwan, UK, Ukraine, USA. [2015.01.07/XD2515/**C**]

♦ International Association of Communication Activists (IACACT) 11791

Contact address not obtained. E-mail: info@iacact.com.
URL: http://www.iacact.com/

History Founded 2012. Registered in accordance with Italian law. **Aims** Assist, develop and support the communication of small non-profit organizations operating in different areas of society. **Structure** Assembly; Board of Directors; Scientific Committee.
Members Organizations, including 7 listed in this Yearbook:
Alliance for Zero Extinction (AZE, #00730); Amphibian Ark (AArk, #00803); CESVI Fondazione; Global Society for Ecology and Sound Economy (ECO2TERRA International); International Rivers; Plastic Pollution Coalition; Rare.
NGO Relations Member of: *Alliance for Zero Extinction (AZE, #00730).* [2018/XM7360/y/**D**]

♦ International Association for Communication in Healthcare (EACH) 11792

Main Office c/o SAS Event & Association Mgt, The Old George Brewery, Rollestone Street, Salisbury, SP1 1DX, UK. T. +441722415154. E-mail: info@each.international.
URL: https://each.international/

History 2001. Founded on the initiative of Jozien Bensing and Sandra van Dulmen. Former names and other names: *European Association for Communication in Healthcare (EACH)* – former (2001). Registration: Charity Commission, No/ID: 1159050, England and Wales. **Aims** Increase quality of healthcare communication through research and education. **Structure** General Meeting; Executive Committee; Advisory Committee. **Languages** English. **Staff** Voluntary. **Finance** Sources: donations; meeting proceeds; members' dues; subsidies. **Activities** Events/meetings; training/education. **Events** *International Conference on Communication in Healthcare* Glasgow (UK) 2022, *International Conference on Communication in Healthcare* 2021, *International Conference on Communication in Healthcare* Salisbury (UK) 2020, *International Conference on Communication in Healthcare* San Diego, CA (USA) 2019, *International Conference on Communication in Healthcare* Porto (Portugal) 2018. **Publications** *Patient Education and Counseling* – journal. Conference proceedings.
Members Individuals (476) in 38 countries:
Australia, Austria, Belgium, Canada, China, Cyprus, Denmark, Finland, France, Germany, Greece, Grenada, India, Indonesia, Ireland, Israel, Italy, Japan, Latvia, Netherlands, New Zealand, Nigeria, Norway, Poland, Portugal, Qatar, Romania, Russia, Slovenia, South Africa, Spain, Sri Lanka, Sweden, Switzerland, Türkiye, UK, United Arab Emirates, USA.
NGO Relations Member of: *European Public Health Association (EUPHA, #08298).* Associated member of: *European Forum for Primary Care (EFPC, #07326).* [2021.09.01/XD8933/v/**C**]

♦ International Association of Communities of Users of Agricultural Equipment (inactive)

♦ International Association for Community Development (IACD) 11793

Pres Baltic Chambers, Suite 305, 50 Wellington Street, Glasgow, G2 6HJ, UK. T. +441142481924. E-mail: info@iacdglobal.org – membership@iacdglobal.org.
URL: http://www.iacdglobal.org/

History Founded 1952, USA. Between 1977-1998 head office in Marcinelle (Belgium), when was registered in accordance with Belgian law, 21 Nov 1978. Former French title: *Association internationale de développement et d'action communautaires (AIDAC).* Moved, Jan 1998, to Edinburgh (UK), and registered in accordance with Scottish law, number: SC036090. **Aims** Promote participative democracy, sustainable development, rights, economic opportunity, equality and social justice through organization, education and empowerment of people within their communities, whether these be of locality, identity or interest, in urban and rural settings. **Structure** General Meeting (annual); Board; Executive Committee; Sub-committees. **Languages** English. **Staff** 0.50 FTE, paid. **Finance** Sources: fees for services; grants; meeting proceeds; members' dues. **Activities** Events/meetings; training/education. **Events** *World Community Development Conference* Nairobi (Kenya) 2021, *World Community Development Conference* Nairobi (Kenya) 2020, *People, place and power* Dundee (UK) 2019, *Conference* Maynooth (Ireland) 2018, *Conference* Auckland (New Zealand) 2017. **Publications** *IACD E-Bulletin* (12 a year) in Arabic, Chinese, English, Hindi, Mandarin Chinese, Spanish; *IACD Newsletter* (2 a year) in Arabic, Chinese, English, Hindi, Mandarin Chinese, Spanish. Conference papers; case studies. **Members** Individuals (about 550) in about 50 countries. Membership countries not specified. **Consultative Status** Consultative status granted from: *ECOSOC (#05331)* (Ros A); *ILO (#11123)* (Special List); *UNICEF (#20332).* **NGO Relations** Member of: *CIVICUS: World Alliance for Citizen Participation (#03962); Scotland's International Development Alliance (the Alliance).* [2020/XB7321/v/**B**]

♦ International Association of Community and Further Education Colleges (IAC) 11794

Pres 9701 Stone Henge Lane, Knoxville TN 37922, USA. T. +18656946616. Fax +18655390864.
URL: http://www.iaoc.org/

History Founded Jun 1998, Bath (UK). **Aims** Provide professional development opportunities for faculty, staff and administrators who serve in community, technical and further education institutions; serve as a forum for the exchange of ideas and resources among higher education institutions; provide consulting and training opportunities for college professionals. **Structure** Executive Board. **Languages** English. **Staff** Voluntary. **Finance** Conference fees. No annual budget. **Activities** Guidance/assistance/consulting; events/meetings. **Events** *Annual Conference* Cape Town (South Africa) 2013, *Conference on developing global partnerships / Annual Conference / World Congress* New York, NY (USA) 2008, *Annual Conference* Knoxville, TN (USA) 2007, *Annual Conference* Cape Town (South Africa) 2006, *Annual Conference* Pretoria (South Africa) 2004.
Members Individuals in 8 countries and territories:
Australia, Canada, Ireland, Netherlands, South Africa, UK, USA, Virgin Is UK. [2018.06.01/XD7912/v/**D**]

♦ International Association of Community TeleService Centres (no recent information)

♦ International Association for Comparative Fascist Studies (COMFAS) 11795

Administrator Pasts – Ctr for Historical Studies, CEU, Nador utca 9, Budapest 1051, Hungary. E-mail: comfas@comfas.org.
URL: http://comfas.org/

History Founded 10 Apr 2015, Amsterdam (Netherlands). **Aims** Promote new multi-disciplinary research approaches in the field of comparative and transnational study of fascism in European and in a global context. **Structure** Board of Directors; Executive Committee. **Finance** Members' dues. **Activities** Events/meetings. **Events** *Convention* Florence (Italy) 2022, *Fascism and violence* Uppsala (Sweden) 2019, *Comparative fascist studies and the transnational turn* Budapest (Hungary) 2018. **Publications** *Journal of Comparative Fascist Studies. Routledge Studies in Fascism and the Far Right* – series. **NGO Relations** *Central European University (CEU, #03717).* [2018/XM7075/**D**]

♦ International Association for Comparative Legislation and Political Economy (inactive)

♦ International Association of Comparative Literature, Society and Culture (IACLSC) 11796

Association internationale de littérature comparée, société et culture – Asociación Internacional de Literature Comparada, la Sociedad y Cultura

Chairman Inst of Advanced Research, Puri Foundation, Koba Institutional Area, Gandhinagar, Gujarat 382426, Gandhinagar GUJARAT 382426, India. T. +917930514204. Fax +917930514110. E-mail: thecomparativereview@gmail.com – info.iaclsc@gmail.com.
URL: https://iaclsc.wixsite.com/iaclsc/publication

History 1 Apr 2014, Gandhinagar (India). **Aims** Revive research scopes in broad areas of *humanities* and *social sciences.* **Structure** Governing Body; Executive. **Languages** Bengali, English, French, German, Hindi, Italian, Odia, Russian, Sanskrit, Serbian, Spanish, Tamil, Ukrainian. **Staff** 17.00 FTE, voluntary. **Finance** Self-financing. Some support from national and international funding agencies. **Activities** Awareness raising; capacity building; conflict resolution; knowledge management/information dissemination; events/meetings; networking/liaising; publishing activities; research/documentation; training/education. **Events** *South Asian Experience and History Congress* Kolkata (India) 2020, *International Seminar on Epic Tradition in World Literature* Ghandinagar (India) 2018, *Post modern nation-state and nationalism – citizenship, history and public sphere* Gandhinagar (India) 2016. **Publications** *The Comparative Review* (2 a year).
Members Individuals (220) in 21 countries:
Australia, Bangladesh, Belarus, Belgium, Brazil, Estonia, Georgia, Germany, India, Jamaica, Jordan, Lebanon, Lithuania, Nepal, Nigeria, Pakistan, Serbia, South Africa, Ukraine, USA, Uzbekistan. [2021/XM5048/**D**]

♦ International Association for Comparative Mythology (IACM) 11797

Pres Dept of South Asian Studies, Harvard Univ, 1 Bow St, 3rd floor, Cambridge MA 02138, USA. T. +16174962990. E-mail: iacm.admin@gmail.com.
Sec Groupe d'Etudes Orientales, Strasbourg University, 22 rue René Descartes, 67084 Strasbourg, France.
URL: http://www.compmyth.org/

History Founded 2006, Beijing (China), during 'Peking University / Harvard Conference on Comparative Myth', following the activities of the Harvard Project on Comparative Myth and the later Harvard Round Table for Comparative Myth and its conferences. **Events** *Annual Conference* Belgrade (Serbia) 2022, *Annual Conference* Chihuahua (Mexico) 2021, *Annual Conference* Chihuahua (Mexico) 2020, *Annual Conference* Tartu (Estonia) 2019, *Annual Conference* Sendai (Japan) 2018. **Publications** Conference proceedings. **Members** Individuals. Membership countries not specified. [2018.09.07/XJ8239/**C**]

♦ International Association of Comparative Physiology and Biochemistry (IACPB) 11798

Chair Dept of Biology, Univ of Ottawa, 30 Marie Curie, Ottawa ON K1N 6N5, Canada.
URL: http://www.iccpb2019.com/

History 1979, Helsinki (Finland), as *International Congress of Comparative Physiology and Biochemistry (ICCPB).* Current title adopted 2009. **Aims** Promote international cooperation in the area of comparative physiology and biochemistry through symposia, conferences, workshops and other means. **Structure** Board. **Languages** English. **Staff** None. **Finance** No budget. **Activities** Events/meetings. **Events** *Congress* Ottawa, ON (Canada) 2019, *From molecules to macrophysiology* Krakow (Poland) 2015, *Congress* Nagoya (Japan) 2011, *Congress* Salvador (Brazil) 2007, *Congress* Mt Buller, VIC (Australia) 2003.
Members Organizations in 8 countries:
Australia, Canada, France, Germany, Japan, New Zealand, Russia, USA.
NGO Relations Scientific member of: *International Union of Biological Sciences (IUBS, #15760).* [2019.06.28/XD6723/**D**]

♦ International Association for Comparative Research on Leukemia and Related Diseases (CRLRD) 11799

Association internationale pour la recherche comparée dans les leucémies et les maladies voisines

SG Univ of Torino, San Luigi Univ Hosp, 10043 Orbassano TO, Italy. T. +39119026721. Fax +39119026610.
URL: http://www.iacrlrd.org/

History 1960, Philadelphia PA (USA), under the auspices of *WHO (#20950),* which supported financially up to 1975. Original title: *World Committee for Comparative Leukemia Research – Comité mondial pour des recherches comparatives sur la leucémie.* **Aims** Promote coordination of comparative clinical and basic research into leukaemia and related diseases and cooperation among different disciplines to develop new hypotheses. **Structure** Governed by World Committee. **Languages** English. **Staff** Voluntary. **Finance** Sources: grants; members' dues. **Activities** Events/meetings; knowledge management/information dissemination; research/documentation. **Events** *Biennial Symposium* Beirut (Lebanon) 2021, *Biennial Symposium* Seoul (Korea Rep) 2019, *Biennial Symposium* Houston, TX (USA) 2017, *Biennial Symposium* Paris (France) 2015, *Biennial Symposium* Turin (Italy) 2013. **Publications** *Comparative Research in Leukemia and Related Diseases – An Introduction to a Scientific Approach* (1999); *Comparative Research on Leukemia and Related Diseases* (1997).

Members Individuals (400) in 40 countries and territories:
Australia, Austria, Belarus, Belgium, Brazil, Bulgaria, Cameroon, Canada, China, Czechia, Denmark, Egypt, Finland, France, Georgia, Germany, Hungary, India, Ireland, Israel, Italy, Japan, Kuwait, Luxembourg, Morocco, Netherlands, Nigeria, Norway, Poland, Russia, Saudi Arabia, Senegal, Slovakia, South Africa, Sweden, Switzerland, Taiwan, UK, USA, Venezuela.
[2017/XD6383/v/**C**]

♦ International Association for Comparative Semitics (unconfirmed)

♦ International Association for Computational Mechanics (IACM) ... 11800

Exec Dir UPC Campus Nord, Jordi Girona 1-3 B0 Building, 08034 Barcelona, Spain. T. +34663029068.
URL: https://iacm.info/

History 1983. Founded following the setting up of a group of *International Centres of Computational Mechanics*, Apr 1981, Atlanta GA (USA), by R H Gallagher, J T Oden and O C Zienkiewicz. Formally constituted Aug 1986, Austin TX (USA), at 1st World Congress. **Aims** Stimulate and promote education, research and practice in computational mechanics; foster interchange of ideas among the various fields contributing to the discipline and provide fora and meetings for dissemination of knowledge in this field, which comprises computational solid mechanics and computational fluid dynamics plus *thermodynamics, electromagnetics*, rigid body mechanics, control systems and some aspects of particle physics. **Structure** General Council; Executive Council. Regional groupings (3). Standing Committee for Congresses. Secretariat located at *International Centre for Numerical Methods in Engineering (CIMNE)*. World congresses are rotated among these regions. **Languages** English. **Staff** 1.00 FTE, paid. **Finance** Sources: members' dues. Annual budget: 80,000 USD. **Activities** Awards/prizes/competitions; events/meetings; training/education. **Events** *International Conference on Isogeometric Analysis (IGA)* Banff, AB (Canada) 2022, *World Congress on Computational Mechanics* Yokohama (Japan) 2022, *COMPLAS : International Conference on Computational Plasticity* Barcelona (Spain) 2021, *International Conference on Isogeometric Analysis (VIGA)* Lyon (France) 2021, *World Congress on Computational Mechanics* Paris (France) 2021. **Publications** *IACM Newsletter* (12 a year); *IACM Expressions* (2 a year) – bulletin. *Advances in Computational Mechanics* – monograph series. **Members** Individual members (4,430); national/regional associations (30) in 41 countries. Membership countries not specified. [2022/XD5402/y/**C**]

♦ International Association of Computed Tomography (unconfirmed)

♦ International Association for Computer and Information Science (ACIS) 11801

Sec 955 E Millbrook Rd, Mount Pleasant MI 48858, USA. T. +19897733836. E-mail: acis@acisinternational.org.
CEO 735 Meadowbrook Dr, Mount Pleasant MI 48858, USA. T. +19897741175. Fax +19897741174.
URL: http://www.acisinternational.org/

Aims Provide a forum for researchers in education and industry from all over the world to interact with one another and disseminate the latest developments in the fields of computer and information science. **Structure** Board of Directors of 4. Steering Committee. **Activities** Organizes conferences. *International Conference on Computer and Information Science (ICIS); International Conference on Computers, Networks, Systems, and Industrial Engineering (CNSI); International Conference on Software Engineering, Artificial Intelligence, Networking and Parallel/Distributed Computing (SNPD); International Symposium on Software and Network Engineering (SSNE).* **Events** *International Conference on Software Engineering Research Management and Applications* Kanazawa (Japan) 2021, *International Conference on Software Engineering, Artificial Intelligence, Networking and Parallel/Distributed Computing* Busan (Korea Rep) 2018, *International Conference on Computer and Information Science* Singapore (Singapore) 2018, *International Conference on Software Engineering, Artificial Intelligence, Networking and Parallel/Distributed Computing* Kanazawa (Japan) 2017, *International Conference on Software Engineering Research, Management and Applications* London (UK) 2017. **Publications** *International Journal of Computer and Information Science (IJCIS)* (4 a year); *International Journal of Innovative Software (IJIS).* [2020/XJ1306/**D**]

♦ International Association for Computerized Adaptive Testing (internationally oriented national body)

♦ International Association for Computer Methods and Advances in Geomechanics (IACMAG) 11802

Pres Fac of Engineering and Built Environment, Univ of Newcastle, Callaghan NSW 2308, Australia. T. +61249217716. Fax +61249217062.
Gen Sec/Treas College of Engineering, Dept of Civil Eng and Eng Mechanics, Univ of Arizona, PO Box 210072, Tucson AZ 85721-0072, USA. T. +15206216571. Fax +15206216577.
URL: http://www.iacmag.org/

History 1991, following decision of 6th International Conference, 1988, Innsbruck (Austria) and arising from an *International Committee on Numerical Methods in Geomechanics* set up in 1976 to organize triennial conferences. **Aims** Promote and encourage basic and applied research and industrial applications related to computer methods and other advances in the interdisciplinary area of geomechanics; promote and establish procedures for introduction of geomechanics in undergraduate and postgraduate education; establish means of providing appropriate input to national and international agencies having direct impact on funding policies and on encouraging research and teaching in *engineering* and geomechanics. **Structure** Board of Directors. **Languages** English. **Staff** 0.50 FTE, paid. **Finance** Sources: meeting proceeds; members' dues. **Activities** Awards/prizes/competitions; events/meetings; networking/liaising. **Events** *Triennial Conference* Turin (Italy) 2022, *Triennial Conference* Turin (Italy) 2021, *Triennial Conference* Turin (Italy) 2020, *Triennial Conference* Wuhan (China) 2017, *Triennial Conference* Kyoto (Japan) 2014. **Publications** *IACMAG Newsletter* (annual). **Members** Full in 50 countries and territories:
Argentina, Australia, Austria, Belgium, Brazil, Bulgaria, Canada, Chile, China, Croatia, Cyprus, Czechia, Denmark, Egypt, Finland, France, Germany, Greece, Hong Kong, Hungary, India, Israel, Italy, Japan, Korea Rep, Malaysia, Mexico, Netherlands, New Zealand, Norway, Oman, Poland, Portugal, Puerto Rico, Romania, Russia, Saudi Arabia, Singapore, Slovakia, South Africa, Spain, Sweden, Switzerland, Taiwan, Thailand, Türkiye, UK, Ukraine, United Arab Emirates, USA. [2017.03.13/XD2664/**C**]

♦ International Association of Computer Science in Sport (IACSS) ... 11803

Pres TUM – Univ of Vienna, Auf der Schmelz 6, 1150 Vienna, Austria. T. +431427748882. Fax +431427748889. E-mail: office@iacss.org.
URL: http://www.iacss.org/

History 2003, Barcelona (Spain). Founded during 4th International Symposium on Computer Science in Sport. Takes over activities of *Computer Science in Sport (COSISP) Working Group.* **Aims** Improve international cooperation in the field of computer science in sport. **Structure** Board. **Languages** English. **Staff** 2.00 FTE, voluntary. **Finance** Members' dues. **Activities** Research/documentation; knowledge management/information dissemination; networking/liaising; guidance/assistance/consulting; events/meetings. **Events** *International Symposium of Computer Sciences in Sport* Vienna (Austria) 2022, *International Symposium of Computer Sciences in Sport* Vienna (Austria) 2021, *Joint International Performance Analysis Workshop and Conference* Vienna (Austria) 2021, *International Symposium of Computer Sciences in Sport* Moscow (Russia) 2019, *International Symposium of Computer Sciences in Sport* Konstanz (Germany) 2017. **Publications** *Refereed E-Journal: International Journal of Computer Science in Sport* (2 a year) – in cooperation with the National Austrian Association on Computer Science in Sport; *IACSS Newsletter* (irregular). **Information Services** *CSS-Mailinglist* – moderated.
Members Organizations in 8 countries:
Austria, China, Croatia, Germany, India, Portugal, Türkiye, UK.
Individuals in 50 countries and territories:
Argentina, Australia, Austria, Belarus, Belgium, Brazil, Canada, China, Croatia, Cyprus, Czechia, Denmark, Egypt, Estonia, Finland, France, Germany, Greece, Hong Kong, Hungary, India, Indonesia, Iran Islamic Rep, Ireland, Israel, Italy, Japan, Jordan, Korea Rep, Lithuania, Malaysia, Mexico, Netherlands, New Zealand, North Macedonia, Poland, Portugal, Qatar, Romania, Russia, Slovakia, South Africa, Spain, Switzerland, Taiwan, Thailand, Türkiye, UK, USA, Venezuela.
NGO Relations Member of: *International Council of Sport Science and Physical Education (ICSSPE, #13077).* [2017.10.12/XJ4271/**D**]

♦ International Association for Computers and Communications (IACC) ... 11804

Contact 785 Dreese Lab, Ohio State University, 2015 Neil Ave, Columbus OH 43210, USA. T. +16142925199.

Activities *International Conference on Parallel Processing (ICPP).* **Events** *International Conference on Parallel Processing* Kyoto (Japan) 2019, *International Conference on Parallel Processing* Philadelphia, PA (USA) 2016, *Conference* Minneapolis, MN (USA) 2014, *International Conference on Parallel Processing* Lyon (France) 2013, *International conference on parallel processing* Vienna (Austria) 2009. [2015/XJ0131/**D**]

♦ International Association of Computing in Archaeology (no recent information)

♦ International Association for Computing and Philosophy (IACAP) .. 11805

Exec Dir c/o Weltec, Private Bag 39803, Wellington Mail Centre, Lower Hutt 5045, New Zealand.
URL: http://www.iacap.org/

History 2004, following a series of conferences since 1986. **Aims** Promote and advance philosophical study of computing; advance uses of computing that have philosophical significance. **Structure** Executive Committee of up to 12 members. **Activities** Events/meetings. **Events** *CEPE/IACAP Joint Conference* Hamburg (Germany) 2021, *International Conference* Mexico City (Mexico) 2019, *International Conference* Warsaw (Poland) 2018, *Joint Conference* Newark, DE (USA) 2015, *International Conference* Thessaloniki (Greece) 2014. **Publications** *IACAP Newsletter* (2 a year). [2020/XJ3167/**D**]

♦ International Association of Concert and Festival Managers / see International Society for the Performing Arts Foundation (#15350)
♦ International Association of Concert Managers / see International Society for the Performing Arts Foundation (#15350)

♦ International Association of Concrete Drillers and Sawers (IACDS) . 11806

Internationaler Verband der Betonbohr und Sägeunternehmungen (IVBS) – Internationella Föreningen för Betonghåltagare (AIEFSB)

SG Av Rey Juan Carlos 92, Argalia Building 4 RABUSO, Leganés, 28916 Madrid, Spain. E-mail: info@iacds.org.
Brussels Office Rue des Colonies 11, Atrium Bldg Regus Rabuso, 1000 Brussels, Belgium.
URL: http://www.iacds.org/

Aims Provide an international union with the cooperation of *trade* associations to support and promote the development of professional drilling and sawing contractors and their methods. **Events** *Annual Meeting* Munich (Germany) 2022, *Annual Meeting* Munich (Germany) 2019, *Annual Convention* Tokyo (Japan) 2018, *Annual Convention* Vienna (Austria) 2017, *Annual Meeting* Munich (Germany) 2016.
Members Professional drilling and sawing associations from the concrete construction and renovation industry worldwide in 9 countries:
Australia, Austria, Germany, Japan, Spain, Sweden, Switzerland, UK, USA. [2020/XM3815/**F**]

♦ International Association of Conference Centers / see IACC

♦ International Association of Conference Interpreters 11807

Association internationale des interprètes de conférence (AIIC) – Asociación Internacional de Intérpretes de Conferencias – Internationaler Verband der Konferenzdolmetscher

Pres Av Blanc 46, 1202 Geneva, Switzerland. T. +41229081540. Fax +41227324151. E-mail: contact@aiic.org.
URL: http://aiic.org

History 11 Nov 1953, Paris (France). Founded taking over the activities of *International Association of Conference Interpreters and Translators (IACIT, inactive)*, set up 1 Jan 1947. Registration: France. **Aims** Promote high standards of quality and ethics in the profession; represent the interests of practitioners. **Structure** General Assembly (every 3 years); Executive Committee; Advisory Board; Budget Committee; Committee on Admissions and Language Classification. **Languages** English, French. **Staff** 3.00 FTE, paid. **Finance** Sources: members' dues. **Events** *AIIC General Assembly* Geneva (Switzerland) 2022, *Private Market Sector Interregional Meeting (PRIMS)* Lyon (France) 2020, *Private Market Sector Interregional Meeting (PRIMS)* London (UK) 2019, *Private Market Sector Interregional Meeting* Montréal, QC (Canada) 2019, *Triennial General Assembly* Valencia (Spain) 2018. **Publications** *AIIC Webzine*; *AIIC Yearbook.* **Members** Individuals (over 3,000) in 106 countries. Membership countries not specified. **Consultative Status** Consultative status granted from: *ECOSOC (#05331)* (Ros C); *UNESCO (#20322)* (Consultative Status); *ILO (#11123)* (Special List); *World Intellectual Property Organization (WIPO, #21593)* (Permanent Observer Status). **NGO Relations** Member of (2): *European Legal Interpreters and Translators Association (EULITA, #07678)*; *Fédération des Institutions Internationales établies à Genève (FIG, #09599).* Cooperates with (1): *International Organization for Standardization (ISO, #14473).* [2022.10.14/XB1265/v/**B**]

♦ International Association of Conference Interpreters and Translators (inactive)
♦ International Association of Conferences on Psychotechnics (inactive)
♦ International Association for Conference Technology (inactive)
♦ International Association of Conference Translators (#02748)

♦ International Association for Conflict Management (IACM) 11808

Main Office PO Box 71047, Myrtle Beach SC 29572, USA.
URL: https://iafcm.org/

History Founded 1984. First international conference 1988. **Aims** Encourage scholars and practitioners to develop and disseminate theory, research and experience useful for understanding and improving conflict management in family, organizational, societal and international settings. **Structure** Board. **Languages** English. **Staff** Voluntary. **Finance** Members' dues. Other sources: conference registration; donations. **Activities** Events/meetings; awards/prizes/competitions. **Events** *Annual Conference* Thessaloniki (Greece) 2023, *Annual Conference* Ottawa, ON (Canada) 2022, *Annual Conference* 2021, *Annual Conference* Myrtle Beach, SC (USA) 2020, *Annual Conference* Dublin (Ireland) 2019. **Publications** *Negotiation and Conflict Management Research (NCMR) Journal*; *Signal Newsletter.*
Members Academic faculty; professional; student. Members (350) in 62 countries and territories:
Albania, Argentina, Australia, Austria, Barbados, Belgium, Benin, Bermuda, Brazil, Canada, Chile, China, Colombia, Costa Rica, Denmark, Finland, France, Georgia, Germany, Ghana, Greece, Hong Kong, Hungary, India, Ireland, Israel, Italy, Jamaica, Japan, Jordan, Korea Rep, Lebanon, Malaysia, Netherlands, New Zealand, Nigeria, Norway, Pakistan, Peru, Poland, Portugal, Romania, Russia, Saudi Arabia, Singapore, Slovenia, South Africa, Spain, Sweden, Switzerland, Taiwan, Tanzania UR, Thailand, Trinidad-Tobago, Türkiye, UK, United Arab Emirates, USA, Uzbekistan, Vietnam, Virgin Is USA, Zimbabwe. [2019/XD4544/**F**]

♦ International Association of Congress Centres / see International Association of Convention Centres (#11818)

♦ International Association Connecting Technologies for Citizens (INTERACT4C) 11809

Publication Manager 133 avenue du bois des falaises, 78670 Villennes-sur-Seine, France. E-mail: info@interact4c.eu.
URL: http://www.interact4c.eu/

History Registration: RNA, No/ID: W783007149, Start date: 10 Feb 2018, France; EU Transparency Register, No/ID: 303527144692-60, Start date: 17 Nov 2021. **Aims** Facilitate international experts to governments and public administrations; protect security, confidentiality and private data. **Activities** Guidance/assistance/consulting; knowledge management/information dissemination. [2021/XM5212/**D**]

♦ International Association for the Conservation of Animal Breeds in the Danubian Region / see Dunamenti Állatfajták Génmegőrző Nemzetközi Egyesülete (#05146)
♦ International Association for Conservation of Books, Paper and Archival Material / see International Association of Book and Paper Conservators (#11729)

♦ International Association for the Conservation of the Geological Heritage (ProGEO) 11810

Pres c/o Geo Survey, Box 670, SE-751 28 Uppsala, Sweden. E-mail: progeo@progeo.ngo – ewa.glowniak.geo@gmail.com.
URL: http://www.progeo.ngo/

History 1988. June 2021, modifying statutes to expand from a European to an international association. Former names and other names: *European Working Group on Earth Science Conservation* – former (1988 to 1993); *European Association for the Conservation of the Geological Heritage (ProGEO)* – former (1993 to 2021). Registration: No/ID: 817605-8769, Spain. **Aims** Promote a co-ordinated European policy for geoconservation. **Structure** General Assembly; Council; Executive Committee; Regional Working Groups. **Languages** English. **Staff** None. **Finance** Members' dues. **Activities** Events/meetings; politics/policy/regulatory. **Events** *International Symposium* Segovia (Spain) 2021, *International Symposium* Segovia (Spain) 2020, *International Symposium on Conservation of Geoheritage* Checiny (Poland) 2018, *International Symposium on Conservation of Geoheritage* Bari (Italy) 2012, *International conference on geodiversity, natural and cultural heritage of the Kaszuby region* Gdansk (Poland) 2010. **Publications** *Geoheritage* – journal; *ProGEO Newsletter*.
Members Full in 42 countries and territories:
Albania, Argentina, Australia, Belarus, Bosnia-Herzegovina, Brazil, Bulgaria, Croatia, Czechia, Denmark, Estonia, Faeroe Is, Finland, France, Germany, Greece, Hungary, Iran Islamic Rep, Ireland, Italy, Japan, Kazakhstan, Kosovo, Latvia, Lithuania, Morocco, Netherlands, North Macedonia, Norway, Poland, Portugal, Romania, Russia, Serbia, Slovakia, Slovenia, Spain, Sweden, Switzerland, Türkiye, UK, Ukraine.
NGO Relations Member of: *International Union for Conservation of Nature and Natural Resources (IUCN, #15766)*. Affiliated with: *International Union of Geological Sciences (IUGS, #15777)*. Cooperation agreement with: *EuroGeoSurveys (#05686)*. [2022/XD7115/**D**]

♦ International Association for Conservation of Natural Resources and Energy (inactive)

♦ International Association of Constitutional Law (IACL) 11811

Association internationale de droit constitutionnel (AIDC)
Deputy SG c/o Department of Law, School of Business and Law, University of Agder, 4604 Kristiansand, Norway.
SG address not obtained.
URL: http://www.iacl-aidc.org/

History 28 Sep 1981, Belgrade (Serbia). Founded 1981, on signature of the Founding Convention, within the framework of UNESCO. **Aims** Develop a network of constitutionalists from countries throughout the world; provide a forum for exchange of knowledge and information and for development of understanding of constitutional systems; examine and compare common constitutional issues and phenomena; anticipate new ideas and identify approaches which might be taken to them; offer a pool from which teams might be constructed to examine and provide advice on particular issues. **Structure** Congress (every 4 years); Council. Executive Committee; Secretariat, headed by Secretary-General; Commissions (7). **Languages** English, French. **Staff** Voluntary. **Finance** Sources: contributions; members' dues; sponsorship. **Activities** Events/meetings; training/education. **Events** *World Congress of Constitutional Law* Johannesburg (South Africa) 2022, *Quadrennial Congress* Seoul (Korea Rep) 2018, *International Symposium on Korean Public Law* Seoul (Korea Rep) 2017, *Quadrennial Congress* Oslo (Norway) 2014, *Quadrennial Congress* Mexico City (Mexico) 2010. **Publications** *10 ans de l'AIDC*; *5 ans de l'AIDC*. Congress reports.
Members National and regional associations and individuals in 87 countries and territories:
Albania, Algeria, Andorra, Angola, Argentina, Armenia, Australia, Austria, Belarus, Belgium, Bolivia, Bosnia-Herzegovina, Brazil, Bulgaria, Cameroon, Canada, Chile, China, Colombia, Congo DR, Côte d'Ivoire, Croatia, Czechia, Denmark, Ecuador, Egypt, Estonia, Ethiopia, Finland, France, Germany, Greece, Hong Kong, Hungary, India, Iraq, Ireland, Israel, Italy, Japan, Jordan, Kenya, Korea Rep, Kuwait, Lebanon, Lithuania, Luxembourg, Malaysia, Mali, Mauritius, Mexico, Montenegro, Morocco, Mozambique, Nepal, Netherlands, New Zealand, Nigeria, North Macedonia, Norway, Palestine, Paraguay, Peru, Philippines, Poland, Portugal, Romania, Russia, Senegal, Serbia, Sierra Leone, Slovakia, Slovenia, South Africa, Spain, Sri Lanka, Sweden, Switzerland, Taiwan, Tunisia, Türkiye, UK, Ukraine, United Arab Emirates, USA, Venezuela, Zambia.
Included in the above, 1 regional association listed in this Yearbook:
Asociación Latinoamericana de Derecho Constitucional (ALDEC, no recent information).
NGO Relations *African Network of Constitutional Lawyers (ANCL, #00384)*. [2020.07.06/XD1581/**C**]

♦ International Association of Construction, Urbanism, and Environment and Life Style (COBATY International) 11812

Association internationale de la construction, de l'urbanisme et de l'environnement – Internationale Verband des Bauwesens, des Städtebaus, der Umweltplanung und des Lebensbereichs
Address not obtained.
URL: http://www.cobaty-intl.org/

History 1957. **Events** *Congress* Paris (France) 2019, *Congress* Lyon (France) 2015, *Congress* Marseille (France) 2013, *Congress* Tours (France) 2011, *Parcours urbains* Saint-Étienne (France) 2009. **Consultative Status** Consultative status granted from: *Organisation internationale de la Francophonie (OIF, #17809)*. [2018/XD9047/**D**]

♦ International Association of Consultants in Higher Education Institutions (inactive)
♦ International Association of Consultants, Valuators and Analysts / see International Association of Certified Valuation Specialists

♦ International Association of Consulting Actuaries (IACA) 11813

Association internationale des actuaires consultants
Exec Dir c/o International Actuarial Association, 99 Metcalfe Street, Suite 1203, Ottawa ON K1P 6L7, Canada. E-mail: secretariat@actuaries.org.
Chairman address not obtained.
URL: http://www.actuaries.org/

History Founded 13 Jun 1968, Munich (Germany FR). Functions as a section of *International Actuarial Association (IAA, #11586)*. **Aims** Facilitate exchange of views and information among members on matters affecting professional responsibilities. **Structure** Committee. **Languages** English. **Staff** Secretariat provided International Actuarial Association. **Finance** Sources: members' dues. **Events** *International Congress of Actuaries* Tokyo (Japan) 2026, *International Congress of Actuaries* Sydney, NSW (Australia) 2023, *Biennial Conference* Berlin (Germany) 2018, *Biennial Conference* St John's, NL (Canada) 2016, *Colloquium* Sydney, NSW (Australia) 2015. **Publications** Conference reports; professional papers.
Members Individuals (339) in 41 countries and territories:
Australia, Austria, Bahrain, Bangladesh, Brazil, Canada, China, Colombia, Costa Rica, Croatia, Denmark, France, Germany, Ghana, Greece, Hong Kong, India, Indonesia, Ireland, Israel, Italy, Jamaica, Japan, Korea Rep, Kuwait, Lebanon, Malaysia, Mauritius, Mexico, Netherlands, New Zealand, Norway, Pakistan, South Africa, Spain, Sweden, Switzerland, Taiwan, Togo, UK, USA. [2020/XD0197/v/**C**]

♦ International Association for Consumer Law (IACL) 11814

Association internationale de droit de la consommation
Pres Univ of South Africa, Preller St, Muckleneuk, Pretoria, 0002, South Africa. T. +27124298477. E-mail: kellym@unisa.ac.za.
Vice-Pres Univ of Amsterdam, NL-1012 WX, Amsterdam, Netherlands. T. +31205253423.
URL: http://www.iacl.net.au/

History 1997, following a series of conferences. Registered in accordance with Belgian law. **Aims** Develop education and research in the field of consumer law; disseminate on an international level information concerning the rights and policy of consumers. **Structure** General Meeting; Board; Advisory Panel. **Finance** Members' dues. Conference funded by sponsors. **Events** *Conference* Indianapolis, IN (USA) 2019, *Conference* Porto Alegre (Brazil) 2017, *Conference* Amsterdam (Netherlands) 2015, *Conference* Sydney, NSW (Australia) 2013, *Conference* London (UK) 2011. **Publications** *IACL Newsletter*. Conference proceedings.
Members Full: individuals; Associate: organizations and individuals. Members in 21 countries and territories:
Argentina, Australia, Belgium, Brazil, Canada, China, Egypt, Finland, Germany, Hong Kong, Hungary, India, Israel, Japan, Malaysia, Netherlands, New Zealand, Nigeria, South Africa, UK, USA.
NGO Relations *Consumers International (CI, #04773)*. [2019/XD6261/**D**]

♦ International Association of Contact Lens Educators (IACLE) 11815

CEO PMB 172, 3-304 Stone Road West, Guelph ON N1G 4W4, Canada. E-mail: iacle@iacle.org.
Exec Officer address not obtained.
URL: http://www.iacle.org/

History 1979. **Aims** Increase number of qualified contact lens educators and improve quality of contact lens teaching, thereby increasing the number of skilled contact lens practitioners throughout the world and facilitating safe use of contact lenses worldwide, in partnership with Industry. **Structure** General Meeting (annual); Board of Directors; Regional Directors, Executive Managers; Administrators. Membership structured in 3 regional groups. **Languages** Chinese, English, Indonesian, Korean, Portuguese, Spanish. **Finance** Sources: sponsorship. **Activities** Awards/prizes/competitions; events/meetings; training/education. Active in all member countries. **Events** *IACLE Virtual Conference* 2022, *IACLE Virtual Conference* 2021, *IACLE Virtual Conference* 2021, *IACLE Virtual Conference* 2020, *Congress on Contact Less Education* Hyderabad (India) 2017. **Publications** *Member e-Newsletter* (12 a year); *Industry Update e-Newsletter*. Research Update.
Members Individuals (about 800) in over 75 countries. Membership countries not specified. [2022.06.20/XD3302/v/**C**]

♦ International Association of Contemporary History of Europe (#02705)

♦ International Association of Contemporary Mosaicists 11816

Association internationale des mosaïstes contemporains – Associazione Internazionale Mosaicisti Contemporanei (AIMC)
SG Museo d'Arte della Città di Ravenna, Loggetta Lombardesca Via di Roma 13, 48121 Ravenna RA, Italy. T. +39544482766 – +39544215004. Fax +39544215004. E-mail: info@aimcinternational.org.
Pres address not obtained.
URL: http://www.aimcinternational.org/

History 1980, Ravenna (Italy). Previous German title *Internationaler Verband Zeitgenossischer Mosaizisten*. **Aims** Promote contemporary mosaic; coordinate contacts between mosaic artists and professionals in this field of *art*. **Structure** Assembly (at least once a year); Executive Council; President. **Languages** English, Italian. **Staff** Voluntary. **Finance** Sources: members' dues. **Activities** Awards/prizes/competitions; events/meetings. **Events** *Biennial Congress* Ravenna (Italy) 2022, *Biennial Congress* Monreale (Italy) 2020, *Biennial Congress* Paray-le-Monial (France) / Lyon (France) 2018, *Biennial Congress* Spilimbergo (Italy) 2016, *Biennial Congress* Vienna (Austria) 2014. **Publications** *AIMC Newsletter* (12 a year). Books; catalogues.
Members Individual; Corporate; Student. Members (253) in 45 countries and territories:
Albania, Argentina, Australia, Austria, Belgium, Brazil, Bulgaria, Canada, China, Croatia, Curaçao, Czechia, Denmark, Egypt, Estonia, France, Germany, Greece, Iran Islamic Rep, Israel, Italy, Japan, Korea Rep, Kuwait, Lithuania, Mexico, Netherlands, New Zealand, North Macedonia, Norway, Peru, Russia, San Marino, Serbia, Slovenia, Spain, Sweden, Switzerland, Taiwan, Türkiye, UK, Ukraine, United Arab Emirates, Uruguay, USA. [2020.03.04/XD6380/**C**]

♦ International Association for Continuing Education and Training (internationally oriented national body)

♦ International Association for Continuing Engineering Education (IACEE) 11817

SG GIT-GLC, 84 Fifth St NW, Atlanta GA 30308-1031, USA. T. +14048949658. E-mail: info@iacee.org.
URL: http://www.iacee.org/

History 17 May 1989, Beijing (China). Founded at 4th World Conference on Continuing Engineering Education, when bylaws were adopted. Headquarters originally based in Helsinki (Finland); moved to Washington DC (USA), 2001; since 2010, based in Atlanta GA (USA). **Aims** Provide a forum for organizations and providers of continuing engineering education to share lessons learned and address emerging issues through exchange of ideas. **Structure** General Membership Meeting (every 2 years, usually at World Conference); Council; Executive Committee. **Languages** English. **Staff** 0.33 FTE, paid. **Finance** Sources: members' dues. **Activities** Events/meetings; knowledge management/information dissemination; training/education. **Events** *World Conference on Continuing Engineering Education* Buffalo, NY (USA) 2022, *World Conference on Continuing Engineering Education* Trondheim (Norway) 2021, *World Conference on Continuing Engineering Education* Trondheim (Norway) 2020, *World Conference on Continuing Engineering Education* Monterrey (Mexico) 2018, *World Conference on Continuing Engineering Education* Porto (Portugal) 2016. **Publications** *IACEE Newsletter* (3-4 a year). *Tools for Effective Dissemination – A Guide to the Dissemination of the Results of International Educational Projects*.
Members Institutional (59) Regional Leader Organizations (3); Professional Organizations and Societies (5); Industrial Organizations and Companies (12); Academic Institutions and Other Coordinators and Providers of CEE (65). Individuals (137). Individuals in 38 countries:
Argentina, Australia, Austria, Belgium, Brazil, Canada, China, Colombia, Denmark, Estonia, Finland, Germany, Ghana, Guatemala, Guyana, Hungary, India, Israel, Japan, Mexico, Netherlands, Nigeria, Norway, Oman, Philippines, Poland, Portugal, Qatar, Russia, Singapore, Slovakia, Spain, Sweden, Switzerland, Thailand, Türkiye, UK, USA.
Institutional members include the following 3 organizations listed in this Yearbook:
African Network of Scientific and Technological Institutions (ANSTI, #00395); *American Society for Engineering Education (ASEE, #00790)*; *Société européenne pour la formation des ingénieurs (SEFI, #19462)*.
Consultative Status Consultative status granted from: *ECOSOC (#05331)* (Ros C); *UNESCO (#20322)* (Consultative Status); *UNIDO (#20336)*. [2021/XD2415/y/**B**]

♦ International Association for Contract and Commercial Management / see World Commerce and Contracting (#21284)
♦ International Association of Convention Bureaus / see Destinations International (#05046)

♦ International Association of Convention Centres (AIPC) 11818

CEO Rue du Luxembourg 22-24, 1000 Brussels, Belgium. T. +3227616670. E-mail: secretariat@aipc.org.
URL: http://www.aipc.org/

History 9 Aug 1958, Liège (Belgium). Statutes adopted 7 Feb 1959, Düsseldorf (Germany FR). Modified 1961, 1965, 1967, 1986, 1996, 2001, 2003, 2012. Former names and other names: *International Association of Congress Centres* – former; *Association internationale des palais de congrès (AIPC)* – former; *Internationaler Verband der Kongresszentren* – former. Registration: BCE, No/ID: 0866143583, Start date: 1 Jun 2004, Belgium. **Aims** Encourage, support and recognize excellence in convention center management, based on the diverse experience and expertise of its international membership. **Structure** General Assembly (annual); Board of Directors. **Languages** English. **Staff** 1.00 FTE, paid. **Finance** Sources: members' dues. **Activities** Advocacy/lobbying/activism; networking/liaising; research/documentation; standards/guidelines; training/education. **Events** *Annual Conference* Budapest (Hungary) 2022, *Sales and Marketing Summit* Frankfurt-Main (Germany) 2022, *Annual Seminar* La Hulpe (Belgium) 2022, *Annual Conference* Lausanne (Switzerland) 2021, *Annual Conference* Paris (France) 2020. **Publications** *AIPC Communiqué* (4 a year). Research reports; surveys; meeting proceedings; guides. **Members** Congress centres (160) with active involvement of over 900 management-level professionals in 60 countries. Membership countries not specified. **NGO Relations** Member of (2): *Joint Meetings Industry Council (JMIC, #16140)*; *Union of International Associations (UIA, #20414)*. [2022.06.28/XC1268/**C**]

♦ International Association of Convention and Visitor Bureaus / see Destinations International (#05046)

♦ International Association for Convergence Science and Technology (IACST) 11819

Pres Room 536, Intl Education Blg, Silla Univ, 700-Bunkil 140, BaekyangDaero, Busan 46958, Korea Rep. T. +82519995066.
URL: http://iacst.org/

Aims Promote the advancement in convergence science and technology. **Structure** Committee; Board of Directors. **Finance** Members' dues. **Activities** Events/meetings; training/education; knowledge management/information dissemination. **Events** *International Conference on Cultural Technology* Pattaya (Thailand) 2019, *International Conference on Cultural Technology* Shaoxing (China) 2018, *International Symposium on Culture Technology* Busan (Korea Rep) 2017, *International Conference on Cultural Technology* Chiang Mai (Thailand) 2017, *International Symposium on Cultural Technology* Busan (Korea Rep) 2016. **Publications** *International Journal of Culture Technology*. [2019/XM6629/**D**]

♦ International Association for Cooperation and Development in Southern Africa (no recent information)
♦ International Association of Cooperative Banks / see International Cooperative Banking Association (#12945)
♦ International Association for the Coordination of Psychiatry and Psychological Methods (inactive)

♦ International Association for Coptic Studies (IACS) 11820

Association internationale des études coptes

Sec Inst für Ägyptologie und Koptologie, Schlaunstrasse 2, 48143 Münster, Germany. T. +492518324940 – +492518324537. Fax +492518329933. E-mail: emmstel@uni-muenster.de.
URL: http://www.cmcl.it/~iacs/

History Founded 1976, Cairo (Egypt), during the Colloquium on the Future of Coptic Studies, following on the work of the (Egyptian) 'Société d'Archéologie Copte' which was founded in 1934 as 'Association des Amis des Eglises et de l'Art Coptes', and 'Nag Hammadi Codices Editing Project'. **Aims** Encourage and contribute to the progress of all aspects of Coptic studies; promote international cooperation; advance information dissemination; facilitate full access to and the rapid publication of source materials; identify priorities for research. **Structure** Congress (every 4 years); Board. **Languages** English, French, German, Italian. **Staff** None. **Finance** Members' dues. Congress registration fees. **Activities** *'Addition of Coptic to Unicode'* – project to design a standard Coptic computer font based on Unicode. **Events** *Quadrennial Congress* Brussels (Belgium) 2022, *Quadrennial Congress* Brussels (Belgium) 2020, *Quadrennial Congress* Claremont, CA (USA) 2016, *Quadrennial Congress* Rome (Italy) 2012, *Quadrennial Congress* Cairo (Egypt) 2008. **Publications** *IACS Newsletter* (annual) in English; *Journal of Coptic Studies* (annual). *International Directory of Institutions Holding Collections of Coptic Antiquities outside of Egypt* (1990). **Information Services** *COPTIST* – electronic discussion group.
Members Organizations in 12 countries:
Belgium, Canada, Egypt, France, Germany, Ireland, Israel, Italy, Netherlands, Russia, UK, USA.
Individuals in 28 countries:
Argentina, Australia, Austria, Belgium, Canada, China, Czechia, Denmark, Egypt, Finland, France, Germany, Greece, Hungary, Ireland, Israel, Italy, Japan, Netherlands, Nigeria, Norway, Poland, Portugal, Spain, Sweden, Switzerland, UK, USA.
[2017.11.27/XD1795/**D**]

♦ International Association of Coroners and Medical Examiners (internationally oriented national body)
♦ International Association for Correctional and Forensic Psychology (internationally oriented national body)
♦ International Association of Costume (internationally oriented national body)

♦ International Association for Counselling (IAC) 11821

CEO c/o Dept Counselling, Univ of Malta, Achille Ferris Street, Msida, MSD 2080, Malta.
URL: http://www.iac-irtac.org/

History 1966, Neuchâtel (Switzerland). Former names and other names: *International Round Table of Educational Counselling and Vocational Guidance* – former (1966); *Table ronde internationale pour l'orientation scolaire et la guidance professionnelle* – former (1966); *International Round Table for the Advancement of Counselling (IRTAC)* – former; *Table ronde internationale pour le développement de l'orientation (TRIDO)* – former; *Mesa Redonda Internacional para el Desarrollo de la Orientación* – former. Registration: Start date: 13 Apr 1971, Belgium. **Aims** Serve as an international leader and catalyst for counsellors and counselling associations by advancing culturally relevant counselling practice, research and policy to promote wellbeing, respect, social justice and peace worldwide. **Structure** General Assembly (every 2 years); Executive Council. **Languages** English, French. **Staff** Voluntary. **Finance** Members' dues. **Activities** Guidance/assistance/consulting; events/meetings; advocacy/lobbying/activism; certification/accreditation. **Events** *International Counselling Convention (ICC)* Kuching (Malaysia) 2022, *International Counselling Convention (ICC)* Kuching (Malaysia) 2021, *International Counselling Convention (ICC)* Kuching (Malaysia) 2020, *Conference* Moncton, NB (Canada) 2019, *Conference* Rome (Italy) 2018. **Publications** *International Journal for the Advancement of Counselling*. Newsletters.
Members Individuals in 98 countries and territories:
Afghanistan, Algeria, Angola, Argentina, Australia, Austria, Bangladesh, Barbados, Belgium, Benin, Bosnia-Herzegovina, Botswana, Brazil, Bulgaria, Canada, Chad, China, Colombia, Costa Rica, Côte d'Ivoire, Cyprus, Czechia, Denmark, Egypt, Estonia, Ethiopia, Fiji, Finland, France, Gabon, Germany, Ghana, Greece, Grenada, Hong Kong, Hungary, Iceland, India, Indonesia, Iran Islamic Rep, Iraq, Ireland, Israel, Italy, Jamaica, Japan, Jordan, Kenya, Kuwait, Lebanon, Lesotho, Liberia, Lithuania, Luxembourg, Malawi, Malaysia, Mali, Malta, Mauritius, Mexico, Moldova, Morocco, Netherlands, New Zealand, Nigeria, Norway, Pakistan, Philippines, Poland, Portugal, Puerto Rico, Romania, Russia, Saudi Arabia, Serbia, Sierra Leone, Singapore, Slovakia, Slovenia, South Africa, Spain, Sri Lanka, Sudan, Sweden, Switzerland, Tanzania UR, Thailand, Trinidad-Tobago, Tunisia, Türkiye, Uganda, UK, United Arab Emirates, USA, Venezuela, Vietnam, Yemen, Zambia.
Consultative Status Consultative status granted from: *ECOSOC (#05331)* (Ros C); *UNESCO (#20322)* (Consultative Status); *ILO (#11123)* (Special List); *UNICEF (#20332)*. **NGO Relations** Member of: *Conference of Non-Governmental Organizations in Consultative Relationship with the United Nations (CONGO, #04635)*; *NGO Committee on the Status of Women, Geneva (#17117)*; *Committee of NGOs on Human Rights, Geneva (#04275)*; *Vienna NGO Committee on the Family (#20774)*. Joint committee with: *International Association for Educational and Vocational Guidance (IAEVG, #11862)*. [2021/XD2423/v/**F**]

♦ International Association of Counterterrorism and Security Professionals (internationally oriented national body)

♦ International Association of Couple and Family Psychoanalysis (IACFP) 11822

Association Internationale de Psychanalyse de Couple et de Famille (AIPCF) – Asociación Internacional de Psicoanalisis de Pareja y Familia (AIPPF)

SG 24 rue Auguste Comte, 69002 Lyon, France. E-mail: contact@aipcf.net.
URL: http://aipcf.net/

History Founded Aug 2006, Montréal QC (Canada). Registered in accordance with French law, Nov 2006. **Aims** Foster and develop practices and theories of couple and family psychoanalysis. **Structure** General Assembly; Board of Directors; Executive Committee; Scientific Council. **Finance** Sources: members' dues. **Activities** Events/meetings; research/documentation. **Events** *Congress* Lyon (France) 2022, *Congress* Lyon (France) 2020, *Congress* Lyon (France) 2018, *Congress* Sao Paulo (Brazil) 2016, *Congress* Bordeaux (France) 2014. **Publications** *AIPCF Newsletter*, *International Review of Couple and Family Psychoanalysis*. **Members** Individuals; institutions. Membership countries not specified. [2018/XM7379/**C**]

♦ International Association for Court Administration (internationally oriented national body)
♦ International Association of Crafts and Small and Medium-Sized Enterprises (inactive)
♦ International Association for Crafts and the Teaching of Art (inactive)

♦ International Association of Craniofacial Identification (IACI) 11823

Sec address not obtained. E-mail: committee.iaci@gmail.com.
URL: http://www.craniofacial-id.org/

History 1988, Kiel (Germany), as *International Craniofacial Identification Group (CIG)*. Present name adopted, 1992. **Activities** Biennial meeting or congress. **Events** *Meeting* Liverpool (UK) 2022, *Meeting* Baton Rouge, LA (USA) 2019, *Meeting* Brisbane, QLD (Australia) 2017, *Meeting* Tokyo (Japan) 2015, *Meeting* South Africa 2013. [2017/XN9418/**C**]

♦ International Association for Creation and Training (internationally oriented national body)
♦ International Association of Creativity and Innovation (unconfirmed)

♦ International Association of Credit Portfolio Managers (IACPM) ... 11824

Exec Dir 82 Nassau St, Ste 602, New York NY 10038, USA. T. +16465830839. E-mail: somlok@iacpm.org – dara@iacpm.org.
Visiting address 120 Broadway, 2nd Fl, New York NY 10271, USA.
URL: http://www.iacpm.org/

History 2001. EU Transparency Register: 817569436762-48. **Aims** Further understanding and management by *financial* institutions of their credit exposures; create a forum for the discussion of issues of relevance to participants in credit markets. **Structure** Board of Directors; Advisory Council. **Finance** Members' dues. **Activities** Events/meetings; advocacy/lobbying/activism; research/documentation. **Events** *Annual Fall Conference* Chicago, IL (USA) 2023, *Annual Spring Conference* The Hague (Netherlands) 2023, *Annual Spring Conference* Madrid (Spain) 2022, *Annual Risk Management Conference* Singapore (Singapore) 2022, *Annual Fall Conference* Washington, DC (USA) 2022.
Members Banks, including 7 listed in this Yearbook:
African Development Bank (ADB, #00283); *African Export-Import Bank (Afreximbank, #00305)*; *Asian Development Bank (ADB, #01422)*; *European Bank for Reconstruction and Development (EBRD, #06315)*; *European Investment Bank (EIB, #07599)*; *European Investment Fund (EIF, #07601)*; *Inter-American Development Bank (IDB, #11427)*. [2019/XD8869/**D**]

♦ International Association of Crime Victim Compensation Boards (inactive)

♦ International Association of Crime Writers (IACW) 11825

Association internationale des auteurs de romans policiers – Asociación Internacional de Escritores Policiacos (AIEP)

Pres address not obtained. E-mail: info@crimewritersna.org.
North American Branch 328 Eighth Ave, Suite 114, New York NY 10001, USA. E-mail: info@crimewritersna.org.
URL: http://www.iacw.org/

History 1986. Also referred to in French as *Association internationale du roman policier*. **Aims** Encourage crime writing, in all its forms; promote the translation of crime writing in all languages. **Structure** Worldwide officers: President, 4 Regional Vice-Presidents. National branches (24), each headed by President. **Activities** Organizes international conference of crime writers. Instrumental in setting up *Crime Writers of Scandinavia (CWS, #04955)*. **Events** *Annual Meeting* Oxford (UK) 2013, *Annual Meeting* Toronto, ON (Canada) 2012, *Annual meeting* Frontignan la Peyrade (France) 2008, *Annual Meeting* Berlin (Germany) 2007, *Annual meeting* Amsterdam (Netherlands) 2004. **Publications** *Detective* (4 a year) in Russian; *Enigma* (4 a year) in Spanish.
Members Professional crime writers in 23 countries:
Argentina, Austria, Bulgaria, Canada, Chile, Cuba, Czechia, Denmark, Estonia, Finland, France, Germany, Hungary, Italy, Japan, Mexico, Norway, Poland, Serbia, Spain, Uruguay, USA, Vietnam.
Members also in the former USSR; countries not specified. [2022/XD1304/v/**C**]

♦ International Association for Criminal Identification / see International Association for Identification
♦ International Association of Critical Infrastructure Protection Professionals / see International Association of CIP Professionals (#11772)

♦ International Association for Critical Realism (IACR) 11826

Gen Sec Dept of Education, Norges Arktiske Universitet, Teorifagbygget hus 1, Office TEO H1-1-560, 9037 Tromsø, Norway. T. +4777645254.
Pres KCL School of Law, Strand, London, WC2R 2LS, UK.
URL: http://www.criticalrealismblog.blogspot.be/

History Founded 1997, on the initiative of the (UK) Centre for Critical Realism (CCR). **Aims** Promote the study of realist philosophy and social theory. **Structure** Council. **Languages** English. **Events** *Annual Conference* The Hague (Netherlands) 2022, *Annual Conference* South Africa 2021, *Annual Conference* Warsaw (Poland) 2020, *Annual Conference* Southampton (UK) 2019, *Annual Conference* Lillehammer (Norway) 2018. **Publications** *Journal of Critical Realism* (2 a year).
Members Individuals. Members in 10 countries:
Botswana, Finland, India, Ireland, Netherlands, Norway, Portugal, Sweden, UK, USA. [2015/XD8361/v/**D**]

♦ International Association for Cross-Cultural Communication (inactive)

♦ International Association of Cross-Cultural Competence and Management (IACCM) 11827

SG WU Vienna (Vienna Univ of Economics and Business), Welthandelsplatz 1 D2-B, 1020 Vienna, Austria. T. +431313364553. Fax +43131336724. E-mail: iaccm@wu.ac.at – barbara.covarrubias@sietar.at.
URL: http://www.wu.ac.at/iaccm/

History 1997. **Aims** Establish a network of researchers and practitioners interested in and concerned with cross-cultural subjects. **Structure** Council. **Finance** Members' dues. **Events** *Conference* Paris (France) 2019, *Annual Conference* Vienna (Austria) 2015, *Annual Conference* Warwick (UK) 2014, *Annual Conference / Conference* Rotterdam (Netherlands) 2013, *Annual Conference / Conference* Naples (Italy) 2012. **Publications** *European Journal of Cross-Cultural Competence and Management (EJCCM)*. **Members** Full in 24 countries. Membership countries not specified. [2019.10.24/XJ1339/**E**]

♦ International Association for Cross-Cultural Psychology (IACCP) .. 11828

SG Inst of Cognitive Neuroscience and Psychology, Hungarian Ac of Sciences, Magyar Tudósk krt 2, Budapest 1117, Hungary. T. +36703138718.
Pres Jacobs Univ Bremen, Campus Ring 1, 28759 Bremen, Germany. T. +494212003401. Fax +494212003303.
URL: http://www.iaccp.org/

History 1 Mar 1972, Hong Kong. Constitution adopted 29 Jul 1978, Munich (Germany FR); corrected and updated Jan 1983; amended Jul 1993; revised Jul 2011. **Aims** Facilitate communication among cross-cultural psychologists; further advancement of research and methodology in cross-cultural psychology and in all branches of psychology and related disciplines worldwide; test more effectively the universal validity of psychological theories; evolve guidelines for ethical standards in cross-cultural research. **Structure** General Meeting (every 2 years); Regional Representatives; Regional and National Committees; Standing Committees; International Conference (every 2 years). **Languages** English. **Staff** 1.00 FTE, paid. **Finance** Sources: members' dues. Other sources: grants; revenues and royalties. **Activities** Awards/prizes/competitions; events/meetings; networking/liaising. **Events** *International Conference* Prague (Czechia) 2022, *Biennial International Conference* Prague (Czech Rep) 2021, *Biennial International Conference* Olomouc (Czechia) 2020, *Latin American Regional Conference* San José (Costa Rica) 2019, *Biennial International Conference* Guelph, ON (Canada) 2018. **Publications** *Journal of Cross-Cultural Psychology (JCCP)* (8 a year); *Directory of Cross-Cultural Research and Researchers*; *Online Readings in Psychology and Culture*. Conference proceedings.
Members Individuals (over 540): Honorary Fellow; Member; National Associations. Members in 67 countries and territories:
Argentina, Australia, Austria, Bangladesh, Belgium, Brazil, Bulgaria, Cameroon, Canada, Chile, China, Colombia, Costa Rica, Croatia, Denmark, Egypt, Estonia, Finland, France, Germany, Ghana, Greece, Hong Kong, Hungary, India, Indonesia, Iran Islamic Rep, Israel, Italy, Jamaica, Japan, Jordan, Kenya, Korea Rep, Libya, Lithuania, Malaysia, Mexico, Namibia, Nepal, Netherlands, New Zealand, Nigeria, Norway, Pakistan, Peru, Philippines, Poland, Portugal, Romania, Saudi Arabia, Singapore, Slovakia, Slovenia, South Africa, Spain, Sweden, Switzerland, Taiwan, Thailand, Trinidad-Tobago, Türkiye, UK, USA, Venezuela, Vietnam, Zimbabwe.
NGO Relations Member of: *International Union of Psychological Science (IUPsyS, #15807)*.
[2019.09.26/XB4619/**B**]

♦ International Association of Cryospheric Sciences (IACS) 11829

SG Geosciences – Crew Bldg, King's Buildings, Alexander Crum Brown Road, Edinburgh, EH9 3FF, UK.
URL: http://www.cryosphericsciences.org/

History 13 Jul 2007, Perugia (Italy). Founded as a constituent association of *International Union of Geodesy and Geophysics (IUGG, #15776)*. Replaces *IUGG Union Commission for the Cryospheric Sciences (IUGG CCS, inactive)*. **Aims** Promote studies and research of cryospheric subsystems of the Earth solar systems; provide opportunities for international exchange on cryospheric research; facilitate standardization of measurements on cryospheric systems and archiving and publication of cryospheric data; promote education and public awareness on the cryosphere. **Structure** Assembly; Bureau; Divisions (5); Standing Groups (3); Working Groups. **Languages** English. **Staff** Voluntary. **Finance** Annual funding allocation from *International Union of Geodesy and Geophysics (IUGG, #15776)*; small additional donations. **Events** *Joint Assembly* Busan (Korea Rep) 2025, *Joint Assembly* Busan (Korea Rep) 2021, *Workshop on Cryospheric Changes and their Regional and Global Impacts* Dunhuang (China) 2018, *Assembly* Auckland (New Zealand) 2017, *International Symposium on the Cryosphere in a Changing Climate* Wellington (New Zealand) 2017. **Publications** Service: *World Glacier Monitoring Service (WGMS, #21539)*. [2021/XM3254/**D**]

♦ International Association for Cryptologic Research (IACR) 11830

Sec c/o NXP Semiconductors, Interleuvenlaan 80, 3001 Leuven, Belgium.
URL: http://www.iacr.org/

History 1983. **Aims** Further research in cryptology and related fields. **Structure** Elected Officers: President; Vice-President; Secretary; Treasurer. Elected Directors (9). Appointed Officers: Membership Secretary; Communications Secretary. **Languages** English. **Activities** Events/meetings. **Events** *Public Key Cryptography Conference* Atlanta, GA (USA) 2023, *International Conference on Fast Software Encryption* Beijing (China) 2023, *Eurocrypt – International Conference on the Theory and Applications of Cryptographic Techniques* Lyon (France) 2023, *CRYPTO: Annual International Cryptology Conference* Santa Barbara, CA (USA) 2023, *Real World Crypto Symposium* Tokyo (Japan) 2023. **Publications** *Journal of Cryptology*. **Members** Membership countries not specified. [2022/XD5128/**D**]

♦ International Association for Crystal Growth / see International Organization for Crystal Growth (#14443)
♦ International Association for Cultivated Plant Taxonomy (inactive)
♦ International Association for Cultural Freedom (inactive)
♦ International Association for Customs Duty Reforms (inactive)

♦ International Association of Customs Museums (IACM) 11831

Association internationale des musées des douanes (AIMD)

Pres Belasting and Douane Museum, Parklaan 14-16, 3016 BB Rotterdam, Netherlands.
Sec Customs Natl Museum, 1 quai Douane, 33000 Bordeaux, France. E-mail: communication@musee-douanes.fr.
URL: http://www.customsmuseums.org/

History 1993, Denmark. **Aims** Promote collection, preservation, documentation and display of customs artefacts. **Structure** General Assembly (annual). **Languages** English, French. **Events** *Conference* Hamburg (Germany) 2020, *Conference* Luxembourg (Luxembourg) 2019, *Conference* Vilnius (Lithuania) 2018, *Conference* Lugano (Switzerland) 2017, *Conference* Vienna (Austria) 2016. **Publications** *IACM Newsletter* in English.
Members Museums in 23 countries:
Austria, Azerbaijan, Belgium, China, Czechia, Finland, France, Germany, Hungary, Iceland, Ireland, Italy, Korea Rep, Lithuania, Luxembourg, Netherlands, Norway, Portugal, Slovakia, Sweden, Switzerland, UK, USA.
NGO Relations Member of (1): *International Council of Museums (ICOM, #13051)*. [2021.04.12/XD8949/**D**]

♦ International Association for Cyanophyte Research (inactive)
♦ International Association of Cybercrime Prevention (#02714)
♦ International Association for Cybernetics (inactive)

♦ International Association of CyberPsychology, Training, and Rehabilitation (IACToR) 11832

SG c/o VRMC Scripps Campus, 9834 Genesee Ave, Ste 427, La Jolla CA 92037, USA. E-mail: frontoffice@vrphobia.com.
Sec/Treasurer 6540 Lusk Blvd, Ste C115, San Diego CA 92121, USA.
URL: http://iactor.ning.com/

Aims Bring together top researchers, policy makers, funders, decision-makers and clinicians, pooling collective knowledge to improve the quality, affordability, and availability of existing healthcare. **Structure** Managing Board, comprising President, Vice President, Secretary General, Treasurer, Secretary and 5 members. **Events** *Annual Conference* Brussels (Belgium) 2013, *Annual Conference* Brussels (Belgium) 2012.
Members Individuals in 49 countries and territories:
Argentina, Australia, Austria, Belgium, Brazil, Bulgaria, Canada, Chile, China, Croatia, Cuba, Denmark, Finland, Georgia, Germany, Greece, Hong Kong, Hungary, India, Iran Islamic Rep, Ireland, Israel, Italy, Japan, Korea Rep, Luxembourg, Malaysia, Mexico, Netherlands, New Zealand, Norway, Pakistan, Peru, Poland, Portugal, Puerto Rico, Romania, Russia, Serbia, Spain, Sweden, Switzerland, Taiwan, Türkiye, UK, Ukraine, USA, Uzbekistan, Venezuela.
NGO Relations *EuroXR (#09197)*; *International Society for Telemedicine and e-Health (ISfTeH, #15504)*. [2019/XJ6854/v/**C**]

♦ International Association of Cycling Journalists (#02708)
♦ International Association of Cystic Fibrosis Adults (inactive)

♦ International Association for Dance Medicine and Science (IADMS) 11833

Exec Dir 13918 E Mississippi Ave, Ste 61846, Aurora CO 80012, USA. E-mail: research@iadms.org – support@iadms.org.
URL: http://www.iadms.org/

History 1990. Registration: 501(c)3, Start date: 1996, USA. **Aims** Enhance health, well-being, training and performance in dance by cultivating medical, scientific and educational excellence. **Structure** Officers: President; Vice-President/President-Elect; Treasurer; Past President. Committees (4): Media; Development; Education; Research. **Languages** English. **Staff** 2.00 FTE, paid. **Events** *Annual Conference* Columbus, OH (USA) 2023, *Annual Conference* Limerick (Ireland) 2022, *Annual Meeting* Denver, CO (USA) 2021, *Annual Meeting* Chiba (Japan) 2020, *Annual Meeting* Montréal, QC (Canada) 2019. **Publications** *IADMS Newsletter* (4 a year); *IADMS Bulletin*; *Journal of Dance Medicine and Science*. *Annual Meeting Proceedings and Abstract Books*. **Members** Individuals (over 1,400) in over 40 countries. Membership countries not specified. [2022/XD7343/**D**]

♦ International Association for Danube Research 11834

Internationale Arbeitsgemeinschaft Donauforschung (IAD)

Main Office c/o IHG, Gregor-Mendel-Str 33, 1180 Vienna, Austria. E-mail: office@oen-iad.org.
URL: https://www.oen-iad.org/

History 1956. Incorporated, 1959, as a section of *International Society of Limnology (#15232)*. Registered in accordance with Austrian law. **Aims** Research the Danube *river* basin, by establishing *environmental* sciences networks, promoting multidisciplinary research and coordinating scientific data; promote and coordinate activities in the fields of limnology, basin management and sustainable development in the Danube river *basin*. **Structure** Praesidium, comprising President, General Secretary and Conference President. National committees (12), each with one country representative. Permanent working groups (12). **Languages** English. **Staff** Voluntary. **Finance** Members' dues. Other sources: government contributions; private sponsorship. Budget (annual): euro 30,000. **Activities** Permanent working groups (12): Chemistry/Physics; Biotic Processes; Microbiology/Hygiene; Phytoplankton/Phytobentos; Macrophytes; Floodplain-Ecology; Zooplankton/Zoobenthos; Fish Biology/Fishery; Saprobiology; Ecotoxicology; Delta/Fore-Delta; Sustainable Development and Public Participation. Key initiatives on a Sturgeon Action Plan; pilot studies on river morphology; integrated scientific cooperation in the Mures catchment. **Events** *The Danube and Black Sea region – unique environment and human well being under conditions of global change* Sofia (Bulgaria) 2014, *Conference* Szentendre (Hungary) 2012, *Conference* Dresden (Germany) 2010, *Interfacing the past and the futur of ecology and water management in a large European river* Vienna (Austria) 2006, *Conference* Novi Sad (Serbia-Montenegro) 2004. **Publications** *Danube News* in English – bulletin. *Large Rivers* – series; *Limnologische Berichte Donau* – series. *Bibliographie der Donau* (1986); *Limnologie der Donau* (1967); *Ergebnisse der Donau-Forschung* – 4 vols to date. Monographs; conference proceedings.
Members Bodies connected by tributaries with the Danube in 12 countries:
Austria, Bulgaria, Croatia, Czechia, Germany, Hungary, Moldova, Romania, Serbia, Slovakia, Switzerland, Ukraine.
Individuals, mainly from Danube and Blac Sea Region countries. Membership countries not specified.
IGO Relations Observer status with *International Commission for the Protection of the Danube River (ICPDR, #12720)*. [2018/XE9441/**E**]

♦ International Association of Dealers in Ancient Art (IADAA) 11835

Chairman c/o Archea Ancien Art, Jacob Marisstraat 59, 1017 DC Amsterdam, Netherlands. E-mail: chairman@iadaa.org.
URL: http://www.iadaa.org/

History 1993, London (UK). Registration: Swiss Civil Code, Switzerland. **Aims** Encourage study of and interest in ancient art; encourage protection and preservation of ancient sites; in particular, address issues concerning works of ancient art from Mediterranean civilizations and other civilizations directly in contact with them; encourage contacts among *museums*, *archaeologists*, *collectors* and the trade and with intergovernmental and international non-governmental organizations. **Structure** General Assembly (annual); Administrative Board; Membership Committee; Ethics Committee; Special Commissions. **Languages** English, German. **Finance** Sources: members' dues. Extraordinary fees; voluntary payments. **Activities** Guidance/assistance/consulting; knowledge management/information dissemination; networking/liaising. Subscribes to the view put forward in the preamble to *Convention for the Protection of Cultural Property in the Event of Armed Conflict (The Hague Convention, 1954, 1954)* that "damage to cultural property belonging to any people whatsoever means damage to cultural heritage of all mankind". In this light, organizes mutual assistance between dealers in works of ancient art and official institutions by communicating to members the information needed to apply strictly to the IADAA Code of Ethics and Practice. **Events** *Annual Symposium* New York, NY (USA) 1998.
Members Individuals in 8 countries:
Belgium, France, Germany, Israel, Netherlands, Switzerland, UK, USA.
NGO Relations Negotiating membership of: *International Confederation of Art Dealers (#12848)*. [2022.02.15/XD4976/v/**D**]

♦ International Association for the Defence of Artists (inactive)
♦ International Association for the Defence of Menaced Languages and Cultures / see Association pour les Langues et Cultures Européennes Menacées (#02782)
♦ International Association for the Defence of Religious Liberty (#02681)
♦ International Association of the Deinking Industry (#13233)

♦ International Association for Democracy in Africa 11836

Association internationale pour la démocratie en Afrique (AID-Afrique)

Contact Cocody Lycée Technique, 216 Logements, en face du Groupe scolaire SAFAK, Rue B52, Bât O2 – 1er étage – Porte 218, BP 803, Abidjan 08, Côte d'Ivoire. T. +22522440050. Fax +22507075983. E-mail: kaudjhisoffoumou@yahoo.fr.

History Founded 16 Aug 1993, Atlanta GA (USA), at constitutive congress, by African participants at a seminar organized by *United States Agency for International Development (USAID)*, when statutes were adopted. Internal rules adopted 14 Oct 1993. Registered in accordance with the law of Niger, 7 Jan 1994. **Aims** Defend and promote: democracy and human rights in a governance society for sustainable development in Africa; government by the majority; respect of human, minority and individual rights and the right to differ; responsible government for just and transparent management of public affairs; people's sovereignty, freedom of the press and other freedoms to counterbalance other powers; independence of the judicial system and an acute sense of its responsibilities by the citizen; monitor democracy and the achievement of the rule of law in Africa. **Structure** Congress (every 3 years); International Executive Bureau of 9 members; Monitoring Committee (meets every 3 years before Congress), consisting of President and 2 Assessors; National Chapters; Committees. **Languages** French. **Finance** Members' dues. **Activities** Advocacy/lobbying/activism; training/education; events/meetings; networking/liaising; research/documentation; projects/programmes; knowledge management/information dissemination. Acts as observer to elections. **Events** *Conference* Agboville (Côte d'Ivoire) 1997, *Human rights, democracy and governance* Abidjan (Côte d'Ivoire) 1996, *La formation des Elus* Abidjan (Côte d'Ivoire) 1996, *Le code électoral en régime de démocratie multipartite* Conakry (Guinea) 1996, *Une constitution en régime de démocratie multipartite* Niamey (Niger) 1995. **Publications** Papers; articles; communications; press statements; declarations; conference proceedings.
Members National chapters (of at least 15 individuals) in 13 countries:
Benin, Burkina Faso, Cape Verde, Central African Rep, Chad, Congo Brazzaville, Congo DR, Côte d'Ivoire, Gabon, Mauritania, Niger, Senegal, Togo.
Consultative Status Consultative status granted from: *African Commission on Human and Peoples' Rights (ACHPR, #00255)* (Observer); *ECOSOC (#05331)* (Special). **NGO Relations** Member of: *EarthAction (EA, #05159)*. Supports: *Global Call for Action Against Poverty (GCAP, #10263)*. [2016.09.07/XD4118/v/**D**]

♦ International Association of Democratic Lawyers (IADL) 11837

Association internationale des juristes démocrates (AIJD) – Asociación Internacional de Juristas Demócratas – Internationale Vereinigung Demokratischer Juristen – Mezdunarodnaja Associacija Juristov-Demokratov

SG Rue Brialmont 21, 1210 Brussels, Belgium. T. +3222233310. E-mail: info@iadllaw.org.
Pres Montague Terrace 3, Apt 2, Brooklyn NY 11201, USA. T. +12124738700. Fax +12124738705.
URL: https://iadllaw.org/

History Oct 1946, Paris (France). Statutes most recently amended at 15th Congress, Apr 2001, Havana (Cuba). **Aims** Facilitate contact and exchange of views between and among lawyers and lawyers' associations of all countries; foster understanding and goodwill among them; work together to achieve the aims set out in the United Nations Charter; ensure common action by lawyers in the study and practice of *democratic principles*, making for maintenance of peace and cooperation among nations; restore, defend and develop democratic rights and liberties in legislation and its practice; promote independence of all peoples and oppose any restriction on this independence whether in law or in practice; defend and promote human rights and peoples' rights; promote preservation of ecology and healthy environment; work for strict adherence to rule of law and independence of the judiciary and legal profession; defend peoples' rights to development and to conditions of economic equality, enjoyment of the fruits of scientific progress and of natural resources. **Structure** General Assembly (every 4 years, at Congress). Council (meets once a year), comprising all members of the Bureau, all other office bearers and one representative appointed by and from each member association. Bureau, comprising up to 18 members. Current Officers: 3 Presidents Emeriti, President, 3 Vice Presidents; Secretary General, 3 Deputy Secretaries General, Treasurer, 2 Deputy Treasurers, 3 Permanent Invitees. Congress open. **Languages** English, French. **Staff** 4.00 FTE, paid; 12.00 FTE, voluntary. **Finance** Sources: contributions; donations; grants; meeting proceeds; members' dues; sale of publications. Other sources: savings and investments. **Activities** Events/meetings. Main areas: research on legal issues affecting human, political and economic rights; study and practice of democratic principles for maintenance of peace and peaceful problem solving, and cooperation among nations; defence and development of democratic rights and liberties in legislation and in the practice of law. Organizes international commissions of enquiry and conferences; topics have included: the new economic order; racism and apartheid; human rights; decolonization and self-determination. Provides observer missions to trials. **Events** *International Peaceful Unification Forum* Seoul (Korea Rep) 2016, *Lawyering for people's rights* Brussels (Belgium) 2014, *Conference of Lawyers in the Asia and the Pacific* Manila (Philippines) 2010, *Law and lawyers in the context of globalization – for peace, development and independence of the judiciary* Hanoi (Vietnam) 2009, *Conference of lawyers of Asia and the Pacific* Seoul (Korea Rep) 2005. **Publications** *Review of Contemporary Law* (2 a year). Reports on all aspects of international law; news bulletins; congress reports; various legal works.
Members Sections, groups and individuals, representing about 200,000 members in all. Organizations in 50 countries and territories:
Argentina, Austria, Bangladesh, Bolivia, Bulgaria, China, Colombia, Cuba, Cyprus, Egypt, El Salvador, Finland, France, Germany, Ghana, Hungary, Iraq, Italy, Japan, Jordan, Korea DPR, Laos, Lebanon, Libya, Madagascar, Mauritania, Mexico, Namibia, Nepal, Nicaragua, Nigeria, Pakistan, Palestine, Peru, Philippines, Portugal, Romania, Russia, Senegal, Serbia, Somalia, South Africa, Spain, Sudan, Syrian AR, Tunisia, UK, Uruguay, USA, Vietnam.
Individuals in 45 countries:
Afghanistan, Algeria, Angola, Australia, Belgium, Benin, Botswana, Brazil, Cambodia, Canada, Cape Verde, Chile, Congo DR, Costa Rica, Côte d'Ivoire, Dominican Rep, Ecuador, Eritrea, Eswatini, Ethiopia, Gabon, Greece, Guatemala, Guinea-Bissau, Indonesia, Iran Islamic Rep, Ireland, Israel, Jamaica, Kenya, Korea Rep, Malta, Morocco, Mozambique, Netherlands, Nicaragua, Poland, Puerto Rico, Romania, Sri Lanka, Switzerland, Thailand, Türkiye, Venezuela, Yemen.
Intercontinental and regional organizations (3):
African Jurists' Association (AJA, #00351); *Arab Lawyers' Union (ALU, #01002)*; *Asociación Americana de Juristas (AAJ, #02110)*.
Consultative Status Consultative status granted from: *ECOSOC (#05331)* (Special); *UNESCO (#20322)* (Consultative Status); *UNICEF (#20332)*. **IGO Relations** Accredited by (1): *United Nations Office at Vienna (UNOV, #20604)*. Associated with Department of Global Communications of the United Nations. **NGO Relations** Member of (6): *Committee of NGOs on Human Rights, Geneva (#04275)*; *EarthAction (EA, #05159)*; *International Centre for Trade Union Rights (ICTUR, #12525)*; *NGO Committee for Disarmament, Geneva (#17105)*; *Vienna NGO Committee on the Status of Women (#20775)*; *World Organisation Against Torture (OMCT, #21685)*. [2022/XB1270/y/**B**]

♦ International Association for Dental Research (IADR) 11838

Association internationale de recherches dentaires

CEO 1619 Duke St, Alexandria VA 22314-3406, USA. T. +17035480066. Fax +17035481883. E-mail: research@iadr.org.
URL: http://www.iadr.org/

History 10 Dec 1920, New York, NY (USA). Founded by William J Gies. Incorporated in the Commonwealth of Virginia (USA). Constitution and Bylaws adopted 14 Mar 1957; most recent revision: Mar 1999. **Aims** Advance research and increase knowledge for improvement of oral health worldwide; support and represent the oral health research community; facilitate communication and application of research findings. **Structure** General Session (annual); Board; Council; Regions (5); Divisions (34); Sections (12); Standing Committees (12); Groups; Networks. Regional Divisions include: *Continental European Division of the International Association for Dental Research (CED-IADR, #04780)*; *Scandinavian Association for Dental Research (#19070)*; *South East Asian Association for Dental Education (SEAADE, #19757)*. **Languages** English. **Staff** 20.00 FTE, paid. **Finance** Sources: donations; meeting proceeds; members' dues; sale of publications. **Activities** Awards/prizes/competitions; events/meetings; knowledge management/information dissemination; networking/liaising; research and development. **Events** *General Session* Kyoto (Japan) 2027, *General Session* San Diego, CA (USA) 2026, *General Session* Barcelona (Spain) 2025, *General Session* New Orleans, LA (USA) 2024, *World Congress on Preventive Dentistry* Bogota (Colombia) 2023. **Publications** *Global Research Update* (12 a year); *JDR Clinical and Tranlational Research* (4 a year); *Journal of Dental Research* (13 a year); *Advances in Dental Research* (irregular). **Members** Individuals (over 11,000). Membership countries not specified. **Consultative Status** Consultative status granted from: *WHO (#20950)* (Official Relations). **NGO Relations** Member of (3): *FDI – World Dental Federation (#09281)* (as Affiliate member association); *International Organization for Standardization (ISO, #14473)* (as Liaison member); *The NCD Alliance (NCDA, #16963)*. [2021/XB1188/**B**]

♦ International Association for Dental Research – Pan European Federation / see Continental European Division of the International Association for Dental Research (#04780)

♦ International Association of Dental Students (IADS) 11839

Contact FDI World Dental Federation, Tour de Cointrin, Ave Louis Casai 71, 1216 Geneva, Switzerland.
URL: https://iads-web.com/

History 26 Aug 1951, Copenhagen (Denmark). Founded at 1st Congress. Constitution adopted: Aug 1967, Paris (France); amended: Aug 1971, Malta; Aug 1981, Alexandria (Egypt); revised Aug 1983, Puerto Rico; 1996, London (UK); 2003, Turkey; 2008, Egypt; 2009, Ljubljana (Slovenia); 2010, Ohrid (Macedonia). Registration: Swiss Civil code, Start date: 2018, Switzerland. **Aims** Represent student of the dental profession on a global level; promote contact, cooperation and exchange among dental students; establish and encourage international programmes to stimulate the interest of dental students in the advancement of the science and art of dentistry. **Structure** General Assembly of delegates (twice a year, at Congress and Mid-Year Meeting). Executive Committees: Internal Bureau; Editorial Board; Science and Research (SCORE); Exchange Board; Finances. Standing Committees: Public Health; Voluntary; Training. Regional Ambassadors (5). Advisory Board (5). **Languages** English. **Staff** Voluntary, part-time. **Finance** Sources: grants; meeting proceeds; members' dues. **Activities** Events/meetings; networking/liaising; projects/programmes. Active in all member countries. **Events** *Annual Congress* Almaty (Kazakhstan) 2022, *Congress* Geneva (Switzerland) 2020, *Congress* St Petersburg (Russia) 2020, *Annual Congress* Mahdia (Tunisia) 2019, *Annual Congress* Kaohsiung (Taiwan) 2018. **Publications** *IADS Magazine* (4 a year); *IADS Newsletter* (2 a year); *International Dental Students Journal (IJDS)* (every 2 years) – Editor-in-Chief Dr. Huthaifa Abdul Qader. *Information/Exchange Guide*.
Members National associations of dental students (Full Country Members) in 20 countries:
Armenia, Bulgaria, Czechia, Denmark, Egypt, Finland, Ghana, Greece, Hungary, India, Malta, Moldova, Mongolia, Nigeria, North Macedonia, Poland, Slovenia, Sudan, Türkiye, UK.
Local associations of dental students or universities; dentistry students' clubs; student leagues. Members in 5 countries:
Australia, Belgium, Greece, Indonesia, Malaysia, Netherlands, Romania, Serbia, Slovakia, Thailand.
Affiliate member:
Young Dentists Worldwide (YDW, #21981).
IGO Relations Takes part in oral health activities of: *WHO (#20950)*. **NGO Relations** Memorandum of Understanding with (1): *Asian Pacific Dental Students Association (APDSA, #01607)*. Member of (2): *FDI – World Dental Federation (#09281)* (Affiliate); *World Health Students' Alliance (WHSA, #21559)*. Instrumental in setting up (1): *Young Dentists Worldwide (YDW, #21981)*. [2022.09.01/XC1271/y/**C**]

♦ International Association of Dental Traumatology (IADT) 11840

Association internationale de traumatologie dentaire

Admin Office c/o RES Inc, 4425 Cass St, Ste A, San Diego CA 92109, USA. T. +18582721018. Fax +18582727687. E-mail: res@res-inc.com.
URL: http://www.iadt-dentaltrauma.org/

History Founded 1989. **Aims** Promote optimal prevention and treatment service in the field of traumatic dental injuries through interaction with dental and medical colleagues, the public and interested parties in education, sports, industry and appropriate government agencies. **Structure** General Assembly. Council, consisting of 12 representatives and Executive Committee, comprising President, President-Elect, Secretary/ Treasurer, Immediate Past-President and Executive Director. **Languages** English. **Staff** 0.50 FTE, paid. **Finance** Members' dues. Budget (annual): US$ 10,000. **Events** *World Congress on Dental Traumatology* Tokyo (Japan) 2024, *World Congress on Dental Traumatology* Lisbon (Portugal) 2022, *World Congress on Dental Traumatology* Lisbon (Portugal) 2021, *World Congress on Dental Traumatology* Lisbon (Portugal) 2020, *World Congress* San Diego, CA (USA) 2018. **Publications** *Dental Traumatology* – official journal.
Members Active; Associate; Honorary; Life; Corporate Sponsors; Student. Members in 36 countries:
Argentina, Australia, Austria, Belgium, Brazil, Canada, Chile, Colombia, Croatia, Denmark, El Salvador, Finland, France, Germany, Greece, Honduras, Ireland, Israel, Italy, Japan, Mexico, Netherlands, Norway, Paraguay, Portugal, Saudi Arabia, Singapore, Slovenia, Spain, Sweden, Switzerland, Türkiye, UK, United Arab Emirates, Uruguay, USA. [2020/XD3771/**D**]

♦ International Association of Dentistry for Children / see International Association of Paediatric Dentistry (#12064)

♦ International Association of Dentistry for the Handicapped / see International Association for Disability and Oral Health (#11848)

♦ International Association of Dentists Against War (inactive)

♦ International Association of Dento-Maxillo-Facial Radiology (IADMFR) 11841

Association internationale de radiologie dento-maxillo-faciale

SG Grensstraat 7, 1831 Diegem, Belgium. E-mail: iadmfr@aimgroup.eu.
URL: http://www.iadmfr.one/

History 16 Aug 1968, Santiago (Chile). Constitution amended 23 Jun 1983. Registration: Banque-Carrefour des Entreprises, No/ID: 0685.877.694, Start date: 13 Dec 2017, Belgium. **Aims** Promote the advancement of radiological research, teaching and services; encourage research in allied *diagnostic* fields; develop clinical services in the field; encourage the work of investigators and *clinicians* in order to improve services to patients. **Structure** General Assembly (every 2 years); Board of Directors; Executive Committee; Regional Directors; Committees (11). **Languages** English. **Finance** Sources: members' dues. **Activities** Events/meetings. **Events** *Biennial Congress* Gwangju (Korea Rep) 2021, *Biennial Congress* Philadelphia, PA (USA) 2019, *Biennial Congress* Kaohsiung (Taiwan) 2017, *Biennial Congress* Santiago (Chile) 2015, *Biennial Congress* Bergen (Norway) 2013. **Publications** *Journal of Dento-Maxillo-Facial Radiology* (6 a year); *IADMFR Newsletter* (4 a year).
Members Founding, Honorary and Individual: dentists and doctors; Affiliated: science oriented, interested individuals. Members in 55 countries and territories:
Argentina, Australia, Belgium, Brazil, Canada, Chile, China, Costa Rica, Czechia, Egypt, Finland, France, Germany, Ghana, Greece, Guatemala, Hong Kong, Hungary, India, Indonesia, Iran Islamic Rep, Ireland, Israel, Italy, Japan, Korea Rep, Latvia, Lebanon, Lithuania, Mexico, Netherlands, New Zealand, Nigeria, North Macedonia, Norway, Peru, Poland, Portugal, Qatar, Romania, Saudi Arabia, Singapore, South Africa, Spain, Sri Lanka, Sweden, Switzerland, Syrian AR, Taiwan, Thailand, Türkiye, UK, Uruguay, USA, Venezuela.
NGO Relations Affiliate member association of: *FDI – World Dental Federation (#09281)*.
[2022/XB6855/v/**B**]

♦ International Association of Department Stores (IADS) 11842

Association internationale de grands magasins (AIGM)

Acting Managing Dir 11-13 rue Guersant, 75017 Paris, France. E-mail: iads@iads.org.
URL: http://www.iads.org/

History 14 Sep 1928, Paris (France). Founded as 'Management Research Group of Department Stores', under sponsorship of now defunct *International Management Institute, Geneva (IMI-Geneva, inactive)*. Registration: French Ministerial Decree, Start date: 8 Sep 1955, France. **Aims** Be an international bond between members, facilitating exchange and communication; research the future of the business and anticipate fundamental changes; promote cooperation and best practices. **Structure** General Assembly (annual); Executive Committee; General Secretary. Affinity group: Association Commerciale Internationale. **Languages** English, French. **Staff** 5.00 FTE, paid. **Finance** Sources: members' dues. **Activities** Awareness raising; events/ meetings; guidance/assistance/consulting; knowledge management/information dissemination; monitoring/ evaluation; projects/programmes; publishing activities; research and development; research/documentation. **Events** *General Assembly* Geneva (Switzerland) 2022, *General Assembly* Paris (France) 2021, *Meeting* Madrid (Spain) 1999, *General Assembly* Paris (France) 1987. **Publications** *White Paper: Smarter department stores organisations – Livre Blanc: La quête de l'organisation humaine optimale des grands magasins* (2021); *White Paper: Global pandemic, local department stores – Livre Blanc: Grands Magasins, les enseignements de la pandémie* (2020). Information Services: Centre of documentation and research; Library (over 3,000 vols).
Members Large-scale retail enterprises operating department stores in 12 countries:
Chile, China, France, Germany, Hong Kong, Mexico, Netherlands, Philippines, Spain, Switzerland, Thailand, Venezuela.
Federation of International Retail Associations (FIRA, #09676). [2022.05.10/XD1272/**D**]

♦ International Association of Deposit Insurers (IADI) 11843

SG c/o Bank for Int'l Settlements, Centralbahnplatz 2, 4002 Basel BS, Switzerland. T. +41612809933. Fax +41612809554. E-mail: service.iadi@bis.org.
Deputy SG address not obtained.
URL: http://www.iadi.org/

History 6 May 2002. Registration: Swiss Civil Code, Switzerland. **Aims** Contribute to the stability of financial systems by promoting international cooperation in the field of deposit insurance; provide guidance for establishing new, and enhancing existing, deposit insurance systems; encourage wide international contact among deposit insurers and other interested parties. **Structure** General Meeting (GM); Executive Council (EXCO); Council Committees; Regional Committees; Secretariat led by Secretary General. **Languages** English. **Staff** 13.50 FTE, paid. **Finance** Sources: contributions; meeting proceeds; members' dues; sponsorship. Supported by: *Bank for International Settlements (BIS, #03165)*. **Activities** Capacity building; events/ meetings; guidance/assistance/consulting; knowledge management/information dissemination; networking/ liaising; politics/policy/regulatory; research and development; research/documentation; standards/guidelines; training/education. **Events** *Biennial Research Conference* Basel (Switzerland) 2021, *Research Conference* Basel (Switzerland) 2021, *Annual Meeting and Conference* Kuala Lumpur (Malaysia) 2021, *Annual General Meeting and Conference* Basel (Switzerland) 2020, *Biennial Research Conference* Basel (Switzerland) 2019. **Publications** *IADI Newsletter*. Annual Report; briefs and notes; core principles and guidance papers; research papers.
Members Full (91); Associate (9); Partner (17). Members in 92 countries and territories:
Albania, Angola, Argentina, Armenia, Australia, Azerbaijan, Bahamas, Bangladesh, Barbados, Belarus, Belize, Bermuda, Bosnia-Herzegovina, Botswana, Brazil, Brunei Darussalam, Bulgaria, Cambodia, Canada, Colombia, Croatia, Czechia, Ecuador, El Salvador, Finland, France, Germany, Ghana, Greece, Guatemala, Honduras, Hong Kong, Hungary, India, Indonesia, Iran Islamic Rep, Italy, Jamaica, Japan, Jordan, Kazakhstan, Kenya, Korea Rep, Kosovo, Kyrgyzstan, Lebanon, Libya, Malaysia, Mexico, Mongolia, Montenegro, Morocco, Netherlands, Nicaragua, Nigeria, Norway, Oman, Pakistan, Palestine, Paraguay, Peru, Philippines, Poland, Portugal, Romania, Russia, Rwanda, Saudi Arabia, Serbia, Singapore, Slovenia, South Africa, Spain, Sudan, Sweden, Switzerland, Taiwan, Tanzania UR, Thailand, Trinidad-Tobago, Tunisia, Türkiye, Uganda, UK, Ukraine, Uruguay, USA, Uzbekistan, Venezuela, Vietnam, Virgin Is UK, Zimbabwe.
IGO Relations Partner of (7): *Arab Monetary Fund (AMF, #01009)*; *Asian Development Bank Institute (ADB Institute, #01423)*; *European Bank for Reconstruction and Development (EBRD, #06315)*; *Inter-American Development Bank (IDB, #11427)*; *International Bank for Reconstruction and Development (IBRD, #12317)*; *International Monetary Fund (IMF, #14180)*; *South East Asian Central Banks Research and Training Centre (SEACEN Centre, #19760)*. Located at: *Bank for International Settlements (BIS, #03165)*. **NGO Relations** Partner of (9): *Alliance for Financial Inclusion (AFI, #00679)*; *Association of Supervisors of Banks of the Americas (ASBA, #02944)*; *Center for Latin American Monetary Studies (#03648)*; *Consultative Group to Assist the Poor (CGAP, #04768)*; *European Forum of Deposit Insurers (EFDI, #07308)*; *International Federation of Restructuring, Insolvency and Bankruptcy Professionals (INSOL International, #13530)*; Toronto Centre; *Union of Arab Banks (UAB, #20349)*; United States Department of the Treasury. [2022.05.18/XM0093/**D**]

♦ International Association of Deputy Managers and Reception Heads of Luxury Hotels (#00798)

♦ International Association of Designers (IAD) 11844

Secretariat Via Manara 9, 22100 Como CO, Italy. T. +39314491918. E-mail: secretariat@ worlddesignconsortium.com.
URL: http://www.worlddesignconsortium.com

History 2009. Former names and other names: *World Design Consortium* – legal name. **Aims** Promote good design practices and principles worldwide so as to push designers worldwide to come up with designs to improve the quality of life. **Structure** Board. **Languages** English. **Staff** 12.00 FTE, voluntary. **Finance** Financed by A' Design Award. Annual budget: 180,000 EUR. **Activities** Awards/prizes/competitions; events/ meetings.
Members Individuals (about 450) in 77 countries and territories:
Albania, Argentina, Australia, Austria, Belarus, Belgium, Brazil, Bulgaria, Canada, Chile, China, Colombia, Croatia, Cyprus, Czechia, Denmark, Egypt, Estonia, Faeroe Is, Finland, France, Germany, Greece, Guatemala, Hong Kong, Hungary, Iceland, India, Indonesia, Iran Islamic Rep, Ireland, Israel, Japan, Jordan, Kazakhstan, Korea Rep, Kuwait, Kyrgyzstan, Latvia, Lebanon, Lithuania, Malaysia, Mexico, Moldova, Netherlands, New Zealand, North Macedonia, Norway, Oman, Palestine, Peru, Philippines, Poland, Portugal, Puerto Rico, Romania, Russia, Saudi Arabia, Serbia, Singapore, Slovakia, Slovenia, South Africa, Spain, Sri Lanka, Sweden, Switzerland, Taiwan, Thailand, Türkiye, UK, Ukraine, United Arab Emirates, Uruguay, USA, Venezuela, Vietnam. [2015.07.29/XJ8374/v/**C**]

♦ International Association for the Development of Advances in Technology (internationally oriented national body)

♦ International Association of Developmental Biology / see International Society of Developmental Biologists (#15052)

♦ International Association for Development of Apnea / see International Association for the Development of Freediving (#11845)

♦ International Association for Development Cooperation / see Associazione per la Cooperazione Internazionale allo Sviluppo

♦ International Association for the Development of Documentation, Libraries and Archives in Africa (inactive)

♦ International Association for the Development of Freediving (AIDA International) 11845

Pres address not obtained. E-mail: president@aidainternational.org – secretary@aidainternational.org.
URL: http://www.aida-international.org/

History 2 Nov 1992, Saint-Louis (France). 2 Nov 1992, St Louis (France), as *International Association for Development of Apnea (AIDA) – Association internationale pour le développement de l'apnée*. Present name adopted 1999. **Aims** Advance *free diving* in leisure and competition; assist medical and scientific research in the field. **Structure** General Assembly. Board, comprising President, 6 Vice-Presidents, Secretary, Treasurer and 3 further members. **Activities** Develops education in free diving. Organizes world championships. Trains instructors and judges. Develops rules and guidelines. Supports medical research. **Publications** *AIDA Journal*.
Members National organizations in 35 countries:
Australia, Austria, Belgium, Brazil, Canada, Colombia, Croatia, Czechia, Denmark, Egypt, Finland, France, Germany, Greece, Hungary, Israel, Italy, Japan, Mexico, Morocco, Netherlands, New Zealand, Norway, Poland, Portugal, Russia, Serbia, Slovenia, South Africa, Sweden, Switzerland, UK, Ukraine, USA, Venezuela. [2016/XD8171/**D**]

♦ International Association for the Development of Human Resources (inactive)

♦ International Association for the Development of International and World Universities (no recent information)

♦ International Association for the Development and Management of Existing and New Towns / see International Urban Development Association (#15832)

♦ International Association for the Development of Natural Gums / see Association for International Development of Natural Gums (#02662)

♦ International Association for the Development of Tropical Odonto-Stomatology (no recent information)

♦ International Association of the Diabetes and Pregnancy Study Groups (IADPSG) 11846

SG address not obtained.
URL: http://www.iadpsg.org/

History 1998. **Aims** Encourage and facilitate research and advance education in the field of diabetes in pregnancy. **Structure** General Meeting/Congress (every 4 years). International Council, consisting of 2 Councillors of each Affiliated Society, one from each Associated Society and up to 4 members at large. Executive Committee, comprising Chair, Vice-Chair, Immediate Past Chair, Secretary-General and Treasurer. **Events** *Scientific Meeting* Kyoto (Japan) 2020, *Scientific Meeting* Buenos Aires (Argentina) 2016, *Scientific Meeting* Chennai (India) 2012, *Research Meeting* Pasadena, CA (USA) 2010. **Members** Regular; Honorary; Senior; Junior; Associate; Industry/Foundation. Membership countries not specified. **NGO Relations** Associated organizations: *Australasian Diabetes in Pregnancy Society (ADIPS)*; *European Association of Perinatal Medicine (EAPM, #06148)*; Diabetes Pregnancy Study Group of *European Association for the Study of Diabetes (EASD, #06228)*. [2019/XJ2402/**C**]

♦ International Association for Dialogue Analysis (IADA) 11847

Pres Univ de Montréal, Dépt de Communication, Pavillon Marie Victorin CP 6128, Succursale Centre-Ville, Montréal QC H3C 3J7, Canada. T. +15143437819.
Sec Sterkrader Str 120C, 46242 Bottrop, Germany. T. +492041559339.
URL: http://www.iada-web.org/

History 1990, Bologna (Italy), during 3rd Congress on Dialogue Analysis. **Aims** Promote and undertake research focusing on a dialogic view of *language* use. **Structure** Executive Board; Honorary Board. **Languages** English, French, German, Italian, Spanish. **Staff** None. **Finance** Members' dues. **Activities** Events/meetings; research/documentation; publishing activities. **Events** *Conference* Moscow (Russia) 2022, *Conference* Montréal, QC (Canada) 2021, *Conference* Warsaw (Poland) 2020, *Conference* Milwaukee, WI (USA) 2019, *Conference* Taipei (Taiwan) 2018.
Members Full in 11 countries:
Argentina, Australia, Canada, Denmark, Finland, France, Germany, Italy, Mexico, Switzerland, USA.
NGO Relations Member of: *International Federation for Modern Languages and Literatures (#13480)*. [2019/XD9381/**D**]

♦ International Association for the Diffusion of Cultures and Languages (inactive)

♦ International Association for Disability and Oral Health (iADH) 11848

Sec Spoorstraat 94, 6591 GV Gennep, Netherlands. E-mail: secretary@iadh.org.
URL: http://www.iadh.org/

History 1976, Stockholm (Sweden). Founded at 3rd International Congress. Constitution adopted 1978, London (UK). Former names and other names: *International Association of Dentistry for the Handicapped (IADH)* – former; *Association internationale de dentisterie pour les handicapés* – former. **Aims** Improve oral health and quality of life for people with *special needs*. **Structure** General Meeting (every 2 years); Executive; Council of Committee Members. **Languages** English. **Staff** Voluntary. **Finance** Sources: members' dues. **Activities** Awards/prizes/competitions; events/meetings; training/education. **Events** *Biennial Congress* Paris (France) 2022, *Biennial Congress* Acapulco (Mexico) 2020, *Biennial Congress* Dubai (United Arab Emirates) 2018, *Biennial Congress* Chicago, IL (USA) 2016, *Biennial Congress* Berlin (Germany) 2014. **Publications** *iADH Magazine*; *iADH Newsletter*; *Journal of Disability and Oral Health (JDOH)*. Abstracts.
Members Associate: national academies/associations; Individual. Members in 41 countries and territories:
Argentina, Australia, Belgium, Brazil, Canada, Chile, Costa Rica, Denmark, Egypt, Finland, France, Germany, Greece, Hong Kong, Iceland, India, Indonesia, Ireland, Israel, Italy, Japan, Korea Rep, Malaysia, Mexico, Nepal, Netherlands, New Zealand, Norway, Pakistan, Peru, Philippines, Romania, Saudi Arabia, Spain, Sweden, Switzerland, Taiwan, Tanzania UR, Türkiye, UK, USA.
NGO Relations Affiliated with (1): *FDI – World Dental Federation (#09281)*. [2020/XD9270/**C**]

♦ International Association for Disabled Sailing (IFDS) 11849

Chairperson address not obtained.
URL: http://www.sailing.org/disabled/

History 1992, The Hague (Netherlands), when constitution was formally adopted. Previously referred to as *International Handicap Sailing Committee (IHSC)*. Registered in accordance with Dutch law. **Aims** Exchange knowledge, experience and information on disabled sailing and instruction in disabled sailing; stimulate and coordinate international sailing *competitions* and draw up uniform rules for such competitions. **Structure** Members' Meeting (annual). Executive Board, comprising Chairman, Vice-President, Treasurer and 4 members. Committees (4): Development; Fundraising; Medical; Technical. **Languages** English. **Finance** Members' dues. **Activities** Maintains an international programme of regattas; supports the *'World Disabled Sailing Championships'*; acts as the governing body for Paralympic Sailing. **Events** *Annual General Meeting* Palma (Spain) 2014, *Annual conference* Paris (France) 2007, *Annual Conference* Helsinki (Finland) 2006, *Annual conference* Singapore (Singapore) 2005, *Annual conference* Copenhagen (Denmark) 2004. **Publications** *IFDS Bulletin* (6 a year). *Functional Classification System* – manual; *Race Management Manual*; *Sailing Manual*. Conference Minutes. Information Services: Information for members: IFDS address list; Functional Classification System; Notice of Race; criteria for the choice of a disabled sailing boat.
Members Recognized national associations and contacts in 22 countries:
Argentina, Australia, Canada, Denmark, Estonia, Finland, France, Germany, Greece, Ireland, Israel, Italy, Japan, Netherlands, New Zealand, Norway, Poland, Singapore, Spain, Sweden, UK, USA.
Contacts in 6 countries:
Belgium, Iran Islamic Rep, Pakistan, Poland, Qatar, South Africa.
NGO Relations Secretarial support provided by: *World Sailing (#21760)*. [2014/XK0493/**F**]

♦ International Association for Discourse Studies (DiscourseNet) ... 11850

Association internationale des Études du discours – Asociación Internacional de Estudios del Discurso – Internationale Gesellschaft für Diskursforschung – Associação Internacional de Estudos do Discurso – Associazione Internazionale di Studi sul Discorso

Sec address not obtained. E-mail: contact@discourseanalysis.net.
URL: https://discourseanalysis.net/

History 14 Sep 2019, Paris (France). Former names and other names: *DiscourseNet (DN)* – former. Registration: Bavaria District court, No/ID: VR 200493, Germany, Fürth. **Aims** Provide a pluralist, multilingual, inclusive and non-hierarchical space for discourse researchers from all disciplinary and geographic backgrounds. **Structure** General Assembly; Board. **Finance** Sources: members' dues. **Activities** Events/meetings. **Events** *DiscourseNet Congress* Valencia (Spain) 2023, *DiscourseNet Congress* Budapest (Hungary) 2021, *DiscourseNet Conference* Giessen (Germany) 2021, *DiscourseNet Conference* Milton Keynes (UK) 2021, *DiscourseNet Conference* Tyumen (Russia) 2020. **Members** Individuals. Membership countries not specified. [2022/AA2478/**D**]

♦ International Association for Distance Learning (internationally oriented national body)
♦ International Association for the Distribution of Food Products and General Consumer Goods / see International Association for the Distributive Trade (#11851)

♦ International Association for the Distributive Trade 11851

Association internationale de la distribution (AIDA) – Internationale Vereinigung des Handels

Admin-SG c/o CRBD, Bd Paepsem 11B, Boîte 1, 1070 Brussels, Belgium. T. +3223459923. Fax +3223460204.
URL: http://www.cbd-bcd.be/fr/other/

History Apr 1952, Paris (France), following 1st Congress, Jun 1950, Paris. Statutes adopted 18 Nov 1963, Copenhagen (Denmark). Formerly known: as *International Association of Food Distribution*; as *International Association for the Study and Development of Marketing and the Distribution of Food Products and Consumer Goods – Association internationale de la distribution des produits alimentaires pour le progrès des techniques et des services*; and, from 1 Jun 1970, Paris, as *International Association for the Distribution of Food Products and General Consumer Goods – Association internationale de la distribution des produits alimentaires et des produits de grande consommation – Internationale Vereinigung der Verteilung von Lebensmitteln und Gebrauchsgütern*. New Statutes adopted on registration in accordance with Belgian law, 6 Dec 1977. **Aims** Raise *living standards* of *consumers*, especially in the domain of nutrition, by stimulating technical progress, improving services and increasing *productivity* of enterprises active in the field of food distribution, developing international trade in *food products* and improving public health. **Structure** General Assembly (annual); Board; Bureau; Honorary Presidents and Secretaries-General; Secretary-General/Administrator; Committees (3). **Languages** English, French, German. **Staff** 8.00 FTE, paid. **Finance** Sources: members' dues. **Activities** Awards/prizes/competitions; events/meetings; training/education. **Events** *Annual Congress* Parma (Italy) 2006, *Annual Symposium* Brussels (Belgium) 2005, *Annual Congress* Sofia (Bulgaria) 2005, *Annual Congress* Vilnius (Lithuania) 2004, *Annual Congress* Florence (Italy) 2003. **Publications** *AIDA International Bulletin* (4 a year). *Sectorial Analysis of the Retail Trade*. Statistics. Information Services: Documentation service.
Members Enterprises; national and international organizations in food economics; national committees; national correspondents. Represented in 56 countries and territories:
Andorra, Argentina, Australia, Austria, Belgium, Brazil, Bulgaria, Canada, Chile, China, Cyprus, Czechia, Denmark, Egypt, Estonia, Finland, France, Gabon, Germany, Greece, Hong Kong, Hungary, India, Indonesia, Ireland, Israel, Italy, Japan, Jordan, Kuwait, Latvia, Lithuania, Luxembourg, Malta, Mexico, Monaco, Morocco, Netherlands, New Zealand, Norway, Poland, Portugal, Romania, Russia, Slovakia, South Africa, Spain, Sweden, Switzerland, Syrian AR, Thailand, Tunisia, Türkiye, UK, Uruguay, USA.
IGO Relations Recognized by: *European Commission (EC, #06633)*. **NGO Relations** In liaison with technical committees of: *International Organization for Standardization (ISO, #14473)*. [2019.04.24/XC1233/t/**C**]

♦ International Association for District Heating, District Cooling and Combined Heat and Power / see Euroheat and Power (#05694)
♦ International Association of Dock, Wharf and Riverside Workers / see International Transport Workers' Federation (#15726)
♦ International Association of Documentalists and Information Officers (inactive)
♦ International Association of Documentary Film Makers (inactive)

♦ International Association of Dredging Companies (IADC) 11852

Association internationale des compagnies de dragage

SG PO Box 80521, 2508 GM The Hague, Netherlands. T. +31703523334. Fax +31703512654. E-mail: info@iadc-dredging.com.
Street address Stationsplein 4, 2275 AZ Voorburg, Netherlands.
URL: http://www.iadc-dredging.com/

History 21 May 1965, Paris (France). Registered in accordance with Dutch law. **Aims** Promote the professional interests of international private dredging contractors. **Languages** Dutch, English. **Staff** 9.00 FTE, paid. **Events** *Seminar on Dredging and Reclamation* Delft (Netherlands) 2020, *Seminar on Dredging and Reclamation* Mumbai (India) 2019, *Dredging for sustainable infrastucture* Amsterdam (Netherlands) 2018, *Seminar on Dredging and Reclamation* Delft (Netherlands) 2018, *Seminar on Dredging and Reclamation* Panama (Panama) 2018. **Publications** *Terra et Aqua* (periodical). *Dredging for Development*, *Environmental Aspects of Dredging*. Books.
Members Private dredging contractors in 45 countries and territories:
Argentina, Australia, Bahrain, Belgium, Brazil, China, Curaçao, Cyprus, Estonia, Finland, France, Germany, Hong Kong, India, Indonesia, Ireland, Italy, Japan, Korea Rep, Latvia, Luxembourg, Malaysia, Mexico, Netherlands, New Zealand, Nigeria, Oman, Panama, Philippines, Portugal, Qatar, Russia, Saudi Arabia, Singapore, South Africa, Spain, Sweden, Taiwan, Thailand, Tunisia, UK, United Arab Emirates, Uruguay, USA, Venezuela.
NGO Relations Member of Port Environment Committee of: *International Association of Ports and Harbors (IAPH, #12096)*. In liaison with technical committees of: *International Organization for Standardization (ISO, #14473)*. [2019.11.05/XC1274/**C**]

♦ International Association of Drilling Contractors (internationally oriented national body)
♦ International Association of Drilling Engineers and Technicians (inactive)
♦ International Association for Driver Education (inactive)
♦ International Association of Druggists (inactive)

♦ International Association of Dry Cargo Shipowners (INTERCARGO) . 11853

Association internationale des transporteurs de marchandises solides – Asociación Internacional de Armadores de Buques de Carga Seca

SG 4th Floor – 123 Minories, London, EC3N 1NT, UK. T. +442081068480. E-mail: info@intercargo.org.
URL: http://www.intercargo.org/

History 23 Apr 1980, London (UK). Founded at first General Meeting. Registration: Companies House, No/ID: 2588658, Start date: 5 Mar 1991, England and Wales; EU Transparency Register, No/ID: 27793056659-68, Start date: 13 Sep 2011. **Aims** Unite and promote quality dry bulk shipping; provide a forum where dry bulk shipowners, managers and operators are informed about, discuss and share concerns on key topics and regulatory challenges, especially in relation to safety, the environment and operational excellence. **Structure** Annual General Meeting; Executive Committee; Management Committee; Technical Committee; Secretariat in London (UK). **Languages** English. **Staff** 6.00 FTE, paid. **Finance** Sources: members' dues. **Activities** Events/meetings; guidance/assistance/consulting; knowledge management/information dissemination; networking/liaising; politics/policy/regulatory; projects/programmes. **Events** *Bi-annual Meeting* London (UK) 2022, *Executive and Technical Committees Meeting* 2021, *Bi-annual Meeting* London (UK) 2021, *Bi-annual Meeting* 2020, *Executive and Technical Committees Meeting* Singapore (Singapore) 2020. **Publications** *Benchmarking Bulk Carriers Report* (annual); *Annual Bulk Carrier Casualty Report*; *INTERCARGO Annual Review*. **Members** Full (about 150) and Associate (about 90) from 30 countries. Membership countries not specified. **Consultative Status** Consultative status granted from: *ECOSOC (#05331)* (Roster); *UNCTAD (#20285)* (Special Category); *International Maritime Organization (IMO, #14102)*. [2022.11.08/XD0274/**C**]

♦ International Association of Dutch Studies 11854

Internationale Vereniging voor Neerlandistiek (IVN)

Dir Paleisstraat 9, 2514 JA The Hague, Netherlands. T. +31648429070. E-mail: bureau@ivn.nu.
URL: http://www.ivn.nu

History 1970. Founded at 4th Colloquium of Professors and Lecturers in Dutch Studies at Foreign Universities, taking over the tasks of *Working Party of Professors and Lecturers in Dutch Studies at Foreign Universities – Werkcommissie van Hoogleraren en Lectoren in de Neerlandistiek aan Buitenlandse Universiteiten*, set up 1961, at 1st Colloquium. **Aims** Promote teaching of Dutch *language*, literature, *history* and cultural history at academic institutions outside the Netherlands and Belgium; contribute to a greater knowledge and understanding of Dutch studies, and of Dutch culture in general, outside the Dutch language-area. **Languages** Dutch. **Staff** 1.00 FTE, paid. **Finance** Sources: members' dues; subsidies. Subsidies from Dutch and Belgian governments. **Activities** Events/meetings; training/education. **Events** *Triennial Colloquium* Nijmegen (Netherlands) 2022, *Triennial Colloquium* Leuven (Belgium) 2018, *Triennial Colloquium* Leiden (Netherlands) 2015, *Triennial Colloquium* Antwerp (Belgium) 2012, *Triennial Colloquium* Utrecht (Netherlands) 2009. **Publications** *IVN-Nieuwsbrief* (5 a year); *VakTaal* (4 a year); *Internationale Neerlandistiek* (3 a year). *Lage Landen Studies* – (approx 2 a year) series. List of teachers and members (every 2 years).
Members Ordinary; Extraordinary; Contributors. Members in 39 countries:
Australia, Austria, Belarus, Belgium, Bulgaria, Canada, China, Czechia, Denmark, Estonia, Finland, France, Germany, Hungary, Indonesia, Italy, Japan, Korea Rep, Latvia, Lithuania, Malaysia, Netherlands, Norway, Poland, Portugal, Romania, Russia, Serbia, Slovakia, Slovenia, South Africa, Spain, Sweden, Switzerland, Türkiye, UK, Ukraine, USA, Uzbekistan.
NGO Relations Instrumental in setting up (1): *Stichting Promotie Internationale Neerlandistiek (SPIN, see: #11854)*. [2021.06.15/XD5377/**D**]

♦ International Association of Dynamic Psychotherapy (internationally oriented national body)
♦ International Association of Early Childhood Education (internationally oriented national body)

♦ International Association for Earthquake Engineering (IAEE) 11855

Association internationale de génie séismique

SG Kenchiku kaikan 4F, 26-20 Shiba 5-chome, Minato-ku, Tokyo, 108-0014 Japan. Fax +81357302830. E-mail: info@iaee.or.jp – secretary@iaee.or.jp.
URL: http://www.iaee.or.jp/

History 1 Feb 1963, Tokyo (Japan), a Preparatory Committee having been set up at 2nd World Conference on Earthquake Engineering, Jul 1960, Tokyo. **Aims** Promote international cooperation among scientists and engineers in the field of earthquake engineering through exchange of knowledge, ideas and results of research and practical experience. **Structure** General Assembly of Delegates; Executive Committee. Includes: *International Strong Motion Array Council (ISMAC, no recent information)*; *'Monograph Committee for Non-Engineered Construction'*; *'IAEE Committee on WSSI'*; *World Seismic Safety Initiative (WSSI, see: #11855)*. **Languages** English. **Staff** No FTE. **Finance** No dues or assessments to member national organizations. **Events** *World Conference on Earthquake Engineering (WCEE)* Milan (Italy) 2024, *World Conference on Earthquake Engineering (WCEE)* Sendai (Japan) 2021, *World Conference on Earthquake Engineering (WCEE)* Sendai (Japan) 2020, *Quadrennial World Conference* Santiago (Chile) 2017, *Quadrennial World Conference* Lisbon (Portugal) 2012. **Publications** *International Journal of Earthquake Engineering and Structural Dynamics* (6 a year); *Earthquake Resistant Regulations – A World List* (every 4 years). *Basic Concepts of Seismic Codes, Vols I and II*; *International Directory of Earthquake Engineering Research*. Monographs; conference proceedings.
Members National committees of 58 countries:
Algeria, Argentina, Armenia, Australia, Austria, Bangladesh, Bulgaria, Canada, Chile, China, Colombia, Costa Rica, Croatia, Dominican Rep, Ecuador, Egypt, El Salvador, Ethiopia, France, Georgia, Germany, Ghana, Greece, Hungary, Iceland, India, Indonesia, Iran Islamic Rep, Israel, Italy, Japan, Korea Rep, Mexico, Montenegro, Myanmar, Nepal, New Zealand, Nicaragua, North Macedonia, Norway, Pakistan, Peru, Philippines, Portugal, Romania, Russia, Singapore, Slovenia, Spain, Switzerland, Taiwan, Thailand, Türkiye, Uganda, UK, Ukraine, USA, Venezuela.
NGO Relations Works with: *International Association of Seismology and Physics of the Earth's Interior (IASPEI, #12157)* through ISMAC. Cooperates with UNESCO through: *International Advisory Committee on Earthquake Risk (no recent information)*. [2020/XC1189/C]

♦ International Association for East Slavonic Lexicography (no recent information)
♦ International Association of Eclectical Psychoanalysis (inactive)
♦ International Association for Ecological Design (no recent information)

♦ International Association for Ecology (INTECOL) 11856

Association internationale d'écologie – Asociación Internacional de Ecologia – Internationale Vereinigung für Ökologie

Pres Myers Ecology Ltd, 62 Onewa Road, Northcote, Auckland 0627, New Zealand.
SG address not obtained.
URL: https://intecol.online/

History 17 Sep 1967, Montreux (Switzerland). Founded to take over the work of former Commission on Applied Ecology of *International Union of Biological Sciences (IUBS, #15760)*. Currently part of the IUBS Section of the Environment. Registration: Lower Saxony District court, No/ID: VR 2204, Start date: 2 Sep 1987, Germany, Osnabrück. **Aims** Promote development of the science of ecology and application of ecological principles to global needs, particularly through international cooperation and major meetings; collect, evaluate, and disseminate information about ecology; promote national, regional and international action in ecological research; train personnel; coordinate large-scale application of ecological principles; encourage public awareness of the economic and social importance of ecology. **Structure** Board of Officers, elected every 4 years, comprises President, Vice-President, Secretary-General, Treasurer and Past-President (who together form the Executive Committee) plus 6 members-at-large. Council of nominated representatives of national societies. Working Groups (8). **Languages** English. **Staff** 1.50 FTE, paid. **Finance** Members' dues (currently under review). Other sources: contributions from national societies; grants from *UNESCO (#20322)*; *International Union of Biological Sciences (IUBS, #15760)*, other agencies; research contracts. **Activities** Advocacy/lobbying/activism; events/meetings; publishing activities; training/education. **Events** *Frontiers in ecology – science and society* Geneva (Switzerland) 2022, *International Wetlands Conference* Christchurch (New Zealand) 2021, *Frontiers in ecology – science and society* Geneva (Switzerland) 2021, *International Wetlands Conference* Christchurch (New Zealand) 2020, *Ecology and civilization in a changing world* Beijing (China) 2017. **Publications** *INTECOL Newsletter* (4 a year); *INTECOL Directory* (every 3 years); *Ecology International* (periodical). Books; reports.
Members Regular (1,200 individuals and institutions), affiliated national societies (32) and affiliated professional organizations (7), in 115 countries and territories:
Afghanistan, Algeria, Argentina, Australia, Austria, Bangladesh, Barbados, Belgium, Benin, Bermuda, Bolivia, Brazil, Bulgaria, Burundi, Cameroon, Canada, Central African Rep, Chad, Chile, China, Colombia, Congo Brazzaville, Congo DR, Costa Rica, Côte d'Ivoire, Croatia, Cuba, Czechia, Denmark, Dominican Rep, Ecuador, Egypt, Ethiopia, Finland, France, Gabon, Gambia, Germany, Ghana, Greece, Guinea, Guyana, Haiti, Hungary, Iceland, India, Indonesia, Iran Islamic Rep, Iraq, Ireland, Israel, Italy, Japan, Jordan, Kenya, Korea Rep, Kuwait, Libya, Madagascar, Malaysia, Maldives, Mali, Malta, Mauritius, Mexico, Mongolia, Montenegro, Morocco, Myanmar, Nepal, Netherlands, New Caledonia, New Zealand, Nigeria, Norway, Pakistan, Panama, Papua New Guinea, Paraguay, Peru, Philippines, Poland, Puerto Rico, Qatar, Romania, Rwanda, Saudi Arabia, Senegal, Serbia, Sierra Leone, Singapore, Slovakia, Somalia, South Africa, Spain, Sri Lanka, Sudan, Suriname, Sweden, Switzerland, Syrian AR, Taiwan, Tanzania UR, Thailand, Trinidad-Tobago, Tunisia, Türkiye, Uganda, UK, United Arab Emirates, Uruguay, USA, Venezuela, Zambia, Zimbabwe.
Members also in the former USSR; countries not specified.
Regional affiliated societies (4), listed in this Yearbook:
Asian Ecological Society (inactive); *European Ecological Federation (EEF, #06956)*; *International Society for Tropical Ecology (ISTE, #15521)*; *Southeast Asian Regional Centre for Tropical Biology (SEAMEO BIOTROP, #19782)*.
NGO Relations Commission on Ecology of: *International Union for Conservation of Nature and Natural Resources (IUCN, #15766)*. Partner of: *International Network of Next-Generation Ecologists (INNGE)*. [2022/XC1190/y/B]

♦ International Association for Ecology and Health / see Ecohealth International (#05294)

♦ International Association for the Economics of Beer and Brewing (Beeronomics Society) 11857

Pres Fac of Economics and Business – KUL, Office WA 02-58, Waaistraat 6, 3000 Leuven, Belgium. T. +3216326556. E-mail: info@beeronomics.org.
URL: http://www.beeronomics.org/

History Jan 2009. **Aims** Capture the issues and challenges associated with the economics of beer by providing an open platform for discussions and debates. **Structure** Executive Committee. **Activities** Events/meetings; research/documentation. **Events** *Conference* Pilsen (Czechia) 2019, *Conference* Copenhagen (Denmark) 2017, *Conference* Seattle, WA (USA) 2015, *Conference* York (UK) 2013, *Conference* Freising (Germany) 2011. **Publications** Monographs; books. [2019/XM6287/C]

♦ International Association of Economic and Social Councils and Similar Institutions (IAESCSI) 11858

Association internationale des conseils économiques et sociaux et institutions similaires (AICESIS)

SG Av d'Auderghem 20, 1040 Brussels, Belgium. T. +3222302878.
URL: http://www.aicesis.org/

History Founded 1 Jul 1999, Port Louis (Mauritius). **Aims** Develop cooperation between members by promoting exchange of experiences and good practices; promote social dialogue and participatory democracy at a wider level; encourage and support the creation of ESCs in countries which do not yet possess them, in accordance with the principles of the United Nations and the Universal Declaration of Human Rights, as well as the fundamental principles and rights at work endorsed by all members of the ILO. **Structure** General Assembly (annual) in one of the member countries. Board of Directors of 18 members representing a balanced geographical distribution (currently 3 for Latin America and the Caribbean, 6 for Africa, 5 for Europe, 3 for Asia – Eurasia – Middle East). General Secretariat. **Languages** English, French. **Staff** 5.00 FTE, paid. **Finance** Members' dues. Also in-kind contributions from some members. Thus, according to their means, most of them strive to participate in AICESIS expenses, for instance by holding and supporting expenditure related to organization of a conference, working group meetings, general assembly, board, etc. **Activities** Main working theme (2015): National human capital and new sources of national competitiveness. Events/meetings; training/education; awards/prizes/competitions; knowledge management/information dissemination. **Events** *General Assembly* Moscow (Russia) 2015, *International Conference on Promoting Workplace Compliance including in the Global Supply Chains* The Hague (Netherlands) 2015, *Joint Conference with ILO* The Hague (Netherlands) 2015, *General Assembly* Bucharest (Romania) 2014, *Joint Conference on Social Protection Floors for All / Joint Conference with ILO* Seoul (Korea Rep) 2014. **Publications** *Annual AICESIS Newsletter* in Arabic, English, French, Italian, Russian, Spanish. Reports; speeches.

Members Ordinary; Associate; Observer. Ordinary members (62) in 62 countries and territories (not specified).
Included in the above, 2 organizations listed in this Yearbook:
Included in the above, 2 organizations listed in this Yearbook:
European Economic and Social Committee (EESC, #06963); *Union of Economic and Social Councils of Africa (UCESA, no recent information)*.
Associate members (6) in 6 countries and territories (not specified).
Included in the above, 2 organizations listed in this Yearbook:
Foro Económico y Social del MERCOSUR (no recent information); *Union des Conseils Economiques et Sociaux et Institutions Similaires Francophones (UCESIF)*.
Observers (4) in 4 countries and territories:
Argentina, Israel, Mexico, Palestine.
IGO Relations Permanent observer status with: *ECOSOC (#05331)*. Reciprocal invitation to meetings with: *ILO (#11123)*. **NGO Relations** Cooperates with: *United Nations Informal Regional Network of Non-Governmental Organizations (UN-NGO-IRENE, #20573)*. [2019/XD8198/y/D]

♦ International Association for the Economics of Participation (IAFEP) 11859

Association internationale d'économie de la participation

Pres c/o Dept of International Economics and Management, Copenhagen Business School, Porcelænshaven 24A, Room POR/24A-2 58, 2000 Frederiksberg, Denmark. T. +4538152504. E-mail: agr.int@cbs.dk.
URL: http://www.iafep.org/

History 13 Oct 1978, Cavtat (Yugoslavia), as *International Association for the Economics of Self-Management (IAFESM)*, at 1st International Conference on the Economics of Worker Management. Present name adopted Aug 1994. **Aims** Promote scholarly exchange among persons interested in the economics of *self-management*, democratic firms and economic participation – in the economic theory, policy, *planning* and development of societies employing worker management; contribute to growth of knowledge in this area. **Structure** Council; President and Vice-President. **Languages** English. **Staff** 1.00 FTE, paid. **Finance** Members' dues. **Activities** Awards/prizes/competitions; events/meetings. **Events** *Biennial Conference* Copenhagen (Denmark) 2016, *Biennial Conference* Montevideo (Uruguay) 2014, *Biennial Conference* New Brunswick, NJ (USA) 2012, *Biennial Conference* Paris (France) 2010, *Biennial Conference* Clinton, NY (USA) 2008. **Publications** *Advances in the Economic Analysis of Participatory and Labor-Managed Firms*.
Members Institutions; Individuals, in 50 countries:
Algeria, Argentina, Australia, Austria, Belgium, Bolivia, Brazil, Canada, Chile, China, Croatia, Czechia, Denmark, Egypt, Estonia, Finland, France, Georgia, Germany, Ghana, Greece, Hungary, India, Ireland, Italy, Japan, Korea Rep, Mexico, Netherlands, New Zealand, Nigeria, North Macedonia, Norway, Peru, Poland, Portugal, Russia, Senegal, Serbia, Slovenia, Spain, Sweden, Tanzania UR, Tunisia, Türkiye, UK, Ukraine, Uruguay, USA, Venezuela. [2018/XC1376/F]

♦ International Association for the Economics of Self-Management / see International Association for the Economics of Participation (#11859)

♦ International Association of Educating Cities (IAEC) 11860

Association internationale des ville éducatrices (AIVE) – Asociación Internacional de Ciudades Educadoras – Associació Internacional de Ciutats Educadores (AICE)

Secretariat Avinyó 15, 4a planta, 08002 Barcelona, Spain. T. +34933427720. Fax +34933427729. E-mail: edcities@bcn.cat.
URL: http://www.edcities.org/

History 1990, Barcelona (Spain). Association formalized, 1994, during Bologna congress. **Structure** General Assembly; Executive Committee. **Activities** Events/meetings. **Events** *International Congress of Educating Cities* Andong (Korea Rep) 2022, *International Congress of Educating Cities* Katowice (Poland) 2020, *Meeting* Dangjin (Korea Rep) 2019, *International Congress of Educating Cities* Cascais (Portugal) 2018, *General Assembly* Changwon (Korea Rep) 2018.
Members Cities in 35 countries:
Argentina, Australia, Belgium, Benin, Bolivia, Brazil, Cape Verde, Colombia, Costa Rica, Croatia, Denmark, Ecuador, Finland, France, Germany, Greece, Italy, Korea Rep, Mexico, Morocco, Nepal, Netherlands, Palestine, Philippines, Poland, Portugal, Puerto Rico, Romania, Senegal, Spain, Sweden, Thailand, Togo, Uruguay, Venezuela. [2023.02.14/XD7821/D]

♦ International Association for Educational Assessment (IAEA) 11861

Association internationale pour l'évaluation éducative (AIEE)

Exec Sec c/o IEB, PO Box 875, Highlands North 2037, Johannesburg, South Africa. T. +27114839700. Fax +27114839797. E-mail: info@iaea.info.
URL: http://www.iaea.info/

History 21 Apr 1974, Princeton NJ (USA). First meeting: May 1975, Geneva (Switzerland). **Aims** Assist educational agencies in the development and appropriate application of educational assessment techniques to improve the quality of education through: international cooperation; facilitation of development of closer ties amongst relevant agencies and individuals worldwide. **Structure** Executive Committee, comprising President, Vice-President, Executive Secretary, Treasurer/Membership Secretary and 4 members. **Languages** English. **Staff** None. **Finance** Sources: members' dues. **Activities** Professional interchange; conferences; workshops; publications and electronic dissemination. **Events** *Conference* Accra (Ghana) 2020, *Conference* Baku (Azerbaijan) 2019, *Conference* Oxford (UK) 2018, *Conference* Batumi (Georgia) 2017, *Conference* Cape Town (South Africa) 2016.
Members Primary members (85); Individual (94); Associate (6); Affiliate (10); Honorary (1). Primary in 60 countries. Membership countries not specified. Included in the above, 4 organizations listed in this Yearbook:
Caribbean Examinations Council (CXC, #03500); *International Baccalaureate (IB, #12306)*; *South Pacific Board for Educational Assessment (SPBEA, inactive)*; *West African Examinations Council (WAEC, #20879)*.
Individuals in 17 countries and territories:
Australia, Brazil, Canada, Cyprus, France, Germany, Japan, Jordan, Malta, Netherlands, New Zealand, Nigeria, Saudi Arabia, Scotland, Slovenia, UK, USA.
Associate members in 5 countries:
Netherlands, Philippines, South Africa, UK, USA.
Included in the above, 3 organizations listed in this Yearbook:
Association for Educational Assessment – Europe (AEA Europe, #02483); *Association for Educational Assessment in Africa (AEAA, #02482)*; *Association of Commonwealth Examination and Accreditation Bodies (ACEAB, #02438)*.
Consultative Status Consultative status granted from: *ECOSOC (#05331)* (Ros C); *UNESCO (#20322)* (Consultative Status). **IGO Relations** Accredited by: *United Nations Office at Vienna (UNOV, #20604)*. [2021/XC8427/y/C]

♦ International Association of Educational and Discovery Television Companies (no recent information)

♦ International Association for Educational and Vocational Guidance (IAEVG) 11862

Association internationale d'orientation scolaire et professionnelle (AIOSP) – Asociación Internacional para la Orientación Educativa y Profesional (AIOEP) – Internationale Vereinigung für Schul- und Berufsberatung (IVSBB)

SG 2395, rue de Rome, Sainte-Julie QC J3E 2K2, Canada. E-mail: membership@iaevg.com – secretarygeneral@iaevg.com – president@iaevg.com.
URL: https://iaevg.com/

History 27 Apr 1951, Paris (France). Founded at a meeting when a provisional committee was set up. Formally constituted 16 Jan 1953, Brussels (Belgium), following meetings 1952, Geneva (Switzerland). Current title and statutes adopted, 1963. Statutes revised: 1991; 2005; 2010; 2015. Former names and other names: *Association internationale d'orientation scolaire et professionnelle* – former. Registration: Start date: Jan 2015, Luxembourg. **Aims** Provide global leadership in and advocates for Educational and Vocational Guidance by promoting ethical, socially just, and best practices throughout the world. **Structure** General Assembly (annual); Board of Directors; Executive Committee; General Secretariat, headed by President (currently serving as UNESCO Representative). **Languages** English, French, German, Spanish. **Staff** 0.10 FTE, paid; 1.00 FTE, voluntary. **Finance** Sources: gifts, legacies; grants; members' dues. **Activities** Events/meetings; research/documentation; standards/guidelines. **Events** *Conference* The Hague (Netherlands) 2023, *Conference* Seoul

(Korea Rep) 2022, *Conference* Riga (Latvia) 2021, *Conference* Riga (Latvia) 2020, *Career guidance for inclusive society* Bratislava (Slovakia) 2019. **Publications** *International Journal for Educational and Vocational Guidance* (annual) in English, French, German; *IAEVG Newsletter* in English, French, German, Spanish. *IAEVG Research Studies* – published by UNESCO. *Glossary of Terms Used in Educational and Vocational Guidance* in English, French, German, Italian, Spanish. Bibliographic bulletin; conference and seminar reports; case studies in liaison with UNESCO. Information Services: Documentation Centre and Archive.
Members National/regional associations of guidance counsellors or associations whose aims involve educational and vocational guidance (current membership represents about 20,000 individuals); individual members (about 200); institutions and other associations with direct interest in guidance (about 40); supportive members, including educational and/or labour departments of national governments and other organizations supporting IAEVG aims. National associations (38) in 24 countries and territories:
Austria, Canada, Denmark, Faeroe Is, Finland, France, Germany, Greece, Iceland, India, Ireland, Japan, Mauritius, Mexico, Netherlands, Nigeria, Norway, Peru, Saudi Arabia, Spain, Sweden, Switzerland, UK, USA.
Consultative Status Consultative status granted from: *UNESCO (#20322)* (Consultative Status); *ILO (#11123)* (Special List). **IGO Relations** Liaises with: *European Commission (EC, #06633)*. **NGO Relations** Member of NGO Standing Committee of: *International Conference of NGOs (#12883)*. Joint committee with: *International Association for Counselling (IAC, #11821)*. [2023.02.16/XC1191/**B**]

♦ International Association for Educational and Vocational Information (inactive)
♦ International Association for Education of the Deaf-Blind / see Deafblind International (#05014)
♦ International Association for the Education of Deaf-Blind People / see Deafblind International (#05014)

♦ International Association for Education in Ethics (IAEE) 11863

Exec Sec Duquesne Univ Fisher Hall 300, 600 Forbes Avenue, Pittsburgh PA 15282, USA. T. +14123964504. E-mail: iaee@duq.edu.
URL: http://www.ethicsassociation.org/

History Legally established Apr 2011. Current bylaws approved 2012. Registered in the State of Pennsylvania (USA) as a 501(c)(3) nonprofit charity: 45-2797707. **Aims** Exchange and analyse experience with the teaching of ethics in various educational settings; promote development of knowledge and methods of ethics education; function as a global center of contact for experts in the field, and promote contacts among members from countries worldwide; enhance and expand teaching of ethics at national, regional and international levels. **Structure** General Assembly; Board of Directors; Secretariat. **Languages** English. **Finance** Sources: members' dues. **Activities** Events/meetings; networking/liaising; research/documentation. **Events** *Conference* Lisbon (Portugal) 2019, *Conference* Stellenbosch (South Africa) 2018. **Publications** *International Journal for Ethics Education*. **Members** Ordinary; Institutional; Honorary. Membership countries not specified. [2018/XM7356/**C**]

♦ International Association for Education to a Life without Drugs (inactive)

♦ International Association of Education in Science and Snowsports (IAESS) 11864

Pres c/o Sport & Exercise Sci Dept, Allmandring 28, 70569 Stuttgart, Germany. E-mail: info@iaess.org.
URL: https://iaess.org/

History 14 Jan 1965, Bad Gastein (Austria). Founded during 7th INTERSKI Congress. Former names and other names: *International Association Skiing in Schools and Universities* – former (Jan 1965 to 1993); *Internationaler Verband Skilauf an Schulen und Hochschulen (IVSS)* – former (Jan 1965 to 1993); *Internationaler Verband Schneesport an Schulen und Hochschulen (IVSS)* – former (1993 to Mar 2022); *International Association for Snowsports at Schools and Universities* – former (1993 to Mar 2022). **Aims** Contribute to the development of snowsports at educational system and to bridge the gap between theory and practice. **Structure** General Assembly. Board, comprising President, Vice-President, Secretary-General and 5 members. **Events** *Congress* Rovaniemi (Finland) 2009, *Congress* Pyeongchang (Korea Rep) 2007, *Congress* Bad Hindelang (Germany) 2005, *Congress* St Christoph am Arlberg (Austria) 2001, *Congress* Vuokatti (Finland) 1997. **Publications** *IVSS Newsletter*.
Members Full in 29 countries:
Argentina, Australia, Austria, Belgium, Bulgaria, Canada, Chile, Croatia, Czechia, Denmark, Finland, France, Germany, Hungary, Israel, Japan, Korea Rep, Montenegro, Netherlands, North Macedonia, Norway, Poland, Serbia, Slovakia, Slovenia, Sweden, Switzerland, UK, USA.
NGO Relations A working body of: *Interski International (INTERSKI, #15975)*. [2022/XN8139/**D**]

♦ International Association of Educators for Peace (internationally oriented national body)
♦ International Association of Educators for World Peace (internationally oriented national body)

♦ International Association of Egyptologists (IAE) 11865

Association internationale des égyptologues – Internationaler Ägyptologen-Verband

SG Inst für Altertumswissenschaften/Ägyptologie, Johannes Gutenberg-Uni Mainz, 55099 Mainz, Germany. E-mail: secretary@iae-egyptology.org.
URL: http://www.iae-egyptology.org/

History Aug 1947, Copenhagen (Denmark). **Aims** Unite the efforts of persons, scholars and supporters for the promotion of Egyptology. **Structure** General Assembly (every 4 years); Council; Presidium; Committees; General Secretary. **Languages** English, French, German. **Staff** 1.00 FTE, paid. **Finance** Sources: members' dues. **Activities** Events/meetings. **Events** *Congress* Leiden (Netherlands) 2023, *Congress* Cairo (Egypt) 2019, *Congress* Florence (Italy) 2015, *Congress* Alexandria (Egypt) 2014, *Congress* Alexandria (Egypt) 2013. **Publications** *Museum Newsletter*. *Online Egyptological Bibliography (OEB)* (2009-); *Annual Egyptological Bibliography* – until 2008. Abstracts; congress proceedings.
Members Professional; Associate; Student. Individuals in 56 countries and territories:
Argentina, Australia, Austria, Belgium, Bosnia-Herzegovina, Brazil, Bulgaria, Canada, China, Congo DR, Costa Rica, Croatia, Cuba, Czechia, Denmark, Egypt, Estonia, Finland, France, Germany, Greece, Guyana, Hong Kong, Hungary, India, Ireland, Israel, Italy, Japan, Kenya, Latvia, Luxembourg, Mexico, Monaco, Netherlands, New Zealand, Norway, Pakistan, Peru, Poland, Portugal, Romania, Russia, Saudi Arabia, Serbia, Singapore, Slovakia, South Africa, Spain, Sweden, Switzerland, Tunisia, UK, Ukraine, Uruguay, USA. [2017.10.26/XD3025/v/**C**]

♦ International Association for Eidetics / see Eidetics Academy (#05400)
♦ International Association of Electrical Contractors / see EuropeOn (#09166)
♦ International Association on Electricity Generation, Transmission and Distribution – Afro-Asian Region (no recent information)
♦ International Association Pro Electron (inactive)

♦ International Association of Elevator Engineers (IAEE) 11866

Chairman Hallmark House, 25 Downham Road, Ramsden Heath, Ramsden Heath, CM11 1PU, UK. Fax +448701300790. E-mail: iaee@elevcon.com.
Brussels Office Av Winston Churchill 119, 1180 Brussels, Belgium.
URL: http://www.elevcon.com/

History 14 Feb 1986, Nice (France). **Aims** Promote scientific knowledge in elevator engineering. **Structure** Administrative Board. Steering Committee, consisting of 5 members. Regional Coordinators. Standards Sub-Committee. **Languages** English. **Staff** Voluntary. **Finance** Sources: contributions; members' dues. **Activities** Organizes ELEVCON World Congress and Asian ELEVCON. **Events** *World Congress* Prague (Czechia) 2022, *World Congress* Prague (Czechia) 2020, *World Congress* Berlin (Germany) 2018, *World Congress* Madrid (Spain) 2016, *World Congress* Paris (France) 2014. **Publications** *IAEE Newsletter*. *IAEE Conference Series*; *IAEE Design Series*; *IAEE Information Series*. Standards; congress proceedings.
Members Individuals in 50 countries and territories:
Australia, Austria, Brazil, Canada, Chile, China, Colombia, Costa Rica, Cyprus, Czechia, Denmark, Finland, France, Germany, Ghana, Greece, Hong Kong, India, Indonesia, Iran Islamic Rep, Ireland, Israel, Italy, Japan, Jordan, Korea Rep, Kuwait, Malaysia, Malta, Netherlands, New Zealand, Norway, Paraguay, Philippines, Puerto Rico, Qatar, Romania, Saudi Arabia, Singapore, South Africa, Spain, Sweden, Switzerland, Thailand, Tunisia, Türkiye, UK, Uruguay, USA, Venezuela. [2019/XD1463/v/**C**]

♦ International Association of Emergency Managers (internationally oriented national body)
♦ International Association for Emergency Psychiatry (no recent information)

♦ International Association of Empirical Aesthetics (IAEA) 11867

Association internationale d'esthétique expérimentale (AIEE) – Internationale Gesellschaft für Empirische Ästhetik – Associazione Internazionale di Estetica Empirica

SG Educational Sciences UniRoma, Via del Castro Pretorio 20, 00185 Rome RM, Italy. T. +39657339818. Fax +39644703879.
Pres address not obtained.
URL: http://www.science-of-aesthetics.org/

History 1965, Paris (France). Statute adopted 16 May 1967. Registered in accordance with French law. **Aims** Bring together specialists of different countries for the scientific study of aesthetic phenomena by means of empirical or experimental verification. **Structure** General Assembly (at the occasion of a Congress). Board of Direction, consisting of President, Secretary-General, Treasurer and Vice-Presidents responsible for different regions. **Languages** English. **Staff** None. **Finance** Members' dues: euro 40. Donations; subsidies. **Activities** Organizes congresses and symposia. Awards: *'Gustav Theodor Fechner Award'*; *'Sir Frances Galton Award'*; *'Alexander Gottlieb Baumgarten Award'*. Offers fellowships. **Events** *Congress* London (UK) 2021, *Congress* London (UK) 2020, *Congress* Toronto, ON (Canada) 2018, *Congress* Vienna (Austria) 2016, *Congress* New York, NY (USA) 2014. **Publications** *Empirical Studies of the Arts* (2 a year). Congress proceedings.
Members Honour; Benefactor; Founding; Fellow; Titular researchers studying aesthetic phenomena in 39 countries and territories:
Argentina, Australia, Austria, Azerbaijan, Belgium, Brazil, Canada, China, Croatia, Czechia, Denmark, Estonia, Finland, France, Germany, Greece, Hong Kong, Hungary, Iraq, Israel, Italy, Japan, Korea Rep, Mexico, Netherlands, New Zealand, Norway, Poland, Portugal, Russia, Serbia, Slovakia, South Africa, Spain, Sweden, Switzerland, Taiwan, UK, USA. [2014/XD9194/v/**C**]

♦ International Association of Endocrine Surgeons (IAES) 11868

Association Internationale de Chirurgie Endocrine

Sec-Treas c/o Foothills Med Ctr, Surgery Dept, 1403 29th St NW, Calgary AB T2N 2T9, Canada. T. +14039442491. Fax +14032834130. E-mail: iaes_jp@icloud.com.
URL: http://www.iaes-endocrine-surgeons.com/

History Founded 1979, San Francisco CA (USA). Integrated Society of: *International Society of Surgery (ISS, #15496)*. **Aims** Be a forum for exchange of views of those who are involved in expanding the frontiers of endocrine surgery whether by clinical experience, laboratory investigation or in any other way. **Structure** Council; Executive Committee; Committees (4). **Languages** English. **Staff** 1.00 FTE, paid. **Finance** Sources: international organizations. Supported by: *International Society of Surgery (ISS, #15496)*. **Events** *Biennial Meeting* Kuala Lumpur (Malaysia) 2024, *Biennial Meeting* Vienna (Austria) 2022, *Biennial Meeting* Krakow (Poland) 2019, *Biennial Meeting* Basel (Switzerland) 2017, *Biennial Meeting* Bangkok (Thailand) 2015.
Members Individuals in 60 countries and territories:
Argentina, Australia, Austria, Azerbaijan, Belgium, Brazil, Bulgaria, Canada, Chile, China, Colombia, Cyprus, Czechia, Denmark, Egypt, Finland, France, Germany, Greece, Guatemala, Hong Kong, Hungary, India, Ireland, Israel, Italy, Japan, Kazakhstan, Kenya, Korea Rep, Kuwait, Lithuania, Luxembourg, Malaysia, Mexico, Nepal, Netherlands, New Zealand, Norway, Philippines, Poland, Portugal, Puerto Rico, Russia, Saudi Arabia, Serbia, Singapore, Slovenia, South Africa, Spain, Sweden, Switzerland, Taiwan, Tajikistan, Türkiye, UK, Ukraine, USA, Uzbekistan, Yemen.
NGO Relations Umbrella organization for: American Association of Endocrine Surgeons (AAES); *Asian Association of Endocrine Surgeons (AsAES, #01321)*; *European Society of Endocrine Surgeons (ESES, #08593)*. [2020/XD2754/v/**C**]

♦ International Association for Energy Economics (IAEE) 11869

Main Office 28790 Chagrin Blvd, Ste 350, Cleveland OH 44122, USA. T. +12164645365. Fax +12164642737. E-mail: iaee@iaee.org.
URL: http://www.iaee.org/

History 1977, as *International Association of Energy Economists*. Has also been unofficially referred to in French as *Association internationale des économistes de l'énergie (AIEE)*. **Aims** Advance the understanding and application of economics across all aspects of energy and foster communication amongst energy concerned professionals. **Structure** Council. International affiliates (34) and USA national chapters (8), each organizing its own meetings and other activities. Branch: *Benelux Association for Energy Economics (BAEE, #03198)*. **Languages** English. **Finance** Sources: contributions; members' dues. Annual budget: 200,000 USD. **Activities** Awards/prizes/competitions; events/meetings. **Events** *European Conference* Athens (Greece) 2022, *Annual International Conference* Tokyo (Japan) 2022, *European Conference* Athens (Greece) 2021, *Annual North American Conference* Austin, TX (USA) 2021, *Annual International Conference* Tokyo (Japan) 2021. **Publications** *The Energy Journal* (4 a year); *IAEE Energy Forum* (4 a year) – newsletter; *Economics of Energy and Environmental Policy* (2 a year). Membership directory (annual); conference proceedings. Most publications, including directory, online.
Members Professionals (over 3,400, of whom 1,100 in North America). International affiliates in 37 countries and territories:
Australia, Austria, Azerbaijan, Barbados, Belarus, Belgium, Canada, Czechia, Denmark, Estonia, Finland, France, Germany, Hungary, India, Indonesia, Iran Islamic Rep, Italy, Japan, Korea Rep, Latvia, Lithuania, Luxembourg, Mexico, Netherlands, Norway, Poland, Russia, Saudi Arabia, Singapore, Spain, Sweden, Switzerland, Taiwan, UK, Ukraine, USA.
Individuals and institutions in 25 countries and territories where there is no international affiliate:
Argentina, Colombia, Ecuador, Guinea, Guyana, Iceland, Ireland, Israel, Kuwait, Malaysia, Nepal, New Zealand, Nigeria, Pakistan, Papua New Guinea, Philippines, Qatar, Senegal, Spain, Sri Lanka, Sudan, Thailand, Trinidad-Tobago, United Arab Emirates, Uruguay. [2021/XD5401/v/**C**]

♦ International Association of Energy Economists / see International Association for Energy Economics (#11869)
♦ International Association for Energy-Efficient Lighting (inactive)

♦ International Association for the Engineering Analysis Community (NAFEMS) 11870

CEO 46 Campbell Street, Hamilton, ML3 6AS, UK. T. +441355225688.
URL: http://www.nafems.org/

History 1990, following activities of the (UK) 'National Agency for Finite Element Methods and Standards'. **Aims** Promote safe and reliable use of finite element and related technology. **Structure** Council of Management; Executive. **Activities** Meeting activities. **Events** *Biennial World Congress* Salzburg (Austria) 2021, *Biennial World Congress* Québec, QC (Canada) 2019, *Nordic Seminar* Helsinki (Finland) 2018, *Nordic seminar on Increasing the Confidence in Numerical Simulation* Oslo (Norway) 2017, *Biennial World Congress* Stockholm (Sweden) 2017. **Members** Corporate (700) in 30 countries (not specified). [2018/XD5195/**D**]

♦ International Association for Engineering and Food (IAEF) 11871

Exec Sec Depto Ingenieria Quimica, Univ de las Américas-Puebla, Exhacienda Santa Catarina Martir, Cholula, 72820 Puebla, Mexico. T. +5222292409. Fax +5222292009.
URL: http://www.icef12.com/

Aims Advance the subject of engineering and food, including education and training, international support for progress, and exchange of information. **Structure** General Meeting. Executive Committee, consisting of President, Secretary, Treasurer and 3 to 5 other members. **Languages** English. **Finance** Conference' registration fees. Members responsible for own expenses except for out-of-pocket expenses of officers. **Activities** Organizes quadrennial congresses on engineering and food (ICEF), equally spaced between congresses of IUFoST. **Events** *Quadrennial Congress* Nantes (France) 2023, *Quadrennial Congress* Melbourne, VIC (Australia) 2019, *Quadrennial Congress* Québec, QC (Canada) 2015, *International Congress on Contemporary Food Science and Engineering* Guangzhou (China) 2013, *Quadrennial Congress* Athens (Greece) 2011.
Members Full in 10 countries:
Canada, Finland, France, Germany, Ireland, Japan, Portugal, Sweden, UK, USA.
NGO Relations *International Union of Food Science and Technology (IUFoST, #15773)*. [2015/XD2456/**D**]

♦ International Association of Engineering Geology / see International Association of Engineering Geology and the Environment (#11872)

♦ International Association of Engineering Geology and the Environment (IAEG) 11872

SG Shaoxing University, No 508 Huanchengxilu, Shaoxing, Chaoyang District, 312010 Zhejiang, China. T. +86057588346551. Fax +86057588346551.
Pres Aristotle University of Thessaloniki, Faculty of Sciences, School of Geology, 541 24 Thessaloniki, Greece.

URL: http://www.iaeg.info/
History 1964, Delhi (India). Founded at 22nd International Geological Congress.Constitution adopted 11 Jan 1967, Paris (France). Constitution revised: Aug 1975, Sao Paulo (Brazil); Sep 1992, Kyoto (Japan). Former names and other names: *International Association of Engineering Geology (IAEG)* – former; *Association internationale de géologie de l'ingénieur (AIGI)* – former. **Aims** Encourage research, training and dissemination of knowledge by developing international cooperation in the field of engineering geology; encourage and promote the application of *earth sciences* to engineering, planning, construction, prospecting, environmental protection and the testing and processing of related materials. **Structure** General Assembly (every 2 years, to coincide with International Geological Congress and IAEG International Congress); Council; Executive Committee; National Groups; Commissions (6); Joint Technical Committee: IAEG-ISRM-ISSMGE Committee on Landslides and Engineered Slopes; Joint European Working Group – IAEG-ISRM-ISSMGE – Professional tasks, responsibilities and cooperation. **Languages** English, French. **Staff** 4.00 FTE, paid. Voluntary. **Finance** Sources: members' dues; revenue from activities/projects. **Activities** Awards/prizes/competitions; events/meetings; financial and/or material support. **Events** *Congress* Chengdu (China) 2023, *Congress* Chengdu (China) 2022, *Africa Regional Congress* Lagos (Nigeria) 2022, *WMESS : World Multidisciplinary Earth Sciences Symposium* Prague (Czechia) 2022, *Asian Regional Conference* Singapore (Singapore) 2021. **Publications** *Bulletin of Engineering Geology and the Environment* (4 a year); *IAEG Newsletter* (2 a year).
Members National Groups, totalling more than 5,200 individual members, in 56 countries and territories:
Albania, Algeria, Argentina, Australia, Austria, Belgium, Brazil, Bulgaria, Canada, China, Colombia, Croatia, Cyprus, Czechia, Denmark, Estonia, Finland, France, Georgia, Germany, Greece, Hungary, Iceland, India, Indonesia, Iran Islamic Rep, Ireland, Italy, Japan, Korea Rep, Lithuania, Malaysia, Mexico, Nepal, Netherlands, New Zealand, Norway, Paraguay, Peru, Poland, Portugal, Romania, Russia, Serbia, Singapore, Slovakia, Slovenia, South Africa, Spain, Sweden, Switzerland, Thailand, Türkiye, UK, USA, Vietnam.
Individuals in 51 other countries and territories:
Angola, Armenia, Azerbaijan, Bahamas, Bangladesh, Belarus, Bosnia-Herzegovina, Cameroon, Congo Brazzaville, Congo DR, Croatia, Cuba, Egypt, Estonia, Gabon, Georgia, Guinea, Honduras, Iran Islamic Rep, Iraq, Jamaica, Kazakhstan, Kenya, Kuwait, Kyrgyzstan, Latvia, Lebanon, Libya, Lithuania, Madagascar, Malaysia, Mali, Mongolia, Mozambique, Nepal, Nicaragua, Pakistan, Sao Tomé-Principe, Saudi Arabia, Senegal, Singapore, Slovenia, Sri Lanka, Sudan, Syrian AR, Taiwan, Tajikistan, Ukraine, United Arab Emirates, Uzbekistan, Zambia.
Regional constituent member:
Southeast Asian Geotechnical Society (SEAGS, #19769).
NGO Relations Member of (5): *Federation of International Geo-Engineering Societies (FedIGS, #09673); International Society for Rock Mechanics and Rock Engineering (ISRM, #15428); International Society for Soil Mechanics and Geotechnical Engineering (ISSMGE, #15452); International Union for Quaternary Research (INQUA, #15811); International Union of Geological Sciences (IUGS, #15777).* Cooperates with (2): *International Association for Promoting Geoethics (IAPG, #12107); International Association of Hydrogeologists (IAH, #11953).* [2023/XB1278/**B**]

♦ International Association for Engineering Graphics (BALTGRAF) . . . 11873

Pres Vilnius Gediminas Technical Univ, Saulėtekio al 11, LT-10223 Vilnius, Lithuania.
URL: http://www.baltgraf.org/
History 1991, Vilnius (Lithuania). **Aims** Establish a new scientific journal; organize scientific conferences; coordinate efforts; exchange ideas in the field of engineering background education dealing with various engineering graphics matters. **Structure** Council of 13, including President. **Languages** English. **Staff** Voluntary. **Finance** Conference registration fees. Occasional conference co-funding. **Events** *Conference* Riga (Latvia) 2013, *Conference* Tallinn (Estonia) 2011, *Conference* Vilnius (Lithuania) 2009, *Conference* Riga (Latvia) 2008, *Conference* Tallinn (Estonia) 2006. **Publications** Conference proceedings.
Members Full in 12 countries:
Austria, Croatia, Estonia, Germany, Japan, Latvia, Lithuania, Poland, Russia, Slovakia, Ukraine, USA. [2017/XJ6521/**D**]

♦ International Association of Engineering Insurers, The (IMIA) 11874

Association internationale d'assurance technique – Internationale Vereinigung der Technischen Versicherer
Business Office c/o Traviss Co, Newtown House, 38 Newtown Road, Liphook, GU30 7DX, UK. E-mail: mss.sec@imia.com.
URL: http://www.imia.com/
History 1968, Munich (Germany). Former names and other names: *International Machinery Insurers' Association* – former; *Association internationale d'assurance technique* – former; *Internationale Vereinigung der Technischen Versicherer* – former. Registration: Companies House, No/ID: 13629672, Start date: 18 Sep 2021, England. **Aims** Promote understanding and best practice in the field of engineering insurance; allow engineering insurers around the world to share experiences, discuss and develop new ideas, investigate and share knowledge on emerging and critical issues; analyse advances in technology, causes of loss, changes in the maintenance and operation of machinery and other technological innovations. **Structure** Annual Conference; Executive Committee; Secretariat. **Languages** English. **Staff** 2.00 FTE, voluntary. **Finance** Sources: members' dues. **Activities** Events/meetings; networking/liaising. **Events** *Annual Conference* Singapore (Singapore) 2023, *Annual Conference* Dún Laoghaire (Ireland) 2022, *Annual Conference* 2021, *Annual Conference* 2020, *Annual Conference* Vienna (Austria) 2019.
Members National associations, invited reinsurers and invited insurers in 25 countries and territories:
Australia, Austria, Canada, Denmark, France, Germany, India, Ireland, Italy, Japan, Korea Rep, Mexico, Netherlands, Norway, Pakistan, Russia, Singapore, South Africa, Spain, Sweden, Switzerland, Taiwan, Türkiye, UK, USA.
Associate members: brokers; adjusters; experts. Membership countries not specified.
[2023.01.24/XD6595/**D**]

- ♦ International Association of Engine Rebuilders and Remanufacturers (#09654)
- ♦ International Association of English Speaking Directors' Organizations (inactive)

♦ International Association of Entertainment Lawyers (IAEL) 11875

Association internationale des avocats du monde et des industries du spectacle
Sec c/o DLA Piper UK LLP, 160 Aldersgate Street, London, EC1A 4HT, UK. T. +442073490296.
URL: http://www.iael.org/
History Founded Jan 1977, Cannes. Registered in accordance with French law. **Aims** Organize meetings between lawyers interested in entertainment *law*; encourage and promote studies to improve the knowledge of the law, rules and regulations governing entertainment. **Structure** Executive Committee. **Languages** English, French. **Finance** Members' dues. **Activities** Events/meetings. **Events** *Conference* Cannes (France) 2001, *Annual conference on international audiovisual law* Cannes (France) 1999, *Annual meeting* Cannes (France) 1995, *Annual meeting* Cannes (France) 1994, *Annual meeting* Cannes (France) 1993. **Publications** *Newsletter of International Association of Entertainment Lawyers* (2 a year) – for members. *Multimedia Deals in the Music Industry* (1996); *Moral Rights* (1995); *Digital Cable Radio* (1994); *Enforcement of Copyright and Related Rights Affecting the Music Industry* (1993); *Mechanical Rights* (1992); *Music in New Markets* (1991); *Rights of Artists and Producers* (1990); *Collecting Societies in the Music Business* (1989); *Music and the New Technologies* (1988); *Limitation of Free Bargaining and Sanctity of Contracts with performing Artists and Composers* (1987); *Merchandising and Sponsorship in the Music Business* (1986).
Members Active (lawyers); Subscribing (any individual or legal entity directly or indirectly concerned with entertainment). Members (over 150) in 21 countries and territories:
Australia, Belgium, Canada, Denmark, Finland, France, Germany, Hong Kong, India, Ireland, Italy, Lebanon, Luxembourg, Mexico, Netherlands, Norway, Spain, Sweden, Switzerland, UK, USA.
Consultative Status Consultative status granted from: *World Intellectual Property Organization (WIPO, #21593)* (Permanent Observer Status). [2020/XD6923/t/**D**]

♦ International Association of Environmental Analytical Chemistry (IAEAC) 11876

Association internationale de la chimie environnementale analytique
Sec Institut F A Forel, Univ of Geneva, 66 Carl-Vogt, 1211 Geneva 4, Switzerland. T. +41223790385. Fax +41223790329.
Pres Inst for Inorganic and Applied Chemistry, Univ of Hamburg, Martin-Luther-King-Platz 6, 20146 Hamburg, Germany. T. +4940428383111. Fax +4940428384381.
Administrative Assistant IAEAC – EPFL, PO Box 52, 1015 Lausanne VD, Switzerland. T. +41793470022. E-mail: iaeac@bluewin.ch.
URL: http://www.iaeac.com/
History 1 Feb 1977, Basel (Switzerland). Derived from *Annual Symposium on the Analytical Chemistry of Pollutants*, first organized 1971, Halifax (Canada), subsequently *Annual Symposium on Environmental Analytical Chemistry*. Registration: Switzerland. **Aims** Support regular exchange of experience among experts in the analytical chemistry of pollutants and related areas; orient members on recent advances in the field; take issue on relevant problems of environmental analysis and on questions related to environmental protection and control; familiarize analytical chemists with environmental issues in a wider sense; provide a basis for interdisciplinary contacts with scientists in other areas. **Structure** General Assembly (every 2 years at regular symposium); Executive Committee. Regional branch: *Red Latinoamericana para el Análisis de la Calidad Ambiental en América Latina (RACAL, #18701).* **Languages** English. **Staff** 1.00 FTE, paid; 3.00 FTE, voluntary. **Finance** Sources: members' dues. **Activities** Events/meetings; training/education. **Events** *Annual International Symposium on the Environment and Analytical Chemistry* Amsterdam (Netherlands) 2023, *Symposium on Chemistry and Fate of Modern Pesticides* Ioannina (Greece) 2022, *Annual International Symposium on the Environment and Analytical Chemistry* Regensburg (Germany) 2021, *Symposium on Chemistry and Fate of Modern Pesticides* Ioannina (Greece) 2020, *Symposium on Chemistry and Fate of Modern Pesticides* Bologna (Italy) 2018. **Publications** *IAEAC Newsletter* (annual); *International Journal of Environmental Analytical Chemistry Environment*; *Journal of Chromatography*. Symposia proceedings.
Members Individuals in 26 countries and territories:
Austria, Costa Rica, Czechia, Denmark, El Salvador, Finland, France, Germany, Greece, Hungary, Ireland, Italy, Netherlands, Nicaragua, Norway, Poland, Portugal, Puerto Rico, Romania, Russia, Slovakia, Spain, Sweden, Switzerland, UK, USA.
[2018/XD0027/v/**C**]

- ♦ International Association for Environmental Communication (internationally oriented national body)

♦ International Association of Environmental Mutagenesis and Genomics Societies (IAEMGS) 11877

Association internationale des sociétés de la mutagenèse de l'environnement
Exec Dir 12627 San Jose Blvd, Ste 202, Jacksonville FL 32223-8638, USA. T. +19042893410. Fax +12816644744.
URL: http://www.iaemgs.org/
History 1973, Asilomar, CA (USA). Founded at 1st International Congress on Environmental Mutagens. New constitution drawn up in 1998; revised 2008 and 2013. Original title: *International Association of Environmental Mutagen Societies (IAEMS) – Association internationale des sociétés de la mutagenèse de l'environnement*. Current title adopted 2013. **Aims** Promote collaboration and communication among member societies; help in training and fostering of research in the fields of environmental mutagenesis and genetic toxicology worldwide. **Structure** General Assembly (every 4 years, at Conference); Council; Executive Board. **Languages** English. **Staff** 2.00 FTE, paid. **Finance** Sources: donations; grants; members' dues. Annual budget: 30,000 USD. **Activities** Events/meetings; knowledge management/information dissemination; training/education. **Events** *ICEM : International Conference on Environmental Mutagens* Ottawa, ON (Canada) 2021, *ICEM : International Conference on Environmental Mutagens* Incheon (Korea Rep) 2017, *International Conference on Environmental Mutagens in Human Populations* Chiang Mai (Thailand) 2016, *ICEM : International Conference on Environmental Mutagens* Foz do Iguaçu (Brazil) 2013, *ICMAA : International Conference on Mechanisms of Antimutagens and Anticarcinogens* Vienna (Austria) 2013.
Members Regional and national societies; individuals. National societies in 94 countries and territories:
Albania, Andorra, Antigua-Barbuda, Argentina, Armenia, Australia, Austria, Azerbaijan, Bahamas, Barbados, Belarus, Belgium, Belize, Bolivia, Bosnia-Herzegovina, Brazil, Bulgaria, Canada, Chile, China, Colombia, Costa Rica, Croatia, Cuba, Cyprus, Czechia, Denmark, Dominica, Dominican Rep, Ecuador, El Salvador, Estonia, Finland, France, Georgia, Germany, Greece, Grenada, Guatemala, Guyana, Haiti, Holy See, Honduras, Hungary, Iceland, India, Ireland, Italy, Jamaica, Jordan, Korea Rep, Latvia, Liechtenstein, Lithuania, Luxembourg, Malta, Mexico, Moldova, Monaco, Montenegro, Netherlands, New Zealand, Nicaragua, North Macedonia, Norway, Panama, Paraguay, Peru, Philippines, Poland, Portugal, Puerto Rico, Romania, Russia, San Marino, Serbia, Slovakia, Slovenia, Spain, St Kitts-Nevis, St Lucia, St Vincent-Grenadines, Suriname, Sweden, Switzerland, Thailand, Trinidad-Tobago, Türkiye, UK, Ukraine, Uruguay, USA, Venezuela.
Regional organizations (5), listed in this Yearbook:
Environmental Mutagenesis and Genomics Society (EMGS); European Environmental Mutagenesis and Genomics Society (EEMGS, #07000); Latin American Association of Environmental Mutagens, Carcinogens and Teratogens (#16240); Molecular and Experimental Pathology Society of Australasia (MEPSA); Pan-African Environmental Mutagen and Genomic Society (PAEMGS, #18048).
IGO Relations Links with *International Programme on Chemical Safety (IPCS, #14650); WHO (#20950).* **NGO Relations** Member of: *International Union of Biological Sciences (IUBS, #15760).* [2020/XC8971/y/**C**]

- ♦ International Association of Environmental Mutagen Societies / see International Association of Environmental Mutagenesis and Genomics Societies (#11877)
- ♦ International Association of Environmental Planning and Management (unconfirmed)
- ♦ International Association – Epics of the World's Peoples (no recent information)
- ♦ International Association for Equality of Women (unconfirmed)
- ♦ International Association of Esperantist Jurist (inactive)
- ♦ International Association of Esperantist Mathematicians (no recent information)
- ♦ International Association of Esperantist Police Employees (inactive)
- ♦ International Association of Esperanto Bankers (inactive)
- ♦ International Association of Esperanto Pharmacists (inactive)
- ♦ International Association of Esperanto Railway Employees (inactive)

♦ International Association of Esperanto-Speaking Cyclists 11878

Association internationale des cyclistes espérantophones – Biciklista Esperantista Movado Internacia (BEMI)
Sec Bloemenweg 102, 6221 TX Maastricht, Netherlands.
URL: http://bemi.free.fr/eo.htm
History Founded 1 Jan 1980, Germany FR. Previously referred to as *International Esperantist Cyclist Movement – Mouvement international de cyclistes espérantistes.* **Finance** Members' dues. **Activities** Events/meetings. Cycling tours by Esperantists, or organized by Esperantists to/from Esperantist conferences. **Events** *Annual young people congress* Sweden 1991. **Publications** *BEMI-Revuo* (2 a year).
Members Individuals in 27 countries:
Belarus, Belgium, Brazil, Canada, Croatia, Czechia, Denmark, Estonia, France, Germany, Hungary, Italy, Japan, Latvia, Lithuania, Netherlands, Norway, Poland, Russia, South Africa, Spain, Sweden, Switzerland, UK, Ukraine, Uruguay, USA.
[2015/XD8328/v/**F**]

- ♦ International Association of Esperanto-Speaking Scientists / see International Esperantist Scientific Association (#13301)

♦ International Association for Ethical Literary Criticism (IAELC) 11879

Sec Fac of Foreign Languages, Ningbo Univ, 818 Fenghua Road, Ningbo, Jianbei District, 315211 Zhejiang, China. E-mail: elc2013@163.com – iaelc_seoul2015@163.com.
History 2012. **Aims** Provide a forum and resource for scholars and advanced students all over the world an opportunity to share their findings in the study of literature and ethics. **Structure** Executive Committee. **Events** *Conference* Manila (Philippines) 2019, *Conference* Kitakyushu (Japan) 2018, *Ethical literary criticism, comparative literature, and world literature* Tartu (Estonia) 2016, *Conference* Seoul (Korea Rep) / Busan (Korea Rep) 2015, *Conference* Shanghai (China) 2014. **Publications** *Ethical Literary Criticism: The Journal of IAELC.*
[2016/XM4403/**C**]

- ♦ International Association for Ethnopsychiatry and Ethnopsychoanalysis (inactive)

♦ International Association of Ethnopsychologists and Ethnopsychotherapists (IAEE) 11880

Pres Mental Health Research Inst, Aleutskaya Street 4, TOMSK, Russia, 634014. T. +73822724379. Fax +73822724425. E-mail: niipzso@yandex.ru – mental@tnimc.ru.
Acting Sec address not obtained.
URL: https://niipz.wordpress.com/

History 1998. Founded for coordination of screening/diagnosis of mental disorders in various ethnic populations of Russia, Mongolia, Hungary and Germany. **Aims** Study interrelations of norm and psychopathology for specialized medical assistance rendering and improvement of health of peoples of the world; work to achieve unity of language through psychiatric classifications through integration of basic scientific investigations in psychotherapy and pharmacotherapy; ascertain statistical compatibility and optimization of diagnostic criteria in various ethnoses. **Structure** Committees (3). **Languages** English, German, Russian. **Staff** 4.00 FTE, paid. **Activities** Advocacy/lobbying/activism; awards/prizes/competitions; awareness raising; events/meetings; guidance/assistance/consulting; healthcare; humanitarian/emergency aid; knowledge management/information dissemination; politics/policy/regulatory; projects/programmes; research and development; research/documentation; training/education. **Events** *Symposium* Berlin (Germany) 2017, *Symposium* Puerto Vallarta (Mexico) 2015, *Symposium* Madrid (Spain) 2014, *Symposium* London (UK) 2012, *Symposium* Buenos Aires (Argentina) 2011. **Publications** *Siberian Hearld of Psychiatry and Addiction Psychiatry* (4 a year) – peer-reviewed journal. *Ethnocultural paradigm of the formation of alcohol dependence* (2016) by Acad Prof Nikolay Bokhan and Prof Dr Anna Mandel et al in Russian; *Dissociative Model of Addictions Formation: Saint-Louis, MO, USA* (2014) by N A Bokhan and A A Ovchinnikov; *Transcultural Narcology and Psychotherapy* (2011) by V Ya Semke et al in Russian; *Comorbidity in Addiction Psychiatry* (2009) by N A Bokhan and V Ya Semke in Russian; *Mental Health of Indigenous People of the East of Russia* (2009) by V Ya Semke et al in Russian; *Transcultural Addictology* (2008) by V Ya Semke and N A Bokhan in Russian; *Drug Addiction in Adolescents under Conditions of Far North* (2005) by Bokhan et al in Russian; *Sketches of Ethnopsychology and Ethnopsychotherapy* (1999) by V Ya Semke et al in Russian. *Alcohol use and resilience among the indigenous Tuvinians of Siberia* (2022) in English.
Members Individuals in 16 countries:
Austria, Canada, China, Egypt, Germany, India, Israel, Italy, Kazakhstan, Mexico, Mongolia, Netherlands, Russia, Sweden, UK, USA.
NGO Relations Accredited by (2): *World Association of Cultural Psychiatry (WACP, #21130)*; *World Psychiatric Association (WPA, #21741)*. [2022.05.12/XD9396/v/**D**]

- ♦ International Association of Eurasian Business Schools (unconfirmed)
- ♦ International Association 'Europe 2000' (inactive)
- ♦ International Association for European Cooperation on Justice and Home Affairs (inactive)
- ♦ International Association of European General Average Adjusters / see Association mondiale de dispacheurs (#02809)

♦ International Association of the European Heritage Network (HEREIN Association) 11881

Association internationale du réseau européen du patrimoine

Contact Rue dees Brigades d'Irlande 1, 5100 Jambes, Belgium. E-mail: hereinaisbl@gmail.com.
URL: http://www.coe.int/herein/

History 17 Nov 2010. Founded in support of *European Information Network on Cultural Heritage Policies (HEREIN Project, #07533)*. Registration: Banque-Carrefour des Entreprises, No/ID: 0831.895.754, Start date: 15 Dec 2010, Belgium; EU Transparency Register, No/ID: 320631435475-78, Start date: 18 Jul 2019. **Aims** Promote experience exchange and foster information exchange of information on cultural heritage policies.
Members Full in 7 countries:
Belgium, Finland, France, Greece, Slovenia, Switzerland, UK.
Consultative Status Consultative status granted from: *Council of Europe (CE, #04881)* (Participatory Status). **NGO Relations** Member of (1): *Conference of INGOs of the Council of Europe (#04607)*. *Association of the Compendium of Cultural Policies and Trends (CCPT Association, #02442)*. [2019/XM4296/**E**]

- ♦ International Association of European Manufacturers of Glass Beads for Safety Road Markings and Other Industrial Purposes (inactive)
- ♦ International Association of the European Manufacturers of Major, Trace and Specific Feed Materials / see European Manufacturers of Feed Minerals Association (#07733)
- ♦ International Association of European Mining Industries, Metal Ores and Industrial Minerals / see European Association of Mining Industries, Metal Ores and Industrial Minerals (#06122)
- ♦ International Association of European Travel Insurers / see International Travel Insurance Alliance e.V. (#15728)

♦ International Association for the Evaluation of Educational Achievement (IEA) 11882

Association internationale pour l'évaluation du rendement scolaire

Chair Keizersgracht 311, 1016 EE Amsterdam, Netherlands. T. +31206253625. Fax +31204207136. E-mail: secretariat@iea.nl.
Exec Dir address not obtained.
URL: http://www.iea.nl/

History 1958. Former names and other names: *Stichting IEA Secretariaat Nederland* – legal name. Registration: Banque-Carrefour des Entreprises, No/ID: 0408.297.843, Start date: 30 May 1967, Belgium. **Aims** Research, understand and improve education worldwide. **Structure** General Assembly (annual); Standing Committee; Sub-Committees; Offices in Amsterdam (Netherlands) and Hamburg (Germany). Study Centers: *TIMSS and PIRLS International Study Center (ISC)*; International Civic and Citizenship Study (ICCS) centre at Australian Council for Educational Research (ACER); International Computer and Information Literacy Study (ICILS) center at ACER. **Languages** English. **Staff** 175.00 FTE, paid. **Finance** Sources: government support; grants; international organizations; members' dues. **Activities** Awards/prizes/competitions; capacity building; events/meetings; monitoring/evaluation; publishing activities; training/education. **Events** *International Research Conference* Dublin (Ireland) 2023, *General Assembly Meeting* Split (Croatia) 2022, *Annual General Assembly* 2021, *International Research Conference* Dubai (United Arab Emirates) 2021, *Annual General Assembly* 2020. **Publications** *IEA Newsletter* (annual); *Large-scale Assessments in Education* – journal. *IEA Compass: Briefs in Education*; *IEA Research for Education Series* – open access books. Reports; user guides; technical documentation. **Information Services** *IEA Data Repository*.
Members Institutions in 69 countries and territories:
Armenia, Australia, Austria, Azerbaijan, Bahrain, Belgium/Flemish Region, Belgium/Wallonia Region, Botswana, Brazil, Bulgaria, Canada, Chile, China, Colombia, Croatia, Cyprus, Czechia, Denmark, Egypt, England, Estonia, Finland, France, Georgia, Germany, Greece, Hong Kong (SAR), Hungary, Indonesia, Iran Islamic Rep, Ireland, Israel, Italy, Japan, Jordan, Kazakhstan, Korea Rep, Kuwait, Latvia, Lithuania, Luxembourg, Malaysia, Mexico, Morocco, Netherlands, New Zealand, North Macedonia, Norway, Oman, Palestine, Philippines, Poland, Portugal, Qatar, Romania, Russia, Saudi Arabia, Serbia, Singapore, Slovakia, Slovenia, South Africa, Spain, Sweden, Taiwan (Chinese Taipei), Thailand, Türkiye, United Arab Emirates, USA.
Consultative Status Consultative status granted from: *UNESCO (#20322)* (Consultative Status). **NGO Relations** Member of (5): American Educational Research Association (AERA); *Comparative and International Education Society (CIES)*; *European Educational Research Association (EERA, #06967)*; *European Network of Policy Makers for the Evaluation of Education Systems (#07971)*; *World Education Research Association (WERA, #21372)*. [2022.06.28/XC1217/v/**C**]

- ♦ International Association of Evangelical Chaplains (internationally oriented national body)

♦ International Association of Evidence Science (IAES) 11883

Contact China Univ of Political Science and Law, 25 Western Tucheng Road, Haidian District, 100088 Beijing, China. E-mail: zhongzh@cupl.edu.cn.
URL: http://www.theiaes.com/

History Constitution adopted 2011, Beijing (China), at 3rd International Conference on Evidence Law and Forensic Science. Incorporated as a not-for-profit, Chicago IL (USA), with Executive Committee located in Beijing (China). **Aims** Promote international development of the study of evidence science; promote interdisciplinary and international communication. **Structure** General Meeting. Council, including President, 5 Vice-Presidents and Executive Committee. Executive Director. **Languages** Chinese, English. **Staff** 3.00 FTE, voluntary. **Finance** Members' dues. Gifts from national and international organizations or individuals. **Activities** Organizes congresses and colloquia; encourages collaboration between evidence scholars and lawyers and forensic scientists, and information exchange concerning data, publications and documents; facilitates research and the preparation of reports. **Events** *International Conference on Evidence Law and Forensic Science* Beijing (China) 2013, *International Conference on Evidence Law and Forensic Science* Beijing (China) 2011, *International Conference on Evidence Law and Forensic Science* Beijing (China) 2009, *International Conference on Evidence Law and Forensic Science* Beijing (China) 2007. **Publications** *China Law Brief: Evidence Science* (2 a year).
Members Full in 13 countries:
Australia, China, Fiji, Hungary, India, Israel, Italy, Japan, Korea Rep, Switzerland, Tanzania UR, USA, Vietnam.
NGO Relations Cooperates with: *International Association for Procedural Law (IAPL, #12102)*. [2013.06.06/XJ6862/**E**]

- ♦ International Association of Exchanges of CIS Countries / see International Association of Exchanges of the Commonwealth of Independent States Countries (#11884)

♦ International Association of Exchanges of the Commonwealth of Independent States Countries (IAEx of CIS) 11884

Exec Dir Moscow Exchange, 13 Bolshoy Kislovskiy, Moscow MOSKVA, Russia, 125009. T. +74953633232ext25084. E-mail: iaex.cis@gmail.com.

History Founded Apr 2000, Moscow (Russia). Also referred to as *International Association of CIS Exchanges* and *International Association of Exchanges of CIS Countries (IAE CIS)*. **Aims** Coordinate development of organized financial markets in accordance with international standards. **Structure** General Meeting; Council; Committees; Working Groups. **Languages** Russian. **Staff** 3.00 FTE, paid. **Finance** Members' dues. Entrance fees. Annual budget (2017): US$ 45,312. **Events** *General Meeting* Almaty (Kazakhstan) 2014, *General Meeting* Alushta (Ukraine) 2013, *General Meeting* Chisinau (Moldova) 2012, *General Meeting* Yerevan (Armenia) 2011, *General Meeting* Kazan (Russia) 2010. **Publications** *Bulletin of Exchanges Statistics* (annual). Annual handbook.
Members Full in 9 countries:
Armenia, Azerbaijan, Belarus, Kazakhstan, Kyrgyzstan, Moldova, Russia, Ukraine, Uzbekistan.
IGO Relations *Commonwealth of Independent States (CIS, #04341)* Secretariat. [2018.08.09/XJ0397/**D**]

♦ International Association for the Exchange of Students for Technical Experience (IAESTE) 11885

Association internationale pour l'échange d'étudiants en vue de l'acquisition d'une expérience technique – Asociación Internacional de Intercambio de Estudiantes para favorecer su Experiencia Técnica

Pres 51 Rue Albert 1er, L-1117 Luxembourg, Luxembourg. T. +35220331699. E-mail: info@iaeste.org.
URL: http://www.iaeste.org/

History Jan 1948, London (UK). Founded on the initiative of James Newby and the Imperial College Vacation Work Committee, as an ad hoc association under its current name. Registration: RCS Luxembourg, No/ID: F1180, Start date: 2005, Luxembourg. **Aims** Operate a high quality practical training exchange programme between members and cooperating institutions so as to enhance technical and professional development and promote international understanding and goodwill amongst students, academic institutions, employers and the wider community. **Structure** General Conference (annual); Board; National Committees; Secretariats. Meetings closed. **Languages** English. **Staff** 4.00 FTE, paid; 5.00 FTE, voluntary. **Finance** Sources: donations; fees for services; fundraising; grants; in-kind support; meeting proceeds; members' dues; revenue from activities/projects; sponsorship; subscriptions. Annual budget: 241,885 EUR (2022). **Activities** Capacity building; events/meetings; guidance/assistance/consulting; knowledge management/information dissemination; networking/liaising; projects/programmes; training/education. **Events** *Annual Conference* Vienna (Austria) 2022, *Annual Conference* Vienna (Austria) 2021, *IAESTE Connect Conference* Oslo (Norway) 2020, *Annual Conference* Vysoké Tatry (Slovakia) 2020, *Central European Convention* Neum (Bosnia-Herzegovina) 2019. **Publications** *IAESTE Newsletter*. Annual Review; Activity Report.
Members Full: National Committees representing academic, industrial and student interests in 53 countries:
Argentina, Australia, Austria, Belarus, Belgium, Bosnia-Herzegovina, Brazil, Canada, Colombia, Croatia, Cyprus, Czechia, Denmark, Ecuador, Egypt, Germany, Ghana, Greece, Hungary, India, Iran Islamic Rep, Japan, Jordan, Kazakhstan, Korea Rep, Lebanon, Malta, Mongolia, North Macedonia, Norway, Oman, Pakistan, Panama, Philippines, Poland, Portugal, Romania, Russia, Serbia, Slovakia, Slovenia, Spain, Sweden, Switzerland, Syrian AR, Tajikistan, Tanzania UR, Thailand, Tunisia, Türkiye, United Arab Emirates, USA, Uzbekistan.
Associate: National Committees representing academic, industrial and student interests in 6 countries:
Bangladesh, Kenya, Nepal, Nigeria, Peru, Qatar.
Cooperating institutions in 24 countries and territories:
Afghanistan, Bolivia, Botswana, Chile, China, France, Gambia, Hong Kong, Iceland, Indonesia, Iraq, Jamaica, Kyrgyzstan, Luxembourg, Macau, Mexico, Nicaragua, Palestine, Saudi Arabia, South Africa, Sri Lanka, Uganda, Vietnam, Yemen.
Consultative Status Consultative status granted from: *ECOSOC (#05331)* (General); *UNESCO (#20322)* (Consultative Status); *ILO (#11123)* (Special List); *UNIDO (#20336)*. **IGO Relations** *Colombo Plan for Cooperative Economic and Social Development in Asia and the Pacific (CPS, #04120)*; *European Commission (EC, #06633)*; *FAO (#09260)*; *OAS (#17629)*; *United Nations Economic Commission for Africa (ECA, #20554)*; *United Nations Office at Vienna (UNOV, #20604)*. Associated with Department of Global Communications of the United Nations. **NGO Relations** *Deutscher Akademischer Austauschdienst (DAAD)*; *The European Law Students' Association (ELSA, #07660)*; *European Students' Union (ESU, #08848)*; *Institution of Engineering and Technology (IET, #11320)*; *International Association of Civil Engineering Students (IACES, #11776)*; *International Association of Students in Agricultural and Related Sciences (IAAS, #12191)*; *International Federation of Automotive Engineering Societies (#13369)*; *International Federation of Medical Students' Associations (IFMSA, #13478)*. [2022.06.14/XC1218/y/**C**]

- ♦ International Association for Exhibition Management / see International Association of Exhibitions and Events
- ♦ International Association of Exhibitions and Events (internationally oriented national body)

♦ International Association of Exhibitions in Latin America 11886

Association des foires internationales d'Amérique – Asociación Internacional de Ferias de América (AFIDA)

Exec Dir Av de Las Américas 406, 090513 Guayaquil, Ecuador. E-mail: informacion@afida.org.
URL: https://afida.org/

History 15 Apr 1969, Lima (Peru). Former names and other names: *Association of International Trade Fairs of America* – former. **Aims** Represent and promote the interests of the Latin American exhibition industry; educate and inform members on latest trends and developments; generate qualified contact and business opportunities. **Structure** General Assembly (annual); Board of Directors. **Languages** English, Spanish. **Staff** 3.00 FTE, paid. **Finance** Members' dues. Other sources: subsidies from private organizations; technical support from international organizations. **Activities** Advocacy/lobbying/activism; events/meetings; knowledge management/information dissemination; training/education. **Events** *Annual General Assembly and Congress* Barcelona (Spain) 2019, *Annual General Assembly and Congress* Mexico City (Mexico) 2015, *Annual General Assembly and Congress* Bogota (Colombia) 2014, *Annual General Assembly and Congress* Santa Cruz (Bolivia) 2013, *Annual General Assembly and Congress / Annual General Assembly* Porto (Portugal) 2012. **Publications** *Buenas Noticias AFIDA* (2 a year).
Members Active in 18 countries:
Argentina, Bolivia, Chile, Colombia, Costa Rica, Cuba, Dominican Rep, Ecuador, El Salvador, Guatemala, Honduras, Mexico, Panama, Peru, Portugal, Spain, Uruguay, USA.
Honorary members (3):
Asociación de Ferias Españolas (AFE); Asociación Portuguese de Ferias y Congresos (APCF); *Federación de Entidades Organizadoras de Congresos y Afines de América Latina (COCAL, #09299)*.
NGO Relations Member of: *International Association of Exhibitions and Events (IAEE)*; *UFI – The Global Association of the Exhibition Industry (#20276)*. [2021/XD8422/y/**D**]

- ♦ International Association of Exorcists (internationally oriented national body)
- ♦ International Association for the Exploration of Central Asia and the East (inactive)

♦ International Association of Facilitators (IAF) 11887

Manager Global Headquarters, 411 Richmond Street East Suite 200, Toronto ON M5S 3S5, Canada. T. +114169443183. E-mail: office@iaf-world.org.
URL: http://www.iaf-world.org/

History Jan 1994, Alexandria, VA (USA). **Aims** Set internationally accepted industry standards; provide accreditation; support a community of practice; advocate and educate on the power of facilitation; embrace the diversity of facilitators. **Structure** Association Coordinating Team; Executive Team; Strategic Initiative Co-ordinators; Regional Representatives; Executive Director. **Languages** Chinese, English, French, Portuguese, Spanish. **Activities** Certification/accreditation; events/meetings; networking/liaising; publishing activities; research/documentation. **Events** *Global Facilitation Summit* 2021, *Global Facilitation Summit* Stockholm (Sweden) 2020, *Annual Asia Regional Conference* Kuala Lumpur (Malaysia) 2019, *Africa Regional Conference* Lomé (Togo) 2019, *Conference of the Americas* Sao Paulo (Brazil) 2019. **Publications** *Group Facilitation Journal*. *IAF Handbook*. Information Services: Maintains database. **Members** Individuals (1,950) in over 65 countries. Membership countries not specified. [2022.10.19/XD5765/v/**F**]

♦ International Association of Factory Inspectors (inactive)
♦ International Association of Fairs and Expositions (internationally oriented national body)

♦ International Association for Falconry and Conservation of Birds of Prey (IAF) 11888

Association internationale de la fauconnerie et de la conservation des oiseaux de proie

Exec Officer Rue de Flandre 31, 1000 Brussels, Belgium. T. +353871330922. E-mail: info@iaf.org.
URL: https://iaf.org/

History 6 Apr 1968, Germany FR. Registration: Banque-Carrefour des Entreprises, No/ID: 0469.046.666, Start date: 18 Jan 2000, Belgium; EU Transparency Register, No/ID: 94837329683-94, Start date: 24 Sep 2012. **Aims** Preserve the ancient art of falconry, a hunting tradition defined as "taking quarry in its natural state and habitat by means of trained birds of prey". **Structure** General Meeting (annual); Council; Board; Advisory Committee; Working Groups. **Languages** English, French. **Staff** 5.00 FTE, paid; 10.00 FTE, voluntary. **Finance** Members' dues. Donations. **Events** *International Conference on Stewardship of Biodiversity and Sustainable Use* Ireland 2016, *Annual General Meeting* Doha (Qatar) 2014, *Annual General Meeting* Valkenswaard (Netherlands) 2013, *Annual General Meeting* Kearney, NE (USA) 2012, *Annual General Meeting* Al Ain (United Arab Emirates) 2011. **Publications** *International Journal of Falconry* (annual).
Members Associations and groups of associations (110) in 79 countries:
Algeria, Argentina, Armenia, Australia, Austria, Azerbaijan, Bahrain, Belarus, Belgium, Brazil, Brunei Darussalam, Bulgaria, Canada, Chile, China, Colombia, Croatia, Cuba, Czechia, Denmark, Ecuador, Egypt, El Salvador, Estonia, France, Georgia, Germany, Guatemala, Hungary, India, Indonesia, Iran Islamic Rep, Ireland, Italy, Japan, Kazakhstan, Korea Rep, Kyrgyzstan, Libya, Lithuania, Malta, Mexico, Mongolia, Morocco, Namibia, Netherlands, New Zealand, North Macedonia, Pakistan, Paraguay, Peru, Philippines, Poland, Portugal, Qatar, Romania, Russia, Saudi Arabia, Serbia, Slovakia, Slovenia, South Africa, Spain, Sweden, Switzerland, Taiwan, Thailand, Tunisia, Türkiye, Turkmenistan, UK, Ukraine, United Arab Emirates, Uruguay, USA, Uzbekistan, Venezuela, Vietnam, Zimbabwe.
Included in the above, 2 international organizations:
Falconry Heritage Trust; *International Council for Game and Wildlife Conservation (#13024).*
IGO Relations Observer status with: *Standing Committee to the Bern Convention on the Conservation of European Wildlife and Natural Habitats (#19949).* **NGO Relations** Member of: *International Union for Conservation of Nature and Natural Resources (IUCN, #15766).* [2021/XD6537/**D**]

♦ International Association of Family Movements for Rural Training (#02719)
♦ International Association of Family Sociology (no recent information)
♦ International Association for Farming Systems Research and Extension / see International Farming Systems Association (#13332)

♦ International Association for Feminist Economics (IAFFE) 11889

Asociación Internacional para la Economía Feminista

Business Manager and Conference Coordinator c/o Feminist Economics MS-9, Rice Univ, PO Box 1892, Houston TX 77251-1892, USA. T. +1405801533.
URL: http://www.iaffe.org/

History 1992, Lewisburg, PA (USA). **Aims** Further gender-aware and inclusive economic inquiry and policy analysis with the goal of enhancing the well-being of children, women and men in local, national and transnational communities. **Structure** Board of Directors. **Staff** 2.00 FTE, paid. **Finance** Sources: donations; grants; meeting proceeds; members' dues. **Activities** Events/meetings. **Events** *Annual Conference* Geneva (Switzerland) 2022, *Annual Conference* Quito (Ecuador) 2021, *Annual Conference* Quito (Ecuador) 2020, *Annual Conference* Glasgow (UK) 2019, *Annual Conference* New Paltz, NY (USA) 2018. **Publications** *Feminist Economics* – scholarly journal. Bibliographies; course syllabi; list of working papers; membership directory.
Members Individuals in 65 countries and territories:
Argentina, Australia, Austria, Barbados, Belgium, Brazil, Canada, Chad, Chile, China, Colombia, Congo Brazzaville, Côte d'Ivoire, Cyprus, Czechia, Denmark, Dominican Rep, Ecuador, Egypt, Finland, France, Georgia, Germany, Ghana, Iceland, India, Iran Islamic Rep, Ireland, Italy, Jamaica, Jordan, Kenya, Korea Rep, Liechtenstein, Luxembourg, Malaysia, Mauritius, Mexico, Micronesia FS, Nepal, Netherlands, New Zealand, Norway, Peru, Philippines, Poland, Portugal, Romania, Russia, Slovakia, South Africa, Spain, Sri Lanka, Sweden, Switzerland, Taiwan, Tanzania UR, Thailand, Trinidad-Tobago, Türkiye, Uganda, UK, Uruguay, USA, Zimbabwe.
NGO Relations Member of (1): *International Confederation of Associations for Pluralism in Economics (ICAPE, #12849).* [2021.06.09/XD6375/**D**]

♦ International Association for the Ferrous and Non-Ferrous Tube and Pipe Industries / see International Tube Association (#15741)
♦ International Association of Film and Television Schools / see International Association of Cinema, Audiovisual and Media Schools (#11771)

♦ International Association of Financial Executives Institutes (IAFEI) . 11890

Internationale Vereinigung von Finanzwirtschaftler-Instituten

Area Pres, Americas c/o FINEX, Unit 1901 19/F, 139 Corporate Center, Valero St, Salcedo Village, 1226 Makati, Philippines. T. +16328114189. Fax +16328114185. E-mail: secretariat@iafei.org – m.vinluan@iafei.org.
Area Pres, Asia address not obtained.
URL: http://www.iafei.org/

History 1969. Registration: Swiss Civil Code, Switzerland. **Aims** Promote networking opportunities for Member Institutes to build a wider understanding of financial practices throughout the world and further their international compatibility and evolution; promote ethical and best practices of financial management. **Structure** Board of Directors; Executive Committee. **Languages** English. **Finance** Sources: members' dues. **Activities** Events/meetings; publishing activities. **Events** *World Congress* Mexico City (Mexico) 2021, *World Congress* 2020, *World Congress* Matera (Italy) 2019, *World Congress* Ho Chi Minh City (Vietnam) 2018, *World Congress* Sao Paulo (Brazil) 2017. **Publications** *IAFEI Quarterly* (4 a year); *IAFEI Bulletin* (2 a year); *IAFEI Directory* (2 a year); *IAFEI Report* (every 2 years).
Members Institutes in 18 countries and territories:
Argentina, Brazil, Cambodia, China, Germany, Greece, Indonesia, Italy, Japan, Mexico, Philippines, Poland, Portugal, South Africa, Spain, Taiwan, Tunisia, Vietnam.
IGO Relations *European Commission (EC, #06633).* [2021/XD1614/**C**]

♦ International Association for Financial Participation (IAFP) 11891

Association internationale pour la participation financière (AIPF)

SG 18 rue de Chazelles, 75017 Paris, France.
URL: http://aipf-association.fr/en/iafp-the-edito/

History 1987. **Aims** Promote wider employee financial participation and share ownership in an employer's business through support and information sharing among national associations, employers and interested academics. **Structure** Executive Committee. Secretary General. **Finance** Endowment. **Activities** Events/meetings; financial and/or material support; guidance/assistance/consulting. **Events** *Conference* Brussels (Belgium) 2005, *Profit sharing 2000 – innovations and best practices in the field of employee participation* Berlin (Germany) 2000. **Publications** Information Services: Mantains an information centre.
Members National organizations in 9 countries:
Australia, Czechia, France, Germany, Ireland, Netherlands, Norway, UK, USA.
Individual members in 10 countries:
Belgium, France, Greece, Ireland, Italy, Japan, Latvia, Malta, Portugal, Spain.
IGO Relations *European Commission (EC, #06633); OECD (#17693).* [2020/XD9426/**D**]

♦ International Association of Fire Chiefs (internationally oriented national body)
♦ International Association of Fire Engineers / see International Association of Fire Chiefs
♦ International Association of Fire Fighters (internationally oriented national body)

♦ International Association for Fire Safety Science (IAFSS) 11892

IAFSS Secretariat Interscience Communications, West Yard House, Guildford Grove, Greenwich, London, SE10 8JT, UK. T. +442086925050. Fax +442086925155. E-mail: office@iafss.org.
Chairman address not obtained.
URL: http://www.iafss.org/

History 9 Oct 1985, Gaithersburg, MD (USA). Founded at *1st Symposium on Fire Safety Science* at (USA) National Bureau of Standards. Registration: Charity Commission, No/ID: 800306, England and Wales. **Aims** Promote research into the science of preventing and mitigating adverse effects of fires; provide a forum for disseminating results of such research. **Structure** General Meeting; Committee; Executive Committee. **Languages** English. **Finance** Sources: members' dues. **Activities** Awards/prizes/competitions; events/meetings. **Events** *International Symposium* Tsukuba (Japan) 2023, *Asia-Oceania Symposium on Fire Science and Technology* Brisbane, QLD (Australia) 2021, *International Symposium* Waterloo, ON (Canada) 2021, *International Symposium* Waterloo, ON (Canada) 2020, *Asia-Oceania Symposium on Fire Science and Technology* Taipei (Taiwan) 2018. **Publications** *Fire Safety Journal*; *IAFSS Newsletter*. Symposium proceedings.
Members Individuals in 29 countries and territories:
Australia, Austria, Belgium, Brazil, Canada, Chile, China, Denmark, Finland, France, Germany, Hong Kong, Iceland, India, Italy, Japan, Korea Rep, New Zealand, Norway, Poland, Portugal, Russia, Singapore, Slovenia, Sweden, Switzerland, Thailand, UK, USA. [2020/XD1416/v/**C**]

♦ International Association of Fishing Industry Workers' Unions 11893

Pres 42 Leninsky Prospekt, Moscow MOSKVA, Russia, 119119. T. +74959387782 – +74959380027. Fax +74959388385.

Members Trade unions in the CIS region (membership countries not specified). **IGO Relations** *Commonwealth of Independent States (CIS, #04341).* **NGO Relations** Member of: *General Confederation of Trade Unions (GCTU, #10108).* [XM2470/t/**D**]

♦ International Association of Fish Inspectors (IAFI) 11894

Exec Dir 1568 Merivale Road Box 225, Ottawa ON K2G 5Y7, Canada. Fax +16137267778.
URL: http://www.iafi.net/

History Oct 1999, Halifax (Canada), at inaugural meeting. **Aims** Promote fish, seafood and associated products that are safe, of acceptable quality and readily available for sale in the world's marketplaces. **Structure** Board, consisting of Executive Committee and 6 members representing geographic zones and 10 members at-large. Executive Committee, comprising President, Past-President, Secretary, Treasurer and 3 members at-large. **Languages** English, French, Spanish. **Staff** 3.00 FTE, paid. **Events** *World Seafood Congress* Penang (Malaysia) 2019, *General Meeting* Reykjavik (Iceland) 2017, *World Seafood Congress* Reykjavik (Iceland) 2017, *World Seafood Congress* Grimsby (UK) 2015, *World Seafood Congress* St John's, NL (Canada) 2013. **IGO Relations** Participates as observer in the activities of: *Codex Alimentarius Commission (CAC, #04081).* [2012.06.01/XD7492/**D**]

♦ International Association of Fish Meal Manufacturers / see The Marine Ingredients Organisation (#16579)
♦ International Association of Flagmakers (inactive)
♦ International Association of Food and Agro-industrial Economy (inactive)
♦ International Association of Food Distribution / see International Association for the Distributive Trade (#11851)
♦ International Association of Football Agents (no recent information)
♦ International Association for Football Lawyers (#02672)

♦ International Association for Forensic Institutes (IAFI) 11895

Contact address not obtained. T. +903124629341.
URL: http://www.interforensic.org/

Aims Provide further development in the area of forensics by means of coordination, cooperation and collaboration among member forensic institutes and scientists. **Structure** General Council (annual); Executive Board; President; Secretariat. Scientific Board. **Activities** Certification/accreditation; events/meetings; training/education. **Events** *Congress* Istanbul (Turkey) 2013, *Congress* Ankara (Turkey) 2012.
Members Institutes (46) in 39 countries and territories:
Albania, Azerbaijan, Bahrain, Bosnia-Herzegovina, Burundi, Central African Rep, Egypt, Ghana, Guinea-Bissau, India, Jordan, Kazakhstan, Kenya, Kosovo, Kuwait, Kyrgyzstan, Liberia, Malawi, Mali, Mexico, Morocco, Niger, Nigeria, Northern Cyprus, Oman, Pakistan, Qatar, Romania, Somalia, Sri Lanka, Sudan, Tanzania UR, Thailand, Türkiye, Turkmenistan, Uganda, United Arab Emirates, Vietnam, Zambia.
IGO Relations *ASEANAPOL (#01138).* [2014/XJ8884/**C**]

♦ International Association of Forensic Linguists (IAFL) 11896

Sec RMIT Univ, School of Global Studies, GPO Box 2476, Melbourne VIC 3001, Australia.
URL: http://www.iafl.org/

Aims Improve administration of the legal systems throughout the world by means of a better understanding of the interaction between language and the law. **Structure** Executive Committee, including President, Vice-President, Treasurer and Secretary. **Finance** Sources: members' dues. **Activities** Events/meetings. **Events** *Biennial Conference* Manila (Philippines) 2023, *European Conference* Porto (Portugal) 2022, *Biennial Conference* Birmingham (UK) 2021, *European Conference* Porto (Portugal) 2020, *Biennial Conference* Melbourne, VIC (Australia) 2019. **Publications** *International Journal of Speech, Language and the Law*. **Members** Individual; Institutional. Membership countries not specified. [2015/XJ8064/**C**]

♦ International Association of Forensic Mental Health Services (IAFMHS) 11897

Mailing address RCB 5246, 8888 University Drive, Burnaby BC V5A 1S6, Canada. T. +16049245026. Fax +16049245027. E-mail: iafmhs@sfu.ca.
URL: http://www.iafmhs.org/

History 21 Apr 2001, Vancouver, BC (Canada). **Aims** Enhance standards of forensic mental health services in the international community; promote an international dialogue about forensic mental health in all its aspects, including violence and family violence; promote education, training and research in forensic mental health; inform professional communities and the public about current issues; promote and utilize advance technologies. **Structure** General Meeting (annual); Board of Directors. **Languages** English. **Staff** 1.00 FTE, paid. **Finance** Members' dues. Conference registration. **Events** *Annual Conference* Sydney, NSW (Australia) 2023, *Annual Conference* Berlin (Germany) 2022, *Annual Conference* Krakow (Poland) 2021, *Annual Conference* Krakow (Poland) 2020, *Annual Conference* Montréal, QC (Canada) 2019. **Publications** *Journal of Forensic Mental Health* (2 a year).
Members Individuals in 25 countries:
Argentina, Australia, Austria, Belgium, Brazil, Canada, Denmark, Finland, France, Germany, Ireland, Japan, Kuwait, Netherlands, New Zealand, Norway, Portugal, Romania, Singapore, South Africa, Spain, Sweden, Switzerland, UK, USA. [2021/XD3718/v/**D**]

♦ International Association of Forensic Nurses (internationally oriented national body)
♦ International Association of Forensic Phonetics / see International Association for Forensic Phonetics and Acoustics (#11898)

♦ International Association for Forensic Phonetics and Acoustics (IAFPA) 11898

Pres c/o JP French Associates, 86 The Mount, York, YO24 1AR, UK. T. +441904634821. E-mail: enquiries@jpfrench.com.
Chair c/o Dutch immigration service IND, PO Box 17, 9560 AA Ter Apel, Netherlands. E-mail: gm.cambier.langeveld@ind.nl – g.m.cambier@hum.leidenuniv.nl.
URL: http://www.iafpa.net/

History 1988, as *International Association of Forensic Phonetics (IAFP)*. 2003, present name adopted. **Aims** Foster basic research in forensic phonetics; provide a forum for the interchange of ideas and information of its practice, development and research. **Structure** Board. Executive Committee. Officers: President; Chair; Secretary; Treasurer. **Languages** English. **Staff** None. **Finance** Members' dues. **Activities** Funds small-scale research projects; organizes Annual Meeting. **Events** *Annual Conference* Prague (Czechia) 2022, *Annual Conference* Marburg (Germany) 2021, *Annual Conference* Istanbul (Türkiye) 2019, *Annual Conference* Huddersfield (UK) 2018, *Annual Conference* Split (Croatia) 2017. **Publications** *The International Journal of Speech, Language and the Law: Forensic Linguistics.*
Members Full; Student. Individuals in 18 countries:
Australia, Austria, Canada, Finland, Germany, Israel, Italy, Korea Rep, Morocco, Netherlands, New Zealand, Poland, Romania, Russia, Sweden, Switzerland, UK, USA. [2019/XD4415/v/**D**]

♦ International Association for Forensic Psychotherapy (IAFP) 11899

Main Office c/o Respond, 24-32 Stephenson Way, London, NW1 2HD, UK.
URL: https://www.forensicpsychotherapy.org/
History Jun 1991, Leuven (Belgium), by members of European Symposium, during 17th International Congress on Law and Mental Health. **Aims** Initiate and promote psychodynamic psychotherapy with offender patients; promote scientific research into causes and prevention of crime; establish observation centres and clinics for diagnosis and treatment of delinquency and crime; co-ordinate and consolidate existing scientific work; secure cooperation between all bodies engaged in similar work; assist and advise the judiciary, hospitals and governmental departments; promote educational and training facilities; promote discussion within and educate public. **Structure** Officers: President, Honorary Life President, Past Presidents (4), Vice-President, Secretary, Treasurer, Executive Council (12 members). **Languages** English. **Finance** Members' dues. **Activities** Events/meeting. **Events** *Annual Conference* Turin (Italy) 2023, *Annual Conference* London (UK) 2022, *Annual Conference* Norwich (UK) 2021, *Annual Conference* Konstanz (Germany) 2019, *Annual Conference* Belfast (UK) 2018. **Publications** *IAFP Newsletter.*
Members Individuals (about 120) in 17 countries:
Australia, Austria, Canada, Croatia, Denmark, Finland, Germany, Ireland, Israel, Italy, Netherlands, Peru, Portugal, Romania, Sweden, UK, USA.
NGO Relations Member of: *Alliance of NGOs on Crime Prevention and Criminal Justice (#00709).*
[2019/XD6285/v/**D**]

♦ International Association of Forensic Radiographers (internationally oriented national body)

♦ International Association of Forensic Sciences (IAFS) 11900

Association internationale des sciences et de la médecine légale
Pres address not obtained.
History 1956. Founded on an informal basis, to provide liaison between Congresses; officially constituted at 5th Congress, 1969, Toronto ON (Canada). An earlier effort was known as *International Association of Forensic Sciences and Criminalistics.* **Aims** Develop forensic sciences; assist forensic scientists and other professionals to exchange scientific and technical information. **Structure** Triennial Congress. Comprises the organizing committee of the following Congress; Council, comprised of past presidents. **Languages** English. **Staff** 4 FTE, paid for IAFS 2017 conference; varies by hosting organization/city. **Finance** Financed by city government of the forensic organization that is hosting the IAFS conference. **Events** *IAFS Congress* 2026, *Triennial Congress* Sydney, NSW (Australia) 2023, *Triennial Congress* Sydney, NSW (Australia) 2021, *Triennial Congress* Sydney, NSW (Australia) 2020, *Triennial Congress* Toronto, ON (Canada) 2017. **Publications** Conference proceedings. **Members** No regular membership, simply participation at congresses.
[2022/XD4868/**F**]

♦ International Association of Forensic and Security Metrology (IAFSM) 11901

Main Office 3416 Primm Ln, Birmingham AL 35216, USA. E-mail: info@iafsm.org.
URL: http://www.iafsm.org/
History Registered in the State of Delaware (USA). **Aims** Further the development of forensic and security metrology – the science of using measurement technologies to document and reconstruct crime and accident scenes and for security planning. **Structure** Board of Directors, comprising President, Vice-President, Secretary/Treasurer, Past President and 3 Directors. Committees (3): Best Practices; Outreach; Membership and Sponsorship. **Activities** Organizes webinars. **Events** *Forensic Metrology and Crime Scene Reconstruction Conference* Westminster, CO (USA) 2022. [2022/XJ6861/**D**]

♦ International Association of Forensic Toxicologists (TIAFT) 11902

Association internationale de toxicologie légale
Pres Grad School of Analytical Science and Technology, Chungnam National Univ, 99 Daehangno, Yseong-gu, Daejeon 305764, Korea Rep. T. +82428218540. Fax +82428218541.
Immediate Past-Pres Dept Laboratory Medicine, Toxicology, Ghent Univ Hospital, De Pintelaan 185, 9000 Ghent, Belgium.
URL: http://www.tiaft.org/
History Founded 23 Apr 1963, London (UK). First constitution adopted 1963 and modified in 1981 and 1995. New constitution established in Jul 2002; modified 2008; 2017. **Aims** Promote cooperation and coordination of efforts among members; encourage research in forensic toxicology. **Structure** Congress (annual, election of officers every 3 years); Board. **Languages** English. **Staff** Voluntary. **Finance** Sources: members' dues. **Activities** Events/meetings; networking/liaising; research/documentation. **Events** *Annual Meeting* Chicago, IL (USA) 2026, *Annual Meeting* Auckland (New Zealand) 2025, *Annual Meeting* St Gallen (Switzerland) 2024, *Annual Meeting* Rome (Italy) 2023, *Annual Meeting* Versailles (France) 2022. **Publications** *TIAFT Bulletin* (3 a year). Books. **Members** Full; DCF; Honorary. Individuals in 100 countries and territories. Membership countries not specified. [2020/XB1284/v/**B**]

♦ International Association for Forest Resources Management (inactive)

♦ International Association of Former Child Migrants and their Families (IAFCMandF) 11903

Contact Child Migrants Trust, 124 Musters Road, West Bridgford, NG2 7PW, UK. T. +441159822811. E-mail: cmtnottingham@aol.com.
History Founded Oct 1997. **Aims** Express and promote the common interests of former British child migrants worldwide; educate and raise issues relating to their needs and those of their families; raise funds to assist them. **Events** *International congress on child migration / Congress* New Orleans, LA (USA) 2002. **Publications** *International Focus* (2 a year). **Members** Membership countries not specified. [2013.06.01/XD8709/**D**]

♦ International Association of Former OEEC and OECD Staff 11904

Association internationale des anciens de l'OECE et de l'OCDE
Secretariat c/o OECD, 2 rue André Pascal, 75775 Paris CEDEX 16, France. T. +33145248594. E-mail: aia@oecd.org.
History 1972, Paris (France), to represent retired staff members of OEEC and *OECD (#17693).* Statutes modified 17 Mar 1980; 30 Mar 2001. Previously referred in English as *International Association of Retired Staff of OEEC and OECD.* Registered in accordance with French law. **Aims** Uphold interests and ensure meetings of *retired* staff. **Structure** General Assembly (annual, in Paris); Administrative Council. **Languages** French. **Staff** Voluntary. **Finance** Entry fee: euro 30. **Events** *Annual General Assembly* Paris (France) 2002, *Annual General Assembly* Paris (France) 2001, *Annual General Assembly* Paris (France) 2000, *Annual General Assembly* Paris (France) 1999, *Annual General Assembly* Paris (France) 1998. **Publications** Newsletter (4 a year).
Members Full in 21 countries:
Australia, Austria, Belgium, Costa Rica, France, Germany, Greece, Hungary, Ireland, Italy, Japan, Luxembourg, Mexico, Monaco, Paraguay, Portugal, Spain, Sweden, Switzerland, UK, USA.
NGO Relations Cooperates with: *Association des agents pensionnés des organisations coordonnées et de leurs ayants droit (AAPOCAD, #02363)*; other associations of retired staff. [2015.09.04/XE7871/v/**E**]

♦ International Association of Former Officials of EUROCONTROL (#02666)
♦ International Association of Former Officials of the European Communities / see Association internationale des anciens de l'Union Européenne (#02667)
♦ International Association of Former Officials of the European Union (#02667)
♦ International Association of Former Soviet Political Prisoners and Victims of the Communist Regime (internationally oriented national body)

♦ International Association on Fracture Mechanics of Concrete and Concrete Structures (IA-FramCoS) 11905

Pres ETH Baustoffe IfB, Schafmattstrasse 6, 8093 Zurich ZH, Switzerland. E-mail: gonzalo.ruiz@uclm.es.
URL: http://framcos.org/
History 1991, USA. Registered in the State of Illinois (USA). **Aims** Promote use of fracture mechanics in the analyses and design of concrete materials and structures, towards safer and more durable infrastructures. **Structure** Board of Directors; Advisory Committee. **Languages** English. **Activities** Organizes international conference (every 3 years). **Events** *Triennial Conference* Bayonne (France) 2019, *Triennial Conference* Berkeley, CA (USA) 2016, *Triennial Conference / Conference* Toledo (Spain) 2013, *Triennial Conference / Conference* Jeju (Korea Rep) 2010, *Triennial Conference / Conference* Catania (Italy) 2007.
Members Individuals (480) in 33 countries and territories:
Argentina, Australia, Belgium, Brazil, Canada, China, Czechia, Denmark, Egypt, France, Germany, Hong Kong, India, Iran Islamic Rep, Israel, Italy, Japan, Korea Rep, Liechtenstein, Netherlands, Norway, Poland, Portugal, Slovenia, South Africa, Spain, Sri Lanka, Sweden, Switzerland, Taiwan, Türkiye, UK, USA. [2015/XD8111/**C**]

♦ International Association for Francophone Solidarity (inactive)
♦ International Association of Francophone Women (no recent information)

♦ International Association of Free Thought (AIFT) 11906

Association Internationale de Libre Pensée (AILP) – Asociación Internacional de Libre Pensamiento (AILP) – Internationale Vereinigung der Freidenker – Associação Internacional do Livre Pensamento – Associazione Internazionale di Libero Pensiero – Internationale Vereniging van Vrije Gedachte – Miedzynarodowe Stowarzyszenie Wolnej Mysli – Asociatia Internationalaa a gândirii libere – Serbest Düsünce Uluslarasi Birligi – Internacia Asocio de Liberpenso
Contact 10-12 rue des Fossés-Saint-Jacques, 75005 Paris, France. T. +33146342150. E-mail: libre.pensee@wanadoo.fr.
URL: http://www.internationalfreethought.org/
History 2011, Oslo (Norway). Provisional statutes adopted 2011; modified 2014. **Aims** Coordinate members' actions and principles on an international level, respecting their independence. **Structure** International Council. **Languages** English, French, Spanish. **Staff** Voluntary. **Finance** Members pay their own expenses. **Activities** Events/meetings. **Events** *Congress* Paris (France) 2017, *Congress* Montevideo (Uruguay) 2015, *Congress* London (UK) 2014, *Congress* Concepción (Chile) 2013. **Publications** None.
Members Full in 24 countries:
Argentina, Australia, Bangladesh, Belgium, Canada, Chile, Ecuador, France, Germany, Hungary, India, Ireland, Italy, Lebanon, Nigeria, Poland, Romania, Senegal, Spain, Switzerland, Tunisia, UK, Uruguay, USA.
Consultative Status Consultative status granted from: *ECOSOC (#05331)* (Special). **NGO Relations** None.
[2019.02.19/XM6179/**E**]

♦ International Association of French-Language University Presses (inactive)
♦ International Association of French-Language Writers (inactive)
♦ International Association of French-Speaking Aircrews (inactive)
♦ International Association of French-Speaking Anaesthetist-Reanimators (inactive)
♦ International Association of French-Speaking Congress Towns / see Coésio – Destinations Francophone de Congrès (#04082)
♦ International Association of French-Speaking Criminologists (#02678)
♦ International Association of French-speaking Demographers (#02682)
♦ International Association of French-Speaking Directors of Educational Institutions (inactive)
♦ International Association of French-Speaking Parliamentarians / see Assemblée parlementaire de la Francophonie (#02312)
♦ International Association of French-Speaking Scientific African Publishers (no recent information)
♦ International Association of French-Speaking Sociologists (#02744)
♦ International Association of French Studies (#02690)
♦ International Association Futuribles / see Futuribles International (#10052)
♦ International Association for Fuzzy Set Management and Economy (#19386)
♦ International Association of Galician Studies (#02164)

♦ International Association of Gaming Advisors (IAGA) 11907

Exec Dir PO Box 92495, Henderson NV 89009, USA. T. +17023541057. E-mail: director@theiaga.org.
URL: http://www.theiaga.org/
History 1980, Las Vegas, NV (USA). Founded as (US) National Association of Gaming Attorneys (NAGA), through Gaming Law Committee of *'American Bar Association'.* Former names and other names: *International Association of Gaming Attorneys (IAGA)* – former (1985 to 2007). **Aims** Unite in common organization those professionally engaged in the gaming industry; facilitate negotiations in the gaming industry; protect and promote the mutual interests of the corporation's members; encourage education in the gaming industry. **Structure** Board of Trustees; Officers; Council of past Presidents; Counselors. **Finance** Sources: members' dues; sponsorship. **Activities** Events/meetings. **Events** *International Gaming Summit* Belfast (UK) 2023, *International Gaming Summit* Boston, MA (USA) 2022, *International Gaming Summit* Half Moon Bay, CA (USA) 2019, *International Gaming Summit* Macau 2018, *International Gaming Summit* Philadelphia, PA (USA) 2014. **Publications** *The Gaming Lawyer* (4 a year) – magazine. Directory. **Members** Gaming attorneys and government attorneys and regulators; associate and corporate members (more than 500) in 23 countriesMembership countries not specified. [2022/XD3282/**D**]

♦ International Association of Gaming Attorneys / see International Association of Gaming Advisors (#11907)

♦ International Association of Gaming Regulators (IAGR) 11908

Pres 7881 W Charleston Blvd, Suite 155, Las Vegas NV 89117, USA. T. +16362776665. E-mail: iagr@iagr.org.
URL: http://www.iagr.org/
Aims Advance the effectiveness and efficiency of gaming regulation. **Structure** Officers: President; Treasurer; Secretary. **Events** *Annual Conference* Melbourne, VIC (Australia) 2022, *Annual Conference* Boston, MA (USA) 2021, *Annual Conference* Boston, MA (USA) 2020, *Annual Conference* Copenhagen (Denmark) 2018, *Annual Conference* Sydney, NSW (Australia) 2016.
Members Regulatory bodies (30) in 6 countries:
Australia, Canada, New Zealand, South Africa, UK, USA. [2020/XD7813/**D**]

♦ International Association for Gastrointestinal Motility in Children (inactive)
♦ International Association of Gay and Lesbian Martial Artists (internationally oriented national body)

♦ International Association of Gay Square Dance Clubs (IAGSDC) ... 11909

Archivist PO Box 9176, Denver CO 80209-0176, USA. T. +13037781937.
URL: http://www.iagsdc.org/
History Founded Feb 1983, Miami FL (USA), an outgrowth of gay rodeo. Original title: (US) National Association of Lesbian and Gay Square Dance Clubs, 13 Feb 1983, Hollywood FL (USA). Current title adopted, 8 Apr 1984. **Aims** Promote Modern Western Square Dancing; enhance the image of gay people, especially in the international square dance community; provide an opportunity for the social and dancing interchange of individual members as well as provide a forum for exchange of ideas among member clubs; support and encourage the growth of membership. **Structure** Executive Board. **Languages** English. **Staff** 6.00 FTE, paid. **Finance** Members' dues. Other sources: All Join Hands Foundation; All Join Hands Canada Foundation. **Activities** Events/meetings. **Events** *Annual Convention* Minneapolis, MN (USA) 2022, *Annual Convention* Houston, TX (USA) 2021, *Annual Convention* Denver, CO (USA) 2020, *Annual Convention* Philadelphia, PA (USA) 2019, *Annual Convention* Seattle, WA (USA) 2018. **Publications** *Newsletter* (2-3 a year).
Members Clubs in 3 countries:
Canada, Japan, USA. [2019.07.20/XD7565/**D**]

♦ International Association on the Genesis of Ore Deposits (IAGOD) . . 11910

Association internationale d'études de la genèse des minerais

SG address not obtained. E-mail: president@iagod.org – treasurer@iagod.org.
Exec Officer address not obtained.
URL: http://www.iagod.org/

History 19 Dec 1964, Delhi (India). Founded during 22nd *International Geological Congress (IGC)*, a provisional Commission having been set up following a symposium, Sep 1963, Prague (Czechoslovakia). **Aims** Promote international cooperation in study of the genesis of ore deposits; further growth of knowledge in this field. **Structure** General Assembly (every 2 years, at quadrennial symposium and at IGC); Council; Executive Committee; Commissions (7): *IAGOD Commission on Industrial Minerals and Rocks (COIMR, see: #11910)*; *IAGOD Commission on Ore Deposits in Mafic and Ultramafic Rocks (CODMUR, see: #11910)*; *IAGOD Commission on Paragenesis (PaC, see: #11910)*; *IAGOD Commission on Placer Deposits (see: #11910)*; *IAGOD Commission on Tectonics of Ore Deposits (CTOD, see: #11910)*; *IAGOD Commission on Thermodynamics of Ore Forming Fluids (see: #11910)*; *International Uranium Group (IUG, see: #11910)*. **Languages** English, French, German, Italian, Russian, Spanish. **Staff** Voluntary. **Finance** Sources: members' dues. **Activities** Events/meetings. **Events** *Symposium* Dublin (Ireland) 2022, *Quadrennial Symposium* Salta (Argentina) 2018, *Quadrennial Symposium* Urumqi (China) 2014, *Quadrennial symposium* Adelaide, SA (Australia) 2010, *International symposium on large igneous provinces of Asia, mantle plumes and metallogeny* Novosibirsk (Russia) 2009. **Publications** *Ore Geology Reviews* (6 a year); *IAGOD Newsletter* (annual); *IAGOD Membership Directory*. Symposium abstracts and proceedings; circulars.

Members National associations and qualified individuals (by election) in 59 countries – "" indicates self-organized national group of individuals:
Albania, Argentina, Armenia, Australia, Austria, Belgium, Bosnia-Herzegovina, Brazil, Bulgaria, Cameroon, Canada, Chile, China, Czechia, Denmark, Egypt, Finland, France, Georgia (*), Germany, Hungary, Indonesia, Iran Islamic Rep, Italy, Japan, Kazakhstan (*), Kenya, Korea Rep, Kyrgyzstan (*), Mexico, Mongolia, Morocco, Mozambique, Namibia, Netherlands, New Zealand, Nigeria, North Macedonia, Norway, Pakistan, Peru, Philippines, Poland, Portugal, Romania, Russia (*), Serbia-Montenegro, Slovakia, South Africa, Spain, Sweden, Switzerland, Tajikistan (*), Türkiye, UK, Ukraine (*), USA, Uzbekistan (*), Venezuela.
Institutional members (11) in 4 countries:
Canada, South Africa, UK, USA.

IGO Relations *International Geoscience Programme (IGCP, #13715)*. **NGO Relations** Affiliated member of: *International Union of Geological Sciences (IUGS, #15777)*. [2022/XC1378/**B**]

♦ International Association for Genetics in Aquaculture (IAGA) 11911

Contact Acuigen Research Group, Genetics Dept – Fac of Veterinary Science, Avda/Carvallo Calero s/n, 27002 Lugo, Spain. T. +34982922428. Fax +34982822428. E-mail: isga@uchile.cl.
URL: http://isga.uchile.cl/

History 1985, Davis, CA (USA). Founded during Symposium Genetics in Aquaculture. **Aims** Promote communication and constructive service concerning all aspects of genetics of aquatic species relevant to aquaculture; provide a mechanism for holding a triennial meeting – International Symposium on Genetics in Aquaculture (ISGA); ensure publication of symposium proceedings. **Events** *International Symposium of Genetics in Aquaculture* Puerto Varas (Chile) 2022, *International Symposium of Genetics in Aquaculture* Puerto Varas (Chile) 2021, *International Symposium of Genetics in Aquaculture* Cairns, QLD (Australia) 2018, *International Symposium on Genetics in Aquaculture – ISGA* Santiago de Compostela (Spain) 2015, *International Symposium on Genetics in Aquaculture – ISGA* Auburn, AL (USA) 2012. **Publications** Proceedings. [2019/XJ9274/c/**E**]

♦ International Association of Geneva Zones for the protection of civilian populations and historic buildings in times of armed conflicts / see International Civil Defence Organization (#12582)
♦ International Association of Genocide Scholars (internationally oriented national body)

♦ International Association of Geoanalysts (IAG) 11912

Contact Inorganic and Isotope Geochemistry, Helmholtz Centre Potsdam, GFZ German Research Centre for Geosciences, 14473 Potsdam, Germany. E-mail: michawi@gfz-potsdam.de.
URL: http://geoanalyst.org/

History Jun 1997, Vail CO (USA). **Aims** Serve as a forum for advancing geoanalytical science; promote interests and support professional needs of those involved in the analysis of geological and environmental materials; support and encourage early career geochemists to pursue careers devoted to metrology and quality assurance as applied to the chemical analysis of geomaterials; promote identification, characterization and distribution of Certified Reference Materials having geologic compositions. **Structure** Council, including President, Vice-President, Immediate Past-President, Honorary Secretary and Honorary Treasurer. **Languages** English. **Staff** Voluntary. **Finance** Members' dues. Subscriptions to proficiency testing programmes; marketing of quality control materials and Certified Reference Materials; sponsoring of workshops and courses. **Activities** Programmes: *'GeoPT'* and *'G-Probe'* – proficiency testing programmes; reference material certification programmes. Production and marketing of Certified Reference Materials. Early career researcher awards. Support of other Reference Material producers who are producing materials relevant for the needs of the geoanalyst. Geoanalysis Conference (every 3 years); meetings; workshops. **Events** *GEOANALYSIS : International Conference on the Analysis of Geological and Environmental Materials* Sydney, NSW (Australia) 2018, *GEOANALYSIS : international conference on the analysis of geological and environmental materials / Conference* Leoben (Austria) 2015, *GEOANALYSIS : international conference on the analysis of geological and environmental materials / Conference* Armação de Búzios (Brazil) 2012, *GEOANALYSIS : international conference on the analysis of geological and environmental materials / Conference* Central Drakensberg (South Africa) 2009, *GEOANALYSIS : international conference on the analysis of geological and environmental materials / Conference* Beijing (China) 2006. **Publications** *Elements Magazine* (6 a year) – joint publication; *Geostandards and Geoanalytical Research* (4 a year) – official journal.

Members Voting; Associate; Student; Corporate. Members in 28 countries:
Australia, Austria, Brazil, Canada, China, Colombia, Czechia, Denmark, Estonia, Finland, France, Germany, Italy, Japan, Mexico, Mongolia, Netherlands, New Zealand, Norway, Poland, Portugal, Russia, Slovakia, South Africa, Spain, Tanzania UR, UK, USA. [2012.06.01/XD8501/**D**]

♦ International Association of GeoChemistry (IAGC) 11913

Office Manager 275 Mendenhall Laboratory, 125 South Oval Mall, Columbus OH 43210, USA. T. +16146884700. Fax +16142927688. E-mail: businessoffice@iagc-society.org.
URL: http://www.iagc-society.org/

History 8 May 1967, Paris (France). Founded at 1st Council meeting during 1st international symposium, following cooperation commencing with 21st *International Geological Congress (IGC)*, 1960, Copenhagen (Denmark), and culminating in a meeting Nov 1965, Paris, when statutes were completed, temporary officers nominated and affiliation requested with *International Union of Geological Sciences (IUGS, #15777)*. Previous work carried out through Commission on the Abundance of Elements, subsequently Commission on Geochemistry, of *International Union of Pure and Applied Chemistry (IUPAC, #15809)*. Statutes last amended 2005. Former names and other names: *International Association of Geochemistry and Cosmochemistry (IAGC)* – former (1967 to 2004); *Association internationale de géochimie et de cosmochimie (AIGC)* – former (1967 to 2004). **Aims** Foster cooperation in, and the advancement of, geochemistry in its broadest sense. **Structure** Council, consisting of Executive Committee members – President, Vice-President, Secretary, Treasurer and Past-President – and 10 further members. Business Office. **Languages** English, French, German, Russian. **Staff** 1.00 FTE, paid. **Finance** Financial support provided by Elsevier and Individual Members. Annual budget: 55,500 USD. **Activities** Working groups (8): Applied Isotope Geochemistry; Geochemical Training in Developing Countries; Geochemistry of the Earth Surface; Geochemistry of Health and Disease; Global Geochemical Mapping; Thermodynamics of Natural Processes; Water-Rock Interaction; Urban Geochemistry. Organizes symposia and conference series, many by working groups (about 2 such meetings a year); co-sponsors meetings in related topics. **Events** *International Symposium on the Geochemistry of the Earth's Surface* Zurich (Switzerland) 2022, *International Symposium on the Geochemistry of the Earth's Surface* Zurich (Switzerland) 2021, *International Symposium on the Geochemistry of the Earth's Surface* Zurich (Switzerland) 2020, *Triennial international symposium on water-rock interaction* Guanajuato (Mexico) 2010, *Triennial international symposium on water-rock interaction* Kunming (China) 2007. **Publications** *International Association of Geochemistry Newsletter* (2 a year); *Applied Geochemistry* (8 a year); *ELEMENTS* – magazine.

Members Individual; Sustaining; Honorary Associate Society. Organizations () and individuals in 47 countries and territories:
Argentina, Australia (*), Austria, Belgium, Bolivia, Brazil, Canada (*), China (*), Colombia, Czechia (*), Denmark, Egypt, Finland (*), France, Gambia, Germany (*), Greece, Hong Kong, Hungary (*), Iceland, India, Israel, Italy, Japan (*), Korea Rep, Mexico (*), Monaco, Mozambique, Netherlands, New Zealand, Norway, Poland, Portugal, Romania, Russia (*), Saudi Arabia, Serbia, South Africa, Spain, Sweden, Switzerland (*), Taiwan, Türkiye, UK (*), USA, Venezuela, Vietnam.

IGO Relations *International Geoscience Programme (IGCP, #13715)*. **NGO Relations** Associated organization of IUPAC. Links and joint events, often through working groups, with: *Committee on Data for Science and Technology (CODATA, #04247)*; *International Association of Hydrogeologists (IAH, #11953)*; *International Mineralogical Association (IMA, #14165)*. [2020/XC1290/**C**]

♦ International Association of Geochemistry and Cosmochemistry / see International Association of GeoChemistry (#11913)

♦ International Association of Geodesy (IAG) 11914

Association internationale de géodésie (AIG) – Asociación Internacional de Geodesia – Internationale Assoziation für Geodäsie

SG c/o FGI, Geodeetinrinne 2, FI-02430 Masala, Finland. T. +358407182152. E-mail: iag.office@nls.fi.
Pres c/o IGN, Bât Lamarck A, 35 rue Hélène Brion, 75013 Paris, France. T. +33157275328.
URL: http://www.iag-aig.org/

History 24 Apr 1862. First session of the Central European Arc Measurement 15 Oct 1864, Berlin (Germany). 1st General Conference of the Central European Arc Measurement, 1886, extended to *International Geodetic Association – Association géodésique internationale*. 1992, became, the Geodesy Section, and subsequently a constituent association under the name *International Union of Geodesy and Geophysics (IUGG, #15776)*. Most recently restructured in 2003. **Aims** Advance geodesy by furthering geodetic theory through research and teaching, by collecting, analysing, modelling and interpreting observational data, by stimulating technological development and by providing a consistent representation of the figure, rotation and gravity field of the Earth and *planets* and their temporal variations.

Structure General Assembly (every 4 years); Scientific Assembly (every 4 years in between); Council; Executive Committee; Office; Communication and Outreach Branch (COB); Commissions (4); Inter-Commission Committees (4); *Global Geodetic Observing System (GGOS, see: #11914)*.
International Scientific Services (12):
– *International Centre for Global Earth Models (ICGEM, #12495)*;
– International Digital Elevation Models Service (IDEMS);
– *International DORIS Service (IDS, #13192)*;
– *International Earth Rotation and Reference Systems Service (IERS, #13216)*; International Service for the Geoid (ISG);
– *International GNSS Service (IGS, #13724)*;
– *Bureau gravimétrique international (BGI, #03361)*;
– International Geodynamics and Earth Tides Service (IGETS);
– International Gravity Field Service (IGFS);
– *International Laser Ranging Service (ILRS, see: #11914)*;
– *International VLBI Service for Geodesy and Astrometry (IVS, #15860)*;
– *Permanent Service for Mean Sea Level (PSMSL, #18333)*.

In 1899, as *Internationale Erdmessung*, instrumental in setting up: *International Latitude Service (ILS, inactive)*, and in 1912: *Bureau International de l'Heure (BIH)*.

Languages English, French. **Staff** 0.50 FTE, paid. **Finance** Sources: contributions; grants; meeting proceeds; members' dues; sale of publications. Allocation from IUGG. **Activities** Events/meetings; research/documentation. **Events** *General Assembly* Beijing (China) 2021, *General Assembly* Montréal, QC (Canada) 2019, *International Symposium on Gravity, Geoid and Height Systems* Copenhagen (Denmark) 2018, *Analyst Centres Workshop* Brussels (Belgium) 2017, *Analyst Centres Workshop* Brussels (Belgium) 2017. **Publications** *Journal of Geodesy* (12 a year); *IAG Newsletter*. *IAG Symposia Series*. *Geodesist's Handbook*; *Travaux de l'Association internationale de géodésie* – comprising general and national reports. Special publications.

Members IUGG Countries; Candidate Members; Individual Members; Fellows. Members in 70 countries and territories:
Albania, Argentina, Armenia, Australia, Austria, Azerbaijan, Belgium, Bolivia, Bosnia-Herzegovina, Brazil, Bulgaria, Canada, Chile, China, Colombia, Congo DR, Costa Rica, Croatia, Czechia, Denmark, Egypt, Estonia, Finland, France, Georgia, Germany, Ghana, Greece, Hungary, Iceland, India, Indonesia, Iran Islamic Rep, Ireland, Israel, Italy, Japan, Jordan, Korea Rep, Luxembourg, Mauritius, Mexico, Morocco, Mozambique, Netherlands, New Zealand, Nicaragua, Nigeria, North Macedonia, Norway, Pakistan, Peru, Philippines, Poland, Portugal, Romania, Russia, Saudi Arabia, Slovakia, Slovenia, South Africa, Spain, Sweden, Switzerland, Taiwan, Thailand, Türkiye, UK, USA, Vietnam.

IGO Relations Cooperates with (8): *Bureau international des poids et mesures (BIPM, #03367)*; *Committee on the Peaceful Uses of Outer Space (COPUOS, #04277)*; *Group on Earth Observations (GEO, #10735)*; *International Committee on Global Navigation Satellite Systems (ICG, #12775)*; *International Hydrographic Organization (IHO, #13825)*; *Pan American Institute of Geography and History (PAIGH, #18113)*; *Regional Committee of United Nations Global Geospatial Information Management for Asia and the Pacific (UN-GGIM-AP, #18766)*; *United Nations Committee of Experts on Global Geospatial Information Management (UN-GGIM, #20540)*. **NGO Relations** Constituent association of International Union of Geodesy and Geophysics, which is one of the Scientific Unions grouped within: *International Council for Science (ICSU, inactive)*. Cooperates with: *International Organization for Standardization (ISO, #14473)*. Member of: *UN-GGO: Geospatial Societies (UN-GGIM GS, #20324)*. [2023.02.15/XB1291/**B**]

♦ International Association for Geoethics (IAGETH) 11915

Pres C/ José Antonio Novais 2, Ciudad Universitaria, 28040 Madrid, Spain. E-mail: j.m.frias@igeo.ucm-csic.es.
URL: http://www.icog.es/iageth/

History Founded following activities initiated in 1992, and that of the *Working Group for Geoethics* under AGID. **Aims** Promote and encourage advancement of geoethics; foster geoethical ways of thinking and acting; improve teaching and training in geoethics. **Structure** Executive Committee; Council; Senior Advisory Board. **Languages** English. **Staff** 3.00 FTE, paid. **Finance** Sources: members' dues. **Activities** Events/meetings; research/documentation. **Publications** *Geoethics in LatinAmerica* by Prof R Daniel Acevedo and J Martinez-Frias; *Geoethics: Theory, Principles, Problems* by Prof Nataliya Nikitina. Articles.

Members National chapters in 48 countries:
Algeria, Argentina, Australia, Belgium, Botswana, Brazil, Canada, Cape Verde, China, Colombia, Costa Rica, Cuba, Ecuador, Egypt, Ethiopia, Greece, Hungary, Iceland, India, Italy, Japan, Kazakhstan, Kenya, Libya, Malawi, Mexico, Mongolia, Morocco, Mozambique, Namibia, New Zealand, Niger, Nigeria, Paraguay, Peru, Portugal, Romania, Russia, South Africa, Spain, Sri Lanka, Tajikistan, UK, Uruguay, USA, Venezuela, Yemen, Zimbabwe.

NGO Relations Affiliate to: *International Union of Geodesy and Geophysics (IUGG, #15776)*; *International Union of Geological Sciences (IUGS, #15777)*. Special Memorandum of Understanding with: *African Network for Geo-Education (ANGE, #00387)*; *European Federation of Geologists (EFG, #07133)*; *Geological Society of Africa (GSAf, #10135)*; *International Geoscience Education Organization (IGEO, #13714)*. Links with numerous NGOs, including: *Arabian Geosciences Union (ArabGU, #00975)*; *Association of Geoscientists for International Development (AGID, #02623)*; *Earth Science Matters Foundation (ESM, #05169)*; *International Association for Geoscience Diversity (IAGD)*; *Promoting Earth Science for Society (YES Network, #18541)*. [2018.10.08/XJ8438/**B**]

♦ International Association of Geo-Informatics (unconfirmed)
♦ International Association of Geoinformation and Communication Technologies (internationally oriented national body)

♦ International Association of Geomagnetism and Aeronomy (IAGA) . 11916

Association internationale de géomagnetisme et d'aéronomie (AIGA)

SG GFZ German Research Centre for Geosciences, Telegrafenberg, 14473 Potsdam, Germany. T. +493312881268. E-mail: sg@iaga-aiga.org.
URL: http://www.iugg.org/IAGA/

History 18 Jul 1919, Brussels (Belgium). New Statutes and By-laws adopted by Extraordinary Assembly, 1977, Seattle WA (USA). Modified by Conference of Delegates: 1983, Hamburg (Germany FR); 1987, Vancouver (Canada); 1999, Birmingham (UK), 2007, Perugia (Italy). Former names and other names: *Association of Terrestrial Magnetism and Electricity of the IUGG* – former (1919 to 1930); *Association de magnétisme et électricité terrestres de l'UISG* – former (1919 to 1930); *International Association of Terrestrial Magnetism and Electricity* – former (1930 to 1954); *Association internationale de magnétisme et électricité terrestre* – former (1930 to 1954). **Aims** Promote study of magnetism and aeronomy of the earth and other bodies of

the solar system, and of interplanetary medium and its interaction with these bodies, where such studies have international interest; encourage research in these subjects by individual countries, institutions or persons and facilitate its international coordination; provide an opportunity for international discussion and publication of research results; promote appropriate standardization of observational programmes, data acquisition systems, data analysis and publication. **Structure** General and Scientific Assemblies (each every 4 years); Executive Committee; Committees (2); Divisions (5); Interdivisional Commissions (2). **Languages** English, French. **Staff** 1.00 FTE, voluntary. **Finance** Sources: members' dues. **Activities** Awards/prizes/competitions; events/meetings; knowledge management/information dissemination; standards/guidelines; training/education. **Events** *Workshop on Long Term Changes and Trends in the Atmosphere* Helsinki (Finland) 2022, *VERSIM : Workshop on Linear and Non-Linear Wave Phenomena at Audible Frequencies, their Generation, Propagation and Effects* Sodankylä (Finland) 2022, *Joint Scientific Assembly* Hyderabad (India) 2021, *Joint Assembly* Cape Town (South Africa) 2017, *VERSIM : Workshop on Linear and Non-Linear Wave Phenomena at Audible Frequencies, their Generation, Propagation and Effects* Hermanus (South Africa) 2016. **Publications** *IAGA News* (annual); *IAGA Bulletin* (irregular). Books; manuals.
Members National correspondents in 61 countries and territories:
Albania, Argentina, Armenia, Australia, Austria, Azerbaijan, Belgium, Bolivia, Bosnia-Herzegovina, Brazil, Bulgaria, Canada, China, Colombia, Congo DR, Croatia, Czechia, Denmark, Egypt, Estonia, Finland, France, Georgia, Germany, Ghana, Greece, Hungary, Iceland, India, Indonesia, Iran Islamic Rep, Ireland, Israel, Italy, Japan, Korea Rep, Luxembourg, Mauritius, Mexico, Mozambique, Nigeria, Norway, Pakistan, Peru, Philippines, Poland, Portugal, Romania, Russia, Slovakia, Slovenia, South Africa, Spain, Sweden, Switzerland, Taiwan, Thailand, Türkiye, UK, USA, Vietnam.
NGO Relations Constituent association of: *International Union of Geodesy and Geophysics (IUGG, #15776)*, which is one of the 20 scientific Unions grouped within *International Council for Science (ICSU, inactive)*. Joint Working Groups with: *International Association of Volcanology and Chemistry of the Earth's Interior (IAVCEI, #12259)*; *International Association of Seismology and Physics of the Earth's Interior (IASPEI, #12157)*; *Union radio-scientifique internationale (URSI, #20475)*. Member of: *Scientific Committee on Solar-Terrestrial Physics (SCOSTEP, #19151)*. [2022.02.02/XB1292/**B**]

♦ International Association of Geomorphologists (IAG) 11917

SG Geomorphological Field Laboratory (GFL), Strandvegen 484, 7584 Selbu, Norway. T. +4793204443. E-mail: iag.secretarygeneral@gmail.com.
Contact Capitán Haya No. 1-15, 28020 Madrid, Spain.
URL: http://www.geomorph.org/

History 1989, Frankfurt-Main (Germany). Founded during the 2nd International Geomorphology Conference, when officially recognized. Former names and other names: *Working Committee for Collaboration in Geomorphology* – former. **Aims** Develop geomorphology through international collaboration; promote its study and development; foster dissemination of knowledge. **Structure** International Conference (every 4 years); Council; Executive Committee. **Languages** English. **Staff** 7.00 FTE, paid. **Finance** Sources: members' dues; sale of publications. Royalties. **Activities** Events/meetings; knowledge management/information dissemination; publishing activities; research/documentation. Active in all member countries. **Events** *International Conference on Geomorphology* Christchurch (New Zealand) 2026, *International Conference on Geomorphology* Coimbra (Portugal) 2022, *Regional Conference* Mashhad (Iran Islamic Rep) 2022, *International Conference on Geomorphology* Coimbra (Portugal) 2021, *Regional Conference* Mashhad (Iran Islamic Rep) 2020. **Publications** *IAG/AIG Newsletter* (4 a year). *IAG Publication Series*; *IAG Special Series*. *Geomorphological Mapping: Methods and Applications* (2011); *Geomorphological Hazards and Disaster Prevention* (2010); *Geomorphological Landscapes of the World* (2010); *Encyclopedia of Geomorphology* (2004); *Spaces, Environments and Landscapes of Terroirs* (2003); *Geomorphology: the Research Frontier and Beyond* (1993); *Geomorphology and Changing Environments in Central Europe*. Conference research monographs; abstract volumes for conferences; collection of conference research papers; field guides; report series; proceedings.
Members National adhering bodies in 70 countries and territories:
Argentina, Australia, Austria, Bangladesh, Belarus, Belgium (Brazil), Brazil, Bulgaria, Cameroon, Canada, China, Colombia, Congo Brazzaville, Costa Rica, Côte d'Ivoire, Croatia, Czechia, Denmark, Egypt, Estonia, Fiji, Finland, France, Germany, Ghana, Greece, Hungary, Iceland, India, Indonesia, Iran Islamic Rep, Iraq, Ireland, Israel, Italy, Jamaica, Japan, Korea Rep, Lithuania, Malta, Mexico, Myanmar, Nepal, Netherlands, New Zealand, Nigeria, Norway, Poland, Portugal, Romania, Russia, Rwanda, Senegal, Serbia, Singapore, Slovakia, Slovenia, South Africa, Spain, Sri Lanka, Sweden, Switzerland, Taiwan, Tunisia, Türkiye, UK, Ukraine, USA, Venezuela, Vietnam.
NGO Relations Member of (2): *International Geographical Union (IGU, #13713)*; *International Union of Geological Sciences (IUGS, #15777)*. [2022.12.15/XD3390/y/**B**]

♦ International Association of Geophysical Contractors (IAGC) 11918

Contact 1225 North Loop West, Ste 220, Houston TX 77008, USA. T. +17139578080. Fax +17139570008. E-mail: iagc@iagc.org.
URL: http://www.iagc.org/

History 1971. **Events** *Annual Conference* Houston, TX (USA) 2017, *Annual Conference* Houston, TX (USA) 2016, *Annual Conference* Houston, TX (USA) 2015, *Annual Conference* Houston, TX (USA) 2014, *Annual Conference* Houston, TX (USA) 2013. **Members** 205 companies worldwide. Membership countries not specified. [2016.06.20/XN2350/**D**]

- ♦ International Association for Geoscience Diversity (internationally oriented national body)
- ♦ International Association for Germanic Studies (#13317)
- ♦ International Association for German-Speaking Media (inactive)

♦ International Association of Gerodontology (IAG) 11919

Association internationale de gérodontologie (AIG)

Contact 9 rue Quatrefages, 75005 Paris, France. T. +33145350159. Fax +33147077952. E-mail: ag.finet@wanadoo.fr.
URL: http://aigerodontologie.free.fr/

History 1985, by Charles Berenholc. **Aims** Develop knowledge and carry out studies in the field of odontology of the aged; secure contacts with governmental bodies in order to improve the care for the elderly people. **Structure** International Bureau of 22. Commissions (7). **Languages** English, French. **Staff** Paid. **Finance** Members' dues. **Activities** Congresses. **Events** *Congress* Monastir (Tunisia) 2006, *Congress* Barcelona (Spain) 2005, *Congress* Paris (France) 2004, *Congress* Monastir (Tunisia) 2002, *Gérontologie et gérodontologie au service du patient* Montrouge (France) 2001.
Members Full Individuals in 7 countries and territories:
Austria, Canada, France, Spain, Switzerland, Tunisia, UK. [2013/XD7020/**D**]

- ♦ International Association of Gerontology / see International Association of Gerontology and Geriatrics (#11920)

♦ International Association of Gerontology and Geriatrics (IAGG) 11920

Secretariat Columnbia University, Mailman School of Public Health, Columbia Aging Center, 722 West 168th Street, New York NY 10032, USA. T. +12123050294. E-mail: msph-iagg@cumc.columbia.edu.
URL: http://www.iagg.info/

History 3 Dec 1950, Liège (Belgium), as *International Association of Gerontology (IAG) – Association Internationale de Gérontologie (AIG) – Asociación Internacional de Gerontologia – Internationaler Verein für Gerontologie*, at 1st International Congress of Gerontology, in continuation of 'Club for Research on Ageing', set up in 1938, UK, by V Korenshevsky. By-laws recently amended: 1981, 1985, 2013. Registered in accordance with Belgian law, 15 Mar 1952. Present name adopted 2005. **Aims** Promote gerontological research in the biological, medical, *behavioural* and social policy and practice fields; promote training of highly qualified personnel in the field of ageing; promote issues of member gerontological organizations in all questions relating to foreign or international matters. **Structure** Council; Executive Committee; Standing Committees (4): *African Research on Ageing Network (AFRAN, #00440)*; IAGG-Gerontology Students Organization (IAGG-GSO); *International Network for the Prevention of Elder Abuse (INPEA, #14307)*; *International Society for Gerontechnology (#15142)*. **Languages** English. **Staff** 2.00 FTE, paid. **Finance** Sources: meeting proceeds; members' dues. **Activities** Awards/prizes/competitions; events/meetings. **Events** *World Congress of Gerontology and Geriatrics* Amsterdam (Netherlands) 2026, *Asia-Oceania Regional Congress* Yokohama (Japan) 2023, *World Congress of Gerontology and Geriatrics* Buenos Aires (Argentina) 2022, *Conference* New York, NY (USA) 2021, *Asia-Oceania Regional Congress* Taipei (Taiwan) 2019. **Publications** *IAGG Newsletter*.
Members National societies (82) in 69 countries and territories:
Argentina, Australia, Austria, Belarus, Belgium, Bolivia, Brazil, Bulgaria, Canada, Chile, China, Colombia, Costa Rica, Cuba, Czechia, Denmark, Ecuador, Estonia, Finland, France, Georgia, Germany, Greece, Hong Kong, Hungary, India, Indonesia, Ireland, Israel, Italy, Japan, Kazakhstan, Kenya, Korea Rep, Luxembourg, Malaysia, Malta, Mexico, Mongolia, Netherlands, New Zealand, Norway, Panama, Paraguay, Peru, Philippines, Poland, Portugal, Puerto Rico, Romania, Russia, San Marino, Serbia, Singapore, Slovakia, Slovenia, South Africa, Spain, Sweden, Switzerland, Taiwan, Thailand, Tunisia, Türkiye, UK, Ukraine, Uruguay, USA, Venezuela.
Consultative Status Consultative status granted from: *ECOSOC (#05331)* (Special). **IGO Relations** Accredited by: *United Nations Office at Geneva (UNOG, #20597)*; United Nations Office at New York; *United Nations Office at Vienna (UNOV, #20604)*. Associated with Department of Global Communications of the United Nations. **NGO Relations** Member of: *European Nutrition for Health Alliance, The (ENHA, #08069)*; *Global Alliance for the Rights of Older People (#10226)*; *NGO Forum on Environment (FOE, #17125)*. Member of: *Conference of Non-Governmental Organizations in Consultative Relationship with the United Nations (CONGO, #04635)*. [2020/XC1293/**B**]

- ♦ International Association for Gesture Research / see International Society for Gesture Studies (#15143)

♦ International Association for Gnotobiology (IAG) 11921

Exec Sec Dept of Infectious Diseases, Kyorin Univ School of Medicine, 6-20-2 Shinkawa Mitaka, Tokyo, 181-8611 Japan. T. +81422475511 – +81422475512. Fax +81422447325.
URL: http://square.umin.ac.jp/JAGG/IAG.html

History Founded 30 Jun 1981. Constitution and bylaws adopted 1 Apr 1982. Incorporated 17 May 1984, Wilmington DE (USA). **Aims** Promote scientific knowledge and encourage research and technology in the field of gnotobiology; disseminate information; unify efforts of those concerned in the field. **Structure** Board of Directors; Councillors; Nominating Committee. **Finance** Sources: members' dues. **Events** *International Symposium on Gnotobiology* Chicago, IL (USA) 2022, *International Symposium on Gnotobiology* Tokyo (Japan) 2017, *Symposium* St Petersburg (Russia) 2014, *Triennial Symposium* Stockholm (Sweden) 2008, *Triennial Symposium* Tokyo (Japan) 2005.
Members All members of the following organizations (3):
Association for Gnotobiotics (#02628); European Gnotobiotics Association (EGA); Japanese Association for Germfree Life and Gnotobiology (JAGG).
NGO Relations Member of: *AAALAC International*. Joint meeting with: *Society for Microbial Ecology and Disease (SOMED, #19596)*. [2019.12.18/XJ0016/**C**]

- ♦ International Association of Golf Administrators (internationally oriented national body)

♦ International Association of Golf Tour Operators (IAGTO) 11922

Chief Executive Concorde House, Grenville Place, London, NW7 3SA, UK. T. +442089063377. Fax +442089068181. E-mail: info@iagto.com.
URL: http://www.iagto.com/

History Jan 1998. **Aims** Represent the interests of golf travel industry; create business opportunities for operators and industry partners; improve access to valuable market information. **Languages** English, Spanish. **Staff** 7.00 FTE, paid. **Finance** Members' dues. **Activities** Sponsors *International Golf Travel Market (IGTM)*, an annual trade show; commissions trade-related surveys; industry awards. Administers Golf Travel Writers Association. **Events** *Asia Golf Tourism Convention* Haikou City (China) 2014, *Asia Golf Tourism Convention* Kuala Lumpur (Malaysia) 2012, *International Golf Travel Market* Malaga (Spain) 2009, *International Golf Travel Market* Marbella (Spain) 2008, *International Golf Travel Market* Cancún (Mexico) 2007.
Members Golf Tour Operators; Golf Resorts; Golf Courses; Hotels; Inbound Operators; Tourist Boards. Member companies and organizations (1,450) in 77 countries and territories:
Argentina, Australia, Austria, Bahrain, Barbados, Belgium, Bermuda, Brazil, Bulgaria, Cambodia, Canada, China, Colombia, Costa Rica, Croatia, Cuba, Cyprus, Czechia, Denmark, Dominican Rep, Egypt, England, Estonia, Eswatini, Fiji, Finland, France, Germany, Gibraltar, Greece, Guatemala, Hong Kong, Hungary, Iceland, India, Ireland, Italy, Jamaica, Japan, Kenya, Latvia, Lithuania, Malaysia, Mauritius, Mexico, Morocco, Nepal, Netherlands, New Zealand, Nigeria, Northern Cyprus, Northern Ireland, Norway, Oman, Paraguay, Peru, Poland, Portugal, Puerto Rico, Qatar, Russia, Scotland, Seychelles, Singapore, Slovakia, Slovenia, South Africa, Spain, Sweden, Switzerland, Thailand, Tunisia, Türkiye, United Arab Emirates, USA, Vietnam, Wales. [2015/XD6746/**D**]

♦ International Association for Gondwana Research (IAGR) 11923

SG China Univ of Geosciences Beijing, No 29 Xueyuan Road, Haidian District, 100083 Beijing, China. T. +861082323117. Fax +861082323117.
URL: http://bm.cugb.edu.cn/iagr/

History 1996, Japan. Incorporated *Gondwana Research Group*, previously active in Japan and India since 1990. **Aims** Promote international research, collaboration and information exchange, organization of seminars/symposia and publication of research results related to the assembly, evolution and dispersal of *super-continents* with specific reference to Gondwana; promote a better understanding of *earth* resources by advancing scientific knowledge. **Structure** Officers: Emeritus President; President; Secretary General; Vice Presidents (6); Secretaries (5); Treasurer; Headquarters Secretary. **Languages** English. **Staff** 2.00 FTE, paid. Several voluntary. **Finance** Grant-in-aid from academic bodies; publication proceeds. **Activities** Events/meetings. **Events** *Annual Convention and International Symposium* Kochi (Japan) 2019, *Annual Convention and International Symposium* Xian (China) 2018, *Gondwana International Conference on Puzzling Out Gondwana* Bangkok (Thailand) 2017, *Annual Convention and International Symposium* Thiruvananthapuram (India) 2016, *Annual Convention and International Symposium* Tsukuba (Japan) 2015. **Publications** *Gondwana Research* – journal.
Members Full in 47 countries and territories:
Argentina, Australia, Austria, Bangladesh, Belgium, Botswana, Brazil, Cameroon, Canada, Chile, China, Congo DR, Eritrea, Ethiopia, Finland, France, Germany, Guyana, India, Italy, Japan, Kenya, Korea Rep, Kuwait, Madagascar, Malawi, Mozambique, Nepal, Netherlands, New Zealand, Norway, Pakistan, Papua New Guinea, Russia, South Africa, Spain, Sri Lanka, Sweden, Switzerland, Tanzania UR, Thailand, Türkiye, UK, USA, Vietnam, Zambia, Zimbabwe. [2019.02.12/XE4755/**E**]

♦ International Association for Greek and Latin Epigraphy 11924

Association internationale d'épigraphie Grecque et Latine (AIEGL) – Asociación Internacional de Epigrafía Griega y Latina – Internationale Gesellschaft für Griechische und Lateinische Epigraphik – Associazione Internazionale di Epigrafia Greca e Latina

SG Univ de Zaragoza, Dpto de Ciencias de la Antigüedad-Área de Historia Antigua, Corona de Aragón 42, 50009 Saragossa, Spain.
Pres Sapienza Univ de Roma, Piazzale Aldo Moro 5, 00185 Rome RM, Italy.
URL: http://www.aiegl.org/

History 1972, Munich (Germany). Constituted 1977, Constantza (Romania). Former names and other names: *International Association for Latin Epigraphy* – former; *Association internationale d'épigraphie latine (AIEL)* – former. **Aims** Promote communication and cooperation among students and scholars of epigraphy throughout the world. **Structure** Administrative Council; Bureau. **Languages** English, French, German, Italian, Spanish. **Staff** Voluntary. **Finance** Sources: members' dues. **Activities** Awards/prizes/competitions; events/meetings; financial and/or material support. **Events** *Epigraphy at the 21st century* Bordeaux (France) 2022, *Languages, culture of writing, identities in antiquity* Vienna (Austria) 2017, *Congress* Berlin (Germany) 2012, *Congress* Oxford (UK) 2007, *Roman Empire provinces through epigraphy* Barcelona (Spain) 2002. **Publications** *Internationalen Kongresses für Griechische und Lateinische Epigraphik* (2019) by Petra Amann et al; *Sprachen – Schriftkulturen – Identitäten der Antike : Beiträge des XV. Internationalen Kongresses für Griechische und Lateinische Epigraphik : Wien, 28. August bis 1. September 2017* (2019) by Petra Amann and Thomas Corsten et al – Verlag Holzhausen GmbH; *CIL Auctarium, vol 4* (2014); *Epigraphy and the historical sciences : 13th International Congress of Greek and Latin Epigraphy, Oxford, 2 – 7 September 2007* (2012) by John Davies – Oxford Univ. Press; *XII Congressus Internationalis Epigraphiae Graecae et Latinae; Provinciae Imperii Romani Inscriptionibus Descriptae; Barcelona, 3 – 8 septembris 2002, 1-2* (2007) by M Mayer – Barcelona; *Actes du Xe Congrès International d'Épigraphie Greque et Latine. Nîmes, 4–9 octobre 1992* (1997) by M Christol and O Masson; *Öffentlichkeit – Monument – Text*.
Members Organizations and individuals in 32 countries:
Algeria, Australia, Austria, Belgium, Bosnia-Herzegovina, Bulgaria, Canada, Croatia, Cyprus, Denmark, Finland, France, Germany, Greece, Holy See, Hungary, Israel, Italy, Japan, Netherlands, Nigeria, Poland, Portugal, Romania, Russia, Slovenia, Spain, Switzerland, Tunisia, Türkiye, UK, USA.
NGO Relations Member of (1): *Fédération internationale des associations d'études classiques (FIEC, #09607)*. [2023.02.16/XD1194/v/**C**]

♦ **International Association for Greek Philosophy (IAGP)** **11925**

Contact 5 Simonidou Str, 174 56 Alimos, Greece. T. +302107277545 – +302109956955. Fax +302107248979 – +302109923281. E-mail: kboud714@ppp.uoa.gr.
URL: http://www.iagp.gr/

History 1987. **Aims** Cultivate and promote the study of Greek philosophy and *culture*, and philosophy in general. **Structure** Governing Body; International Academic Committee; Administrative Committee. **Languages** English, French, German, Irish Gaelic. **Staff** 5.00 FTE, voluntary. **Activities** Events/meetings; publishing activities. **Events** *International Conference* Athens (Greece) / Vouliagmeni (Greece) 2014, *Conference / International Conference* Athens (Greece) 2013, *Conference* Pythagorion (Greece) 2012, *International Conference* Samos (Greece) / Pythagorion (Greece) 2012, *Conference / International Conference* Athens (Greece) / Vouliagmeni (Greece) 2011. **Publications** *IONIA Publications* – in 70 vols. Brochures.
Members Regular, Extraordinary/Probationary and Honorary members. Individuals and organizations (about 450) in 27 countries:
Argentina, Australia, Austria, Belgium, Brazil, Canada, China, Denmark, Finland, France, Germany, Greece, India, Ireland, Italy, Japan, Korea Rep, Luxembourg, Mexico, Netherlands, Portugal, Russia, South Africa, Spain, Sweden, UK, USA.
NGO Relations Member of: *International Federation of Philosophical Societies (FISP, #13507)*. Cooperates with national and international societies and academic institutions. [2014.06.22/XD5618/**D**]

♦ International Association for Green Energy (unconfirmed)

♦ **International Association for Group Psychotherapy and Group Processes (IAGP)** **11926**

Sec address not obtained. E-mail: office@iagp.com – secretary@iagp.com – info@iagp.com.
Registered address Besnerstrasse 27, Kreuzlingen TG, Switzerland.
URL: http://www.iagp.com/

History Aug 1954, Toronto, ON (Canada). Former names and other names: *International Committee on Group Psychotherapy* – former; *International Council of Group Psychotherapy* – former. **Aims** Promote professional cross fertilization of ideas and practices from different cultures, disciplines and methodologies. **Structure** Voluntary Executive; Board; Consultative Assembly of Organizational Affiliates; Sections (6). **Languages** English. **Staff** 40.00 FTE, voluntary. **Finance** Sources: members' dues. **Activities** Events/meetings; projects/programmes; training/education. **Events** *Triennial Congress* Pescara (Italy) 2022, *Triennial Congress* Vancouver, BC (Canada) 2021, *Africa Regional Conference* Cairo (Egypt) 2020, *International Psychodrama Conference* Iseo (Italy) 2019, *Triennial Congress* Malmö (Sweden) 2018. **Publications** *Forum*; *Globeletter*.
Members Individuals and associations with professional involvement in group psychotherapy in 50 countries and territories:
Argentina, Australia, Austria, Belarus, Belgium, Bolivia, Brazil, Bulgaria, Canada, China, Croatia, Czechia, Denmark, Egypt, Estonia, Finland, France, Georgia, Germany, Greece, Hungary, Iceland, India, Ireland, Israel, Italy, Japan, Kenya, Latvia, Lithuania, Mexico, Netherlands, New Zealand, Norway, Palestine, Poland, Portugal, Romania, Russia, Serbia, Slovenia, South Africa, Spain, Sweden, Switzerland, Taiwan, Tunisia, Türkiye, UK, USA. [2020/XD7315/**C**]

♦ International Association of Growers of Rubber Oil Palms and other Tropical Crops / see Tropical Growers' Association (#20250)
♦ International Association of Growers of Tropical Crops / see Tropical Growers' Association (#20250)
♦ International Association of Hail Insurance Companies / see Association internationale des assureurs de la production agricole (#02671)
♦ International Association of Hail Insurers / see Association internationale des assureurs de la production agricole (#02671)

♦ **International Association of Hairdressing Schools (IAHS)** **11927**

Pres address not obtained. E-mail: rsap@bredband.net.
Hon Pres Burgårdens Utbildningscentrum, Skåneg 20, Box 5440, SE-402 29 Gothenburg, Sweden. T. +46313670275. Fax +46313670201.
URL: http://iahs-org.com/

History Apr 1998, Gothenburg (Sweden). **Aims** Increase cooperation between hairdressing schools, promote exchanges between schools and trainee internships; increase availability and quality of teaching materials and methods for the benefit of hairdressing education. **Structure** General Meeting (annual). Board, including Chairman, Secretary and Treasurer. **Languages** English. **Finance** Members' dues. **Activities** Organizes annual meeting; competitions. **Events** *Annual Meeting* Reykjavik (Iceland) 2015, *Annual Meeting* Varberg (Sweden) 2012, *Annual Meeting* Cork (Ireland) 2011, *Annual Meeting* Australia 2010, *Annual Meeting* Melbourne, VIC (Australia) 2010. **Publications** *IAHS Newsletter*.
Members Full Schools (27) in 6 countries:
Denmark, Finland, Iceland, Norway, Sweden, UK.
Support members individuals in 2 countries:
Sweden, UK. [2014/XD8786/**D**]

♦ International Association for Halitosis Research (unconfirmed)

♦ **International Association for Handicapped Divers (IAHD)** **11928**

Managing Dir PO Box 171, 7940 AD Meppel, Netherlands. T. +31522242593. Fax +31522242591.
URL: http://www.iahd.org/

History Founded Apr 1993, Sweden. Registered in accordance with Dutch, UK and Japanese law. **Aims** Promote access to *scuba* diving opportunities for physically handicapped individuals through training and networking activities. **Languages** Dutch, English, French, German, Hebrew, Italian, Japanese, Spanish, Swedish. **Staff** 4.00 FTE, paid. **Finance** Members' dues. Donations; sponsors. **Activities** Training/education; projects/programmes. **Events** *Symposium* Cardiff (UK) 1998. **Publications** *IAHD Newsletter* (6 a year). Training manuals.
Members Professional (Divemasters and Instructors) and non-professional (Dive Partner and Open Water Divers) in 36 countries and territories:
Andorra, Argentina, Australia, Austria, Brazil, Cayman Is, Costa Rica, Cyprus, Denmark, Egypt, France, Germany, Greece, Indonesia, Ireland, Israel, Italy, Japan, Malaysia, Maldives, Malta, Netherlands, Norway, Philippines, Portugal, Seychelles, Singapore, South Africa, Spain, Sweden, Switzerland, Thailand, Türkiye, UK, USA. [2016/XD6478/v/**D**]

♦ **International Association of Hand Papermakers and Paper Artists (IAPMA)** **11929**

Contact address not obtained. E-mail: president@iapma.info.
URL: http://www.iapma.info/

History Founded 1986. Aims and objectives established at 1st General Meeting, Jun 1987, Capellades (Spain). **Aims** Facilitate international exchange of artistic ideas and information; provide the opportunity for members to work together, collaborate on artistic projects and exhibitions, share solutions to technical problems, explore different paper-related cultural backgrounds and encourage new approaches to paper arts. **Structure** General Meeting (biennial, prior to Congress); Executive Committee. **Languages** English. **Staff** 5.00 FTE, voluntary. **Finance** Sources: members' dues. **Activities** Events/meetings; knowledge management/information dissemination; networking/liaising. **Events** *Congress* Toyota (Japan) 2021, *Congress* Toyota (Japan) 2020, *Congress* Sofia (Bulgaria) 2018, *Congress* Brasilia (Brazil) 2016, *Congress* Fabriano (Italy) 2014. **Publications** *IAPMA Newsletter* (6 a year); *IAPMA Bulletin* (annual) – journal. Members' address list.
Members Institutional in 17 countries:
Australia, Bulgaria, Ecuador, Germany, Italy, Japan, Korea Rep, Netherlands, New Zealand, Poland, Slovakia, Spain, Sweden, Switzerland, Türkiye, UK, USA.
Individual (Regular; Student) in 43 countries and territories. Membership countries not specified.
Argentina, Australia, Austria, Bahamas, Belgium, Brazil, Bulgaria, Canada, Chile, China, Colombia, Denmark, Finland, France, Germany, Hungary, Israel, Italy, Japan, Korea Rep, Latvia, Liechtenstein, Luxembourg, Mexico, Netherlands, Norway, Peru, Philippines, Poland, Puerto Rico, Slovakia, Slovenia, Sweden, Switzerland, Taiwan, UK, USA. [2022/XD0867/**C**]

♦ International Association of Headwater Control (no recent information)
♦ International Association of Healthcare Central Service Material Management (internationally oriented national body)
♦ International Association of Healthcare Practitioners (internationally oriented national body)
♦ International Association of Health Insurance Funds / see International Federation of Health Plans (#13442)

♦ **International Association of Health Policy (IAHP)** **11930**

Asociación Internacional de Politicas de Salud

Exec UBA Fac de Psicologia, Av Independencia 3065, C1225AAM Buenos Aires, Argentina. E-mail: stolkin@psi.uba.ar.
Vice-Pres address not obtained. E-mail: josejoj@idecnet.com.
Coordinator for North America Johns Hopkins Univ, School of Hygiene and Public Health, Dept of Health Policy and Management, Hampton House – 4th Floor, 624 North Broadway, Baltimore MD 21205-1901, USA.
URL: http://www.healthp.org/

History 1975, Amsterdam (Netherlands). **Aims** Promote debate, exchange of experiences and knowledge regarding international comparisons in health policies and the scientific analysis of topics related to *public health*. **Structure** Executive Board, comprising President, Vice-President and 4 members. Advisory Board of 12 members. **Languages** English, Spanish. **Staff** 1.00 FTE, voluntary. **Events** *Conference* Montevideo (Uruguay) 2012, *Conference* Madrid (Spain) 2009, *Health, ethics and equity – a call for policies and action* Salvador (Brazil) 2007, *Challenging health inequalities – forging progressive partnerships for public health* Durban (South Africa) 2004, *Conference* Palma (Spain) 2002. **Publications** *International Association of Health Policy Newsletter*.
Members Individual scientists and activists in 18 countries and territories.
Argentina, Brazil, Chile, Colombia, Cuba, Germany, Greece, Italy, Mexico, Peru, Serbia, Spain, Sweden, Türkiye, UK, USA, Venezuela, Wales.
NGO Relations *International Association of Health Policy in Europe (IAHPE, #11931)*; *Asociación Latinoamericana de Medicina Social (ALAMES, #02241)*. [2014/XD0578/v/**D**]

♦ **International Association of Health Policy in Europe (IAHPE)** **11931**

Pres address not obtained. E-mail: iahp.online@gmail.com.
Vice-Pres address not obtained.
URL: http://iahponline.wordpress.com/

History 1982, Frankfurt-Main (Germany). **Aims** Promote health, the struggle against health inequalities and development of social solidarity. **Structure** Executive Board. **Activities** Events/meetings. **Events** *European health policies in the era of capitalist crisis and restructuring* Thessaloniki (Greece) 2017, *Conference* Ankara (Turkey) 2011, *Conference* Coventry (UK) 2009, *European Conference* Frankfurt-Main (Germany) 2008, *Health policy in Europe – contemporary dilemmas and challenges* Thessaloniki (Greece) 2005. [2018.09.09/XM3695/**D**]

♦ International Association of Heat and Frost Insulators and Allied Workers (internationally oriented national body)
♦ International Association of Heat and Frost Insulators and Asbestos Workers / see International Association of Heat and Frost Insulators and Allied Workers
♦ International Association Hegel-Marx for Dialectical Thought (no recent information)
♦ International Association of High Performance Sports Training Centers / see Association of Sport Performance Centres (#02929)
♦ International Association of High Performance Sport Training Centres / see Association of Sport Performance Centres (#02930)
♦ International Association of High Pressure Bioscience and Biotechnology (unconfirmed)
♦ International Association of Hispanists (#02165)

♦ **International Association of Historians of Asia (IAHA)** **11932**

Association internationale des historiens de l'Asie

Contact Centre for General Studies, UUM College of Arts and Sciences, Universiti Utara Malaysia, 06010 UUM Sintok, Kedah, Malaysia. T. +609285584. Fax +609285616. E-mail: sulia@uum.edu.my.
URL: http://www.iaha2014.uum.edu.my/index.php/contact.html

History Founded 1961. Absorbed the *Conference of Southeast Asian Historians (inactive)*, 1964. **Aims** Promote historical research on Asia; encourage historians to exchange ideas and experience on research, leading to academic progress and international cooperation. **Structure** Executive Committee. **Activities** Events/meetings. **Events** *Conference* Kedah (Malaysia) 2014, *Conference* Singapore (Singapore) 2010, *Conference* Singapore (Singapore) 2010, *Conference* Delhi (India) 2008, *Conference* Quezon City (Philippines) 2006. **Members** Membership countries not specified. [2010/XD4955/**D**]

♦ **International Association of Historical Societies for the Study of Jewish History (IAHSSJH)** **11933**

SG PO Box 10477, 2 Beitar Street, 9110401 Jerusalem, Israel. T. +972256504445. Fax +97226712388. E-mail: shazar@shazar.org.il.
The Historical Society of Israel 2 Betar St, 9110401 Jerusalem, Israel. E-mail: history@history.org.il.
URL: http://www.shazar.org.il/

History 1979. **Aims** Encourage the study of Jewish history in all countries in order to advance the knowledge of the subject; encourage foundation and initiation of Jewish historical societies in different countries; encourage cooperation in education, the exchange of students and scholars, the support and establishment of chairs and departments in Jewish history in institutions of higher learning. **Structure** Officers: President; Secretary-General. **Activities** Participates in: CISH activities, international conferences. **Events** *Jewish communities at the center and at the periphery through the ages – from dependence to independence* Sydney, NSW (Australia) 2005, *Comparative perspectives on the interplay of continuity and innovation in the history of jews and other minorities* Oslo (Norway) 2000, *The Spanish expulsion* Jerusalem (Israel) 1992, *Religion and economy* Jerusalem (Israel) 1990, *Sephardic Jewry and its dispersions* Madrid (Spain) 1990.
Members Societies in 14 countries:
Argentina, Australia, Brazil, Canada, France, Germany, Israel, Italy, Mexico, Netherlands, Poland, Spain, UK, USA.
Individuals in 8 countries:
Australia, Canada, France, Israel, Italy, Mexico, UK, USA.
NGO Relations International Affiliate Organization of: *International Committee of Historical Sciences (ICHS, #12777)*. [2018/XD0514/**D**]

♦ International Association of the History and Civilization of Sugar (internationally oriented national body)
♦ International Association for History and Computing (no recent information)

♦ **International Association for the History of Crime and Criminal Justice (IAHCCJ)** **11934**

Association internationale pour l'histoire de la justice et de la criminalité

Contact Dept of History, Univ of Dundee – Nethergate, Dundee, DD1 4HN, UK.
URL: http://www.h-net.org/~iahccj/

History 1978, on the initiative of Herman Diederiks. **Structure** Executive Committee. **Activities** Organizes and participates in conferences, colloquia and sessions. Runs a project on the history of social control. Awards the Herman Diederiks Prize. **Events** *Conference on working as a policeman / Colloquium* Caen (France) 2007, *Annual colloquium / Colloquium* Budapest (Hungary) 2004, *Annual colloquium / Colloquium* Geneva (Switzerland) 2002, *Annual colloquium / Colloquium* Les Treilles (France) 2001, *Session* Oslo (Norway) 2000. **Publications** *Crime, History and Societies/Crime, Hitoire et Sociétés* (2 a year) – journal.
Members Individuals in 28 countries (" indicates national correspondent):
Argentina, Australia, Austria (*), Belgium (*), Brazil, Canada (*), Croatia, Czechia, Denmark (*), France (*), Germany (*), Hungary (*), Israel, Italy (*), Netherlands (*), Norway (*), Poland (*), Portugal, Russia, Spain, Sweden (*), Switzerland (*), Tunisia, UK (*), Ukraine, USA (*), Venezuela, Vietnam. [2011.08.23/XD4659/v/**F**]

♦ International Association of the History of Dentistry (no recent information)
♦ International Association for the History of Glass (#02706)
♦ International Association for the History of Law and Institutions (inactive)

♦ **International Association for the History of Nephrology (IAHN)** **11935**

Sec-Treas Univ of Southern California, 2020 Zonal Ave IRD Ste 806, Los Angeles CA 90033-1029, USA. E-mail: smogorze@usc.edu.
URL: http://iahn.info/

History Officially set up 1994. **Aims** Promote, stimulate and encourage research, study, interest and writing in the history of *medicine* as it pertains to all aspects related to the *kidney* and urinary tract; give support to and cooperate with local, national or international organizations with similar purposes. **Structure** Officers: President; President Elect; Past President; Secretary-Treasurer. **Languages** English. **Staff** 1.00 FTE, voluntary. **Finance** Members' dues. **Activities** Awards/prizes/competitions; events/meetings. **Events** *Congress* Larissa (Greece) 2019, *Congress* Wloclawek (Poland) 2017, *Congress* Milazzo (Italy) 2015, *Congress* Patras (Greece) 2013, *Congress* Paestum (Italy) 2012. **Publications** Conference proceedings.
Members Individuals in 10 countries:
Australia, France, Germany, Greece, Italy, Poland, Serbia, Slovakia, UK, USA.
NGO Relations Links with national and international organizations. [2015.06.29/XJ6125/**D**]

♦ International Association for the History of Physical Education and Sport (inactive)
♦ International Association for the History of Psychoanalysis / see International Association Interactions of Psychoanalysis (#11968)

♦ International Association for the History of Religions (IAHR) 11936

Association internationale pour l'histoire des religions – Asociación Internacional para la Historia de las Religiones – Internationale Vereinigung für Religionsgeschichte

SG Dept of Religious Studies, Fac of Letters, Univ of Tokyo, 7-3-1 Hongo, Bunkyo-ku, Tokyo, 113-0033 Japan. T. +819054328112.
Pres Inst of Philosophy/Education and Study of Religion, Univ of Southern Denmark, Odense – Campusvej 55, 5230 Odense M, Denmark. T. +4565503315. Fax +4565502668.
URL: http://www.iahrweb.org/

History 4 Sep 1950, Amsterdam (Netherlands). Founded at 7th International Congress for the Study of the History of Religions, taking over the activities of *Standing Commission for International Congresses on the History of Religions (inactive)*, set up 18 Sep 1909. Former names and other names: *International Association for the Study of History of Religions* – former (4 Sep 1950). **Aims** Promote academic study of religions through international collaboration of scholars whose research has a bearing on the subject. **Structure** General Assembly; International Committee; Executive Committee. **Languages** English, French. **Finance** Sources: members' dues. **Activities** Events/meetings; networking/liaising. **Events** *Quinquennial Congress* Dunedin (New Zealand) 2020, *Quinquennial Congress* Erfurt (Germany) 2015, *Special Conference* Liverpool (UK) 2013, *Special Conference* Stockholm (Sweden) 2012, *Special Conference* Trondheim (Norway) 2012. **Publications** *Numen – International Review for the History of Religions* (5 a year) – journal; *IAHR Bulletin* (1-2 every 5 years); *IAHR e-Bulletin Supplement* (occasional). Proceedings of congresses and conferences.
Members Associations in 40 countries:
Australia, Austria, Belgium, Brazil, Canada, China, Cuba, Czechia, Denmark, Estonia, Finland, France, Germany, Greece, Hungary, India, Ireland, Italy, Japan, Korea Rep, Latvia, Lithuania, Mexico, Netherlands, New Zealand, Nigeria, Norway, Philippines, Poland, Romania, Russia, Slovakia, South Africa, Spain, Sweden, Switzerland, Türkiye, UK, Ukraine, USA.
Affiliate members (6):
European Society for the Study of Western Esotericism (ESSWE, #08749); *International Association for the Cognitive Science of Religion (IACSR, #11784)*; *International Society for the Study of Religion, Nature and Culture (ISSRNC, #15485)*; *International Study of Religion in Eastern and Central Europe Association (ISORECEA, #15620)*; *Society for Ancient Mediterranean Religions (SAMR)*; *Society of Biblical Literature (SBL)*.
Regional associations (5), listed in this Yearbook:
African Association for the Study of Religions (AASR, #00217); *Asociación Latinoamericana para el Estudio de las Religiones (ALER, #02216)*; *Eastern African Association for the Study of Religions (EAASR, no recent information)*; *European Association for the Study of Religions (EASR, #06235)*; *South and Southeast Asian Association for the Study of Culture and Religion (SSEASR, #19892)*.
NGO Relations Member of: *International Council for Philosophy and Human Sciences (CIPSH, #13061)*.
[2020.03.03/XC1221/y/**C**]

♦ International Association for the History of South-East Europe / see Association internationale d'études du Sud-Est européen (#02693)

♦ International Association for the History of Transport, Traffic and Mobility (T2M Association) 11937

Exec Sec Inst For Social Futures, Lancaster Univ, County South, Lancaster, LA1 4YB, UK. E-mail: secretary@t2m.org.
URL: http://www.t2m.org/

History Launched 8 Nov 2003, Eindhoven (Netherlands), during 1st International Conference on the History of Transport, Traffic and Mobility. Officially set up 2006, when statutes were adopted. **Aims** Be a a collegial association of scholars, practitioners and concerned citizens to encourage and promote an understanding of the historical interaction between transport, traffic and the mobility of people, material objects and ideas. **Structure** Executive Committee. **Activities** Awards/prizes/competitions; events/meetings. **Events** *Conference* Padua (Italy) 2022, *Conference* Lisbon (Portugal) 2021, *Conference* Shanghai (China) 2020, *Conference* Paris (France) 2019, *Conference* Montréal, QC (Canada) 2018. **Publications** *Journal of Transport History* (2 a year).
Members Institutional in 12 countries:
Argentina, Belgium, Canada, Denmark, Finland, France, Germany, Netherlands, Portugal, Switzerland, UK, USA.
Included in the above, 1 organization listed in this Yearbook:
European Centre for Mobility Documentation (ECMD). [2021.02.17/XM1832/y/**D**]

♦ International Association of Holiday Inns / see IHG Owners Association (#11112)

♦ International Association of Homes and Services for the Ageing (IAHSA) 11938

Exec Dir 2519 Connecticut Ave NW, Washington DC 20008-1520, USA. T. +12025089468. Fax +12022200041. E-mail: info@globalageing.org.
URL: http://globalageing.org/

History 1994, Washington, DC (USA). Former names and other names: *The Global Ageing Network* – trading name. **Aims** Promote quality services to assist the ageing, frail elderly and disabled; connect and support care and service provides worldwide to enhance the quality of life for the ageing. **Structure** Board of Directors. **Languages** English. **Staff** 3.00 FTE, paid. **Finance** Members' dues. **Activities** Knowledge management/information dissemination; monitoring/evaluation; guidance/assistance; awards/prizes/competitions. **Events** *Global Ageing Conference* Glasgow (UK) 2023, *Global Ageing Network Summit* Seoul (Korea Rep) 2021, *Global Ageing Conference* Toronto, ON (Canada) 2019, *Biennial Conference* Montreux (Switzerland) 2017, *Biennial Conference* Perth, WA (Australia) 2015. **Publications** *Alliance* (periodical); *IAHSA Newsletter* – online. **Members** Corporate/Business; Facility/Organization; Individual professionals in aging care and service settings in over 35 countries. Membership countries not specified. **Consultative Status** Consultative status granted from: *ECOSOC (#05331)* (Special). **NGO Relations** Member of: *Global Alliance for the Rights of Older People (#10226)*. Set up: *European Association of Homes and Services for the Ageing (EAHSA, inactive)*; *'China Association of Association and Homes for the Ageing (IAHSA-China)'*. Partner of: *International Federation on Ageing (IFA, #13345)*. [2022/XD5818/**D**]

♦ International Association for Horse Assisted Education (EAHAE) ... 11939

Pres G and K HorseDream, Lichtenhagener Str 8, 34593 Knüllwald, Germany. T. +4956859224233. Fax +4956859224234. E-mail: office@eahae.org.
URL: http://www.eahae.org/

History Founded 2004, on the initiative of Gerhard Krebs, as *European Association for Horse Assisted Education (EAHAE)*. **Aims** Serve as a platform for information, communication, education, certification, research and publication on horse assisted education. **Structure** Board of Directors; Advisory Board. **Languages** English. **Staff** 4.00 FTE, voluntary. **Finance** Members' dues. Annual budget: euro 30,000. **Events** *Conference* Lajosmizse (Hungary) 2017, *Conference* Novato, CA (USA) 2016, *Annual Conference* Knüllwald (Germany) 2015, *Annual Conference* Poland 2014, *Annual Conference* Cleveland, OH (USA) 2013. **Publications** Newsletter (12 a year).
Members in 36 countries:
Argentina, Australia, Austria, Belgium, Brazil, Canada, Chile, Costa Rica, Czechia, Denmark, Ecuador, Finland, France, Germany, Hungary, India, Ireland, Israel, Italy, Kazakhstan, Mexico, Netherlands, Norway, Poland, Portugal, Romania, Russia, Singapore, Slovakia, Spain, Sweden, Switzerland, Türkiye, UK, Ukraine, USA. [2017.10.11/XM3623/**D**]

♦ International Association of Horticultural Producers 11940

Association internationale des producteurs de l'horticulture (AIPH) – Asociación Internacional de Productores Horticolas – Internationaler Verband des Erwerbsgartenbaues

SG Horticulture House, Chilton, Didcot, OX11 0RN, UK. E-mail: sg@aiph.org – info@aiph.org.
URL: http://www.aiph.org/

History Statutes adopted 7 Sep 1948, Zurich (Switzerland). Registration: Banque-Carrefour des Entreprises, Start date: Oct 2013, Belgium; EU Transparency Register, No/ID: 873862119851-81, Start date: 4 Dec 2015. **Aims** Represent horticultural producers' organizations around the world; re-ignite and uphold an appreciation of plants; support the work of grower associations globally; champion a prosperous industry, growing plants that enhance lives, advance societies and sustain our planet. **Structure** General Meeting; Board; Specialized Committees (6). **Languages** English. **Staff** 8.00 FTE, paid. **Finance** Sources: meeting proceeds; members' dues; revenue from activities/projects; sale of publications. **Activities** Events/meetings. **Events** *Annual Congress* Almere (Netherlands) 2022, *Spring Meeting* Dubai (United Arab Emirates) 2022, *Annual Congress* Didcot (UK) 2021, *International Plant Health Conference* Didcot (UK) 2021, *Annual Congress* Didcot (UK) 2020. **Publications** *FloraCulture International (FCI)* (6 a year) in English; *International Statistics Yearbook – Flowers and Plants*.
Members Horticultural trade organizations in 30 countries and territories:
Australia, Belgium, Brazil, Canada, China, Colombia, Czechia, Denmark, Finland, France, Germany, Hungary, Indonesia, Ireland, Italy, Japan, Korea Rep, Mexico, Netherlands, Pakistan, Poland, Qatar, Sweden, Switzerland, Taiwan, Tanzania UR, Thailand, Türkiye, UK, USA.
Consultative Status Consultative status granted from: *ECOSOC (#05331)* (Ros C); *FAO (#09260)* (Special Status). **IGO Relations** Observer status with (1): *Union internationale pour la protection des obtentions végétales (UPOV, #20436)*. [2022/XD1295/**C**]

♦ International Association for Hospice and Palliative Care (IAHPC) .. 11941

Contact 5535 Memorial Dr, Ste F-509, Houston TX 77007, USA. T. +18326237650. E-mail: info@iahpc.com.
URL: http://hospicecare.com/

History Founded 2000. **Aims** Collaborate and work to improve the quality of life of patients with advanced life-threatening conditions, and their families, by advancing hospice and palliative care programmes, education, research and favourable policies around the world. **Structure** Board; Executive Committee. **Languages** English. **Staff** 7.00 FTE, paid. **Finance** Sources: donations; grants; members' dues. **Activities** Advocacy/lobbying/activism; knowledge management/information dissemination; training/education. **Events** *Biennial international congress on palliative care* Montréal, QC (Canada) 2010, *Biennial international congress on palliative care* Montréal, QC (Canada) 2008. **Publications** *IAHPC Newsletter* (12 a year). Articles; guidelines; manuals; directories; calendar; fact sheets.
Members Individuals and institutions in 110 countries and territories:
Albania, Argentina, Armenia, Australia, Austria, Bangladesh, Barbados, Belarus, Belgium, Belize, Benin, Bhutan, Bolivia, Brazil, Bulgaria, Burkina Faso, Cameroon, Canada, Cayman Is, Chile, China, Colombia, Congo DR, Costa Rica, Curaçao, Czechia, Dominican Rep, Ecuador, Egypt, El Salvador, Ethiopia, Finland, France, Georgia, Germany, Ghana, Guatemala, Guinea, Guyana, Haiti, Honduras, India, Indonesia, Iran Islamic Rep, Iraq, Ireland, Israel, Italy, Jamaica, Japan, Jordan, Kazakhstan, Kenya, Korea Rep, Kuwait, Kyrgyzstan, Lebanon, Liberia, Lithuania, Malawi, Malaysia, Mauritania, Mauritius, Mexico, Moldova, Mongolia, Morocco, Mozambique, Myanmar, Nepal, Netherlands, New Zealand, Nicaragua, Nigeria, Norway, Panama, Paraguay, Peru, Philippines, Poland, Portugal, Qatar, Romania, Rwanda, Saudi Arabia, Senegal, Singapore, Slovakia, South Africa, Spain, Sri Lanka, St Vincent-Grenadines, Sudan, Sweden, Switzerland, Tanzania UR, Thailand, Togo, Trinidad-Tobago, Türkiye, Uganda, UK, Ukraine, Uruguay, USA, Uzbekistan, Venezuela, Vietnam, Zambia, Zimbabwe.
Consultative Status Consultative status granted from: *WHO (#20950)* (Official); *ECOSOC (#05331)* (Special). **IGO Relations** *Pan American Health Organization (PAHO, #18108)*. **NGO Relations** Member of: *Geneva Global Health Hub (G2H2, #10122)*. [2022.06.14/XC0128/**C**]

♦ International Association of Hospital Central Service Material Management / see International Association of Healthcare Central Service Material Management
♦ International Association of Hospitality Financial Management Education (unconfirmed)
♦ International Association of Hotel Executives (internationally oriented national body)
♦ International Association of Hotel General Managers (unconfirmed)
♦ International Association of Hotel Management Schools (inactive)

♦ International Association of Hotel School Directors 11942

Association internationale des directeurs d'écoles hôtelières (EUHOFA International)

Sec Koningin Marialaan 9, 2595 GA The Hague, Netherlands. T. +31886665513. Fax +31703045233.
URL: http://www.euhofa.org/

History Aug 1955, Germany FR. Aug 1955, Bad Wiessee (Germany FR), as *European Association of Hotel School Directors – Association européenne des directeurs d'écoles hôtelières (EUHOFA) – Asociación Europea de Directores de Escuelas Hoteleras*; officially registered as a European association, 1974; became international, new statutes and current title adopted, 14 Sep 1980, Antwerp (Belgium). Registered under the Swiss Civil Code. **Aims** Contribute directly to continuing improvement and advancement of hotel and catering training and education and to development of members' activities; promote and improve professional training and education; develop good relations among members; facilitate exchange of ideas and experience; obtain information concerning members' professional activities; create a register of the profession. **Structure** General Assembly of full members (annual, in conjunction with Congress). Committee comprises President, Vice-President, Secretary-General, President of Congress and at least 7 members, meets at least once between congresses. President of Congress. **Languages** English, French, German. **Finance** Sources: gifts, legacies; meeting proceeds. Other sources: Members' entrance fees and annual subscriptions. **Events** *Annual Congress* Santiago de Compostela (Spain) 2022, *Annual Congress* Copenhagen (Denmark) 2020, *Annual Congress* Kathmandu (Nepal) 2019, *Annual Congress* Lausanne (Switzerland) 2018, *Annual Congress* Lucca (Italy) 2017. **Publications** *EUHOFA Journal* (2 a year).
Members Active; Directors of European hotel schools. Members in 33 countries and territories:
Argentina, Australia, Austria, Bahamas, Bahrain, Belgium, Canada, Denmark, Egypt, Finland, France, Germany, Iceland, Ireland, Israel, Italy, Japan, Jordan, Kenya, Luxembourg, Malaysia, Mexico, Netherlands, Norway, Poland, Portugal, Slovenia, South Africa, Spain, Switzerland, Thailand, UK, USA.
NGO Relations Member of: *World Association for Hospitality and Tourism Education and Training (WAHTT, #21144)*. [2020/XD0567/**C**]

♦ International Association for Housing Science (IAHS) 11943

Association internationale pour la science du logement – Asociación Internacional para la Ciencia de la Vivienda – Internationale Vereinigung für Wohnungsbauwissenschaften

Pres-Founder PO Box 340254, Coral Gables FL 33134, USA. T. +13054469462. Fax +13054610921.
Sec College of Engineering, Univ of Miami, 1251 Memorial Drive, McArthur Engineering Bldg, Coral Gables FL 33146, USA.
URL: http://www.housingscience.org/

History 24 Apr 1972, St Louis, MO (USA). Founded during 2nd International Symposium on Lower-Cost Housing Problems. Goals, constitution and bylaws adopted 10 Sep 1972. Former names and other names: *International Institute for Housing and Building* – alias. Registration: USA, Missouri. **Aims** Generate interest in improving housing technology and production; generate new knowledge through research and assemble all other available information on housing science; develop means to disseminate this to all concerned; emphasize the interdisciplinary nature of housing problems and the use of an integrated systems approach in the decision process at every phase of planning and construction; incorporate scientific knowledge and methods into the housing industry; create opportunities for all concerned in housing problems to obtain innovative ideas and methods; assemble, compile, publish and disseminate information; cooperate with other organizations in sponsoring and financing research; seek and support innovation with potential to solve the world shortage of decent housing; establish means of avoiding duplication of research. **Structure** General Business Meeting (every 2 years). Board of 6 members, including President. Advisory Board, consisting of 1 member from each country. Executive Secretary; Treasurer. Technical Committees (13). Committees (6): Membership; Publications; Meetings Organization; Data Collection; Public Relations; Research Coordination. **Languages** English, French, German, Spanish. **Staff** 2.50 FTE, paid. **Finance** Sources: members' dues. **Activities** Sponsors and organizes international conferences and workshops. Technical Committees (13): Systems Approach; Construction Methods; Environment Coordination; Materials; Industrialized Production; Human Factors; Codes and Specifications; Economics; Mobile Homes; Basic Utilities; Foundations; Analysis

and Design; Education. **Events** *World Congress* Cochabamba (Bolivia) 2020, *World Congress* Naples (Italy) 2018, *World Congress* Albufeira (Portugal) 2016, *World Congress* Funchal (Portugal) 2014, *World Congress* Milan (Italy) 2013. **Publications** *IAHS Newsletter* (4 a year); *International Journal for Housing Science and its Applications* (4 a year). *Industrial Housing Systems*; *New Trends in Lower-Cost Housing Problems*. Meeting proceedings.
Members An interdisciplinary association open to all interested in various aspects of housing as human habitat. Individual and corporate (sustaining) members in 46 countries and territories:
Argentina, Australia, Austria, Belgium, Brazil, Cameroon, Canada, China, Colombia, Dominican Rep, Egypt, Finland, France, Germany, India, Jamaica, Japan, Kenya, Kuwait, Libya, Malaysia, Mexico, Montenegro, Netherlands, New Zealand, Nigeria, Panama, Peru, Poland, Saudi Arabia, Senegal, Serbia, Singapore, Slovenia, South Africa, Sudan, Switzerland, Taiwan, Tanzania UR, Thailand, Trinidad-Tobago, Türkiye, UK, United Arab Emirates, USA, Venezuela.
Consultative Status Consultative status granted from: *ECOSOC (#05331)* (Ros A). **IGO Relations** Accredited by: *United Nations Office at Vienna (UNOV, #20604)*. Associated with Department of Global Communications of the United Nations. **NGO Relations** Member of: *Conference of Non-Governmental Organizations in Consultative Relationship with the United Nations (CONGO, #04635)*; *International Centre for Earth Construction (#12485)*. [2020/XC4386/**C**]

♦ International Association of Human-Animal Interaction Organizations (IAHAIO) 11944

Main Office 220 W Mercer St, Ste W-430, Seattle WA 98119-3968, USA.
URL: http://www.iahaio.org/

History Apr 1990, Toronto, ON (Canada). Founded at meeting of human-animal bond organizations from 6 countries, an *International Society for the Study of the Human-Companion Animal Bond (ISSHCAB)* having been set up in 1989. Registration: Start date: 1992, USA, Washington State. **Aims** Provide international leadership in advancing the field of human animal interaction through research, education and collaboration among members, policy makers, clinical practitioners, other human animal interaction organizations and the general public. **Structure** General Assembly of national members. Board of Directors, consisting of President, Secretary, Treasurer and 3 Vice-Presidents, each heading a Sub-committee: Conferences; Policy and Finance; Membership. **Languages** English. **Staff** Voluntary. **Finance** Members' dues. Grants. **Activities** Projects include: Animal Assisted Activities/Therapy, including programmes to train volunteers to provide animal-assisted therapy and activities; travelling exhibition on responsible pet ownership; human-animal interaction in veterinary practice; study of human-wildlife interactions; assistance to persons with disabilities, including service animals for individuals with disabilities and consequent changes in quality of life. Organizes: international conference (every 3 years); study programmes; training courses; animal education programmes. Confers 'International Distinguished Scholar' award (every 3 years). Urges international bodies and national governments to consider and activate: the 5 resolutions of the *'IAHAIO Geneva Declaration'*, adopted 5 Sep 1995, Geneva (Switzerland); other relevant treaties – Prague Declaration, adopted 1998, Rio Declaration, adopted 2001, Tokyo Declaration, adopted 2007. **Events** *Anniversary Conference* Strömsholm (Sweden) 2022, *Triennial Congress* Brewster, NY (USA) 2019, *Symposium* Davis, CA (USA) 2017, *Annual Meeting and Symposium* Paris (France) 2016, *Triennial Congress* Paris (France) 2016.
Members Full national organizations (46) in 18 countries:
Australia, Austria, Belgium, China, France, Germany, Italy, Japan, Korea Rep, Luxembourg, Netherlands, Norway, Poland, Spain, Sweden, Switzerland, UK, USA.
Included in the above, 3 organizations listed in this Yearbook:
Federation of Horses in Education and Therapy International (HETI, #09593); *Society for Companion Animal Studies (SCAS)*; *World Animal Protection (#21092)*.
Affiliate related profit and non-profit national and international organizations (11) in 5 countries and territories:
Israel, Japan, Switzerland, Taiwan, USA.
Included in the above, 1 organization listed in this Yearbook:
International Society for Anthrozoology (ISAZ, #14923). [2021/XD1399/y/**D**]

♦ International Association of Human Auxology (no recent information)

♦ International Association of Human Biologists (IAHB) 11945

Association internationale des anthropobiologistes

Pres Northwestern Univ, Dept of Anthropology, 1810 Hinman Ave, Evanston IL 60208-1310, USA.
History 21 Jul 1967, following preliminary meeting, Jun 1967, Wartenstein (Austria), sponsored by *Wenner-Gren Foundations*. **Aims** Advance research and education and facilitate communication on all aspects of human biology on an international basis. **Structure** General Meeting (2 a year). Council of 18 members. Officers: President; Past President; Secretary-General; Past Secretary-General; Membership Secretary. **Languages** English. **Staff** 1.00 FTE, voluntary. **Finance** Sources: members' dues. Annual budget: 3,000 USD. **Activities** Provides expert advice in planning and analysis of research, particularly field studies; distributes information on items of current interest. **Events** *Annual General Meeting* Calgary, AB (Canada) 2014, *General Meeting* Rome (Italy) 2003, *General Meeting* Rome (Italy) 2003, *General Meeting* USA 2002, *International conference on human biodiversity and human origin / General Meeting* Kansas City, MO (USA) 2001. **Publications** *IAHB Newsletter* (annual). Occasional papers.
Members Affiliated national societies (marked ") and individuals in 44 countries and territories:
Algeria, Argentina (*), Australia, Austria, Belgium (*), Bosnia-Herzegovina, Brazil (*), Bulgaria (*), Canada, Chile, China, Croatia (*), Cuba, Czechia, Ecuador, Egypt, France (*), Germany, Greece (*), Hong Kong, Hungary, India (*), Israel, Italy (*), Japan, Kenya, Lithuania (*), Mexico (*), Netherlands (*), New Zealand, Norway, Poland (*), Russia, Slovenia, South Africa, Spain (*), Sweden, Switzerland, Taiwan, Türkiye, UK (*), Ukraine, USA (*), Venezuela.
Included in the above, 4 organizations listed in this Yearbook:
Asociación Latinoamericana de Antropologia Biológica (ALAB, #02180); *European Anthropological Association (EAA, #05904)*; *International Association of Human Auxology (no recent information)*; *Society for the Study of Human Biology*.
NGO Relations Scientific member of: *International Union of Biological Sciences (IUBS, #15760)*. [2013/XB1296/y/**C**]

♦ International Association for Humane Habitat (internationally oriented national body)
♦ International Association of Humanist Educators, Counsellors and Leaders (inactive)
♦ International Association for Humanitarian Medicine Brock Chisholm / see International Association for Humanitarian Medicine Chisholm-Gunn (#11946)

♦ International Association for Humanitarian Medicine Chisholm-Gunn (IAHM) 11946

Admin Office Div Chirurgia Plastica MBC, Ospedale Civico, 90127 Palermo PA, Italy. T. +39916663631. Fax +3991596404. E-mail: contact@iahm.org.
Contact Place du Village 3, 1279 Bogis-Bossey VD, Switzerland. T. +41227762161.
URL: http://www.iahm.org/

History 1984. Founded at *WHO (#20950)* as *Brock Chisholm Trust*.Named after Dr Brock Chisholm, the first WHO Director-General. Registration: Start date: Apr 1998, Italy, Palermo. **Aims** Promote *healthcare* on the principles of humanitarian medicine; cooperate with developing countries in improving their health services. **Structure** Board. **Languages** English, French, Italian. **Staff** 1.00 FTE, paid; 2.00 FTE, voluntary. **Finance** Sources: donations; members' dues; sale of publications. **Activities** Healthcare; humanitarian/emergency aid. **Events** *Conference* Turin (Italy) 2014, *Conference* Palermo (Italy) 2012, *Conference* Tokyo (Japan) 2008, *Conference* Tokyo (Japan) 2007, *Conference* Palermo (Italy) 2005. **Publications** *Journal of Humanitarian Medicine*. *Concepts and Practice of Humanitarian Medicine* in Chinese, English; *Dictionary of Disaster Medicine and Humanitarian Relief*, *Understanding the Global Dimensions of Health*.
Members Full in 52 countries and territories:
Albania, Australia, Austria, Belgium, Bulgaria, Canada, China, Congo DR, Cuba, Cyprus, Czechia, Denmark, Egypt, Finland, France, Germany, Greece, Holy See, Iceland, India, Ireland, Israel, Italy, Japan, Jordan, Lebanon, Libya, Malta, Mexico, Netherlands, New Zealand, Nigeria, Norway, Oman, Palestine, Poland, Portugal, Russia, San Marino, Saudi Arabia, Slovakia, Slovenia, South Africa, Spain, Sweden, Switzerland, Syrian AR, Tunisia, Türkiye, UK, United Arab Emirates, USA.
Consultative Status Consultative status granted from: *ECOSOC (#05331)* (Special). **NGO Relations** Member of (2): *Academic Council on the United Nations System (ACUNS, #00020)*; *International Federation of Surgical Colleges (IFSC, #13560)*. [2023/XD7219/**D**]

♦ International Association on Human Reproduction / see International Academy of Human Reproduction (#11551)

♦ International Association of Human Rights Teachers and Researchers (inactive)
♦ International Association of Human Trafficking Investigators (internationally oriented national body)

♦ International Association for Human Values (IAHV) 11947

Exec Dir Rue des Bains 31, 1205 Geneva, Switzerland. T. +41227382888. E-mail: geneva@iahv.org.
URL: http://www.iahv.org/

History 1997, Geneva (Switzerland). Founder: His Holiness Sri Sri Ravi Shankar. **Aims** Promote and support development of universal human values worldwide. **Structure** International Board, comprising President, Executive Director, Treasurer and 3 members. Regional offices (11): India; USA; Canada; South Africa; Netherlands; UK; Italy; France; Denmark; United Arab Emirates; Morocco. **Languages** English. **Activities** Claims to serve, in collaboration with partners, in programmes and projects in over 140 countries, based on: raising public awareness of the key role of human values in achieving a global society of peace, justice and well-being for all; promoting and supporting the re-vitalization of human values in the society, including in communities, institutions, corporations, organizations and families; inspiring people to live human values in daily life through voluntary, selfless service to society, at all levels and in all paths of life; serving and integrating other institutions and organizations on all levels of society in implementation of programmes and projects to promote and support development of human values. *'5H Programme'* (Health, Hygiene, Homes, Harmony in Diversity and Human Values) – aims towards uplifting poor and disadvantaged communities in developing countries from poverty and empowering them to become socially and economically self-reliant. **Events** *Conference on Ethics in Business* Brussels (Belgium) 2012, *Conference on ethics in business* Brussels (Belgium) 2010, *Conference on ethics in business* Brussels (Belgium) 2009. **Members** Membership countries not specified. **Consultative Status** Consultative status granted from: *ECOSOC (#05331)* (Special). **NGO Relations** Associate member of: *NGO Committee on Financing for Development, New York (#17108)*. Founder also founder of: *World Forum for Ethics in Business (WFEB, #21516)*. [2017/XD9480/s/**F**]

♦ International Association of Humorists (inactive)

♦ International Association for Hungarian Studies (IAHS) 11948

Association internationale des études hongroises – Internationale Gesellschaft für Ungarische Philologie – Nemzetközi Magyarsagtudomanyi Tàrsasàg – Mezdunarodnoe Obscestvo po Hungarologii

Secretariat Tóth Kalman u 4, B 8 41, Budapest 1097, Hungary. T. +3613214407. Fax +3613214407. E-mail: nmtt@iif.hu.
URL: http://www.hungarologia.net/

History 25 Aug 1977. Statutes: approved at 1st General Assembly, 14 Aug 1981, Budapest (Hungary); modified by 3rd General Assembly, 16 Aug 1991, Szeged (Hungary); 5th Assembly, 14 Aug 2001, Jyväskylä (Finland). **Aims** Support scholarly and public interest/activity in the fields of Hungarian *language*, literature, ethnography and cultural history; encourage cooperation and assist scholars, teachers and other specialists working in these fields. **Structure** General Assembly (every 5 years, at Congress). Committee (meeting annually) includes President, 6 Vice-Presidents, General-Secretary, Deputy Secretary-General. **Languages** English, French, German, Hungarian, Italian. **Staff** 0.50 FTE, paid. **Finance** Members' dues: euro 30. Other sources: subsidy from Hungarian Academy of Sciences; support of international organizations. **Activities** Organizes: lectures; discussions; conferences; congresses. Maintains contacts with and involves Hungarian higher education institutions and research centres. Award: John Lotz Commemorative Medal; Klaniczay Prize. **Events** *Quinquennial Congress* Cluj-Napoca (Romania) 2011, *Quinquennial Congress* Debrecen (Hungary) 2006, *Quinquennial congress* Jyväskylä (Finland) 2001, *Quinquennial Congress* Rome (Italy) 1996, *Quinquennial congress* Rome (Italy) 1996. **Publications** *Hungarian Studies* (2 a year) – journal; *Lymbus: Sources of the Hungarian Intellectual History* (annual). *Essential Hungarian Studies Library* (1986) – bibliography. Congress proceedings.
Members Ordinary; Honorary; Supporting. As of 10 Aug 2001, 870 individuals and institutions in 36 countries:
Austria, Belgium, Bulgaria, Canada, China, Croatia, Czechia, Denmark, Estonia, Finland, France, Georgia, Germany, Greece, Hungary, Italy, Japan, Kazakhstan, Korea Rep, Latvia, Lithuania, Netherlands, Norway, Poland, Romania, Russia, Serbia, Slovakia, Slovenia, Sweden, Switzerland, Türkiye, UK, Ukraine, USA, Vietnam. [2020/XD3864/v/**D**]

♦ International Association of Hydatid Disease / see International Association of Hydatidology (#11949)

♦ International Association of Hydatidology (IAH) 11949

Association internationale d'hydatidologie – Asociación Internacional de Hidatidologia (AIH)

Contact 137 Liyushan South Rd, First Affiliated Hosp of Xinjiang Univ, Urumqi, Xinjiang, China. T. +8699144330047. E-mail: turgunbay@163.com.
Pres Estrada da Luz 59 – 8 dto, 1600-152 Lisbon, Portugal. T. +351919851695.
URL: http://www.echinoworld.org/

History 21 Sep 1911, Colonia del Sacramento (Uruguay). Founded 21 Sep 1941, Colonia (Uruguay). Also referred to in English as: *International Association of Hydatid Disease*; *International Hydatidological Association*; *International Hydatidology Association*. **Aims** Contribute to the control and eventual eradication of hydatid disease; carry out and coordinate research work and efforts to combat the *zoonosis hidatica* in all countries. **Structure** General Assembly (in conjunction with Congress); Directive Council; Executive Board; Audit Board. **Languages** English, French, Portuguese, Spanish. **Staff** Voluntary. **Finance** Sources: grants; members' dues. Congress expenses met by host country. **Activities** Advocacy/lobbying/activism; events/meetings; financial and/or material support; research/documentation. **Events** *Congress* Algiers (Algeria) 2017, *Cystic and alveolar echinococcosis old diseases – new challenges* Bucharest (Romania) 2015, *Congress* Khartoum (Sudan) 2013, *Congress* Urumqi (China) 2011, *Congress* Colonia del Sacramento (Uruguay) 2009. **Publications** *Archivos Internacionales de la Hidatidosis* (every 2 years).
Members Individuals (over 600) in 36 countries:
Algeria, Argentina, Australia, Belgium, Bolivia, Brazil, Bulgaria, Canada, Chile, China, Cyprus, France, Germany, Greece, India, Iran Islamic Rep, Iraq, Italy, Kenya, Lebanon, Morocco, New Zealand, Peru, Poland, Portugal, Romania, Saudi Arabia, Serbia, Spain, Sudan, Switzerland, Tunisia, Türkiye, UK, Uruguay, USA.
Consultative Status Consultative status granted from: *ECOSOC (#05331)* (Ros A). [2014.10.02/XC2548/v/**C**]

♦ International Association of Hydraulic Engineering and Research / see International Association for Hydro-Environment Engineering and Research (#11950)
♦ International Association for Hydraulic Research / see International Association for Hydro-Environment Engineering and Research (#11950)
♦ International Association for Hydraulic Structures Research / see International Association for Hydro-Environment Engineering and Research (#11950)

♦ International Association for Hydro-Environment Engineering and Research (IAHR) 11950

Association internationale d'ingénierie et de recherches hydrauliques et environmentales (AIRH)

Contact Paseo Bajo Virgen Del Puerto 3, 28005 Madrid, Spain. T. +34913357908. Fax +34913357935.
Contact A-1 Fuxing Road, Haidian District, 100038 Beijing, China. T. +861068781128. Fax +861068781890.
URL: http://www.iahr.org/

History 3 Sep 1935, Delft (Netherlands). Former names and other names: *International Association for Hydraulic Structures Research* – former; *Association internationale de recherches pour travaux hydrauliques* – former; *International Association for Hydraulic Research* – former; *Association internationale de recherches hydrauliques* – former; *Asociación Internacional de Investigaciones Hidraulicas (AIIH)* – former; *International Association of Hydraulic Engineering and Research* – former; *Association internationale d'ingénierie et de recherches hydrauliques* – former. **Aims** Stimulate and promote *water* and *environmental* engineering research and its application, and by so doing strive to contribute to sustainable development, the optimisation of the world's water resources management and industrial flow processes. **Structure** General Members Assembly (annual); Council; Executive Committee; Technical Divisions (3); Committees, including: *Joint Committee of IAHR and IAW on Urban Drainage (JCUD, #16124)*; Regional Divisions (4). **Languages** English, French. **Staff** 10.00 FTE, paid. **Finance** Sources: members' dues. **Activities** Events/meetings; projects/programmes; publishing activities; research/documentation; training/education. **Events** *World Congress* Vienna (Austria) 2023, *World Congress* Granada (Spain) 2022, *International Symposium on Ice* Montréal, QC (Canada) 2022, *ICUD : Triennial International Conference on Urban Drainage* Melbourne, VIC (Australia) 2021, *International Symposium on Environmental Hydraulics* Seoul (Korea Rep) 2021. **Publications** *NewsFlash* (12

a year); *Journal of Hydraulic Research* (6 a year); *Hydrolink* (4 a year); *Journal of Hydro-Environment Research* (4 a year); *Journal of River Basin Management* (4 a year); *Journal of Ecohydraulics* (2 a year); *Ribagua* (2 a year). *IAHR Monograph Series.* Membership Directory; design manuals; monographs; congress proceedings. **Members** Individuals (5,000); Institutes (about 130). Members in 94 countries and territories:
Algeria, Argentina, Armenia, Australia, Austria, Bahrain, Bangladesh, Belarus, Belgium, Bolivia, Brazil, Bulgaria, Canada, Chile, China, Colombia, Congo DR, Costa Rica, Croatia, Cuba, Czechia, Denmark, Ecuador, Egypt, Estonia, Ethiopia, Finland, France, Georgia, Germany, Ghana, Greece, Guinea, Hong Kong, Hungary, Iceland, India, Indonesia, Iran Islamic Rep, Ireland, Israel, Italy, Japan, Jordan, Kenya, Korea Rep, Kuwait, Lebanon, Libya, Lithuania, Luxembourg, Malaysia, Mauritius, Mexico, Morocco, Mozambique, Namibia, Netherlands, New Zealand, Nigeria, North Macedonia, Norway, Oman, Pakistan, Paraguay, Peru, Poland, Portugal, Puerto Rico, Romania, Russia, Saudi Arabia, Serbia, Singapore, Slovakia, Slovenia, South Africa, Spain, Sri Lanka, Sudan, Sweden, Switzerland, Tanzania UR, Thailand, Türkiye, Uganda, UK, Ukraine, Uruguay, USA, Venezuela, Vietnam, Zambia, Zimbabwe.
Consultative Status Consultative status granted from: *ECOSOC (#05331)* (Ros C); *UNIDO (#20336).* **NGO Relations** Member of (1): *International Science Council (ISC, #14796).* Cooperates with (13): *European Research Community on Flow, Turbulence and Combustion (ERCOFTAC, #08361); Global Water Partnership (GWP, #10653); International Association of Hydrogeologists (IAH, #11953); International Association of Hydrological Sciences (IAHS, #11954); International Commission on Irrigation and Drainage (ICID, #12694); International Commission on Large Dams (ICOLD, #12696); International Research and Training Centre on Erosion and Sedimentation (IRTCES, #14745); International Society of Limnology (#15232); International Union of Pure and Applied Chemistry (IUPAC, #15809); International Water Association (IWA, #15865); International Water-Related Associations' Liaison Committee (IWALC, #15869); International Water Resources Association (IWRA, #15871); PIANC (#18371).* In liaison with technical committees of: *International Organization for Standardization (ISO, #14473).* [2022.01.20/XB1193/**B**]

♦ International Association for Hydrogen Energy (IAHE) 11951

Association internationale pour l'énergie hydrogène – Asociación Internacional para la Energia del Hidrógeno

Main Office 5794 SW 40 St, Ste 303, Miami FL 33155, USA. E-mail: info@iahe.org.
URL: http://www.iahe.org/

History Mar 1974, Miami, FL (USA). Founded at *'The Hydrogen Economy Miami Energy (THEME)'* Conference. **Aims** On a worldwide scale, coordinate efforts to develop a hydrogen-based energy system; inform and educate the public on all areas relating to hydrogen energy and its ultimate benefits, specifically the role of hydrogen energy in planning an inexhaustible and clean energy system. **Structure** Board of Directors. **Languages** English. **Staff** 15.00 FTE, paid. **Finance** Sources: members' dues. **Activities** Awards/prizes/competitions; events/meetings; knowledge management/information dissemination; training/education. **Events** *World Hydrogen Technologies Convention (WHTC)* Foshan (China) 2023, *World Hydrogen Energy Conference (WHEC)* Istanbul (Türkiye) 2022, *World Hydrogen Technologies Convention (WHTC)* Montréal, QC (Canada) 2021, *Biennial World Conference* Istanbul (Turkey) 2020, *World Hydrogen Technologies Convention (WHTC)* Tokyo (Japan) 2019. **Publications** *International Journal of Hydrogen Energy (IJHE)* (60 a year).
Members Individuals and institutions in 93 countries and territories:
Afghanistan, Algeria, Argentina, Armenia, Australia, Austria, Azerbaijan, Bahamas, Belgium, Bermuda, Bolivia, Bosnia-Herzegovina, Brazil, Canada, Chile, China, Colombia, Congo DR, Costa Rica, Croatia, Czechia, Denmark, Dominican Rep, Ecuador, Egypt, Estonia, Finland, France, Georgia, Germany, Greece, Guatemala, Hong Kong, Hungary, Iceland, India, Indonesia, Iran Islamic Rep, Ireland, Israel, Italy, Jamaica, Japan, Jordan, Kazakhstan, Korea Rep, Kuwait, Kyrgyzstan, Malaysia, Mexico, Myanmar, Netherlands, New Zealand, Nicaragua, Nigeria, Norway, Pakistan, Panama, Philippines, Poland, Portugal, Puerto Rico, Qatar, Romania, Russia, Rwanda, Saudi Arabia, Serbia, Sierra Leone, Singapore, Slovakia, Slovenia, South Africa, Spain, Sweden, Switzerland, Syrian AR, Taiwan, Tajikistan, Thailand, Trinidad-Tobago, Türkiye, Turkmenistan, UK, Ukraine, United Arab Emirates, Uruguay, USA, Uzbekistan, Venezuela, Yemen, Zambia, Zimbabwe.
Consultative Status Consultative status granted from: *ECOSOC (#05331)* (Ros A). **IGO Relations** Accredited by (1): *United Nations Office at Vienna (UNOV, #20604).* **NGO Relations** Supports (1): *International Conference on Clean Energy (ICCE).* [2021/XB4531/**B**]

♦ International Association for Hydrogen Safety (HySafe) 11952

Sec Rue du Trône 98, 1050 Brussels, Belgium.
URL: http://www.hysafe.info/

History 26 Feb 2009, Brussels (Belgium). Founded following the activities of the European Network of Excellence 'HySafe – Safety of Hydrogen as an Energy Carrier'. **Aims** Facilitate international coordination, development and dissemination of hydrogen safety knowledge by being the focal point for hydrogen safety research, education and training. **Structure** General Assembly; Coordination Committee. **Languages** English. **Staff** None. **Finance** Members' dues. **Activities** Events/meetings; research and development; knowledge management/information dissemination; standards/guidelines; publishing activities. **Events** *International Conference on Hydrogen Safety (ICHS)* Québec, QC (Canada) 2023, *International Conference on Hydrogen Safety* Edinburgh (UK) 2021, *International Conference on Hydrogen Safety* Adelaide, SA (Australia) 2019, *International Conference on Hydrogen Safety (ICHS)* Hamburg (Germany) 2017, *International Conference on Hydrogen Safety* Yokohama (Japan) 2015. **Publications** *International Journal of Hydrogen Energy. Hydrogen Safety Handbook.*
Members Full; Associate; Honorary. Founding members in 12 countries:
Canada, France, Germany, Greece, Italy, Japan, Norway, Poland, Spain, Sweden, UK, USA. [2020/XJ8197/**E**]

♦ International Association of Hydrogeologists (IAH) 11953

Association internationale des hydrogéologues (AIH)

Exec Manager PO Box 4130, Goring, Reading, RG8 6BJ, UK. E-mail: info@iah.org.
URL: http://www.iah.org/

History 1956, Mexico City (Mexico). Founded during 21st *International Geological Congress (IGC)*, a Provisional Organizing Committee having been formed during 20th Congress, 1952, Algiers (Algeria). Former names and other names: *International Association of Hydrology* – former. **Aims** Further understanding, wise use and protection of *groundwater resources* throughout the world. **Structure** General Assembly (annual); Council; Commissions (8); Networks (7). **Languages** English, French. **Staff** 2.00 FTE, paid. **Finance** Sources: grants; members' dues; sale of publications; sponsorship. **Activities** Awards/prizes/competitions; events/meetings; knowledge management/information dissemination; research/documentation; training/education. **Events** *IAH Congress* Cape Town (South Africa) 2023, *WMESS : World Multidisciplinary Earth Sciences Symposium* Prague (Czechia) 2022, *IAH Congress* Wuhan (China) 2022, *IAH Congress* Brussels (Belgium) 2021, *Congress* Sao Paulo (Brazil) 2021. **Publications** *IAH News and Information* (3 a year); *Hydrogeology Journal* (8 a year); *IAH E-news* (3-5 a year). *International Contributions to Hydrogeology.* Hydrogeological reports; papers; congress reports.
Members National Committees in 49 countries:
Argentina, Australia, Belgium, Brazil, Canada, Chile, China, Colombia, Croatia, Czechia, Denmark, Egypt, France, Georgia, Germany, Greece, Hungary, India, Iraq, Ireland, Italy, Japan, Kazakhstan, Korea Rep, Lebanon, Mexico, Mongolia, Morocco, Netherlands, New Zealand, Nigeria, Norway, Oman, Poland, Portugal, Romania, Russia, Serbia, Slovakia, Slovenia, South Africa, Spain, Sweden, Switzerland, Thailand, Tunisia, Türkiye, UK, USA.
Individual professional scientists and engineers (over 4,000) in 128 countries and territories:
Albania, Algeria, Andorra, Antigua-Barbuda, Argentina, Australia, Austria, Bahamas, Bahrain, Bangladesh, Belgium, Benin, Bolivia, Bosnia-Herzegovina, Botswana, Brazil, Bulgaria, Burkina Faso, Cambodia, Cameroon, Canada, Cape Verde, Chile, China, Colombia, Costa Rica, Côte d'Ivoire, Croatia, Cuba, Cyprus, Czechia, Denmark, Djibouti, Dominican Rep, Ecuador, Egypt, Eritrea, Estonia, Ethiopia, Fiji, Finland, France, Georgia, Germany, Ghana, Greece, Guinea, Haiti, Hong Kong, Hungary, Iceland, India, Indonesia, Iran Islamic Rep, Ireland, Israel, Italy, Jamaica, Japan, Jordan, Kazakhstan, Kenya, Kiribati, Korea Rep, Kuwait, Latvia, Lebanon, Lesotho, Libya, Lithuania, Malawi, Malta, Mauritania, Mauritius, Mexico, Moldova, Mongolia, Morocco, Mozambique, Myanmar, Namibia, Nepal, Netherlands, New Zealand, Nicaragua, Nigeria, Norway, Oman, Pakistan, Palestine, Papua New Guinea, Peru, Philippines, Poland, Portugal, Romania, Russia, Samoa, Saudi Arabia, Senegal, Serbia, Sierra Leone, Singapore, Slovakia, Slovenia, Solomon Is, South Africa, Spain, Sri Lanka, Sweden, Switzerland, Taiwan, Tanzania UR, Trinidad-Tobago, Tunisia, Türkiye, Uganda, UK, Ukraine, United Arab Emirates, Uruguay, USA, Uzbekistan, Vanuatu, Vietnam, Yemen, Zambia, Zimbabwe.
Consultative Status Consultative status granted from: *ECOSOC (#05331)* (Ros A); *UNESCO (#20322)* (Consultative Status). **IGO Relations** Partner of (1): *UN-Water (#20723).* Participates in: *International Hydrological Programme (IHP, #13826).* **NGO Relations** Memorandum of Understanding with (1): *Latin American Association for Groundwater Hydrology Development (#16242).* Member of (3): *Global Water Partnership (GWP, #10653); International Union of Geological Sciences (IUGS, #15777)* (Affiliated member); *World Water Council (WWC, #21908).* Partner of (1): *Internationally Shared Aquifer Resources Management (ISARM, #14071).* Cooperates with (2): *International Association of Hydrological Sciences (IAHS, #11954); International Water Association (IWA, #15865).* [2022/XC1297/**B**]

♦ International Association of Hydrological Sciences (IAHS) 11954

Association internationale des sciences hydrologiques (AISH)

SG UMR SAS, Agrocampus Ouest, CS 84215, 35042 Rennes CEDEX, France. T. +33223485558.
Exec Sec c/o UKCEH Maclean Bldg, Benson Lane, Crowmarsh Gifford, Wallingford, OX10 8BB, UK.
URL: http://iahs.info/

History 1922, Madrid (Spain). Founded incorporating *International Commission of Glaciers (inactive).* A constituent association of *International Union of Geodesy and Geophysics (IUGG, #15776)*, which is one of the 20 scientific Unions grouped within *International Council for Science (ICSU, inactive).* Former names and other names: *International Association of Scientific Hydrology* – former (1922 to 1971); *Association internationale de l'hydrologie scientifique* – former (1922 to 1971). **Aims** Be the foremost international learned society dealing with the pressing problems of water resources, floods, droughts, water pollution, erosion, etc, together with the science and technology to address them. **Structure** General Assembly (every 4 years, at the same time as IUGG); Bureau (meets annually); Commissions (10); Working Groups. **Languages** English, French. **Staff** 3.50 FTE, paid. **Finance** Government grants through IUGG; grants from different specialized UN agencies; sale of publications. **Activities** Awards/prizes/competitions; research/documentation. **Events** *Scientific Assembly* Montpellier (France) 2022, *Scientific Assembly* Port Elizabeth (South Africa) 2017, *International Water Resources Management Conference* Bochum (Germany) 2016, *NOVATECH : International Conference on Sustainable Techniques and Strategies in Urban Water Management* Lyon (France) 2016, *George Kovacs Colloquium* Paris (France) 2016. **Publications** *IAHSNewsletter* (3 a year); *Hydrological Sciences Journal (HSJ)* (8 a year). *Benchmark Papers in Hydrology Series. Blue Books; Red Books.* Proceedings and reports series.
Members National Committees (unofficial IAHS National Committees as not member countries of IUGG) in 92 countries and territories:
Albania (*), Algeria, Argentina, Armenia, Australia, Austria, Bangladesh (*), Belgium, Benin (*), Bosnia-Herzegovina (*), Brazil, Bulgaria, Burkina Faso (*), Cameroon (*), Canada, Chile, China, Colombia, Croatia, Czechia, Denmark, Egypt, Estonia, Ethiopia (*), Finland, France, Germany, Ghana (*), Greece, Hungary, Iceland, India, Indonesia, Iran Islamic Rep, Ireland, Israel, Italy, Jamaica (*), Japan, Jordan, Kenya (*), Korea DPR (*), Korea Rep, Lebanon, Luxembourg, Madagascar (*), Malaysia (*), Mauritius (*), Mexico, Monaco, Mongolia (*), Montenegro, Morocco, Mozambique, Myanmar, Nepal (*), Netherlands, New Zealand, Nigeria, North Macedonia (*), Norway, Pakistan, Palestine (*), Peru, Philippines, Poland, Portugal, Romania, Russia, Samoa (*), Senegal (*), Serbia, Seychelles (*), Slovakia, Slovenia, South Africa, Spain, Sudan (*), Sweden, Switzerland, Syrian AR (*), Taiwan, Tanzania UR (*), Thailand, Trinidad-Tobago (*), Türkiye, UK, Uruguay, USA, Venezuela, Vietnam, Zimbabwe (*).
About 5,500 Individual members worldwide.
IGO Relations Cooperates with: *International Atomic Energy Agency (IAEA, #12294); International Hydrological Programme (IHP, #13826); UNESCO (#20322); UN-Water (#20723); WMO Hydrology and Water Resources Programme (HWRP, #20977); World Meteorological Organization (WMO, #21649); World Water Assessment Programme (WWAP, #21907).* **NGO Relations** Member of: *ISC World Data System (ISC-WDS, #16024); International Water-Related Associations' Liaison Committee (IWALC, #15869).* Cooperates with: *International Association for Hydro-Environment Engineering and Research (IAHR, #11950); International Association of Hydrogeologists (IAH, #11953); International Organization for Standardization (ISO, #14473); World Climate Research Programme (WCRP, #21279).* [2020/XB1340/**B**]

♦ International Association of Hydrology / see International Association of Hydrogeologists (#11953)

♦ International Association for Hydromagnetic Phenomena and Applications (HYDROMAG) 11955

SG Ilmenau Univ of Technology, Dept of Mechanical Engineering, PO Box 10 05 65, 98684 Ilmenau, Germany. T. +493677692445. Fax +493677692411.
Chair Research Center Dresden-Rossendorf, PO Box 510119, 01314 Dresden, Germany. T. +493512603484. Fax +493512602007.
URL: http://hydromag.wordpress.com/

History Aug 1995, Riga (Latvia), during the 14th International Conference on Magnetohydrodynamics. **Aims** Promote and advance the science of hydromagnetics, dealing with fluid flows in electromagnetic fields. **Structure** Chair; 2 Co-Chairs; Secretary; Newsletter Editor. **Languages** English. **Staff** Voluntary. **Events** *Conference* Giens (France) 2000. **Publications** *HYDROMAG Newsletter.*
Members Individuals (personal and institutional) in 31 countries:
Austria, Belgium, Brazil, Bulgaria, Canada, Chile, China, Czechia, France, Germany, Greece, India, Ireland, Israel, Italy, Japan, Korea Rep, Latvia, Mexico, Netherlands, Norway, Poland, Romania, Russia, Slovakia, Spain, Sweden, Switzerland, UK, Ukraine, USA.
NGO Relations Affiliated with: *International Union of Theoretical and Applied Mechanics (IUTAM, #15823).* [2014/XD5725/**D**]

♦ International Association for Hyperthermic Oncology (inactive)
♦ International Association of Ice Cream Manufacturers / see International Ice Cream Association
♦ International Association for Identification (internationally oriented national body)
♦ International Association for Identification, Voice Identification and Acoustic Analysis / see International Association for Identification
♦ International Association of Immunization Trials (no recent information)

♦ International Association for Impact Assessment (IAIA) 11956

Association internationale pour l'évaluation d'impacts (AIEI) – Associação Internacional para Avaliação de Impactos Ambientais

Exec Dir 1330 23rd St S, Suite C, Fargo ND 58103, USA. T. +17012977908. Fax +17012977917. E-mail: info@iaia.org.
URL: http://www.iaia.org/

History Jan 1981, Atlanta, GA (USA). **Aims** Provide the international forum to advance best practice and innovation in impact assessment and advocate for its expanded use for the betterment of society and the environment. **Structure** Board of Directors; Sections (12); Headquarters in Fargo ND (USA). **Languages** English. **Staff** 6.00 FTE, paid. **Finance** Sources: meeting proceeds; members' dues; sponsorship. **Activities** Awards/prizes/competitions; events/meetings; publishing activities; training/education. **Events** *Annual Conference* Kuching (Malaysia) 2023, *Celsius 1.5 Impact Assessment and Climate Change Symposium* Cape Town (South Africa) 2022, *Annual Conference* Vancouver, BC (Canada) 2022, *Smartening Impact Assessment in Challenging Times* Seville (Spain) 2021, *Special Symposium* Washington, DC (USA) 2020. **Publications** *IAIA enews announcements* (12 a year); *Impact Assessment and Project Appraisal (IAPA)* – journal. *Best Practice Principles; FasTips; Key Citation Series Updates.* Glossary. Information Services: Membership database. **Information Services** *EIA Training Database; IAIAConnect; IAIA Meeting/Networking Database.*
Members Individual corporate planners and managers, public interest advocates, private consultants, university teachers and students in 120 countries and territories. Membership countries not specified.
Affiliate (17) in 15 countries and territories:
Brazil, Canada, China, Germany, Ghana, Iran Islamic Rep, Italy, Korea Rep, Mozambique, New Zealand, Nigeria, Portugal, South Africa, Spain, Zambia.
Associate (7) in 8 countries:
Australia, Canada, China, India, New Zealand, Philippines, Türkiye, USA.
Included in the above, 1 organization listed in this Yearbook:
International Society of City and Regional Planners (ISOCARP, #15012).
NGO Relations Member of (1): *International Union for Conservation of Nature and Natural Resources (IUCN, #15766).* Cooperates with (2): *International Organization for Standardization (ISO, #14473); Southern African Institute for Environmental Assessment (SAIEA, #19846).* Instrumental in setting up (1): *Secrétariat international francophone pour l'évaluation environnementale (SIFÉE, #19201).* [2022.10.12/XD0270/**B**]

♦ International Association of Inades-Formation / see Institut Africain pour le Développement Economique et Social – Centre Africain de Formation (#11233)

♦ International Association of Independent Art and Design Schools (AIAS) 11957

SG c/o AKI ArtEZ, Academy for Art and Design, Hulsmaatstraat 35, 7523 WB Enschede, Netherlands. T. +31534824400. E-mail: aki@artez.nl.
URL: http://www.aias-artdesign.org/

History 30 Nov 1990, Dessau (Germany). **Aims** Re-enforce and strengthen the contacts between the participating institutions, so they can contribute to the internationalization of education in the arts. **Structure** General Assembly (annual). Board, comprising President, Vice-President, Treasurer, Secretary General and 2 members. Secretariat. **Languages** English. **Finance** Members' dues. **Activities** Awards 'AIAS Prize of Honour'. Organizes workshops. Runs Exchange Programmes. **Events** *General Assembly* Zurich (Switzerland) 2007, *General Assembly* Enschede (Netherlands) 2004, *General Assembly* Florence (Italy) 2003, *General Assembly* Seoul (Korea Rep) 2002, *General Assembly* London (UK) 2001. **Publications** *AIAS Newsfax*; *AIAS Newsletter*.
Members Schools (18) in 13 countries:
Austria, China, France, Germany, Italy, Japan, Korea Rep, Malaysia, Netherlands, Norway, Portugal, Switzerland, UK.
[2014/XD8146/**D**]

♦ International Association of Independent Corporate Monitors (internationally oriented national body)
♦ International Association of Independent Journalists (internationally oriented national body)

♦ International Association of Independent Law Firms (Interlaw) 11958

Secretariat 1900 Avenue of the Stars, 7th Flo, Los Angeles CA 90067, USA. E-mail: interlawsecretariat@interlaw.org.
URL: http://www.interlaw.org/

History Registered in accordance with UK law. **Aims** Gather lawyers working together on a worldwide basis to provide quality, cost effective, value-added legal and business solutions. **Structure** Board of Directors. **Activities** Awards/prizes/competitions; events/meetings. **Events** *Asia Pacific Regional Meeting* Auckland (New Zealand) 2020, *Annual Global Meeting* Beijing (China) 2019, *Regional Meeting of the Americas* Belo Horizonte (Brazil) 2018, *Europe Middle East Africa and Asia Pacific Meeting* London (UK) 2018, *Annual Global Meeting* Paris (France) 2018.
Members Firms in 58 countries:
Algeria, Argentina, Australia, Austria, Bahrain, Belgium, Bolivia, Brazil, Bulgaria, Canada, Chile, China, Cyprus, Denmark, Dominican Rep, Ecuador, England, Finland, France, Germany, India, Indonesia, Israel, Italy, Japan, Korea Rep, Liechtenstein, Luxembourg, Malaysia, Malta, Mauritius, Mexico, Morocco, Netherlands, New Zealand, Nigeria, Norway, Oman, Panama, Peru, Philippines, Poland, Portugal, Puerto Rico, Romania, Russia, Scotland, Singapore, Spain, Sweden, Switzerland, Thailand, United Arab Emirates, Uruguay, USA, Venezuela, Vietnam, Virgin Is UK. [2017/XM4467/**C**]

♦ International Association of Independent Producers of the Mediterranean (#02731)

♦ International Association of Independent Tanker Owners (INTERTANKO) 11959

Association internationale des armateurs indépendants de pétroliers – Asociación Internacional de Propietarios Independientes de Buques Cisterna

Managing Dir INTERTANKO London Secretariat, St Clare House, 30-33 Minories, London, EC3N 1DD, UK. T. +442079777010. Fax +442079777011. E-mail: london@intertanko.com.
URL: http://www.intertanko.com/

History 1970. Registration: EU Transparency Register, No/ID: 59416811798-38. **Aims** Further the interests of independent tanker owners; promote a free and competitive tanker market and *free enterprise*; improve maritime safety, protection of the marine environment and pollution control. **Structure** General Meeting (annual); Council (meets twice a year); Executive Committee (meets at least 3 times a year); Management Committee; Specialist (technical) Committees (13); Regional Panels (5 – Asian, North American, Latin American, Hellenic Mediterranean, North European). **Languages** English, French, German, Norwegian, Spanish. **Staff** 19.00 FTE, paid. **Finance** Sources: members' dues; sale of publications. **Activities** Advocacy/lobbying/activism; events/meetings; networking/liaising; research/documentation. **Events** *Annual General Meeting* Singapore (Singapore) 2019, *Annual General Meeting* Singapore (Singapore) 2016, *Annual Tanker Summit* Singapore (Singapore) 2016, *Annual General Meeting* Athens (Greece) 2015, *European Panel Meeting* Barcelona (Spain) 2015. **Publications** *Weekly News Bulletin* (50 a year). Annual Report; books; guidelines; commentaries; best practice documents.
Members Full: independent tanker owners and operators (220, not government or oil company controlled), in 40 countries worldwide. Membership countries not specified. Associate (over 300). Membership countries not specified.
Associate (over 300). Membership countries not specified. Included in Associate Members, international organizations (10), including 6 organizations listed in this Yearbook:
Included in Associate Members, international organizations (10), including 6 organizations listed in this Yearbook:
Federation of National Associations of Shipbrokers and Agents (FONASBA, #09694); *Institute of Chartered Shipbrokers (#11247)*; *International Association of Ports and Harbors (IAPH, #12096)*; *International Bunker Industry Association (IBIA, #12411)*; *International Salvage Union (ISU, #14779)*; *Liberian Shipowners Council (LSC, #16455)*.
Consultative Status Consultative status granted from: *ECOSOC (#05331)* (Ros C); *International Maritime Organization (IMO, #14102)*; *UNCTAD (#20285)* (Special Category). **IGO Relations** Observer status with (1): *International Oil Pollution Compensation Funds (IOPC Funds, #14402)*. Associated with Department of Global Communications of the United Nations. **NGO Relations** Cooperates with (7): *Advisory Committee on Protection of the Sea (ACOPS, #00139)*; *BIMCO (#03236)*; *International Association of Dry Cargo Shipowners (INTERCARGO, #11853)*; *International Association of Oil and Gas Producers (IOGP, #12053)*; *International Chamber of Shipping (ICS, #12535)*; *Nordisk Defence Club (#17501)*; *Oil Companies International Marine Forum (OCIMF, #17709)*. Instrumental in setting up (1): *Maritime Industry Foundation*. Consultative member of: *Comité maritime international (CMI, #04192)*. [2020/XC9011/y/**C**]

♦ International Association of Individual Psychology (IAIP) 11960

Association Internationale de la Psychologie Adlérienne (AIPA) – Internationale Vereinigung für Individualpsychologie (IVIP)

Main Office c/o AACI, Hernalser Hauptstr 15/1/2, 1170 Vienna, Austria. E-mail: generalsecretary@adler-iaip.net.
URL: https://adler-iaip.net/

History 1930, on an official basis, the first local group having been set up in 1911, Vienna (Austria), and the organization itself having actually existed since 1922. Known until 1932 as *International Society for Individual Psychology*, when dissolved. Founded again under present title, 28 Jul 1954. Constitution adopted 1963, Paris (France). Constitution revised 1996, Oxford (UK). **Aims** Coordinate and integrate internationally all efforts toward developing and promulgating the individual psychology of Alfred Adler. **Structure** Delegate Conference (every 3 years). Board. Sections (5): Therapy; Counselling; Psychotherapy of Children and Adolescent; Education and Pedagogics; Theory and Research. **Languages** English. **Staff** 10.00 FTE, voluntary. **Finance** Member societies' dues, in proportion to their membership. Budget (annual): about US$ 15,000. **Activities** Events/meetings. **Events** *Triennial Congress* Vienna (Austria) 2021, *Triennial Congress* Lviv (Ukraine) 2020, *Triennial Congress* Minneapolis, MN (USA) 2017, *Triennial Congress* Paris (France) 2014, *Triennial Congress* Vienna (Austria) 2011.
Members International and national societies, associations and institutes in 17 countries:
Austria, Bulgaria, Canada, France, Germany, Hungary, Israel, Italy, Japan, Lithuania, Malta, Netherlands, Romania, Switzerland, UK, Uruguay, USA.
International organization (1): [2019/XC1298/y/**D**]

♦ International Association of Industrial Accident Boards and Commissions (internationally oriented national body)

♦ International Association of Infant Food Manufacturers (IFM) 11961

Association internationale des fabricants d'aliments pour l'enfance

Contact address not obtained. T. +41225606405.
URL: http://www.ifm.net/

History 1984. **Aims** Promote sound infant *nutrition* and high ethical standards. **Structure** General Assembly; Executive Committee. **Languages** English. **Staff** 4.00 FTE, paid. **Finance** Members' dues.
Members Manufacturers (15) in 9 countries:
Denmark, France, Germany, Japan, Netherlands, New Zealand, Sweden, Switzerland, USA. [2014/XD6450/**D**]

♦ International Association of Infant Massage (IAIM) 11962

Association Internationale en Massage pour Bébé – Asociación Internacional de Masaje Infantil – Internationale Gesellschaft für Babymassage – Associação Internacional de Massagem Infantil – Associazione Internazionale di Massagio Infantile

International Office Heidenstams Gata 9, S-422 47 Hisings Backa, Gothenburg, Sweden. T. +46702566693. E-mail: info@iaim.net.
URL: http://www.iaim.net/

History 1981. Incorporated 1986. Former names and other names: *International Association of Infant Massage Instructors* – former (1986 to 1993); *Association internationale d'instructeurs et instructrices en massage pour bébé (AIIMB)* – former (1986 to 1993). **Aims** Promote nurturing touch and communication through training, education and research so that parents, caregivers and children are loved, valued and respected throughout the world community. **Structure** General Assembly (every 2 years); International Board. **Languages** English. **Activities** Certification/accreditation; events/meetings; training/education. **Events** *Virtual General Assembly* Gothenburg (Sweden) 2020, *Conference and General Assembly* Taipei (Taiwan) 2020, *Conference and General Assembly* Madrid (Spain) 2018, *Conference and General Assembly* Paris (France) 2016, *Conference and General Assembly* San José (Costa Rica) 2014. **Publications** Newsletters (online).
Members Chapter Representatives and Country Contact Persons in 74 countries and territories:
Argentina, Barbados, Belgium, Brazil, Brunei Darussalam, Canada, Chad, Chile, Colombia, Costa Rica, Croatia, Cyprus, Czechia, Denmark, Dominican Rep, Ecuador, Finland, France, Germany, Ghana, Greece, Guatemala, Haiti, Hong Kong, Hungary, India, Indonesia, Iran Islamic Rep, Ireland, Israel, Italy, Japan, Jordan, Kenya, Korea Rep, Lithuania, Luxembourg, Malaysia, Malta, Mexico, Namibia, Netherlands, New Zealand, Norway, Oman, Panama, Peru, Philippines, Poland, Portugal, Qatar, Romania, Russia, Saudi Arabia, Serbia, Singapore, Slovakia, Slovenia, South Africa, Spain, Sweden, Switzerland, Taiwan, Thailand, Trinidad-Tobago, Türkiye, UK, Ukraine, United Arab Emirates, Uruguay, USA, Venezuela, Vietnam, Zimbabwe.
[2021.09.09/XN7606/**C**]

♦ International Association of Infant Massage Instructors / see International Association of Infant Massage (#11962)
♦ International Association for Infant Mental Health (inactive)

♦ International Association of Inflammation Societies (IAIS) 11963

Pres address not obtained.
URL: http://www.inflammationsocieties.org/

History 1991, Rome (Italy). **Aims** Relieve sickness, protect and preserve public health and advance education in the field of inflammatory diseases, in particular but not exclusively by organizing and supporting research conferences and local scientific societies for research into inflammatory diseases. **Languages** English. **Staff** None. Run by voluntary trustees of the charity. **Finance** Self-financing through organization of educational meetings. **Events** *World Congress on Inflammation* Rome (Italy) 2022, *World Congress* Sydney, NSW (Australia) 2019, *World Congress* London (UK) 2017, *World Congress* Boston, MA (USA) 2015, *World Congress* Natal (Brazil) 2013. **Publications** *Inflammation Research*.
Members in 13 countries:
Australia, Brazil, Canada, Croatia, Denmark, France, Germany, India, Japan, Sweden, Switzerland, UK, USA.
[2021/XD3793/**D**]

♦ International Association for Information and Data Quality / see Information Quality International (#11197)
♦ International Association of Information and Documentation in Public Administration (inactive)
♦ International Association for Inland Waterways / see Inland Waterways International (#11217)

♦ International Association of Insolvency Regulators (IAIR) 11964

Chair IAIR Secretariat, 1 Pennyburn Road, Kilwinning, KA13 6SA, UK. T. +443002002900. Fax +443002002902. E-mail: secretariat@insolvencyreg.org.
URL: http://www.insolvencyreg.org/

History 1995, Hong Kong. Founded following activities begun in 1993. **Structure** General Meeting (annual, at Conference). **Staff** 4.00 FTE, paid. **Finance** Sources: members' dues. **Activities** Events/meetings. **Events** *Conference* Belgrade (Serbia) 2023, *Conference and Annual General Meeting* Helsinki (Finland) 2022, *Conference and Annual General Meeting* Stratford-upon-Avon (UK) 2022, *Conference and Annual General Meeting* Helsinki (Finland) 2021, *Conference and Annual General Meeting* Kowloon (Hong Kong) 2020. **Publications** Annual Report; handbook; working papers.
Members Government departments, ministries and agencies and public authorities (28) in 26 countries and territories:
Australia, Canada, China, Colombia, Czechia, Finland, Hong Kong, India, Ireland, Jersey, Latvia, Malaysia, Mauritius, Mexico, New Zealand, Pakistan, Peru, Romania, Russia, Serbia, Singapore, South Africa, Thailand, UK, USA, Virgin Is UK.
[2022/XJ8168/**C**]

♦ International Association of Institutes of Export / see International Association of Trade Training Organizations (#12233)

♦ International Association of Institutes of Navigation (IAIN) 11965

Association internationale des instituts de navigation

SG c/o Arab Inst of Navigation, Sebaei Bldg, Cross Road of Sebaei St & 45 Str, Miami, Alexandria, Egypt.
Registered Office c/o Netherlands Inst of Navigation, Seattleweg 7, 3195 ND Rotterdam, Netherlands.
URL: http://www.iainav.org/

History First General Assembly held in London (UK); first Statutes adopted 15 Oct 1975. Registration: Netherlands. **Aims** Unite national and multinational institutes and organizations which foster human activities at sea, in the air, in space and on land and which many benefit from development of the science and practice of navigation and related information techniques, to the general benefit of mankind. **Structure** General Assembly (at least every 3 years); Officers' Committee. **Languages** English. **Staff** 2.00 FTE, paid; 2.00 FTE, voluntary. **Finance** Sources: gifts, legacies; grants; members' dues. **Activities** Events/meetings; networking/liaising; research and development; standards/guidelines; training/education. **Events** *World Congress* Poland 2027, *World Congress* China 2024, *World Congress* Chiba (Japan) 2018, *European Navigation Conference* Bordeaux (France) 2015, *World Congress* Prague (Czech Rep) 2015. **Information Services** *Online news database*.
Members Full: national and international (non-profit) institutes of navigation; Corporate: companies or groups of companies; Honorary. Members (" indicates member of the Nordic Institute) in 21 countries:
Austria, China, Czechia, Denmark (*), Egypt, Finland (*), France, Germany, Israel, Italy, Japan, Korea DPR, Korea Rep, Netherlands, Norway (*), Poland, Russia, Sweden (*), Switzerland, UK, USA.
Included in the above, 2 regional organizations:
Arab Institute of Navigation (AIN, #00985); *Nordic Institute of Navigation (#17323)*.
Associate: associations in 4 countries:
Canada, Nigeria, Russia, UK.
Included in the above, 1 association listed in this Yearbook:
International Public Association – Academy of Navigation and Motion Control.
Corresponding: associations in 6 countries:
Australia, France, India, Ireland, UK, USA.
Included in the above, 2 associations listed in this Yearbook:
Comité International Radio-Maritime (CIRM, #04186); *International Association of Marine Aids to Navigation and Lighthouse Authorities (IALA, #12013)*.
Consultative Status Consultative status granted from: *ECOSOC (#05331)* (Ros C); *International Maritime Organization (IMO, #14102)*. [2022.06.15/XD4779/y/**C**]

♦ International Association of the Institut Marey (inactive)
♦ International Association of Insurance Fraud Agencies (no recent information)
♦ International Association of Insurance and Reinsurance Intermediaries / see BIPAR – European Federation of Insurance Intermediaries (#03263)

♦ International Association of Insurance Supervisors (IAIS) 11966

Association internationale des contrôleurs des assurances (AICA)

SG c/o Bank for Intl Settlements, Centralbahnplatz 2, 4002 Basel BS, Switzerland. T. +41612257300. Fax +41612809151. E-mail: iais@bis.org.
URL: http://www.iaisweb.org/

History 1992. Founded following international participation at meetings of the USA *'National Association of Insurance Commissioners (NAIC)'* since the mid-1980s. Registration: USA, Illinois; Switzerland, 1994. **Aims** Promote effective and globally consistent supervision of the insurance industry in order to develop and maintain fair, safe and stable insurance markets for the benefit and protection of policy holders; contribute to global *financial* stability. **Structure** General Meeting; Executive Committee; Committees (5); Subcommittees. Secretariat housed at *Bank for International Settlements (BIS, #03165)*. **Languages** English. **Staff** 25.00 FTE, paid. 5 staff are seconded. **Finance** Members' dues and assistance. Special support from international organizations. **Activities** Events/meetings; monitoring/evaluation; standards/guidelines. **Events** *Global Seminar* Seattle, WA (USA) 2023, *Annual Conference* Tokyo (Japan) 2023, *Global Seminar* Dubrovnik (Croatia) 2022, *Annual Conference* Santiago (Chile) 2022, *Annual Confernce* 2021. **Publications** *IAIS Newsletter* (12 a year); *Global Insurance Market Report (GIMAR). Insurance Core Principles, Standards, Guidance and Assessment Methodology* (2nd ed revised 2013). Annual Report; Issues papers; Application papers; reports; policy statements.
Members Insurance supervisors and regulators from over 200 jurisdictions in 133 countries and territories:
Albania, Argentina, Armenia, Aruba, Australia, Austria, Azerbaijan, Bahamas, Bahrain, Bangladesh, Barbados, Belarus, Belgium, Belize, Bermuda, Bhutan, Botswana, Brazil, Brunei Darussalam, Bulgaria, Burundi, Cambodia, Canada, Cape Verde, Cayman Is, Chile, China, Colombia, Costa Rica, Curaçao, Cyprus, Czechia, Denmark, Ecuador, Egypt, El Salvador, Estonia, Eswatini, Finland, France, Georgia, Germany, Ghana, Gibraltar, Guatemala, Guernsey, Guinea, Hong Kong, Hungary, Iceland, India, Indonesia, Ireland, Isle of Man, Israel, Italy, Jamaica, Japan, Jersey, Jordan, Kazakhstan, Kenya, Korea Rep, Kosovo, Latvia, Lebanon, Lesotho, Liechtenstein, Lithuania, Luxembourg, Macau, Malawi, Malaysia, Maldives, Malta, Mauritius, Mexico, Moldova, Mongolia, Montenegro, Morocco, Namibia, Nepal, Netherlands, New Zealand, Nigeria, North Macedonia, Norway, Oman, Pakistan, Palestine, Panama, Papua New Guinea, Paraguay, Peru, Philippines, Poland, Portugal, Qatar, Romania, Russia, Rwanda, Samoa, San Marino, Saudi Arabia, Serbia, Singapore, Slovakia, Slovenia, South Africa, Spain, Sri Lanka, St Maarten, Suriname, Sweden, Switzerland, Taiwan, Tanzania UR, Thailand, Trinidad-Tobago, Tunisia, Türkiye, Turks-Caicos, Uganda, UK, United Arab Emirates, Uruguay, USA, Uzbekistan, Vanuatu, Vietnam, Virgin Is UK, Zambia.
Included in the above, 6 organizations listed in this Yearbook:
European Commission (EC, #06633); European Insurance and Occupational Pensions Authority (EIOPA, #07578); Inter-African Conference on Insurance Markets (#11385); International Bank for Reconstruction and Development (IBRD, #12317) (World Bank); *International Monetary Fund (IMF, #14180); OECD (#17693).*
IGO Relations Member of: *Asian Forum of Insurance Regulators (AFIR, #01492).* **NGO Relations** Founding partner of: *Access to Insurance Initiative (A2ii, #00051).* [2018.10.09/XD6029/y/**B**]

♦ International Association for Integration, Dignity and Economic Advancement (IDEA) 11967

Intl Coordinator 32 Fall St, Ste A, PO Box 651, Seneca Falls NY 13148, USA. T. +13155685838. Fax +13155685891.
Admin Coordinator 699 Main St, Ashby MA 01431-2309, USA. T. +19783860048.
URL: http://www.idealeprosydignity.org/

History 1994. **Aims** Foster empowerment, address human rights issues and promote self-sufficiency through an international support network of people affected by *leprosy*. **Activities** include: psychological support and counselling; empowerment workshops; children's scholarships; socio-economic programmes; women's support groups. **Consultative Status** Consultative status granted from: *ECOSOC (#05331)* (Special). **NGO Relations** Member of (1): *Global Partnership for Zero Leprosy (#10543).* [2012/XG9933/**D**]

- ♦ International Association for Integrative Education (inactive)
- ♦ International Association for Integrative Nervous Functions: Neurobiology of Behaviour and Psychosomatics / see Collegium Internationale Activitatis Nervosae Superioris (#04113)
- ♦ International Association of Intellectual Property Professors / see International Association for the Advancement of Teaching and Research in Intellectual Property (#11690)
- ♦ International Association 'Interaction' – East-West Partnerships for a Better World (inactive)

♦ International Association Interactions of Psychoanalysis (IAIP) . . . 11968

Association internationale interactions de la psychanalyse (A2IP) – Internationale Vereinigung Interaktionen der Psychoanalyse

Pres 16 rue de l'Assomption, 75016 Paris, France. T. +33611536618.
Contact 8 rue de Cdt Mouchotte, 75014 Paris, France. E-mail: interactions.psychanalyse@gmail.com.
URL: http://www.a2ip-psychanalyse.org/

History 25 Jun 1985, Paris (France). Reconstituted under current title, 12 Jun 2011, Paris (France). Former names and other names: *International Association for the History of Psychoanalysis (IAHP)* – former; *Association internationale d'histoire de la psychanalyse (AIHP)* – former. **Aims** Foster research and organize scientific meetings and debates on contemporary themes linking the psychoanalytic approach with other fields of knowledge. **Structure** Assembly of active members; Board of Directors; International Scientific Committee; Working Groups; Associate Groups. **Languages** English, French, German, Portuguese, Spanish. **Staff** 5.00 FTE, voluntary. **Finance** Members' dues. **Activities** Research/documentation; events/meetings; knowledge management/information dissemination. **Events** *General Assembly* Paris (France) 2021, *Conference* Villeneuve-lès-Avignon (France) 2017, *Writing the history of a peculiar science – psychoanalysis* Aix-en-Provence (France) 2006, *History and function of the myth in the psychoanalytic relation between mythology, tragedy and clinic* Athens (Greece) 2006, *Psychoanalysts and psychiatrists – a long and complex story* Paris (France) 2004. **Publications** *Topique* in English, French – journal.
Members International affiliated groups in 3 countries:
Brazil, Greece, Türkiye.
Correspondents in 12 countries:
Austria, Belgium, Brazil, France, Germany, Greece, Italy, Luxembourg, Portugal, Switzerland, Türkiye, USA.
Active (limited, 74) and corresponding (387) members. Membership countries not specified. [2022/XD1230/v/**D**]

♦ International Association for Intercultural Education (IAIE) 11969

Association internationale pour l'éducation interculturelle (AIEI)

Pres Mient 201 G, 2564 KL The Hague, Netherlands. T. +31651960525. Fax +528124785. E-mail: info@iaie.org.
URL: http://iaie.org/

History Sep 1984, London (UK). Founded at 2nd conference, following 1st international conference, Nov 1982, Utrecht (Netherlands). **Aims** Examine the implications of societal contexts of education and the relationship between society, nation state and international contexts and the situation of individuals, groups and minorities within them; contribute to development of intercultural education and issues of education in multicultural societies; promote exchange of information, knowledge and materials among teachers, teacher trainers and professionals working in curriculum development, research and educational policy; initiate, react and respond to activities of international organizations. **Structure** Assembly of national/regional coordinators; Organizing Committee (meets annually); Board; Secretariat. **Languages** English, Spanish. **Staff** 0.50 FTE, paid. **Finance** Sources: grants; members' dues. Annual budget: 15,000 EUR. **Activities** Events/meetings; research/documentation. **Events** *Conference* Athens (Greece) 2022, *Conference* Tel Aviv (Israel) 2021, *Conference* Athens (Greece) 2020, *Another brick in the wall – transforming education* Amsterdam (Netherlands) 2019, *Education theory and practice in challenging times* Angers (France) 2017. **Publications** *Intercultural Education* (6 a year) – academic journal; *Intercultural Times* (3 a year) – members' bulletin. Occasional papers; working papers.
Members Institutional and individuals members (400) in 56 countries:
Algeria, Australia, Austria, Belarus, Belgium, Bolivia, Bosnia-Herzegovina, Bulgaria, Canada, Chile, China, Costa Rica, Côte d'Ivoire, Croatia, Cuba, Czechia, Denmark, Finland, France, Germany, Greece, Guatemala, Hungary, India, Ireland, Israel, Italy, Japan, Kenya, Latvia, Lithuania, Luxembourg, Mexico, Morocco, Netherlands, New Zealand, North Macedonia, Norway, Pakistan, Peru, Philippines, Poland, Portugal, Romania, Russia, Singapore, Slovakia, Slovenia, Spain, Sweden, Switzerland, Türkiye, UK, USA, Vanuatu, Vietnam.
IGO Relations *European Commission (EC, #06633); International Bureau of Education (IBE, #12413); Organization for Security and Cooperation in Europe (OSCE, #17887); UNESCO (#20322); UNICEF (#20332).* **NGO Relations** Member of: *EDEN Digital Learning Europe (EDEN, #05356).* [2021/XD1476/**C**]

♦ International Association of Internet Hotlines (INHOPE) 11970

Exec Dir Jan van Galenstraat 335, 1061 AZ Amsterdam, Netherlands. T. +31872399550. E-mail: info@inhope.org.
URL: http://www.inhope.org/

History 23 Nov 1999. Former names and other names: *Internet Hotline Providers in Europe Association* – full title. Registration: Handelsregister, No/ID: KVK 34124277, Netherlands; EU Transparency Register, No/ID: 098793947944-83, Start date: 20 Oct 2022. **Aims** Support and enhance the performance of Internet hotlines around the world, ensuring swift action is taken in responding to reports of *illegal* content making the Internet a safer place. **Structure** General Assembly (annual); Board of Directors. **Staff** 0.50 FTE, paid. **Finance** Sources: grants; members' dues. **Activities** Events/meetings. **Events** *Summit* Amsterdam (Netherlands) 2022, *Summit* Amsterdam (Netherlands) 2021, *Law Enforcement and Industry Conference* Amsterdam (Netherlands) 2012, *Conference* Amsterdam (Netherlands) 2010. **Publications** *INHOPE Newsletter.*
Members Hotlines (47) in 42 countries and territories:
Australia, Austria, Belgium, Bosnia-Herzegovina, Brazil, Bulgaria, Canada, Croatia, Cyprus, Czechia, Denmark, Estonia, Finland, France, Germany, Greece, Hungary, Iceland, Ireland, Italy, Japan, Korea Rep, Latvia, Lithuania, Luxembourg, Malta, Netherlands, New Zealand, Poland, Portugal, Romania, Russia, Serbia, Slovakia, Slovenia, South Africa, Spain, Sweden, Taiwan, Türkiye, UK, USA.
Provisional (2) in 2 countries:
Romania, Slovakia.
IGO Relations Cooperates with (1): *Virtual Global Taskforce (VGT, #20788).* **NGO Relations** Member of (1): *European Financial Coalition against Commercial Sexual Exploitation of Children Online (EFC, #07249).* [2022/XD9408/**D**]

♦ International Association of Investors in the Social Economy (INAISE) 11971

Association internationale des investisseurs dans l'économie sociale – Asociación Internacional de los Inversores en la Economia Social

Pres c/o SIDI, 12 rue Guy de la Brosse, 75005 Paris, France. E-mail: secretariat@inaise.org – coordination.inaise@gmail.com – gerenciageneral@redfasco.org.gt.
URL: http://www.inaise.org/

History 15 Nov 1989, Barcelona (Spain). Launching conference Apr 1990, Brussels (Belgium). Registered in accordance with Belgian law. Previously also referred to as *Association européenne de banques et organismes financiers interpellés par les questions d'écologie, de culture, de gestion démocratique de l'économie sociale.* **Aims** Facilitate development of and international cooperation among *financial* institutions involved in community banking, social investment and other ethical saving activities which encourage a more conscious handling of savings and which invest in ethical, ecological and self-managing undertakings; help develop trust and cooperation among finance organizations so as to enable joint investment across boundaries by members; provide information on policy and practice of investment and banking in members' countries and at European and international level. **Structure** General Meeting of Members (annual) and Board of Directors are decision-making bodies. Secretariat carries day-to-day operations. **Languages** English, French, Spanish. **Staff** 1.00 FTE, paid. **Finance** Members' dues. **Activities** Guidance/assistance/consulting; events/meetings; training/education. **Events** *Annual Conference* Antigua (Guatemala) 2022, *Annual General Meeting and Seminar* Montréal, QC (Canada) 2016, *Annual General Meeting and Seminar* Lima (Peru) 2015, *Annual General Meeting and Seminar* Bochum (Germany) 2014, *Annual General Meeting and Seminar* Paris (France) 2012. **Publications** Newsletter (12 a year).
Members Full financial institutions and networks of social finance organizations; Associate non-financial institutions. Full (46) in 31 countries:
Australia, Bangladesh, Belgium, Bolivia, Brazil, Burkina Faso, Canada, Congo DR, Costa Rica, Denmark, Ethiopia, Finland, France, Germany, Haiti, India, Ireland, Italy, Japan, Luxembourg, Netherlands, Norway, Peru, Poland, Slovakia, South Africa, Spain, Sweden, Togo, Uganda, UK.
Full members also in Latin America.
Included in the above, 1 organization listed in this Yearbook:
Microfinance Centre (MFC, #16745).
Associate (17) in 11 countries:
Canada, Finland, France, Germany, India, Netherlands, Nicaragua, Philippines, Senegal, UK, Venezuela.
Included in the above, 1 organization listed in this Yearbook:
International Solidarity for Development and Investment (SIDI).
NGO Relations Member of: *Intercontinental Network for the Promotion of the Social Solidarity Economy (INPSSE, #11463); European Inter-Network of Ethical and Responsible Initiatives (#07593); RIPESS Europe – Economy Solidarity Europe (RIPESS Europe, #18952).* [2022/XD2181/y/**D**]

- ♦ International Association of Islamic Banks (no recent information)

♦ International Association of IT Lawyers (IAITL) 11972

Address not obtained.

History Registration: No/ID: 29569711, Denmark. **Aims** Promote study and research in *computer* law through international conferences, networking, publication of member's research works, job announcements and the provision of internet resources. **Structure** Executive Board. **Activities** Events/meetings. **Events** *International Conference on Legal, Security and Privavy Issues in IT Law* Lisbon (Portugal) 2014, *International Law and Trade Conference* Lisbon (Portugal) 2014, *International Private Law Conference / Legal Conference Series* Lisbon (Portugal) 2014, *International Public Law Conference* Lisbon (Portugal) 2014, *International Private Law Conference* Bangkok (Thailand) 2013. **Publications** *International Journal of Private Law (IJPL); International Journal of Public Law and Policy (IJPLAP); Journal of International Commercial Law and Technology (JICLT).*
Members Individual; Institutional. Membership countries not specified. **Consultative Status** Consultative status granted from: *World Intellectual Property Organization (WIPO, #21593)* (Observer Status). **IGO Relations** Member of (1): *International Telecommunication Union (ITU, #15673)* (Telecommunication Standardization Sector). [2014/XJ8407/**C**]

- ♦ International Association IUS Primi Viri (internationally oriented national body)
- ♦ International Association for Japanese Philosophy (internationally oriented national body)

♦ International Association of Jaspers Societies (IAJS) 11973

Dir Studium Generale, Joh Gutenberg Uni Mains, Colonel Kleinman Weg 2, 55099 Mainz, Germany. Fax +496136850835.
Contact Univ of Massachusetts, Amherst Campus Dept of Philosophy, Bartlett Hall, Amherst MA 01003, USA. T. +14132533257.

History 21 Feb 2001. **Aims** Promote research and study on *psychologist* and *philosopher* Karl Jaspers. **Structure** Board of Trustees. Directorate, comprising Director and 3 members. **Finance** Members' dues. Contributions from sponsoring societies. **Activities** Organizes conferences. **Events** *Conference / Congress* Athens (Greece) 2013, *Congress* Seoul (Korea Rep) 2008, *Congress* Istanbul (Turkey) 2003. **Publications** Conference papers. **NGO Relations** Organizes conferences in conjunction with those of: *International Federation of Philosophical Societies (FISP, #13507).* [2017/XJ2520/**E**]

- ♦ International Association of Jazz Schools / see International Association of Schools of Jazz (#12148)

♦ International Association of Jesuit Business Schools (IAJBS) 11974

Asociación Internacional de Escuelas de Negocios Jesuitas

Exec Dir College of Business Adminstration, Univ of Detroit Mercy, 4001 West McNichols Rd, Detroit MI 48221, USA. T. +13139931219. Fax +13139931673. E-mail: ulfertgw@udmercy.edu.
Pres Albers School of Business and Economics, Seattle Univ, 901 12th Ave, Seattle WA 98122, USA. T. +12062965699.
URL: http://www.iajbs.org/

History within the framework of *Society of Jesus (SJ).* **Aims** Enhance the ability of members to create and transmit knowledge about, and prepare persons for the profession and vocation of business leadership in a global economy. **Structure** General Council; Board; Representatives for Asia (5), Europe, Africa and Lebanon (5), Latin America (5) and USA (5); Associate Member School Representative; Representative for Jesuit Secretariat. **Languages** English, Spanish. **Staff** 1.00 FTE, paid. **Events** *World Forum* Tlaquepaque (Mexico) 2021, *World Forum* Tlaquepaque (Mexico) 2020, *World Forum* Bhubaneswar (India) 2019, *World Forum* Seattle, WA (USA) 2018, *World Forum* Namur (Belgium) 2017. **Publications** *IAJBS Newsletter.* **Members** Worldwide. Membership countries not specified. **NGO Relations** *Colleagues in Jesuit Business Education (CJBE); Global Jesuit Business Student Association (GJBSA, #10442).* Member of: *Principles for Responsible Management Education (PRME, #18500).* [2018.03.08/XN8468/**D**]

♦ International Association of Jesuit Universities (IAJU) 11975

Contact Curia Generalizia, Soc Gesu Sec Higher Education – Society of Jesus, 4 Borgo Santo Santo Spirito 4, 00193 Rome RM, Italy.
URL: http://www.iaju.org/

History Jul 2018. Approved by Father General Arturo Sosa of the Society of Jesus. Recognized as the international advisory and coordination body to the Secretariat of Jesuit Higher Education and, through him, to Father General and his Assistants in matters related to higher education and the intellectual apostolate. Bylaws adopted summer 2018. **Aims** Contribute to the progress of the Society's apostolate of higher education through the application of its decrees and documents; promote collaboration between and among higher education institutions whether they are part of the Society, Jesuit or secular; represent members at international events and collaborate with other institutions with common purpose; expand Jesuit higher education to the marginalized and the poor. **Structure** Assembly; Board of Directors. **Languages** English, Spanish. **Staff** 1.00 FTE, paid. Voluntary. **Activities** Events/meetings; networking/liaising; projects/programmes. **Events** *General Assembly* Boston, MA (USA) 2022, *General Assembly* Bilbao (Spain) 2018, *General Assembly* Melbourne, VIC (Australia) 2015, *General Assembly* Mexico City (Mexico) 2010. **Members** Institutions (195); Students; Alumni in 66 countries. Membership countries not specified.
[2022.05.11/XM5988/**E**]

♦ International Association of Jewish Genealogical Societies (IAJGS) 11976

Pres PO Box 3624, Cherry Hill NJ 08034-0556, USA. E-mail: president@iajgs.org.
URL: http://www.iajgs.org/

History Founded 1988. Previously known as *Association of Jewish Genealogical Societies*. **Aims** Provide a common voice for issues of significance to members; advance genealogical avocation; coordinate activities of Jewish Genealogical Societies around the world. **Structure** Board. **Languages** English. **Staff** None. **Finance** Members' dues. Other sources: donations; conference proceeds. Annual budget: about US$ 25,000. **Activities** Knowledge management/information dissemination; research/documentation. **Events** *Annual Conference* Philadelphia, PA (USA) 2021, *Annual Conference* Cherry Hill, NJ (USA) 2020, *Annual Conference* Cleveland, OH (USA) 2019, *Annual Conference* Warsaw (Poland) 2018, *Annual Conference* Orlando, FL (USA) 2017.
Members Jewish genealogical organizations (over 70) in 14 countries:
Argentina, Australia, Belgium, Canada, Denmark, France, Germany, India, Israel, Sweden, Switzerland, UK, USA, Venezuela.
[2016.10.31/XD3131/**D**]

♦ International Association of Jewish Lawyers and Jurists (IJL) 11977

Association internationale des avocats et juristes juifs

CEO 10 Daniel Frisch Street, 6473111 Tel Aviv, Israel. T. +97236910673. Fax +97236953855. E-mail: office@ijl.org.
URL: http://www.ijl.org/

History Set up at 1st International Congress of Jewish Lawyers and Jurists. Former names and other names: *IAJLJ* – former. Registration: EU Transparency Register, No/ID: 526505337843-20, Start date: 15 Apr 2020. **Aims** Promote and protect the essential interests of the Jewish people and defend human rights in general; combat racism, xenophobia, anti-Semitism, Holocaust denial, unjust attacks against the State of Israel and violations of international law. **Structure** Congress (serves as General Meeting, every 3 years); Board of Governors; Executive Committee. **Languages** English, French, Hebrew, Spanish. **Staff** 4.00 FTE, paid. **Finance** Sources: contributions; members' dues. **Activities** Events/meetings. **Events** *Triennial Congress* Tel Aviv (Israel) 2020, *Conference* Tel Aviv (Israel) 2019, *Controversial multiculturalism* Rome (Italy) 2018, *Triennial Congress* Jerusalem (Israel) 2017, *Triennial Congress* Eilat (Israel) 2014. **Publications** *Justice* (2 a year). **Members** Individual lawyers and jurists of whatever race, colour or creed who identify with aims of the association, in about 30 countries and territories. Membership countries not specified. **Consultative Status** Consultative status granted from: *ECOSOC (#05331)* (Special). **IGO Relations** Associated with Department of Global Communications of the United Nations. **NGO Relations** Member of (1): *Conference of Non-Governmental Organizations in Consultative Relationship with the United Nations (CONGO, #04635)*. Affiliated with: *World Jewish Congress (WJC, #21599)*. [2021.02.24/XD5317/v/**C**]

♦ International Association of Jewish Studies and Jewish Culture (no recent information)
♦ International Association of Journalists accredited to the League of Nations (inactive)

♦ International Association of Judges (IAJ) 11978

Union internationale des magistrats (UIM) – Unión Internacional de Magistrados – Internationale Vereinigung der Richter – Unione Internazionale dei Magistrati

SG Palazzo di Giustizia, Piazza Cavour, 00193 Rome RM, Italy. T. +390668832213. Fax +39066871195. E-mail: secretariat@iaj-uim.org.
URL: http://www.iaj-uim.org/

History 6 Sep 1953, Salzburg (Austria). Founded by representatives of Austria, Brazil, France, Germany FR, Italy and Luxembourg, following a decision taken at a congress, 1952, Venice (Italy). New statutes adopted 16 Oct 1965, Vienna (Austria); entered into force 1 Mar 1966; most recently amended 2012, Washington DC (USA). **Aims** Defend the independence of the judiciary, as an essential requirement of the judicial function and guarantee of human rights and freedom; protect constitutional and moral position of the judiciary; promote exchange of cultural relations; organize and intensify cordial relations among judges of different countries. **Structure** Central Council (meets annually); Presidency Committee; General Secretariat. Study Commissions (4), each composed of President and 2 Vice-Presidents. Regional Groups (4): Europe (*European Association of Judges (EAJ, #06100)*); Iberoamerica; Africa; Asia, North America and Oceania. **Languages** English, French, German, Italian, Spanish. **Staff** 0.50 FTE, paid; 6.00 FTE, voluntary. **Finance** Sources: members' dues. **Activities** Events/meetings; knowledge management/information dissemination; networking/liaising. **Events** *Annual Meeting* Tel Aviv (Israel) 2022, *Annual Meeting* Rome (Italy) 2021, *Annual Meeting* Nur-Sultan (Kazakhstan) 2019, *Annual Meeting* Marrakech (Morocco) 2018, *Annual Meeting* Santiago (Chile) 2017. **Publications** Congress reports and proceedings; reports and resolutions of study commissions; books.
Members National associations or representative groups in 94 countries and territories:
Albania, Algeria, Angola, Argentina, Armenia, Australia, Austria, Azerbaijan, Belgium, Benin, Bermuda, Bolivia, Bosnia-Herzegovina, Brazil, Bulgaria, Canada, Chile, Colombia, Congo DR, Costa Rica, Côte d'Ivoire, Croatia, Cyprus, Czechia, Denmark, Dominican Rep, Ecuador, Egypt, El Salvador, Estonia, Finland, France, Gabon, Georgia, Germany, Greece, Guatemala, Guinea, Guinea-Bissau, Hungary, Iceland, Iraq, Ireland, Israel, Italy, Japan, Kazakhstan, Latvia, Lebanon, Liberia, Liechtenstein, Lithuania, Luxembourg, Mali, Malta, Mauritania, Mexico, Moldova, Mongolia, Montenegro, Morocco, Mozambique, Netherlands, New Zealand, Nicaragua, Niger, North Macedonia, Norway, Panama, Paraguay, Peru, Philippines, Poland, Portugal, Puerto Rico, Romania, Sao Tomé-Principe, Senegal, Serbia, Slovakia, Slovenia, South Africa, Spain, Sweden, Switzerland, Taiwan, Timor-Leste, Togo, Tunisia, Türkiye, UK, Ukraine, Uruguay, USA.
Consultative Status Consultative status granted from: *ECOSOC (#05331)* (Special); *ILO (#11123)* (Special List); *Council of Europe (CE, #04881)* (Participatory Status). **IGO Relations** Accredited by (1): *United Nations Office at Vienna (UNOV, #20604)*. Associated with Department of Global Communications of the United Nations. **NGO Relations** Member of (2): *Alliance of NGOs on Crime Prevention and Criminal Justice (#00709)*; *Conference of Non-Governmental Organizations in Consultative Relationship with the United Nations (CONGO, #04635)*. Cooperates with (2): *International Commission of Jurists (ICJ, #12695)*; *International Union of Notaries (#15795)*. [2022.02.02/XC2730/**C**]

♦ International Association of Jungian Studies (IAJS) 11979

Contact 30 Dorset House, Gloucester Place, London, NW1 5AD, UK. Fax +442086090347.
URL: http://www.jungianstudies.org/

History Jul 2002, Essex (UK), during 1st International Academic Conference of Analytical Psychology. Sub-title: A Forum for Jungian and Post-Jungian Research. **Aims** Promote and develop Jungian and post-Jungian studies and scholarship on an international basis; promote scholarship relating analytical psychology to the arts and humanities, religious studies, the social sciences, psychology, philosophy, medicine, science and clinical, methodological and theoretical research. **Structure** General Meeting (every 3 years). Executive Committee, including Chair, Honorary Secretary, Membership Secretary and Honorary Treasurer. **Languages** English. **Staff** 9.00 FTE, voluntary. **Finance** No fixed budget. Income from subscriptions, conferences and journal. **Events** *Conference* Phoenix, AZ (USA) 2014, *International Academic Conference of the Analytical Psychology and Jungian Studies* Braga (Portugal) 2012, *International academic conference of the analytical psychology and Jungian studies* Zurich (Switzerland) 2008, *Conference on psyche and imagination* Greenwich (UK) 2006, *International academic conference of analytical psychology and Jungian studies* College Station, TX (USA) 2005. **Publications** *International Journal Jungian Studies*.

Members in 13 countries:
Australia, Brazil, Canada, France, Germany, Italy, Mexico, Poland, South Africa, Spain, Switzerland, UK, USA.
[2015/XM0018/**E**]

♦ International Association of Juvenile Court Judges / see International Association of Youth and Family Judges and Magistrates (#12283)
♦ International Association of Juvenile and Family Court Magistrates / see International Association of Youth and Family Judges and Magistrates (#12283)

♦ International Association for the Karlstad Model (IAKM) 11980

Sec PPR Koge Torvet 1, 4600 Køge, Denmark.
URL: http://www.iakm.org/

History 2009. **Aims** Provide a forum for sharing information, working experience and training around the Karlstad model of language intervention for people with *language disorders*. **Structure** Board of 9. **Events** *Conference* Vaasa (Finland) 2010.
Members Full in 4 countries:
Denmark, Finland, Norway, Sweden.
[2011/XJ4528/**E**]

♦ International Association of Kinesiology (internationally oriented national body)

♦ International Association for Knowledge Management (IAKM) 11981

Contact address not obtained.
URL: http://iakm.weebly.com/

History 16 Apr 2012, Padua (Italy). **Aims** Promote the central role of knowledge and knowledge management in modern organizations; strengthen the "roots" of this field and boost the development of KM as a scientific discipline. **Structure** General Assembly; Board. **Publications** *IAKM Newsletter*.
Members Individuals. Full in 25 countries and territories:
Australia, Austria, Bosnia-Herzegovina, Bulgaria, Canada, China, Colombia, Denmark, Finland, Germany, Hong Kong, Hungary, India, Ireland, Italy, Korea Rep, Lithuania, Netherlands, Poland, Portugal, Romania, South Africa, Spain, UK, USA.
Associate in 14 countries and territories:
France, Germany, Greece, Hong Kong, India, Italy, Kenya, Morocco, Pakistan, Romania, Russia, South Africa, UK, USA.
[2021/AA1386/v/**D**]

♦ International Association Kosmopolit (inactive)
♦ International Association of Kung Fu Toa 21 (unconfirmed)

♦ International Association of Labour History Institutions (IALHI) 11982

Association internationale d'institutions d'histoire ouvrière

Contact c/o International Inst of Social History, PO Box 2169, 1000 CD Amsterdam, Netherlands. E-mail: info@ialhi.org.
URL: http://www.ialhi.org/

History 7 Dec 1970, London (UK). Constitution adopted, Barcelona (Spain), 15 Sep 1981; revised, Zurich (Switzerland), 12 Sep 1988; Copenhagen (Denmark), 24 Sep 1993. **Aims** Foster closer cooperation between member institutions; issue bibliographies and holding lists; encourage interchange of material; study labour history. **Structure** General Meeting (annual); Board; Working Groups. IALHI Foundation, set up Jan 2012. **Languages** English, French. **Staff** Part-time voluntary. **Finance** Sources: members' dues. **Activities** Events/meetings; knowledge management/information dissemination; projects/programmes. **Events** *Annual Conference* Nanterre (France) 2024, *Annual Conference* Buenos Aires (Argentina) 2023, *Annual Conference* Zurich (Switzerland) 2022, *Annual Conference* Zurich (Switzerland) 2021, *Special Conference* Amsterdam (Netherlands) 2020. **Information Services** *Labour History News Service*.
Members Libraries and archives established in organizations of the labour movement, documentation and research institutes, trade Union organizations, Socialist parties, cooperative and other organizations and individuals in 34 countries:
Argentina, Australia, Austria, Belgium, Bolivia, Brazil, Canada, Chile, Cuba, Czechia, Denmark, Finland, France, Germany, Greece, Hungary, Indonesia, Ireland, Italy, Japan, Mexico, Nepal, Netherlands, Norway, Portugal, Russia, South Africa, Spain, Sweden, Switzerland, Türkiye, UK, USA, Vietnam. [2023.02.17/XD0078/**C**]

♦ International Association of Labour Inspection (IALI) 11983

Association internationale de l'inspection du travail (AIIT) – Asociación Internacional de la Inspección de Trabajo – Internationale Vereinigung für Arbeitsinspektion – Mezdunarodnaja Associacija Inspekcii po Trudu

Secretariat c/o Ministry of Manpower, 1500 Bendemeer Rd, Singapore 339946, Singapore. T. +6566924939.
Registered Office Rue du Stand 26, 1204 Geneva, Switzerland. T. +41223278856. Fax +41223275060.
URL: http://www.iali-aiit.org/

History 20 Jun 1972, Geneva (Switzerland). Founded when Statutes were adopted. Statutes modified by the General Assemblies of: 10 May 1977; 17 Jun 1980; 22 Jun 1984; 15 Jun 1990; 7 May 2000; 19 Jun 2002; 15 Jun 2005; 11 Jun 2008. **Aims** Provide a professional foundation for building strong, modernized and effective labour inspection worldwide, principally through: development and implementation of a Global Code of Integrity for labour inspection; promotion and establishment of international labour inspectorate alliances and regional cooperation; demonstration and evaluation of the effectiveness of labour inspection and intervention techniques; provision of information and technical expertise in labour inspection; exchange of good practice and experience in the field. **Structure** General Assembly (every 3 years, at IALI Congress); Executive Committee; General Secretariat; Regional Delegates. **Languages** English, French, Spanish. **Staff** 6.00 FTE, paid. Voluntary. **Finance** Members' dues, calculated in accordance with rates agreed with membership. **Activities** Events/meetings; knowledge management/information dissemination. **Events** *General Assembly* 2021, *Workshop on International Benchmarking on OSH Regulations* Seoul (Korea Rep) 2018, *Triennial Congress and General Assembly* Geneva (Switzerland) 2017, *Triennial Congress and General Assembly* Geneva (Switzerland) 2017, *Triennial Congress and General Assembly* Geneva (Switzerland) 2014. **Publications** *IALI Forum* (annual) – newsletter. *Global Code of Integrity for Labour Inspection*; *IALI Action Plan: 2011-2014 and Beyond*; *IALI Common Principles for Labour Inspection*. Handbook; conference proceedings; reports.
Members Membership open to: national and regional labour departments (Directorates of Labour Inspection, Occupational Safety and Health Directorates, etc); national groups of labour inspectorates (associations, unions, etc). Member organizations (119) in 102 countries and territories:
Albania, Algeria, Argentina, Armenia, Australia, Austria, Azerbaijan, Barbados, Belarus, Belgium, Benin, Bosnia-Herzegovina, Botswana, Brazil, Bulgaria, Burkina Faso, Burundi, Cameroon, Canada, Central African Rep, Chad, Chile, China, Congo Brazzaville, Costa Rica, Côte d'Ivoire, Croatia, Cyprus, Czechia, Denmark, Dominican Rep, Egypt, Estonia, Fiji, Finland, France, Gabon, Georgia, Germany, Ghana, Guinea, Haiti, Hong Kong, Hungary, Iceland, Indonesia, Iran Islamic Rep, Ireland, Israel, Italy, Jamaica, Japan, Jordan, Kenya, Korea Rep, Kyrgyzstan, Latvia, Lesotho, Lithuania, Luxembourg, Macau, Malawi, Malaysia, Mali, Malta, Mauritania, Mexico, Moldova, Morocco, Namibia, Nepal, Netherlands, New Zealand, Niger, North Macedonia, Norway, Pakistan, Peru, Poland, Portugal, Romania, Russia, Senegal, Serbia, Seychelles, Singapore, Slovakia, Slovenia, Spain, Suriname, Sweden, Switzerland, Thailand, Togo, Trinidad-Tobago, Tunisia, Türkiye, Uganda, UK, Vietnam, Zambia, Zimbabwe.
Included in the above, one organization listed in this Yearbook:
African Regional Labour Administration Centre, Harare (ARLAC, #00435).
Consultative Status Consultative status granted from: *ILO (#11123)* (Special List). [2020/XD4516/y/**B**]

♦ International Association for Labour Legislation, 1889 (inactive)

♦ International Association for Ladakh Studies (IALS) 11984

Pres 2001 5-2-15 Oe, Kumamoto, 862-0971 Japan.
Sec F-2601 Palam Vihar, Gurgaon, Gurugram, Haryana 122017, Gurugram HARYANA 122017, India. E-mail: secretaryials@gmail.com.
URL: http://ladakhstudies.org/

History 1987, German DR. 1987, Herrnhut (German DR). **Aims** Increase contacts between those interested in the study of Ladakh; disseminate information on research and publications in the field. **Structure** Executive Committee, comprising President, Honorary Secretary, Honorary Treasurer and Honorary Editor. Advisory Committee. **Finance** Subscriptions. **Events** *Conference* Aberdeen (UK) 2011, *Conference* Leh (India) 2009, *Biennial Colloquium* Rome (Italy) 2007, *Conference* Rome (Italy) 2007, *Biennial colloquium / Conference* Leh (India) 2005. **Publications** *Ladakh Studies* (2 a year). Conference proceedings; special publications.
Members Individuals in 17 countries:
Austria, Belgium, Bhutan, Denmark, France, Germany, Hungary, India, Japan, Netherlands, Norway, Pakistan, Poland, Sweden, Switzerland, UK, USA.
[2010/XD8673/v/**E**]

♦ International Association of Landscape Archaeology (IALA) 11985

Sec VU – Office Research Inst CLUE+, Main Bldg – room 12A-83, De Boelelaan 1105, 1081 HV Amsterdam, Netherlands. E-mail: contact@iala-lac.org.
Pres address not obtained.
URL: https://iala-lac.org/

History 5 Jul 2017, Amsterdam (Netherlands). Founded as part for CLUE+ of the Vrije Universiteit Amsterdam (Netherlands). Built on earlier Landscape Archaeology Conferences. Current statutes adopted 2017. **Aims** Promote interdisciplinary research in the field of landscape archaeology. **Structure** General Assembly; Board; Advisory Board. **Activities** Awards/prizes/competitions; events/meetings. **Events** *Landscape Archaeology Conference* Madrid (Spain) 2021, *Landscape Archaeology Conference* Madrid (Spain) 2020, *LAC – Landscape Archaeology Conference* Durham (UK) / Newcastle upon Tyne (UK) 2018, *Landscape Archaeology Conference* Uppsala (Sweden) 2016, *Landscape Archaeology Conference* Rome (Italy) 2014. [2022/AA1871/**D**]

♦ International Association for Landscape Ecology (IALE) 11986

SG USGS Research Unit, Dept of Wildland Resources, Utah State Univ, Logan UT 84322-5230, USA. T. +14357972529. Fax +14357974025.
URL: http://www.landscape-ecology.org/

History 29 Oct 1982, Czechoslovakia. 29 Oct 1982, Piestany (Czechoslovakia), during 6th International Symposium on Problems of Landscape Ecological Research. **Aims** Further communication between scientists, organizations and planners and managers in the field of landscape ecology; advance interdisciplinary research in landscape ecology; promote development of knowledge in the field and its application and further interaction between scientists and planners. **Structure** General Assembly (every 4 years). Executive Committee, consisting of President, Past President, 4 Vice Presidents, Secretary-General, Treasurer and Bulletin Editor/Deputy Secretary-General. Council, consisting of Executive Committee, one ordinary member representing each Region, the Chairmen of Commissions and Working Groups, Honorary Members. Regions, each Region consisting of either a group of countries or of one country. Working Groups. **Languages** English. **Staff** Voluntary. **Finance** Sources: donations; grants; members' dues. Other sources: contracts. **Activities** Advocacy/lobbying/activism; events/meetings; research/documentation. **Events** *Quadrennial World Congress* Nairobi (Kenya) 2023, *Quadrennial World Congress* Milan (Italy) 2019, *Quadrennial World Congress* Portland, OR (USA) 2015, *European Urban Green Infrastructure Conference* Vienna (Austria) 2015, *European Congress* Manchester (UK) 2013. **Publications** *IALE Bulletin* (6 a year); *IALE Directory* (annual); *Landscape Ecology* – journal.

Members Regional contacts/organizations in 37 countries:
Australia, Belgium, Bulgaria, Canada, Chile, China, Colombia, Czechia, Denmark, Estonia, Finland, France, Germany, Guatemala, Hungary, India, Ireland, Italy, Japan, Latvia, Netherlands, New Zealand, Norway, Peru, Poland, Portugal, Russia, Slovakia, Slovenia, Spain, Sweden, Switzerland, Thailand, UK, Ukraine, USA, Vietnam.
Individuals in 60 countries and territories:
Argentina, Australia, Austria, Belarus, Belgium, Brazil, Bulgaria, Canada, Chile, China, Colombia, Côte d'Ivoire, Cuba, Czechia, Denmark, Estonia, Ethiopia, Finland, France, Germany, Greece, Guatemala, Hong Kong, Hungary, India, Iran Islamic Rep, Ireland, Israel, Italy, Japan, Kenya, Korea Rep, Latvia, Lithuania, Malta, Mexico, Morocco, Netherlands, New Zealand, Nigeria, Norway, Peru, Poland, Portugal, Russia, Slovakia, Slovenia, South Africa, Spain, Sweden, Switzerland, Syrian AR, Taiwan, Thailand, Uganda, UK, USA, Venezuela, Vietnam, Zimbabwe.
NGO Relations Affiliated to: *International Association for Ecology (INTECOL, #11856).* [2018/XD8540/**C**]

♦ International Association Language and Business (IALB) 11987

Association internationale langue et économie – Internationale Vereinigung Sprache und Wirtschaft

Address not obtained.
URL: https://ialb.asso-web.com/

History 1972. Registration: Germany, Nürnberg. **Aims** Improve the general level of foreign language knowledge and application of the same in trade and industry through close cooperation between trade, industry, education and research. **Structure** General Assembly (annual). Council of up to 10 members. **Languages** English, French, German. **Staff** 1.00 FTE, voluntary. **Finance** Members' dues. Conference fees. **Events** *Annual Conference* Warsaw (Poland) 2011, *Annual Conference* Lisbon (Portugal) 2010, *Annual Conference* Geneva (Switzerland) 2009, *Annual Conference* Berlin (Germany) 2008, *Annual Conference* Riga (Latvia) 2007. **Publications** Newsletter; meeting reports.

Members Full in 16 countries:
Austria, Belgium, Canada, Colombia, Denmark, Finland, France, Germany, Ireland, Italy, Japan, Netherlands, Norway, Poland, Switzerland, UK. [2012.06.01/XD7028/**D**]

♦ International Association of Language Centres (IALC) 11988

Contact 12-17 Lombard House, Upper Bridge Street, Canterbury, CT1 2NF, UK. T. +441227769007. E-mail: info@ialc.org.
URL: http://www.ialc.org/

History 1983. Registration: Companies House, No/ID: 09158586, England and Wales. **Aims** Promote cultural and professional exchange through studying modern languages in the countries where they are spoken; represent and convey professionalism and expertise in the teaching of foreign languages; protect and maintain the existence of high quality independent language schools. **Structure** General Assembly (annual); Executive Board. **Languages** English. **Staff** 4.50 FTE, paid; 5.00 FTE, voluntary. **Finance** Sources: members' dues; sponsorship. **Activities** Certification/accreditation; guidance/assistance/consulting. **Events** *Annual General Meeting and Agent Workshop* Leeds (UK) / York (UK) 2016, *Annual General Meeting and Agent Workshop* Rouen (France) 2015, *Central European Workshop* Vienna (Austria) 2015, *Annual General Meeting and Agent Workshop / Annual General Meeting* Brisbane, QLD (Australia) 2014, *Annual General Meeting and Agent Workshop / Annual General Meeting* Lisbon (Portugal) 2013. **Publications** *IALC Directory of Members.* Research reports.

Members Full; Associate. Schools (161) in 20 countries:
Argentina, Australia, Austria, Canada, China, Colombia, Ecuador, France, Germany, Ireland, Italy, Japan, Malta, New Zealand, Portugal, Russia, South Africa, Spain, UK, USA.
NGO Relations Member of: *Global Alliance of Education and Language Associations (GAELA).* [2020/XD6645/**C**]

- ♦ International Association for Language Learning Technology (internationally oriented national body)

♦ International Association for Languages and Intercultural Communication (IALIC) 11989

Sec Univ of Valencia, Fac de Filologia, Traducción y Comunicación, Avenida Blasco Ibañez 32, 46010 Valencia, Spain. T. +34963983421. Fax +34963864253.
Chair Durham Univ, School of Education, Leazes Road, Durham, DH1 1TA, UK. T. +441913348310. Fax +441913348311.
URL: http://ialic.net/

History Dec 2000, Leeds (UK). **Aims** Provide support to scholars in their academic life within the field of languages and intercultural communication; promote languages and intercultural communication as an academic field. **Structure** General Meeting (annual); Executive Committee. **Languages** English. **Staff** None. **Finance** Members' dues. **Activities** Events/meetings. **Events** *Annual Conference* Valencia (Spain) 2019, *Annual Conference* Helsinki (Finland) 2018, *Annual conference* Edinburgh (UK) 2017, *Annual Conference* Barcelona (Spain) 2016, *Annual Conference* Beijing (China) 2015. **Publications** *Language and Intercultural Communication (LAIC)* (6 a year) – journal. [2020.03.04/XM1831/**D**]

♦ International Association of Language and Social Psychology (IALSP) 11990

Pres School of Applied Psychology – Mt Gravatt Campus, Psychology Bldg M24, Room 4 17, Griffith Univ, Messines Ridge Road, Mount Gravatt QLD 4122, Australia.
URL: http://www.ialsp.org/

History 1997, Ottawa ON (Canada), during 6th annual conference. **Aims** Advance scholarship concerning the role of language in society as it relates to group and individual behaviour. **Structure** Executive Officers: President; President-Elect; Immediate Past-President; Treasurer; Officer of Records; Secretary. **Languages** English. **Staff** Voluntary. **Finance** Members' dues. **Activities** Events/meetings. *International Conference on Language and Social Psychology (ICLASP)*.. **Events** *International Conference on Language and Social Psychology* Hong Kong (Hong Kong) 2022, *Conference* Hong Kong (Hong Kong) 2020, *Conference* Edmonton, AB (Canada) 2018, *Conference* Bangkok (Thailand) 2016, *Conference* Honolulu, HI (USA) 2014. **Publications** *IALSP Newsletter.* **Members** Individuals (300) in 32 countries. Membership countries not specified. **NGO Relations** *International Communication Association (ICA, #12814).* [2020/XM3971/**F**]

- ♦ International Association of Lasallian Universities / see International Association of La Salle Universities (#12142)
- ♦ International Association for Laser and Sports Medicine (inactive)
- ♦ International Association for Latin American Air Transport / see Latin American and Caribbean Air Transport Association (#16263)
- ♦ International Association for Latin Epigraphy / see International Association for Greek and Latin Epigraphy (#11924)

♦ International Association of Law and Forensic Sciences (IALFS) ... 11991

Pres address not obtained. E-mail: info@ialfs.org.
URL: http://ialfs.org/

Aims Develop and exchange information and collaboration among forensic sciences and law experts. **Structure** Board of Directors. General Committee. Committees (8): Financial; Medical Education; Law; International Affairs; Research; Training; Ethics; Students Activities. **Events** *Annual Conference* Cairo (Egypt) 2017, *Middle East Congress* Istanbul (Turkey) 2016, *Middle East Congress* Dubai (United Arab Emirates) 2014. **NGO Relations** *Arab Union of Forensic Physicians (AUFP).* [2014/XJ7961/**C**]

♦ International Association of Law Libraries (IALL) 11992

Association internationale des bibliothèques juridiques

Sec Inst of Advanced Legal Studies, Univ of London, 17 Russell Square, London, WC1B 5DR, UK. T. +442078625822. Fax +442078625770.
Pres c/o Peace Palace Library, Carnegieplein 2, 2517 KJ The Hague, Netherlands. T. +31703024242.
URL: http://www.iall.org/

History 1959, New York NY (USA), at a meeting of law librarians held under the auspices of American Association of Law Libraries. Statutes amended in 2002; 2015. **Aims** Promote the law library profession and access to legal information. **Structure** Board of Directors. **Languages** English. **Finance** Sources: members' dues. **Activities** Events/meetings; knowledge management/information dissemination; publishing activities; training/education. **Events** *Conference* Stanford, CA (USA) 2022, *Conference* Stanford, CA (USA) 2021, *Conference* Toulouse (France) 2021, *Conference* Toulouse (France) 2020, *Law down under – Australia's Legal Landscape* Sydney, NSW (Australia) 2019. **Publications** *International Journal of Legal Information* (3 a year). Monographs; course proceedings.

Members Individual; Retired; Student. Persons interested in legal information emanating from sources other than their own jurisdictions, in 42 countries and territories:
Argentina, Australia, Austria, Belgium, Bhutan, Canada, Chile, Denmark, Finland, France, Germany, Greece, Hong Kong, Hungary, India, Ireland, Israel, Italy, Japan, Korea Rep, Luxembourg, Malaysia, Mexico, Montenegro, Netherlands, New Zealand, Norway, Papua New Guinea, Philippines, Poland, Portugal, Serbia, Singapore, South Africa, Spain, Sweden, Switzerland, Thailand, Trinidad-Tobago, Türkiye, UK, USA.
Also members in West Indies. Membership countries not specified. [2017.10.12/XC1300/**B**]

♦ International Association of Law Schools (IALS) 11993

Gen Sec/Treas c/o Cornell Law School, 124 Myron Taylor Hall, Ithaca NY 14853-4901, USA. E-mail: ials@ialsnet.org.
URL: http://www.ialsnet.org/

History Oct 2005, Washington DC (USA). **Aims** Foster mutual understanding of, and respect for, the world's varied and changing legal systems and cultures as a contribution to justice and a peaceful world; enhance and strengthen the role of law in development of societies through legal education; serve as an open and independent forum for discussion of diverse ideas about legal education; contribute to development and improvement of law schools and conditions of legal education throughout the world; contribute to better preparation of lawyers as they increasingly engage in transnational or global legal practice and when they pursue careers other than private practice, including governmental, non-governmental, academic and corporate careers; share experience and practices regarding legal education. **Events** *Global Law Deans Forum* Madrid (Spain) 2015, *Conference on labour law and labour market in the new world economy* Milan (Italy) 2010, *General Assembly* Milan (Italy) 2010, *General Assembly* Canberra, ACT (Australia) 2009, *Conference on constitutional law / Conference* Washington, DC (USA) 2009.

Members Law school deans in 17 countries:
Argentina, Australia, Belgium, Brazil, Canada, Chile, China, Ghana, India, Italy, Japan, Kuwait, Malaysia, Russia, South Africa, UK, USA.
NGO Relations *African Institute of International Law (AIIL, #00341).* [2015/XM0066/**D**]

- ♦ International Association of Lawyer Pilots (inactive)
- ♦ International Association of Lawyers (inactive)
- ♦ International Association of Lawyers (#20422)

♦ International Association of Lawyers Against Nuclear Arms (IALANA) 11994

Head Office Marienstrasse 19-20, 10117 Berlin, Germany. T. +493020654857. E-mail: mail@ialana.info.
URL: https://www.ialana.info/

History 8 Apr 1988, Stockholm (Sweden). 8-9 Apr 1988, Stockholm (Sweden), at inaugural meeting, following initiatives of USA and USSR national bodies and conference 29-31 Aug 1987. Statutes amended 18 Jan 1992, Amsterdam (Netherlands). **Aims** Work for: complete elimination of nuclear arms; prevention of nuclear war; engendering respect by all nations for international law, especially arms control treaties and other associated arrangements. Encourage the steady development of effective mechanisms for peaceful settlement of international disputes. Provide coordination among existing national and regional organizations of lawyers working for the prevention of nuclear war. **Structure** General Assembly (every 3 years). Board of Directors (meets annually) of up to 12 members, including 3 Co-Presidents, Secretary, Treasurer and Counsellor (ex officio). Executive Committee (meets at least once a year), comprising Co-Presidents, Secretary and Treasurer. UN Liaison. International Secretariat in the Hague, headed by Executive Director. **Languages** English. **Staff** 1.00 FTE, paid. **Finance** Member Organizations' dues. Other sources: voluntary contributions from individual members; donations. Annual budget: 8,000 EUR. **Activities** Events/meetings; monitoring/evaluation; publishing activities. **Events** *International medical conference on small arms, gun violence, and injury* Helsinki (Finland) 2001, *The Hague appeal for peace conference* The Hague (Netherlands) 1999, *Conference* Rome (Italy) 1998, *Arms trade* Florence (Italy) 1995, *General Assembly* Florence (Italy) 1995. **Publications** *IALANA Newsletter* (3 a year). *Security and Survival – The Case for a Nuclear Weapons Convention* (1999) by Merav Datan et al; *WHO, Nuclear Weapons and the International Court of Justice* (1994) in English, German; *Nonproliferation / Nichtweiterverbreitung von Atomwaffen – Saving NPT and Abolishing Nuclear Weapons* (1993) in English, German; *World Court Project on Nuclear Weapons and International Law* (1993) by Nicholas Grief in English, Spanish – legal memorandum, together with Nuclear Age Peace Foundation; *Towards Post-Cold War Global Security: a Legal Perspective* (1992) by Burns Weston; *Nuclear Arms and the Law – Lawyers are Uniting* (1990) in Dutch, English; *The (Il) Legality of Threat and Use of Nuclear Weapons: a Guide to the Historic Opinion of the International Court of Justice* by John Burroughs. Conference reports; congress papers; statements; press reports; memoranda, especially within the framework of the World Court Project.

Members National or regional associations of lawyers in 18 countries:
Belgium, Canada, Costa Rica, Germany, India, Italy, Japan, Netherlands, New Zealand, Norway, Poland, Russia, Spain, Sri Lanka, Sweden, Switzerland, UK, USA.
Observers in 4 countries:
Romania, South Africa, Switzerland, UK.
Included in the above, 2 organizations listed in this Yearbook:
Institute for Law and Peace, London (INLAP); International Peace Bureau.

Consultative Status Consultative status granted from: *ECOSOC (#05331)* (Special). **IGO Relations** Associated with Department of Global Communications of the United Nations. **NGO Relations** A founding organization of: *International Coalition for Nuclear Non-Proliferation and Disarmament (inactive)*, together with *International Network of Engineers and Scientists for Global Responsibility (INES, #14260)*; *International Peace Bureau (IPB, #14535)*; *International Physicians for the Prevention of Nuclear War (IPPNW, #14578)*. German office member of: *International Coalition to Ban Uranium Weapons (ICBUW, #12609)*. Instrumental in setting up: *World Court Project (WCP, inactive)*. Initiated and co-founded: *Hague Appeal for Peace (HAP, #10848)*.
[2017.10.26/XD1460/y/**C**]

- ♦ International Association of Lawyers of the Commonwealth of Independent States (inactive)
- ♦ International Association of Lawyers, Jurists and Experts in Air Law (inactive)
- ♦ International Association on Layered and Graded Materials (inactive)
- ♦ International Association for Learning Laboratories / see International Association for Language Learning Technology

♦ International Association of Legal Ethics (IAOLE) 11995

Pres c/o Univ Calgary, University Drive, Calgary AB T2N 1N4, Canada.
Sec address not obtained.
URL: http://www.iaole.org/

History Proposed 2010, Stanford CA (USA), at 4th International Legal Ethics Conference (ILEC). **Aims** Promote teaching, research, vocational training programmes and policy initiatives concerning legal ethics. **Structure** Steering Committee. **Events** *International Legal Ethics Conference* New York, NY (USA) 2016, *International Legal Ethics Conference* London (UK) 2014, *International Legal Ethics Conference* Banff, AB (Canada) 2012, *International Legal Ethics Conference* Banff, AB (Canada) 2012, *International Legal Ethics Conference* Stanford, CA (USA) 2010. **Members** Individuals. Membership countries not specified.
[2018.09.22/XM4466/**C**]

♦ International Association of Legal Methodology 11996

Association internationale de méthodologie juridique

Pres Fac de droit, Bureau A9-211, Pavillon Albert-Leblanc, Univ de Sherbrooke, 2500 blv Université, Sherbrooke QC J1K 2R1, Canada. T. +18198218000ext65023. Fax +18198217578.

History Founded 7 Jan 1986. **Events** *International Congress* Geneva (Switzerland) 2014, *La sécurité juridique* Québec, QC (Canada) 2007, *International Congress* Sherbrooke, QC (Canada) 2007, *Congress / International Congress* Aix-en-Provence (France) 2003, *The recourse to the objectives of the law for its application* Louvain-la-Neuve (Belgium) 1990.
Members National committees in 21 countries:
Argentina, Belgium, Brazil, Canada, Finland, France, Germany, Greece, Italy, Japan, Morocco, Poland, Puerto Rico, Romania, Spain, Switzerland, Tunisia, UK, Uruguay, USA, Venezuela. [2014/XD2051/**D**]

- ♦ International Association of Legal Protection Insurance / see Legal Protection International (#16440)
- ♦ International Association for the Legal Protection of Workers, 1901 (inactive)
- ♦ International Association of Legal Research and Investigators (no recent information)

♦ International Association of Legal Science (IALS) 11997

Association internationale des sciences juridiques (AISJ) – Asociación Internacional de Ciencias Juridicas – Internationaler Verband für Rechtswissenschaft – Mezdunarodnaja Associacija Juridiceskih Nauk

SG Maastricht Univ, Fac of Law, PO Box 616, 6200 MD Maastricht, Netherlands. T. +31135400620. Fax +31433884907. E-mail: secretary-general@aisj-ials.net – info@aisj-ials.net.
URL: http://www.aisj-ials.net/

History 19 Jul 1950, London (UK). Founded under the auspices of *UNESCO (#20322)*. Enlarged Mar 1955. Former names and other names: *International Committee of Comparative Law* – former (1950 to 1955); *Comité international de droit comparé (CIDC)* – former (1950 to 1955). Registration: France. **Aims** Foster development of legal science worldwide through study of foreign law and use of the comparative method; assist international exchange and meetings among jurists and access to legal sources, publications and documents; encourage development in every country of institutions devoted to the study of *law* and comparative law, and stimulate their creation in countries where they do not exist. **Structure** Council; *International Committee of Comparative Law (CIDC)*, functioning as Executive Board. **Languages** English, French. **Staff** 2.00 FTE, voluntary. **Finance** Sources: members' dues. **Activities** Active in all member countries. **Events** *Comparative Law and the Covid-19 Pandemic* Maastricht (Netherlands) 2021, *Symposium on Law and Language* Maastricht (Netherlands) 2019, *Globalisation and private international law* St Petersburg (Russia) 2017, *Legislators, Judges, and Profesors* Hamburg (Germany) 2015, *Conference on Legal Pluralism* Turin (Italy) 2014. **Publications** *Comparative Perspectives on Law and Language* (2022) by Agustín Parise and Olivier Moréteau; *Globalisation and Private International Law* (2019) by Dr Agustin Parise and Prof Evgeny Popov in English – proceedings of the 2017 annual symposium of the International Association of Legal Science (IALS) hosted by the Russian Academy of Legal Sciences (RALS); *Association internationale des sciences juridiques/International Association of Legal Science* – booklet; *Catalogue des sources de documentation juridique dans le monde*; *International Encyclopedia of Comparative Law*; *Legal Education in Africa, South of the Sahara*; *Manual on Environmental Legislation*.
Members National Committees in 30 countries:
Argentina, Australia, Austria, Brazil, Canada, China, Colombia, Czechia, Denmark, Finland, France, Germany, Greece, Israel, Italy, Japan, Lebanon, Luxembourg, Mexico, Netherlands, Norway, Romania, Russia, South Africa, Spain, Sweden, Switzerland, Türkiye, USA, Uzbekistan.
Associate members (6):
Centre de droit de la famille, Louvain-la-Neuve (Belgium); *European Consortium for Church and State Research (#06752)*; *Institut de droit européen (no recent information)*; *International Association of Penal Law (IAPL, #12074)*; *International Society for Labour and Social Security Law (ISLSSL, #15226)*; *International Union of Anthropological and Ethnological Sciences (IUAES, #15755)* (Commission on Legal Pluralism).
IGO Relations Observer status with (2): *International Institute for the Unification of Private Law (UNIDROIT, #13934)*; *United Nations Commission on International Trade Law (UNCITRAL, #20531)*. Cooperates with (2): *FAO (#09260)*; *UNEP (#20299)*. **NGO Relations** Member of (2): *International Science Council (ISC, #14796)*; *ISC World Data System (ISC-WDS, #16024)*. [2022.10.21/XA1302/y/**C**]

♦ International Association of Legislation (IAL) 11998

Internationale Gesellschaft für Gesetzgebung

Pres UCL Fac of Laws, 4-8 Endsleigh Gardens, London, WC1H 0EG, UK. T. +442031088410.
Treas Fac of Law – Univ of Stockholm, Stockholm Ctr for Commercial Law, SE-106 91 Stockholm, Sweden. T. +4608162241.
URL: http://www.ial-online.org/

History 1991, Bad Homburg (Germany), as *European Association of Legislation (EAL) – Europäische Gesellschaft für Gesetzgebung*. **Aims** Promote study of legislation and law-making; enhance quality of legislation at municipal, national, EU and international legislative arenas. **Structure** General Assembly (every 2 years); Board; Advisory Council. **Languages** English, French, German. **Staff** 1.50 FTE, paid. **Finance** Sources: members' dues. Annual budget: 3,000 EUR. **Activities** Events/meetings; knowledge management/information dissemination; publishing activities; training/education. **Events** *Conference* Athens (Greece) 2021, *Conference* Zurich (Switzerland) 2021, *Conference* Rome (Italy) 2019, *Conference* Antwerp (Belgium) 2018, *International Conference* Seoul (Korea Rep) 2017. **Publications** *Legislation in Europe: A Handbook for Scholars and Practitioners* (2017) by Ulrich Karpen and Helen Xanthaki (eds). Information Services: Online information and legislative studies news. **Members** Associations. Membership countries not specified. **IGO Relations** *Council of Europe (CE, #04881)*; *European Parliament (EP, #08146)*; national executives; national parliaments. **NGO Relations** *Commonwealth Association of Legislative Counsel (CALC, #04304)*; Korean Institute for Legislative Research; national branches of IAL. [2021/XU5985/**C**]

- ♦ International Association of Lesbian, Gay, Bisexual and Transgender Pride Coordinators / see InterPride (#15965)
- ♦ International Association of Lesbian and Gay Pride Coordinators / see InterPride (#15965)
- ♦ International Association for Liberal Christianity and Religious Freedom / see International Association for Religious Freedom (#12130)

♦ International Association of Liberal Religious Women (IALRW) 11999

Union internationale des femmes libérales chrétiennes (UFLC)

Contact Dornacherstrasse 286, 4053 Basel BS, Switzerland.
Pres address not obtained.
Main Website: https://ialrw.org

History Aug 1910, Berlin (Germany). Formally organized 1913, Paris (France). Former names and other names: *International Union of Liberal Christian Women (IULCW)* – former (1913 to 1975). **Aims** Promote a link between liberal religious women throughout the world, including groups and individuals; promote friendship and cooperation among such women individually and in organized groups in all countries; open and maintain communications with women who are striving for a liberal religious life. **Structure** Conference (every 3 to 4 years) elects Officers. **Languages** English, Japanese. **Staff** None. **Finance** Sources: meeting proceeds; members' dues. **Activities** Events/meetings; projects/programmes. **Events** *Conference* Washington, DC (USA) 2018, *Conference* Birmingham (UK) 2014, *Conference* Kochi (India) 2010, *Conference* Kaohsiung (Taiwan) 2006, *Conference* Budapest (Hungary) 2002. **Publications** *IALRW Newsletter* (annual). Questionnaires for discussion; articles.
Members National organizations and Groups; Individuals (about 2,000) in 28 countries and territories:
Australia, Austria, Belgium, Canada, China, Czechia, France, Germany, Hungary, India, Ireland, Japan, Korea Rep, Malaysia, Mexico, Mongolia, Nepal, Netherlands, New Zealand, Nigeria, Philippines, Romania, Singapore, Slovakia, Switzerland, Taiwan, UK, USA.
NGO Relations Member of (1): *International Association for Religious Freedom (IARF, #12130)*.
[2021.07.01/XC2735/**D**]

- ♦ International Association of Libraries and Museums of the Performing Arts (#19475)
- ♦ International Association of Library Centres (inactive)

♦ International Association for Lichenology (IAL) 12000

Sec c/o Dept of Life Sciences, Univ of Trieste, via L Giorgieri 10, 34127 Trieste TS, Italy.
Pres Dept of Biology, Duke Univ, Box 90338, Durham NC 27708, USA.
URL: http://www.lichenology.org/

History 1969, Seattle, WA (USA). Conceived 1967; officially launched 1969, at Botanical Congress. **Aims** Promote study and conservation of lichens. **Structure** General Meeting (every 4 years, during Congress); Council; Nominating Committee; Communications Committee; Inclusion, Diversity, Equity, and Access (IDEA) Committee. **Languages** English. **Staff** 9.00 FTE, voluntary. **Finance** Sources: donations; members' dues. **Activities** Awards/prizes/competitions; events/meetings. **Events** *Symposium* Bonito (Brazil) 2021, *Symposium* Bonito (Brazil) 2020, *Symposium* Helsinki (Finland) 2016, *Symposium* Bangkok (Thailand) 2012, *Symposium* Monterey, CA (USA) 2008. **Publications** *IAL Newsletter* (2 a year). **Members** Full (308) in over 60 countries. Membership countries not specified. **NGO Relations** Member of (3): *International Association of Botanical and Mycological Societies (IABMS, #11730)*; *International Botanical Congress (IBC)*; *International Union of Biological Sciences (IUBS, #15760)*. [2022.05.25/XD4571/**D**]

♦ International Association for Life-Cycle Civil Engineering (IALCCE) . 12001

SG Dept Civil/Environmental Engineering, Politecnico di Milano, Piazza L da Vinci 32, 20133 Milan MI, Italy. T. +39223994394. Fax +39223994220.
Pres Dept of Civil and Environmental Engineering, ATLSS Ctr – Lehigh Univ, Imbt Labs, 117 ATLSS Drive, Bethlehem PA 18015-4729, USA. T. +16107586103 – +16107586123. Fax +16107584115 – +16107585553.
URL: http://www.ialcce.org/

History 2006. **Aims** Become the premier international organization for advancement of state-of-the-art in the field of life-cycle civil engineering; promote international cooperation in the field of life-cycle civil engineering to enhance the welfare of society. **Structure** Executive Board. **Events** *International Symposium* Shanghai (China) 2020, *International Symposium* Ghent (Belgium) 2018, *International Symposium* Delft (Netherlands) 2016, *International Symposium / Symposium* Tokyo (Japan) 2014, *International Symposium / Symposium* Vienna (Austria) 2012. **Publications** *Structure and Infrastructure Engineering – Maintenance, Management and Life-Cycle Design and Performance* – scientific journal. Proceedings.
Members Individuals (418) in 52 countries and territories:
Algeria, Australia, Austria, Bangladesh, Belgium, Brazil, Canada, China, Colombia, Croatia, Czechia, Denmark, Finland, France, Germany, Greece, Hong Kong, India, Indonesia, Iran Islamic Rep, Ireland, Israel, Italy, Japan, Korea Rep, Kosovo, Lebanon, Malaysia, Malta, Mexico, Netherlands, New Zealand, Nigeria, North Macedonia, Norway, Pakistan, Palestine, Poland, Portugal, Qatar, Romania, South Africa, Spain, Sweden, Switzerland, Taiwan, Thailand, Türkiye, UK, United Arab Emirates, USA, Vietnam.
Collective (20) in 12 countries:
Austria, Brazil, China, Czechia, Germany, Italy, Korea Rep, Netherlands, Romania, Spain, UK, USA. [2021/XJ1034/**C**]

- ♦ International Association of Lighthouse Authorities / see International Association of Marine Aids to Navigation and Lighthouse Authorities (#12013)
- ♦ International Association of Lighting Designers (internationally oriented national body)
- ♦ International Association of Lighting Management Companies (internationally oriented national body)
- ♦ International Association of Lightning Maintenance Companies / see International Association of Lighting Management Companies
- ♦ International Association of Linear Garden Cities (inactive)

♦ International Association of Linguistics Students (IALS) 12002

Association internationale des étudiants linguistiques – Asociación Internacional de Estudiantes de Lingüística – Internationale Assoziation für Linguistikstudenten

Contact address not obtained. E-mail: ials.linguistics@gmail.com.
URL: https://linguisticsstudents.wordpress.com/

History Jan 2011, Edinburgh (UK). Founded as an online organisation. Revived after a six year period of dormancy. **Aims** Provide a forum for a linguistics students' community; be a central hub for national and university student associations; bridge the gap between academic societies, universities, and students. **Structure** Committee. Director. **Staff** 0.50 FTE, paid. Voluntary. **Finance** Donations.
Members Organizations in 4 countries:
Australia, Germany, UK, USA. [2015/XJ4444/**F**]

- ♦ International Association of Lions Clubs / see Lions Clubs International (#16485)
- ♦ International Association of Literary Critics / see Association internationale de la critique littéraire (#02679)

♦ International Association for Literary Journalism Studies (IALJS) . . 12003

Sec Kent State Univ School of Journalism and Mass Communication, PO Box 5190, Kent OH 44242, USA. T. +13306728285. Fax +13306724064.
Pres Univ of St Thomas, Dept of Communication and Journalism, 2115 Summit Ave, St Paul MN 55105, USA. T. +16514978887.
URL: http://www.ialjs.org/

History 14 Jul 2006. Founded following 1st International Conference on Literary Journalism, Nancy (France). **Aims** Improve scholarly research and education in Literary Journalism and Reportage. **Structure** Officers (7). **Finance** Sources: members' dues. **Events** *International Conference for Literary Journalism Studies* Santiago (Chile) 2022, *International Conference for Literary Journalism Studies* Copenhagen (Denmark) 2021, *International Conference* Copenhagen (Denmark) 2020, *International Conference* Stony Brook, NY (USA) 2019, *International Conference* Vienna (Austria) 2018. **Publications** *IALJS Newsletter* (2 a year); *LJS Journal* (2 a year). **Members** Individuals (147) in 27 countries. Membership countries not specified.
[2019.02.14/XJ7883/**C**]

♦ International Association of Literary Semantics (IALS) 12004

Pres School of European Culture, Univ of Kent, Canterbury, CT2 7NZ, UK.
URL: http://literarysemantics.wordpress.com/

History Founded 1990, Canterbury (UK). **Aims** Support the exchange of ideas among academics and scholars who are interested in advancing the understanding of the bases of literary meaning. **Structure** Executive Committee of 7 members; Board. **Languages** English. **Activities** Events/meetings. Loosely associated with the *'Journal of Literary Semantics'*. **Events** *Conference* Vilnius (Lithuania) 2021, *Symposium* Krakow (Poland) 2018, *Conference* Huddersfield (UK) 2017, *Literary semantics – past, present, future?* Canterbury (UK) 2014, *Conference* Genoa (Italy) 2010.

Members Individuals from a variety of disciplines, but chiefly linguistics, literary studies, philosophy and psychology, and use a range of theoretical perspectives and empirical methods. Members in 48 countries and territories:
Algeria, Argentina, Australia, Austria, Brazil, Cameroon, Canada, China, Czechia, Denmark, Ecuador, Finland, France, Germany, Greece, Hong Kong, Hungary, India, Indonesia, Iran Islamic Rep, Iraq, Ireland, Israel, Italy, Japan, Jordan, Luxembourg, Malaysia, Netherlands, New Zealand, Pakistan, Philippines, Poland, Portugal, Puerto Rico, Russia, Singapore, South Africa, Spain, Sri Lanka, Sweden, Switzerland, Thailand, Türkiye, UK, Ukraine, USA, Yemen.
NGO Relations Cooperates with: *Poetics and Linguistics Association (PALA).* [2018/XD5761/v/**D**]

♦ International Association of Logopedics and Phoniatrics (IALP) . . . 12005

CEO 32 Fl 1 Francesco Buhagiar St, Birkirkara, BKR 1151, Malta. E-mail: office@ialp.info – ceo@ialp.info.
Pres Seton Hall University, South Orange, New Jersey, New York NY 07079, USA.
URL: http://www.ialp.info/

History 1924, Vienna (Austria). Most recent statutes adopted Aug 2022. Former names and other names: *Association internationale de logopédie et phoniatrie* – former; *Asociación Internacional de Logopedia y Foniatria* – former; *Internationale Gesellschaft für Logopädie und Phoniatrie* – former. Registration: Malta Business Registry, No/ID: LPA-154, Start date: 11 Nov 2021, Malta. **Aims** Improve the quality of life of individuals with disorders of communication, speech, language, voice, hearing and swallowing. **Structure** General Assembly (annual); International Board of Directors; Standing Committees (14). **Languages** English. **Staff** Voluntary. **Finance** Sources: meeting proceeds; members' dues. **Activities** Guidance/assistance/consulting; research and development; training/education. **Events** *Triennial Congress* Tel Aviv (Israel) 2025, *Triennial Congress* Auckland (New Zealand) 2023, *Triennial Congress* Taipei (Taiwan) 2019, *Triennial Congress* Dublin (Ireland) 2016, *Triennial Congress* Turin (Italy) 2013. **Publications** *Folia Phoniatrica et Logopedica* (6 a year). Congress reports.
Members Affiliated Organizations and Individual Members in 52 countries and territories:
Australia, Austria, Belgium, Brazil, Bulgaria, Canada, Chile, China, Croatia, Cyprus, Czechia, Denmark, Egypt, Finland, France, Germany, Greece, Hong Kong, Hungary, Iceland, India, Indonesia, Ireland, Israel, Italy, Japan, Korea Rep, Kuwait, Lithuania, Macau, Malaysia, Malta, Netherlands, New Zealand, Norway, Peru, Philippines, Poland, Portugal, Romania, Russia, Saudi Arabia, Singapore, Slovenia, South Africa, Spain, Sweden, Switzerland, Taiwan, UK, United Arab Emirates, USA.
Consultative Status Consultative status granted from: *ECOSOC (#05331)* (Ros C); *WHO (#20950)* (Official Relations); *UNICEF (#20332).* **IGO Relations** Accredited by (1): *United Nations Office at Vienna (UNOV, #20604).* Associated with Department of Global Communications of the United Nations. **NGO Relations** Memorandum of Understanding with (2): European Speech-Language Therapy Association (ESLA); *World Federation for NeuroRehabilitation (WFNR, #21464).* Member of (2): *Hearing International (#10895); NGO Committee on UNICEF (#17120).* [2022.10.28/XC1306/**C**]

♦ International Association of Lusitanists 12006

Associação Internacional de Lusitanistas (AIL)
SG Fac de Letras, Univ de Coimbra, CODEX, 3000-447 Coimbra, Portugal. T. +351239410088. Fax +351239410088. E-mail: secretaria@lusitanistasail.org.
URL: http://www.lusitanistasail.org/

Events *Congress* Rome (Italy) 2021, *Congress* Mindelo (Cape Verde) 2014, *Congress* Faro (Portugal) 2011, *Congress* Funchal (Portugal) 2008, *Congress* Santiago de Compostela (Spain) 2005. [2021/XG6552/**D**]

♦ International Association of Lyceum Clubs (IALC) 12007

Association internationale des Lyceum Clubs
Intl Pres address not obtained.
Intl Sec address not obtained.
URL: http://www.lyceumclubs.org/

History 1903, London (UK). First Lyceum Club having been formed in 1903. Current Rules and Regulations adopted 20 May 2007, Lyon (France); came into force 1 Jul 2007. Rules and regulations modified and entered into force, 8 May 2013. Registration: Switzerland. **Aims** Develop and enhance the spirit of international *friendship* and *understanding* among Lyceum Clubs worldwide; promote formation of Lyceum Clubs grouping *women* of all nations who are dedicated to or actively interested in arts, sciences, social concerns and pursuit of lifelong learning; nurture an environment of openness, discussion and exchange among Clubs; act as a catalyst for inter-Federation and inter-Club contact, thus promoting the international spirit of Lyceum and contributing to intellectual, artistic and social enrichment of individual Clubs and their members. **Structure** International Council (meeting every 3 years at Congress); International Central Bureau (BCI). **Languages** English, French, German. **Finance** Sources: donations; members' dues. **Activities** Events/meetings. **Events** *Triennial Congress* Tauranga (New Zealand) 2025, *Triennial Congress* Rabat (Morocco) 2022, *Triennial Congress* Stockholm (Sweden) 2019, *Triennial Congress* Amsterdam (Netherlands) 2016, *Triennial Congress* Perth, WA (Australia) 2013. **Publications** *International Bulletin* (2 a year).
Members National federations (17) covering 74 active Lyceum Clubs in 17 countries:
Australia, Austria, Belgium, Cyprus, Finland, France, Germany, Greece, Italy, Netherlands, New Zealand, Portugal, Russia, Sweden, Switzerland, UK, USA.
NGO Relations Member of (1): *Federation of International Women's Associations in London (FIWAL).* [2022/XD3651/**C**]

♦ International Association for Machine Translation (IAMT) 12008

Sec Univ of Sheffield, Western Bank, Sheffield, S10 2TN, UK.
Pres address not obtained.
URL: http://www.eamt.org/iamt.php

History 1992. Registered in accordance with the laws of the District of Columbia (USA). **Aims** Bring together users, developers and researchers of automated translation technology. **Structure** General Assembly; Council; Executive Committee; Office, headed by representative organizing next Summit conference. **Languages** English. **Staff** None. **Finance** Sources: members' dues. **Events** *Biennial Machine Translation Summit* Dublin (Ireland) 2019, *Biennial Machine Translation Summit* Nagoya (Japan) 2017, *Annual Conference* Riga (Latvia) 2016, *Biennial Machine Translation Summit* Miami, FL (USA) 2015, *Biennial Machine Translation Summit* Xiamen (China) 2011.
Members Regional organizations (3):
Asia-Pacific Association for Machine Translation (AAMT, #01845); Association for Machine Translation in the Americas (AMTA); European Association for Machine Translation (EAMT, #06115). [2019/XD6308/y/**C**]

♦ International Association of Machinists / see International Association of Machinists and Aerospace Workers
♦ International Association of Machinists and Aerospace Workers (internationally oriented national body)
♦ International Association of Magnetic and Optical Media Manufacturers and Related Industries / see Content Delivery and Storage Association (#04779)

♦ International Association of Management, Spirituality & Religion (IAMSR) 12009

Founder address not obtained. E-mail: info@www.iamsr.org.
URL: https://www.iamsr.org/

History 2010. Founded by Yochanan Altman, bringing together the Journal of Management, Spirituality & Religion (JMSR) – founded 2002 – and the biennial conferences and workshops held worldwide. **Aims** Initiate, facilitate, produce and deliver academic and evidence-based knowledge on the role and place of spirituality in today's world of work. **Structure** Board. **Activities** Events/meetings. **Events** *Conference* Vienna (Austria) 2022, *Conference* Vienna (Austria) 2020, *Conference* Fayetteville, AR (USA) 2017. **Publications** *Journal of Management, Spirituality and Religion (JMSR). Management, Spirituality & Religion.* [2022/AA2950/**C**]

♦ International Association for Management of Technology (IAMOT) . 12010

Main Office College of Engineering, PO Box 248294, Coral Gables FL 33124, USA. T. +13052842344. Fax +13052844040. E-mail: iamot@miami.edu.
URL: http://www.iamot.com/

History 1992, Miami FL (USA). **Aims** Encourage education and act as an information resource centre in the field of Management of Technology. **Structure** Executive Council, comprising President, President-Elect, Secretary, Treasurer, 3 Directors and Immediate Past President. Standing Committees (10): International Advisory; Scientific; Meetings; Membership; Publications; Nominating; Education; Issues of Developing Countries; Industry Liaison; Committee Awards. **Finance** Members' dues. Other sources: conference proceeds; legacies; gifts; interest income from investment of reserves. **Activities** Sponsors and co-sponsors international conferences on Management of Technology and other relevant conferences; supports research and application projects world-wide, either in cooperation with government of private organizations or on its own initiative; exchanges information with other individuals and organizations; establishes research priorities in the field on the basis of current and future needs. **Events** *Annual Conference* Nancy (France) 2022, *Annual Conference* Alexandria (Egypt) 2021, *Annual Conference* Cairo (Egypt) 2020, *Annual Conference* Mumbai (India) 2019, *Annual Conference* Birmingham (UK) 2018. **Publications** *IAMOT News.* Conference proceedings. Information Services: Message board; website searches.
Members Full; Associate; Student; Honorary. Associations, research institutes, universities, industries in 22 countries and territories:
Australia, Belgium, Brazil, Canada, Finland, France, Germany, Hong Kong, Hungary, Israel, Japan, Korea Rep, Mexico, New Zealand, Nigeria, Singapore, Sweden, Switzerland, Taiwan, Türkiye, UK, USA. [2014/XF3897/**F**]

♦ International Association of Manichaean Studies (IAMS) 12011

Sec Dept of Ancient History, Macquarie University, Sydney NSW 2109, Australia.
Pres School Culture and Society – Church History/Practical Theology, Aarhus University, Jens Chr Skous Vej 3 – bldg 1421, 8000 Aarhus C, Denmark.
URL: http://www.manichaeism.de/

History Founded Aug 1987, Lund (Sweden), during 1st International Conference of Manichaean Studies. **Aims** Promote the study of Manichaeism. **Structure** Board. **Languages** English, French, German. **Finance** Sources: members' dues. **Activities** Events/meetings. **Events** *Conference* Aarhus (Denmark) 2022, *Conference* Aarhus (Denmark) 2021, *Conference* Turin (Italy) 2017, *Conference* London (UK) 2013, *Conference* Dublin (Ireland) 2009. **Publications** *Manichaean Studies Newsletter* (annual).
Members in 24 countries:
Australia, Austria, Belgium, Canada, China, Czechia, Denmark, Finland, France, Germany, Greece, Hungary, Iran Islamic Rep, Italy, Japan, Netherlands, Norway, Russia, Spain, Sweden, Switzerland, Türkiye, UK, USA. [2017.10.21/XD7177/**C**]

♦ International Association of Margaret Morris Method (MMM) 12012

Association internationale pour la méthode Margaret Morris
Admin Brook Cottage, Buildwas, TF8 7DA, UK. T. +441952433738. E-mail: admin@margaretmorrismovement.com.
URL: http://www.margaretmorrismovement.com/

History 1939, Glasgow (UK). Registered in Edinburgh (UK) according to UK law. **Aims** Promote the system of movement, *exercises* and *recreational dance* evolved by Margaret Morris and known as *'Margaret Morris Movement'.* **Structure** Board of Directors, comprising Chairman and 9 members. **Languages** English, French. **Finance** Receives annual grant from MMM Movement Therapy. **Activities** Events/meetings. **Events** *Annual Congress* Chichester (UK) 2011, *Annual Congress* Chichester (UK) 2010, *Annual Congress* Chichester (UK) 2009, *Annual Congress* Chichester (UK) 2008, *Annual Congress* Roehampton (UK) 2007. **Publications** *MMM Bulletin* (2 a year); *MMM Magazine* (2 a year); *MMM Newsletter* (2 a year). Text books; records; CDs; DVDs.
Members Individuals (ordinary, associate, class, registered teacher) represented in 12 countries:
Australia, Canada, France, Germany, Japan, Malta, South Africa, Spain, Sweden, Switzerland, UK, USA. [2020/XE0643/v/**E**]

♦ International Association of Marine Aids to Navigation and Lighthouse Authorities (IALA) 12013

Association internationale de signalisation maritime (AISM) – Asociación Internacional de Señalización Maritima
Main Office 10 rue des Gaudines, 78100 Saint-Germain-en-Laye, France. T. +33134517001. Fax +33134518205. E-mail: contact@iala-aism.org.
URL: http://www.iala-aism.org/

History 1 Jul 1957, as *International Association of Lighthouse Authorities – Association internationale de signalisation maritime,* on approval by 20 countries of Constitution drafted after 5th Conference on Lighthouses and other Aids to Navigation, 1955, Scheveningen (Netherlands). Most recent Constitution adopted 27 May 2014, La Coruña (Spain). In 2013, initiated process to begin status change to an IGO; process is ongoing as of 2020. **Aims** Foster safe, economic and efficient movement of vessels by improving and harmonizing aids to navigation worldwide and by other appropriate means, for the benefit of the maritime community and protection of the environment; encourage, support and communicate recent developments; develop international cooperation by promoting close working relationships and assistance among members; enhance mutual exchange of information with organizations representing users of aids to navigation. **Structure** General Assembly (every 4 years, usually during Conference); Council; Committees (4); Ad-hoc Council Working Groups; Policy Advisory Panel; Technical Committees (4); Heritage Forum; Secretariat. **Languages** English, French. **Staff** 8.00 FTE, paid. **Finance** Sources: gifts, legacies; grants; members' dues. **Activities** Capacity building; events/meetings; guidance/assistance/consulting; knowledge management/information dissemination; standards/guidelines; training/education. **Events** *Marine Aids to Navigation – Innovation for a Sustainable Future* Rio de Janeiro (Brazil) 2023, *International Vessel Traffic Services Symposium* Rotterdam (Netherlands) 2021, *Digital@Sea Asia-Pacific Conference* Sejong (Korea Rep) 2021, *International Vessel Traffic Services Symposium* Rotterdam (Netherlands) 2020, *E-Navigation Underway Asia Pacific Conference* Seoul (Korea Rep) 2019. **Publications** *IALA Bulletin* (4 a year) in English, French, Spanish. *IALA 1957-1990: 33 Years of International Cooperation* by Ville; *International Cooperation in Aids to Navigation 1989-1985* by Dr G Wiedmann; *International Dictionary of Aids to Marine Navigation* in English, French, German, Spanish. Recommendations; guidelines; manuals; lists of radionavigation services; specifications; practical notes; reports; proceedings.
Members National; Associate; Industrial; Honorary. Members in 80 countries and territories:
Algeria, Argentina, Australia, Austria, Bahrain, Belgium, Benin, Bermuda, Brazil, Bulgaria, Cameroon, Canada, Chile, China, Colombia, Congo Brazzaville, Côte d'Ivoire, Croatia, Cuba, Czechia, Denmark, Djibouti, Ecuador, Egypt, Estonia, Fiji, Finland, France, Gabon, Germany, Greece, Guinea, Hong Kong, Iceland, India, Indonesia, Iran Islamic Rep, Iraq, Ireland, Israel, Italy, Jamaica, Japan, Kenya, Korea Rep, Kuwait, Latvia, Malaysia, Malta, Mexico, Mozambique, Netherlands, New Zealand, Nigeria, Norway, Oman, Panama, Papua New Guinea, Peru, Philippines, Poland, Portugal, Romania, Russia, Senegal, Singapore, South Africa, Spain, Sweden, Tanzania UR, Thailand, Tunisia, Türkiye, UK, Ukraine, United Arab Emirates, Uruguay, USA, Venezuela, Vietnam.
Consultative Status Consultative status granted from: *International Maritime Organization (IMO, #14102).* **IGO Relations** Working relations with: *International Telecommunication Union (ITU, #15673),* especially its Radiocommunication Sector. Cooperates with: *International Hydrographic Organization (IHO, #13825).* **NGO Relations** Working relations with: *International Association of Institutes of Navigation (IAIN, #11965).* In liaison with technical committees of: *International Organization for Standardization (ISO, #14473).* Observer of: *Asia-Pacific Heads of Maritime Safety Agencies (APHoMSA, #01922).* [2021/XB1303/**B**]

♦ International Association for Marine Electronics Companies (#04186)
♦ International Association of Marine Investigators (internationally oriented national body)
♦ International Association of Marine Radio Interests (inactive)
♦ International Association of Marine Science Libraries and Information Centers / see International Association of Aquatic and Marine Science Libraries and Information Centers (#11707)

♦ International Association of Maritime Economists (IAME) 12014

Sec Texas A&M Univ at Galveston, Dept. of Maritime Administration, 1001 Texas Clipper Road, Galveston TX 77554, USA. T. +14097404451. E-mail: iame-info@tamug.edu.
Pres Univ of Athens, Athens 157 72, 157 72 Athens, Greece. T. +302107277000. Fax +302107277000.
URL: http://www.mar-economists.org/

History Jun 1991, Rotterdam (Netherlands). **Aims** Promote development of maritime economics as a distinct discipline, encourage rational and reasoned discussion within it; facilitate international exchange of ideas and research. **Structure** Annual Conference; General Meeting (every 2 years); Council. **Languages** English. **Staff** 1.00 FTE, paid. **Finance** Sources: members' dues. **Events** *Annual Conference* Busan (Korea Rep) 2022, *Annual Conference* Rotterdam (Netherlands) 2021, *Annual Conference* Hong Kong (Hong Kong) 2020, *Annual Conference* Athens (Greece) 2019, *Annual Conference* Mombasa (Kenya) 2018. **Publications** *IAME*

Newsletter – electronic; *Maritime Economics and Logistics* – journal; *Maritime Policy and Management* – journal. **Members** Individual; Corporate; Student; Retired. Individuals (about 300) in 35 countries. Membership countries not specified. [2022.05.11/XD9049/v/**D**]

♦ International Association of Maritime Institutions (IAMI) 12015

Hon Gen Sec c/o Bilbeck Bus Serv, 19 Janson Road, Southampton, SO15 5FU, UK. T. +441914474160.
Chair address not obtained.
URL: http://www.iami.info/

History 1993. Founded by merger of (UK) Association of Marine Engineering Schools and *International Association of Navigation Schools (inactive)*. **Aims** Promote education and training of all *seafarers* and students in related disciplines; provide a forum for discussion and information exchange across the field of maritime education; provide examination and assessment services to industry and maritime regulators. **Structure** General Meeting (annual, in May); Board of Directors; Specialist Sub-Committees (4): Navigation, Marine Engineering, Restricted Certification (small vessels), Marine Hospitality. **Languages** English. **Staff** 38.00 FTE, paid. **Finance** Sources: fees for services; members' dues. **Activities** Certification/accreditation; events/meetings; standards/guidelines; training/education. **Members** Full; Associate. Members in 18 countries. Membership countries not specified. **NGO Relations** Member of (1): UK Maritime Skills Alliance (MSA). [2022.04.20/XD4303/**D**]

♦ International Association of Maritime Universities (IAMU) 12016

Contact Meiwa Bldg 8F, 1-15-10 Toranomon, Minato-ku, Tokyo, 105-0001 Japan. E-mail: info@iamu-edu.org.
URL: http://www.iamu-edu.org/

History 12 Nov 1999, Istanbul (Turkey), by 7 universities. **Aims** Develop a comprehensive maritime education system for following generations; establish and effective maritime safety management system for the international maritime community; prepare and develop standardized undergraduate curricula and an international system for competency. **Structure** General Assembly (annual); International Executive Board; Standing Committees; Secretariat. **Languages** English. **Events** *Annual General Assembly* Batumi (Georgia) 2022, *Annual General Assembly* Alexandria (Egypt) 2021, *Annual General Assembly* Tokyo (Japan) 2019, *Annual General Assembly* Barcelona (Spain) 2018, *Annual General Assembly* Varna (Bulgaria) 2017.
Members Institutions (60) in 23 countries:
Australia, Bulgaria, Canada, China, Croatia, Egypt, Finland, France, Germany, Iran Islamic Rep, Japan, Korea Rep, Netherlands, Poland, Romania, Russia, Spain, Sweden, Türkiye, UK, Ukraine, USA, Vietnam.
Included in the above, 4 organizations listed in this Yearbook:
Arab Academy for Science, Technology and Maritime Transport (AASTMT, #00891); Baltic Fishing Fleet State Academy; Nippon Foundation; World Maritime University (WMU, #21633).
Consultative Status Consultative status granted from: *International Maritime Organization (IMO, #14102).*
NGO Relations Associate Member of: *International Association of Ports and Harbors (IAPH, #12096).* [2019/XD7425/y/**D**]

- ♦ International Association for Materials Testing (inactive)
- ♦ International Association for Maternal and Neonatal Health (inactive)
- ♦ International Association for Mathematical and Computer Modelling and Scientific Computing (no recent information)
- ♦ International Association for Mathematical Geology / see International Association for Mathematical Geosciences (#12017)

♦ International Association for Mathematical Geosciences (IAMG) . . . 12017

Main Office 661 Pennsylvania Ave SE, Ste 440, Washington DC 20003-4303, USA. T. +18323808833. E-mail: support@iamgmembers.org.
URL: http://www.iamg.org/

History Aug 1968, Prague (Czechia). Founded at *International Geological Congress (IGC)*. Former names and other names: *International Association for Mathematical Geology (IAMG)* – former (1968); *Association internationale pour la géologie mathématique* – former (1968). **Aims** Promote international cooperation in the application and use of all branches of mathematics in geological research and technology. **Structure** Meeting; Council; Committees (6): Distinguished Lecturer, Student Grant, Membership, Education, Publications, Awards. **Languages** English. **Staff** None. **Finance** Sources: members' dues; sale of publications. Travelling expenses met by individual members. **Activities** Scientific meetings, symposia and seminars (commonly held in association with International Geological Congress and International Statistical Institute); independent conferences held during non-IGC years. **Events** *Annual Conference* Trondheim (Norway) 2023, *Annual Conference* Nancy (France) 2022, *Quadrennial Symposium* Delhi (India) 2021, *Quadrennial Symposium* Delhi (India) 2020, *Annual Conference* State College, PA (USA) 2019. **Publications** *Computers and Geosciences* (10 a year); *Applied Computing & Geosciences* (4 a year) – online-only Open Access journal focused on all aspects of computing in the geosciences; *Natural Resources Research* (4 a year); *IAMG Newsletter* (2 a year); *Mathematical Geology* (8 a year). Monograph series; studies in mathematical geology; brochures.
Members Individuals (about 700) in 53 countries and territories:
Argentina, Australia, Austria, Belarus, Belgium, Bolivia, Brazil, Bulgaria, Canada, Chile, China, Colombia, Costa Rica, Czechia, Denmark, Egypt, Fiji, Finland, France, Germany, Greece, Guam, Hungary, India, Indonesia, Israel, Italy, Japan, Korea Rep, Kuwait, Mexico, Netherlands, New Zealand, Norway, Oman, Pakistan, Peru, Philippines, Poland, Portugal, Puerto Rico, Russia, South Africa, Spain, Sweden, Switzerland, Taiwan, Türkiye, UK, Ukraine, USA, Venezuela, Vietnam.
NGO Relations Affiliate member of: *American Association of Petroleum Geologists (AAPG); International Union of Geodesy and Geophysics (IUGG, #15776); International Union of Geological Sciences (IUGS, #15777).* Partner of: *Earth Science Matters Foundation (ESM, #05169).* [2023.02.20/XC3895/v/**C**]

♦ International Association of Mathematical Physics (IAMP) 12018

Association internationale de physique mathématique

Sec Inst for Mathematics, Univ of Zurich, Winterthurerstrasse 190, 8057 Zurich ZH, Switzerland. T. +41446355842. Fax +41446355706. E-mail: secretary@iamp.org.
URL: http://www.iamp.org/

History 1 Oct 1975, Geneva (Switzerland). **Aims** Promote international cooperation in mathematical physics; encourage and coordinate activities and scientific exchanges. **Structure** General Assembly; Executive Committee. **Languages** English. **Staff** 1.00 FTE, voluntary. **Finance** Sources: gifts, legacies; grants; members' dues; subsidies. Other sources: bequests. **Events** *Congress* Geneva (Switzerland) 2021, *Congress* Montréal, QC (Canada) 2018, *Congress* Santiago (Chile) 2015, *Congress* Aalborg (Denmark) 2012, *Congress* Aalborg (Denmark) 2012. **Publications** *IAMP News Bulletin* (4 a year).
Members Individuals Ordinary; Organizations Associate. Members in 54 countries and territories:
Argentina, Armenia, Australia, Austria, Belarus, Belgium, Brazil, Bulgaria, Canada, Chile, China, Costa Rica, Czechia, Denmark, Egypt, Finland, France, Germany, Greece, Hungary, Iceland, India, Indonesia, Iran Islamic Rep, Ireland, Israel, Italy, Japan, Korea Rep, Lithuania, Mexico, Morocco, Netherlands, New Zealand, Nigeria, Norway, Peru, Poland, Portugal, Romania, Russia, Serbia, Slovakia, South Africa, Spain, Sweden, Switzerland, Taiwan, Türkiye, UK, Ukraine, USA, Venezuela, Zimbabwe.
IGO Relations *UNESCO (#20322).* [2015.01.07/XD8254/**C**]

♦ International Association for Mathematics and Computers in Simulation (IMACS) 12019

Association internationale pour les mathématiques et calculateurs en simulation

Office Chaussée de Waterloo 72, 1630 St-Genesius-Rode, Belgium. E-mail: imacs@iac.cnr.it.
Gen Sec Dept of Computer Science, Univ of Toronto, 10 King's College Road, Toronto ON M5S 3G4, Canada.
Pres Inst App Calcolo, Viale del Policlinico 137, 00161 Rome RM, Italy.

History 2 Oct 1955, Brussels (Belgium), as *International Association for Analogue Computation – Association internationale pour le calcul analogique (AICA)*. Present name adopted 1976. Registered in accordance with Belgian law, 10 Feb 1956. New Statutes registered 19 Apr 1979; modified: 8 Apr 1986; 13 Apr 1989. **Aims** Promote exchange of scientific information among specialists interested in analogue computation and hybrid computation methods, by organizing international meetings and displays of equipment, by issuing scientific publications and establishing frequent contacts with scientific associations for the study of arithmetical computation methods. **Structure** General Assembly (every 3 years); Board of Directors. **Languages** English, French. **Staff** 0.50 FTE, paid. **Finance** Sources: members' dues. **Activities** Events/meetings. **Events** *Triennial Congress* Rome (Italy) 2021, *Triennial Congress* Rome (Italy) 2020, *Triennial Congress* Xiamen (China) 2016, *IMACS Seminar on Monte Carlo Methods (MCM 2015)* Linz (Austria) 2015, *MATHMOD : International Symposium on Mathematical Modelling* Vienna (Austria) 2015. **Publications** *Applied Numerical Mathematics* (6 a year); *Mathematics and Computer in Simulation* (6 a year); *Journal of Computation Acoustics*. Proceedings of international meetings and symposia.
Members Regular (individuals); Associate Scientific (academic institutions); Associate Industrial (industrial, public and private firms). Members in 32 countries:
Argentina, Australia, Austria, Belgium, Brazil, Bulgaria, Canada, China, Czechia, Denmark, Finland, France, Germany, Greece, Hungary, India, Ireland, Israel, Italy, Japan, Mexico, Netherlands, Norway, Poland, Romania, Russia, Serbia-Montenegro, Spain, Sweden, Switzerland, UK, USA. [2021/XB1174/**B**]

- ♦ International Association for Maxillo-Facial Surgery / see International College for Maxillo-Facial Surgery (#12645)
- ♦ International Association of Mayors of Northern Cities / see World Winter Cities Association for Mayors (#21940)

♦ International Association for Measurement and Evaluation of Communication (AMEC) 12020

CEO Communications House, 26 York Street, London, W1U 6PZ, UK. T. +442081444465.
URL: http://www.amecorg.com/

History Founded 1996, London (UK). **Aims** As an international trade association for public relations measurement and evaluation, define and develop the industry on an international scale with better professional standards and education. **Structure** Board. **Languages** English. **Staff** 2.00 FTE, paid. Several voluntary. **Activities** Awards/prizes/competitions; events/meetings. **Events** *Virtual Global Summit* London (UK) 2021, *International Summit* London (UK) 2020, *International Summit* Prague (Czechia) 2019, *International Summit* Barcelona (Spain) 2018, *International Summit* Bangkok (Thailand) 2017.
Members Full; Associate; International Research. Members in 32 countries:
Argentina, Australia, Belgium, Bosnia-Herzegovina, Brazil, Canada, China, Croatia, France, Germany, Hungary, Iceland, Ireland, Italy, Japan, Malaysia, Netherlands, North Macedonia, Norway, Portugal, Romania, Russia, Serbia, Slovakia, Slovenia, Spain, Sweden, Switzerland, Türkiye, UK, United Arab Emirates, USA.
Also members in Scandinavian countries. Membership countries not specified. [2020/XJ1262/**C**]

♦ International Association on Mechanization of Field Experiments (IAMFE) 12021

Association internationale de mécanisation des essais en plein champ

Exec Sec Qungdao Agricultural Univ, No 700 Changcheng Road, Chengyang, Qingdao, Shandong, China. T. +8653286080842. Fax +8653286080452.
Pres address not obtained. E-mail: sqingnong@126.com.
URL: http://www.iamfe.org/

History 19 Jun 1964, Ås (Norway), on the initiative of Egil Oyjord, at first international conference, exhibition and demonstration of scientific equipment for field experiments. Constitution adopted 1968, Braunschweig (Germany FR). Constitution amended: Oct 1971, Ås (Norway); Mar 2001, Uppsala (Sweden). **Aims** Inform agronomists, plant breeders and others working in seed and related industries about new machinery, equipment, instruments and other technologies for increasing capacity, accuracy and application of experimental work. **Structure** General Assembly (every 4 years); Executive Committee; Consultative Board. **Languages** English. **Staff** 1.00 FTE, paid; 1.00 FTE, voluntary. **Finance** Sources: gifts, legacies; members' dues. Other sources: support from Qingdao Agricultural University. **Activities** Events/meetings; knowledge management/information dissemination. **Events** *Conference* Beijing (China) 2022, *Conference* Moscow (Russia) 2017, *Conference* Qingdao (China) 2012, *Nordic Regional Conference* St Petersburg (Russia) 2010, *Quadrennial Assembly* Aarhus (Denmark) 2008. **Publications** *IAMFE News* (irregular). *International Directory of Manufacturers of Machinery, Equipment and Instruments for Agricultural Research (IAMFE Directory)*. Reports; conference proceedings.
Members Branches (10) in 14 countries:
Belarus, Belgium, China, Estonia, France, Hungary, India, Latvia, Lithuania, Luxembourg, Netherlands, Norway, Russia, Ukraine.
Institutional members institutions, companies, organizations; Individual membership research workers. Members in 36 countries and territories:
Argentina, Australia, Austria, Belarus, Belgium, Canada, China, Côte d'Ivoire, Cyprus, Denmark, Estonia, Finland, France, Germany, Greece, Hungary, India, Japan, Korea Rep, Latvia, Lithuania, Luxembourg, Netherlands, New Zealand, Norway, Portugal, Romania, Russia, Sweden, Switzerland, Syrian AR, Taiwan, UK, Ukraine, Uruguay, USA.
Correspondents in 83 countries and territories:
Algeria, Argentina, Australia, Austria, Belarus, Belgium, Bolivia, Botswana, Brazil, Bulgaria, Burundi, Canada, Chile, China, Colombia, Côte d'Ivoire, Cuba, Cyprus, Czechia, Denmark, Ecuador, Egypt, Eritrea, Estonia, Ethiopia, Finland, France, Germany, Greece, Hungary, Iceland, India, Indonesia, Iran Islamic Rep, Ireland, Israel, Italy, Japan, Jordan, Kenya, Korea Rep, Latvia, Lithuania, Luxembourg, Madagascar, Mexico, Moldova, Morocco, Netherlands, New Zealand, Niger, Nigeria, Norway, Pakistan, Paraguay, Peru, Philippines, Poland, Portugal, Romania, Russia, Saudi Arabia, Senegal, Serbia, South Africa, Spain, Sri Lanka, Sudan, Sweden, Switzerland, Syrian AR, Taiwan, Thailand, Tunisia, Türkiye, UK, Ukraine, Uruguay, USA, Uzbekistan, Venezuela, Zimbabwe.
IGO Relations *FAO (#09260); International Seed Testing Association (ISTA, #14829).* **NGO Relations** In liaison with technical committees of: *International Organization for Standardization (ISO, #14473)*; other NGOs. [2019/XB1377/**B**]

♦ International Association for Media and Communication Research (IAMCR) 12022

Association internationale des études et recherches sur l'information (AIERI) – Asociación Internacional de Investigación sobre la Comunicación Social (AIICS)

Exec Dir Pablo de Maria 1036, 11-200 Montevideo, Uruguay.
Pres School of Journalism and Communication, Univ of Oregon, Eugene OR 97403, USA.
URL: https://iamcr.org/

History 6 Dec 1956, Strasbourg (France). Interim Committee set up following preparatory work undertaken in collaboration with UNESCO since 1947. Constitutive Assembly: 18-19 Dec 1957, Paris (France). Statutes modified: 6 Oct 1959; 4 Sep 1976; 28 Jul 1988; 20 Jun 2018. **Aims** Support and develop media and communication research throughout the world. **Structure** General Assembly (every 2 years at Scientific Conference); Executive Board; International Council; Standing Committees. **Languages** English, French, Spanish. **Staff** 2.50 FTE, paid. Voluntary. **Finance** Sources: donations; grants; members' dues. Other sources: awards. **Activities** Events/meetings; research/documentation. **Events** *Annual Conference* Lyon (France) 2023, *Annual Conference* Beijing (China) 2022, *Annual Conference* Nairobi (Kenya) 2021, *Annual Conference* Tampere (Finland) 2020, *Annual Conference* Madrid (Spain) 2019. **Publications** *IAMCR Newsletter*. Reports of meetings. Monographs, book series.
Members Individual; Institutional; Associate: over 2,300 in all. Individuals in 72 countries and territories:
Argentina, Australia, Austria, Bangladesh, Belarus, Belgium, Brazil, Bulgaria, Cameroon, Canada, Chile, China, Colombia, Costa Rica, Croatia, Denmark, Egypt, Estonia, Finland, France, Germany, Ghana, Greece, Guatemala, Hong Kong, Hungary, India, Indonesia, Iran Islamic Rep, Ireland, Israel, Italy, Jamaica, Japan, Korea Rep, Kuwait, Laos, Lebanon, Malaysia, Mauritania, Mexico, Nepal, Netherlands, New Zealand, Nigeria, Norway, Pakistan, Peru, Philippines, Poland, Portugal, Romania, Russia, Saudi Arabia, Serbia-Montenegro, Singapore, Slovenia, South Africa, Spain, Sri Lanka, Sweden, Switzerland, Taiwan, Tajikistan, Thailand, Türkiye, UK, Ukraine, United Arab Emirates, Uruguay, USA, Venezuela.
Institutional in 29 countries:
Australia, Austria, Belgium, Brazil, Canada, Czechia, Denmark, Egypt, Estonia, Finland, France, Germany, Greece, Hungary, India, Ireland, Italy, Jamaica, Mexico, Netherlands, Norway, Peru, Portugal, Russia, Singapore, Spain, Sweden, UK, USA.
Included in the above, 4 institutes listed in this Yearbook:
Asian Media Information and Communication Centre (AMIC, #01536); Caribbean School of Media and Communication (CARIMAC, #03552); Nordicom (#17374); Universidad Iberoamericana, México (UIA).
Associate in 20 countries:
Australia, Austria, Brazil, Denmark, Finland, France, Iran Islamic Rep, Italy, Jamaica, Kenya, Latvia, Mexico, Netherlands, Norway, Peru, Singapore, Spain, Switzerland, UK, USA.
Included in the above, 14 organizations listed in this Yearbook:
African Council for Communication Education (ACCE, #00273); Ahl-Ul-Bait World Assembly; Asociación Latinoamericana de Investigadores de la Comunicación (ALAIC, #02237); Baltic Association for Media Research (BAMR, #03098); Caribbean Association for Communication Research (CACR, no recent information); Commonwealth Association for Education in Journalism and Communication (CAEJAC, no recent

information); European Audiovisual Observatory (#06294); International Communication Association (ICA, #12814); International Institute of Communications (IIC, #13870); International Institute of Human Rights – Fondation René Cassin (IIHR, #13887); IPS – Inter Press Service International Association (#16013); Muslim Home (no recent information); World Association for Christian Communication (WACC, #21126); World Association for Public Opinion Research (WAPOR, #21180).
Consultative Status Consultative status granted from: *ECOSOC (#05331)* (Special); *UNESCO (#20322)* (Consultative Status); *World Intellectual Property Organization (WIPO, #21593)* (Permanent Observer Status); *ILO (#11123)* (Special List). **IGO Relations** Invited to sessions of Intergovernmental Council of: *International Programme for the Development of Communication (IPDC, #14651).* **NGO Relations** Member of (3): *Conference of Non-Governmental Organizations in Consultative Relationship with the United Nations (CONGO, #04635); International Federation of Communication Associations; World Journalism Education Council (WJEC, #21602).* [2019.09.25/XB1197/y/**B**]

♦ International Association for Media and History (IAMHIST) 12023

Pres KU Leuven, Fac of Arts, Blijde-Incomststraat 21 – box 3301, 3000 Leuven, Belgium.
URL: http://www.iamhist.net/

History Aug 1975, Brandjberg (Denmark), as *International Association for Audio-Visual Media in Historical Research and Education*, at 6th International Conference on History and Audio-Visual Media. Statutes adopted Sep 1977. Admitted as an internal commission of *International Committee of Historical Sciences (ICHS, #12777)*, 30 Sep 1977. **Aims** Further the use of *audiovisual* media for teaching and research in history. **Structure** Council. **Languages** English, French, German. **Staff** None. **Finance** Sources: members' dues. **Activities** Events/meetings; research and development; training/education. **Events** *Biennial Conference* Newcastle upon Tyne (UK) 2019, *Conference* Paris (France) 2017, *Biennial Conference* Bloomington, IN (USA) 2015, *Biennial Conference* Warwick (UK) 2013, *Biennial Conference* Copenhagen (Denmark) 2011. **Publications** *Historical Journal of Film, Radio and Television* (4 a year) – jointly with Taylor and Francis (UK). Information Services: Preservation of audio-visual materials as documents; international exchange of information.
Members Institutional; Individual. Member institutions (55) in 21 countries:
Australia, Austria, Belgium, Canada, Denmark, Finland, France, Germany, India, Ireland, Israel, Italy, Netherlands, Poland, Romania, Russia, Spain, Sweden, Switzerland, UK, USA. [2019/XD7203/**C**]

♦ International Association for Media in Science (IAMS) 12024

Association internationale pour les media dans la science (AIMS)
Gen Sec c/o St George's Univ of London, Cranmer Terrace, London, SW17 0RE, UK. T. +442072748268.
Registered Office c/o Inst de cinématographie scientifique, 1 Place Aristide Briand, 92195 Meudon CEDEX, France. T. +33145075198.
URL: http://www.media-in-science.org/

History Apr 1992, Saragossa (Spain). Constitution adopted 24 Apr 1992, Saragossa (Spain); amended 8 Jun 1993, Göttingen (Germany). Registered according to French law. Took over activities of the previous *International Scientific Film Association (ISFA, inactive)*, which was set up Oct 1947, Paris (France), and which ceased to exist 18 Jul 1992. **Aims** Promote the production, documentation, preservation, distribution and use of audiovisual media and materials for growth and communication of knowledge in natural and human sciences, technology and medicine. **Structure** General Assembly (annual). Board of 6 members, including President, General Secretary and Treasurer. Special interest and project groups. **Languages** English, French. **Staff** 0.50 FTE, paid. **Finance** Members' dues. Other sources: donations; subsidies; sponsorships. **Activities** Organizes conferences, screenings and workshops. Provides consultancy services. **Events** *Annual Congress* Badajoz (Spain) 2006, *Annual Congress* Hradec Kralové (Czech Rep) 2005, *Annual Congress* Paris (France) 2004, *Annual Congress* Milan (Italy) 2002, *Annual Congress* Vila Real (Portugal) 2001. **Publications** Information Services: Network of databases, including one on members' details.
Members Universities, foundations, associations, institutions, individuals plus corporate bodies and broadcasting organizations which have an interest in the aims of the Association. Organizations in 11 countries:
Belgium, China, France, Germany, Italy, Japan, Netherlands, Poland, Russia, Spain, UK.
Individuals in 13 countries:
Belgium, Chile, Finland, Germany, Greece, Hungary, Italy, Mexico, Netherlands, Portugal, Spain, UK, USA.
NGO Relations Member of: *International Council for Film, Television and Audiovisual Communication (IFTC, #13022).* [2014/XC0015/**D**]

♦ International Association for Medical Assistance to Travellers (internationally oriented national body)
♦ International Association of Medical Colleges (no recent information)
♦ International Association of Medical Esperantists / see Universala Medicina Esperanto-Asocio (#20672)
♦ International Association of Medical Experts for Insurance Companies / see International Committee for Insurance Medicine (#12780)

♦ International Association of Medical Genetics (MAGI) 12025

Contact Laboratorio di Biotecnologie, Via delle Maioliche 57/D, 38068 Rovereto MO, Italy. T. +39464662771. Fax +39464425634.
URL: http://www.assomagi.org/

History 2006. **Events** *International congress* Brussels (Belgium) 2010, *International conference on reliability and quality in design* St Louis, MO (USA) 2005. [2016/XJ2052/**D**]

♦ International Association of Medical Inspectors of Schools (inactive)
♦ International Association of Medical Laboratory Technologists / see International Federation of Biomedical Laboratory Science (#13372)
♦ International Association of Medical Licensing Authorities / see International Association of Medical Regulatory Authorities (#12026)
♦ International Association of Medical Museums / see International Academy of Pathology (#11567)
♦ International Association of Medical Oceanography (inactive)
♦ International Association of Medical Press (inactive)
♦ International Association of Medical Prosthesis Manufacturers (inactive)
♦ International Association of Medical, Psychology and Religious Studies / see International Association for Medico-Psychological and Religious Studies (#12028)

♦ International Association of Medical Regulatory Authorities (IAMRA) 12026

Main Office 400 Fuller Wiser Rd, Ste 300, Euless TX 76039, USA. T. +18178684044. Fax +18178684097. E-mail: secretariat@iamra.com.
URL: http://www.iamra.com/

History 2000. Founded following ongoing conference series. Former names and other names: *International Association of Medical Licensing Authorities (IAMLA)* – former (2000 to 2002). **Aims** Support medical regulatory authorities worldwide in protecting the public interest by: promoting high standards for physician education, licensure and regulation; facilitating the ongoing exchange of information among medical regulatory authorities. **Structure** Management Committee, comprising Chairman, Deputy Chairman and 5 further members. **Languages** English. **Staff** 2.00 FTE, paid. **Finance** Members' dues. **Activities** *International Conference on Medical Regulation.* **Events** *International Conference on Medical Regulation* 2022, *International Conference on Medical Regulation* Johannesburg (South Africa) 2020, *International Conference on Medical Regulation* Dubai (United Arab Emirates) 2018, *International Conference on Medical Regulation* Melbourne, VIC (Australia) 2016, *International Conference on Medical Regulation* London (UK) 2014.
Members in 19 countries and territories:
Australia, Belgium, Canada, Cape Verde, Croatia, Denmark, Egypt, Germany, India, Ireland, Korea Rep, Mauritius, Namibia, Netherlands, New Zealand, Nigeria, Norway, Pakistan, Portugal, Sierra Leone, South Africa, Spain, Sudan, Sweden, Switzerland, Taiwan, UK, USA, Zimbabwe.
NGO Relations *European Accessible Information Network (EUAIN, inactive)* is member. [2021/XM0002/**D**]

♦ International Association for Medical Research and Cultural Exchanges (no recent information)
♦ International Association for Medical Research in West Africa (inactive)

♦ International Association of Medical Science Educators (IAMSE) .. 12027

Contact c/o JulNet Solutions LLC, 1404 1/2 Adams Ave, Huntington WV 25704, USA. T. +13045221270. Fax +13045239701. E-mail: support@iamse.org.
URL: http://www.iamse.org/

History 1993, Charleston SC (USA), as (US) Basic Science Education Forum (BSEF). Present name adopted 1997. **Aims** Promote medical education through faculty development. **Structure** Board of Directors, comprising President/Chairman, Past President, Vice President, Secretary, Treasurer and 11 Directors. **Events** *Annual Meeting* Denver, CO (USA) 2022, *Annual Meeting* Denver, CO (USA) 2021, *Annual Meeting* Denver, CO (USA) 2020, *Annual Meeting* Roanoke, VA (USA) 2019, *Annual Meeting* Las Vegas, NV (USA) 2018. **Publications** *Basic Science Educator* (2 a year); *Journal of the IAMSE* (periodical). [2020/XN9370/**C**]

♦ International Association of Medicine and Biology of the Environment (inactive)

♦ International Association for Medico-Psychological and Religious Studies 12028

Association Internationale d'études medico-psychologiques et religieuses (AIEMPR) – Asociación Internacional de Estudios Médicos-Psicológicos y Religiosos – Associazione Internazionale di Studi Medico-Psicologici e Religiosi
Pres 130 rue Théoret, St Laurent QC H4N 2J5, Canada. T. +15148082101. E-mail: benoit@abbaye-de-leffe.be.
Registered Office 11 Chemin de Tattes-Fontaine, 1353 Vandoeuvres GE, Switzerland.
URL: http://aiempr.net/

History Previously referred to as *International Association of Medical, Psychology and Religious Studies – Association internationale d'études médicales psychologiques et religieuses (AIEMPR).* **Events** *Congress* Rome (Italy) 2022, *Congress* Mexico City (Mexico) 2019, *Congress* Montréal, QC (Canada) 2016, *Congress* Assisi (Italy) 2013, *Congress* St-Maurice (Switzerland) / Lausanne (Switzerland) / St Moritz (Switzerland) 2009. [2016/XD9902/**D**]

♦ International Association for Mediterranean Forests (#02699)
♦ International Association for Mediterranean and Oriental Studies (internationally oriented national body)

♦ International Association of Meiobenthologists (IAM) 12029

Chairperson PP Shirshov Inst of Oceanology, Russian Ac of Sciences, 36 Nakhimovskiy Prospect, Moscow MOSKVA, Russia, 117218.
Treas Lab Morfologie, RUG, Ledeganckstraat 35, 9000 Ghent, Belgium. Fax +3292645344.
URL: http://www.meiofauna.org/

History 1968 at first meeting of founders, as *Association of Meiobenthologists.* Present name adopted, 1974. **Aims** Advance and promote research in the study of meiobenthos in all its branches. **Structure** Executive Committee; Board of Correspondents. **Events** *Triennial Meiofauna Conference* Evora (Portugal) 2019, *Triennial Meiofauna Conference* Heraklion (Greece) 2016, *International Copepoda Conference* Seoul (Korea Rep) 2014, *Triennial Meiofauna Conference / Triennial Conference* Seoul (Korea Rep) 2013, *Triennial meiofauna conference / Triennial Conference* Ghent (Belgium) 2010. **Publications** *Psammonalia* (2 a year) – newsletter.
Members Individuals (over 300) in 46 countries:
Argentina, Australia, Austria, Belgium, Bermuda, Brazil, Canada, Chile, China, Colombia, Cuba, Denmark, Ecuador, Egypt, Finland, France, Germany, Greece, Icèland, India, Indonesia, Italy, Japan, Korea Rep, Malaysia, Mexico, Monaco, Netherlands, New Zealand, Norway, Philippines, Poland, Portugal, Romania, Russia, Saudi Arabia, Serbia, South Africa, Spain, Sweden, Tanzania UR, Thailand, Trinidad-Tobago, UK, Ukraine, USA. [2019.06.27/XC0090/**C**]

♦ International Association of Memory (IAM) 12030

Chairman Claude-Lorrain-Str 31, 81543 Munich, Germany. T. +491176249174. E-mail: info@iam-memory.org.
URL: http://www.iam-memory.org/

History Launched 2016. Registered in accordance with German law. **Aims** Bring memory *sports* to everybody; provide a free and democratic environment for the memory community. **Structure** International Board. **Activities** Sporting activities. **Publications** *IAM Newsletter.* [2020/XM7530/**B**]

♦ International Association for Mentoring (inactive)
♦ International Association of Meteorology / see International Association of Meteorology and Atmospheric Sciences (#12031)
♦ International Association of Meteorology and Atmospheric Physics / see International Association of Meteorology and Atmospheric Sciences (#12031)

♦ International Association of Meteorology and Atmospheric Sciences (IAMAS) 12031

Association internationale de météorologie et de sciences de l'atmosphère (AIMSA)
SG SSEC, Univ of Wisconsin-Madison, 1225 W Dayton St, Madison WI 53706, USA. E-mail: stevea@ssec.wisc.edu.
URL: http://www.iamas.org/

History 1919, Brussels (Belgium), as *International Association of Meteorology – Association internationale de météorologie.* Subsequently name changed to *International Association of Meteorology and Atmospheric Physics (IAMAP) – Association internationale de météorologie et de physique de l'atmosphère (AIMPA).* Present name adopted 1993. Constituent association of *International Union of Geodesy and Geophysics (IUGG, #15776).* **Aims** Promote meteorological research and investigation on all aspects of atmospheric sciences, particularly in fields requiring international cooperation; provide a forum for discussion of results and trends in research, and of those subjects of atmospheric research and investigation which overlap fields of other sciences. **Structure** General Assembly; Executive Committee; Bureau. Commissions (10): *International Commission on Atmospheric Chemistry and Global Pollution (ICACGP, #12664); International Commission on Atmospheric Electricity (ICAE, #12665);* International Commission on Climate; *International Commission on Clouds and Precipitation (ICCP, #12672); International Commission on Dynamical Meteorology (ICDM, #12679); International Commission on Middle Atmosphere Science (ICMA, #12704); International Commission on Planetary Atmospheres and their Evolution (ICPAE, #12715); International Commission on Polar Meteorology (ICPM, #12718); International Ozone Commission (IO3C, #14495); International Radiation Commission (IRC, #14684).* **Languages** English, French. **Staff** 3.00 FTE, voluntary. **Finance** Sources: annual allocation and occasional grants from IUGG. Annual budget: about US$ 46,000. **Activities** Events/meetings; knowledge management/information dissemination. **Events** *Joint Assembly* Busan (Korea Rep) 2025, *Joint Assembly* Busan (Korea Rep) 2021, *Joint Assembly* Cape Town (South Africa) 2017, *Biennial Scientific Assembly* Prague (Czech Rep) 2015, *DACA : Davos Atmospheric and Cryospheric Assembly* Davos (Switzerland) 2013. **Publications** *Advances in Atmospheric Sciences; IAMAS Info-Email. IAMAS Publication Series.* Assembly abstracts; national reports.
Members The same adhering bodies as for IUGG, in 71 countries and territories:
Albania, Algeria, Argentina, Armenia, Australia, Austria, Azerbaijan, Belgium, Bolivia, Bosnia-Herzegovina, Brazil, Bulgaria, Canada, Chile, China, Colombia, Congo DR, Costa Rica, Croatia, Czechia, Denmark, Egypt, Estonia, Finland, France, Georgia, Germany, Ghana, Greece, Hungary, Iceland, India, Indonesia, Iran Islamic Rep, Ireland, Israel, Italy, Japan, Jordan, Korea Rep, Luxembourg, Mauritius, Mexico, Morocco, Mozambique, Netherlands, New Zealand, Nicaragua, Nigeria, North Macedonia, Norway, Pakistan, Peru, Poland, Portugal, Romania, Russia, Saudi Arabia, Serbia, Slovakia, Slovenia, South Africa, Spain, Sweden, Switzerland, Taiwan, Thailand, Türkiye, UK, USA, Vietnam.
NGO Relations Represented in: *Committee on Space Research (COSPAR, #04287); Scientific Committee on Oceanic Research (SCOR, #19149); Scientific Committee on Solar-Terrestrial Physics (SCOSTEP, #19151).* Member of: *International Forum of Meteorological Societies (IFMS, #13644).* [2020/XB1312/**B**]

♦ International Association of Methodist Schools, Colleges and Universities (internationally oriented national body)
♦ International Association for Metropolitan Research and Development (inactive)
♦ International Association of Microbiological Societies / see International Union of Microbiological Societies (#15794)
♦ International Association for Microcircuit Cards (inactive)
♦ International Association of Microscopy (inactive)

♦ International Association for Microstates Studies (inactive)
♦ International Association for Micro-Surgery (inactive)
♦ International Association of Military Flight Surgeon Pilots (no recent information)

♦ International Association for Mission Studies (IAMS) 12032
Association internationale d'étude de la mission – Internationale Vereinigung für Missionswissenschaft – Asociación Internacional de Estudios de la Misión
Gen Sec c/o CTR LUX, Lunds universitet, Box 192, SE-221 00 Lund, Sweden. E-mail: iams@missionstudies.org.
URL: http://www.missionstudies.org/
History 23 Aug 1972, Driebergen (Netherlands). Established following preliminary meetings of European and North American missiologists: 1968, Birmingham (UK); 1970, Oslo (Norway). Constitution adopted 29 Aug 1972, Driebergen; amended 31 Jul 1974, Frankfurt-Main (Germany FR); further amended 15 Aug 2016, Seoul (South Korea). Former names and other names: *Association internationale d'études missionnaires* – former. **Aims** Promote scholarly study of Christian witness and its impact in the world and the related field of intercultural theology. **Structure** General Meeting (every 4 years); Executive Committee; Regional Representatives (6); Study Groups. **Languages** English, French, German, Spanish. **Finance** Sources: donations; grants; members' dues. **Activities** Events/meetings; publishing activities; research/documentation. **Events** *Quadrennial Conference* Sydney, NSW (Australia) 2022, *Quadrennial Conference* Sydney, NSW (Australia) 2020, *Quadrennial Conference* Seoul (Korea Rep) 2016, *Quadrennial Conference* Toronto, ON (Canada) 2012, *Quadrennial Conference* Balatonfüred (Hungary) 2008. **Publications** *Mission Studies* (3 a year). **Information Services** *Membership Database.*
Members Institutional and individual (about 620) in 61 countries and territories:
Angola, Argentina, Australia, Austria, Barbados, Belgium, Bolivia, Botswana, Brazil, Cameroon, Canada, Congo DR, Costa Rica, Côte d'Ivoire, Denmark, Fiji, Finland, France, Germany, Ghana, Guatemala, Hong Kong, Hungary, India, Indonesia, Ireland, Israel, Italy, Jamaica, Japan, Kenya, Korea Rep, Malawi, Malaysia, Mexico, Mozambique, Netherlands, New Caledonia, Nicaragua, Nigeria, Norway, Pakistan, Papua New Guinea, Peru, Philippines, Poland, Russia, Senegal, Serbia, Singapore, South Africa, Sri Lanka, Sweden, Switzerland, Taiwan, Tanzania UR, Thailand, Uganda, UK, USA, Zimbabwe.
Included in the above, 8 organizations listed in this Yearbook:
Association francophone oecuménique de missiologie (AFOM, #02616); Association of Protestant Churches and Missions in Germany (EMW); Commission on World Mission and Evangelism of the World Council of Churches (CWME, inactive); Institute for Scientific Research on Missions (no recent information); Nordic Institute of Mission and Ecumenical Research (NIME, #17322); Overseas Ministries Study Center (OMSC); Società del Verbo Divino (Verbiti); The Lutheran World Federation (LWF, #16532). [2022/XC4597/y/**B**]

♦ International Association for Mobile Learning (IAmLearn) 12033
Pres PO Box 60699, Pierre Van Ryneveld, 0045, South Africa. T. +27123825044.
URL: http://www.iamlearn.org/
History 2008. **Aims** Promote excellence in research, development and application of mobile and contextual learning. **Structure** Executive Committee; Special Interest Groups. **Languages** English. **Staff** 6.00 FTE, paid. **Finance** Sources: members' dues. **Activities** Events/meetings; knowledge management/information dissemination; research and development. **Events** *Annual mLearn Conference* Sydney, NSW (Australia) 2016, *Annual mLearn Conference* Venice (Italy) 2015, *Annual mLearn Conference* Istanbul (Turkey) 2014, *Annual mLearn Conference* Doha (Qatar) 2013, *Annual mLearn Conference* Helsinki (Finland) 2012. **Publications** *IAmLearn Newsletter. IAmLearning: Mobilizing and Supporting Educator Practice* – ebook. Conference proceedings. [2019.04.26/XJ8705/**C**]

♦ International Association of Money Transfer Networks (IAMTN) ... 12034
Contact Kronprinsessegade 26, 1306 Copenhagen, Denmark. E-mail: hello@iamtn.org.
URL: https://www.iamtn-network.org/
History Founded Nov 2005. **Aims** Represent the money transfer industry worldwide; cooperate with regional money transfer trade bodies. **Structure** Advisory Board. **Activities** Events/meetings. **Events** *Global Summit* London (UK) 2022, *Global Summit* London (UK) 2019, *Money transfer singapore conference* Singapore (Singapore) 2010. **Publications** *IAMTN Newsletter.* [2022/XJ2700/**D**]

♦ International Association for Mongol Studies (IAMS) 12035
Association internationale des études mongoles – Mezdunarodnaja Associacija Mongolovedenija – Olon Ulsyn Mongol Sudlalyn Holboo (OUMSH)
Main Office PO Box 20-A, 14200 Sukhbaatar Square 11, Ulaanbaatar, Mongolia. E-mail: iamsmongolia@gmail.com.
URL: https://iams.org.mn/
History 18 Sep 1987, Ulaanbaatar (Mongolia). Founded at 5th International Congress of Mongolists, when constitution was adopted. Revised statutes approved during 7th Congress, 1997, Ulaanbaatar (Mongolia). Former names and other names: *Nariin Bicgiin Darga Naryn Gazar* – alias. **Aims** Promote Mongol studies on an international scale; assist activities of Mongolists, centres and associations for Mongol studies and encourage cooperation and expansion of contacts among them; familiarize the world public with Mongolian culture, language, literature, arts and history, and with the social, economic, political and legal systems; advance scholarly qualifications of young Mongolists. **Structure** Congress (every 5 years); Advisory Board; Secretariat. **Languages** English, Mongolian, Russian. **Staff** 7.00 FTE, paid. **Finance** Sources: donations; members' dues; subsidies. Financial assistance from centres of Mongol studies, organizations and individuals. **Activities** Events/meetings; research/documentation; training/education. **Events** *European Seminar* Ankara (Turkey) 2020, *Quinquennial Congress* Ulaanbaatar (Mongolia) 2011, *Quinquennial Congress* Ulaanbaatar (Mongolia) 2002, *Quinquennial congress* Ulaanbaatar (Mongolia) 1997, *Quinquennial Congress* Ulaanbaatar (Mongolia) 1992. **Publications** *IAMS Bulletin* (2 a year) in English, Mongolian, Russian; *Mongolica* (annual) in English – Journal. *Mongolian Heritage Spread Around the World* – 20 vols – catalogue. Proceedings of international conferences, symposia and seminars sponsored by IAMS.
Members Individual Mongolists in 29 countries and territories:
Afghanistan, Austria, Belgium, Bulgaria, Canada, China, Czechia, Denmark, Finland, France, Germany, Hungary, India, Israel, Italy, Japan, Kazakhstan, Korea Rep, Kyrgyzstan, Mongolia, Norway, Poland, Russia, Sweden, Taiwan, Türkiye, UK, USA, Vietnam.
Full; Associate; Honorary, in 6 countries and territories:
Japan, Korea Rep, Mongolia, Russia, UK, USA.
Corporate membership: centres and associations of Mongol studies in 9 countries:
China, Germany, India, Japan, Korea Rep, Mongolia, Russia, UK, USA.
Consultative Status Consultative status granted from: *UNESCO (#20322)* (Consultative Status).
[2021.06.21/XE0922/**C**]

♦ International Association for Monitoring and Quality Assurance in the Total Food Supply Chain (MoniQA) 12036
Contact Technologiezentrum, Europastr 1, 7540 Gussing, Austria. E-mail: moniqa@moniqa.org.
URL: http://www.moniqa.org/
History Launched 2011, resulting from EU-funded Network of Excellence on Monitoring and Quality Assurance in the Total Food Supply Chain (MoniQA, 2007-2012). Registration: Austria. **Aims** Provide solutions to promote a safer and secure food supply worldwide. **Structure** General Assembly; Supervisory Board; Scientific Advisory Committee. **Activities** Events/meetings. **Events** *International Seminar of Food Fraud Prevention and Effective Food Allergen Management* Vienna (Austria) 2018. **Publications** *e-News Alert*; *QAS Journal.*
Members Founder in 9 countries:
Austria, Belgium, China, Germany, Hungary, Italy, Türkiye, UK.
Full in 10 countries:
Australia, Austria, Bulgaria, Canada, France, Germany, Italy, Russia, UK, USA.
Ordinary in 9 countries:
Austria, Canada, China, Germany, Italy, Spain, Switzerland, UK, USA. [2023.02.16/XM7896/**C**]

♦ International Association of Movers (internationally oriented national body)

♦ International Association for Multibody System Dynamics (IMSD) . 12037
Sec Univ of La Coruña, Lab de Ingenieria Mecanica, Mendizabal s/n, 15403 Ferrol, La Coruña, Spain.
URL: http://info.itm.uni-stuttgart.de/imsd/index.html
History Set up as a successor to the Joint International Conference on Multibody System Dynamics formed 26 May 2010. Current bylaws adopted 1 Jul 2014, Busan (Korea Rep). **Aims** Address computational mechanics, nonlinear dynamics and control design; foster research on the dynamics of multibody systems and related fields; promote international cooperation between scientists and engineers in industry. **Structure** Steering Committee. **Languages** English. **Activities** Events/meetings. **Events** *Asian Conference on Multibody Dynamics* Delhi (India) 2022, *International Conference on Multibody Systems Dynamics* Delhi (India) 2022, *Asian Conference on Multibody Dynamics* Delhi (India) 2020, *International Conference on Multibody Systems Dynamics* Delhi (India) 2020, *International Conference on Multibody Systems Dynamics* Lisbon (Portugal) 2018. **Publications** *Multibody System Dynamics* – journal. **NGO Relations** Affiliate organization of: *International Union of Theoretical and Applied Mechanics (IUTAM, #15823).* [2021/XM5466/**E**]

♦ International Association of Multilingualism (IAM) 12038
Pres Univ Jaume I, Departament d'Estudis Anglesos, Avda de Vicent Sos Baynat s/n, 12071 Castellón de la Plana, Spain. E-mail: pilar.safont@uji.es.
Vice-Pres Université de Fribourg, Département de Plurilinguisme et des langues étrangères, Rue de Rome 1, 1700 Fribourg, Switzerland.
URL: http://www.iam.wildapricot.org/
History Sep 2003, Tralee (Ireland) at the 3rd International Conference on Third Language Acquisition and Trilingualism. **Aims** Establish a network for professionals interested in multilingualism and multiple language acquisition and learning. **Structure** Meeting (every 2 years, at Conference); Executive Committee. **Languages** English. **Staff** None. **Finance** Members' dues. **Activities** Events/meetings. **Events** *Conference* Zagreb (Croatia) 2021, *Conference* Zagreb (Croatia) 2020, *Conference* Lisbon (Portugal) 2018, *Conference* Vienna (Austria) 2016, *Conference* Uppsala (Sweden) 2014. **Publications** *International Journal of Multilingualism* (4 a year). *Multilingualism* – book series. *The Exploration of Multilingualism: Development of Research on L3, Multilingualism and Multiple Language Acquisition.*
Members Full in 17 countries:
Austria, Belgium, Canada, Finland, France, Hungary, Ireland, Israel, Italy, Malaysia, Netherlands, Poland, Spain, Sweden, Switzerland, UK, USA.
IGO Relations *European Centre for Modern Languages (ECML, #06491).* [2020.01.21/XJ5127/**D**]

♦ International Association of Municipal, Sports and Multipurpose Centres / see European Association of Event Centers (#06032)
♦ International Association of Municipal Statisticians / see International Association for Official Statistics (#12052)
♦ International Association for Musculoskeletal Problems in Haemophilia and Related Disorders (inactive)

♦ International Association of Museum Facility Administrators (IAMFA) 12039
Sec 1 Burston Gardens, Lingfield Road, East Grinstead, RH19 2HD, UK. T. +447799690174.
URL: http://www.iamfa.org/
History 1990, Chicago IL (USA). **Aims** Serve members and their *cultural* institutions through educational programmes, advancement of the facilities and security administration profession and through meaningful partnerships with suppliers of products, services and specialized expertise. **Structure** Board of Directors. **Languages** English. **Staff** Voluntary. **Finance** Members' dues. **Events** *Annual Conference* San Francisco, CA (USA) 2022, *Annual Conference* 2021, *Annual Conference* 2020, *Annual Conference* Pittsburgh, PA (USA) 2019, *Annual Conference* Los Angeles, CA (USA) 2018. **Publications** *Papyrus* – magazine.
Members Full in 9 countries and territories:
Australia, Canada, Denmark, France, Hong Kong, Italy, New Zealand, UK, USA.
NGO Relations Affiliated member of: *International Council of Museums (ICOM, #13051).* [2021/XJ1557/**D**]

♦ International Association of Museum Officials (inactive)
♦ International Association of Museums of Arms and Military History / see International Committee of Museums and Collections of Arms and Military History (#12790)
♦ International Association for Museums and Collections of Musical Instruments (inactive)

♦ International Association of Museums of History (IAMH) 12040
Association internationale des musées d'histoire (AIMH)
SG Musée Historique, Pl de la Cathédrale 4, 1005 Lausanne VD, Switzerland.
Registered address c/o Conseil International des Musées (ICOM), Maison de l'UNESCO, 1 rue Miollis, 75732 Paris CEDEX 15, France.
URL: http://www.iamh-aimh.org/
History 1991, Paris (France). Registered in accordance with French law. **Aims** Support the activities of museums of history; encourage curators to focus on the organization of museums and their role; endorse their function of disseminating information to the public in the spirit of remembrance, so as to provide a connection among international institutions. **Structure** Annual General Assembly; Council; Board. **Languages** English. **Finance** Members' dues. **Activities** Networking/liaising; events/meetings. **Events** *Biennial congress / Congress* Berlin (Germany) 2010, *Biennial congress / Congress* Belgrade (Serbia) 2008, *Biennial congress / Congress* Rio de Janeiro (Brazil) / Sao Paulo (Brazil) 2004, *Biennial congress / Congress* Lahti (Finland) 2002, *Biennial congress / Congress* Luxembourg (Luxembourg) 2000. **Publications** Various editions on International History and Museums; acts of conferences.
Members Full in 18 countries:
Belgium, Brazil, Canada, Denmark, Finland, France, Germany, Greece, Italy, Latvia, Lithuania, Luxembourg, Netherlands, Russia, Serbia, Switzerland, UK, USA.
NGO Relations Affiliated to: *International Council of Museums (ICOM, #13051).* [2017.11.23/XD8411/**D**]

♦ International Association of Music Information Centres (IAMIC) ... 12041
Contact Ravensteingalerij 38, 1000 Brussels, Belgium. T. +302103310129. E-mail: office@iamic.net – iamic@iamic.net.
URL: http://www.iamic.net/
History Founded 1958 as a grouping of 'National Music Centre Representatives' under the aegis of *International Music Council (IMC, #14199).* In 1962, member organizations became a constituent branch of *International Association of Music Libraries, Archives and Documentation Centres (IAML, #12042).* In 1986, growing activity and membership led to the setting up of the Association under its current name and under its own bylaws and Board of Directors. Affiliation with AIML ended in 1991 when IAMIC became a fully independent association. Registration: Banque-Carrefour des Entreprises, Start date: 2 Feb 2009, Belgium. **Aims** Encourage and enhance access to information, materials and products provided by members; encourage performance, broadcast, dissemination and export of local music from members; encourage exchange, collaboration and exchange of ideas, experiences and skills amongst members; play an active role in the broader international music environment. **Structure** General Assembly; Board; Research Committees; Working Groups; Executive Manager or Administrator. **Languages** English. **Staff** 1.00 FTE, paid. **Finance** Sources: members' dues. Support from: European Union operational grant; Flemish Authorities. **Activities** Awards/prizes/competitions; events/meetings; networking/liaising; projects/programmes. **Events** *Annual Meeting and General Assembly* 2021, *Annual Conference* Tallinn (Estonia) 2019, *Annual Conference* Rotterdam (Netherlands) 2018, *Annual Conference* Paphos (Cyprus) 2017, *Annual Conference* Galway (Ireland) 2016. **Publications** *IAMIC Newsletter.* Annual Report; conference proceedings; brochure.
Members Music centres in 33 countries:
Australia, Austria, Belgium, Canada, Croatia, Cyprus, Czechia, Denmark, Estonia, Finland, France, Germany, Greece, Iceland, India, Ireland, Israel, Italy, Latvia, Lithuania, Luxembourg, New Zealand, Norway, Poland, Portugal, Slovakia, Slovenia, South Africa, Spain, Sweden, Switzerland, UK, USA.
IGO Relations Member of (1): *Anna Lindh Euro-Mediterranean Foundation for the Dialogue between Cultures (Anna Lindh Foundation, #00847).* **NGO Relations** Member of (3): *Culture Action Europe (CAE, #04981); European Music Council (EMC, #07837); International Music Council (IMC, #14199).*
[2021.06.19/XD5821/**D**]

♦ International Association of Music Libraries / see International Association of Music Libraries, Archives and Documentation Centres (#12042)

♦ International Association of Music Libraries, Archives and Documentation Centres (IAML) 12042

Association internationale des bibliothèques, archives et centres de documentation musicaux (AIBM) – Internationale Vereinigung der Musikbibliotheken, Musikarchive und Musikdokumentationszentren (IVMB)

SG c/o Danish Agency for Culture, Hammerichsgade 14, 1611 Copenhagen, Denmark. E-mail: secretary@iaml.info.
URL: http://www.iaml.info/

History 23 Jul 1951, Paris (France). New Constitution and present name adopted Aug 1980, Cambridge (UK). Most recent Constitution adopted Jul 2014, Antwerp (Belgium). Former names and other names: *International Association of Music Libraries* – former (1951 to 1980); *Association internationale des bibliothèques musicales* – former (1951 to 1980); *Internationale Vereinigung der Musikbibliotheken* – former (1951 to 1980). **Aims** Encourage and promote activities of libraries, archives and documentation centres concerned with music and music materials; strengthen cooperation among institutions and individuals in these fields; publish information concerning their work. **Structure** General Assembly (annual); Board; Forum of Sections; Forum of National Representatives. Bibliographical series for music scholars and librarians (4): *Répertoire international d'iconographie musicale (RIdIM, #18844)*; *Répertoire International de Littérature Musicale (RILM, #18845)*; *International Inventory of the Musical Press (RIPM)*; *International Inventory of Musical Sources (#13949)*. **Languages** English, French, German. **Staff** 12.00 FTE, voluntary. **Finance** Sources: members' dues. **Activities** Events/meetings; knowledge management/information dissemination. **Events** *Congress* Thessaloniki (Greece) 2026, *Congress* Salzburg (Austria) 2025, *Congress* Stellenbosch (South Africa) 2024, *Congress* Cambridge (UK) 2023, *Annual Conference* Prague (Czechia) 2022. **Publications** *Fontes Artis Musicae* (4 a year).

Members Honorary; Individual; Institutional. National branches. Members in 48 countries:
Argentina, Australia, Austria, Belgium, Brazil, Bulgaria, Cameroon, Canada, China, Croatia, Cuba, Czechia, Denmark, Estonia, Finland, France, Germany, Greece, Hungary, Iceland, Indonesia, Ireland, Israel, Italy, Japan, Korea Rep, Latvia, Lithuania, Luxembourg, Netherlands, New Zealand, Nigeria, Norway, Poland, Portugal, Romania, Russia, Singapore, Slovakia, Slovenia, South Africa, Spain, Sweden, Switzerland, Türkiye, UK, Ukraine, USA.

NGO Relations Member of (4): *European Music Council (EMC, #07837)*; *International Council on Archives (ICA, #12996)*; *International Federation of Library Associations and Institutions (IFLA, #13470)*; *International Music Council (IMC, #14199)*. [2022.10.12/XC1318/**C**]

♦ International Association for Music and Medicine (IAMM) 12043

Communications Officer address not obtained.
URL: http://www.iammonline.com/

History 2009, Limerick (Ireland). **Aims** Encourage and support the use of music in medical contexts including research into the benefits of music, and its specialized applications in healthcare. **Structure** General Members' Meeting; Board of Directors; Executive Committee. **Finance** Sources: members' dues. **Activities** Events/meetings. **Events** *Conference* Athens (Greece) 2022, *Conference* Boston, MA (USA) 2020, *Conference* Barcelona (Spain) 2018, *International Conference* Toronto, ON (Canada) 2017, *International Conference* Beijing (China) 2016. **Publications** *Music and Medicine* – journal. [2021/XM5883/**C**]

♦ International Association of Musicology (inactive)
♦ International Association of Muslim Psychologists (unconfirmed)
♦ International Association for Muslim Scholars / see International Union of Muslim Scholars
♦ International Association of Mutual Benefit Societies (#02721)
♦ International Association of Mutual Insurance Companies (inactive)
♦ International Association of Mythcriticism and Acis (internationally oriented national body)
♦ International Association on Natality and Conception (inactive)
♦ International Association of National Motor Insurers' Bureaux / see Council of Bureaux (#04873)

♦ International Association of National Public Health Institutes (IANPHI) 12044

SG c/o Santé Publique France, 12 rue du Val d'Osne, 94415 Saint-Maurice Cedex, France. T. +33141796700. E-mail: info@ianphi.org.
US Office Emory University Global Health Institute, 1599 Clifton Road, Atlanta GA 30322, USA. T. +14047271416.
URL: http://www.ianphi.org/

History First envisioned 2001 and chartered 2006, with initial grants from *The Rockefeller Foundation (#18966)* and *Bill and Melinda Gates Foundation (BMGF)*. Formally launched, 2006, Rio de Janeiro (Brazil). **Aims** Link and strengthen government agencies responsible for public health; improve the world's health by leveraging experiences and expertise of member institutes to build robust public health systems. **Structure** Executive Board of 3 officers and 9 members; Secretariat, co-located in Cuernavaca (Mexico), Paris (France) and Atlanta GA (USA). **Languages** English, French, Portuguese, Spanish. **Staff** 10.00 FTE, paid. **Finance** US$ 20 million initial 5-year grant from *Bill and Melinda Gates Foundation (BMGF)* via Emory University; 2011: US$ 6 million grant from Gates Foundation for projects. **Activities** Advocacy/lobbying/activism; events/meetings; projects/programmes; training/education. **Events** *Annual Meeting* Addis Ababa (Ethiopia) 2019, *Annual Meeting* London (UK) 2018, *Annual Meeting* Rome (Italy) 2017, *Annual Meeting* Shanghai (China) 2016, *International Workshop on Simulation at the System Level for Industrial Applications* Paris (France) 2015. **Publications** *IANPHI World* (4 a year) – electronic newsletter. Annual Report; brochure; fact sheets.

Members Institutes (81) in 74 countries and territories:
Afghanistan, Albania, Angola, Argentina, Bangladesh, Belgium, Brazil, Cambodia, Canada, Chile, China, Colombia, Costa Rica, Côte d'Ivoire, Croatia, Cuba, Czechia, Denmark, El Salvador, Estonia, Ethiopia, Finland, France, Germany, Ghana, Guinea, Guinea-Bissau, Hong Kong, Hungary, Iceland, India, Indonesia, Iran Islamic Rep, Ireland, Israel, Italy, Japan, Jordan, Kenya, Latvia, Libya, Malawi, Mexico, Moldova, Mongolia, Morocco, Mozambique, Myanmar, Nepal, Netherlands, Nigeria, Norway, Pakistan, Panama, Papua New Guinea, Peru, Poland, Portugal, Russia, Saudi Arabia, Serbia, Slovenia, South Africa, Spain, Sudan, Sweden, Tanzania UR, Thailand, Togo, Türkiye, Uganda, UK, USA, Vietnam. [2020/XJ8191/**B**]

♦ International Association for National Youth Service (IANYS) 12045

Contact address not obtained. T. +12027750290. Fax +12023559317. E-mail: stroud@icicp.org.
URL: http://www.icicp.org/ianys/

History 1996, Papua New Guinea, during the 3rd Global Conference on National Youth Service. **Aims** Stimulate and facilitate exchange of information about national youth service (NYS); offer technical assistance to governments or private institutions that seek to develop or reshape NYS programmes; encourage youth to play an active role in their communities. **Structure** Global Council is the governing body, comprising experts in the field of youth service from around the world; currently 11 countries are represented on the Council. Global Council Chairman; Founder/Honorary President; Director. Secretariat provided by Innovations in Civic Participation (ICP), whose Executive Director is the Director of IANYS. **Languages** English, French, Spanish. **Staff** 3.00 FTE, paid. **Finance** Limited to operating costs, currently coming from within the secretariat's core budget. Additional funds are raised for the biannual conferences. The 2008 Global Conference has received the support of the US Embassy in Paris. The conference will also be funded through sponsorship from corporations, foundations, organizations and individuals. **Activities** Knowledge management/information dissemination; guidance/assistance/consulting; training/education; events/meetings; networking/liaising; research/documentation. **Events** *Global Conference* Alexandria (Egypt) 2010, *Biennial global conference / Global Conference* Paris (France) 2008, *Biennial global conference* Montréal, QC (Canada) 2006, *Biennial global conference / Global Conference* Accra (Ghana) 2004, *Biennial global conference / Global Conference* Buenos Aires (Argentina) 2002. **Publications** Conference reports. **Members** No formal membership structure. Since its inception, the Association has grown to include members in 48 countries on 6 continents. Categories State; Organizational; Individual; Cooperative; national and international organizations representatives dealing with youth and youth service issues; national youth service corps programme leaders; university and school-based service-learning programme leaders; scholars and researchers on national youth service; national public officers and international organization officers; young people taking part in NYS programmes; IANYS regional delegates and other related organizations. Membership countries not specified. [2015/XD7835/**D**]

♦ International Association for Natural Gas Vehicles / see NGV Global (#17131)
♦ International Association for Natural Textile Industry / see International Natural Textile Association (#14217)

♦ International Association of Nature Pedagogy (IANP) 12046

Contact Living Classrooms CIC, The Old School, Fowlis Wester, PH7 3NL, UK. E-mail: info@naturepedagogy.com.
URL: http://www.naturepedagogy.com/

History Founded Apr 2016. **Aims** Promote and support all forms of nature-based education and associated activity and research worldwide. **Structure** Board. **Activities** Advocacy/lobbying/activism; events/meetings; knowledge management/information dissemination; networking/liaising; training/education. **Events** *Annual Conference* Sao Paulo (Brazil) 2019.

Members Full in 7 countries:
Australia, Brazil, Canada, Netherlands, New Zealand, UK, USA. [2018/XM7070/**C**]

♦ International Association for Near-Death Studies (IANDS) 12047

Association internationale pour l'étude des états proches de la mort

Mailing Address 2741 Campus Walk Ave, Building 500, Durham NC 27705-8878, USA. T. +19193837940.
URL: http://www.iands.org/

History 1978, St Louis, MO (USA). Former names and other names: *Association for the Scientific Study of Near-Death Phenomena* – former (1978 to 1981). **Aims** Promote responsible, multi-disciplinary exploration of near death experiences (NDE) and near-death-like experiences, their effects on people's lives, and their implications for people's beliefs about life, death and human purpose; encourage research and discussion on and spread information about near-death studies and their implications, especially among hospitals, hospices, nursing homes, religious organizations and other institutions concerned with death and bereavement; provide support to those having had a near-death experience with their families. **Structure** Board of Directors. **Languages** English. **Finance** Members' dues. Other sources: private contributions; program activities. **Activities** Publishing activity; meeting activities; research. **Events** *Conference* Newport Beach, CA (USA) 2014, *Conference* Arlington, VA (USA) 2013, *Conference* Scottsdale, AZ (USA) 2012, *Conference* Durham, NC (USA) 2011, *Conference* Denver, CO (USA) 2010. **Publications** *Journal of Near-Death Studies* (4 a year); *Vital Signs* (4 a year) – newsletter. *Near-Death Experiences: Index to the Periodical Literature through 2001* – CD-ROM.

Members General; Professional; Sustaining. Members (also branches) in 11 countries:
Australia, Belgium, Canada, France, Germany, Hungary, Israel, Netherlands, Slovenia, South Africa, USA. [2021/XE0857/**D**]

♦ International Association for Neo-Latin Studies (IANLS) 12048

Association Internationale d'Études néo-latines (AIENL) – Internationale Gesellschaft für Neulateinische Studien – Associazione Internazionale degli Studi Latini Umanistici e Moderni – Societas Internationalis Studiis Neolatinis Provehendis

Sec Kohtu 6, 10130 Tallinn, Estonia. T. +3725275561.
URL: http://www.ianls.com/

History 1971, Leuven (Belgium). **Aims** Promote interest in Neo-Latin – writings since the beginnings of *Renaissance humanism* (around 1300AD) – and advancement of Neo-Latin studies. **Structure** Executive Committee; Advisory Board; Committee for Digital Resources; Committee on the Teaching of Neo-Latin. **Languages** English, French, German, Italian, Latin, Spanish. **Staff** 10.00 FTE, voluntary. **Finance** Sources: members' dues. **Activities** Events/meetings; knowledge management/information dissemination; research/documentation; training/education. **Events** *Triennial Congress* Leuven (Belgium) 2022, *Triennial Congress* Leuven (Belgium) 2021, *Triennial Congress* Albacete (Spain) 2018, *Triennial Congress* Vienna (Austria) 2015, *Triennial Congress* Münster (Germany) 2012. **Publications** *IANLS Newsletter* (periodical). *Acta Conventus Neolatini Albasitensis: – Proceedings of the Seventeenth International Congress of Neo-Latin Studies (Albacete 2018)* (2020) by Assoc Prof Florian Schaffenrath and Prof María Teresa Santamaría Hernández in English, French, German, Latin, Spanish; *Repertoire of Neo-Latinists* (1998). Circular letter; congress proceedings.

Members Individuals: Full; Student; Retired; Institutional. Members in 47 countries and territories:
Australia, Austria, Belgium, Brazil, Bulgaria, Canada, China, Croatia, Cuba, Czechia, Denmark, Estonia, Finland, France, Georgia, Germany, Greece, Haiti, Holy See, Hungary, Iceland, Ireland, Israel, Italy, Japan, Latvia, Lithuania, Luxembourg, Mexico, Netherlands, New Zealand, Norway, Poland, Polynesia Fr, Portugal, Romania, Serbia, Slovakia, Slovenia, South Africa, Spain, Sweden, Switzerland, Taiwan, UK, Ukraine, USA.

NGO Relations Member of (3): *Fédération internationale des associations d'études classiques (FIEC, #09607)*; *International Federation of Societies and Institutes for the Study of the Renaissance (#13549)*; Renaissance Society of America (RSA). [2022.10.13/XD7837/**C**]

♦ International Association of Neuromuscular Neurologists (no recent information)

♦ International Association for Neuropterology (IAN) 12049

Pres Entomology Dept, Texas A and M Univ, College Station TX 77843-2475, USA.
URL: http://www.neuropterology.org/

History 1994, Cairo (Egypt), during 5th International Symposium on Neuropterology, as an informal, scientific association of entomologists. **Aims** Provide continuity for the triennial International Symposium of Neuropterology; provide a forum for the study of neuropteroidea (insecta). **Structure** Board, comprising 2 Presidents, Vice-President, Secretary, Treasurer and 8 members. No formal office. **Languages** English. **Staff** 12.00 FTE, voluntary. **Finance** Members' dues. **Activities** Organizes symposia. Maintains electronic discussion board. **Events** *Symposium* Ponta Delgada (Portugal) 2011, *Symposium* Piran (Slovenia) 2008, *Symposium* 2006, *Symposium* Ferrara (Italy) 2005, *Symposium* College Station, TX (USA) 2003.

Members Individuals in 26 countries:
Australia, Austria, Brazil, Bulgaria, Canada, Egypt, Finland, France, Germany, Hungary, Iran Islamic Rep, Italy, Mexico, Moldova, Norway, Poland, Portugal, Romania, Russia, Slovenia, South Africa, Spain, Switzerland, UK, Ukraine, USA. [2010/XD7871/**E**]

♦ International Association of Neurorestoratology (unconfirmed)

♦ International Association of NLP Institutes (IN) 12050

Contact NLP and Coachng Inst Berlin, Winterfeldstr 97, 10777 Berlin, Germany. T. +493021478174.
URL: http://www.nlp-institutes.net/

History Founded 2001. Former names and other names: *Neuro Linguistic Programming* – former. **Aims** Develop the highest ethics and quality *standards* in *Neuro Linguistic Programming* (NLP); bridge effective practical applications of NLP with academic education, theory and research. **Structure** Board of Directors; Presidents in Countries; Ambassadors. Developmental Commission (9); Standard Commission (3). **Finance** Sources: members' dues. **Activities** Events/meetings; standards/guidelines; training/education. **Events** *NLP and Coaching World Congress* Hammamet (Tunisia) 2019, *NLP and Coaching World Congress* Paris (France) 2017. **Publications** *IN Newsletter*.

Members Individuals in 52 countries and territories:
Afghanistan, Argentina, Austria, Belgium, Bosnia-Herzegovina, Brazil, Canada, Chile, China, Costa Rica, Croatia, Egypt, Germany, Guadeloupe, Hungary, India, Iran Islamic Rep, Ireland, Israel, Italy, Japan, Kenya, Liechtenstein, Luxembourg, Malaysia, Martinique, Mauritius, Mongolia, Montenegro, Morocco, Netherlands, New Zealand, Nicaragua, Norway, Peru, Poland, Portugal, Romania, Russia, Serbia, Singapore, Sweden, Switzerland, Tanzania UR, Thailand, Türkiye, UK, United Arab Emirates, Uruguay, USA, Venezuela, Vietnam.

NGO Relations *European Coaching Association (ECA)*; *International Association of Coaching Institutes (ICI, #11780)*. [2018/XM6480/v/**C**]

♦ International Association for Non-Violent Sport (no recent information)
♦ International Association for Nuclear Law and Economics / see International Nuclear Law Association (#14379)

♦ International Association for Obsidian Studies (IAOS) 12051

Sec-Treas c/o Far Western Anthropological Research Group, 1180 Center Point Drive, Suite 100, Henderson NV 89074, USA. E-mail: iaos.editor@gmail.com.
Pres address not obtained.
URL: https://www.deschutesmeridian.com/IAOS/index.html

History 1989. **Aims** In the framework of physical and chemical properties of natural glasses and processes that affect them, promote multidisciplinary study of obsidian and obsidian characterization, obsidian hydration dating, geoarchaeological obsidian studies, lithic technology and prehistoric obsidian procurement and utilization; disseminate information regarding advances in obsidian research. **Languages** English. **Staff** Voluntary. **Finance** Sources: members' dues. **Activities** Standards/guidelines; guidance/assistance/consulting; training/education; events/meetings; knowledge management/information dissemination. **Events** *International Obsidian Conference* Berkeley, CA (USA) 2021. **Publications** *IAOS Bulletin* (2 a year). Obsidian bibliography.

Members Regular; Institutional. Individuals, facilities, libraries, institutions and students in 11 countries:
Argentina, Australia, Costa Rica, France, Greece, Guatemala, Mexico, New Zealand, UK, Ukraine, USA. [2021/XD4948/**D**]

♦ International Association of Occitan Studies (#02691)
♦ International Association of Official Human Rights Agencies (internationally oriented national body)

♦ International Association for Official Statistics (IAOS) 12052

Association internationale pour les statistiques officielles

Contact address not obtained. E-mail: contactiaos@gmail.com.
URL: http://isi.cbs.nl/iaos/

History Founded 1985, Amsterdam (Netherlands), at 45th Session of *International Statistical Institute (ISI, #15603)*, as a specialized section of ISI. Absorbed, 1989, *International Association for Regional and Urban Statistics (IARUS, inactive)*, which had been set up 22 Oct 1958, Geneva (Switzerland), following recommendations of ISI, as *International Association of Municipal Statisticians – Association internationale de statisticiens municipaux.* **Aims** Promote understanding and advancement of official statistics and related subjects; foster development of effective and efficient official statistical services through international contacts among individuals and organizations, including users of official statistics, as well as research institutes. **Structure** General Assembly; Executive Committee (EC). **Languages** English. **Staff** Voluntary. **Finance** Members' dues. Other sources: donations; contributions; income, if any, from other sources. **Activities** Events/meetings; awards/prizes/competitions. **Events** *IAOS-ISI Conference* Livingstone (Zambia) 2023, *Conference* Krakow (Poland) 2022, *Conference* Livingstone (Zambia) 2021, *Conference* Livingstone (Zambia) 2020, *Better Statistics for Better Lives* Paris (France) 2018. **Publications** *IAOS Newsletter*; *Statistical Journal of the IAOS (SJIAOS).* **Members** Individuals (437); Institutions (47). Membership countries not specified. **NGO Relations** Sister organization of: *Bernoulli Society for Mathematical Statistics and Probability (BSMSP, #03212)*; *Global Partnership for Sustainable Development Data (Data4SDGS, #10542)*; *International Association for Statistical Computing (IASC, #12183)*; *International Association for Statistics Education (IASE, #12184)*; *International Association of Survey Statisticians (IASS, #12218)*; *International Environmetrics Society (TIES, #13284)*; *International Society on Business and Industrial Statistics (ISBIS, #14989).* [2020.01.03/XB0101/v/**E**]

♦ International Association of Offshore Diving Contractors / see IMCA International Marine Contractors Association (#11127)

♦ International Association of Oil and Gas Producers (IOGP) 12053

Exec Sec City Tower, 40 Basinghall Street, London, EC2V 5DE, UK. T. +442037639700. Fax +442037639701. E-mail: reception@iogp.org.
Brussels Office Bd du Souverain 165 – 4th Floor, 1160 Brussels, Belgium. T. +3225669150. Fax +3225669159.
Houston Office 10777 Westheimer Road, Suite 1100, Houston TX 77042, USA. T. +17134700315.
URL: http://www.iogp.org/

History Aug 1974, London (UK). Former names and other names: *E and P Forum* – former; *OGP* – former. Registration: Companies House, No/ID: 01832064, Start date: 11 Jul 1984, England and Wales. **Aims** Work on behalf of the world's oil and gas exploration and production (E and P) companies to promote safe, responsible and sustainable operations. **Structure** General Meeting (2 a year); Management Committee; Standing Committees; Secretariat. **Languages** English. **Staff** 21.00 FTE, paid. **Finance** Sources: members' dues. **Activities** Awards/prizes/competitions; events/meetings; knowledge management/information dissemination; networking/liaising; projects/programmes; standards/guidelines. **Events** *Annual General Meeting* London (UK) 2022, *Annual General Meeting* London (UK) 2016, *Regional Forum* Mexico City (Mexico) 2016, *European General Meeting* Milan (Italy) 2016, *European General Meeting* The Hague (Netherlands) 2015. **Publications** *Highlights newsletter*. Report series; data reports; activity reports; position papers; fact sheets; posters. **Members** Oil and gas companies (84) involved in exploration or production. Membership countries not specified. **Consultative Status** Consultative status granted from: *ECOSOC (#05331)* (Ros C); *International Maritime Organization (IMO, #14102)*; *World Meteorological Organization (WMO, #21649).* **IGO Relations** Observer to: *OSPAR Commission for the Protection of the Marine Environment of the North-East Atlantic (OSPAR Commission, #17905).* Associated with Department of Global Communications of the United Nations. **NGO Relations** Member of (3): *European Energy Forum (EEF, #06986)* (Associate); *GasNaturally (#10074)*; *Industry4Europe (#11181).* In liaison with: *International Organization for Standardization (ISO, #14473)*; *International Regulators' Forum (IRF, #14710).* [2022/XD4478/**C**]

♦ International Association of Olympic Medical Officers (inactive)

♦ International Association of Online Engineering (IAOE) 12054

Contact Kirchengasse 10/200, 1070 Vienna, Austria. T. +4366473621196. Fax +49891488294752. E-mail: info@online-engineering.org.
URL: http://www.online-engineering.org/

History 2006. Registration: Austria. **Aims** Encourage wider development, distribution and application of Online Engineering (OE) technologies and its influence on society. **Structure** Executive Committee; Scientific Advisory Board. **Languages** English. **Activities** Events/meetings; publishing activities. **Events** *International Conference on Interactive Collaborative Learning* Vienna (Austria) 2022, *Annual Symposium* Dresden (Germany) 2021, *International Conference on Interactive Collaborative Learning* Dresden (Germany) 2021, *International Conference on Interactive Collaborative Learning* Tallinn (Estonia) 2020, *International Conference on Interactive Collaborative Learning* Bangkok (Thailand) 2019. **Publications** *International Journal of Online & Biomedical Engineering* (12 a year). **Members** Individual (over 1,000); Institutional. Members in over 60 countries. Membership countries not specified. **NGO Relations** Member of (1): *International Federation of Engineering Education Societies (IFEES, #13412).* [2021.06.15/XJ0343/**C**]

♦ International Association for Ontology and its Applications (IAOA) 12055

Pres Semantic Technologies Lab, Dept of Mechanical and Industrial Engineering, Univ of Toronto, 5 King's College Road, Toronto ON M5S, Canada. T. +14169468853.
URL: http://www.iaoa.org/

History 29 Apr 2009, Trento (Italy). Registered in accordance with Italian law. Statutes revised 25 May 2012. **Aims** Promote interdisciplinary research and international collaboration at the intersection of philosophical ontology, linguistics, logic, cognitive science, and computer science, as well as in the applications of ontological analysis to conceptual modelling, knowledge engineering, knowledge management, information-systems development, library and information science, scientific research, and semantic technologies in general. **Structure** Executive Council, comprising President, Secretary, Treasurer and 6 members. **Languages** English. **Staff** 2.00 FTE, voluntary. **Finance** Members' dues. Budget (2010): about euro 4,000. **Activities** Events/meetings; networking/liaising; research and development; financial and/or material support; awards/prizes/competitions. **Events** *FOIS : International Conference on Formal Ontology in Information Systems / Conference* Rio de Janeiro (Brazil) 2014, *Conference* Graz (Austria) 2012, *Conference* Toronto, ON (Canada) 2010, *FOIS : international conference on formal ontology in information systems* Toronto, ON (Canada) 2010, *FOIS : international conference on formal ontology in information systems / Conference* Saarbrücken (Germany) 2008. **Members** Individuals and institutions. Membership countries not specified. [2015.03.02/XJ8254/**D**]

♦ International Association of Opera Directors (inactive)
♦ International Association of Operative Millers (internationally oriented national body)
♦ International Association of Ophthalmic Pathology / see International Society of Ophthalmic Pathology
♦ International Association for the Optimization of Plant Nutrition (inactive)

♦ International Association of Oral and Maxillofacial Pathologists (IAOP) 12056

Sec address not obtained.
Pres address not obtained.
URL: https://iaop.com/

History 1976. **Aims** Develop and promote the practice and science of oral pathology; advance under and postgraduate education; further knowledge of clinical aspects, laboratory diagnosis and applied and translational research in the field. **Structure** Council; Executive Committee. **Languages** English. **Staff** Voluntary secretariat. **Finance** Sources: meeting proceeds; members' dues. **Events** *International Congress on Oral Pathology and Medicine* Taipei (Taiwan) 2022, *Biennial International Congress* London (UK) 2021, *Biennial International Congress* London (UK) 2020, *Joint Congress* Cape Town (South Africa) 2019, *Biennial International Congress* Vancouver, BC (Canada) 2018. **Publications** *Newsletter* (2 a year).
Members Individuals (368) in 45 countries and territories:
Argentina, Australia, Belgium, Brazil, Canada, Chile, China, Denmark, Egypt, El Salvador, Finland, France, Germany, Greece, Guatemala, Hong Kong, Iceland, India, Ireland, Italy, Japan, Kenya, Malaysia, Mexico, Netherlands, New Zealand, Nigeria, Norway, Pakistan, Peru, Poland, Portugal, Saudi Arabia, Singapore, South Africa, Spain, Sri Lanka, Sudan, Sweden, Switzerland, Tanzania UR, Thailand, Türkiye, UK, USA. [2021/XD2639/v/**C**]

♦ International Association of Oral and Maxillofacial Surgeons (IAOMS) 12057

Association internationale de chirurgie buccale et maxillo-faciale

Address not obtained.
URL: http://www.iaoms.org/

History 5 Jul 1962, London (UK). Regulations confirmed 24 Jun 1965; revised May 1986, Jan 1993. **Aims** Promote the art and science of oral and maxillofacial surgery. **Structure** Council; Executive Committee; Board of Directors. IAOMS Foundation. Committees. **Languages** English. **Staff** 6.00 FTE, paid. **Finance** Sources: members' dues. **Activities** Events/meetings; training/education. **Events** *International Conference* Kyoto (Japan) 2025, *International Conference* Vancouver, BC (Canada) 2023, *International Conference* Glasgow (UK) 2021, *International Symposium on Orthognathic Surgery* Vienna (Austria) 2020, *Biennial International Conference* Rio de Janeiro (Brazil) 2019. **Publications** *International Journal of Oral and Maxillofacial Surgery (IJOMS).* Newsletters.
Members Affiliated National Societies; Fellows. Members in 82 countries and territories:
Albania, Argentina, Armenia, Australia, Austria, Bahrain, Belarus, Belgium, Bolivia, Brazil, Brunei Darussalam, Bulgaria, Canada, Chile, China, Colombia, Costa Rica, Cuba, Cyprus, Czechia, Denmark, Dominican Rep, Egypt, Estonia, Finland, France, Georgia, Germany, Ghana, Gibraltar, Greece, Hong Kong, Hungary, Iceland, India, Indonesia, Iran Islamic Rep, Ireland, Israel, Italy, Kenya, Korea Rep, Latvia, Libya, Lithuania, Luxembourg, Malaysia, Mexico, Moldova, Netherlands, Nigeria, North Macedonia, Norway, Panama, Paraguay, Peru, Philippines, Poland, Portugal, Qatar, Romania, Saudi Arabia, Serbia, Singapore, Slovakia, South Africa, Spain, Sweden, Switzerland, Syrian AR, Taiwan, Tanzania UR, Thailand, Tunisia, Türkiye, UK, Ukraine, United Arab Emirates, Uruguay, USA, Venezuela, Zimbabwe.
Members also in the Caribbean region (countries not specified). [2022/XB1320/**B**]

♦ International Association of Organizational Innovation (internationally oriented national body)
♦ International Association of the Organizations and Congress Cities of the States Interested in the Mediterranean (inactive)
♦ International Association of Organizers of Cyclo-Cross Organizers (inactive)
♦ International Association of Orientalist Librarians (inactive)
♦ International Association of Original Art Diffusers / see Federation of European Art Galleries Associations (#09492)

♦ International Association for Orthodontics (IAO) 12058

Association internationale d'orthodontie

Exec Dir 750 North Lincoln Memorial Dr, Ste 422, Milwaukee WI 53202, USA. T. +14142722757. Fax +14142722754. E-mail: worldheadquarters@iaortho.org.
URL: http://www.iaortho.org/

History 1961, Los Angeles CA (USA), as *International Academy of Orthodontics.* **Aims** Promote cooperation in the field of orthodontic *dentistry.* **Structure** Executive Board; Committee Chairs; Section Representatives. **Languages** English. **Staff** 4.50 FTE, paid. **Finance** Budget (annual): about US$ 900,000. **Events** *Annual Meeting* New Orleans, LA (USA) 2019, *Annual Meeting* Kauai Is (USA) 2018, *Annual Meeting* Memphis, TN (USA) 2017, *Annual Meeting* Tucson, AZ (USA) 2016, *Annual Meeting* Austin, TX (USA) 2015. **Publications** *International Journal of Orthodontics* (4 a year); *Straight Talk Newsletter* (4 a year); *Membership Directory* (annual).
Members Sections and individuals (mainly in USA) in 62 countries:
Antigua-Barbuda, Argentina, Australia, Austria, Bangladesh, Belize, Benin, Brazil, Canada, China, Colombia, Costa Rica, Denmark, Dominican Rep, Ecuador, Egypt, Ethiopia, France, Germany, Greece, Hong Kong, India, Indonesia, Iran Islamic Rep, Ireland, Israel, Italy, Jamaica, Japan, Jordan, Kenya, Korea Rep, Malaysia, Mexico, Nepal, Netherlands, New Zealand, Nicaragua, Norway, Oman, Pakistan, Peru, Philippines, Poland, Portugal, Qatar, Russia, Saudi Arabia, Singapore, South Africa, Spain, Sri Lanka, St Kitts-Nevis, Switzerland, Taiwan, Thailand, UK, United Arab Emirates, USA, Venezuela, Yemen. [2019/XF1319/**F**]

♦ International Association of Orthopaedic Footwear 12059

Association internationale des podo-orthésists – Internationaler Verband der Orthopädie-Schuhtechniker (IVO)

Secretariat c/o Bundesinnungsverband Orthopädieschuhtechnik, Ricklinger Stadtweg 92, 30459 Hannover, Germany. T. +49511421051. Fax +49511425151. E-mail: info@biv-os.de.
URL: http://www.ivonet.org/

History 1973, Cologne (Germany FR), as *International Association of Orthopaedic Shoe Technicians – Association internationale des techniciens de chaussures orthopédiques.* **Aims** Exchange experience among members concerning the profession. **Languages** German. **Finance** Members' dues. **Events** *IVO Congress* Cologne (Germany) 2022, *IVO Congress* Cologne (Germany) 2021, *Triennial Congress* Toronto, ON (Canada) 2018, *Triennial Congress* Paris (France) 2015, *Triennial Congress* Sydney, NSW (Australia) 2012.
Members National organizations in 14 countries:
Australia, Austria, Belgium, Canada, Denmark, France, Germany, Israel, Italy, Luxembourg, Netherlands, Norway, Switzerland, UK. [2012/XD0229/**D**]

♦ International Association of Orthopaedic Shoe Technicians / see International Association of Orthopaedic Footwear (#12059)

♦ International Association for Otto Gross Studies 12060

Association internationale pour l'étude d'Otto Gross – Associação Internacional para Estudos Otto Gross – Internationale Assoziation für Otto Gross Studien – Asociación Internacional de Estudios de Otto Gross – Internasjonal Forening for Otto Gross Studier – Associazione Internazionale di Studi su Otto Gross – Miedzynarodowe Towarzystwo Studiów o Otto Grossie – Otto Gross Tanulmanyok Nemzetközi Tarsasaga – Internationale vereniging voor Otto Gross studies

Contact c/o Otto Gross Archive, 13 Mansell Rd, London, W3 7QH, UK. T. +442087494388.

History 1999, Germany. Successor to *International Otto Gross Society (inactive).* **Aims** Research the life, work and influence of the medical doctor, pyschoanalist, psychiatrist, revolutionary, *philosopher*, Dr Otto Gross. **Languages** English, French, German, Italian, Portuguese. **Staff** None paid. **Finance** Self-financing. **Activities** Events/meetings; research/documentation. **Events** *Congress* Berlin (Germany) 2020, *Congress* Moscow (Russia) 2017. **Publications** Proceedings; books; articles.
Members Full in 12 countries:
Australia, Austria, Brazil, Chile, France, Germany, Hungary, Italy, Poland, Russia, Switzerland, UK.
IGO Relations None. **NGO Relations** None. [2021.05.25/XM8418/**E**]

♦ International Association for Ottoman Social and Economic History (IAOSEH) 12061

SG address not obtained.
Adjunct Sec address not obtained.
URL: https://iaoseh.wordpress.com/

History 1977. Current statutes adopted June 1998, Bursa (Turkey). **Aims** Provide a scientific platform for the international community of Ottomanists to exchange the results of current research and discuss the historiography, contributing to professional collaboration and solidarity in the field of Ottoman Studies. **Structure** Board; Executive Committee. **Activities** Events/meetings. **Events** *International Congress of Ottoman Social and Economic History* Zagreb (Croatia) 2022, *International Congress of Ottoman Social and Economic History* Zagreb (Croatia) 2020, *International Congress of Ottoman Social and Economic History* Sofia (Bulgaria) 2017, *International Congress of Ottoman Social and Economic History* Alcala de Henares (Spain) 2013, *International Congress of Ottoman Social and Economic History* Retz (Austria) 2011. [2022.10.18/AA1854/**E**]

♦ International Association of Outsourcing Professionals (IAOP) 12062

Contact 2600 South Rd, Ste 44-240, Poughkeepsie NY 12601, USA. T. +18454520600. Fax +18454526988.
URL: http://www.iaop.org/

History Jan 2005. **Structure** Strategic Advisory Board. Committees (4): Advocacy and Outreach; Member Services; Research; Training and Certification. **Events** *Outsourcing World Summit* 2022, *Outsourcing World Summit* Orlando, FL (USA) 2020, *European Outsourcing Summit (EOS18)* Brussels (Belgium) 2018, *Outsourcing World Summit* Lake Buena Vista, FL (USA) 2014, *Asia-Pacific Outsourcing Summit* Singapore (Singapore) 2014.
Members Geographical Chapters (36) and Topical and Industry Chapters (18) in 18 countries and territories:
Australia, Brazil, Canada, China, Colombia, Denmark, Germany, Hong Kong, India, Ireland, Italy, Malaysia, Philippines, Russia, Spain, Switzerland, UK, USA.
NGO Relations Member of: *Emerging Europe Alliance for Business Services, Innovation and Technology (Emerging Europe Alliance).* [2012.07.31/XM0624/t/**D**]

♦ International Association of Oxygen Management in Wine (inactive)

♦ International Association of Packaging Research Institutes (IAPRI) 12063

Association internationale des instituts de recherche sur l'emballage – Internationale Vereinigung der Forschungsinstitute für Verpackung

SG 6200 W Golfridge Drive, East Lansing MI 48823, USA. E-mail: sg@iapri.org.
URL: https://www.iapri.org/

History 1971. Initiated 1969, following biennial meetings dating from 1960. Headquartered in UK until 2017 when moved to USA. Registration: Section 501(c)(6), USA. **Aims** Enhance the effectiveness of packaging research, design and performance testing. **Structure** Board of Directors; President; Secretary General. **Languages** English. **Staff** 2.00 FTE, paid. **Finance** Sources: members' dues. **Activities** Events/meetings; knowledge management/information dissemination; networking/liaising; projects/programmes; publishing activities; research and development; research/documentation. **Events** *World Conference on Packaging* Bangkok (Thailand) 2022, *Symposium on Packaging* East Lansing, MI (USA) 2021, *World Conference on Packaging* Monterrey (Mexico) 2020, *Symposium on Packaging* Enschede (Netherlands) 2019, *World Conference on Packaging* Zhuhai (China) 2018. **Publications** *IAPRI Global Packaging Research E-Newsletter* (12 a year). Annual Conference research papers and presentations.
Members Scientific institutes, academic organizations, packaging testing and commercial organizations (90) in 28 countries:
Australia, Austria, Belgium, Brazil, Canada, Chile, China, Denmark, Finland, France, Germany, Hungary, India, Israel, Japan, Netherlands, New Zealand, Norway, Philippines, Poland, Singapore, Spain, Sweden, Switzerland, Thailand, Türkiye, UK, USA. [2022.06.14/XD1255/**C**]

♦ International Association of Paediatric Dentistry (IAPD) 12064

Sec c/o Paragon, Avenue Louis Casai 18, 1209 Geneva, Switzerland. T. +41225330948. Fax +41225802923. E-mail: iapd@iapdworld.org.
URL: http://www.iapdworld.org/

History Jun 1969, Siena (Italy). Founded at 2nd International Symposium of Child Dental Health, an *'International Forum of Dentistry for Children'* having been held in Feb 1968, London (UK). Former names and other names: *International Association of Dentistry for Children (IADC)* – former (Jun 1969); *Association internationale d'odonto-stomatologie infantile* – former (Jun 1969); *Association internationale de dentisterie pédiatrique (AIDP)* – former; *Association internationale d'odonto-stomatologie pédiatrique* – former. **Aims** Comprise a forum for exchange of international information concerning paediatric dentistry; contribute to progress and promotion of dental health for children and encourage research in the field. **Structure** Council (meets every 2 years in conjunction with general scientific session); Executive Committee. **Languages** English. **Staff** 1.00 FTE, paid. **Finance** Sources: members' dues. **Activities** Awards/prizes/competitions; events/meetings; training/education. **Events** *Biennial Congress* Cape Town (South Africa) 2025, *Biennial Congress* Maastricht (Netherlands) 2023, *Global Summit* Rome (Italy) 2022, *Biennial Congress* Geneva (Switzerland) 2021, *Biennial Congress* Cancún (Mexico) 2019. **Publications** *International Journal of Paediatric Dentistry* (6 a year); *IAPD Newsletter* in English.
Members Member Nations: national societies of children's dentistry, or sections of national dental societies dealing specifically with children's dentistry. Supporting Membership: individuals who possess a recognized dental qualification and wish to support the concept of international dentistry for children. Members in 64 countries and territories:
Algeria, Argentina, Australia, Austria, Belgium, Bolivia, Brazil, Bulgaria, Cambodia, Canada, Chile, China, Colombia, Costa Rica, Croatia, Cyprus, Denmark, Ecuador, Egypt, Finland, France, Germany, Greece, Hong Kong, Hungary, India, Iran Islamic Rep, Ireland, Israel, Italy, Japan, Jordan, Kenya, Korea Rep, Malaysia, Mexico, Netherlands, Nigeria, North Macedonia, Norway, Panama, Paraguay, Peru, Philippines, Poland, Portugal, Romania, Russia, Serbia, Slovenia, South Africa, Spain, Sweden, Switzerland, Taiwan, Thailand, Tunisia, Türkiye, UK, Ukraine, United Arab Emirates, Uruguay, USA, Venezuela.
NGO Relations Member of (1): *FDI – World Dental Federation (#09281).* [2023.02.14/XB4080/**B**]

♦ International Association for Pain and Chemical Dependency (inactive)

♦ International Association of Pancreatology (IAP) 12065

Association internationale de pancréatologie

Sec Dept Gastroenterology, All India Inst of Medical Sciences, Ansari Hagar, Delhi 110029, DELHI 110029, India. T. +919810038116. Fax +911126588663. E-mail: pgarg10@hotmail.com.
URL: http://www.internationalpancreatology.org/

History 1984, Estoril, Portugal. **Aims** Promote and encourage the advancement and exchange of knowledge of normal and diseased exocrine and endocrine pancreas and of basic basic and clinical research in pancreatology; promote public interest in and understanding of the subject. **Structure** Council. **Languages** English. **Staff** None. **Finance** Members' dues. Other sources: grants from industry; journal activity. **Activities** Events/meetings. **Events** *Meeting* Cape Town (South Africa) 2019, *Meeting* Miami, FL (USA) 2018, *Meeting* Buenos Aires (Argentina) 2017, *Meeting* Sendai (Japan) 2016, *Meeting* Shanghai (China) 2015. **Publications** *Pancreatology* (6 a year).
Members Clinical and basic pancreatic researchers in 28 countries:
Argentina, Australia, Austria, Belgium, Brazil, Canada, China, Denmark, France, Germany, Greece, Hong Kong, Hungary, India, Italy, Japan, Mexico, Netherlands, New Zealand, Poland, Portugal, South Africa, Spain, Sweden, Switzerland, Taiwan, UK, USA. [2017.06.01/XD5759/v/**D**]

♦ International Association of Paper Historians (IPH) 12066

Association internationale des historiens du papier – Internationale Arbeitsgemeinschaft der Papierhistoriker

Pres Stenhoejgaardsvej 57, 3460 Birkerød, Denmark. T. +4545816803.
Treas address not obtained.
URL: http://www.paperhistory.org/

History 1959, Germany FR. Founded 1959, Bamberg (Germany FR). Registered in Basle (Switzerland) in accordance with Swiss Civil Code. **Aims** Assist communication between individual research workers; facilitate introduction of valid international descriptions and definitions; collate documentation about paper; propagate knowledge of the history of paper-making and *watermarks*; generally arouse interest in paper history. **Structure** Governing Committee; Executive Council. **Languages** English, French, German. **Staff** Voluntary. **Finance** Sources: members' dues. **Activities** Events/meetings; publishing activities. **Events** *Biennial Congress* Krems (Austria) 2022, *Biennial Congress* Washington, DC (USA) 2021, *Biennial Congress* Washington, DC (USA) 2020, *Biennial Congress* Ghent (Belgium) 2018, *Biennial Congress* Valencia (Spain) 2016. **Publications** *IPH Paper History* (2 a year); *IPH Congress Book* (every 2 years).
Members Individuals (researchers and others); companies; libraries and archives; institutes. Membership totalling 234 in 33 countries:
Argentina, Australia, Austria, Belgium, Belize, Brazil, Canada, Chile, Denmark, Estonia, Finland, France, Germany, Greece, Hungary, Indonesia, Ireland, Italy, Japan, Luxembourg, Netherlands, Norway, Poland, Portugal, Qatar, Russia, Saudi Arabia, Slovenia, Spain, Sweden, Switzerland, UK, USA. [2022/XC1322/**C**]

♦ International Association of Papyrologists (#02725)

♦ International Association of Paratuberculosis 12067

Sec-Treas c/o New Bolton Ctr, 382 West St Rd, Kennett Square PA 19348, USA. T. +16104445800 ext 6132. Fax +16109258100.
URL: http://www.paratuberculosis.net/

History Jan 1989. **Aims** Contribute to the advancement of scientific progress on Mycobacterium avium subspecies paratuberculosis, related mycobacteria and related diseases in livestock. **Structure** Board of Directors; Executive Board. **Languages** English. **Staff** 4.00 FTE, voluntary. **Finance** Sources: members' dues. **Events** *International Colloquium on Paratuberculosis* Jaipur (India) 2024, *Colloquium* Dublin (Ireland) 2022, *Colloquium* Dublin (Ireland) 2021, *Colloquium* Dublin (Ireland) 2020, *Colloquium* Cancún (Mexico) 2018. **Publications** *Paratuberculosis Newsletter* (2 a year). Proceedings.
Members Individuals (140) in 29 countries:
Argentina, Australia, Austria, Belgium, Brazil, Canada, Chile, Colombia, Czechia, Denmark, France, Germany, Greece, India, Ireland, Italy, Japan, Mexico, Netherlands, New Zealand, Norway, Panama, Saudi Arabia, Slovenia, Spain, Switzerland, Thailand, UK, USA. [2021/XD5889/**D**]

♦ International Association of Parkinsonism and Related Disorders (IAPRD) 12068

Exec Dir Van Eeghenstraat 83, 1071 EX Amsterdam, Netherlands. E-mail: iaprd@interplan.de.
URL: https://www.iaprd.info/

History Set up during 1960s, by *World Federation of Neurology (WFN, #21461).* Functions as an independent organization. Current bylaws adopted Dec 2010. Former names and other names: *Association of Parkinsonism and Related Disorders (APRD)* – alias; *Vereniging Parkinsonism and Related Disorders (PRD)* – legal name. Registration: Netherlands. **Aims** Promote and monitor research developments in movement disorders; foster communication among neuroscientists, neurologists and other healthcare professionals. **Structure** Rotating Committees. **Languages** English. **Activities** Events/meetings. **Events** *World Congress on Parkinson's Disease and Related Disorders* Chicago, IL (USA) 2023, *World Congress on Parkinson's Disease and Related Disorders* Prague (Czechia) 2022, *World Congress on Parkinson's Disease and Related Disorders* Amsterdam (Netherlands) 2021, *World Congress on Parkinson's Disease and Related Disorders* Prague (Czechia) 2020, *World Congress on Parkinson's Disease and Related Disorders* Montréal, QC (Canada) 2019. **Publications** *Parkinsonism and Related Disorders* – official journal. **Members** Full; Associate; Honorary. Membership countries not specified. [2022/XJ8614/**C**]

♦ International Association of Partially or Wholly French-Language Schools (inactive)
♦ International Association for Participatory Development (internationally oriented national body)
♦ International Association of Patristic Studies (#02692)

♦ International Association for Pattern Recognition (IAPR) 12069

Association internationale pour la reconnaissance des formes

Contact 18 Albright Circle, Madison NJ 07940, USA. E-mail: secretariat@iapr.org.
URL: http://www.iapr.org/

History Jan 1978. Founded following proposals of a Standing Committee set up following 2nd International Conference on Pattern Recognition, 1974, Copenhagen (Denmark) and approval of Constitution, 1976, Coronado CA (USA). **Aims** Promote pattern recognition and allied branches of *engineering*, together with related arts and science; advance international cooperation in the field to stimulate research, development and the application of pattern recognition in science and human activity; further the dissemination and exchange of information on pattern recognition; encourage education in all aspects of the field. **Structure** Governing Board; Executive Committee. Standing Committees (10): Awards (2); Conferences and Meetings; Advisory; Constitution and Bylaws; Education; Fellow; Industrial Liaison; Membership; Nominating; Publications and Publicity. **Languages** English. **Staff** Secretariat, paid; officers, voluntary. **Finance** Members' dues, depending on size of member society. 10 percent of ICPR conference registration fees. **Activities** Technical Committees (20): Statistical Pattern Recognition Techniques; Structural and Syntactical Pattern Recognition; Neural Networks and Computational Intelligence; Biometrics; Benchmarking and Software; Special Hardware and Software Environments; Remote Sensing and Mapping; Machine Vision Applications; Biomedical Image Analysis; Graphics Recognition; Reading Systems; Multimedia and Visual Information Systems; Pattern Recognition in Astronomy and Astrophysics; Signal Analysis for Machine Intelligence; Graph-based Representations; Algebraic and Discrete Mathematical Techniques in Pattern Recognition; Machine Learning and Data Mining; Discrete Geometry; Computer Vision for Cultural Heritage Applications; Pattern Recognition for Bioinformatics. Technical Committees also arrange workshops. Awards: King Sun-Fu; J K Aggarwal; Best Paper (every 2 years, at Conference). **Events** *International Joint Conference on Biometrics* Abu Dhabi (United Arab Emirates) 2022, *International Conference on Pattern Recognition* Montréal, QC (Canada) 2022, *Asian Conference* Jeju (Korea Rep) 2021, *International Conference on Document Analysis and Recognition* Lausanne (Switzerland) 2021, *International Conference on Pattern Recognition* Milan (Italy) 2021. **Publications** *Pattern Recognition Letters* (12 a year); *Machine Vision and Applications* (6 a year); *IAPR Newsletter* (4 a year). Conference proceedings.
Members National societies in 41 countries and territories:
Australia, Austria, Belarus, Brazil, Bulgaria, Canada, China, Cuba, Czechia, Denmark, Finland, France, Germany, Greece, Hong Kong, Hungary, India, Ireland, Israel, Italy, Japan, Korea Rep, Mexico, Morocco, Netherlands, New Zealand, Norway, Poland, Portugal, Russia, Singapore, Slovenia, South Africa, Spain, Sweden, Switzerland, Taiwan, Türkiye, UK, Ukraine, USA.
NGO Relations Cooperates with (1): *International Society for Photogrammetry and Remote Sensing (ISPRS, #15362).* Supports (1): *Pacific-Rim Symposium on Image and Video Technology (PSIVT).* [2020/XD6418/**C**]

♦ International Association 'Peace through Culture' (PTC) 12070

Association internationale 'Paix par la culture' – Internationale Gesellschaft 'Frieden durch Kultur' – Mezdunarodnaja Associacija 'Mir cerez Kulturu'

Contact 10/1 Orynbor Street, Yesil District, Nur-Sultan, Kazakhstan, 010000. E-mail: astanaforum@bk.ru – info@peace-through-culture.org.
URL: http://astanaforum.kz/en/

History 12 Jul 1989, Moscow (USSR), by Russian writer and philosopher Valentin Sidorov. Became legally international 22 Feb 1991. **Aims** As successor to the spiritual behests of the family of Nicholas Roerich, and believing that the only way out of the global crisis through spiritual-cultural revolution, recreate the movement 'peace through culture' on a new basis by unification and consolidation of spiritual-cultural forces; while identifying with all ethical principles in social and religious teaching, strive for constructive cooperation and unification on ethical grounds of concrete initiatives of Christians, Buddhists, Muslims, Hindus, "believers" and "non-believers"; promote the worldwide movement of spiritual concord on ethical fundamentals, unity in diversity and in cultural ethical unity. **Structure** International Association based in Moscow (Russia). European Branch based in Germany and Switzerland. Local branches. **Languages** English, German, Russian. **Staff** Mostly voluntary. **Finance** Members' dues. Voluntary subsidies. **Activities** Co-organizes international conferences, seminars and congresses. **Events** *World Congress* Rishikesh (India) 1993, *World congress for holistic medicine* Yalta, Crimea (Ukraine) 1993, *World Congress* Almaty (Kazakhstan) 1992, *World Congress* USSR 1990, *World Congress* Crimea (USSR) 1989. **Publications** *Internationale Gesellschaft 'Frieden durch Kultur' Europa-Zentrale Mitteilungsblatt* in German; *Vestnik* in Russian. Books.
Members Membership is open to individuals and associations working on a spiritual and cultural level. Associations and registered branches in 14 countries:
Austria, Bulgaria, Germany, India, Italy, Kazakhstan, Mongolia, Nepal, Poland, Russia, Slovakia, Switzerland, Ukraine, USA.
NGO Relations Links with universities, organizations and associations in social-cultural and other areas of science. [2022/XF5148/**F**]

♦ International Association of Peace Foundations (IAPF) 12071

Mezdunarodnaja Associacija Fondov Mira

Pres 10 Prechistenka St, Moscow MOSKVA, Russia, 119889. T. +79851728548. E-mail: peace.association@yandex.ru.
URL: http://peace-international.org/

History Founded 18 Mar 1992, Moscow (Russia). Has taken over activities of *Soviet Peace Fund*, set up 1961. **Aims** Promote efforts to strengthen the ideals of peace, humanism, democracy, civil and inter-ethnic conciliation and friendship between nations, particularly in CIS countries; safeguard human rights; protect the environment. **Structure** Conference (every 5 years); Board of Founders; Executive Committee; Advisory Board. **Languages** Russian. **Staff** 10.00 FTE, paid. **Finance** Endowment defined by founding conference. Other sources: members' dues; revenues from activities; donations from sponsors. Annual budget: Roubles 1,200,000. **Activities** Projects/programmes; research/documentation; publishing activity. **Events** *Conference* Almaty (Kazakhstan) 2004, *Conference* Moscow (Russia) 2000, *Peace and cooperation in the Caspian sea region* Moscow (Russia) 1996. **Publications** *Forum Magazine* (12 a year); *Facts, Events, Documents* (12 a year); *Bulletin* in Russian.

Members Founding and Associate. Peace foundations in 17 countries:
Armenia, Australia, Austria, Azerbaijan, Belarus, Estonia, Georgia, Kazakhstan, Kyrgyzstan, Latvia, Lithuania, Moldova, Russia, Tajikistan, Turkmenistan, Ukraine, Uzbekistan.
Consultative Status Consultative status granted from: *ECOSOC (#05331)* (General). **IGO Relations** *Asian and Pacific Training Centre for Information and Communication Technology for Development (APCICT, #01645); UNICEF (#20332); United Nations Economic and Social Commission for Asia and the Pacific (ESCAP, #20557); United Nations Office at Geneva (UNOG, #20597).* Associated with Department of Global Communications of the United Nations. [2022/XD4897/D]

♦ International Association of Peacekeeping Training Centres (IAPTC) 12072

Secretariat Ctr for UN Peacekeeping, West Block 3, Wing 5 (FF), RK Puram, Delhi 110066, DELHI 110066, India. T. +919818412170. E-mail: dir.cunpk@gmail.com – iaptc.cunpk@gmail.com.
URL: http://www.iaptc.org/

History 2 Jul 1995, Clementsport (Canada), at inaugural meeting, by 'Lester B Pearson Canadian International Peacekeeping Training Centre' – *Pearson Peacekeeping Centre (PPC, inactive).* Secretariat transferred to Centre for UN Peacekeeping in Delhi (India), Oct 2005. **Aims** Facilitate communication and information exchange between peacekeeping and other related training centres and/or among people responsible for, and interested in, peacekeeping training. **Structure** Executive Committee. **Finance** No members' dues. **Activities** Training/education; standards/guidelines; networking/liaising. **Events** *Annual Conference* Nairobi (Kenya) 2023, *Annual Conference* Gazipur (Bangladesh) 2022, *Seminar* 2021, *Annual Conference* Gazipur (Bangladesh) 2020, *Annual Conference* Lima (Peru) 2019. **Publications** *IAPTC Newsletter* (4 a year) – published and on-line. Meeting reports. Information Services: Information exchange through the Internet.
Members Members/correspondents in 61 countries:
Argentina, Australia, Austria, Bangladesh, Bosnia-Herzegovina, Bulgaria, Canada, Chile, China, Côte d'Ivoire, Croatia, Czechia, Denmark, Egypt, Ethiopia, Fiji, Finland, France, Germany, Ghana, Greece, Guatemala, Hungary, India, Indonesia, Ireland, Italy, Japan, Jordan, Kenya, Latvia, Lebanon, Malaysia, Mali, Malta, Nepal, Netherlands, New Zealand, Nigeria, Norway, Pakistan, Peru, Poland, Romania, Russia, Senegal, Singapore, Slovakia, South Africa, Spain, Sudan, Sweden, Switzerland, Tanzania UR, Türkiye, UK, Ukraine, Uruguay, USA, Zambia, Zimbabwe.
Included in the above, 9 organizations listed in this Yearbook:
Austrian Study Centre for Peace and Conflict Resolution (ASPR); Institute for Peace and Conflict Studies, Malta (IPCS, no recent information); International Fellowship of Reconciliation (IFOR, #13586); Mediterranean Academy of Diplomatic Studies (MEDAC); Norwegian Institute of International Affairs (NUPI); Norwegian Refugee Council (NRC); Peace Research Centre, Canberra (PCR, no recent information); South African Institute of International Affairs (SAIIA); Zentrum für Internationale Friedenseinsätze (ZIF). [2015.09.11/XC0056/y/F]

♦ International Association of Peace Messenger Cities (IAPMC) 12073

Association internationale des villes messagères de la paix (AIVMP)

SG Mestna obcina, Solska ulica 5, 2380 Slovenj Gradec, Slovenia. E-mail: secretary-general@iapmc.org.
URL: http://www.iapmc.org/

History 8 Sep 1988, Verdun (France). Statutes adopted Jun 1992, Marrakech (Morocco). Registration: Start date: 17 Dec 1992, France. **Aims** Facilitate understanding among peoples; allow them to demonstrate their solidarity; propagate a spirit of peace, tolerance and mutual respect; combat war, hunger and natural disasters so as to serve mankind in dignity and respect; make governments aware of the prime necessity for nuclear disarmament and of the importance of human rights, liberty and freedom of individual movement. **Structure** General Assembly (annual); Executive Board; Officers. **Languages** English, French. **Staff** 6.00 FTE, voluntary. **Finance** Sources: members' dues. **Activities** Advocacy/lobbying/activism; awareness raising; events/meetings; networking/liaising; projects/programmes. **Events** *Assembly of Peace Messenger Cities* Volgograd (Russia) 2021, *Assembly of Peace Messenger Cities* Slovenj Gradec (Slovenia) 2020, *Assembly of Peace Messenger Cities* Sarajevo (Bosnia-Herzegovina) 2019, *Assembly of Peace Messenger Cities* Volgograd (Russia) 2018, *Assembly of Peace Messenger Cities* Orestiada (Greece) 2017.
Members Membership open to cities designated by the United Nations as messengers of peace. Members in 49 countries:
Argentina, Australia, Austria, Bangladesh, Belgium, Bolivia, Brazil, Canada, China, Colombia, Costa Rica, Côte d'Ivoire, Cuba, Cyprus, Czechia, El Salvador, Finland, France, Germany, Greece, Guatemala, India, Indonesia, Italy, Japan, Korea Rep, Mexico, Montenegro, Morocco, Mozambique, North Macedonia, Pakistan, Peru, Philippines, Poland, Portugal, Russia, Senegal, Serbia, Sierra Leone, Slovenia, Spain, Sri Lanka, Sweden, Switzerland, Togo, UK, Ukraine, USA.
Consultative Status Consultative status granted from: *ECOSOC (#05331)* (Special). **NGO Relations** Member of (1): *International Campaign to Abolish Nuclear Weapons (ICAN, #12426).* [2022.02.02/XD3733/C]

♦ International Association of Penal Law (IAPL) 12074

Association internationale de droit pénal (AIDP) – Asociación Internacional de Derecho Penal – Internationale Vereinigung für Strafrecht

Officer c/o The Siracusa Intl Inst, Via Logoteta 27, 96100 Siracusa SR, Italy. T. +390931414515. E-mail: secretariat@penal.org.
Pres Willem Pompe Inst for Criminal Science, Utrecht Univ, Boothstraat 6, 3512 BW Utrecht, Netherlands.
URL: http://www.penal.org/

History Mar 1924, Paris (France). Founded as successor to *International Union of Penal Law (IUPL, inactive),* set up 7 Aug 1889, Brussels (Belgium). Current Statutes adopted 4 Oct 1969, Rome (Italy), by General Assembly of 10th International Congress of Penal Law; amended 10 Sep 1994, Rio de Janeiro (Brazil), by General Assembly at 15th International Congress, 19 Sep 2004, Beijing (China) at 17th International Congress, 6 Sep 2014, Rio de Janeiro (Brazil) at 19th International Congress, and 16 Nov 2019, Rome (Italy) at 20th International Congress. **Aims** Harmonize criminal law with scientific data by encouraging exchange of ideas and close collaboration among those who, in different countries, are concerned with the study or application of criminal law or with research on *crime* and its causes; promote theoretical and practical development of international penal law and rules of procedure. **Structure** General Assembly (every 5 years); Board of Directors; Executive Committee; Scientific Committee; Editorial Board; Committee of Young Penalists. Membership open; meetings closed. **Languages** English, French, German, Spanish. **Staff** 0.50 FTE, paid. **Finance** Sources: members' dues. **Activities** Events/meetings; networking/liaising. **Events** *Quinquennial Congress* Rome (Italy) 2019, *Quinquennial Congress* Rio de Janeiro (Brazil) 2014, *Quinquennial Congress* Istanbul (Turkey) 2009, *International colloquium on criminal law theory in transition* Helsinki (Finland) 2006, *Quinquennial Congress* Beijing (China) 2004. **Publications** *Revue internationale de droit pénal* (2 a year) in English, French; *eRIDP. RIDP libri.*
Members National groups in 41 countries:
Albania, Argentina, Austria, Belgium, Brazil, Chile, China, Croatia, Czechia, Denmark, Dominican Rep, Egypt, Finland, France, Germany, Greece, Hungary, Iran Islamic Rep, Italy, Japan, Korea Rep, Kosovo, Luxembourg, Mexico, Montenegro, Morocco, Netherlands, Peru, Poland, Portugal, Romania, Russia, Serbia, Slovenia, Spain, Sweden, Switzerland, Tunisia, Türkiye, Ukraine, USA.
Collective and individual members in 45 countries. Membership countries not specified.
Consultative Status Consultative status granted from: *ECOSOC (#05331)* (Special); *Council of Europe (CE, #04881)* (Participatory Status). [2022.10.11/XB1324/B]

♦ International Association of Pension and Social Funds / see Association of Pension and Social Funds of the CIS (#02856)

♦ International Association for People-Environment Studies (IAPS) .. 12075

Association internationale pour l'étude des relations homme-environnement

Pres Univ of A Coruna, Fac of Education Sciences – Psychology, Campus de Elvina s/n, 15071 La Coruña, Spain. T. +34981167000ext1792 – +34981167000ext1881. Fax +34981167153.
URL: http://www.iaps-association.org/

History Founded 1981, following European conference series initiated in 1969, as *International Association for the Study of People and their Physical Surroundings.* **Aims** Facilitate communication among those concerned with the relationships between people and their physical environment; stimulate research and innovation for improving human well-being and the physical environment; promote integration of research, education, policy and practice. **Structure** Executive Committee; Board. **Languages** English. **Staff** 12.00 FTE, voluntary. **Finance** Members' dues. **Activities** Events/meetings. **Events** *Biennial Conference* Québec, QC (Canada) 2020, *Biennial Conference* Rome (Italy) 2018, *Biennial Conference* Lund (Sweden) 2016, *Biennial Conference* Timisoara (Romania) 2014, *Biennial Conference* Glasgow (UK) 2012. **Publications** *Bulletin of People-Environment Studies.*

Members in 50 countries and territories:
Algeria, Australia, Austria, Belgium, Brazil, Canada, Croatia, Czechia, Denmark, Egypt, Estonia, Finland, France, Germany, Greece, Hong Kong, Hungary, India, Indonesia, Ireland, Israel, Italy, Japan, Kenya, Korea Rep, Kuwait, Lebanon, Malaysia, Mexico, Netherlands, Nigeria, Norway, Pakistan, Poland, Portugal, Romania, Russia, Saudi Arabia, Slovenia, Spain, Sweden, Switzerland, Taiwan, Tanzania UR, Türkiye, Uganda, UK, United Arab Emirates, USA, Venezuela. [2020/XD3710/D]

♦ International Association of People's Lawyers (IAPL) 12076

Contact Hildebranddreef 13, 3561 VD Utrecht, Netherlands. E-mail: info@iapl.net.
URL: https://iapl.net/

History Founded 10 Dec 2000, Doorn (Netherlands). **Structure** General Assembly (every 3 years). Board of Directors, including President, Vice-President, Secretary-General and Treasurer. **Events** *Congress* Philippines 2006, *Congress* Istanbul (Turkey) 2003.
Members Individuals in 10 countries:
Afghanistan, Belgium, Colombia, Greece, India, Mexico, Nepal, Netherlands, Philippines, Türkiye.
NGO Relations Supports: *International Campaign Against Mass Surveillance (ICAMS, no recent information).* [2022/XJ2263/D]

♦ International Association of Performance Art Organizers (no recent information)
♦ International Association of Perlite Producers / see Perlite Institute (#18317)
♦ International Association of Personnel in Employment Security / see International Association of Workforce Professionals (#12278)
♦ International Association for Pharmaceutical Technology (#01082)

♦ International Association for Phenomenology and the Cognitive Sciences (IAPCS) 12077

Co-Dir Univ of Memphis, Dept of Philosophy, 331 Clement Hall, Memphis TN 38152, USA. T. +19016782535. Fax +19016784365.
Co-Dir Center for Subjectivity Research, Univ of Copenhagen, Njalsgade 140-142, 2300 Copenhagen S, Denmark. T. +4535323723 – +4535323721. Fax +4535323751.
URL: http://www.ummoss.org/pcs/

History 1 Oct 2000. Founded by five individuals. **Aims** Organize colloquia and larger conferences devoted to themes that explore the intersection of phenomenology and the cognitive sciences. **Structure** Board of Advisors; Directors (3). **Languages** English. **Staff** None. **Finance** Institutional support from: Center for Subjectivity Research, University of Copenhagen; Dept of Philosophy, University of Memphis. **Events** *Embodied Cognition and Dance* Memphis, TN (USA) 2021, *Workshop* Memphis, TN (USA) 2015, *Workshop* Memphis, TN (USA) 2014, *Workshop* Memphis, TN (USA) 2013, *Conference* Copenhagen (Denmark) 2010. **Publications** *Phenomenology and the Cognitive Sciences* (5 a year) – journal.
Members in 12 countries:
Belgium, Canada, Denmark, France, India, Ireland, Japan, Spain, Sweden, Switzerland, UK, USA. [2021.05.19/XJ3295/F]

♦ International Association of Philatelic Experts (#02696)
♦ International Association of Philatelic Journalists (#02709)
♦ International Association for Philosophy of Law and Social Philosophy (#13318)

♦ International Association for the Philosophy of Sport (IAPS) 12078

Pres NIH, Dept of Teacher Education and Outdoor Studies, Postboks 4014 Ullevål stadion, 0806 Oslo, Norway. T. +4723262259. E-mail: cue113@psu.edu.
Sec/Treas 110W Smith Bldg, 3000 Ivyside Drive, Penn State Altoona, Altoona PA 16601, USA. T. +19495238. E-mail: pmh12@psu.edu.
Events Chair address not obtained.
URL: http://www.iaps.net/

History 28 Dec 1972, Boston, MA (USA). Former names and other names: *Philosophical Society for the Study of Sport (PSSS)* – former (28 Dec 1972 to 1999). **Aims** Stimulate, encourage and promote study, research and writing in the philosophy of sporting and related activity; demonstrate the relevance of philosophic thought concerning sport to matters of professional concern; engender national, regional and continental affiliates devoted to philosophic study of sport. **Structure** Executive. **Languages** English. **Staff** None. **Finance** Sources: members' dues. **Activities** Events/meetings; financial and/or material support; networking/liaising. **Events** *Annual Meeting* Split (Croatia) 2023, *Annual Meeting* State College, PA (USA) 2022, *Annual Meeting* 2021, *Annual Meeting* Split (Croatia) 2020, *Annual Meeting* Kyoto (Japan) 2019. **Publications** *Journal of the Philosophy of Sport (JPS)* (4 a year); *IAPS Newsletter.*
Members Individuals (170) in 30 countries and territories:
Australia, Brazil, Bulgaria, Canada, China, Czechia, Denmark, Finland, Germany, Greece, India, Israel, Italy, Japan, Korea Rep, Mongolia, Namibia, Netherlands, Norway, Poland, Portugal, Slovenia, South Africa, Spain, Sweden, Switzerland, Taiwan, Türkiye, UK, USA.
NGO Relations Member of (2): *International Council of Sport Science and Physical Education (ICSSPE, #13077); International Federation of Philosophical Societies (FISP, #13507).* [2023.02.13/XF2994/v/F]

♦ International Association for the Philosophy of Time (IAPT) 12079

Contact Centre for Philosophy of Time, Dept of Philosophy – Univ degli Studi di Milano, Via Festa del Perdono 7, 20122 Milan MI, Italy.
URL: http://www.centreforphilosophyoftime.it/iapt-4/

Structure Steering Committee; Board of Advisors. **Activities** Events/meetings. **Events** *Annual Conference* Barcelona (Spain) 2022, *Annual Conference* Barcelona (Spain) 2020, *Annual Conference* Boulder, CO (USA) 2019, *Annual Conference* Seoul (Korea Rep) 2018, *Annual Conference* Gargnano (Italy) 2017. **Publications** *IAPT Monthly Newsletter.*
Members Centres/societies (5) in 5 countries:
Australia, Germany, Ireland, Italy, USA. [2020/AA0642/C]

♦ International Association of Phonosurgeons / see International Association of Phonosurgery (#12080)

♦ International Association of Phonosurgery (IAP) 12080

Gen Sec Mont-Godinne Univ Hosp, Dept of Otorhinolaaryngology, Thereasse Avenue 1, 5530 Yvoir, Belgium. T. +3281423710. Fax +3281423703. E-mail: contactiap@intasph.com.
URL: http://www.intasph.com/

History 1990, Belgrade (Serbia). Former names and other names: *International Association of Phonosurgeons* – former (1990). **Aims** Promote better *voice* care around the world by means of organizing and supporting educational and training activities, and also by cooperating with different international entities in order to facilitate the access to state of the art technology and training in areas areas of the world in need of progress. **Structure** Board of Directors. **Activities** Events/meetings. **Events** *World Phonosurgery Congress* Kyoto (Japan) 2022, *World Phonosurgery Congress* Kyoto (Japan) 2021, *World Phonosurgery Congress* Buenos Aires (Argentina) 2019, *World Phonosurgery Congress* Gurugram (India) 2017, *Symposium* Philadelphia, PA (USA) 2015. [2020/XD7994/C]

♦ International Association for Physical Education in Higher Education (#02685)

♦ International Association of Physical Education and Sport for Girls and Women (IAPESGW) 12081

Association internationale d'éducation physique et sportive féminine – Asociación Internacional de Educación Fisica y Deportes para la Joven y la Mujer – Internationaler Verband für Leibeserziehung und Sport der Mädchen und Frauen

Sec-Treas Barry Univ Nursing, 11300 NE 2nd Ave, Miami Shores FL 33161-6695, USA.
URL: http://www.iapesgw.org/

History 27 Jul 1953, Paris (France). Founded at 2nd International Congress on Physical Education for Girls and Women, following resolution at 1st Congress, 1949, Copenhagen (Denmark). Constitution adopted 15 Jul 1957, London (UK). Revised constitution approved Aug 1993. **Aims** Bring together women of many countries working in the field of physical education and sport; strengthen international contacts; provide opportunities for discussion of mutual problems; promote exchange of persons and ideas among member countries and research into problems affecting physical education and sport for girls and women; cooperate with other organizations which encourage particular services of and to women in society; represent the interests of girls and women at all levels and in all areas of physical education and sport. **Structure** Congress (every 4 years);

Council of Representatives; Executive Board. **Languages** English, French, German, Japanese, Portuguese, Spanish. **Staff** Voluntary. **Finance** Sources: members' dues. **Activities** Advocacy/lobbying/activism; capacity building; events/meetings; research/documentation; training/education. **Events** *Quadrennial Congress* Cebu City (Philippines) 2025, *Quadrennial Congress* Tianjin (China) 2021, *European Regional Congress* Madrid (Spain) 2019, *Quadrennial Congress* Miami, FL (USA) 2017, *Quadrennial Congress* Havana (Cuba) 2013. **Publications** *Bulletin of IAPESGW* (annual). Books; handbooks; congress proceedings.
Members Individuals in 67 countries and territories:
Argentina, Australia, Austria, Bahrain, Bangladesh, Barbados, Bosnia-Herzegovina, Botswana, Brazil, Cameroon, Canada, China, Colombia, Costa Rica, Croatia, Cuba, Cyprus, Czechia, Denmark, Egypt, Estonia, Finland, Germany, Ghana, Greece, Hungary, Iceland, India, Indonesia, Iran Islamic Rep, Iraq, Israel, Italy, Japan, Kenya, Korea Rep, Kuwait, Latvia, Lithuania, Malaysia, Malta, Mexico, Morocco, Namibia, Netherlands, New Zealand, Nigeria, Norway, Palestine, Philippines, Poland, Portugal, Puerto Rico, Russia, Sierra Leone, Singapore, Slovakia, South Africa, Spain, Sweden, Switzerland, Taipei, Türkiye, Uganda, UK, USA, Venezuela.
NGO Relations Member of (2): *International Council of Sport Science and Physical Education (ICSSPE, #13077)*; *Sport Association of Arab Women (SAAW, no recent information).* Consultative status with: *International Olympic Committee (IOC, #14408).* [2021.09.02/XB1326/v/**B**]

♦ International Association of Physical Oceanography / see International Association for the Physical Sciences of the Oceans (#12082)

♦ International Association for the Physical Sciences of the Oceans (IAPSO) 12082

Association internationale des sciences physiques de l'océan (AISPO) – Asociación Internacional para las Ciencias Fisicas del Oceano

SG Inst of Marine Sciences, National Research Council of Italy, Viale Romolo Gessi 2, 34123 Trieste TS, Italy. T. +3940305312. Fax +3940308941. E-mail: iapso.sg@gmail.com.
URL: http://iapso.iugg.org/

History Founded 1919, Monaco, as 'Oceanographic Section' of IUGG. Became *International Association of Physical Oceanography (IAPO) – Association internationale d'océanographie physique (AIOP)* in 1931. Present name adopted 1967. **Aims** Promote study of scientific problems relating to the ocean and interactions taking place at ocean boundaries, chiefly in so far as may be carried out with the aid of mathematics, physics and chemistry; initiate, facilitate and coordinate research into, and investigation of, such problems as require international cooperation; provide for discussion, comparison and publications. **Structure** General Assembly; Bureau; Executive Committee, comprising officer and 6 members, elected by delegates from member countries adhering to IUGG. Commission on Mean Sea Level and Tides; SCOR/IAPSO/IAPWS Joint Committee on the Properties of Seawater; IAHS/IAMAS/IAPSO/IASPEI/IAVCEI Joint Commission on Geophysical Risk and Sustainability; IASPEI/IAPSO/IAGA International Ocean Network. **Languages** English. **Staff** 2.00 FTE, voluntary. **Finance** Sources: grants from IUGG; grants from *UNESCO (#20322)* for special projects. **Activities** Events/meetings; research/documentation. **Events** *Joint Assembly* Busan (Korea Rep) 2025, *Joint Assembly* Busan (Korea Rep) 2021, *Joint Assembly* Cape Town (South Africa) 2017, *General Business Meeting* Prague (Czech Rep) 2015, *Joint Assembly* Gothenburg (Sweden) 2013. **Publications** *Publications scientifiques* (irregular). Proceedings of General Assemblies and other meetings. Information Services: *Permanent Service for Mean Sea Level (PSMSL, #18333).*
Members Adhering Bodies and National Committees in 58 countries:
Argentina, Australia, Azerbaijan, Belgium, Brazil, Bulgaria, Canada, Chile, China, Colombia, Costa Rica, Croatia, Denmark, Egypt, Estonia, Finland, France, Georgia, Germany, Ghana, Greece, Hungary, Iceland, India, Indonesia, Iran Islamic Rep, Ireland, Israel, Italy, Japan, Korea Rep, Luxembourg, Mauritius, Mexico, Morocco, Mozambique, Netherlands, New Zealand, Nigeria, Norway, Pakistan, Peru, Philippines, Poland, Portugal, Romania, Russia, Saudi Arabia, Slovenia, South Africa, Spain, Sweden, Switzerland, Thailand, Türkiye, UK, USA, Vietnam.
Also Observer members. Membership countries not specified.
Consultative Status Consultative status granted from: *ECOSOC (#05331)* (Ros C). **NGO Relations** Constituent association of: *International Union of Geodesy and Geophysics (IUGG, #15776)*, which is one of the scientific Unions grouped within *International Science Council (ISC, #14796)* and represented in: *Scientific Committee on Oceanic Research (SCOR, #19149).* Member of: *Federation of the Staff Associations of the United Nations and its Specialized Agencies and their Affiliated Bodies in Denmark (FUNSA Denmark).* Cooperates with: *International Association of Volcanology and Chemistry of the Earth's Interior (IAVCEI, #12259).* [2019/XB1223/**B**]

♦ International Association for Physical Therapists Working with Older People (IPTOP) 12083

Pres address not obtained. E-mail: president@iptop-physio.org – info@iptop-physio.org.
URL: https://www.iptop-physio.org/

History 2002, Birmingham (UK). Since 2003, a subgroup within *World Confederation for Physical Therapy (WCPT, #21293).* **Aims** Be the international resource for physical therapists working with older people. **Structure** Executive Committee. Committees (2): Communications; Education. **Activities** Awards/prizes/competitions; training/education.
Members Full in 25 countries and territories:
Australia, Austria, Belgium, Canada, Denmark, Finland, Greece, Hong Kong, Iceland, Ireland, Italy, Japan, Malta, Netherlands, New Zealand, Nigeria, Poland, Portugal, Slovenia, Sweden, Switzerland, Taiwan, Türkiye, UK, USA.
Associate: individuals (over 60) in 31 countries and territories:
Bermuda, Brazil, Chile, Egypt, Eswatini, Fiji, Ghana, India, Iraq, Jamaica, Jordan, Korea Rep, Lebanon, Malaysia, Nigeria, Northern Cyprus, Norway, Palestine, Peru, Philippines, Portugal, Saudi Arabia, Slovakia, South Africa, Sri Lanka, St Lucia, Suriname, Tanzania UR, Trinidad-Tobago, Uganda, Zambia. [2023/XM1094/**E**]

♦ International Association of Physicians in AIDS Care / see International Association of Providers of AIDS Care

♦ International Association of Physicians in Audiology (IAPA) 12084

Association internationale des médecins audiologistes

Hon Sec c/o UCL Ear Inst, 332 Grays Inn Road, London, WC1X 8EE, UK.
URL: http://www.iapa-audiovestibularmedicine.com/

History 1980, Germany FR. 1980, Wiesbaden (Germany FR). **Aims** Provide a forum for discussion of problems of mutual interest to audiological physicians in different countries; develop the speciality on a worldwide basis. **Structure** General Assembly. Officers: President, Vice-President, Past-President, Treasurer, Assistant Treasurer and General Secretary. **Languages** English. **Staff** Voluntary. **Finance** Sources: members' dues. **Events** *Symposium* Beijing (China) 2020, *Symposium* Hurghada (Egypt) 2018, *Biennial Symposium* Odense (Denmark) 2016, *Biennial Symposium* Pattaya (Thailand) 2014, *Biennial Symposium* Beijing (China) 2012. **Publications** *Audiological Medicine.*
Members Audiological physicians in 40 countries:
Australia, Belgium, Brazil, Canada, Chile, China, Costa Rica, Croatia, Czechia, Denmark, Egypt, Finland, France, Germany, Greece, Hungary, Iceland, India, Ireland, Israel, Italy, Japan, Malaysia, Mexico, Netherlands, New Zealand, Nigeria, Norway, Poland, Portugal, Slovakia, Spain, Sri Lanka, Sudan, Sweden, Switzerland, Tanzania UR, Thailand, UK, USA.
NGO Relations Member of: *Hearing International (#10895).* [2014/XD7401/v/**C**]

♦ International Association of Physics Students (IAPS) 12085

Pres c/o EPS, 6 rue des Frères Lumière, 68200 Mulhouse, France. T. +33389329440. Fax +33389389329449. E-mail: president@iaps.info.
Vice-Pres address not obtained.
URL: https://www.iaps.info/

History 12 Sep 1987, Debrecen (Hungary). Founded during 2nd *International Conference for Students Physics.* Revised Charter and Regulations approved by General Meeting, 1990, Amsterdam (Netherlands); Charter amended and approved 2007, London (UK). Regulations amended and approved: 2008, Krakow (Poland); 2013, Edinburgh (UK); 2015, Zagreb (Croatia); 2019, Cologne (Germany); 2020 at virtual AGM. Registration: Tribunal Judiciaire de Mulhouse, France, Alsace-Moselle. **Aims** Encourage physics students in their academic and professional work in an international context; promote peaceful relations among physics students around the world; introduce physics students to the international community, help them to build professional relations and foster a collaborative attitude among young physicists; organize international conferences and events run by physics students for physics students. **Structure** General Meeting (annual, usually at Conference); Executive Committee of 9 officers and Regular Members. **Languages** English. **Staff** Voluntary. **Finance** Sources: contributions; donations; grants; members' dues. **Activities** Events/meetings; networking/liaising. **Events** *International Conference of Physics Students (ICPS)* Manila (Philippines) / Baguio (Philippines) 2023, *International Conference of Physics Students* Puebla (Mexico) 2022, *International Conference of Physics Students* Copenhagen (Denmark) 2021, *International Conference of Physics Students* Puebla (Mexico) 2020, *Annual Conference* Cologne (Germany) 2019. **Publications** *Journal of the International Association of Physics Students (jIAPS).* Annual Report. Annual conference proceedings. **Information Services** *IRC Channel* – real-time communication; *Network of Contact Persons* – list of information providers.
Members National Committees (22) in 23 countries – UK and Republic of Ireland representing one NC:
Austria, Croatia, Cuba, Czechia, Denmark, Finland, France, Georgia, Germany, Hungary, India, Ireland, Italy, Mexico, Morocco, Netherlands, North Macedonia, Norway, Poland, Portugal, Spain, UK, USA.
Local Committees (23) in 19 countries:
Belgium, Cameroon, Costa Rica, Dominican Rep, Ecuador, Ghana, Greece, Guatemala, Indonesia, Iran Islamic Rep, Malta, Nepal, Pakistan, Philippines, Romania, Russia, Serbia, Türkiye, Ukraine.
Individual Members (about 100) in 28 countries and territories:
Angola, Argentina, Australia, Bahrain, Bolivia, Brazil, Canada, China, Colombia, Greece, Hong Kong, Israel, Japan, Kazakhstan, Kenya, Lebanon, Mauritius, Mozambique, Nigeria, Palestine, Peru, Romania, Russia, Singapore, South Africa, Sudan, Switzerland, Uruguay.
NGO Relations Memorandum of Understanding with (6): African School of Fundamental Physics and Applications (ASP); *International Association of Geomagnetism and Aeronomy (IAGA, #11916)*; *International Association of Volcanology and Chemistry of the Earth's Interior (IAVCEI, #12259)*; *International Astronomical Union (IAU, #12287)*; *International Union of Crystallography (IUCr, #15768)*; International Union of Pure and Applied Biophysics (IUPAB). Member of (1): *Informal Forum of International Student Organizations (IFISO, #11193).* Partner of (1): *European Physical Society (EPS, #08207).* Cooperates with (2): *Federación Iberoamericana de Sociedades de Fisica (FEIASOFI, #09321)*; International Particle Physics Outreach Group (IPPOG). [2022.05.16/XD2561/**D**]

♦ International Association of Physiological Anthropology (IAPA) . . . 12086

SG Forest Research and Management Org, 1 Matsunosato, Tsukuba IBARAKI, 305-8687 Japan. Fax +81298743720.
URL: http://www.intlphysiolanth.org/

History Founded 1996, Nara (Japan), at 3rd International Congress of Physiological Anthropology. Original title: *International Society of Physiological Anthropology (ISPA).* **Aims** Promote research exchange and collaboration the field of physiological anthropology. **Structure** Council; Executive Committee. **Languages** English. **Staff** Voluntary. **Finance** Donations by Executive Committee members and the President of the past congress. Annual budget: 9,000 USD. **Activities** Events/meetings; research/documentation. **Events** *International Congress* Singapore (Singapore) 2019, *International Congress* Loughborough (UK) 2017, *Joint Symposium* Loughborough (UK) 2017, *International Congress* Chiba (Japan) 2015, *International Congress* Banff, AB (Canada) 2013. **Publications** *Physiological Anthropology* (6 a year) – journal.
Members Full in 15 countries and territories:
Australia, China, Croatia, Finland, France, Germany, Japan, Korea Rep, Malaysia, Netherlands, Poland, Singapore, Taiwan, UK, USA. [2017.07.13/XJ0043/**C**]

♦ International Association of Physiotherapy Doctors (inactive)
♦ International Association of Physiotherapy and Physical Medicine (inactive)

♦ International Association of Phytoplankton Taxonomy and Ecology (IAP) 12087

Contact Box 447, 14950 Migdal, Israel. T. +97246721444ext201. Fax +97246724627. E-mail: tamarz@ocean.org.il.

Activities Organizes workshops. **Events** *Workshop* Tiszafured (Hungary) 2021, *Workshop* Tiszafured (Hungary) 2020, *Workshop* Natal (Brazil) 2017, *Workshop* Kastoria (Greece) 2014, *Workshop* San Michele all'Adige (Italy) 2011. **Publications** Conference proceedings. [2017/XD7547/**D**]

♦ International Association of Phytotherapy and Aromatherapy (inactive)

♦ International Association of Piano Builders and Technicians (IAPBT) 12088

Contact c/o Piano Technicians Guild, 4444 Forest Avenue, Kansas City KS 66106-3750, USA. E-mail: exec@ptg.org.
URL: https://my.ptg.org/iapbtw/home

History 1979, Minneapolis, MN (USA). **Aims** Maintain a worldwide fellowship of piano technicians and piano builders; provide a means for and encourage freedom of exchange of technical information and any other subjects of related interest. **Events** *Piano Congress* Warsaw (Poland) 2022, *Biennial Convention* Hamamatsu (Japan) 2019, *Biennial Convention* St Louis, MO (USA) 2017, *Biennial Convention* Moscow (Russia) 2015, *Biennial Convention / Council Meeting and Convention* Shanghai (China) 2013.
Members Individuals; organizations. Members in 24 countries and territories:
Argentina, Australia, China, Cyprus, Denmark, Finland, France, Germany, Greece, Hong Kong, Italy, Japan, Korea Rep, Netherlands, Norway, Russia, South Africa, Spain, Sweden, Switzerland, Taiwan, UK, USA, Uzbekistan. [2021.02.16/XD1365/**D**]

♦ International Association of Pipe Smokers Clubs (IAPSC) 12089

Association internationale de clubs des fumeurs de pipes

Chairman 647 S Saginaw St, Flint MI 48502, USA. E-mail: chairman@iapsc.net.
Sec 1868 Colonial Village Way, Suite 4, Waterford MI 48328, USA. E-mail: secretary@iapsc.net.
URL: http://www.iapsc.net/

History 1949, Schenectady NY (USA). **Aims** Promote friendship through the medium of pipe smoking. **Events** *Annual convention / Annual Meeting* St Louis, MO (USA) 1997, *Annual convention / Annual Meeting* Flint, MI (USA) 1996, *Annual Meeting* Saginaw, MI (USA) 1988.
Members Pipe smokers clubs in 9 countries:
Brazil, Canada, Germany, Israel, Japan, Netherlands, New Zealand, UK, USA.
NGO Relations *Nordic Smokers Guild (NSG)* is member. [2018/XD5415/**D**]

♦ International Association of Planetology (inactive)
♦ International Association of Plant Bakers (#02674)

♦ International Association of Plant Biotechnology (IAPB) 12090

Pres address not obtained.
URL: https://iapbhome.com/

History 1963. Founded at first conference. Former names and other names: *International Association for Plant Tissue Culture (IAPTC)* – former (1963 to 1998); *International Association for Plant Tissue Culture and Biotechnology (IAPTC and B)* – former (1998 to 2006); *Association internationale pour la culture des tissus des plantes* – former (1998 to 2006). **Aims** Promote plant biotechnology, including cell and tissue culture applications. These objectives will be achieved primarily, but not necessarily exclusively. **Structure** Executive Committee; Secretariat. **Languages** English. **Staff** 2.50 FTE, paid. **Finance** Sources: members' dues. Annual budget: 22,500 USD. **Activities** Organizes international congress (every 4 years). **Events** *Congress* Daejeon (Korea Rep) 2023, *Congress* Dublin (Ireland) 2018, *Congress* Melbourne, VIC (Australia) 2014, *Congress* St Louis, MO (USA) 2010, *Meeting* Vienna (Austria) 2008. **Publications** *In Vitro Plant* – journal.
Members Individuals (1,327) in 86 countries and territories:
Australia, Austria, Bangladesh, Belgium, Bolivia, Brazil, Bulgaria, Canada, Chile, China, Colombia, Costa Rica, Croatia, Cuba, Cyprus, Czechia, Denmark, Egypt, Fiji, Finland, France, Germany, Greece, Guatemala, Guyana, Honduras, Hong Kong, Hungary, Iceland, India, Indonesia, Iran Islamic Rep, Iraq, Ireland, Israel, Italy, Jamaica, Japan, Kenya, Korea Rep, Kuwait, Luxembourg, Malawi, Malaysia, Malta, Mexico, Montenegro, Morocco, Myanmar, Nepal, Netherlands, New Zealand, Nigeria, Norway, Pakistan, Palestine, Papua New Guinea, Peru, Philippines, Poland, Portugal, Romania, Russia, Saudi Arabia, Serbia, Sierra Leone, Singapore, Slovakia, Slovenia, South Africa, Spain, Sri Lanka, Sweden, Switzerland, Taiwan, Thailand, Trinidad-Tobago, Tunisia, Türkiye, UK, Ukraine, United Arab Emirates, USA, Venezuela, Vietnam, Zambia. [2020/XD9312/v/**D**]

♦ International Association of Plant Breeders for the Protection of Plant Varieties (inactive)
♦ International Association for Plant Physiologists (inactive)

♦ International Association for the Plant Protection Sciences (IAPPS) 12091

SG 6517 S 19th St, Lincoln NE 68512, USA.
URL: http://www.plantprotection.org/

History Jul 1999, Jerusalem (Israel), at 14th International Plant Protection Congress, by Standing Committee of *International Plant Protection Congresses (IPPC, inactive)*. **Aims** Act as an umbrella organization and hence provide a global forum in order to identify, evaluate, integrate and promote plant protection concepts, technologies and policies that are economically, environmentally and socially acceptable; stimulate development and exchange of plant protection information among researchers, extension specialists, growers, policy makers, administrators, crop protection consultants and environmental and other interested groups. **Structure** General Assembly (every four years); Governing Board; Executive Committee; Regional Centres (15). **Languages** English. **Staff** 2.00 FTE, voluntary. **Finance** Sources: members' dues. **Activities** Awards/prizes/competitions; events/meetings. **Events** *International Plant Protection Congress* Athens (Greece) 2024, *International Plant Protection Congress* Athens (Greece) 2023, *International Plant Protection Congress* Hyderabad (India) 2019, *International Plant Protection Congress* Berlin (Germany) 2015, *International Plant Protection Congress* Honolulu, HI (USA) 2011. **Publications** *Crop Protection* – official journals; *Global Plant Protection Newsletter*.
Members Individual, Affiliate, Associate and Corporate membership. Members in 58 countries and territories:
Argentina, Australia, Belgium, Benin, Brazil, Bulgaria, Burkina Faso, Cameroon, Canada, Chile, China, Colombia, Costa Rica, Czechia, Egypt, France, Germany, Ghana, Greece, Honduras, Hungary, India, Indonesia, Iran Islamic Rep, Iraq, Israel, Italy, Japan, Kenya, Korea Rep, Kuwait, Malaysia, Mali, Mauritius, Mexico, Morocco, Netherlands, New Zealand, Nigeria, Peru, Philippines, Serbia, Sierra Leone, South Africa, Spain, Switzerland, Syrian AR, Taiwan, Thailand, Togo, Türkiye, Uganda, UK, Ukraine, USA, Vietnam, Yemen, Zambia. [2019.12.18/XD7422/**C**]

♦ International Association for Plant Taxonomy (IAPT) 12092

Association internationale pour la taxonomie végétale – Asociación Internacional para la Taxonomia Vegetal – Internationaler Verein für Pflanzen-Taxonomie

Managing Sec Plant Science and Biodiversity Ctr, Slovak Ac of Sciences – Inst of Botany, Dubravska cesta 9, 845 23 Bratislava, Slovakia. T. +421259426151. E-mail: office@iapt-taxon.org.
URL: https://www.iaptglobal.org/

History 18 Jul 1950, Stockholm (Sweden). **Aims** Promote all aspects of botanical systematics and its significance to the understanding and value of biodiversity. **Structure** Congress (every 6 years); Council. Subcommittees (7): Grants; Honours; Nomenclature; Nominating; Membership and Outreach; Publications; Reserve Fund. *International Bureau for Plant Taxonomy and Nomenclature (inactive)* responsible for general administration. Interest groups include: *International Organization of Plant Biosystematists (IOPB, #14463)*. **Languages** English, German. **Staff** 3.00 FTE, paid. **Finance** Sources: members' dues; subscriptions. **Activities** Awareness raising; events/meetings; financial and/or material support; knowledge management/information dissemination; projects/programmes; publishing activities; standards/guidelines. **Events** *International Botanical Congress (IBC)* Madrid (Spain) 2024, *International Botanical Congress (IBC)* Brazil 2023, *Botany Conference* Anchorage, AK (USA) 2022, *Botany Conference* Bratislava (Slovakia) 2020, *Botany Conference* Savannah, GA (USA) 2016. **Publications** *Taxon* (6 a year); *Regnum Vegetabile* (irregular). **Members** Institutes; Individuals (1,000), Supporting and Ordinary. Membership countries not specified. **NGO Relations** Scientific member of: *International Union of Biological Sciences (IUBS, #15760)*. Member of: *International Association of Botanical and Mycological Societies (IABMS, #11730)*. Holds simultaneous conferences with: *International Association of Botanic Gardens (IABG, #11731)*. In liaison with technical committees of: *International Organization for Standardization (ISO, #14473)*. [2021/XC1202/**C**]

- ♦ International Association for Plant Tissue Culture / see International Association of Plant Biotechnology (#12090)
- ♦ International Association for Plant Tissue Culture and Biotechnology / see International Association of Plant Biotechnology (#12090)
- ♦ International Association of the Plastic Arts / see International Association of Art (#11710)
- ♦ International Association of Plastics Distribution (internationally oriented national body)
- ♦ International Association of Plastics Distributors / see International Association of Plastics Distribution
- ♦ International Association of Plumbing and Mechanical Officials (internationally oriented national body)
- ♦ International Association of Poetry (inactive)
- ♦ International Association of Police (internationally oriented national body)

♦ International Association of Police Academies (INTERPA) 12093

Contact Academy, asdasd, 1010, Afghanistan.

History Afghanistan. **Activities** Events/meetings. **Events** *Cyber security and combatting cyber crime* Ahmedabad (India) 2019, *Conference* Doha (Qatar) 2018, *Drug issue and new approaches in police training in combating drugs* Kyrenia (Cyprus) 2017, *Conference* Khartoum (Sudan) 2016, *Conference* Abu Dhabi (United Arab Emirates) 2015. [2023.02.15/XJ8887/**C**]

- ♦ International Association of Police Professors / see Academy of Criminal Justice Sciences
- ♦ International Association of Political Campaign Consultants / see International Association of Political Consultants (#12094)

♦ International Association of Political Consultants (IAPC) 12094

Association internationale de conseils politiques

Treas 1011 S Valentia St, Unit 84, Denver CO 80247, USA. E-mail: info@iapc.org.
URL: http://www.iapc.org/

History Nov 1968, Paris (France), during 1st International Conference of Political Consultants, under the name: *International Association of Political Campaign Consultants – Association internationale conseils en campagnes politiques*. Current title and statutes adopted 1988, San Francisco CA (USA), at 21st Conference. **Aims** Promote, sustain and foster the democratic process as a matter of principle and practice; bring together political consultants, both specialists and generalists, from various countries to exchange views and information about political developments and techniques. **Structure** Founder Presidents (2). Board of Directors (up to 12, 11 currently serving). Officers: President; Vice-Presidents (2); Secretaries (2); Treasurer. Board of Past Presidents. **Languages** English. **Staff** Voluntary. **Finance** Members' dues. **Activities** Organizes annual World Conference where International Democracy Award is made. **Events** *Annual World Conference* London (UK) 2022, *Annual World Conference* Miami, FL (USA) 2020, *Annual World Conference* Passau (Germany) 2019, *Annual World Conference* Sydney, NSW (Australia) 2018, *Annual World Conference* Reykjavik (Iceland) 2017. **Publications** *IAPC Members Register* (every 2 years). Study series.
Members Individuals (over 100) from many spheres of political activity in 34 countries and territories:
Argentina, Australia, Austria, Belgium, Brazil, Canada, Chile, Colombia, Costa Rica, Ecuador, Finland, France, Germany, Guatemala, India, Indonesia, Israel, Italy, Japan, Lithuania, Malta, Philippines, Portugal, Puerto Rico, Romania, Russia, South Africa, Spain, Sweden, Switzerland, Türkiye, UK, USA, Venezuela. [2021/XD4495/v/**D**]

♦ International Association for Political Science Students (IAPSS) . . . 12095

SG 1455 De Maisonneuve Blvd West, Dept of Political Science, Concordia Univ, Montréal QC H3G 1M8, Canada. E-mail: secgen@iapss.org.
Pres address not obtained.
URL: http://www.iapss.org/

History 31 Oct 1998, Leiden (Netherlands). Permanent Seat established 31 Oct 2004, Ljubljana (Slovenia). Permanent Seat relocated to Nijmegen (Netherlands), 10 Mar 2013, and then to Montréal (Canada), 2 Apr, 2021. Registration: Corporations Canada, No/ID: 1285922-0, Start date: 2 Apr 2021, Canada, Quebec. **Aims** Represent political science students around the world as their democratic student government at the global level; provide members with knowledge, information and skills regarding current matters in the field of political science; play a role in the lives of political science students by engaging their potential and stimulating them to become active participants in shaping their local communities and the wider international society. **Structure** General Assembly (at least once a year); Executive Committee (ExCom); Advisory Board. **Languages** English. **Staff** Voluntary. **Finance** Sources: donations; grants; meeting proceeds; revenue from activities/projects; sponsorship. **Activities** Advocacy/lobbying/activism; events/meetings; research/documentation; training/education. **Events** *World Congress* Montréal, QC (Canada) 2023, *World Congress* Montréal, QC (Canada) 2022, *World Congress* Montréal, QC (Canada) 2021, *General Assembly* Montréal, QC (Canada) 2020, *World Congress* Vienna (Austria) 2020. **Publications** *Encuentro Latino Americano* (4 a year) in Spanish; *Journal of Political Theory and Analysis* (4 a year); *POLITIKON* (4 a year); *IAPSS News and Opportunities* (24 a year). **Members** Associations; Individuals. Membership countries not specified. **Consultative Status** Consultative status granted from: *UNESCO (#20322)* (Consultative Status). **IGO Relations** Member of (1): *European Youth Centres (EYCs, #09138)*. **NGO Relations** Member of (7): *CIVICUS: World Alliance for Citizen Participation (#03962)* (Associate); *ECPR European Political Science Network (EpsNet, #05339)*; *European Students' Union (ESU, #08848)* (Associate); Global Student Government; Informal Forum of International Student Organisations (IFISO); *Open Education Consortium (#17751)*; *The Right to Research Coalition (no recent information)*. Partner of (5): *International Student One Health Alliance (ISOHA)*; *International Studies Association (ISA, #15615)*; Leading Women of Tomorriw; The World with MNR; Voters Without Borders. Cooperates with (5): *African Association of Political Science (AAPS)*; *American Political Science Association (APSA)*; *European Consortium for Political Research (ECPR, #06762)*; *International Political Science Association (IPSA, #14615)*; national political science associations. [2022.05.28/XD9444/**D**]

- ♦ International Association on the Political Use of Psychiatry / see Human Rights in Mental Health (#10988)
- ♦ International Association of Port Jurists (no recent information)
- ♦ International Association of Port Police / see InterPortPolice (#15963)

♦ International Association of Ports and Harbors (IAPH) 12096

Association internationale des ports (AIP) – Asociación Internacional de los Puertos – Internationaler Verband der Seehäfen

SG 7th Floor – South Tower New Pier Takeshiba, 1-16-1 Kaigan, Minato-ku, Tokyo, 105-0022 Japan. T. +81354032770. Fax +81354037651. E-mail: info@iaphworldports.org.
Europe Office Spreeuwendal 6, 2914 KK Nieuwerkerk aan den IJssel, Netherlands. T. +31180323399. Fax +31180318569.
URL: http://www.iaphworldports.org/

History 7 Nov 1955, Los Angeles, CA (USA). Founded at 2nd International Port and Harbor Congress, following a resolution at 1st Congress, Oct 1952, Kobe (Japan). Former names and other names: *Association internationale des ports et rades* – former; *World Ports Association (WPA)* – alias. Registration: EU Transparency Register, No/ID: 008739522835-06, Start date: 28 Jul 2016. **Aims** Further knowledge in the fields of port organization, management, administration, operation, development and promotion, and increase efficiency of ports and harbours by development and dissemination of information useful to their administration and providing them with an opportunity of associating together; thereby advance international friendship and understanding and the growth of *waterborne commerce*. **Structure** Conference (annual); Council comprised of Board of Executive Directors and Non-Executive Directors; Legal Counsellors; Internal Committees (4); Technical Committees (3). Regions (6). **Languages** English. **Staff** 6.00 FTE, paid. **Finance** Sources: members' dues. **Activities** Events/meetings; knowledge management/information dissemination; monitoring/evaluation; research/documentation. **Events** *World Ports Conference* Abu Dhabi (United Arab Emirates) 2023, *World Ports Conference* Vancouver, BC (Canada) 2022, *World Ports Conference* Antwerp (Belgium) 2021, *World Ports Conference* Antwerp (Belgium) 2020, *NEVA : International Conference for Shipping, Shipbuiling, Offshore Energy, Ports, Inland Waterways and Oceanography* St Petersburg (Russia) 2019. **Publications** *Ports and Harbors* (6 a year); *IAPH Membership Directory* (annual). Technical Committee reports; conference proceedings; guidelines; occasional reports and papers.
Members Honorary; Founder; Regular (180); Associate (140). Regular and Associate members in 90 countries and territories (not specified). Included in the above Associate members, 12 organizations listed in this Yearbook:
American Association of Port Authorities (AAPA, #00775); *Arab Academy for Science, Technology and Maritime Transport (AASTMT, #00891)*; *Arab Sea Ports Federation (ASPF, #01040)*; *European Sea Ports Organisation (ESPO, #08453)*; *International Association of Dredging Companies (IADC, #11852)*; *International Association of Maritime Universities (IAMU, #12016)*; *International Bank for Reconstruction and Development (IBRD, #12317)* (World Bank); *North African Port Management Association (NAPMA, #17556)*; *Pacific Community (SPC, #17942)* (Regional Maritime Programme of); *Port Management Association of Eastern and Southern Africa (PMAESA, #18462)*; *Port Management Association of West and Central Africa (PMAWCA, #18463)*; *World Maritime University (WMU, #21633)*.
Consultative Status Consultative status granted from: *ECOSOC (#05331)* (Special); *UNCTAD (#20285)* (Special Category); *ILO (#11123)* (Special List); *International Maritime Organization (IMO, #14102)*; *UNEP (#20299)*. **IGO Relations** Memorandum of Understanding signed with: *World Customs Organization (WCO, #21350)*. Close contacts with: *Consultative Meeting of Contracting Parties to the London Convention/Meeting of Contracting Parties to the London Protocol (#04769)*; *International Institute for the Unification of Private Law (UNIDROIT, #13934)*. Observer to: *OSPAR Commission for the Protection of the Marine Environment of the North-East Atlantic (OSPAR Commission, #17905)*. Accredited by: *International Hydrographic Organization (IHO, #13825)*; *United Nations Economic Commission for Europe (UNECE, #20555)*, especially through its *'Working Party on Facilitation of International Trade Procedures'*. Associated with Department of Global Communications of the United Nations.
NGO Relations Consultative member of: *Comité maritime international (CMI, #04192)*. Represented on: *Advisory Committee on Protection of the Sea (ACOPS, #00139)*. In liaison with technical committees of: *International Organization for Standardization (ISO, #14473)*. *North African Port Management Association (NAPMA, #17556)* is member. Close contacts with:
- *Airports Council International (ACI, #00611)*;
- *Association internationale villes et ports – réseau mondial des villes portuaires (AIVP, #02751)*;
- *BIMCO (#03236)*;
- *Bureau international des containers et du transport intermodal (BIC, #03364)*;
- *European Barge Union (EBU, #06318)*;
- *Fédération internationale des associations de transitaires et assimilés (FIATA, #09610)*;
- *ICHCA International Limited (IIL, #11053)*;
- *International Association of Classification Societies (IACS, #11778)*;
- *International Association of Marine Aids to Navigation and Lighthouse Authorities (IALA, #12013)*;
- *International Cargo Handling Coordination Association (ICHCA, inactive)*;
- *International Chamber of Commerce (ICC, #12534)*;
- *International Chamber of Shipping (ICS, #12535)*;
- *International Federation of Shipmasters Associations (IFSMA, #13539)*;
- *International Harbour Masters' Association (IHMA, #13774)* and *European Harbour Masters' Committee (EHMC, #07449)*;
- *International Maritime Pilots' Association (IMPA, #14103)*;
- *Oil Companies International Marine Forum (OCIMF, #17709)*;
- *PIANC (#18371)*;
- *Society of International Gas Tanker and Terminal Operators (SIGTTO, #19582)*. [2022.10.17/XB1329/y/**B**]

- ♦ International Association of Poultry Instructors and Investigators / see World's Poultry Science Association (#21825)
- ♦ International Association of Poultry Pathologists / see World Veterinary Poultry Association (#21902)
- ♦ International Association for Practising Accountants / see IAPA (#11005)

♦ International Association of Practising Lawyers (IAPL) 12097

Sec Seepark – Gartenstrasse 4, Postfach 4819, 6304 Zug, Switzerland. T. +41417287161. Fax +41417287166.
URL: http://www.iapl.org/

History 1982. **Structure** Board, comprising President, Vice-President, Secretary and 2 members.
Members Individuals in 25 countries and territories:
Austria, Belgium, Brazil, Cameroon, Canada, China, Egypt, France, Germany, Hong Kong, Hungary, India, Ireland, Israel, Italy, Lebanon, Netherlands, Poland, Russia, Singapore, Spain, Sweden, Switzerland, UK, USA. [2012.07.23/XD7110/v/**D**]

♦ International Association For Premenstrual Disorders (IAPMD) 12098

Exec Dir 6 Liberty Square, Ste 2077, Boston MA 02109, USA. E-mail: info@iapmd.org.
URL: https://iapmd.org/

History 2013, USA. Founded by Amanda LaFleur and Sandi MacDonald. Former names and other names: *National Association for Premenstrual Dysphoric Disorder (NAPMDD)* – former (2013 to 2018). Registration: No/ID: 47-2480088, USA. **Aims** Provide resources and support for women experiencing Premenstrual Dysphoric Disorder (PMDD) and premenstrual exacerbation of underlying disorders. **Structure** Board of Directors. **Activities** Advocacy/lobbying/activism; events/meetings; guidance/assistance/consulting; research/documentation; training/education. [2023/AA2951/**D**]

- ♦ International Association for Prepress Industry (inactive)

♦ International Association of Press Clubs (IAPC) 12099

Association Internationale des Press Clubs

Gen Secretariat c/o Press Club Polska, Al Ujazdowskie 6A, 00-461 Warsaw, Poland. T. +48222997127. E-mail: secretariat@pressclubs.org.
URL: http://www.pressclubs.org/

History 6 Jan 2002. **Aims** Uphold the ethics of *journalism* and free access to information; support dialogue, cooperation and exchange of experience among journalists worldwide. **Structure** General Assembly; Executive Board. **Languages** English. **Activities** Awards/prizes/competitions; events/meetings. **Events** *International Conference on the Freedom of the Press* Jerusalem (Israel) / Herzliyya (Israel) 2019, *General Assembly* Brussels (Belgium) 2018, *General Assembly* Ulaanbaatar (Mongolia) 2015, *General Assembly* Vienna (Austria) 2014.
Members Press clubs, foreign correspondents' clubs and international press centers in 28 countries and territories:
Australia, Austria, Belarus, Belgium, Cambodia, China, France, Germany, Hong Kong, India, Indonesia, Israel, Italy, Japan, Korea Rep, Malaysia, Mongolia, Netherlands, New Zealand, Poland, Portugal, Singapore, Spain, Switzerland, Taiwan, Thailand, UK, USA.
Included in the above, 3 organizations listed in this Yearbook:
European Federation of Press Clubs (EFPC, #07194); Foreign Correspondents' Club of South Asia (FCC); Overseas Press Club of America (OPC).
Observers in 39 countries:
Angola, Bahamas, Barbados, Benin, Botswana, Burundi, Chad, Congo Brazzaville, Côte d'Ivoire, Ethiopia, Fiji, Gambia, Ghana, Guinea, Guyana, Haiti, Jamaica, Kenya, Liberia, Madagascar, Malawi, Mali, Mauritania, Namibia, Niger, Nigeria, Papua New Guinea, Rwanda, Senegal, Seychelles, South Africa, St Lucia, Sweden, Tanzania UR, Timor-Leste, Togo, Uganda, Zambia, Zimbabwe. [2022.02.21/XM3980/y/**C**]

♦ International Association for the Prevention of Blindness (inactive)
♦ International Association for the Prevention of Smoke / see Air and Waste Management Association
♦ International Association for the Prevention of Unemployment (inactive)
♦ International Association for Preventive Pediatrics (inactive)
♦ International Association of Printing House Craftsmen (internationally oriented national body)
♦ International Association of Privacy Professionals (internationally oriented national body)

♦ International Association of Private Assisted Reproductive Technology Clinics and Laboratories (A-PART) 12100

Secretariat c/o Kato Ladies Clinic, 7-20-3 Nishishinjuku, Shinjuku-ku, Tokyo, 160-0023 Japan. E-mail: info@a-part.jp.
URL: http://www.apartonline.info/

History Founded in 1998. **Aims** Support couples suffering from fertility problems by providing effective, accessible and affordable treatment. **Structure** Board; International Scientific Committee. **Languages** English. **Finance** Members' dues. **Events** *World conference* Tokyo (Japan) 2011, *Scientific meeting* Hong Kong (Hong Kong) 2010, *World conference / World Congress* Las Vegas, NV (USA) 2010, *World conference / World Congress* Geneva (Switzerland) 2009, *World conference / World Congress* Fort Lauderdale, FL (USA) 2008.
Members in 45 countries:
Argentina, Australia, Austria, Belgium, Benin, Bolivia, Brazil, Bulgaria, Canada, Chile, Colombia, Cyprus, Czechia, Denmark, Dominican Rep, Egypt, France, Germany, Ghana, Greece, Hungary, India, Israel, Italy, Japan, Jordan, Korea Rep, Mexico, Nigeria, Pakistan, Poland, Portugal, Russia, Saudi Arabia, South Africa, Spain, Sweden, Switzerland, Togo, Türkiye, UK, Ukraine, United Arab Emirates, Uruguay, USA. [2018.07.28/XD8275/**D**]

♦ International Association of Private Career Colleges (unconfirmed)

♦ International Association for Probabilistic Safety Assessment and Management (IAPSAM) 12101

Sec Computer Science, Boise State Univ, 1910 University Dr, Boise ID 83725, USA.
URL: http://www.iapsam.org/

History Also referred to as *International Association for PSAM*. **Aims** Promote rational decision making to assure *safety* and *reliability* and to optimize the use of resources for complex systems. **Structure** Board of Directors, comprising President, Secretary, Treasurer and 9 members. **Activities** Sponsors and oversees organization of *International Conference on Probabilistic Safety Assessment and Management (PSAM)*. **Events** *Conference* Venice (Italy) 2020, *Conference* Los Angeles, CA (USA) 2018, *Conference* Seoul (Korea Rep) 2016, *Conference* Honolulu, HI (USA) 2014, *Conference* Tokyo (Japan) 2013. [2013/XN7118/**C**]

♦ International Association for Procedural Law (IAPL) 12102

Association internationale de droit processuel – Asociación Internacional de Derecho Procesal – Internationale Vereinigung für Prozessrecht – Associazione Internazionale di Diritto Processuale

Pres Univ Panthéon, 12 place du Panthéon, 75231 Paris CEDEX 05, France. T. +33144077782. Fax +33144077651.
Gen Exec Sec address not obtained. E-mail: fgascon@ucm.es.
URL: http://www.iaplaw.org/

History 30 Sep 1950, Florence (Italy). Founded 30 Sep – 3 Oct 1950, Florence (Italy), as *International Institute of Civil Procedural Law*, during 1st International Congress of Civil Procedure Law. Current name adopted 19 Dec 1955, Bologna. Previously also referred to in French as *Association internationale de droit judiciaire*. Current statutes amended 25 Jul 2011, Heidelberg (Germany). **Aims** Promote the development of the study of procedural law by encouraging collaboration among lawyers and academics in different countries and the exchange of information on sources, publications, practice and adjudication; participate with other juridical experts to promote the study of procedural matters in national and international research institutions. **Structure** General Assembly; Council; Working Groups. **Languages** English, French, German, Italian, Spanish. **Finance** Members' dues. Other sources: gifts from national and international organizations and private persons. **Activities** Events/meetings. **Events** *Annual Congress* Örebro (Sweden) 2022, *World Congress* Kobe (Japan) 2019, *Quadrennial Congress* Istanbul (Turkey) 2015, *Seoul Conference* Seoul (Korea Rep) 2014, *Interim Meeting* Athens (Greece) 2013. **Publications** *International Journal of Procedural Law* (2 a year) in English, French, German, Italian, Spanish.
Members Honorary; Benefactor; Ordinary. Full in 60 countries:
Albania, Argentina, Australia, Austria, Belgium, Benin, Botswana, Brazil, Bulgaria, Canada, Cape Verde, Chile, China, Colombia, Costa Rica, Croatia, Czechia, Denmark, Egypt, Finland, France, Germany, Greece, Guatemala, Hungary, India, Iran Islamic Rep, Israel, Italy, Japan, Korea Rep, Lesotho, Lithuania, Mexico, Moldova, Morocco, Netherlands, New Zealand, Nigeria, Norway, Panama, Peru, Poland, Portugal, Romania, Russia, Senegal, Serbia, Singapore, Slovenia, South Africa, Spain, Sweden, Switzerland, Türkiye, UK, Ukraine, Uruguay, USA, Venezuela. [2017.03.09/XD7741/**D**]

♦ International Association of Process Oriented Psychology (unconfirmed)
♦ International Association of Professional Accountants / see IAPA (#11005)
♦ International Association of Professional Advisers (inactive)
♦ International Association of Professional Base Ball Players (inactive)

♦ International Association of Professional Congress Organisers (IAPCO) 12103

Association internationale des organisateurs professionnels de congrès

CEO Mühlebachstrasse 6, 8008 Zurich ZH, Switzerland.
URL: http://www.iapco.org/

History 5 Jan 1968, Brussels (Belgium). Founded at a meeting under the patronage of *Union of International Associations (UIA, #20414)*. Status finalized Jan 1969, London (UK); official foundation, 30 Jan 1969; Registered Office transferred to Zurich (Switzerland), 1988. Statutes and standing orders adopted Feb 2015, Lisbon (Portugal); Feb 2018, Tokyo (Japan). Registration: Switzerland. **Aims** Raise standards of service among members and other sectors of the *meetings* industry by means of continuing education and interaction with other professionals. **Structure** Annual Meeting and General Assembly; Council Meetings; EDGE Seminars. **Languages** English. **Staff** 3.00 FTE, paid. **Finance** Sources: fees for services; members' dues; sponsorship. **Activities** Certification/accreditation; events/meetings; training/education. **Events** *Annual Meeting and General Assembly* Jerusalem (Israel) 2023, *Council Meeting* Belfast (UK) 2022, *Council Meeting* Florence (Italy) 2022, *Annual Meeting and General Assembly* 2021, *Council Meeting* 2021. **Publications** *The PCO* (5 a year). *Dictionary of Meeting Industry Terminology*. White papers; guidelines; advocacy guides; research findings.
Members Categories: Company; Invited; Honorary; Retirement; International Office; National Office. Members (120) in 41 countries and territories:
Argentina, Australia, Austria, Belgium, Brazil, Bulgaria, Canada, China, Colombia, Czechia, Denmark, Egypt, France, Germany, Greece, India, Ireland, Israel, Italy, Japan, Korea Rep, Lebanon, Malaysia, Mexico, Monaco, Netherlands, New Zealand, Norway, Portugal, Russia, Singapore, Slovenia, South Africa, Spain, Sweden, Switzerland, Taiwan, Türkiye, UK, United Arab Emirates, USA.
Conference officers in the following 6 organizations listed in this Yearbook:
Asian Development Bank (ADB, #01422); European Bank for Reconstruction and Development (EBRD, #06315); European Committee of the Regions (CoR, #06665); European Parliament (EP, #08146); Joint Secretariat of and .
Honorary members (9) in 7 countries. Membership countries not specified.
IGO Relations Also links with United Nations bodies (not specified). **NGO Relations** Member of (2): *Events Industry Council (EIC, #09212); Joint Meetings Industry Council (JMIC, #16140).* [2022.10.12/XC1330/ty/**C**]

♦ International Association of Professional Courier-Drivers (inactive)
♦ International Association of Professional Cyclists (inactive)
♦ International Association of Professional Mercenaries (unconfirmed)

♦ International Association of Professional Numismatists (IAPN) 12104

Association internationale des numismates professionnels (AINP) – Asociación Internacional de Numismaticos Profesionales – Internationaler Verband der Berufs-Numismatiker

SG/Exec Dir Rue de la Bourse 14, 1000 Brussels, Belgium. T. +3225133400. Fax +3225122528. E-mail: secretary@iapn-coins.org.
URL: http://www.iapn-coins.org/

History Founded 12 May 1951, Geneva (Switzerland). Registered in accordance with Swiss Civil code. EU Transparency Register: 99845749094-38. **Aims** Develop a healthy and prosperous numismatic trade conducted according to the highest standards of business ethics and commercial practice; encourage scientific research and the propagation of numismatics and the creation of lasting and friendly relations amongst professional numismatics throughout the world. **Structure** General Assembly (annual); Executive Committee (meets at least twice a year); Special Commissions. Meetings closed. **Languages** English, French. **Finance** Sources: members' dues. **Activities** Awards/prizes/competitions; events/meetings; networking/liaising. **Events** *Annual Congress* Marseille (France) 2020, *Annual Congress* Carefree, AZ (USA) 2019, *Annual Congress* Prague (Czechia) 2018, *Annual Congress* Lucerne (Switzerland) 2017, *Annual Congress* Amsterdam (Netherlands) 2016. **Publications** *Survey of Numismatic Research 2002-2007* (2009); *Survey of Numismatic Research 1995-2000* (2004); *Survey of Numismatic Research 1990-1995* (1997); *Survey of Numismatic Research 1985-1990 – 2 vols* (1991); *Numismatics, Witness to History* (1986); *Survey of Numismatic Research 1978-1984 – 2 vols* (1986); *The Forgotten Forger: Caprara of Smyrna* (1984) by P Kinns; *Le Monete Siciliane dagli Aragonesi ai Borboni* (1982) by R Spahr; *Survey of Numismatic Research 1972-1977* (1979); *Le Monete Siciliane dai Bizantini a Carlo I d'Angio* (1976) by R Spahr; *Die Munzen Saltzburgs* (1959) by G Probszt. Conference proceedings.
Members Numismatic firms in 22 countries:
Australia, Austria, Belgium, Egypt, France, Germany, Hungary, Ireland, Italy, Japan, Monaco, Netherlands, Norway, Poland, Portugal, Spain, Sweden, Switzerland, Thailand, UK, USA, Venezuela.
Corresponding members in 9 countries:
France, Germany, Italy, Netherlands, Singapore, Sri Lanka, Switzerland, UK, USA.
NGO Relations Member of: *International Numismatic Council (INC, #14385)*. Instrumental in setting up: *International Bureau for the Suppression of Counterfeit Coins (IBSCC).* [2019/XC1331/t/**C**]

♦ International Association of Professionals in Disability Management (unconfirmed)
♦ International Association of Professionals in Humanitarian Assistance and Protection / see Professionals in Humanitarian Assistance and Protection (#18515)

♦ International Association of Professionals in Sugar and Integrated Technologies (IAPSIT) 12105

Head Office Guangxi Academy of Agricultural Sciences, 174 East Daxue Road, Nanning, 530007 Guangxi, China. T. +867713277580. Fax +867713276101. E-mail: wsb@gxaas.net.
Satellite Sec Office C-2/278 – Sector F, Jankipuram, Lucknow, Uttar Pradesh 226 021, Lucknow UTTAR PRADESH 226 021, India.
URL: http://www.iapsit.net/

History Founded 2004. **Aims** Promote profitable and sustainable development of the sugar and integrated industries in developing countries encompassing agricultural, industrial, environmental and socio-economic concerns through sharing of scientific knowledge and technological advancement. **Structure** Executive Committee. **Finance** Sources: members' dues. **Activities** Awards/prizes/competitions; events/meetings. **Events** *Conference* Lucknow (India) 2019, *Conference* Udon Thani (Thailand) 2018. **Publications** *IAPSIT Newsletter*, *Sugar Tech* – journal. **Members** Individual; Association; Institutional. Membership countries not specified. [2020/XM8070/t/**B**]

♦ International Association of Professionals in Tourism / see Association Internationale des Skål Clubs (#02743)

♦ International Association of Professional Translators and Interpreters (IAPTI) 12106

Asociación Internacional de Profesionales de la Traducción y la Interpretación (AIPTI)

SG CAECE Univ, Av de Mayo 866, CABA, C1038AAK Buenos Aires, Argentina.
Pres LOGIC 000254, PO Box 02-5780, Miami FL 33102, USA.
URL: http://www.iapti.org/

History 30 Sep 2009, Argentina. **Aims** Promote ethical practices in the field of linguistic translation and interpretation; represent and protect interests of members; stimulate creation of institutional bonds; contribute to training and professional development of translators and interpreters. **Activities** Events/meetings; knowledge management/information dissemination; publishing activities; training/education. **Events** *International Conference* Timisoara (Romania) 2022, *International Conference* Timisoara (Romania) 2020, *International Conference* Valencia (Spain) 2018, *International Conference* Buenos Aires (Argentina) 2017, *International Conference* Bordeaux (France) 2015. **Members** Membership countries not specified. [2022.05.10/XJ7987/t/**D**]

♦ International Association of Professors of Italian (#02989)
♦ International Association for Programmed Instruction (inactive)
♦ International Association for the Progress of Social Science (inactive)

♦ International Association for Promoting Geoethics (IAPG) 12107

Associazione Internazionale per la Promozione della Geoetica

SG INGV, Via di Vigna Murata 605, 00143 Rome RM, Italy. T. +39651860806. E-mail: iapgeoethics@aol.com.
Main Website: https://www.geoethics.org/

History 2012, Brisbane, QLD (Australia). Founded during 34th International Geological Congress (IGC), originating from an idea conceived during General Assembly of *European Geosciences Union (EGU, #07390)*, Apr 2012, Vienna (Austria). Registration: Repubblica Italiana, No/ID: 16255, Start date: 21 Dec 2012, Italy. **Aims** Promote principles and values of geoethics and the geoethical thought within society through international cooperation and by encouraging the involvement and debate of geoscientists on their ethical obligations and social role. **Structure** General Assembly (every 4 years, during International Geological Congress); Executive Council; Board of Experts; National Sections; Task Groups; Delegates; Early Career Scientists Team (ECST). **Languages** English. **Staff** Secretariat: voluntary. **Finance** Sources: donations. Personal funds of members. Supported by: *International Union of Geological Sciences (IUGS, #15777)*. **Activities** Events/meetings; knowledge management/information dissemination; networking/liaising; publishing activities; research/documentation; standards/guidelines; training/education. **Publications** Books; articles; videos; white papers.
Members National sections in 35 countries:
Afghanistan, Argentina, Bangladesh, Bolivia, Brazil, Cameroon, Canada, Chile, Congo DR, Cuba, Egypt, France, Germany, Greece, India, Iran Islamic Rep, Iraq, Italy, Jordan, Lebanon, Malawi, Mexico, Nepal, Nigeria, Pakistan, Paraguay, Peru, Portugal, Romania, Spain, Türkiye, UK, Ukraine, Uruguay, USA.

Individuals (2,988) in 127 countries and territories:
Afghanistan, Albania, Algeria, Angola, Argentina, Australia, Austria, Azerbaijan, Bangladesh, Belgium, Bolivia, Bosnia-Herzegovina, Brazil, Brunei Darussalam, Bulgaria, Burundi, Cambodia, Cameroon, Canada, Chile, China, Colombia, Congo DR, Costa Rica, Côte d'Ivoire, Croatia, Cuba, Cyprus, Czechia, Denmark, Dominican Rep, Ecuador, Egypt, Eritrea, Ethiopia, Finland, France, Gabon, Georgia, Germany, Ghana, Greece, Guatemala, Guinea, Honduras, Hungary, India, Indonesia, Iran Islamic Rep, Iraq, Ireland, Israel, Italy, Jamaica, Japan, Jordan, Kenya, Korea Rep, Kyrgyzstan, Latvia, Lebanon, Libya, Madagascar, Malawi, Malaysia, Mali, Malta, Mexico, Mongolia, Morocco, Mozambique, Myanmar, Namibia, Nepal, Netherlands, New Zealand, Nicaragua, Nigeria, North Macedonia, Norway, Oman, Pakistan, Palestine, Panama, Paraguay, Peru, Philippines, Poland, Portugal, Puerto Rico, Qatar, Romania, Russia, Rwanda, Saudi Arabia, Senegal, Serbia, Sierra Leone, Slovakia, Slovenia, Somalia, South Africa, Spain, Sri Lanka, Sudan, Sweden, Switzerland, Syrian AR, Taiwan, Tanzania UR, Thailand, Togo, Trinidad-Tobago, Tunisia, Türkiye, Uganda, UK, Ukraine, United Arab Emirates, Uruguay, USA, Uzbekistan, Vanuatu, Venezuela, Vietnam, Zambia, Zimbabwe.

NGO Relations Cooperates with (15): *African Association of Women in Geosciences (AAWG, #00219)*; *African Network for Geo-Education (ANGE, #00387)*; *American Geophysical Union (AGU)*; Association of Environmental & Engineering Geologists; *EuroGeoSurveys (#05686)*; *European Federation of Geologists (EFG, #07133)*; Forum for Climate Engineering Assessment; *Geological Society of Africa (GSAf, #10135)*; *Geology for Global Development (GFGD)*; *International Association of Engineering Geology and the Environment (IAEG, #11872)*; *International Association of Geomorphologists (IAG, #11917)*; *International Association of Hydrogeologists (IAH, #11953)*; *International Geoscience Education Organization (IGEO, #13714)*; IUGS-IFG – Initiative on Forensic Geology; *Promoting Earth Science for Society (YES Network, #18541)*. Affiliated with (4): *Geological Society of America (GSA)*; *Geoscience InfoRmation in AFrica (GIRAF)*; *International Council for Philosophy and Human Sciences (CIPSH, #13061)*; *International Union of Geological Sciences (IUGS, #15777)*. Also links with various national organizations. [2023.01.24/XJ8440/**C**]

♦ International Association for the Promotion of Child Welfare (inactive)
♦ International Association for the Promotion of Christian Higher Education / see International Network for Christian Higher Education (#14241)
♦ International Association for the Promotion of Clinical Research in Medicine (inactive)
♦ International Association for the Promotion of Democracy under God (inactive)

♦ International Association for the Promotion and Dissemination of Research on Resilience (RESILIO) 12108

Association Internationale pour la Promotion et a la Diffusion de la Recherche sur la Résilience (RESILIO)

Gen Sec UFR Psychologie/Sciences de l'Education, Maison de la Recherche, Aix-Marseille Univ, 29 avenue Robert Schuman, 13621 Aix-en-Provence CEDEX 1, France.
URL: http://resilio-assocation.com/

Aims Promote, achieve and disseminate theoretical and applied research on resilience; contribute to university and post-university training in this area; encourage collaboration between academics, researchers and practitioners from different countries involved in the field of resilience. **Structure** Board. **Finance** Sources: members' dues. **Activities** Events/meetings. **Events** *World Congress on Resilience* Yaoundé (Cameroon) 2021, *World Congress on Resilience* Yaoundé (Cameroon) 2020, *World Congress on Resilience* Marseille (France) 2018, *General Assembly* Bucharest (Romania) 2017, *Resilio Symposium* Bucharest (Romania) 2017. [2018/XM6429/**C**]

♦ International Association for the Promotion of the Experimental and Clinical Pharmacology (inactive)
♦ International Association for Promotion of Healthcare and Life-Science Research / see Healthcare and Biological Sciences Research Association
♦ International Association for the Promotion and Protection of Private Foreign Investments (inactive)
♦ International Association for the Promotion of Study of Quaternions and Similar Mathematical Systems (inactive)

♦ International Association for the Promotion of Women of Europe (IAPWE) 12109

Association internationale pour la promotion de femmes d'Europe (AIPFE)

Pres address not obtained.
URL: http://www.aipfe.eu/

History 1987, with support from *European Commission (EC, #06633)*. Registered in accordance with Belgian law. **Aims** Encourage the participation of women to the European affairs. **Structure** General Assembly (annual). Board of Directors, including President, Vice-President, Treasurer and Secretary. **Languages** English, French. **Finance** Funding from: *European Commission (EC, #06633)*; *European Parliament (EP, #08146)*; ministries; local and regional authorities. **Activities** Organizes meetings, debates, fora and symposia. Offers biennial 'Women of Europe' award. Set up *'Club de Rhodes'*, 1988, comprising the laureates of the award. Conducts studies. **Members** Founding; Ex officio; Active; Honorary. Membership countries not specified. [2014/XE4276/**E**]

♦ International Association for the Properties of Steam / see International Association for the Properties of Water and Steam (#12110)

♦ International Association for the Properties of Water and Steam (IAPWS) 12110

Association internationale pour les propriétés de l'eau et de la vapeur

Exec Sec address not obtained.
URL: http://www.iapws.org/

History 1929, London (UK), as *International Conference on the Properties of Steam*. Name changed, 1971, New York NY (USA), to *International Association for the Properties of Steam (IAPS) – Association internationale pour les propriétés de la vapeur*. Present name adopted in 1989. **Aims** Provide internationally accepted formulations for properties of light and heavy steam, water and selected aqueous solutions for scientific and industrial applications; define research needs; promote and coordinate research on steam, water and selected aqueous systems important in thermal power cycles, collect and evaluate resulting data, communicate and promulgate findings; provide an international forum for exchange of experience, ideas and results of research. **Structure** General Meeting. Executive Committee, comprising delegates selected by member national organizations, chaired by President. International Secretariat, headed by Executive Secretary. Sub-Committees and Working Groups. **Languages** English. **Finance** Members' dues based on GNP of country concerned. **Activities** Training/education; awards/prizes/competitions; events/meetings. **Events** *International Conference on the Properties of Water and Steam* Boulder, CO (USA) 2024, *Meeting* Turin (Italy) 2023, *Annual Meeting* Rotorua (New Zealand) 2022, *Annual Meeting* Southport (UK) 2021, *Annual Meeting* Turin (Italy) 2020. **Publications** *IAPWS News*. Guidelines and Releases – international Standards; Needs Documents – calling for research on specific topics; relorts; recommendations.
Members Full – National organizations acting through national committees. Full in 14 countries:
Argentina, Brazil, Canada, Czechia, Denmark, France, Germany, Greece, Ireland, Italy, Japan, Russia, UK, USA.
Associate member in 1 country:
Switzerland.
Individuals in 5 countries:
Austria, India, Netherlands, South Africa, Switzerland. [2021/XD1687/**D**]

♦ International Association of Prosecutors (IAP) 12111

SG Hartogstraat 13, 2514 EP The Hague, Netherlands. T. +31703630345. Fax +31703630367. E-mail: sg@iap-association.org – info@iap-association.org.
Exec Dir address not obtained. E-mail: ed@iap-association.org.
URL: http://www.iap-association.org/

History 6 Jun 1995, Vienna (Austria). Founded at *United Nations Office at Vienna (UNOV, #20604)*. Formally inaugurated at 1st meeting, Sep 1996, Budapest (Hungary). **Aims** Set and raise standards of professional conduct and ethics for Prosecutors worldwide; promote the rule of law, fairness, impartiality and respect for human rights and improving international co-operation to combat crime. **Structure** General Meeting; Executive Committee; Secretariat & IAP officials; The Senate; The Financial Review Committee. **Languages** English. **Staff** 5.50 FTE, paid. **Finance** Sources: members' dues. Annual budget: 400,000 EUR. **Activities** Events/meetings; guidance/assistance/consulting; networking/liaising; standards/guidelines. **Events** *Annual Conference* Tbilisi (Georgia) 2022, *Annual Conference* Tbilisi (Georgia) 2021, *Annual Conference* Athens (Greece) 2020, *Annual Conference* Buenos Aires (Argentina) 2019, *Eastern European and Central Asian Regional Conference* Minsk (Belarus) 2019. **Publications** *IAP Newsletter* (4 a year). *Best Practice Series* – 5 vols. *IAP Human Rights Manual* (2nd ed); *Standards for Prosecutors*; *Standards for the Protection of Prosecutors*; *World Directory of Prosecution Services*. Brochures.
Members Individual prosecutors (1,300). Organizational: prosecution services, associations of prosecutors and crime prevention agencies (183). Membership represents over 250,000 prosecutors. Organizational members in 78 countries and territories:
Albania, Angola, Argentina, Armenia, Australia, Austria, Azerbaijan, Barbados, Bolivia, Bosnia-Herzegovina, Brazil, Brunei Darussalam, Bulgaria, Canada, Cape Verde, Chile, China, Congo DR, Croatia, Cyprus, Czechia, Denmark, Ecuador, Estonia, Eswatini, Ethiopia, Fiji, Finland, France, Ghana, Guatemala, Guinea-Bissau, Hong Kong, Hungary, Iceland, India, Ireland, Isle of Man, Japan, Kazakhstan, Korea Rep, Kyrgyzstan, Liechtenstein, Lithuania, Malawi, Moldova, Mongolia, Mozambique, Namibia, Netherlands, New Zealand, Nigeria, North Macedonia, Norway, Oman, Peru, Philippines, Poland, Romania, Rwanda, Saudi Arabia, Senegal, Serbia, Slovakia, Slovenia, South Africa, Spain, Sri Lanka, Sweden, Switzerland, Tanzania UR, Thailand, Togo, Uganda, UK, Ukraine, USA, Zambia.
Individuals in 88 countries and territories:
Angola, Argentina, Australia, Austria, Azerbaijan, Bahamas, Bangladesh, Barbados, Belgium, Benin, Brazil, Bulgaria, Burundi, Cameroon, Canada, Chile, China, Colombia, Côte d'Ivoire, Cyprus, Czechia, Denmark, Djibouti, Estonia, Fiji, Finland, France, Gambia, Germany, Ghana, Guinea, Guyana, Haiti, Hong Kong, Hungary, Iceland, India, Indonesia, Ireland, Israel, Italy, Kenya, Korea Rep, Lesotho, Liberia, Madagascar, Malawi, Malaysia, Mali, Mauritania, Mauritius, Morocco, Mozambique, Namibia, Nepal, Netherlands, New Zealand, Nigeria, Norway, Palau, Palestine, Panama, Papua New Guinea, Poland, Portugal, Romania, Russia, Rwanda, Sao Tomé-Principe, Senegal, Singapore, Slovakia, Slovenia, Solomon Is, South Africa, St Vincent-Grenadines, Sweden, Switzerland, Taiwan, Thailand, Timor-Leste, Togo, Uganda, UK, Ukraine, Venezuela, Yemen, Zambia.
Regional members (3), listed in this Yearbook:
Asia Crime Prevention Foundation (ACPF, #01263); *Eurojust (#05698)*; *Naif Arab University for Security Sciences (NAUSS, #16929)*.
IGO Relations Observer status with (1): *Council of Europe (CE, #04881)*. Committee of Experts on the Role of the Public Prosecution in the Criminal Justice System. **NGO Relations** Member of (1): *International Legal Assistance Consortium (ILAC, #14025)*. Partner of (1): *Global Forum on Law, Justice and Development (GFLJD, #10373)*. [2022.10.20/XD5913/y/**B**]

♦ International Association for the Protection of the Environment in Africa (no recent information)
♦ International Association for the Protection of Human Rights in Cyprus (internationally oriented national body)
♦ International Association for the Protection of Industrial Property / see International Association for the Protection of Intellectual Property (#12112)

♦ International Association for the Protection of Intellectual Property 12112

Association internationale pour la protection de la propriété intellectuelle (AIPPI) – Internationale Vereinigung für den Schutz des geistigen Eigentums

Exec Dir Toedistrasse 16, 8002 Zurich ZH, Switzerland. T. +41442805880. Fax +41442805885. E-mail: mail@aippi.org.
Events Dir address not obtained.
URL: http://www.aippi.org/

History 8 May 1897, Brussels (Belgium). Statutes revised: 1926; 1952; 11 Apr 1966, Tokyo (Japan); 13 Jun 1969, Venice (Italy); 17 Nov 1972, Mexico City (Mexico); 19 May 1978, Munich (Germany FR); 27 May 1983, Geneva (Switzerland); 13 Jun 1986, London (UK); 30 Jun 1995, Montréal QC (Canada); 30 Mar 2001, Melbourne (Australia); 2018, Cancun (Mexico). Former names and other names: *International Association for the Protection of Industrial Property* – former; *Association internationale pour la protection de la propriété industrielle* – former; *Asociación Internacional para la Protección de la Propiedad Industrial* – former; *Internationale Vereinigung für Gewerblichen Rechtsschutz* – former; *IAPIP* – alias; *IVfgR* – alias. Registration: Swiss Civil Code, Switzerland. **Aims** Develop and improve laws for the protection of intellectual property. **Structure** General Assembly; Executive Committee; Council of Presidents; General Secretariat; Permanent Committees, including Statutory Committees. **Languages** English, French, German. **Finance** Sources: members' dues. **Activities** Advocacy/lobbying/activism; events/meetings; guidance/assistance/consulting; management of treaties and agreements; research/documentation. Manages the following treaties/agreements: *Paris Convention for the Protection of Industrial Property, 1883 (1883)*. **Events** *World Congress* Dubai (United Arab Emirates) 2025, *World Congress* Yokohama (Japan) 2024, *World Congress* Istanbul (Türkiye) 2023, *World Congress* San Francisco, CA (USA) 2022, *World Congress* Zurich (Switzerland) 2021. **Publications** *AIPPI Summary Yearbook* (1-2 a year) in English, French, German, German. Working guidelines for new questions; national and regional group reports – comparative law studies; summary reports – syntheses of group reports; reports of international meetings; annual membership list.
Members National groups, regional groups and independent members (individuals). National/regional groups in 62 countries:
Argentina, Australia, Austria, Belarus, Belgium, Bolivia, Brazil, Bulgaria, Canada, Chile, China, Colombia, Croatia, Czechia, Denmark, Ecuador, Egypt, Estonia, Finland, France, Georgia, Germany, Greece, Hungary, Iceland, India, Indonesia, Ireland, Israel, Italy, Japan, Korea Rep, Latvia, Lithuania, Luxembourg, Malaysia, Mexico, Netherlands, New Zealand, Nigeria, Norway, Panama, Paraguay, Peru, Philippines, Poland, Portugal, Romania, Russia, Serbia, Singapore, Slovakia, Slovenia, South Africa, Spain, Sweden, Switzerland, Thailand, UK, Ukraine, USA, Venezuela.
Consultative Status Consultative status granted from: *ECOSOC (#05331)* (Special); *UNCTAD (#20285)* (Special Category); *UNIDO (#20336)*; *World Intellectual Property Organization (WIPO, #21593)* (Permanent Observer Status). **IGO Relations** Observer status with (1): *Union internationale pour la protection des obtentions végétales (UPOV, #20436)*. Cooperates with (3): *Eurasian Patent Office (EAPO, #05612)*; *European Commission (EC, #06633)*; *European Union Intellectual Property Office (EUIPO, #08996)*. Associated with Department of Global Communications of the United Nations. **NGO Relations** Member of (1): *Conference of Non-Governmental Organizations in Consultative Relationship with the United Nations (CONGO, #04635)*. [2023.02.15/XB1227/**B**]

♦ International Association for the Protection of the Mother and for the Reform of Sexual Life (inactive)
♦ International Association for the Protection of Private Rights (inactive)

♦ International Association of Protective Structures (IAPS) 12113

Pres Univ of Bundeswehr München, Inst for Engineering Mechanics and Structural Analysis, Lab for Computational Engineering, RISC Research Ctr, Werner-Heisenberg-Weg 39, 85577 Neubiberg, Germany. T. +498960043239. Fax +498960044549.
URL: http://www.protectivestructures.org/

History By-laws adopted, 29 Sep 2010, Manchester (UK). **Aims** Promote research and development associated with protective structures in *civil engineering*. **Structure** Board. **Languages** English. **Staff** Part-time, voluntary. **Finance** No budget. **Activities** Awards/prizes/competitions; events/meetings. **Events** *International Conference on Protective Structures* Auburn, AL (USA) 2021, *International Conference on Protective Structures* Auburn, AL (USA) 2020, *International Conference on Protective Structures* Poznań (Poland) 2018, *International Conference on Protective Structures* Beijing (China) 2016, *International Conference on Protective Structures* Newcastle, NSW (Australia) 2015. **Publications** *International Journal of Protective Structures* (4 a year). **Members** Full in 40 countries. Membership countries not specified. **IGO Relations** Cooperates with ministries and federal offices. **NGO Relations** Informal contacts with NGOs. [2016.06.01/XM4685/**C**]

♦ International Association for Protein Structure Analysis and Proteomics (IAPSAS) 12114

Address not obtained.
URL: http://www.bnl.gov/iapsap/default.asp

History 1999. Founded to facilitate the *Methods in Protein Structure Analysis (MPSA)* meetings series, which originated in 1974. Registration: Start date: 14 Sep 1999, USA, Virginia. **Aims** Promote the discovery and exchange of new methods and techniques for the analysis of protein structure; facilitate the application of methods in protein structure analysis in the pursuit of solutions to biological problems; support and foster the education of researchers in the techniques of protein chemistry, protein structure analysis, and proteomics. **Structure** Board. Executive Committee, comprising President, Secretary, Treasurer and 3 members. **Activities** Organizes the 'Methods in Protein Structure Analysis (MPSA) Meeting. **Events** *Methods in Protein Structure Analysis Meeting (MPSA2012)* Ottawa, ON (Canada) 2012, *International Conference on Methods in Protein Structural Analysis (MPSA)* Uppsala (Sweden) 2010, *Meeting of methods in protein* *structural analysis / MPSA Meeting* Sapporo (Japan) 2008, *Meeting of Methods in Protein Structural Analysis / MPSA Meeting* Lille (France) 2006, *Meeting od Methods in Protein Structural Analysis / MPSA Meeting* Seattle, WA (USA) 2004. [2012/XJ0059/**E**]

- ♦ International Association of Providers of AIDS Care (internationally oriented national body)
- ♦ International Association for PSAM / see International Association for Probabilistic Safety Assessment and Management (#12101)
- ♦ International Association of Psychoanalytic Gerontology (inactive)
- ♦ International Association for the Psychology of Food and Nutrition (inactive)

♦ International Association for the Psychology of Language Learning (IAPLL) 12115

Pres CBU Psychology Dept, PO Box 5300, 1250 Grand Lake Rd, Sydney NS B1P 6L2, Canada. E-mail: office@iapll.com.
URL: http://www.iapll.com/

History 2013, Jyväskylä (Finland). **Aims** Bring together language teachers and academics with an interest in diverse aspects of the psychology involved in *teaching* and learning foreign languages. **Structure** Executive Board; Advisory Board. **Activities** Events/meetings; knowledge management/information dissemination. **Events** *International Conference* Sydney, NS (Canada) 2022, *International Conference* Sydney, NS (Canada) 2021, *International Conference* Sydney, NS (Canada) 2020, *International Conference* Tokyo (Japan) 2018, *International Conference* Jyväskylä (Finland) 2016. **Publications** *Journal for the Psychology of Language Learning* (annual). [2022/XM6382/**C**]

♦ International Association for the Psychology of Religion (IAPR) . . . 12116

Internationale Gesellschaft für Religionspsychologie

Pres Kopernika St 26, 31-501 Krakow, Poland.
Gen Sec/Treas Johannisstrasse 1, 48143 Münster, Germany.
URL: http://www.iaprweb.org/

History 1914, Nuremberg (Germany). New statutes adopted, 28-30 Sep 2001, Soesterberg (Netherlands). Former names and other names: *International Association for Psychology of Religion and the Science of Religion* – former; *Internationale Gesellschaft für Religionspsychologie und Religionswissenschaft* – former. **Aims** Promote psychology of religion by: stimulating study of the psychology of religion in its widest sense; providing a forum for exchange of scholarly information. **Structure** General Meeting (every 2 years); Board. **Languages** English. **Staff** 3.50 FTE, voluntary. **Finance** Sources: members' dues. **Activities** Awards/prizes/competitions; events/meetings. **Events** *Conference* Netherlands 2023, *Conference* 2021, *Conference* Gdansk (Poland) 2019, *Conference* Hamar (Norway) 2017, *Conference* Istanbul (Turkey) 2015. **Publications** *Archiv für Religionspsychologie – Archive for the Psychology of Religion* in English, French, German; *IAPR Newsletter*.
Members Regular; Student; academically trained persons (more than 300) who share the objectives of the Society in more than 31 countries:
Australia, Belgium, Bosnia-Herzegovina, Brazil, Canada, Czechia, Denmark, Finland, Georgia, Germany, India, Indonesia, Iran Islamic Rep, Israel, Italy, Lithuania, Netherlands, New Zealand, Norway, Poland, Portugal, Romania, Russia, Slovakia, Spain, Sweden, Switzerland, Thailand, Türkiye, UK, USA. [2022.10.19/XF3792/**D**]

- ♦ International Association for Psychology of Religion and the Science of Religion / see International Association for the Psychology of Religion (#12116)
- ♦ International Association of Psychotechnics / see International Association of Applied Psychology (#11705)
- ♦ International Association for Psychotronic Research (no recent information)
- ♦ International Association of Pteridologists (no recent information)
- ♦ International Association of Public Cleansing / see International Solid Waste Association (#15567)
- ♦ International Association of Public Employment Services / see International Association of Workforce Professionals (#12278)
- ♦ International Association for Public Finance and Fiscal Law / see International Fiscal Association (#13608)

♦ International Association for Public Participation (IAP2) 12117

Exec Dir PO Box 270723, Louisville CO 80027, USA. E-mail: iap2hq@iap2.org.
URL: http://www.iap2.org/

History 1990, as *International Association of Public Participation Practitioners (IAPPP)*, also referred to as *IAP3*. New name adopted at annual conference, Denver CO (USA) 1996. Process initiated to become international federation of Affiliates, 2010. As of 1 Jan 2011 *Federation of IAP2* was set up, with founding Affiliates in Australasia, North America, Europe and Southern Africa. **Aims** Build an international community of public participation practitioners committed to excellence in enabling quality decision-making that involves the public effected by the decisions. **Structure** Board of Directors, selected from Affiliated Members; Executive Director. **Languages** Afrikaans, English, French, Italian, Spanish. **Staff** Voluntary. **Finance** Income through training services, products and advice. **Activities** Awards/prizes/competitions; certification/accreditation; projects/programmes; publishing activities. **Events** *Australasian Conference* Brisbane, QLD (Australia) 2021, *Latin American Conference* Bucaramanga (Colombia) 2020, *International Forum on Public Participation and Stakeholder Engagement for the Sustainable Development Goals* Bangkok (Thailand) 2019, *Australasian Conference* Sydney, NSW (Australia) 2019, *Australasian Conference* Gold Coast, QLD (Australia) 2018. **Publications** *Journal of Public Deliberation*. [2021/XN6634/**C**]

- ♦ International Association of Public Participation Practitioners / see International Association for Public Participation (#12117)
- ♦ International Association of Public Pawnbroking Institutions (inactive)

♦ International Association of Public Transport 12118

Union internationale des transports publics (UITP) – Unión Internacional de Transportes Públicos – Internationaler Verband für Öffentliches Verkehrswesen

SG Rue Sainte-Marie 6, 1080 Brussels, Belgium. T. +3226736100. Fax +3226601072. E-mail: info@uitp.org.
URL: http://www.uitp.org/

History 17 Aug 1885, Brussels (Belgium). Former names and other names: *International Union of Tramways, Local Railways and Public Motor Transport* – former (1885 to 1939); *Union internationale de tramways, de chemins de fer d'intérêt local et de transports publics automobiles* – former (1885 to 1939). Registration: Banque-Carrefour des Entreprises, No/ID: 0544.198.506, Start date: 10 May 1938, Belgium; EU Transparency Register, No/ID: 06869148182-50, Start date: 28 Feb 2012. **Aims** Enhance quality of life and economic well-being by supporting and promoting sustainable transport in urban areas worldwide. **Structure** General Assembly (at biennial Congress); Policy Board; Executive Board; Divisions; Commissions; Regional Offices (16); General Secretariat, headed by Secretary General. **Languages** English, French, German, Spanish. **Staff** 130.00 FTE, paid. **Finance** Sources: fees for services; meeting proceeds; members' dues; sale of publications. **Activities** Advocacy/lobbying/activism; knowledge management/information dissemination; networking/liaising. **Events** *Global Public Transport Summit* Barcelona (Spain) 2023, *Global Public Transport Summit* Melbourne, VIC (Australia) 2021, *Conference on Sustainable Urban Mobility* Brussels (Belgium) 2020, *SITCE (Singapore International Transport Congress) Seminar* Singapore (Singapore) 2020, *International Bus Conference* Brussels (Belgium) 2019. **Publications** Statistics; policy briefs; action points; reports. **Information Services** *MyLibrary* – documentation centre.
Members Full membership is open to all legal entities, associations and public authorities, eligible for membership of a UITP division. There is no statutory limit to the number of members. Full: operating companies; transport authorities; public transport associations; industry (including consultants). Associate and Academic: universities and research institutes; associations/organizations with an interest in public transport. Personal: senior staff of Full Members. Members (about 3,500) in 97 countries and territories:
Albania, Algeria, Argentina, Armenia, Australia, Austria, Azerbaijan, Bahrain, Belarus, Belgium, Bermuda, Bolivia, Brazil, Bulgaria, Burkina Faso, Burundi, Cameroon, Canada, Chile, China, Colombia, Costa Rica, Côte d'Ivoire, Croatia, Czechia, Denmark, Egypt, Estonia, Ethiopia, Finland, France, Georgia, Germany, Greece, Hong Kong, Hungary, Iceland, India, Indonesia, Iran Islamic Rep, Ireland, Israel, Italy, Japan, Jordan, Kazakhstan, Kenya, Korea DPR, Korea Rep, Kuwait, Liechtenstein, Lithuania, Luxembourg, Malaysia, Maldives, Malta, Mauritius, Mexico, Moldova, Monaco, Morocco, Namibia, Netherlands, New Zealand, Nigeria, Norway, Oman, Panama, Philippines, Poland, Portugal, Qatar, Réunion, Romania, Russia, Rwanda, Saudi Arabia, Senegal, Serbia, Singapore, Slovakia, Slovenia, South Africa, Spain, Sri Lanka, Sweden, Switzerland, Taiwan, Thailand, Tunisia, Türkiye, UK, Ukraine, United Arab Emirates, Uruguay, USA, Uzbekistan.

Included in the above, 1 organization listed in this Yearbook:
International Institute for Information Design (IIID).
Consultative Status Consultative status granted from: *ECOSOC (#05331)* (Special); *UNEP (#20299)*. **IGO Relations** Accredited by (1): *United Nations Framework Convention on Climate Change – Secretariat (UNFCCC, #20564)*. Cooperates with (1): *International Telecommunication Union (ITU, #15673)*. **NGO Relations** Member of (4): *Climate and Clean Air Coalition (CCAC, #04010)*; *ERTICO ITS Europe (#05532)*; *European Road Transport Research Advisory Council (ERTRAC, #08396)*; *Federation of European and International Associations Established in Belgium (FAIB, #09508)*. Partner of (2): *Covenant of Mayors for Climate and Energy (#04939)*; *Partnership on Sustainable, Low Carbon Transport Foundation (SLoCaT Foundation, #18244)*. Cooperates with (1): *International Union of Railways (#15813)*. Instrumental in setting up (2): *European Rail Research Advisory Council (ERRAC, #08325)*; *Youth For Public Transport (Y4PT, #22024)*. Associate member of: *European Federation for Transport and Environment (T and E, #07230)*; *Rail Forum Europe (RFE, #18607)*. Links with technical committees of: *Comité européen de normalisation (CEN, #04162)*; *European Committee for Electrotechnical Standardization (CENELEC, #06647)*; *International Organization for Standardization (ISO, #14473)*. Represented in: *European Citizens' Mobility Forum (ECMF, #06559)*. [2022/XB2765/**B**]

- ♦ International Association of Public Works Officials (inactive)
- ♦ International Association of Publishers of Applied Linguistics (inactive)
- ♦ International Association of Publishers of Postage Stamp Catalogues / see ASCAT – International Association of Stamp Catalogue, Stamp Album and Philatelic Magazine Publishers (#01130)
- ♦ International Association of Pure and Applied Experimental or Academic Sciences, for Objective Humanism (inactive)
- ♦ International Association for Quality / see International Academy for Quality (#11573)
- ♦ International Association for Quality Assurance in Higher Education (internationally oriented national body)
- ♦ International Association for Quality Research on Food Plants (inactive)
- ♦ International Association on Quaternary Research / see International Union for Quaternary Research (#15811)

♦ International Association for Radiation Research (IARR) 12119

Association internationale de recherche sur les radiations

Sec-Treas University of Sussex, Sussex House, Falmer, Brighton, BN1 9RH, UK.
URL: http://www.radres.org/page/IARR

History 9 Aug 1962, Harrogate (UK), following a first international congress 1958, Burlington VT (USA). Statutes approved 16 Jul 1974, Seattle WA (USA). **Aims** Promote research in radiation physics, chemistry, medicine and biology. **Structure** General Assembly (every 4 years). Council, comprising President, Vice-President (President-elect), Secretary-Treasurer, one councillor for each discipline (Physics; Chemistry; Biology; Medicine), one councillor appointed by each member organization with over 100 active members and 3 Councillors-at-large. **Languages** English. **Staff** Voluntary. **Finance** Sources: members' dues. **Activities** Teaching workshops in different areas of radiation science. Organizes International Congress (every 4 years). **Events** *Quadrennial Congress* Manchester (UK) 2019, *Quadrennial Congress* Kyoto (Japan) 2015, *Quadrennial Congress* Warsaw (Poland) 2011, *International Congress of Radiation Research (ICRR)* San Francisco, CA (USA) 2007, *Quadrennial Congress* Brisbane, QLD (Australia) 2003. **Publications** Congress proceedings.
Members National associations in 13 countries:
Australia, Canada, China, Germany, Ireland, Italy, Japan, Korea Rep, Netherlands, Poland, South Africa, UK, USA.
Regional associations (2):
Asian Association for Radiation Research (AARR, #01335); *European Radiation Research Society (ERRS, #08319)*.
NGO Relations Scientific member of: *International Union of Biological Sciences (IUBS, #15760)*. [2018/XD2500/y/**C**]

- ♦ International Association of Radiolarian Micropalaeontologists / see International Association of Radiolarian Palaeontologists (#12120)

♦ International Association of Radiolarian Palaeontologists (INTERRAD) 12120

Pres Dept of Geology, Niigata Univ, Niigata, 950-2181 Japan.
Sec CNR Ist de Geoscienwe e Georisorse, Via G L Pira 4, 50121 Florence FI, Italy.
URL: http://www.radiolaria.org/interrad/

History as an International Research Group of *International Palaeontological Association (IPA, #14501)*. Previous titles: *International Association for the Study of Radiolarians*; *International Association of Radiolarian Micropalaeontologists*. **Aims** Promote research on all aspects of radiolarian biology, ecology, taxonomy, evolution, paleobiology, paleoecology, paleobiogeography and biostratigraphy. **Structure** Officers: President; Past-President; Secretary; Assistant Secretary; Treasurer; Working Group Chairpersons. **Finance** Members' dues: US$ 15. **Activities** Working Groups (3): Cenozoic-Recent; Mesozoic; Paleozoic. **Events** *Meeting* Ljubljana (Slovenia) 2021, *Meeting* Ljubljana (Slovenia) 2020, *Meeting* Niigata (Japan) 2017, *Meeting* Antalya (Turkey) 2015, *Meeting* Cadiz (Spain) 2012. **Publications** *Radiolaria Newsletter*.
Members Individual palaeontologists in 28 countries:
Argentina, Australia, Austria, Brazil, Canada, China, Czechia, France, Germany, Hungary, India, Iran Islamic Rep, Italy, Japan, Mexico, Morocco, New Zealand, Norway, Philippines, Poland, Russia, Slovenia, Spain, Switzerland, Thailand, Türkiye, UK, USA. [2016/XE0708/**E**]

♦ International Association of Radiopharmacology (IAR) 12121

Contact 3243 Wilshire Blvd Ste 203, Los Angeles CA 90010, USA.

History 1980. Currently inactive (2012). **Aims** Foster communication among *practitioners* of radiopharmacology; promote knowledge and uses of *radiotracers* in *biology* and *medicine*. **Structure** General Assembly Meeting (every 2 years). Officers: President; Executive Secretary. **Languages** English. **Staff** 1.00 FTE, voluntary. **Finance** Members' dues. Symposia. Budget (annual) US$ 5,000. **Events** *Biennial Symposium* Interlaken (Switzerland) 2001, *Biennial Symposium* St Louis, MO (USA) 1999, *Biennial Symposium* Genoa (Italy) 1997, *Biennial Symposium* Ann Arbor, MI (USA) 1995, *Biennial Symposium* Ghent (Belgium) 1993. **Publications** *International Association of Radiopharmacology Newsletter* (2 a year); *Quarterly Journal of Nuclear Medicine* – jointly with Italian Society Nuclear Medicine.
Members Full membership open to any individual. Members in 12 countries:
Argentina, Austria, Belgium, Brazil, Canada, Czechia, France, Germany, Greece, Italy, Switzerland, UK.
NGO Relations Instrumental in setting up: *Society of Radiopharmaceutical Sciences (SRS, #19627)*. [2012/XD9346/d/**D**]

- ♦ International Association of Radio Women / see International Association of Women in Radio and Television (#12271)
- ♦ International Association of Railway Journalists (no recent information)

♦ International Association of Railway Radio Amateurs 12122

Fédération internationale des radio-amateurs cheminots (FIRAC) – Internationale Vereinigung der Eisenbahner-Funkamateure

Office Jean Baptist Tassynsstraat 162, 2070 Zwijndrecht, Belgium. T. +32476232508. E-mail: on4cir@proximus.be – on4cir@gmail.com.
URL: http://www.firac.de/

History 20 Sep 1964, Hamburg (Germany). **Aims** Under the motto 'Friendship without Borders', maintain contacts by way of the mutual hobby of amateur radio. **Structure** Officers: President; Vice-President; Secretary; Treasurer; Public Relations Officer. **Languages** English, French, German. **Staff** 5.00 FTE, voluntary. **Activities** Awards/prizes/competitions; events/meetings. **Events** *Annual International Congress* Suceava (Romania) 2022, *Annual International Congress* Bad Salzuflen (Germany) 2021, *Annual International Congress* Suceava (Romania) 2020, *Annual International Congress* Caserta (Italy) 2019, *Annual International Congress* Tapolca (Hungary) 2018. **Publications** *FIRAC Handbook*.
Members Individual radio amateurs (about 2,200) in countries. National groups in 19 countries:
Austria, Belgium, Bulgaria, Czechia, Denmark, Finland, France, Germany, Hungary, Italy, Luxembourg, Netherlands, North Macedonia, Norway, Romania, Slovakia, Sweden, Switzerland, UK. [2022.05.12/XD7046/**D**]

- ♦ International Association of Railway Special Agents and Police (inactive)

♦ International Association of the Raoul Follereau Foundations / see Raoul Follereau International Union (#18618)
♦ International Association for the Rational Destruction of Rats (inactive)

♦ International Association of Rebekah Assemblies (IARA) 12123

Main Office 422 Trade St, Winston-Salem NC 27101, USA. T. +13367256037. Fax +13367731066. E-mail: iarasec2016@outlook.com.
URL: http://www.ioof.org/
History Founded 20 Sep 1851, USA, on adoption by *Independent Order of Odd Fellows (IOOF)* of the *'Rebekah Degree'* for women, written by Schuyler Colfax and based on biblical teachings. **Aims** Establish homes for senior members and for orphaned children. **Structure** Sovereign Grand Lodge; Grand Lodge; Rebekah Assembly; Rebekah Lodge. **Languages** English. **Staff** 1.00 FTE, paid. **Finance** Members' dues. **Events** *Annual Meeting* Winston-Salem, NC (USA) 2019, *Annual Meeting* Baltimore, MD (USA) 2018, *Annual Meeting* 2017, *Annual Meeting* Rapid City, SD (USA) 2016, *Annual Meeting* Fort Worth, TX (USA) 2015. **Publications** *IOOF News*.
Members Women's assemblies in 13 countries:
Australia, Belgium, Canada, Denmark, Estonia, Finland, Germany, Iceland, Netherlands, New Zealand, Norway, Sweden, USA.
[2016.12.14/XE4553/v/**E**]

♦ International Association for Reconciliation Studies (IARS) 12124

Sec Leutragraben 1, 07743 Jena, Germany.
URL: https://mir-nikita.wixsite.com/website
History 10 Aug 2020, Jena (Germany). Statutes ratified 10 Aug 2020. **Aims** Convene activists, academics and politicians from all segments of society regardless of ethnicity, nationality, region, race or gender and support the advancement of peace and reconciliation. **Structure** General Assembly; Administrative Board. **Languages** English, German, Hebrew, Russian, Ukrainian. **Finance** Sources: members' dues. **Activities** Publishing activities. **Events** *World Conference on Reconciliation Studies* Washington, DC (USA) 2022. **Publications** *Critical & Cultural Perspectives for Reconciliation Studies and Practices* – journal. **NGO Relations** Cooperates with (3): Friedrich Schiller University Jena; *Jimmy and Rosalynn Carter School for Peace and Conflict Resolution*; The Center for International Reconciliation Studies at Waseda University.
[2022.03.16/AA2241/**C**]

♦ International Association of Red Sports and Gymnastics Associations (inactive)

♦ International Association of Refrigerated Warehouses (IARW) 12125

Chairman c/o Premier Refrigerated Warehouse, 1101 NE 23rd Street, Fort Worth TX 76164, USA. E-mail: email@gcca.org.
URL: https://www.gcca.org/iarw/vision-mission-history
History 1891, USA. Earlier name: (US) National Association of Refrigerated Warehouses. **Aims** Promote interests of the public refrigerated warehousing industry; address members' problems in technical, operational and regulatory areas. **Structure** Board of Directors; Committees (7). **Languages** English. **Staff** 15.00 FTE, paid. **Finance** Primarily members' dues based on volume of refrigerated space. Annual budget: US$ 2,000,000. **Activities** Events/meetings. **Events** *Annual Meeting* Orlando, FL (USA) 2015, *Annual Meeting* San Diego, CA (USA) 2014, *Annual Meeting* Hollywood, FL (USA) 2013, *Annual Meeting* Tucson, AZ (USA) 2012, *Assembly of the committees* Washington, DC (USA) 2011. **Publications** *International Directory of Public Refrigerated Warehouses* (annual). Bulletins; guides; manuals.
Members Refrigerated warehouses (over 1,000) in 56 countries and territories:
Albania, Argentina, Australia, Austria, Bahamas, Barbados, Belgium, Bermuda, Brazil, Canada, Chile, China, Colombia, Denmark, Dominican Rep, Egypt, Finland, France, Germany, Greece, Hong Kong, India, Indonesia, Ireland, Italy, Jamaica, Japan, Kuwait, Lithuania, Malaysia, Mauritius, Mexico, Morocco, Netherlands, New Zealand, Norway, Peru, Philippines, Poland, Portugal, Qatar, Romania, Russia, Singapore, South Africa, Spain, Sri Lanka, Sweden, Switzerland, Türkiye, UK, Ukraine, United Arab Emirates, USA, Venezuela, Vietnam.
NGO Relations Core Partner in: *Global Cold Chain Alliance (GCCA, #10299)*. [2021/XD0198/**F**]

♦ International Association of Refrigeration (inactive)
♦ International Association of Refugee Law Judges / see International Association of Refugee and Migration Judges (#12126)

♦ International Association of Refugee and Migration Judges (IARMJ) 12126

Mailing Address Postbus 1621, 2003 BR Haarlem, Netherlands. T. +31615042782. E-mail: office@iarmj.org – info@iarmj.org.
URL: http://www.iarmj.org/
History 1997, Warsaw (Poland). Founded following 8 conferences. Initial constitution ratified Oct 1998. Current constitution endorsed Nov 2018. Former names and other names: *International Association of Refugee Law Judges (IARLJ)* – former (1997 to Mar 2019); *Association internationale des juges en matière de droit des réfugiés* – former (1997 to Mar 2019). Registration: Netherlands. **Aims** Foster recognition that protection from persecution on account of race, religion, nationality, membership in a particular social group, or political opinion, is an individual *right* established under international law; and that determination of refugee status and its cessation should be subject to the rule of law. **Structure** General Meeting; Supervisory Council; Management Board. Regional Chapters (4): Africa; Americas; Asia Pacific; European. **Languages** Dutch, English, French. **Staff** 0.20 FTE, paid. **Finance** Sources: members' dues. **Events** *World Conference* The Hague (Netherlands) 2023, *Africa Chapter Conference* Arusha (Tanzania UR) 2022, *Asia Pacific Chapter Conference* Newcastle, NSW (Australia) 2022, *World Conference* San José (Costa Rica) 2020, *World Conference* Athens (Greece) 2017. **Publications** Global and regional newsletter; conference proceedings.
Members Judges in 60 countries:
Albania, Algeria, Armenia, Australia, Austria, Belgium, Benin, Brazil, Bulgaria, Burundi, Cameroon, Chad, Costa Rica, Côte d'Ivoire, Croatia, Cyprus, Czechia, Denmark, Egypt, Fiji, Finland, France, Germany, Ghana, Hungary, India, Ireland, Japan, Kenya, Latvia, Lesotho, Liechtenstein, Lithuania, Malta, Mozambique, Netherlands, New Zealand, Nigeria, Norway, Panama, Philippines, Poland, Romania, Russia, Rwanda, Senegal, Slovakia, South Africa, Spain, Sri Lanka, Sudan, Sweden, Switzerland, Tanzania UR, Tunisia, Uganda, UK, Ukraine, USA, Zambia.
Consultative Status Consultative status granted from: *Council of Europe (CE, #04881)* (Participatory Status). **IGO Relations** Memorandum of Understanding signed with: *UNHCR (#20327)*. [2023.02.16/XC0098/v/**C**]

♦ International Association for Regional Cooperation and Revitalisation (inactive)
♦ International Association for Regional and Urban Statistics (inactive)
♦ International Association for Regression Research and Therapies (internationally oriented national body)
♦ International Association for Relational Psychoanalysis and Psychotherapy (internationally oriented national body)

♦ International Association for Relationship Research (IARR) 12127

Pres U-MN Psychology Dept, 215 Johnston Hall, 101 Pleasant St SE, Minneapolis MN 55455, USA. E-mail: simps108@umn.edu.
URL: http://www.iarr.org/
History 2 Apr 2004, by merger of *International Network on Personal Relationships (INPR, inactive)* and *International Society for the Study of Personal Relationships (ISSPR, inactive)*. **Aims** Stimulate and support the scientific study of *personal relationships*; encourage cooperation among *social scientists* worldwide. **Events** *Biennial Conference* Boston, MA (USA) 2024, *Biennial Conference* 2022, *Biennial Conference* 2021, *Biennial Conference* London (UK) 2020, *Biennial Conference* Fort Collins, CO (USA) 2018. **Publications** *Journal of Social and Personal Relationships* (6 a year); *Personal Relationships* (4 a year); *Relationship Research News* (2 a year). *Advances in Personal Relationships* – series. [2016/XJ4508/**D**]

♦ International Association for Relativistic Dynamics (IARD) 12128

Sec Dept of Physics, Howard Univ, 2400 Sixth St NW, Washington DC 20059, USA.
URL: http://www.iard-relativity.org/
History 1998, Houston TX (USA). **Aims** Facilitate acquisition and dissemination of knowledge about research programmes in classical and quantum relativistic dynamics of particles and fields. **Structure** Standing Committee; Officers: President, Vice-President, Secretary, Treasurer. **Languages** English. **Staff** Part-time, voluntary. **Finance** Members' dues. Donations. **Events** *Biennial Conference* Storrs, CT (USA) 2014, *Biennial Conference* Florence (Italy) 2012, *Biennial Conference* Hualien (Taiwan) 2010, *Biennial Conference* Thessaloniki (Greece) 2008, *Biennial Conference* Storrs, CT (USA) 2006. **Publications** Conference proceedings.

Members Full in 12 countries and territories:
Argentina, Canada, Chile, Croatia, Greece, Ireland, Israel, Italy, Netherlands, Slovenia, Taiwan, USA. [2018/XD7765/**D**]

♦ International Association of Religion Journalists (IARJ) 12129

Exec Dir c/o The Jakarta Post Print, Jl Palmerah Barat 142-143, Jakarta 10270, Indonesia. T. +18604364856. E-mail: dbriggs@theiarj.org.
URL: http://www.theiarj.org/
History Launched by *International Center for Journalists (ICFJ)*, in partnership with Association of Religion Data Archives (ARDA). Inaugural meeting, Mar 2012, Bellagio (Italy), at *The Rockefeller Foundation (#18966)*. **Aims** Offer collegial forums for dialogue and cooperation, online and in-person training, and resources and data to promote better coverage of religious issues. **Structure** Board of Directors. **Languages** Arabic, English. **Staff** 4.00 FTE, paid. **Activities** Events/meetings; networking/liaising. **Members** Individuals (over 600). Membership countries not specified. [2019.12.31/XJ5503/**C**]

♦ International Association for Religious Freedom (IARF) 12130

Association internationale pour la liberté religieuse – Asociación Internacional para la Libertad de Religión – Weltbund für Religiöse Freiheit – Internationaal Verbond voor Geloofsvrijheid – Mezinarodni Svaz pro Nabozenskou Svobodu – Szabadelvü Vallasok Nemzetközi Szövetsege
Main Office Essex Hall, 1-6 Essex St, London, WC2R 3HY, UK. E-mail: luke@iarf.net.
URL: http://www.iarf.net/
History 25 May 1900, Boston MA (USA), as *International Council of Unitarian and other Liberal Religious Thinkers and Workers*. Name changed, 1910, to *International Congress of Free Christians and other Religious Liberals – Congrès international des chrétiens libéraux et d'autres libre-croyants*; reconstituted, 1930, Arnhem (Netherlands), as *International Association for Liberal Christianity and Religious Freedom – Association internationale pour le christianisme libéral et la liberté religieuse*. From 1950, groups from other than Christian tradition joined the Association; the exclusive reference to Christianity in the title was revised and present name adopted, 1969, Boston MA (USA). Registration: Charity Commission, No/ID: 1026699, England and Wales. **Aims** Work for freedom of religion and belief, as a *human right*, through: freedom from oppressive interference or discrimination by the state, government or society's institutions on the grounds of religion or belief; mutual understanding, respect and the promotion of harmony, or at least *tolerance*, among communities or individuals of different religions or beliefs; accountability of religious communities to ensure that their own practices uphold the fundamental dignity and human rights of their members and others. **Structure** General Assembly (every 4 years) at Congress. Council, consisting of President, Vice-President, Treasurer/Secretary and 17 members. Regional Coordinators: South Asia; East Asia; North America; Europe and the Middle East. Meetings open. **Languages** English, French, German, Japanese. **Staff** 5.00 FTE, paid. **Finance** Sources: grants; members' dues. **Activities** Supporting affected communities; Non-formal diplomacy; Young adult programmes; Codes of conduct; Preventive strategies. Organizes Quadrennial Congress, Regional (Continental) Conferences, Commissions and Chapters. **Events** *Quadrennial Congress* Washington, DC (USA) 2018, *Quadrennial Congress* Birmingham (UK) 2014, *Quadrennial Congress* Kochi (India) 2010, *Quadrennial Congress* Kaohsiung (Taiwan) 2006, *Triennial congress / Congress* Budapest (Hungary) 2002. **Publications** Announcements; reports; congress proceedings.
Members Constituent members include Bahais, Buddhists, Christians, Hindus, Muslims, Jews, Shintoists, Sikhs, Unitarians, Universalists, Zoroastrians and members of tribal religious traditions. Full Group; Associate Group; Individual. Members in 30 countries and territories:
Australia, Austria, Bahrain, Bangladesh, Canada, Czechia, Denmark, Finland, France, Germany, Hungary, India, Indonesia, Israel, Japan, Kenya, Malawi, Nepal, Netherlands, Nigeria, Pakistan, Philippines, Poland, Romania, South Africa, Sri Lanka, Switzerland, Taiwan, UK, USA.
International associations (2):
International Association of Liberal Religious Women (IALRW, #11999); *World Congress of Faiths (WCF, #21304)*.
Consultative Status Consultative status granted from: *ECOSOC (#05331)* (General); *UNICEF (#20332)*. **IGO Relations** *UNESCO (#20322)*. Accredited by: *International Whaling Commission (IWC, #15879)*. Associated with Department of Global Communications of the United Nations. **NGO Relations** United Nations non-governmental advisory groups (not specified). Member of: *Conference of Non-Governmental Organizations in Consultative Relationship with the United Nations (CONGO, #04635)*; *International Interfaith Organizations Network (IION, #13945)*; *Committee of NGOs on Human Rights, Geneva (#04275)*. [2020/XC1205/y/**C**]

♦ International Association of Religious Journalism and Publishing / see International Christian Organisation of the Media (#12563)

♦ International Association for the Representation of the Mutual Interests of the Inland Shipping and the Insurance and for Keeping the Register of Inland Vessels in Europe 12131

Association Internationale pour la sauvegarde des intérêts communs de la navigation intérieure européenne et de l'assurance et pour la tenue d'un registre des bateaux intérieurs en Europe – Internationale Vereinigung zur Wahrnehmung der Gemeinsamen Interessen der Binnenschiffahrt und der Versicherung und zur Führung des Binnenschiffsregisters in Europa – Internationale Vereniging voor de Behartiging van de Gemeenschappelijke Belangen van de Binnenvaart en de Verzekering en voor het Houden van het Register van Binnenschepen in Europa (IVR)
SG Vasteland 78, 3011 BN Rotterdam, Netherlands. T. +31104116070. Fax +31104129091. E-mail: info@ivr-eu.com.
URL: http://www.ivr-eu.com/
History 14 Nov 1947, Rotterdam (Netherlands). Founded under the aegis of registre des bateaux intérieurs en Europe *Association du registre des bateaux du Rhin (inactive)*, set up 1874. Former names and other names: *International Association for the Rhine Ships Register* – former; *Association internationale du registre des bateaux du Rhin* – former; *Internationale Vereinigung des Rheinschiffsregisters* – former; *Internationale Vereniging het Rijnschepenregister* – former; *International Association for Rhine Vessels Register* – former. Registration: Eu Transparency Register, No/ID: 052415726522-61, Start date: 27 Mar 2017; KVK, No/ID: 40341965, Start date: 26 May 1948, Netherlands. **Aims** Publish an inland *navigation* ships database; recommend surveyors and vessel *damage* prevention and knowledge transfer. **Structure** General Assembly; Council; Board of Directors; Commissions (3). **Languages** Dutch, English, French, German. **Finance** Members' dues. Other sources: official fees; proceeds of Register and deliveries of IVR; attestations (certificates). **Activities** Knowledge management/information dissemination; events/meetings; advice/assistance/consulting. **Events** *Annual General Assembly and Congress* Ghent (Belgium) 2021, *Annual General Assembly and Congress* Ghent (Belgium) 2020, *Annual General Assembly* Ghent (Belgium) 2020, *Annual General Assembly and Congress* Prague (Czechia) 2019, *Annual General Assembly and Congress* Strasbourg (France) 2018. **Publications** *IVR Report* (2 a year) in Dutch, French, German. *Liability Rules for Inland Navigation on Rhine and Danube* (2008); *General Average IVR 2007*; *Technical Descriptions for Inland Navigation Vessels*. Lists of surveyors; maps.
Members Shipowners and their associations; insurers and their associations; shipbuilding engineers' average adjusters and all interested in Rhine navigation. Members in 12 countries:
Austria, Belgium, France, Germany, Hungary, Luxembourg, Netherlands, Poland, Serbia, Slovakia, Switzerland, UK.
IGO Relations Observer to: *Commission du Danube (CD, #04210)*. **NGO Relations** Consultative member of: *Comité maritime international (CMI, #04192)*. [2020/XE1231/**E**]

♦ International Association for Research in Economic Psychology (IAREP) 12132

Association internationale de recherche en psychologie économique – Internationale Gesellschaft für Forschung in Ökonomischer Psychologie
Sec Univ of Leeds, Maurice Keyworth Bldg, Moorland Road, Leeds, LS6 1AN, UK. E-mail: secretary@iarep.org.
URL: http://www.iarep.org/
History Jul 1982, Edinburgh (UK). Founded at a colloquium on applied psychology, arising from a series of such colloquia of which the 1st was held in 1976, Tilburg (Netherlands). **Aims** Serve as a meeting point for all those interested in the areas where psychology and economics intersect. **Structure** General Assembly (annual, at colloquium); Board; Managing Committee. **Languages** English. **Finance** Sources: meeting proceeds; members' dues. **Activities** Events/meetings; networking/liaising; publishing activities;

training/education. **Events** *Joint Conference on Economic Psychology and Behavioural Economics* Nice (France) 2023, *Annual Conference* Kristiansand (Norway) 2022, *Joint Conference on Economic Psychology and Behavioural Economics* 2021, *Joint Conference on Economic Psychology and Behavioural Economics* Kristiansand (Norway) 2020, *Joint Conference on Economic Psychology and Behavioural Economics* Dublin (Ireland) 2019. **Publications** *Journal of Economic Psychology* (6 a year); *IAREP Newsletter* (2 a year).
Members Academics, practitioners and students, including psychologists, economists and specialists in business administration and consumer behaviour. Individuals in 52 countries and territories:
Argentina, Armenia, Australia, Austria, Belarus, Belgium, Bosnia-Herzegovina, Brazil, Canada, Chile, China, Colombia, Croatia, Czechia, Denmark, Finland, France, Germany, Greece, Hong Kong, Hungary, Indonesia, Ireland, Israel, Italy, Japan, Korea Rep, Kuwait, Latvia, Lithuania, Luxembourg, Malaysia, Netherlands, New Zealand, Norway, Philippines, Poland, Portugal, Romania, Russia, Singapore, Slovenia, South Africa, Spain, Sweden, Switzerland, Taiwan, Türkiye, UK, Ukraine, USA, Venezuela.
NGO Relations With *Society for the Advancement of Behavioral Economics (SABE, #19514)* instrumental in setting up: *International Confederation for the Advancement of Behavioral Economics and Economic Psychology (ICABEEP, #12842)*. [2022.10.25/XD1380/**D**]

♦ International Association for Research on Epstein-Barr Virus and Associated Diseases (EBV Association) 12133

Pres School of Life Sciences, Univ of Sussex, Falmer, Brighton, BN1 9QG, UK. T. +441273678404.
URL: http://www.sussex.ac.uk/ebvassociation/
Aims Promote and stimulate the exchange of ideas, knowledge and research materials among research workers throughout the world who study the Epstein-Barr virus (EBV) and related diseases. **Structure** Board, including President, Vice-President, Treasurer and Secretary. **Finance** Sources: members' dues. **Activities** Events/meetings. **Events** *International Symposium on Epstein-Barr Virus and Associated Diseases* Asahikawa (Japan) 2021, *International Symposium on Epstein-Barr Virus and Associated Diseases* Madison, WI (USA) 2018, *International Symposium on Epstein-Barr Virus and Associated Diseases* Zurich (Switzerland) 2016, *International Symposium on Epstein-Barr Virus and Associated Diseases* Brisbane, QLD (Australia) 2014, *International Symposium on EBV Research* Philadelphia, PA (USA) 2012.
Members Full in 34 countries:
Algeria, Australia, Austria, Belgium, Canada, China, Croatia, Denmark, France, Germany, Greece, Hong Kong, Hungary, Indonesia, Ireland, Israel, Italy, Japan, Malaysia, Morocco, Netherlands, Norway, Portugal, Russia, Saudi Arabia, Serbia, Singapore, Spain, Sweden, Switzerland, Taiwan, Türkiye, UK, USA. [2020/XN4759/**C**]

- ♦ International Association for Research in Favour of Persons with Mental Handicap (#02738)
- ♦ International Association of Research Fellows and Scholars (internationally oriented national body)
- ♦ International Association for Research in Hospital Hygiene (no recent information)

♦ International Association for Research in Income and Wealth (IARIW) 12134

Association internationale de recherches sur le revenu et la richesse – Asociación Internacional de Investigaciones sobre Rentas y Riqueza
Exec Dir 170 Laurier Ave W, Ste 604, Ottawa ON K1P 5V5, Canada. T. +16132338891. E-mail: info@iariw.org.
General: http://www.iariw.org/
History 15 Sep 1947, Washington, DC (USA). Founded at meeting of the International Statistical Institute. Former names and other names: *Association internationale de recherches sur le revenu et la fortune* – former. **Aims** Further research on national and economic and social accounting, including: development of concepts and definitions for measurement and analysis of income and wealth; development and further integration of systems of economic and social *statistics*; related problems of statistical methodology; bring together academic and government scholars in the field of economic and social statistics for communication and exchange. **Structure** Council; Executive Committee. Meetings closed. **Languages** English. **Staff** 1.00 FTE, paid. **Finance** Sources: members' dues; sale of publications. **Activities** Events/meetings; knowledge management/information dissemination. **Events** *Conference on Central Banks, Financial Markets and Inequality* Naples (Italy) 2023, *Conference on the Valuation of Data* Waterloo, ON (Canada) 2023, *Conference on Measurement of Income, Wealth and Well-being in Africa* Arusha (Tanzania UR) 2022, *General Conference* Luxembourg (Luxembourg) 2022, *IARIW – ESCoE Conference* London (UK) 2021. **Publications** *The Review of Income and Wealth* (4 a year) – journal. Conference proceedings.
Members Institutions and individuals in 47 countries and territories:
Argentina, Australia, Austria, Belgium, Brazil, Bulgaria, Canada, Colombia, Croatia, Cuba, Czechia, Denmark, Dominica, Finland, France, Germany, Greece, Hong Kong, Hungary, India, Ireland, Israel, Italy, Japan, Korea Rep, Lesotho, Luxembourg, Mexico, Netherlands, New Zealand, Nigeria, North Macedonia, Norway, Philippines, Poland, Portugal, Romania, Russia, Slovenia, South Africa, Spain, Sweden, Switzerland, Trinidad-Tobago, UK, USA, Venezuela.
Included in the above, organizations listed in this Yearbook (3):
International Monetary Fund (IMF, #14180); *OECD (#17693)*; *Statistical Office of the European Union (Eurostat, #19974)*.
Consultative Status Consultative status granted from: *ECOSOC (#05331)* (Ros A). **IGO Relations** Accredited by (1): *United Nations Office at Vienna (UNOV, #20604)*. Associated with Department of Global Communications of the United Nations. [2023.02.22/XC1206/y/**C**]

- ♦ International Association of Research Institutes for the Graphic Arts Industry / see International Association of Research Organizations for the Information, Media and Graphic Arts Industries (#12136)
- ♦ International Association for Research into Juvenile Criminology (no recent information)

♦ International Association for Research in L1 Education (ARLE) 12135

Sec address not obtained. E-mail: info@arle.be.
URL: http://www.arle.be/
History Nov 2014. Founded as successor to *International Association for the Improvement of Mother Tongue Education (IAIMTE, inactive)*. Registration: No/ID: VR 200959, Germany, Hildesheim. **Aims** Build and maintain a network of specialists in research on L1 education; create an international network of national and regional associations of similar associations. **Structure** Board. **Languages** English. **Staff** 4.00 FTE, paid. **Activities** Events/meetings; research/documentation; training/education. **Events** *Conference* Melbourne, VIC (Australia) 2024, *Conference* Nicosia (Cyprus) 2022, *Conference* Melbourne, VIC (Australia) 2021, *Conference* Lisbon (Portugal) 2019, *Conference* Tallinn (Estonia) 2017. **Publications** *L1 – Educational Studies in Language and Literature* – journal.
Members Individuals in 86 countries and territories:
Albania, Algeria, Argentina, Australia, Austria, Bangladesh, Belgium, Botswana, Brazil, Bulgaria, Cameroon, Canada, China, Colombia, Curaçao, Cyprus, Czechia, Denmark, Dominican Rep, Egypt, Estonia, Ethiopia, Faeroe Is, Finland, France, Gambia, Germany, Greece, Guinea, Hong Kong, Hungary, Iceland, India, Indonesia, Iran Islamic Rep, Ireland, Israel, Italy, Japan, Kenya, Korea Rep, Latvia, Lithuania, Macau, Malawi, Malaysia, Malta, Mexico, Montenegro, Morocco, Namibia, Nepal, Netherlands, New Zealand, Nigeria, Northern Cyprus, Northern Ireland, Norway, Pakistan, Peru, Philippines, Poland, Portugal, Romania, Russia, Saudi Arabia, Scotland, Senegal, Serbia, Singapore, Slovakia, Slovenia, South Africa, Spain, Sweden, Switzerland, Taiwan, Tanzania UR, Thailand, Türkiye, Uganda, UK, United Arab Emirates, USA, Venezuela, Yemen. [2021/XM7349/v/**D**]

♦ International Association of Research Organizations for the Information, Media and Graphic Arts Industries (IARIGAI) 12136

SG Fac of Graphic Arts, Getaldiceva 2, HR-10000 Zagreb, Croatia. T. +38512371080ext157. E-mail: office@iarigai.org.
Pres PAGORA, 461 rue de la Papeterie, Domaine Univ, BP 65, 38402 Saint-Martin-d'Hères, France.
URL: http://www.iarigai.org/
History Jun 1965, Finland, as *International Association of Research Institutes for the Graphic Arts Industry – Association internationale des instituts de recherches des industries graphiques* as a result of biennial international conferences of graphic arts research institutes, first held in 1951, UK, hosted by the Printing, Packaging and Allied Trades Research Association (PATRA), subsequently the (now commercial) *Pira International (inactive)*. Subsequently changed title to *International Association of Research Organizations for the Printing, Information and Communication Industries – Association internationale des instituts de recherches des industries graphiques*. Present name adopted 2000. **Aims** Cultivate and promote international cooperation and networking among research workers on science and technology of the printing, media and allied industries; support evolutionary process towards the comprehensive information society, as well as dissemination of knowledge and scientific information. **Structure** General Assembly (annual); Board. **Languages** English. **Staff** 0.50 FTE, paid. **Finance** Members' dues (annual): euro 850. **Activities** Networking/liaising; knowledge management/information dissemination; publishing activities. **Events** *Research Conference* Helsinki (Finland) 2015, *Research Conference* Swansea (UK) 2014, *Research conference* Budapest (Hungary) / Debrecen (Hungary) 2011, *Research conference* Montréal, QC (Canada) 2010, *Research conference* Montréal, QC (Canada) 2010. **Publications** *Journal of Print and Media Technology Research* (4 a year); *Advances in Printing and Media Technology* (annual). Information Services: Members' bibliographic databases available online.
Members Regular members (44) in 19 countries:
Belgium, Canada, Croatia, Czechia, Finland, France, Germany, Hungary, India, Norway, Russia, Serbia, Slovenia, Sweden, Switzerland, Taiwan, Thailand, UK, USA.
NGO Relations In liaison with technical committees of: *International Organization for Standardization (ISO, #14473)*. [2014.09.23/XD1334/ty/**D**]

- ♦ International Association of Research Organizations for the Printing, Information and Communication Industries / see International Association of Research Organizations for the Information, Media and Graphic Arts Industries (#12136)
- ♦ International Association for Research on Plantain and Bananas (inactive)
- ♦ International Association for Research in Public Management (internationally oriented national body)
- ♦ International Association of Research, Scientific and Technical Libraries (inactive)

♦ International Association for Research on Textbooks and Educational Media (IARTEM) 12137

Sec c/o USN, PO Box 235, 3603 Kongsberg, Norway.
URL: http://iartem.org/
History 1991. **Aims** Promote research on, and understanding of textbooks and educational media. **Structure** General Assembly; Board; Nominating Committee. **Activities** Events/meetings. **Events** *International Conference on Textbooks and Educational Media* Florence (Italy) 2022, *Conference* Odense (Denmark) 2019, *IARTEM Regional Conference* Buenos Aires (Argentina) 2018, *Conference* Lisbon (Portugal) 2017, *IARTEM Regional Conference* Pereira (Colombia) 2016. **Publications** *IARTEM eJournal*. Conference reports. [2021/XM6442/**D**]

- ♦ International Association for Research in Toxicological Information (inactive)
- ♦ International Association of Residential and Community Alternatives / see International Community Corrections Association (#12822)
- ♦ International Association for the Respect of Autochthonous Peoples' Rights (inactive)
- ♦ International Association of Retired NATO Civilian Staff and their Dependents (#02665)
- ♦ International Association of Retired Staff of OEEC and OECD / see International Association of Former OEEC and OECD Staff (#11904)
- ♦ International Association for the Rhine Ships Register / see International Association for the Representation of the Mutual Interests of the Inland Shipping and the Insurance and for Keeping the Register of Inland Vessels in Europe (#12131)
- ♦ International Association for Rhine Vessels Register / see International Association for the Representation of the Mutual Interests of the Inland Shipping and the Insurance and for Keeping the Register of Inland Vessels in Europe (#12131)
- ♦ International Association for the Rights of Needy and Suffering Children (internationally oriented national body)

♦ International Association of Risk Management in Medicine (IARMM) 12138

Pres IARMN Head Office, 4-7-12-102 Hongo, Bunkyoku, Tokyo, 113-0033 Japan. T. +81338176770. Fax +81338176670. E-mail: head.office01@iarmm.org – manager@iarmm.org.
URL: http://www.iarmm.org/
History 2002, Tokyo (Japan). Former names and other names: *Union of Risk Management for Preventive Medicine (URMPM)* – former (2002 to 2013). **Aims** Encourage research and exchange of information related to health risk management. **Structure** International Directory Board, including Chairperson. International Advisory Board. President; 3 Vice-Presidents. **Languages** English. **Staff** 5.00 FTE, paid. 5 FTE, paid. **Finance** Members' dues: OECD countries – US$ 100; non-OECD countries – US$ 30. **Activities** Organizes international academic conference. Includes: *World Health Risk Management Centre (WHRMC, #21558)*. **Events** *World Congress of Clinical Safety* Tokyo (Japan) 2021, *World Congress of Clinical Safety* Prague (Czechia) 2019, *World Congress of Clinical Safety* Bern (Switzerland) 2018, *World Congress of Clinical Safety* Rome (Italy) 2017, *World Congress of Clinical Safety* Boston, MA (USA) 2016. **Publications** *Journal of Medical Safety (JMS)*. **Members** in 70 countries in 4 regions Europe; America; Asia-Pacific; Africa. Membership countries not specified. **NGO Relations** Links with national academies. [2021/XJ4477/**D**]

- ♦ International Association of Road Safety Organizations (inactive)
- ♦ International Association of Rolling Stock Builders (inactive)

♦ International Association of Ropeway Manufacturers (IARM) 12139

Association internationale des constructeurs de transporteurs aériens
Pres Leitner SpA, Via Brennero, 34, 39049 Vipiteno, Italy.
Events *Meeting* Grenoble (France) 2014. **NGO Relations** *International Organization for Transportation by Rope (#14481)*. [2014/XD1248/**D**]

- ♦ International Association of Rotary Clubs / see Rotary International (#18975)
- ♦ International Association for Rural Development (inactive)

♦ International Association of Rural Health and Medicine (IARM) 12140

SG JA Toride Medical Center, Hongo 2-1-1, Toride City, Ibaraki OSAKA, 302-0022 Japan. T. +81297745551. Fax +81297720120. E-mail: iarm@live.jp – shihochristopher@gmail.com.
Pres address not obtained. E-mail: iarm@live.jp.
URL: http://www.iarm-jrm.org/
History 12 Jul 1961, Tours (France), at 1st International Congress of Rural Medicine, as *International Association of Agricultural Medicine*. Subsequently changed title to *International Association of Agricultural Medicine and Rural Health (IAAMRH) – Association internationale de médecine agricole et de santé rurale*, 1978. Current title adopted, 13 Oct 2009, when association was revived with relocation of Secretariat to Japan. Original statutes legally approved 23 Jun 1962; amended Nov 1991, Beijing (China). Current statutes adopted Mar 2009, Cartagena de Indias (Colombia). **Aims** Support the WHO goal of "Health for All in the 21st Century"; help improve the status of health of rural communities and protect the health of agricultural workers; help member organizations adopt a scientific approach in the field of agricultural medicine and rural health and assist in its practical application; establish effective collaboration with other branches of medicine, health, agricultural, environmental and other related sciences; study the effects of social, physical and environmental conditions on human health. **Structure** General Assembly (every 3 years at Congress); Executive Board; Presidency; Specialized Commissions. **Languages** English. **Staff** 1.00 FTE, paid. **Finance** Sources: members' dues. **Activities** Events/meetings. **Events** *Congress* Pécs (Hungary) 2020, *Triennial Congress* Tokyo (Japan) 2018, *Triennial Congress* Lodi (Italy) 2015, *Triennial international congress / Triennial Congress* Goa (India) 2012, *Triennial Congress* Cartagena de Indias (Colombia) 2009. **Publications** *Journal of Rural Medicine* (2 a year).
Members Honorary; Full. Individuals or groups in 44 countries:
Albania, Armenia, Australia, Belgium, Benin, Botswana, Brazil, Bulgaria, Canada, China, Colombia, Croatia, Denmark, Egypt, Finland, France, Germany, Greece, Hungary, India, Indonesia, Iran Islamic Rep, Israel, Italy, Japan, Kazakhstan, Korea Rep, Kyrgyzstan, Mexico, Montenegro, Nepal, New Zealand, North Macedonia, Philippines, Poland, Romania, Serbia, Slovakia, Sweden, Switzerland, Tanzania UR, Thailand, Togo, USA.
Consultative Status Consultative status granted from: *ILO (#11123)* (Special List). **IGO Relations** Cooperates with a number of United Nations organizations, including: *FAO (#09260)*; *UNESCO (#20322)*; *WHO (#20950)*. [2019.12.12/XC1248/**C**]

- ♦ International Association of Safe Injection Technology (inactive)
- ♦ International Association of Safety Professionals (internationally oriented national body)

♦ International Association for Safety and Survival Training (IASST) . 12141

Main Office Oceana House, 39-49 Commercial Rd, Southampton, S015 1GA, UK. E-mail: iasst@iasst.com.
URL: http://www.iasst.com/

History Founded 1980. **Aims** Facilitate exchange of information on matters relating to safety in the *maritime* environment; promote continuous improvement in safety and survival training internationally. **Structure** Management Committee, including Chairman, Vice-Chairman, Secretary and Treasurer. **Languages** English. **Staff** 4.00 FTE, voluntary. **Finance** Sources: members' dues. **Events** *International Meeting and Safety Seminar* Halifax, NS (Canada) 2022, *International Meeting and Safety Seminar* Ålesund (Norway) 2019, *International Meeting and Safety Seminar* Reykjavik (Iceland) 2018, *International Meeting and Safety Seminar* Baku (Azerbaijan) 2015, *International Meeting and Safety Seminar* Halifax, NS (Canada) 2014.
Members Representatives in 37 countries and territories:
Australia, Azerbaijan, Brazil, Brunei Darussalam, Canada, Croatia, Cyprus, Denmark, Estonia, Faeroe Is, Finland, France, Germany, Greece, Iceland, India, Indonesia, Ireland, Italy, Lithuania, Malaysia, Netherlands, New Zealand, Norway, Philippines, Poland, Qatar, Singapore, South Africa, Spain, Sri Lanka, Sweden, Taiwan, Türkiye, Ukraine, United Arab Emirates, USA.
[2020/XC0096/**C**]

♦ International Association of La Salle Universities (IALU) 12142

Asociación Internacional de Universidades La Salle (AIUL)
Exec Dir Gastao Gonçalves 79, Niterói RJ, 24240-030, Brazil. E-mail: ialu@lasalle.org.
URL: http://ialu.org/

History 1998. Also referred to as *International Association of Lasallian Universities (IALU)*. **Aims** Actively support the promotion of the educational vision of St John Baptist de La Salle by facilitating innovative opportunities for collaboration, research, exchange and development of member institutions. **Structure** Board of Directors, comprising President, Vice-President, Regional members (North America, Bethlehem, and English-speaking Africa; Europe and French-speaking Africa; Asia and Pacific Islands; Center and South America; Mexico), 2 members-at-large and Executive Secretary. **Publications** *Star fraternity* – newsletter.
Members Institutions in 22 countries and territories:
Andorra, Argentina, Bolivia, Brazil, Canada, Colombia, Costa Rica, Côte d'Ivoire, France, Haiti, Indonesia, Italy, Kenya, Mexico, Nicaragua, Palestine, Peru, Philippines, Singapore, Spain, USA, Venezuela. [2017/XJ7505/**E**]

♦ International Association of Sanskrit Studies (IASS) 12143

Association internationale pour les études sanskrites
SG Poltenweg 4, Vill, 6080 Innsbruck, Austria. T. +43512376121.
URL: http://www.sanskritassociation.org/

History 1973. First International Conference held 1972, as a fork from the *International Congress of Asian and North African Studies (ICANAS, #12891)*. Statutes adopted 25 Jun 1977. **Aims** Promote, diversify, intensify and coordinate Sanskrit studies in all countries; foster research, studies and exchange of views in the field of Sanskrit and Sanskrit-based *literature*. **Structure** Board; Consultative Committee; Regional Directors. **Languages** English, Sanskrit. **Staff** Voluntary. **Finance** Sources: members' dues. **Activities** Events/meetings; research/documentation. **Events** *World Sanskrit Conference (WSC)* Mumbai (India) 2027, *World Sanskrit Conference (WSC)* Kathmandu (Nepal) 2024, *World Sanskrit Conference (WSC)* Canberra, ACT (Australia) 2023, *World Sanskrit Conference (WSC)* Canberra, ACT (Australia) 2022, *World Sanskrit Conference (WSC)* Canberra, ACT (Australia) 2021. **Publications** *Indologica Taurinensia* (periodical); *IASS Online News*; *Newsletter of the IASS*. Reports.
Members National associations in 10 countries:
Austria, Belgium, France, Germany, India, Italy, Japan, Nepal, Netherlands, USA.
Individuals in 38 countries:
Argentina, Australia, Austria, Belgium, Brazil, Bulgaria, Canada, China, Croatia, Czechia, Denmark, Finland, France, Germany, Hungary, India, Indonesia, Iran Islamic Rep, Italy, Japan, Korea Rep, Malaysia, Mexico, Mongolia, Nepal, Netherlands, Norway, Philippines, Poland, Romania, Russia, South Africa, Sri Lanka, Sweden, Switzerland, Thailand, UK, USA.
NGO Relations Cooperates with: Organizing Committee of *International Congress of Asian and North African Studies (ICANAS, #12891)*. [2022/XC5371/**C**]

♦ International Association to Save Tyre (IAST) 12144

Association Internationale pour la Sauvegarde de Tyr (AIST)
SG 35 avenue Foch, 75116 Paris, France. T. +33145002014. Fax +33145002015. E-mail: aist.france@fondationtyr.org – fondation@fondationtyr.org.
Lebanon National Committee/Pres Akhtal El Saghir Str, Baltagi Blg, Beirut, Lebanon. T. +9611851351. Fax +9611833601. E-mail: fondation@fondationtyr.org.
URL: http://www.fondationtyr.org/

History 6 May 1980, Paris (France), following Resolution 459, adopted 19 Dec 1979, by *United Nations Security Council (UNSC, #20625)*, put forward by Lebanon government on behalf of the "Committee of Tyre International Festival" and Resolution 4/13, adopted by *UNESCO (#20322)* and decisions of *European Parliament (EP, #08146)* and the US Senate. Statutes adopted 6 May 1980, Paris; modified by General Assembly 18 Apr 1983; ratified 30 Dec 1992. Previously also referred to as *International Committee for the Safeguard of Tyre – Comité international pour la sauvegarde de Tyr*. **Aims** Protect and preserve the *archaeological sites* of Tyre; make recommendations to national and international bodies. **Structure** General Assembly (annual). Executive Board, comprising Honorary President, Present, Secretary General, Treasurer, Legal Counsel and Archaeological Consultant. **Languages** Arabic, English, French. **Staff** 4.00 FTE, paid. **Finance** Members' dues. Other sources: private donations; fundraising activities. **Activities** Programme consisting of national and international activities to implement UNESCO's International Campaign for Tyre. Organizes exhibitions, conferences and annual International Forum. **Events** *Forum* Cadiz (Spain) 2012, *Forum* Larnaca (Cyprus) 2011, *Forum* Byblos (Lebanon) 2010, *Forum* Paris (France) 2009, *Annual General Assembly* Paris (France) 1996. **Publications** Proceedings; catalogues.
Members National committees and individuals in 15 countries:
Austria, Belgium, Egypt, France, Germany, Italy, Japan, Lebanon, Morocco, Netherlands, Spain, Syrian AR, Tunisia, UK, USA.
Consultative Status Consultative status granted from: *UNESCO (#20322)* (Consultative Status). **IGO Relations** Operational relations with: *UNDP (#20292)*. Networking with: *Anna Lindh Euro-Mediterranean Foundation for the Dialogue between Cultures (Anna Lindh Foundation, #00847)*; Cultural Council of *Union for the Mediterranean (UfM, #20457)*; *Organisation internationale de la Francophonie (OIF, #17809)*.
[2012.11.01/XE8218/**E**]

♦ International Association for Scandinavian Studies (IASS) 12145

Association internationale d'études scandinaves
Pres Centre of Scandinavian Studies, Vilnius Univ, Universiteto g 3, LT-01513 Vilnius, Lithuania. T. +37061408058. E-mail: ieva.steponaviciute@flf.vu.lt.
Sec Dept Nordic Studies and Linguistics, Univ of Copenhagen, KUA1 – Bldg 22 3 34, 2300 Copenhagen, Denmark.

History Founded 1962, Århus (Denmark), as a result of Conferences on Scandinavian Studies: 1956, Cambridge (UK); 1958, Lillehammer (Norway); 1960, Oosterbeek (Netherlands). **Aims** Promote, develop and encourage Scandinavian studies, especially the scholarly study of the *literature* of the Scandinavian countries. **Structure** Conference (every 2 years); Committee. **Languages** Danish, English, Faroese, French, German, Icelandic, Norwegian, Swedish. **Finance** Conferences financed through fees, government and academic grants, FILLM, local bodies. **Events** *Biennial Conference* Tromsø (Norway) 2023, *Biennial Conference* Vilnius (Lithuania) 2021, *Biennial Conference* Vilnius (Lithuania) 2020, *Biennial Conference* Copenhagen (Denmark) 2018, *Biennial Conference* Groningen (Netherlands) 2016. **Publications** Conference proceedings.
Members Individuals (180) in 31 countries and territories:
Australia, Austria, Belarus, Belgium, Canada, Croatia, Czechia, Denmark, Estonia, Faeroe Is, Finland, France, Germany, Hungary, Iceland, India, Israel, Italy, Japan, Latvia, Lithuania, Netherlands, Norway, Poland, Romania, Russia, Slovakia, Sweden, Switzerland, UK, USA.
NGO Relations Member of: *International Federation for Modern Languages and Literatures (#13480)*.
[2019/XC4512/v/**D**]

♦ International Association of Scholarly Publishers (inactive)
♦ International Association of School Doctors (inactive)

♦ International Association of School Librarianship (IASL) 12146

Association internationale des bibliothécaires scolaires
Exec Dir c/o C2C Assn Management Solutions, 124 E High St, Jefferson City MO 65102, USA.
Pres address not obtained.
URL: http://www.iasl-online.org/

History Founded 1971, following international conferences: 1967, Vancouver BC (Canada); 1968, Dublin (Ireland); 1970, Sydney (Australia), and in succession to an ad hoc committee of WCOTP. By-Laws adopted Jul 1971, Kingston (Jamaica); new constitutions adopted 2013. Previously also referred to in French as *Association internationale de bibliothéconomie scolaire (AIBS)*. **Aims** Provide an international forum for those interested in promoting effective school library media programmes as viable instruments in the educational process; provide guidance and advice for development of school library programs and the school library profession. **Structure** Board; Executive Committee; Regional Directors. **Languages** English. **Staff** 0.50 FTE, paid. **Finance** Sources: donations; fundraising; members' dues. **Activities** Awards/prizes/competitions; events/meetings; projects/programmes; publishing activities. **Events** *Annual Conference* Dubrovnik (Croatia) 2019, *Annual Conference* Istanbul (Turkey) 2018, *Annual Conference* Long Beach, CA (USA) 2017, *Annual Conference* Tokyo (Japan) 2016, *Annual Conference* Maastricht (Netherlands) 2015. **Publications** *IASL Newsletter* (4 a year); *School Libraries Worldwide* (2 a year) – journal. Conference proceedings; monographic series; specialized bibliographies. **Information Services** *IASL-Link* – international electronic discussion group.
Members Individuals and organizations in 79 countries and territories:
Australia, Austria, Bahamas, Bangladesh, Belgium, Botswana, Brazil, Cambodia, Cameroon, Canada, Chile, China, Croatia, Denmark, Dominican Rep, Egypt, Ethiopia, Finland, France, Germany, Ghana, Hong Kong, Hungary, Iceland, India, Indonesia, Ireland, Israel, Italy, Jamaica, Japan, Jordan, Kazakhstan, Kenya, Korea Rep, Kuwait, Latvia, Lebanon, Macau, Malaysia, Malta, Mauritius, Micronesia FS, Montenegro, Namibia, Nepal, Netherlands, New Zealand, Nigeria, Norway, Oman, Pakistan, Palestine, Papua New Guinea, Philippines, Poland, Portugal, Romania, Russia, Saudi Arabia, Serbia, Singapore, Slovenia, South Africa, Spain, Sri Lanka, Sweden, Switzerland, Syrian AR, Taiwan, Thailand, Trinidad-Tobago, Türkiye, UK, Ukraine, United Arab Emirates, USA, Vietnam, Zimbabwe.
NGO Relations Member of: *International Federation of Library Associations and Institutions (IFLA, #13470)*.
[2019/XB4601/**B**]

♦ International Association of Schools in Advertising (inactive)
♦ International Association of Schools or Higher Institutes of Physical Education / see Association internationale des écoles supérieures d'éducation physique (#02685)

♦ International Association of Schools and Institutes of Administration (IASIA) 12147

Association internationale des écoles et instituts d'administration (AIEIA) – Asociación Internacional de Escuelas e Institutos de Administración – Internationale Vereinigung der Verwaltungsschulen und -institute
Exec Sec c/o IISA, 6 étage – bloc C, Rue du Commerce 96, 1040 Brussels, Belgium. E-mail: info@iias-iisa.org.
URL: https://iasia.iias-iisa.org/

History 1961, Lisbon (Portugal). Founded as a constituent organ of *International Institute of Administrative Sciences (IIAS, #13859)*. New regulations adopted Jul 1984. **Aims** Strengthen administrative capacity building to advance excellence in public administration education and training; conduct, discuss and disseminate research and smart practices on governance and administration. **Structure** General Meeting (annual); Board of Management; Working Groups (10); Secretariat. **Languages** English, French. **Staff** 1.00 FTE, paid. **Finance** Sources: meeting proceeds; members' dues. **Activities** Capacity building; events/meetings; knowledge management/information dissemination; publishing activities; research/documentation. **Events** *IASIA Conference* Manila (Philippines) 2023, *IASIA Conference* Rabat (Morocco) 2022, *Conference* Bela-Bela (South Africa) 2021, *Conference* Bela-Bela (South Africa) 2020, *Conference* Lisbon (Portugal) 2019. **Publications** *Developments in Administration* – journal; *International Review of Administrative Sciences*. Annual Report; reports; books; circulars.
Members A network of schools and institutes and international organizations covering 86 countries and territories:
Albania, Algeria, Argentina, Australia, Austria, Azerbaijan, Bahrain, Bangladesh, Belgium, Benin, Botswana, Brazil, Brunei Darussalam, Bulgaria, Cameroon, Canada, Chad, Chile, China, Croatia, Czechia, Dominican Rep, Egypt, Estonia, Ethiopia, Fiji, Finland, France, Gabon, Germany, Greece, Hungary, India, Indonesia, Iraq, Italy, Kazakhstan, Kenya, Korea Rep, Kosovo, Kyrgyzstan, Latvia, Lebanon, Libya, Lithuania, Luxembourg, Madagascar, Malaysia, Mali, Malta, Mauritania, Mexico, Mongolia, Montenegro, Morocco, Netherlands, Nigeria, Oman, Palestine, Peru, Poland, Portugal, Qatar, Romania, Russia, Rwanda, Saudi Arabia, Senegal, Serbia, Seychelles, Slovakia, South Africa, Spain, Switzerland, Tanzania UR, Thailand, Togo, Tunisia, Türkiye, Uganda, UK, Ukraine, United Arab Emirates, USA, Vietnam, Zimbabwe.
Included in the above, 1 organization listed in this Yearbook:
European Association for Public Administration Accreditation (EAPAA, #06177).
International members (5):
Arab Administrative Development Organization (ARADO, #00893); *Association of Management Training Institutions of Eastern and Southern Africa (AMTIESA, no recent information)*; *ILO (#11123)*; *International Bank for Reconstruction and Development (IBRD, #12317)* (World Bank); *West African Management Development Institutes Network (WAMDEVIN, #20886)*. [2021.05.27/XE5372/y/**E**]

♦ International Association of Schools of Jazz (IASJ) 12148

Exec Dir address not obtained. E-mail: info@iasj.com.
Sec address not obtained.
URL: http://www.iasj.com/

History 1989. Previously referred to as *International Association of Jazz Schools*. **Aims** Increase communication between institutions engaged in the teaching of jazz. **Structure** Artistic Director. Board, comprising Chairman, Secretary, Treasurer and 2 members. Service Bureau. **Languages** English. **Staff** 2.00 FTE, paid. **Finance** Member' dues. **Events** *Annual Meeting* New York, NY (USA) 2022, *Annual Meeting* Munich (Germany) 2021, *Annual Meeting* New York, NY (USA) 2020, *Annual Meeting* Zagreb (Croatia) 2019, *Annual Meeting* Viljandi (Estonia) 2018. **Publications** *IASJ Newsletter* (4 a year).
Members Ordinary; Associate; Individual. Members in 33 countries:
Argentina, Australia, Austria, Belgium, Brazil, Canada, Denmark, Estonia, Finland, France, Germany, Greece, Hungary, Ireland, Israel, Italy, Japan, Latvia, Mexico, Netherlands, New Zealand, Norway, Poland, Portugal, Russia, South Africa, Spain, Sweden, Switzerland, Türkiye, UK, Ukraine, USA.
NGO Relations Member of: *European Music Council (EMC, #07837)*; *International Music Council (IMC, #14199)*. Collaborates with: *Association Européenne des Conservatoires, Académies de Musique et Musikhochschulen (AEC, #02560)*. [2020/XD2746/**D**]

♦ International Association of Schools of Social Work (IASSW) 12149

Association internationale des écoles de travail social (AIETS) – Asociación Internacional de Escuelas de Trabajo Social
Pres address not obtained.
Exec Officer address not obtained.
URL: http://www.iassw-aiets.org/

History 1929, Berlin (Germany). The first International Conference on Social Work was held in 1928, Paris (France). Constitution completely revised, 1956, Munich (Germany). New Constitution approved 1994. Former names and other names: *International Committee of Schools of Social Work* – former; *Comité international des écoles de service social* – former. Registration: Start date: 1971, USA, State of New York. **Aims** Ensure international leadership and encourage high standards in social work *education* and research; provide an international forum; collect and disseminate information; represent the interests of social work education in connection with activities of other international governmental and nongovernmental bodies; encourage exchange of teachers and students. **Structure** General Assembly (every 2 years); Board of Directors (meets twice annually); Executive Committee; Committees; Task Forces. Congresses open; Assemblies open to representatives of all schools of social work, but vote limited to member schools. Regional committee: *Nordic Association of Schools of Social Work (NASSW, #17204)*. **Languages** Chinese, English, French, Japanese, Spanish. **Staff** 1.50 FTE, paid. **Finance** Sources: fees for services; gifts, legacies; meeting proceeds; members' dues; sale of publications; subscriptions. **Activities** Events/meetings; guidance/assistance/consulting; research/documentation. **Events** *Joint World Conference on Social Work Education and*

Social Development Seoul (Korea Rep) 2022, *Joint World Conference on Social Work, Education and Social Development* Seoul (Korea Rep) 2022, *Joint World Conference on Social Work and Social Development* Rimini (Italy) 2020, *Joint World Conference on Social Work and Social Development* Dublin (Ireland) 2018, *General Assembly* Seoul (Korea Rep) 2016. **Publications** *International Social Work* (3 a year); *IASSW News* (2 a year); *Social Dialogue Magazine* (2-3 a year). Directory; congress and seminar proceedings.
Members Institutions and organizations classified under 2 categories: Full; Affiliate. Individual associates and constituent membership (full members) in 100 countries and territories:
Albania, Argentina, Australia, Austria, Bangladesh, Barbados, Belgium, Bolivia, Bosnia-Herzegovina, Botswana, Brazil, Bulgaria, Burundi, Cambodia, Canada, Chile, China, Costa Rica, Croatia, Czechia, Denmark, Ecuador, England, Ethiopia, Fiji, Finland, France, Germany, Ghana, Greece, Greenland, Guyana, Haiti, Honduras, Hong Kong, Hungary, Iceland, India, Indonesia, Iran Islamic Rep, Ireland, Israel, Italy, Jamaica, Japan, Jordan, Kenya, Korea Rep, Kosovo, Kyrgyzstan, Latvia, Lebanon, Lithuania, Macau, Madagascar, Malawi, Malaysia, Mauritania, Mexico, Mongolia, Namibia, Nepal, Netherlands, New Zealand, Nicaragua, Nigeria, Norway, Oman, Pakistan, Peru, Philippines, Poland, Portugal, Puerto Rico, Qatar, Romania, Russia, Senegal, Serbia, Singapore, Slovakia, Slovenia, South Africa, Spain, Sri Lanka, Sweden, Switzerland, Taiwan, Tanzania UR, Thailand, Trinidad-Tobago, Türkiye, Uganda, UK, Ukraine, United Arab Emirates, USA, Venezuela, Vietnam, Zimbabwe.
Affiliate in 4 countries and territories:
Canada, Italy, Puerto Rico, South Africa.
Regional member associations (5):
Asian and Pacific Association for Social Work Education (APASWE, #01601); Asociación Latinoamericana de Escuelas de Trabajo Social (ALAETS, inactive); Association of Schools of Social Work in Africa (ASSWA, inactive); European Association of Schools of Social Work (EASSW, #06200); North American and Caribbean Association of Schools of Social Work (NACASSW, #17562).
Consultative Status Consultative status granted from: *ECOSOC (#05331)* (Special); *UNICEF (#20332)*. **IGO Relations** Accredited by (1): *United Nations Office at Vienna (UNOV, #20604)*. *UNESCO (#20322)*. Official Relations with: *OAS (#17629)*. Associated with Department of Global Communications of the United Nations. **NGO Relations** Member of (3): *Conference of Non-Governmental Organizations in Consultative Relationship with the United Nations (CONGO, #04635); NGO Committee on UNICEF (#17120); Nordiska Socionomförbunds Samarbetskommitté (NSSK, #17495).* [2022.10.12/XB1337/y/**B**]

♦ International Association for Science and Cultural Diversity (IASCUD) 12150

Asociación Internacional de Ciencia y Diversidad Cultural
SG address not obtained. E-mail: secretary@iascud.org.
URL: http://iuhpst.org/pages/inter-division-commissions/iascud.php
History 30 Nov 2000, Pachuca de Soto (Mexico). 30 Nov 2000, Pachuca (Mexico). Scientific Section within the Division of the History of Science (DHS) of *International Union of History and Philosophy of Science and Technology (IUHPST, #15779)*. **Aims** Promote the history of science by establishing and extending the scholarly bases for the study of science and cultural diversity. **Structure** General Assembly; Council; Executive Committee. **Activities** Events/meetings. [2019/XD8718/**E**]

♦ International Association for the Science and Information on Coffee / see Association for the Science and Information on Coffee (#02905)
♦ International Association of Science Parks / see International Association of Science Parks and Areas of Innovation (#12151)

♦ International Association of Science Parks and Areas of Innovation (IASP) 12151

CEO Málaga TechPark, C/Maria Curie 35, Campanillas, 29590 Malaga, Málaga, Spain. T. +34952028303. E-mail: iasp@iasp.ws.
Events Manager address not obtained.
URL: http://www.iasp.ws/
History 5 Jul 1984, France. Former names and other names: *International Association of Science Parks (IASP)* – former; *Club international des technopoles* – former; *Asociación Internacional de Parques Tecnológicos* – former. **Aims** Be the global network for science parks and areas of innovation; drive growth, internationalization and effectiveness for members. **Structure** General Meeting (annual, at Conference); International Board; Executive Board. **Languages** English, French, Italian, Spanish. **Staff** 8.00 FTE, paid. **Finance** Sources: fees for services; meeting proceeds; members' dues; sale of publications. **Activities** Knowledge management/information dissemination. **Events** *European Division Workshop* Budapest (Hungary) 2022, *World Conference on Science Parks and Areas of Innovation* Seville (Spain) 2022, *World Conference on Science Parks and Areas of Innovation* Malaga (Spain) 2021, *World Conference on Science Parks and Areas of Innovation* Malaga (Spain) 2020, *World Conference* Nantes (France) 2019. **Publications** *Electronic On-line Bulletin*. Books.
Members Full fully operational science parks and incubators. Affiliate science parks at the conceptual stage of development. Associate universities; technology institutes; development agencies. Consultants brokers and professionals related to economic development, technology and innovation. Discretionary honorary, emeritus, patrons. Science parks in 76 countries and territories:
Argentina, Australia, Austria, Azerbaijan, Barbados, Belarus, Belgium, Botswana, Brazil, Bulgaria, Canada, China, Colombia, Croatia, Cuba, Cyprus, Denmark, Ecuador, Egypt, Estonia, Eswatini, Finland, France, Germany, Greece, Hungary, Iceland, India, Iran Islamic Rep, Italy, Japan, Kazakhstan, Kenya, Korea Rep, Kosovo, Latvia, Lithuania, Luxembourg, Malaysia, Mexico, Mongolia, Morocco, Netherlands, Nigeria, Oman, Pakistan, Palestine, Panama, Paraguay, Peru, Poland, Portugal, Qatar, Romania, Russia, Saudi Arabia, Serbia, Singapore, Slovakia, Slovenia, South Africa, Spain, Sudan, Sweden, Switzerland, Taiwan, Thailand, Türkiye, Turkmenistan, UK, Ukraine, United Arab Emirates, Uruguay, USA, Uzbekistan, Venezuela.
NGO Relations Member of (1): *World Alliance for Innovation (WAINOVA, #21082).* [2022.02.02/XD2035/**B**]

♦ International Association for the Sciences related to History (inactive)

♦ International Association for Science and Technology of Building Maintenance and Monuments Preservation 12152

Association technique et scientifique pour la conservation et la restauration des bâtiments et des monuments – Wissenschaftlich-Technische Arbeitsgemeinschaft für Bauwerkserhaltung und Denkmalpflege (WTA) – Wetenschappelijk-Technische Groep voor Aanbevelingen inzake Bouwenrenovatie en Monumentenzorg
Main Office Ingolstädter Str 102, 85276 Pfaffenhofen, Germany. T. +498957869727. Fax +498957869729. E-mail: wta@wta.de.
URL: http://www.wta-international.org/
History 1977, Munich (Germany). Former names and other names: *Scientific and Technological Association for the Restoration and Preservation of Monuments* – former alias. Registration: Germany. **Aims** Increase knowledge and transfer of knowledge in the field of building maintenance and monuments preservation. **Structure** General Assembly. Executive Committee. Technical Committees. Regional branches (5): Austrian; Czech; Dutch-Flemish; German; Swiss. **Activities** Organizes conferences, seminars and workshops. **Events** *Colloquium* Delft (Netherlands) 2022. **Publications** *International Journal for Restoration of Buildings and Monuments; International Journal for Technology and Applications in the Building Maintenance and Monuments Preservation.* [2022/XD9288/**D**]

♦ International Association for the Science of Tobacco (inactive)
♦ International Association of Scientific Experts in Tourism (#02697)
♦ International Association of Scientific Hydrology / see International Association of Hydrological Sciences (#11954)
♦ International Association of Scientific Paper Makers (inactive)

♦ International Association for the Scientific Study of Intellectual and Developmental Disabilities (IASSIDD) 12153

International Office address not obtained. E-mail: office@iassidd.org.
Pres Dept of Psychiatry and Mental Health, Fac of Health Sciences, UCT, J-Block, Groote Schuur Hospital, Observatory, Cape Town, 7925, South Africa.
URL: http://www.iassidd.org/
History 11 Aug 1964, Copenhagen (Denmark). Founded following 3 international congresses. Former names and other names: *International Association for the Scientific Study of Mental Deficiency (IASSMD)* – former; *Association internationale pour l'étude scientifique de l'arriération mentale* – former; *Asociación Internacional para el Estudio Científico de la Deficiencia Mental* – former; *Internationale Vereinigung zum Wissenschaftlichen Studium der Geistigen Zurückgebliebenheit* – former; *International Association for the Scientific Study of Intellectual Disabilities (IASSID)* – former; *Association internationale pour l'étude scientifique de la déficience intellectuelle* – former; *Asociación Internacional para el Estudio Científico del Deficiencia Intelectual* – former; *Internationale Vereinigung zum Wissenschaftlichen Studium von Intelligenzstörungen* – former. **Aims** Promote development of new knowledge, research and other scholarly activities, as well as the application of knowledge, to improve the lives of people with intellectual and developmental disabilities, their families and those who support them. **Structure** Assembly (every 3 years, at Congress); Council; Executive; Special Interest Research Groups: Committees (7); Ad-hoc committees as required. **Languages** English. **Staff** 0.50 FTE, paid. **Finance** Sources: members' dues. **Activities** Events/meetings; research and development; training/education. **Events** *IASSIDD World Conference* Chicago, IL (USA) 2024, *IASSIDD Europe Congress* Amsterdam (Netherlands) 2021, *IASSIDD Asia Pacific Regional Congress* Hyderabad (India) 2020, *World Congress* Glasgow (UK) 2019, *Asia Pacific Regional Congress* Bangkok (Thailand) 2017. **Publications** *Journal of Intellectual Disability Research* (12 a year); *Journal of Policy and Practice in Intellectual Disability* (4 a year); *IASSID News Update* (irregular).
Members Individual; Organizational. Individual subscribing members in 33 countries and territories:
Australia, Austria, Belgium, Canada, Czechia, Finland, France, Germany, Hong Kong, Iceland, Iraq, Ireland, Israel, Italy, Japan, Korea Rep, Kuwait, Mexico, Netherlands, New Zealand, Norway, Papua New Guinea, Philippines, Poland, Singapore, Slovenia, South Africa, Spain, Sweden, Switzerland, Taiwan, UK, USA.
Organizational subscribing members in 19 countries and territories:
Argentina, Australia, Belgium, Canada, Croatia, Finland, Germany, Ireland, Israel, Netherlands, New Zealand, Norway, Singapore, Spain, Sweden, Switzerland, Taiwan, UK, USA.
Consultative Status Consultative status granted from: *WHO (#20950)* (Official Relations). [2022/XC1232/y/**C**]

♦ International Association for the Scientific Study of Intellectual Disabilities / see International Association for the Scientific Study of Intellectual and Developmental Disabilities (#12153)
♦ International Association for the Scientific Study of Mental Deficiency / see International Association for the Scientific Study of Intellectual and Developmental Disabilities (#12153)

♦ International Association of Scientific, Technical and Medical Publishers (STM) 12154

Association internationale d'éditeurs scientifiques, techniques et médicaux
CEO Prins Willem Alexanderhof 5, 2595 BE The Hague, Netherlands. E-mail: info@stm-assoc.org.
Admin Office Prama House, 267 Banbury Road, Oxford, OX2 7HT, UK. T. +441865339323.
URL: http://www.stm-assoc.org/
History 7 Oct 1969, Frankfurt-Main (Germany). Former names and other names: *International Group of Scientific, Technical and Medical Publishers* – former (7 Oct 1969); *Groupement international d'éditeurs scientifiques, techniques et médicaux* – former (7 Oct 1969); *STM Group* – alias. Registration: EU Transparency Register, No/ID: 98356852465-08; No/ID: 41200219, Start date: 24 Aug 1970, Netherlands. **Aims** Assist publishers and their *authors* in disseminating research results in the fields of science, technology and medicine; assist national and international organizations concerned with improving the dissemination, storage and retrieval of such information; carry on such work in conjunction with the International Publishers Association and other governmental, international and national professional bodies. **Structure** General Assembly; Executive Board. **Languages** Dutch, English, French, German. **Staff** 8.00 FTE, paid. **Finance** Sources: members' dues. **Activities** Events/meetings; knowledge management/information dissemination; training/education. **Events** *Frankfurt Annual Conference* Frankfurt-Main (Germany) 2022, *JST-STM Seminar* Tsukuba (Japan) 2022, *Frankfurt Annual Conference* Frankfurt-Main (Germany) 2021, *Frankfurt Annual Conference* Frankfurt-Main (Germany) 2020, *Frankfurt Annual Conference* Frankfurt-Main (Germany) 2019. **Publications** *STM Newsletter* (2 a month); *STM Report*. Best practice and guidance notes. **Members** Learned societies, university presses, private companies, new starts and established commercial players (120) in 21 Countries. Membership countries not specified. **Consultative Status** Consultative status granted from: *World Intellectual Property Organization (WIPO, #21593)* (Observer Status). **NGO Relations** Affiliated member of: *International Publishers Association (IPA, #14675)*. Member of: *Alliance for Permanent Access (#00712); International Council for Scientific and Technical Information (ICSTI, #13070)*. Associate member of: *ISC World Data System (ISC-WDS, #16024)*. Cooperates, among others, with: *Association of Learned and Professional Society Publishers (ALPSP, #02786); International Council for Science (ICSU, inactive); International Federation of Library Associations and Institutions (IFLA, #13470); International Federation of Scientific Editors (IFSE, no recent information)*; Society for Scholarly Publishing (SSP). Associate member of: *International Federation of Reproduction Rights Organizations (IFRRO, #13527)*, which was originally a joint working group with IPA. [2023.02.28/XC3910/**C**]

♦ International Association of Scientific and Technological University Libraries / see International Association of University Libraries (#12247)
♦ International Association of Scientologists (see: #03922)
♦ International Association for Scottish Philosophy (internationally oriented national body)
♦ International Association of Secretaries of Ophthalmological and Otolaryngological Societies (inactive)

♦ International Association of Sedimentologists (IAS) 12155

Association internationale de sédimentologistes – Asociación Internacional de Sedimentólogos
Pres c/o Ghent Univ, Dept of Geology, Campus Sterre, Bldg S8, Krijgslaan 281, 9000 Ghent, Belgium.
Gen Sec address not obtained.
URL: http://www.sedimentologists.org/
History 1952, Algiers (Algeria). Founded at International Geological Congress. Discussion for formation of the Association originated at first meeting of British sedimentary petrologists, headed by P Allen, after closing of the 18th International Geological Congress, London (UK). Statutes revised: 30 May 1963, Amsterdam (Netherlands); 11 Aug 1967, Reading (UK); 2 Sep 1971, Heidelberg (Germany FR); 8 Jul 1975, Nice (France); 30 Aug 2006, Fukuoka (Japan); 26 Sep 2010, Mendoza (Argentina); 18-22 Aug 2014, Geneva (Switzerland). Former names and other names: *Association internationale de sédimentologie* – former. Registration: Banque-Carrefour des Entreprises, No/ID: 0665.946.471, Start date: 14 Jun 2016, Belgium. **Aims** Promote sedimentology, especially by facilitating cooperative international research. **Structure** Congress (every 4 years); Bureau; Council. **Languages** English. **Staff** Voluntary. **Finance** Sources: members' dues. **Activities** Events/meetings; training/education. The *IAS Meeting of Sedimentology (IMS)* takes place annually in years in which a Congress is not held. **Events** *International Sedimentological Congress* Wellington (New Zealand) 2026, *IAS Meeting of Sedimentology (IMS)* Aberdeen (UK) 2024, *IAS Meeting of Sedimentology (IMS)* Dubrovnik (Croatia) 2023, *International Sedimentological Congress* Beijing (China) 2022, *Annual Regional Meeting* Prague (Czechia) 2021. **Publications** *Basin Research* (6 a year) – in collaboration with EAGE; *IAS Newsletter* (6 a year); *The Depositional Record* (annual) – open access; *Sedimentology* (7 a year) – journal. *IAS Special Publications*. Reprint series; field guides.
Members Individuals (over 2,000) in 95 countries and territories:
Albania, Algeria, Argentina, Australia, Austria, Bangladesh, Belgium, Bolivia, Botswana, Brazil, Brunei Darussalam, Bulgaria, Cameroon, Canada, Chile, China, Colombia, Congo Brazzaville, Costa Rica, Croatia, Cuba, Cyprus, Czechia, Denmark, Ecuador, Egypt, Estonia, Ethiopia, Finland, France, Gabon, Germany, Ghana, Greece, Hungary, India, Indonesia, Iran Islamic Rep, Iraq, Ireland, Israel, Italy, Japan, Jordan, Korea Rep, Kuwait, Latvia, Liberia, Libya, Luxembourg, Madagascar, Malawi, Malaysia, Mexico, Morocco, Myanmar, Namibia, Nepal, Netherlands, New Zealand, Nigeria, Norway, Oman, Pakistan, Papua New Guinea, Peru, Poland, Portugal, Romania, Russia, Saudi Arabia, Senegal, Singapore, Slovakia, Slovenia, South Africa, Spain, Sri Lanka, Sudan, Sweden, Switzerland, Syrian AR, Taiwan, Tanzania UR, Thailand, Tunisia, Türkiye, UK, Ukraine, United Arab Emirates, USA, Venezuela, Vietnam, Yemen, Zambia.
NGO Relations Member of (2): *Federation of European and International Associations Established in Belgium (FAIB, #09508); International Union of Geological Sciences (IUGS, #15777)*. Cooperates with (1): *European Association of Geoscientists and Engineers (EAGE, #06055)*. Supports (2): *International Conference on Fluvial Sedimentology (ICFS); International Meeting of Carbonate Sedimentologists (Bathurst Meeting)*. Instrumental in setting up (1): *International Association for Sediment Water Science (IASWS, #12156).* [2023/XB1342/v/**B**]

♦ International Association for Sediment Water Science (IASWS) 12156

Pres Joseph Stephan Institute, Dept Environmental Sciences, Jamova 39, 1000 Ljubljana, Slovenia.
Sec University Mediterranea, Dept Agraria, Feo di Vito, 89123 Reggio Calabria RC, Italy.
URL: https://www.ufz.de/iasws/

History 1984, Geneva (Switzerland). Founded at 3rd *International Symposium on the Interactions Between Sediment and Fresh Water*, when statutes were adopted, discussions having been held since 1st Symposium, Nov 1976, Amsterdam (Netherlands), and encouraged by *International Association of Sedimentologists (IAS, #12155)*. **Aims** Promote, encourage and recognize excellence in scientific research related to sediments and their interaction with water and biota in fluvial, lacustrine and marine systems, with particular reference to environmental concerns; foster collaborative research among earth scientists, biologists, chemists and environmental engineers whose interests pertain to sediment-water interactions in all aquatic systems. **Structure** General Assembly (every 3 years, at Symposium). Board of Directors, comprising the Executive – President, Past President, Vice-President, Secretary and Treasurer – plus 5 Directors-at-large and Convenor of the upcoming and of the past Symposium (ex officio). **Languages** English. **Staff** Voluntary. **Finance** Members' dues: US$ 50, incorporated in conference registration and covering the period commencing the first day of the symposium for which they are registered until the day before the following triennial conference. **Activities** Provides continuity in the holding of triennial conferences and a financial base for underwriting them. **Events** *International Symposium* Portoroz (Slovenia) 2021, *Triennial International Symposium* Portoroz (Slovenia) 2020, *Triennial International Symposium* Taormina (Italy) 2017, *Triennial International Symposium* Grahamstown (South Africa) 2014, *Triennial international symposium* Totnes (UK) 2011. **Publications** Newsletter. Symposium proceedings. **Members** Full and student in 34 countries. Membership countries not specified. [2020/XD2896/**C**]

- ♦ International Association of Seed Crushers (inactive)
- ♦ International Association of Seismology / see International Association of Seismology and Physics of the Earth's Interior (#12157)

♦ International Association of Seismology and Physics of the Earth's Interior (IASPEI) 12157

Association internationale de séismologie et de physique de l'intérieur de la Terre (AISPIT)

SG c/o NORSAR, PO Box 53, Gunnar Randers vei 15, 2027 Kjeller, Norway. T. +4741614946. E-mail: iaspei@norsar.no.
Pres address not obtained.
URL: http://www.iaspei.org/

History 1901, Strasbourg (France). Founded as *Central Bureau of Seismology – Bureau central de séismologie*. Original organization dissolved and present body formed 1922, Rome (Italy), as constituent association of *International Union of Geodesy and Geophysics (IUGG, #15776)*. Current statutes adopted by General Assembly, 1975, Grenoble (France), and amended by General Assembly, 1981, London ON (Canada), 2011, Melbourne (Australia), 2015, Prague (Czech Rep), and 2017, Kobe (Japan). Former names and other names: *International Association of Seismology (IAS)* – former (1930 to 1951); *Seismology Section of IUGG* – former (1921 to 1930); *Association Internationale de Séismologie (ISA)* – former (1904 to 1921). **Aims** Promote study of the structure, properties and processes of the Earth; advance theoretical and observational development of seismology and its applications to Earth structure, resource exploration, earthquake science, earthquake hazards, nuclear testing, related treaty monitoring and environmental monitoring.
Structure General Assembly (every 2 years, alternate assemblies being held with a full assembly of IUGG); Executive Committee; Bureau; Secretariat, headed by Secretary General.
IASPEI Commissions (7); Joint Association Activities (6):
- IASPEI/IAVCEI/IAPSO
- *IAPSO/IASPEI/IAVCEI Joint Tsunami Commission*;
- *IASPEI/IAVCEI Joint Commission on Physics and Chemistry of Earth Materials (#11009)*;
- *IASPEI/IAVCEI Commission on Volcano Seismology (#11008)*;
- Structure of the Earth's Deep Interior (SEDI);
- *'IAGA/IASPEI/IAVCEI Working Group on Electromagnetic Studies of Earthquakes and Volcanoes'*.

Regional Commissions (4):
- *Africa Seismological Commission (AfSC)*;
- *Latin American and Caribbean Seismological Commission (LACSC, #16285)*;
- *European Seismological Commission (ESC, #08461)*;
- *Asian Seismological Commission (ASC, see: #12157)*.

Commission Status (2):
- *International Federation of Digital Seismograph Networks (FDSN, #13407)*;
- *International Heat Flow Commission (IHFC, #13786)*.

Languages English. **Staff** None. **Finance** Sources: grants; sale of publications; subscriptions. Expenses met by IUGG. Contracts from UNESCO and other organizations. **Activities** Knowledge management/information dissemination; research/documentation. **Events** *General Assembly* Hyderabad (India) 2021, *Joint Scientific Assembly* Hyderabad (India) 2021, *General Assembly* Montréal, QC (Canada) 2019, *General Assembly* Kobe (Japan) 2017, *Joint Scientific Assembly* Kobe (Japan) 2017. **Publications** *IASPEI Newsletter*. Conference proceedings; reports; resolutions and statements.
Members Adhering organizations in 64 countries and territories:
Albania, Argentina, Armenia, Australia, Austria, Azerbaijan, Belgium, Bolivia, Bosnia-Herzegovina, Brazil, Bulgaria, Canada, Chile, China, Colombia, Congo DR, Costa Rica, Croatia, Czechia, Denmark, Egypt, Estonia, Finland, France, Georgia, Germany, Greece, Hungary, Iceland, India, Indonesia, Iran Islamic Rep, Ireland, Israel, Italy, Japan, Korea Rep, Luxembourg, Mexico, Morocco, Mozambique, Netherlands, New Zealand, Nicaragua, North Macedonia, Norway, Peru, Poland, Portugal, Romania, Russia, Saudi Arabia, Slovakia, Slovenia, South Africa, Spain, Sweden, Switzerland, Taiwan, Thailand, Türkiye, UK, USA, Vietnam.
NGO Relations Constituent association of IUGG, which is one of the 20 scientific Unions grouped within: *International Council for Science (ICSU, inactive)*. Joint commissions with: *International Association of Geomagnetism and Aeronomy (IAGA, #11916)*; *International Association for the Physical Sciences of the Oceans (IAPSO, #12082)*; *International Association of Volcanology and Chemistry of the Earth's Interior (IAVCEI, #12259)*. Through IUGG, cooperates with: *International Union of Geological Sciences (IUGS, #15777)*; *International Lithosphere Program (ILP, #14059)*. [2021.11.30/XB1344/**B**]

- ♦ International Association of Selectors (inactive)

♦ International Association on Self-Propagating High-Temperature Synthesis (SHS-AS) 12158

Contact Inst of Structural Macrokinetics and Materials Science, Chernogolovka, Moscow MOSKVA, Russia, 142432. T. +7959628000. Fax +7959628040.
URL: http://www.waceramics.org/itamembers.shtml

History 2002. A unit of the Institute of Topical Associations within *World Academy of Ceramics (WAC, #21067)*. **Aims** Maintain *ceramic*-related activities in the field of self-propagating high-temperature (SHS). **Structure** Council of Founders (meets once a year). Officers: President; Executive Director; Executive Secretary. **Finance** Members' dues. Symposium fees. **Activities** Awards/prizes/competitions; events/meetings. **Events** *Symposium* Moscow (Russia) 2019, *Symposium* Dijon (France) 2007, *Symposium* Quartu Sant'Elena (Italy) 2005, *Symposium* Krakow (Poland) 2003. **Publications** *International Journal of Self-Propagating High-Temperature Synthesis* in English, Russian. [2018/XM2195/**D**]

- ♦ International Association for the Semiotics of Law (inactive)
- ♦ International Association for the Semiotics of Space / see International Association for the Semiotics of Space and Time (#12159)

♦ International Association for the Semiotics of Space and Time (IASSp+T) 12159

Association Internationale de Sémiotique de l'Espace et du Temps (AISE + T)

SG address not obtained.
Pres address not obtained.
URL: https://www.ias-st.com/

History 1989, Urbino (Italy). Former names and other names: *Association internationale de sémiotique de l'espace (AISE)* – former; *International Association for the Semiotics of Space (IASSP)* – former. **Aims** Promote semiotic research in the field of disciplines treating space – *architecture*, urbanism, environment, painting, *design*, publicity, cinema, television; enrich these disciplines through decompartmentalization and through homogenization of methodology. **Structure** General Assembly (every 2 years); Scientific Board; Executive Board. **Languages** English, French. **Staff** 6.00 FTE, voluntary. **Finance** Sources: members' dues. **Activities** Events/meetings. **Events** *Congress* Lisbon (Portugal) 2005, *The sense of forms and temporalities of space – towards a semiotics of space and time* Vaulx-en-Velin (France) 2004, *Congress* Dresden (Germany) 1999, *Conference* Thessaloniki (Greece) 1997, *Conference* Urbino (Italy) 1997. **Publications** Conference proceedings.
Members Individuals in 15 countries:
Argentina, Canada, Chile, Estonia, Finland, France, Greece, Italy, Lithuania, Portugal, Russia, Serbia, Spain, Switzerland, USA. [2019/XC0012/**C**]

♦ International Association for Semiotic Studies (IASS-AIS) 12160

Association internationale de sémiotique (AIS) – Asociación Internacional de Sémiotica – Internationale Vereinigung für Semiotik

Pres address not obtained. E-mail: info@iass-ais.org.
SG address not obtained.
URL: http://www.iass-ais.org/

History Founded 22 Jan 1969, Paris (France). Also referred to by combined acronym *IASS-AIS*. Registered in accordance with French Law. **Aims** Promote scientific semiotic research and strengthen international cooperation in the field. **Structure** General Assembly (every 5 years at Congress); Executive Committee; Bureau; Secretariat at address of Secretary-General (5-year term). **Languages** English, French, German, Spanish. **Finance** Sources: members' dues. **Activities** Events/meetings; networking/liaising; training/education. **Events** *International Congress on Musical Signification* Barcelona (Spain) 2022, *World Congress* Thessaloniki (Greece) 2022, *International Congress on Musical Signification* Barcelona (Spain) 2021, *World Congress* Buenos Aires (Argentina) 2019, *World Congress* Kaunas (Lithuania) 2017. **Publications** *Semiotica* (5 a year).
Members Individual; collective (associations, libraries and institutes). Members in 65 countries and territories:
Argentina, Australia, Austria, Belgium, Bosnia-Herzegovina, Brazil, Bulgaria, Cameroon, Canada, Chile, China, Colombia, Costa Rica, Croatia, Cyprus, Czechia, Denmark, Estonia, Finland, France, Gabon, Georgia, Germany, Greece, Hong Kong, Hungary, India, Israel, Italy, Japan, Korea Rep, Lebanon, Lesotho, Malaysia, Malta, Mexico, Moldova, Morocco, Netherlands, Nigeria, North Macedonia, Norway, Peru, Poland, Portugal, Puerto Rico, Romania, Russia, San Marino, Serbia, Slovakia, Slovenia, South Africa, Spain, Sweden, Switzerland, Taiwan, Tunisia, Türkiye, UK, Ukraine, Uruguay, USA, Venezuela, Vietnam.
NGO Relations Member of (1): *International Pragmatics Association (IPrA, #14634)*. [2021/XC4413/**C**]

- ♦ International Association of Settlements (inactive)
- ♦ International Association of Severe Weather Specialists (no recent information)

♦ International Association of Sexual Plant Reproduction Research (IASPRR) 12161

Pres Mc Gill Univ, Dept of Plant Sciences, Raymond Building, 845 Sherbrooke Street West, Montréal QC H3A 0G4, Canada. T. +5143987594.
Sec Gen Wageningen Univ, Lab of Biochemistry, Dreijenlaan 3, 6703 HA Wageningen, Netherlands.
URL: http://www.iasprr.org/

History Founded 6 Jul 1990, Leningrad (USSR). **Aims** Stimulate scientific research in the field of plant reproduction and related subjects; promote application of the results of such research in *agricultural* and *forestry* practice. **Structure** International Board. **Languages** English. **Staff** No permanent staff. **Finance** Sources: members' dues. Annual budget: 5,000 EUR. **Activities** Events/meetings; knowledge management/information dissemination. **Events** *Biennial Congress* Prague (Czechia) 2022, *Biennial Congress* Prague (Czechia) 2020, *Biennial Congress* Gifu (Japan) 2018, *Biennial Congress* Tucson, AZ (USA) 2016, *Biennial Congress* Porto (Portugal) 2014. **Publications** *IASPRR Membership Newsletter* (annual); *Sexual Plant Reproduction* – journal. Congress proceedings.
Members Full in 44 countries, and territories:
Argentina, Australia, Austria, Belarus, Belgium, Brazil, Bulgaria, Canada, China, Costa Rica, Czechia, Denmark, France, Georgia, Germany, Greece, Hungary, India, Iran Islamic Rep, Ireland, Israel, Italy, Japan, Korea Rep, Mexico, Netherlands, New Zealand, Norway, Pakistan, Peru, Philippines, Poland, Portugal, Russia, Slovakia, South Africa, Spain, Sweden, Switzerland, Taiwan, Türkiye, UK, Ukraine, USA.
IGO Relations None. **NGO Relations** Member of: *International Union of Biological Sciences (IUBS, #15760)*. [2018/XC0039/**C**]

- ♦ International Association of Sheet Metal, Air, Rail and Transportation Workers (internationally oriented national body)

♦ International Association for Shell and Spatial Structures (IASS) .. 12162

Association internationale pour les voiles minces et les voiles spatiaux (AIVM) – Asociación Internacional de Estructuras Laminares y Espaciales (AIEL) – Internationale Verbindung für Schalentragwerke und Raumtragwerke (IVS)

Sec Lab Central de Estructuras y Materiales, CEDEX, C/ Alfonso XII 3, 28014 Madrid, Spain. T. +34913357409. Fax +34913357422. E-mail: iass@iass-structures.org.
Pres address not obtained.
URL: http://www.iass-structures.org/

History 18 Sep 1959, Madrid (Spain). Founded by Eduardo Torroja, on taking over the activities of *International Committee for Shell Structures (ICSS)*, previously set up in Oslo (Norway). Registration: Switzerland. **Aims** Advance development of technology of *construction* of shells or three dimensional continuous or discontinuous structures, whose thickness is small compared to their other two dimensions, and in which the forces acting in the middle plane are fundamental; achieve further progress through interchange of ideas among all interested in lightweight structural systems such as lattice, tension, membrane and shell structures. **Structure** Executive Council (meets at least annually); Advisory Board; Technical Working Groups (12). **Languages** English. **Staff** 1.50 FTE, paid. **Finance** Members' dues. Assistance from the Spanish Administration for secretariat hosting. **Activities** Awards/prizes/competitions; events/meetings. **Events** *Annual Symposium* Melbourne, VIC (Australia) 2023, *IASS Annual Symposium and Asia-Pacific Conference on Spatial Structures (APCS)* Beijing (China) 2022, *Annual Symposium* Guildford (UK) 2021, *Annual Symposium* Guildford (UK) 2020, *Annual Symposium* Barcelona (Spain) 2019. **Publications** *Journal of the IASS* (4 a year) in English.
Members Individual; Collective; Honorary; Student; Chapters; Exchanges; Subscribers. Members (about 830) in 66 countries and territories:
Algeria, Argentina, Australia, Austria, Bangladesh, Belgium, Brazil, Canada, China, Colombia, Congo DR, Costa Rica, Cuba, Czechia, Denmark, Ecuador, Egypt, El Salvador, Finland, France, Germany, Greece, Hong Kong, Hungary, India, Iran Islamic Rep, Ireland, Israel, Italy, Japan, Jordan, Korea Rep, Kuwait, Lebanon, Luxembourg, Malaysia, Malta, Mexico, Monaco, Mozambique, Netherlands, New Zealand, Nigeria, Norway, Panama, Peru, Poland, Portugal, Romania, Russia, Saudi Arabia, Singapore, Slovakia, Slovenia, Spain, Sweden, Switzerland, Taiwan, Thailand, Tunisia, Türkiye, UK, Ukraine, United Arab Emirates, USA, Zimbabwe. [2021/XC1207/**B**]

- ♦ International Association of Sheriff Officers and Judicial Officers / see International Union of Judicial Officers (#15785)

♦ International Association of Shin Buddhist Studies (IASBS) 12163

North American Office c/o Inst of Buddhist Studies, 2140 Durant Ave, Berkeley CA 94704, USA.
Exec Sec Ryukoku Univ, 125-1 Daiku-cho, Shichijo-Dori Ohmiya Higashi-iru, Shimogyo-ku, Kyoto, 600-8268 Japan. E-mail: iasbs@msn.com.
URL: http://www.iasbs.org/

History 30 Apr 1982, Kyoto (Japan). By-laws came into effect 1 May 1982; amended 10 Aug 1987, 1 Jan 1989, 10 Sep 1991, 23 Aug 1995. **Aims** Develop international Shin Buddhist studies and Pure Land Buddhist Studies; facilitate exchange among members. **Structure** Steering Committee. Officers: President; Vice-President; Executive Secretary; Treasurer; Advisors; Steering Committee members; 2 Auditors. Academic association in contact with universities having members. **Languages** English, French, German, Japanese. **Staff** Part-time, voluntary. **Finance** Members' dues. Donations. **Activities** Events/meetings; publishing activities. **Events** *Biennial Conference* Taipei (Taiwan) 2019, *Biennial Conference* Tokyo (Japan) 2017, *Biennial Conference* Berkeley, CA (USA) 2015, *Biennial Conference* Kyoto (Japan) 2011, *Biennial Conference* Tokyo (Japan) 2005. **Publications** *The Pure Land: Journal of Pure Land Buddhism* (annual).
Members Regular, student and supporting. Individuals in 14 countries and territories:
Argentina, Australia, Austria, Belgium, Brazil, Canada, Germany, Japan, Korea Rep, Poland, Switzerland, Taiwan, UK, USA. [2018.04.06/XD0461/**D**]

♦ International Association of Shipowners of the Black Sea Region / see International Black Sea Region Association of Shipowners (#12359)
♦ International Association for Shock Wave Research / see International Shock Wave Institute (#14851)
♦ International Association of Shoe Industry Technicians / see Union internationale des techniciens de l'industrie de la chaussure (#20439)
♦ International Association Skiing in Schools and Universities / see International Association of Education in Science and Snowsports (#11864)
♦ International Association for Ski Instruction / see International Ski Instructors Association (#14870)
♦ International Association of Ski Journalists (#02710)
♦ International Association of Ski Writers / see Association internationale des journalistes du ski (#02710)
♦ International Association of Slavonic Languages and Literatures (inactive)

♦ International Association of Sleep Research in Gerontology (IASRG) 12164

Pres Hôp Bichat, 46 rue Henri-Huchard, 75877 Paris CEDEX 18, France.

History 2008, by Dr Fannie Onen. **Structure** International Scientific Committee. **Events** *Aging and Sleep Conference* USA 2020, *Aging and Sleep Biennial Meeting* Lyon (France) 2017, *Aging and Sleep Biennial Meeting* Lyon (France) 2014, *Aging and Sleep Biennial Meeting / Biennial International Meeting* Paris (France) 2012, *Aging and Sleep Biennial Meeting / Biennial International Meeting* Lyon (France) 2010. [2020/XJ2397/c/**E**]

♦ International Association for Small Hydro (IASH) 12165

SG CBIP Bldg, Malcha Marg, Chanakyapuri, Delhi 110021, DELHI 110021, India. T. +911126115984 – +911126876229ext133. Fax +911126116347. E-mail: batra@cbip.org – cbip@cbip.org.
URL: http://cbip.org/iash/iash.html

History Founded Sep 1994, Delhi (India). **Aims** Promote information exchange and technical expertise for accelerated development of small hydro, including mini hydro; provide a forum for specialists planners, designers, manufacturers and users for interaction on the latest development of SHP sector. **Structure** Governing Council. **Languages** English. **Finance** Members' dues. Conference fees. **Activities** Events/meetings; training/education. **Events** *International conference on renewable energy / Conference* Mauritius 1999, *International conference on renewable energy* Hyderabad (India) 1997, *Conference* Nepal 1997, *Conference* Delhi (India) 1996. **Publications** *IASH Newsletter*. Journal. Conference proceedings.
Members Full in 15 countries and territories:
Australia, Austria, Belgium, China, Croatia, Germany, India, Mauritius, Nepal, Norway, Polynesia Fr, Serbia, Solomon Is, Sri Lanka, UK. [2018.06.01/XD7646/**D**]

♦ International Association of Y's Men's Clubs / see Y's Men International (#19326)
♦ International Association on Smoking Control & Harm Reduction (unconfirmed)
♦ International Association for Snowsports at Schools and Universities / see International Association of Education in Science and Snowsports (#11864)
♦ International Association of the Soap and Detergent Industry (inactive)
♦ International Association of the Soap, Detergent, and Maintenance Products Industry / see International Association for Soaps, Detergents and Maintenance Products (#12166)

♦ International Association for Soaps, Detergents and Maintenance Products 12166

Association internationale de la savonnerie, de la détergence et des produits d'entretien (AISE)

Dir Gen Bd du Souverain 165, 4th Floor, 1160 Brussels, Belgium. T. +3226796260. E-mail: aise.main@aise.eu.
URL: http://www.aise.eu/

History Dec 1995, Belgium. Founded on merger of *International Association of the Soap and Detergent Industry (AIS, inactive)* and *International Federation of Associations of Cleaning Products Manufacturers (FIFE, inactive)*. Former names and other names: *International Association of the Soap, Detergent, and Maintenance Products Industry* – former. Registration: Banque-Carrefour des Entreprises, No/ID: 0538.183.615, Start date: 1 Jan 1974, Belgium; EU Transparency Register, No/ID: 6168551998-60, Start date: 22 Jan 2009. **Aims** Act as the industry's expert and valued voice in Europe of the cleaning and hygiene products industry; ensure and maintain open dialogue with EU institutions, international organizations, NGOs, industry partners and other stakeholders to enable the cleaning and maintenance products industry to achieve its vision of a sustainable future for all while improving the environment in which the industry operates. **Structure** General Assembly; Board; National Associations Committee; Management Committee; Steering Groups: Working Groups; Task Forces; Advisory Groups; Secretariat. **Languages** English. **Staff** 14.00 FTE, paid. **Finance** Sources: members' dues. Annual budget: 3,500,000 EUR. **Activities** Advocacy/lobbying/activism; events/meetings; politics/policy/regulatory; research and development. **Events** *General Assembly* 2021, *Cleaning & Hygiene Forum* Brussels (Belgium) 2021, *General Assembly* Brussels (Belgium) 2018, *General Assembly* Paris (France) 2017, *General Assembly* Brussels (Belgium) 2016. **Publications** Annual Report; activity and sustainability report; brochures, posters; promotional material.
Members Ordinary: national associations in 26 countries:
Austria, Belgium, Croatia, Czechia, Denmark, Estonia, Finland, France, Germany, Greece, Hungary, Ireland, Italy, Latvia, Lithuania, Luxembourg, Netherlands, Norway, Poland, Portugal, Romania, Slovakia, Spain, Sweden, Switzerland, UK.
Extraordinary members in 3 countries:
Russia, Serbia, Türkiye.
Associate members (10), include the following 3 listed in this Yearbook:
Association of Manufacturers and Formulators of Enzyme Products (AMFEP, #02793); European Committee of Organic Surfactants and their Intermediates (#06660); European Engineering Industries Association (EUnited, #06991).
Ordinary Company Members (8) in 8 countries:
Belgium, France, Germany, Italy, Netherlands, Spain, Switzerland, UK.
Supporting corporate members (8). Membership countries not specified.
IGO Relations Associated with Department of Global Communications of the United Nations. **NGO Relations** Member of (7): *Circular Plastics Alliance (#03936); Conseil européen de l'industrie chimique (CEFIC, #04687)* (Affiliate); *Downstream Users of Chemicals Co-ordination group (DUCC, #05127); European Biocidal Product Forum (EBPF, #06332); European Partnership for Alternative Approaches to Animal Testing (EPAA, #08155); Federation of European and International Associations Established in Belgium (FAIB, #09508); Industry4Europe (#11181).* In liaison with technical committees of: *Comité européen de normalisation (CEN, #04162); International Organization for Standardization (ISO, #14473).* [2022/XD4941/y/**D**]

♦ International Association of Social Educators 12167

Association internationale des éducateurs sociaux (AIEJI) – Asociación Internacional de Educadores Sociales

Gen Sec c/o Socialpaedagogerne, Brolaeggerstraede 9, 1211 Copenhagen, Denmark. T. +4572486862. E-mail: mhn@sl.dk.
Pres address not obtained. E-mail: forbundsformanden@sl.dk.
URL: http://www.aieji.net/

History 19 Mar 1951, Germany FR. Founded at 4th international meeting. Declaration accepted at 12th World Congress, Jul 1990, New York NY (USA). New statutes and current title adopted 13 Jun 1997, Brescia (Italy), when activities widened to include all age-groups. Former names and other names: *International Association of Workers for Troubled Children and Youth* – former (19 Mar 1951); *Association internationale des éducateurs de jeunes inadaptés* – former (19 Mar 1951); *Asociación Internacional de Educadores de Jóvenes Inadaptados* – former (19 Mar 1951); *Internationale Vereinigung von Erziehern Gefährdeter Jugend* – former (19 Mar 1951); *Associazione Internazionale degli Educatori della Gioventù in Difficoltà* – former (19 Mar 1951); *Associação Internacional de Educadores de Jovens Inadaptados* – former (19 Mar 1951); *Associazione Internazionale degli Educatori dei Giovani Disadattati* – alias (19 Mar 1951). Registration: Start date: 2 May 1953, Netherlands; Start date: 1971, Switzerland. **Aims** Emphasize and promote the philosophy of social education and its uniqueness in being actively involved in partnership with clients, working with them not only individually but in groups, families, communities and social environments towards development of their strengths and in resolving personal, social and community difficulties. **Structure** General Assembly (every 4 years); Executive Committee; Regional Offices (4); International Congress Committee; International Technical Committee. **Languages** English, French, German, Spanish. **Staff** 19.00 FTE, voluntary. **Finance** Sources: members' dues. **Activities** Capacity building; events/meetings; networking/liaising. **Events** *World Congress* Lausanne (Switzerland) 2022, *World Congress* Lausanne (Switzerland) 2021, *World Congress* Sao Paulo (Brazil) 2017, *World Congress* Luxembourg (Luxembourg) 2013, *World Congress* Copenhagen (Denmark) 2009. **Publications** Congress reports; pamphlets on technical problems. Information Services: Documentation centre.
Members Active national associations (over 20); private and public organizations; qualified social educators and other interested professionals in countries with no national member association. Associate qualified individuals not wishing to be member of a national association. Members in 25 countries:
Algeria, Austria, Belgium, Brazil, Canada, Congo DR, Côte d'Ivoire, Denmark, France, Germany, Honduras, India, Israel, Italy, Luxembourg, Portugal, South Africa, Spain, Switzerland, Togo, Tunisia, UK, Uruguay, USA, Venezuela.
Included in the above, 4 organizations listed in this Yearbook:
Groupe européen d'échanges et de recherches en éducation sociale (GEERES, no recent information); Institut méditerranéen de formation et recherche en travail social (IMF); International Learning Exchange in Social Education (ILEX); International Organization of Psychomotricity and Relaxation (#14465).
Consultative Status Consultative status granted from: *Council of Europe (CE, #04881)* (Participatory Status). **IGO Relations** *UNESCO (#20322); UNICEF (#20332).* **NGO Relations** Member of: *European Network for Social Action (ENSACT, #08003).* [2019/XC1374/y/**C**]

♦ International Association for Social Progress (inactive)
♦ International Association for Social Psychiatry / see World Association for Social Psychiatry (#21190)

♦ International Association on Social Quality (IASQ) 12168

Main Office Bredeweg 8, 1098 BP Amsterdam, Netherlands. T. +31206654923. E-mail: info@socialquality.org.
URL: http://www.socialquality.org/

History 10 Jun 1997, Amsterdam (Netherlands), starting as an independent juridical construction of three scientific networks: *'SIWO'*, *'The European Union's Observatory on Older People'* and *'The European Union's Observatory on Social Exclusion'*. Adopted the 'Amsterdam Declaration on the Social Quality of Europe'. Subsequently changed title to *European Foundation on Social Quality (EFSQ).* **Aims** Develop the social quality theory, methodology and approach by exploring dynamics and evolution of contemporary societies and their impact on economic, socio-political, socio-cultural and environmental dimensions of daily circumstances. **Structure** Board. **Languages** English. **Staff** 0.50 FTE, paid; 1.00 FTE, voluntary. **Finance** Project funds. **Activities** Research/documentation; events/meetings; politics/policy/regulatory. **Events** *SQ Workshop* Hangzhou (China) 2014, *Open Forum* Hangzhou (China) 2013, *International Conference* Hong Kong (Hong Kong) 2012, *International Conference* Hong Kong (Hong Kong) 2012, *International Conference* Seoul (Korea Rep) 2011. **Publications** *International Journal of Social Quality* (2 a year). *Social Quality: From Theory to Indicators* (2012) – Palgrave Macmillan ; *Social Quality: a Vision for Europe* (2001); *Social Quality of Europe* (1997).
Members Universities and university professors (198), signatories of the Amsterdam Declaration on the Social Quality of Europe, from 26 countries:
Austria, Belgium, Canada, Czechia, Denmark, Finland, France, Germany, Greece, Hungary, Ireland, Italy, Lithuania, Luxembourg, Netherlands, Norway, Poland, Portugal, Romania, Slovakia, Slovenia, Spain, Sweden, Switzerland, UK, USA.
Network of scientists collaborating with the Asian Steering Committee on Social Quality in 11 countries and territories:
Australia, China, Hong Kong, India, Indonesia, Japan, Korea Rep, Malaysia, Singapore, Taiwan, Thailand. [2015/XF4972/fv/**D**]

♦ International Association for Social Science Information Service and Technology (IASSIST) 12169

Association internationale pour les services et techniques d'information en sciences sociales

Sec Univ of Pennsylvania, Philadelphia PA 19104, USA.
Pres address not obtained.
URL: http://www.iassistdata.org/

History 1976. **Aims** Foster and promote a network of excellence for data services; advance infrastructure in the social sciences; provide opportunities for collegial exchange of sound professional practices related to data services. **Structure** General Assembly (annual) Officers; Ex-Officio Officers; Administrative Committee; Regional Secretaries (5); Committees (5); IASSIST Fellows. **Languages** English. **Staff** Part-time, voluntary. **Finance** Sources: members' dues. **Activities** Events/meetings; knowledge management/information dissemination; networking/liaising; training/education. **Events** *Annual Conference* Philadelphia, PA (USA) 2023, *Annual Conference* Gothenburg (Sweden) 2022, *Annual Conference* 2021, *Joint Meeting* Stockholm (Sweden) 2021, *Annual Conference* Gothenburg (Sweden) 2020. **Publications** *IQ* (4 a year). Conference abstracts; reports; peer reviewed articles.
Members Individuals (about 300) in 27 countries:
Australia, Canada, Czechia, Denmark, Finland, France, Germany, Greece, Hungary, Ireland, Israel, Italy, Japan, Latvia, Netherlands, Norway, Poland, Romania, Russia, Slovakia, Slovenia, South Africa, Spain, Sweden, Switzerland, UK, USA.
NGO Relations Member of (1): *centerNet.* Joint activities with: *International Federation of Data Organizations for the Social Sciences (IFDO, #13402).* [2023.02.14/XC0051/v/**C**]

♦ International Association of Social Scientists, Architects and Planners (inactive)
♦ International Association for Social Tourism (no recent information)
♦ International Association for Social Work with Groups (unconfirmed)
♦ International Association of Societies for Autistic Children and Adults (inactive)

♦ International Association of Societies of Design Research (IASDR) . 12170

Pres address not obtained.
SG address not obtained.
URL: http://www.iasdr.net/

History 1 Nov 2005, Korea Rep. **Aims** Promote research in and study into or about the activity of design and its many applications through encouraging collaboration on an international level among independent societies of design research. **Structure** Executive Board. **Languages** English. **Staff** 10.00 FTE, voluntary. **Finance** Sources: members' dues. **Activities** Events/meetings; networking/liaising; research/documentation. **Events** *Biennial Congress* Hong Kong (Hong Kong) 2021, *Biennial Congress* Manchester (UK) 2019, *Biennial Congress* Cincinnati, OH (USA) 2017, *Biennial Congress* Brisbane, QLD (Australia) 2015, *Biennial Congress* Tokyo (Japan) 2013. **Publications** Conference proceedings.
Members Societies in 5 countries and territories:
China, Japan, Korea Rep, Taiwan, UK.
Included in the above, 2 organizations listed in this Yearbook:
Design Research Society (DRS, #05044); Design Society, the (#05045).
IGO Relations None. **NGO Relations** None. [2021.09.01/XM3756/y/**C**]

♦ International Association for Society and Natural Resources (IASNR) 12171

Exec Dir University of Illinois Urbana-Champaign, College of Health Sciences – 110 Huff Hall, 1206 South Fourth St., Champaign IL 61820, USA. E-mail: info@iasnr.org.
URL: http://www.iasnr.org/

History 2001. **Aims** Foster interdisciplinary social scientific understanding of the relationships between humans and natural resources; further the application of social science information in natural resource decision-making; provide a mechanism for dialogue and information exchange. **Structure** Council; Executive. Organizes *International Symposium on Society and Resource Management (ISSRM).* **Languages** English. **Staff** 2.00 FTE, paid. **Finance** Sources: meeting proceeds; members' dues. **Activities** Events/meetings. **Events** *Conference* Portland, ME (USA) 2023, *Conference* San José (Costa Rica) 2022, *Conference* Champaign, IL (USA) 2021, *Annual International Symposium on Society and Resource Management* Cairns, QLD (Australia) 2020, *Conference* Champaign, IL (USA) 2020. **Publications** *Keeping in Touch; Society and Natural Resources.*
Members Individuals (about 600). Membership countries not specified. [2022/XJ3819/**D**]

♦ International Association for Software Architects / see Iasa Global
♦ International Association for Solar Energy Education (inactive)

♦ International Association of Soldiers for Peace / see Soldiers of Peace International Association (#19678)
♦ International Association of Somatotherapy (no recent information)
♦ International Association of Sound Archives / see International Association of Sound and Audiovisual Archives (#12172)

♦ International Association of Sound and Audiovisual Archives (IASA) 12172

Association internationale d'archives sonores et audiovisuelles – Asociación Internacional de Archivos Sonoros y Audiovisuales – Internationale Vereinigung der Schall- und Audiovisuellen Archive

SG etv Pty Ltd, Block B – Longkloof Studios, Darters Road Gardens, Cape Town, 8001, South Africa. T. +27214814414. E-mail: secretary-general@iasa-web.org.
Pres M-Net, MultiChoice, Randburg, South Africa. T. +27116866176. E-mail: president@iasa-web.org.
URL: http://www.iasa-web.org/

History 1969, as *International Association of Sound Archives – Association internationale d'archives sonores – Internationale Vereinigung der Schallarchive*. Constitution of 1978, amended 12 May 1983, Washington DC (USA). Current Constitution and By-Laws adopted 9 Sep 1985, Berlin (German DR); amended: 12 Sep 1988, Vienna (Austria); 29 Sep 1992, Canberra (Australia); 8 Dec 1995, by postal ballot; 22 Sep 1999, Vienna. **Aims** Strengthen cooperation between archives and other institutions which preserve sound and audiovisual documents; initiate and encourage activities to develop and improve the organization, administration and contents of recorded sound and audiovisual collections. **Structure** General Assembly (annual); Executive Board. **Languages** English, French, German, Spanish. **Staff** None. **Finance** Sources: members' dues. **Activities** Events/meetings; knowledge management/information dissemination; networking/liaising; research/documentation. **Events** *Annual Conference* Mexico City (Mexico) 2022, *Annual Conference* 2021, *Annual Conference* Cape Town (South Africa) 2020, *Annual Conference* Amsterdam (Netherlands) 2019, *Annual Conference* Accra (Ghana) 2018. **Publications** *IASA Journal* (2 a year); *IASA Newsletter* (annual). Standards; guidelines.

Members Full; Honorary; Sustaining; Sponsoring. Members (336) in 70 countries and territories:
Albania, Andorra, Australia, Austria, Barbados, Belgium, Botswana, Brazil, Bulgaria, Burkina Faso, Canada, China, Congo DR, Croatia, Cuba, Czechia, Denmark, Djibouti, Egypt, Estonia, Finland, France, Germany, Ghana, Greece, Hungary, Iceland, India, Iran Islamic Rep, Ireland, Israel, Italy, Japan, Kenya, Latvia, Lithuania, Malawi, Malaysia, Mexico, Mozambique, Myanmar, Namibia, Netherlands, New Zealand, Nigeria, Norway, Oman, Pakistan, Papua New Guinea, Poland, Portugal, Puerto Rico, Russia, Singapore, Slovakia, Slovenia, South Africa, Spain, Sudan, Sweden, Switzerland, Tanzania UR, Thailand, Türkiye, UK, Uruguay, USA, Venezuela, Yemen, Zimbabwe.
International and regional organizations (8):
Archive of Maori and Pacific Sound (AMPS); International Institute of Social History (IISG); International Library of African Music (ILAM); School of Oriental and African Studies (SOAS); Stiftung Mozarteum Salzburg; UNESCO; *Union of International Associations (UIA, #20414); United Nations (UN, #20515).*

Consultative Status Consultative status granted from: *UNESCO (#20322)* (Consultative Status). **NGO Relations** Member of: *Co-ordinating Council of Audiovisual Archives Associations (CCAAA, #04820).* Participant in: *Europeana Foundation (#05839).* [2019/XC5129/y/**B**]

♦ International Association of Soup Industries (inactive)

♦ International Association for Southeast European Anthropology (InASEA) 12173

Association internationale d'anthropologie du sudest européen – Internationale Gesellschaft für die Anthropologie Südosteuropas

Pres Dept of Ethnology and Anthropology, Univ of Zadar, Franje Tudmana 24i, HR-23000 Zadar, Croatia.
URL: http://inasea.net/contacts/

History 2000, Sofia (Bulgaria). Successor to *Association of Balkan Anthropology (ABA, inactive)*, founded 1996. **Aims** Facilitate communication among scholars engaged in Southeast European studies; encourage understanding and development of this field of scholarship through professional communication and cooperation; facilitate international and interdisciplinary cooperation and the development of common projects. increase the presence of Southeast European anthropology in international anthropological discourse. **Structure** General Assembly (every 2 years). Executive Committee; Electoral Committee; Advisory Board; Editorial Board; special committees. **Languages** English, French, German. **Finance** Members' dues. Other sources: grants. **Activities** Areas of interest: Southeast European ethnology, cultural and social anthropology, folklore, ethnography, historical anthropology and cognate fields and disciplines. Organizes conferences, seminars, workshops and educational activities. **Events** *Biennial Conference* Regensburg (Germany) 2011, *Biennial Conference* Ankara (Turkey) 2009, *Conference / Biennial Conference* Timisoara (Romania) 2007, *Conference / Biennial Conference* Belgrade (Serbia-Montenegro) 2005, *Conference / Biennial Conference* Graz (Austria) 2003. **Publications** *Ethnologia Balkanica* (annual).

Members in 25 countries:
Albania, Austria, Belgium, Bulgaria, Canada, Croatia, Czechia, Finland, France, Germany, Greece, Hungary, Italy, Moldova, Netherlands, North Macedonia, Poland, Romania, Serbia, Slovenia, Sweden, Switzerland, Türkiye, UK, USA.

NGO Relations Member of: *World Council of Anthropological Associations (WCAA, #21317).* [2020/XM2261/**D**]

♦ International Association of South-East European Studies (#02693)
♦ International Association of Speakers Bureaus (internationally oriented national body)

♦ International Association for Special Education (IASE) 12174

Contact PO Box 170061, Milwaukee WI 53217, USA. E-mail: presidentiase@gmail.com.
URL: http://www.iase.org/

History 1985. Also referred to as *International Association for the Advancement of Special Education.* **Aims** Improve the quality of life and service delivery for all individuals with special needs. **Structure** Governing Committee. **Staff** Voluntary. **Finance** Members' dues. Other sources: conference fees; fundraising. **Activities** Awareness raising; networking/liaising; research and development; training/education; publishing activities; projects/programmes. **Events** *Biennial Conference* Tanzania UR 2019, *Biennial Conference* Perth, WA (Australia) 2017, *Biennial Conference* Wroclaw (Poland) 2015, *Biennial Conference* Vancouver, BC (Canada) 2013, *Biennial Conference* Windhoek (Namibia) 2011. **Publications** *Annuntiatus* (4 a year) – newsletter; *International Journal of Special Education* (annual). **Members** Regular; Institutional; Student. Membership countries not specified. **NGO Relations** Participates in: *Global Partnership on Children with Disabilities (GPcwd, #10529).* [2019.02.12/XD1313/**D**]

♦ International Association of Specialists in Energy (no recent information)

♦ International Association of Specialized Kinesiologists (IASK) 12175

Association internationale de kinésiologistes spécialisés

Contact 320 chemin de Labourdette, 31380 Gragnague, France. E-mail: iaskboard@gmail.com – home-office@iask.org.
Pres Kristinavägen 26, SE-141 32 Huddinge, Sweden.
URL: http://www.iask.org/

History 4 Jun 1987. Registration: USA, State of Nevada; France. **Aims** Establish the professional image of kinesiology worldwide; offer a platform for international exchange of personal and professional experiences; be a forum for the introduction and discussion of new kinesiology techniques; provide guidance to allow practitioners to assume their personal responsibility. **Structure** General Meeting (annually); Board of Directors; Executive Board. **Languages** English. **Staff** 9.00 FTE, voluntary. **Finance** Sources: members' dues. **Events** *Roots and Innovations* 2021, *Stress and the Immune System* 2020, *Conference* Moscow (Russia) 2019, *Annual General Meeting* Bergamo (Italy) 2017, *Meeting of Kinesiology Associations* Bergamo (Italy) 2017. **Publications** *News from the Board* in English. **Members** Regular; Honorary; Supporting; Associate. Membership countries not specified. [2023.02.15/XD8087/**D**]

♦ International Association for Spectral Imaging (IASIM) 12176

Editor BurgerMetrics, SIA, Peldu iela 7, Jelgava LV-3002, Latvia. T. +37129174908.
General: http://iasim14.iasim.net/

History Founded 2006, Umeå (Sweden), when proposed at NIR-Nord meeting, as *European Association for Spectral Imaging (EASIM).* Current title adopted, Mar 2009, Gembloux (Belgium). **Events** *Conference* Esbjerg (Denmark) 2022, *Conference* Skagen (Denmark) 2020, *Conference* Seattle, WA (USA) 2018, *Conference* Chamonix (France) 2016, *Conference* Rome (Italy) 2014. **Publications** *Journal of Spectral Imaging (JSI)* – online. **Members** Membership countries not specified. [2014/XJ0742/**D**]

♦ International Association of Spiritual Psychiatry (inactive)

♦ International Association of Sport Economists (IASE) 12177

Association internationale des économistes du sport

Headquarters c/o CDES, 13 rue de Genève, 87100 Limoges, France. T. +33555457600. Fax +33555457601. E-mail: iase@cdes.fr.
URL: http://www.iase-sport.org/

History 1999, Limoges (France). **Structure** General Meeting (annually); Board of Directors; Executive Committee. **Languages** English, French. **Events** *International Conference in Sport Economics* Rio de Janeiro (Brazil) 2014, *Conference* Prague (Czech Rep) 2013, *Conference* London (UK) 2012, *Conference* New Zealand 2011, *Conference* Portland, OR (USA) 2010. **Members** Individuals (100) in 20 countries. Membership countries not specified. [2016/XJ8080/v/**D**]

♦ International Association of Sport Kinetics (IASK) 12178

Internationale Gesellschaft für Sportmotorik – Miedzynarodowe Stowarzyszenie Motoryki Sportowej

Pres ul Trylogii 2/16, 01-982 Warsaw, Poland. Fax +48228350977. E-mail: insp@insp.waw.pl.
URL: http://www.internationalsportkinetics.org/

History Founded 28 Apr 1990, Rogi (Poland). **Aims** Create appropriate conditions for further development of human movement science and sport kinetics as a scientific discipline which constitutes a fundamental element in sciences related to sport. **Structure** General Assembly; Praesidium. **Languages** English, German, Polish. **Staff** Voluntary. **Finance** Members' dues. Private finance of President. **Activities** Events/meetings. **Events** *Biennial Conference* Biala Podlaska (Poland) 2015, *Biennial Conference* Rimini (Italy) 2013, *Biennial conference* Krakow (Poland) 2011, *Biennial Conference* Chalkidiki (Greece) 2009, *Biennial conference* Kallithea (Greece) 2009. **Publications** Books; conference proceedings. **Members** Full (241) in 31 countries. Membership countries not specified. **NGO Relations** Member of: *International Council of Sport Science and Physical Education (ICSSPE, #13077).* [2016.11.07/XD6167/**D**]

♦ International Association of Sport Research (inactive)

♦ International Association for Sports Information (IASI) 12179

Contact c/o National Sport Information Centre, Australian Sports Commission, Po Box 176, Belconnen ACT 2616, Australia. E-mail: nsic@ausport.gov.au.
URL: http://www.iasi.org/

History 1 Sep 1960, Rome (Italy), as a Committee of *International Council of Sport Science and Physical Education (ICSSPE, #13077).* **Aims** Encourage and support *documentation* and information on *physical education* and sport in all countries; coordinate efforts in this area following UNISIST guidelines; make projects of general interest known and assist in their realization; offer services to members and organs of ICSSPE, to other organizations working in the area of physical education and sport, to their members and to other interested persons and institutions; stimulate participation among members in international *databases.* **Structure** General Assembly (at least every 4 years). Praesidium, consisting of President, Vice-Presidents and Managerial Unit (Executive Secretary, Treasurer and Publications Officer). Secretariat. Executive Committee, comprising 25 members. Regional Bureaux in: Africa, Asia, Europe, Latin America, North America, Oceania. Ad Hoc Working Groups. **Languages** English. **Finance** Members' dues. Other sources: occasional grants from ICSSPE and other organizations; sale of publications. **Activities** Research/documentation; training/education; events/meetings; knowledge management/information dissemination. **Events** *Annual Meeting* San Juan (Puerto Rico) 2015, *Annual Meeting* Canberra, ACT (Australia) 2014, *Annual Meeting* Paris (France) 2013, *Annual Meeting* Leipzig (Germany) 2011, *Congress* Canberra, ACT (Australia) 2009. **Publications** *IASI Newsletter. Manual for a Sports Information Centre* in English, French, Spanish. Bibliographies on sport science and physical education; congress proceedings. **Information Services** *SPORT/IASI* – database.

Members National sport information centres, offices and libraries in 74 countries:
Argentina, Australia, Austria, Bahrain, Belarus, Belgium, Bolivia, Brazil, Canada, Chile, China, Colombia, Costa Rica, Cuba, Cyprus, Czechia, Denmark, Ecuador, Egypt, El Salvador, Estonia, Fiji, Finland, France, Germany, Greece, Guatemala, Honduras, Hong Kong, Hungary, Iceland, India, Iran Islamic Rep, Ireland, Israel, Italy, Japan, Jordan, Korea DPR, Latvia, Luxembourg, Macau, Malaysia, Mauritius, Mexico, Netherlands, New Zealand, Nigeria, Norway, Panama, Paraguay, Peru, Poland, Portugal, Romania, Russia, Saudi Arabia, Singapore, Slovakia, Slovenia, South Africa, Spain, Suriname, Sweden, Switzerland, Taiwan, Tanzania UR, Thailand, UK, United Arab Emirates, USA, Venezuela, Zimbabwe.
Individuals in 28 countries:
Australia, Austria, Belgium, Brazil, Canada, China, Ecuador, Egypt, France, Germany, India, Italy, Japan, Jordan, Macau, Mexico, Netherlands, Norway, Portugal, Romania, Russia, Saudi Arabia, South Africa, Spain, Switzerland, Taiwan, Tanzania UR, USA.

NGO Relations Recognized by: *International Olympic Committee (IOC, #14408).* [2017/XE3985/y/**E**]

♦ International Association of Sports Law (IASL) 12180

Association internationale du droit des sports (ASSIDS) – Asociación Internacional de Derecho Deportivo (ASIDD) – Internationale Vereinigung für Sportrecht (IVFS) – Internationale Vereniging voor Sportrecht (IVSR) – Associació Internacional del Dret de l'Esport (IASL)

Main Office 13 Veranzerou St, 106 77 Athens, Greece. T. +302103839440. Fax +302103839540. E-mail: info@iasl.org.
URL: http://iasl.org/

History 11 Dec 1992, Athens (Greece). 11-13 Dec 1992, Athens (Greece), during first International Congress. Originally referred to by French and Spanish initials *ASSIDS – AIDD.* Statutes adopted 12 Dec 1993, Athens. Registered in accordance with Greek law, 25 Jan 1994, Pyrgos (Greece), number: 17/3.12.92. **Aims** Promote cultivation and development of the science, research and teaching of sports law and the institution of the Olympic Games; promote studies of the international sports jurisprudence, programming and consultative in the legislative, administrative, organizational and practical section of sports law and the institution of the Olympic Games. **Structure** General Assembly (annual, at Congress); Board of Directors. **Languages** English, French, Irish Gaelic. **Staff** 2.00 FTE, paid. **Finance** Sources: contributions; donations; members' dues; subscriptions. **Activities** Events/meetings; research/documentation. **Events** *Congress* Athens (Greece) 2019, *Congress* Athens (Greece) 2018, *Congress* Rome (Italy) 2017, *Congress* Sochi (Russia) 2016, *Congress* Marrakech (Morocco) 2015. **Publications** *International Sports Law Review, PANDEKTIS* (2 a year) – official journal; *IASL Bulletin – Information* in English, Greek; *IASL Information Bulletin. Sports Law – Lex Sportiva and Lex Olympica, Theory and Praxis* (2011) by Dimitrios Panagiotopoulos. Congress proceedings.

Members Individual academics, teachers, students, lawyers, sport administrative personnel and government representatives together with organizations (marked ") in the field of sport. Members in 42 countries:
Albania, Algeria, Angola, Argentina, Australia, Belgium (*), Bulgaria, Chile, China, Costa Rica, Cyprus, Egypt, Estonia, Eswatini, Finland, France, Germany, Greece (*), Hungary, India, Iran Islamic Rep, Italy, Japan (*), Kenya, Latvia, Malaysia, Mexico, Netherlands, New Zealand, Nigeria, Poland (*), Portugal (*), Puerto Rico, Russia, Senegal, Spain, Sri Lanka, Suriname, Switzerland, Tunisia, UK, USA.
International organization (1):
Fédération internationale de basketball (FIBA, #09614).

NGO Relations Cooperates with: *International Bar Association (IBA, #12320).* [2020.03.03/XD4598/y/**C**]

♦ International Association for Sports and Leisure Facilities (#13319)

♦ International Association for Sports Surface Sciences (ISSS) 12181

Treas Hintergasse 15, 8253 Diessenhofen TG, Switzerland. T. +41527403005. E-mail: info@isss-sportsurfacescience.org.
URL: http://www.isss-sportsurfacescience.org/

History Founded 1985. Most recent statutes adopted 6 Nov 2003, Cologne (Germany). Registered in accordance with Swiss Civil Code. **Aims** Advance scientific and practical investigation of sport surfaces; disseminate information on the results to members and interested and concerned people. **Structure** General Meeting (annual); Executive Board; Working Groups; Secretariat. **Languages** English. **Staff** 1.00 FTE, paid. **Finance** Members' dues. **Activities** Networking/liaising; knowledge management/information dissemination; events/meetings. **Events** *Conference* Florence (Italy) 2016, *Conference* San Francisco, CA (USA) 2014, *Conference* Shanghai (China) 2012, *Conference* Paris (France) 2010, *Conference* Rome (Italy) 2008. **Publications** Papers of Technical Meetings – online.
Members Scientific institutes, testing laboratories, design professionals, sports federations and public authorities in 15 countries:
Australia, Austria, China, Denmark, France, Germany, Italy, Netherlands, New Zealand, Norway, Spain, Sweden, Switzerland, UK, USA.
Individuals in 7 countries:
Australia, Canada, Germany, Ireland, Norway, Switzerland, USA. [2017.10.11/XD7201/**D**]

♦ International Association for Stability and Handling of Liquid Fuels / see International Association for Stability, Handling and Use of Liquid Fuels (#12182)

♦ International Association for Stability, Handling and Use of Liquid Fuels (IASH) 12182

Administrator c/o Meeting Expectations, 3525 Piedmont Rd, Bldg 5 Ste 300, Atlanta GA 30305, USA. T. +17709495861. Fax +17709494566.
URL: http://www.iash.net/
History 1986, as *International Association for Stability and Handling of Liquid Fuels*. Incorporated in the State of Georgia (USA). **Aims** Promote research and experimentation on the scientific and operational factors affecting the stability and handling of fuels during their manufacture, blending, *transportation, storage* and use; provide a forum for the exchange of ideas and information. **Structure** Board of Directors, comprising Chairman, First and Second Vice-Chairs, Secretary, Treasurer and at least 10 members-at-large. **Languages** English. **Staff** Volunteers. **Finance** Members' dues (individual and sponsor). Other sources: conference registration fees. **Events** *International Conference* Dresden (Germany) 2021, *Biennial Conference* Rome (Italy) 2017, *Biennial Conference* Charleston, SC (USA) 2015, *Biennial Conference* Rhodes Is (Greece) 2013, *Biennial Conference* Sarasota, FL (USA) 2011. **Publications** Newsletter (2 a year); conference proceedings; CD-ROMs.
Members Individuals in 31 countries:
Australia, Austria, Belgium, Brazil, Bulgaria, Canada, China, Colombia, Czechia, Denmark, Finland, France, Germany, Greece, Israel, Italy, Korea Rep, Kuwait, Netherlands, Norway, Philippines, Poland, Saudi Arabia, South Africa, Spain, Sweden, Switzerland, UK, United Arab Emirates, USA, Venezuela. [2020/XD3601/v/**C**]

♦ International Association of the Staff of the European Organization for the Safety of Air Navigation / see AIPE-International Association of EUROCONTROL Staff (#00597)
♦ International Association of State Lotteries (inactive)

♦ International Association for Statistical Computing (IASC) 12183

Association internationale pour l'informatique statistique (AIIS)
Permanent Office PO Box 24070, 2490 AB The Hague, Netherlands. T. +31703375737. Fax +31703860025.
URL: http://www.iasc-isi.org/
History Dec 1977, Delhi (India). Founded as a section of *International Statistical Institute (ISI, #15603)*. **Aims** Promote the theory, methods and practice of statistical computing; foster interest and knowledge in effective and efficient statistical computing. **Structure** General Assembly (normally every 2 years); Council; Executive Committee; Regional Sections (3). **Languages** Arabic, Chinese, English, French, German, Italian, Japanese, Korean, Portuguese, Russian, Spanish. **Staff** Administered by the ISI Permanent Office. **Finance** Members' dues. Other sources: governmental and institutional subventions; corporate membership dues. **Events** *STATCOMP: Asian Regional Conference on Statistical Computing* Kyoto (Japan) 2022, *Data, Science, Statistics and Visualisation Conference (DSSV)* Tainan (Taiwan) 2022, *COMPSTAT : Biennial Symposium on Computational Statistics* Bologna (Italy) 2021, *Latin American Conference on Statistical Computing* Mexico City (Mexico) 2021, *Data, Science, Statistics and Visualisation Conference (DSSV)* Rotterdam (Netherlands) 2021. **Publications** *Computational Statistics and Data Analysis* (periodical); *Statistical Software Newsletter* (periodical). Proceedings of COMPSTAT Symposia; Proceedings of ARS Conferences.
Members Individuals (511) in 58 countries and territories:
Albania, Algeria, Argentina, Australia, Austria, Belgium, Brazil, Bulgaria, Canada, Chile, China, Colombia, Croatia, Czechia, Denmark, Estonia, Finland, France, Germany, Ghana, Greece, Hong Kong, Hungary, India, Iran Islamic Rep, Ireland, Italy, Japan, Korea Rep, Kuwait, Lithuania, Luxembourg, Malaysia, Mexico, Netherlands, New Zealand, Norway, Peru, Philippines, Poland, Portugal, Romania, Russia, Saudi Arabia, Serbia, Singapore, Slovakia, Slovenia, South Africa, Spain, Sweden, Switzerland, Syrian AR, Tanzania UR, Trinidad-Tobago, Türkiye, UK, USA. [2022/XD1976/v/**E**]

♦ International Association for Statistics Education (IASE) 12184

Association internationale pour l'enseignement statistique (AIES)
Operations Manager PO Box 24070, 2490 AB The Hague, Netherlands. T. +31703375728. Fax +31703860025.
URL: https://iase-web.org/
History 1991, Cairo (Egypt). Founded as a section of *International Statistical Institute (ISI, #15603)*. First elected Executive Committee took office 1993. **Aims** Develop and improve statistics education on a worldwide basis, particularly in *developing countries*; provide a forum for those concerned with statistics education; take the lead in and respond to issues in statistics education and training. **Structure** Executive Committee, including President, President-elect, 4 Vice-Presidents, 3 Co-opted members and Executive Director. President is member *'ex officio'* of ISI Council. **Finance** Members' dues. Finance managed by ISI office. **Activities** Responsible for all ISI education meetings, including: International Conference on the Teaching of Statistics (ICOTS) (every 4 years); roundtables; scientific meetings; meetings on education at ISI World Statistics Congress. Subgroups include those of university staff teaching statistics and of researchers on teaching and learning. **Events** *International Conference on Teaching Statistics (ICOTS)* Rosario (Argentina) 2022, *International Conference on Teaching Statistics* Kyoto (Japan) 2018, *International Conference on Teaching Statistics* Flagstaff, AZ (USA) 2014, *international conference on teaching statistics* Ljubljana (Slovenia) 2010, *International conference on applied statistics for development in Africa* Cotonou (Benin) 2007. **Publications** *IASE Newsletter* (3 a year); *IASE Review* (occasional); *Journal of Statistics Education* – electronic journal on Internet (ARIS). Electronic archive of information, software, and discussions related to statistics and statistics education. **Members** Individuals (302) in 58 countries. Membership countries not specified. **IGO Relations** *UNESCO (#20322)*. **NGO Relations** Sponsors roundtable at quadrennial conference of: *International Commission on Mathematical Instruction (ICMI, #12700)*. Sister organization of: *International Association for Statistical Computing (IASC, #12183)*. [2022/XE2125/v/**E**]

♦ International Association for Statistics in Physical Sciences / see Bernoulli Society for Mathematical Statistics and Probability (#03212)

♦ International Association for Steiner/Waldorf Early Childhood Education (IASWECE) 12185

Contact PO Box 34, SE-161 26 Stockholm, Sweden. T. +46855170250. Fax +4686949350. E-mail: info@iaswece.org.
Registered Address Neuarlesheimerstrasse 15, 4143 Dornach SO, Switzerland.
URL: https://iaswece.org/
History 19 Oct 1969, Stuttgart (Germany). Former names and other names: *Internationale Vereinigung der Waldorfkindergärten* – former; *International Waldorf Kindergarten Association* – former. **Aims** Support and deepen the work of Waldorf early *childhood* centres around the world and the work of Waldorf training programmes for early childhood educators; coordinate the work of Waldorf early childhood education with related organizations; promote research in child development and early childhood education. **Structure** Council; Coordinating Group; Board. **Finance** Sources: gifts, legacies; members' dues. **Activities** Events/meetings; projects/programmes; training/education. **Events** *World Early Childhood Conference* Dornach (Switzerland) 2019, *Unfolding Conference* Brussels (Belgium) 2013, *Conference* Hannover (Germany) 2006, *Playing, encountering and learning* Dornach (Switzerland) 2005, *Summer meeting* Vienna (Austria) 1999. **Publications** *IASWECE Newsletter*. Books.
Members Country associations in 40 countries and territories:
Australia, Austria, Belgium, Brazil, Canada, China, Czechia, Denmark, Estonia, Finland, France, Germany, Hungary, India, Ireland, Israel, Italy, Japan, Kenya, Korea Rep, Lithuania, Mexico, Netherlands, New Zealand, Norway, Poland, Romania, Russia, Slovenia, South Africa, Spain, Sweden, Switzerland, Taiwan, Tanzania UR, Uganda, UK, Ukraine, USA, Vietnam.
IGO Relations *UNESCO (#20322)*; *UNICEF (#20332)*. **NGO Relations** Member of (1): *Alliance ELIANT (#00672)*. Partner of (2): *European Council for Steiner Waldorf Education (ECSWE, #06844)*; *International Forum for Steiner/Waldorf-Education (Hague Circle, #13653)*. [2023/XN8597/**B**]

♦ International Association for Structural Control / see International Association for Structural Control and Monitoring (#12186)

♦ International Association for Structural Control and Monitoring (IASCM) 12186

SG USC Civil Engineering, 3620 S Vermont Ave, KAP210 MC2531, Los Angeles CA 90089-2531, USA. T. +12137400602. Fax +12137441426.
URL: http://www.usc.edu/dept/civil_eng/structural/welcome.html
History 1994. Former names and other names: *International Association for Structural Control (IASC)* – former. Registration: USA, State of California. **Aims** Advance the science and practice of structural control, and monitoring, by means of education, research and application of knowledge, including the response of structures to earthquakes, wind and man-made forces. **Structure** Board of Directors. **Languages** English. **Activities** Events/meetings. **Events** *World Conference* Orlando, FL (USA) 2022, *World Conference* Qingdao (China) 2018, *World Conference* Barcelona (Spain) 2014, *World conference* Tokyo (Japan) 2010, *World Conference* San Diego, CA (USA) 2006. **Publications** *IASC Newsletter*.
Members Regional Organizations of Structural Control and Monitoring Panels in 6 countries:
Australia, China, India, Japan, Korea Rep, USA.
Members also in Europe. Membership countries not specified.
NGO Relations Affiliated organization of: *International Union of Theoretical and Applied Mechanics (IUTAM, #15823)*. [2022.10.19/XD9352/**D**]

♦ International Association of Structural Engineering and Mechanics (internationally oriented national body)

♦ International Association for Structural Mechanics in Reactor Technology (IASMiRT) 12187

Contact NC State Univ, Campus Box 7908, Raleigh NC 27695-7908, USA. T. +19195155277. Fax +19195155301. E-mail: iasmirtinfo@gmail.com.
Vice-Pres/Sec c/o KINGS, KEPCO International Nuclear Graduate School, 658-91 Haemaji-ro, Seosaeng-myeon, Ulju-gun, Ulsan 689-882, Korea Rep.
URL: http://www.iasmirt.org/
History 1971, Berlin West (Germany FR). **Aims** Promote and foster international scientific engineering communication in the field; promote the technological goals of safe and economic exploitation of fission nuclear power and of eventually bringing fusion nuclear power into being. **Structure** Officers: President; Vice-President; Treasurer; Secretary; Advisor General. Regional Divisions (4): American; European; Japanese; Chinese. **Languages** English. **Staff** None. **Finance** Conference registration fees. **Activities** Organizes International SMiRT Conferences (every 2 years). Assists in organizing international seminars. **Events** *Biennial Conference* Yokohama (Japan) 2024, *Biennial Conference* Berlin (Germany) 2022, *Biennial Conference* Berlin (Germany) 2021, *Biennial Conference* Charlotte, NC (USA) 2019, *Conference* Tokyo (Japan) 2017. **Publications** *Nuclear Engineering and Design* – official journal. Conference Transactions (every 2 years).
Members Individuals in 29 countries:
Algeria, Australia, Austria, Belgium, Brazil, Bulgaria, Canada, China, Czechia, Finland, France, Germany, Greece, India, Iran Islamic Rep, Italy, Japan, Korea Rep, Netherlands, Portugal, Romania, Russia, Slovakia, Slovenia, Spain, Sweden, Switzerland, UK, USA.
IGO Relations *International Atomic Energy Agency (IAEA, #12294)*. [2014/XD5794/v/**D**]

♦ International Association for Structural Safety and Reliability (IASSAR) 12188

Pres College of Civil Engineering, Tongji University, 1239 Siping Road, 200092 Shanghai, China.
URL: http://iassar.net/
History 1985. **Aims** Promote and sponsor the *International Conferences on Structural Safety and Reliability (ICOSSAR)*. **Structure** Executive Board, comprising Chairman, 2 immediate Past-Presidents and 7 members. Other officers: President; Executive Vice President. **Activities** Award Committee grants Senior and Junior Research Awards. Committee on Stochastic Methods in Structural Engineering, comprising 5 subcommittees. **Events** *International Conference on Structural Safety & Reliability (ICOSSAR)* Shanghai (China) 2022, *International Conference on Structural Safety & Reliability (ICOSSAR)* Shanghai (China) 2021, *International Symposium on Reliability Engineering and Risk Management* Singapore (Singapore) 2018, *International Conference on Structural Safety & Reliability (ICOSSAR)* Vienna (Austria) 2017, *Quadrennial Conference* New York, NY (USA) 2013. [2020/XD7685/**D**]

♦ International Association of Structural / Tectonic Geologists (inactive)

♦ International Association of Student Affairs and Services (IASAS) . 12189

Main Office Rue de Treves 49 bte 3, 1040 Brussels, Belgium. E-mail: enquiries@iasas.global.
Sec Pace Univ, 207 Kessel Ctr, 861 Bedford Rd, Pleasantville NY 10570, USA.
URL: http://iasas.global/
History 2000. Founded on the initiative of Roger Luderman, as an informal network of student affairs professionals. Founded with legal structure 1 Mar 2010. Registration: Banque-Carrefour des Entreprises, No/ID: 0537.228.659, Start date: 1 Aug 2013, Belgium. **Aims** Act as a global advocate for higher education institutions and students, student affairs and services professionals and practitioners, and for the profession, research and scholarship itself. **Structure** General Assembly; Board of Management; Regional Coordinators. **Languages** English. **Staff** None. **Finance** Sources: donations; honorariums. **Activities** Advocacy/lobbying/activism; events/meetings; guidance/assistance/consulting. **Publications** *Student Affairs and Services in Higher Education: Global Foundations, Issues and Best Practices* (2009); *The Role of Student Affairs and Services in Higher Education: A Practical Manual for Developing, Implementing, and Assessing Student Affairs Programmes and Services* (2002); *Supporting Students Globally in Higher Education*.
Members Effective; Adherent. Individuals and organizations. Membership countries not specified. Included in the above, 1 organization listed in this Yearbook:
Included in the above, 1 organization listed in this Yearbook:
European University College Association (EucA, #09028). [2020.04.01/XM3935/y/**B**]

♦ International Association for Student Insurance Services (IASIS) .. 12190

Manager Keizersgracht 174-176, 1016 DW Amsterdam, Netherlands. T. +31204212800. Fax +31204212810.
URL: http://www.iasis-insure.org/
History Set up within *International Student Travel Confederation (ISTC, inactive)*, as *ISTC Commission on International Student Insurance Service (ISIS)*. Subsequently became independent under ISTC umbrella, originally with the title *International Student Insurance Services Association (ISIS Association)*; present title adopted Oct 1993, Vienna (Austria), on revision of statutes. Previously a sector association within *World Youth Student and Educational Travel Confederation (WYSE Travel Confederation, #21959)*. **Aims** Fulfil young peoples' global travel ambitions by ensuring the best possible risk protection to meet travel, study and adventure needs. **Structure** Annual General Meeting; Executive Board. **Languages** English. **Staff** 1.00 FTE, paid. **Finance** Members' dues. **Activities** Advocacy/lobbying/activism; financial and/or material support; research/documentation. **Events** *Annual general meeting / General Meeting* Miami, FL (USA) 1998, *Annual general meeting / General Meeting* Paris (France) 1997, *General Meeting* Gold Coast, QLD (Australia) 1996, *Annual general meeting / General Meeting* Sitges (Spain) 1995, *General Meeting* Vancouver, BC (Canada) 1994. **Members** Distributors of insurance cover operating in the youth, student and education travel market. Membership countries not specified. **NGO Relations** *International Social Security Association (ISSA, #14885)*. [2019.02.13/XE1451/**E**]

♦ **International Association of Students in Agricultural and Related Sciences (IAAS)** 12191

Pres c/o IAAS Headquarters, Kasteelpark Arenberg 20, Bus 4020, 3001 Leuven, Belgium. E-mail: president@iaasworld.org – info@iaasworld.org.
URL: http://www.iaasworld.org/

History 15 Jul 1957, Tunis (Tunisia). Established following initial meetings of students in agriculture in Bucharest (Romania), 1954, Paris (France), 1956. Founding World Congress, Tunis (Tunisia), 1957, after particular cooperation between students from NSR (Netherlands) and UGET (Tunisia). Former names and other names: *Association Internationale des Etudiants en Agriculture (AIEA)* – former (1957); *International Association of Agricultural Students* – former; *Asociación Internacional de Estudiantes de Agricultura* – former; *Mezdunarodnyj Sojuz Selskohozjajstvennyh Studentov* – former. Registration: Banque-Carrefour des Entreprises, No/ID: 0443.807.266, Start date: 4 Apr 1991, Belgium. **Aims** Promote exchange of experience, knowledge, and ideas and improve cooperation and mutual understanding between students in the field of agriculture and related sciences all over the world; encourage formation and development of local organizations of Students in Agricultural and Related Sciences; promote sustainable agriculture, economics and food production. **Structure** Global Executives; Global Control Boards; Global Quality Boards; Regional Boards; National Committee; Local Committee. **Languages** Dutch, English, French, Spanish. **Staff** Voluntary. **Finance** Sources: contributions; fundraising; members' dues; revenue from activities/projects; sponsorship. Annual budget: 25,000 EUR. **Activities** Events/meetings; training/education. Active in all member countries. **Events** *International Conference for Youth in Agriculture* Bonn (Germany) 2022, *Annual Congress and General Assembly* Alanya (Turkey) 2021, *Annual Congress and General Assembly* Leuven (Belgium) 2020, *Annual Congress and General Assembly* Abidjan (Côte d'Ivoire) 2019, *International Conference for Youth in Agriculture* Leuven (Belgium) 2019. **Publications** *IAAS World* (annual). Annual review; congress, meeting and seminar reports.

Members Student and youth associations representing 100,000 students of agronomy, agricultural economics and technology, food science, landscape architecture, forestry and environmental studies. Full members in 55 countries and territories:
Afghanistan, Argentina, Austria, Bangladesh, Belgium, Benin, Bulgaria, Chile, Colombia, Costa Rica, Côte d'Ivoire, Croatia, Czechia, Ecuador, Finland, France, Gambia, Germany, Ghana, Greece, Guatemala, India, Indonesia, Iran Islamic Rep, Italy, Kenya, Madagascar, Mali, Mexico, Montenegro, Morocco, Nepal, Netherlands, Niger, Nigeria, Panama, Paraguay, Peru, Poland, Portugal, Rwanda, Serbia, Slovenia, Spain, Sweden, Switzerland, Taiwan, Tajikistan, Togo, Tunisia, Türkiye, Uganda, Ukraine, USA, Zimbabwe.
Candidate members in 10 countries:
Australia, Azerbaijan, Brazil, China, Hungary, Japan, Malta, Pakistan, Uzbekistan, Venezuela.

Consultative Status Consultative status granted from: *ECOSOC (#05331)* (Ros C); *UNESCO (#20322)* (Consultative Status); *FAO (#09260)* (Liaison Status); *UNEP (#20299)*. **NGO Relations** Member of (1): *The Right to Research Coalition (no recent information)*. Partner of (2): *Informal Forum of International Student Organizations (IFISO, #11193)*; *International Student One Health Alliance (ISOHA)*. Contacts with individual faculty student organizations, youth organizations and other organizations in related fields, in particular: *AIESEC (#00593)*; *Association for European Life Science Universities (ICA, #02519)*; *Board of European Students of Technology (BEST, #03294)*; *Europe de l'enseignement agronomique (Eurõpea, #09153)*; *European Geography Association for Students and Young Geographers (EGEA, #07388)*; *The European Law Students' Association (ELSA, #07660)*; *European Students' Union (ESU, #08848)*; *International Association of Dental Students (IADS, #11839)*; *International Federation of Medical Students' Associations (IFMSA, #13478)*; *International Forestry Students' Association (IFSA, #13628)*; *International Pharmaceutical Students' Federation (IPSF, #14568)*.
[2022/XC1249/**C**]

♦ International Association of Student Television and Radio (no recent information)
♦ International Association of Studies on Mecanography (inactive)
♦ International Association of Studies on Mediterranean Civilizations (inactive)
♦ International Association for Studies of Men (no recent information)
♦ International Association for the Studies of South-East Asia (inactive)
♦ International Association for the Study of Ancient Mosaics (#02689)
♦ International Association for the Study of Anglo-Irish Literature / see International Association for the Study of Irish Literatures (#12201)
♦ International Association for the Study of Antisemitism (inactive)

♦ **International Association for the Study of Attention and Performance** 12192

Sec Leiden Univ, Cognitive Psychology Unit, Wassenaarseweg 52, 2333 AK Leiden, Netherlands.
URL: http://home.planet.nl/~homme247/AP/Main.html

History 1976, Netherlands, following symposium series begun in 1966. **Aims** Increase and disseminate scientific information in the area of human attention, performance and *information processing*; foster international communication in the area; provide an international forum for both established and young and promising scientists to present their work. **Structure** Advisory Council. Executive Committee, comprising Chair, Secretary, Treasurer and up to 6 members. **Languages** English. **Staff** Voluntary. **Finance** Not financed. **Activities** Organizes Bi-Annual Attention And Performance Symposia (invitation only). **Publications** Proceedings. **Members** No membership. [2014.06.01/XU8748/**E**]

♦ International Association for the Study of Cancer (inactive)

♦ **International Association for the Study of Canon Law** 12193
Association internationale pour l'étude du droit canon – Consociatio Internationalis Studio Iuris Canonici Promovendo

Pres Pontificia Univ della Santa Croce, Piazza di Sant'Apollinare 49, Via die Farnesi 83, 00186 Rome RM, Italy. E-mail: presidente@consociatio.org – info@consociatio.org.
URL: http://www.consociatio.org/

History Mar 1973, Rome (Italy). Registration: Italy. **Events** *International Congress* Paris (France) 2022, *International Congress* Paris (France) 2021, *Webinaire* Paris (France) 2021, *International Congress* Rome (Italy) 2017, *International Congress* Washington, DC (USA) 2014. **Members** Membership countries not specified. [2021/XD5341/**D**]

♦ **International Association for the Study of Child Language (IASCL)** 12194
Association Internationale pour l'Etude du Langage Enfantin

Treas Coupland Bldg 1, Psychological Sciences, Univ of Manchester, Oxford Road, Manchester, M13 9PL, UK.
URL: https://iascl.talkbank.org/

History 1970, Brno (Czechia). Statutes adopted 1970 and amended 1993, 1996 and 2008. Registration: Charity Commission, No/ID: SC038873, Scotland. **Aims** Promote international and interdisciplinary cooperation in the study of child language. **Structure** Executive Committee. Nominating and Appointing Committee. Officers: President; Vice-President; Secretary; Assistant Secretary; Treasurer; Assistant Treasurer. **Languages** English, French. **Finance** Sources: members' dues. **Events** *Triennial Congress* 2021, *Triennial Congress* Philadelphia, PA (USA) 2020, *Triennial Congress* Lyon (France) 2017, *Triennial Congress* Amsterdam (Netherlands) 2014, *Triennial Congress* Montréal, QC (Canada) 2011. **Publications** *Child Language Bulletin* (2 a year).
Members Individuals in 42 countries and territories:
Australia, Austria, Belgium, Brazil, Canada, China, Cyprus, Czechia, Denmark, Finland, France, Germany, Greece, Hong Kong, Hungary, Iceland, Iran Islamic Rep, Ireland, Israel, Italy, Japan, Kenya, Malta, Mexico, Netherlands, New Zealand, Norway, Pakistan, Poland, Portugal, Russia, Saudi Arabia, Singapore, Slovakia, Slovenia, Spain, Sweden, Switzerland, Taiwan, Türkiye, UK, USA. [2021/XJ3019/**C**]

♦ International Association for the Study of Clays (#02688)
♦ International Association for the Study of Common Property / see International Association for the Study of the Commons (#12195)

♦ **International Association for the Study of the Commons (IASC)** 12195

Exec Dir c/o Global Biosocial Complexity Initiative, PO Box 872701, Tempe AZ 85287-2701, USA. E-mail: iasc@iasc-commons.org.
Registered Office 513 N Park Ave, Bloomington IN 47408, USA.
URL: http://www.iasc-commons.org/

History 1989. Former names and other names: *International Association for the Study of Common Property (IASCP)* – former (1989 to 2006). **Aims** Bring together interdisciplinary researchers, practitioners and policy makers so as to foster better understandings, improvements and *sustainable* solutions for environmental, electronic and any other type of *shared resource* that is a commons or a common pool resource. **Structure** General Meeting (annual); Executive Council. **Finance** Members' dues. Donations from institutions. **Activities** Publishing activities; events/meetings; knowledge management/information dissemination. **Events** *Biennial Conference* Tempe, AZ (USA) 2021, *Biennial Conference* Lima (Peru) 2019, *Biennial Conference* Utrecht (Netherlands) 2017, *Thematic Conference on Knowledge Commons* Paris (France) 2016, *Biennial Conference* Edmonton, AB (Canada) 2015. **Publications** *Commons Digest* (4 a year); *International Journal of the Commons* (2 a year). **Members** Institutions and individuals (over 1,000). Membership countries not specified.
[2021/XG3718/**D**]

♦ **International Association for the Study of Controversies (IASC)** 12196

Vice-Pres Dipto Studi Umanistici, Univ del Salento, Via V M Stampacchia 45, 73100 Lecce BT, Italy. T. +39832294662. E-mail: vicepresident@iasc.me.
URL: http://www.iasc.me/

History 1995. **Aims** Engage in the study of actual controversies; encourage development of appropriate tools for controversy study and management; seek actively to apply results of studies to conflict management in areas of practical activity, therefore not limiting them to theoretical purposes. **Structure** Assembly. **Staff** None. **Activities** Events/meetings; research/documentation. **Events** *International Conference* Beijing (China) 2018, *International Conference* Lisbon (Portugal) 2017, *International Conference* Pisa (Italy) 2016, *International Conference* Tel Aviv (Israel) 2015, *International Conference* Lecce (Italy) 2014. **Publications** *Parardoxes of Conflicts* (2016); *Perspectives on Theories of Controversies and the Ethics of Communication* (2014).
Members Light; Full; Honorary. Individuals in 27 countries and territories:
Argentina, Australia, Austria, Belgium, Benin, Brazil, Burkina Faso, Chile, China, Denmark, Finland, France, Germany, Greece, Hungary, Israel, Italy, Mexico, Netherlands, Palestine, Poland, Portugal, Romania, Spain, Switzerland, Taiwan, UK.
NGO Relations Accredited by (1): *International Federation of Philosophical Societies (FISP, #13507)*.
[2021/XD8871/**D**]

♦ International Association for the Study and Development of Marketing and the Distribution of Food Products and Consumer Goods / see International Association for the Distributive Trade (#11851)
♦ International Association for the Study of Disorders of Iron Metabolism (inactive)

♦ **International Association for the Study of Dreams (IASD)** 12197

Contact 1672 University Avenue, Berkeley CA 94703, USA. T. +12097240889. Fax +12097240889. E-mail: office@asdreams.org.
URL: http://www.asdreams.org/

History 1983. Registration: USA, California. **Aims** Promote scientific research and personal exploration of the study of dreams; provide an educational forum for the interdisciplinary exchange and discussion of such information among the scientific and professional communities and the general public. **Structure** Board of Directors; Executive Committee. Advisory Committees (19): Advertising and Public Relations; Arts; Procedures and Bylaws; Conference; Continuing Education; Development; Education; Ethics Global Advisory; Heritage Fund; Nominating; Membership; Regionals, including Membership Registrations and Communications Team; Past Presidents Advisory; Publications; Regional Events; Research Grant; Research; Social Networking, including subcommittee; Student Awards. **Activities** Advocacy/lobbying/activism; awareness raising; events/meetings; knowledge management/information dissemination. **Events** *Annual Conference* 2021, *Annual Conference* Scottsdale, AZ (USA) 2020, *Annual Conference* Kerkrade (Netherlands) 2019, *Annual Conference* Scottsdale, AZ (USA) 2018, *Annual Conference* Anaheim, CA (USA) 2017. **Publications** *Dream Time* (3 a year) – magazine; *Dreaming* – journal; *IASD Newsletter*. [2021/XM2601/**C**]

♦ International Association for the Study of the European Quaternary / see International Union for Quaternary Research (#15811)

♦ **International Association for the Study of Forced Migration (IASFM)** 12198

Address not obtained.
URL: http://www.iasfm.org/

History Jan 1994. **Aims** promote and increase scientific knowledge of forced migration; advance the understanding of appropriate and effective practice concerning forced migration. **Structure** General Meeting (annual); Executive Committee. Working Groups (3): International Refugee Law; International Relations; Internally Displaced Persons. **Languages** English. **Staff** 2.00 FTE, voluntary. **Finance** Sources: donations; members' dues. **Activities** Awards/prizes/competitions; events/meetings. **Events** *Conference* Accra (Ghana) 2021, *Conference* Accra (Ghana) 2020, *Conference* Thessaloniki (Greece) 2018, *Conference* Cartagena de Indias (Colombia) 2014, *Contested spaces and cartographic challenges* Kolkata (India) 2013. **Publications** *IASFM Newsletter*. Annual Report.
Members Full in 42 countries and territories:
Australia, Austria, Bangladesh, Belgium, Bosnia-Herzegovina, Canada, Congo DR, Croatia, Denmark, Egypt, Estonia, France, Germany, Ghana, Greece, India, Indonesia, Italy, Japan, Jordan, Kenya, Latvia, Mexico, Morocco, Mozambique, Netherlands, Nigeria, Norway, Pakistan, Palestine, Philippines, Russia, Singapore, South Africa, Spain, Sudan, Sweden, Switzerland, Thailand, Uganda, UK, USA.
NGO Relations Secretariat at: *Refugee Studies Centre, Oxford (RSC)*. [2021/XD5014/**C**]

♦ International Association for the Study of Fossil Cnidaria / see International Association for the Study of Fossil Cnidaria and Porifera (#12199)

♦ **International Association for the Study of Fossil Cnidaria and Porifera (IASFCP)** 12199

Sec Univ Paul Sabatier, GET, 14 av E Belin, 31400 Toulouse, France. E-mail: tom-asz.wrzolek@us.edu.pl.
URL: http://www.cnidaria.nat.uni-erlangen.de/IASFCP/

History 1971, Novosibirsk (USSR), as an international research group of *International Palaeontological Association (IPA, #14501)*. Previously referred to as *International Association for the Study of Fossil Cnidaria*. **Aims** Promote international exchange of information on research on fossil *corals* and *sponges*. **Structure** General Assembly; Council. **Languages** English. **Staff** 2.00 FTE, voluntary. **Finance** Members' dues. **Events** *Quadrennial Symposium* Muscat (Oman) 2015, *Quadrennial Symposium* Liège (Belgium) 2011, *Quadrennial Symposium* St Petersburg (Russia) 2007, *Quadrennial Symposium* Graz (Austria) 2003, *Quadrennial Symposium* Sendai (Japan) 1999. **Publications** *Fossil Cnidaria and Porifera* (annual) – online.
Members Individuals in 46 countries:
Argentina, Armenia, Australia, Austria, Belgium, Brazil, Bulgaria, Canada, China, Croatia, Czechia, Denmark, Dominican Rep, Egypt, Estonia, France, Germany, Hungary, India, Iran Islamic Rep, Ireland, Italy, Japan, Kazakhstan, Korea Rep, Mexico, Morocco, Netherlands, Nigeria, Norway, Panama, Poland, Portugal, Romania, Russia, Slovenia, Spain, Sweden, Switzerland, Taiwan, Tajikistan, Türkiye, UK, Ukraine, USA, Vietnam. [2019.02.12/XD1823/v/**E**]

♦ **International Association for the Study of German Politics (IAGSP)** 12200

Sec POLCES Dept, Univ of Sussex, Falmer, Brighton, BN1 9SN, UK. T. +441273877648.
URL: http://www.iasgp.org/

History 1974, as *Association for the Study of German Politics (ASGP) – Association pour l'étude de la politique allemande – Asociación para el Estudio de la Politica Alemana – Vereinigung für das Studium der Deutschen Politik*. Present name and structure adopted, 2007, upon merger with (USA) 'German Politics Association'. **Aims** Encourage teaching and research in the politics and society of the Federal Republic of *Germany*, *Austria* and *Switzerland*. **Languages** English, German. **Staff** 4.00 FTE, paid; 8.00 FTE, voluntary. **Finance** Members' dues. Royalties from books. Budget (annual): about pounds2,000. **Activities** Holds annual conferences, with invited speakers from German-speaking countries. Organizes and sponsors other conferences, seminars and especially research workshops. **Events** *Annual Conference* London (UK) 2014, *Annual Conference* London (UK) 2013, *Annual Conference* London (UK) 2012, *Annual Conference* London (UK) 2011, *Annual Conference* London (UK) 2010. **Publications** *German Politics* (4 a year). Books.
Members Individuals in 6 countries:
Austria, France, Germany, Netherlands, UK, USA. [2010/XE5881/v/**E**]

♦ International Association for the Study of History of Religions / see International Association for the History of Religions (#11936)
♦ International Association for the Study of Human Palaeontology (no recent information)
♦ International Association for the Study of Insurance Economics / see Geneva Association (#10119)

♦ International Association for the Study of Irish Literatures (IASIL) . 12201

Chairperson An Foras Feasa, National Univ Ireland – Maynooth, Maynooth, CO. KILDARE, Ireland.
URL: http://www.iasil.org/

History 1969, as *International Association for the Study of Anglo-Irish Literature (IASAIL)*. **Aims** Encourage teaching and study of Irish *writing* in *higher education education* worldwide; facilitate international contact among scholars already teaching and doing research in this field; serve as a vehicle for bringing Irish writing to a wider audience. **Structure** Officers: Chairperson, Secretary, Treasurer, 2 Sub-Treasurers, 14 International Representatives. **Languages** English, Irish Gaelic. **Staff** None. **Finance** Members' dues. **Events** *Annual Conference* Dublin (Ireland) 2019, *United Nations/Argentina Workshop on Applications of Global Navigation Satellite Systems* Falda del Carmen (Argentina) 2018, *Annual Conference* Nijmegen (Netherlands) 2018, *Annual Conference* Singapore (Singapore) 2017, *Annual Conference* Cork (Ireland) 2016.
Members IASIL-Japan (a federated branch with 250 members) and individuals. Members in 39 countries:
Argentina, Australia, Austria, Belgium, Brazil, Bulgaria, Canada, China, Croatia, Czechia, Denmark, Egypt, Finland, France, Germany, Greece, Hungary, India, Ireland, Israel, Italy, Japan, Lithuania, Monaco, Netherlands, New Zealand, Norway, Poland, Portugal, Russia, Serbia, Singapore, Slovakia, South Africa, Spain, Sweden, Switzerland, UK, USA. [2012.06.01/XE0868/E]

♦ International Association for the Study of the Italian Language and Literature (AISLLI) 12202

Association internationale pour l'étude de la langue et la littérature italienne – Associazione Internazionale per gli Studi di Lingua e Letteratura Italiana (AISLLI)
Sec/Treas Univ of Pensylvania, Center for Italian Studies, 549 Williams Hall, 255 South 36th St, Philadelphia PA 19104-6305, USA. T. +12158986040. Fax +12158980933. E-mail: italians@sas.upenn.edu.
Pres address not obtained.
URL: http://www.sas.upenn.edu/italians/aislli/

History 1950, Florence (Italy). Founded at 1st International Congress of Modern Languages and Literatures. **Aims** Promote knowledge of Italian language and literature worldwide. **Structure** International Board. Officers: International President; Italian President; Secretary/Treasurer; Honorary President. **Events** *Triennial Congress* Philadelphia, PA (USA) 2016, *Triennial Congress* Philadelphia, PA (USA) 2013, *Triennial Congress* Philadelphia, PA (USA) 2009, *Triennial Congress* Trieste (Italy) 2006, *Triennial congress* Louvain-la-Neuve (Belgium) / Antwerp (Belgium) / Brussels (Belgium) 2003.
Members Individuals (about 1,200) in 32 countries:
Argentina, Australia, Austria, Belgium, Brazil, Canada, Croatia, Denmark, Finland, France, Germany, Hungary, India, Ireland, Israel, Italy, Japan, Malta, Mexico, Netherlands, Norway, Poland, Romania, Slovakia, Slovenia, Spain, Sweden, Switzerland, Tunisia, UK, Uruguay, USA.
NGO Relations Member of: *International Council for Philosophy and Human Sciences (CIPSH, #13061)*; *International Federation for Modern Languages and Literatures (#13480)*. [2020.09.08/XD3849/v/C]

♦ International Association for the Study of the Liver (IASL) 12203

Association internationale pour l'étude du foie – Internationale Gesellschaft zum Studium der Leberkrankheiten – Asociación Internacional para el Estudio del Hígado
Office Hanshin Bldg 12, Suite 1711, Mapo-daero, Mapo-gu, Seoul 04175, Korea Rep. T. +8223731005. Fax +8223731106. E-mail: iasl@hbni.co.kr.
Pres Klinikum Klagenfurt am Wörthersee, Feschnigstrasse 11, 9020 Klagenfurt am Wörthersee, Austria.
URL: http://www.iasliver.org/

History 1958, Washington, DC (USA). By-laws approved by General Assembly, Sep 17 1986, Caracas (Venezuela). **Aims** Foster the training of experts in *hepatology*; encourage basic and clinical research on the liver and its diseases; facilitate internationally the prevention, recognition and treatment of diseases of the liver and biliary tract. **Structure** General Assembly (every 2 years). Council (meets at General Assembly), consisting of President, President-elect, Vice-President, Secretary-Treasurer (elected at General Membership Meeting and at biennial meeting), 9 councillors (elected by regional associations) and Immediate Past-President. Members are proposed by regional associations or by Council. **Languages** English. **Staff** Voluntary. **Finance** Sources: members' dues. **Activities** Events/meetings; knowledge management/information dissemination; networking/liaising. Organizes international study groups; encourages exchange of research workers, study materials and information. **Events** *Annual Conference* Seoul (Korea Rep) 2021, *Congress* Beijing (China) 2019, *International Workshop on HIV Pediatrics* Mexico City (Mexico) 2019, *Annual Congress* Dubai (United Arab Emirates) 2018, *International Workshop on HIV Pediatrics* Paris (France) 2017. **Publications** *Liver International* (6 a year) – journal.
Members Individuals in 65 countries and territories:
Albania, Algeria, Argentina, Australia, Austria, Bangladesh, Belgium, Bolivia, Brazil, Bulgaria, Canada, Chile, China, Colombia, Costa Rica, Czechia, Denmark, Egypt, Estonia, Finland, France, Germany, Ghana, Greece, Hong Kong, Hungary, India, Indonesia, Ireland, Israel, Italy, Japan, Kenya, Korea DPR, Korea Rep, Kuwait, Mexico, Myanmar, Netherlands, New Zealand, Nigeria, Norway, Pakistan, Peru, Philippines, Poland, Portugal, Romania, Saudi Arabia, Singapore, Slovakia, South Africa, Spain, Sri Lanka, Sweden, Switzerland, Syrian AR, Taiwan, Thailand, Türkiye, Uganda, UK, Uruguay, USA, Venezuela.
Constituent Associations (5):
African Association for the Study of Liver Diseases (AFASLD, no recent information); *American Association for the Study of Liver Diseases (AASLD)*; *Asian Pacific Association for the Study of the Liver (APASL, #01602)*; *European Association for the Study of the Liver (EASL, #06233)*; *Latin American Association for the Study of the Liver (LASL, #16252)*. [2021/XB1240/y/A]

♦ International Association for the Study of Lung Cancer (IASLC) . . . 12204

Association internationale pour l'étude du cancer du poumon
Headquarters 999 17th Street, Suite 200, Denver CO 80202-2725, USA. T. +18554642752. E-mail: info@iaslc.org.
URL: http://www.iaslc.org/

History 26 Oct 1974, Florence (Italy). Founded during 9th International Cancer Congress, the idea of setting up such an association having been launched at 1st International Workshop for the Therapy of Lung Cancer, 20 Oct 1972, Washington DC (USA). Statutes adopted Oct 1974, Florence; most recently revised Jul 2005. **Aims** Promote the study of *etiology*, *epidemiology*, prevention, diagnosis, treatment and all other aspects of lung cancer. **Structure** World Conference (annual); Board; Executive Committee. **Languages** English. **Staff** 16.00 FTE, paid. **Finance** Sources: members' dues. **Activities** Events/meetings; knowledge management/information dissemination. **Events** *World Conference on Lung Cancer* San Diego, CA (USA) 2024, *World Conference on Lung Cancer* Singapore (Singapore) 2023, *World Conference on Lung Cancer* Vienna (Austria) 2022, *World Conference on Lung Cancer* 2021, *ELCC : European Lung Cancer Conference* Lugano (Switzerland) 2021. **Publications** *Journal of Thoracic Oncology (JTO)*. **Members** Individuals (about 5,000) in 85 countries. Membership countries not specified. [2022/XC6831/v/C]

♦ International Association for the Study of Maritime Mission (IASMM) 12205

Exec Dir 123 Haven Street, PO Box 160, Reading MA 01867, USA.
URL: http://iasmm.org/

History 3 Jun 1990, Leeds (UK). Became operational at 1st International Conference, 7 Apr 1991, Tilbury (UK). Current constitution approved 27 Apr 1995, Liverpool. **Aims** Provide a forum for debate, dissemination of information and ideas in maritime mission; promote preservation, cataloguing and publicizing of sources for research; encourage maritime mission studies in places of learning. **Structure** General Meeting (every 2 years, after Conference); General Committee. **Languages** English. **Staff** Voluntary. **Finance** Sources: donations. **Activities** Events/meetings. **Events** *Biennial Conference* Barcelona (Spain) 2007, *Biennial Conference* England (UK) 2004, *Biennial Conference* UK 2004, *Biennial Conference* Ireland 2002, *Biennial conference* South Africa 1999. **Publications** *Maritime Mission Studies – The Journal of the International Association for the Study of Maritime Mission* (periodically). Occasional papers; books.
Members Organizations and individuals in 17 countries:
Australia, Brazil, Canada, Finland, France, Germany, Holy See, Ireland, Italy, Korea DPR, Netherlands, Norway, Philippines, South Africa, Spain, Türkiye, UK. [2022.02.15/XD2977/D]

♦ International Association for the Study of Medieval and Modern Period Mediterranean Ceramics (#02711)
♦ International Association for the Study of Obesity / see World Obesity (#21678)
♦ International Association for the Study of Organized Crime (internationally oriented national body)

♦ International Association for the Study of Pain (IASP) 12206

Association internationale pour l'étude de la douleur
CEO FASAE CAE, 1510 H St NW, Ste 600, Washington DC 20005, USA. T. +12025245300. Fax +12025245301. E-mail: iaspdesk@iasp-pain.org.
URL: http://www.iasp-pain.org/

History May 1973, Washington, DC (USA). Founded on the initiative of Prof John J Bonica (1917-1994). Registration: Start date: 9 May 1974, USA, Washington DC. **Aims** Foster research, improve patient management, promote education and training in the field of chronic pain, acute pain and cancer pain. **Structure** General Assembly; Council; Executive Committee; Task Forces and Working Groups; National Chapters (89); Special Interest Groups. Advocacy group: *Global Alliance of Partners for Pain Advocacy (GAPPA, #10217)*. **Languages** English. **Staff** 17.00 FTE, paid. **Finance** Sources: grants; meeting proceeds; members' dues; sale of publications. Other sources: royalties. Annual budget: US$ 4,000,000 – 8,000,000. **Activities** Advocacy/lobbying/activism; awards/prizes/competitions; events/meetings; training/education. **Events** *International Symposium on Pediatric Pain* Halifax, NS (Canada) 2023, *International Congress on Neuropathic Pain* Lisbon (Portugal) 2023, *International Symposium on Pediatric Pain* Auckland (New Zealand) 2022, *World Congress on Pain* Toronto, ON (Canada) 2022, *World Congress on Pain* Washington, DC (USA) 2021. **Publications** *PAIN* (12 a year) – journal; *PAIN e-monthly* (12 a year) – newsletter; *PAIN Reports* (12 a year) – journal; *Pain: Clinical Updates* (8 a year). Numerous titles published through IASP Press. **Members** Individuals (8,000) Regular; Trainee; Retired; Contributing; Honorary. Members in 126 countries. Membership countries not specified.
Consultative Status Consultative status granted from: *ECOSOC (#05331)* (Ros C); *WHO (#20950)* (Official Relations). **NGO Relations** Member of (1): *Global Health Council (GHC, #10402)*. Instrumental in setting up (3): *Association of South-East Asian Pain Societies (ASEAPS, #02922)*; *European Pain Federation (EFIC, #08131)*; *Federación Latinoamericana de Asociaciones para el Estudio del Dolor (FEDELAT, #09343)*. [2022/XB4589/v/B]

♦ International Association for the Study of Peace and Prejudice (no recent information)
♦ International Association for the Study of People and their Physical Surroundings / see International Association for People-Environment Studies (#12075)
♦ International Association for the Study of Persian-Speaking Societies / see Association for the Study of Persianate Societies

♦ International Association for the Study of Popular Music (IASPM) . . 12207

Association internationale pour l'étude de la musique populaire
Gen Sec PO Box 80, SE-901 03 Umeå, Sweden. E-mail: secretary@iaspm.net.
URL: http://www.iaspm.net/

History Sep 1981. **Aims** Promote inquiry, scholarship and analysis in the area of popular music. **Structure** General Meeting; Executive Committee. Branch Committees at national and regional levels. **Languages** English. **Staff** Voluntary. **Finance** Sources: members' dues. **Activities** Events/meetings; research/documentation. **Events** *Biennial Conference* Daegu (Korea Rep) 2022, *Latin America Congress (IASPM-AL)* Valparaiso (Chile) 2022, *Biennial Conference* Daegu (Korea Rep) 2021, *Biennial Conference* Canberra, ACT (Australia) 2019, *Biennial Conference* Kassel (Germany) 2017. **Publications** *Review of Popular Music (RPM)* (periodical) – newsletter; *Journal of Popular Music Studies*. *Encyclopedia of Popular Music of the World (EPMOW)* – in 6 vols. Conference proceedings. Information Services: database.
Members Individual, Institutional and Supporting in 54 countries and territories:
Argentina, Australia, Bahrain, Belgium, Brazil, Bulgaria, Canada, Chile, China, Croatia, Cuba, Czechia, Denmark, Finland, France, Germany, Ghana, Greece, Hong Kong, India, Indonesia, Iran Islamic Rep, Ireland, Israel, Italy, Japan, Kenya, Korea Rep, Lithuania, Mexico, Montenegro, Netherlands, New Zealand, Nigeria, Norway, Pakistan, Papua New Guinea, Philippines, Poland, Puerto Rico, Russia, Serbia, Singapore, Slovenia, South Africa, Spain, Sweden, Taiwan, Türkiye, Uganda, UK, Uruguay, USA, Venezuela. [2022/XD9606/D]

♦ International Association for the Study of Pre-Columbian Cultures of the Lesser Antilles / see International Association for Caribbean Archaeology (#11756)
♦ International Association for the Study of Psychiatric Disorders of Childbearing / see International Marcé Society for Perinatal Mental Health (#14089)
♦ International Association for the Study of Questions Relating to Higher Technical Education (inactive)
♦ International Association for the Study of Racism (inactive)
♦ International Association for the Study of Radiolarians / see International Association of Radiolarian Palaeontologists (#12120)

♦ International Association for the Study of Scottish Literatures (IASSL) 12208

Contact address not obtained. E-mail: iassl@glasgow.ac.uk.
URL: https://www.iassl.org/

History 2014, Glasgow (UK). Registration: Scottish Charity Regulator, No/ID: SC044410, Scotland. **Aims** Cultivate the study of Scottish languages, literatures and cultures across the globe. **Structure** Executive Committee. **Finance** Sources: members' dues. **Activities** Awards/prizes/competitions; events/meetings. **Events** *World Congress of Scottish Literatures* Prague (Czechia) 2022, *World Congress of Scottish Literatures* Prague (Czechia) 2021, *World Congress of Scottish Literature* Prague (Czechia) 2020, *World Congress of Scottish Literatures* Glasgow (UK) 2014. [2022/AA2087/j/E]

♦ International Association for the Study of Sexuality, Culture and Society (inactive)
♦ International Association for the Study of Spiritual and Theological Teachings (inactive)

♦ International Association for the Study of Traditional Asian Medicine (IASTAM) 12209

Pres Chinazentrum Univ Kiel, Leibnizstrasse 10, 24118 Kiel, Germany.
URL: http://www.iastam.org/

History 1977. **Aims** Promote and encourage the study of traditional medicine, including classical systems and local and tribal traditions, in all their aspects. **Structure** General Meeting; Council. **Languages** English. **Staff** None. **Finance** Sources: members' dues. **Activities** Events/meetings. **Events** *Conference* Taipei (Taiwan) 2023, *Conference* Kiel (Germany) 2017, *Conference* Changwon (Korea Rep) 2013, *Congress / Conference* Thimphu (Bhutan) 2009, *Authenticity, best practice, and the evidence mosaic, the challenge of integrating traditional East Asian medicines into Western health care* London (UK) 2007. **Publications** *Asian Medicine Newsletter* (6 a year); *Asian Medicine – Tradition and Modernity*. **NGO Relations** Also links with national organizations. [2020.06.23/XU6012/D]

♦ International Association for the Study of Traditional Environments (IASTE) 12210

Coordinator 207 E 5th Ave, Suite 258, Eugene OR 97401, USA. T. +15417127832 – +15412212495. E-mail: coordinator@iaste.org.
URL: http://iaste.org/

History Apr 1988, Berkeley CA (USA), at 1st International Symposium on Traditional Dwellings and Settlements. **Aims** Serve as an umbrella association for all scholars studying vernacular, indigenous, popular and traditional environments; emphasize and foster the need for an interdisciplinary approach to the study of traditional environments; encourage use of comparative and *cross-cultural* methods. **Languages** English. **Finance** Members' dues. **Activities** Events/meetings; publishing activities; knowledge management/information dissemination; research/documentation. **Events** *Biennial Conference* Nottingham (UK) 2021, *Biennial Conference* Nottingham (UK) 2020, *Biennial Conference* Coimbra (Portugal) 2018, *Biennial Conference* Kuwait (Kuwait) 2016, *Biennial Conference* Kuala Lumpur (Malaysia) 2014. **Publications** *Traditional Dwellings and Settlements Review* (2 a year). *Traditional Dwellings and Settlements Working Papers Series* – papers presented at IASTE conferences.
Members Individuals and institutions in 64 countries and territories:

Algeria, Argentina, Australia, Austria, Bahrain, Bangladesh, Belgium, Brazil, Canada, Chile, China, Colombia, Costa Rica, Croatia, Cyprus, Denmark, Egypt, Eritrea, Finland, France, Germany, Greece, Guatemala, Hong Kong, India, Indonesia, Iran Islamic Rep, Ireland, Israel, Italy, Japan, Jordan, Korea Rep, Kuwait, Lebanon, Malaysia, Malta, Mexico, Morocco, Nepal, Netherlands, New Zealand, Nigeria, Norway, Pakistan, Palestine, Portugal, Puerto Rico, Saudi Arabia, Singapore, South Africa, Spain, Sri Lanka, Sweden, Switzerland, Syrian AR, Taiwan, Thailand, Tunisia, Türkiye, UK, United Arab Emirates, USA, Venezuela.
[2020.02.26/XF1366/v/F]

♦ International Association for the Study of Traumatic Brain Injury (inactive)

♦ International Association for the Study of Youth Ministry (IASYM) . 12211

Conference Academic Chair address not obtained.
URL: http://iasym.net/

History Constitution adopted Jan 2015, London (UK). Registered as Charity in England and Wales: 1114169. **Aims** Further the international study, research and teaching of ministry; work with youth, rooted in the *Christian* theological tradition. **Structure** Executive Committee. **Finance** Sources: members' dues. **Activities** Awareness raising; events/meetings; knowledge management/information dissemination. **Events** *Biennial European Conference* Copenhagen (Denmark) 2023, *Biennial European Conference* Helsinki (Finland) 2021, *Biennial European Conference* Helsinki (Finland) 2020, *Biennial Conference* Sydney, NSW (Australia) 2017. **Publications** *Journal of Youth and Theology* (2 a year). **Members** Individuals; Affiliate institutions. Membership countries not specified. [2018/XM6507/C]

♦ International Association of Sufism (IAS) 12212

Contact 14 Commercial Blvd, Ste 101, Novato CA 94949, USA. E-mail: ias@ias.org.
URL: http://www.ias.org/

History 1983, USA. **Aims** Introduce Sufism to the public; make known the inter-relation between Sufi principles and scientific principles; provide a forum for continuing dialogue between the different schools of Sufism; preserve and advance the study and goals of Sufism. **Languages** English, Persian. **Staff** 50.00 FTE, voluntary. **Finance** Sources: contributions; fundraising; members' dues; subscriptions. **Activities** Events/meetings; projects/programmes. **Events** *Annual Symposium* San Rafael, CA (USA) 2011, *Annual Symposium* San Rafael, CA (USA) 2010, *Annual Symposium* San Rafael, CA (USA) 2009, *Annual Symposium* Cairo (Egypt) 2008, *Annual Symposium* California (USA) 2001. **Publications** *Sufi Women* (4 a year) – newsletter; *Insight* (2 a year); *Sufism: An Inquiry* (2 a year); *Sufism and Psychology* (annual) – newsletter. *Shah Maghsoud: Life and Legacy* (1st ed 2022) by Dr Nahid Angha; *Caravan:Biographies from Sufism Symposia1994-2014* (2nd ed, 2022 2015) by Dr Nahid Angha in English; *Sufi Women: the Journey towards the Beloved: Collected Essays* (1st ed 1998) by Dr Hamaseh Kianfar and Dr Sahar Kianfar. **Members** Membership countries not specified. **IGO Relations** Associated with Department of Global Communications of the United Nations.
[2022.05.18/XD5981/v/D]

♦ International Association for Suicide Prevention / see International Association for Suicide Prevention and Crisis Intervention (#12213)

♦ International Association for Suicide Prevention and Crisis Intervention (IASP) 12213

Association internationale pour la prévention du suicide et l'intervention en cas de suicide (AIPS) – Internationale Vereinigung für Selbstmordprophylaxe und Krisenintervention (IVSP)

Coordinator c/o AAS, 5221 Wisconsin Ave NW, Washington DC 20015, USA. E-mail: admin@iasp.info.
Events Manager address not obtained.
URL: http://www.iasp.info/

History 1960, Vienna (Austria). Former names and other names: *International Association for Suicide Prevention* – former; *Association internationale pour la prévention du suicide* – former; *Asociación Internacional para la Prevención del Suicido* – former; *Internationale Vereinigung für Selbstmordprophylaxe* – former. Registration: 501(c)(3) non-profit charitable, No/ID: EIN 20-4701041, USA. **Aims** Prevent suicidal behaviour; alleviate its effects; provide a forum for academics, mental health professionals, crisis workers, volunteers and suicide survivors. **Structure** General Assembly (every 2 years, at Congress); Executive Board; Central Administrative Office. **Languages** English, French, German. **Staff** 1.20 FTE, paid. **Finance** Sources: contributions; members' dues; subsidies. **Activities** Events/meetings. **Events** *World Congress* Piran (Slovenia) 2023, *Asia Pacific Regional Conference* Gold Coast, QLD (Australia) 2022, *World Congress* Gold Coast, QLD (Australia) 2021, *Asia Pacific Regional Conference* Taipei (Taiwan) 2020, *Biennial International Congress* Londonderry (UK) 2019. **Publications** *Crisis – International Journal of Crisis Intervention and Suicide Prevention* (4 a year); *IASP Newsletter*. Congress proceedings.
Members Individuals; Organizations. Members in over 50 countries. Membership countries not specified.
International organization (1):
International organization (1):
International Federation of Telephone Emergency Services (IFOTES, #13567).
Consultative Status Consultative status granted from: *ECOSOC (#05331)* (Ros C); *WHO (#20950)* (Official Relations). **IGO Relations** Accredited by: *United Nations Office at Vienna (UNOV, #20604).* Associated with Department of Global Communications of the United Nations. [2021/XC1210/y/C]

♦ International Association of Supercomputing Centers (IASC) 12214

Contact address not obtained. E-mail: helloworld@supercomputingcenters.org.
URL: https://www.supercomputingcenters.org/

History 2022, Hamburg (Germany). Officially launched at ISC High Performance. Founded by Lawrence Livermore National Laboratory (LLNL), Science and Technology Council (STFC), Hartree Centre, National Center for Supercomputing Applications (NCSA) and Leibniz Supercomputing Centre (LRZ). **Aims** Examine and communicate best practice for centre management; study and suggest solutions for common challenges; foster communication and collaboration among centres, collaborators and users. **Activities** Events/meetings. **Members** Centres in 3 countries:
Germany, UK, USA. [2022/AA3258/C]

♦ International Association of Supreme Administrative Jurisdictions (IASAJ) 12215

Association internationale des hautes juridictions administratives (AIHJA)

Sec c/o Conseil d'Etat, Place du Palais Royal, 75100 Paris, France. T. +33140208011. Fax +33140208134. E-mail: aihja@conseil-etat.fr.
Contact address not obtained.
URL: http://www.aihja.org/

History 9 Dec 1983, Paris (France). Established at Constitutive Congress, following recommendations, 1 Jul 1980, Madrid (Spain), of Congress of the International Institute of Administrative Sciences (IIAS). Registered in accordance with French law. Registration: France. **Aims** Contribute to development of *law* by encouraging exchange of views and experience among jurisdictions. **Structure** General Assembly (every 3 years at Congress); Board; Council of Administration. **Languages** English, French. **Staff** 2.00 FTE, voluntary. **Finance** Sources: donations; grants; members' dues. Other sources: cost of Congress defrayed by host country. **Activities** Events/meetings; networking/liaising; publishing activities. **Events** *Congress* Brussels (Belgium) 2022, *Congress* Mexico 2019, *Congress* Istanbul (Turkey) 2016, *Triennial Congress* Cartagena de Indias (Colombia) 2013, *Meeting* Abidjan (Côte d'Ivoire) 2012. **Publications** *Recueils des Décisions des hautes juridictions administratives – Selections of Decisions of Supreme Administrative jurisdictions.* Congress reports.
Members Jurisdictions in 55 countries:
Algeria, Australia, Austria, Belgium, Benin, Burkina Faso, Cameroon, Canada, Cape Verde, Chad, Chile, China, Colombia, Costa Rica, Côte d'Ivoire, Cyprus, Czechia, Egypt, Finland, France, Germany, Greece, Guinea, Hungary, Ireland, Israel, Italy, Korea Rep, Lebanon, Lithuania, Luxembourg, Madagascar, Mali, Malta, Mexico, Morocco, Mozambique, Netherlands, Norway, Poland, Portugal, Romania, Senegal, Slovakia, Slovenia, Spain, Suriname, Sweden, Switzerland, Thailand, Togo, Tunisia, Türkiye, Ukraine, Uruguay.
International jurisdiction:
Observers in 25 countries:
Angola, Bangladesh, Bolivia, Brunei Darussalam, Cambodia, Congo DR, Denmark, Gambia, Holy See, Iceland, Japan, Kenya, Laos, Malaysia, Monaco, New Zealand, Niger, Pakistan, Panama, Paraguay, Philippines, Singapore, UK, USA, Vietnam.
International Observers (4):
Council of Europe (CE, #04881); ILO (#11123); International Institute of Administrative Sciences (IIAS, #13859); United Nations (UN, #20515). [2022/XD9556/y/C*]

♦ International Association of Surgeons and Gastroenterologists / see International Association of Surgeons, Gastroenterologists and Oncologists (#12216)

♦ International Association of Surgeons, Gastroenterologists and Oncologists (IASGO) 12216

Contact 64-103 Higashiyama, Kamitakano, Sakyo-ku, Kyoto, 601-1255 Japan. E-mail: office@iasgo.org.
URL: http://www.iasgo.org/

History 1988, Amsterdam (Netherlands). Founded following the Medical Faculty of Amsterdam University's acceptance of a proposal by Prof Lygidakis and Prof Vanderheiden to initiate an international medical foundation. Former names and other names: *International Surgical Club* – former (1988); *International Gastro-Surgical Club (IGSC)* – former (1988); *International Association of Surgeons and Gastroenterologists (IASG)* – former. **Aims** Improve standards of medical care; globalize current medical knowledge; pioneer and innovate steps for further progress of knowledge; bridge the gap that exists in quality and standard of medical care worldwide. **Languages** English. **Activities** Events/meetings; training/education. **Events** *World Congress* Taipei (Taiwan) 2021, *Annual World Congress* Taipei (Taiwan) 2020, *Annual World Congress* Bangkok (Thailand) 2019, *Annual World Congress* Moscow (Russia) 2018, *Regional Meeting* Tokyo (Japan) 2018. **Publications** *Surgery Gastroenterology and Oncology (SGO)* (6 a year) – journal. **Members** Full in 90 countries. Membership countries not specified. **NGO Relations** Instrumental in setting up: *International School of Surgical Oncology, Strasbourg (ISSO, no recent information).* [2021/XF4403/F]

♦ International Association for the Surgery of Trauma and Surgical Intensive Care / see International Association for Trauma Surgery and Intensive Care (#12239)
♦ International Association of Surgical Blade Manufacturers (inactive)

♦ International Association for Surgical Metabolism and Nutrition (IASMEN) 12217

Sec-Treas c/o ISS-SIC, Seefeldstrasse 88, 8008 Zurich ZH, Switzerland. T. +41445337650. Fax +41445337659. E-mail: surgery@iss-sic.com.
Pres address not obtained.
URL: http://www.iasmen.org/

History Aug 1993, Hong Kong, at 35th World Congress of Surgery of *International Society of Surgery (ISS, #15496)*, when statutes were adopted. **Aims** Promote the theoretical and practical aspects of surgical nutrition as a field of primary importance in surgical care; promote scientific exchange and communication among surgeons and organizations having a prime interest in research, education and training in surgical metabolism and nutrition. **Structure** General Assembly (biennial, at ISS/SIC World Congress); Executive Board; Advisory Council; Regional Council; National Delegates; International Committee. **Finance** Sources: donations; grants; members' dues. **Events** *Meeting* Yokohama (Japan) 2011, *Meeting* Adelaide, SA (Australia) 2009, *Meeting* Montréal, QC (Canada) 2007, *Meeting* Durban (South Africa) 2005, *Meeting* Bangkok (Thailand) 2003.
Members Individuals in 35 countries and territories:
Argentina, Belgium, Brazil, Canada, Chile, China, Colombia, Costa Rica, Cuba, Ecuador, El Salvador, Finland, France, Germany, Greece, Guatemala, Hong Kong, India, Italy, Japan, Korea Rep, Mexico, New Zealand, Norway, Panama, Paraguay, Peru, Portugal, Spain, Sweden, Switzerland, Thailand, Uruguay, USA, Venezuela.
NGO Relations Integrated Society of International Society of Surgery. [2020.03.13/XD4116/v/C]

♦ International Association of Survey Statisticians (IASS) 12218

Association internationale des statisticiens d'enquêtes (AISE)

Scientific Secretary c/o ISI Permanent Office, PO Box 24070, 2490 AB The Hague, Netherlands. T. +31703375737. Fax +31703860025.
Pres address not obtained. E-mail: sheering@umich.edu.
URL: http://isi-iass.org/

History 1973, Vienna (Austria), during 39th Session of *International Statistical Institute (ISI, #15603)*, as a section of ISI. **Aims** Promote study and development of the theory and practice of statistical censuses and surveys and associated subjects; foster interest in these subjects among statisticians, organizations, institutions, governments and the general public all over the world. **Structure** Council; Executive Committee. **Languages** English, French. **Staff** Voluntary. **Finance** Members' dues. **Activities** Training/education; awards/prizes/competitions; knowledge management/information dissemination; networking/liaising; events/meetings. **Events** *Biennial General Assembly* Durban (South Africa) 2009, *Baltic-Nordic conference on survey sampling* Kuusamo (Finland) 2007, *Biennial General Assembly* Lisbon (Portugal) 2007, *ICES : international conference on establishment surveys* Montréal, QC (Canada) 2007, *Conference on complex sampling, retrospective sampling and missing data* Auckland (New Zealand) 2005. **Publications** *Survey Statistician* (2 a year) in English, French, Spanish. Directory of members; conference booklets.
Members Individuals (999) in 118 countries and territories:
Albania, Algeria, Antigua-Barbuda, Argentina, Armenia, Australia, Austria, Bangladesh, Barbados, Belgium, Benin, Bhutan, Bosnia-Herzegovina, Botswana, Brazil, Burkina Faso, Burundi, Canada, Cape Verde, Central African Rep, Chad, Chile, China, Colombia, Comoros, Congo Brazzaville, Congo DR, Costa Rica, Côte d'Ivoire, Croatia, Czechia, Denmark, Dominican Rep, Ecuador, Egypt, El Salvador, Estonia, Ethiopia, Fiji, Finland, France, Gabon, Gambia, Germany, Ghana, Greece, Guatemala, Haiti, Honduras, Hungary, India, Indonesia, Iran Islamic Rep, Ireland, Israel, Italy, Jamaica, Japan, Jordan, Kenya, Korea Rep, Latvia, Lebanon, Lesotho, Liberia, Lithuania, Luxembourg, Madagascar, Malaysia, Mali, Mauritania, Mauritius, Mexico, Morocco, Myanmar, Netherlands, New Zealand, Niger, Nigeria, Norway, Oman, Pakistan, Palestine, Panama, Paraguay, Peru, Philippines, Poland, Portugal, Romania, Russia, Rwanda, Sao Tomé-Principe, Saudi Arabia, Senegal, Sierra Leone, Singapore, Slovakia, Slovenia, South Africa, Spain, Sweden, Switzerland, Taiwan, Tanzania UR, Thailand, Togo, Trinidad-Tobago, Türkiye, Uganda, UK, Ukraine, United Arab Emirates, Uruguay, USA, Venezuela, Zambia, Zimbabwe.
IGO Relations *UNESCO (#20322).* [2017.06.01/XE3673/v/E]

♦ International Association for Sustainable Aviation (internationally oriented national body)
♦ International Association of Sylviculturists and Users of Forest and Wood Products (inactive)
♦ International Association of Synthesis of Knowledge (no recent information)
♦ International Association of Tamil Research (no recent information)
♦ International Association of Tariff-Specialists / see International Association of Tariff-Specialists – Organization of Tariff and Transport Experts (#12219)

♦ International Association of Tariff-Specialists – Organization of Tariff and Transport Experts 12219

Association internationale des tarifeurs – Organisation des experts des tarifs et des transports – Internationaler Verband der Tarifeure – Organisation der Tarif- und Transportexperten (IVT)

Contact Postfach 55, Europaplatz 1, 1150 Vienna, Austria. E-mail: office@ivt-int.org.
URL: http://www.ivt-int.org

History 21 Sep 1911, Trieste (Italy). Formal foundation 1930, Vienna (Austria). Discontinued during World War II and refounded in 1970, Vienna. Current Statutes adopted 1984. Original title: *International Association of Tariff-Specialists – Association internationale des tarifeurs – Internationaler Verband der Tarifeure.* **Aims** Unite national and regional groups working in the field of tariffs for *traffic* and transport organizations; promote tariff specialists as a *professional* group; promote technical interests of members acting at the international level in the field of *transportation* and *logistics*. **Structure** General Assembly (every 4 years); Presidency; Court of Arbitration. **Languages** English, French, German, Russian. **Staff** 4.00 FTE, voluntary. **Finance** Members' dues. **Activities** Events/meetings; training/education; guidance/assistance/consulting. **Events** *Meeting of the Presidency* Leoben (Austria) 2018, *Meeting of the Presidency* Košice (Slovakia) 2017, *General Assembly* Vienna (Austria) 2016, *Meeting* Sopron (Hungary) 2015, *Meeting of the Presidency* Belgrade (Serbia) 2014. **Publications** *100 Jahre Internationaler Verband der Tarifeure IVT* (2011).
Members Full (national associations and individuals); Affiliated; Subscribing; Associate; Honorary. Members in 19 countries:
Austria, Bosnia-Herzegovina, Bulgaria, Croatia, Czechia, France, Germany, Hungary, Italy, Liechtenstein, Montenegro, Netherlands, North Macedonia, Poland, Serbia, Slovakia, Slovenia, Switzerland, UK.
IGO Relations *Organisation intergouvernementale pour les transports internationaux ferroviaires (OTIF, #17807).* **NGO Relations** *Comité international des transports ferroviaires (CIT, #04188); International Union of Railways (#15813).* [2017.10.27/XD2933/D]

♦ International Association for Task-Based Language Teaching (IATBLT) 12220

Contact address not obtained. E-mail: info@tblt.org.
URL: http://www.tblt.org/

History Registered in accordance with Belgian law. **Aims** Promote principled approaches to Task-Based Language Teaching (TBLT). **Structure** Executive Board. **Finance** Sources: members' dues. **Activities** Events/meetings. **Events** *Conference* Innsbruck (Austria) 2022, *Conference* Ottawa, ON (Canada) 2019, *Conference* Barcelona (Spain) 2017, *Biennial Conference* Leuven (Belgium) 2015, *Biennial Conference* Banff, AB (Canada) 2013. [2017/XM5851/**C**]

♦ International Association of Tax Judges (IATJ) 12221

Pres Tax Court Canada, 200 Kent St, Ottawa ON K1A 0M1, Canada. T. +16139922159. Fax +16139965863. E-mail: iatj.net@gmail.com.
URL: http://www.iatj.net/

History Statutes adopted, 2010. Registered in accordance with Dutch law. **Aims** Promote the exchange of views and experiences on matters submitted to tax Judges around the world, including information on the organization and functioning of Tax Courts or Tribunals and the rules of law in jurisdictions worldwide. **Structure** General Assembly; Board of Directors; Executive. **Languages** English. **Finance** Sources: members' dues. **Events** *Assembly* Madrid (Spain) 2016, *Assembly* Washington, DC (USA) 2014, *Assembly* Amsterdam (Netherlands) 2013, *Assembly* Munich (Germany) 2012, *Assembly* Paris (France) 2011. **Publications** *IATJ Newsletter* (3 a year).

Members Courts; Tribunals; Administrative Bodies; (retired) Judges. Members in 38 countries and territories:
Argentina, Australia, Austria, Belgium, Brazil, Canada, Colombia, Denmark, England, Estonia, Finland, France, Germany, Hong Kong, Hungary, India, Indonesia, Ireland, Israel, Italy, Kenya, Korea Rep, Lithuania, Malaysia, Mexico, Morocco, Netherlands, Nigeria, Norway, Poland, South Africa, Spain, Sweden, Switzerland, Trinidad-Tobago, UK, Ukraine, USA.
[2019.03.08/XM3970/**C**]

♦ International Association of Teachers of English as a Foreign Language (IATEFL) 12222

Association internationale des professeurs d'anglais comme langue étrangère

Journal Editor 2-3 The Foundry, Seager Road, Faversham, ME13 7FD, UK. T. +441795591414. Fax +441795538951. E-mail: info@iatefl.org.
URL: http://www.iatefl.org/

History 17 Mar 1967. Registration: Charity Commission, No/ID: 1090853, England and Wales. **Aims** Draw together teachers of English as a foreign or second language in all countries and at all age-levels so that, by exchange of experience, views and information, the teaching of English may be improved. **Structure** Conference (annual). Board of Trustees; Advisory Council. Executive Committees (5): Conference; Finance; Publications; Membership; Electronic. Special Interest Groups. **Languages** English. **Staff** 7.00 FTE, paid. **Finance** Members' dues: pounds40. **Activities** Awards/prizes/competitions; events/meetings. **Events** *International Conference* 2024, *International Conference* Harrogate (UK) 2023, *International Conference* Belfast (UK) 2022, *BESIG Annual Conference* Gdansk (Poland) 2022, *Developing Learner Autonomy in Language Learning* Mexico City (Mexico) 2021. **Publications** *IATEFL Newsletter* (6 a year). SIG Newsletters.

Members Institutional in 56 countries and territories:
Argentina, Australia, Austria, Azerbaijan, Bangladesh, Belgium, Brazil, Brunei Darussalam, Canada, China, Colombia, Congo DR, Cyprus, Czechia, Egypt, Ethiopia, Finland, France, Gabon, Georgia, Germany, Greece, Hong Kong, India, Ireland, Italy, Japan, Korea Rep, Kosovo, Lebanon, Libya, Malaysia, Malta, Mexico, Morocco, Netherlands, Palestine, Peru, Philippines, Portugal, Romania, Serbia, Singapore, Spain, Sri Lanka, Sweden, Switzerland, Taiwan, Thailand, Tunisia, Türkiye, UK, Ukraine, United Arab Emirates, Uruguay, USA.

Associate in 91 countries:
Albania, Angola, Argentina, Australia, Azerbaijan, Bangladesh, Belarus, Belgium, Bosnia-Herzegovina, Brazil, Bulgaria, Cameroon, Canada, Chile, China, Congo DR, Costa Rica, Côte d'Ivoire, Croatia, Cuba, Cyprus, Czechia, Denmark, Ecuador, Egypt, Estonia, Ethiopia, Finland, France, Georgia, Germany, Ghana, Greece, Haiti, Hungary, Iceland, India, Indonesia, Iran Islamic Rep, Ireland, Israel, Italy, Japan, Korea Rep, Kuwait, Kyrgyzstan, Latvia, Lebanon, Libya, Lithuania, Malta, Mexico, Moldova, Montenegro, Morocco, Nepal, Netherlands, New Zealand, Nigeria, North Macedonia, Peru, Poland, Portugal, Qatar, Russia, Rwanda, Saudi Arabia, Senegal, Serbia, Slovakia, Slovenia, Spain, Sri Lanka, Sudan, Sweden, Switzerland, Tanzania UR, Thailand, Tunisia, Türkiye, Uganda, UK, Ukraine, United Arab Emirates, Uruguay, USA, Uzbekistan, Venezuela, Yemen, Zambia, Zimbabwe.

Included in the above, 1 organization listed in this Yearbook:
Global Educators Network Inc. (#10338).

NGO Relations Affiliated to: *International Federation of Language Teacher Associations (#13468).*
[2020/XC2433/**C**]

- ♦ International Association of Teachers of German (#13228)
- ♦ International Association of Teachers of Hungarian (no recent information)
- ♦ International Association of Teachers and Researchers in Intellectual Property / see International Association for the Advancement of Teaching and Research in Intellectual Property (#11690)
- ♦ International Association of Teachers of Russian Language and Literature (#16739)
- ♦ International Association of Teachers of Veterinary Preventive Medicine (inactive)
- ♦ International Association for the Teaching of Comparative Law (inactive)
- ♦ International Association for the Teaching of Living Languages by Modern Methods (inactive)
- ♦ International Association for Technical Issues Related to Wood (internationally oriented national body)

♦ International Association of Technical Survey and Classification Institutions (TSCI) 12223

Secretariat 15 bld 2, Okruzhnoy prozd, Moscow MOSKVA, Russia, 105187. T. +79160759879. Fax +74957854358.
URL: http://www.tsci.rivreg.ru/

History Memorandum of establishment and first Statutes signed 17 Dec 1998. Registered in accordance with Russian law, 7 Oct 2002. **Aims** Improve activities aimed at determination of safety operation conditions of inland and river-sea *vessels* and other floating objects, protection of human life on inland waterways and at seas, safety of cargoes carried by the vessels including dangerous good, environmental protection; develop and harmonize requirements for ships and other supervised objects; improve technical survey over transport, industrial and construction objects; improve quality of rendered services in the field. **Structure** Council; Working Groups; Commissions; Secretariat; other working bodies. **Languages** English, Russian. **Staff** 3.00 FTE, paid. **Finance** Members' dues. **Activities** Research and development; research/documentation; standards/guidelines; events/meetings. **Publications** None.

Members Full in 6 countries:
Cuba, Kazakhstan, Korea Rep, Russia, Slovakia, Vietnam.

Consultative Status Consultative status granted from: *ECOSOC (#05331)* (Special).
[2019.12.12/XM5405/**D**]

- ♦ International Association of Technicians, Experts and Researchers (#02745)
- ♦ International Association of Technological University Libraries / see International Association of University Libraries (#12247)
- ♦ International Association of Technologists in Biology / see Association Internationale des Technologistes Biomédicaux (#02747)
- ♦ International Association for Technology Assessment and Forecasting Institutions (inactive)
- ♦ International Association of Technology, Education and Development (internationally oriented national body)
- ♦ International Association of Telecommunications Dealers (no recent information)
- ♦ International Association of Television Editors (inactive)
- ♦ International Association of Terminology (inactive)
- ♦ International Association of Terrestrial Magnetism and Electricity / see International Association of Geomagnetism and Aeronomy (#11916)
- ♦ International Association for Textile Care Labelling (#10761)
- ♦ International Association of Textile Dyers (inactive)
- ♦ International Association of Textile Dyers and Printers (inactive)

♦ International Association of Textile and Light Industry Workers' Unions 12224

Pres 42 Leninsky Prospekt, Moscow MOSKVA, Russia, 119119. T. +7959388564.

Members Trade unions in the CIS region (membership countries not specified). **NGO Relations** Member of: *General Confederation of Trade Unions (GCTU, #10108).* [2014/XM2475/t/**D**]

- ♦ International Association of Thalassotherapy (no recent information)

♦ International Association of Theatre for Children and Young People 12225

Association internationale du théâtre pour l'enfance et la jeunesse (ASSITEJ)

SG Nørregade 26 – 1st Floor, 1165 Copenhagen, Denmark. E-mail: sg@assitej-international.org – president@assitej-international.org.
Pres address not obtained.
URL: http://www.assitej-international.org/

History 28 May 1965, Paris (France). Statutes changed: Oct 1996, Rostov on Don (Russia); Sep 2005, Montréal QC (Canada); 2017, Cape Town (South Africa); 2021, Tokyo (Japan). **Aims** Unite theatres, organizations and individuals dedicated to theatre for children and young people. **Structure** General Assembly (every 3 years); Executive Committee. **Languages** English. **Staff** 1.00 FTE, paid. **Finance** Sources: members' dues. **Activities** Awards/prizes/competitions; events/meetings; training/education. **Events** *World Congress* Havana (Cuba) 2024, *World Congress* Tokyo (Japan) / Nagano (Japan) 2021, *World Congress* Tokyo (Japan) 2020, *Meeting* Kristiansand (Norway) 2019, *World Congress* Cape Town (South Africa) 2017. **Publications** *ASSITEJ e-Newsletter* (12 a year); *ASSITEJ Magazine* (annual).

Members National centres; professional networks; individuals. Members in 75 countries:
Angola, Argentina, Armenia, Australia, Austria, Azerbaijan, Bangladesh, Belgium, Botswana, Brazil, Bulgaria, Cameroon, Canada, Chile, China, Côte d'Ivoire, Croatia, Cuba, Cyprus, Czechia, Denmark, Ecuador, Estonia, Finland, France, Germany, Haiti, Hungary, Iceland, India, Iran Islamic Rep, Ireland, Israel, Italy, Japan, Jordan, Kazakhstan, Korea Rep, Latvia, Lebanon, Liechtenstein, Lithuania, Luxembourg, Mali, Mexico, Nepal, Netherlands, New Zealand, Nigeria, Norway, Pakistan, Poland, Romania, Russia, Rwanda, Saudi Arabia, Senegal, Serbia, Singapore, Slovakia, Slovenia, South Africa, Spain, Sri Lanka, Sweden, Switzerland, Togo, Türkiye, UK, Uruguay, USA, Uzbekistan, Vietnam, Zambia, Zimbabwe. [2022.06.14/XC1181/**C**]

♦ International Association of Theatre Critics (IATC) 12226

Association internationale des critiques de théâtre (AICT)

SG 987 route Marie-Victorin, Verchères, Montréal QC J01 2R0, Canada. T. +15142785764. E-mail: contact@aict-iatc.org.
Pres Strykerskev 6, SE-112 64 Stockholm, Sweden. T. +4686579770. Fax +4686579770.
URL: http://www.aict-iatc.org/

History Founded 1956, Paris (France), deriving from *Theatre of Nations – Théâtre des Nations*, which had been established in 1954, by resolution of UNESCO. **Aims** Bring together national or representative associations of drama, *opera* and *dance* critics anxious to develop international cooperation in the performing arts; foster criticism as a discipline and contribute to its methodological basis; protect the professional interests of critics and promote their common rights; promote ethical and professional awareness and cultural understanding by encouraging international meetings and exchanges. **Structure** General Assembly (every 2 years); Executive Committee. **Languages** English, French. **Staff** 4.00 FTE, voluntary. **Finance** Sources: members' dues. **Activities** Awards/prizes/competitions; events/meetings. **Events** *Biennial Congress* Montréal, QC (Canada) 2021, *Biennial Congress* St Petersburg (Russia) 2018, *Biennial Congress* Belgrade (Serbia) 2016, *Biennial Congress* Beijing (China) 2014, *Biennial Congress* Warsaw (Poland) 2012. **Publications** *Critical Stages*; *World Encyclopedia of Contemporary Theatre* – together with UNESCO, IFTR and SIBMAS. Congress and conference proceedings.

Members National Sections and individuals in 69 countries and territories:
Albania, Argentina, Azerbaijan, Barbados, Belarus, Belgium, Brazil, Bulgaria, Canada, Chile, China, Colombia, Croatia, Cuba, Czechia, Denmark, Ecuador, Estonia, Finland, France, Georgia, Germany, Greece, Guadeloupe, Haiti, Hong Kong, Hungary, India, Iran Islamic Rep, Ireland, Italy, Jamaica, Japan, Kenya, Korea Rep, Latvia, Lithuania, Malta, Martinique, Mexico, Moldova, Morocco, Nepal, Netherlands, New Zealand, Nigeria, North Macedonia, Norway, Poland, Portugal, Puerto Rico, Romania, Russia, Serbia, Singapore, Slovakia, Slovenia, South Africa, Spain, St Lucia, Sweden, Switzerland, Taiwan, Thailand, Türkiye, UK, Ukraine, Uruguay, USA.

NGO Relations Cooperates with: *International Theatre Institute (ITI, #15683).* [2017/XD1361/**C**]

- ♦ International Association of Theatre Public Organization (inactive)
- ♦ International Association of Theatre Technicians (inactive)
- ♦ International Association of Theological Libraries (inactive)
- ♦ International Association of Theoretical and Applied Limnology / see International Society of Limnology (#15232)

♦ International Association for Therapeutic Drug Monitoring and Clinical Toxicology (IATDMCT) 12227

Business Office PO Box 1570, 4 Cataraqui Street, Ste 310, Kingston ON K7L 5C8, Canada. T. +16135318166. Fax +18663030626. E-mail: office@iatdmct.org.
URL: http://www.iatdmct.org/

History 1990. Founded on the initiative of Charles E Pippenger and Irving Sunshine. **Events** *International Congress of Therapeutic Drug Monitoring & Clinical Toxicology* 2026, *Congress* Oslo (Norway) 2023, *International Congress of Therapeutic Drug Monitoring and Clinical Toxicology* Prague (Czechia) 2022, *Congress* Rome (Italy) 2021, *Congress* Banff, AB (Canada) 2020. [2022/XD4059/**D**]

♦ International Association for Tibetan Studies (IATS) 12228

SG MIASU, University of Cambridge, The Mond Building, Free School Lane, Cambridge, CB2 3RF, UK. E-mail: iatsub2013@gmail.com.
URL: http://www.iats.info/

History 1979, Oxford (UK). **Aims** Develop the study of Tibetan culture in all its aspects, through international cooperation between institutions, individual scholars and working groups; encourage interdisciplinary exchange. **Structure** Board of Advisers, consisting of 12 members. President, who represents IATS. Secretary General. Convenor is appointed to host each Conference. **Languages** English, French, German, Tibetan. **Activities** Organizes (every 3 years) international conferences, known as International Seminars on Tibetan Studies. **Events** *Seminar* Paris (France) 2019, *Seminar* Bergen (Norway) 2016, *Seminar / International Seminar on Tibetan Studies* Ulaanbaatar (Mongolia) 2013, *Seminar* Vancouver, BC (Canada) 2010, *Seminar / International Seminar on Tibetan Studies* Königswinter (Germany) 2006. **Publications** Seminar papers.

Members Associated (300) in 37 countries and territories:
Argentina, Australia, Austria, Belgium, Bhutan, Bulgaria, Canada, China, Czechia, Denmark, Estonia, Finland, France, Germany, Hungary, India, Israel, Italy, Japan, Korea Rep, Luxembourg, Nepal, Netherlands, New Zealand, Norway, Poland, Romania, Russia, Slovakia, Slovenia, Spain, Sweden, Switzerland, Taiwan, Thailand, UK, USA. [2015/XE1432/**E**]

♦ International Association for Time Use Research (IATUR) 12229

Address not obtained.
Main: http://www.iatur.org/

History 1970, as *International Research Group on Time Budgets and Social Activities*. Present name adopted 1988. **Aims** Foster exchange of ideas and promote analysis of time-use, utilizing tools, methods and theoretical frameworks specifically designed for such analysis; promote and encourage adoption of methodology ensuring international and diachronic *comparability* of time-use studies; strive to establish basic methodological standards to ensure such comparability; foster acquaintance and discussion among members and with scholars in related fields. **Structure** General Meeting (annual). Council, comprising President, Vice-President, Secretary, Treasurer and 8 Council members representing the following areas: Africa; Central and South America; Eastern Europe; North America; North and East Asia; Oceania; South Asia and Middle East; Western Europe. **Languages** English. **Staff** None. **Finance** Sources: donations; members' dues. **Activities** Serves primarily as a hub for networks of people interested in studying daily activity patterns; promotes best practice in data collection and analysis through conferences and publications; promotes the wider use of time diary data in policy and academic research applications. More recently, conducts training courses to increase capacity to use time use data in developing countries. **Events** *Annual Conference* Tokyo (Japan) 2023, *Annual Conference* Montréal, QC (Canada) 2022, *Annual Conference* Barcelona (Spain) 2021, *Annual Conference* Tokyo (Japan) 2020, *Annual Conference* Washington, DC (USA) 2019. **Publications** *Electronic International Journal of Time Use Research*. Twitter news.

Members Individuals (over 250 dues paying members and 1,000 participants) in 77 countries and territories:
Argentina, Australia, Austria, Bangladesh, Belgium, Bhutan, Bolivia, Brazil, Burkina Faso, Cambodia, Canada, Chile, China, Czechia, Denmark, Djibouti, Egypt, Estonia, Ethiopia, Fiji, Finland, France, Gambia, Germany, Ghana, Greece, Guinea, Hong Kong, Hungary, India, Indonesia, Iran Islamic Rep, Ireland, Israel, Italy, Japan, Kenya, Kiribati, Korea Rep, Latvia, Luxembourg, Malawi, Malaysia, Malta, Mexico, Moldova, Mongolia, Nepal, Netherlands, New Zealand, Nigeria, North Macedonia, Norway, Pakistan, Palestine, Philippines, Poland, Portugal, Romania, Russia, Singapore, Slovakia, Slovenia, South Africa, Spain, Sri Lanka, Sweden, Switzerland, Taiwan, Thailand, Türkiye, Uganda, UK, Ukraine, USA, Venezuela, Zimbabwe. [2011.06.01/XC0041/v/**C**]

♦ International Association of Tontine Development (internationally oriented national body)
♦ International Association of Toto and Lotto Organizations (inactive)

♦ International Association for Tourism Economics (IATE) 12230

Gen Sec Victoria Univ of Wellington, VMS Rutherford House, 23 Lambton Quay, Pipitea Campus, Wellington 6011, New Zealand.
Pres North-West University, School of Economics, Private Bag X6001, Potchefstroom, 2521, South Africa.
URL: http://www.tourism-economics.net/

History Sep 2007. Constituent Assembly met 26 Oct 2007, Palma (Spain). Registration: Spain. **Aims** Promote the value and profile of tourism economics studies worldwide. **Structure** General Assembly; Council; Executive Committee. **Finance** Sources: members' dues. **Activities** Events/meetings. **Events** *Conference* Perpignan (France) 2022, *Conference* La Plata (Argentina) 2019, *Conference* Rimini (Italy) 2017, *Conference* Hong Kong (Hong Kong) 2015, *Biennial Conference* Ljubljana (Slovenia) 2013. **Publications** *IATE Newsletter*. **Members** Individual; Institutional. Membership countries not specified. [2022/XJ5969/**C**]

♦ International Association of Tourism Guides, Interpreters and Couriers (inactive)
♦ International Association for Tourism Policy (unconfirmed)
♦ International Association of Tourist Organizations Operating in Central Asia (inactive)
♦ International Association for Tourists' Information Bureaux and Similar Groups (inactive)

♦ International Association of Tour Managers (IATM) 12231

Association internationale de tour managers

Central Office 46 Arthur Road, New Malden, KT3 6LX, UK. T. +442089424338. Fax +442089492247. E-mail: iatm@iatm.co.uk.
URL: http://www.iatm.co.uk/

History 1962, London (UK). **Aims** Promote and maintain the highest standards of competence, integrity and professional conduct on the part of all tour managers; promote, protect and improve the welfare and status of tour managers. **Structure** General Meeting (annual); Board of Directors; President (2-year-term); General Manager, in charge of Central Office in London (UK). Each Chapter is geographically determined. **Staff** 2.00 FTE, paid. **Finance** Sources: members' dues. Annual budget: 70,000 GBP. **Activities** Events/meetings. **Events** *Annual General Meeting* San Sebastian (Spain) 2020, *Annual General Meeting* Palermo (Italy) 2019, *Annual General Meeting* Taipei (Taiwan) 2018, *Annual General Meeting* Oslo (Norway) 2017, *Annual General Meeting* Valencia (Spain) 2016. **Publications** *IATM Newsletter* (4 a year); *Membership Handbook* (annual). *Ethics and Principles of the Tour Manager*.
Members Active professional tour managers; Associates major tour operators, travel agents, airlines, rail and coach operators; hotels, national tourist boards, restaurants, local guide associations; Allied services not in transport or accommodation but connected with the travel industry. Members (800) in 41 countries and territories:
Australia, Austria, Belgium, Brazil, Canada, China, Croatia, Czechia, Denmark, Estonia, Finland, France, Germany, Greece, Hong Kong, Hungary, Iceland, India, Indonesia, Ireland, Israel, Italy, Jordan, Latvia, Lithuania, Netherlands, New Zealand, Norway, Poland, Portugal, Serbia, Singapore, Slovakia, Slovenia, South Africa, Spain, Sweden, Switzerland, Taiwan, UK, USA.
IGO Relations Recognized by: *European Commission (EC, #06633)*. **NGO Relations** Member of (2): *European Tourism Manifesto (#08921)*; *European Travel and Tourism Advisory Group (ETAG, #08946)*. Affiliated with (1): *American Society of Travel Advisors*. [2020.08.18/XC4078/**C**]

♦ International Association Town Planning and Distribution (URBANICOM) 12232

Association internationale urbanisme et commerce – Internationale Vereinigung Städtebau und Handel

Dir Gen c/o CRBD, Bd Paepsem 11B, Boîte 1, 1070 Brussels, Belgium. T. +3223459923. Fax +3223460204. E-mail: info@cbd-bcd.be.

History Nov 1966, Brussels (Belgium). Registered in accordance with Belgian law. **Aims** Organize congresses, symposia and international study days concerning commerce and service activities in the areas of town and regional planning; coordinate relevant initiatives. **Structure** General Assembly (every 2 years); Board of Directors; Executive Committee. **Languages** English, French, German. **Finance** Members' dues. Other sources: grants; donations. **Activities** Events/meetings; training/education. **Events** *Congress* Brussels (Belgium) 2011, *Congress* Brussels (Belgium) 2005, *Congress* Brussels (Belgium) 2002, *Seminar* Barcelona (Spain) 1993, *Town planners and distribution; the essential partnership* Brussels (Belgium) 1990.
Members Individuals and federations (250) in 28 countries:
Austria, Belgium, Bulgaria, Canada, China, Czechia, Denmark, Finland, France, Germany, Greece, Hungary, Ireland, Italy, Japan, Lithuania, Luxembourg, Netherlands, Norway, Portugal, Romania, South Africa, Spain, Sweden, Switzerland, Tunisia, UK, USA. [2019.08.24/XD4521/**D**]

♦ International Association of Towns of the Future (inactive)

♦ International Association of Trade Training Organizations (IATTO) .. 12233

Secretariat ITRISA, PO Box 2475, Rivonia, 2128, South Africa. T. +27118075317. Fax +27118075321. E-mail: info@iatto.org.
Registered Office 26 York Street, London, W1U 6PZ, UK.
URL: http://www.iatto.org/

History 1973, Helsinki (Finland), as *International Association of Institutes of Export*. 1994, present name adopted. **Aims** Advance professional standards in the field of international trade education and training; encourage assistance with, supporting of and engaging in research and development activities. **Structure** General Assembly elects Board, Chairman and Vice-Chairman. Secretary appointed by the Board. **Languages** English. **Staff** 0.50 FTE, paid. **Finance** Members' dues. **Activities** Offers international accreditation of educational and training courses in international trade; networks on a member-to-member basis. Launched international trade professional designation WTP (World Trade Professional). **Events** *Annual Conference* Thessaloniki (Greece) 2013, *Annual Conference* Tallinn (Estonia) 2012, *Annual Conference* Chengdu (China) 2011, *Annual Conference* Cannes (France) 2009, *Annual Conference* Stockholm (Sweden) 2008. **Publications** Newsletter.
Members Organizations in 22 countries:
Argentina, Australia, Belgium, Canada, Finland, France, Greece, India, Ireland, Israel, Italy, Korea Rep, Malaysia, Netherlands, New Zealand, Norway, South Africa, Sweden, Taiwan, Türkiye, UK, USA.
Individuals in 7 countries and territories:
Brazil, Canada, Finland, Hong Kong, Jordan, Nigeria, USA. [2013.08.21/XD4468/t/**D**]

♦ International Association of Trade Unions of Workers in Scientific Research and Production Cooperatives and Enterprises 12234

Pres 42 Leninsky Prospekt, Moscow MOSKVA, Russia, 119119. T. +74959387503. Fax +74959301056. E-mail: profppck@yandex.ru.
URL: http://en.vkp.ru/

Members Trade unions in the CIS region (membership countries not specified). **NGO Relations** Member of: *General Confederation of Trade Unions (GCTU, #10108)*. [2014/XM2466/t/**D**]

♦ International Association of Trading Organizations for a Developing World (inactive)
♦ International Association of Traditional Wrestling Sports (no recent information)

♦ International Association of Traffic and Safety Sciences (IATSS) ... 12235

Association internationale des sciences de la circulation et de la sécurité routières – Kokusai Koutsu Anzen Gakkai

Pres 6-20, 2-chome, Uaesu, Chuo-ku, Tokyo, 104-0028 Japan. T. +81332737884. Fax +81332727054.
URL: https://www.iatss.or.jp/

History 17 Sep 1974, Tokyo (Japan). **Aims** Promote practical application of research in various fields to realize a better traffic society. **Structure** Board of Councillors; Board of Directors. **Languages** English, Japanese. **Staff** 13 directors; 19 secretariat (paid). **Finance** Endowment. **Activities** Major types of activities (5): Research; Symposia; Publicity and Publications; Awards; International Exchange. **Events** *Global Interactive Forum on Traffic and Safety* Tokyo (Japan) 2022, *Global Interactive Forum on Traffic and Safety* Tokyo (Japan) 2021, *International Perspective to the New Traffic System with Autonomous Vehicle* Tokyo (Japan) 2021, *Global Interactive Forum on Traffic and Safety* Tokyo (Japan) 2018, *Global Interactive Forum on Traffic and Safety* Tokyo (Japan) 2017. **Publications** *IATSS Review* (4 a year) in Japanese – with English abstracts; *IATSS RESEARCH* (2 a year) in English. **Members** Individuals (Japan). [2019/XD9092/**F**]

♦ International Association for Training, Education and Development (inactive)
♦ International Association of Training and Research in Family Education (#02700)
♦ International Association of Trampoline Parks (internationally oriented national body)
♦ International Association for Transformation (internationally oriented national body)

♦ International Association for Translation and Intercultural Studies (IATIS) 12236

Chair address not obtained.
URL: http://www.iatis.org/

History Officially launched, 12-14 Aug 2004, Seoul (Korea Rep). **Aims** Provide an internationally-based platform for scholars and institutions to exchange information and insights on various topical translation and interpreting issues. **Events** *Conference* Barcelona (Spain) 2021, *Regional Workshop* Osaka (Japan) 2020, *IATIS International Conference* Hong Kong 2018, *Conference* Belo Horizonte (Brazil) 2015, *Conference* Belfast (UK) 2012. **NGO Relations** Member of (1): *International Network of Translation and Interpreting Studies Associations (INTISA, #14335)*. [2020/XD9382/**D**]

♦ International Association of Transport and Communications Museums (IATM) 12237

Association internationale des musées de transports et de communications – Asociación Internacional de Museos de Transportes y Comunicaciones

Treas c/o DB Museum, Lessingstrasse 6, 90443 Nuremberg, Germany. T. +493512799103. E-mail: office@iatm.museum.
Pres c/o London Transport Museum, 39 Wellington Street, London, WC2E 7BB, UK.
URL: http://www.iatm.museum/

History Aug 1968, Cologne (Germany). Originally operated as a Committee of *International Council of Museums (ICOM, #13051)*. **Aims** Work for active collaboration across national borders between museums within its special field. **Structure** Meeting (annual); Board; Advisory Committee. **Languages** English. **Staff** 1.00 FTE, paid. Voluntary. **Finance** Sources: members' dues. **Activities** Projects/programmes. **Events** *Conference* Prague (Czechia) 2022, *Sustaining our Museums through and beyond Covid-19* 2020, *Sustainable Museums* Berlin (Germany) 2019, *Museums in a digital world* Ottawa, ON (Canada) 2018, *Museum 4.0 – Digital opportunities for Transport and Communications Museums* Lucerne (Switzerland) / Bern (Switzerland) 2017. **Publications** *IATM Journal*; *IATM Newsletter*.
Members Institutional transport museums covering the following categories railways; road traffic; aeronautics; ships; post; telecommunications. Individual. Members in 27 countries and territories:
Australia, Austria, Canada, Czechia, Denmark, Estonia, Finland, France, Germany, Hungary, India, Italy, Japan, Latvia, Liechtenstein, Luxembourg, Netherlands, Norway, Poland, Portugal, Russia, Spain, Sweden, Switzerland, Taiwan, UK, USA.
NGO Relations Member of: *International Council of Museums (ICOM, #13051)*. [2022/XC4614/**C**]

♦ International Association for Transport Properties (IATP) 12238

Sec Fac Chemical Engineering, Aristotle Univ, 541 24 Thessaloniki, Greece. T. +302310996163. Fax +302310996170.
Chairman Univ of Southampton, Highfield, SO17 1BJ, UK. T. +442380592801. Fax +442380593159.
URL: http://transp.cheng.auth.gr/

History Founded 1981, as the Subcommittee on Transport Properties within IUPAC Commission on Thermodynamics. Present name adopted when IUPAC was reorganized, 2001. **Aims** Advance the transport properties of materials. **Languages** English. **Finance** None. **Activities** Networking/liaising; knowledge management/information dissemination; events/meetings. **Events** *Scientific Meeting* Venice (Italy) 2023, *Scientific Meeting* Lisbon (Portugal) 2022, *Scientific Meeting* Erlangen (Germany) 2019, *Scientific Meeting* Boulder, CO (USA) 2018, *Scientific Meeting* Graz (Austria) 2017. **Publications** *Experimental Thermodynamics – vol IX: Advances in Transport Properties of Fluids* (2014); *Transport Properties of Fluids: Their Correlation, Prediction and Estimation* (1996); *Experimental Thermodynamics – vol III: Measurement of the Transport Properties of Fluids* (1991).
Members Scientists (52) in 20 countries:
Australia, China, France, Germany, Greece, Iran Islamic Rep, Japan, Korea Rep, Mexico, Netherlands, New Zealand, Portugal, Russia, Singapore, Slovakia, Spain, Türkiye, UK, Ukraine, USA. [2018.08.28/XM0056/v/**D**]

♦ International Association of Trauma Counseling / see Association of Traumatic Stress Specialists (#02961)

♦ International Association for Trauma Surgery and Intensive Care (IATSIC) 12239

Secretariat c/o ISS/SIC, Seefeldstrasse 88, 8008 Zurich ZH, Switzerland. T. +41445337650. Fax +41445337659. E-mail: surgery@iss-sic.com.
URL: http://www.iatsic.org/

History Founded 1987, Toronto (Canada), as *International Association for the Surgery of Trauma and Surgical Intensive Care (IATSIC)*, as an Integrated Society of *International Society of Surgery (ISS, #15496)*. **Aims** Provide a forum for exchanging information and developing new knowledge in the field of trauma surgery and surgical intensive care, whether by clinical experience or laboratory investigation. **Structure** Board of Directors; Executive Committee; National Chapters. **Languages** English. **Staff** 3.00 FTE, paid. **Finance** Members' dues. **Activities** Training/education; meeting activities. **Events** *Congress* Kuala Lumpur (Malaysia) 2024, *Congress* Vienna (Austria) 2022, *Congress* Krakow (Poland) 2019, *Congress* Basel (Switzerland) 2017, *Workshop on Visceral Trauma* Graz (Austria) 2015. **Publications** *Guidelines for Essential Trauma Care in Conjunction with the World Health Organization* (2004); *Manual of Definitive Surgical Trauma Care* (2003).
Members Full (303) in 53 countries and territories:
Argentina, Australia, Austria, Bangladesh, Belgium, Bulgaria, Canada, Chile, Colombia, Czechia, Egypt, El Salvador, Finland, France, Germany, Greece, Honduras, Hong Kong, India, Iran Islamic Rep, Ireland, Israel, Italy, Japan, Korea Rep, Kuwait, Libya, Lithuania, Luxembourg, Mexico, Mozambique, Myanmar, Netherlands, New Zealand, Nigeria, Panama, Peru, Poland, Portugal, Romania, Russia, Saudi Arabia, South Africa, Spain, Sweden, Switzerland, Taiwan, Tunisia, Türkiye, UK, USA, Venezuela, Yemen. [2020/XD3808/**E**]

♦ International Association for Travel Behaviour Research (IATBR) ... 12240

Sec-Treas Indian Institute of Science – IISc, CV Raman Road, Bangalore, Karnataka 560012, Bangalore KARNATAKA 560012, India. E-mail: iatbr.secretary@gmail.com.
URL: http://iatbr.org/

History Founded 1970. Previously also referred to in French as *Association internationale sur les comportements de déplacements*. **Aims** Promote research on understanding and analysis of travel behaviour; provide a forum for debate and a mechanism for dissemination of travel behaviour research. **Structure** Board. **Languages** English. **Staff** None. **Finance** Members' dues. Other sources: congresses proceedings; sale of publications. **Activities** Awards/prizes/competitions; knowledge management/information dissemination; events/meetings. **Events** *Triennial Conference* Santa Barbara, CA (USA) 2018, *Triennial Conference* Windsor (UK) 2015, *Triennial Conference* Toronto, ON (Canada) 2012, *Triennial Conference* Jaipur (India) 2009, *Triennial Conference* Kyoto (Japan) 2006. **Publications** Books of congress papers (every 3 years). Special issues of papers presented at the congress in scientific journals. **Members** Full (350) from various countries. Membership countries not specified. **NGO Relations** Transportation Research Board (TRB). [2019.04.21/XD8121/**D**]

♦ International Association of Travel Officials / see US Travel Association

♦ International Association of Travel Research and Marketing Professionals / see Travel and Tourism Research Association

♦ International Association for the Treatment of Sexual Offenders (IATSO) 12241

Internationale Gesellschaft zur Behandlung von Sexualstraftätern

Main Office Gerichtsgasse 4/5, 1210 Vienna, Austria. T. +431278530031. Fax +431278530032. E-mail: office@iatso.org.

URL: http://www.iatso.org/

History 24 Mar 1998, Caracas (Venezuela). Founded during the 5th International Conference on the Treatment of Sex Offenders. **Aims** Promote humane, dignified, comprehensive, ethical and effective treatment of sexual offenders throughout the world. **Structure** Governing Board; General Assembly; Advisory Committee. **Activities** Events/meetings; standards/guidelines. **Events** *IATSO Conference* Trondheim (Norway) 2023, *IATSO Conference* Frankfurt-Main (Germany) 2021, *IATSO Conference* Frankfurt-Main (Germany) 2020, *IATSO Conference* Vilnius (Lithuania) 2018, *Conference* Copenhagen (Denmark) 2016. [2022/XD8380/**D**]

♦ International Association of Trichologists (IAT) 12242

Dir 185 Elizabeth Street, Ste 919, Sydney NSW 2000, Australia. T. +61882964098.

URL: http://www.trichology.edu.au/

History 1974. **Aims** Promote study, research and legitimate practice in all aspects pertaining to the treatment and care of human *hair* and *scalp* in *health* and disease; supply comprehensive instruction, training and aid in professional application of these scientific specialities. **Languages** English. **Staff** 1.00 FTE, paid; 1.50 FTE, voluntary. **Finance** Members' dues. Other sources: sales of educational materials; fees from trichology courses. **Activities** Training/education. **Events** *World Conference* Reykjavik (Iceland) 2021, *World Conference* Reykjavik (Iceland) 2020, *World Conference* Toronto, ON (Canada) 2019, *World Conference* Washington, DC (USA) 2018, *Annual Conference* Sao Paulo (Brazil) 2012. **Publications** *Hairy Tales – Trichologists from Around the World Tell Their Stories* (2018); *Hair Loss Handbook* (2014); *Picture Guide to Scalp and Hair Problems* (1997); *IAT Guide to Hairloss* (1995). DVDs.

Members Individuals in 40 countries and territories:

Argentina, Australia, Bahrain, Bangladesh, Botswana, Brazil, Canada, Chile, China, Colombia, Egypt, France, Hong Kong, India, Indonesia, Ireland, Israel, Jamaica, Japan, Kenya, Korea Rep, Latvia, Malaysia, Mauritius, Mexico, Mongolia, New Zealand, Nigeria, Puerto Rico, Russia, Singapore, South Africa, Sri Lanka, Sweden, Taiwan, Trinidad-Tobago, UK, United Arab Emirates, USA, Vietnam. [2018.09.06/XD3482/v/**D**]

♦ International Association of Trusted Blockchain Applications (unconfirmed)

♦ International Association of Ukrainian Studies (IAUS) 12243

Miznarodna Asociacija Ukrainistiv (MAU)

Contact address not obtained. E-mail: mau-nau@ukr.net.

URL: http://mau-nau.org.ua/

History 1 Jun 1989, Naples (Italy), when statutes were approved; revised 29 Aug 1996, Kharkiv (Ukraine). Registered in accordance with the law of Ukraine. **Aims** Promote the development of Ukrainian studies, mainly in the area of humanities and social sciences; facilitate international cooperation between scholars and institutions in the field. **Structure** Congress. Office, comprising President, 5 Vice-Presidents, 2 scholarly Secretaries and 6 members. Revisionary Committee. **Finance** Members' dues. Other sources: grants; donations. **Events** *Triennial Congress* Yalta, Crimea (Ukraine) 2008, *Triennial Congress* Donetsk (Ukraine) 2005, *Triennial Congress* Chernivtsi, Vinnytsia (Ukraine) 2002, *Triennial Congress* Odessa (Ukraine) 1999, *Triennial congress* Kharkiv (Ukraine) 1996. **Publications** *Ukrainian History – A Bibliographic Yearbook* (annual); *Ukrainian Studies Abstracts* (annual); *Visnyk MAU* (periodical) in Ukrainian. Conference proceedings; monographs.

Members National organizations in 21 countries:

Australia, Austria, Belarus, Belgium, Bulgaria, Canada, China, Czechia, France, Germany, Hungary, Israel, Japan, Lithuania, Poland, Romania, Russia, Slovakia, UK, Ukraine, USA. [2013/XE2181/**E**]

♦ International Association of Ultrarunners (IAU) 12244

Association internationale de courses de grand fond

Main Office 6-8, Quai Antoine 1er, BP 359, CEDEX, 98007 Monte Carlo, Monaco. E-mail: info@iau-ultramarathon.org.

URL: http://www.iau-ultramarathon.org/

History 1984, Austria. **Aims** Develop ultra-distance running internationally. **Structure** Congress (every 2 years). General Council, consisting of Representatives for: Asia; Europe; North America, Central America and Caribbean; Oceania. Executive Council of up to 13 members and including President, Vice-President and 4 Directors (Development; Competitions; Organizations; Asian Affairs). Committees (2): Records; Technical. Arbitration Panel. Commissions (3); Veterans; Medical; Website. **Languages** English. **Staff** 6.00 FTE, voluntary. **Finance** Members' dues. **Activities** Organizes: annual IAU 100 Km World Cup; European 100 Km Championships. Organizes congresses and technical meetings. **Publications** *IAU Newsletter* (4 a year). Fixture list.

Members National associations and individuals in 60 countries and territories:

Argentina, Australia, Austria, Belarus, Belgium, Bosnia-Herzegovina, Botswana, Brazil, Canada, China, Croatia, Cuba, Czechia, Denmark, Estonia, Eswatini, Ethiopia, Finland, France, Germany, Greece, Hong Kong, Hungary, Iceland, India, Ireland, Italy, Japan, Kazakhstan, Kenya, Korea Rep, Liechtenstein, Lithuania, Luxembourg, Mexico, Monaco, Mongolia, Namibia, Nepal, Netherlands, New Zealand, Norway, Pakistan, Poland, Portugal, Russia, Serbia, Slovakia, South Africa, Spain, Sweden, Switzerland, Taiwan, Tajikistan, Trinidad-Tobago, UK, Ukraine, Uruguay, USA.

NGO Relations Recognized by: *World Athletics (#21209).* [2019/XD7056/**D**]

♦ International Association for the Union of Democracies (inactive)

♦ International Association of Unions of Architects (IAUA) 12245

Secretariat Granatny per 3 str 2, Moscow MOSKVA, Russia, 123001. T. +74956903047 – +74956904702. E-mail: nva@co.ru – masa4arch@gmail.com.

URL: http://www.maca.ru/

History 1992. **Aims** Promote protection of creative, social and economic rights and professional interests of architects and others that participate in development of architecture and their associations; promote aesthetic education of domestic and world architecture; promote creative cooperation and achievement of mutual understanding among architects. **Structure** Conference; Council; Bureau. **Languages** Russian. **Staff** 11.00 FTE, paid. **Finance** Annual budget: 9,000,000 RUB. **Activities** Awards/prizes/competitions; events/meetings; knowledge management/information dissemination; training/education. **Publications** *Architecture, Construction, Design* – journal.

Members National organizations in 13 countries:

Armenia, Azerbaijan, Belarus, Georgia, Kazakhstan, Kyrgyzstan, Moldova, Russia, Serbia, Tajikistan, Turkmenistan, Ukraine, Uzbekistan. [2022.05.11/XM2612/**D**]

♦ International Association for Universal Design (internationally oriented national body)

♦ International Association of Universities (IAU) 12246

Association internationale des Universités (AIU) – Asociación Internacional de Universidades – Internationaler Universitätsverband – Mezdunarodnaja Associacija Universitetov

SG USESCO House, 1 rue Miollis, 75732 Paris CEDEX 15, France. T. +33145684800. Fax +33147347605. E-mail: iau@iau-aiu.net.

URL: http://www.iau-aiu.net/

History 4 Dec 1950, Nice (France). Prior to creation, a preparatory university conference was convened by UNESCO and the Dutch government, 1948, Utrecht (Netherlands). Statutes adopted 9 Dec 1950, Nice (France); amended: 24 Sep 1955, Istanbul (Turkey); 12 Sep 1960, Mexico City (Mexico); 20 Aug 1975, Moscow (USSR); 12 Aug 1985, Los Angeles CA (USA); 25 Aug 2000, Durban (South Africa); 28 July 2004, Sao Paulo (Brazil); 5 July 2008, Utrecht (Netherlands). **Aims** Be the most representative and influential global association of diverse higher education institutions and their organizations, promoting and advancing a dynamic leadership role for higher education in society. **Structure** General Conference (every 4 years); Administrative Board; Executive Committee; International Universities Bureau; International Secretariat. **Languages** English, French. **Staff** 12.00 FTE, paid. **Finance** Sources: grants; members' dues. **Activities** Advocacy/lobbying/activism; events/meetings; guidance/assistance/consulting; knowledge management/information dissemination; monitoring/evaluation; publishing activities; training/education. **Events** *General Conference* Dublin (Ireland) 2022, *General Conference* Dublin (Ireland) 2021, *World Sustainability Forum* Tokyo (Japan) 2021, *General Conference* Dublin (Ireland) 2020, *Biennial Global Meeting of Associations of Universities* Paris (France) 2020. **Publications** *Higher Education Policy Journal* (4 a year); *IAU Horizons Magazine* (2 a year). *IAU Global Survey on Internationalization of Higher Education.* **Information Services** *HESD Global Portal* – sustainable development initiatives; *IDEA-PHD Portal* – institutional profiles, announcement calls and offers of interest to members in Africa; *WHED* – information on higher education systems, credentials and institutions. **Members** Institutions; Organizations; Affiliates; Associates. Over 650 members from 130 countries. Membership countries not specified. **Consultative Status** Consultative status granted from: *ECOSOC (#05331)* (Ros C); *UNESCO (#20322)* (Associate Status); *Council of Europe (CE, #04881)* (Participatory Status). **IGO Relations** *International Bank for Reconstruction and Development (IBRD, #12317)* (World Bank); *OECD (#17693)*; *UNESCO (#20322).* **NGO Relations** Works with various organizations in the field of higher education (not specified). [2023.02.14/XB1363/y/**B**]

♦ International Association of Universities and Colleges of Art, Design and Media / see The Global Association of Art and Design Education and Research (#10241)

♦ International Association of Universities of the Third Age (#02749)

♦ International Association of University Libraries (IATUL) 12247

Association internationale des bibliothèques d'universités – Asociación Internacional de Bibliotecas de las Universidades – Internationaler Verband der Universitätsbibliotheken

Pres Zum Ehrenhain 34, 22885 Barsbüttel, Germany. T. +494067088280. E-mail: iatul@cpo-hanser.de.

URL: http://www.iatul.org/

History 16 Sep 1955, Brussels (Belgium). Former names and other names: *International Association of Technological University Libraries (IATUL)* – former (1995 to 2009); *International Association of Scientific and Technological University Libraries (IATUL)* – former (2009 to 2014); *Association internationale des bibliothèques d'universités polytechniques* – former (2009 to 2014); *Asociación Internacional de Bibliotecas de las Universidades Tecnológicas* – former (2009 to 2014); *Internationale Vereinigung der Bibliotheken Technischer Hochschulen* – former (2009 to 2014); *Mezdunarodnoe Obedinenie Bibliotek Vyssih Tehniceskih Skol* – former (2009 to 2014). Registration: No/ID: VR 200449, Start date: 30 Aug 2006, Germany, Munich. **Aims** Act as organ for international cooperation among member libraries to stimulate and develop library projects which are of international and regional importance; provide a forum for library directors to exchange views and develop a collaborative approach to problems. **Structure** Board of Directors. Libraries represented by their directors. Membership open. **Languages** English. **Staff** Voluntary. **Finance** Sources: members' dues. Other sources: donor funding; cooperation agreements. **Activities** Awards/prizes/competitions; events/meetings. **Events** *Annual Conference* Dubai (United Arab Emirates) 2023, *Annual Conference* Miami, FL (USA) 2022, *Annual Conference* Porto (Portugal) 2021, *Annual Conference* Porto (Portugal) 2020, *Annual Conference* Perth, WA (Australia) 2019. **Publications** *IATUL Proceedings.*

Members Ordinary – libraries of universities offering doctoral degrees; Associate – academic libraries and sustaining organizations. Members (238) in 68 countries and territories:

Australia, Austria, Bahrain, Bangladesh, Belarus, Belgium, Botswana, Brazil, Brunei Darussalam, Bulgaria, Cambodia, Canada, China, Colombia, Czechia, Denmark, Estonia, Ethiopia, Finland, France, Georgia, Germany, Ghana, Greece, Hungary, India, Indonesia, Iran Islamic Rep, Ireland, Israel, Italy, Jamaica, Kenya, Latvia, Lebanon, Lithuania, Malaysia, Mali, Namibia, Netherlands, New Zealand, Norway, Pakistan, Philippines, Poland, Portugal, Qatar, Romania, Russia, Saudi Arabia, Singapore, Slovakia, Slovenia, Solomon Is, South Africa, Spain, Sweden, Switzerland, Tanzania UR, Thailand, Türkiye, Uganda, UK, Ukraine, United Arab Emirates, USA, Uzbekistan, Zambia.

NGO Relations Member of (2): *International Council for Scientific and Technical Information (ICSTI, #13070); International Federation of Library Associations and Institutions (IFLA, #13470).* Cooperates with (1): *International Organization for Standardization (ISO, #14473).* [2022.06.14/XC1351/**C**]

♦ International Association of University Presidents (IAUP) 12248

Association internationale des recteurs d'universités

SG Institute of International Education., One World Trade Center, 36th Floor., New York NY 10007, USA. E-mail: office@iaup.org – secretarygeneral@iaup.org.

Pres address not obtained.

URL: http://www.iaup.org/

History 15 Jun 1964, Rutherford, NJ (USA). Inaugural conference Jun 1965, Oxford (UK). Articles most recently amended: Jul 1996, San Francisco CA (USA); 2014, Japan; 2017, Vienna (Austria). **Aims** Provide a worldwide vision of higher *education*; strengthen the international mission of institutions worldwide; promote academic exchange and collaboration; promote networking and collaboration between university leaders, supporting sustainable development in a context of global competency; promote peace and international understanding through education. **Structure** General Assembly (every 3 years); Board of Directors; Executive Committee (meets twice a year); Advisory Council. Special Commissions: IAUP/UN Commission for Disarmament, Conflict Resolution and Peace; United Nations Representation. **Languages** English. **Staff** 1.00 FTE, paid. Several voluntary. **Finance** Sources: donations; fees for services; members' dues. **Activities** Events/meetings; networking/liaising; training/education. **Events** *Innovation and Inclusion – Key Priorities for Universities in a Complex World* Mexico City (Mexico) 2021, *Triennial Conference* Mexico City (Mexico) 2020, *Half-Yearly Meeting* Tbilisi (Georgia) 2020, *Half-Yearly Meeting* Vancouver, BC (Canada) 2019, *Joint Conference* Xinzheng (China) 2019. **Publications** *IAUP Newsletter* (4 a year) – electronic; *Academe – Journal on Higher Education Leadership.* Minutes of special academic programmes; abstracts on Regional Council and National Chapter meetings.

Members Presidents/Rectors/Vice-Chancellors of Universities; Heads of institutions of higher education; Associate. Membership continues after the member retires. Members in 74 countries and territories:

Angola, Antigua-Barbuda, Argentina, Armenia, Australia, Austria, Azerbaijan, Bahrain, Bangladesh, Belgium, Bolivia, Botswana, Brazil, Brunei Darussalam, Cambodia, Canada, Cayman Is, Chile, China, Colombia, Costa Rica, Cyprus, Czechia, Denmark, Dominican Rep, Ecuador, El Salvador, Estonia, Fiji, Gambia, Georgia, Germany, Ghana, Greece, Hong Kong, India, Indonesia, Iran Islamic Rep, Ireland, Jamaica, Japan, Kenya, Korea Rep, Lebanon, Liberia, Lithuania, Malaysia, Mexico, Moldova, Morocco, Nigeria, Pakistan, Panama, Papua New Guinea, Philippines, Puerto Rico, Romania, Russia, Rwanda, Saudi Arabia, Slovenia, South Africa, Spain, Switzerland, Taiwan, Tanzania UR, Thailand, Türkiye, UK, Ukraine, United Arab Emirates, USA, Zambia, Zimbabwe.

Consultative Status Consultative status granted from: *ECOSOC (#05331)* (Special); *UNESCO (#20322)* (Consultative Status). **IGO Relations** Instrumental in setting up (1): *University for Peace (UPEACE, #20702).* Associated with Department of Global Communications of the United Nations. **NGO Relations** Member of (1): *Conference of Non-Governmental Organizations in Consultative Relationship with the United Nations (CONGO, #04635).* Cooperates with (4): *Association of Universities of Latin America and the Caribbean (#02970); Mediterranean Universities Union (UNIMED, #16687); United Nations Academic Impact (UNAI, #20516); WISE Initiative.* Also links with universities. [2022.02.17/XD1364/v/**B**]

♦ International Association of University Professors of English (IAUPE) 12249

SG/Treas English Dept, Univ of Calgary, 2500 University Dr NW, Calgary AB T2N 1N4, Canada. T. +14036070215. Fax +14032891123. E-mail: iaupe.secretarygeneral@gmail.com.

URL: http://www.iaupe.net/

History 1951. Founded by an international consultative committee, set up Aug 1950, Oxford (UK). Constitution adopted 29 Aug 1959, Bern (Switzerland); revised Jul 1992, Peterborough (Canada). Former names and other names: *Association internationale des professeurs d'anglais des universités* – former; *Asociación Internacional de los Profesores de Inglés de la Universidades* – former. **Aims** Make information accessible to members, in particular that relating to English studies and to the teaching of English in universities. **Structure** General Meeting (every 3 years); International Committee; Executive Committee. **Languages** English. **Staff** 1.00 FTE, voluntary. **Finance** Sources: members' dues. Supported by: *UNESCO (#20322)* (grants for traveling expenses). **Activities** Events/meetings. **Events** *Triennial Conference* Sydney, NSW (Australia) 2023, *Triennial Conference* Poznań (Poland) 2019, *Triennial Conference* London (UK) 2016, *Triennial Conference* Beijing (China) 2013, *Triennial Conference* Malta 2010. **Publications** Occasional.

Members Individuals (480) – full professors of English language and/or literature in universities of international reputation and other scholars of distinction in these or related fields, in 42 countries and territories:

Albania, Australia, Austria, Belgium, Botswana, Canada, China, Czechia, Denmark, Finland, France, Georgia, Germany, Hungary, India, Ireland, Israel, Italy, Japan, Korea Rep, Kuwait, Malaysia, Malta, Netherlands, New Zealand, Norway, Pakistan, Poland, Russia, Saudi Arabia, Serbia, Slovakia, Slovenia, South Africa, Spain, Sweden, Switzerland, Taiwan, UK, Ukraine, United Arab Emirates, USA. [2022/XC1366/v/C]

♦ International Association of University Professors and Lecturers (IAUPL) 12250

Association internationale des professeurs et maîtres de conférences des universités – Asociación Internacional de Profesores y Conferenciantes Universitarios

SG 1 rue Guy de la Brosse, 75005 Paris, France. T. +33681629808. E-mail: libertes.universitaires@orange.fr.

URL: http://www.iaupl.org/

History 1 Jul 1945, Oxford (UK), as *World Association of University Professors – Association mondiale des professeurs d'université*, on merging of *International University Conference (inactive)*, inaugurated Jul 1934, Oxford (UK), and *Association of Professors and Lecturers of the Allied Countries in Great Britain*, set up Jan 1942, London (UK). Statutes adopted Apr 1947, Brussels (Belgium); amended: 7 Sep 1956, Munich (Germany FR); 28 Sep 1962, Ghent (Belgium); 11 Sep 1964, Heidelberg (Germany FR); Sep 1990, Paris (France). Registered in accordance with French law, 3 Feb 1971. **Aims** Develop *academic* fraternity among university teachers and research workers and further their interests; protect the independence and freedom of teaching and research; defend academic freedom; consider academic problems and questions referred by governments, university authorities, or any other appropriate body; collaborate with bodies having similar interests. **Structure** Council (normally every 4 years, at International University Conference), constituted by elected representatives of every National Section and of every Group. Executive Committee, composed of 8 members elected from members of Council and one additional co-opted member; President and 2 Vice-Presidents, elected by Council from the countries of membership in rotation; Honorary Secretary-General and Treasurer, elected for 4 years. European Liaison Committee. Meetings closed. **Languages** English, French. **Finance** Sources: donations; members' dues; sale of publications. Other sources: payments under contract for work undertaken; Unesco subvention. **Activities** Maintains reference documentation; prepares specialist reports and studies on academic topics. Completes studies for Unesco into status of university teachers, their recruitment, training and prospects of career service. Organizes conferences and seminars. **Events** *Assembly* Malta 1988. **Publications** *Le Bilan social de l'université* (1984); *Déclaration sur la liberté académique* (1982); *The Recruitment and Training of University Teachers* (1967) by Armand Hacquaert; *The Status of University Teachers* (1961) by R H Shryock.

Members National sections, Federations of national sections, or groups of university teachers; Organizations interested in university matters. Members in 17 countries:

Barbados, Denmark, Finland, France, Gabon, Germany, Ireland, Israel, Italy, Madagascar, Malta, Netherlands, Serbia, South Africa, Switzerland, USA, Venezuela.

Correspondents in 23 countries and territories:

Argentina, Australia, Brazil, Canada, Ecuador, Guyana, Hong Kong, Hungary, India, Japan, Kenya, Malaysia, Mexico, New Zealand, Norway, Peru, Philippines, Poland, Portugal, Singapore, Sri Lanka, Sweden, Türkiye.

Consultative Status Consultative status granted from: *UNESCO (#20322)* (Consultative Status); *ECOSOC (#05331)* (General). [2023/XC1365/C]

♦ International Association of University Women (inactive)

♦ International Association for Urban Climate (IAUC) 12251

Sec address not obtained. E-mail: iauc-secretary@rub.de.

Pres address not obtained.

URL: http://www.urban-climate.org/

History 2000. Founded following the initial event series known as International Conference on Urban Climatology (ICUC). **Aims** Bring together those with scientific, scholarly and technical interests and responsibilities in the field of urban climate. **Structure** Board, comprising President, Past-President, Secretary and 8 members; Committees (5). **Languages** English. **Staff** Voluntary. **Finance** Sources: meeting proceeds. **Activities** Knowledge management/information dissemination; publishing activities; training/education. **Events** *International Conference on Urban Climate (ICUC11)* Sydney, NSW (Australia) 2023, *International Conference on Urban Climate (ICUC11)* Sydney, NSW (Australia) 2021, *International Conference on Urban Climate* New York, NY (USA) 2018, *International Conference on Urban Climate (ICUC9)* Toulouse (France) 2015, *International Conference on Urban Climate* Dublin (Ireland) 2012. **Publications** *Urban Climate News*. **Members** in over 80 countries. Membership countries not specified. **IGO Relations** Support from: *World Meteorological Organization (WMO, #21649)*. **NGO Relations** Member of (1): *International Forum of Meteorological Societies (IFMS, #13644)*. Affiliated with (1): *International Society of Biometeorology (ISB, #14969)*. [2023.02.26/XD9331/D]

♦ International Association for Urban and Regional Research and Education (inactive)
♦ International Association of Used Equipment Dealers (inactive)
♦ International Association for the Use of Regional Languages at School (no recent information)
♦ International Association of Users of Artificial and Synthetic Filament Yarns and of Natural Silk (#02750)

♦ International Association of Users and Developers of Electronic Libraries and New Information Technologies (ELNIT Association) 12252

Pres 7-9 bl 2 Khokhlovskiy per, Moscow MOSKVA, Russia, 10100. T. +74956463605. Fax +74956463605. E-mail: shra@gpntb.ru.

URL: http://www.elnit.org/

History 1996, as *International Association of CDS/ISIS Systems and New Information Technologies Users and Developers (ISIS-NIT)*. New title adopted, 1999. **Aims** Serve and stimulate the interests of professional libraries and information specialists; organize professional cooperation between libraries of FSU territory in computer and digital environment. **Structure** Governing Board, consisting of President, Vice-Presidents and Executive Director. Executive Board. **Languages** Russian. **Finance** Members' dues. **Activities** Events/meetings. **Events** *Libcom Conference* Suzdal (Russia) 2014, *Crimea Conference* Sudak (Ukraine) 2013, *Libcom Conference* Suzdal (Russia) 2013, *Libcom Conference* Moscow (Russia) 2012, *Crimea conference* Sudak (Ukraine) 2012.

Members Libraries (395) and other organizations in 9 countries:

Armenia, Azerbaijan, Belarus, Kazakhstan, Kyrgyzstan, Russia, Tajikistan, Ukraine, Uzbekistan.

NGO Relations International association member of: *International Federation of Library Associations and Institutions (IFLA, #13470)*. [2015.02.11/XD8499/D]

♦ International Association of Users of Man-Made Fibres Filament Yarns and of Natural Silk / see Association internationale des utilisateurs de fils de filaments artificiels et synthétiques et de soie naturelle (#02750)
♦ International Association of Users of Private Sidings / see Cargo Rail Europe (#03431)
♦ International Association of Users of Yarn of Man-Made Fibres / see Association internationale des utilisateurs de fils de filaments artificiels et synthétiques et de soie naturelle (#02750)
♦ International Association of Users of Yarn of Man-Made Fibres and of Natural Silk / see Association internationale des utilisateurs de fils de filaments artificiels et synthétiques et de soie naturelle (#02750)

♦ International Association for Vegetation Science (IAVS) 12253

Pres Landcare Research, PO Box 69040, Lincoln 7640, New Zealand. E-mail: president@iavs.org.

Sec Natl Taiwan Univ, No 1 Sect 4 Roosevelt Rd, Da'an District, New Taipei City 10617, Taiwan.

URL: http://iavs.org/

History 1939. Present name adopted at General Assembly, 7 Apr 1982, Prague (Czechoslovakia). Statutes revised and adopted at General Assembly, 7 Mar 2002, Porto Alegre (Brazil). Former names and other names: *International Phytosociological Society* – former (1939 to 1982); *AIEV* – former; *AJCV* – former; *IVV* – former. **Aims** Facilitate personal contacts among vegetation scientists all over the world; promote research in all aspects of vegetation science and its applications. **Structure** Council (meets annually at Symposium); Governing Board. Working Groups: Circumboreal Vegetation Map (CBVM); EcoInformatics; Eurasian Dry Grassland Group (EDGG); European Vegetation Survey (EVS); Group for Phytosociological Nomenclature (GPN); Historical Vegetation Ecology; Vegetation Classification Working Group (VCWG); Young Scientists. **Languages** English. **Finance** Sources: meeting proceeds; members' dues; sale of publications. Annual budget: 50,000 EUR. **Activities** Events/meetings; projects/programmes. **Events** *European Vegetation Survey Meeting* Perugia (Italy) 2026, *European Vegetation Survey Meeting* Kiev (Ukraine) 2025, *European Vegetation Survey Meeting* Funchal (Portugal) 2024, *Annual Symposium* Coffs Harbour, NSW (Australia) 2023, *European Vegetation Survey Meeting* Rome (Italy) 2023. **Publications** *Journal of Vegetation Science* (6 a year) in English; *Applied Vegetation Science* (4 a year) in English; *IAVS Bulletin* (4 a year) in English; *Palaearctic Grasslands* (4 a year) in English; *Vegetation Classification and Survey* (continuous publishing) in English.

Members Individuals (666) in 79 countries and territories:

Albania, Algeria, Argentina, Australia, Austria, Belgium, Bosnia-Herzegovina, Botswana, Brazil, Bulgaria, Canada, Canaries, Chile, China, Colombia, Costa Rica, Croatia, Cuba, Czechia, Denmark, Egypt, Estonia, Ethiopia, Faeroe Is, Finland, France, Georgia, Germany, Greece, Greenland, Hungary, Iceland, India, Iran Islamic Rep, Ireland, Italy, Japan, Jordan, Korea DPR, Korea Rep, Latvia, Lithuania, Malaysia, Mexico, Mongolia, Namibia, Nepal, Netherlands, New Zealand, Nigeria, Norway, Peru, Poland, Portugal, Romania, Russia, Rwanda, Saudi Arabia, Scotland, Senegal, Serbia, Singapore, Slovakia, Slovenia, South Africa, Spain, Sri Lanka, Sweden, Switzerland, Taiwan, Tanzania UR, Türkiye, UK, Ukraine, Uruguay, USA, Venezuela, Zambia, Zimbabwe.

IGO Relations Cooperates with (1): *Conservation of Arctic Flora and Fauna (CAFF, #04728)*. **NGO Relations** Scientific Member and Commission on Vegetation Science of: *International Union of Biological Sciences (IUBS, #15760)*. [2021.02.24/XC2497/v/C]

♦ International Association for Vehicle Design (IAVD) 12254

Contact c/o Inderscience Publishers Editorial Office, PO Box 735, Olney, MK46 5WB, UK. E-mail: editor@inderscience.com – support@inderscience.com.

URL: http://www.inderscience.com/ijvd/

Events *International Congress on Vehicle Design and Components* Geneva (Switzerland) 1989, *International congress on vehicle and components* Geneva (Switzerland) 1989, *Buses : design, manufacture and operation* Liverpool (UK) 1989, *International Congress on Vehicle Design and Components* Liverpool (UK) 1989, *International Congress on Vehicle Design and Components* Geneva (Switzerland) 1987. **Publications** *International Journal of Vehicle Design* (4 a year). **Members** Membership countries not specified. [2016/XD1330/D]

♦ International Association for Vehicle System Dynamics (IAVSD) ... 12255

SG Dept of Mechanics/Biomechanics and Mechatronics, Fac of Mechanical Engineering, Czech Technical Univ, Karlovo Namesti 13, 121 35 Prague 2, Czechia. T. +420224357361. Fax +420224916709.

URL: http://www.iavsd2015.org/

History 1968, Vienna (Austria). Founded Sep 1977, Vienna (Austria), symposia on vehicle dynamics having been inaugurated in 1968, Detroit MI (USA). **Aims** Further the advance of vehicle dynamics; encourage *engineering* applications. **Structure** Board of Officers and Trustees served by Secretary General. **Languages** English. **Staff** None. **Finance** Sources: members' dues. **Activities** Organizes symposia and workshops. **Events** *Biennial Symposium* St Petersburg (Russia) 2021, *Biennial Symposium* Gothenburg (Sweden) 2019, *Biennial Symposium* Rockhampton, QLD (Australia) 2017, *Biennial Symposium* Graz (Austria) 2015, *International Symposium on Advanced Vehicle Control* Tokyo (Japan) 2014. **Publications** *Vehicle System Dynamics* (12 a year); *IAVSD Newsletter*. Symposium proceedings; reports as supplements to the journal.

Members Full in 35 countries and territories:

Algeria, Australia, Austria, Belgium, Brazil, Bulgaria, Canada, China, Croatia, Czechia, Denmark, Egypt, Finland, France, Germany, Hungary, India, Italy, Japan, Korea Rep, Latvia, Netherlands, New Zealand, Poland, Russia, Serbia, Slovakia, South Africa, Spain, Sweden, Switzerland, Taiwan, UK, Ukraine, USA.

NGO Relations Affiliated organization to: *International Union of Theoretical and Applied Mechanics (IUTAM, #15823)*. [2014/XD9339/C]

♦ International Association of Venue Managers (internationally oriented national body)
♦ International Association of Veterinary Anatomists / see World Association of Veterinary Anatomists (#21202)
♦ International Association of Veterinary Editors (unconfirmed)
♦ International Association of Veterinary Food Hygienists / see World Association of Veterinary Food Hygienists (#21204)

♦ International Association for Veterinary Homeopathy (IAVH) 12256

Gen Sec Gregorygasse 49/11, 1230 Vienna, Austria. T. +436648618964.

Pres 5 St Davids Way, Marlborough, SN8 1DH, UK. T. +441672513863.

URL: http://www.iavh.org/

History 1986. **Aims** Promote worldwide experience in the field of veterinary homeopathy. **Structure** Board; Subcommittees (3). **Languages** English. **Staff** Voluntary. **Finance** Members' dues. **Activities** Events/meetings; politics/policy/regulatory; training/education; research/documentation. **Events** *Annual Congress* Colombia 2019, *Joint Homeopathic Symposium* Sofia (Bulgaria) 2018, *Workshop on homoeopathy in organic farming* Cirencester (UK) 2003. **Publications** *IAVH Newsletter* (4 a year) in English. *Materia Medica der Homöopathischen Veterinärmedizin* (2001).

Members in 33 countries:

Argentina, Australia, Austria, Belgium, Brazil, Canada, Colombia, Cyprus, Denmark, Estonia, Finland, France, Germany, Greece, Hungary, Ireland, Israel, Italy, Japan, Latvia, Netherlands, New Zealand, Russia, Serbia, Slovenia, South Africa, Spain, Sweden, Switzerland, Thailand, Türkiye, UK, USA. [2017.10.20/XD1311/D]

♦ International Association of Veterinary Rehabilitation and Physical Therapy (IAVRPT) 12257

Treas 8309 Birch Run Lane, Knoxville TN 37919, USA. E-mail: rehab@iavrpt.org.

URL: http://www.iavrpt.org/

History Incorporated in the State of Tennessee (USA). **Aims** Promote the practice, teaching and research of veterinary rehabilitation and physical therapy; further scientific investigation; provide better patient care based on sound scientific study. **Structure** Board of Directors of 7, including President, President-Elect, Secretary and Treasurer. **Events** *International Symposium* Cambridge (UK) 2022, *International Symposium* Cambridge (UK) 2020, *International Symposium* Knoxville, TN (USA) 2018, *International Symposium* Uppsala (Sweden) 2016, *International Symposium* Corvallis, OR (USA) 2014. **Members** Active; Associate. Membership countries not specified. [2015/XJ5771/C]

♦ International Association for Video in Arts and Culture (inactive)
♦ International Association for Vine, Fruit, and Vegetable-Growing Mechanization (inactive)

♦ International Association for Visual Semiotics (IAVS) 12258

Association internationale de sémiotique visuelle (AISV) – Asociación Internacional de Semiótica Visual

Pres Secretaria de Investigaciones, Fac de Arquitectura, Univ de Buenos Aires, Ciudad Universitaria Pab 3 piso 4, C1428BFA Buenos Aires, Argentina.

SG Avd för Semiotik, Inst för Konst- och Musikvetenskap, Lund Univ, Box 117, SE-221 00 Lund, Sweden. T. +46462229531. Fax +46462224204.

URL: http://aisviavs.wordpress.com/

History 1989, Blois (France), as *Association internationale de sémiologie de l'image (AISIM)*. **Aims** Gather semioticians interested in images and visual signification, without privileging any particular interpretation of semiotics and without favoring any semiotic tradition. **Structure** Officers: Honorary President; President; 6 Vice-Presidents; Secretary-General; Treasurer. **Languages** English, French, Spanish. **Events** *Biennial Congress* Lund (Sweden) 2019, *Biennial Congress* Liège (Belgium) 2015, *Regional Conference* Urbino (Italy) 2014, *Biennial Congress* Buenos Aires (Argentina) 2012, *Conference* Lisbon (Portugal) 2011. **Publications** *Bibliotheque Visio* – 6 vols published to date.

Members Full in 34 countries:

Argentina, Australia, Austria, Belgium, Brazil, Bulgaria, Canada, Chile, Colombia, Czechia, France, Germany, Greece, Ireland, Israel, Italy, Korea Rep, Luxembourg, Mexico, Morocco, Netherlands, Peru, Poland, Portugal, Romania, Russia, Spain, Sweden, Switzerland, Türkiye, UK, Uruguay, USA, Venezuela. [2014.06.24/XD6426/D]

♦ International Association of Voice Identification / see International Association for Identification
♦ International Association for Voice Mail and Voice Processing Services (inactive)

♦ International Association of Volcanology and Chemistry of the Earth's Interior (IAVCEI) 12259

Association internationale de volcanologie et de chimie de l'intérieur de la Terre (AIVCIT)

Pres Inst de Physique du Globe de Paris, 1 rue Jussieu, 75005 Paris, France. T. +33183957630.
SG Dipto di Scienze della Terra e Geoambientali, Univ di Bari, Via Orabona 4, 70125 Bari BA, Italy. T. +39805442589. Fax +39805442625.
URL: https://www.iavceivolcano.org/

History 1919, Brussels (Belgium). Founded as a constituent association of *International Union of Geodesy and Geophysics (IUGG, #15776)*. Statutes and By-Laws adopted 1960, Helsinki (Finland); revised: 1967, Zurich (Switzerland); 1979, Canberra (Australia). Constituent association of IUGG, which is one of the 20 Scientific Unions grouped within: *International Council for Science (ICSU, inactive)*. Former names and other names: *International Association of Vulcanology* – former; *Association internationale de volcanologie* – former. **Aims** Study scientific problems related to volcanoes and volcanic processes, past and present, and to the chemistry of the Earth's interior; encourage, initiate and coordinate research and promote international cooperation in these studies; arrange for the discussion and publication of results of scientific research on volcanology and on the chemistry of the Earth's interior; encourage volcanologists to alert appropriate authorities to the importance of adequate surveillance of active and potentially active volcanoes and of volcanic risk assessment. **Structure** Executive Committee; Bureau. IAVCEI Commissions (25), including: *IASPEI/IAVCEI Commission on Volcano Seismology (#11008)*; *IASPEI/IAVCEI Joint Commission on Physics and Chemistry of Earth Materials (#11009)*; *International Volcanic Health Hazard Network (IVHHN, see: #12259)*; *World Organization of Volcano Observatories (WOVO, #21696)*; *International Heat Flow Commission (IHFC, #13786)*. **Languages** English, French, Italian, Japanese, Spanish. **Staff** None. **Finance** Provided by IUGG and personal memberships. **Activities** Events/meetings; research/documentation. **Events** *Conference on Cities on Volcanoes* Heraklion (Greece) 2022, *Scientific Assembly* Rotorua (New Zealand) 2022, *Scientific Assembly* Rotorua (New Zealand) 2021, *Conference on Cities on Volcanoes* Naples (Italy) 2018, *Scientific Assembly* Portland, OR (USA) 2017. **Publications** *Bulletin of Volcanology* – continuation of 'Bulletin volcanologique', since 1933; *IAVCEI News*. *Catalogue of Active Volcanoes of the World Including Solfatara Fields* – in 18 parts; *Proceedings in Volcanology*. Videos. **Members** Individuals. Membership countries not specified. **NGO Relations** Cooperates with (1): *International Association for the Physical Sciences of the Oceans (IAPSO, #12082)*. [2023.02.15/XB1369/**B**]

♦ International Association for Volunteer Effort (IAVE) 12260

Contact c/o CSC Group, 805 15th St NW, Ste 100, Washington DC 20005, USA. T. +12029641133. E-mail: info@iave.org.
URL: http://www.iave.org/

History 1970, Los Angeles, CA (USA). **Aims** Enable leaders of volunteering worldwide to stand in solidarity with one another to promote, support and celebrate volunteering in the many ways it happens throughout the world. **Structure** Board of Directors; Secretariat. **Languages** English. **Staff** 7.00 FTE, paid. **Finance** Sources: contributions; fees for services; grants; members' dues; sponsorship. **Activities** Advocacy/lobbying/activism; capacity building; events/meetings; knowledge management/information dissemination; networking/liaising; projects/programmes; research and development. **Events** *Biennial Conference* Abu Dhabi (United Arab Emirates) 2022, *Biennial Conference* Abu Dhabi (United Arab Emirates) 2020, *Asia Pacific Regional Conference* Bangkok (Thailand) 2019, *Biennial Conference* Augsburg (Germany) 2018, *Asia Pacific Regional Conference* Kuala Lumpur (Malaysia) 2017. **Publications** *Volunteering Together Magazine* (3 a year) in English. *The Big Tent: Corporate Volunteering in the Global Age* by Dr Kenn Allen in Chinese, English, Spanish. **Information Services** *Corporate Engagement with the Sustainable Development Goals* in English; *Global Companies Volunteering Globally* in English, Portuguese, Spanish.

Members Individual; Organizational; Corporate; Global Friends of Volunteering; Global Network of Volunteering Leadership. Members in 127 countries and territories:
Afghanistan, Albania, Algeria, Argentina, Armenia, Australia, Austria, Bahrain, Bangladesh, Belgium, Benin, Bolivia, Bosnia-Herzegovina, Botswana, Brazil, Burundi, Cambodia, Cameroon, Canada, Central African Rep, Chad, Chile, China, Colombia, Cook Is, Costa Rica, Côte d'Ivoire, Croatia, Cyprus, Czechia, Denmark, Dominican Rep, Ecuador, Egypt, Fiji, Finland, France, Georgia, Germany, Ghana, Guatemala, Haiti, Hong Kong, India, Indonesia, Ireland, Israel, Italy, Jamaica, Japan, Jordan, Kenya, Korea Rep, Kuwait, Lebanon, Lesotho, Macau, Madagascar, Malawi, Malaysia, Maldives, Mali, Mauritius, Mexico, Moldova, Mongolia, Morocco, Mozambique, Namibia, Nepal, Netherlands, New Zealand, Nicaragua, Niger, Nigeria, Northern Ireland, Norway, Oman, Pakistan, Palestine, Panama, Papua New Guinea, Paraguay, Peru, Philippines, Poland, Portugal, Puerto Rico, Romania, Russia, Rwanda, Saudi Arabia, Scotland, Senegal, Sierra Leone, Singapore, Slovakia, Slovenia, South Africa, South Sudan, Spain, Sri Lanka, St Lucia, Sudan, Sweden, Switzerland, Taiwan, Tajikistan, Tanzania UR, Thailand, Togo, Trinidad-Tobago, Tunisia, Türkiye, Uganda, UK, Ukraine, United Arab Emirates, Uruguay, USA, Uzbekistan, Venezuela, Vietnam, Wales, Yemen, Zambia, Zimbabwe.

IGO Relations Cooperates with (1): *United Nations Volunteers (UNV, #20650)*. Associated with Department of Global Communications of the United Nations. **NGO Relations** Member of (4): *CIVICUS: World Alliance for Citizen Participation (#03962)*; *Conference of Non-Governmental Organizations in Consultative Relationship with the United Nations (CONGO, #04635)*; *New York NGO Committee on Drugs (NYNGOC, #17097)*; *NGO Committee on Disarmament, Peace and Security, New York, NY (#17106)*. Partner of (1): *International Communications Volunteers (ICVolunteers, #12817)*. Special links with: *International Council on Social Welfare (ICSW, #13076)*. *Centre for European Volunteering (CEV, #03743)* is member. [2021.03.03/XC3670/**B**]

♦ International Association of Vulcanology / see International Association of Volcanology and Chemistry of the Earth's Interior (#12259)

♦ International Association of the Wagner Societies 12261

Association internationale des cercles Richard Wagner – Richard Wagner Verband International

Pres Geschäftsstelle Am Eichelberg 27, 95448 Bayreuth, Germany. T. +49921910911. Fax +49921980851.
URL: http://www.richard-wagner.org/

History 1909. Became international in 1991. **Aims** Create interest in, and support the works of, Richard Wagner. **Languages** English, French, German. **Activities** Events/meetings; awards/prizes/competitions; financial and/or material support. **Events** *Annual Congress* Munich (Germany) 2021, *Annual Congress* Bonn (Germany) 2020, *Annual Congress* Venice (Italy) 2019, *Annual Congress* Innsbruck (Austria) 2018, *Annual Congress* Budapest (Hungary) 2017. **Publications** *Wagner Weltweit*.

Members National and local societies (148) with total of 40,000 members in 40 countries and territories:
Australia, Austria, Belgium, Brazil, Bulgaria, Canada, Chile, China, Czechia, Denmark, England, Estonia, Finland, France, Germany, Greece, Hawaii, Hong Kong, Hungary, Iceland, India, Italy, Japan, Korea Rep, Latvia, Netherlands, New Zealand, Poland, Portugal, Russia, Scotland, Singapore, Slovakia, Slovenia, South Africa, Spain, Sweden, Switzerland, Ukraine, Uruguay, USA. [2021/XE4388/**E**]

♦ International Association of the Wallpaper Trade (inactive)

♦ International Association for Walser 12262

Association internationale des Walser – Internationale Vereinigung für Walsertum (IVfW) – Associazione internationale per i Walser

Sec Bielstrasse 46, 3912 Termen VS, Switzerland. T. +41279239670.
Pres Gasse 1, 1950 Sion VS, Switzerland. T. +41273211332.
URL: http://www.wir-walser.ch/

History Also referred to previously by English title *International Association for Walser Culture*. **Aims** Promote and protect Walser culture and *folklore*.

Members Full in 5 countries:
Austria, Germany, Italy, Liechtenstein, Switzerland. [2014/XE2187/**E**]

♦ International Association for Walser Culture / see International Association for Walser (#12262)
♦ International Association of Waterborne Emergency Response Activities (inactive)

♦ International Association for Water Law 12263

Asociación Internacional de Derecho de Aguas (AIDA) – Association internationale du droit des eaux

Chairman Via Faa di Bruno 52, 00195 Rome RM, Italy. T. +393923406624. E-mail: info@aida-waterlaw.org.
URL: http://www.aida-waterlaw.org/

History 30 May 1967, Washington, DC (USA). Founded during the international conference 'Water for Peace'. Charter finalized and adopted 25 Mar 1968, Valencia (Spain), as amended 30 June 1997, 31 Oct 2001, 25 June 2003 and 29 Dec 2008. Charter replaced by Articles of Association adopted 31 May 2022. Former names and other names: *IAWL* – former; *AIDE* – former. Registration: Italy. **Aims** Foster evolution, study, knowledge, understanding and application of water law, national and international, with a view to raising awareness and the knowledge and practice of this field of the law of natural resources. **Structure** General Conference (usually once every 3 years); Executive Council. **Languages** English, French, Italian, Spanish. **Staff** Voluntary. **Finance** Sources: donations; members' dues. Other sources: patronage; trust funds. **Activities** Events/meetings; training/education. **Events** *Global Conference* Cancún (Mexico) 2017, *Global Conference* Edinburgh (UK) 2015, *Global Conference* Porto de Galinhas (Brazil) 2011, *Regional conference* Teslic (Bosnia-Herzegovina) 2001, *Conference* Paris (France) 1996. **Publications** *AquaForum-Newsletter* (2 a year); *Annales Juris Aquarum* – reports and proceedings of conferences.

Members (a) Regular: lawyers, or holders of law and/or other degrees with an active professional interest in water law, who are admitted to regular membership by Executive Council under the sponsorship of a regular member; (b) Institutional: corporate or other legal entities which are admitted to institutional membership by the Executive Council upon proposal of a member of the Association; (c) Student. Members in 106 countries:
Albania, Algeria, Argentina, Australia, Austria, Bangladesh, Belgium, Benin, Bolivia, Bosnia-Herzegovina, Botswana, Brazil, Bulgaria, Burkina Faso, Cambodia, Canada, Chad, Chile, China, Colombia, Costa Rica, Cyprus, Czechia, Dominican Rep, Ecuador, Egypt, El Salvador, Eswatini, Ethiopia, Finland, France, Germany, Ghana, Greece, Guatemala, Guinea-Bissau, Haiti, Honduras, Hungary, India, Indonesia, Iran Islamic Rep, Iraq, Ireland, Israel, Italy, Japan, Jordan, Kenya, Kuwait, Kyrgyzstan, Laos, Lebanon, Libya, Lithuania, Madagascar, Malaysia, Mali, Malta, Mauritania, Mauritius, Mexico, Montenegro, Morocco, Mozambique, Nepal, Netherlands, Nicaragua, Nigeria, Oman, Pakistan, Panama, Paraguay, Peru, Philippines, Portugal, Qatar, Russia, Senegal, Serbia, Sierra Leone, Slovakia, Somalia, South Africa, Spain, Sudan, Sweden, Switzerland, Syrian AR, Tajikistan, Tanzania UR, Thailand, Tunisia, Türkiye, Turkmenistan, Uganda, UK, United Arab Emirates, Uruguay, USA, Uzbekistan, Venezuela, Vietnam, Yemen, Zambia, Zimbabwe.

Consultative Status Consultative status granted from: *ECOSOC (#05331)* (Special); *FAO (#09260)* (Liaison Status). **IGO Relations** Accredited by (2): *United Nations Office at Geneva (UNOG, #20597)*; *United Nations Office at Vienna (UNOV, #20604)*. Partner of (3): *OECD (#17693)*; *UN-Water (#20723)*; Water Governance Initiative. Reciprocal Information Status with: *UNESCO (#20322)*. Consultative Status with: *WHO (#20950)*. Associated with Department of Global Communications of the United Nations. **NGO Relations** Partner of (1): *Global Forum on Law, Justice and Development (GFLJD, #10373)*. [2022.12.04/XB4230/**B**]

♦ International Association of Water Polo Referees (inactive)
♦ International Association on Water Quality (inactive)
♦ International Association of Water Resources / see International Water Resources Association (#15871)

♦ International Association of Water Service Companies in the Danube River Catchment Area (IAWD) 12264

Internationale Arbeitsgemeinschaft der Wasserwerke im Donaueinzugsgebiet (IAWD)

Office c/o Vienna Waterworks, Grabnergasse 4-6, 1061 Vienna, Austria. T. +436642125453. E-mail: office@iawd.at.
URL: http://www.iawd.at/

History 28 Oct 1993. Statutes adopted at foundation meeting. Former names and other names: *International Association of Water Supply Companies in the Danube River Catchment Area* – former. Registration: Austria. **Aims** Promote joint efforts at national and international level to improve and safeguard water quality of the Danube, its tributaries and related groundwater sources, to conserve the purity of surface water and groundwater resources and to avoid/eliminate dangers to water supply such as arise from pollution and other types of impairment; encourage all measures and efforts aimed at avoiding and eliminating all contamination of, and hazards to, raw water quality in order to ensure reliable drinking water supply; represent interests of member water supply companies and promote and facilitate exchange of experience among them; develop a uniform, internationally agreed, water monitoring programme. **Structure** General Assembly (annual). Board of up to 20 members, including Chairman, 2 Vice-Chairmen and Treasurer. Technical-Scientific Advisory Committee; Board; Headquarters in Vienna (Austria); Technical Economic Advisory Committee. **Languages** English, German. **Finance** Sources: members' dues. **Activities** Programme for scientific measuring and analysis jointly agreed by members gathers and evaluates data to assess water quality and analyse qualitative and quantitative changes over time. **Events** *Danube Water Forum* Tirana (Albania) 2022, *International River Symposium* Vienna (Austria) 2022, *Danube Water Conference* Vienna (Austria) 2021, *European River Symposium* Vienna (Austria) 2021, *Danube Water Conference on Water Services* Vienna (Austria) 2019. **Publications** Annual Report.

Members Ordinary; extraordinary; supporting. Water companies in 12 countries:
Austria, Bosnia-Herzegovina, Croatia, Czechia, Germany, Hungary, Netherlands, Romania, Serbia, Slovakia, Slovenia, Switzerland. [2022.11.10/XD7617/**D**]

♦ International Association of Water Supply Companies in the Danube River Catchment Area / see International Association of Water Service Companies in the Danube River Catchment Area (#12264)
♦ International Association of Waterworks in the Rhine Catchment Area (#13215)
♦ International Association of Wholesale Markets within IULA / see World Union of Wholesale Markets (#21889)

♦ International Association of Wildland Fire (IAWF) 12265

Exec Dir 1418 Washburn St, Missoula MT 59801, USA. T. +14065318264. E-mail: execdir@iawfonline.org.
URL: http://www.iawfonline.org/

History 1991. **Aims** Create an international community of wildland fire professionals; promote dialogue among the different groups involved in wildlife fire issues, including; fire researchers, fire managers, fire ecologists, firefighters, fire educators, media, land-use planners, and conservationists; act as a clearinghouse for wildland fire information. **Structure** Board of Directors. **Activities** Events/meetings. **Events** *IAWF Fire and Climate Conference* Pasadena, CA (USA) / Melbourne, VIC (Australia) 2022, *International Fire Behavior and Fuels Conference* Marseille (France) / Sydney, NSW (Australia) / Albuquerque, NM (USA) 2019, *Human Dimensions of Wildland Fire Conference* Asheville, NC (USA) 2018, *International Wildland Fire Safety Summit* Asheville, NC (USA) 2018, *International Wildland Fire Safety Summit* Barcelona (Spain) 2017. **Publications** *Current Titles in Wildland Fire* (12 a year) – bulletin on paper, disk or electronic mail; *International Journal of Wildlife Fire* (4 a year); *Wildfire Magazine* (4 a year). Software package; directory searches; bibliography searches; printing facilities, including book reprinting; translations. **Information Services** *International Bibliography of Wildland Fire*; *International Directory of Wildland Fire*. **Members** Individuals, mostly in USA but worldwide. Membership countries not specified. **NGO Relations** Member of (1): *International Society of Tropical Foresters (ISTF, #15522)*. [2022/XF4174/v/**F**]

♦ International Association of Wind Engineering (IAWE) 12266

Association internationale d'ingénierie éolienne

SG State Key Lab for Disaster Risk Reduction in Civil Engineering, Tongji Univ, Siping Road 1239, 200032 Shanghai, China.
Pres NatHaz Modeling Lab, Dept of Civil Engineering and Geological Sciences, Univ of Notre Dame, 156 Fitzpatrick Hall, Notre Dame IN 46556, USA. T. +12196315380. Fax +12196319236.
URL: http://www.iawe.org/

History Founded 1975. **Aims** Promote international cooperation among scientists, engineers and other professionals for the advancement of knowledge in the broad field of wind engineering. **Structure** General Assembly; Executive Board; International Group for Wind-Related Disaster Risk Reduction (IG-WRDRR). Regions (3): Europe and Africa; North and South America; Asia and Australia. **Languages** English. **Staff** Voluntary. **Finance** Sources: contributions; grants. Other sources: Voluntary contributions; percentage of registration fees at conferences; royalty revenues from publications. **Activities** Events/meetings; networking/liaising. **Events** *Quadrennial Conference* Beijing (China) 2019, *International Symposium on Computational Wind Engineering* Seoul (Korea Rep) 2018, *Quadrennial Asia-Pacific Conference on Wind Engineering* Auckland (New Zealand) 2017, *Americas Conference* Gainesville, FL (USA) 2017, *European and African Conference on Wind Engineering* Liège (Belgium) 2017. **Publications** *Journal of Wind Engineering and Industrial Aerodynamics (JWEIA)* – official journal.

Members Organizations (23) and Corporate Supporting (5). Organizations representing 24 countries and territories:
Austria, Belgium, Brazil, China, Cuba, Czechia, Denmark, France, Germany, Greece, Hong Kong, India, Italy, Japan, Korea Rep, Netherlands, Norway, Poland, Spain, Switzerland, Taiwan, UK, Ukraine, USA.
Included in the above, one organization listed in this Yearbook:
Australasian Wind Engineering Society (AWES).
Corporate Supporting members in 4 countries:
Canada, Italy, Japan, USA.
NGO Relations Cooperates with: *World Wind Energy Association (WWEA, #21937).*
[2015.07.05/XD2464/y/**C**]

♦ International Association of Women in the Arts (internationally oriented national body)

♦ International Association of Women Judges (IAWJ) 12267

Association internationale des femmes juges – Asociación Internacional de Mujeres Jueces
Exec Dir 1800 Massachusetts Ave NW, Suite 401, Washington DC 20036, USA. T. +12022234455. Fax +12022234480. E-mail: office@iawj.org.
URL: http://www.iawj.org/
History 1991. *International Women Judges Foundation (IWJF, inactive)* merged into IAWJ, 2002. **Aims** Promote and empower women judges to help uproot gender bias, end discriminatory laws, advance gender-responsive courts and promote human rights for all. **Structure** Board of Managerial Trustees; International Executive Council; Board of Directors. **Languages** English, French, Spanish. **Staff** 6.00 FTE, paid. **Finance** Sources: international organizations. Supported by: *Arca Foundation*; *Commonwealth Foundation (CF, #04330)*; *DANIDA*; Dutch Ministry of Foreign Affairs; *Ford Foundation (#09858)*; *Friedrich-Ebert-Stiftung (FES)*; *German Marshall Fund of the United States (GMF)*; *International Bank for Reconstruction and Development (IBRD, #12317)*; *Mertz Gilmore Foundation*; *Swedish International Development Cooperation Agency (Sida)*; *United Nations Democracy Fund (UNDEF, #20551)*; *United States Agency for International Development (USAID)*; United States Department of State. **Activities** Capacity building; networking/liaising; training/education. **Events** *Biennial Conference* Marrakech (Morocco) 2023, *Biennial Conference* Auckland (New Zealand) 2021, *Biennial Conference* Auckland (New Zealand) 2020, *Europe, Middle East and North Africa Regional Conference* Madrid (Spain) 2019, *Asia Pacific Regional Conference* Panglao Is (Philippines) 2019. **Publications** *Counterbalance International* (2 a year) in English, Spanish – newsletter. Membership directory. **Members** Individuals (over 6,000) and Associations (49) in 85 countries and territories. Membership countries not specified. **Consultative Status** Consultative status granted from: *ECOSOC (#05331)* (Special). **IGO Relations** Associated with Department of Global Communications of the United Nations. **NGO Relations** Member of: *International Legal Assistance Consortium (ILAC, #14025).* [2020/XC0125/**C**]

♦ International Association of Women Ministers (IAWM) 12268

Treas 1921 Palm St, Reading PA 19604, USA.
Pres address not obtained.
URL: http://www.womenministers.org/
History 1919, St Louis, MO (USA). Former names and other names: *American Association of Women Ministers* – former. **Aims** Urge women to educate themselves for *Christian* ministry; promote international and ecumenical advocacy for women's ordination; encourage women to grow professionally in ministry. **Structure** Assembly (biennial); Executive Board; Regional Directors; Committee Chairs. **Languages** English, German, Spanish. **Staff** Voluntary. **Finance** Sources: contributions; investments; members' dues. **Events** *Assembly* Karlsruhe (Germany) 2022, *Assembly* 2021, *Assembly* Pittsburgh, PA (USA) 2019, *Assembly* Matanzas (Cuba) 2017, *Assembly* Stony Point, NY (USA) 2015. **Publications** *The Woman's Pulpit* (4 a year). Prayer calendar; assembly proceedings.
Members Active; student; retired; fraternal; sustaining. Women ministers of the church in 43 countries and territories:
Anguilla, Australia, Bahamas, Botswana, Cameroon, Canada, Cuba, Czechia, England, Eswatini, Ethiopia, France, Germany, Ghana, Guatemala, Haiti, Hungary, India, Indonesia, Jamaica, Japan, Kenya, Korea Rep, Lesotho, Liberia, Malawi, Mexico, Namibia, New Zealand, Nicaragua, Nigeria, Northern Ireland, Pakistan, Peru, Philippines, Scotland, Sierra Leone, South Africa, Sweden, Switzerland, Uganda, USA, Zambia. [2022.10.25/XC0369/v/**C**]

♦ International Association of Women Philosophers 12269

Association internationale de femmes philosophes – Internationale Assoziation von Philosophinnen (IAPh)
Sec Center History of Women Philosophers and Scientists, Univ Paderborn, Warburger Str 100, 33098 Paderborn, Germany. T. +495251602309.
Treas address not obtained.
URL: http://www.women-philosophy.org/
History 1976, Würzburg (Germany). Registration: Amtsgericht Berlin, No/ID: VR 12895 B, Germany. **Aims** Support communication and cooperation among women who are philosophically active or interested; encourage feminist research in the fields of philosophy and of the history of philosophy in particular; improve working conditions and the reputation of women philosophers by drawing attention to historical as well as current discrimination against them as individuals and against their work. **Structure** Board. **Languages** English, German, Spanish. **Staff** 9.00 FTE, voluntary. **Finance** Sources: members' dues. **Activities** Events/meetings. **Events** *Biennial Symposium* Paderborn (Germany) 2021, *Biennial Symposium* Paderborn (Germany) 2020, *Biennial Symposium* Beijing (China) 2018, *Biennial Symposium* Melbourne, VIC (Australia) 2016, *Biennial Symposium* Alcala de Henares (Spain) 2014. **Members** Women philosophers in over 35 countries. Membership countries not specified. **IGO Relations** Member of (1): *UNESCO (#20322)* (International Network of Women Philosophers). **NGO Relations** Member of (1): *International Federation of Philosophical Societies (FISP, #13507).* [2022.07.28/XD2650/v/**C**]

♦ International Association of Women Police (IAWP) 12270

Pres Lowell Massachusetts Police Dept, 12600 Kavanaugh Lane, Bowie MD 20715, USA. T. +13014641402. E-mail: president@iawp.org – carolpaterick@gmail.com.
URL: http://www.iawp.org/
History 1915, Los Angeles, CA (USA). Reorganized 1956, San Diego CA (USA) and adopted current name, 25 Oct 1969; amended Oct 1977, Oct 1979, Oct 1982, Sep 1984, Sep 1985, Sep 1987, Sep 1988. Current constitution, Sep 2007. Former names and other names: *International Policewomen's Association* – former. Registration: 501(c)(6) organization, No/ID: 51-0200042, Start date: 1926, USA, Washington DC. **Aims** Strengthen, unite and raise capacity of women in policing internationally. **Structure** Board of Directors (meets twice a year); Regional Coordinators (26); Board of Trustees; Standing Committees (8); Affiliates (30). **Languages** English. **Finance** Sources: fundraising; members' dues; revenue from activities/projects; sponsorship. **Activities** Education/training; events/meetings; financial and/or material support; awards/prizes/competitions; networking/liaising. **Events** *Annual Conference* Abu Dhabi (United Arab Emirates) 2025, *Annual Conference* Chicago, IL (USA) 2024, *Annual Conference* Auckland (New Zealand) 2023, *Annual Conference* Niagara Falls, ON (Canada) 2022, *Annual Conference* Yogyakarta (Indonesia) 2021. **Publications** *WomenPolice* (4 a year) – magazine; *IAWP Speaker's Bureau* (annual). Brochures and historical information available online. Information Services: Member Mentor Directory; Member Seeking-a-mentor Directory. **Members** Categories: Active; Associate; Honorary; Affiliate; Life. Membership countries not specified. **IGO Relations** Cooperates with: *South Eastern and Eastern Europe Clearinghouse for the Control of Small Arms and Light Weapons (SEESAC, #19804).* Associated with Department of Global Communications of the United Nations. **NGO Relations** Cooperates with: *Australasian Council of Women and Policing (ACWAP).* [2020/XD3868/**F**]

♦ International Association of Women in Radio and Television (IAWRT) 12271

Association internationale de femmes à la radio et à la télévision – Asociación Internacional de Mujeres de Radio y Televisión
Sec 14 Robbinsdale Residences, G. Araneta Avenue corner Palanza Street, 1113 Quezon City, Philippines. E-mail: contact@iawrt.org – secretariat@iawrt.org.
URL: http://www.iawrt.org/
History 30 Sep 1951. New statutes adopted 1956, to include television. New statutes, 2003, include new media. Former names and other names: *International Association of Radio Women* – former. **Aims** Network with and support professional women in integrating and extending their position in the *media*; aware of the responsibility of the mass media towards society as a whole, work to bring a woman's viewpoint to all aspects of world development, human rights and peace. **Structure** Board; Local Chapters (7). No physical headquarters. **Languages** English. **Staff** 3.00 FTE, paid. **Finance** Sources: donations; members' dues. Other sources: broadcasting companies. Supported by: *Forum for Kvinner og Utviklingsspørsmål (FOKUS)*. **Activities** Awards/prizes/competitions; events/meetings; financial and/or material support; projects/programmes. **Events** *Biennial Conference* Zanzibar (Tanzania UR) 2022, *Biennial Conference* Quezon City (Philippines) 2017, *Biennial Conference* Delhi (India) 2015, *Biennial Conference* Casablanca (Morocco) 2013, *Biennial Conference* Kuala Lumpur (Malaysia) 2011. **Publications** *IAWRT E-mail Bulletin* (4-6 a year).
Members Women professionals (400) in radio, television, electronic media and research work in 61 countries and territories:
Afghanistan, Australia, Belgium, Bhutan, Brazil, Bulgaria, Burundi, Cambodia, Cameroon, Canada, China, Czechia, Denmark, Ethiopia, Finland, Gambia, Germany, Ghana, Guatemala, Guyana, Hungary, Iceland, India, Ireland, Jamaica, Kenya, Laos, Lithuania, Madagascar, Malawi, Malaysia, Moldova, Mongolia, Nepal, Netherlands, Niger, Nigeria, Norway, Pakistan, Palestine, Peru, Philippines, Romania, Russia, Rwanda, Serbia, Sierra Leone, South Africa, Sri Lanka, Sweden, Switzerland, Taiwan, Tanzania UR, Thailand, Trinidad-Tobago, Uganda, UK, USA, Vietnam, Zambia, Zimbabwe.
Consultative Status Consultative status granted from: *ECOSOC (#05331)* (Special). **IGO Relations** Accredited by (1): *United Nations Office at Vienna (UNOV, #20604)*. Associated with Department of Global Communications of the United Nations. **NGO Relations** Member of (1): *Ethical Journalism Network (EJN, #05554).* [2022/XD0278/**C**]

♦ International Association for Women in the Seafood Industry (inactive)

♦ International Association for Women's Mental Health (IAWMH) 12272

Exec Dir 8213 Lakenheath Way, Potomac MD 20854, USA. T. +13019836282. Fax +13019836288. E-mail: info@iawmh.org.
URL: http://www.iawmh.org/
History 2001. Registration: 501(c)(3) organization, No/ID: EIN: 16-1614585, Start date: 2002, USA, State of Maryland. **Aims** Improve mental health of women worldwide by promoting gender-sensitive and autonomy-enhancing mental health services for women. **Structure** Board of Directors; Executive Committee. **Languages** English. **Staff** 1.00 FTE, paid. **Activities** Advocacy/lobbying/activism; awareness raising; events/meetings; networking/liaising; projects/programmes; publishing activities. **Events** *World Congress on Women's Mental Health* Bangalore (India) 2025, *World Congress on Women's Mental Health* Maastricht (Netherlands) 2022, *World Congress on Women's Mental Health* Melbourne, VIC (Australia) 2021, *World Congress on Women's Mental Health* Paris (France) 2019, *World Congress on Women's Mental Health* Dublin (Ireland) 2017. **Publications** *Archives of Women's Mental Health*. **Consultative Status** Consultative status granted from: *ECOSOC (#05331)* (Special). **NGO Relations** Member of (1): *Global Alliance for Maternal Mental Health (GAMMH, #10208).* [2023.01.31/XM3522/**D**]

♦ International Association of Women Writers (inactive)

♦ International Association of Wood Anatomists (IAWA) 12273

Association internationale des anatomistes du bois – Asociación Internacional de Anatomistas de la Madera – Internationaler Verband der Holzanatomen
Exec Sec c/o Research Inst of Wood Industry, Chinese Ac of Forestry, 1 Dongxiaofu, Haidian District, 100091 Beijing, China. E-mail: iawa.financial.office@gmail.com.
URL: http://www.iawa-website.org/
History 4 Jul 1931, Paris (France). Established following a meeting of wood anatomists at *International Botanical Congress (IBC)*, 1930, Cambridge (UK). **Aims** Create awareness of the place of wood anatomy in science, technology and conservation of *natural resources*; exchange ideas and information; encourage and assist study and teaching of wood anatomy and related fields and promote research; facilitate collection, storage and exchange of research materials; provide rational bases for consistent terminology descriptions; cooperate with others having similar aims in related fields of *plant* anatomy. **Structure** International Council. Regional groups: Africa; Americas; Asia-Pacific; Europe. Membership and meetings open. **Languages** English. **Staff** 2.00 FTE, voluntary. **Finance** Sources: members' dues. **Activities** Events/meetings; standards/guidelines. **Events** *Fossil Wood Symposium* Prague (Czechia) 2024, *International Symposium on Challenges and Opportunities for Udating Wood Identification* Beijing (China) 2019, *Pacific Regional Wood Anatomy Conference (PRWAC)* Bali (Indonesia) 2017, *Pacific Regional Wood Anatomy Conference (PRWAC)* Nanjing (China) 2013, *International Symposium on Wood Structure in Plant Biology and Ecology* Naples (Italy) 2013. **Publications** *IAWA Journal* (4 a year). *Wood Anatomy of the Mimosoideae (Heguminorae)* (2006) by J E Evans et al; *IAWA List of Microscopic Features for Softwood Identification* (2004); *Wood Atlas of the Euphorbiaceae* (2004) by L Y Th Westra and J Koek-Noorman; *Woods of the Middle Eocene Nut Beds Flora, Clarno Formation* (2002) by E A Wheeler and S R Manchester; *Wood Anatomy of the Sapindaceae* (1999) by R Klaassen; *Bibliography of Systematic Wood Anatomy of Dicotyledons* (1994) by Mary Gregory; *IAWA List of Microscopic Features for Hardwood Identification* (1989).
Members Full; Student; Library. Individuals (550) in 69 countries and territories:
Argentina, Australia, Austria, Bangladesh, Belgium, Brazil, Bulgaria, Canada, Chile, China, Colombia, Croatia, Cuba, Czechia, Denmark, Dominican Rep, Egypt, Finland, France, Gabon, Georgia, Germany, Ghana, Greece, Guyana, Honduras, Hungary, India, Indonesia, Iran Islamic Rep, Ireland, Israel, Italy, Japan, Kenya, Korea Rep, Lithuania, Malaysia, Mexico, Montenegro, Myanmar, Nepal, Netherlands, New Zealand, Norway, Panama, Papua New Guinea, Paraguay, Peru, Philippines, Poland, Portugal, Russia, Serbia, Slovakia, Slovenia, South Africa, Spain, Sweden, Switzerland, Taiwan, Tanzania UR, Thailand, Türkiye, UK, Uruguay, USA, Venezuela, Vietnam. [2021/XB1372/v/**B**]

♦ International Association of Wood Products Societies (IAWPS) 12274

Contact Japan Wood Research Society, Takasakiya-Bld 4F, 1-1-17 Mukogaoka, Bunkyo-ku, Tokyo, 113-0023 Japan. T. +81368785195. E-mail: office@jwrs.org.
URL: http://www.jwrs.org/iawps/
History 1995. **Aims** Support the continuing development of the science and technology of wood and the optimization of its utilization. **Activities** Organizes conferences, symposia. **Events** *International Symposium on Wood Science and Technology* Tokyo (Japan) 2015, *Pacific Rim Bio-Based Composites Symposium* Shizuoka (Japan) 2012, *Biennial Conference* Madison, WI (USA) 2010, *International Symposium on Wood Science and Technology* Harbin (China) 2008, *Biennial Conference* Yokohama (Japan) 2005.
Members Societies (15) in 10 countries and territories:
Australia, Brazil, China, Indonesia, Japan, Korea Rep, Malaysia, Mexico, Taiwan, USA. [2023/XD6874/**D**]

♦ International Association of Wool Textile Laboratories (INTERWOOLLABS) 12275

Association internationale de laboratoires textiles lainiers – Internationale Gesellschaft der Wolltextillaboratorien
SG 7 Southway, Bingley, Bradford, BD16 3EW, UK. E-mail: info@interwoollabs.org.
URL: http://www.interwoollabs.org/
History 4 Jun 1969, Paris (France). **Aims** Develop harmonization among member laboratories to ensure correct and uniform application of IWTO *test methods*, thus obtaining coordinated analyses with maximum benefit to the wool trade; aid member laboratories in solving disputes arising from differences in measurements by discovering the reason for the recorded discrepancy. **Structure** General Assembly (annual, at Conference); Board of Directors; Executive Council. **Languages** English, French. **Staff** 2.00 FTE, paid; 7.00 FTE, voluntary. **Finance** Sources: members' dues. **Activities** Conducts: comparative tests on fibre fineness and length measurements; confidential tests for accreditation of laboratories and for continued membership-awards seals, indicating the methods of analysis for which the laboratory is recognized. **Events** *Annual general assembly / Annual Conference* Buenos Aires (Argentina) 2003, *Annual general assembly / Annual Conference* Barcelona (Spain) 2002, *Annual general assembly / Annual Conference* Shanghai (China) 2001, *Annual general assembly / Annual Conference* Christchurch (New Zealand) 2000, *Annual general assembly / Annual Conference* Florence (Italy) 1999.
Members Laboratories reaching stipulated standards (125) in 36 countries and territories:
Argentina, Australia, Austria, Belgium, Brazil, Canada, Chile, China, Czechia, Egypt, Falklands/Malvinas, France, Germany, Hong Kong, Hungary, India, Ireland, Italy, Japan, Korea Rep, Mexico, Netherlands, New Zealand, Peru, Portugal, Russia, Serbia, South Africa, Spain, Switzerland, Taiwan, Thailand, Türkiye, UK, Uruguay, USA. [2020/XC1373/**C**]

♦ **International Association of Word and Image Studies (IAWIS)** 12276
Association internationale pour l'étude des rapports entre texte et image (AIERTI)
Sec address not obtained.
Pres address not obtained.
URL: http://wmaforum.org/
History 1987, Amsterdam (Netherlands). Registered in accordance with Dutch law. **Aims** Act as an international forum for different disciplines and approaches to exchange ideas about the way visual and verbal work interact; expand interdisciplinary interaction on the basis of local associations. **Structure** General Assembly; Advisory Board; Executive Board; Administrative Offices (2). **Languages** English, French. **Staff** None. **Finance** Members' dues. **Events** *Triennial Conference* Esch-sur-Alzette (Luxembourg) 2021, *Triennial Conference* Esch-sur-Alzette (Luxembourg) 2020, *Triennial Conference* Lausanne (Switzerland) 2017, *Triennial Conference* Dundee (UK) 2014, *Triennial conference* Montréal, QC (Canada) 2011. **Publications** *IAWIS Newsletter* (2 a year). Conference proceedings.
Members Individuals in 28 countries and territories:
Argentina, Austria, Belgium, Brazil, Canada, China, Colombia, Czechia, Denmark, Finland, France, Germany, Hungary, Ireland, Israel, Italy, Japan, Mexico, Netherlands, New Zealand, Poland, Portugal, Spain, Sweden, Switzerland, Taiwan, UK, USA.
[2020.03.10/XD4011/v/**D**]

♦ **International Association for Word and Music Studies (WMA)** 12277
Treas Univ of Graz, Dept of English Studies, Heinrichstrasse 36/2, 8010 Graz, Austria. T. +433163802472.
Sec address not obtained.
URL: http://www.wordmusicstudies.net/
History 1997. Registration: Austria. **Aims** Promote transdisciplinary scholarly inquiry devoted to relations between literature/verbal texts/language and music. **Structure** General Assembly; Executive Board; Advisory Board; Court of Arbitration. **Languages** English. **Staff** No full-time staff. **Finance** Sources: members' dues. **Activities** Events/meetings; training/education. **Events** *Conference* Munich (Germany) 2023, *Conference* Leipzig (Germany) 2022, *Conference* Leipzig (Germany) 2021, *Conference* Graz (Austria) 2019, *Conference* Stockholm (Sweden) 2017. **Publications** *Word and Music Studies (WMS).*
Members Individuals in 26 countries and territories:
Australia, Austria, Azerbaijan, Belgium, Canada, China, Finland, France, Germany, Hong Kong, Hungary, India, Ireland, Italy, Japan, Lithuania, Norway, Philippines, Poland, Russia, Slovenia, Spain, Sweden, Türkiye, UK, USA. [2022.06.24/XJ5420/**C**]

♦ International Association for the Work of Doctor Albert Schweitzer of Lambaréné (#02723)
♦ International Association of Workers Movement Study Centres (inactive)
♦ International Association of Workers for Troubled Children and Youth / see International Association of Social Educators (#12167)

♦ **International Association of Workforce Professionals (IAWP)** 12278
Main Office 3267 Bee Caves Rd, Ste 107-104, Austin TX 78746, USA. E-mail: info@iawponline.org.
URL: https://iawponline.org/
History 20 Dec 1913, as *'American Association of Public Employment Offices'.* 1920, with the affiliation of Canada, name changed to *International Association of Public Employment Services.* Name changed 1952 to *International Association of Personnel in Employment Security (IAPES) – Association internationale du personnel de la sécurité de l'emploi.* 2003, current name adopted. **Aims** Enhance the individual competence, knowledge and proficiency of members engaged in all occupations in the field of employment security, training and related programs. **Structure** Officers: President, President-elect, Vice-President, Secretary-Treasurer. Committees; Executive Board's subcommittees. Chapters: 53 in USA and Canada; 10 in other countries. Districts: 15 in USA (including possessions) and one each for Canada, Japan, Taiwan, Europe plus one all other nations with organized chapters. *IAPES Foundation.* **Staff** 1.00 FTE, paid. **Finance** Members' dues. **Events** *Annual Conference* San Antonio, TX (USA) 2019, *Annual Conference* Cincinnati, OH (USA) 2018, *Annual Conference* Costa Mesa, CA (USA) 2017, *Annual Conference* Buffalo, NY (USA) 2016, *Annual Conference* Savannah, GA (USA) 2015. **Publications** *Workforce* (8 a year) – professional newsletter. Resource Guides.
Members Based in North America but covers 10 countries and territories:
Israel, Japan, Latvia, Mexico, Nigeria, Poland, Puerto Rico, Russia, Senegal, Taiwan. [2022/XF0938/**F**]

♦ **International Association on Workplace Bullying and Harassment (IAWBH)** 12279
Pres address not obtained. E-mail: contact@iawbh.org.
URL: http://www.iawbh.org/
History Jun 2008, Montréal, QC (Canada). Founded during 6th International Workplace Bullying Conference. **Aims** Stimulate, generate, integrate and disseminate research and evidence-based practice in the field of workplace bullying and harassment. **Structure** Board. **Languages** English. **Staff** Voluntary. **Finance** Sources: members' dues. **Activities** Events/meetings; research/documentation. **Events** *International Conference on Workplace Bullying and Harassment* San Diego, CA (USA) 2022, *International Conference on Workplace Bullying and Harassment* Dubai (United Arab Emirates) 2021, *Biennial Conference* Dubai (United Arab Emirates) 2020, *Biennial Conference* Bordeaux (France) 2018, *Biennial Conference* Auckland (New Zealand) 2016. **Publications** *IAWBH Newsletter* (4 a year).
Members Individuals (approx 200) in 27 countries and territories:
Albania, Australia, Belgium, Canada, Denmark, Finland, France, Germany, Greece, Hong Kong, India, Ireland, Japan, Mexico, Netherlands, New Zealand, Norway, Poland, Portugal, Saudi Arabia, Spain, Sweden, Switzerland, Türkiye, UK, United Arab Emirates, USA. [2022/XM8156/**C**]

♦ International Association of Work Psychology in French Language (#02734)
♦ International Association of World Counsellors For Better Tomorrow (internationally oriented national body)

♦ **International Association for World Englishes (IAWE)** 12280
Sec Univ of Michigan-Dearborn, 4901 Evergreen Rd, Dearborn MI 48128, USA.
URL: http://www.iaweworks.org/
History 1978. **Aims** Provide a forum for the study, research and teaching of world Englishes. **Structure** Executive Committee; Commissions (2). **Languages** English. **Staff** 1.00 FTE, voluntary. **Finance** Members' dues. **Activities** Events/meetings. **Events** *Annual Conference* Stony Brook, NY (USA) 2023, *Annual Conference* Limerick (Ireland) 2019, *Annual Conference* Quezon City (Philippines) 2018, *Annual Conference* Syracuse, NY (USA) 2017, *Annual Conference* Istanbul (Turkey) 2015. **Publications** *World Englishes* – journal.
Members Individuals (over 200) in 42 countries and territories:
Australia, Austria, Bahrain, Brazil, Brunei Darussalam, Canada, Chile, China, Czechia, Finland, France, Germany, Greece, Hong Kong, India, Iran Islamic Rep, Ireland, Israel, Italy, Japan, Korea Rep, Lithuania, Macau, Malaysia, Mexico, Netherlands, New Zealand, Nigeria, Philippines, Russia, Saudi Arabia, Singapore, South Africa, Spain, Sweden, Switzerland, Taiwan, Thailand, Türkiye, UK, United Arab Emirates, USA. [2020.03.03/XD7537/**D**]

♦ **International Association of World Peace Advocates (IAWPA)** 12281
Contact Apartment 5, Plot 885, Olatuse St, Jabi, Abuja, Federal Capital Territory, Nigeria. E-mail: uninfodesk@rocketmail.com.
URL: https://iawpa.org/
Aims Promote universal peace, just and inclusive society within the United Nations; ensure that all classes of people in society are carried along on the schemes, programmes and policies of the United Nations. **Structure** International Governing Council. **NGO Relations** Partner of (1): *International Campaign to Abolish Nuclear Weapons (ICAN, #12426).* [2019/XM8974/**C**]

♦ International Association of Yoga Science Centres (no recent information)

♦ **International Association of Young Lawyers** 12282
Association internationale des jeunes avocats (AIJA) – Asociación Internacional de Jóvenes Abogados – Internationale Vereinigung Junger Rechtsanwälte – Associação Internacional dos Jovens Advogados – Associazione Internazionale dei Giovani Avvocati – Internationale Vereniging van Jonge Advokaten
Office Manager Av de Tervueren 231, 1150 Brussels, Belgium. T. +3223473334. E-mail: office@aija.org.
URL: http://www.aija.org/
History Jul 1962, Toulouse (France). Founded in Toulouse (France) and Luxembourg (simultaneously). Objectives extended in the *'Declaration of Athens'*, adopted at 4th Congress, 27 Aug 1966, Athens. Registration: Banque-Carrefour des Entreprises, No/ID: 0850.829.857, Start date: 1 Jan 1996, Belgium. **Aims** Provide outstanding international opportunities for young lawyers to network, learn and develop. **Structure** General Assembly (annual); Bureau; Extended Bureau; Executive Committee; Committees; Standing Commissions (20); Secretariat. **Languages** English, French. **Staff** 7.00 FTE, paid. **Finance** Sources: meeting proceeds; members' dues. **Activities** Events/meetings; networking/liaising; training/education. **Events** *Annual Congress* Rio de Janeiro (Brazil) 2023, *Half-Yearly Conference* The Hague (Netherlands) 2023, *Annual Labour Law Conference* Amsterdam (Netherlands) 2022, *Half-Yearly Conference* Edinburgh (UK) 2022, *Annual Congress* Singapore (Singapore) 2022. **Publications** Archives; annual directory; books; publications of Commissions; other publications. Publishes books written by members.
Members Collective. Associations/bars of lawyers and corporate counsels in 25 countries and territories:
Argentina, Australia, Austria, Belgium, Canada, Chad, Finland, France, Germany, Hong Kong, Hungary, Italy, Japan, Luxembourg, Mexico, Netherlands, Portugal, Senegal, Slovakia, Spain, Sweden, Switzerland, Tunisia, UK, USA.
Individuals (about 4,000) in over 90 countries. Membership countries not specified.
Consultative Status Consultative status granted from: *African Commission on Human and Peoples' Rights (ACHPR, #00255)* (Observer). **IGO Relations** Represented with: *European Court of Human Rights (#06855); International Institute for the Unification of Private Law (UNIDROIT, #13934).* Accredited by: *United Nations Office at Vienna (UNOV, #20604).* Associated with Department of Global Communications of the United Nations. **NGO Relations** Represented with: American Bar Association; *The European Law Students' Association (ELSA, #07660); Inter-American Bar Association (IABA, #11401); International Bar Association (IBA, #12320); International Commission of Jurists (ICJ, #12695) International Legal Assistance Consortium (ILAC, #14025); Inter-Pacific Bar Association (IPBA, #15957).* Member of: *Federation of European and International Associations Established in Belgium (FAIB, #09508).* [2022.10.12/XC3615/**B**]

♦ International Association of Young Philosophers (inactive)

♦ **International Association of Youth and Family Judges and Magistrates (IAYFJM)** 12283
Association internationale des magistrats de la jeunesse et de la famille (AIMJF) – Asociación Internacional de Magistrados de la Juventud y de la Familia
Pres c/o IDE, Case Postale 4176, 1950 Sion VS 4, Switzerland. E-mail: president@aimjf.org.
URL: http://www.aimjf.org/
History Founded 1930, Brussels (Belgium), as *International Association of Juvenile Court Judges – Association internationale des juges des enfants.* Name changed, 1958, to *International Association of Youth Magistrates – Association internationale des magistrats de la jeunesse (AIMJ).* Previously also referred to in English as *International Association of Juvenile and Family Court Magistrates (IAJFCM).* Present name adopted at 10th World Congress, Montréal QC (Canada), 21 Jul 1978. Statutes adopted 1930, Brussels (Belgium); revised: 1963, 1966; 1978; 1992; 1998. Registered in accordance with Belgian law. **Aims** Promote research on international problems facing the operation of the courts and various laws relating to youth and family. **Structure** General Assembly (every 4 years); Council; Executive Committee; General Committee; Sub-Committees. **Languages** English, French, Spanish. **Staff** None. **Finance** Sources: members' dues. **Activities** Events/meetings. **Events** *Latin American Regional Conference* Buenos Aires (Argentina) 2019, *American Regional Conference* Mérida (Mexico) 2019, *European Section Meeting* Paris (France) 2018, *World Congress on Justice for Children* Paris (France) 2018, *European Section Meeting* London (UK) 2016. **Publications** *IAYFJM Chronicle* (2 a year) in English, French, Spanish.
Members Ordinary: judges, magistrates and other persons who hold or have held office in a youth or family court or are performing similar functions; Affiliated National Associations; Associate; Honorary. Individuals in 31 countries and territories:
Argentina, Australia, Austria, Bangladesh, Belgium, Canada, Chile, Croatia, France, Germany, India, Italy, Kosovo, Mexico, New Zealand, North Macedonia, Northern Ireland, Peru, Poland, Portugal, Samoa, Scotland, South Africa, Spain, Sweden, Switzerland, Tajikistan, Türkiye, UK, USA, Venezuela.
National associations in 12 countries:
Argentina, Austria, Belgium, Brazil, France, Germany, Italy, Japan, Netherlands, Poland, Switzerland, USA.
Also included in the above, South Pacific Council for Youth and Children's Courts.
Consultative Status Consultative status granted from: *Council of Europe (CE, #04881)* (Participatory Status). **IGO Relations** Accredited by: *Interagency Panel on Juvenile Justice (IPJJ, #11390).* Associated with Department of Global Communications of the United Nations. **NGO Relations** Member of: *Alliance of NGOs on Crime Prevention and Criminal Justice (#00709);* Child Justice Advocacy Group; *Child Rights Connect (#03884).* [2020/XC1375/**C**]

♦ International Association of Youth Magistrates / see International Association of Youth and Family Judges and Magistrates (#12283)

♦ **International Association for Youth Mental Health (IAYMH)** 12284
Contact C/- Locked Bag 10, 35 Poplar Road, Parkville VIC 3052, Australia.
URL: https://www.iaymh.org/
History Founded 2012. Registered in accordance with Australian law. **Aims** Improve mental health outcomes for 12-25 year olds. **Structure** Executive Committee. **Activities** Events/meetings. **Events** *International Youth Mental Health Conference* Copenhagen (Denmark) 2022, *International Youth Mental Health Conference* Brisbane, QLD (Australia) 2019, *International Youth Mental Health Conference* Dublin (Ireland) 2017, *International Youth Mental Health Conference* Montréal, QC (Canada) 2015, *International Youth Mental Health Conference* Brighton (UK) 2013. [2019/XM8649/**C**]

♦ International Association for Youth Transportation Safety (#02742)
♦ International Association 'Znanie' (internationally oriented national body)
♦ International Association of Zoo Educators / see International Zoo Educators Association (#15944)

♦ **International Asteroid Warning Network (IAWN)** 12285
Contact UMD-Dept of Astronomy, 1113 Physical Sciences Complex, Bldg 415, College Park MD 20742, USA.
Contact address not obtained.
URL: http://iawn.net/
History 2013. **Aims** Establish a worldwide effort to detect, track and physically characterize near-earth objects to determine those that are potential impact threats to earth. **Structure** Steering Committee. **Events** *Meeting* College Park, MD (USA) 2019, *Meeting* Garching (Germany) 2019, *Meeting* Vienna (Austria) 2019, *Meeting* Knoxville, TN (USA) 2018, *Meeting* Vienna (Austria) 2018. **IGO Relations** Sanctioned by *United Nations (UN, #20515).* [2022/XM7274/**F**]

♦ International Asthma Council (inactive)

♦ **International Astronautical Federation (IAF)** 12286
Fédération internationale d'astronautique
Exec Dir 100 Avenue de Suffren, 75015 Paris, France. T. +33145674260. Fax +33142732120. E-mail: info@iafastro.org.
URL: http://www.iafastro.org/
History Sep 1951, France. Founded when scientists from the field of space research gathered in an attempt to ensure a constant dialogue between the space nations, regardless of political turmoil. Former names and other names: *Federación Astronautica Internacional* – former; *Internationaler Astronautischer Föderation* – former. Registration: France. **Aims** Promote cooperation through collaborative platforms for experts from space agencies, industry and research; advance international development by bringing together experts from experienced and emerging space nations alike; nurture new talents through activities targeting students and young professionals. **Structure** General Assembly (annual, at International Astronautical Congress); Bureau; Steering Committee; Administrative and Technical Committees; International Programme Committee. **Languages** English, French, German, Russian, Spanish. **Staff** 13.00 FTE, paid; 2.00 FTE, voluntary. **Finance** Sources: donations; meeting proceeds; members' dues. **Activities** Awards/prizes/competitions; awareness raising; events/meetings; knowledge management/information dissemination. **Events** *International Astronautical Congress* 2025, *International Astronautical Congress* Baku (Azerbaijan) 2023, *Spring Meeting* Paris (France) 2023, *International Astronautical Congress (IAC)* Paris (France) 2022, *Spring Meeting* Paris (France) 2022. **Publications** Reports; technical paper archive; books; congress and scientific meeting proceedings.

Members Space organizations (433) in 72 countries. Membership countries not specified.
Included among membership, 11 organizations listed in this Yearbook:
Association of European Space Industry (EUROSPACE, #02544); Eurisy (#05625); European Conference for Aero-Space Sciences (EUCASS, #06728); International Association for the Advancement of Space Safety (IAASS, #11689); Internationaler Förderkreis für Raumfahrt Hermann Oberth-Wernher von Braun (IFR); International Lunar Observatory Association (ILOA, #14067); Secure World Foundation (SWF); Space Foundation; Space Generation Advisory Council in Support of the United Nations Programme on Space Applications (SGAC, #19898); Women in Aerospace Europe (WIA Europe, #20984).
Members map: https://www.iafastro.org/membership/iaf-members-map.html.
Consultative Status Consultative status granted from: *UNESCO (#20322)* (Consultative Status); *World Meteorological Organization (WMO, #21649).* **IGO Relations** Observer status with (1): *Committee on the Peaceful Uses of Outer Space (COPUOS, #04277).* Partner of (1): *Group on Earth Observations (GEO, #10735).* Associated with Department of Global Communications of the United Nations. **NGO Relations** Member of (1): *Asia-Pacific Regional Space Agency Forum (APRSAF, #02010).* Cooperates with (3): *Committee on Space Research (COSPAR, #04287); International Academy of Astronautics (IAA, #11536); International Institute of Space Law (IISL, #13926).* [2022.06.24/XC1381/y/**C**]

♦ International Astronomical Union (IAU) 12287
Union astronomique internationale (UAI)
Gen Sec 98bis Blvd Arago, 75014 Paris, France. T. +33143258358. E-mail: iauinfos@iap.fr – iau-general.secretary@iap.fr.
Assistant address not obtained. E-mail: iau-assistant.general.secretary@iap.fr.
URL: http://www.iau.org/
History Jul 1919, Brussels (Belgium). Founded at Constitutive Assembly of the then *'International Research Council (IRC) – Conseil international des recherches (CIR)'*, subsequently, since 1931, *International Council for Science (ICSU, inactive).* Merged, May 1922, with *International Permanent Committee for the Production of a Photographic Map of the Sky (inactive)*, set up 24 Apr 1887, Paris (France). Statutes revised: 1961; 1964; 1970; 2003; 2012. **Aims** Promote and safeguard the science of astronomy in all its aspects through international cooperation. **Structure** General Assembly (every 3 years); Executive Committee; Secretariat. Meetings closed. Direct involvement of individual members is encouraged. Divisions (9); Commissions (currently 38); Centres (2). Also includes: *Office of Astronomy for Development (OAD); Office for Astronomy Outreach (OAO).* **Languages** English, French. **Finance** Dues from adhering countries. Annual budget: 233,333 USD. **Activities** Events/meetings; knowledge management/information dissemination; research/documentation; training/education. **Events** *Asian-Pacific Regional Meeting* Kōriyama (Japan) 2023, *Triennial General Assembly* Busan (Korea Rep) 2022, *Communicating Astronomy with the Public International Conference* Sydney, NSW (Australia) 2022, *Dark and Quiet Skies for Science and Society* 2021, *Triennial General Assembly* Busan (Korea Rep) 2021. **Publications** *IAU/UAI Information Bulletin* (2 a year); *Highlights of Astronomy. IAU Colloquia; IAU Symposia; Reports on Astronomy.* Proceedings of General Assemblies.
Members National members in 67 countries and territories:
Argentina, Armenia, Australia, Austria, Belgium, Brazil, Bulgaria, Canada, Chile, China, Colombia, Costa Rica, Croatia, Czechia, Denmark, Egypt, Estonia, Ethiopia, Finland, France, Germany, Greece, Holy See, Honduras, Hungary, Iceland, India, Indonesia, Ireland, Israel, Italy, Japan, Kazakhstan, Korea DPR, Korea Rep, Latvia, Lebanon, Lithuania, Malaysia, Mexico, Mongolia, Netherlands, New Zealand, Nigeria, Norway, Panama, Philippines, Poland, Portugal, Romania, Russia, Slovakia, South Africa, Spain, Sweden, Switzerland, Taiwan, Tajikistan, Thailand, Türkiye, UK, Ukraine, Uruguay, USA, Venezuela, Vietnam.
Individuals (over 12,000) in 22 other countries:
Albania, Algeria, Azerbaijan, Colombia, Ecuador, Ethiopia, Georgia, Honduras, Iraq, Kazakhstan, Korea DPR, Malta, Mauritius, North Macedonia, Pakistan, Singapore, Slovenia, Sri Lanka, Trinidad-Tobago, United Arab Emirates, Uzbekistan, Vietnam.
Consultative Status Consultative status granted from: *World Meteorological Organization (WMO, #21649); UNESCO (#20322)* (Consultative Status). **IGO Relations** Observer status with (1): *Committee on the Peaceful Uses of Outer Space (COPUOS, #04277).* Instrumental in setting up (1): *World Space Observatory – Ultraviolet (WSO-UV, #21819).* **NGO Relations** Member of (6): *Arab Union for Astronomy and Space Sciences (AUASS, #01063); Committee on Space Research (COSPAR, #04287); International Science Council (ISC, #14796); Scientific Committee on Antarctic Research (SCAR, #19147); Scientific Committee on Problems of the Environment (SCOPE, #19150); Scientific Committee on Solar-Terrestrial Physics (SCOSTEP, #19151).* Instrumental in setting up (2): *European Astronomical Society (EAS, #06288); International Square Kilometre Array Project (SKA, inactive).* Represented in: *Committee on Data for Science and Technology (CODATA, #04247).* Maintains: *Solar Influences Data Analysis Centre (SIDC, #19675).* Instrumental with and cooperates on: *International Earth Rotation and Reference Systems Service (IERS, #13216); International Space Environment Service (ISES, #15572); Scientific Committee on Frequency Allocations for Radio Astronomy and Space Science (IUCAF, #19148).* [2022/XC1382/v/**B**]

♦ International Astronomical Youth Camp / see International Workshop for Astronomy (#15913)

♦ International Atherosclerosis Society (IAS) 12288
Société internationale d'athérosclérose
Sec 2020 K Street NW, Suite 505, Washington DC 20006, USA. T. +3929006267. E-mail: info@athero.org.
URL: http://www.athero.org/
History 29 Nov 1978, Philadelphia, PA (USA). **Aims** Promote scientific understanding of the *aetiology*, prevention and treatment of atherosclerosis. **Structure** Officers: President; Secretary; Treasurer; President Elect; Past President; Members at Large; Chairs IAS Federations. **Languages** English. **Staff** 5.00 FTE, voluntary. **Finance** Sources: grants; members' dues. **Activities** Awards/prizes/competitions; events/meetings; research/documentation; standards/guidelines; training/education. **Events** *Triennial Symposium* Muscat (Oman) 2024, *Triennial Symposium* Kyoto (Japan) 2021, *Satellite Symposium* Muscat (Oman) 2021, *Triennial Symposium* Toronto, ON (Canada) 2018, *Triennial Symposium* Amsterdam (Netherlands) 2015. **Publications** *IAS e-literature* (12 a year); *IAS e-Newsletter* (12 a year). Online slide libraries.
Members Membership Groups – organizations in 50 countries and territories:
Argentina, Australia, Austria, Belgium, Brazil, Canada, Chile, China, Croatia, Cuba, Czechia, Egypt, Finland, France, Georgia, Germany, Greece, Hungary, India, Indonesia, Iran Islamic Rep, Iraq, Israel, Italy, Japan, Korea Rep, Kuwait, Mexico, Morocco, Netherlands, New Zealand, Oman, Philippines, Poland, Portugal, Romania, Russia, Saudi Arabia, Serbia, Slovakia, South Africa, Spain, Switzerland, Taiwan, Tunisia, Türkiye, UK, United Arab Emirates, USA, Venezuela.
Regional organizations (8), listed in this Yearbook:
Asian-Pacific Society of Atherosclerosis and Vascular Diseases (APSAVD, #01630); Commonwealth of Independent States Atherosclerosis Society (CIS AS, no recent information); European Atherosclerosis Society (EAS, #06289); IAS Asia Pacific Federation (#11007); Lipid and Atherosclerosis Society of Southern Africa (LASSA); Scandinavian Society for Atherosclerosis Research (SSAR, #19102); Sociedad Iberolatinoamericana de Aterosclerosis (SILAT, #19379); Sociedad Latinoamericana de Aterosclerosis (SOLAT, #19391).
Individuals in 4 countries:
Cyprus, Mongolia, North Macedonia, Vietnam.
NGO Relations Affiliated with (2): *International Chair on Cardiometabolic Risk (#12533); World Heart Federation (WHF, #21562).* [2023/XD8442/y/**B**]

♦ International Atherosclerosis Society Regional Federation for Alia-Pacific / see IAS Asia Pacific Federation (#11007)

♦ International Athletic Association for Persons with Down Syndrome (IAADS) 12289
SG X strada 5, Castelnuovo di Porto, 00060 Rome RM, Italy.
Pres address not obtained.
URL: http://www.iaads.info/
History Founded 12 Nov 2009, when statutes were adopted. Registered in accordance with Italian law. **Aims** Develop and spread throughout the world the practice of sport in athletics as a means of psychological, physical and moral training of persons with Down syndrome; promote the knowledge and practice in athletics among people with Down syndrome. **Structure** General Assembly; Executive Board; Secretariat based in Italy. **Languages** English. **Staff** All voluntary. **Finance** Members' dues (every 2 years): US$ 300. **Events** *General Assembly* Nymburk (Czechia) 2022, *General Assembly / World Championships* Portugal 2012, *Open European Championships* Cagliari (Italy) 2011, *General Assembly* Puerto Vallarta (Mexico) 2010, *World Championships* Puerto Vallarta (Mexico) 2010. **Publications** None.
Members Full in 19 countries and territories:
Austria, Brazil, Cameroon, China, Colombia, Costa Rica, Dominican Rep, Finland, Great Britain, Guatemala, Italy, Macau, Mexico, Nicaragua, Portugal, South Africa, Türkiye, Turkmenistan, Venezuela.
IGO Relations None. **NGO Relations** Member of: *Sports Union for athletes with Down Syndrome (SU-DS, #19930).* [2013.09.23/XJ6950/**C**]

♦ International Athletic Footwear and Apparel Manufacturers Association (inactive)

♦ International Athletics Foundation (IAF) 12290
Gen Sec c/o IAAF, 6 Quai Antoine 1er, BP 359, 98007 Monte Carlo, Monaco. T. +37792057068. E-mail: iaf@iaaf.org.
Pres address not obtained.
URL: http://www.iaaf.org/about-iaaf/foundation/
History Founded 1986, Monaco, by *World Athletics (#21209).* **Aims** Assist the IAAF and its affiliated national governing bodies in perpetuating the development and promotion of athletics worldwide. **Structure** Council. Honorary President: Prince Albert II of Monaco (Monaco). **Languages** English, French. **Staff** 1.00 FTE, paid. **Finance** Donations. Annual budget: US$ 1,000,000. **Activities** Projects/programmes; financial and/or material support; events/meetings. **Members** Individuals. Membership countries not specified. [2018.10.20/XF2276/fv/**F**]

♦ International Atlantic Committee (inactive)

♦ International Atlantic Economic Society (IAES) 12291
Exec VP 230 Peachtree St NW, Ste 1640, Atlanta GA 30303, USA. T. +14049651555. Fax +14049651556. E-mail: iaes@iaes.org.
URL: http://www.iaes.org/
History Nov 1973, Richmond, VA (USA). Former names and other names: *Atlantic Economic Society (AES)* – former. Registration: Start date: 13 Aug 1974, USA. **Aims** Provide an educational and scientific forum for the global community of economists and others in related disciplines. **Structure** Executive Committee; Program Committee. **Languages** English. **Staff** 3.00 FTE, paid; 1.00 FTE, voluntary. **Finance** Sources: grants; meeting proceeds; members' dues; sale of publications. Annual budget: 500,000 USD. **Activities** Awards/prizes/competitions; events/meetings; financial and/or material support; publishing activities. **Events** *Annual Spring Conference* Atlanta, GA (USA) 2022, *Annual Fall Conference* Atlanta, GA (USA) 2021, *Annual Spring Conference* Rome (Italy) 2020, *Annual Fall Conference* Washington, DC (USA) 2020, *Annual Fall Conference* Miami, FL (USA) 2019. **Publications** *Atlantic Economic Journal* (4 a year); *International Advances in Economic Research* (4 a year).
Members Class A – General; Class B – Distinguished Associates; Class C – Organizations. Individuals (mainly in USA) in 53 countries and territories:
Argentina, Australia, Austria, Bahrain, Barbados, Belgium, Brazil, Canada, China, Colombia, Croatia, Czechia, Denmark, Estonia, Finland, France, Germany, Greece, Hong Kong, Hungary, Iceland, India, Iran Islamic Rep, Ireland, Israel, Italy, Japan, Korea Rep, Malaysia, Mexico, Netherlands, New Zealand, Nigeria, Norway, Oman, Poland, Portugal, Romania, Russia, Saudi Arabia, Serbia, Slovenia, South Africa, Spain, Sweden, Switzerland, Taiwan, Trinidad-Tobago, Türkiye, UK, Ukraine, United Arab Emirates, USA. [2022.02.09/XF0248/v/**F**]

♦ International Atlantic Salmon Research Board (IASRB) 12292
Address not obtained.
URL: http://www.nasco.int/sas/index.htm
History 2001, by *North Atlantic Salmon Conservation Organization (NASCO, #17574).* **Aims** Promote collaboration and cooperation on research into the causes of marine mortality of Atlantic salmon and the opportunities to counteract this mortality. **Structure** Officers: Chairman; Chairman Scientific Advisory Group; Secretary. **Activities** Runs the SALSEA Programme – international programme of cooperative research designed to improve understanding of the migration and distribution of salmon at sea in relation to feeding opportunities and predation. **Events** *Symposium on salmon at sea* La Rochelle (France) 2011. [2011.03.01/XJ2189/**E***]

♦ International Atmospheric Circulation Reconstructions over the Earth Initiative (ACRE) 12293
Project Manager Met Office Hadley Ctr, Exeter, EX1 3PB, UK.
URL: http://www.met-acre.org/
History 2006-2007. **Aims** Undertake and facilitate historical global surface terrestrial and marine *weather* data recovery, imaging and digitization, feeding these data into the international repositories responsible for such material. **Finance** Government support. **Activities** Projects/programmes; research/documentation; knowledge management/information dissemination. **Events** *Workshop* Maynooth (Ireland) 2016, *New data, improved reanalyses and wilder applications* Santiago (Chile) 2015, *Expanding applications of reanalysis products* Toronto, ON (Canada) 2014, *Workshop* Lisbon (Portugal) 2013, *Workshop* Toulouse (France) 2012. **Publications** Books.
Members Consortium of 9 core partners in 5 countries:
Australia, Germany, Switzerland, UK, USA.
Included in the above, 1 organization listed in this Yearbook:
International Environmental Data Rescue Organization (IEDRO).
IGO Relations *Joint WMO-IOC Technical Commission for Oceanography and Marine Meteorology (JCOMM, #16151).* **NGO Relations** *Global Precipitation Climatology Centre (GPCC); World Climate Research Programme (WCRP, #21279).* [2016.06.01/XJ9303/**F**]

♦ International Atomic Energy Agency (IAEA) 12294
Agence internationale de l'énergie atomique (AIEA) – Organismo Internacional de Energía Atómica (OIEA) – Mezdunarodnoe Agenstvo po Atomnoj Energii
Dir Gen IAEA Headquarters – Vienna Intl Centre, PO Box 100, 1400 Vienna, Austria. T. +43126000. Fax +43126007. E-mail: official.mail@iaea.org.
URL: http://www.iaea.org/
History 29 Jul 1957. Based on a decision of the General Assembly of the United Nations, after 18 states had deposited the necessary instruments of ratification with the United States Government. Preparatory Commission, set up by Statute Conference, met in 1956 and 1957 in New York NY (USA) and Vienna (Austria) to prepare the initial programme and make arrangements to bring it into operation. Statute amended: 31 Jan 1963; 1 Jun 1973; 28 Dec 1989. An autonomous organ linked to the General Assembly of *United Nations (UN, #20515)* within *United Nations System (#20635).* Received the Nobel Peace Prize, 2005.
Aims Foster, encourage and advise on development of *peaceful uses* of atomic energy worldwide; accelerate and enlarge the contribution of atomic energy to peace, health and prosperity; as far as possible ensure that assistance provided, requested, supervised or controlled is not used in such a way as to further any military purpose; promote wider use of *radioisotopes* and radiation sources in research, industry, agriculture, medicine and hydrology.
Under Article III (Functions) of the Statute, as amended 1 Jun 1973, the Agency is authorized to:
- Encourage and assist research on, and development and practical application of, atomic energy for peaceful uses throughout the world; act as an intermediary for the purposes of securing performance of services or supplying of materials, equipment or facilities by one member of the Agency for another; perform any operation or service useful in research on, or development or practical application of, atomic energy for peaceful purposes;
- Make provision, for materials, services, equipment and facilities to meet the needs of research on, and development and practical application of, atomic energy for peaceful purposes, including production of electric power, with due consideration for the needs of under-developed areas of the world;
- Foster exchange of scientific and technical information on peaceful uses of atomic energy;
- Encourage exchange and training of scientists and experts in the field of peaceful uses of atomic energy;
- Establish and administer safeguards designed to ensure that special fissionable and other materials, services, equipment, facilities and information made available by the Agency or at its request or under its supervision or control are not used in such a way as to further any military purpose; apply safeguards, at the request of the parties, to any bilateral or multilateral arrangement, or at the request of a state, to any of that state's activities in the field of atomic energy;
- Establish or adopt, in consultation and, where appropriate, in collaboration with the competent organs of the United Nations and with the specialized agencies concerned, standards of safety for protection of health and minimization of danger to life and property (including such standards for labour conditions); provide for application of these standards to own operations as well as to operations making use of materials, services, equipment, facilities and information made available by the Agency or at its request or under its control or supervision; provide for application of these standards, at the request of the parties, to operations under any bilateral or multilateral arrangement, or, at the request of a state, to any of that state's activities in the field of atomic energy;

– Acquire or establish any facilities, plant and equipment useful in carrying out authorized functions, whenever the facilities, plant, and equipment otherwise available in the area concerned are inadequate or available only on terms deemed unsatisfactory.

In carrying out these functions, the Agency has to:
– Conduct its activities in accordance with the purposes and principles of the United Nations to promote peace and international cooperation, and in conformity with policies of the United Nations furthering the establishment of safeguarded worldwide disarmament and in conformity with any international agreements entered into pursuant to such policies;
– Establish control over the use of special fissionable materials received by the Agency, in order to ensure that these materials are used only for peaceful purposes;
– Allocate its resources in such a manner as to secure efficient utilization and the greatest possible general benefit in all areas of the world, bearing in mind the special needs of the under-developed areas of the world;
– Submit reports on activities annually to the General Assembly of the United Nations and, when appropriate, to the Security Council: if in connection with the activities of the Agency questions arise that are within the competence of the Security Council the Agency has to notify the Security Council, as the organ bearing the main responsibility for the maintenance of international peace and security, and may also take the measures open to it under the Statute;
– Submit reports to the Economic and Social Council and other organs of the United Nations on matters with the competence of these organs.

Structure General Conference (annual) approves programmes and budget for each year and elects President and Officers for the duration of the session. Board of Governors (meeting about 5 times a year) consists of 35 members, of which 13 are designated by the Board and 22 are elected by the General Conference; it is responsible for carrying out the functions of the Agency and approves states for membership.

Secretariat is headed by Director General, who is responsible for programme administration and implementation and is assisted by 6 Deputy Directors General, who head the 6 Departments:
– *'Management'* – Budget and Finance, Conference and Document Services, General Services, Information Technology, Personnel, Public Information;
– *'Nuclear Energy'* – Nuclear Fuel Cycle and Waste Technology, Nuclear Power;
– *'Nuclear Safety and Security'* – Nuclear Installation Safety, Radiation, Transport and Waste Safety, including 4 Safety Standards Commissions: Nuclear (NUSSC); Radiation (RASSC); Transport (TRANSSC); Waste (WASSC).
– *'Nuclear Sciences and Applications'* – Joint FAO/IAEA Division of Nuclear Techniques in Food and Agriculture, Human Health, Physical and Chemical Sciences, Agency Laboratories,
– *IAEA Environment Laboratories (IAEA-EL, #11004)* (with UNEP and IOC).

Isotope Hydrology Section includes *Global Network of Isotopes in Precipitation (GNIP, #10491)*.
– *'Safeguards'* – Concepts and Planning, Operations A, Operations B, Operations C, Technical Support, Safeguards Information Technology;
– *'Technical Cooperation'* – Africa, Asia and the Pacific, Europe, Latin America, Programme Support and Coordination.
– *International Fusion Research Council (IFRC, see: #12294)*;
– Secretariat of the Policy-Making Organs;
– Office of External Relations and Policy Coordination;
– Office of Internal Oversight Services;
– Office of Legal Affairs.

Headquarters: Vienna (Austria). Liaison Offices (2): New York NY (USA); Geneva (Switzerland). Laboratories and Research Centres (3): Seibersdorf (Austria); Monaco; *Abdus Salam International Centre for Theoretical Physics (ICTP, #00005)*. Regional Safeguards Offices (2): Toronto ON (Canada); Chiyoda (Japan). Also includes: *Global Nuclear Safety and Security Network (GNSSN, #10509)*.

Languages Arabic, Chinese, English, French, Russian, Spanish. **Staff** 2200.00 FTE, paid. Negotiations through *Staff Association of the International Atomic Energy Agency (#19938)*. The *Administrative Tribunal of the International Labour Organization (ILO Tribunal, #00118)* is competent to settle disputes. **Finance** Regular and voluntary contributions from member states. Technical assistance financed by: voluntary contributions from member states; funds from UNDP; gifts in kind such as equipment grants, cost-free fellowships and cost-free expert services; funds in trust.

Activities Establishes safety standards for all types of nuclear activity; prepares feasibility and market studies; operates 2 laboratories; advises governments on atomic energy programmes; awards fellowships for advanced study; arranges the loan of equipment; finances research; acts as an intermediary in arranging the supply of nuclear materials. Work is carried out in close cooperation with many other national and international organizations.

Main pillars (3):
1. *'Promoting Safeguards and Verification'*, coordinated at Department of Safeguards:
– /Safeguards/ – Inspects nuclear and related facilities under safeguards agreements with member states.

Most agreements concluded pursuant to *Treaty on the Non-proliferation of Nuclear Weapons (NPT, 1968)*, under which states commit themselves internationally not to possess nuclear weapons.

2. *'Promoting Safety and Security'*, coordinated at Department of Nuclear Safety and Security:
– /Safety/ – Covers nuclear installations, radioactive sources, radioactive materials in transport and radioactive waste. Aims to set up and promote application of international safety standards for management and regulation of activities involving nuclear and radioactive materials.
– /Security/ – Covers nuclear installations and nuclear and radioactive materials. Focus is on helping states prevent, detect and respond to terrorist or other malicious acts and protect nuclear installations and transport against sabotage.

3. *'Promoting Science and Technology'*, programmes led by Departments of Technical Cooperation, Nuclear Sciences and Applications, and Nuclear Energy:
– /Energy and Electricity/ – Helps countries assess and plan their energy needs, including nuclear generation of electricity.
– /Research and Development/ – Supports research and development on critical problems facing developing countries.
– /Technical Cooperation/ – Supports cooperative projects achieving tangible social and economic benefits for people in developing countries.

Conventions negotiated and adopted under the auspices of the Agency and for which the Director General is the depositary, in the field of:

'Safety and Security':
– *Convention on Early Notification of a Nuclear Accident (1986)*, in force since 27 Oct 1986;
– *Convention on Assistance in the Case of Nuclear Accident or Radiological Emergency (1986)*, in force since 26 Feb 1987;
– *Convention on Nuclear Safety (1994)*, opened for signature at the IAEA on 20 Sep 1994, in force 24 Oct 1996;
– *Joint Convention on the Safety of Spent Fuel Management and on the Safety of Radioactive Waste Management (1997)*, adopted 5 Sep 1997 and opened for signature on 29 Sep 1997;
– *Convention on the Physical Protection of Nuclear Material (1979)*, in force since 8 Feb 1987;
– *Vienna Convention on Civil Liability for Nuclear Damage (1963)*, adopted May 1963, in force since 12 Nov 1977, and *Optional Protocol Concerning the Compulsory Settlement of Disputes (1963)*, in force since 13 May 1999, updated by *Protocol to Amend the Vienna Convention on Civil Liability for Nuclear Damage (1997)* and *Convention on Supplementary Compensation for Nuclear Damage (1997)*, both adopted 12 Sep 1997 and opened for signature on 28 Sep 1997;
– *Joint Protocol Relating to the Application of the Vienna Convention and the Paris Convention (1988)*, in force since 27 Apr 1992;
– *Nordic Mutual Emergency Assistance Agreement in Connection with Radiation Accidents (1973)*;
– *Convention on the Prevention of Marine Pollution by Dumping of Wastes and other Matter (LDC, 1972)*.

'Science and Technology':
– *African Regional Cooperative Agreement for Research, Development and Training Related to Nuclear Science and Technology (AFRA)* – second extension entered into force of 4 Apr 2000;
– *Regional Cooperation Agreement for the Promotion of Nuclear Science and Technology in Latin America and the Caribbean (ARCAL Agreement, #18772)*, opened for signature 25 Sep 1998;
– Second agreement to extend *Regional Cooperative Agreement for Research, Development and Training Related to Nuclear Science and Technology in Asia (RCA, #18774)*, entered into force 12 Jun 1997;
– *revised guiding principles and general operating rules to govern the provision of technical assistance by the Agency*;
– *Revised supplementary agreement concerning provision of technical assistance by the IAEA (RSA)*;
– *Cooperative Agreement for Arab States in Asia for Research, Development and Training Related to Nuclear Science and Technology (ARASIA, 2002)*, in force since 2002;
– Agreement on the Establishment of *ITER International Fusion Energy Organization (ITER Organization, #16072)* for the Joint Implementation of the ITER Project;
– Agreement on the Privileges and Immunities of the ITER International Fusion Energy Organization for the Joint Implementation of the ITER.

'Safeguards and Verification':
– Structure and Content of Agreements between the Agency and States Required in Connection with the Treaty on the non-proliferation of nuclear weapons.
– *Application of Safeguards on Implementation of Article III 1 and 4 of the Treaty on the Non-proliferation of Nuclear Weapons (1973)*;
– Model Protocol Additional to the Agreement(s) between State(s) and the Agency for the Application of Safeguards, Sep 1997;
– Agency's Safeguards System, 1965, Provisionally Extended, 1966 and 1968.

'Organization and Cooperative Agreements':
– IAEA Agreements with the United Nations, 30 Oct 1959;
– *Agreement on the Privileges and Immunities of the International Atomic Energy Agency (1959)*;
– IAEA Headquarters Agreement with Austria and Related Agreements;
– IAEA Relationship Agreements with Specialized Agencies;
– Cooperation Agreements with Intergovernmental Organizations.

'Other Agreements' related to IAEA:
– *Treaty for the Prohibition of Nuclear Weapons in Latin America and the Caribbean (Treaty of Tlatelolco, 1967)* and *Amendment to the Treaty for the Prohibition on Nuclear Weapons in Latin America (1990)*;
– *African Nuclear-weapon-free-zone Treaty (Pelindaba Treaty, 1996)*, including Annexes and Protocols and Cairo Declaration;
– *South Pacific Nuclear Free Zone Treaty (Treaty of Rarotonga, 1985)* and Protocols;
– *Treaty on the Southeast Asia Nuclear Weapon-free Zone (Bangkok Treaty, 1995)*;
– Agreement between the Republic of Argentina, Federative Republic of Brazil, Brazilian-Argentine Agency for Accounting and Control of Nuclear Materials (ABACC) and IAEA for the Application of Safeguards;
– Verification Agreement between IAEA and *European Atomic Energy Community (Euratom, inactive)*;
– Guidelines for Nuclear Transfers, 1993 Revision of NSG London Guidelines;
– *International Convention for the Safety of Life at Sea, 1974 (SOLAS, 1974)*;
– *Convention Relating to Civil Liability in the Field of Maritime Carriage of Nuclear Material (NUCLEAR, 1971)*;
– *Treaty Banning Nuclear Weapon Tests in the Atmosphere, in Outer Space and under Water (1963)*;
– *Paris Convention on Third Party Liability in the Field of Nuclear Energy (1960)*;
– *Convention Supplementary to the Paris Convention on Third Party Liability in the Field of Nuclear Energy (Brussels supplementary convention, 1963)*;
– Code of Practice on the International Transboundary Movement of Radioactive Waste: the IAEA Code of Practice;
– Code of Conduct on the Safety of Research Reactors;
– *Comprehensive Nuclear-Test-Ban Treaty (CTBT, 1996)*;
– *International Convention for the Suppression of Acts of Nuclear Terrorism (2005)*.

'Events' Annual General Conference Session in Vienna (Austria). Board of Governors meets in quarterly sessions in Vienna. About 12 scientific conferences, symposia or seminars annually.

Events *DEMO Workshop* Aomori (Japan) 2022, *Management System Event* Helsinki (Finland) 2022, *DEMO Workshop* Vienna (Austria) 2022, *ICARST : International Conference on Applications of Radiation Science and Technology* Vienna (Austria) 2022, *Regional Workshop on Threat Assessment and a Risk Informed Approach for Nuclear and other Radioactive Material out of Regulatory Control* Zagreb (Croatia) 2022. **Publications** *INIS CD-ROM* (bi-weekly); *Nuclear Fusion* (12 a year); *IAEA Bulletin* (2 a year) in Arabic, Chinese, English, French, Russian, Spanish. *IAEA Nulcear Security Series*; *IAEA Safety Standards Series*; *IAEA Technical Technical Documents (IAEA-TECDOCs)*. Annual Report; books; reports. Information Services: *International Nuclear Information System (INIS, #14378)* – established 1970, Vienna (Austria), collects and merges references to technical literature in the nuclear field and redistributes them to national information centres – currently includes 3 million records to which 122 countries and 24 international organizations have provided input. **Information Services** *Nuclear Information System (NDIS)* – with nuclear data centres in Brookhaven NY (USA) and Paris (France) and 22 other centres worldwide; *Power Reactor Information System (PRIS)* – with 33 member states.

Members Initial members: states which were members of the United Nations or of one of its specialized agencies and which had signed the Statute within 90 days of its opening for signature and had deposited an instrument of ratification. Other members: states, whether or not members of the United Nations or of any of the specialized agencies, which have deposited an instrument of acceptance of the Statute after their membership has been approved by General Conference on the recommendation of the Board of Governors.

As of Jul 2009: Member states (150):
Afghanistan, Albania, Algeria, Angola, Argentina, Armenia, Australia, Austria, Azerbaijan, Bahrain, Bangladesh, Belarus, Belgium, Belize, Benin, Bolivia, Bosnia-Herzegovina, Botswana, Brazil, Bulgaria, Burkina Faso, Burundi, Cameroon, Canada, Central African Rep, Chad, Chile, China, Colombia, Congo Brazzaville, Congo DR, Costa Rica, Côte d'Ivoire, Croatia, Cuba, Cyprus, Czechia, Denmark, Dominican Rep, Ecuador, Egypt, El Salvador, Eritrea, Estonia, Ethiopia, Finland, France, Gabon, Georgia, Germany, Ghana, Greece, Guatemala, Haiti, Holy See, Honduras, Hungary, Iceland, India, Indonesia, Iran Islamic Rep, Iraq, Ireland, Israel, Italy, Jamaica, Japan, Jordan, Kazakhstan, Kenya, Korea Rep, Kuwait, Kyrgyzstan, Latvia, Lebanon, Lesotho, Liberia, Libya, Liechtenstein, Lithuania, Luxembourg, Madagascar, Malawi, Malaysia, Mali, Malta, Marshall Is, Mauritania, Mauritius, Mexico, Moldova, Monaco, Mongolia, Montenegro, Morocco, Mozambique, Myanmar, Namibia, Nepal, Netherlands, New Zealand, Nicaragua, Niger, Nigeria, North Macedonia, Norway, Oman, Pakistan, Palau, Panama, Paraguay, Peru, Philippines, Poland, Portugal, Qatar, Romania, Russia, Saudi Arabia, Senegal, Serbia, Seychelles, Sierra Leone, Singapore, Slovakia, Slovenia, South Africa, Spain, Sri Lanka, Sudan, Sweden, Switzerland, Syrian AR, Tajikistan, Tanzania UR, Thailand, Tunisia, Türkiye, Uganda, UK, Ukraine, United Arab Emirates, Uruguay, USA, Uzbekistan, Venezuela, Vietnam, Yemen, Zambia, Zimbabwe.

Member States whose membership has been approved by IAEA General Conference and will take effect once States deposit the necessary legal instruments (5):
Cambodia, Cape Verde, Papua New Guinea, Rwanda, Togo.

IGO Relations United Nations bodies, including: *FAO (#09260)*; *ILO (#11123)*; *Intergovernmental Oceanographic Commission (IOC, #11496)*; *UNEP (#20299)*; *UNESCO (#20322)*; *UNIDO (#20336)*; *United Nations Group on the Information Society (UNGIS, #20570)*; *United Nations Office for Disarmament Affairs (UNODA, #20594)*; *WHO (#20950)*. Permanent observer status with: *World Intellectual Property Organization (WIPO, #21593)*. Observer to: *Generation IV International Forum (GIF, #10115)*; *Global Initiative to Combat Nuclear Terrorism (GICNT, #10424)*; *International Framework for Nuclear Energy Cooperation (IFNEC, #13681)*. Member of: *UN-OCEANS (#20711)*; *UN-Water (#20723)*. Partner of: *Regional Seas Programme (#18814)*. Represented on: *United Nations System Chief Executives Board for Coordination (CEB, #20636)*. Memorandum of Understanding signed with: *World Customs Organization (WCO, #21350)*.

Entitled to be represented at sessions of the General Conference: *African Union (AU, #00488)*; *Agency for the Prohibition of Nuclear Weapons in Latin America and the Caribbean (#00554)*; *Arab Atomic Energy Agency (AAEA, #00901)*; *European Atomic Energy Community (Euratom, inactive)*; *ITER International Fusion Energy Organization (ITER Organization, #16072)*; *League of Arab States (LAS, #16420)*; *Nuclear Energy Agency (NEA, #17615)*; *Foro Iberoamericano de Organismos Reguladores Radiológicos y Nucleares (FORO, #09878)*.

NGO Relations Rule 13 of the Rules on the Consultative Status of Non-Governmental Organizations provides for the Director-General to submit annually to the General Conference a list of organizations to which consultative status has been granted – as of 2009, 10 nongovernmental organizations:
– *nucleareurope (#17616)*;
– *International Air Transport Association (IATA, #11614)*;
– *International Chamber of Commerce (ICC, #12534)*;
– *International Commission on Radiation Units and Measurements (ICRU, #12722)*;
– *International Commission on Radiological Protection (ICRP, #12724)*;
– *International Co-operative Alliance (ICA, #12944)*;
– *International Organization for Standardization (ISO, #14473)*;
– *Japan Atomic Industrial Forum (JAIF)*;
– *World Energy Council (WEC, #21381)*;
– *World Federation of United Nations Associations (WFUNA, #21499)*.

Organizations invited to send observers to General Conference in 2009 (38):
– *American Nuclear Society (ANS)*;
– Canadian Nuclear Association;
– Conference of Radiation Control Program Directors;
– Conference of Radiation Control Program Directors;
– *Contractors International Group on Nuclear Liability (CIGNL)*;
– Council on Radionuclides and Radiopharmaceuticals;
– *Environmentalists for Nuclear Energy (EFN)*;
– *European Nuclear Society (ENS, #08059)*;
– *European Physical Society (EPS, #08207)*;
– German Atomic Forum;
– Health Physics Society;
– Institute of Nuclear Materials Management;
– International Economic Association for the Organization of Cooperation in the Production and Supply of Equipment and for the Provision of Technical Assistance in the Construction of Nuclear Power Plants;
– *International Institute for Applied Systems Analysis (IIASA, #13861)*;
– *International Irradiation Association (iiA, #13954)*;
– *International Nuclear Energy Academy (#14377)*;
– *International Nuclear Law Association (INLA, #14379)*;
– *International Nuclear Societies Council (INSC, #14382)*;
– *International Organization for Medical Physics (IOMP, #14453)*;
– *International Radiation Protection Association (IRPA, #14686)*;
– *International Society of Radiographers and Radiological Technologists (ISRRT, #15410)*;
– *International Society of Radiology (ISR, #15412)*;
– *International Source Suppliers and Producers Association (ISSPA, #15571)*;
– *International Trade Union Confederation (ITUC, #15708)*;

– *International Union of Radioecology (IUR, #15812)*;
– *James Martin Center for Nonproliferation Studies (CNS)*;
– Korean Nuclear Society;
– Moroccan Association of Nuclear Engineers;
– Nuclear Energy Institute;
– *Pacific Nuclear Council (PNC, inactive)*;
– *Sovereign Military Hospitaller Order of St John of Jerusalem, of Rhodes and of Malta (SMOM)*;
– US Civilian Research and Development Foundation (CRDF);
– *Verification Research, Training and Information Centre (VERTIC)*;
– *World Association of Nuclear Operators (WANO, #21168)*;
– *World Council of Nuclear Workers (WONUC, inactive)*;
– *World Federation of Nuclear Medicine and Biology (WFNMB, #21467)*;
– *World Nuclear Association (WNA, #21674)*;
– *World Nuclear Transport Institute (WNTI, #21676)*. [2020.02.18/XB1383/**B***]

♦ International Atomic and Molecular Data Centre Network 12295

Head c/o IEAE, Atomic and Molecular Data Unit, Nuclear Data Section, NAPC Div, Vienna Intl Ctr, PO Box 100, 1400 Vienna, Austria. T. +431260021731. Fax +43126007. E-mail: nds.contact-point@iaea.org.
URL: http://www-amdis.iaea.org/

History Within the Nuclear Data Section of *International Atomic Energy Agency (IAEA, #12294)*. **Aims** Establish and maintain internationally recommended numerical databases on atomic and molecular collision and radiative processes, atomic and molecular structure characteristics, particle-solid surface interaction processes and physico-chemical and thermo-mechanical material properties for use in *fusion* energy research and other plasma science and technology applications. **Events** *Technical Meeting* Vienna (Austria) 2017. **Information Services** *ALADDIN*; *AMBDAS – Atomic and Molecular Database*; *GENIE – GENeral Internet*. **Members** National data centres (11) in 9 countries. Membership countries not specified. [2018/XF6867/**E***]

♦ International Auditing and Assurance Standards Board (IAASB) . . . 12296

Managing Dir 529 Fifth Ave, 6th Floor, New York NY 10017, USA.
URL: https://www.iaasb.org/

History 1977, New York, NY (USA). Founded as a Standing Committee within the framework of *International Federation of Accountants (IFAC, #13335)*. Currently overseen by *Public Interest Oversight Board (PIOB, #18566)*. Former names and other names: *International Auditing Practices Committee (IAPC)* – former (1977). **Aims** Set, independently and under its own authority, high quality standards dealing with auditing, review, other assurance, quality control and related services; facilitate the convergence of national and international standards, so as to enhance quality and uniformity of practice throughout the world and strengthen public confidence in financial reporting. **Structure** Board, comprising Chair, Vice-Chair, 3 Public Members and 13 members. Consultative Advisory Group; Technical Advisors; Task Forces. **Staff** 8.00 FTE, paid; 18.00 FTE, voluntary. **Finance** Members' dues. Direct funding from Forum of Firms. **Activities** Standards/guidelines; events/meetings. **Events** *Meeting* New York, NY (USA) 2019, *Meeting* New York, NY (USA) 2019, *Meeting* New York, NY (USA) 2018, *Meeting* New York, NY (USA) 2018, *Meeting* Madrid (Spain) 2017. **Publications** *International Standards on Auditing* – translated into 20 languages. Annual Report; supplements to standards. **Members** Full; Associate; Affiliate: national accountancy bodies (159), representing over 2.5 million accountants. Full in 106 countries and territories:
Argentina, Australia, Austria, Bahamas, Bahrain, Bangladesh, Barbados, Belgium, Bolivia, Botswana, Brazil, Bulgaria, Cameroon, Canada, Chile, China, Colombia, Costa Rica, Côte d'Ivoire, Croatia, Cyprus, Czechia, Denmark, Dominican Rep, Egypt, El Salvador, Eswatini, Fiji, Finland, France, Georgia, Germany, Ghana, Greece, Guyana, Haiti, Honduras, Hong Kong, Hungary, Iceland, India, Indonesia, Iran Islamic Rep, Iraq, Ireland, Israel, Italy, Jamaica, Japan, Jordan, Kazakhstan, Kenya, Korea Rep, Kuwait, Lebanon, Lesotho, Liberia, Libya, Luxembourg, Madagascar, Malawi, Malaysia, Malta, Mexico, Namibia, Netherlands, New Zealand, Nicaragua, Nigeria, Norway, Pakistan, Panama, Paraguay, Peru, Philippines, Poland, Portugal, Romania, Russia, Saudi Arabia, Serbia-Montenegro, Sierra Leone, Singapore, Slovakia, Slovenia, South Africa, Spain, Sri Lanka, Sudan, Sweden, Switzerland, Syrian AR, Taiwan, Tanzania UR, Thailand, Trinidad-Tobago, Tunisia, Türkiye, Uganda, UK, Uruguay, USA, Venezuela, Vietnam, Zambia, Zimbabwe.
Associate in 15 countries:
Albania, Azerbaijan, Ireland, Kyrgyzstan, Lithuania, Moldova, Mongolia, Nepal, Pakistan, Russia, Serbia-Montenegro, Sri Lanka, UK, Ukraine, Uzbekistan.
Affiliate in 3 countries:
Bahrain, France, USA.
Regional member (1), listed in this Yearbook:
International Arab Society of Certified Accountants (IASCA, #11665).
IGO Relations *European Commission (EC, #06633)* through EU Committee on Auditing; *Financial Stability Board (FSB, #09770)*. **NGO Relations** *Basel Committee on Banking Supervision (BCBS, #03183)*; *International Organization of Securities Commissions (IOSCO, #14470)*. [2020/XE6625/y/**E**]

♦ International Auditing Practices Committee / see International Auditing and Assurance Standards Board (#12296)
♦ International Auditor Training Certification Association / see International Personnel Certification Association (#14560)

♦ International Auschwitz Committee (IAC) 12297

Comité international d'Auschwitz (CIA) – Comité Internacional de Auschwitz – Internationales Auschwitz-Komitee (IAK) – Mezdunarodnyj Komitet Byvsi Uznikov Osvencima – Miedzynarodowy Komitet Oswiecimski

Coordinating Office c/o German Resistance Memorial, Stauffenbergst 13-14, 10785 Berlin, Germany. T. +493026392681. Fax +493026392683. E-mail: kontakt@auschwitz.info.
Chairman Centre of Organizations of Holocaust Survivors in Israel (COHSI), 4 Emile Botta St, PO Box 7218, Jerusalem, Israel. T. +97226231737. Fax +97226222743.
URL: http://www.auschwitz.info/

History May 1946. **Aims** Erect a monument to the memory of the *victims* of the *concentration camp* of Auschwitz; defend the social rights of *detainees*; act to bring justice to bear on those who are to blame; preserve Auschwitz-Birkenau area and site. **Structure** Meeting (twice a year). General Assembly at Auschwitz (every 3 years) for elections. Executive Committee, consisting of 6 members. Steering Committee, comprising 18 members. **Finance** Members' dues. Grants. **Activities** Invitation of several Nobel prizewinners of Peace to celebrate the liberation of Auschwitz, 27 Jan 1995, Auschwitz (Poland). **Events** *Meeting* Oswiecim (Poland) 1995, *Steering Committee Meeting* Vienna (Austria) 1994.
Members National organizations (32) in 20 countries:
Australia, Austria, Belgium, Bulgaria, Czechia, France, Germany, Greece, Hungary, Israel, Italy, Luxembourg, Netherlands, Poland, Romania, Russia, Serbia, Slovakia, Slovenia, USA. [2020/XE1384/**E**]

♦ International Australian Football Confederation / see Aussie Rules International
♦ International Australian Football Council / see Aussie Rules International
♦ International Authority for the Ruhr (inactive)

♦ International Authors Forum (IAF) 12298

Administrator Barnard's Inn – 1st Floor, 86 Fetter Lane, London, EC4A 1EN, UK. T. +442072645707.
URL: http://www.internationalauthors.org/

History Registered in accordance with UK law: 8496616, 19 Apr 2013. **Aims** Provide authors' organizations worldwide with an international platform to exchange information, develop positions and provide support in authors' rights. **Structure** General Meeting; Steering Committee.
Members National authors' organizations (33) in 17 countries:
Australia, Canada, Finland, Germany, Hungary, Ireland, Korea Rep, Malawi, Netherlands, South Africa, Sudan, Sweden, Tanzania UR, Uganda, UK, USA, Zimbabwe.
Regional organizations (2) listed in this Yearbook:
Conseil européen des associations de traducteurs littéraires (CEATL, #04686); *Pyramide Europe (#18585)*.
Consultative Status Consultative status granted from: *ECOSOC (#05331)* (Special); *World Intellectual Property Organization (WIPO, #21593)* (Observer Status). [2014.11.13/XJ7506/**F**]

♦ International Autistic Research Organization (inactive)

♦ International Auto/Biography Association (IABA) 12299

Contact address not obtained.
URL: https://sites.google.com/ualberta.ca/iaba/home/

History Jun 1999, Beijing (China). Former names and other names: *International Association for Biography and Autobiography* – former. **Aims** Broaden the world vision of auto/biographers, scholars and *readers*; deepen cross-cultural understanding of self, identity and experience; increase global dialogues on life *writing*. **Structure** Organizing Committee. Includes *IABA Africa*, *IABA Chapter of the Americas*, *IABA Asia-Pacific* and *IABA Europe*. **Languages** English. **Staff** None. **Finance** No annual budget. **Activities** Events/meetings; networking/liaising; publishing activities. **Events** *Conference* Turku (Finland) 2022, *Conference* Turku (Finland) 2020, *Biennial Americas Conference* Jamaica 2019, *European Conference* Madrid (Spain) 2019, *Conference* São João Del Rey (Brazil) 2018. **Publications** *a/b: auto/biography studies* (4 a year); *Biography* (4 a year); *Life Writing* (4 a year). *Framing Lives* (2014) – special issue of Auto/Biography journal; *Life Writing and Critical-Creative Practice* (2011) – special issue of Literature Compass, online; *Life Writing and Intimate Publics* (2011) – special issue of Biography journal; *Autobiography and Mediation* (2010); *Life Writing and Translation* (2009); *Inhabiting Multiple Worlds: Auto/Biography in an (Anti-) Global Age* (2005); *Autobiography and the Generations* (2004); *Autobiography and Changing Identities* (2001). Conference proceedings.
Members Individuals in 59 countries and territories:
Argentina, Australia, Austria, Belgium, Benin, Brazil, Canada, China, Colombia, Cuba, Curaçao, Cyprus, Czechia, Denmark, Estonia, Finland, France, Germany, Hungary, Iceland, India, Iran Islamic Rep, Ireland, Israel, Italy, Jamaica, Japan, Kenya, Korea Rep, Latvia, Lebanon, Lithuania, Malaysia, Mexico, Morocco, Namibia, Netherlands, New Zealand, Nigeria, Norway, Philippines, Poland, Portugal, Puerto Rico, Romania, Russia, Singapore, South Africa, Spain, Sweden, Switzerland, Thailand, Türkiye, UK, United Arab Emirates, Uruguay, USA, Vietnam, Zambia. [2021.11.13/XD8696/**B**]

♦ International Automobile Federation (#09613)
♦ International Automobile Recycling Congress (meeting series)

♦ International Automotive Glass Federation (InterAutoGlass) 12300

Contact Beechavenue 54-80, 1119 PW Schiphol, Netherlands. T. +31206586499. Fax +31206586111.

History 30 Nov 2007, Zurich (Switzerland). Registration: Netherlands. **Aims** Act as the international representative in the field and promote professional interests; identify and promote health and safety legislation; organize national and international competitions; develop technical standards. **Structure** Committees (3): Training; Technical; Master Fitter Competition. **Languages** English. **Activities** Organizes the International Master Fitter Competition and its national preparatory competitions.
Members Full in 7 countries:
Australia, Ireland, Italy, Japan, Netherlands, New Zealand, USA. [2015/XM1895/**D**]

♦ International Automotive Institute (inactive)

♦ International Automotive Lighting and Light Signalling Expert Group (GTB) 12301

Sec-Gen c/o Regus, Via Confienza 10, 10121 Turin TO, Italy. T. +390117538670. E-mail: secretary@gtb-lighting.org.
Registered Address Via Don Giovanni Minzoni 14, 10121 Turin TO, Italy.
URL: http://www.gtb-lighting.org/

History Sep 1951, Lucerne (Switzerland). Launched as a joint Working Party of *International Organization for Standardization (ISO, #14473)*, *Commission Internationale de l'Eclairage (CIE, #04219)* and *International Electrotechnical Commission (IEC, #13255)*. Became a legally established association 26 Jan 2011, Turin (Italy). Former names and other names: *Groupe de Travail "Bruxelles 1952 (GTB")* – former. Registration: EU Transparency Register, No/ID: 152358748147-30, Start date: 17 Nov 2022. **Aims** Prepare proposals for new and amended UNECE *Regulations*, taking into account technical development, actual testing experience and safety and economic implications, with a view to practical application. **Structure** General Assembly; Administrative Committee; Technical Steering Committee; Committee of Experts; Working Groups and Taskforces. **Languages** English, Spanish. **Staff** 1.20 FTE, paid. **Finance** Annual budget: 250,000 EUR. **Activities** Events/meetings. **Events** *Meeting* Spain 2014, *Meeting* Austria 2013, *Meeting* Sweden 2013, *Meeting* Copenhagen (Denmark) 2012, *Meeting* USA 2012.
Members Associations (17) in 16 countries:
Austria, Belgium, Czechia, Denmark, France, Germany, Hungary, Italy, Japan, Netherlands, Poland, Slovenia, Spain, Sweden, UK, USA.
Included in the above, 1 organization listed in this Yearbook:
International Motorcycle Manufacturers Association (IMMA, #14186).
Consultative Status Consultative status granted from: *ECOSOC (#05331)* (Special). [2022/XJ9917/**E**]

♦ International Autonautique Federation (inactive)

♦ International Auto Sound Challenge Association (IASCA Worldwide) 12302

Pres 2129 South Ridgewood Ave, South Daytona FL 32119, USA. T. +13863221551. Fax +13867611740. E-mail: memberservices@iasca.com.
URL: http://www.iasca.com/

History 1987.
Members Affiliates in 26 countries:
Belgium, Brazil, Canada, China, Colombia, Dominican Rep, France, Guatemala, Indonesia, Ireland, Italy, Japan, Korea Rep, Malaysia, Mexico, Panama, Philippines, Russia, Singapore, South Africa, Spain, Taiwan, Thailand, Türkiye, UK, Ukraine. [2018/XN0522/**D**]

♦ International Auxiliary Language Association (inactive)
♦ International Avaya Users Group (internationally oriented national body)

♦ International Aviation Fire Protection Association (IAFPA) 12303

Headquarters PO Box 6269, Thatcham, RG19 9JX, UK. T. +442081661690. E-mail: webmaster@iafpa.org.uk.
Chairman address not obtained.
URL: http://www.iafpa.org.uk/

History 2000, as a fraternal and professional body. **Aims** Promote greater international understanding of safety to life and property relating to aircraft fire fighting and rescue and airport facilities. **Structure** Executive Board of 4 members. **Events** *Aircraft Rescue and Fire-Fighting Conference* Singapore (Singapore) 2020, *International Airport Water Rescue Working Group Meeting* Singapore (Singapore) 2019, *Aircraft Rescue and Fire-Fighting Conference* Singapore (Singapore) 2018, *Aircraft Rescue and Fire-Fighting Conference* Singapore (Singapore) 2015, *Aircraft Rescue and Fire Fighting Conference / Annual Conference* Dubai (United Arab Emirates) 2013. **Publications** *IAFPA Bulletin*. **NGO Relations** Joint conference with: *Aircraft Rescue and Fire Fighting Working Group (ARFFWG)*. [2020/XD8318/**D**]

♦ International Aviation Training and Education Organisation (unconfirmed)

♦ International Avocado Society (IAS) 12304

Sociedad Internacional del Aguacate

Contact PO Box 8005, Woolloongabba QLD 4102, Australia. T. +61738466566. Fax +61738466577. E-mail: congress@avocado.org.au.
URL: http://ias2011.wordpress.com/

History 1987, South Africa. **Aims** Interchange information and experiences on the avocado industry. **Structure** Officers: President; President Elect; Past President; Secretary/Treasurer. **Languages** English, Spanish. **Staff** 0.50 FTE, voluntary. **Finance** No budget as yet. **Events** *World Avocado Congress* Auckland (New Zealand) 2023, *World Avocado Congress* Medellin (Colombia) 2019, *World Avocado Congress* Lima (Peru) 2015, *World Avocado Congress* Cairns, QLD (Australia) 2011, *Quadrennial world congress* Viña del Mar (Chile) 2007. **Publications** Congress proceedings.
Members Participants to previous World Congress. Members in 23 countries:
Argentina, Australia, Brazil, Chile, China, Colombia, Costa Rica, Cuba, Dominican Rep, Eswatini, France, Germany, Guatemala, Israel, Italy, Kenya, Mexico, New Zealand, Peru, South Africa, Spain, UK, USA. [2020/XD7856/**C**]

♦ International Baby Food Action Network (IBFAN) 12305

Réseau international des groupes d'action pour l'alimentation infantile – Red Internacional de Grupos pro Alimentación Infantil

European Office c/o GIFA, Avenue de la Paix 11, 1202 Geneva, Switzerland. T. +41227989164. Fax +41227984443. E-mail: info@gifa.org.
URL: http://www.ibfan.org/

History Oct 1979, by international organizations, including *International Coalition for Development Action (ICDA, inactive)*, following a WHO/UNICEF meeting on infant and young child feeding. **Aims** Promote and protect *breastfeeding* worldwide; challenge activities of the baby food industry which violate international recommendations and do not respect children's and women's rights; work toward full implementation of WHO/UNICEF International Code of *Marketing* of *Breastmilk* Substitutes and subsequent relevant World Health Assembly resolutions. **Structure** Network of 8 Regional Coordinating Offices (ROCs), each with regional Board or Advisory Committees: Africa; Francophone Africa; Arab World; Asia; Europe; Latin America and Caribbean; North America; Oceania. Global Program Offices (4): Penang – *International Code Documentation Centre (ICDC, see: #12305)*; *Geneva Infant Feeding Association (GIFA)* (Liaison); Codex Alimentarius Global Programme; Baby Milk Action. **Languages** Arabic, English, French, Portuguese, Spanish. **Finance** Donations, except from manufacturers or distributors of infant and young child feeding and related products. **Activities** Advocacy/lobbying/activism; knowledge management/information dissemination; events/meetings. **Events** *World Breastfeeding Conference* Johannesburg (South Africa) 2016, *International forum on the infant feeding crisis* Manila (Philippines) 1989. **Publications** *Breastfeeding Briefs* (periodical) in Arabic, English, French, Portuguese, Spanish; *Courrier de l'IBFAN*; *IBFAN Africa News*; *IBFAN Info. Breaking the Rules, Stretching the Rules* in English, French, Spanish; *State of the Code by Company and Country*; *The Code Handbook: A guide to implementating the international code of marketing of breastmilk substitutes* in English, French, Portuguese, Spanish. Guides; reports; briefings.

Members Organizations (273) in 168 countries. Membership countries not specified. Included in the above, 2 organizations listed in this Yearbook:
Included in the above, 2 organizations listed in this Yearbook:
Geneva Infant Feeding Association (GIFA); *Nordic Work Group for International Breastfeeding Issues (#17470)*.
Consultative Status Consultative status granted from: *African Commission on Human and Peoples' Rights (ACHPR, #00255)* (Observer); *WHO (#20950)* (Official). **IGO Relations** Participates as observer in the activities of: through WHO Official Status for NGOs, *Codex Alimentarius Commission (CAC, #04081)*. **NGO Relations** Joint programmes with: *Consumers International (CI, #04773)*; *Geneva Infant Feeding Association (GIFA)*; *FIAN International (#09743)*; *International Nestlé Boycott Committee (INBC)*; *WEMOS*. Founding member of: *World Alliance for Breastfeeding Action (WABA, #21079)*. Member of: *Conference of Non-Governmental Organizations in Consultative Relationship with the United Nations (CONGO, #04635)*; *ETO Consortium (ETOs, #05560)*; *Right to Food and Nutrition Watch Consortium (#18943)*; *NGO Committee on the Status of Women, Geneva (#17117)*; *Child Rights Connect (#03884)*; *PMNCH (#18410)*. European office is signatory to Founding Statement of: *Alliance for Lobbying Transparency and Ethics Regulation (ALTER-EU, #00705)*.
[2017/XF1134/y/**F**]

♦ International Baccalaureate (IB) 12306

Baccalauréat International (BI) – Bachillerato Internacional

Head Office Route des Morillons 15, Le Grand-Saconnex, 1218 Geneva, Switzerland. T. +41223092540. Fax +41227882380. E-mail: ibid@ibo.org – support@ibo.org.
URL: http://www.ibo.org/

History 1968, Geneva (Switzerland). Founded in succession to *International Schools Examination Syndicate (ISES)* – *Service d'examens des écoles internationales*, which had been set up, 5 Jun 1964, as an autonomous service of *International Schools Association (ISA, #14789)*. Former names and other names: *International Baccalaureate Office* – former; *Office du baccalauréat international* – former; *Oficina Bachillerato Internacional* – former; *International Schools Examination Syndicate (ISES)* – former; *Service d'examens des écoles internationales* – former; *International Baccalaureate Organization (IBO)* – former; *Organisation du baccalauréat international (OBI)* – former; *Organización del Bachillerato Internacional* – former. Registration: Switzerland. **Aims** Develop inquiring, knowledgeable and caring *young* people who help to create a better and more peaceful world through intercultural understanding and respect. **Structure** Board of Governors; Director General; Senior Leadership Team. **Languages** English, French, Spanish. **Staff** 674.00 FTE, paid. **Finance** Sources: authorization and evaluation fees; workshops and conferences; publications; annual school fee; examination fees; other fees, including donations. **Activities** Training/education. **Events** *Global Conference* Adelaide, SA (Australia) 2023, *IB Heads World Conference* 2022, *Global Conference* San Diego, CA (USA) 2022, *Global Conference* Singapore (Singapore) 2022, *Global Conference* The Hague (Netherlands) 2022. **Publications** *IB World* (annual) – magazine. **Members** As of Nov 2018: 4,954 schools in 153 countries. Membership countries not specified. **Consultative Status** Consultative status granted from: *ECOSOC (#05331)* (Ros C); *UNESCO (#20322)* (Consultative Status). **NGO Relations** Member of: *Fédération des Institutions Internationales établies à Genève (FIIG, #09599)*; *International Association for Educational Assessment (IAEA, #11861)*.
[2022/XC1389/**B**]

- ♦ International Baccalaureate Office / see International Baccalaureate (#12306)
- ♦ International Baccalaureate Organization / see International Baccalaureate (#12306)
- ♦ International Back Pain Society (inactive)
- ♦ International Badminton Federation / see Badminton World Federation (#03060)

♦ International Balint Federation (IBF) 12307

Fédération internationale Balint

Gen Sec Mail Stop F-496 Ac Office, 112631 East 17th Ave, Aurora CO 80045, USA.
URL: http://www.balintinternational.com/

History 4 Oct 1975, Paris (France). First congresses held in London (UK) 1972. **Aims** Promote group training and practice according to principles elaborated by Michael Balint (1896-1970) with the object of improving understanding of the *patient-physician* relationship and its therapeutic potential. **Structure** International Congress (every 2 years); Board. **Languages** English. **Staff** Voluntary. **Finance** Members' dues. **Activities** Events/meetings; training/education. **Events** *Congress* Brussels (Belgium) 2022, *Congress* Brussels (Belgium) 2021, *Congress* Porto (Portugal) 2019, *Biennial Group Leadership Conference* Helsinki (Finland) 2018, *Congress* Oxford (UK) 2017. **Publications** *Balint-Journal* (4 a year) in German; *La bulletin societé medical Balint* (2 a year) in French; *Journal of the Balint Society* (annual) in English. Other journals; congress proceedings. **Information Services** *Balint Documentation Centre – Centre de documentation Balint*.

Members Affiliate member societies in 26 countries:
Armenia, Australia, Austria, Belgium, Brazil, Bulgaria, China, Croatia, Denmark, Finland, France, Germany, Greece, Hungary, Israel, Italy, Netherlands, Poland, Portugal, Romania, Russia, Serbia, Sweden, Switzerland, UK, USA.
Individuals in several countries. Membership countries not specified.
[2021/XD5319/**E**]

- ♦ International Ballistics Committee / see International Ballistics Society (#12308)

♦ International Ballistics Society (IBS) 12308

Sec address not obtained. E-mail: poc-ibs@ballistics.org.
URL: http://www.ballistics.org/

History Set up to organize the *International Symposium on Ballistics*. Original title: *International Ballistics Committee (IBC)*. Current constitution adopted 25 Jan 2010. **Aims** Promote the international ballistics community through international conferences as well as through professional development. **Structure** Board of Directors. **Finance** Members' dues. **Activities** Awards/prizes/competitions; events/meetings. **Events** *Symposium* Edinburgh (UK) 2016, *Symposium* Atlanta, GA (USA) 2014, *Symposium* Freiburg-Breisgau (Germany) 2013, *Symposium* Miami, FL (USA) 2011, *Symposium* Beijing (China) 2010. **Publications** *IBS Newsletter*.

Members Individual; Corporate. Points of contact in 32 countries:
Australia, Austria, Belgium, Brazil, Canada, China, Czechia, Denmark, Finland, France, Germany, Greece, India, Israel, Italy, Jordan, Korea Rep, Mexico, Netherlands, Norway, Poland, Portugal, Russia, Serbia, Singapore, South Africa, Spain, Sweden, Switzerland, Türkiye, UK, USA.
[2015/XM0318/**E**]

- ♦ International Baltic Sea Fishery Commission (internationally oriented national body)
- ♦ International Baltic Sea Foundation for Nature Conservation / see Baltic Sea Conservation Foundation
- ♦ International Balut Federation (no recent information)

♦ International Balzan Prize Foundation 12309

Fondation Internationale Prix Balzan – Internationale Stiftung Balzan Preis – Fondazione Internazionale Premio Balzan

Sec – Prize Piazzetta Umberto Giordano 4, 20122 Milan MI, Italy. T. +39276002212. E-mail: balzan@balzan.it.
Sec – Fund Claridenstrasse 20, 8002 Zurich ZH, Switzerland. T. +41442014822. E-mail: balzan@balzan.ch.
URL: https://www.balzan.org/

History 1956, Lugano (Switzerland). Acts jointly through: *International Balzan Foundation – Fund*, Zurich (Switzerland), registered in accordance with Swiss law; *International Balzan Foundation – Prize*, based in Milan (Italy). Former names and other names: *International E Balzan Foundation* – former. Registration: Italy. **Aims** Commemorate Eugenio Balzan; foster *culture*, *science* and outstanding *humanitarian* initiatives worldwide. **Structure** *'International E Balzan Prize Foundation – Prize'*: Board; General Prize Committee. *'International E Balzan Prize Foundation – Fund'* – manages the funds: Board. **Languages** English, French, German, Italian. **Finance** Self-financed. **Activities** Awards/prizes/competitions; events/meetings. **Events** *Meeting of meeting of linteR-La+b* Bern (Switzerland) 2019. **Publications** *Balzan Prizes* (annual) in English, French, German, Italian; *The Balzan Prizewinners' Research Projects: An Overview* (every 2 years). *Balzan Papers*; *The Annual Balzan Lecture*.

Members Full in 13 countries:
Austria, Denmark, Egypt, France, Germany, Italy, Luxembourg, Netherlands, Norway, Portugal, Sweden, Switzerland, UK.
[2023.03.06/XF3909/f/**F**]

- ♦ International Bamboo Association / see World Bamboo Organization (#21214)
- ♦ International Banana Association (no recent information)
- ♦ International Ban Asbestos Secretariat (internationally oriented national body)
- ♦ International Band of Hope Council (inactive)
- ♦ International Bandy Federation / see Federation of International Bandy (#09601)
- ♦ International Bank for Arms Regulation (unconfirmed)

♦ International Bank for Economic Co-operation (IBEC) 12310

Banque internationale pour la coopération économique – Mezdunarodnyj Bank Ekonomicheskogo Sotrudnicestva (MBES)

Contact 11 Masha Poryvaeva Street, GSP-6, Moscow MOSKVA, Russia, 107996. T. +74956047668. E-mail: fvi@ibec.int – info@ibec.int.
URL: http://www.ibec.int/

History 22 Oct 1963, Moscow (USSR), on signature of Intergovernmental Agreement and Statutes, including: multilateral settlements and IBEC organization; the Statutes of the Bank (an integral part of the Agreement). These were registered with the Secretariat of the United Nations on 20 Aug 1964, No 7388. Agreement and Statutes amended: Dec 1970; Nov 1977; Dec 1990. Registration: Secretariat of the United Nations, No/ID: 7388, Start date: 20 Aug 1964. **Aims** Contribute to economic growth and sustainable development of member states; promote trade and economic cooperation and integration among member states and beyond; support interregional trade and assist in expansion to new markets. **Structure** Council; Board of Management; Departments. **Languages** English, Russian. **Finance** Authorized capital: euro 400,000,000. Paid-up capital: euro 200,000,000. **Activities** Events/meetings; financial and/or material support; networking/ liaising; projects/programmes. **Publications** Annual Report in English, Russian.

Members Governments of 5 countries:
Bulgaria, Mongolia, Romania, Russia, Vietnam.

IGO Relations Participates in the activities of: *International Bank for Reconstruction and Development (IBRD, #12317)* (World Bank); *OECD (#17693)*; *UNCTAD (#20285)*. **NGO Relations** Member of (4): *Banking Association for Central and Eastern Europe (BACEE, #03163)*; *International Chamber of Commerce (ICC, #12534)*; *International Swaps and Derivatives Association (ISDA, #15638)*; *Society for Worldwide Interbank Financial Telecommunication (SWIFT, #19661)*.
[2023.02.14/XF1392/**F***]

- ♦ International Bankers Association (no recent information)
- ♦ International Banking Assocdiation / see IBOS Association (#11038)

♦ International Banking Federation (IBFed) 12311

Managing Dir UK Finance, 5th Floor, 1 Angel Court, London, EC2R 7HJ, UK.
URL: http://www.ibfed.org/

History 30 Mar 2004. Former names and other names: *IBF* – former. Registration: EU Transparency Register, No/ID: 002208439307-92, Start date: 26 Aug 2020. **Aims** Address legislative, regulatory and other issues affecting the banking industry globally. **Structure** Board; Secretariat. Working Groups. **Languages** English. **Staff** 3.00 FTE, paid. **Events** *Meeting* Seoul (Korea Rep) 2011.

Members Founding members (6) in 6 countries:
Australia, Canada, Japan, South Africa, USA.
European Banking Federation (EBF, #06312).
Associate members (4) in 4 countries:
Brazil, China, India, Korea Rep.
[2020/XJ3296/**D**]

- ♦ International Banking Institute, Sofia (internationally oriented national body)
- ♦ International Banking Institute, St Petersburg (internationally oriented national body)
- ♦ International Banking – One Solution / see IBOS Association (#11038)
- ♦ International Banking Research Institute / see International Banking Study Institute (#12313)

♦ International Banking Security Association (IBSA) 12312

Chairman address not obtained. E-mail: info@globalibsa.org.
URL: http://www.globalibsa.org

History 1981, Illinois (USA). **Aims** Prevent and investigate financial crimes; work towards security and continuity of banking business within global financial operations. **Events** *General Membership Meeting* Helsinki (Finland) 2011, *Meeting* Beijing (China) 2008, *Meeting* Moscow (Russia) 2003, *General meeting / Meeting* Sydney, NSW (Australia) 1997, *Meeting* Sydney, NSW (Australia) 1995. **Members** Global financial security leaders (over 50). Membership countries not specified. **IGO Relations** Memorandum of Understanding signed with: *World Customs Organization (WCO, #21350)*.
[2015/XD5681/**D**]

♦ International Banking Study Institute 12313

Institut international d'études bancaires (IIEB) – Instituto Internacional de Estudios Bancarios – Internationales Institut für Bankforschung – Istituto Internazionale di Studi Bancari

Address not obtained.

History 6 Apr 1951, Paris (France). Also referred to as *International Banking Research Institute*. Founders included: Pierre de Bonvoisin (1903-1982). **Events** *Conference* Vienna (Austria) 2011, *Conference* Stockholm (Sweden) 2010, *Conference* Athens (Greece) 2006, *Conference* Dublin (Ireland) 2005, *Conference* Naples (Italy) 1998.
[2011/XF5523/j/**F**]

♦ International Banking Summer School 12314

Dir Indian Inst of Banking and Finance, Kohinoor City, Commercial II – Tower I – 2nd Fl, Kirol road, Off L B S Marg, Kurla (W), Mumbai, Maharashtra 400 070, Mumbai MAHARASHTRA 400 070, India.

History 1948, within the framework of *Institute of Bankers, London*. **Aims** Promote study of major developments in banking; develop personal relations among banking *executives*, chosen for the school as likely to occupy top positions within a few years. **Languages** English. **Events** *Summer School* Russia 2010, *Summer School* India 2009, *Summer School* Melbourne, VIC (Australia) 2006, *Summer School* Dublin (Ireland) 2005, *Summer School* Greece 2004.
[2011.07.01/XK1160/c/**E**]

♦ International Banknote Designers Association (IBDA) 12315

Main Office Chemin des Humberts 5b, 1073 Savigny VD, Switzerland. E-mail: info@ibd-association.com.
URL: http://www.ibd-association.com/

History 2010. Former names and other names: *International Banknotes Designers Association* – alias. Registration: Switzerland. **Aims** Represent designers active in banknote design across over 70 countries. **Structure** Committee, headed by President. **Events** *International Banknote Designers Conference (IBDC)* Dubrovnik (Croatia) 2022, *International Banknote Designers Conference (IBDC)* Lisbon (Portugal) 2018, *International Banknote Designers Conference (IBDC)* Paris (France) 2016, *International Banknote Designers Conference (IBDC)* Montréal, QC (Canada) 2014, *International Banknote Designers Conference (IBDC)* Stockholm (Sweden) 2012. **NGO Relations** Member of: *International Currency Association (ICA, #13123)*.
[2021/XJ6617/**D**]

♦ International Banknotes Designers Association / see International Banknote Designers Association (#12315)

♦ International Bank Note Society (IBNS) 12316

Société internationale pour les billets de banque

Gen Sec PO Box 289, St James NY 11780, USA. E-mail: general-secretary@theibns.org – us-secretary@theibns.org.
URL: http://www.theibns.org/

History 1961, UK. Registration: USA, District of Columbia. **Aims** Promote, stimulate and advance educational, scientific and historical study and knowledge of bank notes and paper *currencies* worldwide. **Structure** General Meeting (annual at International Paper Money Show); Directors (19) and Officers, elected for two-year terms. **Languages** English. **Staff** None. **Finance** Sources: donations; members' dues; revenue from activities/projects. Other sources: auctions; advertising. **Activities** Events/meetings; knowledge management/ information dissemination. **Events** *Board Meeting* Milwaukee, WI (USA) 2022, *European meeting* London (UK) 1999, *European meeting* Maastricht (Netherlands) 1999, *Annual General Meeting* Memphis, TN (USA) 1999, *European meeting* London (UK) 1998. **Publications** *IBNS Journal* (4 a year). Books; newsletters. **Members** Regular; Junior; Group; Family; Life. Individuals (over 2,000) in 90 countries and territories. Membership countries not specified. [2021.05.31/XB4259/**F**]

♦ International Bank for Reconstruction and Development (IBRD) ... 12317

Banque internationale pour la reconstruction et le développement (BIRD) – Banco Internacional de Reconstrucción y Fomento (BIRF)

Vice-Pres Europe/Central Asia IBRD Headquarters, 1818 H St NW, Washington DC 20433, USA. T. +12024771234. Fax +12024776391.
URL: http://www.worldbank.org/

History 27 Dec 1945, Washington DC (USA), when Bank's Charter, or *'Articles of Agreement'*, was signed by 28 nations; commenced operations 25 Jun 1946. IBRD was conceived at *Bretton Woods Conference*, 22 Jul 1944, when representatives of 44 nations met to lay plans for international economic and financial cooperation in postwar years. Most nations attending the Conference later ratified the Bank's Charter and became the first members. Although the USSR never became a member, after its dissolution its component republics individually applied for admission in 1991 and 1992. The Bank is a specialized agency of *United Nations (UN, #20515)* within *United Nations System (#20635)* and linked to *ECOSOC (#05331)*. Formal relations between the Bank and the UN are governed by an agreement approved by the Bank's Board of Governors in Sep 1947 and by the UN General Assembly in Nov 1947. Relations with the United Nations are maintained through the *The World Bank Group (#21218)*, which is an umbrella organization comprising the IBRD with its affiliates: *International Development Association (IDA, #13155)*, *International Finance Corporation (IFC, #13597)* and *Multilateral Investment Guarantee Agency (MIGA, #16888)*. The IBRD is also known popularly as *World Bank – Banque mondiale – Banco Mundial*, although the expression *'World Bank'* in fact technically refers to IBRD and IDA together. **Aims** Help reduce global poverty and promote the economic development of member countries by making loans to governments, or with a government guarantee, below conventional rates of interest for high-priority productive projects in cases where capital is not obtainable from other sources on reasonable terms; provide member countries with technical assistance on matters relating to their economic development; try to increase the effectiveness of the international development effort by fostering cooperation with and among other donors of financial and technical assistance.
Structure Board of Governors, consisting of one Governor appointed by each member nation, delegates most authority to (currently 24) Executive Directors, 5 appointed by the nations having the largest capital subscription (USA, Germany, Japan, UK, France) and 19 elected for 2-year terms by the Governors of the remaining member countries. Each Director appoints an Alternate. Directors are resident in Washington DC (USA) and meet in weekly session plus other meetings as required. They are responsible for matters of policy and approve all the loans made by the Bank. Appointed Directors cast the votes of the appointing country; elected Directors cast the total votes of the electing countries. Voting power is proportionate to a nation's capital subscription. Executive Directors select President who is their Chairman, ex officio, is responsible for day-to-day operations, including making recommendations to Executive Directors on loans and questions of policy, and is also the President of each IBRD affiliate. The same Executive Directors govern IBRD, IFC and IDA (MIGA has a separate Board of Directors, most members of which are also IBRD Executive Directors). The Board of Governors normally meets once a year in the Autumn jointly with the annual meeting of the Board of Governors of *International Monetary Fund (IMF, #14180)*; the two organizations were established together as complementary institutions and are often referred to as *Bretton Woods Institutions (BWIs, #03322)*. The Executive Directors and Alternate Directors of the Fund in some cases also serve on the Executive Board of the Bank, and the same is true of some Governors.
/Officers/:
- President;
- Managing Directors (4);
- Senior Vice-President/Chief Financial Officer;
- Senior Vice-President, Development Economics/Chief Economist;
- Regional Vice-Presidents and Offices (6):
- Africa,
- East Asia and the Pacific,
- Europe and Central Asia,
- Latin America and the Caribbean,
- Middle East and North Africa,
- South Asia;
- Further Vice-Presidents (17):
- Chief Information Officer,
- Controller,
- Corporate Secretary,
- External Affairs, Europe,
- External Affairs and UN Affairs,
- Financial Sector,
- General Counsel,
- Human Resources,
- Network Head, Environmentally and Socially Sustainable Development,
- Network Head, Human Development,
- Network Head, Operations Policy and Country Services,
- Network Head, Poverty Reduction and Economic Management,
- Private Sector Development and Infrastructure/Network Head, Private Sector and Infrastructure,
- Resource Mobilization and Cofinancing,
- Strategy and Resource Management,
- Treasurer,
- World Bank Institute;
- Director-General, Operations Evaluation.

World Bank Institute (WBI, #21220), established 1955, is an autonomous unit within the Bank.
Languages English. **Staff** Staff recruited from over 100 nations. Staff questions negotiated with *World Bank Group Staff Association (#21219)*. **Finance** Funds for loans are obtained from: (a) payments made by members on account of their capital subscriptions; (b) borrowings in the various capital markets of the world; (c) net earnings. In addition, the Bank sells portions of its loans to financial institutions (usually instalments that are due to be repaid within a fairly short time) and thus replenishes its cash resources. The Bank also uses repayments of principal on earlier loans for lending purposes. Subscribed capital was originally US$ 10,000 million; in 2002, subscriptions totalled US$ 189,505 million. Of this total, US$ 11,476 million was paid in; the remainder was subject to call only if required by the Bank to meet its obligations on borrowings or on loans guaranteed by it; most of the capital is, in effect, a guarantee fund for the Bank's obligations. The Bank makes a profit and thus maintains high credit standing. Figures for 2002: US$ 23,000 million in medium- to long-term maturities raised in international markets as part of regular financing operations; operating income US$ 1,924 million, of which US$ 1,291 million retained in general reserve; liquid asset portfolio US$ 25,000 million; loan commitments US$ 11,452 million; loan disbursements US$ 11,256.
Activities The initial emphasis of Bank activity was on urgent problems in reconstruction of the war-damaged economies in Western Europe, for which it made loans totalling US$ 497 million in 1947. When Marshall Aid came into operation in 1948, the Bank turned its attention to financing development worldwide. It plays a catalytic role through encouraging cofinancing of its loans with official agencies and commercial banks. The interest rate on loans to developing countries changes every 6 months. A small fee is charged (0.5% over Bank's borrowing costs on capital markets, reducing to 0.25% or even 0.15% for current borrowers). Loans usually have a 5-year grace period and must be repaid within 15 to 20 years. In providing guarantees, IBRD aims to cover the minimum risk possible to make a project finance-able. Partial risk guarantees are used mainly for limited recourse project finance, where lenders attach more importance to revenues and assets of a project than to the sponsor's credit and can cover risks associated with government contractual commitment; partial credit guarantees, however, cover only a part of the term of the financing and aim to improve borrowing terms through a lengthening maturity. *Enhanced Heavily Indebted Poor Countries Initiative (HIPC Initiative, #05483)*, enhanced framework commenced Oct 1999, is a response to the world debt crisis and the need for poverty reduction.
Of the US$ 11,500 million lent by IBRD in fiscal year 2002, regional distribution was as follows: Europe and Central Asia – 42%; Latin America and the Caribbean – 37%; East Asia and Pacific – 9%; South Asia – 8%; Middle East and North Africa – 4%; Sub-Saharan Africa – less than 1%. Emphasis is on investment that can directly affect the well-being of the masses of poor people in developing countries by making them more productive and integrating them as active partners in the developing process. Current focus is on assisting clients to improve development strategies, implement reform policies and build institutional capacity and on strengthening the financial and private sector regulatory framework and improving public sector governance. The Bank also supports economic management and urban development. For 2002, lending was aimed at the following sectors: Law, justice and public administration – 31%; Finance – 18%; Transportation – 13%; Health and other social services – 12%; Education – 7%; Energy and mining – 6%; Industry and trade – 5%; Agriculture, fishing and forestry – 5%; Water, sanitation and flood protection – 2%; Information and communication – 1%.
Regional and resident missions abroad assist member countries to identify and prepare projects for presentation to the Bank and IDA. Projects normally go through 6 stages: identification; preparation; appraisal; negotiation and Board presentation; implementation and supervision; evaluation, although some project ideas never get beyond identification and others may be fundamentally reworked during preparation and appraisal stages. *'Operations Evaluation Department (OED)'*, an independent department within IBRD, carries out the final (evaluation) stage. Development assistance is coordinated through Consultative Groups, Aid Groups and Aid Consortia of capital-providing countries and international agencies, which coordinate the flow of finance and technical assistance. The Bank supports the reforms taking place in Eastern Europe and is carrying out activities to ease the transition of the republics of the former USSR to market-oriented economies. These include a technical assistance programme, design of economic and sector work programmes and intensive development-training efforts in preparation for lending for reform programmes. It is a partner in *Environmental Action Programme for Central and Eastern Europe (EAP, inactive)* and organizes its own *World Bank Baltic Sea Programme*, providing investment and support to protection of the environment in the Baltic Sea region, assisting transition policies of national governments and creating a Baltic fund for the social sector.
To be eligible to apply for membership of the Bank a country must first be a member of IMF. However, while the IMF may lend to any member country lacking sufficient foreign currency to cover short-term obligations to creditors in other countries, the Bank may lend only to poor countries. From 1 Apr 1989, the World Bank requires IMF approval for some of its loans to developing countries.
The Bank is co-sponsor with FAO and UNDP of *CGIAR System Organization (CGIAR, #03843)*, providing Chairman and Executive Secretariat. Together with UNDP and UNEP, it jointly manages *Global Environment Facility (GEF, #10346)*. With UNDP and a number of bilateral donors, it runs the *Energy Sector Management Assistance Programme (ESMAP)* to increase use of natural gas in developing countries, help them devise sound energy strategies and make the necessary institutional and policy reforms to facilitate the transition. *'Foreign Investment Advisory Service (FIAS)'* advises governments wanting to attract foreign direct investment. IBRD acts as Secretariat for and cooperates with governments and other international agencies in *Consultative Group to Assist the Poor (CGAP, #04768)*; it functioned as a component of *Urban Management Programme for Asia and the Pacific (UMPAP, inactive)* through *Metropolitan Environment Improvement Programme (MEIP, no recent information)*.
Events *Innovation Workshop* Stockholm (Sweden) 2020, *Workshop on SDG Indicator 10.7.1* Istanbul (Turkey) 2019, *International Conference on Migration and Development* Madrid (Spain) 2019, *Annual Conference on Land and Poverty* Washington, DC (USA) 2019, *Conference on Perspectives on Poverty Measurement* Washington, DC (USA) 2019. **Publications** *Evaluation Results* (annual). *Information Briefs* – 12 series set. *World Bank Atlas*; *World Debt Tables*; *World Development Report*. Annual Report. Summary proceedings of Annual Meetings; speeches; sector and working papers; technical books. Information Services: *infoDev (#11190)* – global multilateral donor program administered by the IBRD to assist developing countries in taking advantage of the emerging information society. **Information Services** *Public Information Centre (PIC)* – offices in Washington DC (USA) Headquarters, in London (UK), Paris (France) and Tokyo (Japan) and in resident missions worldwide.
Members As of 2007, IBRD has 183 member countries:
Afghanistan, Albania, Algeria, Angola, Antigua-Barbuda, Argentina, Armenia, Australia, Austria, Azerbaijan, Bahamas, Bahrain, Bangladesh, Barbados, Belarus, Belgium, Belize, Benin, Bhutan, Bolivia, Bosnia-Herzegovina, Botswana, Brazil, Brunei Darussalam, Bulgaria, Burkina Faso, Burundi, Cambodia, Cameroon, Canada, Cape Verde, Central African Rep, Chad, Chile, China, Colombia, Comoros, Congo Brazzaville, Congo DR, Costa Rica, Côte d'Ivoire, Croatia, Cyprus, Czechia, Denmark, Djibouti, Dominica, Dominican Rep, Ecuador, Egypt, El Salvador, Equatorial Guinea, Eritrea, Estonia, Eswatini, Ethiopia, Fiji, Finland, France, Gabon, Gambia, Georgia, Germany, Ghana, Greece, Grenada, Guatemala, Guinea, Guinea-Bissau, Guyana, Haiti, Honduras, Hungary, Iceland, India, Indonesia, Iran Islamic Rep, Iraq, Ireland, Israel, Italy, Jamaica, Japan, Jordan, Kazakhstan, Kenya, Kiribati, Korea Rep, Kuwait, Kyrgyzstan, Laos, Latvia, Lebanon, Lesotho, Liberia, Libya, Lithuania, Luxembourg, Madagascar, Malawi, Malaysia, Maldives, Mali, Malta, Marshall Is, Mauritania, Mauritius, Mexico, Micronesia FS, Moldova, Mongolia, Morocco, Mozambique, Myanmar, Namibia, Nepal, Netherlands, New Zealand, Nicaragua, Niger, Nigeria, North Macedonia, Norway, Oman, Pakistan, Palau, Panama, Papua New Guinea, Paraguay, Peru, Philippines, Poland, Portugal, Qatar, Romania, Russia, Rwanda, Samoa, San Marino, Sao Tomé-Principe, Saudi Arabia, Senegal, Serbia, Seychelles, Sierra Leone, Singapore, Slovakia, Slovenia, Solomon Is, Somalia, South Africa, Spain, Sri Lanka, St Kitts-Nevis, St Lucia, St Vincent-Grenadines, Sudan, Suriname, Sweden, Switzerland, Syrian AR, Tajikistan, Tanzania UR, Thailand, Timor-Leste, Togo, Tonga, Trinidad-Tobago, Tunisia, Türkiye, Turkmenistan, Uganda, UK, Ukraine, United Arab Emirates, Uruguay, USA, Uzbekistan, Vanuatu, Vietnam, Yemen, Zambia, Zimbabwe.
IGO Relations Cooperates with: *Egmont Group of Financial Intelligence Units (#05396)*; *Programme on Man and the Biosphere (MAB, #18526)*; *United Nations Economic Commission for Latin America and the Caribbean (ECLAC, #20556)*. Permanent observer status with: *World Intellectual Property Organization (WIPO, #21593)*. Observer to: *Eurasian Group on Combating Money Laundering and Financing of Terrorism (EAG, #05608)*; *International Organization for Migration (IOM, #14454)*; *Secretariat for Eastern African Coastal Area Management (SEACAM, no recent information)*. Represented on: *United Nations System Chief Executives Board for Coordination (CEB, #20636)*. Member of Steering Committee of: *Caspian Environment Programme (CEP, #03596)*. Joint programme with: *UNDP (#20292)*. Member of: *Collaborative Partnership on Forests (CPF, #04100)*; *Congo Basin Forest Partnership (CBFP, #04662)*; *Inter-Agency Working Group on Desertification (IAWGD, inactive)*; *Inter-Agency Standing Committee (IASC, #11393)*; *United Nations Group on the Information Society (UNGIS, #20570)*; *UN-OCEANS (#20711)*; *UN-Water (#20723)*. Observer member of: *United Nations Sustainable Development Group (UNSDG, #20634)*. Partner of: *Northern Dimension Environmental Partnership (NDEP, #17584)*; *United Nations Forum on Forests (UNFF, #20562)*; *World Water Assessment Programme (WWAP, #21907)*. Partnership agreement with: *OECD (#17693)*. Instrumental in setting up: *Black Sea Action Plan (BSAP, no recent information)*; *Mediterranean Environment Programme (MEP, inactive)* and *Mediterranean Environmental Technical Assistance Programme (METAP, inactive)*; *Onchocerciasis Control Programme (OCP, inactive)* (with UNDP, FAO and WHO); *Prototype Carbon Fund (PCF, #18552)*; *Water and Sanitation Programme (WSP, #20837)*.

NGO Relations Although the Bank has no formal mechanism for consultative status, there are clear operational rules for collaboration with NGOs working at a project level, usually in a tripartite arrangement with the Bank and the host government. *'World Bank NGO Unit'* supports and guides Bank staff in improving and strengthening their relations with NGOs, which collaborate in over one third of Bank-supported projects. *World Bank – Civil Society Joint Facilitation Committee (JFC, #21217)* which is serviced by IBRD and which promotes collaboration in joint-sponsored development activities, provides an ongoing forum within which senior World Bank officials and developed and developing country NGO leaders exchange ideas.
Honorary member of: *World Federation of Development Financing Institutions (WFDFI, #21428)*. Member of: *Bellagio Forum for Sustainable Development (BFSD, no recent information)*; *International Institute of Administrative Sciences (IIAS, #13859)*; *World Road Association (PIARC, #21754)*. Instrumental in setting up: *Community Development Carbon Fund (CDCF, #04395)* – with *International Emissions Trading Association (IETA, #13262)*; *Joint Africa Institute (JAI, inactive)* (with AfDB and IMF); *World Bank – WWF Alliance for Forest Conservation and Sustainable Use (WB – WWF Forest Alliance, #21221)*. [2017/XF1393/**F***]

♦ International Bank for West Africa (inactive)

♦ International Baptist Convention (IBC) 12318

Address not obtained.
URL: http://www.ibc-churches.org/

History Founded 1957, as *European Baptist Convention (EBC)*. **Aims** Provide the framework and available resources for member churches and their missions to: proclaim the gospel of Jesus Christ; plant new churches; strengthen member churches; enhance fellowship among member churches; support other Baptist groups; promote worldwide Christian missions. **Structure** Summer Assembly (annual), always in Interlaken (Switzerland). **Languages** English. **Staff** 3.00 FTE, paid. **Finance** Voluntary donations. **Activities** Organizes: men's, women's, singles, youth and leadership conferences; seminars; study courses; teacher training; missionary preparation; prayer campaigns; special events for men, women and children; support and training for pastors and church leaders; funds. **Events** *Women Conference* Berlin (Germany) 2016, *Annual Convention* Sofia (Bulgaria) 2013, *Women Leadership Conference* Stuttgart (Germany) 2013, *Annual Convention* Berlin (Germany) 2012, *Singles Conference* Madrid (Spain) 2011. **Publications** *Highlights* (3 a year).
Members Churches and missions (74) in 27 countries:
Argentina, Austria, Belgium, Brazil, Bulgaria, Costa Rica, Czechia, Denmark, France, Germany, Greece, Hungary, Italy, Netherlands, Norway, Portugal, Romania, Russia, Slovakia, South Africa, Spain, Switzerland, Tanzania UR, Türkiye, UK, Ukraine, United Arab Emirates.
NGO Relations *Baptist World Alliance (BWA, #03176)*; *European Baptist Federation (EBF, #06316)*; *EBM International (#05270)*; *European Baptist Women United (EBWU, #06317)*. [2014/XD5262/**D**]

♦ International Baptist Theological Study Centre, Amsterdam (IBTSC) 12319

Administrator Baptist House, Postjesweg 175, 1061 AX Amsterdam, Netherlands. T. +31202103025. E-mail: administrator@ibts.eu – librarian@ibts.eu.
URL: http://www.ibts.eu/

History Successor to *International Baptist Theological Seminary (Prague)*, set up 1949. Also referred to as *IBTS Centre Amsterdam*. Owned by members of *European Baptist Federation (EBF, #06316)*. **Aims** Provide research, researchers, educators, and leaders who can serve the mission and ministry of churches in Europe, the Middle East and beyond. **Structure** General Meeting. **Activities** Training/education; research/documentation; events/meetings. **Publications** *Journal of European Baptist Studies*. **NGO Relations** Member of: *Consortium of European Baptists Theological Schools (CEBTS, #04738)*. [2022/XM5214/**E**]

♦ International Bar Association (IBA) 12320

Association internationale du barreau

Exec Dir 5 Chancery Lane, London, WC2A 1LG, UK. T. +442078420090. E-mail: iba@int-bar.org.
URL: http://www.ibanet.org/

History 17 Feb 1947, New York, NY (USA). Founded as a federation of national bar associations. Constitution modified: 1947; 1958; 1966; 1968; 1972; 1976; 1982; 1984; 1986; 1988; 1991; 2000; 2002; 2005; 2007; 2009; 2010; 2012; 2016. Restructured 24 Oct 2004, Auckland (New Zealand). Registration: Start date: 2007, USA, New York; EU Transparency Register, No/ID: 55828722666-53, Start date: 26 Nov 2009. **Aims** Support the independence of the *judiciary*, the right of *lawyers* to practise their profession without interference, and *human rights* of lawyers worldwide; establish and maintain permanent relations and exchanges among bar associations and law societies and individual member lawyers; discuss problems of professional organization and status; advance the science of *jurisprudence* in all its phases; promote uniformity and definition in appropriate fields of *law* by common study of practical legal problems; promote administration of justice under law among peoples of the world; promote legal aspects of the principles and aims of the United Nations in executing these objectives; cooperate with, and promote coordination among, international juridical organizations having similar purposes. **Structure** IBA Council (meeting twice a year), comprises one representative of each member organization and, ex officio, the officers: President; Vice-President; Secretary-General; Treasurer. Management Board. IBA Office. Standing Committees. From 24 Oct 2004, two divisions replace *International Bar Association – Section on Business Law (SBL, inactive)*, *International Bar Association – Section on Legal Practice (inactive)* and *International Bar Association – Section on Energy and Natural Resources Law (inactive)*: Legal Practice Division comprises: LPD Council; LPD Officers – Chair, Vice-Chair, Secretary-Treasurer (who is also IBA Treasurer) and Honorary President Founder; Sections – SBL Committees, SERL Committees and SLP commercially-focused committees. PUblic and Professional Interest Division (PPID) comprises: PPID Council; PPID Officers – Chair, Vice-Chair and Secretary-Treasurer (who is Assistant Treasurer of IBA); Bar Issues Commission; professional and public interest committees; some IBA Standing Committees; *International Bar Association's Human Rights Institute (IBAHRI, #12322)*. Meetings closed. **Languages** English, French, German, Spanish. **Staff** 55.00 FTE, paid. **Finance** Members' dues, with 40% discount for lawyers from developing countries. Full: includes membership of IBA, LPD and PPID (including membership of one LPD committee and one PPID constituent, with extra LPD committees and PPID constituents at extra cost); General: includes membership of IBA and PPID (including membership of one PPID constituent, with extra PPID constituents at extra cost). **Activities** Events/meetings. **Events** *Annual Joint Conference on International Franchising* Washington, DC (USA) 2024, *Annual Conference* Paris (France) 2023, *Annual Joint Conference on International Franchising* Washington, DC (USA) 2023, *Biennial Global Immigration Conference* London (UK) 2022, *Annual Conference* Miami, FL (USA) 2022. **Publications** *IBA E-News for Members* (12 a year); *International Bar News (IBN)* (6 a year); *Journal of Energy and Natural Resources Law* (4 a year); *The In-House Persepctive* (4 a year) – magazine; *Competition Law International* (3 a year) – journal; *Dispute Resolution International* (2 a year) – journal; *Insolvency and Restructuring International* (2 a year) – journal; *Convergence* – journal. Books.
Members Bar associations and law societies (nearly 200) in 122 countries and territories:
Afghanistan, Algeria, Angola, Argentina, Armenia, Australia, Austria, Bahamas, Bahrain, Bangladesh, Barbados, Belgium, Bermuda, Botswana, Brazil, Bulgaria, Cameroon, Canada, Cayman Is, Channel Is, Chile, China, Costa Rica, Cyprus, Czechia, Denmark, Dominica, Ecuador, Egypt, England, Equatorial Guinea, Estonia, Eswatini, Ethiopia, Fiji, Finland, France, Gambia, Germany, Ghana, Gibraltar, Greece, Guyana, Hong Kong, Hungary, Iceland, India, Indonesia, Iran Islamic Rep, Iraq, Ireland, Isle of Man, Israel, Italy, Jamaica, Japan, Jordan, Kenya, Korea Rep, Kosovo, Kuwait, Latvia, Lesotho, Liberia, Libya, Liechtenstein, Lithuania, Luxembourg, Malawi, Malaysia, Malta, Mauritius, Mexico, Mongolia, Morocco, Namibia, Nepal, Netherlands, New Zealand, Nigeria, Norfolk Is, North Macedonia, Northern Ireland, Norway, Pakistan, Panama, Papua New Guinea, Peru, Philippines, Poland, Portugal, Puerto Rico, Romania, Russia, Rwanda, Scotland, Sierra Leone, Singapore, Slovakia, Solomon Is, South Africa, Spain, Sri Lanka, St Lucia, St Vincent-Grenadines, Sweden, Switzerland, Syrian AR, Tanzania UR, Thailand, Tonga, Trinidad-Tobago, Tunisia, Türkiye, Uganda, Ukraine, Uruguay, USA, Venezuela, Zambia, Zimbabwe.
Individual lawyers (about 30,000) in 182 countries and territories:
Afghanistan, Albania, Algeria, Andorra, Angola, Anguilla, Antigua-Barbuda, Argentina, Armenia, Aruba, Australia, Austria, Azerbaijan, Bahamas, Bahrain, Bangladesh, Barbados, Belarus, Belgium, Belize, Benin, Bermuda, Bolivia, Botswana, Brazil, Brunei Darussalam, Bulgaria, Burkina Faso, Cambodia, Cameroon, Canada, Cayman Is, Channel Is, Chile, China, Colombia, Congo DR, Cook Is, Costa Rica, Côte d'Ivoire, Croatia, Cuba, Cyprus, Czechia, Denmark, Dominica, Dominican Rep, Ecuador, Egypt, El Salvador, England, Estonia, Eswatini, Ethiopia, Fiji, Finland, France, Gabon, Gambia, Georgia, Germany, Ghana, Gibraltar, Greece, Grenada, Guatemala, Guyana, Haiti, Honduras, Hong Kong, Hungary, Iceland, India, Indonesia, Iran Islamic Rep, Iraq, Ireland, Isle of Man, Israel, Italy, Jamaica, Japan, Jordan, Kazakhstan, Kenya, Korea Rep, Kuwait, Kyrgyzstan, Latvia, Lebanon, Lesotho, Liberia, Libya, Liechtenstein, Lithuania, Luxembourg, Macau, Madagascar, Malawi, Malaysia, Mali, Malta, Mauritania, Mauritius, Mexico, Micronesia FS, Moldova, Monaco, Montserrat, Morocco, Mozambique, Myanmar, Namibia, Nepal, Netherlands, New Zealand, Niger, Nigeria, Norfolk Is, North Macedonia, Northern Ireland, Norway, Oman, Pakistan, Panama, Papua New Guinea, Paraguay, Peru, Philippines, Poland, Portugal, Puerto Rico, Qatar, Romania, Russia, Sabah, Sarawak, Saudi Arabia, Scotland, Senegal, Serbia, Sierra Leone, Singapore, Slovakia, Slovenia, Solomon Is, South Africa, Spain, Sri Lanka, St Kitts-Nevis, St Lucia, St Vincent-Grenadines, Sudan, Sweden, Switzerland, Syrian AR, Taiwan, Tanzania UR, Thailand, Togo, Tonga, Trinidad-Tobago, Tunisia, Türkiye, Turks-Caicos, Tuvalu, Uganda, Ukraine, United Arab Emirates, Uruguay, USA, Uzbekistan, Vanuatu, Venezuela, Vietnam, Virgin Is UK, Virgin Is USA, Wales, Yemen, Zambia, Zimbabwe.
Consultative Status Consultative status granted from: *ECOSOC (#05331)* (Special); *UNCTAD (#20285)* (General Category); *World Intellectual Property Organization (WIPO, #21593)* (Permanent Observer Status); *Council of Europe (CE, #04881)* (Participatory Status). **IGO Relations** Participates in the work of: *United Nations Economic Commission for Europe (UNECE, #20555)*. Recognized by: *European Commission (EC, #06633)*. Accredited by: *United Nations Office at Vienna (UNOV, #20604)*. Member of: *Convention against Torture Initiative (CTI, #04786)*. Associated with Department of Global Communications of the United Nations. **NGO Relations** Member of: *International Council of Environmental Law (ICEL, #13018)*; *International Criminal Bar (ICB, #13107)*. Consultative member of: *Comité maritime international (CMI, #04192)*. Observer to: *Presidents of Law Associations in Asia (POLA, #18486)*. Instrumental in setting up: *Southern Africa Litigation Centre (SALC, #19832)*; *South Pacific Lawyers' Association (SPLA, #19887)*. [2021/XB1396/**B**]

♦ International Bar Association – Public and Professional Interest Division (PPID) 12321

Exec Dir 4th Floor, 10 St Bride Street, London, EC4A 4AD, UK. T. +442078420090. Fax +442078420091. E-mail: iba@int-bar.org.
URL: https://www.ibanet.org/Committees/Divisions/Public_Professional_Interest_Div/ ppidhome.aspx

History 24 Oct 2004, Auckland (New Zealand). Founded within the framework of *International Bar Association (IBA, #12320)*, together with *International Bar Association – Legal Practice Division (LPD)* taking over activities of the previous *International Bar Association – Section on Business Law (SBL, inactive)*, *International Bar Association – Section on Legal Practice (inactive)* and *International Bar Association – Section on Energy and Natural Resources Law (inactive)*. **Aims** Promote exchange of information and views on public and professional interest activities of the *legal profession* worldwide; support and promote those activities, the rule of law and defence of *human rights*. **Structure** Steering Group. *'Bar Issues Commission (BIC)'*; *International Bar Association's Human Rights Institute (IBAHRI, #12322)*; *'Section on Public and Professional Interest (SPPI)'*. **Activities** Constituents (13): Academics; Access to Justice; Barristers and Advocates; Client Protection; Development of the Legal Profession, including MDP, WTO, Cross-Border, 2020 Commission and Anti-Corruption, these sub-constituents not being open to membership; Judges; Law Firm Management Committee; Legal Education; Professional Ethics, including *'Code of Ethics Working Group'* (not open to membership); Senior Lawyers; UNWOC (not open to membership); Women Lawyers; Young Lawyers. **Publications** Who's who; handbook. [2014/XJ7043/**E**]

♦ International Bar Association's Human Rights Institute (IBAHRI) . . . 12322

Dir 10 St Bride Street, 4th floor, London, EC4A 4AD, UK. T. +442078420090. Fax +442078420090. E-mail: hri@int-bar.org.
URL: http://www.ibanet.org/IBAHRI.aspx

History Founded 5 Dec 1995, by *International Bar Association (IBA, #12320)*, under the Honorary Presidency of Nelson Mandela. **Aims** Work with the global legal community to promote and protect human rights and the independence of the legal profession worldwide. **Structure** Council. **Languages** Arabic, English, French, Portuguese, Russian, Spanish. **Staff** 10.00 FTE, paid. **Finance** Grant funding, including from the following organizations listed in this Yearbook: *Open Society Foundations (OSF, #17763)*; *Swedish International Development Cooperation Agency (Sida)*; UK Foreign and Commonwealth Office; *United States Agency for International Development (USAID)*. **Activities** Training/education; guidance/assistance/consulting; knowledge management/information dissemination; research/documentation; advocacy/lobbying/activism; capacity building. **Events** *Rule of law fact-finding by NGOs* London (UK) 2015, *Conference* London (UK) 2000. **Publications** Books. Annual Report; country reports; thematic papers; training manuals. [2020.01.02/XE3348/j/**E**]

♦ International Barcode of Life (iBOL) 12323

Secretariat Biodiversity Inst of Ontario, Univ of Guelph, 50 Stone Road East, Guelph ON N1G 2W1, Canada. T. +15198244120ext56393. Fax +15198245703. E-mail: info@ibol.org.
Head Office 150 Metcalfe Str, Suite 2100, Ottawa ON K2P 1P1, Canada.
URL: http://ibol.org/

History Administrative structures started Jul 2009; formal activation of the *International Barcode of Life Project*, Oct 2010. Registered in accordance with Canadian law. **Aims** Extend the geographic and taxonomic coverage of the barcode reference library – Barcode of Life Data Systems (BOLD) – storing the resulting barcode records, providing community access to the knowledge they represent and promoting new applications of *DNA barcoding* that provide social, economic and environmental benefits. **Structure** Board of Directors; Research Oversight Committee; International Scientific Collaboration Committee; Secretariat. **Activities** Working Groups: DNA Barcode Library; Methods and Technologies; Informatics; Coordination; GE3LS. **Events** *Conference* 2019. **Publications** *Barcode Bulletin* – newsletter.
Members National, regional and central nodes Researchers and biodiversity organizations. Members in 29 countries:
Argentina, Australia, Brazil, Canada, China, Colombia, Costa Rica, Finland, France, Germany, India, Kenya, Korea Rep, Madagascar, Mexico, Netherlands, New Zealand, Norway, Pakistan, Panama, Papua New Guinea, Peru, Portugal, Russia, Saudi Arabia, South Africa, Switzerland, UK, USA.
IGO Relations *Global Biodiversity Information Facility (GBIF, #10250)*. [2013.07.26/XJ5267/**F**]

♦ International Barents Secretariat / see Barents Euro-Arctic Council (#03177)
♦ International Bariatric Endoscopic Surgical Trends Congress (meeting series)
♦ International Barley Genetics Symposium (meeting series)

♦ International Bartenders Association (IBA) 12324

Registered Office 218 Orchard Road, Level 6 / 7, Singapore 238851, Singapore.
URL: http://www.iba-world.com/

History 24 Feb 1951, UK. Registration: Registry of Societies, No/ID: T06SS0054C, Singapore. **Aims** Promote and maintain international relations among Guild Members; make available the opportunity for exchange of news, views, proposals and ideas; promote a close relationship and liaison between Guild Members and the kindred industry; promote customer service and encourage the knowledge of the international guests, habits and customs in relation to drinking; encourage standardization of mixed drinks recipes; promote educational facilities for bartenders of the Association. **Structure** Annual General Meeting; Council. **Languages** English. **Staff** None. **Finance** Payment by per country basis, decided at Annual General Meeting. **Activities** Awards/prizes/competitions; events/meetings; training/education. **Events** *Annual Conference* St Petersburg (Russia) 2020, *Annual Conference* Chengdu (China) 2019, *Annual Conference* Tallinn (Estonia) 2018, *Annual Conference* Copenhagen (Denmark) 2017, *Annual Conference* Tokyo (Japan) 2016.
Members Full in 59 countries and territories:
Argentina, Armenia, Australia, Austria, Belgium, Brazil, Bulgaria, China, Colombia, Croatia, Cuba, Cyprus, Czechia, Denmark, Dominican Rep, Estonia, Finland, France, Germany, Greece, Hong Kong, Hungary, Iceland, Ireland, Israel, Italy, Japan, Korea Rep, Luxembourg, Malta, Mexico, Montenegro, Netherlands, New Zealand, North Macedonia, Norway, Peru, Philippines, Poland, Portugal, Puerto Rico, Romania, Russia, Serbia, Singapore, Slovakia, Slovenia, South Africa, Spain, Sweden, Switzerland, Taiwan, Türkiye, UK, Ukraine, Uruguay, USA, Venezuela, Vietnam. [2021/XD1794/v/**F**]

♦ International Basal Ganglia Society (IBAGS) 12325

Chair 954 Gatewood Rd NE, Atlanta GA 30329-4208, USA. E-mail: contact@ibags.global – webmaster@ibags.global.
Treas address not obtained.
URL: http://www.ibags.global/

History 1983. **Aims** Promote understanding of normal and abnormal basal ganglia function including pathophysiology of their disorders such as *Parkinson's disease*, *L-DOPA* induced *Dyskinesia*, *Huntington's disease*, *depression* and *schizophrenia*. **Structure** Council. **Languages** English. **Finance** Sources: members' dues; sponsorship. **Activities** Events/meetings. **Events** *Triennial Meeting* Stockholm (Sweden) 2023, *Triennial Meeting* Blenheim (New Zealand) 2022, *Triennial Meeting* Biarritz (France) 2019, *Triennial Meeting* Mérida (Mexico) 2017, *Triennial Meeting* Eilat (Israel) 2013. **Members** Regular; Student; Lifetime; Emeritus. Membership countries not specified. [2022.05.16/XJ3109/**D**]

♦ International Baseball Federation (inactive)

♦ International Basel-Karlsruhe Media-Forum Foundation (internationally oriented national body)
♦ International Basement Tectonics Association (inactive)
♦ International Basimetric Society (inactive)
♦ International Basketball Federation (#09614)

♦ International Basketball Federation – North American Zone 12326
SG PO Box 8925, Santurce PR 00907, USA. T. +17879774999. Fax +17879774007. E-mail: info-americas@fiba.com.
Street Address 952 Ave Fernandez Juncos Parada 15, Santurce PR 00910, USA.
URL: http://www.fibaamerica.com/
History within the framework of: *Fédération internationale de basketball (FIBA, #09614)*. **Structure** Part of: *FIBA Americas (#09745)*. No permanent Secretariat.
Members National federations (members of FIBA) in 2 countries:
Canada, USA. [2016.06.01/XE0580/**E**]

♦ International Bat Research Conference (meeting series)
♦ International Battery and Energy Storage Alliance (unconfirmed)

♦ International Battery Materials Association (IBA) 12327
Chairman MEET – Room M-1-003, Corrensstr 46, 48149 Münster, Germany. T. +492518336033. Fax +492518336032.
Contact 22416 Yarrow Trl, Strongsville OH 44149, USA.
URL: http://www.international-battery-association.org/
History Registered in accordance with US law: EIN 34-1434869. **Aims** Foster and promote science and technology of batteries and related electrochemical energy storage systems on all levels. **Structure** Board of Directors. Award Committee. **Activities** Awards/prizes/competitions; events/meetings. **Events** *Annual meeting* San Diego, CA (USA) 2019, *Annual Meeting* Jeju (Korea Rep) 2018, *Meeting* Nara (Japan) 2017, *Meeting* Brisbane, QLD (Australia) 2014, *Meeting* Barcelona (Spain) 2013. [2018/XN8089/**C**]

♦ International Bauxite Association (inactive)

♦ International B Conference Steering Committee 12328
Association de pilotage des conférences B (APCB)
Sec IUT – Dept Informatique, 3 rue du Maréchal Joffre, BP 34103, 44041 Nantes CEDEX 1, France. T. +33240306056. Fax +33240306047. E-mail: mery@loria.fr.
URL: http://www.lina.sciences.univ-nantes.fr/apcb/
History Founded 16 Aug 1997, when registered in accordance with French law. **Aims** Promote the B-method for specifying, designing and coding *software* systems, dealing essentially with central aspects of the software lifecycle: technical specification; design by successive refinement steps; layered architecture; executable code generation. **Structure** Board. **Languages** English, French. **Events** *ABZ Conference* Toulouse (France) 2014, *ABZ Conference* Pisa (Italy) 2012, *ABZ Conference* Québec, QC (Canada) 2010, *ABZ conference* London (UK) 2008, *International conference on the B method* Nantes (France) 2008.
Members Individuals in 8 countries:
Australia, Canada, Finland, France, Israel, Italy, UK, USA.
NGO Relations Liaises with: *B Formal Method Users Group (BUG, no recent information)*; *Z User Group (ZUG, #22041)*. [2014.06.24/XE3859/v/**E**]

♦ International Beach Volleyball Players' Association (IBVPA) 12329
Pres Neunbrunnenstr 38, 8050 Zurich ZH, Switzerland. E-mail: office@ibvpa.org.
URL: https://ibvpa.org/
History Constituent General Assembly held 26 July 2017. **Aims** Develop the sport of beach volleyball and create an environment in which the professional athletes can earn a stable living. **Structure** General Assembly; Managment Board. **Languages** English. **Finance** Sources: members' dues. **Activities** Sporting activities.
Members Individuals in 24 countries:
Argentina, Australia, Austria, Belgium, Brazil, Canada, Chile, Czechia, Finland, France, Germany, Italy, Kenya, Latvia, Mexico, Netherlands, Norway, Poland, Qatar, Russia, Slovenia, Spain, Switzerland, USA.
NGO Relations Member of (1): *European Elite Athletes Association (EU Athletes, #06977)*.
[2020/AA1283/v/**D**]

♦ International Bear Association / see International Association for Bear Research and Management (#11722)
♦ International Bear Foundation / see Bears in Mind

♦ International Bee Research Association (IBRA) 12330
Association internationale de recherche apicole
Registered Office 1 Agincourt Street, Monmouth, NP25 3DZ, UK. E-mail: mail@ibra.org.uk.
URL: https://www.ibra.org.uk/
History 1949. Former names and other names: *Bee Research Association (BRA)* – former (1949 to 1976). Registration: Charity Commission, No/ID: 209222, England and Wales. **Aims** Promote the value of bees by providing information on bee science and beekeeping worldwide. **Structure** General Assembly (annual); Council. **Languages** English. **Staff** 1.00 FTE, voluntary. **Finance** Sources: donations; grants; members' dues; sale of publications. **Activities** Events/meetings; guidance/assistance/consulting; research/documentation. **Events** *International conference on recent trends in apicultural science / European Bee Conference* Mikkeli (Finland) 2007, *Quadrennial international conference* Ribeirão Preto (Brazil) 2004, *European bee conference* Cardiff (UK) 2002, *Quadrennial international conference / Quadrennial Conference on Tropical Apiculture* Chiang Mai (Thailand) 2000, *Quadrennial international conference / Quadrennial Conference on Tropical Apiculture* San José (Costa Rica) 1996. **Publications** *Journal of Apicultural Research* (5 a year); *Bee World* (4 a year) – journal. *Form and Function in the Honey Bee* by Lesley Goodman. Textbooks; other books, pamphlets; directories; educational aids; bibliographies and multilingual dictionaries of major beekeeping terms; catalogues; technical works; reprints..
Members Associations; individual members; subscribers. Members in 132 countries and territories:
Afghanistan, Algeria, Angola, Argentina, Australia, Austria, Azores, Bahamas, Bangladesh, Barbados, Belgium, Belize, Bolivia, Bosnia-Herzegovina, Botswana, Brazil, Brunei Darussalam, Bulgaria, Burkina Faso, Burundi, Canada, Chile, China, Colombia, Congo Brazzaville, Congo DR, Costa Rica, Côte d'Ivoire, Croatia, Cuba, Cyprus, Czechia, Denmark, Dominican Rep, Ecuador, Egypt, Eswatini, Ethiopia, Fiji, Finland, France, Gambia, Germany, Ghana, Greece, Guatemala, Guyana, Honduras, Hong Kong, Hungary, India, Indonesia, Iran Islamic Rep, Iraq, Ireland, Israel, Italy, Jamaica, Japan, Kenya, Kiribati, Korea Rep, Lebanon, Lesotho, Liberia, Libya, Liechtenstein, Luxembourg, Malawi, Malaysia, Malta, Martinique, Mauritania, Mauritius, Mexico, Montserrat, Morocco, Mozambique, Myanmar, Nepal, Netherlands, New Caledonia, New Zealand, Nigeria, Niue, Norway, Oman, Pakistan, Papua New Guinea, Paraguay, Peru, Philippines, Poland, Portugal, Puerto Rico, Romania, Russia, Samoa, Sao Tomé-Principe, Saudi Arabia, Senegal, Serbia, Seychelles, Sierra Leone, Slovakia, Slovenia, South Africa, Spain, Sri Lanka, St Lucia, St Vincent-Grenadines, Sudan, Suriname, Sweden, Switzerland, Taiwan, Tanzania UR, Thailand, Tonga, Trinidad-Tobago, Tunisia, Türkiye, Tuvalu, Uganda, UK, Ukraine, Uruguay, USA, Vanuatu, Venezuela, Zambia, Zimbabwe.
IGO Relations Close cooperation and joint projects with: FAO. **NGO Relations** Scientific member of: *International Union of Biological Sciences (IUBS, #15760)*. [2022.10.11/XB0188/**B**]

♦ International Behavioral Ecology Association / see International Society for Behavioral Ecology (#14954)

♦ International Behavioral Neuroscience Society (IBNS) 12331
Exec Dir IBNS Central Office, 1123 Comanche Path, Bandera TX 78003, USA. T. +18307969393. Fax +18307969394. E-mail: ibns@ibnsconnect.org.
URL: http://www.ibnsconnect.org/
History 1992. **Aims** Encourage research and education in the field of behavioural neuroscience. **Structure** Council; Committees. **Activities** Awards/prizes/competitions; events/meetings. **Events** *Annual Meeting* Glasgow (UK) 2022, *Annual Meeting* Puerto Vallarta (Mexico) 2021, *Online Poster Sessions* Bandera, TX (USA) 2020, *Annual Meeting* Glasgow (UK) 2020, *Annual Meeting* Cairns, QLD (Australia) 2019. **Publications** *IBNS News*. **Members** Scientists, clinicians, teachers and others (575) in 33 countries. Membership countries not specified. **NGO Relations** Member of: *AAALAC International*; *International Brain Research Organization (IBRO, #12392)*. [2020.08.18/XG6288/**C**]

♦ International Behavioural Insights Conference Behavioural Exchange (meeting series)

♦ International Behavioural and Neural Genetics Society (IBANGS) .. 12332
Contact 321 Main Street, PO Box 352, Wakefield MA 01880, USA. E-mail: administrator@ibangs.org.
URL: http://www.ibangs.org/
History Founded 1996, as *European Behavioural and Neural Genetics Society (EBANGS)*. Also referred to as *IBANGS Society*. **Aims** Promote research and learning in the field of behavioural and neural genetics. **Structure** Executive Committee; (5). **Languages** English. **Staff** 1.00 FTE, voluntary. **Finance** Members' dues. **Events** *Annual Meeting* Memphis, TN (USA) 2022, *Annual Meeting* Edinburgh (UK) 2019, *Annual Meeting* Rochester, NY (USA) 2018, *Annual Meeting* Madrid (Spain) 2017, *Annual Meeting* Bar Harbor, ME (USA) 2016. **Publications** *Genes, Brain and Behavior* (8 a year) – journal. **Information Services** *BANGNet* – listserv.
Members Individuals in 12 countries:
Australia, Belgium, Brazil, Canada, France, Germany, Italy, Netherlands, Russia, Switzerland, UK, USA.
NGO Relations Founding member of: *Federation of European Neuroscience Societies (FENS, #09522)*.
[2022/XD7239/v/**D**]

♦ International Behavioural Trials Network (IBTN) 12333
Co-lead address not obtained.
Co-lead address not obtained.
URL: https://www.ibtnetwork.org/
History 2014. **Aims** Facilitate the global improvement of the quality of behavioural trials; provide networks and capacity to undertake more and higher quality trials; develop a repository for existing recommendations, tools, and methodology papers on behavioural trials and intervention development. **Structure** Executive Committee. **Activities** Awards/prizes/competitions; events/meetings; research/documentation; training/education. **Events** *Conference* Montréal, QC (Canada) 2022, *Conference* 2020, *International Behavioural Trials Network Meeting* Montréal, QC (Canada) 2018, *Conference* Montréal, QC (Canada) 2016. **Publications** *IBTN Newsletter*. **Members** Members (over 800) in over 50 countries. Membership countries not specified.
[2022/AA2603/**F**]

♦ International Belt Wrestling Association 12334
Pres st 54a Beibitshilik, d 54a, Nur-Sultan, Kazakhstan.
Gen Sec 8 Maly Tatarsky Pereulok street, Moscow MOSKVA, Russia.
URL: https://ibwa-w.com/
Aims Serve as a platform for cultural exchange and sports among belt wrestling sports associations. **Structure** Executive Board, including President, Vice-Presidents and General Secretary. **Activities** Sporting activities.
Members National federations in 42 countries and territories:
Afghanistan, Armenia, Austria, Azerbaijan, Belarus, Bulgaria, Canada, Cuba, Cyprus, Estonia, Georgia, Germany, Hong Kong, Hungary, Iran Islamic Rep, Ireland, Israel, Italy, Japan, Kazakhstan, Korea Rep, Kuwait, Kyrgyzstan, Latvia, Lithuania, Malaysia, Mauritius, Moldova, Netherlands, Pakistan, Poland, Russia, Slovakia, Slovenia, Sri Lanka, Tajikistan, Togo, Turkmenistan, Ukraine, United Arab Emirates, USA, Uzbekistan.
Continental federations (5):
African Confederation of Traditional Wrestling Sports (AFCTWS, #00263); *Asian Jujitsu Belt Wrestling Federation (AJJBWF, #01523)*; *European Belt Wrestling Confederation*; *Oceanian Belt Wrestling Confederation*; *Panamerican Belt Wrestling Confederation*.
NGO Relations Member of (1): *International Association of Traditional Wrestling Sports (IATWS, no recent information)*. [2020/XM2362/y/**D**]

♦ International Benefits Network (unconfirmed)
♦ International Bentham Society / see International Society for Utilitarian Studies
♦ International B.E.S.T. Congress – International Bariatric Endoscopic Surgical Trends Congress (meeting series)

♦ International BFM Study Group (I-BFM-SG) 12335
Chairman Dept Paedriatrics, Univ of Milano-Bicocca, Hosp S Gerardo, Via Pergolesi 33, 20900 Monza MB, Italy. T. +39392336816. E-mail: cmanganini@fondazionembbm.it.
URL: https://bfminternational.wordpress.com/
History 1987. BFM stands for: Berlin-Frankfurt-Münster. **Aims** Improve lives of children and adolescents with *leukaemia* and *lymphoma*; better understand and translate research findings into better cures; foster information exchange among dedicated research groups; make clinical research the key to better and safer treatments. **Structure** Executive Board; SG Committees; Associated Working Groups. **Events** *Annual Meeting* Helsinki (Finland) 2018, *Annual Meeting* Jerusalem (Israel) 2017, *Annual Meeting* Athens (Greece) 2016, *Annual Meeting* Budapest (Hungary) 2015, *Annual Meeting* Prague (Czech Rep) 2014.
Members Oncology groups and societies in 30 countries and territories:
Argentina, Austria, Belgium, Chile, Croatia, Czechia, Denmark, Finland, France, Germany, Greece, Hong Kong, Hungary, Iceland, Israel, Italy, Japan, Netherlands, Norway, Poland, Portugal, Serbia, Slovakia, Slovenia, Spain, Sweden, Türkiye, UK, Ukraine, Uruguay.
Included in the above, 2 organizations listed in this Yearbook:
European Organisation for Research and Treatment of Cancer (EORTC, #08101); *Nordic Society for Pediatric Hematology and Oncology (NOPHO, #17424)*.
NGO Relations Member of: *Industry Technology Facilitator (ITF)*. [2022/XM3208/y/**E**]

♦ International Biathlon Union (IBU) 12336
Internationale Biathlon Union
SG Sonystr 20, Anif b Salzburg, 5081 Salzburg, Austria. T. +4366285505013. E-mail: biathlon@ibu.at.
URL: https://www.biathlonworld.com/
History 2 Jul 1993, Heathrow (UK). Amendments to Constitution adopted by Congress: 1994; 1996; 1998; 2000; 2004; 2006; 2008; 2010; 2012; 2014. United with *World Penthathlon (UIPM, #21720)* as umbrella organization until 26 Sep 1998, when decision of 26 Jun 1998, to exist autonomously came into effect. The sport had been represented from 1960 by UIPM, which from 1960 to 1998 was referred to as *'International Modern Pentathlon and Biathlon Union – Union internationale de pentathlon moderne et biathlon (UIPMB)'*. Registered in accordance with Austrian law, 26 Jan 2000. **Aims** Develop the sport of biathlon and promote it worldwide. **Structure** Congress (every 2 years); Executive Board; Committees (6). **Languages** English. **Staff** 12.00 FTE, paid. **Activities** Events/meetings; sporting activities. **Events** *Biennial Congress* Salzburg (Austria) 2022, *Biennial Congress* Salzburg (Austria) 2020, *Extraordinary Congress* Munich (Germany) 2019, *Biennial Congress* Porec (Croatia) 2018, *Meeting* Salzburg (Austria) 2018. **Publications** *Biathlonworld* – magazine; *IBU Guide*; *IBU Rules*. *50 Years of Biathlon 1958-2008*.
Members Full: national federations (54) in 54 countries and territories:
Argentina, Armenia, Australia, Austria, Belarus, Belgium, Bosnia-Herzegovina, Brazil, Bulgaria, Canada, Chile, China, Croatia, Cyprus, Czechia, Denmark, Estonia, Finland, France, Georgia, Germany, Greece, Greenland, Hungary, India, Ireland, Italy, Japan, Kazakhstan, Korea Rep, Kyrgyzstan, Latvia, Liechtenstein, Lithuania, Moldova, Mongolia, Netherlands, New Zealand, North Macedonia, Norway, Poland, Romania, Serbia, Slovakia, Slovenia, Spain, Sweden, Switzerland, Taiwan, Türkiye, UK, Ukraine, USA, Uzbekistan.
Provisional (2) in 2 countries:
Dominican Rep, Russia.
IGO Relations Cooperates with: *UNESCO (#20322)*. **NGO Relations** Member of (4): *Association of the International Olympic Winter Sports Federations (AIOWF, #02757)*; *International Committee for Fair Play (#12769)*; *International Masters Games Association (IMGA, #14117)*; *Olympic Movement (#17719)*. Recognized by: *International Olympic Committee (IOC, #14408)*. [2022/XB0001/**B**]

♦ International Bible Reading Association (IBRA) 12337
Association internationale pour la lecture de la Bible – Asociación Internacional de Lectores de la Biblia
Headquarters Imperial Court, Sovereign Road, Birmingham, B30 3FH, UK. T. +441214583313. Fax +441212851816. E-mail: ibra@christianeducation.org.uk.
URL: http://www.ibraglobal.org/
History 1882, London (UK). Founded following evangelistic work with children from 1867, and foundation of a national organization in 1879, UK. **Aims** Promote daily Bible reading, give a greater understanding of the contents of the Bible and explore it's relevance to daily life. **Languages** English, Ewe, Fante, French, Ga, Hindi, Kongo, Lingala, Portuguese, Samoan, Spanish, Telugu, Tokelau, Tokelau, Twi, Yoruba. **Finance** Sources:

donations; gifts, legacies. **Activities** Financial and/or material support; knowledge management/information dissemination. **Publications** *Fresh from the Word: the Bible for a Change*. Bible notes; daily bible readings; annual bible readings with notes.
Members Offices in 12 countries and territories:
Cameroon, Congo DR, Fiji, Ghana, India, Kiribati, New Zealand, Nigeria, Samoa, Samoa USA, South Africa, UK.
[2020.04.29/XC1399/**F**]

♦ International Bible Society / see Biblica

♦ International Bible Students Association (IBSA) 12338

Contact IBSA House, The Ridgeway, London, NW7 1RN, UK. T. +442089062211.
URL: http://www.internationalbiblestudents.com/index.html

History Founded 1914, London (UK). A corporation associated with *Jehovah's Witnesses (#16096)*, the latter legally represented by *Watch Tower Bible and Tract Society of Pennsylvania*. Registered in accordance with UK law, 30 Jun 1914. **Aims** Act as legal agency for Jehovah's Witnesses, *Christian* Bible students who preach the Gospel of God's kingdom; print and distribute Bibles and Bible literature in various languages; establish and maintain free Bible classes and schools. **Languages** English. **Staff** Voluntary. **Finance** Voluntary contributions. **Activities** Events/meetings; networking/liaising; training/education. **Events** *International conference on indigenous place names* Kautokeino (Norway) 2010, *Convention* Dalfsen (Netherlands) 1990, *International convention* Dalfsen (Netherlands) 1988. **Publications** *Insight on the Scriptures*; *Jehovah's Witnesses: Proclaimers of God's Kingdom*; *New World Translation of the Holy Scriptures*; *Questions Young People Ask – Answers That Work*; *The Greatest Man Who Ever Lived*; *The Origin of Life – Five Questions Worth Asking*; *The Secret of Family Happiness*; *What Does the Bible Really Teach?*. Bible literature in over 950 languages.
Members in 236 lands, including the following 204 countries and territories:
Albania, Andorra, Angola, Anguilla, Antigua, Argentina, Armenia, Aruba, Australia, Austria, Azerbaijan, Azores, Bahamas, Bangladesh, Barbados, Belarus, Belgium, Belize, Benin, Bermuda, Bolivia, Bonaire Is, Bosnia-Herzegovina, Botswana, Brazil, Bulgaria, Burkina Faso, Burundi, Cambodia, Cameroon, Canada, Cape Verde, Cayman Is, Central African Rep, Chad, Chile, Chuuk, Colombia, Congo Brazzaville, Congo DR, Cook Is, Costa Rica, Côte d'Ivoire, Croatia, Cuba, Curaçao, Cyprus, Czechia, Denmark, Dominica, Dominican Rep, Ecuador, El Salvador, Equatorial Guinea, Estonia, Eswatini, Ethiopia, Faeroe Is, Falklands/Malvinas, Fiji, Finland, France, Gabon, Gambia, Georgia, Germany, Ghana, Gibraltar, Greece, Greenland, Grenada, Guadeloupe, Guam, Guatemala, Guiana Fr, Guinea, Guinea-Bissau, Guyana, Haiti, Honduras, Hong Kong, Hungary, Iceland, India, Indonesia, Ireland, Israel, Italy, Jamaica, Japan, Kazakhstan, Kenya, Kiribati, Korea Rep, Kosovo, Kosrae, Kyrgyzstan, Latvia, Lebanon, Lesotho, Liberia, Liechtenstein, Lithuania, Luxembourg, Macau, Madagascar, Madeira, Malawi, Malaysia, Mali, Malta, Marshall Is, Martinique, Mauritius, Mayotte, Mexico, Moldova, Mongolia, Montenegro, Montserrat, Mozambique, Myanmar, Namibia, Nauru, Nepal, Netherlands, Nevis Is, New Caledonia, New Zealand, Nicaragua, Niger, Nigeria, Niue, Norfolk Is, North Macedonia, Northern Mariana Is (Rota; Saipan; Tinian), Norway, Pakistan, Palau, Palestine, Panama, Papua New Guinea, Paraguay, Peru, Philippines, Pohnpei, Poland, Portugal, Puerto Rico, Réunion, Rodriguez Is, Romania, Russia, Rwanda, Saba, Samoa, Samoa USA, San Marino, Sao Tomé-Principe, Senegal, Serbia, Seychelles, Sierra Leone, Slovakia, Slovenia, Solomon Is, South Africa, Spain, Sri Lanka, St Eustatius, St Helena, St Kitts Is, St Lucia, St Maarten, St Pierre-Miquelon, St Vincent-Grenadines, Sudan, Suriname, Sweden, Switzerland, Tahiti Is, Taiwan, Tanzania UR, Thailand, Timor-Leste, Togo, Tonga, Trinidad-Tobago, Türkiye, Turks-Caicos, Tuvalu, Uganda, UK, Ukraine, Uruguay, USA, Vanuatu, Venezuela, Virgin Is UK, Virgin Is USA, Wallis-Futuna, Yap, Zambia, Zimbabwe.
[2015.11.09/XD4605/v/**E**]

♦ International Bicycle Fund (internationally oriented national body)

♦ International Biennial Association (IBA) 12339

Office PO Box 20123, Bait Obaid Al Shamsi, Al Shuwaihean, Sharjah, United Arab Emirates. T. +97165554012. E-mail: info@biennialassociation.org.
URL: http://www.biennialassociation.org/

History 2014, Gwangju (Korea Rep). Founded as an initiative taken at World Biennial Forum, Oct 2012, Seoul (Korea Rep); moved to Sharjah (United Arab Emirates) 2018. **Aims** Expand and share activities of curatorial, artistic creation and knowledge through cooperation and exchange among biennials around the world; create a horizontal network within the broader biennial world to develop further cultural and artistic production; create a space for communication, cooperation and information exchange by providing strategies, methodologies and vision. **Structure** General Assembly; Board; Executive; Office. **Languages** English. **Staff** 4.00 FTE, paid. **Finance** Sources: contributions; donations; government support; members' dues. **Activities** Awareness raising; capacity building; events/meetings; knowledge management/information dissemination; networking/liaising; projects/programmes; publishing activities; research and development; research/documentation; standards/guidelines. Active in: United Arab Emirates. **Events** *General Assembly* Pristina (Kosovo) 2022, *General Assembly* 2021, *General Assembly* 2020, *General Assembly* Santiago (Chile) 2019, *General Assembly* Kochi (India) 2018. **Publications** *IBA Newsletter* (12 a year); *PASS: Journal of the International Biennial Association* in English.
Members Organizations in 27 countries:
Argentina, Australia, Bangladesh, Belgium, Brazil, Chile, France, Germany, Greece, Haiti, India, Ireland, Italy, Japan, Korea Rep, Lithuania, Morocco, Netherlands, Norway, Poland, Romania, Senegal, Slovenia, Sweden, UK, United Arab Emirates, USA.
Individuals in 34 countries:
Bangladesh, Bermuda, Bolivia, Brazil, Canada, China, Colombia, Congo DR, Cuba, Czechia, Denmark, France, Germany, Indonesia, Italy, Japan, Korea Rep, Lebanon, Mali, Netherlands, Nigeria, Pakistan, Romania, Russia, Senegal, Singapore, Slovenia, Spain, Sri Lanka, Switzerland, Türkiye, UK, United Arab Emirates, USA.
[2023.03.01/XM6166/**C**]

♦ International Big History Association (unconfirmed)
♦ International Biliary Association / see International Hepato-Pancreato-Biliary Association (#13790)
♦ International Billiards Federation (inactive)

♦ International Billiards and Snooker Federation (IBSF) 12340

Gen Sec PO BOX 8996, Rawdat Al-Khayl Street, Mansoura, Doha, Qatar. T. +97444356099.
URL: http://www.ibsf.info/

History 1971. Former names and other names: *World Billiards and Snooker Council* – former. **Aims** Coordinate, promote and develop the sports of billiards and snooker on a *non-professional* level worldwide. **Structure** General Meeting (annual); Board of Directors. Committees (6): Finance; Constitution and International Affairs; Championship; Referee and Rules; Promotion and Sponsorship; Billiards. Regional federations: *African Billiards and Snooker Confederation (ABSC, #00221)*; *Asian Confederation of Billiards Sports (ACBS, #01396)*; *Confederación Panamericana de Billar (CPB, #04469)*; *European Billiards and Snooker Association (EBSA, #06330)*; *Asia Pacific Snooker & Billiards Federation (APSBF)*. **Languages** English. **Staff** None. **Finance** Sources: members' dues; sponsorship. Annual budget: 80,000 GBP. **Activities** As the world governing body for non-professional snooker and billiards, determines championship conditions, formats, dates and venues for the following: IBSF World Snooker Championships; IBSF Under-21 World Snooker Championships; IBSF World Ladies Snooker Championships; IBSF World Billiard Championships. **Events** *Meeting* Bulgaria 2012, *Meeting* Syrian AR 2010, *Meeting* Austria 2008, *Meeting* Jordan 2006, *Annual meeting / Meeting* Netherlands 2004.
Members Full in 91 countries and territories:
Afghanistan, Australia, Austria, Bahrain, Bangladesh, Belarus, Belgium, Brazil, Brunei Darussalam, Bulgaria, Cambodia, Canada, China, Croatia, Cyprus, Czechia, Denmark, Egypt, England, Estonia, Fiji, Finland, France, Germany, Gibraltar, Greece, Guatemala, Guernsey, Hong Kong, Hungary, Iceland, India, Indonesia, Iran Islamic Rep, Iraq, Ireland, Isle of Man, Israel, Italy, Japan, Jersey, Jordan, Kazakhstan, Korea Rep, Kuwait, Latvia, Lebanon, Libya, Lithuania, Macau, Malaysia, Malta, Mauritius, Moldova, Morocco, Myanmar, Nepal, Netherlands, New Zealand, Northern Ireland, Norway, Oman, Pakistan, Papua New Guinea, Philippines, Poland, Qatar, Romania, Russia, Saudi Arabia, Scotland, Singapore, South Africa, Spain, Sri Lanka, Sudan, Sweden, Switzerland, Syrian AR, Taiwan, Tanzania UR, Thailand, Türkiye, Ukraine, United Arab Emirates, USA, Venezuela, Vietnam, Wales, Yemen, Zimbabwe.
Regional Associations (5):
African Billiards and Snooker Confederation (ABSC, #00221); *Asian Confederation of Billiards Sports (ACBS, #01396)*; *Asia Pacific Snooker & Billiards Federation (APSBF)*; *Confederación Panamericana de Billar (CPB, #04469)*; *European Billiards and Snooker Association (EBSA, #06330)*.
NGO Relations Is the snooker division of: *World Confederation of Billiards Sports (WCBS, #21291)*.
[2022/XD5147/y/**B**]

♦ International Bioacoustics Council / see International Bioacoustics Society (#12341)

♦ International Bioacoustics Society (IBAC) 12341

Société Internationale de Bioacoustique
Sec British Library Sound Archive, 96 Euston Road, London, NW1 2DB, UK.
Chair Univ of Lyon/Saint-Etienne, 23 rue Michelon, 42023 Saint-Étienne CEDEX 2, France.
URL: http://www.ibac.info/

History 1969, Aarhus (Denmark). Former names and other names: *International Bioacoustics Council (IBAC)* – former (1969); *IBAC Society* – alias. Registration: France, Saint-Etienne. **Aims** Bring together biologists, engineers, sound archivists, computer scientists and other interested parties to foster discussion, share knowledge and exchange ideas surrounding the subject of *vocal communication* in *animals*. **Structure** Executive Committee. **Languages** English. **Staff** Voluntary. **Finance** No budget. **Activities** Knowledge management/information dissemination; events/meetings. **Events** *International Congress* Sapporo (Japan) 2022, *International Congress* Brighton (UK) 2019, *International Congress* Haridwar (India) 2017, *International Congress* Murnau am Staffelsee (Germany) 2015, *International Congress* Pirenópolis (Brazil) 2013. **Publications** *Bioacoustics* – journal.
[2021/XD5634/**D**]

♦ International Biochar Initiative (IBI) 12342

Exec Admin 1211 Connecticut Ave NW, Suite 650, Washington DC 20036, USA. T. +12024570868 ext 309. E-mail: info@biochar-international.org.
URL: http://www.biochar-international.org/

History Founded Jul 2006, Philadelphia PA (USA), as *International Agrichar Initiative (IAI)*, during side meeting held at World Soil Science Congress of *International Union of Soil Sciences (IUSS, #15817)*. Present name adopted 2007. **Aims** Provide a platform for the international exchange of information and activities in support of biochar *charcoal* research, development, demonstration and commercialization. **Structure** Steering Committee; Advisory Committee. **Activities** Networking/liaising; research/documentation; training/education; knowledge management/information dissemination; events/meetings. **Events** *International Conference on Technical and Engineering Challenges of Addressing Sustainable Development* Seoul (Korea Rep) 2019, *Asia Pacific Conference* Chuncheon (Korea Rep) 2016, *Forebiom Workshop* Vienna (Austria) 2013, *International Conference* Beijing (China) 2012, *Asia Pacific Conference* Kyoto (Japan) 2011. **Publications** *IBI Newsletter* (12 a year). White papers. **Members** Individuals (120). Membership countries not specified. **IGO Relations** Accredited to the Conference of the Parties of: *Secretariat of the United Nations Convention to Combat Desertification (Secretariat of the UNCCD, #19208)*.
[2019.12.11/XM3332/**F**]

♦ International Biocontrol Manufacturers Association (IBMA) 12343

Advocacy and Communication Manager Rue de Trèves 61, 1040 Brussels, Belgium. T. +32471873724. E-mail: administration@ibma-global.org.
Exec Dir address not obtained.
URL: http://www.ibma-global.org/

History 1995. Registration: EU Transparency Register, No/ID: 06818218065-85, Start date: 1 Mar 2012; Belgium. **Aims** Promote biocontrol technologies and bring to the market via proportionate regulation these innovative and effective technologies for sustainable agriculture, allowing the farmers to grow healthy, productive and profitable crops. **Structure** General Assembly; Board; Executive Committee; Council of National Associations. **Languages** English. **Staff** 3.00 FTE, paid. **Finance** Sources: members' dues. **Activities** Events/meetings; knowledge management/information dissemination; networking/liaising; research and development. **Events** *ABIM: Annual Biocontrol Industry Meeting* Basel (Switzerland) 2023, *ABIM: Annual Biocontrol Industry Meeting* Basel (Switzerland) 2022, *ABIM : Annual Biocontrol Industry Meeting* Basel (Switzerland) 2021, *ABIM : Annual Biocontrol Industry Meeting* Basel (Switzerland) 2020, *ABIM : Annual Biocontrol Industry Meeting* Basel (Switzerland) 2019. **Publications** *Members Directory*. **Members** Active (183); Associate (66). Members in 42 countries. Membership countries not specified.
[2022.05.11/XM1430/**D**]

♦ International Biodegradable Products Manufacturers Association (inactive)

♦ The International Biodeterioration and Biodegradation Society (IBBS) 12344

Hon Sec 161 Gloucester Place, Flat 8, London, NW1 6DX, UK. T. +447505681654. E-mail: secretary@ibbsonline.org.
Main Website: https://www.ibbsonline.org

History 1969, Southampton (UK). Former names and other names: *The Biodeterioration Society* – former (1969); *International Biodeterioration Society* – former. Registration: Charity Commission, England and Wales. **Aims** Promote the science of biodeterioration and biodegradation. **Structure** Annual General Meeting; Council. **Languages** English. **Staff** None. **Finance** Sources: meeting proceeds; members' dues. **Activities** Events/meetings; financial and/or material support; guidance/assistance/consulting; publishing activities. **Events** *International Biodeterioration and Biodegradation Symposium* 2021, *International Biodeterioration and Biodegradation Symposium* Bozeman, MT (USA) 2020, *International Biodeterioration and Biodegradation Symposium* Manchester (UK) 2017, *Conference on Biodeterioration and Protection of Culture Heritage* Lódz (Poland) 2016, *Latin American Biodeterioration Symposium* Rio de Janeiro (Brazil) 2016. **Publications** *IBBS Newsletter* (2-3 a year); *International Biodeterioration and Biodegradation* (8 a year) – journal. *Atlas of Biodeterioration*.
Members Full in 39 countries and territories:
Argentina, Australia, Austria, Belgium, China, Czechia, Denmark, Estonia, France, Germany, Greece, Hong Kong, Hungary, India, Iran Islamic Rep, Israel, Italy, Japan, Malaysia, Mexico, Netherlands, New Zealand, Nigeria, Norway, Pakistan, Poland, Portugal, Qatar, Romania, Russia, Saudi Arabia, South Africa, Spain, Sweden, Switzerland, Türkiye, UK, United Arab Emirates, USA.
[2022.06.15/XD0528/**C**]

♦ International Biodeterioration Research Group (IBRG) 12345

Contact Pale Lane, Hartley Wintney, RG27 8DH, UK.
URL: http://www.ibrg.org/

History 1968. Statutes revised 1985. **Aims** Facilitate cooperation among members; harmonize cooperative research programmes agreed upon by members and facilitate the dissemination and application of research results; promote the exchange of technical information. **Structure** Plenary Meeting (annual). Bureau, consisting of President of IBRG (Bureau Chairman), Vice-President, General Secretary (Bureau Secretary), Treasurer, Chairman of each Project Group, Technical Secretary of each Project Group, a representative from the Council of Biodeterioration Society and National Representatives. **Languages** English. **Finance** Members' dues. **Activities** Project Groups (7): Paints; Metal-working Fluid; Plastics; Taxonomy Ecology; Constructional Materials; Microbial Corrosion; Polymer Emulsions. **Events** *Spring Meeting* Athens (Greece) 2019, *Autumn meeting* Ghent (Belgium) 2007, *Spring meeting* Kendal (UK) 2007, *Joint meeting* Manchester (UK) 2003, *Annual Plenary Meeting* Belgium 1996. **Publications** *International Biodeterioration and Biodegradation* (8 a year).
Members Individuals in 13 countries:
Belgium, Denmark, France, Germany, Kuwait, Netherlands, New Zealand, Norway, Spain, Sweden, Switzerland, UK, USA.
[2019/XE5896/v/**E**]

♦ International Biodeterioration Society / see The International Biodeterioration and Biodegradation Society (#12344)

♦ International BioDynamic Association (IBDA) 12346

Internationaler Verein für Biologisch-Dynamische Landwirtschaft (IBDA)
Sec Goetheanum Section for Agriculture, Hügelweg 59, 4143 Dornach SO, Switzerland. T. +41617064212. E-mail: agriculture@goetheanum.ch.
Conference Organisation address not obtained.
URL: http://www.ibda.ch/

Structure Board. **Publications** Annual Report.
Members Organizations in 21 countries:
Argentina, Brazil, Chile, Denmark, France, Germany, Greece, India, Italy, Korea Rep, Luxembourg, Netherlands, Norway, Serbia, Slovenia, South Africa, Spain, Sweden, Switzerland, UK, USA.
Included in the above, 1 organization listed in this Yearbook:
NGO Relations *Demeter International (#05029)*. Member of: *Alliance ELIANT (#00672)*.
[2022/XM3380/**D**]

♦ International Bioenergy Platform (IBEP) 12347

Plateforme internationale sur la bioénergie – Plataforma Internacional de Bioenergia
Address not obtained.

History 9 May 2006, New York NY (USA), by *FAO (#09260)*. **Aims** Coordinate bioenergy information and support throughout the global community.
[2008/XM2111/**F**]

♦ International Bioenergy Professionals Association / see Bioenergy Institute

♦ International Bioethics Committee of UNESCO (IBC) 12348

Comité international de bioéthique de l'UNESCO (CIB)

Main Office UNESCO, 7 place Fontenoy, 75732 Paris 07 SP, France. T. +33145684994. Fax +33145685552. E-mail: ibc@unesco.org.
URL: https://en.unesco.org/themes/ethics-science-and-technology/ibc

History 1993. Founded by *UNESCO (#20322)*. Statutes of permanent committee adopted at 154th Session of UNESCO Executive Board, 7 May 1998. Former names and other names: *UNESCO International Committee of Bioethics* – alias. **Aims** Promote reflection on *ethical* and *legal* issues raised by research in *life sciences* and their applications; encourage exchange of ideas and information, particularly through education; encourage action to heighten awareness among specialized groups, public and private decision-makers and the general public; in contribute to dissemination and promotion of principles set out in the normative instruments adopted by UNESCO (Universal Declaration on the Human Genome and Human Rights, 1997; International Declaration on Human Genetic Data, 2003; Universal Declaration on Bioethics and Human Rights, 2005). **Structure** Annual session, convened by UNESCO Director-General; Committee; Working Groups. An *Intergovernmental Bioethics Committee (IGBC) – Comité intergouvernemental de bioéthique (CIGB)* is also set up under 1998 Statutes, comprising 36 representatives of UNESCO Member States, elected by UNESCO General Conference. Secretariat ensured by Section for Bioethics and Ethics of Science, Division of Ethics, Youth and Sport of UNESCO. **Languages** Arabic, Chinese, English, French, Russian, Spanish. **Staff** 5.00 FTE, paid. **Finance** Part of a UNESCO programme. Budget (biannual): US$ 320,000. **Activities** Standards/guidelines; events/meetings. Management of treaties and agreements: *International Declaration on Human Genetic Data (2003)*; *Universal Declaration on Bioethics and Human Rights (2005)*; *Universal Declaration on the Human Genome and Human Rights (1997)*. **Events** *Session* Paris (France) 2021, *Session* Paris (France) 2019, *Session* Paris (France) 2018, *Session* Paris (France) 2014, *Session / Annual Session* Seoul (Korea Rep) 2013. **Publications** *International Declaration on Human Genetic Data* in Arabic, Chinese, English, French, Hebrew, Portuguese, Russian; *Universal Declaration of the Human Genome and Human Rights* in Arabic, Chinese, English, French, Russian, Spanish; *Universal Declaration on Bioethics and Human Rights* in Arabic, Chinese, English, French, Russian, Spanish; *Women's Rights and Bioethics* in English, French. Proceedings of annual sessions, in French, English; reports.

Members Individuals in their personal capacity from 36 countries:
Austria, Brazil, Canada, Cuba, Czechia, Egypt, Finland, France, Gabon, Georgia, Germany, Ghana, India, Iran Islamic Rep, Israel, Italy, Jamaica, Japan, Kenya, Korea Rep, Kuwait, Malaysia, Mexico, Netherlands, Oman, Panama, Poland, Russia, Senegal, Singapore, Spain, Switzerland, Togo, Tunisia, Uruguay, USA. [2021/XK0459/v/**E**]

♦ International Biogeography Society (IBS) 12349

Contact PO Box 476, Charleston SC 29402, USA. E-mail: crahbek@bio.ku.dk – biogeography.ibs@gmail.com.
URL: http://biogeography.org/

History 2000. **Aims** Foster communication and collaboration between biogeographers in disparate academic fields; increase both awareness and interests of the scientific community and the lay public in the contributions of biogeographers; promote training and education of biogeographers so that they may develop sound strategies for studying and conserving the world's biota. **Structure** Elected officers: President; President Elect; 3 Vice-Presidents; Secretary; Treasurer; 2 Directors-at-large; Student-at-large. **Finance** Members' dues. Conference registration. **Events** *Biennial Conference* Vancouver, BC (Canada) 2022, *Early Career Biogeographers Conference* 2021, *Biennial Conference* Malaga (Spain) 2019, *Biennial Conference* Tucson, AZ (USA) 2017, *Biennial Conference* Bayreuth (Germany) 2015. **Publications** *Frontiers of Biogeography* – journal.

Members Individuals in 47 countries:
Argentina, Armenia, Australia, Austria, Azerbaijan, Belarus, Belgium, Brazil, Bulgaria, Chile, China, Costa Rica, Czechia, Denmark, Estonia, Finland, France, Georgia, Germany, Greece, Hungary, Iceland, India, Ireland, Israel, Italy, Luxembourg, Mexico, Netherlands, New Zealand, Norway, Panama, Philippines, Poland, Portugal, Russia, Slovakia, Slovenia, South Africa, Spain, Sri Lanka, Sweden, Switzerland, Thailand, UK, USA, Venezuela. [2019.04.24/XM0331/**D**]

♦ International Biographical Association (IBA) 12350

Association biographique internationale

Address not obtained.
URL: http://www.ibassociation.com/

History 1970, Dartmouth (UK), to commemorate sailing of the 'Mayflower' to the New World, 1620. **Aims** Bring people together in friendship and understanding following their being cited in a recognized biographical reference work. **Activities** Carries out biographical research. Maintains *International Biographical Centre (IBC)*. **Events** *International congress on arts and communications / Annual Congress* Cambridge (UK) 2001, *International congress on arts and communications / Annual Congress* Washington, DC (USA) 2000, *International congress on arts and communications / Annual Congress* Lisbon (Portugal) 1999, *International congress on arts and communications / International Congress* New Orleans, LA (USA) 1998, *Annual Congress* USA 1998. **Publications** *Biographical Directory*; *IBA Newsletter*.

Members Individuals in 115 countries and territories:
Albania, Andorra, Argentina, Armenia, Australia, Austria, Azerbaijan, Bahamas, Bahrain, Bangladesh, Barbados, Belarus, Belgium, Bosnia-Herzegovina, Botswana, Brazil, Bulgaria, Cambodia, Cameroon, Canada, Chile, China, Croatia, Cyprus, Czechia, Denmark, Egypt, Estonia, Fiji, Finland, France, Gambia, Georgia, Germany, Ghana, Greece, Hong Kong, Hungary, Iceland, India, Indonesia, Iran Islamic Rep, Ireland, Israel, Italy, Jamaica, Japan, Jordan, Kazakhstan, Kenya, Korea Rep, Kuwait, Latvia, Lebanon, Libya, Lithuania, Luxembourg, Malawi, Malaysia, Malta, Mauritius, Mexico, Monaco, Mongolia, Morocco, Mozambique, Myanmar, Namibia, Nepal, Netherlands, New Zealand, Niger, Nigeria, North Macedonia, Norway, Pakistan, Papua New Guinea, Peru, Philippines, Poland, Portugal, Romania, Russia, Saudi Arabia, Senegal, Serbia, Sierra Leone, Singapore, Slovakia, Slovenia, Solomon Is, South Africa, Spain, Sri Lanka, Sudan, Sweden, Switzerland, Taiwan, Tanzania UR, Thailand, Togo, Trinidad-Tobago, Tunisia, Türkiye, Uganda, UK, Ukraine, United Arab Emirates, Uruguay, USA, Vanuatu, Venezuela, Vietnam, Zambia, Zimbabwe. [2010/XE1217/v/**F**]

♦ International Biographical Centre (internationally oriented national body)
♦ International Biohydrometallurgy Symposium (meeting series)

♦ International Bioiron Society (IBIS) 12351

Contact Two Woodfield Lake, 1100 E Woodfield Rd, Ste 520, Schaumburg IL 60173, USA. T. +18475177225. Fax +18475177229. E-mail: info@bioiron.org.
URL: http://www.bioiron.org/

History 2003. Assumed activities of *International Association for the Study of Disorders of Iron Metabolism (inactive)*. **Aims** Advance knowledge about biological and medical roles of iron and the processes in which it participates, with particular reference to those processes of industrial and medical importance. **Structure** General Meeting (every 2 years). Board of Directors, including President, President Elect, Immediate Past President, Secretary, Treasurer and Director. **Events** *Meeting* Darwin, NT (Australia) 2023, *Meeting* Heidelberg (Germany) 2019, *Meeting* Los Angeles, CA (USA) 2017, *Biennial Meeting* China 2015, *Biennial Meeting* London (UK) 2013. [2021/XM3244/**D**]

♦ International Biology and Environment Research Institute (unconfirmed)

♦ International Biomass Torrefaction Council (IBTC) 12352

Contact Place du Champ de Mars 2, 1050 Brussels, Belgium. T. +3223184100. E-mail: info@bioenergyeurope.org.
URL: https://ibtc.bioenergyeurope.org/

History 2012. Founded by *Bioenergy Europe (#03247)*, as one of its networks. **Aims** Promote the use of torrefied biomass; assist the development of its industry, based on fair business conditions. **Structure** Secretariat. **Activities** Advocacy/lobbying/activism; events/meetings; knowledge management/information dissemination; networking/liaising. **Events** *Workshop* Rotterdam (Netherlands) 2016.

Members Companies (over 20). Full in 9 countries:
Austria, Belgium, Canada, Germany, Ireland, Netherlands, Sweden, UK, USA.
Developing members in 2 countries:
Portugal, Russia.
Associated members in 5 countries:
Austria, Belgium, Finland, Netherlands, Spain. [2022/AA1302/**E**]

♦ International Biometals Society (IBS) 12353

Sec Dept of Biology – MSC03 2020, Univ of New Mexico, Albuquerque NM 87131, USA. T. +15052772537. Fax +15052770304.
Contact LCBM/IRIG, CEA-Grenoble, Bât K, 17 avenue des Martyrs, 38054 Grenoble CEDEX 9, France.
URL: https://www.biometals-society.org/

History Jul 2010, Tucson, AZ (USA). Set up at 7th International Biometals Symposium. **Aims** Promote research in the field of *metal* interactions in *biology*; encourage interdisciplinary exchange of information on this subject. **Structure** General Meeting. Board of Directors, including President, Vice-President/President-Elect, Treasurer and Secretary. **Languages** English. **Staff** All voluntary. **Finance** Sources: members' dues. **Activities** Events/meetings. **Events** *International Biometals Symposium* Autrans (France) 2020, *International Biometals Symposium* Ottawa, ON (Canada) 2018, *International Biometals Symposium* Dresden (Germany) 2016, *Biennial Symposium* Durham, NC (USA) 2014, *Biennial Symposium* Brussels (Belgium) 2012. **Publications** *BioMetals* – journal; *IBS Newsletter*. [2020/XJ6532/**C**]

♦ International Biometric Society 12354

Société internationale de biométrie – Sociedad Internacional de Biometria – Internationale Biometrische Gesellschaft

Main Office 1120 20th St NW, Ste 750, Washington DC 20036-3441, USA. T. +12027129049. Fax +12022169646. E-mail: ibs@biometricsociety.org.
URL: https://www.biometricsociety.org/

History 6 Sep 1947, Woods Hole MA (USA). Constitutes biometric section of *International Union of Biological Sciences (IUBS, #15760)*. **Aims** Advance quantitative biological science through development of quantitative theories and application, development and dissemination of effective mathematical and *statistical* techniques. **Structure** Council, consisting of general officers and up to 36 members, one-half replaced at biennial elections. Executive Committee, comprising President, Vice-President, Secretary, Treasurer and Editorial Representative. **Languages** English, French, German. **Staff** 2.00 FTE, paid. **Finance** Sources: members' dues. Other sources: Journal subscriptions. **Activities** Regional meeting held regularly for reading of papers and discussions. **Events** *Biennial International Biometric Conference* Riga (Latvia) 2022, *Biennial International Biometric Conference* Seoul (Korea Rep) 2020, *Biennial International Biometric Conference* Barcelona (Spain) 2018, *Nordic-Baltic Biometric Conference* Copenhagen (Denmark) 2017, *Conference* Vienna (Austria) 2017. **Publications** *Biometric Bulletin* (4 a year); *Biometrics* (4 a year); *Biometrische Zeitschrift* (4 a year); *Biométrie-Praximétrie* (4 a year).

Members Sustaining institutions and corporations in 5 countries:
Belgium, Germany, Netherlands, Switzerland, USA.
Individuals (over 5,200) in 76 countries and territories:
Argentina, Australia, Austria, Bahamas, Bangladesh, Belgium, Botswana, Brazil, Bulgaria, Burkina Faso, Cameroon, Canada, Chile, China, Colombia, Costa Rica, Côte d'Ivoire, Croatia, Cyprus, Czechia, Denmark, Egypt, Estonia, Ethiopia, Finland, France, Germany, Ghana, Greece, Guatemala, Hong Kong, Hungary, Iceland, India, Indonesia, Ireland, Israel, Italy, Japan, Jordan, Kenya, Korea Rep, Kuwait, Latvia, Lithuania, Malaysia, Mexico, Namibia, Netherlands, New Zealand, Niger, Nigeria, Norway, Pakistan, Papua New Guinea, Portugal, Puerto Rico, Russia, Saudi Arabia, Singapore, South Africa, Spain, Sri Lanka, Sweden, Switzerland, Taiwan, Thailand, Trinidad-Tobago, Türkiye, Uganda, UK, United Arab Emirates, Uruguay, USA, Venezuela, Zimbabwe.

NGO Relations Member of: *International Statistical Institute (ISI, #15603)*. In liaison with technical committees of: *International Organization for Standardization (ISO, #14473)*. [2019/XD0192/**C**]

♦ International Bioprocessing Association – An International Forum on Industrial Bioprocesses / see International Forum on Industrial Bioprocesses (#13640)
♦ International Biosafety Working Group / see International Federation of Biosafety Associations (#13373)
♦ International Biotechnology Foundation – International Foundation For Biotechnology Research and Early Stimulation in the Culture of Health, Nutrition, Sport, Art, Science, Technology and Society (internationally oriented national body)

♦ International Biotherapy Society (IBS) 12355

Sec 10274 Alliance Rd, Cincinnati OH 45242, USA. T. +15138919991. Fax +15138919947.
Pres 442-17 Ssangyong IT Twin Tower A-805, Sangdaewondong, Jungwongu, Seongnam GYEONGGI, Korea Rep. T. +82317320800. Fax +82317320207. E-mail: cmk@apimeds.com.
URL: http://www.biotherapysociety.org/

History Founded 1996. **Aims** Support the use and understanding of living organisms in the treatment of human and animal diseases. **Structure** General Meeting (annual); Executive Committee; Scientific Committee. **Languages** English. **Staff** 11.00 FTE, voluntary. **Finance** None. **Activities** Events/meetings; knowledge management/information dissemination. **Events** *Conference* Kuala Lumpur (Malaysia) 2015, *Conference* Los Angeles, CA (USA) 2010, *Conference* Seoul (Korea Rep) 2007, *Conference* Sivas (Turkey) 2003, *Conference* Würzburg (Germany) 2000. **Publications** *IBS Newsletter*. **Members** Fellow; Regular; Associate; Honorary. Individuals (about 300) in 68 countries. Membership countries not specified. **IGO Relations** None. **NGO Relations** None. [2014.06.30/XD8905/**D**]

♦ International Bird Rescue (internationally oriented national body)
♦ International Bird Rescue Research Center / see International Bird Rescue
♦ International Bird Strike Committee (inactive)

♦ International Bitumen Emulsion Federation (IBEF) 12356

Fédération internationale de l'emulsion de bitume

SG c/o USIRF, 9 rue de Berri, 75008 Paris, France. T. +33144133281. E-mail: ibef@usirf.com.
URL: http://www.ibef.net/

Aims Promote the use of bitumen emulsion; increase information exchange concerning promotional means, standardization, safety and the developments of bitumen emulsion applications. **Structure** General Meeting (annual). **Events** *Pavement Preservation and Recycling World Summit* Paris (France) 2015, *Emulsion producers day* Lyon (France) 2010, *World congress on emulsions* Lyon (France) 2010, *Symposium of world road bitumen emulsion producers* Lyon (France) 2002, *World congress of emulsions* Lyon (France) 2002. **Publications** *IBEF Bulletin*.

Members in 9 countries:
Algeria, Bulgaria, France, Italy, Japan, Netherlands, Norway, UK, USA. [2014/XD9117/**D**]

♦ International Blackcurrant Association (IBA) 12357

Main Office 1 rue Charles Lacretelle, 49070 Beaucouzé, France. E-mail: info@blackcurrant-iba.com.
URL: https://www.blackcurrant-iba.com/

History 2008, Christchurch (New Zealand). Founded following the European Conference organized since 1995. **Structure** Board, comprising Executive (President and Vice-President) and 5 members. **Finance** Funded by grower associations. **Events** *International Blackcurrant Conference* Lviv (Ukraine) 2022, *International Blackcurrant Grower Meeting* Miltenberg (Germany) 2022, *International Blackcurrant Conference* Lviv (Ukraine) 2020, *International Blackcurrant Conference* Angers (France) 2018, *International Blackcurrant Conference* Ashford (UK) 2016.

Members Full in 8 countries:
Denmark, France, Germany, Japan, Netherlands, New Zealand, Norway, UK.
Observing in 9 countries:
Australia, Canada, Estonia, Latvia, Lithuania, Poland, Sweden, Ukraine, USA.

NGO Relations Cooperates with: *The James Hutton Institute*. [2021/XJ5570/**C**]

♦ International Black Rhino Foundation / see International Rhino Foundation (#14752)

♦ International Black Sea Club (IBSC) 12358

Gen Sec Boyan Bachvarov 55, 9000 Varna, Bulgaria. T. +359879020000. E-mail: ibscsecretarygeneral@gmail.com.
URL: http://www.ibsc-net.com/

History 1992. Statutes adopted at Constituent Assembly, 7-10 Dec 1993, Varna (Bulgaria). Registration: Start date: Feb 1994, Bulgaria. **Aims** Address problems of rational utilization of the Black Sea resources and its environmental protection; strengthen the system of organizational, economic, scientific, technological research, business and cultural relations among Black Sea municipalities and regions; coordinate efforts of *cities / municipalities* of the Black Sea countries for solving common tasks related to the Black Sea *coast* and of regional clubs in the priority fields of economics, science, ecology, transport, free zones,

tourism, journalism, culture and telecommunications; participate in programmes and projects for preserving *environmental* equilibrium of the Black Sea and its adjacent (coastal) territory; organize exchange of *economic-commercial* information; assist in development of *tourism*; participate in national and international events on exploration, research and *preservation* of the Black Sea; establish contacts between business units and governmental administrative bodies of the corresponding countries. **Structure** General Meeting (Assembly) (at least once a year); Executive Board, consisting of mayors of 6 cities from 6 countries, headed by Chairman; Executive Director (rotating every 3 years with Executive Board); Permanent Executive Office in Varna (Bulgaria), headed by Managing Director. **Finance** Sources: donations; gifts, legacies; members' dues; revenue from activities/projects. Other sources: dividends; interests. **Activities** Approves, develops and promotes commercial, production and other proposals for cooperation in various fields and recommends projects. Assists enterprises and organizations in developing technical, economic, ecological, social and cultural cooperation when conducting negotiations and concluding contracts. Develops and assists in the implementation of joint projects on the use of natural resources, environmental protection and restoration, scientific and research potential, and spiritual, cultural and religious communication in the region. Holds workshops and other meetings in such fields as ecology, transport, communications, customs regulations, tourism, SMEs and port activities. **Events** *General Assembly* Azov (Russia) 2011, *General Assembly* Kavala (Greece) 2010, *General Assembly* Yalta, Crimea (Ukraine) 2007, *General assembly* Nikolaev (Ukraine) 1999, *General Assembly* Ukraine 1999. **Publications** *International Black Sea Club Newsletter* (4 a year).
Members Cities (20) in 7 countries:
Bulgaria, Greece, Italy, Romania, Russia, Türkiye, Ukraine.
Consultative Status Consultative status granted from: *ECOSOC (#05331)* (Special). **IGO Relations** Observer status with (1): *Organization of Black Sea Economic Cooperation (BSEC, #17857)*. **NGO Relations** Member of (1): *World Organization of United Cities and Local Governments (UCLG, #21695)*. [2022.10.18/XF3363/**F**]

♦ International Black Sea NGO Network / see Black Sea NGO Network (#03276)

♦ International Black Sea Region Association of Shipowners (BINSA) 12359

Contact Office 31, Build 3, 30 Pionerska Str, Odessa, 65009, Ukraine. T. +38482428087. Fax +38482219358.
History 1993. Also referred to as *International Association of Shipowners of the Black Sea Region*. **Events** *Meeting / Council Meeting* Odessa (Ukraine) 2009, *Meeting / Council Meeting* Baku (Azerbaijan) 2008, *Joint conference / Conference* Varna (Bulgaria) 1997. **IGO Relations** Member of: *Organization of Black Sea Economic Cooperation (BSEC, #17857)*. [2016/XD8597/**D**]

♦ International Black Sea University (internationally oriented national body)
♦ International Black Yoga Teachers Association (internationally oriented national body)

♦ International Bladder Cancer Network (IBCN) 12360

Pres Univ Clinic Urology, Krankenhausstr 12, 91054 Erlangen, Germany. T. +4991318223122. Fax +4991318223179. E-mail: ibcn1997@gmail.com.
SG Level 6, 2775 Laurel St, Vancouver BC V5Z 1M9, Canada.
URL: http://ibcnweb.net/
Aims Improve diagnosis, prevention and treatment of bladder cancer through the application of biologic markers. **Languages** English, French, German. **Activities** meeting held in conjunction with that of ESUR. **Events** *Meeting* Aarhus (Denmark) 2019, *Meeting* Rotterdam (Netherlands) 2018, *Meeting* Lisbon (Portugal) 2017, *Meeting* Bochum (Germany) 2016, *Meeting* Athens (Greece) 2015. **Publications** Articles. **NGO Relations** Links with national organizations. [2017/XF6700/**F**]

♦ International Blaise Users Group (IBUG) 12361

Chairperson Univ of Michigan, Survey Research Center, PO Box 1248, Ann Arbor MI 48106-1248, USA. E-mail: qianyang@umich.edu.
URL: http://www.blaiseusers.org/
History Founded 1992, Voorburg (Netherlands), at first conference. **Aims** Promote the use of the Blaise *software*; serve as a forum for discussion and exchange of ideas and experience. **Structure** Informal group, headed by Chair. **Languages** English. **Staff** None. **Finance** Conferences paid by participants' fees. **Activities** Events/meetings. **Events** *Conference* The Hague (Netherlands) 2016, *Conference / IBUC Conference* Beijing (China) 2015, *Conference / IBUC Conference* Washington, DC (USA) 2013, *IBUC Conference* London (UK) 2012, *IBUC Conference* Baltimore, MD (USA) 2010. **Members** in all countries with Blaise users (not specified). [2015.06.01/XJ7011/c/**E**]

♦ International Blind Golf Association (IBGA) 12362

Chairman address not obtained. E-mail: office@internationalblindgolf.com.
URL: http://www.internationalblindgolf.com/
History 1998. **Aims** Promote golf as a sport for blind and vision impaired persons. **Structure** General Meeting (every 2 years). Board of Directors, comprising President, Vice-President, Secretary-Treasurer and 3 further members. **Finance** Members' dues. **Activities** Organizes championships. **Members** in 10 countries. Membership countries not specified. [2019/XD8775/**D**]

♦ International Blind Sports Association / see International Blind Sports Federation (#12363)

♦ International Blind Sports Federation (IBSA) 12363

Federación Internacional de Deportes para Ciegos
Exec Dir Nijemheim 24-19, 3704 VJ Zeist, Netherlands. T. +31644830820. E-mail: secgen@ibsasport.org – ibsa@ibsasport.org.
Registered Address Adenauer Allee 212-214, 53113 Bonn, Germany.
URL: http://www.ibsasport.org/
History 24 Apr 1981, Paris (France). Founded following the meeting of a preparatory Committee, 1980, London (UK). Statutes approved at General Assembly, 29 May 1985, Hurdal (Norway); revised at General Assemblies: 2-4 Jun 1989, Forma (Italy); 24-25 Jun 1993, San José (Costa Rica); Jun 1997, Casablanca (Morocco); 2005, Beijing (China). Former names and other names: *International Sports Association of the Blind* – former; *International Blind Sports Association* – former; *Association internationale pour le sport des aveugles (AISA)* – former; *Asociación Internacional de Deportes para Ciegos* – former; *Internationaler Blindensportverband (IBSV)* – former. Registration: North Rhine-Westphalai District court, No/ID: VR 9793, Start date: 16 Apr 2014, Germany, Bonn; Start date: Mar 1996, End date: 2014, Spain. **Aims** Organize sports competitions and activities where blind and partially sighted can compete in equal conditions with their peers. **Structure** General Assembly (every 4 years); Executive Committee. Regions have their own committee: America; Europe; Africa; Asia; Oceania. **Languages** English. **Finance** Sources: contributions; grants; members' dues. **Activities** Sporting activities. **Events** *General Assembly* Jordan 2021, *General assembly* Fort Wayne, IN (USA) 2019, *General assembly* Cluj-Napoca (Romania) 2017, *Delegation Coordinating Meeting* Seoul (Korea Rep) 2015, *General Assembly* Copenhagen (Denmark) 2013.
Members National organizations, institutions and committees Full and Associate in 131 countries and territories:
Albania, Algeria, Andorra, Angola, Argentina, Armenia, Australia, Austria, Azerbaijan, Bahrain, Barbados, Belarus, Belgium, Benin, Bolivia, Bosnia-Herzegovina, Brazil, Brunei Darussalam, Bulgaria, Burkina Faso, Cambodia, Cameroon, Canada, Central African Rep, Chile, China, Colombia, Congo DR, Costa Rica, Côte d'Ivoire, Croatia, Cuba, Cyprus, Czechia, Denmark, Dominican Rep, Ecuador, Egypt, El Salvador, Estonia, Faeroe Is, Fiji, Finland, France, Georgia, Germany, Ghana, Great Britain, Greece, Guatemala, Honduras, Hong Kong, Hungary, Iceland, India, Indonesia, Iran Islamic Rep, Iraq, Ireland, Israel, Italy, Japan, Jordan, Kazakhstan, Kenya, Korea Rep, Kuwait, Kyrgyzstan, Latvia, Lebanon, Lesotho, Liberia, Libya, Lithuania, Macau, Madagascar, Malaysia, Mali, Mauritius, Mexico, Moldova, Mongolia, Montenegro, Morocco, Mozambique, Nepal, Netherlands, New Zealand, Nicaragua, Niger, Norway, Pakistan, Panama, Paraguay, Peru, Philippines, Poland, Portugal, Puerto Rico, Qatar, Romania, Russia, Rwanda, Samoa, Saudi Arabia, Senegal, Serbia, Singapore, Slovakia, Slovenia, Solomon Is, South Africa, Spain, Sweden, Switzerland, Taiwan, Tanzania UR, Thailand, Tonga, Trinidad-Tobago, Tunisia, Türkiye, Turkmenistan, Uganda, Ukraine, United Arab Emirates, Uruguay, USA, Uzbekistan, Vanuatu, Venezuela.
NGO Relations Member of (2): *Association of Paralympic Sports Organisations (APSO, #02850)*; *International Paralympic Committee (IPC, #14512)*. Recognized by: *World Blind Union (WBU, #21234)*. Cooperates with other International Sport Federations, not specified. [2021/XB0094/**B**]

♦ International Blue Crescent (internationally oriented national body)
♦ International Blue Crescent Humanitarian Relief and Development Foundation / see International Blue Crescent

♦ International Blue Cross (IBC) 12364

Gen Sec Lindenrain 5a, 3012 Bern, Switzerland. T. +41313019804. Fax +41313019805. E-mail: office@internationalbluecross.org.
URL: http://www.internationalbluecross.org
History Founded 1886, on expansion of the scope of a Swiss national temperance society set up 1877, Geneva (Switzerland). Constitution adopted 4 Jun 1909, Hamburg (Germany); modified: 14 Aug 1955, Copenhagen (Denmark); 21 Sep 1971, Holzhausen (Germany FR); 9 Jul 1981, Seeboden (Austria); 26 Jul 1987, Haslev (Denmark); 24 Jul 1989, Holstein (Switzerland). First official seat of General Secretariat 1980, Geneva (Switzerland); subsequently relocated to Bern (Switzerland). Restructured 2008 and 2016. Former names and other names: *International Federation of the Temperance Blue Cross Societies* – former; *Fédération internationale des sociétés de tempérance de la Croix-Bleue* – former; *International Federation of the Blue Cross Societies* – former; *Fédération internationale des sociétés de la Croix-Bleue* – former; *International Blue Cross Union* – alias; *International Federation of Blue Cross Organizations* – former; *International Federation of the Blue Cross (IFBC)* – former; *Fédération internationale de la Croix-Bleue* – former; *Internationaler Bund des Blauen Kreuzes* – former; *Federação Internacional da Cruz Azul* – former. **Aims** As a health development organization of professionals, care for people harmed by *alcohol* and/or *drug* dependence. **Structure** General Assembly; Network Committee; Secretariat in Bern (Switzerland). **Languages** English, French, German. **Staff** 5.00 FTE, paid. Several voluntary. **Finance** Sources: donations; members' dues. **Activities** Healthcare; research and development; training/education. **Events** *European seminar* Stuttgart (Germany FR) 1990, *European seminar / Biennial Conference* Leuenberg (Switzerland) 1989, *Biennial Conference* Haslev (Denmark) 1987, *Biennial Conference* Denmark 1985, *Biennial Conference* Germany FR 1983. **Publications** Annual Report; newsletters; factsheets.
Members Affiliated societies in 37 countries and territories:
Austria, Botswana, Brazil, Burkina Faso, Cameroon, Chad, Chile, Congo Brazzaville, Congo DR, Côte d'Ivoire, Czechia, Denmark, Faeroe Is, Finland, France, Germany, Ghana, Hungary, India, Japan, Kenya, Lesotho, Madagascar, Nigeria, Norway, Paraguay, Poland, Portugal, Romania, Russia, South Africa, Sweden, Switzerland, Tanzania UR, Togo, Uganda, Ukraine.
Consultative Status Consultative status granted from: *ECOSOC (#05331)* (Special). **NGO Relations** Member of (3): *European Alcohol Policy Alliance (Eurocare, #05856)*; *European Mutual-Help Network for Alcohol-Related Problems (EMNA, #07843)*; *International Christian Federation for the Prevention of Alcoholism and Drug Addiction (ICF-PADA, no recent information)*. [2022.10.20/XC2031/**C**]

♦ International Blue Cross Union / see International Blue Cross (#12364)
♦ International Bluegrass Music Association (internationally oriented national body)

♦ International Board on the Applications of the Mössbauer Effect (IBAME) 12365

Chair Deutsches Electron-Synchrotron DESY, Notkestr 85, 22607 Hamburg, Germany. T. +444089984503.
Vice Chairman address not obtained.
URL: http://www.ibame.org/
History 1979. Current Constitution adopted 2015. Former names and other names: *International Commission on the Applications of the Mössbauer Effect (ICAME)* – former (1979 to 1993). **Aims** Advance diffusion of knowledge in the field of Mössbauer effect and its applications. **Structure** Chair; Vice-Chair; Secretary. **Languages** English. **Staff** None. **Finance** Donation of euro 1 per participant at ICAME Conference. **Activities** Events/meetings. **Events** *Biennial International Conference* Brasov (Romania) 2021, *Biennial International Conference* Dalian (China) 2019, *Biennial International Conference* St Petersburg (Russia) 2017, *Biennial International Conference* Hamburg (Germany) 2015, *Biennial International Conference* Opatija (Croatia) 2013.
Members Individuals Elected; Honorary; Executive. Members in 31 countries:
Argentina, Australia, Austria, Belgium, Brazil, Canada, China, Colombia, Croatia, Czechia, Denmark, Egypt, Finland, France, Germany, Hungary, Israel, Italy, Japan, Netherlands, Oman, Poland, Portugal, Romania, Russia, Slovakia, South Africa, Spain, Sweden, UK, USA.
NGO Relations Associated organization of: *International Union of Pure and Applied Chemistry (IUPAC, #15809)*. [2022/XE0883/v/**E**]

♦ International Board for Aquatic, Sports and Recreation Facilities (#13211)
♦ International Board of Aviation Medicine (inactive)

♦ International Board on Books for Young People (IBBY) 12366

Union internationale pour les livres de jeunesse – Organización Internacional para el Libro Juvenil – Internationales Kuratorium für das Jugendbuch
Exec Dir Nonnenweg 12, Postfach, 4009 Basel BS, Switzerland. T. +41612722917. Fax +41612722757. E-mail: ibby@ibby.org.
URL: http://www.ibby.org/
History 4 Oct 1953, Zurich (Switzerland). Registration: Switzerland. **Aims** Represent an international network of people from all over the world who are committed to bringing books and children together. **Structure** General Assembly of National Sections (every 2 years, at Congress); Executive Committee. **Languages** English, French, German, Spanish. **Staff** 2.00 FTE, paid. **Finance** Sources: contributions; members' dues. Other sources: IBBY Foundation. Annual budget: 200,000 CHF. **Activities** Awards/prizes/competitions; events/meetings; financial and/or material support; publishing activities. **Events** *World Congress* Ottawa, ON (Canada) 2026, *World Congress* Trieste (Italy) 2024, *World Congress* Putrajaya (Malaysia) 2022, *Biennial Congress* Moscow (Russia) 2021, *Biennial Congress* Moscow (Russia) 2020. **Publications** *Bookbird* (4 a year) – journal; *IBBY Honour List* (every 2 years); *IBBY Biennial Report*. Newsletters; directories; booklists; scientific works; congress proceedings; catalogues; information brochure; posters.
Members National sections in 80 countries and territories:
Afghanistan, Albania, Argentina, Armenia, Australia, Austria, Azerbaijan, Belgium, Bolivia, Brazil, Cambodia, Canada, Chile, China, Colombia, Costa Rica, Croatia, Cuba, Cyprus, Czechia, Denmark, Ecuador, Egypt, El Salvador, Estonia, Finland, France, Germany, Ghana, Greece, Haiti, Hungary, Iceland, India, Indonesia, Iran Islamic Rep, Ireland, Israel, Italy, Japan, Jordan, Korea Rep, Kuwait, Latvia, Lebanon, Lithuania, Malaysia, Mexico, Moldova, Mongolia, Nepal, Netherlands, New Zealand, Norway, Pakistan, Palestine, Peru, Poland, Russia, Rwanda, Slovakia, Slovenia, South Africa, Spain, Sri Lanka, Sweden, Switzerland, Tanzania UR, Thailand, Tunisia, Türkiye, Uganda, UK, Ukraine, United Arab Emirates, Uruguay, USA, Venezuela, Zambia, Zimbabwe.
Individuals in 4 countries and territories:
Morocco, Sri Lanka, Syrian AR, Taiwan.
Consultative Status Consultative status granted from: *ECOSOC (#05331)* (Ros C); *UNICEF (#20332)*. **NGO Relations** Member of: *International Conference of NGOs (#12883)*; *International Federation of Library Associations and Institutions (IFLA, #13470)* (consultative status); *NGO Committee on UNICEF (#17120)*. [2022/XC1400/**B**]

♦ International Board for Career Management Certification / see Institute of Career Certification International
♦ International Board of Chelation Therapy / see International Board of Clinical Metal Toxicology (#12368)

♦ International Board of Chiropractic Examiners (IBCE) 12367

Contact address not obtained. T. +19703569100.
URL: http://www.ibce.org/
Aims Establish the worldwide acceptance of a chiropractic standard of health care as well as an acceptable level of education and competence. **Structure** Council. **NGO Relations** *Eastern Mediterranean and Middle East Chiropractic Federation (EMME Chiro Fed, no recent information)*; *Federación Latinoamericana de Quiropractica (FLAQ, #09367)*; *International Federation of the Phonographic Industry (IFPI, #13508)*. [2017/XM7741/**C**]

♦ International Board of Clinical Metal Toxicology (IBCMT) 12368

Chairman Renheide 2, 5595 XJ Leende, Netherlands. T. +31495592232. Fax +31495592418.
Secretariat 5267 Warner Ave, Suite 226, Huntington Beach CA 92649, USA. T. +17148403830. Fax +17148405951.
URL: http://www.ibct.info/

History 1994, as *International Board of Chelation Therapy (IBCT)*. **Aims** Set international standards for: the administration of clinical metal chelation therapy; examining and certifying applicants for clinical metal toxicologist; training accumulating and exchanging scientific data to enhance the acceptance of clinical metal toxicology as an approved medical speciality. **Structure** Board of Directors. **Languages** English. **Finance** Members' dues. **Activities** Events/meetings; certification/accreditation. **Events** *Conference* Goa (India) 2014, *Conference* Goa (India) 2013, *International workshop* Eindhoven (Netherlands) 2010, *India workshop of advanced clinical metal toxicology / Conference* Goa (India) 2010, *Annual meeting* Cape Town (South Africa) 2006. **Publications** *Textbook of Clinical Metal Toxicology – 15th ed* by Peter J Van Der Schaar.
Members in 15 countries and territories:
Australia, Bahamas, Belgium, Denmark, Germany, Hong Kong, India, Indonesia, Japan, Mexico, Netherlands, New Zealand, South Africa, Spain, UK. [2018.08.20/XF7018/**F**]

♦ International Board of Cooperation for the Developing Countries (inactive)

♦ International Board of Cosmetic Surgery (IBCS) 12369

Pres 43 Cambridge Road, Wimpole, SG8 5QD, UK. T. +441223208268. Fax +441223207131.
Chair Clinica Krulig Int'l, Centro San Ignacio, Copernico no 9, La Castellana, Caracas 01060 DF, Venezuela. T. +582122666050. Fax +582122667770.
History 2003. **Aims** Develop, promote, support and encourage the science and art of cosmetic surgery; plan and execute examinations; promote postgraduate education in the field. **Structure** Board, comprising President, Chairman and 7 members. **Activities** Board Examinations held worldwide. **Events** *Abu Dhabi International Conference on Dermatology and Aesthetics* Abu Dhabi (United Arab Emirates) 2022, *Abu Dhabi International Conference on Dermatology and Aesthetics* Abu Dhabi (United Arab Emirates) 2020, *Abu Dhabi International Conference on Dermatology and Aesthetics* Abu Dhabi (United Arab Emirates) 2019, *Abu Dhabi International Conference on Dermatology and Aesthetics* Abu Dhabi (United Arab Emirates) 2018, *Abu Dhabi International Conference on Dermatology and Aesthetics* Abu Dhabi (United Arab Emirates) 2017. [2014/XJ8001/**C**]

♦ International Board of Forensic Engineering Sciences (internationally oriented national body)

♦ International Board of Heart Rhythm Examiners (IBHRE) 12370

Main Office 1325 G St NW, Ste 400, Washington DC 20005, USA. T. +12024643400. Fax +12024643401. E-mail: info@ibhre.org – ibhre@hrsonline.org.
URL: http://www.ibhre.org/
History 1985, as NASPExAM, an affiliate of NASPE, currently *Heart Rhythm Society (HRS)*. Current title adopted 2006. **Aims** Improve the quality of knowledge of heart rhythm professionals. **Structure** Board of Governors, comprising President, 1st Vice-President/Treasurer, Secretary and 8 members. **Publications** *IBHRE Newsletter*. [2017/XJ7179/**E**]

♦ International Boarding and Pet Services (unconfirmed)

♦ International Board of Lactation Consultant Examiners (IBLCE) 12371

Int'l Office 10301 Democracy Ln, Ste 400, Fairfax VA 22030, USA. T. +17035607330. Fax +17035607332. E-mail: international@iblce.org.
URL: http://www.iblce.org/
History Founded 1985, USA, with initial financial support from *La Leche League International (LLLI, #16433)*. **Aims** Determine the knowledge of practitioners in lactation and breastfeeding care. **Structure** International Office. Regional offices (3): Americas (serving North, Central and South America and Israel); Australia (serving Australia, Asia Pacific and Africa); Austria (serving Europe, Middle East and North Africa). **Activities** Certification examination for lactation consultants. **Events** *European regional conference* Basel (Switzerland) 2010, *European regional conference* Vienna (Austria) 2008, *European regional conference* Berlin (Germany) 2004.
Members Individuals (International Board Certification Lactation Consultants) in 90 countries and territories:
Argentina, Australia, Austria, Bahrain, Bangladesh, Belarus, Belgium, Bermuda, Bosnia-Herzegovina, Brazil, Bulgaria, Canada, Cayman Is, Chile, China, Colombia, Costa Rica, Croatia, Cyprus, Czechia, Denmark, Dominican Rep, Ecuador, Egypt, Estonia, Ethiopia, Faeroe Is, Finland, France, Germany, Gibraltar, Greece, Guatemala, Haiti, Hong Kong, Hungary, Iceland, India, Indonesia, Ireland, Israel, Italy, Japan, Korea Rep, Kuwait, Latvia, Lebanon, Liechtenstein, Lithuania, Luxembourg, Malawi, Malaysia, Malta, Mexico, Monaco, Netherlands, New Zealand, Nigeria, Norway, Oman, Pakistan, Panama, Peru, Philippines, Poland, Portugal, Puerto Rico, Qatar, Romania, Russia, Rwanda, Saudi Arabia, Singapore, Slovenia, South Africa, Spain, Sri Lanka, St Lucia, Sweden, Switzerland, Taiwan, Thailand, Trinidad-Tobago, Türkiye, UK, Ukraine, United Arab Emirates, Uruguay, USA, Venezuela. [2020/XF6179/**F**]

♦ International Board for Plant Genetic Resources / see Bioversity International (#03262)

♦ International Board of Shoulder and Elbow Surgery (IBSES) 12372

Sec address not obtained.
URL: https://www.ibses.org/
History 1980, London (UK). Re-established, 1992. Former names and other names: *International Board of Shoulder Surgery* – former (1980); *International Shoulder Society* – alias. **Aims** Foster and facilitate the development of International Congresses of Shoulder Surgery; provide continuity in activities between the times of congresses. **Structure** Board, comprising Chair, Secretary, Treasurer, 7 Directors and 2 ex-officio members. **Languages** English. **Staff** None. **Finance** Congress proceeds. **Activities** *International Congress of Shoulder and Elbow Surgery (ICSS)*. **Events** *International Congress on Shoulder and Elbow Surgery (ICSES)* Vancouver, BC (Canada) 2025, *International Congress on Shoulder and Elbow Surgery (ICSES)* Rome (Italy) 2023, *International Congress on Shoulder and Elbow Surgery (ICSES)* Rome (Italy) 2022, *Triennial Congress* Buenos Aires (Argentina) 2019, *Triennial Congress* Jeju (Korea Rep) 2016.
Members Organizations in 34 countries and territories:
Australia, Austria, Belgium, Brazil, Canada, Denmark, Finland, France, Germany, Greece, Hong Kong, Hungary, Iceland, Ireland, Israel, Italy, Japan, Korea Rep, Netherlands, New Zealand, Norway, Poland, Portugal, Russia, Singapore, South Africa, Spain, Sweden, Switzerland, Taiwan, Thailand, Türkiye, UK, USA. [2021/XD6536/**D**]

♦ International Board of Shoulder Surgery / see International Board of Shoulder and Elbow Surgery (#12372)
♦ International Boatmen's Linesmen's Association (unconfirmed)
♦ International Bobath Instructors Association Adult Hemiplegia / see International Bobath Instructors Training Association (#12373)
♦ International Bobath Instructors Training Association / see International Bobath Instructors Training Association (#12373)

♦ International Bobath Instructors Training Association (IBITA) 12373

Chairperson address not obtained.
Exec Sec address not obtained.
URL: https://ibita.org/
History 1984. Former names and other names: *International Bobath Instructors Association Adult Hemiplegia (IBITAH)* – alias; *International Bobath Instructors Training Association (IBITA – An international association for adult neurological rehabilitation)* – full title. Registration: Switzerland. **Aims** Assure adults with *neurological* dysfunction of the services of an interdisciplinary team trained in neurological rehabilitation, originating in the Bobath concept and developed in accordance with current knowledge. **Structure** General Assembly (annual); Executive Committee; Verification Committee. Standing Committees (6): Appeals/Grievance; Education; Developing Countries; Nominating; Research; Website Editorial. **Languages** English. **Staff** Voluntary. **Finance** Members' dues. **Events** *Annual General Meeting* Ljubljana (Slovenia) 2021, *Annual General Meeting* 2020, *Annual General Meeting* Buenos Aires (Argentina) 2019, *Annual General Meeting* Basel (Switzerland) 2018, *Annual General Meeting* Dublin (Ireland) 2017.
Members Physiotherapists and occupational therapists, representing more than 250 members in 26 countries:
Argentina, Australia, Austria, Belgium, Brazil, Canada, Czechia, Denmark, Finland, Germany, Hong Kong, Hungary, Ireland, Israel, Italy, Japan, Korea Rep, Netherlands, Norway, Portugal, South Africa, Spain, Sweden, Switzerland, UK, USA.
National organizations in 9 countries:
Australia, Belgium, Canada, Germany, Italy, Netherlands, South Africa, UK, USA. [2021/XD8524/**D**]

♦ International Bobbin and Needle Lace Organization 12374

Organisation internationale de la dentelle au fuseau et l'aiguille (OIDFA)
Pres 5 Pamburra Ct, Melbourne VIC 3088, Australia. E-mail: president@oidfa.com – feedback@oidfa.com – secretary@oidfa.com.
URL: http://www.oidfa.com/
History 1982, France. **Aims** Promote, coordinate and increase efforts for the study, practice and quality of bobbin and needle lace in traditional techniques as well as modern interpretations and use. **Structure** General Assembly (every 2 years, at Congress); Executive Committee; Administrative Council. **Languages** English, French. **Staff** Voluntary. **Finance** Sources: members' dues; sale of products. **Activities** Events/meetings; knowledge management/information dissemination; networking/liaising; research/documentation. **Events** *Biennial Congress* Nova Gorica (Slovenia) / Gorizia (Italy) 2023, *Biennial Congress* Tartu (Estonia) 2021, *Biennial Congress* Tartu (Estonia) 2020, *Biennial Congress* Zaandam (Netherlands) 2018, *Biennial Congress* Ljubljana (Slovenia) 2016. **Publications** *OIDFA Bulletin* (4 a year). Brochures; books; pattern folders.
Members Individuals; national organizations; schools; groups. Members in 39 countries:
Argentina, Australia, Austria, Belarus, Belgium, Bulgaria, Canada, Croatia, Czechia, Denmark, Estonia, Finland, France, Germany, Greece, Hungary, Ireland, Israel, Italy, Japan, Luxembourg, Malta, Moldova, Netherlands, New Zealand, Norway, Poland, Russia, Slovakia, Slovenia, South Africa, Spain, Sri Lanka, Sweden, Switzerland, Türkiye, UK, Ukraine, USA. [2022/XD2599/**D**]

♦ International Bobsleighing and Tobogganing Federation / see International Bobsleigh and Skeleton Federation (#12375)

♦ International Bobsleigh and Skeleton Federation (IBSF) 12375

Internationales Bob- und Skeletonverband
SG Maison du Sport, Ave de Rhodanie 54, 1007 Lausanne VD, Switzerland. T. +41216015101. Fax +41216012677. E-mail: office@ibsf.org.
Pres Salzburger Strasse 678, 5084 Grossgmain, Austria. T. +4362472023210. Fax +4362472023211.
URL: http://www.ibsf.org/
History 23 Nov 1923, Paris (France). Founded as *International Bobsleighing and Tobogganing Federation – Fédération internationale de bobsleigh et de tobogganing (FIBT) – Federación Internacional de Bobsleigh y Toboganing*. Previously also referred to in German as *Internationale Vereinigung des Bobsleigh und Rodelsportes*. Present titles adopted Jun 2015. **Aims** Develop the *sport* of bobsleigh and skeleton. **Structure** Congress (annual); Executive Committee. **Languages** English, German. **Finance** Members' dues. **Activities** Sporting events. **Events** *Annual Congress* 2021, *Annual Congress* 2020, *Annual Congress* Prague (Czechia) 2019, *Annual Congress* Rome (Italy) 2018, *Annual Congress* Salt Lake City, UT (USA) 2017. **Publications** Annual Report in English, German.
Members National federations in 72 countries and territories:
Andorra, Argentina, Armenia, Australia, Austria, Azerbaijan, Belgium, Bermuda, Bosnia-Herzegovina, Brazil, Bulgaria, Canada, Chile, China, Colombia, Côte d'Ivoire, Croatia, Czechia, Denmark, Dominican Rep, Finland, France, Gambia, Germany, Ghana, Great Britain, Greece, Hungary, India, Iraq, Ireland, Israel, Italy, Jamaica, Japan, Kazakhstan, Korea Rep, Latvia, Liechtenstein, Lithuania, Luxembourg, Mexico, Monaco, Mongolia, Netherlands, New Zealand, Nigeria, Norway, Panama, Poland, Portugal, Puerto Rico, Romania, Russia, Samoa, Samoa USA, San Marino, Serbia, Slovakia, Slovenia, South Africa, Spain, Sweden, Switzerland, Taiwan, Togo, Trinidad-Tobago, Türkiye, Ukraine, USA, Venezuela, Virgin Is USA.
NGO Relations Member of (2): *Association of the International Olympic Winter Sports Federations (AIOWF, #02757)*; *International Committee for Fair Play (#12769)*. Cooperates with (1): *International Testing Agency (ITA, #15678)*. Recognized by: *International Olympic Committee (IOC, #14408)*. [2022/XC1401/**D**]

♦ International Bocce Association / see Fédération internationale de boules (#09616)
♦ International Bocce Federation (#09616)
♦ International Bodyflight Association (unconfirmed)

♦ International Bodyguard Association (IBA) 12376

International Secretariat IBAHQ Ste 206, 33 Parkway, London, NW1 7PN, UK. T. +353871940787 – +35387(447720823855. E-mail: sg@ibabodyguards.com.
Dir Gen Castle Cosey, Castlebellingham, CO. LOUTH, Ireland. T. +353871940787. E-mail: dg@ibabodyguards.com.
URL: http://www.ibabodyguards.com/
History 1957, Paris (France). **Aims** Advance knowledge of protective service agents; maintain high standards and ethics; promote efficiency of agents and the services they perform; aid in establishment of effective security programs; emphasize a professional approach to the bodyguard function. **Structure** General Meeting (annual); Executive Council; International Bodyguard Service; Women's Bureau. **Languages** Arabic, English, French, Russian. **Staff** 2.00 FTE, paid. **Activities** Awards/prizes/competitions; events/meetings; training/education. **Events** *Annual General Meeting* Oslo (Norway) 2014, *Annual General Meeting* London (UK) 2013, *Annual General Meeting* Ireland 2012, *Annual General Meeting* Ireland 2011, *Annual General Meeting* Castlebellingham (Ireland) 2010. **Publications** *Sword and Shield* (periodical).
Members Full; Associate. Organizations and individuals in 130 countries and territories:
Afghanistan, Albania, Algeria, Argentina, Armenia, Australia, Austria, Azerbaijan, Bangladesh, Barbados, Belarus, Belgium, Bosnia-Herzegovina, Brazil, Bulgaria, Cambodia, Cameroon, Canada, China, Congo DR, Costa Rica, Côte d'Ivoire, Croatia, Cuba, Cyprus, Czechia, Denmark, Dominican Rep, Ecuador, Egypt, Estonia, Ethiopia, Fiji, Finland, France, Gambia, Germany, Ghana, Greece, Guatemala, Guinea, Haiti, Holy See, Honduras, Hong Kong, Hungary, Iceland, India, Indonesia, Iran Islamic Rep, Iraq, Ireland, Israel, Italy, Jamaica, Japan, Kazakhstan, Kenya, Korea Rep, Kosovo, Kuwait, Laos, Latvia, Lebanon, Libya, Liechtenstein, Lithuania, Luxembourg, Malaysia, Malta, Mauritius, Mexico, Moldova, Mongolia, Montenegro, Morocco, Mozambique, Myanmar, Namibia, Nepal, Netherlands, New Zealand, Nicaragua, Nigeria, North Macedonia, Norway, Pakistan, Palestine, Panama, Papua New Guinea, Paraguay, Peru, Philippines, Poland, Portugal, Qatar, Romania, Russia, Rwanda, Samoa, San Marino, Sao Tomé-Principe, Saudi Arabia, Serbia, Seychelles, Sierra Leone, Singapore, Slovakia, Slovenia, South Africa, Spain, Sri Lanka, St Kitts-Nevis, St Lucia, Sudan, Sweden, Switzerland, Syrian AR, Taiwan, Thailand, Trinidad-Tobago, Türkiye, Uganda, UK, Ukraine, United Arab Emirates, USA, Venezuela, Zambia, Zimbabwe.
Also membership in East, South, West and North Africa regions (not specified). [2022/XD5133/**C**]

♦ International Bodyguard and Security Services Association (IBSSA) 12377

Gen Sec 11 Mizrachi St, 49501 Petach Tiqva, Israel. T. +97239308150. Fax +97239309504. E-mail: secretary@ibssa.org.
URL: http://www.ibssa.org/
History Registered in accordance with French law. **Structure** Board of Directors, comprising Honorary President, Executive President, 3 Vice-Presidents and General Secretary. **Events** *Congress* Belgrade (Serbia) 2007. **Members** Associated; Corporate; Honorary; Individual. Membership countries not specified. **NGO Relations** Member of: *International Federation of Non-Government Organizations for the Prevention of Drug and Substance Abuse (IFNGO, #13490)*. [2010/XD8941/**D**]

♦ International Body Image Association (inactive)

♦ International BodyTalk Association (IBA) 12378

Office Manager 2750 Stickney Pt Rd, Ste 203, Sarasota FL 34231, USA. T. +19419217443. Fax +19419243779.
URL: http://www.ibaglobalhealing.com/
History 2000, Sarasota FL (USA). **Aims** Be the official governing organization for the BodyTalk System – the use of *biofeedback* to communicate with the body and discover its healing needs and priorities – and its related modalities. **Structure** Leadership Team. Offices (3): USA; Europe; Australasia. *International BodyTalk Foundation (IBF)*. **Staff** 6.00 FTE, paid. **Activities** Training/education. **Publications** *IBA Newsletter*. [2014/XJ8368/**C**]

♦ International Boethius Society (internationally oriented national body)

♦ International Bone and Mineral Society (IBMS) 12379

Exec Dir 330 N Wabash, Ste 1900, Chicago IL 60611, USA. T. +13123215113. Fax +13126736934.
URL: http://www.ibmsonline.org/
History 1980, as *International Conferences on Calcium Regulating Hormones (ICCRH)*, following the Parathyroid Conference series. Current name adopted 1995. **Aims** Promote generation and dissemination of knowledge of basic biology and clinical science of the *skeleton* and mineral *metabolism*. **Structure** Executive Committee, consisting of President, Vice-President, Immediate Past President and Secretary-Treasurer. Board of Directors. **Activities** Developed and maintains 'Bonekey IBMS' – a knowledge environment dedicated to improving bone health. **Events** *International Conference on Cancer-Induced Bone Disease* Rotterdam (Netherlands) 2015, *Joint Meeting* Rotterdam (Netherlands) 2015, *International Conference on Progress in Bone and Mineral Research* Vienna (Austria) 2015, *ICOBR : International Conference on Osteoporosis and Bone Research* Xiamen (China) 2014, *Joint Meeting* Kobe (Japan) 2013. **Publications** *Bone* (12 a year) – journal.

Members Individuals in 55 countries:
Albania, Australia, Austria, Belgium, Brazil, Bulgaria, Canada, China, Croatia, Czechia, Denmark, Egypt, El Salvador, France, Georgia, Germany, Guyana, Honduras, Hong Kong, India, Israel, Italy, Japan, Lebanon, Liechtenstein, Luxembourg, Malaysia, Mali, Malta, Mexico, Nepal, Netherlands, New Zealand, Nigeria, Norway, Pakistan, Peru, Poland, Puerto Rico, Romania, Russia, Samoa, Senegal, Sierra Leone, Slovenia, South Africa, Spain, Sri Lanka, Sweden, Switzerland, Taiwan, Thailand, Türkiye, UK, USA. [2017/XF7210/v/**F**]

♦ International Bone Research Association (IBRA) 12380

Main Office Hochbergerstr 60E, 4057 Basel BS, Switzerland. T. +41613190505. Fax +41613190519. E-mail: info@ibra.ch.
USA Office 224 Valley Creek Blvd, Ste 100, Exton PA 19341, USA.
URL: http://www.ibra.ch/

History 25 Sep 2004, Zurich (Switzerland). Registration: Switzerland, Basel. **Aims** Advance bone-tissue research and management. **Structure** General Assembly. Board of Directors. Administration Office. **Activities** Meeting activities; support; education. **Events** *From the Finger Tip to the Elbow Seminar* Vienna (Austria) 2013. [2021/XJ7980/**D**]

- ♦ International Bone Ultrasound Society (unconfirmed)
- ♦ International Book Bank (internationally oriented national body)
- ♦ International Book Information Service (internationally oriented national body)
- ♦ International Booksellers Federation (inactive)
- ♦ International Border Management and Technologies Association (unconfirmed)

♦ International Bordetella Society 12381

Contact Damron-Barbier Lab, One Medical Center Drive, Morgantown WV 26506, USA.
URL: https://www.bordetella.org/

History 8 Apr 2016, Argentina. Founded at 11th Symposium on Bordetella. **Structure** Board of Directors. **Activities** Events/meetings. **Events** *International Symposium on Bordetella* Brussels (Belgium) 2019. [2020/AA0075/c/**E**]

♦ International Boreal Forest Research Association (IBFRA) 12382

Secretariat Forest Sciences, SLU, Petrus Lestadius väg, SE-901 83 Umeå, Sweden. T. +46907868100. Fax +46907868102. E-mail: info@ibfra.org.
URL: http://www.ibfra.org/

History 1991, as a result of meeting of International Panel on Boreal Forests. **Aims** Promote and coordinate research to increase the understanding of the role of the circumpolar boreal forest in the global environment and the influence of resource management and environmental change on that role. **Structure** Cooperators. Coordinator. **Languages** English. **Staff** 1.00 FTE, paid. **Finance** No formal funding mechanism. **Activities** Working groups (4): Carbon; Fire; Inventory; Insect and Disease. Research priorities: classification, monitoring, and inventory of boreal forests; climate and ecosystem monitoring (of boreal forests), including carbon modelling, and the impact of change factors such as fire, pests and air pollution; forest management and biodiversity. **Events** *Changing Boreal Biome* Fairbanks, AK (USA) 2021, *Cool forests at risk? The critical role of boreal and mountain ecosystems for people, bioeconomy and climate* Laxenburg (Austria) 2018, *Towards a new era of forest science in boreal region* Rovaniemi (Finland) 2015, *Boreal forests at risk* Edmonton, AB (Canada) 2013, *Conference* Krasnoyarsk (Russia) 2011. **Publications** Conference proceedings.
Members Cooperators in 6 countries:
Canada, Finland, Norway, Russia, Sweden, USA. [2021/XD4891/**D**]

♦ International Borzoi Council (IBC) 12383

Address not obtained.
URL: https://internationalborzoicouncil.org/

History 1986. **Aims** Group breeders and those interested in Borzoi *dogs*; encourage the standardization of the *breed*. **Structure** Board. **Finance** Sources: members' dues. **Events** *Conference* Amsterdam (Netherlands) 2023, *Conference* 2020, *Conference* England (UK) 2017, *Triennial Conference* Pleasanton, CA (USA) 2014, *Triennial Conference* Fribourg (Switzerland) 2011. **Publications** Newsletter.
Members Individuals in 19 countries:
Argentina, Australia, Belgium, Canada, Denmark, Finland, France, Germany, Ireland, Japan, Mexico, Netherlands, New Zealand, Norway, Puerto Rico, Sweden, Switzerland, UK, USA. [2022/XF0878/v/**C**]

- ♦ International Botanical Congress (meeting series)
- ♦ International Bottled Water Association (internationally oriented national body)
- ♦ International Bottling Congress (meeting series)
- ♦ International Boundaries Research Unit (internationally oriented national body)
- ♦ International Boundary Commission / see International Boundary and Water Commission
- ♦ International Boundary Commission (inactive)
- ♦ International Boundary and Water Commission (internationally oriented national body)
- ♦ International Bowling Federation / see International Bowling Federation (#12384)

♦ International Bowling Federation (IBF) 12384

CEO Maison du Sport International, Avenue de Rhodanie 54, 1007 Lausanne VD, Switzerland. E-mail: info@bowling.sport.
Secretary General 2004 Olympic House, 1 Stadium Path, So Kon Po, Causeway Bay, Hong Kong.
URL: https://bowling.sport/

History 27 Jan 1952, Hamburg (Germany). Founded reviving the *International Bowling Association (IBA)*, set up 1926. Rebranded 2014, on merger with *World Tenpin Bowling Association (WTBA, inactive)*, a previously independent discipline within FIQ. Statutes adopted 2 Oct 1975, London (UK); valid since 1 Jan 1976; 20 Jul 1995, Reno NV (USA). Former names and other names: *International Bowling Federation* – former (1952); *Fédération internationale des quilleurs (FIQ)* – former (1952); *International Skittles Federation* – former; *World Bowling* – former (2014 to 2020). Registration: Switzerland. **Aims** Foster worldwide interest in and development of amateur tenpin bowling and ninepin bowling; promote international friendship among bowlers of different countries through world and zone tournaments and bowling *competitions*; establish rules for the uniform practice of bowling worldwide; promote the Olympic Movement and ensure that official bowling activities meet the requirements of the Olympic Charter. **Structure** Executive Board; Committees (7). Zones: Bowling Federation of Africa; *Asian Bowling Federation (ABF, #01362)*; *European Tenpin Bowling Federation (ETBF, #08899)*; Oceania Bowling Federation; *Pan American Bowling Confederation (PABCON, #18085)*. **Languages** English. **Staff** 1.00 FTE, paid. **Finance** Sources: members' dues. Annual budget: 210,000 USD. **Activities** Awards/prizes/competitions; events/meetings; sporting activities. **Events** *Biennial Congress* Las Vegas, NV (USA) 2019, *Biennial Congress* Las Vegas, NV (USA) 2017, *Biennial Congress* Abu Dhabi (United Arab Emirates) 2015, *Biennial Congress* Hong Kong (Hong Kong) 2011, *Congress* Monterrey (Mexico) 2007. **Publications** *World Bowling Newsletter*. Circulars.
Members National federations, totaling about 12 million individuals, in 114 countries and territories:
Afghanistan, Argentina, Aruba, Australia, Austria, Azerbaijan, Bahamas, Bahrain, Belarus, Belgium, Bermuda, Bolivia, Brazil, Brunei Darussalam, Bulgaria, Cambodia, Canada, Catalunya, Chile, China, Colombia, Costa Rica, Croatia, Curaçao, Cyprus, Czechia, Denmark, Dominican Rep, Ecuador, Egypt, El Salvador, England, Estonia, Ethiopia, Finland, France, Germany, Gibraltar, Greece, Guam, Guatemala, Honduras, Hong Kong, Hungary, Iceland, India, Indonesia, Iran Islamic Rep, Iraq, Ireland, Israel, Italy, Japan, Jersey, Jordan, Kazakhstan, Korea DPR, Korea Rep, Kosovo, Kuwait, Latvia, Lithuania, Luxembourg, Macau, Malaysia, Malta, Mexico, Moldova, Mongolia, Nepal, Netherlands, New Zealand, Northern Ireland, Northern Mariana Is, Norway, Oman, Pakistan, Panama, Paraguay, Peru, Philippines, Poland, Portugal, Puerto Rico, Qatar, Romania, Russia, San Marino, Saudi Arabia, Scotland, Serbia, Singapore, Slovakia, Slovenia, Somalia, South Africa, Spain, Sweden, Switzerland, Syrian AR, Taiwan, Thailand, Tunisia, Türkiye, Turkmenistan, Ukraine, United Arab Emirates, Uruguay, USA, Uzbekistan, Venezuela, Vietnam, Virgin Is USA, Wales.
NGO Relations Member of (5): *Association of the IOC Recognized International Sports Federations (ARISF, #02767)*; *International Masters Games Association (IMGA, #14117)*; *International Paralympic Committee (IPC, #14512)*; *International World Games Association (IWGA, #15914)*; *Olympic Movement (#17719)*. Recognized by: *International Olympic Committee (IOC, #14408)*. [2022/XB6056/**B**]

♦ International Boxing Association (IBA) 12385

Association internationale de boxe

SG Maison du Sport International, Av de Rhodanie 54, 1007 Lausanne VD, Switzerland. T. +41213212777. Fax +41213212772. E-mail: info@aiba.org – communication@aiba.org.
Head of Administration address not obtained.
URL: https://www.iba.sport/

History 28 Nov 1946, London (UK). Replaced the previous *International Amateur Boxing Federation – Fédération internationale de boxe amateur*, which was set up in 1920, Paris (France), and ceased to function during World War II. Former names and other names: *International Amateur Boxing Association* – former (28 Nov 1945); *Association internationale de boxe amateur* – former (28 Nov 1945). **Aims** Regulate boxing in all its forms in accordance with AIBA Statutes, Bylaws, Technical and Competition Rules, Code of Ethics, Disciplinary Code and Procedural Rules. **Structure** Congress (every 2 years); Executive Committee; Commissions (9); Continental Confederations (5): *African Boxing Confederation (ABC, #00228)*; *American Boxing Confederation (AMBC, #00776)*; *Asian Boxing Confederation (ASBC, #01363)*; *European Boxing Confederation (EUBC, #06387)*; *Oceania Boxing Confederation (OCBC, #17653)*. **Languages** Arabic, English, French, Russian, Spanish. **Staff** 16.00 FTE, paid. **Finance** Sources: members' dues. Other sources: hosting fees; international tv rights; product licensee programs. **Activities** Sporting activities. **Events** *Congress* Abu Dhabi (United Arab Emirates) 2022, *Extraordinary Congress* Istanbul (Turkey) 2022, *Quadrennial Congress* Moscow (Russia) 2018, *Quadrennial Congress* Jeju (Korea Rep) 2014, *Supervisors and R and Js Workshop* Incheon (Korea Rep) 2012. **Publications** *Boxing News Magazine* (2 a year) in English; *WSB Yearbook*. Final Reports; championship results.
Members National federations in 197 countries and territories:
Afghanistan, Albania, Algeria, Andorra, Angola, Antigua-Barbuda, Argentina, Armenia, Aruba, Australia, Austria, Azerbaijan, Bahamas, Bahrain, Bangladesh, Barbados, Belarus, Belgium, Belize, Benin, Bermuda, Bhutan, Bolivia, Bosnia-Herzegovina, Botswana, Brazil, Brunei Darussalam, Bulgaria, Burkina Faso, Burundi, Cambodia, Cameroon, Canada, Cape Verde, Cayman Is, Central African Rep, Chad, Chile, China, Colombia, Comoros, Congo Brazzaville, Congo DR, Cook Is, Costa Rica, Côte d'Ivoire, Croatia, Cuba, Cyprus, Czechia, Denmark, Dominica, Dominican Rep, Ecuador, Egypt, El Salvador, England, Equatorial Guinea, Estonia, Eswatini, Ethiopia, Fiji, Finland, France, Gabon, Gambia, Georgia, Germany, Ghana, Greece, Grenada, Guam, Guatemala, Guinea, Guinea-Bissau, Guyana, Haiti, Honduras, Hong Kong, Hungary, Iceland, India, Indonesia, Iran Islamic Rep, Iraq, Ireland, Israel, Italy, Jamaica, Japan, Jordan, Kazakhstan, Kenya, Kiribati, Korea DPR, Korea Rep, Kosovo, Kuwait, Kyrgyzstan, Laos, Latvia, Lebanon, Lesotho, Liberia, Lithuania, Luxembourg, Macau, Madagascar, Malawi, Malaysia, Mali, Mauritius, Mexico, Micronesia FS, Moldova, Monaco, Mongolia, Montenegro, Morocco, Mozambique, Myanmar, Namibia, Nauru, Nepal, Netherlands, New Zealand, Nicaragua, Niger, Nigeria, North Macedonia, Norway, Oman, Pakistan, Palestine, Panama, Papua New Guinea, Paraguay, Peru, Philippines, Poland, Polynesia Fr, Portugal, Puerto Rico, Qatar, Romania, Russia, Rwanda, Samoa, Samoa USA, San Marino, Saudi Arabia, Scotland, Senegal, Serbia, Seychelles, Sierra Leone, Singapore, Slovakia, Slovenia, Solomon Is, Somalia, South Africa, Spain, Sri Lanka, St Kitts-Nevis, St Lucia, St Vincent-Grenadines, Sudan, Suriname, Sweden, Switzerland, Syrian AR, Taiwan, Tajikistan, Tanzania UR, Thailand, Timor-Leste, Togo, Tonga, Trinidad-Tobago, Tunisia, Türkiye, Turkmenistan, Uganda, Ukraine, United Arab Emirates, Uruguay, USA, Uzbekistan, Vanuatu, Venezuela, Vietnam, Virgin Is USA, Wales, Yemen, Zambia, Zimbabwe.
NGO Relations Member of (3): *Association of Summer Olympic International Federations (ASOIF, #02943)*; *International Committee for Fair Play (#12769)*; *Olympic Movement (#17719)*. Cooperates with (1): *International Testing Agency (ITA, #15678)*. Recognized by: *International Olympic Committee (IOC, #14408)*. [2023/XB1156/y/**B**]

♦ International Boxing Federation (IBF) 12386

Main Office 899 Mountain Ave, Ste 2C, Springfield NJ 07081, USA. T. +19735648046. Fax +19735648751.
URL: http://www.ibf-usba-boxing.com/

History 1982, USA. Derives from *World Boxing Association (WBA, #21241)*. Former names and other names: *International Boxing Federation/United States Boxing Federation (IBF/USBA)* – former (1984 to 2018). [2019/XD9036/**D**]

- ♦ International Boxing Federation/United States Boxing Federation / see International Boxing Federation (#12386)
- ♦ International Boxing Union (inactive)

♦ International Boys' Schools Coalition (IBSC) 12387

Communications Dir 2000 Lee Rd, Unit 242, Cleveland Heights OH 44118, USA. E-mail: ibsc@theibsc.org.
URL: http://www.theibsc.org/

History 1995, USA. Registration: USA, Ohio. **Aims** Promote education and development of boys worldwide, professional growth of those who work with them, and advocacy and advancement of institutions – primarily schools for boys. **Structure** Board of Trustees. **Activities** Events/meetings; projects/programmes; research/documentation. **Events** *Annual Conference* Auckland (New Zealand) 2023, *Annual Conference* Dallas, TX (USA) 2022, *Annual Conference* Barcelona (Spain) 2021, *Conference* La Jolla, CA (USA) 2020, *Annual Conference* Montréal, QC (Canada) 2019. **Publications** *The Compass* (4 a year) – newsletter. Research project reports.
Members Schools in 24 countries and territories:
Argentina, Australia, Bermuda, Canada, China, Costa Rica, France, India, Ireland, Japan, Mexico, New Zealand, Nigeria, Peru, Poland, Singapore, South Africa, Spain, Switzerland, Thailand, UK, Uruguay, USA, Zimbabwe. [2022/XJ6530/**C**]

- ♦ International Boys' Town Trust / see International Children's Trust
- ♦ International Børnehjaelp (internationally oriented national body)

♦ International Braille Chess Association (IBCA) 12388

Association internationale des échecs en Braille – Internationaler Blinden Schach Bund

Pres c/o FIDE, Avenue de Rhodanie 54, 1007 Lausanne VD, Switzerland.
Gen Sec address not obtained.
URL: https://www.ibca-info.org/

History Founded 1958, on the initiative of a British national organization and European players. 1st meeting, 1958, Rhein-Breitbach (Germany FR). **Aims** Further contacts between *blind* chess players all over the world; standardize rules of play and special chess sets and other equipment governing play between blind people and between blind people and sighted people. **Structure** General Assembly; Executive Committee. **Languages** English, French, German, Russian, Spanish. **Staff** Voluntary. **Finance** Sources: donations; members' dues. **Activities** Organizes tournaments and championships by post and "across the board". General, World Championships organized so as to have "across the board" championships: for men every non-olympic even year; for women every year after an olympic year; for teams every olympic year; for juniors (under 21) every odd year. **Events** *Congress* Cagliari (Italy) 2019, *Congress* Chennai (India) 2012, *Congress* Heraklion (Greece) 2008, *Congress* Tarragona (Spain) 2004, *Congress* 2000.
Members National Groups; Individuals. Members in 50 countries:
Argentina, Austria, Belarus, Belgium, Bolivia, Bosnia-Herzegovina, Brazil, Bulgaria, Chile, Colombia, Croatia, Cuba, Czechia, Denmark, Estonia, Finland, France, Germany, Greece, Honduras, Hungary, India, Iran Islamic Rep, Ireland, Israel, Italy, Kazakhstan, Lithuania, Montenegro, Netherlands, North Macedonia, Norway, Peru, Poland, Portugal, Romania, Russia, Serbia, Slovakia, Slovenia, South Africa, Spain, Sweden, Switzerland, Türkiye, Turkmenistan, UK, Ukraine, USA, Venezuela.
NGO Relations Affiliated to: *Fédération internationale des échecs (FIDE, #09627)*. [2020/XC1406/**C**]

♦ International Brain Barriers Society (IBBS) 12389

Pres UM-Medical School Duluth, 251 SMed, 1035 Univ Drive, Duluth MN 55812, USA. T. +12187267925.
URL: http://www.ibbsoc.org/

History Registered in accordance with US law. **Aims** Encourage, promote and advocate scientific and clinical research on the biological barriers in the central nervous system (CNS); accumulate information about barriers in the CNS and promote its dissemination to scientists, physicians, patients, policy makers, public and private funding agencies and other concerned parties; educate the general public and medical profession about the existence, diagnosis and treatment of disorders involving the barriers of the CNS. **Structure** Steering Council. **Activities** Events/meetings. **Events** *International Conference on Cerebral Vascular Biology* Uppsala (Sweden) 2023, *Symposium on Signal Transduction in the Blood Brain Barriers* Bari (Italy) 2022, *Symposium on Signal Transduction in the Blood Brain Barriers* Bari (Italy) 2021, *International Conference on Cerebral Vascular Biology* Uppsala (Sweden) 2021, *International Conference on Cerebral Vascular Biology* Miami, FL (USA) 2019. **Members** Individuals. Membership countries not specified. [2017/XM5444/v/**C**]

♦ International Brain Bee (IBB) 12390

Contact 1121 14th Street NW Suite 1010, Washington DC 20005, USA. E-mail: admin@thebrainbee.org.
URL: https://thebrainbee.org/

History 2018. Registration: 170(b)(1)(A)(vi) Public Charity – 501(c)(3), Start date: 18 Jan 2018, USA. **Aims** Motivate students to learn about the brain and inspire them to pursue careers in neuroscience so they can help treat and find cures for brain disorders. **Structure** Board of Directors. **Staff** 1.00 FTE, paid. **Activities** Awards/prizes/competitions. Active in: Albania, Argentina, Australia, Brazil, Canada, Chile, China, Croatia, Egypt, Ethiopia, France, Germany, Ghana, Grenada, Hungary, India, Iran Islamic Rep, Ireland, Israel, Italy, Japan, Kenya, Korea Rep, Latvia, Lithuania, Macau, Malaysia, Nepal, Netherlands, New Zealand, Nigeria, Poland, Romania, Russia, Sierra Leone, St Kitts-Nevis, St Maarten, UK, Ukraine, USA. **NGO Relations** Partner of (1): *International Youth Neuroscience Association (IYNA, #15937)*. Governing partners include: *Alzheimer's Association*; *Federation of European Neuroscience Societies (FENS, #09522)*; *International Brain Research Organization (IBRO, #12392)*. [2022.10.20/AA0237/C]

♦ International Brain Injury Association (IBIA) 12391

Exec Dir MCC Association Mgt, PO Box 1804, Alexandria VA 22313, USA. E-mail: congress@internationalbrain.org.
URL: http://www.internationalbrain.org/

History 1992. Took over activities of *International Association for the Study of Traumatic Brain Injury (IASTBI, inactive)*, 1998. **Aims** Develop and support multidisciplinary medical and clinical professionals, family members, survivors and others who work to improve outcomes, opportunities and successes for persons with brain injury. **Structure** Executive Committee; Board of Governors. **Finance** Sources: donations; sponsorship. **Activities** Awards/prizes/competitions; events/meetings; networking/liaising; training/education. **Events** *World Congress on Brain Injury* Dublin (Ireland) 2023, *World Congress on Brain Injury* 2021, *Biennial World Congress* Toronto, ON (Canada) 2019, *Biennial World Congress* New Orleans, LA (USA) 2017, *Biennial World Congress* The Hague (Netherlands) 2016. **Publications** *International NeuroTrauma Letter* (4 a year); *Brain Injury* (14 a year) – journal.

Members Full in 17 countries and territories:
Australia, Austria, Canada, Denmark, Germany, Iceland, Israel, Italy, Japan, Netherlands, New Zealand, Norway, Spain, Sweden, Taiwan, UK, USA.
General in 4 countries:
Israel, Romania, UK, USA.
Students in 3 countries:
Canada, Israel, USA.

NGO Relations Cooperates with (1): *International Paediatric Brain Injury Society (IPBIS, #14497)*. [2022/XD4888/B]

♦ International Brain Research Organization (IBRO) 12392

Organisation internationale de recherche sur le cerveau – Organización Internacional de Investigaciones sobre el Cerebro

Exec Dir 255 rue Saint Honoré, 75001 Paris, France. T. +33146479292. E-mail: secretariat@ibro.org.
URL: http://www.ibro.org/

History 4 Oct 1960, Paris (France). Founded at a meeting convened on behalf of *UNESCO (#20322)* by *Council for International Organizations of Medical Sciences (CIOMS, #04905)*, a preliminary meeting having been held 1958, Moscow (USSR). Incorporated as an independent international organization, 1961, Ottawa (Canada). By-laws amended 1983, 2000. *Caribbean Brain Research Organization (CARIBRO, inactive)* and *South American Brain Research Organization (SABRO, inactive)* became part of IBRO Regional Committee for Latin America in 2001. **Aims** Develop, support, coordinate and promote scientific research in all fields concerning the brain; promote international collaboration and exchange of scientific information on brain research throughout the world; provide for and assist in education and dissemination of information relating to brain research. **Structure** Governing Council; Executive Committee; Secretariat. Regional Committees (5); General Committees (10). **Languages** English, French. **Staff** 5.00 FTE, paid. **Finance** Sources: donations; members' dues; sale of publications. Other sources: partnerships with other charitable and non-profit organizations. Supported by: Dana Foundation; Dargut and Milena Kemali Foundation; *Federation of European Neuroscience Societies (FENS, #09522)*; *International Bureau of Education (IBE, #12413)*; Japan Neuroscience Society; RIKEN; *Society for Neuroscience (SfN)*; *UNESCO (#20322)*. **Activities** Events/meetings; publishing activities; training/education. **Events** *IBRO World Congress of Neuroscience* Granada (Spain) 2023, *Meeting for Synaptic Function and Neural Circuitry* Busan (Korea Rep) 2019, *Global Neuroethics Summit* Daegu (Korea Rep) 2019, *World Congress* Daegu (Korea Rep) 2019, *World Congress* Rio de Janeiro (Brazil) 2015. **Publications** *Neuroscience* (28 a year) – official journal; *IBRO Reports* – open access journal.

Members National societies (76) in 65 countries and territories:
Argentina, Armenia, Australia, Austria, Brazil, Bulgaria, Canada, Chile, China, Colombia, Congo DR, Croatia, Cuba, Czechia, Denmark, Egypt, Finland, France, Georgia, Germany, Ghana, Greece, Hong Kong, Hungary, India, Iran Islamic Rep, Ireland, Israel, Italy, Japan, Kenya, Korea Rep, Lithuania, Malaysia, Mexico, Mongolia, Morocco, Netherlands, New Zealand, Nigeria, Norway, Oman, Pakistan, Peru, Philippines, Poland, Portugal, Romania, Russia, Serbia, Singapore, Slovakia, Slovenia, South Africa, Spain, Sri Lanka, Sweden, Switzerland, Türkiye, UK, Ukraine, United Arab Emirates, Uruguay, USA, Venezuela.
International and regional members (16):
Academia de Ciencias de América Latina (ACAL, #00010); Dana Foundation; *European Brain and Behaviour Society (EBBS, #06390)*; *Federation of Asian Oceanian Neuroscience Societies (FAONS, #09439)*; *Federation of European Neuroscience Societies (FENS, #09522)*; *Federation of Latin American and Caribbean Neurosciences (FALAN, #09684)*; *International Behavioral Neuroscience Society (IBNS, #12331)*; *International League Against Epilepsy (ILAE, #14013)*; *International Neuroethics Society (INS, #14350)*; *International Neuroinformatics Coordinating Facility (INCF, #14351)*; *International Society of Neuropathology (ISN, #15300)*; *International Society of Psychoneuroendocrinology (ISPNE, #15399)*; *International Union of Physiological Sciences (IUPS, #15800)*; *Mediterranean Neuroscience Society (MNS, #16667)*; *Society for Neuroscience (SfN)*; *Society of Neuroscientists of Africa (SONA, #19608)*. [2023/XC1407/y/B]

♦ International Brain Tumour Alliance (IBTA) 12393

Chair PO Box 244, Tadworth, KT20 5WQ, UK. E-mail: info@theibta.org.
Registered Address c/o Hamlins Llp Roxburghe House, 273-287 Regent Street, London, W1B 2AD, UK.
URL: http://www.theibta.org/

History May 2005, Edinburgh (UK). Founded during World Conference of *World Federation of Neuro-Oncology Societies (WFNOS, #21462)* and *European Association for Neuro-Oncology (EANO, #06132)*. Registration: Companies House, No/ID: 06031485, Start date: 18 Dec 2006, England and Wales. **Aims** Provide support, advocacy and information groups for brain tumour patients and carers in different countries and for researchers, scientists, clinicians and allied health professionals who work in the field. **Structure** Steering Committee. **Staff** Voluntary. **Activities** Awareness raising; events/meetings. **Publications** *Brain Tumour* (annual) – magazine. Electronic newsletter. **Members** Membership countries not specified. **NGO Relations** Member of (7): *European Cancer Organisation (ECO, #06432)* (Patient Advisory Committee); *European Cancer Patient Coalition (ECPC, #06433)*; *European Federation of Neurological Associations (EFNA, #07177)*; *EURORDIS – Rare Diseases Europe (#09175)* (Associate); *Global Cancer Coalitions Network (GCCN, #10270)*; *Rare Cancers Europe (RCE, #18620)*; *Workgroup of European Cancer Patient Advocacy Networks (WECAN, #21054)*. [2021/XM1255/C]

- ♦ International Branch of the YMCA, New York (internationally oriented national body)
- ♦ International Brangus Breeders Association (internationally oriented national body)
- ♦ International Brassinosteroid Conference (meeting series)
- ♦ International Breast Cancer Screening Database Project / see International Cancer Screening Network (#12435)
- ♦ International Breast Cancer Screening Network / see International Cancer Screening Network (#12435)

♦ International Breast Cancer Study Group (IBCSG) 12394

Contact IBCSG Coordinating Center, Effingerstrasse 40, 3008 Bern, Switzerland. T. +41315119400. Fax +41315119401. E-mail: ibcsgcc@ibcsg.org.
URL: http://www.ibcsg.org/

History 1977, as Ludwig Breast Cancer Study Group. Present name adopted 1985. **Aims** Improve prognosis of women with breast cancer. **Events** *Annual Meeting* 2021, *Annual Meeting* Barcelona (Spain) 2020, *Annual Meeting* Vienna (Austria) 2019, *Annual Meeting* Barcelona (Spain) 2018, *Annual Meeting* Vienna (Austria) 2017.

Members Participating centres in 20 countries:
Australia, Austria, Bosnia-Herzegovina, Brazil, Canada, Chile, China, Finland, Hungary, Italy, New Zealand, Peru, Romania, Russia, Slovenia, South Africa, Spain, Sweden, Switzerland, UK.

NGO Relations Member of: *Breast International Group (BIG, #03319)*. [2019.06.13/XJ3518/E]

♦ International Breast Ultrasound School (IBUS) 12395

Founding Pres PO Box 479, Double Bay NSW 1360, Australia. E-mail: info@ibus.org.
URL: http://www.ibus.org/

History 1991. Registration: Switzerland. **Aims** Improve the standards of breast ultrasound through the provision of high-quality educational programmes. **Structure** Executive Council, consisting of Executive Committee (President, Vice-President, Secretary and Founding President), Administration Board and Advisory Board. **Activities** Organizes: International Breast Ultrasound Seminars; International Breast Ultrasound Courses in Ferrara (Italy). **Events** *Workshop on Hot Topics in Advanced Breast Ultrasound* Glasgow (UK) 2014, *International Breast Ultrasound Seminar* Zurich (Switzerland) 2014, *International Breast Imaging Update – IBIU* Zurich (Switzerland) 2001, *Seminar* Vienna (Austria) 2000, *IBIU : international breast imaging update meeting / International Breast Imaging Update – IBIU* Freiburg (Germany) 1999. **NGO Relations** Affiliated with: *Senologic International Society (SIS, #19230)*. [2021/XD7036/D]

♦ International Breathwork Foundation (IBF) 12396

Pres address not obtained. E-mail: vero@almanacer.es.
URL: http://www.ibfnetwork.com/

Aims Provide an opportunity for people world-wide to learn about breathwork and its practice as a *therapeutic* and transformational tool for attaining *health* in body, mind and spirit; encourage quality in breathwork training and practice; support ethics, integrity and professionalism for breathworkers world-wide; offer recommendations for breathwork sessions and training and ongoing development for breathwork practitioners; promote international cooperation and exchange programmes for research and education. **Structure** Board of Directors. **Finance** Member's dues. **Activities** Events/meetings; research/documentation; knowledge management/information dissemination. **Events** *Global Inspiration Conference* Port Elizabeth (South Africa) 2016, *Annual global inspiration conference* Estonia 2004, *Annual global inspiration conference / Annual Conference* Australia 2003, *Annual global inspiration conference* Porlamar (Venezuela) 2002, *Annual Conference* Venezuela 2002. **Publications** *Breathe magazine* (4 a year); *IBF Newsletter* (4 a year). IBF Directory.

Members National Coordinators in 24 countries:
Argentina, Australia, Austria, Belgium, Canada, Denmark, Ecuador, Estonia, France, Germany, Ireland, Israel, Italy, Netherlands, New Zealand, Poland, Russia, Spain, Sweden, Switzerland, UK, Ukraine, USA, Venezuela.

Consultative Status Consultative status granted from: *ECOSOC (#05331)* (Special). [2016/XD6929/f/F]

♦ International Brecht Society (IBS) 12397

Sec-Treas Univ of West Florida, 11000 University Parkway, Pensacola FL 32514, USA.
Pres Modern Languages, 160 Baker Hall, Carnegie Mellon Univ, Pittsburgh PA 15213-3890, USA. E-mail: smb@andrew.cmu.edu.
URL: http://www.brechtsociety.org/

History Founded 1970, by Brecht scholars. Also referred to in German as *Internationale Brecht-Gesellschaft (IBG)* and in French as *Société Internationale de Brecht*. Constitution amended 30 Apr 1977 and 9 Mar 1985; updated 19 May 2010. Registered in the State of Maryland (USA). **Aims** Support *scholarly* and *theatrical* work on the German *author* Bertolt Brecht, his contemporaries, new productions, new research and his influence. **Structure** Steering Committee. **Languages** English, French, German. **Staff** None. **Finance** Members' dues. Royalties. Annual budget: about US$ 13,000. **Activities** Events/meetings. **Events** *Symposium* Leipzig (Germany) 2019, *Symposium* Oxford (UK) 2016, *Symposium* Porto Alegre (Brazil) 2014, *International Symposium* Porto Alegre (Brazil) 2013, *Symposium* Honolulu, HI (USA) 2010. **Publications** *Brecht Yearbook – Das Brecht-Jahrbuch* (annual); *e-cibs – Communications from the International Brecht Society* – journal.

Members Individuals in 28 countries:
Australia, Austria, Bolivia, Brazil, Canada, Colombia, Denmark, Finland, France, Germany, India, Ireland, Italy, Japan, Korea Rep, Netherlands, New Zealand, Norway, Peru, Poland, Russia, South Africa, Spain, Sri Lanka, Sweden, Switzerland, UK, USA.
Nationals in 2 countries:
Germany, USA.

NGO Relations Universities. [2018.10.31/XN4084/E]

- ♦ International Breeders Association (inactive)

♦ International Brethren in Christ Association (IBICA) 12398

Contact 2700 Bristol Circle, Oakville ON L6H 6E1, Canada. T. +19054832335. E-mail: info@theibica.com.
URL: http://www.theibica.com/

History 2005. **Aims** Nurture a common identity, promote a common mission, and provide a common network for the global community of the Brethren in Christ so as to facilitate communication and provide a framework for addressing issues of mutual concern. **Structure** Executive Committee. **Finance** Sources: members' dues. **Events** *Gathering* Asunción (Paraguay) 2009. [2019/XJ7357/C]

- ♦ International Brethren in Christ Fellowship (meeting series)
- ♦ International Brewers' Guild (internationally oriented national body)
- ♦ International Brick and Block Masonry Conference (meeting series)
- ♦ International Bridge League / see European Bridge League (#06402)

♦ International Bridge Press Association (IBPA) 12399

Sec 1322 Patricia Blvd, Kingston ON N9Y 2R4, Canada. T. +15197339247. Fax +4618521303. E-mail: mail@ibpa.com – ibpaeditor@sympatico.ca.
Pres Apt 8E, 22 West 26th St, New York NY 10010, USA.
URL: http://www.ibpa.com/

History 1958, Oslo (Norway). Current statutes adopted 1994. Former names and other names: *European Bridge Press Association* – former (1958 to 1960). Registration: Section 501(c)(3), USA, State of Montana. **Aims** Assist bridge journalists in their bridge related professional activities. **Structure** General Meeting (annual); Board of Directors; Executive Committee; Control Committee. **Languages** English. **Staff** 1.00 FTE, paid. **Finance** Sources: members' dues; sponsorship. **Events** *Annual Meeting* Australia 2021, *Annual Meeting* Kingston, ON (Canada) 2020, *Annual Meeting* Wuhan (China) 2019, *Annual Meeting* Orlando, FL (USA) 2018, *Annual Meeting* Lyon (France) 2017. **Publications** *IBPA Bulletin* (12 a year).

Members Full; Associate; Honorary; Sponsor. Active bridge journalists (400) in 65 countries and territories:
Algeria, Argentina, Australia, Austria, Belarus, Belgium, Bermuda, Botswana, Brazil, Bulgaria, Canada, Chile, China, Colombia, Croatia, Cyprus, Czechia, Denmark, Egypt, Estonia, Finland, France, Germany, Hong Kong, Hungary, Iceland, India, Indonesia, Ireland, Israel, Italy, Japan, Kenya, Latvia, Lebanon, Lithuania, Luxembourg, Malta, Mauritius, Mexico, Netherlands, New Zealand, Norway, Pakistan, Palestine, Philippines, Poland, Portugal, Réunion, Romania, Russia, Singapore, Slovakia, Slovenia, South Africa, Spain, Sweden, Switzerland, Taiwan, Türkiye, UK, Ukraine, USA, Uzbekistan, Venezuela.

NGO Relations Cooperates with (2): *European Bridge League (EBL, #06402)*; *World Bridge Federation (WBF, #21246)*. [2022/XD4421/v/C]

- ♦ International Bridges to Justice (internationally oriented national body)

♦ International Bridge, Tunnel and Turnpike Association (IBTTA) 12400

Association internationale du pont, du tunnel et de l'autoroute à péage

Exec Dir 1146 19th St NW, Ste 600, Washington DC 20036, USA. T. +12026594620. Fax +12026590500. E-mail: bcramer@ibtta.org.
URL: http://www.ibtta.org/

History Founded 1933, USA, as 'American Toll Bridge Association'. Constitution amended and present title adopted 1964. **Aims** Represent the interests of owners and operators of toll facilities and the businesses that serve them; promote advocacy, thought leadership and education for the implementation by members of state-of-the-art, innovative user-based transportation financing solutions to address critical infrastructure challenges. **Structure** Annual Meeting; Board of Directors; Executive Committee; Functional Committees (13). **Languages** English, French, Italian, Spanish. **Staff** 11.00 FTE, paid. **Finance** Members' dues. Meeting registration fees. Annual budget: US$ 4,000,000. **Activities** Knowledge management/information dissemination; research/documentation; advocacy/lobbying/activism; events/meetings. **Events** *Annual Meeting* Seattle,

WA (USA) 2023, *Annual Meeting* Austin, TX (USA) 2022, *Annual Meeting* Anaheim, CA (USA) 2021, *Annual Meeting* Austin, TX (USA) 2020, *Annual Meeting* Halifax, NS (Canada) 2019. **Publications** *IBTTA SmartBrief.* **Members** Operators; Associate; Honorary; Sustaining. Collective bodies and individuals, totalling about 250, in 26 countries. Membership countries not specified. **NGO Relations** Member of: *International Road Federation (IRF Global, #14759).* Cooperates with: *Association Européenne des Concessionnaires d'Autoroutes et d'Ouvrages à Péage (ASECAP, #02559).* [2018.06.01/XC4044/D]

♦ International Brigades (inactive)
♦ International Broadcasters Society (inactive)
♦ International Broadcasting Association / see IBRA Media
♦ International Broadcasting Bureau (internationally oriented national body)
♦ International Broadcasting Convention / see IBC (#11011)
♦ International Broadcasting Society (inactive)
♦ International Broadcasting Trust (internationally oriented national body)
♦ International Broadcasting Union (inactive)
♦ International Broadcast Institute / see International Institute of Communications (#13870)
♦ International Bromine Council / see Bromine Science and Environmental Forum (#03337)
♦ International Broncho-Esophagological Society / see International Bronchoesophagological Society (#12401)

♦ International Bronchoesophagological Society (IBES) 12401

Société internationale de broncho-oesophagologie

Contact 200 1st Street SW, Rochester MN 55905, USA. T. +12848855. E-mail: inquiry@ibesociety.org.
URL: http://www.ibesociety.org/

History 1951, Atlantic City NJ (USA). Also referred to as *International Broncho-Esophagological Society.* **Aims** Promote by all possible means the progress of *bronchology, esophagology* and *laryngology* including diagnostic techniques and endoscopy therapy and current research; permit specialists of different branches of the science to meet and exchange their points of view. **Structure** Congress (every 2 years). **Languages** English. **Staff** 0.50 FTE, voluntary. **Finance** Members' dues: US$ 25. **Events** *World Congress for Bronchology and Interventional Pulmonology* Marseille (France) 2022, *World congress* Florence (Italy) 2016, *World congress* Kyoto (Japan) 2014, *World congress* Cleveland, OH (USA) 2012, *Biennial Congress* Budapest (Hungary) 2010. **Publications** Congress proceedings.
Members Individuals (approx 300) in 35 countries and territories:
Argentina, Austria, Belgium, Brazil, Canada, China, Czechia, Denmark, Egypt, France, Germany, Greece, Hungary, India, Indonesia, Italy, Japan, Korea DPR, Korea Rep, Mexico, Netherlands, Norway, Philippines, Poland, Puerto Rico, Russia, Singapore, Spain, Sweden, Switzerland, Türkiye, UK, Uruguay, USA, Venezuela. [2020/XC1410/v/C]

♦ International Broncho-Pneumologic Association (inactive)
♦ International Brotherhood of Boilermakers, Iron Shipbuilders, Blacksmiths, Forgers and Helpers (internationally oriented national body)
♦ International Brotherhood of Boilermakers, Iron Ship Builders and Helpers of America / see International Brotherhood of Boilermakers, Iron Shipbuilders, Blacksmiths, Forgers and Helpers
♦ International Brotherhood of Electrical Workers (internationally oriented national body)
♦ International Brotherhood of Locomotive Engineers / see Brotherhood of Locomotive Engineers, International

♦ International Brotherhood of Magicians (IBM) 12402

Fraternité internationale des magiciens

Main Office 13 Point West Blvd, St Charles MO 63301-4431, USA. E-mail: ibmsecretary@magician.org.
URL: http://www.magician.org/

History 1922, Canada. Founded as a correspondence society. Incorporated and Officers elected at first Magic Convention, 1926, Kenton OH (USA). **Aims** Promote and advance the *art* of magic; organize and associate individuals interest in magic; advance the ethics of the *profession*; encourage advancement of literature and invention pertaining to the art of magic. **Structure** National chapters, *'Rings'.* **Languages** English. **Staff** 2.00 FTE, paid. **Finance** Members' dues. Budget (annual): about US$ 275,000. **Activities** Annual Convention; regional conventions sponsored by Rings; annual mid-year business meeting. **Events** *Annual Convention* Scottsdale, AZ (USA) 2019, *Annual Convention* Grand Rapids, MI (USA) 2018, *Annual Convention* Louisville, KY (USA) 2017, *Annual Convention* San Antonio, TX (USA) 2016, *Annual Convention* Jacksonville, FL (USA) 2015. **Publications** *Linking Ring* (12 a year) – magazine.
Members Individuals (12,497), mostly in USA, approximately 10 percent being professional magicians, in 105 countries and territories:
Argentina, Aruba, Australia, Austria, Bahamas, Bahrain, Bangladesh, Belgium, Belize, Bermuda, Bolivia, Botswana, Brazil, Bulgaria, Canada, Chile, China, Colombia, Croatia, Curaçao, Cyprus, Czechia, Denmark, Dominican Rep, Ecuador, Egypt, England, Falklands/Malvinas, Fiji, Finland, France, Germany, Gibraltar, Greece, Guam, Guatemala, Hong Kong, Hungary, Iceland, India, Indonesia, Iran Islamic Rep, Ireland, Isle of Man, Israel, Italy, Jamaica, Japan, Kenya, Korea Rep, Lebanon, Lithuania, Luxembourg, Macau, Malaysia, Malta, Mauritius, Mexico, Mongolia, Mozambique, Myanmar, Namibia, Nepal, Netherlands, New Zealand, Nigeria, Northern Ireland, Norway, Oman, Pakistan, Panama, Peru, Philippines, Poland, Polynesia Fr, Portugal, Puerto Rico, Romania, Russia, Saudi Arabia, Scotland, Serbia, Singapore, Slovakia, Slovenia, South Africa, Spain, Sri Lanka, Sweden, Switzerland, Taiwan, Tanzania UR, Thailand, Tunisia, Türkiye, UK, Ukraine, United Arab Emirates, Uruguay, USA, Venezuela, Vietnam, Wales, Zimbabwe.
Also in West Indies. Membership countries not specified.
NGO Relations Member of: *International Federation of Magic Societies (#13473).* [2021/XD4535/v/F]

♦ International Brotherhood of Painters and Allied Trades / see International Union of Painters and Allied Trades
♦ International Brotherhood of Police Officers (internationally oriented national body)
♦ International Brotherhood of Teamsters (internationally oriented national body)
♦ International Brotherhood of Teamsters, Chauffeurs, Warehousemen and Helpers of America / see International Brotherhood of Teamsters

♦ International Bryozoology Association (IBA) 12403

SG Dept Geological Sciences, Univ of Canterbury, Private Bag 4800, Ilam, Christchurch 8140, New Zealand.
URL: http://bryozoa.net/iba/

History 1965, Stockholm (Sweden), as an International Research Group of *International Palaeontological Association (IPA, #14501).* **Aims** Encourage research and interaction among researchers on the *phylum Bryozoa.* **Structure** Advisory Council to the President. **Languages** English. **Staff** Voluntary. **Finance** Members' voluntary fees. **Events** *Triennial Scientific and Business Conference* Liberec (Czechia) 2019, *Larwood Symposium* Cardiff (UK) 2018, *Larwood Symposium* Vienna (Austria) 2017, *Triennial Scientific and Business Conference* Melbourne, VIC (Australia) 2016, *Triennial Scientific and Business Conference* Catania (Italy) 2013. **Publications** *IBA Bulletin* (4 a year); *IBA Review* (every 3 years).
Members Individuals in 48 countries:
Argentina, Australia, Austria, Belarus, Brazil, Bulgaria, Canada, Chile, China, Colombia, Croatia, Cuba, Czechia, Denmark, Egypt, France, Germany, Hungary, India, Ireland, Israel, Italy, Japan, Jordan, Kazakhstan, Korea Rep, Luxembourg, Mexico, Mongolia, Morocco, Netherlands, New Zealand, Norway, Panama, Poland, Portugal, Romania, Russia, Slovakia, South Africa, Spain, Sweden, Switzerland, Thailand, Tunisia, UK, Ukraine, USA.
NGO Relations Scientific member of: *International Union of Biological Sciences (IUBS, #15760).* [2019.02.11/XC0379/v/E]

♦ International Buchenwald-Dora Committee / see International Committee Buchenwald Dora and Commandos (#12749)

♦ International Buckskin Horse Association (IBHA) 12404

Exec Sec PO Box 268, Shelby IN 46377, USA. T. +12195521013. E-mail: ibhainc@sbcglobal.net.
URL: http://www.ibha.net/

History 1971. **Aims** Record and preserve *pedigree* and show record of buckskin, *dun* and *grulla* coloured horses. **Finance** Members' dues. Registration fees. Budget (annual): US$ 200,000. **Activities** Holds annual convention. Hosts annual World Championship Horse Shows for IBHA registered horses. **Events** *Annual convention* Indianapolis, IN (USA) 1999, *Annual Convention* Indianapolis, IN (USA) 1998, *Annual Convention* Indianapolis, IN (USA) 1997, *Annual Convention* Indianapolis, IN (USA) 1996, *Annual Convention* Indianapolis, IN (USA) 1995. **Publications** *Equine National.*
Members Individuals in 9 countries:
Australia, Canada, Georgia, Hungary, Italy, Japan, Netherlands, New Zealand, USA. [2011.07.08/XE3999/v/E]

♦ International Buckwheat Research Association (unconfirmed)

♦ International Buddhist Confederation (IBC) 12405

CEO Room 330, Vigyan Bhawan Annexe, Delhi 110011, DELHI 110011, India. T. +911125084363. E-mail: secretariat@ibcworld.org.
URL: http://www.ibcworld.org/

History Set up Nov 2011, Delhi (India). **Aims** Create a role for Buddhism on the global stage so as to help to preserve this heritage, share knowledge, and promote values; represent a united front for Buddhism to enjoy meaningful participation in the global discourse. **Structure** General Assembly; Supreme Dhamma Council; Council of Patrons, Permanent Steering Committee; Secretariat. **Activities** Events/meetings; knowledge management/information dissemination. [2019/XM6713/C]

♦ International Buddhist Foundation (internationally oriented national body)
♦ International Buddhist Relief Organization (internationally oriented national body)

♦ International Budget Partnership (IBP) 12406

Main Office 750 First Street NE, Ste 700, Washington DC 20002, USA. T. +12026837171. Fax +12024088173. E-mail: info@internationalbudget.org.
URL: http://www.internationalbudget.org/

History 1997. Founded within the Center on Budget and Policy Priorities (CBPP), Washington DC (USA). **Aims** Work to advance public budget systems that work for people, not special interests. **Structure** Board of Directors; Strategic Advisory Council. Offices in: Kenya; Netherlands, South Africa; USA. **Finance** Sources: international organizations. Institutional support from: *Ford Foundation (#09858)*; Open Society Institute; *The William and Flora Hewlett Foundation.* Dedicated support from: *Bill and Melinda Gates Foundation (BMGF).* Additional support from: *Department for International Development (DFID, inactive)*; *Swedish International Development Cooperation Agency (Sida).* **Activities** Financial and/or material support; knowledge management/information dissemination; training/education. **Events** *Partners Meeting* Bangkok (Thailand) 2012, *Partners Meeting* Dar es Salaam (Tanzania UR) 2011, *Partners Meeting* Siem Reap (Cambodia) 2010, *Partners Meeting* Rio de Janeiro (Brazil) 2009, *Partners Meeting* Washington, DC (USA) 2008. **Publications** *Budget Briefs* (periodical) – electronic; *IBP e-Newsletter* (24 a year). *Our Money, Our Responsibility: A Citizens' Guide to Monitoring Government Expenditures* (2008); *A Guide to Tax Work for NGOs* (2006); *Dignity Counts: A Guide to Using Budget Analysis to Advance Human Rights* (2004) – jointly with Fundar and International Human Rights Internship Program; *A Guide to Budget Work for NGOs* (2001). Reports; key papers; case studies. **NGO Relations** Member of (3): *American Council for Voluntary International Action (InterAction)*; *Financial Transparency Coalition (FTC, #09772)*; *Transparency, Accountability and Participation Network (TAP Network, #20222).* Partner of (1): *Every Woman Every Child (EWEC, #09215).* [2022.02.22/XJ0297/E]

♦ International Budo Federation (inactive)

♦ International Budokai 12407

Pres address not obtained. T. +31703651123. E-mail: info@kamakura.demon.nl – internationalbudokai@gmail.com.
URL: http://www.internationalbudokai.com/

History Registered as a foundation in the Netherlands. **Aims** Promote *martial arts* worldwide. **Structure** Board. **Finance** Members' dues. **Activities** Sporting events; events/meetings.
Members Individuals in 10 countries:
Greece, Hungary, Iran Islamic Rep, Italy, Netherlands, New Zealand, Poland, Romania, Slovakia, Türkiye. [2017/XM6240/D]

♦ International Buffalo Federation (IBF) 12408

Gen Sec c/o CREA/ZA, Via Salaria 31, km 26-700, Monterotondo, 00015 Rome RM, Italy. E-mail: info@internationalbuffalofed.org.
URL: http://internationalbuffalofed.org/

History Founded 1985, Cairo (Egypt). Current constitution and by-laws adopted, Oct 1997, Caserta (Italy); reformatted and adopted, 2004, Manila (Philippines). Registered in accordance with Italian law, 11 Oct 2010. **Aims** Advance research and development of buffaloes worldwide. **Structure** General Assembly (every 3 years); Standing Committee; Executive Committee. Regions (5): America; Asia; Europe; Oceania; Africa. Honorary Committee; Permanent Headquarters in Rome (Italy). **Languages** English. **Finance** Members' dues. Contributions from institutes. **Activities** Projects/programmes; research and development; training/education. Active in: Azerbaijan, Bangladesh, China, Indonesia, Iran Islamic Rep, Japan, Thailand, Türkiye. **Events** *Triennial World Congress* Istanbul (Turkey) 2019, *Triennial World Congress* Cartagena de Indias (Colombia) 2016, *Triennial World Congress* Phuket (Thailand) 2013, *Triennial World Congress* Buenos Aires (Argentina) 2010, *Triennial World Congress* Caserta (Italy) 2007. **Publications** *Buffalo Newsletter. Buffalo Livestock and Products* (2013); *Buffalo Production and Research* (2005).
Members Full in 33 countries:
Argentina, Australia, Bangladesh, Bolivia, Brazil, Bulgaria, Canada, China, Colombia, Costa Rica, Cuba, Ecuador, Egypt, Germany, Greece, Guatemala, Hungary, India, Indonesia, Iran Islamic Rep, Iraq, Italy, Mexico, Pakistan, Philippines, Sri Lanka, Thailand, Trinidad-Tobago, Türkiye, UK, USA, Venezuela, Vietnam.
NGO Relations Member of: *World Veterinary Association (WVA, #21901).* [2019/XD1845/C]

♦ International Buffalo Information Centre (internationally oriented national body)
♦ International Builders' Order / see International Association of Building Companions (#11745)

♦ International Building Performance Simulation Association (IBPSA) 12409

Association internationale de la simulation dans la construction

Vice-Pres Plymouth Univ, R Levinsky Bldg 301A, Drake Circus, Plymouth, PL4 8AA, UK.
Sec address not obtained.
URL: http://www.ibpsa.org/

History Former names and other names: *IBPSA World* – alias. **Aims** Advance and promote the science of building performance simulation so as to improve design, construction, operation and maintenance of new and existing buildings worldwide. **Structure** Board of Directors. Committees. **Activities** Awards/prizes/competitions; events/meetings; knowledge management/information dissemination; publishing activities; research and development; standards/guidelines; training/education. **Events** *Building Simulation* Brisbane, QLD (Australia) 2025, *Building Simulation – International IBPSA Conference and Exhibition* Shanghai (China) 2023, *Building Simulation – International IBPSA Conference and Exhibition* Bruges (Belgium) 2021, *Asia Conference* Osaka (Japan) 2020, *BuidSim Nordic* Oslo (Norway) 2020. **Publications** *IBPSA News*; *Journal of Building Performance Simulation.*
Members Categories Regional Affiliates; Individual; Corporate; IBPSA Fellows. Regional Affiliates in 32 countries and territories:
Argentina, Australia, Brazil, Canada, Chile, China, Czechia, Egypt, England, Flanders, France, Germany, India, Indonesia, Iran Islamic Rep, Ireland, Italy, Japan, Korea Rep, Mexico, Netherlands, Poland, Russia, Scotland, Singapore, Slovakia, Spain, Switzerland, Türkiye, United Arab Emirates, USA, Vietnam.
Affiliates also representing Australasia, Danube and Nordic regions. [2023/XD6944/B]

♦ International Bulb Society (no recent information)

♦ International Bull Evaluation Service (INTERBULL) 12410

Contact Dep Animal Breeding and Genetics SLU, Box 7023, SE-750 07 Uppsala, Sweden.
Chairman Vereinigte Informationssysteme Tierhaltung, Heideweg 1, 27283 Verden, Germany. Fax +494231955166.
URL: http://www.interbull.org/

History 1983, as a joint venture of *European Federation of Animal Science (EAAP, #07046)*, *International Committee for Animal Recording (ICAR, #12746)* and *International Dairy Federation (IDF, #13128).* Since 1988 a permanent subcommittee within ICAR. **Aims** Provide the means for correct evaluation and comparison of *cattle* populations on a global basis thereby facilitating and effectively supporting the international trade of *livestock genetic* material (frozen semen, embryos, live animals) among member organizations. **Structure** General Assembly (annual). Steering Committee, comprising 9 members, including Chairman. **Languages** English. **Staff** 8.00 FTE, paid. **Finance** Members' dues. Funds. **Activities** Carried out at *'INTERBULL Centre'*, Sweden, in collaboration with members. **Events** *Joint International Congress on Animal Science* Lyon (France) 2023, *Annual Meeting* Auckland (New Zealand) 2018, *Annual Meeting* Tallinn (Estonia) 2017, *Annual Meeting*

Orlando, FL (USA) 2015, *Annual Meeting* Berlin (Germany) 2014. **Publications** *INTERBULL Bulletin*. Seminar proceedings; newsletters; reports; review documents. Computation of international genetic evaluations of individual bulls (3 times a year). Information Services: Database of animal pedigree and performance information. Provides technical leadership in standardizing information exchange.
Members Organizations in 39 countries:
Australia, Austria, Belgium, Canada, Czechia, Denmark, Estonia, Finland, France, Germany, Hungary, Ireland, Israel, Italy, Japan, Latvia, Lithuania, Luxembourg, Netherlands, New Zealand, Norway, Poland, Portugal, Slovakia, Slovenia, South Africa, Spain, Sweden, Switzerland, UK, USA.
IGO Relations Supported by: *FAO (#09260)*. Contacts with the Zootechnical Committee of: *European Commission (EC, #06633)*. **NGO Relations** Supported by EAAP and IDF. [2014/XE2079/**E**]

♦ International Bullying Prevention Association (internationally oriented national body)
♦ International Bunker Conference (meeting series)

♦ International Bunker Industry Association (IBIA) 12411

Gen Dir 107 Cheapside, London, EC2V 6DN, UK. T. +442039519615. Fax +442033973865. E-mail: ibia@ibia.net.
URL: http://www.ibia.net/
History Oct 1992. Registration: Start date: 29 Jan 1993, UK. **Aims** Provide an international forum to address concerns of all sectors of the bunker industry; improve and clarify industry practices and documentation; increase professional understanding and competence of those working in the industry. **Structure** Board of Directors. **Staff** 5.00 FTE, paid. **Finance** Sources: members' dues. **Activities** Events/meetings; networking/liaising; training/education. **Events** *IBIA Mediterranean Energy and Shipping Conference* Genoa (Italy) 2023, *Annual Convention* London (UK) 2020, *Africa Conference* Cape Town (South Africa) 2019, *Annual Convention* Istanbul (Turkey) 2019, *Sulphur 2020 Countdown Conference* London (UK) 2019. **Publications** *World Bunkering Magazine* (4 a year). Annual Report.
Members Corporate; Individual. Members in 65 countries and territories:
Argentina, Australia, Barbados, Belgium, Brazil, Bulgaria, Canada, Chile, China, Cyprus, Denmark, Ecuador, Egypt, Estonia, France, Germany, Ghana, Gibraltar, Greece, Guatemala, Hong Kong, India, Indonesia, Iran Islamic Rep, Italy, Japan, Kenya, Kuwait, Latvia, Lebanon, Libya, Lithuania, Malaysia, Maldives, Malta, Monaco, Netherlands, Nigeria, Norway, Oman, Pakistan, Panama, Peru, Philippines, Poland, Portugal, Qatar, Romania, Russia, Saudi Arabia, Serbia, Singapore, South Africa, Spain, Sri Lanka, Suriname, Sweden, Switzerland, Thailand, Türkiye, UK, United Arab Emirates, USA, Venezuela.
Also members in West Indies. Membership countries not specified.
Consultative Status Consultative status granted from: *International Maritime Organization (IMO, #14102)*. **NGO Relations** Member of (1): *International Salvage Union (ISU, #14779)*. [2022.10.12/XC0049/t/**C**]

♦ International Bureau of Abstaining Students (inactive)
♦ International Bureau and Action Committee for Civil Defence in War-Time (inactive)
♦ International Bureau Against Alcoholism / see International Council on Alcohol and Addictions (#12989)
♦ International Bureau of Antivivisection Federations and Societies and for the Protection of Animals (inactive)
♦ International Bureau of Associations of Manufacturers, Wholesalers and Retailers of Jewellery, Gold and Silver Ware / see CIBJO – The World Jewellery Confederation (#03923)
♦ International Bureau of the Association of Socialist Youth Leagues (inactive)
♦ International Bureau for Audiophonology / see Bureau international d'audiophonologie (#03362)
♦ International Bureau of Automobile Manufacturers / see International Organization of Motor Vehicle Manufacturers (#14455)
♦ International Bureau of Automobile Standardization (inactive)
♦ International Bureau of Catholic Youth (inactive)
♦ International Bureau of Chambers of Commerce / see World Chambers Federation (#21269)

♦ International Bureau for Children's Rights (IBCR) 12412

Bureau international des droits des enfants – Oficina Internacional de los Derechos de los Niños
Dir Gen 805 rue Villeray, Montréal QC H2R 1J4, Canada. T. +15149327656. Fax +15149329453. E-mail: info@ibcr.org.
URL: http://www.ibcr.org/
History 20 Nov 1994, Paris (France). Founded by Judge Andrée Ruffo (Canada) and Dr Bernard Kouchner (France). **Aims** Contribute to the protection and promotion of children's rights in line with the 1989 United Nations Convention on the Rights of the Child (CRC) and its optional protocols; strengthen capacities of people who work directly with children, whether social workers, members of defense and security forces, officials in the judicial system, civil society groups, government agencies, and organizations in formal and informal private sectors. **Structure** General Assembly (annual); Board of Directors. **Languages** Arabic, English, French, Spanish. **Staff** 30.00 FTE, paid. Voluntary. **Finance** Private contributions (including religious communities); contributed services; government contributions; international organizations' contributions. **Activities** Capacity building; monitoring/evaluation; research/documentation; training/education; guidance/assistance/consulting; advocacy/lobbying/activism; knowledge management/information dissemination. **Publications** Over 110 publications in English and/or Arabic, French, Spanish. Country profiles; toolkits; reports; guidelines. **IGO Relations** Cooperates with: *African Union (AU, #00488)*; *Deutsche Gesellschaft für Internationale Zusammenarbeit (GIZ)*; *International Organization for Migration (IOM, #14454)*; *Japan International Cooperation Agency (JICA)*; *Organisation internationale de la Francophonie (OIF, #17809)*; *UNICEF (#20332)*; *United Nations (UN, #20515)* – Department of Peace-keeping Operations. **NGO Relations** Cooperates with: Child Protection Working Group; *Save the Children Federation (SCF)*; *Terre des Hommes International Federation (TDHIF, #20133)*; *WAO-Afrique (#20816)*; *War Child International (#20817)*; *World Vision International (WVI, #21904)*; national organizations. [2021/XD6846/**D**]

♦ International Bureau for Declarations of Death (inactive)
♦ International Bureau of Differential Anthropology (inactive)
♦ International Bureau for Economic Research on Thermalism (inactive)

♦ International Bureau of Education (IBE) 12413

Bureau international d'éducation (BIE) – Oficina Internacional de Educación (OIE) – Mezdunarodnoe Bjuro Prosvescenija (MBP)
Dir PO Box 199, 1211 Geneva 20, Switzerland. T. +41229177825 – +41229177800. Fax +41229177801.
Street address 15 route des Morillons, Le Grand-Saconnex, 1218 Geneva, Switzerland.
URL: http://www.ibe.unesco.org/
History Dec 1925, Geneva (Switzerland), as an international nongovernmental organization, under the initiative of *World Association for the School as an Instrument of Peace (#21184)*; became the first intergovernmental organization in the field of education by Statutes signed 25 Jul 1929. Integrated with *UNESCO (#20322)*, 1 Jan 1969. Current Statutes adopted by the General Conference of UNESCO at its 15th session, 1968, and amended at 19th, 21st, 24th, 25th and 29th sessions. Also referred to as *UNESCO: International Bureau of Education – Unesco: Bureau international d'éducation*. Enjoys wide intellectual and functional autonomy within the framework of UNESCO. **Aims** Introduce innovative approaches in curriculum design and implementation to improve practical skills and facilitate international dialogue on educational policies and practices. **Structure** Council, comprising 12 member states designated by the General Conference of UNESCO, and including a President and 5 Vice-Presidents from the 6 regional groupings, meets in ordinary session at least once a year. Director, appointed by the Director-General of UNESCO from a list drawn up by Council. **Languages** Arabic, Chinese, English, French, Russian, Spanish. **Staff** 18.00 FTE, paid. **Finance** Voluntary contributions from member states, international organizations, foundations and other bodies; fees for training and research projects. **Activities** Main functions: Observatory of educational structures, content and methods; Promotion of dialogue on educational policy; Capacity-building in curriculum development at national, sub-regional and regional levels; Dissemination of information. Prepares for and organizes sessions of the *International Conference on Education (ICE)*; provides technical assistance for the organization of training programmes, workshops and seminars in curriculum development; functions as an observatory of educational structures, content and methods. **Events** *International Conference on Education – ICE* Geneva (Switzerland) 2009, *International conference on education session* Geneva (Switzerland) 2008, *Séminaire international conjoint* Ouagadougou (Burkina Faso) 2006, *Seminar on adapting curricula* Cotonou (Benin) 2005, *International conference on education "ICE"* Geneva (Switzerland) 2004. **Publications** *Prospects* (4 a year) – international comparative education review; *Educational Innovation and Information* (3 a year); *World Data on Education* (annual) – CD-ROM. *Educational Practices* – series; *IBEdata* – reference series; *Innodata Monographs* – series; *Studies in Comparative Education* – series. Seminar and workshop reports; projects; working papers. **Information Services** *Country Dossiers* – database; *Global Content Bank on Education for HIV/AIDS Prevention* – commenced 2002; *IBEARCH Database* – IBE archives inventory 1925-1968; *IBEDOCS Database*; *IBETHES Database* – thesaurus; *World Data on Education (WDE)* – databank, CD-ROM and online.
Members Governments of 193 countries and territories:
Afghanistan, Albania, Algeria, Andorra, Angola, Antigua-Barbuda, Argentina, Armenia, Australia, Austria, Azerbaijan, Bahamas, Bahrain, Bangladesh, Barbados, Belarus, Belgium, Belize, Benin, Bhutan, Bolivia, Bosnia-Herzegovina, Botswana, Brazil, Brunei Darussalam, Bulgaria, Burkina Faso, Burundi, Cambodia, Cameroon, Canada, Cape Verde, Central African Rep, Chad, Chile, China, Colombia, Comoros, Congo Brazzaville, Congo DR, Cook Is, Costa Rica, Côte d'Ivoire, Croatia, Cuba, Cyprus, Czechia, Denmark, Djibouti, Dominica, Dominican Rep, Ecuador, Egypt, El Salvador, Equatorial Guinea, Eritrea, Estonia, Eswatini, Ethiopia, Fiji, Finland, France, Gabon, Gambia, Georgia, Germany, Ghana, Greece, Grenada, Guatemala, Guinea, Guinea-Bissau, Guyana, Haiti, Honduras, Hungary, Iceland, India, Indonesia, Iran Islamic Rep, Iraq, Ireland, Israel, Italy, Jamaica, Japan, Jordan, Kazakhstan, Kenya, Kiribati, Korea DPR, Korea Rep, Kuwait, Kyrgyzstan, Laos, Latvia, Lebanon, Lesotho, Liberia, Libya, Lithuania, Luxembourg, Madagascar, Malawi, Malaysia, Maldives, Mali, Malta, Marshall Is, Mauritania, Mauritius, Mexico, Micronesia FS, Moldova, Monaco, Mongolia, Montenegro, Morocco, Mozambique, Myanmar, Namibia, Nauru, Nepal, Netherlands, New Zealand, Nicaragua, Niger, Nigeria, Niue, North Macedonia, Norway, Oman, Pakistan, Palau, Panama, Papua New Guinea, Paraguay, Peru, Philippines, Poland, Portugal, Qatar, Romania, Russia, Rwanda, Samoa, San Marino, Sao Tomé-Principe, Saudi Arabia, Senegal, Serbia, Seychelles, Sierra Leone, Singapore, Slovakia, Slovenia, Solomon Is, Somalia, South Africa, Spain, Sri Lanka, St Kitts-Nevis, St Lucia, St Vincent-Grenadines, Sudan, Suriname, Sweden, Switzerland, Syrian AR, Tajikistan, Tanzania UR, Thailand, Timor-Leste, Togo, Tonga, Trinidad-Tobago, Tunisia, Türkiye, Turkmenistan, Tuvalu, Uganda, UK, Ukraine, United Arab Emirates, Uruguay, USA, Uzbekistan, Vanuatu, Venezuela, Vietnam, Yemen, Zambia, Zimbabwe.
Associate members in 7 countries:
Aruba, Cayman Is, Faeroe Is, Macau, Tokelau, Virgin Is UK.
IGO Relations Liaison with all organizations working in the field of education which maintain contacts with UNESCO (not specified). **NGO Relations** Liaison with all the organizations working in the field of education which maintain contacts with UNESCO (not specified). [2017.06.30/XE1427/**E***]

♦ International Bureau of Educational Documentation (inactive)

♦ International Bureau for Epilepsy (IBE) 12414

Bureau international pour l'épilepsie
Main Office Office 208, Nesta Business Park, 4-5 Burton Hall Road, Sandyford, Dublin, CO. DUBLIN, D18 A094, Ireland. T. +35312108850. E-mail: annlittle@ibe-epilepsy.org – ibeexecdir@gmail.com.
Main: http://www.ibe-epilepsy.org/
History 1961, Rome (Italy). Founded at a meeting of *International League Against Epilepsy (ILAE, #14013)*. **Aims** Collect and distribute information and experience regarding the *care* and social concerns of individuals suffering from epilepsy; provide information on how to organize lay societies and how to finance them. **Structure** General Assembly (every 2 years); Executive Committee; Commissions (6). **Languages** English. **Staff** 2.00 FTE, paid. **Finance** Sources: donations; grants; members' dues. **Activities** Awards/prizes/competitions; events/meetings. **Events** *International Epilepsy Congress* Dublin (Ireland) 2023, *Asian & Oceanian Epilepsy Congress* 2022, *Latin American Congress* 2021, *Asian and Oceanian Epilepsy Congress* Dublin (Ireland) 2021, *International Epilepsy Congress* Dublin (Ireland) 2021. **Publications** *International Epilepsy News (IE News)* (4 a year). Annual Report; eZines.
Members Full – national epilepsy associations; Associate; Donor; Corporate. Full members in 101 countries and territories:
Albania, Argentina, Australia, Austria, Bangladesh, Belgium, Brazil, Bulgaria, Cameroon, Canada, Chile, China, Colombia, Congo DR, Costa Rica, Croatia, Cuba, Cyprus, Czechia, Denmark, Dominican Rep, Ecuador, Egypt, Estonia, Eswatini, Ethiopia, Fiji, Finland, France, Gambia, Georgia, Germany, Ghana, Greece, Guatemala, Guyana, Honduras, Hong Kong, Hungary, Iceland, India, Indonesia, Iran Islamic Rep, Ireland, Israel, Italy, Jamaica, Japan, Kazakhstan, Kenya, Korea Rep, Lebanon, Lesotho, Luxembourg, Malawi, Malaysia, Malta, Mauritius, Mexico, Moldova, Mongolia, Morocco, Namibia, Netherlands, New Zealand, Niger, Nigeria, Norway, Pakistan, Panama, Paraguay, Peru, Philippines, Poland, Portugal, Romania, Rwanda, Senegal, Serbia, Sierra Leone, Singapore, Slovakia, Slovenia, South Africa, Spain, Sri Lanka, Sweden, Switzerland, Taiwan, Tanzania UR, Thailand, Tunisia, Türkiye, Uganda, UK, Ukraine, Uruguay, USA, Venezuela, Zambia, Zimbabwe.
Associate members in 23 countries:
Argentina, Australia, Cameroon, Czechia, Denmark, Ecuador, France, Georgia, Germany, Hong Kong, Indonesia, Italy, Japan, Lebanon, Netherlands, Russia, Singapore, Spain, Switzerland, Togo, Uganda, UK, USA.
Consultative Status Consultative status granted from: *ECOSOC (#05331)* (Special); *WHO (#20950)* (Official Relations). **NGO Relations** Member of (2): *Conference of Non-Governmental Organizations in Consultative Relationship with the United Nations (CONGO, #04635)*; *European Federation of Neurological Associations (EFNA, #07177)*. Instrumental in setting up (2): *Epilepsy Alliance Europe (EAE, #05512)*; *European Concerned Action and Research in Epilepsy (EUCARE, inactive)*. Founding member of: *Associations and Conference Forum (AC Forum, #02909)*. Associate member of: *European Patients' Forum (EPF, #08172)*.
[2021.03.03/XB1413/**B**]

♦ International Bureau of the Federations of Master Printers / see Intergraf (#11505)
♦ International Bureau of Filmology (inactive)

♦ International Bureau of Fiscal Documentation (IBFD) 12415

CEO PO Box 20237, 1000 HE Amsterdam, Netherlands. T. +31205540100. E-mail: info@ibfd.org.
URL: http://www.ibfd.org/
History 1938. Former names and other names: *Bureau international de documentation fiscale* – former; *Internationales Steuerdokumentationsbüro* – former; *Internationaal Belasting Documentatie Bureau* – former; *Stichting Internationaal Belasting Documentatie Bureau* – legal name. Registration: Handelsregister, No/ID: KVK 41197411, Netherlands; EU Transparency Register, No/ID: 135950711071-58, Start date: 2 May 2013. **Aims** Serve the international community by collecting, evaluating and disseminating international *tax* data and studying and documenting international taxation systems, and investment *legislation* in a manner which combines scientific objectivity with practical realism. **Structure** Board of Trustees; Team of Management; Secretariat. Academic Council. **Languages** Arabic, Dutch, English, French, German, Hungarian, Italian, Latvian, Polish, Portuguese, Spanish. **Staff** 200.00 FTE, paid. In 40 countries. **Finance** Sources: fees for services; members' dues; subscriptions. **Activities** Events/meetings; guidance/assistance/consulting; knowledge management/information dissemination; training/education. **Events** *Annual Corporate Tax Summit* Vienna (Austria) 2015, *Joint Seminar on Challenges of Reforming Tax and Customs Administrations* Singapore (Singapore) 2012, *Annual conference* Yaoundé (Cameroon) 2002, *International tax aspects of permanent establishments* Amsterdam (Netherlands) 2001, *International tax law summer conference* Rust (Austria) 2001. **Publications** *Asia-Pacific Tax Bulletin* (12 a year); *Bulletin for International Fiscal Documentation* (12 a year) – offical journal; *European Taxation* (12 a year) – journal; *International Transfer Pricing Journal* (6 a year).
Members Members of Board of Trustees in 14 countries:
Austria, Chile, China, France, Germany, India, Italy, Malaysia, Netherlands, New Zealand, Nigeria, Poland, Switzerland, UK.
NGO Relations Instrumental in setting up: *International Tax Academy (ITA, inactive)*. Provides secretariat for: *European Association of Tax Law Professors (EATLP, #06247)*. [2022.06.16/XC1429/**C**]

♦ International Bureau of Information and Cooperation between Music Publishers (inactive)
♦ International Bureau for Information and Enquiries regarding Relief to Foreigners (inactive)
♦ International Bureau for Jewish Education (inactive)
♦ International Bureau of Local Government / see Local Government International Bureau
♦ International Bureau for Masonic Relations (inactive)
♦ International Bureau of New Schools (inactive)
♦ International Bureau of Physico-Chemical Standards (inactive)
♦ International Bureau for Precast Concrete / see Bureau international du béton manufacturé (#03363)
♦ International Bureau for Professional Development (inactive)
♦ International Bureau of Religious Journalists / see International Christian Organisation of the Media (#12563)
♦ International Bureau for Research on Leisure (inactive)
♦ International Bureau for Rock Mechanics / see International Bureau of Strata Mechanics (#12417)
♦ International Bureau of Social Tourism / see International Social Tourism Organisation (#14889)

◆ **International Bureau of the Societies Administering the Rights of Mechanical Recording and Reproduction** 12416
Bureau international des sociétés gérant les droits d'enregistrement et de reproduction mécanique (BIEM)
Head of Secretariat 20-26 bd du Parc, 92200 Neuilly-sur-Seine, France. T. +33155620840. Fax +33155620841. E-mail: info@biem.org.
URL: https://www.biem.org/index.php?lang=en
History 21 Jan 1929, Paris (France). In 1932, became a constituent federation of *Confédération internationale des sociétés d'auteurs et compositeurs (CISAC, #04563)*. Registered in accordance with Article 1832 and following of the French Civil Code. Has also been referred to as *International Federation of Societies of Mechanical Reproduction Rights – Fédération internationale des sociétés des droits de reproduction mécanique*. Statutes most recently modified May 2019, Tokyo (Japan). **Aims** Promote efficient administration of recording and mechanical reproduction rights by grouping together societies administering such rights; defend and develop *copyright* protection in the field; secure protection and administration of repertoires of associated societies in territories not forming part of their territories of exploitation. **Structure** General Assembly (annual); Management Committee; General Secretariat. **Finance** Members' dues. **Activities** Knowledge management/information dissemination; networking/liaising. **Events** *General Assembly* Brussels (Belgium) 2022, *General Assembly* Paris (France) 2016, *General Assembly* Brussels (Belgium) 2015, *Annual seminar for Central and Eastern Europe on good governance* Budapest (Hungary) 2008, *Joint session* Buenos Aires (Argentina) 2008.
Members Associated and adhering societies in 25 countries:
Argentina, Austria, Belgium, Canada, Chile, Croatia, Czechia, Denmark, Egypt, France, Germany, Greece, Hungary, Israel, Italy, Japan, Netherlands, Poland, Portugal, Serbia, Slovakia, Spain, Switzerland, UK, USA.
Included in the above, 1 regional organization:
Nordisk Copyright Bureau (NCB, #17500).
Adhering societies in 15 countries:
Albania, Australia, Bulgaria, Canada, Hong Kong, Indonesia, Korea Rep, Mexico, Nigeria, Romania, South Africa, Trinidad-Tobago, Türkiye, Uruguay.
Consultative Status Consultative status granted from: *World Intellectual Property Organization (WIPO, #21593)* (Permanent Observer Status). **IGO Relations** Memorandum of Understanding signed with: *World Customs Organization (WCO, #21350).* Observer to: *Intergovernmental Committee of the International Convention of Rome for the Protection of Performers, Producers of Phonograms and Broadcasting Organizations (#11474); Council of Europe (CE, #04881); Union for the International Registration of Audiovisual Works (#20444).* **NGO Relations** Member of: *Culture First Coalition (inactive).* [2022/XD1438/**E**]

◆ International Bureau of Spiritualism (inactive)
◆ International Bureau for the Standardization of Man-Made Fibres (#03369)

◆ **International Bureau of Strata Mechanics (IBSM)** 12417
Bureau international de mécanique des terrains (BIMT) – Oficina Internacional de Mecanica de las Rocas (OIMR) – Internationales Büro für Gebirgsmechanik (IBG) – Mezdunarodnoe Bjuro po Mehanike Gornyh Porod (MBMGP)
Chairman c/o Central Mining Institute, plac Gwarków 1, 40-166 Katowice, Poland. T. +48322592600. Fax +48322592640.
History Nov 1958, German DR. Nov 1958, Leipzig (German DR). Since Oct 1971, operates as a permanent international body affiliated to the *World Mining Congress (WMC, #21654)*. Also referred to as *International Bureau for Rock Mechanics – Bureau international de mécanique des roches – Internationales Büro für Gebirgsmechanik (IBG).* **Aims** Carry out effective *rock mechanics* activities for the *mining* industry; encourage international cooperation in the fields of rock mechanics and mining *geomechanics*; stimulate basic research in the area of rock and strata mechanics; study geomechanical problems which arise in mining practice; encourage application of rock mechanics to planning, design and operation of mines; maintain relations with other organizations dealing with problems related to rock mechanics and rock engineering. **Structure** Maintains an independent Secretariat. **Finance** Supported by Central Mining Institute. **Activities** Task Groups, each of several experts, study detailed scientific and technological problems of concern to the mining industry. **Events** *Biennial Plenary Session* Istanbul (Turkey) 2011, *Biennial plenary session* Krakow (Poland) 2008, *Biennial plenary session* Teheran (Iran Islamic Rep) 2005, *Biennial plenary session* Teheran (Iran Islamic Rep) 2005, *Biennial plenary session* Delhi (India) 2003. **Publications** *Geomechanical Criteria for Underground Coal Mine Design* (1995); *Effect of Geomechanics on Mine Design* (1992); *Strata Control in Deep Mines* (1990); *Catalogue of Geomechanical Underground Measuring Devices*; *Dictionary of Mining Geomechanics* – in 13 languages.
Members Individuals (80), prominent scientists and experts in the fields of rock and strata mechanics, in 32 countries:
Australia, Austria, Bosnia-Herzegovina, Brazil, Bulgaria, Canada, China, Croatia, Czechia, Finland, France, Georgia, Germany, Hungary, India, Italy, Japan, Kazakhstan, Kyrgyzstan, Mexico, Papua New Guinea, Poland, Romania, Russia, Serbia, Slovakia, Slovenia, Spain, Sweden, Türkiye, UK, USA. [2009.08.25/XE5516/v/**E**]

◆ International Bureau for the Suppression of Counterfeit Coins (internationally oriented national body)
◆ International Bureau for the Suppression of Traffic in Persons (inactive)
◆ International Bureau of Teachers' Federations (inactive)
◆ International Bureau for the Unification of Penal Law (inactive)
◆ International Bureau of Weights and Measures / see Bureau international des poids et mesures (#03367)
◆ International Bureau for Youth Tourism and Exchanges (inactive)
◆ International Burmese Monks Organization (unconfirmed)
◆ International Business Aircraft Association – Europe / see European Business Aviation Association (#06415)

◆ **International Business Aviation Council (IBAC)** 12418
Conseil international de l'aviation d'affaires – Consejo Internacional de Aviación de Asuntos
Headquarters 999 Robert-Bourrassa Blvd, Suite 16.33, Montréal QC H3C 5J9, Canada. T. +15149548054. Fax +15149546161. E-mail: info@ibac.org.
URL: http://www.ibac.org/
History 15 Jun 1981. Bylaws ratified by founding members, 14 Sep 1981; amended: 22 Nov 1996; 5 Aug 1997. Registration: USA, Washington. **Aims** Represent, promote and protect the interests of business aviation and concerns of operating aircraft companies for the carriage of passengers or goods. **Structure** Council; Governing Board. Planning and Operations Committee; Technical Committees. Divisions, covering global concerns and the following 8 regions: USA and Canada; Caribbean and Mexico to Colombia; Brazil, Peru and Ecuador southwards; North Atlantic, Greenland and Iceland; Europe plus Algeria to Egypt; Africa south of Algeria, Libya and Egypt; Middle East, Southeast Asia and Australia; Pacific Ocean south of Alaska. Headquarters located with ICAO. **Languages** English. **Staff** 4.00 FTE, paid. **Finance** Costs shared among members. **Activities** Centred on 5 strategic objectives: Safety, Security and Efficiency; Equitable Access; Standards and Planning; Presence; Growth. Issues IBAC Aircrew Identification Card and Standard for Business Aircraft Operations (IS-BAO). **Events** *Half-Yearly Board Meeting* Montréal, QC (Canada) 2006, *Half-Yearly Board Meeting* Orlando, FL (USA) 2006, *Half-Yearly Board Meeting* Geneva (Switzerland) 2005, *Half-Yearly Board Meeting* Orlando, FL (USA) 2005, *Half-Yearly Board Meeting* Las Vegas, NV (USA) 2004. **Publications** *IBAC Update. International Standard for Business Aircraft Operations (IS-BAO).* Annual Report; policy/position papers; Business Plan; Strategic Plan.
Members Member organizations in 13 countries:
Australia, Brazil, Canada, France, Germany, India, Ireland, Italy, Japan, South Africa, UK, USA.
African Business Aviation Association (AfBAA, #00231); Asian Business Aviation Association (AsBAA, #01370); European Business Aviation Association (EBAA, #06415); Middle East and North Africa Business Aviation Association (MEBAA, #16776).
Affiliated organizations (over 7,500 commercial firms) in 59 countries and territories:
Antigua-Barbuda, Argentina, Australia, Austria, Bahamas, Barbados, Belgium, Bermuda, Brazil, Canada, Chile, China, Colombia, Costa Rica, Côte d'Ivoire, Cyprus, Czechia, Denmark, Dominican Rep, Egypt, Finland, France, Germany, Greece, Guatemala, Hong Kong, India, Ireland, Israel, Italy, Japan, Jordan, Korea Rep, Latvia, Luxembourg, Malaysia, Mali, Mexico, Namibia, Netherlands, Nigeria, Norway, Philippines, Portugal, Puerto Rico, Romania, Russia, Saudi Arabia, Singapore, Slovenia, South Africa, Spain, St Lucia, Sweden, Switzerland, UK, USA, Venezuela, Virgin Is USA.
Consultative Status Consultative status granted from: *ECOSOC (#05331)* (Ros C). **IGO Relations** Participates in deliberations of: *International Civil Aviation Organization (ICAO, #12581).* [2021/XD0289/y/**C**]

◆ **International Business Congress (IBC)** 12419
Contact Markgrafenstr 23, 10117 Berlin, Germany. T. +493020672703. Fax +493020672704. E-mail: info@ibc-sekretariat.org.
URL: https://www.international-bc-online.org
History Dec 1997, Bonn (Germany). Founded by participants at the Dec 1997 *OSCE Economic Forum*. Former names and other names: *European Business Congress (EBC)* – former (8 Dec 1997 to 28 May 2015). Registration: Germany. **Aims** Promote economic development in the OSCE countries and worldwide. **Structure** General Meeting (annual); Board of Executive Directors; Presiding Committee; Secretariat. **Languages** English, German, Russian. **Staff** 4.00 FTE, paid. **Finance** Sources: members' dues. **Activities** Events/meetings; financial and/or material support. **Events** *Annual General Meeting* 2023, *Annual General Meeting* 2020, *Annual General Meeting* Bonn (Germany) 2019, *Annual General Meeting* New Delhi (India) 2018, *Annual General Meeting* Vienna (Austria) 2017. **Publications** *IBC Newsletter* (2 a year) in English, Russian.
Members Companies (112) in 23 OSCE members states:
Armenia, Austria, Belarus, Belgium, China, Cyprus, France, Germany, Greece, India, Italy, Japan, Lithuania, Netherlands, North Macedonia, Norway, Russia, Serbia, Slovenia, Switzerland, UK, Ukraine, Vietnam. [2021.06.02/XF6311/**F**]

◆ International Business and Economic Development Center (internationally oriented national body)
◆ International Business, Economic Geography and Innovation (unconfirmed)
◆ International Businesses Standards Organization (internationally oriented national body)

◆ **International Business Law Consortium (IBLC)** 12420
Permanent Sec CILS, Matzenkopfgasse 19, 5020 Salzburg, Austria. T. +43662835399. Fax +4366283539909. E-mail: secretariat@iblc.com.
Street Address Matzenkopfgasse 19, 5020 Salzburg, Austria.
URL: http://www.iblc.com/
History Founded 1996, Salzburg (Austria), by *Center for International Legal Studies, Salzburg (CILS).* A proprietary division of the Center. **Aims** Provide clients with independent advice and concerted advocacy, local knowledge and global perspective, experienced counsel and innovative solutions. **Structure** Annual General Meeting; Council. **Languages** Arabic, Chinese, English, French, German, Russian, Spanish. **Staff** 3.00 FTE, paid. **Finance** Members' dues. **Activities** Events/meetings; networking/liaising. **Events** *Annual General Meeting* Stockholm (Sweden) 2019, *Annual General Meeting* Lisbon (Portugal) 2018, *Annual General Meeting* Cincinnati, OH (USA) 2017, *Annual General Meeting* Cardiff (UK) 2016, *Session on environmental policy and public dialogue* Salzburg (Austria) 2003. **Publications** *Corporate Subsidiaries* – reference book. Judgments Portal.
Members Firms (nearly 100) in 63 countries and territories:
Argentina, Australia, Austria, Bahamas, Barbados, Belgium, Bermuda, Bolivia, Brazil, Canada, Cayman Is, Chile, China, Colombia, Cyprus, Czechia, Denmark, Dominica, Ecuador, Estonia, Finland, France, Germany, Ghana, Grenada, Hong Kong, Hungary, India, Indonesia, Iran Islamic Rep, Ireland, Italy, Japan, Kuwait, Latvia, Lebanon, Luxembourg, Malaysia, Mauritius, Mexico, Montserrat, Netherlands, Nigeria, Oman, Palestine, Panama, Peru, Philippines, Poland, Spain, St Kitts-Nevis, St Lucia, St Vincent-Grenadines, Sweden, Switzerland, Türkiye, UK, United Arab Emirates, USA, Venezuela, Virgin Is UK, Virgin Is USA, Zambia.
IGO Relations Consultative status and Observer status with *UNCTAD (#20285)* via CILS. Also Observer status with *United Nations Commission on International Trade Law (UNCITRAL, #20531)* via CILS. [2017.03.09/XF4773/**F**]

◆ International Business and Management Education Centre (internationally oriented national body)
◆ International Business NLP Association (unconfirmed)
◆ International Bus and Lorry Transport Office / see International Road Transport Union (#14761)

◆ **International Butchers' Confederation (IBC)** 12421
Confédération internationale de la boucherie et de la charcuterie (CIBC) – Internationaler Metzgermeister-Verband (IMV)
Dir Rue Jacques de Lalaing 4, Box 10, 1040 Brussels, Belgium. T. +3222303876. Fax +3222303451. E-mail: info@cibc.be.
URL: http://www.cibc.be/
History 1907, as *International Congress of Butchers' Associations – Congrès international de bouchers.* Reconstituted 13 Sep 1946, Amsterdam (Netherlands). Registered in accordance with Belgian law. Current statutes adopted Jan 1991, Brussels (Belgium). Previously referred to in English as *International Federation of Meat Traders' Associations* and as *International Butchery Organization.* New name adopted 1995. **Aims** Promote knowledge and legislation on foodstuffs, with particular emphasis on meat and meat products; defend common interests of the meat trading and catering industry in the areas of vocational training, economic and social policy and industry, commerce and handicrafts policy; represent the affairs of the meat-cutting and catering industry before institutions of the European Union and other associations and organizations; monitor and analyse developments and relevant information; act as a forum for exchange of ideas and experience; promote cooperation with other European associations; promote a permanent exchange of ideas with scientists and consumers on health and nutrition at the European level. **Structure** General Assembly (once a year). General Council's meeting (twice a year), comprising President and 2 representatives of each member country. Presidency also includes 2 Vice-Presidents. General Secretary and Office Manager. Permanent general secretariat in Brussels (Belgium). **Languages** English, French, German. **Staff** 2.00 FTE, paid. **Finance** Members' dues and entry fees. **Activities** *European Meat Forum* annual in Brussels (Belgium). **Events** *Autumn General Assembly* Brussels (Belgium) 2012, *Spring General Assembly* Luxembourg (Luxembourg) 2012, *Spring General Assembly* Amsterdam (Netherlands) 2011, *Autumn General Assembly* Brussels (Belgium) 2011, *Spring General Assembly* London (UK) 2010.
Members National organizations representing small and medium sized enterprises, butchers legally registered in their own countries. Associations (17) in 16 countries:
Austria, Belgium, Denmark, France (2), Germany, Hungary, Ireland, Italy, Luxembourg, Netherlands, Norway, Poland, Spain, Switzerland, Türkiye, UK.
NGO Relations Founding member of: *European Liaison Committee for Agricultural and Agri-Food Trades (#07687).* [2014/XD1954/**D**]

◆ International Butchery Organization / see International Butchers' Confederation (#12421)
◆ International Byron Society / see International Association of Byron Societies (#11750)
◆ International Cabin Crew Association (inactive)

◆ **International Cablemakers Federation (ICF)** 12422
Sec Am Heumarkt 7/6/44, 1030 Vienna, Austria. T. +4315329640. Fax +4315329769.
Events Manager address not obtained.
URL: http://www.icf.at/
History 2 Jul 1990, Vienna (Austria). **Aims** Promote the use of, and increased security and energy-saving in, cable systems; promote and follow trends in design and use of cables; encourage and coordinate research and development programmes for improved utilization and recovery of cable materials, especially considering ecological aspects; develop and improve contact with related wire and cable industries; analyse and collate international statistical data. **Structure** General Assembly (annual); Council; Standing Commission. **Languages** English. **Staff** 2.00 FTE, paid. **Finance** Sources: members' dues. **Activities** Events/meetings. **Events** *Congress* San Francisco, CA (USA) 2022, *Congress* Tokyo (Japan) 2022, *Congress* 2021, *Congress* Tokyo (Japan) 2021, *Annual Congress* 2020. **Publications** *ICF Newsletter* (4 a year).
Members Full in 38 countries and territories:
Argentina, Australia, Austria, Bahrain, Belgium, Brazil, Canada, China, Croatia, Denmark, France, Germany, Greece, Hungary, India, Italy, Japan, Korea Rep, Mexico, Netherlands, New Zealand, Norway, Oman, Poland, Portugal, Russia, Saudi Arabia, Singapore, South Africa, Spain, Sweden, Switzerland, Taiwan, Türkiye, UK, Ukraine, United Arab Emirates, USA. [2021/XC0017/**C**]

◆ **International Cable Protection Committee (ICPC)** 12423
Comité international pour la protection des cables
Gen Manager PO Box 150, Lymington, SO41 6WA, UK.
URL: http://www.iscpc.org/

History 22 May 1958, London (UK), as *'Cable Damage Committee'*. Present title adopted Jun 1967, London. Incorporated into Limited Company, Jan 2005. Widened membership criteria to include Governments, Sep 2010. **Aims** Safeguard *submarine* cables from man-made and natural hazards by serving as a forum for exchange of technical and legal information pertaining to submarine cables and by taking appropriate steps where necessary; draw the attention of interested parties, such as *fishing* and offshore hydrocarbon industries, to the need to share the *seabed*, particularly crowded continental shelves, and to avoid submarine cables in the common interest of all seabed users. **Structure** Plenary Meeting (annual); Executive Committee. **Languages** English. **Staff** None. **Finance** Members' dues (annual): pounds1,500. Contributions. Annual budget: 165,000 GBP. **Activities** Works with other seabed users – especially those involved in the oil industry, fishing, mining and offshore renewables – to agree on the protection of submarine cables Other activities include: publicity; public relations; information exchange; research on an individual basis through research departments/ laboratories of member organizations. **Events** *Plenary Meeting* Madrid (Spain) 2021, *Plenary Meeting* San Diego, CA (USA) 2019, *Plenary Meeting* Cape Town (South Africa) 2018, *Plenary Meeting* Montevideo (Uruguay) 2017, *Plenary Meeting* Dubai (United Arab Emirates) 2014. **Publications** *Fishing and Submarine Cables* – booklet; *Submarine Cables and the Oceans: Connecting the World* – report jointly produced by ICPC and UNEP. Video; PowerPoint Presentations. **Information Services** *WWW Information Page* – central access point to online submarine cable protection information, including a database of submarine cable systems with links to more detailed information.

Members Subject to satisfying the criteria defined with the Membership Agreement, membership available to Submarine Cable Owners, Submarine Cable Maintenance Authorities, Submarine Cable System Manufacturers, Cable Ship Operators, Submarine Cable Route Survey Companies and Governments. Members (124) in 61 countries:

Angola, Aruba, Australia, Bahamas, Bahrain, Cameroon, Canada, Channel Is, China, Colombia, Comoros, Cyprus, Denmark, Faeroe Is, France, Germany, Ghana, Greece, Greenland, Guadeloupe, Hong Kong, Iceland, India, Ireland, Italy, Japan, Korea Rep, Latvia, Malaysia, Malta, Mauritius, Micronesia FS, Netherlands, New Caledonia, New Zealand, Nigeria, Norway, Oman, Papua New Guinea, Philippines, Poland, Polynesia Fr, Portugal, Qatar, Russia, Saudi Arabia, Senegal, Singapore, Somalia, South Africa, Spain, Sri Lanka, Sudan, Taiwan, Tanzania UR, Trinidad-Tobago, UK, United Arab Emirates, Uruguay, USA.

Consultative Status Consultative status granted from: *ECOSOC (#05331)* (Special). **IGO Relations** Memorandum of Understanding with: *International Seabed Authority (ISBA, #14813)*. [2020/XC1441/**C**]

♦ International CAD Conference (meeting series)
♦ International Cadet Class (see: #21760)

♦ International Cadmium Association (ICdA) 12424

Contact ICdA, Avenue de Tervueren 168, Box 4, 1150 Brussels, Belgium. T. +3227760073. Fax +3227760092. E-mail: contact@cadmium.org.
URL: http://cadmium.org/

History Founded 1994, on merger of *Cadmium Association (CA, inactive)*, set up 1976 and *Cadmium Council (CC, inactive)*, formed 1981. The component organizations no longer exist as such but continue to serve regional needs of their member companies as the European and North American Offices respectively. **Aims** Represent the specific cadmium interests of: nonferrous mining industry; producers, processors and distributors of cadmium; manufacturers and marketers of cadmium products; recyclers of cadmium. Further the interests of the industry by market development and by assessment of and response to regulatory and environmental health issues. Collect and disseminate technical information on the properties and uses of the metal, its alloys and compounds. **Structure** Board of Directors. **Languages** English, French, German. **Staff** 1.50 FTE, paid. **Finance** Producers' dues based on production of cadmium metal; other members pay dues based on consumption of cadmium metal. **Activities** Events/meetings; publishing activities; knowledge management/information dissemination. **Events** *International Conference* Lisbon (Portugal) 2016, *Conference* Kunming (China) 2011, *Conference* Prague (Czech Rep) 1998, *Conference* Barcelona (Spain) 1996, *Conference* Geneva (Switzerland) 1994. **Publications** *Management of the Risks Related to Chronic Occupational Exposure to Cadmium and Its Compounds* (2013); *Cadmium Pigments are Green* (2001); *Cadmium: A Problem of the Past, A Solution for the Future* (2000); *Technical Notes on Cadmium Production, Properties and Uses* (1991). Conference proceedings.

Members Miners and cadmium producers; recyclers of cadmium; transformers; nickel-cadmium battery producers; pigments producers; downstream uses and others. Members (33) in 21 countries:

Australia, Belgium, Brazil, Bulgaria, Canada, Czechia, Finland, France, Germany, Italy, Japan, Korea Rep, Mexico, Netherlands, Norway, Peru, Poland, Spain, Sweden, UK, USA.

NGO Relations Member of: *RECHARGE (#18627)*. [2019/XC0040/**D**]

♦ International Calicivirus Conference (meeting series)
♦ International CALL Research Conference (meeting series)

♦ International Camellia Society (ICS) 12425

Société internationale du camelia

Pres Kunming Inst of Botany, 132 Lanhei Road, Heilongtan, Kunming, 650204 Yunnan, China. E-mail: guanky@mail.kib.ac.cn.
URL: http://www.internationalcamellia.org/

History Apr 1962. **Aims** Promote the genus 'Camellia'. **Structure** Officers: President, 4 Vice-Presidents, Registrar, Secretary, Treasurer, Membership Registrar, Editor; Regional Directors. **Languages** English. **Staff** Voluntary. **Finance** Sources: members' dues. **Activities** Events/meetings; knowledge management/information dissemination. **Events** *International Camellia Congress* Lucca (Italy) 2023, *International Camellia Congress* Japan 2020, *Biennial Congress* Nantes (France) 2018, *Biennial Congress* Dali (China) 2016, *Biennial Congress* Pontevedra (Spain) 2014. **Publications** *International Camellia Journal* (annual). *International Register of the Genus Camellia* (2011).

Members Camellia enthusiasts, nurserymen, scientists (about 2,000) in 33 countries and territories:

Australia, Austria, Belgium, Canada, Channel Is, China, Croatia, Czechia, Denmark, Eswatini, France, Germany, Hungary, India, Ireland, Italy, Japan, Korea Rep, Luxembourg, Netherlands, New Zealand, Norway, Portugal, Slovenia, South Africa, Spain, Sweden, Switzerland, Taiwan, UK, USA, Vietnam, Zimbabwe. [2020/XD5848/v/**C**]

♦ International Campaign to Abolish Nuclear Weapons (ICAN) 12426

Exec Dir Pl de Cornavin 2, 1201 Geneva, Switzerland. T. +41227882063. E-mail: office@icanw.org – info@icanw.org.
Asia Office PO Box 1379, Carlton VIC 3053, Australia.
URL: http://www.icanw.org/

History Apr 2007, Austria. Initial activities began in Australia. Formally launched April 2007, Austria. Recipient of the 2017 Nobel Peace Prize. Registration: Switzerland; EU Transparency Register, No/ID: 139811437603-09. **Aims** Mobilize people in all countries to inspire, persuade and pressure their governments to initiate negotiations for a treaty banning nuclear weapons. **Structure** International Steering Group. **Events** *International Conference on the Humanitarian Impact of Nuclear Weapons* Mexico 2014, *Civil Society Forum* Vienna (Austria) 2014, *International Conference on the Humanitarian Impact of Nuclear Weapons* Vienna (Austria) 2014, *Conference* Oslo (Norway) 2013, *International Conference on the Humanitarian Impact of Nuclear Weapons* Oslo (Norway) 2013.

Members Partners in 197 countries and territories:

Afghanistan, Albania, Algeria, Andorra, Angola, Antigua-Barbuda, Argentina, Armenia, Australia, Austria, Azerbaijan, Bahamas, Bahrain, Bangladesh, Barbados, Belarus, Belgium, Belize, Benin, Bhutan, Bolivia, Bosnia-Herzegovina, Botswana, Brazil, Brunei Darussalam, Bulgaria, Burkina Faso, Burundi, Cambodia, Cameroon, Canada, Cape Verde, Central African Rep, Chad, Chile, China, Colombia, Comoros, Congo Brazzaville, Congo DR, Cook Is, Costa Rica, Côte d'Ivoire, Croatia, Cuba, Cyprus, Czechia, Denmark, Djibouti, Dominica, Dominican Rep, Ecuador, Egypt, El Salvador, Equatorial Guinea, Eritrea, Estonia, Eswatini, Ethiopia, Fiji, Finland, France, Gabon, Gambia, Georgia, Germany, Ghana, Greece, Grenada, Guam, Guatemala, Guinea, Guinea-Bissau, Guyana, Haiti, Holy See, Honduras, Hungary, Iceland, India, Indonesia, Iran Islamic Rep, Iraq, Ireland, Israel, Italy, Jamaica, Japan, Jordan, Kazakhstan, Kenya, Kiribati, Korea DPR, Korea Rep, Kuwait, Kyrgyzstan, Laos, Latvia, Lebanon, Lesotho, Liberia, Libya, Liechtenstein, Lithuania, Luxembourg, Madagascar, Malawi, Malaysia, Maldives, Mali, Malta, Marshall Is, Mauritania, Mauritius, Mexico, Micronesia FS, Moldova, Monaco, Mongolia, Montenegro, Morocco, Mozambique, Myanmar, Namibia, Nauru, Nepal, Netherlands, New Zealand, Nicaragua, Niger, Nigeria, Niue, Norway, Oman, Pakistan, Palau, Palestine, Panama, Papua New Guinea, Paraguay, Peru, Philippines, Poland, Portugal, Qatar, Romania, Russia, Rwanda, Samoa, San Marino, Sao Tomé-Principe, Saudi Arabia, Senegal, Serbia, Seychelles, Sierra Leone, Singapore, Slovakia, Slovenia, Solomon Is, Somalia, South Africa, South Sudan, Spain, Sri Lanka, St Kitts-Nevis, St Lucia, St Vincent-Grenadines, Sudan, Suriname, Sweden, Switzerland, Syrian AR, Tajikistan, Tanzania UR, Thailand, Timor-Leste, Togo, Tonga, Trinidad-Tobago, Tunisia, Türkiye, Turkmenistan, Tuvalu, Uganda, UK, Ukraine, United Arab Emirates, Uruguay, USA, Uzbekistan, Vanuatu, Venezuela, Vietnam, Yemen, Zambia, Zimbabwe.

Included in the above, 2 organizations listed in this Yearbook:
Article 36; *Norwegian Peace Association (NPA)*.

International partners include 27 organizations listed in this Yearbook:
- *Abolition 2000 – Global Network to Eliminate Nuclear Weapons (Abolition 2000, #00006)*;
- *Amplify (#00805)*;
- *European Youth Network for Nuclear Disarmament (BANg, #09143)*;
- *Global Partnership for the Prevention of Armed Conflict (GPPAC, #10538)*;
- *International Association of Lawyers Against Nuclear Arms (IALANA, #11994)*;
- *International Association of Peace Messenger Cities (IAPMC, #12073)*;
- *International Association of World Peace Advocates (IAWPA, #12281)*;
- *International Fellowship of Reconciliation (IFOR, #13586)*;
- *International Network of Engineers and Scientists for Global Responsibility (INES, #14260)*;
- *International Peace Bureau (IPB, #14535)*;
- *International Physicians for the Prevention of Nuclear War (IPPNW, #14578)*;
- *International Trade Union Confederation (ITUC, #15708)*;
- *International Union of Socialist Youth (IUSY, #15815)*;
- *Inter Press Service (IPS, #15964)*;
- *Mayors for Peace (#16605)*;
- *Nobel Women's Initiative (#17144)*;
- *PAX*;
- *Pax Christi – International Catholic Peace Movement (#18266)*;
- *Religions for Peace (RfP, #18831)*;
- *Seguridad Humana en América Latina y el Caribe (SEHLAC, #19218)*;
- *Soka Gakkai International (SGI, #19672)*;
- *UNI Global Union (#20338)*;
- *Women's International League for Peace and Freedom (WILPF, #21024)*;
- *World Council of Churches (WCC, #21320)*;
- *World Federation of Public Health Associations (WFPHA, #21476)*;
- *World Federation of United Nations Associations (WFUNA, #21499)*;
- *World without Wars and Violence (WwW)*. [2021/XJ8305/y/**F**]

♦ International Campaign for Abortion Rights / see Women's Global Network for Reproductive Rights (#21019)

♦ International Campaign to Ban Landmines – Cluster Munition Coalition (ICBL-CMC) 12427

Dir c/o Ecumenical Centre, Route de Ferney 150, PO Box 2100, 1211 Geneva 2, Switzerland. E-mail: info@icblcmc.org.
URL: http://www.icblcmc.org/

History 2011. Founded on merger of *International Campaign to Ban Landmines (ICBL, inactive)* and *Cluster Munition Coalition (CMC, inactive)*. **Aims** Ensure full implementation of the international treaties banning cluster munitions and landmines, stop casualties, and assist survivors. **Structure** Governance Board; Advisory Committee. Consists of: *International Campaign to Ban Landmines*; *Cluster Munition Coalition*; *Landmine and Cluster Munititon Monitor*. **Finance** Sources: contributions; government support; international organizations. Contributions from various governments and organizations, including: Governments of Australia, Austria, Belgium, Canada, Germany, Holy See, Luxembourg, New Zealand, Norway, Sweden, Switzerland, USA. **Activities** Advocacy/lobbying/activism; awareness raising; research/documentation. **Publications** *Cluster Munition Monitor* (annual); *Landmine Monitor* (annual).

Members Organizations in 110 countries and territories:

Afghanistan, Albania, Algeria, Angola, Argentina, Armenia, Australia, Austria, Azerbaijan, Bahrain, Bangladesh, Belarus, Belgium, Bosnia-Herzegovina, Brazil, Cambodia, Cameroon, Canada, Chad, Chile, Colombia, Congo DR, Croatia, Denmark, Djibouti, Egypt, El Salvador, Eritrea, Ethiopia, Fiji, Finland, France, Gambia, Georgia, Germany, Ghana, Grenada, Guinea-Bissau, India, Indonesia, Iran Islamic Rep, Iraq, Ireland, Israel, Italy, Japan, Jordan, Kenya, Korea Rep, Kosovo, Kuwait, Kyrgyzstan, Laos, Latvia, Lebanon, Liberia, Libya, Malawi, Mali, Mexico, Mongolia, Mozambique, Myanmar, Nepal, Netherlands, New Zealand, Nicaragua, Nigeria, North Macedonia, Norway, Pakistan, Palestine, Paraguay, Peru, Philippines, Russia, Rwanda, Sahara West, Senegal, Serbia, Sierra Leone, Slovakia, Slovenia, Somalia, South Africa, South Sudan, Spain, Sri Lanka, Sudan, Sweden, Switzerland, Syrian AR, Taiwan, Tajikistan, Thailand, Togo, Tonga, Trinidad-Tobago, Türkiye, Tuvalu, Uganda, UK, Ukraine, Uruguay, USA, Vanuatu, Venezuela, Vietnam, Zambia, Zimbabwe.

Included in the above, 93 organizations listed in this Yearbook:
- *Action Against Hunger (#00086)*;
- *ADD International*;
- *African Charitable Society for Mother and Child Care (ACSMCC, no recent information)*;
- *Amnesty International (AI, #00801)*;
- *Anti-Persoonsmijnen Ontmijnende Productontwikkeling (APOPO)*;
- *Article 36*;
- *Asian Disaster Preparedness Center (ADPC, #01426)*;
- *Association for Aid and Relief – Japan (AAR)*;
- *Australian Centre for Peace and Conflict Studies (ACPACS, no recent information)*;
- *Australian Council for International Development (ACFID)*;
- *Baltic International Centre of Human Education – Cooperation for Peace (CfP, no recent information)*;
- *Broederlijk Delen*;
- *Brücke-Le pont*;
- *Campaign Against Arms Trade (CAAT)*;
- *Campaign for International Cooperation and Disarmament (CICD)*;
- *Canadian International Demining Corps (CIDC)*;
- *Catholic Organization for Relief and Development (Cordaid)*;
- *Center for Civilians in Conflict (CIVIC)*;
- *Centre for Humanitarian Dialogue (The HD Centre)*;
- *Centre for Peace and Development Studies, Limerick*;
- *Christian World Service (CWS)*;
- *Clear Path International (CPI)*;
- *CNCD Opération 11 11 11*;
- *Commission Tiers-Monde de l'Eglise catholique, Genève (COTMEC)*;
- *Concern Worldwide*;
- *Cooperation Canada*;
- *Coordination SUD*;
- *Délégation catholique pour la coopération (DCC)*;
- *Entraide et fraternité*;
- *Finn Church Aid (FCA)*;
- *Folkekirkens Nødhjaelp (FKN)*;
- *Fonds voor Ontwikkelingssamenwerking – Socialistische Solidariteit (FOS)*;
- *Foundation for Peace*;
- *Foundation for Security and Development in Africa (FOSDA)*;
- *Foundation World Without Mines (WOM)*;
- *Fund for Reconciliation and Development (FRD)*;
- *Geneva Call*;
- *Geneva International Peace Research Institute (GIPRI)*;
- *Global Action to Prevent War (GAWP)*;
- *Global Health Foundation (GHF)*;
- *Groupe de recherche et d'information sur la paix et la sécurité (GRIP)*;
- *Humanity and Inclusion (HI, #10975)*;
- *Human Rights Watch (HRW, #10990)*;
- *Ignitus Worldwide*;
- *International Club for Peace Research (ICPR, no recent information)*;
- *International Coalition to Ban Uranium Weapons (ICBUW, #12609)*;
- *International Peace Bureau (IPB, #14535)*;
- *Islamic Relief Agency (ISRA, inactive)*;
- *Islamic Relief Worldwide (IRWW, #16048)*;
- *Japan International Volunteer Centre (JVC)*;
- *Jesuit Refugee Service Europe (JRS Europe, #16107)*;
- *Landmine Survivors Network (LSN)*;
- *Médecins du Monde – International (MDM, #16613)*;
- *Medicus Mundi International – Network Health for All (MMI, #16636)*;
- *Mercy Corps International (MCI)*;
- *Nonviolence International (NI, #17152)*;
- *Norwegian People's Aid (NPA)*;
- *Observatoire des armements / CDRPC*;
- *Oxfam Australia*;

- *Oxfam GB*;
- *Oxfam International (#17922)*;
- *Oxfam Novib*;
- *Pacific Foundation for the Advancement of Women (PACFAW, #17950)*;
- *Pacific Peace Working Group (PPWG, #17988)*;
- *Parliamentary Forum on Small Arms and Light Weapons (Parliamentary Forum on SALW, #18218)*;
- *Partage – avec les enfants du monde (Partage)*;
- *PAX*;
- *Pax Christi – International Catholic Peace Movement (#18266)*;
- *Peace Union of Finland*;
- *Physicians for Global Survival, Canada (PGS)*;
- *POWER International*;
- *Première Urgence Internationale*;
- *Project Ploughshares*;
- *Refugee Children of the World (ERM)*;
- *Religions for Peace (RfP, #18831)*;
- *Reporters sans frontières (RSF, #18846)*;
- *Servicio Tercer Mundo (SETEM)*;
- *Soldiers of Peace International Association (SPIA, #19678)*;
- *Solidaritätsdienst International (SODI)*;
- *Soroptimist International of Great Britain and Ireland (SIGBI, #19690)*;
- *Southern African Centre for the Constructive Resolution of Disputes (SACCORD)*;
- *Surpaz*;
- *Swedish Peace and Arbitration Society (SPAS)*;
- *Swissaid*;
- *Swiss Interchurch Aid (EPER)*;
- *Trocaire – Catholic Agency for World Development*;
- *Union Aid Abroad-APHEDA*;
- *Voluntary Service Overseas (VSO)*;
- *West Africa Network for Peacebuilding (WANEP, #20878)*;
- *Women's International League for Peace and Freedom (WILPF, #21024)*;
- *World Organisation Against Torture (OMCT, #21685)*;
- *World Renew*.

IGO Relations Supports (1): *Convention on Cluster Munitions (CCM, 2008)*. [2021.12.16/XM4895/y/**F**]

♦ International Campaign to End Genocide / see Alliance Against Genocide (#00655)

♦ International Campaign for Establishment and Development of Oncology Centres (ICEDOC) 12428

Pres Borg Alsafwa Centre, 3 Algeish Str, Port Said, 42111, Egypt. T. +2066332758. Fax +19282442696. E-mail: worldcooperation@gmail.com.
SG 18954 State Hwy 16 North, Medina TX 78055, USA.
URL: http://www.icedoc.org/

History 1996, Vienna (Austria). Registered in the State of Texas (USA), 1999. **Aims** Increase *cancer prevention*, *treatment* and *care* worldwide; decrease *morbidity* and *mortality* of cancer. **Structure** Board, comprising President, Vice-President, Secretary-General and Treasurer. *'ICEDOC Experts in Cancer Without Borders'*, composed of 120 volunteer experts and advisors of cancer worldwide. **Activities** Offers free of charge consultations, workshops and missions to: enhance cancer management programmes and treatment; promote optimal cancer control and care to be tailored according to each different underserved region; share in the efforts for continuing education for professionals and public in underserved regions of the world; help in building a constructive collaboration of oncology professionals and manufacturers of pharmaceuticals and radiation equipment through raising common interests that could result in increasing the fraction of cancer patients receiving reasonable cancer management around the globe. Current programmes: establish and secure organizational viability through solicitation of financial support; broaden the network of expert volunteers in all aspects of cancer prevention, treatment and care; establish and maintain cooperative and collaborative partnerships with professional and non-profit organizations and industry that further the mission of ICEDOC. Launched a campaign to form and *'International Strategy Group for Palliative Care of Cancer and Severe Chronic Illness'* with the objective of helping local professionals around the world in creation of palliative care programmes in many countries that lack such programmes. **Events** *Meeting* Izmir (Turkey) 2002, *Meeting* Vienna (Austria) 2000, *Meeting* Vienna (Austria) 1999, *Meeting* Los Angeles, CA (USA) 1998, *Meeting* Hamburg (Germany) 1997. **Publications** *Cancerologists Without Borders* – online bulletin. Annual (written) Report.

Members Organizations in 4 countries:
Belgium, Egypt, India, USA.
Individuals in 43 countries:
Algeria, Argentina, Australia, Austria, Belgium, Bolivia, Brazil, Canada, China, Czechia, Denmark, Egypt, France, Georgia, Germany, Greece, Honduras, Iceland, India, Italy, Japan, Korea Rep, Kuwait, Lebanon, Lithuania, Mexico, Morocco, Netherlands, Nigeria, Oman, Pakistan, Panama, Poland, Russia, Saudi Arabia, South Africa, Switzerland, Tanzania UR, Thailand, Türkiye, UK, USA, Vietnam.

NGO Relations Affiliate of: *International Psycho-Oncology Society (IPOS, #14665)*. [2018/XE4485/**E**]

♦ International Campaign for Responsible Technology (internationally oriented national body)
♦ International Campaign to Save Lake Chad (inactive)

♦ International Campaign for Tibet (ICT) 12429

Main Office 1825 Jefferson Pl NW, Washington DC 20036, USA. T. +12027851515. Fax +12027854343. E-mail: info@savetibet.org.
URL: http://www.savetibet.org/

History 1988, Washington DC (USA). EU Transparency Register: 40839587237-49. Registration: No/ID: 52-1570071, USA. **Aims** Monitor and promote internationally recognized *human rights*, *democratic freedoms* and *self-determination* for Tibetans and protect their culture and environment. **Structure** Board of Directors of 14 members. Board of Advisors. International Council of Advisors. Offices in: Amsterdam (Netherlands); Berlin (Germany); Brussels (Belgium); London (UK); Washington DC (USA). **Staff** 19.00 FTE, paid. **Finance** Members' dues. Other source: donations. **Activities** Conducts fact-finding missions to Tibet, India and Nepal; monitors and investigates human rights conditions; testifies before national and international bodies; promotes news coverage of issues in Tibet. China Project: networks with exiled Chinese democracy and overseas Chinese organizations, works with Chinese language media, conducts research on Chinese rule of Tibet. Contacts with academic, civic and community groups. **Publications** *Tibet Press Watch (TPW)* (3 a year); *Refugee Report* (annual); *Action Alerts*. Media reports; brochures; videos.

Members Individuals (mostly in USA) Full; International Member; Supporter; Sponsor; Donor; Patron. Members in 67 countries and territories:
Australia, Bahamas, Barbados, Belarus, Belgium, Belize, Brazil, Bulgaria, Canada, Chile, China, Colombia, Costa Rica, Croatia, Cyprus, Czechia, Denmark, Dominican Rep, Ecuador, Egypt, Estonia, Finland, France, Germany, Greece, Guatemala, Honduras, Hong Kong, Hungary, Iceland, India, Ireland, Israel, Italy, Japan, Latvia, Liechtenstein, Lithuania, Mexico, Monaco, Mongolia, Nepal, Netherlands, New Zealand, Norway, Panama, Peru, Philippines, Poland, Portugal, Puerto Rico, Russia, Serbia-Montenegro, Slovakia, Slovenia, South Africa, Spain, Sri Lanka, Sweden, Switzerland, Taiwan, Thailand, Türkiye, UK, Ukraine, USA, Venezuela.

NGO Relations Cooperates with: *Unrepresented Nations and Peoples Organization (UNPO, #20714)*. Member of: *International Federation for Human Rights (#13452)*; *World Heritage Watch (WHW)*. [2020/XF3798/v/**F**]

♦ International Campaign for Women's Right to Safe Abortion 12430

Registered Office c/o Promsex, Av José Pardo 601, Oficina 604, Miraflores, 18, Lima, Peru. E-mail: info@safeabortionwomensright.org.
URL: http://www.safeabortionwomensright.org/

History Launched May 2012, when replaced *International Consortium for Medical Abortion (ICMA, inactive)*. **Aims** Build an international campaign to promote universal access to safe, legal abortion as a women's health and human rights issue; support women's autonomy to make their own decisions whether and when to have children and have access to the means of acting on those decisions without risk to their health and lives. **Languages** English, French, Spanish. **Activities** Advocacy/lobbying/activism; publishing activities; knowledge management/information dissemination. **Publications** Newsletter; guidelines; blog; research reports; statements; social media. **Members** Organizations and individuals (about 1,480) in 126 countries and territories worldwide. [2020.01.15/XM5273/**F**]

♦ International Camping Fellowship (ICF) 12431

Secretariat 1844 Ravenscliffe Road, Huntsville ON P1H 2N2, Canada. T. +17057895612. Fax +17057896624. E-mail: info@icfconnect.net – communications@icfconnect.net.
URL: https://icfconnect.net/

History 1987. *Asia Oceania Camping Fellowship (AOCF, inactive)* merged into ICF to became ICF-Asia Oceania, 2016. **Aims** Coordinate the exchange of news and information between individuals, camps, outdoors experiences and organizations in different countries; encourage and facilitate bilateral and multilateral exchanges; stimulate efforts to achieve international understanding and global living, leadership, and ecological action through organized camping and outdoor experience; encourage the organization of regional and national camping associations. **Structure** Board. **Activities** Events/meetings. **Events** *International Camping Congress* Tarragona (Spain) 2023, *International Camping Congress* Beijing (China) 2020, *International Camping Congress* Sochi (Russia) 2017, *International Camping Congress* Antalya (Turkey) 2014, *International Camping Congress* Hong Kong (Hong Kong) 2011. **Publications** *ICF Newsletter*.

Members Camps and organizations in 36 countries and territories:
Australia, Bermuda, Bosnia-Herzegovina, Brazil, Canada, China, Colombia, Costa Rica, Georgia, Germany, Greece, Hong Kong, Ireland, Italy, Japan, Kenya, Korea Rep, Liberia, Malaysia, Mexico, Mongolia, Nigeria, Pakistan, Palestine, Philippines, Poland, Russia, Serbia, Singapore, Switzerland, Taiwan, Türkiye, UK, Ukraine, USA, Venezuela. [2022/XJ6653/**F**]

♦ International Canals and Waterways Organization (inactive)
♦ International Cancer Advocacy Network (unconfirmed)

♦ International Cancer Genome Consortium (ICGC) 12432

Contact address not obtained. E-mail: info@icgc.org.
URL: http://icgc.org/

Aims Obtain a comprehensive description of genomic, transcriptomic and epigenomic changes in 50 different tumor types and/or subtypes which are of clinical and societal importance across the globe. **Structure** International Scientific Steering Committee; Executive Committee. Committees; Working Groups. **Activities** Knowledge management/information dissemination; research/documentation. **Events** *Scientific Workshop* Beijing (China) 2021, *Scientific Workshop* Goyang (Korea Rep) 2020, *Scientific Workshop* Glasgow (UK) 2019, *Scientific Workshop* Paris (France) 2018, *Scientific Workshop* Seoul (Korea Rep) 2017. **NGO Relations** Member of: *Global Alliance for Genomics and Health (GA4GH, #10199)*. [2019/XM6738/**C**]

♦ International Cancer Imaging Society (ICIS) 12433

Gen Manager 45 Queen Anne St, London, W1G 9JF, UK. T. +442070368805. Fax +442086613901. E-mail: admin@cancerimagingsociety.org.uk.
Events and Marketing Manager address not obtained.
General: http://www.icimagingsociety.org.uk/

History 1998, London (UK). Inaugural meeting 2000, London. UK Registered Charity: 1082082. **Aims** Promote education and research in cancer imaging; foster its role in the multidisciplinary management of malignancy. **Structure** Officers: President; Vice-President; President-Elect; Secretary; Treasurer. **Languages** English. **Staff** 4.00 FTE, paid. **Activities** Training/education. **Events** *Meeting* Lisbon (Portugal) 2019, *Annual Meeting* Verona (Italy) 2019, *Annual Meeting* Menton (France) 2018, *Annual Meeting* Berlin (Germany) 2017, *Annual Meeting* Glasgow (UK) 2016.

Members Fellows (61) in 17 countries and territories:
Australia, Austria, Belgium, Canada, Denmark, France, Germany, Hong Kong, Ireland, Italy, Korea Rep, Netherlands, Singapore, Spain, Switzerland, UK, USA.
Associate members in 32 countries. Membership countries not specified. [2015/XD7858/**D**]

♦ International Cancer Immunotherapy Conference (meeting series)
♦ International Cancer Microenvironment Forum / see International Cancer Microenvironment Society (#12434)

♦ International Cancer Microenvironment Society 12434

Contact 18 Aharon Boxer St, 7405728 Ness Ziona, Israel. T. +972546615108. E-mail: tumic@cancermicroenvironment.org.
URL: http://www.cancermicroenvironment.org/

History Former names and other names: *International Cancer Microenvironment Forum (ICMF)* – former. **Languages** English. **Events** *Conference* Enschede (Netherlands) 2021, *Conference* Lisbon (Portugal) 2018, *Conference* Tel Aviv (Israel) 2015, *Conference* Suzhou (China) 2012, *Conference* Versailles (France) 2009. [2021.06.14/XF6001/**D**]

♦ International Cancer Screening Network (ICSN) 12435

Contact c/o NCI-CGH, 9609 Medical Center Dr, Bethesda MD 20892-9760, USA. E-mail: ncicenterforglobalhe@mail.nih.gov.
URL: https://www.cancer.gov/about-nci/organization/cgh/partnerships-dissemination/icsn-international-cancer-screening-network

History Dec 1988. Former names and other names: *International Breast Cancer Screening Database Project* – former (1988 to 1997); *International Breast Cancer Screening Network (IBSN)* – former (1997). **Aims** Promote collaborative research aimed at identifying and fostering efficient and effective approaches to cancer control worldwide through population-based screening. **Activities** Events/meetings. **Events** *International Cancer Screening Conference* Rotterdam (Netherlands) 2019, *Meeting* Bethesda, MD (USA) 2017, *Biennial Meeting* Rotterdam (Netherlands) 2015, *Biennial Meeting* Sydney, NSW (Australia) 2012, *Biennial Meeting* Oxford (UK) 2010.

Members Participating countries and territories (33):
Australia, Belgium, Brazil, Canada, Czechia, Denmark, Finland, France, Germany, Greece, Hungary, Iceland, Ireland, Israel, Italy, Japan, Korea Rep, Luxembourg, Malaysia, Netherlands, New Zealand, Norway, Poland, Portugal, Saudi Arabia, Spain, Sweden, Switzerland, Taiwan, Türkiye, UK, Uruguay, USA. [2022/XM0263/**F**]

♦ International Canine Federation / see Fédération cynologique internationale (#09477)

♦ International Cannabinoid Research Society (ICRS) 12436

Exec Dir PO Box 12628, Research Triangle Park, Durham NC 27709, USA. E-mail: executive.director@icrs.co – icrs@icrs.co.
Managing Dir address not obtained.
URL: http://icrs.co/

History 1992. **Aims** Foster cannabinoid research; promote exchange of scientific information and perspectives about *cannabis*; serve as a source of information regarding chemistry, pharmacology, therapeutic uses, toxicology and behavioural, psychological and social effects of cannabis and its constituents. **Structure** Officers: President; Executive Director; Managing Director; Past-President; President-Elect; Treasurer; Secretary; International Secretary; Trainee Representative; Grant PI. **Languages** English. **Staff** 3.00 FTE, paid. **Events** *Symposium* Jerusalem (Israel) 2021, *Symposium* Leiden (Netherlands) 2018, *Symposium* Montréal, QC (Canada) 2017, *Symposium* Bukowina (Poland) 2016, *Symposium* Wolfville, NS (Canada) 2015. **Members** Individuals (over 600) in 32 countries. Membership countries not specified. **NGO Relations** Canadian Consortium for the Investigation of Cannabinoids (CCIC); Carolina Cannabinoid Collaborative Conference (CCC); *International Association for Cannabinoid Medicines (IACM, #11754)*. [2018.09.06/XN9816/**D**]

♦ International Cannabis Alliance for Reform (inactive)
♦ International Cannabis and Cannabinoids Institute (internationally oriented national body)

♦ International Canoe Federation (ICF) 12437

Fédération internationale de canoë (FIC)

SG Maison du Sport International, Av de Rhodanie 54, 1007 Lausanne VD, Switzerland. T. +41216120290. E-mail: info@canoeicf.com.
Events Manager address not obtained.
URL: http://www.canoeicf.com/

History 19 Jan 1924, Copenhagen (Denmark). Reconstituted 9 Jun 1946, Stockholm (Sweden). Statutes amended 1974, Mexico City (Mexico); 1992, Madrid (Spain); 1994, Acapulco (Mexico); 1996, Paris (France). Former names and other names: *Internationale Representantschaft für Kanusport (IRK)* – former. **Aims** Develop canoe and kayak activity on national and international level with the priority given to maintaining canoeing as an Olympic discipline; organize international *competitions* in all disciplines of the *sport*: flatwater, slalom, wildwater, marathon, canoe polo, canoe sailing, dragon boat, freestyle; stimulate international touring.

Structure Congress (every 2 years); Board of Directors; Executive Committee. Standing Committees (12). **Languages** English, French, German, Italian, Spanish. **Staff** 10.00 FTE, paid. **Finance** Sources: members' dues. Other sources: TV rights from Olympic games. **Activities** Events/meetings; sporting activities. **Events** *Congress* Pattaya (Thailand) 2022, *Congress* Rome (Italy) 2021, *Congress* Manila (Philippines) 2020, *Congress* Budapest (Hungary) 2018, *Congress* St Petersburg (Russia) 2012. **Publications** *Planet Canoe.*
Members Federations in 166 countries and territories:
Afghanistan, Albania, Algeria, Andorra, Angola, Antigua-Barbuda, Argentina, Armenia, Aruba, Australia, Austria, Azerbaijan, Barbados, Belarus, Belgium, Belize, Bhutan, Bolivia, Bosnia-Herzegovina, Botswana, Brazil, Brunei Darussalam, Bulgaria, Burkina Faso, Burundi, Cambodia, Cameroon, Canada, Chile, China, Colombia, Congo DR, Cook Is, Costa Rica, Côte d'Ivoire, Croatia, Cuba, Cyprus, Czechia, Denmark, Djibouti, Dominica, Dominican Rep, Ecuador, Egypt, El Salvador, Equatorial Guinea, Eritrea, Estonia, Ethiopia, Fiji, Finland, France, Georgia, Germany, Ghana, Great Britain, Greece, Guam, Guatemala, Guinea, Guinea-Bissau, Guyana, Honduras, Hong Kong, Hungary, India, Indonesia, Iran Islamic Rep, Iraq, Ireland, Israel, Italy, Jamaica, Japan, Kazakhstan, Kenya, Kiribati, Korea DPR, Korea Rep, Kuwait, Kyrgyzstan, Laos, Latvia, Lebanon, Liberia, Libya, Lithuania, Luxembourg, Macau, Madagascar, Malawi, Malaysia, Mali, Malta, Mauritius, Mexico, Moldova, Mongolia, Montenegro, Morocco, Mozambique, Myanmar, Namibia, Nepal, Netherlands, New Zealand, Nicaragua, Nigeria, North Macedonia, Norway, Pakistan, Palau, Palestine, Panama, Papua New Guinea, Paraguay, Peru, Philippines, Poland, Portugal, Puerto Rico, Qatar, Romania, Russia, Samoa, Samoa USA, Sao Tomé-Principe, Senegal, Serbia, Seychelles, Singapore, Slovakia, Slovenia, Somalia, South Africa, Spain, Sri Lanka, St Maarten, St Vincent-Grenadines, Sudan, Suriname, Sweden, Switzerland, Tahiti Is, Taiwan, Tajikistan, Thailand, Timor-Leste, Togo, Tonga, Trinidad-Tobago, Tunisia, Türkiye, Turkmenistan, Uganda, Ukraine, United Arab Emirates, Uruguay, USA, Uzbekistan, Vanuatu, Venezuela, Vietnam, Virgin Is UK, Zambia.
NGO Relations Member of (7): *Association of Paralympic Sports Organisations (APSO, #02850); Association of Summer Olympic International Federations (ASOIF, #02943); International Committee for Fair Play (#12769); International Masters Games Association (IMGA, #14117); International Paralympic Committee (IPC, #14512); International World Games Association (IWGA, #15914); Olympic Movement (#17719).* Supports (5): *Asian Canoe Confederation; Confederación Panamericana de Canoas (COPAC, #04471); Confederation of African Canoeing (CAC, #04505); European Canoe Association (ECA, #06438); Oceania Canoe Association (OCA, #17654).* Recognized by: *International Olympic Committee (IOC, #14408).* [2021/XC1442/B]

♦ International Capital Market Association (ICMA) 12438

Zurich Head Office Dreikönigstrasse 8, 8002 Zurich ZH, Switzerland. T. +41443634222. Fax +41443637772. E-mail: info@icmagroup.org.
Brussels Representative Office Avenue des Arts 56, 1000 Brussels, Belgium. T. +3228011388. E-mail: brussels@icmagroup.org.
Hong Kong Representative Office Unit 3603, Tower 2, Lippo Centre, 89 Queensway, Admiralty, Hong Kong, Central and Western, Hong Kong. T. +85225316592. E-mail: apac@icmagroup.org.
URL: http://www.icmagroup.org

History 1969, Zurich (Switzerland). Changed name, 1 Jan 1992, to *International Securities Market Association (ISMA, inactive).* Merged, 1 Jul 2005, with *International Primary Market Association (IPMA, inactive).* Former names and other names: *Association of International Bond Dealers (AIBD)* – former. Registration: Swiss Civil Code, Switzerland; EU Transparency Register, No/ID: 0223480577-59, Start date: 30 Oct 2008. **Aims** Promote resilient well-functioning international and globally coherent cross-border debt securities markets, which are essential to fund sustainable economic growth and development. **Structure** Annual General Meeting; Board; Executive Committee; Representative Offices in London (UK), Paris (France), Brussels (Belgium) and Hong Kong. **Languages** English. **Staff** 54.00 FTE, paid. **Activities** Events/meetings; knowledge management/information dissemination; networking/liaising; politics/policy/regulatory; research/documentation; standards/guidelines; training/education. **Events** *Annual General Meeting and Conference* Paris (France) 2023, *Annual General Meeting and Conference* Vienna (Austria) 2022, *Fixed Income Leaders Summit* Singapore (Singapore) 2021, *Annual General Meeting and Conference* Zurich (Switzerland) 2021, *Annual General Meeting and Conference* Vienna (Austria) 2020. **Publications** *ICMA Quarterly Report.* Recommendations; guidance; position papers; consultation responses; surveys; reports; directories. **Members** Over 600 members located in 65 jurisdictions drawn from both the sell and buy-side of the market. Membership countries not specified. [2023.02.24/XM0737/y/D]

♦ International Carbohydrate Quality Consortium (ICQC) 12439

Office address not obtained. T. +39276006271.
Coordinator address not obtained.
URL: http://www.carbquality.org/

History Created 7 Jun 2013, Stresa (Italy). **Aims** Support, summarize and disseminate the science around *dietary* carbohydrate and health with a focus on quality; harmonize the work of scientists from academia, industry and government. **Structure** 2 Co-Chairs; Scientific Committee. **Activities** Events/meetings. **Events** *Meeting* Palinuro (Italy) 2019, *Meeting – Healthy carbohydrate foods* Rome (Italy) 2017, *Meeting – Update on glycemic index methodology, labelling and guidelines* Toronto, ON (Canada) 2015, *Meeting* Stresa (Italy) 2013. [2019/XM7799/C]

♦ International Carbon Action Partnership (ICAP) 12440

Partenariat International d'Action sur le Carbone

Secretariat Köthener Str 2, 10963 Berlin, Germany. E-mail: info@icapcarbonaction.com.
URL: https://icapcarbonaction.com/

History 2007, Lisbon (Portugal), by leaders of over 15 governments. **Aims** Act a a forum for governments and public authorities that have implemented or are planning to implement *emissions* trading systems (ETS). **Structure** Plenary; Steering Committee; Co-Chairs; Secretariat. **Languages** English. **Finance** Voluntary financial and/or in-kind voluntary contributions. **Activities** Events/meetings; knowledge management/information dissemination; training/education. **Events** *Tokyo Symposium* Tokyo (Japan) 2017, *Annual Meeting* Montréal, QC (Canada) 2014. **Publications** *ICAP Newsletter* (4 a year). Reports; handbook.
Members Governments of or governmental institutions in 17 countries:
Australia, Canada, Denmark, France, Germany, Greece, Ireland, Italy, Japan, Netherlands, New Zealand, Norway, Portugal, Spain, Switzerland, UK, USA.
Regional entity:
Observers (4):
Japan, Kazakhstan, Korea Rep, Ukraine. [2018.03.12/XM5899/F*]

♦ International Carbon Black Association (ICBA) 12441

Address not obtained.
URL: http://www.carbon-black.org/

History Founded 1977. Registered in accordance with Belgian law. **Aims** Encourage and develop international cooperation, communication and research concerning environmental, health and safety matters, standards and nomenclature relevant to carbon black. **Structure** General Assembly (annual). Administrative Council (meeting annually before the General Assembly), comprises no more than the total number of members plus one and includes President and one or more Vice-Presidents. Secretary and Treasurer are not directors. Secretariat in Brussels (Belgium). **Finance** Members' dues.
Members Companies, associations and individuals. Companies (8) in 4 countries:
Canada, Germany, Portugal, USA. [2016/XD5887/D]

♦ International Carbon Reduction and Offset Alliance (ICROA) 12442

Secretariat Rue Merle d'Aubigné 24, 1207 Geneva, Switzerland. T. +41227370500. Fax +41227370508. E-mail: secretariat@ieta.org.
URL: http://www.icroa.org/

History Constitution adopted 20 Mar 2008. Since Jun 2011, functions as a Working Group of *International Emissions Trading Association (IETA, #13262).* **Aims** Promote a credible code of best practice for carbon reduction services; provide a credible, influential and uniform voice on carbon reduction policy and standards; promote a commitment to shared learning and best practice on methods and strategies for effective *emissions* reductions. **Structure** General Meeting (annual); Executive Committee; Secretariat. **Finance** Members' dues. [2019/XJ3422/E]

♦ International Cardiac Pacing and Electrophysiology Society / see World Society of Arrhythmias (#21799)
♦ International Cardiac Pacing Society / see World Society of Arrhythmias (#21799)
♦ International Cardijn Association (internationally oriented national body)
♦ International Cardijn Foundation / see International Cardijn Association
♦ International Cardiovascular Health Alliance (unconfirmed)
♦ International Card Manufacturers Association (internationally oriented national body)
♦ International Career Support Association (internationally oriented national body)
♦ International Care Ethics Observatory (internationally oriented national body)
♦ International Care and Relief / see Build Africa
♦ International Cargo Handling Coordination Association (inactive)
♦ International Caritas Conference / see Caritas Internationalis (#03580)

♦ International Carotenoid Society 12443

Sec Gloval R&D Manager, Fuji Chemical Industry Co Ltd, 2-6-3-12F Shibakoen, Minato-ku, Tokyo, 105-0011 Japan.
URL: http://www.carotenoidsociety.org/

History Aug 1996, Leiden (Netherlands), at 11th International Symposium on Carotenoids. **Aims** Promote, support and encourage all areas of carotenoid science, pure and applied, academic and commercial, research and educational. **Structure** Council, comprising President, President-elect, Secretary, Treasurer, Immediate Past-President, Chairman future Symposium and 7 members. **Events** *International Symposium on Carotenoids* Toyama City (Japan) 2023, *International Symposium on Carotenoids* Salt Lake City, UT (USA) 2014, *International symposium on carotenoids* Krakow (Poland) 2011, *International symposium on carotenoids* Okinawa (Japan) 2008, *International Symposium on Carotenoids* Edinburgh (UK) 2005. **Members** Membership countries not specified. [2020/XJ0050/D]

♦ International Carpet Classification Organization (no recent information)
♦ International Carriage and Brake Van Union (inactive)

♦ International Carrom Federation (ICF) 12444

Address not obtained.
URL: http://www.carrom.org/

History 15 Oct 1988. **Aims** Promote the *sport* of carrom. **Activities** Organizes championships. [2009/XM0590/D]

♦ International Cartel for Peace (inactive)

♦ International Cartilage Regeneration & Joint Preservation Society (ICRS) 12445

Executive Director Spitalstr 190, House 3, 8623 Wetzikon ZH, Switzerland. T. +41445037370. E-mail: office@cartilage.org.
Senior Event Manager address not obtained.
URL: https://www.cartilage.org/

History 1997, Switzerland. Initiated by the organizers of the 1st International Fribourg Symposium on Cartilage Repair. Former names and other names: *International Cartilage Repair Society (ICRS)* – former (2018). **Aims** Advance science and education in the prevention and treatment of cartilage disease worldwide. **Structure** General Assembly; Executive Board; General Board; Committees (10). **Languages** English. **Staff** 2.50 FTE, paid. **Finance** Members' dues. Other sources: sponsorships; meeting registration revenue. **Activities** Events/meetings; training/education; awards/prizes/competitions; knowledge management/information dissemination; financial and/or material support. **Events** *World Congress* Sitges (Spain) 2023, *World Congress* Berlin (Germany) 2022, *Focus Meeting Cartilage and Sports* Thessaloniki (Greece) 2022, *World Congress* Berlin (Germany) 2021, *Focus Meeting on Imaging, Diagnosis and Treatment* Vienna (Austria) 2019. **Publications** *Cartilage* (4 a year) – journal. **Information Services** *Patient Information Platform.* **Members** (1,300) in 67 countries (not specified). [2022/XD8725/D]

♦ International Cartilage Repair Society / see International Cartilage Regeneration & Joint Preservation Society (#12445)

♦ International Cartographic Association (ICA) 12446

Association Cartographique Internationale (ACI) – Asociación Cartografica Internacional (ACI) – Internationale Kartographische Vereinigung (IKV)

SG Fed Dept of Home Affairs (FDHA), Swiss Federal Statistical Office, Espace de l'Europe 10, 2010 Neuchâtel, Switzerland. T. +41584636731.
Acting Pres 10382 Stansfield Road, Laurel MD 20723, USA. T. +14109729922. E-mail: president@icaci.org.
URL: http://icaci.org/

History 9 Jun 1959, Bern (Switzerland). Preparatory conferences prior to creation held: 1956, Stockholm (Sweden); 1957, Chicago IL (USA); 1958, Mainz (Germany FR). Statutes adopted at 1st General Assembly, 30 May 1961, Paris (France). Former names and other names: *Internationale Gesellschaft für Kartographie* – former. Registration: Swiss Civil Code, No/ID: 008.123.502/17, Start date: 1 Jan 2022, Switzerland, Fribourg. **Aims** Advance study of problems in cartographic and *geographical information science*; initiate and coordinate cartographic and GIS research involving cooperation among different nations; exchange ideas and documents; further training in cartography and GIS; encourage disseminating cartography knowledge. **Structure** General Assembly of Delegates (every 4 years, at Conference); Executive Committee; Commissions (28); Working Groups (4); Committees (3). **Languages** English, French. **Staff** Voluntary. **Finance** Sources: members' dues; sale of publications. **Activities** Awards/prizes/competitions; capacity building; events/meetings; knowledge management/information dissemination; networking/liaising; publishing activities; research and development; standards/guidelines; training/education. Active in all member countries. **Events** *International Cartographic Conference* Vancouver, BC (Canada) 2025, *International Cartographic Conference* Cape Town (South Africa) 2023, *International Conference on Location Based Services* Munich (Germany) 2022, *European Cartographic Conference (EuroCarto 2022)* Vienna (Austria) 2022, *International Conference on Location Based Services* Glasgow (UK) 2021. **Publications** *eCarto News* (12 a year); *ICA News* (2 a year); *International Journal of Cartography* (3-4 a year). *Cartography – Maps Connecting the World* (2015); *Abstracting Geographic Information in a Data Rich World* (2014); *Cartography from Pole to Pole* (2013); *History of Cartography* (2012); *Maps for the Future* (2012); *Advances in Cartography and GIScience* (2011). Lecture Notes; conference proceedings; national reports.
Members National Committees in 73 countries and territories:
Algeria, Argentina, Armenia, Australia, Austria, Bangladesh, Belgium, Benin, Botswana, Brazil, Bulgaria, Canada, Chile, China, Colombia, Croatia, Cuba, Cyprus, Czechia, Denmark, Ecuador, Estonia, Finland, France, Georgia, Germany, Greece, Hong Kong, Hungary, India, Indonesia, Iran Islamic Rep, Ireland, Israel, Italy, Japan, Jordan, Kenya, Korea Rep, Latvia, Lithuania, Madagascar, Malaysia, Mexico, Mongolia, Montenegro, Morocco, Mozambique, Netherlands, New Zealand, Nigeria, North Macedonia, Norway, Oman, Pakistan, Poland, Portugal, Romania, Russia, Slovakia, Slovenia, South Africa, Spain, Sri Lanka, Sweden, Switzerland, Thailand, Trinidad-Tobago, Türkiye, UK, Ukraine, Uruguay, USA.
Affiliate members (36) in 28 countries and territories:
Argentina, Australia, Austria, Belgium, Bulgaria, Chile, China, Finland, France, Germany, India, Italy, Jamaica, Japan, Kenya, Lebanon, Netherlands, New Zealand, Nigeria, Poland, Russia, Rwanda, Spain, Taiwan, Türkiye, UK, United Arab Emirates, USA.
Included in the above, 2 organizations listed in this Yearbook:
African Regional Institute for Geospatial Information Science and Technology (AFRIGIST, #00433); Regional Centre for Mapping of Resources for Development (RCMRD, #18757).
Consultative Status Consultative status granted from: *UNESCO (#20322)* (Consultative Status). **IGO Relations** Member of (1): *International Committee on Global Navigation Satellite Systems (ICG, #12775).* Cooperates with (3): *Group on Earth Observations (GEO, #10735); International Hydrographic Organization (IHO, #13825); United Nations Committee of Experts on Global Geospatial Information Management (UN-GGIM, #20540).* **NGO Relations** Member of (3): *International Science Council (ISC, #14796); Open Geospatial Consortium (OGC, #17752); UN-GGO: Geospatial Societies (UN-GGIM GS, #20324).* Cooperates with (2): *Geo-Information for Disaster Management (Gi4DM); International Organization for Standardization (ISO, #14473).* [2023.02.25/XB1447/B]

♦ International Cartridge Collectors Association / see International Ammunition Association
♦ International Carwash Association (internationally oriented national body)
♦ International Casting Federation / see International Casting Sport Federation (#12447)

♦ International Casting Sport Federation (ICSF) 12447

SG Novosuchdolska 37, 165 00 Prague, Czechia. E-mail: info@icsf-castingsport.com.
Pres address not obtained.
URL: http://www.icsf-castingsport.com/

History 1955, Rotterdam (Netherlands). Constitution adopted Sep 1958; revised: 1973, Scarborough (UK); Jul 1984, Toronto (Canada); Jul 1986, Madrid (Spain); Feb 1995, The Hague (Netherlands); Feb 1997, The Hague. Former names and other names: *International Casting Federation (ICF)* – former (1955 to 13 Apr 2003); *Fédération international de lancer* – former (1955 to 13 Apr 2003). **Aims** Promote and encourage the *sport* of casting throughout the World in conformity with Olympic principles; follow and lead the evaluation of casting sport; frame and interpret ICF Rules and Regulations; promote and sanction international *competitions* in bait, fly and surf-casting activities. **Structure** General Assembly (every 2 years). Board of Directors (meets at least 3 times a year) consisting of President, 5 Board members and Secretary General-Treasurer. Executive Officers: President and General Secretary. Permanent Committees, each with Chairman and members: Constitution and Rules Committee; Tournament Rules and Future Committee. Court of Arbitration for Sport. **Languages** English, German. **Staff** Voluntary. **Finance** Sources: members' dues. Other sources: Surplus from championships. **Activities** Arranges dates, events and venues for World (in even years) and Continental Championships (in odd years). Participates in World Games and arranges Casting World Games. Confirms and maintains World Record and Continental Record scores and international judges. The Federation's accepted rules and regulations apply at all international tournaments recognized by the ICF. **Events** *Biennial Congress* Prague (Czechia) 2022, *Biennial Congress* Vienna (Austria) 2019, *Biennial Congress* Tarnowo Podgorne (Poland) 2017, *Biennial Congress* Halle (Saale) (Germany) 2013, *Biennial Congress* Vienna (Austria) 2011. **Publications** *ICF News Flash*.

Members Clubs, federations, associations or unions (one per country) in 35 countries and territories:
Australia, Austria, Belgium, Bosnia-Herzegovina, Bulgaria, Canada, Croatia, Czechia, Denmark, England, Estonia, Finland, France, Germany, Hungary, Italy, Japan, Latvia, Lithuania, Luxembourg, Netherlands, New Zealand, North Macedonia (former Yugoslav Rep of), Norway, Poland, Romania, Russia, Slovakia, Slovenia, South Africa, Spain, Sweden, Switzerland, USA, Wales.
NGO Relations Member of (3): *Alliance of Independent recognised Members of Sport (AIMS, #00690)*; *International World Games Association (IWGA, #15914)*; *Olympic Movement (#17719)*. Recognized by: *International Olympic Committee (IOC, #14408)*. [2020/XC4323/**C**]

♦ International Castles Institute (inactive)
♦ International Catalogue of Scientific Literature (inactive)
♦ The International Cat Association (internationally oriented national body)
♦ International Cat Care (internationally oriented national body)

♦ International Catholic Association of Institutes of Educational Sciences 12448

Association catholique internationale des sciences de l'éducation (ACISE) – Asociación Católica Internacional de Instituciones de Ciencias de la Educación

Pres Fac de Educaçao e Psicologia, Univ Católica Portuguesa, Rua Diogo de Botelho 1327, 4169-005 Porto, Portugal.
Sec Univ Catholique de l'Ouest, BP 10808, 49008 Angers CEDEX 01, France.
URL: https://www.fiuc.org/bdf_recherche-1_en.html

History 1989. Founded as a sectorial group of *International Federation of Catholic Universities (IFCU, #13381)*. Former names and other names: *Association of Catholic Institutes of Education (ACISE)* – alias. **Aims** Provide the opportunity for Catholic institutions concerned with the study of education to explore and develop education inspired by Christian values and principles; foster mutual cooperation among members. **Structure** Administration Council. **Languages** English, French, Spanish. **Staff** 1.00 FTE, voluntary. **Finance** Members' dues. **Events** *Conference* Porto (Portugal) 2021, *Annual Colloquium* Madrid (Spain) 2019, *Conference* Glasgow (UK) 2018, *Annual Colloquium* Krakow (Poland) 2016, *Annual Colloquium* Rome (Italy) 2015.

Members Full in 15 countries:
Belgium, Chile, Colombia, France, Germany, Holy See, Italy, Mexico, Netherlands, Poland, Portugal, Puerto Rico, Slovakia, Spain, UK. [2020/XD6017/**D**]

♦ International Catholic Association for the Study of Medical Psychology (inactive)

♦ International Catholic Centre of Geneva (ICCG) 12449

Centre catholique international de Genève (CCIG) – Centro Católico Internacional de Ginebra (CCIG)

SG Rue de Varembé 1, 1202 Geneva, Switzerland. T. +41227341465. Fax +41227340878. E-mail: secretariat@ccig-iccg.org.
URL: http://www.ccig-iccg.org/

History 1950, Geneva (Switzerland). Founded within the framework of *Conference of International Catholic Organizations (CICO, inactive)*. New statutes registered 1992. Former names and other names: *Information Centre of the International Catholic Organizations* – former; *Centre d'information des organisations internationales catholiques (CIOIC)* – former; *Centro de Información de las Organizaciones Internacionales Católicas* – former. Registration: Swiss Civil Code, Start date: 1992, Switzerland. **Aims** Be the catalyst for NGO commitment, in particular of Catholic inspired international organizations, within the United Nations System. **Structure** Committee. **Languages** English, French. **Staff** 0.50 FTE, paid. **Finance** Sources: members' dues; subsidies. **Activities** Events/meetings; knowledge management/information dissemination; training/education. **Publications** *ADDRESSING IMPLEMENTATION: SAFEGUARDING THE RIGHTS OF CHILDREN, YOUTH AND WOMEN IN BOLIVIA – ABORDANDO LA IMPLEMENTACIÓN: SALVAGUARDANDO LOS DERECHOS DE LOS NIÑOS, JÓVENES Y MUJERES EN BOLIVIA* (1st ed 2019) in English, Spanish; *TRADUCTION DES RECOMMANDATIONS PORTANT SUR LA LUTTE CONTRE LA TORTURE ET AUTRES PEINES OU TRAITEMENTS CRUELS, INHUMAINS OU DÉGRADANTS* (1st ed 2018) in French – with illustration and translations in Togo's three languages: Ewe, Kabye and Ifé; *Building a Future with Decent Work: Youth Employment and Domestic Workers*.

Members Organizations (23):
- *Association Catholique Internationale de Services pour la Jeunesse Féminine (ACISJF/In Via, #02417)*;
- Association des Educatrices Compagnie de Marie Notre-Dame;
- *Association Internationale des Charités (AIC, #02675)*;
- *Association Points-Coeur (#02863)*;
- *Associazione Comunità Papa Giovanni*;
- *Brothers of Charity (FC)*;
- *Caritas Internationalis (CI, #03580)*;
- *Catholic International Education Office (#03604)*;
- *Company of the Daughters of Charity of St Vincent de Paul (DC)*;
- *Crescendo Worldwide Network (#04950)*;
- *Dominicans for Justice and Peace (OP, #05113)*;
- *Edmund Rice International (ERI, #05362)*;
- Fondations Apprentis d'Auteuil;
- *Fondazione Marista per la Solidarietà Internazionale Onlus (#09831)*;
- *Franciscans International (FI, #09982)*;
- *International Confederation of the Society of St Vincent-de-Paul (#12870)*;
- *International Federation of ACATs – Action by Christians for the Abolition of Torture (#13334)*;
- *Istituto Internazionale Maria Ausiliatrice delle Salesiane di Don Bosco (IIMA)*;
- *Mouvement international d'apostolat des milieux sociaux indépendants (MIAMSI, #16864)*;
- *Pax Romana, International Catholic Movement for Intellectual and Cultural Affairs (ICMICA, #18267)*;
- *Sisters of Our Lady of Charity of the Good Shepherd*;
- *Teresian Association*;
- *Volontariato Internazionale Donna Educazione Sviluppo (VIDES, #20806)*.

Consultative Status Consultative status granted from: *ECOSOC (#05331)* (Special). **NGO Relations** Member of (2): *Conference of Non-Governmental Organizations in Consultative Relationship with the United Nations (CONGO, #04635)* (Associate member); *Fédération des Institutions Internationales établies à Genève (FIIG, #09599)*. [2021.09.06/XE2009/y/**E**]

♦ International Catholic Centre for UNESCO / see International Catholic Cooperation Centre for UNESCO (#12454)

♦ International Catholic Child Bureau 12450

Bureau international catholique de l'enfance (BICE) – Oficina Internacional Católica de la Infancia

Office Director 70 bd de Magenta, 75010 Paris, France. T. +33153350100. Fax +33153350119. E-mail: contact@bice.org.
Gen Sec 11 rue Butini, 1202 Geneva, Switzerland. T. +41227313248.
URL: http://www.bice.org/

History 17 Jan 1948, Paris (France). Registration: RNA, No/ID: W751031441, France. **Aims** Promote and protect children's rights and dignity. **Structure** General Assembly (annual); Board of Directors; Bureau. **Languages** English, French, Italian, Russian, Spanish. **Staff** 15.00 FTE, paid. **Finance** Sources: fundraising; gifts, legacies; grants; members' dues. Other sources: co-financing of projects. **Activities** Advocacy/lobbying/activism; events/meetings; projects/programmes; publishing activities; research/documentation; training/education. **Events** *The right to education – Towards a Renewed Commitment to Education* Geneva (Switzerland) 2019, *Annual General Assembly* Paris (France) 2015, *Annual General Assembly* Paris (France) 2014, *Annual General Assembly* Paris (France) 2013, *Annual General Assembly* Brussels (Belgium) 2012. **Publications** *BICE Newsletter* (12 a year); *Enfants de partout* (4 a year) in French; *L'Essentiel* (annual) in French. *Cahiers du BICE* in English, French, Italian, Russian, Spanish. Books; brochures; training manuals; reports.

Members Full; Associate; Individual. Full (13) in 7 countries:
Argentina, Brazil, Congo DR, France, Italy, Mali, Malta.
Included in the above, 1 organization listed in this Yearbook:
Fondazione Marista per la Solidarietà Internazionale Onlus (#09831).
Associate (63) in 31 countries:
Argentina, Armenia, Belgium, Benin, Brazil, Cambodia, Cameroon, Central African Rep, Chile, Congo DR, Côte d'Ivoire, France, Georgia, Guatemala, India, Italy, Kazakhstan, Lebanon, Malawi, Mauritius, Moldova, Mozambique, Nepal, Paraguay, Peru, Russia, Spain, Switzerland, Thailand, Togo, Uruguay.
Individuals (11) in 7 countries:
Argentina, Belgium, France, India, Italy, Lebanon, Portugal.
Consultative Status Consultative status granted from: *ECOSOC (#05331)* (Special); *UNESCO (#20322)* (Consultative Status); *Council of Europe (CE, #04881)* (Participatory Status); *UNICEF (#20332)*; *African Commission on Human and Peoples' Rights (ACHPR, #00255)* (Observer). **IGO Relations** Accredited by (2): *Organisation internationale de la Francophonie (OIF, #17809)*; *United Nations (UN, #20515)*. Maintains relations with: *ILO (#11123)*; *Inter-American Children's Institute (IACI, #11406)*; *WHO (#20950)*. Associated with Department of Global Communications of the United Nations. **NGO Relations** Member of: *Child Rights Connect (#03884)*; *Forum of Catholic Inspired NGOs (#09905)*. Partner of: NGO Platform on the Right to Education. [2022/XC1451/**C**]

♦ International Catholic Commission of Prison Chaplaincies / see International Commission of Catholic Prison Pastoral Care (#12670)
♦ International Catholic Committee of the Blind (inactive)

♦ International Catholic Committee of Nurses and Medico-social Assistants 12451

Comité international catholique des infirmières et des assistantes médico-sociales (CICIAMS) – Comité Internacional Católico de Enfermeras y Asistentas Médico-Sociales – Internationaler Verband Katholischer Kranken-Schwestern

SG Piazza San Calisto 16, 00120 Vatican City, Vatican. T. +39669887372. E-mail: ciciamsinternational12@gmail.com.
Int Pres address not obtained.
URL: http://www.ciciams.org/

History Sep 1933, Lourdes (France). Founded at 1st Congress. Became an international professional Catholic organization, following decision of an international meeting of presidents of Catholic nursing associations, Basel (Switzerland), 1928. Former names and other names: *International Study Committee of Catholic Nursing Associations* – former; *Comité international d'études des associations catholiques d'infirmières* – former; *International Committee of Catholic Associations of Nurses* – former (1928); *Comité international catholique des associations d'infirmières* – former (1928); *Internationale Arbeitsgemeinschaft der Katholischen Pflegeorganisation* – former (1928); *International Committee of Catholic Nurses* – former. **Aims** Endeavour to promote basic and advanced nurse education and professional research; represent professional and *Christian* interest of members; promote enhancement of spiritual welfare and ethical values of members; promote health and social measures following Christian principles and professional development; promote cooperation between member associations. **Structure** General Council (meets every 2 years); Executive Board; Permanent Committees (5). **Languages** English, French, Spanish. **Staff** 2.00 FTE, voluntary. **Finance** Sources: members' dues. *'Solidarity Fund of CICIAMS – Fonds de solidarité du CICIAMS'* set up by decision of General Council, 9 May 1968. **Activities** Events/meetings; research/documentation. **Events** *World Congress of Catholic Nurses* Doylestown, PA (USA) 2022, *African Regional Congress* Nairobi (Kenya) 2020, *Quadrennial World Congress* Kuching (Malaysia) 2018, *African Regional Congress* Manzini (Eswatini) 2016, *Quadrennial World Congress* Dublin (Ireland) 2014. **Publications** *CICIAMS News* in English.

Members Full; Associate. Professional Catholic associations, legally constituted as such under the laws of their respective countries. Members in 25 countries and territories:
Croatia, England, Eswatini, Ghana, Hong Kong, India, Indonesia, Ireland, Italy, Kenya, Malaysia, Mexico, Nigeria, Pakistan, Philippines, Portugal, Scotland, Singapore, South Africa, Spain, Taiwan, Tanzania UR, Thailand, USA, Zambia.
Consultative Status Consultative status granted from: *ECOSOC (#05331)* (Ros C); *ILO (#11123)* (Special List); *WHO (#20950)* (Official Relations); *UNICEF (#20332)*. **IGO Relations** Accredited by (1): *United Nations Office at Vienna (UNOV, #20604)*. Associated with Department of Global Communications of the United Nations. **NGO Relations** Member of (4): *Crescendo Worldwide Network (#04950)*; *Forum of Catholic Inspired NGOs (#09905)*; *New York NGO Committee on Drugs (NYNGOC, #17097)*; *NGO Committee on UNICEF (#17120)*. [2023/XB1605/**B**]

♦ International Catholic Confederation of Hospitals (inactive)

♦ International Catholic Conference of Guiding (ICCG) 12452

Conférence internationale catholique du guidisme (CICG) – Conferencia Internacional Católica del Guidismo (CICG)

Contact c/o SGDF, 65 rue de la Glacière, 75013 Paris, France. T. +33144523737. E-mail: dcussen@gmail.com – iccg.cicg.mondial@gmail.com.
URL: http://cicg-iccg.com/wordpress/

History Jan 1965, Rome (Italy). Founded following regular meetings since 1948. Charter, Constitution and Bye-Laws approved by the Holy See. Structure of the organization changed/updated at extraordinary international meeting, Feb 1994, Mozet (Belgium), although Charter, Constitution and Bye-Laws remained unchanged. **Aims** Help Catholic leaders fulfil their mission of education and service and help them in their task of leading *girl* guides and girl scouts through guiding to attain a higher degree of *Christian* life; bring guiding into the international life of Church and represent member groups on international organizations of Catholic laity; contribute to development of guiding in Catholic circles, in accordance with the directives of the local hierarchy. **Structure** General Council, comprising 2 representatives and one national chaplain per member group and World team members. World team (meets annually), consisting of Coordinator, Ecclesiastic Assistant and one representative for each of the 4 regions (Europe, Africa, Latin America, Middle-East). The World team is assisted by Technical team, composed of Executive Secretary and one person responsible for finances. **Languages** English, French, Spanish. **Staff** None. **Finance** Sources: grants; members' dues. **Activities** Events/meetings. **Events** *International Meeting* Warsaw (Poland) 2006, *World meeting / International Meeting* Buenos Aires (Argentina) 2003, *International Meeting* Toronto, ON (Canada) 2002, *General Assembly* Lomé (Togo) 2000, *World meeting / International Meeting* Lomé (Togo) 2000. **Publications** *Caminos de Reconciliación* in English, French, Spanish; *Caminos de Solidaridad*; *En el Mundo de las Niñas y Las Adolscentes*; *Guidismo: Una Padagogia Inclusiva en Tiempos de Exclusión* in English, French, Spanish; *Haciendo Memoria: 40 Años de la CICG*; *En el Mundo de las Niñas y Las Adolscentes*.

Members Full national organizations in 38 countries:
Argentina, Belgium, Benin, Bolivia, Brazil, Burkina Faso, Cameroon, Canada, Central African Rep, Chile, Colombia, Côte d'Ivoire, Czechia, El Salvador, France, Germany, Guinea, Haiti, Hungary, Ireland, Italy, Jordan, Lebanon, Liechtenstein, Luxembourg, Madagascar, Monaco, Paraguay, Poland, Portugal, Rwanda, Senegal, Spain, Switzerland, Togo, Uganda, UK, Uruguay.
Applicants for membership in 3 countries:
Chad, Costa Rica, Panama.
Contact countries (22):
Belarus, Belize, Burundi, Congo Brazzaville, Egypt, Estonia, Ghana, Greece, Guatemala, Honduras, Jamaica, Latvia, Mali, Malta, Mexico, Peru, Romania, Russia, Slovakia, Slovenia, Ukraine, Venezuela. [2020/XD5218/**B**]

♦ International Catholic Conference of Scouting (ICCS) 12453

Conférence internationale catholique du scoutisme (CICS) – Conferencia Internacional Católica de Escultismo (CICE) – Internationale Katholische Konferenz des Pfadfindertums (IKKP)

Secretariat Piazza Pasquale Paoli 18, 00186 Rome RM, Italy. T. +3966865270. Fax +3966865211. E-mail: cics-iccs@cics.org.

URL: http://www.cics.org/

History 1948, Luxembourg. Founded as successor to *International Office for Catholic Scouting (inactive)*, created in 1920. New Statutes approved by Holy See Jun 1962 and Nov 1975. Former names and other names: *International Catholic Scouting Conference* – former (1948 to 1975); *Conférence internationale du scoutisme catholique* – former (1948 to 1975). **Aims** Contribute to the complete education of *young people* through scouting from the Catholic faith viewpoint; cooperate in developing and enhancing the spiritual dimension of scouting in accordance with unity and diversity of the World Scout Movement; ensure that Catholic scouts are actively present in the Church and guarantee communication between the Catholic Church and the World Scout Movement; promote projects related to the development of the Catholic faith and of society; provide opportunity for members to meet together as friends and for Catholic Scout leaders and officials to share their experience as providers of an educational service from the Catholic faith viewpoint; encourage dialogue with other creeds in scouting; foster relations with national and international institutions; assist associations to develop programmes for education in the Catholic faith, while respecting different religious views and practices. **Structure** World Council (meets every 3 years), comprising members of the Steering Committee, persons in charge of each member organization (or appointed deputy), National Chaplain of each member organization and (ex-officio) a delegate of the World Committee of Scouting. Steering Committee, comprising members of General Secretariat and representatives of the 4 ICCS regions. General Secretariat, consisting of Secretary General (serving as Chair), World Ecclesiastical Assistant, Treasurer, 2 Deputies and others. Members of the Secretariat who are not members of the Steering Committee may attend the meetings of the Council. Regions (4): Africa; America; Asia-Pacific; Europe-Mediterranean, each headed by a Regional Secretary, elected by the Regional Council, in cooperation with an Ecclesiastical Assistant and a Committee. **Languages** English, French, German, Spanish. **Staff** 1.00 FTE, paid. **Finance** Sources: members' dues. Other sources: subsidies from donors and foundations, and particularly from *International Catholic Scout Foundation (ICSF, no recent information)*. **Activities** Events/meetings; knowledge management/information dissemination; research/documentation; training/education. **Events** *World Council Meeting* Fatima (Portugal) 2021, *Triennial World Council Meeting and Seminar* Rome (Italy) 2017, *Triennial World Council Meeting and Seminar* St Louis, MO (USA) 2011, *Meeting* Bangkok (Thailand) 2010, *Triennial world council meeting and seminar* Rome (Italy) 2008. **Publications** *Signes-Signs* (4 a year) in English, French – magazine; *Circular Letter* (3 a year) – electronic. Reports of Seminars; booklet of the official ICCS documents; booklet on inter-religious dialogue; booklet on peace and justice.

Members Associate; Observer. Organizations, in 66 countries and territories:
Argentina, Austria, Belgium, Benin, Bolivia, Brazil, Burundi, Cameroon, Canada, Central African Rep, Chad, Chile, Colombia, Congo DR, Costa Rica, Côte d'Ivoire, Czechia, Ecuador, France, Gabon, Germany, Guinea, Haiti, Hong Kong, Hungary, Ireland, Israel, Italy, Japan, Jordan, Kenya, Korea Rep, Lebanon, Liechtenstein, Lithuania, Luxembourg, Madagascar, Mali, Malta, Netherlands, New Zealand, Niger, Nigeria, Palestine, Paraguay, Peru, Philippines, Poland, Portugal, Romania, Rwanda, Senegal, Singapore, Slovakia, Spain (2), St Lucia, Switzerland (2), Tanzania UR, Thailand, Togo, Uganda, UK, Uruguay, USA, Zimbabwe.

NGO Relations Member of (2): *Laudato Si' Movement (#16403)*; *World Scout Interreligious Forum (see: #21693)*. [2020/XB1683/B]

♦ International Catholic Cooperation Centre for UNESCO (CCIC) 12454

Centre catholique international de coopération avec l'UNESCO (CCIC) – Centro Católico Internacional de Cooperación para la UNESCO

Main Office 67 rue de Sèvres, 75006 Paris, France. T. +33147051759. E-mail: secretariat@ccic-unesco.org – infos@ccic-unesco.org.

URL: http://ccic-unesco.org/

History Jan 1947, Paris (France). Founded following modification of the statutes of *Comité de soutien et de promotion du Centre catholique international pour l'UNESCO (inactive)*, to carry out the activities of this committee. Former names and other names: *International Catholic Coordinating Centre for UNESCO* – former; *Centre catholique de coordination auprès de l'UNESCO* – former; *Centro Católico Internacional de Coordinación ante la UNESCO* – former; *International Catholic Centre for UNESCO* – former (1973 to 2002); *Centre catholique international pour l'UNESCO (CCIC)* – former (1973 to 2002); *Centro Católico Internacional para la UNESCO* – former (1973 to 2002); *Internationales Katholisches Zentrum für die UNESCO* – former (1973 to 2002). Registration: France. **Aims** Facilitate activities of international Catholic organizations having consultative status with UNESCO, of individuals who contribute to the work of UNESCO (including government delegates, members of the Secretariat, field experts, etc) and of the Holy See in its UNESCO-related activities; facilitate the action of *Christians* interested in UNESCO. **Structure** Board, comprising President, Secretary, Treasurer, Ecclesiastical Advisor and 15 members. Secretariat, headed by Delegate. **Languages** English, French. **Staff** 1.00 FTE, paid; 3.00 FTE, voluntary. **Finance** Members' dues. Donations. **Activities** Follows up on and participates in studies and projects of UNESCO in the fields of: Youth; Culture; Social Sciences. Training. Organizes concertation meetings and colloquia; provides documentation service. **Events** *General Assembly* Paris (France) 2011, *General Assembly* Paris (France) 2010, *General Assembly* Paris (France) 2009, *General Assembly* Paris (France) 2008, *General Assembly* Paris (France) 2007. **Publications** *Le mois à l'UNESCO* (4 a year) in English, French, Spanish; *Informations rapides* (24 a year) in English, French, Spanish – online. Books. **Members** Individuals in 122 countries. Membership countries not specified. **Consultative Status** Consultative status granted from: *UNESCO (#20322)* (Consultative Status).

NGO Relations Member of: *Forum of Catholic Inspired NGOs (#09905)*. Collaborates with:
- *Association Catholique Internationale de Services pour la Jeunesse Féminine (ACISJF/In Via, #02417)*;
- *Association Internationale des Charités (AIC, #02675)*;
- *Caritas Internationalis (CI, #03580)*;
- *Catholic International Education Office (#03604)*;
- *Federation of Catholic Family Associations in Europe (#09468)*;
- *Vie montante internationale (VMI, #20769)*;
- *International Catholic Child Bureau (#12450)*;
- *International Christian Organisation of the Media (ICOM, #12563)*;
- *International Christian Union of Business Executives (#12566)*;
- *International Federation of Catholic Universities (IFCU, #13381)*;
- *International Federation of Fe y Alegría (FIFyA, #13425)*;
- *International Federation of Rural Adult Catholic Movements (#13535)*;
- *International Jacques Maritain Institute (#13967)*;
- *International Young Catholic Students (IYCS, #15926)*;
- *International Young Christian Workers (IYCW, #15927)*;
- *Mouvement international d'apostolat des milieux sociaux indépendants (MIAMSI, #16864)*;
- *Mouvement international de la jeunesse agricole et rurale catholique (MIJARC, #16865)*;
- *Organisation mondiale des anciens élèves de l'enseignement catholique (OMAEC, #17816)*;
- *Pax Christi – International Catholic Peace Movement (#18266)*;
- *Pax Romana, International Catholic Movement for Intellectual and Cultural Affairs (ICMICA, #18267)*;
- *Pax Romana, International Movement of Catholic Students (IMCS, #18268)*;
- *UMEC-WUCT (#20280)*;
- *World Catholic Association for Communication (SIGNIS, #21264)*;
- *World Union of Catholic Women's Organisations (WUCWO, #21876)*. [2021/XE0349/v/E]

♦ International Catholic Cooperative Centre (inactive)

♦ International Catholic Coordinating Centre for UNESCO / see International Catholic Cooperation Centre for UNESCO (#12454)

♦ International Catholic Esperantists Union 12455

Union internationale espérantiste catholique – Internacia Katolika Unuigo Esperantista (IKUE)

Pres IKUE, Via di Porta Fabbrica 15, 00165 Rome RM, Italy. E-mail: ikue@ikue.org – ikue.reto@gmail.com.

URL: http://www.ikue.org/

History 1 Apr 1910, Paris (France). **Aims** Proclaim the *gospel* worldwide; give witness to the unity of the *church* by using the international language of Esperanto in the liturgy and in pastoral activities; contribute to understanding, brotherhood and peace among all people. **Languages** Esperanto. **Activities** Events/meetings. **Events** *Congress* Rome (Italy) 2022, *Congress* Rome (Italy) 2021, *Congress* Rome (Italy) 2020, *Congress* Podebrady (Czechia) 2018, *Congress* Nitra (Slovakia) 2016. **Publications** *Espero Katolika* (4 a year).

Members National sections; Individuals (1,300), in 44 countries:
Albania, Algeria, Argentina, Australia, Austria, Belgium, Brazil, Canada, Colombia, Côte d'Ivoire, Croatia, Cuba, Czechia, France, Germany, Hungary, India, Ireland, Italy, Japan, Lithuania, Madagascar, Mexico, Morocco, Netherlands, New Zealand, Nigeria, Norway, Poland, Portugal, Romania, Russia, Serbia, Slovakia, Spain, Switzerland, Taiwan, Thailand, Togo, Tunisia, UK, Ukraine, Uruguay, USA.

NGO Relations Consulting member of: *Universal Esperanto Association (UEA, #20676)*.
[2023.02.13/XE2702/E]

♦ International Catholic Federation of Physical Education and Sports 12456

Fédération internationale catholique d'éducation physique et sportive (FICEP) – Federación Católica Internacional de Educación Física y Deportes – Internationaler Katholiken-Verband für Körpererziehung und Sport

Pres 22 rue Oberkampf, 75011 Paris, France. T. +33143385057. Fax +33143140665. E-mail: info@ficep.org.

URL: http://www.ficep.org/

History 1911, Nancy (France). Former names and other names: *Union internationale des oeuvres catholiques d'éducation physique* – former. Registration: France. **Aims** Link Catholic *gymnastic* and sporting associations in different countries, developing their activities in accordance with Christian precepts; encourage and regulate international meetings, competitions and championships; promote friendly encounters between affiliated groups; promote Christian education within family and professional spheres. **Structure** Congress (annual); Bureau; Executive Committee. Meetings closed. **Languages** English, French, German. **Staff** 1.00 FTE, paid. **Finance** Sources: members' dues. Annual budget: 30,000 CHF. **Activities** Events/meetings; sporting activities. **Events** *Annual Congress and General Assembly* Cologne (Germany) 2022, *Annual Congress and General Assembly* Vienna (Austria) 2021, *Annual Congress and General Assembly* Linz (Austria) 2019, *Annual Congress and General Assembly* Nice (France) 2018, *Annual Congress and General Assembly* Krakow (Poland) 2017.

Members National federations, totalling over 2,500,000 members, in 12 countries:
Austria, Belgium, Cameroon, Congo DR, Czechia, France, Germany, Italy, Madagascar, Poland, Romania, Senegal.

NGO Relations Member of (1): *International Committee for Fair Play (#12769)*. [2022.05.10/XD0221/D]

♦ International Catholic Federation of Young People's Missionary Organizations (inactive)

♦ International Catholic Foundation for the Service of Deaf Persons (ICF) 12457

Exec Dir 7202 Buchanan St, Landover Hills MD 20784, USA. T. +12404419855. E-mail: admin@icfdeafservice.org.

UK Office Hollywood House, Sudell Street, Manchester, M4 4JF, UK.

URL: http://www.icfdeafservice.org/

History Proposed 1971, Dublin (Ireland), at International Conference. UK Registered Charity since Nov 1986. Registered in the USA. **Aims** Support and promote the religious formation and pastoral care of, with and by deaf people within the Catholic community. **Structure** Board, comprising President and 10 members. **Events** *Symposium* Leuven (Belgium) 2009, *Conference* Rome (Italy) 2008, *Conference* Mexico City (Mexico) 2003, *Conference* Fort Lauderdale, FL (USA) 1998, *Symposium* Cologne (Germany) 1997. [2010/XJ2177/t/F]

♦ International Catholic-Jewish Liaison Committee (ILC) 12458

Comité international de liaison catholique-juif – Comitato Internazionale di Collegamento Cattolico-Ebraico

Postal Address c/o Pontifical Council, Via della Conciliazione 5, 00193 Rome RM, Italy. Fax +39669885365. E-mail: office@christianunity.va.

Contact c/o IJCIC, 327 Lexington Ave, New York NY 10016, USA. T. +12026868670.

URL: http://www.christianunity.va/content/unitacristiani/en/commissione-per-i-rapporti-religiosi-con-l-ebraismo.html

History 1970, as an international religious dialogue and study committee between jews and catholics; not an international organization in the strict sense of the world. Also referred to as *International Jewish-Catholic Liaison Committee – Comité international de liaison juif-catholique*. **Structure** The constituencies of the Committee are: *International Jewish Committee on Interreligious Consultations (IJCIC, #13970)*, with its constituencies and delegates; *Commission for Religious Relations with the Jews (#04238)*. Sponsored by: IJCIC; *Pontifical Council for Promoting Christian Unity (PCPCU, #18446)*. **Activities** Since 1971-1972 has organized 15 sessions. **Events** *Meeting* Jerusalem (Israel) 1994, *Meeting* Baltimore, MD (USA) 1992, *Meeting* Prague (Czechoslovakia) 1990. **Publications** *Fifteen Years of Catholic-Jewish Dialogue 1970-1985 – Selected Papers* (1988). [1996.06.10/XE6103/E]

♦ International Catholic League Sobrietas (inactive)

♦ International Catholic Liaison Body for Agricultural and Rural Organizations / see International Catholic Rural Association (#12461)

♦ International Catholic Migration Commission (ICMC) 12459

Commission internationale catholique pour les migrations (CICM) – Comisión Católica Internacional de Migración – Commissione Cattolica Internazionale per le Migrazioni

Pres ICMC Secretariat, Rue Varembé 1, Case postale 96, 1211 Geneva 20, Switzerland. T. +41229191020. Fax +41229191048. E-mail: info@icmc.net.

SG address not obtained.

URL: http://www.icmc.net/

History Founded 1951, in the wake of the human displacement caused by the Second World War. Statutes approved by the Holy See. Registered in accordance with Swiss Civil Code. **Aims** Serve and protect uprooted people – *refugees*, internally *displaced persons* and migrants – regardless of faith, ethnicity or nationality; respond to the challenges of people on the move and their communities; implement and advocate *rights*-based *policies* and durable solutions through membership, and alongside government and non-governmental partners. **Structure** Council, comprising 18 nominees of Catholic Bishops' Conferences and equivalent bodies working specifically with migration and refugee issues. Council elected President who convenes and chairs both Council and Governing Committee meetings. Governing Committee, comprising members selected by regionally based voting. Secretary-General, appointed by Governing Committee. Secretariat located in Geneva (Switzerland). Affiliated offices: *International Catholic Migration Commission – Europe (ICMC – Europe, #12460)*, Brussels (Belgium); US Liaison Office, Washington DC (USA); Development Office, Boston MA (USA). **Languages** English, French, Spanish. **Staff** 425.00 FTE, paid. **Activities** Advocacy/lobbying/activism; events/meetings; humanitarian/emergency aid; projects/programmes. **Events** *Joint seminar* Geneva (Switzerland) 2000, *Regional meeting* 1996, *Asia regional meeting* Manila (Philippines) 1996, *General Assembly* Geneva (Switzerland) 1993, *Meeting* Geneva (Switzerland) 1993. **Publications** Annual Report; brochures; handbooks; reports; guides.

Members Catholic Bishops Conferences and Episcopal assemblies and equivalent bodies that work with migrants and refugees on national and regional levels. Members in 159 countries and territories. Membership countries not specified. Included in the above, 2 organizations listed in this Yearbook:
Included in the above, 2 organizations listed in this Yearbook:
Conférence des évêques de la région du Nord de l'Afrique (CERNA, #04605); *Southern African Catholic Bishops' Conference (SACBC, #19838)*.

Consultative Status Consultative status granted from: *ECOSOC (#05331)* (Special); *ILO (#11123)* (Special List); *UNICEF (#20332)*; *Council of Europe (CE, #04881)* (Participatory Status). **IGO Relations** Observer to: *African Union (AU, #00488)*; *International Organization for Migration (IOM, #14454)*. Implementing Partner of: UNHCR. Member of Consultative Forum of *Frontex, the European Border and Coast Guard Agency (#10005)*. Associated with Department of Global Communications of the United Nations. **NGO Relations** Ensures contact with departments of the Roman Curia according to their area of competence through permanent and active collaboration. Maintains: permanent working relationships with international Catholic organizations and with those working internationally to prevent forced migration and protect and assist migrants and refugees; cooperative relations with Christian and non-Christian international organizations operating in the field. Member of: *American Council for Voluntary International Action (InterAction)*; *European Council on Refugees and Exiles (ECRE, #06839)*; *Fédération des Institutions Internationales établies à Genève (FIIG, #09599)*; *Forum of Catholic Inspired NGOs (#09905)*; Steering Committee of *Global Campaign for Ratification of the Convention on the Rights of Migrant Workers (#10267)*; *International Council of Voluntary Agencies (ICVA, #13092)*. Also close relations with: *Jesuit Refugee Service (JRS, #16106)*. [2020.02.12/XB1457/y/B]

♦ International Catholic Migration Commission – Europe (ICMC – Europe) 12460

Commission Internationale Catholique pour les Migrations – Europe (CICM – Europe)

Head of Office Rue Washington 40, 1050 Brussels, Belgium. T. +3222279729. Fax +3226486369.
URL: http://www.icmc.net/

History Jun 1994, Brussels (Belgium). Statutes adopted, June 1994. A separate legal identity acting as the European office of *International Catholic Migration Commission (ICMC, #12459)*. Registration: Banque-Carrefour des Entreprises, No/ID: 0452.912.992, Start date: 24 Jun 1994, Belgium; EU Transparency Register, No/ID: 304664841672-26, Start date: 9 Mar 2021. **Aims** Act as European liaison office of ICMC; coordinate advocacy actions, cooperation and humanitarian assistance programmes in third countries; follow EU policy-making in asylum and migration and advocate for human rights of all migrants regardless of their status; implement networking, capacity-building and multi-stakeholder collaboration programmes, particularly in areas of refugee resettlement, mixed migration, integration, human trafficking, and migration and development. **Structure** EU policy and programme office, situated in Brussels (Belgium), representing ICMC at European level. **Events** *Regional meeting* Brussels (Belgium) 1996. **Publications** Reports; guides. **IGO Relations** *UNHCR (#20327)* – NGO platform on migration and asylum. *Global Forum on Migration and Development (GFMD, #10376)*. **NGO Relations** Member of: *European Council on Refugees and Exiles (ECRE, #06839)*; *Federation of European and International Associations Established in Belgium (FAIB, #09508)*; *Platform for International Cooperation on Undocumented Migrants (PICUM, #18401)*; *Transparency, Accountability and Participation Network (TAP Network, #20222)*. [2021/XE2443/**E**]

- ♦ International Catholic Organization for Cinema and Audiovisual (inactive)
- ♦ International Catholic Organizations Information Center (internationally oriented national body)
- ♦ International Catholic Organizations Network / see International Catholic Organizations Information Center
- ♦ International Catholic and Pedagogical Federation (inactive)
- ♦ International Catholic Programme of Evangelization / see Institute for World Evangelisation (#11303)

♦ International Catholic Rural Association (ICRA) 12461

Association internationale rurale catholique – Asociación Internacional Rural Católica – Internationale Katholische Bäuerliche und Ländliche Vereinigung – Associazione Internazionale Rurale Cattolica

Contact Palazzo San Calisto, 00120 Vatican City, Vatican. T. +39669887123. Fax +39669887223.
URL: http://www.laici.va/content/laici/fr/sezioni/associazioni/repertorio/associazione-rurale-cattolica-internazionale.html

History Founded Oct 1964, Rome (Italy), an *International Catholic Liaison Body for Agricultural and Rural Organizations – Comité international catholique de liaison pour les organisations agricoles et rurales* having been set up at an international congress of Catholics on rural life, Sep 1962, Rome. Present name adopted 7 Jul 1966, Rome. Statutes most recently revised, 2011, Rome. **Aims** Facilitate contact, exchange and joint endeavour among all Catholic rural and *agricultural* organizations throughout the world; stimulate mutual help on an international level between these organizations; help to find *Christian*-inspired solutions to social, religious and moral aspects of rural problems. **Structure** General Assembly (every 5 years); General Board; Board of Directors. **Languages** English, French, Italian, Spanish. **Staff** 2.00 FTE, paid. **Finance** Sources: gifts, legacies; members' dues. **Events** *European Study Meeting* Hungary 2014, *European Study Meeting* Italy 2013, *European Study Meeting* Greece 2012, *World Congress General Assembly* Rome (Italy) 2012, *Meeting* Malta 2002. **Publications** *ICRA Information* (4 a year) in English – bulletin, including a booklet in English, French, Italian, Spanish. *Vocation of the Agricultural Leader* (2016).

Members Representatives in the General Assembly in 21 countries and territories:
Belgium, Chile, Colombia, Congo DR, El Salvador, France, Greece, Hungary, India, Ireland, Italy, Malta, Peru, Philippines, Poland, Romania, Russia, Taiwan, Thailand, Uganda, USA.

Consultative Status Consultative status granted from: *ECOSOC (#05331)* (Ros C); *FAO (#09260)* (Liaison Status). **NGO Relations** Administers: *Agrimissio (no recent information)*. Member of: *Forum of Catholic Inspired NGOs (#09905)*. [2020.03.06/XC1459/**C**]

- ♦ International Catholic Scouting Conference / see International Catholic Conference of Scouting (#12453)
- ♦ International Catholic Society for Girls (#02417)
- ♦ International Catholics Organisation of the Media / see International Christian Organisation of the Media (#12563)
- ♦ International Catholics Organisation of the Media – The World Forum of Professionals and Institutions in Secular and Religious Media / see International Christian Organisation of the Media (#12563)
- ♦ International Catholic Stewardship Council (internationally oriented national body)
- ♦ International Catholic Union of the Middle Classes (inactive)
- ♦ International Catholic Union of the Press / see International Christian Organisation of the Media (#12563)
- ♦ International Catholic Union for the Study of the Rights of Men according to Christian Principles (inactive)
- ♦ International Catholic University Press Secretariat (inactive)
- ♦ International Catholic Work IKA (inactive)
- ♦ International Catholic Youth Federation (inactive)
- ♦ International Cattle Breeders Federation (inactive)

♦ International Cell Death Society (ICDS) 12462

Pres Dept of Biology, Queens College/Graduate Ctr of CUNY, 65-30 Kissena Blvd, Flushing NY 11367, USA. T. +17189973450. Fax +17189973429. E-mail: secretary@celldeath-apoptosis.org.
URL: http://www.celldeath-apoptosis.org/

History 1995, as a club. **Aims** Promulgate research and clinical information on the broad topic of cell death, including apoptosis, autophagy, necrosis, necroptosis, and other variants. **Structure** Board; Advisory Board. **Activities** Events/meetings. **Events** *Meeting* Johannesburg (South Africa) 2021, *Meeting* Johannesburg (South Africa) 2020, *Meeting* New York, NY (USA) 2019, *Meeting* Seoul (Korea Rep) 2018, *Meeting* Malaga (Spain) 2013.

Members Societies in 5 countries:
Brazil, Iran Islamic Rep, South Africa, Türkiye, USA. [2020/XJ7153/**C**]

- ♦ International Cell Line Authentication Committee (unconfirmed)

♦ International Cell Research Organization (ICRO) 12463

Organisation internationale de recherche sur la cellule – Organización Internacional de Investigaciones Celulares

Pres Univ of Pittsburgh, School of Medicine, Dept of Cell Biology, 3500 Terrace St, S362 Biomedical Science Tower/South, Pittsburgh PA 15261, USA. E-mail: gps15@pitt.edu.
URL: https://icro-unesco.org/dev/

History 22 Jun 1962, Paris (France), under auspices of UNESCO, following recommendations adopted 30 Sep 1961, Istanbul (Turkey). Registered in accordance with Belgian law. **Aims** Foster and facilitate exchange of information on basic research in cell biology and biotechnology; give young scientists of every country equal chance to contribute by creative research to the progress of science and become full members of the scientific community. **Structure** Council (meets every 4 years); Executive Committee. **Activities** Training/education; research/documentation. **Events** *Meeting* Naples (Italy) 2003, *Meeting* Shanghai (China) 2001, *Meeting* Paris (France) 2000, *Meeting* Martonvasar (Hungary) / Budapest (Hungary) 1999, *Meeting* Valdivia (Chile) / Santiago (Chile) 1998.

Members Individual scientists and research workers of international repute (400) in 56 countries. Membership countries not specified. Council and Executive Committee members in 28 countries and territories:
Council and Executive Committee members in 28 countries and territories:
Argentina, Australia, Belgium, Brazil, Bulgaria, Chile, China, Egypt, France, Germany, Hong Kong, Hungary, India, Indonesia, Ireland, Israel, Italy, Japan, Mexico, Netherlands, Poland, Russia, South Africa, Sweden, Switzerland, Tunisia, UK, USA.

Consultative Status Consultative status granted from: *ECOSOC (#05331)* (Ros C); *FAO (#09260)* (Liaison Status); *UNEP (#20299)*. **IGO Relations** Cooperative activities with: *United Nations University (UNU, #20642)*. [2020.03.03/XC1463/v/**D**]

♦ International Cell Senescence Association (ICSA) 12464

Treas Dept of Biosciences – Room 2017, Durham Univ, Durham, DH1 3LE, UK.
URL: http://www.cellsenescence.info/

Aims Promote research, cooperation and information exchange among all interested in any aspect of cellular senescence. **Structure** Steering Committee. **Finance** Members' dues. **Activities** Events/meetings; research/documentation. **Events** *Conference* Groningen (Netherlands) 2022, *Conference* Osaka (Japan) 2021, *Conference* Osaka (Japan) 2020, *Conference* Athens (Greece) 2019, *Conference* Montréal, QC (Canada) 2018. [2018/XM6477/**D**]

♦ International Cellulosics Association (ICA) 12465

SG c/o Kellen, Avenue de Tervueren 188A, Postbox 4, 1150 Brussels, Belgium. T. +3227611673. E-mail: secretariat@icacellulosics.org.
URL: https://ica-cellulosics.org/

History Registration: Banque-Carrefour des Entreprises, No/ID: 0751.923.016, Start date: 10 Aug 2020, Belgium; EU Transparency Register, No/ID: 847599045450-45, Start date: 8 Feb 2022. **Aims** Represent the interests of manufacturers, distributors and users of cellulose and cellulose derivatives. **Structure** General Assembly; Board of Directors; Technical Working Group; Secretariat. **Activities** Knowledge management/information dissemination; research/documentation; training/education. **Members** Full; Associate. Membership countries not specified. [2023.02.20/AA2410/t/**D**]

- ♦ International Celso Furtado Center for Development Policies (internationally oriented national body)
- ♦ International Cemetery Supply Association / see International Memorialization Supply Association
- ♦ International Center for Advanced Materials and raw materials of Castilla y León (internationally oriented national body)
- ♦ International Center for Advanced Mediterranean Agronomic Studies – Mediterranean Agronomic Institute of Montpellier / see Mediterranean Agronomic Institute of Montpellier (#16643)
- ♦ International Center for Advocates Against Discrimination (internationally oriented national body)

♦ International Center for Agricultural Research in the Dry Areas (ICARDA) 12466

Centre international de recherches agricoles dans les régions sèches

Dir Gen PO Box 114/5055, Beirut, Lebanon. T. +9611843472 – +9611813303. Fax +9611804071 – +9611843473. E-mail: icarda@cgiar.org.
Headquarters Dalia Bldg 2nd Floor, Bashir El Kassar Street, Verdun, Beirut, Lebanon.
URL: http://www.icarda.org/

History 1977. A Research Center of *CGIAR System Organization (CGIAR, #03843)*. **Aims** Contribute to improvement of livelihoods of the resource-poor in dry areas by enhancing *food* security and alleviating *poverty* through research and partnerships to achieve sustainable increases in agricultural productivity and income, while ensuring efficient and more equitable use and conservation of natural resources. **Structure** Board of Trustees. **Languages** Arabic, English, French. **Staff** 450.00 FTE, paid.

Finance Annual budget: about US$ 70,000,000. Sources: about 25 governments, including: Australia; Austria; Belgium; Canada; China; Denmark; Egypt; Ethiopia; France; Germany; India; Iran Islamic Rep; Italy; Iraq; Japan; Korea Rep; Morocco; Netherlands; Norway; Pakistan; Portugal; South Africa; Sweden; Switzerland; Syria AR; Turkey; UK; USA. Also from other international organizations and foundations including the following:
- *African Development Bank (ADB, #00283)*;
- *Arab Fund for Economic and Social Development (AFESD, #00965)*;
- *Asian Development Bank (ADB, #01422)*;
- *Common Fund for Commodities (CFC, #04293)*;
- *European Commission (EC, #06633)*;
- *FAO (#09260)*;
- *Fondo Regional de Tecnologia Agropecuaria (FONTAGRO, #09834)*;
- *Global Crop Diversity Trust (Crop Trust, #10313)*;
- *Gulf Cooperation Council (GCC, #10826)*;
- *International Bank for Reconstruction and Development (IBRD, #12317)*;
- *International Development Research Centre (IDRC, #13162)*;
- *International Fund for Agricultural Development (IFAD, #13692)*;
- *Islamic Development Bank (IsDB, #16044)*;
- *Kuwait Fund for Arab Economic Development (KFAED)*;
- *OPEC Fund for International Development (OFID, #17745)*;
- *UNESCO (#20322)*.

Activities Research and development; projects/programmes; events/meetings. **Events** *Regional Consultation on Scoping, Prioritizing and Mapping of Crop Related Neglected and Underutilized Species in Selected Countries in Asia* Bangkok (Thailand) 2016, *Policies for water and food security in the dry areas* Cairo (Egypt) 2013, *Arab water forum* Cairo (Egypt) 2011, *International symposium on medicinal plants* Petra (Jordan) 2010, *International wheat conference* St Petersburg (Russia) 2010. **Publications** *ICARDA Caravan*. Annual Report; books; brochures; proceedings of national and international conferences and workshops; technical reports and manuals; field guides.

Members Regional and country offices in 19 countries:
Afghanistan, Egypt, Ethiopia, Georgia, India, Iran Islamic Rep, Iraq, Jordan, Lebanon, Morocco, Oman, Pakistan, Sudan, Syrian AR, Tunisia, Türkiye, United Arab Emirates, Uzbekistan, Yemen.
Regional mandate covers 42 countries and territories:
Afghanistan, Algeria, Argentina, Armenia, Azerbaijan, Bahrain, Chile, China, Colombia, Cyprus, Egypt, Eritrea, Ethiopia, Georgia, India, Iran Islamic Rep, Iraq, Jordan, Kazakhstan, Kuwait, Kyrgyzstan, Lebanon, Libya, Mauritania, Mexico, Morocco, Oman, Pakistan, Palestine, Peru, Qatar, Saudi Arabia, Somalia, Sudan, Syrian AR, Tajikistan, Tunisia, Türkiye, Turkmenistan, United Arab Emirates, Uzbekistan, Yemen.

IGO Relations Member of: *International Information System for the Agricultural Sciences and Technology (AGRIS, #13848)*. Associate member of: *Asia-Pacific Association of Agricultural Research Institutions (APAARI, #01830)*. Accredited to the Conference of the Parties of: *Secretariat of the United Nations Convention to Combat Desertification (Secretariat of the UNCCD, #19208)*. Sponsoring agency of: *Association of Agricultural Research Institutions in the Near East and North Africa (AARINENA, #02364)*. Partner of: *Global Soil Partnership (GSP, #10608)*. Cooperates with: *CIHEAM – International Centre for Advanced Mediterranean Agronomic Studies (CIHEAM, #03927)*. Special links with: *Arab Centre for the Studies of Arid Zones and Dry Lands (ACSAD, #00918)*. Joint activities with: *Scientific Information Centre of Interstate Coordination Water Commission of Central Asia (SIC ICWC, #19152)*.

Cooperates with national agricultural research organizations, universities, and the other CGIAR supported centres:
- *Africa Rice Center (AfricaRice, #00518)*, Bouaké (Côte d'Ivoire);
- *International Crops Research Institute for the Semi-Arid Tropics (ICRISAT, #13116)*, Patancheru (India);
- *International Livestock Research Institute (ILRI, #14062)*, Nairobi (Kenya);
- *International Rice Research Institute (IRRI, #14754)*, Manila (Philippines).

Instrumental in setting up: *International Center for Agricultural Research in the Dry Areas (ICARDA, #12466)*.
Partner of:
- *Arab Authority for Agricultural Investment and Development (AAAID, #00902)*;
- *Arab Organization for Agricultural Development (AOAD, #01018)*;
- *AVRDC – The World Vegetable Center (#03051)*;
- *CABI (#03393)*;
- *Centre for Environment and Development for the Arab Region and Europe (CEDARE, #03738)*;
- *Economic Cooperation Organization (ECO, #05313)*;
- *Institut de recherche pour le développement (IRD)*;
- *International Atomic Energy Agency (IAEA, #12294)*;
- *International Seed Testing Association (ISTA, #14829)*;
- *Japan International Cooperation Agency (JICA)*;
- *Observatoire du Sahara et du Sahel (OSS, #17636)*;
- *Programme on Man and the Biosphere (MAB, #18526)*;
- *Regional Centre on Agrarian Reform and Rural Development for the Near East (#18755)*;
- *United Nations Economic and Social Commission for Western Asia (ESCWA, #20558)*;
- *United Nations University (UNU, #20642)*.

NGO Relations Member of: *European Forest Institute Mediterranean Facility (EFIMED, #07298)*; *InsideNGO (inactive)*; *International Foundation for Science (IFS, #13677)*; *International Network of Feed Information Centres (INFIC, no recent information)*. Represented with: *Borlaug Global Rust Initiative (BGRI, #03305)*; *Wheat Initiative (#20931)*. Instrumental in setting up: *Central Asia and South Caucasus Consortium of Agricultural*

universities for Development (CASCADE, #03685). Partner of: *Global Call for Climate Action (GCCA, inactive)*; *Japan International Research Centre for Agricultural Sciences (JIRCAS)*. Cooperates with national agricultural research organizations, universities, and the other CGIAR supported centres: *Center for International Forestry Research (CIFOR, #03646)*, Bogor (Indonesia); *International Centre for Tropical Agriculture (#12527)*, Cali (Colombia); *International Food Policy Research Institute (IFPRI, #13622)*, Washington DC (USA); *International Institute of Tropical Agriculture (IITA, #13933)*, Ibadan (Nigeria); *International Maize and Wheat Improvement Center (#14077)*, Mexico City (Mexico); *International Potato Center (#14627)*, Lima (Peru); *International Water Management Institute (IWMI, #15867)*, Colombo (Sri Lanka); *World Agroforestry Centre (ICRAF, #21072)*, Nairobi (Kenya); *WorldFish (#21507)*, Penang (Malaysia).
Partner of:
– *Arab Science and Technology Foundation (ASTF, #01039)*; *Borlaug Global Rust Initiative (BGRI, #03305)*; *Central Asia and the Caucasus Association of Agricultural Research Institutions (CACAARI, #03678)*; *Centre for Legumes in Mediterranean Agriculture (CLIMA)*; *Crops For the Future (CFF, #04968)*; *Institut des régions arides, Tunisia (IRA)*; *International Center for Biosaline Agriculture (ICBA, #12468)*; *International Commission on Irrigation and Drainage (ICID, #12694)*; *International Dryland Development Commission (IDDC, #13208)*; *International Institute for Applied Systems Analysis (IIASA, #13861)*; *ISRIC – World Soil Information (#16068)*; *Mediterranean Agronomic Institute of Zaragoza (MAIZ, #16644)*; *TerrAfrica (#20127)*; *World Overview of Conservation Approaches and Technologies (WOCAT, see: #21192)*. [2022/XE5928/**E***]

- ♦ International Center for AIDS Care and Treatment Programs / see ICAP
- ♦ International Center of Applied Phonetics, Mons (internationally oriented national body)
- ♦ International Center for Appropriate and Sustainable Technology (internationally oriented national body)
- ♦ International Center for Aquaculture / see International Center for Aquaculture and Aquatic Environments
- ♦ International Center for Aquaculture and Aquatic Environments (internationally oriented national body)
- ♦ International Center for Arid and Semiarid Land Studies (internationally oriented national body)

♦ International Center for Banking and Corporate Governance (ICBCG) 12467

Chairman Ukrainian Ac of Banking of Natl Bank of Ukraine, Petropavlivska Str 57, Sumy, 40000, Ukraine. T. +380542619942.
URL: http://uabs.edu.ua/en/international-center-for-banking- and-corporate-governance/
History Founded 2010, as a research institute at the Ukrainian Academy of Banking of the National Bank of Ukraine. **Aims** Conduct and encourage high quality research in banking and corporate governance; engage in interdisciplinary and cross-border research through collaboration with contacts worldwide; consult with professional bodies, banks, corporations and other groups, on banking and corporate governance issues; disseminate research. **Structure** Board of Directors. **Languages** English, Russian, Ukrainian. **Staff** 6.00 FTE, paid. **Finance** Funded by Publishing House Virtus Interpress, Ukraine. **Activities** Research/documentation; training/education; events/meetings; knowledge management/information dissemination. **Events** *International Conference on Corporate Governance* Milan (Italy) 2014, *International Conference on Global Financial Market and Corporate Governance* Nürburg (Germany) 2014, *International Conference on International Competition in Banking / International Conference* Sumy (Ukraine) 2014, *International Conference on Governance and Control in Finance and Banking* Paris (France) 2013, *International Conference on Financial Distress* Rome (Italy) 2013. **Publications** Research books; papers.
Members Individuals (over 80) in 41 countries and territories:
Argentina, Australia, Bahrain, Brazil, Canada, China, Colombia, Egypt, Finland, France, Germany, Greece, India, Italy, Japan, Jordan, Kuwait, Latvia, Malaysia, Mexico, Netherlands, New Zealand, Norway, Peru, Poland, Qatar, Russia, Saudi Arabia, Serbia, South Africa, Spain, Sweden, Switzerland, Taiwan, Thailand, Tunisia, Türkiye, UK, Ukraine, United Arab Emirates, USA.
NGO Relations Partners with several international research organizations and centers.
[2015.08.27/XJ6538/v/**E**]

♦ International Center for Biosaline Agriculture (ICBA) 12468

Headquarters Academic City, Al Ain Rd, Al Ruwayyah, PO Box 14660, Dubai, United Arab Emirates. T. +97143361100. Fax +97143361155. E-mail: icba@biosaline.org.ae.
URL: http://www.biosaline.org/
History Sep 1999. Founded by *Islamic Development Bank (IsDB, #16044)*, *OPEC Fund for International Development (OFID, #17745)* and *Arab Fund for Economic and Social Development (AFESD, #00965)*, with additional support from government of United Arab Emirates through Ministry of Environment and Water (MoEW) and Dubai Municipality. Former names and other names: *Biosaline Agriculture Centre (BAC)* – former. **Aims** Work in partnership to deliver agricultural and water scarcity solutions in marginal environments. **Structure** Board of Directors; Director General; Directors. **Languages** Arabic, English. **Staff** 56.00 FTE, paid. **Finance** Currently supported with core funding from the Government of the United Arab Emirates and *Islamic Development Bank (IsDB, #16044)*. Additional funding secured through projects supported by bilateral agreements. **Activities** Capacity building; knowledge management/information dissemination; politics/policy/regulatory; research and development. **Events** *Global Forum on Innovations for Marginal Environments (GFIME)* Dubai (United Arab Emirates) 2019, *International Date Palm Conference* Abu Dhabi (United Arab Emirates) 2018, *Arab water forum* Cairo (Egypt) 2011. **Publications** *Biosalinity e-newsletter* (12 a year) in Arabic, English. Annual Report; project briefs; success stories. **IGO Relations** Memorandum of Understanding with: *Arab Authority for Agricultural Investment and Development (AAAID, #00902)*; *Arab Organization for Agricultural Development (AOAD, #01018)*; *FAO (#09260)*; *International Crops Research Institute for the Semi-Arid Tropics (ICRISAT, #13116)*. Member of: *Asia-Pacific Association of Agricultural Research Institutions (APAARI, #01830)*; *Association of Agricultural Research Institutions in the Near East and North Africa (AARINENA, #02364)*. Partner of: *CGIAR System Organization (CGIAR, #03843)*; *Global Soil Partnership (GSP, #10608)*; *International Center for Agricultural Research in the Dry Areas (ICARDA, #12466)*. Invited as observer to Governing Council session of: *International Fund for Agricultural Development (IFAD, #13692)*. **NGO Relations** Member of: *Association of International Research and Development Centers for Agriculture (AIRCA, #02760)*. Observer member of: *Arab Forum for Environment and Development (AFED, #00960)*. Partner of: *Global Water Partnership (GWP, #10653)*. Cooperates with: *Stockholm International Water Institute (SIWI)*. Set up: *Global Biosaline Network (GBN)*. [2020.05.06/XE4435/**E**]

- ♦ International Center for Chemical and Biological Sciences (internationally oriented national body)
- ♦ International Center for Climate Governance (internationally oriented national body)
- ♦ International Center for Clubhouse Development / see Clubhouse International (#04035)
- ♦ International Center for Communications, San Diego CA (internationally oriented national body)
- ♦ International Center for Complexity and Conflict (internationally oriented national body)
- ♦ International Center for Conciliation (internationally oriented national body)
- ♦ International Center for Conflict Resolution and Mediation / see Pacific Path Institute
- ♦ International Center for Contemporary Education (internationally oriented national body)
- ♦ International Center for Cooperation and Conflict Resolution (internationally oriented national body)
- ♦ International Center for Development Policy / see International Forum for Innovative Northeast Asia Strategy
- ♦ International Center for the Development of Youth Hostels in Latin America (#03804)
- ♦ International Center for Education and Human Development (internationally oriented national body)
- ♦ International Center for Elementary Particle Physics, Tokyo (internationally oriented national body)
- ♦ International Center for Environmental Technology Transfer (internationally oriented national body)
- ♦ International Center for Epidemiologic and Preventive Ophthalmology / see Dana Center for Preventive Ophthalmology (#04997)
- ♦ International Center for Equal Healthcare Access / see Global Medic Force

♦ International Center for Ethnobotanical Education Research and Service (ICEERS) 12469

Exec Dir c/ Sepúlveda 65 Loca 2, 08015 Barcelona, Spain. T. +34931882099. E-mail: constanzas-anchez@iceers.org – info@iceers.org.
URL: http://www.iceers.org/
Aims Transform society's relations with psychoactive *plants*. **Structure** Board of Directors. **Activities** Advocacy/lobbying/activism; knowledge management/information dissemination; research/documentation. **Publications** *ICEERS Newsletter*. **Consultative Status** Consultative status granted from: *ECOSOC (#05331)* (Special). [2021.06.14/XM6404/**D**]

- ♦ International Center for Ethno-Religious Mediation (internationally oriented national body)
- ♦ International Center for Family Medicine / see Confederación Iberoamericana de Medicina Familiar (#04450)
- ♦ International Center for Glyptics Research / see Centre international de recherches glyptographiques (#03763)
- ♦ International Center for Health, Law and Ethics, University of Haifa (internationally oriented national body)
- ♦ International Center for Health Leadership Development (internationally oriented national body)
- ♦ International Center for Holocaust Studies / see ADL Braun Holocaust Institute
- ♦ International Center for the Human Rights of Migrants (internationally oriented national body)
- ♦ International Center for Infectiology Research (internationally oriented national body)
- ♦ International Center for Integrated Water Resources Management (internationally oriented national body)
- ♦ International Center for Jesuit Higher Education (internationally oriented national body)
- ♦ International Center for Journalists (internationally oriented national body)
- ♦ International Center for Law in Development (internationally oriented national body)
- ♦ International Center of Law, Life, Faith and Family (internationally oriented national body)
- ♦ International Center for Law and Religion Studies, Provo UT (internationally oriented national body)
- ♦ International Center for Letter of Credit Arbitration (internationally oriented national body)
- ♦ International Center for Materials Research (internationally oriented national body)
- ♦ International Center for Mathematical Meetings (internationally oriented national body)
- ♦ International Center for Mental Health (internationally oriented national body)

♦ International Center of Mental Health Policy and Economics (ICMPE) 12470

Dir Via Daniele Crespi 7, 20123 Milan MI, Italy. T. +39258106901. Fax +39258106901. E-mail: info@icmpe.org.
URL: http://www.icmpe.org/
Aims Facilitate the integration of various disciplines whose research focuses on the mental health sector from different perspectives (psychiatry, economics, public health, health services analysis, sociology). **Activities** Organizes meetings and workshops. Grants the 'Adam Smith Award'. Provides training. **Events** *Workshop on costs and assessment in psychiatry* Venice (Italy) 2011. **Publications** *Journal of Mental Health Policy and Economics*. [2010/XJ1742/**D**]

- ♦ International Center for Non-profit Law / see International Center for Not-for-Profit Law (#12471)
- ♦ International Center on Nonviolent Conflict (internationally oriented national body)

♦ International Center for Not-for-Profit Law (ICNL) 12471

Pres 1126 16th St NW, Ste 400, Washington DC 20036, USA. T. +12024528600. Fax +12024528555. E-mail: infoicnl@icnl.org.
URL: http://www.icnl.org/
History 15 Oct 1992, Wilmington DE (USA). Also referred to as *International Center for Non-profit Law*. **Aims** Improve the legal environment for civil society, philanthropy and public participation around the world. **Structure** Advisory Council of 42 members. Board of Directors, comprising Chair, Vice-Chair, Secretary, Treasurer and 2 ex-officio. Office in Washington DC (USA). Affiliate offices in Budapest (Hungary) – *European Center for Not-for-Profit Law (ECNL, #06463)* – and Sofia (Bulgaria). Representative offices in: Azerbaijan; Afghanistan; Kazakhstan; Turkmenistan; Ukraine. LLC offices in Kyrgyzstan, Tajikistan and Russia. **Finance** Supported by various public and private organizations, including: *Charles Stewart Mott Foundation*; *Council on Foundations (CF)*; *Counterpart International (FSP)*; *East-West Management Institute (EWMI)*; *Ford Foundation (#09858)*; *International Bank for Reconstruction and Development (IBRD, #12317)*; *MacArthur Foundation*; *United States Agency for International Development (USAID)*; *World Learning*. **Activities** Advocacy/lobbying/activism; guidance/assistance/consulting. **Events** *Global Forum* Stockholm (Sweden) 2015, *Global forum on civil society law* Istanbul (Turkey) 2005, *Conference* Sinaia (Romania) 1994. **Publications** *Global Trends in NGO Law* (4 a year) – online; *International Journal of Not-for-Profit Law* (4 a year) – online. Philanthropy law reports; country reports; reports and surveys. Information Services: Maintains an online database.
Members Not a membership organization. Standing relationship ith organizations and individuals in 84 countries and territories:
Albania, Algeria, Argentina, Armenia, Azerbaijan, Bahrain, Bangladesh, Belarus, Bosnia-Herzegovina, Brazil, Bulgaria, Canada, Colombia, Cook Is, Croatia, Cyprus, Czechia, Ecuador, Egypt, El Salvador, Estonia, Fiji, France, Georgia, Germany, Ghana, Guatemala, Honduras, Hungary, India, Indonesia, Iraq, Ireland, Japan, Jordan, Kazakhstan, Kenya, Kiribati, Kosovo, Kyrgyzstan, Laos, Latvia, Lebanon, Lithuania, Malta, Mexico, Micronesia FS, Moldova, Mongolia, Morocco, Nauru, Netherlands, New Zealand, Nicaragua, Nigeria, Niue, North Macedonia, Palau, Palestine, Paraguay, Peru, Philippines, Poland, Romania, Russia, Rwanda, Samoa, Saudi Arabia, Serbia, Sierra Leone, Slovakia, Slovenia, Solomon Is, Tajikistan, Tanzania UR, Türkiye, Tuvalu, UK, Ukraine, USA, Uzbekistan, Vanuatu, Venezuela, Vietnam.
Consultative Status Consultative status granted from: *ECOSOC (#05331)* (Special); *African Commission on Human and Peoples' Rights (ACHPR, #00255)* (Observer). **NGO Relations** Member of: *American Council for Voluntary International Action (InterAction)*; *CIVICUS: World Alliance for Citizen Participation (#03962)*; *Extractive Industries Transparency Initiative (EITI, #09229)*; *Worldwide Initiatives for Grantmaker Support (WINGS, #21926)*. Partner of: *Arab NGO Network for Development (ANND, #01016)*. [2017.06.01/XE4219/**E**]

- ♦ International Center for Otologic Training (internationally oriented national body)

♦ International Center for Peace and Development (ICPD) 12472

Exec Dir 2352 Stonehouse Drive, Napa CA 94558, USA. T. +17072524967. Fax +17072528169.
URL: http://www.icpd.org/
History Founded 22 Apr 1989, Napa CA (USA), as *International Commission on Peace and Food (ICPF)*, 1st preliminary meeting having been held 19-20 Oct 1990, Trieste (Italy), under the sponsorship of *TWAS (#20270)*. Converted into a research institution and present name adopted 15 Aug 1996. **Aims** Promote world peace and international development by conducting theoretical research and practical programmes to accelerate economic and social development, eradicate unemployment, double world food production and preserve the environment. **Structure** Plenary Meeting (annual). Secretariat in Napa CA (USA). Working Groups (5): Theory of Peace; Abolition of Nuclear Weapons; Full Employment; Theory of Money; Education. **Languages** English. **Finance** Individual contributions. **Activities** Undertakes research to evolve a comprehensive theoretical framework for development, a theory of peace, a theory of money and strategies to promote full employment. Major projects: Establishment of Human Science Wiki – an integral approach to human accomplishment and development. Recent studies: Strategies for Full Employment in India; Employment Generation in Southeastern Europe; Future of Work; Abolition of Nuclear Weapons. Co-sponsored establishment of an experimental school for early childhood learning, Pondicherry (India). Organizes and co-sponsors conferences and seminars. **Events** *Annual Conference* Delhi (India) 2011, *Annual Conference* Hyderabad (India) 2008, *Annual Conference* New York, NY (USA) 2006, *Annual Conference* Washington, DC (USA) / Zagreb (Croatia) 2005, *Annual Conference* Delhi (India) 2004. **Publications** *Cadmus Journal* (2 a year). *Uncommon Opportunities: An Agenda for Peace and Equitable Development* (1994) – 2nd ed 2004. Working papers. **IGO Relations** Formal contacts with: Secretariat of the *United Nations (UN, #20515)* General Assembly; *UNDP (#20292)*; *UNESCO (#20322)*; *UNICEF (#20332)*. [2012.06.01/XE1589/v/**E**]

- ♦ International Center for Peace and Justice (internationally oriented national body)
- ♦ International Center for Policy and Conflict (internationally oriented national body)
- ♦ International Center for the Political Economy of Sustainable Development (internationally oriented national body)
- ♦ International Center for Professional Development (internationally oriented national body)

♦ International Center on Qanats and Historic Hydraulic Structures, Yazd (ICQHS) 12473

Centre international sur les Qanats et les ouvrages historiques hydrauliques, Yazd
Main Office Mojtame Edarat, Daneshjoo Blvd, Yazd, 9816188117, Iran Islamic Rep. T. +983538258393 – +983538250553. Fax +983538241690. E-mail: info@icqhs.org.
URL: http://www.icqhs.org/

History Founded Mar 2005, under the auspices of *UNESCO (#20322)*. **Aims** Promote information and capacities with regard to all aspects of Qanat technology and other historic hydraulic structures to fulfil sustainable development of *water resources* and public welfare within the communities whose existence depend on the rational exploitation of the resources and preservation of such historical structures; promote research and development to restore Qanats and other traditional historic hydraulic structures for sustainable development objectives through international cooperation and global transfer of knowledge and technology; preserve cultural values regarding materialistic and spiritual frameworks. **Structure** Board, composed of: a representative of the Government: a representative of each of the other Member States that have sent the Director-General notification and make a substantial contribution to the operating budget or running of the Centre; a representative of the Director-General of the Organization; Director of RCUWMM-Teheran; a representative of any other intergovernmental organization or international non-governmental organization making a substantial contribution to the operating budget or running of the Centre. Headquarters based in Yazd (Iran Islamic Rep). **Languages** English, Persian. **Staff** 8.00 FTE, paid. **Finance** Sources: Non-governmental – budget comes from contracts signed with other entities mostly in terms of study and training projects on qanats and historic hydraulic structures, covering a part of salaries and running budget; Governmental – budget comes from the Iranian Ministry of Energy. **Activities** Training/education; events/meetings; research/documentation; knowledge management/information dissemination; publishing activities. **Publications** *A Survey on the Qanats of Bam from Engineering Point of View*; *Qanat in its Cradle*; *Qanat Practitioners of Kerman*; *Quanat from Practitioners' Point of View*; *Veins of Desert*. Proceedings; abstracts. [2020/XJ0861/E]

♦ International Center for Relativistic Astrophysics (ICRA) 12474

Pres address not obtained. E-mail: segreteria@icra.it.
URL: http://www.icra.it/

History 1985. Became a legal entity 1991. Former names and other names: *Centre international d'astrophysique, Rome* – former; *Consorzio Internazionale di Astrofisica Relativistica* – former. **Structure** Assembly; Council; President. **Activities** Events/meetings; training/education. **Events** *MG16 – Triennial Marcel Grossmann Meeting on General Relativity* Rome (Italy) 2021, *MG15 – Triennial Marcel Grossmann Meeting on General Relativity* Rome (Italy) 2018, *MG14 – Triennial Marcel Grossmann Meeting on General Relativity* Rome (Italy) 2015, *MG13 – Triennial Marcel Grossmann Meeting on General Relativity* Stockholm (Sweden) 2012, *MG12 – Triennial Marcel Grossmann Meeting on General Relativity* Paris (France) 2009.
Members Universities and institutes in 4 countries:
China, Holy See, Italy, USA.
Included in the above, 2 organizations listed in this Yearbook:
Abdus Salam International Centre for Theoretical Physics (ICTP, #00005); *TWAS (#20270)*.
NGO Relations National societies; universities; research centres. [2022.05.25/XN0023/D]

♦ International Center for Relativistic Astrophysics Network (ICRANet) 12475

Dir Piazza della Repubblica 10, 65122 Pescara PE, Italy. T. +398523054200. Fax +39854219252. E-mail: secretariat@icranet.org.
URL: http://www.icranet.org/

History Statutes adopted 19 Mar 2003. Registration: Start date: 10 Feb 2005, Italy. **Aims** Promote training, education and research in the fields of relativistic astrophysics, cosmology, theoretical physics and mathematical physics. **Structure** Steering Committee; Scientific Committee; Director. **Finance** Sources: contributions; donations; government support. **Activities** Events/meetings; research/documentation; training/education.
Members Governments of 3 countries:
Armenia, Holy See, Italy.
Universities and research centres (3):
International Center for Relativistic Astrophysics (ICRA, #12474); Stanford University (USA); University of Arizona (USA).
NGO Relations National and international societies; universities; research centres. [2022.10.19/XM4783/F]

- ♦ International Center for Relief to Civilian Populations (inactive)
- ♦ International Center for Religion and Diplomacy (internationally oriented national body)

♦ International Center for Research and Decision Support of the International Federation of Catholic Universities (CIRAD) 12476

Centre International de Recherche et d'Aide à la Décision de la Fédération Internationale des Universités Catholiques – Centro Internacional de Investigación y de Apoyo a la Decisión de la Federación Internacional de Universidades Católicas

Dir c/o FIUC, 21 rue d'Assas, 75270 Paris CEDEX 06, France. T. +33144395227. Fax +33144395228. E-mail: sgfiuc@bureau.fiuc.org – montserrat.alom@bureau.fiuc.org.
URL: http://www.cirad-fiuc.org/

History 1975, Delhi (India), during the General Assembly of *International Federation of Catholic Universities (IFCU, #13381)*, when it took the initiative (almost revolutionary at the time) to turn to concerted research by creating its own Centre of Coordination of Research (CCR). Original title: *Centre for Coordination of Research of the International Federation of Catholic Universities – Centre de coordination de la recherche de la Fédération Internationale des Universités Catholiques – Centro Coordinador de la Investigación de la Federación Internacional de Universidades Católicas*. Statutes drawn up by IFCU Council, Feb 1980, Seattle WA (USA). Previously located in Rome (Italy); Jan 1995, moved to IFCU general secretariat in Paris (France). **Aims** Promote joint inter-institutional initiatives among IFCU affiliated universities and various stakeholders in the fields of research and training, and consultancy and foresight. **Structure** Director; Project Chief; Research Assistant. **Languages** English, French, Spanish. **Staff** 4.00 FTE, paid. **Finance** Funding from national and international institutions; private and public donors; foundations. **Activities** Networking/liaising; knowledge management/information dissemination; training/education. **Events** *General Assembly* Melbourne, VIC (Australia) 2015, *General Assembly* Sao Paulo (Brazil) 2012, *General Assembly* Bangkok (Thailand) 2006, *General Assembly* Kampala (Uganda) 2003, *International seminar on new religious movements in Asia* Manila (Philippines) 1993. **Publications** *Electronic Newsletter* (11 a year); *Analisis* – review; *Journals of the Center*. Symposia proceedings; research reports; publications representing results of projects.
Members Full organizations in 53 countries and territories:
Angola, Argentina, Australia, Belgium, Brazil, Cameroon, Canada, Chile, Colombia, Congo DR, Côte d'Ivoire, Czechia, Dominican Rep, Ecuador, France, Germany, Ghana, Guatemala, Haiti, Honduras, Hungary, India, Indonesia, Ireland, Italy, Japan, Kenya, Korea Rep, Lebanon, Malta, Mexico, Mozambique, Netherlands, Nicaragua, Palestine, Panama, Paraguay, Peru, Philippines, Poland, Portugal, Puerto Rico, Romania, Spain, Switzerland, Taiwan, Thailand, Uganda, UK, Ukraine, Uruguay, USA, Venezuela. [2017.10.26/XE8123/E]

- ♦ International Center for Research on Women (internationally oriented national body)
- ♦ International Center of Social Gerontology (inactive)
- ♦ International Center for the Study of the Herculaneum Papyri (internationally oriented national body)
- ♦ International Center for the Study of Violent Extremism (internationally oriented national body)
- ♦ International Center for Technology Assessment (internationally oriented national body)
- ♦ International Center for Terrorism Studies (internationally oriented national body)
- ♦ International Center for Transitional Justice (internationally oriented national body)
- ♦ International Center for Tropical Ecology, St Louis MO / see Whitney R Harris World Ecology Center
- ♦ International Center for Urban Water Hydroinformatics Research and Innovation (internationally oriented national body)
- ♦ International Center for Work and Family (internationally oriented national body)
- ♦ International Central American Bureau (inactive)
- ♦ International Central American Tribunal (inactive)
- ♦ International Central Office for the Control of the Liquor Traffic in Africa (inactive)
- ♦ International Centre of Advanced Communication Studies for Latin America (#03806)
- ♦ International Centre for Advanced Technical and Vocational Training / see International Training Centre of the ILO (#15717)
- ♦ International Centre for the Advancement of Community-Based Rehabilitation (internationally oriented national body)
- ♦ International Centre for the Advancement of Human Rights (internationally oriented national body)
- ♦ International Centre for Advancement of Manufacturing Technology, Bangalore (see: #20336)
- ♦ International Centre for African Social and Economic Documentation (inactive)
- ♦ International Centre Against Censorship – Article 19 / see ARTICLE 19 (#01121)
- ♦ International Centre for Antarctic Information and Research / see Gateway Antarctica
- ♦ International Centre for Arachnological Documentation / see International Society of Arachnology (#14935)

♦ International Centre for Archival Research (ICARUS) 12477

Communications Manager SPACES Central Station, Turm 9, Gertrude Fröhlich Sander Str 2-4, 1100 Vienna, Austria. E-mail: info@icar-us.eu.
URL: http://www.icar-us.eu/

History 2008. Current statutes adopted 15 Jun 2011, Poznan (Poland)/Vienna (Austria). Registration: Austria. **Aims** Support the archives facing IT challenges; coordinate international and transnational collaboration between archives and other cultural and scientific institutions; support archives through project initiation and processing; supply digital platforms and non-commercial services for project realization. **Structure** General Assembly; Board of Directors. **Activities** Events/meetings. **Events** *Meeting* Paris (France) 2022, *Meeting* St Pölten (Austria) 2022, *Meeting* Helsinki (Finland) 2018, *Meeting* Madrid (Spain) 2017, *Meeting* Madrid (Spain) 2013.
Members Regular; Special; Honorary. Members in 25 countries:
Albania, Austria, Belgium, Bosnia-Herzegovina, Bulgaria, Canada, Croatia, Czechia, Finland, France, Germany, Hungary, Italy, Kosovo, Malta, Montenegro, Netherlands, North Macedonia, Poland, Romania, Serbia, Slovakia, Slovenia, Spain, Switzerland.
Included in the above, 1 organization listed in this Yearbook:
European Research Centre for Book and Paper Conservation-Restoration (ERC, #08359).
NGO Relations *National Movements and Intermediary Structures in Europe (NISE, #16938)*. [2022.10.19/XJ5265/y/D]

- ♦ International Centre for Asian Studies (internationally oriented national body)
- ♦ International Centre for Bamboo and Rattan (internationally oriented national body)
- ♦ International Centre for the Bantu Civilizations (inactive)
- ♦ International Centre for Biological Sciences, Caracas (internationally oriented national body)

♦ International Centre for Black Sea Studies (ICBSS) 12478

Dir Gen 19-21 Arachovis Str, Ippokratous, 106 80 Athens, Greece. T. +302103242321. Fax +302103242244. E-mail: icbss@icbss.org.
URL: http://www.icbss.org/

History 24 Mar 1998, Athens (Greece). Founded as a non-profit organisation, by the Hellenic Ministry of Foreign Affairs, on a decision of the *Organization of Black Sea Economic Cooperation (BSEC, #17857)*. Since, fulfilled a dual function as an independent research and training institution focusing on the wider Black Sea region, and also as a related body of the BSEC and its think-tank. **Aims** Foster multilateral cooperation among BSEC member states as well as with their international partners; pursue applied, policy-oriented research; build capacity; promote knowledge on the Black Sea region both within and outside its boundaries. **Structure** International Board of Directors (BoD), consisting of senior representatives from the diplomatic and academic communities of 12 BSEC Member States, and including BSEC PERMIS Secretary General, ICBSS Director General and Alternate Director General, and three personalities of international standing. **Languages** English. **Staff** 10-15 permanent paid; plus external collaborators, trainees and/or interns. **Activities** Events/meetings; projects/programmes; research/documentation; training/education. **Events** *Annual Conference* Moscow (Russia) 2010, *Annual Conference* Rhodes Is (Greece) 2006. **Publications** *The Black Sea Monitor* (4 a year) – online review. *The Xenophon Papers* (2006 – 2018) in English – series; *Policy Briefs* – series. **NGO Relations** Member of (1): *International Federation for Sustainable Development and Fight to Poverty in the Mediterranean-Black Sea (FISPMED, #13562)*. [2023.02.15/XK1891/E]

♦ International Centre for Career Development and Public Policy (ICCDPP) 12479

Dir 161 B – Av St Marguerite, 06200 Nice, France. E-mail: jmc@iccdpp.org.
URL: http://www.iccdpp.org/

History Proposed at OECD International Review of Career Guidance symposium, Toronto (Canada), 2003. Established 2004, within *European Centre for the Development of Vocational Training (Cedefop, #06474)*. Set up as a separate legal entity, 2006, Strasbourg (France). Moved to Wellington (New Zealand), 2010. Relocated to Nice (France), 2013. Incorporated as a not for profit legal entity in Denmark, 2018. **Aims** Facilitate and promote international policy sharing and policy learning for public career guidance provision through its website, newsletter, and international symposia for career guidance and public policy. **Structure** Executive Board; Director. **Languages** English, French. **Staff** 1.00 FTE, paid. **Finance** Sources: government support. Other sources: support from organizations and companies. Supporters to date have included: education ministries of Australia, Denmark, Ireland, Luxembourg, New Zealand, Canada, and UK; national career delivery organizations and associations; career guidance resources company (USA). Annual budget: 16,000 EUR. **Activities** Events/meetings; guidance/assistance/consulting; knowledge management/information dissemination. Active in all member countries. **Events** *Symposium* Tromsø (Norway) 2019, *Career Development – at the crossroads of relevance and impact* Seoul (Korea Rep) 2017. **Publications** *ICCDPP Newsletter* (12 a year). Information and advice on policy and systems development for career guidance provided on request.
Members Individuals in 8 countries:
Australia, Canada, Chile, Denmark, Finland, Hungary, UK, USA. [2022.06.23/XJ5439/C]

- ♦ International Centre of Chemical Fertilizers and Products Useful for Agriculture / see Centre international scientifique des fertilisants (#03767)
- ♦ International Centre for Choral Music (internationally oriented national body)
- ♦ International Centre for the City, the Architecture and the Landscape (internationally oriented national body)
- ♦ International Centre for Climate Change and Development (internationally oriented national body)
- ♦ International Centre of Climate and Environmental Sciences (internationally oriented national body)
- ♦ International Centre for Coastal and Ocean Policy Studies (internationally oriented national body)
- ♦ International Centre for Coastal Resources Management / see International Centre for Coastal Resources Research (#12480)

♦ International Centre for Coastal Resources Research 12480

Centre Internacional d'Investigació dels Recursos Costaners (CIIRC)

Vice-Pres Jordi Girona 1-3, Campus Nord-UPC, Edif D-1, 08034 Barcelona, Spain. T. +34932806400. Fax +34932806019. E-mail: ciirc@upc.edu.
URL: https://camins.upc.edu/en/research/deps-centres-labs

History Jan 1993. Founded, having been proposed Apr 1989. A coordination centre for interdisciplinary applied coastal research created by the Generalitat de Catalunya (Barcelona), the Universitat Politècnica de Catalunya (Barcelona) and *International Federation of Institutes for Advanced Study (IFIAS, inactive)*, with the support of *UNEP (#20299)*. Former names and other names: *International Centre for Coastal Resources Management* – former; *International Coordinating Centre for Coastal Resources Management* – former. **Aims** Initiate and coordinate: execution of coastal engineering and coastal science studies analysing and resolving coastal zone and *nearshore* problems; execution of coastal resources management studies aiming towards *sustainable development* of coastal zones and resources; education and training programmes on coastal zone problems and resources management. **Structure** Sections (8). **Languages** English, Spanish. **Events** *Conference* Barcelona (Spain) 2012, *COASTLAB international conference* Barcelona (Spain) 2010, *International conference on coastal dynamics* Barcelona (Spain) 2005, *MEDCOAST : international conference on the Mediterranean costal environment / Biennial Conference* Tarragona (Spain) 1995, *International conference on coastal dynamics* Barcelona (Spain) 1994. [2016.10.19/XF5180/E]

♦ International Centre for Coast Ecohydrology (ICCE) 12481

UNESCO Chair c/o CIMA, Science and Technology Faculty, Building 7, University of Algarve, Campus de Gambelas, 8005-139 Faro, Portugal.
Contact Av 16 de Junho, 8700-311 Olhão, Portugal. T. +351289713218. Fax +351289715031.
URL: http://icce-unesco.org/

History Oct 2009, Portugal, with the approval of General Assembly of *UNESCO (#20322)*. **Aims** Contribute to the implementation of UNESCO's programmes, particularly the International Hydrological Program, through the development of scientific knowledge based on the concept of ecohydrology and the establishment of educational strategies and cultural dissemination for the society, which harmonize the sustainable use of aquatic resources with the enhancement of human being, contributing to the improvement of quality of life of society, with special emphasis on Africa and areas of Mediterranean climate. **Structure** Departments (3): Education; Science and Cooperation; Communication. **Publications** *ICCE Newsletter*.
Members Full in 5 countries:
Brazil, Germany, Poland, Portugal, Spain.
International organizations (2):
European Regional Centre for Ecohydrology of the Polish Academy of Sciences, Lodz (ERCE PAS, #08341).
[2017/XJ1671/y/**E**]

♦ International Centre for Comparative Criminology (ICCC) 12482

Centre international de criminologie comparée (CICC)
Dir Univ de Montréal, CP 6128, Succursale Centre Ville, Montréal QC H3C 3J7, Canada. T. +15143437065. Fax +15143432269. E-mail: cicc@umontreal.ca.
URL: http://www.cicc-iccc.org/

History 1 Jun 1969, Montréal, QC (Canada). Founded by agreement between *International Society of Criminology (ISC, #15038)* and the Université de Montréal. Combined with Université du Québec à Trois-Rivières, 2016. **Aims** Unite an interdisciplinary group of experts in the study of crime, and public, private and community institutions that are assembled in reaction to crime. **Structure** Council; Researchers (62). **Languages** English, French. **Staff** 7.00 FTE, paid. **Finance** Sources: government support; grants. Supported by: Canadian government; University of Montréal. Annual budget: 650,000 CAD. **Activities** Events/meetings; research/documentation; training/education. **Events** *Colloque International sur le Rôle des Intervenants dans l'Abandon des Carrières Criminelles* Montréal, QC (Canada) 2020, *OH CANNABIS ! Un an après la légalisation du cannabis au Canada* Montréal, QC (Canada) 2019, *Atelier international sur la participation de la police civile aux opérations de paix* Montréal, QC (Canada) 2011, *Atelier sur les réseaux illicites* Wollongong, NSW (Australia) 2010, *French-speaking international colloquium* Nicolet, QC (Canada) 2005. **Publications** *ICCC Newsletter* (weekly); *Revue Criminologie* (2 a year). Annual Report; research studies; articles; reports.
Members in 13 countries:
Australia, Belgium, Brazil, Côte d'Ivoire, Cyprus, France, Italy, Netherlands, South Africa, Spain, Switzerland, UK, USA.
NGO Relations Member of (1): *Association internationale des criminologues de langue française (AICLF, #02678)*. Cooperates with: African, Canadian and European institutes. [2020.11.17/XF0280/**E**]

♦ International Centre of Comparative Environmental Law 12483

Centre international de droit comparé de l'environnement (CIDCE)
Pres 32 rue Turgot, 87000 Limoges, France. T. +33607730751. E-mail: admin@cidce.org.
URL: http://www.cidce.org/

History 27 Jul 1982, Limoges (France). **Aims** Group *jurists* and national associations specialized in environmental law from various countries worldwide for facilitating a better mutual knowledge of environmental law, exchanging information and harmonizing the rules of the law in order to save the environment. **Structure** Executive Council; Scientific Council. **Languages** English, French, Spanish. **Staff** 1.00 FTE, paid. **Finance** Sources: grants; sale of publications. Research contracts. Annual budget: 52,402 EUR. **Activities** Events/meetings; training/education. **Events** *Meeting* Limoges (France) 2021, *Measuring the Effectiveness of Environmental Law through Legal Indicators* Sceaux (France) 2021, *Meeting* Limoges (France) 2010, *Colloquium on Natural Disasters and the Law* Limoges (France) 2009, *Workshop on legal support for the implementation of the Ramsar Convention in West and Central Africa* Yaoundé (Cameroon) 2006. **Publications** *Revue européenne de droit de l'environnement* (4 a year) in French. Books; reports; recommendations.
Members Individuals and associations in 29 countries:
Argentina, Belgium, Brazil, Cameroon, Canada, Chile, Colombia, Czechia, Finland, France, Germany, Greece, India, Italy, Japan, Mexico, Morocco, Netherlands, Portugal, Romania, Senegal, Spain, Switzerland, Togo, Tunisia, Türkiye, UK, Uruguay, Venezuela.
Regional associations (2), listed in this Yearbook:
African Environmental Law Association, Yaoundé (no recent information); European Environmental Law Association (inactive).
Consultative Status Consultative status granted from: *ECOSOC (#05331)* (Special); *UNEP (#20299)*. **IGO Relations** Observer status with (1): *Codex Alimentarius Commission (CAC, #04081)*. Accredited to the Conference of the Parties of: *Secretariat of the United Nations Convention to Combat Desertification (Secretariat of the UNCCD, #19208)*. **NGO Relations** Member of (4): *International Council of Environmental Law (ICEL, #13018); International Union for Conservation of Nature and Natural Resources (IUCN, #15766); Mediterranean Information Office for Environment, Culture and Sustainable Development (MIO-ECSDE, #16657); Transparency, Accountability and Participation Network (TAP Network, #20222).* [2023/XF1568/**E**]

♦ International Centre of Complex Project Management (ICCPM) 12484

CEO PO Box 327, WEST, Deakin ACT 2600, Australia. T. +61261205110. E-mail: admin@iccpm.com.
URL: http://iccpm.com/

History Establishment 2007 led by Australian Department of Defence (Defence Materiel Organisation), with support from UK Ministry of Defence, US Department of Defense, Canadian National Defence and Defence industry as part of the Australian Department of Defence's Complex Project Management Initiative. Registered in accordance with Australian law. **Aims** Build organizational capability in complex project management. **Structure** Board of Directors. **Languages** English. **Activities** Events/meetings; guidance/assistance/consulting; networking/liaising; research/documentation; training/education. **Events** *Round Table* Brisbane, QLD (Australia) 2018, *Round Table* Canberra, ACT (Australia) 2018, *Round Table* Melbourne, VIC (Australia) 2018. **Publications** *CONNECT Magazine* (4 a year). Reports; ebooks; articles; blogs; podcasts.
Members Full in 7 countries:
Australia, Brazil, Canada, India, Singapore, UK, USA. [2020.03.03/XM6982/**C**]

- ♦ International Centre for Conflict and Human Rights Analysis (internationally oriented national body)
- ♦ International Centre on Conflict and Negotiation (internationally oriented national body)
- ♦ International Centre for Counter-Terrorism – The Hague (internationally oriented national body)
- ♦ International Centre for Criminal Law Reform and Criminal Justice Policy (internationally oriented national body)
- ♦ International Centre of Cultural Development and Cooperation, Rome (internationally oriented national body)
- ♦ International Centre for Cultural Studies (internationally oriented national body)
- ♦ International Centre for Defence and Security (internationally oriented national body)
- ♦ International Centre for Democratic Transition (internationally oriented national body)
- ♦ International Centre for Demonstration and Training in Utilising Rainwater (internationally oriented national body)
- ♦ International Centre for Development Initiatives (internationally oriented national body)
- ♦ International Centre for Development Oriented Research in Agriculture (internationally oriented national body)
- ♦ International Centre for Development and Research (internationally oriented national body)
- ♦ International Centre for Diarrhoeal Disease Research, Bangladesh / see ICDDR,B (#11051)
- ♦ International Centre for Diarrhoeal Disease Research, Centre for Health and Population Research / see ICDDR,B (#11051)
- ♦ International Centre for Diffraction Data (internationally oriented national body)
- ♦ International Centre for the Documentation and Research of Basketball, Alcobendas (internationally oriented national body)

♦ International Centre for Earth Construction 12485

Centre international de la construction en terre (CRATerre-ENSAG)
Pres Maison Levrat, Parc Fallavier, 2 rue de la Buthière, BP 53, 38092 Villefontaine CEDEX, France. T. +33474954391. Fax +33474956421. E-mail: craterre@grenoble.archi.fr.
URL: http://www.craterre.org/

History 1979, as *International Centre for the Research and the Application of Earth Construction – Centre international de recherche et d'application pour la construction en terre*. Since 1986, functions as research centre of the school of architecture of the University of Grenoble. Full title, in French: *Centre international de la construction en terre – Ecole nationale supérieure d'architecture de Grenoble (CRATerre-ENSAG)*. **Aims** Encourage *local authorities* to assume responsibility for *spatial development* and *town planning*; improve *housing* conditions of *underprivileged* populations; promote earth construction; encourage inhabitants to create and control their own *living conditions*. **Languages** English, French. **Staff** 28.00 FTE, paid. **Finance** Budget (annual): about euro 800,000. **Activities** Research and development; training/education; knowledge management/information dissemination; training/education; events/meetings. **Events** *TERRA Conference on the Study and Conservation of Earthen Architectural Heritage* Lyon (France) 2016, *TERRA conference on the study and conservation of earthen architectural heritage* Lima (Peru) 2012, *Conference* Peru 2012, *TERRA Conference on the study and conservation of earthen architecture / Conference* Bamako (Mali) 2008, *Regional seminar on wooden structures conservation* Muscat (Oman) 2003. **Publications** *Building with Earth* (1996) in English, Spanish; *Compressed Earth Blocks* (1995) in English, French – 3 vols; *Earth Construction – A Comprehensive Guide* – (1989) in French, (1994) in English. Technical notebook series; technology guides series; technical and scientific books; monographs; manuals; bibliographies; catalogues; conference and colloquium proceedings; videos; tapes; slides; posters.
Members Principal international member institutes (4), listed in this Yearbook:
International Association for Housing Science (IAHS, #11943); International Council on Monuments and Sites (ICOMOS, #13049); International Foundation for Earth Construction (IFEC, no recent information); UNESCO (#20322).
Individuals in 10 countries:
Australia, Brazil, Colombia, France, Germany, India, Italy, Korea Rep, Netherlands, Spain.
Consultative Status Consultative status granted from: *ECOSOC (#05331)* (Ros C); *UNIDO (#20336)*. **NGO Relations** Member of: *Building Advisory Service and Information Network (BASIN, #03351)*. Partner of: *Global Network for Sustainable Housing (GNSH, #10502); Global Shelter Cluster (GSC, #10594).*
[2019/XE5987/y/**E**]

- ♦ International Centre for Earth Simulation (unconfirmed)

♦ International Centre for Earth Tides (ICET) 12486

Centre international des marées terrestres
Chairman University of French Polynesia, Laboratoire des Sciences de la Terre, BP 6570, 98702 Faaa TAHITI, Polynesia Fr.
URL: http://www.upf.pf/ICET

History Founded 1958, Brussels (Belgium), as a permanent service of *Federation of Astronomical and Geophysical Data Analysis Services (FAGS, inactive)* and *International Union of Geodesy and Geophysics (IUGG, #15776)*. **Aims** Conduct, store, evaluate, interpret and disseminate research on *tidal measurements* worldwide. **Structure** Directing Board; Director. **Languages** English, French. **Staff** 1.50 FTE, paid. **Finance** FAGS: US$1,500; Royal Observatory of Belgium (ROB): US$ 3,000. **Activities** Participates in the *Global Geodynamics Project (GGP)*, for which ICET is responsible of the data preprocessing and analysis and of the scientific maintenance of the database. **Events** *Quadrennial International Symposium on Geodynamics and Earth Tides* Trieste (Italy) 2016, *Quadrennial Symposium* Warsaw (Poland) 2013, *Quadrennial Symposium* Jena (Germany) 2008, *Quadrennial Symposium* Ottawa, ON (Canada) 2004, *Quadrennial Symposium* Mizusawa (Japan) 2000. **Publications** *ICET Bibliography* (annual); *Bulletin d'informations des marées terrestres* (2-3 a year).
Members Full in 89 countries and territories:
Afghanistan, Algeria, Argentina, Australia, Austria, Bahrain, Bangladesh, Belarus, Belgium, Bhutan, Bolivia, Brazil, Brunei Darussalam, Bulgaria, Cambodia, Canada, Chile, China, Côte d'Ivoire, Croatia, Cuba, Czechia, Denmark, Egypt, Estonia, Ethiopia, Finland, France, Germany, Greece, Guatemala, Hong Kong, Hungary, Iceland, India, Indonesia, Iran Islamic Rep, Iraq, Ireland, Israel, Italy, Japan, Kenya, Korea DPR, Korea Rep, Latvia, Lebanon, Libya, Lithuania, Luxembourg, Madagascar, Malaysia, Mexico, Monaco, Morocco, Mozambique, Myanmar, Netherlands, New Zealand, Nigeria, Norway, Pakistan, Philippines, Poland, Portugal, Romania, Russia, Saudi Arabia, Senegal, Serbia, Slovakia, Slovenia, South Africa, Spain, Sudan, Sweden, Switzerland, Syrian AR, Tanzania UR, Thailand, Tunisia, Türkiye, UK, Ukraine, Uruguay, USA, Venezuela, Vietnam, Zimbabwe.
NGO Relations *Global Geodetic Observing System (GGOS, see: #11914); Bureau gravimétrique international (BGI, #03361); Permanent Service for Mean Sea Level (PSMSL, #18333).* [2016/XF4067/**E**]

- ♦ International Centre of Economics, Humanities and Management (unconfirmed)
- ♦ International Centre on Economic, Social and Cultural Rights (internationally oriented national body)
- ♦ International Centre for Educational Research, Sèvres (internationally oriented national body)

♦ International Centre of Educational Systems (ICES) 12487

Centre international des systèmes d'éducation (CISE) – Internationales Zentrum für Ausbildungssysteme (IZAS) – Mezdunarodnyj Centr Obucajuscih Sistem (MCOS)
Pres Prospect Vernadski 125, app 10, Moscow MOSKVA, Russia, 119571. T. +79033638913. Fax +79035932627. E-mail: ices01@mail.ru – ices02@mail.ru.

History 1989, Paris (France), at 25th General Conference of UNESCO. **Aims** Implement the ideals of *international cooperation*; promote educational, cultural, scientific, technological and business multifaceted trans- and *inter-disciplinary* education of man; promote *technology transfer* and educational, cultural, scientific, technological and business cooperation among Russian, international and foreign organizations. **Structure** Council; Branches (7); Administration Units; General and Specialized Departments. Centre comprises: Director General; *International Chair-Network UNESCO/ICES on "Transfer of Technologies for Sustainable Development" (TTSD, no recent information)*, set up Nov 1993; *International Chair-Network UNESCO/ICES on "Technical and Vocational Education and Training" (TVET, see: #12487)*, set up Aug 1996. **Languages** English, French, German, Russian. **Staff** 12.00 FTE, voluntary. International Chair Networks and Branches: 24 FTE, paid; 18 voluntary. **Finance** Self supporting. **Activities** Training/education; events/meetings. **Events** *International conference of young scientists* Moscow (Russia) 2003, *International scientific and practical seminar* Moscow (Russia) 2003, *Man-Earth-space* Russia 2003, *Conference on promoting education for sustainable future in Russia* Moscow (Russia) 2000, *International conference on young scientists* Moscow (Russia) 2000. **Publications** *Magister* (6 a year) in English, German, Russian. Reports; book.
Members Associate: organizations and individuals in 5 countries:
Algeria, France, Morocco, Russia, Tajikistan.
IGO Relations *Council of Europe (CE, #04881)*. United Nations bodies: *International Atomic Energy Agency (IAEA, #12294); UNDP (#20292); UNEP (#20299); UNESCO (#20322); UNIDO (#20336)*. **NGO Relations** Member of: *International Association for Continuing Engineering Education (IACEE, #11817).*
[2018.07.01/XE1937/**E**]

- ♦ International Centre for Education, Capacity Building and Applied Research in Water (internationally oriented national body)
- ♦ International Centre for Education in Development, Coventry (internationally oriented national body)

♦ International Centre for Electronic Commerce (ICEC) 12488

Dir Kyung Hee Univ, 26 Kyungheedae-ro, Dongdaemun-gu, Seoul 02447, Korea Rep. T. +8229610490. Fax +8223250400. E-mail: contact@icec.net.
URL: http://www.icec.net/

History 15 Nov 1996, Seoul (Korea Rep). **Languages** Chinese, English, Korean. **Activities** Events/meetings; research/documentation. **Events** *ICEC Conference* Chengdu (China) 2021, *ICEC Conference* Chengdu (China) 2020, *ICEC Conference* Busan (Korea Rep) 2019, *ICEC Conference* Tianjin (China) 2018, *ICEC Conference* Seongnam (Korea Rep) 2017. **Publications** *Electronic Commerce Research and Applications (ECRA)*.
[2017/XN5169/**E**]

- ♦ International Centre for Environmental Education and Community Development (internationally oriented national body)

♦ International Centre for the Environmental Management of Enclosed Coastal Seas (internationally oriented national body)
♦ International Centre for Environmental and Nuclear Sciences (internationally oriented national body)
♦ International Centre for Environmental Social and Policy Studies (internationally oriented national body)

♦ International Centre for Environment Audit and Sustainable Development (iCED) 12489

Contact RIICO Industrial Area Kant Kalwar, Jaipur, Rajasthan, Jaipur RAJASTHAN, India. E-mail: iced@cag.gov.in.
URL: http://iced.cag.gov.in/

History 1993, Geneva (Switzerland), as *International Centre for Environment and Development (ICED)*. **Aims** Provide advice to government and international organizations and corporations on policy issues in the area of environment and development. **Structure** Founder/President; 3 Vice-Presidents; Secretary General; Treasurer; 4 Partners; 17 Associates. **Finance** Projects funded by several organizations, including: *UNEP (#20299); International Bank for Reconstruction and Development (IBRD, #12317); Ford Foundation (#09858)*. **Activities** Policy-level assistance; Environmental training; Environmental management. **IGO Relations** Accredited by: *Green Climate Fund (GCF, #10714)*. Partner of: *Mediterranean Action Plan (MAP, #16638)*. [2019/XE4236/**E**]

♦ International Centre for Environment and Development / see International Centre for Environment Audit and Sustainable Development (#12489)
♦ International Centre for Eremology (internationally oriented national body)

♦ International Centre for Ethnic Studies (ICES) 12490

Exec Dir 2 Kynsey Terrace, Colombo, 00800, Sri Lanka. T. +9412685085 – +9412679745 – +9412674884. Fax +9412698048. E-mail: admin@ices.lk.
Researcher 554/6A Peradeniya Road, Kandy, 20000, Sri Lanka. T. +94812232381. Fax +94812234892. E-mail: iceskandy@gmail.com.
URL: http://www.ices.lk/

History 1982, Sri Lanka. Registration: Registrar of Companies, No/ID: GA471, Start date: 2007, Sri Lanka. **Aims** Provide an organized institutional focus for the study and understanding of ethnic *conflict* and its management. **Structure** Board of Directors. **Languages** English. **Staff** 18.00 FTE, paid. **Finance** Sources: donations; revenue from activities/projects. **Activities** Advocacy/lobbying/activism; events/meetings; knowledge management/information dissemination; networking/liaising; research/documentation; training/education. **Publications** *Seminar Series*. Workshop reports; monographs; papers; books. **Members** Membership countries not specified. **NGO Relations** Member of (1): *International Dalit Solidarity Network (IDSN, #13129)*. Supports (1): *Global Call for Action Against Poverty (GCAP, #10263)*. [2021.05.26/XE2101/**E**]

♦ International Centre for Evidence in Disability (internationally oriented national body)

♦ International Centre of Excellence in Tourism and Hospitality Education (THE-ICE) 12491

CEO 49 Clover Street, Enoggera, Brisbane QLD 4051, Australia.
Sec address not obtained.
Main Website: http://www.the-ice.org/

History 2004, Australia. Founded as one of five international centres of excellence, funded by Australian government. Transformed into a not-for-profit international agency, 1 Jul 2008. **Aims** Enhance the quality of higher education in tourism, hospitality and events (TH&E) globally. **Events** *International Panel of Experts (IPoE) Forum* Manila (Philippines) 2019, *International Panel of Experts (IPoE) Forum* Bangkok (Thailand) 2018, *International Panel of Experts (IPoE) Forum* Melbourne, VIC (Australia) 2017, *International Panel of Experts (IPoE) Forum* Lucerne (Switzerland) 2016, *International Panel of Experts (IPoE) Forum* Leeuwarden (Netherlands) 2015.
Members Institutions (37) in 19 countries and territories:
Australia, Austria, Fiji, Finland, France, Hong Kong, Italy, Malaysia, Netherlands, Philippines, Poland, Qatar, Singapore, Switzerland, Taiwan, Thailand, UK, United Arab Emirates, USA.
NGO Relations Member of: *Asia-Pacific Quality Network (APQN, #02004)*. Associate member of: *European Alliance of Subject-Specific and Professional Accreditation and Quality Assurance (EASPA, #05887)*. [2022/XJ9471/**F**]

♦ International Centre for Eyecare Education / see Brien Holden Vision Institute
♦ International Centre for Eye Health (internationally oriented national body)

♦ International Centre for Family Studies 12492

Centre international d'études sur la famille – Centro Internazionale Studi Famiglia (CISF)
Dir Via Giotto 36, 20145 Milan MI, Italy. T. +39248072702. Fax +39248072799. E-mail: cisf@stpauls.it.
Registered Address Piazza San Paolo 14, 12051 Alba CN, Italy.
URL: http://www.cisf.it/

History Founded 1973, Milan (Italy), by the Society of Saint Paul. Registration: Italy. **Aims** Promote a culture of the family inspired by *Christian* principles. **Structure** Scientific Committee. **Languages** English, Italian. **Staff** 4.00 FTE, paid. Various collaborations. **Finance** Private donations. **Activities** Events/meetings; knowledge management/information dissemination; monitoring/evaluation. **Events** *Congress on Family and European Citizenship* Milan (Italy) 2004, *Women and family – family as the object of science* Bratislava (Slovakia) 1994, *Family associations – building links between the daily life of the family and new citizenship* Milan (Italy) 1994. **Publications** *Report on Family in Italy* (every 2 years). Books; reports; proceedings; e-newsletter. **IGO Relations** Associated with Department of Global Communications of the United Nations. **NGO Relations** Member of: *International Commission on Couple and Family Relations (ICCFR, #12676); World Family Organization (WFO, #21399)*. [2022/XE0858/**E**]

♦ International Centre of Films for Children and Young People 12493

Centre international du film pour l'enfance et la jeunesse (CIFEJ) – Centro Internacional del Film para Niños y Jóvenes – Internationale Zentrale für Kinder- und Jugendfilme
SG End of Seif St, Phase 3, Shahrak-e Gharb-Sanaat Sq, Teheran, 1466893311, Iran Islamic Rep. T. +982188087870. Fax +982188085847. E-mail: info@cifej.com.
Exec Dir address not obtained.
URL: http://www.cifej.com/

History 29 Mar 1955, Brussels (Belgium), following the Conference organized by Unesco, 1955, Edinburgh (UK). Statutes modified: 1961; 1966; 1971; 1992; 27 Sep 2000, Montréal QC (Canada); 2005, Teheran (Iran Islamic Rep); 2012, Warsaw (Poland). Registered: 29 Jul 1967, Brussels; 27 Feb 1967, Brussels (new statutes); 26 Nov 1971, Paris (France); 1992, Berlin (Germany); 3 Jan 2011, Teheran (Iran Islamic Rep); 21 Feb 2011, Istanbul (Turkey). **Aims** Promote production of films and *audio-visual media* that are culturally diverse, artistic, educational, informative and, at the same time, entertaining, especially designed for children and young people; help children to communicate through cinema. **Structure** General Assembly (every 2 years); Board of Directors; Secretariat. **Languages** English. **Staff** 2.00 FTE, paid. **Finance** Members' dues. Grants. **Activities** Events/meetings; awards/prizes/competitions; training/education; research/documentation. **Events** *General Assembly* Beijing (China) 2014, *General Assembly* Warsaw (Poland) 2012, *General Assembly* Warsaw (Poland) 2011, *General Assembly* Taiwan 2009, *General Assembly* Amsterdam (Netherlands) 2007. **Publications** *CIFEJ Info* (4 a year) in English; *Who's Who in CIFEJ* – online. *Calendar of Festivals* – online.
Members Active (95), representing Professional producers, distributors, broadcasters, writers and directors in the audiovisual industry and cultural educational institutions, festivals, consumer and parents groups, academics and media researchers. Organizations in 40 countries and territories:
Argentina, Austria, Bangladesh, Belarus, Belgium, Bulgaria, Canada, China, Colombia, Egypt, Finland, France, Germany, Greece, India, Iran Islamic Rep, Italy, Japan, Lebanon, Mauritius, Mexico, Netherlands, Nigeria, Norway, Pakistan, Poland, Qatar, Réunion, Serbia, Sierra Leone, Slovakia, Slovenia, South Africa, Spain, Syrian AR, Tajikistan, Tanzania UR, Türkiye, Ukraine, USA.
International/regional members (3):
European Children's Television Centre (ECTC, no recent information); Pan African Federation of Film Makers (FEPACI, no recent information); World Catholic Association for Communication (SIGNIS, #21264).
Consultative Status Consultative status granted from: *ECOSOC (#05331)* (Ros C); *UNICEF (#20332)*. **IGO Relations** Relevant treaty: *United Nations Convention on the Rights of the Child (CRC, 1989)*. Accredited by: *United Nations Office at Vienna (UNOV, #20604)*. [2016.12.14/XE1483/y/**E**]

♦ International Centre for Financial and Economic Development, Moscow (internationally oriented national body)
♦ International Centre for Food Micro-Algae Against Malnutrition (internationally oriented national body)
♦ International Centre for Foreign Journalists / see International Center for Journalists

♦ International Centre for Genetic Engineering and Biotechnology (ICGEB) 12494

Centre international de génie génétique et de biotechnologie (CIGGB)
Dir-Gen AREA Science Park, Padriciano 99, 34149 Trieste TS, Italy. T. +39403757337 – +394037571. Fax +39403757361 – +3940226555. E-mail: icgeb@icgeb.org – director.general@icgeb.org.
Communications Officer address not obtained.
URL: http://www.icgeb.org/

History 13 Sep 1983, Madrid (Spain). Established as a project of *UNIDO (#20336)*. Statutes entered into force in 1994, when ICGEB became an autonomous intergovernmental organization. The Agreement between UNIDO and ICGEB for the transfer of assets was signed 22 Dec 1995 by the two organizations. Part of *United Nations System (#20635)*. **Aims** Undertake research, development and training in *molecular* and *cell biology* for the benefit of *developing countries*; strengthen the research capability of members. **Structure** Board of Governors; ,Council of Scientific Advisers. Components (3): Trieste (Italy); Delhi (India); Cape Town (South Africa). Affiliated Centres in member states. **Languages** English. **Staff** Trieste: 118 researchers; 26 scientific support personnel and 32 administrative staff. Delhi (India): 120 researchers; 47 scientific support personnel and 22 administrative staff. The *Administrative Tribunal of the International Labour Organization (ILO Tribunal, #00118)* is competent to settle disputes. **Finance** Until 1998, voluntary contributions from member states (mainly Italy and India). From 1999, member states' contributions according to scale of assessment. Budget (annual): about US$ 14 million. **Activities** Events/meetings; financial and/or material support; guidance/assistance/consulting; research and development; training/education. **Events** *DNA Tumour Virus Conference* Montréal, QC (Canada) 2020, *Workshop on Plant Stress Biology and Food Security* Delhi (India) 2019, *Meeting on DNA Tumour Virus* Trieste (Italy) 2019, *Workshop on Emerging Issues in Oncogenic Virus Research* Bevagna (Italy) 2018, *Workshop on Human Papillomavirus* Rosario (Argentina) 2014. **Publications** Activity reports (annual). **Information Services** *ICGEBnet* – central biocomputing resource located in Trieste, that currently provides login facilities to over 600 users worldwide via Internet and X.25 connections.
Members Member States (66):
Afghanistan, Algeria, Angola, Argentina, Bangladesh, Bosnia-Herzegovina, Brazil, Bulgaria, Burkina Faso, Burundi, Cameroon, Chile, China, Colombia, Costa Rica, Côte d'Ivoire, Croatia, Cuba, Ecuador, Egypt, Eritrea, Ethiopia, Hungary, India, Iran Islamic Rep, Iraq, Italy, Jordan, Kenya, Kuwait, Kyrgyzstan, Liberia, Libya, Malaysia, Mauritius, Mexico, Montenegro, Morocco, Namibia, Nigeria, North Macedonia, Pakistan, Panama, Peru, Qatar, Romania, Russia, Saudi Arabia, Senegal, Serbia, Slovakia, Slovenia, South Africa, Sri Lanka, Sudan, Syrian AR, Tanzania UR, Trinidad-Tobago, Tunisia, Türkiye, United Arab Emirates, Uruguay, Venezuela, Vietnam, Zimbabwe.
Signatory Countries (43):
Afghanistan, Algeria, Argentina, Bolivia, Brazil, Bulgaria, Chile, China, Colombia, Congo Brazzaville, Congo DR, Costa Rica, Croatia, Cuba, Ecuador, Egypt, Greece, Hungary, India, Indonesia, Iran Islamic Rep, Iraq, Italy, Kuwait, Mauritania, Mauritius, Mexico, Morocco, Nigeria, Pakistan, Panama, Peru, Senegal, Spain, Sri Lanka, Sudan, Syrian AR, Thailand, Trinidad-Tobago, Tunisia, Türkiye, Venezuela, Vietnam.
IGO Relations Consultative Status with: *ECOSOC (#05331)*. Cooperation agreement with: United Nations; *UNESCO (#20322)*; UNIDO; *United Nations University (UNU, #20642)*. Cooperates with: *Commission on Science and Technology for Sustainable Development in the South (COMSATS, #04239)*. Member of: United Nations Inter-Agency Committee on Bioethics; *United Nations Joint Staff Pension Fund (UNJSPF, #20581)*. **NGO Relations** Member of: *Inter-Agency Network for Safety in Biotechnology (IANB, inactive); Consortium for the Barcode of Life (CBOL, #04737)*. Permanent Observer status with: *Red Latinoamericana de Ciencias Biológicas (RELAB, #18706)*. Observer to: *InterAcademy Partnership (IAP, #11376)*. [2022/XE0116/**E***]

♦ International Centre of Genetic Epistemology (inactive)
♦ International Centre for Geohazards (internationally oriented national body)

♦ International Centre for Global Earth Models (ICGEM) 12495

Dir c/o GFZ Helmholtz Centre, Telegrafenberg, 14473 Potsdam, Germany. E-mail: icgem@gfz-potsdam.de.
URL: http://icgem.gfz-potsdam.de/home/

History as a service within *International Association of Geodesy (IAG, #11914)*, a sub-structure of *International Union of Geodesy and Geophysics (IUGG, #15776)*. **Aims** Collect and archive all existing global gravity field models; validate global gravity field models by standardized procedures; collect and archive software for global gravity field models, manipulation and transformation; create a user interface for getting access to global gravity field models, validation results and manipulation software; create web site tutorials on global gravity field models, user interaction with the service and online software applications; contribute to IGeS schools. **Publications** Activity Report (annual). **NGO Relations** Member of: *Global Geodetic Observing System (GGOS, see: #11914)*. [2019/XM3679/**E**]

♦ International Centre on Global-Scale Geochemistry (internationally oriented national body)
♦ International Centre of Health Protection (internationally oriented national body)

♦ International Centre for Heat and Mass Transfer (ICHMT) 12496

Centre international d'études sur le transfert de chaleur et de masse
SG Mechanical Engineering Dept E-104, Middle East Technical Univ, Dumlupinar Bulvari No:1, 06800 Ankara/Ankara, Türkiye. T. +903122105213. E-mail: ichmt@ichmt.org.
Exec Sec address not obtained.
URL: http://www.ichmt.org/

History 16 Sep 1968, Herceg Novi (Montenegro). Statutes adopted 1969. Moved, 1993, to Ankara (Turkey). Statutes and By-Laws revised by General Assembly, 13 Aug 1994. Registration: Turkey. **Aims** Foster the international exchange of science and engineering in all branches of heat and mass transfer through symposia, publications, promotion of research and exchange of personnel. **Structure** General Assembly; Scientific Council; Executive Committee. **Languages** English. **Staff** 4.00 FTE, paid. **Finance** Sources: meeting proceeds; sale of publications. **Activities** Events/meetings. **Events** *International Symposium on Convective Heat and Mass Transfer (CONV-22)* Izmir (Türkiye) 2022, *International Symposium on Turbulence, Heat and Mass Transfer* St Petersburg (Russia) 2022, *International Symposium on Convective Heat and Mass Transfer* 2021, *International Symposium on Advances in Computational Heat Transfer* Rio de Janeiro (Brazil) 2021, *International Symposium on Turbulence, Heat and Mass Transfer* St Petersburg (Russia) 2021. **Publications** Proceedings of meetings.
Members Institutions (41) in 33 countries and territories:
Australia, Austria, Belarus, Belgium, Brazil, Canada, China, Egypt, France, Germany, Hungary, India, Israel, Italy, Japan, Korea Rep, Mexico, Morocco, Netherlands, New Zealand, Poland, Portugal, Romania, Russia, Serbia, South Africa, Spain, Sweden, Switzerland, Thailand, Türkiye, UK, USA.
NGO Relations Affiliated organization to: *International Union of Theoretical and Applied Mechanics (IUTAM, #15823)*. Close cooperation with: American Society of Mechanical Engineers (ASME). Also links with a number of international and national organizations interested in the field. [2022.05.13/XE5809/**E**]

♦ International Centre for Heritage Conservation (internationally oriented national body)
♦ International Centre for Higher Education Management (internationally oriented national body)
♦ International Centre for Human Development (internationally oriented national body)
♦ International Centre for the Humanities and Development, Byblos / see International Centre for Human Sciences, Byblos
♦ International Centre for Human Sciences, Byblos (internationally oriented national body)
♦ International Centre for Hydrogen Energy Technologies (internationally oriented national body)
♦ International Centre for Hydropower (internationally oriented national body)
♦ International Centre for Indoor Environment and Energy (internationally oriented national body)
♦ International Centre for Information on Mutuality / see Association internationale de la mutualité (#02721)
♦ International Centre of Information for Telephonic Help / see International Federation of Telephone Emergency Services (#13567)

♦ International Centre for Innovation in Education (ICIE) 12497

Dir/Co-Chair Heilmeyersteige 93, 89075 Ulm, Germany. T. +497315094494.
Gen Dir Postfach 1240, 89002 Ulm, Germany.
URL: http://icieworld.net/

History 2005. **Aims** Empower every person to become a responsible, self-directed, lifelong learner through a positive partnership of families, teachers, scholars in gifted education, ministries of education and community. **Structure** Board; Branches (7). **Languages** Arabic, Croatian, English, French, German, Portuguese, Turkish. **Staff** 7.00 FTE, paid. **Finance** Self-financed. **Activities** Capacity building; events/meetings; guidance/assistance/consulting; knowledge management/information dissemination; research/documentation; standards/guidelines; training/education. **Events** *International Conference on Excellence in Education* Helsinki (Finland) 2022, *International Conference on Excellence in Education* Prairie View, TX (USA) 2019, *International Conference on Excellence in Education* Paris (France) 2018, *International Conference on Excellence in Education* Lisbon (Portugal) 2017, *International Conference on Excellence in Education* Dubai (United Arab Emirates) 2016. **Publications** *International Journal for Talent Development and Creativity (IJTDC).* Books; handbooks; training kits; tests; proceedings. **Members** Individuals. Membership countries not specified. [2020.08.18/XJ5384/C]

♦ International Centre of Innovation and Exchange in Public Administration (internationally oriented national body)
♦ International Centre for Innovation and Industrial Logistics (internationally oriented national body)

♦ International Centre for Innovation and Knowledge Transfer on the Social and Solidarity Economy 12498

Centre international de transfert d'innovations et de connaissances en économie sociale et solidaire (CITIES) – Centro Internacional de Transferencia de Innovaciones y Conocimientos en Economia Social y Solidaria

Contact 1431 rue Fullum, bureau 209, Montréal QC H2K 0B5, Canada. E-mail: info@cities-ess.org.
URL: http://www.cities-ess.org/

History Set up Sep 2016, Montréal QC (Canada), at 3rd *Global Social Economy Forum (GSEF, #10603).* **Aims** Help social and solidarity economy initiatives to spread around the world by promoting the sharing of knowledge and the adaptation of good practices at an international level. **Languages** English, French, Spanish. **Staff** 1.00 FTE, paid. **Activities** Knowledge management/information dissemination; training/education; monitoring/evaluation; guidance/assistance/consulting.
Members Full in 3 countries:
Canada, Korea Rep, Spain. [2016.10.05/XM5096/E]

♦ International Centre of Insect Physiology and Ecology (ICIPE) 12499

Centre international sur la physiologie et l'écologie des insectes – Centro Internacional de Fisiologia y Ecologia de los Insectos

Dir-Gen PO Box 30772-00100, Nairobi, Kenya. T. +254208632000. Fax +254208632001 – +254208632002. E-mail: icipe@icipe.org – dg@icipe.org.
URL: http://www.icipe.org/

History Apr 1970, Nairobi (Kenya). **Aims** Help alleviate poverty, ensure food security and improve the overall health status of peoples of the tropics by developing and extending management tools and strategies for harmful and useful *arthropods*, while preserving the natural resource base through research and capacity building. **Structure** Governing Council; Directors (3); Senior Management Committee; Units; Support Units; Departments. **Languages** English. **Staff** 78.00 FTE, paid.
Finance Funded by continental unions, international and private charitable organizations, UN organizations and governmental aid agencies. Core funding (2019) from: Ministry of Higher Education, Science and Technology, Kenya; *Swiss Agency for Development and Cooperation (SDC)*; *Swedish International Development Cooperation Agency (Sida)*; *Department for International Development (DFID, inactive)* – UK Aid; Government of the Federal Democratic Republic of Ethiopia. Main grant donors include the following organizations listed in this Yearbook:
- *African Union (AU, #00488)*;
- *Biovision Africa Trust (BvAT)*;
- *Stiftung für Ökologische Entwicklung (Biovision)*;
- *Centre de coopération internationale en recherche agronomique pour le développement (CIRAD, #03733)*;
- *FAO (#09260)*;
- *Global Environment Facility (GEF, #10346)*;
- *Institut de recherche pour le développement (IRD)*;
- *International Atomic Energy Agency (IAEA, #12294)*;
- *International Development Research Centre (IDRC, #13162)*;
- *International Fund for Agricultural Development (IFAD, #13692)*;
- *International Institute of Tropical Agriculture (IITA, #13933)*;
- *McKnight Foundation*;
- *Royal Museum for Central Africa (KMMA)*;
- *UNEP (#20299)*;
- *United States Agency for International Development (USAID)*;
- *Volkswagen Foundation*;
- *Wellcome Trust*;
- *World Federation of Scientists (WFS)*;
- *World Trade Organization (WTO, #21864)*.

Annual budget: 34,300,000 USD (2019).
Activities Capacity building; events/meetings; knowledge management/information dissemination; networking/liaising; research and development; training/education. **Events** *Conference on climate change and food security* Nairobi (Kenya) 2011, *International conference on lepidopterous cereal stem and cob borers in Africa* Nairobi (Kenya) 2005, *International workshop on conservation and utilisation of commercial insects* Nairobi (Kenya) 2002, *Symposium* Nairobi (Kenya) 2002, *Scientific study workshop on recent development in Tsetse* Kenya 1995. **Publications** *External Review Report* (periodical); *Results-Based Management Framework* (periodical); *Vision and Strategy Report* (periodical); *icipe e-bulletin.* Annual Reort; articles manuals; books; project reports; policy briefs. **Information Services** *icipe Digital Repository.*
Members Governing Council includes representatives of scientific institutions, academia and banking in 10 countries:
Australia, Colombia, Ethiopia, France, Japan, Kenya, South Africa, Sweden, Switzerland, USA.
IGO Relations Cooperates with numerous IGOs, including: *Bioversity International (#03262)*; *CGIAR System Organization (CGIAR, #03843)* institutions including *FAO (#09260)*; *Interafrican Bureau for Animal Resources (AU-IBAR, #11382)*; *International Fund for Agricultural Development (IFAD, #13692)*; *International Livestock Research Institute (ILRI, #14062)*; *OIE – World Organisation for Animal Health (#17703)*; *UNEP (#20299)*; *UNDP (#20292).* **NGO Relations** Member of (1): *Association of International Research and Development Centers for Agriculture (AIRCA, #02760).* Instrumental in setting up (1): *African Regional Postgraduate Programme in Insect Science (ARPPIS, see: #12499).* Links with national associations and universities. [2021/XC4494/E]

♦ International Centre for Integrated Assessment and Sustainable Development (internationally oriented national body)

♦ International Centre for Integrated Mountain Development (ICIMOD) 12500

Centre international de mise en valeur intégrée des montagnes

Dir Gen PO Box 3226, Khumaltar, Lalitpur, Kathmandu 44700, Nepal. T. +97715275222. Fax +97715275238. E-mail: info@icimod.org.
URL: http://www.icimod.org/

History Sep 1981. Established by agreement between UNESCO and the Government of Nepal. Inaugurated in Dec 1983; began operating in Sep 1984. **Aims** Enable and facilitate the equitable and sustainable well-being of the people of the *Hindu-Kush Himalayas* by supporting *sustainable* mountain development through active regional cooperation. **Structure** Board of Governors; ICIMOD Support (Donor) Group. **Languages** English. **Staff** 9.00 FTE, paid. **Finance** Programmes and activities funded by long-term sponsors (regional member countries and non-regional financial partners). Contributions of other public and private donors towards specific projects. **Activities** Events/meetings; monitoring/evaluation; research/documentation; training/education. **Events** *Geo4SDGs International Conference* Hyderabad (India) 2018, *International Symposium on Glaciology in High Mountain Asia* Kathmandu (Nepal) 2015, *Global Workshop on Long-Term Observatories of Mountain Social-Ecological Systems* Reno, NV (USA) 2014, *Bhutan + 10 : International Conference on Gender and Sustainable Mountain Development in a Changing World* Thimphu (Bhutan) 2012, *Climate summit for a living Himalayas* Thimphu (Bhutan) 2011. **Publications** Annual Report; books and booklets; workshop/seminar reports; workshop/symposia proceedings; manuals; handbooks; toolkits; information sheets; brochures; flyers. All publication available online.
Members Participating countries of the Hindu Kush-Himalayan (HKH) Region (8):
Afghanistan, Bangladesh, Bhutan, China, India, Myanmar, Nepal, Pakistan.
Consultative Status Consultative status granted from: *FAO (#09260)* (Special Status). **IGO Relations** Member of: Global Earth Observation System of Systems (GEOSS) of *Group on Earth Observations (GEO, #10735).* Observer status with: *Intergovernmental Panel on Climate Change (IPCC, #11499)*; Conference of the Parties (CoP) of *United Nations Framework Convention on Climate Change (UNFCCC, 1992).* Joint management partner with: *European Union (EU, #08967).* Partner of: *Asian Development Bank (ADB, #01422)*; *International Bank for Reconstruction and Development (IBRD, #12317)* and its Abu Dhabi Dialogue Group. Strategic partner of: *International Fund for Agricultural Development (IFAD, #13692).* **NGO Relations** Hosts secretariat of: *South Asian Network for Development and Environmental Economics (SANDEE, #19735).* Member of: *Association of International Research and Development Centers for Agriculture (AIRCA, #02760)*; *Climate and Clean Air Coalition (CCAC, #04010)*; *Global Mountain Biodiversity Assessment (GMBA, #10477)*; *International Union for Conservation of Nature and Natural Resources (IUCN, #15766)*; *Mountain Partnership (MP, #16862).* Affiliate partner of: *Biodiversity Indicators Partnership (BIP, #03242).* Participates in: *Global Center on Adaptation (GCA).* [2021.10.26/XE2467/E*]

♦ International Centre for Integrative Studies / see International Centre for Integrated Assessment and Sustainable Development
♦ International Centre for Intercultural Education Timisoara / see Intercultural Institute Timisoara
♦ International Centre for Island Technology (internationally oriented national body)
♦ International Centre for Law Reform / see International Centre for Criminal Law Reform and Criminal Justice Policy
♦ International Centre for Living Aquatic Resources Management / see WorldFish (#21507)

♦ International Centre for Local Credit (ICLC) 12501

Centre international pour le crédit communal – Centro Internacional para el Crédito Comunal – Internationales Zentrum für Kommunalkredit

Secretariat 1 Passerelle des Reflets, Tour Dexia La Defense 2, TSA 12203, 92919 Paris La Défense CEDEX, France. T. +33158587391. Fax +33158588740.

History 8 Oct 1958, Oslo (Norway), as *International Information Centre for Local Credit – Centre international d'informations pour le crédit communal.* **Aims** Promote local authority credit through: gathering, exchanging and distributing information and advice; gathering, exchanging and distributing information on local authority credit and subjects connected with or affecting the same; studying, jointly if necessary, important subjects in the field of local authority credit; other activities. **Structure** Conference (every 18 months). Executive Committee, comprising President, Secretary General and 2 members. **Languages** English. **Finance** Members' dues. **Activities** Conferences; staff meetings. **Events** *Conference* Paris (France) 2006, *Conference* Vienna (Austria) 2005, *Conference* Victoria, BC (Canada) 2003, *Conference* Rome (Italy) 2002, *Conference* Rome (Italy) 2002. **Publications** *Newsletter* (3 a year); *Bulletin* (irregular). *Credit institutions for local authorities* (1986); *Electronic Data Processing in Banks for Local Credit* (1980); *Economic and Financial Pictures of Cities in Western Europe (including Israel and Japan)* (1978); *Contributions to Human Settlements by Credit Institutions for Local Authorities* (1976); *Simplification de la gestion des titres* (1971); *Economic Policy in Practice* (1969); *Government measures for the promotion of regional economic development* (1964); *Managing Bonds and Interest Coupons by means of Electronic Data Processing*; *The Issue of Securities by Institutions for Local Credit.* Proceedings of meetings and conferences; reports; handbooks.
Members Full institutions (23) in 17 countries:
Austria, Belgium, Canada, China, Denmark, Finland, France, Germany, Ireland, Israel, Italy, Japan, Netherlands, Norway, Portugal, South Africa, Sweden. [2011/XD1468/E]

♦ International Centre for Local Development Studies (internationally oriented national body)
♦ International Centre of Martial Arts (internationally oriented national body)
♦ International Centre of Martial Arts for Youth Development and Engagement under the auspices of UNESCO / see International Centre of Martial Arts
♦ International Centre for Materials Technology Promotion (see: #20336)
♦ International Centre for Mathematical Sciences (internationally oriented national body)
♦ International Centre for Mathematics (internationally oriented national body)
♦ International Centre for Mechanical Sciences (#03766)
♦ International Centre for Medical and Surgical Films (inactive)
♦ International Centre for Migration and Health / see International Centre for Migration, Health and Development (#12502)

♦ International Centre for Migration, Health and Development (ICMHD) 12502

Centre International pour la Migration, la Santé, et le Développement – Centro Internacional para la Migración, la Salud y el Desarrollo

Exec Dir Route du Nant d'Avril 11, 1214 Geneva, Switzerland. T. +41227831080. Fax +41227831087. E-mail: admin@icmhd.ch.
URL: http://www.icmhd.ch/

History 17 Mar 1995. Founded as a joint undertaking of *International Organization for Migration (IOM, #14454)*, the University of Geneva (Switzerland) and *WHO (#20950).* Former names and other names: *International Centre for Migration and Health (ICMH)* – former. Registration: Swiss Civil Code, Switzerland. **Aims** Provide governments, UN agencies, international and national NGOs and the private sector with technical and advocacy support on all aspect of population movement and health. **Structure** Executive Committee; International Scientific Advisory Board. **Languages** English, French, Spanish. **Finance** Sources: grants; revenue from activities/projects. **Activities** Knowledge management/information dissemination; research/documentation; training/education. **Publications** *Clinical outcomes and risk factors for COVID-19 among migrant populations in high-income countries: A systematic review*; *Connaissances, perceptions, attitudes et pratiques des membres de la Police Nationale Congolaise en matière de violences sexuelles dans trois provinces de la République Démocratique du Congo* in French; *Evolving migrant crisis in Europe: implications for health systems*; *Health and Migration in the European Union: Better Health for All in an Inclusive Society*; *Health and Wellbeing of Women, Children and Adolescents on the Move: Introduction and Overview*; *Migration and health in the European Union*; *Migration, hepatitis B and hepatitis C*; *Migration, Refugees, and Health Risks.* A full list of publications is available at: https://icmhd.ch/publications/. **Information Services** *COVID-19 and Community Quarantine – COVID-19 et la quarantaine communautaire* in English, French, Portuguese, Russian, Spanish; *Notes on COVID-19 and Humanitarian Crises* in English; *Notes on COVID-19 and Midwifery* in English; *Notes on COVID-19 and Migrants* in English.
Members Organizations and individuals in 16 countries:
Albania, Bangladesh, Canada, Congo DR, Côte d'Ivoire, El Salvador, France, Italy, Lebanon, Liberia, Norway, Senegal, Spain, Switzerland, UK, USA.
IGO Relations Memorandum of Understanding with (5): China-Maldives Cultural Association; Eminence, Bangladesh; Glasgow Caledonian University; *Joint United Nations Programme on HIV/AIDS (UNAIDS, #16149)*; Kaohsiung Medical University. Cooperates with (7): *European Centre for Disease Prevention and Control (ECDC, #06476)*; *European Commission (EC, #06633)*; *UNESCO (#20322)*; *UNICEF (#20332)*; *United Nations Population Fund (UNFPA, #20612)*; *United States Agency for International Development (USAID)*; *WHO (#20950).* **NGO Relations** Member of (1): *Global Health Workforce Alliance (GHWA, inactive).* Cooperates with (9): *Geneva Forum*; *Global Health Cluster (GHC, #10401)*; *Graduate Institute of International Studies, Geneva (inactive)*; Hepatitis B and C Policy Association; *International Federation of Red Cross and Red Crescent Societies (#13526)*; Istituto Superiore di Sanità (ISS); *Payson Center for International Development and Technology Transfer*; *PMNCH (#18410)*; *Tulane University School of Public Health and Tropical Medicine.* [2021.05.28/XE2391/E]

♦ International Centre for Migration Policy Development (ICMPD) . . . 12503

Centre international pour le développement des politiques migratoires

Headquarters Gonzagagasse 1, 5th floor, 1010 Vienna, Austria. T. +43150446770. Fax +43150446772375. E-mail: icmpd@icmpd.org.

Brussels Office Rue Belliard 159, 2nd floor, 1040 Brussels, Belgium. E-mail: icmpd-brussels@icmpd.org.

Main: http://www.icmpd.org/

History 1 Jun 1993. Established following an initiative by the governments of Austria and Switzerland. The Centre enjoys full diplomatic status with privileges and immunities in accordance with the Headquarters Agreement signed in 1999 with the government of Austria, and the Agreement entered into force in 2000. Headquarters agreement signed with Belgium, 2008. **Aims** Strive for comprehensive, sustainable and future-oriented migration governance based on solid evidence and in partnership with all relevant stakeholders at national, regional and international levels. **Structure** Policy Steering Group; Operational programmes: General Affairs and Research; Financial Resources. Headquarters in Vienna (Austria); mission in Brussels (Belgium) since May 2007. Local representatives in: Albania; Bosnia-Herzegovina; Bulgaria; Georgia; Lebanon and the Middle East; North Macedonia; Moldova; Montenegro; Serbia; Tunisia and Maghreb region. Field project offices in: Ankara (Turkey); Beirut (Lebanon); Bishkek (Kyrgyzstan); Brasilia (Brazil); Chisinau (Moldova); Kiev (Ukraine); Pristina (Kosovo); San Salvador (El Salvador); Sarajevo (Bosnia-Herzegovina); Skopje (North Macedonia); Tbilisi (Georgia); Tunis (Tunisia). **Languages** Arabic, English, French, German, Russian, Spanish. **Staff** As of 20 Dec 2013: 173; 89 in Vienna (Austria); 23 in Brussels (Belgium); 61 local representatives and staff in project offices. **Finance** Project-funded with some contributions by member states for basic infrastructure. Funding of projects primarily from *European Commission (EC, #06633)* and European governments, as well as international organizations, including: *United States Agency for International Development (USAID)*; *UNDP (#20292)*; *ILO (#11123)*. Total budget (2013): euro 18.6 million. **Activities** Work based on 3 interlinked pillars: migration dialogues; capacity building; research. Main areas cover: asylum; border management and visa; illegal migration and return; legal migration and integration; migration and development; trafficking in human beings. **Events** *Vienna Migration Conference* Vienna (Austria) 2018, *Seminar* Vienna (Austria) 2017, *Vienna Migration Conference* Vienna (Austria) 2017, *Prague Process Seniors Officials Meeting* Berlin (Germany) 2014, *Conference on trafficking in human beings* Trier (Germany) 2006. **Publications** Newsletters; reports of projects; studies; training materials. Information Services: Maintains collection of migration-specific literature.

Members Full – governments of 15 countries:

Austria, Bosnia-Herzegovina, Bulgaria, Croatia, Czechia, Hungary, North Macedonia, Poland, Portugal, Romania, Serbia, Slovakia, Slovenia, Sweden, Switzerland.

IGO Relations Observer Status in *United Nations (UN, #20515)* General Assembly. Signatory member of: *International Anti-Corruption Academy (IACA, #11654)*. Memorandum of Understanding signed with: *Common Market for Eastern and Southern Africa (COMESA, #04296)*; *Frontex, the European Border and Coast Guard Agency (#10005)*; *International Criminal Police Organization – INTERPOL (ICPO-INTERPOL, #13110)*; *International Organization for Migration (IOM, #14454)*; International Policy Migration Programme (IMP); *League of Arab States (LAS, #16420)*; *Migration, Asylum, Refugees Regional Initiative (MARRI, #16800)* – Regional Centre (MARRI RC); national organizations; *Southeast European Law Enforcement Center (SELEC, #19815)*; *UNDP (#20292)*; *United Nations Economic and Social Commission for Western Asia (ESCWA, #20558)*; *World Customs Organization (WCO, #21350)*. **NGO Relations** Member of: *European Policy Centre (EPC, #08240)*. [2021/XE3768/**E***]

♦ International Centre for Minority Studies and Intercultural Relations (IMIR) 12504

Intl Projects Coordinator 55 Antim I Street, 1303 Sofia, Bulgaria. T. +35928323112 – +35928324044. Fax +35929310583. E-mail: lubo@lfconsult.org – minority@imir-bg.org.

Chair address not obtained.

URL: http://www.imir-bg.org/

History Dec 1992, Sofia (Bulgaria). **Aims** Study inter-religious and inter-ethnic issues in Bulgaria, the *Balkans* and the *Mediterranean*; analyse zones of compatibility and incompatibility between *Islam* and *Christianity*; disseminate knowledge about the ethnic, religious, cultural and linguistic minorities, so as to overcome *xenophobia* and cultivate mutual confidence and understanding; work for peace and peaceful co-existence of various ethnic and religious communities in these areas and promote *tolerance* and equality among these communities; contribute to creation of open society in the Balkans in order to overcome prejudices towards minorities and Balkan neighbours; combat *discrimination* toward minorities in order to secure their social, cultural and political *inclusion*. **Structure** Board of Directors, including Chairperson. Officers: Programme Director; Project Coordinators; Accountants. **Languages** Bosnian, Bulgarian, Croatian, English, Russian, Serbian, Slovene. **Staff** 6.00 FTE, paid. **Finance** Receives funds from sponsors for projects. **Activities** Research/documentation; events/meetings; publishing activities. **Events** *Forced ethnic migrations on the Balkans – consequences and rebuilding of societies* Sofia (Bulgaria) 2005, *Round table on limitations and possibilities for multi-ethnic co-existence in Kosovo and Macedonia* Sofia (Bulgaria) 2003, *Round table on Albanian national question and the Balkans* Sofia (Bulgaria) 2002, *Avoiding conflicts in the Balkans* Sofia (Bulgaria) 1994, *Compatibility and incompatibility of Christians and Muslims in Bulgaria* Sofia (Bulgaria) 1994. **Publications** *Common Balkans – Young Authors – First Books – vols 2-8* (2006) in Bulgarian – latest vol; *Roma Everyday Life in Bulgaria* (2006) by Alexey Pamporov in Bulgarian; *Immigration in Bulgaria* (2005) in Bulgarian; *Trade Unions against Racism and Discrimination* (2005) in Bulgarian; *Citizens for Human Rights – vol 1* (2004) by Orlin Avramov in Bulgarian; *History and Culture of Early Arabia* (2004) by Pavel Pavlovitch in Bulgarian; *Urgent Anthropology – vol 3* (2004) in Bulgarian, English. Conference proceedings.

Members Full in 4 countries:

Bulgaria, Germany, Slovenia, UK.

NGO Relations Associate member of: *Policy Association for an Open Society (PASOS, #18416)*. [2013/XE1918/**E**]

♦ International Centre for Missing and Exploited Children (ICMEC) . . 12505

Contact 2318 Mill Rd, Ste 1010, Alexandria VA 22314, USA. T. +17038376313. Fax +17035494504. E-mail: information@icmec.org.

URL: http://www.icmec.org/

History Founded 1998 at first meeting. Officially launched Apr 1999. **Aims** Identify gaps in the global community's ability to protect children from abduction, sexual abuse and exploitation, and assemble the people, resources and tools needed to fill those gaps. **Languages** English, German, Portuguese, Russian, Spanish. **Staff** 13.00 FTE, paid. **Activities** Projects/programmes; guidance/assistance/consulting; advocacy/lobbying/activism; training/education; research/documentation. **Events** *Workshop on computer facilitated crimes against children induction* Tokyo (Japan) 2006, *Forum* Lyon (France) 2005, *Forum* Dublin (Ireland) 2002. **Publications** *Global Training Catalogue*. Information Services: Research library. **Members** Not a membership organization. **Consultative Status** Consultative status granted from: *ECOSOC (#05331)* (Special). [2019.02.12/XE4573/**E**]

♦ International Centre for Monetary and Banking Studies (ICMB) 12506

Centre international d'études monétaires et bancaires (CIMB)

Dir Chemin Eugène-Rigot 2A, 1202 Geneva 1, Switzerland. T. +41227349548. E-mail: secretariat@cimb.ch.

URL: http://www.cimb.ch/

History 1973, Geneva (Switzerland). **Aims** Carry out scientific study and promote exchange of ideas and information in the field of international monetary, *financial* and banking studies; provide an international forum for exchange of ideas between policy makers, the private sector and academics. **Structure** Under the supervision of the Swiss Federal Department of the Interior. ICMB Foundation Board; Management Committee; Scientific Committee; Executive Director; Manager. **Languages** English, French. **Staff** 2.00 FTE, paid. **Finance** Contributions from financial institutions. **Activities** Politics/policy/regulatory; events/meetings. **Events** *Living with low inflation* Geneva (Switzerland) 2008, *Conference on international financial stability* Geneva (Switzerland) 2007, *International conference* Geneva (Switzerland) 2003, *International conference* Geneva (Switzerland) 2002, *Meeting* Geneva (Switzerland) 1988. **Publications** *Geneva Reports on the World Economy* – series. Papers.

Members Institutional members financial institutions, central banks and organizations, in 7 countries:

France, Germany, Italy, Netherlands, Spain, Switzerland, UK. [2019.10.08/XD6517/**E**]

♦ International Centre of the Neutral Esperanto Movement (inactive)
♦ International Centre for New Media (internationally oriented national body)
♦ International Centre for a New Water Civilization / see International Centre for a Water Civilization
♦ International Centre for Numerical Methods in Engineering (internationally oriented national body)
♦ International Centre for Parliamentary Studies (internationally oriented national body)
♦ International Centre for Pesticide Safety / see International Centre for Pesticides and Health Risk Prevention
♦ International Centre for Pesticides and Health Risk Prevention (internationally oriented national body)

♦ International Centre for Physical Land Resources (ICPLR) 12507

Contact Coupure Links 653 (ITC), 9000 Ghent, Belgium. T. +3292644638. E-mail: plrprog.adm@ugent.be.

URL: http://www.plr.ugent.be/

History Founded 1998, by Ghent University (Belgium) and the Vrije Universiteit Brussel (Belgium), on reorganization of *International Training Centre for Post-Graduate Soil Scientists (ITC Ghent)*, set up at the Ghent University, 1963. Also integrates *International Training Centre for Eremology (ICE, inactive)*, set up in 1989 at Ghent University to study drylands and desertification. **Aims** Provide an academic training in research and modern applications of physical land resources and prepare students for tasks in *surveying*, development projects, experimental stations and research in government institutes and universities. **Structure** Board of Governors, consisting of Director, Academic Secretary and members of the teaching staff (currently 25). **Languages** English. **Staff** 27.00 FTE, paid. **Finance** Funded by: Ghent University (Belgium); Vrije Universiteit Brussel (Belgium); Vlaamse Interuniversitaire Raad (VLIR-UOS). **Activities** Training/education. **Publications** *Pedon* (annual) – newsletter. **Members** Not a membership organization. **IGO Relations** *UNESCO (#20322)*. [2015.06.01/XE1002/**E**]

♦ International Centre of Physics (#03807)
♦ International Centre for Policy Studies, Kiev (internationally oriented national body)
♦ International Centre for Political Violence and Terrorism Research (internationally oriented national body)
♦ International Centre for Positive Family Therapy and Positive Psychotherapy / see World Association for Positive and Transcultural Psychotherapy (#21174)
♦ International Centre for Positive Psychotherapy / see World Association for Positive and Transcultural Psychotherapy (#21174)
♦ International Centre for Positive Psychotherapy, Transcultural Family Therapy and Psychosomatic Medicine / see World Association for Positive and Transcultural Psychotherapy (#21174)

♦ International Centre for the Prevention of Crime (ICPC) 12508

Centre international pour la prévention de la criminalité (CIPC) – Centro Internacional para la Prevención de la Criminalidad (CIPC)

Dir Gen 3535 avenue du Parc, 4th floor, Montréal QC H2X 2H8, Canada. T. +15142886731. E-mail: info@cipc-icpc.org.

URL: https://cipc-icpc.org/

History 7 Apr 1994, Montréal, QC (Canada). Founded by the governments of France, Canada and Québec, who adopted a declaration on the creation in Montréal of the Centre and joined forces with the Montréal Urban Community (MUC), Federation of Canadian Municipalities (FCM), *European Forum for Urban Security (Efus, #07340)*, and the *'Société du Centre de conférences internationales de Montréal'*, to set up a Constituent Board for ICPC. **Aims** Support development and implementation of practical and effective policies, programmes and projects to reduce crime and delinquency; reinforce feelings of safety in communities, cities and other regional authorities; enhance civic vitality; support concerted action and cooperation among partners in institutional, community, voluntary and private sectors, including citizens, to deal with problems of crime and insecurity; support strategies to mobilize key community stakeholders in crime prevention. **Structure** Board of Directors; Executive Committee; Director General; Governmental Policy and Advisory Committee. **Languages** English, French, Spanish. **Staff** 15.00 FTE, paid. **Finance** Sources: government support. Core programme funded by governments of Province of Québec (Canada), France, Norway, Chile and South Africa. Project funding by government of Canada and others. Annual budget: 950,000 CAD. **Activities** Events/meetings; knowledge management/information dissemination; politics/policy/regulatory; training/education. **Events** *International Conference on the Analysis, Observation and Prevention of Insecurity* Paris (France) 2022, *International Conference on Crime Observation and Criminal Analysis* Brussels (Belgium) 2019, *Annual Colloquium* Montréal, QC (Canada) 2017, *International Conference on Crime Observation and Criminal Analysis* Mexico City (Mexico) 2015, *Annual Colloquium* Palermo (Italy) 2014. **Publications** *ICPC Newsletter* – online. Annual Report; guides; papers; compendium; reports; observatories.

Members Federations and institutes in 23 countries:

Australia, Austria, Belgium, Canada, Chile, Colombia, Costa Rica, El Salvador, France, Germany, Italy, Kenya, Mexico, New Zealand, Nigeria, Norway, Saudi Arabia, South Africa, Spain, Switzerland, Uganda, UK, USA.

International/regional organizations (10):

African Policing Civilian Oversight Forum (APCOF, #00419); *Coalición Centroamericana para la Prevención de la Violencia Juvenil (CCPVJ, #04043)*; *European Forum for Urban Security (Efus, #07340)*; *Instituto Latinoamericano de las Naciones Unidas para la Prevención del Delito y Tratamiento del Delincuente (ILANUD, #11347)*; *International Agency for Crime Prevention, Criminal Law and Jurisdiction*; *Naif Arab University for Security Sciences (NAUSS, #16929)*; *United Nations African Institute for the Prevention of Crime and the Treatment of Offenders (UNAFRI, #20519)*; *United Nations Human Settlements Programme (UN-Habitat, #20572)*; *United Nations Office on Drugs and Crime (UNODC, #20596)*; *World Association of the Major Metropolises (Metropolis, #21158)*.

NGO Relations Member of (1): *Violence Prevention Alliance (VPA, #20781)*. Supports (1): *African Forum for Urban Security (AFUS, #00323)*. [2022.11.09/XE2026/y/**E**]

♦ International Centre for Primary Health Care and Family Medicine (internationally oriented national body)
♦ International Centre for Prison Studies, London (internationally oriented national body)
♦ International Centre of Privatization, Investment and Management / see International Institute of Business
♦ International Centre for the Promotion of Education and Development (internationally oriented national body)

♦ International Centre for Promotion of Enterprises (ICPE) 12509

Centre international de promotion pour les entreprises – Centro Internacional de Promoción de Empresas

Acting Gen Dir Dunajska 104, 1001 Ljubljana, Slovenia. T. +38615682331. E-mail: info@icpe.int.

URL: http://www.icpe.int/

History 1974, Ljubljana (Slovenia). Established as a Yugoslav institution at the initiative of Secretary-General of United Nations. In 1976, at the proposal of developing countries, became a joint intergovernmental organization. Former names and other names: *International Centre for Public Enterprises in Developing Countries* – former; *Centre international pour les entreprises publiques dans les pays en développement* – former; *Centro Internacional para Empresas Públicas de Paises en Desarrollo* – former; *International Centre for Public Enterprises* – former; *Centre international pour les entreprises publiques* – former; *Centro Internacional para Empresas Públicas* – former. **Aims** Promote and support enterprise development in *developing economies* and *transitional economies* with the view of fostering their *economic development* in the regional and global context. **Structure** Assembly; Council; Director General. **Languages** Arabic, English, French, Spanish. **Finance** Sources: contributions; international organizations. **Activities** Capacity building; knowledge management/information dissemination; projects/programmes; research/documentation; training/education. **Events** *Regional meeting* Ljubljana (Slovenia) 1994, *Biennial Assembly* Ljubljana (Slovenia) 1992, *International workshop and seminar on consultancy on strategic information planning* Ljubljana (Slovenia) 1992, *Workshop on information network on public enterprises in developing countries* Ljubljana (Slovenia) 1992, *Seminar on management restructuring of public enterprises* Islamabad (Pakistan) 1991. **Publications** *Public Enterprise Journal* (2 a year) in English. Books; monographs; case studies.

Members Membership open to all states and intergovernmental organizations. Member countries (14):

Algeria, Angola, Bosnia-Herzegovina, Congo Brazzaville, Congo DR, Guinea, Guyana, India, Iraq, North Macedonia, Slovenia, Sri Lanka, Tanzania UR, Zambia.

IGO Relations Observer status with (3): *ECOSOC (#05331)*; *Group of 77 (G-77, #10732)*; *UNCTAD (#20285)*. Member of (1): *Intergovernmental Organizations Conference (IGO Conference, #11498)*. Cooperates with (14): *Central European Free Trade Agreement (CEFTA, 1992)*; *Commonwealth Secretariat (#04362)*; *European Bank for Reconstruction and Development (EBRD, #06315)*; *FAO (#09260)*; *Inter-American Development Bank (IDB, #11427)*; *International Bank for Reconstruction and Development (IBRD, #12317)*; *International Trade Centre (ITC, #15703)*; *OPEC Fund for International Development (OFID, #17745)*; *Regional Cooperation Council (RCC, #18773)*; *South Centre (#19753)*; *United Nations Economic and Social Commission for Asia and the Pacific (ESCAP, #20557)*; *United Nations Economic Commission for Africa (ECA, #20554)*; *United Nations Economic Commission for Europe (UNECE, #20555)*; *United Nations International Research and Training Institute for the Advancement of Women (UN-INSTRAW, inactive)*. Executing agency of: *UNDP (#20292)*. Relationship agreement with: *UNIDO (#20336)* (also official observer at the Industrial Development Board). Special agreement with: *UNESCO (#20322)*. **NGO Relations** Cooperates with (2): *EFMD – The Management Development Network (#05387)*; *Fondation internationale pour le développement (FID, no recent information)*.
[2023.02.14/XE6053/y/**E***]

- ♦ International Centre for the Promotion of Human Rights at the Local and Regional Levels / see European Training- and Research Centre for Human Rights and Democracy
- ♦ International Centre for Public Enterprises / see International Centre for Promotion of Enterprises (#12509)
- ♦ International Centre for Public Enterprises in Developing Countries / see International Centre for Promotion of Enterprises (#12509)
- ♦ International Centre for Pure and Applied Mathematics (#03758)
- ♦ International Centre for Quality Promotion and Consumer Information (inactive)
- ♦ International Centre for Radio Astronomy Research (internationally oriented national body)
- ♦ International Centre for Reconciliation, Coventry (internationally oriented national body)
- ♦ International Centre for Regional Planning and Development (inactive)
- ♦ International Centre of Registration Law / see IPRA-CINDER – International Property Registries Association (#16012)
- ♦ International Centre for the Registration of Serial Publications / see ISSN International Centre (#16069)
- ♦ International Centre for Reproductive Health (internationally oriented national body)
- ♦ International Centre for Reproductive Health and Sexual Rights (internationally oriented national body)
- ♦ International Centre for Research in Accountability and Governance (unconfirmed)
- ♦ International Centre for Research in Agroforestry / see World Agroforestry Centre (#21072)
- ♦ International Centre for the Research and the Application of Earth Construction / see International Centre for Earth Construction (#12485)

♦ International Centre for Research on Delinquency, Marginality and Social Relationships 12510

Centro Internacional de Investigación sobre la Delincuencia, la Marginalidad y las Relaciones Sociales

Dir c/o Universidad del Pais Vasco, Centro Carlos Sanatmaria, Elhuyar Plaza 2, E-20018 San Sebastian, Santa Cruz de Tenerife, Spain. E-mail: dms@ehu.es.
URL: http://www.ehu.eus/es/web/dms/

History 1993, by an agreement between *International Society of Criminology (ISC, #15038)* and the *'Basque Country University'*. Also referred to as *DMS International Research Centre*. **Aims** Promote research and development about *migrations* of populations, mainly in *Europe*, and their connections with marginality and delinquency. **Structure** Board of Directors. **Languages** Basque, English, French, Spanish. **Activities** Training/education; networking/liaising; events/meetings; publishing activities. **NGO Relations** *International Association of Penal Law (IAPL, #12074)*.
[2016.02.16/XE4494/**E**]

- ♦ International Centre on Research Development and Environment / see International Research Centre on Environment and Development
- ♦ International Centre of Research and Information on Collective Economy / see Centre international de recherches et d'information sur l'économie publique, sociale et coopérative (#03764)
- ♦ International Centre of Research and Information on the Public, Social and Cooperative Economy (#03764)
- ♦ International Centre on Research El Niño (internationally oriented national body)

♦ International Centre for Research in Organic Food Systems (ICROFS) 12511

Address not obtained.
URL: http://www.icrofs.org/

History Founded 2008, by the Danish Government, upon deciding to give the former research centre *DARCOF* an international mandate and Board of Directors, thus founding the new Centre. **Aims** Initiate, coordinate and monitor high quality research of international standard in organic food and farming systems; stimulate international and transnational research and secure impact of the research results through support and dissemination in order to achieve optimum benefit from the allocated resources. **Structure** Board, headed by Chairman. **Activities** Research/documentation; monitoring/evaluation. **Publications** *ICROFS news*. Leaflets; books; reports.
[2018.09.21/XJ1196/**E**]

♦ International Centre for Research in Organizational Discourse, Strategy and Change (ICRODSC) 12512

Contact UniMelb Dept of Management, Level 10, 198 Berkeley St, Melbourne VIC 3010, Australia.
URL: http://icrodsc.org.au/

History 2001, Australia. Previously referred to with the acronym *ICROD*. **Aims** Facilitate research and cooperation on organizational discourse, strategy and change; encourage collaborative research projects among leading universities in the field of organizational discourse; disseminate research findings on discourse analysis and its applications; facilitate research and teaching interchanges among scholars. **Activities** *International Conference on Organizational Discourse*. **Events** *Terra firma, terra nova, terra incognita* Cardiff (UK) 2014, *Processes, practices and performance* Amsterdam (Netherlands) 2012, *Conference* Amsterdam (Netherlands) 2010, *Conference* London (UK) 2008, *Identity, ideology and idiosyncrasy* Amsterdam (Netherlands) 2006.

Members Partner universities (8) in 5 countries:
Australia, Canada, Sweden, UK, USA.
[2013/XE4675/**E**]

- ♦ International Centre for Research and Training on Seabuckthorn (internationally oriented national body)

♦ International Centre for Responsible Tourism (ICRT) 12513

Managing Dir address not obtained.
URL: http://responsibletourismpartnership.org/

History Set up 2002, in support of the Cape Town Declaration. **Activities** Advocacy/lobbying/activism; training/education; research/documentation; events/meetings. **Events** *International Conference of Responsible Tourism in Destinations* Helsinki (Finland) 2022, *International Conference of Responsible Tourism in Destinations* Jyväskylä (Finland) 2016, *International Conference on Responsible Tourism in Destinations* Calvia (Spain) 2015, *International Conference on Responsible Tourism in Destinations* Cape Town (South Africa) 2015, *International Conference on Responsible Tourism in Destinations* Dublin (Ireland) 2015. **Publications** *RTP newsletter*.

Members Affiliated centres in 10 countries:
Australia, Brazil, Canada, Finland, India, Ireland, Romania, Russia, Spain, Sweden.
Regional affiliated centres (2):
Better Tourism Africa; *International Centre for Responsible Tourism-West Africa (ICRT-WA)*.
[2016/XJ0491/**F**]

- ♦ International Centre for Responsible Tourism-West Africa (unconfirmed)
- ♦ International Centre of the Roerichs (internationally oriented national body)
- ♦ International Centre of Rural Broadcasting (inactive)
- ♦ International Centre for Science and High Technology (inactive)
- ♦ International Centre for Scientific Culture World Laboratory / see ICSC – World Laboratory (#11088)

♦ International Centre for Scientific and Technical Information (ICSTI) 12514

Centre international pour l'information scientifique et technique (CIPIST) – Centro Internacional de Información Científica y Técnica – Internationales Zentrum für Wissenschaftliche und Technische Information – Mezdunarodnyj Centr Naucnoj i Tehniceskoj Informacii (MCNTI) – Mezdunaroden Centar za Naucna i Tehniceska Informacija – Nemzetközi Tudomanyos és Müszaki Informaciós Központ – Sinzleh Uhoan, Tehnikijn Medellijn Olon Ulsyn Tfb – Miedzynarodowe Centrum Informacji Naukowej i Technicznej – Centrul International de Informare Stiintifica si Tehnica – Mezinarodni Centr Vedeckych a Technickych Informaci

Dir 21-B Kuusinen Street, Moscow MOSKVA, Russia, 125252. T. +74951987021. Fax +74959430089. E-mail: icsti@icsti.int.
URL: http://www.icsti.int/

History 27 Feb 1969, Moscow (Russia). Established on signature of an intergovernmental agreement by 8 contracting parties – German Democratic Republic and 7 members of *Council for Mutual Economic Assistance (CMEA, inactive)*: Bulgaria, Czechoslovakia, Hungary, Mongolia, Poland, Romania, USSR. Agreement subsequently signed, 1973, by the Republic of Cuba and 1979, by the Democratic People's Republic of Korea and the Socialist Republic of Vietnam. In 1992 membership of USSR was succeeded by Russia. Between 1992 and 2006, joined by Belarus, Ukraine, Latvia, Estonia, Moldova, Turkey, Sri Lanka, Georgia, India, South Africa and Egypt. Registered in accordance with USSR law, 23 Jul 1971. Registered with the United Nations, 23 Jun 1971. *Convention on the legal status, privileges and immunities of inter-governmental economic organizations acting within certain fields of cooperation*, 5 Dec 1980. Protocol to the 1969 Agreement, 19 May 1989. Statutes registered in *'UNTS 1/11230'*. **Aims** Facilitate and support international cooperation in science, information exchange, technology transfer and innovations; provide services in the field of scientific and technical information; assist small and medium innovative technology-driven business. **Structure** Committee of Plenipotentiary Representatives (CPR) (meets at least once a year); Directorates (3); Office of the Director. **Languages** English, Russian. **Staff** 250.00 FTE, paid. **Finance** Members' dues. Self financing, non-profit. Operating capital: US$ 1.5 million. **Activities** Knowledge management/information dissemination; research/documentation; events/meetings; training/education. **Events** *Joint annual seminar* Zakopane (Poland) 2001, *Joint annual seminar* Zakopane (Poland) 2000, *International conference on information interchange between ASEAN, Russia, Central and Eastern Europe* Ho Chi Minh City (Vietnam) 1997, *International conference on electronic commerce* Moscow (Russia) 1997, *Mobile systems business forum* Moscow (Russia) 1997. **Publications** *Information and Innovations* (4 a year) in English, Russian – journal; *Diplomatic Corp in Moscow* (annual) in Russian. Information Services: Scientific and technical databases; electronic document delivery systems.

Members Governments of 22 countries:
Azerbaijan, Belarus, Bulgaria, Cuba, Egypt, Estonia, Georgia, Hungary, India, Kazakhstan, Korea DPR, Latvia, Moldova, Mongolia, Poland, Romania, Russia, South Africa, Sri Lanka, Türkiye, Ukraine, Vietnam.
Associate partners in 12 countries:
Austria, China, Cyprus, Czechia, Germany, Hungary, Korea DPR, Korea Rep, Latvia, Türkiye, UK, Vietnam.

IGO Relations Member of: *International Information System for the Agricultural Sciences and Technology (AGRIS, #13848)*; *International Nuclear Information System (INIS, #14378)*. Working contacts with: *European Commission (EC, #06633)*; *FAO (#09260)*; *International Atomic Energy Agency (IAEA, #12294)*; *ISSN International Centre (ISSNIC, #16069)*; *OECD (#17693)*; *UNEP (#20299)*; *UNESCO (#20322)*; *United Nations Institute for Training and Research (UNITAR, #20576)*. **NGO Relations** Working contacts with: *European Association of Information Services (EUSIDIC, no recent information)*. In liaison with technical committees of: *International Organization for Standardization (ISO, #14473)*. Contacts with: *International Institute for Applied Systems Analysis (IIASA, #13861)*; *International Institute of Applied Technologies (IIAT, inactive)*.
[2021/XD4447/**E***]

♦ International Centre for Settlement of Investment Disputes (ICSID) 12515

Centre international pour le règlement des différends relatifs aux investissements (CIRDI) – Centro Internacional de Arreglo de Diferencias Relativas a Inversiones (CIADI)

SG 1818 H St NW, MSN J2-200, Washington DC 20433, USA. T. +12024581534. Fax +12025222615 – +12025222027. E-mail: icsidsecretariat@worldbank.org.
URL: http://icsid.worldbank.org/

History Established by *Convention on the Settlement of Investment Disputes between States and Nationals of other States (1965)*, 18 Mar 1965, Washington DC (USA), formulated by the Executive Directors of *International Bank for Reconstruction and Development (IBRD, #12317)* (World Bank). Entered into force 14 Oct 1966, when ratified by 20 countries. One of 5 organizations that make up *The World Bank Group (#21218)*. **Aims** Provide facilities and services to support *conciliation* and *arbitration* of international investment disputes. **Structure** Administrative Council; Secretariat. **Languages** English, French, Spanish. **Staff** 70.00 FTE, paid. Staff from 32 countries. **Finance** If expenditures of the Centre cannot be met out of charges for use of its facilities, or out of other receipts, the excess is borne by Contracting States. **Activities** Offers services for resolution of international disputes, primarily between investors and states, but also in state-to-state disputes; offers fact-finding proceedings to examine and report on facts before a dispute arises. **Events** *Young ICSID Seminar on Opportunities and Challenges in Light of the Singapore Convention on Mediation* Singapore (Singapore) 2020, *Annual Meeting* Washington, DC (USA) 2013, *Annual Meeting* Tokyo (Japan) 2012, *Investment arbitration conference* Seoul (Korea Rep) 2011, *Annual Meeting* Washington, DC (USA) 2011. **Publications** *ICSID Review – Foreign Investment Law Journal* (3 a year); *Investment Treaties* (3 a year); *Investment Laws of the World* (annual). Annual Report; background papers; decisions.

Members Open for signature to member states of the International Bank for Reconstruction and Development, or any other state which is party to the Statute of the International Court of Justice on invitation of the ICSID Administrative Council. As of 11 Jan 2018, Signatory and Contracting States (159):
Afghanistan, Albania, Algeria, Argentina, Armenia, Australia, Austria, Azerbaijan, Bahamas, Bahrain, Bangladesh, Barbados, Belarus, Belgium, Belize, Benin, Bosnia-Herzegovina, Botswana, Brunei Darussalam, Bulgaria, Burkina Faso, Burundi, Cambodia, Cameroon, Canada, Cape Verde, Central African Rep, Chad, Chile, China, Colombia, Comoros, Congo Brazzaville, Congo DR, Costa Rica, Côte d'Ivoire, Croatia, Cyprus, Czechia, Denmark, Dominican Rep, Egypt, El Salvador, Estonia, Eswatini, Ethiopia, Fiji, Finland, France, Gabon, Georgia, Germany, Ghana, Greece, Grenada, Guatemala, Guinea, Guinea-Bissau, Guyana, Haiti, Honduras, Hungary, Iceland, Indonesia, Iraq, Ireland, Israel, Italy, Jamaica, Japan, Jordan, Kazakhstan, Kenya, Korea Rep, Kosovo, Kuwait, Kyrgyzstan, Latvia, Lebanon, Lesotho, Liberia, Lithuania, Luxembourg, Madagascar, Malawi, Malaysia, Mali, Malta, Mauritania, Mauritius, Mexico, Micronesia FS, Moldova, Mongolia, Montenegro, Morocco, Mozambique, Namibia, Nauru, Nepal, Netherlands, New Zealand, Nicaragua, Niger, Nigeria, North Macedonia, Norway, Oman, Pakistan, Panama, Papua New Guinea, Paraguay, Peru, Philippines, Portugal, Qatar, Romania, Russia, Rwanda, Samoa, San Marino, Sao Tomé-Principe, Saudi Arabia, Senegal, Serbia, Seychelles, Sierra Leone, Singapore, Slovakia, Slovenia, Solomon Is, Somalia, South Sudan, Spain, Sri Lanka, St Kitts-Nevis, St Lucia, St Vincent-Grenadines, Sudan, Syrian AR, Tanzania UR, Thailand, Timor-Leste, Togo, Tonga, Trinidad-Tobago, Tunisia, Türkiye, Turkmenistan, Uganda, UK, Ukraine, United Arab Emirates, Uruguay, USA, Uzbekistan, Yemen, Zambia, Zimbabwe.
Of the above, 149 have also deposited instruments of ratification. Signatory states not having ratified the Convention (9):
Belize, Canada, Dominican Rep, Ethiopia, Guinea-Bissau, Kyrgyzstan, Namibia, Russia, Thailand.

IGO Relations *Gulf Cooperation Council (GCC, #10826)* Commercial Arbitration Centre; *Permanent Court of Arbitration (PCA, #18321)*; *Regional Centre for International Commercial Arbitration, Lagos (LRCICA, #18756)*; *UNCTAD (#20285)*; *United Nations Commission on International Trade Law (UNCITRAL, #20531)*. **NGO Relations** Links with other arbitration institutions, including: *Australian Centre for International Commercial Arbitration (ACICA)*; *Cairo Regional Centre for International Commercial Arbitration (CRCICA, #03398)*; *China International Economic and Trade Arbitration Commission (CIETAC)*; *Hong Kong International Arbitration Centre (HKIAC)*; *International Centre for Dispute Resolution (ICDR)*; *International Chamber of Commerce (ICC, #12534)*; *Singapore International Arbitration Centre (SIAC)*; national organizations.
[2020/XB1476/**E***]

- ♦ International Centre for Sexual Reproductive Rights / see International Centre for Reproductive Health and Sexual Rights
- ♦ International Centre for Shipping, Trade and Finance, London / see Costas Grammenos Centre for Shipping, Trade and Finance, The

♦ International Centre of Sindonology 12516

Centre international d'études sur le Saint Suaire – Centro Internacional de Sindonologia – Internationales Forschungszentrum für das Heiligen Leichentuch Christi – Centro Internazionale di Sindonologia

Main Office Via San Domenico 28, 10122 Turin TO, Italy. T. +39114365832. E-mail: museo@sindone.org.
URL: http://www.sindone.it/

History Founded 23 Dec 1959, on the wake of the "Cultores Sanctae Sindonis", and following the approval in the 1920's of the Archbishop of Turin, Cardinal Maurilio Fossati. The Centre arranged a documentary exhibition (the first nucleus of the Museum of the Shroud) and a library. Following intensification of activity during the latest expositions, some members joined the Commission for the Public Display of the Shroud and contributed on organizational, technical and scientific levels. The Centre built the new seat of the Museum of the Holy Shroud into the crypt of the 18th century church of the Holy Shroud, inaugurated 15 Apr 1998, along with the Public Display. **Aims** Coordinate studies, spread knowledge and collect and preserve anything that concerns the Shroud. **Structure** Central Council, based in seat of the Museum of the Holy Shroud. **Languages** English, French, Italian, Russian, Spanish. **Staff** 1.00 FTE, paid; 80.00 FTE, voluntary. **Finance** Voluntary donations. **Activities** Events/meetings; knowledge management/information dissemination. **Publications** *Sindon* (periodical).

Members Individuals in 53 countries and territories:
Argentina, Australia, Austria, Belgium, Bolivia, Brazil, Bulgaria, Canada, Chile, Congo DR, Costa Rica, Czechoslovakia (unspecified), Denmark, Ecuador, Egypt, El Salvador, Finland, France, Germany, Haiti, Holy See, Hong Kong, Hungary, India, Ireland, Israel, Italy, Japan, Lebanon, Luxembourg, Macau, Mali, Malta, Mexico, Morocco, Netherlands, New Zealand, Peru, Philippines, Poland, Portugal, Romania, Serbia, Spain, Sri Lanka, Sweden, Switzerland, Tunisia, Türkiye, UK, Uruguay, USA, Venezuela.

NGO Relations *Centre International d'Etudes sur le Linceul de Turin (CIELT)*; national sindonology centres.
[2019.12.11/XE6571/E]

♦ International Centre for Small Hydropower / see International Centre on Small Hydro-Power
♦ International Centre on Small Hydro-Power (internationally oriented national body)
♦ International Centre for Social Franchising (internationally oriented national body)
♦ International Centre for South-South Cooperation in Science, Technology and Innovation, Kuala Lumpur / see International Science, Technology and Innovation Centre for South-South Cooperation under the auspices of UNESCO (#14799)

♦ International Centre on Space Technologies for Natural and Cultural Heritage (HIST) 12517

Office No 9 Dengzhuang South Road, Haidian District, 100094 Beijing, China. T. +861082178911. Fax +861082178915.
URL: http://www.unesco-hist.org/

History Proposed May 2007. Approved by *UNESCO (#20322)* General Conference, Oct 2009. Ratified by the State Council of China, Apr 2011. Launched 24 Jul 2011, Beijing (China). A UNESCO Category II Centre. Full title: *International Centre on Space Technologies for Natural and Cultural heritage under the Auspices of UNESCO (HIST)*. **Aims** Monitor and evaluate natural and cultural heritage sites and *biosphere* reserves; combat the effects of *climate change* and natural *disasters*. **Structure** Governing Board; Scientific Committee. **Activities** Research/documentation; training/education. [2017/XM6153/E*]

♦ International Centre on Space Technologies for Natural and Cultural heritage under the Auspices of UNESCO / see International Centre on Space Technologies for Natural and Cultural Heritage (#12517)
♦ International Centre for Space Weather Science and Education (unconfirmed)

♦ International Centre for Sport Security (ICSS) 12518

CEO PO Box 64163, Doha, Qatar. T. +97444308000. Fax +97444308001. E-mail: info@theicss.org.
URL: http://www.theicss.org/

Aims Improve security, safety and integrity in sport by addressing real issues and providing world-leading services, skills, networks and knowledge. **Structure** Board of Directors; Management Board. **Languages** Arabic, English, French, Italian, Portuguese, Spanish. **Activities** Awareness raising; capacity building; certification/accreditation; events/meetings; guidance/assistance/consulting; projects/programmes; research and development; research/documentation; sporting activities; standards/guidelines; training/education. **Events** *Securing Sport* 2020, *Securing Sport* Washington, DC (USA) 2018, *Securing Sport* New York, NY (USA) 2015, *Securing Sport* London (UK) 2014, *Annual International Conference* Doha (Qatar) 2013. **Publications** *Guide on the Security of Major Sporting Events: Promoting Sustainable Security and Legacies* (2021). **IGO Relations** Member of (2): European Union's Expert Group on Sport Integrity (XG Integrity); Europol Platform for Experts and the European Parliament's Intergroup on Sport. Cooperates with (4): *International Anti-Corruption Academy (IACA, #11654)*; *International Bank for Reconstruction and Development (IBRD, #12317)* (World Bank); *UNESCO (#20322)*; *United Nations Office on Drugs and Crime (UNODC, #20596)*. Supports (2): Convention on the Manipulation of Sports Competitions and the Declaration of Berlin; UNESCO's Kazan Action. **NGO Relations** Member of (1): *Sport Integrity Global Alliance (SIGA, #19925)* (Founding). Participant of: *United Nations Global Compact (#20567)*. [2022.02.02/XJ4558/E]

♦ International Centre for Sports History and Culture (internationally oriented national body)
♦ International Centre for Sports Studies (internationally oriented national body)

♦ International Centre for Studies in Religious Education (LUMEN VITAE) 12519

Centre international d'études de la formation religieuse (CIEFR) – Centro Internacional de Estudios de la Formación Religiosa – Internationales Studienzentrum für Religiöse Bildung und Erziehung

Dir Rue Joseph Graffé 4 – bte 2, 5000 Namur, Belgium. T. +328181826255. E-mail: international@lumenvitae.be.
URL: http://www.lumenonline.net

History 1935, Leuven (Belgium). Founded by *Society of Jesus (SJ)*, as *'Centre documentaire catéchétique'*. Transferred to Brussels (Belgium) and present name adopted 1946. Statutes amended: 19 Feb 1955; 13 Mar 1969; 16 May 1974; 21 Apr 2004. Registration: Belgium. **Aims** Contribute methodically to the progress of religious education and religious psychology worldwide, at all levels from early childhood to adult. **Structure** General Assembly (annual), only full members having voting rights. Administrative Council of 7. Includes: educational centre; school of catechism; *International Institute of Catechetics and Pastoral Studies (#13867)*. **Languages** French. **Staff** 14.00 FTE, paid. **Finance** Sources: sale of publications; course fees; donations. **Activities** Training/education. **Events** *Colloquium* Brussels (Belgium) 2008. **Publications** *Revue internationale de catéchèse et de pastorale* (4 a year). Books; manuals. Documentation centre and library (70,000 vols) with 3,500 members in 100 countries. [2019/XC1477/E]

♦ International Centre of Studies on the Tourist Economy (internationally oriented national body)
♦ International Centre for Studies in Urban Architecture / see International Centre for Studies on Urban Design (#12520)

♦ International Centre for Studies on Urban Design (ICSUD) 12520

Centre international d'études sur le projet urbain – Internationales Zentrum für die Stadtgestaltung – Centro Internazionale di Studi sul Disegno Urbano (CISDU)

Main Office via San Niccolo 93, 50122 Florence FI, Italy. E-mail: infocisdu@gmail.com.
URL: http://www.cisdu.org/

History 1986, Florence (Italy), on the initiative of teachers from schools of architecture in Florence, Darmstadt (Germany), Stuttgart (Germany) and Nottingham (UK). Also referred to as *International Centre for Studies in Urban Architecture* and as *Centro Disegno Urbano*. **Aims** Serve as a link between actors of the international scientific community; act as a meeting place to ponder urban problems; promote exchange of information and data; develop cultural relations and cooperation among all working on problems of modern *cities* and *urban space* planning; propose its consultant activity for cities and their administrations in the field of the project of the urban space and of the territory. **Structure** Assembly. Board of Directors, consisting of President, 3 Vice-Presidents, Director, 4 members and 3 Substitute members. Group of Experts. **Languages** English, Italian. **Staff** 9.00 FTE, voluntary. **Finance** Members' dues. Sponsorship for specific events. **Activities** Organizes congresses, conferences, workshops, seminars, exhibitions. Drew up *European Charter for the City – Charte européenne pour la ville – Carta Europea para la Ciudad – Carta Europea per la Città*. **Events** *Meeting / Conference* Florence (Italy) 2006, *International workshop on studies on urban design* Florence (Italy) 2005, *International conference* Bilbao (Spain) 2000, *International seminar* Nantes (France) 2000, *International conference* Glasgow (UK) 1999. **Publications** *Quaderno*. Conference proceedings; papers.

Members Organizations in 7 countries:
Belgium, France, Germany, Greece, Italy, Spain, UK.
Individuals in 16 countries and territories:
Australia, Austria, Belgium, China, Czechia, Denmark, France, Germany, Greece, Italy, Serbia, Spain, Sweden, Switzerland, UK, USA. [2015/XE2493/E]

♦ International Centre for Study and Documentation – Istituto Paolo VI (internationally oriented national body)
♦ International Centre for the Study of East Asian Development, Kitakyushu / see Asian Growth Research Institute
♦ International Centre for the Study of Giftedness (internationally oriented national body)
♦ International Centre for the Study of Languages, Le Relecq-Kerhuon (internationally oriented national body)

♦ International Centre for the Study of the Preservation and Restoration of Cultural Property (ICCROM) 12521

Centre international d'études pour la conservation et la restauration des biens culturels

Dir Gen Via di San Michele 13, 00153 Rome RM, Italy. T. +396585531. Fax +39658553349. E-mail: iccrom@iccrom.org.
URL: https://www.iccrom.org/

History May 1958, Rome (Italy). Established on coming into force of statutes approved, 5 Dec 1956, Delhi (India), at 8th session of General Conference of *UNESCO (#20322)*. Present Statutes adopted 21 Oct 1993, Rome; amended 12 Apr 1973. Official acronym *'ICCROM'* adopted by 10th General Assembly, Apr 1979. Statutes registered in *'UNTS 1/22032'*. **Aims** Provide Member States with tools, knowledge, skills and enabling environment for preserving cultural *heritage* in all its forms for the benefit of all people. **Structure** General Assembly (every 2 years); Council; Secretariat. **Languages** English, French. **Staff** 49.00 FTE, paid. *SEAIAC Press International (no recent information)* is competent to settle disputes. **Finance** Members' dues: derived from the UN scale of assessments. Other sources: contracts; grants. **Activities** Advocacy/lobbying/activism; awards/prizes/competitions; events/meetings; guidance/assistance/consulting; knowledge management/information dissemination; networking/liaising; research/documentation; standards/guidelines; training/education. **Events** *People-Nature Culture Forum* Suwon (Korea Rep) 2022, *International Conference on Sustaining Sound and Image Collections* Brussels (Belgium) 2015, *International Symposium on Disaster Risk Management for Cultural Heritage* Seoul (Korea Rep) 2011, *Biennial General Assembly* Rome (Italy) 2009, *Biennial General Assembly* Rome (Italy) 2007. **Publications** Annual Report; monographs; library catalogue records; conference and symposium proceedings; reports.

Members Members of UNESCO which have sent a formal declaration of accession to the Director-General. Governments of 136 countries:
Afghanistan, Albania, Algeria, Andorra, Angola, Argentina, Armenia, Australia, Austria, Azerbaijan, Bahrain, Bangladesh, Barbados, Belgium, Benin, Bolivia, Bosnia-Herzegovina, Botswana, Brazil, Brunei Darussalam, Bulgaria, Burkina Faso, Cambodia, Cameroon, Canada, Chad, Chile, China, Colombia, Congo Brazzaville, Côte d'Ivoire, Croatia, Cuba, Cyprus, Czechia, Denmark, Dominican Rep, Ecuador, Egypt, Estonia, Eswatini, Ethiopia, Finland, France, Gabon, Gambia, Georgia, Germany, Ghana, Greece, Guatemala, Guyana, Haiti, Honduras, Hungary, India, Iran Islamic Rep, Iraq, Ireland, Israel, Italy, Japan, Jordan, Kenya, Korea Rep, Kuwait, Laos, Latvia, Lebanon, Lesotho, Libya, Lithuania, Luxembourg, Madagascar, Malawi, Malaysia, Maldives, Mali, Malta, Mauritania, Mauritius, Mexico, Monaco, Mongolia, Montenegro, Morocco, Mozambique, Myanmar, Namibia, Nepal, Netherlands, New Zealand, Nicaragua, Nigeria, North Macedonia, Norway, Oman, Pakistan, Paraguay, Peru, Philippines, Poland, Portugal, Qatar, Romania, Russia, Rwanda, Saudi Arabia, Senegal, Serbia, Seychelles, Slovakia, Slovenia, South Africa, Spain, Sri Lanka, Sudan, Sweden, Switzerland, Syrian AR, Tanzania UR, Thailand, Togo, Trinidad-Tobago, Tunisia, Türkiye, UK, Ukraine, United Arab Emirates, Uruguay, USA, Venezuela, Vietnam, Yemen, Zambia, Zimbabwe.

IGO Relations Member of: *United Nations Joint Staff Pension Fund (UNJSPF, #20581)*. Agreement with: *Council of Europe (CE, #04881)*. Observer to: *African World Heritage Fund (AWHF, #00505)*. **NGO Relations** Member of (2): *Forum UNESCO – University and Heritage (FUUH, #09931)*; *International Coordinating Committee on the Safeguarding and Development of the Historic Site of Angkor (ICC-Angkor, #12954)*. Cooperates with (3): *Association internationale pour l'étude de la mosaïque antique (AIEMA, #02689)*; *International Council of Museums (ICOM, #13051)*; *International Council on Monuments and Sites (ICOMOS, #13049)*. Instrumental in setting up (1): *Asian Academy for Heritage Management (AAHM, #01294)*. [2023/XB1478/y/F*]

♦ International Centre for the Study of Radicalisation (unconfirmed)

♦ International Centre for the Study of Radicalization (ICSR) 12522

Exec Dir Dept of War Studies – 6th Floor, King's College London, 138-142 Strand, London, WC2R 1HH, UK. T. +442078482098. Fax +442078482748. E-mail: mail@icsr.info.
URL: http://icsr.info/

History Jan 2008, as a joint project between King's College London (UK), University of Pennsylvania (USA), *International Institute for Counter-Terrorism (ICT)*, and Jordan Institute of Diplomacy. Also known as *International Centre for the Study of Radicalization and Political Violence*. **Aims** Educate the public in relation to diplomacy and strategy, public administration and policy, *security* and counter-terrorism and international *conflict resolution*. **Structure** Trustees; Academic Partners; Affiliates; Board of Advisors. **Activities** Conducts research; facilitates dialogue. **Publications** *ICSR Insight* – newsletter. [2017/XM4014/E]

♦ International Centre for the Study of Radicalization and Political Violence / see International Centre for the Study of Radicalization (#12522)
♦ International Centre for Sustainable Cities, Vancouver (internationally oriented national body)
♦ International Centre for Sustainable Development of Energy, Water and Environment Systems (internationally oriented national body)
♦ International Centre for Sustainable Human Development (internationally oriented national body)
♦ International Centre of Sylviculture (inactive)

♦ International Centre for Tax and Development (ICTD) 12523

CEO c/o Inst of Development Studies, Brighton, BN1 9RE, UK. T. +441273606261. E-mail: info@ictd.ac.
URL: http://www.ictd.ac/

History Formally set up 15 Nov 2010. **Aims** Improve the quality of tax policy and administration in developing countries. **Structure** Centre Advisory Group. **Languages** English, French. **Finance** Initially funded by 5-year grant from *Department for International Development (DFID, inactive)* and *Norwegian Agency for Development Cooperation (Norad)*. Since Apr 2016 funded by DFID and *Bill and Melinda Gates Foundation (BMGF)*. **Activities** Research/documentation; knowledge management/information dissemination. **Publications** *ICTD Research* – series; *ICTD Working Paper* – series; *in ICTD Summary Brief* – series. **NGO Relations** Partners include: *Institute of Development Studies, Brighton (IDS)*; *Chr Michelsen Institute – Development Studies and Human Rights (CMI)*; *Centre for Studies and Research on International Development, Clermont-Ferrand (CERDI)*; *Fondation pour les études et recherches sur le développement international (FERDI)*; *African Tax Administration Forum (ATAF, #00479)*. [2018.02.28/XM5742/F]

♦ International Centre for Terrestrial Antarctic Research (internationally oriented national body)
♦ International Centre for Theoretical Physics / see Abdus Salam International Centre for Theoretical Physics (#00005)

♦ International Centre for Trade and Sustainable Development, Geneva (ICTSD) 12524

Sec Intl Environmental House 2, Chemin de Balexert 7-9, Châtelaine, 1219 Geneva, Switzerland. T. +41229178492. Fax +41229178093. E-mail: info@ictsd.ch.
Chair address not obtained.
URL: http://www.ictsd.org/

History Set up Sep 1996, Geneva (Switzerland). **Aims** Advance sustainable development through trade-related policymaking. **Structure** Governing Board. **Languages** Chinese, English, French, Portuguese, Russian, Spanish. **Finance** Funding and support from donors and partners including: *Department for International Development (DFID, inactive)*; *Swedish International Development Cooperation Agency (Sida)*; DGIS – Ministry of Foreign Affairs Netherlands; Danish, Finnish and Norwegian Ministries of Foreign Affairs. **Activities** Knowledge management/information dissemination; research/documentation; politics/policy/regulatory. **Events** *Trade and Sustainable Development Symposium* Buenos Aires (Argentina) 2017, *Annual Trade and Development Symposium* Nairobi (Kenya) 2015, *Dialogue Meeting on Agricultural Trade Policy and Sustainable Development in East Africa* Nairobi (Kenya) 2015, *Geneva trade and biodiversity day meeting* Geneva (Switzerland) 2010, *Meeting on trade and climate change* Singapore (Singapore) 2009. **Publications** *BioRes* in English; *Bridges* in English; *Bridges Africa* in English; *Passerelles* in French; *Pontes* in Portuguese; *Puentes* in Spanish. Research papers.
Members Founding members (5):
Alliance Sud, Swiss Alliance of Development Organisations Swissaid – Catholic Lenten Fund – Bread for All – Helvetas – Caritas – Interchurch Aid; Consumer Unity and Trust Society, India; *Fundación Futuro Latinoamericano (FFLA, #10022)*; *International Institute for Sustainable Development (IISD, #13930)*; *International Union for Conservation of Nature and Natural Resources (IUCN, #15766)*.
Consultative Status Consultative status granted from: *ECOSOC (#05331)*; *UNCTAD (#20285)* (General Category); *World Intellectual Property Organization (WIPO, #21593)* (Permanent Observer Status); *UNIDO (#20336)*; *UNEP (#20299)*. **IGO Relations** Accredited to the Conference of the Parties of: *Secretariat of the United Nations Convention to Combat Desertification (Secretariat of the UNCCD, #19208)*. Collaborates with: *Agency for International Trade Information and Cooperation (AITIC, #00553)*. Follows the activities of: *OECD (#17693)*; *Secretariat of the Basel Convention (SBC, #19196)*; *Secretariat of the Convention on International Trade in Endangered Species of Wild Fauna and Flora (CITES Secretariat, #19199)*; *Secretariat for the Vienna Convention for the Protection of the Ozone Layer and the Montreal Protocol on Substances that Deplete the Ozone Layer (Ozone Secretariat, #19209)*; *United Nations Commission on Sustainable Development (CSD, inactive)*. Accredited by: *Green Climate Fund (GCF, #10714)*; *United Nations Framework Convention on Climate Change – Secretariat (UNFCCC, #20564)*. Cooperation agreement with: *Development Bank of Latin America (CAF, #05055)*. Agreement with: *European Patent Office (EPO, #08166)*. **NGO Relations** Special links with: *International Organization for Standardization (ISO, #14473)*. Located at: *International Environment House (IEH)*. Partners with a range of NGOs in the field (not specified). [2018/XE2879/ty/**E**]

♦ International Centre for Trade Union Rights (ICTUR) 12525

Centre international pour les droits syndicaux (CIDS) – Centro Internacional para los Derechos Sindicales (CIDS)

Dir CAN Mezzanine, 7-14 Great Dover Street, London, SE1 4YR, UK. E-mail: ictur@ictur.org.
URL: http://www.ictur.org/

History 16 Nov 1987. Current Constitution adopted Jun 2000. Former names and other names: *Centre international des droits et des libertés syndicales* – alias. **Aims** Defend and extend the rights and *freedoms* of trade unions and trade unionists; collect information on, and increase awareness of, trade union rights and freedoms and their violations; carry out activities in the spirit of the UN Charter, Universal Declaration of Human Rights, ILO conventions and recommendations and other appropriate international *treaties*. **Structure** Administrative Council (meets annually, usually in Geneva, Switzerland); Executive Committee; National and Regional Committees. **Languages** English. **Staff** 1.50 FTE, paid. **Finance** Sources: members' dues; revenue from activities/projects; sale of publications. Annual budget: 90,000 EUR. **Activities** Advocacy/lobbying/activism; events/meetings; guidance/assistance/consulting; projects/programmes; research/documentation. **Events** *Annual meeting* Geneva (Switzerland) 2006, *Annual meeting* Geneva (Switzerland) 2005, *Annual meeting* Geneva (Switzerland) 2004, *Annual meeting* Geneva (Switzerland) 2003, *Annual meeting* Geneva (Switzerland) 2002. **Publications** *International Union Rights* (4 a year) in English. *Trade Unions of the World* (8th ed 2021) in English; *World Maps of Freedom of Association and Trade Union Rights* (2012). **Members** Local, national and international organizations including trade unions, lawyers' organizations and human rights NGOs. Membership countries not specified. **Consultative Status** Consultative status granted from: *ECOSOC (#05331)* (Ros A); *ILO (#11123)* (Special List). **IGO Relations** Associated with Department of Global Communications of the United Nations. **NGO Relations** Occasionally cooperates with: *Amnesty International (AI, #00801)*; *International Trade Union Confederation (ITUC, #15708)*. [2022.02.01/XE1065/t/**E**]

♦ International Centre for Training and Exchanges in the Geosciences (#03754)

♦ International Centre for Transdisciplinary Studies and Research . . 12526

Centre international de recherches et études transdisciplinaires (CIRET)

Pres 19 Villa Curial, 75019 Paris, France. T. +33140353694. Fax +33144729427.
URL: http://ciret-transdisciplinarity.org/

History 1987, by 52 personalities of the scientific and cultural world, on the initiative of Basarab Nicolescu. Registered in accordance with French law. **Aims** Develop research into transdisciplinarity as a new approach to the consequences of *information* flow between branches of knowledge; create links between specialists of different branches of *science* and with those from other areas of activity, in particular artists, industrialists and education specialists. **Structure** Administrative Council; Bureau; Advisers. **Languages** English, French. **Staff** 10.00 FTE, voluntary. **Finance** Members' dues. **Activities** Research/documentation; events/meetings. **Events** *International Transdisciplinary-Transnational-Transcultural Conference* Taichung (Taiwan) 2014, *World congress / Congress* Paris (France) 2010, *Congress* Paris (France) 2008, *Congress* Paris (France) 2007, *World congress of transdisciplinarity* Guarapari (Brazil) / Vitória (Brazil) 2005. **Publications** *Rencontres transdisciplinaires* in French – bulletin. Information bank.
Members Individuals (165) in 28 countries:
Argentina, Australia, Austria, Belgium, Brazil, Canada, Cape Verde, France, Germany, Greece, Israel, Italy, Japan, Lebanon, Mexico, Morocco, Netherlands, Portugal, Romania, Spain, Sweden, Switzerland, Syrian AR, Türkiye, UK, Uruguay, USA, Venezuela.
IGO Relations *UNESCO (#20322)*. [2019.02.15/XE2146/v/**E**]

♦ International Centre for Tropical Agriculture 12527

Centre international d'agriculture tropicale – Centro Internacional de Agricultura Tropical (CIAT)

Dir Gen Km 17 Recta Cali-Palmira, A A 6713, Cali 763537, Valle del Cauca, Colombia. T. +5724450027.
URL: http://ciat.cgiar.org/

History 1967, Palmira (Colombia) and became operational 1968. Since 1971, operates under the aegis of *CGIAR System Organization (CGIAR, #03843)*. Established as an International Organization, 28 May 1986. **Aims** Reduce *hunger* and *poverty*; improve human nutrition in the tropics through research aimed at increasing the eco-efficiency of agriculture. **Structure** Board of Trustees; Management Team; Office of the Director General. **Languages** English, Spanish. **Staff** 650.00 FTE, paid. 80 staff are internationally recruited scientists. **Finance** Receives funds through CGIAR or through special projects from 53 countries and organizations, including: *Australian Centre for International Agricultural Research (ACIAR)*; *Bill and Melinda Gates Foundation (BMGF)*; *Deutsche Gesellschaft für Internationale Zusammenarbeit (GIZ)*; *European Commission (EC, #06633)*; *Inter-American Development Bank (IDB, #11427)*; *International Bank for Reconstruction and Development (IBRD, #12317)* (World Bank); *International Fund for Agricultural Development (IFAD, #13692)*; *Irish Aid*; *Kreditanstalt für Wiederaufbau (KfW)*; *Swiss Agency for Development and Cooperation (SDC)*; *Swiss Agency for Development and Cooperation (SDC)*; *United States Agency for International Development (USAID)*. **Activities** Research and development; research/documentation; projects/programmes. Active in: Latin America and Caribbean; Sub-Saharan Africa; Southeast Asia. **Events** *Pedometrics Conference* Nairobi (Kenya) 2013, *Innovation Africa symposium* Kampala (Uganda) 2006, *Workshop on territory and sustainable development* Santa Clara (Cuba) 2004, *International symposium on helping farmers raise soil fertility* Yaoundé (Cameroon) 2004, *Workshop on territory and sustainable development* Cali (Colombia) 2003. **Publications** Annual report; technical books; bulletins; leaflets; policy briefs; audiotutorial training materials. **Information Services** *New World Fruits Database* – in collaboration with IPGRI and CIRAD. **Members** Not a membership organization. **NGO Relations** Partners include: *Association of Amazonian Universities (UNAMAZ, #02366)*; *CARE International (CI, #03429)*; *Catholic Relief Services (CRS, #03608)*; Climate Focus; *The Nature Conservancy (TNC)*; *Pan American Agricultural School 'El Zamorano' (EAP)*; University of Wageningen. Charter member of: *Global Landscapes Forum (GLF, #10451)*. Works with: *Young Professionals for Agricultural Development (YPARD, #21996)*. Together with IFPRI, convenes *HarvestPlus (#10862)*. [2018.06.01/XE4637/**E**]

♦ International Centre for Tropical Ecology (#03805)
♦ International Centre for Underwater Archaeology in Zadar (internationally oriented national body)
♦ International Centre for Urban Safety Engineering (internationally oriented national body)
♦ International Centre for a Water Civilization (internationally oriented national body)
♦ International Centre for Water Cooperation (internationally oriented national body)
♦ International Centre of Water for Food Security (internationally oriented national body)
♦ International Centre for Water Hazard and Risk Management (internationally oriented national body)
♦ International Centre for Water Law, Policy and Science / see UNESCO Centre for Water Law, Policy and Science
♦ International Centre for Water Management Services (internationally oriented national body)

♦ International Centre for Water Resources and Global Change (ICWRGC) 12528

Dir Federal Inst of Hydrology, PO Box 200253, 56068 Koblenz, Germany. T. +4926113065435. E-mail: icwrgc@bafg.de.
Street address Bahnhofstr 40, 56068 Koblenz, Germany.
URL: http://www.icwrgc.org/

History Set up by German Federal Government as national secretariat only for the UNESCO and WMO water programmes in 1975. Since July 2014 renamed ICWRGC and acknowledged as Category 2 Water Centre under the auspices of *UNESCO (#20322)*. **Aims** Estimate impacts of global change to fresh water resources management and provide global hydrological data information through global water data centres; monitor and analyse water quality and world water balance; support the international development agenda; promote international cooperation; support national operational hydrological services in the field of water issues. **Structure** Governing board; Administrative Board; Scientific Advisory Board. **Finance** Financed by German Federal ministries (national committee) **Activities** Capacity building; events/meetings; knowledge management/information dissemination; research/documentation; training/education. **Publications** Papers; reports. **Members** Not a membership organization. **IGO Relations** Cooperates with (7): *FAO (#09260)*; *Global Climate Observing System (GCOS, #10289)*; *Global Runoff Data Centre (GRDC, #10584)*; *International Commission for the Hydrology of the Rhine Basin (#12693)*; *UNEP (#20299)*; *UN-Water (#20723)*; *World Meteorological Organization (WMO, #21649)*. Manages Secretariat of: *International Hydrological Programme (IHP, #13826)*. **NGO Relations** Cooperates with (3): *Global Precipitation Climatology Centre (GPCC)*; *International Association of Hydrogeologists (IAH, #11953)*; *International Association of Hydrological Sciences (IAHS, #11954)*. Also cooperates with other Global Water Centres through GTN-H; national water science institutions. [2022.10.25/XM6000/**E***]

♦ International Centre for Women and Child (internationally oriented national body)

♦ International Centre for Women Playwrights (ICWP) 12529

Contact address not obtained. E-mail: admin@womenplaywrights.org.
URL: https://www.womenplaywrights.org/

History 1989, Buffalo, NY (USA). First International Women Playwrights Conference organized 1988. Registration: Section 501(c)(3), USA, Ohio. **Aims** Support and promote women playwrights worldwide; bring attention to their works. **Structure** Board of Directors. **Activities** Knowledge management/information dissemination; networking/liaising; projects/programmes; publishing activities. **Events** *International Women Playwrights Conference* Montréal, QC (Canada) 2022, *International Women Playwrights Conference* Stockholm (Sweden) 2012. **Publications** *ICWP Newsletter*. *Mother Daughter Monologues*; *Scenes from a Diverse World*.
Members Individuals in 26 countries and territories:
Australia, Bangladesh, Brazil, Canada, China, Costa Rica, Finland, France, India, Indonesia, Israel, Italy, Kenya, Malaysia, New Zealand, Nigeria, Norway, Philippines, Scotland, Singapore, South Africa, Uganda, UK, Uruguay, USA, Zimbabwe. [2022.02.02/XM8956/v/**C**]

♦ International Centre for Workers' Education (inactive)
♦ International Centre for Yoga Education and Research (internationally oriented national body)
♦ International Centre for Youth Development on Information Communication Technology (internationally oriented national body)
♦ International Ceramic Association / see International Ceramic Federation (#12530)

♦ International Ceramic Federation (ICF) 12530

Sec-Treas Materials Research, Tohoku Univ, 2-1-1 Katahira, Aoba-ku, Sendai MIYAGI, 980-8577 Japan.
Secretariat c/o American Ceramic Soc, 600 N Cleveland Ave, Suite 210, Westerville OH 43082, USA. T. +16147945855. Fax +16147945852. E-mail: icfsecretariat@ceramics.org.
URL: http://www.ceramic.or.jp/icf/

History 1991, an *International Ceramic Association (ICA)* having existed since 1985. **Aims** Promote the art, science and technology of ceramics; foster understanding of ceramic materials among users and the public at large; facilitate communication among ceramic societies. **Structure** Executive Committee, consisting of President, President-Elect, Vice-President, Secretary and other members. Executive Secretary. **Activities** Maintains a world calendar of meetings on ceramics and provides a central clearinghouse for their coordination; prepares and issues reports and surveys on topics of international significance. **Events** *International Congress on Ceramics* Montréal, QC (Canada) 2024, *International Congress on Ceramics* Krakow (Poland) 2022, *International Congress on Ceramics* Seoul (Korea Rep) 2021, *International Congress on Ceramics* Seoul (Korea Rep) 2020, *International Congress on Ceramics* Dresden (Germany) 2016.
Members National organizations in 32 countries:
Australia, Belgium, Brazil, China, Czechia, Denmark, Egypt, Finland, France, Georgia, Greece, Hungary, India, Iran Islamic Rep, Italy, Japan, Korea Rep, Latvia, Netherlands, Norway, Poland, Portugal, Romania, Russia, Serbia, Slovakia, Slovenia, Spain, Sweden, Türkiye, UK, USA.
Regional organizations (2):
European Ceramic Society (ECerS, #06507); *World Academy of Ceramics (WAC, #21067)*.
NGO Relations In liaison with technical committees of: *International Organization for Standardization (ISO, #14473)*. [2016/XD4550/y/**C**]

♦ International Cerebral Palsy Society (ICPS) 12531

Secretariat c/o FAPPC, Av Rainha D Amélia, Lumiar, 1600-676 Lisbon, Portugal. E-mail: contact@cpint.org – info@cpint.org.
Registered Office c/o Berkeley Hall, Marshall Ltd, 6 Charlotte Street, Bath, BA1 2NE, UK. E-mail: chairman@cpint.org.
URL: https://www.cpint.org/

History 17 Sep 1954, The Hague (Netherlands), as *World Commission for Cerebral Palsy – Commission mondiale pour l'infirmité motrice cérébrale* of the then *'International Society for Welfare of Cripples'*, currently *RI Global (#18948)*. Constitution amended 25 Jun 1963, Copenhagen (Denmark). Reconstituted and present title adopted Sep 1969, Dublin (Ireland). Constitution amended Oct 1982, Namur (Belgium). Currently an independent organization, an international member of RI. UK Registered Charity: 273102. **Aims** Promote at all times the rights and welfare of people with cerebral palsy and related disorders. **Structure** General Meeting (annual); Executive Committee; Secretary General. **Languages** English. **Staff** 0.50 FTE, paid. **Finance** Sources: members' dues. **Activities** Events/meetings; guidance/assistance/consulting; knowledge management/information dissemination; training/education. **Events** *International Cerebral Palsy Conference* Stockholm (Sweden) 2016, *International Congress on Cerebral Palsy* Bled (Slovenia) 2013, *International Cerebral Palsy Conference* Pisa (Italy) 2012, *Seminar / Conference* Barcelona (Spain) 2011, *International congress on cerebral palsy* Ljubljana (Slovenia) 2010.
Members Organizational; Associate Organizational; Individual. Members in 54 countries and territories:
Argentina, Australia, Austria, Belgium, Brazil, Bulgaria, Cameroon, Chile, China, Croatia, Cyprus, Czechia, Ecuador, Finland, France, Germany, Greece, Hong Kong, Hungary, India, Ireland, Israel, Italy, Japan, Jordan, Korea Rep, Kuwait, Lebanon, Luxembourg, Malaysia, Mexico, Nepal, New Zealand, Nigeria, Norway, Pakistan, Palestine, Poland, Portugal, Saudi Arabia, Singapore, Slovenia, South Africa, Spain, Sweden, Switzerland, Tanzania UR, Türkiye, Uganda, UK, United Arab Emirates, USA, Venezuela, Zimbabwe.
NGO Relations Member of: *European Disability Forum (EDF, #06929)*. Instrumental in setting up: *Cerebral Palsy International Sports and Recreation Association (CPISRA, #03833)*. [2022/XB3485/**B**]

♦ International Certificate Conference / see ICC – the international language association (#11050)

♦ International Certificate Conference – The International Language Association / see ICC – the international language association (#11050)

♦ International Certification Network (IQNet) 12532

Contact Bollwerk 31, 3011 Bern, Switzerland. T. +41313102440. Fax +41313102449. E-mail: headoffice@iqnet.ch.

URL: http://www.iqnet-certification.com/

History Founded 1990, as *European Certification Network (EQNet)*. Present name adopted Jan 1997. Registered in accordance with Swiss Civil Code. **Aims** Promote recognition of *management* system certificates issued by partners; provide 'added value' to national *accreditation* and other recognition systems (such as harmonized accreditation) by means of direct cooperation among colleague certification bodies, including joint audits and certification, 'calibration' of *auditors*, discussion of cases and exchange of experience. **Structure** General Assembly (annual); Board of Directors; Standing Committees (4). **Languages** English. **Staff** 6.00 FTE, paid. **Finance** Members' dues. Annual budtet: Swiss Fr 1,500,000. **Activities** Certification/accreditation; monitoring/evaluation. **Events** *General assembly* Kuala Lumpur (Malaysia) 2018, *General Assembly* Estoril (Portugal) 2015, *General Assembly* Barcelona (Spain) 2006, *Forum* Singapore (Singapore) 2000, *Forum* Porto (Portugal) 1999.

Members National management system certification bodies complying with relevant ISO or EN standards in 33 countries:
Argentina, Austria, Belgium, Brazil, China, Colombia, Costa Rica, Croatia, Cyprus, Czechia, Finland, France, Germany, Greece, Hungary, Ireland, Israel, Italy, Japan, Korea Rep, Malaysia, Mexico, Norway, Poland, Portugal, Romania, Russia, Serbia, Slovenia, Spain, Switzerland, Türkiye, Venezuela.

NGO Relations Member of: *International Accreditation Forum (IAF, #11584).* [2022/XF5603/**F**]

♦ International Cetacean Education Research Centre (internationally oriented national body)
♦ International CFP Council / see Financial Planning Standards Board (#09768)

♦ International Chair on Cardiometabolic Risk 12533

Secretariat Ctr de recherche – Inst univ de cardiologie et de pneumologie de Québec, Pavilion Marguerite-D'Youville, 4th Flr, 2725 chemin Ste-Foy, Québec QC G1V 4G5, Canada. T. +14186568711ext3183. Fax +14186564953. E-mail: chair.cardiometabolic-risk@criucpq.ulaval.ca.

URL: http://www.myhealthywaist.org/

History Founded 2005. **Aims** Help raise awareness of *abdominal* obesity as a new risk factor that, along with traditional risk factors, figures largely in the new concept of global cardiometabolic risk. **Structure** International Academic Board of 26. Executive Board of 5. Scientific Director; Executive Director. Secretariat. **Languages** English, French. **Staff** 3.00 FTE, paid. **Activities** Organizes conferences and symposia; offers expert opinions, reports of scientific and clinical studies and assessment techniques and tools. **Events** *Joint Conference on Obesity and Related Chronic Diseases* Sydney, NSW (Australia) 2019, *International Congress on Abdominal Obesity* Seoul (Korea Rep) 2013, *International congress on abdominal obesity* Québec, QC (Canada) 2012, *International congress on abdominal obesity / International Congress* Buenos Aires (Argentina) 2011, *International Congress* Hong Kong (Hong Kong) 2010.

Members Individuals in 11 countries:
Australia, Belgium, Canada, China, Finland, France, Italy, Japan, Spain, Sweden, USA.

NGO Relations Affiliated with: *International Atherosclerosis Society (IAS, #12288).* Links with national organizations and with: *Education for Health*; *European Society of Cardiology (ESC, #08536)*; *European Society of Hypertension (ESH, #08627)*; *Foundation of European Nurses in Diabetes (FEND, #09953)*; *Inter-American Society of Hypertension (IASH, #11449)*; *International Diabetes Federation (IDF, #13164)*; *International Society of Diabetes and Vascular Disease (ISDVD, inactive)*; *International Union for Health Promotion and Education (IUHPE, #15778)*; *ProCor*, *World Hypertension League (WHL, #21574)*; *World Obesity (#21678).* [2013.07.18/XM4650/**F**]

♦ International Chair-Network UNESCO/ICES on "Technical and Vocational Education and Training" (see: #12487)

♦ International Chamber of Commerce (ICC) 12534

Chambre de commerce internationale – Camara de Comercio Internacional

Main Office 33-43 av du Président Wilson, 75116 Paris, France. T. +33149532828. Fax +33149532859. E-mail: icc@iccwbo.org.

Secretariat: https://iccwbo.org/

History 1919, Paris (France). Founded following decision at International Trade Conference, 1919, Atlantic City NY (USA). Sub-title: *World Business Organization.* Registered by French Ministerial Decree, 24 Jan 1949, Paris. **Aims** Serve world *business* by promoting *trade* and *investment* and the *free market* system; represent the interests of all main business sectors, including banking, financial services, information technology, telecommunications, the environment, arbitration, competition law, intellectual property and transportation; harmonize trade practices and terminology and draw up rules for the conduct of trade and *ethical* codes governing marketing and advertising. **Structure** Council (meets annually), comprising ICC Delegates. Executive Board, comprising at least 15 members plus the Presidency – President, Vice-President, immediate Past President and Chairman of Finance Committee. Policy Commissions, comprising senior business executives and experts delegated by member companies and corporations. International Secretariat, headed by Secretary General. International Court of Arbitration. ICC national committees and groups bring together member companies or sectoral organizations at national level. Specialized division: *ICC Centre for Maritime Cooperation (CMC, see: #12534).* **Languages** English, French. **Staff** About 180 in Paris (France), Hong Kong (Hong Kong), and New York NY (USA). National committee staff in 93 countries. **Finance** Contributions by national committees, determined according to the economic importance of the countries they represent. Other sources: income from services and publications.

Activities *'Commissions'* (12):
- *'ICC Commission on Arbitration'* – drafts and revises the various ICC rules for dispute resolution, including ICC Rules of Arbitration, ICC ADR Rules, IC Dispute Board Rules, and ICC Rules for Expertise; produces reports and guidelines on legal, procedural and practical aspects of dispute resolution; proposes new policies in the interest of efficient and cost-effective dispute resolution; provides useful tools for the conduct of dispute resolution.
- *'Commission on Banking Technique and Practice'* – serves as a global forum and rule-making body for the banking community.
- *'ICC Commission on Commercial Law and Practice'* – facilitates international trade and promotes a balanced self-regulatory and regulatory legal framework for international business-to-business (B2B) transactions. Rules of the CLP Commission have become part of the legal fabric of international commerce.
- *'ICC Commission on Competition'* – ensures that modern business needs and the realities of global markets are taken into account in the formulation and implementation of competition laws and policies.
- *'ICC Commission on Corporate Responsibility and Anti-Corruption'* – aims to define the role of business in the context of globalization and changing societal expectations, to develop world business views on key corporate responsibility issues, to encourage self-regulation by business in confronting issues of extortion and bribery and to provide business input into international initiatives to fight corruption.
- *'ICC Commission on Customs and Trade Facilitation'* – focuses on customs reform and modernization and the implementation of transparent, simplified and harmonized customs policies and procedures
- *'ICC Commission on the Digital Economy'* – seeks to realize the full potential of e-commerce by developing policy and practical tools that encourage competition, growth, predictability, compliance and the secured and free flow of information in cross-border trade, via the Internet and information and communication technologies.
- *'ICC Commission on Environment and Energy'* – aims at developing business recommendations on major environmental and energy regulatory and market issues, and maintaining ICC as the primary business interlocutor and partner in key intergovernmental negotiations and deliberations in these areas.
- *'ICC Commission on Intellectual Property'* – identifies key intellectual property issues facing the international business community and contributes the business voice to debates to resolve these; initiated and continues to actively support and contribute to the Business Action to Stop Counterfeiting and Piracy (BASCAP), a high-level ICC initiative uniting different sectors worldwide to fight against counterfeiting and piracy; through awareness-raising and advocacy initiatives, promotes the positive role of the IP brings together leading, gives guidance on how the system can be made more efficient and cost effective, and helps policymakers adapt the system to new challenges.
- *'ICC Commission on Marketing and Advertising'* – examines major marketing and advertising related policy issues of interest to world business; promotes high ethical standards in marketing by business self-regulation through ICC international marketing codes; elaborates world business views on government initiatives affecting marketing and consumer protection.
- *'ICC Commission on Taxation'* – promotes transparent and non-discriminatory treatment of foreign investment and earnings that eliminates tax obstacles to cross-border trade and investment.
- *'ICC Commission on Trade and Investment Policy'* – promotes an open global economy that encourages cross-border trade and investment by business to foster job creation, sustainable development, and improve living standards.

'Resolution of Disputes':
- *ICC International Court of Arbitration (#11049)* – is a neutral and independent body composed of legal and business specialists from about 85 countries; it administers and supervises worldwide the resolution of international business disputes by means of arbitration under ICC Rules of Arbitration.
- *ICC International Centre for ADR (see: #12534)* – the administrative body that oversees application of the ICC Amicable Dispute Resolution and Dispute Board DOCDEX Rules.

'Other bodies':
- *ICC Commercial Crime Services (CCS, see: #12534)* – the anti-crime arm of the ICC. Based in London (UK). A membership organization tasked ith combating all forms of commercial crime. Specialist divisions offer a range of services dedicated to meeting individual needs of members, and tackle all types of commercial crime such as fraud in international trade, insurance fraud, financial instrument fraud, money laundering, shipping fraud and product counterfeiting.
- *ICC Institute of World Business Law (#11047)* – encourages study of legal problems of international trade, fosters wider knowledge of international commercial law and strengthens links among international trade practitioners, scholars and researchers.
- *World Chambers Federation (WCF, #21269)* – acts as world spokesman for Chambers of Commerce vis-à-vis intergovernmental and other international bodies; provides a world forum for discussions among Chambers on policy and technical issues of topical and common interest; provides technical assistance to Chambers, specifically on organizational structure, management and services; operates *World Chambers Network (WCN, #21270)*, facilitating increased SME competitiveness and participation in global trade by exploiting internet opportunities.

'ICC Training and Conferences' – promotes ICC's expertise to a wider audience through events such as training seminars and conferences.

'Special Projects':
- *'Business Action for Responsible Marketing and Advertising (BARMA)'* – facilitates the spread of self-regulation and reinforces its effectiveness by promoting greater application and reach of ICC's internationally-agreed codes for advertising and marketing practice, and providing training resources to foster better understanding of code compliance.
- *'Business Action to Stop Counterfeiting and Piracy (BASCAP)'* – raises public awareness of the economic and social harm of counterfeiting and piracy and encourages governmental efforts to combat them.
- *'Business Action to Support the Information society (BASIS)'* – promotes global business priorities on the range of Internet governance and information and communications technologies (ICTs) issues that contribute to economic and social development, in forums established by the UN World Summit on the Information Society (WSIS), and preserves the multi-stakeholder approach to these issues.

Also includes: *International Maritime Bureau (IMB, #14097)*; *Piracy Reporting Centre, Kuala Lumpur (#18373)*; *ICC Financial Investigation Bureau (FIB, #11046)*; *ICC Counterfeiting Intelligence Bureau (CIB, #11043).* **Events** *World Chambers Congress* 2025, *World Chambers Congress* Geneva (Switzerland) 2023, *ICC – FIDIC Conference on International Construction Contracts and Dispute Resolution* Dubrovnik (Croatia) 2022, *World Chambers Congress* Dubai (United Arab Emirates) 2021, *Asia Pacific ADR Conference* Seoul (Korea Rep) 2021. **Publications** *Documentary Credits Insight* (4 a year). Publications related to banking and finance, international trade contracts, commercial fraud and counterfeiting, arbitration, international law, environment, marketing/advertising, etc.

Members National committees and groups in 93 countries and territories:
Albania, Algeria, Argentina, Australia, Austria, Bahrain, Bangladesh, Belgium, Bolivia, Brazil, Bulgaria, Burkina Faso, Cameroon, Canada, Chile, China, Colombia, Costa Rica, Croatia, Cuba, Cyprus, Czechia, Denmark, Dominican Rep, Ecuador, Egypt, Estonia, Finland, France, Georgia, Germany, Ghana, Greece, Guatemala, Hong Kong, Hungary, Iceland, India, Indonesia, Iran Islamic Rep, Ireland, Israel, Italy, Japan, Jordan, Kenya, Korea Rep, Kuwait, Lebanon, Lithuania, Luxembourg, Macau, Malaysia, Mexico, Monaco, Morocco, Netherlands, New Zealand, Nigeria, Norway, Pakistan, Palestine, Panama, Paraguay, Philippines, Poland, Portugal, Qatar, Romania, Russia, Saudi Arabia, Senegal, Serbia, Singapore, Slovakia, Slovenia, South Africa, Spain, Sri Lanka, Sweden, Switzerland, Syrian AR, Taiwan, Thailand, Trinidad-Tobago, Tunisia, Türkiye, UK, Ukraine, United Arab Emirates, Uruguay, USA, Venezuela.

Direct members in countries with no national committee or group in 36 countries and territories:
Afghanistan, Andorra, Armenia, Azerbaijan, Bahamas, Belarus, Bermuda, Bosnia-Herzegovina, Botswana, Congo DR, Eritrea, Ethiopia, Gibraltar, Haiti, Iraq, Korea DPR, Latvia, Liberia, Libya, Malta, Mauritania, Mauritius, Moldova, Mongolia, Montenegro, Mozambique, Myanmar, Nicaragua, North Macedonia, Oman, Peru, Sudan, Tajikistan, Tanzania UR, Uganda, Vietnam.

Consultative Status Consultative status granted from: *FAO (#09260)*; *International Atomic Energy Agency (IAEA, #12294)*; *UNIDO (#20336)*; *World Intellectual Property Organization (WIPO, #21593)* (Permanent Observer Status); *International Maritime Organization (IMO, #14102)*; *Council of Europe (CE, #04881)* (Participatory Status); *UNCTAD (#20285)* (General Category); *UNEP (#20299).* **IGO Relations** Privileged access to: *World Trade Organization (WTO, #21864)*, including annual working Cooperates with: *European Union Intellectual Property Office (EUIPO, #08996).* session with WTO ambassadors. Official consultations with: *European Commission (EC, #06633).* Accredited by: *United Nations Framework Convention on Climate Change – Secretariat (UNFCCC, #20564).* Memorandum of Understanding signed with: *International Telecommunication Union (ITU, #15673)*; *World Customs Organization (WCO, #21350).* Agreement with: *International Criminal Police Organization – INTERPOL (ICPO-INTERPOL, #13110).* Associated with Department of Global Communications of the United Nations. **NGO Relations** Close working relations with a number of international nongovernmental bodies concerned with economic and legal affairs (not specified). [2020/XB1490/**B**]

♦ International Chamber of Educational Films (inactive)
♦ International Chamber of Law (inactive)
♦ International Chambers of Expert Advisers on Transport (inactive)

♦ International Chamber of Shipping (ICS) 12535

Chambre internationale de la marine marchande

SG 38 St Mary Axe, London, EC3A 8BH, UK. T. +442070901460. Fax +442070901464. E-mail: info@ics-shipping.org.

URL: http://www.ics-shipping.org/

History Founded 23 Nov 1921, London (UK), as *International Shipping Conference – Conférence internationale des armateurs.* Present name adopted 1948. New constitution adopted Nov 1987. Registered under UK law, Aug 1990. EU Transparency Register: 90104608462-14. **Aims** Promote internationally the interests of members in matters of shipping *policy* and ship operation; encourage high standards of operation and provision of high quality and efficient shipping services; strive for a *regulatory* environment which supports safe shipping operations, protection of the environment and adherence to internationally adopted standards and procedures; promote properly considered international regulation of shipping and oppose unilateral and regional action by governments; press for recognition of *commercial* realities of shipping and the need for quality to be rewarded by a proper commercial return; promote industry guidance on best operating practices. **Structure** General Meeting (annual); ICS Board of Directors. Committees (4); Sub-Committees (4); Panels (6). *International Shipping Federation (ISF, inactive)*, set up 1909, is the identity used by ICS when acting as the international employers' association for ship operators. **Languages** English. **Staff** 20.00 FTE, paid. Provided by MARISEC. **Finance** Members' dues, based in the main on their gross tonnage entry. **Activities** Advocacy/lobbying/activism; events/meetings; management of treaties and agreements; standards/guidelines. Manages the following treaties/agreements: *International Convention for the Prevention of Pollution from Ships (MARPOL, 1973)*; *International Convention for the Safety of Life at Sea, 1974 (SOLAS, 1974).* **Events** *Annual General Meeting* London (UK) 2020, *Annual conference* London (UK) 2017, *World Ocean Summit* Nusa Dua (Indonesia) 2017, *Annual General Meeting* Tokyo (Japan) 2016, *Annual General Meeting* Rotterdam (Netherlands) 2015. **Publications** *ICS Annual Review*, *ICS Circular Letter* – for members only; *Mariscene* – newsletter. *Ship to Ship Transfer Guide (Petroleum)* (4th ed 2005) – jointly with OCIMF; *Model Ballast Water Management Plan and Guidance on IMO 'Ballast Winter' Convention* (3rd ed 2005) – jointly with Intertanko; *Shipping and the Environment: A Code of Practice* (2005); *Pirates and Armed Robbers: Guidelines on Prevention for Masters and Ship Security Officers* (4th ed 2004) – jointly with ISF; *ICS Model Ship Security Plan* (2003) – with CD-ROM; *Maritime Security: Guidance for Ship Operators on the IMO International Ship and Port Facility (ISPS) Code* (2003); *Tanker Safety Guide (Chemicals)* (3rd ed 2002); *Guidelines on Good Employment Practice* (2001); *Environmental Criminal Liability in the United States* (2000); *Ship/Shore Safety Checklist for Bulk Carriers* (2000); *Contingency Planning and Crew Response Guide for Gas Carrier Damage at Sea and in Port Approaches* (3rd ed 1999) – jointly with OCIMF/SIGTTO; *Contingency Planning for the Gas Carrier Alongside and Within Port Limits* (2nd ed 1999) – jointly with OCIMF/SIGTTO; *Garbage Management Plans* (1998); *Bridge Procedures Guide* (3rd ed 1998); *Peril at Sea and Salvage: A Guide for Masters* (5th ed 1998) – jointly with OCIMF; *Assessment and Development of Safety Management Systems* (1997) – in 2 parts; *International Safety Guide for Oil Tankers and Terminals (ISGOTT)* (4th ed 1996) – jointly with OCIMF/IAPH; *Guidelines on the Application of the IMO International Safety Management (ISM) Code* (3rd ed 1996) – jointly with ISF; *Ship to Ship Transfer Guide (Liquefied Gases)* (2nd ed 1995) – jointly with OCIMF/SIGTTO; *Tanker Safety Guide (Liquefied Gas)* (2nd ed 1995); *Clean Seas Guide for Oil Tankers (Retention of Oil Residues on Board)* (4th ed 1994) – jointly with OCIMF; *Prevention of Oil Spillages Through Cargo Pumproom Sea Valves*

(2nd ed 1991) – jointly with OCIMF; *Guide to Helicopter/Ship Operations* (3rd ed 1989); *Safety in Liquefied Gas Tankers* (1978); *Safety in Oil Tankers* (2nd ed 1978); *Safety in Chemical Tankers* (1977). Posters; brochures.
Members Full national associations of shipowners and operators; Associate regional associations and individual shipping companies where there is no national organization, where the national organization is not a member of ICS or where the national organization is not representative of owners and operatives in that country. Full members in 34 countries and territories:
Australia, Austria, Belgium, Bulgaria, Canada, Chile, Croatia, Cyprus, Denmark, Faeroe Is, Finland, France, Germany, Greece, Hong Kong, Iceland, Ireland, Italy, Japan, Kuwait, Liberia, Luxembourg, Mexico, Netherlands, New Zealand, Norway, Pakistan, Singapore, Spain, Sweden, Switzerland, Türkiye, UK, USA.
Associate in 4 countries:
Australia, Russia, United Arab Emirates, USA.
Consultative Status Consultative status granted from: *ECOSOC (#05331)* (Special); *UNCTAD (#20285)* (Special Category); *International Maritime Organization (IMO, #14102)*.
IGO Relations Consultative Status with: *ILO (#11123)*. Cooperates with:
- *International Mobile Satellite Organization (IMSO, #14174)*;
- *International Telecommunication Union (ITU, #15673)*;
- *OECD (#17693)*;
- United Nations Division of Ocean Affairs and the Law of the Sea (DOALAS);
- *United Nations Economic Commission for Europe (UNECE, #20555)* and its *'Working Party on Facilitation of International Trade Procedures'*;
- *World Meteorological Organization (WMO, #21649)*;
- *World Trade Organization (WTO, #21864)*.

Observer status with: *Baltic Marine Environment Protection Commission – Helsinki Commission (HELCOM, #03126)*; *International Oil Pollution Compensation Funds (IOPC Funds, #14402)*.
NGO Relations Works closely with IACS, insurance underwriters and other specialized maritime bodies and nongovernmental institutions whose policies and procedures have an impact on shipping. Also has close relationship with national maritime authorities throughout the world and with relevant departments and agencies of the European Union.
Member of: *High Level Panel for a Sustainable Ocean Economy (Panel, #10917)* – Advisory Network. Consultative member of: *Comité maritime international (CMI, #04192)*. Cooperates with: *International Organization for Standardization (ISO, #14473)*; *International Support Vessel Owners' Association (ISOA, #15628)*. Instrumental in setting up: *Maritime Industry Foundation*; *Piracy Reporting Centre, Kuala Lumpur (#18373)*. [2020/XC1492/**C**]

♦ International Chamber of the Transport Industry 12536
Cámara Internacional de la Industria de Transportes (CIT) – Câmara Internacional da Indústria de Transportes

Headquarters SAS – Quadra 1, Bloco J – Ed CNT, Torre A – 7o Andar, Sl 702, Brasilia DF, 70070-010, Brazil. T. +556132250055 – +556132250112. Fax +556132250055 – +556132250112. E-mail: cit@citamericas.org.
URL: http://www.citamericas.org/

History 25 May 2002. 2002. Former names and other names: *Camara Interamericana de Transportes (CIT)* – former (2002 to 2021); *Interamerican Transportation Chamber* – former (2002 to 2021); *Inter-American Transport Chamber* – former (2002 to 2021); *Câmara Interamericana de Transporte* – former (2002 to 2021); *Câmara Interamericana de Transportes* – former (2002 to 2021). **Aims** Provide an open forum for discussion and identification of the main trends and issues regarding the transportation sector. **Structure** General Assembly; Chapters; Regional Directors. **Languages** English, Portuguese, Spanish. **Staff** 6.00 FTE, paid. **Events** *General Assembly* Montevideo (Uruguay) 2021, *General Assembly* Quito (Ecuador) 2015, *General Assembly* Geneva (Switzerland) 2014, *General Assembly* Montevideo (Uruguay) 2014, *General Assembly* New York, NY (USA) 2013. **Publications** *InterAmericas Magazine* (annual).
Members Full in 18 countries:
Argentina, Bolivia, Brazil, Chile, Colombia, Costa Rica, Dominican Rep, Ecuador, El Salvador, Guatemala, Honduras, Mexico, Nicaragua, Panama, Paraguay, Peru, Uruguay, Venezuela.
Consultative Status Consultative status granted from: *UNCTAD (#20285)* (General Category). **IGO Relations** Registered as Civil Society Organization of: *OAS (#17629)*. Member of Executive Committee of: *Inter-American Committee on Ports (#11415)*. Cooperation Agreement with: *Latin American Integration Association (LAIA, #16343)*. **NGO Relations** Cooperation Agreement with: *International Road Transport Union (IRU, #14761)*. [2021/XJ6084/**D**]

♦ International Charismatic Consultation (ICC) 12537
Address not obtained.
URL: http://www.iccowe.com/

History 1989, UK, *International Charismatic Consultation on World Evangelization (ICCOWE)*. Since 2004, includes *European Charismatic Consultation (ECC, inactive)*. Also officially referred to by the initials *ICC*. UK Registered Charity: 1003378. Activities currently infrequent and by invitation only, 2016. **Aims** Bring together Christians from all churches and ecclesial communities; foster fruitful consultation on the task of world evangelization. **Structure** Executive Committee, consisting of 12 members representative of major streams in the Pentecostal/Charismatic Renewal. Advisory Council, comprising about 80 members. **Languages** English. **Staff** 0.50 FTE, paid. **Finance** Donations. Budget: pounds10,000. **Events** *International Conference* Malta 2004, *International Conference* Malaysia 2000, *Conference* Penang (Malaysia) 2000, *Conference* Prague (Czech Rep) 2000, *Theological conference / International Conference* Prague (Czech Rep) 2000.
Members Advisory Council Members individuals in 35 countries:
Argentina, Australia, Austria, Barbados, Canada, Chile, Czechia, Denmark, Finland, France, Germany, Ghana, Hungary, India, Ireland, Italy, Kenya, Latvia, Malaysia, Netherlands, New Zealand, Nigeria, Norway, Panama, Philippines, Romania, Russia, Singapore, South Africa, Spain, Sweden, Thailand, UK, USA, Venezuela. [2016.06.01/XF4156/dv/**F**]

- ♦ International Charismatic Consultation on World Evangelization / see International Charismatic Consultation (#12537)
- ♦ International Charitable Foundation for Political and Legal Research / see International Public Foundation (#14667)
- ♦ International Charity Association (inactive)
- ♦ International Charter of Physical Education and Sport (1978 treaty)

♦ International Charter "Space and Major Disasters" 12538
Executive Secretariat address not obtained. E-mail: executivesecretariat@disasterscharter.org – webmaster@disasterscharter.org.
URL: http://www.disasterscharter.org/

History 1999, Vienna (Austria). Founded when *European Space Agency (ESA, #08798)* and the French space agency CNES initiated the International Charter. Formally operational since 1 Nov 2000. **Aims** Provide space-based data and information in support of relief efforts during emergencies caused by major disasters. **Activities** Knowledge management/information dissemination. **Events** *Meeting* Daejeon (Korea Rep) 2022, *Meeting* Hyderabad (India) 2015, *Meeting* Daejeon (Korea Rep) 2014. **Publications** *International Charter Newsletter*.
Members Signatories (13):
Argentina, Brazil, Canada, China, France, Germany, India, Japan, Korea Rep, Russia, UK, USA, Venezuela.
Regional organizations (2):
European Organisation for the Exploitation of Meteorological Satellites (EUMETSAT, #08096); *European Space Agency (ESA, #08798)*. [2023/XJ9507/**F**]

♦ International Cheer Union (ICU) 12539
Membership Committee 2574 Sam Cooper Blvd, Memphis TN 38112, USA. T. +19012073010. Fax +19013874358. E-mail: info@cheerunion.org.
URL: https://cheerunion.org/

History 26 Apr 2004. Registration: USA, Texas. **Aims** Manage, direct, promote, organize, and assist the activities and disciplines associated with Cheer worldwide. **Structure** General Assembly; Governing Council; Bureau. Committees: Technical; Sector. Commissions (6): Medical; Ethical; Athlete; Entourage; Sports For All; Gender Equity. Doping Panel. **Activities** Sporting activities. **Events** *General Assembly* Orlando, FL (USA) 2019, *General Assembly* Orlando, FL (USA) 2018, *General Assembly* Orlando, FL (USA) 2017, *General Assembly* Orlando, FL (USA) 2016, *General Assembly* Orlando, FL (USA) 2015.
Members National federations in 111 countries and territories:
Argentina, Armenia, Australia, Austria, Azerbaijan, Bahamas, Barbados, Belarus, Belgium, Bolivia, Bosnia-Herzegovina, Brazil, Burundi, Cameroon, Canada, Chile, China, Colombia, Costa Rica, Croatia, Czechia, Denmark, Dominican Rep, Ecuador, Egypt, El Salvador, England, Estonia, Finland, France, Georgia, Germany, Ghana, Gibraltar, Great Britain, Greece, Guam, Guatemala, Guernsey, Haiti, Honduras, Hong Kong, Hungary, India, Indonesia, Ireland, Isle of Man, Israel, Italy, Jamaica, Japan, Kazakhstan, Kenya, Korea Rep, Kyrgyzstan, Laos, Latvia, Luxembourg, Macau, Malaysia, Mali, Mexico, Moldova, Mongolia, Montenegro, Morocco, Namibia, Netherlands, New Zealand, Nigeria, North Macedonia, Northern Ireland, Norway, Pakistan, Panama, Peru, Philippines, Poland, Puerto Rico, Romania, Russia, Rwanda, Samoa USA, San Marino, Saudi Arabia, Scotland, Serbia, Singapore, Slovenia, South Africa, Spain, Sri Lanka, St Kitts-Nevis, Suriname, Sweden, Switzerland, Taiwan, Tanzania UR, Thailand, Trinidad-Tobago, Uganda, Ukraine, United Arab Emirates, USA, Venezuela, Vietnam, Virgin Is UK, Virgin Is USA, Wales, Zambia, Zimbabwe.
NGO Relations Member of (6): *Alliance of Independent recognised Members of Sport (AIMS, #00690)* (Associate); *Association of the IOC Recognized International Sports Federations (ARISF, #02767)*; *Fédération Internationale de Savate (FISav, #09656)*; *International Council of Sport Science and Physical Education (ICSSPE, #13077)*; *Olympic Movement (#17719)*; *The Association for International Sport for All (TAFISA, #02763)*. Recognized by: *International Olympic Committee (IOC, #14408)*. [2023/XM4458/**B**]

♦ International Chemical Biology Society (ICBS) 12540
Chair 5111 Rollins Research Ctr, 1510 Clifton Rd, Atlanta GA 30322, USA.
URL: http://www.chemical-biology.org/

Aims Promote research and educational opportunities at the interface of *chemistry* and biology. **Structure** Board of Directors; International Advisory Board. **Events** *Annual Conference (ICBS 2022)* Brisbane, QLD (Australia) 2022, *Conference* 2021, *Conference* 2020, *Annual Conference* Hyderabad (India) 2019, *Annual Conference* Vancouver, BC (Canada) 2018. [2021/XM4601/**C**]

♦ International Chemical Employers Labour Relations Committee (LRC) 12541
SG c/o BAVC, Abraham-Lincoln-Str 24, 65189 Wiesbaden, Germany. E-mail: lrc@bavc.de.
History As an informal network. Also referred to as *Chemical Industry Labour Relations Committee*. **Members** Membership countries not specified. **NGO Relations** *European Chemical Employers Group (ECEG, #06521)*; *IndustriALL Global Union (IndustriALL, #11177)*; *International Organisation of Employers (IOE, #14428)*. [2016/XE0758/**F**]

♦ International Chemical Information Network (ChIN) 12542
Réseau international d'information chimique

Dir Laboratory of Computer Chemistry, Institute of Chemical Metallurgy, Chinese Academy of Sciences, 100190 Beijing, China. T. +861062554066. Fax +861062561822.
Co-Dir Dept Information Engineering, Toyohashi Univ, 1-1 Hibarigaoka, Tempaku-cho, Toyohashi AICHI, 441 Japan. T. +81532446878. Fax +81532446873. E-mail: taka@mis.tutkie.tut.ac.jp.
URL: http://www.chinweb.com.cn/

History Jun 1988, Ljubljana (Yugoslavia), within *Federation of Asian Chemical Societies (FACS, #09431)*, at a meeting organized by *International Centre for Chemical Studies (ICCS, no recent information)*, with support from the General Information Programme (PGI) of *UNESCO (#20322)*, following proposal of 23rd Session UNESCO's General Conference, 1985. Launched in 1990. Also referred to as *International Network for Chemical Information (INCI)*. **Aims** Improve awareness of network members concerning new developments and applications of databases, information systems and information handling software in chemistry and related fields, through exchange of experience and ideas; promote establishment and use of chemical information systems to solve specific problems, particularly those related to national development; provide a framework for international cooperative projects aimed at elaborating and applying information strategies for solving developmental problems involving chemical science and technology. Promote: establishment of national and regional information networks; access to and exchange of information experience on information handling methods in chemistry; free or low-cost exchange of information and improved access to databases; access to primary information, including core journals, patents, grey literature and translation facilities. **Structure** Steering Committee (meets every 2 years), consisting of 7 members plus the Executive Secretary; Advisory Committee; Secretariat, headed by Executive Secretary. An autonomous, self-sufficient, flexible association of institutions dealing with chemical information. Intention is for each country to be represented by at least one national institution. **Languages** English. **Activities** Promotion of access to, and the exchange of information and experience on chemistry information sources, methods and techniques. Setting up of cooperative schemes for the exchange of primary documentation, including core journals, patents, grey literature and translations, among ChIN members. Advice in the building of specialized chemical information systems at the national level and in linking them internationally. Exchange of information on training programmes in chemical information, cooperation in development of core curricula and methodologies for training users and specialists in chemical information, and promotion of recommended training programmes (training of trainers). Organizes academic symposiums. **Publications** *ChIN Directory*. **Members** Not a membership organization; works as a virtual community. **IGO Relations** *UNIDO (#20336)*. **NGO Relations** *Asian Coordinating Group for Chemistry (ACGC, no recent information)*; *Asian Network of Analytical Chemistry (ANAC, #01546)*. [2008/XF0811/**F**]

- ♦ International Chemical Secretariat (internationally oriented national body)

♦ International Chemical Trade Association (ICTA) 12543
Contact c/o FECC, Rue du Luxembourg 16B, 1000 Brussels, Belgium. T. +3226790260. E-mail: info@icta-chem.org.
Pres c/o NACD, 1560 Wilson Bld, Suite 1100, Arlington VA 22209, USA. E-mail: ebyer@nacd.com.
URL: http://www.icta-chem.org/

History Founded 1991, as *International Council of Chemical Trade Associations (ICCTA)*. Current title adopted 1 Feb 2016. Current statutes adopted Apr 2016. Registered in accordance with Belgian law. **Aims** Coordinate among associations worldwide on the strategy and representation of chemical distribution and trade before international stake holders on key issues of common interest and on chemical industry programmes, through dialogue and cooperation. **Structure** General Assembly; Board. Secretariat hosted by: *Fédération européenne du commerce chimique (Fecc, #09563)*. **Languages** English. **Activities** Awareness raising. **Events** *Meeting* Nice (France) 2018, *Meeting* Naples, FL (USA) 2017, *Meeting* Warsaw (Poland) 2017, *Meeting / Biannual Meeting* Athens (Greece) 2015, *Meeting / Biannual Meeting* Bonita Springs, FL (USA) 2015.
Members National associations of chemical distributors and traders in 9 countries:
Belgium, Brazil, Germany, Ireland, Italy, Mexico, Netherlands, UK, USA.
NGO Relations Cooperates with: *International Council of Chemical Associations (ICCA, #13003)*. [2019/XE3524/t/**E**]

- ♦ International Chemical Workers Union / see International Chemical Workers Union Council
- ♦ International Chemical Workers Union Council (internationally oriented national body)
- ♦ International Chemistry Conference in Africa (meeting series)
- ♦ International Chemistry Office (inactive)
- ♦ International Chemometrics Society (inactive)

♦ International Chess Committee of the Deaf (ICCD) 12544
SG Velkika Vasylkivska str 74, apt 31, Kiev, 03150, Ukraine. E-mail: iccd.gensec@gmail.com.
URL: http://chessdeaf.org/

History 14 Aug 1949, Copenhagen (Denmark). New statutes adopted 1 Oct 2012, Almaty (Kazakhstan). Former names and other names: *International Committee of Silent Chess (ICSC)* – former (14 Aug 1949 to 1 Oct 2012); *Weltausschuss für Gehörlosenschach* – former (14 Aug 1949 to 1 Oct 2012). **Aims** Promote chess among deaf people of all nations. **Structure** Congress; Board; Executive Board. **Languages** English. **Finance** Sources: members' dues. **Activities** Sporting activities. **Events** *Biennial Congress* Manchester (UK) 2018, *Biennial Congress* Yerevan (Armenia) 2016, *Biennial Congress* Opatija (Croatia) 2014, *Biennial Congress* Almaty (Kazakhstan) 2012, *Congress* Almaty (Kazakhstan) 2012.
Members National chess organizations in 34 countries:
Armenia, Azerbaijan, Bangladesh, Belarus, Bulgaria, Croatia, Czechia, England, Germany, Hungary, India, Israel, Italy, Kazakhstan, Kyrgyzstan, Latvia, Lithuania, Moldova, Mongolia, Netherlands, Poland, Portugal, Romania, Russia, Scotland, Serbia, Slovakia, Slovenia, Spain, Sweden, Switzerland, Turkmenistan, Ukraine, Uzbekistan.
NGO Relations Member of (1): *Fédération internationale des échecs (FIDE, #09627)*. [2020/XM4755/**D**]

♦ International Chess Problem Board (inactive)

♦ International Chewing Gum Association (ICGA) 12545

Contact c/o Keller-Heckman, 1001 G St NW, Ste 500 West, Washington DC 20001, USA. E-mail: icga@gumassociation.org.
URL: http://www.gumassociation.org/

History 10 Jun 2005, Athens (Greece). Founded by merger of *European Association of the Chewing Gum Industry (EACGI, inactive)* and (US) National Association of Chewing Gum Manufacturers. Registration: 501(c)(6) Organization, No/ID: 30-0630080, Start date: 2010, USA, Washington DC; EU Transparency Register, No/ID: 124900116844-06, Start date: 20 Apr 2015. **Aims** Promote harmonization of the various international and national chewing gum regulations and standards applicable worldwide to chewing gum and its primary constituent ingredients. **Structure** General Assembly; Board of Directors; Secretariat. Various committees. Administered through Keller and Heckman LLP. **Languages** English. **Finance** Sources: members' dues. **Activities** Events/meetings. **Events** *Annual Meeting* Baveno (Italy) 2013, *Annual Meeting* Seoul (Korea Rep) 2012, *Annual Meeting* Hong Kong (Hong Kong) 2011, *Annual Meeting* New York, NY (USA) 2010, *Annual Meeting* Rome (Italy) 2009.

Members Categories A, B, C and D. Companies producing chewing gum and primary and intermediate ingredients in 18 countries:
Argentina, Belgium, Brazil, China, Denmark, Egypt, France, Germany, India, Italy, Japan, Mexico, Netherlands, Spain, Switzerland, Türkiye, UK, USA.

IGO Relations Participates as observer in the activities of: *Codex Alimentarius Commission (CAC, #04081)*. **NGO Relations** Works with organizations representing food, confectionery or ingredient producing companies and, where relevant, their respective national associations. Relations include the following organizations listed in this Yearbook: *Association of the Chocolate, Biscuit and Confectionery Industries of the EU (CAOBISCO, #02427)*; *Calorie Control Council (CCC)*; *Conseil européen de l'industrie chimique (CEFIC, #04687)*; *EU Specialty Food Ingredients (#09200)*; *FoodDrinkEurope (#09841)*; *International Confectionery Association (ICA, #12840)*; *International Council of Grocery Manufacturers Associations (ICGMA, #13026)*; *International Organization of the Flavor Industry (IOFI, #14446)*. [2020/XM1657/**C**]

♦ International Child Abduction Center (internationally oriented national body)
♦ International Child Art Foundation (internationally oriented national body)

♦ International Childbirth Education Association (ICEA) 12546

Exec Dir 110 Horizon Drive, Ste 210, Raleigh NC 27615, USA. T. +19196744183. Fax +19194592075. E-mail: info@icea.org.
URL: http://www.icea.org/

History 1960. **Aims** Unite those who support *family*-centred *maternity care* and those who believe in freedom of choice based on knowledge of alternatives in birth. **Structure** Board of Directors. **Activities** Certification/accreditation; events/meetings; training/education. **Events** *Freedom of choice based on knowledge of alternatives* Minneapolis, MN (USA) 1989, *International convention* Los Angeles, CA (USA) 1987, *International convention* Washington, DC (USA) 1987, *International convention* Chicago, IL (USA) 1986. **Members** Individuals (over 8,000) in 42 countries. Membership countries not specified. **NGO Relations** Member of (1): *International Childbirth Initiative (ICI, #12547)*. [2022.10.18/XG2695/v/**F**]

♦ International Childbirth Initiative (ICI) 12547

Exec Dir address not obtained.
Chair address not obtained.

History 2018. Launched by *International MotherBaby Childbirth Organization (IMBCO, #14185)* and *Fédération Internationale de Gynécologie et d'Obstétrique (FIGO, #09638)*. Former names and other names: *International Childbirth Initiative (ICI): 12 Steps to Safe and Respectful MotherBaby-Family Maternity Care* – full title. **Aims** Provide guidance and support for safe and respectful maternity care. **Structure** Executive Board.

Members Organizations which have endorsed the initiative include 11 organizations listed in this Yearbook: *Council of International Neonatal Nurses (COINN, #04904)*; *DONA International (#05115)*; *Every Mother Counts*; *Fédération Internationale de Gynécologie et d'Obstétrique (FIGO, #09638)*; *International Childbirth Education Association (ICEA, #12546)*; *International Confederation of Midwives (ICM, #12863)*; *International Council of Nurses (ICN, #13054)*; *International MotherBaby Childbirth Organization (IMBCO, #14185)*; *International Pediatric Association (IPA, #14541)*; *Lamaze International*; *White Ribbon Alliance for Safe Motherhood (WRA, #20934)*. [2021/AA1483/y/**E**]

♦ International Childbirth Initiative (ICI): 12 Steps to Safe and Respectful MotherBaby-Family Maternity Care / see International Childbirth Initiative (#12547)
♦ International Child Development Initiatives (internationally oriented national body)

♦ International Child Development Programme (ICDP) 12548

Chair 46 Mildred Ave, Watford, WD18 7DZ, UK. E-mail: icdpoffice@gmail.com.
URL: https://www.icdp.info/

History Development started 1985; formally set up 1992. Registration: No/ID: 92/04227, Start date: 1992, Norway, Oslo. **Aims** Provide for human care by activating empathy and education of both caregivers and their children; implement recent knowledge from scientific research in child development for the benefit of *disadvantaged* and *neglected* children. **Structure** Board. **Languages** English. **Staff** Voluntary. **Activities** Projects/programmes; training/education. **Publications** Programme evaluation; articles.

Members Partners and national bodies in 39 countries:
Australia, Bolivia, Botswana, Brazil, Burkina Faso, China, Colombia, Denmark, Ecuador, El Salvador, Ethiopia, Finland, Ghana, Guatemala, India, Israel, Japan, Kenya, Korea Rep, Lebanon, Lesotho, Malawi, Mexico, Mozambique, Nepal, Nicaragua, Norway, Paraguay, Peru, Philippines, Portugal, Russia, Somalia, South Africa, Sweden, Tanzania UR, Ukraine, USA, Zambia.

IGO Relations Cooperates with: *UNICEF (#20332)*; ministries and local governments and municipalities. Allied partner of UNICEF Colombia. **NGO Relations** Member of: *Susila Dharma International Association (SDIA, #20048)*. Cooperates with: *Plan International (#18386)*; *Save the Children International (#19058)*; universities; local NGOs. [2021/XF3175/**F**]

♦ International Child Health and Diarrhoeal Disease Foundation / see Child Health Foundation
♦ International Child Health Foundation / see Child Health Foundation
♦ International Child Health Group (internationally oriented national body)

♦ International Childhood and Youth Research Network (ICYRnet) ... 12549

Sec School of Sociology/Social Policy/Social Work, Belfast 6 College Park, Belfast, BT7 1LP, UK. T. +442890973375.
Pres Ctr for the Study of Childhood and Adolescence, Diogenes Street 6, Engomi PO Box 22006, CY-1516 Nicosia, Cyprus. T. +35722713167. Fax +35722713048.
URL: http://www.icyrnet.net/

Aims Promote, internationally, the inter-disciplinary study of children and young people so as to further awareness and understanding of issues that affect their well being. **Structure** General Assembly; Executive Board. **Activities** Organizes: research programmes; staff exchanges; seminars; information dissemination.

Members Organizations in 28 countries and territories:
Australia, Austria, Belgium, Bulgaria, Cyprus, Ethiopia, Germany, India, Ireland, Israel, Liberia, Malawi, Malta, Nepal, Netherlands, New Zealand, Norway, Palestine, Romania, Russia, Serbia, Slovenia, South Africa, Spain, Sweden, Thailand, UK, USA.

Included in the above, 6 international organizations:
Aflatoun International (#00152); *Children's Rights European Academic Network (CREAN, #03878)*; *European Centre for Social Welfare Policy and Research (European Centre, #06500)*; *International Child Development Initiatives (ICDI)*; *International Rescue Committee (IRC, #14717)*; *UCL Institute for Global Health (IGH)*. [2015/XJ1084/y/**D**]

♦ International Child Neurology Association (ICNA) 12550

Association internationale de neurologie infantile

Main Office c/o Child-Neurology.Net, 466 Fullwell Ave, London, IG5 0RL, UK. E-mail: office@icnapedia.org.
URL: http://www.icnapedia.org/

History 12 Sep 1973. Registration: Start date: 14 Aug 1974, Belgium. **Aims** Advance the care of children with neurological problems throughout the world. **Structure** Council of the Future Leaders of ICNA. **Languages** English. **Staff** 0.50 FTE, paid. **Finance** Sources: meeting proceeds; sale of publications. Other sources: contracts. **Activities** Events/meetings; financial and/or material support; knowledge management/information dissemination; networking/liaising; research/documentation; training/education. **Events** *International Child Neurology Congress* Antalya (Türkiye) 2022, *Congress* San Diego, CA (USA) 2020, *International Child Neurology Congress* Mumbai (India) 2018, *International Child Neurology Congress* Amsterdam (Netherlands) 2016, *International Child Neurology Congress* Foz do Iguaçu (Brazil) 2014. **Publications** *Newsletter* (2 a year); *Journal of the International Child Neurology Association (JICNA)*. *International Review of Child Neurology Series*. *Textbook of Child Neurology*. **Information Services** *ICNApedia®* – knowledge environment portal.

Members Individuals in 63 countries and territories:
Argentina, Australia, Austria, Bangladesh, Belgium, Brazil, Bulgaria, Canada, Chile, China, Colombia, Croatia, Cuba, Cyprus, Czechia, Denmark, Estonia, Finland, France, Germany, Greece, Hong Kong, Hungary, India, Indonesia, Ireland, Israel, Italy, Japan, Korea Rep, Kuwait, Lithuania, Mexico, Netherlands, New Zealand, Nigeria, Norway, Paraguay, Peru, Philippines, Poland, Portugal, Puerto Rico, Qatar, Romania, Russia, Saudi Arabia, Serbia, Singapore, Slovenia, South Africa, Spain, Sweden, Switzerland, Taiwan, Thailand, Tunisia, Türkiye, UK, United Arab Emirates, Uruguay, USA, Venezuela.

NGO Relations Cooperates with (1): *Asian Oceanian Child Neurology Association (AOCNA, #01575)*. [2022/XD6941/v/**C**]

♦ International Children's Alliance (internationally oriented national body)

♦ International Children's Care (ICC) 12551

Secours international d'enfants

CEO PO Box 820610, Vancouver WA 98682-0013, USA. T. +13605730429. Fax +13605730491. E-mail: info@forhiskids.org.
Street Address 2711 NE 134th Way, Vancouver WA 98686, USA.
URL: http://www.forhiskids.org/

History Founded 1978. Chartered in the States of Oregon and Washington (USA). **Aims** Work on behalf of *orphaned, abandoned* and *needy* children; champion *Christian* ideals that each individual reflects the image of God, each person has dignity. **Structure** Board of Trustees; Executive Committee; Administrative Office in Vancouver WA (USA). Departments: Administration; Director of Development; International Operations; Children's Services; Publications and Graphics; Accounting; International Development and Industries; Sponsorship. **Staff** 14.00 FTE, paid. **Finance** Funded through: sponsorships; public donations. **Activities** Humanitarian/emergency aid. **Publications** *ICC Newsletter* (12 a year) in English; *Que Pasa* in English – newsletter.

Members Affiliate projects or organizations in 24 countries and territories:
Belgium, Brazil, Canada, Colombia, Congo DR, Dominican Rep, El Salvador, France, Germany, Ghana, Guatemala, Hong Kong, Iceland, India, Korea Rep, Mexico, Netherlands, Nicaragua, Romania, Spain, Switzerland, UK, USA, Zambia. [2014.12.04/XE1474/**E**]

♦ International Children's Center (internationally oriented national body)

♦ International Children's Continence Society (ICCS) 12552

Gen Sec St Louis Children's Hospital, Washington Univ, School of Medicine, 1 Childrens Pl, St Louis MO 63110, USA. T. +13144546034. Fax +13144542876.
Pres Nephrology Unit, Univ Children's Hospital, SE-751 85 Uppsala, Sweden. T. +46186110000. Fax +46186115853.
URL: http://www.i-c-c-s.org/

History Jun 1997, Paris (France). **Aims** Improve the quality of life and life expectancy for individuals with deficient *bladder* function, expressed as problems of storage and evacuation of *urine*. **Structure** Board, comprising President, Past-President, General Secretary, Treasurer, Scientific Chairman and 5 members. **Languages** English. **Events** *Congress* Aarhus (Denmark) 2021, *Congress* Gdansk (Poland) 2019, *Congress* Rome (Italy) 2018, *Meeting* Kyoto (Japan) 2016, *Congress* Prague (Czech Rep) 2015. **Publications** Reports. [2015/XD6389/**D**]

♦ International Children's Dream Foundation (internationally oriented national body)
♦ International Children's Health and Environment Network / see International Network on Children's Health, Environment and Safety (#14240)
♦ International Children's Heart Foundation (internationally oriented national body)

♦ International Children's Palliative Care Network (ICPCN) 12553

Chief Exec 13 Assagay Road, Assagay, Durban, 3610, South Africa. T. +447751879310. E-mail: chiefexec@icpcn.org.
URL: http://www.icpcn.org/

History 2005, Seoul (Korea Rep). Registration: Companies and Intellectual Propert Commission, No/ID: 2011/001648/08, Start date: 1 May 2011, South Africa. **Aims** Achieve the best quality of life and care for children and young people with life-limiting conditions, their families and carers worldwide, by raising awareness of children's palliative care, lobbying for the global development of children's palliative care services, and sharing expertise, skills and knowledge. **Structure** International Board of Trustees; Executive Board; Chief Executive. **Languages** English. **Staff** 5.00 FTE, paid. **Finance** Sources: donations; grants. **Activities** Advocacy/lobbying/activism; awareness raising; knowledge management/information dissemination; research/documentation; training/education. **Events** *Conference* Durban (South Africa) 2018, *Conference* Buenos Aires (Argentina) 2016, *Conference* Mumbai (India) 2014. **Publications** *Children's Palliative Care – an international case-based manual* (1st ed 2020) by Julia Downing in English – ebook for download – various contributing authors; *Touching Rainbows – Acknowledging the child's voice in palliative care* by Julia Downing and Sue Boucher. Reports; position papers; journal papers.

Members Full (2011) in 83 countries and territories:
Afghanistan, Angola, Armenia, Australia, Austria, Bangladesh, Belarus, Benin, Botswana, Brazil, Cameroon, Canada, Chile, China, Colombia, Congo Brazzaville, Côte d'Ivoire, Czechia, Denmark, Ecuador, Estonia, Eswatini, Ethiopia, France, Gambia, Georgia, Germany, Ghana, Greece, Guatemala, Honduras, Hong Kong, Hungary, India, Indonesia, Iran Islamic Rep, Ireland, Israel, Italy, Japan, Kazakhstan, Kenya, Kuwait, Kyrgyzstan, Latvia, Lesotho, Liberia, Malawi, Malaysia, Mexico, Namibia, Nepal, Netherlands, New Zealand, Nigeria, Norway, Pakistan, Peru, Poland, Portugal, Romania, Russia, Rwanda, Serbia, Sierra Leone, Singapore, South Africa, Spain, Sri Lanka, Sweden, Switzerland, Taiwan, Tajikistan, Tanzania UR, Thailand, Togo, Uganda, UK, Ukraine, United Arab Emirates, USA, Zambia, Zimbabwe.

NGO Relations Member of (1): *World Patients Alliance (WPA)*. [2022.05.09/XM4908/y/**F**]

♦ International Children's Peace Council (internationally oriented national body)
♦ International Children's Rights Protection Network / see Children's Rights International (#03879)
♦ International Children's Trust (internationally oriented national body)
♦ International Child Resource Institute, Berkeley (internationally oriented national body)
♦ International Child Rights Center (internationally oriented national body)
♦ International Child Support / see ICS
♦ International Child Welfare Organization (internationally oriented national body)
♦ International Child Welfare Service (internationally oriented national body)
♦ International Child and Youth Care Network (unconfirmed)

♦ International China Concern (ICC) 12554

CEO Room 1208, Tung Che Commercial Centre, 246 Des Voeux Road, Sai Ying Pun, Central and Western, Hong Kong. T. +85225292192. E-mail: international@chinaconcern.org.
URL: http://www.chinaconcern.org/

History 1993. Founded by David Gotts. Registration: Australia; Tax Exempt Charity, No/ID: 91/04700, Hong Kong; Canada; Netherlands; Singapore; Charity Commission, No/ID: 1164736, England and Wales; USA. **Aims** Provide love, hope and opportunity to children with disabilities; strive to end abandonment by keeping families together. **Structure** International offices (7): Australia; Canada; Hong Kong; Netherlands; Singapore; UK; USA. Development office based in China. **Languages** Dutch, English, Mandarin Chinese. **Staff** 315.50 FTE, paid; 50.00 FTE, voluntary. 30 FTE, self-funded. **Finance** Annual budget: 3,500,000 USD. **Activities** Financial and/or material support; guidance/assistance/consulting; training/education. **Publications** *ICC Newsletter* (2 a year). Annual Summary; regular donor correspondence.

Members Representative offices in 8 countries and territories:
Australia, Canada, China, Hong Kong, Netherlands, Singapore, UK, USA. [2020.11.17/XE4563/**E**]

- ♦ International Chinese Hard Tissue Society / see International Chinese Musculoskeletal Research Society
- ♦ International Chinese Kuo Shu Federation (inactive)
- ♦ International Chinese Musculoskeletal Research Society (internationally oriented national body)
- ♦ International Chiropractors Association (internationally oriented national body)

♦ International Cholangiocarcinoma Research Network (ICRN) 12555

Contact c/o Cholangiocarcinoma Foundation, 5526 West 13400 S, Ste 510, Herriman UT 84096, USA. E-mail: info@cholangiocarcinoma.org.
URL: https://cholangiocarcinoma.org/icrn/

Aims Accelerate the clinical translation of scientific discoveries to impact the lives of *patients* with cholangiocarcinoma. **Structure** Executive Committee. **Events** *Conference* Busan (Korea Rep) 2018. **Publications** *ICRN Newsletter*.
Members Institutions in 14 countries and territories:
Canada, China, France, Germany, Ireland, Italy, Japan, Korea Rep, Netherlands, Taiwan, Thailand, Türkiye, UK, USA.
[2018/XM8304/**F**]

- ♦ International Chornobyl Centre (internationally oriented national body)
- ♦ International Christian Aid Relief Enterprises (internationally oriented national body)

♦ International Christian Association (ICA) 12556

Association chrétienne internationale – Internationale Christliche Vereinigung
Address not obtained.
URL: http://www.internationalchristianassociation.org/

History within the framework of *The Voice of the Martyrs (VOM, #20804)*, under the guidance of the founder, Rev Richard Wurmbrand, to act as the umbrella organization for Wurmbrand-established missions. **Aims** Coordinate worldwide ministry. **Structure** About 30 offices worldwide established as a result of Pastor Richard and Sabina Wurmbrand's international travels after their arrival in USA from Romania.
Members Offices in 13 countries:
Australia, Belgium, Canada, Costa Rica, Czechia, Finland, Germany, Korea Rep, Netherlands, New Zealand, South Africa, UK, USA.
Included in the above, 1 organization listed in this Yearbook:
Hulp aan de Verdrukte Kerk (HVK). [2014.06.19/XD3369/**D**]

- ♦ International Christian Broadcasters (inactive)

♦ International Christian Centre for Research on Information about and Analysis of the Strip Cartoon 12557

Centre international chrétien de recherche, d'information et d'analyse de la bande dessinée (CRIABD)
Admin Office Bvd St Michel 24, 1040 Brussels, Belgium. T. +32478269728.
URL: http://www.criabd.be/

History 20 Jun 1985, Brussels (Belgium). Became a non-profit making association 23 Aug 1986. Also referred to as *Religious Centre for Information and Analysis of Comics – Centre religieux d'information et d'analyse de la bande dessinée – Christelijke Raad voor Informatie en Analyse van Beeldverhalen*. **Aims** Promote Christian strip cartoons and their distribution; appreciate the value of strip cartoons from a Christian point of view; promote education and training in reading strip cartoons. **Structure** General Assembly (annual); Board; International Correspondents. **Languages** Dutch, English, French, Spanish. **Staff** 2.50 FTE, voluntary. **Finance** Sources: Commission chrétienne des médias et de la culture; subsidies and gifts. Annual budget: euro 20,000. **Activities** Knowledge management/information dissemination; events/meetings; training/education; awards/prizes/competitions. **Events** *Annual General Assembly* Brussels (Belgium) 2012, *Annual General Assembly* Brussels (Belgium) 2011, *Annual General Assembly* Brussels (Belgium) 2010, *Annual General Assembly* Brussels (Belgium) 2009, *Annual General Assembly* Brussels (Belgium) 2008. **Publications** *Gabriel, échos de la bande dessinée chrétienne* (4 a year); *Gabriël – Informatieblad over het Christelijk Beeldverhaal* (annual). *Panorama '97 de la bande dessinée chrétienne* (1997); *La BD chrétienne* (1994).
Members Teams and international correspondents in 18 countries:
Australia, Belgium, Canada, Ecuador, France, Germany, Holy See, Hungary, India, Italy, Lebanon, Luxembourg, Netherlands, Portugal, Romania, Spain, Switzerland, USA. [2018.02.15/XE0505/**E**]

♦ International Christian Chamber of Commerce (ICCC) 12558

International Office Hjälmarbergets Företagscenter, Grusgropvagen 5, SE-702 36 Örebro, Sweden. T. +4619247000. Fax +4619247001. E-mail: international.office@iccc.net.
URL: http://www.iccc.net/

History 1985, The Hague (Netherlands). Registered in accordance with Belgian law, 1986. **Aims** Teach and unite Christians in business and professional life; undertake development aid projects. **Structure** General Meeting (every 2 years); International Board of Directors, comprising Chairman/Founder, President, Vice-President, Vice-President/Secretary, Vice-President/Treasurer and 3 Vice-Presidents-at-Large. **Languages** English. **Finance** Members' dues. Other sources: donations. **Activities** Conference/General Meeting (every 2 years); local events. **Events** *Youth conference* Vaasa (Finland) 2010, *Africa regional conference* Johannesburg (South Africa) 2009, *Asian regional conference* Singapore (Singapore) 2009, *Approaching a new era – serving the nations* Jerusalem (Israel) 2008, *Youth conference* Vaasa (Finland) 2007. **Publications** *The Market Calling*.
Members Individuals and companies in over 100 countries. Membership countries not specified.
[2016/XD0428/**F**]

♦ International Christian Dance Fellowship (ICDF) 12559

Joint-Coordinator address not obtained.
Joint-Coordinator address not obtained.
URL: https://www.icdf.com/

History Jan 1988, Australia. Founded at International Christian Dance and Movement Conference, as an interdenominational fellowship. **Aims** Help initiate, support and guide the formation and continued growth of Christian Dance Fellowships (CDF) in interested countries; provide resources and teaching related to Dance Ministry. **Structure** ICDF Wider Committee; Steering Committee; Board of Reference; Pastoral Advisers; Regional Committees; Specialist Dance Networks. **Languages** English, Spanish. **Staff** Voluntary. **Finance** Sources: donations; members' dues. **Activities** Events/meetings; networking/liaising; training/education. **Events** *Conference* Halmstad (Sweden) 2022, *Conference* Accra (Ghana) 2016, *Conference / International Conference* San Juan (Puerto Rico) 2013, *Conference / International Conference* St Andrews (UK) 2009, *Conference / International Conference* Kuala Lumpur (Malaysia) 2006. **Publications** *ICDF e-Monthly Newsletter for Networks* (12 a year); *ICDF e-Newsletter* (annual); *ICDF e-Newsflash* (11 a year).
Members Members in 28 countries and territories:
Australia, Brazil, Canada, Costa Rica, Cuba, Fiji, France, Ghana, India, Indonesia, Ireland, Jamaica, Japan, Kenya, Korea Rep, Malaysia, Netherlands, New Zealand, Nigeria, Puerto Rico, Singapore, South Africa, Suriname, Sweden, Trinidad-Tobago, Uganda, UK, USA. [2023.02.20/XF1407/**F**]

♦ International Christian Embassy Jerusalem (ICEJ) 12560

Pres PO Box 1192, 91010 Jerusalem, Israel. T. +97225399700. Fax +97225399723. E-mail: icej@icej.org.
URL: http://www.icej.org/

History 30 Sep 1980. Founded at a gathering of Christians from many countries for the biblical Feast of Tabernacles. Registration: Israel. **Aims** Stand with Israel in support and friendship; equip and teach the world wide Church regarding God's purposes with Israel and the nations of the Middle East; be an active voice of reconciliation between Jews, Christians and Arabs, and support churches and congregations in the Holy Land. **Structure** Global Board of Trustees; Branches; Representatives. Headquarters in Jerusalem (Israel). **Languages** English, Finnish, German, Mandarin Chinese, Norwegian, Portuguese, Spanish. **Staff** 50.00 FTE, paid. **Finance** Sources: donations. **Activities** Events/meetings; guidance/assistance/consulting; training/education. **Events** *Convention of the Feast of Tabernacles* Jerusalem (Israel) 2014, *Convention of the Feast of Tabernacles* Jerusalem (Israel) 2013, *International Christian Zionist congress / Christian Zionist Congress* Jerusalem (Israel) 2000, *Convention of the Feast of Tabernacles* Jerusalem (Israel) 1999, *Convention of the Feast of Tabernacles* Jerusalem (Israel) 1998. **Publications** *A Word from Jerusalem* (12 a year); *ICEJ News Services*. **Members** Branch offices and representatives in about 95 countries. Membership countries not specified. **Consultative Status** Consultative status granted from: *UNEP (#20299)*.
[2022.05.04/XF2609/**F**]

- ♦ International Christian Federation for the Prevention of Alcoholism and Drug Addiction (no recent information)
- ♦ International Christian Fellowship / see Vineyard International Consortium (#20778)

♦ International Christian Maritime Association (ICMA) 12561

Association maritime chrétienne internationale – Asociación Marítima Cristiana Internacional – Associação Marítima Cristão Internacional
Gen Sec address not obtained. E-mail: gensec@icma.as.
Registered Office The Mission to Seafarers, St Michael Paternoster Royal, College Hill, London, EC4R 2RL, UK.
URL: http://www.icma.as/

History 1969. **Aims** Promote and encourage collaboration and mutual assistance among members; coordinate their activities; speak on their behalf within and outside the *shipping* industry; provide liaison with other bodies whose activities affect the lives and *welfare* of merchant *seafarers* and *fishermen*, their families and dependants. **Structure** General Meeting (annual). Executive Committee, comprising Chairman, Vice-Chairman, Treasurer and 4 other members. Regions (9): East Asia; West Africa; Black Sea, Mediterranean and Middle East; Western Europe; Northern Europe; Southern Africa; North America; UK and Ireland; Brazil. **Languages** English. **Staff** 1.00 FTE, paid; 0.05 FTE, voluntary. **Finance** Contributions from member societies. **Activities** Certification/accreditation; events/meetings; monitoring/evaluation; training/education. **Events** *World conference* Kaohsiung (Taiwan) 2019, *Annual General Meeting* London (UK) 2017, *Black Sea Mediterranean and Middle East Regional Conference* Odessa (Ukraine) 2013, *Northern Europe conference* Helsingborg (Sweden) 2012, *Annual General Meeting* Rome (Italy) 2012. **Publications** *ICMA Directory* – online. Manuals.
Members Organizations in 113 countries and territories:
Algeria, Angola, Antigua-Barbuda, Argentina, Australia, Bahamas, Bahrain, Bangladesh, Barbados, Belgium, Benin, Botswana, Brazil, Cameroon, Canada, Chile, Colombia, Congo Brazzaville, Congo DR, Costa Rica, Côte d'Ivoire, Croatia, Cyprus, Denmark, Ecuador, Egypt, Estonia, Fiji, Finland, France, Gabon, Gambia, Germany, Ghana, Greece, Guatemala, Guinea, Guyana, Haiti, Holy See, Honduras, Hong Kong, Iceland, India, Indonesia, Ireland, Israel, Italy, Jamaica, Japan, Jordan, Kenya, Kiribati, Korea Rep, Latvia, Liberia, Lithuania, Madagascar, Malaysia, Malta, Mauritania, Mauritius, Mexico, Morocco, Mozambique, Myanmar, Namibia, Netherlands, New Zealand, Nicaragua, Nigeria, Norway, Pakistan, Papua New Guinea, Peru, Philippines, Poland, Portugal, Réunion, Romania, Russia, Samoa, Senegal, Seychelles, Sierra Leone, Singapore, Slovenia, Solomon Is, South Africa, Spain, Sri Lanka, St Lucia, St Vincent-Grenadines, Sudan, Sweden, Switzerland, Taiwan, Tanzania UR, Thailand, Togo, Tonga, Trinidad-Tobago, Tunisia, Türkiye, Uganda, UK, Ukraine, United Arab Emirates, Uruguay, USA, Vanuatu, Venezuela, Yemen.
Included in the above, 6 organizations listed in this Yearbook:
Apostleship of the Sea – Stella Maris (AOS); *Korea International Seamen's Mission (KISMA, no recent information)*; *North America Maritime Ministry Association (NAMMA)*; *Seamen's Mission – Norwegian Church Abroad*; *The Mission to Seafarers*.
Consultative Status Consultative status granted from: *ILO (#11123)* (Special List); *International Maritime Organization (IMO, #14102)*. **IGO Relations** Close relations with: *Nordic Council (NC, #17256)*. **NGO Relations** Member of: *International Seafarers' Welfare and Assistance Network (ISWAN, #14815)*; *Maritime Piracy Humanitarian Response Programme (MPHRP, #16583)*. Close relations with: North American Maritime Ministry Association. [2019/XB5864/y/**B**]

♦ International Christian Medical and Dental Association (ICMDA) ... 12562

International Office Suite 8, Censeo House, 6 St Peters St, St Albans, AL1 3LF, UK. T. +441727227514. E-mail: office@icmda.net.
URL: http://www.icmda.net/

History 1986, Cancún (Mexico). 1986, under present title, a conference series with the title *International Conference of Christian Physicians (ICCP)* having existed since 1963, Amsterdam (Netherlands). An international student movement, including a number of conferences, which developed alongside ICCP/ICMDA, merged with ICMDA as its Student Section in 1990. **Aims** Start and strengthen national Christian medical and dental movements. **Structure** General Committee. **Languages** Arabic, English, French, Mandarin Chinese, Portuguese, Russian, Spanish. **Staff** 3.00 FTE, paid. **Finance** Sources: donations; subscriptions. **Activities** Events/meetings; healthcare; knowledge management/information dissemination; networking/liaising; training/education. **Events** *Quadrennial World Congress* Arusha (Tanzania UR) 2023, *Quadrennial World Congress* Hyderabad (India) 2018, *Quadrennial World Congress* Rotterdam (Netherlands) 2014, *Quadrennial world congress* Punta del Este (Uruguay) 2010, *Quadrennial world congress* Sydney, NSW (Australia) 2006.
Members National societies in 84 countries and territories:
Albania, Argentina, Armenia, Australia, Austria, Bangladesh, Belgium, Benin, Bolivia, Botswana, Brazil, Bulgaria, Burkina Faso, Burundi, Cambodia, Cameroon, Canada, Congo DR, Costa Rica, Denmark, Ecuador, Egypt, El Salvador, Estonia, Eswatini, Ethiopia, Finland, France, Gambia, Germany, Ghana, Greece, Guatemala, Haiti, Honduras, Hong Kong, Hungary, India, Indonesia, Ireland, Japan, Kenya, Korea Rep, Lithuania, Madagascar, Malawi, Mali, Mexico, Mongolia, Nepal, Netherlands, New Zealand, Niger, Nigeria, Norway, Pakistan, Panama, Peru, Poland, Portugal, Romania, Russia, Rwanda, Serbia, Singapore, South Africa, South Sudan, Spain, Sri Lanka, Sudan, Sweden, Switzerland, Taiwan, Tanzania UR, Thailand, Togo, Uganda, UK, Ukraine, Uruguay, USA, Venezuela, Zambia, Zimbabwe. [2021.09.02/XD0131/**D**]

♦ International Christian Organisation of the Media (ICOM) 12563

Organisation chrétienne internationale des Médias – Organización Cristiana internacional de los medios – Internationale Christliche Organisation der Medien
General Secretariat CP 197, 1211 Geneva 20, Switzerland. E-mail: icom@bluewin.ch.
URL: http://www.icomworld.info/

History Founded 15 Dec 1889, as *International Federation of Associations of Religious Journalists*. Subsequently changed title to: *International Association of Religious Journalism and Publishing*, 1905; *International Bureau of Religious Journalists*, 1917; *International Union of the Catholic Press – Union internationale de la press catholique (UIPC)*, 15 Dec 1927 (Belgium); *International Catholic Union of the Press – Union catholique internationale de la presse (UCIP) – Unión Católica Internacional de la Prensa – Katholische Weltunion der Presse*, 1966, following 7th World Congress, 1965, New York NY (USA); *International Catholics Organisation of the Media (ICOM) – Organisation internationale de catholiques dans les Médias – Organización internacional de católicos en los medios – Internationale Organisation der Katholiken in den Medien*, 2011, with full title *International Catholics Organisation of the Media – The World Forum of Professionals and Institutions in Secular and Religious Media – Organisation internationale de catholiques dans les Médias – Le forum mondial des professionnels et institutions dans le journalisme séculier et religieux – Organización internacional en los medios – El Foro Mundial de los Profesionales e Instituciones en el Periodismo Secular y Religioso – Internationale Organisation der Katholiken in den Medien – Weltforum von Medienschaffenden und Einrichtungen im säkularen und religiösen Journalismus*. Previously also referred to by English acronym *ICUP*. Current statutes approved 22 Sep 2001, Fribourg (Switzerland). Registered in accordance with Swiss Civil Code. **Aims** Link all who exercise an influence on *public opinion* through the press and the media, with a view to intensifying their efforts; inspire a high standard of professional conscience in journalists; develop friendship and exchange of information among *journalists*; represent and promote journalism at international institutions and events worldwide. **Structure** General Assembly (annual); Board; Directing Committee; Regions (8). Launched *International Network of Young Journalists (#14346)*, Oct 1987. **Languages** English, French, German, Spanish. **Staff** 8.00 FTE, paid. **Finance** Sources: contributions; government support. **Activities** Awards/prizes/competitions; events/meetings; publishing activities; research/documentation. **Events** *World Congress* Tagaytay (Philippines) 2016, *Triennial Congress and General Assembly* Panama (Panama) 2013, *Triennial congress and general assembly* Ouagadougou (Burkina Faso) 2010, *Triennial congress and general assembly* Sherbrooke, QC (Canada) 2007, *Triennial congress and general assembly / Triennial Congress* Bangkok (Thailand) 2004. **Publications** *ICOM Information* (4 a year) – articles in original languages. Series of books; documents.
Members Institutional; Individual. Associates in 172 countries and territories:
Afghanistan, Albania, Algeria, Andorra, Angola, Argentina, Armenia, Australia, Austria, Bangladesh, Barbados, Belarus, Belgium, Belize, Benin, Bolivia, Bosnia-Herzegovina, Botswana, Brazil, Bulgaria, Burkina Faso, Burundi, Cambodia, Cameroon, Canada, Cape Verde, Central African Rep, Chile, China, Colombia, Congo Brazzaville, Congo DR, Costa Rica, Côte d'Ivoire, Croatia, Cuba, Cyprus, Czechia, Denmark, Dominica, Dominican Rep, Ecuador, Egypt, El Salvador, Eritrea, Estonia, Eswatini, Ethiopia, Fiji, Finland, France, Gabon, Gambia, Georgia, Germany, Ghana, Greece, Grenada, Guatemala, Guinea, Guinea-Bissau, Guyana, Haiti, Honduras, Hong Kong, Hungary, Iceland, India, Indonesia, Iran Islamic Rep, Iraq, Ireland, Israel, Italy, Jamaica, Japan, Jordan, Kazakhstan, Kenya, Kiribati, Korea Rep, Laos, Latvia, Lebanon, Lesotho, Liberia, Liechtenstein, Lithuania, Luxembourg, Madagascar, Malawi, Malaysia, Maldives, Mali, Malta, Marshall Is, Mauritania, Mauritius, Mexico, Moldova, Monaco, Mongolia, Morocco, Mozambique, Myanmar, Namibia, Nepal, Netherlands, New Zealand, Nicaragua, Niger, Nigeria, North Macedonia, Norway, Oman, Pakistan, Palau, Palestine, Panama, Papua New Guinea, Paraguay, Peru, Philippines, Poland, Portugal, Puerto Rico, Romania, Russia, Rwanda, Samoa, Sao Tomé-Principe, Saudi Arabia, Senegal, Serbia, Seychelles, Sierra Leone,

Singapore, Slovakia, Slovenia, Solomon Is, Somalia, South Africa, Spain, Sri Lanka, St Lucia, St Vincent-Grenadines, Sudan, Suriname, Sweden, Switzerland, Syrian AR, Taiwan, Tanzania UR, Thailand, Timor-Leste, Togo, Tonga, Trinidad-Tobago, Türkiye, Turkmenistan, Uganda, UK, Ukraine, United Arab Emirates, Uruguay, USA, Vanuatu, Venezuela, Vietnam, Zambia, Zimbabwe.
Consultative Status Consultative status granted from: *ECOSOC (#05331)* (Special); *UNESCO (#20322)* (Consultative Status). **IGO Relations** Accredited by: *United Nations Office at Vienna (UNOV, #20604)*. Invited to sessions of Intergovernmental Council of: *International Programme for the Development of Communication (IPDC, #14651)*. Associated with Department of Global Communications of the United Nations. **NGO Relations** Founding organization of: *Catholic Media Council (CAMECO, #03605)*. [2022/XA1458/y/**B**]

♦ International Christian Peace Fellowship (inactive)

♦ International Christian Peace Service (EIRENE) 12564

Service chrétien international pour la paix – Servicio Cristiano Internacional por la Paz – Internationaler Christlicher Friedensdienst

Main Office Engerser Str 81, 56564 Neuwied, Germany. T. +49263183790. Fax +492631837990. E-mail: empfang@eirene.org – eirene-int@eirene.org.
URL: http://www.eirene.org/

History Aug 1957. Founded by representatives of the historic peace Churches of the Mennonites and the Brethren, *International Fellowship of Reconciliation (IFOR, #13586)* and European Christians who advocate non-violence. Former names and other names: *International Christian Service for Peace* – alias; *Mezdunarodnaja Hristianskaja Sluzba Delu Mira* – alias. Registration: Germany. **Aims** Promote peace and better understanding among peoples by combating poverty, falsely-directed development, social injustice, political tensions and cultural oppression, in a non-violent and ecumenical spirit based on love of one's neighbour and in willingness to face the consequences of acting non-violently; encourage the building of democratic civilian societies in which non-violent means of conflict resolution replace violent confrontation. **Structure** General Meeting, comprising 6 representatives of institutional member organizations and 268 individual members. board of trustees of 7. President; General Secretary. Secretariat in Neuwied (Germany). **Languages** English, French, German, Spanish. **Staff** 19.00 FTE, paid. Voluntary. **Finance** Members' contributions. Private and government grants. Budget (annual): about euro 5.5 million. **Activities** Activism/lobbying/activism; conflict resolution; events/meetings. **Events** *Congress* France 2001, *Congress* Vallendar (Germany) 2000, *Annual meeting* Bonn (Germany) 1997, *Contributions to the ecumenical programme – to overcome violence* Hamminkeln (Germany) 1997, *Was tragen Friedensdienste zu Lösungen von Konflikten in Süd und Nord bei?* Mülheim (Germany) 1996. **Publications** *EIRENE Newsletter* (4 a year). *EIRENE: Quo Vadis ?*. Annual report in German/English/French. **Members** Institutional members (6); individual members (268). Membership countries not specified. **IGO Relations** Partner of: *UNHCR (#20327)*. **NGO Relations** Member of (8): *Arbeitsgemeinschaft der Entwicklungsdienste (AGdD)*; *Church and Peace (#03916)*; *German Platform for Peaceful Conflict Management (PZK)*; *Network of European Voluntary Service Organisations (NEVSO)*; *United4Rescue*; *Verband Entwicklungspolitik und Humanitäre Hilfe e.V. (VENRO)*; *Ziviler Friedensdienst (ZFD)*; *Ökumenisches Netz Zentralafrika (ÖNZ)*. [2020/XD0526/**D**]

♦ International Christian Police Association (inactive)
♦ International Christian Relief / see Build Africa
♦ International Christian Service for Peace / see International Christian Peace Service (#12564)
♦ International Christian-Social Union (inactive)

♦ International Christian Studies Association (ICSA) 12565

Pres 1065 Pine Bluff Drive, Pasadena CA 91107, USA. T. +16263510419. E-mail: info@jis3.org.
URL: https://www.jis3.org/icsamembership/

History 1 Jan 1983, Santa Monica, CA (USA). 1st World Congress: 24-26 Aug 1984, Pasadena CA (USA). **Aims** Further exploration of knowledge and its integration with Judaeo-Christian ethical and spiritual values within an open forum of international, interdisciplinary and interfaith dialogue, seeking to expand our understanding of God, man and the universe to the greater glory of God and the dignity of man. **Structure** General Assembly (every 4 years); Governing Council. **Languages** English, French, German. **Staff** 1.50 FTE, voluntary. **Finance** Sources: contributions; grants; meeting proceeds; sale of publications. **Activities** Events/meetings; publishing activities. **Events** *JIS Symposium* Pasadena, CA (USA) 2022, *JIS Symposium* Pasadena, CA (USA) 2021, *Quadrennial Congress* Pasadena, CA (USA) 2016, *Freedom and virtue – reinventing free institutions in an era of globalization* Pasadena, CA (USA) 2015, *Symposium* Pasadena, CA (USA) 2014. **Publications** *ICSA Newsletter* (annual); *Journal of Interdisciplinary Studies (JIS): An International Journal of Interdisciplinary and Interfaith Dialogue* (annual) – co-sponsored and published by the Institute for Interdisciplinary Research. *JIS Computerized Bibliography 1989-2009*. **Members** Regular; Associate; Affiliate (institutional); Student. Membership countries not specified. [2022.05.10/XD7320/**D**]

♦ International Christian Support Fund / see ICS
♦ International Christian Technologists' Association (internationally oriented national body)

♦ International Christian Union of Business Executives 12566

Union internationale chrétienne des dirigeants d'entreprise (UNIAPAC) – Unión Internacional Cristiana de Dirigentes de Empresa

SG 26 rue de l'Amiral Hamelin, 75116 Paris, France. T. +33155730754.
Project Coordinator address not obtained.
URL: https://uniapac.org/

History Founded 1931, Rome (Italy), as *International Conference of Catholic Employers' Associations – Conférence internationale des associations patronales catholiques*, national bodies grouping Catholic employers having been formed in the Netherlands, 1915, and in Belgium and France, 1925-1926. Name changed, 13 Dec 1949, to *International Union of Catholic Employers' Associations – Union internationale des associations patronales catholiques (UNIAPAC)*. Subsequently became ecumenical and, 19 Nov 1962, Brussels (Belgium), adopted present name. Registered under Belgian law and statutes adopted 25 Jul 1959. Statutes modified: 30 May 1963; 16 Dec 1971; 12 Sep 1974; 10 Aug 1978. New statutes adopted Dec 1994. Current statutes adopted Oct 2004. **Aims** Study, maintain and propagate the principles and applications of Christian social teaching in economic and social life, in the context both of individual business corporations and of national and international economies; act as a link among associations of Christian *employers* having the same aims; promote such organizations in countries where they do not exist; work with other international associations to achieve these aims. **Structure** General Assembly (annual). Board of 20-25 members, including representatives of each regional association, plus up to 8 co-opted members. Past Presidents, Secretary-General and the organization's Spiritual Advisers participate in Board meetings. Executive Committee, consisting of President assisted by Vice-Presidents representing regional organizations (4): Europe; Latin America; Africa; Asia. Bureau, comprising President; Honorary President, Past President, Presidents of Programme and Finance Committees, Secretary-General, Executive Secretary and 2 members. Secretariat. Secretariat-General for Latin America. **Languages** English, French, Spanish. **Staff** 2.00 FTE, paid. **Finance** Sources: donations; meeting proceeds; members' dues. **Activities** Events/meetings. **Events** *Triennial Congress* Rome (Italy) 2022, *Triennial Congress* Manila (Philippines) 2021, *Triennial Congress* Lisbon (Portugal) 2018, *Triennial Congress* Belo Horizonte (Brazil) 2015, *Meeting* Zurich (Switzerland) 2014. **Publications** *Socio-Economic Papers*.
Members Active associations of business executives; Associate individuals and legal entities. Member associations in 33 countries and territories:
Angola, Argentina, Belgium (2), Benin, Bolivia, Brazil, Burkina Faso, Cameroon, Chile, Congo DR, Croatia, Ecuador (2), France (2), Germany (2), Hong Kong, Hungary, Italy, Korea Rep, Mexico, Netherlands, Paraguay, Poland, Portugal, Senegal, Singapore, Slovakia, Slovenia, Spain, Switzerland, Thailand, Uganda, UK, Uruguay.
Consultative Status Consultative status granted from: *UNCTAD (#20285)* (General Category); *FAO (#09260)* (Liaison Status). **IGO Relations** Cooperates with: *ECOSOC (#05331)*; *ILO (#11123)*; *OECD (#17693)*; *UNCTAD (#20285)*; *UNESCO (#20322)*; World Trade Council. **NGO Relations** Member of: *European Sunday Alliance (#08856)*; *Forum of Catholic Inspired NGOs (#09905)*. [2021/XC1502/**C**]

♦ International Christian University (internationally oriented national body)
♦ International Christian Women's Fellowship / see International Disciples Women's Ministries
♦ International Christian Youth Exchange / see International Cultural Youth Exchange (#13122)

♦ International Chromium Development Association (ICDA) 12567

Exec Dir 43 rue de la Chaussée d'Antin, 75009 Paris, France. T. +33140760689.
URL: http://www.icdacr.com/

History 1984, Paris (France). Registered under French law. **Aims** Foster and encourage the growth and development of worldwide use of chromium. **Structure** Council of 19 members; President; Vice-President. **Languages** English. **Staff** 3.00 FTE, paid. Consultants. **Finance** Sources: members' dues. **Activities** Specific research and development projects. Semi-annual meetings and global and regional industry forums. Collects and disseminates statistical information. Health, Safety and Environment Committee advises on all chromium-related aspects of environmental issues. **Events** *Members Meeting* Kyoto (Japan) 2021, *CHROMIUM Conference* 2020, *Members Meeting* Kyoto (Japan) 2020, *CHROMIUM Conference* Victoria Falls (Zimbabwe) 2019, *CHROMIUM Conference* Baotou (China) 2018. **Publications** *ICDA Statistical Bulletin* (annual); *Health, Safety and Environment* (regular). DVDs; brochures.
Members Representatives of the chromium industry. Ordinary in 19 countries and territories:
Australia, China, Finland, France, Germany, India, Japan, Korea Rep, Luxembourg, Madagascar, Slovenia, South Africa, Spain, Sweden, Switzerland, Taiwan, Türkiye, UK, Zimbabwe.
Associate in 17 countries and territories:
Canada, Czechia, France, Germany, Italy, Japan, Luxembourg, Mauritius, Netherlands, South Africa, Spain, Sweden, Switzerland, Türkiye, United Arab Emirates, USA, Zimbabwe.
Affiliate in 6 countries:
China, Finland, France, Germany, South Africa, USA.
Consultative Status Consultative status granted from: *UNCTAD (#20285)* (Special Category). **NGO Relations** Member of: *TEAM STAINLESS (#20113)*. [2021/XC0025/**C**]

♦ International Chromosome and Genome Society (ICGS) 12568

Pres Biosciences Dept, Univ of Kent, Canterbury, CT2 7AF, UK.
SG Herbert Wertheim College of Medicine, 11200 SW 8th St, HLS II 693, Miami FL 33199, USA.
URL: https://www.kent.ac.uk/icgs/

History 2002, by Harold Klinger and Michael Schmid, as *International Cytogenetics and Genome Society (ICGS)*. Registered, 2003, Basel (Switzerland). Re-registered in accordance with Dutch law. **Aims** Foster exchange of knowledge and collaboration between investigators of different disciplines of cytogenetics. **Events** *International Chromosome Conference* Prague (Czechia) 2018, *International Chromosome Conference* Foz do Iguaçu (Brazil) 2017, *International chromosome conference* Amsterdam (Netherlands) 2007, *Congress* Canterbury (UK) 2006, *Congress* Granada (Spain) 2005. **Publications** *Cytogenetics and Genome Research*.
Members Individuals in 14 countries:
Australia, Brazil, Czechia, France, Germany, India, Israel, Japan, Netherlands, Russia, Spain, Sweden, UK, USA.
[2019/XJ4326/**D**]

♦ International Chronic Myeloid Leukemia Foundation (iCMLf) 12569

Chief Exec 20 Eversley Road, Bexhill-on-Sea, TN40 1HE, UK. E-mail: info@cml-foundation.org.
URL: http://www.cml-foundation.org/

History 2009. Former names and other names: *International CML Foundation* – alias. Registration: Charity Commission, No/ID: 1132984, England and Wales. **Aims** Improve the outcomes for patients with CML globally. **Structure** Board of Directors. **Languages** English. **Staff** 3.00 FTE, paid. **Finance** Sources: Grants; donations; sponsorship. **Activities** Awards/prizes/competitions; capacity building; events/meetings; healthcare; projects/programmes; research and development; training/education. **Events** *Annual John Goldman Conference on Chronic Myeloid Leukemia* 2021, *Annual John Goldman Conference on Chronic Myeloid Leukemia* 2020, *Annual John Goldman Conference on Chronic Myeloid Leukemia* Estoril (Portugal) 2017, *Annual John Goldman Conference on Chronic Myeloid Leukemia* Houston, TX (USA) 2016, *Annual John Goldman Conference on Chronic Myeloid Leukemia* Estoril (Portugal) 2015. **Publications** *iCMLf Newsletter*. Annual Report. **NGO Relations** Cooperates with (2): *European School of Haematology (ESH, #08430)*; The Max Foundation. [2022/XJ6440/f/**F**]

♦ International Chrysanthemum Council (no recent information)

♦ International Chrysotile Association (ICA) 12570

Association internationale du chrysotile (AIC)

Contact address not obtained. T. +3222307042. Fax +3222310822. E-mail: info@2019ica.com.
URL: https://chrysotileassociation.com/

History Nov 1976, London (UK). Former names and other names: *International Asbestos Information Committee* – former; *Asbestos International Association (AIA)* – former (1977); *Association internationale de l'amiante* – former (1977). **Aims** Ensure safe use of chrysotile *asbestos*; create awareness of health problems associated with those fibres; provide information service covering medical, scientific and technical matters both occupational and environmental; defend the industry from unwarranted attack. **Structure** Governing Council (meets annually); Executive Committee. **Languages** English, French. **Staff** 2.00 FTE, paid. **Finance** Sources: members' dues. Annual budget: 200,000 USD. **Activities** Advocacy/lobbying/activism; standards/guidelines. **Events** *International Scientific Conference on Chrysotile* Delhi (India) 2013, *Biennial Meeting* Delhi (India) 2000, *Biennial Meeting* Montréal, QC (Canada) 1997, *Biennial Meeting* Montréal, QC (Canada) 1995, *Biennial Meeting* Paris (France) 1993. **Publications** *Recommended Control Procedures*. *Reference Technical Methods*. Learned and technical papers.
Members Associations representing groups in 21 countries:
Bolivia, Brazil, Canada, China, Colombia, El Salvador, India, Indonesia, Kazakhstan, Mexico, Pakistan, Philippines, Russia, Senegal, Sri Lanka, Thailand, United Arab Emirates, USA, Vietnam, Zambia, Zimbabwe.
Consultative Status Consultative status granted from: *ECOSOC (#05331)* (Roster). **IGO Relations** Accredited by (1): *United Nations Office at Vienna (UNOV, #20604)*. **NGO Relations** *International Organization for Standardization (ISO, #14473)* (Category B liaisons with Technical Committees 77 and 147).
[2023/XC3279/**C**]

♦ International Churches of Christ (internationally oriented national body)
♦ International Church Film Organization / see International Interchurch Film Organization (#13943)
♦ International Church of the Foursquare Gospel (internationally oriented national body)
♦ International Churchill Societies / see Churchill Centre, The (#03914)

♦ International Church of the Nazarene 12571

Global Ministry Center 17001 Prairie Star Parkway, Lenexa KS 66220, USA. T. +19135770500. E-mail: info@nazarene.org.
URL: http://www.nazarene.org/

History Founded 1908, USA. **Aims** Respond to the Great Commission of Christ to "go and make disciples of all nations"; advance God's Kingdom by the preservation and propagation of Christian Holiness set forth in the Scriptures. **Structure** Promotional, educational, fund-raising and programme arm of missions: *Nazarene Missions International (NMI, no recent information)*. Also includes: *Nazarene Compassionate Ministries (NCM, see: #12571)*; *European Nazarene College (see: #12571)*. **Events** *Third wave conference* Bangkok (Thailand) 2011, *Third wave conference* Johannesburg (South Africa) 2007, *Third wave conference* Quito (Ecuador) 2004. [2015.11.16/XF6527/**F**]

♦ International Cinema Technology Association (unconfirmed)

♦ International Cinema and Television School 12572

Escuela Internacional de Cine y Televisión (EICTV)

Dir Finca San Tranquilino, KM 41/2 Carretera a Vereda Nueva, AP Aéreo 40/41 CP 32500, San Antonio de los Baños, Artemisa, Cuba. T. +5347383102 – +5347383152ext502. E-mail: susana@eictv.org.cu.
URL: http://www.eictv.org/

History 15 Dec 1986, by *Foundation of New Latin American Cinema (#09967)*. **Aims** Train *professionals* from Latin America, the Caribbean, Europe, Africa and Asia with the best resources of modern technology. **Structure** Councils (Rector, Academic and Administrative), headed by General Director. **Languages** Spanish. **Staff** 400.00 FTE, paid. **Finance** Sources: subscription fees; donations and grants from governmental and non-governmental organizations all over the world. **Activities** Training/education. **Events** *Conference of Latin American producers and distributors* Havana (Cuba) 1996. **Publications** *ENFOCO Magazine* (12 a year). Books. **NGO Relations** Member of: *CILECT Ibero América (CIBA, see: #11771)*; *International Association of Cinema, Audiovisual and Media Schools (#11771)*. Agreements of collaboration with many schools and institutions worldwide. [2018.08.29/XF2251/**E**]

♦ International Cinematograph Bureau (inactive)

♦ International Circle of Educational Institutes for Graphic Arts Technology and Management (ICEIGATM) 12573

Internationale Kreis der Lehrinstitute für die Polygrafische Industrie

Pres Industrieweg 232, 9030 Mariakerke, Belgium.

URL: http://www.internationalcircle.net/

History Founded 1957, Lausanne (Switzerland). Also referred to by acronym *IC*. **Aims** Serve as an international network and forum for sharing experience and ideas on teaching graphic arts, printing technology, and media production in general; develop partnerships at research work; encourage exchanges of students and faculty staff members. **Structure** General Assembly at Annual Conference; Presidium; Advisory Board. **Languages** Chinese, English, French, German, Russian. **Staff** 0.20 FTE, paid. **Finance** Sponsorship; volunteerism. **Activities** Events/meetings; networking/liaising; knowledge management/information dissemination. **Events** *Annual Conference* Tashkent (Uzbekistan) 2019, *Annual Conference* Warsaw (Poland) 2018, *Annual Conference* Beijing (China) 2017, *Annual Conference* Leipzig (Germany) 2016, *Annual Conference* San Luis Obispo, CA (USA) 2015. **Publications** *IC Journal*.

Members Educational institutes' rectors, presidents, deans, headmasters or similar. Individuals (162) in 45 countries and territories:

Argentina, Austria, Belgium, Brazil, Bulgaria, Canada, Chile, China, Croatia, Czechia, Denmark, Egypt, Estonia, Finland, France, Germany, Greece, Hungary, Iceland, India, Ireland, Italy, Japan, Kazakhstan, Kenya, Korea Rep, Latvia, Lithuania, Netherlands, Norway, Pakistan, Paraguay, Poland, Portugal, Russia, Serbia, Slovenia, Spain, Sweden, Switzerland, Taiwan, UK, Ukraine, USA, Uzbekistan.

NGO Relations *Intergraf (#11505)*; *European Graphic/Media Industry Network (EGIN, #07405)*; *International Association of Research Organizations for the Information, Media and Graphic Arts Industries (IARIGAI, #12136)*. [2018.06.01/XF4686/tv/**F**]

♦ International Circle of Hotel Managers (unconfirmed)

♦ International Circle of Penal Abolitionists (ICOPA) 12574

Contact c/o Justice Action, Trades Hall-Lv 2, Ste 204, 4 Goulburn St, Sydney NSW 2000, Australia. T. +61292830123. Fax +61292830112. E-mail: ja@justiceaction.org.au.

URL: http://www.actionicopa.org/

History 1982, as *International Conference on Prison Abolition (ICOPA)*. 1987, name changed to *International Conference on Penal Abolition*. **Events** *Conference* London (UK) 2018, *Conference* Dartmouth, MA (USA) 2017, *Conference* Quito (Ecuador) 2016, *Conference* Ottawa, ON (Canada) 2014, *Conference* St Augustine (Trinidad-Tobago) 2012. **Publications** *JustRitt News*. [2016.06.01/XJ0662/**F**]

♦ International Circle for Philosophical Research by Computer (inactive)

♦ International Circle for the Promotion of the Creation 12575

Cercle international pour la promotion de la création (CIPCRE)

Dir Gen BP 1256, Bafoussam, Cameroon. T. +2373446267 – +2373446668. Fax +2373446669. E-mail: cipcre_dg@cipcre.org.

Benin Office BP 287, Porto-Novo, Benin. T. +229222249. Fax +229223050. E-mail: cipcre.benin@cipcre.org.

URL: http://www.cipcre.org/

History 26 May 1990. Statutes adopted 25 May 1991. Registration: Start date: Jul 1990, Cameroon. **Aims** Contribute to the thriving of all human beings by promoting lasting, harmonious and responsible *human development* in a healthy, efficient and prosperous environment. **Structure** General Assembly (every 3 years). Management Board (meets once a year), consisting of Director and 9 members. Directorate General. National Offices. Operational Units and Cells. **Languages** English, French. **Staff** 40.00 FTE, paid. **Finance** Members' dues. Other sources: contributions from donors; income from consultations; sale of publications. **Activities** Information, education and sensitization on environmental issues; assistance to micro-projects in environmental field. Organizes international seminars and conferences (2-3 a year). Instrumental in setting up *Wagon africain de gestion de nouvelles électroniques (Réseau WAGNE, see: #12575)*. **Events** *Ecologie et citoyenneté* Yaoundé (Cameroon) 2000, *Ecologie et evangélisation* Porto-Novo (Benin) 1997, *Ethique écologique et reconstruction de l'Afrique* Bati (Cameroon) 1996. **Publications** *Eco-Jeunes* (4 a year); *ECOVOX* (4 a year) in French – newspaper. *Ouvrages de la Collection Foi et Action*.

Members Individuals in 5 countries:

Benin, Cameroon, Germany, Netherlands, Switzerland.

NGO Relations Member of: *EarthAction (EA, #05159)*; *Forum of African Voluntary Development Organizations (FAVDO, inactive)*; *Mouvement Nord-Sud pour l'environnement et le développement (MONSED, no recent information)*. [2019/XF5522/v/**F**]

♦ International Circle of Sea Captains who have rounded the Cape Horn / see International Association of Cape Horners (#11755)

♦ International Circuits and Computers Conference (meeting series)

♦ International Circulation Directors Association (ICDA) 12576

Pres address not obtained.

History 1973. Replaced *International Circulation Managers' Commission (inactive)*. **Events** *Meeting* Istanbul (Turkey) 2014, *Meeting* Madrid (Spain) 2014, *Meeting* London (UK) 2013, *Meeting* Nice (France) 2013, *Meeting* Milan (Italy) 2012. **Members** Publishing companies (about 20). Membership countries not specified. [2014/XN3534/**D**]

♦ International Circulation Managers' Commission (inactive)

♦ International Cities of Peace (ICP) 12577

Exec Dir 1740 E Stroop Rd, Box 291-761, Dayton OH 45402, USA. T. +19377081335. E-mail: info@internationalcitiesofpeace.org.

URL: http://www.internationalcitiesofpeace.org/

History Feb 2009. **Aims** Network, encourage, document, and provide resources and information for leaders and organizations working to make peace a consensus value through the global Cities of Peace movement. **Structure** Advisory Council; Board. **Languages** English, Spanish. **Publications** *ICP Newsletter* (4 a year).

Members Cities of peace in 45 countries and territories:

Afghanistan, Argentina, Barbados, Bosnia-Herzegovina, Burundi, Cameroon, Canada, Colombia, Congo DR, Costa Rica, Cyprus, Ethiopia, Gambia, Germany, Ghana, Guinea, Haiti, India, Kenya, Lebanon, Liberia, Libya, Malawi, Mexico, Moldova, Nepal, Netherlands, Nigeria, Pakistan, Palestine, Philippines, Rwanda, Sierra Leone, Somalia, South Sudan, Sudan, Switzerland, Tanzania UR, Thailand, Tunisia, Uganda, UK, United Arab Emirates, Uruguay, USA. [2020/XJ5447/**F**]

♦ International Cities of Refuge Network (ICORN) 12578

Exec Dir Sílvberget KF, Stavanger Cultural Ctr, PO Box 310, 4002 Stavanger, Norway. T. +4751507465. Fax +4751507025. E-mail: icorn@icorn.org.

Street Address Sílvberggt 2, 4006 Stavanger, Norway.

URL: http://www.icorn.org/

History Current statutes approved 22 Apr 2009, Barcelona (Spain), and in effect as of 1 Jan 2010. Registered in accordance with Norwegian law. **Aims** Promote the value of freedom of expression. **Structure** General Assembly; Board; Administration Centre. **Activities** Member cities and regions offer safe havens for persecuted writers. **Events** *General Assembly* Gdansk (Poland) 2022, *Joint Conference* Rotterdam (Netherlands) 2019, *Meeting* Krakow (Poland) 2013. **Publications** *ICORN Newsletter*.

Members Cities hosting writers in 14 countries:

Belgium, Denmark, France, Germany, Iceland, Italy, Mexico, Netherlands, Norway, Poland, Slovenia, Spain, Sweden, USA.

NGO Relations Agreement with: *International PEN (#14552)*. [2021/XJ2622/**F**]

♦ International Citizen debt Audit Network (unconfirmed)

♦ International City / County Management Association (ICMA) 12579

Association internationale de l'administration des villes – Asociación Internacional de Administración de Ciudades

Exec Dir 777 N Capitol St NE, Ste 500, Washington DC 20002-4201, USA. T. +12022894262. Fax +12029623500.

URL: http://icma.org/

History Founded 1914, as *International City Managers' Association*. Known from 1969 as *International City Management Association*. New name adopted, 1991. **Aims** Create excellence in *local* governance by developing and fostering professional local government management worldwide. **Structure** Executive Board. **Languages** English. **Staff** 106.00 FTE, paid. Contract employees; volunteers. **Finance** Members' dues. Other sources: professional development; proceeds of technical assistance; grants; contracts; publications. Budget (annual): US$ 36 million. **Activities** Guidance/assistance/consulting; training/education; capacity building; knowledge management/information dissemination; publishing activities. **Events** *Annual Conference* Pittsburgh, PA (USA) 2024, *Annual Conference* Austin, TX (USA) 2023, *Annual Conference* Columbus, OH (USA) 2022, *Annual Conference* Portland, OR (USA) 2021, *Annual Conference* Washington, DC (USA) 2020. **Publications** *ICMA Newsletter* (weekly); *Public Management* (12 a year) – magazine; *Municipal Year Book*. *Municipal Management Series* – textbooks and manuals. Training manuals; survey research; grant- and contract-funded publications. **Information Services** *Knowledge Network* – online community cosponsored by ICMA and the Alliance for Innovation.

Members Individuals, mainly in North America, in 35 countries and territories:

Argentina, Australia, Austria, Canada, China, Cyprus, Denmark, France, Germany, India, Iraq, Ireland, Italy, Japan, Jordan, Korea Rep, Mexico, Namibia, Nepal, Netherlands, New Zealand, Nigeria, Norway, Peru, Romania, Saudi Arabia, Serbia, Slovakia, South Africa, Sweden, Taiwan, Trinidad-Tobago, UK, USA, Zimbabwe.

NGO Relations Member of: *Extractive Industries Transparency Initiative (EITI, #09229)*; *International Housing Coalition (IHC Global)*; *Volunteers for Economic Growth Alliance (VEGA)*; *World Historic and Cultural Canal Cities Cooperation Organization (WCCO, #21570)*. [2017/XD0641/v/**F**]

♦ International City Leaders (unconfirmed)

♦ International City Management Association / see International City / County Management Association (#12579)

♦ International City Managers' Association / see International City / County Management Association (#12579)

♦ International Civil Airports Association (inactive)

♦ International Civil Aviation English Association (ICAEA) 12580

Gen Sec address not obtained.

Pres address not obtained.

URL: http://www.icaea.pansa.pl/

History 12 Nov 1991, Paris (France), following Forums organized since 1984. Current statutes adopted 5 Nov 2007, Paris (France). Registered in accordance with French law. **Aims** Bring together people and organizations concerned by or interested in the use of English in the aviation and aeronautical world; promote the exchange of information as regards English, English training, standards, qualifications, translation, documents etc, between people working within aviation in different countries; centralize information useful to the airlines, authorities, air traffic services, manufacturers, pilots, engineers, universities, research institutes, training centers and teachers. **Structure** Board (up to 25 members), including President, Vice-Presidents, General Secretary and Treasurer. **Languages** English, French. **Staff** 5.00 FTE, voluntary. **Finance** Forum registration fees. **Activities** Training/education. **Events** *Forum* Istanbul (Turkey) 2013, *Forum* Paris (France) 2013, *Forum* Bangkok (Thailand) 2012, *Forum* Brasilia (Brazil) 2011, *Forum* Toulouse (France) 2011. **Publications** ICAO Circulars.

Members include one organization listed in this Yearbook:

International Civil Aviation Organization (ICAO, #12581).

Consultative Status Consultative status granted from: *ECOSOC (#05331)* (Ros A). [2014/XJ2609/y/**C**]

♦ International Civil Aviation Organization (ICAO) 12581

Organisation de l'aviation civile internationale (OACI) – Organización de Aviación Civil Internacional (OACI)

Headquarters 999 Blvd Robert-Bourassa, Montréal QC H3C 5H7, Canada. T. +15149548219. Fax +15149546077. E-mail: icaohq@icao.int.

URL: http://www.icao.int/

History The *Convention on International Civil Aviation (Chicago Convention, 1944)* was signed 7 Dec 1944, Chicago IL (USA). Pending ratification of the Convention by 26 States, the *Provisional International Civil Aviation Organization (PICAO) – Organisation provisoire de l'aviation civile internationale* was established and functioned from 6 Jun 1945 to 4 Apr 1947. By 5 Mar 1947, the 26th Ratification having been received, ICAO came into being on 4 Apr 1947. In Oct 1947, became a specialized agency of *United Nations (UN, #20515)* in the framework of *United Nations System (#20635)*, linked to *ECOSOC (#05331)*. **Aims** Serve as a platform of cooperation among national governments who cooperate together on international civil aviation matters under the Chicago Convention. **Structure** Regional offices (8). Plenary Assembly (at least every 3 years). Permanent Council (meets 3 times a year), comprising 36 members serving 3-year term. Air Navigation Commission of 15 members; Air Transport Committee of 36 members; Joint Support Committee of 13 members; Finance Committee of 17 members; Committee on Unlawful Interference with International Aviation and its Facilities Committee of 21 members; Technical Cooperation Committee of 19 members. Special panels appointed from time to time as required. Meetings of main bodies normally open. /Secretariat Structure/ – reporting to Secretary General I. Office of Secretary General II. Air Navigation Bureau III. Air Transport Bureau IV. Technical Cooperation Bureau V. Bureau of Administration and Services VI. Legal Bureau. **Languages** Arabic, Chinese, English, French, Russian, Spanish. **Staff** 700.00 FTE, paid. **Finance** Sources: contributions of member/participating states.

Activities Capacity building; events/meetings; guidance/assistance/consulting; management of treaties and agreements; politics/policy/regulatory; research/documentation; standards/guidelines; training/education.

- *Convention for the Unification of Certain Rules Regarding International Carriage by Air, 1929 (1929)*;
- *Interim Agreement on International Civil Aviation (1944)*;
- *International Air Services Transit Agreement (1944)*;
- *International Air Transport Agreement (1944)*;
- *Convention on the Privileges and Immunities of the Specialized Agencies (1947)*;
- *Protocol Relating to an Amendment to the Convention on International Civil Aviation, Article 93bis (1947)*;
- *Convention on the International Recognition of Rights in Aircraft (1948)*;
- *Convention on Damage Caused by Foreign Aircraft to Third Parties on the Surface (1952)*;
- *Protocol Relating to an Amendment to the Convention on International Civil Aviation, Article 45 (1954)*;
- *Protocol Relating to an Amendment to the Convention on International Civil Aviation, Articles 48a, 49e, 61 (1954)*;
- *Protocol to Amend the Convention for the Unification of Certain Rules Relating to International Carriage by Air (1955)*;
- *Agreement on the Joint Financing of Certain Air Navigation Services in Greenland and the Faeroe Islands (1956)*;
- *Agreement on the Joint Financing of Certain Air Navigation Services in Iceland (1956)*;
- *Multilateral Agreement on Commercial Rights of Non-scheduled Air Services in Europe (1956)*;
- *EUROCONTROL International Convention Relating to Cooperation for the Safety of Air Navigation (1960)*;
- *Multilateral Agreement Relating to Certificates of Airworthiness for Imported Aircraft (1960)*;
- *Convention, Supplementary to the Warsaw Convention, for the Unification of Certain Rules Relating to International Carriage by Air Performed by a Person other Than the Contracting Carrier (1961)*;
- *Protocol Relating to an Amendment to the Convention on International Civil Aviation, Article 50a (1961)*;
- *Protocol Relating to an Amendment of the Convention on International Civil Aviation, Article 48a (1962)*;
- *Convention on Offences and Certain other Acts Committed on Board Aircraft (Tokyo convention, 1963)*;
- *International Agreement on the Procedure for the Establishment of Tariffs for Scheduled Air Services (1967)*;
- *Protocol on the Authentic Trilingual Text of the Convention on International Civil Aviation (1968)*;
- *Additional Protocol to the EUROCONTROL International Convention Relating to Cooperation for the Safety of Air Navigation (1970)*;
- *Convention for the Suppression of Unlawful Seizure of Aircraft (1970)*;
- *Multilateral Agreement Relating to the Collection of Route Charges (1970)*;
- *Convention for the Suppression of Unlawful Acts Against the Safety of Civil Aviation (1971)*;
- *Multilateral Agreement on Commercial Rights of Non-scheduled Air Services among the Association of South-East Asian Nations (1971)*;
- *Protocol to Amend the Convention for the Unification of Certain Rules Relating to International Carriage by Air Signed Warsaw on 12 October 1929 as Amended by the Protocol Done at The Hague on 28 September 1955 (1971)*;
- *Protocol Relating to an Amendment to the Convention on International Civil Aviation, Article 50a (1971)*;
- *Protocol Relating to an Amendment to the Convention on International Civil Aviation, Article 56 (1971)*;
- *Agreement Relating to Governmental Supervision of Airworthiness, Operation and Maintenance of Aeroplanes Involved under the Technical Cooperation Agreements between KLM, SAS, Swissair and UTA (1972)*;
- *Multilateral Agreement on Search and Rescue (SAR, 1973)*;
- *Protocol Relating to an Amendment of the Convention on International Civil Aviation, Article 50a (1974)*;
- *Agreement on Governmental Supervision of the Operation of the Aeroplanes Involved under Technical Cooperation Agreements between Air France, Lufthansa and Sabena (1976)*;

- *Agreement Regarding Monitoring of the Stratosphere (1976)*;
- *Protocol to an Amendment to the Convention on International Civil Aviation – Final Clause, Russian Text (1977)*;
- *Protocol on the Authentic Quadrilingual Text of the Convention on International Civil Aviation, Chicago 1944 (1977)*;
- *Protocol to Amend the Convention on Damage Caused by Foreign Aircraft to Third Parties on the Surface (1978)*;
- *Protocol for the Amendment of the Additional Protocol to the "Eurocontrol" International Convention Relating to Cooperation for the Safety of Air Navigation, 1978 (1978)*;
- *Protocol Relating to an Amendment to the Convention on International Civil Aviation, Article 83bis (1980)*;
- *Multilateral Agreement Relating to Route Charges (1981)*;
- *Protocol Amending of the Additional Protocol to the "Eurocontrol" International Convention Relating to Cooperation for the Safety of Air Navigation, 1981 (1981)*;
- *Protocol for the Amendment of the 1956 Agreement on the Joint Financing of Certain Air Navigation Services in Greenland and the Faeroe Islands (1982)*;
- *Protocol for the Amendment of the 1956 Agreement on the Joint Financing of Certain Air Navigation Services in Iceland (1982)*;
- *Agreement on the Practical Application of the Provisions of Article 83bis of the Convention on International Civil Aviation (1994)*;
- *Protocol Relating to an Amendment to the Convention on International Civil Aviation, Article 3bis (1984)*;
- *International Agreement on the Procedure for the Establishment of Tariffs for Intra-European Scheduled Air Services (1987)*;
- *International Agreement on the Sharing of Capacity on Intra-European Scheduled Air Services (1987)*;
- *Protocol for the Suppression of Unlawful Acts of Violence at Airports Serving International Civil Aviation (1988)*;
- *Protocol Relating to an Amendment to the Convention on International Civil Aviation, Article 56 (1989)*;
- *Protocol Relating to an Amendment to the Convention of International Civil Aviation, Article 50a (1990)*;
- *Convention on the Marking of Plastic Explosives for the Purpose of Identification (1991)*;
- *Agreement to Ban Smoking on International Passenger Flights (1994)*;
- *Verdrag Inzake de Bescherming van de Schelde, 1994 (1994)*;
- *Arrangement on the Joint Financing of a North Atlantic Height Monitoring System (1995)*;
- *Ilopango Agreement Concerning Inspection Procedures with the Objective of Guaranteeing the Safety of Flight Operations in Central America, Panama and Belize (1995)*;
- *Protocol on the Authentic Quinquelingual Text of the Convention on International Civil Aviation, Chicago 1944 (1995)*;
- *Protocol Relating to an Amendment to the Convention on International Civil Aviation – Final Clause, Arabic Text (1995)*;
- *Protocol on the Authentic Six-language Text of the Convention on International Civil Aviation, Chicago 1944 (1998)*;
- *Protocol Relating to an Amendment to the Convention on International Civil Aviation – Final Clause, Chinese Text (1998)*;
- *Convention for the Unification of Certain Rules for International Carriage by Air, 1999 (1999)*.

Events *Meeting of the Directors General of Civil Aviation-Middle East Region* Abu Dhabi (United Arab Emirates) 2022, *Conference of Directors General of Civil Aviation Asia and Pacific Region* Incheon (Korea Rep) 2022, *Council Session* Montréal, QC (Canada) 2022, *High-level Meeting on the Feasibility of a Long-Term Aspirational Goal for International Aviation CO2 Emissions Reductions* Montréal, QC (Canada) 2022, *Legal Seminar* Seoul (Korea Rep) 2022. **Publications** UnitingAviation.com; ICAO.TV.

Members Contracting States (193):
Afghanistan, Albania, Algeria, Andorra, Angola, Antigua-Barbuda, Argentina, Armenia, Australia, Austria, Azerbaijan, Bahamas, Bahrain, Bangladesh, Barbados, Belarus, Belgium, Belize, Benin, Bhutan, Bolivia, Bosnia-Herzegovina, Botswana, Brazil, Brunei Darussalam, Bulgaria, Burkina Faso, Burundi, Cambodia, Cameroon, Canada, Cape Verde, Central African Rep, Chad, Chile, China, Colombia, Comoros, Congo Brazzaville, Congo DR, Cook Is, Costa Rica, Côte d'Ivoire, Croatia, Cuba, Cyprus, Czechia, Denmark, Djibouti, Dominica, Dominican Rep, Ecuador, Egypt, El Salvador, Equatorial Guinea, Eritrea, Estonia, Eswatini, Ethiopia, Fiji, Finland, France, Gabon, Gambia, Georgia, Germany, Ghana, Greece, Grenada, Guatemala, Guinea, Guinea-Bissau, Guyana, Haiti, Honduras, Hungary, Iceland, India, Indonesia, Iran Islamic Rep, Iraq, Ireland, Israel, Italy, Jamaica, Japan, Jordan, Kazakhstan, Kenya, Kiribati, Korea DPR, Korea Rep, Kuwait, Kyrgyzstan, Laos, Latvia, Lebanon, Lesotho, Liberia, Libya, Lithuania, Luxembourg, Madagascar, Malawi, Malaysia, Maldives, Mali, Malta, Marshall Is, Mauritania, Mauritius, Mexico, Micronesia FS, Moldova, Monaco, Mongolia, Montenegro, Morocco, Mozambique, Myanmar, Namibia, Nauru, Nepal, Netherlands, New Zealand, Nicaragua, Niger, Nigeria, North Macedonia, Norway, Oman, Pakistan, Palau, Panama, Papua New Guinea, Paraguay, Peru, Philippines, Poland, Portugal, Qatar, Romania, Russia, Rwanda, Samoa, San Marino, Sao Tomé-Principe, Saudi Arabia, Senegal, Serbia, Seychelles, Sierra Leone, Singapore, Slovakia, Slovenia, Solomon Is, Somalia, South Africa, South Sudan, Spain, Sri Lanka, St Kitts-Nevis, St Lucia, St Vincent-Grenadines, Sudan, Suriname, Sweden, Switzerland, Syrian AR, Tajikistan, Tanzania UR, Thailand, Timor-Leste, Togo, Tonga, Trinidad-Tobago, Tunisia, Türkiye, Turkmenistan, Tuvalu, Uganda, UK, Ukraine, United Arab Emirates, Uruguay, USA, Uzbekistan, Vanuatu, Venezuela, Vietnam, Yemen, Zambia, Zimbabwe.

IGO Relations *World Trade Organization (WTO, #21864)* (Observer Status). Agreement, signed 3 Oct 1947, with the United Nations. Represented on: *United Nations System Chief Executives Board for Coordination (CEB, #20636)*. Member of: *Intergovernmental Organizations Conference (IGO Conference, #11498)*. Participates in: *Inter-Agency Task Force on Enabling Environment for Economic and Social Development (inactive)*. Liaises with: *Economic Community of West African States (ECOWAS, #05312)*; *Intergovernmental Panel on Climate Change (IPCC, #11499)*; *United Nations Office on Drugs and Crime (UNODC, #20596)*. Liaison with ITU Radiocommunication Sector. Cooperates with: *Common Market for Eastern and Southern Africa (COMESA, #04296)*; *International Transport Forum (ITF, #15725)*; *Southern African Development Community (SADC, #19843)*.

/Organizations which may be invited to attend ICAO meetings/:

I. *'United Nations and Subsidiary Bodies'* -
- *International Atomic Energy Agency (IAEA, #12294)*;
- *UNEP (#20299)*;
- *UNCTAD (#20285)*;
- *UNDP (#20292)*;
- *UNHCR (#20327)*;
- *UNICEF (#20332)*;
- *United Nations Economic Commission for Africa (ECA, #20554)*;
- *United Nations Economic Commission for Europe (UNECE, #20555)*;
- *United Nations Economic Commission for Latin America and the Caribbean (ECLAC, #20556)*;
- *United Nations Economic and Social Commission for Asia and the Pacific (ESCAP, #20557)*;
- *United Nations Economic and Social Commission for Western Asia (ESCWA, #20558)*;
- *United Nations Institute for Training and Research (UNITAR, #20576)*;
- *United Nations University (UNU, #20642)*;
- *World Food Programme (WFP, #21510)*.

II. *'Specialized Agencies'* -
- *FAO (#09260)*;
- *ILO (#11123)*;
- *International Bank for Reconstruction and Development (IBRD, #12317)*;
- *International Fund for Agricultural Development (IFAD, #13692)*;
- *International Maritime Organization (IMO, #14102)*;
- *International Monetary Fund (IMF, #14180)*;
- *International Telecommunication Union (ITU, #15673)*;
- *UNESCO (#20322)*;
- *UNIDO (#20336)*;
- *Universal Postal Union (UPU, #20682)*;
- *WHO (#20950)*;
- *World Intellectual Property Organization (WIPO, #21593)*;
- *World Meteorological Organization (WMO, #21649)*;
- WTO.

III. *'Other inter-governmental organizations'* -
- *Agency for the Safety of Aerial Navigation in Africa and Madagascar (#00556)*;
- *Corporación Centroamericana de Servicios de Navegación Aérea (COCESNA, #04837)*;
- *Council of Europe (CE, #04881)*;
- *EUROCONTROL (#05667)*;
- *European Space Agency (ESA, #08798)*;
- *European Union (EU, #08967)*;
- *International Criminal Police Organization – INTERPOL (ICPO-INTERPOL, #13110)*;
- *International Hydrographic Organization (IHO, #13825)*;
- *International Institute for the Unification of Private Law (UNIDROIT, #13934)*;
- *League of Arab States (LAS, #16420)*;
- *OAS (#17629)*;
- *Pan American Institute of Geography and History (PAIGH, #18113)*;
- *World Tourism Organization (UNWTO, #21861)*.

/Close working relationships with autonomous regional civil aviation bodies/:
- *African Civil Aviation Commission (AFCAC, #00248)*;
- *European Civil Aviation Conference (ECAC, #06564)*;
- *Latin American Civil Aviation Commission (LACAC, #16297)*.

/Also links with/:
- *African Development Bank (ADB, #00283)*;
- *African Development Bank Group (ADB Group, #00284)*;
- *Agencia Centroamericana de Seguridad Aeronautica (ACSA, see: #04837)*;
- *Arab Civil Aviation Organization (ACAO, #00920)*;
- *ASEAN (#01141)*;
- *Asia-Pacific Telecommunity (APT, #02064)*;
- *Asociación Latinoamericana de Derecho Aeronautico y Espacial (ALADA, #02202)*;
- *Association of Caribbean States (ACS, #02411)*;
- *Caribbean Meteorological Organization (CMO, #03524)*;
- *Commonwealth Secretariat (#04362)*;
- *Convention on Long-range Transboundary Air Pollution (#04787)*;
- *East African Community (EAC, #05181)*;
- *Eastern and Southern African Management Institute (ESAMI, #05254)*;
- *ESCAP/WMO Typhoon Committee (TC, #05534)*;
- *European Union Aviation Safety Agency (EASA, #08978)*;
- *Intergovernmental Oceanographic Commission (IOC, #11496)*;
- *Organisation intergouvernementale pour les transports internationaux ferroviaires (OTIF, #17807)*;
- *International Bird Strike Committee (IBSC, inactive)*;
- *International Civil Service Commission (ICSC, #12587)*;
- *International Cospas-Sarsat Programme (#12975)*;
- *International Mobile Satellite Organization (IMSO, #14174)*;
- *International Seabed Authority (ISBA, #14813)*;
- *Joint Aviation Authorities Training Organisation (JAA TO, #16122)*;
- *Joint Inspection Unit of the United Nations (JIU, #16133)*;
- *Office of the United Nations Special Coordinator for the Middle East Process (UNSCO, #17698)*;
- *Pacific Islands Forum (#17968)*;
- *Pacific Islands Forum Secretariat (#17970)*;
- *Regional Centre for Mapping of Resources for Development (RCMRD, #18757)*;
- *Secretariat for the Vienna Convention for the Protection of the Ozone Layer and the Montreal Protocol on Substances that Deplete the Ozone Layer (Ozone Secretariat, #19209)*;
- *Southeast Asian Agency for Regional Transport and Communications Development (SEATAC, inactive)*;
- *Southern African Transport and Communications Commission (SATCC, no recent information)*;
- *United Nations Commission on Narcotic Drugs (CND, #20532)*;
- *United Nations Committee of Experts on Public Administration (CEPA, #20542)*;
- *United Nations Committee of Experts on the Transport of Dangerous Goods and on the Globally Harmonized System of Classification and Labelling of Chemicals (Committee of Experts on TDG and GHS, #20543)*;
- *United Nations Framework Convention on Climate Change – Secretariat (UNFCCC, #20564)*;
- *United Nations Joint Staff Pension Fund (UNJSPF, #20581)*;
- *United Nations Volunteers (UNV, #20650)*;
- *WHO Regional Office for Europe (#20945)*;
- *WMO Applications of Meteorology Programme (AMP, see: #21649)*;
- *WMO/ESCAP Panel on Tropical Cyclones (PTC, #20976)*;
- *World Customs Organization (WCO, #21350)*.

NGO Relations Organizations which may be invited to attend ICAO meetings:
- Aeronautical Radio Inc (ARINC);
- *Aerospace Medical Association (ASMA)*;
- *SITA (#19299)*;
- *Airports Council International (ACI, #00611)*, in its capacity of taking over from *Airport Associations Coordinating Council (AACC, inactive)*, itself taking over from *International Civil Airports Association (ICAA, inactive)*;
- *Alliance internationale de tourisme (AIT, #00694)*;
- *Association internationale des traducteurs de conférence (AITC, #02748)*;
- *Comité International Radio-Maritime (CIRM, #04186)*;
- *Commission Internationale de l'Eclairage (CIE, #04219)*;
- *Fédération aéronautique internationale (FAI, #09397)*;
- *Fédération Internationale de l'Automobile (FIA, #09613)*;
- *Global Express Association (GEA, #10351)*;
- *Institute of Air Transport (ITA, inactive)*;
- *Institute of International Law (#11276)*;
- *Inter-American Statistical Institute (IASI, #11452)*;
- *International Academy of Aviation and Space Medicine (IAASM, #11537)*;
- *International Air Safety Association (IASA, inactive)*;
- *International Air Transport Association (IATA, #11614)*;
- *International Association of Aircraft Brokers and Agents (IABA, inactive)*;
- *International Association for the Physical Sciences of the Oceans (IAPSO, #12082)*;
- *International Chamber of Commerce (ICC, #12534)*;
- *International Coalition for Sustainable Aviation (ICSA, #12623)*;
- *International Coordinating Council of Aerospace Industry Associations (ICCAIA, #12956)*;
- *International Council of Aircraft Owner and Pilot Associations (IAOPA, #12988)*;
- *International Federation of Air Line Pilots' Associations (IFALPA, #13349)*;
- *International Federation of Helicopter Associations (IFHA, #13444)*;
- *International Geographical Union (IGU, #13713)*;
- *International Law Association (ILA, #14003)*;
- *International Organization for Standardization (ISO, #14473)*;
- *International Transport Workers' Federation (ITF, #15726)*;
- *International Union of Aerospace Insurers (IUAI, #15750)*;
- *International Union of Geodesy and Geophysics (IUGG, #15776)*;
- *International Union of Railways (#15813)*.

Member of: *Association for Human Resources Management in International Organizations (AHRMIO, #02634)*; *International Council on Archives (ICA, #12996)*. Cooperates with: *Informing Science Institute (ISI, #11201)*. Instrumental in setting up: *Gulf Centre for Aviation Studies (GCAS)*. [2022.02.23/XB1505/**B***]

♦ International Civil and Commercial Law Centre Foundation (internationally oriented national body)

♦ International Civil Defence Organization (ICDO) 12582

Organisation internationale de protection civile (OIPC) – Organización Internacional de Protección Civil (OIPC)

SG Chemin de Surville 10-12 BP 172, Petit-Lancy 1, 1213 Geneva, Switzerland. T. +41228796969. Fax +41228796979. E-mail: icdo@icdo.org.
URL: http://www.icdo.org/

History Originates from Association *Les Lieux de Genève*, founded 1931, Paris (France). Association transferred to Geneva (Switzerland), 1937, when renamed *International Association of Geneva Zones for the protection of civilian populations and historic buildings in times of armed conflicts – Association internationale pour la protection des populations civiles, des monuments historiques et oeuvres d'art en temps de guerre*. Reconstituted under current title, Jan 1958, as a non-governmental organization. Present constitution adopted, Oct 1966, Monaco, at Constituent Assembly; entered into force 1 Mar 1972, when ICDO became and intergovernmental organization. Constitution registered with the *United Nations (UN, #20515)* under 'UNTS I/14376', 10 Oct 1975, New York NY (USA), according to Article 102 of the UN Charter. Headquarters agreement concluded 10 Mar 1976 with Swiss Federal Council. Established 1 Mar 1972, Geneva (Switzerland), on entry into force of constitution which had been adopted by Plenipotentiary Conference 17 Oct 1966, Monaco. Mandate is based on its Constitution and the *Universal Declaration on Civil Protection (Amman Declaration)* adopted Apr 1994, Amman. Supplemented by texts adopted during major conferences, including: *Beijing Declaration*, 1998; Framework Convention on Civil Defence Assistance (Geneva, May 2000); Declaration of the Conference for Follow-up of the Framework Convention (Geneva, Oct 2002); Bishkek Declaration, 12 May 2016; ICDO Strategic Programme 2015-2025, adopted 2014. **Aims** Contribute to development by states of structures known as civil *protection*, civil defence or civil safety, ensuring protection and assistance of populations, and *safeguarding* property and the environment in the face of natural or man-made *disasters*; federate these national structures and favour cooperation and mutual solidarity among them. **Structure** General Assembly (every 2 years); Executive Council (meets annually). Permanent Secretariat and International Monitoring and Coordination Centre (IMCC) (established 2015) located at Headquarters in Geneva (Switzerland); E-Learning Centre in Tunis (Tunisia) (established 2014). ICDO Emergency Relief Warehouses in Kyrgyzstan and Togo. **Languages** Arabic, Chinese, English, French, Russian, Spanish. **Staff** 11.00 FTE, paid. Numerous consultants and international experts. **Finance** Sources: contributions of member/participating states. **Activities** Awards/prizes/competitions; guidance/assistance/consulting; humanitarian/emergency aid; monitoring/evaluation; projects/programmes; training/education. **Events** *Ministerial Meeting* Geneva (Switzerland) 2002, *Ministerial Meeting* Geneva (Switzerland) 2001, *Ministerial Meeting* Geneva (Switzerland) 2000, *Ministerial Meeting* Tunis (Tunisia) 1999, *Ministerial Meeting* Beijing (China) 1998. **Publications** *International Civil Defence Journal* – temporarily discontinued. *International Directory of National Structures of Civil Protection, Defence and Safety,*

and Emergency Management (1999); *Community Emergency Preparedness Guide* – together with WHO, IFRC, UNITAR; *Disaster Management Guide*; *ICDO Guide to Preparedness and Conduct in Case of Disaster*; *ICDO Manual*. Conférence and meeting proceedings and reports; monographs; training and technical documents; IMCC disaster situation status reports; declarations; recommendations. Information Services: Information clearing house; Documentation Centre and Library on disaster management and civil protection. Collects and disseminates information, including laws, regulations, official reports and statistical details concerning protection and safety of populations and properties published in member countries. **Information Services** *Civl Defence Expo* – internet platform on modern civil defence/civil protection technology; *International Civil Defence Academy* – internet platform for exchange of information about training and scientific research.
Members Governments of 58 states represented by national authorities in charge of implementing protection and safety measures (" indicates original member):
Algeria, Armenia, Azerbaijan, Bahrain, Benin (*), Bosnia-Herzegovina, Burkina Faso, Burundi, Cameroon, Central African Rep, Chad (*), China, Congo Brazzaville, Congo DR, Côte d'Ivoire, Cuba, Cyprus (*), Egypt (*), El Salvador, Gabon (*), Georgia, Ghana, Guinea, Guinea-Bissau, Haiti, Iraq, Jordan, Kazakhstan, Korea Rep, Kuwait, Kyrgyzstan, Lebanon (*), Lesotho, Liberia (*), Libya, Malaysia, Mali, Mauritania (*), Mongolia, Morocco, Niger, Nigeria, Oman, Pakistan, Palestine, Qatar (*), Russia, Saudi Arabia (*), Senegal, Serbia, South Sudan, Sudan, Syrian AR, Tajikistan, Togo, Tunisia (*), United Arab Emirates, Yemen.
Observers in 17 countries:
Belarus, Chile, Comoros, France, Indonesia, Malta, Mauritius, Monaco, Nicaragua, Portugal, Rwanda, Slovakia, South Africa, Switzerland, Ukraine, Uzbekistan, Zimbabwe.
As of Feb 2020, Affiliate members (26) – international organizations and private, commercial or industrial concerns whose mandates relate closely to that of ICDO, in 16 countries:
Belgium, France, Hungary, Italy, Kazakhstan, Norway, Qatar, Russia, Saudi Arabia, Serbia, Spain, Switzerland, Thailand, Tunisia, UK, USA.
Included in the above, 4 organizations listed in this Yearbook:
Arab Interior Ministers' Council (AIMC, #00990); *International Emergency Management Society (TIEMS, #13261)*; *Naif Arab University for Security Sciences (NAUSS, #16929)*; *World Agency of Planetary Monitoring and Earthquake Risk Reduction (WAPMERR)*.
IGO Relations Observer status with (1): *United Nations (UN, #20515)* (General Assembly). Cooperates with (8): *ECOSOC (#05331)*; *International Search and Rescue Advisory Group (INSARAG, #14816)*; *United Nations Institute for Training and Research (UNITAR, #20576)*; *United Nations Office at Geneva (UNOG, #20597)*; *United Nations Office for Disaster Risk Reduction (UNDRR, #20595)*; *United Nations Office for the Coordination of Humanitarian Affairs (OCHA, #20593)*; *WHO (#20950)*; *WHO Regional Office for Europe (#20945)*. **NGO Relations** Joint meetings and other links with: *Arab Red Crescent and Red Cross Organization (ARCO, #01033)*; *International Committee of the Red Cross (ICRC, #12799)*; *International Federation of Red Cross and Red Crescent Societies (#13526)*. [2020.02.11/XC1506/y/**C***]

♦ International Civil Engineering Risk and Reliability Association (CERRA) 12583

Pres CEME – Room 2014, Civil and Mechanical Engineering Bldg, Univ of British Columbia, 6250 Applied Science Lane, Vancouver BC V6T 1Z4, Canada. T. +16048275557. E-mail: terje@civil.ubc.ca.
Chairman Dept of Civil and Environmental Engineering, Seoul Natl Univ, 1 Gwanak-ro, Gwanak-gu, Seoul 151-742, Korea Rep. T. +8228807369. Fax +8228732684.
URL: http://icasp.snu.ac.kr/
History Set up to organize the *International Conference on Applications of Statistics and Probability in Soil and Structural Engineering (ICASP)*. Bylaws approved 27 May 1987; amended 15 Dec 1999, Sydney (Australia), and 7 Jul 2003, San Francisco CA (USA). **Aims** Promote professional analysis of risk and reliability associated with Civil Engineering Systems. **Structure** General Meeting; Board of Directors; Secretariat. **Activities** Events/meetings; awards/prizes/competitions. **Events** *ICASP : Quadrennial International Conference on Applications of Statistics and Probability in Civil Engineering* Seoul (Korea Rep) 2019, *International Symposium on Reliability Engineering and Risk Management* Singapore (Singapore) 2018, *ICASP : Quadrennial International Conference on Applications of Statistics and Probability in Civil Engineering* Vancouver, BC (Canada) 2015, *ICASP : Quadrennial International Conference on Applications of Statistics and Probability in Civil Engineering* Zurich (Switzerland) 2011, *ICASP : quadrennial international conference on applications of statistics and probability in civil engineering* Chiba (Japan) 2007. [2018.03.20/XJ1063/c/**E**]

♦ International Civil Liberties Alliance (ICLA) 12584

Alianza Internacional pro Derechos Civiles – Internationale Bürgerrechts-Allianz
Contact Postfach 1403, 4001 Basel BS, Switzerland. E-mail: info@libertiesalliance.org.
URL: http://www.libertiesalliance.org/
History 1 Jun 2012, Basel (Switzerland), as a project of *Center for Vigilant Freedom*, which was disbanded prior to ICLA being registered in accordance with Swiss Civil Code. **Aims** Uphold democracy, freedom and individual liberties. **Structure** General Assembly. Board. **Languages** English, German. **Staff** Voluntary. **Finance** Sources: donations; members' dues. **Activities** Education and campaigns; conferences. **Events** *International Conference for Free Speech and Human Rights* Brussels (Belgium) 2012. **IGO Relations** *Organization for Security and Cooperation in Europe (OSCE, #17887)*. [2016/XJ6839/**C**]

♦ International Civil Liberties Monitoring Group (internationally oriented national body)
♦ International Civil-Military Air Traffic Control Centre / see EUROCONTROL Maastricht Upper Area Control Centre (#05670)

♦ International Civil Servants Mutual Association 12585

Association mutuelle des fonctionnaires internationaux (AMFI)
Sec Palais des Nations, Office B-214, Library Bldg – Door 20 – Lift 19 – 2nd Floor, 1211 Geneva 10, Switzerland. T. +41229173510. Fax +41229170071. E-mail: lamutuelle@un.org.
URL: https://www.lamutuelle.org/
History 1959. Also referred to as *Mutuelle d'épargne et de crédit (MEC)* and as *MUTUELLE*. **NGO Relations** *Groupement de prévoyance et d'assurance des fonctionnaires internationaux (GPAFI, #10764)*. [2008/XF0509/**F**]

♦ International Civil Service 12586

Address not obtained.
History The first international civil servants, as opposed to those serving in the administration of a single state, were those employed: in Universal Postal Union (UPU), established 9 Oct 1874, Bern (Switzerland); by the League of Nations, set up 10 Jan 1920; and by the International Labour Organisation (ILO) formed 28 Jun 1919. The scope was greatly expanded with the establishment of the United Nations (UN) and its specialized agencies after World War II, and subsequently by bodies such as the Organisation for Economic Co-operation and Development (OECD) and the European Commission. Such civil servants owe their allegiance to the international agency in which they are employed and not to their respective national governments, from whom they are not allowed to take instruction. **Structure** Not a formally organized body. Organizations which exist to coordinate or regulate international activity at this level include: *International Civil Service Commission (ICSC, #12587)*, which deals with conditions of service within the United Nations Common System; and *Federation of International Civil Servants' Associations (FICSA, #09603)*, which deals principally with the staff associations of the United Nations, acting at inter-Agency level. [2009/XF2043/**F**]

♦ International Civil Service Commission (ICSC) 12587

Commission de la fonction publique internationale (CFPI) – Comisión de Administración Pública Internacional (CAPI)
Exec Sec Two United Nations Plaza, 10th Floor – Room DC2-1070, New York NY 10017, USA. T. +12129635465. Fax +12129630159. E-mail: icscmail@un.org.
URL: http://icsc.un.org/
History 18 Dec 1974, New York, NY (USA). Established by UN General Assembly resolution 3357 (XXIX), as a commission of *United Nations (UN, #20515)*. Rules of procedure adopted at 1st Session, May 1975. **Aims** Regulate and coordinate the conditions of service of the *United Nations* common system of organizations. **Structure** Commission meets twice a year and comprises 15 members appointed by UN General Assembly for 4-year terms in their personal capacity, 2 of whom are designated Chairman and Vice-Chairman. Divisions (3): Cost-of-Living; Salaries and Allowances; Human Resources Policies. Secretariat, headed by Executive Secretary. **Languages** English, French, Russian. **Staff** 47.00 FTE, paid. **Finance** Established by UN Secretary-General and approved by UN General Assembly, after consultation with Chief Executives Board for Coordination (CEB), on the basis of proposals by Secretary-General. Contributors include UNESCO. **Activities** Within the general framework of the *International Civil Service (#12586)*, coordinates and regulates working conditions of personnel working for the United Nations and its agencies. **Events** *Session* New York, NY (USA) 2010, *Session* Santiago (Chile) 2010, *Session* Montréal, QC (Canada) 2009, *Session* New York, NY (USA) 2009, *Session* New York, NY (USA) 2008.
Members Independent experts, nationals of 15 countries (expiry dates in brackets):
Algeria (2024), China (2024), France (2022), Germany (2021), Italy (2021), Jamaica (2022), Japan (2021), Korea Rep (2024), Libya (2022), Mexico (2021), Morocco (2024), Poland (2022), Russia (2024), Sierra Leone (2022), USA (2021).
IGO Relations Reports to United Nations General Assembly Fifth Committee. In consultation with: *United Nations System Chief Executives Board for Coordination (CEB, #20636)*; CEB High Level Committee on Management.
In addition to the United Nations, 13 organizations have accepted the Commission's statute:
- *FAO (#09260)*;
- *ILO (#11123)*;
- *International Atomic Energy Agency (IAEA, #12294)*;
- *International Civil Aviation Organization (ICAO, #12581)*;
- *International Maritime Organization (IMO, #14102)*;
- *International Telecommunication Union (ITU, #15673)*;
- *UNESCO (#20322)*;
- *UNIDO (#20336)*;
- *Universal Postal Union (UPU, #20682)*;
- *WHO (#20950)*;
- *World Intellectual Property Organization (WIPO, #21593)*;
- *World Meteorological Organization (WMO, #21649)*;
- *World Tourism Organization (UNWTO, #21861)*.

Organization which has not formally accepted the statute but which participates fully in the Commission's work:
- *International Fund for Agricultural Development (IFAD, #13692)*.

NGO Relations In consultation with: *Federation of International Civil Servants' Associations (FICSA, #09603)*; *Coordinating Committee for International Staff Unions and Associations of the United Nations System (CCISUA, #04818)*. [2021/XE0128/**E***]

♦ International Civil Society Action Network (ICAN) 12588

Main Office 1775 Mass Ave NW, Ste 524, Washington DC 20036, USA. T. +12029860952. Fax +12029860952. E-mail: info@icanpeacework.org.
URL: http://www.icanpeacework.org/
History 2006, USA, on the initiative of Sanam Naraghi-Anderlini and Sussan Tahmasebi. Registration: USA. **Aims** Strengthen *women's* participation and influence in conflict prevention, social justice, coexistence, and peacebuilding efforts, in situations of closed political space and conflict affected states; elevate the voices and impact of women's civil society groups in issues of rights, security and peace in countries undergoing transitions affected by rising militarism and extremism targeting women. **Structure** Board of Directors. **Languages** Arabic, English, French, Persian, Spanish. **Finance** Supported by: independent foundations; *United Nations (UN, #20515)*; governments of Norway and Switzerland. **Activities** Collection and dissemination of objective information on the situation of women in conflict-affected countries, to the international policy community; Provision of trainings to locally based organizations in transition and conflict-affected countries; Provision of concrete recommendations to the international community; Connection of on-the-ground civil society activists with counterparts regionally, international media, organizations and governments. Organizes: annual Forum; regional events, training and strategy meetings. **Events** *Forum* Istanbul (Turkey) 2014, *Building movements, promoting plurality* Istanbul (Turkey) 2013, *Civil Society Forum / Forum* Oslo (Norway) 2013. **Publications** *What the Women Say* – country briefs. Video interviews.
Members Full in 14 countries:
Afghanistan, Egypt, Iran Islamic Rep, Iraq, Lebanon, Libya, Pakistan, Palestine, Saudi Arabia, Sri Lanka, Syrian AR, Tunisia, Türkiye, Yemen.
NGO Relations Instrumental in setting up: *Global Network of Women Peacebuilders (GNWP, #10503)*. [2020/XJ4564/**F**]

♦ International Civil Society Centre 12589

Contact Agricolastr 26, 10555 Berlin, Germany. T. +49302062469711. Fax +49302062469719. E-mail: mail@icscentre.org.
URL: http://www.icscentre.org/
History 2007, as *Berlin Civil Society Center*, on the initiative of Burkhard Gnärig. Current title adopted 2013. **Aims** Help the world's leading ICSOs maximize their impact for a sustainable and more equitable world. **Structure** Shareholders' Meeting (annual); Board of Trustees. **Languages** English. **Staff** 15.00 FTE, paid. **Finance** Supported by civil society organizations and grants from donors. Annual budget (2018): euro 1,769,409. **Activities** Projects/programmes; events/meetings; knowledge management/information dissemination; guidance/assistance/consulting; networking/liaising. **Events** *Annual Innovators Forum* Berlin (Germany) 2019, *Annual Innovators Forum* Berlin (Germany) 2018, *Navigating disruptive change – how civil society organisations can survive and thrive in an increasingly disruptive world* Johannesburg (South Africa) 2013. **Publications** *Diversify, Adapt and Innovate – Changing ICSO Business Models* (2014); *Riding the Wave*; *The Hedgehog and the Beetle – Disruption and Innovation in the Civil Society Sector* by Burkhard Gnärig.
Members Shareholders (14):
Adventist Development and Relief Agency International (ADRA, #00131); *Amnesty International (AI, #00801)*; *CARE International (CI, #03429)*; *ChildFund Alliance (#03868)*; *Christian Blind Mission (CBM)*; *HelpAge International (#10904)*; *Islamic Relief Worldwide (IRWW, #16048)*; *Oxfam International (#17922)*; *Plan International (#18386)*; *Sightsavers International (#19270)*; *SOS-Kinderdorf International (#19693)*; *Transparency International (TI, #20223)*; *Voluntary Service Overseas (VSO)*; *World Vision International (WVI, #21904)*.
Consultative Status Consultative status granted from: *ECOSOC (#05331)* (Special). **IGO Relations** *International Bank for Reconstruction and Development (IBRD, #12317)* (World Bank); *OECD (#17693)*; *United Nations (UN, #20515)*. [2019/XJ7435/y/**E**]

♦ International Civil Society Support (internationally oriented national body)

♦ International Clarinet Association (ICA) 12590

Exec Dir 829 Bethel Rd, Ste 216, Columbus OH 43214, USA. T. +18889835441. E-mail: edo@clarinet.org.
URL: http://www.clarinet.org/
History Aug 1974. Former names and other names: *International Clarinet Society (ICS)* – former (1974 to 1988); *International Clarinet Society/ClariNetwork International (ICS/CI)* – former (1988 to 1992). **Aims** Support projects which benefit clarinet performance; provide opportunities for exchange of ideas, material and information among members; foster composition, publication, recording and distribution of music for the clarinet; encourage research and manufacture of a more definitive clarinet; further communication and cooperation between clarinettists and the music industry. **Structure** Board of Directors. **Languages** English. **Finance** Sources: donations; members' dues; revenue from activities/projects; sale of publications. Annual budget: 200,000 USD. **Activities** Awards/prizes/competitions; events/meetings; financial and/or material support. **Events** *Annual Congress* Reno, NV (USA) 2022, *Annual Congress* 2021, *Annual Congress* Knoxville, TN (USA) 2019, *Annual Congress* Ostend (Belgium) 2018, *Annual Congress* Orlando, FL (USA) 2017. **Publications** *The Clarinet* (4 a year). Membership directory. **Information Services** *Klarinet* – online discussion group.
Members Active (individual membership with voting rights); Associate (non-voting membership for libraries, institutions, publishers and dealers). Membership covers 56 countries and territories:
Argentina, Armenia, Australia, Austria, Belarus, Belgium, Brazil, Bulgaria, Canada, Chile, China, Colombia, Costa Rica, Croatia, Cyprus, Czechia, Denmark, Ecuador, Finland, France, Germany, Greece, Hungary, Iceland, India, Ireland, Israel, Italy, Japan, Korea Rep, Luxembourg, Mexico, Moldova, Netherlands, New Zealand, Norway, Panama, Peru, Poland, Portugal, Puerto Rico, Russia, Serbia, Singapore, Slovakia, Slovenia, South Africa, Spain, Sweden, Switzerland, Thailand, Türkiye, UK, Uruguay, USA, Venezuela. [2023.02.13/XF1352/**F**]

♦ International Clarinet Society / see International Clarinet Association (#12590)
♦ International Clarinet Society/ClariNetwork International / see International Clarinet Association (#12590)
♦ International Class 'A' Yacht Association / see International Maxi Association (#14122)

♦ **International Classic Cosmoenergy Federation (ICCF)** **12591**

Contact Staiceles iela 1 / 3 – 31, Riga, Latvia. E-mail: iccfworld@gmail.com.
URL: http://www.iccfworld.com/

Aims Promote research, training, and treatment in the fields of *energy physiology* and complementary *bioenergetics*. **NGO Relations** Member of: *Global Health Workforce Alliance (GHWA, inactive)*. [2010/XJ1582/**D**]

♦ **International Classified Marketplace Association (ICMA)** **12592**

Conference and Marketing Manager Coen van Boshuizenlaan 74, 1191 TB Ouderkerk aan de Amstel, Netherlands. E-mail: communications@icmaonline.org.
Chairperson c/o Russmedia, Gutenbergstrasse 1, 6858 Schwarzach, Austria.
URL: http://www.icmaonline.org/

History 1986, as *Free Ads Papers International Association (FAPIA)*. Subsequently changed title to *International Classified Media Association (ICMA)*, Apr 2003, to reflect acceptance of broader membership. **Structure** General Meeting (twice a year); Board of Directors. **Languages** English. **Staff** 3.00 FTE, paid. **Activities** Events/meetings. **Events** *Online Markets Place Conference* Helsinki (Finland) 2022, *Half-Yearly General Meeting* 2021, *Half-Yearly General Meeting* Helsinki (Finland) 2021, *Half-Yearly General Meeting* Helsinki (Finland) 2020, *Half-Yearly General Meeting* Istanbul (Turkey) 2019. **Publications** *ICMA Newsletter* (12 a year) – online, also paper (4 a year).

Members Newspapers (over 200) in 35 countries:
Argentina, Australia, Austria, Belarus, Belgium, Brazil, Canada, Croatia, Czechia, Denmark, Estonia, Finland, Germany, Greece, Hungary, India, Ireland, Italy, Kazakhstan, Latvia, Lithuania, Malta, Mexico, Netherlands, New Zealand, Portugal, Romania, Russia, Slovakia, South Africa, Spain, Sweden, Switzerland, Ukraine, USA.

NGO Relations Member of: *World Association of Newspapers and News Publishers (WAN-IFRA, #21166)*. [2019/XD6994/**D**]

♦ International Classified Media Association / see International Classified Marketplace Association (#12592)

♦ International Cleaning and Restoration Association (internationally oriented national body)

♦ **International Cleantech Network (ICN)** **12593**

Head of Secretariat Rådhuspladsen 59 – 4, 1550 Copenhagen V, Denmark. T. +4561243316. E-mail: lrv@cleancluster.dk.
Secretariat Assistant address not obtained.
URL: http://www.internationalcleantechnetwork.com/

History 2009. Launched by Copenhagen Capacity, as a loose network. Secretariat founded 1 Jan 2016. Registration: Denmark. **Aims** Stimulate project development among members; support the SMEs of cluster members; share best practice knowledge *business* intelligence. **Structure** General Meeting; Board of Directors; Steering Committee. Working Groups; Task Forces. **Languages** English. **Staff** 1.00 FTE, paid. **Finance** Sources: members' dues. **Activities** Events/meetings; knowledge management/information dissemination; networking/liaising; projects/programmes. **Events** *Annual Meeting* Graz (Austria) 2021, *Annual Meeting* Abu Dhabi (United Arab Emirates) 2020, *Annual Meeting* London (UK) 2019, *Annual Meeting* Raleigh, NC (USA) 2018, *Annual Meeting* Lyon (France) 2017. **Publications** *ICN Newsletter* (4 a year); *ICN Annual Booklet* (annual).

Members Clusters (16) in 15 countries:
Argentina, Austria, Belgium, Bulgaria, Canada, Denmark, France, Netherlands, Norway, South Africa, Spain, Sweden, Switzerland, UK, USA.

NGO Relations Member of (1): *World Alliance for Efficient Solutions*. [2021.05.20/XM7293/**F**]

♦ International Clearinghouse for Birth Defects Monitoring Systems / see International Clearinghouse for Birth Defects Surveillance and Research (#12594)

♦ **International Clearinghouse for Birth Defects Surveillance and Research (ICBDSR)** **12594**

Gen Manager Div of Medical Genetics, Dept of Pediatrics, Univ of Utah, 295 Chipeta Way, Salt Lake City UT 84108, USA. T. +18015818943. E-mail: centre@icbdsr.org.
URL: http://www.icbdsr.org/

History 1974, Helsinki (Finland). Formally constituted 1982. Former names and other names: *International Clearinghouse for Birth Defects Monitoring Systems (ICBDMS)* – former; *Organisation internationale des systèmes pour la surveillance des malformations congénitales* – former. Registration: No/ID: K206101, USA, State of Georgia; No/ID: 6054248, USA, State of Utah. **Aims** Bring together birth defect programmes from around the world with the aim of conducting worldwide surveillance and research to prevent birth defects and ameliorate their consequences. **Structure** Plenary Session (at Annual Meeting); Executive Committee. **Languages** English. **Staff** 1.00 FTE, paid; 4.00 FTE, voluntary. **Finance** Sources: members' dues. Annual budget: 30,000 USD (2019). **Activities** Events/meetings; guidance/assistance/consulting; healthcare; knowledge management/information dissemination; projects/programmes; training/education. **Events** *Annual Meeting* St Julian's (Malta) 2023, *Annual Meeting* Bologna (Italy) 2022, *Annual Meeting* Salt Lake City, UT (USA) 2021, *Annual Meeting* Bologna (Italy) 2020, *Annual Meeting* Bratislava (Slovakia) 2019. **Publications** *ICBDSR Newsletter* (12 a year). *Birth Defects Surveillance: A Manual for Programme Managers* (2014); *Atlas of Selected Congenital Anomalies* (1997) in English, French, Spanish; *Congenital Malformations Worldwide* (1991). *Atlas of Selected Congenital Anomalies* and *Birth Defects Surveillance: A Manual for Programme Managers* (2014) in collaboration with *WHO (#20950)* and US Centers for Disease Control and Prevention (CDC). Annual Report; scientific papers; video.

Members Full: Surveillance Systems (43) in 27 countries:
Australia, Canada, Chile, Colombia, Costa Rica, Cuba, Czechia, Finland, France, Germany, Hungary, India, Iran Islamic Rep, Israel, Italy, Japan, Malta, Mexico, Netherlands, New Zealand, Norway, Saudi Arabia, Spain, Sweden, UK, Ukraine, USA.
Included in the above, 1 regional member:
Estudio Colaborativo Latino Americano de Malformaciones Congénitas (ECLAMC, #05552).
Affiliate (19) in 10 countries:
China, India, Italy, Nicaragua, Nigeria, Paraguay, South Africa, UK, Uruguay, USA.

Consultative Status Consultative status granted from: *WHO (#20950)* (Official Relations). **IGO Relations** Affiliated with (1): *WHO (#20950)*. **NGO Relations** Cooperates with (2): *Estudio Colaborativo Latino Americano de Malformaciones Congénitas (ECLAMC, #05552)*; *EUROCAT – European Surveillance of Congenital Anomalies (#05655)*. [2021.08.31/XF2103/y/**F**]

♦ International Clearinghouse on Children, Youth and Media (internationally oriented national body)

♦ International Cleft Lip and Palate Foundation / see Cleft-Children International (#03994)

♦ **International Cleft Lip and Palate Foundation (ICPF)** **12595**

Sec/Treas Himeike-dori, Chikusa-ku, Nagoya AICHI, 464-0055 Japan. T. +81527574465. E-mail: office@icpfweb.org.
URL: http://www.icpfweb.org/

History 23 Oct 1997, Kyoto (Japan). **Aims** Advance the care for cleft lip and palate patients, worldwide; strengthen care activity in cleft lip and palate treatment through volunteer activity, charity missions and fund raising; establish a network system of information exchange, regardless of fields and organization. **Structure** Board of Trustees, including President and Secretary-Treasurer. **Finance** Members' dues. **Events** *World Congress* Seoul (Korea Rep) 2023, *World Congress* Osaka (Japan) 2022, *World Congress* St Petersburg (Russia) 2020, *Congress* Nagoya (Japan) 2019, *Congress* Leipzig (Germany) 2018. [2020/XJ0641/f/**F**]

♦ **International Clematis Society** **12596**

Sec 3 Cuthberts Close, Waltham Cross, EN7 5RB, UK. T. +441992636524. E-mail: secretary@clematisinternational.com – clematis@clematisinternational.com.
URL: http://www.clematisinternational.com/

History 1984. **Aims** Improve and extend cultivation of Clematis; disseminate knowledge of Clematis and Clematis *horticulture*; stimulate scientific research and international cooperation. **Structure** Council. **Languages** English. **Staff** Voluntary. **Finance** Sources: members' dues. **Activities** Events/meetings; knowledge management/information dissemination; networking/liaising. **Events** *Conference* Aarhus (Denmark) / Hamburg (Germany) 2022, *Conference* Aarhus (Denmark) / Hamburg (Germany) 2021, *Conference* Aarhus (Denmark) / Hamburg (Germany) 2020, *Conference* Portland, OR (USA) 2019, *Conference* Edinburgh (UK) / St Andrews (UK) 2018. **Publications** *International Clematis Society Journal* (annual); *International Clematis Society Newsletter*. Articles.

Members Individuals and organizations in 26 countries and territories:
Australia, Austria, Belgium, Canada, China, Denmark, Estonia, Finland, France, Germany, Hong Kong, Ireland, Italy, Japan, Latvia, Netherlands, New Zealand, Norway, Poland, Russia, Sweden, Switzerland, Türkiye, UK, Ukraine, USA.

NGO Relations Affiliated with (1): Royal Horticultural Society, UK. [2022.10.18/XD6638/**D**]

♦ **International Climate Change Information Programme (ICCIP)** **12597**

Internationales Klimawandel-Informationsprogramm

Secretariat Research and Transfer Ctr "Applications of Life Sciences", Hamburg Univ of Applied Sciences, Fac of Life Sciences, Lohbrügger Kirchstr 65, 21033 Hamburg, Germany. T. +4940428756324. Fax +4940428756079. E-mail: info@iccip.net.
URL: http://www.iccip.net/

History Set up following the "Climate 2008" conference. **Aims** Disseminate the latest findings from scientific research on climate change; undertake education, communication and awareness-raising projects on matters related to climate change in both industrialized and developing countries in cooperation with UN agencies, universities, scientific institutions, government bodies, NGOs and other stakeholders; network with people and organizations to discuss problems, barriers, challenges and chances. **Activities** Advocacy/lobbying/activism; events/meetings. *World PhD Students Climate Change Network*. **Publications** *International Journal of Climate Change Strategies and Management*. Books.

Members Founding members universities. Members in 20 countries:
Australia, Bangladesh, Bolivia, Brazil, Canada, Chile, Denmark, Egypt, France, Germany, India, Italy, Kenya, Latvia, Senegal, South Africa, Sweden, Türkiye, UK, USA.
Included in the above, 2 organizations listed in this Yearbook:
International Research Centre on Environment and Development (CIRED); *The Baltic University Programme (BUP, #03155)*.

IGO Relations Cooperates with: *Caribbean Community Climate Change Centre (CCCCC, #03477)*; *European Commission (EC, #06633)*; *European Environment Agency (EEA, #06995)*; *European Space Agency (ESA, #08798)*; *FAO (#09260)*; *Global Environment Facility (GEF, #10346)*; *Observatoire du Sahara et du Sahel (OSS, #17636)*; *UNEP (#20299)*; *UNESCO (#20322)*; *World Meteorological Organization (WMO, #21649)*. **NGO Relations** Cooperates with: *International Centre for Integrated Mountain Development (ICIMOD, #12500)*. [2020/XJ4977/y/**F**]

♦ International Climate Change Partnership (internationally oriented national body)

♦ International Climate Development Institute (internationally oriented national body)

♦ International Climate Initiative (internationally oriented national body)

♦ **International Climate Science Coalition (ICSC)** **12598**

Exec Dir Suite 203, 900 Lady Ellen Pl, Ottawa ON K1Z 5L5, Canada. T. +16137289200.
URL: http://www.climatescienceinternational.org/

Aims Promote better public understanding of *climate change* science and policy worldwide. **Structure** Science Advisory Board; Policy Advisory Board. Administrative Group, comprising Executive Director, Secretary and 3 Directors. Chairman. **Events** *ICCC : international conference on climate change* Chicago, IL (USA) 2010, *ICCC : international conference on climate change* New York, NY (USA) 2009, *ICCC : international conference on climate change* New York, NY (USA) 2009, *ICCC : international conference on climate change* New York, NY (USA) 2008. [2020/XJ1331/**F**]

♦ International Clinical Cytometry Society (internationally oriented national body)

♦ International Clinical Epidemiology Network / see INCLEN Trust International (#11142)

♦ **International Clinical Epidemiology Network – Asia (INCLEN-ASIA)** . **12599**

Regional Coordinator Dept of Clinical Pathology, School of Medicine, Gadjah Mada University, Yogyakarta, Indonesia.
Admin Officer Dept of Clinical Epidemiology, College of Medicine, University of the Philippines – Rm 6, Dr Paz Mendoza Bldg, 547 Pedro Gil Street, Ermita, 1000 Manila, Philippines.
URL: http://inclentrust.org/inclen/inclenasia/

History Founded as *International Clinical Epidemiology Network – Southeast Asia (INCLEN-SEA)*. Previously referred to as *South East Asia Clinical Epidemiology Network (SEACLEN)*. Present name adopted, 2008. Regional network of: *INCLEN Trust International (#11142)*. **Aims** Improve quality of *health* in Southeast Asia through promotion of quality research, practice of evidence based *health care*, research capacity building and creation of strategic partnerships. **Structure** General Assembly (annual, during INCLEN-SEA Scientific Meeting). Board of Coordinators (meets annually) of maximum 11 members elected by the General Assembly, comprising 2 Founding Members from each founding country, 3 representatives from Regular membership and 2 representatives from Associate membership. Secretariat, headed by Coordinator. **Finance** Members' dues. **Activities** Promotes and supports advancement of health research; promotes and supports education and training in Clinical Epidemiology, Health Social Sciences, Health Economics, Biostatistics and related areas; cooperates with health professionals, health care providers, policy makers, institutions and organizations whose objectives complement those of INCLEN-SEA. Offers: Graduate Programmes in Clinical Epidemiology and Related Disciplines; Distance Learning Programme. Also offers training courses on: Research Methodology; Biostatistics; Clinical Trials; Good Clinical Practices; Data Management; Quality Improvement in Health Care; Clinical Economics; Evidence-Based Medicine; Research Management. Organizes Annual Scientific Meeting. **Events** *Meeting / Annual Scientific Meeting* Manila (Philippines) 2003, *Annual Scientific Meeting* Khon Kaen (Thailand) 2001, *Annual Scientific Meeting* Bangkok (Thailand) 2000, *Annual Scientific Meeting* Khon Kaen (Thailand) 1998, *Annual Scientific Meeting* Indonesia 1997. **Publications** *Guiding Lights for Antihypertensive Treatment in Patients with Nondiabetic Chronic Renal Disease: Proteinuria and Blood Pressure Levels* (2003) by Cynthia D Mulrow and Raymond R Townsen; *Progression of Chronic Kidney Disease: The Role of Blood Pressure Control, Proteinuria and Angiotensin-Converting Enzyme Inhibition: A Patient-Level Meta-Analysis* (2003) by Tazeen H Jafar et al.

Members Founding; Regular; Associate. Institutes and universities in 7 countries:
Australia, Indonesia, Malaysia, Pakistan, Philippines, Thailand, Vietnam. [2015/XF5909/**F**]

♦ International Clinical Epidemiology Network – Southeast Asia / see International Clinical Epidemiology Network – Asia (#12599)

♦ **International Clinical Hyperthermia Society (ICHS)** **12600**

Contact Belgische Allee 9, 53842 Troisdorf, Germany. T. +4922413199223. Fax +4922413199211. E-mail: info@ichs.eu.
USA Dr James I Bicher, Blvd 304, Los Angeles CA 90066, USA. T. +13103980013. E-mail: info@ichs-conference.org.
URL: http://www.ichs-conference.org/

History 1980, Indianapolis, IN (USA). **Aims** Provide a forum for members to discuss their ideas on the use of hyperthermia and present their clinical experience at meetings. **Structure** Board of Directors. **Languages** English, German. **Staff** 5.00 FTE, paid. **Finance** Members' dues. **Activities** Events/meetings. **Events** *Conference* 2021, *ICHS Conference* Troisdorf (Germany) 2020, *Conference* Thessaloniki (Greece) 2019, *Conference* Budapest (Hungary) 2018, *Annual Symposium* Mumbai (India) 2007. **Publications** *International Clinical Hyperthermia Society Newsletter*.

Members Individuals (active membership); associate membership. Members (mainly in USA) in 18 countries:
Australia, Canada, China, France, Germany, India, Iran Islamic Rep, Israel, Italy, Japan, Netherlands, Russia, Sweden, Switzerland, Taiwan, Türkiye, Ukraine, USA. [2020/XF1356/**F**]

♦ **International Clinical Phonetics and Linguistics Association (ICPLA)** **12601**

Sec/Treas University of Strathclyde, Speech and Language Therapy, Room GH676, Graham Hills Bldg, 40 George Street, Glasgow, G1 1QE, UK. T. +441415482700.
URL: http://www.icpla.info/

History Mar 1991, Cardiff (UK). **Aims** Stimulate the application of linguistics and phonetics to the study of disordered speech and language; facilitate interaction and communication between researchers and clinicians. **Structure** Officers: President; Vice-President; Secretary/Treasurer. **Languages** English. **Activities** Events/meetings. **Events** *Biennial Symposium* Salzburg (Austria) 2023, *Biennial Symposium* Glasgow (UK) 2021, *Biennial Symposium* St Julian's (Malta) 2018, *Biennial Symposium / Symposium* Stockholm (Sweden) 2014, *Biennial Symposium / Symposium* Cork (Ireland) 2012. **Publications** *Clinical Linguistics and Phonetics* (12 a year) – official journal.

Members Full in 19 countries and territories:
Australia, Belgium, Canada, Finland, France, Germany, Hong Kong, Hungary, Ireland, Israel, Italy, Japan, Netherlands, Norway, South Africa, Sweden, Türkiye, UK, USA. [2021/XD3777/**D**]

♦ International Club for Horse Races (inactive)

♦ International Club of Young Laparoscopic Surgeons (ICYLS) 12602

Pres 24 avenue Bouisson Bertrand, 34000 Montpellier, France. T. +33623761778. E-mail: david.nocca@sfr.fr.
URL: http://www.icyls.com/

History 2002, New York NY (USA). **Aims** Connect young surgeons who are interested in laparoscopic procedures worldwide. **Structure** Board, including Honorary President, President, Founder President, Vice-President, Past President and Treasurer. **Events** *Congress / Meeting* Porto Alegre (Brazil) 2014, *Meeting* Buenos Aires (Argentina) 2011, *Congrès International de Coelio-Chirurgie* Lyon (France) 2011, *Congrès international de coelio-chirurgie* Lyon (France) 2010, *Congress* New York, NY (USA) 2010. [2020/XJ2363/**C**]

♦ International Cluttering Association (ICA) 12603

Sec address not obtained. E-mail: icacluttering@gmail.com.
URL: https://sites.google.com/view/icacluttering

History May 2007, Bulgaria. Formed during 1st International Cluttering Conference. **Aims** Increase awareness and understanding of cluttering; improve treatment and quality of life for people who clutter. **Structure** Executive Committee. Committees (7): Consumer Issues; Family Issues; Clinical Issues; Research/Academic; Membership; Website & Communications; International Representatives. **Events** *Joint World Congress on Stuttering and Cluttering* Montréal, QC (Canada) 2022. **Publications** *The T.R.A.D.E.*. **NGO Relations** Cooperates with (2): *International Fluency Association (IFA, #13617)*; *International Stuttering Association (ISA, #15621)*. [2022/AA2599/**C**]

♦ International CML Foundation / see International Chronic Myeloid Leukemia Foundation (#12569)

♦ International Coach Federation (ICF) 12604

Exec Dir 2365 Harrodsburg Rd, Ste A325, Lexington KY 40504, USA. T. +18884233131. Fax +18592264411. E-mail: icfheadquarters@coachfederation.org.
URL: http://www.coachfederation.org/

History Founded 1992, USA, as "National Association of Professional Coaches". Current title adopted, 1995. **Aims** Advance the coaching profession by setting high standards, providing independent certification and building a worldwide network of credentialed coaches. **Structure** Global Board of Directors; Global Committees; Taskforces; Core Teams; Communities of Practice; Chapter Regulatory Liaisons Network; Local ICF Chapters; ICF Foundation. **Languages** English. **Staff** 35.00 FTE, paid. **Finance** Sources: members' dues. **Activities** Certification/accreditation. **Events** *Fitness Check or Environmental Monitoring Conference* Brussels (Belgium) 2016, *Regional Conference* Cleveland, OH (USA) 2014, *Regional Conference* Malmö (Sweden) 2014, *Regional Conference* Rio de Janeiro (Brazil) 2014, *Australasia Coaching Conference* Sydney, NSW (Australia) 2013. **Publications** *Coaching World* – digital magazine. *ICF Global Coaching Study* (2007, 2012, 2015). **Members** Individuals (over 24,000) in over 100 countries. Membership countries not specified. [2015.09.17/XN7455/v/**C**]

♦ International Coaching Community (internationally oriented national body)
♦ International Coach Tourism Federation (internationally oriented national body)
♦ International Coal Development Institute / see World Coal Association (#21280)
♦ International Coalition for Advocacy on Nutrition (unconfirmed)

♦ International Coalition against Enforced Disappearances (ICAED) . . 12605

Pres Chemin de Mont Rose 24, Genthod, 1294 Geneva, Switzerland. T. +41227742320. E-mail: icaed2020@gmail.com – fpicaed@gmail.com.
URL: http://www.icaed.org/

History 26 Sep 2007, Geneva (Switzerland). Launched during *United Nations Human Rights Council (HRC, #20571)* Session. **Aims** Establish a global network of organizations of families of disappeared and NGOs working in a non-violent manner against the practice of enforced disappearances at local, national and international levels. **Structure** Steering Committee. **Languages** English, French, Spanish. **Activities** Advocacy/lobbying/activism.

Members Organizations (54). National organizations in 22 countries:
Algeria, Argentina, Bangladesh, Belarus, Cyprus, Ecuador, El Salvador, Georgia, Guatemala, Iraq, Morocco, Namibia, Nepal, Nigeria, Peru, Philippines, Russia, South Africa, Spain, Sri Lanka, Switzerland, Zimbabwe.
International organizations include the following 12 listed in this Yearbook:
Amnesty International (AI, #00801); *Asian Federation Against Involuntary Disappearances (AFAD, #01453)*; *Asociación de Familiares de Presos y Desaparecidos Saharauis (AFAPREDESA, no recent information)*; *Brot für die Welt*; *Federación Latinoamericana de Asociaciones de Familiares de Detenidos-Desaparecidos (FEDEFAM, #09344)*; *Fédération Euro-Méditerranéenne contre les Disparitions Forcées (FEMED, #09487)*; *Human Rights Watch (HRW, #10990)*; *International Commission of Jurists (ICJ, #12695)*; *International Federation for Human Rights (#13452)*; *International Federation of ACATs – Action by Christians for the Abolition of Torture (#13334)*; *Nonviolence International (NI, #17152)*; *TRIAL International*.
IGO Relations *International Convention for the Protection of all Persons from Enforced Disappearance (2006)*. [2022.02.15/XM4210/y/**E**]

♦ International Coalition for Aging and Physical Activity (ICAPA) 12606

Contact c/o HKUSA AACC, PO Box 5076, Champaign IL 61825-5076, USA.
URL: http://journals.humankinetics.com/japa

History as *International Society for Aging and Physical Activity (ISAPA)*. **Aims** Promote physical activity, exercise science and fitness in the health and well-being of older persons; promote international initiatives in research, clinical practice and public policy in the area of aging and physical activity. **Structure** General Assembly (every 4 years). Executive Committee, comprising 13 voting and 12 non-voting members, including and Programme on Aging and Health of *WHO (#20950)*. Officers: President; President-Elect; Secretary-Treasurer. **Activities** Committees (5): Membership; Nominating; Publication; Scientific; World Congress Liaison. **Events** *Quadrennial World Congress* Melbourne, VIC (Australia) 2016, *Quadrennial World Congress* Glasgow (UK) 2012, *Quadrennial World Congress* Tsukuba (Japan) 2008, *Quadrennial World Congress* London, ON (Canada) 2004, *Quadrennial World Congress* Orlando, FL (USA) 1999. **Publications** *Journal of Aging and Physical Activity* (4 a year); *ISAPA Newsletter* (2 a year). **Members** Membership countries not specified. **IGO Relations** *United Nations Programme on Ageing (inactive)*. [2015/XD9251/**D**]

♦ International Coalition for Agunah Rights (internationally oriented national body)

♦ International Coalition for Animal Welfare (ICFAW) 12607

Sec c/o World Animal Protection, 5th Floor, 222 Grays Inn Road, London, WC1X 8HB, UK. T. +442072390572. Fax +442072390653.
URL: http://icfaw.org/

History 2002. Former names and other names: *International Coalition for Farm Animal Welfare* – former. **Aims** Represent animal welfare organizations at World Organisation for Animal Health. **Structure** Loose coalition of international animal welfare organizations; not a formal or legal coalition. **Languages** English. **Staff** None. **Finance** None.

Members National organizations (6) in 6 countries:
Australia, Belgium, Japan, South Africa, UK, USA.
International organizations (9), listed in this Yearbook:
Coalition of African Animal Welfare Organisations (CAAWO); *Compassion in World Farming (CIWF, #04414)*; *Donkey Sanctuary, The (#05120)*; *Eurogroup for Animals (#05690)*; *Humane Society International (HSI, #10966)*; *International Fund for Animal Welfare (IFAW, #13693)*; *Vier Pfoten International (#20776)*; *World Animal Protection (#21092)*; *World Horse Welfare*.
IGO Relations *OIE – World Organisation for Animal Health (#17703)*. [2020/XJ3554/y/**F**]

♦ International Coalition of Art Deco Societies (ICADS) 12608

Pres address not obtained.
URL: http://www.icads.info/

History 1990, as (US) National Coalition of Art Deco Societies. **Aims** Promote preservation and education of Art Deco. **Events** *World Congress* Buenos Aires (Argentina) 2019, *World Congress* Cleveland, OH (USA) 2017, *World Congress* Shanghai (China) 2015, *World Congress* Havana (Cuba) 2013, *World congress* Rio de Janeiro (Brazil) 2011. [2016.06.01/XM3553/**F**]

♦ International Coalition to Ban Uranium Weapons (ICBUW) 12609

ICBUW spokesperson Marienstrasse 19-20, 10117 Berlin, Germany. T. +493020654857. E-mail: info@icbuw.eu.
ICBUW spokesperson (Belgium) address not obtained.
Coordinator address not obtained.
URL: http://www.icbuw.eu/

History 13 Oct 2003, Berlaar (Belgium). Subsequently based in Manchester (UK); Berlin (Germany). **Aims** Coordinate campaign to ban DU ammunition worldwide within the framework of the United Nations; eliminate the environmental damage caused by uranium weapons use, help the victims, and prevent future damage from such weapons and actions; seek to bring peace, human rights and environmental movements closer together on the uranium weapons issue. **Structure** Steering Committee; Rotating Chair. **Languages** English, German. **Staff** 1.00 FTE, paid. **Finance** Sources: donations. **Activities** Advocacy/lobbying/activism; events/meetings; guidance/assistance/consulting; knowledge management/information dissemination; networking/liaising. Active in: Belgium, Germany, Japan, Netherlands, UK, USA. **Publications** *Laid to Waste: Depleted Uranium Contaminated Military Scrap in Iraq* (2014); *In a State of Uncertainty: Impact and Implications of the Use of Depleted Uranium in Iraq* (2013); *Critique of the European Commission's SCHER Risk Assessment on Depleted Uranium* (2012); *Hazard Aware: Lessons Learned from Military Field Manuals on Depleted Uranium and How to Move Forward for Civilian Protection Norms* (2012); *Managing Acceptability: UK Policy on Depleted Uranium* (2012); *Overstating the Case: an Analysis of the Utility of Depleted Uranium in Kinetic Energy Penetrators* (2012); *Precaution in Practice – Challenging the Acceptability of Depleted Uranium Weapons* (2012); *A Question of Responsibility – the Legacy of Depleted Uranium Use in the Balkans* (2010). *IPPNW-Report "The health effects of uranium weapons: The social debate on the use of a controversial weapon"* in English.

Members Founding partners (14) in 6 countries:
Belgium, Germany, Japan, Netherlands, UK, USA.
Organizations/Groups (160) in 33 countries and territories:
Australia, Austria, Bahrain, Belgium, Bosnia-Herzegovina, Canada, Costa Rica, Finland, France, Germany, Greece, Iceland, India, Iran Islamic Rep, Iraq, Ireland, Italy, Japan, Korea Rep, Kosovo, Netherlands, New Zealand, Norway, Pakistan, Puerto Rico, Romania, Serbia, Sweden, Switzerland, Syrian AR, UK, Ukraine, USA.
Included in the above, 12 organizations listed in this Yearbook:
Bertrand Russell Peace Foundation (BRPF, #03213); *Coalition for a Strong United Nations (CSUN)*; *Global Network Against Weapons and Nuclear Power in Space*; *Indian Institute for Peace, Disarmament and Environmental Protection (IIPDEP)*; *International Action for Liberation (INTAL)*; *International Peace Bureau (IPB, #14535)*; *Islamic Foundation for Ecology and Environmental Sciences (IFEES)*; *Medact*; *Pax Christi – International Catholic Peace Movement (#18266)*; *Project Ploughshares*; *Scientists for Global Responsibility (SGR)*; *Women's International League for Peace and Freedom (WILPF, #21024)*.
Consultative Status Consultative status granted from: *ECOSOC (#05331)* (Special). **IGO Relations** Cooperates with (2): *European Parliament (EP, #08146)*; *United Nations (UN, #20515)*. **NGO Relations** Member of (1): *International Campaign to Ban Landmines – Cluster Munition Coalition (ICBL-CMC, #12427)*. Partner of (1): *International Campaign to Abolish Nuclear Weapons (ICAN, #12426)*. [2023.02.14/XM3150/y/**F**]

♦ International Coalition of Cities against Racism 12610

Contact UNESCO Social and Human Sciences Sector, UNESCO, 1 rue Miollis, 75732 Paris CEDEX 15, France. Fax +33145685724. E-mail: l.tinio@unesco.org.
URL: http://www.unesco.org/shs/citiesagainstracism/

History Mar 2004, Nürburg (Germany). Mar 2004, Nuremberg (Germany), by *UNESCO (#20322)*. **Aims** Set up a network of cities interested in sharing experiences so as to improve their policies to fight racism, discrimination, xenophobia and exclusion. **Activities** So as to take into account the specificities and priorities of each region, created regional coalitions: *African Coalition of Cities against Racism and Discrimination*, launched Sep 2006, Nairobi (Kenya); Arab coalition, launched 25 Jun 2008; Casablanca (Morocco); *Coalition of Cities against Discrimination in Asia and the Pacific*, launched Oct 2007, Jeju (Korea Rep); *European Coalition of Cities Against Racism (see: #12610)*, launched Dec 2004, Nuremberg (Germany); *Coalition of Latin American and Caribbean Cities against Racism*, launched Oct 2006, Montevideo (Uruguay); Canadian Coalition of Municipalities against Racism and Discrimination (CMARD) – for North America, in the process of creation. **Events** *Conference* Bandung (Indonesia) 2009, *Meeting* Bandung (Indonesia) 2009, *Sub-regional conference* Durban (South Africa) 2009, *Working meeting* Nürburg (Germany) 2009, *Annual general conference* Sao Paulo (Brazil) 2008. [2014.10.30/XM1797/**F**]

♦ International Coalition to Combat Anti-Semitism / see Inter-parliamentary Coalition for Combating Antisemitism (#15960)
♦ International Coalition for the Decade for the Promotion of a Culture of Peace and Non-violence for the Children of the World / see International Network for a Culture of Nonviolence and Peace (#14247)

♦ International Coalition to Eliminate HBV (ICE-HBV) 12611

Contact address not obtained. E-mail: info@ice-hbv.org.
URL: https://ice-hbv.org/

Aims Fast track the discovery of a safe, effective, affordable and scalable cure to benefit all people living with CHB, including children and people living with HCV, HDV and HIV co-infection. **Structure** Governing Board. **Activities** Events/meetings; networking/liaising; research and development; training/education. [2023/AA3280/**B**]

♦ International Coalition to End Torture (ICET) 12612

Exec Dir Rue du Mont-Blanc 14, 1201 Geneva, Switzerland. E-mail: info@endtorture.org.
URL: http://endtorture.org/

History 2003. Founded as a programme by *Amnesty International (AI, #00801)*. Programme set up in Teheran (Iran Islamic Rep), 2005, with offices set up in New York NY (USA) after that. **Aims** Promote the United Nations Convention against Torture and Other Cruel, Inhuman or Degrading Treatment or Punishment and thus raise human rights awareness around the world by knowing them, demanding them and defending them. **Structure** International Council; International Executive Committee. **Languages** Arabic, Azerbaijani, English, French, German, Persian, Turkish. **Staff** 48.00 FTE, paid; 230.00 FTE, voluntary. **Finance** Primarily through donations. **Activities** Training/education; guidance/assistance/consulting; advocacy/lobbying/activism; capacity building; publishing activities; knowledge management/information dissemination. **Publications** *Breaking News*; *Weekly News*. Press releases.

Members Full in 3 countries:
Iran Islamic Rep, Türkiye, USA.
IGO Relations *UNESCO (#20322)*; *United Nations Human Rights Council (HRC, #20571)*. **NGO Relations** *Association for the Prevention of Torture (APT, #02869)*; *Human Rights Watch (HRW, #10990)*; *World Organisation Against Torture (OMCT, #21685)*. [2020/XJ5891/**E**]

♦ International Coalition for Energy Storage and Innovation (ICESI) . . 12613

Contact address not obtained. E-mail: icesi2020@raci.org.au.
URL: https://www.icesi2020.com/

History 2018. **Aims** Establish an international forum to connect and industry in the world to address the long term scientific and technological challenges for the development and deployment of scalable energy storage technologies for electric grid and emerging market applications; serve as the authority, spokesperson and advocator for supporting energy storage research. **Structure** Working Committee. **Activities** Events/meetings. **Events** *Annual Conference* Sydney, NSW (Australia) 2020, *Annual Conference* Waikoloa, HI (USA) 2019, *Annual Conference* Dalian (China) 2018. [2020/AA1735/c/**E**]

♦ International Coalition for Farm Animal Welfare / see International Coalition for Animal Welfare (#12607)

♦ International Coalition of Fisheries Associations (ICFA) 12614

Sec PO Box 1544, McLean VA 22102, USA. T. +17037528892. E-mail: icfa@fishcoalition.org.
URL: https://aboutseafood.com/international-coalition-of-fisheries-associations-3/

History 1988. Registration: USA. **Aims** Preserve and maintain the *oceans* as a major *food source* for people worldwide. **Events** *Annual meeting* St John's, NL (Canada) 1997, *International conference on fish inspection and quality control* Washington, DC (USA) 1996.

Members National associations in 17 countries and territories:
Australia, Canada, Chile, China, Denmark, France, Iceland, Ireland, Japan, Morocco, Netherlands, New Zealand, Norway, Peru, Taiwan, UK, USA.
NGO Relations Participates in: *Global Partnership for Oceans (GPO, #10537)*. Member of: *High Level Panel for a Sustainable Ocean Economy (Panel, #10917)* – Advisory Network. [2022.05.04/XF0786/**F**]

♦ International Coalition for Genital Integrity (unconfirmed)
♦ International Coalition of Historic Site Museums of Conscience / see International Coalition of Sites of Conscience (#12621)
♦ International Coalition for Human Rights in the Philippines (unconfirmed)
♦ International Coalition for Jewish Prisoner Services / see Jewish Prisoner Services International

♦ International Coalition of Library Consortia (ICOLC) 12615

Recorder LYRASIS, 1438 W Peachtree St NW, Ste 150, Atlanta GA 30309, USA.
URL: http://icolc.net/

History Founded 1997, as *Consortium of Consortia (COC)*, as a voluntary organization of consortial leaders and directors. **Aims** Provide: information on *licensing* of *electronic* resources to academic libraries; a forum for exchange of ideas and information and discussion on topics related to activities of library consortia. **Structure** Informal structure. **Languages** English. **Staff** Voluntary. **Finance** None. **Activities** Events/meetings. **Events** *European Meeting* London (UK) 2018, *European Meeting* Amsterdam (Netherlands) 2016, *European Meeting* Oslo (Norway) 2015, *European Meeting* Lisbon (Portugal) 2014, *Annual Meeting* Toronto, ON (Canada) 2013. **Publications** Statements.
Members Organizations, libraries and universities in 66 countries and territories. Membership countries not specified. Included in the above, 4 organizations listed in this Yearbook:
Included in the above, 4 organizations listed in this Yearbook:
American International Consortium of Academic Libraries (AMICAL, #00783); Association of European Research Libraries (#02540); Commonwealth Scientific and Industrial Research Organization (CSIRO); Electronic Information for Libraries (EIFL, #05425). [2018.09.28/XF5570/y/**F**]

♦ International Coalition of Medicines Regulatory Authorities (ICMRA) 12616

Secretariat address not obtained. E-mail: icmracoordination@ema.europa.eu.
URL: https://icmra.info/

History Proposed May 2012, and further developed at meetings Oct and Dec 2012. **Aims** Safeguard public health by facilitating strategic leadership and greater cooperation of international medicines authorities on shared regulatory issues and challenges. **Structure** Plenary; Executive Committee; Secretariat. **Activities** Capacity building; events/meetings; healthcare; knowledge management/information dissemination. **Events** *Summit* Brazil 2021.
Members Medicines regulatory authorities of 21 countries:
Australia, Brazil, Canada, China, France, Germany, India, Ireland, Italy, Japan, Korea Rep, Mexico, Netherlands, New Zealand, Nigeria, Singapore, South Africa, Sweden, Switzerland, UK, USA.
European Medicines Agency (EMA, #07767); European Union (EU, #08967) (DG Health and Food Safety – DG SANTE).
Associate in 15 countries:
Argentina, Austria, Colombia, Cuba, Denmark, Egypt, Ghana, Iceland, Israel, Poland, Portugal, Russia, Saudi Arabia, Spain, Ukraine.
Observer (1):
WHO (#20950).
IGO Relations Partner of (2): *Asia-Pacific Economic Cooperation (APEC, #01887); International Medical Device Regulators Forum (IMDRF, #14132).* **NGO Relations** Partner of (3): *International Council on Harmonisation of Technical Requirements for Registration of Pharmaceuticals for Human Use (ICH, #13027); International Pharmaceutical Regulators Programme (IPRP, #14567); Pharmaceutical Inspection Co-operation Scheme (PIC/S, #18353).* [2022/AA2860/y/**C**]

♦ International Coalition for the Optional Protocol to the Convention on the Rights of the Child on a Communications Procedure (Ratify OP3CRC) 12617

Secretariat address not obtained. E-mail: info@ratifyop3.org.
URL: http://www.ratifyop3crc.org/

History Replaced NGO Working Group that coordinated the international campaign for the drafting and adoption of the OP3CRC, under Child Rights Connect (then the NGO Group for the CRC), based in Geneva (Switzerland). **Aims** As a coalition of international, regional and national non-governmental organizations and networks, human rights institutions and other non-governmental bodies, achieve rapid ratification and entry into force of the OPCRC on a Communications Procedure (OP3CRC); raise awareness about the OP3CRC; disseminate information, tools and ideas to enable interested partners to engage in the ratification campaign. **Structure** Steering Committee of 10 organizations and headed by 2 Co-Chairs. **Languages** English, French, Spanish. **Publications** *Advocacy Toolkit* in English, French, Spanish; *Answers to Key Questions About the Optional Protocol* in Arabic, English, French, Russian, Spanish; *Rules of Procedure* in English; *Text of the Optional Protocol* in Arabic, Chinese, English, French, Russian, Spanish.
Members Organizations (78). National organizations in 36 countries and territories:
Angola, Argentina, Austria, Belgium, Bolivia, Bosnia-Herzegovina, Burkina Faso, Chile, Costa Rica, Croatia, Denmark, Egypt, Greece, Guatemala, Guinea, Honduras, Ireland, Italy, Kenya, Kuwait, Lebanon, Mexico, Moldova, Netherlands, Palestine, Peru, Qatar, Serbia, Slovenia, Spain, Switzerland, Türkiye, UK, Uruguay, Yemen, Zimbabwe.
Regional/International include 16 organizations listed in this Yearbook:
African Child Policy Forum (ACPF, #00246); Child Rights Connect (#03884); Child Rights International Network (CRIN, #03885); Defence for Children International (DCI, #05025); End Child Prostitution, Child Pornography and Trafficking of Children for Sexual Purposes (ECPAT, #05456); End Corporal Punishment (#05457); Help for Children in Need (KNH); International Foster Care Organization (IFCO, #13663); International Juvenile Justice Observatory (IJJO); International Movement ATD Fourth World (#14193); International Planned Parenthood Federation (IPPF, #14589); Plan International (#18386); Red Latinoamericana y Caribeña por la Defensa de los Derechos de los Niños, Niñas y Adolescentes (REDLAMYC, #18705); Save the Children Federation (SCF); Terre des Hommes International Federation (TDHIF, #20133); World Vision International (WVI, #21904). [2015.08.06/XJ7694/y/**E**]

♦ International Coalition for Organizations Supporting Endocrine Patients (ICOSEP) 12618

Contact 4200 Cantera Dr, Ste 106, Warrenville IL 60555, USA. E-mail: contactus@icosep.org.
URL: http://www.icosep.org/

History Started Sep 2012, as the international division of The MAGIC Foundation (USA). **Aims** Enhance early identification of children with any type of *medical* condition impacting their physical growth; coordinate a public education with all charitable organizations and medical societies to unite and share the message that growth is a medical symptom and not a cosmetic issue. **Structure** Advisory Board; Ambassadors Board; Medical Advisors. **Languages** English. **Staff** 2.00 FTE, paid. **Finance** Funded by The MAGIC Foundation. **Activities** Events/meetings; knowledge management/information dissemination; awareness raising. **Publications** *ICOSEP Newsletter*. Weekly email. [2019.12.12/XM7440/**E**]

♦ International Coalition for Religious Freedom (ICRF) 12619

Exec Dir 3600 New York Avenue NE, Third Floor, Washington DC 20002, USA. T. +12025585462.

History Founded within the framework of *Holy Spirit Association for the Unification of World Christianity (HSA-UWC)*, deriving from the US national *Coalition for Religious Freedom* set up in 1983. **Aims** Promote the vision of religious freedom found in Article 18 of the Universal Declaration of Human Rights, that everyone regardless of creed, gender or ethnic origin, has the right to freedom of thought, conscience and religion, including freedom to change his religion or belief and, alone or in community with others, in public or private, to manifest his religion or belief in teaching, practice, worship and observance as his conscience leads – balanced against the requirements of generally applicable criminal law. **Finance** Funding from institutions and individuals related to the Unification Church community. **Activities** Organizes international conferences of religious leaders, scholars, human rights leaders and government officials from a wide variety of religious faiths. [2013/XF4618/**F**]

♦ International Coalition for the Responsibility to Protect (ICRtoP) . . . 12620

Contact c/o Global Centre for the Responsibility to Protect, Ralph Bunche Inst for Intl Studies, 365 Fifth Ave, Suite 5203, New York NY 10016, USA. T. +12128171929. E-mail: jpittalwala@globalr2p.org – info@globalr2p.org.
URL: https://www.globalr2p.org/international-coalition-for-the-responsibility-to-protect/

History 28 Jan 2009. Founded by representatives of: *International Refugee Rights Initiative (IRRI, #14708); West Africa Civil Society Institute (WACSI); Oxfam International (#17922); World Federalist Movement – Movement for a Just World Order through a Strengthened United Nations (WFM, #21404); Initiatives for International Dialogue; Human Rights Watch (HRW, #10990); East Africa Law Society (EALS, #05173); Coordinadora Regional de Investigaciones Económicas y Sociales (CRIES, #04812).* Founding follows the work of WFM's Responsibility to Protect-Engaging Civil Society (R2PCS), initiated in 2003. **Aims** Unite NGOs from all world regions to strengthen consensus for responsibility to protect (RtoP), further understanding of the norm, push for strengthened capacities to prevent and halt genocide, war crimes, ethnic cleansing and crimes against humanity; mobilize NGOs to push for action to save lives in RtoP country-specific situations. **Structure** Steering Committee; Secretariat, based at *Global Centre for the Responsibility to Protect (GCR2P, #10277).* **Languages** English, French, Spanish. **Staff** 3.50 FTE, paid; 3.00 FTE, voluntary. **Finance** Support from: governments of Australia, Netherlands, Sweden, UK; *MacArthur Foundation*; Oak Foundation; Arsenault Family Foundation; individual donations. **Activities** Capacity building; events/meetings; publishing activities. **Publications** Listserv; reports; educational tools.
Members National and international organizations (over 90) in 40 countries and including 41 organizations listed in this Yearbook:
Argentina, Australia, Belgium, Brazil, Burundi, Canada, Colombia, Congo DR, Costa Rica, Denmark, Georgia, Germany, Ghana, Greece, Guatemala, Hungary, Indonesia, Iraq, Kenya, Lebanon, Liberia, Mali, Nepal, Netherlands, Nigeria, Paraguay, Philippines, Portugal, Serbia, Sierra Leone, South Africa, Spain, Sudan, Sweden, Switzerland, Syrian AR, Tanzania UR, Thailand, Trinidad-Tobago, USA.
- *Act for Peace;*
- *AEGIS Trust;*
- *African Centre for Justice and Peace Studies (ACJPS);*
- *African Women's Development and Communication Network (FEMNET, #00503);*
- *Asia-Pacific Centre for the Responsibility to Protect (#01868);*
- *Auschwitz Institute for the Prevention of Genocide and Mass Atrocities;*
- *Budapest Centre for the International Prevention of Genocide and Mass Atrocities;*
- *Canadian Lawyers for International Human Rights (CLAIHR);*
- *Center for Euro-Atlantic Studies (CEAS);*
- *Citizens for Global Solutions;*
- *Coordinadora Regional de Investigaciones Económicas y Sociales (CRIES, #04812);*
- *Cyrus R Vance Center for International Justice (Vance Center);*
- *East Africa Law Society (EALS, #05173);*
- *Euro-Mediterranean Human Rights Monitor (Euro-Med Monitor, #05721);*
- *Genocide Alert;*
- *Genocide Watch;*
- *Global Centre for the Responsibility to Protect (GCR2P, #10277);*
- *Human Rights Watch (HRW, #10990);*
- *Initiatives for International Dialogue;*
- *International Centre on Conflict and Negotiation (ICCN);*
- *International Crisis Group (Crisis Group, #13111);*
- *International Justice Project (IJP);*
- *International Refugee Rights Initiative (IRRI, #14708);*
- *International Relations and Peace Research Institute (IRIPAZ);*
- *Kofi Annan International Peacekeeping Training Centre (KAIPTC);*
- *Minority Rights Group International (MRG, #16820);*
- *Montreal Institute for Genocide and Human Rights Studies (MIGS);*
- *NATO Watch (#16949);*
- *Oxfam International (#17922);*
- *Pan-African Lawyers Union (PALU, #18054);*
- *PAX;*
- *Permanent Peace Movement (PPM);*
- *The Hague Institute for Global Justice (The Hague Institute);*
- *United to End Genocide;*
- *Vision GRAM-International;*
- *West Africa Civil Society Forum (WACSOF, #20864);*
- *West Africa Civil Society Institute (WACSI);*
- *West Africa Network for Peacebuilding (WANEP, #20878);*
- *Women's Refugee Commission (WRC);*
- *World Federalist Movement – Movement for a Just World Order through a Strengthened United Nations (WFM, #21404)* (Institute for Global Policy);
- *World Federation of United Nations Associations (WFUNA, #21499).*

IGO Relations Partner of (1): *United Nations Office on Genocide Prevention and the Responsibility to Protect (#20598).* **NGO Relations** Member of (1): *Global Action Against Mass Atrocity Crimes (GAAMAC, #10164).* Founded by: *World Federalist Movement – Movement for a Just World Order through a Strengthened United Nations (WFM, #21404).* [2021/XJ8127/y/**E**]

♦ International Coalition of Sites of Conscience (ICSC) 12621

Coalition Internationale des Sites de Conscience – Coalición Internacional de Sitios de Conciencia – Coalizão Internacional de Sites de Consciência

Exec Dir 55 Exchange Place, Suite 404, New York NY 10005, USA. E-mail: coalition@sitesofconscience.org.
URL: http://www.sitesofconscience.org/

History 1999. Former names and other names: *International Coalition of Historic Site Museums of Conscience* – former. Registration: 501c(3), USA. **Aims** Connect past struggles to today's movements for human rights. **Structure** Board of Trustees; Ambassador's Circle. **Activities** Projects/programmes. Projects and programmes include: *Global Initiative for Justice, Truth and Reconciliation (GIJTR).* **Publications** *Building a Learning Community: Lessons for a Holistic and Sustainable Approach to Transitional Justice; Pathways of Innovation: Civil Society Advancing Transitional Justice.*
Members Over 300 members in 55 countries and territories:
Afghanistan, Algeria, Argentina, Australia, Austria, Bahrain, Bangladesh, Belgium, Bosnia-Herzegovina, Brazil, Cambodia, Canada, Chile, Colombia, Croatia, Czechia, Dominican Rep, Egypt, El Salvador, France, Guatemala, Italy, Japan, Kenya, Korea Rep, Kosovo, Lebanon, Liberia, Mexico, Morocco, Norway, Paraguay, Peru, Philippines, Poland, Portugal, Puerto Rico, Russia, Rwanda, Senegal, Sierra Leone, South Africa, Spain, Sri Lanka, Sweden, Syrian AR, Tanzania UR, Thailand, Tunisia, Türkiye, Uganda, UK, Uruguay, USA, Yemen.
Consultative Status Consultative status granted from: *ECOSOC (#05331)* (Special). [2022.11.29/XJ9920/y/**B**]

♦ International Coalition to Stop Crimes Against Humanity in North Korea (ICNK) 12622

Contact Human Rights Watch, 350 Fifth Avenue, 34th Floor, New York NY 10118-3299, USA. E-mail: kekyoung@gmail.com.
URL: http://www.stopnkcrimes.org/

History 8 Sep 2011, by *Amnesty International (AI, #00801), Human Rights Watch (HRW, #10990)* and *International Federation for Human Rights (#13452).* **Aims** Establish a UN Commission of Inquiry to investigate crimes against humanity in North Korea; raise public understanding and awareness of the human rights situation in North Korea. **Events** *International Conference on Advancing the Human Rights Movement and Adapting to Change in North Korea* Seoul (Korea Rep) 2018, *International Conference on Rights to Information in North Korea* Seoul (Korea Rep) 2016, *Inaugural Conference* Tokyo (Japan) 2011.
Members Participants include:
Advocates International; Amnesty International (AI, #00801); Asian Federation Against Involuntary Disappearances (AFAD, #01453); Conectas Human Rights; CSW; Freedom House; Human Rights Watch (HRW, #10990); Human Rights without Frontiers International (HRWF, #10983); International Federation for Human Rights (#13452); Simon Wiesenthal Center (SWC). [2014/XJ5501/y/**E**]

♦ International Coalition for Sustainable Aviation (ICSA) 12623

Contact c/o T and E, 2nd floor, Square de Meeus 18, 1050 Brussels, Belgium. T. +3228510221.
URL: http://www.icsa-aviation.org/

History 1998. **Aims** Campaign on sustainable transport at EU level. **IGO Relations** Observer Status with: *International Civil Aviation Organization (ICAO, #12581).* **NGO Relations** Coordinated by: *European Federation for Transport and Environment (T and E, #07230).* Cooperates with: *Carbon Market Watch (#03423); Environmental Defense Fund (EDF); International Council on Clean Transportation (ICCT, #13007); World Wide Fund for Nature (WWF, #21922).* [2018/XM1922/F]

♦ International Coalition for Trachoma Control (ICTC) 12624

Vice Chair The Carter Center, 453 John Lewis Freedom Pkwy NE, Atlanta GA 30307, USA. E-mail: info@cartercenter.org.
URL: http://www.trachomacoalition.org/

History 2004. **Aims** Contribute to the global effort to eliminate *blinding* trachoma; advocate and implement the SAFE strategy, endorsed by the World Health Organization (WHO). **Structure** Executive Group, comprising Chair, Vice Chair and Past Chair.
Members Organizations (25), including the following listed in this Yearbook (18):
Amref Health Africa (#00806); Christian Blind Mission (CBM); Eyes of the World Foundation; Fred Hollows Foundation; Helen Keller International (HKI, #10902); IMA World Health (IMA); International Agency for the Prevention of Blindness (IAPB, #11597); International Trachoma Initiative (ITI, #15701); Light for the World (#16474); Lions Clubs International (LCI, #16485); London School of Hygiene and Tropical Medicine (LSHTM); Operation Eyesight Universal; ORBIS International (#17786); Organisation pour la prévention de la cécité (OPC); Sightsavers International (#19270); The Carter Center; WaterAid (#20822).
Observers include the following 5 organizations listed in this Yearbook:
Bill and Melinda Gates Foundation (BMGF); Conrad N Hilton Foundation (CNHF); International Centre for Eye Health (ICEH); United States Agency for International Development (USAID). [2019/XJ5216/y/C]

♦ International Coal Testing Conference (meeting series)

♦ International Coastal and Ocean Organization (ICO) 12625

Head of Secretariat c/o Gerard J Mangone Center for Marine Policy, Univ of Delaware, Newark DE 19716, USA. T. +13028318086. Fax +13028318086. E-mail: bcs@udel.edu.
URL: https://globaloceanforum.com/contact-us/

History Jul 1989, Charleston, SC (USA). Incorporated in the State of Massachusetts (USA). Registration: No/ID: 501(c)(3), USA. **Aims** Link professional planners, policy specialists, managers, institutions, and organizations around the world concerned with the management, protection, and development of coastal and ocean resources and space. **Structure** Board of Directors (meets once a year) of 12 members; International Advisory Committee, comprising marine management professionals. Committees (3): Publications, Programs and Events; Exchange of Technical Data and Information; Marine Conservation and Protected Areas. **Finance** Sources: fees for services; grants; private foundations. The University of Massachusetts at Boston MA (USA) contributes to the support of the Organization. Annual budget: 200,000 USD. **Activities** Events/meetings; guidance/assistance/consulting; publishing activities. **Events** *Global Oceans Conference* Hanoi (Vietnam) 2008, *Global Oceans Conference* Paris (France) 2006, *Global Oceans Conference* Paris (France) 2003, *Global conference on oceans and coasts at Rio+10* Paris (France) 2001, *EMECS conference* Baltimore, MD (USA) 1993. **Publications** *ICO Report* (4 a year).
Members Individuals; institutions and corporations. Members in 73 countries and territories:
Argentina, Australia, Bahamas, Bangladesh, Barbados, Belgium, Belize, Brazil, Brunei Darussalam, Bulgaria, Canada, Chile, China, Colombia, Costa Rica, Côte d'Ivoire, Croatia, Denmark, Ecuador, Egypt, Fiji, Finland, France, Georgia, Germany, Greece, Honduras, Hong Kong, India, Indonesia, Israel, Italy, Jamaica, Japan, Jordan, Kenya, Kuwait, Latvia, Malaysia, Maldives, Mexico, Netherlands, New Zealand, Nigeria, Norway, Oman, Pakistan, Panama, Papua New Guinea, Peru, Philippines, Poland, Portugal, Puerto Rico, Romania, Russia, Saudi Arabia, Serbia, Singapore, South Africa, Spain, Sri Lanka, Sweden, Taiwan, Tanzania UR, Thailand, Türkiye, UK, Ukraine, Uruguay, USA, Venezuela.
Consultative Status Consultative status granted from: *ECOSOC (#05331)* (Special). **NGO Relations** Provides Secretariat for: *Global Forum on Oceans, Coasts and Islands (GOF, #10377). European Coastal Association For Science And Technology (Federation EUROCOAST, no recent information).* [2020.06.22/XD2895/D]

♦ International Cocoa Agreement, 1972 (1972 treaty)
♦ International Cocoa Agreement, 1975 (1975 treaty)
♦ International Cocoa Agreement, 1980 (1980 treaty)
♦ International Cocoa Agreement, 1986 (1986 treaty)
♦ International Cocoa Agreement, 1993 (1993 treaty)
♦ International Cocoa Agreement, 2001 (2001 treaty)
♦ International Cocoa Agreement, 2010 (2010 treaty)

♦ International Cocoa Initiative (ICI) 12626

Exec Dir Chemin de Balexert 9, 1219 Geneva, Switzerland. T. +41223414725. Fax +41223414726. E-mail: info@cocoainitiative.org.
URL: http://www.cocoainitiative.org/

History 1 Jul 2002, Geneva (Switzerland). Founded following signing of agreement, known as *'Harkin-Engel Protocol'*, by chocolate and cocoa industry representatives. Registration: Swiss Civil Code, Switzerland; EU Transparency Register, No/ID: 554053241397-60, Start date: 15 Feb 2021. **Aims** Work to ensure a better future for children in cocoa-growing communities; advance elimination of child labour and forced labour by uniting the forces of the cocoa and chocolate industry, civil society, farming communities, governments, international organizations and donors. **Structure** Board; Executive Secretariat, in Geneva (Switzerland); National Offices in Abidjan (Côte d'Ivoire) and Accra (Ghana). **Languages** English, French. **Staff** 148.00 FTE, paid. **Finance** Sources: contributions. Contributions from Industry and Civil Society Members. Annual budget: 9,948,284 CHF (2020). **Activities** Capacity building; networking/liaising; politics/policy/regulatory; research and development.
Members Civil society board members (6):
Free the Slaves; General Agricultural Workers' Union of Ghana (GAWU); *Global March Against Child Labour (#10463); Jacobs Foundation (JF, #16084); Rainforest Alliance; Save the Children International (#19058); SOLIDARIDAD Network (#19681); WAO-Afrique (#20816).*
IGO Relations Advisors: *ILO (#11123); UNICEF (#20332);* US Department of Labor. [2021.08.31/XF6710/y/F]

♦ International Cocoa Organization (ICCO) 12627

Organisation internationale du cacao – Organización Internacional del Cacao – Mezdunarodnaja Organizacija po Kakao

Exec Dir 06 BP 1166 06, Abidjan 06, Côte d'Ivoire. T. +22522514950 – +22522514951. Fax +22522514979. E-mail: info@icco.org.
URL: http://www.icco.org/

History 1973. Established to implement the *International Cocoa Agreement, 1972 (1972).*
This Agreement, was succeeded by the *International Cocoa Agreement, 1975 (1975)*, which entered into force on 1 Oct 1976, expired on Mar 31 1980.
The *International Cocoa Agreement, 1980 (1980)* entered into force on 1 Aug 1981, and was succeeded by the *International Cocoa Agreement, 1986 (1986)*, which entered into force 20 Jan 1987 and remained in force for three cocoa years; it was extended, without its economic provisions, for a further period of two years from 1 Oct 1990 and was further extended for one year from 1 Oct 1992.
The *International Cocoa Agreement, 1993 (1993)* was successfully negotiated under the auspices of the United Nations Cocoa Conference, 1992, and was concluded 16 Jul 1993. Entered into force on 22 Feb 1994; extended until 1 Oct 2003. *International Cocoa Agreement, 2001 (2001)* provisionally entered into force 1 Oct 2003; by 30 Sep 2008, it will have reached the end of the 5th full cocoa year; Council approved to extend it for a period of 2 years, until 30 Sep 2010; extended until 30 Sep 2012, when *International Cocoa Agreement, 2010 (2010)* came into force. *Intergovernmental Group on Cocoa (inactive)*, set up 1956, worked in setting up ICCO but has been inactive since.
ICCO Statutes registered under *'UNTS 1/15033'*.
Designated International Commodity Body of: *Common Fund for Commodities (CFC, #04293).*
Aims Promote international cooperation in the world cocoa industry; provide an appropriate framework for the discussion of all matters relating to all sectors thereof; help strengthen national cocoa economies of member countries, in particular through preparing appropriate projects to be submitted to the relevant institutions for financing and implementation. Contribute to a balanced development of the world cocoa economy, including through promoting: a sustainable cocoa economy; the carrying out of research and implementation of its findings; transparency, through collection, analysis and dissemination of relevant statistics and undertaking appropriate studies; consumption of *chocolate* and cocoa-based products in order to increase demand for cocoa, in close cooperation with the private sector. **Structure** *International Cocoa Council*, highest authority, consists of all members and holds 2 regular sessions in each cocoa year, which runs from 1 Oct to 30 Sep. Voting powers in the Council are evenly divided between exporting and importing members. Committees (3); Expert Working Group. Consultative Board on the World Cocoa Economy is composed of experts from all sectors of the cocoa economy. Secretariat comprises Office of the Executive Director, including Personnel and Administration Section and Information and Conference Section. Economics and Statistics Division, consisting of Statistics and Market Review Section and Economics and Development Section. **Languages** English, French, Russian, Spanish. **Staff** 19.00 FTE, paid. **Finance** Members' contributions to the administrative budget; sale of publications; conference proceeds. **Activities** Events/meetings; guidance/assistance/consulting; knowledge management/information dissemination; projects/programmes. **Events** *World Cocoa Conference* Brussels (Belgium) 2024, *World Cocoa Conference* Bali (Indonesia) 2022, *International Symposium on Cocoa Research* Montpellier (France) 2022, *World Cocoa Conference* Bali (Indonesia) 2021, *World Cocoa Conference* Bali (Indonesia) 2020. **Publications** *Quarterly Bulletin of Cocoa Statistics; World Cocoa Directory.* Annual Report; cocoa briefs; country studies.
Members Contracting parties to the 2010 Agreement, in force 1 Oct 2012 – Exporting Members (21):
Brazil, Cameroon, Congo DR, Costa Rica, Côte d'Ivoire, Dominican Rep, Ecuador, Gabon, Ghana, Guinea, Indonesia, Liberia, Madagascar, Malaysia, Nicaragua, Papua New Guinea, Peru, Sierra Leone, Togo, Trinidad-Tobago, Venezuela.
Contracting parties to the 2010 Agreement, Importing Members (30):
Austria, Belgium, Bulgaria, Croatia, Cyprus, Czechia, Denmark, Estonia, Finland, France, Germany, Greece, Hungary, Ireland, Italy, Latvia, Lithuania, Luxembourg, Malta, Netherlands, Poland, Portugal, Romania, Russia, Slovakia, Slovenia, Spain, Sweden, Switzerland, UK.
Regional economic integration importing organization, 1 listed in this Yearbook:
European Union (EU, #08967).
IGO Relations Cooperates with: *European Development Fund (EDF, #06914); FAO (#09260); UNCTAD (#20285).* Observer status with: *Codex Alimentarius Commission (CAC, #04081).* **NGO Relations** Cooperates with: *Association of the Chocolate, Biscuit and Confectionery Industries of the EU (CAOBISCO, #02427); European Cocoa Association (ECA, #06599); International Confectionery Association (ICA, #12840); World Cocoa Foundation (WCF).* Staff association is member of: *Federation of International Civil Servants' Associations (FICSA, #09603).* [2022/XC2404/y/B*]

♦ International Cocoa Trades Federation (inactive)

♦ International Coconut Community (ICC) 12628

Exec Dir 8th Fl BAPPEBTI Bldg, Jl Kramat Raya No 172, Kenari, Senen, Jakarta 10430, Indonesia. T. +62213100557 – +62213100557. Fax +62213101007. E-mail: icc@coconutcommunity.org – apcc@indo.net.id.
URL: https://coconutcommunity.org/

History Nov 1968, Jakarta (Indonesia). Established by Agreement drafted by representatives of participating governments in two series of intergovernmental consultations, held in Oct and Nov 1968, following a proposal resulting from a study prepared by the secretariat of United Nations Economic Commission for Asia and the Far East (ESCAFE), now *United Nations Economic and Social Commission for Asia and the Pacific (ESCAP, #20557).* The Agreement was adopted 1 Dec 1968 and entered into force 30 Jul 1969. Rules of procedure were adopted 2-8 Sep 1969, Colombo (Sri Lanka); amended 27-31 Jul 1976, Davao (Philippines). Name changed at 13th session, 17-20 Dec 1975, Bali (Indonesia). 33rd Session, 28-31 Oct 1996, decided that the associate membership of the Community be extended to other developing countries outside the region. Former names and other names: *Asian Coconut Community (ACC)* – former (1968 to 1975); *Asian and Pacific Coconut Community (APCC)* – former (1975 to 2018); *Communauté asiatique et pacifique de la noix de coco* – former (1975 to 2018). **Aims** Promote, coordinate and harmonize all activities of the coconut industry with a view to achieving maximum economic development of the industry through better production, processing, marketing and research. **Structure** Each member State Contracting Party has 1 representative with plenipotentiary authority (in addition, members may designate 1 or more advisers). Each representative in turn holds Chairmanship (1-year term). Secretariat, headed by Executive Director (appointed for a 3-year term, extendable for another 3 years). The Community meets annually but may also be called to extra sessions when necessary. Secretariat Divisions (4): Trade and Market/Statistical; Publication; Administration and Finance; Documentation. **Languages** English. **Staff** 11.00 FTE, paid. **Finance** Sources: contributions of member/participating states. **Activities** Advocacy/lobbying/activism; knowledge management/information dissemination; projects/programmes; research/documentation; standards/guidelines; training/education. **Events** *International COCOTECH Conference* Kuala Lumpur (Malaysia) 2022, *International COCOTECH Conference* Jakarta (Indonesia) 2021, *ICC Session and Ministerial Meeting* Port Moresby (Papua New Guinea) 2021, *ICC Session and Ministerial Meeting* Apia (Samoa) 2020, *ICC Session and Ministerial Meeting* Manila (Philippines) 2019. **Publications** *Cocommunity* (12 a year) – newsletter; *Cocoinfo International* (2 a year); *Coconut Research and Development (CORD)* (2 a year); *Coconut Statistical Yearbook* (annual). Reports; proceedings; studies; directories; assessments; videos; CD-Roms.
Members Governments of 20 countries:
Fiji, Guyana, India, Indonesia, Jamaica, Kenya, Kiribati, Malaysia, Marshall Is, Micronesia FS, Papua New Guinea, Philippines, Samoa, Solomon Is, Sri Lanka, Thailand, Timor-Leste, Tonga, Vanuatu, Vietnam.
IGO Relations Cooperation agreement with: *UNIDO (#20336).* Participates as observer in the activities of: *Codex Alimentarius Commission (CAC, #04081).* Member of: *Bioversity International (#03262); Intergovernmental Group on Oilseeds, Oils and Fats (#11492).* **NGO Relations** Member of: *ASEAN Vegetable Oils Club (AVOC, inactive).* [2022.02.15/XD3933/D*]

♦ International Code of Conduct Association (ICoCA) 12629

Exec Dir Geneva Nations 3rd Floor, Rue du Pré-de-la-Bichette 1, 1202 Geneva 2, Switzerland. E-mail: secretariat@icoca.ch.
URL: http://www.icoca.ch/

History Sep 2013. Set up as a mechanism for governance and oversight of the International Code of Conduct for Private Security Service Providers (the Code), finalised Nov 2010. Articles of Association adopted Feb 2013. Former names and other names: *International Code of Conduct for Private Security Service Providers' Association (ICoCA)* – full title. Registration: Swiss Civil Code, Switzerland; EU Transparency Register, No/ID: 366427819671-47, Start date: 25 Nov 2015. **Aims** Promote, govern and oversee implementation of the Code; promote responsible provision of security services and respect for human rights and national and international law in accordance with the Code; reduce risk in the security supply chain by conducting due diligence on Members & Affiliates, monitoring their activities, certifying their operations, providing guidance and handling complaints. **Structure** Annual General Assembly; Board of Directors; Secretariat, headed by Executive Director. **Languages** English, French, Spanish. **Staff** 7.90 FTE, paid. **Finance** Sources: donations; grants; members' dues. **Activities** Certification/accreditation; monitoring/evaluation; politics/policy/regulatory. **Publications** *ICoCA Newsletter.*
Members Governments of 7 countries:
Australia, Canada, Norway, Sweden, Switzerland, UK, USA.
Private Security Companies (115) in 46 countries and territories:
Albania, Australia, Belgium, Brazil, Canada, China, Colombia, Congo DR, Côte d'Ivoire, Cyprus, Egypt, Finland, France, Germany, Ghana, Guatemala, Haiti, Honduras, Iraq, Ireland, Italy, Kenya, Lebanon, Libya, Malaysia, Mauritius, Mexico, Nigeria, Papua New Guinea, Peru, Philippines, Seychelles, Somalia, South Sudan, Sri Lanka, Sweden, Switzerland, Tanzania UR, Uganda, UK, Ukraine, United Arab Emirates, USA, Virgin Is UK, Yemen, Zimbabwe.
Civil Society Organizations (50) in 21 countries:
Cameroon, China, Colombia, Congo Brazzaville, Congo DR, France, Guatemala, Guinea, Iraq, Kenya, Malawi, Myanmar, Niger, Nigeria, Peru, Rwanda, Senegal, South Africa, Tanzania UR, UK, USA.
Included in the above, 4 organizations listed in this Yearbook:
Human Rights First; Human Rights Watch (HRW, #10990); International Corporate Accountability Roundtable (ICAR, #12968); One Earth Future Foundation (OEF).
IGO Relations Cooperates with (1): *Geneva Centre for Security Sector Governance (DCAF, #10121).* [2023.02.16/XJ8591/y/E]

♦ International Code of Conduct for Private Security Service Providers' Association / see International Code of Conduct Association (#12629)
♦ International Code Council (internationally oriented national body)
♦ International Code Documentation Centre (see: #12305)
♦ International Code of Marketing of Breast-milk Substitutes (1981 treaty)
♦ International Coffee Agreement, 1962 (1962 treaty)
♦ International Coffee Agreement, 1968 (1968 treaty)
♦ International Coffee Agreement, 1976 (1976 treaty)
♦ International Coffee Agreement, 1982 (1982 treaty)
♦ International Coffee Agreement, 1994 (1994 treaty)
♦ International Coffee Agreement, 2001 (2000 treaty)

♦ International Coffee Organization (ICO) 12630

Organisation internationale du café (OIC) – Organización Internacional del Café – Organização Internacional do Café

Exec Dir 222 Gray's Inn Road, London, WC1X 8HB, UK. T. +442076120600. Fax +442076120630. E-mail: info@ico.org.
Personal Assistant to Exec Dir address not obtained. T. +442076120618.
URL: http://www.ico.org/

History Aug 1963, on entry into force (for a 5-year period) of *International Coffee Agreement, 1962 (1962)*, registered under *'UNTS 1/9262'*. Operations continued under provisions of: *International Coffee Agreement, 1968 (1968)*, registered under *'UNTS 1/6791'*; International Coffee Agreement 1968 as Extended; *International Coffee Agreement, 1976 (1976)*, in force from 1 Oct 1976 until 30 Sep 1983; *International Coffee Agreement, 1982 (1982)*, which entered into force on 1 Oct 1983 and was extended until 30 Sep 1994; *International Coffee Agreement, 1994 (1994)*, which entered into force on 1 Oct 1994 for 5 years; *International Coffee Agreement, 2001 (2000)*, which entered into force on 1 Oct 2001 for 6 years; *International coffee agreement, 2007*, which entered into force on 2 Feb 2011 for 10 years. **Aims** Promote enhanced international cooperation and provide a forum for intergovernmental consultations on coffee matters; facilitate expansion and transparency of international *trade* in coffee; encourage development of a sustainable coffee economy; promote quality; analyse and advise on the preparation of coffee development projects; promote training and information programmes to assist the transfer of relevant technology to members; act as a centre for the collection, analysis and dissemination and publication of economic and technical information, statistics and studies; encourage and increase the *consumption* of coffee. **Structure** *International Coffee Council – Conseil international du café* (meeting twice a year), the highest authority, comprises all members. Private Sector Consultative Board (meeting 2 times a year) comprises 8 representatives of private sector associations in exporting countries and 8 from associations in importing countries. Executive Director, appointed by Council. Headquarters Agreement with the UK Government accords privileges and immunities to representatives of ICO member countries, ensuring complete independence in the exercise of functions connected with the ICO; members of the staff of the Executive Director thus have privileges and immunities granted by the UK to international organizations. **Languages** English, French, Portuguese, Spanish. **Staff** 14.00 FTE, paid. **Finance** Contributions from member governments pro rata to their position in world coffee trade. **Activities** Since 1963, administers provisions of the Agreement and supervises its operation. The 2007 Agreement: strengthens the Organization's role as a forum for intergovernmental consultations; facilitates international trade through increased transparency and access to relevant information; promotes a sustainable coffee economy for the benefit of all stakeholders and particularly of small-scale farmers in coffee producing countries. It is an important instrument for development cooperation and will provide the legal framework for core activities undertaken by the Organization. About 15 of the 45 Exporting Members are least-developed countries, adn the 25 million small coffee farmers and their families who produce 70% of the world's coffee are particularly affected by fluctuations in market prices and imbalances in supply and demand. The Preamble specifically acknowledges the contribution of a sustainable coffee sector to the achievement of internationally agreed development goals, including the Millennium Development Goals, particularly with respect to poverty eradication. Other activities include promotion of coffee consumption, quality improvement, project development, statistics, development of coffee policy. **Events** *World Coffee Leaders Forum* Seoul (Korea Rep) 2020, *Session* London (UK) 2019, *Session* Nairobi (Kenya) 2019, *Session* London (UK) 2018, *World Coffee Leaders Forum* Seoul (Korea Rep) 2018. **Publications** Annual Review; Coffee Statistics; reports; economic studies. **Information Services** *Coffeeline*.

Members belonging to the International Coffee Agreement 2007. As of 1 Oct 2017: Exporting members (44):
Angola, Bolivia, Brazil, Burundi, Cameroon, Central African Rep, Colombia, Congo DR, Costa Rica, Côte d'Ivoire, Cuba, Ecuador, El Salvador, Ethiopia, Gabon, Ghana, Guatemala, Honduras, India, Indonesia, Kenya, Liberia, Madagascar, Malawi, Mexico, Nepal, Nicaragua, Panama, Papua New Guinea, Paraguay, Peru, Philippines, Rwanda, Sierra Leone, Tanzania UR, Thailand, Timor-Leste, Togo, Uganda, Venezuela, Vietnam, Yemen, Zambia, Zimbabwe.
Importing members (31):
Austria, Belgium, Bulgaria, Croatia, Cyprus, Czechia, Denmark, Estonia, Finland, France, Germany, Greece, Hungary, Ireland, Italy, Latvia, Lithuania, Luxembourg, Malta, Netherlands, Norway, Poland, Portugal, Romania, Slovakia, Slovenia, Spain, Sweden, Switzerland, Tunisia, UK.

IGO Relations Relationship agreement with: *FAO (#09260)*; *International Trade Centre (ITC, #15703)*. Participates in the activities of: *UNCTAD (#20285)*. Participates as observer in the activities of: *Codex Alimentarius Commission (CAC, #04081)*. Designed International Commodity Body of: *Common Fund for Commodities (CFC, #04293)*. Supports: *CABI (#03393)*. **NGO Relations** Member of: *Global Alliance for Climate-Smart Agriculture (GACSA, #10189)*. Memorarndum of Understanding with: *Conservation International (CI)*; *Global Coffee Platform (GCP, #10298)*; International Women's Coffee Alliance. In liaison with technical committees of: *International Organization for Standardization (ISO, #14473)*. [2019.03.07/XB1509/**B***]

♦ International Coffee Organization Staff Association (ICOSA) 12631

Contact c/o ICO, 222 Gray's Inn Road, London, WC1X 8HB, UK. T. +442076120600. Fax +442076120630.

History Founded to represent staff of *International Coffee Organization (ICO, #12630)*. Former names and other names: *ICO Staff Association* – former alias. **NGO Relations** Member of: *Federation of International Civil Servants' Associations (FICSA, #09603)*. [2018/XE2809/**E**]

♦ International Cogeneration Alliance / see World Alliance for Decentralized Energy (#21081)
♦ International Cogeneration Society (inactive)

♦ International Cognition and Cancer Task Force (ICCTF) 12632

Address not obtained.
URL: http://www.icctf.com/

Aims Advance understanding of the impact of cancer and cancer-related treatment on cognitive and behavioral functioning in patients with central nervous system cancer and non-central nervous system cancer. **Structure** Steering Committee. **Activities** Events/meetings. **Events** *Conference* Denver, CO (USA) 2020, *Conference* Sydney, NSW (Australia) 2018. [2019/XM8003/**F**]

♦ International Cognitive Linguistics Association (ICLA) 12633

Sec/Treas Lund Univ, Centre for Languages and Literature, PO Box 201, SE-221 00 Lund, Sweden.
URL: http://www.cognitivelinguistics.org/

History 1989, Duisburg (Germany FR). **Aims** Support and develop cognitive linguistic theory of language and grammar. **Structure** Board. **Languages** English. **Staff** None. **Finance** Members' dues. **Activities** Events/meetings. Online Regulatory and Tax Resource. **Events** *Biennial Conference* Nishinomiya (Japan) 2019, *Biennial Conference* Tartu (Estonia) 2017, *Biennial Conference / International Cognitive Linguistics Conference – ICLC* Newcastle upon Tyne (UK) 2015, *Biennial Conference* Edmonton, AB (Canada) 2013, *International Cognitive Linguistics Conference – ICLC* Edmonton, AB (Canada) 2013. **Publications** *Cognitive Linguistics Journal* (4 a year). **Information Services** *Electronic Cognitive Bibliography (CogBIB)*.

Members Individuals (400) in 33 countries and territories:
Australia, Austria, Belgium, Brazil, Canada, China, Croatia, Denmark, Estonia, Finland, France, Germany, Greece, Hungary, Italy, Japan, Korea Rep, Malaysia, Mexico, Netherlands, New Zealand, Norway, Poland, Portugal, Serbia, South Africa, Spain, Sweden, Switzerland, Taiwan, Tunisia, UK, USA. [2019/XD5782/v/**D**]

♦ International Cognitive Load Theory Association (unconfirmed)
♦ International Coiled Tubing Association / see Intervention and Coiled Tubing Association
♦ International Coke Association (no recent information)
♦ International Coke Association (inactive)
♦ International Cold Chain Technology (internationally oriented national body)

♦ International Cold Forging Group (ICFG) 12634

Secretariat Egerlandstr 13, 91058 Erlangen, Germany. T. +4991318528309. Fax +4991318527141. E-mail: icfg@lft.uni-erlangen.de.
URL: http://www.icfg.info/

History 15 Nov 1967. **Aims** Promulgate the economic advancement of cold forging by encouraging and coordinating national and international cooperation, by stimulating research and disseminating knowledge of relevant processes and sciences. **Structure** Advisory Board, comprising Chair, Vice-Chair, Treasurer and 5 members. Secretariat in Germany. Subgroups (3). **Languages** English. **Finance** Members' dues. **Activities** Subgroups (3): Process Simulation; Tool Life and Tool Quality; Cold Forging 2050. Organizes meetings. **Events** *Plenary Meeting* Stuttgart (Germany) 2016, *Plenary Meeting* Daejeon (Korea Rep) 2015, *Plenary Meeting* Ankara (Turkey) 2014, *Plenary Meeting* Paris (France) 2013, *Plenary Meeting* Nagoya (Japan) 2012. **Publications** Documents and data sheets; papers.

Members Full; Corresponding; Emeritus; Honorary; Companies. Individuals (90) in 26 countries and territories:
Australia, Brazil, Bulgaria, China, Denmark, Finland, France, Germany, Hungary, India, Italy, Japan, Korea Rep, Liechtenstein, Mexico, Netherlands, Norway, Poland, Slovenia, Spain, Sweden, Switzerland, Taiwan, Türkiye, UK, USA. [2017/XE3902/v/**E**]

♦ International Collaboration on ADHD and Substance Abuse (ICASA) . 12635

Dir Postbus 725, 3500 AS Utrecht, Netherlands. T. +313053456301.
URL: http://www.adhdandsubstanceabuse.org/

History 2 Sep 2010. Registered in accordance with Dutch law. **Aims** Contribute to a substantial decrease in the proportion of Attention Deficit Hyperactivity Disorder (ADHD) patients developing Substance Use Disorders (SUD); substantially improve the detection, diagnosis and treatment of patients having both ADHD and SUD. **Structure** Board; Advisory Board. Office, based in Utrecht (Netherlands). **Languages** English. **Activities** Projects/programmes; research/documentation. **Events** *Conference* Berlin (Germany) 2011, *International conference on ADHD and substance use disorder / Conference* Bergen (Norway) 2010, *Conference* Budapest (Hungary) 2009, *Meeting* Stockholm (Sweden) 2009, *Conference* Barcelona (Spain) 2008.

Members Full (45) in 14 countries:
Australia, Belgium, Bulgaria, Finland, France, Hungary, Netherlands, Norway, South Africa, Spain, Sweden, Switzerland, UK, USA.

NGO Relations Cooperates with: *ADHD-Europe (#00113)*. [2018/XJ1588/**C**]

♦ International Collaboration on Advanced Neutron Sources (ICANS) . 12636

Contact MS 6466, Oak Ridge National Laboratory, Oak Ridge TN 37831, USA. T. +18652415702.
URL: http://www.neutron.anl.gov/ipns/icans.html

History 1977, as an informal network of laboratories. **Aims** Facilitate the exchange of technical information; provide for review of results and designs; reduce duplication of efforts; identify areas for collaborative efforts; provide means for informing participants about plans for activities relating to pulsed and steady spallation neutron source development. **Structure** Responsibility for meetings and publications rotates amongst participating laboratories on the basis of agreements reached following each meeting. **Languages** English. **Staff** None. **Finance** Host organizations. **Activities** Advanced Cold Moderators (ACOM) collaboration; International Collaboration on High-Power Spallation Targets; Union of Compact Accelerator-based Neuron Sources. **Events** *Meeting* Mito (Japan) 2014, *Meeting* Bariloche (Argentina) 2012, *Meeting* Grindelwald (Switzerland) 2010, *Meeting* UK 2009, *Meeting* Beijing (China) 2007. **Publications** Proceedings.

Members Laboratories (11) in 13 countries:
Argentina, Australia, Austria, Canada, China, Germany, Japan, Russia, Spain, Sweden, Switzerland, UK, USA. [2011.06.01/XF6265/**F**]

♦ International Collaboration on Cancer Reporting (ICCR) 12637

Contact address not obtained. T. +61283565828. E-mail: admin@iccr-cancer.org.
URL: http://www.iccr-cancer.org/

History 2011. Registration: No/ID: ABN 69 601 723 960, Australia. **Aims** Reduce the global burden of cancer dataset development and reduplication of effort by the different international institutions that commission, publish and maintain standardised cancer reporting datasets. **Structure** Board; Dataset Steering Committee; Editorial Review Committee; Dataset Authoring Committees. **Finance** Sources: members' dues.

Members Organizations in 4 countries:
Australia, Canada, UK, USA.
Regional associations (2):
European Society of Pathology (ESP, #08689); *Royal College of Pathologists of Australasia (RCPA)*.

NGO Relations *African Strategies for Advancing Pathology (ASAP, #00476)*; *International Society of Gynecological Pathologists (ISGyP, #15151)*; *International Society of Urological Pathology (ISUP, #15531)*; *Union for International Cancer Control (UICC, #20415)*. [2021/XM5510/y/**C**]

♦ International Collaboration for Community Health Nursing Research (internationally oriented national body)

♦ International Collaboration for Essential Surgery (ICES) 12638

Chair c/o Quai Santé, Ave des Alpes 74, 1820 Montreux VD, Switzerland.
URL: http://www.essentialsurgery.com/

Aims Promote the effective use of low-cost surgical care to save lives and prevent disability around the world. **Structure** Board of Directors. [2017/XJ9661/**F**]

♦ International Collaboration for Health (internationally oriented national body)
♦ International Collaboration for Hypermesis Gravidarum Research (unconfirmed)
♦ International Collaborative for Best Care for the Dying Person (unconfirmed)
♦ International Collaborative Society for Supportive Care in Oncology (inactive)

♦ International Collective in Support of Fishworkers (ICSF) 12639

Collectif international d'appui aux travailleurs de la pêche – Colectivo Internacional en Apoyo al Pescador Artesanal (CIAPA)

Exec Sec No 22 First Floor, Venkatrathinam Nagar, Adyar, Chennai, Tamil Nadu 600 020, Chennai TAMIL NADU 600 020, India. T. +914424451216 – +914424451217. Fax +914424450216. E-mail: icsf@icsf.net.
URL: http://www.icsf.net/

History Nov 1986, Thiruvananthapuram (India). Registered in accordance with Swiss Civil Code. Previously also referred as *Collectif international d'appui à la pêche artisanale (CIAPA) – Colectivo Internacional de Apoyo a los Pescadores Artesanales*. **Aims** Work towards the establishment of equitable, gender-just, self-reliant and sustainable fisheries, particularly in the small-scale, artisanal sector. **Structure** General Body; Animation Team. Secretariat, headed by Executive Secretary. Offices (2): Chennai (India); Brussels (Belgium). **Languages** English, French, Spanish. **Staff** 7.00 FTE, paid. **Finance** Financed by governmental and non-governmental development organizations. Annual budget: US$ 250,000 – 500,000. **Activities** Research/documentation; training/education; advocacy/lobbying/activism; knowledge management/information dissemination. **Events** *Conference* Cebu City (Philippines) 1994, *Global fisheries trends and the future of fishworkers* Bangkok (Thailand) 1990. **Publications** *Samudra Report* (3 a year) in English, French, Spanish; *Yemaya – Women in Fisheries Newsletter* (3 a year) in English, French, Spanish. *Samudra Monographs/Dossiers* – series. Reports; occasional papers; proceedings; documentary films and CDs. **Members** Regular (24); Associate (14); Honorary (5). Membership countries not specified. **Consultative Status** Consultative status granted from: *ECOSOC (#05331)* (Ros A); *ILO (#11123)* (Special List); *FAO (#09260)* (Liaison Status). **IGO Relations** Accredited to: *United Nations Conference on Environment and Development (UNCED)*. Cooperates with: *Asia-Pacific Fishery Commission (APFIC, #01907)*. **NGO Relations** Member of: *Deep Sea Conservation Coalition (DSCC, #05024)*; *High Level Panel for a Sustainable Ocean Economy (Panel, #10917)*; *ICCA Consortium (#11041)*; *International NGO/CSO Planning Committee for Food Sovereignty (IPC, #14365)*. Instrumental in setting up *Coalition for Fair Fisheries Agreements (CFFA, #04060)*. [2017.03.09/XF0127/**F**]

♦ International College of Angiology (ICA) 12640

Collège international d'angiologie – Collegium Internationale Angiologiae

Exec Dir 161 Morin Drive, Jay VT 05859, USA. T. +18029884065. Fax +18029884066.
URL: http://www.intlcollegeofangiology.org/

History Founded 1958. **Aims** Encourage, support and facilitate research and education in problems of *cardiovascular medicine* and *surgery*. **Structure** Board of Directors; Advisory Board; Scientific Council. **Languages** English. **Staff** 1.00 FTE, paid. **Finance** Members' dues. **Activities** Research/documentation; training/education; events/meetings. **Events** *Annual Congress* Vienna (Austria) 2020, *Annual Congress* Columbus, OH (USA) 2019, *Annual Congress* Tokyo (Japan) 2018, *Annual Congress* Vienna (Austria) 2017, *Annual Congress* Prague (Czech Rep) 2016. **Publications** *International Journal of Angiology*.
Members Full; Associate Fellow; Affiliate Fellow; Members; Students. Fellows, by invitation of the Board of Directors, Membership Committee or Officers. Members in 58 countries and territories:
Argentina, Australia, Austria, Bangladesh, Belgium, Brazil, Bulgaria, Canada, Chile, China, Côte d'Ivoire, Czechia, Denmark, Dominican Rep, Egypt, Finland, France, Georgia, Germany, Greece, Haiti, Hong Kong, Hungary, India, Indonesia, Ireland, Israel, Italy, Japan, Jordan, Korea Rep, Kuwait, Malaysia, Netherlands, New Zealand, Nigeria, Norway, Pakistan, Peru, Poland, Portugal, Romania, Russia, Saudi Arabia, Singapore, South Africa, Spain, Sweden, Switzerland, Taiwan, Thailand, Trinidad-Tobago, Türkiye, UK, Ukraine, United Arab Emirates, USA, Venezuela.
NGO Relations Member of: *Council for International Organizations of Medical Sciences (CIOMS, #04905).* [2016.10.18/XF2139/v/F]

♦ International College of Applied Kinesiology (ICAK) 12641

Exec Sec UK address not obtained. E-mail: info@icak.co.uk.
Sec address not obtained.
ICAK-USA Central Office 4919 Lamar Ave, Mission KS 66202, USA. T. +19133845336. Fax +19133845112. E-mail: icak@dci-kansascity.com.
URL: http://www.icak.com/

History 1976. **Aims** Advance manual muscle testing as a system of diagnosis for evaluating areas of dysfunction within the body. **Structure** Board; Chapters (14), including *International Association of Kinesiology*. **Languages** English. **Staff** Voluntary. **Finance** Members' dues. **Events** *Annual Conference* Montréal, QC (Canada) 2023, *Annual Conference* Bruges (Belgium) 2022, *Annual Conference* Montréal, QC (Canada) 2021, *Annual Conference* Bruges (Belgium) 2020, *Annual Conference* Brisbane, QLD (Australia) 2019. **Publications** *A K Review* (2 a year). **NGO Relations** *International Medical Society for Applied Kinesiology (IMAK, #14139).* [2018.06.01/XN6296/E]

♦ International College of Cardiology (ICC) 12642

Founder/Pres Halberg Hosp and Research Inst, Civil Lines, Moradabad, Uttar Pradesh 244001, Moradabad UTTAR PRADESH 244001, India. T. +915912417437. Fax +915912410092.
Exec Dir Dept of Sports Medicine, Fac of Medicine, P J Safaric Univ, Trieda SNP 1, 040 66 Košice, Slovakia. Fax +421917725118.
URL: https://icc-world.org/

History 2000, Slovakia. **Aims** Educate cardiologists and physicians on research and education on prevention of cardiovascular diseases by lifestyle changes and drug therapy; develop guidelines on food, nutraceuticals, nutrients and drug therapy for industry and doctors. **Structure** Board of Directors; President; Secretary General; Secretary. **Languages** English. **Staff** 3.00 FTE, voluntary. **Finance** Sources: donations; meeting proceeds; members' dues. **Activities** Events/meetings; standards/guidelines. **Events** *International Congress of Cardiology and Diabetes (ICCD)* Košice (Slovakia) 2022, *Congress of Cardiology and Diabetes* Košice (Slovakia) 2020, *Congress of Cardiology and Diabetes* Košice (Slovakia) 2018, *Congress on Cardiovascular Diseases* Dubai (United Arab Emirates) 2017, *Congress on Cardiovascular Diseases* Recife (Brazil) 2015. **Publications** *World Heart Journal*. Proceedings; abstract book; research articles.
Members Full in 29 countries and territories:
Argentina, Australia, Belgium, Brazil, Bulgaria, Canada, China, Egypt, Finland, Germany, Hong Kong, India, Iran Islamic Rep, Iraq, Italy, Japan, Korea Rep, New Zealand, Philippines, Poland, Russia, Serbia, Singapore, Slovakia, South Africa, Taiwan, Thailand, UK, USA.
NGO Relations Also links with national organizations. [2022/XF6914/F]

♦ International College of Cranio-Mandibular Orthopedics (ICCMO) 12643

Main Office PO Box 1491, Cannon Beach OR 97110, USA. T. +15034360703. Fax +15034360612. E-mail: info@iccmo.org.
URL: http://www.iccmo.org/

History 1979. **Aims** Alleviate widespread human suffering of those afflicted with the varied symptomatology of *head* and *neck pain* and dysfunction. **Structure** International Officers: President; President-Elect; Vice-President; Treasurer and Secretary. Sections (7): Canada; France; Germany; Italy; Japan; South America; USA. **Activities** Events/meetings; awards/prizes/competitions. **Events** *Annual International Congress* Moscow (Russia) 2019, *Annual Meeting* Vienna (Austria) 2018, *Biennial Congress* Buenos Aires (Argentina) 2017, *Biennial Congress* Kyoto (Japan) 2015, *Biennial Congress* Munich (Germany) 2013. **Publications** *ICCMO Newsletter. Anthology of Craniomandibular Orthopedics.*
Members Full in 16 countries:
Argentina, Australia, Austria, Bolivia, Brazil, Canada, Finland, France, Germany, Italy, Japan, New Zealand, Portugal, Singapore, South Africa, USA.
NGO Relations Supporting member of: *FDI – World Dental Federation (#09281).* [2018/XD7136/F]

♦ International College of Dentists (ICD) 12644

Collège international de chirurgiens-dentistes

SG 615 S Saginaw St, Suite 3008, Flint MI 48502, USA. T. +18108203087. E-mail: office@icd.org – chelsea@icd.org.
URL: http://www.icd.org/

History Nov 1920, Tokyo (Japan). Conceived 1920, by Dr Louis Ottofy (USA) and Dr Tsurukichi Okumura (Japan). Central Office established 1927, Chicago IL (USA); moved to Oakland CA (USA), 1928; Minneapolis MN (USA) Feb 1935. Became inactive 1939, during World War II; reorganized 1947. Central Office moved to Washington DC (USA), Jan 1989. 2001, Constitution and Bylaws revised. Central Office moved to Rockville MD (USA) 2010. Registration: Start date: 31 Dec 1927, USA, Chicago IL; No/ID: 41-0797196, Start date: 9 Jul 1928, USA, District of Columbia; Start date: 29 Dec 1929, USA, District of Columbia. **Aims** Uphold the highest standard of professional competence and personal ethics; recognize distinguished service to the profession and the public worldwide; foster measures for the prevention and treatment of oral disease by encouraging and supporting humanitarian projects; contribute to the advancement of the profession of dentistry by fostering the growth and diffusion of dental knowledge worldwide; provide a universal international forum for the cultivation of cordial relations within the profession and to assist in preserving the highest perception of the profession worldwide. **Structure** International Council; Executive Committee; virtual World Headquarters; Operations Center; Standing and ad hoc Committees. Sections (16); Regions (15). **Languages** English. **Staff** 4.00 FTE, paid. **Finance** Annual budget: 400,000 USD (2020). **Activities** Events/meetings; humanitarian/emergency aid; networking/liaising; standards/guidelines; training/education. **Events** *Centennial Symposium on ICD Humanitarian and Educational Programs* Nagoya (Japan) 2021, *International Council Meeting* Nagoya (Japan) 2021, *Annual Meeting* Porto (Portugal) 2021, *International Council Meeting* 2020, *Annual Meeting* Porto (Portugal) 2020. **Publications** *The College Today* (2 a year) – e-newsletter; *The Globe* – journal. *Orientation and Leadership Manual* – leadership manual. **Members** Fellows (over 12,000) in over 122 countries. Membership countries not specified. **IGO Relations** Partner of (2): U.S. Centers for Disease Control and Prevention; *WHO (#20950).* **NGO Relations** Member of (1): *Alliance for Oral Health Across Borders (#00710).* Affiliated with (1): *FDI – World Dental Federation (#09281).* [2022.10.24/XE1956/v/E]

♦ International College of Experimental Phonology (inactive)
♦ International College for Family History Studies (internationally oriented national body)
♦ International College of Foot Medicine and Surgery of the Foot / see International Federation of Foot and Ankle Societies (#13431)
♦ International College for Health Cooperation in Developing Countries / see CUAMM – Medici con l'Africa
♦ International College of Literary Translators (internationally oriented national body)

♦ International College for Maxillo-Facial Surgery (ICMFS) 12645

SG Weissenfelser Strasse 15, 04229 Leipzig, Germany. T. +493414772679. Fax +493414229554. E-mail: post@icmfs.com.
URL: http://www.icmfs.com/

History 1970, German DR. 1970, Leipzig (German DR), as *International Association for Maxillo-Facial Surgery (IAMFS) – Association internationale de chirurgie maxillo-faciale.* Statutes adopted: 2 Oct 1975, Budapest (Hungary); 8 May 1985, Leipzig (German DR); 31 Jul 1993, Leuven (Belgium). New name adopted, 1993, Leuven (Belgium). **Aims** Stimulate and exchange scientific experiences in the field of maxillofacial surgery. **Structure** Praesidium; Executive. **Languages** English. **Staff** Voluntary. **Finance** Sources: members' dues. **Activities** Events/meetings. **Events** *World Congress* Tel Aviv (Israel) 2019, *World Congress* Boston, MA (USA) 2017, *World Congress* Limassol (Cyprus) 2015, *World Congress* Cancún (Mexico) 2014, *World Congress* Bad Hofgastein (Austria) 2013.
Members Surgeons with recognized qualifications in maxillo-facial surgery in 61 countries and territories:
Argentina, Australia, Austria, Belgium, Brazil, Bulgaria, Canada, Chile, China, Congo DR, Costa Rica, Côte d'Ivoire, Cuba, Cyprus, Czechia, Denmark, Ecuador, Egypt, Finland, France, Germany, Greece, Guatemala, Hungary, India, Iraq, Ireland, Israel, Italy, Korea Rep, Kuwait, Lebanon, Lithuania, Nepal, Netherlands, Nigeria, Norway, Pakistan, Panama, Philippines, Poland, Portugal, Puerto Rico, Romania, Russia, Saudi Arabia, Singapore, Slovakia, Slovenia, South Africa, Spain, Switzerland, Syrian AR, Taiwan, Tunisia, Türkiye, UK, United Arab Emirates, Uruguay, USA, Vietnam.
Corporate members in 4 countries:
Japan, Mexico, Philippines, Serbia. [2017.12.03/XD6394/v/C]

♦ International College of Medicine and Surgery of the Foot / see International Federation of Foot and Ankle Societies (#13431)
♦ International College of Neuropsychopharmacology (#04115)

♦ International College of Nuclear Medicine Physicians (ICNMP) 12646

Colegio Internacional de Médicos Nucleares

Pres FACNM, Zacatecas 230-502, Col Rome, CP 06700, 06700 Mexico City CDMX, Mexico. T. +525555648244. Fax +525555744885.

History 1995. **Aims** Expand knowledge in nuclear medicine among medical specialists. **Structure** Officers: President; Past President; 3 Honorary Presidents; Vice-President. **Languages** English, Spanish. **Activities** Organizes symposia.
Members Full; Honorary. Members in 20 countries:
Argentina, Australia, Brazil, Chile, Finland, Germany, India, Japan, Kuwait, Mexico, Netherlands, Norway, Pakistan, Peru, Saudi Arabia, South Africa, Spain, Türkiye, UK, USA. [2012.06.01/XD6405/D]

♦ International College of Nutrition (internationally oriented national body)
♦ International College of Oral Implantologists / see International Congress of Oral Implantologists (#12899)
♦ International College of Oriental Medicine (internationally oriented national body)

♦ International College of Person-Centered Medicine (ICPCM) 12647

SG Mount Sinai School of Medicine, New York Univ, Fifth Avenue and 100th St, Box 1093, New York NY 10029, USA. E-mail: icpcmsecretariat@aol.com.
Pres Thimble Hall, 108 Blean Common, Blean, Canterbury, CT2 P66, UK. T. +441227781771. Fax +441227781771.
URL: http://www.personcenteredmedicine.org/

History Set up, 2009, New York NY (USA), following *'Geneva Conferences on Person-Centered Medicine'*, 2008 and 2009, Geneva (Switzerland). Original title: *International Network on Person-Centered Medicine (INPCM).* Current title and by-laws adopted, 2 May 2011. **Aims** Promote health as a state of physical, mental, social and spiritual wellbeing; reduce disease. **Structure** General Assembly; Board; Advisory Council. **Events** *Geneva Conference on Person-Centered Medicine* 2021, *International Congress of Person Centered Medicine* Montevideo (Uruguay) 2020, *International Congress of Person Centered Medicine* Tokyo (Japan) 2019, *International Congress of Person Centered Medicine* Delhi (India) 2018, *International Congress of Person Centered Medicine* Zagreb (Croatia) 2017. **Publications** *International Journal of Person Centered Medicine (IJPCM).* **Members** Membership countries not specified. [2017/XJ0330/C]

♦ International College of Philosophy, Paris (internationally oriented national body)

♦ International College of Prosthodontists (ICP) 12648

Exec Dir 4525 Cass St, Ste A, San Diego CA 92109, USA. T. +18582701814. Fax +18582727687. E-mail: icp@icp-org.com.
Sec Univ of BAsel, Clinic of Periodontology/Endodontology/Cariology, Hebelstr 3, 4056 Basel BS, Switzerland. T. +41612672613.
URL: http://www.icp-org.com/

Structure Councilor Board. Standing Committees. **Events** *Biennial Meeting* Amsterdam (Netherlands) 2019, *Biennial Meeting* Santiago (Chile) 2017, *Biennial Meeting* Seoul (Korea Rep) 2015, *Biennial Meeting* Turin (Italy) 2013, *Biennial Meeting* Waikoloa, HI (USA) 2011. **Publications** *ICP Newsletter, International Journal of Prosthodontics.* [2014/XE3894/E]

♦ International College of Psychosomatic Medicine (ICPM) 12649

Collège international de médecine psychosomatique – Colegio Internacional de Medicina Psicosomatica – Internationales Collegium der Psychosomatischen Medizin

Address not obtained.
URL: http://www.icpmonline.org/

History 1970, Guadalajara (Mexico). **Aims** Promote and advance principles of psychosomatic medicine worldwide and achieve highest standards of research, education practice and exchange of scientific information; promote psychosomatic medicine as a core approach to clinical medicine. **Structure** Executive Board; Advisory Board. Committees (3): Membeship; Nominating; Psychosomatic Specialist Evaluation. **Languages** English. **Staff** 1.00 FTE, paid. **Finance** Sources: members' dues. **Activities** Events/meetings. **Events** *Biennial Congress* Rochester, NY (USA) 2021, *Biennial Congress* Florence (Italy) 2019, *Biennial Congress* Beijing (China) 2017, *Biennial Congress* Glasgow (UK) 2015, *Biennial Congress* Lisbon (Portugal) 2013. **Publications** *Journal of Psychosomatic Research.* **Members** Medical professionals, psychologists and members of other branches involved in psychosomatic research, teaching or clinical practice. Individuals (about 200) in 2 classes of membership: Fellow; Corresponding Fellow. Members in 40 countries and territoires. Membership countries not specified. **NGO Relations** *Asian College of Psychosomatic Medicine (ACPM, #01386).* [2019/XC4072/v/C]

♦ International College of Spiritual and Psychic Sciences (internationally oriented national body)

♦ International College of Surgeons (ICS) 12650

Collège international des chirurgiens – Colegio Internacional de Cirujanos

Exec Dir 1516 N Lake Shore Dr, Chicago IL 60610, USA. T. +13126423555. Fax +13127871624.
URL: http://www.icsglobal.org/

History 1935, Geneva (Switzerland). Incorporated in 1940, Washington DC (USA), according to USA law. Registration: USA. **Aims** Improve the lives of *patients* through development and education of members and advancement of the field. **Structure** International Board of Governors, consisting of International Executive Council and delegates elected by component Sections and comprising about 120 members from 75 countries. Officers: World President; President-Elect; Immediate Past President; First Vice-President; Corporate Secretary; Treasurer. National Sections (70) each with president and other officers. Regional federations (6): *African Federation of the International College of Surgeons (see: #12650); Asia Federation of the International College of Surgeons (see: #12650); European Federation of the International College of Surgeons (EUROFED, see: #12650); Latin American Federation of the International College of Surgeons (no recent information); North American Federation of the International College of Surgeons (see: #12650); Pacific Federation of the International College of Surgeons (see: #12650).* **Languages** English. **Staff** 3.00 FTE, paid. **Finance** Sources: members' dues. **Activities** *'Surgical Teams'* – teams of highly qualified surgeons and surgical specialists teach and demonstrate surgical techniques at medical schools and hospitals in developing countries on request. *'Research and Scholarships'* – provides scholarship grants and postgraduate training to young practising surgeons and members of teaching staff. Fund-raising programme. Organizes international conferences. **Events** *ICS World Congress* Ankara (Türkiye) 2023, *ICS World Congress* Bangkok (Thailand) 2021, *ICS World Congress* Bangkok (Thailand) 2020, *Biennial World Congress* Kaohsiung (Taiwan) 2018,

International Oncoplastic Breast Surgery Symposium Bangkok (Thailand) 2016. **Publications** *ICS Newsletter* (12 a year); *Journal of International Surgery* (6 a year). **Members** Junior Members; Fellows; Honorary Fellows; Emeritus; Benefactors. General surgeons and physicians who work with surgeons in over 100 countries. Membership countries not specified. **Consultative Status** Consultative status granted from: *UNICEF (#20332); WHO (#20950)* (Official Relations). **IGO Relations** Associated with Department of Global Communications of the United Nations. **NGO Relations** Member of (1): *NGO Committee on UNICEF (#17120)*. Instrumental in setting up (1): *Global Academy of Tropical Health and Culture (GATH-INTERNATIONAL, #10162)*.
[2020/XB1513/B]

♦ International College of Thermology (no recent information)
♦ International Collegium of Radiology in Otorhinolaryngology (inactive)

♦ International Collegium of Rehabilitative Audiology (ICRA) 12651

SG ExpORL, KU L Neurosciences, Onderwijs en Navorsing 2, Herestraat 49 bus 721, 3000 Leuven, Belgium.
URL: http://icra-audiology.org/

History 1988. **Structure** Executive Board. **Events** *Meeting* Berkeley, CA (USA) 2015, *Meeting* Helsingør (Denmark) 2013, *Meeting* Toronto, ON (Canada) 2011, *Meeting* Oldenburg (Germany) 2009, *Meeting* Leuven (Belgium) 2007. **NGO Relations** Member of: *International Society of Audiology (ISA, #14948)*.
[2015/XE1990/E]

♦ International Collie Society (ICS) 12652

Sec Tan-Y-FFridd Farm, Llangyniew, Welshpool, Powys, SY21 0JZ, UK. E-mail: ingledenecollies@btinternet.com.
Pres address not obtained.
URL: http://internationalcolliesociety.net/

History 1984. **Aims** Unite collie breeders worldwide. **Structure** Committee, including President, Chairman, Secretary and Treasurer. **Languages** English. **Finance** Subscriptions; income from activities. **Events** *Annual Meeting* Ry (Denmark) 2010, *Annual Meeting* Sydney, NSW (Australia) 2009, *Annual Meeting* Hungary 2008, *Annual Meeting* Ireland 2007, *Annual Meeting* Italy 2006. **Publications** *International Collie Handbook*.
Members Full in 22 countries:
Argentina, Australia, Belgium, Brazil, Croatia, Denmark, Estonia, Finland, Germany, Hungary, Ireland, Israel, Japan, New Zealand, Norway, Portugal, Russia, Serbia, South Africa, Spain, Sweden, UK. [2020/XD7612/D]

♦ International Colloquium on Ancient Greek Linguistics (meeting series)
♦ International Colloquium on Apterygota (meeting series)
♦ International Colloquium – Biology of the Soricidae (meeting series)

♦ International Colloquium on Conflict and Aggression 12653

Coloquios Internacionales sobre Cerebro y Agresión (CICA)
Vice-Pres C/ Enrique Larreta 10, 2º G, 28036 Madrid, Spain. E-mail: info@cicainternational.org – vicepresident@cicainternational.org.
URL: http://www.cicainternational.org/

History 1983. "Seville Statement of Violence" finalized in 1986; endorsed by General Conference of UNESCO in 1989. Former names and other names: *CICA International Foundation (CICA)* – legal name (1 Jan 2018). **Aims** Promote and support a multidisciplinary understanding of aggression and its many expressions, including conflict, violence and terrorism, as well as resolution of conflicts and achievement of peace. **Structure** Council of Trustees; Scientific Committee; Research Area Centers; National Committees. **Languages** English. **Staff** Voluntary. **Finance** Public and private sponsors. **Activities** Awareness raising; conflict resolution; events/meetings; knowledge management/information dissemination; networking/liaising; projects/programmes; publishing activities; research and development; research/documentation; training/education. **Events** *CICA International Conference on Security* Madrid (Spain) 2022, *Conference on Mental Health* Madrid (Spain) 2021, *Conference on Security and Defense* Madrid (Spain) 2021, *Colloquium* Krakow (Poland) 2020, *Conference* Krakow (Poland) 2020. **Publications** Books; articles.
Members National Committees in 7 countries:
Colombia, Egypt, Greece, Italy, Mexico, Poland, Spain.
NGO Relations Joint conferences with: *International Society for Research on Aggression (ISRA, #15419); Pugwash Conferences on Science and World Affairs (#18574); Society for Terrorism Research (STR, #19653)*; universities. [2022.02.21/XJ0117/E]

♦ International Colloquium on Graph Theory and Combinatorics (meeting series)
♦ International Colloquium on Group Theoretical Methods in Physics (meeting series)
♦ International Colloquium on Magnetic Films and Surfaces (meeting series)
♦ International Colloquium on Prospective Biology (meeting series)
♦ International Colloquium on Structural Information and Communication Complexity (meeting series)
♦ International Color Consortium (internationally oriented national body)

♦ International Colorectal Cancer Club (ICRCC) 12654

Pres Universitätsklinikum Ulm, Klinik für Allgemein- und Viszeralchirurgie, Albert-Einstein-Allee 23, 89081 Ulm, Germany.
URL: http://www.icrcc.com/

History 2001, Wiesbaden (Germany). **Aims** Promote the hightest standard for research, diagnosis and treatment of colorectal cancer. **Activities** Events/meetings. **Events** *International Colorectal Cancer Club Annual Congress* Nanjing (China) 2019, *Meeting* Shanghai (China) 2009, *Congress* Shanghai (China) 2008, *Congress / Meeting* Wiesbaden (Germany) 2007, *Joint meeting* Stockholm (Sweden) 2006.
[2020/XM3068/F]

♦ International Colour Association (AIC) 12655

Association Internationale de la Couleur – Internationale Vereinigung für die Farbe
Sec/Treas School of Design, Univ of Leeds, Leeds, LS2 9JT, UK. E-mail: treasurer@aic-color.org.
Pres address not obtained.
URL: https://aic-color.org/

History 21 Jun 1967, Washington, DC (USA). Statutes amended 10 Aug 1988; latest statutes adopted 2013. **Aims** Promote research and education in all aspects of colour; disseminate colour knowledge; encourage co-operation with industries. **Structure** Executive Committee. **Languages** English, French, German. **Staff** 10.00 FTE, voluntary. **Activities** Awards/prizes/competitions; events/meetings; training/education. **Events** *Interim Meeting* Taipei (Taiwan) 2025, *Midterm Meeting* Sao Paulo (Brazil) 2024, *Congress* Chiang Rai (Thailand) 2023, *Midterm Meeting* Toronto, ON (Canada) 2022, *Quadrennial Congress* Milan (Italy) 2021. **Publications** *Journal of the International Colour Association (JAIC)*. Annual Review; proceedings.
Members Regular – national or regional colour associations in 28 countries and territories:
Argentina, Australia, Belgium, Brazil, Bulgaria, Canada, Chile, China, Croatia, Finland, France, Germany, Hungary, Italy, Japan, Korea Rep, Mexico, Netherlands, Norway, Portugal, Slovenia, Spain, Sweden, Switzerland, Taiwan, Thailand, UK, USA.
Associate: 2 organizations listed in this Yearbook:
Color Marketing Group (CMG); International Association of Colour Consultants/Designers (IACC) (North America).
NGO Relations Statutory cooperation with: *Commission Internationale de l'Eclairage (CIE, #04219)*.
[2022/XC1515/C]

♦ International Colour Consortium / see International Color Consortium

♦ International Colour Vision Society (ICVS) 12656

Gen Sec College of Biological Sciences, UC Davis, One Shields Ave, Davis CA 95616, USA. T. +19167346817.
URL: https://www.icvs.info/

History 1971, Ghent (Belgium), as *International Research Group on Colour Vision Deficiencies (IRGCVD)*. 1997, present name adopted. **Structure** Directors Board. Verriest Medal Committee. **Finance** Members' dues. Sponsors. Budget (annual): euro 7,500. **Activities** Awards Verriest Medal. **Events** *Biennial Symposium* Riga (Latvia) 2019, *Biennial Symposium* Erlangen (Germany) 2017, *Biennial Symposium / Biennial International Symposium* Sendai (Japan) 2015, *Biennial Symposium / Biennial International Symposium* Winchester (UK) 2013, *Biennial symposium / Biennial International Symposium* Kongsberg (Norway) 2011. **Publications** *Daltoniana Newsletter* (periodical). Symposium proceedings.
Members Honorary, Student and Regular in 29 countries:
Argentina, Australia, Austria, Belgium, Brazil, Canada, China, Finland, France, Germany, Hungary, Iceland, Israel, Italy, Japan, Korea Rep, Lithuania, Netherlands, New Zealand, Norway, Slovenia, Spain, Sweden, Switzerland, UK, USA.
[2019/XF0085/v/F]

♦ International Combined Orthopaedic Research Societies (I-CORS) .. 12657

Sec c/o ORS, 9400 West Higgins Rd, Ste 225, Rosemont IL 60018-4976, USA.
URL: https://www.ors.org/icors/

History Combined Meeting launched 1992. New alliance formed under current title, 15 Oct 2013, Venice (Italy). Former names and other names: *ICORS* – alias. **Aims** Promote orthopaedic and musculoskeletal research, including the fields of engineering, biology, and clinical research; monitor organizational progress and educational content. **Structure** Steering Committee. **Activities** Events/meetings; networking/liaising. **Events** *I-CORS World Orthopaedic Research Congress (WORC)* Adelaide, SA (Australia) 2025, *World Orthopaedic Research Congress (WORC)* Edinburgh (UK) 2022, *Combined World Orthopaedic Research Congress* Montréal, QC (Canada) 2019, *Combined World Orthopaedic Research Congress* Xian (China) 2016, *Combined Meeting of Orthopaedic Research Societies* Venice (Italy) 2013.
Members Constituent members (10) in 9 countries and territories:
Australia, Canada, China, Japan, Korea Rep, New Zealand, Taiwan, UK, USA.
Included in the above, 2 regional associations:
Asia Pacific Orthopaedic Association (APOA, #01987); European Orthopaedic Research Society (EORS, #08119).
Associate Scientific Members (2):
AO Foundation (#00866); International Chinese Musculoskeletal Research Society (ICMRS).
[2022/XM8658/y/C]

♦ International Commercial Property Associates (inactive)
♦ International Commissie voor de Hydrologie van het Rijngebied / see International Commission for the Hydrology of the Rhine Basin (#12693)
♦ International Commission on Acoustics / see International Commission for Acoustics (#12658)

♦ International Commission for Acoustics (ICA) 12658

Registered Office Calle Serrano 144, 28006 Madrid, Spain. E-mail: icasecgen@icacommission.org.
Pres Walker Department of Mechanical Engineering, The University of Texas at Austin, 204 E Dean Keeton Street – ETC 4.146C, Austin TX 78712-1591, USA. T. +15124713055.
URL: http://www.icacommission.org/

History 1951. Founded as a sub-committee of *International Union of Pure and Applied Physics (IUPAP, #15810)*. New statutes adopted 31 Mar 1996, Antwerp (Belgium) and approved at IUPAP General Assembly, 20 Sep 1996, Uppsala (Sweden). By-laws adopted by member societies, 1998, at first General Assembly. Former names and other names: *International Commission on Acoustics (ICA)* – former (1951 to 1998); *Commission internationale sur l'acoustique* – former alias. **Aims** Promote international development and collaboration in all fields of acoustics, including research, development, education and standardization. **Structure** General Assembly (every 3 years, at Congress); Board; Executive. **Languages** English. **Staff** Voluntary. **Finance** Sources: members' dues. Other sources: levy from congress; special donations or grants. **Activities** Awards/prizes/competitions; events/meetings; financial and/or material support. **Events** *International Congress on Acoustics* New Orleans, LA (USA) 2025, *International Congress on Acoustics* Gyeongju (Korea Rep) 2022, *International Congress on Acoustics* Aachen (Germany) 2019, *International Congress on Acoustics* Buenos Aires (Argentina) 2016, *International Symposium on Nonlinear Acoustics* Lyon (France) 2015. **Publications** Congress proceedings.
Members Member Societies (47) in 46 countries and territories (indicates two Member Societies):
Argentina, Australia, Austria, Belgium, Brazil, Canada, Chile, China, Croatia, Czechia, Denmark, Egypt, Finland, France, Germany, Greece, Hong Kong, Hungary, Iceland, India, Iran Islamic Rep, Israel, Italy, Japan, Korea Rep, Lithuania, Mexico, Netherlands, New Zealand, Nigeria, Norway, Peru, Poland, Portugal, Russia, Serbia, Singapore, Slovakia, Slovenia, Spain, Sweden, Switzerland, Taiwan, Türkiye, UK, USA (*).
Observers in 5 countries:
Belarus, Indonesia, Latvia, Morocco, South Africa.
International affiliate members (8):
Audio Engineering Society (AES, #03014); European Acoustics Association (EAA, #05824); Ibero-American Federation of Acoustics (#11021); International Commission on Biological Effects of Noise (ICBEN, #12668); International Congress on Ultrasonics (ICU, #12901); International Institute of Acoustics and Vibration (IIAV, #13858); International Institute of Noise Control Engineering (IINCE, #13903); Western Pacific Commission for Acoustics (WESPAC, #20918).
NGO Relations Member of: *ISC World Data System (ISC-WDS, #16024); International Science Council (ISC, #14796)*. [2022/XE4650/y/C]

♦ International Commission of Aerial Navigation (inactive)

♦ International Commission against the Death Penalty (ICDP) 12659

Comisión Internacional contra la Pena de Muerte
SG Serrano Galvache 26, Torre Sur – 10 planta, Despacho 10-78, 28071 Madrid, Spain. T. +34913799458. E-mail: info@icomdp.org.
URL: http://www.icomdp.org/

History 7 Oct 2010, Madrid (Spain), on the initiative of the Spanish Government. **Aims** Promote, complement or support any action which aims at obtaining the abolition of the death penalty in all regions of the world. **Structure** Commission, chaired by President; Support Group; Secretariat. **Activities** Advocacy/lobbying/activism; events/meetings. **Publications** *ICDP Newsletter*. Annual Review; Reports. [2016/XM4677/C]

♦ International Commission against Impunity in Guatemala 12660

Comisión Internacional contra la Impunidad en Guatemala (CICIG)
Contact Apartado Postal 934 "A", Guatemala, Guatemala. T. +50223680455. E-mail: prensa@cicig.org.
URL: https://www.cicig.org/

History Established 12 Dec 2006, when government of Guatemala and *United Nations (UN, #20515)* signed the Agreement establishing CICIG. Operations began 2008. Mandate extended, 15 apr 2009, to run until 4 Sep 2011; mandate extended again to run until 4 Sep 2013; new mandate until 4 Sep 2015. **Aims** Investigate the existence of illicit security forces and clandestine security organizations that commit crimes that affect the fundamental human rights of the citizens of Guatemala, and identify the illegal group structures, activities, modes of operation and sources of financing; support the work of Guatemalan institutions, principally the Attorney General; make recommendations to the Government for the adoption of new public policies mechanisms and procedures directed at the eradication of these groups and strengthen the State's capacity to protect the basic human rights of its citizens; provide technical assistance to Justice Sector institutions in order to leave the Public Prosecutors Office and National Civilian Police better equipped to fight organized crime even after the conclusion of CICIG's mandate. [2019/XJ1652/E*]

♦ International Commission of Agricultural and Biosystems Engineering 12661

Commission internationale du génie rural (CIGR) – Comisión Internacional de Ingenieria Rural – Internationale Kommission für Agrartechnik
SG Tigert 1, Univ of Florida, Gainesville FL 32611, USA. E-mail: secretarygeneral@cigr.org.
URL: http://www.cigr.org/

History Founded Aug 1930, Liège (Belgium), at 1st International Congress of Agricultural Engineering. Originally referred to in English as *International Commission of Agricultural Engineering (CIGR)*. Current English title adopted, 1 Jan 2009. Statutes changed 2 Oct 1958, Brussels (Belgium); modified: 9 Mar 1964, Lausanne (Switzerland); 1969, Baden-Baden (Germany FR); 26 Sep 1974, Flevohof (Netherlands); 12 Jul 1979, East Lansing MI (USA); 7 Sep 1989, Dublin (Ireland); 1994, Milan (Italy) – effective 1 Jan 1995; 2000, Tsukuba (Japan) – effective 1 jan 2001. Present statutes adopted, 3 Sep 2008, Iguaçu (Brazil) – effective 1 Jan 2009. **Aims** Promote the art, science and technology of agricultural engineering; encourage and coordinate research; promote creation and activities of national and regional associations of agricultural engineers, technicians and architects; facilitate relations and exchange of research results and technology

among specialists in the field; encourage education, training and mobility of young professionals; constitute a documentation source and assist in publishing information useful for members. **Structure** General Assembly (every 2 years); Presidium; Executive Board. Technical Sections; Working Groups; Academy. **Languages** English. **Staff** 9.00 FTE, voluntary. **Finance** Sources: grants; members' dues. **Activities** Events/meetings; research/documentation. **Events** *Quadrennial Congress* Kyoto (Japan) 2022, *Joint AgEng Biennial Conference* Evora (Portugal) 2021, *Quadrennial International Conference on Agricultural Engineering* Québec, QC (Canada) 2021, *Joint AgEng Biennial Conference* Evora (Portugal) 2020, *Quadrennial International Conference on Agricultural Engineering* Québec, QC (Canada) 2020. **Publications** *CIGR Newsletter* (4 a year) in Arabic, Chinese, English, French, Russian, Spanish – also serves EurAgEng; *Agricultural Engineering International: The CIGR Journal of Scientific Research and Development* – electronic. *The University Structure and Curricula on Agricultural Engineering – An Overview of 25 countries* (1994); *CIGR Handbook of Agricultural Engineering* – 6 vols published to date. Section reports; congress and symposium proceedings.
Members Regional associations (6):
American Society of Agricultural and Biological Engineers; *Asian Association for Agricultural Engineering (AAAE, #01313)*; *Asociación Latinoamericana y del Caribe de Ingeniería Agrícola (ALIA, #02190)*; *Euro-Asian Association of Agricultural Engineers (EAAAE, #05636)*; *European Society of Agricultural Engineers (EurAgEng, #08513)*; *Southern and Eastern Africa Society of Agricultural Engineers (SEASAE, no recent information)*.
National members in 18 countries:
Australia, Brazil, Canada, China, Czechia, France, Ghana, India, Indonesia, Iran Islamic Rep, Israel, Japan, Korea Rep, Morocco, Poland, Slovakia, South Africa, Türkiye.
Corporate members (6):
Arab Organization for Agricultural Development (AOAD, #01018); Association of Overseas Chinese Agriculture, Biological, and Food Engineers (AOC); *Centre for Sustainable Agricultural Mechanization (CSAM, #03789)*; *FAO (#09260)*; *Institut International d'Ingénierie de l'Eau et de l'Environnement (2iE, #11313)*; *UNIDO (#20336)*.
Consultative Status Consultative status granted from: *ECOSOC (#05331)* (Ros C); *FAO (#09260)* (Special Status). **NGO Relations** *Club of Bologna (#04031)*; *Commission internationale pour organisation scientifique du travail en agriculture (CIOSTA, #04226)*; *European Federation of Animal Science (EAAP, #07046)*; *International Association of Rural Health and Medicine (IARM, #12140)*; *International Commission on Irrigation and Drainage (ICID, #12694)*; *International Organization for Standardization (ISO, #14473)*; *International Society for Horticultural Science (ISHS, #15180)*; *International Soil Tillage Research Organization (ISTRO, #15562)*; *International Union of Forest Research Organizations (IUFRO, #15774)*. [2020/XC1548/y/**C**]

♦ International Commission of Agricultural Engineering / see International Commission of Agricultural and Biosystems Engineering (#12661)
♦ International Commission for Agricultural Teaching (inactive)
♦ International Commission of Agriculture (inactive)

♦ International Commission for Alpine Rescue (ICAR) 12662

Commission internationale de sauvetage alpin (CISA) – Internationale Kommission für Alpines Rettungswesen (IKAR)

Office c/o Swiss Alpine Rescue SAR, Rega-Center, PO Box 1414, Zurich Airport, 8058 Zurich ZH, Switzerland. T. +41446543554. Fax +41446543842. E-mail: office@alpine-rescue.org.
URL: http://www.alpine-rescue.org/

History 1948. Founded as a result of the first international rescue course held in Obergurgl (Austria). **Aims** Provide a platform for mountain rescue and related organizations to disseminate knowledge with the prime goal of improving mountain rescue services and their safety. **Structure** Assembly of Delegates (annual); Executive Board; Technical Commissions (4); Sub-Commission. **Languages** English, French, German. **Staff** 0.30 FTE, paid. **Finance** Sources: meeting proceeds; members' dues. **Activities** Guidance/assistance/consulting; knowledge management/information dissemination; networking/liaising; research and development; training/education. **Events** *Annual Assembly* Montreux (Switzerland) 2022, *Annual Assembly* Thessaloniki (Greece) 2021, *Annual Assembly* Thessaloniki (Greece) 2020, *Annual Assembly* Zakopane (Poland) 2019, *Annual Assembly* Chamonix (France) 2018. **Publications** Surveys; guidelines; checklists.
Members Representatives from mountain rescue organizations in 40 countries and territories:
Andorra, Argentina, Australia, Austria, Belgium, Bosnia-Herzegovina, Bulgaria, Canada, China, Croatia, Cyprus, Czechia, France, Germany, Greece, Iceland, Ireland, Italy, Japan, Korea Rep, Liechtenstein, Montenegro, Nepal, Netherlands, New Zealand, North Macedonia, Norway, Poland, Romania, Scotland, Serbia, Slovakia, Slovenia, South Africa, Spain, Sweden, Switzerland, Tanzania UR, UK, USA.
NGO Relations Cooperates with (1): *Union internationale des associations d'alpinisme (UIAA, #20420)*. [2020.06.23/XD1521/**D**]

♦ International Commission on Antigens and Molecular Diagnostics (see: #15794)
♦ International Commission on the Applications of the Mössbauer Effect / see International Board on the Applications of the Mössbauer Effect (#12365)

♦ International Commission on Astroparticle Physics 12663

Chairperson address not obtained.
URL: https://iupap.org/commissions/c4-commission-on-astroparticle-physics/

History 1947. Founded as a Commission (C 4) of *International Union of Pure and Applied Physics (IUPAP, #15810)*. Currently serves as an internal commission. Former names and other names: *International Commission on Cosmic Rays* – former; *Commission internationale sur les rayons cosmiques* – former; *IUPAP Commission on Cosmic Rays* – alias; *Commission de l'UIPPA sur les rayons cosmiques* – alias. **Aims** Promote exchange of information and views among members of the international scientific community in the general field of Astroparticle Physics. **Structure** Chairman; Vice-Chairman; Secretary. **Finance** Supported by: *International Union of Pure and Applied Physics (IUPAP, #15810)*. **Events** *International Cosmic Ray Conference – ICRC* Nagoya (Japan) 2023, *Biennial International Cosmic Ray Conference* Berlin (Germany) 2021, *Biennial International Cosmic Ray Conference* Madison, WI (USA) 2019, *Biennial International Cosmic Ray Conference* Busan (Korea Rep) 2017, *International Meeting for Large Neutrino Infrastructures* Tsukuba (Japan) 2016. **Publications** Proceedings.
Members Individuals in 14 countries:
China, France, Germany, India, Italy, Japan, Netherlands, Norway, Poland, Russia, South Africa, Sweden, UK, USA.
Associate members (3) in 2 countries:
Finland, Switzerland. [2022.02.01/XE2394/v/**E**]

♦ International Commission on Astrophysics / see IUPAP Commission on Astrophysics (#16082)

♦ International Commission on Atmospheric Chemistry and Global Pollution (ICACGP) 12664

Commission internationale de chimie atmosphérique et de pollution globale

Pres Inst of Environmental Physics and Remote Sensing IUP/IFE, Univ of Bremen – FB1, Postfach 330440, 28334 Bremen, Germany. T. +4942121862100. Fax +494212184555.
Scientific Sec Dept of Physics/Atmospheric Science, Sir James Dunn Bldg – Room 130, Dalhousie Univ, Halifax NS B3H 3J5, Canada. T. +19024942324. Fax +19024945191.
URL: http://www.icacgp.org/

History 1957, as *Commission on Atmospheric Chemistry and Radioactivity*. Present name adopted 1971. Parent organization: *International Association of Meteorology and Atmospheric Sciences (IAMAS, #12031)*. Also referred to as *IAMAP International Commission on Atmospheric Chemistry and Global Pollution – Commission internationale de chimie atmosphérique et de pollution globale de l'AIMPA* and as *Commission on Atmospheric Chemistry and Global Pollution of the International Association of Meteorology and Atmospheric Physics (CACGP)*. **Aims** Promote research on the chemistry and composition of the global *troposphere*, exchange of gases and particulate material between the atmosphere and the underlying surface and climate change; initiate, facilitate and coordinate in this field, the research programs which require, or benefit from, international cooperation; stimulate discussion and provide publication of the results of such research programs. **Structure** Officers. **Languages** English. **Staff** 30.00 FTE, voluntary. **Finance** Support by IAMAS. Annual budget: about euro 10,000. **Activities** Events/meetings; research/documentation. **Events** *Quadrennial Symposium* Natal (Brazil) 2014, *Quadrennial Symposium* Halifax, NS (Canada) 2010, *Quadrennial Symposium* Halifax, NS (Canada) 2010, *Joint symposium on atmospheric chemistry at the interfaces* Cape Town (South Africa) 2006, *Clouds, aerosols, radiation and climate symposium* Sapporo (Japan) 2003. **Publications** Conference abstracts.
Members Individuals in 18 countries and territories:
Australia, Brazil, Canada, Chile, China, France, Germany, India, Italy, Japan, Norway, Puerto Rico, Russia, South Africa, Spain, Taiwan, UK, USA.
NGO Relations Joint projects with: *Future Earth (#10048)*; *Scientific Committee on Oceanic Research (SCOR, #19149)*. Instrumental in setting up: *International Global Atmospheric Chemistry Project (IGAC, #13721)*. [2018.06.01/XE3837/v/**E**]

♦ International Commission on Atmospheric Electricity (ICAE) 12665

Commission internationale de l'Electricité Atmosphérique – Comisión Internacional de Electricidad Atmosférica – Internationale Luftelektrische Kommission – Mezdunarodnaja Komissija po Atmosfernomu Elektricestvu

Pres Dept of Electrical and Electronic Engineering, Gifu Univ, Yanagido 1-1, Gifu, 501-1193 Japan. T. +81582932702. Fax +81582301894.
Sec Tokyo Metropolitan Univ, Asahigaoka 6-6, Hino-shi, Tokyo, 191-0065 Japan.
URL: http://icae.jp/

History as a commission of *International Association of Meteorology and Atmospheric Sciences (IAMAS, #12031)*, itself a constituent international association of *International Union of Geodesy and Geophysics (IUGG, #15776)*. Also referred to as *IAMAP International Commission on Atmospheric Electricity – Commission internationale de l'électricité atmosphérique de l'AIMPA*. **Aims** Promote the study of atmospheric electricity by making a scientific and human community whose work will benefit all humanity. **Structure** Officers: President, Secretary, Honorary members and members. **Languages** English. **Staff** Voluntary. **Finance** Budget (annual): US$ 1,250. **Activities** Events/meetings; research/documentation. **Events** *Quadrennial Conference on Atmospheric Electricity* Nara (Japan) 2018, *Quadrennial Conference on Atmospheric Electricity* Norman, OK (USA) 2014, *Quadrennial Conference on Atmospheric Electricity* Rio de Janeiro (Brazil) 2011, *Quadrennial Conference on Atmospheric Electricity* Beijing (China) 2007, *Quadrennial Conference on Atmospheric Electricity* Paris (France) 2003. **Publications** *ICAE Newsletter* (2 a year). Conference Proceedings.
Members Individuals in 11 countries:
Brazil, China, Estonia, France, Israel, Japan, Poland, Russia, Sweden, UK, USA. [2018/XE3842/v/**E**]

♦ International Commission on Atomic, Molecular and Optical Physics 12666

Commission internationale sur la physique atomique, moléculaire et optique

Chair address not obtained.
URL: https://iupap.org/commissions/c15-atomic-molecular-and-optical-physics/

History 1966. Established as a Commission (C 15) of *International Union of Pure and Applied Physics (IUPAP, #15810)*. Currently serves as an internal commission. Former names and other names: *International Commission on Atomic and Molecular Physics and Spectroscopy* – former (1966 to 1994); *Commission internationale sur la physique atomique et moléculaire et la spectroscopie* – former (1966 to 1994); *IUPAP Commission on Atomic and Molecular Physics and Spectroscopy* – former; *Commission de l'UIPPA sur la physique atomique et moléculaire et la spectroscopie* – former. **Aims** Promote information exchange in the general field of atomic, molecular and optical physics, including: properties of charged and neutral atoms and molecules; dynamics of these entities; applications of optical and laser techniques to the manipulation of atomic and molecular species; application of atomic and molecular physics to technology. **Structure** Chair, Vice-Chair, Secretary and 11 members. **Languages** English. **Staff** 3.00 FTE, voluntary. **Finance** Supported by: *International Union of Pure and Applied Physics (IUPAP, #15810)*. **Activities** Events/meetings. **Events** *ICPEAC : International Conference on Photonic, Electronic and Atomic Collisions* 2021, *ICPEAC : Biennial International Conference on Photonic, Electronic and Atomic Collisions* Caen (France) / Deauville (France) 2019, *ICPEAC : Biennial International Conference on Photonic, Electronic and Atomic Collisions* Cairns, QLD (Australia) 2017, *ICPEAC : Biennial International Conference on Photonic, Electronic and Atomic Collisions* Madrid (Spain) 2015, *ICAP : International Conference on Atomic Physics* Washington, DC (USA) 2014.
Members Individuals (14) in 14 countries:
Argentina, Australia, Austria, Canada, China, Czechia, France, Germany, India, Japan, Korea Rep, Spain, Sweden, UK. [2022.05.06/XE0903/v/**E**]

♦ International Commission on Atomic and Molecular Physics and Spectroscopy / see International Commission on Atomic, Molecular and Optical Physics (#12666)
♦ International Commission for Bee Botany / see International Commission for Plant-Pollinator Relationships (#12716)
♦ International Commission on Bio-indicators / see International Commission on Bioindicators (#12667)

♦ International Commission on Bioindicators 12667

Chair Dept of Physiology, Univ of Kuopio, PO Box 1627, FI-70211 Kuopio, Finland.

History Founded 1988, Canberra (Australia). Also referred to as *Interdisciplinary Commission on Bioindicators* and *IUBS Commission for Bioindicators*. **Aims** Facilitate, encourage and stimulate research on bioindicators; support and organize cooperation and exchange of information between *laboratories*; promote practical application of *biological indicators* for monitoring the state of the *environment*. **Languages** English. **Staff** Voluntary. **Finance** Commission itself has no funding; event often funded by Academy of hosting country and university or research institute. **Events** *International Conference* St Petersburg (Russia) 2008, *International Conference* Hong Kong (Hong Kong) 2007, *Biennial symposium / International Conference* Linthicum Heights, MD (USA) 2006, *International Conference* Prague (Czech Rep) 2005, *Biennial Symposium* Hong Kong (Hong Kong) 2003. **Publications** *Environmental Bioindicators* – journal. *Biological Monitoring of the Environment – A Manual of Methods* (1994) by J Salanki, et al. Symposium and conference proceedings.
Members Individuals in 23 countries and territories:
Australia, Canada, China, Czechia, Estonia, Finland, France, Germany, Hong Kong, Hungary, India, Ireland, Italy, Japan, Malaysia, Netherlands, Philippines, Poland, Russia, Taiwan, UK, Ukraine, USA.
NGO Relations Scientific member of *International Union of Biological Sciences (IUBS, #15760)*. Instrumental in setting up: *International Society of Environmental Indicators (ISEI, #15095)*. [2015/XD2772/v/**F**]

♦ International Commission for Biological Control / see International Organisation for Biological Control (#14424)
♦ International Commission for Biological Education / see IUBS Commission for Biological Education (#16079)

♦ International Commission on Biological Effects of Noise (ICBEN) . . 12668

Commission internationale sur les effets biologiques du bruit

Sec Min of Infrastructure and Water Management, D-G Environment and International Affairs, PO Box 20901, 2500 EX The Hague, Netherlands. T. +31611155608.
Chairperson Unit for Experimental Psychiatry, Div of Sleep & Chronobiology, Dept of Psychiatry, Perelman School of Medicine, Univ of Pennsylvania, 1013 Blockley Hall, 423 Guardian Drive, Philadelphia PA 19104-6021, USA. T. +12155735866. Fax +12155736410.
URL: http://www.icben.org/

History Founded 1968, Washington DC (USA). **Aims** Promote a high level of scientific research concerning all aspects of noise-induced effects on human beings and animals including preventive regulatory measures; keep alive a vivid communication among scientists working in the field. **Structure** Congress (every 3 years); Executive Committee; International Noise Teams (9). **Languages** English. **Staff** None. **Finance** Officers supply funds. **Activities** Events/meetings. **Events** *Congress* Stockholm (Sweden) 2021, *Congress* Stockholm (Sweden) 2020, *Noise as a public health problem* Zurich (Switzerland) 2017, *Congress* Nara (Japan) 2014, *Congress* London (UK) 2011. **Publications** Conference proceedings.
Members Individuals in 33 countries and territories:
Australia, Austria, Belgium, Canada, China, Czechia, Denmark, Finland, France, Germany, Greece, Hong Kong, India, Israel, Italy, Japan, Korea Rep, Malaysia, Montenegro, Netherlands, New Zealand, Nigeria, Norway, Poland, Portugal, Russia, Serbia, Spain, Sweden, Switzerland, Türkiye, UK, USA.
NGO Relations Cooperates with: *International Organization for Standardization (ISO, #14473)*. Member of: *International Commission for Acoustics (ICA, #12658)*. [2021/XE2564/v/**E**]

♦ International Commission on Biological Physics 12669

Chair address not obtained.
URL: https://iupap.org/commissions/c6-biological-physics/

History 1990, as a Commission (C 6) of *International Union of Pure and Applied Physics (IUPAP, #15810)*. Also referred to as *IUPAP Commission on Biological Physics*. Currently serves as an internal commission. **Aims** Promote information exchange in the field, including experimental, theoretical and computational studies of *biomolecules* and other biological systems. **Structure** Chairman, Vice-Chairman, Secretary and 10 members. **Languages** English. **Finance** Source: IUPAP. **Activities** Organizes several series of international conferences and symposia. **Events** *International conference on biological physics* Montevideo (Uruguay) 2007, *International conference on biological physics / Triennial International Symposium on Biological Physics – ICBP* Gothenburg (Sweden) 2004, *International conference on biological physics* Kyoto (Japan) 2001, *Meeting on biological physics and synchrotron radiation* Grenoble (France) 2000, *International conference on biological physics / Triennial International Symposium on Biological Physics – ICBP* Santa Fe, NM (USA) 1998.
Members Individuals in 13 countries:
Argentina, Belgium, France, Germany, Hungary, India, Italy, Japan, New Zealand, Russia, Slovakia, Sweden, USA.
Associate members (2) in 2 countries:
Brazil, Germany. [2019/XK0033/v/**E**]

♦ International Commission on Bionomenclature / see International Committee on Bionomenclature (#12748)
♦ International Commission for Botanical Maps (inactive)
♦ International Commission of the Cape Spartel Light in Tanger (inactive)

♦ International Commission of Catholic Prison Pastoral Care (ICCPPC) 12670

Commission internationale de la pastorale catholique des prisons – Comisión Internacional de la Pastoral Penitenciaria Católica – Internationale Kommission der Katholischen Gefängnisseelsorge
Gen Sec Eikvarenlaan 1, 5646 AL Eindhoven, Netherlands. T. +31620953014.
URL: http://www.iccppc.org/
History 1950. Statutes adopted, 1974. Officially recognized by Vatican, 2014. Former names and other names: *International Commission of Prison Chaplains* – former; *Commission internationale des aumôniers des prisons* – former; *International Commission of General Prison Chaplains* – former; *International Commission of Principal Prison Chaplains* – former; *International Catholic Commission of Prison Chaplaincies* – former; *Commission internationale des aumôniers généraux de prison* – former; *Comisión Internacional de Capellanes Generales de Prisión* – former; *Internationale Kommission der Katholische Hauptgefängnisseelsorger* – former. **Aims** Promote training of prison *chaplains* and coordinate their work; contribute towards reformation of the penal system; support human *rights* and defend freedom of religious assistance in prisons. **Structure** General Meeting (every 5 years, in conjunction with Congress); Executive Board. **Languages** English, French, Spanish. **Staff** 0.50 FTE, voluntary. **Finance** Sources: donations; gifts, legacies; members' dues. **Activities** Advocacy/lobbying/activism; networking/liaising. **Events** *Congress* Panama (Panama) 2017, *Congress* Yaoundé (Cameroon) 2011, *Conference* Esztergom (Hungary) 2009, *Congress* Rome (Italy) 2007, *Congress* Dublin (Ireland) 2003. **Publications** *Newsletter*. *For Mercy and Justice – International Reflections on Prison Chaplaincy* (2016); *Guide for Prison Chaplains to Prevent Torture* (2010); *UN and EU Recommendations on the Treatment of Foreigners in Prison* (2007); *Discover the Face of Life* (2006); *Human Rights and the Catholic Church* (2001). Congress reports; country reports; booklets.
Members Head chaplains or their representatives who are responsible for catholic prison chaplaincy in 115 countries and territories:
Albania, Algeria, Andorra, Antigua-Barbuda, Argentina, Australia, Austria, Barbados, Belarus, Belgium, Belize, Benin, Bolivia, Bosnia-Herzegovina, Botswana, Brazil, Bulgaria, Burundi, Cameroon, Canada, Cape Verde, Central African Rep, Chad, Chile, China, Colombia, Congo Brazzaville, Congo DR, Côte d'Ivoire, Croatia, Cuba, Curaçao, Czechia, Denmark, Dominica, Dominican Rep, Ecuador, Egypt, El Salvador, Equatorial Guinea, Estonia, Ethiopia, Finland, France, Gabon, Gambia, Germany, Ghana, Greece, Grenada, Guinea-Bissau, Guyana, Haiti, Holy See, Honduras, Hong Kong, Hungary, India, Indonesia, Ireland, Italy, Jamaica, Japan, Kenya, Korea Rep, Latvia, Lebanon, Lesotho, Liberia, Lithuania, Luxembourg, Madagascar, Malawi, Mali, Malta, Mauritania, Mauritius, Mexico, Mozambique, Netherlands, New Zealand, Nicaragua, Nigeria, Panama, Paraguay, Peru, Philippines, Poland, Portugal, Romania, Russia, Rwanda, Singapore, Slovakia, Slovenia, South Africa, Spain, Sri Lanka, Suriname, Sweden, Switzerland, Taiwan, Tanzania UR, Thailand, Togo, Tonga, Uganda, UK, Ukraine, Uruguay, USA, Venezuela, Vietnam, Zambia, Zimbabwe.
Consultative Status Consultative status granted from: *ECOSOC (#05331)* (Special). **NGO Relations** Member of (1): *Forum of Catholic Inspired NGOs (#09905)*. [2022.03.01/XD4776/v/**D**]

♦ International Commission on Chemical Crop Protection (inactive)
♦ International Commission for the Chemical Study of the Soil (inactive)

♦ International Commission on Civil Status (ICCS) 12671

Commission internationale de l'état civil (CIEC)
Secretariat 3 place Arnold, 67000 Strasbourg, France. T. +33388611862. E-mail: ciec-sg@ciec1.org.
URL: http://www.ciec1.org/
History Sep 1948, Amsterdam (Netherlands). Recognized in Bern (Switzerland) by protocol dated 25 Sep 1950; further protocol dated 25 Sep 1952. **Aims** Promote international treaties on civil status problems and international family law; encourage exchange of legislative texts and regulations; advise authorities and administrations of member States; research means of simplifying or unifying the rights of individuals and administrative techniques concerning civil status. **Structure** General Assembly (annual); Bureau; National Sections (7). Membership open to governments only. Meetings closed. **Languages** English, French. **Staff** 1.00 FTE, paid. **Activities** Guidance/assistance/consulting; knowledge management/information dissemination; events/meetings; projects/programmes. **Events** *Annual General Assembly* Brussels (Belgium) 2011, *Annual General Assembly* Lódz (Poland) 2010, *Annual General Assembly* Strasbourg (France) 2009, *Annual General Assembly* Luxembourg (Luxembourg) 2008, *Annual General Assembly* Munich (Germany) 2007. **Publications** Conventions; recommendations; guides.
Members Governments of 7 countries:
Belgium, France, Greece, Luxembourg, Spain, Switzerland, Türkiye.
IGO Relations Member of: *European Committee on Legal Cooperation (#06655)*. Special agreement with: *Council of Europe (CE, #04881)*; *The Hague Conference on Private International Law (HCCH, #10850)*; *Parliamentary Assembly of the Council of Europe (PACE, #18211)*; *UNHCR (#20327)*.
[2018.09.14/XD1559/**D***]

♦ International Commission on Cloud Physics / see International Commission on Clouds and Precipitation (#12672)

♦ International Commission on Clouds and Precipitation (ICCP) 12672

Commission internationale des nuages et des précipitations
Sec address not obtained.
URL: http://www.iccp-iamas.org/
History 4 Oct 1967, Lucerne (Switzerland), as a successor to *'Ad Hoc Committee on Cloud Physics'*, under the name *International Commission on Cloud Physics* and as a Commission of *International Association of Meteorology and Atmospheric Sciences (IAMAS, #12031)*. Also referred to as *IAMAP International Commission on Clouds and Precipitation*. **Aims** Stimulate scientific research throughout the world in the area of clouds and precipitation through organization of conferences, workshops and symposia; encourage transfer of scientific ideas to scientists worldwide and facilitate international collaboration. **Structure** Executive Committee, comprising President, Vice-President, Secretary, Honorary Members and members. **Languages** English. **Staff** None. **Finance** Financed via: quadrennial conference registration fees; IAMAS; *World Meteorological Organization (WMO, #21649)*. Budget (annual): about euro 4,000, mostly to support travel grants to quadrennial conference. **Activities** Events/meetings. **Events** *Quadrennial Conference* Manchester (UK) 2016, *International Conference* Fort Collins, CO (USA) 2013, *Quadrennial Conference* Leipzig (Germany) 2012, *International conference* Prague (Czech Rep) 2009, *Quadrennial conference / Quadrennial Conference on Clouds and Precipitation* Cancún (Mexico) 2008. **Publications** Proceedings of quadrennial conference.
Members Experts in 17 countries:
Australia, Brazil, Canada, China, France, Germany, Hungary, India, Israel, Italy, Japan, Mexico, Poland, Russia, Sweden, UK, USA.
IGO Relations Co-sponsors conferences with: WMO. [2015/XE3841/v/**E**]

♦ International Commission on Communication, Information and Informatics (no recent information)

♦ International Commission on Computational Physics 12673

Chair address not obtained.
URL: https://iupap.org/commissions/computational-physics/
History 20 Sep 1996, Uppsala (Sweden), at IUPAP 22nd General Assembly, following a 2-year activity by a working group, as a Commission (C 20) of *International Union of Pure and Applied Physics (IUPAP, #15810)*. Currently serves as an internal commission. **Aims** Promote information exchange in the area of computational studies of problems originating in or relevant to physics, including: numerical and symbolic models and *algorithms* for the *simulation* of physical systems; computational control and *data processing* of experiments; physical basis of *computer* machinery. **Structure** Officers: Chair; Vice-Chair; Secretary. **Languages** English. **Staff** 12.00 FTE, paid. **Activities** Presents recommendations related to advancement of Computational Physics, including improved education, exchange of information and sponsorship of international conferences related to the field; may designate Associate Members working in the industry or universities to improve contact with people working in the field. Organizes several international conference series, including Annual International Conference on Computational Physics (CCP), successor of EPS-APS Joint Conferences "Physics Computing" (PC) organized annually since 1989. **Events** *IUPAP Conference on Computational Physics* Guwahati (India) 2015, *IUPAP Conference on Computational Physics / Annual International Conference on Computational Physics (CCP)* Boston, MA (USA) 2014, *IUPAP Conference on Computational Physics / Annual International Conference on Computational Physics (CCP)* Moscow (Russia) 2013, *Conference on Computational Physics / Annual International Conference on Computational Physics (CCP)* Kobe (Japan) 2012, *Conference on Computational Physics* Gatlinburg, TN (USA) 2011.
Members Individuals in 12 countries:
Australia, Austria, Canada, Cuba, Finland, Germany, Hungary, Japan, Russia, Spain, UK, USA.
Associated members (5) in 4 countries:
Czechia, Germany (2), Switzerland, USA.
NGO Relations Collaborates with: Group of Computational Physics (CPG) of *European Physical Society (EPS, #08207)*; Division of Computational Physics (DCP) of the American Physical Society; similar organizations in Asia, Africa and America. [2019/XK1341/v/**E**]

♦ International Commission for Conformity Certification of Electrical Equipment / see IEC System of Conformity Assessment Schemes for Electrotechnical Equipment and Components (#11096)

♦ International Commission of the Congo-Ubangui-Sangha Basin . . . 12674

Commission internationale du Bassin Congo-Oubangui-Sangha (CICOS)
SG Bldg Kilou, croisement avenues Poids Lourds et Wagenia, 3e étage, BP 12645, Kinshasa, Congo DR.
URL: http://www.cicos.info/
History 16 Nov 1999. **Aims** Support sustainable development, reduce poverty and reinforce regional integration in the countries of the Congo-Ubangui-Sangha Basin. **Structure** Committee of Ministers, Management Committee; Secretariat. **Finance** Supported by: *Deutsche Gesellschaft für Technische Zusammenarbeit (GTZ, inactive)*.
Members Governments of 4 countries:
Cameroon, Central African Rep, Congo Brazzaville, Congo DR.
Observer (1):
Angola.
IGO Relations Memorandum of Cooperation with: *Secretariat of the Convention of Wetlands (#19200)*. Memorandum of Understanding with: *Lake Chad Basin Commission (LCBC, #16220)*. Partner of: *Niger Basin Authority (NBA, #17134)*. Participates in: *ECA Sub-Regional Office for Central Africa (ECA/SRO-CA, #05274)*. **NGO Relations** Member of: *African Network for Basin Organizations (ANBO, #00381)*. [2016/XM1737/**E***]

♦ International Commission for Congresses of Agricultural Associations and for Rural Demography (inactive)

♦ International Commission for the Conservation of Atlantic Tunas (ICCAT) 12675

Commission internationale pour la conservation des thonidés de l'Atlantique (CICTA) – Comisión Internacional para la Conservación del Atún Atlantico (CICAA)
Exec Sec Calle Corazon de Maria 8, 6th floor, 28002 Madrid, Spain. T. +34914165600. Fax +34914152612. E-mail: info@iccat.int.
URL: http://www.iccat.int/
History Established 21 Mar 1969, following ratification or adherence by 7 countries to *International Convention for the Conservation of Atlantic Tunas (1966)*, signed 14 May 1966, Rio de Janeiro (Brazil), at a conference convened by *FAO (#09260)*. Protocol to amend the Convention finalized, Nov 2019. **Aims** Under the provisions of the International Convention for the Conservation of Atlantic Tunas, maintain the populations of tunas and tuna-like species found in the Atlantic Ocean and the adjacent seas at levels which will permit the maximum *sustainable* catch for food and other purposes. **Structure** Commission (meet annually), composed of Contracting Party Delegations. Standing Committees (2): Finance and Administration (STACFAD); Research and Statistics (SCRS), including sub-committees on statistics and ecosystems. Compliance Committee; Permanent Working Group on the Improvement of ICCAT Statistics and Conservation Measures (PWG); Standing Working Group on Dialogue between Fisheries Scientists and Managers (SWGSM); Panels (4); Headquarters in Madrid (Spain). **Languages** English, French, Spanish. **Staff** 39.00 FTE, paid. **Finance** Member countries' contributions, assessed on the basis of the Madrid Protocol, in force since Mar 2005, and dividing Contracting Parties into 4 groups, based on classification of market economies and per capita GNP, and on tuna catch and canned production. Other sources: voluntary contributions; observer participation in meetings. **Activities** Knowledge management/information dissemination; research/documentation; advocacy/lobbying/activism; events/meetings. **Events** *Meeting* Sapporo (Japan) 2016, *Meeting* Madrid (Spain) 2015, *Annual Meeting* Madrid (Spain) 2014, *Atlantic Bluefin Tuna Stock Assessment Meeting* Madrid (Spain) 2014, *Intersessional Meeting* Madrid (Spain) 2014. **Publications** *ICCAT Statistical Bulletin* (annual). Collective volume of scientific papers; annual report for biennial period, in English, French, Spanish.
Members Contracting Parties (53 including European Community serving as 1 party):
Albania, Algeria, Angola, Barbados, Belize, Brazil, Canada, Cape Verde, China, Côte d'Ivoire, Curaçao, Egypt, El Salvador, Equatorial Guinea, Gabon, Gambia, Ghana, Grenada, Guatemala, Guinea, Guinea-Bissau, Honduras, Iceland, Japan, Korea Rep, Liberia, Libya, Mauritania, Mexico, Morocco, Namibia, Nicaragua, Nigeria, Norway, Panama, Philippines, Russia, Sao Tomé-Principe, Senegal, Sierra Leone, South Africa, St Pierre-Miquelon, St Vincent-Grenadines, Syrian AR, Trinidad-Tobago, Tunisia, Türkiye, UK Overseas Territories, Uruguay, USA, Vanuatu, Venezuela.
Regional entity (1):
European Union (EU, #08967).
IGO Relations Cooperates with:
- *Agreement on the Conservation of Albatrosses and Petrels (ACAP, 2001)*;
- *Commission for the Conservation of Antarctic Marine Living Resources (CCAMLR, #04206)*;
- *Commission for the Conservation of Southern Bluefin Tuna (CCSBT, #04207)*;
- *Convention for the Protection on the Marine Environment for the North-East Atlantic (OSPAR Convention, 1992)*;
- *FAO (#09260)*;
- *General Fisheries Commission for the Mediterranean (GFCM, #10112)*;
- *Indian Ocean Tuna Commission (IOTC, #11162)*;
- *Inter-American Tropical Tuna Commission (IATTC, #11454)*;
- *International Council for the Exploration of the Sea (ICES, #13021)*;
- *International Whaling Commission (IWC, #15879)*;
- *North-East Atlantic Fisheries Commission (NEAFC, #17581)*;
- *Northwest Atlantic Fisheries Organization (NAFO, #17606)*;
- *Secretariat of the Convention on International Trade in Endangered Species of Wild Fauna and Flora (CITES Secretariat, #19199)*;
- *South East Atlantic Fisheries Organization (SEAFO, #19801)*;
- *Statistical Office of the European Union (Eurostat, #19974)*;
- *Western Central Atlantic Fishery Commission (WECAFC, #20911)*;
- *Western and Central Pacific Fisheries Commission (WCPFC, #20912)*;
- *World Trade Organization (WTO, #21864)*. [2019.12.15/XC3899/**E***]

♦ International Commission on Cosmic Rays / see International Commission on Astroparticle Physics (#12663)

♦ International Commission on Couple and Family Relations (ICCFR) . 12676

Commission internationale des relations du couple et de la famille (CIRCF)

Admin 16 Myddelton Gardens, London, N21 2PA, UK. E-mail: secretariat@iccfr.org – administrator@iccfr.org.
Chair address not obtained.
URL: http://www.iccfr.org/

History 1953. Founded within *World Family Organization (WFO, #21399)*. Former names and other names: *International Commission on Marriage and Marriage Guidance* – former; *International Commission on Marriage and Interpersonal Relations (CIMRI)* – former. **Aims** Advance and disseminate knowledge about couple and family relationships; support activities promoting their well-being; provide a forum for dialogue. **Structure** Council; Board of Trustees. **Languages** English, French. **Staff** 0.20 FTE, paid. **Finance** Sources: members' dues. **Activities** Events/meetings; networking/liaising; publishing activities. **Events** *Poland in Solidarity with Ukrainian Refugees* London (UK) 2022, *Couple and Family Relationships in Times of Crisis* London (UK) 2021, *Seminar* London (UK) 2020, *Annual Conference* Rome (Italy) 2019, *Couple relationships in the 21st century – evolving contexts and emergent meanings* Valletta (Malta) 2018. **Publications** Conference papers and proceedings; reports.
Members Organizations and individuals in 40 countries and territories:
Argentina, Australia, Austria, Belgium, Bulgaria, Canada, China, Congo DR, Czechia, Denmark, Egypt, Estonia, Finland, France, Germany, Hong Kong, Hungary, India, Ireland, Italy, Latvia, Luxembourg, Malta, Netherlands, New Zealand, Norway, Portugal, Russia, Saudi Arabia, Singapore, Slovenia, South Africa, Spain, Sri Lanka, Sweden, Switzerland, Thailand, Tunisia, UK, USA.
NGO Relations Links with numerous NGOs including: *International Centre for Family Studies (#12492)*; national associations. [2022.10.19/XE2956/E]

- ♦ International Commission CV-AV Apostolic Movement for Children / see International Movement of Apostolate of Children (#14192)
- ♦ International Commission of the Danube (inactive)
- ♦ International Commission for the Decennial Revision of the International Lists of Diseases and Causes of Death (inactive)
- ♦ International Commission on Diplomatics (see: #12777)

♦ International Commission on Distance Education 12677

Exec Pres C/ Monasterio del Escorial 11, 28300 Aranjuez, Madrid, Spain. T. +34913599233. E-mail: info@intcode.org.
URL: http://www.intcode.org/

History Founded 1997, Geneva (Switzerland). **Aims** Promote open, distance and online education. **Structure** Board. **Languages** English, French, Spanish. **Finance** Members' dues. **Activities** Training/education; publishing activitites; networking/lilaising. **Members** Institutions offering post-secondary and/or adult education; research institutions; educational authorities; individuals. Membership countries not specified. **Consultative Status** Consultative status granted from: *ECOSOC (#05331)* (Special). [2015.08.26/XE4704/E]

♦ International Commission for Driver Testing (CIECA) 12678

Commission internationale des examens de conduite automobile (CIECA) – Internationale Kommission für Fahrerlaubnisprüfungen (CIECA)

Managing Dir Av de la Toison d'Or 77, 1060 Brussels, Belgium. T. +3227327230. E-mail: info@cieca.eu.
Pres address not obtained.
URL: http://www.cieca.eu/

History 15 Nov 1956, The Hague (Netherlands). Former names and other names: *International Driving Tests Committee (CIECA)* – former; *Internationale Kommission für Kraftfahrzeug-Führerprüfungen* – former; *International Commission for Driver Testing Authorities (CIECA)* – former. **Aims** Improve driving standards; contribute to road traffic education; improve road safety; protect the environment; facilitate mobility. **Structure** General Assembly (annual); Permanent Bureau (Board); Expert Advisory Group; Theory Test Advisory Group; Secretariat. **Languages** English. **Staff** 4.00 FTE, paid. **Finance** Sources: members' dues. **Activities** Events/meetings; knowledge management/information dissemination; networking/liaising; research/documentation; standards/guidelines; training/education. **Events** *General Assembly and Congress* Vienna (Austria) 2023, *General Assembly and Congress* Naples (Italy) 2022, *General Assembly and Congress* 2021, *General Assembly* 2020, *Annual General Assembly and Congress* Tbilisi (Georgia) 2019. **Publications** *CIECA Newsletter*. Annual Report; expert reports.
Members Effective; Associate; Affiliate. Effective: national organizations responsible for regulation, execution or auditing of driving tests in 37 countries and territories:
Austria, Bulgaria, Croatia, Cyprus, Czechia, Denmark, Estonia, Faeroe Is, Finland, Flanders, France, Georgia, Germany, Great Britain, Greece, Hungary, Iceland, Ireland, Korea Rep, Kosovo, Latvia, Lithuania, Luxembourg, Malta, Monaco, Netherlands, New Zealand, Northern Ireland, Norway, Poland, Portugal, Romania, Spain, Sweden, Switzerland, United Arab Emirates, Wallonia.
Associate in 10 countries:
Austria, Belgium, France, Germany, Ireland, Norway, Poland, Spain, UK, United Arab Emirates.
IGO Relations Accredited by (2): *European Commission (EC, #06633)* (DG Mobility and Transport); *United Nations Office at Vienna (UNOV, #20604)*. Associated with Department of Global Communications of the United Nations. **NGO Relations** Affiliated with (5): American Association of Motor Vehicle Administrators (AAMVA); *Association européenne des formateurs du transport (EuroTra, #02571)*; *Fédération européenne des auto-écoles (EFA, #09560)*; *MOVING International Road Safety Association (MOVING, #16874)*; *Nordisk Trafikskole Union (NTU, #17541)*. [2023.02.13/XD9844/y/F]

- ♦ International Commission for Driver Testing Authorities / see International Commission for Driver Testing (#12678)

♦ International Commission on Dynamical Meteorology (ICDM) 12679

Commission internationale de la météorologie dynamique

Sec ARC Centre of Excellence for Climate Extremes, Univ of Melbourne, Parkville VIC 3010, Australia. T. +8316565715. Fax +8316564789.
Pres Geophysical Inst, Univ of Bergen, Allegaten, 70, Postboks 7800, 5020 Bergen, Norway. T. +4755589846. Fax +4755589883.
URL: https://www.iamas.org/icdm/

History 1967. Founded as a commission of *International Association of Meteorology and Atmospheric Sciences (IAMAS, #12031)*. Also referred to as *IAMAS International Commission on Dynamical Meteorology – Commission internationale de la météorologie dynamique de l'AIMSA*. **Aims** Promote scientific observation and research of the atmosphere and its dynamics; initiate, facilitate and coordinate international cooperation in the study and investigation of atmospheric dynamics, and application of the research to practical problems; stimulate presentation and publication of scientific studies and assessments; stimulate, facilitate and assist in continuing development and education of scientists in the field. **Structure** Officers; Working Groups (4). **Languages** English. **Staff** None paid. **Finance** No budget. **Activities** Events/meetings. **Events** *Workshop on Dynamics and Predictability of High-Impact Weather and Climate Events* Kunming (China) 2012, *Workshop on sustainable future modelling* Singapore (Singapore) 1988.
Members As of Aug 2020, individuals in 14 countries:
Australia, Austria, Brazil, Canada, China, France, Germany, Japan, Korea Rep, Norway, Russia, Sweden, UK, USA. [2021/XE3839/v/E]

- ♦ International Commission for Educational and Pastoral Reflection (see: #15589)
- ♦ International Commission on the Educational Use of Films and Broadcasting (inactive)
- ♦ International Commission of the Elbe (inactive)

♦ International Commission for Electromagnetic Safety (ICEMS) 12680

Commissione Internazionale per la Sicurezza Elettromagnetica

Address not obtained.
URL: http://www.icems.eu/

History 18 Dec 2002, Venice (Italy), for an initial period of 9 years. Registered in accordance with Italian law. **Aims** Promote research to protect public health from electromagnetic fields; develop the scientific basis and strategies for assessment, prevention, management and communication of risk. **Structure** Steering Committee; Board. **Finance** Members' dues. **Activities** Organizes workshops. **Events** *Congress* Vienna (Austria) 2006, *Workshop* Venice (Italy) 2003, *Workshop* Venice (Italy) 2002. [2007/XM2747/E]

♦ International Commission on English in the Liturgy (ICEL) 12681

Commission internationale pour l'emploi de l'anglais dans la liturgie

Exec Dir 1100 Connecticut Ave NW, Ste 710, Washington DC 20036, USA. T. +12023470800. Fax +12023471839. E-mail: icel@eliturgy.org.
URL: http://www.icelweb.org/

History 1963. Founded as a joint commission of Catholic Bishops' Conferences. **Aims** Prepare an English translation of liturgical texts for approval by the Bishops of the *Roman Catholic Church*. **Structure** Board of Directors (meets annually); Ad-hoc Committees. **Languages** English. **Staff** 6.00 FTE, paid.
Members Episcopal conferences in 31 countries and territories:
Australia, Barbados, Canada, Fiji, Gambia, Ghana, India, Ireland, Kenya, Liberia, Malawi, Malaysia, Neth Antilles, New Zealand, Nigeria, Pakistan, Papua New Guinea, Philippines, Sierra Leone, Singapore, Solomon Is, South Africa, Sri Lanka, St Lucia, Tonga, Trinidad-Tobago, Uganda, UK, USA, Zambia, Zimbabwe. [2021.02.16/XD3477/D]

- ♦ International Commission for the European Mycological Congresses (inactive)
- ♦ International Commission for Fashion and Textile Colours (#04218)

♦ International Commission on Financing Global Education Opportunity (Education Commission) 12682

Dir 6 West 48th St, 12th Floor, New York NY 10036, USA. T. +12128430346. E-mail: info@educationcommission.org.
URL: http://educationcommission.org/

History Announced Jul 2015, Oslo (Norway) at Summit on Education for Development. **Aims** Reinvigorate the case for investing in education; chart a pathway for increased investment so as to develop the potential of all of the world's young people. **Structure** Commission Leadership; Team. **Activities** Research/documentation. **Members** Individuals. Membership countries not specified. **IGO Relations** Partner of (1): *School Meals Coalition*. [2021/XM5633/v/E]

- ♦ International Commission on Folk Arts and Folklore / see Société internationale d'ethnologie et de folklore (#19481)
- ♦ International Commission for Food Industries (inactive)
- ♦ International Commission on Food Mycology (see: #15794)
- ♦ International Commission of General Prison Chaplains / see International Commission of Catholic Prison Pastoral Care (#12670)
- ♦ International Commission on General Relativity and Gravitation / see International Society on General Relativity and Gravitation (#15138)
- ♦ International Commission of Geographic History (inactive)
- ♦ International Commission of Glaciers (inactive)

♦ International Commission on Glass (ICG) 12683

Commission internationale du verre (CIV) – Comisión Internacional del Vidrio – Internationale Kommission für Glas

Exec Sec China Triumph International Engineering Co., Ltd, 26F Bldg Zhongqi 2000 North Zhongshan Rd, 200063 Shanghai, China.
Pres UniglassAC, Nizzaallee 75, 52072 Aachen, Germany.
URL: http://www.icglass.org/

History 23 Sep 1933, Venice (Italy). Founded when constitution was signed by 6 founding members. New constitution approved 1950, Bern (Switzerland); revised 1964, Copenhagen (Denmark); 5 Nov 1974; 18 Dec 1978. Legal status under Belgian law of 25 Oct 1919, granted by Royal Decree 11 Apr 1968. Former names and other names: *Union of Scientific and Technical Organizations* – alias (1967). Registration: Banque-Carrefour des Entreprises, No/ID: 0407.575.786, Start date: 11 Apr 1968, Belgium. **Aims** Stimulate cooperative effort in glass *technology*, serve as an international centre for the exchange of information on the art, science and technology of glass. **Structure** Assembly (annual); Council; Steering Committee; Technical Committees (21). Membership, congresses and meetings open. **Languages** English. **Staff** Voluntary. **Finance** Sources: members' dues. **Activities** Awards/prizes/competitions; events/meetings. **Events** *Triennial Congress* Berlin (Germany) 2022, *Annual Meeting* Incheon (Korea Rep) 2021, *Annual Meeting* Krakow (Poland) 2020, *Triennial Congress* Boston, MA (USA) 2019, *Annual Meeting* Yokohama (Japan) 2018. **Publications** Congress proceedings; reports; surveys; technical handbooks, dictionaries and bibliographies produced by sub-committees. **Information Services** *GLASSFILE* – scientific and technical database.
Members National societies and/or institutes in 32 countries:
Argentina, Australia, Belgium, Brazil, Bulgaria, Canada, China, Czechia, Denmark, Finland, France, Germany, Hungary, India, Iran Islamic Rep, Italy, Japan, Korea Rep, Liechtenstein, Mexico, Netherlands, Poland, Portugal, Romania, Russia, Slovakia, Spain, Sweden, Thailand, Türkiye, UK, USA.
IGO Relations *UNESCO (#20322)*. **NGO Relations** In liaison with technical committees of: *Comité européen de normalisation (CEN, #04162)*; *International Organization for Standardization (ISO, #14473)*. [2022/XC1560/C]

♦ International Commission on Historical Demography (ICHD) 12684

Commission internationale de démographie historique (CIDH)

Gen Sec Francis Marion Univ, 4822 E Palmetto St, Florence SC 29506, USA.
Assistant Gen Sec Radboud Univ, Houtlaan 4, 6525 XZ Nijmegen, Netherlands.
Facebook: https://www.facebook.com/historicaldemography/

History 1960, Stockholm (Sweden). Accepted as an internal commission of *International Committee of Historical Sciences (ICHS, #12777)*, 1964. Reorganized as an independent association, affiliated to ICHS, 2000, Oslo (Norway). **Aims** Promote studies concerning the *history* of the *population* and of the *human society* throughout the world; favour exchanges between researchers; encourage any initiative which leads to the development, spreading and teaching of historical demography as a science. **Structure** Board. **Languages** English, French. **Staff** 1.00 FTE, voluntary. **Finance** Members' dues. Grants. **Activities** Conferences. **Events** *Conference* Amsterdam (Netherlands) 2010, *Conference* New Delhi (India) 2005, *Colloquium / Conference* Montréal, QC (Canada) 1995, *Conference* Milan (Italy) 1994, *Conference* Santiago de Compostela (Spain) 1993. **Publications** *Bibliographie internationale de la démographie historique – International Bibliography of Historical Demography* (1978 -).
Members National Committees of the International Committee of Historical Sciences in 47 countries:
Albania, Andorra, Argentina, Australia, Austria, Belgium, Bulgaria, Canada, China, Cyprus, Czechia, Denmark, Finland, France, Germany, Greece, Guinea, Holy See, Hungary, Iceland, India, Ireland, Israel, Italy, Japan, Korea DPR, Korea Rep, Luxembourg, Mexico, Mongolia, Netherlands, Norway, Poland, Portugal, Romania, Russia, Slovakia, Spain, Sweden, Switzerland, Tunisia, Türkiye, UK, Uruguay, USA, Venezuela, Vietnam.
NGO Relations International Affiliation Organization of: *International Committee of Historical Sciences (ICHS, #12777)*. [2022/XE7846/E]

- ♦ International Commission for the History of the French Revolution (#04222)

♦ International Commission on the History of Geological Sciences (INHIGEO) 12685

Commission internationale d'histoire des sciences géologiques – Internationale Kommission für Geschichte der Geologischen Wissenschaften

SG Luisenstrass 37, Earth Sciences Dept, University of of Munich, 80333 Munich, Germany.
URL: http://www.inhigeo.com/

History 1967. Founded as a Commission of *International Union of Geological Sciences (IUGS, #15777)* and the Division of History of Science and Technology (DHST) of *International Union of History and Philosophy of Science and Technology (IUHPST, #15779)*. By-laws most recently amended 2012, Brisbane (Australia). **Aims** Promote study of the history of the geological sciences; stimulate and coordinate activities of national and regional organizations with the same purpose. **Structure** Board. **Languages** English. **Staff** 2.00 FTE, voluntary. **Finance** Funded by IUGS and IUHPS. Budget (annual): US$ 3,000-4,000. **Activities** Events/meetings; publishing activity. **Events** *Symposium* Krakow (Poland) 2023, *Symposium* Les Eyzies (France) 2022, *Symposium* Krakow (Poland) 2021, *Geoscience for societyco* Delhi (India) 2020, *Symposium* Como (Italy) / Varese (Italy) 2019. **Publications** *Annual Record*. *History of Geoscience: Celebrating 50 Years of INHIGEO*. Symposium proceedings.
Members Individuals (291) in 49 countries:

Argentina, Australia, Austria, Belarus, Belgium, Bolivia, Brazil, Bulgaria, Canada, Chile, China, Colombia, Costa Rica, Czechia, Denmark, Estonia, France, Germany, Greece, Hungary, India, Ireland, Israel, Italy, Japan, Latvia, Lithuania, Malawi, Malta, Mexico, Montenegro, Namibia, Netherlands, New Zealand, Norway, Poland, Portugal, Romania, Russia, Serbia, South Africa, Spain, Sweden, Switzerland, Türkiye, UK, USA, Uzbekistan, Venezuela. [2022/XD2495/v/E]

♦ International Commission of History of International Relations / see Commission of History of International Relations (#04217)

♦ International Commission on the History of Mathematics (ICHM) .. 12686

Sec Dept Mathematics and Computer Science, Western Carolina Univ, Cullowhee NC 28723, USA. E-mail: ichm.info@mathunion.org.
Chair School of Mathematics and Statistics, Fac of STEM, The Open Univ, Walton Hall, Milton Keynes, MK7 6AA, UK.
URL: https://www.mathunion.org/ichm

History Jan 1974. Founded as a commission of the History of Science Division (DHS) of *International Union of History and Philosophy of Science and Technology (IUHPST, #15779)*; established as a joint Commission with *International Mathematical Union (IMU, #14121)* in 1987. **Aims** Encourage the study of the history of mathematics; promote a high level of historically and mathematically sophisticated scholarship in the field. **Structure** Executive Committee. **Languages** English. **Staff** None. **Finance** Conference organization expenses covered by IUHPS History of Science Division. Other sources: sale of publications; gifts. **Activities** Awards/prizes/competitions; events/meetings; knowledge management/information dissemination. **Events** *History of mathematics* Liège (Belgium) 1997, *The history of reading the ancients in mathematics* Marseille (France) 1995. **Publications** *Historia Mathematica* (4 a year). *Writing the History of Mathematics: Its Historical Development* (2002) – Birkhäuser Verlag; *World Directory of Historians of Mathematics* (3rd ed 1995). Annual Report.
Members Individuals in 56 countries and territories:
Algeria, Australia, Austria, Bangladesh, Belarus, Belgium, Brazil, Canada, Chile, China, Costa Rica, Croatia, Czechia, Denmark, Estonia, Finland, France, Germany, Greece, Guatemala, Hungary, Iceland, India, Iran Islamic Rep, Israel, Italy, Japan, Kazakhstan, Korea Rep, Luxembourg, Mexico, Mozambique, Netherlands, New Zealand, Nigeria, Norway, Poland, Portugal, Puerto Rico, Russia, Saudi Arabia, Singapore, Slovakia, South Africa, Spain, Sweden, Switzerland, Syrian AR, Taiwan, Tunisia, Türkiye, UK, Ukraine, USA, Uzbekistan, Vietnam. [2021/XE1421/v/E]

♦ International Commission on History of Meteorology (ICHM) 12687

Sec George Mason Univ, 4400 Univ Drive, Fairfax VA 22030, USA.
URL: http://meteohistory.org/

History Set up 2001, Mexico City (Mexico). Bylaws adopted 11 Jul 2001, Mexico City (Mexico); amended 27 Jul 2004 and 27 May 2009. An official commission of *International Union of History and Philosophy of Science and Technology (IUHPST, #15779)*. **Aims** Promote the scholarly study of the history of meteorology, climatology, and related sciences including their social and cultural aspects. **Activities** Events/meetings. **Publications** *History of Meteorology* – journal. **Members** Individuals (over 300) in 49 countries. Membership countries not specified. [2017/XM5525/v/E]

♦ International Commission on the History of the October Revolution in Russia / see International Commission on the History of the Russian Revolution (#12688)
♦ International Commission for the History of Representative and Parliamentary Institutions / see International Commission for the History of State Assemblies (#12689)

♦ International Commission on the History of the Russian Revolution 12688

Commission internationale pour l'histoire de la Révolution russe – Mezdunarodnaja Kommissija po Istorii Rossiiskoj Revoljucii

SG Profsouznaya 97-207, Moscow MOSKVA, Russia, 117279. Fax +74953361303. E-mail: rusrevref@mail.ru.

History 1985. Founded as an internal commission of *International Committee of Historical Sciences (ICHS, #12777)*. Ceased to be a commission of CISH, prior to 2012. Former names and other names: *International Commission on the History of the October Revolution in Russia* – former (1985 to 2000); *Commission internationale pour l'histoire de la Révolution d'octobre en Russie* – former (1985 to 2000); *Mezdunarodnaja Kommissija po Istorii Oktjabrskoj Revoljucii v Rossii* – former (1985 to 2000). **Aims** Promote effective contacts with scientists of different countries and facilitate research of the history of the Russian revolutions and reforms (20th century). **Languages** English, Russian. **Staff** None. **Finance** No financial support. **Activities** Events/meetings. **Events** *Scientific Conference* Moscow (Russia) 2019, *Scientific Conference* Russia 2017, *Scientific Conference* Samara (Russia) 2014, *Scientific Conference* Gatchina (Russia) 2013, *Scientific Conference* Samara (Russia) 2012. **Publications** *1917 in Eurasia* (2017); *Russia and the World War I* (2014); *The Fall of the Empire, Revolution and the Civil War in Russia* (2010); *The Crimea* (2006); *Political Parties in the evolutions in the Beginning of XX Century* (2005); *Tragedy of the Great State: National Question and Disintegration of the Soviet Union* (2005); *Russia in the 20th Century – Reforms and Revolutions* (2002) – in 2 vols.
Members Individuals (15) in 13 countries:
Azerbaijan, France, Georgia, Germany, Kazakhstan, Korea Rep, Netherlands, Poland, Russia, Türkiye, UK, Ukraine, USA. [2022.05.05/XE0381/v/E]

♦ International Commission for the History of State Assemblies 12689

Commission internationale pour l'histoire des assemblées d'Etats (CIHAE)

SG Camera dei Deputati, Palazzo Montecitorio, 00186 Rome RM, Italy.
Pres address not obtained.
URL: http://www.ichrpi.com/

History 1936, as a result of a resolution passed at 8th International Congress of Historical Sciences, 1933, Warsaw (Poland). Originally also referred to as *International Commission for the History of Representative and Parliamentary Institutions (ICHRPI) – Internationale Kommission für die Geschichte des Ständewesens und der Parlamente.* **Aims** Engage in wide and comparative study of the development of representative institutions at all periods; encourage international cooperation in research. **Structure** Statutory Business Meeting (every 4 years). Officers: President; 3 Honorary Presidents; 10 Vice-Presidents; Secretary General; Treasurer; 4 Councillors; Director of Publications. **Languages** English, French, German. **Finance** Members' dues: Swiss Fr 60 (pounds25). Other sources: sale of publications; grants. **Activities** Annual Conference (at the invitation of national sections, or of other academic or parliamentary bodies); Annual Business Meetings (held during the Annual Conference). **Events** *Annual Conference* Poznań (Poland) 2022, *Annual Conference* Athens (Greece) 2021, *Annual Conference* Poznań (Poland) 2020, *Annual Conference* Andorra la Vella (Andorra) 2019, *Annual Conference* Vienna (Austria) 2018. **Publications** *Parliaments, Estates and Representation/Parlements, Etats et représentation* (annual). *Separation of Powers and Parliamentarism, the past and the present: law, doctrine, practice* (2007); *The Scottish Parliament under Charles II* (2007); *Contributions to European Parliamentary History* (1999) by Agirreaz Kuenaga; *Contributi alla Storia Parlamentare Europea (secoli XIII-XX)* (1996) by M S Corciulo; *Louis XV and the Parlement of Paris 1737-55* (1995) by J Rogister; *Medieval France and her Pyrenean Neighbours* (1989) by T N Bisson. Conference proceedings.
Members National sections and individuals. Members in 21 countries:
Austria, Azerbaijan, Belgium, Brazil, Bulgaria, Croatia, Czechia, Finland, France, Germany, Hungary, Ireland, Italy, Netherlands, Poland, Portugal, Slovenia, Spain, Switzerland, UK, USA.
NGO Relations Affiliate member of: *International Committee of Historical Sciences (ICHS, #12777).* [2019/XC1533/D]

♦ International Commission for the History and Theory of Historiography (ICHTH) 12690

Commission international de l'histoire et de la théorie de l'historiographie

SG Rowan University, 201 Mullica Hill Rd, Glassboro NJ 08028, USA.
URL: http://www.historiographyinternational.org/

History 1980, as *Commission of the History of Historiography – Commission d'histoire de l'historiographie.* New name adopted 1995. **Aims** Promote study of the history and theory of historiography. **Structure** Board, consisting of President, Vice-President, Secretary General, Programme Chair, Treasurer and 8 members. **Languages** English, French, German, Italian, Spanish. **Finance** Occasional grants. **Events** *Annual Congress* Amsterdam (Netherlands) 2010, *Annual Congress* Shanghai (China) 2007, *Annual Congress* Kofu (Japan) 2006, *Annual Congress* Sydney, NSW (Australia) 2005, *Annual Congress* St Andrews (UK) 2004. **Publications** *Storia della Storiografia* (2 a year).
Members Individuals (95) in 29 countries:
Argentina, Australia, Austria, Belgium, Brazil, Canada, China, Czechia, Finland, France, Germany, Hungary, India, Israel, Italy, Japan, Montenegro, Netherlands, Norway, Poland, Portugal, Romania, Serbia, Spain, Sweden, Switzerland, UK, USA.
NGO Relations Affiliated to: *International Committee of Historical Sciences (ICHS, #12777).* [2012/XD3612/v/E]

♦ International Commission for the History of Towns 12691

Commission internationale pour l'histoire des villes

Pres Nicolaus-Copernicus-Univ, ul Bojarskiego 1, 87-100 Torun, Poland. E-mail: rc@umk.pl.
Gen Sec address not obtained.
URL: http://www.historiaurbium.org/

History 1955, Rome (Italy). **Aims** Promote international cooperation in the field of town history. **Structure** General Assembly; Bureau. **Languages** English, French, German. **Staff** None. **Finance** Sources: members' dues. Annual budget: 1,200 EUR. **Activities** Events/meetings; publishing activities. **Events** *Annual Meeting* Dublin (Ireland) 2022, *Conference* Split (Croatia) 2021, *Annual Meeting* Budapest (Hungary) 2019, *Annual Meeting* Salzburg (Austria) 2018, *Annual Meeting* Krakow (Poland) 2017. **Publications** *Newsletter*; *Nouvelles. Elenchus Fontium Historiae Urbanae*; *European Town Atlas*; *Guide international d'histoire urbaine.* Conference proceedings.
Members Individuals in 34 countries:
Austria, Belgium, Bulgaria, Canada, China, Croatia, Czechia, Denmark, Estonia, Finland, France, Germany, Greece, Hungary, Ireland, Italy, Japan, Latvia, Lithuania, Luxembourg, Netherlands, Norway, Poland, Portugal, Romania, Russia, Serbia, Slovakia, Slovenia, Spain, Sweden, Switzerland, UK, Ukraine.
NGO Relations Member of (1): *International Committee of Historical Sciences (ICHS, #12777).* [2023.02.14/XE7281/v/E]

♦ International Commission for the History of Travel and Tourism (ICHTT) 12692

Commission internationale sur l'histoire du voyage et du tourisme

Gen Sec Mills College, PO Box 9962, Oakland CA 94613, USA.

History 2002, Amsterdam (Netherlands). Founded as an internal commission of *International Committee of Historical Sciences (ICHS, #12777).* Subsequently became an independent Affiliated Organization. **Aims** Represent scholars interested in the history of travel and tourism; create an effective network and profitable exchange of information and ideas between historians of different countries; promote research in the field. **Structure** General Assembly; Bureau. **Languages** English, French. **Staff** 5.00 FTE, voluntary. **Finance** Sources: government support; members' dues; private foundations; subsidies. **Activities** Events/meetings. **Events** *Session* Jinan (China) 2015.
Members Individuals (21) in 11 countries:
Australia, France, India, Italy, New Zealand, Poland, Russia, Sweden, Switzerland, UK, USA. [2021.09.06/XK2344/E]

♦ International Commission for the History of Universities (#04223)

♦ International Commission for the Hydrology of the Rhine Basin ... 12693

Commission internationale de l'hydrologie du bassin du Rhin (CHR) – Internationale Kommission für die Hydrologie des Rheingebietes (KHR) – Internationale Commissie voor de Hydrologie van het Rijnstroomgebied

Exec Sec PO Box 2232, 3500 GE Utrecht, Netherlands. T. +31627118101. E-mail: info@chr-khr.org.
Contact Zuiderwagenplein 2, 8224 AD Lelystad, Netherlands.
URL: http://www.chr-khr.org/

History 1970. Established in the framework of UNESCO's *International Hydrological Decade (IHD).* Between 1975-1977, continuation of activities in the framework of UNESCO' International Hydrological Programme (IHP) and the Hydrology and Water Resources Programme (HWRP) of WMO. Since 1978, activities comprise exchange of verbal notes between participating countries. Former names and other names: *International Commissie voor de Hydrologie van het Rijngebied* – alias. **Aims** Support cooperation between hydrological institutes and services active in the catchment area of the Rhine; execute hydrological studies in the Rhine basin and exchange research results; promote exchange of hydrological data and information in the Rhine (eg current data, forecasts); develop standardized methods for collecting and processing hydrological data in the Rhine riparian states. **Structure** Permanent representatives (meeting twice a year); Permanent Secretariat. **Languages** English, German. **Staff** 2.00 FTE, paid. **Finance** Sources: members' dues. Annual budget: 30,000 EUR. **Activities** Knowledge management/information dissemination; projects/programmes. **Events** *Symposium* Bern (Switzerland) 2022, *Annual CHRs Meeting* Lelystad (Netherlands) 2022, *CHR 51 Years Jubilee Conference* Wageningen (Netherlands) 2021, *Meeting* Kampen (Netherlands) 2018, *Meeting* Metz (France) 2018. **Publications** Annual Report; monographs; scientific reports.
Members Governments of 6 countries:
Austria, France, Germany, Luxembourg, Netherlands, Switzerland.
IGO Relations Observer status with (1): *International Commission for the Protection of the Rhine (ICPR, #12721).* Cooperates with (1): *International Centre for Water Resources and Global Change (ICWRGC, #12528).* [2022.02.16/XD8313/D*]

♦ International Commission on Illumination (#04219)
♦ International Commission of Inquiry for the Investigation of Arms Flows to Former Rwandan Government Forces in the Great Lakes Region (inactive)
♦ International Commission on Intellectual Cooperation (inactive)
♦ International Commission on Irrigation and Canals / see International Commission on Irrigation and Drainage (#12694)

♦ International Commission on Irrigation and Drainage (ICID) 12694

Commission internationale des irrigations et du drainage (CIID) – Comisión Internacional de la Irrigación y el Saneamiento

SG 48 Nyaya Marg, Chanakyapuri, Delhi 110021, DELHI 110021, India. T. +911126116837 – +911126115679. Fax +911126115962. E-mail: icid@icid.org.
Pres ARC, Institute for Agricultural Engineering, Private Bag X 519, Silverton, Pretoria, 0127, South Africa. T. +27128424009. Fax +27128424317.
URL: http://icid-ciid.org/

History Founded 24 Jun 1950, Delhi (India), on adoption of a provisional constitution and with the title *International Commission on Irrigation and Canals – Commission internationale des irrigations et des canaux.* Constitution and current title adopted 12 Jan 1951, Delhi. Scope widened, 1957, to include flood control and river training. By-laws adopted 11-12 Apr 1969, Mexico City (Mexico). Current constitution and by-laws incorporate all amendments made by the International Executive Council from time to time, including those adopted by its 44th meeting, Sep 1983, The Hague (Netherlands). Registered under the Government of India Societies Registration Act XXV of 1860. **Aims** Promote sustainable agriculture *water* management to achieve water secure world, free of poverty and hunger through sustainable rural development; stimulate and promote development and application of engineering, agriculture, economics, ecology, and social science to the management of water and land *resources* for irrigation, drainage and *flood* control, and river training, and/or for research in a more comprehensive manner adopting up-to-date techniques. **Structure** International Executive Council (meets annually); Management Board; Central Office (permanent secretariat); Committees (3); Working Groups (30). **Languages** English, French. **Staff** 16.00 FTE, paid. **Finance** Subscriptions from National Committees. **Activities** Events/meetings; knowledge management/information dissemination; training/education. **Events** *World Irrigation Forum* Beijing (China) 2027, *World Irrigation Forum* Kuala Lumpur (Malaysia) 2025, *World Irrigation Forum* Beijing (China) 2023, *ICID International Congress on Irrigation and Drainage* Visakhapatnam (India) 2023, *International Executive Committee Meeting* Visakhapatnam (India) 2023. **Publications** *News Update* (12 a year); *Irrigation and Drainage* (5 a year) – technical journal; *ICID News* (4 a year); *e-Bulletins.* Technical dictionaries; manuals; surveys; global reviews; guides; transactions; proceedings. Information Services: Technical library; text delilvery services.
Members National Committees in 77 countries and territories:
Afghanistan, Australia, Austria, Bangladesh, Brazil, Bulgaria, Burkina Faso, Canada, Chad, China, Croatia, Czechia, Egypt, Estonia, Ethiopia, Fiji, Finland, France, Georgia, Germany, Greece, Guyana, Hungary, India, Indonesia, Iran Islamic Rep, Iraq, Ireland, Israel, Italy, Japan, Kazakhstan, Korea Rep, Kyrgyzstan, Lithuania, Madagascar, Malawi, Malaysia, Mali, Mexico, Morocco, Mozambique, Myanmar, Nepal, Netherlands, Niger, Nigeria, North Macedonia, Pakistan, Philippines, Poland, Portugal, Romania, Russia, Saudi Arabia, Serbia, Slovakia, Slovenia, Somalia, South Africa, Spain, Sri Lanka, Sudan, Switzerland, Syrian AR, Taiwan, Tajikistan, Tanzania UR, Thailand, UK, Ukraine, Uruguay, USA, Uzbekistan, Vietnam, Zambia, Zimbabwe.

Consultative Status Consultative status granted from: *ECOSOC (#05331)* (Special); *FAO (#09260)* (Special Status); *World Meteorological Organization (WMO, #21649).*
IGO Relations
- *African Development Bank Group (ADB Group, #00284);*
- *European Investment Bank (EIB, #07599);*
- *Inter-State Commission for Water Coordination of Central Asia (ICWC, #15979);*
- *International Bank for Reconstruction and Development (IBRD, #12317);*
- *International Center for Agricultural Research in the Dry Areas (ICARDA, #12466);*
- *International Development Research Centre (IDRC, #13162);*
- *International Fund for Agricultural Development (IFAD, #13692);*
- *International Hydrological Programme (IHP, #13826);*
- *Joint WHO/FAO/UNEP/UNCHS Panel of Experts on Environmental Management for Vector Control (PEEM, no recent information);*
- *Scientific Information Centre of Interstate Coordination Water Commission of Central Asia (SIC ICWC, #19152);*
- *UNEP (#20299);*
- *UN-Water (#20723);*
- *UNDP (#20292);*
- *UNESCO (#20322);*
- *United Nations Economic Commission for Africa (ECA, #20554);*
- *United Nations Economic Commission for Europe (UNECE, #20555);*
- *United Nations Economic Commission for Latin America and the Caribbean (ECLAC, #20556);*
- *United Nations Economic and Social Commission for Asia and the Pacific (ESCAP, #20557);*
- *United Nations Office at Vienna (UNOV, #20604);*
- *United States Agency for International Development (USAID);*
- *WHO (#20950);*
- *World Water Assessment Programme (WWAP, #21907).*

Associated with Department of Global Communications of the United Nations.
NGO Relations
- *European Water Association (EWA, #09080);*
- *European Water Resources Association (EWRA, #09085);*
- *Ford Foundation (#09858);*
- *IHE Delft Institute for Water Education (#11110);*
- *International Association for Hydro-Environment Engineering and Research (IAHR, #11950);*
- *International Association of Hydrological Sciences (IAHS, #11954);*
- *International Commission of Agricultural and Biosystems Engineering (#12661);*
- *International Commission on Large Dams (ICOLD, #12696);*
- *International Council for Science (ICSU, inactive);*
- *International Geosynthetics Society (IGS, #13716);*
- *International Hydropower Association (IHA, #13828);*
- *International Organization for Standardization (ISO, #14473);*
- *International Water Management Institute (IWMI, #15867);*
- *International Water-Related Associations' Liaison Committee (IWALC, #15869);*
- *International Water Resources Association (IWRA, #15871);*
- *PIANC (#18371);*
- *World Water Council (WWC, #21908).* [2021/XB1562/**B**]

♦ International Commission of Jurists (ICJ) 12695
Commission internationale de juristes (CIJ) – Comisión Internacional de Juristas (CIJ)
SG Rue des Bains 33, PO Box 91, 1211 Geneva 8, Switzerland. T. +41229793800. Fax +41229793801. E-mail: info@icj.org.
Dir Media and Communications address not obtained.
URL: http://www.icj.org/

History 1952, Berlin (Germany). Current statutes adopted 1 Jan 2002. Registration: Swiss Civil Code, Switzerland; EU Transparency Register, No/ID: 941916711102-62, Start date: 13 May 2013. **Aims** Ensure progressive development and effective implementation of international human rights and international humanitarian law; secure the realization of civil, cultural, economic, political and social rights; safeguard separation of powers; guarantee independence of the judiciary and legal profession. **Structure** Commission (meets every 2 years) comprising 60 eminent jurists representing the world's different legal systems; National Sections (21); Executive Committee. International Secretariat, headed by Secretary-General. **Languages** Arabic, English, French, Russian, Spanish. **Staff** 60-80 paid. **Finance** Contributions from: private bodies; foundations; development organizations; governments; individuals. **Activities** Guidance/assistance/consulting; knowledge management/information dissemination; advocacy/lobbying/activism, awards/prizes/competitions. **Events** *World Congress* Tunis (Tunisia) 2019, *Annual Jurists Conference* Durban (South Africa) 2016, *World Congress* Geneva (Switzerland) 2012, *World Congress* Geneva (Switzerland) 2008, *Annual seminar for chairpersons and members of parliamentary human rights bodies* Geneva (Switzerland) 2006. **Publications** E-Bulletin. Annual Report; reports; studies; legal briefs; reports of congresses, conferences and seminars.
Members National Sections (21) and Affiliates (39) in 46 countries and territories:
Argentina, Australia, Austria, Bangladesh, Barbados, Bolivia, Burkina Faso, Canada, Chad, Chile, Colombia, Denmark, Ecuador, Egypt, Fiji, France, Germany, Hong Kong, India, Indonesia, Italy, Japan, Jordan, Kenya, Malaysia, Morocco, Nepal, Netherlands, Niger, Nigeria, Norway, Pakistan, Palestine, Peru, Philippines, Poland, Russia, Slovenia, Sweden, Switzerland, Tunisia, UK, Uruguay, USA, Zambia, Zimbabwe.
Included in the above, 2 organizations listed in this Yearbook:
Arab Centre for the Independence of the Judiciary and the Legal Profession (ACIJLP); Global Rights.
Consultative Status Consultative status granted from: *UNESCO (#20322)* (Consultative Status); *ILO (#11123)* (Special List); *World Intellectual Property Organization (WIPO, #21593)* (Permanent Observer Status); *Council of Europe (CE, #04881)* (Participatory Status); *African Commission on Human and Peoples' Rights (ACHPR, #00255)* (Observer). **IGO Relations** Involved in setting up of *African Court on Human and Peoples' Rights (AfCHPR, #00278).* Accredited by: *United Nations Office at Vienna (UNOV, #20604).* Consultation Status with: *United Nations Population Fund (UNFPA, #20612).* Cooperation agreement with: *International Institute for Democracy and Electoral Assistance (International IDEA, #13872).* Member of the Advisory Board of: *United Nations Democracy Fund (UNDEF, #20551).* Member of Consultative Forum of *Frontex, the European Border and Coast Guard Agency (#10005).* Member of: *Convention against Torture Initiative (CTI, #04786).* Participant in Fundamental Rights Platform of: *European Union Agency for Fundamental Rights (FRA, #08969).* Associated with Department of Global Communications of the United Nations. **NGO Relations** Accredited by (13): *Alliance of NGOs on Crime Prevention and Criminal Justice (#00709); Coalition for an Effective African Court on Human and Peoples' Rights (African Court Coalition, #04055); Committee of NGOs on Human Rights, Geneva (#04275); Conference of Non-Governmental Organizations in Consultative Relationship with the United Nations (CONGO, #04635); EarthAction (EA, #05159); ETO Consortium (ETOs, #05560); European Implementation Network (EIN, #07521); Fédération des Institutions Internationales établies à Genève (FIIG, #09599); International Coalition against Enforced Disappearances (ICAED, #12605); International Legal Assistance Consortium (ILAC, #14025); International Network for Economic, Social and Cultural Rights (ESCR-Net, #14255); Sudan Consortium (#20031); UNCAC Coalition (#20283).* Kenya Section member of: *World Organisation Against Torture (OMCT, #21685).* [2022/XB1550/y/**B**]

♦ International Commission on Large Dams (ICOLD) 12696
Commission internationale des grands barrages (CIGB)
Acting Gen Sec 61 av Kléber, 75116 Paris, France. T. +33147041780. Fax +33153751822. E-mail: secretaire.general@icold-cigb.org.
Communications Officer address not obtained.
URL: http://www.icold-cigb.org/

History 7 Jul 1928, Paris (France). Founded following the congress of *UNIPEDE – International Union of Producers and Distributors of Electrical Energy (inactive),* and at the instigation of the 5th Conference on hydro-electric power, 1925, Grenoble (France) and of World Power Conference, 1926, Basel (Switzerland). Completely independent since 1967. **Aims** Advance the art and science of dam engineering; promote wise and sustainable development and management of world's water and *hydropower* resources. **Structure** General Assembly (annual); Officers; National and Technical Committees. **Languages** English, French. **Staff** 4.00 FTE, paid. **Finance** Sources: meeting proceeds; members' dues; sale of publications. Annual budget: 700,000 EUR (2019). **Activities** Capacity building; events/meetings; knowledge management/information dissemination; publishing activities; standards/guidelines; training/education. **Events** *Annual Executive Meeting* Chengdu (China) 2025, *Triennial Congress* Chengdu (China) 2025, *Annual Executive Meeting* New Delhi (India) 2024, *Annual Executive Meeting* Gothenburg (Sweden) 2023, *East Asian Dam Conference* Seoul (Korea Rep) 2022. **Publications** *ICOLD Technical Bulletin* (3-4 a year). *Deterioration of Dams and Reservoirs*; *Technical Dictionary on Dams* in English, French, German, Italian, Portuguese, Spanish; *World Register of Dams.* Technical books; congresses and symposia proceedings; pamphlets.
Members National Committees, totalling about 7,000 individual members, including practising engineers, geologists and scientists from governmental and private organizations, consulting firms, universities, laboratories and construction companies. National Committees in 98 countries:
Albania, Algeria, Argentina, Armenia, Australia, Austria, Belgium, Bhutan, Bolivia, Bosnia-Herzegovina, Brazil, Bulgaria, Burkina Faso, Cameroon, Canada, Chile, China, Colombia, Congo DR, Costa Rica, Côte d'Ivoire, Croatia, Cyprus, Czechia, Denmark, Dominican Rep, Egypt, Ethiopia, Finland, France, Georgia, Germany, Ghana, Greece, Guatemala, Guinea-Bissau, Honduras, Iceland, India, Indonesia, Iran Islamic Rep, Iraq, Ireland, Italy, Japan, Kenya, Korea Rep, Latvia, Lebanon, Lesotho, Libya, Luxembourg, Madagascar, Malaysia, Mali, Mexico, Morocco, Mozambique, Myanmar, Nepal, Netherlands, New Zealand, Niger, Nigeria, North Macedonia, Norway, Pakistan, Panama, Paraguay, Peru, Philippines, Poland, Portugal, Romania, Russia, Serbia, Slovakia, Slovenia, South Africa, Spain, Sri Lanka, Sudan, Sweden, Switzerland, Syrian AR, Tajikistan, Thailand, Tunisia, Türkiye, UK, Ukraine, Uruguay, USA, Uzbekistan, Venezuela, Vietnam, Zambia, Zimbabwe.
IGO Relations Cooperates with (1): *International Hydrological Programme (IHP, #13826).* **NGO Relations** Member of (1): *World Water Council (WWC, #21908).* [2021.11.08/XB1563/**B**]

♦ International Commission on Laser Physics and Photonics 12697
Chair address not obtained.
URL: https://iupap.org/commissions/c17-laser-physics-and-photonics/

History 1975, as a Commission (C 17) of *International Union of Pure and Applied Physics (IUPAP, #15810),* under the title *International Commission on Quantum Electronics – Commission internationale sur l'électronique quantique.* Previously also referred to as *IUPAP Commission on Quantum Electronics – Commission de l'UIPPA sur l'électronique quantique.* Currently serves as an internal commission. **Aims** Promote information exchange in the general field of quantum electronics, including: *physics* of coherent *electromagnetic energy* generation and transmission; physics of interaction of coherent electromagnetic *radiation* with matter; application of quantum electronics to technology. **Structure** Chairman, Vice-Chairman, Secretary and 10 members. **Finance** Source: IUPAP. **Events** *International Quantum Electronics Conference (IQEC)* Moscow (Russia) 2002, *Conference on Laser Applications in Life Sciences (LALS)* Vilnius (Lithuania) 2002, *International Conference on Raman Spectroscopy (ICORS)* Beijing (China) 2000, *International Conference on Coherent and Nonlinear Optics (ICONO)* Moscow (Russia) 1998, *International conference on multiphoton processes / International Conference on Multiphoton Processes (ICOMP)* Garmisch-Partenkirchen (Germany) 1996.
Members Individuals (13) in 13 countries:
Belgium, Brazil, Canada, China, Germany, Hungary, India, Israel, Japan, Poland, Russia, UK, USA.
Associate members (2) in 2 countries:
Italy, USA.
NGO Relations Joint meetings with: *European Physical Society (EPS, #08207).* [2019/XE2200/v/**E**]

♦ International Commission on Low Temperature Physics 12698
Commission internationale sur la physique des très basses températures
Sec address not obtained.
URL: https://iupap.org/commissions/c5-low-temperature-physics/

History 1949, as a Commission (C 5) of *International Union of Pure and Applied Physics (IUPAP, #15810).* Also referred to as *IUPAP Commission on Low Temperature Physics – Commission de l'UIPPA sur la physique des très basses températures.* Currently serves as an internal commission. **Aims** Promote information exchange in the general field of low temperature physics, including: low temperature properties of solids; *quantum solids* and *liquids*; basic mechanisms and physics of *superconductivity*; low temperature techniques; practical applications of low temperature physics; promote free circulation of scientists. **Structure** Chairman, Vice-Chairman, Secretary and 10 members. **Languages** English. **Staff** None. **Finance** Source: IUPAP. **Events** *International Conference on Low Temperature Physics* Sapporo (Japan) 2022, *International Conference on Low Temperature Physics* Sapporo (Japan) 2020, *International Conference on Low Temperature Physics* Gothenburg (Sweden) 2017, *International Conference on Low Temperature Physics* Buenos Aires (Argentina) 2014, *International Conference on Low Temperature Physics* Beijing (China) 2011.
Members Individuals (13) in 13 countries and territories:
Argentina, China, Finland, France, Germany, Israel, Japan, Netherlands, Poland, Russia, Taiwan, UK, USA.
Associate members in 3 countries:
Canada, India, Japan. [2019/XE1114/v/**E**]

♦ International Commission on Magnetism 12699
Commission internationale sur magnétisme
Chair address not obtained.
URL: https://iupap.org/commissions/c9-magnetism/

History 1957. Founded as a Commission (C 9) of *International Union of Pure and Applied Physics (IUPAP, #15810).* Currently serves as an internal commission. Former names and other names: *IUPAP Commission on Magnetism* – alias; *Commission de l'UIPPA sur magnétisme* – alias. **Aims** Promote information exchange in the general field of magnetism, including: phenomena which result in the determination of magnetic interactions at the atomic level; magnetic properties of matter; technical applications of magnetic materials and generation of magnetic fields. **Structure** Chair, Vice-Chair, Secretary. **Activities** Events/meetings. **Events** *International Conference on Magnetism (ICM)* Bologna (Italy) 2024, *ICM : Triennial International Conference on Magnetism* Shanghai (China) 2022, *ICM : Triennial International Conference on Magnetism* Shanghai (China) 2021, *ICM : Triennial International Conference on Magnetism* San Francisco, CA (USA) 2018, *ICM : Triennial International Conference on Magnetism* Barcelona (Spain) 2015.
Members Individuals in 13 countries:
Brazil, Canada, China, Czechia, Denmark, France, India, Ireland, Israel, Japan, Russia, UK, USA.
Associate members in 4 countries:
Austria, Brazil, Germany, Japan. [2022/XE1820/v/**E**]

♦ International Commission of Marine Meteorology (inactive)
♦ International Commission on Marriage and Interpersonal Relations / see International Commission on Couple and Family Relations (#12676)
♦ International Commission on Marriage and Marriage Guidance / see International Commission on Couple and Family Relations (#12676)

♦ International Commission on Mathematical Instruction (ICMI) 12700
Commission internationale de l'enseignement mathématique (CIEM) – Comisión Internacional de Educación Matematica
Secretariat c/o IMU, Hausvogteiplatz 11-A, 10117 Berlin, Germany. E-mail: imu.info@mathunion.org.
SG Dept of Science Teaching, Weizmann Inst of Science, 76100 Rehovot, Israel.
URL: http://www.mathunion.org/ICMI/

History 1908. Founded at the Fourth International Congress of Mathematicians. Reconstituted 1952, following the interruption of the World Wars, as a commission of *International Mathematical Union (IMU, #14121).* **Aims** Conduct activities bearing on mathematical or *scientific education*; inaugurate research and development programmes to further sound development of mathematical education at all levels and secure public appreciation of its importance. **Structure** General Assembly, comprising one representative of each member nation plus the Executive Committee. Executive Committee, consisting of President, 2 Vice-Presidents, Secretary, 4 Members and 2 Ex-Officio Members (President and Secretary of IMU). Affiliated study groups: *International Group for the Psychology of Mathematics Education (PME, #13753); International Organization of Women and Mathematics Education (IOWME, #14483); International Study Group for the Relations between the History and Pedagogy of Mathematics (ISGHPM, see: #14121); World Federation of National Mathematical Competitions (WFNMC, #21460).* National Sub-Commissions. **Languages** English. **Staff** 1.00 FTE, paid. **Finance** Funded by IMU. Grants for projects. **Activities** Events/meetings; research/documentation; financial and/or material support; awards/prizes/competitions. **Events** *International Congress on Mathematics Education (ICME)* Sydney, NSW (Australia) 2024, *EMF : Colloque Espace Mathématique Francophone* Cotonou (Benin) 2021, *EARCOME : East Asia Regional Conference on Mathematics Education* Seoul (Korea Rep) 2021, *International Congress on Mathematical Education (ICME-14)* Shanghai (China) 2021, *Quadrennial Congress* Shanghai (China) 2020. **Publications** *ICMI News* (3 a year).
Members National societies, which may be in non-IMU countries. Members in 88 countries and territories:

Argentina, Armenia, Australia, Austria, Bangladesh, Belgium, Bosnia-Herzegovina, Botswana, Brazil, Brunei Darussalam, Bulgaria, Cameroon, Canada, Cape Verde, Chile, China, Colombia, Costa Rica, Côte d'Ivoire, Croatia, Cuba, Czechia, Denmark, Ecuador, Egypt, Estonia, Eswatini, Finland, France, Georgia, Germany, Ghana, Greece, Hong Kong, Hungary, Iceland, India, Indonesia, Iran Islamic Rep, Ireland, Israel, Italy, Japan, Kazakhstan, Kenya, Korea Rep, Kuwait, Kyrgyzstan, Latvia, Lithuania, Luxembourg, Malawi, Malaysia, Mexico, Mozambique, Netherlands, New Zealand, Nigeria, Norway, Pakistan, Paraguay, Peru, Philippines, Poland, Portugal, Romania, Russia, Saudi Arabia, Senegal, Serbia, Singapore, Slovakia, Slovenia, South Africa, Spain, Sweden, Switzerland, Taiwan, Thailand, Tunisia, Türkiye, UK, Ukraine, Uruguay, USA, Venezuela, Vietnam, Zambia.

IGO Relations *UNESCO (#20322).* **NGO Relations** Activities coordinated with: *Unión Matematica de América Latina y el Caribe (UMALCA, #20456).* Recognizes: *Espace Mathématique Francophone (EMF, #05541).* [2022/XD4995/**F**]

♦ International Commission on Mathematical Physics 12701

Commission internationale sur la physique mathématique

Chair address not obtained.

URL: https://iupap.org/commissions/c18-mathematical-physics/

History 1981, as a Commission (C 18) of *International Union of Pure and Applied Physics (IUPAP, #15810).* Also referred to as *IUPAP Commission on Mathematical Physics – Commission de l'UIPPA sur la physique mathématique.* Currently serves as an internal commission. **Aims** Promote the exchange of information and views in the area of mathematical studies of problems originating in or relevant to physics, including: mathematical models of physical systems; mathematical aspects of physical theories; computational techniques. **Structure** Chair, Vice-Chair, Secretary and 10 members. **Finance** Source: IUPAP. **Activities** Organizes a number of international conference and colloquium series and one-off events. **Events** *Triennial International Congress on Mathematical Physics* Prague (Czech Rep) 2009, *International colloquium on group theoretical methods in physics* Yerevan (Armenia) 2008, *Triennial International Congress on Mathematical Physics* Rio de Janeiro (Brazil) 2006, *International colloquium on group theoretical methods in physics* Cocoyoc (Mexico) 2004, *Von Neumann centennial conference* Budapest (Hungary) 2003. **Publications** Scientific papers.

Members Individuals (13) in 13 countries:
Australia, Belgium, Czechia, Denmark, Finland, France, Ireland, Israel, Japan, Netherlands, Portugal, Russia, USA.
Associate members (4) in 4 countries:
Austria, Brazil, France, Japan. [2019/XE2210/v/**E**]

♦ International Commission on the Meteorology of the Upper Atmosphere / see International Commission on Middle Atmosphere Science (#12704)

♦ International Commission of the Meuse 12702

Commission internationale de la Meuse (CIM) – Internationale Maaskommission (IMK) – Internationale Maascommissie (IMC)

SG CIM Permanent Secretariat, Palais des Congrès, Esplanade de l'Europe 2, 4020 Liège, Belgium. T. +3243401140. Fax +3243490083. E-mail: secr@meuse-maas.be.

URL: http://www.cipm-icbm.be/

History 1 Jan 1998, Liège (Belgium), as *International Commission for the Protection of the Meuse River – Commission internationale pour la protection de la Meuse (CIPM) – Internationale Kommission zum Schutz der Maas (IKSM) – Internationale Commissie voor de Bescherming van de Maas (ICBM)* when *Accord Concernant la Protection de la Meuse (1994)* entered into force. The 1994 treaty was replaced by *Accord International sur la Meuse (2002)*, signed Dec 2002. **Aims** Achieve lasting and comprehensive water management of the Meuse river basin. **Structure** Plenary Meeting; Rotating Presidency. **Languages** Dutch, French, German. **Staff** 3.00 FTE, paid. **Finance** Member parties. Budget (annual): euro 450,000. **Activities** Monitoring/evaluation; research/documentation; projects/programmes; knowledge management/information dissemination. **Events** *International scientific symposium* Maastricht (Netherlands) 2002. **Publications** Annual Report.

Members Governments of 7 countries and territories:
Belgium/Brussels Capital Region, Belgium/Flemish Region, France, Germany, Luxembourg, Netherlands, Wallonia.

IGO Relations Observer to: *International Commission of the Schelde River (#12727).* **NGO Relations** National organizations. [2019/XE3411/**E***]

♦ International Commission on Microbiological Specifications for Foods (ICMSF) 12703

Commission Internationale pour la Définition des Caractéristiques Microbiologiques des Aliments

Secretariat Unilever R and D, Olivier van Noortlaan 120, 3133 AT Vlaardingen, Netherlands.

Chairman Food and Nutritional Sciences, CSIRO, PO Box 52, North Ryde NSW 1670, Australia.

URL: http://www.icmsf.org/

History Aug 1962, Montréal (Canada), as a Standing Committee of the permanent Section on Food Microbiology and Hygiene of the then *'International Association of Microbiological Societies'* currently, since Sep 1980, *International Union of Microbiological Societies (IUMS, #15794).* Became an independent Commission of IUMS in 1970, Mexico City (Mexico). Comes within *IUMS Division of Bacteriology and Applied Microbiology (BAM, see: #15794).* **Aims** Be a leading source for independent and impartial scientific concepts that will reduce the incidence of microbiological foodborne illness and food spoilage worldwide and facilitate global trade. **Structure** General Conference; Executive, consisting of Chairman, Secretary and Treasurer. **Languages** Chinese, English, French, Indonesian, Japanese, Portuguese, Spanish. **Staff** No permanent staff. **Finance** Donations from governments, academia and industry organizations; royalties from book sales. **Activities** Capacity building; events/meetings; publishing activities; research/documentation; training/education; knowledge management/information dissemination. **Events** *Annual Meeting* Sydney, NSW (Australia) 2019, *Annual Meeting* Foz do Iguaçu (Brazil) 2014, *Annual Meeting / General Conference* Melbourne, VIC (Australia) 2011, *General Conference* Annecy (France) 2010, *General Conference* Punta del Este (Uruguay) 2009. **Publications** *A Simplified Guide to Understanding and Using Food Safety Objectives and Performance Objectives* (2015) in English, French, Portuguese, Spanish – also illustrated version, also in Bahasa Indonesia. Books; papers; spreadsheet tools; videos.

Members Main Commission members from 12 countries:
Australia, Brazil, Canada, Indonesia, Italy, Japan, Netherlands, New Zealand, South Africa, Switzerland, UK, USA.
LAS Sub-Commission members in 8 countries:
Argentina, Brazil, Chile, Colombia, Mexico, Peru, Uruguay, Venezuela. [2018.10.19/XE4271/v/**E**]

♦ International Commission on Middle Atmosphere Science (ICMA) . . 12704

Past Pres Dept of Geophysics, Graduate School of Science, Kyoto Univ, Kyoto, 606-8502 Japan. T. +81757533932. Fax +81757533715.

URL: http://www.icma-iamas.org/

History as a Commission of *International Association of Meteorology and Atmospheric Sciences (IAMAS, #12031).* Original title: *International Commission on the Meteorology of the Upper Atmosphere (ICMUA) – Commission internationale de la météorologie de l'atmosphère haute.* Also referred to as *IAMAP International Commission on the Meteorology of the Upper Atmosphere – Commission internationale de la météorologie de l'atmosphère haute de l'AIMPA.* **Aims** Stimulate research on the structure, composition, dynamics, general circulation and *climatology* of the middle atmosphere and interactions of this region with the *troposphere* and *thermosphere*; arrange symposia and workshops; encourage archiving, processing and checking of data; compare techniques data and new observations. **Structure** Executive. **Events** *Workshop on Long Term Changes and Trends in the Atmosphere* Helsinki (Finland) 2022, *Meeting* Toulouse (France) 2005, *Workshop on vertical coupling in the atmosphere/ionosphere system* Bath (UK) 2004, *Workshop on Long Term Changes and Trends in the Atmosphere* Sozopol (Bulgaria) 2004, *International workshop on long-term changes and trends in the upper atmosphere* Prague (Czech Rep) 2001.

Members Individuals of 7 countries:
Australia, France, Germany, India, Japan, UK, USA. [2015/XE3838/v/**E**]

♦ International Commission of Military History (ICMH) 12705

Commission internationale d'histoire militaire (CIHM) – Internationale Kommission für Militärgeschichte – Commissione Internazionale di Storia Militare – Comisión Internacional de Historia Militar

Pres Dept Political Qciences, Univ Cattolica del Sacro Cuore, Largo A Gemelli 1, 20123 Milan MI, Italy.

SG Royal Military Ac, Av de la Renaissance 30, 1000 Brussels, Belgium.

URL: http://www.icmh-cihm.org/en/

History 1938, Zurich (Switzerland). Set up during International Congress of Historical Sciences, as a commission of ICHS; last statutes in this role adopted 1971. Became an autonomous international organization, Jul 1972. New constitution adopted 15 Aug 1973, Stockholm (Sweden), at International Symposium on Military History; amended 1980, Bucharest (Romania), 2005, Madrid (Spain) and 2012, Sofia (Bulgaria). Current statutes adopted 8 Sep 2017, Douala (Cameroon). Also referred to as *Commission internationale d'histoire militaire comparée.* Previously also referred to as *Mezdunarodnaja Komissija Voennoj Istorii.* **Aims** Foster and coordinate studies and research in the field of military history. **Structure** General Assembly (annual); Board; Executive Board; National Commissions (41); Specialized Committees (3). **Languages** English, French, German, Italian, Spanish. **Staff** None. **Finance** Sources: contributions; members' dues. **Activities** Events/meetings; publishing activities. **Events** *Congress* Wroclaw (Poland) / Opole (Poland) 2022, *Independence Wars since the XVIII Century* Athens (Greece) 2021, *Unsettled Problems after the 1919 Peace Conference: Military Conflicts and Diplomatic Negotiations* Sofia (Bulgaria) 2019, *The Creation of New States and Collapse of Old Empires in the XXth Century* Jerusalem (Israel) 2018, *World Wars and Colonies in History* Douala (Cameroon) 2017. **Publications** *ICMH Newsletter* (2 a year) in English, French; *The International Journal of Military History and Historiography* (2 a year); *The International Review of Military History* (annual). Congress proceedings working documents.

Members National commissions in 41 countries:
Argentina, Austria, Belgium, Brazil, Bulgaria, Cameroon, Canada, China, Cyprus, Czechia, Denmark, Finland, France, Germany, Greece, Hungary, Indonesia, Ireland, Israel, Italy, Japan, Jordan, Korea Rep, Morocco, Netherlands, Norway, Poland, Portugal, Romania, Senegal, Slovakia, Slovenia, South Africa, Spain, Sweden, Switzerland, Tunisia, Türkiye, UK, United Arab Emirates, USA.

NGO Relations Affiliate member of: *International Committee of Historical Sciences (ICHS, #12777).* [2021/XC4544/**C**]

♦ International Commission on Missing Persons (ICMP) 12706

Dir Gen Koninginnegracht 12, 2514 AA The Hague, Netherlands. T. +31639405703. E-mail: icmp@icmp.int.

URL: https://www.icmp.int/

History 29 Jun 1996, Lyon (France). Established by United States President Bill Clinton, during Annual Summit Meeting of the G-7, currently *Group of Eight (G-8, #10745)*, to address the issue of persons missing as a result of the different conflicts relevant to Bosnia and Herzegovina, the Republic of Croatia and Serbia and Montenegro from 1991 to 1995. Following the conflict in Kosovo and the crisis in Macedonia, operations were expanded to address missing persons cases from these areas. As a consequence of ICMP's success in former Yugoslavia, and with the financial support of a growing number of donor governments, in 2003 ICMP's mandate and sphere of activity were extended by supporting governments to address the global issue of missing persons, including cases arising from natural disasters. Original title: *International Commission on Missing Persons in the former Yugoslavia.* Framework Agreement on ICMP, signed 15 Dec 2014, Brussels (Belgium), by Netherlands, UK, Sweden, Belgium and Luxembourg, represents an international Treaty constituting ICMP as a formal International Organization with its own structure of governance and international capacities. Other states are invited to accede to the Agreement. As of 2022, eight States – Afghanistan, Chile, Cyprus, Luxembourg, Serbia, Sweden, the Netherlands and the United Kingdom – are Parties to the ICMP Agreement, and Belgium and El Salvador are Signatory States. **Aims** Help governments guild rule-of-law institutions that successfully and impartially search for and identify missing persons; support efforts to develop legislation to enable families of the missing to assert their rights. **Structure** Board of Commissioners; Conference of State Parities; Panel of Experts; Financial Committee; Cross Cutting Programs; Director General. **Languages** English. **Staff** 133.00 FTE, paid. **Finance** Funded primarily by governments; in-kind donations. Project supporters include: G-XG2773 – Charles Stewart Mott Foundation; EULEX; B-XB1775 – International Criminal Police Organization – INTERPOL (ICPO-INTERPOL); Netherlands Forensic Institute (NFI); G-XN3299 – Robert Bosch Foundation; South African Police; University of California, Berkeley. **Activities** Advocacy/lobbying/activism; capacity building; knowledge management/information dissemination; monitoring/evaluation; research and development; training/education. Helps states build institutional capacity and create legislation on missing persons; helps families of the missing assert and advocate their rights; facilitates collection, analysis, storage and secure sharing of missing persons data; maintains leading DNA human identification laboratory; provides learning and development resources to governments, international organizations, CSOs academic institutions and scientific agencies. **Publications** *Missing Persons from the Armed Conflicts of the 1990s: A Stocktaking* (2014); *The Missing: An Agenda for the Future* (2013). ICMP Conference Report. [2022.02.03/XE4141/**E***]

♦ International Commission on Missing Persons in the former Yugoslavia / see International Commission on Missing Persons (#12706)

♦ International Commission on Mushroom Science / see International Society for Mushroom Science (#15286)

♦ International Commission for the Navigation of the Congo (inactive)

♦ International Commission for the Nomenclature of Cultivated Plants (see: #15760)

♦ International Commission on Non-Ionizing Radiation Protection (ICNIRP) 12707

Commission internationale de protection contre les rayonnements non-ionisants

Scientific Sec c/o Bundesamt für Strahlenschutz, Ingolstädter Landstrasse 1, 85764 Oberschleissheim, Germany. T. +4989316032142 – +4989316032156. Fax +4989316032155. E-mail: info@icnirp.org.

URL: http://www.icnirp.org/

History Apr 1977, Paris (France). Founded during 4th International Congress of, and within the framework of, *International Radiation Protection Association (IRPA, #14686).* Became independent, current name and structure adopted at 8th Congress of IRPA, 1992. Former names and other names: *International Non-Ionizing Radiation Committee (INIRC)* – former (1977 to 1992). Registration: Germany. **Aims** Advance non-ionizing radiation (NIR) protection for the benefit of people and the environment. **Structure** Scientific Expert Groups (5); Project Groups (9). **Languages** English. **Staff** 1.00 FTE, paid. **Finance** Sources: contributions; grants. Other sources: German Federal Ministry for the Environment, Nature Conservation and Nuclear Safety (BMU); other international organizations and national radiation protection societies. Supported by: *European Union (EU, #08967); International Radiation Protection Association (IRPA, #14686).* **Activities** Events/meetings; guidance/assistance/consulting; knowledge management/information dissemination; networking/liaising; research/documentation. **Events** *International NIR Workshop* Seoul (Korea Rep) 2020, *Annual Meeting* Paris (France) 2018, *International NIR Workshop* Cape Town (South Africa) 2016, *Annual Meeting* Wollongong, NSW (Australia) 2014, *Annual Meeting* Thessaloniki (Greece) 2013. **Publications** Annual Report; books; Exposure Guidelines; Occupational Practical Guides; proceedings; statements; reviews of published scientific literature; general documents; reports; joint publications.

Members Individuals in 10 countries:
Australia, Austria, Italy, Japan, Netherlands, Norway, Sweden, Switzerland, UK, USA.

Consultative Status Consultative status granted from: *WHO (#20950)* (Official Relations); *ILO (#11123)* (Special List). **IGO Relations** Cooperates with (1): *UNEP (#20299).* **NGO Relations** Cooperates with (8): *Commission Internationale de l'Eclairage (CIE, #04219); European BioElectromagnetics Association (EBEA, #06335); European Committee for Electrotechnical Standardization (CENELEC, #06647); European Society of Skin Cancer Prevention (EUROSKIN, #08735); International Commission on Occupational Health (ICOH, #12709); International Commission on Radiation Units and Measurements (ICRU, #12722); International Electrotechnical Commission (IEC, #13255); Union radio-scientifique internationale (URSI, #20475).* [2023.02.14/XE1592/v/**D**]

♦ International Commission for the Northwest Atlantic Fisheries (inactive)

♦ International Commission on Nuclear Physics 12708

Commission internationale sur la physique nucléaire

Chair address not obtained.

URL: http://iupap.org/commissions/

History 1960, as a Commission (C 12) of *International Union of Pure and Applied Physics (IUPAP, #15810).* Also referred to as *IUPAP Commission on Nuclear Physics – Commission de l'UIPPA sur la physique nucléaire.* Currently serves as an internal commission. **Aims** Promote information exchange in the general field of nuclear physics, including: properties and characteristics of the *atomic nucleus* and its constituents; interaction of

atomic nuclei with other nuclei, with particles and with *radiation*; apparatus and *technology* used in nuclear investigation; applications of nuclear physics to technology. **Structure** Chairman, Vice-Chairman, Secretary and 10 members. **Finance** Source: IUPAP. **Activities** Organizes several series of international conferences and symposia. **Events** *INPC : Triennial International Nuclear Physics Conference* Adelaide, SA (Australia) 2016, *INPC : Triennial International Nuclear Physics Conference* Florence (Italy) 2013, *Triennial International Conference on Cyclotrons and their Applications* Vancouver, BC (Canada) 2013, *Symposium on nuclei in the cosmos* Heidelberg (Germany) 2010, *INPC : triennial international nuclear physics conference* Vancouver, BC (Canada) 2010.
Members Individuals in 13 countries and territories:
Austria, Canada, China, Finland, France, Germany, Italy, Japan, Korea Rep, Russia, Switzerland, Taiwan, USA.
Associate member (4) in 3 countries:
Australia, Canada, USA (2). [2019/XE9142/v/E]

♦ International Commission on Occupational Health (ICOH) 12709

Commission internationale de la santé du travail (CIST) – Comisión Internacional de Medicina del Trabajo (CIMT)

SG c/o INAIL, Dept of Occupational Medicine, Via Fontana Candida 1, 00040 Monteporzio PU, Italy. T. +39694181506. Fax +39694181556. E-mail: icoh@inail.it.
Registered Address via San Barnaba 8, 20122 Milan MI, Italy.
URL: http://www.icohweb.org/

History 13 Jun 1906, Milan (Italy), at 1st International Conference, as *Commission internationale permanente pour l'étude des maladies professionnelles*. Subsequent name changes: 1929 to *Permanent International Commission on Industrial Medicine – Commission internationale permanente pour la médecine du travail*; 1957 to *Permanent Commission and International Association on Occupational Health (PCIAOH) – Commission permanente et Association internationale pour la médecine de travail*. Present name adopted 1984. Registration: Italy. **Aims** Foster scientific progress, knowledge and development of occupational health and *safety*, in all its aspects, on an international basis.
Structure General Assembly (every 3 years, at International Congress); Board. Scientific Committees (37):
- Accident Prevention;
- Aging and Work;
- Allergy and Immunotoxicology;
- Cardiology in OH;
- Education and Training in OH;
- Effectiveness in Occupation Health Services (EOHS);
- Emergency Preparedness and Response in Occupational Health;
- Epidemiology in OH;
- History of Prevention of Occupation and Environmental Diseases;
- Indoor Air Quality and Health;
- Industrial Hygiene;
- Mining Occupational Safety and Health;
- Musculoskeletal Disorders;
- Nanomaterial Workers' Health;
- Neurotoxicology and Psychophysiology;
- Occupational and Environmental Dermatoses;
- Occupational Health Nursing;
- Occupational Medicine;
- Occupational Toxicology;
- OH and Development;
- OH for Health Workers;
- OH in the Chemical Industry (MEDICHEM);
- OH in the Construction Industry;
- Radiation and Work;
- Reproductive Hazards in the Workplace;
- Respiratory Disorders;
- Rural Health: Agriculture, Pesticides and Organic Dusts;
- Shiftwork and Working Time;
- Small-Scale Enterprises and the Informal Sector;
- Thermal Factors;
- Toxicology of Metals;
- Unemployment, Job Insecurity and Health;
- Vibration and Noise;
- Women Health and Work;
- Work and Vision;
- Work Disability Prevention and Integration;
- Work Organisation and Psychosocial Factors.

Secretariat in Rome (Italy).
Languages English, French. **Finance** Sources: members' dues. Annual budget: 581,519 CHF. **Activities** Advocacy/lobbying/activism; events/meetings; networking/liaising; research and development. **Events** *International Congress on Occupational Health* Marrakech (Morocco) 2024, *International Congress on Occupational Health* 2022, *International Symposium on Epidemiology in Occupational Health* 2021, *International Congress on Occupational Health* Melbourne, VIC (Australia) 2021, *International Symposium on Epidemiology in Occupational Health* Montréal, QC (Canada) 2020. **Publications** *ICOH Newsletter*. *Code of Ethics for Occupational Health Professionals*; *International Directory of Research Institutions in Occupational Health*; *Membership Directory*. Congress reports; Scientific Committee reports.
Members Individual Membership, includes categories Honorary, Active, Emeritus, and Retired (occupational physicians, industrial hygienists, engineers, epidemiologists, psychologist, toxicologist, ergonomists and occupational nurses). Collective Membership, includes categories: Sustaining (organizations, societies, industries, enterprises); Affiliate (professional organizations or scientific societies pursuing the same objectives).
Members (1,666) in 99 countries and territories:
Algeria, Argentina, Australia, Austria, Bahrain, Belgium, Benin, Botswana, Brazil, Bulgaria, Cameroon, Canada, Chile, China, Colombia, Costa Rica, Côte d'Ivoire, Croatia, Cuba, Czechia, Denmark, Egypt, Estonia, Ethiopia, Finland, France, Gabon, Germany, Ghana, Greece, Guinea, Hong Kong, Hungary, Iceland, India, Indonesia, Iran Islamic Rep, Ireland, Israel, Italy, Jamaica, Japan, Kenya, Korea DPR, Korea Rep, Kuwait, Latvia, Liberia, Libya, Lithuania, Luxembourg, Malaysia, Mali, Mauritius, Mexico, Monaco, Morocco, Namibia, Nepal, Netherlands, New Zealand, Nicaragua, Nigeria, Norway, Pakistan, Panama, Papua New Guinea, Philippines, Poland, Portugal, Romania, Russia, Rwanda, Saudi Arabia, Senegal, Seychelles, Singapore, Slovenia, South Africa, Spain, Sri Lanka, Sweden, Switzerland, Taiwan, Tanzania UR, Thailand, Togo, Tunisia, Türkiye, Uganda, UK, Ukraine, United Arab Emirates, Uruguay, USA, Venezuela, Vietnam, Zambia, Zimbabwe.
Affiliate members include 2 organizations listed in this Yearbook:
International Institute of Risk and Safety Management (IIRSM, #13920); *International SOS Foundation (ISOS Foundation, #15570)*.
Consultative Status Consultative status granted from: *ECOSOC (#05331)* (Ros C); *ILO (#11123)* (Special List); *WHO (#20950)* (Official Relations). **IGO Relations** Member of: *European Agency for Safety and Health at Work (EU-OSHA, #05843)*. Associated with Department of Global Communications of the United Nations. [2021/XB3092/y/B]

♦ International Commission of the Oder (inactive)

♦ International Commission for Optics (ICO) 12710

Commission Internationale d'Optique (CIO)

SG Inst d'Optique Graduate School, 2 avenue Augustin Fresnel, 91127 Palaiseau CEDEX, France. E-mail: secretariat@e-ico.org.
Pres Dipto di Fisica, Politecnico di Milano, Piazza Leonardo da Vinci 32, 20133 Milan MI, Italy. T. +39223996150.
URL: https://www.e-ico.org/

History 12 Jul 1948, Delft (Netherlands). Founded following preparatory meeting, Jun 1947, Prague (Czechoslovakia). Constitution revised Oct 1972. New statutes adopted 1999, San Francisco CA (USA); amended 2008, Sidney (Australia); Article I amended Aug 2014, Santiago de Compostela (Spain). **Aims** Contribute to progress and diffusion of knowledge in the fields of optics and photonics and their applications. **Structure** General Meeting (every 3 years, at Congress); Bureau; Commission; Sub-committees. Meetings open. **Languages** English, French. **Staff** 21.00 FTE, voluntary. **Finance** Subscriptions from territorial committees according to optics activity. Other sources: occasional grants from UNESCO, official and private bodies. **Activities** Awards/prizes/competitions; events/meetings; research/documentation; training/education. **Events** *Triennial Congress* Dresden (Germany) 2022, *General Meeting* 2021, *Triennial Congress* Dresden (Germany) 2021, *Triennial Congress and General Meeting* Dresden (Germany) 2020, *Triennial Congress and General Meeting* Tokyo (Japan) 2017. **Publications** *ICO Newsletter* (4 a year); *ICO Green Book* (every 3 years). *ICO, Its Constitution, History and Statutes* (1957, 1969); *ICO Topical Volumes*. Conference proceedings.
Members Territorial committees, representing individuals and organizations, in 51 countries and territories:
Argentina, Australia, Belarus, Belgium, Brazil, Canada, China, Colombia, Cuba, Czechia, Denmark, Ecuador, Estonia, Finland, France, Germany, Ghana, Greece, Hungary, India, Indonesia, Iran Islamic Rep, Ireland, Israel, Italy, Japan, Korea Rep, Latvia, Lithuania, Mexico, Moldova, Morocco, Netherlands, New Zealand, Norway, Poland, Romania, Russia, Singapore, Slovakia, Spain, Sudan, Sweden, Switzerland, Taiwan, Tunisia, Türkiye, UK, Ukraine, USA, Venezuela.
International Societies (5), listed in this Yearbook:
African Laser, Atomic and Molecular Sciences Network (LAM Network, #00356); *European Optical Society (EOS, #08091)*; *Institute of Electrical and Electronics Engineers (IEEE, #11259)* (Photonics Society); *OWLS Society (#17921)*; *SPIE (#19919)*.
NGO Relations Member of (1): *International Science Council (ISC, #14796)* (Affiliate). Affiliated Commission of: *International Union of Pure and Applied Physics (IUPAP, #15810)*. Contacts with: *Commission Internationale de l'Eclairage (CIE, #04219)*. In liaison with technical committees of: *International Organization for Standardization (ISO, #14473)*. [2022/XC1525/y/C]

♦ International Commission for Orders of Chivalry (ICOC) 12711

Commission internationale permanente d'études des ordres de chevalerie – Comisión Internacional para las Ordenes de Caballeria – Commissione Internazionale per lo studio degli Ordini Cavallereschi

Sec Via Baronio 14, 47899 Serravalle, San Marino. E-mail: icoc1960@gmail.com.
Contact Via Battisti 3, 40123 Bologna BO, Italy.
URL: http://www.icocregister.org/

History 21 Aug 1960, Stockholm (Sweden). 21-28 Aug 1960, Stockholm (Sweden), at 5th International Congress of Genealogy and Heraldry, according to decision of 3rd Congress of Madrid (Spain), 1955. Established as a permanent international autonomous body at 6th International Congress, 14 Sep 1962, Edinburgh (UK). Outwardly inactive during 1970s while reviewing criteria for acceptance of orders, following criticism that it ignored the different historical development of honours systems in different countries. Restructured as a strictly academic body, Nov 1999. Nov 2000, London (UK), re-examined all chivalric matter. Jan 1996. **Aims** Study, report on, promote exchange of ideas regarding, and provide advice on legal and historic matters connected with assessing the validity of Orders of Chivalry and of bodies granting honours, distinction or awards, irrespective of culture. **Structure** General Assembly (every 2 years); Executive Committee (meeting annually) comprises 4 members. **Languages** English, French, Italian, Spanish. **Finance** Self-financing. **Events** *International Colloquium on Nobility* Madrid (Spain) 2022, *International Colloquium on Nobility* Madrid (Spain) 2019, *International Colloquium on Nobility* Madrid (Spain) 2017, *International Colloquium on Nobility* Madrid (Spain) 2015, *Meeting* Agrigento (Italy) 2007. **Publications** *Il Mondo del Cavaliere* (4 a year); *Register of Orders of Chivalry* (annual). Reports.
Members Members in 15 countries:
Czechia, Denmark, Finland, Germany, Greece, Holy See, Ireland, Italy, Poland, Portugal, Russia, San Marino, Spain, Sweden, UK.
NGO Relations Associazione Insigniti Onorificenze Cavalleresche (AIOC); *International Institute for the Study of Chivalric Orders (IISCO, no recent information)*. [2021/XD1526/v/D]

♦ International Commission on Palaeozoic Microflora (#04225)
♦ International Commission for Palynology / see International Federation of Palynological Societies (#13498)

♦ International Commission on Particles and Fields 12712

Commission internationale sur les particules et champs

Chair address not obtained.
URL: https://iupap.org/commissions/c11-particles-and-fields/

History 1957, as a Commission (C 11) of *International Union of Pure and Applied Physics (IUPAP, #15810)*. Also referred to as *IUPAP Commission on Particles and Fields – Commission de l'UIPPA sur les particules et champs*. Currently serves as an internal commission. **Aims** Promote information exchange in the general field of particles and fields, including: theory and experiment concerned with the nature and properties of the fundamental constituents of matter and the forces acting between these constituents; maintaining of liaison with ICFA; accelerators, detectors and techniques used in these investigations; industrial applications of relevant technologies. **Structure** Chairman, Vice-Chairman, Secretary and 10 members. **Finance** Source: IUPAP. **Activities** Organizes several series of international conferences and symposia. **Events** *ICHEP : Biennial international conference on high energy physics* Valencia (Spain) 2014, *IPAC : International Particle Accelerator Conference* Shanghai (China) 2013, *ICHEP : Biennial international conference on high energy physics* Melbourne, VIC (Australia) 2012, *International conference in neutrino physics and astrophysics* Athens (Greece) 2010, *ICHEP : Biennial international conference on high energy physics* Paris (France) 2010.
Members Individuals (13) in 12 countries:
Argentina, China, France, Germany, India, Italy, Japan, Norway, Poland, Russia, UK, USA (2).
Associate members in 2 countries:
Finland, Spain.
NGO Relations Maintains close liaison with Commissions and Committees of other Unions, other scientific associations and other IUPAP commissions, including *International Committee for Future Accelerators (ICFA, #12774)*. [2019/XE9515/v/E]

♦ International Commission on Peace and Food / see International Center for Peace and Development (#12472)
♦ International Commission for Peace in the Minds of Men (no recent information)
♦ International Commission on Penicillium and Aspergillus (see: #15794)
♦ International Commission on Photometry (inactive)

♦ International Commission on Physics for Development (ICPD) 12713

Commission internationale sur la physique pour le développement

Chairperson address not obtained.
URL: https://iupap.org/commissions/c13-physics-for-development/

History 1981. Founded as a subunit of *International Union of Pure and Applied Physics (IUPAP, #15810)*. Currently serves as an internal commission (C 13). Former names and other names: *IUPAP Commission on Physics for Development* – former; *Commission de l'UIPPA sur la physique pour le développement* – former. **Aims** Promote information exchange in the field by: helping to improve conditions of physics and physicists in *development countries*; proposing and supporting initiatives to promote the contribution of physics to *industrial development*; collecting and distributing relevant information. **Structure** Chairman, Vice-Chairman, Secretary and 10 members. **Finance** Supported by: *International Union of Pure and Applied Physics (IUPAP, #15810)*. **Activities** Events/meetings. **Events** *Workshop on Electron Microscopy in Materials* Tunis (Tunisia) 2013, *International meeting on photodynamics* Havana (Cuba) 2010, *Meeting on new trends in conducting material* Sousse (Tunisia) 2010, *International meeting on photodynamics* Havana (Cuba) 2008, *Conference on optics and laser applications in medicine and environmental monitoring for sustainable development* Cape Coast (Ghana) 2007.
Members Individuals in 13 countries:
Argentina, Brazil, France, Germany, Italy, Japan, Korea Rep, Latvia, Senegal, Spain, Taiwan, UK, USA.
Associate members (2) in 2 countries:
Egypt, Tunisia.
NGO Relations Links with other several scientific commission. [2021.05.25/XE3219/v/E]

♦ International Commission on Physics Education (ICPE) 12714

Commission internationale sur l'éducation en physique (CIEP)

Co-Sec c/o School of Physics A28, Physics Road, University of Sydney, Sydney NSW 2006, Australia.
URL: http://iupap.org/commissions/physics-education/

History 1960, as a Commission (C 14) of *International Union of Pure and Applied Physics (IUPAP, #15810)*. Also referred to as *IUPAP Commission on Physics Education – Commission de l'UIPPA sur l'éducation en physique*. Currently serves as an internal commission. **Aims** Promote information exchange in the general field of physics education, including: the collection, evaluation, coordination and distribution of information education in the physical sciences at all levels; information relating to the assessment of standards of physics

teaching and learning; suggesting ways to improve facilities for physics studies, stimulating experiments and giving help to physics teachers. **Structure** Chairman, Vice-Chairman, Secretary and 12 members. **Languages** English. **Staff** None. **Finance** Source: IUPAP. **Activities** Organizes a number of conference series in the field. **Events** *World Conference on Physics Education* Hanoi (Vietnam) 2021, *World Conference on Physics Education* Hanoi (Vietnam) 2020, *Joint Conference* Budapest (Hungary) 2019, *GIREP-ICPE-EPEC Conference* Dublin (Ireland) 2017, *World Conference on Physics Education* Sao Paulo (Brazil) 2016. **Publications** *International Newsletter on Physics Education* (2 a year); *Physics Now. Connecting Research in Physics Education with Teacher Education* (1998) by A Tiberghien et al; *Niels Bohr – A Centenary Volume* (1985) by A P French and P J Kennedy. Conference proceedings.
Members Individuals in 14 countries:
Argentina, China, Czechia, Ethiopia, Germany, India, Italy, Japan, Poland, Romania, South Africa, Sweden, UK, USA.
Associate members (4) in 4 countries:
Australia, Cyprus, France, Mexico.
NGO Relations Cooperates with (3): *International Commission on Physics for Development (ICPD, #12713)*; *International Research Group on Physics Teaching (#14731)*; *International Science Council (ISC, #14796)*.
[2020/XE1566/v/**E**]

♦ International Commission on Planetary Atmospheres and their Evolution (ICPAE) 12715

Pres Space Science and Engineering Center, 1225 West Dayton St, Madison WI 53706, USA. E-mail: sanjayl@ssec.wisc.edu.
URL: http://icpae.iaps.inaf.it/
History 1977 as a Standing Commission of *International Association of Meteorology and Atmospheric Sciences (IAMAS, #12031)*. Also referred to as *IAMAP International Commission on Planetary Atmospheres and their Evolution*. **Aims** Promote scientific work into the field of planetology in general and of the atmospheres found in the planetary systems. **Structure** Executive Committee; Bureau. **Languages** English. **Staff** 2.00 FTE, paid. **Activities** Events/meetings; awards/prizes/competitions; networking/liaising. **Events** *Symposium on meteorology and climate of Mars* Reading (UK) 1989.
Members Individuals in 13 countries:
Australia, Austria, China, Finland, France, Germany, Greece, India, Japan, Russia, Spain, UK, USA.
[2018.07.31/XE0134/v/**E**]

♦ International Commission for Plant-Bee Relationships / see International Commission for Plant-Pollinator Relationships (#12716)

♦ International Commission for Plant-Pollinator Relationships (ICPPR) 12716

Sec Hasselstr 23, 29223 Celle, Germany.
Pres School of Environmental Sciences, Univ of Guelph, 95 Stone Rd W, Guelph ON N1G 1A1, Canada. T. +15198244120ext52479. Fax +15198370442.
URL: https://www.icppr.com/
History 1951, Leamington Spa (UK). 1951, Leamington (UK), by Anna Maurizio (first President), at International Beekeeping Congress, following decision at International Botanical Congress, 1950, Stockholm (Sweden). Original title: *International Commission for Bee Botany (ICBB) – Commission internationale de botanique apicole – Internationale Kommission für Bienenbotanik*. Subsequently referred to as *International Commission for Plant-Bee Relationships (ICPBR)*. **Aims** Promote and coordinate research on the relationships between plants and bees of all types, including studies of insect *pollinated* plants, bee foraging behaviour, effects of pollinator visits on plants, management and protection of insect pollinators, bee collected materials from plants and products derived from plants and modified by bees. **Structure** General Assembly (every 4 years). Council, consisting of 30 members, including Chairman, Vice-Chairman and Secretary. Executive, comprising Chairman, 2 Vice-Chairmen and Secretary. Working Groups (3). **Languages** English. **Staff** Voluntary. **Finance** Sources: gifts, legacies; grants; meeting proceeds; sale of publications. **Activities** Organizes meetings, colloquia and symposia and publishes and disseminates proceedings; collaborates with other national and international institutions with similar interests. Research include studies of: studies of insect pollinated plants; bee foraging behaviour; effects of pollinator visits on plants; management and protection of pollinators; bee collected materials (honey and pollen from plants); products derived from plants (honeydew, was, royal jelly) and elaborated by bees. Working groups (3): Pollination; Bee Protection; Nectar. **Events** *International symposium on pollination / Symposium* Cholula (Mexico) 2011, *Hazards of pesticides to bees* Wageningen (Netherlands) 2011, *International symposium on pollination / Symposium* Ames, IA (USA) 2006, *Quadrennial General Assembly* Masonmagyarovar (Hungary) 2000, *International symposium on pollination* Mosonmagyaróvar (Hungary) 2000. **Publications** *Bee World*; *Bumblebee Quest* – newsletter; *ICPBR Circular*; *ICPBR Newsletter* – also by e-mail. World directory of bee and pollination scientists; directory of members; symposia proceedings. **Members** Individuals (257) in 42 countries. Membership countries not specified.
NGO Relations Scientific member of: *International Union of Biological Sciences (IUBS, #15760)*. Member of: *International Association of Botanical and Mycological Societies (IABMS, #11730)*. [2015/XD1522/v/**C**]

♦ International Commission on Plasma Physics (ICPP) 12717

Commission internationale sur la physique des plasmas
Chair address not obtained.
URL: https://iupap.org/commissions/c16-plasma-physics/
History 1969, as a Commission (C 16) of *International Union of Pure and Applied Physics (IUPAP, #15810)*. In this respect, referred to as *IUPAP Commission on Plasma Physics – Commission de l'UIPPA sur la physique des plasmas*. Currently serves as an internal commission. **Aims** Promote information exchange in the general field of plasma physics, including: physics of ionized gases, of partially ionized gases and of gaseous electronics; applications of such physics. **Structure** Chairman, Vice-Chairman, Secretary and 10 members. **Finance** Source: IUPAP. **Activities** Organizes a number of international and regional conference and workshop series. **Events** *Biennial International Congress on Plasma Physics* Gyeongju (Korea Rep) 2021, *Biennial International Congress on Plasma Physics* Gyeongju (Korea Rep) 2020, *Biennial International Congress on Plasma Physics* Lisbon (Portugal) 2014, *Biennial International Congress in Plasma Physics* Stockholm (Sweden) 2012, *International Conference on the Physics of Dusty Plasmas* Munich (Germany) 2011.
Members Individuals in 13 countries:
Australia, Belgium, Canada, France, Germany, India, Japan, Netherlands, Poland, South Africa, Spain, Taiwan, USA.
Associate member (4) in 4 countries:
Belgium, Brazil, Russia, USA. [2020/XE1810/v/**E**]

♦ International Commission on Polar Meteorology (ICPM) 12718

Commission internationale de la météorologie polaire (CIMP)
Pres British Antarctic Survey, High Cross, Madingley Road, Cambridge, CB3 0ET, UK. E-mail: tlc@bas.ac.uk.
Sec UWI Madison, Space Sciences, 1225 West Dayton St, Madison WI 53706, USA. E-mail: mattl@ssec.wisc.edu.
URL: http://www.icpm-iamas.aq/
History as a commission of *International Association of Meteorology and Atmospheric Sciences (IAMAS, #12031)*. Also referred to as *IAMAP International Commission on Polar Meteorology – Commission internationale de la météorologie polaire de l'AOMPA*. **Events** *Atmospheric Model Parameterization in the Polar Regions Workshop* Boulder, CO (USA) 2012, *Session on polar regional climate modeling and global impacts* Montréal, QC (Canada) 2009, *Joint workshop on recent high latitude climate change* Seattle, WA (USA) 2007, *Meeting* Vienna (Austria) 1991. **Members** Individuals. Membership countries not specified.
[2016/XE3840/v/**E**]

♦ International Commission for the Prevention of Alcoholism and Drug Dependency (ICPA) 12719

Commission internationale pour la prévention de l'alcoolisme – Comisión internacional para la Prevención del Alcoholismo – Internationaler Ausschuss für die Verhütung der Trinksucht
Exec Dir 12501 Old Columbia Pike, Silver Spring MD 20904, USA. T. +13016806719. Fax +13016806707.
URL: http://icpaworld.org/
History 1952, Washington, DC (USA). **Aims** Encourage scientific research on all forms of intoxication by drink, *tobacco* and drugs, their physiological, mental and moral effects on the individual and their social, economic, political and religious consequences. **Structure** Commission, consisting of 250 prominent men and women, by invitation, representing worldwide geographical regions (number of representatives depending on population). Executive Council, consisting of Executive Director, Vice Presidents (rotate each year, one serving as President), Associate Directors, Treasurers and Honorary Presidents. National Committees. Meetings open. **Languages** English. **Staff** Voluntary. **Finance** Sources: contributions. Annual budget: 200,000 USD. **Activities** Organizes: conferences; two-day national seminars; other seminars; courses; prevention programmes. Sets up national committees. Institutes of Scientific Studies for the Prevention of Alcoholism established in: Mumbai (India); Loma Linda CA (USA); Manila (Philippines); Sydney (Australia); Washington DC (USA); Europe (location not specified). **Events** *World Prevention Congress* Geneva (Switzerland) 2009, *World Prevention Congress* Seoul (Korea Rep) 2008, *World Prevention Congress* Manila (Philippines) 2006, *World prevention congress* Salzburg (Austria) 2004, *World prevention congress* Salzburg (Austria) 2004. **Publications** *Dispatch International*; *ICPA Reporter*. Congress reports. Information Services: Library (2,500 vols).
Members National Committees (66); individuals. Members in 112 countries and territories:
Afghanistan, Algeria, Argentina, Australia, Austria, Bahrain, Belgium, Benin, Bermuda, Bolivia, Brazil, Bulgaria, Burkina Faso, Burundi, Cameroon, Canada, Central African Rep, Chile, China, Colombia, Comoros, Congo DR, Costa Rica, Côte d'Ivoire, Cyprus, Czechia, Denmark, Dominica, Ecuador, Egypt, Eswatini, Ethiopia, Fiji, Finland, France, Germany, Ghana, Greece, Guatemala, Haiti, Hong Kong, Hungary, Iceland, India, Indonesia, Iran Islamic Rep, Iraq, Ireland, Israel, Italy, Jamaica, Japan, Jordan, Kenya, Korea Rep, Kuwait, Latvia, Lebanon, Lesotho, Liberia, Libya, Lithuania, Madagascar, Malawi, Malaysia, Mali, Mauritius, Mexico, Morocco, Nepal, Netherlands, New Zealand, Nigeria, Norway, Oman, Pakistan, Papua New Guinea, Paraguay, Peru, Philippines, Poland, Portugal, Qatar, Romania, Russia, Rwanda, Samoa, Saudi Arabia, Senegal, Serbia-Montenegro, Sierra Leone, Singapore, Solomon Is, South Africa, Spain, Sri Lanka, Sudan, Sweden, Switzerland, Tanzania UR, Thailand, Togo, Tonga, Trinidad-Tobago, Tunisia, Türkiye, UK, United Arab Emirates, Uruguay, USA, Zambia, Zimbabwe.
IGO Relations Accredited by (1): *United Nations Office at Vienna (UNOV, #20604)*. Associated with Department of Global Communications of the United Nations. **NGO Relations** Located at the World Headquarters of: *General Conference of Seventh-Day Adventists (SDA, #10109)*. [2020/XB1538/**B**]

♦ International Commission of Principal Prison Chaplains / see International Commission of Catholic Prison Pastoral Care (#12670)
♦ International Commission of Prison Chaplains / see International Commission of Catholic Prison Pastoral Care (#12670)
♦ International Commission for Protection Against Environmental Mutagens and Carcinogens (inactive)
♦ International Commission for the Protection of the Alps / see CIPRA International (#03930)

♦ International Commission for the Protection of the Danube River (ICPDR) 12720

Internationale Kommission zum Schutz der Donau (IKSD)
Exec Sec VIC – D0412, PO 500, 1400 Vienna, Austria. T. +431260605738. Fax +431260605895. E-mail: icpdr@unvienna.org.
URL: http://www.icpdr.org/
History 1998, to implement the *Convention on Cooperation for the Protection and Sustainable Use of the Danube River (1994)*, also referred to as the Danube River Protection Convention, and to make it a living tool. **Aims** Promote and coordinate *sustainable* and equitable *water* management, including *conservation*, improvement and rational use of waters for the benefit of the Danube River Basin countries and their people. **Structure** Contracting countries' national delegations; Permanent Secretariat; Expert and Task Groups. **Languages** English. **Staff** 10.00 FTE, paid. **Finance** Contributions by contracting parties; funds; partnerships with businesses. **Activities** Politics/policy/regulatory; projects/programmes; awareness raising; knowledge management/information dissemination. **Events** *European River Symposium* Vienna (Austria) 2021, *European River Symposium* Vienna (Austria) 2016, *Ministerial Meeting* Vienna (Austria) 2016, *Meeting* Vienna (Austria) 2010, *Seminar on international water law and cross-border water management* Vienna (Austria) 2009. **Publications** *Danube Watch* – magazine. Annual Report; brochures; posters; technical reports.
Members Contracting parties (15). Governments (14) in 14 countries:
Austria, Bosnia-Herzegovina, Bulgaria, Croatia, Czechia, Germany, Hungary, Moldova, Montenegro, Romania, Serbia, Slovakia, Slovenia, Ukraine.
Included in the above, one regional entity, listed in this Yearbook:
European Commission (EC, #06633).
IGO Relations Based at: *Vienna International Centre (VIC)*. [2017/XE2659/y/**E***]

♦ International Commission for the Protection of the Elbe River (#13249)
♦ International Commission for the Protection of Lake Constance (#13244)
♦ International Commission for the Protection of the Meuse River / see International Commission of the Meuse (#12702)
♦ International Commission for the Protection of the Moselle (inactive)
♦ International Commission for the Protection of the Oder / see Internationale Kommission zum Schutz der Oder gegen Verunreinigung (#13250)
♦ International Commission for the Protection of the Odra River against Pollution (#13250)
♦ International Commission for the Protection of Planets Against Microbes from Earth (inactive)

♦ International Commission for the Protection of the Rhine (ICPR) 12721

Commission internationale pour la protection du Rhin (CIPR) – Internationale Kommission zum Schutz des Rheins (IKSR) – Internationale Commissie ter Bescherming van de Rijn (ICBR)
Head of Secretariat Postfach 20 02 53, 56002 Koblenz, Germany. T. +49261942520. Fax +492619425252. E-mail: sekretariat@iksr.de.
Chair Kaiserin-Augusta-Anlagen 15, 56068 Koblenz, Germany.
URL: http://www.iksr.org/
History 29 Apr 1963, Bern (Switzerland). Established on signature of Convention by the Governments of France, Germany FR, Luxembourg, Netherlands, Switzerland; Convention entered into force 1 May 1965. A supplementary agreement, signed 3 Dec 1976, Bonn (Germany FR) and entered into force 1 Feb 1979, made the European Economic Community (EEC) full member of the Commission. Governmental delegates had first met 1 Jul 1950, Basel (Switzerland), following steps taken by *Central Commission for the Navigation of the Rhine (CCNR, #03687)* and the 'Salmon Commission'. *Rhine Action Programme (RAP)* adopted 1 Oct 1987. Statutes registered in *'UNTS 1/14538'*. Former names and other names: *International Commission for the Protection of the Rhine Against Pollution* – former (1998); *Commission internationale pour la protection du Rhin contre la pollution* – former (1998); *Internationale Kommission zum Schutze de Rheins gegen Verunreinigung* – former (1998); *Internationale Commissie ter Bescherming van de Rijn tegen Verontreiniging* – former (1998); *Internationale Rijn Commissie* – alias; *ICPRP* – alias; *ICRAP* – alias. **Aims** Prepare and carry out research to determine the nature, quantity and origin of pollution in the Rhine; submit proposals to signatory Governments for measures contributing to sustainable development of the Rhine; work out details of possible arrangements between signatory Governments for protecting the waters of the Rhine; improve not only water quality but also the ecosystem; develop and implement an action plan for prevention of flooding. **Structure** Each Contracting Party is represented by a delegation of up to 4 members; President is appointed for 3-year term in rotation from Contracting Parties. Permanent Working Group for Current Research; about 20 Working Parties, including Emissions, Security of Industrial Plants, Legal Questions, Surveillance of the Quality Status of the Rhine, Improvement of the Ecosystem, Flooding Protection, Sustainable Development. Technical/Scientific Secretariat. **Languages** Dutch, English, French, German. **Staff** 12.00 FTE, paid. **Finance** Contracting Parties meet costs of their representation and of current research in their own territory. Other expenses are met: 32.5% each by France, Germany FR, Netherlands; 12% by Switzerland; 2.5% by Luxembourg (Luxembourg); 2.5% by European Community. Budget (annual): about euro 1.2 million. **Activities** Research/documentation; knowledge management/information dissemination; monitoring/evaluation; projects/programmes. **Events** *European River Symposium* Vienna (Austria) 2021, *International Symposium on Low Flows in the Rhine Catchment* Basel (Switzerland) 2017, *European River Symposium* Vienna (Austria) 2016, *Annual Plenary Assembly* Vienna (Austria) 2015, *Rhine-Mekong Symposium on Climate Change and its Influence on Water and Related Sectors* Koblenz (Germany) 2014. **Publications** *Topic Rhine* in English, French, German – newsletter. Statistical reports; general reports; brochures.
Members Governments of 5 countries:

France, Germany, Luxembourg, Netherlands, Switzerland.
Participating regional integration EU entity (1):
European Union (EU, #08967).
IGO Relations Observer to: *Internationale Kommission zum Schutz der Elbe (IKSE, #13249); OSPAR Commission for the Protection of the Marine Environment of the North-East Atlantic (OSPAR Commission, #17905).* **NGO Relations** Observer status granted to 19 NGOs, including: *BirdLife International (#03266); Conseil européen de l'industrie chimique (CEFIC, #04687); European Federation of National Associations of Water and Waste Water Services (#07170); Greenpeace International (#10727); Internationale Arbeitsgemeinschaft der Wasserwerke im Rheineinzugsgebiet (IAWR, #13215).* [2021/XD1540/D*]

- International Commission for the Protection of the Rhine Against Pollution / see International Commission for the Protection of the Rhine (#12721)
- International Commission for the Protection of the Saar (inactive)
- International Commission for the Protection of the Schelde River / see International Commission of the Schelde River (#12727)
- International Commission for the Protection of the Water Lake Geneva (internationally oriented national body)
- International Commission on Protozoology (no recent information)
- International Commission on Quantum Electronics / see International Commission on Laser Physics and Photonics (#12697)

♦ International Commission on Radiation Units and Measurements (ICRU) 12722

Commission internationale des unités et des mesures de radiation
Exec Sec 7910 Woodmont Ave, Ste 400, Bethesda MD 20814-3095, USA. T. +13016572652ext31. Fax +13019078768. E-mail: icru@icru.org.
URL: http://www.icru.org/

History 1925, London (UK), under the auspices of *International Congress of Radiology (ICR)*, as *International X-Ray Unit Committee.* Name changed to: *International Committee on Radiological Units*, 1931, Paris (France); *International Commission on Radiological Units*, 1950, London; *International Commission on Radiological Units and Measurements* 1956, Geneva (Switzerland). Present name adopted 1965, Rome (Italy). Structure modified: 1962, Montreux, to permit establishment of Planning Boards and Task Groups; and 1969, Hakone, to permit establishment of Report Committees working in various Technical Areas. An international commission of *International Society of Radiology (ISR, #15412).* **Aims** Develop a common framework of scientific concepts based on international consensus on matters related to assessing safe and effective use of radiation; assist uniformity in reporting by developing internationally acceptable recommendations regarding quantities and *units* of radiation and *radioactivity*, procedures suitable for measuring and applying these quantities in clinical *radiology*, and physical data needed in applying these procedures; formulate recommendations on radiation quantities, units and measurement in the field of radiation *protection.* **Structure** Commission comprises Chairman and not more than 15 members, including Vice-Chairman and Secretary. Executive Secretary; Executive for Development; Honorary Chairmen; Principal Scientific Counsellor; 2 Senior Advisors. Commission selects Consultants for Technical Areas and members of Report Committees. Meetings closed. **Languages** English. **Finance** Grants from official and private bodies; contribution from the ISR. **Activities** Knowledge management/information dissemination. **Events** *Annual Meeting* Japan 2023, *Annual Meeting* Singapore (Singapore) 2019, *Workshop on Radiation Monitoring for Protection of the Public after Major Radioactive Releases to the Environment* Chiba (Japan) 2016, *International conference on advances in radiation oncology* Vienna (Austria) 2009, *International symposium on hadrontherapy* Geneva (Switzerland) / Villigen (Switzerland) 1996. **Publications** Reports series.
Members Organizations and individuals in 12 countries:
Argentina, Austria, Belgium, Canada, Denmark, France, Germany, Japan, Netherlands, Sweden, UK, USA.
Consultative Status Consultative status granted from: *ECOSOC (#05331)* (Ros C); *International Atomic Energy Agency (IAEA, #12294).* [2018/XC1567/E]

♦ International Commission on Radiological Education (ICRE) 12723

Main Office c/o ISR, 1891 Preston White Drive, Reston VA 20191, USA. T. +17036488360. Fax +17036488361. E-mail: info@isradiology.org.
URL: http://www.isradiology.org/

History 1953, Copenhagen (Denmark), as an international commission of *International Society of Radiology (ISR, #15412)*, during the 7th *International Congress of Radiology (ICR)*, when the structure of IRS was adopted and several other working groups were started. ICRE is the only surviving commission, and is currently the major working commission of ISR. Subsequent name change: *International Commission on Radiological Education and Information*, 1999. **Aims** Encourage and develop educational materials relating to diagnostic imaging in connection with regional and national radiology societies and with international scientific and political organizations; develop material relating to safe and efficacious use of ionizing radiation to the education of specialists in diagnostic radiology, the training of radiation physicists and of radiographers. **Structure** International Committee (meets twice a year), consisting of national delegations of member countries. Executive Committee (meets at least annually), comprising President, President-Elect, Past President, Secretary-General, Treasurer, Executive Director and 10 members. Committees set up by ISR, mostly to provide education content for the website; a separate sub-committee plans scientific programmes for ISR international congresses. Advisory Board for International Affairs in Radiology (ABIAR) performs liaison with other international medical organizations. **Languages** English. **Staff** 0.50 FTE, paid. **Finance** Members' dues from national societies (principal source), which covers their individual members. At times, obtains funds for specific projects from other sources. **Activities** Awards/prizes/competitions; events/meetings; training/education. **Publications** *ISR Newsletter* (2-3 a year). Electronic publications. **Members** National radiology societies (86), representing individual radiologists on all continents except Antarctica. Regional organizations (5) in Europe, North America, South America, Asia and Africa. Membership countries not specified. **IGO Relations** *International Atomic Energy Agency (IAEA, #12294); WHO (#20950).* [2015/XD2539/C]

- International Commission on Radiological Education and Information / see International Commission on Radiological Education (#12723)

♦ International Commission on Radiological Protection (ICRP) 12724

Commission internationale de protection contre les radiations (CIPR) – Comisión Internacional de Protección Radiológica – Internationale Kommission für Strahlenschutz
Scientific Sec PO Box 1046, Station B, 280 Slater Str, Ottawa ON K1P 5S9, Canada. T. +16139479750. Fax +16139441920. E-mail: sci.sec@icrp.org – lynn.lemaire@icrp.org.
URL: http://www.icrp.org/

History 1928, Stockholm (Sweden). Founded at 2nd *International Congress of Radiology (ICR).* Reorganized 1950, London (UK). An international commission of *International Society of Radiology (ISR, #15412).* Former names and other names: *International X-Ray and Radium Protection Committee* – former (1928 to 1950); *Commission internationale de protection en radiologie* – former (1928 to 1950). Registration: Charity Commission, No/ID: 1166304, England and Wales. **Aims** Help prevent cancer and other diseases and effects associated with exposure to ionizing radiation; protect the environment. **Structure** Commission (meets annually); Committees (4); ad hoc Task Groups and Working Parties; Secretariat, headed by Scientific Secretary. **Languages** English. **Staff** 4.00 FTE, paid. **Finance** Sources: contributions; government support; grants. Supported by: *International Society of Radiology (ISR, #15412).* **Activities** Guidance/assistance/consulting. **Events** *International Symposium on the System of Radiological Protection* Tokyo (Japan) 2023, *International Symposium on the System of Radiological Protection* Vancouver, BC (Canada) 2022, *International Symposium on the System of Radiological Protection* Vancouver, BC (Canada) 2021, *International Conference on Recovery after Nuclear Accidents* Ibaraki (Japan) 2020, *International Symposium on the System of Radiological Protection* Adelaide, SA (Australia) 2019. **Publications** *Annals of the ICRP* (4 a year). *ICRP Publication* – series. Recommendations; reviews.
Members Individuals in Commission and its committees in 37 countries:
Argentina, Australia, Austria, Belarus, Brazil, Canada, Chile, China, Colombia, Czechia, Egypt, Finland, France, Germany, Greece, Hungary, Iceland, India, Ireland, Italy, Japan, Korea Rep, Luxembourg, Netherlands, Norway, Peru, Poland, Russia, South Africa, Spain, Sweden, Switzerland, UK, Ukraine, United Arab Emirates, USA, Vietnam.
Consultative Status Consultative status granted from: *ECOSOC (#05331)* (Ros C); *International Atomic Energy Agency (IAEA, #12294); WHO (#20950)* (Official Relations). **IGO Relations** Close working relationships with: *European Commission (EC, #06633); ILO (#11123); Nuclear Energy Agency (NEA, #17615); UNEP (#20299).* Accredited by: *United Nations Office at Vienna (UNOV, #20604).* **NGO Relations** Close cooperation with: *International Commission on Radiation Units and Measurements (ICRU, #12722); International Electrotechnical Commission (IEC, #13255); International Radiation Protection Association (IRPA, #14686).* In liaison with technical committees of: *International Organization for Standardization (ISO, #14473).* [2022.05.04/XC1568/v/E]

- International Commission on Radiological Units / see International Commission on Radiation Units and Measurements (#12722)
- International Commission on Radiological Units and Measurements / see International Commission on Radiation Units and Measurements (#12722)
- International Commission on Radium Standards (inactive)

♦ International Commission for Research into European Food History (ICREFH) 12725

Pres Univ Toulouse Jean Jaurès, Allées A Machado, 31058 Toulouse CEDES 09, France.
URL: http://icrefh.hypotheses.org/

History 1989, Münster (Germany). **Aims** Study the history of food and nutrition in Europe since the late eighteenth century. **Structure** Biennial General Meeting; Committee; Officers. **Languages** English, French, German. **Finance** No financing. **Activities** Events/meetings. **Events** *Food and the life – span in Europe 1800-2000* Copenhagen (Denmark) 2015, *Food at major exhibitions in the 19th and 20th centuries* Brussels (Belgium) 2013, *History of the European food industry in the 19th and 20th centuries* Bologna (Italy) 2011, *Food and war in Europe in the 19th and 20th centuries* Paris (France) 2009, *From undernutrition to obesity – changes in food consumption in twentieth-century Europe* Oslo (Norway) 2007. **Publications** *ICREFH Newsletter.* **Members** Symposium members. Membership countries not specified. [2017.12.20/XM5121/F]

- International Commission for the Revision of Nomenclature of Causes of Death (inactive)

♦ International Commission for the Rights of Aboriginal Peoples (ICRA International) 12726

Commission internationale pour les droits des peuples indigènes
Pres 236 avenue Victor Hugo, 94120 Fontenay-sous-Bois, France. T. +33148778602. Fax +33143940245. E-mail: info@icrainternational.org.
ICRA Belgium Rue Eugène Castaigne 29, 1310 La Hulpe, Belgium. T. +3226446522. E-mail: belgique@icrainternational.org.
ICRA Switzerland Route de Crevel 167, 1468 Cheyres FR, Switzerland. T. +41792738985. E-mail: suisse@icrainternational.org.
URL: http://www.icrainternational.org/

History 1988. Registration: Start date: 21 Apr 1988, France. **Aims** Conscious of *human rights* but also of human *responsibilities*, furnish a source of information on problems of *ethnic minorities* and aboriginal populations, for coordination of cooperative activities and campaigns launched by *humanitarian* organizations or in defence of human rights; sensitize public opinion and mobilize activities to ensure that peoples which have maintained harmonious equilibrium with nature and have much to teach the so-called civilized nations are not swallowed up or neglected; contribute to the promotion of indigenous *cultures* and to the protection of fundamental rights of people and peoples to exist, to assert their differences, to use their land and to *self-determination.* **Structure** Headquarters in France with International Office in Paris (France). Network of indigenous correspondents. Autonomous affiliated departments (3): *'ICRA Info-Action'; AKASSA ONG Internationale (see: #12726); World Fund for the Safeguard of Indigenous Cultures (WOFIC, no recent information).* National sections (3). Regional and local groups in France. Commissions dealing with specific peoples (13): Karenni; Tuareg; Central America; Indonesia; Tibet; Nagaland; Mlabri; Ladakh; Australian Aborigines; Mountain People of Vietnam; Chile; Guyana; Pygmies; Nagaland. **Languages** English, French, Spanish. **Staff** 1.00 FTE, paid. **Finance** Members' dues. Donations. **Activities** Activities are centred on the 3 autonomous affiliated departments. Collects and disseminates information and testimonies on the difficulties and problems currently being faced by ethnic minorities and aboriginal populations; mobilizes human rights, humanitarian and environment associations; draws the attention of international organizations to the most serious cases; pressurizes economic and political policy-makers; lobbies United Nations and European Union bodies and supports indigenous delegations; sets up support and solidarity programmes for educational and cultural humanitarian action and development; organizes information campaigns, letter campaigns, petitions, conferences and exhibitions. **Events** *General Assembly* Belgium 2007, *General Assembly* France 2006, *General Assembly* Switzerland 2005, *General Assembly* Brussels (Belgium) 2004, *General Assembly* Paris (France) 2003. **Publications** *IKEWAN* (4 a year) – journal. Bulletins on urgent activities; petitions; press releases; discussion papers.
Members Members in 33 countries and territories (" indicates regional, national or local sections):
Algeria, Argentina, Australia, Austria, Belgium (*), Benin, Brazil, Burkina Faso, Cambodia, Cameroon, Canada (*), Chile, Colombia, Comoros, Denmark, France (*), Germany, Guatemala, Italy, Luxembourg, Mali, Mauritania, Myanmar, Niger, Palestine, Peru, Philippines (*), South Africa, Spain, Switzerland (*), Thailand, Timor-Leste, USA.
IGO Relations *European Commission (EC, #06633); United Nations Commission on Human Rights (inactive).* [2021/XE2212/E]

- International Commission on Rules for the Approval of Electrical Equipment / see IEC System of Conformity Assessment Schemes for Electrotechnical Equipment and Components (#11096)

♦ International Commission of the Schelde River 12727

Commission internationale de l'Escaut (CIE) – Internationale Scheldecommissie (ISC)
SG Italiëlei 124, 19e verdieping, 2000 Antwerp, Belgium. T. +3232060680. Fax +3232060681. E-mail: sec@isc-cie.org.
URL: http://www.isc-cie.org/

History 11 May 1995, Antwerp (Belgium), as *International Commission for the Protection of the Schelde River – Commission internationale pour la protection de l'Escaut (CIPE) – Internationale Commissie voor de Bescherming van de Schelde (ICBS)*, following signing of *Verdrag Inzake de Bescherming van de Schelde, 1994 (1994)*, 26 Apr 1994. Subsequently also known in Dutch as *Internationale Commissie van de Schelde (ICS).* Officially launched 1 Jan 1998, Antwerp (Belgium), when treaty entered into force. New name adopted when *Scheldeverdrag, 2002 (2002)* was signed. **Aims** Coordinate all politics on water of the rivers, lakes, groundwaters and coastal waters of the international district of the Schelde river (water treatment, drinking water, transport, environment, fishing, recreation, industry, agriculture, flooding, pollution, dryness, etc); international implementation of the EU water framework directive, flood directive, marine strategy framework directive, climate change policy within the international district of the Schelde. **Structure** Plenary Assembly (annual); Working Groups (8); General Secretariat. **Languages** Dutch, French. **Staff** 5.00 FTE, paid. **Finance** by Parties, following Treaty of Ghent. Additional financing by parties and EU through *INTERREG V (#15966).* **Activities** Politics/policy/regulatory. **Publications** Annual Report. Technical reports.
Members Governments of 6 countries and territories:
Belgium (Federal), Belgium/Brussels Capital Region, Belgium/Flemish Region, France, Netherlands, Wallonia.
IGO Relations Observers: *International Commission of the Meuse (#12702);* BENELUX. Cooperates with: *Common Wadden Sea Secretariat (CWSS, #04297); European Commission (EC, #06633); International Commission for the Protection of the Danube River (ICPDR, #12720); International Commissions for the Protection of the Moselle and Saar (ICPMS, #12729); International Commission for the Protection of the Rhine (ICPR, #12721); Internationale Kommission zum Schutz der Oder gegen Verunreinigung (IKSOgV, #13250); OSPAR Commission for the Protection of the Marine Environment of the North-East Atlantic (OSPAR Commission, #17905); United Nations Economic Commission for Europe (UNECE, #20555).* **NGO Relations** Cooperates with: *International Commission for the Protection of the Water Lake Geneva (CIPEL).* Observers: *Association européenne des métaux (EUROMETAUX, #02578); Conseil européen de l'industrie chimique (CEFIC, #04687);* World Youth Parliament for Water (WYPW); national organizations. [2019.02.12/XE3751/E*]

- International Commission for the Scientific Exploration of the Atlantic (inactive)
- International Commission for Scientific Exploration of the Mediterranean Sea / see The Mediterranean Science Commission (#16674)

♦ International Commission on Scientific Radio Telegraphy / see Union radio-scientifique internationale (#20475)

♦ International Commission on Semiconductors 12728

Commission internationale sur les semiconducteurs

Chairperson address not obtained.
URL: https://iupap.org/commissions/c8-semiconductors/

History 1957, as a Commission (C 8) of *International Union of Pure and Applied Physics (IUPAP, #15810)*. Also referred to as *Commission on Semiconductors – IUPAP – Commission sur les semiconducteurs – UIPPA*. Currently serves as an internal commission. **Aims** Promote exchange of information and views among members of the international scientific community in the general field of Semiconductor *Physics*; promote free circulation of scientists, assist conference organizers in ensuring such free circulation and resolve potential infringements. **Structure** Commission (meets every 2 years, during International Conference in Semiconductor Physics), comprises Chair, Vice-Chair, Secretary, 10 Full members and 2 Associate members. **Finance** Funded by IUPAP. **Activities** Areas covered include: electronic states; lattice dynamics and properties of matter in bulk at surfaces and interfaces and in systems or reduced dimensionality (in collaboration with other commissions as appropriate); defects, imperfections, impurities and amorphous semiconductors; application of semiconductor physics to technology. Organizes: international series of conferences and workshops; award of medals or other testimonials of excellence in the field. **Events** *International Conference on the Physics of Semiconductors* Sydney, NSW (Australia) 2022, *International Conference on the Physics of Semiconductors* Sydney, NSW (Australia) 2020, *International Conference on the Physics of Semiconductors* Montpellier (France) 2018, *International Conference on the Physics of Semiconductors* Beijing (China) 2016, *International Conference on the Physics of Semiconductors* Austin, TX (USA) 2014.

Members Individuals in 13 countries:
Australia, Austria, Brazil, Canada, Croatia, France, Germany, Japan, Poland, Russia, Spain, UK, USA.
Associate individuals in 2 countries:
Switzerland, USA. [2020/XE4745/v/**E**]

♦ International Commission of Slavic Historical Studies (#04220)
♦ International Commission for Slavonic Studies / see Commission internationale des études historiques slaves (#04220)
♦ International Commission of Solar Radiation (inactive)
♦ International Commission for the Southeast Atlantic Fisheries (inactive)

♦ International Commissions for the Protection of the Moselle and Saar (ICPMS) 12729

Commissions internationales pour la protection de la Moselle et de la Sarre (CIPMS) – Internationale Kommissionen zum Schutze von Mosel und Saar (IKSMS)

Sec IKSMS/CIPMS Sekretariat, Schillerarkaden 2, 54329 Konz-Saarburg, Germany. T. +4965016070900. Fax +4965016070909. E-mail: mail@iksms-cipms.org.
Pres Fed Ministry for Environment / Nature Conservation / Nuclear Safety, Rubert-Schuman-Platz 3, 5317 Bonn, Germany.
URL: http://www.iksms-cipms.org/

History 20 Dec 1961, Paris (France). Established in fulfillment of Article 55 of *Convention on the Canalization of the Moselle (1956)*, adopted 27 Oct 1956, Luxembourg, on signature of protocols setting up the two Commissions. The two protocols entered into force, 1 Jul 1962. First meeting of Commissions: 29 Jan 1963, Paris. Office in Trier (Germany) established by a complementary protocol, signed Mar 1990. A second complementary protocol, signed Nov 1992, conferred legal capacity and legal competence to the Commissions. Former names and other names: *International Commissions for the Protection of the Moselle and Saar against Pollution* – former; *Commissions internationales pour la protection de la Moselle et de la Sarre contre la pollution* – former; *Internationale Kommissionen zum Schutze von Mosel und Saar gegen Verunreinigung* – former. **Aims** Coordinate members' work to protect the *rivers* and their whole *drainage* area against *pollution* and *flooding*; provide a platform in view of the implementation of the 'European Water Framework Directive'. **Structure** Plenary Assembly (annual, meetings closed); Commissions; Working Groups. **Languages** French, German. **Staff** 3.50 FTE, paid. **Finance** Sources: government support. Governments of Germany, Luxembourg and France. Annual budget: 316,250 EUR (2020). **Activities** Monitoring/evaluation; projects/programmes. **Publications** *ICPMS Report on Water Quality* – annual 1964-1997; *ICPMS Results of Water Quality Analysis* – annual 1964-1997. *Low water in the Moselle and Saar catchment area* (2019); *Management Plan 2016 – 2021 for the Moselle-Saar Management Area*. **Information Services** *Database of Results of Water Quality Analysis* – since 1980; *Low water in the Moselle and Saar catchment area*; *Low water level survey*; *Pilot programme to measure the contamination of biota with SChadants in the catchment areas of the Moselle and Saar rivers*.

Members Governments of 3 countries:
France, Germany, Luxembourg. [2021.02.25/XE2804/**E***]

♦ International Commissions for the Protection of the Moselle and Saar against Pollution / see International Commissions for the Protection of the Moselle and Saar (#12729)
♦ International Commission for the Standardization of Colours for the Fashion and Textile Industries / see Commission internationale pour la couleur dans la mode et le textile (#04218)
♦ International Commission for Standardization of Sanitary Material (inactive)

♦ International Commission on Stratigraphy (ICS) 12730

SG Scott Polar Research Inst, Univ of Cambridge, Lensfield Road, Cambridge, CB2 1ER, UK. T. +441223333924. E-mail: plg1@cam.ac.uk.
Chair Earth Sciences and Principal Van Mildert College, Durham Univ, Durham, DH1 3LE, UK. T. +441913347143.
URL: http://www.stratigraphy.org/

History A Commission of *International Union of Geological Sciences (IUGS, #15777)*. **Aims** Promote and coordinate long-term international cooperation and and establish and maintain standards in stratigraphy. Establish an international *chrono-stratigraphic* standard scale of relative ages for the subdivision of *earth* history, with boundaries defined by *boundary-stratotypes*. **Structure** Executive Committee; Subcommissions (16); Awards Committee; Task Groups. **Languages** English. **Staff** Voluntary. **Finance** Through *International Union of Geological Sciences (IUGS, #15777)*. **Activities** Knowledge management/information dissemination; standards/guidelines; awards/prizes/competitions. **Events** *International Congress on the Jurassic System* Budapest (Hungary) 2022, *International Congress on Stratigraphy* Milan (Italy) 2019, *International Congress on the Jurassic System* San Luis Potosí (Mexico) 2018, *International Congress on Stratigraphy* Graz (Austria) 2015, *Congress* Oslo (Norway) 2008. **Publications** *Episodes* (4 a year) – official journal; *Carnets de Géologie – Notebooks on Geology* in English, French – e-journal; *GeoArabia* – journal; *Lethaia* – official journal; *Newsletters on Stratigraphy* – peer-reviewed journal; *Stratigraphy* – journal. *Concise Geologic Time Scale* (2008).

Members Individuals in 79 countries and territories:
Argentina, Australia, Austria, Barbados, Belgium, Bermuda, Brazil, Bulgaria, Canada, Chile, China, Colombia, Cyprus, Czechia, Denmark, Ecuador, Egypt, Estonia, Fiji, Finland, France, Germany, Ghana, Greece, Guyana, Hong Kong, Hungary, India, Indonesia, Iran Islamic Rep, Iraq, Ireland, Italy, Jamaica, Japan, Kenya, Korea Rep, Kuwait, Liberia, Luxembourg, Malawi, Malaysia, Mexico, Mongolia, Morocco, Myanmar, Namibia, Nepal, Netherlands, New Zealand, Nigeria, Norway, Pakistan, Peru, Philippines, Poland, Portugal, Romania, Samoa, Saudi Arabia, Serbia, Sierra Leone, Singapore, South Africa, Spain, Sri Lanka, Sweden, Switzerland, Tanzania UR, Thailand, Trinidad-Tobago, Tunisia, Türkiye, Uganda, UK, Uruguay, USA, Venezuela, Zimbabwe. [2018.03.08/XE1770/v/**E**]

♦ International Commission on the Structure and Dynamics of Condensed Matter 12731

Commission internationale sur la structure et la dynamique de la matière condensée

Chair address not obtained.
URL: https://iupap.org/commissions/c10-structure-and-dynamics-of-condensed-matter/

History 1960, and re-organized 1981, as a Commission (C 10) of *International Union of Pure and Applied Physics (IUPAP, #15810)*. Also referred to as *IUPAP Commission on the Structure and Dynamics of Condensed Matter – Commission de l'UIPPA sur la structure et la dynamique de la matière condensée*. Currently serves as an internal commission. **Aims** Promote information exchange in the field, including: properties and behaviour of *atoms* and *molecules* in *liquid* and *solid* states; characteristics of solid and liquid states of matter; *modelling* of condensed matter; application of condensed matter *physics* to technology. **Structure** Chairman, Vice-Chairman, Secretary and 10 members. **Finance** Source: IUPAP. **Activities** Organizes an number of international conference series and other meetings. **Events** *Symposium on triple lines in metals and ceramics* Les Houches (France) 2010, *International conference on ion beam modification of materials* Montréal, QC (Canada) 2010, *International conference on materials and mechanisms of superconductivity* Tokyo (Japan) 2009, *International conference on hyperfine interactions* Foz do Iguaçu (Brazil) 2007, *International symposium on nuclear quadrupole interaction* Foz do Iguaçu (Brazil) 2007.

Members Individuals in 13 countries:
Canada, China, Egypt, France, Germany, Hungary, India, Japan, Korea Rep, Mexico, Slovenia, UK, USA.
Associate member (4) in 4 countries:
Canada, Denmark, Israel, Russia. [2019/XE6692/v/**E**]

♦ International Commission for the Study of Communication Problems (inactive)

♦ International Commission for the Study and Improvement of Mathematics Teaching 12732

Commission internationale pour l'étude et l'amélioration de l'enseignement des mathématiques (CIEAEM)

Pres Frei Universität Berlin, Habelschwerdter Allee 45, Room KL 23/237, 14195 Berlin, Germany.
URL: http://www.cieaem.org/

History Founded 1950, Debden (UK). Also referred to as *Commission internationale pour l'étude et l'amélioration des mathématiques (CIEAM)*. **Aims** Improve quality of teaching and learning of mathematics. **Structure** Executive Committee; Advisory Board; Commission. **Languages** English, French. **Staff** None. **Finance** Conferences; donations. **Events** *Annual Meeting* Braga (Portugal) 2019, *Annual Meeting* Mostaganem (Algeria) 2018, *Annual Meeting* Berlin (Germany) 2017, *Annual Meeting* Prague (Czechia) 2016, *Annual Meeting* Aosta (Italy) 2015. **Publications** *CIEAEM Newsletter*. **Members** Individuals. Membership countries not specified. [2014.11.18/XF0843/v/**E**]

♦ International Commission for the Study of Soil Mechanics (inactive)
♦ International Commission of Sugar Technology (inactive)

♦ International Commission on Symbols, Units, Nomenclature, Atomic Masses and Fundamental Constants (SUNAMCO) 12733

Commission internationale sur les symboles, les unités, la nomenclature, les masses atomiques et les constantes fondamentales

Chairperson address not obtained.
URL: https://iupap.org/commissions/commission-on-symbols-units-nomenclature-atomic-masses-and-fundamental-constants/

History 1931, as a Commission (C 2) of *International Union of Pure and Applied Physics (IUPAP, #15810)*. Also referred to as *IUPAP Commission on Symbols, Units, Nomenclature, Atomic Masses and Fundamental Constants – Commission de l'UIPPA sur les symboles, les unités, la nomenclature, les masses atomiques et les constantes fondamentales*. Currently serves as an internal commission. **Aims** Promote the exchange of information and views among the members of the international scientific community in the general field of fundamental constants including: *physical measurements*; pure and applied *metrology*; nomenclature and symbols for physical quantities and units; encouragement of work contributing towards improved recommended values of atomic masses and fundamental physical constants and facilitation of their universal adoption. **Structure** Chairman, Vice-Chairman, Secretary and 10 members. **Finance** Source: IUPAP. **Activities** Organizes triennial 'International Conference on Exotic Nuclei and Atomic Masses (ENAM)', up till 1995 called 'International Conference on Atomic Masses (SUN-AMCO)'. **Events** *Biennial conference on precision electromagnetic measurements* Daejeon (Korea Rep) 2010, *International workshop on precision physics of simple atomic systems* Les Houches (France) 2010, *International conference on exotic nuclei and atomic masses* Ryn (Poland) 2008, *Biennial conference on precision electromagnetic measurements* London (UK) 2004, *International conference on exotic nuclei and atomic masses* Pine Mountain, GA (USA) 2004.

Members Individuals in 13 countries:
Belgium, Brazil, Canada, China, Finland, France, Germany, Japan, Korea Rep, Russia, Sweden, UK, USA.
Associate members (4) in 3 countries:
France, UK, USA.

NGO Relations *International Commission on Particles and Fields (#12712)*; *International Union of Pure and Applied Chemistry (IUPAC, #15809)*. [2020/XE5923/v/**E**]

♦ International Commission on the Taxonomy of Fungi (ICTF) 12734

Exec Vice Pres Biodiversity and Climate Research Centre, Senckenberg Gesellschaft für Naturforschung, Senckenberganlage 25, 60325 Frankfurt-Main, Germany. Fax +496975421800.
Pres Natl Center for Biotechnology Information, Natl Library of Medicine, Natl Inst of Health, Bethesda MD 20892, USA. T. +13014021502. Fax +13014802918.
URL: http://www.fungaltaxonomy.org/

History 1982. Founded as a joint commission of the Division of Mycology of *International Union of Microbiological Societies (IUMS, #15794)*, *IUMS Division of Mycology (see: #15794)*, and *International Mycological Association (IMA, #14203)*, the Section for General Mycology of *International Union of Biological Sciences (IUBS, #15760)*. Statutes adopted, 19 Aug 1994; modified 14 Aug 2002; 15 Apr 2018. **Aims** Promote work on taxonomy and nomenclature of fungi, especially fungi of economic importance; encourage dissemination of results; develop and support working groups and subcommissions focused on specific taxonomic groups; develop good taxonomic practice. **Structure** Commission. **Languages** English. **Finance** No budget. **Activities** Knowledge management/information dissemination. **Events** *General Meeting* Amsterdam (Netherlands) 2015, *General Meeting* Bangkok (Thailand) 2014, *General Meeting* Amsterdam (Netherlands) 2012, *General Meeting* Utrecht (Netherlands) 2012, *General Meeting* Amsterdam (Netherlands) 2011. **Publications** *Fungal taxonomy and sequence-based nomenclature* (2021) – by Lücking, R., Aime, M.C., Robbertse, B. et al. in Nat Microbiol 6, 540–548 (2021); *How to publish a new fungal species, or name, version 3.0* (2021) – by Aime, M.C., Miller, A.N., Aoki, T. et al. in IMA Fungus 12, 11 (2021); *Setting scientific names at all taxonomic ranks in italics facilitates their quick recognition in scientific papers* (2020) – by Thines, M., Aoki, T., Crous, P.W. et al. by IMA Fungus 11, 25 (2020); *Unambiguous identification of fungi: where do we stand and how accurate and precise is fungal DNA barcoding?* (2020) – by Lücking, R., Aime, M.C., Robbertse, B. et al. in IMA Fungus 11, 14 (2020).

Members Individuals appointed by IUMS Division of Mycology. Members in 16 countries and territories:
Australia, Brazil, Canada, China, Estonia, Germany, India, Japan, Netherlands, New Zealand, South Africa, Spain, Taiwan, Thailand, UK, USA.

NGO Relations Member of (3): *International Mycological Association (IMA, #14203)*; *International Union of Biological Sciences (IUBS, #15760)*; *International Union of Microbiological Societies (IUMS, #15794)*. [2022.10.18/XE1175/v/**E**]

♦ International Commission for the Translation of Masterworks (inactive)

♦ International Commission on Trichinellosis 12735

Commission internationale de la trichinellose

Pres c/o Fed Inst for Risk Assessment, Diedersdorfer Weg 1, 12277 Berlin, Germany.
URL: http://www.trichinellosis.org/

History 1958, Budapest (Hungary). Rules and regulations adopted at 2nd International Conference for Trichinellosis, 28 June 1969, Wroclaw (Poland). **Aims** Advise national and international bodies about all aspects of trichinella and trichinellosis in animals and man by developing and distributing recommendations/guidelines based on scientific knowledge using a one health concept; promote scientific research relating to all phases of trichinella and trichinellosis; develop and elaborate statements and responsible opinions relating to the *parasite* and *disease*. **Structure** Conference (every 4 years); Executive Committee. **Languages** English. **Staff** Voluntary. **Finance** No annual budget; conferences funded by registration fees as well as contributions from governmental and private sources. **Activities** Events/meetings; guidance/assistance/consulting; knowledge management/information dissemination; standards/guidelines. **Events** *Conference* Cluj-Napoca (Romania) 2019, *Conference* Berlin (Germany) 2015, *Conference* Changchun (China) 2011, *Conference* Zagreb (Croatia) 2007, *Conference* San Diego, CA (USA) 2004. **Publications** Conference proceedings; guidelines and recommendations.

Members Individuals (1-10 per country) in 47 countries and territories:
Argentina, Australia, Austria, Belgium, Bulgaria, Canada, China, Croatia, Cuba, Czechia, Denmark, Egypt, Estonia, Finland, France, Georgia, Germany, Greece, Guatemala, Honduras, Hungary, India, Italy, Japan, Kazakhstan, Latvia, Lithuania, Mexico, Nepal, Netherlands, Norway, Panama, Papua New Guinea, Poland, Romania, Russia, Serbia, Slovakia, Slovenia, South Africa, Spain, Sweden, Switzerland, Thailand, Türkiye, UK, USA.
NGO Relations Member of: *World Federation of Parasitologists (WFP, #21471)*, through which affiliated to *International Union of Biological Sciences (IUBS, #15760)*. Liaises with national and international organizations and institutions (not specified). [2022.02.02/XC1572/v/**C**]

♦ International Commission for the Unification of Agro-Geological Cartography (inactive)

♦ International Commission for Uniform Methods of Sugar Analysis (ICUMSA) 12736

Commission internationale pour l'unification des méthodes d'analyse du sucre
Address not obtained.
URL: http://www.icumsa.org/
History Founded 1897. Current constitution adopted at 9th session, 1936, London (UK); revised at 21st session, 1994. Company limited by guarantee in England and Wales – Registration No: 9152519. **Aims** Develop uniform methods of analysing sugar products and recommend their use; determine physical constants of sugar and sugar solutions. **Structure** Executive Committee; Administration; Committees (4). **Languages** English. **Staff** 1.00 FTE, paid; 30.00 FTE, voluntary. **Finance** Sources: members' dues. Annual budget: 25,000 EUR. **Activities** Events/meetings; monitoring/evaluation; research/documentation. **Events** *Biennial Session* Berlin (Germany) 2021, *Biennial Session* Warsaw (Poland) 2016, *Biennial Session* Ribeirão Preto (Brazil) 2014, *Biennial Session* Cambridge (UK) 2012, *Biennial Session* Berlin (Germany) 2010. **Publications** *ICUMSA News* (3 a year). *Supplement Methods Book* (2015); *ICUMSA – Methods Book* (1994); *Sugar Analysis – ICUMSA Methods* by F Schneider. Meeting reports.
Members National Committees in 23 countries:
Australia, Austria, Belgium, Brazil, Canada, Czechia, Denmark, Finland, France, Germany, Hungary, India, Indonesia, Japan, Mauritius, Netherlands, Philippines, Poland, South Africa, Sweden, Türkiye, UK, USA.
Also a national committee in the Caribbean (West Indies). Membership country not specified.
IGO Relations Observer status with: *Codex Alimentarius Commission (CAC, #04081)*. Cooperates with: *International Organization of Legal Metrology (#14451)*. **NGO Relations** Cooperates with: *International Organization for Standardization (ISO, #14473)*. [2019/XC1546/**C**]

♦ International Commission on Workforce Development (internationally oriented national body)
♦ International Commission on Yeasts (see: #15794)

♦ International Commission on Zoological Nomenclature (ICZN) 12737

Commission internationale de nomenclature zoologique
Exec Sec c/o Lee Kong Chian Natural History Museum, Fac of Science – NUS, 2 Conservatory Drive, Singapore 117377, Singapore. T. +6565188364. E-mail: iczn@nus.edu.sg.
URL: http://www.iczn.org/
History 1895, Leiden (Netherlands). Founded at 3rd International Zoological Congress. Currently under the auspices of *International Union of Biological Sciences (IUBS, #15760)*, of which it is a Scientific Member. **Aims** Promote stable and uniform nomenclature in zoology, by developing and improving the International Code of Zoological Nomenclature, to provide a set of rules and recommendations for the guidance of zoologists and by giving advice and rulings on individual nomenclature problems. **Structure** Commission; Council; Secretary. Secretariat located at Lee Kong Chian Natural History Museum, Singapore. **Languages** English. **Staff** 1.00 FTE, paid. **Finance** Sources: contributions; donations; sale of publications. Funded by Lee Foundation (Singapore). **Activities** Knowledge management/information dissemination; publishing activities. **Events** *Meeting* Singapore (Singapore) 2019, *Meeting* Singapore (Singapore) 2013, *General Session* Athens (Greece) 2000, *General Session* Budapest (Hungary) 1996, *General Session* Amsterdam (Netherlands) 1991. **Publications** *Bulletin of Zoological Nomenclature*. *International Code of Zoological Nomenclature* (4th ed 1999); *Towards Stability in the Names of Animals* (1995); *Official Lists and Indexes of Names and Works in Zoology* (last ed 1987) – with supplement 1986-2000 (2001). Information Services: ICZN discussion list; Zoo Bank discussion list.
Members Zoologists and palaeontologists (27) in 20 countries and territories:
Argentina, Australia, Austria, Brazil, Canada, China, Denmark, France, Germany, Italy, Japan, New Zealand, Portugal, Russia, Singapore, Sweden, Switzerland, Taiwan, UK, USA.
NGO Relations Cooperates with: Section of Zoology of IUBS, acting as IUBS Section of Zoological Nomenclature. *International Federation of Mammalogists (IFM, see: #15760)* is Affiliate Member. [2022.03.01/XD1573/v/**E**]

♦ International Committee for Abrasive Technology (ICAT) 12738

Contact Southern Univ of Science and Technology, 1088 Xueyuan Ave, Nanshan Qu, Shenzhen, 518055 Guangdong, China. E-mail: isaat2019@163.com.
URL: http://icat-isaat.org/
History 17 Nov 2002, Hong Kong. 17 Nov 2002 Hong Kong, during ISAAT 2002. **Aims** Provide a forum for professionals in manufacturing technology with a particular focus on precision engineering and nano/micro manufacturing using abrasives and other advanced technologies; facilitate development of the discipline globally. **Structure** General Assembly. Board, comprising Chairperson and 2 Vice-Chairpersons. Secretariat. **Events** *Symposium* Shenzhen (China) 2019, *Symposium* Toronto, ON (Canada) 2018, *Symposium* Stockholm (Sweden) 2016, *Symposium* Jeju (Korea Rep) 2015, *Symposium* Singapore (Singapore) 2012. [2019/XM0068/**E**]

♦ International Committee of Abstaining Priests (inactive)

♦ International Committee on Activation Analysis (ICAA) 12739

Sec Inst of Isotope and Surface Chemistry, Dept of Nuclear Research, PO Box 77, Budapest 1525, Hungary. T. +3612754349.
Pres Dalhousie Univ, Dept of Chemistry, Trace Analysis Research Ctr, Halifax NS B3H 4J3, Canada. T. +19024942474.
URL: http://www.icaa-mtaa.org/
History Set up during 4th MTAA Conference, May 1972, Saclay (France). **Structure** Committee of 21, including President and Secretary. **Activities** Organizes: Modern Trends in Activation Analysis Conference (MTAA). Grants Hevesy Medal Award. **Events** *International Conference on Modern Trends in Activation Analysis / MTAA Conference* Delft (Netherlands) 2015, *International Conference on Modern Trends in Activation Analysis / MTAA Conference* College Station, TX (USA) 2011, *MTAA Conference* Tokyo (Japan) 2007, *MTAA Conference* Guildford (UK) 2004, *MTAA Conference* Bethesda, MD (USA) 1999.
Members Individuals (21) in 15 countries:
Brazil, Canada, China, Czechia, Germany, Ghana, Hungary, India, Japan, Netherlands, Portugal, Russia, Slovenia, UK, USA. [2013/XJ6711/cv/**E**]

♦ International Committee for Adlerian Summer Schools and Institutes (ICASSI) 12740

Address not obtained.
URL: http://www.icassi.net/
History Founded 1962, Copenhagen (Denmark), to serve as a training institute for *International Association of Individual Psychology (IAIP, #11960)*. **Aims** Promulgate the work in individual *psychology* of Alfred Adler and Rudolf Dreikurs. **Structure** Board of Directors; Administrator; Faculty. **Languages** English, German. **Staff** 1.50 FTE, paid. voluntary. **Finance** Sources: tuition; donations. Annual budget: US$ 75,000. **Activities** Training/education; events/meetings. **Events** *Annual Summer Institute* Bonn (Germany) 2018, *Annual Summer Institute* Indianapolis, IN (USA) 2017, *Annual Summer Institute* Trencianske Teplice (Slovakia) 2016, *Annual Summer Institute* Dublin (Ireland) 2015, *Annual Summer Institute* Canterbury (UK) 2014. **Publications** *Achi Yotam* (1995); *Equality and Social Interest: Chios Lectures of ICASSI* (1989); *Adlerian Theory: An Introduction* (1982).
Members Individuals in 31 countries:
Australia, Austria, Belarus, Brazil, Canada, China, Czechia, Denmark, France, Germany, Greece, Hungary, Ireland, Israel, Italy, Jamaica, Japan, Korea Rep, Latvia, Lithuania, Luxembourg, Malta, Netherlands, Nigeria, Romania, Singapore, Slovakia, South Africa, Switzerland, UK, USA. [2017.10.24/XE5104/v/**E**]

♦ International Committee for the Advancement of Audio-Visual Media in Education / see International Council for Educational Media (#13014)
♦ International Committee on Aeronautical Fatigue / see International Committee on Aeronautical Fatigue and Structural Integrity (#12741)

♦ International Committee on Aeronautical Fatigue and Structural Integrity (ICAF) 12741

Gen Sec Swedish Defence Research Agency (FOI), SE-164 90 Stockholm, Sweden.
URL: http://www.icaf2015.org/
History Originally set up 1951, as *International Committee on Aeronautical Fatigue (ICAF) – Comité international de la fatigue du dessin aéronautique*. **Aims** Stimulate personal contact among people actively engaged in *aircraft* fatigue and structural integrity problems; exchange information, experience, opinions and ideas concerning such problems. **Structure** Governing Body, consisting of national delegates and General Secretary. **Languages** English. **Finance** None. **Activities** Events/meetings. **Events** *Conference* Krakow (Poland) 2019, *Conference* Nagoya (Japan) 2017, *Conference* Helsinki (Finland) 2015, *Symposium / Biennial Conference* Helsinki (Finland) 2015, *Symposium / Biennial Conference* Jerusalem (Israel) 2013. **Publications** Minutes of conferences – restricted; proceedings of symposia.
Members National Delegates in 15 countries:
Australia, Canada, China, Finland, France, Germany, Israel, Italy, Japan, Netherlands, Poland, Sweden, Switzerland, UK, USA. [2015.08.24/XD1627/**E**]

♦ International Committee for Aesthetics (inactive)

♦ International Committee Against Mental Illness (ICAMI) 12742

Comité international contre la maladie mentale
Pres 118 McLain St, Bedford Corners NY 10549, USA. T. +19142411131. Fax +66684052638709.
Connecticut Office 110 Richmond Hill Road, New Canaan CT 06840, USA.
URL: http://www.icami.us/
History 1958, New York NY (USA), by Dr Nathan Kline (1916-1982). **Aims** Promote *psychosocial rehabilitation* and mental health services and research. **Languages** English. **Staff** 3.00 FTE, paid. **Finance** Members' dues. **Activities** Symposia; workshops; conferences; training programmes. Community mental health services; information systems; research. **Events** *Seminar* Moscow (Russia) 1995, *Seminar* St Petersburg (Russia) 1995. **Members** Membership countries not specified. [2013.10.06/XD0415/**D**]

♦ International Committee Against Rheumatism / see International League of Associations for Rheumatology (#14016)
♦ International Committee on Agricultural Co-operation / see International Co-operative Agricultural Organisation (#12943)
♦ International Committee of Agricultural Librarians (inactive)

♦ International Committee for Airspace Standards and Calibration (ICASC) 12743

Chairman c/o Orlando-Stanford International Airport (KSFB), 100 StarPort way, Sanford FL 32773, USA. T. +14075853434. E-mail: joe@starportusa.com – info@icasc.co.
URL: http://www.icasc.co/
History 25 May 1995, Brussels (Belgium). Founded by delegates at the 8th and 9th editions of the *International Flight Inspection Symposium (IFIS)*. **Aims** Promote interests of the global flight inspection family worldwide; promote optimization of professional standards and value to the customer; serve as a bridge between editions of the IFIS. **Structure** Steering Committee; Secretariat. Working Groups. **Events** *International Flight Inspection Symposium* Nagoya (Japan) 2024, *International Flight Inspection Symposium* Durban (South Africa) 2022, *Biennial International Flight Inspection Symposium* Durban (South Africa) 2020, *Biennial International Flight Inspection Symposium* Monterey, CA (USA) 2018, *Biennial International Flight Inspection Symposium* Belgrade (Serbia) 2016. [2023/XM0019/**E**]

♦ International Committee on Allergic Diseases of Animals (ICADA) .. 12744

Co-Chair Dept of Veterinary Clinical Sciences, School of Veterinary Medicine, Louisiana State Univ, Baton Rouge LA 70803, USA. E-mail: cpucheu@lsu.edu.
CO-Chair Zentrum für klinische Tiermedizin, Ludwig-Maximilians-Uni München, Veterinärstr 13, 80539 Munich, Germany. E-mail: r.mueller@medizinische-kleintierklinik.de.
URL: http://icada.org/
History 1999, as Task Force on Canine Atopic Dermatitis (AD) of the American College of Veterinary Dermatology (ACVD). When membership expanded, became the *International Task Force on Canine Atopic Dermatitis (ITFCAD)*. Group dissolved and restructured under current title, 2010. **Aims** Publish critical reviews on atopic dermatitis, and other allergic conditions affecting the skin and other organ systems of all domestic animal species; encourage and foster development of research projects; advance the practice of veterinary dermatology as applied to allergic diseases. **Structure** Co-Chairs (Americas; Europe/Asia). **Languages** English. **Staff** None paid. **Finance** Subsidies from: *World Association for Veterinary Dermatology (WAVD, #21203)*. **Activities** Knowledge management/information dissemination; events/meetings. **Publications** Articles.
Members Individuals (25) in 9 countries:
Australia, Austria, France, Germany, Greece, Japan, Switzerland, UK, USA.
NGO Relations Affiliate member of: *World Association for Veterinary Dermatology (WAVD, #21203)*. [2022/XJ9411/v/**E**]

♦ International Committee of Analysis for Steel and Iron Industry (ICASI) 12745

Secretariat Box 14 – No 76 Xueyuan Nanlu, Haidian District, 100081 Beijing, China. T. +861062181064. Fax +861062181163. E-mail: icasi@ncschina.com.
History 12 Jun 1992, Scarborough (UK). Former names and other names: *International Committee of Analysts in Steel and Iron Industry* – former. **Aims** Continuously enhance competence of analysts and laboratory personnel involved; promote concepts related to laboratory management, international standardization and international system for accreditation and reference materials. **Structure** Executive Committee, comprising Chairman, 2 Vice-Chairman, Secretary General, Honorary Chairman and members. **Activities** Events/meetings. **Events** *Progress Forum for Instruments and Testing Technology / General Meeting* Beijing (China) 2012, *General Meeting* Beijing (China) 2010, *General Meeting* Beijing (China) 2008. [2016/XJ6718/t/**C**]

♦ International Committee of Analysts in Steel and Iron Industry / see International Committee of Analysis for Steel and Iron Industry (#12745)

♦ International Committee for Animal Recording (ICAR) 12746

Comité international pour le contrôle des performances en élevage – Internationales Komitee für Leistungsprüfungen in der Tierproduktion
Secretariat Arthur van Schendelstraat 650, 3511 MJ Utrecht, Netherlands. E-mail: icar@icar.org.
Registered Office c/o Institut de l'Elevage, 149 rue de Bercy, 75012 Paris, France.
URL: http://www.icar.org/
History 15 Jul 1951, The Hague (Netherlands). Founded on the basis of *'European Agreement on the Standardization of Milk-Butterfat Recording Practices'*, signed 9 Mar 1951, Rome (Italy). Current constitution adopted 16 May 2000, Rome. Former names and other names: *European Committee on Milk-Butterfat Recording* – former (15 Jul 1951); *Comité européen de contrôle laitier-beurrier* – former (15 Jul 1951); *International Committee for Recording the Productivity of Milk Animals (ICRPMA)* – former (1992); *Comité international pour le contrôle de la productivité laitière du bétail (CICPLB)* – former (1992); *Internationales Komitee zur Ermittlung der Wirtschaftlichkeit von Milchtieren (IKEWM)* – former (1992); *Comité Internacional para el Control de la Producción Lechera del Ganado* – former (1992). Registration: France. **Aims** Develop and improve identification, performance recording and genetic evaluation of *farm* animals, through definitions and standards for measuring animal characteristics having economic importance. **Structure** General Assembly (annual). Board of 3 to 11 members. Executive Board, comprising President, 1 or 2 Vice-Presidents, Treasurer and Secretary. Bureau. Meetings closed. Sub-Committees; Working Groups; Task Forces. **Languages** English, French, German. **Staff** None. **Finance** Members' dues: euro 451 or more, depending on number of

animals recorded. **Activities** Studies current questions of animal identification and performance recording and genetic evaluations; awards Certificate of Quality to organizations operating according to the ICAR International Standards. Sub-Committees (4): *International Bull Evaluation Service (INTERBULL, #12410)* – establishes methods for international conversion of breeding values; *'Recording Devices'* – establishes standards for performance recording devices and gives approval to recording tools produces by industries; *'Animal Identification'* – establishes standards for identification devices and gives approval to identification systems produced by industries; *'Milk Analysis'* – aims to improve efficiency and effectiveness of mild testing laboratories. Working Groups (11): Lactation Calculation Methods; Artificial Insemination and Relevant Technologies; Animal Recording Data; Functional Traits; Beef Performance Recording; Conformation Recording; Milk Recording of Sheep; Milk Recording of Buffaloes; Milk Recording in Goats; Animal Fibre; Genetic Analysis. Task Forces (3): Development Fund; Milk Recording Practices; Pig Recording. **Events** *Conference* Toledo (Spain) 2023, *Conference* Montréal, QC (Canada) 2022, *World Congress on Genetics Applied To Livestock Production* Rotterdam (Netherlands) 2022, *Conference* Leeuwarden (Netherlands) 2021, *Conference* Leeuwarden (Netherlands) 2020. **Publications** *ICAR Newsletter. ICAR Technical Series.* Annual milk recordings; ad hoc reports.

Members Active; Associate. Organizations in 46 countries:
Argentina, Australia, Austria, Belgium, Bulgaria, Canada, Croatia, Cyprus, Czechia, Denmark, Egypt, Estonia, Finland, France, Germany, Greece, Hungary, India, Ireland, Israel, Italy, Japan, Korea Rep, Latvia, Lithuania, Luxembourg, Mexico, Netherlands, New Zealand, Norway, Poland, Portugal, Romania, Serbia, Slovakia, Slovenia, South Africa, Spain, Sudan, Sweden, Switzerland, Tunisia, Türkiye, UK, USA, Zimbabwe.

Consultative Status Consultative status granted from: *ECOSOC (#05331)* (Ros C); *FAO (#09260)* (Special Status). **NGO Relations** *European Federation of Animal Science (EAAP, #07046); International Dairy Federation (IDF, #13128); World Association for Animal Production (WAAP, #21117).* In liaison with technical committees of: *International Organization for Standardization (ISO, #14473).* [2022/XD0660/**C**]

♦ International Committee for the Anthropology of Food and Food Habits (inactive)
♦ International Committee for Architectural Photogrammetry – ICOMOS and ISPRS Committee for Documentation of Cultural Heritage / see CIPA Heritage Documentation (#03929)

♦ International Committee on Automation of Mines and Quarries (ICAMC) 12747

Address not obtained.

History 1967. **Aims** Organize conferences. **Structure** National Committee in Poland, with others currently inactive. **Finance** None. **Events** *Conference* Krakow (Poland) 2008, *Conference* Teheran (Iran Islamic Rep) 2005, *Conference* Delhi (India) 2003, *Computer applications in the mineral industries* Tampere (Finland) 2001, *Conference* Vysoké Tatry (Slovakia) 1998. **Publications** Conference proceedings.

Members Full in 7 countries:
Czechia, Finland, India, Poland, Russia, Slovakia, USA.

NGO Relations Independent affiliate of: *World Mining Congress (WMC, #21654).* [2014/XE1199/**E**]

♦ International Committee on Bacteriological Nomenclature / see International Committee on Systematics of Prokaryotes (#12807)
♦ International Committee for Biochemistry (inactive)

♦ International Committee on Bionomenclature (ICB) 12748

Chairman Dept of Botany, Natural History Museum, Cromwell Road, London, SW7 5BD, UK.
Sec Marine Biological Laboratory, Woods Hole MA 02543, USA.
URL: http://www.bionomenclature.net/

History Founded 1995, as *International Commission on Bionomenclature*, within the framework of *International Union of Biological Sciences (IUBS, #15760)* and *International Union of Microbiological Societies (IUMS, #15794)*, and with support of *International Association for Plant Taxonomy (IAPT, #12092)* and *CABI (#03393)*. Also referred to as: *Inter-Union IUBS/IUMS International Commission on Bionomenclature*; *BioCode*. Organization created following considerable international debate, culminating in a meeting, 16-18 Mar 1994, Egham (UK), of interested parties. **Aims** Serve as the scientific body that will develop the framework for future organismal *nomenclature* within ICSU and both founding unions; provide a forum for discussion between representatives of the various organizations and committees responsible for the international rules governing the scientific names of extant and fossil organisms; explore issues of common concern to founding organizations and committees so as to identify and implement common solutions; promote understanding of organismal nomenclature amongst biologists as a whole. **Structure** Committee comprises representatives of member bodies, and includes Chair, Vice-Chair, Secretary and Deputy Secretary. **Languages** English. **Finance** Sources: IUBS/IUMS. Budget (annual): up to US$ 10,000. **Activities** Works on harmonization in terminology: prospective international rules for the scientific names of organisms (revised 2011); promotes establishment of infrastructure for the registration of new names and nomenclatural acts. Currently in charge of IUBS programme on Bionomenclature Across All Organism Groups (2010-2012). Organizes workshops and symposia. **Events** *ISSE : Information Security Solutions Europe Conference* Paris (France) 2016, *ISSE : Information Security Solutions Europe Conference* Berlin (Germany) 2015, *Meeting* Berlin (Germany) 2012, *Meeting* Berlin (Germany) 2009, *Meeting* Patras (Greece) 2002. **Publications** *Draft BioCode* (3rd ed 2011) – online.

Members Individuals (16), representing various organizations (5):
General Committee on Botanical Nomenclature; *International Commission for the Nomenclature of Cultivated Plants (ICNCP, see: #15760); International Commission on Zoological Nomenclature (ICZN, #12737); International Committee on Systematics of Prokaryotes (ICSP, #12807)*; PhyloCode Organization. [2012.06.01/XE2444/y/**E**]

♦ International Committee for Bird Protection / see BirdLife International (#03266)
♦ International Committee of the Blue Shield / see Blue Shield International (#03286)

♦ International Committee Buchenwald Dora and Commandos (IBDC) 12749

Comité international Buchenwald-Dora et Kommandos (CIBD) – Internationales Komitee Buchenwald-Dora und Kommandos (IKBD) – Mezhdunarodnyj Komitet Byvsih Uznikov Buhenvalda-Dora

Pres c/o Ass française Buchenwald Dora et Kommandos, 3/5 rue de Vincennes, 93100 Montreuil, France. T. +33143626204. Fax +33143626308. E-mail: cibd@buchenwald-dora.fr – contact@buchenwald-dora.fr.
URL: http://www.buchenwald-comite.org/

History Apr 1952, Weimar (German DR). Also known as *International Buchenwald-Dora Committee – Comité international des camps de concentration de Buchenwald*; *Dora et Kommandos*. **Aims** Group *survivors* of the *nazi concentration camps* of Buchenwald, Dora and their 'Kommandos', their families and their descendants, in order to safeguard places of remembrance, the memory of History, and the struggle of the *antifascist Resistance* for *liberty* and human *solidarity*. **Structure** Executive Board. Meeting of representatives of national organizations; Bureau. **Finance** Members' dues. Grants, including from: *European Commission (EC, #06633)*. **Events** *Annual Session* Buchenwald (Germany) 2013, *Annual Session* Buchenwald (Germany) 2012, *Annual Session* Buchenwald (Germany) 2011, *Annual Session* Weimar (Germany) 2008, *Annual Session* Weimar (Germany) 2007.

Members Individuals in 19 countries:
Austria, Belarus, Belgium, Canada, Croatia, Czechia, France, Germany, Hungary, Israel, Italy, Norway, Poland, Romania, Russia, Slovenia, Spain, Ukraine, USA.

NGO Relations *International Concentration Camp Committee (ICCC, no recent information).* Also links with a number of other organizations active in the field. [2018/XE9435/v/**E**]

♦ International Committee of Carbide and Acetylene (inactive)
♦ International Committee of Catholic Associations of Nurses / see International Catholic Committee of Nurses and Medico-social Assistants (#12451)
♦ International Committee of Catholic Nurses / see International Catholic Committee of Nurses and Medico-social Assistants (#12451)
♦ International Committee of Cellulose Film Producers (no recent information)
♦ International Committee for Child Psychiatry / see International Association for Child and Adolescent Psychiatry and Allied Professions (#11766)
♦ International Committee of Children's and Adolescents' Movements (inactive)
♦ International Committee on Christian Literature for Africa (inactive)

♦ International Committee for Coal and Organic Petrology (ICCP) 12750

Comité international de pétrographie des charbons – Internationale Kommission für Kohlenpetrologie – Mezdunarodnyj Komitet po Petrologii Uglja

Pres c/o INC CSIC, Francisco Pintado Fe 26, 33011 Oviedo, Asturias, Spain. T. +34985119090. Fax +34985297662. E-mail: angeles@incar.csic.es.
Gen Sec c/o Organic Petrology Services Pty Ltd, PO Box 672, Rozelle NSW 2039, Australia.
URL: http://www.iccop.org/

History Jun 1953, Geleen (Netherlands), at 1st meeting, following recommendations of 3rd Conference on Carboniferous Stratigraphy, 1951, Heerlen (Netherlands). Statutes adopted 1978; revised 1991 and 1999. Statutes written in accordance with UK law. **Aims** Ensure continuing international exchange of scientific information directly or indirectly related to organic petrology; develop international nomenclature on coal petrology and organic matter in sediments; develop and publish definitive descriptions and refine and standardize analytical methods in these fields; develop new applications in geology and industry. **Structure** General Assembly (annual, 2 sessions at each Annual Meeting). Council, comprising: President; Vice President; General Secretary; Treasurer; Chairmen and Secretaries of Commissions; Editor of Newsletter. Executive Committee, consisting President, General Secretary and Treasurer. 'Commission 1' – General Coal and Organic Petrology; 'Commission 2' – Application of Coal and Organic Petrology to Geology, including Prospecting for Oil and Gas; 'Commission 3' – Application of Coal Petrology to Utilization. Thiessen Medal Award Committee. **Languages** English, French, German. **Staff** None. **Finance** Sources: members' dues. Annual budget: 5,000 GBP. **Activities** cover: definition of constituents of lignite (brown coal), of bituminous coal and of dispersed organic matter; development of internationally standardized analytical methods using reflected light and fluorescence microscopy; SCAP – vitrinite reflectance measurement and maceral analysis of single coals; DOMVR – dispersed organic matter vitrinite reflectance measurement; CBAP – petrographic analysis of coal blends. Accreditation programme for organic petrography analysts (reflectivity and maceral analysis). Awards: Thiessen Medal; Organic Petrology Award. Offers training courses on Organic Petrology. **Events** *Annual meeting* Patras (Greece) 2023, *Annual meeting* Delhi (India) 2022, *Annual meeting* Prague (Czechia) 2021, *Annual meeting* Beijing (China) 2020, *Annual meeting* The Hague (Netherlands) 2019. **Publications** *ICCP Newsletter* (3 a year). *International Handbook of Coal Petrology* (1963) in English, French, German, Russian – replaces the Glossary – supplements in 1971, 1976, 1993, 1995; *International Glossary of Coal Petrology* (1957); *Atlas of Anthropogenic Particles* – CD-Rom; *Qualifying Vitrinite for Dispersed Organic Matter Reflectance Analsis* – CD-Rom. Brochure.

Members Full; Associate; Retired; Honorary; Institutional. Individuals and institutions in 38 countries:
Australia, Austria, Belgium, Brazil, Bulgaria, Canada, China, Colombia, Czechia, Denmark, Egypt, France, Germany, Greece, Hungary, India, Indonesia, Japan, Korea Rep, Malaysia, Mozambique, Netherlands, New Zealand, Norway, Peru, Philippines, Poland, Portugal, Romania, Russia, Serbia, South Africa, Spain, Tanzania UR, Thailand, Türkiye, UK, USA.

NGO Relations In liaison with technical committees of: *International Organization for Standardization (ISO, #14473).* Close contacts with: *International Congress of Carboniferous and Permian Stratigraphy and Geology*; *Society for Organic Petrology (TSOP).* [2018/XD7200/**C**]

♦ International Committee for Coal Research (no recent information)
♦ International Committee for Commercial Arbitration / see International Council for Commercial Arbitration (#13010)
♦ International Committee for a Community of Democracies (inactive)
♦ International Committee of Comparative Law / see International Association of Legal Science (#11997)

♦ International Committee on Composite Materials (ICCM) 12751

Pres Dept Mechanical Engineering, Seoul Natl Univ, 1 Gwanak-ro, Gwanak-gu, Seoul 08826, Korea Rep. T. +8228807116.
Senior Vice-Pres Dept Mechanical Engineering, McGill Univ, 817 Sherbrooke Street West, Montréal QC H3A 0C3, Canada. T. +15143896303.
URL: http://www.iccm-central.org/

Aims Encourage free interchange of information on all aspects related to composite materials which are of interest to the global scientific and engineering community; provide a world-wide forum for discussion of such topics; guide and foster understanding and utilization of the science and technology of composite materials; promote international cooperation and education in composite materials science and technology; recognize individuals of outstanding achievement in the science, technology, engineering, and application of composite materials. **Structure** General Assembly; Executive Council; Executive Advisory Board; Conference Organizing Committee. **Languages** English. **Staff** None. **Finance** Mainly from conference fees. **Activities** Awards/prizes/competitions; events/meetings; knowledge management/information dissemination. **Events** *International Conference* Belfast (UK) 2023, *Conference* Belfast (UK) 2021, *Conference* Melbourne, VIC (Australia) 2019, *Conference* Xian (China) 2017, *Conference* Copenhagen (Denmark) 2015. **Publications** None.

Members Full in 36 countries:
Australia, Austria, Belgium, Brazil, Canada, China, Czechia, Denmark, Finland, France, Germany, Greece, Hungary, India, Ireland, Israel, Italy, Japan, Korea Rep, Latvia, Lithuania, Malaysia, Netherlands, New Zealand, Norway, Portugal, Russia, Singapore, South Africa, Spain, Sweden, Switzerland, Türkiye, UK, United Arab Emirates, USA. [2021/XJ1433/**C**]

♦ International Committee on Computational Linguistics (ICCL) 12752

Chairman Dept of Linguistics – Stanford Univ, Margaret Jacks Hall – Room 124, Stanford CA 94305-2150, USA. T. +16507234284. Fax +16507235666.
URL: http://nlp.shef.ac.uk/iccl/

History 1965, New York NY (USA). **Aims** Arrange an international conference on computational linguistics every 2 years. **Structure** Committee. **Staff** None. **Finance** None. **Activities** Events/meetings. **Events** *COLING : International Conference on Computational Linguistics* Gyeongju (Korea Rep) 2022, *COLING : International Conference on Computational Linguistics* Barcelona (Spain) 2020, *COLING : International Conference on Computational Linguistics* Santa Fe, NM (USA) 2018, *COLING : International Conference on Computational Linguistics* Osaka (Japan) 2016, *COLING : International Conference on Computational Linguistics / International Conference* Dublin (Ireland) 2014.

Members Full in 11 countries and territories:
Canada, Czechia, France, Germany, Italy, Japan, Norway, Russia, Taiwan, UK, USA. [2015/XF1239/**F**]

♦ International Committee for Concerted Action Against Potato Blight (inactive)

♦ International Committee on Concrete Model Code for Asia (ICCMC) 12753

Contact c/o Hokkaido Univ Graduate School of Engineering, Lab of Engineering for Maintenance System, Kita 13 Jo, Nishi 8 Chome, Kita-ku, Sapporo HOKKAIDO, 060-8628 Japan.

History 1992. **Aims** Develop and maintain a concrete model code for Asia; promote cooperation on concrete in the Asia-Pacific region. **Structure** General Meeting (annual). Executive Council, including Chairman and 2 Vice-Chairmen. **Activities** Working Groups (4): Design; Editorial; Maintenance; Materials and Construction. Task Groups. **Publications** *ICCMC News* (2 a year).

Members Individuals; corporations. Members in 14 countries:
Australia, China, India, Indonesia, Japan, Korea Rep, Malaysia, Netherlands, Pakistan, Philippines, Singapore, Sri Lanka, Thailand, Vietnam. [2008/XE4510/**E**]

♦ International Committee of the Congresses on Family Education (inactive)
♦ International Committee of the Congress of Peoples Against Imperialism (inactive)

♦ International Committee for the Conservation of the Industrial Heritage (TICCIH) 12754

Comité international pour la conservation du patrimoine industriel

Pres Historic Environment Scotland, Longmore House, Edinburgh, EH9 1SH, UK. T. +441316688611. E-mail: ticcih.president@gmail.com.
SG Pontificia Univ Católica de Valparaiso, Inst de Geografia, Av Brasil 2241, 234 0000 Valparaiso, Valparaíso, Chile. T. +56322274174.
URL: http://www.ticcih.org/

History 1978, Sweden. Founded during 3rd general international meeting on the study and preservation of the industrial heritage, such meetings having been held since 1973. Registration: Charity, No/ID: 1079809, England and Wales; EU Transparency Register, No/ID: 099805734908-77, Start date: 21 May 2019. **Aims** Promote international cooperation concerning safeguarding, conservation, investigation, documentation, scientific research and preservation of the industrial heritage; promote education in these matters. **Structure** General Assembly; Executive Board. **Languages** English, French, German, Spanish. **Staff** Part-time, voluntary. **Finance** Sources: contributions; grants; members' dues. Annual budget: 10,000 GBP. **Activities** Events/ meetings; guidance/assistance/consulting. **Events** *Triennial General Conference* Montréal, QC (Canada) 2022, *Oil Heritage Seminar* Ontario (Canada) 2022, *Triennial General Conference* Montréal, QC (Canada) 2021, *Oil Heritage Seminar* Ontario (Canada) 2020, *Triennial General Conference* Santiago (Chile) 2018. **Publications** *TICCIH Bulletin* (4 a year). Conference proceedings; national reports.
Members National correspondents in 80 countries and territories:
Algeria, Argentina, Australia, Austria, Belgium, Bosnia-Herzegovina, Brazil, Burkina Faso, Canada, Canaries, Chile, China, Colombia, Croatia, Cyprus, Czechia, Denmark, Egypt, England, Finland, France, Germany, Greece, Guatemala, Guyana, Honduras, Hungary, India, Indonesia, Iran Islamic Rep, Ireland, Israel, Italy, Jamaica, Japan, Jordan, Kenya, Latvia, Lithuania, Luxembourg, Malta, Mexico, Morocco, Netherlands, New Zealand, Nigeria, North Macedonia, Northern Ireland, Norway, Pakistan, Panama, Peru, Philippines, Poland, Portugal, Romania, Russia, Saudi Arabia, Scotland, Serbia, Sierra Leone, Slovakia, Slovenia, South Africa, Spain, Sri Lanka, Sweden, Switzerland, Taiwan, Tanzania UR, Thailand, Türkiye, UK, Ukraine, Uruguay, USA, Venezuela, Wales, Zambia, Zimbabwe.
NGO Relations Member of (1): *European Heritage Alliance 3.3 (#07477)*. Joint agreement with: *International Council on Monuments and Sites (ICOMOS, #13049)*. [2022.06.20/XD5741/C]

♦ International Committee for the Conservation of Mosaics (ICCM) . . 12755
Comité international pour la conservation de la mosaïque
Pres c/o Centro di Conservazione Archeologica CCA, Via del Gambero 19, 00187 Rome RM, Italy. E-mail: info@iccm-mosaics.org.
URL: http://www.iccm.ac.cy/
History 1977, by *International Centre for the Study of the Preservation and Restoration of Cultural Property (ICCROM, #12521)*. **Aims** Preserve mosaics through promotion of studies on the technology of mosaics and practices of their conservation and maintenance; encourage international exchange of experience; provide advice to scholars and professionals interested in mosaic conservation. **Structure** Board, comprising President, Honorary President, a representative each of *International Centre for the Study of the Preservation and Restoration of Cultural Property (ICCROM, #12521)* and *Association internationale pour l'étude de la mosaïque antique (AIEMA, #02689)*, and 11 members. **Languages** English, French. **Staff** 14.00 FTE, voluntary. **Finance** Members' dues. Other sources: sales of proceedings; sponsoring; funding from Getty Foundation. **Events** *General Conference* Plovdiv (Bulgaria) 2021, *General Conference* Plovdiv (Bulgaria) 2020, *General Conference* Barcelona (Spain) 2017, *General Conference* Bosa (Italy) 2014, *General Conference* Meknès (Morocco) 2011. **Publications** *ICCM Newsletter* in English, French – online. *Mosaics* – series. Conference proceedings.
Members Full in 47 countries and territories:
Albania, Algeria, Australia, Austria, Belgium, Benin, Bulgaria, Canada, Colombia, Croatia, Cyprus, Czechia, Denmark, Egypt, Finland, France, Georgia, Germany, Greece, Hungary, India, Iran Islamic Rep, Israel, Italy, Jordan, Lebanon, Libya, Malta, Mexico, Morocco, Netherlands, North Macedonia, Palestine, Peru, Poland, Portugal, Saudi Arabia, Serbia, Slovenia, Spain, Sweden, Switzerland, Syrian AR, Togo, Tunisia, Türkiye, UK, USA. [2021/XD9420/D]

♦ International Committee on Contaminated Land (ICCL) 12756
Gen Sec Altlasten Umweltbundesamt, Spittelauer Lände 5, 1090 Vienna, Austria.
URL: http://www.iccl.ch/
History 1993, as *Ad Hoc International Working Group on Contaminated Land*. **Aims** Be a platform for exchange of knowledge and experience for initiating and following-up of international projects among members; establish a discussion platform on policy, research, technical and managerial concepts of contaminated land; offer exchange of expertise to other stakeholders via collaboration with European and international networks. **Activities** Events/meetings. **Events** *Biennial Meeting* Copenhagen (Denmark) 2017, *Common Forum on Contaminated Land* Copenhagen (Denmark) 2017, *Biennial Meeting* Melbourne, VIC (Australia) 2015, *Biennial Meeting* Durban (South Africa) 2013, *Biennial Meeting* Washington, DC (USA) 2011. **NGO Relations** *Network for Industrially Contaminated Land in Europe (NICOLE, #17036)*. [2018.10.15/XM1654/E]

♦ International Committee of Contamination Control Societies / see International Confederation of Contamination Control Societies (#12855)
♦ International Committee For the Convention Against Offensive Microwave Weapons / see International Committee on Offensive Microwave Weapons
♦ International Committee for Co-operation in the History of Technology / see International Committee for the History of Technology (#12778)
♦ International Committee for Cooperation of Journalists (inactive)
♦ International Committee to Coordinate Activities of Technical Groups in the Coatings Industry / see Coatings Societies International (#04075)
♦ International Committee for the Coordination of Agriculture (inactive)
♦ International Committee for the Coordination and Standardization of Speech Databases and Assessment Techniques for Speech Input-Output (unconfirmed)

♦ International Committee of Creole Studies 12757
Comité international des études créoles (CIEC)
Address not obtained.
History Nov 1976, Nice (France), by *Centre international d'études françaises (CIDEF, inactive)*. Acts as the scientific committee of *Association pour la promotion et la diffusion des études créoles (APRODEC)*. **Aims** Promote, develop and coordinate interdisciplinary studies on the Creole-operating regions. **Structure** Committee, consisting of 20 members. Executive Board, consisting of President and 3 Vice-Presidents. **Languages** French. **Staff** Voluntary. **Finance** Members' dues. Other sources: grants; research contracts. **Activities** Organizes international symposia (every 3 years). **Events** *Triennial Colloquium / Colloquium* Aix-en-Provence (France) 2014, *Colloquium* Mauritius 2012, *Triennial Colloquium* Réduit (Mauritius) 2012, *Colloquium* Port-au-Prince (Haiti) 2008, *Triennial Colloquium* Port-au-Prince (Haiti) 2008. **Publications** *Etudes créoles* (2 a year). *Bibliographie des études créoles: langues et littératures – vols 1-2* (1997). Etymological dictionary; conference proceedings.
Members Individuals in 45 countries:
Australia, Austria, Belgium, Belize, Brazil, Burkina Faso, Canada, Cape Verde, Congo Brazzaville (Brazzaville), Côte d'Ivoire, Denmark, Dominica, Finland, France, Germany, Guinea-Bissau, Guyana, Haiti, Hungary, India, Italy, Jamaica, Luxembourg, Madagascar, Mali, Mauritius, Morocco, Netherlands, New Zealand, Nigeria, Portugal, Romania, Rwanda, Senegal, Seychelles, Sierra Leone, Spain, St Lucia, Suriname, Sweden, Switzerland, Tunisia, UK, USA. [2014/XD8290/v/E]

♦ International Committee for Crimea (ICC) 12758
Contact PO Box 15078, Washington DC 20003, USA. E-mail: icc2009@iccrimea.org.
URL: http://www.iccrimea.org/
History Set up 1997, as an Internet group of individuals. Incorporated in Washington DC (USA), Apr 2012. **Aims** Raise awareness of the *historical* and cultural aspects of uprooted *indigenous* people of Crimea and the independent states of the former *Soviet Union*; support the revival of *culture* and native language of people subjected to *forced migration* and political repression. **Structure** Board of Directors. Executive Committee, comprising President, Financial Officer and Secretary. **Languages** English. **Activities** Disseminates information about ongoing social and cultural developments in Crimea; Participates in professional conferences and public programs; Organizes public programs; Supports projects that help restore culture and native language. **Members** Not a membership organization. [2012.07.24/XE4679/E]

♦ International Committee on Databases in Multiple Sclerosis (ICODIMS) 12759
Contact Univ of Colorado School of Medicine, 12631 East 17th Ave, Mail Stop B185, Aurora CO 80045, USA.
History 2000. **Members** Databases in 12 countries. Membership countries not specified. [2008/XJ3110/E]

♦ International Committee of the Decorative Laminates Industry (ICDLI) 12760
Comité international des fabricants de panneaux décoratifs stratifiés – Internationales Komitee der Hersteller dekorativer Schichtstoffplatten
Gen Sec Städelstrasse 10, 60596 Frankfurt-Main, Germany. T. +49692710529. Fax +4969239827.
URL: http://www.icdli.com/
History Registered in accordance with Belgian law. **Aims** Prepare and promote technical and scientific studies in the field of decorative laminates. **Structure** General Assembly (annual); Committee of Presidents. **Events** *Plenary Assembly* Barcelona (Spain) 2016.
Members Full in 8 countries:
Austria, Belgium, France, Germany, Italy, Netherlands, Portugal, Switzerland.
NGO Relations Member of: *European Plastics Converters (EuPC, #08216)*. [2020/XE2907/t/E]

♦ International Committee for the Defence of the Breton Language (ICDBL) 12761
Comité international pour la sauvegarde de la langue bretonne (CISLB) – Comité Internacional para la Salvaguardia de la Lengua Bretona – Internationaler Ausschuss für die Erhaltung der Bretonischen Sprache – Comitato Internazionale per la Difesa della Lingua Bretone – Internationaal Comité ter Bescherming van de Bretonse Taal
Address not obtained.
USA Branch: https://icdbl.org/
History Oct 1975, Brussels (Belgium). **Aims** Promote the survival of the Breton language and obtain greater knowledge of the problems attaching to it; act as a pressure group for inclusion of the Breton language in education, the media and the civil service. **Structure** Central Committee in Brussels (Belgium) (meets annually); Executive Council (meets 3 times a year); National Committees in 17 countries, plus autonomous groups in Wales (UK) and Flanders (Belgium). Establishment of national committees limited to countries with fundamental respect for human rights. **Languages** Dutch, English, Esperanto, French, German, Italian, Spanish. **Staff** 10.00 FTE, voluntary. **Finance** Members' contributions as necessary. **Activities** Organizes petitions. **Events** *Recent restrictive measures of the French Government regarding beton schools and TV* Brussels (Belgium) 1987. **Publications** Fact-finding reports; press releases; publications by National Committees.
Members Individuals (about 300). National Committees in 17 countries:
Australia, Austria, Belgium, Canada, Costa Rica, Denmark, France, Germany, Greece, Ireland, Israel, Italy, Netherlands, Spain, Switzerland, UK, USA. [2010/XD4681/E]

♦ International Committee for the Defence of the Interests of the Oil Industry in Europe (inactive)
♦ International Committee for Democratic Action (inactive)

♦ International Committee for Dermatopathology (ICDP) 12762
Comité international pour la dermatopathologie
Sec-Treas Kempf und Pfaltz Histologische Diagnostik, Affolternstrasse 56, 8050 Zurich ZH, Switzerland.
URL: http://www.icdermpath.org/
History 1980, UK. In Statutes *International League of Dermatopathology Societies (ILDS)* is used. **Aims** Encourage advancement of dermatopathology as a scientific discipline; stimulate research in dermatopathology; promote personal relations among dermatologists; encourage exchange of information in the field through various means. **Structure** Committee; Executive Committee; Nominating Committee; Task Force on Research. **Languages** English. **Staff** Voluntary. **Finance** Members' dues. **Events** *Annual Meeting* San Francisco, CA (USA) 2015, *Annual Meeting* Denver, CO (USA) 2014, *Annual Meeting* Miami, FL (USA) 2013, *Annual Meeting* San Diego, CA (USA) 2012, *Annual Meeting* New Orleans, LA (USA) 2011.
Members National societies or clubs devoted to the field of dermatopathology in 30 countries and territories:
Argentina, Australia, Austria, Belgium, Bolivia, Brazil, Bulgaria, Canada, Chile, China, Czechia, Finland, France, Germany, Iceland, Italy, Japan, Mexico, Netherlands, Panama, Peru, Portugal, Puerto Rico, Singapore, South Africa, Spain, Switzerland, Türkiye, UK, USA.
Regional society:
African Society of Dermatopathology (#00461).
NGO Relations Member of: *International League of Dermatological Societies (ILDS, #14018)*. [2019.12.15/XF2360/D]

♦ International Committee on Design History and Studies (ICDHS) . . . 12763
Address not obtained.
URL: http://www.ub.edu/icdhs/
History Founded 1999, Barcelona (Spain), when first conference was organized. **Structure** Board. **Activities** Events/meetings. **Events** *Lessons to learn? Past design experiences and contemporary design practices* Zagreb (Croatia) 2020, *Conference* Barcelona (Spain) 2018, *Conference* Taipei (Taiwan) 2016, *Conference* Aveiro (Portugal) 2014, *Conference* Aveiro (Portugal) 2012. [2021/XM8356/c/E]

♦ International Committee for the Development of Peoples (internationally oriented national body)
♦ International Committee of Dietetic Associations / see International Confederation of Dietetic Associations (#12856)
♦ International Committee for the Diffusion of Arts and Literature through the Cinema (no recent information)
♦ International Committee for the Dignity of Children (internationally oriented national body)
♦ International Committee for Documentation of Cultural Heritage / see CIPA Heritage Documentation (#03929)
♦ International Committee for Dyeing and Dry Cleaning (inactive)

♦ International Committee on EDI for Serials (ICEDIS) 12764
Contact c/o EDItEUR Ltd, United House, North Road, London, N7 9DP, UK. E-mail: info@editeur.org.
URL: http://www.editeur.org/59/ICEDIS/
History Formerly an independent organization. Now a Special Interest Group of: *EDItEUR (#05361)*. **Aims** Promote use of e-commerce standards and protocols between trading partners in the serials supply chain to facilitate rapid, accurate and automated communications about subscription products. **Structure** 2 Co-Chairs; Consultant from EDItEUR; *ad hoc* Working Groups. **Languages** English. **Staff** 0.50 FTE, paid. **Finance** Administered as part of EDItEUR. **Activities** Events/meetings; knowledge management/information dissemination; standards/guidelines. **Events** *Meeting* Bournemouth (UK) 2016, *Meeting* Charleston, SC (USA) 2015, *Meeting* Frankfurt-Main (Germany) 2015, *Meeting* Glasgow (UK) 2015, *Meeting* Charleston, SC (USA) 2014. **Publications** Technical standards. **Members** Membership though EDItEUR. [2022.02.11/XE4460/E]

♦ International Committee of Editors of Diplomatic Documents (ICEDD) 12765
SG Diplomatic Documents of Switzerland, Archivstrasse 24, 3003 Bern, Switzerland.
URL: https://diplomatic-documents.org/
History 1988. Former names and other names: *International Network of Editors of Diplomatic Documents* – former (1988 to 2013). **Aims** Bring together scholars with a common interest in the editing of contemporary diplomatic documents, enabling them to engage in a wider discussion and investigate common concerns, concepts, problems and methodologies over a diverse range of historical and historiographical areas. **Structure** General Assembly; Bureau. **Activities** Events/meetings. **Events** *Conference* Warsaw (Poland) 2022, *Conference* Berlin (Germany) 2019, *Conference* London (UK) 2017, *Conference* Washington, DC (USA) 2015, *Conference* Geneva (Switzerland) 2013. **Publications** Multivolume series of scholarly editions of documents on foreign relations.
Members Individuals in 13 countries:
Austria, Belgium, France, Germany, Ireland, Israel, Italy, Netherlands, Poland, Portugal, Romania, Switzerland, UK.
NGO Relations Member of (1): *International Committee of Historical Sciences (ICHS, #12777)*. [2021/AA0938/C]

♦ International Committee of Educational Psychology (inactive)
♦ International Committee of Educators to Combat Racism, Anti-Semitism and Apartheid (inactive)

♦ International Committee of Electro-Chemical Thermodynamics and Kinetics / see International Society of Electrochemistry (#15079)

♦ International Committee on Electronic Information and Communication (CEIC) 12766

Chair Dept of Computer Science, Univ of Bath, Bath, BA2 7AY, UK.
URL: http://www.mathunion.org/ceic/

History as a commission of *International Mathematical Union (IMU, #14121)*. **Aims** Advise the International Math Union on electronic matters.
Members in 4 countries:
Australia, Canada, Germany, USA. [2015/XE4521/**E**]

♦ International Committee for Enteric Phage Typing / see International Federation for Enteric Phage Typing (#13413)
♦ International Committee of Entertainment and Media Unions (inactive)

♦ International Committee on Equine Exercise Physiology (ICEEP) . . . 12767

Contact Veterinary Clinical Science, Equine Hosp – Leahurst Campus, Chester High Road, Neston, CH64 7TE, UK. T. +441517946016. E-mail: cpdvets@liverpool.ac.uk.
URL: http://www.iceep.org/

Aims Advance understanding of the physiology, function and health of athletic horses through promotion of scientific research. **Structure** Committee, comprising Chair, 7 members and ex-officio Treasurer. **Events** *Conference* Lorne, NSW (Australia) 2018, *Conference* Chester (UK) 2014, *Conference* Cape Town (South Africa) 2010, *Conference* Fontainebleau (France) 2006. **Publications** Proceedings. [2014/XJ6709/c/**E**]

♦ International Committee for Ethnic Freedoms / see Internacia Komitato por Etnaj Liberecoj (#11523)
♦ International Committee for European Security and Cooperation (inactive)

♦ International Committee of Experimental Ulcer 12768

Address not obtained.

Structure Standing Committee. Chairman; General Secretary. **Events** *ICUR : International Conference on Ulcer Research* Tokyo (Japan) 2012, *ICUR : international conference on ulcer research / International Conference on Ulcer Research (ICUR)* Split (Croatia) 2009, *ICUR : international conference on ulcer research / International Conference on Ulcer Research (ICUR)* Osaka (Japan) 2006, *ICUR : international conference on ulcer research / International Conference on Ulcer Research (ICUR)* Dubrovnik (Croatia) 2003, *ICUR : international conference on ulcer research / International Conference on Ulcer Research (ICUR)* Budapest (Hungary) 2000. [2009/XU1734/**E**]

♦ International Committee of Experts for the Campaign Against the Revival of Neo-Nazism and Antisemitism (inactive)
♦ International Committee of Ex-Service Men (inactive)
♦ International Committee for Eye Research / see International Society for Eye Research (#15111)

♦ International Committee for Fair Play 12769

Comité international pour le fair play (CIFP) – Internationales Fairplay-Komitee

Main Office c/o Hungarian Olympic Committee, Csörsz utca 49-51, Budapest 1124, Hungary. T. +3613868000. E-mail: cifp@fairplayinternational.org.
Paris Office c/o Maison du Sport Français, 1 av Pierre de Coubertin, 75640 Paris CEDEX 13, France.
URL: http://www.fairplayinternational.org/

History 5 Dec 1963, Paris (France). After present name adopted, the Trophies continued to be called *'Trophées du fair play Pierre de Coubertin'*. Statutes adopted 3 Mar 1977, Paris; modified 9 Nov 1993, Paris. Former names and other names: *Comité international provisoire d'organisation des trophées du fair play Pierre de Coubertin* – former (5 Dec 1963 to 25 Jan 1965); *Comité international d'organisation des trophées du fair play Pierre de Coubertin* – former; *International Fair Play Committee* – alias (25 Jan 1965 to 29 May 1973). **Aims** Defend and promote fair play worldwide with: national and international organizations working for *sport* and education; high level athletes; children, adolescents and those in charge of training them – coaches and educationists. **Structure** General Assembly (every 2 years); Administration Council; Bureau. **Languages** English, French. **Finance** Sources: donations; members' dues. **Activities** Awards/prizes/competitions; projects/programmes; training/education. **Events** *General Assembly* Vilnius (Lithuania) 1997, *General Assembly* Rome (Italy) 1995, *General Assembly* Paris (France) 1993, *General Assembly* Acapulco (Mexico) 1992, *General Assembly* Paris (France) 1988.
Members National Olympic Committees in 91 countries and territories:
Algeria, Andorra, Argentina, Armenia, Australia, Austria, Azerbaijan, Belarus, Belgium, Bolivia, Brazil, Bulgaria, Burkina Faso, Cameroon, Chile, China, Colombia, Congo Brazzaville, Côte d'Ivoire, Croatia, Cuba, Cyprus, Czechia, Denmark, Dominican Rep, Ecuador, Egypt, Ethiopia, Fiji, Finland, France, Gabon, Gambia, Georgia, Germany, Greece, Guam, Guatemala, Guinea, Honduras, Hong Kong, Hungary, India, Indonesia, Israel, Italy, Jamaica, Japan, Kenya, Laos, Latvia, Libya, Liechtenstein, Lithuania, Luxembourg, Mauritania, Mauritius, Mexico, Moldova, Monaco, Morocco, Nepal, New Zealand, Nigeria, Norway, Pakistan, Papua New Guinea, Peru, Poland, Portugal, Romania, Russia, Saudi Arabia, Senegal, Slovakia, Slovenia, South Africa, Spain, Suriname, Sweden, Switzerland, Syrian AR, Togo, Tunisia, Türkiye, UK, Ukraine, Uruguay, USA, Uzbekistan.
Other National Organizations (19) in 15 countries:
Argentina, Burkina Faso, Canada (2), France, Germany (2), Israel, Italy (2), Japan, Korea Rep, Malta, Mexico, Netherlands, Portugal, Spain, USA (2).
Individual Members (49) in 30 countries:
Argentina, Australia, Belgium, Canada, Denmark, Ethiopia, France, Germany, Greece, Guatemala, Italy, Japan, Korea Rep, Kuwait, Luxembourg, Malta, Mexico, Netherlands, Norway, Poland, Portugal, Russia, Serbia, Spain, Switzerland, Togo, Türkiye, UK, USA, Venezuela.
Honorary members (3) in 2 countries:
Belgium, France.
Former Benefactor members (4) in 3 countries:
France, Germany, USA.
Founder Members (2):
Association internationale de la presse sportive (AIPS, #02729); *International Council of Sport Science and Physical Education (ICSSPE, #13077)*.
International Sports Federations (23):
- *Fédération internationale de gymnastique (FIG, #09636)*;
- *Fédération Internationale de Motocyclisme (FIM, #09643)*;
- *Fédération internationale d'escrime (FIE, #09629)*;
- *Fédération internationale de volleyball (FIVB, #09670)*;
- *Federation of International Polo (FIP, #09675)*;
- *International Biathlon Union (IBU, #12336)*;
- *International Bobsleigh and Skeleton Federation (IBSF, #12375)*;
- *International Boxing Association (IBA, #12385)*;
- *International Canoe Federation (ICF, #12437)*;
- *International Federation of Association Football (#13360)*;
- *International Handball Federation (IHF, #13771)*;
- *International Hockey Federation (#13802)*;
- *International Luge Federation (FIL, #14066)*;
- *International Shooting Sport Federation (ISSF, #14852)*;
- *International Table Tennis Federation (ITTF, #15650)*;
- *International Tennis Federation (ITF, #15676)*;
- *International Weightlifting Federation (IWF, #15876)*;
- *Union Cycliste Internationale (UCI, #20375)*;
- *United World Wrestling (UWW, #20665)*;
- *World Athletics (#21209)*;
- *World Karate Federation (WKF, #21608)*;
- *World Penthathlon (UIPM, #21720)*;
- *World Taekwondo (#21844)*.

Other International Organizations (6):
Conseil international du sport militaire (CISM, #04695); *International Association for Non-Violent Sport (IANVS, no recent information)*; *International Catholic Federation of Physical Education and Sports (#12456)*; *International Council for Health, Physical Education, Recreation, Sport and Dance (ICHPER-SD, #13028)*; *International University Sports Federation (FISU, #15830)*; *Panathlon International (PI, #18170)*.
NGO Relations Recognized by: *International Olympic Committee (IOC, #14408)*. [2022/XA4499/y/**A**]

♦ International Committee for the Fellowship of the Least Coin / see Fellowship of the Least Coin (#09728)
♦ International Committee of Film Education and Culture (inactive)

♦ International Committee on Food Microbiology and Hygiene (ICFMH) 12770

Comité international de microbiologie et d'hygiène alimentaires

Sec Microbiologia Alimentària IRTA, Finca Camps i Armet, Monells, 17121 Girona, Spain. T. +34972630052. Fax +34972630373. E-mail: contact@icfmh.org.
Pres School of Life and Food Sciences, Handong Global Univ, Pohang NORTH GYEONGSANG 791-708, Korea Rep. T. +82542601314.
URL: http://icfmh.org/

History 1953, Rome (Italy). Founded at 6th World Congress of Microbiology, as branch of *International Union of Microbiological Societies (IUMS, #15794)*. Comes within *IUMS Division of Bacteriology and Applied Microbiology (BAM, see: #15794)*. Constitution approved Sep 1953. **Aims** Promote all international activities related to food microbiology, with special focus on developing countries. **Structure** Executive, consisting of at least President, up to 2 Vice-Presidents, Secretary, Treasurer and one Counsellor-at-large. **Languages** English. **Staff** Voluntary. **Finance** Basic financing relies on income from sale of publication. **Activities** Research and development; events/meetings. **Events** *FoodMicro Conference* Athens (Greece) 2022, *FoodMicro Conference* Athens (Greece) 2021, *FoodMicro Conference* Athens (Greece) 2020, *Symposium* Berlin (Germany) 2018, *Symposium* Dublin (Ireland) 2016. **Publications** *International Journal of Food Microbiology* (12 a year).
Members Individuals in 50 countries:
Australia, Austria, Bangladesh, Belgium, Brazil, Bulgaria, Burkina Faso, Canada, Chile, China, Croatia, Cyprus, Czechia, Denmark, Egypt, Finland, France, Germany, Ghana, Greece, Guatemala, Hungary, Iceland, India, Indonesia, Iran Islamic Rep, Ireland, Israel, Italy, Japan, Korea DPR, Morocco, Netherlands, New Zealand, Nigeria, Norway, Poland, Romania, Russia, Slovakia, Slovenia, South Africa, Spain, Sweden, Switzerland, Thailand, Türkiye, UK, Uruguay, USA, Venezuela.
NGO Relations Founder of: *International Commission on Microbiological Specifications for Foods (ICMSF, #12703)*. [2020/XE3397/v/**E**]

♦ International Committee of Food Science and Technology (inactive)
♦ International Committee on Food for the Small Democracies (inactive)
♦ International Committee of Foundry Technical Associations / see World Foundry Organization (#21528)

♦ International Committee of the Fourth International (ICFI) 12771

Comité international de la Quatrième internationale (CIQI) – Comité Internacional de la Cuarta Internacional (CICI) – Internationale Komitee der Vierten Internationale (IKVI)

Contact US Socialist Equality Party, PO Box 48377, Oak Park MI 48237, USA.
Contact Canada Socialist Equality Party, PO Box 183, Station B, Montréal QC H3B 3J7, Canada.
Contact UK Socialist Equality Party, PO Box 3978, Sheffield, S1 9BP, UK. E-mail: sep@socialequality.org.uk.
URL: https://www.wsws.org/

History 1953. Founded as a result of a split within the original *Fourth International (inactive)* which also gave rise to the *International Secretariat of the Fourth International (no recent information)*. **Aims** Provide leadership for the world *socialist* movement. **Information Services** *World Socialist Web Site*.
Members Sections in 6 countries:
Australia, Canada, Germany, Sri Lanka, UK, USA. [2022/XF2250/**E**]

♦ International Committee of the Francophone Games (#04178)

♦ International Committee for a Free Vietnam (ICFV) 12772

Comité international pour un Vietnam libre (CIVL)

European Chapter Bisschopsdreef 13, 8310 Bruges, Belgium. T. +3250354411. Fax +3250362702.
URL: http://www.lmdcvn.org/

History 4 Dec 1986, Brussels (Belgium). **Structure** Chapters: Asia, Australia, Canada, Europe, USA. Honorary members. **Activities** Annual conference. **Members** Membership countries not specified. [2012.06.12/XE4318/**E**]

♦ International Committee of French-Language Amateur Dramatic Federations (inactive)
♦ International Committee on Fund Raising Control (inactive)

♦ International Committee on Fundraising Organizations (ICFO) 12773

Administration c/o Fundación Lealtad, Calle Velázquez 100, 1ºDcha, 28006 Madrid, Spain. T. +34917890123. E-mail: contact@icfo.org.
URL: http://www.icfo.org/

History 10 Sep 1990, Strasbourg (France). Founded at meeting of accrediting agencies, taking over activities of *International Committee on Fund Raising Control (inactive)*, founded 1958. Current title, sub-title 'and constitution adopted 1989. Constitution amended in Amsterdam (Netherlands): 1995; 1999; 2001; 2002; 2006; 2011. Former names and other names: *Association of National Charity Monitoring Agencies* – alias (1989). Registration: Start date: 10 Sep 1990, Netherlands. **Aims** Ensure that fundraising for charitable purposes are being organized and performed in a satisfactory manner and that administration of collected funds are adequate. **Structure** General Meeting (annual); Board of 5 members. **Languages** English. **Staff** None. **Finance** Sources: members' dues. **Activities** Capacity building; knowledge management/information dissemination; monitoring/evaluation. **Events** *Annual General Meeting* Madrid (Spain) 2020, *Annual General Meeting* Prague (Czechia) 2019, *Annual General Meeting* Mexico City (Mexico) 2018, *Annual General Meeting* Berlin (Germany) 2017, *Annual General Meeting* Oslo (Norway) 2016. **Publications** *IFCO Principles. 50 Years of Informed Trust, Engaging Donors' Trust* (2008). Survey; brochures.
Members Ordinary; Supporting. Organizations (20) which monitor more than 6,500 charities, in 21 countries and territories:
Austria, Belgium, Brazil, Canada, China, Czechia, France, Germany, India, Italy, Japan, Luxembourg, Mexico, Netherlands, Norway, Spain, Sweden, Switzerland, Taiwan, Ukraine, USA. [2020.06.25/XD5671/**D**]

♦ International Committee for Future Accelerators (ICFA) 12774

Comité international pour les futurs accélérateurs

Sec Director's Office, FERMI Natl Accelerator Lab, PO Box 500 MS 121, Batavia IL 60510, USA. T. +16308408302. E-mail: pushpa@fnal.gov.
URL: http://icfa.fnal.gov/

History Founded 1976, Tbilisi (USSR), by *International Union of Pure and Applied Physics (IUPAP, #15810)*. Members approved 1977, Hamburg (Germany FR). **Aims** Promote international collaboration in all phases of the construction and exploitation of very high energy accelerators. **Structure** Committee (meets about twice a year), comprises: 3 members each from member states of *European Organization for Nuclear Research (CERN, #08108)* and from USA; 2 members each from Russia and Japan; 1 member each from China and Canada; 3 members from other countries; Chairman of IUPAP Commission on Particles and Fields, ex officio. Panels (8). **Languages** English. **Activities** Events/meetings. **Events** *Advanced Beam Dynamics Workshop on Energy Recovery Linacs* Berlin (Germany) 2019, *Meeting* Tokyo (Japan) 2019, *Advanced Beam Dynamics Workshop on High-Intensity and High-Brightness Hadron Beams* Daejeon (Korea Rep) 2018, *Meeting* Seoul (Korea Rep) 2018, *International Meeting for Large Neutrino Infrastructures* Tsukuba (Japan) 2016. **Publications** Guidelines. **Members** Membership countries not specified. [2016.10.27/XE6051/**E**]

♦ International Committee of Futuribles / see Futuribles International (#10052)
♦ International Committee on General Relativity and Gravitation / see International Society on General Relativity and Gravitation (#15138)
♦ International Committee for Genetics of Industrial Microorganisms / see Global Society for Industrial Microbiology (#10606)
♦ International Committee for Georgia (inactive)

♦ International Committee on Global Navigation Satellite Systems (ICG) 12775

Comité international sur les systèmes mondiaux de navigation par satellite – Comité Internacional sobre los Sistemas Mundiales de Navegación por Satélite

Executive Secretariat Office for Outer Space Affairs, United Nations Office at Vienna, PO Box 500, 1400 Vienna, Austria. T. +431260604950. Fax +431260605830.

URL: http://www.unoosa.org/oosa/en/ourwork/icg/icg.html
History 1 Dec 2005, Vienna (Austria). Established 1-2 Dec 2005, Vienna (Austria), at an international meeting at *United Nations Office at Vienna (UNOV, #20604)*, as an informal, voluntary forum. Establishment followed the Third United Nations Conference on the Exploration and Peaceful Uses of Outer Space (UNISPACE III), held in 1999, and recommendations made by the 'Action Team on Global Navigation Satellite Systems', established by *Committee on the Peaceful Uses of Outer Space (COPUOS, #04277)* in 2001. Plan of Action endorsed in *United Nations (UN, #20515)* Resolution 59/2, 2004. Providers' Forum set up Sep 2007, Bangalore (India). **Aims** Encourage and facilitate compatibility, interoperability and transparency between all satellite navigation systems to promote and protect the use of their open service applications. **Structure** Plenary; Rotating Chairperson; Working Groups; Executive Secretariat. **Languages** Arabic, Chinese, English, French, Russian, Spanish. **Staff** United Nations Office for Outer Space Affairs serves as Executive Secretariat. **Finance** Voluntary contributions in kind or direct determined by Members and Associate Members. **Activities** Knowledge management/information dissemination; capacity building. **Events** *Annual Meeting* Abu Dhabi (United Arab Emirates) 2022, *Annual Meeting* United Arab Emirates 2021, *Annual Meeting* Vienna (Austria) 2021, *Providers Forum* Vienna (Austria) 2021, *Annual Meeting* Geneva (Switzerland) 2020. **Publications** *International Committee on Global Navigation Satellite Systems: The Way Forward, 10 Years of Achievement, 2005-2015, ST/SPACE/67*. Meeting reports.
Members in 9 member states of the United Nations:
China, India, Italy, Japan, Malaysia, Nigeria, Russia, United Arab Emirates, USA.
Associate Members (11):
Civil Global Positioning System Service Interface Committee (CGSIC); European Position Determination System (EUPOS, #08256); Fédération aéronautique internationale (FAI, #09397); IAG Reference Frame Sub-Commission for Europe (EUREF); *International Association of Geodesy (IAG, #11914); International Cartographic Association (ICA, #12446); International Earth Rotation and Reference Systems Service (IERS, #13216); International Federation of Surveyors (FIG, #13561); International GNSS Service (IGS, #13724); International Society for Photogrammetry and Remote Sensing (ISPRS, #15362); United Nations Office for Outer Space Affairs (UNOOSA, #20601).*
Observers (9):
Arab Institute of Navigation (AIN, #00985); Asia-Pacific Space Cooperation Organization (APSCO, #02051); Bureau international des poids et mesures (BIPM, #03367); Committee on Space Research (COSPAR, #04287); European Space Policy Institute (ESPI, #08801); Interagency Operations Advisory Group (IOAG, #11389); International Association of Institutes of Navigation (IAIN, #11965); International Telecommunication Union (ITU, #15673); Union radio-scientifique internationale (URSI, #20475). [2018.04.23/XM0467/y/**E***]

♦ International Committee on Group Psychotherapy / see International Association for Group Psychotherapy and Group Processes (#11926)
♦ International Committee of Hard-of-Hearing Young People / see International Federation of Hard-of-Hearing Young People (#13436)

♦ International Committee for Historical Metrology (ICHM) 12776

Comité international pour la métrologie historique (CIMH) – Internationales Komitee für Historische Metrologie
SG Historisches Seminar, Univ Leipzig, Postfach 100 920, 04009 Leipzig, Germany. T. +493419737100. Fax +493419737149.
Chairman 34 Allée de la Comédie, 59650 Villeneuve d'Ascq, France. T. +33320053305. Fax +33320336361.
History 1975, Zagreb (Yugoslavia), as an international institution, a scientific section of the Division of History of Science (DHS) of *International Union of History and Philosophy of Science and Technology (IUHPST, #15779)* and of *International Committee of Historical Sciences (ICHS, #12777)*. Currently only an internal commission of ICHS. **Aims** Promote development of scientific research and dissemination of its results and works on the history of *weights* and *measurements* of metrical systems. **Structure** General Assembly (held during the International Congress). Permanent Council of 15 members. Board, consisting of President, 2 Vice-Presidents, Secretary-General and Treasurer. **Finance** Members' dues; Sale of publications. Budget (annual): euro 200. **Events** *Congress* Tübingen (Germany) 2005, *Science et diversité culturelle* Mexico City (Mexico) 2001, *Meeting* Beijing (China) 1999, *Meeting* Munich (Germany) 1997, *Congress* Siegen (Germany) 1996. **Publications** *CIMH – Bulletin* (periodical). *Acta Metrologiea Historicae V* (1999); *Acta Metrologiae Historicae IV* (1994); *Acta Metrologiae Historicae III* (1992); *Acta Metrologiae Historicae II* (1989); *Acta Metrologiae Historicae I* (1985).
Members National Committees; Affiliated Institutes. Individuals. Members in 27 countries:
Austria, Belgium, China, Croatia, Czechia, Denmark, France, Germany, Hungary, Iraq, Israel, Italy, Japan, Mexico, Netherlands, Norway, Poland, Portugal, Serbia, Slovakia, Slovenia, South Africa, Spain, Sweden, Switzerland, UK, USA. [2005/XE0480/**E**]

♦ International Committee of Historical Sciences (ICHS) 12777

Comité international des sciences historiques (CISH) – Comité Internacional de Ciencias Históricas – Internationaler Ausschuss der Geschichtswissenschaften – Mezdunarodnyj Komitet Istoriceskih Nauk
Gen Sec c/o Fondazione Luigi Eianudi, via principe Amedeo 34, 10134 Turin TO, Italy. T. +3911835656.
Treas c/o Diplomatic Documents of Switzerland, Hallwylstrasse 4, 3003 Bern, Switzerland. Fax +41584651236. E-mail: treasurer@cish.org.
URL: http://www.cish.org/
History 14 May 1926, Geneva (Switzerland). Founded in accordance with Congress of Historical Sciences resolution, 15 Apr 1923, Brussels (Belgium). First Statutes adopted 1926; amended: 1933, 1950, 1957, 1960. Current Statutes adopted by General Assembly, 4 Sep 1992, Prague (Czech Rep), superseding constitution voted 21 Aug 1975, San Francisco CA (USA), and modifications introduced 28 Jul 1977, Puerto de la Cruz (Spain). Current statutes amended 2005, Sydney (Australia). Registration: Swiss Civil Code, Switzerland. **Aims** Promote advancement of historical sciences by means of international cooperation. **Structure** General Assembly (at least every 3 years, including every 5 years at Congress); Board (meets annually); Specialized Commissions (16); Internal Commissions (6): *Association of African Historians (#02357); Comité international de paléographie latine (CIPL, #04180); International Committee for Historical Metrology (ICHM, #12776); Commission internationale de diplomatique (CID, see: #12777); International Association for Media and History (IAMHIST, #12023); Peace History Society (PHS).* **Languages** English, French, Spanish. **Staff** 1.00 FTE, voluntary. **Finance** Sources: grants; members' dues. **Activities** Awards/prizes/competitions; events/ meetings. **Events** *Quinquennial Congress* Poznań (Poland) 2022, *Quinquennial Congress* Poznań (Poland) 2021, *Quinquennial Congress* Poznań (Poland) 2020, *General Assembly* Moscow (Russia) 2017, *Joint Round Table* Jinan (China) 2015. **Publications** *ICHS Newsletter*.
Members National Committees in 54 countries:
Albania, Argentina, Australia, Austria, Belarus, Belgium, Brazil, Bulgaria, Canada, Chile, China, Croatia, Cyprus, Czechia, Denmark, Finland, France, Georgia, Germany, Greece, Guinea, Holy See, Hungary, Iceland, India, Ireland, Israel, Italy, Japan, Korea Rep, Latvia, Lithuania, Luxembourg, Mexico, Morocco, Netherlands, Norway, Peru, Poland, Portugal, Romania, Russia, Slovakia, Slovenia, South Africa, Spain, Sweden, Switzerland, Tunisia, Türkiye, UK, Ukraine, USA, Vietnam.
Affiliated international organizations (26):
- *Association internationale d'études du Sud-Est européen (AIESEE, #02693);*
- *Association internationale d'histoire contemporaine de l'Europe (AICHE, #02705);*
- *Association internationale pour l'histoire de l'État et de l'administration;*
- *Commission internationale des études historiques slaves (CIEHS, #04220);*
- *Commission internationale d'histoire de la Révolution française (CIHRF, #04222);*
- *Commission Internationale d'Histoire et d'Etudes du Christianisme (CIHEC, #04221);*
- *Commission internationale pour l'histoire des universités (CIHU, #04223);*
- *Commission of History of International Relations (CHIR, #04217);*
- *International Association for Byzantine Studies (#11751);*
- *International Association of Historical Societies for the Study of Jewish History (IAHSSJH, #11933);*
- *International Commission for the History and Theory of Historiography (ICHTH, #12690);*
- *International Commission for the History of State Assemblies (#12689);*
- *International Commission for the History of Towns (#12691);*
- *International Commission for the History of Travel and Tourism (ICHTT, #12692);*
- *International Commission of Military History (I10H, #12705);*
- *International Commission on Historical Demography (ICHD, #12684);*
- *International Committee of Editors of Diplomatic Documents (ICEDD, #12765);*
- *International Federation for Public History (IFPH, #13524);*
- *International Federation for Research in Women's History (IFRWH, #13528);*
- *International Federation of Societies and Institutes for the Study of the Renaissance (#13549);*
- *International Social History Association (ISHA);*
- *International Society for History Didactics (ISHD, #15167);*
- *International Union of Institutes of Archaeology, History and Art History in Rome (#15782);*
- *Network of Global and World History Organizations (NOGWHISTO, #17033);*
- *Pan American Institute of Geography and History (PAIGH, #18113).*

NGO Relations Partner of (1): *International Students of History Association (ISHA, #15613).* Instrumental in setting up (1): *International Commission for the Application of Quantitative Methods in History (INTERQUANT, no recent information).* Founder member of: *International Council for Philosophy and Human Sciences (CIPSH, #13061).* [2022.12.09/XA1582/y/**A**]

♦ International Committee for the History of Art (#04177)
♦ International Committee of the History of Science / see International Academy of History of Science (#11550)

♦ International Committee for the History of Technology (ICOHTEC) . . 12778

SG c/o Inst for the History of Science, Polish Academy of Sciences, ul Nowy – wiat 72 – pok 9, 00-330 Warsaw, Poland.
Treas 20 Haatzmaut St, 46789 Herzliyya, Israel.
URL: http://www.icohtec.org/
History 27 Aug 1968, Paris (France), at 12th International Conference for the History of Science, Technology and Medicine. Constitutes a Scientific Section within the Division of the History of Science and Technology (DHST) of *International Union of History and Philosophy of Science and Technology (IUHPST, #15779)*. Statutes amended: 22 Aug 1974; 1 Aug 1985; 24 Aug 1993; 17 Aug 2007; 26 Jul 2013. Registered Office moved to: Canada 1977; Britain 1981. Also referred to as *International Committee for Co-operation in the History of Technology*. **Aims** Establish close working relationships among specialists of different disciplines in order to foster international cooperation for the study and development of the history of technology; promote the study of appropriate historical subjects by establishing and extending scholarly bases and by contributing to the resolution of national or international problems; facilitate research and documentation for scholars in all countries by exchange of information and the creation of necessary material means. **Structure** General Assembly (every 4 years); Executive Committee. **Finance** Members' dues. Grants; payment for services rendered. **Events** *History of high-technologies and their socio-cultural contexts* Tel Aviv (Israel) 2015, *Symposium* Brasov (Romania) 2014, *Symposium* Manchester (UK) 2013, *Symposium* Barcelona (Spain) 2012, *Consumer choice and technology* Glasgow (UK) 2011. **Publications** *ICON* (annual); *ICOHTEC Newsletter* (10-12 a year).
Members Honorary; Ordinary; Benefactor (individuals and legal entities). Members in 27 countries:
Argentina, Australia, Austria, Brazil, Bulgaria, Canada, China, Czechia, Finland, France, Germany, Hungary, India, Italy, Japan, Mexico, Netherlands, Norway, Poland, Portugal, Romania, Russia, Spain, Sweden, Switzerland, UK, USA. [2015/XE1709/**E**]

♦ International Committee of Homeopathic Pharmacists (#04183)
♦ International Committee for Horticultural Congresses (inactive)
♦ International Committee of ICOM for Museums and Collections of Modern Art (see: #13051)

♦ International Committee for Imaging Science (ICIS) 12779

Sec Beijing Inst of Graphic Communication, No 1 Xinghua Dajie Er-duan, Daxing District, 102600 Beijing, China. T. +861060261003. Fax +861060261014.
URL: http://www.icisimaging.org/
History 1962, as *International Committee for the Science of Photography (ICSP)*. Since 1975, affiliated to *International Union of Pure and Applied Chemistry (IUPAC, #15809)* and status changed in 1976. Current name adopted 1999. **Aims** Build a platform for scientists and researchers in imaging areas to exchange information on the latest developments of imaging science and technology, and promote friendship and cooperation among them; further scientific and technical discussions on the science and applications of imaging technologies through organization of an international congress. **Structure** Committee (meeting in session every 2 years). **Languages** English. **Staff** Voluntary. **Finance** No budget – members financed by national organizations. **Activities** Offers advice to local groups and imaging organizations on specialized symposia; organizes International Congress (every 4 years); awards Berg and Chibisov Prizes. **Events** *International Congress* Tel Aviv (Israel) 2014, *International Congress* Beijing (China) 2010, *International Congress* Rochester, NY (USA) 2006, *International Congress* Tokyo (Japan) 2002, *International Congress* Antwerp (Belgium) 1998.
Members National photographic-scientific organizations (52) in 25 countries:
Australia, Austria, Belarus, Belgium, Canada, China, Czechia, Finland, France, Germany, India, Israel, Italy, Japan, Korea Rep, Netherlands, Poland, Russia, Sweden, Switzerland, Thailand, UK, Ukraine, USA, Vietnam.
NGO Relations Associated organization of: *International Union of Pure and Applied Chemistry (IUPAC, #15809).* [2019/XD1228/**D**]

♦ International Committee for the Improvement of the Amenities of Rural Life (inactive)
♦ International Committee for the Indians of the Americas / see International Committee for the Indigenous Peoples of the Americas
♦ International Committee for the Indigenous Peoples of the Americas (internationally oriented national body)
♦ International Committee on Industrial Chimneys (#04173)
♦ International Committee of Information and Computing Science (unconfirmed)

♦ International Committee for Insurance Medicine (ICLAM) 12780

Admin address not obtained. E-mail: foundation@iclam.org.
URL: https://www.iclam.org/
History 24 Sep 1901, Amsterdam (Netherlands). Fell apart late 1909. Revitalized 1928 and restarted Aug 1931, Geneva (Switzerland). First official meeting held 11 Sep 1932, Brussels (Belgium), when Statutes were approved. Current statutes adopted 26 May 2013, Madrid (Spain). Former names and other names: *International Association of Medical Experts for Insurance Companies* – former (24 Sep 1901 to Aug 1931); *Association internationale des médecins-experts de compagnies d'assurance (AIMECA)* – former (24 Sep 1901 to Aug 1931); *Permanent International Committee for the study of Life Assurance Medicine* – former (Aug 1931 to 11 Sep 1932); *International Committee for Life Assurance Medicine* – former (11 Sep 1932); *Comité international de médecine d'assurances sur la vie* – former (11 Sep 1932); *International Committee for Life, Disability and Health Assurance Medicine (ICLAM)* – former; *Comité international de médecine d'assurances sur la vie* – former. **Aims** Secure organization of congresses and support implementation of their decisions; promote teaching of insurance medicine; encourage scientific research into related problems; foster personal relations of members. **Structure** Congress (every 3 years); Bureau; Board. **Languages** English. **Staff** 7.00 FTE, voluntary. **Finance** Contributions from national life insurance organizations, particularly for congresses. **Activities** Events/meetings. **Events** *Triennial Congress* Tokyo (Japan) 2022, *Triennial Congress* Mumbai (India) 2019, *Triennial Congress* Maastricht (Netherlands) 2016, *Triennial Congress / International Congress of Insurance Medicine* Madrid (Spain) 2013, *Triennial Congress* Cape Town (South Africa) 2010. **Publications** Congress reports; presentations.
Members Individuals in 53 countries and territories:
Argentina, Aruba, Australia, Austria, Bahrain, Belgium, Brazil, Canada, China, Colombia, Croatia, Czechia, Denmark, Estonia, Finland, France, Germany, Greece, Hong Kong, Hungary, India, Indonesia, Ireland, Israel, Italy, Japan, Korea Rep, Malaysia, Malta, Mauritius, Netherlands, New Zealand, Norway, Pakistan, Poland, Portugal, Romania, Russia, Saudi Arabia, Senegal, Singapore, Slovakia, Slovenia, South Africa, Spain, Sudan, Sweden, Switzerland, Thailand, UK, USA, Venezuela, Vietnam.
IGO Relations None. **NGO Relations** None. [2020/XC1583/v/**C**]

♦ International Committee of the International Congresses on Free Trade (inactive)
♦ International Committee on Laboratory Animals / see International Council for Laboratory Animal Science (#13039)
♦ International Committee of Lawyers for Tibet / see Tibet Justice Center (#20159)
♦ International Committee of the Left for Peace in the Middle East (inactive)
♦ International Committee for Life Assurance Medicine / see International Committee for Insurance Medicine (#12780)
♦ International Committee for Life, Disability and Health Assurance Medicine / see International Committee for Insurance Medicine (#12780)

♦ International Committee for Lift Regulations (inactive)
♦ International Committee on Light (inactive)
♦ International Committee on Management of Population Programmes / see International Council on the Management of Population Programs (#13043)

♦ International Committee for Marine Conservation (ICMC) 12781

Contact Donauschwabenstrasse 20, 65239 Hochheim am Main, Germany. T. +491705457186. Fax +496146846439.
URL: http://my-icmc.eu/

History Founded Sep 1997. **Aims** combine diving and environmental protection. **Activities** Training/education. [2016/XE3753/E]

♦ International Committee on Measurements and Instrumentation (ICMI) 12782

Gen Sec Dept of Mechanical and Aerospace Engineering, Hong Kong Univ of Science and Technology, Clear Water Bay, Kowloon, Hong Kong. T. +85223588649. Fax +85223581543.
URL: http://ihome.ust.hk/~meygao/ICMI/

History 1993. **Aims** Promote and disseminate research in measurement science and technology. **Structure** Council; Board. **Languages** English. **Staff** 1.50 FTE, voluntary. **Events** *International Symposium on Measurement Technology and Intelligent Instruments* Nottingham (UK) 2021, *International Symposium on Measurement Technology and Intelligent Instruments* Niigata (Japan) 2019, *International Symposium on Measurement Technology and Intelligent Instruments* Xian (China) 2017, *International Symposium on Measurement Technology and Intelligent Instruments* Taipei (Taiwan) 2015, *International Symposium on Precision Engineering Measurements and Instrumentation* Zhangjiajie (China) 2014. [2021/XM3069/E]

♦ International Committee for Medical Extension Courses (inactive)
♦ International Committee of Medical Journal Editors (unconfirmed)

♦ International Committee of the Mediterranean Games (ICMG) 12783

Comité International des Jeux Méditerranéens (CIJM)

SG c/o OAKA, Ave Spirou Loui – Aquatic Center, 151 23 Athens, Greece. T. +302106850206. Fax +302106850207. E-mail: info@cijm.org.gr.
Pres address not obtained.
URL: http://www.cijm.org.gr/

History 16 Jun 1961, Athens (Greece). **Aims** Promote sport and olympism as well as the ideals and values they embody in the countries of the Mediterranean Basin. **Structure** General Assembly; Executive Bureau; Executive Committee; Permanent and Ad hoc Commissions; Headquarters located in Athens (Greece). **Languages** Arabic, English, French. **Activities** Sporting activities; training/education. **Events** *Mediterranean Beach Games* Patras (Greece) 2019, *Mediterranean Games* Tarragona (Spain) 2018, *Mediterranean Beach Games* Pescara (Italy) 2015, *Mediterranean Games* Mersin (Turkey) 2013, *Mediterranean Games* Pescara (Italy) 2009. **Publications** Manuals; guides; final reports.
Members Full in 26 countries:
Albania, Algeria, Andorra, Bosnia-Herzegovina, Croatia, Cyprus, Egypt, France, Greece, Italy, Kosovo, Lebanon, Libya, Malta, Monaco, Montenegro, Morocco, North Macedonia, Portugal, San Marino, Serbia, Slovenia, Spain, Syrian AR, Tunisia, Türkiye.
NGO Relations Accredited by (1): *International Olympic Committee (IOC, #14408)*. Member of (1): *Olympic Movement (#17719)*. [2020.05.06/XE0257/E]

♦ International Committee of Memorial Museums for the Remembrance of Victims of Public Crimes (IC MEMO) 12784

Comité international pour les musées à la mémoire des victimes de crimes publics – Comité Internacional de los Museos Conmemorativos de las Victimas de Crimenes Públicos

Chairperson Leo Baeck Institute, Center for Jewish History, 15 West 16th St, New York NY 10011, USA.
Sec Kreismuseum Wewelsburg, Burgwall 19, 33142 Büren, Germany.
URL: https://icmemo.mini.icom.museum/

History Jul 2001. Founded as one of 31 committees of *International Council of Museums (ICOM, #13051)*. **Aims** Foster a responsible memory of history; further cultural cooperation through education and through using knowledge in the interests of peace; facilitate and enhance communication among staff members working at memorial museums dealing with victims of state, socially determined and ideologically motivated crimes. **Structure** Board. **Languages** English. **Finance** Supported by: *International Council of Museums (ICOM, #13051)*. **Events** *Congress* Prague (Czechia) 2022, *Meeting* Milan (Italy) 2016, *Meeting* Munich (Germany) 2015, *Meeting* Ekne (Norway) 2014, *Conference* Tallinn (Estonia) 2013.
Members Full in 26 countries:
Austria, Brazil, Chile, Czechia, Dominican Rep, Estonia, France, Germany, Iran Islamic Rep, Israel, Japan, Latvia, Lithuania, Morocco, Namibia, Netherlands, Norway, Poland, Russia, South Africa, Spain, Sweden, Switzerland, UK, USA, Zambia. [2019/XK2277/v/E]

♦ International Committee for Mental Hygiene (inactive)

♦ International Committee of Military Medicine (ICMM) 12785

Comité International de Médecine Militaire (CIMM)

Exec Sec Hôpital Militaire Reine Astrid, Rue Bruyn 1, 1120 Brussels, Belgium. T. +3224432645. E-mail: info@cimm-icmm.org.
URL: http://www.cimm-icmm.org/

History 21 Jul 1921, Brussels (Belgium). Statutes adopted 1930; modified: 1938, Liège (Belgium); 1954, Luxembourg; 1996, Beijing (China); 2007, Tunis (Tunisia); 2009, Kuala Lumpur (Malaysia); 2013, Jeddah (Saudi Arabia). Former names and other names: *Standing Committee for International Congresses of Military Medicine and Pharmacy* – former (21 Jul 1921 to 1938); *Comité permanent des congrès internationaux de médecine et de pharmacie militaires* – former (21 Jul 1921 to 1938); *International Committee of Military Medicine and Pharmacy (ICMMP)* – former (1938 to 1990); *Comité International de Médecine et de Pharmacie Militaires (CIMPM)* – former (1938 to 1990); *Comité Internacional de Medicina Militar (CIMM)* – former. **Aims** In the spirit of the Geneva Conventions, and with neutrality, impartiality and independence: maintain and strengthen the bonds of continuous professional collaboration between persons worldwide whose missions consist in caring for the sick and wounded of the Armed Forces and in seeking to improve their condition and relieve their pain in times of peace or conflict. **Structure** General Assembly; Regional Assemblies; International Working Group; Regional Working Group; Center of Reference for Education on International Humanitarian Law and Ethics; Scientific Council; Technical Commissions (6). **Languages** English, French. **Staff** 12.00 FTE, paid. **Finance** Sources: contributions of member/participating states; donations; sale of publications. **Activities** Events/meetings; knowledge management/information dissemination; networking/liaising; training/education. **Events** *World Congress on Military Medicine* Brisbane, QLD (Australia) 2024, *World Congress on Military Medicine* Adelaide, SA (Australia) 2023, *Maghrebian Regional Congress* Rabat (Morocco) 2022, *Pan Arab Regional Congress* Rabat (Morocco) 2022, *Pan European Regional Congress* Thessaloniki (Greece) 2022. **Publications** *International Review of the Armed Forces Medical Services* (4 a year) in English, French. Congress proceedings.
Members Governments (" indicates Founder States) of 118 countries:
Afghanistan, Albania, Algeria, Angola, Argentina, Armenia, Australia, Austria, Azerbaijan, Bahrain, Bangladesh, Belgium (*), Bolivia, Brazil (*), Bulgaria, Burkina Faso, Burundi, Cameroon, Canada, Central African Rep, Chad, Chile, China, Comoros, Congo Brazzaville, Congo DR, Côte d'Ivoire, Croatia, Cyprus, Czechia, Denmark, Djibouti, Dominican Rep, Egypt, El Salvador, Estonia, Finland, France (*), Gabon, Germany, Ghana, Greece, Guinea, Haiti, Holy See, Honduras, Hungary, India, Indonesia, Iran Islamic Rep, Iraq, Ireland, Israel, Italy (*), Japan, Jordan, Kenya, Korea Rep, Kuwait, Latvia, Lebanon, Liberia, Libya, Lithuania, Luxembourg, Madagascar, Malaysia, Mali, Malta, Mauritania, Mexico, Morocco, Mozambique, Myanmar, Namibia, Netherlands, New Zealand, Nicaragua, Nigeria, North Macedonia, Norway, Oman, Pakistan, Palestine, Paraguay, Peru, Philippines, Poland, Portugal, Qatar, Romania, Russia, Saudi Arabia, Senegal, Serbia, Singapore, Slovakia, Slovenia, South Africa, Spain (*), Sri Lanka, Sudan, Sweden, Switzerland (*), Syrian AR, Thailand, Togo, Tunisia, Türkiye, Uganda, UK (*), United Arab Emirates, Uruguay, USA (*), Venezuela, Vietnam, Yemen, Zambia.
Included in the above:
Sovereign Military Hospitaller Order of St John of Jerusalem, of Rhodes and of Malta (SMOM).
Observer states (3):
Belarus, Cambodia, Rwanda.
IGO Relations Formal agreements with: *WHO (#20950)*. **NGO Relations** Veterinary Technical Commission is member of: *World Veterinary Association (WVA, #21901)*. [2023/XB1612/B*]

♦ International Committee of Military Medicine and Pharmacy / see International Committee of Military Medicine (#12785)

♦ International Committee of Mine Safety Science and Engineering (ICMSSE) 12786

Sec No 30 Xueyuan Road, Haidian District, 100083 Beijing, China. T. +861062333758. Fax +861062333758.
International Sec address not obtained.
URL: https://www.icmsse.com/

History Apr 2017, Beijing (China). Set following earlier International Symposia on Mine Safety Science and Engineering (ISMSSE) since 2011. Established as a permanent exchange platform for mine safety science and engineering. **Aims** Promote mine safety science and engineering research and education for the well being of the global mining industry and its workforce through the organization of various international events. **Structure** Committee consisting of: Chairperson; International Chairperson; International Members; Secretariat; Officer. **Languages** Chinese, English. **Activities** Events/meetings; projects/programmes; publishing activities. Active in all member countries. **Events** *International Symposium on Mine Safety and Engineering* Beijing (China) 2023, *International Symposium on Mine Safety Science and Engineering* Katowice (Poland) 2021, *International Symposium on Mine Safety Science and Engineering* Katowice (Poland) 2020, *International Symposium on Mine Safety Science and Engineering* Beijing (China) 2018, *International Symposium on Mine Safety Science and Engineering* Montréal, QC (Canada) 2016.
Members Individuals (15~25) in 11 countries:
Australia, Belgium, Canada, China, Czechia, Japan, Poland, Portugal, Russia, South Africa, USA. [2022/AA1608/c/E]

♦ International Committee on the Minority Situation and Human Rights in the USSR (inactive)
♦ International Committee on Modern Literary History / see International Federation for Modern Languages and Literatures (#13480)

♦ International Committee Monitoring Assisted Reproductive Technologies (ICMART) 12787

Dir c/o ICS, Suite 300, 1201 West Pender St, Vancouver BC V6E 2V2, Canada. E-mail: chris@icsevents.com.
Chair USA 540 University Ave, Ste 200, Palo Alto CA 94301, USA.
URL: http://www.icmartivf.org/

History 2003. **Aims** Develop, collect and disseminate worldwide data on assisted reproductive technology (ART); develop a glossary of standard definitions. **Structure** Board; regional representatives. **Languages** English. **Staff** 1.00 FTE, paid; 70.00 FTE, voluntary. **Finance** Sources: contributions; international organizations. Supported by: American Society for Reproductive Medicine (ASRM); *European Society of Human Reproduction and Embryology (ESHRE, #08625)*; Fertility Society of Australia (FSA); Japan Society of Fertilization and Implantation (JSFI); *Latin America Network of Assisted Reproduction (#16315)*; Society for Assisted Reproductive Technology (SART). **Activities** Knowledge management/information dissemination; networking/liaising; publishing activities. **Publications** World Reports on ART; glossaries; articles; presentations. **Members** Representatives in 60 countries. Membership countries not specified. **Consultative Status** Consultative status granted from: *WHO (#20950)* (Official Relations). [2019/XJ1807/C]

♦ International Committee for Moriscos Studies 12788

Comité international d'études morisques (CIEM)

Pres c/o FTERSI, BP 50, 1118 Zaghouan, Tunisia. T. +21672676446680110. Fax +21672676710.

History 1983. Located at *Fondation Temimi pour la recherche scientifique et l'information (FTERSI, #09829)*, together with *Arab Committee for Ottoman Studies (ACOS, no recent information)*. **Aims** Strengthen complementarity and interchange among researchers and *historians* studying the 'Moriscos' *Arab Muslim culture* remaining in Spain after the fall of Granada. **Structure** Bureau; President; Vice-President. **Activities** Events/meetings; research/documentation. **Events** *Congress* Tunis (Tunisia) 2015, *Congress* Tunis (Tunisia) 2009, *Symposium / Congress* Zaghouan (Tunisia) 2003, *Symposium / Congress* Zaghouan (Tunisia) 2001, *Symposium international d'études morisques* Zaghouan (Tunisia) 1999.
Members Individuals in 11 countries:
Algeria, Argentina, Egypt, France, Ireland, Morocco, Puerto Rico, Spain, Tunisia, UK, USA. [2009/XE0825/v/E]

♦ International Committee on Morphological Sciences (ICSMS) 12789

Pres Universidade de Santo Amaro, Rua Profr Enéas de Siqueira Neto 340, Jardim das Imbuias, Santo Amaro, Sao Paulo SP, Brazil.
URL: http://ismsxxii.blogspot.com

Events *Symposium* Almaty (Kazakhstan) 2021, *Symposium* Aktobe (Kazakhstan) 2020, *Symposium* Prague (Czechia) 2018, *Symposium* Xian (China) 2017, *Symposium* Istanbul (Turkey) 2015. **Members** Membership countries not specified. **NGO Relations** *International Federation of Associations of Anatomists (IFAA, #13361)*. [2012/XE2359/E]

♦ International Committee for Mountain Running / see World Mountain Running Association (#21659)
♦ International Committee of the Movements for European Unity / see European Movement International (#07825)

♦ International Committee of Museums and Collections of Arms and Military History (ICOMAM) 12790

Comité internationale des musées et collections d'armes et d'histoire militarie – Internationaler Ausschuss der Waffen- und Militärhistorischen Museen und Sammlungen – Internationaal Comité van Wapen- en Militair-Historische Musea en Verzamelingen

Chair c/o Natl Militaire Museum, Verlengde Paltzerweg 1, 3768 MX Soesterberg, Netherlands. E-mail: icomam.president@gmail.com.
Sec address not obtained.
URL: https://icomam.mini.icom.museum/

History 25 May 1957, Copenhagen (Denmark). Previously, 1957 to June 2002, an Affiliated member of *International Council of Museums (ICOM, #13051)*. Currently an International Committee of ICOM. Former names and other names: *International Association of Museums of Arms and Military History (IAMAM)* – former (25 May 1957); *Association internationale des musées d'armes et d'histoire militaire* – former (25 May 1957); *Internationale Vereinigung der Waffen- und Militärhistorischen Museen* – former (25 May 1957); *Internationale Vereniging van Wapen- en Militair-Historische Musea* – former (25 May 1957). **Aims** Establish contact between said museums and similar institutions; promote study of relevant groups of objects; further the aims of International Council of Museums (ICOM). **Structure** General Assembly (every 3 years, from 2007 onwards in same year as that of ICOM); Executive Board. **Languages** English, French. **Staff** Part-time, volontary. **Activities** Awards/prizes/competitions; events/meetings; knowledge management/information dissemination. **Events** *Congress* Toledo (Spain) 2021, *Symposium* Kyoto (Japan) 2019, *Congress* Ljubljana (Slovenia) 2018, *Congress* Koblenz (Germany) 2017, *Cooperation and sharing in the decorative arts – cultural landscapes from arts and crafts to decorative arts and design* Milan (Italy) 2016. **Publications** *ICOMAM Magazine* (2 a year). Newsletter (irregular); congress proceedings.
Members Museums (over 300). Active and voting members (96) in 34 countries:
Australia, Austria, Belarus, Belgium, Brazil, Canada, Chile, Czechia, Denmark, Finland, France, Germany, Greece, Guatemala, Ireland, Latvia, Luxembourg, Malta, Netherlands, Nigeria, Norway, Poland, Portugal, Romania, Russia, Senegal, Slovenia, South Africa, Spain, Sweden, Switzerland, UK, USA, Vietnam.
IGO Relations *UNESCO (#20322)*. [2023.02.15/XC1317/C]

♦ International Committee for Museums and Collections of Decorative Arts and Design (see: #13051)
♦ International Committee for Museums and Collections of Fine Arts (see: #13051)

♦ International Committee on Nanostructured Materials (ICNM) 12791

Chair Northeastern Univ, 3-11 Wenhua Rd, Shenyang, Liaoning, China.
Vice-Chair Laboratoire Léon Brillouin, UMR 12 CEA/CNRS – bat 563 CEA Saclay, 91191 Gif-sur-Yvette CEDEX, France. T. +33169083684.
URL: http://www.icnm-nano.com/

History 1990, Atlantic City, NJ (USA). **Aims** Promote and organize International nanostructured materials conferences, offering scientists and engineers worldwide a forum to present state-of-the-art research and advanced discoveries in the field of nanostructured materials including nanomaterials. **Structure** Committee. **Languages** English. **Staff** 8.50 FTE, voluntary. **Finance** No budget. **Events** *International Conference on Nanostructured Materials* Seville (Spain) 2022, *International Conference on Nanostructured Materials* Melbourne, VIC (Australia) 2020, *International Conference on Nanostructured Materials* Hong Kong (Hong Kong) 2018, *International Conference on Nanostructured Materials* Québec, QC (Canada) 2016, *Colloquium on Fatigue Mechanisms* Vienna (Austria) 2016. [2022.05.12/XJ6920/c/**E**]

♦ International Committee for Near Infrared Spectroscopy / see International Council for Near Infrared Spectroscopy (#13053)

♦ International Committee On New Integrated Climate change assessment Scenarios (ICONICS) 12792

Co-Chair address not obtained.
Co-Chair c/o IIASA, Schlossplatz 1, 2361 Laxenburg, Austria.
URL: https://depts.washington.edu/iconics/

History 2006. **Aims** Develop, facilitate, and promote the use of socioeconomic development pathways to support interdisciplinary research and assessment of climate change-related risks; support exploration of the effectiveness of adaptation and mitigation policies and actions across spatial and temporal scales to reduce those risks within the context of the Sustainable Development Goals. **Structure** Steering Committee; Working Groups. **Activities** Events/meetings. **Events** *Scenarios Forum for Climate and Societal Futures* Denver, CO (USA) 2019. [2022.10.13/XM8583/**C**]

♦ International Committee on Non-Destructive Testing (ICNDT) 12793

Sec c/o Bindt, Midsummer House, Riverside Way, Northampton, NN1 5NX, UK. T. +441604438300. Fax +441604438301.
Registered Office Jochen-Rindt-Str 33, 1230 Vienna, Austria.
URL: http://www.icndt.org/

History 1955, Brussels (Belgium). Terms of Reference adopted May 1967, Montréal (Canada); revised Nov 1979, Melbourne (Australia); Aug 1982, Moscow (USSR). Registration: Austria. **Aims** Promote international collaboration in all matters relating to development and use of all methods of non-destructive testing. **Structure** General Assembly; Executive Committee; International Advisory Committee; Regional Boards; Committees and Working Groups; Secretariat. **Languages** English. **Staff** 10.00 FTE, voluntary. **Finance** Expenses incurred in relation to an International Conference borne by the host country. **Activities** Awards/prizes/competitions; events/meetings; standards/guidelines. **Events** *World Conference on Non-Destructive Testing* Incheon (Korea Rep) 2024, *Asia-Pacific Conference* Adelaide, SA (Australia) 2023, *World Conference on Non-Destructive Testing* Incheon (Korea Rep) 2022, *World Conference on Non-Destructive Testing* Seoul (Korea Rep) 2020, *Asia-Pacific Conference* Singapore (Singapore) 2017. **Publications** *The ICNDT Journal*.
Members One accredited national representative from each country, nominated by an appropriate national body in that country which has registered its intention to collaborate and cooperate in the work of the International Committee. Members in 70 countries and territories:
Algeria, Argentina, Australia, Austria, Bangladesh, Belarus, Belgium, Bosnia-Herzegovina, Brazil, Bulgaria, Canada, China, Colombia, Costa Rica, Croatia, Czechia, Denmark, Ecuador, Egypt, Finland, France, Germany, Greece, Hungary, India, Indonesia, Israel, Italy, Japan, Kazakhstan, Kenya, Korea Rep, Latvia, Lebanon, Lithuania, Malaysia, Mexico, Moldova, Mongolia, Netherlands, New Zealand, Nigeria, Norway, Pakistan, Philippines, Poland, Portugal, Romania, Russia, Serbia, Singapore, Slovakia, Slovenia, South Africa, Spain, Sri Lanka, Sudan, Sweden, Switzerland, Taiwan, Thailand, Tunisia, Türkiye, UK, Ukraine, Uruguay, USA, Uzbekistan, Venezuela, Vietnam.
Regional Groups (4):
African Federation of Non Destructive Testing; *Asia Pacific Federation for Non Destructive Testing (APFNDT, #01902)*; *European Federation for Non-Destructive Testing (EFNDT, #07179)*; *Pan-American Federation For Nondestructive Testing (PANNDT, #18103)*.
NGO Relations Member of (1): *World Council of Isotopes (WCI, #21331)*. In liaison with technical committees of: *International Organization for Standardization (ISO, #14473)*. Formal contacts with: *International Institute of Welding (IIW, #13935)*. [2022.10.11/XD4702/y/**B**]

♦ International Committee on Occupational Mental Health (inactive)
♦ International Committee on Offensive Microwave Weapons (internationally oriented national body)
♦ International Committee of Onomastic Sciences / see International Council of Onomastic Sciences (#13055)
♦ International Committee on Open Air Education (inactive)
♦ International Committee of the Order of Malta / see Campagne Internationale de l'Ordre de Malte contre la lèpre (#03403)
♦ International Committee of the Order of Malta for Leprosy Relief / see Campagne Internationale de l'Ordre de Malte contre la lèpre (#03403)
♦ International Committee of Paper and Board Converters in the Common Market / see International Confederation of Paper and Board Converters in Europe (#12866)
♦ International Committee of Papyrology (inactive)

♦ International Committee on Pavement Technology (ICPT) 12794

Chair c/o Ctr for Transportation Research, Dept of Civil & Env Engineering, Natl Univ of Singapore, 10 Kent Ridge Crescent, Singapore 119260, Singapore. T. +6565162185. Fax +6567770994. E-mail: ceefwatf@nus.edu.sg.
URL: http://www.pavement.org.sg/

History 1992, Singapore (Singapore). Registration: Registry of societies, No/ID: No. 3491, Start date: 14 Oct 1994, Singapore. **Aims** Promote pavement technological advancement worldwide, with special emphasis on pavement technological development in developing countries. **Structure** International Executive Committee. **Languages** English. **Staff** 11.00 FTE, voluntary. **Finance** Supported by: Pavement Engineering Society (Singapore). Annual budget: 20,000 SGD. **Activities** Events/meetings. **Events** *International Conference on Road and Airfield Pavement Technology* Beijing (China) 2023, *International Conference on Road and Airfield Pavement Technology* Colombo (Sri Lanka) 2021, *International Conference on Road and Airfield Pavement Technology* Kuala Lumpur (Malaysia) 2019, *International Conference on Road and Airfield Pavement Technology* Hong Kong (Hong Kong) 2017, *International Conference on Road and Airfield Pavement Technology* Dalian (China) 2015. **Publications** Conference proceedings.
Members Full in 11 countries:
Australia, China, India, Indonesia, Japan, Korea Rep, Malaysia, Singapore, Sri Lanka, Thailand, Vietnam.
[2023.02.14/XM4380/**E**]

♦ International Committee of Photobiology / see International Union of Photobiology (#15798)
♦ International Committee on Plant Analysis and Fertilizer Problems / see International Plant Nutrition Council (#14592)
♦ International Committee on Plant Nutrition / see International Plant Nutrition Council (#14592)
♦ International Committee for Plastics in Agriculture (#04185)

♦ International Committee for Pre-Ottoman and Ottoman Studies ... 12795

Comité international d'études pré-ottomanes et ottomanes (CIEPO)

SG Inst für Orientalistik, Univ Vienna, Spitalgasse 2, Hof 4, 1090 Vienna, Austria.
Pres Seminar für Sprachen und Kulturen des Vorderen Orients, Universität Heidelberg, Sandgasse 7, 69117 Heidelberg, Germany.
URL: http://www.univie.ac.at/ciepo/

History Founded Sep 1974, Naples (Italy). **Aims** Promote research on *turkology* related to the periods of the *Seljuks*, *Principalities* and *Ottomans*. **Structure** General Assembly (every 4 years); Executive Board. **Languages** English, French, Turkish. **Staff** None. **Finance** Members' dues. **Activities** Research/documentation; events/meetings; awards/prizes/competitions. **Events** *Biennial Symposium* Thessaloniki (Greece) 2022, *Biennial Symposium* Thessaloniki (Greece) 2021, *Biennial Symposium* Thessaloniki (Greece) 2020, *Biennial Symposium* Sofia (Bulgaria) 2018, *Biennial Symposium* Trabzon (Turkey) 2016. **Publications** Symposia proceedings.
Members Individuals in 33 countries and territories:
Albania, Algeria, Austria, Bosnia-Herzegovina, Bulgaria, Canada, Croatia, Cyprus, Czechia, Egypt, Germany, Greece, Hungary, Israel, Italy, Japan, Jordan, Lebanon, Morocco, Netherlands, North Macedonia, Norway, Palestine, Poland, Romania, Russia, Serbia, Spain, Syrian AR, Tunisia, Türkiye, UK, USA.
NGO Relations Member of: *International Council for Philosophy and Human Sciences (CIPSH, #13061)*; *International Union for Oriental and Asian Studies (IUOAS, inactive)*. [2018/XE0983/v/**E**]

♦ International Committee for the Prevention of Charlatanism (inactive)

♦ International Committee for the Prevention of Work Accidents in Inland Navigation 12796

Comité international de prévention des accidents du travail de la navigation intérieure (CIPA) – Internationaler Ausschuss für die Verhütung von Arbeitsunfällen in der Binnenschiffahrt

Secretariat Berufsgenossenschaft Verkehrswirtschaft Post-Logistik, Telekommunikation – Geschäftsbereich Prävention, Fachbereich Binnenschifffahrt, Düsseldorfer Str 193, 47053 Duisburg, Germany. T. +492032952142. Fax +492032952115.
URL: http://www.cipa-online.org/

History 10 Feb 1972, Luxembourg. **Structure** President; Vice President. **Languages** German. **Events** *Annual meeting* Klagenfurt am Wörthersee (Austria) 2009, *Annual meeting* Lucerne (Switzerland) 2008, *Annual meeting* Duisburg (Germany) 2007, *Annual meeting* Vienna (Austria) 2006, *Annual meeting* Vienna (Austria) 2005.
Members Associations, national bodies and ministries in 6 countries:
Austria, Belgium, France, Germany, Luxembourg, Switzerland.
NGO Relations In liaison with technical committees of: *International Organization for Standardization (ISO, #14473)*. [2021/XE6125/**E**]

♦ International Committee for Private and Public Assistance (inactive)
♦ International Committee to Promote Universal Free Trade (inactive)

♦ International Committee for Promotion of Research in Bio-Impedance (ICPRBI) 12797

Chairman Dept Physics, Univ Oslo, PO Box 1048, 0316 Blindern, Norway.
URL: http://www.isebi.org/

History 1981, Tokyo (Japan), during 5th *International Conference on Electrical Bio-Impedance (ICEBI)*. **Aims** Promote research, development, use and understanding of electrical impedance measurements as a means of assessing normal or abnormal *physiological* states in *medicine* and *biology*. **Structure** Committee of national representatives. **Finance** Conference fee covers mailing of information between conferences. **Activities** Set up: *International Society for Electrical Bio-Impedance (ISEBI, #15077)*. **Events** *International conference on electrical bio-impedance / Conference* Heiligenstadt (Germany) 2013, *International conference on electrical bio-impedance / Conference* Gainesville, FL (USA) 2010, *International conference on electrical bio-impedance / Conference* Graz (Austria) 2007, *International conference on electrical bio-impedance / Conference* Gdansk (Poland) 2004, *International conference on electrical bio-impedance / Conference* Oslo (Norway) 2001. **Publications** Conference proceedings.
Members Individuals in 20 countries:
Australia, Austria, China, Estonia, Finland, France, Germany, Ireland, Italy, Japan, Korea Rep, Netherlands, Norway, Poland, Romania, Russia, Spain, Sweden, UK, USA. [2010.07.05/XF5545/v/**F**]

♦ International Committee for the Promotion of Trade (inactive)
♦ International Committee on Proteolysis (inactive)
♦ International Committee for the Publication of Annual Tables of Chemical, Physical, Biological and Technological Constants (inactive)
♦ International Committee for the Publication of Documents on European History (no recent information)
♦ International Committee of Purchasing (inactive)
♦ International Committee on Radio-Electricity (inactive)
♦ International Committee on Radiological Units / see International Commission on Radiation Units and Measurements (#12722)

♦ International Committee for Radionuclide Metrology (ICRM) 12798

Sec c/o Jožef Stefan Institute, Jamova 39, 1000 Ljubljana, Slovenia.
Pres address not obtained.
URL: http://physics.nist.gov/ICRM/index.html

History Sep 1972, Herceg-Novi (Montenegro). Founded as an informal association of scientists representing national laboratories engaged in the field of radionuclide metrology, and also international organizations such as: BIPM; IAEA; *Joint Research Centre (JRC, #16147)* – Institute for Reference Materials and Measurements of the European Commission (EC-JRC-IRMM). May 1974, Paris (France), founded as association of radionuclide metrology laboratories including international organizations engaged in the study and applications of radioactivity. Statutes revised: 2015. **Aims** Serve as the international forum for dissemination of information on techniques, applications and data in the field of radionuclide metrology. **Structure** General Meeting (every 2 years); Executive Board; Working Groups. **Languages** English. **Staff** None. **Finance** No operating funds; member laboratories contribute leadership and services. **Activities** Knowledge management/information dissemination; events/meetings. **Events** *International Conference on Radionuclide Metrology and its Applications* Bucharest (Romania) 2023, *International Conference on Radionuclide Metrology and its Applications* Bucharest (Romania) 2021, *International Conference on Radionuclide Metrology and its Applications* Salamanca (Spain) 2019, *International Conference on Radionuclide Metrology and its Applications* Buenos Aires (Argentina) 2017, *International Conference* Seattle, WA (USA) 2016. **Publications** *ICRM Newsletter* (annual). *ICRM Technical Series* (every 2 years). Annual Report; progress reports; conference proceedings.
Members Delegates: appointed representatives of an institute, agency or laboratory which actively pursues the objectives of ICRM. Associates: persons who are recognized for their special contributions to the work of ICRM working groups or who indicated their willingness to serve in ICRM. Members (47) in 39 countries and territories:
Argentina, Australia, Austria, Belgium, Brazil, Bulgaria, Canada, China, Croatia, Cuba, Czechia, Denmark, Finland, France, Germany, Greece, Hungary, India, Indonesia, Ireland, Italy, Japan, Korea Rep, Mexico, Poland, Portugal, Romania, Russia, Serbia, Slovakia, Slovenia, South Africa, Spain, Sweden, Switzerland, Taiwan, Türkiye, UK, USA.
International organizations (4), listed in this Yearbook:
Bureau international des poids et mesures (BIPM, #03367); *Comprehensive Nuclear-Test-Ban Treaty Organization (CTBTO, #04420)*; *International Atomic Energy Agency (IAEA, #12294)*; *Joint Research Centre (JRC, #16147)* (Geel Belgium). [2021/XE0291/y/**E**]

♦ International Committee for Recording the Productivity of Milk Animals / see International Committee for Animal Recording (#12746)

♦ International Committee of the Red Cross (ICRC) 12799

Comité international de la Croix-Rouge (CICR) – Comité Internacional de la Cruz Roja (CICR) – Internationales Komitee vom Roten Kreuz (IKRK)

Dir Gen 19 av de la Paix, 1202 Geneva, Switzerland. T. +41227346001. Fax +41227332057.
URL: http://www.icrc.org/

History 17 Feb 1863, Geneva (Switzerland), following an appeal made by Henry Dunant for relief societies to be formed to care for the wounded in wartime that would be recognized and protected through and international agreement. In 1863, a charitable association known as *'Geneva Society for Public Welfare'* set up a 5 member commission to consider Dunant's appeal. The commission founded the ICRC under its original name: *International Committee for Relief of Wounded Soldiers – Comité international de secours aux militaires blessés*. Present name adopted 1875. Registered in accordance with Swiss Civil Code.
Its mandate to protect and assist the victims of armed conflict has been conferred on it by States through the four Geneva Conventions of 1949 – *Geneva Convention for the Amelioration of the Condition of Wounded, Sick and Shipwrecked Members of Armed Forces at Sea (1949)*, *Geneva Convention Relative to the Treatment of Prisoners of War (1949)*, *Geneva Convention Relative to the Protection of Civilian Persons in Time of War (1949)* and *Geneva Convention on Torture (1949)* -and their Additional Protocols of 1977 and 2005 – *Protocol Additional to the Geneva Conventions of 12 August 1949 and Relating to the Protection of Victims of International Armed Conflicts (Protocol I, 1977)*, *Protocol II Additional to the Four 1949 Geneva Conventions*

Relating to the Protection of Victims of Non-international Armed Conflicts (1977) and *Protocol III additional to the Geneva Conventions of 12 August 1949, and relating to the Adoption of an Additional Distinctive Emblem (Protocol III), 8 December 2005*, as well as *Convention on Cluster Munitions (CCM, 2008)* – successors to *Convention for the Amelioration of the Condition of the Wounded in Armies in the Field, 1864 (Geneva convention, 1864)*. The ICRC's mandate and legal status set it apart both from intergovernmental agencies, such as UN organizations, and from non-governmental organizations (NGOs). In most of the countries in which it works, the ICRC has concluded headquarters agreements with the authorities. Through these agreements, which are subject to international law, the ICRC enjoys the privileges and immunities usually only granted to intergovernmental organizations, such as immunity from legal process, which protects it from administrative and judicial proceedings, and inviolability of its premises, archives and other documents. The organization has concluded such an agreement with Switzerland, thus guaranteeing its independence and freedom of action from the Swiss government.
Aims Protect and assist civilian and military victims of armed conflicts and internal disturbances on a strictly neutral and impartial basis. **Structure** Assembly (supreme governing body) and Assembly Council (subsidiary body of the Assembly), composed of 5 members elected by the Assembly; both are chaired by ICRC President. Director (executive body). Presidency: President; 2 Vice-Presidents. Offices in 80 countries. **Languages** English, French, Spanish. **Staff** 12000.00 FTE, paid. **Finance** Sources: voluntary contributions from: governments; national societies; supranational organizations; other public and private sources; appeals for funds.
Activities Works to ensure civilians no taking part in hostilities are spared and protected, more specifically: visits prisoners of war and security detainees; transmits messages to reunite family members separated by armed conflict; helps find missing persons; offers or facilitates access to basic health care services; provides urgently needed food, safe drinking water, sanitation and shelter; promotes respect for international humanitarian law; monitors compliance with and contributes to further development of international humanitarian law; helps reduce the impact of mines and explosive remnants of war on people; supports national Red Cross and Red Crescent Societies to prepare for and respond to armed conflict and other situations of violence.
Conventions with which the ICRC is associated and which are not mentioned above:
- *Convention de Genève pour la Protection des Blessés dans les Armées en Campagne, 1906 (Convention de Genève, 1906)*;
- *Convention for the Protection of Cultural Property in the Event of Armed Conflict (The Hague Convention, 1954, 1954)*;
- *Convention on the Prohibition of the Development, Production and Stockpiling of Bacteriological – Biological – and Toxin Weapons and on Their Destruction (1972)*;
- *Convention on Prohibitions or Restrictions on the Use of Certain Conventional Weapons Which May be Deemed to be Excessively Injurious or to Have Indiscriminate Effects, with Annexed Protocols (CCW, 1980)*;
- *Convention Relative to the Treatment of Prisoners of War (1929)*;
- *Geneva Convention for the Amelioration of the Condition of the Wounded and Sick in Armies in the Field, 1929 (1929)*;
- *United Nations Convention on the Rights of the Child (CRC, 1989)*;
- *Convention on the Prohibition of the Development, Production, Stockpiling and Use of Chemical Weapons and on Their Destruction (CWC, 1992)*.

Events *Humanitarian Congress Tokyo* Tokyo (Japan) 2022, *Seminar on International Humanitarian Law* Seoul (Korea Rep) 2020, *Seminar on Armed Conflict and the Environment* Singapore (Singapore) 2020, *Humanitarian Activities Seminar* Seosan (Korea Rep) 2019, *Seminar on International Humanitarian Law* Seoul (Korea Rep) 2018. **Publications** *International Review of the Red Cross* (4 a year) – with annual selections of articles also published on regional level in Arabic, Chinese, French, Russian, Spanish; *National Implementation of International Humanitarian Law* (every 2 years); *ICRC News* in Arabic, English, French, German, Spanish – by fax; *Red Cross Red Crescent* in English, French, Russian, Spanish – magazine of the International Red Cross and Red Crescent Movement. *Handbook of the International Red Cross and Red Crescent Movement* in English, French, Spanish. Annual Report.
Members ICRC delegations in 35 countries:
Afghanistan, Algeria, Angola, Armenia, Azerbaijan, Burundi, Central African Rep, Chad, Colombia, Congo Brazzaville, Congo DR, Egypt, Eritrea, Ethiopia, Georgia, Guinea, Haiti, Iran Islamic Rep, Iraq, Israel, Jordan, Lebanon, Liberia, Myanmar, Nepal, Pakistan, Philippines, Rwanda, Sierra Leone, Somalia, Sri Lanka, Sudan, Syrian AR, Uganda, Yemen.
Included in the above, the Occupied Territories and the Autonomous Territories of Israel.
Also included, delegation to 3 organizations:
African Union (AU, #00488); *European Union (EU, #08967)*; United Nations.
Consultative Status Consultative status granted from: *African Commission on Human and Peoples' Rights (ACHPR, #00255)* (Observer); *International Maritime Organization (IMO, #14102)*; *United Nations (UN, #20515)*; *UNEP (#20299)*. **IGO Relations** Cooperation agreement with: *OAS (#17629)*; *Organisation of Islamic Cooperation (OIC, #17813)*; *UNESCO (#20322)*. Memorandum of Understanding with: *UNHCR (#20327)*. Agreement with: *Council of Europe (CE, #04881)*. Cooperates with: *United Nations Institute for Training and Research (UNITAR, #20576)*. Observers include: *FAO (#09260)*; *UNDP (#20292)*. Follows the activities of and Permanent Observer to: *ECOSOC (#05331)*. Observer status with: *Committee of Legal Advisers on Public International Law (CAHDI, #04267)*; *International Organization for Migration (IOM, #14454)*; *Parliamentary Union of the OIC Member States (PUIC, #18220)*. Official observer of: *Pacific Islands Law Officers' Network (PILON, #17972)*. Guest status with: *Coordinating Bureau of the Non-Aligned Countries (#04815)* and *Non-Aligned Movement (NAM, #17146)* – represented at *Conference of Heads of State or Government of Non-Aligned Countries*. Manages: *Arolsen Archives – International Center on Nazi Persecution (#01112)*. Regular contacts with: *European Commission (EC, #06633)*; *WHO (#20950)*. Signatory to the Framework Partnership Agreement of: ECHO. Invited to sessions of Intergovernmental Council of: *International Programme for the Development of Communication (IPDC, #14651)*. Collaborates with: *International Civil Defence Organization (ICDO, #12582)*. Partner in: *Peace Implementation Council (#18279)*. Represented on: *International Commission on Missing Persons (ICMP, #12706)*. Supported the setting up of: *International Criminal Court (ICC, #13108)*. Member of: *Inter-Agency Standing Committee (IASC, #11393)*. Agreement with: *Interparliamentary Assembly of Member Nations of the Commonwealth of Independent States (IPA CIS, #15958)*. **NGO Relations** The ICRC, *International Federation of Red Cross and Red Crescent Societies (#13526)* and the 178 National Societies constitute the *International Red Cross and Red Crescent Movement (#14707)*. Permanent observer of: *International Council of Voluntary Agencies (ICVA, #13092)*. Member of: *Active Learning Network for Accountability and Performance in Humanitarian Action (ALNAP, #00101)*; *Centre for Information, Counseling and Training Professions Relating to International Cooperation and Humanitarian Aid (CINFO)*; *Digital Radio Mondiale Consortium (DRM, #05082)*; *European Policy Centre (EPC, #08240)*; *Global Partnership for the Prevention of Armed Conflict (GPPAC, #10538)*; *International Council on Archives (ICA, #12996)*; *World Water Council (WWC, #21908)*. Institutional member of: *Centre for European Policy Studies (CEPS, #03741)*. Participates in: *Business Humanitarian Forum (BHF, #03383)*. Represented on the Organizing Committee of: *Hague Appeal for Peace (HAP, #10848)*. Represented on the Steering Committee of: *Global Humanitarian Platform (GHP, #10413)*. In liaison with technical committees of: *International Organization for Standardization (ISO, #14473)*. Partner of: *WorldFish (#21507)*. Supports: *Asia-Pacific Network of People Living with HIV/AIDS (APN+, #01973)*; *International News Safety Institute (INSI, #14364)*. Cooperates with: *College of Europe (#04105)*. Instrumental in setting up: *Paul Reuter Fund*; *Institut Henry-Dunant (IHD, inactive)*. [2020/XF1623/v/**F**]

♦ International Committee on Regulatory Authority Research and Development (ICRARD) 12800

Australia Contact address not obtained.
URL: http://www.icrard.org/
History 1994. **Aims** Coordinate research activities in the field of offshore *oil* and *gas* industry; exchange information in the area of health, safety and environment in the *petroleum* sector; promote research cooperation. **Finance** Primarily sponsored by: USA; UK; Canada; Norway. **Activities** Events/meetings; research/documentation.
Members Governmental institutions of 9 countries:
Australia, Brazil, Canada, Mexico, Netherlands, New Zealand, Norway, UK, USA. [2017/XM5900/**C***]

♦ International Committee for Rehabilitation Aid to Afghanistan (internationally oriented national body)
♦ International Committee for Relief of Wounded Soldiers / see International Committee of the Red Cross (#12799)
♦ International Committee for Research on Processional Giants (inactive)

♦ International Committee for Research and Study of Environmental Factors (ICEF) 12801

Comité international de recherche et d'étude de facteurs de l'ambiance (CIFA)
Gen Sec c/o Montevenda Engineering International Association, PO Box 729, 6903 Lugano TI, Switzerland. T. +41788242622. Fax +41919600562.
URL: http://www.cifafondation.org/
History Founded 7 Sep 1969, Brussels (Belgium), after having existed informally since 1957, Florence (Italy), as *Comitato Internazionale Fenomeni Fluttuanti (CIFF)*. Registered in accordance with Belgian law, 28 Aug 1969. **Aims** Organize, on an international scale, *interdisciplinary* cooperation in research and scientific investigation of environmental factors responsible for fluctuating phenomena in exact, natural and human sciences. **Structure** Board of Directors of 4 members. **Languages** English, French, Italian, Russian, Spanish. **Finance** Members' dues. **Activities** Research/documentation. **Events** *Triennial General Assembly* Florence (Italy) 2006, *Triennial General Assembly* Crimea (Ukraine) 2003, *International Crimean seminar* Partenit (Ukraine) 2001, *General Assembly* Partenit (Ukraine) 1999, *International Crimean seminar* Partenit (Ukraine) 1999. **Publications** *CIFA News* (4 a year).
Members Full in 23 countries:
Austria, Belgium, Canada, Czechia, France, Germany, Hungary, Israel, Italy, Japan, Kazakhstan, Kenya, Latvia, Lithuania, Netherlands, Poland, Romania, Russia, Slovenia, Switzerland, UK, Ukraine, USA.
NGO Relations Supports: *Global Alliance for Improved Nutrition (GAIN, #10202)*. [2016.06.01/XF0105/v/**F**]

♦ International Committee for Research and Technical Support for Hollow Section Structures / see Committee for International Development and Education on Construction of Tubular Structures (#04266)

♦ International Committee on Rheology (ICR) 12802

Comité international de rhéologie
Chairman Pontifícia Univ Católica – RJ, Dept of Mechanical Engineering, Rua Marquês de São Vicente 225, Rio de Janeiro RJ, 22451-900, Brazil. T. +552135271177.
URL: http://icrheology.org/
History Founded 29 Jul 1953, Oxford (UK). **Aims** Promote rheology worldwide. **Structure** Officers: Chairman; Secretary. **Languages** English. **Staff** 2.00 FTE, paid. **Finance** No budget. **Events** *International Congress on Rheology* Athens (Greece) 2023, *Quadrennial Congress* Rio de Janeiro (Brazil) 2020, *Quadrennial Congress* Kyoto (Japan) 2016, *Quadrennial Congress* Lisbon (Portugal) 2012, *Quadrennial Congress* Monterey, CA (USA) 2008.
Members National societies, representing 6,100 rheologists, in 32 countries:
Argentina, Australia, Austria, Belgium, Brazil, Canada, China, Czechia, Denmark, Finland, France, Germany, Greece, India, Iran Islamic Rep, Israel, Italy, Japan, Korea Rep, Mexico, Netherlands, Norway, Portugal, Romania, Russia, Slovenia, South Africa, Spain, Sweden, Switzerland, UK, USA.
Regional society:
Nordic Rheology Society (NRS, #17400).
NGO Relations Member of: *International Union of Theoretical and Applied Mechanics (IUTAM, #15823)*. [2022/XD1637/**C**]

♦ International Committee on the Rights of Sex Workers / see European Sex Workers' Rights Alliance (#08472)
♦ International Committee on the Rights of Sex Workers in Europe / see European Sex Workers' Rights Alliance (#08472)

♦ International Committee for Robot Arms Control (ICRAC) 12803

Chair Computer Science Room 105, Regent Court, 211 Portobello, Sheffield, S1 4DP, UK. T. +441142221803.
URL: http://www.icrac.net/
History Sep 2009, Sheffield (UK). **Aims** Debate about an arms control regime to reduce the threat posed by the rapid pace of development of military robotics and the pressing dangers that these pose to peace and international security and to civilians in war.
Members Individuals in 4 countries:
Australia, Germany, UK, USA.
NGO Relations Member of: *Campaign to Stop Killer Robots (#03405)*. [2019/XJ0783/**E**]

♦ International Committee for the Safeguard of Tyre / see International Association to Save Tyre (#12144)
♦ International Committee on Sarcoidosis / see World Association of Sarcoidosis and other Granulomatous Disorders (#21183)
♦ International Committee of Schools of Social Work / see International Association of Schools of Social Work (#12149)
♦ International Committee for the Science of Photography / see International Committee for Imaging Science (#12779)
♦ International Committee to Secure Employment for Refugee Professional Workers (inactive)
♦ International Committee of Silent Chess / see International Chess Committee of the Deaf (#12544)
♦ International Committee of the Silent Sports / see International Committee of Sports for the Deaf (#12805)
♦ International Committee of Social Insurance (inactive)
♦ International Committee of Sociology of Sport / see International Sociology of Sport Association (#15554)

♦ International Committee for Solvent Extraction (ICSE) 12804

Comité international pour la chimie et la technologie de l'extraction des solvants
SG Technische Uni Kaiserslautern, Gottlieb-Daimler-Str, 67663 Kaiserslautern, Germany. T. +496312052414. Fax +496312052119.
URL: http://www.solventextract.org/
History Founded 1974, to ensure continuity of *International Solvent Extraction Conferences (ISEC)*. Also referred to as *International Solvent Extraction Committee* or *International Committee for Solvent Extraction Chemistry and Technology*. **Aims** Develop and disseminate the science and practice of solvent extraction. **Structure** Honorary Committee. **Languages** English. **Staff** 18.00 FTE, voluntary. **Finance** Donations. **Activities** Events/meetings. **Events** *ISEC : International Solvent Extraction Conference* Gothenburg (Sweden) 2022, *ISEC : International Solvent Extraction Conference* Gothenburg (Sweden) 2020, *ISEC : International Solvent Extraction Conference* Miyazaki (Japan) 2017, *ISEC : International Solvent Extraction Conference* Würzburg (Germany) 2014, *ISEC : International Solvent Extraction Conference* Santiago (Chile) 2011. **Publications** Conference proceedings.
Members Individuals in 14 countries:
Australia, Brazil, Canada, China, France, Germany, India, Israel, Japan, Russia, South Africa, Sweden, UK, USA.
NGO Relations National associations. [2017.03.17/XD9747/cv/**E**]

♦ International Committee for Solvent Extraction Chemistry and Technology / see International Committee for Solvent Extraction (#12804)
♦ International Committee for Soviet and East European Studies / see International Council for Central and East European Studies (#13002)
♦ International Committee of Speech (inactive)

♦ International Committee of Sports for the Deaf (ICSD) 12805

Comité International des Sports des Sourds (CISS)
CEO Maison du Sport Intl, Av de Rhodanie 54, 1007 Lausanne VD, Switzerland. E-mail: office@ciss.org.
URL: http://www.ciss.org/
History 24 Aug 1924, Paris (France). Current Statutes and Regulations adopted by 48th Extraordinary Congress, Nov 2021, Lausanne (Switzerland). Former names and other names: *International Committee of the Silent Sports* – former; *Comité international des sports silencieux (CISS)* – former. Registration: Registre du Commerce du Canton de Vaud, No/ID: CHE-375.811.133, Start date: 24 Jul 2017, Switzerland, Canton de Vaud; French Ministerial Decree, Start date: 27 Mar 1937. **Aims** Develop and control physical education in general and the practice of *sports* in particular among the *deaf* of the world; promote relations between countries practising sports for the deaf and initiate and then give guidance to the practice of these sports in countries where it is unknown; supervise the regular celebration of Deaflympics, World *Championships*

and Regional Championships. **Structure** Congress (every 2 years); Executive Board; Organizing Committee; Technical Directors; Medical and several Commissions; Secretariat. **Languages** English. **Staff** 3.00 FTE, paid. **Finance** Sources: members' dues. **Activities** Events/meetings; sporting activities. **Events** *Biennial Congress* Vienna (Austria) 2022, *Extraordinary Congress* Lausanne (Switzerland) 2021, *Biennial Congress* Verceia (Italy) 2019, *Biennial Congress* Samsun (Turkey) 2017, *Biennial Congress* Khanty-Mansiysk (Russia) 2015.
Members Full; Associate. Full in 120 countries and territories:
Afghanistan, Algeria, Argentina, Armenia, Australia, Austria, Azerbaijan, Bahrain, Bangladesh, Belarus, Belgium, Bolivia, Bosnia-Herzegovina, Botswana, Brazil, Bulgaria, Cameroon, Canada, Chile, China, Colombia, Côte d'Ivoire, Croatia, Cuba, Cyprus, Czechia, Denmark, Ecuador, Egypt, Estonia, Eswatini, Ethiopia, Fiji, Finland, France, Gabon, Gambia, Georgia, Germany, Ghana, Great Britain, Greece, Guinea, Hong Kong, Hungary, Iceland, India, Indonesia, Iran Islamic Rep, Iraq, Ireland, Israel, Italy, Jamaica, Japan, Jordan, Kazakhstan, Kenya, Korea Rep, Kosovo, Kuwait, Kyrgyzstan, Latvia, Lebanon, Libya, Lithuania, Macau, Macedonia, Malaysia, Mali, Malta, Mauritius, Mexico, Moldova, Mongolia, Montenegro, Mozambique, Nepal, Netherlands, New Zealand, Nigeria, North Macedonia, Norway, Pakistan, Palestine, Paraguay, Peru, Philippines, Poland, Portugal, Romania, Russia, Saudi Arabia, Senegal, Serbia, Seychelles, Sierra Leone, Singapore, Slovakia, Slovenia, South Africa, Spain, Sweden, Switzerland, Taiwan, Tanzania UR, Thailand, Tunisia, Türkiye, Uganda, UK, Ukraine, United Arab Emirates, Uruguay, USA, Uzbekistan, Venezuela, Yemen, Zambia, Zimbabwe.
Associate (4), listed in this Yearbook:
Deaf International Basketball Federation (DIBF, #05017); Deaf International Football Association (DIFA, #05018); International Chess Committee of the Deaf (ICCD, #12544); World Deaf Golf Federation (WDGF, #21356).
NGO Relations Accredited by (1): *International Olympic Committee (IOC, #14408).* Member of (1): *Olympic Movement (#17719).* [2022.11.29/XC1624/y/**B**]

- ♦ International Committee for Standardization in Haematology / see International Council for Standardization in Haematology (#13078)
- ♦ International Committee for Standardization in Human Biology (inactive)
- ♦ International Committee for the Standardization of Physical Fitness Tests / see International Council for Physical Activity and Fitness Research (#13062)

♦ International Committee for the Study of Bauxite, Alumina and Aluminium (ICSOBA) 12806

Comité international pour l'étude des bauxites, de l'alumine et de l'aluminium
Registered Office 128 Des Fauvettes, Saint Colomban, Québec QC J5K 0E2, Canada. E-mail: info@icsoba.org.
URL: https://icsoba.org/
History 1963, Yugoslavia. 1963, Zagreb (Yugoslavia). Seat previously registered in Zagreb (Croatia), Budapest (Hungary) and Nagpur (India). Registered in accordance with Canadian law, since Dec 2011. Registration: Corporations Canada, No/ID: 802906-7, Canada, Ontario; Registraire d'Entreprises, No/ID: 1167982181, Canada, Quebec. **Aims** Promote collaboration in the field of bauxite, alumina and aluminium *production* from primary and secondary sources. **Structure** General Meeting; Council; Board of Directors. **Languages** English. **Staff** 1.00 FTE, paid. Voluntary. **Finance** Members' dues: individual – Canadian $ 100; corporate – Canadian $ 500. Other sources: conference fees; sponsorship. **Activities** Events/meetings. **Events** *Conference* Québec, QC (Canada) 2020, *Conference* Krasnoyarsk (Russia) 2019, *Conference* Belém (Brazil) 2018, *Conference* Hamburg (Germany) 2017, *Conference* Québec, QC (Canada) 2016. **Publications** *ICSOBA Newsletter* (2 a year) – electronic. *ICSOBA Travaux* – congress/conference proceedings. **Members** Individual; Corporate in about 30 countries. Membership countries not specified. [2020/XN1734/**E**]

- ♦ International Committee for the Study of Clays / see Association internationale pour l'étude des argiles (#02688)
- ♦ International Committee for the Study of Clouds (inactive)
- ♦ International Committee for the Study of Gliding (inactive)
- ♦ International Committee on Surface Active Agents (inactive)
- ♦ International Committee on Systematic Bacteriology / see International Committee on Systematics of Prokaryotes (#12807)

♦ International Committee on Systematics of Prokaryotes (ICSP) 12807

Chair address not obtained.
URL: http://www.the-icsp.org/
History 1930, Paris (France). Founded at 1st International Microbiological Congress, as *Commission on Nomenclature and Taxonomy* of the then *'International Association of Microbiologists'*, later known as *'International Association of Microbiological Societies (IAMS)'*, and currently, since Sep 1980, *International Union of Microbiological Societies (IUMS, #15794).* Commission subsequently became *International Committee on Bacteriological Nomenclature (ICBN) – Comité international de nomenclature bactériologique.* 1966, Moscow (USSR), name changed to *International Committee on Systematic Bacteriology (ICSB) – Comité international de bactériologie systématique.* Comes within *IUMS Division of Bacteriology and Applied Microbiology (BAM, see: #15794)* since Sep 1986. **Aims** Provide stability in the *nomenclature* of prokaryotes, through publication of an 'International Code of Nomenclature of Prokaryotes'; promote study of taxonomy of prokaryotes and make recommendations relating to *taxonomy*; provide an avenue of publication of research on *microorganisms.* **Structure** Committee; Judicial Commission; Taxonomic Subcommittees (33). **Languages** English. **Staff** Voluntary. **Finance** Grants from International Union of Microbiological Societies. Income (held by IUMS) from investment of Royalties. **Activities** Standards/guidelines. **Events** *Congress* Montréal, QC (Canada) 2014, *Congress* Sapporo (Japan) 2011, *Microbes, then now and hereafter* Istanbul (Turkey) 2008, *Microbes in a changing world* San Francisco, CA (USA) 2005, *Congress* Paris (France) 2002. **Publications** *International Journal of Systematic and Evolutionary Microbiology. The International Code of Nomenclature of Prokaryotes.*
Members Full nominated by member Societies and co-opted, in 14 countries:
Austria, Belgium, Croatia, Germany, Hungary, Israel, Italy, Japan, Korea Rep, Luxembourg, Nepal, Spain, UK, USA.
NGO Relations Cooperates in related fields of interest (directly or through the Union) with: *European Culture Collections' Organization (ECCO, #06872); International Union of Biological Sciences (IUBS, #15760); WFCC-MIRCEN World Data Centre for Microorganisms (WDCM, #20929).* [2021/XD4327/**E**]

- ♦ International Committee on Taxonomy of Viruses (see: #15794)
- ♦ International Committee on the Teaching of Philosophy / see Association internationale des professeurs de philosophie (#02732)

♦ International Committee on Technical Interchange for Space Mission Operations (SpaceOps) 12808

Secretariat c/o Intl Astronautical Federation, av de Suffren 100, 75015 Paris, France. T. +33145674260.
URL: http://www.spaceops.org/
History 1990. Also referred to as *SpaceOps Organization.* **Aims** Foster continuous technical interchange on all aspects of space mission operations and ground data systems; promote and maintain an international community of space operations experts. **Structure** Committee-at-Large; Executive Committee. **Languages** English. **Staff** 0.50 FTE, paid. **Finance** Sources: members' dues. Annual budget: 50,000 USD. **Events** *SPACEOPS – International Conference on Space Operations* Dubai (United Arab Emirates) 2023, *SpaceOps Biennial International Conference on Space Operations* Paris (France) 2021, *SpaceOps Biennial International Conference on Space Operations* Cape Town (South Africa) 2020, *Biennial International Conference on Space Operations* Marseille (France) 2018, *Biennial International Conference on Space Operations* Daejeon (Korea Rep) 2016. **Publications** *SpaceOps Update* (irregular) – newsletter; *Journal of Space Operations and Communicator.* Books.
Members Organizations in 14 countries:
Brazil, Canada, France, Germany, India, Italy, Japan, Korea Rep, Russia, South Africa, Sweden, UK, United Arab Emirates, USA.
Regional organizations (2):
European Organisation for the Exploitation of Meteorological Satellites (EUMETSAT, #08096); European Space Agency (ESA, #08798). [2019/XJ6934/y/**C**]

♦ International Committee of Textile Care 12809

Comité international de l'entretien du textile (CINET) – Internationales Komitee für Textilpflege
Main Office PO Box 10, 4060 GA Ophemert, Netherlands. T. +31344650430. Fax +31344652665. E-mail: cinet@cinet-online.com.
Managing Dir address not obtained.
URL: https://www.cinet-online.com/
History 1994. Also referred to in English as: *International Drycleaning Trade Association*; *International Textile Care and Rental Association.* Registered in accordance with Belgian law. **Aims** Promote the textile care industry and represent its interests with the institutions of the European Union and with other international public and private institutions; advance interests of textile care professionals, in particular as regards administrative, environmental, social and tax laws and regulations; promote cooperation among research institutions; improve professional relations. **Structure** General Assembly, comprising 2 representatives of each member country. Board, consisting of President, and 4 members. Commissions (3): Environment; Care Labelling; Marketing. Temporary working groups. **Languages** English, French, German. **Staff** 1.00 FTE, paid. **Finance** Members' dues. **Activities** Organizes workshops; participates in exhibitions and other events. Exchange of information; international exchange among young members of the profession. **Events** *Meeting* Frankfurt-Main (Germany) 2010, *Meeting* Milan (Italy) 2010, *Meeting* Milan (Italy) 2006, *Meeting* Frankfurt-Main (Germany) 2004, *Meeting* Milan (Italy) 2002. **Publications** *CINET Info* – bulletin. *CINET Echo* – press release.
Members National professional textile care organizations in 19 countries:
Austria, Belgium, China, Denmark, Finland, France, Germany, Greece, Ireland, Italy, Japan, Luxembourg, Moldova, Netherlands, Norway, Russia, Sweden, UK, Ukraine.
Associate member organizations (10) in 8 countries:
Australia, Czechia, France, Germany, Hungary, Netherlands, UK, USA.
Regional associate member (1):
European Chlorinated Solvent Association (ECSA, #06540).
NGO Relations In liaison with technical committees of: *International Organization for Standardization (ISO, #14473).* Cooperates with: *Groupement International de l'Etiquetage pour l'Entretien des Textiles (GINETEX, #10761).* [2022/XD4802/y/**D**]

- ♦ International Committee of Tourism Film Festivals (unconfirmed)
- ♦ International Committee of Toy Industries / see International Council of Toy Industries (#13086)
- ♦ International Committee of Trade of Wines, Ciders, Spirits and Liqueurs (inactive)

♦ International Committee on Ultrahigh Intensity Lasers (ICUIL) 12810

Sec Group Leader Optics and Imaging Sciences, Lab for Laser Energetics, Univ of Rochester, Rochester NY 14627, USA. T. +15872752315. E-mail: jude@lle.rochester.edu.
Chair Univ of California – Irvine, 4162 Frederick Reines Hall, Irvine CA 92697-4575, USA.
URL: http://www.icuil.org/
History 11 Oct 2003, Vancouver BC (Canada), by *International Union of Pure and Applied Physics (IUPAP, #15810).* **Aims** Serve as a forum for representatives of the ultrahigh intensity lasers facilities and members of the user communities; promote unity and coherence in the field. **Structure** Officers: Chair; Secretary; 2 Co-Chairs; Treasurer. **Events** *Conference* Canada 2016, *Conference* Goa (India) 2014, *Conference* Mamaia (Romania) 2012, *Conference* Rochester, NY (USA) 2010, *Development, science and emerging applications* Shanghai (China) 2008. [2018.07.26/XE4707/**E**]

- ♦ International Committee for the Unification of Analytical Methods for Food Products (inactive)
- ♦ International Committee for the Unification of Anthropological Methods (inactive)
- ♦ International Committee of the Union of Bondholders (inactive)
- ♦ International Committee of the United States of the World (inactive)
- ♦ International Committee of Women for Permanent Peace / see Women's International League for Peace and Freedom (#21024)
- ♦ International Committee of Women Trade Unionists (inactive)
- ♦ International Committee of Work Study and Labour Management in Agriculture (#04226)
- ♦ International Committee for a World Conference on Human Rights (inactive)

♦ International Committee for World Day of Prayer 12811

Chairperson 475 Riverside Dr, Suite 729, New York NY 10115, USA. T. +12128703049. E-mail: wdpic@worlddayofprayer.net – admin@worlddayofprayer.net.
URL: http://www.worlddayofprayer.net/
History 22 Jul 1968, Vällingby (Sweden). Founded to take over administrative functions in connection with the World Day of Prayer previously undertaken by the USA national committee, following decision of International Consultation, 1967, Anderson IN (USA). Present statutes revised and adopted May 1986. *World Day of Prayer* commenced 1927, Jerusalem (Israel), at an International Missionary Conference, growing from the Day of Prayer started in the USA, originally, 1887, as a Day of Prayer for Home Missions of the Presbyterian Church and, 1890, as Day of Prayer for Foreign Missions of the Baptist Church. Former names and other names: *Women's World Day of Prayer, Central Committee* – former. **Aims** Establish the policy and planning of the World Day of Prayer, enabling *women* worldwide to affirm their *faith* in Jesus Christ, and to share their hopes and fears, joys and sorrows, opportunities and needs. **Structure** International Committee; Executive Committee; National Committees. **Languages** English, French, Spanish. **Staff** 2.00 FTE, paid. **Finance** National committees contribute towards cost of meetings and secretariat expenses. **Activities** Events/meetings. **Events** *Quadrennial Meeting* Foz do Iguaçu (Brazil) 2017, *Quadrennial meeting* Toronto, ON (Canada) 2007, *Quadrennial meeting* UK 2003, *Quadrennial meeting* South Africa 1999, *Quadrennial meeting* Melbourne, VIC (Australia) 1995. **Publications** *International Committee for World Day of Prayer Journal. World Day of Prayer Service* – TV documentaries. **Members** Not a membership organization. **NGO Relations** Supports (1): *World Young Women's Christian Association (World YWCA, #21947).* [2022.02.15/XC1641/**E**]

♦ International Common Disease Alliance (ICDA) 12812

Address not obtained.
URL: https://www.icda.bio/
Aims Improve prevention, diagnosis, and treatment of common diseases by accelerating discovery from genetic maps to biological mechanisms to physiology and medicine, to benefit people around the world. **Structure** Organizing Committee; Executive Office. **Activities** Events/meetings; networking/liaising. **Events** *Scientific Plenary and Launch* Helsinki (Finland) 2019. **Members** Scientists. Membership countries not specified. [AA0511/v/**C**]

- ♦ International Common Law Exchange Society (inactive)

♦ International Communal Studies Association (ICSA) 12813

Administrator Yad Tabenkin, 5296000 Ramat Efal, Israel. T. +97235358 ext 4. Fax +97235346376. E-mail: contact@icsacommunity.org.
Co-Chair address not obtained.
Co-Chair address not obtained.
URL: https://www.icsacommunity.org/
History 1985. Founded during the first international conference held at Yad Tabenkin (Israel). **Aims** Provide a common framework for scholarly exchange of information on *communes*, international communities, collective settlements and *kibbutz.* **Structure** Joint Chairs; Secretary. **Languages** English. **Staff** 0.20 FTE, paid; 1.00 FTE, voluntary. **Finance** Sources: members' dues. Financial support from kibbutz institutes. **Activities** Events/meetings. **Events** *Conference* Skanderborg (Denmark) 2022, *Triennial Conference* Hudson, NY (USA) 2019, *Triennial Conference* Colos (Portugal) 2016, *Triennial conference* Findhorn (UK) 2013, *Triennial Conference* Afula (Israel) 2010. **Publications** *Bulletin of the International Communal Studies Association* (2 a year) – digital.
Members Individuals in 23 countries:
Australia, Belgium, Bosnia-Herzegovina, Brazil, Canada, China, Croatia, Czechia, France, Germany, Hungary, Israel, Italy, Japan, Korea Rep, Netherlands, New Zealand, Poland, Russia, Serbia, Spain, UK, USA. [2022.05.07/XF2932/v/**F**]

- ♦ International Communes Desk (internationally oriented national body)

♦ International Communication Association (ICA) 12814

Exec Dir 1500 21st ST NW, Washington DC 20036, USA. T. +12029551444. Fax +12029551448. E-mail: icahdq@icahdq.org.
URL: http://www.icahdq.org/

History 1950. **Aims** Advance the scholarly study of human communication by encouraging and facilitating excellence in academic research worldwide. **Structure** Board of Directors; Executive Committe. **Events** *Annual Conference* Denver, CO (USA) 2025, *Annual Conference* Gold Coast, QLD (Australia) 2024, *Annual Conference* Toronto, ON (Canada) 2023, *Central and Eastern Europe Regional Conference* Helsinki (Finland) 2022, *Annual Conference* Paris (France) 2022. **Publications** *ICA Newsletter* (10 a year); *Annals of the International Communication Association* (4 a year); *Communication, Culture, & Critique*; *Communication Theory*; *Human Communication Research*; *Journal of Communication*; *Journal of Computer-Mediated Communication*. Handbooks. **Members** Researchers (over 3,500) in 65 countries. Membership countries not specified. **NGO Relations** Member of (2): *International Association for Media and Communication Research (IAMCR, #12022)*; *International Federation of Communication Associations*. Cooperates with (1): *World Association for Public Opinion Research (WAPOR, #21180)*. Journalism Division is member of: *World Journalism Education Council (WJEC, #21602)*. *LIRNEasia (#16489)* is a member. [2022/XG1545/**C**]

♦ International Communication Enhancement Center (inactive)
♦ International Communications Agency Network (internationally oriented national body)
♦ International Communication Sciences and Technology Association / see Institute for Computer Sciences, Social-Informatics and Telecommunications Engineering (#11248)

♦ International Communications Consultancy Organisation (ICCO) . . . 12815

Gen Manager 82 Great Suffolk Street, London, SE1 0BE, UK. T. +442072336026. Fax +442078284797. E-mail: info@iccopr.com.
Chief Exec address not obtained.
URL: http://www.iccopr.com/

History Founded 1986, by leading PR agencies of the time. **Aims** Provide a forum for senior management of the world's best PR consultancies to meet and address issues of mutual interest and concern. **Structure** Board of Management; Executive Committee; Regional Groups. **Languages** English. **Staff** 2.00 FTE, paid. **Finance** Sources: fees for services; meeting proceeds; members' dues. Other sources: partnerships; training. **Activities** Awards/prizes/competitions; events/meetings; knowledge management/information dissemination; networking/liaising; research/documentation; training/education. **Events** *Global Summit* Lisbon (Portugal) 2019, *Global Summit* Dublin (Ireland) 2018, *Global Summit* Helsinki (Finland) 2017, *Global Summit* Oxford (UK) 2016, *Global Summit* Milan (Italy) 2015. **Publications** *World PR Report* (annual).
Members National associations representing about 4,000 public relations firms in 54 countries:
Algeria, Armenia, Australia, Austria, Bahrain, Belgium, Botswana, Brazil, Bulgaria, Canada, Cyprus, Czechia, Denmark, Egypt, Eswatini, Finland, France, Georgia, Germany, Greece, Hungary, India, Iran Islamic Rep, Ireland, Italy, Jordan, Kazakhstan, Kuwait, Lebanon, Lesotho, Mexico, Morocco, Namibia, Netherlands, Nigeria, Norway, Oman, Poland, Portugal, Qatar, Romania, Russia, Saudi Arabia, Serbia, Slovakia, South Africa, Spain, Sweden, Switzerland, Tunisia, Türkiye, UK, United Arab Emirates, USA.
NGO Relations Instrumental in setting up: *Global Women in PR (GWPR, #10658)*. [2019/XM3949/**C**]

♦ International Communications Forum (ICF) 12816

Forum internationale de la communication
Chairman Angwinack, Ludgvan, Penzance, TR20 8BN, UK.
URL: http://www.icforum.org/

History 1991, UK, by William Erasmus Porter (1920-2009). Registered as a Company Limited by Guarantee in accordance with UK law. **Aims** Promote *media* ethics and *freedom of expression* and information. **Structure** Officers: Founder President; President; 5 Vice-Presidents; Executive Director; Executive Secretary; Director. **Staff** Voluntary. **Events** *Conference / Forum* Caux (Switzerland) 2014, *Conference / Forum* London (UK) 2014, *Conference / Forum* London (UK) 2008, *Conference / Forum* London (UK) 2007, *Conference* Caux (Switzerland) 2006. [2018/XM0135/**F**]

♦ International Communications Industries Association / see Audiovisual and Integrated Experience Association
♦ International Communications and Information Security Association (inactive)

♦ International Communications Volunteers (ICVolunteers) 12817

ICVolontaires – ICVoluntarios
Exec Dir PO Box 755, 1211 Geneva 4, Switzerland. T. +41228001436. Fax +41228001437. E-mail: info@icvolunteers.org.
URL: http://www.icvolunteers.org/

History 1999, Geneva (Switzerland). Adopted of a new organizational structure to become an international federation, Oct 2005. Former names and other names: *International Conference Volunteers (ICVolunteers)* – former (1999 to Oct 2005). **Aims** Be a network of skilled volunteers to support projects and local, national and international communications projects and events worldwide; create opportunities for development and commitment on personal and professional levels through *volunteerism*; through direct action and networking, support partners in implementing social and educational programmes. **Structure** Managing Board; Regional Offices. **Activities** Training/education. **Events** *International symposium on volunteering* Geneva (Switzerland) 2001. **Publications** *ICVNews Flash*. **Members** Individuals (about 15,000) in 179 countries. Membership countries not specified. **Consultative Status** Consultative status granted from: *UNESCO (#20322)* (Consultative Status). **IGO Relations** Partner of (9): *European Organization for Nuclear Research (CERN, #08108)*; *Institut de la Francophonie numérique (IFN, inactive)*; *International Telecommunication Union (ITU, #15673)*; *Organisation internationale de la Francophonie (OIF, #17809)*; *UNDP (#20292)*; *UNESCO (#20322)*; *United Nations Institute for Training and Research (UNITAR, #20576)*; *United Nations Volunteers (UNV, #20650)*; *WHO (#20950)*. Cooperates with (3): *European Commission (EC, #06633)*; *OECD (#17693)*; *United Nations Office at Geneva (UNOG, #20597)*. Associated with Department of Global Communications of the United Nations. **NGO Relations** Member of (1): *World Network for Linguistic Diversity (Maaya, #21671)*. Partner of (8): *African Academy of Languages (ACALAN, #00192)*; *Agence universitaire de La Francophonie (AUF, #00548)*; *Centre for European Volunteering (CEV, #03743)*; *CIVICUS: World Alliance for Citizen Participation (#03962)*; *Fondation des immeubles pour les organisations internationales (FIPOI)*; *International Association for Volunteer Effort (IAVE, #12260)*; *International Federation of Red Cross and Red Crescent Societies (#13526)*; *Université européenne du volontariat (UEV, see: #02978)*. [2019/XJ0406/**E**]

♦ International Communicology Institute (internationally oriented national body)

♦ International Communist Current (ICC) 12818

Courant communiste international – Corriente Comunista Internacional – Internationale Kommunistische Strömung – Corrente Comunista Internacional – Corrente Comunista Internazionale – Internationale Kommunistische Stroming (IKS) – Internationella Kommunistiska Strömningen
Contact address not obtained. E-mail: international@internationalism.org.
URL: http://world.internationalism.org/

History Jan 1975, by communist organizations in 6 countries. **Publications** Books, pamphlets.
Members Sections in 13 countries:
Belgium, France, Germany, India, Italy, Mexico, Netherlands, Spain, Sweden, Switzerland, UK, USA, Venezuela. [2012/XM1434/**F**]

♦ International Communist Esperantist Collective 12819

Collectif espérantiste communiste internationale – Internacia Komunista Esperantista Kolektivo (IKEK)
Pres BCM Box 8932, London, WC1N 3XX, UK. T. +447817379568.
URL: http://www.ikek.org/

History 1973, Austria, as *Communist Esperantist Collective – Collectif espérantiste communiste – Komunista Esperantista Kolektivo (KEK)*. **Aims** Organize communist esperantists; discuss and promote communist ideas in the esperanto language; promote esperanto in the communist and workers' movement; contribute to the linguistic debate in the communist and progressive parties. **Structure** Committee, elected at conference; Officers elected by Committee. **Finance** Subscriptions; donations. **Activities** Holds discussion forums during World Esperanto Congress; organizes annual or biennial conference. **Events** *Conference* Prague (Czech Rep) 2007, *Conference* Vilnius (Lithuania) 2005, *Conference* Lisbon (Portugal) 1996, *International conference / Conference* Vordernberg (Austria) 1988. **Publications** *Internaciisto* (6 a year). **Members** Individuals (members/subscribers) on all continents. Membership countries not specified. **NGO Relations** Member of: *Universal Esperanto Association (UEA, #20676)*. [2018/XF0980/v/**F**]

♦ International Community for Auditory Display (ICAD) 12820

Address not obtained.
URL: http://www.icad.org/

History 1994. **Aims** Act as a forum for presenting research on the use of *sound* to display data, monitor systems and provide enhanced user interfaces for *computers* and *virtual reality* systems; focus on auditory displays and the array of perception, technology and application areas that these encompass. **Structure** Board. **Languages** English. **Staff** None. **Finance** Conference financed by attendance fees and sponsorship. **Activities** Knowledge management/information dissemination; research/documentation; events/meetings. **Events** *International Conference on Auditory Display* 2022, *International Conference on Auditory Display* 2021, *Annual Conference* Newcastle upon Tyne (UK) 2019, *Annual Conference* Houghton, MI (USA) 2018, *Annual Conference* College Park, MD (USA) 2017. **Publications** *NSF Sonification Report*. Bibliography; bulletin board; conference proceedings; community E-mail list; jobs board; online dissertations; surf board. **Information Services**: Electronic fora. **Information Services** *Demonstrations Auditory Browsing (NextWAVe)*. **Members** Membership countries not specified. **NGO Relations** *European Acoustics Association (EAA, #05824)*; National Science Foundation (NSF). [2020/XF6494/**F**]

♦ International Community of Breeders of Asexually Reproduced Ornamental and Fruit Plants / see International Community of Breeders of Asexually Reproduced Ornamental and Fruit Varieties (#12821)
♦ International Community of Breeders of Asexually Reproduced Ornamental and Fruit Trees Varieties / see International Community of Breeders of Asexually Reproduced Ornamental and Fruit Varieties (#12821)

♦ International Community of Breeders of Asexually Reproduced Ornamental and Fruit Varieties 12821

Communauté internationale des obtenteurs de plantes ornementales et fruitières à reproduction asexuée (CIOPORA) – Comunidad Internacional de Fitomejoradores de Plantas Ornamentales y Frutales de Reproducción Asexuada – Internationale Gemeinschaft der Züchter Vegetativ Vermehrbarer Zier- und Obstpflanzen – Comunità Internazionale de Ottenitori di Piante Ornamentali e Fruttifere a Riproduzione Asessuata
Admin Office Diechstr 29, 20459 Hamburg, Germany. T. +494055563702. Fax +494055563703. E-mail: info@ciopora.org.
URL: http://www.ciopora.org/

History Feb 1961, Geneva (Switzerland). Founded by 18 breeders of ornamental plants. Name later changed to reflect inclusion of fruit breeders. Establishment directly connected with, and preceded, Paris Diplomatic Conference of 1961, where *International Convention for the Protection of New Varieties of Plants, 1961 (1961)* was first adopted. Former names and other names: *International Community of Breeders of Asexually Reproduced Ornamentals* – former (Feb 1961); *Communauté internationale des obtenteurs de plantes ornementales de reproduction asexuée* – former (Feb 1961); *Internationale Gemeinschaft der Züchter Vegetativ Vermehrbarer Zierpflanzen* – former (Feb 1961); *International Community of Breeders of Asexually Reproduced Ornamental and Fruit Trees Varieties* – former; *Communauté internationale des obtenteurs de plantes ornementales et fruitières de reproduction asexuée (CIOPORA)* – former; *Comunidad International de los Obtentores de Plantas Ornementales y Frutales de Reproducción Asexuada* – former; *International Community of Breeders of Asexually Reproduced Ornamental and Fruit Plants* – alias. **Aims** Develop and enhance systems of Intellectual Property (IP) Protection for plant innovation, which include Plant Breeders' Rights, Patents, Plant Patents and Trademarks; develop, improve and harmonize national and international regulations of Plant Variety Protection (PVP); establish effective IP protection systems for ornamental and fruit plant varieties worldwide. **Structure** General Assembly (annual); Board; Crop and Topic Groups; Administrative Office, headed by Secretary-General, located in Hamburg (Germany). **Languages** English, French, German, Spanish. **Finance** Members' and supporters' contributions. **Activities** Advocacy/lobbying/activism; training/education; awareness raising; events/meetings. **Events** *Annual General Meeting* Marrakech (Morocco) 2020, *Annual General Meeting* Stellenbosch (South Africa) 2019, *Annual General Meeting* Ghent (Belgium) 2018, *Annual General Assembly* Lisbon (Portugal) 2016, *Annual General Assembly* Hamburg (Germany) 2015. **Publications** *IPisodes* – newsletter. Position papers; articles; press releases.
Members Plant breeders of asexually reproduced ornamental and fruit varieties, breeder associations, patent attorneys and IP consultants in 26 countries:
Australia, Belgium, Brazil, Bulgaria, Canada, China, Colombia, Cyprus, Denmark, Ecuador, France, Germany, India, Israel, Italy, Japan, Mexico, Netherlands, New Zealand, South Africa, Spain, Switzerland, Türkiye, UK, Ukraine, USA.
IGO Relations Observer to: *Union internationale pour la protection des obtentions végétales (UPOV, #20436)*. [2021/XD4233/**D**]

♦ International Community of Breeders of Asexually Reproduced Ornamentals / see International Community of Breeders of Asexually Reproduced Ornamental and Fruit Varieties (#12821)

♦ International Community Corrections Association (ICCA) 12822

Pres 2100 Stella Court, Columbus OH 43215, USA. T. +16142528417. Fax +16142527987. E-mail: staff@iccalive.org.
URL: http://www.iccalive.org/

History 1963, USA. Former names and other names: *International Halfway House Association* – former (1963); *International Association of Residential and Community Alternatives (IARCA)* – former (Oct 1995). Registration: Start date: 1964, USA. **Aims** Promote, commission and disseminate research into evidence-based best practices in community corrections and effective management of systematic change to implement best practices. **Structure** Board of Directors of 26 members. **Languages** English. **Staff** 1.00 FTE, paid. **Finance** Members' dues. Other sources: Conference registration fees; grants from foundations and federal governments. **Activities** Projects/programmes; training/education; events/meetings. **Events** *Annual Research Conference* San Antonio, TX (USA) 2018, *Annual Research Conference* Seattle, WA (USA) 2017, *Annual Research Conference* Toronto, ON (Canada) 2016, *Annual Research Conference* Boston, MA (USA) 2015, *Annual Research Conference* Cleveland, OH (USA) 2014. **Publications** *ICCA Journal of Community Corrections* (4 a year); *Doing What Works* (51 a year) – newsletter. Series of books comprised of annual research conference papers.
Members Categories Agency; Individual; Associate; Affiliate; Corporate. Individuals and associations or agencies (mostly in USA) in 13 countries and territories:
Australia, Canada, China, Italy, Netherlands, New Zealand, Norway, Puerto Rico, Singapore, Spain, UK, USA, Virgin Is USA.
Consultative Status Consultative status granted from: *ECOSOC (#05331)* (Ros A). **IGO Relations** Associated with Department of Global Communications of the United Nations. **NGO Relations** Member of: *Alliance of NGOs on Crime Prevention and Criminal Justice (#00709)*. Affiliated with: *International Prisoners Aid Association (IPAA, inactive)*; national organizations. [2020/XF5038/**F**]

♦ International Community of Defence Industry Workers' Unions (ICDIWU) 12823

Pres 42 Leninsky Prospekt, Moscow MOSKVA, Russia, 119119. T. +7959388313. Fax +7959388923. E-mail: vprop@aport.ru.
Members Trade unions in the CIS region (membership countries not specified). **IGO Relations** *Commonwealth of Independent States (CIS, #04341)*. **NGO Relations** Member of: *General Confederation of Trade Unions (GCTU, #10108)*. [2018/XM2469/t/**D**]

♦ International Community Education Association (inactive)
♦ International Community Foundation (internationally oriented national body)

♦ International Community on Information Systems for Crisis Response and Management (ISCRAM) 12824

Registered Address Avenue des Saisons 100-102 (box30), 1050 Brussels, Belgium. E-mail: contact@iscram.org.
URL: https://iscram.org/

History First workshop organized 2004, Brussels (Belgium). Registration: Banque-Carrefour des Entreprises, No/ID: 0812.335.210, Start date: 17 Jun 2009, Belgium. **Aims** Foster a community dedicated to promoting research and development, exchange of knowledge and deployment of information systems for crisis management, including the social, technical and practical aspects of all information and communication systems used or to be used in all phases of management of emergencies, disasters and crises. **Structure** General Assembly. Board. **Activities** Events/meetings; training/education. **Events** *Annual Global conference* Omaha, NE (USA) 2023, *International Conference* Tarbes (France) 2022, *Annual World Conference* Blacksburg, VA (USA) 2021, *Annual World Conference* Blacksburg, VA (USA) 2020, *Annual World Conference* Valencia (Spain) 2019. **Publications** Conference proceedings. **NGO Relations** Cooperates with (1): *Geo-Information for Disaster Management (Gi4DM).* [2023/XM3160/C]

♦ International Community of NLP (ICNLP International) 12825

Contact Rua Helena 280, cjs 408/409, CEP 04552-050, Sao Paulo SP, 04552-050, Brazil. E-mail: info@slh.nu.
URL: http://www.icnlp.org/

History by Joseph O'Connor. **Aims** Promote standards, ethics and training requirements for the teaching and practice of neuro-linguistic programming (NLP). **NGO Relations** *International Coaching Community (ICC).* [2021/XM8255/D]

- ♦ International Community for Open Research and Education (unconfirmed)
- ♦ International Community for the Relief of Starvation and Suffering (internationally oriented national body)

♦ International Community of Women Living with HIV/AIDS (ICW) . . . 12826

Communauté internationale des femmes vivant avec le VIH/SIDA – Comunidad Internacional de Mujeres con VIH/SIDA

Global Chairperson address not obtained. E-mail: info@wlhiv.org.
URL: https://www.wlhiv.org/

History Jul 1992, Amsterdam (Netherlands). Founded during 8th International Conference on AIDS. **Aims** Raise awareness of HIV positive women's issues and promote effective action to address them; reduce the *isolation* of these women and overcome the stigma of HIV/AIDS; promote *human rights* of HIV positive women globally; empower HIV positive women to address and promote change in issues of importance to their lives. **Structure** International Steering Committee; Global Office, currently bases in Nairobi (Kenya). Independent regional networks operate autonomously. Networks include: *International Community of Women living with HIV Eastern Africa (ICWEA, #12827).* **Finance** Donors include: *Department for International Development (DFID, inactive); Ford Foundation (#09858); Global Fund for Women (GFW, #10384); Joint United Nations Programme on HIV/AIDS (UNAIDS, #16149); Norwegian Agency for Development Cooperation (Norad); WHO (#20950).* **Activities** Knowledge management/information dissemination; networking/liaising; events/meeting; advocacy/lobbying/activism. **Events** *International AIDS conference* Washington, DC (USA) 2012, *International AIDS conference* Vienna (Austria) 2010, *International AIDS conference* Mexico City (Mexico) 2008, *International women summit on HIV and AIDS* Nairobi (Kenya) 2007, *International AIDS Conference* Toronto, ON (Canada) 2006. **Publications** *ICW News* (4 a year) – newsletter. *A Positive Woman's Survival Kit* (1999) in English, French, Spanish. Biennial Report in English/French/Spanish; reports. Information Services: Database of HIV positive women in ICW network.

Members Individuals in 84 countries and territories:
Argentina, Australia, Austria, Bahamas, Bangladesh, Barbados, Belgium, Botswana, Brazil, Bulgaria, Burkina Faso, Burundi, Cameroon, Canada, Central African Rep, Chile, Colombia, Congo Brazzaville, Congo DR, Côte d'Ivoire, Cuba, Cyprus, Czech Rep, Denmark, Dominican Rep, Ecuador, Egypt, Estonia, Eswatini, Fiji, Finland, France, Germany, Ghana, Greece, Guam, Hawaii, Hong Kong, Hungary, Iceland, India, Indonesia, Ireland, Israel, Italy, Jamaica, Japan, Kenya, Latvia, Liechtenstein, Lithuania, Malawi, Malaysia, Mexico, Morocco, Mozambique, Namibia, Nepal, Netherlands, New Zealand, Nicaragua, Nigeria, Norway, Pakistan, Philippines, Poland, Portugal, Russia, Senegal, Singapore, South Africa, Spain, Suriname, Sweden, Switzerland, Tanzania UR, Thailand, Trinidad-Tobago, Uganda, UK, Ukraine, USA, Zambia, Zimbabwe.

IGO Relations *European Commission (EC, #06633).* **NGO Relations** Member of: *ATHENA Network (ATHENA, #03004); International Peace Bureau (IPB, #14535); Robert Carr civil society Networks Fund (RCNF, #18956). Global Coalition on Women and AIDS (GCWA, #10297); International Treatment Preparedness Coalition (ITPC, #15729).* Latin America Chapter is partner of: *Horizontal Technical Cooperation Group of Latin America and the Caribbean on HIV/AIDS (HTGC, #10945).* Instrumental in setting up: *Mas Paz Menos SIDA Fundación (+ Paz – sida Fundación, #16594).* Works on greater involvement of people living with HIV/AIDS together with: *Global Health Council (GHC, #10402); Global Network of People Living with HIV/AIDS (GNP+, #10494); ICASO (#11040).* [2022/XF2697/v/F]

♦ International Community of Women living with HIV Eastern Africa (ICWEA) 12827

Contact PO Box 32252, Kampala, Uganda. T. +256414531913. Fax +256414533341. E-mail: admin@icwea.org.
Street Address Plot 1106 Ssenge Road, Wakiso District, Kampala, Uganda.
URL: http://www.icwea.org/

History Created by group of HIV positive women attending 8th International Conference on AIDS, Jul 1992, Amsterdam (Netherlands). Properly set up Feb 2005. Became and autonomous organization of *International Community of Women Living with HIV/AIDS (ICW, #12826),* 2007. Registered in accordance with the laws of Uganda, 2009. Also referred to as *ICW Eastern Africa.* **Aims** Promote voices of women living with HIV; advocate for changes that improve their lives. **Structure** General Assembly; Board. Special Interest Groups. **Languages** English, French, Swahili. **Staff** 14.00 FTE, paid. **Finance** Donations, including from: *Commonwealth Foundation (CF, #04330); UN Women (#20724).* **Activities** Advocacy/lobbying/activism; projects/programmes. **Publications** Reports; toolkits; policy briefs; press statements; position papers.

Members Full in 5 countries:
Burundi, Kenya, Rwanda, Tanzania UR, Uganda.

NGO Relations Partner with: *Center for Health, Human Rights and Development (CEHURD);* national associations. [2017.03.13/XJ9331/E]

♦ International Companion Animal Management Coalition (ICAM) . . . 12828

Registered Address 4 Westcroft, Comberton, Cambridge, CB23 7EJ, UK. E-mail: info@icam-coalition.org.
URL: https://www.icam-coalition.org/

History 2006. Registration: Charity Commission, No/ID: 1192921, England and Wales. **Aims** Share ideas and data; discuss issues relevant to population management and welfare; agree definitions and hence improve understanding; provide guidance as a collegial and cohesive group. **Activities** Events/meetings; guidance/assistance/consulting; knowledge management/information dissemination. **Events** *International Conference on Dog Population Management* Mombasa (Kenya) 2019, *International Conference on Dog Population Management* Istanbul (Turkey) 2015, *International Conference on Dog Population Management* York (UK) 2012.

Members Organizations (8):
Battersea; *Dogs Trust Worldwide; Global Alliance for Rabies Control (GARC); International Cat Care (iCatCare);* RSPCA International; *Vier Pfoten International (#20776); World Animal Protection (#21092); World Small Animal Veterinary Association (WSAVA, #21795).* [2020/AA2385/y/C]

- ♦ International Company for the Development of Combined Transport and of Controlled-Temperature Transport (inactive)
- ♦ International and Comparative Librarianship Group of the Library Association / see International Library and Information Group (#14037)

♦ International Comparative Literature Association (ICLA) 12829

Association internationale de littérature comparée (AILC)

Pres 17 rue de la Sorbonne, 75005 Paris, France.
Sec address not obtained.
URL: http://ailc-icla.org/

History Founded at congress of *International Federation for Modern Languages and Literatures (#13480),* Sep 1954, Oxford (UK). Statutes adopted during General Assembly, 28 Sep 1955, Venice (Italy); modified: 5 Sep 1964, Fribourg (Switzerland); 5 Sep 1970, Bordeaux (France); 20 Aug 1979, Innsbruck (Austria); 28 Aug 1982, New York NY (USA); 20 Aug 1985, Paris (France); 1997, Leiden (Netherlands); 2016, Vienna (Austria); 28 July 2022, Tbilisi (Georgia). Registration: French Ministerial Decree, Start date: 19 Dec 1995, France; Préfecture de Paris, au Registre National des Associations, No/ID: W751032865, Start date: 3 Jan 1956. **Aims** Sponsor research in comparative literature with the goal of furthering international exchange and cooperation among comparatists. **Structure** General Assembly (every 3 years, during Congress); Executive Council; Executive Committee; Honorary Committee; Standing Committees, Advisory Committees and Commissions. Meetings open to non-members on approval of Bureau. **Languages** English, French. **Staff** Voluntary. **Finance** Sources: grants; members' dues. **Activities** Events/meetings; knowledge management/information dissemination; research/documentation. **Events** *International Congress* Seoul (Korea Rep) 2025, *International Congress* Tbilisi (Georgia) 2022, *Triennial Congress* Macau (Macau) 2019, *Triennial Congress* Vienna (Austria) 2016, *Triennial Congress* Paris (France) 2013. **Publications** *Literary Research/Recherches littéraires* (annual). *Histoire comparée des littératures en langues européennes. Research Directory of the International Comparative Literature Association* (1993); *Théorie littéraire: Problèmes et perspectives* (1989); *Renewals in the Theory of Literary History/Renouvellements dans la théorie de l'histoire littérair, Ottawa* (1984). Congress proceedings.

Members National or Regional Associations; individuals. Member and Supporting Associations in 32 countries and territories:
Azerbaijan, Brazil, Bulgaria, Canada, China, Croatia, Czechia, Egypt, Estonia, France, Georgia, Germany, Greece, Hungary, India, Italy, Japan, Korea Rep, Luxembourg, Morocco, North Macedonia, Portugal, Romania, Slovakia, Slovenia, South Africa, Spain, Switzerland, Taiwan, UK, Ukraine, USA.

IGO Relations *UNESCO (#20322).* **NGO Relations** Member of (1): *International Federation for Modern Languages and Literatures (#13480)* (FILLM). [2023.02.10/XB1644/B]

♦ International Comparative Policy Analysis Forum (ICPA-Forum) . . . 12830

Conatact address not obtained. E-mail: courtneyscottjcpaicpa@gmail.com.
URL: https://www.tandfonline.com/toc/fcpa20/current

Aims Promote the field of comparative policy analysis studies. **Structure** Board. **Finance** Sponsorship. **Activities** Workshops. **Events** *Workshop* Sydney, NSW (Australia) 2012. **Publications** *Journal of Comparative Policy Analysis (JCPA)* (5 a year). [2020.01.15/XJ7773/E]

- ♦ International Comparative Virology Organization (inactive)

♦ International Competence Network for Tourism Research and Education (ICNT) 12831

Address not obtained.
URL: http://icnt.weebly.com/

History Heide, Germany. **Activities** Organizes annual meetings. **Events** *Conference* Potchefstroom (South Africa) 2018, *Conference* Auckland (New Zealand) 2017, *Conference* Heide (Germany) 2016, *Conference* Sheffield (UK) 2015, *Conference* Mexico City (Mexico) 2014. [2018/XJ5388/F]

♦ International Competition Network (ICN) 12832

Réseau international de la concurrence

Chairman Steering Group c/o Bundeskartellamt, Kaiser Friedrich Strasse 16, 53113 Bonn, Germany. E-mail: icn-chair@bundeskartellamt.bund.de.
Secretariat address not obtained. E-mail: ic.icnsecretariatcb-bc.ic@canada.ca.
URL: http://www.internationalcompetitionnetwork.org/

Aims Advocate adoption of superior standards and procedures in competition policy around the world; formulate proposals for procedural and substantive convergence; seek to facilitate effective international cooperation to benefit member agencies, consumers and economies. **Structure** Steering Group; Working Groups; Secretariat. A virtual organization. **Languages** English. **Activities** Advocacy/lobbying/activism; standards/guidelines; networking/liaising; events/meetings. **Events** *Annual Conference* Berlin (Germany) 2022, *Annual Conference* Budapest (Hungary) 2021, *Cartel Workshop* Lisbon (Portugal) 2021, *Annual Conference* Bonn (Germany) 2020, *Annual Conference* Cartagena de Indias (Colombia) 2019. **Publications** Recommendations. **Members** Member agencies from over 135 jurisdictions. Membership countries not specified. **IGO Relations** *OECD (#17693); UNCTAD (#20285).* [2019.06.24/XF6739/F]

♦ International Complement Society 12833

Main Office 9037 Ron Den Ln, Windermere FL 34786-8328, USA. E-mail: ics@complement.org.
URL: http://www.complement.org/

History Jul 2000. **Aims** Promote advances of complement research and development through by encouraging cooperative educational programmes, clinical applications and professional standards. **Structure** Board, including President, President-Elect, Immediate Past-President, Secretary, Treasurer and 8 Councillors. **Languages** English. **Staff** Voluntary. **Finance** Members' dues. **Activities** Organizes meetings and workshops; writes and publishes articles in various journals. **Events** *Biennial International Complement Workshop* Newcastle upon Tyne (UK) 2023, *Biennial International Complement Workshop* 2021, *Biennial International Complement Workshop* Berlin (Germany) 2020, *Biennial International Complement Workshop* Santa Fe, NM (USA) 2018, *Biennial International Complement Workshop* Kanazawa (Japan) 2016.

Members Individuals in 38 countries:
Argentina, Australia, Austria, Belgium, Brazil, Bulgaria, Canada, China, Colombia, Czechia, Denmark, Finland, France, Germany, Greece, Hungary, Iceland, India, Ireland, Israel, Italy, Japan, Mexico, Netherlands, New Zealand, Norway, Poland, Portugal, Romania, Russia, Singapore, South Africa, Spain, Sweden, Switzerland, Türkiye, UK, USA.

NGO Relations Member of: *Federation of Clinical Immunology Societies (FOCIS, #09472).* [2017/XD8911/v/D]

- ♦ International Complex for Research and Higher Education in Agriculture, Montpellier / see Agropolis International
- ♦ International Compliance Association (internationally oriented national body)
- ♦ International Compressed Air and Allied Machinery Committee / see International Compressor Applications And Machinery Committee (#12834)

♦ International Compressor Applications And Machinery Committee (ICAAMC) 12834

Contact address not obtained. E-mail: office@icaamc.org.
URL: http://www.icaamc.org/

History Former names and other names: *International Compressed Air and Allied Machinery Committee (ICAAMC)* – former. **Aims** Promote a spirit of cooperation amongst manufacturers in such a way that free and legal competition is preserved; further the application of compressors and pneumatic tools to serve customers in the most optimal way. **Structure** Plenary Meeting (at least annually); Executive Committee; Secretariat. Sub-Committees; Working Groups. **Activities** Events/meetings. **Events** *Conference* Germany 2022, *Conference* Hiroshima (Japan) 2020, *Conference* Stockholm (Sweden) 2017, *Conference* Limassol (Cyprus) 2013, *Conference* Vienna (Austria) 2012. [2020.08.18/XJ6699/C]

♦ International Compumag Society (ICS) 12835

Sec/Treas ECS-EPE Group, Univ of Southampton, Highfield, Southampton, SO17 1BJ, UK. T. +442380593448. Fax +442380593709.
URL: http://www.compumag.org/wp/

History 1993. **Aims** Advance and disseminate knowledge about the application of *computer* methods to field problems having significant electric, magnetic or electromagnetic components; encourage improvements in methods for field computation as defined above and in their verification and validation; promote information exchange. **Structure** Board (meets at least annually); Executive Committee. **Languages** English. **Staff** Voluntary. **Finance** Sources: members' dues. **Activities** Events/meetings; knowledge management/information dissemination. Database on fertilizers for the Arab region. **Events** *COMPUMAG : Conference of Electromagnetic Fields* Cancún (Mexico) 2027, *COMPUMAG : Conference of Electromagnetic Fields* Naples (Italy) 2025, *COMPUMAG : Conference of Electromagnetic Fields* Kyoto (Japan) 2023, *COMPUMAG : Conference of Electromagnetic Fields* Cancún (Mexico) 2022, *COMPUMAG : Conference of Electromagnetic Fields* Paris (France) 2019. **Publications** *ICS Newsletter* (3 a year). **Information Services** *Electronic Bulletin Board Service – Electromagnetic Forum.*

Members Full: individuals (600) in 40 countries and territories:
Australia, Austria, Belgium, Brazil, Bulgaria, Canada, China, Croatia, Czechia, Finland, France, Germany, Greece, Hong Kong, Hungary, India, Ireland, Israel, Italy, Japan, Korea Rep, Malaysia, Netherlands, New Zealand, North Macedonia, Poland, Portugal, Romania, Russia, Singapore, Slovakia, Slovenia, Spain, Sweden, Switzerland, Taiwan, Türkiye, UK, Ukraine, USA.
IGO Relations None. **NGO Relations** None. [2023.02.14/XD7412/v/**D**]

♦ International Computer Chess Association / see International Computer Games Association (#12836)

♦ International Computer Games Association (ICGA) 12836

Sec-Treas Research Center for Entertainment Science, JAIST, 1-1 Asahidai, Nomi, Ishikawa, 923-1292 Japan. E-mail: info@icga.org.
Pres Dept of Computing Science, Univ of Alberta, 2-32 Athabasca Hall, Edmonton AB T6G 2E8, Canada.
URL: http://www.icga.org/

History 1977. Former names and other names: *International Computer Chess Association (ICCA)* – former. **Aims** Strengthen ties and promote cooperation among researchers interested in *artificial intelligence* algorithms applied to strategy games; represent computer game researchers, developers and home hobbyists to computer science organizations; support organizations and tournament organizers with an interest in artificial intelligence and strategy games. **Structure** Board. **Languages** English. **Staff** 11.00 FTE, voluntary. **Finance** Sources: members' dues. **Activities** Events/meetings. **Events** *Conference on Advances in Computer Games* 2022, *Conference on Advances in Computer Games* 2021, *Conference on Computers and Games* Santiago de Compostela (Spain) 2020, *Conference on Advances in Computer Games* Macau (Macau) 2019, *Conference on Advances in Computer Games* Leiden (Netherlands) 2017. **Publications** *International Computer Games Association (ICGA) Journal* (4 a year). **Members** Individual; University; Industrial. Over 100 members in over 30 countries and territories. Membership countries not specified. [2022.07.08/XD1594/**C**]

♦ International Computer Music Association (ICMA) 12837

Admin Dir c/o Housing IT, 1318 Markley Hall, 1503 Washington Heights, Ann Arbor MI 48109-2015, USA. E-mail: icma@umich.edu.
URL: http://www.computermusic.org/

History 1979. Registration: Start date: 1980, USA, California. **Aims** Serve composers, computer software and hardware developers, researchers and musicians interested in the integration of music and technology. **Structure** Board of Directors. **Finance** Members' dues. Publications. **Activities** Networking/liaising; research/documentation; events/meetings; awards/prizes/competitions. **Events** *International Computer Music Conference* Limerick (Ireland) 2022, *International Computer Music Conference* Santiago (Chile) 2021, *International Computer Music Conference* 2020, *International Computer Music Conference* New York, NY (USA) 2019, *Annual Conference* Daegu (Korea Rep) 2018. **Publications** *Array* – newsletter. *ICMA Recording Series*. Membership Directory – online. Information Services: Database of all musical works performed at ICMC and/or commissioned by ICMA.

Members Individual; Student; Senior; Sustaining; Non-profit Institutional; Corporate: involved in the technical, creative and performance aspects of computer music. Members in 69 countries and territories:
Argentina, Austria, Belgium, Belize, Brazil, Canada, Chile, China, Colombia, Cuba, Czechia, Denmark, Dominica, Dominican Rep, Finland, France, Germany, Greece, Guatemala, Honduras, Hong Kong, Hungary, Iceland, India, Indonesia, Iraq, Ireland, Israel, Italy, Japan, Jordan, Korea DPR, Laos, Lebanon, Malaysia, Malta, Mexico, Mongolia, Nepal, Netherlands, New Zealand, North Macedonia, Norway, Pakistan, Papua New Guinea, Paraguay, Philippines, Poland, Portugal, Russia, Samoa, Singapore, Spain, Sri Lanka, Suriname, Sweden, Switzerland, Syrian AR, Taiwan, Thailand, Trinidad-Tobago, Türkiye, UK, Uruguay, USA, Venezuela, Vietnam. [2021/XF5838/**F**]

♦ International Computer Room Experts Association (ICREA) 12838

Contact Vallarta No 7, Col Barrio La Concepción Coyacan CP 04020, Mexico City CDMX, Mexico. T. +525556599657 – +525556587650. E-mail: paulina@icrea-international.org.
URL: http://www.icrea-international.org/

History 1999, Mexico City (Mexico). Registered in accordance with Mexican law. **Aims** Create and implement standards and best practices for design, construction, management, operation, maintenance, acquisition and installation of infrastructure for information technology environments. **Structure** General Assembly; Board of Directors. **Languages** English, Spanish. **Finance** Sources: members' dues. **Activities** Awards/prizes/competitions; certification/accreditation; events/meetings; standards/guidelines; training/education.
Members Chapters in 24 countries:
Argentina, Bolivia, Brazil, Canada, Chile, Colombia, Costa Rica, Ecuador, El Salvador, Guatemala, Honduras, Italy, Mexico, Nicaragua, Panama, Peru, Philippines, Singapore, Spain, Switzerland, UK, Uruguay, USA, Venezuela. [2019.07.08/XM5570/**C**]

♦ International Computer Science Conventions (internationally oriented national body)

♦ International Computing Centre (ICC) 12839

Centre international de calcul (CIC)

Dir Palais des Nations, 1211 Geneva 10, Switzerland. T. +41229291411. Fax +41229291412. E-mail: business@unicc.org – servicedesk@unicc.org.
URL: http://www.unicc.org/

History 1 Mar 1971, Geneva (Switzerland). Founded by *United Nations (UN, #20515)*, *UNDP (#20292)* and *WHO (#20950)*. Created as an inter-organization facility pursuant to General Assembly Resolution 2741 (XXV), 17 Dec 1970. Former names and other names: *United Nations International Computing Centre (UNICC)* – alias. **Aims** Provide shared, trusted services and digital business solutions; deliver cost-effective, highly available and secure computer systems and network services. **Structure** Management Committee (meeting twice a year); Executive Committee; UNICC Transformation Team. Headquarters in Geneva (Switzerland). Offices in: Valencia (Spain); New York NY (USA); Brindisi (Italy); Rome (Italy). **Languages** English, French. **Staff** 500.00 FTE, paid. **Finance** Self-funding. Operates on the basis of recovering the full cost of service provision. **Activities** Guidance/assistance/consulting; knowledge management/information dissemination; training/education. **Publications** *UNICC Newsletter*. *UNICC Director's Report 2018-2019*.
IGO Relations Partners:
- *OECD (#17693)*;
- *OPEC Fund for International Development (OFID, #17745)*;
- *Organisation for the Prohibition of Chemical Weapons (OPCW, #17823)*;
- *Organization for Security and Cooperation in Europe (OSCE, #17887)*;
- *Special Tribunal for Lebanon (STL, #19911)*;
- *Joint United Nations Programme on HIV/AIDS (UNAIDS, #16149)*;
- *Comprehensive Nuclear-Test-Ban Treaty Organization (CTBTO, #04420)*;
- *Green Climate Fund (GCF, #10714)*;
- *Global Green Growth Institute (GGGI, #10392)*;
- *International Civil Aviation Organization (ICAO, #12581)*;
- *International Court of Justice (ICJ, #13098)*;
- *International Centre for Migration Policy Development (ICMPD, #12503)*;
- *International Organization for Migration (IOM, #14454)*;
- *FAO (#09260)*;
- *ILO (#11123)*;
- *International Atomic Energy Agency (IAEA, #12294)*;
- *International Bank for Reconstruction and Development (IBRD, #12317)* (World Bank);
- *International Fund for Agricultural Development (IFAD, #13692)*;
- *International Maritime Organization (IMO, #14102)*;
- *International Monetary Fund (IMF, #14180)*;
- *International Telecommunication Union (ITU, #15673)*;
- *International Trade Centre (ITC, #15703)*;
- *Office of the United Nations High Commissioner for Human Rights (OHCHR, #17697)*;
- *Pan American Health Organization (PAHO, #18108)*;
- *Preparatory Commission for the Comprehensive Nuclear-Test-Ban Treaty Organization (CTBTO, #18482)*;
- *Secretariat of the United Nations Convention to Combat Desertification (Secretariat of the UNCCD, #19208)*;
- *United Nations Economic Commission for Africa (ECA, #20554)*;
- *UNIDO (#20336)*;
- *United Nations Institute for Training and Research (UNITAR, #20576)*;
- *United Nations Office at Vienna (UNOV, #20604)*;
- *Universal Postal Union (UPU, #20682)*;
- *World Tourism Organization (UNWTO, #21861)*;
- *UNEP (#20299)*;
- *UN Women (#20724)*;
- *UNCTAD (#20285)*;
- *UNDP (#20292)*;
- *UNESCO (#20322)*;
- *UNHCR (#20327)*;
- *UNICEF (#20332)*;
- *United Nations (UN, #20515)*;
- *United Nations Economic Commission for Europe (UNECE, #20555)*;
- *United Nations Framework Convention on Climate Change (UNFCCC, 1992)*;
- *United Nations Joint Staff Pension Fund (UNJSPF, #20581)*;
- *United Nations Office for the Coordination of Humanitarian Affairs (OCHA, #20593)*;
- *United Nations Office at Geneva (UNOG, #20597)*;
- *United Nations Office for Project Services (UNOPS, #20602)*;
- *United Nations Population Fund (UNFPA, #20612)*;
- *United Nations Relief and Works Agency for Palestine Refugees in the Near East (UNRWA, #20622)*;
- *United Nations System Chief Executives Board for Coordination (CEB, #20636)*;
- *United Nations Volunteers (UNV, #20650)*;
- *WHO (#20950)*;
- *World Food Programme (WFP, #21510)*;
- *World Intellectual Property Organization (WIPO, #21593)*;
- *World Meteorological Organization (WMO, #21649)*.

NGO Relations Partner of (3): *Diplo Foundation*; *International Committee of the Red Cross (ICRC, #12799)*; *International Federation of Red Cross and Red Crescent Societies (#13526)*. [2022/XE5305/**E***]

♦ International Concealed Carry Federation (internationally oriented national body)
♦ International Concentration Camp Committee (no recent information)

♦ International Confectionery Association (ICA) 12840

Main Office c/o CAOBISCO, Ave des Nerviens 9-31, 1040 Brussels, Belgium.

History 31 Jan 1986, Brussels (Belgium), on merger of *International Office of Cocoa and Chocolate (IOCC, inactive)*, set up 8 Sep 1930, Antwerp (Belgium), as *'International Office of Chocolate and Cocoa Manufacturers'*, and *International Sugar Confectionery Manufacturers Association (ISCMA, inactive)*, formed 13 Apr 1953, Paris (France). Statutes adopted 2 Jun 1994, Capri (Italy), when focus redefined as a group of regional members rather than countries. Name changed to *International Office of Cocoa, Chocolate and Sugar Confectionery – Office international du cacao, du chocolat et de la confiserie (OICCC)*. Present name adopted 2002. Registered in accordance with Belgian law. **Aims** Encourage scientific research to further development of the industry; safeguard worldwide interests of members and consumers; maintain a position as recognized authority on the industry, particularly in scientific, technical, statistical and health fields. **Structure** General Assembly (annual); Executive Council, comprising 2 accredited representatives of each member. **Languages** English. **Finance** Sources: sale of publications. **Activities** Events/meetings; monitoring/evaluation; publishing activities; research/documentation. **Events** *The sweet future – our consumers, our supplies, our new markets* Cologne (Germany) 1999, *How sweet is the future? – A global view of the opportunities and challenges for the confectionery industry as it moves into the 21st century* Cologne (Germany) 1996, *Conference* Capri (Italy) 1994, *General Assembly* Helsinki (Finland) 1993, *Conference* Sydney, NSW (Australia) 1992. **Publications** *Cocoa Archives*; *IOCCC Analytical Methods*; *IOCCC Annual Statistical Bulletin* – worldwide production and consumption. *Hazard Analysis Critical Control Point (HACCP)* – reference material; *Hygiene and Food Safety Best Practice (GMP)* – reference material. Congress proceedings; nutrition factsheets.
Members Organizations in 31 countries:
Australia, Austria, Belgium, Brazil, Canada, Cyprus, Czechia, Denmark, Estonia, Finland, France, Germany, Greece, Hungary, Ireland, Italy, Japan, Latvia, Lithuania, Luxembourg, Malta, Mexico, Netherlands, Poland, Portugal, Slovakia, Slovenia, Spain, Sweden, UK, USA.
Regional groups representing the industry (2):
Association of the Chocolate, Biscuit and Confectionery Industries of the EU (CAOBISCO, #02427); National Confectioners Association (NCA), USA.
IGO Relations Participates as observer in the activities of: *Codex Alimentarius Commission (CAC, #04081)*. **NGO Relations** Contacts with trade organizations in relevant fields. In liaison with technical committees of: *International Organization for Standardization (ISO, #14473)*. Works with: *International Chewing Gum Association (ICGA, #12545)*. [2017/XC2294/y/**C**]

♦ International Confederation of Accordionists (ICA) 12841

Confédération Internationale des Accordéonistes (CIA)

SG Kyrösselänkatu 3, FI-39500 Ikaalinen, Finland. T. +35834400221. Fax +35834589071. E-mail: secretariat_cia@harmonikkaliitto.net.
URL: http://accordions.com/cia/

History 1935, Paris (France), with the title *Association internationale des accordéonistes*. From May 1948, Lausanne (Switzerland), referred to as *Confédération mondiale de l'accordéon (CMA)*. **Aims** Raise the status of the accordion in the world of *music* generally; encourage composers to write original music for the instrument and manufacturers to improve and widen the scope of the instrument itself; create and develop friendly and cooperative relations between accordion players of every nationality; encourage international exchange of cultural, musical and artistic experience. **Structure** General Assembly (annual); Executive Committee of 8 members. **Languages** English, French. **Staff** 1.00 FTE, paid. **Finance** Sources: members' dues. Other sources: Entry fee for competitions. **Activities** Organizes: annual world championship – *'Coupe mondiale'*; conferences on the musical development of the accordion and its literature. **Events** *Winter Congress* Kungsbacka (Sweden) 2022, *Winter Congress* Basel (Switzerland) 2021, *Winter Congress* Prague (Czechia) 2020, *Winter Congress* Tallinn (Estonia) 2019, *Winter Congress* Kokkola (Finland) 2018. **Publications** *Bulletin de la CIA* (annual).
Members Associations in 28 countries:
Australia, Austria, Bosnia-Herzegovina, Brazil, Bulgaria, China, Croatia, Denmark, Estonia, Finland, France, Germany, Italy, Luxembourg, Netherlands, New Zealand, North Macedonia, Norway, Poland, Portugal, Serbia, Slovakia, Spain, Sweden, Switzerland, UK, USA, Vietnam.
NGO Relations Member of: *European Music Council (EMC, #07837)*; *International Music Council (IMC, #14199)*. [2020/XC1652/**C**]

♦ International Confederation for the Advancement of Behavioral Economics and Economic Psychology (ICABEEP) 12842

Chairman Guilford Glazer Faculty of Business and Management, The Marcus Family Campus, Ben-Gurion Univ of the Negev, PO Box 653, 84105 Beersheba, Israel. T. +972546626077.
URL: http://iarep.org/ICABEEP.htm

History Founded 2009, by *International Association for Research in Economic Psychology (IAREP, #12132)* and Society for the Advancement of Behavioral Economics (SABE). **Structure** Executive Committee of 6 members. [2015.11.29/XJ7310/**C**]

♦ International Confederation of Agricultural Cooperative Societies (inactive)
♦ International Confederation for Agricultural Credit (#04560)
♦ International Confederation of Agriculture (inactive)

♦ International Confederation of Alcohol, Tobacco and other Drug Research Associations (ICARA) 12843

Contact address not obtained.
URL: https://www.icara.info

History Also referred to as *International Confederation of ATOD Research Associations*. Registered in accordance with Finnish law. **Aims** Promote in all nations the scientific understanding of addiction and related problems linked to psychoactive substances. **Structure** General Assembly; Board. **Finance** Sources: members' dues. **Activities** Events/meetings; knowledge management/information dissemination; research/documentation. **Events** *Annual Meeting* 2021, *Annual Meeting* Prague (Czechia) 2018, *Annual Meeting* Washington, DC (USA) 2017, *Annual Meeting* Windsor (UK) 2016, *Annual Meeting* Budapest (Hungary) 2015. **Members** Full; Affiliate. Membership countries not specified. Included in the above, 4 organizations listed in this Yearbook:
Centre for Research and Information on Substance (CRISA); *International Network on Brief Interventions for Alcohol and Other Drugs (INEBRIA, #14236)*; *International Society of Addiction Journal Editors (ISAJE, #14895)*; *Substance Abuse Librarians and Information Specialists (SALIS, #20028)*. [2015/XM4252/**C**]

♦ International Confederation Apostolic Union of Clergy 12844

Confederazione Internazionale Unione Apostolica del Clero (UACI)

International Pres Via Alberico II 4, 00193 Rome RM, Italy. T. +39668806737. Fax +39668803183. E-mail: unioapostolica@gmail.com.
URL: http://www.uac-int.org/

History 26 Aug 1862, Paris (France), as *Apostolic Union of Secular Presbyters – Unione Apostolica dei Presbiteri Secolari – Unionis Apostolicae Sacerdotum Saecularium.* Received first Pontifical recognition, 31 May 1880; further Pontifical recognition by Pope Benedict XI and denomination as *Apostolic Union of Diocesan Presbyters – Unione Apostolica dei Presbiteri Diocesani*, 17 Apr 1921. Name changed to *Apostolic Union of Clergy – Union apostolique du clergé – Unione Apostolica del Clero (UAC)* in 1975. Most recent recognition and present name adopted, 18 Oct 1995, when recognized by the Italian state. Recent statutes recognized by Clergy Congregation, 9 Apr 1998; updated 2007. **Aims** As an association of diocesan ordained ministers (bishops, presbyters and deacons) in the diocesan presbytery: help one another in acquiring personal sanctification for an efficient exercise of their ministry and to live in fraternal communion our diocesan spirituality proper of the diocesan clergy; help ordained ministers. **Structure** International Assembly (every 5 years, in Rome, Italy). Organized in 3 levels: (1) International level – International Confederation of Diocesan Unions of Clergy, Rome (Italy) and including International President, International Treasurer, International Secretary, Seat Director and International Council; (2) different Catholic dioceses Unions with Diocesan Director, Diocesan Treasurer and Secretary; (3) national level – Unions create a national AUC with Treasurer, national Secretary and Councillors. **Languages** English, French, German, Italian, Portuguese, Spanish. **Finance** Members' dues (annual): euro 8. Budget (annual): euro 24,000. **Activities** Organizes: visits to animate AUC members and serve in other Dioceses training for animators for the Clergy's pastoral; retreats for presbyters and deacons; other services. **Events** *General Assembly* 2012, *Assembly* Rome (Italy) 2007. **Publications** *Notitiae Unionis Apostolicae Cleri* (4 a year) in English, French, French, German, Italian, Portuguese, Spanish; *Brothers and Servers* in English, French, Italian, Portuguese, Spanish; *Disciples and Pastors* in English, French, Italian, Portuguese, Spanish.

Members Ordained Diocesan Ministers (Bishops, Priests and Deacons), 10,000 individuals in 66 countries and territories:
Angola, Argentina, Austria, Bangladesh, Belgium, Benin, Bolivia, Brazil, Burkina Faso, Burundi, Cameroon, Central African Rep, Chad, Chile, Colombia, Congo Brazzaville, Congo DR, Costa Rica, Côte d'Ivoire, Cuba, Dominican Rep, Equatorial Guinea, France, Gabon, Germany, Ghana, Greece, Guatemala, Guinea, Guinea-Bissau, Haiti, Honduras, Hungary, India, Indonesia, Kenya, Lebanon, Luxembourg, Madagascar, Mali, Malta, Mexico, Mozambique, Myanmar, Nepal, Nigeria, Pakistan, Panama, Papua New Guinea, Paraguay, Peru, Philippines, Poland, Portugal, Puerto Rico, Rwanda, Senegal, Spain, Sri Lanka, Sudan, Switzerland, Tanzania UR, Togo, Uganda, Uruguay, Venezuela. [2018/XF5640/F]

♦ International Confederation of Arab Trade Unions (ICATU) 12845

Confédération internationale des syndicats arabes (CISA)

SG PO Box 3225, Sahat Al-Tahrir, Damascus, Syrian AR. T. +963114444974. Fax +963114420323. E-mail: icatu-cisa@hotmail.com.
URL: http://www.wftucentral.org/tag/icatu-en/

History Mar 1956, Damascus (Syrian AR). **Aims** Regroup trade union organizations of Arab working people into one central confederation. **Structure** General Congress (every 4 years); General Council; Specialized Departments; General Secretariat, headed by Secretary General. **Languages** Arabic. **Staff** Paid. **Finance** National organizations' contributions. **Events** *International trade union symposium* Athens (Greece) 2008, *Congress* Damascus (Syrian AR) 2004, *Congress* Damascus (Syrian AR) 1999, *Congress* Tunis (Tunisia) 1994, *Congress* Tunisia 1994. **Publications** *Al Amal Al Arab* (12 a year).

Members National trade unions, totalling over 40 million workers, in 18 countries:
Algeria, Bahrain, Djibouti, Egypt, Iraq, Jordan, Kuwait, Lebanon, Libya, Mauritania, Morocco, Oman, Palestine, Somalia, Sudan, Syrian AR, Tunisia, Yemen.

Affiliate member organizations (Arab professional unions) (2):
Arab Federation of Transport Workers (AFTW, no recent information); Fédération arabe des travailleurs des institutions métallurgiques, mécaniques et électriques (no recent information).

Consultative Status Consultative status granted from: *ILO (#11123)* (Regional). **NGO Relations** Proposed setting up: *Arab Centre for Trade Union Rights and Freedoms, Damascus (ACTURF, no recent information).* [2018.07.25/XD1655/t/D]

♦ International Confederation of Architectural Museums (ICAM) 12846

Confédération internationale des musées d'architecture

Pres Historic Environment Scotland, Longmore House, Salisbury Place, Edinburgh, EH9 1SH, UK.
SG Vlaams Architectuurinstituut, Jan Van Rijswijcklaan 155, 2018 Antwerp, Belgium.
URL: http://www.icam-web.org/

History 22 Aug 1979, Helsinki (Finland), when Charter was formulated. **Aims** Foster links between those interested in promoting better understanding of architecture. **Structure** General Assembly; Executive Committee. **Languages** English. **Staff** None. **Finance** Sources: members' dues. **Activities** Events/meetings; knowledge management/information dissemination; networking/liaising. **Events** *Biennial Congress* Munich (Germany) 2021, *Biennial Congress* Munich (Germany) 2020, *Biennial Congress* Copenhagen (Denmark) 2018, *Biennial Congress* Ljubljana (Slovenia) 2016, *Biennial Congress* Montréal, QC (Canada) 2014. **Publications** *Icamprint* (every 2 years).

Members Museums of architecture; similar institutions concerned with promoting architecture and architectural history, associated with a museum function and available to the public. Members (over 100) in 32 countries:
Australia, Austria, Belgium, Bulgaria, China, Croatia, Czechia, Denmark, Estonia, Finland, France, Germany, Greece, Hungary, Indonesia, Ireland, Italy, Japan, Korea Rep, Latvia, Luxembourg, Netherlands, New Zealand, Norway, Poland, Slovenia, Spain, Sweden, Switzerland, Türkiye, UK, USA.

Individuals in 10 countries:
Argentina, Australia, Austria, Canada, France, Netherlands, Spain, Switzerland, UK, USA.

NGO Relations Affiliated member of: *International Council of Museums (ICOM, #13051).* [2018.06.01/XD6291/C]

♦ International Confederation of Art Cinemas 12847

Confédération Internationale des Cinémas d'Art-et-d'Essai (CICAE)

Managing Dir Rankestrasse 31, 10789 Berlin, Germany. T. +493025760841. Fax +493025760843. E-mail: info@cicae.org.
Head Office 12 rue Vauvenargues, 75018 Paris, France. T. +33156331320. Fax +33143804114.
URL: http://www.cicae.org/

History 21 Jul 1955, Paris (France). Statutes modified: 8 May 1983, Cannes (France); 20 Oct 1989, Annecy (France); 13 May 1999, Cannes (France); 18 may 2006, Cannes; 17 May 2012, Cannes (France); 18 May 2017, Cannes (France). Previously also referred to in English *International Art Cinemas Confederation* and *International Confederation of Arthouse Cinemas.* **Aims** Promote international cooperation in the field of research and showing of film masterpieces, old or recent, of recognized quality and destined to make up experimental and art film programmes, as agreed by the Confederation or its national federations; encourage national and international authorities to recognize art cinema; promote cultural activities to widen the audience for such cinema. **Structure** General Assembly (annual); Executive Committee. **Languages** English, French, German, Italian. **Staff** 2.00 FTE, paid. **Finance** Members' dues. Grants from: *European Commission (EC, #06633) Creative Europe Programme*; national film boards of France, Germany and Italy. **Activities** Networking/liaising; training/education; events/meetings; awards/prizes/competitions. **Events** *General Assembly* Cannes (France) 2019, *General Assembly* Cannes (France) 2015, *Ordinary general assembly* Cannes (France) 2002, *Ordinary general assembly* Cannes (France) 1988. **Publications** *Bulletin d'information de la CICAE*; *Courrier de l'Art et Essai.*

Members National federations of cinemas; individual cinemas (where no national federation exists); corresponding members (principally festivals). Members in 51 countries and territories:
Algeria, Austria, Belarus, Belgium, Bosnia-Herzegovina, Bulgaria, Canada, Chile, Croatia, Cyprus, Czechia, Denmark, Ecuador, Egypt, Estonia, Finland, France, Germany, Greece, Greenland, Hungary, Iceland, Iran Islamic Rep, Iraq, Ireland, Israel, Italy, Latvia, Lebanon, Lithuania, Mali, Malta, Morocco, Netherlands, Peru, Poland, Portugal, Romania, Russia, Senegal, Serbia, Slovenia, South Africa, Spain, Sudan, Sweden, Switzerland, Tunisia, UK, USA, Venezuela.

NGO Relations Member of: *International Council for Film, Television and Audiovisual Communication (IFTC, #13022); MEDIA Salles (#16620).* [2020.03.18/XC1820/D]

♦ International Confederation of Art Dealers 12848

Confédération internationale des négociants en oeuvres d'art (CINOA) – Confederación Internacional de los Comerciantes de Obras de Arte – Internationale Kunsthändler-Vereinigung

SG Rue Ernest Allard 32, 1000 Brussels, Belgium.
Pres address not obtained.
URL: http://www.cinoa.org/

History 1935, Amsterdam (Netherlands). Statutes approved by General Assembly, 1996, Salzburg (Austria). Registration: Start date: 1936, Belgium. **Aims** Coordinate the work of chambers, unions, associations or federations of dealers in objets d'art and paintings or their members; contribute by all available legal means to artistic and economic expansion in the world. **Structure** General Assembly (annual). Administrative Council, comprising President, immediate Past-President and 5 Officers. Special Commissions. Meetings closed. **Languages** English, French. **Staff** Part-time. **Finance** Members' dues. **Activities** Serves as central enquiry and research bureau for objets d'art, including Art Loss Register; awards annual CINOA Prize; organizes conferences. **Events** *Annual General Assembly* Paris (France) 2016, *Annual General Assembly* Vienna (Austria) 2013, *Annual general assembly / International Exhibition* Paris (France) 2008, *Annual general assembly / International Exhibition* Sorrento (Italy) 2007, *Annual general assembly / International Exhibition* Utrecht (Netherlands) 2006. **Publications** *Handbook* (2004). Member directory.

Members Affiliated associations (31), totalling over 5,000 individual members, in 20 countries:
Australia, Austria, Belgium, Czechia, Denmark, France, Germany, Ireland, Italy, Netherlands, New Zealand, Norway, Poland, Portugal, South Africa, Spain, Sweden, Switzerland, UK, USA. [2019/XD1656/D]

♦ International Confederation of Arthouse Cinemas / see International Confederation of Art Cinemas (#12847)
♦ International Confederation of Artists Associations (inactive)
♦ International Confederation of Arts, Letters and Sciences (inactive)
♦ International Confederation of Associations of Experts and Consultants (inactive)
♦ International Confederation of Associations of French-Speakers (inactive)
♦ International Confederation of Associations of Graduates in Economic and Commercial Sciences (inactive)

♦ International Confederation of Associations for Pluralism in Economics (ICAPE) 12849

Exec Dir 226 S 16th Street, Lewisburg PA 17837, USA. T. +15705771666.
Sec-Treas Economics, Bucknell Univ, 1 Dent Drive, Lewisburg PA 17837, USA.
URL: http://icape.org/

History 1993. Former names and other names: *International Confederation of Associations for the Reform of Economics (ICARE)* – former (1993 to 2000). **Aims** Promote the idea that pluralism and intellectual progress are complements and remove obstacles to pluralism so as to render a service to the community of economists worldwide. **Languages** English. **Staff** None. **Finance** Sources: members' dues. Annual budget: 2,300 USD. **Events** *Conference* New Orleans, LA (USA) 2023, *Conference* Boston, MA (USA) 2022, *Conference* Chicago, IL (USA) 2021, *Conference* San Diego, CA (USA) 2020, *Conference* Atlanta, GA (USA) 2019. **Publications** *Economic Pluralism* (2009); *Future Directions for Heterodox Economics* (2008). Conference proceedings.

Members Associations (42), including the following 8 organizations listed in this Yearbook:
Association for Evolutionary Economics (AFEE); Economists for Peace and Security (EPS, #05322); European Association for Evolutionary Political Economy (EAEPE, #06033); Global Development and Environment Institute (GDAE); International Association for Feminist Economics (IAFFE, #11889); International Nuclear Track Society (INTS, #14384); Latin American Center of Social Ecology (#16292); Society for the Advancement of Socio-Economics (SASE, #19516). [2021.06.08/XD7644/y/D]

♦ International Confederation of Associations for the Reform of Economics / see International Confederation of Associations for Pluralism in Economics (#12849)
♦ International Confederation of ATOD Research Associations / see International Confederation of Alcohol, Tobacco and other Drug Research Associations (#12843)

♦ International Confederation of Cardiorespiratory Physical Therapists (ICCrPT) 12850

Pres address not obtained. E-mail: info@cardioresp.physio.
URL: https://world.physio/subgroups/cardiorespiratory

History Jun 2011, Amsterdam (Netherlands). A subgroup of *World Confederation for Physical Therapy (WCPT, #21293).*

Members Full in 15 countries and territories:
Australia, Canada, Denmark, Greece, Hong Kong, Iran Islamic Rep, Japan, Namibia, New Zealand, Norway, Singapore, South Africa, Sweden, Taiwan, UK. [2023/XJ5276/E]

♦ International Confederation of Childhood Cancer Parent Organizations / see Childhood Cancer International (#03871)

♦ International Confederation of Christian Family Movements (ICCFM) 12851

Confédération internationale des mouvements des familles chrétiennes – Confederación Internacional de Movimientos Familiares Cristianos – Confederazione Internazionale dei Movimenti delle Famiglie Cristiane

Pres address not obtained. E-mail: office@iccfm.org.
URL: http://www.iccfm.org/

History 1966. Founded during 1st Latin American meeting as an extension to the movement created in 1950 in Argentina and Uruguay, following the work of men's Catholic Action groups set up 1943, Chicago IL (USA) and transformed, 1947, into a couples' organization. Former names and other names: *Christian Family Movement* – alias; *Mouvement familial chrétien* – alias; *Movimiento Familiar Cristiano (MFC)* – alias. **Aims** Improve the quality of family life; develop a consciousness (both a family and a social consciousness) based on Christian principles and examples; develop responsible, concerned and happy families that are part of supportive and affirming network of families within every community who will individually and collectively reach out to others in need; offer opportunities for families to grow in their personal relationships with one another as well as with their friends, neighbours and co-workers; develop a caring society that not only recognizes, but actively supports family life; initiate and encourage research that impacts on the actual needs of families; continue to foster the international spirit of the Christian Family Movements. **Structure** General Assembly (every 3 years). World President Couple; Continental President Couple; National President Couple. Local groups. Regional chapter: *Christian Family Movement Europe (CFM Europe, see: #12851).* **Languages** English, Spanish. **Finance** Members' dues. **Activities** Training/education; advocacy/lobbying/activism; events/meetings. **Events** *Triennial World Congress and Assembly* Bucaramanga (Colombia) 2013, *Triennial World Congress and Assembly* Goa (India) 2010, *Triennial European Convention* Hungary 2009, *Triennial Latin American Convention* Querétaro (Mexico) 2009, *Triennial Asian Convention* Thailand 2009. **Publications** *LINK-LAZO* (2 a year) – newsletter. Study booklets; pamphlets.

Members Individuals (over 120,000), constituting National Groups. Groups in 42 countries and territories:
Angola, Argentina, Bolivia, Brazil, Cameroon, Canada, Chile, Colombia, Costa Rica, Croatia, Cuba, Czechia, Dominican Rep, Ecuador, El Salvador, Ghana, Guatemala, Honduras, Hong Kong, Hungary, India, Japan, Latvia, Malawi, Malta, Mexico, Nigeria, Panama, Paraguay, Peru, Philippines, Portugal, Romania, Singapore, Slovakia, Spain, Sri Lanka, Thailand, Uganda, Uruguay, USA, Venezuela.

Individuals in 5 countries:
Australia, Ireland, Malaysia, Sweden, UK.

Consultative Status Consultative status granted from: *ECOSOC (#05331)* (Special). **IGO Relations** Accredited by: *United Nations Office at Vienna (UNOV, #20604).* Associated with Department of Global Communications of the United Nations. **NGO Relations** Member of: *Vienna NGO Committee on the Family (#20774).* [2018/XD0269/F]

♦ International Confederation of Cleft Lip and Palate and Related Craniofacial Anomalies (ICCPCA) 12852

Contact address not obtained. T. +914424765614. E-mail: cleft2021@in-conference.org.uk – contacticcpca@gmail.com.

URL: http://www.iccpca.org/
History 1969. Constitution adopted at 7th Congress, 1997. **Aims** Promote and facilitate management of cleft lip and palate and related craniofacial anomalies throughout the world. **Structure** General Business Meeting; Executive Committee. **Languages** English. **Activities** Events/meetings; standards/guidelines; research/documentation. **Events** *International Congress of Cleft Lip and Palate and Related Craniofacial Anomalies* Kyoto (Japan) 2025, *International Congress of Cleft Lip and Palate and Related Craniofacial Anomalies* Edinburgh (UK) 2022, *International Congress on Cleft Lip/Palate and Related Craniofacial Anomalies* Edinburgh (UK) 2021, *International Congress on Cleft Lip/Palate and Related Craniofacial Anomalies* Chennai (India) 2017, *International Congress on Cleft Lip/Palate and Related Craniofacial Anomalies* Orlando, FL (USA) 2013. **Members** Active; Honorary. Membership countries not specified. [2020.01.24/XJ9797/v/**E**]

♦ International Confederation of Construction and Building Materials Industry Workers' Unions 12853

Pres 42 Leninsky Prospekt, Moscow MOSKVA, Russia, 119119. T. +7959520364.
Members Trade unions in the CIS region (membership countries not specified). **IGO Relations** *Commonwealth of Independent States (CIS, #04341).* **NGO Relations** Affiliated with: *General Confederation of Trade Unions (GCTU, #10108).* [2008.09.09/XM2473/t/**D**]

♦ International Confederation of Container Reconditioners (ICCR) . . . 12854

Secretariat Mr Lawrence W Bierlein, 1101 30th Street NW, Washington DC 20007, USA. T. +12026258355. E-mail: larry@hazmat-lawyer.com.
Contact c/o SERRED Secretariat, Boval House, 24 Mount Parade, Harrogate, HG1 1BX, UK. T. +447770633320. E-mail: info@serred.org.
URL: http://iccr.biz/
History Previously referred to as *International Confederation of Drum Reconditioners (ICDR).* Also known as *Association of Container Reconditioners (ACR).* **Events** *International Conference on Industrial Packaging* Ghent (Belgium) 2023, *International Conference on Industrial Packaging* Tokyo (Japan) 2018, *International Conference on Industrial Packaging* Vancouver, BC (Canada) 2015, *International Conference on Industrial Packaging* Amsterdam (Netherlands) 2013, *International conference on industrial packaging* San Francisco, CA (USA) 2006.
Members Organizations in 4 countries:
Australia, Japan, UK, USA.
Included in the above, 2 organizations listed in this Yearbook:
Australasian Container Reconditioners Association (ACRA); European Reconditioners of Industrial Packaging (#08333). [2018/XD9055/**D**]

♦ International Confederation of Contamination Control Societies (ICCCS) 12855

Sec VDI Society Building Services, VDI-Platz 1, 40468 Düsseldorf, Germany. T. +492116214500. Fax +492116214177.
Permanent Office PO Box 311, 3830 AJ'Leusden, Netherlands. T. +31334345752. Fax +31334321581.
URL: http://www.icccs.net/
History 1972, as *International Committee of Contamination Control Societies – Comité international des sociétés de contrôle de la contamination.* Present name adopted in 1991. **Aims** Further and promote contamination control technologies. **Languages** English. **Staff** 0.50 FTE, paid. **Finance** Budget (annual): Swiss Fr 15,000. **Events** *International Symposium on Contamination Control* Antalya (Türkiye) 2022, *International Symposium on Contamination Control* Antalya (Turkey) 2020, *International Symposium on Contamination Control* The Hague (Netherlands) 2018, *International Symposium on Contamination Control* Sao Paulo (Brazil) 2016, *International Symposium on Contamination Control* Seoul (Korea Rep) 2014.
Members Societies in 18 countries:
Australia, Belgium, Brazil, China, Denmark, Finland, France, Germany, Ireland, Italy, Japan, Korea Rep, Netherlands, Norway, Russia, Sweden, Switzerland, USA.
Regional organization (1):
Nordic Association of Cleanroom Technology (#17183).
NGO Relations In liaison with technical committees of: *International Organization for Standardization (ISO, #14473).* [2013/XD5138/**D**]

♦ International Confederation of Dairy Retailers (inactive)

♦ International Confederation of Dietetic Associations (ICDA) 12856

Confédération internationale des associations de diététique
Main Office 1 Eglinton Ave E, Suite 705, Toronto ON M4P 3A1, Canada. E-mail: icda@internationaldietetics.org.
URL: https://internationaldietetics.org/
History 1952. Former names and other names: *International Committee of Dietetic Associations* – former. **Aims** Improve understanding and strengthen links among dieticians and *nutritionists* around the world. **Structure** Committee of Members. Organizations (national dietetic associations). Board of Directors. **Languages** English. **Finance** Sources: members' dues. **Events** *International Congress of Nutrition and Dietetics* Toronto, ON (Canada) 2024, *International Congress of Dietetics* Cape Town (South Africa) 2021, *International Congress of Dietetics* Cape Town (South Africa) 2020, *Quadrennial Congress* Granada (Spain) 2016, *International Conference on Violence in the Health Sector* Vancouver, BC (Canada) 2012. **Publications** Congress proceedings; newsletter; manual of work and training of dietitians.
Members Associations in 36 countries and territories:
Australia, Austria, Canada, Chile, Cyprus, Denmark, Finland, France, Germany, Greece, Iceland, India, Ireland, Israel, Italy, Japan, Korea Rep, Luxembourg, Malaysia, Mexico, Netherlands, New Zealand, Norway, Philippines, Singapore, Slovenia, South Africa, Spain, Sudan, Sweden, Switzerland, Taiwan, Trinidad-Tobago, Türkiye, UK, USA.
Regional member (1), listed in this Yearbook:
Caribbean Association of Nutritionists and Dietitians (CANDI, #03456).
NGO Relations Affiliate of: *International Union of Nutritional Sciences (IUNS, #15796).* [2022/XD3804/**C**]

♦ International Confederation for Disarmament and Peace (inactive)

♦ International Confederation of Drum Manufacturers (ICDM) 12857

Chair address not obtained.
Sec address not obtained.
URL: http://www.icdm.org/
Aims Coordinate the communication and actions to promote general interest of the industry worldwide. **Activities** Events/meetings. **Events** *International conference on industrial packaging* San Francisco, CA (USA) 2006, *Conference* Tokyo (Japan) 2004.
Members Organizations (3):
Asia-Oceania Steel Drum Manufacturers (AOSD, no recent information); European Association of Steel Drum Manufacturers (#06222).
IGO Relations *United Nations Committee of Experts on the Transport of Dangerous Goods and on the Globally Harmonized System of Classification and Labelling of Chemicals (Committee of Experts on TDG and GHS, #20543).* [2021/XD4799/y/**D**]

♦ International Confederation of Drum Reconditioners / see International Confederation of Container Reconditioners (#12854)

♦ International Confederation for Electroacoustic Music (ICEM) 12858

Confédération internationale de musique électroacoustique (CIME)
Treas 7 rue de la Croix Blanche, Le Puy, 77460 Chaintreaux, France. E-mail: cime.icem@gmail.com.
Pres c/o PSeME, PO Box 40, 31-045 Krakow, Poland. E-mail: pseme@pseme.com.
URL: http://www.cime-icem.net/
History 1982, following annual meetings of composers from 1974, Bourges (France), at International Festival of Experimental Music. **Aims** Promote at an international level the various aspects of electroacoustic music. **Structure** Annual General Assembly; Executive Bureau. **Languages** English, French. **Staff** Voluntary. **Finance** Members' dues. **Activities** Events/meetings; training/education; knowledge management/information dissemination; standards/guidelines; networking/liaising. **Events** *General Assembly* Krakow (Poland) 2019, *General Assembly* Beijing (China) 2018, *General Assembly* Moscow (Russia) 2017, *General Assembly* Lisbon (Portugal) 2015, *General Assembly* Denton, TX (USA) 2014. **Publications** Documentation; CD-ROMs. Information Services: Bank of programme notes.
Members National federations in 14 countries:
Argentina, Belgium, Chile, China, Cuba, Finland, Greece, Mexico, Poland, Portugal, Spain, Switzerland, UK, Ukraine.
Organizations in 9 countries:
Colombia, France, Hungary, Iran Islamic Rep, Mexico, Russia, Spain, Switzerland, USA.
NGO Relations Member of: *International Music Council (IMC, #14199).* [2017.06.01/XD0425/**D**]

♦ International Confederation of Energy Regulators (ICER) 12859

Secretariat c/o CEER, Cours Saint-Michel 30-A, Box F 5th fl, Securex Bldg, 1040 Brussels, Belgium. E-mail: office@icer-regulators.net.
Chair address not obtained.
URL: http://www.icer-regulators.net/
History 19 Oct 2009, Athens (Greece). Officially constituted at 4th *World Forum on Energy Regulation (WFER, inactive)*, for which framework it is now responsible. Set up as a voluntary framework for cooperation between energy regulators worldwide. Assumed the activities of *International Energy Regulation Network (IERN, inactive).* **Aims** Improve public and policy-maker awareness and understanding of energy regulation and its role in addressing a wide spectrum of socio-economic, environmental and market issues. **Structure** Steering Committee; Virtual Working Groups. **Languages** English. **Activities** Awards/prizes/competitions; events/meetings; healthcare. **Events** *World Forum on Energy Regulation (WFER)* Lima (Peru) 2023, *World Forum on Energy Regulation (WFER)* Cancún (Mexico) 2018, *World Forum on Energy Regulation (WFER)* Istanbul (Turkey) 2015, *World Forum on Energy Regulation* Québec, QC (Canada) 2012. **Publications** *The ICER Chronicle* (2 a year) in English. Reports.
Members Full (13):
African Forum for Utility Regulators (AFUR, #00324); Asociación Iberoamericana de Entidades Reguladoras de la Energia (ARIAE, #02139); Association of Mediterranean Energy Regulators (MEDREG, #02800); Australian Energy Market Commission (AEMC); CAMPUT, Canada; *Council of European Energy Regulators (CEER, #04888); East Asia and Pacific Infrastructure Regulatory Forum (EAPIRF, #05212); Energy Regulators Regional Association (ERRA, #05476);* National Association of Regulatory Utility Commissioners (NARUC), USA; *Organisation of Caribbean Utility Regulators (OOCUR, #17800); Regional Association of Energy Regulators for Eastern and Southern Africa (RAERESA, #18751); Regional Electricity Regulators Association of Southern Africa (RERA, #18779); South Asia Forum for Infrastructure Regulation (SAFIR, #19716).* [2019.06.21/XJ4632/y/**F**]

♦ International Confederation of European Beet Growers (CIBE) 12860

Confédération internationale des betteraviers européens – Internationale Vereinigung Europäischer Rübenanbauer – Confederazione Internazionale dei Bieticoltori Europei – Internationale Confederatie van Europese Suikerbietkwekers – Miedzynarodowa Konfederacja Europejskich Plantatorów Buraka
SG Bd Anspach 111/9, 1000 Brussels, Belgium. T. +3225046090. Fax +3225046099. E-mail: cibeoffice@cibe-europe.eu.
URL: http://www.cibe-europe.eu/
History 20 Jun 1925, Warsaw (Poland). Reorganized in 1947. Statutes modified: 1952, 1960, 1964, 1971, 1989, 1995, 1997. Formerly referred to in Spanish as *Confederación International de los Remolacheros Europeos.* EU Transparency Register: 89930126483-54. **Aims** Represent interests of sugar beet growers in the international sphere; centralize information on economic and technical questions concerning sugar beet growing and its bearing on the sugar industry. **Structure** General Assembly (annual), comprising 5 members per country. Board of Directors (meets 3-4 times a year) of up to 3 members per country. Praesidium includes President, First Vice-President, 7 Vice-Presidents and Secretary General. Special Committees (2): Economic and General Affairs; Technical and Reception Control. **Languages** English, French, German, Italian, Polish. **Staff** 4.00 FTE, paid. **Finance** Members' dues according to annual white beet sugar production. **Activities** Issues: European Community sugar regulations; international negotiations at WTO on agriculture; Common Agricultural Policy of the EC; links with OIS; reception control; cooperation; technical beet issues; the environment. Organizes Triennial Congress (Biennial Congress up to 2006). **Events** *Triennial Congress* Gdansk (Poland) 2022, *General Assembly* Vienna (Austria) 2019, *Triennial Congress* Ghent (Belgium) 2018, *General Assembly* Utrecht (Netherlands) 2016, *Triennial Congress* Berlin (Germany) 2015.
Members National associations in 17 countries:
Austria, Belgium, Czechia, Denmark, Finland, France, Germany, Greece, Hungary, Italy, Netherlands, Poland, Romania, Slovakia, Sweden, Switzerland, UK.
Observers in 1 country:
Türkiye.
Consultative Status Consultative status granted from: *ECOSOC (#05331)* (Ros C); *UNCTAD (#20285)* (Special Category); *FAO (#09260)* (Liaison Status). **IGO Relations** Accredited by: *United Nations Office at Vienna (UNOV, #20604).* **NGO Relations** Appoints members to the Executive Board of: *World Association of Beet and Cane Growers (WABCG, #21120).* Member of: *International Institute of Sugar Beet Research (IIRB, #13928).* Liaison Committee with: *COPA – european farmers (COPA, #04829); Comité européen des fabricants de sucre (CEFS, #04159). General Confederation of Agricultural Cooperatives in the European Union (#10107).* [2016/XD1663/**D**]

♦ International Confederation for Family Support (inactive)
♦ International Confederation of Film Technical Industries (inactive)
♦ International Confederation of Former Prisoners of War (inactive)
♦ International Confederation of Free Trade Unions (inactive)
♦ International Confederation of Genealogy and Heraldry (#04561)
♦ International Confederation of the Hairdressing Trade / see World Hairdressers' Organization (#21550)

♦ International Confederation of Health Workers' Unions 12861

Pres 42 Leninsky Prospekt, Moscow MOSKVA, Russia, 119119. T. +7959388443. Fax +7959388143. E-mail: ckprz@mail.ru.
Members Trade unions in the CIS region (membership countries not specified). **NGO Relations** Affiliated with: *General Confederation of Trade Unions (GCTU, #10108).* [2014/XM2462/**D**]

♦ International Confederation of Installers of Refrigeration and Air-Conditioning Equipment (inactive)
♦ International Confederation of Jewellery, Silverware, Diamonds, Pearls and Stones / see CIBJO – The World Jewellery Confederation (#03923)

♦ International Confederation of Joint Venture Workers' Unions 12862

Chairman 42 Leninsky Prospekt, Moscow MOSKVA, Russia, 119119. T. +7959388462. Fax +7959388195.
Members Trade unions in the CIS region (membership countries not specified). **NGO Relations** Affiliated with: *General Confederation of Trade Unions (GCTU, #10108).* [2014/XM2472/**D**]

♦ International Confederation of the Kneipp Movement / see Kneipp Worldwide (#16197)
♦ International Confederation of Manufacturers of Furnishing Fabrics (inactive)

♦ International Confederation of Midwives (ICM) 12863

Confédération internationale des sages-femmes – Confederación Internacional de Matronas
Secretariat Koninginnegracht 60, 2514 AE The Hague, Netherlands. T. +31703060520. E-mail: admin@internationalmidwives.org – info@internationalmidwives.org.
URL: http://www.internationalmidwives.org/
History 1919, Belgium. Founded following conference of European midwives, 1919, Bruges (Belgium). All activities ceased and records lost during World War II; restarted 1949. Former names and other names: *International Midwives Union* – former; *Union internationale des sages-femmes* – former; *International Federation of Midwives* – former. **Aims** Strengthen member associations and advance the profession of midwifery globally by promoting autonomous midwives as the most appropriate caregivers for childbearing women and in keeping *childbirth* normal, so as to enhance the *reproductive health* of women and the health of the *newborn* and their families. **Structure** Council (meets in 2 types of meetings: annual; triennial together

with ICM Congress); Board; Executive Committee. Secretary-General is CEO, responsible for day-to-day affairs. **Languages** English, French, Spanish. **Staff** 14.00 FTE, paid. **Finance** Sources: government support; members' dues. **Activities** Events/meetings. **Events** *Triennial Conference* Bali (Indonesia) 2023, *Triennial Congress* The Hague (Netherlands) 2021, *Triennial Congress* Bali (Indonesia) 2020, *Eastern Mediterranean/ Southeast Asia and Western Pacific Regional Conference* Dubai (United Arab Emirates) 2018, *Triennial Congress* Toronto, ON (Canada) 2017. **Publications** *International Code of Ethics for Midwives.* Annual Report; congress, workshop and regional conference reports.
Members Midwifery Associations (140), totaling over 250,000 professional members in 119 countries and territories:
Argentina, Australia, Austria, Bangladesh, Barbados, Belgium, Benin, Brazil, Bulgaria, Burkina Faso, Burundi, Cambodia, Cameroon, Canada, Central African Rep, Chile, Comoros, Congo Brazzaville, Congo DR, Costa Rica, Côte d'Ivoire, Croatia, Cyprus, Czechia, Denmark, Ecuador, Estonia, Ethiopia, Fiji, Finland, France, Gabon, Gambia, Germany, Ghana, Greece, Guinea, Guinea-Bissau, Guyana, Haiti, Hong Kong, Hungary, Iceland, India, Indonesia, Iran Islamic Rep, Iraq, Ireland, Israel, Jamaica, Japan, Jordan, Kenya, Korea Rep, Kosovo, Kyrgyzstan, Latvia, Lebanon, Lesotho, Liberia, Luxembourg, Madagascar, Malawi, Malaysia, Mali, Malta, Mexico, Mongolia, Morocco, Mozambique, Myanmar, Namibia, Nepal, Netherlands, New Zealand, Niger, Nigeria, Norway, Pakistan, Palestine, Papua New Guinea, Paraguay, Peru, Philippines, Poland, Portugal, Romania, Rwanda, Saudi Arabia, Senegal, Sierra Leone, Slovenia, Somalia, South Africa, South Sudan, Spain, Sri Lanka, Sweden, Switzerland, Taiwan, Tajikistan, Tanzania UR, Timor-Leste, Togo, Trinidad-Tobago, Tunisia, Türkiye, Uganda, UK, United Arab Emirates, Uruguay, USA, Yemen, Zambia, Zimbabwe.
Consultative Status Consultative status granted from: *ECOSOC (#05331)* (Ros A); *ILO (#11123)* (Special List); *WHO (#20950)* (Official Relations); *UNICEF (#20332)*. **IGO Relations** Accredited by (1): *United Nations Office at Vienna (UNOV, #20604)*. Partner of (1): *United Nations Population Fund (UNFPA, #20612)*. Associated with Department of Global Communications of the United Nations. **NGO Relations** Member of (4): *Global Health Workforce Alliance (GHWA, inactive)*; *International Childbirth Initiative (ICI, #12547)*; *NGO Committee on UNICEF (#17120)*; *PMNCH (#18410)*. Partner of (4): *Amref Health Africa (#00806)*; *Fédération Internationale de Gynécologie et d'Obstétrique (FIGO, #09638)*; *Healthy Newborn Network (HNN, #10894)*; *White Ribbon Alliance for Safe Motherhood (WRA, #20934)*. Affiliates: *Catholic Organization for Relief and Development (Cordaid)*; *Save the Children Federation (SCF)*. Collaborates with: *World Medical Association (WMA, #21646)*.
[2023.01.19/XB1669/**B**]

♦ International Confederation of Musicians (inactive)

♦ International Confederation of Music Publishers (ICMP) 12864

Confédération internationale des éditeurs de musique (CIEM)

European Office 40 Square de Meeûs, 1000 Brussels, Belgium. E-mail: info@icmp-ciem.org.
URL: http://www.icmp-ciem.org/

History Founded 1991, to confederate *International Federation of Popular Music Publishers (IFPMP, inactive)* and *International Federation of Serious Music Publishers (IFSMP, inactive)*, both then being based at ICMP offices for secretariat purposes. From 1999, IFPMP and IFSMP ceased to exist as independent bodies, functioning rather as popular and serious music bureaux in the *ICMP/CIEM* framework. Registered in accordance with Swiss Civil Code. EU Transparency Register: 65684839099-72. **Aims** Increase the level of copyright protection internationally; encourage a better environment for the music publishing business; influence legislation; act as an industry forum for consolidating global positions. **Structure** General Assembly (annual); Board of Directors. Bureaux (2): Secretariat. **Languages** English, French, German, Spanish. **Staff** 4.00 FTE, paid. **Finance** Sources: members' dues. **Activities** Events/meetings. **Events** *MusicMinds Europe Conference* Paris (France) 2022, *Latin America Regional Music Publishers Conference* Antigua (Guatemala) 2018, *Working groups meeting* Brussels (Belgium) 2008, *Annual general congress* Cannes (France) 2005, *Annual general congress* Cannes (France) 2004. **Publications** *Global Briefing* (12 a year) – newsletter.
Members Active and Associate (68) in 51 countries:
Argentina, Australia, Austria, Belgium, Brazil, Bulgaria, Canada, Chile, China, Colombia, Croatia, Cyprus, Czechia, Denmark, Finland, France, Germany, Greece, Hungary, Iceland, India, Indonesia, Ireland, Israel, Italy, Japan, Kenya, Korea Rep, Latvia, Lebanon, Lithuania, Mexico, Netherlands, Norway, Peru, Poland, Portugal, Romania, Russia, Serbia, Slovenia, South Africa, Spain, Sweden, Switzerland, Tanzania UR, Türkiye, UK, Ukraine, United Arab Emirates, USA.
Included in the above, 2 organizations listed in this Yearbook:
Independent Music Publishers Forum (IMPF, #11152); *International Music Publishers Association (IMPA, inactive)*.
Consultative Status Consultative status granted from: *World Intellectual Property Organization (WIPO, #21593)* (Permanent Observer Status).
[2019/XD0499/**C**]

♦ International Confederation of Music Societies (CISM) 12865

Confédération internationale des sociétés musicales (CISM) – Internationaler Musikbund (CISM)

Pres Weiherweidstr 9, 9000 St Gallen, Switzerland.
URL: http://www.cism-online.com/

History 1949. Former names and other names: *International Confederation of Popular Societies of Music* – former; *Confédération internationale des sociétés populaires de musique* – former. **Aims** Preserve, foster and promote music culture; represent the common interests of members vis-à-vis government and society; promote music education and training; organise international (youth) exchanges. **Structure** Board: President; Vice-President; Treasurer; Presidents of Expert Commissions (Music, Communication and Network). **Languages** English, French, German. **Staff** 10.00 FTE, voluntary. **Finance** Sources: members' dues; sponsorship. Annual budget: 30,000 EUR (2020). **Activities** Events/meetings; networking/liaising; projects/programmes; training/ education. **Events** *Annual Meeting* St Gallen (Switzerland) 2020, *Annual Meeting* Rome (Italy) 2018, *Annual Meeting* Trossingen (Germany) 2017, *Annual Meeting* Stuttgart (Germany) 2016, *Annual Meeting* Basel (Switzerland) 2015. **Publications** *Score and Sound* – including CD-ROM. Catalogues of recommended band music; catalogues of experts.
Members National and regional societies (11) representing about 18,000 bands and ensembles in 9 countries:
Austria, France, Germany (2 – one association represents Saar), Italy (2 associations), Liechtenstein, Malta, Slovenia, Spain, Switzerland.
[2022/XD1561/**D**]

♦ International Confederation of Nutrition Support Organizations (inactive)
♦ International Confederation of Paper and Board Converters in the Common Market / see International Confederation of Paper and Board Converters in Europe (#12866)

♦ International Confederation of Paper and Board Converters in Europe (CITPA) 12866

Confédération internationale des transformateurs de papier et carton en Europe (CITPA) – Confederación internacional de los Transformadores de Papel y Cartón en Europa – Internationale Konföderation der Verarbeiter von Papier und Pappe in Europa

SG Ave Louise 250, Box 108, 1050 Brussels, Belgium. T. +3226269838. Fax +3226466460. E-mail: johanna.kloeck@fefco.org – info@citpa-europe.org.
URL: http://www.citpa-europe.org/

History 15 Dec 1961, Frankfurt-Main (Germany FR). Original title: *International Committee of Paper and Board Converters in the Common Market – Comité international des transformateurs de papier et carton dans la Communauté européenne – Internationales Komitee der Verarbeiter von Papier und Pappe in der Europäischen Gemeinschaft.* Title subsequently changed to *International Confederation of Paper and Board Converters in the Common Market – Confédération internationale des transformateurs de papier et carton dans la Communauté européenne – Internationale Konföderation der Verarbeiter von Papier und Pappe in der Europäischen Gemeinschaft*, and then to listed title. Neither previous nor currently listed French, Spanish and German titles are now considered "official". EU Transparency Register: 82090737179-17. **Aims** Represent the interests of industry. **Structure** General Assembly; Board of Directors; Committees. **Finance** Members' dues. **Activities** Knowledge management/information dissemination; politics/policy/regulatory; standards/ guidelines. **Events** *Annual Meeting* Lisbon (Portugal) 2007, *Annual Meeting* Brussels (Belgium) 2006, *Annual meeting* Pultusk (Poland) 2005, *Annual meeting* Zurich (Switzerland) 2004, *Annual meeting* Milan (Italy) 2003.
Members Branch members (6):
European Carton Makers Association (ECMA, #06453); *European Core and Tube Association (ECTA, #06797)*; *European Federation of Corrugated Board Manufacturers (#07091)*; *EUROSAC (#09177)*; *EUROWAXPACK – European Association of Manufacturers of Waxed Packaging Materials (EUROWAXPACK, #09195)*; *FINAT (#09773)*.
National members in 6 countries:
Austria, Belgium, Germany, Italy, Portugal, UK.
Associate members (3):
Association of European Cartonboard and Carton Manufacturers (PRO CARTON, #02502); *European Kraft Paper Producers for the Flexible Packaging Industry (CEPI Eurokraft, #07630)*; *European Manufacturers Paper Honeycomb Association (EMPHA)*.
IGO Relations Recognized by: *European Commission (EC, #06633)*. **NGO Relations** Signatory to Declaration of on Paper Recovery, maintained by *European Paper Recycling Council (EPRC, #08139)*. Cooperates with: *European Organization for Packaging and the Environment (EUROPEN, #08110)*. Member of: *European Platform for Chemicals Using Manufacturing Industries (CheMI, #08223)*; *Industry4Europe (#11181)*.
[2020/XE1614/y/**E**]

♦ International Confederation of Parents (no recent information)
♦ International Confederation for Plastic, Reconstructive and Aesthetic Surgery (inactive)
♦ International Confederation of Plastics Packaging Manufacturers (internationally oriented national body)

♦ International Confederation of Popular Banks 12867

Confédération internationale des banques populaires – Confederación Internacional de Bancos Populares – Internationale Volksbankenvereinigung – Confederazione Internazionale delle Banche Popolari (CIBP)

SG Av des Arts 3-4-5, 1210 Brussels, Belgium. T. +3222091680. Fax +3222091689.
URL: http://www.cibp.eu/

History 24 Jun 1950, Saint-Malo (France). 24 Jun 1950, St Malo (France), as *International Confederation of Popular Credit (ICPC) – Confédération internationale du crédit populaire (CICP) – Confederación Internacional de Crédito Popular – Confederazione Internazionale del Credito Popolare.* Registered in accordance with Belgian law. **Aims** Link financial and banking institutions whose specific aim is to favour the growth, in the widest sense of the word, of small and medium-sized enterprises – SMEs – and of private customers; support members, the majority of them having a cooperative structure, as they grant loans and provide financial services adapted to the needs of individual clients and carry out an advisory role, thus assisting people setting up in business, with particular emphasis on innovation. **Structure** General Assembly; Executive Committee; Presidential Committee; Audit Committee; General Secretariat. Working Groups. **Languages** English, French, German, Italian, Spanish. **Staff** 3.00 FTE, paid. **Finance** Members' dues. **Activities** Events/ meetings; knowledge management/information dissemination; research/documentation. **Events** *European Forum on Co-operative Banks & SMEs* Brussels (Belgium) 2016, *Innovation strengthening cooperative and popular banks* Rio de Janeiro (Brazil) 2015, *European Forum on Co-operative Banks & SMEs* Brussels (Belgium) 2014, *Triennial Congress* Marrakech (Morocco) 2012, *Triennial congress* Québec, QC (Canada) 2010. **Publications** *CIBP Newsletter*. Studies – in English, French, German.
Members Nationally-based popular credit organizations. Members in 8 countries:
Argentina, Austria, Belgium, Brazil, Canada, France, Germany, Morocco.
IGO Relations Recognized by: *European Commission (EC, #06633)*; *United Nations (UN, #20515)*.
[2018.09.25/XD1650/**D**]

♦ International Confederation of Popular Credit / see International Confederation of Popular Banks (#12867)
♦ International Confederation of Popular Societies of Music / see International Confederation of Music Societies (#12865)

♦ International Confederation of Principals (ICP) 12868

Exec Sec 31 Stewart Street – Level 1, Devonport TAS 7310, Australia. T. +61409954462. E-mail: admin@icponline.org.
Pres Lawrence Sheriff School, Clifton Road, Rugby, CV21 3AG, UK. E-mail: president@icponline.org.
URL: http://www.icponline.org/

History Founded by representatives of UK, USA, Switzerland, Australia, Canada, Germany, Japan, Netherlands and USSR. Former names and other names: *International Principals Association – International Confederation of School Principals* – former. **Aims** Offer resources, training, support and networking opportunities to National Principal Organizations and, by so doing, act as a catalyst creating and international synergy for Principal Organizations Worldwide. **Structure** Council; Executive Committee; Ad-hoc Working Groups; Secretariat in Devonport (Australia) headed by Executive Secretary. **Languages** English. **Staff** 0.20 FTE, paid; 7.00 FTE, voluntary. **Finance** Sources: meeting proceeds; members' dues. **Activities** Capacity building; events/ meetings; financial and/or material support; guidance/assistance/consulting; networking/liaising; projects/ programmes. **Events** *Biennial Convention* Toronto, ON (Canada) 2021, *Biennial Convention* Shanghai (China) 2019, *Biennial Convention* Cape Town (South Africa) 2017, *Biennial Convention* Helsinki (Finland) 2015, *Meeting* Helsinki (Finland) 2015. **Publications** *ICP Member Magazine* (4 a year). Position papers.
Members Organizations (43, representing over 200,000 school principals) in 27 countries and territories:
Australia, Canada, China, Finland, Germany, Ghana, Iceland, India, Ireland, Israel, Japan, Kenya, Korea Rep, Lesotho, Namibia, Netherlands, New Zealand, Nigeria, Saudi Arabia, Singapore, South Africa, Switzerland, Uganda, UK, USA, Zambia, Zimbabwe.
Individuals in 13 countries and territories:
Belgium, Fiji, France, Hong Kong, Nauru, Nepal, Oman, Papua New Guinea, Russia, Samoa, Solomon Is, Tonga, Ukraine.
Included in the above, 2 organizations listed in this Yearbook:
Council of British International Schools (COBIS, #04872); *European School Heads Association (ESHA, #08431)*.
IGO Relations Cooperates on projects with: *OECD (#17693)*; *UNESCO (#20322)*; *WHO (#20950)*.
[2022.11.25/XD5615/y/**D**]

♦ International Confederation for Printing and Allied Industries / see Intergraf (#11505)
♦ International Confederation of Private Employment Agencies / see World Employment Confederation (#21376)
♦ International Confederation of Professional and Intellectual Workers (#04564)
♦ International Confederation of Public Servants (no recent information)
♦ International Confederation of Railwaymen and Transport Builders' Trade Unions / see International Confederation of Railway Workers' and Transport Builders' Unions (#12869)

♦ International Confederation of Railway Workers' and Transport Builders' Unions 12869

Confédération internationale des syndicats de cheminots et de constructeurs de matériel de transport

Pres 42 Leninsky Prospekt, Moscow MOSKVA, Russia, 119119. T. +74952628811. Fax +74952621200. E-mail: icturwtb@yandex.ru – org.otdel@mkpz.org.
SG address not obtained.
URL: http://www.mkpz.org/

History Founded 14 May 1992. In English also referred to as *International Confederation of Railwaymen and Transport Builders' Trade Unions*. **Languages** Russian. **Finance** Members' dues. **Members** CIS and Baltic railway unions in 14 countries. Membership countries not specified. **NGO Relations** Affiliated with: *General Confederation of Trade Unions (GCTU, #10108)*.
[2020.03.03/XM2460/**D**]

♦ International Confederation of Societies of Authors and Composers (#04563)

♦ International Confederation of the Society of St Vincent-de-Paul .. 12870

Confédération internationale de la Société de Saint Vincent-de-Paul

SG 65 rue de la Glacière, 75013 Paris, France. T. +33153458753. Fax +33142617256. E-mail: sgssvp.cgi@gmail.com – cgi.communication@ssvpglobal.org.
URL: http://www.ssvpglobal.org/

History 23 Apr 1833, Paris (France). Foudned by a group of students, including Frédéric Ozanam, under the influence of Emmanuel Bailly. Former names and other names: *Society of St Vincent-de-Paul* – former (23 Apr 1833); *Société de Saint Vincent-de-Paul* – former (23 Apr 1833); *Sociedad de San Vicente de Paul* – former (23 Apr 1833); *Vinzenzgemeinschaft* – former (23 Apr 1833). **Aims** Follow *Christ* through service to those in need. **Structure** Council General Assembly (every 6 years); Board; Council General; Superior Councils; Assimilated Councils; Territorial Vice-Presidents; Zone Coordinators; Central Councils; Local Councils (towns); Conferences; Headquarters based in Paris (France). **Languages** Chinese, English, French, Mandarin Chinese,

Portuguese, Spanish. **Staff** 8.00 FTE, paid. **Finance** Sources: contributions; donations; meeting proceeds; subsidies. **Activities** Events/meetings; humanitarian/emergency aid; religious activities. **Events** *Meeting of the International Territorial Vice-Presidents* Paris (France) 2017, *International Plenary Assembly* Rome (Italy) 2016, *Plenary Assembly* Rome (Italy) 2015, *General Assembly* Sao Paulo (Brazil) 2015, *General Assembly* Lisbon (Portugal) 2014. **Publications** *Frederic Ozanam, l'engagement d'un intellectuel catholique au XIXème siècle* by Gérard Cholvy; *La Société de St Vincent de Paul au XIXe siècle – Un fleuron du catholicisme social* by Matthieu Bréjon de Lavergnée; *La Société de St Vincent de Paul – Une mémoire des origines en mouvement – 1833-1914* by Charles Mercier. Annual Report; bulletins. **Members** Individuals (about 720,000), distributed among some 47,000 conferences, in 150 countries and territories. Membership countries not specified. **Consultative Status** Consultative status granted from: *ECOSOC (#05331)* (Special). **IGO Relations** Representative to: *United Nations (UN, #20515)*. **NGO Relations** Member of (2): *Forum of Catholic Inspired NGOs (#09905)*; *International Catholic Centre of Geneva (ICCG, #12449)*. [2023.02.28/XF3242/**F**]

- ♦ International Confederation of Students (inactive)
- ♦ International Confederation of Technical Agricultural Engineers (inactive)
- ♦ International Confederation of Temporary Work Businesses / see World Employment Confederation (#21376)
- ♦ International Confederation of Temporary Work Organizations / see World Employment Confederation (#21376)
- ♦ International Confederation of Theatre Unions (no recent information)
- ♦ International Confederation for Thermal Analysis / see International Confederation for Thermal Analysis and Calorimetry (#12871)

♦ International Confederation for Thermal Analysis and Calorimetry (ICTAC) 12871

Confédération internationale d'analyse thermique et calorimétrie

Pres address not obtained.
Sec address not obtained.
URL: http://www.ictac.org/

History Founded 22 Aug 1968, Worcester MA (USA), as *International Confederation for Thermal Analysis (ICTA)*, at 2nd International Conference on Thermal Analysis, 1st Congress having been held 1965, Aberdeen (UK). Present title adopted, 28 Aug 1992, Hatfield (UK). Statutes established 11 Jul 1974; most recently revised Aug 2016. **Aims** Promote international understanding and cooperation in thermal analysis and calorimetry. **Structure** Congress (every 4 years); Council; Executive Committee; Scientific Commission; Congress Organizing Committee; Standing Committees; Working Groups. Legal domicile at office of Secretary. **Languages** English. **Staff** Voluntary. **Finance** Sources: members' dues. **Activities** Awards/prizes/competitions; events/meetings; standards/guidelines. **Events** *Quadrennial Congress* Krakow (Poland) 2021, *Quadrennial Congress* Krakow (Poland) 2020, *Quadrennial Congress* Orlando, FL (USA) 2016, *Quadrennial Congress* Osaka (Japan) 2012, *Quadrennial Congress* São Pedro (Brazil) 2008. **Publications** *ICTAC News* (2 a year). Proceedings of international congresses; reprints of recommendations and reports.

Members Affiliated national societies and groups in 27 countries:
Australia, Brazil, Bulgaria, Canada, China, Czechia, Denmark, Finland, France, Germany, Greece, Hungary, India, Israel, Italy, Japan, Netherlands, Norway, Poland, Romania, Slovakia, South Africa, Spain, Sweden, Switzerland, UK, USA.
Included in the above, 2 organizations listed in this Yearbook:
Nordic Society for Thermal Analysis and Calorimetry (NOSTAC, #17430); *North American Thermal Analysis Society (NATAS)*.
Individuals in 45 countries (not specified).
NGO Relations Member of: *International Union of Pure and Applied Chemistry (IUPAC, #15809)*. [2021/XC1651/y/**C**]

♦ International Confederation of Trade Unions of Workers in the Oil and Gas Industries, and Construction Workers in the Oil and Gas Complex 12872

Pres 42 Leninsky Prospekt, Moscow MOSKVA, Russia, 119119. T. +7951378159. Fax +7959388702. E-mail: inter@rogwu.ru.

History 1992, Moscow (Russia). **Aims** Further development of the industrial trade union movement in CIS countries in new political and economic conditions; maintain social stability in the labour forces; solve issues of social protection of employees. **Members** Trade unions in the CIS region. Membership countries not specified. **IGO Relations** *Commonwealth of Independent States (CIS, #04341)*. **NGO Relations** Affiliated with: *General Confederation of Trade Unions (GCTU, #10108)*. [2017.12.15/XM2467/t/**D**]

- ♦ International Confederation of Universities of the People (inactive)

♦ International Confederation of Water Transport Workers' Unions (ICWTWU) 12873

Chairman Zemlyanoi Val 64, Bldg 2, Office 329, Moscow MOSKVA, Russia, 109004. T. +74959152517 – +74959155685. Fax +74959152953. E-mail: nicksuh@mail.ru.
URL: http://www.icwtwu.ru/

History 1992. **Aims** Ensure cooperation and coordination of the affiliates' actions so as to protect labour and social-economic rights of workers and legal guarantees of unions' activities; strengthen solidarity. **Structure** Chairman. **Languages** English, Russian. **Staff** 4.50 FTE, paid. **Finance** Members' dues. Other sources: voluntary donations; proceeds from commercial and publishing activities. **Activities** Guidance/assistance/consulting; events/meetings.

Members Trade unions in the CIS region. Affiliates (12) in 7 countries:
Azerbaijan, Belarus, Georgia, Kyrgyzstan, Russia, Turkmenistan, Ukraine.
Cooperating organizations in 4 countries:
Estonia, Latvia, Lithuania, Ukraine.
IGO Relations *Commonwealth of Independent States (CIS, #04341)*; *ILO (#11123)*. **NGO Relations** Affiliated with: *General Confederation of Trade Unions (GCTU, #10108)*. Member of: *International Seafarers' Welfare and Assistance Network (ISWAN, #14815)*. [2020/XG9646/**D**]

- ♦ International Conference on Accelerator and Large Experimental Physics Control Systems (meeting series)
- ♦ International Conference on Accelerator Mass Spectrometry (meeting series)
- ♦ International Conference on Acid Deposition (meeting series)
- ♦ International Conference on Adaptive Structures and Technologies (meeting series)
- ♦ International Conference on the Adjuvant Therapy of Cancer (meeting series)
- ♦ International Conference on the Adjuvant Therapy of Malignant Melanoma (meeting series)
- ♦ International Conference on Adoption Research (meeting series)
- ♦ International Conference on Adult Education (meeting series)
- ♦ International Conference on Advanced Composite Materials (meeting series)
- ♦ International Conference on Advanced Computational Engineering and Experimenting (meeting series)
- ♦ International Conference on Advanced Infocomm Technology (meeting series)
- ♦ International Conference on Advanced Material Engineering & Technology (meeting series)
- ♦ International Conference on Advanced Steels (meeting series)
- ♦ International Conference on Advanced Structural Steels (meeting series)
- ♦ International Conference on Advanced Systems in Public Transport (meeting series)
- ♦ International Conference on Advanced Technologies and Treatments for Diabetes (meeting series)
- ♦ International Conference on the Advances in Fusion and Processing of Glass (meeting series)
- ♦ International Conference on Advances in Liquid Scintillation Spectrometry (meeting series)
- ♦ International Conference on Advances in Quantitative Laryngology, Voice and Speech Research (meeting series)
- ♦ International Conference on Advances in Solidification Processes (meeting series)
- ♦ International Conference on Advances in Steel Structures (meeting series)
- ♦ International Conference of African States on Insurance Supervision (inactive)
- ♦ International Conference on Agreement Technologies (meeting series)
- ♦ International Conference on Agricultural and Biological Sciences (meeting series)
- ♦ International Conference on Agriculture and Biotechnology (meeting series)
- ♦ International Conference on Air Quality – Science and Application (meeting series)
- ♦ International Conference on Algebra and Coalgebra in Computer Science (meeting series)
- ♦ International Conference on Algebraic Methods in Dynamical Systems (meeting series)
- ♦ International Conference on Alkali Aggregate Reaction in Concrete (meeting series)
- ♦ International Conference on Aluminium Alloys (meeting series)
- ♦ International Conference on Alzheimer's and Parkinson's Diseases (meeting series)
- ♦ International Conference on Amorphous and Nano-crystalline Semiconductors (meeting series)
- ♦ International Conference on Analysis and Optimization of Systems (meeting series)
- ♦ International Conference on Animal Health Surveillance (meeting series)
- ♦ International Conference on Antennas and Electromagnetic Systems (meeting series)
- ♦ International Conference on Applied Biochemistry and Biotechnology (meeting series)
- ♦ International Conference on Applied Energy (meeting series)
- ♦ International Conference on Applied Human Factors and Ergonomics (meeting series)
- ♦ International Conference on Applied Robotics for the Power Industry (meeting series)
- ♦ International Conference on Aquatic Invasive Species (meeting series)
- ♦ International Conference on Architecture of Computing Systems (meeting series)
- ♦ International Conference on Architecture, Materials and Construction (meeting series)
- ♦ International Conference on Architecture, Research, Care and Health (meeting series)
- ♦ International Conference on Arctic Margins (meeting series)
- ♦ International Conference on Artificial Intelligence and Statistics (meeting series)
- ♦ International Conference on Artificial Reefs and Related Aquatic Habitats (meeting series)
- ♦ International Conference on Asian Marine Geology (meeting series)
- ♦ International Conference of Asian-Pacific Planning Societies (meeting series)

♦ International Conference of Asian Political Parties (ICAPP) 12874

Secretariat 911 Doryeom Building, Doryeom-dong, Jongro-ku, Seoul, Korea Rep. T. +827088005536. Fax +8227025535. E-mail: secretariat@theicapp.org.
URL: http://www.theicapp.org/

History Sep 2000, Manila (Philippines). Constitution adopted during 4th Biennial Meeting, Seoul (Korea Rep) 2006. **Aims** Promote exchanges and cooperation between political parties from different Asian countries and with various ideologies; enhance mutual understanding and trust between Asian countries. **Structure** General Assembly. Standing Committee, including 2 Co-Chairmen. **Activities** Proposes setting up of: *Asian Union*. **Events** *Biennial General Assembly* Moscow (Russia) 2018, *Media Forum Meeting* Seoul (Korea Rep) 2017, *Biennial General Assembly* Kuala Lumpur (Malaysia) 2016, *Biennial General Assembly* Colombo (Sri Lanka) 2014, *Biennial General Assembly* Baku (Azerbaijan) 2012. [2015/XM2872/c/**F***]

- ♦ International Conference of Associations of War Cripples and Ex-Servicemen (inactive)
- ♦ International Conference on Atmospheric Dust (meeting series)
- ♦ International Conference on Atomic Collisions in Solids (meeting series)
- ♦ International Conference on Atomic Physics (meeting series)
- ♦ International Conference on Automated People Movers (meeting series)
- ♦ International Conference on Automatic Fire Detection (meeting series)
- ♦ International Conference on Availability, Reliability and Security (meeting series)
- ♦ International Conference on Axiomatic Design (meeting series)
- ♦ International Conference on Baltic Sea System Analysis – Environment, Energy and Natural Resource Management in the Baltic Region (meeting series)
- ♦ International Conference on Basement Tectonics (meeting series)
- ♦ International Conference on Beam Injection Assessment of Microstructures in Semiconductors (meeting series)
- ♦ International Conference on the Bearing Capacity of Roads, Railways and Airfields (meeting series)
- ♦ International Conference on Behavior of Offshore Structures (meeting series)
- ♦ International Conference of Benzol Producers (inactive)
- ♦ International Conference on Bio-based Polymers (meeting series)
- ♦ International Conference for the Biochemistry of Lipids / see International Conference on the Bioscience of Lipids (#12875)
- ♦ International Conference on Biological Inorganic Chemistry (meeting series)
- ♦ International Conference on Biological Waste as Resource (meeting series)
- ♦ International Conference on Biology, Environment and Chemistry (meeting series)
- ♦ International Conference on the Biology of Vibrios (meeting series)
- ♦ International Conference on Biomagnetism (meeting series)
- ♦ International Conference on Biomedical and Bioinformatics Engineering (meeting series)

♦ International Conference on the Bioscience of Lipids (ICBL) 12875

Sec Dipto di Scienze Farmacologiche e Biomolecolari-DiSFeB, Univ degli Studi di Milano, via Balzaretti 9, 20133 Milan MI, Italy. T. +39250318393. Fax +39250318397.
URL: http://www.icbl.info/

History Founded 1953, as *International Conference for the Biochemistry of Lipids*. Present name adopted 2001. **Aims** Gather scientists from all continents with common interest in lipid research; provide a forum for the exchange of ideas, communication of novel developments and discussion of a broad variety of aspects related to lipid bioscience; support research of young scientist, giving them the opportunity to meet renowned scientists, and thus providing the scientific inspiration for future careers in lipid research. **Structure** Steering Committee. **Languages** English. **Staff** 18.00 FTE, voluntary. **Finance** None. **Activities** Research/documentation. **Events** *International Conference on the Bioscience of Lipids (ICBL)* Montréal, QC (Canada) 2022, *International Conference on the Bioscience of Lipids (ICBL)* Utrecht (Netherlands) 2021, *International Conference on the Bioscience of Lipids (ICBL)* Tokyo (Japan) 2019, *Annual Conference* Helsinki (Finland) 2018, *Annual Conference* Zurich (Switzerland) 2017. **Publications** *ICBL Newsletter* (annual). [2019.12.11/XF6633/c/**F**]

- ♦ International Conference on Boar Semen Preservation (meeting series)
- ♦ International Conference on Bridges in the Danube Basin (meeting series)
- ♦ International Conference on Broadband Dielectric Spectroscopy and its Applications (meeting series)
- ♦ International Conference On Building Energy & Environment (meeting series)
- ♦ International Conference for Building Envelope Systems and Technology (meeting series)
- ♦ International Conference on Building Materials and Materials Engineering (meeting series)
- ♦ International Conference on Building Resilience (meeting series)
- ♦ International Conference on Bulk Metallic Glasses (with High Entropy Alloys) (meeting series)
- ♦ International Conference on Business, Economics and Information Technology (meeting series)
- ♦ International Conference on Business Process Management (meeting series)

♦ International Conference on Canadian, Chinese and African Sustainable Urbanization (ICCCASU) 12876

Conférence internationale sur l'urbanisation durable au Canada, en Chine et en Afrique

Organizing Committee 60 University St (030), Simard Hall / Pavillion Simard, Univ of Ottawa, Ottawa ON K1N 6N5, Canada. Fax +16135625145. E-mail: icccasu4@uottawa.ca.
URL: https://icccasu2021.org/

History 2014. Founded as a joint initiative of *United Nations Human Settlements Programme (UN-Habitat, #20572)* and the University of Ottawa (Canada). Functions as an international think-tank. **Aims** Promote sustainable and inclusive urban development in a forum based on the diverse but complementary experiences of Canada, China, and African nations. **Finance** Also several national supporting partners and sponsors. Supported by: *Association des Centres de recherche sur l'Utilisation Urbaine du Sous-sol (ACUUS, #02420)*; *Munk School of Global Affairs & Public Policy, University of Toronto (Munk School)*; *United Nations Human Settlements Programme (UN-Habitat, #20572)*. **Activities** Events/meetings; training/education. **Events** *ICCCASU: International Conference on Canadian, Chinese and African Sustainable Urbanization* Montréal, QC (Canada) 2021, *ICCCASU: International Conference on Canadian, Chinese and African Sustainable Urbanization* Chengdu (China) 2019, *ICCCASU: International Conference on Canadian, Chinese and African Sustainable Urbanization* Yaoundé (Cameroon) 2017, *ICCASU: International Conference on Chinese and African Sustainable Urbanization* Ottawa, ON (Canada) 2015. [2021/AA2592/c/**F**]

- ♦ International Conference on Carbonaceous Particles in the Atmosphere (meeting series)
- ♦ International Conference on Carbon for Energy Storage and Environment Protection (meeting series)
- ♦ International Conference on Case-Based Reasoning (meeting series)
- ♦ International Conference of Catholic Employers' Associations / see International Christian Union of Business Executives (#12566)
- ♦ International Conference on the Cell and Molecular Biology of Chlamydomonas (meeting series)
- ♦ International Conference on Cellular Automata for Research and Industry (meeting series)
- ♦ International Conference Centers Consultants (inactive)

♦ International Conference Centre of the International Police Association 12877

Centre international d'études et de formation de l'IPA – Informations- und Bildungszentrum Schloss Gimborn (IBZ)

Dir Schloss Gimborn, Schloss-Strasse 10, 51709 Marienheide, Germany. T. +492264404330. Fax +4922643713. E-mail: info@ibz-gimborn.de.
URL: http://www.ibz-gimborn.de/

History 1969, as an international association of *International Police Association (IPA, #14612)*. **Aims** Promote international cooperation and education of civil and professional affairs. **Structure** General Assembly (annual). Board of Governors (currently 48 members). Board of 11 members. Executive Board, composed of Chairman and 3 Vice-Chairmen. Auditing Committee. **Languages** Dutch, English, French, German, Hungarian, Italian, Polish, Spanish. **Staff** 9.00 FTE, paid. **Finance** Members' dues. Other sources: public funding; contributions of IPA. **Activities** Educational work, mainly through courses and seminars. **Events** *Children in danger* Marienheide (Germany) 2000, *Destructive psychocoulte* Marienheide (Germany) 2000, *Digital world* Marienheide (Germany) 2000, *Gewaltige Verhältnisse* Marienheide (Germany) 2000, *Modern traffic managements systems* Marienheide (Germany) 2000.

Members (a) International Police Association Permanent Executive Bureau (PEB); International Executive Committee (IEC); 28 national sections; 232 regions and branches; (b) Communal authorities (2). (c) Individuals (271). Members in 31 countries:
Austria, Cameroon, Canada, Cyprus, Czechia, Denmark, Finland, France, Germany, Greece, Hungary, Iceland, Ireland, Italy, Latvia, Luxembourg, Monaco, Netherlands, New Zealand, Norway, Poland, Romania, Russia, San Marino, Slovakia, Spain, Sweden, Switzerland, Türkiye, UK, USA. [2011.06.01/XE1361/E]

- ♦ International Conference on Characterization and Control of Interfaces for High Quality Advanced Materials (meeting series)
- ♦ International Conference on Chemical Education (meeting series)
- ♦ International Conference on Chemical Reactors (meeting series)
- ♦ International Conference on Chemistry for Protection of the Environment (meeting series)
- ♦ International Conference on the Chemistry of Selenium and Tellurium (meeting series)
- ♦ International Conference on the Chemistry and Uses of Molybdenum (meeting series)
- ♦ International Conference on Chicano Literature and Latino Studies (meeting series)
- ♦ International Conference on Child and Adolescent Psychopathology (meeting series)
- ♦ International Conference on Chiroptical Spectroscopy (meeting series)
- ♦ International Conference of Christian Physicians / see International Christian Medical and Dental Association (#12562)
- ♦ International Conference of Chronopharmacology and Chronotherapeutics (meeting series)
- ♦ International Conference on Circuits, Systems, Communications and Computers (meeting series)
- ♦ International Conference on Clays in Natural and Engineered Barriers for Radioactive Waste Confinement (meeting series)
- ♦ International Conference on Clean Energy (meeting series)
- ♦ International Conference on Clean and Green Energy (meeting series)
- ♦ International Conference on Clinical Ethics and Consultation (meeting series)
- ♦ International Conference on Coastal Dynamics (meeting series)
- ♦ International Conference on Coastal Engineering (meeting series)
- ♦ International Conference on Coastal and Port Engineering in Developing Countries (meeting series)
- ♦ International Conference on Cochlear Implants and Other Implantable Auditory Technology (meeting series)
- ♦ International Conference of Cognitive Neuroscience (meeting series)
- ♦ International Conference on Coherent Multidimensional Spectroscopy (meeting series)
- ♦ International Conference on Collaboration Technologies and Social Computing (meeting series)
- ♦ International Conference on Collision and Grounding of Ships and Offshore Structures (meeting series)
- ♦ International Conference on Combustion & Energy Utilization (meeting series)
- ♦ International Conference for Community Health Nursing Research / see International Collaboration for Community Health Nursing Research
- ♦ International Conference on Competitive Materials and Technology Processes (meeting series)
- ♦ International Conference on Complex, Intelligent, and Software Intensive Systems (meeting series)
- ♦ International Conference on Complex Network and their Applications (meeting series)
- ♦ International Conference on Composite Structures (meeting series)
- ♦ International Conference on Computational Data and Social Networks (meeting series)
- ♦ International Conference on Computational Design in Engineering (meeting series)
- ♦ International Conference on Computational & Experimental Engineering and Sciences (meeting series)
- ♦ International Conference on Computational Fluid Dynamics (meeting series)
- ♦ International Conference on Computational Heat, Mass and Momentum Transfer (meeting series)
- ♦ International Conference on Computational Methods (meeting series)
- ♦ International Conference "Computational Methods in Applied Mathematics" (meeting series)
- ♦ International Conference on Computational Methods in Water Resources (meeting series)
- ♦ International Conference on Computational Science and Applications (meeting series)
- ♦ International Conference on Computer Law (meeting series)
- ♦ International Conference on Computers Helping People with Special Needs (meeting series)
- ♦ International Conference on Computers in Urban Planning and Urban Management (meeting series)
- ♦ International Conference on Computing Education Research (meeting series)
- ♦ International Conference on Computing in High Energy and Nuclear Physics (meeting series)
- ♦ International Conference on Computing and Informatics (meeting series)
- ♦ International Conference on Computing Methods in Applied Sciences and Engineering (meeting series)
- ♦ International Conference on Computing and Missions (meeting series)
- ♦ International Conference on Conceptual Modeling (meeting series)
- ♦ International Conference on Concurrency Theory (meeting series)
- ♦ International Conference on Condensed Matter Nuclear Science (meeting series)
- ♦ International Conference on the Conservation and Management of Lakes (meeting series)
- ♦ International Conference on Construction in the 21st Century (meeting series)
- ♦ International Conference on Construction Grammar (meeting series)
- ♦ International Conference on Construction History (meeting series)
- ♦ International Conference on Convergence Technology (meeting series)
- ♦ International Conference for Conveying and Handling of Particulate Solids (meeting series)
- ♦ International Conference on Coordination Chemistry (meeting series)
- ♦ International Conference on Coordination on Organometallic Chemistry of Germanium, Tin and Lead (meeting series)
- ♦ International Conference on Coupled THMC Processes in Geosystems (meeting series)
- ♦ International Conference on Culinary Arts and Science (meeting series)
- ♦ International Conference on Cultural Heritage and New Technologies (meeting series)
- ♦ International Conference on Cultural Policy Research (meeting series)
- ♦ International Conference on Culture and History (meeting series)
- ♦ International Conference on Cyber Warfare and Security (meeting series)
- ♦ International Conference on Cyclotrons and their Applications (meeting series)
- ♦ International Conference on Cytochromes (meeting series)
- ♦ International Conference on Database Theory (meeting series)
- ♦ International Conference on Data-Driven Plasma Science (meeting series)
- ♦ International Conference of Deans of French-Speaking Faculties of Medicine (#04616)
- ♦ International Conference on Defects-Recognition, Imaging and Physics in Semiconductors (meeting series)
- ♦ International Conference on Defects in Semiconductors (meeting series)
- ♦ International Conference on Dependency Linguistics (meeting series)
- ♦ International Conference on Desalination using Membrane Technology (meeting series)
- ♦ International Conference on Design and Analysis of Protective Structures (meeting series)
- ♦ International Conference on Design Science Research in Information Systems and Technology (meeting series)
- ♦ International Conference on Diet and Activity Methods (meeting series)
- ♦ International Conference on Diffusion in Solids and Liquids (meeting series)
- ♦ International Conference on Digital Audio Effects (meeting series)
- ♦ International Conference on Digital Preservation (meeting series)
- ♦ International Conference on Digital Satellite Communications (meeting series)
- ♦ International Conference on Direct Reactions with Exotic Beams (meeting series)
- ♦ International Conference on Disability, Virtual Reality and Associated Technologies (meeting series)
- ♦ International Conference on Doctors' Unions (meeting series)
- ♦ International Conference on Driver Distraction and Inattention (meeting series)
- ♦ International Conference on Dynamical Processes in Excited States of Solids (meeting series)
- ♦ International Conference on Dynamics of Disasters (meeting series)
- ♦ International Conference on Dynamics of Rotating Machines (meeting series)
- ♦ International Conference on Earthquake Geotechnical Engineering (meeting series)
- ♦ International Conference on Ecodesign and Sustainable Engineering (meeting series)
- ♦ International Conference Economics and Philosophy (meeting series)
- ♦ International Conference on Economics and Security (meeting series)
- ♦ International Conference Economies of the Balkan and Eastern European Countries (meeting series)
- ♦ International Conference on Education (meeting series)
- ♦ International Conference of Educators of Blind Youth / see International Council for Education of People with Visual Impairment (#13015)
- ♦ International Conference on EEG and EMG Data Processing (meeting series)
- ♦ International Conference on Electrical Fuses and their Applications (meeting series)
- ♦ International Conference on Electrical Impedance Tomography (meeting series)
- ♦ International Conference on Electrical Insulation and Dielectric Phenomena (meeting series)

♦ International Conference on Electrical Machines Steering Committee (ISC) 12878

Contact address not obtained. E-mail: office@icem.cc.
URL: https://icem.cc/

History 1974. Former names and other names: *ICEM Steering Committee* – former. Registration: Switzerland. **Structure** Steering Committee, including Chair, Secretary and Awards Chair. **Activities** Organizes International Conference on Electrical Machines (ICEM). **Events** *International Conference on Electrical Machines (ICEM)* Turin (Italy) 2024, *International Conference on Electrical Machines (ICEM)* Valencia (Spain) 2022, *International Conference on Electrical Machines (ICEM)* Gothenburg (Sweden) 2020, *International Conference on Electrical Machines* Alexandroupoli (Greece) 2018, *International Conference on Electrical Machines (ICEM)* Lausanne (Switzerland) 2016. [2021/XJ6454/c/E]

- ♦ International Conference on Electrical Machines and Systems (meeting series)

♦ International Conference on Electricity Distribution 12879

Congrès international des réseaux électriques de distribution (CIRED)

General Secretariat c/o AIM, Rue des Homes 1, 4000 Liège, Belgium. T. +3242222946.
URL: http://www.cired.net/

History Founded May 1971, Liège (Belgium). **Aims** Increase the business relevant competencies, skills and knowledge of those who see themselves as a part of the electricity distribution community, whether they are from the utility, product, research, regulatory, consultancy, private networks operator, service, business or academic sector. **Structure** Directing Committee (DC); Technical Committee; Advisory Committee; Permanent Secretariat in Liège (Belgium), supported jointly by Belgium and UK. **Languages** English. **Finance** Conference delegates' registration fees. **Activities** Events/meetings. **Events** *Biennial Conference* Rome (Italy) 2023, *Biennial Conference* 2021, *Biennial Conference* Madrid (Spain) 2019, *Biennial Conference* Glasgow (UK) 2017, *Workshop* Helsinki (Finland) 2016. **Publications** Conference proceedings; working group reports.

Members Directing members with national committees represented on Directing Committee, in 20 countries:
Austria, Belgium, China, Croatia, Czechia, Denmark, Finland, France, Germany, Iran Islamic Rep, Italy, Netherlands, Norway, Portugal, Slovenia, Spain, Sweden, Switzerland, UK, USA.
Associate members with liaison committees, in 17 countries:
Argentina, Australia, Bahrain, Bosnia-Herzegovina, Brazil, Canada, Egypt, Greece, Hungary, India, Korea Rep, Malaysia, Montenegro, Poland, Romania, Russia, Serbia. [2017.06.01/XD8266/F]

- ♦ International Conference on Electroluminescence and Optoelectronic Devices (meeting series)
- ♦ International Conference on Electron Dynamics in Semiconductors, Optoelectronics and Nanostructures (meeting series)
- ♦ International Conference on Electronic Properties of Two-Dimensional Systems (meeting series)
- ♦ International Conference on Electronic Publishing (meeting series)
- ♦ International Conference for Electronic Voting (meeting series)
- ♦ International Conference on Electrorheological Fluids and Magnetorheological Suspensions (meeting series)
- ♦ International Conference on Electrostatics (meeting series)
- ♦ International Conference on Embedded Wireless Systems and Networks (meeting series)
- ♦ International Conference on Emerging Contaminants (meeting series)
- ♦ International Conference on Emerging Internet, Data & Web Technologies (meeting series)
- ♦ International Conference on End-of-Life Law, Ethics, Policy, and Practice (meeting series)
- ♦ International Conference on Endothelin (meeting series)
- ♦ International Conference on Energy, Materials and Photonics (meeting series)
- ♦ International Conference on Engineering for Waste and Biomass Valorisation (meeting series)
- ♦ International Conference of English as a Lingua Franca (meeting series)
- ♦ International Conference on Enhancement and Promotion of Computational Methods in Engineering and Science (meeting series)
- ♦ International Conference on Enterprise Information Systems (meeting series)
- ♦ International Conference on Environmental Catalysis (meeting series)
- ♦ International Conference on Environmental Contamination (meeting series)
- ♦ International Conference on the Environmental Effects of Nanoparticles and Nanomaterials (meeting series)
- ♦ International Conference on Environmental Systems (meeting series)
- ♦ International Conference on the Epididymis (meeting series)
- ♦ International Conference on Evaluation and Assessment in Software Engineering (meeting series)
- ♦ International Conference on Evaluation for Practice (meeting series)
- ♦ International Conference on the Exact Renormalization Group (meeting series)
- ♦ International Conference on Excitonic and Photonic Processes in Condensed Matter and Nano Materials (meeting series)
- ♦ International Conference on Exotic Aoms and Related Topics (meeting series)
- ♦ International Conference on Experimental Stress Analysis (meeting series)
- ♦ International Conference on Fetal Breathing and other Movements / see Fetal and Neonatal Physiological Society (#09740)
- ♦ International Conference on Field-Programmable Logic and Applications (meeting series)
- ♦ International Conference on Field Programmable Technology (meeting series)
- ♦ International Conference on Fish Telemetry (meeting series)

♦ International Conference on Flexible and Printed Electronics (meeting series)
♦ International Conference on Flood Management (meeting series)
♦ International Conference on Fluvial Sedimentology (meeting series)
♦ International Conference on the FMR1 Premutation (meeting series)
♦ International Conference on Food Bioactives and Health (meeting series)
♦ International Conference on Food Oral Processing (meeting series)
♦ International Conference on Forensic Inference and Statistics (meeting series)
♦ International Conference on Formal Engineering Methods (meeting series)
♦ International Conference on Formal Modeling and Analysis of Timed Systems (meeting series)
♦ International Conference on Fracture Fatigue and Wear (meeting series)
♦ International Conference on Frontier Computing (meeting series)
♦ International Conference on Functional Imaging and Modeling of the Heart (meeting series)
♦ International Conference of Funeral Service Examining Boards (internationally oriented national body)
♦ International Conference on Future Energy Concepts (meeting series)
♦ International Conference on Gas Discharges and their Applications (meeting series)
♦ International Conference on Gas Hydrates (meeting series)
♦ International Conference on Gas-Liquid and Gas-Liquid-Solid Reactor Engineering (meeting series)
♦ International Conference on Gender Research (meeting series)
♦ International Conference on Geographic Information Science (meeting series)
♦ International Conference on Geometric Modeling and Processing (meeting series)
♦ International Conference on Goat Production and Disease (meeting series)
♦ International Conference on Governance and Accountability (meeting series)
♦ International Conference on Graph Transformation (meeting series)

♦ International Conference on the Great Lakes Region (ICGLR) 12880

Conférence internationale sur la région des Grands Lacs

Exec Sec Boulevard du Japon no 38, PO Box 7076, Bujumbura, Burundi. T. +25722256824 – +25722256825 – +25722256827. Fax +25722256828. E-mail: secretariat@icglr.org.
Communication Officer address not obtained.
URL: http://www.icglr.org/

History Established following *United Nations Security Council (UNSC, #20625)* Resolutions 1291 and 1304, which called for an international conference. Secretariat set up 2000, under the umbrella of *United Nations (UN, #20515)* and *African Union (AU, #00488)*. Eleven Heads of State and Government adopted Declaration of Peace, Security and Development in the Great Lakes Region, Nov 2004, Dar es Salaam (Tanzania UR). Pact on Security Stability and Development in the Great Lakes Region signed 2006, Nairobi (Kenya), when preparatory phase ended and implementation period began. Executive Secretariat inaugurated May 2007, Bujumbura (Burundi). **Aims** Be an effective and dynamic institution which coordinates, facilitates, monitors and ensures implementation of the Pact and other initiatives, so as to attain peace, security, stability and development in the Great Lakes Region. **Structure** Heads of State Summit; Regional Interministerial Committee; National Coordination and Collaboration Mechanism. Executive Secretariat, headed by Executive Secretary. **Activities** Politics/policy/regulatory; training/education. **Events** *Ordinary Summit of Heads of State and Governments* Bujumbura (Burundi) 2020, *Forum on Responsible Mineral Supply Chains* Paris (France) 2016, *Meeting* Brazzaville (Congo Brazzaville) 2011, *Heads of state summit* Kinshasa (Congo DR) 2010, *Capacity building workshop for civil society women organizations on the promotion of domestication of the protocol on prevention and suppression of sexual violence against women and children in the Great Lakes region, and on the follow-up of its implementation* Brazzaville (Congo Brazzaville) 2009.
Members Member States (12):
Angola, Burundi, Central African Rep, Congo Brazzaville, Congo DR, Kenya, Rwanda, South Africa, Sudan, Tanzania UR, Uganda, Zambia.
IGO Relations Observer status with (1): *United Nations (UN, #20515)* (General Assembly). **NGO Relations** Observer status with: *Inter-Parliamentary Union (IPU, #15961)*. Member of: *Tantalum-Niobium International Study Center (T.I.C., #20095)*. [2022/XM0819/c/**E***]

♦ International Conference on Han Characters Education and Research (meeting series)
♦ International Conference on Hard X-ray Photoelectron Spectroscopy (meeting series)
♦ International Conference on Harmonisation of Technical Requirements for Registration of Pharmaceuticals for Human Use / see International Council on Harmonisation of Technical Requirements for Registration of Pharmaceuticals for Human Use (#13027)
♦ International Conference on Head-Driven Phrase Structure Grammar (meeting series)
♦ International Conference on Health Care Systems Engineering (meeting series)
♦ International Conference on Heterocycles in Bioorganic Chemistry (meeting series)
♦ International Conference on High Energy Density Laboratory Astrophysics (meeting series)
♦ International Conference on High Energy Density Sciences (meeting series)
♦ International Conference on High Performance Computing in Asia-Pacific Region (meeting series)
♦ International Conference on High Pressure Semiconductor Physics (meeting series)
♦ International Conference on High Temperature Ceramic Matrix Composites (meeting series)
♦ International Conference of Historians of the Labour Movement / see International Conference of Labour and Social History (#12881)
♦ International Conference of Historical Geographers (meeting series)
♦ International Conference on the History of Cartography (meeting series)
♦ International Conference on the History of the Language Sciences (meeting series)
♦ International Conference on "Hot Sheet Metal Forming of High-Performance Steel" (meeting series)
♦ International Conference on Hydrodynamics (meeting series)
♦ International Conference on Hydroelasticity in Marine Technology (meeting series)
♦ International Conference on Hydrogenases and other redox biocatalysts for energy conversion (meeting series)
♦ International Conference on Hydrotransport (meeting series)
♦ International Conference on Immunofluorescence and Related Staining Techniques (meeting series)
♦ International Conference on Immunotherapy Radiotherapy Combinations (meeting series)
♦ International Conference on Indium Phosphide and Related Materials (meeting series)
♦ International Conference on Indoor Air Quality, Ventilation and Energy Conservation in Buildings (meeting series)
♦ International Conference on Information and Communications Security (meeting series)
♦ International Conference for the Information Community (meeting series)
♦ International Conference on Information Integration Theory and Functional Measurement (meeting series)
♦ International Conference on Information Management and Processing (meeting series)
♦ International Conference on Information Processing and Management of Uncertainty (meeting series)
♦ International Conference on Information Systems / see Association for Information Systems (#02645)
♦ International Conference on Information Systems, Logistics and Supply Chain (meeting series)
♦ International Conference Information Visualisation (meeting series)
♦ International Conference on Ingot Casting, Rolling and Forging (meeting series)
♦ International Conference on Innovation in Computer Science and Artificial Intelligence (meeting series)
♦ International Conference on Innovation, Knowledge, and Management (meeting series)
♦ International Conference on Innovative Computing, Information and Control (meeting series)
♦ International Conference on Innovative Mobile and Internet Services in Ubiquitous Computing (meeting series)
♦ International Conference on Inorganic Membranes (meeting series)
♦ International Conference of Institutions for Christian Higher Education / see International Network for Christian Higher Education (#14241)
♦ International Conference on integrated Formal Methods (meeting series)
♦ International Conference for Integrated Pest Management for Cultural Heritage (meeting series)
♦ International Conference on the Integration of Constraint Programming, Artificial Intelligence, and Operations Research (meeting series)
♦ International Conference on the Integration of Renewable and Distributed Energy Resources (meeting series)
♦ International Conference on Intelligent Data Analysis (meeting series)
♦ International Conference on Intelligent Data Engineering and Automated Learning (meeting series)
♦ International Conference on Intelligent Human Computer Interaction (meeting series)
♦ International Conference on Intelligent Software Methodologies, Tools, and Techniques (meeting series)
♦ International Conference on Intelligent Systems, Metaheuristics & Swarm Intelligence (meeting series)
♦ International Conference on Intelligent Technologies and Applications (meeting series)
♦ International Conference on Intelligent Textiles and Mass Customization (meeting series)
♦ International Conference on Intelligent Transport Systems Telecommunications (meeting series)
♦ International Conference on Interactive Digital Storytelling (meeting series)
♦ International Conference on Intergranular and Interphase Boundaries (meeting series)
♦ International Conference on Internet Pragmatics (meeting series)
♦ International Conference on Ion Beam Analysis (meeting series)
♦ International Conference on Ion Beam Modification of Materials (meeting series)
♦ International Conference on Iranian Linguistics (meeting series)
♦ International Conference on Kansei Engineering and Emotion Research (meeting series)
♦ International Conference of Labour Historians / see International Conference of Labour and Social History (#12881)

♦ International Conference of Labour and Social History 12881

Internationale Tagung der Historikerinnen der Arbeiter- und Anderer Sozialer Bewegungen (ITH)

Gen Sec Altes Rathaus, Wipplingerstr 6-8, Stg 3, 1010 Vienna, Austria. T. +4312289469316. Fax +4312289469319. E-mail: office.vienna@ith.or.at.
Pres address not obtained.
URL: http://www.ith.or.at/

History 1964, Vienna (Austria). Established following recommendations of international conference held on centennial of First International Workers' Association, organized by *Labor Movement's History Study Group (inactive)*, set up 1957/1958. Former names and other names: *International Conference of Historians of the Labour Movement* – former (1964 to 1990); *Conférence internationale des historiens des mouvements ouvriers* – former (1964 to 1990); *Internationale Tagung der Historiker der Arbeiterbewegung* – former (1964 to 1990); *International Conference of Labour Historians* – former (1990); *Conférence internationale des historiennes et historiens du mouvement ouvrier* – former (1990); *Internationale Tagung der Historikerinnen und Historiker der Arbeiterinnen- und Arbeiterbewegung* – former (1990). **Aims** Encourage scholarly interest in, and further international exchange of information pertaining to research on the history of the labour movement and other social movements within the research field of Global Labour History. **Structure** General Meeting (annual); Executive Committee; Board of Trustees; Honorary Committee; International Scientific Committee. **Languages** English, German. **Staff** 0.50 FTE, voluntary. **Finance** Sources: donations; members' dues. Other sources: state and private institutions in Austria. **Activities** Awards/prizes/competitions; events/meetings; knowledge management/information dissemination. **Events** *ITH Conference* Linz (Austria) 2022, *ITH Conference* Linz (Austria) 2021, *ITH Conference* Linz (Austria) 2019, *Annual Conference* Steyr (Austria) 2016, *Annual Conference* Berlin (Germany) 2015. **Publications** Conference proceedings.
Members University departments, political and private institutions in 33 countries:
Argentina, Australia, Austria, Belgium, Brazil, Bulgaria, Canada, China, Cuba, Czechia, Denmark, Finland, France, Germany, Hungary, India, Ireland, Italy, Japan, Korea Rep, Lithuania, Netherlands, Norway, Poland, Portugal, Russia, Slovakia, Slovenia, South Africa, Spain, Sweden, Switzerland, UK.
IGO Relations Associated with Department of Global Communications of the United Nations.
[2022/XD5171/**C**]

♦ International Conference on Large Chemical Plants (meeting series)
♦ International Conference on Large Electric Systems / see International Council on Large Electric Systems (#13040)
♦ International Conference on Large High Voltage Electric Systems / see International Council on Large Electric Systems (#13040)
♦ International Conference on Laser Ablation (meeting series)
♦ International Conference on Laser-Induced Breakdown Spectroscopy (meeting series)
♦ International Conference on Law Enforcement and Public Health (meeting series)
♦ International Conference on Learning Representations (meeting series)
♦ International Conference of Legal Regulators (meeting series)
♦ International Conference on Light-Emitting Devices and Their Industrial Applications (meeting series)

♦ International Conference on Lightning Protection (ICLP) 12882

Technical Sec Dept of Electrical Engineering, La Sapienza, Via Eudossiana 18, 00184 Rome RM, Italy. T. +393332011312. Fax +393334883235.
URL: http://www.iclp-centre.org/

Aims Stimulate and support research concerning lightning phenomena and effects of lightning; further exchange of information in the field. **Structure** Board, comprising President, Vice-President; Scientific Secretary and Secretary. Steering Committee; Scientific Committee; Local Organizing Committees; Referee Groups. **Events** *Conference* Colombo (Sri Lanka) 2021, *Conference* Rzeszów (Poland) 2018, *Conference* Estoril (Portugal) 2016, *Conference* Shanghai (China) 2014, *Conference* Vienna (Austria) 2012. [2008/XS6024/c/**F**]

♦ International Conference on Linguistics and Nordic Languages (meeting series)
♦ International Conference on Liquid Metal Technology in Energy Production (meeting series)
♦ International Conference on Local Government (meeting series)
♦ International Conference on Logistics and Maritime Systems (meeting series)
♦ International Conference of Long Term Care Directors and Administrators (meeting series)
♦ International Conference on Long-Term Complications of Treatment of Children and Adolescents for Cancer (meeting series)
♦ International Conference on Low Volume Roads (meeting series)
♦ International Conference on Luminescent Detectors and Transformers of Ionizing Radiation (meeting series)
♦ International Conference on Lymphatic Tissues and Germinal Centres in Immune Reactions (meeting series)
♦ International Conference on Lymphocyte Engineering (meeting series)
♦ International Conference on Machine Learning, Optimization, and Data Science (meeting series)
♦ International Conference on Magnetic Fluids (meeting series)
♦ International Conference on Magnetic Resonance Microscopy (meeting series)
♦ International Conference on Magnet Technology (meeting series)
♦ International Conference on the Management of Liver Diseases (meeting series)
♦ International Conference on Manipulation, Automation and Robotics at Small Scales (meeting series)
♦ International Conference on Manufacturing Engineering and Processes (meeting series)
♦ International Conference on Manufacturing, Machine Design and Tribology (meeting series)
♦ International Conference on Marine Waste Water Discharges and Coastal Environment (meeting series)
♦ International Conference on Maritime Autonomous Surface Ship (meeting series)
♦ International Conference on Material Engineering and Manufacturing (meeting series)
♦ International Conference on Material Science and Engineering Technology (meeting series)
♦ International Conference on Materials Design and Applications (meeting series)
♦ International Conference on Materials and Mechanisms of Superconductivity (meeting series)
♦ International Conference on Materials and Nanomaterials (meeting series)
♦ International Conference on Materials and Reliability (meeting series)
♦ International Conference on Mathematical Methods for Curves and Surfaces (meeting series)
♦ International Conference on Mathematical Neuroscience (meeting series)
♦ International Conference on Mathematical and Numerical Aspects of Wave Propagation (meeting series)
♦ International Conference on Mathematical and Statistical Methods for Actuarial Sciences and Finance (meeting series)

- ♦ International Conference on Mathematical Views / see Mathematical Views (#16603)
- ♦ International Conference On Matrix Analysis and Applications (meeting series)
- ♦ International Conference On Matrix Vesicles (meeting series)
- ♦ International Conference on Mechanical Ventilation (meeting series)
- ♦ International Conference on Mechanics of Composites (meeting series)
- ♦ International Conference on Mechanics in Medicine and Biology (meeting series)
- ♦ International Conference on Mechanisms of Action of Nutraceuticals (meeting series)
- ♦ International Conference on Mechatronics Technology (meeting series)
- ♦ International Conference for Media in Education (meeting series)
- ♦ International Conference on Megagauss Magnetic Field Generation and Related Topics (meeting series)
- ♦ International Conference on Membrane Science and Technology (meeting series)
- ♦ International Conference on Membrane Science and Technology (meeting series)
- ♦ International Conference on Memory (meeting series)
- ♦ International Conference on Men and Equal Opportunities (meeting series)
- ♦ International Conference on Mercury as a Global Pollutant (meeting series)
- ♦ International conference on Metal-Binding Peptides (meeting series)
- ♦ International Conference on Metal Forming (meeting series)
- ♦ International Conference on Metal Organic Frameworks and Porous Polymers (meeting series)
- ♦ International Conference on Metal Organic Vapor Phase Epitaxy (meeting series)
- ♦ International Conference on Metamaterials, Photonic Crystals and Plasmonics (meeting series)
- ♦ International Conference on Methods and Techniques in Behavioral Research (meeting series)
- ♦ International Conference on Metrology and Properties of Engineering Surfaces (meeting series)
- ♦ International Conference on Microbial Food and Feed Ingredients (meeting series)
- ♦ International Conference on Microelectronics and Plasma Technology (meeting series)
- ♦ International Conference on Micro and Nano Engineering (meeting series)
- ♦ International Conference of Microreaction Technology (meeting series)
- ♦ International Conference on Microwave Materials and their Applications (meeting series)
- ♦ International Conference on Mobility and Transport for Elderly and Disabled Persons (meeting series)
- ♦ International Conference on Modeling and Diagnostics for Advanced Engine (meeting series)
- ♦ International Conference on Modelling and Optimisation of Ship Energy Systems (meeting series)
- ♦ International Conference on Modelling, Optimization and Simulation (meeting series)
- ♦ International Conference on Modern Approach in Humanities (meeting series)
- ♦ International Conference on Modulated Semiconductor Structures (meeting series)
- ♦ International Conference on Molecular Systems Biology (meeting series)
- ♦ International Conference on Monitoring and Management of Visitors in Recreational and Protected Areas (meeting series)
- ♦ International Conference on Monitoring Molecules in Neuroscience / see International Society for Monitoring Molecules in Neuroscience (#15279)
- ♦ International Conference on Monte Carlo Methods and Applications (meeting series)
- ♦ International Conference in Monte Carlo & Quasi-Monte Carlo Methods in Scientific Computing (meeting series)
- ♦ International Conference on Monte Carlo Techniques for Medical Applications (meeting series)
- ♦ International Conference on Multimedia in Physics Teaching and Learning (meeting series)
- ♦ International Conference on Multi-Organisational Partnerships, Alliances and Networks (meeting series)
- ♦ International Conference on Multiphase Flow (meeting series)
- ♦ International Conference on Multiscale Materials Modeling (meeting series)
- ♦ International Conference on Music Perception and Cognition (meeting series)
- ♦ International Conference on Nanogenerators and Piezotronics (meeting series)
- ♦ International Conference on Nanoimprint and Nanoprint Technologies (meeting series)
- ♦ International Conference on Nanomaterials and Biomaterials (meeting series)
- ♦ International Conference on Nanomaterials and Materials Engineering (meeting series)
- ♦ International Conference of National Unions of Mutual Benefit Societies (inactive)
- ♦ International Conference on Networking and Network Applications (meeting series)
- ♦ International Conference on Neutrons and Food (meeting series)
- ♦ International Conference on New Business Models (meeting series)
- ♦ International Conference on New Diamond and Nano Carbons (meeting series)
- ♦ International Conference on the New Diamond Science and Technology (meeting series)
- ♦ International Conference on New Information Technology (meeting series)
- ♦ International Conference on New Interfaces for Musical Expression (meeting series)
- ♦ International Conference on New or Restored Democracies (meeting series)

♦ International Conference of NGOs 12883

Conférence internationale des ONG

Contact c/o Comité de Liaison ONG-UNESCO, UNESCO House, 1 rue Miollis, 75732 Paris CEDEX 15, France. T. +33145683668. Fax +33145660337. E-mail: comite.liaison.ong@unesco.org.
URL: http://www.ngo-unesco.net/

History 23 May 1950, Florence (Italy), as *Conference of International Non-Governmental Organizations in Consultative Relations – Categories A and B – with UNESCO – Conférence des organisations internationales non gouvernementales entretenant des relations de consultation – catégories A et B – avec l'UNESCO*, at 1st Conference, convened by UNESCO following a recommendation, Jan 1950, of *Temporary International Council for Educational Reconstruction (TICER, inactive)*. Subsequently changed title to *Conference of International Non-Governmental Organizations in Consultative Relations with UNESCO – Conférence des organisations internationales non gouvernementales entretenant des relations de consultation avec l'UNESCO*; *Conference of International Non-Governmental Organizations in Official Relations with UNESCO – Conférence des organisations internationales non gouvernementales entretenant des relations officielles avec l'UNESCO*. **Aims** Study and improve arrangements for consultation with UNESCO; seek practical means of cooperation in the implementation of UNESCO programmes. **Structure** Conference (every 3 years, always in Paris), convened by UNESCO. Represented between conferences by *NGO-UNESCO Liaison Committee (#17127)*, consisting of President and 9 representative NGOs, elected at Conference by NGOs maintaining formal relations with UNESCO. **Languages** English, French. **Finance** NGOs' voluntary contributions. Contract with UNESCO covers financing of activities; UNESCO also provides secretarial and technical facilities. **Activities** Engages in collective consultations on aspects of UNESCO's programme. Joint programme commissions carry out in-depth studies on particular subjects: poverty; human rights and culture of peace; Habitat II; Science and ethics. **Events** *Biennial conference* Paris (France) 2009, *Biennial conference* Paris (France) 2007, *Biennial Conference* Paris (France) 2005, *Biennial Conference* Paris (France) 2003, *Biennial conference* Paris (France) 2001. **Members** Open to all NGOs in official partnership with UNESCO; these may attend meetings during the General Conference. **IGO Relations** *UNESCO (#20322)*. **NGO Relations** Members of Liaison Committee elected by Conference, Nov 1998, Paris (France): *Conseil international des radios-télévisions d'expression française (CIRTEF, #04694)*; *Coordinating Committee for International Voluntary Service (CCIVS, #04819)*; *International Council for Open and Distance Education (ICDE, #13056)*; *International Council for Philosophy and Human Sciences (CIPSH, #13061)*; *International Council for Science (ICSU, inactive)*; *International Federation for Information Processing (IFIP, #13458)*; *International PEN (#14552)*; *World Confederation of Teachers (WCT, inactive)*; *World Federation of UNESCO Clubs, Centres and Associations (WFUCA, #21498)*. Informal relations and communication exchange with: *NGO Committee on UNICEF (#17120)*; other groupings of non-governmental organizations (not specified). [2016/XE0407/y/**E**]

- ♦ International Conference on Nightlife, Substance Use and Related Health Issues (meeting series)
- ♦ International Conference on Nitride Semiconductors (meeting series)
- ♦ International Conference on Non-Aqueous Solutions (meeting series)
- ♦ International Conference on Non-contact Atomic Force Microscopy (meeting series)
- ♦ International Conference on Noncovalent Interactions (meeting series)
- ♦ International Conference on Nondestructive Evaluation in the Nuclear Industry (meeting series)
- ♦ International Conference on Nuclear Engineering (meeting series)
- ♦ International Conference of Nuclear-Free Zone Authorities (meeting series)
- ♦ International Conference on the Numerical Analysis of Semiconductor Devices and Integrated Circuits (meeting series)
- ♦ International Conference on Numerical Modeling of Space Plasma Flows (meeting series)
- ♦ International Conference on Numerical Ship Hydrodynamics (meeting series)
- ♦ International Conference on Nutrition & Growth (meeting series)

♦ International Conference of Occlusion Medicine (ICOM) 12884

Contact address not obtained. E-mail: greven@rheinzahn-bonn.de.
URL: http://www.iaaidentistry.com/

History 2006 as *International Academy of Interdisciplinary Dentistry (iAAID)*. **Aims** Provide an academy dedicated to doctors treating complex cases demanding extensive diagnoses and treatment plans; provide educational meetings to promote interdisciplinary research and clinical excellence. **Structure** Council of 9 members. Executive Committee, comprising President, Secretary, Treasurer, Webmaster and Past President. **Events** *Congress* Munich (Germany) 2015, *Asian Congress* Sapporo (Japan) 2014, *Congress* Vienna (Austria) 2012, *Asian Congress* Yokohama (Japan) 2012, *Congress* Nice (France) 2010. **Publications** *International Journal of Stomatology and Occlusion Medicine*. [2020.03.03/XJ6476/v/**C**]

- ♦ International Conference on Open Magnetic Systems for Plasma Confinement (meeting series)
- ♦ International Conference on Ophthalmic Photography (meeting series)
- ♦ International Conference on Optical Angular Momentum (meeting series)
- ♦ International Conference on Optical Fiber Sensors (meeting series)
- ♦ International Conference on Optical, Optoelectronic and Photonic Materials and Applications (meeting series)
- ♦ International Conference on Optics-photonics Design & Fabrication (meeting series)
- ♦ International Conference on Organizational Learning, Knowledge and Capabilities (meeting series)
- ♦ International Conference on Organometallic Chemistry (meeting series)

♦ International Conference on Oriental Carpets (ICOC) 12885

SG PO Box 4312, Philadelphia PA 19118, USA. T. +12152480494. Fax +12152480496.
URL: http://www.icoc-orientalrugs.org/

History 1976, London (UK). Registered in the USA. **Aims** Advance understanding and appreciation of hand-woven carpets and related *textile* arts, primarily of the Eastern hemisphere – the aesthetics, history, traditions and culture of the people who made them. **Structure** International Committee; Executive Committee. **Languages** English. **Staff** 8.00 FTE, voluntary. **Finance** Fees from conferences, tours, seminars and other related activities; book sales. **Events** *Conference* Washington, DC (USA) 2018, *Conference* Washington, DC (USA) 2015, *Conference* Stockholm (Sweden) 2011, *Conference* Istanbul (Turkey) 2007, *Regional conference* Sydney, NSW (Australia) 2004. **Publications** *Oriental Carpet and Textile Studies* – series. *A World of Carpets and Textiles*; *Oriental Rugs from Atlantic Collections*; *Oriental Rugs from Pacific Collections*; *Weaving Traditions of Anatolia* – in 2 vols.
Members International Committee with members in 16 countries:
Australia, Austria, France, Germany, Iran Islamic Rep, Italy, Morocco, Poland, Portugal, Romania, Russia, Sweden, Switzerland, Türkiye, UK, USA. [2018.09.04/XF7111/c/**F**]

- ♦ International Conference on Oxygen Binding and Sensing Proteins (meeting series)
- ♦ International Conference on Paleoceanography (meeting series)
- ♦ International Conference on Parallel Computational Fluid Dynamics (meeting series)
- ♦ International Conference on Parallel and Distributed Computing, Applications and Technologies (meeting series)
- ♦ International Conference on Particle Induced X-ray Emission (meeting series)
- ♦ International Conference of Peace Researchers and Peace Activists / see International Nonviolent Initiatives
- ♦ International Conference on Pediatric Mechanical Circulatory Support Systems and Pediatric Cardiopulmonary Perfusion (meeting series)
- ♦ International Conference on Penal Abolition / see International Circle of Penal Abolitionists (#12574)
- ♦ International Conference on Perspectives in Business Informatics Research (meeting series)
- ♦ International Conference on Petroleum Phase Behavior and Fouling (meeting series)
- ♦ International Conference on Photonic, Electronic and Atomic Collisions (meeting series)
- ♦ International Conference on the Physical Properties and Application of Advanced Materials (meeting series)
- ♦ International Conference on Physician Health (meeting series)
- ♦ International Conference on Physico-Chemical Hydrodynamics (meeting series)
- ♦ International Conference on Physics and Applications of Spin Related Phenomena in Semiconductors (meeting series)
- ♦ International Conference on the Physics of Highly Charged Ions (meeting series)
- ♦ International Conference on the Physics of Non-Crystalline Solids (meeting series)
- ♦ International Conference on Physiology of Food and Fluid Intake (meeting series)
- ♦ International Conference on Planarization/CMP Technology (meeting series)
- ♦ International Conference on Plant Pathogenic Bacteria (meeting series)
- ♦ International Conference on Plasma Surface Interactions in Controlled Fusion Devices (meeting series)
- ♦ International Conference on Plasmodium vivax Research (meeting series)
- ♦ International Conference on Plastics in Medicine and Surgery (meeting series)
- ♦ International Conference on Poisson Geometry (meeting series)
- ♦ International Conference on Political Warfare of the Soviet (meeting series)
- ♦ International Conference on Polymyxins (meeting series)
- ♦ International Conference on Polyol Mediated Synthesis (meeting series)
- ♦ International Conference on Polyphenols and Health (meeting series)
- ♦ International Conference on Population Balance Modelling (meeting series)
- ♦ International Conference on Population Balance Modelling (meeting series)
- ♦ International Conference on Positron Annihilation (meeting series)
- ♦ International Conference on Power and Energy Systems Engineering (meeting series)
- ♦ International Conference on Practical Aspects of Memory (meeting series)
- ♦ International Conference on Precision Physics of Simple Atomic Systems (meeting series)
- ♦ International Conference of the Principal High-Tension Electrical Systems / see International Council on Large Electric Systems (#13040)
- ♦ International Conference on Principles and Practice of Multi-Agent Systems (meeting series)
- ♦ International Conference on Prison Abolition / see International Circle of Penal Abolitionists (#12574)
- ♦ International Conference on Privacy, Security and Trust (meeting series)
- ♦ International Conference on Probabilistic Graphical Models (meeting series)
- ♦ International Conference on Processing and Manufacturing of Advanced Materials (meeting series)
- ♦ International Conference of Producer Organisations (meeting series)
- ♦ International Conference on on Product-Focused Software Process Improvement (meeting series)
- ♦ International Conference on Progress in Vaccination Against Cancer (meeting series)
- ♦ International Conference on the Properties of Steam / see International Association for the Properties of Water and Steam (#12110)
- ♦ International Conference on Prospective Memory (meeting series)
- ♦ International Conference on Proteoglycans (meeting series)
- ♦ International Conference on Provable Security (meeting series)
- ♦ International Conference on Psychology and the Arts (meeting series)
- ♦ International Conference on Quantitative Evaluation of Systems (meeting series)
- ♦ International Conference on Quantitative InfraRed Thermography (meeting series)
- ♦ International Conference on Quantum Communication, Measurement and Computing (meeting series)
- ♦ International Conference on Quantum Dots (meeting series)
- ♦ International Conference on Quarks and Nuclear Physics (meeting series)
- ♦ International Conference Rail Tourism (inactive)
- ♦ International Conference for Railway Technical Unity (inactive)

♦ International Conference on Raman Spectroscopy (meeting series)
♦ International Conference on Rapidly Quenched and Metastable Materials (meeting series)

♦ International Conference on Rare Diseases and Orphan Drugs (ICORD Society) 12886

Pres attn Joan Comella / VHIR, Passeig de la Vall d'Hebron 119-129, 2a planta Ed Mediterrània, 08035 Barcelona, Spain. E-mail: icord@icord.es.
URL: http://icord.es/

History 13 Sep 2007, Brussels (Belgium). Founded following proposal during 1st ICORD conference in 2005, Stockholm (Sweden). **Aims** Improve the welfare of patients with rare diseases and their families worldwide through better knowledge, research, care, information, education and awareness. **Structure** General Assembly (annual); Board. **Languages** English. **Staff** Voluntary. **Finance** Sources: members' dues. **Events** *Conference* Tel Aviv (Israel) 2019, *Conference* Stockholm (Sweden) 2018, *Conference* Cape Town (South Africa) 2016, *Conference* Mexico City (Mexico) 2015, *The societal value of prevention, diagnosis and treatments of rare diseases* Ede (Netherlands) 2014. **Members** Membership countries not specified.
[2022/XJ8273/**E**]

♦ International Conference on Rare Earths and Actinides 82 (meeting series)
♦ International Conference on Reachability Problems (meeting series)
♦ International Conference on Reactive Plasmas (meeting series)
♦ International Conference on Reactive Sputter Deposition (meeting series)
♦ International Conference on Real Options (meeting series)
♦ International Conference on Receptive Ecumenism (meeting series)
♦ International Conference on Relational and Algebraic Methods in Computer Science (meeting series)
♦ International Conference on Reliability and Maintainability (meeting series)
♦ International Conference on Renewable Energy Gas Technology (meeting series)
♦ International Conference on Renewable Energy Research and Applications (meeting series)
♦ International Conference on Renewable Mobility (Fuels of the Future) (meeting series)
♦ International Conference on Renewable Resources and Biorefineries (meeting series)
♦ International Conference on Representations of Algebras (meeting series)
♦ International Conference on Reproduction, Pregnancy and Rheumatic Diseases (meeting series)
♦ International Conference on Research in Computational Molecular Biology (meeting series)
♦ International Conference on Retranslation in Context (meeting series)
♦ International Conference on Reversal Theory (meeting series)
♦ International Conference of RF Superconductivity (meeting series)
♦ International Conference on Risk Assessment of Pharmaceuticals in the Environment (meeting series)
♦ International Conference on Robust Statistics (meeting series)
♦ International Conference on Rock Dynamics and Applications (meeting series)
♦ International Conference on Rodent Biology (meeting series)
♦ International Conference on Rodent Biology and Management (meeting series)
♦ International Conference on Romanticism (internationally oriented national body)
♦ International Conferences on Calcium Regulating Hormones / see International Bone and Mineral Society (#12379)
♦ International Conference on Science, Technology and Innovation for Sustainable Well-Being (meeting series)
♦ International Conference on the Science and Technology of Synthetic Metals (meeting series)
♦ International Conference on the Scientific Basis of Health Services (meeting series)
♦ International Conference on the Scientific and Clinical Applications of Magnetic Carriers (meeting series)
♦ International Conference on Second Language Pedagogies (meeting series)
♦ International Conference on Second Messengers and Phosphoproteins (meeting series)
♦ International Conferences on Environmental Future (meeting series)
♦ International Conference Series on Competition and Ownership in Land Passenger Transport (meeting series)
♦ The International Conference Series on Human Computer Interaction with Mobile Devices and Services (meeting series)
♦ International Conference on Shellfish Restoration (meeting series)
♦ International Conference of Ship Tank Superintendents / see International Towing Tank Conference (#15698)
♦ International Conference for Short and Documentary Film / see International Short Film Conference (#14854)
♦ International Conference of Sickness Insurance Funds and Mutual Benefit Societies / see International Social Security Association (#14885)
♦ International Conference on Silicon Carbide and Related Materials (meeting series)
♦ International Conference on Similarity Search and Applications (meeting series)
♦ International Conference on Sino-Tibetan Langauges and Linguistics (meeting series)
♦ International Conference on Small Gap Semiconductors (meeting series)
♦ International Conference for Social Leagues of Purchasers (inactive)
♦ International Conference on Social Responsibility, Ethics and Sustainable Business (meeting series)
♦ International Conference on Social Robotics (meeting series)
♦ International Conference on Social Science and Medicine (meeting series)
♦ International Conference of Social Theory, Politics and the Arts (meeting series)
♦ International Conference for the Sociology of Religions / see International Society for the Sociology of Religions (#15451)
♦ International Conference on Software Business (meeting series)
♦ International Conference on Software Engineering (meeting series)
♦ International Conference on Software Security and Assurance (meeting series)
♦ International Conference on Solid Compounds of Transition Elements (meeting series)
♦ International Conference on Solid Films and Surfaces (meeting series)
♦ International Conference on Solution Chemistry (meeting series)
♦ International Conference on Southern Hemisphere Meteorology and Oceanography (meeting series)
♦ International Conference on Spectral and High Order Methods (meeting series)
♦ International Conference on Spectroscopic Ellipsometry (meeting series)
♦ International Conference on Speech and Computer (meeting series)
♦ International Conferences of People with HIV/AIDS / see Global Network of People Living with HIV/AIDS (#10494)
♦ International Conferences on Philosophical Practice (meeting series)
♦ International Conference on Spontaneous Coherence in Excitonic Systems (meeting series)
♦ International Conference on Squeezed States and Uncertainty Relations (meeting series)
♦ International Conference on the Stability of Ships and Ocean Vehicles (meeting series)
♦ International Conference on Stable Isotopes in Medicine and Biology (meeting series)
♦ International Conference on Steel Drums (meeting series)
♦ International Conference on Strangeness in Quark Matter (meeting series)
♦ International Conference on the Strength of Metals and Alloys (meeting series)
♦ International Conference on Strongly Correlated Electrons systems (meeting series)
♦ International Conference on Structural Analysis of Historical Constructions (meeting series)
♦ International Conference on Structural Health Assessment of Timber Structures (meeting series)
♦ International Conference on the Structure of Surfaces (meeting series)
♦ International Conference of Students of Systematic Musicology (meeting series)
♦ International Conference on Sublobar Resections for Lung Cancer (meeting series)
♦ International Conference on Superlattices, Nanostructures and Nanodevices (meeting series)
♦ International Conference on Supersymmetry and Unification of Fundamental Interactions (meeting series)
♦ International Conference for Supportive Care in Cancer / see Multinational Association of Supportive Care in Cancer (#16895)
♦ International Conference on Surface Modification of Materials by Ion Beams (meeting series)
♦ International Conference on Surface Plasmon Photonics (meeting series)
♦ International Conference on the Survivors of Rape (meeting series)
♦ International Conference on Sustainable Development in the Minerals Industry (meeting series)
♦ International Conference on Sustainable Energy and Environmental Protection (meeting series)
♦ International Conference on Sustainable Energy and Green Technology (meeting series)
♦ International Conference on Sustainable Solid Waste Management (meeting series)
♦ International Conferences on Waste Minimization and Clean Technology (meeting series)
♦ International Conference of Symphony and Opera Musicians (internationally oriented national body)
♦ International Conference on Synchrotron Radiation Instrumentation (meeting series)
♦ International Conference on Synthesis, Modeling, Analysis and Simulation Methods and Applications to Circuit Design Conference (meeting series)
♦ International Conference on Systems Science (meeting series)
♦ International Conference on Tangible, Embedded and Embodied Interaction (meeting series)
♦ International Conference on Taphonomy and Fossilisation (meeting series)
♦ International Conference for the Teaching of History (inactive)
♦ International Conference on Technologies for Music Notation and Representation (meeting series)
♦ International Conference on Technology Education in the Asia-Pacific Region (meeting series)
♦ International Conference on Technology in Mathematics Teaching (meeting series)
♦ International Conference on Ternary and Multinary Compounds (meeting series)
♦ International Conference on Tethers in Space (meeting series)
♦ International Conference on the Tetrapyrrole Photoreceptors of Photosynthetic Organisms (meeting series)
♦ International Conference on Textures of Materials (meeting series)
♦ International Conference on Thai Studies (meeting series)
♦ International Conference on Theoretical Aspects of Catalysis (meeting series)

♦ International Conference on Theory and Practice of Digital Libraries (TPDL) 12887

Chair Archives/Library/Science/Museology Dept, Fac of Information Science and Informatics, Ionian Univ, 72 Ioannou Theotoki St, 491 00 Corfu, Greece. E-mail: papatheodor@ionio.gr.
Deputy Chair KUL Univ Library, Mgr Ladeuzeplein 21, Bte 5591, 3000 Leuven, Belgium.
URL: http://www.tpdl.eu/

History 1997, as *European Conference on Digital Libraries (ECDL)*, following the activities of *DELOS – Association for Digital Libraries (DELOS, inactive)*. Present name adopted, 2011. **Aims** Promote research and development in the area of digital libraries and other digital collections. **Structure** Steering Committee; Executive Board; Committees (2). **Events** *Conference* Lyon (France) 2020, *Conference* Oslo (Norway) 2019, *Conference* Poznań (Poland) 2015, *Conference* London (UK) 2014, *Conference* Valletta (Malta) 2013. **Publications** Conference proceedings. [2014.06.23/XM4023/c/**E**]

♦ International Conference on Thermal, Mechanical and Multi-Physics Simulation and Experiments in Microelectronics and Microsystems (meeting series)
♦ International Conference on Thin-Walled Structures (meeting series)
♦ International Conference of Tissue-Engineering Heart Valves (meeting series)
♦ International Conference on Tourism Research (meeting series)
♦ International Conference on Toxic Cyanobacteria (meeting series)
♦ International Conference on Toxic Marine Phytoplankton (meeting series)
♦ International Conference on Transdisciplinary Imaging at the intersections between Art, Science and Culture (meeting series)
♦ International Conference on the Transportation, Handling and Storage of Bulk Chemicals (meeting series)
♦ International Conference on Transport Theory (meeting series)
♦ International Conference on Tube Hydroforming (meeting series)
♦ International Conference on Types for Proofs (meeting series)
♦ International Conference on Ubiquitous Information Management and Communication (meeting series)
♦ International Conference on Ultrafast Structural Dynamics (meeting series)
♦ International Conference on Ultra-relativistic Nucleus-Nucleus Collisions (meeting series)
♦ International Conference on Unconventional Computation and Natural Computation (meeting series)
♦ International Conference on Universal Design (meeting series)
♦ International Conference on University Education for Public Relations (inactive)
♦ International Conference of University Teaching and Innovation (meeting series)
♦ International Conference on Urban Pests (meeting series)
♦ International Conference on the Use of Computers in Radiation Therapy (meeting series)
♦ International Conference on UV and Skin Cancer Prevention (meeting series)
♦ International Conference on Vacuum Metallurgy (meeting series)
♦ International Conference on the Valuation of Plant, Machinery and Equipment (meeting series)
♦ International Conference on Vapour Growth and Epitaxy (meeting series)
♦ International Conference on Verification and Evaluation of Computer and Communication Systems (meeting series)
♦ International Conference on Vibration Engineering and Technology of Machinery (meeting series)
♦ International Conference on Violence in the Health Sector (meeting series)
♦ International Conference on Virtual Machining Process Technology (meeting series)
♦ International Conference on Visual Storytelling (meeting series)
♦ International Conference on In Vivo Methods / see International Society for Monitoring Molecules in Neuroscience (#15279)
♦ International Conference on Vocational Guidance (meeting series)
♦ International Conference Volunteers / see International Communications Volunteers (#12817)
♦ International Conference on Water and Environmental Engineering (meeting series)
♦ International Conference on Water Jetting (meeting series)
♦ International Conference on Water Resource and Environment (meeting series)
♦ International Conference on Wearable, Micro and Nano Technologies for Personalized Health (meeting series)
♦ International Conference on Web-based Learning (meeting series)
♦ International Conference and Workshop on Numerical Simulation of 3D Sheet Metal Forming Processes (meeting series)
♦ International Conference on World Peace (meeting series)
♦ International Conference on WT1 in Human Neoplasia (meeting series)
♦ International Conference on XeCT and Related CBF Techniques (meeting series)
♦ International Conference on X-Ray Lasers (meeting series)
♦ International Conference on X-ray Optics and Applications (meeting series)
♦ International Conference on Yeast Genetics and Molecular Biology (meeting series)
♦ International Conference of Young Researchers in Heritage (meeting series)
♦ International Conference of Young Social Workers (inactive)
♦ International Conflict Research Institute (see: #20642)
♦ International Confocal Working Group (unconfirmed)

♦ International Confucian Association 12888

Main Office 26 Yuetan N St, Xicheng District, 100045 Beijing, China. E-mail: icaica@126.com.
URL: http://www.ica.org.cn/

Activities Congress. **Events** *International Conference on Confucius* Seoul (Korea Rep) 2011.
[2015/XE2691/**E**]

♦ International Confucian Ecological Alliance (unconfirmed)
♦ International Congo Aid-Smile African Children (internationally oriented national body)
♦ International Congo Association (inactive)
♦ International Congregational Council (inactive)

♦ **International Congregational Fellowship (ICF)** **12889**

Association congrégationaliste internationale

Communications Dir Olivet College, 320 S Main St, Olivet MI 49076, USA. T. +12697497624.
URL: http://www.intercong.org/

History Jul 1975, Chislehurst (UK), as a successor to *International Congregational Council (ICC, inactive)*, which was set up Jul 1891, London (UK), and absorbed 1970, London, by *World Alliance of Reformed Churches (WARC, inactive)*. **Aims** Serve continuing congregational churches and foster fellowship between them. **Structure** Assembly (every 4 years). Executive Committee. Commissions (5): Theological; Youth; Communications; Finance; Structures. **Languages** English. **Staff** 0.50 FTE, paid. **Finance** Sources: contributions; grants. **Activities** Organize seminars and conferences. **Events** *Conference* Olivet, MI (USA) 2021, *Conference* Cape Town (South Africa) 2017, *Conference* Oxford (UK) 2013, *Quadrennial Conference* Milwaukee, WI (USA) 2009, *Ever family conference* Corfu (Greece) 2005. **Publications** *International Congregational Journal* (2 a year); *ICF Newsletter* (periodical). Conference proceedings.

Members Congregational churches in about 50 countries and territories, including in the following 47:
Angola, Argentina, Armenia, Australia, Botswana, Brazil, Bulgaria, Cambodia, Canada, China, Congo DR, Czechia, Fiji, France, Germany, Greece, Guyana, Honduras, Hong Kong, India, Italy, Japan, Kenya, Kiribati, Korea Rep, Liberia, Marshall Is, Mexico, Micronesia FS, Myanmar, Nauru, New Zealand, Nigeria, Niue, North Macedonia, Paraguay, Philippines, Portugal, Samoa, Samoa USA, South Africa, Taiwan, Tuvalu, UK, USA, Vietnam, Zimbabwe.
Included in the above, 1 church listed in this Yearbook:
United Congregational Church of Southern Africa (UCCSA, #20503). [2014/XD8132/**C**]

♦ International Congress of Acarology (meeting series)
♦ International Congress of Accountants (meeting series)
♦ International Congress of African Studies (inactive)

♦ **International Congress of Americanists (ICA)** **12890**

Congrès international des américanistes – Congreso Internacional de Americanistas – Internationaler Amerikanistenkongress

Sec Inst for History, Univ of Vienna, Universiteitsring 1, 1010 Vienna, Austria.

History Founded 1875, Nancy (France). **Aims** Study man and science in the Americas, particularly the *humanities* and *social sciences* as applied to *Latin America*. **Structure** International and national committees. **Languages** English, French, German, Italian, Portuguese, Spanish. **Staff** 20.00 FTE, voluntary. **Finance** Members' dues. Grants from academic bodies and commercial sources. **Activities** Events/meetings; awards/prizes/competitions. **Events** *Congress* Foz do Iguaçu (Brazil) 2021, *Congress* San Salvador (El Salvador) 2015, *Congress* Vienna (Austria) 2012, *Congress* Mexico City (Mexico) 2009, *Congress* Seville (Spain) 2006. **Publications** Congress proceedings.

Members Archaeologists, anthropologists, historians, linguists, sociologists, political scientists, geographers and other scholars interested in the study of man in the Americas. Members in 96 countries and territories:
Albania, Algeria, Andorra, Antigua-Barbuda, Argentina, Armenia, Australia, Austria, Azerbaijan, Bahamas, Barbados, Belarus, Belgium, Belize, Bolivia, Bosnia-Herzegovina, Brazil, Bulgaria, Canada, Chile, China, Colombia, Costa Rica, Croatia, Cuba, Cyprus, Czechia, Denmark, Dominica, Dominican Rep, Ecuador, Egypt, El Salvador, Estonia, Finland, France, Georgia, Germany, Greece, Grenada, Guatemala, Guyana, Haiti, Holy See, Honduras, Hungary, Iceland, India, Ireland, Israel, Italy, Jamaica, Japan, Latvia, Liechtenstein, Lithuania, Luxembourg, Malta, Mexico, Moldova, Monaco, Netherlands, New Zealand, Nicaragua, Nigeria, North Macedonia, Norway, Pakistan, Panama, Paraguay, Peru, Poland, Portugal, Romania, Russia, San Marino, Serbia, Slovakia, Slovenia, South Africa, Spain, St Kitts-Nevis, St Lucia, St Vincent-Grenadines, Suriname, Sweden, Switzerland, Taiwan, Trinidad-Tobago, Türkiye, UK, Ukraine, Uruguay, USA, Venezuela. [2015/XD1691/v/**F**]

♦ International Congress of Anthropology and Prehistoric Archaeology (inactive)
♦ International Congress on Anti-Cancer Treatment (meeting series)
♦ International Congress on Antiphospholipid Antibodies (meeting series)
♦ International Congress on the Application of Mathematics in Engineering (meeting series)
♦ International Congress on the Application of the Theory of Probability in Telephone Engineering and Administration / see International Teletraffic Congress (#15674)
♦ International Congress of Art Critics / see Association internationale des critiques d'art (#02680)

♦ **International Congress of Asian and North African Studies (ICANAS)** **12891**

Congrès international des études asiatiques et nord-africaines

Address not obtained.

History 1873, Paris (France). Former names and other names: *International Congress of Orientalists* – former (1873 to 1976); *Congrès international des orientalistes* – former (1873 to 1976); *International Congress of Human Sciences in Asia and North Africa* – former (1976 to 1986); *Congrès international des sciences humaines en Asie et en Afrique du Nord* – former (1976 to 1986). **Aims** Encourage and promote Asian and North African studies. by bringing together academicians from different countries to discuss subjects in fields such as language, history, literatures, religion, philosophy, anthropology, culture, ecology, economics and international relations. **Structure** Congress, being a periodical event, has no permanent body or board, and, therefore, the *International Union for Oriental and Asian Studies (IUOAS, inactive)* is responsible for insuring continuity between two Congresses, while having an advisory role. **Events** *Congress* Morocco 2012, *Congress* Ankara (Turkey) 2007, *Congress* Moscow (Russia) 2004, *Oriental and Asian studies in the era of globalization – heritage and modernity, opportunities and challenges* Montréal, QC (Canada) 2000, *International congress of Asian and North African studies* Budapest (Hungary) 1997. **Publications** *Acta Asiatica: Bulletin of the Institute of Eastern Culture* (2 a year); *Transactions of the International Conference of Eastern Studies* (annual). *The Edo Period: Early Modern and Modern in Japanese History* (2006); *History of Protestantism in China: The Indigenization of Christianity* (2000); *An Introduction to Buddhims* (1987). **NGO Relations** Instrumental in setting up: *Permanent International Altaistic Conference (PIAC, #18324).* [2011/XF0372/c/**F**]

♦ International Congress of Assyriology and Near Eastern Archaeology (meeting series)
♦ International Congress on Autoimmunity (meeting series)
♦ International Congress for Battery Recycling (meeting series)
♦ International Congress of Butchers' Associations / see International Butchers' Confederation (#12421)
♦ International Congress of Carboniferous and Permian Stratigraphy and Geology (meeting series)
♦ International Congress on Catalysis / see International Association of Catalysis Societies (#11757)
♦ International Congress on Catalysis and Automotive Pollution Control (meeting series)
♦ International Congress on Catalysis for Biorefineries (meeting series)
♦ International Congress on Catalyst Deactivation (meeting series)
♦ International Congress of Celtic Studies (meeting series)
♦ International Congress of Central American Students (inactive)
♦ International Congress of Chemical Equipment Design and Automation / see International Congress of Chemical and Process Engineering
♦ International Congress of Chemical and Process Engineering (internationally oriented national body)
♦ International Congress on Cinematography and its Applications (inactive)
♦ International Congress on Combustion Engines / see Conseil international des machines à combustion (#04693)
♦ International Congress on Comparative Endocrinology (meeting series)
♦ International Congress of Comparative Physiology and Biochemistry / see International Association of Comparative Physiology and Biochemistry (#11798)
♦ International Congress on Controversies in Rheumatology and Autoimmunity (meeting series)

♦ **International Congress and Convention Association (ICCA)** **12892**

CEO Alpha Tower, De Entree 57, 1101 BH Amsterdam, Netherlands. T. +31203981919.
URL: http://www.iccaworld.org/

History 21 Oct 1963, Amsterdam (Netherlands). New Articles of Association and By-Laws most recently adopted 2008, Victoria (Canada). Registration: Dutch Civil Code, Netherlands. **Aims** Act as the global community for the meetings industry; provide a top quality organization for members through: maximizing business opportunities; raising and encouraging professional standards in line with client expectations; developing members' skills and understanding of the industry; facilitating information exchange among members. **Structure** General Assembly (annual, during Congress); Board of Directors; CEO; Regional Offices (5); Chapters (11). **Languages** English. **Staff** 40.00 FTE, paid. **Finance** Sources: members' dues; sponsorship. **Activities** Events/meetings; networking/liaising; training/education. **Events** *ICCA Congress* Bangkok (Thailand) 2023, *ICCA Congress* Krakow (Poland) 2022, *Europe Summit* Amsterdam (Netherlands) 2021, *ICCA Congress* Cartagena de Indias (Colombia) 2021, *ICCA Asia Pacific Summit* Yokohama (Japan) 2020. **Publications** *ICCA Statistics* (annual). *ICCA Membership Directory* – hardcopy and online. **Information Services** *Association Database* – online.

Members Sectors (6): Destination Marketing; Meetings Management; Meetings Support; Transport; Venues; Honorary. Members (1,100) in 97 countries and territories:
Algeria, Argentina, Australia, Austria, Azerbaijan, Bahrain, Belgium, Bolivia, Botswana, Brazil, Bulgaria, Canada, Chile, China, Colombia, Costa Rica, Croatia, Cuba, Cyprus, Czechia, Denmark, Dominican Rep, Ecuador, Egypt, El Salvador, Estonia, Ethiopia, Faeroe Is, Finland, France, Georgia, Germany, Greece, Guatemala, Honduras, Hong Kong, Hungary, Iceland, India, Indonesia, Ireland, Israel, Italy, Jamaica, Japan, Jordan, Kazakhstan, Kenya, Korea Rep, Latvia, Lithuania, Luxembourg, Macau, Malaysia, Malta, Mexico, Monaco, Montenegro, Morocco, Mozambique, Netherlands, New Zealand, Norway, Oman, Panama, Paraguay, Peru, Philippines, Poland, Portugal, Puerto Rico, Qatar, Russia, Rwanda, Saudi Arabia, Serbia, Singapore, Slovakia, Slovenia, South Africa, Spain, Sri Lanka, Sweden, Switzerland, Taiwan, Tanzania UR, Thailand, Trinidad-Tobago, Türkiye, UK, Ukraine, United Arab Emirates, Uruguay, USA, Uzbekistan, Zambia, Zimbabwe.

IGO Relations Affiliated with (1): *World Tourism Organization (UNWTO, #21861).* **NGO Relations** Member of (3): *Events Industry Council (EIC, #09212)*; *Joint Meetings Industry Council (JMIC, #16140)*; *Union of International Associations (UIA, #20414)* (as Associate member). [2023/XB3539/**B**]

♦ International Congress on the Cultivation of Edible Fungi (meeting series)
♦ International Congress of Dermatology (meeting series)
♦ International Congress on the Deterioration and Conservation of Stone (meeting series)
♦ International Congress on Diplomatic Studies (meeting series)
♦ International Congress of Druggists (inactive)
♦ International Congress on Early Onset Scoliosis and the Growing Spine (meeting series)
♦ International Congress of Engineering Geology (meeting series)
♦ International Congresses on the Communication of Culture through Architecture, Arts and Mass Media (inactive)
♦ International Congresses of Experts on Social Insurance (inactive)
♦ International Congresses of Mathematicians (inactive)
♦ International Congresses for Modern Architecture (inactive)

♦ **International Congresses on Thermal Stresses (ICTS)** **12893**

SG UK College of Engineering, Mechanical Engineering Dept, 263 Ralph G Anderson Bldg, Lexington KY 40506-0503, USA. Fax +18592573304.
Pres Rochester Inst of Technology, One Lomb Memorial Drive, Rochester NY 14623-5603, USA. T. +15854752411.

Aims Create and advance cooperation between those engaged in scientific and industrial research in the area of thermal stresses and related areas. **Structure** International Committee (meets every 2 years). Executive Committee, including President, Secretary-General and Treasurer. **Events** *Biennial Congress* Nanjing (China) 2013, *Biennial Congress* Budapest (Hungary) 2011, *Biennial Congress* Champaign, IL (USA) 2009, *The challenges of internal auditing – developing skills and improving results* Lima (Peru) 2009, *Biennial Congress* Urbana, IL (USA) 2009. **NGO Relations** Affiliated member of: *International Union of Theoretical and Applied Mechanics (IUTAM, #15823).* [2009/XJ4396/c/**F**]

♦ International Congress for Finno-Ugirc Studies (meeting series)
♦ International Congress of Forensic, Social and Industrial Medicine (inactive)

♦ **International Congress on Fracture (ICF)** **12894**

CEO/ 221-1111 27th St East, Vancouver BC V7J 1S3, Canada. T. +17788796040. E-mail: coliemore@hotmail.com.
SG Fracture Research Inst, Engineering Dept, Tohoku Univ, 1-1 Katahira 2-chome, Aoba-ku, Sendai MIYAGI, 980-8577 Japan.
Registered Office Ishikawajimaharami Heavy Industries, Technology Developemnt, Business Development, Intl Operations, 3-2-16 Toyosu Kotuku, Tokyo, 135-8733 Japan. T. +81335342310. Fax +81335342207.
URL: http://www.icfweb.org/

History Dec 1965, Sendai (Japan), on the initiative of T Yokobori. Statutes and By-Laws adopted 16 Apr 1969, Brighton (UK). Revised 12 Apr 1973, Munich (Germany FR). Also referred to as *International Congress on Fracture – World Academy of Structural Integrity (ICF-WASI)*. **Aims** Foster research in the *mechanics* and phenomena of fracture, fatigue and strength of materials for development of better failure-resistant materials; promote international and interdisciplinary cooperation; publish the results of research. **Structure** Conference (every 4 years); Council, consisting of national delegations; Executive Committee. **Languages** English. **Staff** Voluntary. **Finance** Registration fee. **Activities** Awards/prizes/competitions; events/meetings. **Events** *International Quadrennial Conference* Atlanta, GA (USA) 2021, *Quadrennial Conference* Rhodes Is (Greece) 2017, *Quadrennial conference / International Quadrennial Conference* Beijing (China) 2013, *International conference on strength and fracture* Sendai (Japan) 2010, *Quadrennial Conference* Ottawa, ON (Canada) 2009. **Publications** *IJSFC* – journal. Conference proceedings.

Members Organizations; Individuals. Members in 43 countries:
Algeria, Australia, Austria, Belgium, Brazil, Bulgaria, Canada, China, Croatia, Czechia, Denmark, Ecuador, Egypt, Finland, France, Germany, Hungary, India, Ireland, Israel, Italy, Japan, Latvia, Libya, Mexico, Morocco, Netherlands, New Zealand, Pakistan, Poland, Portugal, Russia, Serbia, Singapore, South Africa, Spain, Sweden, Switzerland, Türkiye, UK, Ukraine, USA, Venezuela.
Regional organizations (3):
European Structural Integrity Society (ESIS, #08844); *Far East Oceanic Fracture Society (FEOFS, #09271)*; *Fracture Group of the Americas (FGA, inactive).*

NGO Relations Affiliated to: *International Union of Theoretical and Applied Mechanics (IUTAM, #15823).* [2019/XC1696/y/**C**]

♦ International Congress on Fracture – World Academy of Structural Integrity / see International Congress on Fracture (#12894)
♦ International Congress of Free Christians and other Religious Liberals / see International Association for Religious Freedom (#12130)
♦ International Congress of Furniture Manufacturers (meeting series)
♦ International Congress on Group Medicine (meeting series)
♦ International Congress of Head and Neck Radiology (meeting series)
♦ International Congress on High Speed Photography and Photonics (meeting series)
♦ International Congress on Hormonal Steroids (meeting series)
♦ International Congress of Human Sciences in Asia and North Africa / see International Congress of Asian and North African Studies (#12891)
♦ International Congress on Hydrogen and Materials (meeting series)

♦ **International Congress of Industrialists and Entrepreneurs (ICIE)** .. **12895**

Contact Bolshaya Yakimanka, Moscow MOSKVA, Russia, 119180. T. +74952491251. E-mail: office@ic-ie.com.
URL: http://www.ic-ie.com/

History 21 Feb 1992. **Aims** Consolidate efforts of public associations of industrialists, entrepreneurs and commodity producers in implementation of economic policy that contributes to development of industrial and business activity and establishment of mutually beneficial economic relations. **Structure** Assembly; Council; Praesidium. **Languages** English, Russian. **Events** *Assembly* Vilnius (Lithuania) 2009. **Members** National unions of industrialists and entrepreneurs from 28 countries. Membership countries not specified. **Consultative Status** Consultative status granted from: *ECOSOC (#05331)* (Ros C); *UNIDO (#20336).* **IGO Relations** Partner of: *Eurasian Economic Community (EurAseC, inactive)*; *Interparliamentary Assembly of Member Nations of the Commonwealth of Independent States (IPA CIS, #15958)*; *International Science and Technology Center (ISTC, #14798).* **NGO Relations** Partner of: *European Economic Chamber of Trade, Commerce and Industry (#06959)*; *International Road Federation (IRF Global, #14759)*; *Union of Black Sea and Caspian Business (BCB, #20369).* [2018.09.06/XG9060/t/**C**]

♦ International Congress of Infant Studies (internationally oriented national body)
♦ International Congress on Information Processing and Chemical Engineering (meeting series)
♦ International Congress on Insurance: Mathematics and Economics (meeting series)
♦ International Congress on Luso-Brazilian Construction History (meeting series)

♦ International Congress for Luther Research (meeting series)
♦ International Congress on Malaria (inactive)
♦ International Congress of Maritime Arbitrators (meeting series)

♦ International Congress of Maritime Museums (ICMM) 12896

Congrès international des musées maritimes
SG PO Box 513, Oxford MD 21654, USA.
URL: http://icmmonline.org/

History 1972. **Aims** Facilitate communication among maritime museums throughout the world. **Structure** Congress (every 3 years). Executive Council, including President, Vice-President, Secretary General and Treasurer. Standing Committees (3): Archaeology; Site Selection; Programme. **Finance** Members' dues: Full pounds70; Associate pounds20. **Activities** Brings professional counterparts together from all over the world for regular conferences; provides a focal point of contact and professional help for museums; offers technical assistance on ship and boat preservation; offers opportunities to exchange collections or staff; loans exhibitions; provides planning, research, educational programming, public relations and procurement of supplies for maritime preservation projects; develops guidelines for documentation and preservation of historic ships and boats; provides standards and guidelines for underwater archaeology; monitors and nurtures maritime museums and maritime preservation activities on an international scale; provides formal and informal networks of communication, information and advice to members; develops strategies to ensure long-term public awareness and appreciation of the significance of maritime preservation. Organizes: week-long International Congress (every three years); interim congress; lectures; workshops; discussions; site visits. **Events** *Biennial Conference* Stockholm (Sweden) / Mariehamn (Finland) 2019, *Biennial Conference* Valparaiso (Chile) 2017, *Biennial Conference* Hong Kong (Hong Kong) 2015, *Biennial Conference* Cascais (Portugal) 2013, *Biennial conference* Washington, DC (USA) / Newport News, VA (USA) 2011. **Publications** *ICMM News* (2 a year). *Sources for Maritime History – Library Directory* (1984); *Historic Ship Register* (1981, 1984). Conference proceedings.

Members Full museums substantially concerned with matters of maritime history in 38 countries and territories:
Argentina, Australia, Belgium, Bermuda, Brazil, Bulgaria, Cameroon, Canada, Chile, China, Colombia, Denmark, Estonia, Finland, France, Germany, Greece, India, Ireland, Israel, Italy, Japan, Jordan, Macau, Malta, Monaco, Netherlands, New Zealand, Norway, Poland, Portugal, South Africa, Spain, Sweden, Switzerland, Türkiye, UK, USA.
Associate individuals on staff of museums or other institutions concerned with maritime history in 24 countries:
Australia, Belgium, Bermuda, Cameroon, Canada, Denmark, Finland, France, Germany, Greece, India, Ireland, Italy, Japan, Kenya, Monaco, Netherlands, Norway, Poland, Portugal, Spain, Sweden, UK, USA.
IGO Relations *UNESCO (#20322).* **NGO Relations** Affiliated member of: *International Council of Museums (ICOM, #13051).* [2011/XF9701/**F**]

♦ International Congress of Maxillofacial Prosthetics / see International Society for Maxillofacial Rehabilitation (#15249)
♦ International Congress of Meat Science and Technology (meeting series)

♦ International Congress on Mechanical Behaviour of Materials (ICM) 12897

Conference Chair Aerospace and Aviation, School of Engineering, RMIT Univ, Bundoora Campus, 264 Plenty Rd, Mill Park, Melbourne VIC 3000, Australia. T. +61399256123.
URL: https://www.icm-13.com/

History 1971, Kyoto (Japan), at 1st Conference on Mechanical Behaviour of Materials. **Aims** Foster research on mechanical behaviour of materials; promote related international cooperation among scientists and engineers; provide means for the public dissemination of the results from these efforts. **Structure** Board of Governors; Executive Committee; Secretariat, headed by Secretary. **Languages** English. **Staff** 1.00 FTE, voluntary. **Finance** National members are responsible for meeting their own expenses. Financial arrangements connected with holding the International Conference and other meetings are the responsibility of the host country. **Activities** Events/meetings. **Events** *International Conference* Milan (Italy) 2011, *International Conference* Busan (Korea Rep) 2007, *International conference* Geneva (Switzerland) 2003, *International conference* Victoria, BC (Canada) 1999, *International Conference* The Hague (Netherlands) 1995. **Publications** Conference proceedings.

Members Organizations, societies, bodies and individuals in 26 countries:
Australia, Austria, Brazil, Canada, China, Czechia, Denmark, Finland, France, Germany, India, Ireland, Israel, Italy, Japan, Korea Rep, Malaysia, Netherlands, Poland, Portugal, Romania, Serbia, Sweden, Switzerland, UK, USA.
Members also in the former USSR. Membership countries not specified.
NGO Relations *International Congress on Fracture (ICF, #12894).* Joint symposia organized with and member of: *International Union of Theoretical and Applied Mechanics (IUTAM, #15823).* [2019.02.12/XF2840/c/**F**]

♦ International Congress on Medical Librarianship (meeting series)
♦ International Congress on Medicinal Plants (meeting series)
♦ International Congress on Medieval Studies (internationally oriented national body)
♦ International Congress of Mediterranean-climate Ecosystems / see International Society of Mediterranean Ecology (#15259)
♦ International Congress on Membranes and Membrane Processes (meeting series)
♦ International Congress on Multiple System Atrophy (meeting series)
♦ International Congress on Musical Signification (meeting series)

♦ International Congress on Naturopathic Medicine (ICNM) 12898

Headquarters ICNM Headquarters, 75008 Paris, France. T. +33603231111. Fax +33155620307. E-mail: president@icnm.eu.
URL: http://icnmnaturopathy.eu/

History 2010, Paris (France). Registration: No/ID: W922008631, Start date: 2010, France. **Aims** Provide recurrent, high quality continuing medical education for healthcare professionals worldwide. **Structure** Executive Committee, Organizing Committee; Ambassadors. **Languages** Chinese, English, French, German, Greek, Hindi, Italian, Japanese, Portuguese, Russian, Spanish. **Staff** 8.00 FTE, paid; 25.00 FTE, voluntary. **Activities** Training/education; events/meetings. **Events** *World Congress on Naturopathic Medicine* Paris (France) 2021, *World Congress on Naturopathic Medicine* Paris (France) 2019, *World Congress on Naturopathic Medicine* London (UK) 2017, *World Congress on Naturopathic Medicine* London (UK) 2016. **Members** Membership countries not specified. [2020.05.06/XM7977/c/**E**]

♦ International Congress of Neuromuscular Diseases (meeting series)
♦ International Congress on Neuronal Ceroid Lipofuscinoses (meeting series)
♦ International Congress for de New Evangelization (meeting series)
♦ International Congress on Nitrogen Fixation (meeting series)
♦ International Congress of Ophthalmology (meeting series)

♦ International Congress of Oral Implantologists (ICOI) 12899

Congrès international des implantologistes de la bouche – Collegium Internationale Oris Implantatorum
Main Office 55 Lane Rd, Ste 305, Fairfield NJ 07004, USA. T. +19737836300. Fax +19737831175.
URL: http://www.icoi.org/

History 1975. Assumed activities of *International Association of Dental Implant Technicians (IADIT, inactive).* Former names and other names: *International College of Oral Implantologists* – former (1975 to 1976). **Aims** Link *dentists* and oral *surgeons* concerned with the teaching of and research in oral implantology, with emphasis on *continuing education.* **Staff** 5.50 FTE, paid. **Activities** Training/education; events/meetings. **Events** *ICOI World Congress* Orlando, FL (USA) 2024, *ICOI Winter Implant Symposium* San Diego, CA (USA) 2024, *ICOI World Congress* Dallas, TX (USA) 2023, *ICOI Winter Implant Symposium* New Orleans, LA (USA) 2023, *ICOI World Congress* Sydney, NSW (Australia) 2023. **Publications** *ICOI International Newsletter* (4 a year); *Implant Dentistry* (4 a year) – journal. *Bibliographic Reference Guides.* Course calendars; annual membership and study club directories; auxiliary training manuals.

Members Component and affiliated societies (50) serving over 20,000 members – dentists and other individuals – in 66 countries and territories:
Albania, Argentina, Australia, Austria, Azerbaijan, Bahamas, Barbados, Belgium, Bermuda, Bolivia, Brazil, Bulgaria, Cambodia, Canada, Chile, China, Colombia, Cyprus, Denmark, Dominican Rep, Ecuador, Egypt, Finland, France, Germany, Greece, Hong Kong, Hungary, India, Indonesia, Iraq, Ireland, Israel, Italy, Jamaica, Japan, Korea Rep, Lebanon, Malaysia, Mexico, Netherlands, New Zealand, Norway, Pakistan, Paraguay, Peru, Philippines, Portugal, Puerto Rico, Qatar, Saudi Arabia, Serbia, Singapore, South Africa, Spain, Sri Lanka, Sweden, Switzerland, Syrian AR, Taiwan, Thailand, Türkiye, UK, Uruguay, USA, Venezuela.
NGO Relations Member of: *FDI – World Dental Federation (#09281).* [2022/XC6205/**F**]

♦ International Congress of Orientalists / see International Congress of Asian and North African Studies (#12891)
♦ International Congress on Pediatric Pulmonology (meeting series)
♦ International Congress on Personal Construct Psychology (meeting series)
♦ International Congress PHYTOPHARM (meeting series)
♦ International Congress of Plant Molecular Biology (meeting series)
♦ International Congress of Prehistoric and Protohistoric Sciences / see International Union of Prehistoric and Protohistoric Sciences (#15801)
♦ International Congress on Preparation and Assistance in case of Disaster (meeting series)
♦ International Congress on Prospective Analysis, Forecasting and Planning in Public Services (meeting series)
♦ International Congress on Quality in Laboratory Medicine (meeting series)
♦ International Congress of Radiology (meeting series)
♦ International Congress on Radiology in Oto-Rhino-Laryngology (meeting series)
♦ International Congress on Rapid Methods and Automation in Microbiology and Immunology (meeting series)
♦ International Congress on Rehabilitation in Psychiatry (meeting series)
♦ International Congress of Roman Frontier Studies (meeting series)

♦ International Congress for School Effectiveness and Improvement (ICSEI) 12900

Exec Dir c/o Gonski Institute for Education, University of New South Wales, Sydney NSW 2052, Australia. E-mail: admin@icsei.net.
URL: http://www.icsei.net/

History Jan 1988, London (UK). **Aims** Provide a forum for researchers, school and district leaders, teachers, local and national policy makers and politicians, NGO personnel and consultants to share ideas, promote research and encourage practices that will enhance quality and equity of education for all young people. **Structure** General Meetings (annual); Board. **Languages** English. **Staff** 2.00 FTE, paid. **Finance** Members' dues. Conference proceeds. **Activities** Events/meetings; awards/prizes/competitions. **Events** *Annual Congress* Auckland (New Zealand) 2021, *Annual Congress* Marrakech (Morocco) 2020, *Annual Congress* Stavanger (Norway) 2019, *Annual Congress* Singapore (Singapore) 2018, *Annual Congress* Ottawa, ON (Canada) 2017. **Publications** *ICSEI Express and Digest. ICSEI Monograph.* [2020/XM0598/c/**F**]

♦ International Congress on Science and Skiing (meeting series)
♦ International Congress on Science and Skiing (meeting series)
♦ International Congress on Science and Technology of Ironmaking (meeting series)
♦ International Congress of Sleep Research (meeting series)
♦ International Congress for the Study of Classical Languages (meeting series)
♦ International Congress on Systemic Lupus Erythematosus (meeting series)
♦ International Congress of Theoretical Chemists of Latin Expression (meeting series)
♦ International Congress for Town Hygiene (inactive)
♦ International Congress for Tropical Medicine and Malaria (meeting series)

♦ International Congress on Ultrasonics (ICU) 12901

SG Rehbachstraße 126, 66125 Saarbrücken, Germany. T. +496897764407.
URL: http://www.icultrasonics.org/

History 2005. Founded on merger of *World Congress on Ultrasonics (WCU),* first being held in 2003, Paris (France), and *Ultrasonics International (UI).* **Aims** Promote international exchange and advancement of the general field of ultrasonics. **Structure** Board. **Languages** English. **Staff** Voluntary. **Finance** Sources: meeting proceeds. **Activities** Events/meetings. **Events** *Congress* Beijing (China) 2023, *Congress* Beijing (China) 2021, *Congress* Bruges (Belgium) 2019, *Congress* Honolulu, HI (USA) 2017, *Congress* Metz (France) 2015. **Publications** *Ultrasonics.* Proceedings. **NGO Relations** Member of (1): *International Commission for Acoustics (ICA, #12658).* [2022.06.15/XM1548/**C**]

♦ International Congress for Underwater Archaeology (meeting series)
♦ International Congress for the Unity of Science (inactive)
♦ International Congress of University Adult Education (inactive)
♦ International Congress of Voice Teachers (meeting series)
♦ International Congress on Water, Waste and Energy Management (meeting series)
♦ International Congress on Whole Person Care (meeting series)
♦ International Congress of Writers in Defence of Culture (inactive)
♦ International Congress on X-Ray Optics and Microanalysis (meeting series)
♦ International Congress on Yeasts (meeting series)

♦ International Congress of Zookeepers (ICZ) 12902

Exec Officer c/o AAZK, 8476 E Speedway Blvd, Suite 204, Tucson AZ 85710-1728, USA. E-mail: info@iczoo.org.
URL: https://www.iczoo.org/

History 2000. **Aims** Contribute to the highest standard of professional animal care and the role of zoos today. **Structure** Steering Committee. **Activities** Advocacy/lobbying/activism; events/meetings; financial and/or material support. **Events** *International Congress on Zookeeping* Barcelona (Spain) 2022, *Seminar* 2021, *International Congress on Zookeeping* Wellington (New Zealand) 2021, *International Congress on Zookeeping* Buenos Aires (Argentina) 2018, *International Conference of Zookeepers* Leipzig (Germany) 2015.

Members Professional zookeeper associations (8) covering 10 countries:
Argentina, Australia, France, Germany, Ireland, Netherlands, Philippines, Portugal, Spain, UK.
Australasian Society of Zoo Keeping (ASZK, #03031).
Associate memberes (3) in 3 countries:
Denmark, Italy, USA.
NGO Relations Partner of (6): *International Association of Avian Trainers and Educators (IAATE); International Rhino Keeper Association (IRKA); Pan-African Association of Zoos and Aquaria (PAAZA, #18039); The Shape of Enrichment; Wild Welfare; World Association of Zoos and Aquariums (WAZA, #21208).* [2021/AA1934/y/**C**]

♦ International Consciousness Research Laboratories (ICRL) 12903

Headquarters 211 N Harrison St, Princeton NJ 08540, USA. E-mail: info@icrl.org.
URL: http://www.icrl.org/

History 1990. Registered in the State of New Jersey, 1996. **Aims** Explore the nature of consciousness and its role in the establishment of physical reality. **Structure** Board of Trustees. **Languages** English. **Staff** 2.00 FTE, voluntary. **Finance** Contributions; grants. **Activities** Research/documentation; publishing activities; events/meetings. **Publications** *Journal of Non-Locality* (2 a year). Books; technical reports.

Members Associates (about 80) in 15 countries:
Australia, Belgium, Brazil, Canada, Chile, Czechia, Denmark, France, Greece, India, Italy, Netherlands, Norway, UK, USA.
[2014.07.11/XF4672/**F**]

♦ International Conservation Caucus Foundation / see The ICCF Group (#11045)

♦ International Consortium on Applied Bioeconomy Research (ICABR) 12904

SG Dept of Economics – CEIS, Univ of Rome "Tor Vergata", Via Volumbia 2, 00133 Rome RM, Italy. T. +39672595639. E-mail: icabr@economia.uniroma2.it.
URL: http://www.icabr.org/

History 1998, Rome (Italy). **Aims** Promote and stimulate improvement in the quality and relevance of international bioeconomy research and *policy* analysis. **Structure** President; Secretary General. **Events** *Role of the Bioeconomy in Generating Resilience and Sustainable Development* Ravello (Italy) 2021, *Accelerating the bioeconomy growth through applied research and policy change* Rome (Italy) 2020, *Regulations and Finance of Innovations for a Sustainable Economy* Ravello (Italy) 2019, *Disruptive Innovations, Value Chains and Rural Development* Washington, DC (USA) 2018, *Bioeconomy in Transition: New Players and New Tools* Washington, DC (USA) 2017. [2015/XJ6809/C]

♦ International Consortium for Brain Mapping (ICBM) 12905

Contact UCLA Neuro/Radiol Sci/Pharma, Box 957085, 247 Brain Mapping, Los Angeles CA 90095-7085, USA.
URL: http://www.loni.usc.edu/ICBM/

History 1993. **Aims** Continually develop a probablistic reference system for the human brain. **Structure** Principal Investigator; 4 Co-Principal Investigators. **Finance** Grants from national institutions. **Activities** Over the course of the project, built and expanded the tools available to establish a reference system for structural and functional anatomy on both macroscopic (in vivo) and microscopic (post mortem) levels. To date, data from over 7,000 subjects have been incorporated. Organizes 2 annual meetings.
Members Investigators at 8 institutions in 7 countries:
Canada, Finland, France, Germany, Japan, Netherlands, USA. [2010/XF7041/F]

♦ International Consortium for Civic Education / see CIVITAS International (#03973)

♦ International Consortium on Combating Wildlife Crime (ICCWC) . . . 12906

Contact c/o CITES, Int Environment House, Chemin des Anémones 11, Châtelaine, 1219 Geneva, Switzerland. T. +41229178139 – +41229178140. Fax +41227973417. E-mail: info@cites.org.
URL: http://cites.org/eng/prog/iccwc.php

History Formally launched 23 Nov 2010, St Petersburg (Russia), during International Tiger Forum, by *Secretariat of the Convention on International Trade in Endangered Species of Wild Fauna and Flora (CITES Secretariat, #19199)*, *International Criminal Police Organization – INTERPOL (ICPO-INTERPOL, #13110)*; *United Nations Office on Drugs and Crime (UNODC, #20596)*, *International Bank for Reconstruction and Development (IBRD, #12317)* (World Bank) and *World Customs Organization (WCO, #21350)*. **Aims** Strengthen criminal justice systems and provide coordinated support at national, regional and international level to combat wildlife and *forest* crime. **Activities** Capacity building; training/education. **Events** *Global Meeting of Wildlife Enforcement Networks* Johannesburg (South Africa) 2016, *Global Meeting of Wildlife Enforcement Networks* Bangkok (Thailand) 2013. **Publications** *World Wildlife Crime Report* (2016). Guides; guidelines. [2019/XM4764/y/E]

♦ International Consortium for Cooperation on the Nile (ICCON) 12907

Consortium international de coopération sur le Nil

Address not obtained.

History 26 Jun 2001. **Aims** Encourage dialogue on cooperation, sustainable development and poverty alleviation in the Nile Basin. **Events** *Meeting* Geneva (Switzerland) 2001.
Members Governments of 10 countries:
Burundi, Congo DR, Egypt, Eritrea, Ethiopia, Kenya, Rwanda, Sudan, Tanzania UR, Uganda.
IGO Relations *International Bank for Reconstruction and Development (IBRD, #12317)*; *Nile Basin Initiative (NBI, #17140)*. [2010/XF6411/F*]

♦ International Consortium for Court Excellence (ICCE) 12908

Officer c/o AIJA, Ground Floor, 555 Lonsdale Str, Melbourne VIC 3000, Australia. T. +61396001311.
URL: http://www.courtexcellence.com/

Aims Act as a resource for assessing the performance of a court against detailed areas of excellence; provide guidance tocourts so as to improve their performance. **Structure** Executive Committee; Secretariat. **Events** *Dubai Conference on Court of Excellence and Innovations* Dubai (United Arab Emirates) 2018. **Publications** *ICCE Newsletter*.
Members Full in 20 countries:
Australia, Brazil, Canada, Eswatini, Guam, Indonesia, Kenya, Malaysia, Marshall Is, Namibia, Nepal, New Zealand, Palau, Papua New Guinea, Philippines, Seychelles, Singapore, Ukraine, United Arab Emirates, USA.
Included in the above, 1 organization listed in this Yearbook:
Australasian Institute of Judicial Administration (AIJA).
IGO Relations *Commission européenne pour l'efficacité de la justice (CEPEJ, #04213)*; *International Bank for Reconstruction and Development (IBRD, #12317)* (World Bank). [2018/XM5325/C]

♦ International Consortium on EDS and Related Disorders – International Consortium on Ehlers-Danlos Syndromes and Related Disorders (unconfirmed)

♦ International Consortium for Educational Development (ICED) 12909

Admin c/o ACU, Woburn House, 20-24 Tavistock Square, London, WC1H 9HF, UK.
Pres address not obtained.
URL: http://icedonline.net/

History Founded 1993, Oxford (UK). UK Registered Charity: 1145272. **Aims** Help partner organizations develop their capacity for educational development in higher education through sharing of good practice, problems and solutions. **Structure** Council (meets annually); Board. **Languages** English. **Finance** Members' dues. Events are self-financed. **Activities** Events/meetings; networking/liaising; capacity building. **Events** *Biennial Conference* Zurich (Switzerland) 2020, *Biennial Conference* Atlanta, GA (USA) 2018, *Biennial Conference* Cape Town (South Africa) 2016, *Biennial Conference* Stockholm (Sweden) 2014, *Biennial Conference* Bangkok (Thailand) 2012. **Publications** *The International Journal for Academic Development (IJAD)* (4 a year).
Members Organizations in 26 countries:
Australia, Belgium, Canada, Chile, China, Croatia, Denmark, Estonia, Ethiopia, Finland, Germany, India, Ireland, Israel, Japan, Kenya, Netherlands, Norway, South Africa, Spain, Sri Lanka, Sweden, Switzerland, Thailand, UK, USA. [2019.04.30/XF4092/F]

♦ International Consortium on Ehlers-Danlos Syndromes and Related Disorders (unconfirmed)

♦ International Consortium for Electronic Business (ICEB) 12910

Contact Room 902 Cheng Yu Tung Bldg, Chinese Univ of Hong Kong, Shatin, Hong Kong. T. +85239437816. Fax +85226035104.
URL: http://www.icebnet.org/

History 21 Dec 2001, Hong Kong. **Aims** Promote research and education in electronic business; provide a forum for depositing and sharing knowledge related to electronic business. **Structure** General Meeting (annual); Board; Steering Committee; Advisory Council. **Finance** Members' dues. **Events** *Conference* Dubai (United Arab Emirates) 2017, *Conference* Hong Kong (Hong Kong) 2015, *Creating business values through innovation in cloud services* Taipei (Taiwan) 2014, *Conference* Singapore (Singapore) 2013, *Conference* Xian (China) 2012. [2015.01.21/XM1425/F]

♦ International Consortium for Emergency Contraception (ICEC) 12911

Consortium international pour la contraception d'urgence

Coordinator c/o Mgt Sci for Health, 25 Broadway, 9th Floor, New York NY 10006, USA. T. +17035246575. E-mail: info@cecinfo.org.
URL: http://www.cecinfo.org/

History Founded by 7 international organizations working in the field of family planning, following a meeting convened in 1995 by *The Rockefeller Foundation (#18966)*. Former names and other names: *Consortium for Emergency Contraception* – former. **Aims** Expand access to and ensure safe and locally appropriate use of emergency contraception worldwide within the context of *family planning* and *reproductive health* programmes, with an emphasis on developing countries. **Structure** Steering Committee; Technical Advisory Group. **Languages** English. Many documents translated into French and Spanish. **Staff** 2.50 FTE, paid. **Finance** Sources: grants. **Activities** Advocacy/lobbying/activism; awards/prizes/competitions; capacity building; guidance/assistance/consulting; knowledge management/information dissemination; research and development; training/education. **Publications** Fact sheets; guidelines; case studies.
Members Organizations (22):
- Association of Reproductive Health Professionals;
- British Pregnancy Advisory Service;
- *Catholics for Choice (#03609)*;
- Center for Reproductive Rights;
- *CONRAD*;
- *DKT International*;
- *FHI 360*;
- *Guttmacher Institute*;
- Gynuity Health Projects;
- *Ibis Reproductive Health*;
- *International Planned Parenthood Federation (IPPF, #14589)*;
- *IPAS (#16010)*;
- JSI Research and Training Center for Women's Health;
- Meridian Group International;
- *PAI (#18025)*;
- *PATH (#18260)*;
- *Pathfinder International (#18261)*;
- *Population Council (#18458)*;
- *Prosalud Inter Americana Foundation (PSIA, #18542)*;
- *PSI (#18555)*;
- WHO Special Programme of Research, Development and Research Training in Human Reproduction;
- *WomanCare Global (WCG)*.

NGO Relations Member of (1): *Reproductive Health Supplies Coalition (RHSC, #18847)*. Cooperates with (5): American Society for Emergency Contraception; *Arab World Regional EC Network (AWRN)*; *ECafrique (#05272)*; *European Consortium for Emergency Contraception (ECEC, #06754)*; *Latin American Consortium on Emergency Contraception (LACEC, #16306)*. [2019/XJ7162/y/C]

♦ International Consortium of Environmental History Organizations (ICEHO) 12912

Admin Forest History Society, 2925 Academy Road, Durham NC 27705, USA. T. +19196829319. Fax +19196822349.
URL: http://www.iceho.org/

Aims Foster international communication among environmental history organizations. **Structure** General Assembly (at least once every two years and at World Congress of Environmental History); Board of Directors. **Finance** Members' dues. Sponsors: American Society for Environmental History; *European Society for Environmental History (ESEH, #08596)*; (US) Forest History Society. **Activities** Events/meetings; networking/liaising; standards/guidelines; training/education; awareness raising. **Events** *World Congress of Environmental History* Florianópolis (Brazil) 2019, *World Congress of Environmental History* Guimarães (Portugal) 2014, *World congress of environmental history* Copenhagen (Denmark) 2009.
Members National organizations (24) in 13 countries:
Australia, Austria, Canada, Colombia, Czechia, Germany, India, Italy, Netherlands, New Zealand, Norway, UK, USA.
International organizations (5):
Association for East Asian Environmental History (AEAEH, #02476); *European Society for Environmental History (ESEH, #08596)*; *International Union of Forest Research Organizations (IUFRO, #15774)* (Forest History Society); *International Water History Association (IWHA, #15866)*; *Sociedad Latinoamericana y Caribeña de Historia Ambiental (SOLCHA, #19396)*. [2020/XM2047/y/F]

♦ International Consortium for Executive Development Research (ICEDR) 12913

Founder and Pres 1666 Massachusetts Ave, Lexington MA 02420, USA. T. +17818626633. Fax +17818626211.
URL: http://www.icedr.org/

History 1991.
Members Corporations (40) and academic institutions (25). Included in the above, 3 organizations listed in this Yearbook:
IESE Business School, University of Navarra (IESE); *INSEAD (#11228)*; *Management Centre Europe (MCE, #16561)*. [2010/XF5590/y/F]

♦ International Consortium on Geo-disaster Reduction (ICGdR) 12914

Pres Dept of Geoscience, Fac of Sci/Engr, Shimane Univ, 1060 Nishikawatsu-cho, Matsue SHIMANE, 690-8504 Japan. T. +81852329878. Fax +81852326469. E-mail: 2305246374@qq.com.
URL: http://icgdr.com/

History Registration: Start date: 2013, Japan. **Aims** Promote geo-disaster reduction for the benefit of human society and the natural environment, and capacity development, including education; combine international expertise and coordinate efforts in geo-disaster reduction, thereby resulting in an effective international organization which will act as a partner in various projects; promote regional and global, multidisciplinary activity on geo-disaster reduction. **Structure** Board of Representatives; Officers; Committees (5); Secretariat. **Activities** Awards/prizes/competitions; events/meetings; training/education. **Events** *International Symposium on Geo-Disaster Reduction* Kanazawa (Japan) 2022, *International Symposium on Risk Assessment and Sustainable Stability Design of Slopes* Sendai (Japan) 2022, *International Symposium on Geo-Disaster Reduction* Xining (China) 2021, *International Symposium on Geo-Disaster Reduction* Beijing (China) 2020, *International Symposium on Geo-Disaster Reduction* Issyk-Kul Lake (Kyrgyzstan) 2019. **Publications** *Geoenvironmental Disasters* – journal.
Members Intergovernmental organizations; nongovernmental organizations; governmental and public organizations; other organizations and entities. Members in 15 countries and territories:
Belgium, China, Czechia, France, India, Indonesia, Italy, Japan, Korea Rep, Kyrgyzstan, Nepal, Switzerland, Taiwan, UK, USA. [2022/XM4219/C]

♦ International Consortium on Governmental Financial Management (ICGFM) 12915

Consortium international sur la gestion financière gouvernementale – Consorcio Internacional de Gestión Financiera Gubernamental

Managing Dir 6312 Seven Corners Center, Suite 264, Falls Church VA 22044, USA. T. +15714011687. E-mail: icgfm@icgfm.org.
URL: http://www.icgfm.org/

History 1978. **Aims** Foster strong and effective stewardship of public funds and assets that earns and sustains the trust of citizens around the world; promote best practices in public financial management globally. **Structure** Board of Directors; Executive Committee. **Languages** English, French, Spanish. **Staff** 2.00 FTE, paid. **Finance** Sources: meeting proceeds; members' dues. Annual budget: 350,000 USD. **Activities** Advocacy/lobbying/activism; events/meetings; knowledge management/information dissemination; training/education. **Events** *Conference* Washington, DC (USA) 2022, *Transforming development finance – PFM's role in meeting sustainable development goals* Miami, FL (USA) 2016, *Conference* Miami, FL (USA) 2014, *Winter Conference* Washington, DC (USA) 2014, *Joining forces for responsible leadership to enhance good governance – citizens, public officials, private sector and the press* Miami, FL (USA) 2008. **Publications** *International Journal on Governmental Financial Management*.
Members Corporate; Institutional/Governmental; Sustaining Basic; Organizational Large and Small; Individual. International and national organizations, government institutions, private organizations and individuals in over 50 countries and territories. Membership countries not specified.
Included in the above, 4 major, international and other organization members:
International Monetary Fund (IMF, #14180); Millennium Challenge Corporation; *United States Agency for International Development (USAID)*; US Government Accountability Office.
IGO Relations *International Bank for Reconstruction and Development (IBRD, #12317)* (World Bank); *International Monetary Fund (IMF, #14180)*; *United States Agency for International Development (USAID)*. [2022.05.05/XE3901/y/E]

♦ International Consortium for Health Outcomes Measurement (internationally oriented national body)
♦ International Consortium on Integral Methods in Science and Engineering / see International Steering Committee on Integral Methods in Science and Engineering (#15604)

♦ International Consortium for Intergenerational Programmes (ICIP) . 12916

Contact address not obtained. E-mail: alanyeo@btinternet.com.

History Oct 1999, Netherlands. Registered in accordance with Dutch law. **Aims** Promote intergenerational programmes, strategies and public policy from a global perspective. **Structure** General Meeting (every 2 years). Management Committee of up to 15 members, including Chairman, Vice-Chairman, Secretary and Treasurer. **Languages** English. **Staff** 0.50 FTE, paid. **Finance** None. **Events** *Biennial conference* Singapore (Singapore) 2010, *Biennial conference* Melbourne, VIC (Australia) 2006, *Biennial Conference* Victoria, BC (Canada) 2004, *Biennial conference* Victoria, BC (Canada) 2004, *Biennial Conference* Keele (UK) 2002. **Publications** *ICIP Newsletter*, *Journal of Intergenerational Relationships*.

Members Full in 13 countries:
Australia, Belgium, Botswana, Canada, Denmark, France, Germany, India, Israel, New Zealand, Spain, UK, USA.
[2013.06.01/XF7167/**F**]

♦ International Consortium of Investigative Journalists (internationally oriented national body)
♦ International Consortium for Jellyfish Stings (internationally oriented national body)
♦ International Consortium of Landscape and Ecological Engineering (unconfirmed)

♦ International Consortium on Landslides (ICL) 12917

SG/Treas 138-1 Tanaka-Asukai cho, Sakyo-ku, Kyoto, 606-8226 Japan. T. +81757230640. Fax +81759500910. E-mail: secretariat@iclhq.org.
URL: http://icl.iplhq.org/

History Jan 2002, Kyoto (Japan). Registration: National Tax Agency, No/ID: 1130005005237, Start date: 5 Aug 2002, Japan, Kyoto. **Aims** Promote landslide research and capacity building in developing countries; evaluate landslide risk in urban, rural and developing areas; combine and coordinate international expertise in landslide risk assessment and mitigation studies. **Structure** World Landslide Forum (WLF, every 3 years); Board of Representatives of the International Consortium on Landslides (BOR/ICL); Global Promotion Committee of the International Programme on Landslides and Kyoto Landslide Commitment (GPC/IPL-KLC). **Languages** English, Japanese. **Staff** 6.00 FTE, paid. **Finance** Sources: contributions; donations; members' dues. Other sources: funds; subventions. Supported by: *FAO (#09260)*; Government of Japan; *International Science Council (ISC, #14796)*; *UNESCO (#20322)*; *United Nations Office for Disaster Risk Reduction (UNDRR, #20595)*; *United Nations University (UNU, #20642)*; *World Federation of Engineering Organizations (WFEO, #21433)*. **Activities** Capacity building; certification/accreditation; events/meetings; networking/liaising; projects/programmes; publishing activities; research and development; training/education. Active in all member countries. **Events** *World Landslide Forum (WLF7)* 2026, *World Landslide Forum (WLF6)* Florence (Italy) 2023, *Symposium on Offshore Wind Development in Active Margins* Tokyo (Japan) 2023, *ICL-KLC Hybrid Conference* Japan 2022, *Symposium of Offshore Wind Power Generation at Active Margins* Tokyo (Japan) 2022. **Publications** *Landslides: Journal of the International Consortium on Landslides* (12 a year). *World Landslide Forum Books* – in 7 vols. Teaching tools.

Members Full in 34 countries and territories:
Belgium, Bosnia-Herzegovina, Brazil, Canada, China, Colombia, Croatia, Czechia, Egypt, Georgia, Germany, Honduras, Hong Kong, India, Indonesia, Italy, Japan, Korea Rep, Kyrgyzstan, Malaysia, Mexico, Nepal, North Macedonia, Russia, Serbia, Slovakia, Slovenia, Sri Lanka, Switzerland, Taiwan, Thailand, Ukraine, USA, Vietnam.

Consultative Status Consultative status granted from: *UNESCO (#20322)* (Consultative Status). **NGO Relations** Member of (1): *Global Alliance of Disaster Research Institutes (GADRI, #10194)*. Affiliate Member of: *International Union of Geodesy and Geophysics (IUGG, #15776)*; *International Union of Geological Sciences (IUGS, #15777)*. [2022.02.09/XM3097/y/**F**]

♦ International Consortium for Law and Religion Studies (ICLARS) . . 12918

Contact Univ Milan Fac Law, Dept Cesare Beccaria, Via Festa del Perdono 7, 20122 Milan MI, Italy. Fax +39250312612. E-mail: info@iclars.org – iclars@unimi.it.
URL: http://www.iclars.org/

History 2008. Registration: Italy. **Aims** Provide a place where information, data and opinions can be exchanged and made available to members and the broader scientific community. **Structure** Steering Committee; Secretariat. **Languages** English. **Staff** 7.00 FTE, voluntary. **Finance** Sources: members' dues. Other sources: Event sponsorship. **Events** *Conference* Córdoba (Spain) 2022, *Conference* Córdoba (Spain) 2020, *Conference* Rio de Janeiro (Brazil) 2018, *Freedom of/for/from/in religion – differing dimensions of a common right?* Oxford (UK) 2016, *Conference* Richmond, VA (USA) 2013. **Publications** Newsletter; conference proceedings. **Members** Individuals worldwide; also open to associations. Membership countries not specified. **NGO Relations** Cooperates with (1): *G20 Interfaith Forum Association (IF20, #10055)*. Also links with national organizations. [2020/XM4022/**C**]

♦ International Consortium for Male Contraception (ICMC) 12919

Coordinator 9 rue de Villersexel, 75007 Paris, France. T. +33145483132.
URL: http://www.ic-mc.info/

History 13 Sep 2013. **Aims** Create an international research organization focusing on male contraception; actively promote this type of contraception. **Activities** Events/meetings. **Events** *Congress* Paris (France) 2022, *Congress* Paris (France) 2020, *Congress* Paris (France) 2018, *Congress* Paris (France) 2016.

Members Individuals (119) in 45 countries:
Algeria, Australia, Austria, Belgium, Benin, Bulgaria, Burkina Faso, Cameroon, Canada, Chile, China, Côte d'Ivoire, Cyprus, Denmark, Finland, France, Gabon, Germany, Greece, Guinea, Hungary, India, Indonesia, Israel, Italy, Kenya, Lebanon, Mali, Malta, Mauritania, Morocco, Netherlands, Nigeria, Poland, Portugal, Senegal, Serbia, Spain, Sweden, Switzerland, Tunisia, Türkiye, UK, USA, Vietnam.

NGO Relations Under the auspices of: Association Française de Contraception (AFC); *European Academy of Andrology (EAA, #05780)*; *European Society of Contraception and Reproductive Health (ESC, #08568)*; *European Society of Endocrinology (ESE, #08594)*; *European Society of Gynecology (ESG, #08613)*; *International Society of Andrology (ISA, #14918)*; *Male Contraceptive Initiative (MCI)*; *Population Council (#18458)*; *Société Francophone de Contraception (SFC, #19466)*. [2021.09.13/XM8446/**C**]

♦ International Consortium for Medical Abortion (inactive)

♦ International Consortium for Personalised Medicine (ICPerMed) . . . 12920

Secretariat address not obtained. E-mail: icpermed@dlr.de.
URL: http://www.icpermed.eu/

History Initiated during workshops organized 2016. **Aims** Provide a platform to initiate and support communication and exchange on personalised medicine research, funding and implementation. **Structure** Executive Committee; Steering Board; Secretariat. Challenge Groups; Action Item Groups. **Activities** Events/meetings; training/education. **Events** *Conference* Paris (France) 2021, *Conference* Paris (France) 2020, *Citizens, patients and implementation* Madrid (Spain) 2019, *Meeting* Tallinn (Estonia) 2019, *Personalised medicine in action* Berlin (Germany) 2018. **Publications** *ICPerMed Newsletter*.

Members Funding bodies (over 40) in 29 countries:
Austria, Brazil, Canada, Croatia, Cyprus, Czechia, Denmark, Estonia, Finland, France, Germany, Hungary, Iran Islamic Rep, Ireland, Israel, Italy, Lithuania, Luxembourg, Moldova, Netherlands, Norway, Poland, Portugal, Romania, Slovenia, Spain, Sweden, Switzerland, Türkiye.

Observer:
European Commission (EC, #06633). [2019/XM8378/**E**]

♦ International Consortium of Real Estate Associations (internationally oriented national body)
♦ International Consortium on Rehabilitation Robotics (unconfirmed)

♦ International Consortium for Rehabilitation Technology (ICRT) 12921

Address not obtained.
URL: https://www.rehabweek.org/

History Feb 2018, Zurich (Switzerland). Created to allow organization of RehabWeek. **Events** *RehabWeek* Rotterdam (Netherlands) 2022.

Members Organizations (4):
International Consortium on Rehabilitation Robotics (ICORR); *International Functional Electrical Stimulation Society (IFESS, #13690)*; *International Industry Society in Advanced Rehabilitation Technology (IISART, #13840)*; *International Society for Virtual Rehabilitation (ISVR, #15543)*. [2022/AA2685/cy/**C**]

♦ International Consortium for Salt Lake Research / see International Society for Salt Lake Research (#15431)

♦ International Consortium for Social Development (ICSD) 12922

SG School of Social Work, Arizona State Univ, 411 N Central Ave, Ste 800, Mail Code 3920, Phoenix AZ 85004, USA. T. +16024961195.
URL: http://socialdevelopment.net/

History Founded as *Inter-University Consortium on International Social Development (IUCISD) – Consorcio de Inter-Universidades para el Desarrollo Social Internacional*. Current title adopted, 2006. **Aims** Influence local, national and international systems, promoting world peace and social justice; fight economic and political oppression; improve access to adequate health care and education; overcome discrimination against women and minorities; create sustainable income and economic structure. **Structure** Board; Executive Council; Regional Representatives. **Languages** English. **Finance** Members' dues. **Activities** Guidance/assistance/consulting. **Events** *Biennial International Conference* Johannesburg (South Africa) 2021, *Biennial International Conference* Yogyakarta (Indonesia) 2019, *Biennial International Conference* Zagreb (Croatia) 2017, *Biennial International Conference* Singapore (Singapore) 2015, *Biennial International Conference* Kampala (Uganda) 2013. **Publications** *ICSD Newsletter* (2 a year); *Social Development Issues* – journal. **Members** Individual; Student; Institutional. Membership countries not specified. [2018.09.07/XF2979/**F**]

♦ International Consortium for Social Well-Being Studies (unconfirmed)

♦ International Consortium for Telemetry Spectrum (ICTS) 12923

Chairman 20 allée de la durance, 31770 Colombiers, France.
Vice-Chairman Mid-Atlantic Area Frequency Coordination Office, 5 2 2 2 – Unit 4 – Bldg 2118, 23013 Cedar Point Road, NAVAIRWARCENACDIV, Patuxent River MD 20670-1183, USA.
Sec/Treas 1218 Pasteur Dr, Lancaster CA 93535, USA. E-mail: tcshrek42@gmail.com.
URL: http://www.telemetryspectrum.org/

History 1999, by *International Foundation for Telemetering (IFT)*. **Aims** Ensure the future availability of *electromagnetic* spectrum for telemetering; promote and stimulate technical growth in telemetering and its allied arts and sciences. **Structure** General and Business Meeting (2 a year); Regional Coordinators (3); Committees (2); Working Groups. **Languages** English. **Staff** voluntary. **Finance** Funded by: *International Foundation for Telemetering (IFT)*. **Activities** Knowledge management/information dissemination; guidance/assistance/consulting; events/meetings. **Events** *Conference* Las Vegas, NV (USA) 2021, *Conference* Glendale, AZ (USA) 2020, *Conference* Las Vegas, NV (USA) 2017, *International telemetering conference* Las Vegas, NV (USA) 2011, *Biannual Meeting* San Diego, CA (USA) 2010.

Members Full organizations and individuals in 10 countries:
Australia, Brazil, France, Germany, Italy, New Zealand, South Africa, Switzerland, UK, USA. [2021/XF6677/**F**]

♦ International Consortium for Uncertainty Theory (ICUT) 12924

Address not obtained.
URL: http://www.orsc.edu.cn/icut/

History 2010. **Structure** Board. **Activities** Awards/prizes/competitions; events/meetings. **Events** *International Conference on Uncertainty Theory* Jeju (Korea Rep) 2014, *International Conference on Uncertainty Theory* Tokyo (Japan) 2013, *International Conference on Uncertainty Theory* Phuket (Thailand) 2012, *International Conference on Uncertainty Theory* Lhasa (China) 2011, *International Conference on Uncertainty Theory* China 2010. [2014/XJ9516/**C**]

♦ International Consortium for Universities of Education in East Asia (unconfirmed)

♦ International Construction Information Society (ICIS) 12925

Sec URS PRAHA, Sumavska 35, 602 00 Brno, Czechia. T. +420725988535.
URL: http://www.icis.org/

History Founded 1994, Banff (Canada), by founding organizations STABU (Netherlands), Construction Specifications Canada and Swedish Building Centre. **Aims** Improve communication among participants in the construction process internationally; represent common members' interests in dealings with national and international organizations, authorities and associations; support, investigate and promote efforts and developments in the field of construction information leading to worthwhile international harmonization and standardization; set principles for organizing and preparing construction information. **Structure** Assembly; Technical Committees. **Languages** English. **Staff** 0.50 FTE, voluntary. **Finance** Members' dues. **Activities** Research/documentation; events/meetings. **Events** *Assembly* Portland, ME (USA) 2019, *Assembly* Cologne (Germany) 2018, *Assembly* Newcastle upon Tyne (UK) 2017, *Assembly* Auckland (New Zealand) 2016, *Assembly* Brno (Czech Rep) 2015. **Publications** ICIS Newsletters; reports; technical papers.

Members Organizations (17) in 15 countries:
Australia, Belgium, Canada, Czechia, Denmark, Finland, Germany, Japan, New Zealand, Norway, Singapore, South Africa, Switzerland, UK, USA.

Included in the above, 1 organization listed in this Yearbook:
Institute of International Harmonization for Building and Housing (IIBH). [2018.08.13/XD6427/y/**D**]

♦ International Construction Law Association (ICLA) 12926

Contact Time – Quantum Expert Forensics Ltd, 99 Bishopsgate, London, EC2M 3XD, UK. T. +442033557078. Fax +442033557095.
Contact Breyer Rechtsanwälte, Flughafenstr 32, Ebene 7, 70629 Stuttgart, Germany. T. +497113418000. Fax +4971134180020.
URL: http://www.icl-assoc.com/

History Founded May 2015. **Aims** Gather leading lawyers, barristers, construction professionals, judges, academics, universities and institutions specializing in the field. **Structure** Board. **Languages** English. **Staff** 2.00 FTE, paid. **Finance** Sources: members' dues. **Activities** Events/meetings. **Events** *Building for Change* Auckland (New Zealand) 2021, *Force Majeure Revisited: Dealing with the Unpredictable* Brazil 2020, *Conference* Tokyo (Japan) 2019, *Conference* London (UK) 2018, *Conference* Moscow (Russia) 2018. **Members** Student; Individual; Corporate. Membership countries not specified. [2019.04.25/XM7627/**C**]

♦ International Construction Measurement Standards Coalition / see International Cost Management Standard Coalition (#12978)

♦ International Construction Project Management Association (ICPMA) 12927

Pres c/o Axa-Winterthur, Monbijoustr 114, 3000 Bern 14, Switzerland. E-mail: icpmamembers@gmail.com – office@icpma.net.
URL: https://www.icpma.net/

History 2003. Current constitution adopted 2009, Prague (Czech Rep); amended May 2012, Porto (Portugal); Jun 2013, Wiesbaden (Germany); Jun 2017, Hamburg (Germany). **Aims** Spread best practice in construction and project management. **Structure** Steering Committee. Includes *Young International Construction Project Management Association (YICPMA)*. **Languages** English, French, German, Hungarian, Italian, Japanese, Portuguese, Russian. **Finance** Sources: members' dues. **Activities** Awards/prizes/competitions; events/meetings. **Events** *Annual Conference* Munich (Germany) 2023, *Annual Conference* Porto (Portugal) 2022, *Annual Conference* Lausanne (Switzerland) 2019, *Annual Conference* London (UK) 2018, *Annual Conference* Hamburg (Germany) 2017. **Publications** *ICMPA Newsletter*.

Members Full in 17 countries:
Austria, Finland, Germany, Hungary, Ireland, Japan, Korea Rep, Malta, Nigeria, Philippines, Portugal, South Africa, Spain, Switzerland, UK, United Arab Emirates, USA. [2022/XM4614/**C**]

♦ International Consultation on Urological Diseases (ICUD) 12928

Consultation internationale sur les maladies urologiques (CIMU)

Chairman c/o Bristol Urological Inst, Southmead Hospital, Bristol, BS10 5NB, UK.
URL: http://www.icud.info/

History 28 Jun 1994, following consultation and consensus meetings of national and international urological associations, supported by *WHO (#20950)* and *Union for International Cancer Control (UICC, #20415)*, from 1981 onwards. Registered in accordance with Belgian law. **Aims** Promote improvement in management of urological diseases worldwide. **Structure** General Assembly (annual). Steering Committee (meets at least once a year), comprising: Executive (3-year terms, once renewable), consisting of Chairman, 2 Vice-Chairmen, Treasurer and Secretary; 2 representatives (2-6 year terms) of American Urological Association, *European Association of Urology (EAU, #06264)*, *Société Internationale d'Urologie (SIU, #19499)*; one representative (2-6 year terms) of *Urological Association of Asia (UAA, #20733)*, *Confederación Americana de Urologia (CAU,*

#04440), Japanese Urological Association, *Pan African Urological Surgeons' Association (PAUSA, #18072)*. Executive recommends proposals for consultations and other business to the Steering Committee. **Languages** English, French. **Finance** Members' dues. **Activities** Organizes consultations among experts representing major urological organizations worldwide in order to produce recommendations. Consultations are based on a transparent process where experts examine and analyse available literature according to the principles of evidence-based medicine. Resulting recommendations must be suitable for use in all parts of the world, recognizing that the health services' resources differ widely between countries. Recommendations are not intended to be used as guidelines, although they can be used as part of the production of guidelines. Organizes global consultations on main urological diseases, including cancer, incontinence, impotence and benign prostate hyperplasia. **Events** *Consultation* Marseille (France) 2013, *Consultation on Upper Tract Transitional Cell Carcinoma, Congenital Anomalies in Children* Vancouver, BC (Canada) 2013, *Consultation* Vancouver, BC (Canada) 2013, *Consultation* Fukuoka (Japan) 2012, *Consultation* Paris (France) 2012. **Publications** *Bladder Cancer* (2012); *Incontinence* (2009); *Penile Cancer* (2009); *Stone Disease* (2008); *Bladder Tumors* (2006); *Male Lower Urinary Tract Dysfunction* (2006); *Prostate Cancer* (2006); *Sexual Dysfunctions in Men and Women* (2004).
Members Effective; Associate; Patron individuals and organizations in 6 countries:
Australia, Canada, Israel, New Zealand, Türkiye, USA.
Also members in European Union and the Middle East. Membership countries not specified.
[2013/XF3424/**F**]

- ♦ International Consultative Association of Retired Generals and Admirals / see Strategies for Peace (#20008)
- ♦ International Consultative Commission for the Protection of Nature (inactive)
- ♦ International Consultative Committee of Organizations for Christian – Jewish Cooperation / see International Council of Christians and Jews (#13006)

♦ International Consultative Group on Non Ferrous Metals Statistics . 12929

Address not obtained.
Structure Informal grouping on which non-ferrous metals bodies have representatives. **NGO Relations** *International Wrought Copper Council (IWCC, #15917)*. [2011/XF5205/**F**]

- ♦ International Consultative Group for Peace and Disarmament (inactive)
- ♦ International Consultative Research Group on Rapeseed (#10736)
- ♦ International Consumer Co-operatives Organization / see Consumer Co-operatives Worldwide (#04770)
- ♦ International Consumer Product Health and Safety Organization (internationally oriented national body)
- ♦ International Consumer Product Safety Caucus (inactive)

♦ International Consumer Protection and Enforcement Network (ICPEN) 12930

Réseau international de contrôle et de protection des consommateurs (RICPC)
Contact Stresemannstraße 128 – 130, 10117 Berlin, Germany. E-mail: icpen-secretariat@bmuv.bund.de.
URL: http://www.icpen.org/
History 1992. Former names and other names: *International Marketing Supervision Network (IMSN)* – former (1992 to 2002); *Réseau international de contrôle de la commercialisation (RICC)* – former (1992 to 2002). **Aims** Share information about cross-border commercial activities that may affect consumer interests; encourage international cooperation among law enforcement agencies. **Structure** Presidency (rotating); Steering groups (3). **Languages** English, French. **Finance** No common budget. **Activities** Events/meetings; training/education. **Events** *Conference* Gatineau, QC (Canada) 2021, *Conference* Portugal 2021, *Conference* Bogota (Colombia) 2020, *Conference* Bogota (Colombia) 2020, *Conference* Gatineau, QC (Canada) 2020.
Members Governmental organizations (* indicates Partners status) in 70 countries:
Angola, Australia, Austria, Azerbaijan, Barbados, Belgium, Botswana (*), Bulgaria, Canada, Chile, China, Colombia, Costa Rica, Cyprus, Czechia, Denmark, Dominican Rep, Egypt, El Salvador, Estonia, Eswatini, Finland, France, Gambia, Germany, Greece, Hungary, India (*), Ireland, Israel, Italy, Japan, Kenya, Korea Rep, Kosovo, Latvia, Lithuania, Luxembourg, Malawi, Malta, Mexico, Mongolia, Morocco, Netherlands, New Zealand, Nigeria, Norway, Panama, Papua New Guinea, Peru, Philippines, Poland, Portugal, Qatar, Saudi Arabia, Seychelles, Singapore (*), Slovakia, South Africa, Spain, Sri Lanka, Suriname, Sweden, Switzerland, Türkiye, UK, United Arab Emirates, USA, Vietnam, Zambia.
Observers status (6):
Common Market for Eastern and Southern Africa (COMESA, #04296); *European Commission (EC, #06633)*; *Foro Iberoamericano de Agencias Gubernamentales de Protección al Consumidor (FIAGC, #09877)*; Global Privacy Enforcement Network (GPEN); *OECD (#17693)*; *UNCTAD (#20285)*. [2022.10.20/XF2443/**F***]

♦ International Consumer Research and Testing (ICRT) 12931

Chief Exec 24 Highbury Crescent, London, N5 1RX, UK. T. +442075639170. Fax +442075639171. E-mail: secretariat@international-testing.org.
Brussels Office Hollandstraat 13, 1060 Brussels, Belgium. T. +3225423494. Fax +3225423502.
URL: http://www.international-testing.org/index.html
History Formally set up 1990. Cooperation started 1968, with a group called *European Testing Group (ETG)* set up 1972. Registered in accordance with UK law. **Aims** Be the world-leading organization empowering members to provide high quality and independent information to consumers worldwide. **Structure** Board.
Members Consumer organizations in 32 countries and territories:
Australia, Austria, Belgium, Brazil, Bulgaria, Canada, Chile, China, Czechia, Denmark, Finland, France, Germany, Hong Kong, Hungary, Iceland, Ireland, Italy, Korea Rep, Netherlands, New Zealand, Poland, Portugal, Romania, Serbia, Slovenia, Spain, Sweden, Switzerland, Thailand, UK, USA.
NGO Relations Member of: *European New Car Assessment Programme (EURO NCAP, #08046)*. Supports: *Global New Car Assessment Programme (Global NCAP, #10506)*; *New Car Assessment Programme for Latin America and the Caribbean (Latin NCAP, #17077)*. [2016/XM1918/**F**]

- ♦ International Consumers for Civil Society (no recent information)

♦ International Consumer Support for Infertility Community (iCSi) . . . 12932

CEO c/o Access Australia, PO Box 6769, Silverwater NSW 2128, Australia. T. +61297370245.
URL: http://www.icsicommunity.org/
History 1999. Previously also referred to as *International Consumer Support to Infertility Network*. **Aims** Partner with patient associations worldwide so as to promote equity of access to high quality, affordable infertility health care services; increase involvement of patients in all aspects of treatment and public policy decision making. **Structure** Sub-Groups of Infertility Alliances (4): Africa; Americas; Asia-Pacific; Europe. **Staff** Voluntary. **Activities** Conducts international meetings for patient leaders. Brings patients perspectives to governments and scientific meetings. **Events** *Conference* Kyoto (Japan) 2012, *Conference* Osaka (Japan) 2012, *Conference* Istanbul (Turkey) 2011, *Conference* Istanbul (Turkey) 2010, *Conference* Kampala (Uganda) 2010. **Publications** Factsheets.
Members National organizations in 36 countries:
Argentina, Australia, Belgium, Canada, China, Czechia, Denmark, Finland, Germany, Greece, India, Ireland, Israel, Italy, Japan, Kenya, Korea Rep, Malawi, Malaysia, Mexico, Netherlands, New Zealand, Nigeria, Norway, South Africa, Spain, Sweden, Switzerland, Türkiye, Uganda, UK, Ukraine, Uruguay, USA, Zambia, Zimbabwe.
NGO Relations Member of: *International Alliance of Patients' Organizations (IAPO, #11633)*.
[2013/XM2537/**F**]

- ♦ International Consumer Support to Infertility Network / see International Consumer Support for Infertility Community (#12932)

♦ International Contact Dermatitis Research Group (ICDRG) 12933

Main Office 80 Drummond St, Carlton VIC 3053, Australia. T. +61396239402. E-mail: rnixon@occderm.asn.au.
Chairman Dept Occupational and Environmental Dermatology, Skane Univ Hosp Malmo, SE-20502 Malmö, Sweden. T. +4640331760. Fax +4640336213.
URL: http://www.icdrg.org/
History 1967. **Aims** Promote understanding of contact dermatitis. **Structure** Informal structure. **Languages** English. **Staff** None. **Finance** Sources: meeting proceeds; sale of publications. **Activities** Events/meetings; standards/guidelines. **Events** *Biennial international symposium* Chandigarh (India) 2011, *Biennial International Symposium* Kyoto (Japan) 2009, *Biennial international symposium* Surfers Paradise, QLD (Australia) 2007, *Biennial international symposium* Paphos (Cyprus) 2005, *International symposium on irritant contact dermatitis* Paphos (Cyprus) 2005. **Publications** *ICDRG Standard Series. Patch Testing and Prick Testing: A Practical Guide* (3rd ed 2012) by J M Lachapelle and H I Maibach; *Giant Steps in Patch Testing – A Historical Memoir* (2010) by J M Lachapelle.
Members Individuals (researchers) in 17 countries:
Argentina, Australia, Belgium, Canada, Croatia, Denmark, Germany, India, Japan, Korea Rep, Portugal, Singapore, Sweden, Thailand, UK, Uruguay, USA.
NGO Relations *Asia-Pacific Environmental and Occupational Dermatology Group (APEOD, #01892)*; *European Environmental and Contact Dermatitis Research Group (EECDRG, #06998)*; *European Society of Contact Dermatitis (ESCD, #08567)*; North American Contact Dermatitis Group (NACDG). [2022/XE3907/**E**]

- ♦ International Contact Lens Society of Ophthalmologists / see International Medical Contact Lens Council (#14131)
- ♦ International Contender Association (see: #21760)

♦ International Continence Society (ICS) 12934

Admin Dir 19 Portland Square, Bristol, BS2 8SJ, UK. T. +441179444881. Fax +441179444882. E-mail: info@ics.org.
URL: http://www.ics.org/
History 1971. Former names and other names: *Continence Club* – former (1971). Registration: Charity Commission, No/ID: 1074929, England and Wales. **Aims** Improve the quality of life of people affected by urinary, bowel and pelvic floor disorders by advancing basic and clinical science through education, research and advocacy. **Structure** Board of Trustees; Committees (12). **Languages** English. **Staff** 7.00 FTE, paid. **Finance** Sources: members' dues. **Activities** Events/meetings. **Events** *Annual Meeting* Madrid (Spain) 2024, *Annual Meeting* Toronto, ON (Canada) 2023, *Annual Meeting* Vienna (Austria) 2022, *Annual Meeting* Melbourne, VIC (Australia) 2021, *Annual Meeting* Bristol (UK) 2020. **Publications** *Neurourology and Urodynamics* – journal. **Members** Medical professionals (about 3,000) from over 65 countries. Membership countries not specified. **NGO Relations** In liaison with technical committees of: *International Organization for Standardization (ISO, #14473)*. [2021.02.18/XD8067/**D**]

♦ International Continental Scientific Drilling Program (ICDP) 12935

Exec Sec GFZ German Research Centre for Geosciences, Telegrafenberg, 14473 Potsdam, Germany. T. +493312881085.
Exec Dir address not obtained.
URL: http://www.icdp-online.org/
History 1996, Tokyo (Japan). Operational since 1998. An international programme of the German Research Centre for Geosciences (GFZ). **Aims** Provide funding and support for *geoscientific* research projects where drilling is essential to achieve scientific goals related to societal needs. **Structure** Assembly of Governors; Executive Committee; Science Advisory Group; Operational Support Group. **Languages** English. **Staff** 6.00 FTE, paid. Voluntary. **Finance** Sources: members' dues. **Activities** Financial and/or material support; knowledge management/information dissemination; events/meetings; training/education. **Events** *International Workshop* Manaus (Brazil) 2015, *International Workshop* Utrecht (Netherlands) 2015, *International Workshop* Heimaey Is (Iceland) 2014, *International Workshop* Iceland 2014, *International Workshop* Sao Paulo (Brazil) 2014. **Publications** *Scientific Drilling* (2 a year) – journal.
Members Full: national scientific research organizations in 20 countries:
Austria, Belgium, China, Czechia, Finland, France, Germany, Iceland, India, Israel, Italy, Japan, Netherlands, New Zealand, Norway, Spain, Sweden, Switzerland, UK, USA.
Consultative member:
UNESCO (#20322). [2021/XF3347/y/**F**]

- ♦ International Continuing Committee towards Disarmament (inactive)
- ♦ International Contraception, Abortion and Sterilization Campaign / see Women's Global Network for Reproductive Rights (#21019)

♦ International Contraceptive Access Foundation (ICA Foundation) . . 12936

Address not obtained.
URL: http://www.ica-foundation.org/
History Set up Dec 2003, as a collaboration between Bayer and *Population Council (#18458)*. **Aims** Provide local service-delivery organizations with the levonorgestrel releasing intrauterine system (LNG IUS) contraceptive devices on a not-for-profit basis and ultimately serve the reproductive needs of *women* in resource-poor settings, primarily in developing countries. **Structure** Board of Directors; Advisory Members; Secretariat. **Languages** English. **Staff** Employees from Bayer seconded. **Activities** Financial and/or material support. **Publications** None. **Members** Not a membership organization. **IGO Relations** Formal contacts with: *United Nations Population Fund (UNFPA, #20612)*. **NGO Relations** Member of: *Reproductive Health Supplies Coalition (RHSC, #18847)*. Agreements with: *Americares Foundation*; *International Planned Parenthood Federation (IPPF, #14589)*; *MSI Reproductive Choices*; *Partners in Health (PIH)*. [2017/XJ7493/f/**F**]

- ♦ International Contractors' Group / see European International Contractors (#07586)
- ♦ International Controlled Release Society / see Controlled Release Society (#04784)
- ♦ International Convention for the Abolition of Import and Export Prohibitions and Restrictions (1927 treaty)
- ♦ International Convention for Adapting to Maritime Warfare the Principles of the Geneva Convention of 22 Aug 1864 (1899 treaty)
- ♦ International Convention Against Apartheid in Sports, 1985 (1985 treaty)
- ♦ International Convention Against Apartheid in Sports, 1988 (1988 treaty)
- ♦ International Convention Against Doping in Sport (2005 treaty)
- ♦ International Convention Against the Recruitment, Use, Financing and Training of Mercenaries (1989 treaty)
- ♦ International Convention Against the Taking of Hostages (1979 treaty)
- ♦ International Convention on Arrest of Ships (1999 treaty)
- ♦ International Convention of Asia Scholars (internationally oriented national body)
- ♦ International Convention for the Campaign Against Contagious Diseases of Animals (1935 treaty)
- ♦ International Convention on Certain Rules Concerning Civil Jurisdiction in Matters of Collision (1952 treaty)
- ♦ International Convention on Civil Liability for Bunker Oil Pollution Damage (2001 treaty)
- ♦ International Convention on Civil Liability for Damage Caused by Motor Vehicles (1973 treaty)
- ♦ International Convention on Civil Liability for Oil Pollution Damage (1969 treaty)
- ♦ International Convention Concerning the Carriage of Goods by Rail (1890 treaty)
- ♦ International Convention Concerning the Carriage of Goods by Rail, 1961 (1961 treaty)
- ♦ International Convention Concerning the Carriage of Goods by Rail, 1970 (1970 treaty)
- ♦ International Convention Concerning the Carriage of Passengers and Luggage by Rail (1924 treaty)
- ♦ International Convention Concerning the Carriage of Passengers and Luggage by Rail, 1953 (1953 treaty)
- ♦ International Convention Concerning the Carriage of Passengers and Luggage by Rail, 1961 (1961 treaty)
- ♦ International Convention Concerning the Carriage of Passengers and Luggage by Rail, 1970 (1970 treaty)
- ♦ International Convention Concerning the Carriage of Passengers and Luggage by Rail, with Additional Protocol, 1970 (1970 treaty)
- ♦ International Convention Concerning the Export and Import of Animal Products other Than Meat, Meat Preparations, Fresh Animal Products, Milk and Milk Products (1935 treaty)
- ♦ International Convention Concerning the Laws and Customs of War on Land (1907 treaty)
- ♦ International Convention Concerning the Traffic of Goods by Rail, 1924 (1927 treaty)

♦ International Convention Concerning the Transport of Passengers and Baggage by Rail, 1927 (1927 treaty)
♦ International Convention for the Conservation of Atlantic Tunas (1966 treaty)
♦ International Convention on the Control of Harmful Anti-fouling Systems on Ships (2001 treaty)
♦ International Convention for the Control and Management of Ships' Ballast Water and Sediments (2004 treaty)
♦ International Convention on the Elimination of all Forms of Racial Discrimination (1965 treaty)

♦ International Convention of Exhibition and Fine Art Transporters (ICEFAT) 12937

Secretariat PO Box 875, Hudson OH 44236, USA. E-mail: secretariat@icefat.org – webmaster@icefat.org.
URL: http://www.icefat.org/

Aims Promote the highest standards of professionalism in the field of museum and gallery shipping. **Structure** Steering Committee; Secretariat. **Activities** Events/meetings. **Events** *Convention* Washington, DC (USA) 2019, *Convention* Lisbon (Portugal) 2018, *Convention* Delhi (India) 2017, *Convention* Geneva (Switzerland) 2016, *Convention* Rio de Janeiro (Brazil) 1989. **Publications** *ICEFAT Newsletter*.
Members Companies in 34 countries and territories:
Argentina, Australia, Austria, Brazil, Bulgaria, Canada, China, Czechia, Denmark, Ecuador, Finland, France, Germany, Greece, India, Ireland, Israel, Italy, Japan, Korea Rep, Malaysia, Mexico, Norway, Peru, Portugal, Singapore, South Africa, Spain, Sweden, Switzerland, Taiwan, Türkiye, UK, USA. [2021/XM7488/**C**]

♦ International Convention to Facilitate the Crossing of Frontiers for Goods Carried by Rail (1952 treaty)
♦ International Convention to Facilitate the Crossing of Frontiers for Passengers and Baggage Carried by Rail (1952 treaty)
♦ International Convention to Facilitate the Importation of Commercial Samples and Advertising Material (1952 treaty)
♦ International Convention on the Harmonization of Frontier Controls of Goods (1982 treaty)
♦ International Convention on the Harmonized Commodity Description and Coding System (1983 treaty)
♦ International Convention of Heraldry (inactive)
♦ International Convention for the High Seas Fisheries of the North Pacific Ocean (1952 treaty)
♦ International Convention for the International Catalogue of Scientific Literature (inactive)
♦ International Convention on Liability and Compensation for Damage in Connection with the Carriage of Hazardous and Noxious Substances by Sea (1996 treaty)
♦ International Convention on Load Lines (1966 treaty)
♦ International Convention on Maritime Liens and Mortgages (1993 treaty)
♦ International Convention on Maritime Search and Rescue (1979 treaty)
♦ International Convention for the Marking of Eggs in International Trade (1931 treaty)
♦ International Convention on Mutual Administrative Assistance for the Prevention, Investigation and Repression of Customs Offences (1977 treaty)
♦ International Convention for the Mutual Protection Against Dengue Fever (1934 treaty)
♦ International Convention for the Northwest Atlantic Fisheries (1949 treaty)
♦ International Convention on Oil Pollution Preparedness Response and Cooperation (1990 treaty)
♦ International Convention for the Permanent Control of Outbreak Areas of the Red Locust (1949 treaty)
♦ International Convention for the Prevention of Pollution of the Sea by Oil (1954 treaty)
♦ International Convention for the Prevention of Pollution from Ships (1973 treaty)
♦ International Convention for the Prevention of Pollution from Ships as Modified by the Protocol of 1978 (1978 treaty)
♦ International Convention for the Protection of all Persons from Enforced Disappearance (2006 treaty)
♦ International Convention for the Protection of Birds (1950 treaty)
♦ International Convention for the Protection of New Varieties of Plants, 1961 (1961 treaty)
♦ International Convention for the Protection of Performers, Producers of Phonograms and Broadcasting Organizations (1961 treaty)
♦ International Convention for the Protection of Plants, 1929 (1929 treaty)
♦ International Convention on the Protection of the Rights of all Migrant Workers and Members of Their Families (1990 treaty)

♦ International Convention of Puppetry Schools 12938

Convention internationale des écoles de marionnettes (CIEM)

Contact 7 place Winston Churchill, 08000 Charleville-Mézières, France. T. +33324337250. Fax +33324337269. E-mail: institut@marionnette.com.
URL: http://www.marionnette.com/

History Jun 1990, Charleville-Mézières (France), by 'Ecole nationale supérieure des arts de la marionnette' of *Institut international de la marionnette (IIM, #11314)*, as an international encounter open to all art forms, audiovisual arts, new technologies, dance, music and drama. **Aims** Generate thought about educative methods; encourage cooperation among schools through student and teacher exchange; encourage contacts with other *art* schools; increase knowledge by organizing festivals, debates and meetings.
Members Art schools (20) in 12 countries:
Bulgaria, Czechia, Finland, France, Germany, Israel, Norway, Poland, Romania, Russia, Spain, UK. [2011.09.30/XD6024/**D**]

♦ International Convention on the Recognition of Studies, Diplomas and Degrees in Higher Education in the Arab States and European States Bordering on the Mediterranean (1976 treaty)
♦ International Convention Regarding the Establishment of Uniform Regulations for the Reciprocal Recognition of Official Proof Marks on Fire-arms (1914 treaty)
♦ International Convention Regarding the Regime of the Straits between the Mediterranean and the Black Sea (1936 treaty)
♦ International Convention Regarding the Standardisation of the Methods of Presenting the Results of the Analysis of Foodstuffs for Human Consumption and for Animals (1931 treaty)
♦ International convention for the regulation of the North Sea fisheries (1882 treaty)
♦ International Convention for the Regulation of Whaling (1946 treaty)
♦ International Convention Relating to Economic Statistics, 1928 (1928 treaty)
♦ International Convention Relating to Economic Statistics, 1950 (1948 treaty)
♦ International Convention Relating to Intervention on the High Seas in Cases of Oil Pollution Casualties (1969 treaty)
♦ International Convention Relating to the Limitation of the Liability of Owners of Sea-going Ships (1957 treaty)
♦ International Convention Relating to Road Traffic (1926 treaty)
♦ International Convention Relating to Stowaways (1957 treaty)
♦ International Convention Relative to Bounties on Sugar (1902 treaty)
♦ International Convention Relative to Motor Traffic (1926 treaty)
♦ International Convention Relative to the Opening of Hostilities (1907 treaty)
♦ International Convention Relative to the Status of Enemy Merchant Ships at the Outbreak of Hostilities (1907 treaty)
♦ International Convention Respecting Bombardments by Naval Forces in Time of War (1907 treaty)
♦ International Convention Respecting the Limitation of the Employment of Force for the Recovery of Contract Debts (1907 treaty)
♦ International Convention Respecting the Prohibition of the Use of White, Yellow, Phosphorus in the Manufacture of Matches (1906 treaty)
♦ International Convention with Respect to the Laws and Customs of War by Land (1899 treaty)
♦ International convention on responsibility and compensation for damage linked to marine transport of noxious and potentially dangerous substances (1996 treaty)
♦ International Convention for Safe Containers (1972 treaty)
♦ International Convention for the Safety of Fishing Vessels (1977 treaty)
♦ International Convention for the Safety of Life at Sea, 1914 (1914 treaty)
♦ International Convention for the Safety of Life at Sea, 1933 (1929 treaty)
♦ International Convention for the Safety of Life at Sea, 1948 (1948 treaty)
♦ International Convention for the Safety of Life at Sea, 1960 (1960 treaty)
♦ International Convention for the Safety of Life at Sea, 1974 (1974 treaty)
♦ International Convention on Salvage (1989 treaty)
♦ International Convention on the Simplification and Harmonization of Customs Procedures (1973 treaty)
♦ International Convention on the Standardization of Methods of Wine Analysis and Evaluation (1954 treaty)
♦ International Convention on Standards of Training, Certification and Watchkeeping for Fishing Vessel Personnel (1995 treaty)
♦ International Convention on Standards of Training, Certification and Watchkeeping for Seafarers (1978 treaty)
♦ International Convention for the Suppression of Acts of Nuclear Terrorism (2005 treaty)
♦ International Convention for the Suppression of the Financing of Terrorism (1999 treaty)
♦ International Convention on the Suppression and Punishment of the Crime of Apartheid (1973 treaty)
♦ International Convention for the Suppression of Terrorist Bombings (1997 treaty)
♦ International Convention for the Suppression of the Traffic in Women and Children (1921 treaty)
♦ International Convention for the Suppression of the Traffic in Women of Full Age (1933 treaty)
♦ International Convention for the Suppression of the White Slave Traffic, 1910 (1910 treaty)
♦ International Convention for the Suppression of the White Slave Traffic, 1949 (1949 treaty)
♦ International Convention on Tonnage Measurement of Ships (1969 treaty)
♦ International convention on travel contracts (1970 treaty)
♦ International Convention for the Unification of Certain Rules of Law Relating to Collision between Vessels and Protocol of Signature (1910 treaty)
♦ International Convention for the Unification of Certain Rules Relating to Arrest of Sea-going Ships (1952 treaty)
♦ International Convention for the Unification of Certain Rules Relating to the Assistance and Rescue of Aircraft or by Aircraft at Sea (1938 treaty)
♦ International Convention for the Unification of Certain Rules Relating to Bills of Lading (1924 treaty)
♦ International Convention for the Unification of Certain Rules Relating to Carriage of Passenger Luggage by Sea (1967 treaty)
♦ International Convention for the Unification of Certain Rules Relating to the Immunity of State-owned Vessels (1926 treaty)
♦ International Convention for the Unification of Certain Rules Relating to the Limitation of the Liability of Owners of Seagoing Vessels (1924 treaty)
♦ International Convention for the Unification of Certain Rules Relating to Maritime Liens and Mortgages, 1926 (1926 treaty)
♦ International Convention for the Unification of Certain Rules Relating to Penal Jurisdiction in Matters of Collision or other Incidents of Navigation (1952 treaty)
♦ International Convention for the Unification of Certain Rules Relative to Maritime Liens and Mortgages, 1967 (1967 treaty)
♦ International Convention for the Unification of Certains Rules Relating to the Carriage of Passengers by Sea (1961 treaty)
♦ International Convention for the Unification of Methods of Sampling and Analysing Cheeses (1934 treaty)
♦ International Convergence of Capital Measurement and Capital Standards (1988 treaty)
♦ International Convocation of Unitarian Universalist Women / see International Women's Convocation (#15896)
♦ International Cooperation (internationally oriented national body)
♦ International Cooperation Agency for Maternal and Infant Health (internationally oriented national body)
♦ International Cooperation Centre for Agricultural Education (internationally oriented national body)
♦ International Cooperation Centre of Agricultural Research for Development (#03733)
♦ International Cooperation Coordinating Council on Transsiberian Transportation / see Coordinating Council on Trans-Siberian Transportation (#04821)

♦ International Cooperation on Cosmetics Regulation (ICCR) 12939

Contact c/o MHLW, 1-2-2 Kasumigaseki, Chiyoda-ku, Tokyo, 100-8916 Japan. E-mail: grow-iccrnet@ec.europa.eu.
URL: http://www.iccr-cosmetics.org/

History 2007, as a voluntary international group of cosmetics regulatory authorities. **Aims** Provide a multilateral framework to maintain and enable the highest level of global consumer protection by working towards and promoting regulatory convergence, while minimizing barriers to international trade. **Structure** Rotating Chair; rotating Secretariat. **Finance** Members' representatives carry own costs. **Activities** Politics/policy/regulatory; events/meetings. **Events** *Annual Meeting* Washington, DC (USA) 2021, *Annual Meeting* Tokyo (Japan) 2020, *Annual Meeting* Montréal, QC (Canada) 2019, *Annual Meeting* Tokyo (Japan) 2018, *Annual Meeting* Brasilia (Brazil) 2017.
Members Authorities of 4 countries:
Brazil, Canada, Japan, USA.
Regional entity: [2021/XM5992/**F***]

♦ International Cooperation Council / see Unity-and-Diversity World Council (#20670)
♦ International Cooperation and Development Fund (internationally oriented national body)
♦ International Cooperation for Development and Solidarity / see CIDSE (#03926)

♦ International Cooperation on Education About Standardization (ICES) 12940

Secretariat c/o KSA, 19F 20F, Korea Technology Center Bldg, 305 Teheran-ro, Gangnam-gu, Seoul 135-780, Korea Rep.
Chair PO Box 1738, 3000 DR Rotterdam, Netherlands.

History Feb 2006, Tokyo (Japan). **Aims** Promote education about standardization and improve its quality and attractiveness for all stakeholders. **Structure** Board, comprising Chair and 2 Vice-Chairs. **Events** *Conference* Yogyakarta (Indonesia) 2018, *Conference* Frankfurt-Main (Germany) 2016, *Towards competency requirements for standards professionals* Seoul (Korea Rep) 2015, *Conference / Annual Workshop* Sophia Antipolis (France) 2013, *Annual Workshop* Bali (Indonesia) 2012. [2018/XJ4846/**F**]

♦ International Cooperation Foundation / see Mandat International

♦ International Cooperation on Harmonization of Technical Requirements for the Registration of Veterinary Medicinal Products (VICH) 12941

Secretariat c/o HealthforAnimals, Avenue de Tervueren 168 – Box 8, 1150 Brussels, Belgium. T. +3225437572. Fax +3225737585. E-mail: sec@vichsec.org.
Coordinator address not obtained.
URL: http://www.vichsec.org/

History Apr 1996, Paris (France), under the auspices of *OIE – World Organisation for Animal Health (#17703)*. **Aims** Provide a forum for constructive dialogue between regulatory authorities and the veterinary medicinal products industry on differences in technical requirements for product registration in *European Union*, Japan and the USA; enable this process to serve as a catalyst for a wider international harmonization; identify areas where modifications in technical requirements or greater mutual acceptance of research and development procedures could lead to a more economic use of human, animal and material resources, without compromising safety; make recommendations on practical ways to achieve harmonization in technical requirements affecting registration of veterinary products and to implement these recommendations in the 3 regions. **Structure** Steering Committee, composed of 2 delegates of the regulatory authorities and 2 delegates of representative industry associations from each of the 3 regions. Australia/New Zealand and Canada have observer status with 1 delegate representing government authorities and 1 delegate representing industry associations. **Languages** English. **Activities** Expert Working Groups (9): Antimicrobial

Resistance; Ecotoxicity/Environmental Impact Assessment; Efficacy Requirements for Anthelmintics; Good Clinical Practice; Pharmacovigilance; Quality; Quality Monitoring of Biologicals; Safety; Target Animal Safety, Metabolism and Residue Kinetics. **Events** *VICH conference* Tokyo (Japan) 2015, *VICH conference* Paris (France) 2010, *VICH conference* Washington, DC (USA) 2005, *VICH conference* Tokyo (Japan) 2002, *Vich conference* Brussels (Belgium) 1999. **Members** Steering Committee members from 3 regions European Union; USA; Japan. Observers from Australia, New Zealand and Canada. **IGO Relations** Represented on Steering Committee: *European Medicines Agency (EMA, #07767)*; *European Commission (EC, #06633)*. **NGO Relations** Secretariat provided by: *Health for Animals (#10870)*. [2015/XE3821/y/**E**]

♦ International Cooperation, Milan / see Cooperazione Internazionale
♦ International Cooperation Moroccan Agency (internationally oriented national body)
♦ International Cooperation Networking Association (inactive)
♦ International Cooperation Research Association (internationally oriented national body)
♦ International Cooperation Service Center / see Japan International Cooperation Center
♦ International Cooperation in Ship Research / see European Council for Maritime Applied R and D (#06829)
♦ International Cooperation for Socio-Economic Development / see CIDSE (#03926)
♦ International Cooperation and Solidarity Organization (internationally oriented national body)
♦ International Cooperation South-South (internationally oriented national body)

♦ International Cooperation on Theories and Concepts in Traffic Safety (ICTCT) 12942

Sec c/o FACTUM OG, Hermann-Bahr Strasse 9/11, 1210 Vienna, Austria. T. +4315041546. Fax +4315041548.
Pres address not obtained.
URL: http://www.ictct.org/

History 1987, Vienna (Austria), developed out of an international working group of safety experts. **Aims** Promote cooperation in the identification and analysis of potentially dangerous situations in *road* traffic, and their causes, on the basis of relevant safety data derived from observation techniques; achieve deeper understanding of problems in the area; harmonize future research activities; provide for means for an optimal utilization of research results from different countries. **Structure** General Assembly. Steering Committee, comprising President, Vice-President, Secretary, Vice-Secretary, Cashier and Vice-Cashier. Auditors (2). **Languages** English. **Staff** 3.00 FTE, voluntary. **Finance** Members' dues. **Activities** Organizes: European workshop (annual, end of October); workshop outside Europe (every 2 years). **Events** *Conference* Györ (Hungary) 2022, *Conference* Berlin (Germany) 2021, *Extra Workshop* Accra (Ghana) 2020, *Annual Workshop* Warsaw (Poland) 2019, *Annual Workshop* Porto (Portugal) 2018. **Publications** *ICTCT Newsletter*. Handbooks; brochures; guidelines; workshop proceedings.
Members Institutions in 15 countries:
Austria, Belgium, Brazil, Czechia, Denmark, Estonia, France, Greece, Hungary, Italy, Netherlands, Poland, Sweden, Switzerland, UK.
Included in the above, 1 organization listed in this Yearbook:
International Federation of Pedestrians (IFP, #13502).
Individuals in 32 countries:
Austria, Bangladesh, Belarus, Belgium, Brazil, Canada, Chile, China, Croatia, Czechia, Denmark, Estonia, Finland, France, Germany, Ghana, Greece, Hungary, India, Israel, Italy, Japan, Jordan, Latvia, Nigeria, Norway, Pakistan, Poland, Romania, Spain, Sweden, UK.
NGO Relations Member of: *Confederation of Organizations in Road Transport Enforcement (CORTE, #04574)*. [2018/XM0368/**F**]

♦ International Co-operative Agricultural Organisation (ICAO) 12943

SG 6th floor, 16 Saemunan-Ro, Jung-Gu, Seoul 04516, Korea Rep. T. +82220806125. Fax +82220806130. E-mail: secretariat@icao.coop.
URL: http://icao.coop/

History 1951. Founded within the framework of *International Co-operative Alliance (ICA, #12944)*. A Sector of ICA. Former names and other names: *ICA Agricultural Committee* – former; *Comité agricole de l'ACI* – former; *International Committee on Agricultural Co-operation* – former; *Comité international de la coopération agricole* – former; *ICA Specialized Organization on Agricultural Co-operation* – former (1984). **Aims** Exchange experience on specific activity fields by hosting international seminars; promote the establishment of agricultural co-operatives in *developing countries* and the *transition economies* in order to increase *food security*; improve the distribution of agricultural products; take concrete action for preserving the *environment*. **Structure** General Assembly; Executive Committee; Secretariat. **Languages** English, French. **Finance** Sources: members' dues. **Activities** Events/meetings. **Events** *Annual General Meeting* Seoul (Korea Rep) 2021, *General Assembly* Seoul (Korea Rep) 2021, *Capacity Building for Agricultural Cooperatives Programe Meeting* Seoul (Korea Rep) 2019, *Joint Workshop* Seoul (Korea Rep) 2019, *General Assembly* Antalya (Turkey) 2015.
Members Organizations (38) in 33 countries:
Argentina, Brazil, Bulgaria, Canada, China, Cyprus, Finland, Ghana, Haiti, India, Iran Islamic Rep, Italy, Japan, Korea Rep, Malaysia, Malta, Mongolia, Mozambique, Nepal, Norway, Paraguay, Philippines, Poland, Slovakia, Somalia, South Africa, Sri Lanka, Tanzania UR, Thailand, Türkiye, Uganda, Uruguay, Vietnam. [2022.02.10/XE2305/**E**]

♦ International Co-operative Alliance (ICA) 12944

Alliance coopérative internationale (ACI) – Alianza Cooperativa Internacional (ACI) – Internationaler Genossenschaftsbund (IGB) – Mezdunarodnyj Kooperativnyj Alians (MKA)

Dir Gen Avenue Milcamps 105, 1030 Brussels, Belgium. T. +3227431030. E-mail: ica@ica.coop.
URL: http://www.ica.coop/

History 19 Aug 1895, London (UK). Founded with a mixed membership of individuals and cooperative organizations. Individual membership abolished in 1902. Previously also referred to as *Internationaler Genossenschaftsbund (IGB) – Mezdunarodnyj Kooperativnyj Alians (MKA)*. Registration: Banque-Carrefour des Entreprises, No/ID: 0535.539.869, Start date: 7 Jun 2013, Belgium. **Aims** Be prized as the organization of reference which provides an effective and efficient global voice and forum of knowledge, expertise and coordinated action for and about cooperatives.
Structure General Assembly; Regional Assemblies; ICA Board; Europe Region: *Cooperatives Europe (#04801)*; Regional Offices (4); Project Office in Singapore (Singapore); Secretariat based in Brussels (Belgium).
Specialized organizations (8):
– *Consumer Co-operatives Worldwide (CCW, #04770)*;
– *International Co-operative Agricultural Organisation (ICAO, #12943)*;
– *International Cooperative Banking Association (ICBA, #12945)*;
– *International Cooperative Fisheries Organization (ICFO, #12946)*;
– *Co-operative Housing International (CHI, #04799)*;
– *International Cooperative and Mutual Insurance Federation (ICMIF, #12948)*;
– *International Health Cooperative Organization (IHCO, #13779)*;
– *International Organisation of Industrial and Service Cooperatives (CICOPA, #14429)*.
Board committees (8): Governance; Membership; Audit and Risk; Human Resources; Principles; International Accounting and Regulatory Affairs; Elections; Grant Oversight.
Alliance committees and networks (5):
Thematic Committees (4): Gender Equality Committee; Committee on Co-operative Research; Co-operative Law Committee; Youth Network; Communications Committee.
Languages English, French, Spanish. **Staff** 37.50 FTE, paid. **Finance** Subscriptions of member organizations. Other sources: grants from international and national agencies for specific technical assistance projects. **Activities** Events/meetings; guidance/assistance/consulting; networking/liaising; projects/programmes; research/documentation. **Events** *Asia and Pacific Regional Assembly* Seoul (Korea Rep) 2021, *Cooperative Research Conference on the Cooperative Identity* Seoul (Korea Rep) 2021, *International Forum on Cooperative Law* Seoul (Korea Rep) 2021, *World Cooperative Congress* Seoul (Korea Rep) 2021, *International Forum on Cooperative Law* Seoul (Korea Rep) 2020. **Publications** *ICA Digest* (3 a year) – newsletter; *Review of International Cooperation* (irregular). Books; pamphlets; reports; videos; slides. Regional offices issue their own publications.
Members Full (250); Associate (45). Affiliated organizations in 103 countries and territories:
Argentina, Armenia, Australia, Austria, Bangladesh, Belarus, Belgium, Bhutan, Bolivia, Botswana, Brazil, Bulgaria, Canada, Chile, China, Colombia, Congo DR, Costa Rica, Côte d'Ivoire, Croatia, Cyprus, Czechia, Denmark, Dominican Rep, Ecuador, El Salvador, Ethiopia, Fiji, Finland, France, Germany, Ghana, Greece, Guatemala, Guinea, Haiti, Honduras, Hungary, India, Indonesia, Iran Islamic Rep, Ireland, Israel, Italy, Jamaica, Japan, Kazakhstan, Kenya, Korea Rep, Kuwait, Lithuania, Malaysia, Maldives, Malta, Mauritius, Mexico, Moldova, Mongolia, Morocco, Mozambique, Myanmar, Namibia, Nepal, Netherlands, New Zealand, Niger, Nigeria, Norway, Pakistan, Palestine, Panama, Papua New Guinea, Paraguay, Peru, Philippines, Poland, Portugal, Puerto Rico, Romania, Russia, Rwanda, Saudi Arabia, Singapore, Slovakia, South Africa, Spain, Sri Lanka, Sweden, Switzerland, Tanzania UR, Thailand, Timor-Leste, Türkiye, Uganda, UK, Ukraine, United Arab Emirates, Uruguay, USA, Vanuatu, Vietnam, Zambia, Zimbabwe.
International affiliated organizations (5):
African Confederation of Cooperative Savings and Credit Associations (ACCOSCA, #00261); *Association of Asian Confederation of Credit Unions (ACCU, #02377)*; *Caribbean Confederation of Credit Unions (CCCU, #03478)*; *European Association of Co-operative Banks (EACB, #05990)*; *Latin American Confederation of Credit Unions (#16302)*.
Consultative Status Consultative status granted from: *ECOSOC (#05331)* (General); *ILO (#11123)* (General); *UNCTAD (#20285)* (General Category); *FAO (#09260)*; *UNICEF (#20332)*; *UNIDO (#20336)*. **IGO Relations** Accredited by (1): *United Nations Office at Vienna (UNOV, #20604)*. Participates as observer in the activities of: *Codex Alimentarius Commission (CAC, #04081)*. Associated with Department of Global Communications of the United Nations. **NGO Relations** Member of (4): *Committee for the Promotion and Advancement of Cooperatives (COPAC, #04279)*; *Conference of Non-Governmental Organizations in Consultative Relationship with the United Nations (CONGO, #04635)*; *Federation of European and International Associations Established in Belgium (FAIB, #09508)*; *Fédération des Institutions Internationales établies à Genève (FIIG, #09599)*. Instrumental in setting up (1): *Network for the Development of Agricultural Cooperatives in Asia and the Pacific (NEDAC, #17004)*. Participant of: *United Nations Global Compact (#20567)*. [2021/XA1710/y/**A**]

♦ International Co-operative Alliance Central Banking Committee / see International Cooperative Banking Association (#12945)

♦ International Cooperative Banking Association (ICBA) 12945

Association internationale des banques coopératives – Asociación Internacional de Bancos Cooperativos

Address not obtained.
URL: http://www.icba.coop/

History 1922, as *International Cooperative Banking Committee – Comité international des banques coopératives*, with membership from 7 European consumer cooperative banks. In 1964 membership was opened to all cooperative banks and central cooperative credit organizations directly or indirectly affiliated to *International Co-operative Alliance (ICA, #12944)*, of which it is a specialized body. Following 28th ICA Congress, 1984, Hamburg (Germany FR), became an international specialized organization of ICA, with the title *International Co-operative Alliance Central Banking Committee – Comité central des banques coopératives de l'Alliance coopérative internationale* or *ICA Central Banking Committee – Comité central bancaire de l'ACI*; also sometimes referred to as *International Association of Cooperative Banks – Association internationale coopérative bancaire*. Present name adopted 1992. **Aims** Exchange information; promote cooperation among cooperative banks; advise and assist the development of new cooperative banks; carry out studies and research on subjects of common interest – *capital* formation, cooperative *values* as applied to banking. **Structure** Plenary Session (members' meeting, annual). Executive Committee (meets twice a year). Regional Committees (5): Europe; East, Central and South Africa; North Africa and Middle East; Asia and the Pacific – *Regional Co-operative Banking Association for Asia and the Pacific (RCBA, no recent information)*; Latin America. **Languages** English, French, Polish, Portuguese. **Finance** Members' dues. **Activities** Organizes: plenary sessions; seminars. Regional committees organize their own meetings. **Events** *Annual plenary session* Geneva (Switzerland) 2009, *Seminar* Geneva (Switzerland) 2009, *International co-operative dialogue* Montabaur (Germany) 2008, *Annual plenary session* Singapore (Singapore) 2007, *Annual plenary session* Cartagena de Indias (Colombia) 2005. **Publications** *International Co-operative Banking Association Journal* (annual).
Members Cooperatives (38) and institutions (9) in 38 countries:
Argentina, Bangladesh, Bolivia, Brazil, Canada, Chile, Cyprus, Denmark, Ethiopia, France, Germany, Greece, Hungary, India, Indonesia, Ireland, Italy, Japan, Kenya, Korea DPR, Korea Rep, Luxembourg, Morocco, Netherlands, Paraguay, Poland, South Africa, Sri Lanka, Switzerland, Tanzania UR, Thailand, Türkiye, Uganda, UK, Ukraine, Uruguay, USA, Zambia.
Included in the above 1 organization listed in this Yearbook:
Association of Asian Confederation of Credit Unions (ACCU, #02377).
NGO Relations Member of: *World Council of Credit Unions (WOCCU, #21324)*. Close contact with: EACB; *Internationale Raiffeisen Union e.V. (IRU, #13291)*. [2010/XE1855/y/**E**]

♦ International Cooperative Banking Committee / see International Cooperative Banking Association (#12945)
♦ International Cooperative Biodiversity Groups (internationally oriented national body)
♦ International Cooperative Federation of Dyers and Cleaners (inactive)

♦ International Cooperative Fisheries Organization (ICFO) 12946

Chairman 62 Ogeum-ro, Shincheon-dong, Songpa-ku, Seoul 138-730, Korea Rep. T. +82222400425. E-mail: newyork1@suhyup.co.kr.
URL: http://www.icfo.coop/

History 1966, as a sub-committee of the Agricultural Committee of *International Co-operative Alliance (ICA, #12944)*. Became an independent body, with the name *ICA Fisheries Committee*, in 1976. A specialized body of ICA. **Aims** Create new cooperative fishery organizations; promote cooperative training and education by cooperative movements of advanced countries, including production of educational material; promote exchange of technical information and *human resources* between movements on a regional basis. **Structure** Plenary Session (annual, at Seminar). Executive Committee, consisting of Chairman, 5 Vice-Chairmen, Honorary Chairman, 2 Auditors, Secretary-General, Secretary and 3 members. Auditors. Secretariat, headed by Secretary General. **Languages** English. **Finance** Members' dues. Other sources: grants; contributions. **Activities** Organizes annual seminars on fishery cooperatives. **Events** *Annual Meeting* Bali (Indonesia) 2014, *Annual Meeting* Cape Town (South Africa) 2013, *Annual Meeting* Cancún (Mexico) 2011, *Annual Meeting* Beijing (China) 2010, *Annual Meeting* Geneva (Switzerland) 2009. **Publications** Reports; surveys; studies.
Members Cooperative organizations (27) in 23 countries:
Bangladesh, Canada, Chile, Colombia, Fiji, France, Ghana, Greece, Hungary, Iceland, India, Indonesia, Italy, Japan, Korea Rep, Malaysia, Nigeria, Pakistan, Philippines, Sri Lanka, Tanzania UR, Thailand, Vietnam. [2015/XE2383/**E**]

♦ International Cooperative Group on Environmentally-Assisted Cracking (ICG-EAC) 12947

Administrator 56 Bradford Farm Rd, Mills River NC 28759, USA. E-mail: administrator@icg-eac.org.
Sec Paul Scherrer Inst, 5232 Villigen AG PSI, Switzerland. E-mail: secretary@icg-eac.org.
URL: http://www.icg-eac.org/

History 1978. Former names and other names: *International Cooperative Group on Environmentally Assisted Cracking of Water Reactor Materials (ICG-EAC)* – full title. **Aims** Coordinate international efforts on avoiding environmentally-assisted cracking (EAC) of structural materials in various aqueous reactor service environments. **Structure** Annual Meeting. **Languages** English. **Activities** Events/meetings. **Events** *Annual meeting* Kingston, ON (Canada) 2023, *Annual meeting* Tampere (Finland) 2022, *Annual meeting* 2021, *Annual meeting* Tainan (Taiwan) 2019, *Annual Meeting* Knoxville, TN (USA) 2018. **Members** Organizations (83) in 17 countries. Membership countries not specified. [2022.05.04/XE3938/**E**]

♦ International Cooperative Group on Environmentally Assisted Cracking of Water Reactor Materials / see International Cooperative Group on Environmentally-Assisted Cracking (#12947)
♦ International Cooperative Housing Committee / see Co-operative Housing International (#04799)
♦ International Cooperative Housing Development Association (inactive)
♦ International Co-operative Housing Organization / see Co-operative Housing International (#04799)
♦ International Cooperative Insurance Federation / see International Cooperative and Mutual Insurance Federation (#12948)

♦ **International Cooperative and Mutual Insurance Federation (ICMIF)** 12948
Fédération internationale des coopératives et mutuelles d'assurances – Federación Internacional de Cooperativas y Mutuales de Seguros – Internationaler Verband Genossenschaftlicher und Wechselseitiger Versicherungen – Kokusai Kyodokumiai Hoken Rengo

Main Office Denzell House, Denzell Gardens, Dunham Road, Bowdon, WA14 4QE, UK. T. +441619295090. Fax +441619295163. E-mail: shaun@icmif.org.
URL: http://www.icmif.org/

History 1922, Brussels (Belgium), as 'Auxiliary Insurance Committee' of *International Co-operative Alliance (ICA, #12944)*. Name changed, 1972, Warsaw (Poland), to *International Cooperative Insurance Federation (ICIF) – Fédération internationale des coopératives d'assurances (FICA) – Federación Internacional de Seguros Cooperativos (FISC) – Internationale Genossenschaftliche Versicherungs-Föderation (IGVF)*. A specialized body of ICA as from 28th Congress of ICA, 1984, Hamburg (Germany FR). Present name adopted 1992, Tokyo (Japan). **Aims** Provide a global platform for cooperative and mutual insurers operating in domestic markets in different countries worldwide; foster cooperation among them. **Structure** Conference (every 2 years). Board of Directors, comprising Chairman, 3 Vice-Chairmen, 14 members and the Chief Executive (ex officio). Committees (4): Executive; Development; Intelligence; Reinsurance. Regional bodies (3): *International Cooperative and Mutual Insurance Federation / Regional Association for The Americas (ICMIF/Americas, #12949)*; *Asia and Oceania Association of the ICMIF (AOA, see: #12948)*; *Association Middle East and North Africa (AMENA, no recent information)*. **Languages** English, French, Japanese, Spanish. **Staff** 23.00 FTE, voluntary. Staff includes seconded longterm from member organizations), plus a number of voluntary experts and consultants. **Finance** Members' dues (48%). Services fees. Budget (annual): pounds1.5 million. **Activities** Events/meetings; training/education; networking/liaising; research and development. **Events** *Centenary Conference* Rome (Italy) 2022, *Achievements and lessons of ICMIF 5-5-5 Strategy* Tokyo (Japan) 2022, *Seminar on SDGs: Protecting & building resilience across Coastal communities in Asia Pacific* Tokyo (Japan) 2022, *The ICMIF Foundation – The secret of our success so far* Tokyo (Japan) 2022, *The ICMIF mutual and cooperative sustainability model – How our members are taking action towards a better future* Tokyo (Japan) 2022. **Publications** *NewsByte* (12 a year); *Voice* (4 a year). *ICMIF Member Directory*. Research reports.

Members Cooperative (47%) and mutual (34%) insurance groups and stock (19%) companies. Full in 70 countries and territories:
Algeria, Argentina, Australia, Bahrain, Bangladesh, Barbados, Belgium, Brazil, Burkina Faso, Cameroon, Canada, Colombia, Costa Rica, Denmark, Dominican Rep, Egypt, El Salvador, Finland, France, Germany, Ghana, Greece, Guatemala, Honduras, Hungary, Iceland, India, Indonesia, Italy, Jamaica, Japan, Kenya, Korea Rep, Lebanon, Luxembourg, Malawi, Malaysia, Mexico, Morocco, Netherlands, New Zealand, Nigeria, Norway, Panama, Paraguay, Peru, Philippines, Poland, Portugal, Puerto Rico, Qatar, Russia, Senegal, Singapore, South Africa, Spain, Sri Lanka, Sudan, Sweden, Switzerland, Taiwan, Thailand, Trinidad-Tobago, Tunisia, Türkiye, UK, United Arab Emirates, Uruguay, USA, Venezuela.
International members include:
International Insurance Society (IIS, #13939); *World Council of Credit Unions (WOCCU, #21324)*.

IGO Relations Development partnerships with: *ILO (#11123)*. **NGO Relations** Works closely with *International Co-operative Alliance (ICA, #12944)* and its affiliated organizations and partners. Development partnerships with: *Société de coopération pour le développement international (SOCODEVI)*. [2018/XC4563/y/**E**]

♦ **International Cooperative and Mutual Insurance Federation / Regional Association for The Americas (ICMIF/Americas)** 12949
Fédération Internationale des Coopératives et Mutuelles d'Assurance / Association Régionale pour les Amériques (ICMIF/Amériques) – Federación Internacional de Cooperativas y Mutuales de Seguros / Asociación Regional para Las Américas (ICMIF/Américas) – Federação internacional de Cooperativas e Mutualidades de Seguros / Associação Regional para As Américas (ICMIF/Américas)

Chair 1775 Eye St NW, 8th Floor, Washington DC 20006, USA. T. +12024422305. Fax +12023180753. E-mail: gdiaz@segurosdelmagisterio.com.
Vice Pres Operations address not obtained.
URL: http://www.icmifamericas.org/

History 1992, as *Americas Association of Cooperative / Mutual Insurance Societies (AAC/MIS) – Association des coopératives et mutuelles d'assurances d'Amérique – Asociación de Cooperativas y Mutuales de Seguros de las Américas – Associação de Cooperativas e Mutuais de Seguros das Américas*, as an independent regional association of The Americas affiliated with *International Cooperative and Mutual Insurance Federation (ICMIF, #12948)*. Created on merger of 'North American Association (NAA)', set up 1979, and 'American Hemisphere Association', set up 1984. **Aims** Support and develop effective and viable cooperative, popular-based insurance organizations throughout the Americas. **Structure** General Meeting (annual); Board of Trustees. **Languages** English, Spanish. **Staff** 1.00 FTE, paid. **Finance** Members' dues. Other sources: corporate donations; private and government grants. **Activities** Training/education; projects/programmes; events/meetings; knowledge management/information dissemination. **Events** *Conference* Mendoza (Argentina) 2019, *Conference* Lima (Peru) 2016, *Conference* Mexico City (Mexico) 2015, *Conference* San Juan (Puerto Rico) 2014, *Conference* Panama (Panama) 2013. **Publications** Case studies in English, Spanish.

Members Organizations (61). Full members – cooperatively oriented insurance organizations in 21 countries:
Argentina, Barbados, Brazil, Canada, Colombia, Costa Rica, Dominican Rep, El Salvador, Guatemala, Honduras, Jamaica, Mexico, Nicaragua, Panama, Paraguay, Peru, Puerto Rico, Trinidad-Tobago, Uruguay, USA, Venezuela.
[2016.06.01/XE1702/y/**E**]

♦ **International Cooperative of Plastic Optical Fiber (ICPOF)** 12950

Chairman Photonics Research Inst, Keio K2 Town Campus Bldg E, 7-1 Shin-Kawasaki, Saiwai-ku, Kawasaki-shi, Yokohama KANAGAWA, 212-0032 Japan.

Languages English. **Activities** Events/meetings. **Events** *International Conference on Plastic Optical Fibers* Yokohama (Japan) 2019, *International Conference on Plastic Optical Fibers* Seattle, WA (USA) 2018, *International Conference on Plastic Optical Fibers* Aveiro (Portugal) 2017, *International Conference on Plastic Optical Fibers* Birmingham (UK) 2016, *International Conference on Plastic Optical Fibers* Nuremberg (Germany) 2015.
[2020.03.23/XM1725/**F**]

♦ **International Cooperative Programme on Integrated Monitoring of Air Pollution Effects on Ecosystems (ICP-IM)** 12951

Programme Manager SLU, Dept Aquatic Sciences and Assessment, Box 7050, SE-750 07 Uppsala, Sweden.
URL: https://www.slu.se/en/Collaborative-Centres-and-Projects/integrated-monitoring/

History Belongs to a group of 6 specialist International Cooperative Programmes (ICPs), under the *United Nations Economic Commission for Europe (UNECE, #20555)* Working Group on Effects. **Aims** Determine and predict the state and change of terrestrial and *freshwater* ecosystems in a long-term perspective with respect to the impact of air pollutants, especially nitrogen and sulphur; determine the ecological effects of *tropospheric* ozone, heavy metals and persistent organic substances; provide a major contribution to the international data requirements for examining the ecosystem impacts of *climatic change*, changes in *biodiversity* and depletion of *stratospheric* ozone. **Activities** Monitoring/evaluation; research and development; research/documentation.

Members Participating countries (21):
Austria, Belarus, Canada, Czechia, Denmark, Estonia, Finland, Germany, Iceland, Ireland, Italy, Latvia, Lithuania, Netherlands, Norway, Poland, Portugal, Russia, Spain, Sweden, UK.
National Focal Points in 22 countries and territories:
Austria, Belarus, Canada, Czechia, Denmark, Estonia, Faeroe Is, Finland, Germany, Iceland, Ireland, Italy, Lithuania, Netherlands, Norway, Poland, Portugal, Russia, Spain, Sweden, Switzerland, UK.

NGO Relations Cooperates with (2): *European Long-Term Ecosystem Research Network (LTER-Europe, #07712)*; *Global Terrestrial Observing Network (GT-Net, no recent information)*. [2022.03.23/XE3426/**E**]

♦ International Cooperative Reinsurance Bureau (inactive)
♦ International Cooperatives Consumer Organization / see Consumer Co-operatives Worldwide (#04770)
♦ International Cooperative Trading Organization (inactive)

♦ **International Cooperative University (ICU)** 12952
Université coopérative internationale (UCI) – Universidad Cooperativa Internacional (UCI)

Dir Apdo 1785, Correo 2050, San José, San José, San José, Costa Rica.
Registered Office c/o IRED, Rue Varembé 3, Case 116, 1211 Geneva 20, Switzerland. Fax +41227400011.
URL: http://www.uci.fr.st/

History Sep 1977. Currently being restructured. **Aims** Promote the exchange of studies and research in issues related to social economics, universities and nongovernmental organizations; encourage specialized cooperation in issues related to research and action destined to social and economic development; carry out research in self-development. **Structure** Multicentre of 2nd degree. **Languages** English, French, Spanish. **Staff** Central office – 4 part-time; other offices: 6 full-time; 16 part-time. **Finance** Members' dues. Other sources: subsidies; consultancies; studies; research. **Activities** Carries out technical cooperation on social and participative development; executes projects and programmes; promotes self-education. **Events** *Meeting* Lima (Peru) 2011, *Meeting* Caracas (Venezuela) 2010, *Meeting* Lima (Peru) 2009, *Meeting* Caracas (Venezuela) 2008, *Meeting* Lima (Peru) 2006. **Publications** *International Cooperative University* in French, Spanish – bulletin. Books.

Members Organizations and individuals in 16 countries:
Argentina, Bolivia, Brazil, Canada, Colombia, Costa Rica, Ecuador, El Salvador, France, Guatemala, Honduras, Mexico, Nicaragua, Peru, Spain, Venezuela.

NGO Relations Since 1995, joint meetings with *Asociación Latinoamericana de Centros de Educación Cooperativa (ALCECOOP, no recent information)*. Member of: *International Union for Conservation of Nature and Natural Resources (IUCN, #15766)*. Technical cooperation with: *South North Development Initiative (SNDI, #19881)*; various universities and national NGOs. Also has conventions with universities in Argentina, Bolivia, Colombia, Costa Rica, Paraguay and Peru, as well as other national associations. [2012.06.01/XF7722/**F**]

♦ International Cooperative Wholesale Society (inactive)
♦ International Cooperative Women's Guild (inactive)
♦ International Coordinating Centre for Coastal Resources Management / see International Centre for Coastal Resources Research (#12480)
♦ International Coordinating Committee / see Global Alliance of National Human Rights Institutions (#10214)
♦ International Coordinating Committee of Financial Analysts Associations / see International Council of Investment Associations (#13034)
♦ International Coordinating Committee of National Institutions for the Promotion and Protection of Human Rights / see Global Alliance of National Human Rights Institutions (#10214)
♦ International Coordinating Committee for Peace Movements (inactive)

♦ **International Coordinating Committee for the Presentation of Science and the Development of Out-of-School Scientific Activities (ICC)** 12953
Comité international de coordination pour l'initiation à la science et le développement des activités scientifiques extra-scolaires (CIC) – Comité Internacional de Coordinación para la Iniciación a la Ciencia y al Desarrollo de Actividades Cientificas Extraescolares (CIC) – Internationales Komitee für die Einführung in die Wissenschaft und die Förderung der Wissenschaftlichen Tätigkeit ausserhalb der Schule

Treas and Head Office Avenue des Citronniers 74 – Bte 4, 1020 Brussels, Belgium. T. +3224760516.
SG Toekomstlaan 43, 1640 St-Genesius-Rode, Belgium.

History Nov 1962, Brussels (Belgium). Founded as an interim coordinating committee by the '*Jeunesses scientifiques de Belgique*', under the patronage of the Belgian National Commission for Unesco. Statutes adopted by Constituent General Assembly, 4-6 Oct 1966; modified: 13 Feb 1969; 16 Sep 1976. Registration: Start date: 9 Feb 1967, Belgium. **Aims** Initiate, promote and coordinate, at international level, actions in the field of out-of-school scientific and technical activities for *youth* and the public understanding of science and *technology*, in cooperation with other appropriate governmental or non-governmental international organizations. **Structure** General Assembly (every 2 years); Administrative Council of 10-30 members (of whom at least 1 must be of Belgian nationality) for a term of 4 years; Administrative Council, including President, 4 Vice-Presidents, Treasurer and Secretary-General. Meetings open to members and observers. **Languages** English, French, Spanish. **Finance** Members' dues. Annual subventions from: Council for Cultural Cooperation of the Council of Europe; Department of Scientific Research (Belgium); Administration of International Cultural Relations (Belgium). **Activities** Monitoring/evaluation; knowledge management/information dissemination; events/meetings; projects/programmes; research/documentation. **Events** *Annual Conference* Bruges (Belgium) 2010, *Annual Conference* London (UK) 2009, *Annual Conference* Paris (France) 2008, *Annual Conference* London (UK) 2007, *Annual Conference* Brussels (Belgium) 2006. **Publications** *ICC Journal* in Arabic, English, French, Spanish. List of representative organizations; Handbook.

Members National organizations in 28 countries:
Argentina, Australia, Belgium, Brazil, Canada, Chile, Denmark, Egypt, Finland, France, Germany, Hungary, India, Ireland, Italy, Japan, Kenya, Netherlands, New Zealand, Philippines, Portugal, Spain, Sweden, Switzerland, Thailand, Tunisia, UK, USA.
Individuals in 45 countries:
Argentina, Australia, Austria, Belgium, Brazil, Cameroon, Canada, Chile, China, Czechia, Egypt, France, Gabon, Germany, Greece, Israel, Italy, Kenya, Korea Rep, Kuwait, Luxembourg, Malaysia, Malta, Mexico, Morocco, Netherlands, New Zealand, Norway, Oman, Peru, Poland, Qatar, Romania, Russia, Senegal, Singapore, Slovenia, Spain, Switzerland, Tunisia, Türkiye, UK, Ukraine, USA, Venezuela.

IGO Relations *UNESCO (#20322)*. Collaborates in the working programmes of: *OAS (#17629)*.
[2018.06.01/XB1714/**F**]

♦ **International Coordinating Committee on the Safeguarding and Development of the Historic Site of Angkor (ICC-Angkor)** 12954
Comité international de coordination pour la sauvegarde et le développement du site historique d'Angkor (CIC-Angkor)

Permanent Secretariat Head UNESCO Office – Phnom Penh, 38 Samdech Sothearos Blvd, PO Box 29, Phnom Penh, Cambodia. T. +85523723054. E-mail: n.nou@unesco.org – m.hong@unesco.org – phnompenh@unesco.org.
Contact Cambodian Natl Commission for UNESCO, No 74 Preah Sihanouk Avenue, BP 29, Phnom Penh, Cambodia. T. +85523210369. Fax +85523210369.
URL: http://www.unesco.org/new/en/phnompenh/

History Founded 1993, Phnom Penh (Cambodia), following first Intergovernmental Conference on Safeguarding the Angkor Site, co-chaired by Japan and France, at the appeal of His Majesty King Norodom Sihanouk. The conference adopted the "Tokyo Declaration", the founding document defining the spirit, framework and conditions for international action implemented and coordinated by ICC-Angkor. Action plan outlined during Second Intergovernmental Conference, Paris (France), in accord with Cambodia and Japan and the assistance of UNESCO. **Aims** Conserve and promote sustainable development of the Angkor World Heritage Site; serve as a forum for exchange of ideas, information and research methodologies to conserve and promote sustainable development of the Site. **Structure** Plenary Session (in December); Technical Session (in Jun and December). Co-chaired by France and Japan, in close liaison with Royal Government of Cambodia, and in collaboration with APSARA Authority. Standing Secretariat services provided by *UNESCO (#20322)*. Ad hoc groups of experts (2). **Languages** English, French, Mon-Khmer languages. **Staff** 6.00 FTE, paid. **Finance** Financed by: France; Japan; APSARA; *UNESCO (#20322)*. **Activities** Events/meetings; projects/programmes. **Events** *Plenary Session* Phnom Penh (Cambodia) 2001, *Meeting* Siem Reap (Cambodia) 2001, *Plenary Session* Phnom Penh (Cambodia) 2000, *Meeting* Siem Reap (Cambodia) 2000, *Plenary Session* Phnom Penh (Cambodia) 1999. **Publications** Technical and Plenary session reports (annual).

Members Architects, engineers, restorers, archaeologists, researchers, anthropologists, and technical experts in various fields. Members in 37 countries:
Australia, Belgium, Brunei Darussalam, Canada, China, Denmark, Egypt, France, Germany, Greece, Hungary, India, Indonesia, Italy, Japan, Korea Rep, Laos, Luxembourg, Malaysia, Mexico, Netherlands, New Zealand, Norway, Philippines, Poland, Portugal, Russia, Singapore, Spain, Sri Lanka, Sweden, Switzerland, Thailand, Tunisia, UK, USA, Vietnam.
Included in the above, 13 organizations listed in this Yearbook:
Asian Development Bank (ADB, #01422); *European Union (EU, #08967)*; *FAO (#09260)*; *International Bank for Reconstruction and Development (IBRD, #12317)* (World Bank); *International Centre for the Study of the Preservation and Restoration of Cultural Property (ICCROM, #12521)*; *International Council of Museums (ICOM, #13051)*; *International Council on Monuments and Sites (ICOMOS, #13049)*; *International Monetary Fund (IMF,*

#14180); SEAMEO Regional Centre for Archaeology and Fine Arts (SEAMEO SPAFA, #19169); UNDP (#20292); United Nations Volunteers (UNV, #20650); World Monuments Fund (WMF, #21657); World Trade Organization (WTO, #21864). [2019/XE4210/y/E]

♦ International Coordinating Committee on Solid-State Sensors, Actuators and Microsystems 12955

Chair Dept Electrònica – Univ Barcelona, Diagonal Sud – Fac Fisica/Quimica, Marti Franquès 1, 08028 Barcelona, Spain. E-mail: jrmorante@ub.edu.
URL: http://transducers-eurosensors2013.org/

History 1981, as *International Coordinating Committee on Solid State Transducers Research.* Took over activities of *International Coordinating Committee on Solid-State Sensors and Actuators Research.* **Aims** Promote developments in *microtransducing systems.* **Structure** Subcommittees (3): Europe; North America; Asia. **Finance** Conference fees. **Activities** Organizes the International Conference on Solid-State Sensors, Actuators and Microsystems. **Events** *TRANSDUCERS : International Conference on Solid-State Sensors, Actuators and Microsystems / Biennial Transducers Conference* Barcelona (Spain) 2013, *TRANSDUCERS : International Conference on Solid-State Sensors, Actuators and Microsystems / Biennial Transducers Conference* Beijing (China) 2011, *TRANSDUCERS : biennial international conference on solid-state sensors and actuators / Biennial Transducers Conference* Denver, CO (USA) 2009, *TRANSDUCERS : biennial international conference on solid-state sensors, actuators and microsystems / Biennial Transducers Conference* Lyon (France) 2007, *TRANSDUCERS : biennial international conference on solid-state sensors and actuators / Biennial Transducers Conference* Seoul (Korea Rep) 2005. **Publications** *Tech Digest* (every 2 years).
Members Full in 26 countries and territories:
Australia, Belgium, China, Denmark, Finland, France, Georgia, Germany, Hong Kong, Hungary, Ireland, Israel, Japan, Korea Rep, Netherlands, New Zealand, Norway, Poland, Russia, Singapore, Spain, Sweden, Switzerland, Türkiye, UK, Ukraine.
NGO Relations *Institute of Electrical and Electronics Engineers (IEEE, #11259); International Measurement Confederation (IMEKO, #14124).* [2020/XE0701/c/E]

♦ International Coordinating Committee on Solid State Transducers Research / see International Coordinating Committee on Solid-State Sensors, Actuators and Microsystems (#12955)

♦ International Coordinating Council of Aerospace Industry Associations (ICCAIA) 12956

Comité international des associations d'industriels aérospatiaux (CICAIA) – Consejo Coordinador Internacional de Asociaciones de Industrias Aeroespaciales – Mezdunarodnyj Koordinacionnyj Sovet Associacij Aviacionno-Kosmiceskih Otraslej Promyslennosti
Main Office c/o ICAO, 999 Robert-Bourassa Blvd, Box 65, Montréal QC H3C 5H7, Canada. T. +16139838146.
URL: http://iccaia.org/

History 1972. **Events** *ATAG Global Sustainable Aviation Forum* 2021, *ATAG Global Sustainable Aviation Forum* Montréal, QC (Canada) 2019, *ATAG Global Sustainable Aviation Summit* Geneva (Switzerland) 2018, *ATAG Global Sustainable Aviation Summit* Geneva (Switzerland) 2017, *ATAG Global Sustainable Aviation Summit* Geneva (Switzerland) 2014.
Members Associations in 5 countries:
Belgium, Canada, Japan, UK, USA.
Regional organization:
Aerospace and Defence Industries Association of Europe (ASD, #00146).
Consultative Status Consultative status granted from: *ECOSOC (#05331)* (Ros C). **IGO Relations** *International Civil Aviation Organization (ICAO, #12581).* **NGO Relations** Member of: *International Industry Working Group (IIWG, #13841).* [2019/XE3710/ty/E]

♦ International Coordination of Anthroposophic Medicine 12957

Internationale Koordination Anthroposophische Medizin (IKAM)
Coordination c/o Goetheanum, Rüttiweg 45, 4143 Dornach SO 1, Switzerland. E-mail: michaela.gloeckler@goetheanum.ch.
URL: http://www.medsektion-goetheanum.org/en/home/ikam/

History Set up as the international managing committee of the Medical Section of *School of Spiritual Science (#19134).* **Aims** Form a community and a style of leadership that leaves each individual free to act out of his own initiative, but at the same time allows for common action and responsibility. **Structure** Coordinators (24). **Publications** *IKAM News* (6 a year). [2020/XM4250/E]

♦ International Coordination Bureau of Theatre Schools (#03370)
♦ International Coordination Committee for the Accountancy Profession (inactive)

♦ International Coordination Committee for Immunology of Reproduction (ICCIR) 12958

Comité international de coordination d'immunologie de la reproduction – Mezdunarodnyj Koordinacionnyj Komitet po Immunologii Reprodukcii (MKKIR)
Pres c/o IBIR-BAN, 73 Tzarigradsko Shosse Blvd, 1113 Sofia, Bulgaria. T. +3592722386. Fax +3592720022.
URL: http://www.iccir1967.com/

History Founded 1967, Sofia (Bulgaria), by participants in 1st International Symposium on Immunology of Spermatozoa and Fertilization, held in Varna (Bulgaria). *International Society for Immunology of Reproduction (ISIR, #15193)* set up during 3rd International Symposium on Immunology of Reproduction, 1975, Varna (Bulgaria). **Aims** Coordinate research and educational activities. **Languages** English, French, Russian. **Staff** 2.00 FTE, paid. **Finance** Subsidies by sponsors; symposium registration fees. **Activities** Training/education; knowledge management/information dissemination; guidance/assistance/consulting. **Events** *Triennial Symposium* Varna (Bulgaria) 2015, *Triennial Symposium* Varna (Bulgaria) 2012, *International symposium for immunology of reproduction / Triennial Symposium* Varna (Bulgaria) 2009, *International symposium for immunology of reproduction / Triennial Symposium* Varna (Bulgaria) 2006, *International symposium of immunology of reproduction / Triennial Symposium* Varna (Bulgaria) 2003. **Publications** Symposium Proceedings.
Members Individuals in 20 countries:
Argentina, Australia, Bulgaria, China, Czechia, Denmark, Egypt, France, Germany, Hungary, India, Israel, Italy, Japan, Netherlands, Poland, Serbia, Thailand, UK, USA. [2016/XD5236/v/E]

♦ International Coordination Council of Educational Institutions Alumni (INCORVUZ-XXI) 12959

Dir Gen Akademika Volgina street 6, Moscow MOSKVA, Russia, 117485. T. +74957729325. E-mail: mks@incorvuz.ru.
Council Chair address not obtained.

History 1989, Moscow (Russia). Founded as *International Corporation of Graduates of Soviet Educational Institutions – Association internationale des diplômés des institutions éducatives soviétiques – Mezdunarodnaja Korporacija Vypusknikov Sovetskih Ucebnyh Zavedenij.* Name changed: Nov 1996, to *International Non-Governmental Organization – INCORVUZ Corporation – Organisation internationale non-gouvernementale – Corporation INCORVUZ – Mezdunarodnaja Nepravitelstvennaja Organizacija – Korporacija INCORVUZ*; 26 Mar 2001, to current title. **Aims** Promote humanitarian, scientific and technological contacts, particularly in the field of *higher education*; assist educational institutions in modernizing and increasing their teaching, technical and scientific facilities and in working out advanced and efficient systems of education; assist graduates and alumni in improving and upgrading their professional training in educational and scientific-research institutions and production units; provide assistance to developing countries by transfering and sharing knowledge for their economic and social advancement; promote activities of NGOs and their networking. **Structure** General Meeting; Partnership Board; General Directorate. Includes *'Commission on Recognition of Study Courses, Diplomas and Graduation Certificates, Academic Degrees and Titles'*; *'Alumni World League'*. **Languages** English, Russian. **Staff** 7.00 FTE, paid. **Finance** Members' dues. **Activities** Networking/liaising; events/meetings; guidance/assistance/consulting; projects/programmes; certification/accreditation. **Events** *World Forum* Moscow (Russia) 2012, *All-Arab Regional Meeting* Beirut (Lebanon) 2011, *South-East Asian Regional Meeting* Beijing (China) 2010, *All-Arab Regional Meeting* Lebanon 2010, *Latin-American Regional Meeting* San José (Costa Rica) 2010. **Publications** *Current Information in Federation Eduction On-line System. 3rd World Forum of Foreign Alumni of Russian (Soviet) Higher Educational Institutions* (2012) – collected articles; *National Associations of Alumni of the Russian (Soviet) Universities* (2006).
Members Organizations (42); Individuals (14). Full in 66 countries and territories:
Afghanistan, Algeria, Armenia, Azerbaijan, Bangladesh, Belarus, Benin, Bolivia, Brazil, Bulgaria, Burkina Faso, Burundi, Cameroon, Canada, Chad, China, Colombia, Congo Brazzaville, Côte d'Ivoire, Czechia, Dominican Rep, Egypt, Equatorial Guinea, Ethiopia, Georgia, Ghana, Greece, Haiti, India, Indonesia, Iran Islamic Rep, Iraq, Israel, Jordan, Kazakhstan, Kyrgyzstan, Lebanon, Lithuania, Mali, Mexico, Moldova, Mongolia, Montenegro, Morocco, Nepal, Nigeria, Pakistan, Palestine, Poland, Romania, Russia, Senegal, Slovakia, Spain, Sudan, Syrian AR, Tajikistan, Tanzania UR, Tunisia, Turkmenistan, Uganda, Ukraine, Uzbekistan, Venezuela, Vietnam, Yemen.
Consultative Status Consultative status granted from: *UNESCO (#20322)* (Consultative Status); *ECOSOC (#05331)* (Special). [2021/XE2041/jy/E]

♦ International Coordination Group for the Tsunami Warning System in the Pacific / see Intergovernmental Coordination Group for the Pacific Tsunami Warning and Mitigation System (#11481)

♦ International Coordination of Young Christian Workers (ICYCW) 12960

Coordination Internationale de la Jeunesse Ouvrière Chrétienne (CIJOC) – Coordinación Internacional de la Juventud Obrera Cristiana (CIJOC) – Coordinamento Internazionale della Gioventù Operaia Cristiana (CIGiOC)
Pres Via del Casaletto, 125, 00151 Rome RM, Italy. T. +393271138223. E-mail: cijoc.icycw@gmail.com – int.president@cijoc.org.

History 1986. Founded by YCW movements wanting to promote Cardinal Joseph Cardijn's fundamental vision of the YCW. Officially recognized by the Holy See as an International Catholic Organization, since 1989. **Aims** Facilitate exchanges between YCW National Movements; support the development of new and existing movements; build solidarity. **Structure** International Council; International Secretariat; Commissions. **Languages** English, French, Spanish. **Staff** 4.00 FTE, paid. **Activities** Events/meetings; training/education. Asia, Central Africa, East Africa, Europe, Indian Ocean Islands, Latin America, Middle-East, West Africa (8). **Events** *Meeting* Alton (UK) 2012, *Coming to life* Paris (France) 2008, *International congress* Paris (France) 2008, *International Council* Barcelona (Spain) 2007, *Together let's make the difference* Rome (Italy) 2004. **Publications** *ICYCW News*; *IS Live.*
Members National movements in 54 countries and territories:
Argentina, Benin, Bolivia, Burkina Faso, Burundi, Cambodia, Cameroon, Central African Rep, Chad, China, Congo Brazzaville, Congo DR, Côte d'Ivoire, Cuba, Dominican Rep, Ecuador, England, Ethiopia, France, Guatemala, Guinea, Haiti, Hungary, India, Israel, Italy, Japan, Jordan, Kenya, Korea Rep, Lebanon, Madagascar, Malawi, Mali, Malta, Mauritius, Niger, Nigeria, Paraguay, Peru, Philippines, Poland, Portugal, Réunion, Rodriguez Is, Rwanda, Senegal, Spain, Syrian AR, Tanzania UR, Togo, Uganda, United Arab Emirates, Wales.
Consultative Status Consultative status granted from: *ILO (#11123)* (Special List). **NGO Relations** Observer status with (1): *European Youth Forum (#09140).* Member of (1): *Forum of Catholic Inspired NGOs (#09905).* [2023.02.14/XE1619/F]

♦ International COPD Coalition (ICC) 12961

Exec Dir 8316 86th Ave NW, Gig Harbor WA 98332, USA.
URL: http://www.internationalcopd.org/

History 1999, by member patients organizations of *Global Initiative for Chronic Obstructive Lung Disease (GOLD, #10423).* **Aims** Improve the health and access to care of patients with chronic obstructive pulmonary disease. **Structure** Executive Committee, comprising 2 Co-Chairs and 11 members. **Events** *World Conference* Shanghai (China) 2011, *Meeting* Munich (Germany) 2006.
Members National organizations in 46 countries and territories:
Albania, Argentina, Australia, Austria, Bangladesh, Brazil, Bulgaria, Canada, Chile, China, Costa Rica, Czechia, Denmark, Falklands/Malvinas, Finland, France, Georgia, Germany, Hungary, India, Iran Islamic Rep, Italy, Japan, Kazakhstan, Korea Rep, Kyrgyzstan, Lithuania, Nepal, Netherlands, New Zealand, Norway, Pakistan, Peru, Poland, Portugal, Russia, Serbia, Singapore, Slovenia, South Africa, Sweden, Syrian AR, Thailand, Ukraine, USA, Vietnam.
Regional organizations (2):
Asian Pacific Society of Respirology (APSR, #01643); European Federation of Allergy and Airways Diseases Patients' Associations (EFA, #07045).
NGO Relations Member of: *Global Alliance Against Chronic Respiratory Diseases (GARD, #10182).* [2013/XM1889/y/C]

♦ International Copper Association (ICA) 12962

Association internationale pour le cuivre
Pres 260 Madison Ave, 16th floor, New York NY 10016-2401, USA. T. +12122517240. Fax +12122517245. E-mail: info@copperalliance.org.
URL: http://copperalliance.org/

History Founded 11 Dec 1959, New York NY (USA), as 'Copper Products Development Association'. Name changed to *International Copper Research Association (INCRA)*, 1 Jun 1962, New York NY. Present name adopted 29 Feb 1989, when restructuring added market development to research sponsorship activities. Also trades as *Copper Alliance.* Registered in accordance with the laws of New York State (USA). **Aims** Unite the global copper industry to develop and defend markets for copper and to make a positive contribution to society's sustainable development goals. **Structure** Board of Directors; Executive Committee; Management Team. Offices in 4 primary regions: Asia; Europe and Africa – *European Copper Institute (ECI, #06796)*; Latin America; North America. **Languages** English. **Staff** 10.00 FTE, paid. **Activities** Advocacy/lobbying/activism; politics/policy/regulatory. **Events** *Meeting* Montréal, QC (Canada) 2019, *International conference on environmental pollution, restoration, and management* Ho Chi Minh City (Vietnam) 2010, *Joint session* Tokyo (Japan) 2009, *Meeting* Madrid (Spain) 1998, *Conference* Santiago (Chile) 1995. **Publications** Reports; technical brochures; monographs.
Members Companies representing the copper industry. Full members (29) in 17 countries:
Australia, Belgium, Canada, Chile, Finland, Germany, Greece, Japan, Korea Rep, Mexico, Papua New Guinea, Poland, Portugal, South Africa, Sweden, UK, USA.
Associate members (6) in 4 countries:
Finland, Germany, UK, USA.
NGO Relations Member of: *International Council on Mining and Metals (ICMM, #13048).* Instrumental in setting up: *International Copper Association Southeast Asia (ICASEA).* Supports: *CLASP (#03979).* [2018/XF1716/F]

♦ International Copper Association Southeast Asia (internationally oriented national body)
♦ International Copper Development Council (inactive)
♦ International Copper Research Association / see International Copper Association (#12962)

♦ International Copper Study Group (ICSG) 12963

SG Rua Almirante Barroso 36, 6th Floor, 1000-013 Lisbon, Portugal. T. +351213513870. Fax +351213524035. E-mail: mail@icsg.org.
URL: http://www.icsg.org/

History 23 Jan 1992, Geneva (Switzerland). Terms of reference adopted at inaugural meeting, 22 Jun 1992, Geneva. Former names and other names: *International Study Group on Copper* – alias. **Aims** Increase copper market transparency; promote international cooperation on issues concerning copper, by improving the information available on the international copper economy and providing a global forum where industry and governments can meet over common issues. **Structure** General Session; Standing Committee; Secretariat; Committees (3); Industry Advisory Panel. **Languages** English. **Staff** 5.00 FTE, paid. **Finance** Sources: contributions of member/participating states. **Activities** Guidance/assistance/consulting; knowledge management/information dissemination; monitoring/evaluation; research/documentation. **Publications** *Copper Bulletin* (12 a year); *Statistical Yearbook* (annual); *World Copper Factbook* (annual). Directories; press releases. **Information Services** *ICSG Online Statistical Database.*
Members Open to any country involved in copper production, consumption or trade. Member countries (25):
Australia, Belgium, Brazil, Chile, China, Congo DR, Finland, France, Germany, Greece, India, Iran Islamic Rep, Italy, Japan, Luxembourg, Mexico, Mongolia, Peru, Poland, Portugal, Russia, Serbia, Spain, Sweden, USA.
Regional integration EU organization:
European Union (EU, #08967).

International organization:
International Wrought Copper Council (IWCC, #15917).
IGO Relations Participates in the activities of: *UNCTAD (#20285).* Designed International Commodity Body of: *Common Fund for Commodities (CFC, #04293).* [2020.08.27/XF5468/y/**F***]

♦ International Copyright Society (no recent information)

♦ International Coral Reef Action Network (ICRAN) 12964

Contact c/o UNEP WCMC, 219 Huntingdon Rd, Cambridge, CB3 0DL, UK. T. +441223277314. Fax +441223277136.
URL: https://www.icriforum.org/about-icri/members-networks/international-coral-reef -action-network-icran/

History 2000, as a public private response to the Call of Action of *International Coral Reef Initiative (ICRI, #12965).* **Aims** As a global partnership of coral reef experts, halt and reverse the decline of the health of the world's coral reefs; respond to conservation needs at the global scale by recognizing both traditional and scientific perspectives of coral reef dynamics and respective social dependency. **Structure** Steering Committee of 16 members. Board of 9 members, including Chair. Coordinating Unit. **Activities** Components (3): Reef management; Global coral reef monitoring and assessment; Communications and knowledge dissemination. Engaged in: *Mesoamerican Reef Alliance*; *Coral Reef Advocacy Initiative.* **Publications** *ICRAN Newsletter.* **IGO Relations** Participates in development and implementation of: *Action Plan for the Protection and Management of the South Asia Seas Region (SASP, #00094).* Partners: *South Asia Cooperative Environment Programme (SACEP, #19714)*; *Secretariat of the Pacific Regional Environment Programme (SPREP, #19205)*; *UNEP (#20299)*; *UN Environment Programme World Conservation Monitoring Centre (UNEP-WCMC, #20295).* Involved in development and participation of: *Caribbean Action Plan (CAR, #03432)*; *Regional Seas Programme (#18814).* **NGO Relations** Partners: *The Coral Reef Alliance (CORAL)*; *Global Coral Reef Monitoring Network (GCRMN, #10306)*; *Marine Aquarium Council (MAC, inactive)*; *The Nature Conservancy (TNC)*; *United Nations Foundation (UNF, #20563)*; *World Resources Institute (WRI, #21753)*; *World Wide Fund for Nature (WWF, #21922)*; *WorldFish (#21507).* Participates in: *Global Island Partnership (GLISPA, #10436).* [2014/XF6866/**F***]

♦ International Coral Reef Initiative (ICRI) 12965

Initiative internationale pour les récifs coralliens

Contact Ministry of Foreign Affairs and Cooperation, Place de la Visitation, 98000 Monte Carlo, Monaco.
Contact GBRMPA, 280 Flinders St, PO Box 1379, Townsville QLD 4810, Australia. E-mail: international@gbrmpa.gov.au – dirjenprl@kkp.go.id.
URL: http://www.icriforum.org/

History Established 1994, by 8 governments: Australia; France; Japan; Jamaica; Philippines; Sweden; UK; USA. Announced at First Conference of the Parties of the Convention on Biological Diversity, Dec 1994, and at the high level segment of the Intersessional Meeting of the UN Commission on Sustainable Development, Apr 1995. **Aims** Encourage the adoption of best practice in *sustainable* management of coral reefs and associated ecosystems; build capacity; raise awareness at all levels on the plight of coral reefs around the world. **Structure** General Meeting of Members (at least annual). Coordination and Planning Committee (CPC), is the advisory body, meeting twice a year and comprising representatives from the founding countries, multilateral banks, international agencies, NGOs, scientific bodies, the private sector, one representative from each ICRI region (usually the coordinator at the UNEP Regional Seas Office) and at least one representative of one other country from that region. Includes *Global Coral Reef Monitoring Network (GCRMN, #10306).* International Secretariat co-chaired by UK and Seychelles. **Languages** English. **Staff** None. **Finance** Financed by Secretariat hosts (usually a partnership of 2 member countries); continuous support from US State Department. **Activities** Secretariat progresses objectives through specific Plan of Action; may organize side events at major international summits and conferences; operates through networks and committees which organize regional meetings and workshops. Members may choose to implement ICRI's objectives through National Coral Reef Initiatives. **Events** *General Meeting* Paris (France) 2016, *General Meeting* Pattaya (Thailand) 2015, *General Meeting* Okinawa (Japan) 2014, *General Meeting* Belize City (Belize) 2013, *East Asia Regional Workshop* Singapore (Singapore) 2013. **Publications** *Status of Coral Reefs in the World (and Regions).* Workshop reports; posters; other documents. All available on website.
Members Governments of 35 countries:
Australia, Barbados, Belize, Brazil, Colombia, Costa Rica, Cuba, Dominican Rep, Egypt, Fiji, France, Grenada, Honduras, India, Indonesia, Jamaica, Japan, Kenya, Korea Rep, Madagascar, Maldives, Mexico, Monaco, Palau, Panama, Philippines, Samoa, Seychelles, South Africa, Sweden, Tanzania UR, Thailand, UK, USA, Vietnam.
Included in the above, 9 organizations listed in this Yearbook:
Coastal Oceans Research and Development – Indian Ocean (CORDIO East Africa, #04073); *Conservation International (CI)*; *International Union for Conservation of Nature and Natural Resources (IUCN, #15766)*; *Project AWARE Foundation*; *SeaWeb*; *The Nature Conservancy (TNC)*; *Wildlife Conservation Society (WCS)*; *World Resources Institute (WRI, #21753)*; *World Wide Fund for Nature (WWF, #21922).*
IGO Relations Partners: *Caribbean Environment Programme (CEP, #03497)*; *Coordinating Body on the Seas of East Asia (COBSEA, #04814)*; *Regional Organization for the Conservation of the Environment of the Red Sea and Gulf of Aden (PERSGA, #18804)*; *Regional Organization for the Protection of the Marine Environment (ROPME, #18805)*; *Regional Seas Programme (#18814)*; *Secretariat of the Convention of Wetlands (#19200)*; *Secretariat of the Convention on Biological Diversity (SCBD, #19197)*; *Pacific Community (SPC, #17942)*; *Secretariat of the Pacific Regional Environment Programme (SPREP, #19205)*; *South Asia Cooperative Environment Programme (SACEP, #19714)*; *UNEP (#20299)*; *UN Environment Programme World Conservation Monitoring Centre (UNEP-WCMC, #20295)*; *UNESCO (#20322).* [2019/XF4399/y/**F***]

♦ International Coral Reef Society 12966

Corresponding Secretary address not obtained.
URL: http://www.coralreefs.org/

History Dec 1980, Cambridge (UK). Former names and other names: *International Society for Reef Studies (ISRS)* – former; *International Society for Reef Studies Corporation* – legal name. **Aims** Promote global awareness of, and concern for, *coral* reefs and similar and associated habitats; promote the production of scientific knowledge and understanding of coral reefs, both living and fossil. **Structure** General Meeting (every 4 years); Council; Committees (4); Special Topic Chapter. **Languages** Arabic, Chinese, English, French, Spanish. **Staff** 0.00 FTE, paid. **Finance** Sources: members' dues. **Activities** Awards/prizes/competitions; events/meetings; knowledge management/information dissemination; publishing activities. **Events** *International Coral Reef Symposium (ICRS)* Bremen (Germany) 2022, *International Coral Reef Symposium (ICRS)* Bremen (Germany) 2021, *Quadrennial International Coral Reef Symposium* Bremen (Germany) 2020, *European Coral Reef Symposium* Oxford (UK) 2017, *Quadrennial International Coral Reef Symposium* Honolulu, HI (USA) 2016. **Publications** *Coral Reefs* (4 a year) – journal; *REEF ENCOUNTER* (2 a year) – news bulleting. Symposium proceedings.
Members Full; Student; Family; Sustaining. Individuals (about 2,000) in 70 countries and territories:
Australia, Barbados, Belgium, Belize, Bermuda, Brazil, Brunei Darussalam, Canada, Cayman Is, China, Colombia, Costa Rica, Cuba, Curaçao, Czechia, Denmark, Dominica, Egypt, Fiji, France, Germany, Grenada, Guam, Hong Kong, India, Indonesia, Ireland, Israel, Italy, Jamaica, Japan, Kenya, Korea Rep, Malaysia, Maldives, Mauritius, Mexico, Monaco, Mozambique, Netherlands, New Caledonia, New Zealand, Norway, Palau, Panama, Papua New Guinea, Philippines, Poland, Polynesia Fr, Portugal, Puerto Rico, Russia, Samoa USA, Saudi Arabia, Singapore, South Africa, Spain, Sri Lanka, Sweden, Switzerland, Taiwan, Tanzania UR, Thailand, Trinidad-Tobago, UK, USA, Venezuela, Vietnam, Virgin Is USA, Yemen.
NGO Relations Member of: *Global Coral Reef Monitoring Network (GCRMN, #10306).* Affiliated to: *International Coral Reef Initiative (ICRI, #12965).* [2020/XD1373/v/**C**]

♦ International Corn Foundation (internationally oriented national body)
♦ International Coronary Congress (internationally oriented national body)
♦ International Coronelli Society / see International Coronelli Society for the Study of Globes (#12967)

♦ International Coronelli Society for the Study of Globes 12967

Internationale Coronelli-Gesellschaft für Globenkunde

SG c/o Austrian National Library, Globe Museum, Josefsplatz 1, 1015 Vienna, Austria. T. +43153410-298. Fax +43153410319.
URL: http://www.coronelli.org/

History 1952, Vienna (Austria), as *Coronelli World League of Friends of the Globe* Also referred to as *International Coronelli Society (ICS).* **Aims** Carry out scientific investigation of questions relating to *terrestrial* and *celestial* globes, globes of the moon and of planets, globe related instruments as armillary spheres, *planetaria*, lunaria and star finder; publish the results of these investigations. **Structure** Annual General Meeting; Active Board; Extended Board. **Languages** English, German. **Staff** Voluntary. **Finance** Members' dues. **Activities** Research/documentation; events/meetings. **Events** *Symposium / International Coronelli Symposium* Dresden (Germany) 2015, *Symposium / International Coronelli Symposium* Jena (Germany) 2011, *Symposium / International Coronelli Symposium* Venice (Italy) 2007, *Annual General Assembly* Vienna (Austria) 2003, *Symposium / International Coronelli Symposium* Nürburg (Germany) 2002. **Publications** *Der Globusfreund: Globe Studies* (every 2 years).
Members Individuals in 28 countries:
Argentina, Australia, Austria, Belgium, Bulgaria, Canada, Czechia, Denmark, Finland, France, Germany, Hungary, Israel, Italy, Japan, Luxembourg, Malta, Netherlands, Norway, Poland, Portugal, Romania, Russia, Spain, Sweden, Switzerland, UK, USA. [2016.11.02/XE5899/v/**E**]

♦ International Corporate Accountability Roundtable (ICAR) 12968

Exec Dir 1612 K St NW, Ste 1400, Washington DC 20006, USA.
URL: http://www.icar.ngo/

History 2010, as a project for the Tides Center. **Aims** Harness the collective power of progressive organizations to push governments to create and enforce rules over corporations that promote human rights and reduce inequality. **Structure** Board, including: *Amnesty International (AI, #00801)*; *EarthRights International (ERI)*; *Global Witness (GW)*; *Human Rights Watch (HRW, #10990).* **Languages** English, French, Mandarin Chinese, Spanish. **Staff** 8.00 FTE, paid. **Finance** Annual budget: about US$ 1,100,000. **Events** *Annual Meeting* Washington, DC (USA) 2011.
Members Organizations, including the following 21 listed in this Yearbook:
– *Access Now (#00052)*;
– *Accountability Counsel*;
– *American Jewish World Service (AJWS)*;
– *Center for International Environmental Law (CIEL)*;
– *Corporate Accountability International*;
– *CorpWatch*;
– *Due Process of Law Foundation (DPLF, #05144)*;
– *Earthworks*;
– *End Child Prostitution, Child Pornography and Trafficking of Children for Sexual Purposes (ECPAT, #05456)*;
– *Free the Slaves*;
– *Global Financial Integrity (GFI, #10358)*;
– *Global Labor Justice-International Labor Rights Forum (GLJ-ILRF)*;
– *GoodWeave International (#10681)*;
– *Greenpeace International (#10727)*;
– *Human Rights First*;
– *Interfaith Center on Corporate Responsibility (ICCR)*;
– *Palestine Human Rights Campaign (PHRC, no recent information)*;
– *Peace Brigades International (PBI, #18277)*;
– *Pesticide Action Network (PAN, #18336)*;
– *Solidarity Center*;
– *United to End Genocide.*

NGO Relations Partners include: *Enough – Project to End Genocide and Crimes Against Humanity.* Member of: *International Code of Conduct Association (ICoCA, #12629).* Cooperates with: *European Coalition for Corporate Justice (ECCJ, #06591)*; national organizations. [2017.06.19/XJ5878/y/**F**]

♦ International Corporate Chefs Association (internationally oriented national body)

♦ International Corporate Governance Network (ICGN) 12969

CEO Saffron House, 6-10 Kirby Street, London, EC1N 8TS, UK. T. +442076127011.
Events Manager address not obtained.
URL: http://www.icgn.org/

History 29 Mar 1995, Washington, DC (USA). Registration: Company registry, No/ID: 6467372, England and Wales. **Aims** Promote effective standards of corporate governance and investor stewardship to advance efficient markets and sustainable economies worldwide. **Structure** General Meeting (annual); Board of Governors; Departments (3); Secretariat based in London (UK). **Languages** English. **Staff** 10.00 FTE, paid. **Finance** Members' dues. Other sources: conference fees; education programmes fees. **Activities** Advocacy/lobbying/activism; standards/guidelines; events/meetings; knowledge management/information dissemination; networking/liaising; awards/prizes/competitions; training/education. **Events** *Annual Toronto Conference* Toronto, ON (Canada) 2023, *Seoul Conference* Seoul (Korea Rep) 2022, *ICGN Global Virtual Summit* London (UK) 2021, *Annual Conference* Toronto, ON (Canada) 2021, *Global Virtual Summit* Dubai (United Arab Emirates) 2020. **Publications** Guidance; position papers; yearbooks; viewpoints.
Members Asset Owners; Asset Managers; Corporations; Professional Advisors; Accountants; Banks/Brokers; Governance Consultants; Law; Proxy; Ratings; Registrars; Academic; Associations; Regulators/Stock Exchanges. Members in 45 countries and territories:
Australia, Belgium, Bermuda, Brazil, Canada, China, Denmark, France, Germany, Ghana, Hong Kong, India, Indonesia, Iran Islamic Rep, Israel, Italy, Japan, Korea Rep, Luxembourg, Malaysia, Mauritius, Mexico, Monaco, Morocco, Namibia, Netherlands, New Zealand, Nigeria, Norway, Pakistan, Peru, Portugal, Russia, Singapore, South Africa, Spain, Sweden, Switzerland, Thailand, Trinidad-Tobago, Türkiye, UK, United Arab Emirates, USA, Zambia. [2022/XF6579/**F**]

♦ International Corporate Governance Society (unconfirmed)
♦ International Corporate Health Leadership Council (internationally oriented national body)
♦ International Corporation of Graduates of Soviet Educational Institutions / see International Coordination Council of Educational Institutions Alumni (#12959)

♦ International Corrections and Prisons Association for the Advancement of Professional Corrections (ICPA) 12970

Association internationale des affaires correctionnelles et des pénitenciers pour l'avancement des services correctionnels professionnels – Asociación Internacional de Correccionales y Prisiones para el Avance de Profesionales de las Correcciones

Main Office Av Louise 132-A, 1050 Brussels, Belgium. T. +18197431755. E-mail: contacticpa@icpa.org.
URL: http://www.icpa.org/

History 20 Nov 1998, Canada. Former names and other names: *International Corrections and Prisons Association for the Advancement of Professional Corrections: Centre for Exchanging Best Correctional Practices (ICPA)* – former; *Association internationale des affaires correctionnelles et des pénitenciers pour l'avancement des services correctionnels professionnels: Centre pour l'échange des meilleures pratiques correctionnelles* – former; *Asociación Internacional de Correccionales y Prisiones para el Avance de Profesionales de las Correcciones: Centro para el Intercambio de Mejores Practicas de las Correccionales* – former. Registration: EU Transparency Register, No/ID: 734904645710-40, Start date: 4 Mar 2022. **Aims** Contribute to public safety and healthier communities by encouraging and enabling best correctional practices in prisons and outside communities. **Structure** General Meeting (annual); Board of Directors; Executive Committee; Executive Team; Network Groups. **Languages** English. **Staff** 5.00 FTE, paid. **Finance** Sources: meeting proceeds; members' dues. **Activities** Events/meetings; knowledge management/information dissemination; networking/liaising; training/education. **Events** *Conference and Annual General Meeting* Antwerp (Belgium) 2023, *Annual General Meeting and Conference* Fort Collins, CO (USA) 2022, *Annual General Meeting and Conference* 2021, *International Correctional Research Symposium (CRS)* Porto (Portugal) 2021, *Annual General Meeting and Conference* Hong Kong (Hong Kong) 2020. **Publications** *Advancing Corrections* (2 a year) – journal; *Beyond the Wall* (2 a year) – newsletter. **Members** Public Sector Agencies (37); Corporate Agencies (24); Non-profit and Academic Agencies (15); Individuals (2,563). Membership countries not specified. **Consultative Status** Consultative status granted from: *ECOSOC (#05331)* (Special). **NGO Relations** Member of (2): *Alliance of NGOs on Crime Prevention and Criminal Justice (#00709)*; *Conference of Non-Governmental Organizations in Consultative Relationship with the United Nations (CONGO, #04635).* Instrumental in setting up (1): *Asociación Internacional de Prisiones y Correcciones Capitulo Latinoamericano (ICPALA, #02168).* Links with a wide range of organizations including: *African Correctional Services Association (ACSA, #00269)*; *Confederation of European Probation (CEP, #04530)*; *The Duke of Edinburgh's International Award Foundation*

(#05145); *International Association for Correctional and Forensic Psychology (IACFP)*; *International Community Corrections Association (ICCA, #12822)*; *International Network to Promote the Rule of Law (INPROL, #14310)*; *Prison Fellowship International (PFI, #18503)*; US Department of State (INL-CAP); national associations.
[2023.02.15/XD7044/y/**D**]

♦ International Corrections and Prisons Association for the Advancement of Professional Corrections: Centre for Exchanging Best Correctional Practices / see International Corrections and Prisons Association for the Advancement of Professional Corrections (#12970)
♦ International Correspondence Chess Association / see International Correspondence Chess Federation (#12971)

♦ International Correspondence Chess Federation (ICCF) 12971

Fédération internationale des échecs par correspondance – Weltfernschachbund – Mezdunarodnaja Federacija Igry v Sahmaty po Perepiske

Pres 5 Rue Denis Papin, 91220 Brétigny-sur-Orge, France.
Gen Sec address not obtained. E-mail: pjboogie@yahoo.com.
URL: http://www.iccf.com/

History 12 Feb 1928, Berlin (Germany), as *Internationaler Fernschachbund*. Reconstituted in 1945 as *International Correspondence Chess Association*. Present name adopted 1951, Stockholm (Sweden). **Aims** Promote study and practice of international correspondence chess; organize and carry out world *championships* for individuals and teams; promote and arrange international individual and team tournaments. **Structure** Congress (annual). Executive Board, comprising President, General Secretary, Finance Director, World Tournament Director, Marketing Director, Services Director and up to 4 zonal directors. Management Committee, comprising Executive Board and all functional Commissioners. Appeals Commissions (3): Playing Rules; Other ICCF Rules; Arbitration. **Languages** English, French, German, Russian, Spanish. **Staff** Voluntary. **Finance** Sources: members' dues. Other sources: Tournament fees; commercial sponsors. **Activities** Organizes: World Championships (individual); Correspondence Chess Olympiad; Continental Championships (teams and individuals); promotional tournaments. **Events** *Congress* Glasgow (UK) 2022, *Conference* Brétigny-sur-Orge (France) 2021, *ICCF Virtual Conference* Brétigny-sur-Orge (France) 2020, *Congress* Glasgow (UK) 2020, *Congress* Vilnius (Lithuania) 2019. **Publications** *Amici Sumus* (6 a year) in English.
Members National federations representing over 100,000 individuals members, in 67 countries and territories:
Algeria, Argentina, Australia, Austria, Belarus, Belgium, Brazil, Bulgaria, Burkina Faso, Canada, Chile, Colombia, Croatia, Cuba, Czechia, Denmark, Ecuador, England, Estonia, Finland, France, Germany, Ghana, Greece, Guatemala, Hong Kong, Hungary, Iceland, India, Indonesia, Ireland, Israel, Italy, Japan, Kazakhstan, Kenya, Latvia, Lithuania, Luxembourg, Malta, Mexico, Netherlands, New Zealand, Nicaragua, Norway, Panama, Peru, Poland, Portugal, Qatar, Romania, Russia, Scotland, Singapore, Slovakia, Slovenia, South Africa, Spain, Sweden, Switzerland, Tunisia, Türkiye, Turkmenistan, Ukraine, Uruguay, USA, Venezuela.
[2020/XB1718/**B**]

♦ International Correspondence of Corkscrew Addicts (ICCA) 12972

Contact address not obtained. E-mail: right@the-icca.net – webmaster@the-icca.net.
URL: http://www.the-icca.net/index.htm/

History 1974, London (UK). **Events** *Annual meeting* Williamsburg, VA (USA) 2008, *Annual Meeting* Austria 2007, *Annual Meeting* Budapest (Hungary) 2007, *Annual Meeting* Australia 2006, *Annual Meeting* USA 2005. **Publications** *Bottle Scrue Times*.
Members Individuals (mainly in North America) in 13 countries:
Canada, Denmark, France, Germany, Italy, Netherlands, Norway, Portugal, Spain, Sweden, Switzerland, UK, USA.
[2016/XN3246/**F**]

♦ International Correspondence for Peace (inactive)
♦ International Correspondence Society of Allergists (no recent information)
♦ International Corrosion Committee / see European Committee for the study of corrosion and protection of pipes and pipeline systems (#06670)

♦ International Corrosion Council (ICC) 12973

Conseil international de la corrosion

Pres DISAT, Politecnico di Torino, Corso Duca degli Abruzzi 24, 10129 Turin TO, Italy.
Sec address not obtained.
URL: http://www.icc-net.org/

History 15 Apr 1961, London (UK). Founded at first *International Congress on Metallic Corrosion (ICMC) – Congrès internationale de corrosion métallique*. Current bye-laws adopted in 1963. **Aims** Stimulate international research in corrosion science and *engineering* and encourage broad dissemination of results; promote cooperation and friendship among and between corrosion scientists and engineers in every country; foster practical application of research results through education; facilitate communication between corrosion specialists and engineers. **Structure** Congress (normally every 3 years); Council; Executive Committee. **Languages** English. **Staff** None. **Finance** Congress host. **Activities** Events/meetings. **Events** *International Corrosion Congress* Xian (China) 2024, *International Corrosion Congress* Rio de Janeiro (Brazil) 2021, *International Corrosion Congress* Sao Paulo (Brazil) 2020, *International Corrosion Congress* Prague (Czechia) 2017, *International Corrosion Congress* Jeju (Korea Rep) 2014. **Publications** *Sources of Corrosion Information*; *Survey of Corrosion Research Laboratories*. Congress proceedings.
Members Individuals in 68 countries and territories:
Albania, Algeria, Argentina, Australia, Austria, Belgium, Bolivia, Brazil, Bulgaria, Burkina Faso, Canada, Chile, China, Colombia, Costa Rica, Croatia, Cuba, Czechia, Denmark, Ecuador, Egypt, Finland, France, Germany, Greece, Hong Kong, Hungary, Iceland, India, Indonesia, Israel, Italy, Japan, Jordan, Korea Rep, Kuwait, Latvia, Libya, Lithuania, Mexico, Netherlands, New Zealand, Nigeria, Norway, Pakistan, Panama, Peru, Philippines, Poland, Portugal, Romania, Russia, Saudi Arabia, Singapore, South Africa, Spain, Sweden, Switzerland, Taiwan, Thailand, Tunisia, Türkiye, UK, Ukraine, Uruguay, USA, Venezuela, Vietnam.
[2022/XC5294/v/**B**]

♦ International Corrugated Case Association (ICCA) 12974

Association internationale des fabricants de caisses en carton ondulé

Main Office 500 Park Blvd, Suite 985, Itasca IL 60143, USA. T. +18473649600. Fax +18473649639.
URL: http://www.iccanet.org/

History 1961, Paris (France). Founded by *'Fibre Box Association (FBA)'* and *European Federation of Corrugated Board Manufacturers (#07091)*. Bylaws amended: 2017. **Aims** Provide members those services and activities that can be most effectively conducted by an international organization; provide services that support and enhance the work of members and contribute to the well-being of the corrugated packaging industry worldwide. **Structure** General Meeting; Global Summit (every 2 years) in the country where the Chairman is located; Board of Directors; Secretariat. **Languages** English. **Finance** Sources: members' dues. **Activities** Events/meetings; knowledge management/information dissemination; research and development; research/documentation. **Events** *WCO / ICCA Global Summit* 2021, *Biennial Summit* Palm Beach, FL (USA) 2019, *Biennial Summit* Guajará (Brazil) 2017, *Biennial Summit* Taipei (Taiwan) / Shanghai (China) 2015, *Biennial Summit* Paris (France) 2013. **Publications** *Worldwide Corrugated Packaging Industry Statistics* (4 a year); *Global Corrugated Forecast* (annual).
Members National and regional trade associations, federations and companies. Members in 61 countries and territories:
Argentina, Australia, Austria, Belgium, Bolivia, Brazil, Canada, Chile, China, Colombia, Costa Rica, Côte d'Ivoire, Czechia, Denmark, Ecuador, Egypt, El Salvador, Finland, France, Germany, Greece, Guatemala, Honduras, Hong Kong, Hungary, India, Indonesia, Ireland, Israel, Italy, Japan, Korea Rep, Kuwait, Malaysia, Mexico, Netherlands, New Zealand, Nicaragua, Nigeria, Norway, Panama, Paraguay, Peru, Philippines, Poland, Portugal, Puerto Rico, Russia, Singapore, South Africa, Spain, Sweden, Switzerland, Taiwan, Thailand, Türkiye, UK, Uruguay, USA, Venezuela, Vietnam.
Also in Caribbean region. Membership countries not specified.
Included in the above, 3 organizations listed in this Yearbook:
Asian Corrugated Case Association (ACCA, #01407); *Association of Caribbean, Central and South American Corrugators (ACCCSA, #02402)*; *European Federation of Corrugated Board Manufacturers (#07091)*.
[2021/XB1719/y/**B**]

♦ International Cosmetic and Device Association (unconfirmed)

♦ International Cospas-Sarsat Programme 12975

Head of Secretariat 1250 René-Lévesque Bvd West – Ste 4215, Montréal QC H3B 4W8, Canada. T. +15145007999. Fax +15145007996. E-mail: mail@cospas-sarsat.int.
URL: http://www.cospas-sarsat.int/

History 1979, as *Cospas-Sarsat*, under a Memorandum of Understanding (MOU) signed in Leningrad (USSR), by Canada, France, USSR and USA. The first satellite was launched in 1982 and the system has been operational since 1985, after a second MOU was signed in 1984, Leningrad, to allow for the transition into an operational system. Subsequently, the four founding countries signed, 1 Jul 1988, Paris (France), an intergovernmental Agreement committing them to providing long term support for the Cospas-Sarsat satellite system for search and rescue; the Agreement entered into force 30 Aug 1988. Under-titles: *International Satellite System for Search and Rescue – Système international de satellites pour les recherches et le sauvetage – Mezhdunarodnaja Sputnikovaja Sistema Poiska i Spasanija*. On 9 Jan 1992, the Russian Federation notified *International Maritime Organization (IMO, #14102)* that it was assuming all responsibilities of the former USSR in Cospas-Sarsat. The International Cospas-Sarsat Programme Agreement is deposited with both the Secretary General of *International Civil Aviation Organization (ICAO, #12581)* and the Secretary Secretary General of IMO. Statutes registered in ICAO 3380 and IMO. New intergovernmental agreement between Canada, France, Russia and USA (2005) established programme as an international organization with headquarters in Montréal (Canada). **Aims** As a satellite-based search and *rescue* (SAR) distress alert detection and information distribution system, detect and locate *emergency* beacons activated by aircraft, ships and backcountry hikers in distress. **Structure** Council (normally meets twice a year); Joint Committee (normally meets annually); Secretariat located in Montréal QC (Canada). **Languages** English, French, Russian. **Staff** 12.00 FTE, paid. **Finance** Space Segment and Ground Segment: funding of facilities provided by Parties and Ground Segment Provider States. Secretariat funded by contributions of Parties and Participants (associated states that are Ground Segment Providers and/or User-States). **Activities** Implements, maintains, coordinates and operates a satellite-based system and ground network for receiving and distributing distress alert and location data to search-and-rescue agencies during maritime, aviation and terrestrial distress incidents. Distress alert data provided at no cost to over 220 countries and territories. Provides an international facility for registration of 406 MHz distress beacons. **Events** *Council Session* Montréal, QC (Canada) 2020, *Experts Working Group* Montréal, QC (Canada) 2020, *Northwest Pacific data distribution region meeting* Tokyo (Japan) 2007, *Regional workshop for Central and South American countries* Miami, FL (USA) 2003, *Seminar* Québec, QC (Canada) 2000. **Publications** *Cospas-Sarsat Information Bulletin* (periodical) – online; *Cospas-Sarsat System Data* (periodical) – online. System Documents.
Members Parties to the Agreement (and Space Segment Providers) (4) in 5 countries:
Canada, France, India, Russia, USA.
Participating States (Ground Segment Providers) (27) in 27 countries:
Algeria, Argentina, Australia, Brazil, Chile, China, Cyprus, Greece, India, Indonesia, Italy, Japan, Korea Rep, New Zealand, Nigeria, Norway, Pakistan, Peru, Saudi Arabia, Singapore, South Africa, Spain, Thailand, Türkiye, UK, United Arab Emirates, Vietnam.
Participating States (User-States) (9) in 9 countries:
Denmark, Finland, Germany, Netherlands, Poland, Serbia, Sweden, Switzerland, Tunisia.
Participating Organizations (2) in 2 territories:
Hong Kong, Taiwan.
Non-State Inter-governmental Space Segment Providers (2), listed in this Yearbook:
European Organisation for the Exploitation of Meteorological Satellites (EUMETSAT, #08096); *European Union (EU, #08967)*.
IGO Relations Extensive cooperation with: *International Civil Aviation Organization (ICAO, #12581)*; *International Maritime Organization (IMO, #14102)*, including its Global Maritime Distress and Safety System (GMDSS). Formal cooperation agreements related to the provision of space facilities with: *European Commission (EC, #06633)*; *European Organisation for the Exploitation of Meteorological Satellites (EUMETSAT, #08096)*. Mutual meeting participation and also cooperates with: *Committee on the Peaceful Uses of Outer Space (COPUOS, #04277)*; *International Telecommunication Union (ITU, #15673)*. **NGO Relations** Cospas-Sarsat Secretariat liaises with several organizations, including: *EUROCAE (#05652)*; *International Chamber of Shipping (ICS, #12535)*; *International Federation of Air Line Pilots' Associations (IFALPA, #13349)*; *Comité International Radio-Maritime (CIRM, #04186)*; *Radio Technical Commission for Aeronautics (RTCA)*; *Radio Technical Commission for Maritime Services (RTCM)*.
[2020/XF4717/**F***]

♦ International Cost Engineering Council (ICEC) 12976

Gen Sec c/o Aus Inst Quantity Surveyors, Ste 303 Level 3, 70 Pitt Street, Sydney NSW 2000, Australia. T. +61282344000. Fax +61282344044. E-mail: contact@icoste.org.
URL: http://www.icoste.org/

History 1976. **Aims** Promote cooperation between national and multinational cost engineering/project management/quantity surveying organizations worldwide for their mutual wellbeing and that of their individual members. **Structure** Officers: Chairman; Senior Vice-Chairman; Administrative Vice-Chairman; Technical Vice-Chairman; Past-Chairman; Secretary-Treasurer; Assistant Secretary. **Languages** English. **Activities** Events/meetings; financial and/or material support; awards/prizes/competitions. **Events** *Joint Conference / World Congress* Accra (Ghana) 2024, *World Congress & Council Meeting* Rotterdam (Netherlands) 2022, *Joint Conference* Accra (Ghana) 2020, *World Congress* Sydney, NSW (Australia) 2018, *World Congress* Rio de Janeiro (Brazil) 2016. **Publications** *International Roundup* – electronic journal.
Members National organizations in 40 countries:
Australia, Austria, Brazil, Canada, China, Cyprus, Czechia, Denmark, Fiji, Finland, France, Ghana, Greece, Hong Kong, Hungary, Iceland, India, Italy, Japan, Kenya, Malaysia, Mauritius, Mexico, Namibia, Netherlands, New Zealand, Nigeria, Norway, Romania, Singapore, Slovakia, Slovenia, South Africa, Spain, Sri Lanka, Sweden, Tanzania UR, UK, USA, Venezuela.
Consultative Status Consultative status granted from: *ECOSOC (#05331)* (Ros A). **IGO Relations** *United Nations Human Settlements Programme (UN-Habitat, #20572)*. **NGO Relations** Member of: *International Cost Management Standard Coalition (ICMS Coalition, #12978)*. Cooperates with: *Africa Association of Quantity Surveyors (AAQS, #00156)*; *International Federation of Surveyors (FIG, #13561)*; *International Project Management Association (IPMA, #14655)*; *Pacific Association of Quantity Surveyors (PAQS, #17934)*.
[2022/XF2190/**F**]

♦ International Cost Estimating and Analysis Association (internationally oriented national body)

♦ International Cost Institute 12977

Institut international des coûts – Instituto Internacional de Custos (IIC)

Head Office Paraguay 2067-1C, Buenos Aires, Argentina. T. +541149612013. E-mail: info@iapuco.org.ar.
URL: http://www.intercostos.org/

History 27 Nov 1987, Paraná (Argentina). 27 Nov 1987, Parana (Argentina). Previously also referred to as *International Institute of Costs*. **Aims** Improve quality of management and direction of entreprises through the interchange of ideas and experiences. **Structure** Chief Board Council. Executive Council, comprising President, Executive Vice-President, Secretary-General, 3 Vice-Presidents (Institutional Relations; Communications; Publications) and Technical Secretary. **Events** *Congress* Lyon (France) 2017, *A pathway in time of crisis* Porto (Portugal) 2013, *Congress* Trelew (Argentina) 2009, *Management control, costs control and worldwide competition* Lyon (France) 2007, *Congress* Florianópolis (Brazil) 2005. **Publications** *Revista del Instituto Internacional de Costas*.
Members in 10 countries:
Argentina, Brazil, Colombia, Cuba, France, Mexico, Paraguay, Portugal, Spain, Uruguay.
[2017/XM2676/j/**E**]

♦ International Cost Management Standard Coalition (ICMS Coalition) 12978

Chair Parliament Square, London, SW1P 3AD, UK. T. +442076951602. E-mail: information@icms-coalition.org – standards@rics.org.
URL: http://icms-coalition.org/

History 17 Jun 2015. Launched following a meeting held Jun 2015, Washington DC (USA), at *International Monetary Fund (IMF, #14180)*. Former names and other names: *International Construction Measurement Standards Coalition (ICMS Coalition)* – former. **Aims** Create overarching international standards that will harmonize cost, classification and measurement definitions so as to enhance comparability, consistency, statistics, and benchmarking of capital projects. **Structure** Standards Setting Committee; Board of Trustees. **Languages** Chinese, English, Spanish. **Activities** Standards/guidelines.

Members Organizations in 25 countries and territories:
Australia, Brazil, Canada, China, France, Ghana, Hong Kong, India, Ireland, Italy, Japan, Kenya, Mexico, New Zealand, Nigeria, Philippines, Portugal, Singapore, South Africa, Spain, Switzerland, Türkiye, UK, United Arab Emirates, USA.
Regional organizations include:
Africa Association of Quantity Surveyors (AAQS, #00156); Commonwealth Association of Surveying and Land Economy (CASLE, #04313); European Council of Construction Economists (#06812); European Federation of Engineering Consultancy Associations (EFCA, #07109); Institution of Engineering and Technology (IET, #11320); International Cost Engineering Council (ICEC, #12976); International Federation of Surveyors (FIG, #13561); Pacific Association of Quantity Surveyors (PAQS, #17934); Royal Institution of Chartered Surveyors (RICS, #18991).
For a full list of members: https://icms-coalition.org/list-of-partners/. [2021/XM4328/y/**C**]

♦ International Cotton Advisory Committee (ICAC) 12979

Comité consultatif international du coton (CCIC) – Comité Consultivo Internacional del Algodón (CCIA)

Exec Dir 1629 K St NW, Ste 702, Washington DC 20006-1636, USA. T. +12024636660. Fax +12024636950. E-mail: secretariat@icac.org.
URL: http://www.icac.org/

History 5 Sep 1939, Washington, DC (USA). Established in accordance with a resolution of International Cotton Meeting of 12 principal cotton exporting countries. Executive Committee, later Standing Committee, and Secretariat organized 1947. Rules and Regulations adopted in 1952; revised Oct 1999. Recognized in USA as a public international organization by Executive Order 9911, 19 Dec 1947. **Aims** Observe and keep in close touch with developments affecting the world cotton situation; collect and disseminate complete, authentic and timely statistics on world cotton production, *trade*, consumption, stocks and *prices*; suggest to governments suitable and practicable measures for furthering international collaboration, with due regard to maintaining and developing a sound world cotton economy; act as the forum for international discussion on matters related to cotton prices. **Structure** Plenary Meeting (annual); Standing Committee; Secretariat in Washington DC (USA); coordinating agencies in member countries; Private Sector Advisory Panel (PSAP); Technical Information Section. **Languages** Arabic, English, French, Russian, Spanish. **Staff** 8.00 FTE, paid. **Finance** Contributions of member governments in proportion to international trade in cotton. Annual budget: 1,800,000 USD. **Activities** Knowledge management/information dissemination; research/documentation; training/education. **Events** *World Cotton Research Conference* Sharm el Sheikh (Egypt) 2022, *Annual Plenary Meeting* Washington, DC (USA) 2021, *World Cotton Research Conference* Izmir (Turkey) 2020, *Annual Plenary Meeting* Brisbane, QLD (Australia) 2019, *Annual Plenary Meeting* Abidjan (Côte d'Ivoire) 2018. **Publications** *Cotton This Week* (weekly); *Cotton this Month* (12 a year); *Cotton: Review of the World Situation* (6 a year) in English, French, Spanish – plenary meeting separate issue in Arabic/Russian; *ICAC Recorder* (4 a year) in English, French, Spanish; *Cotton: World Statistics* (annual) – hardcopy updated each October and CD updated each May; *World Cotton Trade* (annual) – hardcopy updated each October and CD updated each May; *World Textile Demand* (annual) – hardcopy updated each October and CD updated each May. *Outlook for Cotton Supply*; *Rules and Regulations*; *World Cotton Market*. Review articles on cotton production research; proceedings of plenary meetings; surveys; technical seminar papers.
Members Open to all UN and FAO member countries which have substantial interest in cotton, on acceptance of standing invitation; others if approved by Committee. Current membership: governments of 29 countries and territories:
Argentina, Australia, Bangladesh, Brazil, Burkina Faso, Cameroon, Chad, Côte d'Ivoire, Egypt, India, Kazakhstan, Kenya, Korea Rep, Mali, Mozambique, Nigeria, Pakistan, Russia, South Africa, Sudan, Switzerland, Taiwan, Tanzania UR, Togo, Türkiye, Uganda, USA, Uzbekistan, Zimbabwe.
Regional member:
European Union (EU, #08967).
IGO Relations Cooperates with (2): *FAO (#09260)*; *UNCTAD (#20285)*. **NGO Relations** Instrumental in setting up (2): *Asian Cotton Research and Development Network (#01408)*; *International Forum for Cotton Promotion (IFCP, inactive).* [2021.09.06/XB1720/**B***]

♦ International Cotton Association (ICA) 12980

Managing Dir 6th Floor, Walker House, Exchange Flags, Liverpool, L2 3YL, UK. T. +441512366041. Fax +441512550174. E-mail: info@ica-ltd.org.
URL: http://www.ica-ltd.org/

History 1841. Founded as *Liverpool Cotton Brokers' Association*. Name changed, 1882, to *Liverpool Cotton Association*. Registration: Companies House, No/ID: 00744445, Start date: 18 Dec 1962, England and Wales. **Aims** Facilitate safe trading of raw cotton internationally through a network based on shared principles and values; pursue equitable trading practices; provide an impartial and effective dispute resolution service in order to ensure contract sanctity in the global trade of cotton. **Structure** Annual General Meeting; Board of Directors; Executive Committee; Committees; Permanent Management Team based in Liverpool (UK). **Languages** English. **Staff** 11.50 FTE, paid. **Finance** Members' dues. Income from services. **Activities** Monitoring/evaluation; standards/guidelines; events/meetings; training/education. **Events** *Trade Event* Las Vegas, NV (USA) 2022, *Annual Trade Event* Singapore (Singapore) 2022, *Annual Trade Event* Singapore (Singapore) 2021, *Annual Trade Event* Singapore (Singapore) 2020, *Annual Trade Event* Liverpool (UK) 2019. **Publications** *ICA Articles Rulebook*. Annual Report; manual; membership directory. **Members** Companies and individuals in over 50 countries. Membership countries not specified. **IGO Relations** Close links with: *International Cotton Advisory Committee (ICAC, #12979)*. **NGO Relations** Provides secretariat for: *Committee for International Cooperation between Cotton Associations (CICCA, #04265)*. Close links with: *International Textile Manufacturers Federation (ITMF, #15679).* [2021/XJ4484/**D**]

♦ International Cotton Federation / see International Textile Manufacturers Federation (#15679)

♦ International Cotton Genome Initiative (ICGI) 12981

Chairperson TAMU, Dept Soil and Crop Sciences, 370 Olsen Blvd, College Station TX 77843-2474, USA.
Co-Chairperson USDA-ARS, 2765 F and B Road, College Station TX 77845, USA.
URL: http://www.cottongen.org/

History Current constitution and by-laws ratified 12 May 2005. **Aims** Increase knowledge of the structure and function of the cotton genome for the benefit of the global community. **Structure** Steering Committee, comprising Chairperson, Co-Chairperson and 9 members. Work groups (5). **Activities** Work groups (5): Bioinformatics; Evolutionary and Comparative Genomics; Functional Genomics; Germplasm and Genetic Stocks; Structural Genomics. Organizes meetings and workshops. **Events** *Workshop* San Diego, CA (USA) 2015, *Research Conference / Conference* Wuhan (China) 2014, *Research Conference / Conference* Raleigh, NC (USA) 2012, *Research conference / Conference* Canberra, ACT (Australia) 2010, *Conference* Anyang (China) 2008.
Members Full (512) in 29 countries:
Argentina, Australia, Bangladesh, Belgium, Brazil, Bulgaria, Canada, China, Egypt, France, Greece, India, Iran Islamic Rep, Israel, Kazakhstan, Kenya, Korea Rep, New Zealand, Nigeria, Pakistan, Peru, Senegal, Singapore, South Africa, Sudan, Türkiye, USA, Uzbekistan, Zimbabwe. [2015/XJ1994/**F**]

♦ International Cotton Producers Association (inactive)

♦ International Council of Academies of Engineering and Technological Sciences (CAETS) 12982

Sec/Treas 3004 The Mall, Williamsburg VA 23185, USA. T. +17035275782.
URL: http://www.caets.org/

History 1978. Governing Rules adopted 4 Oct 1985. Incorporated in the Washington DC (USA), Jun 2000. By-laws approved, Oct 2000. Also referred to as: *Council of Academies of Engineering and Technological Sciences*. **Aims** Promote development of engineering and technology; provide an international forum for discussion of technological and engineering issues; foster cooperative international engineering efforts; foster establishment of additional national engineering academies; contribute to strengthening of engineering and technological activities so as to promote economic growth and social welfare throughout the world. **Structure** Council (meets annually); Board of Directors; Executive Committee. **Languages** English. **Staff** 0.50 FTE, paid. **Finance** Members' dues. Local academy hosts annual meeting. Budget (annual): US$ 78,000. **Activities** Events/meetings. **Events** *Meeting* Seoul (Korea Rep) 2020, *Meeting* Stockholm (Sweden) 2019, *Meeting* Montevideo (Uruguay) 2018, *Meeting* Madrid (Spain) 2017, *Engineering for a better world – capacity building in the developing world* London (UK) 2016. **Publications** Statements; reports.
Members National Non-Governmental Academies in 26 countries (" indicates founding member):
Argentina, Australia (*), Belgium, Canada, China, Croatia, Czechia, Denmark, Finland, France, Germany, Hungary, India, Japan, Korea Rep, Mexico (*), Netherlands, Norway, Slovenia, South Africa, Spain, Sweden (*), Switzerland, UK (*), Uruguay, USA (*).
Consultative Status Consultative status granted from: *ECOSOC (#05331)* (Special). **NGO Relations** Observer of: *InterAcademy Partnership (IAP, #11376).* [2015.09.17/XD4090/**D**]

♦ International Council of Accrediting Agencies / see International Council for Evangelical Theological Education (#13020)
♦ International Council on Active Aging (internationally oriented national body)
♦ International Council for ADP in Government Administration / see International Council for Information Technology in Government Administration (#13033)

♦ International Council for Adult Education (ICAE) 12983

Conseil international d'éducation des adultes (CIEA) – Consejo Internacional de Educación de Adultos

SG Garsije Lorke 9, Belgrade, PAK 11060, Serbia. E-mail: sec.general@icae.global.
URL: http://icae.global/

History 14 Feb 1973, Montréal, QC (Canada). Constitution amended: June 1979, Helsinki (Finland); Oct 2019, Belgrade (Serbia). **Aims** Promote learning and education for adults and young people in pursuit of social justice within the framework of human rights in all its dimensions, to secure healthy, sustainable and democratic development of individuals, communities and societies. **Structure** General Assembly (at least every 4 years); Executive Committee comprised of President, Treasurer, Vice Presidents (representatives of 7 world regions + 3 members), Past President and Secretary General; Secretariat. **Languages** English, French, Spanish. **Staff** 3.00 FTE, paid; 15.00 FTE, voluntary. **Finance** Sources: grants; international organizations; members' dues; revenue from activities/projects. **Activities** Advocacy/lobbying/activism; capacity building. **Events** *Civil Society Forum* Marrakech (Morocco) 2022, *World General Assembly* Belgrade (Serbia) 2020, *World General Assembly* Montréal, QC (Canada) 2015, *World General Assembly* Malmö (Sweden) 2011, *Regional conference in Latin America and the Caribbean on literacy* Mexico City (Mexico) 2008. **Publications** *Voices Rising*. Articles. **Information Services** *ICAE Resource Centre*.
Members Regional and national associations (about 80) in 75 countries. Membership countries not specified. Included in the above, 3 organizations listed in this Yearbook:
African Development Education Network (ADEN, no recent information); International Association 'Znanie'; ProLiteracy Worldwide.
Regional associations include 15 organizations listed in this Yearbook:
Africa Network Campaign on Education for All (ANCEFA, #00302); African Women's Development and Communication Network (FEMNET, #00503); Arab League Educational, Cultural and Scientific Organization (ALECSO, #01003); Arab Network for Civic Education (ANHRE, #01011); Arab Network of Literacy and Adult Education (ANLAE, no recent information); Asia South Pacific Association for Basic and Adult Education (ASPBAE, #02098); Association of African Women for Research and Development (AAWORD, #02362); Campaña Latinoamericana por el Derecho a la Educación (CLADE, #03407); Consejo de Educación de Adultos de América Latina (CEAAL, #04707); Development Alternatives with Women for a New Era (DAWN, #05054); European Association for the Education of Adults (EAEA, #06018); North America Alliance for Popular and Adult Education (NAAPAE, no recent information); PAMOJA West Africa (#18031); Pan African Association for Literacy and Adult Education (PAALAE, no recent information); Red de Educación Popular entre Mujeres de América Latina y el Caribe (REPEM LAC, #18647).
Consultative Status Consultative status granted from: *ECOSOC (#05331)* (General); *UNESCO (#20322)* (Associate Status); *FAO (#09260)* (Liaison Status); *ILO (#11123)* (Special List); *UNICEF (#20332)*; *UNEP (#20299).*
IGO Relations Partner of (1): UN DESA.
Associated with Department of Global Communications of the United Nations. Cooperating United Nations Agencies:
- *International Bureau of Education (IBE, #12413);*
- *International Institute for Educational Planning (IIEP, #13874);*
- *UNDP (#20292);*
- *UNESCO Asia and Pacific Regional Bureau for Education (#20301);*
- *UNESCO Institute for Lifelong Learning (UIL, #20305);*
- *UNESCO Regional Bureau for Education in Latin America and the Caribbean (#20318);*
- *UNESCO Regional Office for Education in the Arab States (UNEDBAS, #20320);*
- *United Nations (UN, #20515);*
- *United Nations Commission on Human Rights (inactive);*
- *United Nations Commission for Social Development (CSocD, #20535);*
- *United Nations Commission on the Status of Women (CSW, #20536);*
- *United Nations Commission on Sustainable Development (CSD, inactive);*
- *United Nations Economic Commission for Africa (ECA, #20554);*
- *United Nations Economic Commission for Europe (UNECE, #20555);*
- *United Nations Economic Commission for Latin America and the Caribbean (ECLAC, #20556);*
- *United Nations Economic and Social Commission for Asia and the Pacific (ESCAP, #20557);*
- *United Nations Economic and Social Commission for Western Asia (ESCWA, #20558);*
- *United Nations International Research and Training Institute for the Advancement of Women (UN-INSTRAW, inactive);*
- *United Nations University (UNU, #20642);*
- *WHO (#20950).*

NGO Relations Member of (2): CCNGO/EFA; *World Social Forum (WSF, #21797).* [2023.02.19/XB4416/y/**B**]

♦ International Council for Advertising Self-Regulation (ICAS) 12984

Dir c/o EASA, Rue des Deux Eglises 26, 1000 Brussels, Belgium. E-mail: info@icas.global.
URL: http://icas.global/

History 2008. Founded by *European Advertising Standards Alliance (EASA, #05829)*, as an informal network operating under the umbrella of EASA. Launched as an independent platform, 2016. Secretariat opened Jun 2017. **Aims** Promote ethical standards in advertising. **Structure** Annual General Assembly; Executive Committee. **Languages** English. **Staff** 0.80 FTE, paid. **Finance** Members' dues. **Activities** Advocacy/lobbying/activism; awards/prizes/competitions; awareness raising; capacity building; knowledge management/information dissemination; events/meetings; monitoring/evaluation; networking/liaising; publishing activities; standards/guidelines; training/education. **Publications** *International Guide to Developing a Self-Regulatory Organisation* (2017).
Members Full in 24 countries:
Australia, Belgium, Brazil, Canada, Chile, Colombia, El Salvador, France, India, Ireland, Italy, Mexico, Netherlands, New Zealand, Peru, Philippines, Portugal, Romania, South Africa, Spain, Sweden, UK, United Arab Emirates, USA.
Included in the above, 5 organizations listed in this Yearbook:
European Advertising Standards Alliance (EASA, #05829); European Publishers Council (EPC, #08304); International Advertising Association (IAA, #11590); World Federation of Advertisers (WFA, #21407); World Out of Home Organization (WOO, #21702). [2021/XM6019/y/**E**]

♦ International Council of the Aeronautical Sciences (ICAS) 12985

Conseil international des sciences de l'aéronautique

Exec Sec c/o DGLR, Godesberger Allee 70, 53175 Bonn, Germany. T. +492283080519. Fax +492283080524. E-mail: icas@icas.org.
Coordinator address not obtained.
URL: http://www.icas.org/

History 30 May 1957, Paris (France). Founded 1957, as a provisional Council. First international congress held Sep 1958, Madrid (Spain). **Aims** Provide opportunities for exchange of knowledge and discussion of aeronautical research, technology and related issues; promote international awareness, cooperation and collaboration. **Structure** Council; Executive Committee; Programme Committee; Secretariat in Bonn (Germany), hosted by Deutsche Gesellschaft für Luft-und Raumfahrt Lilienthal-Oberth (DGLR), German national society. **Languages** English. **Staff** 2.00 FTE, paid. **Finance** Sources: meeting proceeds; members' dues. **Activities** Events/meetings. **Events** *Biennial Congress* Florence (Italy) 2024, *Biennial Congress* Stockholm (Sweden) 2022, *Biennial Congress* Shanghai (China) 2021, *Biennial Congress* Shanghai (China) 2020, *Emerging Technology Forum* Melbourne, VIC (Australia) 2019. **Publications** *The Aeronautical Journal: Covering all aspects of aerospace*. *ICAS Proceedings* (every 2 years) – CD-ROM. Congress reports.
Members National associations in 29 countries:

Australia, Belgium, Brazil, Canada, China, Czechia, Finland, France, Germany, Greece, Hungary, India, Indonesia, Israel, Italy, Japan, Korea Rep, Lithuania, Netherlands, Poland, Portugal, Romania, Russia, Serbia, South Africa, Sweden, Switzerland, UK, USA.
Associate members in 17 countries and territories:
Australia, Belgium, Canada, Czechia, France, Germany, Italy, Japan, Lithuania, Netherlands, Poland, Russia, South Africa, Spain, Sweden, Taiwan, USA. [2020.08.25/XC1759/**C**]

♦ International Council of African Museums (AFRICOM) 12986

Conseil international des musées africains

Exec Dir Kipande Rd, PO Box 38706, Ngara, Nairobi, 00600, Kenya. T. +254721392891. Fax +254203748928.
URL: http://icom.museum/

History 1999, Lusaka (Zambia). Evolved from *AFRICOM Programme (inactive)* of *International Council of Museums (ICOM, #13051)*. Registered in accordance with Kenyan law. **Aims** Promote the development of museums and museum-related institutions in Africa in the context of global development; promote the development of professions on which museum activities are built; strengthen collaboration and cooperation among museums and museum professionals in Africa, and develop exchanges with museum professionals abroad; promote participation of all of society's components to protect and enhance cultural and natural heritage; fight against illicit traffic of African heritage. **Structure** General Assembly. Board, comprising President, Vice-President, Treasurer, 5 Regional Representatives (North Africa, East Africa, Central Africa, Southern Africa and Indian Ocean Islands) and 4 Deputies (North Africa, West Africa, Central Africa and Indian Ocean Islands). **Languages** English, French. **Staff** 9.00 FTE, paid. **Finance** Core funding from: *Swedish International Development Cooperation Agency (Sida)*; *J Paul Getty Trust*; *Ford Foundation (#09858)*. **Activities** Priority areas: Intangible Heritage; Professional Development; Continental Networking. **Events** *Conference and General Assembly* Ouagadougou (Burkina Faso) 2009, *Conference and general assembly / General Assembly* Cape Town (South Africa) 2006, *Conference and general assembly / General Assembly* Nairobi (Kenya) 2003. **Publications** *AFRICOM News* (annual). *Directory of Museum Professionals in Africa* (2003). Conference proceedings.

Members Individual; Institutional; Associated; Student; Honorary. Museums in 55 countries and territories:
Algeria, Angola, Australia, Belgium, Benin, Bolivia, Botswana, Burkina Faso, Burundi, Cameroon, Canada, Central African Rep, Chad, Comoros, Congo Brazzaville, Congo DR, Côte d'Ivoire, Egypt, Eswatini, Ethiopia, France, Gabon, Gambia, Ghana, Guinea, Guinea-Bissau, Italy, Kenya, Korea Rep, Liberia, Madagascar, Malawi, Mali, Mauritania, Morocco, Mozambique, Namibia, Netherlands, Niger, Nigeria, Norway, Réunion, Rwanda, Senegal, Sierra Leone, South Africa, Sudan, Sweden, Tanzania UR, Tunisia, Uganda, UK, USA, Zambia, Zimbabwe.

IGO Relations *African Union (AU, #00488)*; *European Commission (EC, #06633)*; *UNESCO (#20322)*. **NGO Relations** Participates in General Assemblies of and Affiliated Organization of *International Council of Museums (ICOM, #13051)*. [2012/XM2122/**E**]

♦ International Council Against Bullfighting (inactive)
♦ International Council of AIDS Mexico City / see ICASO (#11040)

♦ International Council of Air-Conditioning, Refrigeration, and Heating Manufacturers Associations (ICARHMA) 12987

Secretariat 2311 Wilson Blvd, Ste 400, Arlington VA 22201, USA. T. +17035248800. Fax +17035283816. E-mail: icarhma@icarhma.org.
URL: https://icarhma.ahrinet.org/Home.aspx

History 1991. Founded by *European Committee of Air Handling and Air Conditioning Equipment Manufacturers (EUROVENT, inactive)* and *European Committee of Manufacturers of Refrigeration Equipment (CECOMAF, inactive)*, as *International Council of Air Conditioning and Refrigeration Manufacturers Associations (ICARMA)*. **Aims** Provide a standing consultative body for discussing matters of mutual interest, including possible cooperative actions which council members may agree to recommend to their respective associations. **Structure** Secretariat, provided by *Air-conditioning, Heating, and Refrigeration Institute (AHRI)*, USA. **Languages** English. **Staff** AHRI staff. **Finance** Supported by AHRI. **Activities** Events/meetings; publishing activities. **Events** *Annual Meeting* Arlington, VA (USA) 2021, *Annual Meeting* Arlington, VA (USA) 2020, *Annual Meeting* Boston, MA (USA) 2019, *Annual Meeting* Tokyo (Japan) 2018, *Annual Meeting* Seoul (Korea Rep) 2017.

Members National and international associations. National associations in 8 countries:
Australia, Brazil, Canada, China, India, Japan, Korea Rep, USA.
Regional associations (2):
European Partnership for Energy and the Environment (EPEE, #08157); *Eurovent (#09194)*.

IGO Relations No formal relations. **NGO Relations** No formal relations. [2022/XG4581/**C**]

♦ International Council of Air Conditioning and Refrigeration Manufacturers Associations / see International Council of Air-Conditioning, Refrigeration, and Heating Manufacturers Associations (#12987)

♦ International Council of Aircraft Owner and Pilot Associations (IAOPA) 12988

Conseil international des associations de propriétaires et pilotes d'aéronefs – Consejo Internacional de Asociaciones de Propietarios y Pilotos de Aeronaves

SG 421 Aviation Way, Frederick MD 21701, USA. T. +12027377950. E-mail: iaopa@aopa.org.
Pres address not obtained.
URL: https://www.iaopa.org/

History 22 Oct 1964, Washington, DC (USA). Founded 1964, when accredited status by ICAO, an interim organization having been set up 2 Feb 1962. **Aims** Advance interests of general aviation and facilitate international movement of general *aviation* aircraft for peaceful purposes; increase utility of general aviation *airplanes* as a means of personal and business transportation; coordinate with other international and national organizations and integrate views and requirements of member organizations with regard to international standards, recommended practices, procedures, facilities and services for international general aviation; encourage implementation of planned systems, facilities, services and procedures in order to promote flight safety, efficiency and utility. **Structure** World Assembly (every 2 years); Executive Board; Headquarters Secretariat in Frederick MD (USA); European and Pacific Regional Secretariats; European EC Liaison; Standing Committees (2). **Languages** English. **Staff** 2.00 FTE, paid. **Finance** Sources: members' dues. **Activities** Projects/programmes. **Events** *Biennial World Assembly* Montréal, QC (Canada) 2022, *Biennial World Assembly* Montréal, QC (Canada) 2020, *Biennial World Assembly* Queenstown (New Zealand) 2018, *Biennial World Assembly* Chicago, IL (USA) 2016, *Biennial World Assembly* Beijing (China) 2014. **Publications** *IAOPA Information Bulletin* (4 a year); *IAOPA eNews* (9 a year). Variety of tutorials and interactive computer programmes available on website, designed to provide access to aviation safety materials and programmes.

Members National organizations, one per country, representing 425,000 pilots in 80 countries and territories:
Andorra, Argentina, Australia, Austria, Bangladesh, Belarus, Belgium, Belize, Bermuda, Botswana, Brazil, Bulgaria, Canada, Chile, China, Colombia, Costa Rica, Croatia, Cyprus, Czechia, Denmark, Egypt, Estonia, Finland, France, Germany, Ghana, Greece, Guyana, Hungary, Iceland, India, Ireland, Israel, Italy, Jamaica, Japan, Jordan, Kenya, Korea Rep, Latvia, Lebanon, Liberia, Lithuania, Luxembourg, Malaysia, Malta, Mauritius, Mexico, Moldova, Monaco, Namibia, Netherlands, New Zealand, Nigeria, Norway, Pakistan, Panama, Peru, Philippines, Poland, Portugal, Qatar, Romania, Russia, Saudi Arabia, Singapore, Slovenia, South Africa, Spain, Sweden, Switzerland, Thailand, Trinidad-Tobago, Türkiye, UK, Ukraine, United Arab Emirates, USA, Venezuela.

Consultative Status Consultative status granted from: *ECOSOC (#05331)* (Ros C); *International Civil Aviation Organization (ICAO, #12581)* (Observer Status). **IGO Relations** Working relationship with: *European Civil Aviation Conference (ECAC, #06564)*; *EUROCONTROL (#05667)*; *World Meteorological Organization (WMO, #21649)*. Accredited by: *United Nations Office at Vienna (UNOV, #20604)*. Associated with Department of Global Communications of the United Nations. **NGO Relations** In liaison with technical committees of: *International Organization for Standardization (ISO, #14473)*. Instrumental in setting up: *European General Aviation Safety Foundation (EGASF, inactive)*. [2020.08.25/XC1733/**C**]

♦ International Council on Alcohol and Addictions (ICAA) 12989

Conseil international sur les problèmes de l'alcoolisme et des toxicomanies (CIPAT)

Main Office PO Box 189, 1001 Lausanne VD, Switzerland. E-mail: secretariat@icaa.ch – icaamailbox@aol.com.
URL: http://www.icaa.ch/

History Founded 1 Aug 1907, Stockholm (Sweden), as *International Bureau Against Alcoholism – Bureau international contre l'alcoolisme – Oficina Internacional Contra el Alcoholism – Internationales Bureau zur Bekämpfung des Alkoholismus*. Previously also referred to as *International Temperance Bureau*. In 1935, Montreux (Switzerland), the Bureau became secretariat of *International Union Against Alcoholism – Union internationale contre l'alcoolisme*, sometimes referred to as *International Temperance Union*. Name changed: 1964, to *International Council on Alcohol and Alcoholism – Conseil international sur les problèmes de l'alcool et de l'alcoolisme*; 1968, to present name, widening activities to cover all addictions. Previously also referred to in Spanish and German as *Consejo Internacional sobre el Problema del Alcoholismo y las Toxicomanias – Internationaler Rat zur Bekämpfung des Alkoholismus und der Suchtgefahren*. Current constitution approved 20 Sep 2014. Registered in accordance with Swiss Civil Code. **Aims** Prevent the use and reduce the harmful effects of alcohol, *tobacco* and other *drugs* and of addictive behaviour on individuals, families, communities and society; sensitize, empower and educate organizations and individuals and advocate for effective partnerships in prevention, treatment, research and policy development in the interest of public health and personal and social well-being. **Structure** General Assembly (annual); Management Committee; Secretariat. Sections (8): Alcohol Education; Alcohol Policy; Alcohol Epidemiology; Women and Alcohol; Treatment; Ethnic Dimensions; Workplace; Nicotine. **Languages** English, French, German, Spanish. **Staff** 13.00 FTE, paid. **Finance** Sources: donations; members' dues; sale of publications. Other sources: grants from governments and private organizations. **Activities** Events/meetings; knowledge management/information dissemination; research/documentation; training/education. **Events** *International Symposium on Women and Addiction* New Brunswick (Canada) 2022, *Convention on Women in Addiction in the 2020s* Stockholm (Sweden) 2016, *International Conference on Alcohol and Addiction* Montréal, QC (Canada) 2012, *International conference on the prevention and treatment of dependencies / International Conference on Dependencies* Cancún (Mexico) 2010, *International conference on the prevention and treatment of dependencies / International Conference on Dependencies* Estoril (Portugal) 2009. **Publications** *ICAA News* (4 a year).

Members Organizational; Individual; Student. Membership countries not specified. International and regional member:
International and regional member:
European Treatment Centers for Drug Addiction (EURO-TC, #08947).

Consultative Status Consultative status granted from: *ECOSOC (#05331)* (Special); *ILO (#11123)* (Special List). **IGO Relations** NGO Committee on Narcotic Drugs at: *United Nations Office at Vienna (UNOV, #20604)*. Associated with Department of Global Communications of the United Nations. **NGO Relations** Member of: *Alliance of NGOs on Crime Prevention and Criminal Justice (#00709)*; *New York NGO Committee on Drugs (NYNGOC, #17097)*; *Vienna NGO Committee on Drugs (VNGOC, #20773)*; *Vienna NGO Committee on the Family (#20774)*. Instrumental in setting up: *World Federation of Therapeutic Communities (WFTC, #21491)*. [2018/XB1765/y/**B**]

♦ International Council on Alcohol and Alcoholism / see International Council on Alcohol and Addictions (#12989)

♦ International Council on Alcohol, Drugs and Traffic Safety (ICADTS) 12990

Comité international sur l'alcool, les drogues et la sécurité routière

Sec Univ of Western Ontario, 1151 Richmond St, London ON N6A 3K7, Canada. E-mail: admin@icadtsinternational.com.
Pres c/o NORC, Univ of Chicago, 4350 East-West Highway, 8th Fl, Bethesda MD 20814, USA. T. +13016349576. Fax +13016349301.
URL: http://www.icadtsinternational.com/

History 7 Sep 1962, London (UK). Founded by Robert Borkenstein during 3rd International Conference on Alcohol and Road Traffic, initial discussion having been held following 1st Conference, 30 Aug 1950, Stockholm (Sweden). **Aims** Reduce mortality and morbidity brought about by misuse of alcohol and drugs by operators of vehicles in all modes of transportation; collect, disseminate and share essential information among professionals in the fields of law, medicine, public health, economics, law enforcement, pharmacy, forensics, public information and education, human factors and public policy. **Structure** International Conference (every 3 years); Executive Board; Committees (3); Working Groups (7). **Languages** English. **Staff** Voluntary. **Finance** Sources: grants; members' dues. **Activities** Awards/prizes/competitions; events/meetings; financial and/or material support; knowledge management/information dissemination; politics/policy/regulatory; research/documentation. **Events** *International Conference on Alcohol, Drugs and Traffic Safety* Alcobaça (Portugal) 2025, *International Conference on Alcohol, Drugs and Traffic Safety (ICADTS)* Rotterdam (Netherlands) 2022, *International Council on Alcohol, Drugs and Traffic Safety Conference* Edmonton, AB (Canada) 2019, *International Conference on Alcohol, Drugs and Traffic Safety* Gramado (Brazil) 2016, *IALM Intersocietal Symposium* Venice (Italy) 2016. **Publications** *Traffic Injury Prevention* (6 a year) – journal; *ICADTS Reporter* (4 a year) – newsletter. Conference proceedings.

Members 270 in 32 countries:
Australia, Austria, Bangladesh, Belgium, Brazil, Canada, China, Denmark, Finland, France, Germany, Hungary, India, Ireland, Israel, Italy, Japan, Mexico, Netherlands, New Zealand, Nigeria, Norway, Poland, Slovenia, South Africa, Spain, Sri Lanka, Sweden, Switzerland, UK, USA, Vietnam.

IGO Relations Provides expertise to: *European Commission (EC, #06633)* (DG VII). [2023.02.15/XC1628/**C**]

♦ International Council of Amateur Dancers / see World DanceSport Federation (#21354)

♦ International Council on Amino Acid Science (ICAAS) 12991

ICAAS Japan 3F, 3-11-8 Hatchobori Chuo-ku, Tokyo, 104-0032 Japan. T. +81335377021. Fax +81335377022.
URL: http://www.icaas-org.com/

History 2000, Tokyo (Japan). Registered in accordance with Belgian law, 2008. **Aims** Explore and resolve scientific concerns related to safety, quality and use of amino acids, with emphasis on *dietary* use in humans; establish a framework for assessing and predicting consequences of differing levels of amino acid intake in humans under various conditions; develop quality *specifications* for amino acid products on the market so as to ensure consumer safety.

Members Companies (10) in 7 countries:
Belgium, France, Germany, Hong Kong, Japan (5), UK, USA.

IGO Relations Participates as observer in the activities of: *Codex Alimentarius Commission (CAC, #04081)*. [2015.03.09/XJ6216/**D**]

♦ International Council on Animal Protection in OECD Programmes (ICAPO) 12992

Secretariat Physicians Committee for Responsible Medicine, 5100 Wisconsin Ave NW, Ste 400, Washington DC 20016, USA. E-mail: icapo@pcrm.org.
URL: http://www.icapo.org/

History 2002. **Aims** Ensure the widest possible integration of alternative methods in the OECD's influential guidelines and programmes. **Activities** Working Group of National Coordinators of the Test Guidelines Programme; Task Force on Endocrine Disrupter Testing and Assessment; Task Force on Existing Chemicals; Validation Management Group for Non-animal testing; Validation Management Group for Mammalian testing.

Members National and regional organizations. National organizations (8) in 5 countries:
Canada, Germany, Japan, UK, USA.
Regional organizations (3):
Eurogroup for Animals (#05690); *European Coalition to End Animal Experiments (ECEAE, #06594)*; *People for the Ethical Treatment of Animals (PETA, #18297)*. [2014/XJ6071/y/**E**]

♦ International Council for Applied Mineralogy (ICAM) 12993

SG Fed Inst of Geosciences and Natural Resources (BGR), Stilleweg 2, 30655 Hannover, Germany. T. +495116432565. Fax +495116433664.
Pres IMAA-CNR, C de Santa Loja, Tito Scalo, 85050 Potenza PZ, Italy. T. +39805442618.

History 1981, Johannesburg (South Africa). Constitution adopted 1984, Los Angeles CA (USA). **Aims** Organize interdisciplinary congresses bringing together mineralogists, chemistry specialists, engineers specializing in processing and enrichment of minerals, metallurgists, ceramists, specialists in their disciplines with minerals and with their application in the everyday life; encourage use of mineralogy and mineralogical techniques in exploration, mining, beneficiation and metallurgy, and also such areas as forensic science, environmental optimization and health, mineral resource recovery and utilization of solid waste. **Structure** General Meeting (at Congress). **Languages** English. **Staff** 3.00 FTE, paid. **Finance** No budget. Logistics supplied by BGR (Germany). Congresses funded by organizing committee. **Events** *International Congress* Belgorod Oblast (Russia) 2019, *Congress / Regular Congress* Istanbul (Turkey) 2015, *Congress / Regular Congress* Mianyang (China) 2013, *Congress / Regular Congress* Trondheim (Norway) 2011, *Congress / Regular Congress* Brisbane, QLD (Australia) 2008. **Publications** Congress proceedings.

Members Organizations in 22 countries:
Australia, Belgium, Brazil, Canada, China, Egypt, Finland, France, Germany, Italy, Japan, Korea Rep, Mexico, Netherlands, Norway, Poland, Russia, South Africa, Spain, UK, Ukraine, USA.

NGO Relations Cooperates with the Commission on Applied Mineralogy (CAM) of: *International Mineralogical Association (IMA, #14165)*; national mineralogical associations. [2019/XD7026/**D**]

♦ International Council of the Arabic Language / see Arabic Language International Council (#00978)

♦ International Council of Arbitration for Sport (ICAS) 12994

Conseil international de l'arbitrage en matière de Sport (CIAS)

Secretariat Av de Beaumont 2, 1012 Lausanne VD, Switzerland. T. +41216135000. Fax +41216135001. E-mail: media@tas-cas.org – info@tas-cas.org.
URL: http://www.tas-cas.org/

History Nov 1994, in the framework of *Court of Arbitration for Sport (CAS, #04933)*, of which it is the supreme organ. **Aims** Supervise the Court of Arbitration for Sport and its funding, safeguard its independence and the rights of parties before CAS. **Structure** Comprises 20 high-level lawyers, of which 4 designated by IOC, 4 by International Federations, 4 by National Olympic Committees, 4 representatives of athletes and 4 co-opted independent personalities. **Languages** English, French. **Activities** Standards/guidelines; events/meetings.

Members High level lawyers in 15 countries:
Australia, Austria, Brazil, Canada, China, France, Kuwait, Netherlands, Russia, Slovenia, South Africa, Spain, Sweden, Switzerland, USA. [2019.02.18/XK0381/v/**E**]

♦ International Council for Archaeozoology (ICAZ) 12995

Conseil international d'archéozoologie

Sec c/o Classics – Archaeology, Humanities Bldg, University Park, Nottingham, NG7 2RD, UK. E-mail: icaz@alexandriaarchive.org.
Contact c/o Alexandria Archive Inst, 125 El Verano Way, San Francisco CA 94127, USA.
URL: https://alexandriaarchive.org/icaz/

History 1976, Nice (France). Founded following activities initiated during International Symposium on "Domestikations-forschung und Geschichte der Haustiere", Budapest (Hungary) 1971. **Aims** Develop and stimulate archaeological research; strengthen cooperation among archaeozoologists; foster cooperation with archaeologists and other scientists working in the field of *archaeology* and related fields; promote high ethical and scientific standards for archaeozoological work. **Structure** International Committee; Committee of Honour; Executive Committee. Working Groups. **Languages** English, French, German, Russian, Spanish. **Finance** Members' dues. Budget (annual): US$ 6,000 – US$ 7,000. **Activities** Organizes congresses, conferences and working group meetings; standardizes data recording, nomenclature, measurements and policies relating to archaeozoology; supports scientific publications of international importance. Working Groups (7): Fish Remains (FRWG); Bird Remains (BRWG); Southeast Asia (ASWA); North Atlantic (NABO); Veterinary Pathology (PALPATH); Worked Bone (WBWG); Camelid (CAMWG). **Events** *International Conference* Cairns, QLD (Australia) 2023, *International Conference* Cairns, QLD (Australia) 2022, *ICAZ-ASWA International Meeting* Tokyo (Japan) 2022, *Archaeozoology, Genetics, Proteomins and Morphometrics Working Group Meeting* Oulu (Finland) 2021, *Worked Bone Research Group Meeting* Montréal, QC (Canada) 2019. **Publications** *ICAZ Newsletter* (2 a year). *Animals and Archaeology I – IV* (1983-1984) by J Clutton-Brock and C Grigson; *Archaeozoology* (1983) by M Kubasiewicz; *Archaeozoological Studies* (1975) by A T Clason; *Bibliography of Archaeozoology* by Jorg Schibler.

Members Individuals interested in archaeozoological research in 38 countries:
Argentina, Austria, Belgium, Brazil, Canada, China, Colombia, Czechia, Denmark, Estonia, Finland, France, Germany, Greece, Hungary, India, Ireland, Israel, Italy, Japan, Jordan, Mexico, Netherlands, Norway, Panama, Peru, Poland, Portugal, Puerto Rico, Romania, Russia, South Africa, Spain, Sweden, Switzerland, Türkiye, UK, USA. [2022/XF5646/v/**F**]

♦ International Council of the Architects of Historical Monuments (inactive)

♦ International Council on Archives (ICA) 12996

Conseil international des archives – Consejo Internacional de Archivos – Internationaler Archivrat

Exec Dir 60 rue des Francs-Bourgeois, 75003 Paris, France. T. +33181705562. Fax +33181705561. E-mail: ica@ica.org.
Pres address not obtained. E-mail: president@ica.org.
URL: http://www.ica.org/

History Jun 1948, Paris (France). Founded by professional archivists meeting under the auspices of UNESCO. Definitively established, Aug 1950, Paris, at 1st *International Archives Congress*. Constitution adopted at the Inaugural Meeting of the Provisional Council, convened by UNESCO, 9-11 Jun 1948; amended by Constituent Assembly on 20 Aug 1950, and by General Assemblies on: 16 Aug 1960; 1 Sep 1964; 3 Sep 1968; 25 Aug 1972; 29 Sep 1976; 19 Sep 1980; 19-21 Sep 1984; 24-26 Aug 1988. Constitution revised and adopted at General Assembly on 7-11 Sep 1992; amended by General Assembly on 4-7 Sep 1996; amended and approved by General Assembly 22-26 Sep 2000, Seville (Spain); amended and adopted by General Assembly Aug 2004, Vienna (Austria); amended and approved at Annual General Meeting, Nov 2007; amended and adopted by General Assembly Aug 2012, Brisbane (Australia). **Aims** Promote the management and use of records and archives and the preservation of the archival *heritage* of humanity worldwide, through sharing of experience, research and ideas on professional archival and records management matters and on management and organization of archival institutions.

Structure General Meeting (annual); Executive Board (meets annually); Elected Officer-Holders Meeting. Commissions (2): Audit; Programme. *Fund for the International Development of Archives (FIDA, no recent information)*.

Regional branches (13):
- *Asociación Latinoamericana de Archivos (ALA, #02183)*;
- *Arab Regional Branch of the International Council on Archives (ARBICA, see: #12996)*;
- *Caribbean Regional Branch of the International Council on Archives (CARBICA, see: #12996)*;
- *Regional Branch for Central Africa of the International Council on Archives (CENARBICA, see: #12996)*;
- *East Asian Regional Branch of the ICA (EASTICA, see: #12996)*;
- *Eastern and Southern Africa Regional Branch of the International Council on Archives (ESARBICA, see: #12996)*;
- *Eurasian Regional Branch of the International Council on Archives (EURASICA, see: #12996)*;
- *European Regional Branch of the International Council on Archives (EURBICA, see: #12996)*;
- North American Archival Network (NAANICA);
- *Pacific Regional Branch of the International Council on Archives (PARBICA, see: #12996)*;
- *Southeast Asian Regional Branch of the International Council on Archives (SARBICA, see: #12996)*;
- *South and West Asian Regional Branch of the International Council on Archives (SWARBICA, see: #12996)*;
- *West African Regional Branch of the International Council on Archives (WARBICA, see: #12996)*.

Sections (12):
- Archival Education and Training (SAE);
- Notarial Records (SAN);
- Architectural Records (SAR);
- Business Archives (SBA);
- International Organizations (SIO);
- Archives of Faith Traditions (SAFT);
- Literature and Art Archives (SLA);
- Local, Municipal and Territorial Archives (SMLT);
- Professional Associations (SPA);
- Sports Archives (SPO);
- Archives of Parliaments and Political Parties (SPL);
- University and Research Institution Archives (SUV).

Others (8):
- Expert Group on Archival Description (EGAD);
- Working Group on Archives and Human Rights (HRWG);
- Working Group on Intellectual Property (WGIP);
- Photographic and Audiovisual Archives Group (PAAG);
- Publications Review Working Group (PWRG);
- Archive Buildings and Environment (EGABE);
- Advocacy (AEG);
- International Journal on Archives (COMMA).

Languages English, French, Spanish. **Staff** 5.00 FTE, paid. **Finance** Sources: contributions; members' dues. Other sources: support for projects from other organizations; voluntary contributions from members. **Activities** Advocacy/lobbying/activism; awareness raising; capacity building; events/meetings; networking/liaising; training/education. **Events** *International Congress on Archives* Barcelona (Spain) 2025, *International Congress on Archives* Abu Dhabi (United Arab Emirates) 2023, *Annual Conference* Rome (Italy) 2022, *Annual Conference* 2021, *International Congress on Archives* Abu Dhabi (United Arab Emirates) 2021. **Publications** *Enewsletter* (12 a year); *Comma – International Journal on Archives* (2 a year); *Flash* (2 a year). *Guide to the Sources of the History of Nations/Guide des sources de l'histoire des nations* – 1st series Latin America, 2nd series Africa South of the Sahara, 3rd series North Africa, Asia and Oceania, 4th series Asian History, 5th series Other Guides; *ICA Studies. Capitals of Europe/Les capitales d'Europe.* Regional journals – ALA, ARBICA, CARBICA, ESARBICA, PARBICA, SARBICA, SWARBICA, WARBICA. Handbooks and studies on archival terminology, archives buildings, arrangement and description, disposition of government records, preservation of microfilms.

Members /Category A/: National Archives (197) in 199 countries and territories (not specified). /Category B/: professional associations of archivists (79). Membership countries not specified. Includes 3 associations listed in this Yearbook:

/Category B/: professional associations of archivists (79). Membership countries not specified. Includes 2 associations listed in this Yearbook:

Association internationale des archives francophones (AIAF, #02669); *International Association of Music Libraries, Archives and Documentation Centres (IAML, #12042)*.

/Category C/: institutional members (696) – institutions concerned with administration or preservation of records and archives, or with professional training of archivists. Membership countries not specified. Included in the above, 54 institutions and/or library, archives, records or documentation departments of these institutions:

Included in the above, 54 institutions and/or library, archives, records or documentation departments of these institutions:
- *All Africa Conference of Churches (AACC, #00640)*;
- *Arab League Educational, Cultural and Scientific Organization (ALECSO, #01003)*;
- *ARMA International*;
- *Assemblée parlementaire de la Francophonie (APF, #02312)*;
- *Black Sea Trade and Development Bank (BSTDB, #03278)*;
- *Centre de coopération internationale en recherche agronomique pour le développement (CIRAD, #03733)*;
- *Commonwealth Scientific and Industrial Research Organization (CSIRO)*;
- *Council of Europe (CE, #04881)*;
- *Council of the European Union (#04895)*;
- *European Bank for Reconstruction and Development (EBRD, #06315)*;
- *European Central Bank (ECB, #06466)*;
- *European Centre for the Development of Vocational Training (Cedefop, #06474)*;
- *European Investment Bank (EIB, #07599)*;
- *European Parliament (EP, #08146)*;
- *European Space Agency (ESA, #08798)*;
- *Friedrich-Ebert-Stiftung (FES)*;
- *Heinrich Böll Foundation*;
- *Historical Archives of the European Union (HAEU, #10927)*;
- *ILO (#11123)*;
- *Institut international d'histoire du notariat (IIHN, #11312)*;
- *International Bank for Reconstruction and Development (IBRD, #12317)*;
- *International Centre for the Study of the Preservation and Restoration of Cultural Property (ICCROM, #12521)*;
- *International Civil Aviation Organization (ICAO, #12581)*;
- *International Committee of the Red Cross (ICRC, #12799)*;
- *International Federation of Red Cross and Red Crescent Societies (#13526)*;
- *International Fund for Agricultural Development (IFAD, #13692)*;
- *International Information Centre for Balkan Studies (CIBAL, #13844)*;
- *International Institute for Archival Science of Trieste and Maribor (IIAS, #13862)*;
- *International Institute of Social History (IISG)*;
- *International Monetary Fund (IMF, #14180)*;
- *International Telecommunication Union (ITU, #15673)*;
- *Islamic Development Bank (IsDB, #16044)*;
- *League of Arab States (LAS, #16420)*;
- *NATO (#16945)*;
- *Nordic Council (NC, #17256)*;
- *OAS (#17629)*;
- *Organisation internationale de la Francophonie (OIF, #17809)*;
- *The Rockefeller Foundation (#18966)*;
- UN Archives;
- UN Department of Humanitarian Affairs;
- *UNESCO (#20322)*;
- *UNHCR (#20327)*;
- *UNICEF (#20332)*;
- *Union of Arab Historians (UAH, no recent information)*;
- *United Nations Joint Staff Pension Fund (UNJSPF, #20581)*;
- *United Nations Office at Geneva (UNOG, #20597)*;
- *United Nations Volunteers (UNV, #20650)*;
- *University of the West Indies (UWI, #20705)*;
- UN Records Management Unit;
- *WHO (#20950)*;
- *World Council of Churches (WCC, #21320)*;
- *World Food Programme (WFP, #21510)*;
- *World Intellectual Property Organization (WIPO, #21593)*.

/Category D/: individual members (522) – present and past members of any archival institution, service or training centre. Membership countries not specified.

Consultative Status Consultative status granted from: *ECOSOC (#05331)* (Ros C); *UNESCO (#20322)* (Associate Status); *World Intellectual Property Organization (WIPO, #21593)* (Permanent Observer Status). **IGO Relations** Cooperates with (6): *Council of Europe (CE, #04881)*; *International Bank for Reconstruction and Development (IBRD, #12317)*; *International Centre for the Study of the Preservation and Restoration of Cultural Property (ICCROM, #12521)*; *Organisation internationale de la Francophonie (OIF, #17809)*; *UNDP (#20292)*; *World Meteorological Organization (WMO, #21649)*. **NGO Relations** Cooperates with (14): *Association internationale des archives francophones (AIAF, #02669)*; *Blue Shield International (BSI, #03286)*; *Conference of Non-Governmental Organizations in Consultative Relationship with the United Nations (CONGO, #04635)*; *Coordinating Council of Audiovisual Archives Associations (CCAAA, #04820)*; *ICOM International Committee for Literary Museums (ICLM, see: #13051)*; *ICOM International Committee for University Museums and Collections (UMAC, #11058)*; *International Association of Sound and Audiovisual Archives (IASA, #12172)*; *International Council for Science (ICSU, inactive)*; *International Council of Museums (ICOM, #13051)*; *International Council on Monuments and Sites (ICOMOS, #13049)*; *International Federation of Film Archives (#13427)*; *International Organization for Standardization (ISO, #14473)*; *International Records Management Trust (IRMT, inactive)*; *Union internationale des architectes (UIA, #20419)*. Consultative status with: *International Federation of Library Associations and Institutions (IFLA, #13470)*. [2022/XB1766/y/**B**]

♦ International Council of Associations for Science Education (ICASE) 12997

Fédération internationale des associations de professeurs de sciences (FIAPS)

Coordinator The Eureka Centre, Ground Floor Kane Bldg, Univ College Cork, Cork, CO. CORK, T12 HF72, Ireland. T. +353861002226.
URL: http://www.icaseonline.net/

History 1972. Founded by *UNESCO (#20322)*. Constitution approved 1973, Baltimore MD (USA), during a conference organized by the Committee on the Teaching of Science of *International Council for Science (ICSU, inactive)*. **Aims** Extend and improve science education throughout the world. **Structure** General Assembly; Management Committee; Executive Committee; Regional Representatives (6); Standing Committees (7). **Languages** English, French, Spanish. **Staff** Voluntary. **Finance** Sources: members' dues. **Activities** Events/meetings; research/documentation. **Events** *World Conference on Science and Technology Education* Pattaya

(Thailand) 2019, *World Conference on Science and Technology Education* Antalya (Turkey) 2016, *World Conference on Science and Technology Education / World Science and Technology Education (STE) Congress* Kuching (Malaysia) 2013, *World conference on science and technology education / World Science and Technology Education (STE) Congress* Tartu (Estonia) 2010, *Regional seminar on the way forward for science and technology education* Penang (Malaysia) 2009. **Publications** *Science Education International* (4 a year); *ICASE Newsletter* (2 a year). Conference declarations; symposia and seminar proceedings. **Members** Science teacher associations, institutions, foundations and companies. Organizations (57) in 28 countries and territories. Membership countries not specified. **Consultative Status** Consultative status granted from: *UNESCO (#20322)* (Consultative Status). **NGO Relations** Also links with ministries and universities worldwide. [2023.02.15/XD4758/y/**B**]

♦ International Council of Authors and Composers of Music / see International Council of Music Authors (#13052)
♦ International Council of Authors of Graphic and Plastic Arts and of Photographers / see International Council of Creators of Graphic, Plastic and Photographic Arts (#13011)

♦ International Council on Badges and Credentials (ICoBC) 12998

Secretariat Leibnizstr 32, 10625 Berlin, Germany. E-mail: info@icobc.net.
URL: https://icobc.net/

History 2020. Registration: EU Transparency Register, No/ID: 494452043164-75, Start date: 15 Jun 2021. **Aims** Promote global exchange, collaboration and development for the recognition of informal, non-formal and formal learning with digital badges (Open Badges) and credentials. **Structure** General Assembly; Board of Directors; Executive Committee. **Languages** English, French, German. **Staff** 15.00 FTE, voluntary. **Activities** Awards/prizes/competitions; awareness raising; certification/accreditation; guidance/assistance/consulting; knowledge management/information dissemination; networking/liaising; politics/policy/regulatory; research and development; standards/guidelines; training/education. **Events** *ICoBC Symposium* Berlin (Germany) 2022, *ICoBC Symposium* Berlin (Germany) 2021. [2022.10.12/XM8900/**C**]

♦ International Council of Ballroom Dancing / see World Dance Council (#21353)

♦ International Council of Beverages Associations (ICBA) 12999

Secretariat 1275 Pennsylvania Avenue NW, Suite 1100, Washington DC 20004, USA. T. +12024636739. Fax +12024638172.
URL: http://www.icba-net.org/

History 1995, as *International Soft Drinks Council (ISDC)*. May 2004, present name adopted. **Aims** Represent the beverage industry on a global level; ensure monitoring of issues which affect the beverage industry on a Codex Alimentarius level; represent the industry's interest relating to packaging, including waste management, recycling, safety and potential limitations. **Structure** Secretariat. **Languages** English. **Events** *Meeting* Orlando, FL (USA) 2010, *Meeting* Rio de Janeiro (Brazil) 2010, *Meeting* Munich (Germany) 2009, *Meeting* Vancouver, BC (Canada) 2009, *Meeting* Gold Coast, QLD (Australia) 2008. **IGO Relations** Participates as observer in the activities of: *Codex Alimentarius Commission (CAC, #04081)*. [2020/XG7435/**E**]

♦ International Council of Biotechnology Associations (unconfirmed)
♦ International Council for Bird Preservation / see BirdLife International (#03266)
♦ International Council for Bird Preservation / see World Working Group on Birds of Prey and Owls (#21945)

♦ International Council of BMW Clubs 13000

Manager Club Organisations Schleissheimer Strasse 416, 80935 Munich, Germany.
Chairman address not obtained.
URL: http://www.bmw-clubs-international.com/

History 1981, Munich (Germany). **Aims** Generate and provide communication media processes and tools, coordinated and customized for the various target groups; steer and manage administration and regulatory organization for club issues worldwide; develop future-orientated structures for the efficient management of the BMW Club organizations worldwide; initiate and mediate a mutual profitable cooperation between the BMW clubs and the BMW AG. **Structure** Umbrella organization for BMW Clubs worldwide. Council (annually). Regional sections (3): Europe; America; Asia-Pacific-Africa. International Section: International BMW Classic and Type clubs Section. **Languages** English. **Staff** 2.00 FTE, paid. **Publications** *Council News* (4 a year) – electronic newsletter. [2010.06.01/XD5186/**E**]

♦ International Council of Botanic Medicine (inactive)

♦ International Council of Bottled Water Associations (ICBWA) 13001

Contact 7357 Woodbine Avenue, Ste 617, Markham ON L3R 6L3, Canada. T. +14166181763. Fax +18663542788. E-mail: info@icbwa.org.
URL: http://www.icbwa.org/

Aims Strengthen and promote the global bottled water industry by: supporting and adhering to rigorous international product quality standards; facilitating learning and providing a flow of information about the bottled water industry, among members, international agencies and stakeholders. **Languages** English.
Members Organizations (7):
Australian Bottled Water Institute; Brazilian Industry Association of Mineral Waters (ABINAM); Canadian Bottled Water Association; China Beverage Industry Association (CBIA); *International Bottled Water Association (IBWA)*; *Latin American Bottled Water Association (LABWA, #16258)*; *Natural Mineral Waters Europe (NMWE, #16955)*.
IGO Relations Observer status with (1): *Codex Alimentarius Commission (CAC, #04081)*.
[2022/XD8917/y/**C**]

♦ International Council for Building Research, Studies and Documentation / see International Council for Research and Innovation in Building and Construction (#13069)
♦ International Council for Canadian Studies (internationally oriented national body)
♦ International Council for Capital Formation (internationally oriented national body)
♦ International Council for Caring Communities (internationally oriented national body)

♦ International Council for Central and East European Studies (ICCEES) 13002

Conseil international d'études de l'Europe centrale et orientale – Internationaler Rat für Mittel- und Osteuropastudien – Mezdunarodnyj Sovet po Izuceniju Srednej i Vostocnoj Evropy

Gen Sec c/o DGO, Schaperstr 30, 10719 Berlin, Germany. T. +493021478412. E-mail: information-centre@iccees.org.
URL: http://www.iccees.org/

History 7 Sep 1974, Banff, AB (Canada). Founded at 1st International Conference on Soviet and East European Studies. Former names and other names: *International Committee for Soviet and East European Studies* – former (1972 to 1988); *Comité international d'études soviétiques et est-européennes* – former (1972 to 1988); *Internationales Komitee für Sowjet- und Osteuropastudien* – former (1972 to 1988); *Mezdunarodnyj Komitet po Izuceniju Sovetskogo Sojuza i Vostocnoj Evropy* – former (1972 to 1988); *International Council for Soviet and East European Studies (ICSEES)* – former (1988 to 1992); *Conseil international d'études soviétiques et est-européennes* – former (1988 to 1992); *Internationaler Rat für Sowjet- und Osteuropastudien* – former (1988 to 1992); *Mezdunarodnyj Sovet po Izuceniju Sovetskogo Sojuza i Vostocnoj Evropy* – former (1988 to 1992). **Aims** Stimulate international exchange of information about central and East European studies; foster international cooperation among scholars specializing in those studies. **Structure** International Council (meets twice in 5 years); Executive Committee (meets annually); International Information Centre. **Languages** English, French, German, Russian. **Finance** Sources: financial support from universities and from Foreign Ministries of Australia, Canada, France, Germany, Japan, Scandinavia, UK and USA. **Activities** Events/meetings; knowledge management/information dissemination; networking/liaising. **Events** *East Asian Conference on Slavic-Eurasian Studies* Shanghai (China) 2022, *World Congress* Berlin (Germany) 2021, *World Congress* Montréal, QC (Canada) 2020, *East Asian Regional Conference on Slavic-Eurasian Studies* Tokyo (Japan) 2019, *East Asian Regional Conference on Slavic-Eurasian Studies* Ulaanbaatar (Mongolia) 2018.
Members Organizations and individuals in 17 countries:
Australia, Austria, Belgium, Canada, Czechia, Finland, France, Germany, Ireland, Italy, Netherlands, New Zealand, Russia, Spain, Sweden, UK, USA.

Included in the above, 18 organizations listed in this Yearbook:
Asociación Española de Eslavistas (no recent information); *Association for Slavic, East European, and Eurasian Studies (ASEEES)*; *Associazione Italiana degli Slavisti (AIS)*; *Australasian Association for Communist and Post-Communist Studies (AACPCS)*; *Australian and New Zealand Slavists' Association (no recent information)*; *Belgian Centre of Slav Studies*; *British Association for Slavonic and East European Studies (BASEES)*; *Canadian Association of Slavists (CAS)*; *Centre for Eastern Studies, Warsaw (OSW)*; *Deutsche Gesellschaft für Osteuropakunde (DGO)*; *Dutch Slavists' Association (DSA, inactive)*; *Irish Association of Russian and East European Studies (IAREES, no recent information)*; *Israeli Association of Slavic and East European Studies (IASEES, no recent information)*; *Korean Association of Slavic-Eurasian Studies (KASEUS)*; *Korean Institute of International Studies (KIIS, no recent information)*; *Slavonic Institute, Warsaw (no recent information)*; *Southeast Europe Association (SOG)*. [2022/XD7710/y/**C**]

♦ International Council of Chemical Associations (ICCA) 13003

Conseil international des associations chimiques – Consejo Internacional de Asociaciones de Fabricantes de Productos Quimicos

Manager c/o CEFIC, Avenue E Van Nieuwenhuyse 4 – box 1, 1160 Brussels, Belgium. T. +3226767415. E-mail: rba@cefic.be.
URL: http://www.icca-chem.org/

History 1989, as a virtual organization. **Aims** Help the global chemical industry improve financial performance and reputation by tackling global issues and by helping the industry to improve continuously its performance. **Structure** Board of Directors; Steering Committee; Global Executive Strategy Group; Extended Secretariat. Groups (4): Communications; Energy and Climate; Chemical Policy and Health; Responsible Care. Trade Policy Network. **Activities** Events/meetings. **Events** *Long Range Research Initiative Workshop* Yokohama (Japan) 2022, *International Conference on Chemicals Management* Bonn (Germany) 2021, *Global Chemical Industry European Convention* Helsinki (Finland) 2019, *Global Chemical Industry European Convention* Rotterdam (Netherlands) 2018, *Global Chemical Industry European Convention* Vienna (Austria) 2017. **Publications** *ICCA newsletter*. *ICCA HPV Working List* (latest ed 1999); *ICCA Briefing Notes on Persistent Organic Pollutants (POPs)*. Technical background sheets in English, French, Spanish, Russian; briefing notes; briefing papers; discussion papers; position papers.
Members Full; Observer. Full in 44 countries:
Argentina, Australia, Austria, Bahrain, Belgium, Brazil, Bulgaria, Canada, Chile, Czechia, Denmark, Estonia, Finland, France, Germany, Greece, Hungary, Ireland, Italy, Japan, Korea Rep, Kuwait, Latvia, Lithuania, Mexico, Netherlands, New Zealand, Norway, Oman, Poland, Portugal, Qatar, Saudi Arabia, Singapore, Slovakia, Slovenia, South Africa, Spain, Sweden, Switzerland, Türkiye, UK, United Arab Emirates, USA.
Observer in 5 countries and territories:
China, Hong Kong, India, Russia, Taiwan.
Consultative Status Consultative status granted from: *ECOSOC (#05331)* (Special); *UNEP (#20299)*. **IGO Relations** Memorandum of Understanding signed with: *World Customs Organization (WCO, #21350)*. **NGO Relations** *Asia Pacific Responsible Care Organization (APRO)*; *Conseil européen de l'industrie chimique (CEFIC, #04687)*; *Conselho da Indústria Química do Mercosul (CIQUIM, no recent information)*; *International Organization for Standardization (ISO, #14473)*. *North American Council of Chemical Associations (no recent information)*. [2013/XD3129/y/**C**]

♦ International Council of Chemical Trade Associations / see International Chemical Trade Association (#12543)

♦ International Council for Children's Play (ICCP) 13004

Conseil international des jeux – Internationaler Rat für Kinderspiel

Pres c/o European Network Childfriendly Cities, St Jozefstraat 8, 2800 Mechelen, Belgium. T. +3215418289.
Vice Pres c/o Common Threads, Wessex House, Upper Market Street, Eastleigh, SO50 9FD, UK. T. +442380629460. E-mail: info@commonthreads.org.uk.
URL: http://www.iccp-play.org/

History Jul 1959, Germany FR. Jul 1959, Ulm (Germany FR), at 1st Conference. Originally referred to in French and German as *Conseil international des jeux et jouets – Internationaler Rat für Kinderspiel und Spielzeug*. **Aims** Encourage research on *toys* and play; promote improvement in the standard of toys; develop public understanding of the value of toys and play in a child's development and education; direct action to safeguard the child's right to play. **Structure** Assembly of delegates (annual). Executive Committee of up to 7 members, including Chairman, Vice-Chairman and Secretary. Expert Committee; Research Committee; Special Committees; National Committees. Permanent Working Groups. **Languages** English, French, German. **Finance** Special appeals. **Activities** Special committees work on: selecting recommended toys; play and toys for handicapped children; playgrounds. Organizes: conferences; exchange of information and research work; bibliographical and documentation work; exhibitions. **Events** *Conference* Madrid (Spain) 2020, *Conference* Vilnius (Lithuania) 2017, *Conference* Tallinn (Estonia) 2012, *Children's play – new goals for the future* Lisbon (Portugal) 2010, *Conference* Brno (Czech Rep) 2007. **Publications** Conference proceedings; publications of national committees.
Members National committees (marked ") and individuals. Members in 29 countries:
Australia, Austria, Belgium, Canada, Colombia, Czechia, Denmark, Estonia, Finland, France (*), Germany (*), Greece (*), Hungary, Ireland, Italy (*), Lithuania, Netherlands (*), New Zealand, Norway, Poland, Portugal, Russia, Serbia, South Africa, Spain, Sweden (*), Switzerland (*), UK, USA. [2018/XC1724/**C**]

♦ International Council of Christian Churches (ICCC) 13005

Conseil international d'Eglises chrétiennes (CIEC) – Internationaler Rat Christlicher Kirchen (IRCK) – Internationale Raad van Christelijke Kerken (IRCK) – Concilio Internacional de Iglesias Cristianas (CIIC) – Concílio Internacional de Igrejas Cristãs (CIIC)

Main Office PO Box 26281, Charlotte NC 28221-6281, USA. E-mail: iccc@bellsouth.net.
URL: https://iccc-churches.org/

History 1 Aug 1948, Amsterdam (Netherlands). **Aims** Promote a world-wide witness "for the Word of God, and for the testimony of Jesus Christ" (Revelation 1:9). **Structure** Plenary Congress (meets at least once every 5 years; Executive Committee. Regional councils; national councils worldwide. **Events** *World Congress* Collingswood, NJ (USA) 2023, *World Congress* Puerto Montt (Chile) 2020, * *World Congress* Coatzacoalcos (Mexico) 2017, *World Congress – Part 1* Manila (Philippines) 2010, *World Congress – Part II* São Paulo (Brazil) 2010. **Publications** *Biblical Missions* (12 a year) in English; *Far Eastern Beacon* (12 a year) in English; *Philippine Christian Beacon* (12 a year) in English; *The Morning Star* (12 a year) in English, Swahili; *O Fundamentalista* (4 a year) in Portuguese; *Redeeming th Time* (4 a year); *Guatemala Faro Cristiano* in Spanish.
Members Associations and churches in all of the inhabited continents. [2022.12.01/XB1737/**B**]

♦ International Council of Christian Churches, European Alliance (inactive)

♦ International Council of Christians and Jews (ICCJ) 13006

Amitié internationale judéo-chrétienne – Internationaler Rat der Christen und Juden – Consejo Internacional de Cristianos y Judios

Gen Sec c/o Martin Buber House, PO Box 11 29, 64629 Heppenheim, Germany. T. +4962526896810. Fax +49625268331. E-mail: office@iccj.org.
URL: http://www.iccj.org/

History Founded 8 May 1955, Saarbrücken (Germany FR), as a 'Liaison Centre', the first international conference of Jews and Christians having been held in 1946, Oxford (UK). Name changed to *Liaison Committee of Secretaries of Organizations for Christian-Jewish Cooperation – Comité de liaison des secrétaires des groupes d'amitié judéo-chrétiennes*, 23 Jan 1958, Paris (France). Subsequently, 9 Dec 1960, London (UK), name changed to *International Consultative Committee of Organizations for Christian – Jewish Cooperation – Comité de liaison international des groupes d'amitié judéo-chrétienne*. Present name adopted 1974. Sometimes referred to in Spanish as *Consejo Internacional de los Grupos de Amistad Judeocristianos*. **Aims** Promote mutual respect and cooperation between Christians and Jews; bring them a clearer perception of their unique historical and religious ties; combat discrimination and prejudice in their mutual relations and in those with others; bring religious and moral principles which form the basis of Jewish and Christian traditions to bear upon problems of interfaith, inter-racial and international relations. **Structure** General Meeting (annual); Council; Executive Board; Committees (3); Councils (4); Secretariat; Advisory Panel. **Languages** English, French, German. **Staff** 1.50 FTE, paid. **Finance** Sources: donations; grants; members' dues. Other sources: subsidies from governments and religious bodies. **Activities** Awards/prizes/competitions; events/meetings. **Events** *International Conference* Heppenheim (Germany) 2022, *International Conference* Budapest (Hungary) 2018, *International Conference* Bonn (Germany) 2017, *International Conference* Philadelphia, PA (USA) 2016, *International Conference* Rome (Italy) 2015. **Publications** *From the Martin Buber House*; *ICCJ Nachrichten*; *ICCJ News*. Information Services: Maintains a documentation centre and library on Christian-Jewish relations.

Members National Councils of Christians and Jews or similar bodies in 34 countries:
Argentina, Australia, Austria, Belarus, Belgium, Brazil, Canada, Chile, Colombia, Costa Rica, Czechia, France, Germany, Hungary, Ireland, Israel, Italy, Latvia, Luxembourg, Netherlands, New Zealand, Norway, Peru, Poland, Russia, Slovakia, Spain, Sweden, Switzerland, UK, Ukraine, Uruguay, USA, Venezuela. [2018/XC1702/**C**]

♦ International Council for Classical Homeopathy (inactive)

♦ International Council on Clean Transportation (ICCT) 13007

Exec Dir 1500 K Street NW, Suite 650, Washington DC 20005, USA. T. +12027983986.
Office – Europe Neue Promenade 6, 10178 Berlin, Germany. T. +4930847129102. E-mail: berlin@theicct.org.
URL: http://www.theicct.org/

History 2001. Former names and other names: *International Council on Clean Transportation Europe* – legal name. Registration: EU Transparency Register, No/ID: 06250094777-73, Start date: 14 Dec 2010; Germany, Berlin-Charlottenburg. **Aims** Provide unbiased research and technical and scientific analysis to environmental regulators. **Structure** Participants Council. Board of Directors. Offices in: Brazil; China; Germany; USA (2). **Finance** Sources: international organizations. Supported by: ; *ClimateWorks Foundation (#04024)* (principal funding); *The William and Flora Hewlett Foundation*. **Activities** Projects/programmes. **Events** *Workshop on Marine Black Carbon Emissions* Finland 2019, *Seminar on air pollution and greenhouse gas emission from maritime transport* Brussels (Belgium) 2007. **Consultative Status** Consultative status granted from: *ECOSOC (#05331)* (Special). **IGO Relations** Accredited by: *Green Climate Fund (GCF, #10714)*. **NGO Relations** Member of: *Climate and Clean Air Coalition (CCAC, #04010)*. Partner in: *1% for the Planet*; *ClimateWorks Foundation (#04024)*; *Global Fuel Economy Initiative (GFEI, #10381)*. [2020/XM3740/**C**]

♦ International Council on Clean Transportation Europe / see International Council on Clean Transportation (#13007)
♦ International Council for Coach Education / see International Council for Coaching Excellence (#13008)

♦ International Council for Coaching Excellence (ICCE) 13008

Technical Project Officer ICCE Global Coaching Office, Leeds Beckett Univ, 106 Cavendish Hall, Headingley Campus, Leeds, LS6 3QS, UK. T. +441138123251 – +44113(447780493008.
Pres address not obtained.
URL: http://www.icce.ws/

History Founded 24 Sep 1997, Netanya (Israel), during second International Coach Education Summit. Original title: *International Council for Coach Education (ICCE)*. **Aims** Lead and develop sport coaching globally. **Structure** General Assembly; Executive Board. Committees. **Languages** English. **Staff** Voluntary. **Finance** Members' dues. **Activities** Events/meetings. **Events** *Global Coach Conference* Lisbon (Portugal) 2021, *Global Coach Conference* Tokyo (Japan) 2019, *Global Coach Conference* Liverpool (UK) 2017, *Global Coach Conference* Vierumäki (Finland) 2015, *Global Coach Conference* Durban (South Africa) 2013. **Publications** *International Sport Coaching Journal*.

Members National representative bodies responsible for coach development; international federations; institutions that deliver coach education or represent coaches; individuals who design and deliver coach education; coaches; international sport community at large. National representative bodies in 30 countries and territories:
Australia, Belgium, Canada, China, Denmark, Finland, France, Germany, Hong Kong, India, Ireland, Israel, Italy, Japan, Malaysia, Netherlands, New Zealand, Norway, Papua New Guinea, Portugal, Romania, Saudi Arabia, Singapore, South Africa, Spain, Sweden, Switzerland, Türkiye, UK, USA.
International federations (15):
Badminton World Federation (BWF, #03060); *European Weightlifting Federation (EWF, #09090)*; *Fédération Équestre Internationale (FEI, #09484)*; *Fédération internationale d'escrime (FIE, #09629)*; *International Fitness and Bodybuilding Federation (IFBB, #13610)*; *International Hockey Federation (#13802)*; *International Ice Hockey Federation (IIHF, #13831)*; *International Mixed Martial Arts Federation (IMMAF, #14173)*; *International Table Tennis Federation (ITTF, #15650)*; *International Tennis Federation (ITF, #15676)*; *Special Olympics International (SOI, #19910)*; *Union Cycliste Internationale (UCI, #20375)*; *World Rugby (#21757)*; *World Sailing (#21760)*; *World Triathlon (#21872)*.
Organizations in 33 countries:
Australia, Austria, Bulgaria, Canada, China, Colombia, Czechia, Estonia, Finland, Greece, Hungary, India, Ireland, Israel, Italy, Japan, Korea Rep, Lithuania, Netherlands, New Zealand, Norway, Poland, Portugal, Romania, Singapore, Slovakia, South Africa, Spain, Sweden, Switzerland, UK, USA, Zimbabwe.
Included in the above, 1 organization listed in this Yearbook:
European Athletics Coaches Association (EACA, #06292).

NGO Relations Member of: *European Network of Sport Education (ENSE, #08012)*; *International Council of Sport Science and Physical Education (ICSSPE, #13077)*. [2020/XE4717/**E**]

♦ International Council of Coloproctology (ICCP) 13009

Chairman Ste 17, Level 7, Prince of Wales Private Hosp, Barker Street, Randwick NSW 2031, Australia. T. +61296504222. Fax +61296505494.
URL: https://www.fascrs.org/international-council-coloproctology/

History Founded 1990, Hamilton Is (Australia), as *World Federation of Coloproctology*. Subsequently changed title to *World Council of Coloproctology (WCCP)*. **Aims** Facilitate training programmes, dissemination of information, development of national societies and communication between national societies of colorectal surgery and colorectal surgeons; arrange outreach programmes for training and education in colorectal surgery; promote bowel cancer screening programmes. **Structure** Council; Executive. Regional federations (3); *Asia Pacific Federation of Coloproctology (APFCP, #01897)*; *European Society of Coloproctology (ESCP, #08556)*; *Latin American Association of Coloproctology (ALACP, #16237)*. **Languages** English. **Staff** 0.50 FTE, paid. Voluntary. **Finance** Subscriptions by supporting national societies. **Activities** Awards/prizes/competitions; events/meetings; knowledge management/information dissemination; training/education. **Events** *Annual Meeting* Boston, MA (USA) 2015, *Annual Meeting* Vancouver, BC (Canada) 2011, *Annual Meeting* Minneapolis, MN (USA) 2010, *Annual meeting* Hollywood, FL (USA) 2009, *Annual meeting* Boston, MA (USA) 2008. **Publications** *Diseases of Colon and Rectum* (12 a year).

Members Executives of international colorectal surgical societies in 57 countries and territories:
Argentina, Australia, Austria, Bangladesh, Belarus, Belgium, Bolivia, Brazil, Canada, Chile, China, Colombia, Croatia, Czechia, Denmark, Egypt, France, Germany, Guatemala, Hong Kong, Hungary, Iceland, India, Iran Islamic Rep, Ireland, Israel, Italy, Japan, Korea Rep, Latvia, Lithuania, Malaysia, Mexico, Mongolia, Montenegro, Netherlands, New Zealand, Norway, Peru, Philippines, Poland, Romania, Russia, Saudi Arabia, Serbia, Singapore, South Africa, Spain, Sweden, Switzerland, Taiwan, Thailand, Türkiye, UK, Uruguay, USA, Venezuela. [2018.06.01/XD3546/**C**]

♦ International Council on Combustion Engines (#04693)
♦ International Council of Commerce Employers (inactive)

♦ International Council for Commercial Arbitration (ICCA) 13010

Conseil international pour l'arbitrage commercial

Address not obtained.
URL: http://www.arbitration-icca.org/

History Founded 1972, as *International Committee for Commercial Arbitration*. Current name adopted 1975. **Aims** Promote the use and improve the processes of arbitration, conciliation and other forms of international dispute resolution worldwide. **Structure** Governing Board; Advisory Members. **Languages** English. **Activities** Events/meetings; publishing activities; standards/guidelines. **Events** *Congress* Edinburgh (UK) 2022, *Congress* Edinburgh (UK) 2020, *Biennial Congress* Sydney, NSW (Australia) 2018, *Biennial Congress* Mauritius 2016, *Biennial Congress / Congress* Miami, FL (USA) 2014. **Publications** *Guide to the Interpretation of the 1958 New York Convention* – in 13 languages; *International Handbook on Commercial Arbitration*; *Yearbook Commercial Arbitration*. *Congress Series*; *The ICCA Reports Series*. **Members** Over 950 in 67 countries. Membership countries not specified. **Consultative Status** Consultative status granted from: *ECOSOC (#05331)* (Ros A). [2020/XD8486/**D**]

♦ International Council for Commonality in Blood Banking Automation / see ICCBBA (#11042)
♦ International Council of Communication Design / see International Council of Design (#13013)
♦ International Council of Community Churches (internationally oriented national body)
♦ International Council of Composers (inactive)
♦ International Council for Control of Iodine Deficiency Disorders / see Iodine Global Network (#16004)
♦ International Council for Correspondence Education / see International Council for Open and Distance Education (#13056)

♦ International Council of Creators of Graphic, Plastic and Photographic Arts 13011

Conseil International des Créateurs des Arts Graphiques, Plastiques et Photographiques (CGIAP) – Consejo Internacional de Creadores de Artes Graficas, Plasticas y Fotograficas

Secretariat c/o CISAC, 20-26 boulevard du Parc, 92200 Neuilly-sur-Seine, France. T. +33155620850. Fax +33155620860. E-mail: cisac@cisac.org.
URL: http://www.ciagp.org/

History Set up as an International Council of *Confédération internationale des sociétés d'auteurs et compositeurs (CISAC, #04563)*. Original title: *International Council of Authors of Graphic and Plastic Arts and of Photographers – Conseil international des auteurs des arts graphiques et plastiques et des photographes (CGIAP)*. **Aims** Bring together creators in the field of visual and plastic arts from around the world. **Structure** Executive Committee. **Activities** Events/meetings. **Events** *Meeting* Tokyo (Japan) 2008, *Meeting* Tokyo (Japan) 2008, *Meeting* Lisbon (Portugal) 2007, *Meeting* Mexico City (Mexico) 2005, *Assembly* Madrid (Spain) 1995. [2018/XD5647/**E**]

♦ International Council of Customer Service Organisations (unconfirmed)

♦ International Council for the Day of VESAK (ICDV) 13012

Assistant SG 401 – Zone D, D400 4th Floor, School Bldg, Mahachulalongkornrajavidyalaya Univ Lamsai, Wang Noi, Ayutthaya, Phra Nakhon Si Ayutthaya, 17130, Thailand. T. +6635248098. Fax +6635248099. E-mail: vesak.undv@gmail.com.
URL: http://www.icdv.net/

History Former names and other names: *International Council of United Days of Vesak (INUNDV)* – former. **Aims** Obtain international recognition of the Day of Vesak – Buddha's birthday. **Structure** Council; Office. **Activities** Events/meetings. **Events** *International Buddhist Conference of the United Nations Day of Vesak* Bangkok (Thailand) / Ayutthaya (Thailand) 2015, *International Buddhist conference of the United Nations day of Vesak* Bangkok (Thailand) 2010. **Consultative Status** Consultative status granted from: *ECOSOC (#05331)* (Special). [2016/XJ2793/**E**]

♦ International Council of Design (ICoD) 13013

Conseil international du design

Dir-Gen CP 519 Succ Place d'Armes, Montréal QC H2Y 3H3, Canada. T. +15148757545. E-mail: info@theicod.org – director@theicod.org.
URL: http://www.theicod.org/

History 27 Apr 1963, London (UK). Former names and other names: *International Council of Graphic Design Associations (Icograda)* – former (1963); *Conseil international des associations de design graphique* – former (1963); *Conseil international d'associations graphiques* – former; *Internationaler Rat Grafischer Vereinigungen* – former; *International Council of Communication Design* – former (2011). **Aims** Represent interests of professional designers; define and increase awareness of professional standards and best practices governing design practice; advocate for design as an effective way of advancing best interest of humanity and the environment; foster recognition and respect of design as a valued and vital profession; facilitate knowledge management; cooperation among organizations of designers and allied institutions; support development of design education. **Structure** General Assembly (every 2 years); Executive Board; Secretariat. **Languages** English. **Staff** 6.00 FTE, paid. Voluntary assistance on all projects. **Finance** Sources: contributions; grants; members' dues; private foundations. **Activities** Advocacy/lobbying/activism; events/meetings; networking/liaising; standards/guidelines. **Events** *General Assembly* Kaunas (Lithuania) 2022, *Europe Regional Meeting* Matosinhos (Portugal) 2019, *Meeting* Saint-Étienne (France) 2019, *General Assembly* Vancouver, BC (Canada) 2019, *ASEAN Regional Meeting* Kuala Lumpur (Malaysia) 2018. **Publications** *Worldwide Identity* (2005); *Masters of the 20th Century* (2001); *Graphic Design-World Views – 25 years* (1989). *Professional Code of Conduct for designers* (2019) in English – Presented by the International Council of Design as an international standard and reference. It is an aspirational document, intended to serve as a touchstone for professional associations crafting their own Codes, and to support educational institutions developing curricula. It is a tool for any designer who seeks to adhere to international standards.; *Communication Design* (2015-2017) in English – Communication Design is an international, peer-reviewed publication which aims to develop and critically examine the emerging discourses in research related to contemporary communication and graphic design practice, education and methods as well as their history, theory and criticism. It features theoretical, historical and applied research in communication design, exploring both analogue and digital forms. Areas of emphasis include: craft and critical practice, pedagogy and curriculum development, typography and image-making, book arts and publishing, information visualisation and digital spaces, sustainability and social design, politics and popular culture.; *Iridescent* (2009-2014) in English – ridescent (Icograda Journal of Design Research Volume 1, 2009-2011), the second iteration of the Councils design research journal, Icographic, was about breaking boundaries and was coined the "prism on design research". Considered a new a global take on the future of design, Iridescent was born out of the Council's strategic aim to develop communication design education by merging the interdisciplinary facets of theory, practice and research.; *Icographic* (1971-1978) in English – Icographic was a magazine on visual communication founded by John Halas in 1971 and designed and edited by Patrick Wallis Burke.. Competition regulations/guidelines; bibliographies.

Members Organizations in 50 countries and territories:
Argentina, Australia, Austria, Canada, Chile, China, Colombia, Croatia, Cuba, Cyprus, Czechia, El Salvador, Finland, Germany, Ghana, Hong Kong, Hungary, India, Indonesia, Iran Islamic Rep, Israel, Italy, Japan, Jordan, Korea Rep, Kuwait, Laos, Lebanon, Lithuania, Malaysia, Mexico, New Zealand, North Macedonia, Norway, Peru, Russia, Saudi Arabia, Singapore, Slovenia, South Africa, Spain, Sweden, Switzerland, Taiwan, Türkiye, UK, Ukraine, United Arab Emirates, USA, Zimbabwe.

Consultative Status Consultative status granted from: *ECOSOC (#05331)* (Ros C); *UNIDO (#20336)*; *World Intellectual Property Organization (WIPO, #21593)* (Permanent Observer Status). **IGO Relations** *European Union Intellectual Property Office (EUIPO, #08996)*; *UNESCO (#20322)*. **NGO Relations** International affiliates: *Alliance graphique internationale (AGI, #00684)*; *Association typographique internationale (ATypI, #02965)*; *Bureau of European Design Associations (BEDA, #03359)*; Design Management Institute (DMI); *European Brand and Packaging Design Association (epda, #06396)*; *The Global Association of Art and Design Education and Research (Cumulus Association, #10241)*; *International Federation of Interior Architects / Designers (IFI, #13460)*; *International Federation of Reproduction Rights Organizations (IFRRO, #13527)*; *International Institute for Information Design (IIID)*; *International Society of Typographic Designers (ISTD)*; Women Designers' Forum (WDF); *World Design Organization (WDO, #21358)*. In liaison with technical committees of: *International Organization for Standardization (ISO, #14473)*. [2022.06.14/XC1742/y/**C**]

♦ International Council on Disability (inactive)
♦ International Council for Distance Education / see International Council for Open and Distance Education (#13056)
♦ International Council for Economic and Social Cooperation (inactive)
♦ International Council for Educational Development (inactive)
♦ International Council for Educational Films / see International Council for Educational Media (#13014)

♦ International Council for Educational Media (ICEM) 13014

Conseil international des médias éducatifs (CIME) – Internationale Arbeitsgemeinschaft für Unterrichtsmedien – Consejo Internacional de Medios Educativos

SG Johann Scheidergasse 9, 2201 Gerasdorf bei Wien, Austria. E-mail: info@icem.education.
URL: http://www.icem.education/

History May 1950, Bern (Switzerland), at 2nd International Documentary and Educational Film Congress, as *International Council for Educational Films – Conseil international du film d'enseignement*, continuing activities of *International League for Educational Films – Ligue internationale du film d'enseignement*. Also known as *International Committee for the Advancement of Audio-Visual Media in Education*; *Conseil international des moyens d'enseignement*; *Conseil international des moyens du film d'enseignement*. Statutes adopted 1954; most recently amended 2000. Registered in accordance with Swiss law. **Aims** Provide a channel for exchange and evaluation of information, experience and materials in the field of educational media as they apply to pre-school, primary education, secondary education, technical, vocational, industrial and commercial training, continuing education and and distance education; foster international liaison among individuals and organizations with professional responsibility in the field of educational media; inform manufacturers and producers on needs of education; provide information and consultancy; cooperate in development and application of educational technology with other international organizations involved in research, production, distribution and use; play a leading role in identifying and exploring ongoing and future issues with respect to the role and potential of media in education. **Structure** General Assembly (at least once a year). Executive Committee, composed of President and 4 members. Working Groups. Secretariat. **Languages** English, French. **Staff** 0.50 FTE, paid. **Finance** Members' dues. Sales of publications. **Activities** Co-productions; 'International Media Week'; Study Programmes (in cooperation with UNESCO); consultancy and assistance to underdeveloped countries. **Events** *Conference* Santarém (Portugal) 2021, *Conference* Santarém (Portugal) 2020, *Conference* Memphis, TN (USA) 2019, *Annual Conference* Tallinn (Estonia) 2018, *Annual Conference* Naples (Italy) 2017. **Publications** *Educational Media Internation (EMI)* (4 a year) – journal.

Members Individuals or organizations with a concern for educational technology. Members in 36 countries and territories:

Andorra, Australia, Austria, Belgium, Bulgaria, Canada, China, Cyprus, Czechia, Denmark, Finland, France, Germany, Hong Kong, Hungary, Iceland, Ireland, Israel, Japan, Korea Rep, Luxembourg, Mexico, New Zealand, Norway, Poland, Portugal, Russia, Slovenia, South Africa, Spain, Sweden, Switzerland, Türkiye, UK, United Arab Emirates, USA.

Consultative Status Consultative status granted from: *ILO (#11123)* (Special List). **IGO Relations** Informal links with: *UNESCO (#20322)*. [2020/XD1726/**D**]

♦ International Council for the Education of Exceptional Children / see Council for Exceptional Children

♦ International Council for Education of People with Visual Impairment (ICEVI) 13015

Conseil international pour l'éducation des handicapés de la vue (CIEHV)

Secretariat 3 Professors' Colony, Palamalai Road, SRKV Post, Coimbatore, Tamil Nadu 641 020, Coimbatore TAMIL NADU 641 020, India. T. +914222469104. Fax +914222693414. E-mail: ceo201922@gmail.com.

URL: http://www.icevi.org/

History Founded 1952, Bussum (Netherlands), by 3 national organizations, as *International Conference of Educators of Blind Youth (ICEBY)*, when statutes were adopted. Most recent constitution: Aug 1987, Würzburg (Germany FR). Has been referred to in English as *International Council for Education of the Visually Handicapped (ICEVH)*. Most recent amendment to constitution: Dec 2010, London (UK). **Aims** Ensure access and full participation in education for all children and young people with visual impairment by 2015; promote and assist in building of local capacity to develop *curricula*; provide training and identify and provide equipment and materials for children and young people with visual impairments and for their parents, teachers and others in their communities; collaborate with and make use of networks to ensure that substantially more children and young people with visual impairment receive quality and comprehensive education; disseminate information. **Structure** Council (meets every 4 years at Conference); International Consultative Committee (ICC); Executive Committee. Regional Committees (7): Africa; East Asia; West Asia; Europe; Latin America; North America/Caribbean; Pacific. Secretariat. **Languages** English. **Staff** 6.00 FTE, paid. Voluntary. **Finance** Contributions of international member organizations and others. **Activities** Advocacy/lobbying/activism; events/meetings; training/education. **Events** *Joint General Assembly* Madrid (Spain) 2021, *Joint General Assembly* Madrid (Spain) 2020, *European Conference* Bruges (Belgium) 2017, *European Conference* Istanbul (Turkey) 2013, *Joint General Assembly* Bangkok (Thailand) 2012. **Publications** *The Educator* (2 a year) in English, Japanese, Spanish – also in braille; *ICEVI E-News*.

Members National delegates (with representation depending on total population of country) from 193 countries and territories:

Afghanistan, Albania, Algeria, Andorra, Angola, Antigua-Barbuda, Argentina, Armenia, Australia, Austria, Azerbaijan, Bahamas, Bahrain, Bangladesh, Barbados, Belarus, Belgium, Belize, Benin, Bhutan, Bolivia, Bosnia-Herzegovina, Botswana, Brazil, Brunei Darussalam, Bulgaria, Burkina Faso, Burundi, Cambodia, Cameroon, Canada, Cape Verde, Central African Rep, Chad, Chile, China, Colombia, Comoros, Congo Brazzaville, Cook Is, Costa Rica, Côte d'Ivoire, Croatia, Cuba, Cyprus, Czechia, Denmark, Djibouti, Dominica, Dominican Rep, Ecuador, Egypt, El Salvador, Equatorial Guinea, Eritrea, Estonia, Eswatini, Ethiopia, Fiji, Finland, France, Gabon, Gambia, Georgia, Germany, Ghana, Greece, Grenada, Guatemala, Guinea, Guinea-Bissau, Guyana, Haiti, Honduras, Hong Kong, Hungary, Iceland, India, Indonesia, Iran Islamic Rep, Iraq, Ireland, Israel, Italy, Jamaica, Japan, Jordan, Kazakhstan, Kenya, Kiribati, Korea DPR, Korea Rep, Kuwait, Kyrgyzstan, Laos, Latvia, Lebanon, Lesotho, Liberia, Libya, Liechtenstein, Lithuania, Luxembourg, Macau, Madagascar, Malawi, Malaysia, Maldives, Mali, Malta, Marshall Is, Mauritania, Mauritius, Mexico, Micronesia FS, Moldova, Monaco, Mongolia, Morocco, Mozambique, Myanmar, Namibia, Nauru, Nepal, Netherlands, New Zealand, Nicaragua, Niger, Nigeria, North Macedonia, Norway, Oman, Pakistan, Palau, Palestine, Panama, Papua New Guinea, Paraguay, Peru, Philippines, Poland, Portugal, Qatar, Romania, Russia, Rwanda, Samoa, San Marino, Sao Tomé-Principe, Saudi Arabia, Senegal, Serbia, Seychelles, Sierra Leone, Singapore, Slovakia, Slovenia, Solomon Is, Somalia, South Africa, Spain, Sri Lanka, St Kitts-Nevis, St Lucia, St Vincent-Grenadines, Sudan, Sweden, Switzerland, Syrian AR, Taiwan, Tajikistan, Tanzania UR, Thailand, Timor-Leste, Togo, Tonga, Trinidad-Tobago, Tunisia, Türkiye, Turkmenistan, Tuvalu, Uganda, UK, Ukraine, United Arab Emirates, Uruguay, USA, Uzbekistan, Venezuela, Vietnam, Yemen, Zambia, Zimbabwe.

Founding organizations (3) in 2 countries:

UK, USA.

International organizations include 8 organizations:

Christian Blind Mission (CBM); *Light for the World (#16474)*; Norwegian Association of the Blind and Partially Sighted; ONCE; Perkins School for the Blind; RNIB; Royal Dutch Vision; *Sightsavers International (#19270)*.

Consultative Status Consultative status granted from: *ECOSOC (#05331)* (Special); *UNESCO (#20322)* (Consultative Status); *UNICEF (#20332)*. **NGO Relations** Member of: *Blind Children's Fund (BCF, #03280)*; *Deafblind International (DbI, #05014)*; *European Blind Union (EBU, #06350)*; *International Agency for the Prevention of Blindness (IAPB, #11597)*; *NGO Committee on UNICEF (#17120)*; *Vision Alliance (#20796)*; *World Blind Union (WBU, #21234)*. European region is member of: *European Coalition for Vision (ECV)*. Cooperates with: *Global Partnership on Children with Disabilities (GPcwd, #10529)*. [2018/XD5392/y/**B**]

♦ International Council on Education for Teaching (ICET) 13016

Conseil international de la préparation à l'enseignement (CIPE) – Consejo Internacional de Educación para la Enseñanza (CIEE)

Pres Texas A &M, PH303, 5201 University Blvd, Laredo TX 78042, USA. T. +19563262420. Fax +18473262419. E-mail: contact@icet4u.org.

URL: http://icet4u.org/

History 1953, Oxford (UK). Founded during a conference held by *World Confederation of Organizations of the Teaching Profession (WCOTP, inactive)*. Constitution revised 1958 and 1968. Current constitution adopted 1973. Permanent secretariat created 22 Jul 1968. **Aims** Improve educational experiences and outcomes of learners in all parts of the world by providing opportunities for those involved in their education to share knowledge, practice, resources and expertise, establish active partnerships that are designed to enhance the quality of teaching and learning and improve life opportunities for young people. **Structure** Board of Directors; Executive Committee; Permanent Secretariat, headed by President. **Languages** English. **Staff** 1.00 FTE, voluntary. **Finance** Sources: members' dues. Other sources: grants; endowments; contracts. **Activities** Events/meetings; knowledge management/information dissemination; networking/liaising; training/education. **Events** *World Assembly* Bath (UK) 2022, *World Assembly* Bath (UK) 2021, *World Assembly* Bath (UK) 2020, *World Assembly* Johannesburg (South Africa) 2019, *World Assembly* Laredo, TX (USA) 2018. **Publications** *ICET Newsletter*. Proceedings of World Assemblies and regional conferences; research studies; surveys.

Members Educational Organizations and Institutions; Individuals. Members in 98 countries and territories:

Argentina, Australia, Austria, Bahamas, Bahrain, Bangladesh, Barbados, Belgium, Belize, Benin, Bolivia, Botswana, Brazil, Brunei Darussalam, Bulgaria, Cameroon, Canada, Chile, China, Colombia, Costa Rica, Côte d'Ivoire, Czechia, Denmark, Ecuador, Egypt, Eswatini, Ethiopia, Fiji, France, Germany, Ghana, Greece, Guyana, Haiti, Hong Kong, Hungary, Iceland, India, Indonesia, Iraq, Ireland, Israel, Italy, Jamaica, Japan, Jordan, Kenya, Korea Rep, Kuwait, Lebanon, Lesotho, Liberia, Libya, Malawi, Malaysia, Maldives, Malta, Mexico, Namibia, Nepal, Netherlands, New Zealand, Nigeria, Norway, Oman, Pakistan, Papua New Guinea, Paraguay, Peru, Philippines, Portugal, Puerto Rico, Qatar, Samoa, Saudi Arabia, Senegal, Seychelles, Sierra Leone, Singapore, Somalia, South Africa, Spain, Sweden, Switzerland, Taiwan, Tanzania UR, Thailand, Tonga, Trinidad-Tobago, Türkiye, Uganda, UK, United Arab Emirates, USA, Venezuela, Yemen, Zimbabwe.

Consultative Status Consultative status granted from: *ECOSOC (#05331)* (Ros C); *UNESCO (#20322)* (Consultative Status). **IGO Relations** Cooperates with: *OAS (#17629)*. Accredited by: *United Nations Office at Vienna (UNOV, #20604)*. Associated with Department of Global Communications of the United Nations. **NGO Relations** Member of: *Alliance for International Exchange*. [2021/XB3906/**B**]

♦ International Council for Education of the Visually Handicapped / see International Council for Education of People with Visual Impairment (#13015)

♦ International Council on Electrocardiology / see International Society of Electrocardiology (#15078)

♦ International Council of Electrophoresis Societies (no recent information)

♦ International Council for Elementary and Secondary School Philosophy / see International Council for Philosophical Inquiry with Children (#13060)

♦ International Council of Employers of Bricklayers and Allied Craftsmen / see International Council of Employers of Bricklayers and Allied Craftworkers

♦ International Council of Employers of Bricklayers and Allied Craftworkers (internationally oriented national body)

♦ International Council on Environmental Economics and Development (ICEED) 13017

Address not obtained.

URL: https://i-ceed.org/

Aims Improve the economic, environmental and social conditions of developed and developing countries through mitigating climate change and by developing a new model of economic growth that simultaneously targets economic performance and environmental sustainability, ultimately supporting a global paradigm shift towards a sustainable regenerative economy. **Structure** Board; Executive Committee; Advisory Council. **IGO Relations** Accredited by (2): *UNEP (#20299)* (Governing Body); *United Nations (UN, #20515)*. **NGO Relations** Partner of (1): *Stop Ecocide International (SEI, #19998)*. [2021/AA2673/**C**]

♦ International Council of Environmental Law (ICEL) 13018

Conseil international du droit de l'environnement (CIDE) – Consejo Internacional sobre el Derecho del Medio Ambiente – Internationaler Rat für Umweltrecht

Secretariat Inst P Madoz Del Territorio Urbanizmo y Medioambiente, Universidad Carlos III de Madrid, Campus de Getafe, Calle Madrid 126, 28903 Madrid, Spain.

History 26 Nov 1969, Delhi (India). 26-27 Nov 1969, Delhi (India). Full title: *International Council of Environmental Law – towards sustainable development (ICEL)*. Legal seat in Geneva (Switzerland). Registered in accordance with Swiss law. **Aims** Facilitate professional contact between members, foster the exchange and dissemination of information on the *legal* and policy aspects of environmental *conservation* and cooperate with organizations active in those fields; promote the implementation of sustainable development. **Structure** Council, consisting of elected members and Board of Governors, composed of 19 elected Regional and International Governors. 2 Executive Governors elected for 3 years by Board of Governors. Representatives to the United Nations in New York NY (USA), *United Nations Office at Vienna (UNOV, #20604)* (Austria), Geneva (Switzerland), Nairobi (Kenya) and Beirut (Lebanon). **Languages** English, French, German. **Staff** 2.00 FTE, paid. Voluntary. **Finance** Source: Elizabeth Haub Foundations; Germany, Canada and USA. **Activities** Awards/prizes/competitions. **Publications** *Environmental Policy and Law* (6 a year) – in collaboration with IOS Press. *ICEL Directory*; *International Protection of the Environment and Conservation in Sustainable Development* – loose-leaf service. *Multilateral Treaties* – loose-leaf service.

Members (a) Members (i) Individual; (ii) Corporate. (b) Affiliated Parties public agencies, national and international governmental organizations, which are unable to serve as corporate members. Individuals in 77 countries and territories:

Algeria, Argentina, Armenia, Australia, Austria, Bahrain, Belgium, Brazil, Bulgaria, Cambodia, Cameroon, Canada, Chile, China, Colombia, Croatia, Czechia, Denmark, Egypt, Ethiopia, Finland, France, Georgia, Germany, Ghana, Greece, Guatemala, Hungary, Iceland, India, Indonesia, Iran Islamic Rep, Ireland, Israel, Italy, Japan, Kenya, Korea Rep, Kuwait, Lebanon, Liechtenstein, Mauritius, Mexico, Morocco, Nepal, Netherlands, New Zealand, Nigeria, Norway, Pakistan, Paraguay, Peru, Philippines, Poland, Portugal, Romania, Russia, Samoa, Senegal, Serbia, Seychelles, Singapore, Slovakia, Slovenia, South Africa, Spain, Sweden, Switzerland, Taiwan, Tanzania UR, Thailand, Tunisia, Türkiye, UK, Ukraine, USA, Zambia.

Corporate in 16 countries:

Algeria, Belgium, Canada, Colombia, France, Germany, India, Israel, Italy, Morocco, Peru, Portugal, Spain, Uganda, UK, USA.

Included in the above 5 international organizations listed in this Yearbook:

European Council on Environmental Law (CEDE, no recent information); *Inter-American Commission for Environmental Law and Administration (no recent information)*; *International Association for Water Law (#12263)*; *International Bar Association (IBA, #12320)*; *International Centre of Comparative Environmental Law (#12483)*.

Consultative Status Consultative status granted from: *ECOSOC (#05331)* (General); *UNCTAD (#20285)* (General Category); *UNEP (#20299)*. **IGO Relations** Accredited by: *United Nations Framework Convention on Climate Change – Secretariat (UNFCCC, #20564)*. Entitled to submit collective complaints to: *European Court of Human Rights (#06855)*. Associated with Department of Global Communications of the United Nations. **NGO Relations** Member of: *GEF CSO Network (GCN, #10087)*; *International Union for Conservation of Nature and Natural Resources (IUCN, #15766)*. [2019/XB4097/y/**B**]

♦ International Council of Environmental Law – towards sustainable development / see International Council of Environmental Law (#13018)

♦ International Council of Ethologists (ICE) 13019

Conseil international des éthologie

SG Univ of Zurich, Dept of Evolbiol, Winterthurerstrasse 190, 8057 Zurich ZH, Switzerland.

Sec Biology Dept, NTNU, 7491 Trondheim, Norway.

URL: http://www.ethologycouncil.org/

History 1949, as (biennial) *International Ethological Conference*. Present name adopted 1989. **Aims** Promote the scientific study of *animal behaviour* by organizing the International Ethological Conference. **Structure** International Ethological Conference (every 2 years); Permanent International Committee; Council; Executive Committee; Regional and National Representatives. **Languages** English. **Staff** Voluntary. **Finance** Levy on delegates to International Conferences. **Events** *Biennial Conference* Chicago, IL (USA) 2019, *Biennial Conference* Estoril (Portugal) 2017, *Behaviour Joint Conference* Cairns, QLD (Australia) 2015, *International Conference* Cairns, QLD (Australia) 2015, *Biennial Conference* Newcastle upon Tyne (UK) 2013. **Publications** Conference abstracts.

Members No registered membership. Individuals who attend International Ethological Conferences in 50 countries and territories:

Algeria, Argentina, Australia, Austria, Belgium, Brazil, Cameroon, Canada, Chile, Colombia, Croatia, Czechia, Denmark, Finland, France, Germany, Hungary, India, Indonesia, Israel, Italy, Japan, Kenya, Lithuania, Mexico, Netherlands, New Zealand, Norway, Pakistan, Panama, Peru, Poland, Portugal, Puerto Rico, Romania, Russia, Saudi Arabia, Slovakia, South Africa, Spain, Sweden, Switzerland, Taiwan, Tanzania UR, UK, Ukraine, Uruguay, USA, Venezuela, Vietnam. [2017.03.10/XF1817/**F**]

♦ International Council for Evangelical Theological Education (ICETE) 13020

Executive Assistant PO Box 480, Wheaton IL 60187, USA. T. +13175081024. E-mail: info@icete.info – iceteoffice@gmail.com.

URL: https://icete.info/

History Mar 1980, High Leigh (UK). Founded with the assistance of *Theological Commission of the World Evangelical Alliance*, within the framework of *World Evangelical Alliance (WEA, #21393)*. Former names and other names: *International Council of Accrediting Agencies (ICAA)* – former; *Conseil international des agences accréditantes* – former; *Concilio Internacional de Agencias de Acreditación* – former. **Aims** Enable international interaction and collaboration among all those concerned for the enhancement of evangelical theological education worldwide. **Structure** Board; Executive Committee. **Languages** Arabic, English, French, German, Portuguese, Russian, Spanish, Ukrainian. **Staff** 5.00 FTE, paid. **Finance** Sources: members' dues. External funding. **Activities** Guidance/assistance/consulting. **Events** *Consultation* 2021, *Consultation* Panama (Panama) 2018, *Engaged and effective – the impact of theological education* Antalya (Turkey) 2015, *Consultation* Nairobi (Kenya) 2012, *Consultation* Sopron (Hungary) 2009. **Publications** *Text and Context in*

Theological Education (1994); *Excellence and Renewal – Goals for Accreditation of Theological Education* (1989); *Evangelical Theological Education Today: 1 – An International Perspective* (1982); *Evangelical Theological Education Today: 2 – Agenda for Renewal* (1982); *Manifesto on the Renewal of Evangelical Theological Education*.
Members Regional associations of theological schools, 7 of which listed in this Yearbook:
Asia Theological Association (ATA, #02101); Associação Evangélica de Educação Teológica na América Latina (AETAL, #02326); Association for Biblical Higher Education (ABHE); Association for Christian Theological Education in Africa (ACTEA, #02431); Caribbean Evangelical Theological Association (CETA, #03499); Euro-Asian Accrediting Association of Evangelical Seminaries (EAAA, #05635); European Council for Theological Education (ECTE, #06846).
The above represent over 900 constituency institutions in 109 countries and territories:
Angola, Argentina, Australia, Bangladesh, Barbados, Belgium, Bhutan, Bolivia, Botswana, Brazil, Bulgaria, Burkina Faso, Burundi, Cambodia, Cameroon, Canada, Central African Rep, Chad, Chile, China, Colombia, Congo Brazzaville, Congo DR, Costa Rica, Côte d'Ivoire, Cuba, Cyprus, Czechia, Denmark, Ecuador, Egypt, El Salvador, Eritrea, Eswatini, Ethiopia, Fiji, Finland, France, Gabon, Gambia, Germany, Ghana, Greece, Guatemala, Haiti, Honduras, Hong Kong, India, Indonesia, Israel, Jamaica, Japan, Jordan, Kenya, Korea Rep, Lebanon, Lesotho, Liberia, Madagascar, Malawi, Malaysia, Mali, Mauritius, Mexico, Mozambique, Myanmar, Namibia, Nauru, Netherlands, New Zealand, Nicaragua, Niger, Nigeria, Northern Mariana Is, Norway, Pakistan, Palau, Papua New Guinea, Paraguay, Peru, Philippines, Romania, Samoa, Senegal, Seychelles, Sierra Leone, Singapore, Solomon Is, South Africa, Spain, Sri Lanka, St Lucia, St Vincent-Grenadines, Sudan, Sweden, Switzerland, Taiwan, Tanzania UR, Thailand, Tonga, Trinidad-Tobago, Uganda, UK, Uruguay, USA, Vanuatu, Venezuela, Zambia, Zimbabwe.
NGO Relations Global partner with: *World Evangelical Alliance (WEA, #21393).* [2021.07.15/XD0607/y/**E**]

♦ International Council for Exceptional Children / see Council for Exceptional Children

♦ International Council for the Exploration of the Sea (ICES) 13021

Conseil international pour l'exploration de la mer (CIEM) – International Havundersøgelsesråd
Sec H C Andersens Bvd 44-46, 1553 Copenhagen, Denmark. T. +4533386700. Fax +4533934215. E-mail: info@ices.dk – reception@ices.dk.
URL: http://www.ices.dk/
History 22 Jul 1902, Copenhagen (Denmark). Established by Denmark, Finland, Germany, Netherlands, Norway, Sweden, Russia and UK, to carry out oceanographic research programmes adopted at intergovernmental conferences held in 1899, Stockholm (Sweden), and 1901, Kristiania (Norway). Revised convention signed 12 Sep 1964, in force from 22 July 1968. Protocol to the Convention adopted 13 Aug 1970, in force 12 Nov 1975. Statutes registered in *'UNTS 1/9344'*. Former names and other names: *Permanent International Council for the Exploration of the Sea* – former (1902); *Conseil permanent international pour l'exploration de la mer* – former (1902); *Consejo Internacional para la Exploración del Mar (CIEM)* – former. **Aims** Advance and share scientific understanding of marine ecosystems and the services they provide; generate state-of-the-art advice for meeting conservation, management and sustainability goals. **Structure** Council (annual meeting of Member Countries); Bureau; Finance Committee; Advisory Committee (ACOM); Science Committee (SCICOM); Steering Groups; Secretariat, headed by General Secretary. **Languages** English, French. **Staff** 73.00 FTE, paid. **Finance** Sources: contributions of member/participating states; fees for services. **Activities** Awards/prizes/competitions; events/meetings; knowledge management/information dissemination; projects/programmes; publishing activities; research/documentation; training/education. North Atlantic, North Sea, Baltic Sea, Arctic, strategic partnerships extent to Mediterranean, Black Sea, and Pacific Ocean. **Events** *Annual Science Conference* Dublin (Ireland) 2022, *Annual Science Conference* Copenhagen (Denmark) 2021, *Annual Science Conference* Copenhagen (Denmark) 2020, *Annual Science Conference* Gothenburg (Sweden) 2019, *Annual Meeting* Weymouth (UK) 2019. **Publications** *ICES Journal of Marine Science; ICES Newsletter.* ICES Annual Report; ICES Cooperative Research Reports; Identification Leaflets for Diseases and Parasites of Fish and Shellfish; Identification Leaflets for Plankton; Techniques in Marine Environmental Sciences. Miscellaneous special publications. **Information Services** *Environmental Database* – 1979 to current; *Fisheries Database* – 1903 to current; *Physical Oceanography Database* – 1870 to current.
Members Governments of 20 countries:
Belgium, Canada, Denmark, Estonia, Finland, France, Germany, Iceland, Ireland, Latvia, Lithuania, Netherlands, Norway, Poland, Portugal, Russia, Spain, Sweden, UK, USA.
As per March 2022 Council decision, the Russian Federation has been temporarily suspended from ICES activities.
IGO Relations Observer status with (3): *Arctic Council (#01097); Consultative Meeting of Contracting Parties to the London Convention/Meeting of Contracting Parties to the London Protocol (#04769); United Nations (UN, #20515)* (General Assembly). Memorandum of Understanding with (10): *Baltic Marine Environment Protection Commission – Helsinki Commission (HELCOM, #03126); Convention for the Protection on the Marine Environment for the North-East Atlantic (OSPAR Convention, 1992); European Environment Agency (EEA, #06995); FAO (#09260); General Fisheries Commission for the Mediterranean (GFCM, #10112); North Atlantic Salmon Conservation Organization (NASCO, #17574); North-East Atlantic Fisheries Commission (NEAFC, #17581); North Pacific Marine Science Organization (PICES, #17602); Northwest Atlantic Fisheries Organization (NAFO, #17606); The Mediterranean Science Commission (CIESM, #16674).*
Letters of agreement with:
- *North Atlantic Marine Mammal Commission (NAMMCO, #17573);*
- *OIE – World Organisation for Animal Health (#17703);*
- *Secretariat of the Convention on Biological Diversity (SCBD, #19197).*

Science cooperation agreements with:
- *Arctic Monitoring and Assessment Programme (AMAP, #01100);*
- *Intergovernmental Oceanographic Commission (IOC, #11496).*

Contractual agreements with Advice requesters:
- *European Commission (EC, #06633)* (DG ENV and DG MARE).

Partnership Arrangements with:
- *FAO (#09260)* – International cooperation in the development and maintenance of the Fisheries Resources Monitoring System (FIRMS);
- *Statistical Office of the European Union (Eurostat, #19974).*

Cooperative relations with:
- *European Inland Fisheries and Aquaculture Advisory Commission (EIFAAC, #07540);*
- *International Commission for the Conservation of Atlantic Tunas (ICCAT, #12675);*
- *International Maritime Organization (IMO, #14102);*
- *International Pacific Halibut Commission (IPHC);*
- *International Whaling Commission (IWC, #15879);*
- *Joint Technical Commission of the Marine Front (JTCMF, no recent information);*
- *Nordic Council of Ministers (NCM, #17260).*

NGO Relations Observer status with (1): *Pan-European Infrastructure for Ocean and Marine Data Management (SeaDataNet, #18176).* Memorandum of Understanding with (1): *European Aquaculture Society (EAS, #05909).* Letters of Agreement with: *Baltic Marine Biologists (BMB, #03125); Baltic Organisations' Network for Funding Science EEIG (BONUS EEIG, inactive); International Arctic Science Committee (IASC, #11668); Scientific Committee on Oceanic Research (SCOR, #19149).* In liaison with technical committees of: *International Organization for Standardization (ISO, #14473).* Cooperative relations with: *International Union for Conservation of Nature and Natural Resources (IUCN, #15766).* [2022.10.31/XC1732/**C***]

♦ International Council for Film, Television and Audiovisual Communication (IFTC) 13022

Conseil international du cinéma, de la télévision et de la communication audiovisuelle (CICT)
SG Maison de l'UNESCO, 1 rue Miollis, 75015 Paris, France. T. +33145684878. E-mail: cict.icft@gmail.com.
URL: http://www.cict-icft.org/
History Founded 23 Oct 1958, Paris (France), as *International Film and Television Council – Conseil international du cinéma et de la télévision*, at a meeting convened by UNESCO and attended by representatives of 39 international associations. **Aims** Stimulate creation and promote production and distribution of high standard audiovisual works; advise international organizations and States on implementation of artistic, educational and industrial policies; create a synergy among creators, professionals and media executives by developing collaboration within its members, especially in the service of the broad orientations of UNESCO; set up an arena where different professionals in the field of audiovisual, especially the young people can present their views and suggestions to an international audience; encourage training and research in all audiovisual areas, including media education, and offer a space for reflection on the development of technologies in the service of creation, education and culture; contribute to the efforts of development of communication, especially in the field of digital media and free flow of information. **Structure** General Assembly (every 2 years); Executive Committee (meeting annually); Bureau; Working Commissions (meeting annually). Includes: *International Council of Mediterranean Cinematic Manifestations (no recent information);* national committees. **Languages** English, French. **Staff** Voluntary. **Finance** Sources: members' dues. Other sources: UNESCO contract; grants. **Activities** Advocacy/lobbying/activism; events/meetings; projects/programmes; training/education. **Events** *International assembly of scientific audio-visual media* Paris (France) 1996, *Round table* Paris (France) 1994, *Droit d'auteur en rapport avec les nouvelles technologies* Paris (France) 1993, *Biennial General Assembly* Paris (France) 1989, *Meeting* Paris (France) 1989. **Publications** *Lettre d'information – Letter of Information – Carta Informativa* (4 a year). Information Services: Cooperates in archiving and cataloguing audiovisuals for broadcasting on educational television.
Members (43):
- Act Multimedia;
- *African Union of Broadcasting (AUB, #00490);*
- Archives françaises du film;
- *Association internationale du film d'animation (ASIFA, #02698);*
- Campania Film Commission;
- Canal Club UNESCO;
- Cannes International Film Festival;
- Cinéma du Réel;
- Cinéma Numérique Ambulant (CNA);
- Comité Egyptien du Film et des Traditions (CEIFT);
- Directors Guild of America (DGA);
- *European Broadcasting Union (EBU, #06404);*
- European Cinema Academy;
- *European Space Agency (ESA, #08798);*
- *Fédération internationale de la presse cinématographique (FIPRESCI, #09651);*
- Festival del Popoli;
- Festival International de Programmes Audiovisuels (FIPA);
- Festival International du Film d'Histoire de Pessac;
- Festival Internazionale di Cinema e Televisione (EUROVISIONI);
- Fondation de France;
- Fondation Jean Rouch;
- Fondation Novalia;
- Fondation Pierre Bergé-Yves Saint Laurent;
- Forum Africain du Film Documentaire (FADOC);
- Fundacion de Television Educativa (FUND TV);
- Gaumont-Pathé Archives;
- *International Association for Media in Science (IAMS, #12024);*
- *International Association of Cinema, Audiovisual and Media Schools (#11771);*
- *International Centre of Films for Children and Young People (#12493);*
- *International Confederation of Art Cinemas (#12847);*
- *International Federation of Film Producers' Associations (#13429);*
- Italian National Committee (CNI);
- Manifestations du Cinéma Méditerranéen (MCM);
- Media Education Center (Balkan);
- Museo Nazionale del Cinema (MNC);
- *Observatory for Cultural and Audio-Visual Communication in the Mediterranean (OCCAM, #17643);*
- Pan-African Film Festival of Ouagadougou (FESPACO);
- *Permanent Conference of Mediterranean Audiovisual Operators (COPEAM, #18320);*
- Rencontres internationales Image et Science (RIAVS);
- Satellite Communication for Learning (SCOLA);
- *Union internationale du cinéma (UNICA, #20423);*
- Venice Biennial;
- *World Catholic Association for Communication (SIGNIS, #21264).*

Consultative Status Consultative status granted from: *UNESCO (#20322)* (Associate Status). **IGO Relations** Cooperates with (1): *International Programme for the Development of Communication (IPDC, #14651).* **NGO Relations** Instrumental in setting up (1): *Observatory for Cultural and Audio-Visual Communication in the Mediterranean (OCCAM, #17643).* [2022/XA2054/y/**A**]

♦ International Council of Fine Arts Deans (internationally oriented national body)
♦ International Council of Folklore Festivals and Folk Art / see International Council of Organizations for Folklore Festivals and Folk Art (#13058)

♦ International Council of Forest and Paper Associations (ICFPA) ... 13023

Pres Forest Products Assn of Canada, Suite 410-99 Bank Street, Ottawa ON K1P 6B9, Canada. E-mail: jveale@fpac.ca – info@icfpa.org.
URL: http://www.icfpa.org/
History 17 Jul 2002, Washington, DC (USA). Founded by the *International Forum of Forest and Paper Associations*, an informal meeting of forest and paper associations. **Aims** Serve as a forum of global dialogue among national and regional industry associations and their leadership; represent the forest, paper, wood and forest fibre-based industries with global policy organizations; coordinate action and distribute information. **Structure** Rotating Chairmanship. **Languages** English. **Staff** None. **Finance** No budget. **Activities** Awards/prizes/competitions; events/meetings; knowledge management/information dissemination. **Events** *Annual Meeting* Delhi (India) 2012, *Annual meeting* Montebello, ON (Canada) 2011, *Annual meeting* Tokyo (Japan) 2010, *Environment meeting* Tokyo (Japan) 2010, *Annual meeting* Bakubung (South Africa) 2008. **Publications** *ICFPA Newsletter* (4 a year). *Biennial Sustainability Report of Global Forest and Paper Industry.*
Members Full in 19 countries:
Australia, Belgium, Brazil, Canada, Chile, Finland, France, Germany, Japan, Korea Rep, Lebanon, New Zealand, Portugal, Russia, South Africa, Spain, Sweden, UK, USA.
International organizations (3):
Confédération européenne des industries du bois (CEI Bois, #04545); Confederation of European Paper Industries (CEPI, #04529); Latin American Confederation of the Pulp and Paper Industry (FICEPA, no recent information).
Consultative Status Consultative status granted from: *FAO (#09260)* (Liaison Status); *ECOSOC (#05331)* (Ros A). **NGO Relations** Stakeholder in: *Forest Stewardship Council (FSC, #09869); PEFC Council (#18288).* [2023/XD8766/y/**D**]

♦ International Council for Francophone Studies (#04691)
♦ International Council of the French Language (#04692)
♦ International Council on the Future of the University (inactive)

♦ International Council for Game and Wildlife Conservation 13024

Conseil international de la chasse et de la conservation du gibier (CIC) – Internationaler Rat zur Erhaltung des Wildes und der Jagd
Dir Gen Budakeszi PO Box 82, Budapest 2092, Hungary. T. +3623453830. Fax +3623453832. E-mail: office@cic-wildlife.org.
Street address Telki út, hrsz 0178/9, Erdögazdasag Területén, Budapest 2092, Hungary.
URL: http://www.cic-wildlife.org/
History 1930, Paris (France). Founded by Maxime Ducrocq and a group of well known hunters. New statutes adopted: 26 May 1968, Mamaia (Romania); May 1972, Texel (Netherlands); 1993, Krakow (Poland); 2001, Portoroz (Slovenia); 2005, Abu Dhabi (United Arab Emirates); 2011, St Petersburg (Russia). Former names and other names: *International Hunting Council* – former; *Conseil international de la chasse* – former; *International Hunting and Shooting Council* – former; *Conseil international de la chasse et du tir* – former. Registration: French Ministerial Decree, Start date: 29 May 1969, France; French Ministerial Decree, Start date: 29 Nov 1995, France; Austrian Ministerial Decree, Start date: 28 Jul 2003. **Aims** Promote sustainable *hunting* on a global scale as a tool for conservation while building on valued traditions. **Structure** General Assembly (annual); Council; Executive Committee; Divisions (3); National Delegations (39); Legal seat located in Vienna (Austria). CIC Museum, Palarikovo (Slovakia). **Languages** English, French, German, Russian. **Finance** Sources: members' dues; sponsorship. **Activities** Advocacy/lobbying/activism; awards/prizes/competitions; events/meetings; guidance/assistance/consulting; politics/policy/regulatory; training/

education. **Events** *General Assembly* Budapest (Hungary) 2021, *General Assembly* Windhoek (Namibia) 2019, *General Assembly* Madrid (Spain) 2018, *General Assembly* Montreux (Switzerland) 2017, *General Assembly* Brussels (Belgium) 2016. **Publications** *CIC Newsletter* (4 a year) in English, French, German. *European Charter on Hunting and Biodiversity* in English, French; *National Hunting Museums and Private Collections Open to the Public*. *European Charter on Hunting and Biodiversity* is in cooperation with *Council of Europe (CE, #04881)*. Technical series in cooperation with *FAO (#09260)*. Best practices; guidelines for measurement of trophies.
Members States; government agencies; public institutions; IGOs; NGOs; individuals; experts; sponsors. Members in 82 countries:
Albania, Algeria, Argentina, Austria, Belarus, Belgium, Benin, Bosnia-Herzegovina, Botswana, Brazil, Bulgaria, Burkina Faso, Cameroon, Canada, China, Congo Brazzaville, Côte d'Ivoire, Croatia, Cyprus, Czechia, Denmark, Estonia, Finland, France, Gabon, Germany, Greece, Guinea, Guinea-Bissau, Hungary, India, Iran Islamic Rep, Ireland, Italy, Japan, Kenya, Korea Rep, Latvia, Liechtenstein, Lithuania, Luxembourg, Malawi, Mali, Malta, Mauritania, Mexico, Moldova, Montenegro, Morocco, Namibia, Nepal, Netherlands, New Zealand, Niger, Nigeria, North Macedonia, Norway, Poland, Portugal, Qatar, Romania, Russia, Senegal, Serbia, Slovakia, Slovenia, South Africa, Spain, Sudan, Sweden, Switzerland, Tajikistan, Tanzania UR, Togo, Tunisia, Türkiye, UK, Ukraine, United Arab Emirates, USA, Zambia, Zimbabwe.
Consultative Status Consultative status granted from: *ECOSOC (#05331)* (Special); *FAO (#09260)* (Liaison Status). **IGO Relations** Observer status with (2): *Ministerial Conference on the Protection of Forests in Europe (FOREST EUROPE, #16817)*; *Standing Committee to the Bern Convention on the Conservation of European Wildlife and Natural Habitats (#19949)*. **NGO Relations** Member of (3): *International Partnership for the Satoyama Initiative (IPSI, #14525)*; *International Union for Conservation of Nature and Natural Resources (IUCN, #15766)*; *Mountain Partnership (MP, #16862)*. Instrumental in setting up (1): *Oiseaux migrateurs du paléarctique occidental (OMPO, #17712)*. [2023.02.21/XC2114/**C**]

♦ International Council on Global Conflict Resolution (internationally oriented national body)
♦ International Council for Global Health Progress (no recent information)
♦ International Council of Goodwill Industries / see Goodwill Industries International

♦ International Council on Grapevine Trunk Diseases (ICGTD) 13025

Contact DIBA-Protezione delle piante, P le delle Cascine 28, 50144 Florence FI, Italy. E-mail: icgtdcontact@gmail.com.
Chair address not obtained.
URL: https://icgtd.ucr.edu/

History Jul 1998, USA. **Aims** Serve as a forum for researchers from grape growing countries. **Structure** Committee; Executive Council; Regional Coordinators. **Languages** English. **Staff** None. **Finance** No budget. **Events** *Workshop* Penticton, BC (Canada) 2019, *Workshop* Reims (France) 2017, *Workshop* Adelaide, SA (Australia) 2014, *Workshop* Valencia (Spain) 2012, *Workshop* Santa Cruz (Chile) 2010. **Publications** Workshop papers.
Members Full in 16 countries:
Australia, Brazil, China, Egypt, France, Hungary, Iraq, Italy, Mexico, New Zealand, Pakistan, Peru, Spain, United Arab Emirates, USA, Uzbekistan. [2019/XJ1473/**C**]

♦ International Council of Graphic Design Associations / see International Council of Design (#13013)

♦ International Council of Grocery Manufacturers Associations (ICGMA) 13026

Contact c/o GMA 1001 19th St N, 7th Floor, Arlington VA 22209, USA.
Street Address 1350 I St NW, Ste 300, Washington DC 20005, USA. T. +12026395900.

History 1982. Former names and other names: *International Federation of Grocery Manufacturers Associations (IFGMA)* – former. **Aims** Develop and coordinate world-wide information network among associations of food and drink manufacturers; promote high standards and practices in manufacture and distribution of grocery products, promoting the interests of grocery manufacturers; monitor questions of health, safety, quality, marketing, distribution and systems practices within the industry. **Structure** Informal: Chair rotates to host of the national organization that holds meetings of ICGMA. **Languages** English, French. **Staff** Voluntary. **Finance** Meetings funded by host association; registration fees.
Members Associations of grocery manufacturing companies in 10 countries:
Argentina, Australia, Brazil, Canada, Chile, Mexico, New Zealand, South Africa, UK, USA.
IGO Relations Official recognition by: *Codex Alimentarius Commission (CAC, #04081)*; *OECD (#17693)*. **NGO Relations** Works with: *International Chewing Gum Association (ICGA, #12545)*. [2020/XD9185/**D**]

♦ International Council of Group Psychotherapy / see International Association for Group Psychotherapy and Group Processes (#11926)

♦ International Council on Harmonisation of Technical Requirements for Registration of Pharmaceuticals for Human Use (ICH) 13027

Dir Route Pré-Bois 20, PO Box 1894, 1215 Geneva, Switzerland. E-mail: admin@ich.org.
URL: http://www.ich.org/

History Apr 1990. Former names and other names: *International Conference on Harmonisation of Technical Requirements for Registration of Pharmaceuticals for Human Use* – former (1990 to 23 Oct 2015). Registration: Switzerland. **Aims** Make recommendations towards achieving greater harmonization in interpretation and application of technical guidelines and requirements for pharmaceutical product registration, thereby reducing or obviating duplication of testing carried out during research and development of new human medicines. **Structure** Assembly; Management Committee; MedDRA Management Committee; Coordinators; Working Groups; Secretariat. **Activities** Events/meetings; standards/guidelines; training/education. **Events** *Assembly* Athens (Greece) 2022, *Assembly* Incheon (Korea Rep) 2022, *Meeting* Tokyo (Japan) 2021, *Meeting* Geneva (Switzerland) 2020, *Meeting* Tokyo (Japan) 2020.
Members Founding Regulatory Members (3):
Japan, USA.
European Commission (EC, #06633).
Founding Industry Members (3):
Japan, USA.
European Federation of Pharmaceutical Industries and Associations (EFPIA, #07191).
Standing Regulatory Members (2):
Canada, Switzerland.
Regulatory members (9):
Brazil, China, Korea Rep, Mexico, Saudi Arabia, Singapore, Taiwan, Türkiye, UK.
Industry Members (3):
Biotechnology Innovation Organization (BIO); *Global Self-Care Federation (GSCF, #10588)*; *International Generic and Biosimilar Medicines Association (IGBA, #13708)*.
Standing Observers (2):
International Federation of Pharmaceutical Manufacturers and Associations (IFPMA, #13505); *WHO (#20950)*.
Legislative or Administrative Authorities (20):
Algeria, Argentina, Armenia, Australia, Azerbaijan, Colombia, Cuba, Egypt, India, Indonesia, Iran Islamic Rep, Israel, Jordan, Kazakhstan, Lebanon, Malaysia, Moldova, Russia, South Africa, Ukraine.
Regional Harmonisation Intiatives (6):
ASEAN (#01141); *Asia-Pacific Economic Cooperation (APEC, #01887)*; *East African Community (EAC, #05181)*; *Gulf Health Council (GHC, #10830)*; *Pan American Network for Drug Regulatory Harmonization (PANDRH, #18121)*; *Southern African Development Community (SADC, #19843)*.
International Pharmaceutical Industry Organisation:
Active Pharmaceutical Ingredients Committee (APIC, #00102).
International Organisations regulated or affected by ICH Guideline(s) (6):
Bill and Melinda Gates Foundation (BMGF); *Council for International Organizations of Medical Sciences (CIOMS, #04905)*; European Directorate for the Quality of Medicines and HealthCare; *IPEC Federation (#16011)*; *Pharmaceutical Inspection Co-operation Scheme (PIC/S, #18353)*; *University of the South Pacific (USP, #20703)*.
NGO Relations Partner of (1): *International Coalition of Medicines Regulatory Authorities (ICMRA, #12616)*. [2022/XF4089/c/**F**]

♦ International Council for Health, Physical Education and Recreation / see International Council for Health, Physical Education, Recreation, Sport and Dance (#13028)

♦ International Council for Health, Physical Education, Recreation, Sport and Dance (ICHPER-SD) 13028

Conseil international pour la santé, l'éducation physique, la récréation, le sport et la dance – Consejo Internacional para Salud, Educación Fisica, Recreación, Deporte y Baile – Internationaler Rat für Gesundheit, Leibesüngen, Freizeitgestaltung, Sport und Tanz
Headquarters 1900 Association Dr, Reston VA 20191-1598, USA. T. +17034763462. Fax +17034769527. E-mail: ichper@aahperd.org.
URL: http://www.ichpersd.org/

History Aug 1958, Rome (Italy), as *International Council for Health, Physical Education and Recreation (ICHPER) – Conseil international pour la santé, l'éducation physique et la récréation – Internationaler Rat für Gesundheit, Leibesüngen und Freizeitgestaltung*, by Committee on Health, Physical Education and Recreation of *World Confederation of Organizations of the Teaching Profession (WCOTP, inactive)*. Constitution approved at 2nd World Congress, 1959, Washington DC (USA). **Aims** Unite teachers, administrators, leaders, national departments of physical education and related professional associations concerned with health, physical education, sports and recreation in one organization; present their concerns at international level; foster international understanding and goodwill; encourage development and expansion of educationally sound programmes in all countries. **Structure** Board of Governors; Executive Committee. Committees (9); Commissions (52). **Languages** English, Spanish. **Staff** Voluntary. **Finance** Members' dues: Individual US$ 20 – US$ 40; Life US$ 1,500; Contributing US$ 1,000 or more; Organizations US$ 200 – US$ 2,500; Organizations US$ 100 – US$ 2,500. Other sources: grants from official and private bodies; sale of publications. **Activities** Awards/prizes/competitions; events/meetings; guidance/assistance/consulting. **Events** *World Congress* Manama (Bahrain) 2014, *World Congress* Turkey 2013, *World congress* Cairo (Egypt) 2011, *Forum* San Diego, CA (USA) 2011, *Asia regional congress* Taipei (Taiwan) 2011. **Publications** *Journal of ICHPER-SD* (4 a year) in English – with abstracts in Spanish, German, French, Arabic. Congress proceedings.
Members Individual; Life; Institutional; National; International; Library; Contributing Educational or Business Organization. Members in 203 countries and territories:
Afghanistan, Albania, Algeria, Andorra, Angola, Antigua-Barbuda, Argentina, Armenia, Aruba, Australia, Austria, Azerbaijan, Bahamas, Bahrain, Bangladesh, Barbados, Belarus, Belgium, Belize, Benin, Bermuda, Bhutan, Bolivia, Bosnia-Herzegovina, Botswana, Brazil, Brunei Darussalam, Bulgaria, Burkina Faso, Burundi, Cambodia, Cameroon, Canada, Cape Verde, Cayman Is, Central African Rep, Chad, Chile, China, Colombia, Comoros, Congo Brazzaville, Congo DR, Cook Is, Costa Rica, Côte d'Ivoire, Croatia, Cuba, Cyprus, Czechia, Denmark, Djibouti, Dominica, Dominican Rep, Ecuador, Egypt, El Salvador, Equatorial Guinea, Eritrea, Estonia, Eswatini, Ethiopia, Fiji, Finland, France, Gabon, Gambia, Georgia, Germany, Ghana, Greece, Grenada, Guadeloupe, Guam, Guatemala, Guinea, Guinea-Bissau, Guyana, Haiti, Honduras, Hong Kong, Hungary, Iceland, India, Indonesia, Iran Islamic Rep, Iraq, Ireland, Israel, Italy, Jamaica, Japan, Jordan, Kazakhstan, Kenya, Kiribati, Korea DPR, Korea Rep, Kuwait, Kyrgyzstan, Laos, Latvia, Lebanon, Lesotho, Liberia, Libya, Liechtenstein, Lithuania, Luxembourg, Madagascar, Malawi, Malaysia, Maldives, Mali, Malta, Marshall Is, Mauritania, Mauritius, Mexico, Micronesia FS, Moldova, Monaco, Mongolia, Morocco, Mozambique, Myanmar, Namibia, Nauru, Nepal, Netherlands, New Zealand, Nicaragua, Niger, Nigeria, North Macedonia, Norway, Oman, Pakistan, Palau, Palestine, Panama, Papua New Guinea, Paraguay, Peru, Philippines, Poland, Portugal, Puerto Rico, Qatar, Romania, Russia, Rwanda, Samoa, Samoa USA, San Marino, Sao Tomé-Principe, Saudi Arabia, Senegal, Serbia, Seychelles, Sierra Leone, Singapore, Slovakia, Slovenia, Solomon Is, Somalia, South Africa, Spain, Sri Lanka, St Kitts-Nevis, St Lucia, St Vincent-Grenadines, Sudan, Suriname, Sweden, Switzerland, Syrian AR, Taiwan, Tajikistan, Tanzania UR, Thailand, Togo, Tonga, Trinidad-Tobago, Tunisia, Türkiye, Turkmenistan, Tuvalu, Uganda, UK, Ukraine, United Arab Emirates, Uruguay, USA, Uzbekistan, Vanuatu, Venezuela, Vietnam, Virgin Is UK, Virgin Is USA, Yemen, Zambia, Zimbabwe.
Consultative Status Consultative status granted from: *UNESCO (#20322)* (Consultative Status). **IGO Relations** Member of: Permanent Consultative Council of *Intergovernmental Committee for Physical Education and Sport (#11475)*. **NGO Relations** Recognized by: *International Olympic Committee (IOC, #14408)*. Cooperates with: *International Federation of Sports Medicine (#13554)*. Member of: *International Committee for Fair Play (#12769)*. [2019/XB1769/**B**]

♦ International Council of Hide Sellers' Associations / see International Council of Hides, Skins and Leather Traders Associations (#13029)

♦ International Council of Hides, Skins and Leather Traders Associations (ICHSLTA) 13029

Conseil international des associations de négociants en cuirs et peaux – Consejo Internacional de Asociaciones de Comerciantes de Cueros y Pieles
Sec c/o SG des Cuirs et Peaux, 105 rue du Faubourg St Honoré, 75008 Paris, France. T. +33143598943. E-mail: office@cuirsetpeaux.org – office@french-hides.com.
Registered Office Level 54, Hopewell Centre, 183 Queen's Road, Hong Kong, Central and Western, Hong Kong.
URL: http://www.ichslta.com/

History Founded 1929, London (UK), as *International Council of Hide Sellers' Associations*. **Aims** Establish uniformity in commercial usage, more especially with regard to forms of contract; promote, develop and protect trades in hides, skins and leather. **Structure** General Meeting (annual); Officers. **Languages** English. **Finance** Sources: members' dues. **Events** *Annual General Meeting* Hong Kong (Hong Kong) 2019, *Annual Meeting* Hong Kong (Hong Kong) 2010, *Annual meeting* Hong Kong (Hong Kong) 2007, *Annual meeting* Hong Kong (Hong Kong) 2006, *Annual meeting* Hong Kong (Hong Kong) 2005.
Members National associations in 7 countries:
Australia, China, Ethiopia, France, Italy, Netherlands, USA.
Individuals in 6 countries and territories:
Greece, Namibia, Singapore, Switzerland, Türkiye, UK.
Consultative Status Consultative status granted from: *ECOSOC (#05331)* (Ros C); *FAO (#09260)* (Liaison Status). **NGO Relations** Cooperates with: *International Council of Tanners (ICT, #13084)* and *International Union of Leather Technologists and Chemists Societies (IULTCS, #15788)* on *Global Leather Coordinating Committee (GLCC)*. [2020/XD1598/t/**C**]

♦ International Council for Higher Education (ICHE) 13030

Office Moosbrunnenstrasse 11, 8426 Lufingen ZH, Switzerland. T. +41448135183. E-mail: ichenetwork@gmail.com.
Pres No 54 MIG KHB Colony Koramangala 5th Block, Bangalore, Karnataka 560095, Bangalore KARNATAKA 560095, India. T. +918025531154.
URL: http://ichenetwork.org/

History 1997, Switzerland. **Aims** Advance Christian higher education worldwide. **Structure** Assembly (every 3 years); Executive Board. **Events** *Annual Conference* Nairobi (Kenya) 2023, *Annual Conference* Männedorf (Switzerland) 2020, *Annual Conference* Accra (Ghana) 2018, *Annual Conference* Singapore (Singapore) 2017, *Annual Conference* Johannesburg (South Africa) 2016.
Members Full in 27 countries and territories:
Austria, Bulgaria, Cambodia, Canada, Germany, Haiti, India, Indonesia, Kenya, Korea Rep, Mongolia, Myanmar, Nepal, Netherlands, New Zealand, Nigeria, Palestine, Philippines, Singapore, South Africa, Spain, Switzerland, Taiwan, Uganda, UK, Ukraine, USA. [2023/XD8669/**C**]

♦ International Council of Homehelp Services (inactive)
♦ International Council of Homeopathic Physicians (inactive)

♦ International Council for Homeopathy (ICH) 13031

Secretariat Waidmannsruh 20, 24119 Kronshagen, Germany. T. +49431548535. E-mail: ich@gn.apc.org.
URL: http://www.homeopathy-ich.org/

History Oct 2007. Registration: KvK Kamer van Koophandel, No/ID: 72095504, Start date: 9 Jul 2018, Netherlands. **Aims** Establish and ensure high standards of practice for the benefit of patients through: establishing recommended standards for education and training of homeopaths; establishing recommended regulatory standards and processes for self-regulation; supporting and facilitating research into homeopathic clinical practice. **Structure** Administrator; Secretariat based in Kronshagen (Germany). **Languages** English. **Staff** 0.50 FTE, paid. **Finance** Sources: members' dues. **Events** *Conference* Japan 2011, *International conference* Tsukuba (Japan) 2011. **Publications** *International Guidelines for Homeopathy Education* (2010).
Members Professional associations in 25 countries and territories:
Belgium, Bulgaria, Croatia, Czechia, Denmark, Finland, Germany, Greece, Hong Kong, Ireland, Israel, Italy, Japan, Kenya, Malta, Netherlands, New Zealand, Norway, Portugal, Serbia, Slovakia, Spain, Sweden, Switzerland, USA. [2022/XM0929/**C**]

♦ International Council on Hotel, Restaurant and Institutional Education (internationally oriented national body)

♦ International Council of Human Duties (no recent information)
♦ International Council for Human Rights (internationally oriented national body)

♦ International Council for Industrial and Applied Mathematics (ICIAM) 13032

Exec Sec c/o Math & Comp-Sci Div, Argonne Nat'l Lab, 9700 South Cass Ave, Argonne IL 60439, USA.
URL: http://www.iciam.org/
History Founded on the initiative of four societies: GAMM, IMA, SIAM and SMAI. Former names and other names: *Committee for International Conferences on Industrial and Applied Mathematics (CICIAM)* – former (1999); *Standing Committee of the ICIAM* – former. **Aims** Promote industrial and applied mathematics globally; promote interactions between member societies and promote their goals; coordinate planning for periodic international meetings in the field. **Structure** Board (meets at least annually); Executive Officers. **Languages** English. **Staff** None. **Finance** Sources: meeting proceeds; members' dues. Annual budget: 15,000 USD. **Activities** Awards/prizes/competitions; events/meetings. **Events** *International Congress on Industrial and Applied Mathematics* Tokyo (Japan) 2023, *Quadrennial Congress* Valencia (Spain) 2019, *Quadrennial Congress* Beijing (China) 2015, *Quadrennial Congress* Vancouver, BC (Canada) 2011, *International conference on applied mathematics and informatics* San Andrés (Colombia) 2010. **Publications** *ICIAM Dianoia* (4 a year).
Members Three levels of Full membership (total 21): Small Societies (4); Medium Societies (9); Large Societies (8). Two levels of Associate membership (total 27): Small Associated Societies (15); Large Associated Societies (15). Full – national societies (21) in 18 countries:
Argentina, Australia, Brazil, Canada, China, France, Germany, India, Italy, Japan, Korea Rep, New Zealand, Peru, Romania, Spain, UK, USA, Vietnam.
Included in the above, 2 regional organizations listed in this Yearbook:
European Consortium for Mathematics in Industry (ECMI, #06757); *European Society for Mathematical and Theoretical Biology (ESMTB, #08646)*.
Associate: national societies (30) in 22 countries:
Austria, Canada, China, Czechia, Denmark, Finland, France, Germany, Israel, Italy, Japan, Korea Rep, Mexico, Netherlands, Norway, Poland, Portugal, Singapore, Spain, Sweden, Switzerland, UK, USA, Vietnam.
Also members in Southern African countries. Membership countries not specified. Included in the above, one regional organization listed in this Yearbook:
Included in the above, one regional organization listed in this Yearbook:
European Mathematical Society (EMS, #07755).
NGO Relations Member of (1): *International Science Council (ISC, #14796)*. [2022/XE3485/ty/**E**]

♦ International Council of Infant Food Industries (inactive)
♦ InterNational Council for Infertility Information Dissemination (no recent information)

♦ International Council for Information Technology in Government Administration (ICA) 13033

Address not obtained.
URL: http://www.ica-it.org/
History 1 Aug 1968, Edinburgh (UK). 1-2 Aug 1968, Edinburgh (UK), following consultation amongst participants at International Symposium on Automation of Population Register Files, Sep 1967, Jerusalem (Israel). Original title: *International Council for ADP in Government Administration*. Present title adopted 1986. **Aims** Improve the efficiency and effectiveness of government administration by providing a forum to support senior management in the formulation of automatic data processing / information technology policy; provide officials in national governments with a vehicle to address key issues and information sharing. **Structure** Council, comprising a national representative of each member country. Board, comprising Chairman, Vice Chairman, Treasurer and Programme Committee Chairman. Programme Committee; Study groups. **Languages** English. **Staff** 0.50 FTE, paid; 0.50 FTE, voluntary. **Finance** Sources: members' dues. Annual budget: 3,000 GBP. **Activities** Study groups; annual conference; meetings; online resource section. **Events** *Annual Conference* Brussels (Belgium) 2020, *Annual Conference* Bucharest (Romania) 2019, *Annual Conference* Helsinki (Finland) 2018, *Annual Conference* Tokyo (Japan) 2017, *Annual Conference* Medellin (Colombia) 2016. **Publications** *ICA Information* – online.
Members Government bodies holding prime responsibility for information technology (IT) in 25 countries:
Australia, Austria, Belgium, Canada, Cyprus, Estonia, Finland, Germany, Hungary, Israel, Japan, Korea Rep, Malta, Mexico, Netherlands, New Zealand, Portugal, Singapore, Slovenia, Spain, Sweden, Switzerland, Taiwan, UK, USA.
Regional integration EU entity (1):
European Union (EU, #08967). [2020/XD7890/**C**]

♦ International Council for Innovation in Higher Education (internationally oriented national body)
♦ International Council of Institutes for Liquid Atomization and Spray Systems / see Institute for Liquid Atomization and Spray Systems (#11278)
♦ International Council of Intermediate Bulk Container Associations (internationally oriented national body)
♦ International Council for the International Christian Youth Exchange / see International Cultural Youth Exchange (#13122)

♦ International Council of Investment Associations (ICIA) 13034

Operational Seat Mainzer Landstrasse 47A, 60329 Frankfurt-Main, Germany. T. +4969264848300. Fax +4969264848335.
URL: http://effas.net/index.php?option=com_content&view=article&id=89
History Apr 1974, Los Angeles CA (USA), as *International Coordinating Committee of Financial Analysts Associations (ICCFAA)* – *Comité international de coordination des associations d'analystes financiers*, as an informal consultative group of national and international societies of financial analysts and investment managers. Present name adopted May 1998. **Aims** Further development of the investment profession worldwide; work towards harmonization of investment decision making practices in different countries; enhance links with other organizations in the field. **Structure** Originally an informal consulting committee, has, since 1988, a more formalized structure as regards international relationships: one Co-Chairman and 5 delegates each from ASIF, APIMEC, EFFAS and IASSA. **Languages** English. **Staff** 1.00 FTE, paid. **Finance** No membership fees. **Activities** Initiatives: development of an International Code of Ethics for use by investment professionals and institutions around the world; promotion of the highest ethical and professional standards of practice; promotion of education and training of analysts, including establishment of a common body of knowledge; development of common methodologies and practices of financial analysis and portfolio management; enhancement of global market efficiency, including allocation of capital, through appropriate generation and distribution of information regarding investment-related issues; enhancement of the statutes and influence of the investment management profession in relationship to other international professional and political organizations. Organizes meetings twice a year – once at annual conference of AIMR and once at EFFAS biennial conference or, if there is no EFFAS conference, at ASAF conference. **Events** *Annual meeting* Stockholm (Sweden) 2003, *Annual meeting* Bangkok (Thailand) 1990, *Meeting* Geneva (Switzerland) 1988, *Meeting* San Francisco, CA (USA) 1988, *Council meeting* Taiwan 1987.
Members Delegates (up to 5 each) from 5 organizations which make up ICIA, listed in this Yearbook:
Asian Securities and Investments Federation (ASIF, #01695); Brazilian Association of Capital Market Analysts (APIMEC); *CFA Institute*; *European Federation of Financial Analysts Societies (EFFAS, #07123)*; *Investment Analysts Society of Southern Africa (IASSA)*.
NGO Relations Member of: *International Accounting Standards Board (IASB, #11583)*. [2011/XE8623/y/**E**]

♦ International Council of Iranian Christians / see Iranian Christians International

♦ International Council on Jewish Social and Welfare Services (INTERCO) 13035

Conseil international des services juifs de bienfaisance et d'assistance sociale – Consejo Internacional de los Servicios Judios de Previsión y Asistencia Social – Internationaler Rat der Israelitischen Dienste für Wohltätigkeit und Soziale Fürsorge
Contact address not obtained. T. +12126876200. Fax +12123705467. E-mail: info@jdc.org – press@jdc.org.
URL: http://www.jdc.org/
History 26 Jun 1961, London (UK). **Aims** Facilitate exchange of views and information among members concerning the problems of Jewish social and welfare services, including medical care, old age, welfare, child care, rehabilitation, technical assistance, vocational training, agricultural and other resettlement, economic assistance, refugee, migration, integration and related problems; ensure representation to governments and international organizations on such questions. **Structure** Council (meets twice a year). **Languages** English, French. **Staff** 0.50 FTE, paid. **Finance** Separate operating budgets for member agencies.
Members Organizations in 4 countries:
France, Switzerland, UK, USA.
Consultative Status Consultative status granted from: *ECOSOC (#05331)* (Special); *FAO (#09260)* (Liaison Status); *UNICEF (#20332)*. **IGO Relations** *UNESCO (#20322)*; *UNHCR (#20327)*. Accredited by: *United Nations Office at Vienna (UNOV, #20604)*. Associated with Department of Global Communications of the United Nations. **NGO Relations** Member of: *Conference of Non-Governmental Organizations in Consultative Relationship with the United Nations (CONGO, #04635)*; *NGO Committee on UNICEF (#17120)*. The: *American Jewish Joint Distribution Committee (JDC, #00785)* is a member. [2014/XD1770/y/**D**]

♦ International Council of Jewish Women (ICJW) 13036

Conseil international des femmes juives – Consejo Internacional de Mujeres Judias – Internationaler Rat Jüdischer Frauen
Pres Prolongación bosques reforma 1592 zafiro 502, Colonia Bosques de las Lomas, 05110 Mexico City CDMX, Mexico. E-mail: press@icjw.org – contact@icjw.org.
URL: http://www.icjw.org/
History 1912, Rome (Italy). Reorganized 1949, Paris (France). **Aims** Promote a just society based on human rights and Jewish values; lobby for an end to discrimination against women in all spheres of life; work to upgrade the lives of women and children. **Structure** Convention (every 4 years); Executive Committee; Administrative Committees; Administration Committees (8); Representatives to intergovernmental organizations (31); World Network Committees; Regional Conferences. **Languages** English, French, German, Hebrew, Russian, Spanish. **Staff** 0.20 FTE, paid. **Finance** Sources: donations; gifts, legacies; members' dues. **Activities** Advocacy/lobbying/activism. **Events** *Quadrennial Convention* Jerusalem (Israel) 2022, *European Conference* Athens (Greece) 2019, *Quadrennial Convention* Sydney, NSW (Australia) 2018, *Executive Meeting* Jerusalem (Israel) 2017, *Executive Meeting* London (UK) 2017. **Publications** *ICJW Newsletter* (annual) in English, Russian, Spanish; *Links* in English. *Jewish Women in a Changing World – A History of the International Council of Jewish Women* in English, French, German, Italian, Japanese, Spanish.
Members Affiliate organizations in 36 countries:
Argentina, Australia, Belgium, Bosnia-Herzegovina, Brazil, Bulgaria, Canada, Colombia, Costa Rica, Croatia, Cuba, Czechia, Ecuador, Finland, France, Georgia, Germany, Greece, Hungary, Israel, Mexico, Namibia, New Zealand, Panama, Poland, Russia, Slovakia, South Africa, Spain, Sweden, Switzerland, Uganda, UK, Ukraine, Uruguay, USA.
Associate in 1 country:
Austria.
Consultative Status Consultative status granted from: *ECOSOC (#05331)* (Special); *UNESCO (#20322)* (Consultative Status); *ILO (#11123)* (Special List); *UNICEF (#20332)*; *Council of Europe (CE, #04881)* (Participatory Status). **IGO Relations** Accredited by (5): *Council of Europe (CE, #04881)*; *United Nations Office at Geneva (UNOG, #20597)*; United Nations Office at Paris; *United Nations Office at Vienna (UNOV, #20604)*; *United Nations (UN, #20515)*. Associated with Department of Global Communications of the United Nations. **NGO Relations** Represented at: *African Jewish Congress (AJC, #00349)*; *Committee of NGOs on Human Rights, Geneva (#04275)*; *Conference of Non-Governmental Organizations in Consultative Relationship with the United Nations (CONGO, #04635)*; *European Jewish Congress (EJC, #07609)*; *European Women's Lobby (EWL, #09102)*; *International Conference of NGOs (#12883)*; *Latin American Jewish Congress (LAJC, #16344)*; *NGO Committee on Disarmament, Peace and Security, New York NY (#17106)*; *NGO Committee on the Status of Women, Geneva (#17117)*; *NGO Committee to Stop Trafficking in Persons (NGO CSTIP)*; *NGO Committee on UNICEF (#17120)*; *Religions for Peace (RfP, #18831)*; *Vienna NGO Committee on the Family (#20774)*; *Vienna NGO Committee on the Status of Women (#20775)*; *World Jewish Congress (WJC, #21599)*. [2022/XB1746/**C**]

♦ International Council of Jurists 13037

Registered Office 134 Buckingham Palace Road, London, SW1 W9SA, UK. T. +442081335686. Fax +442077991687. E-mail: international.jurists6@gmail.com.
URL: http://www.internationaljurists.org/
History 2007. **Aims** Promote administration of justice and healthy development of law, suitable to social and economic needs of the people. **Structure** Directors appoint office bearers. **Languages** English. **Staff** 40.00 FTE, voluntary. **Finance** Sources: members' dues. Support from business houses and law firms. Annual budget: 75,000 GBP. **Events** *International Conference of Jurists and Writers* London (UK) 2022, *International Conference of Jurists and Writers* New Delhi (India) 2022, *Conference* Delhi (India) 2014, *Conference* London (UK) 2014, *Conference* Delhi (India) 2013.
Members Individuals in 77 countries:
Algeria, Angola, Argentina, Australia, Austria, Bahrain, Bangladesh, Belarus, Bhutan, Brazil, Brunei Darussalam, Bulgaria, Canada, China, Cuba, Cyprus, Czechia, Denmark, Egypt, Estonia, Fiji, Finland, France, Gambia, Germany, Ghana, Greece, Guyana, Hungary, Iceland, Indonesia, Ireland, Italy, Japan, Jordan, Kazakhstan, Kenya, Laos, Liberia, Lithuania, Malawi, Malaysia, Maldives, Mauritius, Mexico, Mongolia, Myanmar, Nepal, Netherlands, New Zealand, Nigeria, Norway, Oman, Pakistan, Philippines, Poland, Qatar, Romania, Russia, Seychelles, Singapore, South Africa, Spain, Sri Lanka, Switzerland, Tanzania UR, Thailand, Türkiye, Uganda, UK, Ukraine, United Arab Emirates, USA, Vanuatu, Vietnam, Zambia, Zimbabwe.
IGO Relations *International Court of Justice (ICJ, #13098)*; *International Criminal Court (ICC, #13108)*; *United Nations Office on Drugs and Crime (UNODC, #20596)*; Governments of Bangladesh, Bhutan, Malaysia, Maldives, Nepal and Singapore. [2022.02.21/XJ4614/**C**]

♦ International Council of Kinetography Laban (ICKL) 13038

Sec 14 ave des Gobelins, 75005 Paris, France. E-mail: secretary@ickl.org.
URL: http://www.ickl.org/
History 1959, UK, by Lisa Ullmann. Registered in USA. **Aims** Unite professional dancers, teachers and others using the Laban notation system for recording *dance* movements; guide the unified development of the system; encourage consistent standards of practice; act as the authoritative body with regard to *orthography*; promote research into *notation* matters likely to increase the efficiency and international usage of the system. **Languages** English. **Finance** Members' dues. Conference fees. **Events** *Biennial Conference* Tours (France) 2015, *Biennial Conference* Toronto, ON (Canada) 2013, *Biennial Conference* Toronto, ON (Canada) 2013, *Biennial Conference* Budapest (Hungary) 2011, *Biennial Conference* Bangkok (Thailand) 2009. **Publications** *Laban Notation Scores: an International Bibliography* – in 4 vols. Conference proceedings; index of technical matters and technical and non-technical papers from the biennial fora. Information Services: Library and documentation service.
Members Individuals in 22 countries:
Belgium, Brazil, Canada, China, Denmark, France, Germany, Greece, Hong Kong, Hungary, Japan, Mexico, Philippines, Serbia, Singapore, Slovenia, Spain, Sweden, Taiwan, Thailand, UK, USA. [2016/XD4698/v/**E**]

♦ International Council for Laboratory Animal Science (ICLAS) 13039

Conseil international des sciences de l'animal de laboratoire
Main Office Rue Washington 40, 1050 Brussels, Belgium. E-mail: info@iclas.org.
URL: http://www.iclas.org/
History 4 Dec 1956, Paris (France). Founded at meeting of consultants convened by *UNESCO (#20322)*, *Council for International Organizations of Medical Sciences (CIOMS, #04905)* and IUBS. Former names and other names: *International Committee on Laboratory Animals (ICLA)* – former (1956 to 1979); *Comité international sur les animaux de laboratoire* – former (1956 to 1979). Registration: Banque-Carrefour des Entreprises, No/ID: 0833.180.213, Start date: 26 Jan 2011, Belgium. **Aims** Advance human and animal health by promoting ethical care and use of laboratory animals in research worldwide. **Structure** Full General Assembly (every 4 years); abbreviated General Assembly (annual); Governing Board; Executive Committee; Committees (6); Regional Committees (5). **Languages** English. **Staff** Voluntary. **Finance** Sources: donations; members' dues. **Activities** Events/meetings; monitoring/evaluation; training/education. **Events** *Quadrennial International Symposium and General Assembly* Prague (Czechia) 2019, *Quadrennial International Symposium and General Assembly* Montréal, QC (Canada) 2015, *East Mediterranean regional meeting* Istanbul (Turkey)

2011, *Quadrennial international symposium and general assembly* Istanbul (Turkey) 2011, *Regional meeting / Congress* Montevideo (Uruguay) 2009. **Publications** *ICLAS FYI Bulletin. ICLAS Special Reprints. ICLAS/CSIC Working Group on Complimentary Methods.* Guidelines; symposia proceedings; surveys; handbooks; reports. Also joint publications with *Council for International Organizations of Medical Sciences (CIOMS, #04905).*
Members National members in 30 countries and territories:
Argentina, Australia, Austria, Belgium, Brazil, Canada, Costa Rica, Cuba, Denmark, Finland, Germany, Greece, India, Ireland, Israel, Italy, Japan, Korea Rep, Mexico, Netherlands, New Zealand, Norway, Poland, South Africa, Spain, Sri Lanka, Sweden, Thailand, Tunisia, USA.
Union members (6), listed in this Yearbook:
International Union of Basic and Clinical Pharmacology (IUPHAR, #15758); International Union of Biological Sciences (IUBS, #15760); International Union of Immunological Societies (IUIS, #15781); International Union of Nutritional Sciences (IUNS, #15796); International Union of Physiological Sciences (IUPS, #15800); International Union of Toxicology (IUTOX, #15824).
Scientific members in 27 countries and territories:
Argentina, Australia, Bangladesh, Belgium, Brazil, Canada, Chile, China, Croatia, Finland, France, Germany, Israel, Japan, Korea Rep, Mexico, Netherlands, New Zealand, Peru, Spain, Switzerland, Taiwan, Thailand, UK, Uruguay, USA, Venezuela.
Included in the above, 3 organizations listed in this Yearbook:
AAALAC International; Asociación Centroamericana, del Caribe y Mexicana de Animales de Laboratorio (ACCMAL, #02113); Scandinavian Society for Laboratory Animal Science (Scand-LAS, #19112).
Associate members in 14 countries:
Brazil, Denmark, Finland, France, Germany, Greece, India, Italy, Japan, Netherlands, Norway, Slovenia, UK, USA.
Honorary members in 8 countries:
Belgium, Canada, France, Germany, Japan, Norway, UK, USA.
IGO Relations *Council of Europe (CE, #04881); OIE – World Organisation for Animal Health (#17703); WHO (#20950).* **NGO Relations** Member of: *European Animal Research Association (EARA, #05903); Federation of European and International Associations Established in Belgium (FAIB, #09508); International Science Council (ISC, #14796).* Associate member of CIOMS; *International Union of Immunological Societies (IUIS, #15781).* Observer status with: *International Air Transport Association (IATA, #11614); World Veterinary Association (WVA, #21901).* [2020.09.04/XC1632/y/B]

♦ International Council on Large Electric Systems 13040

Conseil international des grands réseaux électriques (CIGRE)

Secretariat 21 rue d'Artois, 75008 Paris, France. T. +33153891290. Fax +33153891299. E-mail: comments@cigre.org.
URL: http://www.cigre.org/

History Mar 1921, Paris (France). Subsequently referred to as *International Conference on Large Electric Systems – Conférence internationale des grands réseaux électriques, International Conference on Large High Voltage Electric Systems – Conférence internationale des grands réseaux électriques à haute tension* and in English as *International Council on Large High Voltage Electric Systems.* Then changed title to *International Council on Large High Electric Systems.* Statutes adopted 18 Jun 1931; modified: 1933, 1939, 1946, 1948, 1966, 1972, 1974, 1982, 1984, 1990, 1992, 1994, 2000, 2002, 2006. Former names and other names: *International Conference of the Principal High-Tension Electrical Systems* – former (Mar 1921); *International Conference on Large Electric Systems* – former; *Conférence internationale des grands réseaux électriques* – former; *International Conference on Large High Voltage Electric Systems* – former; *Conférence internationale des grands réseaux électriques à haute tension* – former; *International Council on Large High Voltage Electric Systems* – former; *International Council on Large High Electric Systems* – former. **Aims** Develop and distribute technical knowledge in the field of the generation and transmission of high voltage electricity. **Structure** General Assembly (every 2 years). Administrative Council, consisting of about 56 members, representing National Committees. Steering Committee of 15, including President, Treasurer and Technical Committee Chairman. Technical Committee, comprising 2 Council members, Secretary-General and Chairmen of the 16 International Study Committees. National committees. Central Office. Membership and congresses open. **Languages** English, French. **Staff** 8.50 FTE, paid. **Finance** Sources: members' dues. **Activities** Deals with all main themes, i e organization of utilities, development and adaptation of grids, optimization of maintenance and life expectancy of electrical equipment, analysis of the impact on the environment, etc. Organizes: Biennial General Session (at even years, always in Paris); biennial Symposium (at odd years); Regional Meetings; local events. Study Committees (16): A1 – Rotating Electrical Machines; A2 – Transformers; A3 – High Voltage Equipment; B1 – Insulated Cables; B2 – Overhead Lines; B3 – Substations; B4 – HVDC and Power Electronics; B5 – Protections and Automations; C1 – System Development and Economics; C2 – System Control and Operation; C3 – System Environmental Performance; C4 – System Technical Performance; C5 – Electricity Markets and Regulation; C6 – Distribution Systems and Dispersed Generation; D1 – Materials and Emerging Test Techniques; D2 – Information Systems and Telecommunications. Working Groups (about 200). **Events** *Colloquium* Sendai (Japan) 2023, *Kyoto Symposium* Kyoto (Japan) 2022, *International Conference on Electric Power Equipment – Switching Technology* Seoul (Korea Rep) 2022, *Biennial General Session* Paris (France) 2021, *South-East European Regional Conference* Vienna (Austria) 2021. **Publications** *Electra* (6 a year) in English, French – journal. Congress proceedings; membership directory; technical brochures; reports.
Members As of 2009: individual (6,146) in the engineering, teaching and others involved in the industry; collective (1,105), including public or private companies, scientific organizations, research institutes and educational bodies. Individuals in 80 countries and territories:
Algeria, Argentina, Australia, Austria, Bahrain, Belgium, Benin, Bolivia, Bosnia-Herzegovina, Brazil, Bulgaria, Cameroon, Canada, Chile, China, Congo DR, Costa Rica, Côte d'Ivoire, Croatia, Cuba, Cyprus, Czechia, Denmark, Dominican Rep, Egypt, Estonia, Finland, France, Germany, Greece, Hungary, Iceland, India, Indonesia, Iran Islamic Rep, Ireland, Israel, Italy, Japan, Jordan, Korea Rep, Kuwait, Latvia, Libya, Malaysia, Mexico, Montenegro, Netherlands, New Zealand, Nigeria, North Macedonia, Norway, Oman, Paraguay, Peru, Philippines, Poland, Portugal, Qatar, Romania, Russia, Saudi Arabia, Serbia, Singapore, Slovakia, Slovenia, South Africa, Spain, Sweden, Switzerland, Syrian AR, Taiwan, Thailand, Türkiye, UK, Ukraine, United Arab Emirates, Uruguay, USA, Venezuela.
Collective members in 75 countries and territories:
Algeria, Argentina, Australia, Austria, Bahrain, Belgium, Bolivia, Bosnia-Herzegovina, Brazil, Burkina Faso, Canada, Chile, China, Côte d'Ivoire, Croatia, Cyprus, Czechia, Denmark, Ecuador, Egypt, Estonia, Finland, France, Germany, Greece, Hungary, Iceland, India, Indonesia, Iran Islamic Rep, Ireland, Israel, Italy, Japan, Jordan, Korea Rep, Kuwait, Lithuania, Malaysia, Malta, Mexico, Montenegro, Mozambique, Namibia, Netherlands, New Zealand, Norway, Oman, Paraguay, Peru, Poland, Portugal, Qatar, Romania, Russia, Saudi Arabia, Serbia, Singapore, Slovakia, Slovenia, South Africa, Spain, Sweden, Switzerland, Taiwan, Thailand, Tunisia, Türkiye, UK, Ukraine, United Arab Emirates, Uruguay, USA, Venezuela, Vietnam.
IGO Relations Working relations with: *International Telecommunication Union (ITU, #15673),* especially its Radiocommunication Sector. [2020/XC1685/C]

- ♦ International Council on Large High Electric Systems / see International Council on Large Electric Systems (#13040)
- ♦ International Council on Large High Voltage Electric Systems / see International Council on Large Electric Systems (#13040)
- ♦ International Council of Legal Enforcement (unconfirmed)
- ♦ International Council for the Life Sciences (unconfirmed)
- ♦ International Council of Literary Authors (inactive)
- ♦ International Council for Local Development (inactive)
- ♦ International Council for Local Environmental Initiatives / see Local Governments for Sustainability (#16507)
- ♦ International Council for Machinery Lubrication (internationally oriented national body)

♦ International Council on Magnetic Resonance in Biological Systems (ICMRBS) 13041

Chair 28 rue du Dr Roux, 75015 Paris, France.
Treas CUNY Advanced Science Research Center, 85 St Nicholas Terrace, New York NY 10031, USA.
URL: http://www.icmrbs.org/index.html

History 1964. Registration: Start date: 1992, USA, State of Wisconsin. **Aims** Foster development of the field of *biomolecular* magnetic resonance *spectroscopy* and magnetic resonance *imaging.* **Structure** Officers: Chairperson; Secretary-General; Treasurer. **Languages** English. **Staff** None. **Finance** Sources: donations. **Activities** Awards/prizes/competitions; events/meetings. **Events** *International Conference on Magnetic Resonance in Biological Systems* Boston, MA (USA) 2022, *International Conference on Magnetic Resonance in Biological Systems* Boston, MA (USA) 2021, *International Conference on Magnetic Resonance in Biological Systems* Boston, MA (USA) 2020, *International Conference on Magnetic Resonance in Biological Systems* Dublin (Ireland) 2018, *International Conference on Magnetic Resonance in Biological Systems* Kyoto (Japan) 2016. **Publications** Meeting abstracts. [2023.02.15/XM0021/E]

♦ International Council of Management Consulting Institutes (ICMCI) 13042

Exec Dir c/o Maurer Stager AG, Fraumünsterstr 17, Postfach 318, 8024 Zurich ZH, Switzerland. E-mail: cmc-global@cmc-global.org.
URL: http://www.cmc-global.org/

History 1987. **Aims** Promote closer working relationships among management consultants or organizations primarily dedicated to the registration or certification of individual management consultants, so as to accelerate achievement of mutual goals of national institutes; in particular assist them in raising standards of the *profession* of management consulting. **Structure** Board; Assembly of Delegates; Committees (4); Working Committees and Task Forces. **Languages** English. **Staff** 2.00 FTE, paid. Several voluntary. **Finance** Sources: members' dues. **Activities** Advocacy/lobbying/activism; awards/prizes/competitions; awareness raising; certification/accreditation; events/meetings; knowledge management/information dissemination; monitoring/evaluation; networking/liaising; politics/policy/regulatory; projects/programmes; research/documentation; standards/guidelines. **Events** *Euro Hub Meeting* Italy 2022, *CMC International Conference* Vienna (Austria) 2022, *General Assembly* Vienna (Austria) 2022, *International Consultants Day Meeting* Zurich (Switzerland) 2022, *Asia Pacific Hub Meeting* Singapore (Singapore) 2021. **Publications** *CMC Today* in English – newsletter. Articles; whitepapers.
Members Institutes of Consultants (46) in 44 countries and territories:
Armenia, Australia, Austria, Bangladesh, Brazil, Bulgaria, Canada, China, Croatia, Cyprus, Finland, Germany, Hong Kong, Hungary, India, Iran Islamic Rep, Ireland, Israel, Italy, Japan, Jordan, Kazakhstan, Korea Rep, Kosovo, Kyrgyzstan, Netherlands, New Zealand, Nigeria, North Macedonia, Philippines, Romania, Russia, Serbia, Singapore, South Africa, Sweden, Switzerland, Taiwan, Thailand, Türkiye, UK, Ukraine, USA, Zimbabwe.
Also members in the Caribbean. Membership countries not specified.
NGO Relations Member of (1): *Conference of Non-Governmental Organizations in Consultative Relationship with the United Nations (CONGO, #04635).* [2022.11.30/XN6552/B]

♦ International Council on the Management of Population Programs (ICOMP) 13043

Contact 534 Jalan Lima, Taman Ampang Utama, Selangor, 68000 Ampang, Malaysia. T. +60342573234 – +60342562358. Fax +60342560029.

History 30 Oct 1973, London (UK). Former names and other names: *International Committee on Management of Population Programmes* – former. Registration: Malaysia; Charity, No/ID: EIN 98-0037433, USA. **Aims** Seek excellence in management of population programmes. **Structure** General Assembly (every 3 years); Executive Committee; Secretariat, headed by Executive Director. **Languages** English. **Staff** 15.00 FTE, paid. **Finance** Support for activities from members and from donor agencies. Current member organizations making annual donations are the organizations from China, India and Indonesia. Current other donors: *European Commission (EC, #06633); Ford Foundation (#09858); International Bank for Reconstruction and Development (IBRD, #12317)* (World Bank); *The William and Flora Hewlett Foundation;* Packard Foundation; Partner's Secretariat; UNFPA; *WHO (#20950).* **Events** *Asia Pacific Conference on Reproductive and Sexual Health and Rights* Beijing (China) 2009, *Asia Pacific Conference on Reproductive and Sexual Health and Rights (APCRSHR)* Hyderabad (India) 2007, *Asia Pacific Conference on Reproductive and Sexual Health and Rights (APCRSHR)* Kuala Lumpur (Malaysia) 2005, *Asia Pacific conference on reproductive and sexual health and rights* Bangkok (Thailand) 2003, *International Conference* Kampala (Uganda) 2003. **Publications** *Series on Upscaling Innovations in Reproductive Health. Innovative Approaches to Population Programme Management.*
Members Full (54) in 32 countries:
Bangladesh, Brazil, Cambodia, China, Colombia, Costa Rica, Ecuador, Egypt, Ethiopia, Gambia, Ghana, India, Indonesia, Kenya, Malaysia, Mauritius, Morocco, Nepal, Nigeria, Pakistan, Philippines, Sri Lanka, Tanzania UR, Thailand, Tunisia, Türkiye, Uganda, UK, Venezuela, Vietnam, Zambia, Zimbabwe.
Consultative Status Consultative status granted from: *ECOSOC (#05331)* (General); *UNICEF (#20332); United Nations Population Fund (UNFPA, #20612).* **NGO Relations** Member of: *Asia Pacific Alliance for Sexual and Reproductive Health and Rights (APA, #01825); Reproductive Health Supplies Coalition (RHSC, #18847); Vienna NGO Committee on the Family (#20774).* [2013/XF1838/F]

♦ International Council of Marine Industry Associations (ICOMIA) ... 13044

Conseil international des associations des industries nautiques – Consejo Internacional de Asociaciones de Industrias Nauticas – Internationale Raad van Verenigingen voor Watersport Industrie

SG The Post House, Kitsmead Lane, Longcross, KT16 0EG, UK.
URL: https://www.icomia.com/

History 1967. Registration: Banque-Carrefour des Entreprises, No/ID: 0420.036.724, Start date: 21 Dec 1979, Belgium; EU Transparency Register, No/ID: 25344966554-43, Start date: 2 Sep 2011. **Aims** Promote *boating* as a leading international recreational activity by establishing a medium for the exchange of information on all matters related to the common interest: pollution, safety, service, quality, marinas, so as to stimulate the sale and use of pleasure boats and their equipment. Break down barriers to trade, including unnecessary or unviable legislation; promote awareness of the recreational marine industry's requirements and objectives. **Structure** Membership Meeting (annual, at Congress); Executive Committee; Working Committees. **Languages** English. **Staff** 4.50 FTE, paid. **Finance** Sources: meeting proceeds; members' dues. **Activities** Events/meetings; guidance/assistance/consulting; research/documentation. **Events** *World Marinas Conference* Dubai (United Arab Emirates) 2021, *Joint Congress* Split (Croatia) 2019, *World Marinas Conference* Athens (Greece) 2018, *Annual Congress* Berlin (Germany) 2018, *Asian Boating Forum* Singapore (Singapore) 2018. **Publications** *Boating Industry Statistics* (annual).
Members Full in 36 countries:
Argentina, Australia, Belgium, Brazil, Canada, China, Colombia, Croatia, Cyprus, Czechia, Denmark, Finland, France, Germany, Greece, Hungary, India, Ireland, Italy, Japan, Korea Rep, Lebanon, Netherlands, New Zealand, Norway, Poland, Portugal, Singapore, South Africa, Spain, Sweden, Switzerland, Thailand, Türkiye, UK, USA.
Consultative Status Consultative status granted from: *ECOSOC (#05331)* (Ros C); *International Maritime Organization (IMO, #14102).* **IGO Relations** Recognized by: *European Commission (EC, #06633).* **NGO Relations** Member of (1): *WATERBORNE (#20823).* Cooperates with (2): *European Boating Industry (EBI, #06377); Leisure Marine Association-MENA (LMA-MENA).* In liaison with technical committees of: *International Organization for Standardization (ISO, #14473).* [2022/XD1747/t/C]

♦ International Council on Materials Education (ICME) 13045

Pres MTSE, Discovery Park, Univ of North Texas, Denton TX 76207, USA. T. +19405653262 – +19405654337. Fax +19405654824. E-mail: icmatered@gmail.com.
URL: https://icme.unt.edu/

History Founded 1979, as US Materials Education Council. Current title adopted 2000. **Aims** Interact with organizations which have a component involving education in Materials Science and Engineering (MSE); organizes workshops and symposia. **Structure** Board; Office. **Languages** English. **Staff** 3.00 FTE, voluntary. **Finance** Subscription fees; participation fees. **Activities** Events/meetings; networking/liaising; publishing activities. **Publications** *Journal on Materials Education.*
Members Individuals in 26 countries:
Argentina, Australia, Austria, Brazil, Canada, China, Colombia, France, Georgia, India, Israel, Italy, Lithuania, Malaysia, Mexico, Poland, Portugal, Romania, Russia, Singapore, Slovakia, Spain, Sweden, Türkiye, UK, USA.
IGO Relations None. **NGO Relations** Cooperates with: *International Council for Science (ICSU, inactive); International Union of Materials Research Societies (IUMRS, #15790);* Materials Research Society; Scientific Committee of *World Forum on Advanced Materials (POLYCHAR).* [2022/XJ7650/v/F]

♦ International Council of Medical Acupuncture and Related Techniques (ICMART) 13046

Sec address not obtained.
Gen Sec address not obtained.
Registered Office Rue de l'Amazone 62, 1000 Brussels, Belgium.
URL: http://www.icmart.org/

History 19 Oct 1983, Vienna (Austria). Founded at First World Congress of Scientific Acupuncture. Registration: Belgium. **Aims** Group associations of acupuncture and similar techniques whose members are qualified through a recognized institute of medicine, dentistry or veterinary practice, strengthening the links between such associations through contacts and exchanges (both personal and of ideas); contribute to cultural and scientific progress in the field, both in research and in practice of therapeutic techniques. **Structure** General Assembly (every 2 years at Congress) elects Officers (who comprise Executive Committee) and Board of Directors (7 to 15 members). **Finance** Sources: members' dues. **Events** *World Congress on Medical Acupuncture* Athens (Greece) 2021, *World Congress on Medical Acupuncture* Athens (Greece) 2020, *World Congress on Medical Acupuncture* Gold Coast, QLD (Australia) 2019, *World Congress on Medical Acupuncture* Munich (Germany) 2018, *World Medical Acupuncture Congress* Mexico City (Mexico) 2017.
Members Effective, Observer, Patron, Honorary. Members in 44 countries:
Armenia, Australia, Austria, Belarus, Belgium, Brazil, Bulgaria, Canada, Croatia, Cyprus, Czechia, Denmark, Estonia, Finland, France, Georgia, Germany, Greece, Hungary, Indonesia, Ireland, Israel, Italy, Japan, Latvia, Lithuania, Luxembourg, Mexico, Netherlands, New Zealand, Norway, Poland, Portugal, Romania, Russia, Serbia, Slovakia, Slovenia, Spain, Sweden, Türkiye, UK, Ukraine, USA.
NGO Relations Member of: *European Public Health Alliance (EPHA, #08297)*; *CAMDOC Alliance (#03402)*. Affiliated with: *EUROCAM (#05653)*. [2020/XF1340/**C**]

♦ International Council for Medicinal and Aromatic Plants (ICMAP) . . 13047

SG Anadolu Univ, Pharmacy Fac, 26470 Eskisehir/Eskisehir, Türkiye.
URL: http://www.icmap.org/

History 8 Jun 1993, Paris (France), following 1st World Congress on Medicinal and Aromatic Plants (WOCMAP) organized by *International Society for Horticultural Science (ISHS, #15180)*, 1992, Maastricht (Netherlands). **Aims** Promote international understanding, cooperation and exchange between national and international organizations on the role of medicinal and aromatic plants in science, medicine and industry, and coordinate their activities; promote knowledge on use of traditional medicine. **Structure** General Meeting (every 2 years); Bureau; Board; Regional Representatives; Committees; Task forces; Secretariat. **Languages** English. **Staff** Voluntary. **Finance** Members' dues. Co-sponsored by: *UNESCO (#20322)*; IUPHAR; IUBS. Other sources: congresses; sale of publications; grants; donations. **Activities** Events/meetings; projects/programmes; standards/guidelines; knowledge management/information dissemination. **Events** *Quinquennial World Congress on Medicinal and Aromatic Plants for Human Welfare* Famagusta (Cyprus) 2019, *Quinquennial World Congress on Medicinal and Aromatic Plants for Human Welfare / Quinquennial World Congress* Brisbane, QLD (Australia) 2014, *International symposium on essential oils* Antalya (Turkey) 2011, *International symposium on medicinal and aromatic plants* Antigua (Guatemala) 2011, *Quinquennial world congress on medicinal and aromatic plants for human welfare* Pretoria (South Africa) 2008. **Publications** *ICMAP Newsletter*. Information Services: establishing an information centre.
Members Council comprises representatives of institutional members; representatives of international or national supporting organizations; representatives of affiliated organizations or institutes; associated individuals. Regional representatives in 17 countries:
Argentina, Austria, Belgium, Ethiopia, France, Germany, Greece, Hungary, India, Italy, Netherlands, Poland, Sri Lanka, Switzerland, Türkiye, UK, USA.
Representatives of the following international bodies (6):
Bioversity International (#03262); *FAO (#09260)*; *International Pharmaceutical Federation (#14566)*; *International Union of Basic and Clinical Pharmacology (IUPHAR, #15758)*; ISHS; *World Agroforestry Centre (ICRAF, #21072)*.
NGO Relations Scientific member of: *International Union of Biological Sciences (IUBS, #15760)*. [2019.02.14/XD4392/y/**D**]

♦ International Council on Metals and the Environment (inactive)

♦ International Council on Mining and Metals (ICMM) 13048

CEO 34-37 Liverpool Street, London, EC2M 7PP, UK. T. +442074675070. E-mail: info@icmm.com.
URL: https://www.icmm.com/

History 24 Oct 2001, London (UK). Founded, taking over activities of *International Council on Metals and the Environment (ICME, inactive)*. Registration: Companies House, No/ID: 08164875, Start date: 1 Aug 2012, England and Wales; EU Transparency Register, No/ID: 578631147955-49, Start date: 21 Oct 2022. **Aims** Improve *sustainable development* performance in the mining, minerals and metals *industry*; represent views and interests of members and serve as a principal point of engagement with the industry's key constituencies in the international arena; promote science-based regulations and material-choice decisions that encourage market access and the safe *production*, use, reuse and *recycling* of metals and minerals; identify and advocate use of good practices to address sustainable development issues within the industry; promote cooperation in the industry to best ensure continued access to land, capital and markets, and to build trust and respect by demonstrating ability to contribute successfully to sustainable development. **Structure** Council (meets twice a year); Principal Liaisons Committee; specialist programme committees; Associations Co-ordination Group; Secretariat. Includes *Committee for Mineral Reserves International Reporting Standards (CRIRSCO, #04272)*. **Languages** Chinese, English, French, Japanese, Portuguese, Russian, Spanish. **Staff** 17.50 FTE, paid. **Finance** Sources: members' dues. **Activities** Guidance/assistance/consulting; networking/liaising. **Events** *Conference on how to manage social and environmental risk and opportunity* London (UK) 2010, *Greenland sustainable mineral and petrolium development conference* Copenhagen (Denmark) 2009, *Conference of metallurgists* Toronto, ON (Canada) 2007, *Annual meeting* London (UK) 2003. **Publications** *Good Practice Newsletter*. *A Practical Guide to Catchment-based Water Management for the Mining and Metals Industry* (2015); *Hazard Assessment of Ores and Concentrates for Marine Transport* (2014); *Health and Safety Performance Indicators* (2014); *The Role of Mining in National Economies – 2nd ed* (2014); *Water Stewardship Framework* (2014). Annual Review; toolkits; reports; discussion papers; guidance papers.
Members Mining and metals companies (21); national and regional mining associations and global commodity associations (35). National associations in 10 countries:
Australia, Brazil, Chile, Colombia, Ghana, India, Peru, Philippines, South Africa, Zambia.
Included in the above, 11 organizations listed in this Yearbook:
Association européenne des métaux (EUROMETAUX, #02578); *CASI Institute (#03595)*; *Cobalt Institute (CI, #04076)*; *European Association of Mining Industries, Metal Ores and Industrial Minerals (EUROMINES, #06122)*; *International Aluminium Institute (IAI, #11643)*; *International Copper Association (ICA, #12962)*; *International Iron Metallics Association (IIMA, #13953)*; *International Lead Association (ILA, #14009)*; *International Manganese Institute (IMnI, #14083)*; *International Molybdenum Association (IMOA, #14178)*; *Nickel Institute (#17133)*.
Consultative Status Consultative status granted from: *UNCTAD (#20285)* (Special Category); *UNEP (#20299)*.
IGO Relations Cooperates with (1): *United Nations Committee of Experts on the Transport of Dangerous Goods and on the Globally Harmonized System of Classification and Labelling of Chemicals (Committee of Experts on TDG and GHS, #20543)*. **NGO Relations** Cooperates with (1): *Business and Industry Advisory Committee to the OECD (BIAC, #03385)*. Supports (1): *Life Cycle Initiative (LCI, #16464)*. Also links with national centres, agencies and companies. [2022/XD8509/y/**B**]

♦ International Council on Monuments and Sites (ICOMOS) 13049

Conseil international des monuments et des sites – Consejo Internacional de Monumentos y Sitios – Mezhdunarodnyj Sovet po Voprosam Pamjatnikov i Dostoprimecatelnyh Mest

Dir Gen 11 rue du Séminaire de Conflans, 94220 Charenton-le-Pont, France. T. +33141941759. Fax +33148931916. E-mail: secretariat@icomos.org.
URL: https://www.icomos.org/

History 21 Jun 1965, Warsaw (Poland). Founded at constituent General Assembly, following 1st *International Congress of Architects and Specialists of Historic Buildings*, 1957, Paris (France) and 2nd such congress, 1964, Venice (Italy), at which the first 2 of 13 resolutions adopted were (1) *International Restoration Charter (Venice Charter) – Charte internationale de la restauration (Charte de Venise)* and (2) (put forward by UNESCO) providing for the creation of ICOMOS. Statues amended by 5th General Assembly, 22 May 1978, Moscow (USSR); 18th General Assembly, 12 Nov 2014, Florence (Italy); Extraordinary General Assembly, 12 Dec 2017, Delhi (India). **Aims** Promote *conservation*, protection, use and enhancement of monuments, building complexes and sites. **Structure** General Assembly (annual); Extraordinary General Assembly (every 3 years); Board; Advisory Committee; Scientific Council; International Secretariat. International Scientific Committees (currently 31); National committees (over 100); Regional Groups. **Languages** English, French, Russian, Spanish. **Staff** 10.00 FTE, paid. **Finance** Sources: members' dues. Other sources: gifts and bequests; subvention from UNESCO and governmental subsidies; voluntary contributions.
Activities Advocacy/lobbying/activism; events/meetings; management of treaties and agreements; research/documentation. International Committees (31):
- *ICOMOS International Committee on Twentieth Century Heritage (ISC20C, see: #13049)*;
- *ICOMOS International Scientific Committee on Analysis and Restoration of Structures of Architectural Heritage (ISCARSAH, #11072)*;
- *ICOMOS International Scientific Committee on Archaeological Heritage Management (ICAHM, #11073)*;
- *ICOMOS – IFLA International Scientific Committee on Cultural Landscapes (ISCCL, #11059)*;
- *ICOMOS International Committee on Cultural Routes (#11060)*;
- *ICOMOS International Cultural Tourism Committee (ICTC, #11070)*;
- *ICOMOS International Committee on Earthen Architectural Heritage (#11061)*;
- *ICOMOS International Committee on Economics of Conservation (#11062)*;
- *ICOMOS International Scientific Committee on Energy and Sustainability (ISCES, #11075)*;
- *ICOMOS International Scientific Committee on Fortifications and Military Heritage (ICOFORT, #11076)*;
- *CIPA Heritage Documentation (CIPA, #03929)*;
- *ICOMOS International Committee on Historic Cities, Towns and Villages (ICOMOS CIVVIH, #11063)*;
- *ICOMOS International Committee on Intangible Cultural Heritage (ICICH, #11064)*;
- *ICOMOS International Committee on Interpretation and Presentation (ICIP, #11065)*;
- *ICOMOS International Scientific Committee on Legal, Administrative and Financial Issues (#11077)*;
- *ICOMOS International Scientific Committee on Mural Paintings (ISCMP, #11078)*;
- *ICOMOS International Scientific Committee on Places of Religion and Ritual (PRERICO, #11079)*;
- *ICOMOS International Polar Heritage Committee (IPHC, #11071)*;
- *ICOMOS International Scientific Committee on Risk Preparedness (ICORP, #11080)*;
- *ICOMOS International Committee on Rock Art (#11066)*;
- *ICOMOS International Scientific Committee for the Conservation of Stained Glass (ISCCSG, #11074)*;
- *ICOMOS International Scientific Committee for Stone (ISCS, #11082)*;
- *ICOMOS International Committee on Theory and Philosophy of Conservation and Restoration (TheoPhilos, #11067)*;
- *ICOMOS International Scientific Committee on Shared Built Heritage (SBH ISC, #11081)*;
- *ICOMOS International Training Committee (#11084)*;
- *ICOMOS International Committee on the Underwater Cultural Heritage (#11068)*;
- *ICOMOS International Committee for Vernacular Architecture (#11069)*;
- *ICOMOS International Wood Committee (IIWC, #11085)*;
- *ICOMOS International c Committee on Industrial Heritage (ISCIH)*;
- *ICOMOS International Scientific Committee on Water and Heritage (ISCWater, #11083)*;
- *ICOMOS International Committee on Aerospace Heritage (ISCoAH)*.

Manages the following treaties/agreements: *Convention Concerning the Protection of the World Cultural and Natural Heritage (World Heritage Convention, 1972)*.
Events *Triennial General Assembly* Sydney, NSW (Australia) 2023, *Heritage and Metropolis International Workshop* Seoul (Korea Rep) 2021, *Integrating Heritage into the SDGs* Seoul (Korea Rep) 2020, *Triennial General Assembly* Sydney, NSW (Australia) 2020, *Modern Asean Architecture International Conference* Singapore (Singapore) 2019. **Publications** *ICOMOS e-News*; *ICOMOS Newsletter* in English, French. Bibliographies produced by ICOMOS Documentation Centre on the 14 areas of ICOMOS research; symposium proceedings.
Information Services *Database on the Conservation of the Architectural Heritage* – financed under a special UNESCO contract; *ICOMOS Documentation Centre Database*; *UNESCO-ICOMOS Documentation Centre – Centre de documentation UNESCO-ICOMOS* – set up 1966, builds and keeps up-to-date a body of reference material on conservation, protection, use and rehabilitation of the architectural heritage.
Members National Committees in 112 countries:
Albania, Andorra, Argentina, Armenia, Australia, Austria, Azerbaijan, Bahrain, Bangladesh, Barbados, Belarus, Belgium, Bolivia, Bosnia-Herzegovina, Brazil, Bulgaria, Burkina Faso, Cameroon, Canada, Chad, Chile, China, Colombia, Comoros, Costa Rica, Côte d'Ivoire, Croatia, Cuba, Cyprus, Czechia, Denmark, Dominican Rep, Estonia, Ethiopia, Finland, France, Georgia, Germany, Greece, Guatemala, Haiti, Honduras, Hungary, Iceland, India, Indonesia, Iran Islamic Rep, Ireland, Israel, Italy, Japan, Jordan, Kazakhstan, Korea Rep, Latvia, Lebanon, Lithuania, Luxembourg, Madagascar, Malaysia, Mali, Malta, Mauritius, Mexico, Moldova, Monaco, Mongolia, Montenegro, Morocco, Myanmar, Nepal, Netherlands, New Zealand, Nicaragua, Nigeria, North Macedonia, Norway, Oman, Pakistan, Palestine, Panama, Peru, Philippines, Poland, Portugal, Qatar, Romania, Russia, Saudi Arabia, Senegal, Serbia, Seychelles, Singapore, Slovakia, Slovenia, South Africa, Spain, Sri Lanka, Sweden, Switzerland, Syrian AR, Thailand, Trinidad-Tobago, Tunisia, Türkiye, UK, Ukraine, United Arab Emirates, Uruguay, USA, Venezuela, Zambia.
Regional group for Pacific islands in 1 country:
Fiji.
Consultative Status Consultative status granted from: *UNESCO (#20322)* (Associate Status).
IGO Relations Accredited by (1): *United Nations Office at Vienna (UNOV, #20604)*.
Cooperates in related fields of interest with:
- *Arab League Educational, Cultural and Scientific Organization (ALECSO, #01003)*;
- *Council of Europe (CE, #04881)*;
- *Intergovernmental Committee for Promoting the Return of Cultural Property to its Countries of Origin or its Restitution in case of Illicit Appropriation (#11476)*;
- *International Centre for the Study of the Preservation and Restoration of Cultural Property (ICCROM, #12521)*;
- *League of Arab States (LAS, #16420)*;
- *Mediterranean Action Plan (MAP, #16638)*;
- *OAS (#17629)*;
- *SEAMEO Regional Centre for Archaeology and Fine Arts (SEAMEO SPAFA, #19169)*;
- *UNEP (#20299)*;
- *UNESCO Regional Bureau for Culture for Latin America and the Caribbean (#20317)*;
- *United Nations Institute for Training and Research (UNITAR, #20576)*;
- *World Heritage Centre (WHC, #21566)*;
- *World Heritage Committee (#21567)*;
- *World Heritage Fund (#21568)*;
- *World Tourism Organization (UNWTO, #21861)*.

NGO Relations Member of (4): *European Heritage Alliance 3.3 (#07477)*; *International Centre for Earth Construction (#12485)*; *International Coordinating Committee on the Safeguarding and Development of the Historic Site of Angkor (ICC-Angkor, #12954)*; *International Federation of Interior Architects / Designers (IFI, #13460)*. Instrumental in setting up (2): *Blue Shield International (BSI, #03286)*; *International Committee of the Blue Shield (ICBS, inactive)*. In liaison with technical committees of: *Comité européen de normalisation (CEN, #04162)*. Contact with: *International Society for Photogrammetry and Remote Sensing (ISPRS, #15362)*. [2023/XB1748/**B**]

♦ International Council of Multiple Birth Organisations (ICOMBO) . . . 13050

Chair 29 Grange Cct, Beaconsfield VIC 3805, Australia. E-mail: chair@icombo.org.
URL: https://icombo.org/

History 1980, Jerusalem (Israel). Founded at Congress of *International Society for Twin Studies (ISTS, #15526)*. Former names and other names: *COMBO* – former. **Aims** Collaborate globally to raise awareness of the unique health, educational, emotional and social needs of all multiples and their families. **Structure** Board of Directors. **Finance** Sources: members' dues. **Activities** Events/meetings; research/documentation.
Publications *ICOMBO Newsletter* (4 a year).
Members Organizations in 21 countries:
Argentina, Australia, Canada, Czechia, Denmark, Finland, France, Germany, Japan, Liberia, Mexico, New Zealand, Nigeria, Norway, Rwanda, Serbia, Sierra Leone, Spain, Trinidad-Tobago, UK, USA.
Twinless Twins Support Group International (TTSGI).
NGO Relations Partner of (2): *European Foundation for the Care of Newborn Infants (EFCNI, #07344)*; *Global Alliance for Newborn Care (GLANCE, #10215)*. [2022/AA3150/y/**C**]

♦ International Council of the Museum of Modern Art (internationally oriented national body)

♦ International Council of Museums (ICOM) 13051

Conseil international des musées – Consejo Internacional de Museos – Internationaler Museumsrat

Dir Gen Maison de l'UNESCO, 1 rue Miollis, 75732 Paris CEDEX 15, France. T. +33147340500. Fax +33143067862. E-mail: secretariat@icom.museum.
Pres address not obtained.
URL: http://icom.museum/

History 16 Nov 1946, Paris (France). EU Transparency Register: 333322034810-67. **Aims** Work for society and its development, ensuring conservation and protection of cultural goods. **Structure** General Assembly (annual); Executive Board; Advisory Council; National and International Committees; Secretariat, headed by Director General. **Languages** English, French, Spanish. **Staff** 24.00 FTE, paid. **Finance** Sources: members'

dues. Other sources: UNESCO subvention; contracts; fund raising activities of the ICOM Foundation and Secretariat General.
Activities Events/meetings; knowledge management/information dissemination; networking/liaising; research/documentation; standards/guidelines. *'National Committees'* provide the principal instrument of communication between ICOM and its members and organize international exchange programmes.
'International Committees' (31, meeting annually) represent different types of museum or particular disciplines and carry out ICOM's major objectives: exchange of scientific information at international level; drawing up of professional standards; adoption of rules and recommendations; realization of joint projects. They are:
- *ICOM International Committee for Architecture and Museum Techniques (ICAMT, see: #13051);*
- *ICOM International Committee for Audiovisual and New Technologies of Image and Sound (AVICOM, see: #13051);*
- *ICOM International Committee for Collecting (COMCOL, #11055);*
- *ICOM International Committee for the Collections and Activities of Museums of Cities (CAMOC, #11056);*
- *ICOM International Committee for Conservation (ICOM-CC, see: #13051);*
- *ICOM International Committee for Documentation (CIDOC, see: #13051);*
- *ICOM International Committee for Education and Cultural Action (CECA, see: #13051);*
- *ICOM International Committee for Egyptology (CIPEG, see: #13051);*
- *ICOM International Committee for Exhibition Exchange (ICEE, see: #13051);*
- *ICOM International Committee for Historic House Museums (DEMHIST, #11057);*
- *ICOM International Committee for Literary Museums (ICLM, see: #13051);*
- *ICOM International Committee for Marketing and Public Relations (MPR, see: #13051);*
- *ICOM International Committee for Money and Banking Museums (ICOMON, see: #13051);*
- *ICOM International Committee for Museology (ICOFOM, see: #13051);*
- *ICOM International Committee for Museum Management (INTERCOM, see: #13051);*
- *ICOM International Committee for Museum Security (ICMS, see: #13051);*
- *ICOM International Committee for Museums and Collections of Archaeology and History (ICMAH, see: #13051);*
- *ICOM International Committee for Museums and Collections of Costume (see: #13051);*
- *ICOM International Committee for Museums and Collections of Ethnography (ICME, see: #13051);*
- *ICOM International Committee for Museums and Collections of Glass (see: #13051);*
- *ICOM International Committee for Museums and Collections of Natural History (ICOM NATHIST, see: #13051);*
- *ICOM International Committee for Museums and Collections of Science and Technology (CIMUSET, see: #13051);*
- *ICOM International Committee of Museums and Collections of Instruments and Music (CIMCIM, see: #13051);*
- *ICOM International Committee for Regional Museums (ICR, see: #13051);*
- *ICOM International Committee for the Training of Personnel (ICTOP, see: #13051);*
- *ICOM International Committee for University Museums and Collections (UMAC, #11058);*
- *International Committee of ICOM for Museums and Collections of Modern Art (CIMAM, see: #13051);*
- *International Committee of Memorial Museums for the Remembrance of Victims of Public Crimes (IC MEMO, #12784);*
- *International Committee of Museums and Collections of Arms and Military History (ICOMAM, #12790);*
- *International Committee for Museums and Collections of Decorative Arts and Design (ICDAD, see: #13051);*
- *International Committee for Museums and Collections of Fine Arts (ICFA, see: #13051).*

'Regional Alliances' (5):
- *ICOM Regional Alliance for South East Europe (ICOM SEE, see: #13051);*
- *ICOM Regional Alliance for Arab Countries (ICOM-ARAB, see: #13051);*
- *ICOM Asia-Pacific Regional Alliance (ICOM-ASPAC, see: #13051);*
- *ICOM European Regional Alliance (ICOM-Europe, see: #13051);*
- *ICOM Latin American and Caribbean Regional Alliance (ICOM-LAC, see: #13051).*

Events *Interim Meeting* Helsinki (Finland) 2022, *General Conference* Prague (Czechia) 2022, *Symposium* Hokkaido (Japan) 2019, *Meeting* Osaka (Japan) 2019, *Tokyo Seminar* Tokyo (Japan) 2019. **Publications** Conference proceedings; technical books and brochures; reports and papers on museums. Information Services: Administers: *UNESCO-ICOM Museum Information Centre (see: #13051)* – repository of information on ICOM publications and activities.
Members Categories: Individual; Institutional; Supporting; Honorary. National Committees in 117 countries:
Afghanistan, Albania, Algeria, Andorra, Angola, Argentina, Armenia, Australia, Austria, Azerbaijan, Bangladesh, Barbados, Belarus, Belgium, Benin, Bolivia, Bosnia-Herzegovina, Botswana, Brazil, Bulgaria, Burkina Faso, Cambodia, Cameroon, Canada, Chile, China, Colombia, Congo Brazzaville, Congo DR, Costa Rica, Côte d'Ivoire, Croatia, Cuba, Cyprus, Czechia, Denmark, Dominican Rep, Ecuador, Egypt, Estonia, Eswatini, Finland, France, Georgia, Germany, Ghana, Greece, Guatemala, Haiti, Hungary, Iceland, India, Indonesia, Iran Islamic Rep, Ireland, Israel, Italy, Japan, Kenya, Korea Rep, Kyrgyzstan, Latvia, Lebanon, Lithuania, Luxembourg, Madagascar, Malaysia, Mali, Malta, Mauritania, Mexico, Moldova, Monaco, Mongolia, Montenegro, Morocco, Namibia, Nepal, Netherlands, New Zealand, Nicaragua, Niger, Nigeria, North Macedonia, Norway, Oman, Panama, Paraguay, Peru, Philippines, Poland, Portugal, Romania, Russia, Senegal, Serbia, Singapore, Slovakia, Slovenia, South Africa, Spain, Sri Lanka, Sweden, Switzerland, Thailand, Togo, Tunisia, Türkiye, UK, Ukraine, United Arab Emirates, Uruguay, USA, Venezuela, Vietnam, Zambia, Zimbabwe.
International Affiliated Organizations (16):
Association internationale des musées d'agriculture (AIMA, #02720); *Association of European Open Air Museums (AEOM, #02527)*; *Commonwealth Association of Museums (CAM, #04305)*; *Hands On ! International Association of Children's Museums (HO!I, #10856)*; International Association of Archaeological Open-Air Museums and Experimental Archaeology, or EXARC; *International Association of Customs Museums (IACM, #11831)*; *International Association of Museum Facility Administrators (IAMFA, #12039)*; *International Association of Museums of History (IAMH, #12040)*; *International Association of Transport and Communications Museums (IATM, #12237)*; *International Confederation of Architectural Museums (ICAM, #12846)*; *International Congress of Maritime Museums (ICMM, #12896)*; *International Council of African Museums (AFRICOM, #12986)*; *Mouvement international pour une nouvelle muséologie (MINOM, #16866)*; *Museums Association of the Caribbean (MAC, #16909)*; *Pacific Island Museums Association (PIMA, #17959)*; *Société internationale des bibliothèques et des musées des arts du spectacle (SIBMAS, #19475)*.
Consultative Status Consultative status granted from: *ECOSOC (#05331)* (Ros C); *UNESCO (#20322)* (Associate Status); *World Intellectual Property Organization (WIPO, #21593)* (Observer Status). **IGO Relations** Memorandum of Understanding signed with: *World Customs Organization (WCO, #21350)*. Agreement with: *Arab League Educational, Cultural and Scientific Organization (ALECSO, #01003)*; *International Criminal Police Organization – INTERPOL (ICPO-INTERPOL, #13110)*. Associated with Department of Global Communications of the United Nations. **NGO Relations** Member of (2): *European Heritage Alliance 3.3 (#07477)*; *NGO-UNESCO Liaison Committee (#17127)*. [2017.09.25/XB1749/y/**B**]

♦ International Council of Music Authors 13052

Conseil International des Créateurs de Musique (CIAM) – Consejo Internacional de Creadores de Música

Secretariat c/o CISAC, 20-26 boulevard du Parc, 92200 Neuilly-sur-Seine, France. T. +33155620850. Fax +33155620860. E-mail: cisac@cisac.org.
URL: http://www.ciamcreators.org/

History Set up 1966, as an International Council of *Confédération internationale des sociétés d'auteurs et compositeurs (CISAC, #04563)*. Original title: *International Council of Authors and Composers of Music – Conseil international des auteurs et compositeurs de musique (CIAM)*. **Aims** Unify the voice of music creators of all repertoires; be the worldwide umbrella organisation for composers and creators of music. **Structure** General Assembly; Executive Committee. **Activities** Events/meetings; advocacy/lobbying/activism; research/documentation. **Events** *Meeting* Amsterdam (Netherlands) 2005, *Composer and technology* Reykjavik (Iceland) 1995. **NGO Relations** Partner organizations: *Alianza Latinoamericana de Compositores y Autores de Música (ALCAM, #00632)*; *Asia-Pacific Music Creators' Alliance (APMA, #01960)*; *European Composer and Songwriter Alliance (ECSA, #06691)*; Music Creators North America (MCNA); *Pan-African Composers' and Songwriters' Alliance (PACSA, #18047)*. [2018/XD3585/**E**]

♦ International Council of the National Academy of Television Arts and Sciences / see International Academy of Television Arts and Sciences

♦ International Council for Near Infrared Spectroscopy (ICNIRS) 13053

Pres Dept Statistical Science, UCL, Gower Street, London, WC1E 6BT, UK. T. +44276791873. Fax +44231083105.
Hon Sec address not obtained.
URL: http://www.icnirs.org/

History Jun 1986, Budapest (Hungary). Founded during the International NIR Meeting organized by Karoly Kaffka. Suggestion to form an international body for NIR spectroscopy came from Prof Vadim Krischenko of the Central Institute of Agrochemical Service, Moscow (USSR). Former names and other names: *International Committee for Near Infrared Spectroscopy* – former (1986 to 2003). **Aims** Advance the theory and practice of near infrared spectroscopy. **Structure** Council Management Committee; Executive Committee; Advisory Committee. **Languages** English. **Staff** Voluntary. **Finance** Sources: members' dues. **Activities** Awards/prizes/competitions; events/meetings; training/education. **Events** *Conference* Beijing (China) 2021, *Conference* Gold Coast, QLD (Australia) 2019, *NIR spectroscopy at work in industry* Copenhagen (Denmark) 2017, *Conference* Foz do Iguaçu (Brazil) 2015, *Picking up good vibrations* Montpellier (France) 2013. **Publications** *Journal of Near Infrared Spectroscopy* (6 a year) – print, electronic and online; *NIR News* (8 a year). **NGO Relations** Also links with multi-national organizations. [2021.09.01/XM2758/**E**]

♦ International Council for New Initiatives in East-West Cooperation / see International Vienna Council (#15853)

♦ International Council of Nurses (ICN) 13054

Conseil international des infirmières (CII) – Consejo Internacional de Enfermeras (CIE)

CEO Place Jean-Marteau 3, 1201 Geneva, Switzerland. T. +41229080100. Fax +41229080101. E-mail: williamson@icn.ch – icn@icn.ch.
Main Website: http://www.icn.ch/

History 1899, London (UK). First Congress and Grand Council meeting held in 1901, Buffalo NY (USA). Accepted into official relations with the World Health Organization, 1948. Registration: Switzerland. **Aims** Represent nursing worldwide; advance the nursing profession; promote the well-being of nurses; advocate for health in all policies. **Structure** Council of National Association Representatives (CNR), meets every 2 years; Board of Directors; Sub-committees. International Council of Nurses Foundation (ICNF). **Languages** English, French, Spanish. **Staff** 25.00 FTE, paid. **Finance** Sources: donations; members' dues; sale of publications. *Florence Nightingale International Foundation (FNIF, #09798)* raises funds to support work of ICN. **Activities** Advocacy/lobbying/activism; certification/accreditation; events/meetings; networking/liaising; politics/policy/regulatory; projects/programmes; training/education. **Events** *Congress* Helsinki (Finland) 2025, *Congress* Montréal, QC (Canada) 2023, *International Nurse Practitioner/Advanced Practice Nursing Network Conference* Dublin (Ireland) 2022, *Congress* Geneva (Switzerland) 2021, *ICN Nurse Practitioner/Advanced Practice Nursing Network Conference* Halifax, NS (Canada) 2021. **Publications** *International Nursing Review* (4 a year). ICN Position Statements; ICN Code of Ethics for Nurses; books; guidelines; monographs; media materials; standards. **Members** National Nursing Associations in 135 countries and territories. Membership countries not specified. **Consultative Status** Consultative status granted from: *ECOSOC (#05331)* (Ros C); *ILO (#11123)* (Special List); *WHO (#20950)* (Official Relations); *UNCTAD (#20285)* (Special Category); *UNICEF (#20332)*. **IGO Relations** Associated with Department of Global Communications of the United Nations. [2022.10.19/XB1750/**F**]

♦ International Council of Onomastic Sciences (ICOS) 13055

Sec Box 135, SE-751 04 Uppsala, Sweden.
URL: http://icosweb.net

History 15 Jul 1949, Brussels (Belgium). Founded at 3rd *International Congress of Toponymy and Anthroponymy*. Current statutes adopted Aug 2002, Uppsala (Sweden). Former names and other names: *International Committee of Onomastic Sciences* – former (1949 to 1993); *Comité international des sciences onomastiques (CISO)* – former (1949 to 1993). **Aims** Promote advancement, representation and coordination of the study of *proper names* on an international level and in an interdisciplinary context. **Structure** General Assembly; Board of Directors; Executive Committee. Working Groups. **Languages** English, French, German. **Staff** 12.00 FTE, voluntary. **Finance** Sources: members' dues. **Activities** Events/meetings. Onomastics Online lecture series (see: https://icosweb.net/onomastics-online/) **Events** *Triennial Congress* Helsinki (Finland) 2024, *Triennial Congress* Krakow (Poland) 2021, *Triennial Congress* Krakow (Poland) 2020, *Triennial Congress* Debrecen (Hungary) 2017, *Triennial Congress* Glasgow (UK) 2014. **Publications** *Onoma* – journal.
Members Specialists in 54 countries:
Albania, Australia, Austria, Azerbaijan, Belgium, Brazil, Bulgaria, Canada, Chile, China, Colombia, Croatia, Czechia, Denmark, Estonia, Finland, France, Germany, Greece, Hungary, Iceland, India, Ireland, Israel, Italy, Japan, Jordan, Kazakhstan, Korea Rep, Kuwait, Latvia, Malta, Mexico, Netherlands, New Zealand, Nigeria, Norway, Paraguay, Peru, Poland, Portugal, Romania, Russia, Serbia, Singapore, Slovakia, South Africa, Spain, Sweden, Switzerland, Türkiye, UK, USA, Venezuela. [2022.06.29/XC1613/v/**C**]

♦ International Council for Open and Distance Education (ICDE) 13056

Main Office Pløens gate 2B, 0181 Oslo, Norway. T. +4722062632. E-mail: icde@icde.org.
URL: http://www.icde.org/

History 1938, Victoria, BC (Canada). Former names and other names: *International Council for Correspondence Education (ICCE)* – former; *Conseil international de l'enseignement par correspondance* – former; *Consejo Internacional de la Enseñanza por Correspondencia* – former; *International Council for Distance Education (ICDE)* – former; *Conseil international de l'enseignement à distance* – former; *Consejo Internacional de la Enseñanza a Distancia* – former. Registration: No/ID: NO971286512, Norway. **Aims** Be the leading global membership organization for open, distance, flexible and online education including e-learning. **Structure** Executive Committee (4-year terms); Board of Trustees; Election Committee; Permanent Secretariat, headed by Secretary-General. **Languages** English. **Staff** 6.00 FTE, paid. **Finance** Sources: government support; grants; in-kind support; meeting proceeds; members' dues. **Events** *International Lillehammer Lifelong Learning ICDE Conference* Lillehammer (Norway) 2023, *Leadership Summit* Seoul (Korea Rep) 2022, *Leadership Summit* Auckland (New Zealand) 2021, *ICDE's Countdown to 2030 – Reiterating Commitments and Redefining Routes* Natal (Brazil) 2021, *Leadership Summit* Seoul (Korea Rep) 2020. **Publications** *Open Praxis* (4 a year). Conference proceedings; ICDE reports; LangOER policy briefs.
Members Institutional (156); Individual (90); Associate (20). Institutions in 69 countries:
Argentina, Australia, Bangladesh, Barbados, Bosnia-Herzegovina, Botswana, Brazil, Burkina Faso, Canada, China, Costa Rica, Cyprus, Ecuador, Fiji, France, Gambia, Germany, Greece, Guyana, Hong Kong, India, Indonesia, Iran Islamic Rep, Ireland, Israel, Italy, Kenya, Korea DPR, Korea Rep, Kuwait, Lebanon, Lithuania, Malaysia, Mauritius, Mexico, Mongolia, Mozambique, Myanmar, Namibia, Netherlands, New Zealand, Nigeria, Norway, Oman, Pakistan, Palestine, Philippines, Poland, Portugal, Romania, Russia, Rwanda, Singapore, South Africa, Spain, Sri Lanka, Sweden, Switzerland, Taiwan, Tanzania UR, Thailand, Trinidad-Tobago, Türkiye, UK, United Arab Emirates, USA, Vietnam, Yemen, Zambia.
Individuals in 29 countries:
Argentina, Australia, Bangladesh, Botswana, Brazil, Cameroon, Canada, China, Germany, India, Italy, Jamaica, Kosovo, Kuwait, Malaysia, Mexico, Netherlands, Nigeria, Norway, Palestine, Philippines, Poland, South Africa, Spain, Sweden, Tanzania UR, Türkiye, UK, USA.
Associate, including 7 regional organizations listed in this Yearbook:
African Council for Distance Education (ACDE, #00274); *Arab Network for Open and Distance Education (ANODE, no recent information)*; *Association of African Distance Learning Centres (AADLC, #02354)*; *Australasian Council on Open, Distance and E-Learning (ACODE)*; *EDEN Digital Learning Europe (EDEN, #05356)*; *European Association of Distance Teaching Universities (EADTU, #06016)*; *Middle East e-Learning Association (MEEA, #16769)*.
Consultative Status Consultative status granted from: *ECOSOC (#05331)* (Roster); *UNESCO (#20322)* (Consultative Status). **IGO Relations** Member of: *Southeast Asian Ministers of Education Organization (SEAMEO, #19774)*. Affiliate member of: *SEAMEO Regional Center for Educational Innovation and Technology (SEAMEO INNOTECH, #19168)*. Partner of: *Commonwealth of Learning (COL, #04346)*. **NGO Relations** Member of: *International Conference of NGOs (#12883)*; *NGO-UNESCO Liaison Committee (#17127)*. Partner of: *International Network of Quality Assurance Agencies in Higher Education (INQAAHE, #14312)*. [2020.09.03/XB1768/y/**B**]

♦ International Council of Ophthalmology (ICO) 13057

Concilium Ophthalmologicum Universale

CEO Tour de Lyon, Rue de Lyon 77, 1203 Geneva, Switzerland. E-mail: info@icoph.org.
Events Liaison address not obtained.
URL: https://icoph.org/

History 14 Jul 1927, Scheveningen (Netherlands). Until 27 Jun 2008, functioned as executive body of *International Federation of Ophthalmological Societies (IFOS, inactive)*, when IFOS was integrated into ICO. Statutes adopted 3 Dec 1962, Delhi (India); modified: 18 May 1974, Paris (France); 4 Nov 1982, San Francisco CA (USA); May 1987, Barcelona (Spain); Sep 1989, Rio de Janeiro (Brazil); 23 Jun 1998, Amsterdam (Netherlands); 22 Apr 2002, Sydney (Australia); 23 Oct 2004, New Orleans LA (USA); 21 Feb 2006, Sao Paulo (Brazil); 5 Jun 2010, Berlin (Germany); 16 Feb 2012, Abu Dhabi (United Arab Emirates); 2 April 2014, Tokyo (Japan); 15 Jun 2018, Barcelona (Spain). Registration: Swiss Civil Code, Switzerland. **Aims** Enhance ophthalmic education and improve access to the highest quality of eye care so as to preserve and restore vision; build a 'World Alliance for Sight' by stimulating and supporting efforts of ophthalmological societies, eye departments and related organizations worldwide. **Structure** Board of Trustees. **Languages** English. **Staff** 6.00 FTE, paid. **Finance** Sources: members' dues. Other sources: proceeds from World Ophthalmology Congress (WOC); support from ICO Foundation. **Activities** Awards/prizes/competitions; events/meetings; financial and/or material support; networking/liaising; research/documentation; standards/guidelines; training/education. **Events** *WOC : World Ophthalmology Congress* Beijing (China) 2022, *WOC : World Ophthalmology Congress* Geneva (Switzerland) 2020, *WOC : World Ophthalmology congress* Barcelona (Spain) 2018, *WOC : World Ophthalmology congress* Guadalajara (Mexico) 2016, *WOC : World Ophthalmology Congress* Tokyo (Japan) 2014. **Publications** *ICO Educator Letter* (12 a year); *Insight* (12 a year) – newsletter.

Members National societies in 123 countries and territories:

Afghanistan, Albania, Argentina, Australia, Austria, Azerbaijan, Bahrain, Bangladesh, Belgium, Benin, Bolivia, Bosnia-Herzegovina, Brazil, Bulgaria, Burkina Faso, Burundi, Cambodia, Cameroon, Canada, Chile, China, Colombia, Congo DR, Costa Rica, Côte d'Ivoire, Croatia, Cuba, Cyprus, Czechia, Denmark, Dominican Rep, Ecuador, Egypt, El Salvador, Estonia, Ethiopia, Finland, France, Gabon, Georgia, Germany, Ghana, Greece, Haiti, Honduras, Hong Kong, Hungary, Iceland, India, Indonesia, Iran Islamic Rep, Iraq, Ireland, Israel, Italy, Jamaica, Japan, Jordan, Korea Rep, Kosovo, Laos, Latvia, Lebanon, Lithuania, Madagascar, Malawi, Malaysia, Mali, Mauritania, Mexico, Mongolia, Morocco, Mozambique, Myanmar, Nepal, Netherlands, New Zealand, Niger, Nigeria, Norway, Oman, Pakistan, Palestine, Panama, Paraguay, Peru, Philippines, Poland, Portugal, Puerto Rico, Romania, Russia, Rwanda, Saudi Arabia, Senegal, Serbia, Singapore, Slovakia, Slovenia, South Africa, South Sudan, Spain, Sri Lanka, Sweden, Switzerland, Syrian AR, Taiwan, Tanzania UR, Thailand, Togo, Tunisia, Türkiye, Uganda, UK, Ukraine, United Arab Emirates, Uruguay, USA, Uzbekistan, Vietnam, Yemen, Zambia, Zimbabwe.

Regional societies (8) include the following 3 listed in this Yearbook:

College of Ophthalmology of Eastern Central and Southern Africa (COECSA, #04108); SAARC Academy of Ophthalmology (SAO, #19013); Société Africaine Francophone d'Ophtalmologie (SAFO, #19453).

International subspecialty societies (45) include the following 26 organizations listed in this Yearbook:

- *Asia-Pacific Glaucoma Society (APGS, #01917);*
- *Asia-Pacific Society of Eye Genetics (APSEG);*
- *Asia Pacific Society of Ophthalmic Plastic and Reconstructive Surgery (APSOPRS, #02041);*
- *Asia-Pacific Strabismus and Paediatric Ophthalmology Society (APSPOS, #02055);*
- *Association for Research in Vision and Ophthalmology (ARVO, #02894);*
- *Cornea Society;*
- *EURETINA – European Society of Retina Specialists (#05623);*
- *EuroLam Retina (#05699);*
- *European Association for Vision and Eye Research (EVER, #06274);*
- *European Board of Ophthalmology (EBO, #06366);*
- *European Paediatric Ophthalmological Society (EPOS, #08127);*
- *European Society of Ophthalmic Plastic and Reconstructive Surgery (ESOPRS, #08673);*
- *European Strabismological Association (ESA, #08840);*
- *Global Alliance of Eye Bank Associations (GAEBA, #10197);*
- *International Medical Contact Lens Council (IMCLC, #14131);*
- *International Ocular Inflammation Society (IOIS, #14397);*
- *International Pediatric Ophthalmology and Strabismus Council (IPOSC, #14544);*
- *International Society for Genetic Eye Diseases and Retinoblastoma (ISGEDR, #15139);*
- *International Society of Geographical and Epidemiological Ophthalmology (ISGEO, #15140);*
- *International Society of Ocular Oncology (ISOO, #15315);*
- *International Society of Oculoplastic, Plastic and Reconstructive Surgery (ISOPRS);*
- *International Society of Ophthalmic Pathology (ISOP);*
- *International Strabismological Association (ISA, #15609);*
- *Jules Gonin Club (#16165);*
- *Pan-American Retina and Vitreous Society (PRVS, #18126);*
- *World Glaucoma Association (WGA, #21540).*

Consultative Status Consultative status granted from: *WHO (#20950).* **NGO Relations** Official structural links with: *Afro-Asian Council of Ophthalmology (AACO, #00536); Asia-Pacific Academy of Ophthalmology (APAO, #01814); European Society of Ophthalmology (SOE, #08674);* IAPB; *Middle East African Council of Ophthalmology (MEACO, #16752); Pan-American Association of Ophthalmology (PAAO, #18081).* Member of Board of Trustees: *Academia Ophthalmologica Internationalis (AOI, #00017).* Cooperates with: *Glaucoma Research Society (GRS, #10159).* Instrumental in setting up: *African Ophthalmology Council (AOC, #00402); International Agency for the Prevention of Blindness (IAPB, #11597); International Glaucoma Committee (no recent information).* Initiates and supervises arrangement for: *International Congress of Ophthalmology.* Official links with members and with: *European Organisation for Research and Treatment of Cancer (EORTC, #08101)* (Ophthalmic Oncology Group); *European VitreoRetinal Society (EVRS, #09072); International Colour Vision Society (ICVS, #12656); International Contact Lens Council of Ophthalmology (ICLCO, no recent information); International Glaucoma Association (IGA, #13719); International Ophthalmology Teacher Training Council (IOTTC); International Organization Against Trachoma (IOAT, #14436); International Society for Low Vision Research and Rehabilitation (ISLRR, #15237); International Society for Ocular Fluorophotometry (ISOF, no recent information); International Society of Ocular Trauma (ISOT, #15317).* [2021/XD7365/y/**B**]

♦ International Council of Organizations for Folklore Festivals and Folk Art 13058

Conseil international des organisations de festivals de folklore et d'arts traditionnels (CIOFF) – Consejo Internacional de Organización de Festivales de Folklore y Arte Tradicional – Internationale Rat für Organisationen von Folklorefestivals und Volkskunst

SG Stockton Business Centre, 70 Brunswick Street, Stockton-on-Tees, TS18 1DW, UK. E-mail: info@cioff.org.

URL: http://www.cioff.org/

History 10 Aug 1970, Confolens (France). Statutes revised: 1983, Italy; 1998, China; 2022 Mexico. Former names and other names: *International Council of Folklore Festivals and Folk Art* – former; *Conseil international des organisations de festivals de folklore* – former; *Consejo Internacional de Organización de Festivales de Folklore y Arte Popular* – former. **Aims** Safeguard, promote and diffuse traditional culture and folklore. **Structure** General Assembly (annual, at World Congress); Council; Executive Committee; Commissions (3); Sectors (6). **Languages** English, French, Spanish. **Staff** Voluntary. **Finance** Sources: members' dues. Annual budget: 70,000 EUR. **Activities** Events/meetings. **Events** *Annual Congress and General Assembly* Budapest (Hungary) 2021, *Quadrennial World Folkloriada* Zacatecas (Mexico) 2016, *Annual Congress and General Assembly* Arequipa (Peru) 2015, *Annual Congress and General Assembly / Annual General Assembly* Bautzen (Germany) 2014, *Annual Congress and General Assembly / Annual General Assembly* Zacatecas (Mexico) 2013. **Publications** *Entre Nous* (2 a year) – newsletter. *International Monograph of Folk Dance* (1986). Annual Report; index of folklore periodicals; brochures; bulletins; conference papers – all in English, French, Spanish.

Members Full – national sections (68); Associate (12); Corresponding (30). Full in 68 countries and territories:

Albania, Argentina, Armenia, Austria, Azerbaijan, Belgium, Bosnia-Herzegovina, Brazil, Bulgaria, Canada, Chile, China, Colombia, Congo DR, Costa Rica, Croatia, Cuba, Cyprus, Czechia, Ecuador, El Salvador, Estonia, Finland, France, Gambia, Georgia, Germany, Greece, Guatemala, Haiti, Honduras, Hungary, India, Indonesia, Israel, Italy, Japan, Korea Rep, Latvia, Lithuania, Luxembourg, Malaysia, Mexico, Montenegro, Netherlands, New Zealand, North Macedonia, Norway, Panama, Paraguay, Peru, Poland, Portugal, Puerto Rico, Romania, Russia, Slovenia, Spain, Sweden, Switzerland, Taiwan, Thailand, Trinidad-Tobago, Türkiye, UK, Ukraine, United Arab Emirates, USA.

Associate in 12 countries and territories:

Antigua-Barbuda, Belize, Egypt, Gabon, Iran Islamic Rep, Ireland, Pakistan, Palestine, Philippines, Polynesia Fr, South Africa, Sri Lanka.

Corresponding in 28 countries and territories:

Algeria, Anguilla, Austria, Belarus, Benin, Brazil, Burkina Faso, Cameroon, Cayman Is, Central African Rep, Côte d'Ivoire, Cyprus, Dominica, Grenada, Guinea, Kuwait, Kyrgyzstan, Mali, Mauritania, Morocco, Niger, Saudi Arabia, Senegal, St Vincent-Grenadines, Syrian AR, Togo, Tunisia, Uzbekistan.

Consultative Status Consultative status granted from: *UNESCO (#20322)* (Associate Status). **NGO Relations** Member of (2): *European Music Council (EMC, #07837); NGO-UNESCO Liaison Committee (#17127).* Affiliated with (1): *International Music Council (IMC, #14199).* [2023.02.15/XD4746/**C**]

♦ International Council on Pastoral Care and Counselling (ICPCC) . . . 13059

Sec address not obtained. E-mail: secretary.icpcc@gmail.com – communications.icpcc@gmail.com.

URL: http://www.icpcc.net/

History 1971. Current title adopted, Edinburgh (UK), during the first International Congress of Reflective Practitioners of Pastoral Care and Counselling. Former names and other names: *World Association of Pastoral Care and Counselling* – former (1971 to 1979). **Aims** Promote reflective practice of pastoral care and counselling; through such care and counselling, respond to current needs and situations faced by people and communities worldwide; inform, educate and inspire practitioners in various contexts; enable practitioners to be resources for one another and to learn from each other's culture and traditions; support and advocate the unique and essential dimension of *spirituality* in *teaching* and practice; develop relevant theories in the field and engage in interdisciplinary discourse. **Structure** Council (meets every 4 years at Congress); Coordinating Committee. **Languages** English. **Staff** 3.00 FTE, voluntary. **Finance** Sources: donations; members' dues. **Activities** Events/meetings; guidance/assistance/consulting; knowledge management/information dissemination. **Events** *Quadrennial World Congress* Potchefstroom (South Africa) 2023, *Quadrennial World Congress* Melaka (Malaysia) 2019, *Quadrennial World Congress* San Francisco, CA (USA) 2015, *Quadrennial world congress* Rotorua (New Zealand) 2011, *Quadrennial world congress* Krzyżowa (Poland) 2007.

Members Organizations (over 40) and individuals organizations in 17 countries:

Australia, Austria, Canada, Finland, Germany, Ghana, Hungary, India, Japan, Netherlands, Nigeria, Norway, South Africa, Sweden, Tanzania UR, UK, USA.

Individuals in 16 countries and territories:

Brazil, Czechia, France, Greece, Hong Kong, Iceland, Indonesia, Ireland, Italy, Korea Rep, New Zealand, Philippines, Poland, Romania, Singapore, Switzerland.

NGO Relations *European Council for Pastoral Care and Counselling (ECPCC, #06836)* organizes European conferences. [2019/XD8644/**C**]

♦ International Council for Peace and Justice (internationally oriented national body)

♦ International Council for Philosophical Inquiry with Children (ICPIC) 13060

Contact address not obtained. E-mail: icpic.website@gmail.com.

URL: http://www.icpic.org/

History 1984, as *International Council for Elementary and Secondary School Philosophy*, within the framework of *'Institute for the Advancement of Philosophy for Children (IAPC)'.* **Aims** Strengthen communication among those in different parts of the world who are engaged in philosophical inquiry with children, in teacher education, in research and for school administrators looking to initiate and develop programmes that would encourage children's philosophical thinking. **Structure** General Assembly (every 2 years); Executive Committee; Public Profile Committee; Advisory Board. **Languages** English. **Finance** Members' dues. Donations. **Events** *Biennial Conference* Tokyo (Japan) 2022, *Biennial Conference* Bogota (Colombia) 2019, *Biennial Conference* Madrid (Spain) 2017, *Biennial Conference* Vancouver, BC (Canada) 2015, *Biennial Conference* Cape Town (South Africa) 2013. **Publications** *Childhood and Philosophy* – journal; *ICPIC Newsletter.*

Members Regular institutions and individuals; Honorary individuals. Members in 52 countries and territories:

Afghanistan, Argentina, Australia, Austria, Bangladesh, Belgium, Brazil, Bulgaria, Canada, Chile, Colombia, Cyprus, Czechia, Denmark, Finland, France, Germany, Greece, Guatemala, Hungary, Iceland, India, Indonesia, Iran Islamic Rep, Ireland, Israel, Italy, Japan, Korea Rep, Latvia, Malta, Mexico, Netherlands, New Zealand, Nigeria, Norway, Peru, Philippines, Poland, Portugal, Russia, Singapore, Slovenia, South Africa, Spain, Sweden, Switzerland, Taiwan, UK, Ukraine, Uruguay, USA.

IGO Relations *UNESCO (#20322).* [2016/XF0081/**F**]

♦ International Council for Philosophy and Humanistic Studies / see International Council for Philosophy and Human Sciences (#13061)

♦ International Council for Philosophy and Human Sciences (CIPSH) . 13061

Conseil international de la philosophie et des sciences humaines (CIPSH) – Consejo Internacional de Filosofía y Ciencias Humanas (CIPSH) – Internationaler Rat für Philosophie und die Geisteswissenschaften (CIPSH) – Mezdunarodnyj Sovet po Filosofii i Gumanitarnym Naukam (CIPSH)

Acting Pres Inst Politecnico de Tomar, Estrada da Serra, Campus da Quinta do Contador, 2300-313 Tomar, Portugal. T. +351249328100 – +351249346363. Fax +351249346366. E-mail: emailcipsh@icphs.org.

Head Office Bonvin-Paris UNESCO, 1, rue de Miollis, 75732 Paris, France. E-mail: emailcipsh@icphs.org.

URL: http://www.cipsh.net/

History 19 Jan 1949, Brussels (Belgium). Founded on the initiative and under the auspices of UNESCO. Constitution amended: 28 Sep 1955, Paris (France); 21 Sep 1963, Mexico City (Mexico); 14 Sep 1973, Rio de Janeiro (Brazil); 23 Sep 1975, Dubrovnik (Yugoslavia); 15 Sep 1977, Montréal (Canada); 21 Nov 1986, Cairo (Egypt); 10 Dec 2010, Nagoya (Japan); 9 Dec 2015, Beijing (China). Former names and other names: *International Council for Philosophy and Humanistic Studies (ICPHS)* – former. Registration: France. **Aims** Extend UNESCO's action in the domain of humanistic studies. **Structure** General Assembly (every 3 years); Board/Executive Committee; Central Secretariat. **Languages** English, French. **Staff** 1.00 FTE, voluntary. **Finance** Sources: members' dues; revenue from activities/projects; subsidies. **Activities** Advocacy/lobbying/activism; knowledge management/information dissemination; projects/programmes; research and development. **Events** *Triennial General Assembly* Lisbon (Portugal) / Tomar (Portugal) 2020, *Triennial General Assembly* Liège (Belgium) 2017, *World Humanities Conference* Liège (Belgium) 2017, *Biennial General Assembly* Beijing (China) 2015, *Biennial General Assembly* Paris (France) 2014. **Publications** *Diogenes* (4 a year) in Chinese, English, French; *CIPSH Bulletin.*

Members Institutional; Individual. Individuals in 150 countries and territories:

Afghanistan, Albania, Algeria, Andorra, Angola, Argentina, Australia, Austria, Bahrain, Bangladesh, Barbados, Belarus, Belgium, Benin, Bolivia, Brazil, Bulgaria, Burkina Faso, Burundi, Cambodia, Cameroon, Canada, Central African Rep, Chad, Chile, China, Colombia, Congo Brazzaville, Congo DR, Costa Rica, Côte d'Ivoire, Croatia, Cuba, Cyprus, Czechia, Denmark, Dominican Rep, Ecuador, Egypt, El Salvador, Equatorial Guinea, Eswatini, Ethiopia, Fiji, Finland, France, Gabon, Gambia, Germany, Ghana, Greece, Guatemala, Guinea, Guyana, Haiti, Holy See, Honduras, Hong Kong, Hungary, Iceland, India, Indonesia, Iran Islamic Rep, Iraq, Ireland, Israel, Italy, Jamaica, Japan, Jordan, Kenya, Korea DPR, Korea Rep, Kosovo, Kuwait, Laos, Lebanon, Lesotho, Liberia, Libya, Liechtenstein, Luxembourg, Madagascar, Malawi, Malaysia, Mali, Malta, Mauritania, Mauritius, Mexico, Monaco, Mongolia, Montenegro, Morocco, Mozambique, Myanmar, Namibia, Nepal, Netherlands, New Zealand, Nicaragua, Niger, Nigeria, Norway, Oman, Pakistan, Panama, Papua New Guinea, Paraguay, Peru, Philippines, Poland, Portugal, Qatar, Romania, Russia, Rwanda, Saudi Arabia, Senegal, Serbia, Sierra Leone, Singapore, Slovakia, Slovenia, Somalia, South Africa, Spain, Sri Lanka, Sudan, Suriname, Sweden, Switzerland, Syrian AR, Tanzania UR, Thailand, Togo, Trinidad-Tobago, Tunisia, Türkiye, Uganda, UK, Ukraine, United Arab Emirates, Uruguay, USA, Venezuela, Vietnam, Yemen, Zambia, Zimbabwe.

Institutions including the following 18 organizations listed in this Yearbook:

APHELEIA – Humanities International Association For Cultural Integrated Landscape Management (#00874); Asian New Humanities Net (ANHN, #01565); Comité international permanent des linguistes (CIPL, #04182); Consortium of Humanities Centers and Institutes (CHCI); European Consortium for Humanities Institutes and Centres (ECHIC, #06755); Fédération internationale des associations d'études classiques (FIEC, #09607); International Association for Aesthetics (IAA, #11692); International Association for Promoting Geoethics (IAPG, #12107); International Association for the History of Religions (IAHR, #11936); International Committee of Historical Sciences (ICHS, #12777); International Federation for Modern Languages and Literatures (#13480); International Federation of Philosophical Societies (FISP, #13507); International Geographical Union (IGU, #13713); International Positive Psychology Association (IPPA); International Union of Anthropological and Ethnological Sciences (IUAES, #15755); International Union of History and Philosophy of Science and Technology (IUHPST, #15779) (Division of History of Science and Technology DHST); *International Union of Prehistoric and Protohistoric Sciences (#15801); Union académique internationale (UAI, #20345); World Network for Linguistic Diversity (Maaya, #21671).*

Consultative Status Consultative status granted from: *ECOSOC (#05331)* (Ros C); *UNESCO (#20322)* (Associate Status). **NGO Relations** Member of (1): *International Conference of NGOs (#12883).* Cooperates with (1): *Commission mondiale d'éthique des connaissances scientifiques et des technologies de l'UNESCO (COMEST, #04235).* [2021.03.03/XA1728/y/**A**]

♦ International Council for Physical Activity and Fitness Research (ICPAFR) 13062

Pres Biomedicine and FISPPA Depts, Univ of Padua, Via Venezia 8, 35131 Padua PD, Italy. T. +394988804668. Fax +39498276600.

Sec-Treas Waikato Univ, Hillcrest, Hamilton 3216, New Zealand.

History 3 Oct 1964, Tokyo (Japan). Inactive as of 2020. Former names and other names: *International Committee for the Standardization of Physical Fitness Tests (ICSPFT)* – former (1964 to 1973); *Comité international pour la normalisation des tests de l'aptitude physique* – former (1964 to 1973); *International Council for Physical Fitness Research (ICPFR)* – former (1973 to 1992). **Aims** Promote *lifestyle* most conducive to realization of highest creative potential through promotion of physical activity and fitness. **Structure** Board. **Languages** English. **Staff** Voluntary. **Finance** Sources: donations. Other sources: Universities. **Activities** Events/meetings; research/documentation; standards/guidelines. **Events** *Symposium* Kaunas (Lithuania)

2016, *Symposium* Thórshavn (Faeroe Is) 2015, *Biennial Scientific Symposium* Hamilton (New Zealand) 2013, *Biennial Scientific Symposium* Louwsburg (South Africa) 2010, *Biennial Scientific Symposium* Loma Linda, CA (USA) 2008. **Publications** *International Journal of Body Composition Research – vol 6* (2010). *Hamilton ICPAFR Symposium Proceeding Book* (2013); *New Horizons* (2006); *Actas Kinesiologiae Universitatis Tartuensis – vol 7* (2002); *Physical Fitness and Activity in the Context of Leisure Education* (2001); *Physical Activity and Health: Physiological, Behavioral and Epidemiological* (1998); *Nutrition and Physical Activity* (1997); *Worldwide Variations in Physical Fitness* (1993); *Fitness for Aged, Disabled and Industrial Workers* (1990); *Physical Fitness and the Ages of Man* (1987); *Physical Fitness Research XIV* (1981); *Physical Fitness Assessment Principles, Practice and Applications* (1978); *Fitness, Health and Work Capacity: International Standards for Assessment* (1974); *International Guide to Fitness and Health* (1973). Seminar and symposium proceedings; guides.
Members Individual researchers (over 300) in 46 countries:
Argentina, Australia, Austria, Belarus, Belgium, Botswana, Brazil, Bulgaria, Canada, China, Croatia, Czechia, Denmark, Egypt, Estonia, Finland, France, Germany, Greece, Hungary, India, Israel, Italy, Japan, Korea Rep, Latvia, Lithuania, Mexico, Mozambique, Netherlands, New Zealand, Nigeria, Norway, Philippines, Poland, Portugal, Senegal, Serbia, Slovakia, Slovenia, South Africa, Spain, Thailand, Tunisia, UK, USA. [2019/XD5457/dv/**C**]

- ♦ International Council for Physical Fitness Research / see International Council for Physical Activity and Fitness Research (#13062)
- ♦ International Council of Physiotherapy in Psychiatry and Mental Health / see International Organization of Physical Therapists in Mental Health (#14461)
- ♦ International Council of Plant Nutrition / see International Plant Nutrition Council (#14592)

♦ International Council of Police Representative Associations (ICPRA) 13063

SG Scottish Police Federation, 5 Woodside Place, Glasgow, G3 7QF, UK. T. +441413325234. Fax +441413312436. E-mail: icpra@icpra.org.
Chairman New Zealand Police Assoc, Level 11, 57 Willis Street, PO Box 12344, Wellington, New Zealand. T. +6444966800. Fax +6444966819.
URL: http://www.icpra.org/
History Founded 1996, Windsor (Canada). **Aims** Promote the rights, efficiency and welfare of police officers worldwide; foster and assist in the establishment of police representative associations across the world; secure the participation of, and influence of members in the administration, development and planning of international policing initiatives; cooperate with similar organizations; promote international improvements in policing methods and the standard of policing; enhance the professional standing of members. **Structure** Executive Committee; Chairman; General Secretary. **Languages** English. **Staff** None. **Finance** Members' dues, based on number of members in their organization. **Activities** Guidance/assistance/consulting. **Events** *Biennial Meeting* Canberra, ACT (Australia) 2018, *Biennial Meeting* 2016, *Biennial Meeting* Cape Town (South Africa) 2014, *Biennial Meeting* Baltimore, MD (USA) 2012, *Biennial Meeting* Copenhagen (Denmark) 2010. **Publications** *ICPRA Newsletter*.
Members Organizations in 10 countries and territories:
Australia, Canada, Cook Is, Denmark, Ireland, New Zealand, Portugal, South Africa, UK, USA.
Included in the above, 1 international organization:
European Confederation of Police (EuroCOP, #06719). [2022/XJ0258/y/**C**]

- ♦ International Council of Portuguese-Speaking Architects (internationally oriented national body)
- ♦ International Council of Practitioners of the International Plan of Accounts (inactive)

♦ International Council for Pressure Vessel Technology (ICPVT) 13064

Conseil international de la technologie de chaudrons sous pression
Co-Chair Haggerty Eng 279, PO Box 1881, Milwaukee WI 53201-1881, USA.
Co-Chair address not obtained.
Co-Chair address not obtained.
History 1969, Delft (Netherlands), during an international conference on pressure vessel technology, with support from several national engineering institutions. **Aims** Further international cooperation and exchange of knowledge on pressure vessel technology. **Structure** Regional Committees (3): European and African; Asian and Oceanic; the Americas. **Languages** English. **Staff** None. **Finance** Conference excess income. **Activities** Arranges international conferences (every 3 to 4 years) and intermediate regional conferences. **Events** *International Conference on Pressure Vessel Technology* Perth, WA (Australia) 2024, *International Conference on Pressure Vessel Technology* Shanghai (China) 2015, *International Conference on Pressure Vessel Technology* London (UK) 2012, *International Conference on Pressure Vessel Technology* Jeju (Korea Rep) 2009, *International Conference on Pressure Vessel Technology* Vancouver, BC (Canada) 2006.
Members Associations in 17 countries and territories:
Australia, Austria, Belgium, Canada, China, Czechia, France, Germany, Hong Kong, Italy, Japan, Netherlands, New Zealand, Poland, Sweden, UK, USA.
Individuals in 23 countries and territories:
Argentina, Bahrain, Brazil, Denmark, Egypt, Finland, India, Iran Islamic Rep, Ireland, Mexico, Norway, Pakistan, Philippines, Portugal, Russia, Saudi Arabia, Singapore, South Africa, Spain, Switzerland, Taiwan, Türkiye, Venezuela.
NGO Relations *International Institute of Welding (IIW, #13935).* Also links with a number of interested national organizations. Instrumental in setting up: *European Pressure Equipment Research Council (EPERC, #08269).* [2015/XD6602/**C**]

- ♦ International Council of Prison Medical Services (no recent information)
- ♦ International Council on Probabilistic Methods Applied to Power Systems / see PMAPS International Society (#18409)
- ♦ International Council of Producers' Organizations (inactive)
- ♦ International Council for the Promotion of Christian Higher Education / see International Network for Christian Higher Education (#14241)

♦ International Council of Psychologists (ICP) 13065

SG 1080 Tantra Park Circle, Boulder CO 80305, USA. T. +13037173024. E-mail: icpincinfo@gmail.com.
URL: http://icpweb.org/
History 1941. Originally founded as a national organization to make services of US women psychologists available to war effort. Name changed, 1946 and 1960, when organization included members from other countries, and when it opened to all psychologists, women or men. Bylaws revised, 2019. Co-founded with EFPA *European Federation of Psychologists Associations (EFPA, #07199)* the *Global Network of Psychologists for Human Rights.* Strategic Plan 2022-2026 adopted in 2021. Former names and other names: *National Council of Women Psychologists* – former (1941 to 1946); *International Council of Women Psychologists* – former (1946 to 1960). Registration: Section 501(c)(3), No/ID: 84-6044463, Start date: 1962, USA, State of Connecticut. **Aims** Promote human rights, dignity, and justice and further international understanding and world peace by facilitating collaborative relationships around the world; provide international networking opportunities, global information exchange, and global resources in matters of psychology and human rights, dignity justice, and peace; value diversity in knowledge and methodological approaches, cultural humility, peer relations, mutual understanding, scientific approaches, critical thinking, and inclusion. **Structure** Board of Directors; Standing Committees; Interest Groups; Ad Hoc Committees; Friends of ICP. **Languages** English. **Staff** 1.00 FTE, voluntary. **Finance** Sources: donations; meeting proceeds; members' dues; sale of publications. Annual budget: 11,800 USD (2021). **Activities** Awards/prizes/competitions; events/meetings; networking/liaising; projects/programmes; training/education. **Events** *Annual Convention* 2021, *Annual Convention* 2020, *Annual Convention* Cadiz (Spain) 2019, *Annual Convention* Montréal, QC (Canada) 2018, *Annual Convention* New York, NY (USA) 2017. **Publications** *International Psychologist (IP)* (2 a year). *Visions and Resources for International Psychology* (2018); *ICP – The First Quarter Century 1942-1967*.
Members Individual; Affiliate; Early Career; Student. Members in 31 countries and territories:
Australia, Austria, Brazil, Canada, Colombia, France, Germany, Greece, Guatemala, Hong Kong, India, Indonesia, Jamaica, Japan, Lebanon, Mexico, Netherlands, Oman, Pakistan, Philippines, Poland, Russia, Rwanda, Serbia, Spain, Sri Lanka, Taiwan, UK, USA, Vietnam, Zambia.
Consultative Status Consultative status granted from: *ECOSOC (#05331)* (Special); *UNICEF (#20332).* **IGO Relations** Accredited by (2): *United Nations Office at Geneva (UNOG, #20597); United Nations Office at Vienna (UNOV, #20604).* Associated with Department of Global Communications of the United Nations. **NGO Relations** Member of (3): *Conference of Non-Governmental Organizations in Consultative Relationship with the United Nations (CONGO, #04635); Vienna NGO Committee on the Family (#20774); World Federation for Mental Health (WFMH, #21455).* Affiliated with (1): *International Union of Psychological Science (IUPsyS, #15807).* Special liaison with: *International Association of Applied Psychology (IAAP, #11705).* Liaison with: *Association for Humanistic Psychology (AHP, #02633); Inter-American Society of Psychology (ISP, #11450); International Literacy Association (ILA, #14057); International Peace Research Association (IPRA, #14537); International School Psychology Association (ISPA, #14788); International School-to-School Experience (ISSE, #14791); NGO Committee on the Family, New York NY (#17107); NGO Committee on Mental Health, New York NY (#17111); Stress, Trauma, Anxiety, and Resilience Society (STAR, #20011).* Also links with a number of national organizations interested in the field. [2022.02.02/XB5216/v/**B**]

♦ International Council for the Publication of the Opera Omnia of Erasmus 13066

Conseil international pour l'édition des oeuvres complètes d'Erasme
Sec c/o Huygens Inst, Dept Renaissance, PO Box 10855, 1001 EW The Hague, Netherlands. T. +31703315825. Fax +31703820546.
History Founded 1963, under patronage of *Union académique internationale (UAI, #20345)*, at a meeting convened by the Royal Netherlands Academy of Arts and Sciences. **Aims** Make available a critical and annotated edition of the complete works of Erasmus, with introductions and commentaries in English, French and German. **Structure** Editorial Board. **Activities** Events/meetings. **Events** *Meeting* Amsterdam (Netherlands) 1989. **Publications** *Erasmi Opera Omnia* (1969-) – in 65 vols.
Members Individuals in 8 countries:
Belgium, Canada, France, Germany, Italy, Netherlands, Switzerland, USA. [2018.07.10/XE2369/v/**E**]

- ♦ International Council on Public Relations in Rehabilitation (inactive)

♦ International Council for Quality Function Deployment (ICQFD) 13067

Exec Dir 1140 Morehead Ct, Ann Arbor MI 48103-6181, USA. T. +17349950847. Fax +17553074637. E-mail: icqfd@qfdi.org.
URL: http://qfdi.org/icqfd/
History 1997 at 3rd International Symposium on QFD. Incorporated in the State of Michigan (USA). **Aims** Provide a unified body to coordinate local QFD organizations, efforts, and events around the world. **Structure** Council. **Languages** English. **Staff** 1.00 FTE, paid. **Finance** Proceeds from events and publications. **Events** *International QFD Symposium* Boise, ID (USA) 2016, *North American Symposium* Charleston, SC (USA) 2014, *International QFD Symposium* Istanbul (Turkey) 2014, *International QFD Symposium* Santa Fe, NM (USA) 2013, *International QFD Symposium* Portland, OR (USA) 2010. **Publications** Symposia proceedings.
Members Organizations in 10 countries and territories:
Australia, Brazil, China, Germany, Hong Kong, Japan, Mexico, Sweden, Türkiye, USA. [2016.06.01/XN8647/c/**E**]

- ♦ International Council for the Quality of Working Life (inactive)
- ♦ International Council of Red Trade Unions (inactive)

♦ International Council of Reflexologists (ICR) 13068

Membership Sec 142 Edmonds Road, Glenwood, Durban, 4001, South Africa. Fax +27880312060600.
URL: http://www.icr-reflexology.org/
History Founded 1990, Toronto (Canada). **Aims** Ensure public safety; promote the study and exchange of the knowledge and art of reflexology within the profession. **Structure** General Council. Board of Directors, comprising President, Vice President, Secretary, Treasurer, 3 Directors at Large, Past President, Membership Secretary, Newsletter Editor. **Languages** English. **Finance** Members' dues. **Activities** Organizes: Biennial International Conference; World Reflexology Week. **Events** *Reflexology out of Africa* Cape Town (South Africa) 2013, *Conference* Castro Verde (Portugal) 2011, *Spotlight on reflexology* Los Angeles, CA (USA) 2009, *Conference* Cairns, QLD (Australia) 2007, *Conference* Amsterdam (Netherlands) 2005. **Publications** *ICR Newsletter* (4 a year).
Members Individuals; associations; educational institutions. Members in 32 countries and territories:
Australia, Austria, Belgium, Canada, Chile, China, Denmark, France, Germany, Greece, India, Ireland, Israel, Italy, Jamaica, Japan, Lebanon, Luxembourg, Malaysia, Mexico, Netherlands, New Zealand, Portugal, Singapore, Slovenia, South Africa, Sweden, Switzerland, Taiwan, Türkiye, UK, USA. [2015/XD7654/**D**]

- ♦ International Council for Reprography (inactive)
- ♦ International Council for Research in Agroforestry / see World Agroforestry Centre (#21072)
- ♦ International Council for Research into the Fetal Origins of Adult Disease / see International Society for Developmental Origins of Health and Disease (#15055)

♦ International Council for Research and Innovation in Building and Construction (CIB) 13069

CEO 11 Warwick House, 21-23 London Road, St Albans, AL1 1PX, UK. E-mail: secretariat@cibworld.org.
URL: https://cibworld.org/
History 25 Jun 1953, Geneva (Switzerland). Replaced *International Council for Building Documentation – Conseil international de documentation du bâtiment (CIDB)*, which had been set up in Oct 1950, Paris (France), on recommendation of a Conference on Building Research convened by *United Nations Economic Commission for Europe (UNECE, #20555).* CIDB was replaced following a suggestion of the Housing Sub-Committee of UN ECE, the sphere of competence being enlarged to include research work. Present name adopted, and current constitution and by-laws approved, 10 Jun 1998, Gävle (Sweden); the acronym 'CIB' is retained. Former names and other names: *International Council for Building Research, Studies and Documentation* – former (1953); *Conseil International du Bâtiment pour la recherche, l'étude et la documentation* – former. Registration: Handelsregister, No/ID: KVK 40346215, Netherlands. **Aims** Provide a global network for international exchange and cooperation in building and construction research and innovation. **Structure** General Assembly (annual); Board; Committees (5); Working Commissions, Task Groups, Student Chapters; General Secretariat. **Languages** English. **Staff** 3.20 FTE, paid. **Finance** Sources: members' dues. **Activities** Advocacy/lobbying/activism; awards/prizes/competitions; awareness raising; capacity building; events/meetings; guidance/assistance/consulting; knowledge management/information dissemination; networking/liaising; projects/programmes; publishing activities; research and development; research/documentation; training/education. Active in all member countries. **Events** *World Sustainable Built Environment (WSBE) Conference* Montréal, QC (Canada) 2023, *World Building Congress* Melbourne, VIC (Australia) 2022, *CIB International Conference on Smart and Sustainable Built Environment* Dubai (United Arab Emirates) 2021, *World Sustainable Built Environment (WSBE) Conference* Gothenburg (Sweden) 2020, *SBE19 SEOUL : Sustainable Built Environment Seoul Conference* Seoul (Korea Rep) 2019. **Publications** *CIB Newsletter* (10 a year); *Research Roadmaps* (every 3 years). Congress and symposium proceedings; technical reports, analyses, registers and recommendations of Working Commissions; best practice reports. **Information Services** *International Construction Database (ICONDA).*
Members Full in 25 countries and territories:
Australia, Belgium, Brazil, Canada, China, Denmark, Finland, France, Hungary, India, Iran Islamic Rep, Israel, Italy, Japan, Korea Rep, Malaysia, Morocco, Netherlands, New Zealand, Poland, South Africa, Sweden, Tanzania UR, UK, USA.
Associate (138) in 50 countries and territories:
Australia, Belgium, Botswana, Brazil, Bulgaria, Canada, Chile, China, Croatia, Czechia, Denmark, Estonia, Finland, France, Germany, Greece, Hungary, Indonesia, Ireland, Italy, Japan, Lithuania, Malaysia, Mexico, Nepal, Netherlands, New Zealand, Nigeria, Norway, Poland, Portugal, Romania, Singapore, Slovakia, Slovenia, South Africa, Spain, Sri Lanka, Sudan, Sweden, Switzerland, Taiwan, Tanzania UR, Thailand, Trinidad-Tobago, Türkiye, UK, United Arab Emirates, USA, Venezuela.
Individuals (184) in 38 countries and territories:
Australia, Austria, Belgium, Brazil, Canada, Czechia, Denmark, Finland, Germany, Greece, India, Indonesia, Ireland, Italy, Japan, Lesotho, Malaysia, Netherlands, New Zealand, Nigeria, Norway, Pakistan, Poland, Portugal, Romania, Saudi Arabia, Seychelles, South Africa, Spain, Sweden, Switzerland, Taiwan, Tanzania UR, Trinidad-Tobago, Türkiye, UK, United Arab Emirates, USA.
Consultative Status Consultative status granted from: *ECOSOC (#05331)* (Special); *UNIDO (#20336).* **IGO Relations** Regular contacts with: *European Commission (EC, #06633); FAO (#09260); International Energy Agency (IEA, #13270); UNESCO (#20322); WHO (#20950).* Working arrangements with: *World Meteorological Organization (WMO, #21649).* **NGO Relations** Founding member of: *Liaison Committee of International Associations of Civil Engineering (#16453)* and member of its *Joint Committee on Structural Safety (JCSS, #16126).* Links with other members of the Liaison Committee: *European Convention for Constructional*

Steelwork (ECCS, #06779); *Fédération internationale du béton (FIB, #09615)*; *International Association for Bridge and Structural Engineering (IABSE, #11737)*; *Réunion internationale des laboratoires d'essais et de recherches sur les matériaux et les constructions (RILEM, #18930)*. In liaison with technical committees of: *Comité européen de normalisation (CEN, #04162)*; *International Organization for Standardization (ISO, #14473)*. [2023.02.16/XB1723/y/**B**]

♦ International Council for Research in the Sociology of Cooperation (inactive)
♦ International Council for Russian Compatriots (internationally oriented national body)
♦ International Council for Science (inactive)
♦ International Council for Scientific Agriculture (inactive)

♦ International Council for Scientific and Technical Information (ICSTI) 13070

Conseil international pour l'information scientifique et technique

Exec Sec 5 Rue Ambroise Thomas, 75009 Paris, France. T. +33614651657. Fax +33642151262. E-mail: icstioffice@gmail.com.
Exec Dir address not obtained.
URL: http://www.icsti.org/

History Jun 1952, and registered by Belgian Royal Decree, 3 Nov 1953, as *International Council of Scientific Unions Abstracting Board (ICSU AB) – Bureau des résumés analytiques du Conseil international des unions scientifiques*. New Statutes and By-Laws adopted together with current name at Extraordinary General Assembly, 20 Jun 1984, Philadelphia PA (USA). **Aims** Increase accessibility to, and awareness of, scientific, technical and *medical* information (STMI); offer a unique forum for interaction between organizations that create, disseminate and use STMI; provide leadership in promoting recognition of the value of STMI to the world's economic, research, scholarly and social progress; enhance access to and delivery of information for all constituencies in business, industry, academia, government and the public through exchange of information and sharing of experience among international peers; develop appropriate tools to better meet the information requirements among all participants in the information flow; provide a unique gathering of the diverse groups interested in and concerned with STMI, from generation through access to archiving. **Structure** General Assembly (annual); Executive Board. Information Trends and Opportunities Committee; Technical Activities Coordinating Committee. **Languages** English, French. **Staff** 2.00 FTE, paid. **Finance** Members' dues. Study contracts. **Activities** Events/meetings; knowledge management/information dissemination; research/documentation. **Events** *Annual Conference* Dublin (Ireland) 2020, *Annual Conference* Shanghai (China) 2019, *Annual Conference* London (UK) 2018, *Annual Conference* Tokyo (Japan) 2014, *General Assembly* Tokyo (Japan) 2014. **Publications** *Forum* (4 a year) – printed and electronic newsletter. *Information and Data in E-Science – Making Seamless Access a Reality* (2006); *Open Access to Scientific and Technical Information* (2003); *Digital Preservation – The Record of Science* (2002).

Members Categories: Full; Associate; Honorary; Fellows. Institutions, compagnies and individuals in 12 countries:
Canada, China, France, India, Japan, Netherlands, Portugal, Russia, South Africa, Sweden, UK, USA.
Included in the above, 8 organizations listed in this Yearbook:
Association of Learned and Professional Society Publishers (ALPSP, #02786); *Committee on Data for Science and Technology (CODATA, #04247)*; *International Association of Scientific, Technical and Medical Publishers (STM, #12154)*; *International Association of University Libraries (IATUL, #12247)*; *International Federation of Library Associations and Institutions (IFLA, #13470)*; *International Nuclear Information System (INIS, #14378)*; *ISC World Data System (ISC-WDS, #16024)*; *ISSN International Centre (ISSNIC, #16069)*.

NGO Relations Member of: *International Science Council (ISC, #14796)*. Associate member of: *ISC World Data System (ISC-WDS, #16024)*. In liaison with technical committees of: *International Organization for Standardization (ISO, #14473)*. [2020/XE1753/y/**E**]

♦ International Council of Scientific Unions Abstracting Board / see International Council for Scientific and Technical Information (#13070)
♦ International Council of Seamen's Agencies / see North America Maritime Ministry Association

♦ International Council of Securities Associations (ICSA) 13071

SG c/o ICMA, 5th floor, 110 Cannon Street, London, EC4N 6EU, UK. T. +447469159049.
URL: http://www.icsa.global/

History 1988, Tokyo (Japan). Present name adopted at 4th Annual Meeting, London (UK). Former names and other names: *International Council of Securities Dealers and Self-Regulatory Associations (ICSDSRA)* – former. **Aims** Aid and encourage the sound growth of the international securities markets by promoting and encouraging harmonization in the procedures and effective regulation of those markets thereby facilitating international securities transactions, and by promoting mutual understanding and the sharing and exchange of information among members of the Councils. **Structure** General Meeting (annual); Board of Directors; Secretariat. Standing Committee on Regulatory Affairs; Emerging Markets Committee; Secretariat. **Languages** English, French, Japanese. **Events** *Annual General Meeting* Washington, DC (USA) 2022, *Annual General Meeting* Washington, DC (USA) 2021, *Annual General Meeting* Washington, DC (USA) 2020, *Annual Meeting* Milan (Italy) 2019, *Annual Meeting* Taipei (Taiwan) 2018.

Members Full; Correspondent. Full in 13 countries and territories:
Australia, Canada, Denmark, France, Germany, India, Italy, Japan, Korea Rep, Sweden, Taiwan, Türkiye, USA.
Association for Financial Markets in Europe (AFME, #02596).
Correspondent members in 3 countries:
Mexico, New Zealand, Thailand.

NGO Relations Some of ICSA members are also members of Consultative Committee of: *International Organization of Securities Commissions (IOSCO, #14470)*. Instrumental in setting up: *International Forum for Investor Education (IFIE, #13642)*. [2021/XF1136/y/**F**]

♦ International Council of Securities Dealers and Self-Regulatory Associations / see International Council of Securities Associations (#13071)
♦ International Council on Security and Development / see ICOS (#11086)

♦ International Council on Shared Parenting (ICSP) 13072

Conseil International sur la Résidence Alternée (CIRA) – Internationaler Rat für die Paritätische Doppelresidenz

SG Stiftsgasse 6, 53111 Bonn, Germany. T. +491708004615.
URL: https://twohomes.org/

History Started as an informal organization with the title *International Platform on Shared Parenting*, 2013. Formalized into an organization registered in accordance with German law, 22 Feb 2014. **Aims** Disseminate and advance scientific knowledge on the needs and rights of children whose parents are living apart; formulate evidence-based recommendations about the legal, judicial and practical implementation of shared parenting. **Structure** General Assembly; Board of Directors. **Languages** English, French, German. **Finance** Sources: members' dues; sponsorship. **Activities** Events/meetings; knowledge management/information dissemination. **Events** *International Conference on Shared Parenting* Vancouver, BC (Canada) 2020, *International Conference on Shared Parenting* Strasbourg (France) 2018, *International Conference on Shared Parenting* Boston, MA (USA) 2017, *International Conference on Shared Parenting* Bonn (Germany) 2015, *International Conference on Shared Parenting* Bonn (Germany) 2014. **Members** in 21 countries. Membership countries not specified. **Consultative Status** Consultative status granted from: *Council of Europe (CE, #04881)* (Participatory Status). [2019.02.12/XJ8502/**C**]

♦ International Council of Sheet Metal Presswork Associations (ICOSPA) 13073

Conseil international des associations de la transformation des métaux en feuilles – Consejo Internacional de Asociaciones de Imprentas Metalúrgicas – Internationaler Rat der Verbände der Blechumformung

SG PMA, 6363 Oak Tree Blvd, Independence OH 44131, USA. T. +12169018800.
URL: http://www.icospa.com/

History 1965. Current bylaws adopted 17 Mar 1993, Chicago IL (USA). **Aims** Provide a forum for exchange of information on the commercial and technical situation and development of the world-wide sheet metal industry; promote sheet metal parts as basic components in industrial and consumer products; enhance the role of sub-contract metal forming in changing manufacturing structures. **Structure** Council (meets annually), consisting of former Presidents of ICOSPA and acting presidents or chairmen of the national associations or their chief executives, chaired by President. Administrative Secretariat, headed by Administrative Secretary. **Languages** English. **Staff** 1.00 FTE, paid. **Finance** Members' dues. Budget (annual): euro 23,000. **Activities** Sponsors Sheet Metal Presswork Congress every 2-3 years. Organizes: annual Council meetings; technical meetings and publications; plant visits and study tours. Represents members' interests in international organizations. **Events** *Triennial Congress* Birmingham (UK) 2020, *Triennial Congress* Suzhou (China) 2017, *Triennial Congress* Strasbourg (France) 2014, *Annual Meeting* Marseille (France) 2013, *Annual Meeting* Bavaria (Germany) 2012.

Members National associations (5) in 5 countries:
France, Germany, Japan, UK, USA.
Company member (1) in 1 country:
Italy. [2014/XD4366/**D**]

♦ International Council of Shopping Centers (ICSC) 13074

Conseil international des centres commerciales

Pres/CEO 1251 Ave of the Americas, 45th Floor, New York NY 10020-1104, USA. T. +16467283800. E-mail: membership@icsc.com – dsherman@icsc.com.
Exec Vice-Pres address not obtained.
URL: https://www.icsc.com/

History 3 Mar 1957, New York NY (USA). **Aims** Enhance exchange of experience and mutual education for and by the shopping center *industry*. **Structure** Board of Trustees. **Languages** English. **Staff** 115.00 FTE, paid. **Finance** Members' dues. Income from publications and meetings. **Activities** Programs, implemented through volunteer officers, include: international and regional conventions; educational institutes; deal-making. **Events** *European Conference* Barcelona (Spain) 2019, *Retail Innovation Forum* London (UK) 2019, *Québec Conference* Montréal, QC (Canada) 2019, *Annual Asia Pacific Conference* Singapore (Singapore) 2019, *Annual conference* Dubai (United Arab Emirates) 2018. **Publications** *Shopping Centers Today* (12 a year). Various publications.

Members Regular; Affiliate. Members (38,000) in 57 countries and territories:
Argentina, Australia, Austria, Bahamas, Bahrain, Barbados, Belgium, Bermuda, Brazil, Canada, Chile, Colombia, Czechia, Denmark, Egypt, El Salvador, Finland, France, Germany, Greece, Hong Kong, Hungary, Iceland, India, Indonesia, Ireland, Israel, Italy, Japan, Kenya, Luxembourg, Malaysia, Malta, Mexico, Monaco, Netherlands, New Zealand, Nigeria, Norway, Oman, Peru, Philippines, Poland, Portugal, Russia, Saudi Arabia, Singapore, South Africa, Spain, Sweden, Switzerland, Türkiye, UK, United Arab Emirates, Uruguay, USA. [2020/XF4964/**F**]

♦ International Council for Ski Mountaineering Competitions / see International Ski Mountaineering Federation (#14871)

♦ International Council for Small Business (ICSB) 13075

Exec Dir Funger Hall Ste 315, 2201 G St NW, GWU School of Business, Washington DC 20052, USA. T. +12029940704. Fax +12029944930. E-mail: info@icsb.org.
URL: http://www.icsb.org/

History 1957, USA. Former names and other names: *National Council for Small Business Management Development* – former (1957 to 1978). **Aims** Advance management development practices for potential entrepreneurs and existing small business owner/managers. **Structure** Board of Directors. **Languages** English. **Activities** Events/meetings; training/education. **Events** *World Congress* Gwangju (Korea Rep) 2023, *World Congress* Washington, DC (USA) 2022, *World Congress* Paris (France) 2021, *Annual Conference* Paris (France) 2020, *Asian SME Conference* Gwangju (Korea Rep) 2019. **Publications** *ICSB Bulletin* (12 a year); *Journal of Small Business Management* (4 a year). Conference proceedings (annual).

Members Affiliates in 19 countries and territories:
Argentina, Australia, Bangladesh, Brazil, Canada, China, Egypt, Indonesia, Japan, Korea Rep, Malaysia, Mexico, Myanmar, New Zealand, Puerto Rico, Russia, Singapore, Taiwan, USA.
Affiliates also include one organization listed in this Yearbook:
European Council for Small Business and Entrepreneurship (ECSB, #06842).

NGO Relations Participant of: *United Nations Global Compact (#20567)*. [2022/XF1395/y/**F**]

♦ International Council of Social Democratic Women / see Socialist International Women (#19341)

♦ International Council on Social Welfare (ICSW) 13076

Conseil international de l'action sociale (CIAS) – Consejo Internacional de Bienestar Social

Exec Dir C/ Obispo Trejo 2, 28040 Madrid, Spain. T. +34913988582. E-mail: icsw@icsw.org.
URL: http://www.icsw.org/

History 1928, Paris (France). Founded at 1st International Conference of Social Work. Reorganized: 1946; 1966. Constitution amended: 4 Sep 1982, Brighton (UK); 1986, Tokyo (Japan); 2007, Utrecht (Netherlands). Former names and other names: *Permanent Committee of the International Conferences of Social Work* – former; *Comité permanent des conférences internationales du service social* – former; *Ständiger Ausschuss der Internationalen Konferenz für Soziale Arbeit* – former. **Aims** Promote forms of social and economic *development* which aim to reduce *poverty*, hardship and vulnerability, especially amongst *disadvantaged* people; strive for recognition and protection and realization of fundamental *rights* to employment, income, food, shelter, education, health care and security; promote equality of opportunity, freedom of expression, freedom of association, participation and access to human services and oppose discrimination; promote policies and programmes which strike an appropriate balance between social and economic goals and which respect *cultural diversity*; strengthen *civil society* worldwide; seek implementation of objects by governments, international organizations and non-governmental agencies in cooperation with member organizations. **Structure** General Assembly; Supervisory and Advisory Board; General Secretariat. **Languages** English, French, Spanish. **Staff** 1.00 FTE, paid; 10.00 FTE, voluntary. **Finance** Sources: government support; grants; international organizations; meeting proceeds; members' dues; private foundations. Annual budget: 100,000 EUR. **Activities** Events/meetings; guidance/assistance/consulting; knowledge management/information dissemination; projects/programmes; research and development. **Events** *Joint World Conference on Social Work Education and Social Development* Seoul (Korea Rep) 2022, *Joint World Conference on Social Work and Social Development* Rimini (Italy) 2020, *Joint World Conference on Social Work and Social Development* Dublin (Ireland) 2018, *Joint World Conference on Social Work, Education and Social Development* Seoul (Korea Rep) 2016, *Joint World Conference on Social Work and Social Development* Melbourne, VIC (Australia) 2014. **Publications** Proceedings of biennial conference (electronic); regional newsletters; selected papers and articles.

Members Category A: national committees in 26 countries and territories:
Armenia, Austria, Brazil, Brunei Darussalam, Eswatini, Fiji, Finland, Germany, Haiti, Hong Kong, India, Indonesia, Jamaica, Korea Rep, Malaysia, Maldives, Mauritius, Mongolia, Morocco, Philippines, Senegal, Taiwan, Thailand, Uruguay, Zambia, Zimbabwe.
Category B: International member organizations (6), of which 5 are listed in this Yearbook:
Association Internationale pour la Formation, la Recherche et l'Intervention Sociale (AIFRIS, #02701); *International Association of Schools of Social Work (IASSW, #12149)*; *International Federation of Social Workers (IFSW, #13544)*; *International Social Service (ISS, #14886)*; *Salvation Army (#19041)*.
Category C: Other organizations in 30 countries:
Armenia, Bangladesh, Cameroon, Cyprus, Czechia, France, Gambia, Georgia, Ghana, Ireland, Italy, Japan, Kenya, Korea Rep, Malaysia, Mauritius, Moldova, Nepal, Netherlands, Norway, Philippines, Portugal, Slovakia, Spain, Sri Lanka, Sweden, Switzerland, USA, Vietnam, Zimbabwe.
Category D: members in 4 countries:
Brazil, Dominican Rep, India, Thailand.
Category E: distinguished persons (26). Membership countries not specified.

Consultative Status Consultative status granted from: *ECOSOC (#05331)* (General); *UNESCO (#20322)* (Consultative Status); *FAO (#09260)* (Liaison Status); *ILO (#11123)* (Special List); *Council of Europe (CE, #04881)* (Participatory Status); *UNICEF (#20332)*; *UNCTAD (#20285)* (General Category). **IGO Relations** Accredited by (1): *United Nations Office at Vienna (UNOV, #20604)*. Consultative Status with: *UNDP (#20292)*. Associated with Department of Global Communications of the United Nations. **NGO Relations** Member of (8): *Alliance for Health Promotion (A4HP, #00687)*; *Committee of NGOs on Human Rights, Geneva (#04275)*; *Conference of Non-Governmental Organizations in Consultative Relationship with the United Nations (CONGO, #04635)*; *European*

Network for Social Action (ENSACT, #08003); International Conference of NGOs (#12883); NGO Committee on the Status of Women, Geneva (#17117); SDG Watch Europe (#19162); Social Platform (#19344). Cooperates with (2): *International Association of Schools of Social Work (IASSW, #12149); International Federation of Social Workers (IFSW, #13544).* [2023.02.23/XA1771/y/**A**]

♦ International Council of Societies of Industrial Design / see World Design Organization (#21358)
♦ International Council of Societies of Industrial Designers / see World Design Organization (#21358)
♦ International Council of Societies of Pathology (no recent information)
♦ International Council for Soviet and East European Studies / see International Council for Central and East European Studies (#13002)
♦ International Council of Sport and Physical Education / see International Council of Sport Science and Physical Education (#13077)

♦ International Council of Sport Science and Physical Education (ICSSPE) 13077

Conseil international pour l'éducation physique et la science du sport (CIEPSS) – Consejo Internacional para la Ciencia del Deporte y la Educación Fisica – Weltrat für Sportwissenschaft und Leibes-/Körpererziehung

Exec Dir Hanns-Braun-Str 1, Friesenhaus I, 14053 Berlin, Germany. T. +4930311023210. Fax +4930311023229. E-mail: icsspe@icsspe.org.
Pres address not obtained.
URL: http://www.icsspe.org/

History 27 Sep 1958, Paris (France). Founded by signatories to first Statutes, both private individuals and representatives of national and international bodies concerned with sport and physical education. First Statutes amended and adopted by the first General Assembly, 12 Sep 1960, Rome (Italy). Statutes subsequently modified by General Assemblies: Oct 1963, Paris; Oct 1964, Tokyo (Japan); Oct 1968, Mexico City (Mexico); Jan 1971, Paris; Aug 1972, Munich (Germany FR); Jul 1976, Québec (Canada); Jul 1982, Helsinki (Finland); Sep 1988, Cheonan (Korea Rep). Current Statutes, adopted by 18th General Assembly, 18 Nov 1998, Barcelona (Spain), came into effect 1 Feb 1999; revised at 20th General Assembly, Jul 2002, Manchester (UK), at 21st General Assembly, Aug 2004, Thessaloniki (Greece), at 22nd General Assembly, Aug 2006, Berlin (Germany), at 23rd General Assembly, Jul 2008, Guangzhou (China), at 24th General Assembly, Jul 2010, Havana (Cuba), at 25th General Assembly, Jul 2012, Glasgow (UK), at 26th General Assembly, Jun 2014, Helsinki (Finland), at 27th General Assembly, April 2016, Santos (Brazil), at 28th General Assembly, April 2017, Frankfurt (Germany), at 29th General Assembly, September 2018, Johannesburg (South Africa), and at 30th General Assembly (online),12 May 2021. Former names and other names: *International Council of Sport and Physical Education (ICSPE-CIEPS)* – former (1958 to 31 Dec 1982); *Conseil international pour l'éducation physique et le sport* – former (1958 to 31 Dec 1982); *Consejo Internacional para la Educación Fisica y el Deporte* – former (1958 to 31 Dec 1982); *Weltrat für Sport und Leibeserziehung* – former (1958 to 31 Dec 1982). Registration: No/ID: VR 28362, Start date: 28 Jan 2009, Germany, Berlin. **Aims** Contribute to a strong sporting sector, high quality physical education and improved health worldwide; maintain an inclusive perspective on the different disciplines of sport, sport science and physical education and of furthering a continuing collaboration between them. **Structure** General Assembly (every 2 years, since 1992); Executive Board; Development Committee; Committees; Executive Office (General Secretariat), based in Berlin (Germany), headed by Executive Director. Seat of the Council is in Berlin (Germany). **Languages** English, French, German, Spanish. **Staff** 6.00 FTE, paid. **Finance** Partnerships. **Activities** Awards/prizes/competitions; awareness raising; events/meetings; knowledge management/information dissemination; projects/programmes; training/education. **Events** *International Conference of Physical Education and Sports Science (ICPESS)* Barcelona (Spain) 2022, *General Assembly* Berlin (Germany) 2021, *International Conference of Physical Education and Sports Science (ICPESS)* Barcelona (Spain) 2020, *World Congress on Science and Fooball* Melbourne, VIC (Australia) 2019, *General Assembly* Johannesburg (South Africa) 2018. **Publications** *ICSSPE News* (12 a year); *Perspectives, the Multidisciplinary Journal of Physical Education and Sport Science. Sport Science Studies. Directory of Sport Science.* Symposia proceedings.

Members Governmental Sport, health and education authorities (9); Non-governmental sport organizations (53); Scientific and educational organizations (104). Members in 73 countries and territories:
Albania, Argentina, Australia, Austria, Bangladesh, Barbados, Belgium, Brazil, Bulgaria, Canada, China, Croatia, Cuba, Czechia, Denmark, Egypt, Finland, France, Georgia, Germany, Ghana, Greece, Hong Kong, Hungary, India, Indonesia, Iran Islamic Rep, Iraq, Ireland, Israel, Italy, Japan, Jordan, Korea Rep, Kuwait, Latvia, Lebanon, Lithuania, Luxembourg, Madagascar, Malaysia, Maldives, Malta, Mexico, Monaco, Mongolia, Nepal, Netherlands, New Zealand, Nigeria, Norway, Oman, Pakistan, Poland, Portugal, Romania, Russia, Sierra Leone, Singapore, Slovakia, South Africa, Spain, Sri Lanka, Sweden, Switzerland, Taiwan, Türkiye, UK, Ukraine, USA, Venezuela, Zambia, Zimbabwe.

Included in the above, 60 organizations listed in this Yearbook:
- *Africa Association for Health, Physical Education, Recreation, Sport and Dance (AFAHPER-SD, no recent information);*
- *Asian Council of Exercise and Sports Science (ACESS, #01409);*
- *Association internationale des écoles supérieures d'éducation physique (AIESEP, #02685);*
- *Conseil international du sport militaire (CISM, #04695);*
- *European Association for Sport Management (EASM, #06219);*
- *European College of Sport Science (ECSS, #06616);*
- *European Fair Play Movement (EFPM, #07025);*
- *European Group for Research into Elderly and Physical Activity (EGREPA, #07432);*
- *European Physical Education Association (EUPEA, #08206);*
- *Fédération internationale de gymnastique (FIG, #09636);*
- *Fundación Red Deporte y Cooperación (Fundación Red Deporte);*
- *Global Council of Sport Science (GCSS);*
- *International Association for the Philosophy of Sport (IAPS, #12078);*
- *International Association of Computer Science in Sport (IACSS, #11803);*
- *International Association of Kung Fu Toa 21;*
- *International Association of Physical Education and Sport for Girls and Women (IAPESGW, #12081);*
- *International Association of Sport Kinetics (IASK, #12178);*
- *International Cheer Union (ICU, #12539);*
- *International Committee of Sports for the Deaf (ICSD, #12805);*
- *International Council for Coaching Excellence (ICCE, #13008);*
- *Internationale Vereinigung Sport- und Freizeiteinrichtungen (IAKS, #13319);*
- *International Federation of Adapted Physical Activity (IFAPA, #13338);*
- *International Federation of Association Football (#13360);*
- *International Federation of Physical and Sport Education (#13510);*
- *International Fitness and Bodybuilding Federation (IFBB, #13610);*
- *International Luge Federation (FIL, #14066);*
- *International Martial Arts Union (IMAU, #14110);*
- *International Paralympic Committee (IPC, #14512);*
- *International School Sport Federation (ISF, #14792);*
- *International Society for Comparative Physical Education and Sport (ISCPES, #15023);*
- *International Society for the Advancement of Kinanthropometry (ISAK, #14901);*
- *International Society for the History of Physical Education and Sport (ISHPES, #15175);*
- *International Society of Olympic Historians (ISOH, #15322);*
- *International Society of Sport Psychology (ISSP, #15455);*
- *International Sociology of Sport Association (ISSA, #15554);*
- *International Sport Lawyers Association (ISLA, #15591);*
- *International Sports Council;*
- *International Tennis Federation (ITF, #15676);*
- *International Traditional Taekwon-Do Federation (ITTAF, #15712);*
- *International University Sports Federation (FISU, #15830);*
- *International Weightlifting Federation (IWF, #15876);*
- *International Workers and Amateurs in Sports Confederation (#15905);*
- *Panathlon International (PI, #18170);*
- *Special Olympics International (SOI, #19910);*
- *Sport Association of Arab Women (SAAW, no recent information);*
- *The Association for International Sport for All (TAFISA, #02763);*
- *United World Wrestling (UWW, #20665);*
- *WomenSport International (WSI, #21033);*
- *World All Styles Kickboxing Organization (WASKO, no recent information);*
- *World Association for Sport Management (WASM, #21194);*
- *World Athletics (#21209);*
- *World Federation of Athletic Training and Therapy (WFATT, #21413);*
- *World Federation of Self Defence, Arme Blanche and Personal Arts (WFSAPA, no recent information);*
- *World Flying Disc Federation (WFDF, #21509);*
- *World Hatha Yog Federation (#21554);*
- *World Kalaripayattu Federation (WKF);*
- *World O-Sport Federation (WOF, #21700);*
- *World Pahuyuth Federation (WPF, #21706);*
- *World Penthathlon (UIPM, #21720).*

Consultative Status Consultative status granted from: *UNESCO (#20322)* (Associate Status). **NGO Relations** Recognized by: *International Olympic Committee (IOC, #14408).* [2021.09.20/XB1757/y/**B**]

♦ International Council of Sqay (internationally oriented national body)

♦ International Council for Standardization in Haematology (ICSH) . . 13078

Conseil international de standardisation en hématologie

Registered Office 2-4 Packhorse Road, Gerrards Cross, SL9 7QE, UK. E-mail: admin@icsh.org.
URL: http://icsh.org/

History 1963. Founded as a standardization committee by *European School of Haematology (ESH, #08430)*, officially constituted by ISH and ESH in 1964. Current constitution ratified, Apr 2007; revised Oct 2013. Registered in accordance with Dutch law. Re-registered in accordance with Dutch law and US law, Apr 2007. Former names and other names: *International Committee for Standardization in Haematology* – former (1963); *Comité international de standardization en hématologie* – former (1963). Registration: Netherlands. **Aims** Achieve reliable and reproducible results in *laboratory* analysis, primarily concerning diagnostic haematology. **Structure** Managing Board. **Languages** English. **Staff** Voluntary. **Activities** Standards/guidelines. **Events** *General Assembly* 2022, *General Assembly* Lund (Sweden) 2019, *General Assembly* Miami, FL (USA) 2018, *General Assembly* Kobe (Japan) 2017, *General Assembly* Lucerne (Switzerland) 2016. **Publications** Standards; guidelines.

Members National committees, or unofficial contacts (A), in 50 countries and territories:
Argentina, Australia, Austria, Belgium, Bolivia, Brazil, Bulgaria, Canada, Chile, China (A), Colombia, Costa Rica, Cuba, Czechia, Denmark, Finland, France, Germany, Ghana, Greece, Hungary, India, Indonesia, Israel, Italy, Jamaica, Japan, Kenya, Korea Rep, Malaysia, Mexico, Netherlands, New Zealand, Nigeria, Norway, Poland, Portugal, Romania, Russia, Slovakia, South Africa, Spain, Sri Lanka, Sweden, Switzerland, Taiwan, Türkiye, UK, USA, Venezuela.

Consultative Status Consultative status granted from: *ECOSOC (#05331)* (Ros C); *WHO (#20950)* (Official Relations). **NGO Relations** Member of: Standardization Committee of *International Union of Immunological Societies (IUIS, #15781).* Member of: *Joint Committee for Traceability in Laboratory Medicine (JCTLM, #16127).* [2021/XC9428/**C**]

♦ International Council for the Study of the Pacific Islands (ICSPI) . . . 13079

Conseil international pour l'étude des îles du Pacifique (CIEIP)

Secretariat c/o UNESCO Office in Apia, PO Box 615, Matautu Uta, Apia, Samoa. T. +68524276. Fax +68526593. E-mail: apia@unesco.org.

History 29 Jun 2001, Apia (Samoa). **Aims** Facilitate mutual cooperation between institutions and organizations dedicated to Pacific Islands studies in order to: promote research and teaching for the benefit of the peoples of the Pacific Islands; maintain a resource base of Pacific Island research; facilitate research; promote recognition of the Pacific Islands' distinctive contributions to knowledge. **Structure** Council (every 2 years); Executive Committee; Secretariat. **Languages** English. **Staff** 1.50 FTE, paid. **Finance** Funding from regional and international organizations (not specified). **Members** in the Pacific (membership countries not specified). **IGO Relations** Secretariat provided by: *UNESCO Office for the Pacific States (#20315).* [2008.10.07/XM0276/**E**]

♦ International Council for the Study of Viruses and Virus Diseases of the Grapevine / see International Council for the Study of Virus and Virus-like Diseases of the Grapevine (#13080)

♦ International Council for the Study of Virus and Virus-like Diseases of the Grapevine (ICVG) 13080

Sec Dept Plant Pathology, Cornell Univ, NY State Agricultural Experiment Station, Geneva NY 14456, USA.
URL: http://web.pppmb.cals.cornell.edu/fuchs/icvg/committee.htm

History Founded 1964, Switzerland, as *International Working Group for the Study of Viruses and Virus Diseases of the Grapevine.* Previously also referred to as *International Council for the Study of Viruses and Virus Diseases of the Grapevine (ICVG).* **Aims** Promote research on viruses and virus-like agents of grapevine diseases, such as phytoplasmas and viroids, on the diseases caused, on control and on prevention methods. **Structure** Committee. **Finance** No annual contribution requested from members. Each meeting financed locally with funds from inviting institutes and private sponsors. **Events** *Congress* Ankara (Turkey) 2015, *Congress* Davis, CA (USA) 2012, *Congress* Dijon (France) 2009, *Congress* Stellenbosch (South Africa) 2006, *Congress* Locorotondo (Italy) 2003. **Publications** *ICVG Newsletter* (periodical). Bibliography on grapevine virus and virus-like diseases; proceedings of meetings.

Members Individuals in 41 countries and territories:
Argentina, Australia, Austria, Brazil, Bulgaria, Canada, Chile, China, Croatia, Cyprus, Czechia, Egypt, France, Germany, Greece, Hungary, India, Iran Islamic Rep, Israel, Italy, Japan, Korea Rep, Mexico, New Zealand, North Macedonia, Palestine, Peru, Portugal, Romania, Russia, Serbia, Slovenia, South Africa, Spain, Switzerland, Syrian AR, Tunisia, Türkiye, Ukraine, Uruguay, USA. [2014.06.01/XE0046/v/**E**]

♦ International Council Supporting Fair Trial and Human Rights (ICSFT) 13081

Conseil international pour le soutien à des procès équitables et aux droits de l'homme

Contact Route de Ferney 150, 1218 Le Grand Saconnex, Case postal 2100, 1211 Geneva 2, Switzerland. T. +41227884808. Fax +41227884807. E-mail: info@icsft.net.
URL: http://www.icsft.net/

History Registered in accordance with Swiss Civil Code. **Aims** Strengthen the human rights movement within the *Middle East* and North Africa. **Structure** General Assembly; Executive Committee; Founders; Board; Auditor. **Languages** Arabic, English. **Activities** Advocacy/lobbying/activism, research/documentation; capacity building; networking/liaising; events/meetings. **Consultative Status** Consultative status granted from: *ECOSOC (#05331)* (Special). [2019.02.18/XM6182/**D**]

♦ International Council for Sustainable Agriculture (ICSA) 13082

Pres c/o IFEED, Kirchweg 4a, 31275 Lehrte, Germany. T. +4953021303. E-mail: info@ifeed.org.

Aims Provide a common international platform for exchange of scientific information and experiences on sustainable agriculture for food, energy and industry, food security and sustainable development on local and global issues. **Structure** Executive Council. **Activities** Research and development; projects/programmes; guidance/assistance/consulting; publishing activities. **Events** *Conference* Kuala Lumpur (Malaysia) 2015, *Conference* Hurup Thy (Denmark) 2014, *Conference* Vechelde (Germany) 2013, *Asia Pacific Symposium on Food Safety* Melbourne, VIC (Australia) 2011, *International conference on sustainable agriculture for food, energy and industry / Conference* Sapporo (Japan) 2008. [2018/XM0116/**D**]

♦ International Council on Systems Engineering (INCOSE) 13083

Operations Mgr 7670 Opportunity Rd, Ste 220, San Diego CA 92111-2222, USA. T. +18585411725. Fax +18585411728. E-mail: info@incose.org.
URL: http://www.incose.org/

History 1991. **Aims** Address complex societal and technical challenges by enabling, promoting and advancing Systems Engineering and systems approaches. **Structure** Board of Directors. Chapters (over 70)in 3 areas: Americas; EMEA; Asia-Oceania. Working Groups. **Activities** Advocacy/lobbying/activism; events/meetings; training/education. **Events** *Annual Symposium* Honolulu, HI (USA) 2023, *International Workshop* Torrance, CA (USA) 2023, *Annual Symposium* Detroit, MI (USA) 2022, *International Workshop* Torrance, CA (USA) 2022, *Annual Symposium* Honolulu, HI (USA) 2021. **Publications** *Insights* (4 a year) – magazine. **Members** Network members (over 18000) in 35 countries. Membership countries not specified. **IGO Relations** Participating organization of: *Group on Earth Observations (GEO, #10735).* **NGO Relations** Member of (2): *ABET; International Federation for Systems Research (IFSR, #13564).* In liaison with technical committees of: *International Organization for Standardization (ISO, #14473).* [2023/XN7601/**C**]

♦ International Council of Tanners (ICT) 13084

Conseil international des tanneurs (CIT) – Consejo Internacional de Curtidores (CIC) – Internationale Gerbervereinigung (IG) – Consiglio Internazionale dei Conciatori (CIC)

Secretariat Leather Trade House, Kings Park Road, Moulton Park, Northampton, NN3 6JD, UK. T. +441604679917. Fax +441604679998. E-mail: sec@tannercouncil.org.

URL: http://www.leather-council.org/

History 6 Jul 1926, London (UK). Most recent statutes adopted 2 Oct 2010. **Aims** Promote interests of the *leather* industry internationally. **Structure** Council (meets 1-2 times a year); Executive Committee; Secretariat, headed by Secretary. **Languages** English. **Staff** 1.00 FTE, paid. **Finance** Sources: members' dues; sale of publications. **Activities** Events/meetings; research/documentation; standards/guidelines. **Events** *World Leather Congress* Addis Ababa (Ethiopia) 2021, *World Leather Congress* New York, NY (USA) 2019, *World Leather Congress* Shanghai (China) 2017, *World Leather Congress* Milan (Italy) 2015, *Meeting* Hong Kong (Hong Kong) 2011. **Publications** *International Glossary of Leather Terms* (1976); *Analytical Methods for Use in Conjunction with the ICT Ecotox Label*; *ICT Eco-Toxguideline*; *International Contract No 6 – Hides and Skins*; *International Contract No 7 – Finished Leather.*

Members National associations in 33 countries and territories:
Brazil, Burundi, China, Comoros, Congo DR, Djibouti, Egypt, Eritrea, Eswatini, Ethiopia, France, Germany, Italy, Japan, Kenya, Libya, Madagascar, Malawi, Mauritius, Netherlands, Rwanda, Seychelles, Spain, Sudan, Sweden, Taiwan, Türkiye, Uganda, UK, USA, Uzbekistan, Zambia, Zimbabwe.

NGO Relations Partner of (1): *Livestock Environmental Assessment and Performance Partnership (LEAP, #16500).* Cooperates with (2): *International Council of Hides, Skins and Leather Traders Associations (ICHSLTA, #13029); International Union of Leather Technologists and Chemists Societies (IULTCS, #15788).* In liaison with technical committees of: *International Organization for Standardization (ISO, #14473).*
[2022.10.12/XC1758/**C**]

♦ International Council for Technical Communication (inactive)

♦ International Council of Theological Library Associations / see European Theological Libraries (#08906)

♦ International Council of Thirteen Indigenous Grandmothers 13085

Contact Center for Sacred Studies, PO Box 2904, Guerneville CA 95446, USA. T. +17076047362. E-mail: info@grandmotherscouncil.com.

URL: http://www.grandmotherscouncil.org/

History Oct 2004, Phoenicia NY (USA), as an alliance of prayer, education and healing. **Aims** *Save the planet* by passing down traditions to younger generations; strive for unity and world *peace.*

Members Individuals (13) in 6 countries:
Brazil, Gabon, Mexico, Nepal, Tibet, USA. [2016/XM2572/**E**]

♦ International Council of Tourism Partners (internationally oriented national body)

♦ International Council of Toy Industries (ICTI) 13086

Conseil international des industries de jouets

Permanent Secretariat c/o Toy Industry Assn, 1375 Broadway, Ste 1001, New York NY 10018, USA. T. +12024590355. E-mail: icti@toyassociation.org.

Pres c/o Asociacion Mexicana de la Industria del Juguete, Rio Rhin 56, Col Renacimiento, Cuauhtémoc, 06500 Mexico City CDMX, Mexico.

URL: http://www.toy-icti.org/

History 1974, as *International Committee of Toy Industries.* New name adopted 1992. **Aims** Act as a center of discussion and information exchange on trends and issues important to the toy industry; promote safety standards; reduce or eliminate barriers to trade; advance social responsibility with programs to address environmental concerns, fair and lawful employment practices and workplace safety. **Structure** President. Executive Committee, comprising 3 Vice-Presidents representing the Americas, Asia and Europe. Secretariat. **Languages** English. **Finance** Members' dues. **Events** *Annual Meeting* Tokyo (Japan) 2014, *Annual Meeting* Washington, DC (USA) 2013, *Annual Meeting* Egham (UK) 2012, *Annual Meeting* Hong Kong (Hong Kong) 2011, *Annual meeting* Hong Kong (Hong Kong) 2011.

Members Full in 20 countries and territories:
Argentina, Australia, Austria, Brazil, Canada, China, Denmark, France, Germany, Hong Kong, India, Italy, Japan, Mexico, Netherlands, Spain, Sweden, Taiwan, UK, USA.

Consultative Status Consultative status granted from: *ECOSOC (#05331)* (Ros A). **NGO Relations** In liaison with technical committees of: *International Organization for Standardization (ISO, #14473).* Affiliated with: *ICTI Ethical Toy Program (#11089).* [2018/XE0410/t/**E**]

♦ International Council of Trade and Industrial Unions (inactive)

♦ International Council for Traditional Music (ICTM) 13087

Conseil international de la musique traditionnelle (CIMT) – Consejo Internacional de Música Tradicional

Exec Sec Lokavec 130 B, 5270 Ajdovscina, Slovenia. E-mail: secretariat@ictmusic.org.

URL: https://www.ictmusic.org/

History Sep 1947, London (UK). Statutes adopted 22 Sep 1947. Most recently amended Jul 2017. Former names and other names: *International Folk Music Council (IFMC)* – former (1947 to 1981); *Conseil international de la musique populaire (CIMP)* – former (1947 to 1981); *Consejo Internacional de Música Popular* – former (1947 to 1981). **Aims** Further the study, practice, documentation, preservation and dissemination of traditional music and dance of all countries. **Structure** General Assembly; Executive Board; World Network; Study Groups; Secretariat, comprising Secretary General and Executive Assistant. **Languages** English. **Staff** 1.00 FTE, paid. **Finance** Members' dues (Individual and Corporate); Institutional subscribers. Other sources: donations; grants from UNESCO, other bodies and governments. Annual budget: US$ 96,000. **Activities** Events/meetings; networking/liaising; research/documentation. **Events** *World Conference* Legon (Ghana) 2023, *World Conference* Lisbon (Portugal) 2022, *Colloquium* Shanghai (China) 2022, *Symposium* Lisbon (Portugal) 2021, *World Conference* Lisbon (Portugal) 2021. **Publications** *Bulletin of the International Council for Traditional Music* (3 a year); *Yearbook for Traditional Music* (annual). *A Select Bibliography of European Folk Music* (1966); *The Collecting of Folk Music and other Ethnomusicological Material* (1958). Proceedings of conferences and colloquia; study group reports; manuals. **Members** in 129 countries and territories. Membership countries not specified. **Consultative Status** Consultative status granted from: *UNESCO (#20322)* (Consultative Status). **NGO Relations** Sponsoring society of: *Répertoire International de Littérature Musicale (RILM, #18845).* Instrumental in setting up: *International Study Group on Music Archaeology (ISGMA).* [2022/XB2061/v/**B**]

♦ International Council of Traditional Sports and Games (ICTSG) 13088

Conseil International pour les Jeux et Sports Traditionnels – Consejo Internacional para los Juegos Tradicionales y Deportes – Conselho Internacional de Esportes e Jogos Tradicionais

Pres 254-H, Street 6, Phase 5, DHA, Lahore 54792, Pakistan. T. +923028405463. Fax +923008405463. E-mail: president@traditionalsportsgames.org – office@traditionalsportsgames.org – office.ictsg@gmail.com.

URL: http://www.traditionalsportsgames.org/

History 2009, Teheran (Iran Islamic Rep). Statutes approved and adopted, 15 Aug 2018, Istanbul (Turkey). **Aims** Contribute to promotion and development of traditional sports and games (TSG), as a distinct and different category to modern sports; facilitate promotion and understanding of TSG as cultural identity and diversity so as to achieve sport for peace in the context of achieving Education for All (EFA) and the Sustainable Development Goals (SDGs). **Structure** World Body; Continental Unions; Regional Associations; National Associations. **Languages** English. **Staff** 5.50 FTE, paid; 10.00 FTE, voluntary. **Finance** Sources: donations; fundraising; gifts, legacies; grants; members' dues. **Activities** Awareness raising; events/meetings; networking/liaising; research and development; sporting activities; standards/guidelines; training/education.

Members Full in 47 countries and territories:
Azerbaijan, Belize, Brazil, Bulgaria, Canada, Cape Verde, Chile, Colombia, Costa Rica, Côte d'Ivoire, Dominican Rep, Egypt, Estonia, France, Gambia, Ghana, Guam, Guatemala, Guinea-Bissau, India, Iran Islamic Rep, Ireland, Kazakhstan, Kenya, Korea Rep, Kuwait, Kyrgyzstan, Malawi, Mexico, Monaco, Mongolia, Niger, Nigeria, North Macedonia, Pakistan, Palau, Panama, Poland, Qatar, Samoa, Saudi Arabia, Senegal, Sierra Leone, South Africa, Sri Lanka, Tanzania UR, Tunisia.

National organizations in 61 countries:
Afghanistan, Armenia, Australia, Azerbaijan, Bangladesh, Belarus, Belgium, Belize, Benin, Bolivia, Bosnia-Herzegovina, Brazil, Bulgaria, Cameroon, Canada, Chile, Comoros, Costa Rica, Côte d'Ivoire, Croatia, Denmark, Dominican Rep, Egypt, France, Honduras, India, Indonesia, Ireland, Italy, Japan, Kazakhstan, Kuwait, Kyrgyzstan, Latvia, Lebanon, Lithuania, Malaysia, Mexico, Micronesia FS, Monaco, Mongolia, Nepal, New Zealand, Norway, Pakistan, Palau, Panama, Philippines, Poland, Samoa, Saudi Arabia, Singapore, Sri Lanka, Tajikistan, Thailand, Timor-Leste, Trinidad-Tobago, Turkmenistan, United Arab Emirates, Uruguay, Uzbekistan.

International Federations (7):
Asian Pencak Silat Federation (APSIF, #01660); International Qazak Kuresi Federation; *International Zurkhaneh Sports Federation (IZSF, #15946)*; Mongolian Traditional Archery Federation; *Sport Jiu-Jitsu International Federation (SJJIF, #19926)*; *World Federation of Kowat Alrami and Self Defense (WFKA, #21450)*; *World Silambam Federation (WSF).*

Individuals in 18 countries:
Belize, Brazil, Costa Rica, Côte d'Ivoire, Denmark, Egypt, France, Gambia, Guinea-Bissau, Kuwait, Malawi, Mexico, Niger, Pakistan, Palau, Russia, Spain, United Arab Emirates.

IGO Relations *Intergovernmental Committee for Physical Education and Sport (#11475).* **NGO Relations** *International Traditional Sports and Games Association (ITSGA, no recent information).*
[2020.05.08/XM8620/**E**]

♦ International Council of Unitarian and other Liberal Religious Thinkers and Workers / see International Association for Religious Freedom (#12130)

♦ International Council of Unitarians and Universalists (ICUU) 13089

Main Office PO Box 1434, Framingham MA 01701, USA.

URL: http://www.icuu.net/

History 25 Mar 1995, Essex MA (USA). **Aims** Foster communication, relationships and understanding within the international Unitarian, Universalist and Unitarian Universalist community; build networks and partnerships among member groups, their congregations, leaders and institutions; identify and nurture emerging groups around the world for mutual inspiration, development and growth. **Structure** Council (meets every 2 years). Executive Committee, comprising President, Vice-President, Secretary, Treasurer and 3 members. **Languages** English. **Staff** 0.50 FTE, paid. **Finance** Members' dues. **Activities** Organizes training seminars, conferences, symposia and spring tours. **Events** *Council Meeting and Conference* Montréal, QC (Canada) 2020, *Conference and Council Meeting / Conference* New York, NY (USA) 2014, *Conference* Dumaguete City (Philippines) 2004, *Conference* Dumaguete City (Philippines) 2004, *Conference* Prague (Czech Rep) 2003. **Publications** *The Global Chalice* (2 a year) – newsletter. *A Global Conversation: Unitarianism/Universalism at the Dawn of the 21st Century.*

Members Congregations (about 2,000) in 18 countries:
Australia, Canada, Czechia, Denmark, Finland, Germany, Hungary, India, New Zealand, Nigeria, Pakistan, Philippines, Poland, Romania, South Africa, Sri Lanka, UK, USA.

Emerging groups in x countries:
Burundi, Cuba, France, Indonesia, Mexico.

Correspondents and Associates in 6 countries:
Argentina, Bolivia, Brazil, Latvia, Russia, Spain. [2020/XD5874/**D**]

♦ International Council of United Days of Vesak / see International Council for the Day of VESAK (#13012)

♦ International Council on United Fund Raising / see United Way Worldwide (#20663)

♦ International Council for United Services to Seamen (inactive)

♦ International Council of Universities in the Spirit of St Thomas Aquinas (ICUSTA) 13090

Exec Dir Universidad Santo Tomas, Ejército 146, 8370003 Santiago, Santiago Metropolitan, Chile.

URL: http://www.icusta.org/

History 1993, as *International Council of Universities of St Thomas Aquinas* by Universidad Santo Tomas, Santiago (Chile). **Aims** Inspired by the life, works and tradition of St Thomas Aquinas, promote international diversity, love and passion for truth; support religious and moral principles that will enable students and faculty to meet global challenges of the 21st century. **Structure** General Assembly (every 2 years); Council of Honor; Executive Committee; Steering Committee. **Languages** English. **Staff** 3.00 FTE, paid. **Finance** Members' dues. Donations. **Activities** Events/meetings; projects/programmes; networking/liaising. **Events** *Biennial Conference* Mar del Plata (Argentina) 2022, *Biennial Conference* Houston, TX (USA) 2019, *Biennial Conference* Avila (Spain) 2017, *Biennial Conference* Santiago (Chile) 2015, *Biennial Conference* La Roche-sur-Yon (France) 2013. **Publications** *ICUSTA Newsletter. ICUSTA: 25 Years Promoting a Passion for Truth in the Service on Humanity.*

Members Institutions (29) in 15 countries and territories:
Argentina, Australia, Canada, Chile, France, Ireland, Italy, Japan, Mozambique, Philippines, South Sudan, Spain, Taiwan, USA, Zimbabwe. [2020.01.02/XJ9760/**E**]

♦ International Council of Universities of St Thomas Aquinas / see International Council of Universities in the Spirit of St Thomas Aquinas (#13090)

♦ International Council on Ventilation Hygiene (no recent information)

♦ International Council of Voluntarism, Civil Society, and Social Economy Researcher Associations (ICSERA) 13091

Pres 4852 11th Ave Cir E, Bradenton FL 34208, USA.

URL: https://icsera.wordpress.com/

History 2010. Registered in the State of Florida, 6 Jun 2010. Registered in USA as 501(c)(3), 2012. **Aims** Foster growth of the emerging academic discipline of voluntarism, civil society and social economy research worldwide (now termed *voluntaristics*) as an organized interdisciplinary field (since 1971) by linking and supporting existing researcher associations and fostering new ones. **Structure** Board; Executive Committee; World Region Vice-Presidents; Specialized Officers. **Languages** English. **Staff** Voluntary. **Finance** Sources: donations. Annual budget: 1,000 USD. **Activities** Events/meetings; publishing activities; research/documentation. **Publications** *Voluntaristics Review: Brill Research Perspectives* (6 a year). *A Dictionary of Nonprofit Terms and Concepts* (2nd ed 2019); *Palgrave Handbook of Volunteering, Civic Participation, and Nonprofit Associations* (2016). **Information Services** *RESOURCES* – online list of voluntaristics researcher associations, academic journals, research centers and institutes. **Members** Voluntaristics Researcher Organizations. Membership countries not specified. [2020.03.16/XJ7574/**C**]

♦ International Council of Voluntary Agencies (ICVA) 13092

Conseil international des agences bénévoles – Consejo Internacional de Organizaciones Voluntarias

Exec Dir La Voie-Creuse 16, 1202 Geneva, Switzerland. T. +41223322971. E-mail: secretariat@icvanetwork.org.

Information Officer address not obtained.

URL: https://www.icvanetwork.org/

History 6 Mar 1962. Established by merger of: *Conference of Non-Governmental Organizations Interested in Migration – Conférence des organisations non-gouvernementales intéressées aux problèmes de migration,* which held its 1st Conference 10-16 Jan 1950, Geneva (Switzerland); *Standing Conference of Voluntary Agencies Working for Refugees – Conférence permanente des agences bénévoles travaillant pour les réfugiés,* set up 16 Jun 1948, Geneva; *International Committee for World Refugee Year – Comité international pour l'Année mondiale du réfugié* – 1959-1961. Statutes amended: 1976; 1989; 1991; 1999; 2003; 2006; 2009; 2012; 2015; 2018; 2021. Completely restructured, 1997, when mandate was reaffirmed and sharpened by members. Regional hubs set up, 2013. **Aims** Make humanitarian action more principled and effective by working collectively and independently to influence policy and practice. **Structure** General Assembly (every 3 years); Board; Committees (3); Regional Hubs (3). **Languages** English. **Staff** Geneva: 14. Regional Hubs: 2 in each. **Finance** Sources: donations; government support; international organizations; members' dues. **Activities** Advocacy/lobbying/activism; knowledge management/information dissemination; networking/liaising; politics/policy/regulatory. **Events** *Annual Conference* Geneva (Switzerland) 2023, *Annual Conference* Geneva (Switzerland) 2021, *General Assembly* Geneva (Switzerland) 2021, *Annual Conference* Geneva (Switzerland) 2020, *Annual Conference* Geneva (Switzerland) 2019. **Publications** *ICVA Bulletin.* Annual Report; conference proceedings; information briefing papers; special reports.

Members Member Agencies (137) in 48 countries and territories:

Afghanistan, Australia, Bangladesh, Canada, Chad, China, Congo DR, Côte d'Ivoire, Denmark, Ethiopia, Finland, France, Germany, Greece, Holy See, India, Indonesia, Iran Islamic Rep, Ireland, Italy, Japan, Jordan, Kenya, Korea Rep, Lebanon, Libya, Malaysia, Mauritius, Mexico, Netherlands, Norway, Pakistan, Palestine, Philippines, Senegal, Somalia, South Africa, South Sudan, Sudan, Sweden, Switzerland, Tanzania UR, Thailand, Türkiye, Uganda, UK, USA, Yemen.

Included in the above, 73 organizations listed in this Yearbook:
- *ACT Alliance (#00081)*;
- *Act for Peace*;
- *Action Against Hunger (#00086)*;
- *ActionAid (#00087)*;
- *Adventist Development and Relief Agency International (ADRA, #00131)*;
- *Africa Humanitarian Action (AHA)*;
- *African Initiatives for Relief and Development (AIRD, #00339)*;
- *African Office for Development and Cooperation (OFADEC)*;
- *Afrique Secours et Assistance (ASA)*;
- *Agency Coordinating Body for Afghan Relief (ACBAR)*;
- *Agency for Technical Cooperation and Development (ACTED)*;
- *AMERA International*;
- *Asia Pacific Refugee Rights Network (APRRN, #02007)*;
- *Asylum Access*;
- *Australian Council for International Development (ACFID)*;
- *Buddhist Tzu Chi Foundation (#03347)*;
- *CARE International (CI, #03429)*;
- *Caritas Internationalis (CI, #03580)*;
- *Catholic Agency for Overseas Development (CAFOD)*;
- *ChildFund Alliance (#03868)*;
- *Christian Aid*;
- *Church World Service (CWS)*;
- *Community and Family Services International (CFSI)*;
- *Community World Service Asia (#04407)*;
- *Concern Worldwide*;
- *Cooperazione Internazionale (COOPI)*;
- *Danish Refugee Council (DRC)*;
- *Dutch Refugee Council*;
- *Finn Church Aid (FCA)*;
- *Finnish Refugee Council (FRC)*;
- *Folkekirkens Nødhjaelp (FKN)*;
- *Globalt Fokus*;
- *Good Neighbors International*;
- *Greek Council for Refugees (GCR)*;
- *HH Humanitarian Relief Foundation*;
- *HIAS*;
- *Human Appeal (#10961)*;
- *Humanity and Inclusion (HI, #10975)*;
- *International Catholic Migration Commission (ICMC, #12459)*;
- *International Detention Coalition (IDC, #13154)*;
- *International Islamic Relief Organization (IIRO)*;
- *International Medical Corps (IMC)*;
- *International Refugee Rights Initiative (IRRI, #14708)*;
- *International Rescue Committee (IRC, #14717)*;
- *INTERSOS*;
- *Irish Association of Non-Governmental Development Organisations (Dóchas)*;
- *Islamic Relief Worldwide (IRWW, #16048)*;
- *Jesuit Refugee Service (JRS, #16106)*;
- *Johanniter-Unfall-Hilfe (JUH, #16120)*;
- *Korea NGO Council for Overseas Development Cooperation (KCOC)*;
- *MEDAIR*;
- *Médecins du Monde – International (MDM, #16613)*;
- *Mercy Corps International (MCI)*;
- *Netherlands Refugee Foundation*;
- *Norwegian Church Aid*;
- *Norwegian People's Aid (NPA)*;
- *Norwegian Refugee Council (NRC)*;
- *Oxfam GB*;
- *Plan International (#18386)*;
- *Refugee Council of Australia (RCOA)*;
- *Refugees International (RI)*;
- *RET International (#18927)*;
- *Save the Children International (#19058)*;
- *Swiss Foundation for Mine Action (FSD)*;
- *Tearfund, UK*;
- *Télécoms sans frontières (TSF)*;
- *Terre des Hommes International Federation (TDHIF, #20133)*;
- *The Lutheran World Federation (LWF, #16532)*;
- *Translators without Borders (#20216)*;
- *Verband Entwicklungspolitik und Humanitäre Hilfe e.V. (VENRO)*;
- *Welthungerhilfe*;
- *Women's Refugee Commission (WRC)*;
- *World Vision International (WVI, #21904)*.

Observers (2), listed in this Yearbook:
Bureau international des Médecins sans frontières (MSF International, #03366); *International Federation of Red Cross and Red Crescent Societies (#13526)*.
Affiliate, (3) includes 2 listed in this Yearbook:
Active Learning Network for Accountability and Performance in Humanitarian Action (ALNAP, #00101); *Refugee Studies Centre, Oxford (RSC)*.
Consultative Status Consultative status granted from: *ECOSOC (#05331)* (General); *ILO (#11123)* (Special List); *UNICEF (#20332)*; *UNEP (#20299)*. **IGO Relations** Observer status with (1): *International Organization for Migration (IOM, #14454)*. Cooperates with (4): *FAO (#09260)*; *United Nations Office for the Coordination of Humanitarian Affairs (OCHA, #20593)*; *United Nations Relief and Works Agency for Palestine Refugees in the Near East (UNRWA, #20622)*; *World Food Programme (WFP, #21510)*. Represented on: *Inter-Agency Standing Committee (IASC, #11393)*. Associated with Department of Global Communications of the United Nations. **NGO Relations** Co-chairs active involvement in: *The Sphere Project (#19918)* on minimum standards in humanitarian assistance. Collaborates with other NGO consortia, not specified. [2022.12.02/XA1762/y/**A**]

♦ International Council of Women (ICW) 13093

Conseil international des femmes (CIF)

Pres 309 Gangnam-daero, Ste 1910, Seocho-gu, Seoul 137-860, Korea Rep. E-mail: icw.secretariat@gmail.com.
Headquarters 19 rue Vignon, 7500 Paris, France. T. +33149240700. Fax +33149240710.
URL: http://www.icw-cif.com/

History 1888, Washington DC (USA). Constitution and Standing Orders drawn up 1888, Washington DC, and revised: 1936, Dubrovnik (Yugoslavia); 1954, Helsinki (Finland); 1973, Vienna (Austria), Ottawa (Canada) 1997, Helsinki 2000. Obtained the status of 'Utilité publique' in France, 1980. **Aims** Unite national councils of women's non-governmental organizations from all parts of the world for action to improve the status of women and the well-being of society. **Structure** General Assembly (every 3 years). Board of Officers, consisting of President, Immediate Past President, 5 Vice-Presidents, Treasurer, Assistant Treasurer, 2 Recording Secretaries, 5 Members and Liaison Officers to the United Nations in New York NY (USA), Geneva (Switzerland) and Vienna (Austria). Executive Committee, comprising members of the Board, Presidents of affiliated National Councils of Women, Coordinators, Advisors of the International Standing Committees, ICW Permanent Representatives at the United Nations and its Specialized Agencies and Members of the Committee of Honour. Regional Councils (3): *'European Centre of ICW (ECICW)'*; *'Asia-Pacific Regional Council (APRC)'*; *'Regional Council of the Americas (RCA)'*; *'African Council of ICW (ACICW)'*. **Languages** English, French. **Staff** Voluntary. **Finance** Annual dues of affiliated National Councils plus additional annual contribution agreed by each National Council at Plenary Assembly. Subscriptions of Life Members and International Triennial Members. Other sources: gifts; legacies; funds. **Activities** Organizes regional seminars on human rights, literacy, education, the advancement of women and their participation in economic and social development. *European Centre of the International Council of Women (ECICW, #06485)* promotes women's interests with the European Union. International Standing Committees (5): *'Status of Women'* Sub-Committees – Legislation; Implementation of Conventions; Human Rights; International Relations and Peace. *'Sustainable Development'* Sub-Committees – Economics; Consumer Affairs; Women in Employment; Rural and Urban Women. *'General Wellbeing'* Sub-Committees – Health; Environment; Habitat; Nutrition. *'Communication'* Sub-Committees – Education; Mass Media; Arts and Letters; Music. *'Social Issues'* Sub-Committees – Child and Family; Youth; Ageing; Migration. **Events** *Triennial General Asssembly* Avignon (France) 2022, *Triennial General Asssembly* Yogyakarta (Indonesia) 2018, *Triennial General Assembly* Izmir (Turkey) 2015, *Triennial General Assembly* Seoul (Korea Rep) 2012, *Triennial General Assembly* Johannesburg (South Africa) 2009. **Publications** *ICW Newsletter* (4 a year). *Women Changing the World* (2005) in English, French; *Anthologie de la poésie féminine mondiale*; *Community Development (Parts I and II)*; *Habitat Compendium*; *Highlights in History of ICW*; *History of ICW and National Councils*; *Literacy – A Social Experience*; *Side by Side: Anthology*; *Women and the UN* in English, French, German, Norwegian; *Women in a Changing World: a History of ICW*; *Women in Modern Life and Work*. *Laruan* – film on prostitution. Congress reports (1888-); ICW Resolutions (1888-).

Members National Councils, composed of national and local women's organizations of different scope in 65 countries and territories:
Argentina, Australia, Austria, Azerbaijan, Bangladesh, Belgium, Benin, Bolivia, Brunei Darussalam, Cambodia, Cameroon, Canada, Colombia, Congo Brazzaville, Cook Is, Denmark, Dominican Rep, Fiji, Finland, France, Germany, Greece, Guatemala, Hungary, India, Indonesia, Israel, Italy, Kenya, Korea Rep, Lebanon, Lesotho, Lithuania, Madagascar, Malaysia, Malta, Monaco, Mongolia, Morocco, Nepal, Netherlands, New Zealand, Nigeria, North Macedonia, Pakistan, Papua New Guinea, Peru, Philippines, Russia, Samoa, Senegal, South Africa, Spain, Suriname, Switzerland, Taiwan, Thailand, Tunisia, Türkiye, Uganda, UK, Ukraine, Uruguay, USA, Vanuatu.

Consultative Status Consultative status granted from: *ECOSOC (#05331)* (General); *UNESCO (#20322)* (Consultative Status); *ILO (#11123)* (Special List); *FAO (#09260)*; *UNCTAD (#20285)* (General Category); *UNEP (#20299)*; *UNIDO (#20336)*. **IGO Relations** Close relations with: *UNDP (#20292)*; *UNHCR (#20327)*; *United Nations Economic Commission for Africa (ECA, #20554)*; *United Nations Economic Commission for Europe (UNECE, #20555)*; *United Nations Economic Commission for Latin America and the Caribbean (ECLAC, #20556)*; *United Nations Economic and Social Commission for Asia and the Pacific (ESCAP, #20557)*; *United Nations Economic and Social Commission for Western Asia (ESCWA, #20558)*; *United Nations Population Fund (UNFPA, #20612)*. Accredited by: *United Nations Framework Convention on Climate Change – Secretariat (UNFCCC, #20564)*; *United Nations Office at Vienna (UNOV, #20604)*. Observer to: *International Fund for Agricultural Development (IFAD, #13692)*. Associated with Department of Global Communications of the United Nations.

NGO Relations With *International Federation of Business and Professional Women (BPW International, #13376)*, *Graduate Women International (GWI, #10688)*, *Soroptimist International (SI, #19686)* and *Zonta International (#22038)* as sponsoring organizations, set up: *Project Five-0 (inactive)*, to train women and girls. Represented on Bureau of: *NGO Committee on Development, Geneva (#17104)*.
Member of:
- *Child Rights Connect (#03884)*; *Child Rights International Network (CRIN, #03885)*; *Committee of NGOs on Human Rights, Geneva (#04275)*; *Conference of Non-Governmental Organizations in Consultative Relationship with the United Nations (CONGO, #04635)*; *Framework Convention Alliance (FCA, #09981)*; *Huairou Commission (#10960)*; *International Institute on Ageing, United Nations – Malta (INIA, #13860)*; *New York NGO Committee on Drugs (NYNGOC, #17097)*; *NGO Committee on the Status of Women, Geneva (#17117)*; *NGO Forum on Environment (FOE, #17125)*; *Union des organisations internationales non-gouvernementales établies en France (UOIF, inactive)*; *Vienna NGO Committee on Drugs (VNGOC, #20773)*; *Vienna NGO Committee on the Family (#20774)*; *Vienna NGO Committee on the Status of Women (#20775)*. [2019/XB1763/**B**]

♦ International Council of Women Psychologists / see International Council of Psychologists (#13065)

♦ International Council on Women's Health Issues (ICOWHI) 13094

Counsel General 525 N. Wolfe St, Baltimore MD 21205, USA. T. +14109557544.
Sec University of Alberta, Faculty of Nursing, 116 St and 85 Ave, Edmonton AB T6G 2R3, Canada.
Pres address not obtained.
URL: https://icowhi.org/

History 1984, at 1st International Congress, Halifax (Canada), being conceived in 1983 by a group of women interested in the health and health care of women throughout the world. By-laws adopted at 2nd International Congress, 1986, Halifax (Canada). Registered in accordance with US law, 2004. **Aims** Explore biological, socio-economic, cultural, political and spiritual factors affecting the health and development of women throughout their life cycle; identify areas of need; facilitate, implement and evaluate solutions to potential and actual health problems of women of all ages; encourage a multi-disciplinary and multi-sectoral approach to promoting women's health and well being; promote and supporte women's health research; influence policy related to women's health worldwide. **Structure** Board of Directors, comprising President, Secretary, Treasurer, Counsel General and 10 members. **Languages** English. **Staff** None. **Finance** Members' dues. Grants. **Activities** Organizes: International Congresses (biennial); Regional Meetings (every 2 years). Maintains Council Archives; provides consultation and advocacy services. Offers financial support in the form of scholarships to women from developing countries. **Events** *Scale and sustainability – moving women's health forward* Baltimore, MD (USA) 2016, *Biennial Congress* Cape Town (South Africa) 2014, *Congress* Bangkok (Thailand) 2012, *Congress / Biennial Congress* Philadelphia, PA (USA) 2010, *Congress / Biennial Congress* Gaborone (Botswana) 2008. **Publications** *Health Care for Women International* (6 a year) – journal.

Members Multidisciplinary network of women's health providers, planners and advocates. Individuals in 33 countries and territories:
Argentina, Australia, Botswana, Brazil, Bulgaria, Canada, China, Denmark, Egypt, Finland, Germany, Hong Kong, Iceland, Ireland, Japan, Kenya, Korea Rep, Lebanon, Mexico, Netherlands, New Zealand, Norway, Oman, Philippines, Sierra Leone, South Africa, Sweden, Taiwan, Tanzania UR, Thailand, UK, United Arab Emirates, USA.

NGO Relations Member of: *Global Health Council (GHC, #10402)*. [2021/XD5819/v/**D**]

♦ International Council of Youth for Christ / see Youth for Christ International (#22009)

♦ International Counterparts Network 13095

Contact c/o CED, 1530 Wilson Blvd, Ste 400, Arlington VA 22209, USA. E-mail: info@ced.org.
URL: http://www.ced.org/about/international-counterparts/

History Set up as *International Network of Private Business Organizations*. Current title adopted 2008. **Events** *Annual Conference* Johannesburg (South Africa) 2009, *Annual Conference* Santa Cruz (Bolivia) 2008, *Annual Conference* Sydney, NSW (Australia) 2007, *Annual Conference* Madrid (Spain) 2006, *Annual Conference* Haikou City (China) 2005.

Members Organizations (11) in 10 countries:
Australia, China, Finland, France, Germany, Japan, Portugal, South Africa, Spain, USA.
Regional organization (1):
Latin American Business Council (#16261). [2014/XM0023/y/**F**]

♦ International Courier Conference / see Global Express Association (#10351)
♦ International Court of the Environment (see: #13097)

♦ International Court of Environmental Arbitration and Conciliation (ICEAC) 13096

Corte Internacional de Arbitraje y Conciliación Ambiental (CIACA)

SG Guadalquivir 94, Col Cuauhtémoc, 06500 Mexico City CDMX, Mexico. T. +526241778960. E-mail: rojedamestre@yahoo.com – ramonojedamestre@gmail.com.

History Nov 1994, Mexico City (Mexico). Registration: Mexico. **Aims** Facilitate, by conciliation and arbitration, the settlement of environmental disputes between States, natural or legal persons and submitted to it by agreement of the parties to the dispute ("Parties"); give consultative opinions on questions of environmental law or on legal aspects of the use or protection of elements of the environment in any case which is of international concern, at the request of any natural of legal person whether national or international, public or private, including States and local authorities ("Petitioner"). **Structure** Members of the Court exercise their functions in Plenary Session, composed of all Members of the Court and, depending on the requests which are submitted to the Court, either in the form of a Commission of Conciliation, a Tribunal of Arbitration or a Chamber for Consultative Opinions. Secretary General, who carries out the functions of Registrar of the Court and is head of its administration, is assisted by Assistant Secretary General and a Secretariat. Permanent seats in Mexico City (Mexico) and San Sebastian (Spain). **Languages** English, Spanish. **Activities** Conflict resolution; guidance/assistance/consulting. **Publications** *ICEAC Newsletter*.

Members Lawyers (29) in 24 countries:
Argentina, Australia, Belgium, Bolivia, Brazil, Canada, Chile, Colombia, Costa Rica, Czechia, France, Germany, Greece, Italy, Japan, Kenya, Luxembourg, Mexico, Peru, Portugal, Spain, Tunisia, UK, USA. [2021.05.19/XF4334/**F**]

♦ International Court of the Environment Foundation (ICEF) 13097

Dir Via Cardinal Pacca 19, 00165 Rome RM, Italy. T. +3966630546. Fax +3966630546.
International Relations Officer Via dei Macci 19, 50122 Florence FI, Italy.

History 22 May 1992, Rome (Italy). Former names and other names: *Foundation for an International Court of the Environment* – alias. Registration: Italy. **Aims** Promote establishment of an International Court of the Environment as a new, specialized and permanent institution on a global level based on the principles of: right of access not only for states but also for individuals and NGOs; erga omnes effect and authority of decisions handed down in the name of the international community; on-going promotion of initiatives to strengthen existing institutions and instruments for resolving environmental disputes. Promote bio-diplomacy to: enhance international cooperation in environmental issues; support efforts to maintain biological and cultural diversity; improve human relations and achieve world peace by replacing current diplomatic attitudes with a complete international, intercultural perspective. **Structure** Board of Directors; Scientific Committee; Committee of Honour. *Organizing Committee for an International Court of the Environment – Comité promoteur pour un Tribunal international de l'environnement.* **Languages** English, French, Italian, Spanish. **Staff** 5.00 FTE, voluntary. **Finance** Sources: donations of founder members; public and private organizations in Italy. Sponsoring bodies include the following organizations listed in this Yearbook: *Habitat International Coalition (HIC, #10845); Institute for Development and Disaster Studies, Ethiopia (no recent information); International Society of Doctors for the Environment (ISDE, #15065); Mandate for Life on Earth (no recent information); Middle East Centre for the Transfer of Appropriate Technology (MECTAT, no recent information); Pacific Institute for Resource Management (PIRM); Rural Development Foundation of Pakistan (RDF, inactive).* **Activities** Events/meetings. **Events** *International Conference* Rio de Janeiro (Brazil) 2012, *International Conference* Rome (Italy) 2010, *International Conference* Verona (Italy) 2008, *International Conference* Venice (Italy) 2007, *International conference* Rome (Italy) 2003. **Publications** Conference proceedings; projects; reports.

Members Organizing committees in 11 countries:
Argentina, Belgium, Canada, Germany, Greece, Japan, Luxembourg, Mexico, Portugal, Spain, USA.
Supporting organizations in 28 countries:
Australia, Bangladesh, Brazil, Chile, Costa Rica, Cyprus, Ecuador, El Salvador, Ethiopia, Gambia, Germany, Greece, Guatemala, India, Indonesia, Italy, Japan, Lebanon, Lesotho, Madagascar, Mauritius, Mexico, New Zealand, Nigeria, Pakistan, Philippines, Spain, UK.

Consultative Status Consultative status granted from: *ECOSOC (#05331)* (Ros A). **IGO Relations** Working towards setting up: *International Court of the Environment (see: #13097); International Environmental Agency (inactive).* [2017.06.01/XF5431/f/**F**]

♦ International Court of Honour (inactive)

♦ International Court of Justice (ICJ) 13098

Cour internationale de Justice (CIJ) – Corte Internacional de Justicia (CIJ) – Internationaal Gerechtshof

Registrar Peace Palace, 2517 KJ The Hague, Netherlands. T. +31703022323. Fax +31703649928. E-mail: information@icj-cij.org.
URL: http://www.icj-cij.org/

History 6 Feb 1946. Established as the principal judicial organ of *United Nations (UN, #20515)*, superseding *Permanent Court of International Justice (inactive)*, set up 13 Dec 1920. Operates under a Statute which is part of the UN Charter (Article 94-1); parties to the Statute include all members of the United Nations. Comes within the *United Nations System (#20635)*, any of the other UN Main Organs (except Secretary-General) and all those Agencies being currently authorized to request opinions of the Court. Based at *Peace Palace*, The Hague (Netherlands). **Aims** Settle in accordance with international *law* the legal *disputes* submitted by states; give advisory opinions on legal questions referred by duly authorized international organs and agencies. **Structure** Court consists of 15 judges elected by UN General Assembly and by UN Security Council, voting independently. Judges serve for a term of 9 years, one third being elected every 3 years, and may be re-elected. No two judges may be of the same nationality. A party to a case may nominate a judge 'ad hoc' if no member of the bench is of its nationality. Questions before the full Court are decided by a majority of the judges present, with 9 judges, plus any judges ad hoc, constituting a quorum. With a view to speedy dispatch of business, a chamber of 5 judges is formed annually and may, at the request of the parties, hear and determine cases by summary procedure. Also at the request of the parties, the Court may constitute an ad-hoc Chamber to deal with a particular case. **Languages** English, French. **Staff** 117.00 FTE, paid. **Finance** Provided by the United Nations. **Activities** Conflict resolution. **Publications** *Reports of Judgments, Advisory Opinions and Orders – Recueil des arrêts, avis consultatifs et ordonnances* (annual). *Handbook* (2014) – online; *A Dialogue at the Court – Un Dialogue à la Cour* (2006); *The International Court of Justice – La Cour internationale de justice* (5th ed 2004) in English, French; *Acts and Documents concerning the Organization of the Court – Actes et documents relatifs à l'organisation de la Cour, Pleadings, Oral Arguments, Documents – Mémoires, plaidoiries et documents* in English, French; *Questions and Answers Handbook: Question and Answers About the ICJ* in English, French – online. Yearbook; Background notes; catalogue; bibliography; press releases; flyer.

Members Judges (15) from 15 countries:
Australia, Brazil, China, France, Germany, India, Jamaica, Japan, Lebanon, Morocco, Russia, Slovakia, Somalia, Uganda, USA.
IGO Relations Principal judicial organ of: *United Nations (UN, #20515).* [2022.12.02/XF3379/**F***]

♦ International Court of Justice for Animal Rights 13099

Cour internationale de justice des droits de l'animal – Internationaler Gerichtshof für Tierrechte

Contact Case postale 1668, 1820 Montreux VD 1, Switzerland. T. +41219642424. Fax +41219645736. E-mail: ffw@ffw.ch.
URL: http://www.ffw.ch/

History 8 Nov 1979, Geneva (Switzerland), by *Franz Weber Foundation*, as a principal organ of *United Animal Nations (UAN, #20497).* Statutes adopted, 9 Nov 1979, Geneva; amended 9 Jun 1983, 9 Nov 1999. **Aims** Punish, following official trials, serious crimes against the animal kingdom which have not been taken up by ordinary courts. **Structure** Court, composed of President, one or 2 alternate judges and jury of 6 to 12 members. **Languages** English, French, German, Spanish. **Activities** Holds trials.

Members Full in 22 countries:
Australia, Austria, Belgium, Bulgaria, Chile, Denmark, France, Germany, Greece, Ireland, Israel, Italy, Luxembourg, Netherlands, New Zealand, Poland, Portugal, Serbia, Spain, Togo, UK, USA.
IGO Relations Relevant convention: *Convention on International Trade in Endangered Species of Wild Fauna and Flora (CITES, 1973).* [2014.10.31/XF6883/**F**]

♦ International Courtly Literature Society (ICLS) 13100

Société internationale de littérature courtoise (SILC)

Pres c/o Leeds – Languages, Cultures and Societies, Michael Sadler Bldg, Univ of Leeds, Leeds, LS2 9JT, UK.
Sec address not obtained.
URL: http://iclsweb.org/

History Dec 1973, Chicago, IL (USA). **Aims** Promote the study of courts and court-related cultures, with particular reference to the written records of *medieval* Europe. **Structure** International Executive Committee. **Languages** English, French, German. **Staff** Part-time, voluntary. **Finance** Sources: members' dues. **Events** *Triennial Congress* Vancouver, BC (Canada) 2023, *Triennial Congress* Exeter (UK) 2019, *Triennial Congress* Lexington, KY (USA) 2016, *Triennial Congress* Lisbon (Portugal) 2013, *Triennial Congress* Montréal, QC (Canada) 2010. **Publications** *Encomia* (annual). Conference proceedings.

Members Life; Contributing; Regular; Student. National branches: North American (USA/Canada; Japan; Australia/New Zealand); British (UK/Ireland; Australia/New Zealand); Belgian (Belgium); Dutch (Netherlands); French (France); German (Germany/Austria); Italian (Italy); Scandinavian (Denmark/Norway/Sweden); Swiss (Switzerland); Tunisian (Tunisia). Societies and individuals (). Members in 19 countries:
Australia (*), Austria (*), Belgium, Canada (*), Denmark, France, Germany, Ireland (*), Italy, Japan (*), Netherlands, New Zealand (*), Norway (*), Russia, Sweden (*), Switzerland, Tunisia, UK, USA. [2021.06.08/XD0151/**D**]

♦ International Covenant on Civil and Political Rights (1966 treaty)
♦ International Covenant on Economic, Social and Cultural Rights (1966 treaty)
♦ International Cover Crop Clearinghouse (internationally oriented national body)

♦ International CPTED Association (ICA) 13101

Main Office 10980 Westdowne Road, No 79, Ladysmith BC V9G 1X4, Canada. E-mail: office@cpted.net.
URL: http://www.cpted.net/

History 1996, Calgary, AB (Canada). **Aims** Create safer environments and improve the quality of life through the use of *crime prevention* through environmental design (CPTED) principles and strategies. **Structure** Officers: Chair; Vice-Chair; Executive Director; 7 Directors. European chapter: *European Designing Out Crime Association (E-DOCA, #06911).* **Languages** English, Spanish. **Staff** 1.00 FTE, paid. **Finance** Members' dues: US$ 50. **Events** *Conference* Helsingborg (Sweden) 2021, *Conference* Quintana Roo (Mexico) 2019, *Annual Conference* Calgary, AB (Canada) 2015, *Annual Conference* Calgary, AB (Canada) 2013, *Annual Conference* Amsterdam (Netherlands) 2003. **Publications** *ICA Newsletter.*

Members Individuals in 24 countries:
Australia, Bahamas, Brazil, Cambodia, Canada, Central African Rep, Costa Rica, Cyprus, Estonia, Hong Kong, Israel, Japan, Mexico, Netherlands, New Zealand, Norway, Russia, Serbia, South Africa, Spain, Sweden, Thailand, UK, USA. [2021/XD7493/**C**]

♦ International Crane Foundation (ICF) 13102

Fondation internationale pour la sauvegarde des grues

Pres E-11376 Shady Lane Rd, PO Box 447, Baraboo WI 53913-0447, USA. T. +16083569462. Fax +16083569465. E-mail: info@savingcranes.org.
URL: http://www.savingcranes.org/

History 1973, Baraboo, WI (USA). **Aims** *Conserve* cranes and the wetland, grassland, and other ecosystems on which they depend; provide experience, knowledge, and inspiration to involve people in resolving threats to these ecosystems. **Structure** Meeting of Members (annual); Board of Directors; Board of Advisors; Emeritus Directors (24). **Languages** English. **Finance** Sources: contributions; grants; investments; revenue from activities/projects; sale of products. **Activities** Events/meetings. **Events** *Global flyways conference* Edinburgh (UK) 2004, *International crane workshop* Beijing (China) 2002, *Cranes and their habitats – what we can do together to protect them* Qiqihar (China) 1987. **Publications** *ICF Bugle* (4 a year) – newsletter. Annual Report.

Members Members in 67 countries and territories:
Australia, Bangladesh, Belgium, Bhutan, Botswana, Burkina Faso, Burundi, Cambodia, Cameroon, Canada, China, Colombia, Cuba, Denmark, Ethiopia, Finland, France, Gabon, Gambia, Germany, Ghana, Guinea-Bissau, Hong Kong, India, Iran Islamic Rep, Israel, Italy, Japan, Kenya, Korea Rep, Laos, Latvia, Lesotho, Malawi, Malaysia, Mauritania, Mexico, Mongolia, Morocco, Mozambique, Namibia, Nepal, Netherlands, Niger, Nigeria, Norway, Pakistan, Philippines, Poland, Portugal, Rwanda, Saudi Arabia, Senegal, Singapore, South Africa, Spain, Sweden, Switzerland, Taiwan, Tanzania UR, Thailand, Türkiye, UK, Uzbekistan, Vietnam, Zambia, Zimbabwe.

IGO Relations Partner of (1): *Secretariat of the Convention on the Conservation of Migratory Species of Wild Animals (UNEP/CMS, #19198).* **NGO Relations** Member of (2): *Alliance for Zero Extinction (AZE, #00730); International Union for Conservation of Nature and Natural Resources (IUCN, #15766).* Partner of (1): *East Asian – Australasian Flyway Partnership (EAAFP, #05198).* [2022/XF4553/f/**F**]

♦ International Craniofacial Identification Group / see International Association of Craniofacial Identification (#11823)
♦ International Craniomandibular Orthopedic Society (inactive)
♦ International Credit Insurance Association / see International Credit Insurance & Surety Association (#13103)

♦ International Credit Insurance & Surety Association (ICISA) 13103

Exec Dir Evert van de Beekstraat 354, 1118 CZ Amsterdam, Netherlands. T. +31206254115. Fax +31205285176. E-mail: secretariat@icisa.org.
URL: http://www.icisa.org/

History Apr 1928, Paris (France). Founded 1928, following first international conference on trade credit insurance, 1926, London (UK). Founding Members: Cobac of Belgium (now Allianz Trade); Crédito y Caución of Spain; Eidgenössische of Switzerland (now Winterthur); Hermes of Germany (now Allianz Trade); NCM of the Netherlands (now Atradius); SFAC of France (now Allianz Trade); SIAC of Italy (now Allianz Trade); Trade Indemnity of the UK (now Allianz Trade). Based in Switzerland from 1928 to 1999; relocated to London, 1999-2003, and then to Amsterdam (Netherlands) in 2003. Former names and other names: *International Credit Insurance Association (ICIA)* – former; *Internationale Kreditversicherungs-Vereinigung* – former; *Association internationale des assureurs-crédit* – former; *Internationale Kreditversicherungs- und Kaution Vereinigung* – former. Registration: Swiss Civil Code, Switzerland; EU Transparency Register, No/ID: 14682974416-46. **Aims** Represent the interests of leading trade credit insurers, sureties and their reinsurers internationally; engage with supranational bodies, governments, regulators, NGOs and the media on their behalf. **Structure** General Meeting (annual); Committees; Working Groups. **Languages** English. **Staff** 5.00 FTE, paid. **Activities** Advocacy/lobbying/activism; events/meetings; knowledge management/information dissemination; networking/liaising; research/documentation. **Events** *Annual General Assembly* Helsinki (Finland) 2022, *Annual General Assembly* Amsterdam (Netherlands) 2020, *Autumn Meeting* Amsterdam (Netherlands) 2019, *Spring Meeting* Rome (Italy) 2019, *Annual General Assembly* Washington, DC (USA) 2019. **Publications** *The ICISA Insider* (4 a year). *A Guide to Trade Credit Insurance; Catalogue of Trade Credit Insurance Terminology.* [2022.06.15/XC1772/**C**]

♦ International Cremation Federation (ICF) 13104

Fédération internationale de crémation – Internationaler Verband für Feuerbestattung

SG PO Box 80532, 2508 GM The Hague, Netherlands. T. +31703518824. Fax +31703518827. E-mail: melanie@facultatieve.com.
Registered Office Van Stolkweg 29a, 2585 JN The Hague, Netherlands.
URL: http://www.int-crem-fed.org/

History 2 Oct 1937, London (UK), at 1st Congress. Rules amended: 12-15 Aug 1957, Zurich (Switzerland); 23-26 May 1966, Vienna (Austria); 25-26 Oct 1991, Brussels (Belgium); Aug 2005, New York NY (USA). **Aims** Spread knowledge of cremation and of its superiority in hygienic, ethical, economic, aesthetic and other respects to the traditional form of *burial*; facilitate the employment of cremation and promote its general adoption; endeavour to have legal regulations in favour of cremation issued in those countries where it suffers from restrictive laws and ordinances. **Structure** Congress (every 2 years); General Council. Executive Committee, consisting of President, 3 Vice-Presidents, Treasurer and Secretary General. **Languages** English, French. **Staff** 0.50 FTE, paid. **Finance** Sources: members' dues. **Activities** Compilation of statistics; circulation of information. **Events** *International Cremation and Burial Conference* Newcastle upon Tyne (UK) 2012, *International cremation and burial conference / Congress* Bristol (UK) 2011, *Congress* Sydney, NSW (Australia) 2009, *Congress* Newcastle upon Tyne (UK) 2007, *Congress* New York, NY (USA) 2005. **Publications** *Pharos International* (4 a year).

Members National societies and organizations (47) in 23 countries and territories:
Australia, Belgium, Czechia, Denmark, Finland, France, Germany, Greece, Guatemala, Hong Kong, Ireland, Israel, Italy, Japan, Netherlands, Serbia, Slovenia, Spain, Sweden, Switzerland, Taiwan, UK, USA.
Consultative Status Consultative status granted from: *ECOSOC (#05331)* (Ros A). [2020/XC1773/**C**]

♦ International Cricket Council (ICC) 13105

Conseil internationale de cricket

Chief Exec PO Box 500 070, Street 69 Dubai Sports City, Sh Mohammed Bin Zayed Road, Dubai, United Arab Emirates. T. +94143828800. Fax +94143828600. E-mail: enquiry@icc-cricket.com.
URL: http://www.icc-cricket.com/

History 1909, London (UK). Assumed activities of *International Women's Cricket Council (IWCC, inactive)* following merger in 2005. Former names and other names: *Imperial Cricket Conference* – former. **Aims** As the global governing body for cricket: represent members; govern and administrate the game; work with members to grow the sport. **Structure** Meeting (annual); Board of Directors; Committees (9). Regional Councils (5): *African Cricket Association (ACA, #00279); Asian Cricket Council (ACC, #01412); Cricket Council of the Americas (ICC Americas, #04952)*; East Asia-Pacific Council (EAP); *International Cricket Council Europe Region (ICC Europe, #13106).* **Languages** English. **Staff** 87.00 FTE, paid. **Finance** Member's dues. Tournaments. **Activities** Events/meetings; sporting activities. **Events** *Annual Conference* London (UK) 2019, *Annual Conference* Dublin (Ireland) 2018, *Annual Conference* London (UK) 2017, *Annual Conference* Kuala Lumpur (Malaysia) 2012, *Meeting* 1995. **Publications** *ICC Official Playing Handbook.* Annual Report; minutes and memoranda for members only.

Members Full in 11 countries and territories (also in West Indies, countries not specified):
Afghanistan, Australia, Bangladesh, England, India, Ireland, New Zealand, Pakistan, South Africa, Sri Lanka, Zimbabwe.
Associate in 92 countries and territories:
Argentina, Austria, Bahamas, Bahrain, Belgium, Belize, Bermuda, Bhutan, Botswana, Brazil, Bulgaria, Cameroon, Canada, Cayman Is, Chile, China, Cook Is, Costa Rica, Croatia, Cyprus, Czechia, Denmark, Estonia, Eswatini, Falklands/Malvinas, Fiji, Finland, France, Gambia, Germany, Ghana, Gibraltar, Greece, Guernsey, Hong Kong, Hungary, Indonesia, Iran Islamic Rep, Isle of Man, Israel, Italy, Japan, Jersey, Kenya, Korea Rep, Kuwait, Lesotho, Luxembourg, Malawi, Malaysia, Maldives, Mali, Malta, Mexico, Morocco, Mozambique, Myanmar, Namibia, Nepal, Netherlands, Nigeria, Norway, Oman, Panama, Papua New Guinea, Peru, Philippines, Portugal, Qatar, Romania, Russia, Rwanda, Samoa, Saudi Arabia, Scotland, Serbia, Seychelles, Sierra Leone, Singapore, Slovenia, Spain, St Helena, Suriname, Sweden, Tanzania UR, Thailand, Türkiye, Turks-Caicos, Uganda, United Arab Emirates, Vanuatu, Zambia.
NGO Relations Member of (3): *Association of the IOC Recognized International Sports Federations (ARISF, #02767)*; *Olympic Movement (#17719)*; *Sports Rights Owners Coalition (SROC, #19929)*. Recognized by: *International Olympic Committee (IOC, #14408)*. Instrumental in setting up: *Cricket West Indies (CWI, #04953)*.
[2019/XC1774/**C**]

♦ International Cricket Council Europe Region (ICC Europe) 13106

Regional Development Manager ICC Europe Office, The Europe Office, Lord's Cricket Ground, London, NW8 8QN, UK. T. +442076168635. Fax +442076168634.
URL: http://www.icc-europe.org/

History 1997, as *European Cricket Council (ECC)*. Regional council of *International Cricket Council (ICC, #13105)*. **Aims** Support the development of cricket at all levels in Europe. **Structure** General Meeting (annual). Committees (2): European Advisory; European Cricket. **Languages** English. **Staff** 8.50 FTE, paid. **Finance** Financed by: ICC; England and Wales Cricket Board. Budget (annual): US$ 1,800,000. **Activities** Organizes: 11 European tournaments at various levels; Coaching conferences; Administration governance and Management conferences. **Publications** *EuropeNews* (12 a year); *Coaches Newsletter*; *Umpires Newletter*.
Members Full in 30 countries and territories:
Austria, Belgium, Bulgaria, Croatia, Cyprus, Czechia, Denmark, Estonia, Finland, France, Germany, Gibraltar, Greece, Guernsey, Ireland, Isle of Man, Israel, Italy, Jersey, Luxembourg, Malta, Netherlands, Norway, Portugal, Scotland, Slovenia, Spain, Sweden, Switzerland, Türkiye.
[2011.06.01/XE4619/**E**]

♦ International Criminal Bar (ICB) 13107

Barreau Pénal International (BPI) – Colegio de Abogados Penal Internacional (CAPI)

Coordinator Avda Diagonal 529 1o 2a, 08029 Barcelona, Spain. T. +34934051424. Fax +34934051424.
International Relations address not obtained.
Coordinator address not obtained.
URL: http://www.bpi-icb.com/

History Founded 15 Jun 2002, Montréal QC (Canada), to act as representative of counsel before *International Criminal Court (ICC, #13108)*. **Aims** Ensure that counsel are able to practice in total independence before the International Criminal Court (ICC), and the right of defence is completely respected in the procedures before the ICC; ensure protection for victims and their reparation; respect human rights and application of the Convention of Rome; promote development of an independent legal profession and practice before the ICC; develop criminal policy and promote core principles of justice; provide assistance to lawyers who defend victims and defendants before the ICC; facilitate effective communication between the Court and lawyers. **Structure** General Assembly; Council; Executive Committee. **Languages** Catalan, English, French, Spanish. **Staff** 2.00 FTE, paid. **Finance** Members' dues. Submits grant proposals to European Commission, Open Society Foundation and others. **Activities** Events/meetings; training/education. **Events** *General Assembly* Valencia (Spain) 2017, *General Assembly* The Hague (Netherlands) 2005, *General Assembly* Berlin (Germany) 2003. **Publications** *BPI-ICB Newsletter*.
Members Bar associations (33) in 21 countries:
Australia, Austria, Belgium, Canada, Congo DR, Costa Rica, Denmark, France, Germany, Japan, Korea DPR, Korea Rep, Lebanon, Mexico, Netherlands, Norway, Spain, Sweden, Switzerland, UK, USA.
International organizations (7):
Arab Lawyers' Union (ALU, #01002); *Arab Organization for Human Rights (AOHR, #01020)*; *Avocats Sans Frontières (ASF, #03050)*; *Coalition for the International Criminal Court (CICC, #04062)*; *Council of Bars and Law Societies of Europe (CCBE, #04871)*; *Inter-American Bar Association (IABA, #11401)*; *International Bar Association (IBA, #12320)*.
[2019.02.12/XJ3678/y/**F**]

♦ International Criminal Court (ICC) 13108

Cour pénale internationale (CPI) – Corte Penal Internacional

Spokesperson PO Box 19519, 2500 CM The Hague, Netherlands. T. +31705158515. E-mail: publicaffairs.unit@icc-cpi.int – otp.informationdesk@icc-cpi.int – otpnewsdesk@icc-cpi.int.
Street address Oude Waalsdorperweg 10, NL-2597 AK, The Hague, Netherlands.
URL: http://www.icc-cpi.int/

History Initially proposed 1948, when the *International Law Commission (ILC, #14004)* was requested by the *United Nations (UN, #20515)* to study the possibility of setting up such a court. Two draft statutes for such a Court were developed by the United Nations in 1951 and 1953, and much international dialogue has ensued, work having been carried out by International Law Commission in particular. Work was suspended during the *'Cold War'* but resumed, 1989, following a suggestion at the 44th General Assembly of the United Nations. A further draft statute, drawn up by the ILC and published in 1992, was submitted to the 48th and 49th General Assemblies in 1993 and 1994, without agreement being reached. Draft statute prepared by a UN Ad Hoc committee, *Preparatory Committee on the Establishment of an International Criminal Court (inactive)*, following review of the ILC draft statute was submitted to the *United Nations Conference of Plenipotentiaries on the Establishment of an International Criminal Court*, 15 Jun to 17 Jul 1998, Rome (Italy), and adopted by 120 of the 148 nations represented at the Conference. The Statute is referred to as *Rome Statute – Statut de la CPI* and includes both crimes covered by international treaties and crimes recognized under international or national law. It particularly refers to *Convention on the Prevention and Punishment of the Crime of Genocide (Genocide Convention, 1948)* and *Geneva Convention on Torture (1949)*. ICC was formally established after 60 ratifications of the Rome Statute on 1 Jul 2002. *Agreement on the Privileges and Immunities of the International Criminal Court (APIC, 2002)* was adopted Sep 2002. Former names and other names: *Cour criminelle internationale (CCI)* – former. **Aims** Governed by an international treaty, the Rome Statute, investigate and, where warranted, try individuals charged with the gravest crimes of concern to the international community: genocide, war crimes, crimes against humanity and the crime of aggression; participate in a global fight to end impunity, and through international criminal justice, hold those responsible accountable for their crimes and help prevent these crimes from happening again; seek to complement, not replace, national Courts as a court of last resort. **Structure** Comprises 4 organs: Presidency; Judicial Divisions (Pre-Trial, Trial and Appeals); Office of the Prosecutor; Registry. Court comprises 18 Judges, each from a different country and with a mandate of 9 years, a Prosecutor with a mandate of 9 years and a Registrar with a mandate of 5 years. The Assembly of States Parties acts as the legislative body of the Court. The Court is seated in The Hague (Netherlands). **Languages** Arabic, Chinese, English, French, Russian, Spanish. **Staff** Elected officials/judges – 18; Staff on established posts – 848; General temporary assistance – 166; Short term appointments – 52; Contractors – 67; Visiting professionals – 21. Staff Union is member of: *Coordinating Committee for International Staff Unions and Associations of the United Nations System (CCISUA, #04818)*. **Finance** Sources: contributions of member/participating states; government support; international organizations. Other sources: individuals, corporations and other entities. **Activities** Events/meetings. Has jurisdiction over the most serious crimes of concern to the international community as a whole committed after 1 Jul 2002, including genocide, crimes against humanity, war crimes and crime of aggression, all of which are defined in the Rome Statute. May exercise jurisdiction if the accused is a national of a State which is a party to the Statute or if the crime is committed on the territory of a State Party (or a State which accepted the Court's jurisdiction). These conditions do not apply when a situation is referred to the Prosecutor by the *United Nations Security Council (UNSC, #20625)*. States Parties, as well as the Security Council, can refer situations to the Prosecutor for investigation. Prosecutor also has the power to initiate investigations on his or her own initiative on the basis of information received from reliable sources. After examining the information, he or she makes the determination that there is a reasonable basis to proceed with investigations. A Pre-Trial Chamber of judges must give prior authorization for the Prosecutor to proceed. Once investigations have been opened, any warrant of arrest or summons to appear may be issued solely by the Judges of the Pre-Trial Chamber. State Parties are obliged to cooperate fully with the Court in relation to its investigations and prosecution of crimes for which it has jurisdiction. Statute includes important provisions concerning the rights and interests of victims. For the first time in the history of international criminal law, participation of victims at all stages of the proceedings is guaranteed and possible reparations are foreseen. Statute based on principle of complementarity, which guarantees sovereignty of the States in justice matters. Accordingly, the Court does not replace national criminal justice systems, but supplements them. It may investigate, and if appropriate prosecute and try, individuals only when the States concerned are unwilling or unable to genuinely do so. In addition to establishing the ICC, the Statute created the Trust fund for Victims to support and implement programmes addressing harms resulting from genocide, crimes of humanity and war crimes. The *Coalition for the International Criminal Court (CICC, #04062)*, based in New York NY (USA) and in The Hague (Netherlands), unites nongovernmental organizations worldwide and is a network of over 2,000 nongovernmental organizations advocating for a fair, effective and independent International Criminal Court. **Events** *Assembly of the States Parties* New York, NY (USA) 2021, *Assembly of the States Parties* The Hague (Netherlands) 2021, *Assembly of the States Parties* The Hague (Netherlands) 2020, *Assembly of the States Parties* The Hague (Netherlands) 2019, *Assembly of the States Parties* The Hague (Netherlands) 2018.
Members State Parties (123) at Aug 2020:
Afghanistan, Albania, Andorra, Antigua-Barbuda, Argentina, Australia, Austria, Bangladesh, Barbados, Belgium, Belize, Benin, Bolivia, Bosnia-Herzegovina, Botswana, Brazil, Bulgaria, Burkina Faso, Cambodia, Canada, Cape Verde, Central African Rep, Chad, Chile, Colombia, Comoros, Congo Brazzaville, Congo DR, Cook Is, Costa Rica, Côte d'Ivoire, Croatia, Cyprus, Czechia, Denmark, Djibouti, Dominica, Dominican Rep, Ecuador, El Salvador, Estonia, Fiji, Finland, France, Gabon, Gambia, Georgia, Germany, Ghana, Greece, Grenada, Guatemala, Guinea, Guyana, Honduras, Hungary, Iceland, Ireland, Italy, Japan, Jordan, Kenya, Kiribati, Korea Rep, Latvia, Lesotho, Liberia, Liechtenstein, Lithuania, Luxembourg, Madagascar, Malawi, Maldives, Mali, Malta, Marshall Is, Mauritius, Mexico, Moldova, Mongolia, Montenegro, Namibia, Nauru, Netherlands, New Zealand, Niger, Nigeria, North Macedonia, Norway, Palestine, Panama, Paraguay, Peru, Poland, Portugal, Romania, Samoa, San Marino, Senegal, Serbia, Seychelles, Sierra Leone, Slovakia, Slovenia, South Africa, Spain, St Kitts-Nevis, St Lucia, St Vincent-Grenadines, Suriname, Sweden, Switzerland, Tajikistan, Tanzania UR, Timor-Leste, Trinidad-Tobago, Tunisia, Uganda, UK, Uruguay, Vanuatu, Venezuela, Zambia.
IGO Relations Observer status with (1): *United Nations (UN, #20515)* (General Assembly). Member of (1): *United Nations Joint Staff Pension Fund (UNJSPF, #20581)*. Concerned organization: *ECHO (inactive)*. Precursors include: *International Criminal Tribunal for the former Yugoslavia (ICTY, inactive)*; *International Criminal Tribunal for Rwanda (ICTR, inactive)*. Permanent Observer to: *ECOSOC (#05331)*. **NGO Relations** Concerned organizations: *Amnesty International (AI, #00801)*; *Foundation for the Establishment of an International Criminal Court (FEICC, inactive)*; *International Association of Penal Law (IAPL, #12074)*; *International Committee of the Red Cross (ICRC, #12799)*; *International Criminal Bar (ICB, #13107)*; *International Criminal Justice and Weapons Control Center (IWCC)*; *No Peace Without Justice (NPWJ, #17155)*; *Nonviolent Radical Party, Transnational and Transparty (PRNTT, #17154)*; *Siracusa International Institute for Criminal Justice and Human Rights (SII, #19289)*; *Women's Initiatives for Gender Justice (Women's Initiatives, #21021)*; *World Federalist Movement – Movement for a Just World Order through a Strengthened United Nations (WFM, #21404)*.
[2022.10.19/XF4580/**F***]

♦ International Criminal Court Bar Association (ICCBA) 13109

Association du Barreau près la Cour Pénale Internationale (ABCPI)

Exec Dir Oude Waalsdorperweg 10, 2597 AK The Hague, Netherlands. E-mail: info@iccba-abcpi.org.
URL: http://www.iccba-abcpi.org/

History Set up Jul 2016. Recognized by Assembly of States Parties of *International Criminal Court (ICC, #13108)*, Nov 2016. Registered as a foundation in accordance with Dutch law. **Aims** Serve as a collective voice for independent Counsel and Support Staff who represent victims, defendants and other actors before the ICC; provide support and services; act as a forum for discussion on all matters pertaining to the ICC. **Structure** General Assembly; Executive Council; Executive Committee; Secretariat. Committees (8): Defence; Victims; Counsel Support Staff; Professional Standards Advisory; Legal Advisory; Membership; Training; Amicus. **Languages** English, French. **Finance** Members' dues. **Activities** Advocacy/lobbying/activism; training/education; guidance/assistance/consulting; networking/liaising. **Publications** *ICCBA Newsletter*. **Members** Full; Associate; Affiliate. Membership countries not specified. **IGO Relations** *International Criminal Court (ICC, #13108)*. **NGO Relations** Member of: *International Legal Assistance Consortium (ILAC, #14025)*.
[2019.12.11/XM7033/**E**]

♦ International Criminal Defence Attorneys Association (inactive)
♦ International Criminal Investigations Foundation / see Institute for International Criminal Investigations (#11274)
♦ International Criminal Justice and Weapons Control Center (internationally oriented national body)
♦ International Criminal Law Network (internationally oriented national body)
♦ International Criminal Police Commission / see International Criminal Police Organization – INTERPOL (#13110)

♦ International Criminal Police Organization – INTERPOL (ICPO-INTERPOL) 13110

Organisation internationale de police criminelle – INTERPOL (OIPC-INTERPOL) – Organización Internacional de Policia Criminal – INTERPOL

Gen Secretariat 200 quai Charles de Gaulle, 69006 Lyon, France. T. +33472447000. Fax +33472447163.
INTERPOL Global Complex for Innovation 18 Napier Road, Singapore 285510, Singapore.
URL: http://www.interpol.int/

History Established Sep 1923, Vienna (Austria), as a nongovernmental body with the title *International Criminal Police Commission – Commission internationale de police criminelle – Internationale Kriminalpolizeiliche Kommission – Commissione Internazionale di Polizia Criminale*. Reconstituted and headquarters transferred from Vienna to Paris (France) in 1946. Emblem adopted, 1949. Constitution modified and present name adopted, 1956, Vienna. Constitution amended: 1962, Madrid (Spain); 1964, Caracas (Venezuela); 1967, Kyoto (Japan); 1968, Teheran (Iran Islamic Rep); 1974, Cannes (France); 1975, Buenos Aires (Argentina); 1977, Stockholm (Sweden). Moved from Paris to Lyon (France), 1989. *INTERPOL* currently functions as an international intergovernmental organization. **Aims** Prevent and fight *crime* through enhanced cooperation and innovation on *police* and security matters. **Structure** General Assembly (annual); Executive Committee; General Secretariat, located in Lyon (France); INTERPOL Global Complex for Innovation (Singapore); Regional Bureaus (7); Special Representative Offices (3). Each member country runs a National Central Bureau (NCB). Commission for the Control of INTERPOL's files (CCF) is an independent body providing advice and supervising the processing of requests from individuals. **Languages** Arabic, English, French, Spanish. **Staff** 850.00 FTE, paid. **Finance** Sources: euro 54,000,000 from member country statutory and euro 70,000,000 from voluntary funding, mostly governments. Total budget (2017): euro 124,000,000. **Activities** Capacity building; events/meetings; guidance/assistance/consulting; knowledge management/information dissemination; projects/programmes; training/education. **Events** *Match-Fixing Task Force (IMFTF) Meeting* Abu Dhabi (United Arab Emirates) 2022, *Regional Intellectual Property Crime Conference in the Middle East and North Africa* Dubai (United Arab Emirates) 2021, *European Regional Conference* Lyon (France) 2021, *INTERPOL-UNICRI Global Meeting on AI for Law Enforcement* Singapore (Singapore) 2020, *LIFE SMART Waste Project Final Conference* Brussels (Belgium) 2019. **Publications** Annual Report; fact sheets; guides and manuals; leaflets and brochures; videos. Information Services: Databases on criminal information, forensics, travel and official documents, stolen property, firearms trafficking, organized crime networks, radiological and nuclear materials.
Members Countries (192) in Dec 2017:
Afghanistan, Albania, Algeria, Andorra, Angola, Antigua-Barbuda, Argentina, Armenia, Aruba, Australia, Austria, Azerbaijan, Bahamas, Bahrain, Bangladesh, Barbados, Belarus, Belgium, Belize, Benin, Bhutan, Bolivia, Bosnia-Herzegovina, Botswana, Brazil, Brunei Darussalam, Bulgaria, Burkina Faso, Burundi, Cambodia, Cameroon, Canada, Cape Verde, Central African Rep, Chad, Chile, China, Colombia, Comoros, Congo Brazzaville, Congo DR, Costa Rica, Côte d'Ivoire, Croatia, Cuba, Curaçao, Cyprus, Czechia, Denmark, Djibouti, Dominica, Dominican Rep, Ecuador, Egypt, El Salvador, Equatorial Guinea, Eritrea, Estonia, Eswatini, Ethiopia, Fiji, Finland, France, Gabon, Gambia, Georgia, Germany, Ghana, Greece, Grenada, Guatemala, Guinea, Guinea-Bissau, Guyana, Haiti, Holy See, Honduras, Hungary, Iceland, India, Indonesia, Iran Islamic Rep, Iraq, Ireland, Israel, Italy, Jamaica, Japan, Jordan, Kazakhstan, Kenya, Korea Rep, Kuwait, Kyrgyzstan, Laos, Latvia, Lebanon, Lesotho, Liberia, Libya, Liechtenstein, Lithuania, Luxembourg, Madagascar, Malawi, Malaysia, Maldives, Mali, Malta, Marshall Is, Mauritania, Mauritius, Mexico, Moldova, Monaco, Mongolia, Montenegro, Morocco, Mozambique, Myanmar, Namibia, Nauru, Nepal, Netherlands, New Zealand, Nicaragua, Niger, Nigeria, North Macedonia, Norway, Oman, Pakistan, Palestine, Panama, Papua

New Guinea, Paraguay, Peru, Philippines, Poland, Portugal, Qatar, Romania, Russia, Rwanda, Samoa, San Marino, Sao Tomé-Principe, Saudi Arabia, Senegal, Serbia, Seychelles, Sierra Leone, Singapore, Slovakia, Slovenia, Somalia, South Africa, South Sudan, Spain, Sri Lanka, St Kitts-Nevis, St Lucia, St Maarten, St Vincent-Grenadines, Sudan, Suriname, Sweden, Switzerland, Syrian AR, Tajikistan, Tanzania UR, Thailand, Timor-Leste, Togo, Tonga, Trinidad-Tobago, Tunisia, Türkiye, Turkmenistan, Uganda, UK, Ukraine, United Arab Emirates, Uruguay, USA, Uzbekistan, Venezuela, Vietnam, Yemen, Zambia, Zimbabwe.

IGO Relations Observer status with (2): *Global Initiative to Combat Nuclear Terrorism (GICNT, #10424)*; *World Intellectual Property Organization (WIPO, #21593)*. Member of (1): *Virtual Global Taskforce (VGT, #20788)*. Cooperates with (6): *Co-operation Group to Combat Drug Abuse and Illicit Trafficking in Drugs (Pompidou Group, #04796)*; *European Commission (EC, #06633)*; *European Committee on Crime Problems (CDPC, #06645)*; *Inter-American Drug Abuse Control Commission (#11429)*; *International Multilateral Partnership Against Cyber Threats (IMPACT, #14196)*; *World Trade Organization (WTO, #21864)*.
Special arrangement with: *ECOSOC (#05331)*.
Agreements with:
- *African Union Mechanism for Police Cooperation (AFRIPOL, #00492)*;
- *Andean Community (#00817)*;
- *Arab Interior Ministers' Council (AIMC, #00990)*;
- *Council of Europe (CE, #04881)*;
- *European Monitoring Centre for Drugs and Drug Addiction (EMCDDA, #07820)*;
- *European Police Office (Europol, #08239)*;
- *International Centre for Migration Policy Development (ICMPD, #12503)*;
- *International Civil Aviation Organization (ICAO, #12581)*;
- *International Maritime Organization (IMO, #14102)*;
- *OAS (#17629)*;
- *Secretariat of the Basel Convention (SBC, #19196)*;
- *Secretariat of the Convention on International Trade in Endangered Species of Wild Fauna and Flora (CITES Secretariat, #19199)*;
- *UNESCO (#20322)*;
- *United Nations (UN, #20515)*;
- *Universal Postal Union (UPU, #20682)*;
- *World Customs Organization (WCO, #21350)*.

Relations with United Nations subsidiary bodies:
- *International Narcotics Control Board (INCB, #14212)*;
- *UNEP (#20299)*;
- *United Nations Commission on Narcotic Drugs (CND, #20532)*.

Relations with specialized agencies of the United Nations:
- *International Telecommunication Union (ITU, #15673)*;
- *United Nations Police (UNPOL, #20611)*;
- *WHO (#20950)*.

NGO Relations Member of (1): *International Network for Environmental Compliance and Enforcement (INECE, #14261)*. Agreements signed with: *Institute of Research Against Counterfeit Medicines (IRACM)*; *International Chamber of Commerce (ICC, #12534)*; *International Council of Museums (ICOM, #13051)* and its *ICOM International Committee for University Museums and Collections (UMAC, #11058)*. [2020/XB1775/**B***]

♦ International Criminal Tribunal (no recent information)
♦ International Criminal Tribunal for the former Yugoslavia (inactive)
♦ International Criminal Tribunal for Rwanda (inactive)
♦ International Crisis Aid (internationally oriented national body)

♦ International Crisis Group (Crisis Group) 13111

Pres/CEO Av Louise 235 – Level 5, 1050 Brussels, Belgium. T. +3225029038. Fax +3225025038. E-mail: brussels@crisisgroup.org.
URL: http://www.crisisgroup.org/

History 1 Jul 1995, USA. Registered in the State of Washington DC. Branch of US entity constituting the operational headquarters is registered in accordance with Belgian law. Former names and other names: *ICG* – former. **Aims** Be an independent, non-partisan source of analysis and advice to governments and intergovernmental bodies on preventing and resolving deadly conflict. **Structure** Board of Trustees. Headquarters in Brussels (Belgium); Advocacy offices in Washington DC (USA), New York NY (USA), London (UK); Liaison offices in Moscow (Russia) and Beijing (China). **Staff** 122.00 FTE, paid. **Finance** Governments; private foundations; private individuals. **Activities** Conflict resolution; guidance/assistance/consulting; research/documentation; advocacy/lobbying/activism. **Events** *Meeting* Brussels (Belgium) 2013, *Meeting* Singapore (Singapore) 2012, *Global Meeting* Brussels (Belgium) 2011. **Publications** *CrisisWatch* (12 a year) – bulletin. Annual Report. Policy reports; briefing papers. **IGO Relations** Regular contact with: *Commonwealth Secretariat (#04362)*; *Council of Europe (CE, #04881)*; *European Commission (EC, #06633)*; *European Parliament (EP, #08146)*; *International Bank for Reconstruction and Development (IBRD, #12317)* (World Bank); *Joint United Nations Programme on HIV/AIDS (UNAIDS, #16149)*; *NATO (#16945)*; *OAS (#17629)*; *Organization for Security and Cooperation in Europe (OSCE, #17887)*; UN DPA; UN DPKO; *UNHCR (#20327)*; *United Nations Security Council (UNSC, #20625)*; *United States Agency for International Development (USAID)*. Associated with Department of Global Communications of the United Nations. **NGO Relations** Member of (6): *Alliance Against Genocide (AAG, #00655)*; *European Policy Centre (EPC, #08240)*; *Extractive Industries Transparency Initiative (EITI, #09229)*; *Global Partnership for the Prevention of Armed Conflict (GPPAC, #10538)*; *International Coalition for the Responsibility to Protect (ICRtoP, #12620)*; *NGO Working Group on the Security Council (#17128)*. Institutional member of: *Centre for European Policy Studies (CEPS, #03741)*. [2020/XE2666/**E**]

♦ International Critical Control Rooms Alliance (ICCRA) 13112

Editor-in-Chief address not obtained. T. +31642108561.
URL: http://www.iccraonline.com/

History Set up as a working group of *TCCA (#20106)*. **Aims** Become the focus and platform for critical service control room discussion, learning and development of proactive measures designed to create constant evolution and ensure best practice. **Structure** Team. Special Interest Groups (4): Operations; Technology; Environment and Ergonomics; People and Performance. **Activities** Events/meetings. **Events** *International Critical Control Rooms Congress* Geneva (Switzerland) 2017, *International Critical Control Rooms Congress* Prague (Czechia) 2016. **Publications** *ICCRA Newsletter*. [2017/XM6255/**E**]

♦ International Critical Geography Group (ICGG) 13113

Contact address not obtained. E-mail: icgg.committee@gmail.com.
URL: http://internationalcriticalgeography.org/

Aims Develop the theory and practice necessary for combating social exploitation and oppression. **Structure** Steering Committee. **Activities** Events/meetings. **Events** *Conference* Hong Kong (Hong Kong) 2013, *International Conference on Social Justice and the City* Hong Kong (Hong Kong) 2013, *Conference* Frankfurt-Main (Germany) 2011, *Conference* Mumbai (India) 2007, *Conference* Mexico City (Mexico) 2005. [2020.03.15/XJ6940/v/**C**]

♦ International Critical Incident Stress Foundation (internationally oriented national body)

♦ International Critical Management Studies Board (ICMS Board) . . . 13114

Sec Alliance Manchester Business School, Booth Str East, Manchester, M13 9SS, UK.
Co-Chair Office 220 – Sobey Bldg, Dept of Management, Sobey School of Business, Saint Mary's Univ, 923 Robie Str, Halifax NS B3H 3C3, Canada.
URL: http://internationalcms.org/

History 2012. Founded to provide a structure for the conferences organized since 1999. **Aims** Tackle power relations, inequalities and the role managing and organizing play in perpetuating repression and domination and/or preventing the development of a sustainable and fairer world. **Structure** Board. **Activities** Events/meetings. **Events** *International Conference in Critical Management Studies* Nottingham (UK) 2023, *International Conference in Critical Management Studies* Delhi (India) 2021, *International Conference in Critical Management Studies* Milton Keynes (UK) 2019, *International Conference in Critical Management Studies* Liverpool (UK) 2017, *International Conference in Critical Management Studies* Leicester (UK) 2015. [2023/XM5416/c/**E**]

♦ International Crop Improvement Association / see Association of Official Seed Certifying Agencies (#02837)

♦ International Crop Science Society (ICSS) 13115

Secretariat 5585 Guilford Rd, Madison WI 53711, USA. T. +16082738080. E-mail: membership@crops.org.
URL: http://www.intlcss.org/

History Founded 2004, Brisbane (Australia) during International Crop Science Congress, Australia. The concept of the Society began at the 1996 Congress in India where it was proposed and discussed, and was approved by the delegates at the 2000 Congress in Germany. **Aims** Facilitate research, education and information exchange on the *sustainable* production of sufficient quality and quantity of crop products to meet the food and industrial feedstock needs of humankind. **Structure** Board, comprising a representative from the previous and next Congresses for an 8-year term spanning three Congresses (the representative from the previous Congress will become the President of the ICSS for a 4-year term until the next Congress), Vice-President and members-at-large. **Activities** Organizes International Crop Science Congress (every 4 years). **Events** *Quadrennial Congress* Beijing (China) 2016, *Quadrennial Congress / International Congress* Bento Gonçalves (Brazil) 2012, *Quadrennial congress / International Congress* Jeju (Korea Rep) 2008, *Quadrennial congress / International Congress* Brisbane, QLD (Australia) 2004. **Publications** Congress proceedings. **Members** Individuals; Corporations; Organizations. Membership countries not specified. **NGO Relations** Member of: *Global Plant Council (#10550)*. [2016/XJ0503/**C**]

♦ International Crops Research Institute for the Semi-Arid Tropics (ICRISAT) 13116

Institut international de recherche sur les cultures des zones tropicales semi-arides – Instituto Internacional de Investigación de Cultivos para las Zonas Tropicales Semiaridas

Dir Gen Patancheru, Hyderabad, Telangana 502 324, Hyderabad TELANGANA 502 324, India. T. +914030713071. Fax +914030713074. E-mail: icrisat@cgiar.org.
Liaison Office CG Centers Block, NASC Complex, Dev Prakash Shastri Marg, Delhi 110 012, DELHI 110 012, India. T. +911132472306 – +911132473307 – +911132472308. Fax +911125841294.
URL: http://www.icrisat.org/

History 28 Mar 1972. Established on signing of an agreement between the Government of India and *Ford Foundation (#09858)*, as one of 15 centres supported by *CGIAR System Organization (CGIAR, #03843)*. Constitution, sponsored by *International Bank for Reconstruction and Development (IBRD, #12317)*, *FAO (#09260)* and *UNDP (#20292)*, signed 5 Jul 1972. **Aims** Innovate to help poor communities in Africa and Asia to fight hunger and poverty, reduce malnutrition and revitalize the environment. **Structure** Governing Board; Management Committee; Regional Hubs (2); Country Offices (8). Includes Intellectual Property Management Office, set up Feb 2002. **Languages** English, French, Portuguese. **Staff** 1100.00 FTE, paid. Plus collaborative staff.
Finance Donors include: governments of UK, USA, Germany, Ireland, Austria, Norway, Belgium, Switzerland, Australia, India, Sweden, Malawi, Niger, Nigeria, Japan, Mozambique, Netherlands, Italy, Denmark, South Africa, Korea Rep, China, Thailand and Philippines; private sector companies; development banks, foundations and charitable organizations, including bilateral funders:
- *Australian Centre for International Agricultural Research (ACIAR)*;
- *Bill and Melinda Gates Foundation (BMGF)*;
- *Catholic Relief Services (CRS, #03608)*;
- *Common Fund for Commodities (CFC, #04293)*;
- *Department for International Development (DFID, inactive)*;
- *European Commission (EC, #06633)*;
- FAO;
- *FAO (#09260)*;
- *Forum for Agricultural Research in Africa (FARA, #09897)*;
- *Global Crop Diversity Trust (Crop Trust, #10313)*;
- *International Fund for Agricultural Development (IFAD, #13692)*;
- *International Technical Cooperation Centre, Korea Rep (ITCC, no recent information)*;
- *McKnight Foundation*;
- *Organization of the Petroleum Exporting Countries (OPEC, #17881)*;
- *Swedish International Development Cooperation Agency (Sida)*;
- *Swiss Agency for Development and Cooperation (SDC)*;
- *UNEP (#20299)*;
- UNDP;
- *United States Agency for International Development (USAID)*;
- World Bank.

Activities Awards/prizes/competitions; research and development. **Events** *ScaleWAYS Project Start-up Workshop* Entebbe (Uganda) 2019, *Regional Consultation on Scoping, Prioritizing and Mapping of Crop Related Neglected and Underutilized Species in Selected Countries in Asia* Bangkok (Thailand) 2016, *ASPA Annual Conference* Hyderabad (India) 2016, *International conference on horticulture* Bangalore (India) 2009, *BioEnergy forum* Singapore (Singapore) 2009. **Publications** Annual Report; research reports; scientific publications; corporate publications. Information Services: Maintains library database.
Members Member States (16):
Australia, Austria, Belgium, Canada, Finland, France, Germany, India, Italy, Japan, Netherlands, Norway, Sweden, Switzerland, UK, USA.
Regional hubs in 2 countries:
Kenya, Mali.
Country offices in 8 countries:
Ethiopia, India, Malawi, Mali, Mozambique, Niger, Nigeria, Zimbabwe.
Also active in 1 country:
Senegal.
IGO Relations Member of: *International Information System for the Agricultural Sciences and Technology (AGRIS, #13848)*. Cooperates with other CGIAR supported centres: *Africa Rice Center (AfricaRice, #00518)*; *Bioversity International (#03262)*; *International Center for Agricultural Research in the Dry Areas (ICARDA, #12466)*; *International Livestock Research Institute (ILRI, #14062)*; *International Rice Research Institute (IRRI, #14754)*. Close cooperation with:
- *African Union Scientific Technical Research Commission (AU STRC, #00493)*;
- *AGRHYMET Regional Centre (#00565)*;
- *Arab Bank for Economic Development in Africa (#00904)*;
- *Arab Organization for Agricultural Development (AOAD, #01018)*;
- *Asia-Pacific Association of Agricultural Research Institutions (APAARI, #01830)*;
- *Australian Aid (inactive)*;
- *CABI (#03393)*;
- *Centre de coopération internationale en recherche agronomique pour le développement (CIRAD, #03733)*;
- *FAO Regional Office for Asia and the Pacific (RAP, #09266)*;
- *Institut de recherche pour le développement (IRD)*;
- *Institut du Sahel (INSAH, #11357)*;
- *Inter-American Development Bank (IDB, #11427)*;
- *Semi-Arid Food Grain Research and Development (AU SAFGRAD, #19226)*;
- *Southern African Development Community (SADC, #19843)*;
- *UNESCO (#20322)*;
- *UNICEF (#20332)*.

NGO Relations Cooperates with other CGIAR supported centres: *Center for International Forestry Research (CIFOR, #03646)*; *International Centre for Tropical Agriculture (#12527)*; *International Food Policy Research Institute (IFPRI, #13622)*; *International Institute of Tropical Agriculture (IITA, #13933)*; *International Maize and Wheat Improvement Center (#14077)*; *International Potato Center (#14627)*; *International Water Management Institute (IWMI, #15867)*; *World Agroforestry Centre (ICRAF, #21072)*; *WorldFish (#21507)*. Memorandum of Understanding with: *International Center for Biosaline Agriculture (ICBA, #12468)*. Cooperates with: *International Fertilizer Development Center (IFDC, #13590)*. *European Cooperative for Rural Development (EUCORD, #06788)*. Close cooperation with:
- *African Technology Policy Studies Network (ATPS, #00481)*;
- *Agricultural Libraries Network (AGLINET, #00571)*;
- *Cereals and Legumes Asia Network (CLAN, no recent information)*;
- *Comisión Latinoamericana de Investigadores en Sorgo (CLAIS, no recent information)*;
- *International Association for the Study of the Commons (IASC, #12195)*;
- *International Benchmark Sites Network for Agrotechnology Transfer (IBSNAT, no recent information)*;
- *International Centre of Insect Physiology and Ecology (ICIPE, #12499)*;
- *International Sorghum, Millet and Other Grains Program (INTSORMIL, inactive)*;

- *Natural Resources Institute (NRI);*
- *West and Central Africa Millet Research Network (WCAMRN, no recent information);*
- *Winrock International.*

Instrumental in setting up: *Soil and Water Management Network (SWMnet, inactive).* [2021/XE4115/j/E*]

♦ International Crossbow Shooting Union 13117
Internationale Armbrustschützen Union (IAU)

Contact Vrbik 22, HR-10000 Zagreb, Croatia. T. +385915147787. E-mail: office@iau-crossbow.org.
URL: http://www.iau-crossbow.org/

History 1956, Germany FR. Founded 1956, Landshut (Germany FR). **Aims** Enter in Sportaccord; seek Olympic recognition for crossbow *sport.* **Structure** General Assembly; Executive Committee; Technical Committees. **Languages** English, German. **Staff** 13.00 FTE, paid. **Finance** Sources: members' dues. **Activities** Sporting activities. **Events** *Annual General Assembly* Frankfurt-Main (Germany) 2014, *Annual General Assembly* Thaon-les-Vosges (France) 2009, *Annual General Assembly* Sulgen (Switzerland) 2008, *Annual General Assembly* Steyr (Austria) 2006, *Annual General Assembly* Zwevegem (Belgium) 2003. **Publications** *IAU Newsletter* – electronic. Rule books; guides.
Members National federations (20) in 20 countries and territories:
Austria, Belgium, Croatia, Czechia, Estonia, Finland, France, Germany, Hungary, India, Iran Islamic Rep, Ireland, Israel, Italy, Japan, Netherlands, Russia, Slovenia, Switzerland, Taiwan. [2020/XD9164/v/C]

- ♦ International Cruise Council Australasia / see CLIA Australasia
- ♦ International Cruise Victims (internationally oriented national body)

♦ International Cryogenic Engineering Committee (ICEC) 13118
Comité international pour l'ingéniérie cryogénique

Chairman Univ of Twente, Fac of Science and Technology, PO Box 217, 7500 AE Enschede, Netherlands.
URL: https://icec.web.cern.ch/

History 18 Mar 1969, Zurich (Switzerland). Registered according to Swiss law. **Aims** Promote development of cryogenic engineering on an international basis; promote exchange of information and collaboration among scientists and engineers in the field. **Structure** Committee; Organizing Committee. **Languages** English. **Staff** No permanent staff. **Finance** Conference proceeds. **Activities** Events/meetings; knowledge management/ information dissemination. **Events** *Biennial Conference* Hangzhou (China) 2020, *Biennial Conference* Oxford (UK) 2018, *Biennial Conference* Delhi (India) 2016, *Biennial Conference* Enschede (Netherlands) 2014, *European Cryogenics Day* UK 2014. **Publications** Conference proceedings.
Members Individuals (20): scientists and engineers in 15 countries:
China, Czechia, France, Germany, India, Italy, Japan, Korea Rep, Netherlands, Poland, Russia, Sweden, Switzerland, UK, USA.
NGO Relations Joint meeting with *International Cryogenic Materials Conference.* [2018.06.01/XD4260/v/D]

- ♦ International Cryogenic Materials Conference (meeting series)

♦ International Cryosphere Climate Initiative (ICCI) 13119
Dir address not obtained.
European Dir address not obtained.
URL: http://iccinet.org/

History 2009. Registered in the US; *ICCI Europe* is registered in accordance with Swedish law. **Aims** Create, shape and implement initiatives designed to preserve as much of the Earth's cryosphere as possible. **Structure** Advisory Board. **Staff** 5.00 FTE, paid. **NGO Relations** Member of (1): *Climate and Clean Air Coalition (CCAC, #04010).* [2013/XJ7584/F]

♦ International Crystal Federation (ICF) 13120
Vice-Chairman PO Box 6250, Avon CO 81620-6250, USA.
Chairman RCR Cristalleria Italiana, Localita Catarelli, 53034 Colle Val d'Elsa SI, Italy.
URL: http://www.internationalcrystalfederation.org/

History Apr 1991, Washington DC (USA). Incorporated "Not For Profit", 7 Feb 1992, Washington DC. **Aims** Serve as an advocate for the crystal industry in the areas of governmental relations, trade relations and consumer education. **Structure** Annual Member Meeting (held on Sunday of the Ambiente Fair), Frankfurt (Germany); Board of Directors; Standing Committees. **Languages** English. **Staff** None. **Finance** Members' dues. **Activities** Standards/guidelines; knowledge management/information dissemination; events/meetings. **Events** *Annual Technical Exchange Conference* Rogaska Slatina (Slovenia) 2016, *Conference* Kosta (Sweden) 2014, *Annual Technical Exchange Conference* Kufstein (Austria) 2013, *Annual Technical Exchange Conference* Arques (France) 2012, *Annual technical exchange conference* Rogaska Slatina (Slovenia) 2011. **Publications** Newsletters; meeting notes; legal announcements and regulatory summaries; technical papers – Technical Exchange Conferences. Information Services: Technical information and testing data exchange with regulatory agencies. **Members** Crystal manufacturers, distributors and associates (160 companies). International membership concentrated in Europe and USA. Membership countries not specified. **NGO Relations** Sister organization: *European Domestic Glass (EDG, #06938).* [2020/XD8735/D]

- ♦ International Culinary Tourism Association / see World Food Travel Association

♦ International Cultic Studies Association (ICSA) 13121
Exec Dir PO Box 2265, Bonita Springs FL 34133, USA. T. +12395143081. Fax +13053938193. E-mail: mail@icsamail.com.
URL: http://www.icsahome.com/

History 1979. Former names and other names: *American Family Foundation (AFF)* – former (1979 to 2004). **Aims** Study cults, cult-like groups and their methodologies. **Activities** Events/meetings; research/ documentation. **Events** *Annual Conference* Montréal, QC (Canada) 2022, *Annual Conference* Montréal, QC (Canada) 2021, *Annual Conference* Montréal, QC (Canada) 2020, *International Conference* Manchester (UK) 2019, *Annual Conference* Stockholm (Sweden) 2015. **Publications** *ICSA Today* (3 a year); *International Journal of Coercion, Abuse, and Manipulation.* [2021.02.17/XM4561/D]

- ♦ International Cultural Centre (internationally oriented national body)
- ♦ International Cultural Diversity Organization (unconfirmed)
- ♦ International Cultural Exchange Organization (internationally oriented national body)

♦ International Cultural Youth Exchange (ICYE Federation) 13122
Intercambio Internacional Cultural Juvenil – Internationaler Kultureller Jugendaustausch – Internationale Jongeren Uitwisseling

SG Grosse Hamburger Str 30, 10115 Berlin, Germany. T. +493028390550. E-mail: icye@icye.org.
URL: http://www.icye.org/

History 1949. Founded as a youth exchange programme. Current constitution adopted 23 Sep 1977, Skalholt (Iceland). Former names and other names: *International Christian Youth Exchange* – former; *International Council for the International Christian Youth Exchange* – former; *Conseil international pour l'Echange international chrétien de jeunesse* – former; *International Christian Youth Exchange (ICYE)* – former; *Echange international chrétien de jeunes* – former; *Intercambio Internacional Cristiano de Jóvenes* – former; *Internationaler Christlicher Jugendaustausch (ICJA)* – former; *Internationale Jongeren Uitwisseling* – former; *Föderation der Nationalkomitees im Internationalen Kulturellen Jugendaustausch (ICYE)* – legal name. Registration: No/ID: VR 5830, Start date: 28 Nov 1978, Germany, Berlin. **Aims** Provide challenging intercultural learning experiences to young people, enhancing their social and personal development through international volunteer programmes. **Structure** General Assembly (every 2 years); Board of Managers; regional structures in Africa, Asia/Pacific, Europe and Americas; International Office. **Languages** English, Spanish. **Staff** 2.00 FTE, paid. **Finance** Sources: donations; grants. Main source: membership and administration fees paid by National Committees. **Activities** Advocacy/lobbying/activism; awareness raising; capacity building; events/ meetings; monitoring/evaluation; networking/liaising; projects/programmes. **Events** *General Assembly* Berlin (Germany) 2022, *Biennial General Assembly* Hôi An (Vietnam) 2019, *Biennial General Assembly* Naestved (Denmark) 2017, *Biennial General Assembly* Goa (India) 2015, *Biennial General Assembly* Kampala (Uganda) 2013. **Publications** *Worlds of Experience* (3 a year).
Members National Committees in 40 countries and territories:
Argentina, Austria, Belgium, Bolivia, Brazil, Colombia, Costa Rica, Denmark, Ecuador, Finland, France, Germany, Ghana, Honduras, Iceland, India, Indonesia, Italy, Japan, Kenya, Korea Rep, Mexico, Morocco, Mozambique, Nepal, New Zealand, Nigeria, Philippines, Poland, Russia, Slovakia, South Africa, Spain, Switzerland, Taiwan, Tanzania UR, Uganda, UK, USA, Vietnam.

Consultative Status Consultative status granted from: *ECOSOC (#05331)* (Ros A); *UNESCO (#20322)* (Consultative Status). **IGO Relations** Accredited by (1): *United Nations Office at Vienna (UNOV, #20604).* Cooperates with (1): *European Commission (EC, #06633)* (DG XXII). Associated with Department of Global Communications of the United Nations. **NGO Relations** Member of (2): *Coordinating Committee for International Voluntary Service (CCIVS, #04819); UNITED for Intercultural Action – European Network Against Nationalism, Racism, Fascism and in Support of Migrants and Refugees (UNITED, #20511).* Instrumental in setting up (1): *European Youth Forum (#09140).* [2021.05.26/XE3178/E]

- ♦ International Culture Service / see International Cultural Centre
- ♦ International Culture University (internationally oriented national body)
- ♦ International Curling Federation / see World Curling Federation (#21348)
- ♦ International Curling Federation, 1898 (inactive)

♦ International Currency Association (ICA) 13123
Main Office 1B The Beacon, Beaufront Park, Anick Road, Hexham, NE46 4TU, UK. T. +441932508803. E-mail: secretariat@currencyassociation.org.
URL: http://www.currencyassociation.org/

History Founded 2016. **Aims** Promote and represent the views of the currency industry. **Structure** Board of Directors. Committees (3): Membership; Communications; Global Cash Alliance. **Finance** Sources: members' dues. **Activities** Advocacy/lobbying/activism; events/meetings. **Events** *Global Currency Forum* Barcelona (Spain) 2022, *Global Currency Forum* Barcelona (Spain) 2021, *Global Currency Forum* Barcelona (Spain) 2020.
Members Full and Associate in 13 countries:
Australia, Austria, Belgium, Canada, France, Germany, Italy, Japan, Netherlands, Russia, Switzerland, UK, USA.
Included in the above, 4 organizations listed in this Yearbook:
ATM Industry Association (ATMIA); European Intelligent Cash Protection Association (EURICPA, #07581); Intergraf (#11505); International Banknote Designers Association (IBDA, #12315); International Hologram Manufacturers Association (IHMA, #13804). [2021/XM7862/y/C]

♦ International Customs Tariffs Bureau 13124
Bureau international des tarifs douaniers (BITD) – Internationaal Bureau voor de Bekendmaking der Toltarieven

Secretariat Rue des Petits Carmes 15, 1000 Brussels, Belgium. T. +3225018774. Fax +3225013147.
Dir address not obtained.
Pres address not obtained.
URL: http://www.bitd.org/

History Established 5 Jul 1890, Brussels (Belgium), as *International Union for the Publication of Customs Tariffs – Union internationale pour la publication des tarifs douaniers,* under an International Convention which came into force 1 Apr 1891, currently modified by a Protocol of 16 Dec 1949, Brussels. **Aims** In the name of the 'International Union for the Publication of Customs Tariffs', translate and *publish,* in English, French, German, Italian and Spanish, the customs tariffs of all countries, together with updated supplements of those tariffs. **Structure** No meetings are held; communication with member states is implemented via those states' embassies in Brussels (Belgium) and the Belgian diplomatic network abroad. **Languages** English, French, German, Italian, Spanish. **Staff** 16.00 FTE, paid. **Finance** Government contributions based on the volume of their foreign trade. **Publications** *International Customs Journal – Bulletin international des douanes* in English, French, German, Italian, Spanish – based on documents forwarded by governments. Annual report.
Members Member States of the International Union for the Publication of Customs Tariffs (52):
Albania, Algeria, Belgium, Bolivia, Brazil, Bulgaria, Burundi, Chile, China, Colombia, Congo DR, Costa Rica, Cuba, Cyprus, Dominican Rep, Ecuador, Egypt, Finland, France, Germany, Greece, Haiti, Iceland, India, Iraq, Israel, Italy, Japan, Jordan, Korea Rep, Lebanon, Libya, Luxembourg, Malaysia, Malta, Morocco, Nicaragua, Pakistan, Panama, Romania, Russia, Rwanda, Saudi Arabia, Senegal, Slovenia, Sudan, Sweden, Switzerland, Syrian AR, Tunisia, USA, Venezuela.
IGO Relations *European Commission (EC, #06633); UNCTAD (#20285); World Customs Organization (WCO, #21350).* [2014.12.04/XB2674/B*]

- ♦ International Cybernetics Congress Committee / see World Organisation of Systems and Cybernetics (#21686)

♦ INTERNATIONAL CYBER POLICING ORGANIZATION (CYBERPOL) 13125
SG Geneva Nations, Pre-de-la-Blechette 1, 1202 Geneva, Switzerland. Fax +41225185854. E-mail: contact@cyberpol.info.
URL: http://www.cyberpol.info

History Originally set up 2014, UK, as *International Cyber Security Organization (ICSO).* Granted international status under current title, when registered in accordance with Belgian law. Registration: Start date: 2 Jul 2015, Belgium. **Aims** Ensure and promote the widest possible mutual international assistance between all international Cyber Criminal police authorities within the limits of the laws existing in the different countries and in the spirit of the "Universal Declaration of Human Rights"; establish and develop all institutions likely to contribute effectively to the prevention and suppression of ordinary and advanced cyber law crimes. **Structure** General Assembly (annual); Executive Committee. **Languages** Dutch, English, French. **Staff** 6.00 FTE, paid. **Finance** Sources: members' dues; revenue from activities/projects. **Activities** Monitoring/evaluation; networking/liaising. **Events** *CYBERPOL Cyber Security Summit* Brussels (Belgium) 2015. **Publications** *CYBERBoK Cyber Body of Knowledge.*
Members States to which the provisions of Article 48 of the Statute of Membership shall apply (57):
Argentina, Australia, Austria, Belgium, Brazil, Cambodia, Canada, Chile, Colombia, Costa Rica, Cuba, Curaçao, Denmark, Dominican Rep, Egypt, Finland, France, Germany, Greece, Guatemala, India, Indonesia, Iran Islamic Rep, Ireland, Israel, Italy, Japan, Jordan, Lebanon, Liberia, Libya, Luxembourg, Mexico, Monaco, Myanmar, Netherlands, New Zealand, Norway, Pakistan, Philippines, Portugal, Saudi Arabia, Serbia, South Africa, Spain, Sri Lanka, Sudan, Suriname, Sweden, Switzerland, Syrian AR, Thailand, Türkiye, UK, Uruguay, USA, Venezuela. [2021.02.23/XM4385/D]

- ♦ International Cyber Security Organization / see INTERNATIONAL CYBER POLICING ORGANIZATION (#13125)
- ♦ International Cyber Security Protection Alliance (internationally oriented national body)

♦ International Cyber University for Health (ICUH) 13126
Contact Yonsei Univ Graduate School of Public Health, 134 Shinchon-dong, Seodaemun-gu, Seoul 120-752, Korea Rep. T. +82222281536. Fax +8223927734.
URL: http://icuh.yonsei.ac.kr/

History 3 May 2004, by *Asia-Pacific Academic Consortium for Public Health (APACPH, #01811)* and Yonsei University, Seoul (Korea Rep). **Aims** Serve as the educational focal point for the provision of public health education in the Asia-Pacific region. **Structure** Board of Governors. Committees (3): Steering; Curriculum; Management. President. **Activities** Provides courses. [2010/XJ1070/E]

- ♦ International Cycling History Conference (meeting series)
- ♦ International Cycling Safety Conference (meeting series)
- ♦ International Cycling Union / see Union Cycliste Internationale (#20375)
- ♦ International Cystic Fibrosis / Mucoviscidosis / Association (inactive)
- ♦ International Cystinuria Foundation (internationally oriented national body)
- ♦ International Cyto-Cybernetic Centre (inactive)
- ♦ International Cytogenetics and Genome Society / see International Chromosome and Genome Society (#12568)

♦ International Cytokine and Interferon Society (ICIS) 13127
Managing Dir 297 Kinderkamack Rd, Suite 348, Oradell NJ 07649, USA. T. +18009471960. Fax +12013221818.
Main: https://cytokinesociety.org/

History 1983. Current title adopted on merger with *International Cytokine Society (inactive).* Former names and other names: *International Society for Interferon Research (ISIR)* – former (1983 to 2013); *International Society for Interferon and Cytokine Research (ISICR)* – former. **Aims** Promote original research in the fields of cytokines, interferons, chemokines, growth factors and their receptors; facilitate communication and interaction between scientists aimed at the multidisciplinary integration of current basic and clinical knowledge and concepts in these areas of research; promote the dissemination of information on, and applications of knowledge of theses areas of biomedical research; promote an awareness with educational programmes of the national and international health communities of the importance of these areas of biomedical research. **Structure** Board of Directors. International Council, consisting of representatives from national chapters. Officers: President, President-Elect, Secretary and Treasurer. **Languages** English. **Staff** 1.00 FTE, paid. **Finance** Sources: contributions; members' dues; sponsorship. **Activities** Events/meetings; knowledge management/information dissemination; networking/liaising; research/documentation; training/education. **Events** *Annual Meeting* Athens (Greece) 2023, *Annual Meeting* Waikoloa, HI (USA) 2022, *Annual Meeting* Cardiff (UK) 2021, *Annual Meeting* Seattle, WA (USA) 2020, *Annual Meeting* Vienna (Austria) 2019. **Publications** *Cytokine* – official journal; *Journal of Interferon and Cytokine Research* – official journal; *Signals Newsletter*.

Members Individuals – scientists (over 600) devoted to research in the fields of cytokine, interferon and chemokine cell biology, molecular biology, biochemistry and the clinical use of these biological response modifiers; organizations. Members in 36 countries and territories:

Algeria, Argentina, Australia, Austria, Belgium, Brazil, Bulgaria, Canada, China, Croatia, Denmark, Egypt, Estonia, Finland, France, Germany, Greece, Ireland, Israel, Italy, Japan, Netherlands, Norway, Poland, Russia, Saudi Arabia, Singapore, Slovakia, Slovenia, South Africa, Spain, Sweden, Switzerland, Taiwan, UK, USA.

NGO Relations Member of (1): *Federation of Clinical Immunology Societies (FOCIS, #09472).* [2022/XD0886/**C**]

♦ International Cytokine Society (inactive)
♦ International Dachau Committee (#04174)
♦ International Dairy Agreement (1979 treaty)
♦ International Dairy Committee (inactive)

♦ International Dairy Federation (IDF) 13128

Fédération Internationale du Lait (FIL) – Federación Internacional de Lecheria – Internationaler Milchwirtschaftverband (IMV)

Dir Gen Blvd Auguste Reyers 70/B, 1030 Brussels, Belgium. T. +3223256740. E-mail: info@fil-idf.org.

URL: http://www.fil-idf.org/

History 1903, Brussels (Belgium). Founded at 1st International Dairy Congress. Status of international organization granted by Belgian Royal Decree, 5 Nov 1955. Present official constitution adopted 16 Oct 2016. Former names and other names: *Federation internationale de laiterie* – alias. Registration: Banque-Carrefour des Entreprises, No/ID: 0407.592.317, Start date: 10 Nov 1955, Belgium. **Aims** Represent the dairy sector as a whole at international level by providing a global source of scientific expertise and knowledge in support of the development and promotion of quality *milk* and milk products so as to deliver consumers with nutrition, health and well-being. **Structure** General Assembly (annual); Council; Scientific Coordination Committee; Secretariat. **Languages** English, French. **Staff** 10.00 FTE, paid. **Finance** Sources: members' dues; sale of publications. Other sources: proportion of congress fees and of other events. **Activities** Advocacy/lobbying/activism; events/meetings; guidance/assistance/consulting; monitoring/evaluation. **Events** *World Dairy Summit* Beijing (China) 2023, *Colloquium* Dublin (Ireland) 2022, *World Dairy Summit* New Delhi (India) 2022, *Global Dairy Conference* Copenhagen (Denmark) 2021, *World Dairy Summit* Puerto Varas (Chile) 2021. **Publications** *Bulletin of the IDF* (10 a year); *IDF News*; *IDF Standards of Composition and Methods of Analysis*; *IDF World Dairy Situation Report*; *ISO/IDF Standards*. Books – special issues; proceedings of sessions, conferences and seminars.

Members National Committees in 47 countries:

Argentina, Australia, Belgium, Brazil, Bulgaria, Canada, Chile, China, Croatia, Cyprus, Czechia, Denmark, Egypt, Finland, France, Germany, Greece, Iceland, India, Iran Islamic Rep, Ireland, Israel, Italy, Japan, Korea Rep, Kuwait, Latvia, Lithuania, Luxembourg, Mexico, Mongolia, Netherlands, New Zealand, Norway, Philippines, Poland, Portugal, Russia, South Africa, Sweden, Switzerland, Türkiye, UK, Ukraine, Uruguay, USA, Zimbabwe.

Consultative Status Consultative status granted from: *ECOSOC (#05331)* (Ros C); *FAO (#09260)* (Special Status); *UNICEF (#20332)*; *UNEP (#20299)*. **NGO Relations** Member of: *Federation of European and International Associations Established in Belgium (FAIB, #09508)*. Partner of: *Livestock Environmental Assessment and Performance Partnership (LEAP, #16500)*. Cooperates with: *Comité européen de normalisation (CEN, #04162)*; *International Organization for Standardization (ISO, #14473).* [2021/XC1784/**C**]

♦ International Dairy Foods Association (internationally oriented national body)

♦ International Dalit Solidarity Network (IDSN) 13129

Exec Dir Farvergade 27D, 1463 Copenhagen K, Denmark. T. +4531493104. E-mail: info@idsn.org.

URL: http://www.idsn.org/

History Mar 2000. Statutes modified 16 Sep 2003, Brussels (Belgium). Current statutes adopted 19 Dec 2014. Registration: Denmark. **Aims** Eliminate *caste discrimination* and similar forms of discrimination based on work and descent. **Structure** Council (meets every three years); Executive Group; Secretariat. **Languages** English. **Staff** 4.00 FTE, paid; 3.00 FTE, voluntary. **Finance** Supported by: *Brot für die Welt*; Norwegian Human Rights Foundation. Annual budget: 265,500 EUR (2021). **Activities** Advocacy/lobbying/activism; awareness raising; capacity building; events/meetings; networking/liaising; projects/programmes; training/education. **Publications** *IDSN Newsletter* (6 a year). Annual Report; thematic publications.

Members National Dalit platforms and solidarity networks in 9 countries:

Bangladesh, Finland, Germany, India, Nepal, Netherlands, Norway, Pakistan, UK.

International and Regional Associates (15):

Anti-Slavery International (#00860); Arisa – Advocating Rights In South Asia; *Asian Centre for Human Rights (ACHR)*; *Asian Forum for Human Rights and Development (FORUM-ASIA, #01491)*; *Asian Human Rights Commission (AHRC, #01507)*; *Commonwealth Human Rights Initiative (CHRI, #04340)*; *Franciscans International (FI, #09982)*; *Human Rights Watch (HRW, #10990)*; *Minority Rights Group International (MRG, #16820)*; *Pax Romana, International Catholic Movement for Intellectual and Cultural Affairs (ICMICA, #18267)*; *Rafto Foundation*; *Robert F Kennedy Human Rights*; *The International Movement Against All Forms of Discrimination and Racism (IMADR, #14191)*; *The Lutheran World Federation (LWF, #16532)*; *World Council of Churches (WCC, #21320).*

Affiliate members (10) include 1 organization listed in this Yearbook:

International Centre for Ethnic Studies (ICES, #12490).

IGO Relations Participant in Fundamental Rights Platform of: *European Union Agency for Fundamental Rights (FRA, #08969)*. **NGO Relations** Member of (1): *Human Rights and Democracy Network (HRDN, #10980).* [2022.10.20/XE4255/y/**E**]

♦ International Dance Council 13130

Conseil international de la danse (CID)

Gen Sec and Headquarters CID – UNESCO, 1 rue Miollis, 75732 Paris 15, France. T. +33145684953. E-mail: execsec@cid-world.org.

Pres Dora Stratou Dance Theatre, Scholiou 8, Plaka, 105 58 Athens, Greece. T. +302103244395. Fax +302103246921.

URL: http://www.cid-world.org

History 12 Nov 1973, Paris (France). Founded with the support and encouragement of UNESCO. Current statutes and rules of procedure adopted 1985. The official umbrella organization for all forms of dance in all countries of the world. Registration: France. **Aims** Protect the heritage of dance throughout the world. **Structure** General Assembly (every 2 years); Executive Committee. Based at UNESCO Headquarters, Paris (France). **Languages** English, French, German, Irish Gaelic, Italian, Russian, Spanish. **Staff** Paid; voluntary. **Finance** Sources: members' dues; subsidies. Supported by: *UNESCO (#20322)*. **Activities** Events/meetings; knowledge management/information dissemination; research/documentation; training/education. **Events** *World Congress on Dance Research* Moscow (Russia) 2021, *World Congress on Dance Research* Athens (Greece) 2020, *World Congress on Dance Research* Yerevan (Armenia) 2020, *World Congress on Dance Research* Athens (Greece) 2019, *World Congress on Dance Research* Athens (Greece) 2018. **Publications** Inventories of dance films; catalogues. CID Sections produce their own publications.

Members CID Sections (over 100); Institutional Members (over 3,000) – federations, schools, companies, associations, museums, institutes, conservatories, etc; Individuals (over 10,000) – choreographers, educators, dance historians, administrators, critics and others. Members in over 170 countries. Membership countries not specified. Included in the above, 2 organizations listed in this Yearbook:

Included in the above, 2 organizations listed in this Yearbook:

European Association of Folklore Festivals (EAFF, #06043); *World Dance Council (WDC, #21353).*

Consultative Status Consultative status granted from: *UNESCO (#20322)* (Partner Status); *World Intellectual Property Organization (WIPO, #21593)* (Permanent Observer Status). [2022.11.10/XD4418/y/**C**]

♦ International Dance Educators / Education Association / see Dance and the Child International (#04999)

♦ International Dance Organization (IDO) 13131

Exec Sec Udsigten 3, Slotsbjergby, 4200 Slagelse, Denmark. T. +4558585920. Fax +4558585677. E-mail: executive.secretary@ido-dance.com – info@ido-dance.com – president@ido-dance.com.

URL: http://www.ido-dance.com/

History 18 Sep 1981, Florence (Italy). Registration: Denmark. **Events** *Annual General Meeting* 2021, *Annual General Meeting* 2020, *Annual General Meeting* Rome (Italy) 2019, *Annual General Meeting* Chuncheon (Korea Rep) 2018, *Annual General Meeting* Athens (Greece) 2017.

Members Organizations in 67 countries and territories:

Armenia, Australia, Austria, Bangladesh, Belarus, Belgium, Bosnia-Herzegovina, Brazil, Bulgaria, Canada, China, Croatia, Cyprus, Czechia, Denmark, England, Estonia, Finland, France, Georgia, Germany, Ghana, Gibraltar, Greece, Haiti, Hong Kong, Hungary, India, Indonesia, Italy, Japan, Kazakhstan, Kenya, Korea Rep, Kyrgyzstan, Latvia, Lithuania, Macau, Mexico, Moldova, Montenegro, Netherlands, New Zealand, Nigeria, North Macedonia, Norway, Philippines, Poland, Portugal, Romania, Russia, Serbia, Sierra Leone, Singapore, Slovakia, Slovenia, South Africa, Spain, Sri Lanka, Sweden, Switzerland, Taiwan, Türkiye, Ukraine, United Arab Emirates, USA, Zimbabwe.

IGO Relations Member of (1): *Enlarged Partial Agreement on Sport (EPAS, #05487)* (Consultative Committee). **NGO Relations** Member of (2): *The Association for International Sport for All (TAFISA, #02763)*; *World DanceSport Federation (WDSF, #21354).* [2020/XF4995/**F**]

♦ International Dance Sport Association (IDSA) 13132

Pres Saksaganskogo str 7/13, Kiev, 01033, Ukraine. T. +380442392335. Fax +380442890251.

Gen Sec address not obtained.

URL: http://idsa.com.ua/

History Registration: No/ID: 2356, Start date: 14 Dec 2005, Ukraine. **Aims** Promote development of dance sport. **Structure** General Meeting; Praesidium. **Languages** English. **Staff** 3.00 FTE, paid. **Finance** Members' dues. Charity funds. No budget. **Activities** Awards/prizes/competitions; events/meetings; training/education. .

Members Continental and sub-continental federations, included in this Yearbook:

East European Dance Sport Federation (EEDSF, #05258); *European Dance Sport Federation (EDSF, #06887).*

Federations in 34 countries:

Armenia, Australia, Belarus, Bulgaria, China, Croatia, Cyprus, Czechia, Georgia, Germany, Greece, Hungary, India, Indonesia, Israel, Italy, Japan, Kazakhstan, Korea Rep, Latvia, Lithuania, Luxembourg, Moldova, Poland, Romania, Russia, Serbia, Slovakia, South Africa, Switzerland, Syrian AR, UK, Ukraine, USA.

NGO Relations Member of: *The Association for International Sport for All (TAFISA, #02763).* [2020/XJ6347/y/**C**]

♦ International Dance Sport Federation / see World DanceSport Federation (#21354)

♦ International Dance Teachers' Association (IDTA) 13133

Association internationale des professeurs de danse

Main Office International House, 76 Bennett Road, Brighton, BN2 5JL, UK. T. +441273685652. Fax +441273674388. E-mail: info@idta.co.uk.

URL: http://www.idta.co.uk/

History 1967. Founded when current title was adopted, on amalgamation of *International Dancing Masters' Association (IDMA, inactive)* and *'Dance Teachers Association'*, these two bodies also being the result of mergers of UK and international organizations including: *Empire Society of Teachers of Dancing*; *Universal Association of Teachers of Dancing*; *Professional Institute of Teachers of Dance*, set up 1903, London (UK). **Aims** Promote and foster the art of dancing in all its forms and uphold the highest ideals of the dance profession; improve and further the technical and general knowledge of members; disseminate information on the conduct of classes, delivery of lectures and other advice beneficial to members in discharging their *profession*; advise government departments, local authorities, education establishments and other interested organizations on all matters relating to the activities in dance performance, training and education of members. **Structure** Board of Directors of 20. Sub-committees of specialists (7): Ballroom Dancing; Freestyle; Latin Dancing; Modern Dance; Sequence Dancing; Tap Dance; Theatre Dance. **Activities** Sporting activities; certification/accreditation; events/meetings; knowledge management/information dissemination. **Events** *Congress and AGM* Blackpool (UK) 2022, *Congress* Blackpool (UK) 1993, *Congress* London (UK) 1993, *Seminar* Leicester (UK) 1992, *Congress* Blackpool (UK) 1991. **Publications** *Dance Teacher* (12 a year) – magazine; *Dancing Year Book* (annual).

Members Individuals in 46 countries:

Australia, Austria, Barbados, Belgium, Canada, China, Croatia, Cyprus, Denmark, Estonia, Finland, France, Germany, Greece, Hungary, Iceland, India, Israel, Italy, Japan, Kenya, Korea Rep, Luxembourg, Malaysia, Malta, Morocco, Nepal, Netherlands, New Zealand, Norway, Poland, Portugal, Russia, Singapore, South Africa, Spain, Sri Lanka, Sudan, Sweden, Switzerland, Taiwan, Thailand, Trinidad-Tobago, UK, United Arab Emirates, USA. [2022/XD2222/v/**F**]

♦ International Dangerous Goods and Containers Association (internationally oriented national body)

♦ International Danube Neurology Association of Central and East Europe 13134

Gen Sec Univ of Szeged, Dept of Neurology, Semmelweis u 6, Szeged 6725, Hungary. T. +3662545348. Fax +3662545597.

URL: http://www.danubeneurology.eu/

History Founded following several symposia organized since 1962. Original title of *International Danube Symposium for Neurological Sciences and Continuing Education*, adopted 1994, combined – for historical reasons – with the title of *Central and East-European Association for Neurology (CEEAN)*. Present name adopted during 36th symposium in 2004, Sofia (Bulgaria). **Aims** Foster and coordinate fellowship programmes for young neurologists from Danube countries. **Structure** Board. **Languages** English. **Staff** 0.50 FTE, paid; 1.00 FTE, voluntary. **Finance** Proceeds from symposia, meetings, teaching courses, etc. **Activities** Events/meetings; networking/liaising; training/education. **Events** *Symposium* Bucharest (Romania) 2019, *Symposium* Debrecen (Hungary) 2018, *Symposium* Budapest (Hungary) 2017, *Symposium* Ljubljana (Slovenia) 2016, *Symposium* Düsseldorf (Germany) 2015. **Publications** *Danube Neurology Newsletter* (annual). Calendar of events.

Members Full in 31 countries:

Austria, Belgium, Bosnia-Herzegovina, Bulgaria, China, Croatia, Czechia, Denmark, France, Germany, Greece, Hungary, Ireland, Israel, Italy, Lithuania, Netherlands, North Macedonia, Norway, Poland, Portugal, Romania, Russia, Serbia, Slovakia, Slovenia, Spain, Sweden, Switzerland, UK, Ukraine. [2018.07.25/XS0299/**D**]

♦ International Danube Symposium for Neurological Sciences and Continuing Education / see International Danube Neurology Association of Central and East Europe (#13134)
♦ International Dark-Sky Association (internationally oriented national body)

♦ International DART 18 Association (IDA) 13135

Pres address not obtained.

URL: https://dart18class.com/

History Around 1970, as *International Dart Association – Association internationale de dart.* **Aims** Promote international dart and catamaran *yacht competitions*. **Structure** Each country has its own country organization, which are coordinated by IDA. **Languages** English. **Staff** All voluntary. **Finance** Members' dues (annual), based on number of active members per country. Country members plan their own budgets. **Activities** Coordinates and supports organization of European and World Championships. **Publications** Most member countries have their own booklets.

Members National organizations in 12 countries and territories:

Aruba, Austria, Canada, France, Germany, Ireland, Italy, Netherlands, Portugal, South Africa, Switzerland, UK. [2017/XD9412/**D**]

♦ International Dart 18 Class Association (see: #21760)
♦ International Dart Association / see International DART 18 Association (#13135)
♦ International Dart Players Association (internationally oriented national body)

♦ International Database Engineering and Applications Symposium (meeting series)

♦ International Database on Longevity (IDL) 13136

Contact c/o Max Planck Inst for Demographic Research, Konrad-Zuse-Strasse 1, 18057 Rostock, Germany. E-mail: info@demogr.mpg.de.
URL: http://www.supercentenarians.org/

History Jun 2000, Rostock (Germany), by institutes in France and Germany. **Aims** Draw up mortality statistics beyond age 110 so as to estimate mortality trajectories at extreme ages. **Structure** Executive Scientific Committee; Advisory Board. **Activities** Organizes workshops. [2019.10.24/XJ4309/F]

♦ International Data Centre on Hydrology of Lakes and Reservoirs (HYDROLARE) 13137

Contact State Hydrological Institute, 2nd Line – 23, St Petersburg SANKT-PETERBURG, Russia, 199053. T. +78123233458. Fax +73231028. E-mail: idc@hydrolare.net.
URL: http://hydrolare.net/

History 2009. Set up under the auspices of *World Meteorological Organization (WMO, #21649)*, in accordance with Agreement between the Russian Service for Hydrometeorology and Environmental Monitoring (ROSHYDROMET) and WMO, signed 5 May 2008, Geneva (Switzerland). **Aims** Establish, develop and regularly update an international database on hydrological regime of lakes and reservoirs, so as to: stimulate development of the global monitoring system of lakes and reservoirs for rational use, preservation and management of their water recourses; improve knowledge of lateral fluxes transformation within lakes and reservoirs; supply data for scientific and education purposes, modelling, development of different global and regional project/programmes. **Structure** International Steering Committee, with representatives from *World Meteorological Organization (WMO, #21649), Global Terrestrial Network – Hydrology (GTN-H, #10624)*, SHI, *International Lake Environment Committee Foundation (ILEC, #13998), Global Runoff Data Centre (GRDC, #10584)* and LEGOS/CNES. **Languages** English, Russian. **Staff** 4.00 FTE, paid. **Finance** Annual budget: about US$ 50,000. **Activities** Events/meetings; knowledge management/information dissemination; publishing activities; research/documentation. **Publications** *HYDROLARE Newsletter* (annual).
[2023.02.19/XM6003/E*]

♦ International Data Exchange Association (inactive)

♦ International Data Links Society (IDLSoc) 13138

Communication Sec The Dyers Bldg, 21 Silver Street, Ilminster, Ilminster, TA19 9DD, UK. T. +441460298090. E-mail: secretariat@idlsoc.com – communication_secretary@idlsoc.com.
URL: http://www.idlsoc.com/

History Founded Jan 2004. **Aims** Bring together and facilitate a network of international professionals in the Data links community; promote increased use and higher quality of standards; become a key liaison with corporate, government, military, research, educational and other organizations concerned with civil and military data links. **Structure** Board of Directors; General Committee; Events Committee; Technical Committee. Active Chapters (3): Australia/new Zealand; Sweden, USA. **Languages** English. **Activities** Events/meetings. **Events** *Annual Symposium* Abu Dhabi (United Arab Emirates) 2017, *Annual Symposium* Maastricht (Netherlands) 2016, *Annual Symposium* Ottawa, ON (Canada) 2015, *Annual Symposium* Berlin (Germany) 2014, *Annual Symposium* Norfolk, VA (USA) 2013. **Publications** *IDLSoc Newsletter* (12 a year). Guides.
Members Members in 34 countries and territories:
Australia, Austria, Belgium, Canada, Chile, Czechia, Denmark, Estonia, Finland, France, Germany, Greece, Hungary, Italy, Japan, Korea Rep, Netherlands, New Zealand, Norway, Oman, Poland, Portugal, Saudi Arabia, Singapore, South Africa, Spain, Sweden, Switzerland, Taiwan, Thailand, Türkiye, UK, United Arab Emirates, USA. [2016.12.15/XM0749/D]

♦ International Data Spaces Association (IDSA) 13139

CEO Emil-Figge-Str 80, 44227 Dortmund, Germany. T. +4923170096501. E-mail: info@internationaldataspaces.org.
Legal Office Fraunhofer FORUM Berlin, Anna-Louisa-Karsch-Str 2, 10178 Berlin, Germany.
URL: https://internationaldataspaces.org/

History Registration: Berlin District court Berlin, No/ID: VR 34791, Start date: 2 Mar 2016, Germany, Charlottenburg; EU Transparency Register, No/ID: 486403441916-47, Start date: 22 Mar 2021. **Aims** Develop and establish a global standard for data spaces and sovereign data sharing; fosters related technologies and business models that will drive the data economy of the future across industries. **Structure** Board. **Activities** Advocacy/lobbying/activism; knowledge management/information dissemination; networking/liaising; training/education. **Members** Over 140 organizations in 22 countries. Membership countries not specified.
[2022.10.18/AA1488/D]

♦ International Day of the African Childhood / see International Day of the African Child and Youth (#13140)

♦ International Day of the African Child and Youth (IDAY) 13140

SG Rue des Jambes 19, 1420 Braine-l'Alleud, Belgium. T. +3223854413. E-mail: info@iday.org.
URL: http://www.iday.org/

History 2005. Former names and other names: *International Day of the African Childhood (IDAY)* – former; *Journée internationale de l'enfance africaine* – former; *Dia internacional de la Criancia Africana* – former; *Internationaler Tag der Afrikanischen Kindheit* – former; *Internationale Dag van de Afrikaanse Jeugd* – former; *Journée internationale de l'enfance et la jeunesse africaine* – former; *Dia internacional del Infante y Yuventud Africanas* – former; *Internationaler Tag der Afrikanischen Kindheit und Jugd* – former; *Internationale Dag van het Kind en de Jeugd van Afrika* – former; *IDAY International* – legal name. Registration: Banque-Carrefour des Entreprises, No/ID: 0895.443.325, Start date: 16 Jan 2008, Belgium; EU Transparency Register, No/ID: 089115517868-76, Start date: 17 Jun 2015. **Aims** Support action by African civil society to promote basic *education* for all in Africa and, in particular, the achievement of the 6 objectives of Education for All in the wider context of the Second Millennium Development Goal. **Structure** General Assembly (annual); Board of Directors; Management Committee; Honorary Committee. **Languages** English, French. **Staff** 2.60 FTE, paid; 1.20 FTE, voluntary. **Finance** Sources: members' dues; private foundations; revenue from activities/projects; sponsorship; subsidies. **Activities** Advocacy/lobbying/activism; awareness raising; events/meetings; financial and/or material support. **Events** *Overcoming the main obstacles to quality basic education for all in Africa* Brussels (Belgium) 2013, *Conference* Brussels (Belgium) 2012, *Conference* Brussels (Belgium) 2011. **Publications** *IDAY Newsletter* (4 a year). Annual Report; position papers; thematic monographs.
Members National coalitions of civil society organizations in 22 countries:
Benin, Burkina Faso, Burundi, Cameroon, Congo Brazzaville, Congo DR, Côte d'Ivoire, Gabon, Ghana, Guinea, Kenya, Liberia, Mali, Mauritania, Nigeria, Rwanda, Senegal, Tanzania UR, Togo, Uganda, Zambia.
IGO Relations Cooperates with (1): *Global Partnership for Social Accountability (GPSA, #10541)*. **NGO Relations** Member of (3): *Belgian Platform for Education and Development (Educaid.be)*; *Fédération des Associations de Solidarité Internationale (FASI)*; *Global Campaign for Education (GCE, #10264)*. Also links with national organizations and universities. [2022.02.10/XJ0334/F]

♦ International DB2 Users Group (IDUG) 13141

Main Office UPS6756, #154, 4403 Oleander Dr, Ste C, Wilmington NC 28403, USA. E-mail: idug@idug.org.
URL: http://www.idug.org/

History 1988. **Aims** Support and strengthen the *information systems* community by providing quality education and services designed to promote the effective utilization of the DB2 family of products. **Structure** Board of Directors; Conference Planning Committees. **Staff** 1.00 FTE, paid. **Finance** Revenues from conferences. Budget (annual): about US$ 2 million. **Events** *North America Db2 Tech Conference* Boston, MA (USA) 2022, *EMEA Db2 Tech Conference* Edinburgh (UK) 2022, *EMEA Conference* Edinburgh (UK) 2021, *EMEA Conference* 2020, *EMEA Conference* Rotterdam (Netherlands) 2019. **Publications** *IDUG eBulletin* (12 a year). Conference proceedings; videos. **Members** About 16,000 members (mostly in USA) in over 80 countries. Membership countries not specified. [2021/XE1879/E]

♦ International Deaf Academics and Researchers Conference (meeting series)
♦ International Deaf Basketball Association / see Deaf International Basketball Federation (#05017)
♦ International Deaf Children's Society / see Deaf Child Worldwide
♦ International Deaf Emergency (internationally oriented national body)
♦ International Deaf Rugby Organization (no recent information)

♦ International Debate Education Association (IDEA) 13142

Exec Dir – IDEA Netherlands Mariahoek 16-17, 3511 LG Utrecht, Netherlands. T. +31634919800. E-mail: info@idebate.nl.
Contact IDEA United Kingdom, Suite 14, Collaboration House, 77-79 Charlotte Street, London, W1T 4PW, UK. E-mail: ahelling@idebate.org.uk.
URL: http://idebate.org/

History 1999, Netherlands. Registration: Netherlands. **Aims** Give young people a voice through education, debate and by raising their awareness about worldwide issues. **Structure** General Assembly (annual); Board of Directors.
Members Organizations in 21 countries:
Albania, Bosnia-Herzegovina, Croatia, Czechia, Estonia, Georgia, Greece, Haiti, Hungary, Italy, Latvia, Lithuania, Netherlands, North Macedonia, Poland, Romania, Serbia, Slovakia, Slovenia, Spain, Ukraine.
NGO Relations IDEA Netherlands is member of: *European Youth Forum (#09140)*. [2021/XD8861/D]

♦ International Declaration on Human Genetic Data (2003 treaty)
♦ International Declaration Prohibiting the Discharge of Projectiles and Explosives from Balloons (1907 treaty)

♦ International Deep Drawing Research Group (IDDRG) 13143

Groupement international de recherches sur l'emboutissage – Internationale Forschungsgruppe für Tiefziehen

SG Jupitervägen 5, SE-291 70 Kristianstad, Sweden. T. +46732704867.
URL: http://www.iddrg.com/

History 20 Mar 1957, Amsterdam (Netherlands). **Aims** Promote cooperation in development of research on deep drawing and pressing of sheet *metals*. **Structure** Executive Committee; Officers: President, Secretary-General, Treasurer. **Languages** English. **Finance** Events are self-supporting. Annual budget: 1,400 EUR. **Activities** Events/meetings. **Events** *Annual Conference* Lorient (France) 2022, *Annual Conference* Stuttgart (Germany) 2021, *Annual Conference* Seoul (Korea Rep) 2020, *Annual Conference* Enschede (Netherlands) 2019, *Annual Conference* Waterloo, ON (Canada) 2018. **Publications** Conference proceedings.
Members National groups in 29 countries:
Australia, Austria, Belgium, Brazil, Canada, China, Cuba, Czechia, Denmark, Finland, France, Germany, Hungary, India, Italy, Japan, Korea Rep, Luxembourg, Netherlands, Norway, Portugal, Slovakia, Slovenia, South Africa, Spain, Sweden, Switzerland, UK, USA. [2022.06.14/XC1786/F]

♦ International Defence Economics Association (inactive)
♦ International Defense Equipment Exhibitors Association (internationally oriented national body)

♦ International Delegates on Filtration (INDEFI) 13144

Chairman address not obtained.
URL: https://www.wfc13.com

History 1990. Founded as an umbrella body to coordinate and widen the competition to organize *World Filtration Congress*. Former names and other names: *International Delegation on Filtration (INDEFI)* – alias.
Members Filtration societies in 11 countries and territories:
Austria, China, France, Germany, Hungary, India, Japan, Korea Rep, Taiwan, UK, USA.
Included in the above, 1 organization listed in this Yearbook:
Nordic Filtration Society (NoFS, #17289). [2021.09.01/XM2208/F]

♦ International Delegation on Filtration / see International Delegates on Filtration (#13144)

♦ International Delphic Committee 13145

Contact address not obtained. T. +74956515400. E-mail: mail@idcworld.org.
URL: http://delphic.world/

History Registered in accordance with Russian law, 2003. **Aims** Hold the Delphic *Games*; popularize and develop the International Delphic Movement; search and support *young* talent; promote and develop common values by means of art, preservation of world cultural heritage and cultural upbringing of the young generation. **Structure** Board.
Members Members and Observers in 65 countries:
Argentina, Armenia, Australia, Austria, Azerbaijan, Bangladesh, Belarus, Benin, Brazil, Bulgaria, Cameroon, Chad, China, Colombia, Côte d'Ivoire, Cyprus, Denmark, Dominica, Ecuador, Egypt, Estonia, Ethiopia, Finland, France, Georgia, Germany, Ghana, Greece, Guinea-Bissau, Haiti, India, Iran Islamic Rep, Italy, Japan, Kazakhstan, Korea DPR, Korea Rep, Kyrgyzstan, Latvia, Lithuania, Maldives, Moldova, Mongolia, Netherlands, Nigeria, Palestine, Peru, Poland, Romania, Russia, Seychelles, Singapore, Slovakia, South Africa, Sri Lanka, Sweden, Tajikistan, Thailand, Togo, Türkiye, UK, Ukraine, USA, Uzbekistan, Vietnam. [2017/XM5916/E]

♦ International Delphic Council (IDC) 13146

Internationaler Delphischer Rat

SG Berliner Str 19-A, 13189 Berlin, Germany. T. +493047300171. Fax +493047300173. E-mail: mail@delphic.org.
URL: http://www.delphic.org/

History 15 Dec 1994, Berlin (Germany). Founding Congress attended by representatives of 20 countries, by *Musica Magna International (MMI, inactive)* and J Christian B Kirsch, 100 years after the re-introduction of the Olympic Games. Registration: No/ID: 15533 Nz, Germany. **Aims** Reintroduce the Delphic Games and introduce the *Youth* Delphic *Games* and Delphiads. **Structure** General Assembly (every 2 years, after the Games); Amphictyony (Executive Board); Commissions (4). **Languages** English, German, Irish Gaelic. **Staff** 4.00 FTE, paid; 6.00 FTE, voluntary. **Finance** Sources: private and public donations; contributions of the NDCs. **Activities** Sporting activities. **Events** *Junior Delphic Games* Port Elizabeth (South Africa) 2011, *Delphic Games (adult)* Jeju (Korea Rep) 2009, *Delphic Congress* Seoul (Korea Rep) / Jeju (Korea Rep) 2009, *Delphic Congress* Jeju (Korea Rep) 2008, *Delphic Congress* Baguio (Philippines) 2007. **Publications** *Delphi Newsletter* (4 a year).
Members National; Regional; Individual. Members in 12 countries:
Albania, China, Georgia, Germany, India, Korea Rep, Malaysia, Philippines, Poland, Russia, South Africa, USA.
[2022.02.06/XF3346/E]

♦ International Democratic Education Conference (meeting series)
♦ International Democratic Education Network (unconfirmed)

♦ International Democrat Union (IDU) 13147

Union démocratique internationale (UDI) – Internationale Demokratische Union

SG CSU-Landesleitung, Franz Josef Strauß Haus, Mies-van-der-Rohe-Str 1, 80807 Munich, Germany. T. +49891243301. E-mail: secretariat@idu.org.
URL: http://www.idu.org/

History Founded 24 Jun 1983, London (UK), at a conference hosted by the then Prime Minister Margaret Thatcher and the UK Conservative Party, as an umbrella organization for *European Democrat Union (EDU, inactive)* and *Asia Pacific Democrat Union (APDU, #01881)*. Currently also includes: *Democrat Union of Africa (DUA, #05036)*; *Caribbean Democrat Union (CDU, #03489)*, set up Jan 1986; *Union of Latin American Parties (UPLA, #20448)*; *European People's Party (EPP, #08185)*; *International Young Democrat Union (IYDU, #15928)*. **Aims** Promote a free, open and democratic society, the free market economy, the rule of law, social justice, the role of the family and a society where conditions are created to enable everyone to reach their full potential and carry out their responsibilities to their fellow men and women; foster the common philosophy of member parties; establish permanent relations at a bilateral and multilateral level and encourage mutual support; provide a forum for the exchange of views and information on matters of interest to all or a considerable number of member parties. **Structure** Party Leaders Conference (every 3 years). Executive Committee (meets twice a year). Standing Committees; Ad Hoc Groups (Committees). Officers: Chairman; Deputy Chairman; Vice-Chairmen (currently 16); Treasurer(s) (currently 1); Assistant Chairmen (currently 2); Executive Secretary; Chairmen of Standing Committee on Foreign Affairs (SCFA) and *International Young Democrat Union (IYDU, #15928)*. **Languages** English. **Staff** Paid. **Finance** Members' dues, calculated on the basis of the number of votes each received in their previous national election. **Activities** Undertakes fact-finding missions, for example to: Central America; South Africa. SCFA develops internal reports on specific international questions, providing the basis for public communiqués and for recommendations to the leadership of member parties. Occasional Ad Hoc Groups monitor important national elections and prepare for future work. **Events** *Executive Committee Meeting* Munich (Germany) 2021, *Executive Committee Meeting* Munich (Germany) 2020, *Executive Committee Meeting* Santiago (Chile) 2019, *Executive Committee Meeting* Marrakech (Morocco) 2015, *Party Leaders' Conference* Seoul (Korea Rep) 2014.

Members Conservative, Centre and like-minded parties (63) in 56 countries and territories:
Albania, Australia, Austria, Azerbaijan, Belarus (2), Bolivia, Bosnia-Herzegovina, Brazil, Bulgaria, Canada, Chile (2), China, Colombia, Croatia, Cuba, Cyprus, Czechia, Denmark, Dominican Rep, Ecuador, El Salvador, Estonia, Finland, France, Georgia (3), Germany (2), Ghana, Greece, Guatemala, Honduras, Hungary, Iceland, Korea Rep, Lithuania, Maldives, Malta, Mongolia, Mozambique, Namibia, New Zealand, Nicaragua, North Macedonia, Norway, Panama, Peru, Portugal, Serbia (2), Slovenia, Spain, Sri Lanka, Sweden, Tanzania UR, Uganda, UK, USA, Venezuela. [2020/XD8078/**C**]

♦ International Dendrimer Symposium (meeting series)

♦ International Dendrology Society (IDS) 13148

Union internationale de dendrologie

Sec Hergest Estate Office, Kington, HR5 3EG, UK. T. +441544232045. E-mail: ids@hergest.co.uk.
URL: http://www.dendrology.org/

History 7 May 1952, Brussels (Belgium). Former names and other names: *International Dendrology Union* – former (1952 to 1965). Registration: Charity Commission, No/ID: 1178252, Start date: 2018, UK, England and Wales. **Aims** Promote study and enjoyment of *trees*, woody *plants* and *shrubs*; conserve and protect those that are rare and endangered. **Structure** General Meeting (annual); Council; Trustees. **Languages** English. **Staff** 1.00 FTE, paid. **Finance** Sources: donations; revenue from activities/projects; subscriptions. **Activities** Events/meetings; publishing activities. **Publications** Yearbook.
Members Full in 49 countries and territories:
Argentina, Australia, Austria, Belgium, Bhutan, Canada, Chile, China, Colombia, Czechia, Denmark, Estonia, Finland, France, Germany, Ghana, Greece, Hong Kong, Iceland, Ireland, Israel, Italy, Japan, Kenya, Latvia, Lithuania, Luxembourg, Madagascar, Mexico, Morocco, Netherlands, New Zealand, Norway, Poland, Portugal, Russia, Singapore, Slovakia, Slovenia, South Africa, Spain, Sweden, Switzerland, Taiwan, Türkiye, UK, Uruguay, USA, Venezuela. [2021.09.01/XD1303/**C**]

♦ International Dendrology Union / see International Dendrology Society (#13148)

♦ International Dental Ethics and Law Society (IDEALS) 13149

Pres UWC Dentistry, Robert Sobukwe Road, Bellville, 7535, South Africa.
URL: http://www.ideals.ac/

History Dec 2000. Registered in accordance with Belgian law. **Aims** Foster an international dialogue on the values guiding the practice of oral health care and dental ethical codes. **Structure** General Assembly. Board of up to 15 members, including President, President-elect, Secretary, Assistant Secretary/Treasurer and Treasurer. **Languages** English. **Staff** All voluntary except for part-time, paid webmaster and paid staff during biannual congress. **Finance** Members' dues. Congress registration fees. **Events** *Biennial Congress* Chicago, IL (USA) 2016, *Biennial congress* Helsinki (Finland) 2010, *Biennial congress* Toronto, ON (Canada) 2007, *Biennial Congress* Florence (Italy) 2005, *Biennial Congress* Omaha, NE (USA) 2003. **Publications** *On-Line Bulletin* (2 a year). Congress proceedings.
Members in 22 countries:
Australia, Belgium, Canada, Croatia, Denmark, Fiji, Finland, Greece, Ireland, Italy, Japan, Latvia, Netherlands, Norway, Philippines, Portugal, Spain, Sweden, Switzerland, Türkiye, UK, USA. [2016/XM0054/**D**]

♦ International Dental Federation / see FDI – World Dental Federation (#09281)
♦ International Dental Hygienists' Federation / see International Federation of Dental Hygienists (#13405)
♦ International Dental Manufacturers / see Association of International Dental Manufacturers (#02661)
♦ International Dental Relief (inactive)

♦ International Dermato-Epidemiology Association (IDEA) 13150

Pres Emory Clinic 'A', 1365-A Clifton Rd NE, Atlanta GA 30322, USA.

History 1996. **Aims** Serve as an international forum on epidemiology and health services research; promote and encourage epidemiologic and health services research related to cutaneous disorders; facilitate education in epidemiology and health services research. **Structure** Board of Directors, comprising President, Secretary, Treasure and 3 further members. Committees (2): Membership; Nominating. **Finance** Members' dues. **Events** *International Congress on Dermato-Epidemiology* Rotterdam (Netherlands) 2022, *International Congress on Dermato-Epidemiology* Denver, CO (USA) 2019, *Meeting* Berlin (Germany) 2018, *International Congress on Dermato-Epidemiology* Malmö (Sweden) 2012, *International Congress on Dermato-Epidemiology* Nottingham (UK) 2008. **Publications** *IDEA Newsletter*. **NGO Relations** *European Dermato-Epidemiology Network (EDEN, #06906)*. [2012/XD8182/**D**]

♦ International Dermatology Nursing Group / see International Skin-Care Nursing Group (#14872)

♦ International Dermoscopy Society (IDS) 13151

Internationale Gesellschaft für Ausflichtmikroskopie

Treas Division of Dermatology, Medical Univ of Graz, Auerbruggerplatz 8, 8036 Graz, Austria. T. +433163852423. Fax +433163852466. E-mail: communication@dermoscopy-ids.org.
URL: http://www.dermoscopy-ids.org/

History 17 Nov 2003, Graz (Austria). **Aims** Expand the use of dermoscopy worldwide; promote clinical research in dermoscopy; improve education in dermoscopy. **Structure** General Assembly (every 3 years); Board of Directors; Arbitration Board. **Languages** English. **Staff** 10.00 FTE, voluntary. **Finance** Sources: members' dues. **Activities** Advocacy/lobbying/activism; training/education. **Events** *World Congress of Dermoscopy* Graz (Austria) 2021, *Triennial Congress* Thessaloniki (Greece) 2018, *Triennial Congress* Vienna (Austria) 2015, *Triennial congress / World Congress* Brisbane, QLD (Australia) 2012, *Annual Meeting* Miami, FL (USA) 2010. **Publications** *Dermatology* – offical publication; *IDS Newsletter* – online; *The Case of the Month* – online. **Members** Individuals (6,579) in 124 countries. Membership countries not specified.
[2022.10.20/XM0219/**D**]

♦ International Desalination Association (IDA) 13152

SG PO Box 387, Topsfield MA 01983, USA. T. +19787740959. E-mail: info@idadesal.org.
URL: http://www.idadesal.org/

History 1984. Founded on merger of the former *International Desalination and Environmental Association (IDEA, inactive)*, set up 1971, with *Water Supply Improvement Association (WSIA)*. Registration: 501(c)(6) organization, No/ID: EIN: 22-2099951, Start date: 1981, USA, State of Massachusettes. **Aims** Promote use of desalination to increase availability of potable *water*; serve the interests of and promote communication among desalting plant owners and operators, suppliers and consumers; monitor progress in the field; work for the development of regional and international specifications and standards; assist in monitoring of thermal and chemical *pollution* and environmentally/ ecologically compatible control of discharges. **Structure** Board of Directors (meets twice a year); Officers: President, First and Second Vice-Presidents, Treasurer, Secretary, Editor, Secretary-General, Comptroller; Standing Committees (9); Special Committees (8). **Languages** English. **Staff** 2.00 FTE, paid. Numerous independent contractors. **Finance** Sources: fees for services; meeting proceeds; members' dues; revenue from activities/projects. **Activities** Awards/prizes/competitions; events/meetings; training/education. **Events** *IDA Water Reuse and Recycling Conference (IDA WRR)* Seville (Spain) 2023, *IDA-SWCC DTRI International Specialty Conference on Innovation in Desalination* Jeddah (Saudi Arabia) 2022, *IDA-SWCC DTRI Ocean Brine Mining for Desalination Conference* Khobar (Saudi Arabia) 2022, *World Congress* Sydney, NSW (Australia) 2022, *World Congress* Sydney, NSW (Australia) 2021. **Publications** *IDA Global Connections* (6 a year). *ABC's of Desalting*; *Desalination by Questions and Answers*; *IDA Water Security Handbook*. Books; white papers; proceedings.
Members Individuals and corporate bodies in 56 countries and territories:
Algeria, Australia, Austria, Bahamas, Bahrain, Barbados, Belgium, Belize, Bermuda, Canada, Cape Verde, Chile, Cyprus, Denmark, Egypt, Finland, France, Germany, Greece, Hong Kong, Iceland, India, Indonesia, Iraq, Israel, Italy, Japan, Jordan, Kenya, Korea Rep, Kuwait, Lebanon, Malaysia, Malta, Mexico, Morocco, Netherlands, New Zealand, Oman, Pakistan, Puerto Rico, Qatar, Russia, Saudi Arabia, Singapore, South Africa, Sweden, Switzerland, Taiwan, Tunisia, UK, United Arab Emirates, USA, Venezuela, Yemen, Zimbabwe.
Affiliate organizations (8), including 3 listed in this Yearbook:
Caribbean Desalination Association (CaribDA, #03491); *European Desalination Society (EDS, #06908)*; *Water Science and Technology Association (WSTA, #20838)*.
Association Affiliate members (8), including 1 organization listed in this Yearbook:
Asia Pacific Desalination Association (APDA, #01883).
Consultative Status Consultative status granted from: *ECOSOC (#05331)* (Ros A). **IGO Relations** Accredited by (1): *United Nations Office at Vienna (UNOV, #20604)*. Associated with Department of Global Communications of the United Nations. **NGO Relations** Member of (2): *Global Clean Water Desalination Alliance (GCWDA, #10285)*; *World Water Council (WWC, #21908)*. [2021.09.07/XD8426/**C**]

♦ International Desalination and Environmental Association (inactive)

♦ International Deserters' Network 13153

Contact Connection e V, Von-Behring-Str 110, 63075 Offenbach, Germany. T. +496982375534. Fax +496982375535. E-mail: office@connection-ev.org.
URL: https://en.connection-ev.org/

History 1994. Founded by Connection eV. **Aims** Support deserters from *war* regions; demand open frontiers and the right to *asylum* for deserters. **Structure** Working Groups. **Languages** English, German. **Activities** Guidance/assistance/consulting. **Events** *Meeting* 1996, *Meeting* 1995.
Members National organizations in 21 countries:
Angola, Austria, Belarus, Belgium, Canada, Colombia, Egypt, Eritrea, France, Germany, Israel, Korea Rep, Russia, Serbia, South Africa, Switzerland, Turkey, Türkiye, UK, Ukraine, USA.
International organization (3), listed in this Yearbook:
European Bureau for Conscientious Objection (EBCO, #06411); *International Fellowship of Reconciliation (IFOR, #13586)*; *War Resisters' International (WRI, #20818)*. [2022.10.19/XF3108/y/**F**]

♦ International Design Center, Berlin (internationally oriented national body)
♦ International Design Centre, Nagoya (internationally oriented national body)
♦ International Destination Management Association (inactive)

♦ International Detention Coalition (IDC) 13154

Dir The Hub, Level 2, Bourke Street 696, Melbourne VIC 3000, Australia. E-mail: info@idcoalition.org.
Admin Dir address not obtained.
URL: http://idcoalition.org/

History Formally launched Jun 2006. Registration: Start date: Mar 2009, Australia, Melbourne VIC. **Aims** Advocate to secure the human rights of people impacted by, and at-risk of, immigration detention. **Structure** Committee; International Advisory Committee; Director and Staff. **Staff** 15.00 FTE, paid; 5.00 FTE, voluntary. **Activities** Advocacy/lobbying/activism; capacity building; networking/liaising; research/documentation.
Members Organizations, groups, individuals and representatives of communities impacted by immigration detention. Members (over 400) in 91 countries and territories:
Australia, Austria, Bangladesh, Belgium, Belize, Botswana, Brazil, Bulgaria, Cameroon, Canada, Costa Rica, Croatia, Cyprus, Czechia, Denmark, Dominican Rep, Ecuador, Egypt, El Salvador, Estonia, Finland, France, Gambia, Germany, Ghana, Greece, Guatemala, Guinea, Honduras, Hong Kong, Hungary, India, Indonesia, Ireland, Israel, Italy, Japan, Jordan, Kenya, Korea Rep, Kosovo, Kuwait, Latvia, Lebanon, Libya, Luxembourg, Malawi, Malaysia, Malta, Mauritania, Mexico, Morocco, Mozambique, Nepal, Netherlands, New Zealand, Nicaragua, Nigeria, North Macedonia, Norway, Pakistan, Palestine, Panama, Peru, Poland, Romania, Saudi Arabia, Serbia, Sierra Leone, Slovakia, Slovenia, South Africa, Spain, Sri Lanka, Sweden, Switzerland, Syrian AR, Taiwan, Tanzania UR, Thailand, Trinidad, Tunisia, Türkiye, Uganda, UK, Ukraine, USA, Venezuela, Yemen, Zambia, Zimbabwe.
Consultative Status Consultative status granted from: *ECOSOC (#05331)* (Special); *Council of Europe (CE, #04881)* (Participatory Status). **NGO Relations** Member of (2): *European NGO Platform Asylum and Migration (EPAM, #08051)*; *International Council of Voluntary Agencies (ICVA, #13092)*. [2022.02.03/XJ8889/y/**C**]

♦ International Developmental Pediatrics Association (unconfirmed)

♦ International Development Association (IDA) 13155

Association internationale de développement (AID) – Asociación Internacional de Fomento (AIF)

Secretariat c/o World Bank, 1818 H St NW, Washington DC 20433, USA. T. +12024771234. Fax +12024776391.
European Office 66 av d'Iéna, 75116 Paris, France. T. +33140693000.
URL: http://www.worldbank.org/ida/

History 24 Sep 1960, Washington DC (USA), being affiliated to the *International Bank for Reconstruction and Development (IBRD, #12317)* and together with the IBRD comprising *World Bank – Banque mondiale – Banco Mundial* – although this title is sometimes used to refer to the IBRD alone. Commenced operations Nov 1960. Together with IBRD and its other affiliates, *International Finance Corporation (IFC, #13597)* and *Multilateral Investment Guarantee Agency (MIGA, #16888)*, comprises *The World Bank Group (#21218)*; through the Group is a specialized agency of *United Nations (UN, #20515)*, within *United Nations System (#20635)* and linked to *ECOSOC (#05331)*. World Bank organizations are part of what are often referred to as *Bretton Woods Institutions (BWIs, #03322)*. **Aims** Reduce *poverty* in the poorest countries and promote *sustainable* economic development, labour-intensive growth and environmental sustainability by providing finance on terms more flexible and bearing less heavily on the balance of payments of recipient countries than those of conventional *loans*, thereby supplementing the World Bank's activities. **Structure** Although a separate legal entity with its own financial resources, IDA has the same Board of Governors and the same Executive Directors representing countries that are members of both IBRD and IDA. The President of the Bank is ex-officio President of IDA and the officers and staff of the Bank also serve IDA. **Languages** English. **Staff** Although legally separate, shares IBRD staff and facilities. Staff negotiations through *World Bank Group Staff Association (#21219)*. **Finance** Unlike the IBRD, IDA cannot rise funds in capital markets. Donor nations replenish resources. Initial subscriptions of all members are in proportion to their subscription to the capital stock of the Bank. However, under the Articles of Agreement, member countries are divided into two groups: Part I and Part II. Part I countries pay their entire subscription in convertible currency, all of which may be used by IDA for lending; Part II countries pay only 10% in convertible form and the remainder in their own currency, which may not be used by IDA without the member's consent. Only countries with annual per capita income of less than US$ 940 may borrow from IDA. Most of IDA's loans are provided to countries with annual per capita income of US$ 805 or less. Initial subscriptions to IDA have totalled about US$ 1,227 million of which US$ 900 million in convertible currencies. In 1964, the then 18 Part I (wealthier) countries agreed to a replenishment of IDA's resources by about US$ 750 million. Subsequent replenishments have covered 3-year periods. Additionally, the World Bank transferred to IDA approximately US$ 2,500 million during the period 1964-1987. The 13th replenishment commenced on 30 Jun 2002, making possible a commitment of about SDR 18,000 million (US$ 23,000 million) of which about SDR 10,000 million (US$ 13,000 million) from new donor contributions. There are currently 41 donor countries, including developing and transition countries, some donors being IBRD and former IDA borrowers. Figures for 2002: total net resources available for development activities – US$ 23,393 million; total development credits – US$ 118,882 million; total lending commitments – US$ 8,068 million.
Activities Of the US$ 8,100 million lent by IDA in fiscal year 2002, regional distribution was as follows: Sub-Saharan Africa – 47%; South Asia – 32%; East Asia and Pacific – 10%; Europe and Central Asia – 8%; Latin America and the Caribbean – 2%; Middle East and North Africa – 1%. For 2002, lending was aimed at the following sectors: Law, justice and public administration – 20%; Energy and mining – 16%; Health and other social services – 13%; Industry and trade – 10%; Transportation – 11%; Finance – 10%; Agriculture, fishing and forestry – 8%; Education – 8%; Water, sanitation and flood protection – 5%; Information and communication – 1%.
'Loans' – Acts as the concessionary loan affiliate of the World Bank, accounting for a quarter of all World Bank lending. Extends credit to the poorest countries, although some recipients are sufficiently creditworthy to borrow from the IBRD as well. Currently a minimum of 45% has been allocated to Sub-Saharan Africa and a maximum of 30% to China and India combined. In the 1960s, IDA financed mainly infrastructure projects; emphasis in the 1970s was more on programmes directly benefiting the poor. Since the 1980s IDA has become more involved in economic policy change and institutional reform, structural adjustment lending now being about one quarter of all lending, although the majority of credits are still extended for specific investments. IDA thus takes an active role in helping governments undertake structural adjustment to protect and expand human development programmes and alleviate short term costs. Adjustment programmes supported by IDA have generally been accompanied by stabilization programmes supported by the IMF, this collaboration being formalized from 1986 in joint Policy Framework Papers.
Credit is extended to help finance development projects and economic restructuring programmes in member countries, especially the poorest countries. Credits have a 10-year grace period and are made for a term of 35 to 40 years. Unlike IBRD loans, no interest is charged; but to meet the administrative costs of IDA, there is a service charge of 0.75% on amounts withdrawn. Credits are made only to governments or to entities with a government guarantee. Repayments are due in foreign exchange. As the largest single source of multilateral concessional funds, IDA also helps coordinate and mobilize aid from other multilateral organizations and donor countries. It assists in determining a country's investment priorities and in rationalizing allocation of external aid, and takes the lead in consultative group discussions between a country and its donors. *Enhanced Heavily Indebted Poor Countries Initiative (HIPC Initiative, #05483)*, set up 1996, enhanced initiative launched Oct 1999, aims to reduce to a sustainable level the external debt of the world's poorest, most heavily indebted

countries, placing debt relief within an overall framework of poverty reduction. It is open only to countries eligible for highly concessional assistance from IDA and from the IMF's Poverty Reduction and Growth Facility (PRGF). *Special Programme of Assistance for African Countries (SPA)*, launched 1987, helps low-income, debt-distressed Sub-Saharan countries implementing economic reform programmes, ensuring such programmes are adequately financed and providing a framework for coordination of donor efforts. The *'IDA Debt Reduction Facility'* helps ease the burden of commercial debt for poorer countries.
'Poverty Reduction' – Sets up social funds and social action programmes in many countries, particularly addressing chronic poverty through immunization and nutrition programmes, funding primary education costs and financing simple income-generating activities. The *'Country Assistance Strategy (CAS)'* is a means of ensuring that the goal of poverty reduction is pursued effectively and tailored to specific country conditions. Debt sustainability for heavily indebted poor countries is an increasing problem; specific additional measures for countries facing such problems and a significant burden of multilateral debt are underway. Social measures to protect the poor have become components of many IDA adjustment loans. IDA supports rural development programmes and projects aiming to increase agricultural productivity and ensure adequate food supplies, finances projects giving special attention to improving women's incomes and status in their communities, and supports population, health and nutrition projects. On the environment, borrowers are assisted in developing their own National Environment Action Plans to identify policy changes, investments and institution building required for environmentally sustainable development. As well as building environmental considerations into project design, many IDA and IDA/IBRD projects have helping the environment or forests as their primary objective. Improvements in infrastructure are still a priority, in particular addressing weaknesses in institutions providing essential services, fostering greater autonomy and insulating them from political interference.
Events *Special high-level meeting* New York, NY (USA) 2006, *Special high-level meeting* New York, NY (USA) 2005, *Annual Meeting of the Board of Governors* Dubai (United Arab Emirates) 2003, *Annual Meeting of the Board of Governors* Washington, DC (USA) 2002, *IDA 13 replenishment meeting* Montreux (Switzerland) 2001. **Publications** *Global Economic Perspectives*; *World Debt Tables*; *World Development Report*.
Members Membership open to member countries of the World Bank. As of 2002, 26 States were Part I members:
Australia, Austria, Belgium, Canada, Denmark, Finland, France, Germany, Iceland, Ireland, Italy, Japan, Kuwait, Luxembourg, Netherlands, New Zealand, Norway, Portugal, Russia, South Africa, Spain, Sweden, Switzerland, UK, United Arab Emirates, USA.
As of 2002, 136 countries were Part II members:
Afghanistan, Albania, Algeria, Angola, Argentina, Armenia, Azerbaijan, Bangladesh, Barbados, Belize, Benin, Bhutan, Bolivia, Bosnia-Herzegovina, Botswana, Brazil, Burkina Faso, Burundi, Cambodia, Cameroon, Cape Verde, Central African Rep, Chad, Chile, China, Colombia, Comoros, Congo Brazzaville, Congo DR, Costa Rica, Côte d'Ivoire, Croatia, Cyprus, Czechia, Djibouti, Dominica, Dominican Rep, Ecuador, Egypt, El Salvador, Equatorial Guinea, Eritrea, Eswatini, Ethiopia, Fiji, Gabon, Gambia, Georgia, Ghana, Greece, Grenada, Guatemala, Guinea, Guinea-Bissau, Guyana, Haiti, Honduras, Hungary, India, Indonesia, Iran Islamic Rep, Iraq, Israel, Jordan, Kazakhstan, Kenya, Kiribati, Korea Rep, Kyrgyzstan, Laos, Latvia, Lebanon, Lesotho, Liberia, Libya, Madagascar, Malawi, Malaysia, Maldives, Mali, Marshall Is, Mauritania, Mauritius, Mexico, Micronesia FS, Moldova, Mongolia, Morocco, Mozambique, Myanmar, Nepal, Nicaragua, Niger, Nigeria, North Macedonia, Oman, Pakistan, Palau, Panama, Papua New Guinea, Paraguay, Peru, Philippines, Poland, Rwanda, Samoa, Sao Tomé-Principe, Saudi Arabia, Senegal, Serbia, Sierra Leone, Slovakia, Slovenia, Solomon Is, Somalia, Sri Lanka, St Kitts-Nevis, St Lucia, St Vincent-Grenadines, Sudan, Syrian AR, Tajikistan, Tanzania UR, Thailand, Togo, Tonga, Trinidad-Tobago, Tunisia, Türkiye, Uganda, Uzbekistan, Vanuatu, Vietnam, Yemen, Zambia, Zimbabwe.
IGO Relations As a specialized agency of the United Nations, formal relationships are covered by an agreement similar to that which the World Bank has with the United Nations. Associated with Department of Global Communications of the United Nations. Permanent observer status with: *World Intellectual Property Organization (WIPO, #21593)*. Member of: *Committee of International Development Institutions on the Environment (CIDIE, no recent information)*. Close cooperation with: *Nordic Development Fund (NDF, #17271)*. Supports: *African Trade Insurance Agency (ATI, #00485)*; *CIS-7 Initiative (no recent information)*. Observer of: *International Fund for Agricultural Development (IFAD, #13692)*. **NGO Relations** No organic relations with nongovernmental organizations, but indirect links through: *World Bank – Civil Society Joint Facilitation Committee (JFC, #21217)*. [2015/XB1791/B*]

♦ International Development Centre for Africa (internationally oriented national body)
♦ International Development Centre of Japan (internationally oriented national body)
♦ International Development Economics Associates (internationally oriented national body)
♦ International Development Education Association of Scotland (internationally oriented national body)

♦ International Development Enterprises (IDE) 13156

CEO 1031 33rd St, Ste 270, Denver CO 80205, USA. T. +17209241227. E-mail: info@ideglobal.org.
Europe Office c/o WeWork, 2 Leman Street, London, E1 8FA, UK. E-mail: europe@ideglobal.org.
URL: https://www.ideglobal.org/

History 1981, Lakewood CO (USA). Incorporated under US law 1 Oct 1992. Registered with the Swiss Civil Code in 2002. Previously also referred to as *IDE-International*. **Aims** Alleviate rural poverty in least developed countries through economic development; enable rural farmers to increase production, generate income and improve living standards; increase and improve rural farmers' abilities to produce wealth-generating, high value crops to sell in the marketplace; develop market environments and equip local private enterprises to meet the needs of the rural poor. **Structure** Board of Directors. **Staff** 500.00 FTE, paid. Staff in more than 12 countries. **Finance** Public, corporate and private grants, including grants from: governments of Netherlands, Germany and Switzerland; *United States Agency for International Development (USAID)*; *German Catholic Bishops' Organisation for Development Cooperation (MISEREOR)*; *Winrock International*; *Plan International (#18386)*; *The Rockefeller Foundation (#18966)*; *UNICEF (#20332)*; private donors worldwide. **Activities** Projects/programmes. **Publications** *IDE Insider* (6 a year) – e-newsletter. Annual Report; articles and concept papers covering topics related to IDE work and staff projects; analysis reports of current projects.
Members National IDE organizations (NIOs) in 3 countries:
Canada, UK, USA.
Consultative Status Consultative status granted from: *ECOSOC (#05331)* (Special). **IGO Relations** Cooperates with: *Asian Development Bank (ADB, #01422)*; *DANIDA*; *Deutsche Gesellschaft für Technische Zusammenarbeit (GTZ, inactive)*; *FAO (#09260)*; *International Fund for Agricultural Development (IFAD, #13692)*; *Swiss Agency for Development and Cooperation (SDC)*; UNICEF; USAID; *World Food Programme (WFP, #21510)*. **NGO Relations** Member of: *Cooperation Committee for Cambodia (CCC)*; *Freshwater Action Network (FAN, inactive)*; *Extractive Industries Transparency Initiative (EITI, #09229)*; *Manitoba Council for International Cooperation (MCIC)*. Cooperates with: *Christian Outreach – Relief and Development (CORD)*; *Church World Service (CWS)*; *ICCO – Interchurch Organization for Development Cooperation*; MISEREOR; PLAN International; Rockefeller Foundation; *Save the Children Federation (SCF)*; Winrock International Institute for Agricultural Development; *World Concern International (#21290)*. Partner of: *1% for the Planet*. [2017/XF6538/F]

♦ International Development Ethics Association (IDEA) 13157

Asociación Internacional de Etica del Desarrollo

Pres Dept of Philosophy, Allegheny College, Meadville PA 16335, USA. T. +18143502652.
Sec Dept of Philosophy and Humanistic Studies, Western Connecticut State Univ, Danbury CT 06810, USA.
URL: http://www.developmentethics.org/

History Founded 1984, San José (Costa Rica), as *'Development Ethics Working Group'*. Present name adopted 1987. **Aims** Apply ethical reflection to development goals and strategies and to relations between "North" and "South"; effect ethically sound development policies, institutions and practices; promote solidarity, mutual support and interchange among development theorists. **Structure** Executive Board; Advisory Council; Members at Large. **Languages** English, French, Spanish. **Finance** Members' dues. **Activities** Research/documentation; events/meetings; networking/liaising. **Events** *A world united – allies in development* Bordeaux (France) 2018, *International Conference on Ethics and Development* Istanbul (Turkey) 2016, *International Conference on Ethics and Development* San José (Costa Rica) 2014, *International Conference on Ethics and Development* Bamako (Mali) 2013, *International Conference on Ethics and Development* Bryn Mawr, PA (USA) 2011. **Publications** *Journal of Global Ethics*. **Members** Individuals (78) researchers and students from a range of academic disciplines pertaining to development; practitioners working with a variety of development NGOs, agencies and institutions. Members in 40 countries (not specified). [2019.12.28/XF0014/v/F]

♦ International Development Evaluation Association (IDEAS) 13158

Admin PontNet Ste 84, Private Bag X12, Cresta, Johannesburg, 2118, South Africa. E-mail: jeanhilburn@telkomsa.net.
URL: http://www.ideas-int.org/

Aims Advance and extend the practice of development evaluation by refining methods, strengthening capacity and expanding ownership. **Structure** Board, comprising President, Vice-President, Treasurer, Secretary and 6 further members. **Finance** Members' dues. **Events** *Global Assembly* Prague (Czechia) 2019, *International Conference on National Evaluation Capacities* Bangkok (Thailand) 2015, *Biennial Conference* Delhi (India) 2005. **NGO Relations** Secretariat located at: *Development Bank of Southern Africa (DBSA)*. Member of: *International Organisation for Cooperation in Evaluation (IOCE, #14426)*. Cooperates with: *EvalPartners (#09208)*. [2014/XM1796/D]

♦ International Development Exchange (internationally oriented national body)

♦ International Development Finance Club (IDFC) 13159

Head Office 5 rue Roland Barthes, 75598 Paris CEDEX 12, France. T. +33153443131. Fax +33144879939. E-mail: secretariat_idfc@afd.fr.
URL: https://www.idfc.org/

History Founded 2011. **Aims** Play a leading role in global development and *climate* agendas. **Structure** Annual Meeting; Steering Group; Sherpas; Working Groups; Secretariat.
Members Development banks (26), including 10 listed in this Yearbook:
Agence française de développement (AFD); *Banque ouest africaine de développement (BOAD, #03170)*; *Black Sea Trade and Development Bank (BSTDB, #03278)*; *Central American Bank for Economic Integration (CABEI, #03658)*; *Development Bank of Latin America (CAF, #05055)*; *Development Bank of Southern Africa (DBSA)*; *International Investment Bank (IIB, #13951)*; *Japan International Cooperation Agency (JICA)*; *Kreditanstalt für Wiederaufbau (KfW)*; *Trade and Development Bank (TDB, #20181)*. [2020/XM8847/y/F]

♦ International Development Group for Corrugated Board (SUW) 13160

Sec c/o RISE, Box 7047, SE-164 07 Kista, Sweden.
Chairman Smurfit Kappa Kraftliner, SE-941 38 Piteå, Sweden.
URL: https://www.ri.se/en/what-we-do/networks/suw

History 1968, as Swedish Development Group for Corrugated Board. Later became *Scandinavian Development Group for Corrugated Board – Skandinaviska Utvecklingsgruppen för Wellpapp (SUW)*. **Aims** Develop and support quality and utilization of corrugated board in order to defend and strengthen its competitiveness on the packaging market; develop cost efficient process techniques for the production and conversion of corrugated board; improve corrugated board raw materials. **Members** Companies and organizations. Membership countries not specified. [2021/XM0824/D]

♦ International Development Innovation Network (internationally oriented national body)
♦ International Development Institute (unconfirmed)
♦ International Development Law Institute / see International Development Law Organization (#13161)

♦ International Development Law Organization (IDLO) 13161

Organisation internationale de droit du développement (OIDD)

Headquarters Viale Vaticano 106, 00165 Rome RM, Italy. T. +39640403200. Fax +39640403232. E-mail: info@idlo.int.
Branch Office Hofweg 9E, 2511 AA The Hague, Netherlands. E-mail: thehague@idlo.int.
URL: http://www.idlo.int/

History 18 Mar 1983, as *International Development Law Institute (IDLI) – Institut international de droit du développement – Instituto Internacional de Derecho para el Desarrollo – Istituto Internazionale di Diritto per lo Sviluppo*, as a nongovernmental organization registered in accordance with Dutch law. Transformed into an intergovernmental organization, 28 Apr 1989, when the *'Agreement for the Establishment of the International Development Law Institute, 5 Feb 1988'* came into force. Commenced operations as an IGO, 1 Jan 1991. Current name adopted 30 Jun 2002. **Aims** Promote the rule of law and good *governance* in developing countries, transition economies and nations emerging from conflict; help these countries establish the legal framework needed to achieve economic, social and institutional *development*; work closely with local groups, addressing their specific needs and empowering them to contribute to their national development. **Structure** Assembly of Parties. Board of Advisers. Standing Committee. Director-General. Headquarters in Rome (Italy); Regional Centres in Cairo (Egypt) and Sydney (Australia); Project Offices in Afghanistan, Kyrgyzstan and Sudan. **Languages** Arabic, English, French. **Staff** 120.00 FTE, paid.
Finance Budget (annual): about US$ 20 million. Main sources: voluntary contributions from governments, multilateral organizations, foundations and the private sector, including the following organizations listed in this Yearbook:
- *America-Mideast Educational and Training Services (AMIDEAST)*;
- *Arab Bank for Economic Development in Africa (#00904)*;
- *Arab Fund for Economic and Social Development (AFESD, #00965)*;
- *Asian Development Bank (ADB, #01422)*;
- *Australian Aid (inactive)*;
- *Canadian International Development Agency (CIDA, inactive)*;
- *Commonwealth Secretariat (#04362)*;
- *DANIDA*;
- *Department for International Development Cooperation*;
- *European Bank for Reconstruction and Development (EBRD, #06315)*;
- *Institute of Development Studies, Brighton (IDS)*;
- *International Bank for Reconstruction and Development (IBRD, #12317)* – World Bank;
- *Irish Aid*;
- *Kuwait Fund for Arab Economic Development (KFAED)*;
- *Libera Università Internazionale degli Studi Sociali, Guido Carli (LUISS)*;
- *MacArthur Foundation*;
- *Norwegian Agency for Development Cooperation (Norad)*;
- *OPEC Fund for International Development (OFID, #17745)*;
- *Swedish International Development Cooperation Agency (Sida)*;
- *United Nations Office for Project Services (UNOPS, #20602)*;
- *United States Agency for International Development (USAID)*.

Activities Training courses and seminars, technical assistance, research and publications. Programmes cover: trade law; investment law; microfinance law and regulation; environmental and natural resources law; health law; land law; justice sector; governance sector; legal education, human rights and gender-related issues. By Aug 2010 had worked with over 20,000 legal professionals in 175 countries. Alumni associations (44 worldwide) provide continuing legal education, assistance, research and publications. **Events** *Meeting* Rome (Italy) 2015, *Meeting* Rome (Italy) 2014, *Meeting* Rome (Italy) 2013, *Meeting* Rome (Italy) 2010, *Strengthened and expanded HIV legal services* Bali (Indonesia) 2009. **Publications** Books; monographs; working papers; policy briefs; manuals.
Members Governments of 21 countries:
Australia, Austria, Bulgaria, Burkina Faso, China, Colombia, Ecuador, Egypt, France, Italy, Jordan, Kenya, Netherlands, Norway, Paraguay, Philippines, Romania, Senegal, Sudan, Tunisia, USA.
Regional Entity:
OPEC Fund for International Development (OFID, #17745).
IGO Relations Permanent Observer to: *ECOSOC (#05331)*. Observer to General Assembly of: *United Nations (UN, #20515)*. Partner of: *Organisation pour l'Harmonisation en Afrique du Droit des Affaires (OHADA, #17806)*. **NGO Relations** Member of: *CIVICUS: World Alliance for Citizen Participation (#03962)*; *Global Development Learning Network (GDLN, #10317)*. Partner of: *Global Forum on Law, Justice and Development (GFLJD, #10373)*. Involved in setting up: *European Law Centre, Romania (no recent information)*. Cooperative agreement with: *European Centre for Peace and Development (ECPD, #06496)*. [2020/XD0003/E*]

♦ International Development Programme of Australian Universities and Colleges / see IDP Education
♦ International Development Programme of the Danish Youth Council (internationally oriented national body)
♦ International Development and Relief Foundation (internationally oriented national body)

♦ International Development Research Centre (IDRC) 13162

Centre de recherches pour le développement international (CRDI)

Pres PO Box 8500, Ottawa ON K1G 3H9, Canada. T. +16132366163. Fax +16132356391. E-mail: info@idrc.ca.
Sec address not obtained. E-mail: info@idrc.ca.
Street address 150 Kent St, Ottawa ON K1P 0B2, Canada.

URL: http://www.idrc.ca/
History Established May 1970, Ottawa ON (Canada), by the Canadian Parliament. **Aims** Initiate, encourage, support and conduct research into the problems of the *developing regions* of the world and into the means for applying and adapting scientific, technical and other knowledge to the *economic* and *social* advancement of those regions. **Structure** Board of Governors; Head office in Ottawa ON (Canada); Regional Offices (4). **Languages** English, French. **Staff** 36.00 FTE, paid. **Finance** Main source: Canadian Parliament. Budget (2016-2017): Canadian $ 149,200,000. **Activities** Projects/programmes; research/documentation; events/meetings. **Events** *Think Tank Initiative Exchange Meeting* Bangkok (Thailand) 2018, *International Open Data Conference* Buenos Aires (Argentina) 2018, *Gender Summit North America* Montréal, QC (Canada) 2017, *International Open Data Conference* Madrid (Spain) 2016, *International Conference on Asian Highland Natural Resources Management* Chiang Mai (Thailand) 2015. **Publications** *The IDRC Bulletin*. Free e-books. Annual Report. **Information Services** *IDRC Digital Library* – open access institutional repository of project outputs; *IDRIS+* – database of IDRC project descriptions. **Members** Crown corporation; not a membership organization. **IGO Relations** Cooperates with: *Department for International Development (DFID, inactive)*; *International Bank for Reconstruction and Development (IBRD, #12317)* (World Bank); *Norwegian Agency for Development Cooperation (Norad)*; national organizations. Instrumental in setting up: *CGIAR System Organization (CGIAR, #03843)*. **NGO Relations** Member of: *Donor Committee for Enterprise Development (DCED, #05122)*; *Global Research Collaboration for Infectious Disease Preparedness (GLOPID-R, #10573)*. Participates in: *Global Center on Adaptation (GCA)*. Cooperates with: *Bill and Melinda Gates Foundation (BMGF)*; *The William and Flora Hewlett Foundation*; Instrumental in setting up: *Asian Institute of Technology (AIT, #01519)*. Supports: *Namati (#16931)*; *Organization for Women in Science for the Developing World (OWSD, #17890)*.
[2016.10.27/XE0390/**E***]

♦ International Development Research Group / see Research Centre on Development and International Relations
♦ International Development, UEA (internationally oriented national body)
♦ International D H Lawrence Conference (meeting series)

♦ International Diabetes Epidemiology Group (IDEG) 13163

Pres address not obtained.
URL: http://www.ideg-diabetes.org/
History 1979. Previously referred to as *International Diabetes Epidemiology Study Group*. **Aims** Forge collaboration and exchange ideas and data on the epidemiology of diabetes to better understand and explore its causes and consequences. **Structure** President; Organizing Committee. **Languages** English. **Staff** None paid. **Finance** Meetings financed by registration fees and donations from sponsors. **Activities** Events/meetings; training/education. **Events** *Symposium* Busan (Korea Rep) 2019, *Symposium* Abu Dhabi (United Arab Emirates) 2017, *Symposium* Vancouver, BC (Canada) 2015, *Symposium* Melbourne, VIC (Australia) 2013, *Symposium* Québec, QC (Canada) 2009. **Members** Full in over 30 countries. Membership countries not specified. **NGO Relations** Cooperates with: 'European Diabetes Epidemiology Group (EDEG)' of *European Association for the Study of Diabetes (EASD, #06228)*; *Grupo Latinoamericano de Epidemiologia de la Diabetes (GLED)*.
[2018.01.31/XE4216/**E**]

♦ International Diabetes Epidemiology Study Group / see International Diabetes Epidemiology Group (#13163)

♦ International Diabetes Federation (IDF) 13164

Fédération internationale du diabète (FID) – Federación Internacional de Diabetes (FID)
Executive Office Av Hermann-Debroux 54, 1160 Brussels, Belgium. T. +3225385511. Fax +3225385114. E-mail: info@idf.org.
Executive Office Chaussée de la Hulpe 166, 1170 Brussels, Belgium.
URL: http://www.idf.org/
History 23 Sep 1950, Amsterdam (Netherlands). Registration: Banque Carrefour des Entreprises, No/ID: 0433.674.528, Start date: 23 Jun 1985, Belgium. **Aims** Promote diabetes care, prevention and a cure worldwide. **Structure** General Council (meets every 2 years); Board; Regions (7): Africa (AFR); *International Diabetes Federation Europe (IDF Europe, #13165)*; Middle East North Africa (MENA); North America and Caribbean (NAC); South and Central America (SACA); South-East Asia (SEA); Western Pacific (WP). **Languages** English, French, Spanish. **Staff** 20.00 FTE, paid. **Finance** Sources: contributions; donations. **Activities** Advocacy/lobbying/activism; awareness raising; events/meetings; humanitarian/emergency aid; publishing activities; training/education. **Events** *Congress* Belgium 2023, *World Diabetes Congress* Lisbon (Portugal) 2022, *Biennial Congress* Brussels (Belgium) 2021, *Diabetes Complications Congress* Lisbon (Portugal) 2021, *Diabetes Complications Congress* Lisbon (Portugal) 2020. **Publications** *IDF Diabetes Atlas* (every 2 years); *Diabetes Voice* – online magazine. *International Standards for Education of Diabetes Health Professionals* (2015); *International Curriculum for Diabetes Health Professional Education* (2008). Annual Report; guidelines and clinical practice recommendations; educational guides; consensus statements.
Members National associations in 155 countries and territories:
Afghanistan, Albania, Algeria, Anguilla, Antigua-Barbuda, Argentina, Armenia, Aruba, Australia, Austria, Azerbaijan, Bahrain, Bangladesh, Barbados, Belarus, Belgium, Belize, Bermuda, Bolivia, Bosnia-Herzegovina, Botswana, Brazil, Bulgaria, Burkina Faso, Burundi, Cambodia, Cameroon, Canada, Cayman Is, Chile, China, Colombia, Congo Brazzaville, Congo DR, Costa Rica, Côte d'Ivoire, Croatia, Cuba, Curaçao, Cyprus, Czechia, Dominica, Dominican Rep, Ecuador, Egypt, El Salvador, Eritrea, Estonia, Eswatini, Ethiopia, Faeroe Is, Fiji, Finland, France, Gambia, Georgia, Germany, Ghana, Greece, Grenada, Guatemala, Guinea, Guyana, Haiti, Honduras, Hong Kong, Hungary, Iceland, India, Indonesia, Iran Islamic Rep, Iraq, Israel, Italy, Jamaica, Japan, Jordan, Kazakhstan, Kenya, Korea Rep, Kuwait, Kyrgyzstan, Latvia, Lebanon, Lesotho, Libya, Lithuania, Luxembourg, Madagascar, Malawi, Maldives, Mali, Malta, Mauritania, Mauritius, Mexico, Moldova, Montserrat, Morocco, Nepal, Nicaragua, Nigeria, North Macedonia, Norway, Oman, Pakistan, Palestine, Papua New Guinea, Paraguay, Peru, Philippines, Poland, Portugal, Puerto Rico, Qatar, Romania, Russia, Rwanda, Saudi Arabia, Senegal, Serbia, Seychelles, Singapore, Slovakia, Slovenia, South Africa, Spain, Sri Lanka, St Kitts-Nevis, St Lucia, St Maarten, Sudan, Suriname, Sweden, Switzerland, Syrian AR, Taiwan, Tanzania UR, Thailand, Togo, Tonga, Trinidad-Tobago, Tunisia, Türkiye, Uganda, Ukraine, United Arab Emirates, Uruguay, USA, Uzbekistan, Venezuela, Virgin Is UK, Yemen, Zambia, Zimbabwe.
Consultative Status Consultative status granted from: *WHO (#20950)* (Official Relations). **IGO Relations** Associated with Department of Global Communications of the United Nations. **NGO Relations** Member of (6): *Associations and Conference Forum (AC Forum, #02909)*; *EU Platform for Action on Diet, Physical Activity and Health (inactive)*; *European Alliance for Personalised Medicine (EAPM, #05878)*; *Global Alliance for the Prevention of Obesity and Related Chronic Disease (#10219)*; *International Alliance of Patients' Organizations (IAPO, #11633)*; *PMNCH (#18410)*. Partner of (1): *Every Woman Every Child (EWEC, #09215)*. Founding member of: *The NCD Alliance (NCDA, #16963)*.
[2023/XB1792/**B**]

♦ International Diabetes Federation Europe (IDF Europe) 13165

Contact Chaussée de la Hulpe 166, 1170 Brussels, Belgium. T. +3225371889. E-mail: idfeurope@idf-europe.org.
URL: https://idf.org/our-network/regions-members/europe/welcome.html
History European chapter of *International Diabetes Federation (IDF, #13164)*. Registration: EU Transparency Register, No/ID: 80267287489-88, Start date: 21 Dec 2011. **Aims** Influence policy, increase public awareness, encourage *health* improvement and promote exchange of best practice and high-quality information about *diabetes* throughout the European region. **Structure** General Assembly (annual); Board; Regional Office. **Languages** English, French. **Staff** 2.00 FTE, paid. **Finance** Through partnerships. **Activities** Advocacy/lobbying/activism; awareness raising; events/meetings; politics/policy/regulatory. **Events** *Annual General Assembly* Lisbon (Portugal) 2012. **Publications** Annual Report; position papers.
Members Organizations (69) in 45 countries and territories:
Albania, Armenia, Austria, Azerbaijan, Belarus, Belgium, Bulgaria, Croatia, Cyprus, Czechia, Estonia, Faeroe Is, Finland, France, Georgia, Germany, Greece, Hungary, Iceland, Ireland, Israel, Italy, Kazakhstan, Kyrgyzstan, Latvia, Lithuania, Luxembourg, Malta, Moldova, Netherlands, North Macedonia, Norway, Poland, Portugal, Romania, Russia, Serbia, Slovakia, Slovenia, Spain, Sweden, Switzerland, Türkiye, Ukraine, Uzbekistan.
Consultative Status Consultative status granted from: *Council of Europe (CE, #04881)* (Participatory Status). **IGO Relations** *European Committee of the Regions (CoR, #06665)*; *Council of Europe (CE, #04881)*; *European Commission (EC, #06633)*; *European Parliament (EP, #08146)*; *WHO (#20950)*. **NGO Relations** Member of (10): *Conference of INGOs of the Council of Europe (#04607)*; *EU Health Coalition*; *European Alliance for Diabetes Research (EURADIA, #05868)*; *European Chronic Disease Alliance (ECDA, #06548)*; *European Coalition for Diabetes (ECD, #06592)*; *European Coalition for Vision (ECV)*; *European Foundation for the Study of Diabetes (EFSD, #07351)*; *European Patients' Forum (EPF, #08172)*; *European Public Health Alliance (EPHA, #08297)*; *Health First Europe (HFE, #10881)*.
[2019.12.11/XJ6311/**E**]

♦ International Diabolo Association (IDA) 13166

Contact address not obtained.
URL: https://www.diabolo-ida.org/
History 4 Jan 2013, Taipei (Taiwan). **Aims** Develop and promote diabolo. **Structure** Executive Board. Committees. **Activities** Advocacy/lobbying/activism; sporting activities.
Members Federations in 13 countries and territories:
China, Finland, Hong Kong, Italy, Japan, Korea Rep, Malaysia, Malta, Norway, Russia, Switzerland, Taiwan, USA.
Asia Diabolo Association (ADA); *European Diabolo Association (EDA)*.
NGO Relations Member of (2): *General Association of Asia Pacific Sports Federations (GAAPSF, #10106)*; *International Sport Network Organization (ISNO, #15592)*.
[2020/AA1073/**C**]

♦ International Diaconate Centre (IDC) 13167

Centre international du diaconat – Centro Internationale del Diaconado – Internationales Diakonatszentrum (IDZ)
Contact Postfach 9, 72101 Rottenburg, Germany. T. +497472169737. Fax +497472169607. E-mail: idz@bo.drs.de.
URL: http://diaconia-idz.org/
History 1959, Germany FR. 1959, Freiburg (Germany FR), as *International Diaconate Circle – Internationale Diakonatskreis*, uniting diaconate groups which had been established from 1951 in a number of towns in Germany and other countries. International Information Centre set up 1965. Reorganized under current title, 1969. Transferred to Rottenburg (Germany) in 1992. **Aims** Animate the spirit of diaconia of *Jesus Christ* in a renewed diaconate through contemporary service for deacons ministering to *suffering* humanity in the *Church* and in society; offer *ecumenical* cooperation with diaconal and other Church communities. **Structure** General Assembly (at least every 4 years). Delegate Assembly, comprising up to 15 internationally-representative individuals. Executive Board, comprising President, 2 Vice-Presidents (one must be a permanent Deacon), a Deacon's wife and Director. Advisors. **Activities** Supplies information and literature about the permanent diaconate; organizes international study conferences. Includes *Centro Internacional do Diaconado Permanente da América Latina (CIDAL)*. **Events** *Conference* Velehrad (Czech Rep) 2013. **Publications** *Diaconia Christi* (periodical) – in several languages. **Members** Diaconate contacts in 18 European and 33 other countries (not specified). **NGO Relations** Cooperates with: *Consejo Episcopal Latinoamericano (CELAM, #04709)*.
[2020/XE3326/**E**]

♦ International Diaconate Circle / see International Diaconate Centre (#13167)
♦ International Diagnostics Centre (internationally oriented national body)
♦ International Dialogue for Environmental Action (internationally oriented national body)

♦ International Dialogues Foundation (IDF) 13168

Address not obtained.
URL: http://www.internationaldialogues.nl/
History 1989, evolving from *Research Institute of Oppressed Peoples (RIOP, inactive)*. **Aims** Enhance dialogue to promote *just international relations*. **Structure** General Board, comprising Chairman, 2 Vice-Chairmen, Treasurer and 15 members. Executive Board, comprising Chairman, Treasurer and 4 members. Advisory Council. **Finance** Supported by: Dutch Government; *European Commission (EC, #06633)*; *European Cultural Foundation (ECF, #06868)*; *Oxfam Novib*. **Activities** Organizes international conferences. Runs *'Religion, State and Civil Society – Freedom Religion Euro-Mediterranean Partnership'*. Coordinates projects on: Kurds; Indonesia; Sudan; Vocational training. **Events** *Meeting on coalitions for justice and peace in Jerusalem* The Hague (Netherlands) 2010, *Meeting* The Hague (Netherlands) 2008, *The Hague international conference on youth and metropolis* The Hague (Netherlands) 2006, *Open European youth parliament conference* Alexandria (Egypt) 2000, *Conference on the elaboration of human rights on the basis of a common understanding of Islam and the West* The Hague (Netherlands) 1996.
[2008/XF6167/f/**F**]

♦ International Dialogue on Underwater Munitions (IDUM) 13169

Chair 584 Leitches Cree, Lietches Creek Highway 223 East, Leitches Creek NS B2A 3Z7, Canada. T. +19025747420. E-mail: info@idum.org.
URL: http://www.underwatermunitions.org/
History 2004. Registered in accordance with Canadian law. **Aims** Promote the creation of an internationally binding treaty on all classes (biological, chemical, conventional, and radiological) of underwater munitions. **Structure** Board of Directors. International Scientific Advisory Board (ISAB) on Sea-Dumped Chemical Weapons (SDCWs) of 16 members; International Technology Advisory Board (ITAB) on Sea Dumped Weapons (SDWs) of 16 members. **Languages** English, French. **Staff** 3.00 FTE, paid; 5.00 FTE, voluntary. **Finance** Funded by private donations and member organizations on a project-to-project basis. **Activities** Organizes: annual dialogues/conferences; Working Groups on Science, Technology and Policy. **Publications** Articles. **IGO Relations** Observer to: *Baltic Marine Environment Protection Commission – Helsinki Commission (HELCOM, #03126)*. **NGO Relations** Member of: *Chemical Weapons Convention Coalition (CWCC)*.
[2018/XJ6846/**F**]

♦ International Diamond Council (IDC) 13170

Conseil international du diamant
Pres c/o SBD, Hovenierstraat 22, 2018 Antwerp, Belgium.
URL: http://www.internationaldiamondcouncil.org/
History 1975, Amsterdam (Netherlands), in the form of a Joint Committee which submitted its report to *International Diamond Manufacturers Association (IDMA, #13171)* and *World Federation of Diamond Bourses (WFDB, #21430)*, at Congress, 1978, Tel Aviv. Subsequently transformed into present organization. **Aims** Investigate possibilities for unification of diamond grading standards. **Structure** Chairman. **Languages** English. **Finance** Members' dues. **Publications** *IDC Rules for Grading Polished Diamonds*.
Members Full in 5 countries:
Belgium, Germany, Israel, Netherlands, UK.
[2018.06.20/XD9422/**D**]

♦ International Diamond Manufacturers Association (IDMA) 13171

Association internationale des fabricants de diamants
Treas c/o SBD, Hovenierstraat 22, 2018 Antwerp, Belgium. T. +3222331129. E-mail: idma.net@gmail.com – sbd@sbd.be.
Pres 580 Fifth Ave, Suite 613-625, New York NY 10036, USA.
URL: http://www.idma.co/
History 1946. **Aims** Foster and promote the highest ideals of honesty and best practice principles throughout the diamond industry, as well as full compliance with all relevant national and international laws. **Structure** Board. **Languages** English. **Staff** 1.00 FTE, voluntary. **Finance** Sources: members' dues. **Activities** Events/meetings. **Events** *Biennial World Congress* Dubai (United Arab Emirates) 2016, *Biennial World Congress / Biennial World Diamond Congress* Antwerp (Belgium) 2014, *WFDB Asian Summit* Singapore (Singapore) 2014, *Biennial World Diamond Congress* Mumbai (India) 2012, *Biennial World Congress / Biennial World Diamond Congress / Biennial World Diamond Congress* Moscow (Russia) 2010. **Publications** *WINC (Weekly Internet News Collection)* (weekly).
Members Associations in 15 countries:
Armenia, Belgium, Botswana, Canada, China, Germany, India, Israel, Namibia, Netherlands, Russia, South Africa, Sri Lanka, Thailand, USA.
NGO Relations Cooperates with: *World Federation of Diamond Bourses (WFDB, #21430)*.
[2020.04.11/XD2659/**D**]

♦ International Diatomite Producers Association (IDPA) 13172

Pres 1200 18th Street NW, Suite 1150, Washington DC 20036, USA. T. +12024570200.
URL: http://www.ima-europe.eu/idpa/
Languages English. **NGO Relations** Member of: *Industrial Minerals Association – Europe (IMA Europe, #11179)*. Shares office staff with: *Calcium Carbonate Association – Europe (CCA-Europe, #03399)*; *European Association of Feldspar Producers (EUROFEL, #06037)*; *European Association of Industrial Silica Producers (EUROSIL, #06082)*; *European Bentonite Producers Association (EUBA, #06328)*; *European Borates Association (EBA, #06382)*; *European Kaolin and Plastic Clays Association (KPC Europe, #07623)*; *European Lime Association (EuLA, #07699)*; *European Speciality Minerals Association (ESMA, #08811)*; *Scientific Association of European Talc Industry (Eurotalc, #19146)*; IMA Europe; IMA North America; National Industrial Sand Association (NISA).
[2019/XD9400/t/**D**]

♦ International Dielectric Society (IDS) 13173

Pres School of Molecular Sciences, Arizona State Univ, Box 871604, Tempe AZ 85287-1604, USA.
URL: http://the-dielectric-society.org/

Aims Serve the community of researchers interested in promotion, development and application of broadband dielectric spectroscopy and related techniques. **Languages** English. **Activities** Events/meetings; financial and/or material support; networking/liaising; research and development; training/education. **Events** *BDS Conference* San Sebastian (Spain) 2022, *IDS Online Workshop* San Sebastian (Spain) 2021, *IDS Online Workshop* Tempe, AZ (USA) 2020, *BDS Conference* Brussels (Belgium) 2018, *BDS Conference* Pisa (Italy) 2016. **Members** Membership countries not specified. [2022.05.10/XJ8070/**D**]

♦ International Digestive Cancer Alliance (IDCA) 13174

Executive Secretariat 555 East Wells St, Ste 1100, Milwaukee WI 53202, USA. T. +14149189798. Fax +14142763349. E-mail: info@worldgastroenterology.org.
URL: http://www.worldgastroenterology.org/

History by *World Gastroenterology Organisation (WGO, #21536), World Endoscopy Organization (WEO, #21380), United European Gastroenterology (UEG, #20506), European Society of Gastrointestinal Endoscopy (ESGE, #08606), Union for International Cancer Control (UICC, #20415)* and Cancer Research and Prevention Foundation (CRPF). Formally inaugurated Mar 2002. An official division within WGO. **Aims** Promote the screening, early detection, and primary prevention of digestive cancers worldwide through an international alliance of organizations that share the same goal. **Structure** Steering Committee, comprising 2 Co-Chairs, 2 Vice-Chairs, Secretary General, Deputy Secretary General, Finance Officer and WGO President. **NGO Relations** *European Society of Digestive Oncology (ESDO, #08582).* [2010/XJ1862/**E**]

♦ International Digital Enterprise Alliance (Idealliance) 13175

Alliance internationale pour l'entreprise digitalisée

Pres/CEO 1800 Diagonal Rd, Ste 320, Alexandria VA 22314, USA. T. +17038371070. Fax +17038371069. E-mail: info@idealliance.org.
URL: http://www.idealliance.org/

History Jan 1966, USA. Former names and other names: *Graphic Communications Association* – former (1981 to 2001); *Computer Section – Printing Industries of America* – former (Jan 1966 to 1969); *Graphic Communications Computer Association (GCCA)* – former (1969 to 1981). **Aims** Lead the industry to continued global process improvement, profitability and standardization through leading specifications, workflow efficiencies, ISO standard developments, leading globally recognized certifications, expert technological consulting in printing and packaging technologies, and workflows and brand strategy consulting. **Structure** Board of Directors. **Languages** Dutch, English, Italian, Portuguese, Spanish. **Activities** Standards/guidelines; certification/accreditation; training/education; guidance/assistance/consulting; research/documentation. **Events** *Experience Annual Conference* Dallas, TX (USA) 2018, *European conference on standard generalized markup language* Barcelona (Spain) 2002, *How XML powers industry applications international conference* Berlin (Germany) 2001, *European conference on standard generalized markup language* Munich (Germany) 1996, *Asia-Pacific conference on standard generalized markup language* Sydney, NSW (Australia) 1996. **Publications** *Printing Markets – State Of The Industry Report* (annual); *Printing Markets – Capital Investment Report.* White Papers; Case Studies. **Information Services** *GAMUT* – printing and packaging podcast. **NGO Relations** Sponsors: *PapiNet (#18192).* [2021/XN3138/**D**]

- ♦ International Digital Games Committee (unconfirmed)
- ♦ International Digital Image Correlation Society (internationally oriented national body)
- ♦ International Diplomatic Academy (#00024)

♦ International Disability Alliance (IDA) 13176

Head Office Route de Ferney 150, PO Box 2100, 1211 Geneva 2, Switzerland. T. +41227884273. Fax +41227884274. E-mail: info@ida-secretariat.org.
New York Office 205 East 42nd St, New York NY 10017, USA. T. +16467760822.
URL: http://www.internationaldisabilityalliance.org/

History 1999, Cape Town (South Africa). Founded as a network of global, and since 2007, regional organizations of persons with disabilities (DPOs) and their families. Registration: Swiss Civil Code, Start date: 7 Jun 2013, Switzerland. **Aims** Promote the rights of persons with disabilities across the United Nations' efforts to advance human rights and sustainable development. **Structure** General Assembly (annual); Board; Secretariat, based in Geneva (Switzerland) and New York (USA), managed by Executive Director. **Languages** English. **Staff** 20.00 FTE, paid. **Finance** Sources: subsidies. Supported by: Australian Department of Foreign Affairs and Trade (DFAT); *Christian Blind Mission (CBM); Disability Rights Fund (DRF, #05096)*; Finnish Ministry of Foreign Affairs; *Humanity and Inclusion (HI, #10975); Open Society Foundations (OSF, #17763); Sightsavers International (#19270); Swedish International Development Cooperation Agency (Sida)*; UK Department for International Development (DFID). Annual budget: 3,000,000 USD. **Activities** Advocacy/lobbying/activism; capacity building; events/meetings; knowledge management/information dissemination; networking/liaising; research/documentation; training/education. **Events** *Global Disability Summit* Oslo (Norway) 2022, *Global Disability Summit* London (UK) 2018, *International Conference on the Promotion of the Rights of Women and Girls with Disability* Seoul (Korea Rep) 2016. **Publications** Reports; statements; position papers; guides.
Members International organizations (8), listed in this Yearbook:
Down Syndrome International (DSi, #05128); Inclusion International (#11145); International Federation for Spina Bifida and Hydrocephalus (IF SBH, #13552); International Federation of Hard of Hearing People (IFHOH, #13435); World Blind Union (WBU, #21234); World Federation of the Deafblind (WFDB, #21426); World Federation of the Deaf (WFD, #21425); World Network of Users and Survivors of Psychiatry (WNUSP, #21672).
Regional organizations (6):
African Disability Forum; *Arab Organization of Disabled People (AODP, #01019)*; ASEAN Disability Forum (ASEAN-DF); *European Disability Forum (EDF, #06929); Latin American Network of Non-Governmental Organizations of Persons with Disabilities and their Families (#16354); Pacific Disability Forum (PDF, #17945).*
Consultative Status Consultative status granted from: *ECOSOC (#05331)* (Special). **NGO Relations** Member of (3): *CBR Global Network (#03618); End Corporal Punishment (#05457); ILO Global Business and Disability Network (GBDN, #11122).* Instrumental in setting up (1): *International Disability Caucus (IDC, inactive).* Co-Chair and member of: *Global Action on Disability Network (GLAD, #10165).* Participates in: *Global Partnership on Children with Disabilities (GPcwd, #10529).* [2023/XF6792/y/**A**]

- ♦ International Disability Consortium / see International Disability and Development Consortium (#13177)

♦ International Disability and Development Consortium (IDDC) 13177

Coordinator Rue de l'Industrie 10, 1000 Brussels, Belgium. T. +3228932490. E-mail: info@iddcconsortium.net.
URL: http://www.iddcconsortium.net/

History 17 Oct 1994, Oslo (Norway), as *International Disability Consortium (IDC)*, taking over the activities of *European Rehabilitation Partners (ERP, inactive).* EU Transparency Register: 26634082731-16. **Aims** Promote inclusive development internationally, with a special focus on promoting the full and effective enjoyment of human rights by all persons with disabilities living in economically poor communities in lower and middle-income countries. **Structure** General Assembly (annual); Board; Task Groups; Working Groups and Consultants; Secretariat. **Languages** English. **Finance** Members' dues. Members pay their own expenses for meetings and fund specific projects. **Activities** Knowledge management/information dissemination; networking/liaising. **Events** *General Assembly* Brussels (Belgium) 2022, *General Assembly* Vienna (Austria) 2013, *General Assembly* Lyon (France) 2012, *General Assembly* Prague (Czech Rep) 2011, *General Assembly* Copenhagen (Denmark) 2010. **Publications** *IDDC Newsflash* (12 a year).
Members Disability and development NGOs, disabled people's organizations (32), including the following 20 organizations listed in this Yearbook:
ADD International; Atlas Alliance; Christian Blind Mission (CBM); Deaf Child Worldwide; European Christian Organisations in Relief and Development (EU-CORD, #06545); HelpAge International (#10904); Inclusion International (#11145); International Agency for the Prevention of Blindness (IAPB, #11597); International Federation for Spina Bifida and Hydrocephalus (IF SBH, #13552); International Federation of Anti-Leprosy Associations (ILEP, #13355); Italian Association Amici di Raoul Follereau (AIFO); Leonard Cheshire Disability (#16443); Leprosy Mission International (TLMI, #16446); Light for the World (#16474); MyRight – Empower People with Disabilities; Organismo di Volontariato per la Cooperazione Internazionale – La Nostra Famiglia (OVCI); Plan International (#18386); Sense International; Sightsavers International (#19270); Stichting Liliane Fonds (SLF).
IGO Relations *European Commission (EC, #06633)*; United Nations; *WHO (#20950).* **NGO Relations** Member of: *CBR Global Network (#03618); Global Action on Disability Network (GLAD, #10165).* Participates in: *Global Partnership on Children with Disabilities (GPcwd, #10529).* Supports: *Global Call for Action Against Poverty (GCAP, #10263).* [2018.06.22/XF3691/y/**F**]

♦ International Disability Management Standards Council (IDMSC) .. 13178

Secretariat NIDMAR, 4755 Cherry Creek Rd, Port Alberni BC V9Y 0A7, Canada. T. +17784210821. E-mail: info@idmsc.org.
URL: http://www.idmsc.org/

History 2003. **Aims** Promote, through a system of policy, programme and professional certification, international acceptance, continued development and broad-based implementation of consensus-based, outcome focused Disability Management policies, programmes and professional standards. **Structure** Governing Board. **Activities** Certification/accreditation; events/meetings. **Events** *International Biennial Congress on Disability Management and Return to Work* Brussels (Belgium) 2022, *Forum* Brussels (Belgium) 2021, *Forum* Brussels (Belgium) 2020, *International Forum on Disability Management (IFDM)* Vancouver, BC (Canada) 2018, *International Forum on Disability Management (IFDM)* Kuala Lumpur (Malaysia) 2016.
Members Individuals in 25 countries and territories:
Australia, Austria, Belgium, Brunei Darussalam, Cambodia, Canada, China, France, Germany, Hong Kong, Iceland, Indonesia, Ireland, Laos, Luxembourg, Malaysia, Myanmar, Netherlands, Philippines, Singapore, Switzerland, Thailand, UK, USA, Vietnam.
NGO Relations *International Association of Professionals in Disability Management (IAPDM).* [2019/XJ6731/**C**]

- ♦ International Disciples Women's Ministries (internationally oriented national body)
- ♦ International Discussion Club – Initiative for International Development and Cooperation (internationally oriented national body)
- ♦ International Discussion Meeting on Relaxations in Complex Systems (meeting series)

♦ International Disk Drive Equipment and Materials Association (IDEMA) 13179

Chair 1226 Lincoln Ave No 100, San Jose CA 95125, USA. T. +14082940082. Fax +14082940087. E-mail: tgressley@idema.org.
IDEMA Asia Pacific c/o Kaifa Technology – Singapore, 2 Kallang Pudding Road, 04-07 Macthech Building, Singapore 349307, Singapore. T. +6567455388. Fax +6567330471.
URL: http://www.idema.org/

History 1986. **Structure** Subsidiaries: USA; Japan; Asia-Pacific (Singapore, Malaysia, Thailand and China). 3 Boards of Directors. **Activities** Provides educational programmes. Organizes: technical conferences; symposia; networking events; active international standards programmes. Initiative: Advanced Storage Technology Consortium (ASTC) – R and D collaboration with leading storage companies and universities and institutes worldwide. Founder and presenter of: DISKCON USA; DISKCON Asia-Pacific; DISKCON Japan. **Events** *Symposium on hard disk and solid state reliability* Sunnyvale, CA (USA) 2008, *Diskcon Asia Pacific conference* Singapore (Singapore) 2007, *Diskcon Asia Pacific conference* Singapore (Singapore) 2006, *Asia computer storage conference* Singapore (Singapore) 1995, *DISKCON conference* Singapore (Singapore) 1994.
Members Corporate, individual and university (over 200, mostly in USA), in 20 countries and territories:
Austria, Belgium, Canada, Chile, China, France, Hong Kong, Indonesia, Italy, Japan, Korea Rep, Malaysia, Norway, Philippines, Singapore, Switzerland, Taiwan, Thailand, UK, USA. [2014/XN6100/**F**]

- ♦ International Dispensary Association / see IDA Foundation (#11091)
- ♦ International Dispute Resolution Institute (unconfirmed)
- ♦ International Distance Learning Centre 'LINK / see International Institute of Management LINK

♦ International Distribution Institute (IDI) 13180

Address not obtained.
URL: http://www.idiproject.com/

History Registered in accordance with Italian law. **Aims** Promote the study of the law of international distribution. **Structure** General Meeting (annual). Council, comprising 5 permanent members (founders) and 2 country experts. President; Vice-President; Secretary. **Activities** through the *IDI Project.* **Events** *Annual Conference* Florence (Italy) 2018, *Annual Conference* Paris (France) 2017, *Annual Conference* Turin (Italy) 2016, *Annual Conference* Porto (Portugal) 2015, *Annual Conference* Turin (Italy) 2014. [2017/XJ0072/j/**F**]

- ♦ International District Energy Association (internationally oriented national body)
- ♦ International District Heating Association / see International District Energy Association
- ♦ International District Heating and Cooling Association / see International District Energy Association

♦ International Divers Alert Network (IDAN) 13181

Main Office 6 West Colony Pl, Durham NC 27705, USA. T. +19196842948. Fax +19194906630. E-mail: dan@diversalertnetwork.org.
URL: http://www.diversalertnetwork.org/

History Feb 1991, when the process to form an international DAN was started. **Aims** Enhance diving safety for recreational scuba divers; provide expert information and advice for the benefit of the diving public, especially regarding emergency medical advice and assistance for underwater diving injuries; work to prevent injuries; promote and support underwater diving research and education particularly as it relates to the improvement of diving safety, medical treatment and first aid; provide the most accurate, up-to-date and unbiased information on issues of common concern to the diving public. **Structure** Network of independent DAN organizations: DAN America, covers North, Central and South America and the Caribbean; *Divers Alert Network Europe (DAN Europe, see: #13181)*, covers all countries in Europe, the Mediterranean, Red Sea, Middle East, Ethiopia and the Maldives; DAN Japan; *Divers Alert Network Asia-Pacific (DAN Asia-Pacific, see: #13181)*, covers Australia, South Pacific Islands, Southeast Asia and New Zealand; *Divers Alert Network Southern Africa (DAN Southern Africa, see: #13181)*, covers South Africa, Eswatini, Lesotho, Namibia, Botswana, Zimbabwe, Mozambique, Angola, Zambia, Malawi, Tanzania, Kenya, Madagascar, Comoros, Seychelles and Mauritius. Head office located in DAN America. **Finance** Members' dues, based on region. **Activities** Provides medical consultations for injured divers; collects and analyses diving injury and fatality information; promotes educational programmes; offers diving accident insurance and *'DAN TravelAssist'*, a worldwide medical evacuation and assistance service; investigates causes and mechanisms of decompression illness (DCI), therapies that are effective for their treatment and diving guidelines that might reduce DCI incidence. *'Project Dive Exploration'* (or Project Safe Dive in Europe) is an international database of dives to study diving practices and how these dives compare to dive accident profiles. Organizes oxygen first aid courses representing entry-level training designed to educate the general diving (and qualified non-diving) public in how to recognize possible dive-related injuries, provide emergency oxygen first aid while activating local emergency medical services and arrange for evacuation to the nearest available medical facility. Independent DAN organizations are based around the world to provide expert emergency medical and referral services to regional diving communities. **Publications** *Alert Diver* (6 a year) – magazine; *On Board* (4 a year); *Sponsor News* (4 a year); *Annual Report on Scuba Diving Injuries and Fatalities. DAN Dive and Travel Medical Guide.* Instructional materials. [2019/XF4949/**F**]

- ♦ International Diving Educators Association (internationally oriented national body)

♦ International Diving Educators Association – Europe (IDEA Europe) 13182

Admin Office Via Antica Arischia 185 P, 67100 L'Aquila AQ, Italy.
President Office Via Mulino di Pile 3, 67100 L'Aquila AQ, Italy. Fax +396233290421.
URL: http://www.idea-eu.org/

History 1995, within *International Diving Educators Association (IDEA).*
Members Regional offices in 11 countries:
Belgium, Croatia, France, Germany, Greece, Italy, Netherlands, Serbia, Spain, Sweden, UK. [2018/XD9063/**D**]

♦ International Diving Schools Association (IDSA) 13183

Secretariat Ambachtsweg 27, 2641 KS Pijnacker, Netherlands. T. +31152512029. E-mail: info@idsaworldwide.org – post@idsaworldwide.org.
URL: http://www.idsaworldwide.org/

History 1982. Former names and other names: *Association of International Diving Schools* – former. **Aims** Create international diving standards, which will contribute to: equating standards worldwide; providing guidance to organizations setting standards for the first time; improving safety; providing contractors with a direct input to the diver training syllabus and enabling them to bid across national borders on a more even playing field; improving the quality of diver education; providing divers with greater job opportunities. **Structure** A branch organization. **Languages** Dutch, English. **Finance** Sources: members' dues. **Activities** Events/meetings; standards/guidelines; training/education. **Events** *Annual Meeting* Bergen (Norway) 2023, *Annual Meeting* Ireland 2022, *Annual Meeting* Oslo (Norway) 2014, *Annual Meeting* Copenhagen (Denmark) 2013, *Annual Meeting* Seattle, WA (USA) 2012. **Publications** *IDSA News* (2 a year).
Members Associations in 25 countries:
Austria, Belgium, Bulgaria, Croatia, Denmark, Egypt, Finland, France, India, Iran Islamic Rep, Italy, Montenegro, Morocco, Namibia, Netherlands, Norway, Poland, Russia, Singapore, South Africa, Spain, Sweden, Switzerland, UK, USA.
NGO Relations Member of (1): *European Diving Technology Committee (EDTC, #06932).*
[2022.10.19/XF6160/**F**]

♦ International DMB Advancement Group (IDAG) 13184

Pres RBM5, Bjírnstjerne Bjírnsons plass 1, 0340 Oslo, Norway. T. +4740000022.
URL: http://www.theidag.org/

History Jun 2009. Registered in accordance with Norwegian law: 995 288 079. **Aims** Promote, facilitate and coordinate DMB initiatives around the world. **Structure** Steering Board. **Finance** Members' dues.
Members Companies in 16 countries:
Australia, Belgium, Germany, Ireland, Italy, Latvia, Malaysia, Malta, Mongolia, Netherlands, Norway, Poland, South Africa, Switzerland, UK, Vietnam.
Associate members in 5 countries:
France, Germany, Netherlands, Norway, UK. [2017/XM5915/**F**]

♦ International DN Ice Yacht Racing Association (IDNIYRA) 13185

IDNIYRA Europe Wingham House, Winchester Road, Bishops Waltham, SO32 1BZ, UK. T. +441489892182. E-mail: c.w.w@btinternet.com.
IDNIYRA North America 2205 California St NE, Suite 101, Minneapolis MN 55418, USA. T. +16124352002. E-mail: us5214@iceboating.net.
URL: https://idniyra.eu/

History Incorporated in the State of Michigan (USA), 1962. **Aims** Promote, protect and perpetuate DN one-design iceboating; advance the art and skill of DN Ice Yacht construction and sailing, as well as future development of DN Class Ice Yacht and the sport of ice yachting on all hard waters of the world. **Structure** Comprises: *International DN Ice Yacht Racing Association – Europe (IDNIYRA – Europe, see: #13185); International DN Ice Yacht Racing Association-North America (IDNIYRA-North America, see: #13185).* **Languages** English. **Staff** None. **Finance** Members' dues. **Activities** Events/meetings. **Events** *World Championship* Estonia 2014, *World Championship* USA 2013, *World Championship* Sweden 2012, *World Championship* Poland 2010, *World Championship* Czech Rep 2008. **Publications** *Runner Tracks* (4 a year). Yearbook.
Members National organizations in 20 countries:
Austria, Belarus, Canada, Czechia, Denmark, Estonia, Finland, Germany, Hungary, Latvia, Lithuania, Netherlands, Norway, Poland, Russia, Sweden, Switzerland, UK, USA. [2018.08.02/XJ3805/**E**]

♦ International DN Ice Yacht Racing Association – Europe (see: #13185)
♦ International DN Ice Yacht Racing Association-North America (see: #13185)
♦ International Doctors for Healthier Drug Policies (internationally oriented national body)

♦ International Doctors – ILDAV 13186

Internationale Ärtze – ILÄAT – Médecins Internationales – ILMAV

SG Via Gian Battista Brocchi 11, 20131 Milan MI, Italy. T. +3926427882. Fax +39178220661. E-mail: secretariat@limav.org – info@limav.org.
URL: http://www.limav.org/

History 1987, Switzerland, as *International League of Doctors for the Abolition of Vivisection (ILDAV).* Known in Italian as *Lega Internazionale Medici per l'Abolizione della vivisezione (LIMAV).* **Aims** Abolish *animal* experimentation. **Finance** Donations. **Activities** Organizes international scientific congresses against vivisection; promotes conferences and debates by agencies, schools and universities worldwide; funds researches that do not use animals; stimulates the development of truly scientific techniques, therefore without the involvement of animals. **NGO Relations** Member of: *EarthAction (EA, #05159).* Secretariat located at: *Organisation internationale pour la protection des animaux (OIPA, #17810).* [2018/XF6398/**F**]

♦ International Documentary Association (IDA) 13187

Exec Dir 3600 Wilshire Blvd, Ste 1810, Los Angeles CA 90010, USA. T. +12132321660. E-mail: info@documentary.org.
URL: http://www.documentary.org/

History 6 Feb 1982, Los Angeles CA (USA). **Aims** Support and promote the work of nonfiction film and documentary film and video makers; improve public awareness of, and increase the market for, this art. **Structure** Board of Directors and Board of Trustees, each comprising about 20 members. **Languages** English. **Staff** 10.00 FTE, paid. Volunteers. **Finance** Members' dues. Other sources: grants; fund-raising activities. Budget (annual): US$ 850,000. **Activities** Educational programmes; screenings; workshops and seminars. Special events: 'IDA Awards Competition'; IDA Awards Gala'; 'Annual Oscar Reception'; 'DocuDAY'; 'DocuFest'. **Events** *Congress* Los Angeles, CA (USA) 2001, *Congress* Los Angeles, CA (USA) 1998, *Documentary film* Los Angeles, CA (USA) 1995, *Meeting* Los Angeles, CA (USA) 1992. **Publications** *International Documentary* (10 a year); *IDA Membership Directory* (every 2 years). Occasional books; transcripts; audiotapes and videotapes.
Members Individuals (mostly in USA) in 49 countries and territories:
Argentina, Armenia, Australia, Austria, Bahamas, Belgium, Brazil, Bulgaria, Canada, Chile, China, Colombia, Denmark, Finland, France, Germany, Greece, Hong Kong, Hungary, Iceland, India, Ireland, Israel, Italy, Japan, Korea Rep, Lebanon, Mexico, Nepal, Netherlands, New Zealand, Norway, Poland, Portugal, Russia, Serbia, Slovakia, Slovenia, South Africa, Spain, Sweden, Switzerland, Taiwan, Türkiye, UK, United Arab Emirates, Uruguay, USA, Vietnam. [2022/XD1582/v/**F**]

♦ International Documentation Centre for Plastic Expressions (inactive)

♦ International DOI Foundation (IDF) 13188

Dir c/o GTC Law Group, 400 Blue Hill Drive, Ste 2, Westwood MA 02090, USA. E-mail: info@doi.org.
URL: http://www.doi.org/

History 1997, at Frankfurt Book Fair (Germany). Registered in the state of Delaware (USA). **Aims** Support the needs of the *intellectual property* community in the *digital* environment through development and promotion of the Digital Object Identifier system as a common infrastructure for content management, setting policies for the system, choosing service providers and overseeing its operation. **Structure** Business Meeting; Board of Directors. **Languages** English. **Staff** 0.50 FTE, paid. **Finance** Members' dues. Franchise fees from Registration Agencies. **Activities** Certification/accreditation; research and development. **Events** *Business Meeting* Oxford (UK) 2015, *Outreach Meeting / Business Meeting* Tokyo (Japan) 2015, *Outreach Conference / Business Meeting* Milan (Italy) 2014, *Meeting / Business Meeting* Oxford (UK) 2014, *Business Meeting* Taipei (Taiwan) 2014. **Publications** *DOI Handbook. DOI Factsheets.*
Members Charter (2); General (5); Affiliate (1); Registration Agency (9). Membership, open to all organizations worldwide with an interest in electronic publishing and its related enabling technologies. Members in 10 countries and territories:
Belgium, China, France, Germany, Italy, Japan, Netherlands, Taiwan, UK, USA.
Including in the above, 2 organizations listed in this Yearbook:
International Federation of Reproduction Rights Organizations (IFRRO, #13527); Publications Office of the European Union (Publications Office, #18562).
Consultative Status Consultative status granted from: *World Intellectual Property Organization (WIPO, #21593)* (Permanent Observer Status). **NGO Relations** Member of standards organizations and maintains liaison or alliances with several national and international organizations, including: *EDItEUR (#05361); International Organization for Standardization (ISO, #14473); Linked Content Coalition (LCC).*
[2016.12.14/XF4383/fy/**F**]

♦ International Doll Association (inactive)

♦ International Dolphin Watch (IDW) 13189

Hon Dir 10 Melton Road, North Ferriby, HU14 3ET, UK. T. +441652637477.
URL: http://www.idw.org/

History 1978, North Ferriby (UK). **Aims** Study and help *conservation* of wild dolphins by gathering information about their population and movements through observation in their natural environment; promote research into the healing power of dolphins. **Languages** English. **Finance** Donations through *International Dolphin Watch Supporters Club.* **Activities** Research/documentation; advocacy/lobbying/activism; training/education; standards/guidelines; knowledge management/information dissemination. **Events** *International dolphin and whale conference* Kailua-Kona, HI (USA) 1992. **Publications** Books; CDRoms; DVDs.
Members Full individuals, mostly in UK but in a total of 15 countries:
Australia, Czechia, Denmark, France, Germany, Greece, Ireland, Italy, Netherlands, Norway, Russia, South Africa, Switzerland, UK, USA.
IGO Relations Accredited by: *International Whaling Commission (IWC, #15879).* [2018.01.29/XF1099/v/**F**]

♦ International Domestic Workers Federation (IDWF) 13190

Gen Sec c/o CTU Training Ctr, 18 Shek Lei Street, Kwai Chung, Hong Kong.
URL: http://www.idwfed.org/

History Launched 2009, Geneva (Switzerland), at International Labour Conference (ILC), as *International Domestic Workers Network (IDWN).* Restructured into a more formal structure under current title, 28 Oct 2013, when Founding Congress was held. **Aims** Build a strong, democratic and united domestic/household workers' global organization to protect and advance domestic workers' rights everywhere. **Structure** Congress (every 5 years); Executive Committee; Secretariat, headed by General Secretary. **Languages** English, French, Spanish. **Staff** 9.00 FTE, paid; 3.00 FTE, voluntary. **Finance** Members' dues. Contributions from funding organizations. **Activities** Events/meetings; knowledge management/information dissemination; politics/policy/regulatory; research/documentation; training/education. **Publications** *IDWF e-Newsletter. IDWF Strategic Plan 2016-2020.* Annual Report; regional reports; manuals; handbooks.
Members Affiliates (67) representing over 600,000 domestic/household workers in 54 countries and territories:
Antigua-Barbuda, Argentina, Bangladesh, Belgium, Benin, Brazil, Burkina Faso, Cambodia, Chile, Colombia, Costa Rica, Côte d'Ivoire, Dominican Rep, El Salvador, Germany, Ghana, Guatemala, Guinea, Hong Kong, India, Indonesia, Italy, Jamaica, Kenya, Korea Rep, Liberia, Malawi, Malaysia, Mali, Mexico, Mozambique, Namibia, Nepal, Netherlands, Nicaragua, Niger, Nigeria, Paraguay, Peru, Philippines, Senegal, South Africa, Sri Lanka, Switzerland, Tanzania UR, Thailand, Togo, Trinidad-Tobago, Türkiye, Uganda, USA, Zambia, Zimbabwe.
IGO Relations Supports: *Domestic Workers Convention, 2011 (C189, 2011).* **NGO Relations** Member of: *International Union of Food, Agricultural, Hotel, Restaurant, Catering, Tobacco and Allied Workers Associations (IUF, #15772); Women in Informal Employment: Globalizing and Organizing (WIEGO, #21003).*
[2018.07.31/XJ8446/**C**]

♦ International Domestic Workers Network / see International Domestic Workers Federation (#13190)

♦ International Dominican Youth Movement (IDYM) 13191

Movimiento Juvenil Dominicano Internacional – Mouvement de la Jeunesse Dominicaine International

Secretariat CG Frati Domenicani, Convento S Sabina, Piazza Pietro d'Illiria 1, 00153 Rome RM, Italy. E-mail: idym@curia.op.org.
URL: http://idymop.org/

History 1996. **Aims** Follow Saint Dominic's path through preaching from youth to youth. **Structure** International Commission; International Coordinator. **Languages** English, French, Spanish. **Finance** Private donations; local fundraising activities. **Activities** Religious activities; training/education; events/meetings. **Events** *International Meeting and Assembly* Nairobi (Kenya) 2021, *International Meeting and Assembly* Nairobi (Kenya) 2020, *Meeting* Bogota (Colombia) 2013, *General Assembly* Fatima (Portugal) 2009, *Meeting* Ocaña (Spain) 2002.
Members Full in 25 countries:
Argentina, Brazil, Cameroon, Central African Rep, Chile, Colombia, Congo DR, Costa Rica, Croatia, Guatemala, Italy, Kenya, Korea Rep, Mexico, Pakistan, Paraguay, Peru, Philippines, Portugal, Spain, Togo, Trinidad-Tobago, USA, Venezuela, Zimbabwe.
[2020/XE3933/**E**]

♦ International DORIS Service (IDS) 13192

Dir CLS, 8-10 rue Hermes, Parc Technologique du Canal, 31526 Ramonville CEDEX, France. T. +33561394849. Fax +33561394806.
URL: http://ids.cls.fr/

History as a *DORIS Pilot Experiment,* Jul 1999, by *International Association of Geodesy (IAG, #11914)* and *International Earth Rotation and Reference Systems Service (IERS, #13216).* Officially started as as IAG Service, 1 Jul 2003, at General Assembly of *International Union of Geodesy and Geophysics (IUGG, #15776),* Sapporo (Japan). DORIS stands for: *Doppler Orbit determination and Radiopositioning Integrated on Satellite.* **Aims** Provide a service to support, through DORIS data and data products, geodetic and geophysical activities. **Structure** Governing Board. Central Bureau. Working Groups. **Members** Permanent tracking stations (56). Membership countries not specified. **NGO Relations** Consortium member of: *Global Geodetic Observing System (GGOS, see: #11914).* Network member of: *ISC World Data System (ISC-WDS, #16024).*
[2014/XM1277/**E**]

♦ International Dostoevsky Society (IDS) 13193

Exec Sec address not obtained. E-mail: starezsozima@yahoo.de.
Pres address not obtained.
URL: http://www.dostoevsky.org/

History Founded 1971. **Aims** Promote study, and facilitate contact between scholars, of the life and work of the *writer* Fyodor Mikhailovich Dostoevsky. **Languages** English, French, German, Russian. **Events** *Triennial Symposium* Moscow (Russia) 2013, *Triennial Symposium* Naples (Italy) 2010, *Triennial Symposium* Moscow (Russia) 2009, *Triennial Symposium* Moscow (Russia) 2008, *Triennial Symposium* Budapest (Hungary) 2007. **Publications** *Dostoevsky Studies* (annual).
Members Societies 17 countries:
Australia, Brazil, Bulgaria, Czechia, Estonia, France, Germany, Hungary, Italy, Japan, New Zealand, Poland, Russia, Spain, Switzerland, UK, USA.
Members also in Scandinavia. [2014.06.01/XE3222/**E**]

♦ International Double Reed Society (IDRS) 13194

Société des anches doubles internationale

Main Office PO Box 490, Riderwood MD 21139-0490, USA.
URL: http://www.idrs.org/

History Founded Aug 1972, Ann Arbor MI (USA). **Aims** Provide a means of fostering world-wide communication and fellowship among double reed *musicians* (oboists and bassoonists), all those interested in the problems and activities of *performers,* teachers, students and manufacturers of double *reed instruments* and accessories. **Structure** General Meeting (annual); Executive Committee. **Languages** English. **Staff** 1.00 FTE, paid. **Finance** Members' dues. Sources: exhibit fees from conference; advertising proceeds. Budget (annual): about US$ 125,000. **Activities** Maintains archives; meeting activities; competitions. **Events** *Annual Conference* Tampa, FL (USA) 2019, *Annual Conference* Granada (Spain) 2018, *Annual Conference* Appleton, WI (USA) 2017, *Annual Conference* Columbus, GA (USA) 2016, *Annual Conference* Tokyo (Japan) 2015. **Publications** *The Double Reed* (4 a year).
Members Double reed musicians, performers, teachers, students, and manufacturers of double reed instruments. Types of membership Regular; Student; Institutional; Contributing. Individuals (4,500, mainly in USA) in 58 countries:
Argentina, Australia, Austria, Belarus, Belgium, Bolivia, Brazil, Canada, Chile, China, Colombia, Costa Rica, Croatia, Cuba, Cyprus, Czechia, Denmark, Egypt, El Salvador, Finland, France, Germany, Greece, Hong Kong, Hungary, Iceland, Ireland, Israel, Italy, Jamaica, Japan, Kazakhstan, Korea Rep, Lithuania, Luxembourg, Mexico, Netherlands, New Zealand, Norway, Oman, Philippines, Poland, Portugal, Puerto Rico, Russia, Singapore, South Africa, Spain, Sweden, Switzerland, Taiwan, Türkiye, UK, Ukraine, United Arab Emirates, Uruguay, USA, Venezuela. [2019/XF1357/v/**F**]

♦ International Down and Feather Bureau (IDFB) **13195**
Bureau international des duvets et des plumes – Internationales Daunen-und Federn-Bureau
Gen Sec Schwalbenweg 15, 6973 Höchst, Austria. T. +436649686030. E-mail: idfb@idfb.net.
URL: http://www.idfb.net/
History 1953, Paris (France). Former names and other names: *International Feather Bureau* – former; *Internationales Federn-Bureau* – former. Registration: No/ID: VR 9132, Germany, Frankfurt-Main. **Aims** Provide a worldwide association for the down/feather industry, down/feather trade, and testing institutes for down/feather as filling material. **Events** *Annual General Meeting* Toronto, ON (Canada) 2022, *Annual General Meeting* Höchst (Austria) 2021, *Annual General Meeting* 2020, *Conference* Lijiang (China) 2010, *Conference* Cape Town (South Africa) 2009.
Members Individuals (over 650) in 29 countries and territories:
Australia, Austria, Belgium, Bulgaria, Canada, China, Czechia, Denmark, Finland, France, Germany, Hungary, Iceland, Ireland, Italy, Japan, Korea Rep, Liechtenstein, Poland, Russia, South Africa, Spain, Switzerland, Taiwan, Thailand, Türkiye, Ukraine, USA, Vietnam. [2022.05.03/XF2330/**F**]

♦ International Downhill Federation (IDF) **13196**
Pres address not obtained.
URL: https://internationaldownhillfederation.org/
History Registered in accordance with French law. **Aims** Organize and promote downhill disciplines, namely, *skateboard*, streetluge and classic *luge*. **Structure** Annual General Meeting; Board. **Finance** Sources: members' dues. **Activities** Sporting activities; standards/guidelines; training/education. [2018/XM6966/**C**]

♦ International Down Syndrome Federation / see Down Syndrome International (#05128)
♦ International Downtown Association (internationally oriented national body)
♦ International Downtown Executives Association / see International Downtown Association
♦ International Draft Animal Consultants (internationally oriented national body)
♦ International Dragon Association (see: #21760)

♦ International Dragon Boat Federation (IDBF) **13197**
SG address not obtained. E-mail: general-secretary@dragonboat.sport – idbfdragon@126.com – admin@dragonboat.sport.
URL: http://www.idbf.org/
History 24 Jun 1991, Hong Kong (Hong Kong). **Aims** Encourage the development of Dragon Boat racing, maintaining its Asian cultural, historical and religious traditions. **Structure** Executive Committee. **Activities** Sporting activities. **Events** *Congress* Busan (Korea Rep) 2013, *Annual Congress* Penang (Malaysia) 1996, *Annual Meeting* Penang (Malaysia) 1996.
Members Full in 61 countries and territories:
Argentina, Armenia, Australia, Austria, Brazil, Bulgaria, Canada, China, Côte d'Ivoire, Cyprus, Czechia, Egypt, Finland, France, Georgia, Germany, Ghana, Great Britain, Guam, Hong Kong, Hungary, India, Indonesia, Iran Islamic Rep, Ireland, Israel, Italy, Jamaica, Japan, Kenya, Korea Rep, Macau, Malaysia, Myanmar, Nepal, Netherlands, New Zealand, Nigeria, Norway, Panama, Philippines, Poland, Puerto Rico, Qatar, Réunion, Russia, Serbia, Singapore, Slovakia, South Africa, Spain, Sweden, Switzerland, Taiwan, Thailand, Trinidad-Tobago, Uganda, Ukraine, United Arab Emirates, USA, Vietnam.
NGO Relations Member of (2): *Alliance of Independent recognised Members of Sport (AIMS, #00690)*; *Olympic Movement (#17719)*. Cooperates with (1): *International Testing Agency (ITA, #15678)*. Recognized by: *International Olympic Committee (IOC, #14408)*. [2021/XN8731/**C**]

♦ International Drama/Theatre and Education Association (IDEA) ... **13198**
Association Internationale d'Art Dramatique/ Théâtre et Education – Asociación Internacional de Drama/Teatro y Educación
Pres School of Education, Murdoch Univ, 90 South Str, Murdoch WA 6150 WA, Australia.
Sec address not obtained.
Sec address not obtained.
URL: http://www.ideadrama.org/
History Jul 1992, Porto (Portugal). Previously also referred to as *Association internationale théâtre et éducation – Asociación Internacional Teatro y Educación* Registered in accordance with Portuguese law, 1994. **Aims** Offer a forum for meeting and discussion to individuals, groups and institutions worldwide, who are working and campaigning for the universal right to arts education and in particular to the place of drama/theatre in the education of each person; facilitate international communication and information dissemination; support the development of research into the theory and practice of drama/theatre and education; promote and encourage regional, national and international initiatives by facilitating the exchange of drama/theatre observers, practitioners and educators. **Structure** General Council; Executive Committee; Accountancy Committee; General Meetings Committee. **Languages** Chinese, English, French, Spanish. **Staff** 15.00 FTE, voluntary. **Finance** Members' dues. **Activities** Events/meetings; research/documentation; liaising/networking. **Events** *Triennial World Congress* Reykjavik (Iceland) 2022, *Triennial World Congress* Ankara (Turkey) 2016, *Triennial World Congress* Paris (France) 2013, *Triennial world congress* Belém (Brazil) 2010, *World conference on arts education* Seoul (Korea Rep) 2010. **Publications** Conference proceedings; research publications.
Members Ordinary in 32 countries and territories:
Australia, Bangladesh, Bosnia-Herzegovina, Brazil, Canada, Croatia, Czechia, Denmark, Finland, France, Germany, Greece, Hong Kong, Hungary, Iceland, India, Ireland, Italy, Korea Rep, Netherlands, New Zealand, North Macedonia, Norway, Philippines, Portugal, Serbia, Singapore, Sweden, Türkiye, Uganda, UK, USA.
Associate in 17 countries and territories:
Bulgaria, Canada, Denmark, France, Greece, Hungary, Japan, Kenya, Lithuania, Macau, Nicaragua, Peru, South Africa, Sudan, Taiwan, UK, Zimbabwe.
IGO Relations *UNESCO (#20322)*. **NGO Relations** Member of: *World Alliance for Arts Education (WAAE, #21078)*. Associate of: *International Association of Theatre for Children and Young People (#12225)*; *International Theatre Institute (ITI, #15683)*. [2017.10.12/XD4039/**D**]

♦ International Draughts Federation (IDF) **13199**
Office Manager Dobrich Region, Chernomorska Str 41, 9649 Kranevo, Bulgaria. E-mail: office@idf64.org.
Pres address not obtained.
URL: http://idf64.org/
History 12 Jul 2012, Balchik (Bulgaria). Founded as as a legal entity of FMJD Section 64 of *Fédération Mondiale du Jeu de Dames (FMJD, #09690)*. Oct 2015 FMJD Section 64, represented by the IDF, left the FMJD and works independently under the IDF brand. Current statutes adopted Aug 2018, Kranevo (Bulgaria). Cooperation agreement with FMJD signed, 13 Feb 2022. Registration: No/ID: 176513387, Start date: 5 Jun 2013, Bulgaria. **Aims** Develop draughts-64 in the world. **Structure** General Meeting; Board. **Languages** English, Russian. **Finance** Support for conducting of competitions from Foundation for the Promotion of Draughts Sports "Russian Draughts". **Activities** Events/meetings; sporting activities. **Events** *General Assembly* Kranevo (Bulgaria) 2022, *General Assembly* Kranevo (Bulgaria) 2021, *Annual Seminar* Kranevo (Bulgaria) 2019, *Seminar for Referees* Kranevo (Bulgaria) 2018, *Annual Seminar* Kranevo (Bulgaria) 2017.
Members Full in 65 countries and territories:
Angola, Armenia, Australia, Austria, Azerbaijan, Barbados, Belarus, Brazil, Bulgaria, Cambodia, Congo Brazzaville, Congo DR, Cyprus, Czechia, Estonia, Ethiopia, Finland, France, Georgia, Germany, Ghana, Greece, Guinea-Bissau, Haiti, India, Iran Islamic Rep, Israel, Jamaica, Japan, Kazakhstan, Korea Rep, Kyrgyzstan, Latvia, Liberia, Lithuania, Malawi, Malta, Moldova, Mongolia, Morocco, Mozambique, Nepal, Nigeria, Northern Ireland, Norway, Pakistan, Philippines, Portugal, Romania, Russia, Singapore, South Africa, Sri Lanka, Syrian AR, Tajikistan, Tanzania UR, Türkiye, Turkmenistan, Uganda, Ukraine, USA, Uzbekistan, Vietnam, Zambia, Zimbabwe.
NGO Relations Member of (1): *The Association for International Sport for All (TAFISA, #02763)*. [2022.02.15/XM5483/**D**]

♦ International Dressage Judges Club / see International Dressage Officials Club (#13200)

♦ International Dressage Officials Club (IDOC) **13200**
Secretariat Van De Reydtlaan 83, 2990 Brecht, Belgium.
URL: http://dressage-officials.com/
History Founded 30 Nov 1990, as *International Dressage Judges Club (IDJC)*. Statutes revised and current title adopted, 2009. Registered in accordance with Belgian law. **Aims** Represent, unite, educate, promote and protect the international dressage officials community; foster higher and more consistent standards in dressage judging. **Structure** General Assembly (annual); Executive Board. **Languages** Dutch, English, French. **Staff** No permanent staff. **Activities** Training/education; events/meetings. **Events** *General Assembly* London (UK) 2014, *General Assembly* London (UK) 2013, *General Assembly* Aachen (Germany) 1993. **Members** FEI International Dressage Officials (Judges and Stewards). Membership countries not specified. **NGO Relations** Member of: *European Equestrian Federation (EEF, #07005)*; *Fédération Équestre Internationale (FEI, #09484)*. [2020/XD2682/**F**]

♦ International Dressage Riders Club (IDRC) **13201**
Club international des cavaliers de dressage
SG Albeck and Albeck Vermögensverwaltung, Kurfürstendamm 63, 10707 Berlin, Germany. T. +4930884770. Fax +493088477263.
Pres address not obtained.
URL: https://www.idrc.me/
History 1986, Aachen (Germany). **Aims** Represent the interests of international dressage riders; promote the interests and image of the dressage sport. **Structure** General Assembly (annual); Executive Board. **Finance** Sources: members' dues. **Events** *General Assembly* Germany 2022, *General Assembly* Germany 2021. **NGO Relations** *Fédération Équestre Internationale (FEI, #09484)*. Associate member of: *European Equestrian Federation (EEF, #07005)*. [2022/XF1707/**F**]

♦ International Dressage Trainers Club (IDTC) **13202**
Secretariat Koestraat 9, 5095 BD Hooge Mierde, Netherlands.
URL: http://www.idtc-online.com/
Aims Promote correct dressage training. **Structure** Board; President; Secretary General. **Languages** English. **Finance** Members' dues. **NGO Relations** Associate member of: *Fédération Équestre Internationale (FEI, #09484)*. [2021/XJ9440/**F**]

♦ International DRH Movement **13203**
Contact Volunteer Progr – DRH South Zealand, Lindersvoldvej 5, 4640 Faxe, Denmark. T. +4523674906. E-mail: info@lindersvold.dk.
URL: https://lindersvold.dk/
History DRH stands for *Den Rejsende Højskole*, meaning *Travelling Folk High School*. First travelling school set up 1970, Denmark. **Aims** Offer people the opportunity to study with practical, autodidactic and traditional courses about *global issues*, *development* work and the fight against *poverty*.
Members Schools (7) in 5 countries:
Denmark, Norway, St Vincent-Grenadines, UK, USA. [2020.04.29/XJ5653/**F**]

♦ International Drivers' Behaviour Research Association (inactive)
♦ International Driving Tests Committee / see International Commission for Driver Testing (#12678)

♦ International Drug Abuse Research Society (IDARS) **13204**
Exec Officer NCTR – HFT 132, 3900 NCTR Rd, Jefferson AR 72079, USA.
URL: http://www.idars.org/
History Registered in accordance with US law. **Aims** Promote and foster research and collaboration of scientists around the world in the area of substances of abuse and addiction. **Structure** Board. **Events** *Conference* Nice (France) 2022, *Conference* Casablanca (Morocco) 2019, *Conference* Dubrovnik (Croatia) 2017, *Conference* Sydney, NSW (Australia) 2015, *Conference* Mexico City (Mexico) 2013. **Publications** *IDARS Newsletter*, *The Journal of Drug and Alcohol Research (JDAR)*. [2016/XM4738/**C**]

♦ International Drug Association / see IDA Foundation (#11091)
♦ International Drug Awareness Research Foundation (internationally oriented national body)
♦ International Drug Enforcement Conference (meeting series)

♦ International Drug Policy Consortium (IDPC) **13205**
Mailing Address 61 Mansell Street, London, E1 8AN, UK. E-mail: contact@idpc.net.
URL: http://www.idpc.net/
History 2006, London (UK). Former names and other names: *IDPC Consortium* – legal name. Registration: Handelsregister, No/ID: KVK 76670260, Netherlands; EU Transparency Register, No/ID: 541865242158-31, Start date: 7 Apr 2021. **Aims** Amplify and strengthen a diverse global movement to repair the harms caused by punitive drug policies, and promote just responses. **Structure** Board of Directors. **Languages** English, French, Spanish, Thai. **Staff** 5.50 FTE, paid. **Activities** Advocacy/lobbying/activism; capacity building; knowledge management/information dissemination; networking/liaising. **Events** *Getting ready for the Global Drug Policy Index* 2021, *International Drug Policy Reform Conference* Denver, CO (USA) 2013. **Members** NGOs (194). Membership countries not specified. **Consultative Status** Consultative status granted from: *ECOSOC (#05331)* (Special). **NGO Relations** Member of (4): *Alliance of NGOs on Crime Prevention and Criminal Justice (#00709)*; *Civil Society Forum on Drugs (CSFD, #03968)*; *New York NGO Committee on Drugs (NYNGOC, #17097)*; *Vienna NGO Committee on Drugs (VNGOC, #20773)*. [2022.10.18/XM1901/y/**F**]

♦ International Dry Bulk Terminals Contact Group / see International Dry Bulk Terminals Group (#13206)

♦ International Dry Bulk Terminals Group (DBTG) **13206**
Exec Dir address not obtained. T. +447779797012. E-mail: info@drybulkterminals.org.
URL: http://www.drybulkterminals.org/
History First meeting Oct 1997, Rotterdam (Netherlands); Working Party set up Apr 1998, London (UK). Final Draft Constitution approved Dec 1998, Amsterdam (Netherlands). Previously also referred to as *International Dry Bulk Terminals Contact Group*. Registered in England and Wales. **Aims** Create mutual information exchange on all aspects of dry bulk *transportation* and handling; offer general support. **Structure** General Assembly (annual). Executive Committee. **Languages** English. **Finance** Members' dues. Event proceeds. **Events** *Annual Meeting* Barcelona (Spain) 2019, *Annual Meeting* Rotterdam (Netherlands) 2016, *Annual Meeting* Panama 2014, *Annual Meeting* Santander (Spain) 2013, *Annual Meeting* New Orleans, LA (USA) 2012. **Consultative Status** Consultative status granted from: *International Maritime Organization (IMO, #14102)*. [2019/XD8497/**D**]

♦ International Drycleaners Congress (IDC) **13207**
Association internationale des nettoyeurs – Congreso Internacional de Tintorerias – Internationaler Chemischer-Reiniger Congress
Exec Dir 256 Sun Valley Drive SE, Calgary AB T2X 2T8, Canada. T. +14036854755. Fax +14032561580. E-mail: interdryclean@shaw.ca.
URL: http://www.idcgroup.org/
History 1959, Tokyo (Japan). Registration: Start date: 1961, USA, State of California. **Aims** Strengthen international understanding and good will in the *textile* care industry by providing opportunities for travel, exchange of information and communication for members. **Structure** Congress (every 2 years); International President and Vice President; Regional Vice Presidents; Executive Director. **Languages** English. **Staff** 1.00 FTE, paid. **Finance** Sources: members' dues. Annual budget: 40,000 USD. **Activities** Awards/prizes/competitions; events/meetings. **Events** *Annual Convention* Melbourne, VIC (Australia) 2021, *Annual Convention* Jakarta (Indonesia) 2018, *Annual Convention* Las Vegas, NV (USA) 2017, *Annual Convention* Osaka (Japan) 2015, *Annual Convention* Vancouver, BC (Canada) 2014. **Publications** *IDC News* (2 a year).
Members Individuals in 22 countries and territories:
Australia, Canada, China, Colombia, Germany, Hong Kong, India, Indonesia, Ireland, Japan, Korea Rep, Malaysia, New Zealand, Nigeria, Romania, Saudi Arabia, Singapore, Sri Lanka, Taiwan, UK, USA, Venezuela. [2022.05.12/XF5354/v/**F**]

♦ International Drycleaning Trade Association / see International Committee of Textile Care (#12809)

♦ International Dryland Development Commission (IDDC) **13208**
Executive Officer 19 Aboul Feda St, Zamalek, Cairo, Egypt. T. +20212222100511. Fax +20227370037.
Chairman address not obtained. E-mail: elbeltagy@optomatica.com.

History 1987. Former names and other names: *International Dry Lands Development Commission* – former. **Aims** Promote all aspects of dryland studies by fostering cooperation, collaboration and networking between various international, regional and national organizations. **Structure** Governing Board; Executive Board. **Languages** English. **Staff** Voluntary. **Finance** Funding from donor agencies. **Activities** Events/meetings. . **Events** *International Conference on Development of Drylands* Jodhpur (India) 2019, *Conference* Alexandria (Egypt) 2016, *Global climate change and its impact on food and energy security in the drylands* Beijing (China) 2013, *Meeting the challenge of sustainable development in drylands under changing climate – moving from global to local* Cairo (Egypt) 2010, *Conference* Alexandria (Egypt) 2008. **Publications** Conference proceedings.
[2021.09.06/XJ3884/**E**]

♦ International Dry Lands Development Commission / see International Dryland Development Commission (#13208)
♦ International DSM Conference (meeting series)

♦ International Dunhuang Project (IDP) 13209

Secretariat British Library, 96 Euston Road, London, NW1 2DB, UK. T. +442074127685.
URL: http://idp.bl.uk/

History 1994. **Aims** Promote international cooperation to study, preserve and make accessible the *archaeological* legacy of the Eastern *Silk* Road. **Structure** Business Meeting (every 2 years); Secretariat at the British Library in London (UK); Regional offices (8). **Languages** Chinese, English, French, German, Japanese, Korean, Russian. **Staff** Secretariat: 8.5 FTE, paid; Regional offices: 20 FTE, paid. **Finance** Donations; grants from: Arts and Humanities Research Council; British Academy; Dunhuang Culture Promotion Foundation; Korea University; *European Commission (EC, #06633)*; *Ford Foundation (#09858)*; *Leverhulme Trust*. British Library provides office space and some overheads. **Activities** Knowledge management/information dissemination; training/education; networking/liaising; events/meetings. **Events** *Conference* London (UK) 2012, *Conference* London (UK) 2007, *Conservation conference / Conference* Beijing (China) 2005, *Conservation conference* London (UK) 2005, *Conservation conference / Conference* Stockholm (Sweden) 2002. **Publications** *IDP Newsletter* (2 a year) in English. Exhibition catalogue; articles; occasional publications on conservation science; conference proceedings.
Members Founder members; libraries and institutes (11) in 10 countries:
China, France, Germany, Hungary, India, Japan, Korea Rep, Russia, Sweden, UK. [2015.08.26/XE4451/**E**]

♦ International Dupuytren Society 13210

Contact Westerbuchberg 60b, 83236 Übersee, Germany.
URL: http://www.dupuytren-online.info/

History Sep 2011, evolving from the former Duputyren eV. **Aims** Support patients and promote research, education and global cooperation to find a cure for Dupuytren *disease* and related conditions. **Structure** Advisory Board; Management Board. **Languages** English. **Staff** 21.00 FTE, voluntary. **Finance** Members' dues. Donations. **Activities** Events/meetings; awards/prizes/competitions. **Events** *International Conference on Dupuytren Disease* Oxford (UK) 2021, *International Conference on Dupuytren Disease* Oxford (UK) 2020, *International Conference on Dupuytren Disease* Groningen (Netherlands) 2015, *International Conference on Dupuytren Disease* Miami, FL (USA) 2010. **Publications** *Dupuytren Disease and Related Diseases – The Cutting Edge* (2017); *Dupuytren's Disease and Related Hyperproliferative Disorders* (2012).
Members Organizations in 7 countries:
Canada, Germany, Italy, Netherlands, Russia, UK, USA.
NGO Relations Full member of: *International Alliance of Patients' Organizations (IAPO, #11633)*.
[2019.06.25/XJ7745/**D**]

♦ International Duty Free Confederation / see European Travel Retail Confederation (#08945)
♦ International Dwarf Sports Federation (unconfirmed)
♦ International Dyslexia Association (internationally oriented national body)
♦ International Dyslexia Association Founded in Memory of Samuel T Orton / see International Dyslexia Association
♦ International Dystrophia Myotonica Consortium (unconfirmed)
♦ Internationale Agrarkredit-Konferenz / see Confédération internationale du crédit agricole (#04560)
♦ Internationale Akademie für Bäderkunde und Bädertechnik / see Internationale Akademie für Bäder-, Sport-, und Freizeitbauten (#13211)
♦ Internationale Akademie für Bäder-, Sport-, und Freizeitbauten / see Internationale Akademie für Bäder-, Sport-, und Freizeitbauten (#13211)

♦ Internationale Akademie für Bäder-, Sport-, und Freizeitbauten (IAB) 13211

Académie internationale de l'équipement des piscines, des sports et des loisirs – International Board for Aquatic, Sports and Recreation Facilities

Main Office Fangstrasse 22-24, 59077 Hamm, Germany. T. +492381438510. Fax +492381438512. E-mail: info@iab-ev.de.
URL: http://www.iab-ev.de/

History 6 Mar 1965, Basel (Switzerland), as *International Aquatic Board – Académie pour la science et la technique des piscines et des bains – Internationale Akademie für Bäderkunde und Bädertechnik*. Also known as *Internationale Akademie für Bäder-, Sport-, und Freizeitbauten*. **Aims** Promote research, planning, design, construction and management of all types of aquatic *buildings*, sports establishments and all recreational facilities related to them. **Structure** General Meeting (at least every 4 years). Executive Council; International and Scientific Advisory Panels. **Events** *Congress* Hamm (Germany) 2009, *Congress* Baden Baden (Germany) 2003, *Congress* Leipzig (Germany) 1995, *Congress* Leipzig (Germany) 1993, *Congress* Neckarsulm (Germany) 1991. **Publications** *Sport Bäder Freizeitbauten* (6 a year). *Bäderbauten Aquatic Buildings* – book.
Members Firms, architects, engineers, communes and towns, in 20 countries:
Austria, Belgium, Czechia, Denmark, Finland, France, Germany, Greece, Iran Islamic Rep, Israel, Italy, Japan, Liechtenstein, Luxembourg, Monaco, Netherlands, Sweden, Switzerland, UK, USA. [2012/XD6415/**F**]

♦ Internationale Akademie für Geschichte der Pharmazie (no recent information)
♦ Internationale Akademie für Innovative Pädagogik, Psychologie und Ökonomie, Freien Universität Berlin (internationally oriented national body)

♦ Internationale Akademie land- und hauswirtschaftlicher Beraterinnen und Berater (IALB) 13212

International Academy of Rural Advisors

Main Office Porschestr 5a, 84030 Landshut, Germany. T. +498719522318. Fax +498719522399. E-mail: ialb@fueak.bayern.de.
URL: http://www.ialb.org/

History 1961. Former names and other names: *Internationaler Arbeitskreis Landwirtschaftlicher Berater* – former; *International Group for Agricultural and Home Economics Extension Officers* – former. **Aims** Provide services to individuals and corporate bodies, in the fields of education and official and private consultancy, as well as to service providers in rural areas. **Structure** Bureau. **Languages** German. **Activities** Events/meetings. **Events** *Meeting* Dresden (Germany) 2023, *Meeting* Lugo (Spain) 2022, *Congress* Hohenems (Austria) 2021, *Congress* Landshut (Germany) 2020, *Congress* Salzburg (Austria) 2019.
Members Full (625) in 13 countries:
Austria, Belgium, Bosnia-Herzegovina, Croatia, Denmark, France, Germany, Hungary, Italy, Luxembourg, Slovenia, Spain, Switzerland.
NGO Relations Cooperates with (2): *European Forum for Agricultural and Rural Advisory Services (EUFRAS, #07303)*; *South Eastern Europe Advisory Service Network (SEASN, #19805)*. [2022/XN4750/**D**]

♦ Internationale Akademie Nürnberger Prinzipien (internationally oriented national body)
♦ Internationale Akademie für Positive und Transkulturelle Psychotherapie (internationally oriented national body)
♦ Internationale Akademie für Tourismus (inactive)
♦ Internationale Akademie der Wissenschaften, San Marino (#00617)
♦ Internationale Akademie der Wissenschaft vom Holz (#11581)
♦ Internationale Akademie für Zytologie (#11544)
♦ Internationale Aktuarvereinigung (#11586)
♦ Internationale Alexander Lernet-Holenia Gesellschaft (#11616)
♦ Internationale Allianz Iranischer Studenten (internationally oriented national body)
♦ Internationale Allianz von Patienten-Organisationen (#11633)
♦ Internationale Alpenschutzkommission / see CIPRA International (#03930)
♦ Internationale Amateur-Theater-Vereinigung / see International Amateur Theatre Association (#11647)
♦ Internationale des amis de l'Ordre spirituel (inactive)
♦ Internationale Anti-Jagd Kommitee (internationally oriented national body)
♦ Internationale Anti-Militaristische Vereeniging (inactive)
♦ Internationale Anwalts-Union / see Union Internationale des Avocats (#20422)
♦ Internationale Arbeiterhilfe, 1925 (inactive)
♦ Internationale der Arbeiter-Kultur-Organisationen (#13285)
♦ Internationale Arbeitsgemeinschaft der Archiv-, Bibliotheks- und Graphikrestauratoren (#11729)
♦ Internationale Arbeitsgemeinschaft für Cannabinoidmedikamente (#11754)
♦ Internationale Arbeitsgemeinschaft Cannabis als Medizin / see International Association for Cannabinoid Medicines (#11754)
♦ Internationale Arbeitsgemeinschaft der Circus-und Schausteller-Seelsorger (#13752)
♦ Internationale Arbeitsgemeinschaft Deutschsprachiger Theater (no recent information)
♦ Internationale Arbeitsgemeinschaft Donauforschung (#11834)
♦ Internationale Arbeitsgemeinschaft Dynamische Osteosynthese / see Osteosynthesis and Trauma Care Foundation (#17911)
♦ Internationale Arbeitsgemeinschaft für Entwicklung und Solidarität / see CIDSE (#03926)

♦ Internationale Arbeitsgemeinschaft für Hymnologie (IAH) 13213

Cercle international d'études hymnologiques – International Society for Hymnological Studies

Secretariat Steinauweg 27, 3007 Bern, Switzerland. T. +41765031105. E-mail: sekretariat@iah-hymnologie.de.
Pres Skindbjerg Høje, 7700 Vestervig, Denmark.
URL: https://www.iah-hymnologie.de/

History 1959, Lüdenscheid (Germany). Current Constitution and By-laws adopted at membership meeting, 12 Aug 2005, Tartu (Estonia). **Aims** Bring together people interested in hymnological research and in promoting sacred song. **Structure** Membership Meeting (every 2 years); Executive Committee; Secretariat. **Languages** Dutch, English, French, German, Swedish. **Finance** Sources: members' dues. **Activities** Events/meetings; research/documentation. **Events** *Extraordinary Conference* Mainz (Germany) 2022, *Joint Conference* Washington, DC (USA) 2022, *Biennial Study Conference* Halle (Saale) (Germany) 2019, *Biennial Study Conference* Løgumkloster (Denmark) 2017, *Biennial Study Conference* Cambridge (UK) 2015. **Publications** *IAH-Bulletin*; *Jahrbuch für Liturgik und Hymnologie*; *Mitteilungen der IAH*.
Members Researchers and practitioners (312) who concern themselves with the systematic consideration of fundamental, historical and practical questions regarding hymns and church music, in 30 countries and territories:
Australia, Austria, Belgium, Canada, Croatia, Czechia, Denmark, Estonia, Finland, France, Germany, Hungary, Iceland, Japan, Latvia, Lithuania, Montenegro, Netherlands, Norway, Poland, Romania, Russia, Serbia, Slovenia, South Africa, Sweden, Switzerland, Taiwan, UK, USA. [2020.05.03/XF0383/v/**F**]

♦ Internationale Arbeitsgemeinschaft für Jugendherbergen / see Hostelling International (#10950)
♦ Internationale Arbeitsgemeinschaft der Katholischen Pflegeorganisation / see International Catholic Committee of Nurses and Medico-social Assistants (#12451)
♦ Internationale Arbeitsgemeinschaft von Organisationen für Qualitätsförderung und Informative Warenkennzeichnung (inactive)
♦ Internationale Arbeitsgemeinschaft der Papierhistoriker (#12066)

♦ Internationale Arbeitsgemeinschaft Sozialmanagement / Sozialwirtschaft (INAS) 13214

Chair c/o FHS St Gallen, Rosenbergstrasse 59, 9000 St Gallen, Switzerland.
URL: http://www.inas-ev.eu/

History 12 Feb 2009. Registered in accordance with German law. **Aims** Promote and network education and training, science and research in the field of *social management* and social *economics*. **Structure** Board. **Languages** German. **Finance** Members' dues. **Activities** Publishing activities; networking/liaising. **Events** *Führen in der Sozial- und Gesundheitswirtschaft – Neue Organisations- und Denkmodelle* Dresden (Germany) 2018, *Future strategies for social economy and social management in theory, research and practice* Feldkirchen in Kärnten (Austria) 2016, *Congress* Olten (Switzerland) 2014, *Congress* Berlin (Germany) 2012, *Congress* Linz (Austria) 2011.
Members Members in 4 countries:
Austria, Germany, Italy, Switzerland. [2018/XJ5269/**D**]

♦ Internationale Arbeitsgemeinschaft für Sozial-Wirtschaftliche Entwicklung / see CIDSE (#03926)
♦ Internationale Arbeitsgemeinschaft für Unterrichtsmedien (#13014)
♦ Internationale Arbeitsgemeinschaft der Wasserwerke im Donaueinzugsgebiet (#12264)

♦ Internationale Arbeitsgemeinschaft der Wasserwerke im Rheineinzugsgebiet (IAWR) 13215

Comité international des services des eaux du bassin rhénan – International Association of Waterworks in the Rhine Catchment Area – Internationaal Samenwerkingsverband van Waterleidingbedrijven in het Rijnstroomgebied

Secretariat c/o Stadtwerke Düsseldorf AG, Wasserwerke Himmelgeister Landstrasse 1, 40589 Düsseldorf, Germany. T. +4921182124944. Fax +49211821772494. E-mail: iawr@iawr.org.
URL: http://www.iawr.org/

History 23 Jan 1970, Düsseldorf (Germany FR), by *Association of River Water Companies (RIWA, #02895)*, *Association of Rhine Waterworks (ARW)* and *Association of Waterworks Lake Constance-Rhine (AWBR)*. **Aims** Protect the Rhine, its tributaries and the pre-Alpine lakes, so that the quality of their waters is good enough to allow drinking water to be produced using only natural methods such as river or bank filtration; safeguard interest of public water supply for its 30 million consumers; promote better methods of pollution control. **Structure** General Assembly; Council. **Languages** Dutch, English, German. **Staff** 1.00 FTE, paid. **Finance** Members' dues. Budget (annual): about euro 70,000. **Activities** Projects/programmes; knowledge management/information dissemination; monitoring/evaluation. **Events** *Working meeting* Amsterdam (Netherlands) 2003, *Working meeting / Meeting* Stuttgart (Germany) 2000, *Meeting* Duisburg (Germany) 1996, *Biennial meeting / Meeting* Zurich (Switzerland) 1993, *Biennial meeting* The Hague (Netherlands) 1991. **Publications** Assembly proceedings; press releases.
Members Associations (about 120) in 6 countries:
Austria, Belgium, France, Germany, Netherlands, Switzerland.
IGO Relations *International Commission for the Protection of the Rhine (ICPR, #12721)*.
[2015.09.03/XD3921/**D**]

♦ Internationale der Arbeitssanger / see Internationale des organisations culturelles ouvrières (#13285)
♦ International Early Psychosis Association / see IEPA Early Intervention in Mental Health (#11097)
♦ Internationale Armbrustschützen Union (#13117)
♦ International Earth Observations Satellite Committee / see Committee on Earth Observation Satellites (#04249)

♦ International Earth Rotation and Reference Systems Service (IERS) 13216

Service international de la rotation de la terre et des systèmes de référence

Dir IERS Central Bureau, c/o Bundesamt für Kartographie und Geodäsie, Richard-Strauss-Allee 11, 60598 Frankfurt-Main, Germany. T. +49696333273. Fax +496963332100. E-mail: central_bureau@iers.org.
URL: http://www.iers.org/

History Aug 1987, Vancouver, BC (Canada). Founded at *International Union of Geodesy and Geophysics (IUGG, #15776)* General Assembly, and, Sep 1987, at *International Astronomical Union (IAU, #12287)* General Assembly, replacing *International Polar Motion Service (IPMS, inactive)* and taking over the earth rotation activities of *Bureau international de l'heure (BIH, inactive)*, while *Bureau international des poids et mesures (BIPM, #03367)* takes over the BIH activities on time scales. Commenced operations on 1 Jan 1988. New structure commenced operations as of 1 Jan 2001. Former names and other names: *International Earth Rotation Service (IERS)* – former; *Service international de la rotation terrestre* – former. **Aims** Serve the astronomical, geodetic, geophysical and space communities by providing data and standards related to Earth rotation and reference frames. **Structure** Directing Board; Central Bureau. Technique Centres (4); Product Centres (6); ITRS Combination Centres; Working Groups. **Languages** English. **Staff** Varying in different institutions. **Finance** Financed by host institutions. **Activities** Events/meetings; knowledge management/ information dissemination; monitoring/evaluation; publishing activities; standards/guidelines. **Events** *IERS Workshop on Local Surveys and Co-locations* Paris (France) 2013, *IERS Workshop on EOP Combination and Prediction* Warsaw (Poland) 2009, *IERS Workshop on Conventions* Paris (France) 2007, *Workshop on global geophysical fluids* San Francisco, CA (USA) 2006, *Workshop on combination research and global geophysical fluids* Munich (Germany) 2002. **Publications** *IERS Bulletin*; *IERS Messages*. Annual Report; technical notes; reports; minutes. **Members** Not a membership organization. **IGO Relations** Member of (1): *International Committee on Global Navigation Satellite Systems (ICG, #12775)* (as Associate member). **NGO Relations** Member of (2): *Global Geodetic Observing System (GGOS, see: #11914)*; *ISC World Data System (ISC-WDS, #16024)*. Technique Centres provided by: *International DORIS Service (IDS, #13192)*; *International GNSS Service (IGS, #13724)*; *International Laser Ranging Service (ILRS, see: #11914)*; *International VLBI Service for Geodesy and Astrometry (IVS, #15860)*. [2022.05.09/XF2144/F]

- ♦ International Earth Rotation Service / see International Earth Rotation and Reference Systems Service (#13216)
- ♦ Internationale Artusgesellschaft (#11671)
- ♦ Internationale Ärtze – ILÄAT (#13186)
- ♦ Internationale Ärztegesellschaft für Applied Kinesiology (#14139)
- ♦ Internationale Ärztegesellschaft für biophysikalische Informationstherapie (#15253)
- ♦ Internationale Ärztegesellschaft für Energiemedizin (no recent information)
- ♦ Internationale Associatie voor Cannabinoïden als Medicijn (#11754)
- ♦ Internationale Associatie voor Cannabis als Medicijn / see International Association for Cannabinoid Medicines (#11754)
- ♦ Internationale Assoziation Deutschsprachiger Medien (inactive)
- ♦ Internationale Assoziation für Geodäsie (#11914)
- ♦ Internationale Assoziation für Linguistikstudenten (#12002)
- ♦ Internationale Assoziation für Medizintechnik (no recent information)
- ♦ Internationale Assoziation für Otto Gross Studien (#12060)
- ♦ Internationale Assoziation von Philosophinnen (#12269)
- ♦ Internationale Assoziation der Touristenorganisationen die sich auf Mittelasien spezialisieren (inactive)
- ♦ Internationale Astronautische Akademie (#11536)
- ♦ International EAV Association (#16689)
- ♦ Internationale Bäderwirtschaftswissenschaftliche Arbeitsstätte (inactive)
- ♦ International E Balzan Foundation / see International Balzan Prize Foundation (#12309)
- ♦ Internationale Begegnung in Gemeinschaftsdiensten (internationally oriented national body)
- ♦ Internationale Bekleidungsarbeiter-Föderation (inactive)
- ♦ Internationale Beleuchtungskommission (#04219)
- ♦ Internationale Bereinigung Alterer Bürger (inactive)
- ♦ Internationale Berufssekretariate / see Global Union Federations (#10638)
- ♦ Internationale Berufsvereinigung der Werktätigen des Handels (inactive)
- ♦ Internationale Beweging van de Katholieke Landelijke Jeugd en Boerenjeugd (#16865)
- ♦ Internationale Beweging voor de Verdediging van het Recht op het Genot (#14194)
- ♦ Internationale Bewegung für den Atlantischen Block (inactive)
- ♦ Internationale Bewegung für eine Brüderliche Vereinigung der Rassen und Völker / see Unis pour l'Equite et la Fin du Racisme (#20490)
- ♦ Internationale Bewegung Wir sind Kirche / see We Are Church International (#20841)
- ♦ Internationale Biathlon Union (#12336)
- ♦ Internationale Bibliothek für Zukunftsfragen, Salzburg – Robert-Jungk Stiftung (internationally oriented national body)
- ♦ Internationale Binnenschiffahrts Union (inactive)
- ♦ Internationale Biometrische Gesellschaft (#12354)
- ♦ Internationale Blindenfederatie (inactive)
- ♦ Internationale Bodenkundliche Gesellschaft / see International Union of Soil Sciences (#15817)
- ♦ Internationale Bodenkundliche Union (#15817)

♦ Internationale Bodenseekonferenz (IBK) 13217

International Lake Constance Conference

Contact Geschäftsstelle der Internationalen Bodensee Konferenz, Benediktinerplatz 1, 78467 Konstanz, Germany. T. +49753152722. Fax +49753152869. E-mail: info@bodenseekonferenz.org.
URL: http://www.bodenseekonferenz.org/

History Established 1972, Konstanz (Germany FR), by the Heads of Government of the countries bordering onto Lake Conference. **Aims** Increase cooperation to solve *cross-border* problems in fields including environment, health, education and science, transport, culture and economy. **Structure** Heads of Government Meeting (annual); Permanent Committee; Commissions of Experts; Secretariat. **Languages** German. **Staff** 4.00 FTE, paid. **Finance** Members' dues. Project funding. Some projects funded by *INTERREG V (#15966)*. Annual budget: euro 1,200,000. **Activities** Events/meetings. **Events** *Meeting* Bregenz (Austria) 2014. **Publications** Annual Report; project reports.
Members in 4 countries:
Austria, Germany, Liechtenstein, Switzerland. [2017.10.25/XF6431/F*]

- ♦ Internationale Bond van Bouw- en Houtarbeiders (inactive)
- ♦ Internationale Bond voor Kunstambacht en Kunstonderwijs (inactive)
- ♦ Internationale Bouworde (#11745)
- ♦ Internationale Brecht-Gesellschaft / see International Brecht Society (#12397)
- ♦ Internationale de Bruxelles des libres-penseurs (inactive)
- ♦ Internationale Buchhändler-Vereinigung (inactive)
- ♦ Internationale Budo Federatie (inactive)
- ♦ Internationale Bund der Blindenführhundeschulen / see International Guide Dog Federation (#13763)
- ♦ Internationale Bund des Kampfes der Völker (#14021)
- ♦ Internationale Bund für Multiple Sklerose (#16899)
- ♦ Internationale Bürgerrechts-Allianz (#12584)
- ♦ Internationale des cadres des industries métallurgiques / see European Federation of Managers in the Steel Industry (#07162)
- ♦ International Echinoderm Conference (meeting series)
- ♦ Internationale Christelijke Sociale Vereniging (inactive)
- ♦ Internationale Christliche Organisation der Medien (#12563)
- ♦ Internationale Christliche Vereinigung (#12556)

♦ Internationale des coiffeurs de dames (Intercoiffure Mondial) 13218

Ladies' Hairdressers International

Main Office 249 rue Saint-Martin, 75003 Paris, France. T. +33156432222. Fax +33156432229. E-mail: paris@intercoiffure.org – info-press@intercoiffure.org.
URL: http://www.intercoiffure-mondial.org/

History 1925, Hamburg (Germany). Restructured 1955, Paris (France). Former names and other names: *Association Internationale des Maîtres Coiffeurs de Dames (ICD)* – former. **Aims** Promote international *hair* techniques, *fashion*, friendship and fraternity to members; assure to the public, the careful vetting of members regarding good hair fashion wherever the 'Intercoiffure' sign is seen. **Activities** Maintains 'Maison des Nations Intercoiffure' and 'Galerie culturelle'. Organizes: World Congresses; a Mondial Performance (annual), always in Paris (France). **Events** *World Congress* Berlin (Germany) 2021, *Europe congress* Interlaken (Switzerland) 2018, *Nordic Congress* Malmö (Sweden) 2018, *World Congress* Kyoto (Japan) / Osaka (Japan) 2017, *World Congress* Shanghai (China) 2016. **Publications** *Intercoiffure Newsletter* (4 a year) in English, French, German, Spanish; *Intercoiffure Magazine* (annual) in English, French, German, Spanish. DVD.
Members High-class hairdressers (3,000) in 54 countries and territories:
Argentina, Australia, Austria, Belgium, Bolivia, Brazil, Bulgaria, Canada, Chile, China, Costa Rica, Denmark, Dubai, Finland, France, Germany, Greece, Hungary, Iceland, India, Indonesia, Ireland, Israel, Italy, Japan, Jordan, Korea Rep, Lebanon, Luxembourg, Mexico, Netherlands, New Zealand, North Macedonia, Norway, Peru, Poland, Portugal, Romania, Russia, Saudi Arabia, Singapore, South Africa, Spain, Sweden, Switzerland, Syrian AR, Taiwan, Tunisia, Türkiye, UK, Ukraine, Uruguay, USA, Venezuela. [2021/XF1942/v/F]

- ♦ International Eco-Labelling Committee / see Global Ecolabelling Network (#10328)

♦ International E coli Alliance (IECA) 13219

Address not obtained.
URL: http://www.uni-giessen.de/ecoli/IECA/index.php

History 2002, London (UK). **Aims** Develop knowledge of the *biochemistry*, molecular *biology* and *genetics* of escherichia coli. **Events** *Conference* Mexico 2011, *Conference* Cambridge (UK) 2008, *Conference on systems biology* Jeju (Korea Rep) 2006, *Conference* Jeju (Korea Rep) 2006, *Conference on systems biology* Banff, AB (Canada) 2004.
Members in 4 countries:
Canada, Japan, UK, USA. [2011/XM2897/F]

♦ International Ecological Engineering Society (IEES) 13220

Co-Pres c/o ZAHW, Grüentalstrasse 14, 8820 Wädenswil ZH, Switzerland. T. +41415206162. E-mail: contact@iees.ch.
URL: http://www.iees.ch/

History 15 Oct 1993, Utrecht (Netherlands). **Aims** Promote the use of ecological engineering; improve cooperation between ecologists and engineers. **Structure** General Meeting (annual); Advisory Board; Activity Group. **Finance** Sources: members' dues. **Activities** Events/meetings; publishing activities; research and development; training/education. **Events** *Closed Cycles and the Circular Society Conference* Chania (Greece) 2023, *Closed Cycles Symposium* Wädenswil (Switzerland) 2020, *Integrating the sciences – understanding and solving environmental problems in the 21st century* Halifax, NS (Canada) 2000, *Conference* Beijing (China) 1996, *Conference* Copenhagen (Denmark) 1996. **Publications** *EcoEng Newsletter*. [2022.10.22/XD7999/D]

♦ International Ecological Safety Collaborative Organization (UN-IESCO) 13221

Executive Office 28 Beauty Asian Gardens, No 8 West Xinglong Street, Tainping Shuang, Chaoyang District, 100123 Beijing, China. T. +861085769558. Fax +861085762956.
Secretariat 8/F Emperor Group Ctr, 288 Hennessy Road, Wan Chai, Wanchai, Hong Kong. T. +85228383673. Fax +85225731363.
URL: https://www.un-iesco.org/

History Feb 2006. Founded by *International Academy of Ecology and Life Protection Sciences (IAELPS)*. **Aims** Eradicate extreme poverty and hunger; ensure environmental sustainability; develop a global partnership for development. **Structure** Global Ecological Safety Council. Presidium. Consultative Committees (2): Expert; Legal. **Publications** *International Ecology and Safety Magazine*. **Consultative Status** Consultative status granted from: *ECOSOC (#05331)* (Special). [2009/XJ0502/E]

- ♦ Internationale Commissie voor de Bescherming van de Maas / see International Commission of the Meuse (#12702)
- ♦ Internationale Commissie voor de Bescherming van de Schelde / see International Commission of the Schelde River (#12727)
- ♦ Internationale Commissie voor de Hydrologie van het Rijnstroomgebied (#12693)
- ♦ Internationale Commissie van de Schelde / see International Commission of the Schelde River (#12727)
- ♦ Internationale Commissie ter Bescherming van de Rijn (#12721)
- ♦ Internationale Commissie ter Bescherming van de Rijn tegen Verontreiniging / see International Commission for the Protection of the Rhine (#12721)
- ♦ Internationale communiste (inactive)
- ♦ Internationale Confederatie van Europese Suikerbietkwekers (#12860)
- ♦ Internationale Confederatie van Meubelstoffabrikanten (inactive)

♦ International Economic Association (IEA) 13222

Association internationale des sciences économiques (AISE) – Asociación Internacional de Economia – Internationale Vereinigung für Wirtschaftswissenschaften – Mezdunarodnaja Associacija Ekonomiceskih Nauk

SG Inst de Analisis Economico – CSIC, Campus UAB, 08193 Barcelona, Spain. T. +34935806612. Fax +3493580145. E-mail: iea@iea-world.org.
Pres address not obtained.
URL: http://www.iea-world.com/

History Aug 1949, Paris (France), on recommendation of the Social Sciences Department of *UNESCO (#20322)*. Statutes adopted at Council meeting, 10 Sep 1950, and amended: 25 Aug 1971; 3 Sep 1983; 29 Nov 1986; 28 Feb 1987; 23 Aug 1992. Registered by French Ministerial decree, 8 Nov 1950. **Aims** Initiate or coordinate international collaborative measures to assist in advancing knowledge of *economics*; secure and develop personal contacts among economists of different countries; encourage provision of international media to disseminate thinking and knowledge in the field. **Structure** Council (meets every 3 years); Executive Committee; Programme Committee Secretariat. **Languages** English, French. **Staff** 1.00 FTE, paid. **Finance** Sources: members' dues. Grants from UNESCO and foundations. **Activities** Events/meetings; knowledge management/information dissemination; training/education. **Events** *World Congress* Bali (Indonesia) 2021, *World Congress* Mexico City (Mexico) 2017, *World Congress* Sweimeh (Jordan) 2014, *Triennial Congress* Beijing (China) 2011, *Triennial Congress* Istanbul (Turkey) 2008. **Publications** *IEA Newsletter* (2 a year). Proceedings of conferences and congresses.
Members National associations and Associate () in 57 countries and territories:
Argentina, Australia, Austria, Bangladesh, Belgium, Brazil, Bulgaria, Canada, China, Colombia, Cuba, Cyprus, Czechia, Denmark, Ecuador, Egypt, Estonia, Finland, France, Germany, Ghana, Greece, Hong Kong, Hungary, India (*), Ireland, Israel, Italy, Japan, Kenya, Korea Rep, Lithuania, Mexico, Mongolia, Morocco, Nigeria, Norway, Pakistan, Paraguay, Peru, Poland, Portugal, Romania, Russia, Slovenia, Spain, Sweden, Switzerland, Tunisia, Türkiye, Uganda, UK, Uruguay, USA, Venezuela, Vietnam, Zimbabwe.
Regional member, one organization listed in this Yearbook:
Federation of ASEAN Economic Associations (FAEA, #09425).
Consultative Status Consultative status granted from: *ECOSOC (#05331)* (Ros C); *FAO (#09260)* (Liaison Status). **NGO Relations** Member of (3): *Global Labor Organization (GLO, #10445)*; *International Committee for Social Science Information and Documentation (ICSSD, no recent information)*; *International Science Council (ISC, #14796)*. Instrumental in setting up: *International Graduate School (SEED, no recent information)*. [2020/XB1794/y/B]

- ♦ International Economic Association for Arranging Co-operation in the Manufacture and Deliveries of Equipment and Technical Assistance in the Construction of Nuclear Power Stations / see International Economic Association Interatomenergo (#13223)

♦ International Economic Association Interatomenergo (IEA Interatomenergo) 13223

Mezdunarodnoe Hozjajstvennoe Obedinenie Interatomenergo

Headquarters Kitajgorodskij pr 7, Moscow MOSKVA, Russia, 109074. T. +7957104604. Fax +7956257559. E-mail: interatomenergo@eesnet.ru.

History Dec 1973, Moscow (Russia). Former names and other names: *International Economic Association for Arranging Co-operation in the Manufacture and Deliveries of Equipment and Technical Assistance in the Construction of Nuclear Power Stations* – full title. **Aims** Resolve matters connected with construction, operation and decommissioning of *nuclear power* stations. **Structure** General Council; Director General; Departments (6); Service Branches. **Staff** 100.00 FTE, paid. **Finance** Financed by profit obtained as a result of economic activities. **Activities** Basic tasks: (1) development of balanced requirements and production capacities for equipment, instruments and materials for Nuclear Power Stations (NPSs); (2) drafting proposals for specialization and cooperation in production, as well as in expanding the production of equipment, instruments and materials for NPSs by the industries in the Contracting Parties' countries; (3) arranging cooperative production of equipment, instruments and materials for NPSs; (4) drafting proposals for joint planning in the production of specified types of equipment, instruments and materials for NPSs; (5) control over the transfer of design and engineering documentation to manufacturers of equipment, instruments and materials; (6) ensuring a reliable supply of equipment, instruments, materials and spare parts for NPSs by the industries in the Contracting Parties' countries and acting as the general contractor at the customer's request; (7) control over cooperative production and supply of spare parts for the NPS equipment; (8) control over cooperation in designing and providing designs for NPSs; (9) certain functions in the commissioning and adjusting NPSs under construction; (10) technical training and brush-up courses for NPS operators and for experts in NPS designing and in the manufacture of equipment and its assembly; (11) repair of certain types of equipment and instruments used at NPSs; (12) technical assistance in the construction of NPSs in the Contracting Parties' countries and in the third countries; (13) organization and carrying out international exhibitions, seminars, conferences and other activities for exchange of the experience in the field of nuclear power; (14) execution of works aimed at the reduction of dangerous effects on environment, modernization, development of systems, reconstruction and decommissioning of NPSs; (15) research works in the field of nuclear power; (16) scientific and research works as well as the works connected with development and implementation into production of new achievements in the field of nuclear power; (17) technical servicing of instruments, equipment, machines and tools to be used in the nuclear power field; (18) information and advertising activities, marketing; (19) consulting. **Publications** *Nuclear Power News* (2 a year).

Members Contracting parties: governments of the following 11 countries:
Bulgaria, Cuba, Czechia, Germany, Hungary, Montenegro, Poland, Romania, Russia, Serbia, Slovakia.

IGO Relations Observer status with (1): *International Atomic Energy Agency (IAEA, #12294)*.
[2006.11.28/XD7611/e/**D***]

♦ International Economic Cooperation Development Fund / see International Cooperation and Development Fund
♦ International Economic Development Council (internationally oriented national body)
♦ International Economic Forum of the Americas (internationally oriented national body)

♦ International Economic History Association (IEHA) 13224

Association internationale d'histoire économique

SG Dept of History, Appalachian State Univ, 224 Joyce Lawrence Lane, Houghton Street, Boone NC 28608, USA. T. +18282626006. Fax +18282624976. E-mail: iehaofficial@gmail.com.
URL: http://www.ieha-wehc.org/

History 27 Aug 1965, Munich (Germany). Founded on adoption of a provisional Constitution which had been agreed at 1st International Congress, 1960, Stockholm (Sweden). Most recent statutes adopted 18 Aug 1978, Edinburgh (UK); modified 29 Aug 1986, Bern (Switzerland), Aug 2002, Buenos Aires (Argentina), Aug 2006, Helsinki (Finland) and Aug 2009, Utrecht (Netherlands). **Aims** Organize periodic academic meetings, and in particular, international congresses of economic history. **Structure** General Assembly (every 3-4 years, at Congress); Executive Committee. **Languages** English, French, German, Russian, Spanish. **Staff** 2.00 FTE, paid. **Finance** Members' dues (annual): euro 200, determined on the basis of a recommendation of the Executive Committee and decided upon by the General Assembly. **Activities** Events/meetings. **Events** *World Economic History Congress* Paris (France) 2022, *World Economic History Congress* Paris (France) 2021, *World Economic History Congress* Boston, MA (USA) 2018, *World Economic History Congress* Kyoto (Japan) 2015, *Meeting* Amsterdam (Netherlands) 2014. **Publications** Newsletter; congress proceedings.

Members National commissions for economic history or history of political economy; national and international societies and organizations (over 40) concerned with particular aspects of these subjects. Members in 37 countries:
Argentina, Australia, Austria, Belgium, Brazil, Canada, China, Colombia, Czechia, Denmark, Finland, France, Germany, Greece, Hungary, India, Ireland, Israel, Italy, Japan, Korea Rep, Mexico, Netherlands, New Zealand, Norway, Poland, Portugal, Romania, Russia, South Africa, Spain, Sweden, Switzerland, Türkiye, UK, Uruguay, USA.

Included in the above, 1 regional organization and 5 international organizations:
Business History Conference; *Cliometric Society*; *European Business History Association (EBHA, #06419)*; *European Historical Economics Society (EHES, #07490)*; *International Social History Association (ISHA)*; *Scandinavian Society for Economic and Social History (SSESH, #19106)*. [2020/XC1795/y/**C**]

♦ Internationale Coronelli-Gesellschaft für Globenkunde (#12967)

♦ The International Ecotourism Society (TIES) 13225

Main Office PO Box 96503, Ste 34145, Washington DC 20090-6503, USA. T. +12025065033. Fax +12027897279. E-mail: david@ecotourism.org – media@ecotourism.org – info@ecotourism.org.
URL: http://www.ecotourism.org/

History 1990. Founded as *The Ecotourism Society (TES)*. Current title adopted 2000. **Aims** Make ecotourism a tool for conservation and sustainable development worldwide. **Structure** Management and Program Team; Advisory Board; Research and Education Council. **Activities** Awards/prizes/competitions; events/meetings; training/education. **Events** *ESTC : Ecotourism and Sustainable Tourism Conference* Tokat (Turkey) 2021, *ESTC : Ecotourism and Sustainable Tourism Conference* Hambantota (Sri Lanka) 2020, *ESTC : Ecotourism and Sustainable Tourism Conference* Florence (Italy) 2019, *ESTC : Ecotourism and Sustainable Tourism Conference* Florence (Italy) 2018, *ESTC : Ecotourism and Sustainable Tourism Conference* Ansan (Korea Rep) 2017. **Publications** *TIES Newsletter* (4 a year). Books.

Members Societies (490); individuals (about 1150). Members in 77 countries and territories:
Argentina, Australia, Austria, Bahamas, Belgium, Belize, Botswana, Brazil, Cambodia, Cameroon, Canada, Chile, Colombia, Costa Rica, Denmark, Dominican Rep, Ecuador, Egypt, Estonia, Ethiopia, Fiji, Georgia, Germany, Ghana, Greece, Guatemala, Honduras, India, Indonesia, Iran Islamic Rep, Israel, Italy, Japan, Jordan, Kenya, Korea Rep, Laos, Luxembourg, Madagascar, Malawi, Malaysia, Mexico, Micronesia FS, Mongolia, Morocco, Nepal, New Zealand, Nicaragua, Norway, Pakistan, Palau, Panama, Papua New Guinea, Peru, Portugal, Puerto Rico, Romania, Russia, Slovakia, South Africa, Spain, Sri Lanka, Sweden, Taiwan, Tajikistan, Tanzania UR, Thailand, Trinidad-Tobago, Türkiye, Turks-Caicos, Uganda, UK, Ukraine, United Arab Emirates, USA, Venezuela, Vietnam.

NGO Relations Member of: *European Network for Sustainable Tourism Development (ECOTRANS, #08018)*; *Global Sustainable Tourism Council (GSTC, #10619)*; *International Union for Conservation of Nature and Natural Resources (IUCN, #15766)*. [2021/XN9586/**C**]

♦ International Ecumenical Fellowship (IEF) 13226

Amitié oecuménique internationale – Asociación Ecuménica Internacional – Internationale Oekumenische Gemeinschaft – Internationale Oecumenische Gemeenschap – Miedzynarodowa Wspólnota Ekumeniczna

Int Pres 8 allée van Gogh, 78160 Marly-le-Roi, France. T. +33139588804.
Registered Address Engelendalelaan 89, 8310 Assebroek, Belgium.
URL: https://i-ecumenical-fellowship.org/EN/indexgb.html

History 1967, Switzerland. Founded at first International Conference. Registration: Crossroads Bank for Enterprises, No/ID: 0451.407.712, Start date: 17 Nov 1993, Belgium. **Aims** Group concerned *Christians* as a means of 'living today the *Church* of tomorrow'; listen to the word of *God*; follow the will of God referring to the unity asked in the prayer of Jesus Christ; give the witness of a reconciled community for the glory of God, Father, Son and Holy Spirit. **Structure** General Assembly (annual), composed of representative members from Regional corporations; International Council of Management; International Theological Commission. **Languages** Czech, Dutch, English, French, German, Hungarian, Polish, Romanian, Slovakian, Spanish. **Staff** 4.00 FTE, paid. **Finance** Sources: members' dues. Annual budget: 8,000 EUR. **Activities** Events/meetings; networking/liaising. **Events** *International Conference* Liverpool (England) 2022, *Love of Christ compels us* Krakow (Poland) 2019, *Mini-Conference* Assisi (Italy) 2018, *International Conference* Lutherstadt Wittenberg (Germany) 2017, *International Conference* Prague (Czech Rep) 2015. **Publications** Regional newsletters in English, German, French, Spanish, Hungarian (usually 2 a year). Conference documents in English, French, German, Spanish.

Members Regional Corporations in 13 countries:
Belgium, Colombia, Czechia, France, Germany, Hungary, Kenya, Poland, Romania, Slovakia, Spain, Uganda, UK.
[2023.02.13/XF5500/**F**]

♦ International Ecumenical Fraternity (internationally oriented national body)

♦ International Eczema Council (IEC) 13227

CEO 8735 W Higgins Road, Suite 300, Chicago IL 60631, USA. E-mail: info@eczemacouncil.org.
Operations Manager address not obtained.
URL: https://www.eczemacouncil.org/

History 2014. Founded by Drs Amy Paller and Emma Guttman. **Aims** Increase the understanding of atopic dermatitis; promote its optimal management through research, education and patient/family care. **Structure** Board of Directors. **Activities** Events/meetings; training/education.

Members Councilors in 22 countries and territories:
Australia, Austria, Brazil, Canada, China, Denmark, France, Germany, India, Ireland, Israel, Italy, Japan, Korea Rep, Netherlands, Poland, South Africa, Switzerland, Taiwan, Tanzania UR, UK, USA.

Associates in 13 countries:
Argentina, Canada, Denmark, France, Germany, Israel, Japan, Korea Rep, Netherlands, Singapore, Spain, Tanzania UR, USA.

NGO Relations Member of (1): *International League of Dermatological Societies (ILDS, #14018)*.
[2023/AA2128/v/**C**]

♦ Internationale Dag van de Afrikaanse Jeugd / see International Day of the African Child and Youth (#13140)
♦ Internationale Dag van het Kind en de Jeugd van Afrika / see International Day of the African Child and Youth (#13140)
♦ Internationale démocrate chrétienne / see Centrist Democrat International (#03792)
♦ Internationale democratique (#05033)
♦ Internationale Demokratische Frauenföderation (#21022)
♦ Internationale Demokratische Union (#13147)

♦ Internationale Deutschlehrerverband / Der (IDV) 13228

International Association of Teachers of German – Association internationale des professeurs d'allemand

Pres Dipto Filologia/Letteratura/Linguistica, Univ degli Studi di Pisa, via S Maria 36, 56126 Pisa PI, Italy.
URL: http://www.idvnetz.org/

History 1968, Yugoslavia. Founded 1968, Zagreb (Yugoslavia). **Aims** Further understanding through international cooperation among *teachers* of German. **Structure** Assembly of Representatives; Executive Committee. **Languages** German. **Staff** 5.00 FTE, voluntary. 3 experts. **Finance** Members' dues. Co-financed by *Goethe-Institut* and Österreichisches Bundesministerium für Bildung (BMB). **Activities** Events/meetings. **Events** *Quadrennial Congress* Vienna (Austria) 2022, *Quadrennial Congress* Vienna (Austria) 2021, *Quadrennial Congress* Fribourg (Switzerland) 2017, *Regional Congress* Helsinki (Finland) 2015, *Quadrennial Congress* Bolzano (Italy) 2013. **Publications** *IDV Aktuell* (periodical); *IDV-Magazin* (periodical).

Members National associations of teachers of German (94) in 85 countries and territories:
Albania, Algeria, Argentina, Armenia, Australia, Austria, Azerbaijan, Belarus, Belgium, Benin, Bolivia, Bosnia-Herzegovina, Brazil, Bulgaria, Burkina Faso, Cameroon, Canada, Chile, Colombia, Côte d'Ivoire, Croatia, Cuba, Czechia, Denmark, Ecuador, Egypt, Estonia, Finland, France, Georgia, Germany, Ghana, Greece, Guatemala, Hungary, Iceland, India, Indonesia, Ireland, Italy, Japan, Kazakhstan, Korea Rep, Kosovo, Kyrgyzstan, Latvia, Lithuania, Luxembourg, Madagascar, Malaysia, Mali, Mexico, Moldova, Mongolia, Morocco, Netherlands, Nigeria, North Macedonia, Norway, Paraguay, Peru, Poland, Portugal, Romania, Russia, Senegal, Serbia, Slovakia, Slovenia, South Africa, Spain, Sweden, Switzerland, Taiwan, Thailand, Togo, Tunisia, Türkiye, UK, Ukraine, Uruguay, USA, Uzbekistan, Venezuela, Vietnam. [2017.10.26/XD0380/**C**]

♦ Internationale Diakonatskreis / see International Diaconate Centre (#13167)
♦ Internationale pour les droits égaux (inactive)
♦ International Educational Cinematographic Institute (inactive)

♦ International Educational Data Mining Society (IEDMS) 13229

Office Dept of Social Science and Policy Studies, Worcester Polytechnic Inst, 100 Institute Rd, Worcester MA 01609, USA. E-mail: admin@educationaldatamining.org.
URL: http://www.educationaldatamining.org/

History Jul 2011, by *International Working Group on Educational Data Mining*. Bylaws approved 9 Dec 2011; last amended 25 Mar 2014. Incorporated in the State of Massachusetts (USA). **Aims** Promote scientific research in the interdisciplinary field of educational data mining. **Structure** Board of Directors. **Events** *International Conference on Educational Data Mining* Montréal, QC (Canada) 2019, *International Conference on Educational Data Mining* Raleigh, NC (USA) 2016, *International Conference on Educational Data Mining* Madrid (Spain) 2015, *International Conference on Educational Data Mining* London (UK) 2014, *International Conference on Educational Data Mining* Memphis, TN (USA) 2013. **Publications** *Journal of Educational Data Mining*. [2015/XM4218/**C**]

♦ International Educational Development – Humanitarian Law Project (internationally oriented national body)
♦ International Education Association (internationally oriented national body)
♦ International Education Association of Australia (internationally oriented national body)
♦ International Education Association of South Africa (internationally oriented national body)
♦ International Education Centre of Svendborg (internationally oriented national body)
♦ International Education Funders Group (unconfirmed)

♦ International Education for Peace Institute (EFP-International) 13230

Dir 208-1875 Lansdowne Road, Victoria BC V8P 1A9, Canada. T. +12503709419. E-mail: director@efpinternational.org – info@efpinternational.org.
Associate Dir Chemin du Pontet 6, 2013 Colombier NE, Switzerland. T. +41327241583. Fax +41327241583.
URL: http://www.efpinternational.org/

History Founded Jun 2000, with the launch of a two-year pilot project of Education for Peace in 3 primary and 3 secondary schools in Bosnia-Herzegovina, with the participation of over 400 teachers and school staff, 6,000 students and their parents/guardians. By 2006, implemented in 112 schools with approximately 80,000 students, 5,000 teachers, schools staff and administrators, and thousands of parents/guardians. Devolved from *Institute of International Education and Development, Landegg Academy*, founded 1988, by *International Landegg Baha'i Foundation (no recent information)*. **Aims** Contribute to the urgent global need for creation of a civilization of peace within the context of the consciousness of the oneness of humanity and the principle of unity in diversity; engage students, teachers, parents/guardians and community leaders in a process of study and application of the universal principles of peace. **Structure** Board of Directors. International Advisory Board. Academic Council. Affiliate institutes (5): *Education for Peace Institute of the Balkans (EFP Balkans)*; Education for Peace – America; International Education for Peace Institute – Canada; Education for Peace – Canada; Education for Peace – Mexico. **Languages** Bosnian, Croatian, English, French, Persian, Serbian, Spanish. **Staff** Varies according to projects. **Finance** Project and research grants; training revenue; donations. Grants, including from: Japanese and Luxembourg governments; UK and Norway embassies in Sarajevo (Bosnia-Herzegovina); *Canadian International Development Agency (CIDA, inactive)*; *Japan International Cooperation Agency (JICA)*; *Rotary International (RI, #18975)*; *Swiss Agency for Development and Cooperation (SDC)*; *United States Institute of Peace (USIP)*; Soros Foundation, OSCE Mission and small businesses in Bosnia-Herzegovina; private and government agencies in Mexico. **Activities** Offers systematic programs of training, research, program implementation, consulting and academic collaboration. Programs include: EFP Intensive; EFP World; Youth Peace-Builders Network; EPF Professional Diploma; EFP Leadership; Violence-Free Environments (VFE); Leadership for Peace (LFP); Peace-Based Governance; Conflict-Free Conflict Resolution (CFCR); EFP Internships; Short-Term Intensive Training Programs; EFP Research Placements; Certificate in Education for Peace; Professional Certificate in Education for Peace. Plan (2007-2012) aims to incorporate the EFP Curriculum into the BiH education reform process, thus involving all BiH primary and secondary

schools with about 500,000 students and 70,000 teachers and school staff in the study of all subjects from grades K to 12 within the parameters of peace. Programmes introduced into several other countries, including: Bermuda; Canada; Cyprus; Malawi; Turkey; USA. **Events** *SERFAC international conference on the family* Bangkok (Thailand) 2011, *Conference* Sarajevo (Bosnia-Herzegovina) 2011, *Conference* Vancouver, BC (Canada) 2007, *International education for peace conference* Vancouver, BC (Canada) 2007, *Culture of healing and leadership for peace seminar* Sarajevo (Bosnia-Herzegovina) 2005. **Publications** *Education for Peace Newsletter* (3-4 a year). Annual Report. Books; CD-ROMs; articles.
Members in 8 countries:
Bermuda, Bosnia-Herzegovina, Canada, Germany, India, Mexico, Switzerland, USA.
IGO Relations Consultative Status with the United Nations. **NGO Relations** Links with NGOs (unspecified) in countries where most active. [2013.06.11/XG4651/j/E]

♦ International Education and Resource Network (iEARN) 13231

Exec Council Member Passeig Anselm Clavé 19, baixos, Callûs, 08262 Barcelona, Spain. E-mail: fb@iearn.org.
URL: http://www.iearn.org/
History 1994. Founded when global constitution adopted, deriving from a US national organization set up in 1988 by the Copen Family Fund. Registration: No/ID: 586513, Spain, Barcelona. **Aims** Empower teachers and young people to work together online using the internet and other new communication technologies to enhance quality of life. **Structure** International Assembly; Executive Council; Country Coordinators and Management Teams. **Staff** Voluntary. **Finance** Individual centres funded by: fees; grants. Some centres have no budget. **Activities** Projects/programmes; research and development; training/education. **Events** *Annual Conference* Winchester, VA (USA) 2018, *Youth Summit* Winchester, VA (USA) 2018, *Annual Conference* Marrakech (Morocco) 2017, *Youth Summit* Marrakech (Morocco) 2017, *Youth Summit* Pune (India) 2016. **Publications** Newsletters; directories; books; educational tools; training CD-ROM. Information Services: Tools to make global on-line project work easier: WWW-based database.
Members IEA centres – schools and youth organizations (over 15,000) in 82 countries and territories:
Albania, Algeria, Andorra, Argentina, Armenia, Azerbaijan, Belarus, Bosnia-Herzegovina, Botswana, Brazil, Bulgaria, Cambodia, Canada, Chile, China, Côte d'Ivoire, Croatia, Czechia, Ecuador, Egypt, El Salvador, Estonia, Finland, France, Georgia, Germany, Ghana, Greece, Guatemala, Hungary, India, Iran Islamic Rep, Israel, Jamaica, Japan, Jordan, Kazakhstan, Kenya, Korea Rep, Kyrgyzstan, Latvia, Lebanon, Lithuania, Malaysia, Mexico, Mongolia, Morocco, Namibia, Nepal, Netherlands, Nigeria, North Macedonia, Pakistan, Palestine, Paraguay, Peru, Poland, Portugal, Qatar, Romania, Russia, Senegal, Serbia, Sierra Leone, Slovakia, Slovenia, South Africa, Spain, Sri Lanka, Suriname, Taiwan, Tanzania UR, Thailand, Trinidad-Tobago, Tunisia, Türkiye, Uganda, Ukraine, USA, Uzbekistan, Zambia, Zimbabwe.
IGO Relations Partner of (1): *Global Learning and Observations to Benefit the Environment (GLOBE).* Associated with Department of Global Communications of the United Nations. **NGO Relations** Member of (1): *Alliance for International Exchange.* Partner of (6): *Global Rivers Environmental Education Network (GREEN); International Student Exchange Program (ISEP); Partners of the Americas; Save the Children Federation (SCF); Sister Cities International (SCI); USC Shoah Foundation Institute for Visual History and Education.* [2022/XF2651/F]

♦ International Education and Training Research Network (#18896)

♦ The International Edvard Grieg Society (IGS) 13232

Det Internasjonale Edvard Grieg Selskap
Secretariat c/o KODE, Vestre Strømkaien 7, 5008 Bergen, Norway. T. +4790128299. E-mail: post@griegsociety.com.
URL: http://griegsociety.com/
History 15 Jun 1996, Oslo (Norway). **Aims** Further development of knowledge and understanding of, and increased accessibility to, the work of composer Edvard Grieg (1843-1907). **Structure** General Assembly; Executive Committee. **Activities** Events/meetings. **Events** *Conference* Bergen (Norway) 2019, *Conference* Bergen (Norway) 2017, *Edvard Grieg and the human voice* Bergen (Norway) 2015, *Conference* Bergen (Norway) 2014, *Conference* Bergen (Norway) 2013. **Publications** Conference papers.
Members Societies in 11 countries and territories:
Belgium, Germany, Italy, Japan, Netherlands, Norway, Russia, Scotland, UK, Ukraine, USA. [2023.02.14/XQ0281/E]

♦ Internationale de l'éducation (#05371)
♦ Internationale Eisenbahn-Kongressvereinigung (inactive)
♦ Internationale Eisenbahn-Presse-Vereinigung (#20434)
♦ Internationale Elektrotechnische Kommission / see International Electrotechnical Commission (#13255)
♦ Internationale Elektrowärme Union / see International Union for Electricity Applications (#15770)
♦ Internationale Entschädigunsfonds für Ölverschmutzungsschäden / see International Oil Pollution Compensation Funds (#14402)
♦ Internationale Erard-Gesellschaft (internationally oriented national body)
♦ Internationale Erdöl Union (inactive)
♦ Internationale Ergophthalmologische Gesellschaft (no recent information)
♦ Internationale Ernst Cassirer Gesellschaft (#13295)
♦ Internationale Esperanto-Vereinigung der Juristen (inactive)
♦ Internationale Etikettenkonferenz (meeting series)
♦ Internationale Europäische Bewegung / see European Movement International (#07825)
♦ Internationale évangélique ouvrière (inactive)
♦ Internationale Expertenorganisation (#17808)
♦ Internationale Pro-Falascha Komitee (inactive)
♦ Internationale Farmaceutische Bijstand / see Orbi-Pharma
♦ Internationale Federatie van Bloed Donorsorganisaties (#13374)
♦ Internationale Federatie van Christelijke Mijnwerkersbonden (inactive)
♦ Internationale Federatie van Jeugd en Muziek / see Jeunesses Musicales International (#16110)
♦ Internationale Federatie van Katholieke Arbeiders Bewegingen (inactive)
♦ Internationale Federatie van Katholieke Parochiale Jeugdgemeenschappen / see International Federation of Catholic Parochial Youth Movements (#13379)
♦ Internationale Federatie van Liberale Jongeren (#13469)
♦ Internationale Federatie van Liberale en Radicale Jongeren / see International Federation of Liberal Youth (#13469)
♦ Internationale Federatie van het Overheidspersoneel (#13410)
♦ Internationale Federatie van de Periodieke Pers / see FIPP (#09776)
♦ Internationale Federatie van Post-, Telegraaf- en Telefoonpersoneel (inactive)
♦ Internationale Federatie voor Speelgoed en Kindertijd (inactive)
♦ Internationale Federatie Textiel en Kleding (inactive)
♦ Internationale Federatie van Vakorganisaties van Vervoerpersoneel (inactive)
♦ Internationale Federation für Medizinische und Biologische Technik (#13477)
♦ Internationale Federation der Nationalen Verbände der Reifenspezialisten und Runderneuerer / see BIPAVER – European Retread Manufacturers Association (#03264)
♦ Internationale Federation für Zervixpathologie und Kolposkopie (#13385)
♦ Internationale des femmes démocrates-chrétiennes (inactive)
♦ Internationale Filmkammer (inactive)
♦ Internationale Filmtheaterunion (#15763)
♦ Internationale Flösservereinigung (#15691)
♦ Internationale Föderation der Agrarjournalisten (#13346)
♦ Internationale Föderation – Aktion der Christen für die Abschaffung der Tortur / see International Federation of ACATs – Action by Christians for the Abolition of Torture (#13334)
♦ Internationale Föderation des Alterns (#13345)
♦ Internationale Föderation der Ausschüsse Normenpraxis / see International Federation of Standards Users (#13558)
♦ Internationale Föderation der Buchbinder und verwandter Berufe (inactive)
♦ Internationale Föderation der Chopin Gesellschaften (#13387)
♦ Internationale Föderation für Chormusik (#13388)
♦ Internationale Föderation des Dachdeckerhandwerks (#13534)
♦ Internationale Föderation für Datenverarbeitung (#13458)
♦ Internationale Föderation der Eisenbahn-Reklame-Gesellschaften (inactive)
♦ Internationale Föderation für Eisstockschiessen / see International Federation Icestocksport (#13455)
♦ Internationale Föderation der Europa-Häuser (inactive)
♦ Internationale Föderation der Fussgängerverbände (#13502)
♦ Internationale Föderation der Gesellschaften der Kosmetik-Chemiker (#13545)
♦ Internationale Föderation der Gesellschaften für Unternehmensforschung (#13493)
♦ Internationale Föderation des Handwerks (inactive)
♦ Internationale Föderation für Hygiene, Präventiv- und Sozialmedizin (inactive)
♦ Internationale Föderation für Informations und Kommunikationsverarbeitung (#09667)
♦ Internationale Föderation für Informationsverarbeitung / see Fédération internationale pour le traitement de l'information et de la communication (#09667)
♦ Internationale Föderation der Innenarchitekten (#13460)
♦ Internationale Föderation Internationaler Möbelspediteure / see FIDI Global Alliance (#09753)
♦ Internationale Föderation der Islandpferde Vereine / see International Federation of Icelandic Horse Associations (#13454)
♦ Internationale Föderation der Katholischen Blindenvereinigungen (#13377)
♦ Internationale Föderation für Kurzschrift und Maschinenschreiben / see Fédération internationale pour le traitement de l'information et de la communication (#09667)
♦ Internationale Föderation der Öffentlich Bediensteten (#13410)
♦ Internationale Föderation von Patentanwälten (#09624)
♦ Internationale Föderation der Plantagen, Land- und Anverwandten Arbeiter (inactive)
♦ Internationale Föderation der Polizeibeamten (inactive)
♦ Internationale Föderation für Psychotherapie (#13523)
♦ Internationale Föderation des Seilerhandwerks (inactive)
♦ Internationale Föderation der Sozialistischen und Demokratischen Presse (no recent information)
♦ Internationale Föderation der Sozial-Kulturellen Nachbarschaftszentren (#13538)
♦ Internationale Föderation der Spediteurorganisationen (#09610)
♦ Internationale Föderation für Spielzeug und Kinderzeit (inactive)
♦ Internationale Föderation im sportlichen Meeresangeln (see: #04562)
♦ Internationale Föderation der Vereine der Textilchemiker und Coloristen (#13365)
♦ Internationale Föderation der Vereinten Schulen (#20660)
♦ Internationale Föderation Verheirateten Katholischen Priester (inactive)
♦ Internationale Föderation Vexillologischer Gesellschaften (#09611)
♦ Internationale Föderation der Widerstandskämpfer (#13529)
♦ Internationale Föderation der Widerstandskämpfer – Bund der Antifaschisten / see International Federation of Resistance Movements (#13529)
♦ Internationale Föderation von Wirkerei- und Strickerei-Fachleuten (#13465)
♦ Internationale Folkehøjskole / see International People's College
♦ Internationale Forening af Forhenvaerende EF-Medarbejdere / see Association internationale des anciens de l'Union Européenne (#02667)
♦ Internationale Forschungsgemeinschaft für Bioelektronische Funktionsdiagnostik und Therapie (internationally oriented national body)

♦ Internationale Forschungsgemeinschaft Deinking-Technik (INGEDE) 13233

International Association of the Deinking Industry
Head of Communications Oetztaler Strasse 5B, 81373 Munich, Germany. T. +49897692332. Fax +49897692338. E-mail: contact@ingede.com.
URL: http://www.ingede.com/
History 1989. Founded by European paper manufacturers. Former names and other names: *International Research Association Deinking Technology* – former. **Aims** Further research in recovered paper *recycling* technology; secure their supply for the *paper* industry; maintain and improve the quality of paper for recycling; consult and test in terms of deinkability for *ecolabel* applications; communicate with other members of the paper chain. **Structure** Board. **Languages** English, German. **Staff** 2.50 FTE, paid. **Finance** Sources: members' dues. Annual budget: 350,000 EUR. **Activities** Certification/accreditation; knowledge management/information dissemination; research and development. **Events** *How print products and white packaging stay a recyclable resource* Munich (Germany) 2022, *Paper Has to Be Recyclable* Munich (Germany) 2021, *Packaging Design in the Fibre Cycle* Munich (Germany) 2020, *Symposium* Munich (Germany) 2019, *Symposium* Munich (Germany) 2018. **Publications** *INGEDE News* (4 a year) in English, German. *Guide to an Optimum Utilization of Recovered Graphic Paper* (2002); *Entry Inspection for Recovered Graphic Paper* – manual; *INGEDE Methods.* Videos.
Members Paper mills operating a deinking plant and research divisions (21) in 7 countries:
Austria, Belgium, Finland, Germany, Italy, Netherlands, Switzerland. [2022.10.18/XD7122/t/D]

♦ Internationale Forschungsgemeinschaft für Mechanische Produktions Technik / see CIRP – The International Academy for Production Engineering (#03945)
♦ Internationale Forschungsgesellschaft für Kinder- und Jugendliteratur (#14742)
♦ Internationale Forschungsgruppe zur Krebsaufspürung und Vorbeugung (inactive)
♦ Internationale Forschungsgruppe für Tiefziehen (#13143)
♦ Internationale Fortschrittsorganization (#14653)
♦ Internationale Forum for Person-Centreret Tilgang (meeting series)
♦ Internationale des forums du champ lacanien / see Internationale des Forums – Ecole de Psychanalyse des Forum du Champ Lacanien (#13234)

♦ Internationale des Forums – Ecole de Psychanalyse des Forum du Champ Lacanien 13234

International of Forums – School of Psychoanalysis of the Forums of the Lacanian Field – Internacional de los Foros – Escuela de Psicoanalisis de los Foros del Campo Lacaniano – Internacional dos Fóruns – Escuela de Psicanalise dos Fóruns do Campo Lacaniano – Internazionale dei Forums – Scuola di Psicoanalisi dei Forums del Campo Lacaniano
Contact FCL, 118 rue d'Assas, 75006 Paris, France. T. +33156242256. Fax +33156242237. E-mail: epfcl.secretariat@orange.fr.
URL: http://www.champlacanienfrance.net/
History Jul 1998, Barcelona (Spain), as *Internationale des forums du champ lacanien (IFCL) – Internacional de los Foros del Campo Lacaniano – Internazionale dei Forum del Campo Lacaniano.* **Aims** Install a *psychoanalytic* community oriented by the teachings of Sigmund Freud and Jacques Lacan and aimed at restoring the primary goals of a School of *Psychoanalysis.* **Events** *Meeting* Barcelona (Spain) 2018, *Meeting* Medellin (Colombia) 2016, *Meeting* Paris (France) 2014, *Les temps du sujet de l'inconscient* Sao Paulo (Brazil) 2008, *Meeting* Paris (France) 2006. **Publications** *Wunsch* – bulletin. [2014/XE4528/E]

♦ Internationale Franz Lehar Gesellschaft 13235

International Franz Lehar Society
Gen Sec Münzwardeingasse 5/8, 1060 Vienna, Austria. E-mail: info@franz-lehar-gesellschaft.com.
URL: http://www.franz-lehar-gesellschaft.com/
History 14 Apr 1949. **Aims** Promote study and appreciation of the work of composer Franz Lehar (1870-1948). **Staff** 3.00 FTE, paid. **Activities** Events/meetings. **Publications** *Lehariana* – magazine. **Members** Individuals (250). Membership countries not specified. **NGO Relations** Universities; orchestras. [2019.11.07/XE2242/E]

♦ Internationale Frauenliga für Frieden und Freiheit / see Women's International League for Peace and Freedom (#21024)
♦ Internationale Freiwilligendienste / see Service Civil International (#19238)
♦ Internationale Freundschaftsliga / see International Friendship League (#13685)
♦ Internationale Friedensbrigaden (#18277)
♦ Internationale Friedensforschungsinstitut, Oslo / see Peace Research Institute Oslo
♦ Internationale Früchtsaft Union / see International Fruit and Vegetable Juice Association (#13687)

- ♦ Internationale Gebedsvereniging (religious order)
- ♦ Internationale Gebetsvereinigung (religious order)
- ♦ Internationale Gemeinschaft des Gebäudereinigungs-Gewerbes (#09628)
- ♦ Internationale Gemeinschaft für Holztechnologie-Transfer / see Combois (#04122)
- ♦ Internationale Gemeinschaft der Züchter Vegetativ Vermehrbarer Zier- und Obstpflanzen (#12821)
- ♦ Internationale Gemeinschaft der Züchter Vegetativ Vermehrbarer Zierpflanzen / see International Community of Breeders of Asexually Reproduced Ornamental and Fruit Varieties (#12821)
- ♦ Internationale Gemeischaft für die Unterstützung von Kriegsopfern (internationally oriented national body)
- ♦ Internationale Gemengde Vrijmetselaarsorde (religious order)
- ♦ Internationale Genossenschaftliche Grosseinkaufsgesellschaft (inactive)
- ♦ Internationale Genossenschaftliche Versicherungs-Föderation / see International Cooperative and Mutual Insurance Federation (#12948)
- ♦ Internationale Geodätische Studentenorganisation (#13712)
- ♦ Internationale Gerbervereinigung (#13084)
- ♦ Internationale Gesellschaft für Aerosole in der Medizin (#14907)
- ♦ Internationale Gesellschaft der Allergologie und Klinische Immunologie / see World Allergy Organization – IAACI (#21077)
- ♦ Internationale Gesellschaft für Allgemeinmedizin (inactive)
- ♦ Internationale Gesellschaft für Analytische Psychologie (#11700)

♦ Internationale Gesellschaft für angewandte Präventionsmedizin (I-GAP) 13236

International Society of Applied Preventive Medicine

Contact Währinger Str 63, 1090 Vienna, Austria. T. +49408313124. Fax +49408313129. E-mail: office@i-gap.org.
URL: http://www.i-gap.org/

Aims Work with nutrition experts to develop and realize inter-regional guidelines for prevention and nutrition. **Structure** Advisory Council; Directory Board; Scientific Board. **Activities** Events/meetings; knowledge management/information dissemination; research/documentation; standards/guidelines; training/education. **Publications** *I-GAP Newsletter* (12 a year).

Members Individuals in 16 countries:
Austria, Belgium, Czechia, Germany, Hungary, Indonesia, Italy, Luxembourg, Malaysia, Romania, Slovakia, Slovenia, Sweden, Switzerland, Thailand, USA. [2018/XM6376/v/**C**]

- ♦ Internationale Gesellschaft von Ärzten für den Umweltschutz (#15065)
- ♦ Internationale Gesellschaft für Ärztliche Psychotherapie / see International Federation for Psychotherapy (#13523)
- ♦ Internationale Gesellschaft für Astmologie / see INTERASMA (#11457)
- ♦ Internationale Gesellschaft für Audiologie (#14948)
- ♦ Internationale Gesellschaft für Ausflichtmikroskopie (#13151)
- ♦ Internationale Gesellschaft für Babymassage (#11962)
- ♦ Internationale Gesellschaft zur Behandlung von Sexualstraftätern (#12241)
- ♦ Internationale Gesellschaft für Behandlung im Voraus Planen und Betreuung am Lebensende (#00126)
- ♦ Internationale Gesellschaft der Bildende Künste (internationally oriented national body)
- ♦ Internationale Gesellschaft der Bildenden Künste (#11710)
- ♦ Internationale Gesellschaft für Bildgebende Verfahren der Haut (inactive)
- ♦ Internationale Gesellschaft für Biospeologie (#14975)
- ♦ Internationale Gesellschaft für Blut-Uberleitung (#14979)
- ♦ Internationale Gesellschaft für Chemo- und Immunotherapie (inactive)
- ♦ Internationale Gesellschaft für Dialektologie und Geolinguistik (#19477)
- ♦ Internationale Gesellschaft für die Anthropologie Südosteuropas (#12173)
- ♦ Internationale Gesellschaft für die Entwicklung des Kombinierten Verkehrs und von Transporten unter Geregelter Temperatur (inactive)
- ♦ Internationale Gesellschaft für die Geschichte der Leibeserziehung und des Sports (#15175)
- ♦ Internationale Gesellschaft für Diskursforschung (#11850)
- ♦ Internationale Gesellschaft für Empirische Ästhetik (#11867)
- ♦ Internationale Gesellschaft für Empirische Literaturwissenschaft (#15085)
- ♦ Internationale Gesellschaft zur Erforschung der Arktis mit Luftfahrzeugen (inactive)

♦ Internationale Gesellschaft zur Erforschung und Förderung der Blasmusik (IGEB) 13237

Association internationale de la recherche et de l'avancement de la musique à vent – Sociedad Internacional para la Investigación y Promoción de la Música de Orquestas de Viento – International Society for the Promotion and Research of Wind Music – Associazione Internazionale per lo Studio e la Promozione della Musica per Fiatti

Treas – IGEB Office Univ für Musik und darstellende Kunst Graz, Institut 12 – Pannonische Forschungsstelle, Hauptplatz 8, 7432 Oberschützen, Austria. E-mail: emailigeb@gmail.com – igeb@uni.lu.
Pres Faculté des sciences humaines, sociales et d'éducation, Maison des Sciences Humaines, Porte des Sciences 11, L-4366 Esch-sur-Alzette, Luxembourg.
URL: http://www.igeb.net/

History 1974, Graz (Austria). Founded following a series of meetings held since 1966. Former names and other names: *International Society for the Promotion and Investigation of Wind Music* – alias. Registration: Austria. **Aims** Explore all aspects of wind music and *wind instruments*. **Structure** Board. Officers: President; Vice-Presidents; Secretary-General; Treasurer; Deputy Treasurer. **Languages** English, French, German, Italian. **Staff** Voluntary. **Finance** Sources: members' dues. **Activities** Events/meetings. **Events** *Congress* Valencia (Spain) 2024, *Congress* Bolzano (Italy) 2022, *Congress* 2021, *Congress* 2020, *Congress* Wadgassen (Germany) 2018. **Publications** *Mitteilungsblatt* (4 a year) – online , in print (2 a year); *IGEB Biographies. Alta Musica* – in 35 vols; *IGEB Reprints und Manuskripte* – in 7 vols.

Members Individuals (about 450) in 24 countries:
Austria, Belgium, Bulgaria, Canada, Czechia, Estonia, Finland, France, Germany, Israel, Italy, Lithuania, Luxembourg, Netherlands, New Zealand, Norway, Poland, Portugal, Spain, Suriname, Sweden, Switzerland, UK, USA. [2022/XD9343/**D**]

- ♦ Internationale Gesellschaft zur Erforschung von Grenzgebieten der Medizin (inactive)
- ♦ Internationale Gesellschaft zur Erforschung von Hirntraumata (inactive)
- ♦ Internationale Gesellschaft zur Erforschung von Zivilisationskrankheiten und Umwelt (inactive)
- ♦ Internationale Gesellschaft für Erzieherische Hilfen (#09622)
- ♦ Internationale Gesellschaft für Ethnologie und Volkskunde (#19481)
- ♦ Internationale Gesellschaft für Extremitätenerhaltung / see International Society of Limb Salvage (#15231)
- ♦ Internationale Gesellschaft für Familienrecht (#15114)
- ♦ Internationale Gesellschaft für Fettwissenschaft (#15115)

♦ Internationale Gesellschaft der Feuerbach Forscher 13238

Societas Ad Studia De Hominis Condicione Colenda

Pres WWU Inst Allgemeine Erziehungswissenschaft, Büro der Geschäftsführung, Bispinghof 5/6, Georgskommende 26, 48143 Münster, Germany.
URL: https://www.uni-muenster.de/EW/forschung/forschungsstellen/feuerbach/kooperationen/international.html

History Founded 1987, Zurich (Switzerland). **Aims** Promote the work of Ludwig Feuerbach (1804-1972). **Structure** Officers: President; Secretary-Treasurer.

Members Individuals in 16 countries:
China, Czechia, Finland, Germany, Hungary, Israel, Italy, Japan, Netherlands, Poland, Portugal, Russia, Spain, Sweden, Switzerland, USA. [2019.10.21/XE4450/v/**E**]

- ♦ Internationale Gesellschaft für Forensische Genetik (#15128)
- ♦ Internationale Gesellschaft der Forschung im ökologischen Landbau (#15331)
- ♦ Internationale Gesellschaft für Forschung in Ökonomischer Psychologie (#12132)
- ♦ Internationale Gesellschaft 'Frieden durch Kultur' (#12070)
- ♦ Internationale Gesellschaft fur Tiefenpsychologie (internationally oriented national body)

♦ Internationale Gesellschaft für Ganzheitliche Zahn-Medizin (GZM) . 13239

Main Office Kloppenheimerstr 10, 68239 Mannheim, Germany. T. +496214824300. Fax +49621473949. E-mail: info@gzm-org.de.
URL: http://www.gzm.org/

History 1985. Registration: Germany. **Aims** Improve *holistic dentistry*. **Languages** German. **Staff** 1.00 FTE, paid. **Finance** Members' dues. **Activities** Events/meetings. **Events** *European Congress* Lindau (Germany) 2015, *European congress* Cologne (Germany) 2010, *European congress* Leipzig (Germany) 2009, *European Congress* Munich (Germany) 2008, *European Congress* Munich (Germany) 2007. **Publications** *Systemische Orale Medizin (SOM)* – magazine.

Members Individuals (1,200) in 16 countries:
Austria, Belgium, Brazil, Canada, Denmark, Finland, France, Germany, Italy, Netherlands, South Africa, Spain, Switzerland, UK, United Arab Emirates, Venezuela.

NGO Relations Member of: *European Council of Doctors for Plurality in Medicine (ECPM, #06816)*. [2022/XD2547/v/**D**]

- ♦ Internationale Gesellschaft für Ganzheitsmedizin (unconfirmed)
- ♦ Internationale Gesellschaft für Gartenbauwissenschaften / see International Society for Horticultural Science (#15180)
- ♦ Internationale Gesellschaft für Geographische Pathologie (inactive)
- ♦ Internationale Gesellschaft für Geschichte der Leibeserziehung und des Sports (inactive)
- ♦ Internationale Gesellschaft für Geschichte der Pharmacie (#15173)
- ♦ Internationale Gesellschaft für Geschichtsdidaktik (#15167)
- ♦ Internationale Gesellschaft für Gesetzgebung (#11998)
- ♦ Internationale Gesellschaft für Getreidechemie / see ICC – International Association for Cereal Science and Technology (#11048)
- ♦ Internationale Gesellschaft für Getreidewissenschaft und -technologie (#11048)
- ♦ Internationale Gesellschaft für Griechische und Lateinische Epigraphik (#11924)
- ♦ Internationale Gesellschaft Hegel-Marx für Dialektisches Denken (no recent information)
- ♦ Internationale Gesellschaft für Heilpädagogik (inactive)

♦ Internationale Gesellschaft heilpädagogischer Berufs- und Fachverbände (IGhB) 13240

International Society of Professional Heilpaedagogic Organizations

Pres Herzbergstr 82-84, 10365 Berlin, Germany. T. +493040605060. Fax +493040605069. E-mail: info@ighb.eu.
URL: https://ighb.eu/

History 2005. **Activities** Events/meetings. **Events** *Internationaler Kongress* Berlin (Germany) 2015.

Members Associations in 7 countries:
Austria, Germany, Hungary, Luxembourg, Netherlands, Slovakia, Switzerland. [2022.06.29/AA1869/**D**]

- ♦ Internationale Gesellschaft für Heimerziehung / see Fédération internationale des communautés éducatives (#09622)
- ♦ Internationale Gesellschaft für historische Alpenforschung (#02990)
- ♦ Internationale Gesellschaft für historische und systematische Schulbuch- und Bildungsmedienforschung / see Internationale Gesellschaft für Schulbuch- und Bildungsmedienforschung (#13242)
- ♦ Internationale Gesellschaft für historische und systematische Schulbuchforschung / see Internationale Gesellschaft für Schulbuch- und Bildungsmedienforschung (#13242)
- ♦ Internationale Gesellschaft für Homöopathie und Homotoxikologie (internationally oriented national body)
- ♦ Internationale Gesellschaft für Homotoxikologie und Antihomotoxische Therapie / see Internationale Gesellschaft für Homöopathie und Homotoxikologie
- ♦ Internationale Gesellschaft für Humane und Animale Mykologie (#15181)
- ♦ Internationale Gesellschaft für Ingenieurpädagogik (#15089)
- ♦ Internationale Gesellschaft für Innere Medizin (#15212)
- ♦ Internationale Gesellschaft für Kartographie / see International Cartographic Association (#12446)
- ♦ Internationale Gesellschaft für Kaufmännisches Bildungswesen (#19479)
- ♦ Internationale Gesellschaft für Landbautechnik / see International Society for Soil Mechanics and Geotechnical Engineering (#15452)
- ♦ Internationale Gesellschaft für Logopädie und Phoniatrie / see International Association of Logopedics and Phoniatrics (#12005)

♦ Internationale Gesellschaft für Logotherapie und Existenzanalyse (GLE International) 13241

International Society of Logotherapy and Existential Analysis

Pres Eduard Suess Gasse 10, 1150 Vienna, Austria. T. +4319859566. E-mail: gle@existenzanalyse.org.
URL: http://www.existenzanalyse.org/

History Founded 1985. Became international in 2002. Registered in accordance with Austrian law. **Aims** Further develop and make known existential-analytical *anthropology* and its application in psychotherapy, education, ministry, social work, industry, work place and management; support and publish scientific research in the field of existential psychotherapy, counselling and coaching. **Structure** Board. **Languages** Czech, English, German, Romanian, Russian, Spanish. **Staff** 19.50 FTE, paid. **Finance** Members' dues. Other sources: training; congress proceeds; publications. Annual budget: euro 150,000. **Activities** Training/education; events/meetings; research/documentation; guidance/assistance/consulting. **Events** *Annual Congress* Vienna (Austria) 2023, *Annual Congress* Lindau (Germany) 2022, *Annual Congress* Vienna (Austria) 2021, *Annual Congress* Lindau (Germany) 2020, *Annual Congress* Salzburg (Austria) 2019. **Publications** *Existenzanalyse* (2 a year) – journal.

Members in 19 countries:
Argentina, Australia, Austria, Canada, Chile, Croatia, Czechia, France, Germany, Israel, Italy, Liechtenstein, Mexico, Netherlands, Poland, Romania, Russia, Switzerland, USA.

NGO Relations *European Association for Psychotherapy (EAP, #06176)*; *International Federation for Psychotherapy (IFP, #13523)*; *International Society of Depth Psychology (IGT)*; *Society for Psychotherapy Research (SPR, #19626)*. [2018/XD9359/**D**]

- ♦ Internationale Gesellschaft für Lymphologie (#15238)
- ♦ Internationale Gesellschaft für Männergesundheit (#15260)
- ♦ Internationale Gesellschaft für Männergesundheit und Geschlechtsspezifische Medizin / see International Society for Men's Health (#15260)
- ♦ Internationale Gesellschaft für Manuelle Medizin (#09642)
- ♦ Internationale Gesellschaft für Markscheidewesen (#15272)
- ♦ Internationale Gesellschaft für Medizinische Balneologie und Klimatologie (#15254)
- ♦ Internationale Gesellschaft für Menschenrechte (#15183)
- ♦ Internationale Gesellschaft für Mittel- und Osteuropaforschung, Wien (internationally oriented national body)
- ♦ Internationale Gesellschaft für Mobile Jugendarbeit (#15276)
- ♦ Internationale Gesellschaft für Moorforschung (inactive)
- ♦ Internationale Gesellschaft für Moor- und Torfkunde (#14538)
- ♦ Internationale Gesellschaft für Musik-Erziehung (#15287)
- ♦ Internationale Gesellschaft für Musik in der Medizin (#15289)
- ♦ Internationale Gesellschaft für Musikwissenschaft / see International Musicological Society (#14201)
- ♦ Internationale Gesellschaft für Nachhaltige Entwicklung und Landwirtschaft (inactive)
- ♦ Internationale Gesellschaft für Nadel-Punktierung (inactive)
- ♦ Internationale Gesellschaft für Neronischen Studien (#19484)

♦ Internationale Gesellschaft für Neue Musik (#15035)
♦ Internationale Gesellschaft für Neulateinische Studien (#12048)
♦ Internationale Gesellschaft für Neuraltherapie nach Huneke / see Internationale Medizinische Gesellschaft für Neuraltherapie nach Huneke-Regulationstherapie
♦ Internationale Gesellschaft für Neuropathologie (#15300)
♦ Internationale Gesellschaft für Normale und Pathologische Ethnopsychologie (inactive)
♦ Internationale Gesellschaft der Notokakteen-Freunde (internationally oriented national body)
♦ Internationale Gesellschaft für Nutztierhaltung (#15236)
♦ Internationale Gesellschaft für Organisationsentwicklung (#14444)
♦ Internationale Gesellschaft für Orientforschung (no recent information)
♦ Internationale Gesellschaft von Pflanzenvermehrern (#14594)
♦ Internationale Gesellschaft für Phonetische Wissenschaften (#15361)
♦ Internationale Gesellschaft für Photogrammetrie / see International Society for Photogrammetry and Remote Sensing (#15362)
♦ Internationale Gesellschaft für Photogrammetrie und Fernerkundung (#15362)
♦ Internationale Gesellschaft für Pränatale und Perinatale Psychologie und Medizin / see International Society for Pre- and Perinatal Psychology and Medicine (#15382)
♦ Internationale Gesellschaft für Prä- und Perinatale Psychologie und Medizin (#15382)
♦ Internationale Gesellschaft für Psychopathologische Ausdrucksformen (#15400)
♦ Internationale Gesellschaft für Quantitative Linguistik (#14678)
♦ Internationale Gesellschaft für Radiologie (#15412)
♦ Internationale Gesellschaft für das Recht der Arbeit und der Sozialen Sicherheit / see International Society for Labour and Social Security Law (#15226)
♦ Internationale Gesellschaft für Regenbogenfische (#14693)
♦ Internationale Gesellschaft für Religionspsychologie (#12116)
♦ Internationale Gesellschaft für Religionspsychologie und Religionswissenschaft / see International Association for the Psychology of Religion (#12116)
♦ Internationale Gesellschaft für Sandspiel Therapie (#15432)
♦ Internationale Gesellschaft für Schädel- und Kieferorthopädie (inactive)
♦ Internationale Gesellschaft der Schriftpsychologie (#15398)

♦ Internationale Gesellschaft für Schulbuch- und Bildungsmedienforschung (IGSBi) 13242

International Society for Research on Textbooks and Educational media

Pres Univ Augsburg, Lehrstuhl für Pädagogik, Universitätsstr 10, 86159 Augsburg, Germany. Fax +498215985630.
URL: http://www.schulbuch-gesellschaft.de/

History 1997, as *Internationale Gesellschaft für historische und systematische Schulbuchforschung – International Society for Historical and Systematic Research On Schoolbooks.* Adopted new name *Internationale Gesellschaft für historische und systematische Schulbuch- und Bildungsmedienforschung (IGSBi) – International Society for Historical and Systematic Research on Textbooks and Educational media* 2013. Current title adopted 2018. **Aims** Further interdisciplinary, historical and systematic research on textbooks and educational media. **Structure** Managing Board. **Languages** English, German. **Staff** Voluntary. **Finance** Members' dues. Donations. **Activities** Events/meetings; awards/prizes/competitions; publishing activities. **Events** *Conference* Würzburg (Germany) 2022, *Annual Conference* Chur (Switzerland) 2019, *Annual Conference* Bressanone (Italy) 2018, *Annual Conference* Augsburg (Germany) 2017, *Annual Conference* Oslo (Norway) 2016. **Publications** *Contributions to the Historical and Systematic Research on Textbooks and Educational Media* – series.
Members Full (112) in 24 countries:
Albania, Austria, Belgium, Czechia, Estonia, Finland, France, Germany, Greece, Hungary, Italy, Japan, Korea Rep, Latvia, Netherlands, Norway, Poland, Russia, Serbia, Slovenia, Spain, Sweden, Switzerland, UK. [2020.03.04/XM4244/**D**]

♦ Internationale Gesellschaft für Seelische Gesundheit in der Frühen Kindheit / see World Association for Infant Mental Health (#21146)
♦ Internationale Gesellschaft für Skitraumatologie und Wintersport-Medizin (#15445)
♦ Internationale Gesellschaft für Soziale Arbeit mit Gruppen (unconfirmed)
♦ Internationale Gesellschaft für Sportmotorik (#12178)
♦ Internationale Gesellschaft der Stadt- und Regionalplaner (#15012)
♦ Internationale Gesellschaft für Sterbebegleitung und Lebensbeistand (inactive)
♦ Internationale Gesellschaft für Studien des Gregorianischen Chorals (#02991)
♦ Internationale Gesellschaft zum Studium der Leberkrankheiten (#12203)
♦ Internationale Gesellschaft für Szientometrie und Informetrie (#15436)

♦ Internationale Gesellschaft für Theologische Mediävistik (IGTM) 13243

International Society for Medieval Theology

Contact c/o FTH, Rathenaustr 5-7, 35394 Giessen, Germany. E-mail: info@medievaltheology.org – info@mittelalterlichetheologie.de.
Chairman address not obtained.
URL: https://medievaltheology.org/

History 2002, Frankfurt-Main (Germany). Registration: Germany. **Aims** Promote study of the history of medieval theology within its cultural context. **Structure** Directors Board. **Languages** English, French, German, Italian, Spanish. **Staff** Voluntary. **Finance** Sources: members' dues. **Activities** Events/meetings; financial and/or material support; research/documentation. **Events** *Annual Conference* Munich (Germany) 2022, *Annual Conference* Copenhagen (Denmark) 2021, *Annual Conference* Copenhagen (Denmark) 2020, *Annual Conference* Linz (Austria) 2019, *Annual Conference* Krakow (Poland) 2018. **Publications** *Archa Verbi* (annual). *Archa Verbi Subsidia* – monograph series.
Members in 23 countries:
Argentina, Australia, Austria, Brazil, Chile, Czechia, Estonia, France, Germany, Holy See, Israel, Italy, Japan, Mexico, Mongolia, Netherlands, Nigeria, Poland, Spain, Sweden, Switzerland, UK, USA. [2022.05.11/XM2739/**D**]

♦ Internationale Gesellschaft für Thymologie und Immunotherapie (inactive)
♦ Internationale Gesellschaft für Tierhygiene (#14922)
♦ Internationale Gesellschaft für Umweltschutz (#15097)
♦ Internationale Gesellschaft für Unfall- und Verkehrsmedizin / see International Traffic Medicine Association (#15713)
♦ Internationale Gesellschaft für Ungarische Philologie (#11948)
♦ Internationale Gesellschaft für Urheberrecht (no recent information)
♦ Internationale Gesellschaft für Warenwissenschaften und Technologie (#11790)
♦ Internationale Gesellschaft für Weltwirtschaft (internationally oriented national body)
♦ Internationale Gesellschaft für Wirtschaftliche Bildung / see Société internationale pour l'enseignement commercial (#19479)
♦ Internationale Gesellschaft für Wissenorganisation (#15224)
♦ Internationale Gesellschaft für Wissenschaftliche Bäderkunde / see International Society of Medical Hydrology and Climatology (#15254)
♦ Internationale Gesellschaft für Wissenschaftliche Ordenskunde (inactive)
♦ Internationale Gesellschaft der Wolltextillaboratorien (#12275)
♦ Internationale Gesellschaft für Zellenbiologie (#13382)
♦ Internationale Gesellschaft für Zwillingsforschung (#15526)

♦ Internationale Gewässerschutzkommission für den Bodensee (IGKB) 13244

International Commission for the Protection of Lake Constance – Commission internationale pour la protection du lac de Constance – Commissione Internazionale per la Protezione del Lago di Costanza

Managing Dir Bayerisches Landesamt für Umwelt, Referat 67, Bürgermeister-Ulrich-Strasse 160, 86179 Augsburg, Germany. T. +4982190715736 – +4982190715897.
Managing Dir address not obtained.
URL: http://www.igkb.org/

History Set up by the Convention signed between the 'Länder' of Baden-Württemberg and Bavaria (Federal Republic of Germany), Austria and Switzerland. Constitution drawn up, 5-6 Nov 1959, St Gallen (Switzerland), and signed, 27 Oct 1960, Steckborn (Switzerland). Convention entered into force, 10 Nov 1961. Former names and other names: *Commission internationale pour la protection des eaux du lac de Constance contre la pollution* – former; *Internationale Kommission zum Schutz des Bodensees gegen Verunreinigung* – former; *Commissione Internazionale per la Protezione delle Acque del Lago di Costanza dall'Inquinamento* – former. **Aims** Determine the sanitary conditions of Lake Constance and causes of its pollution; regularly supervise its sanitary conditions, discuss measures to remedy the present pollution and to prevent future pollution, and make recommendations to the riparian States. **Structure** Commission; Cercle of Experts; Working Groups (4). **Languages** German. **Staff** 20 Delegates; about 60 Experts. **Finance** Supported by governmental institutions of Switzerland, Austria, Bavaria (Germany), Baden-Württemberg (Germany) and Liechtenstein. No fixed budget. **Activities** Monitoring/evaluation; networking/liaising; projects/programmes. **Events** *Annual Conference* Itingen (Switzerland) 2020, *Annual Conference* Kempten (Germany) 2019, *Annual Conference* Schwägalp (Switzerland) 2018, *Annual Conference* Konstanz (Germany) 2017, *Annual Conference* Horn (Switzerland) 2016. **Publications** Reports.
Members Governments of the 3 countries bordering on Lake Constance:
Austria, Germany (through states of Baden-Württemberg and Bavaria), Switzerland.
Participant on a voluntary basis:
Liechtenstein. [2021.07.06/XD5512/**D***]

♦ Internationale Gewerbeunion (inactive)
♦ Internationale Gewerkschaft im Europäischen Patentamt (#19944)

♦ International Egg Commission (IEC) 13245

Commission internationale des oeufs – Comisión Huevera Internacional

CEO Eaton Manor, Church Stretton, SY6 7DH, UK. T. +441694723004. E-mail: info@internationalegg.com.
URL: http://www.internationalegg.com/

History 22 Aug 1962, Sydney, NSW (Australia). Founded at 1st International Egg Marketing Conference, when Steering Committee was appointed to arrange for permanent establishment at 2nd Conference, 11 Sep 1964, Bologna (Italy). Registration: Companies House, No/ID: 07434096, Start date: 9 Nov 2010, England and Wales. **Aims** Keep members up to date with the latest developments in production, nutrition, and marketing to support business decision-making and development. **Languages** English. **Staff** 6.00 FTE, paid. **Finance** Sources: members' dues. **Activities** Awards/prizes/competitions; events/meetings; knowledge management/information dissemination; research/documentation. **Events** *Vision 365 Egg Leaders Strategy Summit* Nice (France) 2022, *Global Leadership Conference* Rotterdam (Netherlands) 2022, *Global Leadership Conference* Copenhagen (Denmark) 2019, *Conference* Monte Carlo (Monaco) 2019, *Global Leadership Conference* Kyoto (Japan) 2018. **Publications** *IEC E-Newsletter. IEC Business Insight Webinars; IEC Country Insights Series.* Chick placement data; industry statistics. **Members** Egg producers, processors and allied industries in 80 countries. Membership countries not specified. **Consultative Status** Consultative status granted from: *ECOSOC (#05331)* (Ros A); *FAO (#09260)* (Liaison Status). **NGO Relations** Memorandum of Understanding with (1): *International Poultry Council (IPC, #14628).* Member of (1): *World Egg Organisation (WEO).* Instrumental in setting up (1): *International Egg Foundation (IEF).* [2022.06.16/XC1797/t/**C**]

♦ International Egg Foundation (unconfirmed)
♦ Internationale Glas-Arbeiter-Föderation (inactive)
♦ Internationale Graphische Föderation (inactive)
♦ Internationale Groepering van de Farmaceutische Industrie van de Landen der EEG (inactive)
♦ Internationale Gruppierung der Pharmazeutischen Industrie der Länder der EWG (inactive)
♦ Internationale Gussasphalt-Vereinigung (#14119)
♦ Internationale Gustav Mahler Gesellschaft (#13765)
♦ Internationale Gutenberg-Gesellschaft in Mainz (#13766)
♦ Internationale Handball Federation (#13771)

♦ Internationale Hanns Eisler Gesellschaft (IHEG) 13246

Chairman Eisenbahnstrasse 21, 10997 Berlin, Germany. T. +493061288461. Fax +493061280463. E-mail: iheg@hanns-eisler.de.
URL: http://www.hanns-eisler.net/

History Jun 1994. **Aims** Promote the works of *composer* Hanns Eisler (1898-1962). **Structure** Governing Board; Board. **Languages** English, German. **Finance** Members' dues. **Activities** Organizes and coordinates a variety of artistic and scholarly events connected with Eisler's life and work. **Events** *Annual Symposium* Leipzig (Germany) 2014, *Annual Symposium* Berlin (Germany) 2013, *Annual Symposium* Berlin (Germany) 2012, *Annual Symposium* Augsburg (Germany) 2011, *Annual Symposium* London (UK) 2010. **Publications** *Eisler Mitteilungen* (2 a year).
Members Individuals in 19 countries:
Australia, Austria, Brazil, Denmark, Finland, France, Germany, Italy, Japan, Korea Rep, Mexico, Netherlands, Norway, Poland, Sweden, Switzerland, UK, Uruguay, USA. [2013.08.12/XE4561/v/**E**]

♦ International eHealth Association (no recent information)
♦ Internationale Hegel-Gesellschaft (#13788)

♦ Internationale Hegel-Vereinigung 13247

International Association for the Advancement of Hegelian Studies – Association internationale pour la promotion des études hégéliennes – Internationale Vereinigung zur Förderung des Studiums der Hegelschen Philosophie – Associazione Internazionale per la Promozione dello Studio della Filosofia di Hegel

Contact Freie Univ Berlin, Inst für Philosophie, Habelschwerdter Allee 30, 14195 Berlin, Germany.
Pres Freie Univ Berlin, Institut für Philosophie, Habelschwerdter Allee 30 Raum 25, 14195 Berlin, Germany.
URL: https://hegelvereinigung.org/

History 1962. Registration: Germany. **Aims** Promote study of the *philosophy* of Georg Wilhelm Friedrich Hegel. **Events** *International Congress* Stuttgart (Germany) 2017, *Congress* Stuttgart (Germany) 2011, *Van der logik zur sprache* Stuttgart (Germany) 2005, *Congress* Stuttgart (Germany) 1999, *Concepts of reason in modern thinking* Stuttgart (Germany) 1993. **Publications** Annual newsletter; conference proceedings.
Members Full (about 260) in 26 countries and territories:
Argentina, Austria, Belgium, Brazil, China, Croatia, Denmark, France, Germany, Hungary, Israel, Italy, Japan, Korea Rep, Luxembourg, Netherlands, Peru, Poland, Slovakia, Spain, Switzerland, Taiwan, Türkiye, UK, USA, Venezuela.
NGO Relations Member of: *International Federation of Philosophical Societies (FISP, #13507).* [2021/XE0405/**E**]

♦ Internationale Heimtier-Handelsorganisation (inactive)

♦ Internationale Heinrich-Schütz-Gesellschaft (ISG) 13248

Société internationale Heinrich Schütz – International Heinrich Schütz Society

Head Office Heinrich-Schütz-Allee 35, 34131 Kassel, Germany. T. +495613164500. Fax +495613164501. E-mail: info@schuetzgesellschaft.de.
Pres Möringstr 15, 37671 Höxter, Germany.
URL: http://www.schuetzgesellschaft.de/

History 1930, Berlin (Germany). New constitution adopted 1976, Kassel (Germany FR). **Aims** Promote interest in the work of Heinrich Schütz and his contemporaries and in the development of old and new sacred *music.* **Structure** General Assembly; Council; Executive Board; Sections (7). **Languages** English, French, German. **Finance** Members' dues. **Activities** Events/meetings. **Events** *Meeting* Zurich (Switzerland) 2018, *International Festival* Copenhagen (Denmark) 2014, *International Festival* Venice (Italy) 2013, *International Festival* Torgau (Germany) 2012, *International Festival* Hannover (Germany) 2011. **Publications** *Acta Sagittariana* in English, French, German – newsletter; *Schütz-Jahrbuch. Heinrich Schütz* – collected works; *Johann Hermann Schein* – collected works; *Leonhard Lechner* – collected works. Records; scores.
Members Individuals and institutions in 17 countries:
Australia, Austria, Canada, Czechia, Denmark, France, Germany, Italy, Japan, Netherlands, Norway, Poland, Slovakia, Sweden, Switzerland, UK, USA. [2020/XE2100/**E**]

- ♦ Internationale Hippokratische Gesellschaft, Zurich (unconfirmed)
- ♦ Internationale Horngesellschaft (#13810)
- ♦ Internationale Højskole (internationally oriented national body)
- ♦ Internationale Humanistische und Ethische Union / see Humanists International (#10972)
- ♦ Internationale Hunde-Union (#20370)
- ♦ Internationale Industriezweigorganisation für Zusammenarbeit auf dem Gebiet Kleintonnagiger Chemischer Erzeugnisse (inactive)
- ♦ Internationale Investitionsbank (#13951)
- ♦ Internationale ISBN-Agentur (#13955)
- ♦ Internationale ISMN-Agentur (#13963)
- ♦ Internationale des jeunes amis de la nature (#15929)
- ♦ Internationale de la jeunesse (inactive)
- ♦ Internationale de la jeunesse communiste (inactive)
- ♦ Internationale de la jeunesse socialiste (inactive)
- ♦ Internationale des jeunes travailleurs (inactive)
- ♦ Internationale Jongeren Uitwisseling (#13122)
- ♦ Internationale Journalisten-Föderation (#13462)
- ♦ Internationale J A Schumpeter Gesellschaft (#13974)
- ♦ Internationale Judo-Föderation (#13975)
- ♦ Internationale Jugendbibliothek (#15936)
- ♦ Internationale Jugendgemeinschaftsdienste (internationally oriented national body)
- ♦ Internationale Kampagne zur Beendigung von Völkermord / see Alliance Against Genocide (#00655)
- ♦ Internationale Kartographische Vereinigung (#12446)
- ♦ Internationale Katholieke Vereniging voor Medisch-Psychologische Studies (inactive)
- ♦ Internationale Katholische Bäuerliche und Ländliche Vereinigung (#12461)
- ♦ Internationale Katholische Konferenz des Pfadfindertums (#12453)
- ♦ Internationale Katholische Land- und Bauernjugendbewegung (#16865)
- ♦ Internationale Katholische Mittelstandsbewegung (inactive)
- ♦ Internationale Katholische Studierende Jugend (#15926)
- ♦ Internationale Katholische Vereinigung für Medizinisch- Psychologische Forschung (inactive)
- ♦ Internationale Katholische Vereinigung für Soziale Arbeit (inactive)
- ♦ Internationale Kirchliche Filmorganisation (#13943)
- ♦ Internationale Klimaschutzinitiative (internationally oriented national body)
- ♦ Internationale Komitee für Photobiologie / see International Union of Photobiology (#15798)
- ♦ Internationale Komitee der Vierten Internationale (#12771)
- ♦ Internationale Kommission für Agrartechnik (#12661)
- ♦ Internationale Kommission für Alpines Rettungswesen (#12662)
- ♦ Internationale Kommission für Bienenbotanik / see International Commission for Plant-Pollinator Relationships (#12716)
- ♦ Internationale Kommission der Detektiv-Verbände (#13364)
- ♦ Internationale Kommission für die Geschichte des Ständewesens und der Parlamente / see International Commission for the History of State Assemblies (#12689)
- ♦ Internationale Kommission für die Hydrologie des Rheingebietes (#12693)
- ♦ Internationale Kommission Einheitlicher Untersuchungsmethoden der Nahrungsmittel (inactive)
- ♦ Internationale Kommissionen zum Schutze von Mosel und Saar (#12729)
- ♦ Internationale Kommissionen zum Schutze von Mosel und Saar gegen Verunreinigung / see International Commissions for the Protection of the Moselle and Saar (#12729)
- ♦ Internationale Kommission für Fahrerlaubnisprüfungen (#12678)
- ♦ Internationale Kommission für Geschichte der Geologischen Wissenschaften (#12685)
- ♦ Internationale Kommission für Glas (#12683)
- ♦ Internationale Kommission der Katholische Hauptgefängnisseelsorger / see International Commission of Catholic Prison Pastoral Care (#12670)
- ♦ Internationale Kommission der Katholischen Gefängnisseelsorge (#12670)
- ♦ Internationale Kommission für Kohlenpetrologie (#12750)
- ♦ Internationale Kommission für Kraftfahrzeug-Führerprüfungen / see International Commission for Driver Testing (#12678)
- ♦ Internationale Kommission der Lebensmittelindustrie (inactive)
- ♦ Internationale Kommission für Militärgeschichte (#12705)
- ♦ Internationale Kommission für Mode- und Textilfarben (#04218)
- ♦ Internationale Kommission zum Schutz des Bodensees gegen Verunreinigung / see Internationale Gewässerschutzkommission für den Bodensee (#13244)
- ♦ Internationale Kommission zum Schutz der Donau (#12720)

♦ Internationale Kommission zum Schutz der Elbe (IKSE) 13249

International Commission for the Protection of the Elbe River (ICPER) – Mezinárodní komise pro ochranu Labe (MKOL)

Exec Sec Fürstenwallstr 20, 39104 Magdeburg, Germany. T. +49391400030. Fax +493914000311. E-mail: sekretariat@ikse-mkol.org.
URL: https://www.ikse-mkol.org/

History 8 Oct 1990. Established on signature of an international convention. Signatories: Germany; Czechoslovakia; *European Community (inactive).* **Aims** Enable use of Elbe *water*, mainly to gain drinking water, by means of bank infiltration, and to gain water and sediments for *agricultural* purposes; obtain a natural environmental system with many species; diminish *pollution* of the North Sea from the Elbe catchment area. **Structure** Working Groups (3); Expert Groups (4). **Languages** Czech, German. **Staff** 8.00 FTE, paid. **Finance** Sources: government support. Financed by the Governments of Germany (66.7%) and Czechia (33.3%). **Activities** Management of treaties and agreements. Agreement on the International Commission for the Protection of the Elbe River (ICPER). **Events** *International Elbe Forum* 2021, *International Elbe Forum* Dresden (Germany) 2019, *International Elbe Forum* Usti nad Labem (Czech Rep) 2015, *International Elbe Forum* Usti nad Labem (Czech Rep) 2013, *International Elbe forum* Usti nad Labem (Czech Rep) 2009. **Publications** Reports; plans; action programmes; research results.

Members Contracting parties governments of 2 countries:
Czechia, Germany.
Observers governments of 2 countries:
Austria, Poland.
Observers – International Organizations (3):
International Commission for the Protection of the Danube River (ICPDR, #12720); International Commission for the Protection of the Rhine (ICPR, #12721); Internationale Kommission zum Schutz der Oder gegen Verunreinigung (IKSOgV, #13250).
European Commission was signatory power until accession of Czech Rep, 1 May 2004.
NGO Relations Also links with national organizations. [2023.02.27/XE3024/y/**E***]

- ♦ Internationale Kommission zum Schutze der Mosel (inactive)
- ♦ Internationale Kommission zum Schutze de Rheins gegen Verunreinigung / see International Commission for the Protection of the Rhine (#12721)
- ♦ Internationale Kommission zum Schutze der Saar (inactive)
- ♦ Internationale Kommission zum Schutz des Genfersees (internationally oriented national body)
- ♦ Internationale Kommission zum Schutz der Maas / see International Commission of the Meuse (#12702)

♦ Internationale Kommission zum Schutz der Oder gegen Verunreinigung (IKSOgV) 13250

Commission internationale pour la protection de l'Oder – International Commission for the Protection of the Odra River against Pollution (ICPO) – Miedzynarodowa Komisja Ochrony Odry przed Zanieczycszczeniem (MKOOpZ) – Mezinarodni Komise pro Ocranu Oddry pvred Znecistenim (MKOOpZ)

Secretariat c/o MKOOpZ, ul M Curie-Sklodowskiej 1, 50-381 Wroclaw, Poland. T. +48713267470. Fax +48713283711. E-mail: sekretariat@mkoo.pl.
URL: http://www.mkoo.pl/

History 11 Apr 1996, Wroclaw (Poland), on signature of an international convention. Convention entered into force 26 Apr 1999. Previously also referred to in English as *International Commission for the Protection of the Oder.* Previously also known under the acronym *IKSO.* Secretariat in Wroclaw (Poland). **Aims** Coordinate implementation of Water Framework Directive and Flood Directive in the Oder river basin; prevent and reduce *pollution* of the Oder and the *Baltic Sea.* **Structure** Presidency rotates among contracting parties. **Languages** Czech, German, Polish. **Staff** 8.00 FTE, paid. **Finance** Contributions from contracting parties: Czech Rep – 20.50%; Germany – 38.75%; Poland – 38.75%. **Activities** Research/documentation; knowledge management/information dissemination; monitoring/evaluation; projects/programmes; awareness raising; events/meetings.

Members Contracting parties governments of 3 countries:
Czechia, Germany, Poland.
Regional economic integration organization (1):
European Union (EU, #08967).
IGO Relations *International Commission for the Protection of the Danube River (ICPDR, #12720); International Commission for the Protection of the Rhine (ICPR, #12721); International Commission of the Schelde River (#12727); International Commissions for the Protection of the Moselle and Saar (ICPMS, #12729); International Sava River Basin Commission (#14783); Internationale Kommission zum Schutz der Elbe (IKSE, #13249).*
[2019.07.10/XE4280/**E***]

- ♦ Internationale Kommission zum Schutz des Rheins (#12721)
- ♦ Internationale Kommission zur Veröffentlichung von Quellen zur Europäischen Geschichte (no recent information)
- ♦ Internationale Kommission für Zuckertechnologie (inactive)
- ♦ Internationale Kommunikation und Kultur (internationally oriented national body)
- ♦ Internationale Kommunistische Ströming (#12818)
- ♦ Internationale Konferenz für die Technische Einheit im Eisenbahnwesen (inactive)
- ♦ Internationale Konferenz Theologischer Mitarbeiter in der Diakonie / see Internationale Konferenz Theologischer Mitarbeiterinnen und Mitarbeiter in der Diakonie
- ♦ Internationale Konferenz Theologischer Mitarbeiterinnen und Mitarbeiter in der Diakonie (internationally oriented national body)
- ♦ Internationale Konferenz über Automatische Brandentdeckung (meeting series)
- ♦ Internationale Konföderation für Abrüstung und Frieden (inactive)
- ♦ Internationale Konföderation der Kneipp-Bewegung / see Kneipp Worldwide (#16197)
- ♦ Internationale Konföderation der Verarbeiter von Papier und Pappe in Europa (#12866)
- ♦ Internationale Konföderation der Verarbeiter von Papier und Pappe in der Europäischen Gemeinschaft / see International Confederation of Paper and Board Converters in Europe (#12866)
- ♦ Internationale Kongress für Tropische Medizin und Malaria (meeting series)
- ♦ Internationale Koordination Anthroposophische Medizin (#12957)

♦ Internationale Krachtbalfederatie (IKBF) 13251

International Powerball Federation

Sec Kluisweg 7, 9255 Buggenhout, Belgium.
URL: http://www.ikbf.eu/

History 29 Jun 1998, Buggenhout (Belgium). Registration: Banque Carrefour des Entreprises, No/ID: 0464.682.062, Start date: 29 Jun 1998, Belgium. **Aims** Promote the *game* of powerball. **Structure** General Assembly (annual). Council, comprising President, Vice-President, Treasurer and Secretary. Commissions. Secretariat. **Languages** Dutch, English. **Staff** 5.00 FTE, voluntary. **Finance** No members' dues. **Activities** Sporting activities.

Members Founding members in 6 countries:
Belgium, France, Netherlands, Norway, Portugal, Sweden. [2011.06.01/XD6683/**D**]

- ♦ Internationale Krankenhaus-Gesellschaft (inactive)
- ♦ Internationale Kreditversicherungs- und Kaution Vereinigung / see International Credit Insurance & Surety Association (#13103)
- ♦ Internationale Kreditversicherungs-Vereinigung / see International Credit Insurance & Surety Association (#13103)
- ♦ Internationale Kreis der Lehrinstitute für die Polygrafische Industrie (#12573)
- ♦ Internationale der Kriegsdienstgegner/innen/ (#20818)
- ♦ Internationale Kriminalistische Vereinigung (inactive)
- ♦ Internationale Kriminalpolizeiliche Kommission / see International Criminal Police Organization – INTERPOL (#13110)
- ♦ Internationale KSJ / see International Young Catholic Students (#15926)
- ♦ Internationale Kulturliga (inactive)
- ♦ Internationale Kunstausstellungsleitertagung (#11116)
- ♦ Internationale Kunsthändler-Vereinigung (#12848)
- ♦ Internationale du Lac de Constance (#16221)

♦ International Elbow Working Group (IEWG) 13252

Pres Utrecht Univ, Fac of Veterinary Medicine, Dept of Clinical Sciences of Companion Animals, Yalelaan 8, 3584 CM Utrecht, Netherlands. E-mail: how@planet.nl.
URL: http://www.vet-iewg.org/

History 1989. **Aims** Disseminate on canine elbow information. **Structure** Officers: President; Vice-President; Secretary; Treasurer. **Events** *Annual Meeting* Barcelona (Spain) 2018, *Annual Meeting* Verona (Italy) 2017, *Annual Meeting* Vienna (Austria) 2016, *Annual Meeting* Bangkok (Thailand) 2015, *Annual meeting* Rhodes Is (Greece) 2004. [2020/XE3514/**E**]

♦ International E-Learning Association (IELA) 13253

Contact c/o Kaleidoscope Learning, 287 Park Ave South, 2nd Floor, New York NY 10010, USA. E-mail: info@ielassoc.org.
URL: http://www.ielassoc.org/

History 2007, USA. Registration: USA, State of New York. **Aims** Advance knowledge and practice of e-learning in the classroom and the workplace. **Structure** Board of Directors; International Advisory Board. **Staff** 4.00 FTE, paid. **Activities** Events/meetings; publishing activities. Sponsors: Learning Ideas Conference (formerly International Conference on E-learning in the Workplace (ICELW)); International Conference on Interactive Collaborative Learning (ICL); International Conference on Interactive Mobile Communications,Technologies, and Learning (IMCL). **Events** *The Learning Ideas Conference* New York, NY (USA) 2022, *International Conference on E-Learning in the Workplace* New York, NY (USA) 2019, *International Conference on E-Learning in the Workplace* New York, NY (USA) 2018, *International Conference on E-Learning in the Workplace* New York, NY (USA) 2017, *International Conference on Computer-Aided and Blended Learning* Riyadh (Saudi Arabia) 2017. **Publications** *International Journal of Advanced Corporate Learning (iJAC); International Journal of Emerging Technologies in E-Learning (iJET); International Journal of Interactive Mobile Technologies (iJIM).*

Members in 35 countries. Membership countries not specified. [2022.06.15/XJ6303/**C**]

- ♦ International La Leche Liga (#16433)
- ♦ International Election Monitors Institute / see Global Democracy Initiative

♦ International Electrical Research Exchange (IERE) 13254

SG 2-11-1 Iwado Kita, Komae-shi, Tokyo, 201-8511 Japan.
URL: https://www.iere.jp/

History Founded Oct 1968, by *UNIPEDE – International Union of Producers and Distributors of Electrical Energy (inactive),* and USA, Japanese and Canadian research organizations for the electricity supply industry throughout the world. Renovated 1 Jan 2001, inviting wide spectrum of members from around the world. Organizational structures, activities and services have thus far been renewed in order to expedite the progress of electricity technologies and to foster cooperative R and D on a global scale. **Aims** Promote cooperation and exchange of information concerning research and development of production, transmission, distribution and

use of electrical *energy.* **Structure** General Meeting (annual); Board. **Languages** English. **Staff** 7.00 FTE, paid. **Finance** Members' dues. **Activities** Knowledge management/information dissemination; networking/liaising; awards/prizes/competitions; events/meetings. **Events** *General Meeting* Tokyo (Japan) 2022, *General Meeting* Kyoto (Japan) 2018, *General Meeting* Vancouver, BC (Canada) 2017, *General Meeting* Beijing (China) 2016, *General Meeting* Berlin (Germany) 2015. **Publications** Newsletter. Annual Report; papers and presentation data submitted at events.
Members Electric power utilities, manufacturers and research and development organizations in 19 countries and territories:
Australia, Canada, China, France, Germany, Hong Kong, Indonesia, Iran Islamic Rep, Japan, Korea Rep, Malaysia, Mexico, Philippines, Singapore, South Africa, Spain, Taiwan, Thailand, USA.
Consultative Status Consultative status granted from: *ECOSOC (#05331)* (Ros A). [2019.06.10/XF1583/**F**]

♦ International Electricians' Society (inactive)
♦ International Electric Propulsion Conference (meeting series)
♦ International Electric Response Audiometry Study Group / see International Evoked Response Audiometry Study Group (#13320)
♦ International Electronic Article Surveillance Manufacturers' Association (no recent information)
♦ International Electronics Association (inactive)
♦ International Electronics Recycling Congress (meeting series)

♦ International Electrotechnical Commission (IEC) 13255

Commission électrotechnique internationale

Gen Sec Rue de Varembé 3, 1202 Geneva, Switzerland. T. +41229190211. E-mail: info@iec.ch.
Pres address not obtained.
URL: http://www.iec.ch/

History 26 Jun 1906, London (UK). Founded as a result of a resolution passed at the International Electrical Congress, Sep 1904, St Louis MO (USA). First Statutes drawn up at Preliminary Meeting, 1906, London, adopted in 1908. Revised Statutes adopted: 1949, Stresa (Italy); 1963, Venice (Italy); 1976, Nice (France); 1991, Madrid (Spain); 1992, Rotterdam (Netherlands); 1997; 2000; 2001 (amended in 2004, 2005, 2008 and 2009). Former names and other names: *Comisión Electrotécnica Internacional* – former; *Internationale Elektrotechnische Kommission* – former; *Mezdunarodnaja Elektrotehniceskaja Komissija* – former. Registration: Swiss Civil Code, Switzerland; EU Transparency Register, No/ID: 825251334263-76. **Aims** Prepare and publish International *Standards* for all *electrical, electronic* and related technologies; administer Conformity Assessment Systems covering equipment, services and personnel. **Structure** Council (General Assembly), meets at least annually; Council Board; Executive Committee; Standardization Management Board (SMB); Conformity Assessment Board (CAB); Marketing Strategy Board (MSB); technical committees and sub-committees managed by SMB; Member National Committees. Administers the following Conformity Assessment Systems: *IEC Quality Assessment System for Electronic Components (IECQ, #11095); IEC System of Conformity Assessment Schemes for Electrotechnical Equipment and Components (IECEE, #11096); International Electrotechnical Commission System for Certification to Standards Relating to Equipment for use in Explosive Atmospheres (IECEx System, #13256)*, IEC System for Certification to Standards Relating to Equipment for Use in Renewable Energy Applications (IECRE System). **Languages** English, French, Russian. **Staff** 121.00 FTE, paid. **Finance** Sources: members' dues; sale of publications. Annual budget: 20,000,000 CHF. **Activities** Certification/accreditation; events/meetings; publishing activities; standards/guidelines. **Events** *Plenary meeting* Osaka (Japan) 2022, *General Meeting* Dubai (United Arab Emirates) 2021, *Subcommittee on Software and Systems Engineering Meeting* Okayama (Japan) 2021, *Plenary meeting* Geneva (Switzerland) 2020, *Annual General Meeting* Seogwipo (Korea Rep) 2020. **Publications** *IEC e-tech* (6 a year). IEC Blog; Catalogue of IEC Publications; Standards in database format. **Information Services** *Electropedia – The International Electrotechnical Vocabulary*; *IEC Glossary*.
Members National Committees. Full in 62 countries:
Algeria, Argentina, Australia, Austria, Belarus, Belgium, Brazil, Bulgaria, Canada, Chile, China, Colombia, Croatia, Czechia, Denmark, Egypt, Finland, France, Germany, Greece, Hungary, India, Indonesia, Iran Islamic Rep, Iraq, Ireland, Israel, Italy, Japan, Korea Rep, Kuwait, Luxembourg, Malaysia, Mexico, Netherlands, New Zealand, Nigeria, Norway, Oman, Pakistan, Peru, Philippines, Poland, Portugal, Qatar, Romania, Russia, Saudi Arabia, Serbia, Singapore, Slovakia, Slovenia, South Africa, Spain, Sweden, Switzerland, Thailand, Türkiye, UK, Ukraine, United Arab Emirates, USA.
Associate in 27 countries:
Albania, Bahrain, Bangladesh, Bosnia-Herzegovina, Côte d'Ivoire, Cuba, Cyprus, Estonia, Ethiopia, Georgia, Ghana, Iceland, Jordan, Kazakhstan, Kenya, Korea DPR, Latvia, Lithuania, Malta, Moldova, Montenegro, Morocco, North Macedonia, Sri Lanka, Tunisia, Uganda, Vietnam.
Affiliate Country Programme participants in 84 countries and territories:
Afghanistan, Angola, Antigua-Barbuda, Armenia, Azerbaijan, Bahamas, Barbados, Belize, Benin, Bhutan, Bolivia, Botswana, Brunei Darussalam, Burkina Faso, Burundi, Cambodia, Cameroon, Cape Verde, Central African Rep, Chad, Comoros, Congo Brazzaville, Congo DR, Costa Rica, Djibouti, Dominica, Dominican Rep, Ecuador, El Salvador, Eritrea, Eswatini, Fiji, Gabon, Gambia, Grenada, Guatemala, Guinea, Guinea-Bissau, Guyana, Haiti, Honduras, Jamaica, Kyrgyzstan, Laos, Lebanon, Lesotho, Liberia, Madagascar, Malawi, Mali, Mauritania, Mauritius, Mongolia, Mozambique, Myanmar, Namibia, Nepal, Nicaragua, Niger, Palestine, Panama, Papua New Guinea, Paraguay, Rwanda, Sao Tomé-Principe, Senegal, Seychelles, Sierra Leone, South Sudan, St Kitts-Nevis, St Lucia, St Vincent-Grenadines, Sudan, Suriname, Syrian AR, Tanzania UR, Togo, Trinidad-Tobago, Turkmenistan, Uruguay, Uzbekistan, Yemen, Zambia, Zimbabwe.
Consultative Status Consultative status granted from: *ECOSOC (#05331)* (General); *International Maritime Organization (IMO, #14102); UNIDO (#20336).*
IGO Relations Associated with Department of Global Communications of the United Nations. Cooperates with:
- *Bank for International Settlements (BIS, #03165);*
- *Bureau international des poids et mesures (BIPM, #03367);*
- *Conférence européenne des administrations des postes et des télécommunications (CEPT, #04602);*
- *Council of Europe (CE, #04881);*
- *EFTA (#05391);*
- *European Commission (EC, #06633)*, via *European Committee for Electrotechnical Standardization (CENELEC, #06647);*
- *European Organization for Nuclear Research (CERN, #08108);*
- *ILO (#11123);*
- *International Atomic Energy Agency (IAEA, #12294);*
- *International Centre for Scientific and Technical Information (ICSTI, #12514);*
- *International Civil Aviation Organization (ICAO, #12581);*
- *International Energy Agency (IEA, #13270);*
- *International Hydrographic Organization (IHO, #13825);*
- *International Mobile Satellite Organization (IMSO, #14174);*
- *International Organization of Legal Metrology (#14451);*
- *International Telecommunication Union (ITU, #15673)* – Radiocommunication, Telecommunication Standardization and Development Sectors;
- *League of Arab States (LAS, #16420);*
- *OECD (#17693);*
- *UNCTAD (#20285);*
- *UNESCO (#20322);*
- *United Nations Economic Commission for Europe (UNECE, #20555);*
- *Universal Postal Union (UPU, #20682);*
- *WHO (#20950);*
- *World Customs Organization (WCO, #21350);*
- *World Intellectual Property Organization (WIPO, #21593);*
- *World Meteorological Organization (WMO, #21649).*

NGO Relations Cooperates with: *European Committee for Electrotechnical Standardization (CENELEC, #06647); International Organization for Standardization (ISO, #14473).* Member of: *Fédération des Institutions Internationales établies à Genève (FIIG, #09599).* [2020.09.07/XC1800/**C**]

♦ International Electrotechnical Commission System for Certification to Standards Relating to Equipment for use in Explosive Atmospheres (IECEx System) 13256

Exec Sec Level 33, Australia Square, 264 George Street, Sydney NSW 2000, Australia. T. +61246284690. Fax +61246275285. E-mail: info@iecex.com.
URL: http://www.iecex.com/

History Founded within *International Electrotechnical Commission (IEC, #13255).* Former names and other names: *IEC System for the Certification to Standards for Electrical Equipment for Explosive Atmospheres* – alias. **Aims** Facilitate international trade in equipment and services intended for use in areas where flammable/combustible liquids, gases and dusts my be present (termed explosive atmospheres, Ex equipment). explosive atmospheres (ex equipment). **Structure** General Meeting (annual). Management Committee of currently 31 members. Executive Committee, including Chairman, Vice-Chairman, Secretary and Treasurer. Technical Committees; Working Groups. Executive Secretariat. **Languages** English. **Staff** Full-time, paid; part-time, paid. **Finance** Members' dues. Fee on certificates issues. **Activities** Provides 3 International Certification Schemes: IECEx Certified Equipment Scheme; IECEx Certified Services Scheme; IECEx Certified Persons Scheme for Personnel Competencies. Organizes annual symposium at General Meeting. **Events** *Meeting of the IECEx System* Tokyo (Japan) 2021, *Meeting of the IECEx System* Durban (South Africa) 2016, *Joint Conformity Assessment Seminar* Accra (Ghana) 2015, *Meeting of the IECEx System* Christchurch (New Zealand) 2015, *International Conference* Gdansk (Poland) 2015. **Publications** *IEC e-Tech Monthly* – magazine.
Members National organizations in 31 countries:
Australia, Brazil, Canada, China, Croatia, Czechia, Denmark, Finland, France, Germany, Hungary, India, Italy, Japan, Korea Rep, Malaysia, Netherlands, New Zealand, Norway, Poland, Romania, Russia, Serbia, Singapore, Slovenia, South Africa, Sweden, Switzerland, Türkiye, UK, USA.
IGO Relations *Asia-Pacific Economic Cooperation (APEC, #01887); ASEAN (#01141); European Commission (EC, #06633); United Nations Economic Commission for Europe (UNECE, #20555); World Trade Organization (WTO, #21864).* [2021/XJ4453/**F**]

♦ International Elephant Foundation (internationally oriented national body)
♦ Internationale Lesegesellschaft / see International Literacy Association (#14057)
♦ Internationale libérale (#16454)
♦ Internationale des libres et penseurs prolétaires (inactive)
♦ Internationale Liga der Dermatologischen Gesellschaften (#14018)
♦ Internationale Liga der Handelsvertreter und Reisenden (inactive)
♦ Internationale Liga gegen Unlauteren Wettbewerb / see Ligue internationale du droit de la concurrence (#16478)
♦ Internationale Liga für Unterricht, Erziehung und Volksbildung (#14023)
♦ Internationale Liga von Vereinigungen für Menschen mit Geistiger Behinderung / see Inclusion International (#11145)
♦ Internationale Liga von Vereinigungen zugunsten Geistig Behinderter / see Inclusion International (#11145)
♦ Internationale Liga für Wettbewerbsrecht (#16478)
♦ Internationale Luftelektrische Kommission (#12665)
♦ Internationale Maascommissie (#12702)
♦ Internationale Maaskommission (#12702)
♦ Internationale Mandel- und Nussvereinigung / see International Nut and Dried Fruit Council Foundation (#14387)
♦ Internationale Martin-Buber-Stiftung (internationally oriented national body)
♦ Internationale Max Scheler Gesellschaft (#14123)
♦ Internationale Mazdaznan Frauen Föderation (inactive)

♦ International Embryo Technology Society (IETS) 13257

Sociedad Internacional sobre la Transmisión de Embriones

Main Office 1800 South Oak St, Ste 100, Champaign IL 61820, USA. T. +12173984697. Fax +12173984119. E-mail: iets@assochq.org.
HQ 2441 Village Green Place, Champaign IL 61822, USA.
URL: http://www.iets.org/

History 1974, Denver CO (USA), as *International Embryo Transfer Society (IETS).* **Aims** Further the science of animal embryo transfer by promoting more effective research, disseminating scientific and educational information, fostering high standards of education, maintaining high standards of ethics and cooperating with other organizations having similar objectives. **Structure** Boards of Governors. Officers: President; Vice-President; Secretary-Treasurer. **Languages** English. **Finance** Members' dues. **Events** *Annual Conference* Lima (Peru) 2023, *Annual Conference* New Orleans, LA (USA) 2019, *Annual Conference* Bangkok (Thailand) 2018, *Annual Conference* Austin, TX (USA) 2017, *Annual Conference* Louisville, KY (USA) 2016. **Publications** *Embryo Transfer Newsletter* (4 a year). Manual; conference proceedings; members directory.
Members Full; Associate; Student; Sustaining. Individuals (mostly in USA) in 50 countries and territories:
Argentina, Australia, Austria, Belgium, Bolivia, Brazil, Canada, Chile, China, Colombia, Costa Rica, Czechia, Denmark, Ecuador, Finland, France, Germany, Hong Kong, Hungary, India, Iran Islamic Rep, Ireland, Israel, Italy, Japan, Korea Rep, Mexico, Netherlands, New Zealand, Norway, Paraguay, Peru, Poland, Portugal, Puerto Rico, Saudi Arabia, Slovakia, Slovenia, South Africa, Spain, Sweden, Switzerland, Taiwan, Thailand, Türkiye, UK, Uruguay, USA, Vietnam, Zimbabwe. [2022/XF3492/v/**F**]

♦ International Embryo Transfer Society / see International Embryo Technology Society (#13257)
♦ International EMECS Centre – International Centre for the Environmental Management of Enclosed Coastal Seas (internationally oriented national body)
♦ Internationale Medienhilfe (internationally oriented national body)
♦ Internationale Medische Hulp aan het Kind (internationally oriented national body)
♦ Internationale Medische Samenwerking / see Artsen Zonder Vakantie
♦ Internationale Medische Samenwerking (internationally oriented national body)
♦ Internationale Medische Samenwerking – Afrika / see Artsen Zonder Vakantie
♦ Internationale Medizinische Gesellschaft für Blut- und Geschwulstkrankheiten (inactive)
♦ Internationale Medizinische Gesellschaft für Elektroakupunktur nach Dr. Voll / see Medizinische Gesellschaft für System- und Regulationsdiagnostik (#16689)
♦ Internationale Medizinische Gesellschaft für Elektroakupunktur nach Voll / see Medizinische Gesellschaft für System- und Regulationsdiagnostik (#16689)
♦ Internationale Medizinische Gesellschaft für Neuraltherapie nach Huneke-Regulationstherapie (internationally oriented national body)
♦ Internationale Ménière Federatie (inactive)

♦ International Emergency Action (IEA) 13258

Action d'urgence internationale (AUI)

Contact c/o Les Terrasses de Montcalm, 1401 rue de Fontcouverte, 34070 Montpellier, France. T. +33467270609.

History Oct 1976, Paris (France). Former names and other names: *Corps mondial de secours en cas de catastrophe naturelle* – former. Registration: France. **Aims** Grouping together associations of volunteers conscious of the problems raised by *natural disasters*, promote, by concrete action, establishment of a supranational aid structure at the time of such disasters. **Structure** Board of Directors. **Languages** Esperanto, French, Spanish. **Staff** 1.00 FTE, paid; 80.00 FTE, voluntary. **Finance** Public funding: French government and local communities. Private funding. **Activities** Works on 3 levels: prevention; emergency relief and rescue; rehabilitation. **Publications** Bulletin (3 a year). **Members** National mouvements in 15 countries. Membership countries not specified. **Consultative Status** Consultative status granted from: *ECOSOC (#05331)* (Ros A). **NGO Relations** Member of: *Registre des Citoyens du Monde (RICM, #18822).* [2012.06.28/XF0252/**F**]

♦ International Emergency and Development Aid (internationally oriented national body)
♦ International Emergency Food Council (inactive)

♦ International Emergency Food Reserve (IEFR) 13259

Réserve alimentaire internationale d'urgence (RAIU) – Reserva Alimentaria Internacional de Emergencia

Contact c/o World Food Programme, Via Cesare Giulio Viola 68/70, 00148 Rome RM, Italy. T. +39665132068.

History 1975, by a special meeting of UN General Assembly. Supplies are handled by *World Food Programme (WFP, #21510).* **Aims** Function as a multilateral source of food. **Activities** Contributions in 1991 amounted to 612,000 tons of commodities (cereals and non-cereals) from 18 donor countries. Since 1989, the Reserve covers only emergency requirements, long-term needs being met by WFP from other sources. *'Immediate Response Account (IRA)'*, established 1991, is used to buy and deliver food as the fastest possible initial response to new emergency situations. The IRA is funded by WFP regular resources – US$ 7.5 million in 1992 – and by voluntary contributions. **IGO Relations** *OPEC Fund for International Development (OFID, #17745).* [2009/XF4341/f/**F***]

♦ International Emergency Management and Engineering Society / see International Emergency Management Society (#13261)

♦ International Emergency Management Organization (IEMO) 13260

Organisation internationale pour l'aménagement des urgences (OIAU)

Pres 144 .E Nord Tevragh Zeina, Nouakchott, Mauritania. E-mail: iemo@iemo.it – iemo@iemo.int.
Executive Assistant address not obtained.
URL: https://www.iemo.int/fr/

History 14 Apr 2006. Established on entering into force of IEMO Establishment Convention, endowed with juridical personality of international law. Convention registered 1 Jun 2006 with the United Nations Secretariat at No 42766 of the United Nations Treat Series (UNTS), published in Volume 2371 (2006) page 5, on the Statement of Treaties and International Agreement registered or filed and recorded with the Secretariat of the United Nations No ST/LEG/SER A-712 of Jun 2006, and on the United Nations Cumulative Index No 44 of the Treaties and International Agreement registered or filed and recorded with the Secretariat of the United Nations (Volumes 2351 to 2400) – (1) Treaties Nos 42198 to 43348 (Registered), and (2) Treaties Nos 1285 to 1298 (Filed and Recorded), page 265. Statutes established as Additional Protocol to the aforesaid Convention, settle the relevant functioning of the IEMO Organization and the rules of procedure and categories of membership. **Aims** Work for emergency prevention, preparedness, mitigation and recovery, with special focus on *humanitarian aid* for underprivileged emergencies and prevention of complex emergencies; network and represent on the topic of emergency prevention the various national emergency management organizations (NEMOs) and national emergency management agencies (NEMAs) providing them with emergency skills as the Integrated Emergency Prevention System (IEPS) as well as counter-emergencies studies and resources. **Structure** Council; Presidency. Departments (5): International Relations (DEIR); Early Warning (DEW); Operations (DOP); Internal Audit (DEIA); Budget and Administration (DEBA). Commissions (3): Early Warning System Data Collection; Experts on Emergency Evaluation; Security Standards in Emergency Operation. **Languages** English, French, Italian, Spanish. **Staff** 50.00 FTE, paid. **Finance** Sources: grants. Annual budget: 500,000 USD. **Activities** Events/meetings; humanitarian/emergency aid. **Events** *International Conference on Emergency Prevention* Milan (Italy) 2019, *International Conference on Emergency Prevention* Rome (Italy) 2014, *International Conference on Emergency Prevention* New York, NY (USA) 2011, *International Conference on Emergency Prevention* Rome (Italy) 2010, *International conference on emergency prevention* Rome (Italy) 2010. **Publications** *IEMO Bulletin* (4 a year). *IEMO Humanitarian Aid Handbook.* Conference proceedings.

Members Full Member States (7):
Benin, Burundi, Guinea, Lebanon, Madagascar, Somalia, St Kitts-Nevis.
Associate Members or Members by Right are endowed with the right to attend as Observers to the Sessions of the Council. Affiliate Members (States possessing one or more NEMA or NEMO or Competent Civil Defense Organization, affiliated to IEMO, possessing the right to attend as Observers to the Council). Members in 132 countries and territories:
Albania, Algeria, Angola, Antigua-Barbuda, Argentina, Armenia, Azerbaijan, Bahamas, Bahrain, Bangladesh, Barbados, Belarus, Belgium, Belize, Bhutan, Bolivia, Bosnia-Herzegovina, Botswana, Burkina Faso, Burundi, Cambodia, Cameroon, Cape Verde, Central African Rep, Chad, Chile, China, Colombia, Congo Brazzaville, Congo DR, Cook Is, Côte d'Ivoire, Croatia, Cuba, Czechia, Djibouti, Dominica, Dominican Rep, Ecuador, Egypt, El Salvador, Equatorial Guinea, Eritrea, Estonia, Ethiopia, Fiji, France, Gambia, Germany, Ghana, Grenada, Guatemala, Guinea, Guinea-Bissau, Holy See, Honduras, Hungary, Iceland, Indonesia, Israel, Jamaica, Jordan, Kazakhstan, Kenya, Kiribati, Korea Rep, Kuwait, Kyrgyzstan, Laos, Latvia, Lebanon, Lesotho, Liberia, Lithuania, Malawi, Malaysia, Mali, Malta, Marshall Is, Mauritania, Micronesia FS, Moldova, Mongolia, Montenegro, Mozambique, Myanmar, Namibia, Nauru, Nepal, Netherlands, New Zealand, Nicaragua, Niger, Nigeria, North Macedonia, Pakistan, Palau, Panama, Papua New Guinea, Paraguay, Peru, Poland, Qatar, Romania, Rwanda, Samoa, Saudi Arabia, Senegal, Seychelles, Sierra Leone, Solomon Is, Spain, Sri Lanka, St Lucia, St Vincent-Grenadines, Syrian AR, Tajikistan, Thailand, Timor-Leste, Tokelau, Tonga, Trinidad-Tobago, Turkmenistan, Tuvalu, Uganda, Ukraine, United Arab Emirates, Uruguay, Venezuela, Yemen, Zambia, Zimbabwe.

NGO Relations Participates in: *United Nations Global Compact (#20567).* Links with national organizations. [2023.02.20/XJ0824/**C***]

♦ International Emergency Management Society (TIEMS) 13261

Pres Ostvangveien 29, 0588 Oslo, Norway. T. +4791693012.
Registered Office Rue des Deux Eglises 39, 1000 Brussels, Belgium.
URL: http://www.tiems.org/

History 1993, as *International Emergency Management and Engineering Society.* Present name adopted 1996. Registered in accordance with Belgian law, 2006. **Aims** Prepare the world for emergencies. **Structure** Officers: President; Vice President; Treasurer; Secretary; Directors (11). **Languages** English. **Staff** Voluntary. **Activities** Training/education; certification/accreditation; events/meetings. **Events** *Annual Conference* South Africa 2023, *Annual Conference* Atlanta, GA (USA) 2022, *New Emergency Management in a Resilience Era Facing Health, Climate and Energy Challenges* Paris (France) 2021, *Annual Conference* Oslo (Norway) 2020, *Annual Conference* Goyang (Korea Rep) 2019. **Publications** Electronic newsletter; conference proceedings. **Members** Individuals (about 3,000). Membership countries not specified. **IGO Relations** Associate member of: *International Civil Defence Organization (ICDO, #12582).* **NGO Relations** Cooperates with: *PfP Consortium of Defence Academies and Security Studies Institutes (#18345).* [2018.09.05/XD7059/**D**]

♦ Internationale Messtechnische Konföderation (#14124)
♦ Internationale Metall-Union / see European Metal Union (#07785)
♦ Internationale Mieterallianz (#15822)
♦ Internationale Militärmusik-Gesellschaft (#14162)

♦ International Emissions Trading Association (IETA) 13262

Association internationale pour l'échange de droits d'émission (AIEDE)

Head Office Rue Merle d'Aubigné 24, 1207 Geneva, Switzerland. T. +41227370500. Fax +41227370508. E-mail: secretariat@ieta.org.
URL: http://www.ieta.org/

History Jun 1999. Registered in accordance with Swiss Civil Code. EU Transparency Register: 7157999502-14. **Aims** Develop an active and consistent global *greenhouse gas* emissions market involving any future international market mechanisms. **Structure** General Meeting (annual); Board; Secretariat; Offices (5); Working Groups. **Languages** English. **Finance** Members' dues. **Activities** Advocacy/lobbying/activism; standards/guidelines; knowledge management/information dissemination; capacity building; events/meetings. **Events** *ACF : Africa Carbon Forum* Accra (Ghana) 2019, *Latin American Carbon Forum* Montevideo (Uruguay) 2018, *Latin American Climate Week* Montevideo (Uruguay) 2018, *ACF : Africa Carbon Forum* Nairobi (Kenya) 2018, *Asia Pacific International Conference on the Implementation of the Paris Agreement* Seoul (Korea Rep) 2017. **Publications** *Annual COP Debrief and Summary*; *Emissions Trading 101*; *IETA Newsletter.* Market and policy reports; surveys. **Members** Companies (140). Membership countries not specified. [2019/XD8178/**D**]

♦ Internationale Montessori Vereinigung (#02812)

♦ Internationale Mosel-Gesellschaft mbH (IMG) 13263

Société internationale de la Moselle – International Moselle Company

Joint Manager Franz-Ludwig-Strasse 21, 54290 Trier, Germany. T. +496519794170. Fax +4965197941620.
Joint Manager address not obtained.

History 29 Jan 1957, Trier (Germany FR). Previously managed by *Moselle Commission (#16857).* Limited liability company under German law, based on Annexe II of *Convention on the Canalization of the Moselle (1956)*, adopted 27 Oct 1956, Luxembourg. Protocols: *Protocol Amending the Convention on the Canalization of the Moselle (1974)*; *Second Protocol Amending the Convention on the Canalization of the Moselle (1983)*; *Third Protocol Amending the Convention on the Canalization of the Moselle (1987).* **Aims** Together with national authorities for *inland navigation*, secure financing and execution of *canalization* of the Moselle river for 1,500 ton *vessels* from Thionville to Koblenz. **Structure** General Meeting of Associates appoints Board of Directors, composed of 5 members (2 German, 2 French, 1 Luxembourg); 2 Managers are appointed, one by German, the other by French Associates. **Languages** French, German. **Staff** 0.50 FTE, paid. **Finance** Capital contributed by member Governments: Germany – euro 50 million, France – euro 50 million, Luxembourg (Luxembourg) – euro 2 million.

Members Governments of 3 countries:
France, Germany, Luxembourg. [2009.09.11/XF2269/e/**F***]

♦ Internationale Moselkommission / see Moselle Commission (#16857)

♦ International Employee Assistance Professionals Association (EAPA) 13264

CEO 4350 North Fairfax Dr, Ste 740, Arlington VA 22203, USA. T. +17033871000. Fax +17035224585. E-mail: info@eapassn.org.
URL: http://www.eapassn.org/

History Founded 27 Apr 1971, as 'Association of Labor – Management, Administrators and Consultants on Alcoholism (ALMACA)', from the work of the USA National Council on Occupational Alcoholism. Present name adopted, 1989. Former names and other names: *Employee Assistance Professionals Association (EAPA)* – former (1989); *Association of Labor and Management Administrators and Consultants on Alcoholism (ALMACA)* – former (1971 to 1989). **Aims** Promote the highest standards of practice and continuing development of employee assistance professionals, programmes and services. **Structure** Board of Directors. **Activities** Events/meetings; certification/accreditation; awareness raising; knowledge management/information dissemination. **Events** *Conference* Houston, TX (USA) 2021, *Conference* Houston, TX (USA) 2020, *Conference* St Louis, MO (USA) 2019, *Conference* Minneapolis, MN (USA) 2018, *Conference* Los Angeles, CA (USA) 2017. **Publications** *EAP Association Exchange* (6 a year); *Journal of Employee Assistance.*

Members Primarily a North American organization. Chapters in 6 countries:
Australia, Brazil, Canada, South Africa, UK, USA. [2021/XG7646/t/**D**]

♦ International Employment Law, Pensions and Employee Benefits Alliance (IUS LABORIS) 13265

Exec Dir Boulevard du Souverain 280, 1160 Brussels, Belgium. T. +3227614610. Fax +3227614615. E-mail: exdi@iuslaboris.com – info@iuslaboris.com.
URL: http://www.iuslaboris.com/

History Jan 2001. **Events** *Congress* Copenhagen (Denmark) 2006.

Members Law firms in 36 countries:
Argentina, Austria, Belgium, Brazil, Canada, Chile, Colombia, Costa Rica, Cyprus, Czechia, Denmark, Dominican Rep, Estonia, Finland, France, Germany, Greece, Ireland, Italy, Latvia, Lithuania, Luxembourg, Mexico, Netherlands, Norway, Panama, Peru, Poland, Portugal, Russia, Spain, Sweden, Switzerland, Türkiye, UK, USA. [2011.07.28/XM0194/**F**]

♦ International Employment Relations Association (IERA) 13266

Contact PO Box 1752, Lane Cove NSW 1595, Australia.
URL: http://iera.net.au/

Aims Represent and serve academics, practitioners, students and others interested in employment relations. **Structure** Committee, comprising President, International Vice-President, 4 Regional Vice-Presidents, Immediate Past President, Secretary, Assistant Secretary, Treasurer, Postgraduate Representative, Webmaster and 7 members. Divisions (4): European; North America; Asian; Pacific – *Pacific Employment Relations Association (PERA, inactive).* **Activities** Events/meetings. **Events** *Annual Conference* Darwin, NT (Australia) 2014, *Biennial Conference* Macau (Macau) 2013, *Biennial Conference / Annual Conference* Singapore (Singapore) 2011, *Annual Conference* Nijmegen (Netherlands) 2008, *Annual Conference* Canterbury (UK) 2007. **Publications** *Employment Relations Record* (2 a year) – journal; *International Employment Relations Review* (2 a year) – journal; *International Journal of Employment Studies.* Conference proceedings. [2016/XN8090/**C**]

♦ Internationale Musiker-Föderation (#13486)
♦ Internationale Musikgesellschaft (inactive)
♦ Internationale Mykologische Gesellschaft (#14203)
♦ Internationalen Altkatholischen Bischofskonferenz (#14403)

♦ International Enamellers Institute (IEI) 13267

Institut international d'émailleurs – Internationales Email-Institut

SG Viale Vincenzo Lancetti 43, 20158 Milan MI, Italy. T. +3923264283 – +392(393488003263. E-mail: info@iei-world.org.
URL: http://www.iei-world.org/

History 25 Nov 1957. **Aims** Promote collation, collection and interchange on an international scale of technical matters relating to the practice of vitreous enamelling; advise on the holding of international conferences. **Structure** Congress (every 3 years). **Languages** English, French, German, Italian. **Staff** 1.00 FTE, voluntary. **Finance** Members' dues. Levy for additional work. **Activities** knowledge management/information dissemination. **Events** *Triennial Congress* Kyoto (Japan) 2023, *Triennial Congress* Kyoto (Japan) 2022, *Triennial Congress* Chicago, IL (USA) 2018, *Triennial Congress* Florence (Italy) 2015, *Triennial Congress* Cologne (Germany) 2012. **Publications** Proceedings.

Members Technical organizations representing vitreous enamelling in 17 countries:
Australia, Austria, China, Czechia, France, Germany, Hungary, Italy, Japan, Netherlands, New Zealand, Slovakia, Spain, Türkiye, UK, Ukraine, USA.

NGO Relations In liaison with technical committees of: *Comité européen de normalisation (CEN, #04162)*; *International Organization for Standardization (ISO, #14473).* [2020/XD1802/j/**D**]

♦ Internationale Naturisten-Föderation (#14219)
♦ International Encephalitis Society (inactive)
♦ International Endohernia Society / see International Endo Hernia Society (#13268)

♦ International Endo Hernia Society (IEHS) 13268

Gen Sec Dept of Surgery, Ctr for Minimal Invasive Surgery, Vivantes Klinikum Spandau, Neue Bergstr 6, 13585 Berlin, Germany. T. +4930130132150. Fax +4930130132154. E-mail: ferdin-and.koeckerling@vivantes.de.
URL: http://www.iehs.de/

History 31 May 2004, Chalkidiki (Greece). Also referred to as *International Endohernia Society.* **Structure** Board, comprising President, General Secretary and Congress President. **Events** *Visceral Surgical Week* Wagrain (Austria) 2013, *Meeting / Annual Meeting* Windhoek (Namibia) 2013, *Meeting / Annual Meeting* Belgrade (Serbia) 2012, *Visceral Surgical Week* Wagrain (Austria) 2012, *Meeting / Annual Meeting* Suzhou (China) 2011. **Members** Membership countries not specified. **NGO Relations** *Asia Pacific Hernia Society (APHS, #01926).* [2013/XJ0828/**E**]

♦ International Endotoxin and Innate Immunity Society (IEIIS) 13269

Sec John Hopkins Univ, School of Medicine, 733 N Broadway, Baltimore MD 21205, USA. E-mail: ieiis@aol.com.
URL: http://www.ieiis.org/

History Founded 1987, as *International Endotoxin Society (IES).* Current name adopted at 8th Biennial Conference, Kyoto (Japan), Nov 2004. **Aims** Promote scientific knowledge on all aspects of endotoxin research; facilitate interactions between scientists worldwide who study *bacterial* endotoxins and related bacterial products. **Structure** Officers: President; President Elect; Past President; Secretary; Treasurer; 4 Scientific Councillors (Chemistry, Microbiology, Immunology and Pathology). Committees (4): Scientific Programme; Local Organizing; Membership; Investment. Fundraising Chair; Editor-in-Chief of Journal of Endotoxin Research; Newsletter Editor; Website Editor. Regional Organizers. **Languages** English. **Staff** Voluntary. **Finance** Sources: members' dues. **Activities** Proposes endotoxin-related nomenclatures and standardized abbreviations as needed; may prepare and distribute pure chemically well-analysed endotoxin samples to use as standards; organizes Biennial International Conference; arranges Memorial Lectures; offers Young Investigator Award. **Events** *Biennial Meeting* Kobe (Japan) 2021, *Biennial Meeting* Kobe (Japan) 2020, *Biennial Meeting* Phoenix, AZ (USA) 2018, *Biennial Meeting* Hamburg (Germany) 2016, *Biennial Meeting* Salt Lake City, UT (USA) 2014. **Publications** *Endotoxin Newsletter* (4 a year); *IES Journal. Endotoxin Research.* Congress proceedings. Information Services: Serves as an information centre for exchange of visiting scientists at pre- or postdoctoral or visiting professor levels.

Members Individuals Active; Emeritus; Supporting; Student. Scientists (over 400) working on endotoxin or related bacterial molecules in the formal disciplines of microbiology, chemistry, pathology and clinical, in 43 countries and territories:

Australia, Austria, Belgium, Bolivia, Bulgaria, Canada, Chile, China, Colombia, Cuba, Czechia, Denmark, Finland, France, Germany, Greece, Hong Kong, Hungary, India, Iran Islamic Rep, Ireland, Israel, Italy, Japan, Korea Rep, Lebanon, Mexico, Netherlands, Nigeria, Norway, Poland, Romania, Russia, Saudi Arabia, Singapore, Slovenia, South Africa, Spain, Sweden, Switzerland, Taiwan, UK, USA. [2021/XC0008/v/**C**]

- ♦ International Endotoxin Society / see International Endotoxin and Innate Immunity Society (#13269)
- ♦ International Endo-Urological Society / see Endourology Society (#05463)

♦ International Energy Agency (IEA) 13270

Agence internationale de l'énergie (AIE)

Exec Dir 31-35 rue de la Fédération, 75739 Paris CEDEX 15, France. T. +33140576500. Fax +33140576509. E-mail: info@iea.org.

URL: http://www.iea.org/

History 15 Nov 1974, Paris (France). Established by decision of the Council of *OECD (#17693)*, as an autonomous agency. The Council Decision and the Agreement on an International Energy Programme (the Agency's operative agreement signed 18 Nov 1974) followed negotiations within *Energy Coordinating Group (inactive)* arising from an intergovernmental conference on energy, Feb 1974, Washington DC (USA). Long Term Cooperation Programme approved by the Governing Board in Jan 1976. **Aims** Provide data, analysis and policy guidance across the energy mix; advise on ensuring energy security, economic growth, environmental sustainability and access to governments and other stakeholders around the world. **Structure** Governing Board; Management Team; Executive Director. **Languages** English. **Staff** 270.00 FTE, paid. **Finance** Members' dues. **Activities** Research/documentation; knowledge management/information dissemination; monitoring/evaluation; guidance/assistance/consulting. Technology Collaboration Programmes (TCPs). Management of treaties and agreements. **Events** *Solar Power and Chemical Energy Systems Conference (SolarPACES)* Albuquerque, NM (USA) 2022, *IEA Energy in Buildings and Communities Programme (EBC) Annex 83 Working Meeting* Espoo (Finland) 2022, *International Conference on Greenhouse Gas Control Technologies* Lyon (France) 2022, *Joint International Conference on Ocean Energy and Ocean Energy Europe Annual Event* San Sebastian (Spain) 2022, *Solar Power and Chemical Energy Systems Conference (SolarPACES)* 2021. **Publications** *CO2 Emissions from Fuel Combustion* (annual); *Energy Balances and Energy Statistics of OECD and Non-OECD Countries* (annual); *Energy Policies of IEA Countries* (annual); *Global Gas Security Review* (annual); *Key World Energy Statistics* (annual); *Oil, Electricity, Coal Natural Gas, Renewables Information* (annual); *World Energy Outlook* (annual); *Energy Technology Perspectives* (every 2 years); *Monthly Oil Market Report* – plus August supplement; *OPEN Energy Technology Bulletin*; *Quarterly Oil, Gas, Coal and Electricity Statistics and Energy Prices and Taxes.* Annual Market Reports; manuals; country studies; monographs; papers. **Information Services** *Online Data Service.*

Members Governments of 29 of the member States of OECD:

Australia, Austria, Belgium, Canada, Czechia, Denmark, Estonia, Finland, France, Germany, Greece, Hungary, Ireland, Italy, Japan, Korea Rep, Luxembourg, Netherlands, New Zealand, Norway, Poland, Portugal, Slovakia, Spain, Sweden, Switzerland, Türkiye, UK, USA.

Participating in the work of IEA:

Association countries (8):

Brazil, China, India, Indonesia, Mexico, Morocco, Singapore, Thailand.

IGO Relations

- *ASEAN Centre for Energy (ACE, #01150)*;
- *Asia-Pacific Economic Cooperation (APEC, #01887)*;
- *Asia-Pacific Partnership for Clean Development and Climate (APPCDC, #01990)*;
- *Baltic Sea Region Energy Cooperation (BASREC, #03148)*;
- *Carbon Sequestration Leadership Forum (CSLF, #03425)*;
- *Centralnoe Dispetcherskoe Upravlenie Obedinennyh Energeticheskih Sistem (CDU OES, no recent information)*;
- *Committee on Sustainable Energy (#04288)*;
- *Convention on Long-range Transboundary Air Pollution (#04787)*;
- *Economic Research Institute for ASEAN and East Asia (ERIA, #05319)*;
- *Energy Charter Conference (#05466)*;
- *Euratom Supply Agency (ESA, #05617)*;
- *European Commission (EC, #06633)*;
- *European Environment Agency (EEA, #06995)*;
- *FAO (#09260)*;
- *Global Bioenergy Partnership (GBEP, #10251)*;
- *Global Green Growth Forum (3GF)*;
- *IEA Clean Coal Centre (#11093)*, set up 1975, London (UK);
- *International Atomic Energy Agency (IAEA, #12294)*;
- *International Bank for Reconstruction and Development (IBRD, #12317)* (World Bank);
- *International Institute of Refrigeration (IIR, #13918)*;
- *International Monetary Fund (IMF, #14180)*;
- *International Partnership for Energy Efficiency Cooperation (IPEEC, #14520)*;
- *International Smart Grid Action Network (ISGAN, #14877)*;
- *Latin American Energy Organization (#16313)*;
- *Organization of the Petroleum Exporting Countries (OPEC, #17881)*;
- *Round Table on Sustainable Development at the OECD (see: #17693)*;
- *Statistical Office of the European Union (Eurostat, #19974)*;
- *United Nations Economic Commission for Europe (UNECE, #20555)*;
- *United Nations Framework Convention on Climate Change – Secretariat (UNFCCC, #20564)*;
- *World Trade Organization (WTO, #21864)*.

NGO Relations

- *Air Infiltration and Ventilation Centre (AIVC, #00603)*;
- *Asociación Regional de Empresas del Sector Petróleo, Gas y Biocombustibles en Latinoamérica y el Caribe (ARPEL, #02296)*;
- *Buildings Performance Institute Europe (BPIE, #03354)*;
- *Climate Technology Centre and Network (CTCN, #04023)* with Greenhouse Gas R and D Programme;
- *Comité européen de normalisation (CEN, #04162)*;
- *Conseil européen de l'industrie chimique (CEFIC, #04687)*;
- *Euroheat and Power (EHP, #05694)*;
- *European Association for Coal and Lignite (EURACOAL, #05978)*;
- *European Gas Research Group (#07380)*;
- *Gas Infrastructure Europe (GIE, #10073)*;
- *Global Alliance for Buildings and Construction (GlobalABC, #10187)*;
- *Global Battery Alliance (GBA, #10249)*
- *Global Fuel Economy Initiative (GFEI, #10381)*;
- *Global Wind Energy Council (GWEC, #10656)*;
- *Greenhouse Gas Protocol (GHG Protocol, #10721)*;
- *International Aluminium Institute (IAI, #11643)*;
- *International Association for Hydrogen Safety (HySafe, #11952)*;
- *International Council of Forest and Paper Associations (ICFPA, #13023)*;
- *International Council on Large Electric Systems (#13040)*;
- *International Council for Research and Innovation in Building and Construction (CIB, #13069)*;
- *International Electrotechnical Commission (IEC, #13255)*;
- *International Energy Forum (IEF, #13272)*;
- *International Fertilizer Association (IFA, #13589)*;
- *International Fuel and Power Association (IFPA, #13688)*;
- *International Gas Union (IGU, #13700)*;
- *International Network for Sustainable Energy (INFORSE, #14331)*;
- *International Organization for Standardization (ISO, #14473)*;
- *International Solar Energy Society (ISES, #15564)*;
- *ITER International Fusion Energy Organization (ITER Organization, #16072)*;
- *Joint Organisations Data Initiative (JODI, #16143)*;
- *Partnership for Clean Fuels and Vehicles (PCFV, #18231)*;
- *Preinsulated Pipe Group (PPG, no recent information)*;
- *REN21 (#18836)*;
- *Union of the Electricity Industry – Eurelectric (#20379)*;
- *WindEurope (#20965)*;
- *World Business Council for Sustainable Development (WBCSD, #21254)*;
- *World Coal Association (WCA, #21280)*;
- World Energy Congress (WEC);
- *World Energy Council (WEC, #21381)*;
- *World LPG Association (WLPGA, #21629)*;
- *World Petroleum Council (WPC, #21722)*;
- *World Steel Association (worldsteel, #21829)*;
- *World Wind Energy Association (WWEA, #21937)*. [2021/XE5314/**E***]

♦ International Energy Credit Association (IECA) 13271

Exec Dir 1120 Route 73, Ste 200, Mount Laurel NJ 08054, USA. T. +18563806849. Fax +18564390525.

Meeting Manager address not obtained. T. +18563806863.

URL: http://www.ieca.net/

History 1923, Tulsa OK (USA), as Petroleum Refiners Bureau of the (US) National Association of Credit Men (NACM). Name changed: 1941, to Petroleum Division of the (US) National Association of Credit Men; 1946, to *American Petroleum Credit Association*; 1992, to *International Petroleum Credit Association (IPCA)*. **Aims** As an international organization of credit and financial professionals, provide a forum for the free and open exchange of ideas and discussion of issues relevant to credit management and the petroleum industry. **Staff** Volunteers. **Finance** Members' dues. Conference fees. **Activities** Standing Committees (14): Advisory, Nomination and Elections; Allied Members; By-Laws; Conference Management; Education; Finance; Fundraising; Journal; Membership – Recruitment; Membership – Renewal; Membership – Retention; Program (Annual Conference); Recognition and Credentials; Scholarships. Credit Education and Interchange Groups (6): Canadian; Commercial; Crude Oil and Refined Products; European Division; Natural Gas and Gas Liquids; Retail Credit Card. **Events** *Annual Conference* St Pete Beach, FL (USA) 2019, *Annual Conference* Naples, FL (USA) 2018, *Annual Conference* Atlanta, GA (USA) 2017, *Annual Conference* Austin, TX (USA) 2016, *European Conference* Lisbon (Portugal) 2016. **Publications** *IPCA Journal* (3 a year). Annual Membership Directory.

Members Regular Membership employees engaged in the credit function of companies whose product is a petroleum derivative or whose business is pipeline transportation of a petroleum derivative. Allied Membership employees of companies providing credit support, finance or legal service to the petroleum and natural gas industry. Members (mostly in USA) in 16 countries:

Belgium, Bulgaria, Canada, Denmark, Finland, France, Germany, Italy, Mexico, Netherlands, Norway, South Africa, Switzerland, Türkiye, UK, USA. [2019/XF4175/v/**F**]

♦ International Energy Forum (IEF) 13272

Mailing Address PO Box 94736, Diplomatic Quarter, Riyadh 11614, Saudi Arabia. T. +966114810033. Fax +966114810055. E-mail: info@ief.org.

URL: http://www.ief.org/

History First meeting, Jul 1991, Paris (France). **Aims** Serve as the neutral facilitator of informal, open, informed and continuing global energy dialogue; foster greater mutual understanding and awareness of common energy interests among members; promote a better understanding of the benefits of stable and transparent energy markets for the health of the world economy, the security of energy supply and demand, and the expansion of global trade and investment in energy resources and technology; identify and promote principles and guidelines that enhance energy market transparency, stability and sustainability; narrow the differences among energy producing, consuming and transit member states on global energy issues and promote a fuller understanding of their interdependency and the benefits to be gained from cooperation through dialogue among them, as well as between them and energy related industries; promote the differences among energy producing, consuming the inter-relationships among energy, technology, environmental issues, economic growth and development; build confidence and trust through improved information sharing among states; facilitate the collection, compilation and dissemination of data, information and analyses that contribute to greater market transparency, stability and sustainability. **Structure** Ministerial Meetings (every 2 years). Executive Board, comprising representatives of Ministers responsible for energy matters from 31 member states; chaired by the host state of the forthcoming Ministerial Meeting. Secretariat, based in the Diplomatic Quarter of Riyadh (Saudi Arabia) since Dec 2003. **Languages** English. **Staff** Funded by member countries, but may receive funding from any source. **Activities** Knowledge management/information dissemination; networking/liaising; training/education; events/meetings. Ministers address issues of energy security and the links between energy, environment and economic development. **Events** *Ministers Forum IEF Ministerial IEF17* Saudi Arabia 2021, *Ministers Forum* China 2020, *Biennial Asian Energy Ministerial Round Table* Abu Dhabi (United Arab Emirates) 2019, *IEF-SHFE Meeting on the Emerging Asian Energy Trading Market* Shanghai (China) 2019, *Round Table on Natural Gas and LNG Market Dynamics in Asia* Singapore (Singapore) 2019.

Members Member countries are signatories to the IEF Charter which outlines the framework of the global energy dialogue through this inter-governmental arrangement, and account for about 90% of global supply and demand for oil and gas. Governments of 75 countries:

Algeria, Angola, Argentina, Australia, Austria, Bahrain, Bangladesh, Belgium, Brunei Darussalam, Bulgaria, Burkina Faso, Canada, Chad, China, Comoros, Cyprus, Czechia, Denmark, Djibouti, Ecuador, Egypt, Eritrea, Ethiopia, Finland, France, Germany, Greece, Guinea, Hungary, India, Iran Islamic Rep, Iraq, Ireland, Italy, Japan, Kazakhstan, Korea Rep, Kuwait, Malaysia, Mali, Mauritania, Mexico, Morocco, Mozambique, Netherlands, New Zealand, Niger, Nigeria, Norway, Oman, Panama, Philippines, Poland, Qatar, Russia, Saudi Arabia, Senegal, Singapore, Somalia, South Africa, Sudan, Sweden, Switzerland, Tanzania UR, Trinidad-Tobago, Tunisia, Türkiye, Uganda, UK, United Arab Emirates, USA, Venezuela, Vietnam, Yemen, Zambia.

IGO Relations Cooperates with: *Asia-Pacific Economic Cooperation (APEC, #01887)*; *European Commission (EC, #06633)*; *Gas Exporting Countries Forum (GECF, #10072)*; *International Energy Agency (IEA, #13270)*; *Latin American Energy Organization (#16313)*; *Organization of the Petroleum Exporting Countries (OPEC, #17881)*; *Statistical Office of the European Union (Eurostat, #19974)*. **NGO Relations** Cooperates with: *International Gas Union (IGU, #13700)*. [2020/XM3690/**F***]

♦ International Energy Foundation (IEF) 13273

Pres 24 December Street – Bldg 192, PO Box 83617, Tripoli, Libya. T. +21821333183034. Fax +218213331231. E-mail: info@ief-ngo.org.

SG Hetton Lawn, Cudnall Street, Cheltenham, GL53 8HU, UK. T. +441242238705. Fax +44124269080.

URL: http://www.ief-ngo.org/

History 26 Mar 1989. **Aims** Facilitate transfer and disbursement of information, knowledge, expertise and advanced technologies in the fields of energy, environment and development. **Structure** Board of Directors; Executive Committee; Standing Committee; Chapters. **Languages** English. **Finance** Contributions; donations; subscriptions; aids; grants. **Activities** Events/meetings; research/documentation; training/education; guidance/assistance/consulting. **Events** *International All Things Energy Congress / International All Energy Congress* Vancouver, BC (Canada) 2012, *International all things energy congress / International All Energy Congress* Sydney, NSW (Australia) 2011, *International Energy Conference ENERGEX* Vancouver, BC (Canada) 2011, *ENERGEX : international energy conference* Singapore (Singapore) 2010, *International Energy Conference ENERGEX* Sydney, NSW (Australia) 2010.

Members Individuals in 129 countries and territories:

Albania, Algeria, Angola, Argentina, Armenia, Australia, Austria, Bangladesh, Belarus, Belgium, Belize, Bolivia, Bosnia-Herzegovina, Botswana, Brazil, Bulgaria, Burkina Faso, Burundi, Cameroon, Canada, Cape Verde, Chad, Chile, China, Colombia, Comoros, Congo Brazzaville, Costa Rica, Croatia, Cuba, Cyprus, Czechia, Denmark, Dominican Rep, Ecuador, Egypt, El Salvador, Eritrea, Estonia, Eswatini, Ethiopia, Fiji, Finland, France, Gabon, Georgia, Germany, Ghana, Greece, Guatemala, Guinea, Hungary, India, Indonesia, Iran Islamic Rep, Iraq, Ireland, Italy, Jamaica, Japan, Jordan, Kazakhstan, Kenya, Korea DPR, Korea Rep, Kuwait, Kyrgyzstan, Laos, Latvia, Lebanon, Lesotho, Libya, Madagascar, Malawi, Malaysia, Maldives, Mali, Malta, Marshall Is, Mauritius, Mexico, Moldova, Mongolia, Morocco, Namibia, New Zealand, Nicaragua, Nigeria, North Macedonia, Norway, Oman, Pakistan, Palestine, Papua New Guinea, Philippines, Poland, Portugal, Puerto Rico, Qatar, Romania, Russia, Rwanda, Saudi Arabia, Senegal, Serbia, Slovenia, Spain, Sri Lanka, St Lucia, Sudan, Syrian AR, Tajikistan, Tanzania UR, Thailand, Tonga, Trinidad-Tobago, Tunisia, Türkiye, Turkmenistan, Uganda, UK, United Arab Emirates, USA, Uzbekistan, Venezuela, Vietnam, Yemen, Zambia, Zimbabwe.

Consultative Status Consultative status granted from: *UNIDO (#20336)*. **NGO Relations** In liaison with technical committees of: *International Organization for Standardization (ISO, #14473)*. Member of: *Mediterranean Information Office for Environment, Culture and Sustainable Development (MIO-ECSDE, #16657)*; *World Wind Energy Association (WWEA, #21937)*. [2018.06.01/XF4962/f/**F**]

♦ International Energy and Mines Organization (IEMO) 13274

Organisation internationale de l'énergie et des mines (OIEM) – Organización Internacional de Energía y Minas

Contact c/o OIEM/FNME, 263 rue de Paris, 93516 Montreuil CEDEX, France. T. +33156932652. Fax +33156932749. E-mail: oiem-iemo@live.fr.

History 18 Jun 1996, Geneva (Switzerland), by *International Miners' Organization (IMO, no recent information)* and *Trade Unions International of Workers in Energy (TUIWE, inactive)*. **Structure** Executive Committee of 26 members; Executive Bureau of 17 members. 2 Co-Presidents of Honour; Secretary General. **Languages** English, French, Russian, Spanish. **Staff** 2.00 FTE, paid. **Finance** Members' dues. **Events** *World Congress* Kochi (India) 2002, *World Congress* Montluçon (France) 1996. **Publications** *IEMO Newsletter – Courrier de* *l'OIEM – Correo de la OIEM* (4 a year). **Members** Organizations (89) in 68 countries. Membership countries not specified. **IGO Relations** Consultative Status with: *ECOSOC (#05331)*; *ILO (#11123)*. [2014/XD5722/**F**]

- ♦ International Energy Workshop (meeting series)
- ♦ Internationale Netz Produktiver Bildungsprojekte und Schulen (#14308)
- ♦ Internationalen Netzwerk für die Verbreitung von Voluntäraktivitäten in Europa / see Volonteurope (#20807)
- ♦ Internationalen Gesellschaft für Forensische Hämogenetik / see International Society for Forensic Genetics (#15128)
- ♦ Internationalen Gesellschaft für Pteridinologie (#15403)

♦ International Engineering Alliance 13275

Secretariat c/o Engineering New Zealand, PO Box 12241, Wellington 6144, New Zealand. E-mail: hello@engineeringnz.org.
URL: http://www.ieagreements.org/

Aims Advance benchmarking and mobility in the engineering profession. **Activities** Oversees 6 international engineering agreements: Washington Accord; Sydney Accord; Dublin Accord; APEC Engineer agreement; Engineers Mobility Forum agreement; Engineering Technologist Mobility Forum agreement. **Events** *General Assembly* Seoul (Korea Rep) 2013, *Meeting* Seoul (Korea Rep) 2013, *Workshop* Sydney, NSW (Australia) 2012, *Meeting* Taipei (Taiwan) 2011, *Meeting* Kyoto (Japan) 2009. [2019/XJ1512/**C**]

- ♦ International Engineering and Technology Publication Association (unconfirmed)
- ♦ Internationalen för Handels- och Kontorsanställda samt Privatanställda Tjänstemän (inactive)
- ♦ Internationalen Institut für Angewandte Ästhetik (internationally oriented national body)
- ♦ Internationalen Kneipp-Konföderation / see Kneipp Worldwide (#16197)
- ♦ Internationalen Lagergemeinschaft des KZ Neuengamme / see International Neuengamme Committee (#14347)

♦ International Enneagram Association (IEA) 13276

Main Office 4100 Executive Park Drive, Ste 16, Cincinnati OH 45241, USA. T. +15132325054. Fax +15135639743. E-mail: administration@internationalenneagram.org.
URL: http://www.internationalenneagram.org/

History Conceived 1994, Stanford CA (USA). A US organization described in RIC Section 501(c)(3). **Aims** Provide opportunities for: engagement with an international community of shared interest and diverse approaches; education in theory and application of the enneagram; developing greater excellence in the use of the enneagram. **Structure** General Assembly of Affiliates (annual); Global Board of Directors. **Activities** Certification/accreditation; events/meetings. **Events** *Nordic Enneagram Conference* Stockholm (Sweden) 2022, *Global Conference* Cincinnati, OH (USA) 2021, *Nordic Enneagram Conference* Stockholm (Sweden) 2020, *International Summit* Lisbon (Portugal) 2019, *Global Conference* Oakland, CA (USA) 2019. **Publications** *IEA Nine Points* – online.
Members Regional affiliates in USA. National affiliates in 12 countries:
Argentina, Brazil, China, Denmark, Finland, France, Korea Rep, Netherlands, Norway, Portugal, Spain, Sweden.
[2018/XN7914/**C**]

- ♦ Internationalen Podologen- und Podiaterverbands / see International Federation of Podiatrists (#13514)
- ♦ Internationalen för Stats- och Kommunalsanställda (#18572)

♦ Internationalen Stauden Union (ISU) 13277

Union internationale des producteurs de plantes vivaces – International Hardy Plant Union

Sec Servatiusstr 53, 53175 Bonn, Germany. T. +492288100255. Fax +492288100277. E-mail: info@isu-perennials.org.
URL: http://www.isu-perennials.org/

History Founded 14 Jan 1965, Hannover (Germany FR). **Aims** Promote contacts among perennial plant growers. **Languages** English, German. **Staff** 0.50 FTE, paid. **Finance** Members' dues. **Activities** Events/meetings. **Events** *Biennial Congress* Horgen (Switzerland) 2014, *Biennial Congress* Netherlands 2012, *Biennial Congress* Baden Baden (Germany) 2010, *Biennial Congress* Gothenburg (Sweden) 2008, *Biennial Congress* Sweden 2008.
Members National Associations (11) in 11 countries:
Austria, Belgium, Denmark, Finland, France, Germany, Netherlands, Norway, Sweden, Switzerland, USA. [2021/XD9040/**D**]

- ♦ Internationalen Symposiums für Textilpflegekennzeichnung / see Groupement International de l'Etiquetage pour l'Entretien des Textiles (#10761)
- ♦ International Entente Against the Third International (inactive)
- ♦ International Entente of Radical and Similar Democratic Parties (inactive)
- ♦ International Enterprise Class Association (see: #21760)
- ♦ International Entertainment Buyers Association (internationally oriented national body)
- ♦ International Entertainment Education Conference (meeting series)
- ♦ International Entomology Association (inactive)
- ♦ Internationale Numismatische Kommission / see International Numismatic Council (#14385)
- ♦ Internationalen Verbandes der Ski-Instruktoren / see International Federation of Snowsport Instructors (#13542)
- ♦ Internationalen Verband der Schneesportinstruktoren (#13542)
- ♦ International Environmental Analysis and Education Center (internationally oriented national body)
- ♦ International Environmental Association of Odour Managers (#02281)
- ♦ International Environmental Association of River Keepers (internationally oriented national body)
- ♦ International Environmental Bureau (inactive)

♦ International Environmental Communication Association (IECA) . . . 13278

Contact address not obtained.
URL: http://theieca.org/

History 2011. Registration: 501(c)(3), USA. **Aims** Foster effective and inspiring communication that alleviates environmental issues and conflicts, and solves the problems that cause them. **Structure** Board of Directors. **Activities** Awards/prizes/competitions; events/meetings; training/education. **Events** *Biennial Conference on Communication and Environment* Harrisonburg, VA (USA) 2023, *Biennial Conference on Communication and Environment* 2021, *Biennial Conference on Communication and Environment* Vancouver, BC (Canada) 2019, *Biennial Conference on Communication and Environment* Leicester (UK) 2017, *Biennial Conference on Communication and Environment* Boulder, CO (USA) 2015. **Publications** *Environmental Communication* – official scholarly journal. Proceedings. **NGO Relations** Member of (1): *Global Call for Climate Action (GCCA, inactive)*. [2023/XM5347/**C**]

- ♦ International Environmental Data Rescue Organization (internationally oriented national body)

♦ International Environmental & Health Sciences Consortium (IEHSC) 13279

Contact address not obtained.
URL: https://www.iehsconsortium.org/

History Mar 2020, USA. Former names and other names: *Environmental & Health Sciences Consortium* – alias. **Aims** Connect and align a network of scientists, public health professionals and organizations so as to develop viable partnerships in environmental, public health and earth sciences research and training. **Structure** Managing Director; Secretary; Treasurer. **Activities** Events/meetings; projects/programmes; training/education.
Members Experts from 13 countries and territories:
Aguadilla, Chile, China, Dar es Salaam, France, Italy, Mayagüez, Mexico, Netherlands, Nigeria, Russia, Sweden, USA.
NGO Relations Cooperates with (4): Entrepreneurial & Leadership Initiative for a Sustainable Africa (ELISA); *International Conference on Atmospheric Dust (DUST)*; *International Medical Geology Association (IMGA, #14133)*; national institutes and universities. [2022.06.14/AA2175/v/**C**]

- ♦ International Environmental Law Research Centre (internationally oriented national body)

♦ International Environmental Modelling and Software Society (IEMSS) 13280

Secretariat iEMSs Seretariat c/- IDSIA, Galleria 2, 6928 Manno TI, Switzerland. E-mail: secretary@iemss.org.
URL: http://www.iemss.org/

History 18 Jun 2000, Halifax, NS (Canada). **Aims** Develop and use environmental modelling and software tools to advance the science and improve decision making with respect to resource and environmental issues; promote transdisciplinary research and contacts between scientists, engineers, economists, software developers, managers, decision makers and other stakeholders; promote information exchange in the field. **Structure** Board of Directors. **Languages** English. **Finance** Sources: members' dues. **Activities** Events/meetings; training/education. **Events** *Conference* Brussels (Belgium) 2022, *Conference* Brussels (Belgium) 2020, *Asian Regional Conference* Nanjing (China) 2019, *Conference* Fort Collins, CO (USA) 2018, *Conference* Toulouse (France) 2016. **Publications** *Environmental Modelling and Software*. Proceedings.
Members Full in 32 countries:
Argentina, Australia, Austria, Belgium, Brazil, Canada, Czechia, Denmark, Finland, France, Germany, Greece, Ireland, Italy, Japan, Lebanon, Luxembourg, Malaysia, Mexico, Nepal, Netherlands, New Zealand, North Macedonia, Poland, Russia, Serbia, Spain, Sweden, Switzerland, UK, USA, Venezuela.
NGO Relations Also links with national organizations. [2022/XD8413/**D**]

♦ International Environmental Specimen Bank Group (IESB) 13281

Contact Umweltbundesamt, Wörlitzer Platz 1, 06844 Dessau-Rosslau, Germany.
URL: http://www.inter-esb.org/

Aims Promote the establishment of high quality standards in collecting, analysing and archiving samples from the environment. **Activities** Advocacy/lobbying/activism; events/meetings. **Events** *The past, present and future of environmental specimen banks* Stockholm (Sweden) 2019. **Members** Environmental specimen banks (about 30). [2020.03.13/XM8334/**C**]

♦ International Environmental Technology Centre (IETC) 13282

Centre international des technologies de l'environnement

Dir 2-110 Ryokuchikoen Tsurumi-ku, Osaka, 538-0036 Japan. T. +81669154581. Fax +81669150304. E-mail: ietc@unep.org.
URL: http://www.unep.or.jp/

History 30 Oct 1992, Japan, when inaugurated, following decision, May 1991, of Governing Council of *UNEP (#20299)*. Based on *Global Action Plan for Environment and Development in the 21st Century (Agenda 21, inactive)*, which emerged from *United Nations Conference on Environment and Development (UNCED)*, 1992. Commenced activities Apr 1994, when offices set up. Also known by acronym *UNEP/IETC*. **Aims** Assist *developing countries* and countries with economies in *transition* to use environmentally sound technology (EST) for *sustainable* management of *urban* and *freshwater resources* and in addressing urban and freshwater basin environmental problems, focusing on: *water supply*; *sewage*; *solid waste*; land contamination. Improve access to quality information and assist in capacity building to improve the ability of decision-makers to use that information. **Structure** Operates from 2 locations, each office supported and augmented by a foundation: Osaka (Japan) Office – *Global Environment Centre (GEC)* – environmental issues in large cities; Shiga (Japan) Office: *International Lake Environment Committee Foundation (ILEC, #13998)* – management of freshwater lake/reservoir basins. **Finance** Sources: Government of Japan; UNEP.
Activities Works closely with international multilateral and bilateral financial institutions, technical assistance organizations, other UNEP units and independent corporations in developing and maintaining information systems and capacity-building initiatives designed to promote EST adoption and use. Work Programme covers 4 objectives:
- Promotion and Transfer of Environmental Sound Technology;
- Urban Environmental Management;
- Cities as Sustainable Ecosystems;
- Freshwater Environmental Management.

Work includes: provision of information and data; training; research and consulting services; public awareness. Current concerns include: environmentally sound technology for air quality management in cities; environmental management systems (EMS) for cities and local authorities; development of post-industrial "brownfield" sites; environmentally sustainable buildings and infrastructure; eco-hydrology and phytotechnology; water convention; *Cities As Sustainable Ecosystems (CASE)*; environmentally sound technology for wastewater treatment and for water resource conservation; groundwater protection and remediation. **Events** *International Electric Vehicle Meeting* Jeju (Korea Rep) 2016, *Seminar on Holistic Waste Management and Eco-Town Models for Sustainable Development in Asia-Pacific* Jeju (Korea Rep) 2015, *Regional Workshop on e-waste/WEEE management* Osaka (Japan) 2010, *International symposium on low carbon society* Tokyo (Japan) 2008, *World lake vision plenary meeting* Kusatsu (Japan) 2003. **Publications** *Insight* (3 a year) in English, Japanese – newsletter; *Sourcebooks of Alternative Technologies for Freshwater Augmentation* – 5 to date, each covering a specific region. *IETC Report Series* – 6 to date; *IETC Technical Publications Series* – 11 to date. *UNEP Survey of Information Systems Related to Environmentally Sound Technologies (ESTs)* (1997). Proceedings of meetings, seminars and fora. **Information Services** *Searchable Directory on Environmentally Sound Technologies (ESTs) and Related Information Systems/Institutions (maESTro)* – information platform in partnership with 110 information providers, comprising data on 1,100 technologies, 467 institutions and 92 information systems. **IGO Relations** Close coordination with: UNEP Division of Environmental Policy Development and Law; UNEP Division of Environmental Policy Implementation. Joint activities with: *ILO (#11123)*; *United Nations Human Settlements Programme (UN-Habitat, #20572)*, especially *United Nations Commission on Sustainable Development (CSD, inactive)*; *UNDP (#20292)*; *UNCTAD (#20285)*; *UNIDO (#20336)*; *UNESCO (#20322)* – regional commissions – *United Nations Economic Commission for Africa (ECA, #20554)*, *United Nations Economic Commission for Europe (UNECE, #20555)*, *United Nations Economic Commission for Latin America and the Caribbean (ECLAC, #20556)*, *United Nations Economic and Social Commission for Asia and the Pacific (ESCAP, #20557)*, *United Nations Economic and Social Commission for Western Asia (ESCWA, #20558)*; *WHO (#20950)*. **NGO Relations** Partner organizations: *Asian Institute of Technology (AIT, #01519)*; *International Council for Research and Innovation in Building and Construction (CIB, #13069)*; *International Solid Waste Association (ISWA, #15567)*; *International Water Association (IWA, #15865)*. [2017.06.01/XE1873/**E***]

♦ International Environment Forum (IEF) 13283

Contact Chemin de Maisonneuve 12B, Chatelaine, 1219 Geneva, Switzerland. E-mail: ief@iefworld.org.
URL: https://iefworld.org/

History 1997. Established as a Baha'i-inspired professional organization. **Aims** Provide a forum for members to deepen understanding of the social and ethical principles in the Baha'i Writings and other scriptures that relate to environmental responsibility and sustainable development and explore the application of those principles in their work and activities; engage with individuals and other groups to apply collective knowledge for the benefit of society; share knowledge and experience; promote environmental awareness and sustainable development through educational materials that empower and contribute to practical action. **Structure** General Assembly; Governing Board. **Languages** English, French, Spanish. **Staff** Part-time, voluntary. **Finance** No budget. **Activities** Awareness raising; events/meetings; knowledge management/information dissemination. **Events** *Annual Conference* Stockholm (Sweden) 2022, *Annual Conference* Glasgow (UK) 2021, *Education for Social Cohesion* Maharashtra (India) 2020, *Annual Conference* Auckland (New Zealand) / Rotorua (New Zealand) 2019, *Annual Conference* New York, NY (USA) 2018. **Publications** *Leaves*. Annual Report.
Members Individuals in 78 countries and territories:
Albania, Angola, Argentina, Australia, Austria, Bangladesh, Belgium, Bolivia, Bosnia-Herzegovina, Brazil, Brunei Darussalam, Bulgaria, Cambodia, Cameroon, Canada, Chile, China, Colombia, Congo DR, Cook Is, Czechia, Denmark, Ecuador, Eritrea, Eswatini, Ethiopia, Fiji, Finland, France, Germany, Ghana, Greece, Guinea-Bissau, Guyana, Hong Kong, Hungary, India, Iran Islamic Rep, Ireland, Israel, Italy, Japan, Kazakhstan, Kenya, Liberia, Malawi, Malaysia, Marshall Is, Namibia, Netherlands, New Zealand, North Macedonia, Norway, Pakistan, Philippines, Poland, Portugal, Serbia, Singapore, Slovakia, South Africa, Spain, Suriname, Sweden, Switzerland, Tanzania UR, Thailand, Timor-Leste, Togo, Tonga, Trinidad-Tobago, Uganda, UK, USA, Vanuatu, Vietnam, Zambia, Zimbabwe. [2021.05.19/XM4735/**F**]

- ♦ International Environment House (internationally oriented national body)
- ♦ International Environment Institute, Malta / see Institute of Earth Systems, Malta

♦ International Environmetrics Society (TIES) **13284**

Sec Dep Economia e Statistica, Lungo Dora Siena 100 A, 10153 Turin TO, Italy. T. +39116703873. Fax +39116703895.
Pres CSIRO EcoSciences Precinct – Dutton Park, 41 Boggo Road, Brisbane QLD 4102, Australia. T. +61408737901.
URL: http://www.environmetrics.org/

History 1989. 11 May 1993, registered in accordance with Canadian law. **Aims** Foster development and use of statistical and other quantitative methods in the environmental sciences, environmental engineering and environmental monitoring and protection. Promote participation of statisticians, mathematicians, scientists and engineers in the solution of environmental problems. Emphasize collaboration and communication between individuals from different disciplines and between researchers and practitioners. **Structure** Board of Directors comprising President, President Elect, Secretary, Treasurer, Publication Officer and Regional Directors (2 for each region – North America/Europe/other geographical areas). **Activities** Conducts meetings; organizes environmetrics conferences. **Events** *Annual Conference* Bologna (Italy) 2009, *North American regional meeting* Corvallis, OR (USA) 2009, *Annual Conference* Kelowna, BC (Canada) 2008, *Annual Conference* Mikulov (Czech Rep) 2007, *North American regional meeting* Seattle, WA (USA) 2007. **Publications** *TIES Newsletter* (2 a year); *Environmetrics* – official journal.
Members Societies in 36 countries:
Argentina, Australia, Austria, Brazil, Canada, Colombia, Czechia, Denmark, Egypt, Finland, France, Germany, Greece, Hungary, Italy, Korea Rep, Kuwait, Malaysia, Mexico, Mozambique, Netherlands, New Zealand, Norway, Paraguay, Portugal, Qatar, Russia, Saudi Arabia, Singapore, Spain, Sweden, Switzerland, UK, USA, Venezuela, Zimbabwe.
NGO Relations Specialized Section of: *International Statistical Institute (ISI, #15603)*. Sister organization to: *International Association for Statistical Computing (IASC, #12183)*. [2014.01.01/XD2578/**C**]

♦ Internationale Oecumenische Gemeenschap (#13226)
♦ Internationale Oekumenische Gemeinschaft (#13226)
♦ Internationale der Öffentlichen Dienste (#18572)
♦ Internationale van Oorlogstegenstanders (#20818)
♦ Internationale Organisatie voor Cognitieve Educatie / see International Association for Cognitive Education and Psychology (#11782)
♦ Internationale Organisatie voor de Handel in Stro, Veevoer, Turf en Aanverwante Produkten (no recent information)
♦ Internationale Organisation der Auflagenkontrollbüros (#13366)
♦ Internationale Organisation für Biologische Bekämpfung (#14424)
♦ Internationale Organisation der Katholiken in den Medien / see International Christian Organisation of the Media (#12563)
♦ Internationale Organisation der Katholiken in den Medien – Weltforum von Medienschaffenden und Einrichtungen im säkularen und religiösen Journalismus / see International Christian Organisation of the Media (#12563)
♦ Internationale Organisation Leitender Polizeibeamter (no recent information)
♦ Internationale Organisation für Medizinische Physik (#14453)
♦ Internationale Organisation für naturnahe Badegewässer (#14457)
♦ Internationale Organisation für Normung (#14473)
♦ Internationale Organisation der Obersten Rechnungskontrollbehörden (#14478)
♦ Internationale Organisation Öffentlicher Verwaltungen für Grünflächen und Erholung (inactive)
♦ Internationale Organisation für Palaeobotanik (#14459)

♦ Internationale des organisations culturelles ouvrières (IDOCO) **13285**

Internationale der Arbeiter-Kultur-Organisationen
Contact Niedersächsischer Chorverband Hannover, Königsworther Str 33, 30167 Hannover, Germany. T. +495117100832. E-mail: office@ndschorverband.de.
Vice-Pres Leuningerstrasse 67, 30457 Hannover, Germany.

History 1926, as *Internationale der Arbeitssanger*. Present name adopted 1946. **Events** *International Music Festival* Germany 2010, *International Music Festival* Vaasa (Finland) 2007, *International Music Festival* Lublin (Poland) 2006, *International Music Festival* Linz (Austria) 2003, *International Music Festival* Aalborg (Denmark) 2000. **Publications** *Fachzeitschriften der Jeweiligen Lander* (4 a year) in English, German.
Members Cultural workers' organizations in 7 countries:
Austria, Denmark, Finland, Germany, Norway, Sweden, Switzerland. [2012.08.31/XF0053/**F**]

♦ Internationale Organisation für das Seilbahnwesen (#14481)
♦ Internationale Organisation für Senioren (#09609)
♦ Internationale Organisation zum Studium der Ermüdungsfestigkeit von Drahtseile (#14474)
♦ Internationale Organisation für Sukkulentenforschung (#14477)
♦ Internationale Organisation für den Tierschutz (#17810)
♦ Internationale Organisation für Vakuum- Physik und -Technik / see International Union for Vacuum Science, Technique and Applications (#15826)
♦ Internationale Organisation für Volkskunst (#14447)
♦ Internationale Orientierungslauf Föderation (#14485)

♦ International Eosinophil Society (IES) **13286**

Exec Dir 555 E Wells, Ste 1100, Milwaukee WI 53202, USA. T. +14142766445. Fax +14142763349. E-mail: info@eosinophil-society.org.
URL: http://www.eosinophil-society.org/

History 2000. **Aims** Bring together scientists who are engaged in research in the field of Eosinophil Biology and Eosinophil Disorders with a view to facilitating exchange of ideas and information about this *inflammatory cell type* and its role in *diseases*. **Languages** English. **Finance** Sponsors; registration; donors. **Events** *Symposium* Hamilton, ON (Canada) 2023, *Virtual Seminar Forum* Milwaukee, WI (USA) 2021, *Biennial Congress* Portland, OR (USA) 2019, *Biennial Congress* Gothenburg (Sweden) 2017, *Biennial Congress* Chicago, IL (USA) 2015. [2022/XM0195/**D**]

♦ Internationale ouvrière catholique (inactive)
♦ Internationale ouvrière de radiodiffusion (inactive)
♦ Internationale ouvrière et socialiste (inactive)
♦ Internationale Ozon-Vereinigung (#14494)
♦ Internationale Paneuropa Union (#14509)
♦ Internationale Pappel-Kommission (#14619)
♦ Internationale des Personals der PTT- Betriebe (inactive)
♦ Internationale Pharmazeutische Föderation (#14566)

♦ International Epidemiological Association (IEA) **13287**

Association Internationale d'épidémiologie – Asociación Internacional de Epidemiologia
Sec address not obtained.
Pres address not obtained.
URL: http://www.ieaweb.org/

History 1954. Legally registered in USA. **Aims** Facilitate communication among those engaged in research and teaching of epidemiology throughout the world; encourage its use in all fields of health including social, community and preventative medicine. **Structure** Council. Regional organization: *IEA European Epidemiology Federation (EEF, #11094)*. **Languages** English. **Staff** 2.00 FTE, paid. **Finance** Sources: grants; members' dues. **Activities** Events/meetings; training/education. **Events** *South East Asia Regional Scientific Meeting* Chiang Rai (Thailand) 2022, *Congress* 2021, *Congress* Melbourne, VIC (Australia) 2020, *European Congress of Epidemiology* Lyon (France) 2018, *Congress* Saitama (Japan) 2017. **Publications** *International Journal of Epidemiology* (6 a year); *IEA Newsletter* (annual). *Development of Modern Epidemiology*; *Dictionary of Epidemiology*.
Members Individuals (over 1,500) in 113 countries and territories:
Algeria, Argentina, Australia, Austria, Bahrain, Bangladesh, Barbados, Belgium, Bolivia, Brazil, Bulgaria, Burkina Faso, Cameroon, Canada, Chile, China, Colombia, Costa Rica, Croatia, Cuba, Cyprus, Czechia, Denmark, Dominican Rep, Egypt, El Salvador, Estonia, Ethiopia, Fiji, Finland, France, Gambia, Georgia, Germany, Ghana, Greece, Guatemala, Guinea-Bissau, Haiti, Honduras, Hong Kong, Hungary, Iceland, India, Indonesia, Iran Islamic Rep, Iraq, Ireland, Israel, Italy, Jamaica, Japan, Jordan, Kenya, Korea Rep, Kuwait, Lebanon, Libya, Lithuania, Luxembourg, Malaysia, Malta, Mexico, Mongolia, Morocco, Namibia, Nepal, Netherlands, New Zealand, Nicaragua, Nigeria, Norway, Oman, Pakistan, Palestine, Panama, Papua New Guinea, Paraguay, Peru, Philippines, Poland, Portugal, Qatar, Romania, Russia, Saudi Arabia, Senegal, Serbia, Seychelles, Singapore, Slovenia, South Africa, Spain, Sudan, Sweden, Switzerland, Syrian AR, Taiwan, Tanzania UR, Thailand, Trinidad-Tobago, Tunisia, Türkiye, Uganda, UK, United Arab Emirates, Uruguay, USA, Venezuela, Vietnam, Yemen, Zambia, Zimbabwe.
Consultative Status Consultative status granted from: *ECOSOC (#05331)* (Ros C); *WHO (#20950)* (Official Relations). **IGO Relations** Accredited by: *United Nations Office at Vienna (UNOV, #20604)*. **NGO Relations** Member of: *International Network for Epidemiology in Policy (INEP, #14264)*. Affiliated with: *Council for International Organizations of Medical Sciences (CIOMS, #04905)* and the Countdown to 2015 Initiative. [2018.06.01/XC1806/v/**C**]

♦ Internationale Plato Gesellschaft (#14603)
♦ Internationale A S Poesjkin Stichting (internationally oriented national body)
♦ Internationale de la porte ouverte, pour l'émancipation économique de la travailleuse (no recent information)
♦ Internationale Posaunenvereinigung (internationally oriented national body)
♦ Internationale Primatologen-Gesellschaft / see International Primatological Society (#14642)
♦ Internationale Primatologische Gesellschaft (#14642)
♦ Internationale Privatgüterwagen-Union (#15827)

♦ International EPR Society (IES) **13288**

Pres MPRC Kobe Univ, 1-1 Rokkodai, Nada, Kobe HYOGO, 657-8501 Japan. Fax +81788035770.
Sec Schulich Fac Chemistry, Technion, 32000 Haifa, Israel. E-mail: ab359@tx.technion.ac.il.
General: http://iepr.org/

History Jul 1989, Denver CO (USA). **Aims** Promote scientific development of electron paramagnetic resonance (EPR) – electron spin resonance (ESR) *spectroscopy*; serve as a clearing house on EPR; encourage application of EPR in a wide variety of fields; promote educational programmes on EPR and related spectroscopies. **Structure** Officers: President; Past-President; 3 Vice-Presidents; Secretary; Treasurer. **Languages** English. **Staff** 7.00 FTE, voluntary. **Finance** Members' dues. Other sources: advertisements. **Activities** Organizes meetings; workshops; awards prizes. **Events** *Annual General Meeting* Turin (Italy) 2016, *Annual General Meeting* Nara (Japan) 2014, *Annual General Meeting* Copper Mountain, CO (USA) 2012, *Annual General Meeting* Frankfurt-Main (Germany) 2011, *Annual General Meeting* Puerto Rico 2010. **Publications** *EPR Newsletter* (4 a year).
Members Full in 15 countries:
Australia, Belgium, Canada, Denmark, France, Germany, Israel, Italy, Japan, Netherlands, Norway, Russia, Sweden, UK, USA.
Also members worldwide. Membership countries not specified. [2015/XD8807/**D**]

♦ Internationale Psychoanalytische Studienorganization (#14663)
♦ Internationale Psychoanalytische Vereinigung (#14662)
♦ Internationale PTT-Sportvereinigung (inactive)
♦ Internationale Quartärvereinigung (#15811)
♦ International Equestrian Federation (#09484)

♦ International Equestrian Organisers' Alliance (IEOA) **13289**

Alliance internationale des organisateurs équestres
SG Belfaststraat 26, B3-1, 8500 Kortrijk, Belgium. T. +32476878730.
URL: http://www.equestrianorganizers.com/

History 29 Jun 1995, Aachen (Germany). Registered in accordance with German law. **Aims** Offer general support to show organizers. **Structure** General Assembly (annual), comprising up to 3 representatives of each Association/Alliance. Executive Board, comprising President, 1st and 2nd Vice-Presidents, Secretary General and members. **Finance** Members' dues. **Events** *General Assembly* Geneva (Switzerland) 2007, *General Assembly* Munich (Germany) 2005, *World Congress* Amsterdam (Netherlands) 2000, *World Congress* Amsterdam (Netherlands) 1999, *General Assembly* Brussels (Belgium) 1998. **Publications** *IEOA Newsletter*.
Members Associations and alliances (4):
Alliance of Jumping Organizers (AJO, #00699); *Alliance of Organizers Concours Attelage International (AOCAI, no recent information)*; *Association of International Dressage Event Organizers (AIDEO, #02663)*; *Eventing Organisers Association (#09211)*.
NGO Relations Associate member of: *European Equestrian Federation (EEF, #07005)*. [2019/XF1681/y/**F**]

♦ International Equine Ophthalmology Consortium (IEOC) **13290**

Office address not obtained. T. +12084462519. E-mail: office@equineophtho.org.
URL: http://www.equineophtho.org/

History 2009. **Aims** Promote knowledge sharing in the study and practice of equine ophthalmology; promote development of multi-center clinical trials and research in equine ophthalmology. **Structure** Board of Directors. **Activities** Events/meetings. **Events** *Annual Symposium* Louisville, KY (USA) 2022, *Annual Symposium* 2021, *Annual Symposium* Lucerne (Switzerland) 2020, *Annual Symposium* Vancouver, BC (Canada) 2019, *Annual Symposium* Reykjavik (Iceland) 2018. **Members** Veterinarians; researchers. Membership countries not specified. [2020/XJ7156/**C**]

♦ Internationale Raad van de Architekten van Historische Monumenten (inactive)
♦ Internationale Raad van Christelijke Kerken (#13005)
♦ Internationale Raad van Verenigingen voor Watersport Industrie (#13044)
♦ Internationaler Abdichtungsverband / see European Waterproofing Association (#09084)
♦ Internationaler Aero-Philatelisten Club (internationally oriented national body)
♦ Internationaler Aero-Philatelisten Club "Otto Lilienthal" eV / see Internationaler Aero-Philatelisten Club
♦ Internationaler Aerosol-Verband (inactive)
♦ Internationaler Ägyptologen-Verband (#11865)

♦ Internationale Raiffeisen Union e.V. (IRU) **13291**

Union internationale Raiffeisen (IRU) – Unión Internacional Raiffeisen (IRU) – International Raiffeisen Union (IRU)
SG Adenauerallee 121, 53113 Bonn, Germany. T. +492288861364. Fax +492288861356. E-mail: info@iru.de.
URL: http://www.iru.de/

History 30 Mar 1968, Neuwied (Germany). Registration: Germany. **Aims** Promote internationally the ideas of Friedrich Wilhelm Raiffeisen with respect to *agricultural* and *credit cooperatives*; bring about the continual exchange of opinions and knowledge between members. **Structure** General Meeting; Board of Directors; Presidium Meetings; Reference Centres (4). **Languages** English, French, German, Spanish. **Staff** 1.00 FTE, paid. **Finance** Sources: members' dues. **Activities** Events/meetings; guidance/assistance/consulting; knowledge management/information dissemination; networking/liaising; publishing activities. **Events** *General Meeting* Delhi (India) 2016, *General Meeting* Istanbul (Turkey) 2014, *International Conference* Bonn (Germany) 2012, *Forum* Paris (France) 2010, *General Meeting* Paris (France) 2010. **Publications** *IRU-Courier* in English, French, German, Spanish. *50 Years of IRU – A Chronicle* (2018) in English, German – The environment of the organisation today is completely different from when it was founded in 1968. By 2018, the reality of life in the member countries, the national and international challenges, have changed significantly. The IRU has managed to assert itself while preserving the tried and tested. Over 50 years, the shared 'Raiffeisen ideology' formed the cohesive kit that held the core group of members together. So it's time to take a look back to honour the development of half a century. The essence of the organisation's history is bundled in the booklet.; *Raiffeisen Today – An Excerpt from the lively Exchange of the IRU Members* (2018) in English – In cooperation with its member organisations from all over the world, many contributions of best practice examples have been compiled in this latest publication showcasing how Raiffeisen and its cooperative principles nowadays are actively lived and practically implemented in the various countries..
Members National and international representative central organizations or institutions established on a voluntary basis (cooperative establishments of the Raiffeisen system); corporate bodies employed in cooperative work. Regular members in 22 countries and territories:
Austria, Belgium, Canada, Colombia, Egypt, France, Germany, India, Italy, Japan, Kenya, Korea Rep, Luxembourg, Mexico, Netherlands, Panama, Paraguay, Portugal, Switzerland, Taiwan, Türkiye, Uruguay.
Promoter members in 18 countries:
Argentina, Bolivia, Congo DR, Egypt, Greece, Hungary, Japan, Jordan, Nigeria, Paraguay, Russia, Rwanda, Senegal, Spain, Sri Lanka, Thailand, Türkiye, USA.

Regular members include 1 organization listed in this Yearbook:
Latin American Confederation of Credit Unions (#16302).
Promoter members include 2 organizations listed in this Yearbook:
Association of Asian Confederation of Credit Unions (ACCU, #02377); World Council of Credit Unions (WOCCU, #21324).
Consultative Status Consultative status granted from: *FAO (#09260)* (Liaison Status).
[2021.09.01/XF3914/y/**E**]

- ♦ Internationaler Amerikanistenkongress (#12890)
- ♦ Internationaler Anti-Militaristischer Verein (inactive)
- ♦ Internationaler Arbeitskreis zur Förderung des Physikunterrichtes (#14731)
- ♦ Internationaler Arbeitskreis Landwirtschaftlicher Berater / see Internationale Akademie land- und hauswirtschaftlicher Beraterinnen und Berater (#13212)
- ♦ Internationaler Arbeitskreis Sicherheit beim Skilauf (#15443)
- ♦ Internationaler Arbeitskreis Sonnenberg (#15569)
- ♦ Internationaler Arbeitskreis Sport- und Freizeitbauten / see Internationale Vereinigung Sport- und Freizeiteinrichtungen (#13319)
- ♦ Internationaler Arbeitskreis Systematische und Vergleichende Musikwissenschaft (inactive)
- ♦ Internationaler Architekten Union (#20419)
- ♦ Internationaler Archivrat (#12996)
- ♦ International Erard Society (internationally oriented national body)
- ♦ Internationaler Astronautischer Föderation / see International Astronautical Federation (#12286)
- ♦ Internationale Rat von AIDS-Service-Organisationen / see ICASO (#11040)
- ♦ Internationale Rat für Kommunale Umweltinitiativen / see Local Governments for Sustainability (#16507)
- ♦ Internationale Rat für Metalle und Umwelt (inactive)
- ♦ Internationale Rat für Organisationen von Folklorefestivals und Volkskunst (#13058)
- ♦ Internationale Rat für Vogelschutz / see BirdLife International (#03266)
- ♦ Internationaler Ausschuss für die Erhaltung der Bretonischen Sprache (#12761)
- ♦ Internationaler Ausschuss für die Verhütung von Arbeitsunfällen in der Binnenschiffahrt (#12796)
- ♦ Internationaler Ausschuss für die Verhütung der Trinksucht (#12719)
- ♦ Internationaler Ausschuss der Geschichtswissenschaften (#12777)
- ♦ Internationaler Ausschuss für Industrieschornsteine (#04173)
- ♦ Internationaler Ausschuss für Kohleforschung (no recent information)
- ♦ Internationaler Ausschuss der Waffen- und Militärhistorischen Museen und Sammlungen (#12790)
- ♦ Internationaler Bauernrat (inactive)
- ♦ Internationaler Bauorden (#11745)
- ♦ Internationaler Beamtenbund (no recent information)
- ♦ Internationaler Bergarbeiterverband (inactive)
- ♦ Internationaler Berufsverband der Frauenärzte und Geburtshelfer (#20473)
- ♦ Internationaler Blinden Schach Bund (#12388)
- ♦ Internationaler Blindensportverband / see International Blind Sports Federation (#12363)
- ♦ Internationaler Bund der Bau- und Holzarbeiter (inactive)
- ♦ Internationaler Bund des Blauen Kreuzes / see International Blue Cross (#12364)
- ♦ Internationaler Bund Christlicher Angestelltenverbände (inactive)
- ♦ Internationaler Bund Christlicher Bergarbeiterverbände (inactive)
- ♦ Internationaler Bund Christlicher Fabrik und Transportarbeiter-Verbände (inactive)
- ♦ Internationaler Bund Christlicher Verbände des Post-, Telegrafen-, und Telephon-Personals (inactive)
- ♦ Internationaler Bund Freier Evangelischer Gemeinden (#13433)
- ♦ Internationaler Bund Freier Gewerkschaften (inactive)
- ♦ Internationaler Bund der Gesellschaften für Augenheilkunde (inactive)
- ♦ Internationaler Bund der Katholischen Pfarrlichen Jugendgemeinschaften / see International Federation of Catholic Parochial Youth Movements (#13379)
- ♦ Internationaler Bund Katholischer Arbeitnehmer-Bewegungen (inactive)
- ♦ Internationaler Bund der Konfessionslosen und Atheisten (#14020)
- ♦ Internationaler Bund der Milcheinzelhandels-Verbände (inactive)
- ♦ Internationaler Bund der Nationalen Verbände der Ingenieur-Studenten (inactive)
- ♦ Internationaler Bund der Opfer des Krieges und der Arbeit (inactive)
- ♦ Internationaler Bund der Privatangestellten (inactive)
- ♦ Internationaler Bund Religiöser Sozialisten (#14022)
- ♦ Internationaler Bund der Sachverständigen und Konsulenten-Vereinigungen (inactive)
- ♦ Internationaler Bund der Schuh- und Lederarbeiter (inactive)
- ♦ Internationaler Bund gegen den Stierkampf (inactive)
- ♦ Internationaler Bund Textil und Bekleidung (inactive)
- ♦ Internationaler Bustouristik Verband (internationally oriented national body)
- ♦ Internationaler Camping, Caravaning- und Motorcaravaningverband (#09618)
- ♦ Internationaler Camping-und Caravaningverband / see Fédération Internationale de Camping, Caravanning et Autocaravaning (#09618)
- ♦ Internationaler Chemischer-Reiniger Congress (#13207)
- ♦ Internationaler Christlicher Bund für Alkohol- und Drogenprobleme (no recent information)
- ♦ Internationaler Christlicher Friedensdienst (#12564)
- ♦ Internationaler Christlicher Jugendaustausch / see International Cultural Youth Exchange (#13122)
- ♦ Internationaler Club der Weltreisenden (#15915)
- ♦ Internationaler Coiffeurmeister-Verband / see World Hairdressers' Organization (#21550)

♦ Internationaler Controller Verein (ICV) 13292

Managing Dir Münchner Str 8, 82237 Wörthsee, Germany. T. +4981538897420. Fax +4981538897431.
URL: http://www.icv-controlling.com/

History 1975, as *Controller Verein.* **Aims** Develop and promote procedures and concepts related to business controller activities. **Structure** General Meeting; Managing Committee; Board of Trustees; Executive Secretary; Working Groups. **Languages** English, German, Polish. **Finance** Members' dues. **Activities** Events/meetings; training/education. **Events** *Congress* Munich (Germany) 2019, *International Controller Health Conference* Vienna (Austria) 2019, *Controlling Insights Meeting* Steyr (Austria) 2018, *Congress* Munich (Germany) 2015, *Controlling Insights Meeting* Steyr (Austria) 2015. **Publications** *Controller Magazine.* **Members** Honorary; Associate; Corporate. Members in 30 countries. Membership countries not specified. **NGO Relations** Member of: *International Group of Controlling (IGC, #13742).* [2018.10.31/XJ5389/**D**]

- ♦ Internationaler Dachverband der Briefmarkenhändelverbände (#13557)
- ♦ Internationaler Dachverband der Medizinischen Gesellschaften für Neuraltherapie (#13476)
- ♦ Internationaler Dachverband der Transportversicherer (#15789)
- ♦ Internationaler Delphischer Rat (#13146)
- ♦ Internationaler Draht und Maschinenverband (#15893)
- ♦ Internationaler Drogisten-Kongress (inactive)
- ♦ Internationale Reederei-Assoziation (inactive)

♦ Internationale Regierungskommission Alpenrhein (IRKA) 13293

Program Officer Unterdorf 17, 7411 Sils im Domleschg GR, Switzerland. T. +41794509836. E-mail: info@alpenrhein.net.
URL: http://www.alpenrhein.net/

History 7 Aug 1995. **Structure** Government Commission. Coordination Group. Working Groups (4): Energy; River Engineering; Water and Fish Ecology; Groundwater. **Languages** German.
Members Governments of 4 regions in 3 countries:
Austria, Liechtenstein, Switzerland.
[2017/XM3417/**D***]

- ♦ Internationaler Eisenbahnverband (#15813)
- ♦ Internationaler Eishockey Verband (#13831)
- ♦ Internationaler Elektronik-Arbeitskreis (inactive)
- ♦ Internationale Religionspsychologische Gesellschaft (inactive)
- ♦ Internationaler Representantschaft für Kanusport / see International Canoe Federation (#12437)
- ♦ Internationale des résistants/résistantes à la guerre (#20818)
- ♦ Internationale Rettungshunde Organisation (#14817)
- ♦ Internationaler Europäischer Bauverband / see European Construction Industry Federation (#06766)
- ♦ Internationaler Fachverband des Unabhängigen Schuheinzelhandels (inactive)
- ♦ Internationaler Faustball-Verband / see International Fistball Association (#13609)
- ♦ Internationaler Feriendienst / see INTERVac – International Home Exchange Holiday Service (#15989)
- ♦ Internationaler Fernschachbund / see International Correspondence Chess Federation (#12971)
- ♦ Internationaler Förderkreis für Raumfahrt Hermann Oberth-Wernher von Braun (internationally oriented national body)
- ♦ Internationaler Frauen-Verband (#11639)
- ♦ Internationaler Fremdenführerklub (inactive)
- ♦ Internationaler Friedens-Pressedienst (inactive)
- ♦ Internationaler Gemeindeverband (inactive)
- ♦ Internationaler Gemischter Freimaurerischer Orden (religious order)
- ♦ Internationaler Genossenschaftsbund (#12944)
- ♦ Internationaler Gerichtshof für Tierrechte (#13099)
- ♦ Internationaler Gewerkschaftsbund (#15708)

♦ International Ergonomics Association (IEA) 13294

Association internationale d'ergonomie – Asociación Internacional de Ergonomia

Vice-Pres/SG address not obtained. E-mail: vpsg@iea.cc – secretariat@iea.cc – office@iea.cc.
Pres address not obtained.
URL: https://iea.cc/

History 20 Aug 1961, Stockholm (Sweden). Founded during 1st Congress, following recommendations of the British national society and *European Productivity Agency (EPA, inactive)* attached to the then *'Organization for European Economic Cooperation (OEEC)'*, currently *OECD (#17693)*, preliminary meetings having started in 1957, Leiden (Netherlands). Initially open to individuals, because so few organizations existed in the field; but, from 1976, national federated societies took control. Articles adopted 6 Apr 1959, Oxford (UK) and revised: 1964, Dortmund (Germany FR); 1967, Birmingham (UK); 1976, Maryland NY (USA). Former names and other names: *Ergonomics Research Society* – former (1961). Registration: Switzerland. **Aims** Elaborate and advance ergonomics science and practice. **Structure** Council of federated society representatives(meets annually); Elected Executives; Standing Committees (6); Technical Committees/Scientific Interest Groups (25). **Languages** English. **Staff** 6.00 FTE, voluntary. External part-time administrator. **Finance** Sources: donations; meeting proceeds; members' dues. Annual budget: 100,000 USD (2023). **Activities** Awards/prizes/competitions; certification/accreditation; events/meetings; networking/liaising; research and development; standards/guidelines; training/education. **Events** *Triennial Congress* Jeju (Korea Rep) 2024, *International Conference on Slips, Trips, and Falls* Sendai (Japan) 2022, *Triennial Congress* Vancouver, BC (Canada) 2021, *HEPS : International Conference on Healthcare Systems Ergonomics and Patient Safety* Lisbon (Portugal) 2019, *Symposium on Analysis, Design and Evaluation of Human-Machine Systems* Tallinn (Estonia) 2019. **Publications** *IEA Checkpoints* (2nd ed 2010). Committee reports and documents; workshop and project reports; guidelines. **Information Services** *IEA Good Practices Database.*
Members Federated societies in 57 countries and territories:
Algeria, Argentina, Australia, Austria, Belgium, Brazil, Canada, Chile, China, Colombia, Croatia, Czechia, Denmark, Ecuador, Finland, France, Germany, Greece, Hong Kong, Hungary, Iceland, India, Indonesia, Iran Islamic Rep, Ireland, Israel, Italy, Japan, Korea Rep, Latvia, Malaysia, Mexico, Netherlands, New Zealand, Nigeria, Norway, Peru, Philippines, Poland, Portugal, Russia, Serbia, Singapore, Slovakia, South Africa, Spain, Sweden, Switzerland, Taiwan, Thailand, Tunisia, Türkiye, UK, Ukraine, Uruguay, USA, Venezuela.
CIEHF; *Human Factors and Ergonomics Society (HFES).*
Regional networks (5):
BRICS Network; *ErgoAfrica; Federation of European Ergonomics Societies (FEES, #09504); South East Asian Network of Ergonomics Societies (SEANES, #19777); Unión Latinoamericana de Ergonomía (ULAERGO, #20450).*
Affiliated society:
Human Ergology Society.
Consultative Status Consultative status granted from: *ECOSOC (#05331)* (Ros C); *ILO (#11123)* (Special List); *WHO (#20950)* (Official Relations). **IGO Relations** Accredited by (1): *United Nations Office at Vienna (UNOV, #20604).* [2023.02.15/XC1808/y/**C**]

- ♦ International Ergophthalmological Society (no recent information)
- ♦ Internationaler Gras Ski Verband (inactive)
- ♦ Internationaler Güterwagen-Verband (inactive)
- ♦ Internationale Rheinregulierung (internationally oriented national body)
- ♦ Internationaler Hilfsfonds (internationally oriented national body)
- ♦ Internationaler Hotelbesitzer-Verein (inactive)
- ♦ Internationaler Hotelverband / see International Hotel and Restaurant Association (#13813)
- ♦ Internationale Rijn Commissie / see International Commission for the Protection of the Rhine (#12721)
- ♦ Internationaler Jugendherbergsverband / see Hostelling International (#10950)
- ♦ Internationaler Kalkverband (#14049)
- ♦ Internationaler Katholiken-Verband für Körpererziehung und Sport (#12456)
- ♦ Internationaler Katholischer Krankenhausverband (inactive)
- ♦ Internationaler Kongress der Möbel Fabrikanten (meeting series)
- ♦ Internationaler Kongress über Anwendungen der Mathematik in den Ingenieurwissenschaften (meeting series)
- ♦ Internationaler Kongreß für Unterwasserarchäologie (meeting series)
- ♦ Internationaler Kultureller Jugendaustausch (#13122)
- ♦ Internationaler Kunsterzieher-Verband / see International Society for Education through Art (#15074)
- ♦ Internationaler Ländlicher Entwicklungsdienst (internationally oriented national body)
- ♦ Internationaler Leichtathletik Verband / see World Athletics (#21209)
- ♦ Internationaler Leichtatletic Lehrer Verband (#15702)
- ♦ Internationaler Limeskongress (meeting series)
- ♦ Internationaler Metallgewerkschaftsbund (inactive)
- ♦ Internationaler Metzgermeister-Verband (#12421)
- ♦ Internationaler Milchwirtschaftverband (#13128)
- ♦ Internationaler Missionsrat (inactive)
- ♦ Internationaler Museumsrat (#13051)
- ♦ Internationaler Musikbund (#12865)
- ♦ Internationaler Musikrat (#14199)

♦ International Ernst Cassirer Society 13295

Société internationale Ernst Cassirer – Internationale Ernst Cassirer Gesellschaft (IECG)

Main Office Unter den Linden 6, 10099 Berlin, Germany. E-mail: moeckelc@philosophie.hu-berlin.de.
URL: https://ernst-cassirer.org/

History 13 Oct 1993. **Aims** Promote the study and dissemination of the works of *philosopher* Ernst Cassirer.
[2012/XE3773/**E**]

- ♦ Internationaler Numismatischer Rat (#14385)

♦ International E-Road Network 13296

Contact UNECE, Transport Div, Palais des Nations, 1211 Geneva 10, Switzerland. T. +41229173259. Fax +41229170039. E-mail: roadtransport@unece.org.
URL: http://www.elbruz.org/eroads/AGR_2.htm

History under the auspices of *United Nations Economic Commission for Europe (UNECE, #20555)*, following signature of *European Agreement on Main International Traffic Arteries (AGR, 1975).* A network of roads in Europe numbered E1 and up. **Aims** Facilitate and develop international road traffic in Europe.
[2008.11.04/XM0930/**F***]

- ♦ Internationale Robert-Musil-Gesellschaft (#14762)
- ♦ Internationaler Ornithologenkongress (#14486)
- ♦ Internationale Rorschach-Gesellschaft (#15430)

♦ International Erosion Control Association (IECA) 13297

Contact 3033 S Parker Rd, Ste 410, Aurora CO 80014, USA. T. +13036407554. E-mail: info@ieca.org.
URL: http://www.ieca.org/

History 1972, Seattle WA (USA), as (US) *'National Erosion Control Association'*, with primarily North American membership. **Aims** Promote erosion and *sediment* control and *soil conservation* through professional *certification*; establish standards for control materials and installation procedures; provide technical expertise to policymakers and contractors; disseminate information. **Structure** Board of Directors; Head office; regional chapters. **Finance** Members' dues. Other sources: conference fees; revenues from professional developm-ent courses. **Activities** Knowledge management/information dissemination; capacity building; networking/liaising; accreditation/certification; events/meetings; training/education. **Events** *Annual conference* Kansas City, MO (USA) 2021, *Annual conference* Raleigh, NC (USA) 2020, *Annual Conference* Denver, CO (USA) 2019, *International Erosion Control Conference* Christchurch (New Zealand) 2018, *Annual Conference* Long Beach, CA (USA) 2018. **Publications** *eNewsletter*, *Environmental Connection* – magazine. Conference proceedings; membership directory. **Members** Membership categories: Cornerstone; Emerald; Corporate; Professional; Professional Plus; Young Professional; Emeritus; Student. Membership countries not specified.
[2019.04.24/XF4561/v/**F**]

- ♦ Internationaler Philatelisten-Verband (#09650)
- ♦ Internationaler Photo- und Kinohändler-Bund (inactive)
- ♦ Internationaler Radio-Wissenschaftlicher Verein (#20475)
- ♦ Internationaler Rat der Architecten der Denkmalpflege (inactive)
- ♦ Internationaler Rat zur Bekämpfung des Alkoholismus und der Suchtgefahren / see International Council on Alcohol and Addictions (#12989)
- ♦ Internationaler Rat der Christen und Juden (#13006)
- ♦ Internationaler Rat Christlicher Kirchen (#13005)
- ♦ Internationaler Rat für die Paritätische Doppelresidenz (#13072)
- ♦ Internationaler Rat zur Erhaltung des Wildes und der Jagd (#13024)
- ♦ Internationaler Rat für Frauen-Cricket (inactive)
- ♦ Internationaler Rat der Gesellschaften für Industrielle Formgebung und Formgestaltung / see World Design Organization (#21358)
- ♦ Internationaler Rat für Gesundheit, Leibesüngen und Freizeitgestaltung / see International Council for Health, Physical Education, Recreation, Sport and Dance (#13028)
- ♦ Internationaler Rat für Gesundheit, Leibesüngen, Freizeitgestaltung, Sport und Tanz (#13028)
- ♦ Internationaler Rat Grafischer Vereinigungen / see International Council of Design (#13013)
- ♦ Internationaler Rat der Hauspflegedienste (inactive)
- ♦ Internationaler Rat der Israelitischen Dienste für Wohltätigkeit und Soziale Fürsorge (#13035)
- ♦ Internationaler Rat Jüdischer Frauen (#13036)
- ♦ Internationaler Rat der Kindernährmittelhersteller (inactive)
- ♦ Internationaler Rat für Kinderspiel (#13004)
- ♦ Internationaler Rat für Kinderspiel und Spielzeug / see International Council for Children's Play (#13004)
- ♦ Internationaler Rat der Landschaftlichen Wirtschaften (inactive)
- ♦ Internationaler Rat für Mittel- und Osteuropastudien (#13002)
- ♦ Internationaler Rat für Philosophie und die Geisteswissenschaften (#13061)
- ♦ Internationaler Rat der Praktiker von dem Internationalen Kontenplan (inactive)
- ♦ Internationaler Rat für Sowjet- und Osteuropastudien / see International Council for Central and East European Studies (#13002)
- ♦ Internationaler Rat für Sozialwissenschaften (inactive)
- ♦ Internationaler Rat für Umweltrecht (#13018)
- ♦ Internationaler Rat der Verbände der Blechumformung (#13073)
- ♦ Internationaler Rat der Vereinigungen theologischer Bibliotheken / see European Theological Libraries (#08906)
- ♦ Internationaler Regenmantelfabrikantenverband (inactive)
- ♦ Internationaler Reisezug- und Gepäckwagenverband (inactive)
- ♦ Internationaler Rennrodelverband / see International Luge Federation (#14066)
- ♦ Internationaler Rodelsportverband / see International Luge Federation (#14066)
- ♦ Internationaler Rodelverband (#14066)
- ♦ Internationaler Rohrverband (#15741)
- ♦ Internationaler Saathandelsverband (inactive)
- ♦ Internationaler Schauspielerverband (#13337)
- ♦ Internationaler Schiess-Sportverband (#14852)
- ♦ Internationaler Schlittensportverband / see International Luge Federation (#14066)
- ♦ Internationaler Schriftstellerkongress zur Verteidigung der Kultur (inactive)
- ♦ Internationaler Seefunk-Ausschuss (#04186)
- ♦ Internationaler Seegerichtshof (#15731)
- ♦ Internationaler Sekretariat der Katholischen Akademischen Presse (inactive)
- ♦ Internationaler Skilehrerverband (#14870)
- ♦ Internationaler Ski Verband (#09659)
- ♦ Internationaler Sozialdienst (#14886)
- ♦ Internationaler Sportpresse-Verband (#02729)
- ♦ Internationaler Stadtentwicklungsverband (#15832)
- ♦ Internationaler Strassenverband (#14758)
- ♦ Internationaler Suchdienst / see Arolsen Archives – International Center on Nazi Persecution (#01112)
- ♦ Internationaler Süsstoff-Verband (#15639)
- ♦ Internationaler Süsswarenhandelsverband (internationally oriented national body)
- ♦ Internationaler Tabakarbeiterverband (inactive)
- ♦ Internationaler Tag der Afrikanischen Kindheit / see International Day of the African Child and Youth (#13140)
- ♦ Internationaler Tag der Afrikanischen Kindheit und Jugd / see International Day of the African Child and Youth (#13140)
- ♦ Internationaler Technischer Vanadium Ausschuss (#20746)
- ♦ Internationaler Technischer Verband Tropenholz (#15668)
- ♦ Internationaler Technischer Verband des Tropischen Holzes / see International Technical Tropical Timber Association (#15668)
- ♦ Internationaler Tonjäger Föderation (inactive)
- ♦ Internationaler Trampolin-Verband (inactive)
- ♦ Internationaler Turnerbund (#09636)
- ♦ Internationale Rundfunk- und Fernsehorganisation (inactive)
- ♦ Internationale Rundfunk- und Fernsehuniversität / see International Radio and Television Union (#14689)
- ♦ Internationaler Universitätsverband (#12246)
- ♦ Internationaler Verband für Abfallbeseitigung (#15567)
- ♦ Internationaler Verband für Abfallbeseitigung und Städtereinigung / see International Solid Waste Association (#15567)
- ♦ Internationaler Verband der ACLI (#13336)
- ♦ Internationaler Verband der Aero-Philatelisten-Vereine (#13342)
- ♦ Internationaler Verband für das Alkoholverbot (inactive)
- ♦ Internationaler Verband der Alpinistenvereine (#20420)
- ♦ Internationaler Verband Anthroposophischer ApothekerInnen / see International Association of Anthroposophic Pharmacists
- ♦ Internationaler Verband für Arbeiterbildung (#13580)
- ♦ Internationaler Verband der Aufbauten- und Anhängerindustrie (#11727)
- ♦ Internationaler Verband für Austausch und Bildung von Kindern und Jugendlichen (no recent information)
- ♦ Internationaler Verband der Bäcker und Bäcker-Konditoren / see International Union of Bakers and Confectioners (#15757)
- ♦ Internationaler Verband der Bäcker und Konditoren (#15757)
- ♦ Internationaler Verband der Bahnärztlichen Dienste (#20437)
- ♦ Internationaler Verband der Bekleidungsindustrie (#11659)
- ♦ Internationaler Verband der Berufs-Numismatiker (#12104)
- ♦ Internationaler Verband der Betonbohr und Sägeunternehmungen (#11806)
- ♦ Internationaler Verband der bibliothekarischen Vereine und Institutionen (#13470)
- ♦ Internationaler Verband der Bibliothekar-Vereine / see International Federation of Library Associations and Institutions (#13470)
- ♦ Internationaler Verband der Bienenzüchter-Vereinigungen (#13370)
- ♦ Internationaler Verband des Blumengrosshandels / see UNION FLEURS (#20408)
- ♦ Internationaler Verband der Blutspenderorganisationen (#13374)
- ♦ Internationaler Verband der Brotindustrie (#02674)
- ♦ Internationaler Verband für Christliche Erziehung und Bildung (#11770)

♦ Internationaler Verband Christlicher Hotels (VCH-International) ... 13298

Christian Hotels/Hospitality International (CHI)

Contact c/o Via Migiome 31, 6616 Losone TI, Switzerland. E-mail: mail@vch.ch.
URL: http://www.christian-hospitality.com/

History 1904, Kassel (Germany).
Members Full in 10 countries:
Denmark, Finland, France, Germany, Israel, Italy, Netherlands, Norway, Sweden, Switzerland. [2016.06.01/XF7205/**F**]

- ♦ Internationaler Verband für Die Wärmebehandlung und Randschichttechnik (#13443)
- ♦ Internationaler Verband von Direktoren Zoologischer Gärten / see World Association of Zoos and Aquariums (#21208)
- ♦ Internationaler Verband der Eisenbahner für Nüchternheit (inactive)
- ♦ Internationaler Verband der Eisenbahner Touristen-Vereinigungen (inactive)
- ♦ Internationaler Verband des Erwerbsgartenbaues (#11940)
- ♦ Internationaler Verband für Erziehung zu Suchmittelfreiem Leben (inactive)
- ♦ Internationaler Verband Evangelischer Erzieher / see International Association for Christian Education (#11770)
- ♦ Internationaler Verband der Fachpresse (inactive)
- ♦ Internationaler Verband für Fernheizung, Fernkühlung und Kraft-Wärme-Kopplung / see Euroheat and Power (#05694)
- ♦ Internationaler Verband der Fernwärmeversorger / see Euroheat and Power (#05694)
- ♦ Internationaler Verband für Feuerbestattung (#13104)
- ♦ Internationaler Verband der Filmarchive (#13427)
- ♦ Internationaler Verband der Filmproduzenten-Vereinigungen (#13429)
- ♦ Internationaler Verband zur Förderung der Gewinnung und Verwertung von Heil-, Gewürz- und Verwandten Pflanzen (inactive)
- ♦ Internationaler Verband Forstlicher Forschungsanstalten (#15774)
- ♦ Internationaler Verband Freier Journalisten (inactive)
- ♦ Internationaler Verband der Führungskrafte des Verkehrswesens (#07730)
- ♦ Internationaler Verband der Führunskräfte der Mettelindustrie / see European Federation of Managers in the Steel Industry (#07162)
- ♦ Internationaler Verband der Gastronomie- und Weinbuau- Presse (inactive)
- ♦ Internationaler Verband der Geistesarbeiter (#04564)
- ♦ Internationaler Verband Genossenschaftlicher und Wechselseitiger Versicherungen (#12948)
- ♦ Internationaler Verband für Geschichte und Philosophie der Wissenschaften / see International Union of History and Philosophy of Science and Technology (#15779)
- ♦ Internationaler Verband der Gesellschaften für Elektronenmikroskopie (#13550)
- ♦ Internationaler Verband der Gewerkschaften des Verkehrspersonals (inactive)
- ♦ Internationaler Verband für Haus Finanzierungen / see International Union for Housing Finance (#15780)
- ♦ Internationaler Verband für Hauswirtschaft (#13447)
- ♦ Internationaler Verband für Hauswirtschaftsunterricht / see International Federation for Home Economics (#13447)
- ♦ Internationaler Verband von Herstellern Gummierter Papiere (#09631)
- ♦ Internationaler Verband der Holzanatomen (#12273)
- ♦ Internationaler Verband der Immobilienberufe (#09653)
- ♦ Internationaler Verband der Ingenieurvereine für Automobiltechnik (#13369)
- ♦ Internationaler Verband für Innere Mission und Diakonie / see European Federation for Diaconia (#07099)
- ♦ Internationaler Verband der Italienischen Lehrer (#02989)
- ♦ Internationaler Verband der Katholischen Ärzte / see International Federation of Catholic Medical Associations (#13378)
- ♦ Internationaler Verband Katholischer Kranken-Schwestern (#12451)
- ♦ Internationaler Verband für Klassiche Archeologie (#02988)
- ♦ Internationaler Verband für Klinische Chemie (#13392)
- ♦ Internationaler Verband der Konditoren, Confiseure und Speiseeishersteller (inactive)
- ♦ Internationaler Verband der Konferenzdolmetscher (#11807)
- ♦ Internationaler Verband für Konferenztechnik (inactive)
- ♦ Internationaler Verband der Konferenz Übersetzer (#02748)
- ♦ Internationaler Verband der Kongresszentren / see International Association of Convention Centres (#11818)
- ♦ Internationaler Verband Körperbehinderter Menschen (#13504)
- ♦ Internationaler Verband des Kraftfahrzeuggewerbes (inactive)
- ♦ Internationaler Verband Krankenhaustechnik (#13439)
- ♦ Internationaler Verband Kulturpflegender Eisenbahner (#09660)
- ♦ Internationaler Verband der Landschafts-Architekten (#13467)
- ♦ Internationaler Verband für Leibeserziehung und Sport der Mädchen und Frauen (#12081)
- ♦ Internationaler Verband Magischer Gesellschaften (#13473)
- ♦ Internationaler Verband für Mess- und Automatisierungstechnik (#13367)
- ♦ Internationaler Verband der Möbelstoff-Fabrikanten (inactive)
- ♦ Internationaler Verband von Museumsbeamten (inactive)
- ♦ Internationaler Verband der nationalen Vereinigungen der Seilbahnen (#09608)
- ♦ Internationaler Verband der Naturtextilwirtschaft (#14217)
- ♦ Internationaler Verband für Öffentliches Verkehrswesen (#12118)
- ♦ Internationaler Verband der Operndirektoren (inactive)
- ♦ Internationaler Verband der Orthopädie-Schuhtechniker (#12059)
- ♦ Internationaler Verband der Pektinproduzenten (#14539)
- ♦ Internationaler Verband der PEN Klubs / see International PEN (#14552)
- ♦ Internationaler Verband der Petroleum- und Chemiearbeiter (inactive)
- ♦ Internationaler Verband der Pflanzenzüchter für den Schutz von Pflanzenzüchtungen (inactive)
- ♦ Internationaler Verband der Philatelistischen Experten (#02696)
- ♦ Internationaler Verband der Photographischen Kunst (#13509)
- ♦ Internationaler Verband de Privatkliniken (no recent information)
- ♦ Internationaler Verband Psychiatrischer Epidemiologie (#13521)

- Internationaler Verband Psychologisch-Medizinischer Organisationen (inactive)
- Internationaler Verband für Rechtswissenschaft (#11997)
- Internationaler Verband der Reinigungsunternehmen / see Fédération internationale des entreprises de nettoyage (#09628)
- Internationaler Verband für Schiffahrt / see PIANC (#18371)
- Internationaler Verband Schneesport an Schulen und Hochschulen / see International Association of Education in Science and Snowsports (#11864)
- Internationaler Verband der Schuhtechniker (#20439)
- Internationaler Verband zum Schutz Bedrohter Sprachen und Kulturen / see Association pour les Langues et Cultures Européennes Menacées (#02782)
- Internationaler Verband zum Schutz von Pflanzenzuechtungen (#20436)
- Internationaler Verband für Schwerhörigenseelsorge (#13500)
- Internationaler Verband der Seehäfen (#12096)
- Internationaler Verband der Seifen- und Waschmittelindustrie (inactive)
- Internationaler Verband für Selbsttätige Regelung und Steuerung / see International Federation of Automatic Control (#13367)
- Internationaler Verband Skilauf an Schulen und Hochschulen / see International Association of Education in Science and Snowsports (#11864)
- Internationaler Verband für Socialtourismus (inactive)
- Internationaler Verband der Sozialtouristischer Reiseorganisationen (inactive)
- Internationaler Verband der Stadt-, Sport- und Mehrzweckhallen / see European Association of Event Centers (#06032)
- Internationaler Verband der Tarifeure / see International Association of Tariff-Specialists – Organization of Tariff and Transport Experts (#12219)
- Internationaler Verband der Tarifeure – Organisation der Tarif- und Transportexperten (#12219)
- Internationaler Verband für Telefonseelsorge (#13567)
- Internationaler Verband der Textilveredlungs- und Stoffdruck-Industrie (inactive)
- Internationaler Verband Theologischer Mitarbeiter in der Diakonie / see Internationale Konferenz Theologischer Mitarbeiterinnen und Mitarbeiter in der Diakonie
- Internationaler Verband der Universitätsbibliotheken (#12247)
- Internationaler Verband der Verarbeiter von Chemiefaser Filament- und Naturseidengaren (#02750)
- Internationaler Verband für Verkehrsschulung und Verkehrserziehung (inactive)
- Internationaler Verband der Wandbekleidungsfabrikanten / see IGI – The Global Wallcoverings Association (#11107)
- Internationaler Verband für Wasserrettung (inactive)
- Internationaler Verband für Wohnungswesen (inactive)
- Internationaler Verband für Wohnungswesen und Städtebau / see International Federation for Housing and Planning (#13450)
- Internationaler Verband für Wohnungswesen, Städtebau und Raumordnung (#13450)
- Internationaler Verband der Yacht-Rennen / see World Sailing (#21760)
- Internationaler Verband Zeitgenossischer Mosaizisten / see International Association of Contemporary Mosaicists (#11816)
- Internationaler Verband der Zeitschriftenpresse / see FIPP (#09776)
- Internationaler Verband der Zeitungsausschnittbüros (#09617)
- Internationaler Verein für Biologisch-Dynamische Landwirtschaft (#12346)
- Internationaler Verein der Biologischen Wissenschaften (#15760)
- Internationaler Verein für die Förderung der Experimentellen und Klinischen Pharmakologie (inactive)
- Internationaler Verein von Europäische Reiseversicherer / see International Travel Insurance Alliance e.V. (#15728)
- Internationaler Verein für Geodäsie und Geophysik / see International Union of Geodesy and Geophysics (#15776)
- Internationaler Verein für Gerontologie / see International Association of Gerontology and Geriatrics (#11920)
- Internationaler Verein des Haus und Grundbesitzer (#15804)
- Internationaler Verein der Homöopathischer Ärzte (#16471)
- Internationaler Verein der Kino-Betreiber / see International Union of Cinemas (#15763)
- Internationaler Verein für Pflanzen-Taxonomie (#12092)
- Internationaler Verein der Prähistorischen und Protohistorischen Wissenschaften (#15801)
- Internationaler Verein für Schlafmedizin (inactive)
- Internationaler Verein der Tapetenfabrikanten / see IGI – The Global Wallcoverings Association (#11107)
- Internationaler Verein für Technische Holzfragen (internationally oriented national body)
- Internationaler Verein Trappist (#15727)
- Internationaler Versehrtensportverband (inactive)
- Internationaler Versöhnungsbund (#13586)
- Internationaler Volkssportverband (#13515)
- Internationaler Zeitungs Marketing-Verband (#14363)
- Internationaler Ziegenzuchtverband (inactive)
- Internationaler Zionistischer Frauenbund (#21030)
- Internationaler Zivildienst / see Service Civil International (#19238)

♦ Internationales Altkatholische Forum 13299

Contact VIAKL, 3000 Bern, Switzerland. T. +4989582785.
Chair address not obtained.
Pres address not obtained.
URL: https://altkatholisches-forum.org/

History 1 Jan 1991. Former names and other names: *Internationales Altkatholische Laienforum* – former; *Verein Internationales AK Laienforum (VIAKL)* – legal name. Registration: Swiss Civil Code, Start date: 13 Aug 2011, Switzerland. **Aims** Unite committed laypeople across Europe to discuss *spiritual* matters and become acquainted with local parishes. **Structure** Assembly; Bureau; Executive Board. **Languages** English, German. **Finance** Sources: members' dues. **Activities** Events/meetings. **Events** *Forum* Wahlwiller (Netherlands) 2012, *Forum* Graz (Austria) 2011, *Forum* Zurich (Switzerland) 2003, *Meeting* Vienna (Austria) 2000, *Forum* Prague (Czech Rep) 1999. **Members** Individuals (about 50) in 6 countries. Membership countries not specified. **NGO Relations** National churches. [2021.09.02/XE3814/**F**]

- Internationales Altkatholische Laienforum / see Internationales Altkatholische Forum (#13299)
- Internationales Amt für Kataster und Grundbuchwesen (#14398)
- Internationales Arbeiter-Hilfswerk / see SOLIDAR (#19680)
- Internationale Sauna-Gesellschaft / see International Sauna Association (#14782)
- Internationales Auschwitz-Komitee (#12297)
- Internationales Begegnungszentrum Friedenshaus / see World House, Bielefeld
- Internationales Bildungs- und Begegnungswerk (internationally oriented national body)
- Internationales Bob- und Skeletonverband (#12375)
- Internationales Bodenkundliches Museum / see ISRIC – World Soil Information (#16068)
- Internationales Bodenreferenz und Informations-Zentrum / see ISRIC – World Soil Information (#16068)
- Internationales Buchdrucker-Sekretariat (inactive)
- Internationales Bureau zur Bekämpfung des Alkoholismus / see International Council on Alcohol and Addictions (#12989)
- Internationales Burgen-Institut (inactive)
- Internationales Büro für Audiophonologie (#03362)
- Internationales Büro der Beton- und Fertigteil-Industrie (#03363)
- Internationales Büro für Differentiale Anthropologie (inactive)
- Internationales Büro der Fabrikanten-, Grossisten- und Einzelhändlerverbände des Juwelen- und Edelmetallfaches / see CIBJO – The World Jewellery Confederation (#03923)
- Internationales Büro für Gebirgsmechanik (#12417)
- Internationales Büro für Jugendtouristik und Jugendaustausch (inactive)
- Internationales Büro der Kleingärtnerorganisationen / see Fédération Internationale des Jardins Familiaux (#09641)
- Internationales Büro der Kleingärtnerverbände / see Fédération Internationale des Jardins Familiaux (#09641)
- Internationales Büro der Schuh- und Lederwirtschaft (inactive)
- Internationales Büro für Sozialtourismus / see International Social Tourism Organisation (#14889)
- Internationales Büro für Wasservogel- und Feuchtgebietforschung (inactive)
- Internationales Centrum für Neue Medien (internationally oriented national body)
- Internationales Centrum für Weltmission (internationally oriented national body)
- Internationale Scheldecommissie (#12727)
- Internationale School van het Gouden Rozenkruis (religious order)
- Internationale Schule des Goldenen Rosenkreuzes (religious order)
- Internationale Schulsport Föderation (#14792)
- Internationale Schützenunion / see International Shooting Sport Federation (#14852)
- Internationales Collegium der Psychosomatischen Medizin (#12649)
- Internationales Daunen-und Federn-Bureau (#13195)
- Internationales Design Zentrum, Berlin (internationally oriented national body)
- Internationales Diakonatszentrum (#13167)
- Internationale Segelschulen Vereinigung (#14777)
- Internationale Seidenbau Kommission (#14837)
- Internationale Seiden-Vereinigung (inactive)
- Internationales Eisenbahntransportkomitee (#04188)
- Internationale Selbstbedienungs-Organisation (no recent information)
- Internationales Email-Institut (#13267)
- Internationale des Services Publics (#18572)
- Internationales Erwin Schrödinger Institut (internationally oriented national body)
- Internationales Fairplay-Komitee (#12769)
- Internationales Federn-Bureau / see International Down and Feather Bureau (#13195)
- Internationales Fernsehsymposium (meeting series)
- Internationales Fluidtechnisches Kolloquium (meeting series)
- Internationales Forschungs- und Informationszentrum für Öffentliche Wirtschaft und Gemeinwirtschaft / see Centre international de recherches et d'information sur l'économie publique, sociale et coopérative (#03764)
- Internationales Forschungs- und Informationszentrum für Öffentliche Wirtschaft, Sozialwirtschaft und Genossenschaftswesen (#03764)
- Internationales Forschungszentrum für das Heiligen Leichentuch Christi (#12516)
- Internationales FORUM für den Entwicklungsdienst (#13659)
- Internationales Forum Junge Chormusik (internationally oriented national body)
- Internationales Forum für Minichirurgie der Varizen (#13645)
- Internationales Forum für System-Aufstellungen in Organisationen und Arbeitskontexten (#13656)
- Internationales Friedensbüro (#14535)
- Internationales Gewerkschaftliches Arbeiterinnenkomitee (inactive)
- Internationales Gewerkschaftsnetzwerk der Solidarität und des Kampfes (unconfirmed)
- Internationales Harfen-Zentrum (internationally oriented national body)
- Internationales Haus Sonnenberg (internationally oriented national body)
- Internationales Hilfskomitee für Intellektuelle (inactive)
- Internationales Hilfswerk für Missions Personal (#14170)
- Internationales Hopfenbaubüro (#13807)
- Internationales Informationszentrum für Terminologie (#13846)
- Internationales Institut für Angewandte Systemanalyse (#13861)
- Internationales Institut für Bankforschung (#12313)
- Internationales Institut für Bienentechnologie und -Wirtschaft / see Fundatia Institutul International de Tehnologie si Economie Apicola
- Internationales Institut für die Vereinheitlichung des Privatrechts (#13934)
- Internationales Institut für Förderung und Ansehen (#11315)
- Internationales Institut für Forschung und Dokumentierung des Handelswettbewerbes (inactive)
- Internationales Institut für den Frieden (#13907)
- Internationales Institut für Informations-Design (internationally oriented national body)
- Internationales Institut für Journalismus und Kommunikation (internationally oriented national body)
- Internationales Institut für Journalistik, Berlin – Brandenburg (internationally oriented national body)
- Internationales Institut für Journalistik 'Werner Lamberz', Schule der Solidarität / see International Institute of Journalism, Berlin – Brandenburg
- Internationales Institut für Jugendliteratur und Leseforschung (#13869)
- Internationales Institut für Kunstwissenschaften (inactive)
- Internationales Institut für Lehrfilmwesen (inactive)
- Internationales Institut für Nachhaltigkeitsanalysen und -strategien (#13929)

♦ Internationales Institut für Nationalitätenrecht und Regionalismus (INTEREG) 13300

Institut international pour les droits des groupes ethniques et pour le régionalisme – Instituto Internacional para los Derechos de Grupos Etnicos y Regionalismo – International Institute for Ethnic Group Rights and Regionalism – Istituto Internazionale per il Diritto dei Gruppi Etnici e il Regionalismo

Sec Postfach 340161, 80098 Munich, Germany. T. +498927294222. Fax +498927294226. E-mail: info@intereg.org.
Street Address Hessstrasse 24, 80799 Munich, Germany.
URL: http://www.intereg.org/

History 29 Oct 1977, Germany FR. 29 Oct 1977, Regensburg (Germany FR). Also referred to as *International Institute for Nationality Rights and Regionalism.* **Aims** Promote nationality rights, regionalist independence and self-determination in order to reduce armed conflicts and maintain peace. **Structure** Advisory Board; Praesidium. **Languages** English, French, German, Italian, Portuguese, Spanish. **Finance** State budget. **Activities** Events/meetings; training/education. **Events** *Congress* Bad Kissingen (Germany) 2014, *Congress* Bad Kissingen (Germany) 2014, *Symposium / Congress* Berlin (Germany) 2014, *Congress* Munich (Germany) 2013, *Congress* Munich (Germany) 2013. **Publications** *in Europäisches Journal für Minderheitenfragen.* Monographs; pamphlets; folders.

Members Individuals in 16 countries and territories:
Austria, Belgium, Croatia, Czechia, Denmark, France, Germany, Hungary, Italy, Liechtenstein, North Macedonia, Poland, Slovakia, Switzerland, Ukraine, USA.

Consultative Status Consultative status granted from: *Council of Europe (CE, #04881)* (Participatory Status).
NGO Relations Joint publication with: *Association of European Border Regions (AEBR, #02499).* [2016.10.19/XD7410/jv/**F**]

- Internationales Institut für Philosophie (#13910)
- Internationales Institut für Rechtsfragen Französisch-sprechenden Staaten (#11310)
- Internationales Institut für Rübenforschung / see International Institute of Sugar Beet Research (#13928)
- Internationales Institut für Sozio-Informatik (internationally oriented national body)
- Internationales Institut für Soziologie (#13925)
- Internationales Institut für Sportwissenschaft (internationally oriented national body)
- Internationales Institut für Terminologieforschung (#13932)
- Internationales Institut für Traditionelle Musik (inactive)
- Internationales Institut der Verschiedenen Kulturstufen (inactive)

- Internationales Institut für Zahnärztliche Arbeitswissenschaft und Technologie (inactive)
- Internationale Situationniste (inactive)
- Internationales Jugendnetzwerk für die Vereinten Nationen (#20652)
- Internationales Kali-Institut (#14626)
- Internationales Katholische Missionswerk / see MISSIO (#16827)
- Internationales Katholisches Büro für Unterricht und Erziehung / see Catholic International Education Office (#03604)
- Internationales Katholisches Zentrum für die UNESCO / see International Catholic Cooperation Centre for UNESCO (#12454)
- Internationales Klimawandel-Informationsprogramm (#12597)
- Internationales Kolpingwerk / see KOLPING INTERNATIONAL (#16203)
- Internationales Komitee Buchenwald-Dora und Kommandos (#12749)
- Internationales Komitee für die Einführung in die Wissenschaft und die Förderung der Wissenschaftlichen Tätigkeit ausserhalb der Schule (#12953)
- Internationales Komitee für die Indianer Amerikas / see International Committee for the Indigenous Peoples of the Americas
- Internationales Komitee für die Inigenen Amerikas (internationally oriented national body)
- Internationales Komitee zur Ermittlung der Wirtschaftlichkeit von Milchtieren / see International Committee for Animal Recording (#12746)
- Internationales Komitee für Ethnische Freiheiten / see Internacia Komitato por Etnaj Liberecoj (#11523)
- Internationales Komitee der Färberei und Chemische Reinigung (inactive)
- Internationales Komitee Giessereitechnischer Vereinigungen / see World Foundry Organization (#21528)
- Internationales Komitee der Hersteller dekorativer Schichtstoffplatten (#12760)
- Internationales Komitee für Historische Metrologie (#12776)
- Internationales Komitee für Leistungsprüfungen in der Tierproduktion (#12746)
- Internationales Komitee für Sowjet- und Osteuropastudien / see International Council for Central and East European Studies (#13002)
- Internationales Komitee für Spendenwesen (inactive)
- Internationales Komitee für Textilpflege (#12809)
- Internationales Komitee der Verarbeiter von Papier und Pappe in der Europäischen Gemeinschaft / see International Confederation of Paper and Board Converters in Europe (#12866)
- Internationales Komitee vom Roten Kreuz (#12799)
- Internationales Kontaktnetz Junger Journalisten (#14346)
- Internationales Konversionszentrum Bonn (#03300)
- Internationales Kuratorium für das Jugendbuch (#12366)
- Internationales Maasübereinkommen (2002 treaty)
- Internationales Mauthausen Komitee (#04179)
- Internationales Musikinstitut Darmstadt (internationally oriented national body)
- Internationales Musikzentrum / see IMZ International Music + Media Centre (#11139)
- Internationales Netz zur Förderung von Rauchfreien Krankenhäusern / see Anti-Smoking International Alliance (#00861)
- Internationales Netz der Strassenzeitungen / see International Network of Street Papers (#14330)
- Internationales Netzwerk der Gesellschaften für Katholische Theologie (#14328)
- Internationales Netzwerk Umweltrecht (#05504)
- Internationales Neuengamme-Komitee (#14347)
- Internationale Socialiste (#19340)
- Internationale socialiste des femmes (#19341)
- Internationales Olympisches Institut (inactive)
- Internationales Ombudsman Institut (#14411)
- Internationale Sozialdemokratische Organisation für Bildung (#14881)
- Internationales Parlament für Sicherheit und Frieden (internationally oriented national body)
- Internationales Patentinstitut (inactive)
- Internationales PCA Forum (meeting series)
- International Esperantist Chess League (inactive)
- International Esperantist Cyclist Movement / see International Association of Esperanto-Speaking Cyclists (#11878)

♦ International Esperantist Scientific Association 13301

Association scientifique internationale des espérantistes – Asociación Cientifica Internacional de Esperantistas – Internationale Wissenschaftliche Esperanto-Organisation – Internacia Scienca Asocio Esperantlingva (ISAE)

Contact Nieuwe Binnenweg 176, 3015 BJ Rotterdam, Netherlands.
Sec Casilla 508, Puerto Montt, Los Lagos, Chile.
URL: https://scienca-revuo.info/

History 30 Aug 1906, Geneva (Switzerland). Reconstructed: Aug 1947, Bern (Switzerland), and Aug 1959, Marseille (France). Also referred to in English as *International Association of Esperanto-Speaking Scientists*. **Aims** Introduce the use of Esperanto in scientific and technological circles. **Structure** Committee of national delegates (elected for 3 years) elects Directing Board. Special Commissions. Board of 5. **Languages** Esperanto. **Staff** Part-time, voluntary. **Finance** Members' dues: Swiss Fr 30. **Activities** Especially in: Astronomy; Chemistry; Computing; Ecology; Geology; Law; Mathematics; Philology; Students. Preparation of technical terminologies and of bibliographical data concerning scientific publications in Esperanto. **Events** *Annual Conference* Hanoi (Vietnam) 2012, *Annual Conference* Copenhagen (Denmark) 2011, *Annual Conference* Havana (Cuba) 2010, *Annual Conference* Bialystok (Poland) 2009, *Annual Conference* Rotterdam (Netherlands) 2008. **Publications** *Bulteno de ISAE* (4 a year); *Science Revuo* (2 a year).
Members National Branches and Societies (3); Special Commission; Individuals, totalling 200 persons, in 30 countries:
Australia, Austria, Belgium, Brazil, Canada, China, Cuba, Czechia, Finland, France, Germany, Hungary, Iran Islamic Rep, Ireland, Italy, Japan, Korea Rep, Netherlands, New Zealand, Norway, Romania, Russia, South Africa, Spain, Sweden, Switzerland, Tajikistan, UK, USA, Uzbekistan.
NGO Relations Affiliated member of: *Universal Esperanto Association (UEA, #20676).* [2015/XC1810/**C**]

- International Esperanto Association of Jurists (inactive)
- International Esperanto Fellowship of Rotarians (#18973)

♦ International Esperanto Institute (IEI) 13302

Institut international d'espéranto (IIE) – Internacia Esperanto-Instituto (IEI)

Sec Riouwstraat 172, 2585 HW The Hague, Netherlands. T. +31703556677. E-mail: iesperanto@versatel.nl.
URL: http://www.iei.nl/

History 24 May 1930, The Hague (Netherlands). **Aims** Study the culture and history of Esperanto; promote study of the Cseh method, an instruction method of Esperanto, editing books and digital products. **Structure** Board. **Languages** Dutch, Esperanto. **Staff** 4.00 FTE, voluntary. **Finance** Gifts and revenues from the selling of books and instruction material. **Activities** Training/education; publishing activities; knowledge management/information dissemination; events/meetings. **Events** *Seminar* The Hague (Netherlands) 2014, *Seminar* Bialystok (Poland) 2009, *Seminar* Rotterdam (Netherlands) 2008, *Seminar* Yokohama (Japan) 2007, *Seminar* Florence (Italy) 2006. **Publications** *Cseh-Kurso: Gvidilo por Instruantoj*; *Esprimo de Sentoj*; *Vivo de Andreo Cseh*. Booklets; leaflets; various books.
Members Individuals in 18 countries:
Australia, Belgium, Canada, Côte d'Ivoire, Cuba, France, Germany, Lithuania, Montenegro, Netherlands, North Macedonia, Poland, Russia, Serbia, Spain, Togo, Ukraine, USA.
NGO Relations Associated with: *Universal Esperanto Association (UEA, #20676).* [2017.10.25/XE1813/jv/**E**]

- International Esperanto Tourist Association (inactive)
- Internationale Spielplatzvereinigung / see International Play Association (#14604)
- Internationale sportive et socialiste ouvrière (inactive)

♦ International Esports Federation (IESF) 13303

SG 615 – 6F, Suyoeonggangbyeon-daero 140, Haendae-gu, Busan 48058, Korea Rep. T. +8227156668. E-mail: info@ie-sf.org.
URL: http://www.ie-sf.org/

History Nov 2008. New statutes adopted: Oct 2016; Dec 2019. **Aims** Promote esports as true sport beyond language, race and culture barriers. **Structure** Board; Secretariat. **Languages** English. **Staff** 4.00 FTE, paid. **Finance** Sources: donations; government support; members' dues. **Activities** Capacity building; networking/liaising; sporting activities. **Events** *Global Executive Summit* Busan (Korea Rep) 2021, *Global Executive Summit* Busan (Korea Rep) 2020, *Global Executive Summit* Busan (Korea Rep) 2019, *Global Executive Summit* Busan (Korea Rep) 2017.
Members Member Federations in 71 countries and territories:
Argentina, Australia, Austria, Azerbaijan, Bahamas, Belarus, Belgium, Bosnia-Herzegovina, Brazil, Brunei Darussalam, Chile, China, Colombia, Costa Rica, Czechia, Denmark, Dominican Rep, Egypt, Finland, Georgia, Germany, Guatemala, Hong Kong, India, Indonesia, Iran Islamic Rep, Ireland, Israel, Italy, Jamaica, Japan, Jordan, Kazakhstan, Korea Rep, Kyrgyzstan, Lebanon, Macau, Malaysia, Maldives, Mexico, Mongolia, Montenegro, Myanmar, Namibia, Nepal, Netherlands, New Zealand, North Macedonia, Norway, Panama, Peru, Philippines, Poland, Portugal, Russia, San Marino, Saudi Arabia, Serbia, Slovakia, South Africa, Sri Lanka, Sweden, Switzerland, Syrian AR, Taiwan, Thailand, Tunisia, United Arab Emirates, USA, Uzbekistan, Vietnam.
NGO Relations Member of: *The Association for International Sport for All (TAFISA, #02763)*; *World Esports Consortium (WESCO, #21391)*. Signatory to: *World Anti-Doping Agency (WADA, #21096)*. Memorandum of Understanding with: *World Athletics (#21209)*; *International Table Tennis Federation (ITTF, #15650)*; *International University Sports Federation (FISU, #15830)*; *International School Sport Federation (ISF, #14792)*. [2022/XM5480/**C**]

♦ International Esports Federation (IESF) 13304

Secretariat 615 – 6F, Suyeonggangbyeon-daero 140, Haeundae-gu, Busan 48058, Korea Rep. T. +8227156668.
URL: https://ie-sf.org/

History Current statutes adopted 13 Dec 2019. **Aims** Promote Esports as a true sport beyond barriers. **Structure** General Meeting; Board; Secretariat. Committees. **Languages** English. **Finance** Sources: members' dues. **Activities** Sporting activities; standards/guidelines; training/education. **Events** *Global e-Sports Executive Summit* Busan (Korea Rep) 2022, *Global e-Sports Executive Summit* Busan (Korea Rep) 2021, *Global e-Sports Conference* Busan (Korea Rep) 2020, *Global e-Sports Executive Summit* Busan (Korea Rep) 2020, *Meeting* Busan (Korea Rep) 2020.
Members Full in 71 countries and territories:
Argentina, Australia, Austria, Azerbaijan, Bahamas, Belarus, Belgium, Bosnia-Herzegovina, Brazil, Brunei Darussalam, China, Colombia, Costa Rica, Czechia, Denmark, Dominican Rep, Egypt, Finland, Georgia, Germany, Guatemala, Hong Kong, India, Indonesia, Iran Islamic Rep, Ireland, Israel, Italy, Jamaica, Japan, Kazakhstan, Korea Rep, Kyrgyzstan, Lebanon, Macau, Malaysia, Maldives, Mexico, Mongolia, Montenegro, Myanmar, Namibia, Nepal, Netherlands, New Zealand, North Macedonia, Norway, Panama, Peru, Philippines, Poland, Portugal, Russia, San Marino, Saudi Arabia, Serbia, Slovakia, South Africa, Sri Lanka, Sweden, Switzerland, Syrian AR, Taiwan, Thailand, Tunisia, Türkiye, Ukraine, United Arab Emirates, USA, Uzbekistan, Vietnam.
Affiliate members (2):
Korea Rep.
eSports Middle East (ESME).
NGO Relations Memorandum of Understanding with (2): *Asian Electronic Sports Federation (AESF, #01435)*; *International School Sport Federation (ISF, #14792)*. Partner of (2): *Maccabi World Union (MWU, #16537)*; *World Esports Consortium (WESCO, #21391).* [2020/AA1026/**B**]

- Internationales Presse Institut (#14636)
- Internationales Quellenlexikon der Musik (#13949)
- Internationales Repertorium der Musikikonographie (#18844)
- Internationales Repertorium der Musikliteratur (#18845)
- Internationales Sachsenhausen-Komitee (#04187)

♦ Internationales Sachsensymposion – Arbeitsgemeinschaft zur Archäologie der Sachsen und ihrer Nachbarvölker in Nordwesteuropa (Internationales Sachsensymposion) 13305

International Sachsensymposion – Research network for the archaeological study of the Saxons and their neighbouring peoples in northwestern Europe

Chair Braunschweigisches Landesmuseen, Friedrich-Wilhelm-Strasse 3, 38100 Braunschweig, Germany.
Sec University College London, Institute of Archaeology, 1-34 Gordon Square, London, WC1H 0PY, UK.
Registered Seat Koning Albert II-laan 19 – bus 5, 1210 Brussels, Belgium.
URL: http://www.sachsensymposion.org/

History 1949, Cuxhaven (Germany). Former names and other names: *Arbeitsgemeinschaft für Sachsenforschung* – former (1949); *Study Group for Saxon Research* – former (1949); *Working Group for the Archaeology of the Saxons and their Neighbours in north-western Europe* – former. Registration: Belgium. **Aims** Study the history and ethnic origins of the Germanic Saxons. **Structure** General Meeting; Executive Council. **Activities** Events/meetings; research/documentation. **Events** *International Symposium* Stavanger (Norway) 2023, *International Symposium* Krakow (Poland) 2022, *International Symposium* Braunschweig (Germany) 2019, *International Symposium* Stockholm (Sweden) 2018.
Members Archaeologists and historians (about 180) in 11 countries:
Belgium, Denmark, Finland, France, Germany, Netherlands, Norway, Poland, Sweden, UK, USA. [2022/XM8328/c/**E**]

- **Internationales Sachsensymposion** Internationales Sachsensymposion – Arbeitsgemeinschaft zur Archäologie der Sachsen und ihrer Nachbarvölker in Nordwesteuropa (#13305)
- Internationales Schiedsgericht der Wirtschaftskammer Österreich / see Vienna International Arbitral Centre
- Internationales Seismologisches Zentrum (#14830)
- Internationales Sekretariat Christlicher Künstler / see International Society of Christian Artists (#15009)
- Internationales Sekretariat der Gewerkschaften für Kunst, Medien und Unterhaltung (inactive)
- Internationales Sekretariat katholischer Sekundarschullehrer / see SIESC – European Federation of Christian Teachers (#19267)
- International Essential Tremor Foundation (internationally oriented national body)
- Internationales Städteforum Graz (internationally oriented national body)
- Internationales Städteforum Graz – Forum der historischen Städte und Gemeinden / see International Forum of Towns and Villages in Graz
- Internationales Ständiges Büro der Automobilhersteller / see International Organization of Motor Vehicle Manufacturers (#14455)
- Internationales Ständiges Sekretariat der Sozialarbeiter / see International Federation of Social Workers (#13544)
- Internationales Statistisches Institut (#15603)
- Internationales Steuerdokumentationsbüro / see International Bureau of Fiscal Documentation (#12415)
- Internationales Studieninstitut des Mittelstandes (inactive)
- Internationales Studienzentrum für Religiöse Bildung und Erziehung (#12519)
- Internationales Symposium über Pflanzenschutz (meeting series)
- Internationale Städtereinigungskongresse (inactive)
- Internationale Standard-Buchnummer / see International ISBN Agency (#13955)
- Internationales Technisches Komitee für Vorbeugenden Brandschutz und Feuerlöschwesen / see CTIF International Association of Fire and Rescue Services (#04979)
- Internationale Stelle des Arbeiterbildungswesens (inactive)
- Internationales Terminologienetz (#14332)
- Internationale Stiftung Balzan Preis (#12309)
- Internationale Stiftung Zur Erhaltung der Fauna (#13667)
- Internationale Stiftung zur Erhaltung des Wildes / see International Foundation for the Conservation of Wildlife (#13667)

- ♦ Internationale Stiftung Hochalpine Forschungsstationen Jungfraujoch und Gornergrat (#13671)
- ♦ Internationale Stiftung Mozarteum / see Stiftung Mozarteum Salzburg
- ♦ Internationale Stiftung für Umwelt und Natur / see Global Nature Fund (#10479)
- ♦ Internationale Strassenteer Konferenz / see International Tar Association (#15655)
- ♦ Internationale Strassentransportunion (#14761)
- ♦ Internationales Treffen für Chemische Technik und Biotechnologie (meeting series)
- ♦ Internationales Treffen der Rechtsschutzversicherer / see Legal Protection International (#16440)
- ♦ International Estuarine Research Federation / see Coastal and Estuarine Research Federation
- ♦ Internationale Studiengemeinschaft für Pränatale Psychologie / see International Society for Pre- and Perinatal Psychology and Medicine (#15382)
- ♦ Internationale Studienkommission für Motorlosen Flug (inactive)
- ♦ Internationales Warnsystem für Arbeits- und Gesundheitsgefahren (inactive)
- ♦ Internationales Wasseramt (#14399)
- ♦ Internationales Weltbürger-Register / see Registre des Citoyens du Monde (#18822)
- ♦ Internationales Wissenschaftliches Komitee Alpenforschung (#14804)
- ♦ Internationales Wissenschaftliches Zentrum für Düngemittel (#03767)
- ♦ Internationales Wissenschaftsforum Bonn (internationally oriented national body)
- ♦ Internationales Woll-Sekretariat (inactive)
- ♦ Internationales Zentrum für Abfüll- und Verpackungstechnik (#15667)
- ♦ Internationales Zentrum für Ausbildungssysteme (#12487)
- ♦ Internationales Zentrum für Chormusik (internationally oriented national body)
- ♦ Internationales Zentrum für die Stadtgestaltung (#12520)
- ♦ Internationales Zentrum für Finanz-und Ökonomische Entwicklung, Moskau (internationally oriented national body)
- ♦ Internationales Zentrum für Glyptographische Forschungen (#03763)
- ♦ Internationales Zentrum für Kommunalkredit (#12501)
- ♦ Internationales Zentrum Wien (internationally oriented national body)
- ♦ Internationales Zentrum für Wissenschaftliche und Technische Information (#12514)
- ♦ Internationale Szondi-Gesellschaft (#15648)
- ♦ Internationale Tabakwissenschaftlichen Gesellschaft (inactive)
- ♦ Internationale Tagung der Historiker der Arbeiterbewegung / see International Conference of Labour and Social History (#12881)
- ♦ Internationale Tagung der Historikerinnen der Arbeiter- und Anderer Sozialer Bewegungen (#12881)
- ♦ Internationale Tagung der Historikerinnen und Historiker der Arbeiterinnen- und Arbeiterbewegung / see International Conference of Labour and Social History (#12881)
- ♦ International Etchells Class Association (see: #21760)
- ♦ Internationale Teerkonferenz / see International Tar Association (#15655)
- ♦ Internationale Teervereinigung (#15655)
- ♦ Internationale Textil-, Bekleidungs- und Lederarbeiter-Vereinigung (inactive)
- ♦ International Ethical Collegium / see Collegium International (#04112)
- ♦ International Ethical, Political and Scientific Collegium / see Collegium International (#04112)

♦ International Ethics Standards Board for Accountants (IESBA) 13306

Dir 529 5th Ave, New York NY 10017, USA. T. +12122869344.
URL: https://www.ethicsboard.org/

History Founded by *International Federation of Accountants (IFAC, #13335)* Board, as an independent standard-setting body under the auspices of IFAC and subject to the oversight of *Public Interest Oversight Board (PIOB, #18566)*. Registration: EU Transparency Register, No/ID: 769888947860-59, Start date: 7 Oct 2022. **Aims** Develop high-quality ethical standards and other pronouncements for professional accountants worldwide. **Structure** Board. **Finance** Sources: members' dues. Annual budget: 4,759,063 EUR (2021). **Activities** Events/meetings; standards/guidelines. [2022/AA0998/**E**]

♦ International Ethics Standards Coalition (IES Coalition) 13307

Chair c/o ICG, Leipziger Platz 9, 10117 Berlin, Germany.
URL: http://ies-coalition.org/

History Oct 2014, New York, NY (USA). Also known under the acronym *IESC*. Current Charter and by-laws adopted 2016. **Aims** Research, develop, publicize and implement International Ethics Standards (IES) for land, property, construction, infrastructure and related professions. **Structure** Board of Trustees; Standard Setting Committee. **Languages** English. **Staff** Voluntary. **Finance** Sources: contributions. No budget.
Members Supporters (around 150): Businesses; Academic bodies; Governmental and Regulatory bodies. Professional bodies and NGOs (over 130) in 44 countries and territories:
Australia, Belgium, Botswana, Brazil, Bulgaria, Canada, China, Colombia, Croatia, Cyprus, Czechia, Estonia, France, Germany, Ghana, Greece, Hong Kong, India, Indonesia, Ireland, Italy, Japan, Kenya, Lebanon, Malaysia, Morocco, Netherlands, New Zealand, Nigeria, Philippines, Poland, Romania, Russia, Senegal, Serbia, Singapore, South Africa, Spain, Switzerland, Thailand, Uganda, UK, United Arab Emirates, USA.
Included in the above, 16 organizations listed in this Yearbook:
Asian Association for Investors in Non-Listed Real Estate Vehicles (ANREV, #01327); Asia Pacific Real Assets Association (APREA, #02006); Association of International Property Professionals (AIPP); Commonwealth Association of Surveying and Land Economy (CASLE, #04313); Council of European Geodetic Surveyors (#04890); European Association for Investors in Non-listed Real Estate Vehicles (INREV, #06093); Fédération internationale des professions immobilières (FIABCI, #09653); International Consortium of Real Estate Associations (ICREA); International Cost Engineering Council (ICEC, #12976); International Facility Management Association (IFMA, #13325); International Federation of Surveyors (FIG, #13561); International Housing Coalition (IHC Global); International Right of Way Association (IRWA); International Society of City and Regional Planners (ISOCARP, #15012); International Valuation Standards Council (IVSC, #15840); Royal Institution of Chartered Surveyors (RICS, #18991). [2021/XM4444/y/**C**]

- ♦ International Ethnographic Bureau (inactive)
- ♦ International Ethnographic Institute (inactive)
- ♦ International Ethological Conference / see International Council of Ethologists (#13019)
- ♦ Internationale Tierärztliche Gesellschaft, Fachgebiet Schweine (#14584)
- ♦ Internationale Tierärztliche Vereinigung für Tierproduktion (inactive)
- ♦ Internationale Touristische Werbegemeinschaft – Die Donau (#05005)
- ♦ Internationale Transpersoonlijke Associatie (#15722)
- ♦ Internationale Transportarbeiter-Föderation (#15726)
- ♦ Internationale des travailleurs du bâtiment et du bois (#03355)
- ♦ Internationale des travailleurs de l'enseignement (inactive)
- ♦ Internationale des travailleurs de l'univers / see Industrial Workers of the World
- ♦ Internationale Unabhangige Universitat fur Okologie und Politilogie (internationally oriented national body)
- ♦ Internationale Unie van Gerechtsdeurwaarders en Gerechtelijke Officieren (#15785)
- ♦ Internationale Unie van Gezinsorganisaties / see World Family Organization (#21399)
- ♦ Internationale Unie van Verenigingen van Artsen-Automobilisten (no recent information)
- ♦ Internationale Unie der Verenigingen van Installateurs in Verwarming, Ventilatie en Luchtbehandeling (inactive)
- ♦ Internationale Union der Anthropologischen und Ethnologischen Wissenschaften / see International Union of Anthropological and Ethnological Sciences (#15755)
- ♦ Internationale Union der Bauzentren (#15761)
- ♦ Internationale Union der Berufskraftfahrer (#15802)
- ♦ Internationale Union für die Freiheit des Unterrichts (inactive)
- ♦ Internationale Union for Engros-Handelen med Blomster / see UNION FLEURS (#20408)
- ♦ Internationale Union der Ernährungswissenschaften (#15796)
- ♦ Internationale Union der Familienverbände / see World Family Organization (#21399)
- ♦ Internationale Union Gastgewerblicher Landesverbände (inactive)
- ♦ Internationale Union für Geologische Wissenschaften (#15777)
- ♦ Internationale Union der Gerichtsvollzieher und Gerichtlichen Beamten (#15785)
- ♦ Internationale Union der Gewerkschaften der Lebens- und Genussmittelbranchen / see International Union of Food, Agricultural, Hotel, Restaurant, Catering, Tobacco and Allied Workers Associations (#15772)
- ♦ Internationale Union für Grundstückbesteuerung und Freihandel / see International Union for Land Value Taxation and Free Trade (#15787)
- ♦ Internationale Union für Grundstückwertbesteuerung und Freihandel (#15787)
- ♦ Internationale Union der Handelsvertreter und Handelsmakler / see Internationally United Commercial Agents and Brokers (#14072)
- ♦ Internationale Union der Hotel-, Restaurant- und Café-Angestellten (inactive)
- ♦ Internationale Union Junger Christlicher Demokraten (inactive)
- ♦ Internationale Union der Kinofachverbände (inactive)
- ♦ Internationale Union der Kreditversicherer (#15767)
- ♦ Internationale Union für Kristallographie (#15768)
- ♦ Internationale Union der Lebens- und Genussmittelarbeiter-Gewerkschaften / see International Union of Food, Agricultural, Hotel, Restaurant, Catering, Tobacco and Allied Workers Associations (#15772)
- ♦ Internationale Union der Lebensmittel-, Landwirtschafts-, Hotel-, Restaurant-, Café- und Genussmittelarbeiter-Gewerkschaften (#15772)
- ♦ Internationale Union der Ledertechniker und -Chemiker Verbände (#15788)
- ♦ Internationale Union af Levneds- og Nydelsesmiddelarbejder-Forbund / see International Union of Food, Agricultural, Hotel, Restaurant, Catering, Tobacco and Allied Workers Associations (#15772)
- ♦ Internationale Union der Organisationen der Arbeiter und Arbeiterinnen der Lebens und Genussmittelindustrien / see International Union of Food, Agricultural, Hotel, Restaurant, Catering, Tobacco and Allied Workers Associations (#15772)
- ♦ Internationale Union für Reine und Angewandte Chemie (#15809)
- ♦ Internationale Union der Schuh Industrie Techniker / see Union internationale des techniciens de l'industrie de la chaussure (#20439)
- ♦ Internationale Union Sozialistischer Demokratischer Erzieher / see International Social Democratic Union for Education (#14881)
- ♦ Internationale Union für Speläologie (#15818)
- ♦ Internationale Union für Spenglerei and Sanitär Installation (inactive)
- ♦ Internationale Union zum Studium der Sozialen Insekten (#15819)
- ♦ Internationale Union für Theoretische und Angewandte Mechanik (#15823)
- ♦ Internationale Union der Touristik Manager (no recent information)
- ♦ Internationale Union für Vakuum-Forschung, -Technik und -Anwendung (#15826)
- ♦ Internationale Union von Verbänden der Privatgüterwagen-Besitzer / see International Union of Wagon Keepers (#15827)
- ♦ Internationale Union der Vereinigungen der Unternehmungen für Heizung, Lüftung und Luftklimatisierung (inactive)
- ♦ Internationale Union zur Wahrung der Sozialethik (inactive)
- ♦ Internationale Union der Widerstandsbewegungen und Deportierten (no recent information)
- ♦ Internationale Union des Zweirad-Handwers und -Handels (inactive)
- ♦ Internationale Universitäre Vereinigung des Weins under der Rebprodukte (unconfirmed)

♦ International Euphorbia Society (IES) 13308

Sec Gangwerf 11-A, 1676 GA Twisk, Netherlands.
Chairman Samuel Gerssenlaan 63, 3861 HB Nijkerk, Netherlands. E-mail: rikus@u4ba.nl.
URL: http://www.euphorbia-international.org/

History 2005, UK. **Aims** Advance *education, cultivation* and *conservation* of the species of the *plant* family *Euphorbiaceae* in general, and of the genus Euphorbia in particular. **Structure** General Meeting (annual); Committee; National Representatives (9). **Languages** English. **Staff** 3.50 FTE, voluntary. **Finance** Sources: members' dues. **Events** *Annual General meeting* Blankenberge (Belgium) 2022, *Annual General Meeting* Blankenberge (Belgium) 2017, *Annual General Meeting* Blankenberge (Belgium) 2016, *Annual General Meeting* Blankenberge (Belgium) 2015, *Symposium* Meise (Belgium) 2015. **Publications** *Euphorbia World* (3 a year) – journal.
Members Individuals and institutions in 24 countries and territories:
Australia, Austria, Belgium, Bolivia, Czechia, Denmark, France, Germany, Hungary, Italy, Japan, Kenya, Monaco, Netherlands, Peru, Poland, Réunion, Slovenia, South Africa, Spain, Switzerland, Türkiye, UK, USA. [2022/XM0262/**E**]

- ♦ International and EU Port Law Centre (internationally oriented national body)

♦ International Eurasia-Press Fund (IEPF) 13309

Chairman 1a M Huseyn Str, AZ 1006, AZ 370000 Baku, Azerbaijan. T. +994124397697. Fax +994124394915. E-mail: office@iepf-ngo.org.
URL: http://www.iepf-ngo.org/

History 22 Jun 1992, Azerbaijan. Registration: Azerbaijan. **Aims** Take active part in strengthening of civil society in the framework of collaboration with international organizations and intensify the role of *mass media* in this process; get true and objective information from the conflict zone and bring it to world community notice. Activity directions: Peacemaking Actions and Conflictology; Media and Civil society Development; Education; Refugees/IDPs problems and studying migration issues and Community Development. **Structure** Board. **Publications** Since 2005, in accordance with the Presidential Order on "Transition of Azerbaijan Literature from Cyril to Latin alphabet", the IEPF joined and more than 81 books were typed, edited and composed and published with more than 2 million circulation. **Consultative Status** Consultative status granted from: *ECOSOC (#05331)* (General); *UNEP (#20299)*. **NGO Relations** Member of (2): *European Council on Refugees and Exiles (ECRE, #06839); UNITED for Intercultural Action – European Network Against Nationalism, Racism, Fascism and in Support of Migrants and Refugees (UNITED, #20511).* Cooperates with (1): *United Nations Global Compact (#20567).* [2021.09.01/XG9038/f/**F**]

♦ International Euro-Asian Aikido Federation (IEAAF) 13310

Central Office Russian Fed, Naberezhnaya Obvodnogo kanala 123 b, St Petersburg SANKT-PETERBURG, Russia. T. +78123164847. Fax +78123871479. E-mail: feedback@aikido.ru.
URL: http://en.aikido.ru/

History 27 Oct 1990, as *USSR Aikido Federation*. Current title adopted 5 Jul 1995. **Aims** Protect common interests and achieve statutory goals and objectives aimed at the development and popularization of Aikido. **Activities** Offers public training courses for instructors; organizes seminars, festivals and sports events.
Members Full in 12 countries:
Azerbaijan, Belarus, Estonia, Georgia, Kazakhstan, Kyrgyzstan, Latvia, Lithuania, Moldova, Russia, Ukraine, Uzbekistan. [2012/XJ5136/**D**]

- ♦ International European Construction Federation / see European Construction Industry Federation (#06766)
- ♦ International/European Federation of Management and Professional Staff in the Chemical and Related Industries / see European Federation of Managerial Staff in the Chemical and Allied Industries (#07160)
- ♦ International and European Forum of Migration Research (internationally oriented national body)
- ♦ International European Movement / see European Movement International (#07825)
- ♦ International European Permanent Commission of Industrial Gases and Calcium Carbide / see European Industrial Gases Association (#07525)

♦ International and European Public Services Organisation (IPSO) ... 13311

Organisation der Beschäftigten bei europäischen und internationalen Einrichtungen in der Bundesrepublik Deutschland

SG Nistergasse 16, 60439 Frankfurt-Main, Germany.
URL: https://www.ipso.de/

History 11 Dec 1997, Germany. Founded by staff members of *European Central Bank (ECB, #06466).* Since 2008, officially recognized by ECB as staff union. **Aims** Represent the professional interests of persons working for the ECB and other international institutions and agencies in Germany. **Structure** Members' Assembly; Board. **NGO Relations** Member of (1): *Union Syndicale Fédérale (USF, #20485).* Affiliated with (1): *European Federation of Public Service Unions (EPSU, #07202).* [2022/AA2365/v/**E**]

♦ **International Europe Class Union (IECU)** **13312**

Pres La Balconada / Es Monestri, 17252 Calonge, Girona, Spain. T. +34972315100. Fax +34972315861. E-mail: president@europeclass.org.
Secretariat Box 10207, SE-434 23 Kungsbacka, Sweden. T. +4630018659. Fax +4630018659. E-mail: info@europeclass.org.
URL: http://www.europeclass.org/

Aims Promote and coordinate international Europe Class *yacht competition* throughout the world under uniform rules in cooperation with ISAF and national associations. **Events** *Annual General Assembly* Helsinki (Finland) 1986. **NGO Relations** International Class Association of: *World Sailing (#21760)*.
[2014.01.16/XE1597/**D**]

♦ Internationale Vegetarier Union (#15842)

♦ **International Eventing Officials Club (IEOC)** **13313**

SG Swan Farm, St Michaels-on-Wyre, Preston, PR3 0TT, UK. T. +447753910832.
URL: http://www.i-eoc.org/

History 1998. Statutes revised Mar 2009. **Aims** Provide a forum for communication between, and education of, members and a pooling of knowledge of the technical aspects of Eventing. **Structure** General Meeting (annual). Board, comprising Chairman, Vice-Chairman, Treasurer, Secretary-General and up to 5 members and 3 advisors. **Languages** English. **Staff** Voluntary. **Finance** Website sponsorship: euro 3,000 a year. **Events** *General Meeting* Stamford (UK) 2013, *Annual General Meeting / General Meeting* Stamford (UK) 2012. **Members** Individuals. Membership countries not specified. **NGO Relations** *Fédération Équestre Internationale (FEI, #09484)*.
[2013.06.14/XM3928/**E**]

♦ Internationale Verband des Bauwesens, des Städtebaus, der Umweltplanung und des Lebensbereichs (#11812)
♦ Internationale Verbindung für Schalentragwerke und Raumtragwerke (#12162)
♦ Internationale Verbindungsstelle der Stickerei-, Gardinen- und Spitzenindustrie (inactive)
♦ Internationale Vereeniging voor Financieel en Fiscal Recht / see International Fiscal Association (#13608)
♦ Internationale Vereinigung der Agrarrmuseen (#02720)
♦ Internationale Vereinigung für Ambulante Chirurgie (#11698)
♦ Internationale Vereinigung der Anschlussgeleise-Benützer / see Cargo Rail Europe (#03431)
♦ Internationale Vereinigung Anthroposophischer Apotheker (internationally oriented national body)

♦ **Internationale Vereinigung Anthroposophischer Ärztegesellschaften (IVAA)** **13314**

Fédération internationale des associations médicales anthroposophiques – International Federation of Anthroposophical Medical Associations

SG Rue du Trône 194, 1050 Brussels, Belgium. T. +3226440022. E-mail: contact@ivaa.info.
URL: http://www.ivaa.info/

History 1993. Former names and other names: *International Association of Anthroposophic Physicians* – former. **Aims** Represent anthroposophic medicine worldwide with respect to political-legal affairs. **Structure** Board. **Languages** English, French, German. **Staff** 3.00 FTE, paid. **Finance** Sources: grants; members' dues; revenue from activities/projects. **Activities** Advocacy/lobbying/activism; networking/liaising; politics/policy/regulatory; training/education. **Publications** *The System of Anthroposophic Medicine*.
Members Organizations in 37 countries and territories:
Argentina, Australia, Austria, Belgium, Brazil, Canada, Chile, Colombia, Czechia, Denmark, Ecuador, Estonia, Finland, France, Georgia, Germany, Hungary, India, Italy, Japan, Latvia, Netherlands, New Zealand, Norway, Peru, Philippines, Poland, Romania, Russia, Serbia, Spain, Sweden, Switzerland, Taiwan, UK, Uruguay, USA.
NGO Relations Member of (4): *Alliance ELIANT (#00672)*; *CAMDOC Alliance (#03402)*; *EUROCAM (#05653)*; *European Public Health Alliance (EPHA, #08297)*.
[2021.06.08/XD8601/**D**]

♦ Internationale Vereinigung der arabischen Ubersetzer und Sprachwissenschaftler (#21118)
♦ Internationale Vereinigung der Arbeiter der Bau-, Holz- und Baumaterialienindustrie (#20185)
♦ Internationale Vereinigung für Arbeitsinspektion (#11983)
♦ Internationale Vereinigung Ärztlicher Kraftfahrer-Verbände (no recent information)
♦ Internationale Vereinigung für Ästhetik (#11692)
♦ Internationale Vereinigung für Ausbildung und Personalentwicklung (inactive)
♦ Internationale Vereinigung für Balneologie und Klimatologie / see Fédération mondiale du thermalisme et du climatisme (#09692)
♦ Internationale Vereinigung zur Beförderung und zum Schutz Privater Ausländischer Investitionen (inactive)
♦ Internationale Vereinigung Beratender Ingenieure (#13399)
♦ Internationale Vereinigung der Bergführerverbände (#15756)
♦ Internationale Vereinigung der Bibliotheken Technischer Hochschulen / see International Association of University Libraries (#12247)
♦ Internationale Vereinigung der Bild-Text-Verarbeitung (inactive)

♦ **Internationale Vereinigung für binokulares Sehen (IVBS)** **13315**

International Association for Binocular Vision

Office Bergstr 10, 65558 Flacht, Germany. T. +496432920320. Fax +496432920321. E-mail: info@ivbs.org.
URL: http://www.ivbs.org/

History Statutes amended: July 2012; May 2020. Registration: Swiss Civil Code, Switzerland. **Aims** Promote the uniform and correct application of the Measuring and Correcting Methodology (MKH). **Structure** Board; Presidium. **Finance** Sources: members' dues. **Events** *Annual Congress* Mainz (Germany) 2021, *Annual Congress* Koblenz (Germany) 2014.
[2022.02.24/XJ7767/**D**]

♦ Internationale Vereinigung Biologischer Landbaubewegungen / see IFOAM – Organics International (#11105)
♦ Internationale Vereinigung Biologischer Landwirtschaftsbewegungen / see IFOAM – Organics International (#11105)
♦ Internationale Vereinigung des Bobsleigh und Rodelsportes / see International Bobsleigh and Skeleton Federation (#12375)
♦ Internationale Vereinigung für Brückenbau und Hochbau (#11737)
♦ Internationale Vereinigung für Chemiefasernormen (#03369)

♦ **Internationale Vereinigung Christlicher Geschäftsleute (IVCG)** **13316**

Association internationale des hommes d'affaires chrétiens – Christian Business Men's Association International

Pres Postfach 1330, 58653 Hemer, Germany. T. +492372555400. Fax +4972221047579. E-mail: mail@ivcg.org.
URL: http://www.ivcg.org/

History 1957, Zurich (Switzerland). **Activities** Events/meetings. **Events** *Crisis as an opportunity* Pforzheim (Germany) 2004, *Meeting* Feldkirch (Austria) 1996, *Congress* Vienna (Austria) 1996, *Congress* Noordwijkerhout (Netherlands) 1988. **Publications** *Geschäftsmann und Christ* (10 a year).
Members Individuals in 6 countries:
Austria, Belgium, France, Germany, Liechtenstein, Switzerland.
[2022/XN3141/**F**]

♦ Internationale Vereinigung für Cybernetik (inactive)
♦ Internationale Vereinigung Demokratischer Juristen (#11837)
♦ Internationale Vereinigung für die Entwicklung des Handelsverkehrs (inactive)
♦ Internationale Vereinigung für die Farbe (#12655)
♦ Internationale Vereinigung für die Geschichte des Glases (#02706)
♦ Internationale Vereinigung für die Pflegekennzeichnung von Textilien (#10761)
♦ Internationale Vereinigung gegen die Politische Verwendung der Psychiatrie / see Human Rights in Mental Health (#10988)
♦ Internationale Vereinigung für die technische Prüfung von Kraftfahrzeugen / see International Motor Vehicle Inspection Committee (#14187)
♦ Internationale Vereinigung der Dokumentalisten und Spezialisten der Information (inactive)
♦ Internationale Vereinigung der Ehemaligen Angehörigen der Europäischen Gemeinschaften / see Association internationale des anciens de l'Union Européenne (#02667)
♦ Internationale Vereinigung des Ehemaligen Beamten und Bediensteten von EUROCONTROL / see Association internationale des anciens d'EUROCONTROL (#02666)
♦ Internationale Vereinigung der Ehemaligen Bediensteten Europäischen Union (#02667)
♦ Internationale Vereinigung der Ehemaligen Kriegsgefangenen (inactive)
♦ Internationale Vereinigung für Einkauf (inactive)
♦ Internationale Vereinigung für Einkauf und Materialwirtschaft / see International Federation of Purchasing and Supply Management (#13525)
♦ Internationale Vereinigung von Einkaufs- und Marketingverbänden (inactive)
♦ Internationale Vereinigung der Eisenbahner-Funkamateure (#12122)
♦ Internationale Vereinigung der Eisenbahnjournalisten (no recent information)
♦ Internationale Vereinigung der Eisenwaren- und Eisenhändlerverbände / see International Federation of Hardware and Housewares Associations (#13437)
♦ Internationale Vereinigung der Erfinder-Verbände (#13461)
♦ Internationale Vereinigung zur Erforschung der Qualität von Nahrungspflanzen (inactive)
♦ Internationale Vereinigung von Erziehern Gefährdeter Jugend / see International Association of Social Educators (#12167)
♦ Internationale Vereinigung der Erziehungsgemeinschaften / see Fédération internationale des communautés éducatives (#09622)
♦ Internationale Vereinigung 'Europa 2000' (inactive)
♦ Internationale Vereinigung Europäischer Rübenanbauer (#12860)
♦ Internationale Vereinigung für Europarecht (#13419)
♦ Internationale Vereinigung von Fachkräften und Verbänden zu Schwangerschaftsabbruch und Kontrazeption (#09612)
♦ Internationale Vereinigung des Feuerwehr- und Rettungswesen CTIF (#04979)
♦ Internationale Vereinigung der Filialbetriebe / see The Consumer Goods Forum (#04772)
♦ Internationale Vereinigung von Finanzwirtschaftler-Instituten (#11890)
♦ Internationale Vereinigung zur Förderung des Studiums der Hegelschen Philosophie (#13247)
♦ Internationale Vereinigung der Forschungsinstitute für Verpackung (#12063)
♦ Internationale Vereinigung der Freidenker (#11906)
♦ Internationale Vereinigung Freier Lehrergewerkschaften (inactive)
♦ Internationale Vereinigung für Friedensforschung (#14537)
♦ Internationale Vereinigung der Friedensgesellschaften (inactive)
♦ Internationale Vereinigung der Geigenbau- und Bogenmacher-Meister (#15542)

♦ **Internationale Vereinigung für Germanistik (IVG)** **13317**

Association internationale des germanistes – International Association for Germanic Studies

Contact Dipto di Scienze Umanistiche, Univ degli Studi di Palermo, Viale delle Scienze – Ed 12, 90128 Palermo PA, Italy. E-mail: ivg2020@unipa.it.
URL: http://ivg2020.unipa.it/

History 1951, Florence (Italy). Previously also referred to as *Association internationale des langues et littératures germaniques*. **Aims** Support international cooperation of the members in teaching and research; organize international congresses. **Structure** President, 2 Vice-Presidents and 20 members. **Languages** Afrikaans, Danish, Dutch, Finnish, German, Germanic languages, Icelandic, Norwegian, Swedish, Yiddish. **Finance** Contributions; subsidies for congress and publications. **Events** *Quinquennial Congress* Palermo (Italy) 2021, *Quinquennial Congress* Palermo (Italy) 2020, *Quinquennial Congress* Shanghai (China) 2015, *Quinquennial Congress* Warsaw (Poland) 2010, *Quinquennial Congress* Paris (France) 2005. **Publications** *Jahrbuch für Internationale Germanistik*. Congress proceedings.
Members Individuals (about 1,900) in 51 countries and territories:
Algeria, Argentina, Australia, Austria, Belgium, Brazil, Bulgaria, Canada, China, Croatia, Czechia, Denmark, Egypt, Finland, France, Germany, Hungary, India, Iran Islamic Rep, Ireland, Israel, Italy, Japan, Korea Rep, Latvia, Luxembourg, Mexico, Montenegro, Morocco, Netherlands, New Zealand, Norway, Poland, Portugal, Romania, Russia, Serbia, Slovakia, Slovenia, South Africa, Spain, Sweden, Switzerland, Taiwan, Thailand, Togo, Tunisia, Türkiye, UK, Ukraine, USA.
[2020.03.03/XD3855/v/**C**]

♦ Internationale Vereinigung von Gesellschaften für Chirurgie (#13560)
♦ Internationale Vereinigung der Gesellschaften für den Kombinierten Verkehr Schiene-Strasse (#15765)
♦ Internationale Vereinigung für Gewerblichen Rechtsschutz / see International Association for the Protection of Intellectual Property (#12112)
♦ Internationale Vereinigung der Gewerkschaften der Chemischen, Erdöl- und Artverwandten Industrien (inactive)
♦ Internationale Vereinigung der Gewerkschaften der Werktätigen der Metallindustrie (inactive)
♦ Internationale Vereinigung der Gewerkschaften der Werktätigen des Öffentlichen Dienstes und Verwandter Berufe (#20191)
♦ Internationale Vereinigung der Glatzenträger (no recent information)
♦ Internationale Vereinigung der Glukoseindustrien (inactive)
♦ Internationale Vereinigung des Gross- und Aussenhandels (inactive)
♦ Internationale Vereinigung der Hagelversicherer / see Association internationale des assureurs de la production agricole (#02671)
♦ Internationale Vereinigung des Handels (#11851)
♦ Internationale Vereinigung der Hersteller von Aluminium-Aerosoldosen (#14437)
♦ Internationale Vereinigung der Hersteller und Verarbeiteiz von Selbstklebenden und Heissiegelfähigen und andere Stoffen / see FINAT (#09773)
♦ Internationale Vereinigung der Huckepackgesellschaften / see International Union for Combined Road – Rail Transport (#15765)
♦ Internationale Vereinigung für Individualpsychologie (#11960)
♦ Internationale Vereinigung der Ingenieur-Agronomen (inactive)
♦ Internationale Vereinigung Interaktionen der Psychoanalyse (#11968)
♦ Internationale Vereinigung für Jugendhilfe (inactive)
♦ Internationale Vereinigung von Jungen Landwirten (#15829)
♦ Internationale Vereinigung Junger Rechtsanwälte (#12282)
♦ Internationale Vereinigung für Kakao und Schokolade (inactive)
♦ Internationale Vereinigung Katholischer Apotheker (#13380)
♦ Internationale Vereinigung Katholischer Männer (#20720)
♦ Internationale Vereinigung für Kinderhilfe (inactive)
♦ Internationale Vereinigung der Klein- und Mittelbetriebe des Handels (inactive)
♦ Internationale Vereinigung der Klein- und Mittelbetriebe der Industrie (inactive)
♦ Internationale Vereinigung für Kognitives Lernen / see International Association for Cognitive Education and Psychology (#11782)
♦ Internationale Vereinigung für Kommunikationswissenschaft (inactive)
♦ Internationale Vereinigung zur Krebsbekämpfung (#20415)
♦ Internationale Vereinigung der Kriegswaisen (inactive)
♦ Internationale Vereinigung für Kunstunterricht, Zeichnen und Angewandte Kunst (inactive)
♦ Internationale Vereinigung für Landentwicklung (inactive)
♦ Internationale Vereinigung für Landwirtschaftskredit (#04560)
♦ Internationale Vereinigung Lehrergewerkschaften (#09662)
♦ Internationale Vereinigung der Lehrer an Öffentlichen Höheren Schulen (inactive)
♦ Internationale Vereinigung der Leprahilfswerke / see International Federation of Anti-Leprosy Associations (#13355)
♦ Internationale Vereinigung der Lions-Club / see Lions Clubs International (#16485)
♦ Internationale Vereinigung für Literatur und Kunst (#14058)

- ♦ Internationale Vereinigung der Mikrobiologischen Gesellschaften (#15794)
- ♦ Internationale Vereinigung für Missionswissenschaft (#12032)
- ♦ Internationale Vereinigung der Motoreninstandsetzungsbetriebe (#09654)
- ♦ Internationale Vereinigung der Musikbibliotheken / see International Association of Music Libraries, Archives and Documentation Centres (#12042)
- ♦ Internationale Vereinigung der Musikbibliotheken, Musikarchive und Musikdokumentationszentren (#12042)
- ♦ Internationale Vereinigung für Mutterschutz und Sexualreform (inactive)
- ♦ Internationale Vereinigung von Nahrungsmittel Import- und Grosshandelsverbänden (inactive)
- ♦ Internationale Vereinigung der Nationalen Briefmarkenhändelverbände / see International Federation of Stamp Dealers' Associations (#13557)
- ♦ Internationale Vereinigung für Neuere Sprachen und Literaturen (#13480)
- ♦ Internationale Vereinigung der Öffentlichen Pfandkreditanstalten (inactive)
- ♦ Internationale Vereinigung für Ökologie (#11856)
- ♦ Internationale Vereinigung von Organisationen der Lebensmittel-Detaillanten (inactive)
- ♦ Internationale Vereinigung Papyrologen (#02725)
- ♦ Internationale Vereinigung der Pfadfinderschaft Europas / see Union Internationale des Guides et Scouts d'Europe – Fédération du Scoutisme Européen (#20426)
- ♦ Internationale Vereinigung der Pharmaberater-Verbände (#15791)
- ♦ Internationale Vereinigung Philosophischer Gesellschaften (#13507)
- ♦ Internationale Vereinigung für Prozessrecht (#12102)
- ♦ Internationale Vereinigung Psychoanalytischer Gesellschaften (#13522)
- ♦ Internationale Vereinigung gegen Qualvolle Tierversuche (#11694)
- ♦ Internationale Vereinigung der Rauhfutter-, Fourage-, und Torfhändler (no recent information)
- ♦ Internationale Vereinigung für das Recht des Kindes zu Spielen (#14604)
- ♦ Internationale Vereinigung für Rechtshilfe (inactive)
- ♦ Internationale Vereinigung der Rechtsschutz-Versicherung / see Legal Protection International (#16440)

♦ Internationale Vereinigung für Rechts- und Sozialphilosophie (IVR) 13318

Association internationale de philosophie du droit et de philosophie sociale – International Association for Philosophy of Law and Social Philosophy

SG address not obtained.
Pres address not obtained.
URL: https://ivronlineblog.wordpress.com

History 1 Oct 1909, Berlin (Germany). Statutes: adopted 26 Aug 1987; amended 24 Aug 1991, 15 Aug 2003. Registration: Germany. **Aims** Cultivate and promote *legal* and *social philosophy* at national and international level. **Structure** General Assembly (every 4 years); Executive Committee; National Sections. **Languages** English, French, German, Spanish. **Staff** 4.00 FTE, voluntary. **Finance** Sources: members' dues. Annual budget: 10,000 USD. **Activities** Awards/prizes/competitions; events/meetings. **Events** *World Congress* Buenos Aires (Argentina) 2023, *World Congress* Bucharest (Romania) 2022, *World Congress* Bucharest (Romania) 2021, *World Congress* Lucerne (Switzerland) 2019, *World Congress* Lisbon (Portugal) 2017. **Publications** *Archives for Philosophy of Law and Social Philosophy* (4 a year) in English, French, German, Spanish; *IVR Newsletter* (2 a year).
Members Full individual scholars and specialists; Supporting associations, federations, institutions, libraries and other bodies. Members in 46 countries and territories:
Argentina, Australia, Austria, Belgium, Brazil, Bulgaria, Canada, Chile, China, Colombia, Czechia, Denmark, Finland, France, Germany, Greece, Honduras, Hungary, Iceland, India, Israel, Italy, Japan, Korea Rep, Lebanon, Lithuania, Mexico, Netherlands, New Zealand, Norway, Poland, Romania, Russia, Serbia, Slovakia, Slovenia, South Africa, Spain, Sweden, Switzerland, Taiwan, Türkiye, UK, Ukraine, USA, Venezuela.
IGO Relations *UNESCO (#20322)*. **NGO Relations** Instrumental in setting up: *European Association for the Teaching of Legal Theory (EATLT, #06250)*. [2021/XC1222/**C**]

- ♦ Internationale Vereinigung für Reine und Angewandte Biophysik (#15808)
- ♦ Internationale Vereinigung für Religionsgeschichte (#11936)
- ♦ Internationale Vereinigung des Rheinschiffsregisters / see International Association for the Representation of the Mutual Interests of the Inland Shipping and the Insurance and for Keeping the Register of Inland Vessels in Europe (#12131)
- ♦ Internationale Vereinigung der Richter (#11978)
- ♦ Internationale Vereinigung der Rugby Amateur / see Rugby Europe (#18998)
- ♦ Internationale Vereinigung für Saatgutprüfung / see International Seed Testing Association (#14829)
- ♦ Internationale Vereinigung der Schallarchive / see International Association of Sound and Audiovisual Archives (#12172)
- ♦ Internationale Vereinigung der Schall- und Audiovisuellen Archive (#12172)
- ♦ Internationale Vereinigung Schmuck, Silberwaren, Diamanten, Perlen und Steine (#03923)
- ♦ Internationale Vereinigung für Schul- und Berufsberatung (#11862)
- ♦ Internationale Vereinigung für den Schutz des geistigen Eigentums (#12112)
- ♦ Internationale Vereinigung für Selbstmordprophylaxe / see International Association for Suicide Prevention and Crisis Intervention (#12213)
- ♦ Internationale Vereinigung für Selbstmordprophylaxe und Krisenintervention (#12213)
- ♦ Internationale Vereinigung für Semiotik (#12160)
- ♦ Internationale Vereinigung der Senioren Universitäten (#02749)
- ♦ Internationale Vereinigung der Sicherheitsingenieure, Sicherheitsdienste und Betriebsärzte (no recent information)
- ♦ Internationale Vereinigung der Ski-Journalisten (#02710)
- ♦ Internationale Vereinigung für Sozialen Fortschritt (inactive)
- ♦ Internationale Vereinigung für Soziale Sicherheit (#14885)
- ♦ Internationale Vereinigung Sozialistischer Ärzte (inactive)
- ♦ Internationale Vereinigung für Soziologie (#15553)
- ♦ Internationale Vereinigung der Sportanwälte (#15591)

♦ Internationale Vereinigung Sport- und Freizeiteinrichtungen (IAKS) 13319

Association internationale équipements de sport et de loisirs – Asociación Internacional para Instalaciones Deportivas y Recreativas – International Association for Sports and Leisure Facilities

SG Eupener Str 70, 50933 Cologne, Germany. T. +492211680230. Fax +4922116802323. E-mail: info@iaks.sport – sb@iaks.sport.
Main Website: http://www.iaks.sport

History May 1965, Cologne (Germany). Statutes amended: 1973, Cologne (Germany FR); 1989, Cologne (Germany FR); 2003, Cologne (Germany). Former names and other names: *International Working Group for the Construction of Sports and Leisure Facilities* – former; *Groupe international de travail pour les équipements de sport et de loisirs* – former; *Grupo Internacional de Trabajo para Instalaciones Deportivas y Recreativas* – former; *Internationaler Arbeitskreis Sport- und Freizeitbauten* – former. Registration: Register of Associations, No/ID: 5754, Germany, Cologne. **Aims** Champion for sustainable and high-quality indoor and outdoor sports and leisure facilities that are fully inclusive, universally accessible and socially relevant. **Structure** General Assembly (every 2 years); Executive Board. **Languages** English, French, German, Spanish. **Staff** 5.00 FTE, paid. **Finance** Sources: meeting proceeds; members' dues; sale of publications; sponsorship; subscriptions. **Activities** Awards/prizes/competitions; events/meetings; knowledge management/information dissemination; networking/liaising. **Events** *Congress* Cologne (Germany) 2023, *Congress* Cologne (Germany) 2021, *International Swimming Pool Conference* Asker (Norway) 2020, *Artificial Ice Rinks Management Conference* Krefeld (Germany) 2020, *Congress* Cologne (Germany) 2019. **Publications** *sb – International Magazine for Sports, Leisure and Recreational Facilities* (6 a year) in English, German; *E-mail Newsletter* (26 a year). Congress reports; manuals.
Members Full: Individual; Association; Associate. Members in 93 countries and territories:
Afghanistan, Algeria, Argentina, Australia, Austria, Bahamas, Barbados, Belgium, Bermuda, Brazil, Cambodia, Cameroon, Canada, Chad, Chile, China, Colombia, Costa Rica, Côte d'Ivoire, Croatia, Cyprus, Denmark, Ecuador, Egypt, Eswatini, Fiji, Finland, France, Germany, Ghana, Greece, Guyana, Haiti, Honduras, Hong Kong, Hungary, Iceland, India, Indonesia, Ireland, Israel, Italy, Japan, Jordan, Kazakhstan, Kenya, Korea Rep, Latvia, Luxembourg, Malawi, Malaysia, Moldova, Monaco, Mongolia, Morocco, Myanmar, Namibia, Nepal, Netherlands, Niger, Norway, Pakistan, Papua New Guinea, Paraguay, Peru, Philippines, Poland, Portugal, Puerto Rico, Romania, Russia, Saudi Arabia, Senegal, Serbia, Singapore, Slovenia, Spain, Suriname, Sweden, Switzerland, Taiwan, Tanzania UR, Thailand, Togo, Trinidad-Tobago, Tunisia, Uganda, UK, Uruguay, USA, Uzbekistan, Venezuela.
Consultative Status Consultative status granted from: *ECOSOC (#05331)* (Ros A). **IGO Relations** *UNESCO (#20322)*. **NGO Relations** Member of (1): *Olympic Movement (#17719)*. Recognized by: *International Olympic Committee (IOC, #14408)*. Cooperation agreement with: *The Association for International Sport for All (TAFISA, #02763)*; *International Paralympic Committee (IPC, #14512)*. [2022.10.11/XB4245/**B**]

- ♦ Internationale Vereinigung für Sportrecht (#12180)
- ♦ Internationale Vereinigung Sprache und Wirtschaft (#11987)
- ♦ Internationale Vereinigung Städtebau und Handel (#12232)
- ♦ Internationale Vereinigung für Steuerrecht (#13608)
- ♦ Internationale Vereinigung der Stiftungen Raoul Follereau / see Raoul Follereau International Union (#18618)
- ♦ Internationale Vereinigung für Strafrecht (#12074)
- ♦ Internationale Vereinigung der Studierenden an Instituten für Übersetzer- und Dolmetscherausbildung (no recent information)
- ♦ Internationale Vereinigung zum Studium der Tone (#02688)
- ♦ Internationale Vereinigung für das Studium der Versicherungswirtschaft / see Geneva Association (#10119)
- ♦ Internationale Vereinigung für Südosteuropäische Studien (#02693)
- ♦ Internationale Vereinigung der Superphosphat-Fabrikanten / see International Fertilizer Association (#13589)
- ♦ Internationale Vereinigung des Tapetenhandels (inactive)
- ♦ Internationale Vereinigung der Technischen Versicherer (#11874)
- ♦ Internationale Vereinigung der Textilarbeiter (inactive)
- ♦ Internationale Vereinigung der Textilindustrie (#15679)
- ♦ Internationale Vereinigung für Thalasso-Therapie (no recent information)
- ♦ Internationale Vereinigung für Theoretische und Angewandte Limnologie / see International Society of Limnology (#15232)
- ♦ Internationale Vereinigung der Toto- und Lotto-Gesellschaften (inactive)
- ♦ Internationale Vereinigung von Touristischen Mittelpunkten (inactive)
- ♦ Internationale Vereinigung Unabhängiger Laboratorien (#20429)
- ♦ Internationale Vereinigung der Verbände des Stahl-, Stahlrohr- und Metall-Handels (inactive)
- ♦ Internationale Vereinigung der Vermessungsingenieure (#13561)
- ♦ Internationale Vereinigung der Versicherer der Landwirtschaftlichen Produktion (#02671)
- ♦ Internationale Vereinigung der Versicherungsgesellschaften auf Gegenseitigkeit (inactive)
- ♦ Internationale Vereinigung für Versicherungsrecht (#02684)
- ♦ Internationale Vereinigung der Verteilung von Lebensmitteln und Gebrauchsgütern / see International Association for the Distributive Trade (#11851)
- ♦ Internationale Vereinigung der Verwaltungsschulen und -institute (#12147)
- ♦ Internationale Vereinigung der Veterinäranatomen / see World Association of Veterinary Anatomists (#21202)
- ♦ Internationale Vereinigung der Waffen- und Militärhistorischen Museen / see International Committee of Museums and Collections of Arms and Military History (#12790)
- ♦ Internationale Vereinigung zur Wahrnehmung der Gemeinsamen Interessen der Binnenschiffahrt und der Versicherung und zur Führung des Binnenschiffsregisters in Europa (#12131)
- ♦ Internationale Vereinigung der Waldorfkindergärten / see International Association for Steiner/Waldorf Early Childhood Education (#12185)
- ♦ Internationale Vereinigung für Walsertum (#12262)
- ♦ Internationale Vereinigung für Wirtschaftswissenschaften (#13222)
- ♦ Internationale Vereinigung für Wissenschaftlichen Film (inactive)
- ♦ Internationale Vereinigung zum Wissenschaftlichen Studium der Geistigen Zurückgebliebenheit / see International Association for the Scientific Study of Intellectual and Developmental Disabilities (#12153)
- ♦ Internationale Vereinigung zum Wissenschaftlichen Studium von Intelligenzstörungen / see International Association for the Scientific Study of Intellectual and Developmental Disabilities (#12153)
- ♦ Internationale Vereinigung Wissenschaftlicher Fremdenverkehrsexperten (#02697)
- ♦ Internationale Vereinigung für Wissenschaft der Politik (#14615)
- ♦ Internationale Vereinigung für Wohnungsbauwissenschaften (#11943)
- ♦ Internationale Vereinigung der Zuckerwarenfabrikanten (inactive)
- ♦ Internationale Vereniging van Afrikaanse Jongeren (unconfirmed)
- ♦ Internationale Vereniging van de Animatiefilm (#02698)
- ♦ Internationale Vereniging voor de Behartiging van de Gemeenschappelijke Belangen van de Binnenvaart en de Verzekering en voor het Houden van het Register van Binnenschepen in Europa (#12131)
- ♦ Internationale Vereniging voor Belastingrecht (#13608)
- ♦ Internationale Vereniging van Europese Scouts en Gidsen / see Union Internationale des Guides et Scouts d'Europe – Fédération du Scoutisme Européen (#20426)
- ♦ Internationale Vereniging van de Industriële Bakkerijen (#02674)
- ♦ Internationale Vereniging van Jonge Advokaten (#12282)
- ♦ Internationale Vereniging van de Kaalhoofdigers (no recent information)
- ♦ Internationale Vereniging voor Maritieme Geneeskunde (#14099)
- ♦ Internationale Vereniging voor Neerlandistiek (#11854)
- ♦ Internationale Vereniging van Oorlogswezen (inactive)
- ♦ Internationale vereniging voor Otto Gross studies (#12060)
- ♦ Internationale Vereniging van Oud-Personeelsleden van EUROCONTROL / see Association internationale des anciens d'EUROCONTROL (#02666)
- ♦ Internationale Vereniging van Oudpersoneelsleden van de Europese Gemeenschappen / see Association internationale des anciens de l'Union Européenne (#02667)
- ♦ Internationale Vereniging voor Plattelandsontwikkeling (inactive)
- ♦ Internationale Vereniging van de Rechtsbijstandverzekering / see Legal Protection International (#16440)
- ♦ Internationale Vereniging het Rijnschepenregister / see International Association for the Representation of the Mutual Interests of the Inland Shipping and the Insurance and for Keeping the Register of Inland Vessels in Europe (#12131)
- ♦ Internationale Vereniging van Somatotherapie (no recent information)
- ♦ Internationale Vereniging voor Spina Bifida en Hydrocephalus (#13552)
- ♦ Internationale Vereniging voor Sportrecht (#12180)
- ♦ Internationale Vereniging Trappist (#15727)
- ♦ Internationale Vereniging voor Voortgezet Tandheelkunding Onderwijs (inactive)
- ♦ Internationale Vereniging van Vrije Gedachte (#11906)
- ♦ Internationale Vereniging van Wapen- en Militair-Historische Musea / see International Committee of Museums and Collections of Arms and Military History (#12790)
- ♦ Internationale Verkehrssicherheitsorganisation (#18493)
- ♦ Internationale Verleger-Union (#14675)
- ♦ Internationale Verzekeringsbibliotheek (internationally oriented national body)
- ♦ Internationale Viola-Gesellschaft / see International Viola Society (#15855)

♦ **International Evoked Response Audiometry Study Group (IERASG) . 13320**
Chair MRC Inst of Hearing Research, Royal South Hants Hosp, Southampton, SO14 0YG, UK. T. +442380637946. Fax +442380825611.
URL: http://www.ierasg.ifps.org.pl/
History 1968. Former names and other names: *ERA Club* – former (1968 to 1970); *International Electric Response Audiometry Study Group* – former (1970 to 1993). **Aims** Provide an open forum for the discussion of *physiological* signals generated within the *auditory* system. **Structure** Officers: Chairman; Vice-Chairman; Treasurer; Secretary; Newsletter Editor; Membership Secretary. **Languages** English. **Staff** Voluntary. **Finance** Members' dues. **Events** *Biennial Symposium* 2021, *Biennial symposium* Sydney, NSW (Australia) 2019, *Biennial Symposium* Busan (Korea Rep) 2015, *Biennial Symposium* New Orleans, LA (USA) 2013, *Biennial Symposium* Moscow (Russia) 2011. **Publications** *IERASG Newsletter*. **Members** Full in 70 countries. Membership countries not specified. [2022/XE3665/**E**]

♦ Internationale Volksbankenvereinigung (#12867)
♦ Internationale Vredesinformatiedienst (internationally oriented national body)
♦ Internationale Vrijmetselaars Unie (#14113)
♦ Internationale Waggonbauvereinigung (inactive)
♦ Internationale Wernicke-Kleist-Leonhard Gesellschaft (#15878)
♦ Internationale Wissenschaftliche Esperanto-Organisation (#13301)
♦ Internationale Wissenschaftliche Vereinigung Weltwirtschaft und Weltpolitik (internationally oriented national body)
♦ Internationale Wochenschau Vereinigung (no recent information)
♦ Internationale Wollvereinigung (#15904)
♦ International Exchange Committee (inactive)
♦ International Exchange Promotion Association (internationally oriented national body)
♦ International Executive Development Centre, Brdo / see IEDC – Bled School of Management
♦ International Executive Development Centre, Kranj / see IEDC – Bled School of Management

♦ **International Executive Search Federation (IESF) 13321**
Global Headquarters Amersfoortsestraat 78 c, 3769 AL Soesterberg, Netherlands. E-mail: info@iesf.com.
URL: http://www.iesf.com/
History 2002. **Aims** Deliver talented leadership as the international executive search partner with global knowledge and reach for clients in emerging and mature markets. **Structure** General Meeting (annual); Leadership Council. **Activities** Events/meetings. **Events** *Annual Global Meeting* Soesterberg (Netherlands) 2020, *Annual Global Meeting* Montréal, QC (Canada) 2019. **Members** Full in 23 countries. Membership countries not specified. [2020.03.11/XM7709/**C**]

♦ International Executive Service Corps (internationally oriented national body)
♦ International Exhibition Logistics Associates / see International Exhibition Logistics Association (#13322)

♦ **International Exhibition Logistics Association (IELA) 13322**
Exec Dir c/o TQ Consulting, Lindenhof 6, 6060 Sarnen OW, Switzerland. T. +41416611781. Fax +41416611719. E-mail: adminiela@iela.org.
Registered Address 4 rue Charles-Bonnet, Box 399, 1211 Geneva 12, Switzerland.
URL: http://www.iela.org/
History 1985, Geneva (Switzerland), as *International Exhibition Logistics Associates (IELA)*. Since 2012, registered in accordance with Swiss Civil Code, when new title was also adopted. **Aims** Provide a forum for people and companies engaged in international transportation of exhibition material. **Structure** General Assembly (annual); Board of Management; Committee; Secretariat. **Languages** English. **Activities** Networking/liaising; standards/guidelines; monitoring/evaluation. **Events** *Annual Congress* Cape Town (South Africa) 2021, *Biennial Operations Summit* Bangkok (Thailand) 2020, *Annual Congress* Cape Town (South Africa) 2020, *Annual Congress* Venice (Italy) 2019, *Annual Congress* San Francisco, CA (USA) 2018. **Publications** *IELA Report* (periodical). *Handbook on International Exhibitions*.
Members Companies (155) in 54 countries and territories:
Argentina, Australia, Austria, Azerbaijan, Belgium, Brazil, Bulgaria, Canada, Chile, China, Colombia, Cyprus, Czechia, Denmark, Egypt, Estonia, Finland, France, Germany, Greece, Hong Kong, Hungary, India, Iran Islamic Rep, Israel, Italy, Japan, Jordan, Korea Rep, Lebanon, Libya, Lithuania, Malaysia, Mexico, Netherlands, Nigeria, Peru, Poland, Portugal, Qatar, Russia, Saudi Arabia, Singapore, South Africa, Spain, Sweden, Switzerland, Syrian AR, Taiwan, Thailand, Türkiye, UK, United Arab Emirates, USA.
IGO Relations Observer to: *World Customs Organization (WCO, #21350)*. **NGO Relations** Member of (1): *Events Industry Council (EIC, #09212)*. [2016.06.13/XF0742/**F**]

♦ International Exhibitions Bureau / see Bureau International des Expositions (#03365)

♦ **International Experiential Dynamic Therapy Association (IEDTA) . . . 13323**
Pres Belmont Center, 68 Leonard St, Belmont MA 02478, USA. T. +16174899090. E-mail: connect@iedta.net.
URL: http://iedta.net/
History Set up 2000, as *International Experiential STDP Association (IESA)*. **Aims** Support, improve, disseminate and research experiential dynamic therapies (EDTs). **Structure** Board of Directors; Advisory Board; Committees (7). **Activities** Certification/accreditation; events/meetings. **Events** *International Conference* Venice (Italy) 2022, *International Conference* Boston, MA (USA) 2019, *International Conference* Amsterdam (Netherlands) 2016, *International Conference* Bethesda, MD (USA) 2014, *International Conference* Oxford (UK) 2012. **Members** Full; Student; Honorary; Advanced; Teacher and Supervisor. Membership countries not specified. [2018/XM5754/**C**]

♦ International Experiential STDP Association / see International Experiential Dynamic Therapy Association (#13323)
♦ International Express Carriers Conference / see Global Express Association (#10351)
♦ International Extranodal Lymphoma Study Group (internationally oriented national body)
♦ International Extruded Concrete Association / see International Prestressed Hollowcore Association (#14638)
♦ International Eye Bank / see International Eye Foundation (#13324)

♦ **International Eye Foundation (IEF) 13324**
Pres and CEO 10801 Connecticut Ave, Kensington MD 20895, USA. T. +12402900263. Fax +12402900269. E-mail: contact@iefusa.org.
Main: http://www.iefusa.org/
History 1961. Founded as a project of CARE/Medico. Former names and other names: *International Eye Bank* – former. **Aims** Reduce blindness and low vision caused by cataract, childhood eye diseases, onchocerciasis (river blindness) and uncorrected refractive error; work with eye hospitals in *developing countries* to build capacity for quality eye care and sustainability by improving clinical, management and financial practices; offer services to provide low cost equipment and supplies for eye care and surgery. **Structure** Board of Directors; Executive Committee. Standing Committees (5): Finance; Nominating; Development; Personnel; Programme Advisory. **Languages** English. **Staff** 7.00 FTE, paid. **Finance** Sources: corporation, foundation and government grants and contracts; Combined Federal Campaign; fundraising events; general contributions; gifts-in-kind. **Activities** Advocacy/lobbying/activism; guidance/assistance/consulting; events/meetings; projects/programmes; awareness raising; knowledge management/information dissemination; healthcare. **Events** *Glaucoma in the developing world* Montego Bay (Jamaica) 1993, *World congress* Rome (Italy) 1986. **Publications** Annual Report; scientific articles; fact sheets; legacy brochure. **Members** Not a membership organization. **Consultative Status** Consultative status granted from: *ECOSOC (#05331)* (Ros C); *WHO (#20950)* (Official Relations). **IGO Relations** Relations with: *African Programme for Onchocerciasis Control (APOC, no recent information)*; *Pan American Health Organization (PAHO, #18108)*; *United States Agency for International Development (USAID)*. [2021/XF1856/f/**F**]

♦ Internationale Zentrale für Kinder- und Jugendfilme (#12493)
♦ Internationale Zentralstelle für Bauernfunk (inactive)
♦ Internationale Zentralstelle von Verbänden der Krankenkassen und Hilfsvereine (inactive)
♦ Internationale Zentrum zur Förderung der Menschenrechte in Gemeinden und Regionen / see European Training- and Research Centre for Human Rights and Democracy
♦ Internationale Zentrum für Glasmalerei (internationally oriented national body)
♦ International Fabricare Institute (internationally oriented national body)
♦ International Facial Nerve Symposium (meeting series)

♦ **International Facility Management Association (IFMA) 13325**
Main Office 800 Gessner Rd, Ste 900, Houston TX 77024-4257, USA. T. +17136234362. Fax +17136236124. E-mail: ifma@ifma.org.
URL: http://www.ifma.org/
History 1980. Code of ethics adopted 1983. **Aims** Advance collective knowledge, value and growth for Facility Management professionals to perform at the highest level. **Structure** Chapters (137); Council (16). **Finance** Sources: members' dues. Other sources: expositions; sales; job placement service. **Activities** Certification/accreditation; events/meetings; research/documentation; training/education. **Events** *World Workplace Conference* Nashville, TN (USA) 2022, *World Workplace Asia Conference* Singapore (Singapore) 2022, *World Workplace Asia Conference* Singapore (Singapore) 2021, *World Workplace Asia Conference* Singapore (Singapore) 2020, *World Workplace Conference* Phoenix, AZ (USA) 2019. **Publications** *IFMA Insider* (weekly); *Facility Management Journal* (6 a year). Books; research reports; white papers; conference proceedings. **Members** Professional; Associate; Student; Retired, Corporate Sustaining. Individuals in 78 countries. Membership countries not specified. **NGO Relations** Member of (3): *ABET*; *Global Facility Management Association (Global FM, #10353)*; *International Property Measurement Standards Coalition (IPMSC, #14656)*. [2021.09.02/XD3968/v/**F**]

♦ International Factoring Association (internationally oriented national body)

♦ **International Faculty for Artificial Organs (INFA) 13326**
Dean c/o BioCon Valley, Friedrich-Barnewitz-Str 8, 18119 Rostock, Germany. T. +4938151964950. Fax +4938151964952. E-mail: hk@bcv.org.
History 1991, within *International Federation for Artificial Organs (IFAO, #13357)*, following activities initiated in 1986. **Aims** Coordinate relevant teaching courses and programmes related to artificial organs. **Events** *Singapore biennial international conference on biomedical engineering* Singapore (Singapore) 2000.
Members Colleges and universities (11) in 8 countries:
Belgium, Denmark, France, Italy, Japan, Singapore, UK, USA. [2018/XE4124/**E**]

♦ International Fair Play Committee / see International Committee for Fair Play (#12769)
♦ International Fair Trade Association / see World Fair Trade Organization (#21396)
♦ International Falcon Mouvement / see International Falcon Movement – Socialist Educational International (#13327)

♦ **International Falcon Movement – Socialist Educational International (IFM-SEI) 13327**
Mouvement international des faucons – Internationale éducative socialiste (MIF/IES)
SG Rue Joseph II 120, 1000 Brussels, Belgium. T. +3222157927. Fax +3222450083. E-mail: contact@ifm-sei.org.
Office Sec address not obtained.
URL: http://www.ifm-sei.org/
History 18 Jun 1922, Salzburg (Austria). Founded, replacing the pre-war *Socialist Educational International (inactive)*, set up in 1922. Current Constitution adopted Nov 1982, Bommersvik (Sweden). Constitution amended: 1985, Castelo de Vide (Portugal); 1988, Vienna (Austria); 1991, Borzée (Belgium); 1995, Oslo (Norway); 1998, Nivelles (Belgium); 2001, Malmö (Sweden); 2004, Nuremberg (Germany); 2007, Vienna (Austria); 2010, Prague (Czech Rep); 2013, Manchester (UK); 2016, Thalmässing (Germany); 2019, Tbilisi (Georgia). Former names and other names: *International Falcon Secretariat* – former (1947 to 1953); *Secrétariat international des faucons* – former (1947 to 1953); *International Falcon Mouvement (IFM)* – former (1953 to 1970); *Mouvement international des faucons (MIF)* – former (1953 to 1970). Registration: Banque-Carrefour des Entreprises, No/ID: 0441.247.654, Start date: 13 Aug 1990, Belgium; EU Transparency Register, No/ID: 59726234027-26, Start date: 19 Aug 2010. **Aims** Empower children and young people to take an active role in society and fight for their rights. **Structure** International Congress; Council of Members; International Committee; Presidium; Regional bodies (5) include: *European Falcon Network (#07027)*; Thematic Networks (4); Secretariat in Brussels (Belgium). **Languages** English, French, Spanish. **Staff** 7.00 FTE, paid; 2.00 FTE, voluntary. **Finance** Sources: contributions of member/participating states; donations; grants; members' dues; sale of products; sale of publications. Annual budget: 90,000 EUR (2022). **Activities** Advocacy/lobbying/activism; events/meetings; training/education. **Events** *Meeting* Brussels (Belgium) 2020, *Congress* Tbilisi (Georgia) 2019, *Meeting* Brussels (Belgium) 2018, *Congress* Manchester (UK) 2013, *Congress* Prague (Czech Rep) 2010. **Publications** *IFM-SEI Newsletter*, *IFM-SEI Report*. Educational manuals in English, French, German, Spanish. Annual Report; policy documents; books; calendars; songbook; training materials.
Members Member; Candidate Member; Fraternal. Organizations in 39 countries:
Armenia, Austria, Belarus, Belgium, Bhutan, Bolivia, Brazil, Cameroon, Chile, Colombia, Czechia, Denmark, Ecuador, Egypt, Finland, Georgia, Germany, Ghana, Hungary, India, Indonesia, Israel, Italy, Lithuania, Mali, Nicaragua, Norway, Palestine, Paraguay, Peru, Senegal, Slovakia, Slovenia, Spain, Sweden, Switzerland, Türkiye, UK, Zimbabwe.
Consultative Status Consultative status granted from: *ECOSOC (#05331)* (Special); *UNICEF (#20332)*; *Council of Europe (CE, #04881)* (Participatory Status). **IGO Relations** Accredited by (1): *United Nations Office at Vienna (UNOV, #20604)*. Basic document: *United Nations Convention on the Rights of the Child (CRC, 1989)*. **NGO Relations** Member of (4): *Espacio Iberoamericano de Juventud (EIJ, no recent information)*; *European Youth Forum (#09140)*; *NGO Committee on UNICEF (#17120)*; *Socialist International (SI, #19340)*. Supports (2): *European Citizens' Initiative Campaign (ECI Campaign, #06558)*; *Global Call for Action Against Poverty (GCAP, #10263)*. Instrumental in setting up (2): *Arab Youth Movement (AYM, see: #13327)*; *Olof Palme Institute (OPI)*. [2022.06.30/XC1821/**C**]

♦ International Falcon Secretariat / see International Falcon Movement – Socialist Educational International (#13327)
♦ International Family Day Care Organization (inactive)
♦ International Family Doctors Association (inactive)

♦ **International Family Enterprise Research Academy (IFERA) 13328**
Main Office c/o UIS College of Business, 1 University Plaza, UHB 4060, Springfield IL 62703, USA. E-mail: office@ifera.org.
URL: http://www.ifera.org/
History Jan 2001, Barcelona (Spain). **Aims** Advance family business research, theory and practice through enhanced collaboration and accelerated learning. **Structure** Board; Fellows. **Languages** English. **Finance** Sources: members' dues. **Activities** Events/meetings. **Events** *IFERA Annual Conference* Santander (Spain) 2022, *IFERA Annual Conference* Santander (Spain) 2021, *Annual Conference* Bergamo (Italy) 2019, *Annual Conference* Hamburg (Germany) 2015, *Annual Research Conference / Annual Conference* Lappeenranta (Finland) 2014. **Publications** *Family Business Review* – online. *Handbook of Research on Family Business*. Information Services: research database. **Members** Full in 36 countries. Membership countries not specified. [2021/XM2900/**D**]

♦ **International Family Forestry Alliance (IFFA) 13329**
Contact Forestry House, Rue du Luxembourg 66, 1000 Brussels, Belgium. T. +3222392305.
Chair address not obtained. T. +15063672503. E-mail: grandpic@nbnet.nb.ca.
URL: http://www.familyforestry.net/
History 1 Jul 2002. Registered in the District of Columbia (USA). **Aims** Serve as an informal alliance between family forest owners' organizations worldwide; promote existence, development and advantage of family forestry and advocate supportive policies; provide a forum for the exchange of experience, ideas and information. **Structure** Board, comprising including Chairman, Vice-Chairman, Secretary-Treasurer and 2 further members. **Events** *Annual Meeting* Brussels (Belgium) 2012, *Annual Meeting* Rio de Janeiro (Brazil) 2010, *Annual meeting* Munich (Germany) 2007, *International forest owners congress* Helsinki (Finland) 2006, *Meeting / Annual Meeting* Helsinki (Finland) 2006. **Publications** *IFFA Newsletter*.
Members National organizations (21) in 21 countries:

Australia, Austria, Belgium, Canada, Czechia, Denmark, Estonia, Finland, France, Germany, Greece, Kenya, Latvia, Lithuania, Luxembourg, Mexico, Norway, Spain, Sweden, Switzerland, USA.
Associate members (3):
Confederation of European Forest Owners (CEPF, #04525); PEFC Council (#18288); Unión de Silvicultores del Sur de Europa (USSE, #20478).
Consultative Status Consultative status granted from: *ECOSOC (#05331)* (Special). [2018/XM3071/y/F]

♦ International Family Health Care Association (inactive)
♦ International Family Ministries and Counseling Association (no recent information)

♦ International Family Nursing Association (IFNA) 13330

Contact 461 Cochran Rd, Box No 246, Pittsburgh PA 15228, USA. T. +14123441414. Fax +14123440599. E-mail: debbie@internationalfamilynursing.org.
URL: http://internationalfamilynursing.org/
History Bylaws adopted Jun 2009, Reykjavik (Iceland). **Aims** Foster the individual and collective development of nurses involved in the promotion of health care to families by providing an international forum of shared responsibility for the advance of family nursing. **Structure** Board of Directors, comprising President, President-Elect, Secretary, Treasurer and Directors. Standing Committees (7): Communications; Conference; Education; Membership; Nominating; Practice; Research. **Finance** Sources: members' dues. **Events** *Conference* Pittsburgh, PA (USA) 2021, *Conference* Washington, DC (USA) 2019, *Improving the art and science of family nursing – transforming health for families* Pamplona (Spain) 2017, *Improving family health globally through research, education, and practice* Odense (Denmark) 2015, *Conference* Minneapolis, MN (USA) 2013. **Members** Individuals (459) in 35 countries. Membership countries not specified. [2016/XJ5473/C]

♦ International Family Office Association (internationally oriented national body)

♦ International Family Therapy Association (IFTA) 13331

Gen Sec Marriage and Family Counseling Service, 1800 3rd Ave, Room 512 Safety Bldg, Rock Island IL 61201, USA. T. +13097864491. Fax +13097860205.
URL: http://www.ifta-familytherapy.org/
History Founded following the East-West Bridging Congress, 1987, Prague (Czech Rep). **Aims** Advance family therapy by promoting research, education and sound practices while promoting international cooperation and exchange of knowledge and ideas that support the health and well-being of families and persons around the world. **Structure** Annual World Conference; Board of Directors. **Languages** English. **Staff** 6.00 FTE, paid. **Finance** Sources: members' dues. **Activities** Certification/accreditation; events/meetings; knowledge management/information dissemination. **Events** *World Family Therapy Congress* Malaga (Spain) 2023, *World Family Therapy Congress* San Juan (Puerto Rico) 2022, *World Family Therapy Congress* 2021, *World Congress* Basel (Switzerland) 2020, *World Congress* Aberdeen (UK) 2019. **Publications** *Systemic Family Therapy e-News* (4 a year) – online newsletter; *International Journal of Systemic Therapy* (4 a year) – online; *International Connection* (2 a year) – online newsletter. Member Directory.
Members Membership Category I, II and III; Institutional/Organizational; Lifetime. Therapists, theorists, researchers, publishers, teachers, trainers and others who work with families and couples. Category I members in 58 countries and territories:
Argentina, Australia, Austria, Bahamas, Bahrain, Barbados, Belarus, Belgium, Bermuda, Brunei Darussalam, Canada, Chile, China, Costa Rica, Cuba, Cyprus, Czechia, Denmark, Estonia, Finland, France, Germany, Greece, Hong Kong, Hungary, Iceland, Ireland, Israel, Italy, Japan, Korea Rep, Kuwait, Latvia, Lithuania, Luxembourg, Malta, Mexico, Netherlands, New Zealand, Norway, Poland, Portugal, Puerto Rico, Qatar, Serbia, Seychelles, Singapore, Slovakia, Slovenia, Spain, St Kitts-Nevis, Sweden, Switzerland, Trinidad-Tobago, UK, United Arab Emirates, Uruguay, USA.
Category II members in 87 countries and territories:
Albania, Algeria, Antigua-Barbuda, Armenia, Azerbaijan, Bangladesh, Belize, Bhutan, Bolivia, Bosnia-Herzegovina, Botswana, Brazil, Bulgaria, Cambodia, Cape Verde, China, Colombia, Comoros, Congo Brazzaville, Dominica, Dominican Rep, Ecuador, Egypt, El Salvador, Equatorial Guinea, Eswatini, Fiji, Gabon, Georgia, Ghana, Grenada, Guatemala, Guyana, Honduras, India, Indonesia, Iran Islamic Rep, Jamaica, Jordan, Kazakhstan, Kyrgyzstan, Laos, Lebanon, Lesotho, Libya, Malaysia, Maldives, Mauritius, Moldova, Mongolia, Morocco, Myanmar, Namibia, Nicaragua, North Macedonia, Oman, Palestine, Panama, Papua New Guinea, Paraguay, Peru, Philippines, Romania, Russia, Samoa, Sao Tomé-Principe, Saudi Arabia, Solomon Is, South Africa, Sri Lanka, St Lucia, St Vincent-Grenadines, Sudan, Suriname, Syrian AR, Taiwan, Tajikistan, Thailand, Togo, Tunisia, Türkiye, Turkmenistan, Ukraine, Uzbekistan, Vanuatu, Venezuela, Vietnam.
Category III members in 35 countries:
Angola, Benin, Burkina Faso, Burundi, Cameroon, Central African Rep, Chad, Congo DR, Côte d'Ivoire, Djibouti, Eritrea, Ethiopia, Gambia, Guinea, Guinea-Bissau, Haiti, Kenya, Liberia, Madagascar, Malawi, Mali, Mauritania, Mozambique, Nepal, Niger, Nigeria, Pakistan, Rwanda, Senegal, Sierra Leone, Tanzania UR, Uganda, Yemen, Zambia, Zimbabwe.
Consultative Status Consultative status granted from: *ECOSOC (#05331)* (Special). [2022.06.14/XD4631/C]

♦ International Farm Comparison Network / see IFCN
♦ International Farmer and Peasant Council (inactive)

♦ International Farming Systems Association (IFSA) 13332

Association internationale sur les systèmes de production – Asociación Internacional de Sistemas Agricolas
IFSA Europe Group Univ für Bodenkultur, Feistmantelstr 4, 1180 Vienna, Austria. E-mail: ika.darnhofer@boku.ac.at.
URL: http://www.ifsa-europe.org/
History Founded 1989, USA, as *Association for Farming Systems Research and Extension (AFSRE)*, following symposia initiated in 1980. Later known as *International Association for Farming Systems Research and Extension (AFSRE)*. 1993, registered in accordance with the laws of the Philippines. **Aims** Foster and support regional farming systems associations and networks; provide a global forum for exchange of information between members and the various regional organizations. **Structure** Steering Committee. **Languages** English. **Finance** Conference fees. **Events** *European Farming Systems Symposium* Evora (Portugal) 2022, *European Farming Systems Symposium* Evora (Portugal) 2021, *European Farming Systems Symposium* Evora (Portugal) 2020, *European Farming Systems Symposium* Chania (Greece) 2018, *European Symposium* Newport (UK) 2016. **Publications** Symposia proceedings. Archive and documentation. **Members** No formal membership. [2019.02.17/XF4146/F]

♦ International Farm Management Association (IFMA) 13333

Association internationale de gestion agricole
Hon Sec Portbury House, Sheepway, Portbury, Bristol, BS20 7TE, UK. T. +447801435772. E-mail: honsecretary@ifmaonline.org.
URL: http://www.ifmaonline.org/
History Founded 1974, Guelph ON (Canada), at 2nd International Congress, following 1st Congress, Warwick (UK). **Aims** Further knowledge and understanding of farm business management; exchange ideas and information about farm management theory and practice. **Structure** Council; Executive Committee. **Languages** English. **Staff** 1.00 FTE, voluntary. **Finance** Sources: members' dues. **Events** *Congress* Copenhagen (Denmark) 2022, *Congress* Copenhagen (Denmark) 2021, *Congress* Launceston, TAS (Australia) 2019, *Congress* Edinburgh (UK) 2017, *Congress* Québec, QC (Canada) 2015. **Publications** *International Journal of Agricultural Management*. Congress papers. **Members** Full; Corporate. Membership countries not specified. [2020/XD8338/B]

♦ International Fashion and Design Congress (meeting series)
♦ International Fatigue Congress (meeting series)
♦ International Feather Bureau / see International Down and Feather Bureau (#13195)
♦ International Federalist Correspondence Club (inactive)

♦ International Federation of ACATs – Action by Christians for the Abolition of Torture 13334

Fédération internationale des ACAT – Action des chrétiens pour l'abolition de la torture (FIACAT)
Exec Dir 96 bd de la Libération, 94300 Vincennes, France. T. +33158641047. E-mail: fiacat@fiacat.org.
Pres address not obtained.
URL: http://www.fiacat.org/
History Feb 1987. Founded by 10 national associations of *Christian Action for the Abolition of Torture – Action des chrétiens pour l'abolition de la torture (ACAT)*, the first national organization having been set up 1974, France. Former names and other names: *Federación Internacional – Acción de los Cristianos para la Abolición de la Tortura* – former; *Internationale Föderation – Aktion der Christen für die Abschaffung der Tortur* – former; *Fédération internationale de l'action des chrétiens pour l'abolition de la torture* – alias. Registration: RNA, No/ID: W751108187, France; EU Transparency Register, No/ID: 428642112183-35, Start date: 4 Nov 2013. **Aims** Work towards abolition of torture and the death penalty. **Structure** International Council; International Bureau; International Secretariat. **Languages** English, French. **Staff** 6.00 FTE, paid; 9.00 FTE, voluntary. **Finance** Sources: donations; grants; members' dues. **Activities** Advocacy/lobbying/activism; awareness raising; capacity building; guidance/assistance/consulting; networking/liaising. **Events** *Symposium* Brussels (Belgium) 2012, *Ban on torture – a principle under threat* Lungern (Switzerland) 2007, *Seminar* Dakar (Senegal) 2002, *Symposium* Paris (France) 1998, *Combating torture and other forms of inhuman treatment, Christians in Central and Eastern Europe take up the challenge* Budapest (Hungary) 1997. **Publications** *Guides sur les garanties judiciaires du prévénu au Congo et à Madagascar* (2018); *Guides sur les garanties judiciaires du prévénu en RDC* (2017); *Sensibiliser à la peine de mort au Burkina Faso* (2016-2018); *Sensibiliser à la peine de mort au Congo* (2016-2018); *Sensibiliser à la peine de mort au Mali* (2016-2018); *Sensibiliser à la peine de mort au Niger* (2016-2018); *Sensibiliser à la peine de mort au Tchad* (2016-2018); *Sensibiliser à la peine de mort en République centrafricaine* (2016-2018); *Guides sur les garanties judiciaires du prévénu au Bénin et en Côte d'Ivoire* (2016). Annual reports; periodicals.
Members National associations (about 30) in 26 countries:
Belgium, Benin, Brazil, Burkina Faso, Burundi, Canada, Central African Rep, Chad, Congo Brazzaville, Congo DR, Côte d'Ivoire, France, Germany, Ghana, Italy, Liberia, Luxembourg, Madagascar, Mali, Niger, Senegal, Spain, Switzerland, Togo, UK, USA.
Consultative Status Consultative status granted from: *African Commission on Human and Peoples' Rights (ACHPR, #00255)* (Observer); *ECOSOC (#05331)* (Special); *Council of Europe (CE, #04881)* (Participatory Status); *Organisation internationale de la Francophonie (OIF, #17809)*. **IGO Relations** Accredited by (1): *Organisation internationale de la Francophonie (OIF, #17809)*. Member of (1): *Convention against Torture Initiative (CTI, #04786)*. Cooperates with (1): *European Union Agency for Fundamental Rights (FRA, #08969)*. **NGO Relations** Member of (4): *Human Rights and Democracy Network (HRDN, #10980); International Catholic Centre of Geneva (ICCG, #12449); International Coalition against Enforced Disappearances (ICAED, #12605); World Coalition Against the Death Penalty (#21281).* [2021/XD1401/C]

♦ International Federation of Accountants (IFAC) 13335

CEO 529 Fifth Ave, New York NY 10017, USA. T. +12122869344. Fax +12122869570. E-mail: communications@ifac.org.
Registered Office Postfach 361, 1211 Geneva 25, Switzerland.
URL: https://www.ifac.org/
History 7 Oct 1977, Munich (Germany). Founded at 11th World Congress of Accountants, to replace *International Coordination Committee for the Accountancy Profession (ICCAP, inactive)*, set up Nov 1972. Registration: Civil Code, No/ID: CHE-102.197.003, Switzerland. **Aims** Serve the public interest by contributing to the development of high-quality *standards* and guidance, facilitating adoption and implementation of high-quality standards and guidance, contributing to the development of strong *professional* accountancy organizations and accounting firms and to high-quality practices by professional accountants, and promoting the value of professional accountants worldwide, and speaking out on public interest issues. **Structure** Board of Directors. *Public Interest Oversight Board (PIOB, #18566)*, which oversees *International Auditing and Assurance Standards Board (IAASB, #12296)*, *International Accounting Education Standards Board (IAESB, #11582)* and *International Ethics Standards Board for Accountants (IESBA, #13306)*. Also provides structure for *International Public Sector Accounting Standards Board (IPSASB, #14673)*. Constituency-focused committees (3). **Languages** English. **Staff** Overall direction and administration is provided by the IFAC Secretariat headquartered in New York NY (USA). IFAC is staffed by accounting professionals from around the world. **Activities** Events/meetings; guidance/assistance/consulting; management of treaties and agreements; standards/guidelines. Management of treaties and agreements: *International Accounting Profession Agreement*, ratified by member organizations of IFAC and Board members and member organizations of the then International Accounting Standards Committee (IASC) (currently IASB), Oct 1982, Mexico City (Mexico). **Events** *World Congress of Accountants* Mumbai (India) 2022, *Conference* New York, NY (USA) 2019, *Conference* Singapore (Singapore) 2018, *World Congress of Accountants* Sydney, NSW (Australia) 2018, *Meeting* Brussels (Belgium) 2017. **Publications** *IFAC Quarterly* (4 a year); *Articles of Merit* (annual) – award booklet; *Handbook of International Auditing, Assurance, and Ethics Pronouncements* (annual); *Handbook of International Public Sector Accounting Pronouncements* (annual). *Code of Ethics for Professional Accountants*; *Codification of International Standards on Auditing*; *Introduction to IFAC Education Committee*; *Introduction to IFAC Public Sector Committee*. Annual Report; statements on auditing, financial and management accounting.
Members Membership: over 170 professional accountancy organizations, representing over 3000000 professional accountants. Full in 117 countries and territories:
Albania, Argentina, Australia, Austria, Azerbaijan, Bahamas, Bangladesh, Barbados, Belgium, Bolivia, Bosnia-Herzegovina, Botswana, Brazil, Bulgaria, Cameroon, Canada, Cayman Is, Chile, China, Colombia, Costa Rica, Côte d'Ivoire, Cyprus, Czechia, Denmark, Dominican Rep, Egypt, El Salvador, Estonia, Eswatini, Fiji, Finland, France, Georgia, Germany, Ghana, Greece, Guatemala, Guyana, Haiti, Honduras, Hong Kong, Hungary, Iceland, India, Indonesia, Iran Islamic Rep, Iraq, Ireland, Israel, Italy, Jamaica, Japan, Jordan, Kazakhstan, Kenya, Korea Rep, Kosovo, Kuwait, Latvia, Lebanon, Lesotho, Liberia, Lithuania, Luxembourg, Madagascar, Malawi, Malaysia, Malta, Mauritius, Mexico, Moldova, Mongolia, Montenegro, Morocco, Namibia, Nepal, Netherlands, New Zealand, Nicaragua, Nigeria, North Macedonia, Norway, Pakistan, Panama, Papua New Guinea, Paraguay, Peru, Philippines, Poland, Portugal, Romania, Saudi Arabia, Senegal, Serbia, Sierra Leone, Singapore, Slovakia, Slovenia, South Africa, Spain, Sri Lanka, Sweden, Switzerland, Taiwan, Tanzania UR, Thailand, Trinidad-Tobago, Tunisia, Türkiye, Uganda, UK, Ukraine, Uruguay, Vietnam, Zambia, Zimbabwe.
Associate: organizations in 26 countries:
Armenia, Benin, Brunei Darussalam, Burkina Faso, Cambodia, Croatia, Ecuador, Guatemala, Honduras, Indonesia, Ireland, Kazakhstan, Kyrgyzstan, Lithuania, Luxembourg, Montenegro, Mozambique, Pakistan, Palestine, Russia, Rwanda, Serbia, Suriname, Togo, Uzbekistan, Vietnam.
Affiliate: organizations (4) in 2 countries:
Netherlands, USA.
IGO Relations Strategic partners include:
- *African Development Bank (ADB, #00283);*
- *Asian Development Bank (ADB, #01422);*
- *Australian Aid (inactive);*
- *Department for International Development (DFID, inactive);*
- *European Commission (EC, #06633);*
- *European Parliament (EP, #08146);*
- *Financial Stability Board (FSB, #09770);*
- *Global Fund to Fight AIDS, Tuberculosis and Malaria (Global Fund, #10383);*
- *Inter-American Development Bank (IDB, #11427);*
- *International Bank for Reconstruction and Development (IBRD, #12317)* (World Bank);
- *International Monetary Fund (IMF, #14180);*
- *New Zealand Ministry of Foreign Affairs and Trade – New Zealand Aid Programme;*
- *OECD (#17693);*
- *Statistical Office of the European Union (Eurostat, #19974);*
- *Swedish International Development Cooperation Agency (Sida);*
- *UNCTAD (#20285);*
- *United Nations (UN, #20515);*
- *United States Agency for International Development (USAID).*

Associate expert of: *COMESA Clearing House (inactive).*
NGO Relations Strategic partners include:
- *Basel Committee on Banking Supervision (BCBS, #03183);*
- *Business and Industry Advisory Committee to the OECD (BIAC, #03385);*
- *Gavi – The Vaccine Alliance (Gavi, #10077);*
- *Global Public Policy Institute (GPPi);*
- *Global Reporting Initiative (GRI, #10567);*
- *Institute of Internal Auditors (IIA, #11272);*
- *Institute of International Finance (IIF, #11275);*
- *International Accounting Standards Board (IASB, #11583);*
- *International Actuarial Association (IAA, #11586);*
- *International Association of Insurance Supervisors (IAIS, #11966);*
- *International Corporate Governance Network (ICGN, #12969);*

- *International Financial Reporting Standards Foundation (IFRS Foundation, #13603)*;
- *International Forum of Independent Audit Regulators (IFIAR, #13639)*;
- *International Integrated Reporting Council (IIRC, inactive)*;
- *International Organization of Securities Commissions (IOSCO, #14470)*;
- *International Organization for Standardization (ISO, #14473)*;
- *International Organization of Supreme Audit Institutions (INTOSAI, #14478)*;
- *International Valuation Standards Council (IVSC, #15840)*;
- *Public Interest Oversight Board (PIOB, #18566)*;
- *SMEunited (#19327)*;
- *World Federation of Exchanges (WFE, #21434)*.

Recognizes 3 regional organizations: *Confederation of Asian and Pacific Accountants (CAPA, #04511)*; *Accountancy Europe (#00061)*; *Inter-American Accounting Association (IAA, #11395)*. Recognizes 6 groupings: *Association of Accountancy Bodies in West Africa (ABWA, #02343)*; *Eurasian Institute of Certified Public Accountants (EICPA, #05610)*; *Fédération des experts comptables méditerranéens (FCM, #09584)*; *Fédération internationale des experts-comptables francophones (FIDEF, #09630)*; *Institute of Chartered Accountants of the Caribbean (ICAC, #11245)*; *South Asian Federation of Accountants (SAFA, #19727)*. [2023/XB5221/y/**B**]

♦ International Federation of ACLI 13336

Fédération internationale des ACLI – Internationaler Verband der ACLI – Federación Internacional de las ACLI – Federazione ACLI Internazionali (FAI)

Head Office Rue Franklin 136, 1000 Brussels, Belgium. T. +3227340897.
SG Via G Marcora 18/20, 00153 Rome RM, Italy.
URL: http://www.aclifai.it/

History 1996, as *Federation of International Christian Workers Associations – Fédération des associations chrétiennes travailleurs internationaux – Bund der Internationalen Christlichen Arbeitnehmerverbände – Federación Asociaciones Cristianas Trabajadores Internacionales – Federazione Associazioni Cristiane Lavoratori Internazionali (FAI)*. **Aims** Connect the "ACLI family" in Europe and worldwide; represent the international vocation of participation in development of transnational partnerships; strengthen international networks within the *third sector*, through solidarity and associative collaboration; contribute to the harmonious edification of a united Europe, promoting freedom, social security and democracy. **Structure** General Assembly (every 4 years). General Council, comprising Presidents and a maximum of 5 representatives for each national association. Presidency, including President, Vice-President, Treasurer and Secretary General. Offices (19), 10 in the EU countries and 9 in the American continent, Australia and South Africa. Secretariat based in Brussels (Belgium). **Languages** English, French, Italian. **Staff** 1.00 FTE, paid. 3 trainees. **Finance** Members'dues. **Activities** Offers permanent representation at the European level; gives consultancy services for the ACLI system; offers a permanent information service; coordinates collaboration and assistance between members. **Events** *Congress and General Assembly* Amsterdam (Netherlands) 2014, *Congress* Brussels (Belgium) 2004, *Congress* Orvieto (Italy) 2004, *Congress* Turin (Italy) 2004, *Congress* Orvieto (Italy) 2003. **Publications** *FAI Newsletter*, *GA Newsletter – Youth ACLI*; *Vocational Training Newsletter*. *Specials on Europe*. Brochure.
Members National organizations, representing more than 800,000 individuals, in 19 countries:
Argentina, Australia, Belgium, Brazil, Canada, Chile, Denmark, France, Germany, Italy, Luxembourg, Netherlands, South Africa, Spain, Switzerland, UK, Uruguay, USA, Venezuela.
NGO Relations Cooperates with: *Commission of the Bishops' Conferences of the European Union (COMECE, #04205)*; *European Trade Union Confederation (ETUC, #08927)*. [2016/XD8377/**D**]

♦ International Federation of Actors 13337

Fédération internationale des acteurs (FIA) – Federación Internacional de Actores – Internationaler Schauspielerverband

Gen Sec Rue Joseph II 40, B/04, 1000 Brussels, Belgium. T. +3222350874 – +3222345653. Fax +3222350870. E-mail: office@fia-actors.com.
URL: http://www.fia-actors.com/

History Jun 1952, London (UK). Constitution amended: 1954, Venice (Italy); 1956, Brussels (Belgium); 1964, Mexico City (Mexico); 1967, Prague (Czechoslovakia); 1970, Amsterdam (Netherlands); 1973, Stockholm (Sweden); 1985, Athens (Greece); 1988, Leningrad (USSR); 1992, Montréal QC (Canada); 1996, Copenhagen (Denmark); 2000, Montevideo (Uruguay), 2004, Budapest (Hungary); 2008, Marrakech (Morocco); 2012, Toronto ON (Canada). Since 25 Sep 1970, incorporates *International Federation of Variety Artists (IFVA, inactive)*. **Aims** Ensure protection and promotion, on a strictly *professional* basis, of the artistic, economic, social and legal interests of actors and performers organized in affiliated unions. **Structure** Congress (every 4 years); Executive Committee; Regional organizations (7). Membership limited to national unions or professional and representative organizations. **Languages** English, French. **Staff** 3.00 FTE, paid. **Finance** Sources: members' dues. **Activities** Advocacy/lobbying/activism; guidance/assistance/consulting; research/documentation. **Events** *European Group Meeting* Berlin (Germany) 2019, *European Group Meeting* Brussels (Belgium) 2018, *Executive Committee Meeting* Tokyo (Japan) 2018, *International Symposium on the Status of the Artist* Tokyo (Japan) 2018, *Meeting* Copenhagen (Denmark) 2017. **Publications** *FIA-The First Thirty Years* in English, French; *The Actors Charter* – in 4 languages; *The Theatre and the Actor in Society* – in 4 languages. Guidelines; handbooks.
Members Affiliated unions in 62 countries and territories:
Argentina, Australia, Austria, Azerbaijan, Belarus, Belgium, Brazil, Bulgaria, Cameroon, Canada, Chile, Colombia, Croatia, Cuba, Cyprus, Czechia, Denmark, Ecuador, Estonia, Finland, France, Georgia, Germany, Ghana, Greece, Hungary, Iceland, India, Ireland, Israel, Italy, Japan, Kazakhstan, Kyrgyzstan, Latvia, Madagascar, Mexico, Moldova, Morocco, Namibia, Netherlands, New Zealand, Nigeria, Norway, Panama, Peru, Poland, Portugal, Romania, Russia, Slovakia, Slovenia, South Africa, Spain, Sweden, Switzerland, Türkiye, UK, Ukraine, Uruguay, USA, Zambia.
Consultative Status Consultative status granted from: *UNESCO (#20322)* (Consultative Status); *Council of Europe (CE, #04881)* (Participatory Status); *World Intellectual Property Organization (WIPO, #21593)* (Permanent Observer Status). **IGO Relations** Observer to: *Intergovernmental Committee of the International Convention of Rome for the Protection of Performers, Producers of Phonograms and Broadcasting Organizations (#11474)*; *Union for the International Registration of Audiovisual Works (#20444)*. **NGO Relations** Member of (3): *European Arts and Entertainment Alliance (EAEA, #05918)*; *International Arts and Entertainment Alliance (IAEA, #11676)*; *On the Move (OTM, #16868)*. [2021/XC1844/**C**]

♦ INternational Federation of Acute Neonatal Transport Services (unconfirmed)

♦ International Federation of Adapted Physical Activity (IFAPA) 13338

Fédération internationale de l'activité physique adaptée (FIAPA) – Federación Internacional del Actividad Fisica Adaptada

Pres Dept Health and Physical Education, Mount Royal Univ, Calgary AB T3E 6K6, Canada. T. +14034406495.
URL: http://ifapa.net/

History 1973, Québec, QC (Canada). **Aims** Give global focus to professionals who use adapted physical activity for instruction and scientific research; promote and disseminate knowledge and information about adapted physical activity, disability sport and all other aspects of sport, movement and exercise science for the benefit of persons who require adaptations to enable their participation. **Structure** Board of Directors. **Languages** English. **Staff** None. **Finance** Sources: members' dues. **Activities** Events/meetings; guidance/assistance/consulting; networking/liaising. International Symposium on Adapted Physical Activity (ISAPA). **Events** *International Symposium on Adapted Physical Activity (ISAPA)* Dunedin (New Zealand) 2023, *International Symposium on Adapted Physical Activity (ISAPA)* Jyväskylä (Finland) 2021, *International Symposium on Adapted Physical Activity (ISAPA)* Charlottesville, VA (USA) 2019, *International Symposium of Adapted Physical Activity (ISAPA)* Daegu (Korea Rep) 2017, *International Symposium on Adapted Physical Activity (ISAPA)* Netanya (Israel) 2015. **Publications** *Adapted Physical Activity Quarterly* (4 a year) – journal; *IFAPA Newsletter* (4 a year). Symposium proceedings.
Members Individual, corporate, student, in 38 countries and territories:
Algeria, Angola, Australia, Austria, Belgium, Brazil, Cameroon, Canada, Colombia, Denmark, Finland, France, Germany, Greece, Hong Kong, Hungary, Iceland, India, Ireland, Israel, Italy, Japan, Korea Rep, Luxembourg, Mexico, Netherlands, New Zealand, Norway, Panama, Poland, Portugal, Spain, Sweden, Switzerland, Taiwan, UK, USA, Venezuela.
NGO Relations Member of (1): *International Council of Sport Science and Physical Education (ICSSPE, #13077)*. Instrumental in setting up (4): *Asian Society for Adapted Physical Education and Exercise (ASAPE, #01703)*; *European Federation of Adapted Physical Activity (EUFAPA, #07038)*; *Federación Sudamericana de Actividad Física Adaptada (FESAFA, #09392)*; *North American Federation of Adapted Physical Activity (NAFAPA)*. [2021/XD1586/**C**]

♦ International Federation for Adipose Therapeutics and Science (IFATS) 13339

Exec Dir 6300 Sagewood Drive, Ste H255, Park City UT 84098, USA. T. +14354290600. Fax +14354872011.
Pres address not obtained.
URL: http://www.ifats.org/

History 2002, Pittsburgh, PA (USA). **Aims** As a global scientific society for adipose derived stem cell biology and applications in regenerative medicine, bring together professionals in the disciplines of reconstructive surgery, cardiovascular biology, neurosciences, orthopaedic surgery, endocrinology, developmental biology, biomaterials, bioengineering, cell therapy, stem cell biology, tissue engineering and many other interested in regenerative medicine. **Structure** Executive Committee; Board of Directors. **Languages** English. **Finance** Sources: meeting proceeds; members' dues. Annual budget: 75,000 USD. **Activities** Events/meetings; networking/liaising. **Events** *Annual Conference* Fort Lauderdale, FL (USA) 2021, *Annual Conference* Marseille (France) 2019, *Annual Conference* Las Vegas, NV (USA) 2018, *Annual Conference* Miami, FL (USA) 2017, *Annual Conference* San Diego, CA (USA) 2016.
Members Full in 38 countries and territories:
Australia, Bahrain, Belgium, Brazil, Canada, China, Denmark, Finland, France, Germany, Greece, Guiana Fr, India, Iran Islamic Rep, Israel, Italy, Japan, Korea Rep, Luxembourg, Malta, Mexico, Mongolia, Netherlands, Norway, Peru, Poland, Portugal, Russia, Serbia, South Africa, Spain, Sweden, Switzerland, Taiwan, Thailand, Türkiye, UK, USA. [2021.08.31/XJ1277/**C**]

♦ International Federation of Adjusting Associations (IFAA) 13340

Secretariat 46-48 East Smithfield, St Katharine Docks, London, E1W 1AW, UK. T. +442076238461. Fax +442076811183. E-mail: sec@theifaa.net.
URL: http://www.theifaa.net/

History 1999. Registration: Companies House, No/ID: 05757371, Start date: 27 Mar 2006, England and Wales. **Aims** Promote the role of loss adjusting associations and their members. **Languages** English. **Events** *Regional Claims Conference* Colombo (Sri Lanka) 2014, *Regional Claims Conference* London (UK) 2011, *Regional Claims Conference* Singapore (Singapore) 2010, *Regional Claims Conference* London (UK) 2009, *Annual general meeting* Johannesburg (South Africa) 2008. **Publications** *Adjusting World* (annual).
Members Organizations and institutes in 11 countries:
Canada, Chile, Japan, Malaysia, Nigeria, Russia, Singapore, South Africa, Spain, UK, USA.
Included in the above, 2 organizations listed in this Yearbook:
Australasian Institute of Chartered Loss Adjusters (AICLA); *European Federation of Loss Adjusting Experts (#07158)*. [2019/XD9378/y/**D**]

♦ International Federation of Advertising Agencies / see International Communications Agency Network
♦ International Federation of Advertising Clubs (inactive)
♦ International Federation of Advertising Managers Associations (inactive)
♦ International Federation of Aeronautical and Astronautical Journalists (inactive)

♦ International Federation of Aeronautical Information Management Associations (IFAIMA) 13341

Exec Sec Rua Norte Júnior 231 – 9H, 1950-206 Lisbon, Portugal. T. +38641601464. E-mail: eb@ifaima.org.
URL: http://www.ifaima.org/

History 2008. Registration: Portugal; EU Transparency Register, No/ID: 48126336216-22. **Aims** Promote safety efficiency and regularity in international air navigation. **Structure** General Assembly; Executive Board; Regional Directors. **Languages** English. **Staff** 13.00 FTE, voluntary. **Finance** Sources: members' dues; sponsorship. Annual budget: 90,000 EUR. **Activities** Events/meetings; knowledge management/information dissemination. **Events** *General Assembly* Lisbon (Portugal) 2022, *Global Aeronautical Information Management Conference (Global AIM)* Warsaw (Poland) 2022, *Global Aeronautical Information Management Conference* 2021, *General Assembly* Lisbon (Portugal) 2020, *Global Aeronautical Information Management Conference* Warsaw (Poland) 2020. **Publications** *IFAIMA Newsletter*.
Members Associations (34); Individuals (1,825); Corporate (15). Members in 85 countries:
Albania, Algeria, Angola, Argentina, Australia, Austria, Belgium, Bolivia, Brazil, Canada, Cape Verde, Chile, Colombia, Comoros, Congo DR, Côte d'Ivoire, Croatia, Czechia, Dominican Rep, Ecuador, Egypt, Estonia, Ethiopia, France, Gambia, Germany, Ghana, Guatemala, Haiti, Honduras, Hungary, India, Indonesia, Iran Islamic Rep, Ireland, Italy, Jamaica, Japan, Jordan, Kenya, Korea Rep, Kuwait, Latvia, Lebanon, Liberia, Libya, Luxembourg, Maldives, Malta, Mexico, Mongolia, Mozambique, Namibia, Nepal, Netherlands, Nigeria, Oman, Pakistan, Panama, Peru, Philippines, Poland, Portugal, Qatar, Saudi Arabia, Senegal, Sierra Leone, Slovakia, Slovenia, Somalia, Spain, Sri Lanka, Sudan, Switzerland, Tanzania UR, Timor-Leste, Trinidad-Tobago, Tunisia, Türkiye, Uganda, UK, United Arab Emirates, USA, Zambia, Zimbabwe. [2022.06.14/XJ9601/**C**]

♦ International Federation of Aero-Philatelic Societies 13342

Fédération internationale des sociétés aérophilatéliques (FISA) – Federación Internacional de Sociedades Aerofilatélicas – Internationaler Verband der Aero-Philatelisten-Vereine

Pres Rallenweg 3, 13505 Berlin, Germany. T. +493043666511. Fax +493043666510.
SG 't Pleintje 13, 2861 Onze-Lieve-Vrouw-Waver, Belgium. T. +3215252888. Fax +3215253686.
URL: http://www.fisa-web.com/

History Founded 10 Jun 1951, Wuppertal-Elberfeld (Germany FR). Constitution adopted 23 Apr 1960, Strasbourg (France). **Structure** General Assembly (biennial). Board of Directors, comprising Patron, President, Vice-President Aero, Vice-President Astro, Treasurer, Secretary General and 5 members. **Languages** English, French, German. **Staff** Voluntary. **Finance** Sources: members' dues. **Activities** Sponsors exhibitions; awards prizes for merit. **Events** *Biennial Congress and General Assembly* Berlin (Germany) 2019, *Biennial Congress and General Assembly* Hirtenberg (Austria) 2017, *Biennial Congress and General Assembly / Biennial General Assembly* London (UK) 2015, *Biennial Congress and General Assembly / Biennial General Assembly* San Francisco, CA (USA) 2013, *Biennial Congress and General Assembly / Biennial General Assembly* Graz (Austria) 2011. **Publications** *Bulletin FISA* – electronically.
Members Clubs and societies in 24 countries:
Argentina, Australia, Austria, Belgium, Canada, Colombia, Czechia, Denmark, France, Germany, Hungary, India, Ireland, Italy, Japan, Netherlands, New Zealand, Poland, Romania, Russia, South Africa, Switzerland, Uruguay, USA.
Included in the above, 4 societies listed in this Yearbook:
Aerophilatelic Society of Southern Africa; *European Aero-Philately Club (no recent information)*; *Internationaler Aero-Philatelisten Club (IAPC)*; *Nordisk Luftpostsamler Forening (NLF, inactive)*.
NGO Relations *Fédération internationale de philatélie (FIP, #09650)*, through its Aerophilatelic Commission. [2018/XC1848/y/**C**]

♦ International Federation of Aerospace Technology and Engineering / see International Federation of Airworthiness (#13352)

♦ International Federation of Aesthetic Group Gymnastics (IFAGG) . . . 13343

Office Hitsaajankatu 22, FI-00810 Helsinki, Finland.
Pres Isokaari 34, FI-45740 Kuusankoski, Finland.
URL: http://www.ifagg.com/

History 12 Oct 2003, Helsinki (Finland). **Aims** Promote the sport of aesthetic group gymnastics. **Structure** General Assembly; Council; Standing Committees (2). **Languages** English. **Finance** Members' dues.
Members Full in 13 countries and territories:
Brazil, Bulgaria, Canada, Czechia, Denmark, El Salvador, Estonia, Faeroe Is, Finland, Israel, Russia, Spain, Ukraine.
Country members in 11 countries:
Austria, Belarus, Belgium, France, Germany, Hungary, Moldova, Poland, South Africa, Türkiye, USA. [2015.01.07/XJ3291/**D**]

♦ International Federation of Aestheticians (INFA) 13344

Fédération internationale de l'esthétique-cosmétique – International Föderation der Kosmetikerinnen

Pres Bd de Waterloo 53, 1000 Brussels, Belgium. T. +3256555789. Fax +3256556310. E-mail: administration@infa.org.
URL: http://www.infa.org

History 18 Feb 1978, Brussels (Belgium). Registration: Belgium. **Aims** Promote the profession of aesthetician and its training. **Structure** Executive Council (meets annually); Board of Directors. **Languages** English, French. **Staff** Voluntary. **Finance** Members' dues. **Activities** Events/meetings; knowledge management/information dissemination; standards/guidelines. **Events** *Annual General Assembly* Brussels (Belgium) 2019, *Annual General Assembly* Brussels (Belgium) 2010, *Annual General Assembly* Neuchâtel (Switzerland) 2009, *Annual General Assembly* Brussels (Belgium) 2002, *Annual General Assembly* Brussels (Belgium) 2001. **Publications** *Médecine et Esthétique* in Dutch, French – bulletin.

Members National groups and individuals in 34 countries and territories:
Argentina, Belgium, Benin, Bolivia, Cameroon, Canada, China, Congo DR, Côte d'Ivoire, France, Germany, Hong Kong, Hungary, Italy, Japan, Korea Rep, Lithuania, Luxembourg, Malaysia, Malta, Morocco, Nigeria, Portugal, Russia, Slovenia, Spain, Switzerland, Syrian AR, Taiwan, Togo, Tunisia, UK, Ukraine, USA.

NGO Relations Member of: *Federation of European and International Associations Established in Belgium (FAIB, #09508).* [2020.03.09/XD6659/**D**]

♦ International Federation on Ageing (IFA) 13345

Fédération internationale du vieillissement (FIV) – Federación Internacional de la Vejez – Internationale Föderation des Alterns

SG 1 Bridgepoint Drive, Suite G-238, Toronto ON M4M 2B5, Canada. T. +14163421655. Fax +14166392165.
URL: http://www.ifa.ngo/

History 26 Dec 1973, London (UK). Founded at a meeting of national voluntary organizations, replacing the American *Association of Retired Persons International (ARPI, inactive)*, set up 1963. Registration: Canada. **Aims** Be the global point of connection and networks of experts and expertise to influence and shape age-related policy. **Structure** Board of Directors; Secretariat headed by Secretary General. **Languages** English, French. **Staff** 17.00 FTE, paid. Several voluntary. **Finance** Sources: grants; members' dues; revenue from activities/projects. **Activities** Advocacy/lobbying/activism; awareness raising; capacity building; events/meetings; guidance/assistance/consulting; healthcare; knowledge management/information dissemination; networking/liaising; politics/policy/regulatory; projects/programmes; publishing activities; research and development; research/documentation; training/education. **Events** *Global Conference on Ageing* Bangkok (Thailand) 2023, *Global Conference on Ageing* Niagara Falls, ON (Canada) 2021, *Global Conference on Ageing* Niagara Falls, ON (Canada) 2020, *Copenhagen Summit on Cognitive Reserve* Copenhagen (Denmark) 2019, *Global Conference on Ageing* Toronto, ON (Canada) 2018. **Publications** *IFA VoltAGE. IFA Global Cafe.* Annual Report; reports; studies; surveys; guidelines; case studies.

Members Full (NGOs, Corporate sector; Individuals and Academia representing or serving older people); Associate; Government associate. Organizations in 60 countries and territories:
Albania, Argentina, Armenia, Australia, Austria, Bangladesh, Barbados, Belgium, Brazil, Cameroon, Canada, Chile, China, Colombia, Congo Brazzaville, Costa Rica, Czechia, Denmark, Finland, France, Germany, Ghana, Greece, Hungary, India, Indonesia, Iran Islamic Rep, Ireland, Israel, Italy, Japan, Korea Rep, Liberia, Lithuania, Malaysia, Malta, Mauritius, Mexico, Nepal, Netherlands, New Zealand, Nigeria, Norway, Pakistan, Peru, Philippines, Russia, Singapore, South Africa, Spain, Sri Lanka, Sweden, Switzerland, Taiwan, Thailand, Türkiye, Uganda, UK, USA, Zambia.

Included in the above, 16 organizations listed in this Yearbook:
AARP International; Age UK; Council of Europe (CE, #04881); ECOSOC (#05331); EURAG – European Federation of Older Persons (#05597); HelpAge International (#10904); Human Rights Committee (CCPR, #10979); ILO (#11123); International Association of Gerontology and Geriatrics (IAGG, #11920); International Association of Homes and Services for the Ageing (IAHSA, #11938); International Longevity Centre Global Alliance (ILC Global Alliance, #14064); International Network for the Prevention of Elder Abuse (INPEA, #14307); New World Hope Organization (NWHO); UNESCO (#20322); United Nations Economic and Social Commission for Asia and the Pacific (ESCAP, #20557); WHO (#20950).

Consultative Status Consultative status granted from: *ECOSOC (#05331)* (General); *ILO (#11123)* (Special List); *WHO (#20950)* (Official Relations). **IGO Relations** Cooperates with (1): *United Nations Population Fund (UNFPA, #20612).* Associated with Department of Global Communications of the United Nations. **NGO Relations** Member of (5): *Geneva Global Health Hub (G2H2, #10122); Global Alliance for the Rights of Older People (#10226); International Institute on Ageing, United Nations – Malta (INIA, #13860); Vienna NGO Committee on the Family (#20774); Vienna NGO Committee on the Status of Women (#20775).* Cooperates with (2): *Global Meeting of Generations (GMG); International Council for Adult Education (ICAE, #12983).* [2023/XC4419/y/**C**]

♦ International Federation of Agricultural Brainworkers (inactive)

♦ International Federation of Agricultural Journalists (IFAJ) 13346

Fédération internationale des journalistes agricoles (FIJA) – Internationale Föderation der Agrarjournalisten

Global Manager PO Box 250, Ormstown QC J0S 1K0, Canada. T. +18777826456. E-mail: globalmanager@ifaj.org – globaloffice@ifaj.org.
URL: http://www.ifaj.org/

History Founded 1957, Paris (France). **Aims** Give agricultural journalists and communicators a platform for professional development and international networking. **Structure** Congress (annual); Executive Committee; Praesidium. **Languages** English. **Staff** 5.00 FTE, voluntary. **Finance** Sources: members' dues; sponsorship. Other sources: registration fees. **Activities** Awards/prizes/competitions; events/meetings; networking/liaising. **Events** *Annual Congress* Interlaken (Switzerland) 2024, *Annual Congress* Calgary, AB (Canada) 2023, *Annual Congress* Bredsten (Denmark) 2022, *Annual Congress* 2021, *Annual Congress* 2020. **Publications** *IFAJ Newsletter.*

Members Full in 50 countries:
Albania, Argentina, Australia, Austria, Bangladesh, Belgium, Burkina Faso, Burundi, Cameroon, Canada, Congo DR, Croatia, Czechia, Denmark, Finland, Gambia, Georgia, Germany, Ghana, Guinea, Hungary, India, Iran Islamic Rep, Ireland, Israel, Italy, Japan, Kenya, Liberia, Madagascar, Netherlands, New Zealand, Nigeria, Norway, Rwanda, Senegal, Serbia, Slovakia, Slovenia, Somalia, South Africa, Spain, Sweden, Switzerland, Tanzania UR, Togo, Türkiye, UK, Ukraine, USA.

Affiliate in 1 country:
Nepal.

Consultative Status Consultative status granted from: *ECOSOC (#05331)* (Ros C); *FAO (#09260)* (Special Status). [2018.09.05/XC2681/**C**]

♦ International Federation of Agricultural Press (inactive)
♦ International Federation of Agricultural Producers (inactive)
♦ International Federation of Agricultural Research Systems for Development (no recent information)
♦ International Federation of Agricultural Staff (inactive)

♦ International Federation of Air Hostesses and Flight Nurses 13347

Fédération Internationale des Hôtesses et Convoyeuses de l'Air (FIHCA)

Pres Sedanstr 42, 12167 Berlin, Germany. T. +49307929340.
Registed Office Aéro-Club de France, 6 rue Galilée, 75116 Paris, France. E-mail: fihca75@gmail.com.

History 19 Aug 1966, Paris (France), as *Fédération internationale des hôtesses de l'air.* Current statutes adopted 27 Jun 1993, Paris, when present title was adopted. Registered in accordance with French law. **Aims** Encourage and develop mutual assistance, friendship, cultural and linguistic exchanges and solidarity among air hostesses of different airlines; promote cultural and family exchanges between countries; highlight the essential aeronautical characteristics common to air hostesses and escorts; provide members with information on professional possibilities open to them. **Structure** General Assembly (annual). Board (meets 4 times a year), comprising President, 8 Vice-Presidents (Presidents of member federations), Secretary-General, Treasurer, 7 Deputy-Secretaries and 10 members. **Languages** English, French. **Staff** 28.00 FTE, paid. **Finance** Members' dues. **Events** *Annual General Assembly* Italy 2014, *Annual General Assembly* St Petersburg (Russia) 2013, *Annual General Assembly* Dubrovnik (Croatia) 2012, *Annual General Assembly* Washington, DC (USA) 2011, *Annual General Assembly* Dresden (Germany) 2010. **Publications** Meeting and convention reports.

Members Honorary; Active; Benefactor. Individuals and associations in 16 countries:
Belgium, Canada, Denmark, Finland, France, Germany, Hungary, Monaco, Norway, Poland, Portugal, Spain, Sweden, Switzerland, UK, USA. [2019/XD5447/**D**]

♦ International Federation of Airline Dispatchers' Associations (IFALDA) 13348

Special Assistant 3364 Thornewood Drive, Doraville GA 30340, USA. T. +14046309568.
Pres address not obtained.
URL: http://www.ifalda.org/

History 1962, Montréal, QC (Canada). **Aims** Promote safety in civil aviation through standardization of operational control. **Structure** General Meeting (annual) elects Officers. **Languages** English. **Staff** 4.00 FTE, voluntary. **Finance** Sources: members' dues. **Activities** Working towards a worldwide licence for flight operations officers. **Events** *Annual General Meeting* Miami, FL (USA) 2024, *Annual General Meeting* Paris (France) 2023, *Annual General Meeting* Toronto, ON (Canada) 2022, *Annual General Meeting* 2021, *Annual General Meeting* Copenhagen (Denmark) 2019. **Publications** *IFLADA News* (3 a year).

Members Regional and local organizations (92) representing 2,200 flight dispatchers/flight operation officers in 53 countries and territories:
Argentina, Australia, Austria, Bahamas, Belgium, Bolivia, Bosnia-Herzegovina, Brazil, Bulgaria, Canada, Chile, Colombia, Cuba, Czechia, Denmark, Finland, France, Germany, Ghana, Greece, Hungary, Iceland, India, Ireland, Israel, Italy, Jamaica, Japan, Latvia, Luxembourg, Malta, Mexico, Netherlands, Norway, Peru, Philippines, Poland, Portugal, Puerto Rico, Russia, Serbia, Spain, Sri Lanka, Sweden, Switzerland, Taiwan, Thailand, Trinidad-Tobago, Türkiye, UK, Uruguay, USA, Venezuela.

IGO Relations Accredited by (1): *International Civil Aviation Organization (ICAO, #12581).* [2021/XD0767/**C**]

♦ International Federation of Air Line Pilots' Associations (IFALPA) .. 13349

Fédération internationale des associations de pilotes de ligne – Federación Internacional de Asociaciones de Pilotos de Linea Aérea

Main Office 485 McGill St, Ste 700, Montréal QC H2Y 2H4, Canada. T. +15144191191. Fax +15144191195. E-mail: ifalpa@ifalpa.org.
URL: http://www.ifalpa.org/

History 7 Apr 1948, London (UK), as *World Federation of Air Line Pilots – Fédération mondiale des pilotes de ligne.* Took over *International Flight Engineers' Organization (IFEO, inactive)*, 13 Oct 2001. **Aims** Promote the highest level of aviation safety worldwide and be the global advocate of the piloting profession, providing representation, services and support to both our members and the *aviation* industry. **Structure** Conference (annual); Executive Board; Standing Committees (11). Regions (5), each led by Executive Vice-President: Africa and Middle East (AFI/MID); Asia and Pacific (ASIA/PAC); Caribbeanand North America (CAR/NAM); Europe (EUR); South America (SAM). Membership open; meetings closed. **Languages** English. **Staff** 12.00 FTE, paid. **Finance** Sources: members' dues. **Events** *Annual Conference* Singapore (Singapore) 2022, *Annual Conference* Montréal, QC (Canada) 2021, *Annual Conference* Singapore (Singapore) 2020, *Annual Conference* Berlin (Germany) 2019, *Annual Conference* Luxembourg (Luxembourg) 2018. **Publications** *InterPilot Magazine* (4 a year) – electronic. Bulletins; reports.

Members Associations in 97 countries and territories:
Algeria, Argentina, Armenia, Australia, Austria, Bahamas, Bangladesh, Belgium, Bolivia, Bosnia-Herzegovina, Brazil, Bulgaria, Canada, Cape Verde, Cayman Is, Chile, China, Colombia, Costa Rica, Croatia, Cyprus, Czechia, Denmark, Dominican Rep, Ecuador, Egypt, Estonia, Ethiopia, Fiji, Finland, France, Georgia, Germany, Greece, Hong Kong, Hungary, Iceland, India, Indonesia, Ireland, Israel, Italy, Jamaica, Japan, Kazakhstan, Kenya, Korea Rep, Kuwait, Latvia, Lebanon, Leeward Is, Lithuania, Luxembourg, Malaysia, Malta, Mauritania, Mauritius, Mexico, Mongolia, Montenegro, Morocco, Namibia, Netherlands, New Zealand, Nigeria, North Macedonia, Norway, Pakistan, Panama, Papua New Guinea, Paraguay, Peru, Philippines, Poland, Portugal, Romania, Russia, Senegal, Serbia, Singapore, Slovakia, Slovenia, South Africa, Spain, Sri Lanka, Suriname, Sweden, Switzerland, Tanzania UR, Thailand, Trinidad-Tobago, Tunisia, Türkiye, UK, Ukraine, Uruguay, USA.

Consultative Status Consultative status granted from: *ECOSOC (#05331)* (Ros C); *World Meteorological Organization (WMO, #21649).* **IGO Relations** Cooperates with: *European Aviation Security Training Institute (EASTI, #06304).* Accredited by: *United Nations Office at Vienna (UNOV, #20604).* Associated with Department of Global Communications of the United Nations. **NGO Relations** Observers exchanged at conferences with: *International Transport Workers' Federation (ITF, #15726). European Cockpit Association (ECA, #06598)* represents European interests. Member of: *Flight Safety Foundation (FSF, #09795).* Maintains relations with: *Airports Council International (ACI, #00611); International Air Transport Association (IATA, #11614); International Federation of Air Traffic Controllers' Associations (IFATCA, #13350).* [2020/XB1851/**B**]

♦ International Federation of Air Traffic Controllers' Associations (IFATCA) 13350

Fédération internationale des associations de contrôleurs du trafic aérien – Federación Internacional de las Asociaciones de Directores del Trafico Aéreo

Office Manager 360 St Jacques, Ste 2002, Montréal QC H2Y 1P5, Canada. T. +15148667040. Fax +15148667612. E-mail: office@ifatca.org.
URL: http://www.ifatca.org/

History 19 Oct 1961, Amsterdam (Netherlands). Registered in accordance with the Swiss Civil Code. Aims and objectives, formulated in 1961, Amsterdam, still in force. **Aims** Promote *safety*, efficiency and regularity in international air *navigation*; promote, advise and assist in developing safe and orderly systems of Air Traffic Control (ATC); promote and uphold a high standard of knowledge and professional efficiency among air traffic controllers; protect and safeguard the interests of the profession; make mutually beneficial affiliations with other international organizations. **Structure** Annual Conference. Executive Board, consisting of: President/Chief Executive Officer; Deputy President; Executive Vice Presidents (7) – Finance, Professional, Technical, Africa and Middle East, Americas, Asia and Pacific, Europe; Conference Executive/Board Secretary. Regions (4): Africa and Middle East (AFM); Americas (AMA); Asia and Pacific (ASP); Europe (EUR). Standing Committees; Committees. **Languages** English. **Staff** 2.00 FTE, paid. All the others voluntary. **Finance** Members' dues – 3 grades based on UN Development categories: (a) US$ 16.63 per member; (b) US$ 9.80 per member; (c) US$ 6.46 per member. **Activities** Collects and studies data on technical subjects. Standing Committees currently in operation: SC1 – Technical and Operational Matters in Air Traffic Control (TOC); SC3 – Finance (FIC); SC4 – Professional and Legal Matters in Air Traffic Control (PLC); SC6 – Constitution and Administrative Policy (CAC). Committee A (Administrative Policy and Constitutional Matters); Committee B (Technical and Operational Matters); Committee C (Human Factors, Legal and Professional Matters). Participates in international meetings, panels and working groups. **Events** *Annual Conference* 2022, *Annual Conference* Montego Bay (Jamaica) 2021, *Asia Pacific Regional Meeting* 2020, *Annual Conference* Singapore (Singapore) 2020, *Asia Pacific Regional Meeting* Kathmandu (Nepal) 2019. **Publications** *The Controller* (4 a year) – journal; *IFATCA Circular* (3 a year) – internal. *IFATCA Manual*; *Information Handbook.* Technical and professional manuals; brochure.

Members Professional; Associate Professional; Corporate; Honorary Associate. National associations, totalling over 50,000 members, in 134 countries and territories:
Albania, Algeria, Angola, Antigua-Barbuda, Argentina, Armenia, Australia, Austria, Bahamas, Barbados, Belarus, Belgium, Benin, Bermuda, Bolivia, Bosnia-Herzegovina, Botswana, Brazil, Bulgaria, Burkina Faso, Burundi, Cameroon, Canada, Cape Verde, Chad, Chile, Comoros, Congo Brazzaville, Congo DR, Costa Rica, Côte d'Ivoire, Croatia, Cyprus, Czechia, Denmark, Djibouti, Dominican Rep, Ecuador, Egypt, El Salvador, Eritrea, Estonia, Eswatini, Ethiopia, Fiji, Finland, France, Gabon, Gambia, Georgia, Germany, Ghana, Greece, Grenada, Guatemala, Guinea, Guinea-Bissau, Guyana, Haiti, Hong Kong, Hungary, Iceland, India, Indonesia, Iran Islamic Rep, Ireland, Israel, Italy, Jamaica, Japan, Jordan, Kenya, Latvia, Liberia, Lithuania, Luxembourg, Macau, Madagascar, Malaysia, Mali, Malta, Mauritania, Mauritius, Mexico, Moldova, Mongolia, Morocco, Namibia, Nepal, Netherlands, New Zealand, Niger, Nigeria, North Macedonia, Norway, Panama, Peru, Philippines, Poland, Portugal, Romania, Russia, Rwanda, Senegal, Serbia-Montenegro, Seychelles, Sierra Leone, Singapore, Slovakia, Slovenia, South Africa, Spain, Sri Lanka, St Lucia, Sudan, Suriname, Sweden, Switzerland, Taiwan, Tanzania UR, Togo, Trinidad-Tobago, Tunisia, Türkiye, Uganda, UK, Ukraine, United Arab Emirates, Uruguay, USA, Yemen, Zambia, Zimbabwe.

Regional member organization:
EUROCONTROL Guild of Air Traffic Services (EGATS, #05669).

Corporate members in 14 countries:
Austria, Canada, Denmark, France, Germany, Israel, Italy, Norway, South Africa, Spain, Sweden, Switzerland, UK, USA.

Associate professional members in 3 countries and territories:
Korea Rep, Kosovo, Pakistan.

IGO Relations *International Civil Aviation Organization (ICAO, #12581)* (Observer Status). **NGO Relations** Active in: *Informal South Pacific Air Traffic Services Group (ISPACG, no recent information); North Atlantic Systems Planning Group (NATSPG, no recent information).* [2020/XB1852/y/**B**]

♦ International Federation of Air Traffic Safety Electronic Associations (IFATSEA) 13351

Fédération internationale des associations de l'électronique de sécurité du trafic aérien

Exec Sec Frankfurt Airport Center 1, Bldg 234 HBK 18, Hugo-Eckener-Ring 1, 60549 Frankfurt-Main, Germany. T. +494251672440. Fax +4942516720525. E-mail: execsec@ifatsea.org – info@ifatsea.org.
URL: http://www.ifatsea.org/

History Oct 1972, London (UK). **Aims** Promote safety, efficiency and regularity in international air navigation; assist and secure development of electronics systems to maintain safe and orderly flow of air traffic; uphold high standard of knowledge and professional efficiency among personnel; protect and safeguard collective professional interests of personnel. **Structure** General Assembly (annual); Council (annual); Executive (meets twice a year). **Languages** English. **Staff** 6.00 FTE, voluntary. **Finance** Sources: members' dues. **Activities** Knowledge management/information dissemination; standards/guidelines. **Events** *Annual General Assembly* Accra (Ghana) 2019, *Annual General Assembly* Hammamet (Tunisia) 2018, *Annual General Assembly* Montréal, QC (Canada) 2017, *Annual General Assembly* Abuja (Nigeria) 2016, *Annual General Assembly* Berlin (Germany) 2015. **Publications** *Navaire* (2 a year) – online.
Members Associations, totalling 12,000 members; Corporate. Members in 68 countries:
Albania, Angola, Argentina, Austria, Belgium, Benin, Bulgaria, Burkina Faso, Cameroon, Canada, Cape Verde, Chile, China, Croatia, Cyprus, Czechia, Djibouti, Ethiopia, Finland, France, Gambia, Germany, Ghana, Greece, Haiti, India, Iran Islamic Rep, Ireland, Italy, Jamaica, Japan, Kenya, Lithuania, Luxembourg, Mali, Malta, Mongolia, Montenegro, Morocco, Nepal, Netherlands, Niger, Nigeria, North Macedonia, Norway, Pakistan, Peru, Portugal, Romania, Russia, Senegal, Serbia, Slovakia, Slovenia, South Africa, Spain, Sri Lanka, Sudan, Sweden, Switzerland, Tanzania UR, Tunisia, Türkiye, Uganda, UK, Ukraine, United Arab Emirates, USA. [2018.09.20/XC4594/**C**]

♦ International Federation of Airworthiness (IFA) 13352
Fédération internationale de navigabilité aérospatiale

Sec 59 Hurst Farm Road, East Grinstead, RH19 4DQ, UK. T. +447746773170. E-mail: sec@ifairworthy.com.
URL: http://www.ifairworthy.com/

History Sep 1964. Former names and other names: *International Federation of Aerospace Technology and Engineering* – former (1964 to 1968); *International Federation of Airworthiness Technology and Engineering (IFATE)* – former (1968 to 1975); *Fédération internationale de technologie et de navigabilité spatiale* – former (1968 to 1975). Registration: No/ID: 296354, UK. **Aims** Ensure safety and economy in *aircraft* operation; encourage cooperative action among bodies concerned with airworthiness to promote practices for standardization and proper maintenance and safe operation of *air transport*; encourage internationally acceptable standards of proficiency and experience through personnel licensing, especially of aircraft maintenance engineers. **Structure** General Meeting (annual); Board; Technical Committee; Working Groups; Permanent Secretariat headed by CEO. **Languages** English. **Staff** 1.00 FTE, paid; 10.00 FTE, voluntary. **Finance** Sources: members' dues. **Activities** Events/meetings; financial and/or material support. **Events** *Annual Conference* Dubai (United Arab Emirates) 2018, *SMS – How can it make a real difference?* Hong Kong (Hong Kong) 2017, *Risk Management* Dubai (United Arab Emirates) 2016, *Continuing Airworthiness – Critical Interface* Hong Kong (Hong Kong) 2015, *Maintaining Airworthiness Standards & Investing in the Most Important Asset 'Human Factors'* Dubai (United Arab Emirates) 2014. **Publications** *IFA News* (annual) – magazine; *IFA News Extra* – electronic newsletter.
Members Corporate airlines; maintenance repair organizations; aerospace manufacturing companies; airworthiness authorities ; aviation insurance; consultancies; professional colleges; professional societies; universities and colleges. Members in 19 countries and territories:
Australia, Canada, China, France, Guyana, Hong Kong, Indonesia, Italy, Kenya, Kuwait, Netherlands, New Zealand, Nigeria, Philippines, Spain, Taiwan, UK, United Arab Emirates, USA.
IGO Relations Observer status with (1): *International Civil Aviation Organization (ICAO, #12581)*. [2021.02.24/XC1854/**C**]

♦ International Federation of Airworthiness Technology and Engineering / see International Federation of Airworthiness (#13352)
♦ International Federation of Allied Ex-Servicemen (inactive)
♦ International Federation for Alternative Trade / see World Fair Trade Organization (#21396)
♦ International Federation Alysh (no recent information)
♦ International Federation of Amateur Theatrical Societies (inactive)

♦ International Federation Amateur Unifight (FIAU) 13353
Pres str Vorontsovskaya, 6 bldg 2, Moscow MOSKVA, Russia, 109004. T. +74959129057. Fax +74959122731. E-mail: unifight1@mail.ru.
URL: http://www.unifight.com/

History Also referred to as *European Continental International Federation Amateur Unifight (ECIFAU)*. **Aims** Promote the *sport* of amateur unifight. **Structure** Executive Committee; Commissions (3). **Languages** English, Russian. **Staff** Voluntary. **Finance** Members' dues. **Activities** Events/meetings; sporting activities. **Events** *Congress* Medyn (Russia) 2013, *Congress* Medyn (Russia) 2012, *Congress* Moscow (Russia) 2011.
Members National organizations (20) in 20 countries:
Armenia, Azerbaijan, Belarus, Bulgaria, Finland, France, Georgia, Germany, India, Iran Islamic Rep, Kazakhstan, Lithuania, Moldova, Nepal, Romania, Russia, Tajikistan, Turkmenistan, Ukraine, Uzbekistan. [2019.12.12/XM2810/**D**]

♦ International Federation of Ambulance Officers (inactive)

♦ International Federation of American Football (IFAF) 13354
Managing Dir 16 Boulevard Saint Germain, CS 70514, 75237 Paris CEDEX 05, France. E-mail: info@americanfootball.sport.
URL: http://www.americanfootball.sport/

History 1998. Registration: Start date: Mar 2001, France. **Aims** Promote the game of American football worldwide; coordinate all matters relating to American football. **Structure** Congress (annual); Executive Board; Presidium; Secretariat. Global Committees (15). Regions (5): Africa; America; Asia; Europe: Oceania. **Languages** English. **Staff** 3.00 FTE, paid; 25.00 FTE, voluntary. **Finance** Sources: members' dues; revenue from activities/projects; sponsorship. **Activities** Sporting activities. **Events** *Congress* USA 2022, *Congress* 2021, *Congress* 2020, *Congress* London (UK) 2019, *Congress* Vienna (Austria) 2011.
Members Full national federations in 74 countries and territories:
Antigua-Barbuda, Argentina, Australia, Austria, Belarus, Belgium, Brazil, Cameroon, Canada, Chile, Colombia, Congo Brazzaville, Côte d'Ivoire, Cuba, Czechia, Denmark, Egypt, El Salvador, Finland, France, Georgia, Germany, Great Britain, Guam, Guatemala, Haiti, Honduras, Hong Kong, Hungary, India, Indonesia, Ireland, Israel, Italy, Jamaica, Japan, Jordan, Kazakhstan, Kenya, Korea Rep, Kuwait, Luxembourg, Malaysia, Malta, Mexico, Morocco, Netherlands, New Caledonia, New Zealand, Nicaragua, Nigeria, Norway, Panama, Papua New Guinea, Philippines, Poland, Russia, Serbia, Singapore, Slovakia, Slovenia, South Africa, Spain, Sweden, Switzerland, Tahiti Is, Tunisia, Türkiye, Uganda, Ukraine, Uruguay, USA, Vietnam, Zimbabwe.
NGO Relations Member of (3): *Alliance of Independent recognised Members of Sport (AIMS, #00690)* (Associate); *Association of the IOC Recognized International Sports Federations (ARISF, #02767)*; *Olympic Movement (#17719)*. Recognized by: *International Olympic Committee (IOC, #14408)*. [2023/XD9365/**B**]

♦ International Federation of 'Amies de la Jeune Fille' (inactive)
♦ International Federation of Angling in Fresh Waters (see: #04562)
♦ International Federation for Animal Health / see Health for Animals (#10870)
♦ International Federation for Animal Health Europe / see AnimalhealthEurope (#00837)
♦ International Federation of Anthroposophical Medical Associations (#13314)
♦ International Federation of Anthroposophic Arts and Eurythmy Therapies (internationally oriented national body)

♦ International Federation of Anti-Leprosy Associations (ILEP) 13355
Fédération internationale des associations contre la lèpre

CEO c/o Quai de l'ile 13, 1204 Geneva, Switzerland. T. +41225962240. E-mail: officer@ilepfederation.org.
URL: http://www.ilepfederation.org/

History 25 Sep 1966, Bern (Switzerland). Constitution adopted 20 Apr 1969, Paris (France); new constitution adopted 12 Dec 1987; current constitution adopted 31 Mar 2006, London (UK). Present title adopted 12 Apr 1975, Bonn (Germany FR). Former names and other names: *European Federation of Anti-Leprosy Associations* – former; *Fédération européenne des associations contre la lèpre* – former; *Internationale Vereinigung der Leprahilfswerke* – former. Registration: No/ID: CHE-179.299.957), Switzerland; Charity, No/ID: 280676, Start date: 21 Jun 1980, End date: 9 Dec 2016, England and Wales. **Aims** Promote and facilitate cooperation and collaboration between members by coordinating support to leprosy programmes, representing common interests and providing technical expertise. **Structure** Members' Assembly; Executive Board; Advisory Panel; Technical Commission; Secretariat. **Languages** English, French. **Staff** 4.00 FTE, paid. **Finance** Sources: donations; members' dues. **Activities** Events/meetings; guidance/assistance/consulting; monitoring/evaluation; networking/liaising; projects/programmes; research and development; standards/guidelines; training/education. **Events** *Cooperation Meeting* London (UK) 2012, *Cooperation Meeting* London (UK) 2011, *Cooperation Meeting* London (UK) 2010, *Cooperation Meeting* London (UK) 2009, *Cooperation Meeting* London (UK) 2008. **Publications** *ILEP Review* (annual) in English, French; *ILEP Statistics – Global Summary of ILEP Support of Anti-Leprosy Projects* (annual). *ILEP Coordinate Budget*; *ILEP Coordinate Expenditure*; *ILEP Learning Guides*; *ILEP Technical Guides*. Technical bulletins; Training Catalogue; Research Directory.
Members NGOs (13) in 12 countries:
Belgium, Canada, France, Germany, Italy, Japan, Luxembourg, Netherlands, Spain, Switzerland, UK, USA.
Included in the above, 5 organizations listed in this Yearbook:
Damien Foundation – Voluntary Organization for Leprosy and TB Control (AF); *LEPRA Health in Action (LEPRA)*; *Leprosy Mission International (TLMI, #16446)*; *Raoul Follereau International Union (#18618)*; *Secours aux lépreux Canada (SLC)*.
Consultative Status Consultative status granted from: *WHO (#20950)* (Official Relations); *ECOSOC (#05331)* (Special). **NGO Relations** Member of (2): *Global Partnership for Zero Leprosy (#10543)*; *Neglected Tropical Diseased NGO Network (NNN, #16969)*. [2020/XD0719/y/**C**]

♦ International Federation for the Application of Standards / see International Federation of Standards Users (#13558)

♦ International Federation of Arabian Horse Racing (IFAHR) 13356
Registered Address 46 place Abel Gance, 92100 Boulogne-Billancourt, France. E-mail: info@ifahr.net.
URL: https://www.ifahr.net/

History 11 Jan 1999, Paris (France). Former names and other names: *International Federation of Arabian Horse Racing Authorities* – legal name. Registration: RNA, No/ID: W923004854, Start date: 1999, France. **Aims** Improve the speed, stamina, soundness and temperament of the Arab horse breed through racing. **Structure** General Meeting; Executive Board.
Members Full in 37 countries:
Algeria, Australia, Austria, Azerbaijan, Brazil, Canada, Chile, Czechia, Denmark, Egypt, France, Germany, Iran Islamic Rep, Italy, Kazakhstan, Kuwait, Lebanon, Libya, Lithuania, Morocco, Netherlands, Norway, Oman, Poland, Portugal, Qatar, Russia, Saudi Arabia, Spain, Sweden, Switzerland, Syrian AR, Tunisia, Türkiye, UK, United Arab Emirates, USA. [2021/AA2475/**C**]

♦ International Federation of Arabian Horse Racing Authorities / see International Federation of Arabian Horse Racing (#13356)
♦ International Federation of Armsports (internationally oriented national body)
♦ International Federation of Aromatherapists (internationally oriented national body)
♦ International Federation for Art Education (inactive)
♦ International Federation for Art Education, Drawing and Arts Applied to Industries (inactive)

♦ International Federation for Artificial Organs (IFAO) 13357
Fédération internationale des organes artificiels

Sec c/o Ash Access Technology Inc, INOK Business Center, 3601 Sagamore Parkway North, Ste B, Lafayette IN 47904, USA.
Main Office c/o Midland Building, 10 West Erie St, Suite 200, Painesville OH 44077, USA.
URL: http://www.ifao.org/

History 1977, as *International Society for Artificial Organs (ISAO) – Société internationale des organes artificiels*. Also previously referred to as *International Society for Artificial Internal Organs (ISAIO)*. Current title adopted when present Federation emerged from the former ISAO, 2004. **Aims** Increase and encourage knowledge and research on artificial organs, apheresis, tissue engineering, regenerative medicine and other related topics; facilitate international exchange of knowledge; provide education related to the improvement and optimal utilization of organ assist devices. **Structure** Board of Directors. **Languages** English. **Staff** None. **Finance** Members' dues. **Activities** Events/meetings; research and development; knowledge management/information dissemination; training/education. **Events** *IFAO Congress* Bergamo (Italy) 2023, *IFAO Congress* Osaka (Japan) 2019, *IFAO Congress* Vienna (Austria) 2017, *IFAO Congress* Chicago, IL (USA) 2015, *IFAO Congress* Yokohama (Japan) 2013. **Publications** *Artificial Organs* – journal.
Members Organizations (3):
American Society for Artificial International Organs; *European Society for Artificial Organs (ESAO, #08525)*; Japanese Society for Artificial Organs.
NGO Relations Joint journal with: *International Society for Mechanical Circulatory Support (ISMCS, #15251)*. [2018.06.01/XD4687/v/**D**]

♦ International Federation of Arts Councils and Culture Agencies (IFACCA) 13358
Fédération Internationale des Conseils des Arts et des Agences Culturelles – Federación Internacional de Consejos de Artes y Agencias Culturales

Exec Dir 405/50 Holt Street, Surry Hills NSW 2070, Australia. T. +61417461675. E-mail: info@ifacca.org.
Main Website: http://www.ifacca.org/

History Dec 2000, Ottawa, ON (Canada). Formally founded 12 Jun 2001. **Aims** Foster a world in which arts and culture thrive and are recognized by governments and peoples for their contribution to society. **Structure** General Assembly; Board; Secretariat. **Languages** English, French, Spanish. **Staff** 4.00 FTE, paid. **Finance** Sources: fees for services; members' dues; private foundations; sponsorship. **Activities** Capacity building; events/meetings; knowledge management/information dissemination; networking/liaising. **Events** *World Summit on the Arts and Culture* Stockholm (Sweden) 2023, *World Summit on the Arts and Culture* Kuala Lumpur (Malaysia) 2019, *World Summit on the Arts and Culture* Valletta (Malta) 2016, *World Summit on Arts and Culture / World Summit on the Arts and Culture* Santiago (Chile) 2014, *World summit on arts and culture / World Summit on the Arts and Culture* Melbourne, VIC (Australia) 2011. **Publications** Discussion papers; reports. **Information Services** *ACORNS – Arts and Culture Online Readers News Service*; *Cultural Policy Quick Facts*; *Information Exchange*.
Members National members in 61 countries and territories:
Argentina, Australia, Bahamas, Belize, Botswana, Bulgaria, Canada, Cayman Is, Chile, China, Colombia, Cook Is, Croatia, Cuba, Cyprus, Denmark, El Salvador, England, Estonia, Eswatini, Fiji, Finland, Georgia, Guyana, Iceland, Ireland, Korea Rep, Lithuania, Luxembourg, Malawi, Maldives, Malta, Mexico, Namibia, Netherlands, New Zealand, Niger, Northern Ireland, Norway, Paraguay, Philippines, Scotland, Seychelles, Singapore, Slovakia, Solomon Is, South Africa, Spain, Sri Lanka, Sweden, Switzerland, Tanzania UR, Togo, Tunisia, Ukraine, Uruguay, USA, Vietnam, Wales, Zambia, Zimbabwe.
Consultative Status Consultative status granted from: *UNESCO (#20322)* (Consultative Status). [2022.10.26/XD8432/**D**]

♦ International Federation of Arts, Letters and Sciences (inactive)
♦ International Federation of Asian and Pacific Associations of Optometrists / see Asia Pacific Council of Optometry (#01876)

♦ International Federation of Asian and Western Pacific Contractors' Associations (IFAWPCA) 13359
Fédération internationale des associations d'entrepreneurs asiatiques et du Pacifique occidental

Contact 3rd Floor Padilla Bldg, F Ortigas Jr Road, Ortigas Center, 1605 Pasig City RIZ, Philippines. Fax +6326312789.

History 10 Mar 1956, Manila (Philippines), as *Federation of Asian and Western Pacific Contractors' Associations – Fédération des associations d'entrepreneurs asiatiques et du Pacifique occidental*. Constitution amended and present title adopted 10 Oct 1959, Melbourne (Australia). Further amendments adopted: 1961, Taipei (Taiwan); 1963, Tokyo (Japan); 1964, Seoul (Korea Rep); 1965, Hong Kong; 1967, New Zealand; 1968, Manila; 1976, Hong Kong; 1978, Indonesia; 1988, Taiwan; 1996, Seoul. **Aims** Promote international fellowship and cooperation; develop relationships between governments and contractors in the region; establish cooperative working arrangements in furtherance of civil and building construction projects. **Structure** General Assembly (every 12-18 months); Executive Board; Standing Committees (8). **Languages** English. **Finance** Members' dues. Other sources: conventions proceeds. **Activities** Awards/prizes/competitions. **Events** *Annual Convention* Malé (Maldives) 2020, *Annual Convention* Kuala Lumpur (Malaysia) 2018, *Annual Convention* Seoul (Korea Rep) 2017, *Annual Convention* Tokyo (Japan) 2015, *Convention* Jakarta (Indonesia) 2014. **Publications** *Asia Pacific Contractor* (regular); *IFAWPCA Information Service* (regular); *IFAWPCA Newsletter* (regular). Convention proceedings.

Members Regular (representing bodies) – national contractor associations – in 18 countries and territories:
Australia, Bangladesh, Bhutan, Cambodia, Hong Kong, India, Indonesia, Japan, Korea Rep, Malaysia, Maldives, Mongolia, Nepal, New Zealand, Philippines, Singapore, Taiwan, Thailand.

IGO Relations *ASEAN (#01141)*; *Asian Development Bank (ADB, #01422)*; *ILO (#11123)*; *International Bank for Reconstruction and Development (IBRD, #12317)* (World Bank). **NGO Relations** Approved and ratified the 'Conditions of Contract (International) for Works of Civil Engineering Construction', in collaboration with: *Associated General Contractors of America (AGC)*; *European Construction Industry Federation (#06766)*; *Federación Interamericana de la Industria de la Construcción (FIIC, #09333)*; *International Federation of Consulting Engineers (#13399)*; *International Road Federation (IRF Global, #14759)*. [2018/XD1855/**D**]

♦ International Federation of Associated Wrestling Styles / see United World Wrestling (#20665)

♦ International Federation of Association Football 13360

Fédération Internationale de Football Association (FIFA) – Federación Internacional de Fútbol Asociación

Headquarters FIFA-Strasse 20, 8044 Zurich ZH, Switzerland. T. +41432227777. E-mail: contact@fifa.org.
URL: http://www.fifa.com/

History 21 May 1904, Paris (France). **Aims** Promote the *game* of football, protect its integrity and bring the game to all. **Structure** Congress; Council; Standing Committees; General Secretariat, located in Zurich (Switzerland). Regulatory body: *International Football Association Board (IFAB, see: #13360)*. **Languages** English, French, German, Spanish. **Staff** 749.00 FTE, paid. **Finance** Majority of revenue from FIFA World Cup: media and broadcasting rights; sponsorship; ticket sales. **Activities** Sporting activities. **Events** *FIFA Congress* Kigali (Rwanda) 2023, *FIFA Congress* Tokyo (Japan) 2021, *Annual Congress* Paris (France) 2019, *Football Conference* London (UK) 2018, *Annual Congress* Moscow (Russia) 2018. **Publications** *1904 Magazine* (12 a year) in English, French, German, Spanish. Financial report; governance report; activity report.

Members National Associations grouped in 6 Continental Confederations, in 211 countries and territories:
Afghanistan, Albania, Algeria, Andorra, Angola, Anguilla, Antigua-Barbuda, Argentina, Armenia, Aruba, Australia, Austria, Azerbaijan, Bahamas, Bahrain, Bangladesh, Barbados, Belarus, Belgium, Belize, Benin, Bermuda, Bhutan, Bolivia, Bosnia-Herzegovina, Botswana, Brazil, Brunei Darussalam, Bulgaria, Burkina Faso, Burundi, Cambodia, Cameroon, Canada, Cape Verde, Cayman Is, Central African Rep, Chad, Chile, China, Colombia, Comoros, Congo Brazzaville, Congo DR, Cook Is, Costa Rica, Côte d'Ivoire, Croatia, Cuba, Curaçao, Cyprus, Czechia, Denmark, Djibouti, Dominica, Dominican Rep, Ecuador, Egypt, El Salvador, England, Equatorial Guinea, Eritrea, Estonia, Eswatini, Ethiopia, Faeroe Is, Fiji, Finland, France, Gabon, Gambia, Georgia, Germany, Ghana, Gibraltar, Greece, Grenada, Guam, Guatemala, Guinea, Guinea-Bissau, Guyana, Haiti, Honduras, Hong Kong, Hungary, Iceland, India, Indonesia, Iran Islamic Rep, Iraq, Ireland, Israel, Italy, Jamaica, Japan, Jordan, Kazakhstan, Kenya, Korea DPR, Korea Rep, Kosovo, Kuwait, Kyrgyzstan, Laos, Latvia, Lebanon, Lesotho, Liberia, Libya, Liechtenstein, Lithuania, Luxembourg, Macau, Madagascar, Malawi, Malaysia, Maldives, Mali, Malta, Mauritania, Mauritius, Mexico, Moldova, Mongolia, Montenegro, Montserrat, Morocco, Mozambique, Myanmar, Namibia, Nepal, Netherlands, New Caledonia, New Zealand, Nicaragua, Niger, Nigeria, North Macedonia, Northern Ireland, Norway, Oman, Pakistan, Palestine, Panama, Papua New Guinea, Paraguay, Peru, Philippines, Poland, Portugal, Puerto Rico, Qatar, Romania, Russia, Rwanda, Samoa, Samoa USA, San Marino, Sao Tomé-Principe, Saudi Arabia, Scotland, Senegal, Serbia, Seychelles, Sierra Leone, Singapore, Slovakia, Slovenia, Solomon Is, Somalia, South Africa, South Sudan, Spain, Sri Lanka, St Kitts-Nevis, St Lucia, St Vincent-Grenadines, Sudan, Suriname, Sweden, Switzerland, Syrian AR, Tahiti Is, Taiwan, Tajikistan, Tanzania UR, Thailand, Timor-Leste, Togo, Tonga, Trinidad-Tobago, Tunisia, Türkiye, Turkmenistan, Turks-Caicos, Uganda, Ukraine, United Arab Emirates, Uruguay, USA, Uzbekistan, Vanuatu, Venezuela, Vietnam, Virgin Is UK, Virgin Is USA, Wales, Yemen, Zambia, Zimbabwe.
Associate members in 11 countries and territories:
Guadeloupe, Guiana Fr, Kiribati, Martinique, Niue, Northern Mariana Is, Réunion, St Maarten, St Martin, Tuvalu.
Continental Confederations (6), listed in this Yearbook:
Asian Football Confederation (AFC, #01487); *Confederación Norte-Centroamericana y del Caribe de Fútbol (CONCACAF, #04465)*; *Confederación Sudamericana de Fútbol (CONMEBOL, #04487)*; *Confédération africaine de football (CAF, #04500)*; *Oceania Football Confederation (OFC, #17662)*; *Union of European Football Associations (UEFA, #20386)*.

NGO Relations Member of (6): *Association of Summer Olympic International Federations (ASOIF, #02943)*; *International Committee for Fair Play (#12769)*; *International Council of Sport Science and Physical Education (ICSSPE, #13077)*; *International Masters Games Association (IMGA, #14117)*; *Olympic Movement (#17719)*; *Sports Rights Owners Coalition (SROC, #19929)*. Affiliated with (1): *EMEA Synthetic Turf Council (ESTC, #05436)*. Recognized by: *International Olympic Committee (IOC, #14408)*. Partner of: *African Union of Broadcasting (AUB, #00490)*. Maintains relations with: *Virtus: World Intellectual Impairment Sport (#20793)*. Instrumental in setting up *Centre international d'étude du sport (CIES)*, Neuchâtel (Switzerland); *European Club Association (ECA, #06579)*. [2022/XB1856/y/**B**]

♦ International Federation of Associations of Anatomists (IFAA) 13361

Fédération internationale des associations d'anatomistes (FIAA)

SG Medical School, Faculdade de Ciências Médicas da UNL, Campo Mártires da Pátria 130, 1169-056 Lisbon, Portugal.
Pres Fac of Health Sciences, Univ of the Witwatersrand, 1 Jan Smuts Avenue,, Braamfontein, 2000, South Africa.
URL: http://www.ifaa.net/

History 1903, Nancy (France), as a federation of national and multinational associations of anatomists; 1st International Anatomical Congress: 6 Aug 1905, Geneva (Switzerland). Current statutes adopted 10 Aug 1989, Rio de Janeiro (Brazil). **Aims** Further the development and promote the progress of all anatomical and *biomorphological* sciences; encourage and increase scientific, technical, educational and administrative exchange among anatomists worldwide; provide general guidelines for educational, technological and scientific purposes and for issues of general interest to anatomical science; coordinate and support preparation, revision and publication of documents on terminology of anatomy and biomorphology; stimulate friendship and cooperation among members; promote international scientific congresses, symposia and other meetings of anatomical and morphological sciences. **Structure** General Assembly of members' representatives (every 4-5 years) at *Federative International Congress of Anatomists*. Executive Committee/Permanent Board, consisting of President, Vice-President, Honorary President, Secretary General, 2 Secretaries and Treasurer. Headquarters/Secretariat in Lübeck (Germany). **Languages** English. **Staff** 2.00 FTE, voluntary. **Finance** Members' dues: US$ 50-800, depending on number of members. **Activities** Committees (4): *Federative International Programme for Anatomical Terminology (FIPAT, #09716)*, reporting to IFAA General Assembly and Executive Committee, has its own Chairman, Secretary and constitution; *Federative Committee on Anatomical and Scientific Press (FCASP)*; *Federative Committee on Comparative and Applied Morphology (FCAM)*; *Federative Committee on Education in the Anatomical Sciences (FCEAS)*. **Events** *Federative International Congress of Anatomists* Istanbul (Türkiye) 2022, *Federative International Congress of Anatomists* Istanbul (Turkey) 2021, *Federative International Congress of Anatomists* London (UK) 2019, *Federative International Congress of Anatomists* Beijing (China) 2014, *Federative international congress of anatomists / Federative International Congress of Anatomy* Cape Town (South Africa) 2009. **Publications** *IFAA Directory* (annual).

Members National associations (47) in 50 countries (as one society Australia and New Zealand, Argentina and Uruguay, UK and Ireland):
Argentina, Australia, Bangladesh, Belarus, Belgium, Bolivia, Brazil, Bulgaria, Canada, Chile, China, Colombia, Costa Rica, Croatia, Czechia, Egypt, Finland, France, Germany, Greece, Hungary, India, Indonesia, Ireland, Israel, Italy, Japan, Korea Rep, Mexico, Netherlands, New Zealand, Nigeria, Pakistan, Panama, Peru, Philippines, Poland, Portugal, Romania, Russia, Serbia, South Africa, Spain, Sweden, Switzerland, Türkiye, UK, Uruguay, USA, Venezuela.
Included in the above, 8 organizations listed in this Yearbook:
Afro-Asia-Oceania Association of Anatomists (AAOAA, no recent information); *Anatomical Society of Southern Africa (ASSA)*; *Anatomical Society of West Africa (no recent information)*; *Anatomische Gesellschaft (AG, #00813)*; *Association of Morphologists (#02814)*; *International Society of Developmental Biologists (ISDB, #15052)*; *Pan American Association of Anatomy (PAAA, #18079)*; *World Association of Veterinary Anatomists (WAVA, #21202)*. [2020/XC1164/y/**C**]

♦ International Federation of Associations of Business Economists (inactive)

♦ International Federation of Associations of Catholic Doctors / see International Federation of Catholic Medical Associations (#13378)

♦ International Federation of Associations of Cleaning Products Manufacturers (inactive)

♦ International Federation of Associations of Computer Users in Engineering, Architecture and Related Fields (no recent information)

♦ International Federation of Associations of Defense in Phytotherapy, Research and Teaching (inactive)

♦ International Federation of Associations of the Elderly (#09609)

♦ International Federation of Associations in the Field of Microwave and RF Power Engineering (MAJIC) 13362

Contact c/o AMPERE Europe, Dpto Tecnologías de la Información y las Comunicaciones, Universidad Politècnica de Cartagena, Plaza del Hospital 1, 30202 Cartagena, Murcia, Spain. E-mail: juan.monzo@upct.es – contact@ampereeurope.org.

History Aug 2006. **Events** *Global congress on microwave energy applications* Otsu, Tokyo (Japan) 2008.
Members Founding members (5):
Association for Microwave Power in Europe for Research and Education (AMPERE Europe, #02806); Chinese Microwave Society; *International Microwave Power Institute (IMPI, #14160)*; Japan Society of Electromagnetic Wave Energy Applications; Microwave Working Group. [2009/XJ0068/y/**E**]

♦ International Federation of Associations of Pharmaceutical Physicians (IFAPP) 13363

Fédération internationale des associations de médecins de l'industrie pharmaceutique

Secretariat Leidsestraatweg 41-D, 3443 BP Woerden, Netherlands. T. +31622911039. E-mail: secretariat@ifapp.org.
Sec address not obtained.
URL: http://www.ifapp.org/

History Sep 1975, Florence (Italy). **Aims** Act as the international forum for associations of pharmaceutical physicians; work towards international recognition and development of pharmaceutical medicine as a separate medical speciality with its specific body of knowledge and distinctive fields of professional responsibility. **Structure** House of Delegates; Board of Officers. **Languages** English. **Staff** 5.00 FTE, paid. **Finance** Sources: members' dues. **Activities** Events/meetings. **Events** *International Conference on Pharmaceutical Medicine (ICPM)* 2022, *ICPM : International Conference on Pharmaceutical Medicine* Rome (Italy) 2020, *ICPM : International Conference on Pharmaceutical Medicine* Tokyo (Japan) 2018, *ICPM : International Conference on Pharmaceutical Medicine* Rio de Janeiro (Brazil) 2016, *ICPM : International Conference on Pharmaceutical Medicine* Berlin (Germany) 2014. **Publications** *IFAPP World* (3 a year).

Members Full national associations in 29 countries:
Argentina, Australia, Austria, Bangladesh, Belgium, Brazil, Denmark, Finland, Germany, Greece, Hungary, Indonesia, Ireland, Italy, Japan, Korea Rep, Mexico, Netherlands, Pakistan, Peru, Portugal, Romania, Serbia, Singapore, South Africa, Spain, Switzerland, UK, USA.

NGO Relations Member of: *Council for International Organizations of Medical Sciences (CIOMS, #04905)*. [2021/XD5991/t/**C**]

♦ International Federation of Associations of Private Detectives 13364

Internationale Kommission der Detektiv-Verbände (IKD)

SG 2nd Floor, Winnington House, 2 Woodberry Grove, London, N12 0DR, UK. T. +442033972715. Fax +442033972714. E-mail: secretarygeneral@i-k-d.com.
URL: http://www.i-k-d.com/

History Registered in accordance with Austrian law. **Structure** Board, including Secretary General, Vice Secretary General and Treasurer. **Events** *Meeting* Vienna (Austria) 2019, *Meeting* Helsinki (Finland) 2017, *General Assembly* Istanbul (Turkey) 2010.

Members Associations and individuals in 21 countries:
Austria, Belgium, Denmark, Finland, France, Germany, Hungary, India, Israel, Italy, Japan, Latvia, Netherlands, Norway, Portugal, Romania, Slovenia, Spain, Switzerland, Türkiye, UK.
Included in the above, 3 organizations listed in this Yearbook:
Bund Internationaler Detektive (BID); *Europäische Detektiv-Akademie (EURODET)*; *World Association of Detectives (WAD, #21131)*. [2015/XJ4927/y/**D**]

♦ International Federation of Associations of Religious Journalists / see International Christian Organisation of the Media (#12563)

♦ International Federation of Associations of Social, Ecological and Culture Aid (#09335)

♦ International Federation of Associations of Specialists in Occupational Safety and Industrial Hygiene (no recent information)

♦ International Federation of Associations of Spinners of Linen and Tow (inactive)

♦ International Federation of Associations of Steel, Tube and Metal Merchants (inactive)

♦ International Federation of Associations of Textile Chemists and Colourists (IAFTCC) 13365

Fédération Internationale des Associations de Chimistes du Textile et de la Couleur – Federación Internacional de las Asociaciones de Quimicos y Coloristas Textiles – Internationale Föderation der Vereine der Textilchemiker und Coloristen (IFVTCC) – Federazione Internazionale delle Associazioni di Chimica Tessile e Coloristica

Headquarters Via Alberto Riva Villasanta 3, 20145 Milan MI, Italy. E-mail: secretary@ifatcc.org.
URL: http://www.ifatcc.org/

History 14 May 1930, Milan (Italy). Activities ceased in 1939; revived 1952. Since 2016, based in Milan (Italy). Current statutes adopted 2017. **Aims** Promote friendly relations among member associations; encourage scientific and technical cooperation with a view to developing the industry. **Structure** Congress (every 3 years); Delegate Assembly;Board; Management Committee. **Languages** English, French, German. **Staff** 2.00 FTE, voluntary. **Finance** Members' dues. **Events** *Congress* 2020, *Congress* Pardubice (Czech Rep) 2016, *Triennial Congress* Stresa (Italy) 2010, *Triennial Congress* Barcelona (Spain) 2008, *Triennial Congress* Weimar (Germany) 2005.

Members National associations in 8 countries:
Austria, Czechia, Denmark, France, Germany, Hungary, Italy, Spain.
Associate members in 4 countries:
Japan, Poland, Romania, Slovenia. [2021/XD1860/**D**]

♦ International Federation of Audit Bureaux of Certification (IFABC) . . 13366

Fédération internationale des bureaux de justification de la diffusion – Internationale Organisation der Auflagenkontrollbüros

Contact c/o Audited Media Assn of Australia, Suite 6/01, 6/127 York Street, Sydney NSW 2000, Australia. T. +61299549800. E-mail: marketing@auditedmedia.org.au.
Pres Inst Verificador de Circulaçao, Alameda Santos 200 cj72, Sao Paulo SP, 01418-000 SP, Brazil. E-mail: info@ivc.org.br.
URL: http://www.ifabc.org/

History 29 May 1963, Stockholm (Sweden). Former names and other names: *International Federation of Audit Bureaux of Circulations (IFABC)* – former. **Aims** Promote uniform verification and reporting of *statistics* on circulation of publications and other *media* brand data; work towards greater standardization and uniformity in reporting such circulation and uniformity and standardization of audit concepts and procedures; encourage establishment of audit bureaux of circulation in countries where none exists; encourage exchange of information and experience among members. **Structure** General Assembly (every 2 years). **Languages** English. **Finance** Sources: members' dues. **Activities** Events/meetings. **Events** *General Assembly* Vienna (Austria) 2020, *General Assembly* San Francisco, CA (USA) 2018, *General Assembly* Ascona (Switzerland) 2016, *General Assembly* Rio de Janeiro (Brazil) 2014, *General Assembly* Madrid (Spain) 2012. **Publications** *Circulation Auditing Around the World*. Conference reports.

Members Full; Affiliate. Full: Country Bureaux in 25 countries and territories:
Australia, Austria, Belgium, Brazil, Croatia, Czechia, Finland, France, Germany, Hungary, India, Italy, Japan, Korea Rep, Malaysia, Netherlands, Poland, Portugal, Serbia, Spain, Sweden, Switzerland, Taiwan, UK, USA.
Affiliate in 1 country:
Norway. [2020.09.07/XC0344/v/**C**]

♦ International Federation of Audit Bureaux of Circulations / see International Federation of Audit Bureaux of Certification (#13366)

♦ International Federation of Automatic Control (IFAC) 13367

Fédération internationale pour la commande automatique – Internationaler Verband für Mess- und Automatisierungstechnik – Federación Internacional de Automatización

Sec Schlossplatz 12, 2361 Laxenburg, Austria. T. +43223671447. E-mail: secretariat@ifac-control.org.

Administration address not obtained.

URL: http://www.ifac-control.org/

History 12 Sep 1957, Paris (France). Founded following Automatic Control Congress, 27 Sep 1956, Heidelberg (Germany FR). Present constitution and by-laws adopted 2 Jul 1984, Budapest (Hungary); amended 1994, 2000, 2008, 2017 and 2020. Former names and other names: *Internationaler Verband für Selbsttätige Regelung und Steuerung* – former. Registration: Swiss Civil Code, Switzerland. **Aims** Promote science and technology of automatic control in all systems, whether for example, engineering, physical, biological, social or economic, in both theory and application. **Structure** General Assembly (every 3 years, at World Congress); Council; Technical Board; Conference Board; Publications Board; Committees; Secretariat. **Languages** English. **Staff** 3.00 FTE, paid. Voluntary. **Activities** Awards/prizes/competitions; events/meetings; financial and/or material support. **Events** *World Congress* Busan (Korea Rep) 2026, *World Congress* Yokohama (Japan) 2023, *SYROCO : International Symposium on Robot Control* Matsumoto (Japan) 2022, *Workshop on Time Delay Systems* Montréal, QC (Canada) 2022, *Symposium on System Structure and Control* Sinaia (Romania) 2022. **Publications** *Automatica* (12 a year) – journal; *Control Engineering Practice* (12 a year) – journal; *Engineering Applications of Artificial Intelligence* (10 a year) – international journal; *Mechatronics* (10 a year) – international journal; *IFAC Journal of Systems and Control* (4 a year); *Nonlinear Analysis: Hybrid Systems* (4 a year) – journal; *Annual Reviews in Control* (2 a year) – journal; *Journal of Process Control* (8 a year). *IFAC Proceedings Volumes.*

Members One national scientific or professional engineering organization (or one council formed by 2 or more such organizations) in each of 49 countries:
Australia, Austria, Azerbaijan, Belgium, Brazil, Bulgaria, Canada, Chile, China, Croatia, Cuba, Czechia, Denmark, Estonia, Finland, France, Germany, Hungary, India, Ireland, Israel, Italy, Japan, Korea Rep, Kosovo, Lithuania, Malaysia, Mexico, Netherlands, North Macedonia, Norway, Pakistan, Peru, Poland, Portugal, Romania, Russia, Singapore, Slovakia, Slovenia, South Africa, Spain, Sweden, Switzerland, Tunisia, Türkiye, UK, Ukraine, USA.

Consultative Status Consultative status granted from: *ECOSOC (#05331)* (Ros C). **IGO Relations** Associated with Department of Global Communications of the United Nations. [2022.10.11/XC1862/**B**]

♦ International Federation of Automobile Electricians, Electrotechnicians and Specialists (inactive)

♦ International Federation of Automobile Engineers and Technicians Associations / see International Federation of Automotive Engineering Societies (#13369)

♦ International Federation of Automobile Experts (IFAE) 13368

Fédération internationale des experts en automobile (FIEA)

Pres 41/43 rue des Plantes, 75014 Paris, France. E-mail: secretariat@fiea.org.

Gen Sec address not obtained.

URL: http://www.fiea.org/

History 1954. Registration: France. **Aims** Undertake any actions and any studies which might be deemed useful for the recognition, organization, promotion, defence and continuity of the profession of the automobile expert. **Structure** Board of Trustees (meets 3 times a year); Directing Committee; Work Commissions (2). **Languages** English, French. **Staff** 1.00 FTE, paid; 5.00 FTE, voluntary. **Finance** Members' dues. **Activities** Events/meetings; standards/guidelines; advocacy/lobbying/activism; networking/liaising. **Events** *General Assembly* Larnaca (Cyprus) 2022, *General Assembly* Spa (Belgium) 2016, *General Assembly* Porto (Portugal) 2015, *General Assembly* Poznań (Poland) 2014, *General Assembly* Milan (Italy) 2013. **Publications** *FIEA Newsletter* (10 a year) in English, French. Topical matters regarding FIEA; initiatives taken in member associations' countries; general relevant information surrounding automotive industry and automotive experts profession.

Members Full: national organizations (23) in 19 countries:
Austria, Belgium, Côte d'Ivoire, Cyprus, France, Germany, Greece, Italy, Latvia, Luxembourg, Morocco, Netherlands, Poland, Portugal, Spain, Switzerland, Tunisia, Türkiye, UK.

Individuals in 2 countries:
Monaco, Romania.

IGO Relations Recognized by: *European Commission (EC, #06633).* **NGO Relations** Member of: *European Council of Liberal Professions (#06828); World Union of Professions (WUP, #21882).* [2022/XD1864/**D**]

♦ International Federation of Automotive Aftermarket Distributors (#09635)

♦ International Federation of Automotive Engineering Societies 13369

Fédération internationale des sociétés d'ingénieurs des techniques de l'automobile (FISITA) – Federación Internacional de Ingenieros en Técnicas Automotrices – Internationaler Verband der Ingenieurvereine für Automobiltechnik

Chief Exec 29 M11 Business Link, Stansted, CM24 8GF, UK. T. +441279883470. E-mail: info@fisita.com.

URL: http://www.fisita.com/

History Jan 1948, Paris (France). Founded following international congress on automotive engineering, Oct 1947, Paris. Former names and other names: *International Federation of Automobile Engineers and Technicians Associations* – former. Registration: France. **Aims** Provide a global platform for knowledge exchange between industry and academia, helping to guide the future direction of the automotive engineering profession. **Structure** Council (meets twice a year); Executive Board; Committees. **Languages** English. **Activities** Events/meetings. **Events** *EuroBrake Annual Forum* Barcelona (Spain) 2023, *EuroBrake Annual Forum* 2022, *Asia Pacific Automotive Engineering Conference* Melbourne, VIC (Australia) 2022, *World Mobility Summit* Paris (France) 2022, *Biennial Congress* Prague (Czechia) 2021.

Members National automotive engineering societies representing over 210,000 automotive engineers in 37 countries:
Argentina, Australia, Austria, Belarus, Belgium, Brazil, China, Croatia, Czechia, Finland, France, Germany, Hungary, India, Indonesia, Iran Islamic Rep, Israel, Italy, Japan, Korea Rep, Latvia, Lithuania, Netherlands, Poland, Romania, Russia, Serbia, Slovakia, Slovenia, Spain, Sri Lanka, Sweden, Switzerland, Thailand, UK, USA, Vietnam. [2021/XC1863/**C**]

♦ International Federation of Bank and Stock Exchange Employees (inactive)

♦ International Federation of Beekeepers' Associations (APIMONDIA) 13370

Fédération internationale des associations d'apiculture – Federación Internacional de Asociaciones de Apicultura – Internationaler Verband der Bienenzüchter-Vereinigungen – Mezdunarodnaja Federacija Pcelovadnym Obedinenij

SG Corso Vittorio Emmanuele 101, 00186 Rome RM, Italy. T. +3966852286. Fax +3966852287. E-mail: apimondia@mclink.it.

URL: http://www.apimondia.org/

History 1897, Belgium. Statutes amended: 22 Sep 1958, Rome (Italy); 25 Aug 1965, Bucharest (Romania); 20 Oct 1973, Buenos Aires (Argentina); 27 Aug 1983, Budapest (Hungary); 22 Sep 1993, Beijing (China); 16 Aug 1995, Lausanne (Switzerland); 16 Sep 2015, Daejeon (Korea Rep). **Aims** Promote scientific, technical, ecological, social and economic apicultural development in all countries and the cooperation of beekeepers' associations, scientific bodies and individuals involved in apiculture worldwide.

Structure General Assembly (every 2 years, during international Congress); Executive Council (meets annually), comprising the 3 members of the Management Board, 7 Presidents of Scientific Commissions and 5 Presidents of Regional Commissions. Scientific Commissions (7): Apitherapy; Bee Health; Biology; Economy; Pollination and Bee Flora; Rural Development; Technology and Quality. Regional Commissions (5): Africa; Americas; Asia; Europe; Oceania. Maintains: *Fundatia Institutul International de Tehnologie si Economie Apicola (FIITEA).*

Working Groups (14):
- International Honey Commission;
- EU Organic Beekeeping Legislation Revision;
- Bees Declared as an Endangered Species;
- Harmonization of Regulations for International Honey Contests;
- Good Beekeeping Practice for Medical Grade Bee Products;
- Ethical Charter for the International Honey Trade;
- Queen Rearing and Impact on the Genetic Variability of Productive Bee Colonies;
- Apimondia and Api-tourism;
- Adverse Effects of Agrochemicals and Bee Medicines on Bees;
- GMOs and Impact on the Beekeeping Sector;
- Definitions and Standardization for the Queen and Package Bee Market;
- Young Beekeepers;
- New EU Honey Directive for Honeys from Asian Bees;
- Melipona and Trigona Honey Categorization.

Languages English, French, German, Spanish. **Staff** 2.00 FTE, voluntary. **Finance** Members' dues, proportional to the number of hives existing in the various countries (annual). **Activities** Events/meetings. **Events** *African Regional Apimondia Symposium* Durban (South Africa) 2023, *Apicultural Congress* Santiago (Chile) 2023, *Apimondia Congress* Istanbul (Türkiye) 2022, *Apimondia Congress* Ufa (Russia) 2022, *Symposium* Abu Dhabi (United Arab Emirates) 2021. **Publications** *Apiacta* (4 a year) in English, French, Spanish – journal. *Thesaurus Agrovoc* (1992) in English, French, German, Italian, Spanish; *Apiculture* by G A Avetisyan in English; *Instrumental Insemination of the Queen Bee* by F Ruttner in English, French, French, German, Spanish; *Varroasis – A Honey Bee Disease* in English, French, Spanish; *Textbook on Melissopalinology* by G Ricciardelli d'Albore in English; *Taste of Honey* by G Vache and M Gonnet in English, Spanish; *South African Mead Notes* by E N Lear in English; *Queen Rearing* by F Ruttner in English, German, Spanish; *Propolis* in English, German, Spanish; *Prophylaxis and Control of Varroa Disease* in English, French, German, Spanish; *Problems of Melliferous Flora and Pollination* in English, French, German, Russian; *New Research in Apitherapy* in English, French, German, Spanish; *Migratory Beekeeping* in Spanish – photostatic version only; *Instrumental Insemination of the Queen Bee* by R F A Moritz in English, German; *Honey – Technological Aspects* in French; *Apitherapy Today* in English, French, German, Spanish; *Honey Plants – the Basis of Apiculture* in English, French, German, Spanish; *History of the Hive* in French, Spanish; *History of Apiculture and Museums of Apiculture* – each report is published in the original language; *Genetics, Selection, and Reproduction of the Honey Bee* in English, French, Spanish; *Dictionary of Beekeeping Terms* – in 4 vols, in 14 languages; *Diagnosis and Therapy of Varroa Disease* in German; *Development of World Apicultural Trade* in English, French, German, Spanish; *Controlled Mating and Selection of the Honey Bee* in English, German, Russian; *Biological Aspects of Nosema Disease* in English, French, German, Russian, Spanish; *Bee's Time* by H Watanabe in English; *Beekeeping in Cold-Climate Zones* in English, French, German, Spanish; *Bases of Beekeeping* by A S Nuzhdin and V P Vinogradov in French; *World Cooking with Honey* in English, German, Russian. Scientific bulletins; congress and symposium proceedings.

Members Full: national organizations (94) in 72 countries:
Algeria, Argentina, Armenia, Australia, Austria, Azerbaijan, Belarus, Belgium, Bosnia-Herzegovina, Brazil, Bulgaria, Cambodia, Canada, Chile, China, Côte d'Ivoire, Croatia, Cuba, Cyprus, Czechia, Denmark, Estonia, Eswatini, Finland, France, Germany, Greece, Haiti, Hungary, Indonesia, Iran Islamic Rep, Ireland, Israel, Italy, Japan, Kazakhstan, Korea Rep, Kyrgyzstan, Latvia, Libya, Lithuania, Luxembourg, Malta, Mexico, Moldova, Montenegro, Morocco, Netherlands, New Zealand, Norway, Philippines, Poland, Romania, Russia, San Marino, Saudi Arabia, Serbia, Slovakia, Slovenia, South Africa, Spain, Sweden, Switzerland, Tanzania UR, Türkiye, Uganda, UK, Ukraine, Uruguay, USA, Venezuela, Vietnam.

Associate: organizations (20) in 15 countries and territories:
Australia, Bulgaria, Germany, Greece, India, Japan, Libya, Romania, Saudi Arabia, Slovakia, Spain, Taiwan, Trinidad-Tobago, Uganda, Ukraine.

Included in the above, 6 organizations listed in this Yearbook:
Asia Pacific Apitherapy Association (APAA); *Association of Caribbean Beekeepers Organisations (ACBO, #02401); Balkan Federation of Apicultural Associations (#03073); European Federation of Honey Packers and Distributors (#07140); European Professional Beekeepers Association (EPBA, #08284); International Honey Export Organization (IHEO, #13806).*

Consultative Status Consultative status granted from: *ECOSOC (#05331)* (Special); *FAO (#09260)* (Special Status); *UNCTAD (#20285)* (Special Category). **IGO Relations** Member of: *International Information System for the Agricultural Sciences and Technology (AGRIS, #13848).* Accredited by: *United Nations Office at Vienna (UNOV, #20604).* Observer status with: *Codex Alimentarius Commission (CAC, #04081).* Associated with Department of Global Communications of the United Nations. [2022/XB1867/**B**]

♦ International Federation of Bike Messenger Associations (IFBMA) . 13371

Address not obtained.

URL: http://www.messengers.org/

History 1994, as *International Federation of Cycle Messengers and Companies (IFCMC).* Present name adopted 1998, Washington DC (USA). **Aims** Foster a spirit of cooperation and community amongst bicycle messengers worldwide; promote the use of pedal power for commercial purposes. **Structure** Council of at least 3. **Activities** Organizes annual 'Cycle Messenger World Championships (CMWC)'. [2011/XD8429/**D**]

♦ International Federation of Biomedical Laboratory Science (IFBLS) 13372

Exec Admin 33 Wellington Street North, Hamilton ON L8R 1M7, Canada. T. +19056678695. Fax +19055284968. E-mail: communications@ifbls.org.

URL: http://www.ifbls.org/

History Jun 1954, Zurich (Switzerland). Current bylaws adopted 2014. Former names and other names: *International Association of Medical Laboratory Technologists (IAMLT)* – former; *Association internationale des technologistes de laboratoire médical* – former; *Asociación Internacional de Técnicos de Laboratorios Médicos* – former; *Association internationale des techniciens de laboratoire médical* – former. Registration: Canada. **Aims** Promote worldwide: maintenance of high quality standards of practice in the delivery of quality *health care*; continuous development of quality biomedical laboratory technologists/scientists so as to meet the needs of their communities; practice of high ethical and professional values by biomedical laboratory technologists/scientists; active professional partnerships in health care at the international level; active participation of members in international activities. **Structure** General Assembly of Delegates (every 2 years); Board of Directors; IFBLS Office, headed by Executive Administrator; Special Committees. **Languages** English. **Staff** Paid. **Finance** Sources: members' dues. Other sources: Corporate sponsorship. **Activities** Awards/prizes/competitions; certification/accreditation; standards/guidelines; training/education. **Events** *World Congress* Suwon (Korea Rep) 2022, *Biennial Congress* Copenhagen (Denmark) 2021, *Biennial Congress* Copenhagen (Denmark) 2020, *Biennial Congress* Florence (Italy) 2018, *Biennial Congress* Kobe (Japan) 2016. **Publications** *IFBLS Newsletter* (4 a year); *International Journal of Biomedical Laboratory Science (IJBLS)* – online. Directories; guidelines; policy statements.

Members National organizations, associations and groups representing 200,000 medical laboratory technologists in 26 countries and territories:
Cameroon, Canada, Denmark, Estonia, Finland, Germany, Ghana, Greece, Hong Kong, Iceland, India, Ireland, Italy, Japan, Kenya, Nigeria, Norway, Philippines, Portugal, Singapore, Spain, Sri Lanka, Sweden, Taiwan, UK, USA.

Consultative Status Consultative status granted from: *ECOSOC (#05331)* (Roster); *WHO (#20950)* (Official Relations). **IGO Relations** Accredited by: *United Nations Office at Vienna (UNOV, #20604).* Links with WHO and its regional offices: *WHO Regional Office for Africa (AFRO, #20943); Pan American Sanitary Bureau (PASB, #18129); WHO Regional Office for the Eastern Mediterranean (EMRO, #20944); WHO Regional Office for Europe (#20945); WHO Regional Office for South-East Asia (SEARO, #20946).* **NGO Relations** In liaison with technical committees of: *International Organization for Standardization (ISO, #14473).* [2023/XC1310/**C**]

♦ International Federation of Biosafety Associations (IFBA) 13373

Exec Dir 102-2460 Lancaster Road, Ottawa ON K1B 4S5, Canada. T. +16132318555. Fax +16132313970. E-mail: secretariat@internationalbiosafety.org.

Sec/Treas address not obtained.

URL: http://www.internationalbiosafety.org/

History 2001, as *International Biosafety Working Group (IBWG).* Current title adopted Jun 2009, Stockholm (Sweden). **Aims** Support and promote biosafety on national and international levels through collaboration among national and regional biosafety organizations worldwide. **Structure** Board of Directors. **Activities** Awards/prizes/competitions; awareness raising; certification/accreditation; events/meetings; standards/guidelines.

Members Full; Observer. Organizations in 34 countries and territories:
Afghanistan, Argentina, Australia, Azerbaijan, Bangladesh, Belgium, Brazil, Cameroon, Canada, Côte d'Ivoire, Egypt, Georgia, Germany, India, Indonesia, Japan, Kenya, Korea Rep, Malaysia, Mexico, Morocco, Netherlands, New Zealand, Nigeria, Pakistan, Philippines, Singapore, South Africa, Spain, Taiwan, Thailand, Trinidad-Tobago, UK, USA.

Included in the above, 14 organizations listed in this Yearbook:
African Biological Safety Association (AfBSA, #00223); African Society for Laboratory Medicine (ASLM, #00463); Asia Pacific Biosafety Association (A-PBA, #01859); Caribbean Med Labs Foundation (CMLF, #03522); CRDF Global; European Biosafety Association (EBSA, #06343); International Council for the Life Sciences (ICLS); International Science and Technology Center (ISTC, #14798); International Society for Biosafety Research (ISBR, #14973); International Veterinary Biosafety Workgroup (IVBW, #15847); Pan American Health Organization (PAHO, #18108); Verification Research, Training and Information Centre (VERTIC); Virtual Biosecurity Centre (VBC); WHO (#20950) (Biosafety Programme). [2019/XJ8866/y/**B**]

♦ International Federation of the Blind (inactive)

♦ International Federation of Blood Donor Organizations (IFBDO) 13374

Fédération internationale des organisations de donneurs de sang (FIODS) – Federación Internacional de las Organizaciones de Donadores de Sangre – Internationaler Verband der Blutspenderorganisationen – Federação Internacional de Organizações de Doadores Voluntarios de Sangre – Federazione Internazionale delle Organizzazioni dei Donatori di Sangue – Internationale Federatie van Bloed Donorsorganisaties – Federasi Internasional Perhimpunan Donor Darah Sukarela

Pres Via Bellini 3, 86170 Isernia IS, Italy.
Headquarters 27 Bvd de Suisse, 98000 Monte Carlo, Monaco. T. +34635631983. E-mail: alexandrubugner@gmail.com.
URL: http://www.fiods.org/

History 27 May 1955, Nancy (France), following recommendations at a Congress, 1954. First Constitution adopted 4 Dec 1955, Luxembourg. New Statutes adopted at 8th Congress, 21-24 Nov 1974, Marrakech (Morocco); modified at: 10th Congress, 11-14 Jun 1981, Madrid (Spain); 13th Congress, May-Jun 1990, Porto (Portugal). Current Statutes adopted at 18th Congress, 2005, Paris (France). Rules of Procedure submitted by Secretary-General (Apr 1975) and accepted with modifications by Executive Committee: Apr 1975, Monaco; May 1978, Liège (Belgium); Jun 1981, Madrid; 1 Jun 1990, Porto (Portugal). Registered Office at the Red Cross Society in Monaco. **Aims** Promote worldwide the voluntary, non-remunerated giving of blood; actively promote the principle that blood is priceless, knows no frontiers and is the common possession of humanity; bring together national groups of blood donors in order to consider at the international level problems of common interest; examine matters of possible interest to blood donors and related to their organization, or to knowledge of medical progress in the area of blood *transfusion*, or of actual situations which might call for measures requiring services of blood donors. **Structure** General Assembly (annual); Congress (every 3 years); Executive Council acts as permanent representative of blood donors and as board of *Order of International Merit for Blood (see: #13374)*. **Languages** English, French, Spanish. **Staff** Voluntary. **Finance** Members' dues, on sliding scale according to situation. **Activities** Events/meetings; knowledge management/information dissemination; networking/liaising. **Events** *Youth Forum* 2020, *Youth Forum* Baku (Azerbaijan) 2019, *General Assembly* Cascais (Portugal) 2019, *Workshop on Blood Donation in the Third Millennium* Rome (Italy) 2019, *Youth Forum* Aveiro (Portugal) 2018. **Publications** *FIODS Review* in English, French, Spanish. Congress proceedings.

Members Active National – national federations, associations, societies and groups of voluntary blood donors. Active Regional – federations, associations, societies and groups of voluntary blood donors working in an autonomous part of their respective countries where there is no national organization. Sympathizers – organizations, societies and private individuals doing scientific or practical work in line with the Federation's aims. Members in 66 countries and territories:
Afghanistan, Algeria, Argentina, Azerbaijan, Belarus, Benin, Bolivia, Brazil, Burkina Faso, Burundi, Cameroon, Central African Rep, Comoros, Congo Brazzaville, Congo DR, Côte d'Ivoire, Denmark, Djibouti, Dominican Rep, Estonia, Faeroe Is, France, Greece, Guinea, Guinea-Bissau, Iceland, India (including West Bengal and Tamilnadu), Indonesia, Italy, Kosovo, Latvia, Libya, Lithuania, Luxembourg, Madagascar, Mali, Malta, Mauritania, Mauritius, Mexico, Monaco, Mongolia, Morocco, Nepal, Netherlands, Nicaragua, Nigeria, Pakistan, Palestine, Philippines, Poland, Portugal, Romania, San Marino, Sao Tomé-Principe, Senegal, Spain, Switzerland, Tahiti Is, Togo, Tunisia, Türkiye, Ukraine, Uruguay, Venezuela, Vietnam.
Individuals in 5 countries:
Canada, Germany, Jordan, Oman, Yemen.

Consultative Status Consultative status granted from: *ECOSOC (#05331)* (Special). **IGO Relations** Consultative status with: WHO. **NGO Relations** Represented on Administrative Council of: *International Society of Blood Transfusion (ISBT, #14979)*. Working relationship with: *International Federation of Red Cross and Red Crescent Societies (#13526)*. [2022/XC1868/**C**]

♦ International Federation of the Blue Cross / see International Blue Cross (#12364)
♦ International Federation of Blue Cross Organizations / see International Blue Cross (#12364)
♦ International Federation of the Blue Cross Societies / see International Blue Cross (#12364)

♦ International Federation of Boat Show Organisers (IFBSO) 13375

Fédération internationale des organisateurs de salons nautiques – Federación Internacional de Organizadores de Salones Naúticos

SG Cherry Tree House, Main Street, Levisham, YO18 7NL, UK. T. +441751460032. E-mail: secgen@ifbso.com – info@ifbso.com.
URL: http://www.ifbso.com/

History Oct 1963, London (UK). Registered in accordance with UK law. **Aims** Further and promote the interests of member organizers of boat shows of international status. **Structure** Executive Committee, comprising President, Past-President, Vice-President, Treasurer, Secretary-General and members. **Languages** English. **Finance** Members' dues. **Activities** Provides for exchanges of views and information with member boat shows. **Events** *Joint Congress* Split (Croatia) 2019, *Annual Congress* Berlin (Germany) 2018, *Annual Congress* Istanbul (Turkey) 2014, *Annual Congress* London (UK) 2013, *Annual Congress* Cape Town (South Africa) 2012. **Members** Organizations in 23 countries:
Australia, Belgium, China, Croatia, Denmark, Finland, Germany, Greece, Italy, Japan, Korea Rep, Netherlands, New Zealand, Norway, Poland, Portugal, Slovenia, Spain, Sweden, Türkiye, UK, United Arab Emirates, USA. [2019/XD1869/**D**]

♦ International Federation of Body-Builders / see International Fitness and Bodybuilding Federation (#13610)
♦ International Federation of Bodybuilding and Fitness / see International Fitness and Bodybuilding Federation (#13610)
♦ International Federation of Bookbinders and Kindred Trades (inactive)
♦ International Federation of Booksellers' Associations (inactive)
♦ International Federation of Brewery Workers (inactive)
♦ International Federation of Building and Public Works / see European Construction Industry Federation (#06766)
♦ International Federation of Building and Wood Workers (inactive)

♦ International Federation of Business and Professional Women (BPW International) 13376

Fédération internationale des femmes de carrières libérales et commerciales – Federación Internacional de Mujeres de Negocios y Profesionales

Pres Office 14 Syria Str, Mohandseen, Cairo, 12611, Egypt. E-mail: presidents.office@bpw-international.org – communication.admin@bpw-international.org.
Registered Address c/o Sabine E Baerlocher, Rue de Carouge 36bis, 1205 Geneva, Switzerland.
URL: http://www.bpw-international.org/

History 22 Aug 1930, Geneva (Switzerland), by Dr Lena Madesin Phillips (USA). Most recent amendments to Constitution and By-Laws adopted at 21st Congress, 5-10 Jul 1993, Nagoya (Japan). Also referred to as *Business and Professional Women International (BPWI)*. Previously also known by the acronym *IFBPW – FIFCLC – FIMNP*. **Aims** Organize business and professional women worldwide to use their combined abilities and strengths for the attainment of high standards in business and the professions; work for *equal opportunities* and status for women in the economic, civil and political life of all countries; encourage women and girls to acquire education, occupational training and advanced education; use their occupational capacities and intelligence to the advantage of others as well as themselves; promote worldwide friendship, cooperation and understanding among business and professional women. **Structure** Congress (every 3 years). Board of Directors (meets every 3 years). International Executive, including President, 1st Vice President, 2nd Vice President, Executive Secretary and Finance Director. Young BPE Representative; Regional Coordinators (5); Standing Committees (13); Ad hoc Committees (2); Task Forces (9). Includes: *BPW Europe – European Region of BPW International (#03309)*. **Languages** English, French, Italian, Spanish. **Finance** Sources: members' dues. Annual budget: 400,000 USD. **Activities** Advocacy/lobbying/activism; events/meetings. **Events** *Triennial Congress* Orlando, FL (USA) 2020, *Asia Pacific Regional Conference* Bangkok (Thailand) 2018, *Triennial Congress* Cairo (Egypt) 2017, *Asia Pacific Regional Conference* Auckland (New Zealand) 2016, *African Regional Congress* Kampala (Uganda) 2016. **Publications** *BPW News International* (6 a year) – newsletter. *A Bus to 42nd Street* by Sylvia G Perry and Livia M Ricci; *A Measure Filled* by Lisa Sergio; *IFBPW – A History, Parts I and II*; *In Pride and with Promise* by Phillis Deakin. IFBPW Handbook; proceedings; reports; public relations leaflets.

Members National Federations and Associate Clubs in 76 countries and territories:
Afghanistan, Algeria, Argentina, Australia, Austria, Bahamas, Bangladesh, Barbados, Belgium, Bolivia, Brazil, Bulgaria, Burkina Faso, Cameroon, Canada, Chile, Colombia, Croatia, Cyprus, Czechia, Ecuador, Egypt, Estonia, Finland, France, Germany, Haiti, Hong Kong, Iceland, India, Indonesia, Ireland, Israel, Italy, Jamaica, Japan, Jordan, Kenya, Korea Rep, Latvia, Lithuania, Mexico, Moldova, Morocco, Nepal, Netherlands, New Zealand, Nigeria, Pakistan, Palestine, Panama, Papua New Guinea, Paraguay, Peru, Philippines, Poland, Romania, Russia, Singapore, South Africa, Spain, Sri Lanka, St Kitts-Nevis, Sudan, Sweden, Switzerland, Thailand, Trinidad-Tobago, UK, Ukraine, Uruguay, USA, Uzbekistan, Venezuela, Zimbabwe.
Individuals in 1 country:
Ethiopia.

Consultative Status Consultative status granted from: *ECOSOC (#05331)* (General); *UNESCO (#20322)* (Consultative Status); *ILO (#11123)* (Special List); *FAO (#09260)* (Liaison Status); *UNIDO (#20336)*; *UNCTAD (#20285)* (General Category); *Council of Europe (CE, #04881)* (Participatory Status); *UNICEF (#20332)*. **IGO Relations** Regular contacts with: *United Nations International Research and Training Institute for the Advancement of Women (UN-INSTRAW, inactive)*; *United Nations Population Fund (UNFPA, #20612)*. Invited to Governing Council sessions of: *International Fund for Agricultural Development (IFAD, #13692)*. Cooperates with and has representatives at: *United Nations Economic Commission for Africa (ECA, #20554)*; *United Nations Economic Commission for Europe (UNECE, #20555)*; *United Nations Economic Commission for Latin America and the Caribbean (ECLAC, #20556)*; *United Nations Economic and Social Commission for Asia and the Pacific (ESCAP, #20557)*; *United Nations Economic and Social Commission for Western Asia (ESCWA, #20558)*. Accredited by: *United Nations Office at Vienna (UNOV, #20604)*. Associated with Department of Global Communications of the United Nations.

NGO Relations Board member of: *Conference of Non-Governmental Organizations in Consultative Relationship with the United Nations (CONGO, #04635)*. Member of:
– NGO Executive Committee of *International Conference of NGOs (#12883)*;
– *NGO Committee on the Status of Women, Geneva (#17117)*;
– *NGO Committee on Sustainable Development, Vienna (#17119)*;
– *NGO Forum on Environment (FOE, #17125)*;
– *NGO Committee on UNICEF (#17120)*;
– *United Nations Global Compact (#20567)*;
– *Vienna NGO Committee on Drugs (VNGOC, #20773)*;
– *Vienna NGO Committee on the Status of Women (#20775)*;
– *Women for Water Partnership (WfWP, #21041)*;
– *World Water Council (WWC, #21908)*. [2021/XB1872/t/**B**]

♦ International Federation of Calvinists (inactive)
♦ International Federation of Camping and Caravanning / see Fédération Internationale de Camping, Caravanning et Autocaravaning (#09618)
♦ International Federation of Camping, Caravanning, and Motorcaravanning (#09618)
♦ International Federation for Camping Trade and Industry (inactive)
♦ International Federation of Cardio HIIT BodyWeight Exercise (internationally oriented national body)
♦ International Federation of Carpenters (inactive)

♦ International Federation for Catholic Associations of the Blind 13377

Fédération internationale des associations catholiques d'aveugles (FIDACA) – Federación Internacional de Asociaciones Católicas de Ciegos – Internationale Föderation der Katholischen Blindenvereinigungen – Federazione Internazionale delle Associazioni Cattoliche Ciechi

Pres address not obtained. T. +33160894946. Fax +33160894946. E-mail: fidacacontact@gmail.com.
URL: http://www.fidaca.org/

History 1981, Landschlacht (Switzerland). Recognized by the Holy See, 1988. **Aims** In compliance with the spirit of the 2nd Vatican Council: promote the blind spiritually, morally, culturally and financially, and by participating in the life and mission of the Church by giving witness for Christianity and performing apostolic mission; create and develop organizations for the blind dealing with religious welfare in dioceses and nationwide in various countries; promote fraternal cooperation with the blind in developing countries. **Structure** General Assembly (every 4 years); Executive Board; General Secretariat in Paris (France). **Languages** French, German, Spanish. **Staff** Voluntary. **Finance** Sources: contributions; gifts, legacies; members' dues. **Activities** Events/meetings; publishing activities. **Events** *General Assembly* Haguenau (France) 2008, *Congress* Haguenau (France) 2003, *General Assembly* Haguenau (France) 2003, *Church life* Lugano (Switzerland) 2001, *General assembly / Conference with East European Countries* Landschlacht (Switzerland) 1999. **Publications** *Bulletin FODACA* (4 a year); *FIDACA INTERNAL Info* (2 a year) in French, German, Spanish.

Members National organizations or groups from countries where no organization exists. Members (15) in 14 countries:
Austria, Belgium, Benin, Chile, Colombia, Congo Brazzaville, Germany, Italy, Latvia, Lithuania, Peru, Spain, Switzerland, Togo.
NGO Relations Member of: *World Blind Union (WBU, #21234)*. [2020/XD0043/**C**]

♦ International Federation of Catholic Journalists (inactive)

♦ International Federation of Catholic Medical Associations 13378

Fédération internationale des associations médicales catholiques (FIAMC) – Federación Internacional de Asociaciones Médicas Católicas

SG Palazzo San Calisto, 00120 Vatican City, Vatican. T. +39669887372.
Exec Sec address not obtained.
URL: http://www.fiamc.org/

History Founded 1936, Vienna (Austria), taking over the activities of *Central Office for the National Societies of Roman Catholic Doctors (inactive)*, set up 1924. Recognized by *Pax Romana, International Catholic Movement for Intellectual and Cultural Affairs (ICMICA, #18267)*, 1957, Rome (Italy). Current organization set up in 1966, at 11th Congress. Previously referred to as *International Secretariat of National Societies of Catholic Doctors* and as *International Federation of Associations of Catholic Doctors – Asociación Internacional de Médicos Católicos – Internationaler Verband der Katholischen Ärzte*. New constitution approved by the Holy See, 1970. **Aims** Study and solve medical *ethical* problems according to *conscience* in the light of Catholic faith and teaching; promote a Catholic medical ethic by providing opportunities for the study of moral problems affecting society and especially medicine; coordinate efforts of Catholic medical associations throughout the world, especially in ethical and pastoral matters. **Structure** General Assembly (every 4 years, at Congress); Executive Committee. **Languages** English, French, Italian, Spanish. **Staff** 1.00 FTE, paid. Several voluntary. **Finance** Sources: members' dues. Other sources: donations and voluntary contributions of doctors. **Activities** Events/meetings; research/documentation; training/education. **Events** *Quadrennial World Congress* Manila (Philippines) 2014, *Quadrennial World Congress* Mumbai (India) 2014, *Asian Congress* Bali (Indonesia) 2012, *European Congress* Rome (Italy) 2012, *Quadrennial world congress* Lourdes (France) 2010.

Members National guilds or associations in 60 countries and territories (Asian countries through AFCMA):
Angola, Argentina, Australia, Austria, Belgium, Benin, Bolivia, Brazil, Bulgaria, Canada, Chile, Colombia, Côte d'Ivoire, Croatia, Cuba, Czechia, Denmark, Dominican Rep, Finland, France, Germany, Ghana, Honduras, Hong Kong, Hungary, India, Indonesia, Ireland, Italy, Jamaica, Japan, Korea Rep, Lithuania, Malaysia, Malta, Mexico, Myanmar, Netherlands, New Zealand, Nigeria, Norway, Panama, Paraguay, Peru, Philippines, Poland, Portugal, Romania, Rwanda, Singapore, Slovakia, Slovenia, Spain, Sweden, Switzerland, Tanzania UR, Thailand, UK, Uruguay, USA.
International organizations (3), listed in this Yearbook:
Asian Federation of Catholic Medical Associations (AFCMA, #01455); European Federation of Catholic Physicians Associations (FEAMC, no recent information); Latin American Federation of Catholic Doctors Associations (FAMCLAM, no recent information).
NGO Relations Member of: *Crescendo Worldwide Network (#04950); Forum of Catholic Inspired NGOs (#09905)*. [2022/XC1857/y/**C**]

♦ International Federation of Catholic News Agencies (inactive)
♦ International Federation of Catholic Parochial Youth Communities / see International Federation of Catholic Parochial Youth Movements (#13379)

♦ International Federation of Catholic Parochial Youth Movements .. 13379

Fédération Internationale des Mouvements Catholiques d'Action Paroissiale (FIMCAP)

Contact Kipdorp 30, 2000 Antwerp, Belgium. T. +3232310795. E-mail: info@fimcap.org.
URL: http://www.fimcap.org/

History 7 Oct 1961, Munich (Germany). 7-8 Oct 1961, Munich (Germany FR), as the result of a proposal adopted, Oct 1959, Lucerne (Switzerland), during the National Presidents' Conference of European Movements affiliated to *International Catholic Youth Federation (ICYF, inactive)*, which subsequently, 25 Apr 1968, merged with *World Federation of Catholic Young Women and Girls (WFCYWG, inactive)* to form *World Federation of Catholic Youth (WFCY, inactive)*, which itself ceased to exist in Jun 1981, its activities being taken over by Fimcap; and following the setting up of a Constitutional Commission by delegates from parochial youth organizations, Aug 1960, Munich, during the World Eucharistic Congress. A previous organization had been set up 1921, Rome (Italy), as *International Secretariat of Catholic Youth*, reorganized 15 Sep 1948, as *International Office of Catholic Youth – Bureau international de la jeunesse catholique*, and subsequently – Oct 1954 – *International Federation of Catholic Youth*. Previously also referred to as *International Federation of Catholic Parochial Youth Communities – Fédération internationale des communautés de jeunesse catholique paroissiales – Federación Internacional de las Comunidades de Juventud Católica Parroquial – Internationaler Bund der Katholischen Pfarrlichen Jugendgemeinschaften – Internationale Federatie van Katholieke Parochiale Jeugdgemeenschappen*. New statutes adopted: 14-18 Oct 1981, London (UK); Oct 1995, Randa (Switzerland); Jul 1998, Botha's Hill (South Africa); Jul 2001, Abokobi (Ghana); Jul 2004, Barcelona (Spain); Jul 2007, Assisi (Italy). **Aims** Group together Catholic youth associations which are not aimed at specific professional groups, but which focus on leading children and young people in integrated development activities in a parish-related context; build a better world and a living Church. **Structure** General Assembly (every 3 years); Bureau. **Languages** English, French, Spanish. **Staff** 0.70 FTE, paid. **Activities** Events/meetings; networking/liaising; training/education. **Events** *General Assembly* Westmalle (Belgium) 2019, *General Assembly* Melchtal (Switzerland) 2016, *General Assembly* Modra (Slovakia) 2013, *General Assembly* Assisi (Italy) 2007, *Afro-conference* Burundi 2005. **Publications** *Link* (4 a year) – newsletter. **NGO Relations** Member of: *Forum of Catholic Inspired NGOs (#09905)*; *Generation Climate Europe (GCE, #10114)*.
[2019.07.09/XC3960/**C**]

♦ International Federation of Catholic Pharmacists 13380

Fédération internationale des pharmaciens catholiques (FIPC) – Federación Internacional de Farmacéuticos Católicos – Internationale Vereinigung Katholischer Apotheker – Federazione Internazionale Farmacisti Cattolici

Contact Square Vergote 43, 1030 Brussels, Belgium. T. +3271877145.
Pres address not obtained.

History Founded 1950, Rome (Italy), as a sub-Secretariat of *Pax Romana, International Catholic Movement for Intellectual and Cultural Affairs (ICMICA, #18267)*. Subsequently became a Secretariat and finally an independent federation. Statutes officially adopted 1962. New statutes registered in accordance with Belgian law, Dec 1998. **Aims** Live the Christian faith in practising the pharmaceutical profession; apprehend and study problems arising from this experience; help shape the growth and future of pharmacy; witness and, through personal initiative, cultivate service to the sick; stimulate international friendship and understanding; be open to exchange and solidarity with the Third World and Eastern Europe. **Structure** International Council/General Assembly. Executive Committee meets twice a year as Administrative Council and comprises President, 1-3 Vice-Presidents, Secretary-General and a representative of each national member association; Treasurer and Ecclesiastical Adviser attend in consultative capacity. Secretariat General; Study Commissions. **Languages** English, French, German, Italian, Spanish. **Staff** Voluntary. **Finance** Members' dues. Donations; subsidies; legacies; proceeds of congresses and publications. **Activities** Events/meetings; training/education. **Events** *Biennial congress* Rome (Italy) 2007, *Biennial congress* Rome (Italy) 2000, *Biennial congress* Bratislava (Slovakia) 1995, *Traditional African medicine, community health and the medicaments, evolution and solidarity, North South relations* Cameroon 1994, *Biennial Congress* Antwerp (Belgium) 1993. **Publications** *FIPC Listing* (2 a year). Recommendations on ethical problems raised by the advance of pharmaceutical science.

Members National associations in 10 countries:
Austria, Belgium, France, Germany, Italy, Mexico, Peru, Switzerland, UK, USA.
Corresponding members in 12 countries:
Australia, Congo DR, Côte d'Ivoire, Czechoslovakia (unspecified), Hungary, Ireland, Luxembourg, Netherlands, Nigeria, Poland, Portugal, Spain.

NGO Relations Member of: *Crescendo Worldwide Network (#04950)*. [2016/XD1875/**D**]

♦ International Federation of Catholic Schools of Journalism (inactive)

♦ International Federation of Catholic Universities (IFCU) 13381

Fédération internationale des universités catholiques (FIUC) – Federación Internacional de Universidades Católicas (FIUC)

SG General Secretariat, 21 rue d'Assas, 75270 Paris, France. T. +33144395226. Fax +33144395228. E-mail: sgfiuc@bureau.fiuc.org.
URL: http://www.fiuc.org/

History 29 Jun 1948, Rome (Italy). Founded by a Decree of the Holy See, after informal negotiations since 1924. Recognized by Pope Pius XII in 1949. First Statutes approved by the *Sacred Congregation of Seminaries and Universities*, 11 Jan 1951. Revised several times including: 1965 Tokyo (Japan); 1970 Boston MA (USA); 1988 Jakarta (Indonesia); 2000, Fremantle (Australia); 2006, Bangkok (Thailand); 2009, Rome (Italy); 2012, Sao Paulo (Brazil). Former names and other names: *Federation of Catholic Universities* – former; *Fédération des universités catholiques* – former; *Foederatio Universitatum Catholicarum* – former; *Sacred Congregation of Seminaries and Universities* – former. **Aims** Contribute to *progress* of *knowledge* and its applications and to development of a more just and humane world in the light of reason and faith through the ferment of the Gospel.

Structure General Assembly of Rectors (every 3 years); Board of Administration; Executive; General Secretariat, headed by Secretary General. *International Center for Research and Decision Support of the International Federation of Catholic Universities (CIRAD, #12476)* connects member universities and research initiatives through interdisciplinary and international cooperation projects, seminars, colloquia and training. Sectoral Groups, composed of faculty members and representatives of various departments of colleges and universities, offer a platform for specialists to work together. They include: *International Catholic Association of Institutes of Educational Sciences (#12448)*; Sciences and Technologies; *Red Europea de Institutos de la Familia (REDIF, #18653)*; Sectoral Group in Political Science; *Conference of Catholic Theological Institutions (COCTI, see: #13381)*; *International Association of Catholic Medical Schools (IACMS, #11759)*; World Conference of Catholic University Institution of Philosophy; Conference of Catholic Institutions of Psychology (FIUCUP/IFCUP); Social Sciences.
Regional associations (6): Association of Catholic Colleges and Universities (ACCU); *Association of Catholic Universities and Higher Institutes of Africa and Madagascar (ACUHIAM, #02416)*; *Association of Southeast and East Asian Catholic Colleges and Universities (ASEACCU, #02923)*; *European Federation of Catholic Universities (#07070)*; *Organization of Catholic Universities in Latin America and the Caribbean (#17858)*; Xavier Board of Higher Education in India.

Languages English, French, Spanish. **Staff** 8.00 FTE, paid. **Finance** Sources: members' dues. **Activities** Networking/liaising; projects/programmes; training/education. **Events** *Triennial General Assembly* Boston, MA (USA) 2022, *Triennial General Assembly* Boston, MA (USA) 2021, *General Assembly and Conference* Lisbon (Portugal) 2020, *Triennial General Assembly* Maynooth (Ireland) 2018, *General Assembly and Conference* Québec, QC (Canada) 2018. **Publications** *E-Bulleting* (weekly); *IDEM ALITER* (12 a year) – newsletter; *The Journal of the Center* (2 a year). Monographs; articles; proceedings; CDs. **Information Services** *ICARIN – IFCU Cooperation and Research Information Network* – programme on Internet.

Members Full; Associate. Catholic universities (217) in 56 countries and territories:
Angola, Argentina, Australia, Belgium, Bolivia, Brazil, Cameroon, Canada, Chile, Colombia, Congo DR, Costa Rica, Côte d'Ivoire, Dominican Rep, Ecuador, France, Germany, Ghana, Guatemala, Haiti, Honduras, Hungary, India, Indonesia, Ireland, Italy, Japan, Kenya, Korea Rep, Lebanon, Mexico, Mozambique, Netherlands, Nicaragua, Nigeria, Palestine, Panama, Paraguay, Peru, Philippines, Poland, Portugal, Puerto Rico, Rwanda, Slovakia, South Africa, Spain, Switzerland, Taiwan, Thailand, Uganda, UK, Ukraine, Uruguay, USA, Venezuela.
Included in the above, 5 organizations listed in this Yearbook:
Pontifical University Antonianum; *Salesian Pontifical University (#19038)*; *Universidad Centroamericana, Managua (UCA)*; *Universidad Iberoamericana, México (UIA)*; *Université catholique d'Afrique centrale (UCAC)*.

Consultative Status Consultative status granted from: *ECOSOC (#05331)* (Ros C); *UNESCO (#20322)* (Consultative Status); *Council of Europe (CE, #04881)* (Participatory Status). **IGO Relations** Accredited by (1): *United Nations Office at Vienna (UNOV, #20604)*. Associated with Department of Global Communications of the United Nations. **NGO Relations** Member of (2): *Crescendo Worldwide Network (#04950)*; *Forum of Catholic Inspired NGOs (#09905)*. Partner of (2): *United Nations Academic Impact (UNAI, #20516)*; *World Catholic Association for Communication (SIGNIS, #21264)*. Instrumental in setting up (1): *Tantur Ecumenical Institute (#20096)*. Links with national bodies and with: *Association of African Universities (AAU, #02361)*; *Association of Universities Entrusted to the Society of Jesus in Latin-America (#02969)*; *International Association of Universities (IAU, #12246)*; *International Catholic Cooperation Centre for UNESCO (CCIC, #12454)*; *International Catholic Organizations Information Center (ICO Center)*. [2022/XC1876/y/**B**]

♦ International Federation for Cell Biology (IFCB) 13382

Fédération internationale de biologie cellulaire – Federación Internacional de Biologia Celular – Internationale Gesellschaft für Zellenbiologie

SG Dept of Structural and Functional Biology, State University of Biology, Charles Darwin St, Campinas SP, 13083-863, Brazil. T. +551935216118. E-mail: contact@ifcbiol.com.
URL: http://www.ifcbiol.com/

History Nov 1972, St Louis, MO (USA). Founded by representatives of *European Cell Biology Organization (ECBO, inactive)*, and American and Japanese national societies, as successor to *International Society of Cell Biology (ISCB, inactive)*, set up in Jul 1947, Stockholm (Sweden), at 6th International Congress of Experimental Cytology, itself replacing *International Society for Experimental Cytology (inactive)*, formed in 1933. **Aims** Promote international cooperation and contribute to advancement of cell biology in all its branches; act as a coordinating body able to initiate special studies and encourage research in areas outside the normal scope of national societies, such as problems of scientific communication. **Structure** General Assembly (every 2 years at International Congress); Executive Committee; Officers: President, Vice-President, Secretary-General. **Languages** English. **Staff** 0.50 FTE, paid. **Finance** Sources: members' dues; sale of publications. **Activities** Events/meetings; financial and/or material support. **Events** *International Congress of Cell Biology* Taipei (Taiwan) 2022, *International Congress of Cell Biology* Hyderabad (India) 2018, *International Congress of Cell Biology* Prague (Czechia) 2016, *International Congress of Cell Biology* Philadelphia, PA (USA) 2014, *International Congress of Cell Biology* Rio de Janeiro (Brazil) 2012. **Publications** *Cell Biology International* (12 a year) – official journal; *Cell Biology International Reports* – online journal. *International Cell Biology 1976-1977* by B R Brinkley and Keith Porter; *International Cell Biology 1980-1981* by H G Schweiger. Reports of past international congresses. Information Services: Databases on cell theory and primary cilia.

Members Associate; Affiliate. National societies and contact persons and individual biologists in 33 countries:
Argentina, Australia, Austria, Belgium, Brazil, Canada, Chile, China, Denmark, Finland, France, Germany, Greece, Hungary, India, Iran Islamic Rep, Israel, Italy, Japan, Latvia, Mexico, Netherlands, New Zealand, Norway, Poland, Romania, Russia, South Africa, Sweden, Switzerland, UK, Ukraine, USA.
Regional members organizations include:
Asian-Pacific Organization for Cell Biology (APOCB, #01619).

NGO Relations Represents cell biology in: *International Union of Biological Sciences (IUBS, #15760)*.
[2022/XC2476/y/**C**]

♦ International Federation of Celtic Wrestling (IFCW) 13383

Fédération internationale des luttes celtiques (FILC)

Gen Sec 4 rue de Kerallan, 29280 Plouzané, France.

History 16 Nov 1985, Cardiff (UK). Registered in France as an international NGO. **Aims** Develop the practice of the 4 styles of Celtic wrestling; help members to develop their native style of wrestling; regulate, control and coordinate the international meetings and competitions of Celtic wrestling. **Languages** English, French, Spanish. **Staff** Voluntary. **Finance** Members' dues. **Activities** Sporting events. **Events** *Championships* St Brieuc (France) 2010, *Championships* East Kilbride (UK) 2009, *Championships* Arona (Spain) 2008, *Championships* León (Spain) 2007, *Championships* Carlisle (UK) 2006.

Members Organizations in 10 countries, with Spain and UK subdivided into regions:
Austria, France, Iceland, Ireland, Italy, Netherlands, Spain (2), Sweden, UK (3), USA.

NGO Relations Member of: *European Traditional Sports and Games Association (ETSGA, #08931)*; *International Sport and Culture Association (ISCA, #15587)*. Cooperation agreement with: *United World Wrestling (UWW, #20665)*. [2013.09.05/XD7918/**D**]

♦ International Federation Centres of CICOP / see Federation of International Centres for the Preservation of the Architectural Heritage (#09602)

♦ International Federation of Centres for Puppetry Arts (IFCPA) 13384

Pres c/o Scottish Mask and Puppet Centre, 8-10 Balcarres Ave, Kelvindale, G12 0QF, UK. T. +441413396185. Fax +441413574484. E-mail: info@maskandpuppet.co.uk.

History 1990, Bilbao (Spain). Previously also known under the acronym *IFIPAC*. Registered in accordance with Dutch law. **Aims** As a federation of professional centres involved with public programmes of work from within buildings containing theatres, museums and education institutes, promote exchange of information, festivals and companies, exhibitions and education projects.

Members Full in 10 countries:
Belgium, Mexico, Netherlands, Poland, Russia, Slovakia, Spain, UK, USA, Venezuela.

NGO Relations *Europees Figurenteatercentrum (no recent information)*. [2015/XF2388/**F**]

♦ International Federation of Ceramic Workers (inactive)

♦ International Federation for Cervical Pathology and Colposcopy (IFCPC) 13385

Fédération internationale de pathologie cervicale et colposcopie – Federación Internacional de Patologia Cervical y Colposcopia – Internationale Federation für Zervixpathologie und Kolposkopie

Administration c/o ASCCP Natl Office, 131 Rollins Ave, Suite 2, Rockville MD 20852, USA. T. +13018577877. Fax +12404337971. E-mail: info@ifcpc.org.
SG 5006 Dickson Bldg, 5820 University Ave, Halifax NS B3H 1V7, Canada. T. +19024734029. Fax +19024737765. E-mail: neerja_bhatla@yahoo.co.in.
URL: http://www.ifcpc.org/

History 6 Nov 1972, Mar del Plata (Argentina), at 1st World Congress for Cervical Pathology and Colposcopy. Current Constitution: approved by General Assembly, 16 Oct 1981, London (UK); modified at 11th World Congress, Jul 2011, Rio de Janeiro (Brazil). **Aims** Stimulate basic and applied research and diffusion of knowledge in matters concerning uterine cervical pathology and colposcopy; contribute to standardization of terminology and evaluation of diagnostic and therapeutic procedures in the field. **Structure** General Assembly (every 3 years, at Congress); Executive Board; Scientific Advisory Committee; Education Committee. **Languages** English. **Finance** Sources: members' dues. **Activities** Events/meetings; financial and/or material support; knowledge management/information dissemination; standards/guidelines. **Events** *Triennial Congress* Rockville, MD (USA) 2021, *Triennial Congress* Hyderabad (India) 2020, *Triennial Congress* Orlando, FL (USA) 2017, *Triennial World Congress* London (UK) 2014, *Triennial World Congress* Rio de Janeiro (Brazil) 2011. **Publications** *Journal of Lower Genital Tract Disease*.

Members National societies in 37 countries:
Argentina, Australia, Austria, Bolivia, Brazil, Canada, Chile, Colombia, Costa Rica, Croatia, Czechia, Ecuador, France, Germany, Greece, Hungary, India, Indonesia, Ireland, Israel, Italy, Korea Rep, Mexico, Netherlands, North Macedonia, Paraguay, Philippines, Poland, Portugal, Serbia, Singapore, Slovakia, Spain, Türkiye, UK, Uruguay, USA.

NGO Relations Recognized by: *Fédération Internationale de Gynécologie et d'Obstétrique (FIGO, #09638).* Joint activities with: *International Gynecologic Cancer Society (IGCS, #13767); International Society for the Study of Vulvovaginal Disease (ISSVD, #15491).* Liaises with: *European Federation for Colposcopy and Pathology of the Lower Genital Tract (EFC, #07081)* and *Federación Latinoamericana de Patologia del Tracto Genital Inferior y Colposcopia (FLPTGIC, #09358).* [2019/XC5847/**C**]

♦ International Federation of Chauffeur-Drivers, Mechanics, Electricians and Automobilists (inactive)

♦ International Federation of Cheerleading (IFC) 13386

Pres Aoyama Success Bldg – 7th Floor, 2-11-13 Minami-Aoyama, Minato-ku, Tokyo, 107-0062 Japan. T. +81357705747.
URL: https://ifccheer.org/

History 5 Jul 1998. Registration: Japan. **Aims** Promote the *sport* of cheerleading worldwide; spread knowledge of cheerleading; develop friendly sporting relations among member associations/federations. **Structure** General Meeting (annual); Executive Committee; Executive Board. Committees (3): Rules; Education; Competition Organizing. Continental federations (3): *Asian Federation of Cheerleading (AFC, #01456); European Cheerleading Association (ECA, #06520); Pan American Federation of Cheerleading (PFC, #18101).* **Activities** Sporting activities. **Events** *Annual General Meeting* Takasaki (Japan) 2019, *Annual General Meeting* Takasaki (Japan) 2018, *Annual General Meeting* Takasaki (Japan) 2017, *Annual General Meeting* Takasaki (Japan) 2016.

Members Full in 54 countries and territories:
Argentina, Armenia, Barbados, Belgium, Bolivia, Brazil, Cambodia, Chile, Colombia, Croatia, Denmark, Ecuador, Georgia, Germany, Gibraltar, Greece, Hungary, India, Indonesia, Ireland, Italy, Japan, Kazakhstan, Korea Rep, Kyrgyzstan, Latvia, Lithuania, Luxembourg, Mali, Mexico, Moldova, Mongolia, Myanmar, Netherlands, North Macedonia, Panama, Philippines, Romania, Russia, Singapore, Slovenia, South Africa, Spain, Switzerland, Taiwan, Thailand, Uganda, UK, Ukraine, Uruguay, USA, Venezuela, Vietnam, Zimbabwe.

NGO Relations Member of: *The Association for International Sport for All (TAFISA, #02763).* Associate member of: *World DanceSport Federation (WDSF, #21354).* [2020/XJ6338/**B**]

♦ International Federation of Chemical, Energy and General Workers' Unions (inactive)
♦ International Federation of Chemical, Energy, Mine and General Workers' Unions (inactive)
♦ International Federation of Chemists (inactive)
♦ International Federation of Chief Editors (inactive)
♦ International Federation of Children of Mary Immaculate (religious order)
♦ International Federation of Children's Communities / see Fédération internationale des communautés éducatives (#09622)
♦ International Federation of Children's Organizations / see International Union of Children's Organizations (#15762)
♦ International Federation of Chiropodists and Podiatrists / see International Federation of Podiatrists (#13514)

♦ International Federation of Chopin Societies (IFCS) 13387

Fédération internationale des sociétés Chopin – Internationale Föderation der Chopin Gesellschaften

Pres Biberstrasse 4, 1010 Vienna, Austria. T. +4315122374. Fax +4315122375. E-mail: office@chopin.at.
URL: http://www.chopin.at/

History 17 Oct 1985, Warsaw (Poland). Registered in accordance with Polish law. **Aims** Disseminate and expand knowledge about Frederic Chopin and in particular about his *artistic* output; support international artistic and *scholarly* endeavours related to Frederic Chopin; popularize Chopin's works in the countries of members and worldwide; create advantageous conditions for actively sharing *musical culture.* **Structure** General Assembly of Members (every 5 years during International Frederic Chopin Piano Competition in Warsaw). Board, including Praesidium of the Board, consisting of President, 2 Vice-Presidents, Treasurer, Secretary General and Members of the Board. Audit Committee, composed of 3-5 members, of whom Chairman and Deputy Chairman are elected. Conciliation Board, consisting of 3-5 members representing different nationalities, of whom Chairman, Deputy Chairman and Secretary are elected. **Finance** Members' dues. **Activities** Initiates, promotes and conducts scholarly research into Chopin's life and artistic output and initiates renditions of his work; animates and conducts international publishing activity; assists member societies in organization of concerts, competitions, festivals, exhibitions, lectures and seminars; endeavours to protect Chopin's relics and artifacts. Organizes General Assembly (every 5 years, always in Warsaw). **Events** *CARME : international conference on correspondence analysis and related methods* Rotterdam (Netherlands) 2007, *Quinquennial General Assembly* Warsaw (Poland) 1995, *Quinquennial General Assembly* Warsaw (Poland) 1990. **Publications** *Chopin in the World* (annual) in English – journal.

Members Chopin societies (41) in 30 countries and territories:
Argentina, Australia, Austria, Belgium, Brazil, Canada, Chile, Croatia, Cuba, Czechia, Denmark, France, Germany, Guatemala, Israel, Italy, Japan, Korea Rep, Mexico, Morocco, Philippines, Poland, Russia, Serbia, Spain, Switzerland, Taiwan, Thailand, USA, Vietnam.

NGO Relations Associate member of: *International Music Council (IMC, #14199).* Member of: *European Music Council (EMC, #07837).* [2011/XE1079/**E**]

♦ International Federation for Choral Music (IFCM) 13388

Fédération internationale de la musique chorale (FIMC) – Federación Internacional para la Música Coral – Internationale Föderation für Chormusik

Pres Rua de Buenos Aires 39, 1200-623 Lisbon, Portugal.
Manager PO Box 42318, Austin TX 78704, USA. E-mail: office@ifcm.net.
Registered Address c/o ACDA, 545 Couch Dr, Oklahoma City OK 73102-2207, USA. E-mail: office@ifcm.net.
URL: http://www.ifcm.net/

History 1982, Namur (Belgium). Founded by 7 national and international choral organizations, representing 88 nations. **Aims** Strengthen cooperation among national and international organizations and individuals interested in all aspects of choral music; encourage formation of choral organizations; foster and promote international exchange programmes for *choirs*, conductors, composers and students of choral music; promote, coordinate and encourage choral festivals, seminars, competitions and meetings; facilitate dissemination of choral repertoire, research, recordings and other appropriate materials; encourage inclusion of choral music in general education. **Structure** Board. Organizes: *World Youth Choir (WYC, #21955).* **Languages** Chinese, English, French, German, Japanese, Korean, Spanish. **Staff** 3.00 FTE, paid. **Activities** Events/meetings; knowledge management/information dissemination. **Events** *World Symposium on Choral Music* Doha (Qatar) 2023, *World Symposium on Choral Music* Auckland (New Zealand) 2020, *World Symposium on Choral Music* Barcelona (Spain) 2017, *World Symposium on Choral Music* Seoul (Korea Rep) 2014, *World choral summit* Beijing (China) 2012. **Publications** *International Choral Bulletin* (4 a year); *World Census of Choral Music* (annual) – online. *Cantemus.*

Members Individuals; individual choirs; institutions; businesses; national organizations of choirs; international organizations; founding organizations. Members in 73 countries and territories:
Algeria, Argentina, Armenia, Australia, Austria, Belgium, Brazil, Bulgaria, Canada, Chile, China, Colombia, Congo DR, Costa Rica, Côte d'Ivoire, Croatia, Cuba, Cyprus, Czechia, Denmark, Estonia, Finland, France, Gabon, Germany, Greece, Guatemala, Hong Kong, Hungary, Iceland, India, Indonesia, Ireland, Israel, Italy, Japan, Kenya, Korea Rep, Latvia, Lebanon, Lithuania, Luxembourg, Malaysia, Maldives, Mexico, Mozambique, Netherlands, New Zealand, Norway, Panama, Peru, Philippines, Poland, Puerto Rico, Romania, Russia, Serbia, Singapore, Slovenia, South Africa, Spain, Sri Lanka, Sweden, Switzerland, Taiwan, Thailand, Türkiye, UK, Ukraine, United Arab Emirates, Uruguay, USA, Venezuela.

Founding members (7), of which 3 international and regional bodies listed in this Yearbook:
Choral Festival Network (CFN, #03894); European Choral Association – Europa Cantat (#06541); Nordisk Korforum (#17521).

IGO Relations *UNESCO (#20322).* **NGO Relations** Member of: *European Music Council (EMC, #07837); International Music Council (IMC, #14199).* [2021/XD0426/y/**C**]

♦ International Federation of Christian Churches (IFCC) 13389

Contact Postnet Ste 521, Private Bag X 10030, Randburg, 2125, South Africa. T. +27117917283. Fax +27117916832. E-mail: ifcc@rhema.co.za.

History 18 Aug 1985, Durban (South Africa), as *International Fellowship of Christian Churches.* Present name adopted 1996. **NGO Relations** Member of: *South African Council of Churches (SACC, #19699).* [2011.06.01/XU8920/**D**]

♦ International Federation of Christian Employees' Trade Unions (inactive)
♦ International Federation of Christian Employees' Unions / see World Organization of Workers (#21697)
♦ International Federation of Christian Factory and Transport Workers Trade Unions (inactive)
♦ International Federation of Christian Miners' Unions (inactive)
♦ International Federation of Christian Postal Workers (inactive)
♦ International Federation of Christians of Salaried Employees, Technicians, Managerial Staff and Commercial Travellers / see World Organization of Workers (#21697)
♦ International Federation of Christian Trades Unions of Railway and Tramway Men (inactive)
♦ International Federation of the Christian Trade Unions of Employees, Technicians and Managerial Staff / see World Organization of Workers (#21697)
♦ International Federation of Christian Trade Unions of Public Services / see International Federation of Employees in Public Services (#13410)
♦ International Federation of Christian Unions of Agricultural Workers (inactive)
♦ International Federation of Christian Workers in Exile (inactive)
♦ International Federation of Christian Workers Movements (inactive)

♦ International Federation of Cinematographers (IMAGO) 13390

Gen Sec Maison Euro des Auteurs, Rue du Prince Royal 85, 1050 Brussels, Belgium. E-mail: generalsecretary@imago.org – president@imago.org.
Pres Bd Général Wahis 16F, 1030 Brussels, Belgium.
URL: http://www.imago.org/

History 13 Dec 1992, Rome (Italy). Statutes revised: 2017; 2019, 2021. Former names and other names: *European Federation of Cinematographers (IMAGO)* – former (1992 to 2019); *Fédération Européenne des Directeurs de la Photographie Cinématographique* – former (1992 to 2019). Registration: No/ID: 0834 948 680, Start date: 13 Feb 2017, Belgium, Brussels. **Aims** Champion and uphold the high standards achieved by the Cinematography Profession; promote the spread of that highly-specialised culture on which the long-standing technical and artistic quality of the European Cinema industry is firmly based. **Structure** Annual General Assembly; Extraordinary General Assembly; Administration Board; Committees (7). **Languages** English. **Staff** 8.00 FTE, voluntary. **Finance** Sources: grants; members' dues; sponsorship. Income from National societies by size of membership. **Activities** Events/meetings; financial and/or material support; training/education. **Events** *Annual General Assembly* Brussels (Belgium) 2022, *Extraordinary General Assembly* Brussels (Belgium) 2022, *General Assembly* Brussels (Belgium) 2021, *General Assembly* Brussels (Belgium) 2020, *General Assembly* Belgrade (Serbia) 2019. **Publications** *International Directory of Cinematographers* (2016); *Making Pictures – A Century of European Cinematography.*

Members Full; Associate. National societies representing over 4,000 individuals in 54 countries and territories:
Argentina, Australia, Austria, Azerbaijan, Belgium, Bosnia-Herzegovina, Brazil, Bulgaria, Canada, Chile, Colombia, Croatia, Cuba, Denmark, Estonia, Finland, France, Greece, Hong Kong, Hungary, Iceland, India, Iran Islamic Rep, Ireland, Israel, Italy, Japan, Korea Rep, Latvia, Lithuania, Malaysia, Mexico, New Zealand, North Macedonia, Norway, Peru, Philippines, Poland, Romania, Russia, Serbia, Singapore, Slovakia, Slovenia, South Africa, Spain, Sweden, Switzerland, Türkiye, UK, Ukraine, Uruguay, USA, Venezuela. [2022.05.11/XD8901/**D**]

♦ International Federation of the Cinematographic Press / see Fédération internationale de la presse cinématographique (#09651)
♦ International Federation of Citizens Opposed to Membership of Turkey in the European Union (unconfirmed)
♦ International Federation of City, Sport and Multipurpose Halls / see European Association of Event Centers (#06032)
♦ International Federation of Civil Servants (inactive)

♦ International Federation of Classification Societies (IFCS) 13391

Sec Wroclaw University of Economics and Business, Komandorska 188/120, 53-345 Wroclaw, Poland.
URL: http://ifcs.boku.ac.at/

History 1985, Cambridge (UK). Founded at 4th Joint Meeting of Classification Societies. **Aims** Promote communication, cooperation and interchange of views among those interested in scientific principles, numerical methods, theory and practice of data science, data analysis and classification. **Structure** Grouping of regional or national societies plus a "group at large" for individuals having no member society. Council; Executive Committee. **Languages** English, French, German, Italian, Japanese, Portuguese, Spanish. **Staff** 45.00 FTE, voluntary. **Finance** Sources: members' dues. Annual budget: 3,000 EUR. **Activities** Events/meetings. **Events** *Biennial Conference* San José (Costa Rica) 2024, *Biennial Conference* Porto (Portugal) 2022, *Biennial Conference* Porto (Portugal) 2021, *Biennial Conference* Thessaloniki (Greece) 2019, *Biennial Conference* Tokyo (Japan) 2017. **Publications** *IFCS Newsletter.*

Members Societies (14), representing 26 countries:
Belgium, Canada, Colombia, Costa Rica, Cuba, France, Germany, Greece, Guatemala, Honduras, Hungary, Ireland, Italy, Japan, Korea Rep, Mexico, Morocco, Netherlands, Nicaragua, Poland, Portugal, Slovenia, South Africa, Spain, UK, USA.

In the above, 2 organizations listed in this Yearbook:
Sociedad Centroamericana y del Caribe de Clasificación y Analisis de Datos (SoCCCAD, #19352); Société francophone de classification (SFC, #19465). [2022.12.09/XD0648/y/**D**]

♦ International Federation of Clinical Chemistry / see International Federation of Clinical Chemistry and Laboratory Medicine (#13392)

♦ International Federation of Clinical Chemistry and Laboratory Medicine (IFCC) 13392

Fédération Internationale de Chimie Clinique (FICC) – Federación Internacional de Química Clínica – Internationaler Verband für Klinische Chemie

Coordinator Via Carlo Farini 81, 20159 Milan MI, Italy. T. +390266809912. E-mail: ifcc@ifcc.org.
Registered Office c/o Seedamm Business Center, Churerstrasse, 135, 8808 Pfaeffikon SZ, Switzerland.
URL: http://www.ifcc.org/

History 24 Jul 1952, Paris (France). Founded at 2nd International Congress of Biochemistry, under the auspices of *International Union of Pure and Applied Chemistry (IUPAC, #15809).* Statutes modified, 1955, Brussels (Belgium); next modification: 1963, Detroit MI (USA). Initially closely connected with IUPAC through its Commission (later Section and now Division) of Clinical Chemistry, but became independent in 1967 although still an Associate Member. Present statutes adopted 18 Jun 1972, Copenhagen (Denmark); most recently amended 1996, London (UK). Articles approved 18 Jun 1972 and amended 13 Jul 1975, 29 Apr 1984, 14 Nov 1993, 20 Oct 2002, 24 Jul 2005, 15 May 2011, 30 Jun 2013, 1 Apr 2016. Former names and other names: *International Association of Clinical Biochemists* – former (1952 to 1955); *International Federation of Clinical Chemistry (IFCC)* – former (1955); *Fédération internationale de chimie clinique (FICC)* – former (1955); *Federación Internacional de Quimica Clinica* – former (1955); *Internationaler Verband für Klinische Chemie* – former (1955). **Aims** Advance excellence in laboratory medicine for better healthcare worldwide. **Structure** Council; Executive Board. Divisions (4); Other Committees liaised to Executive Board (4); Task Forces (10); Technical Secretariat in Milan (Italy). **Languages** English. **Staff** 4.80 FTE, paid. **Finance** Sources: grants; members' dues; sale of publications; sponsorship. **Activities** Awards/prizes/competitions; events/meetings; knowledge management/information dissemination; publishing activities; standards/guidelines. **Events** *International Congress of Clinical Chemistry and Laboratory Medicine – WorldLab* Dubai (United Arab Emirates) 2024, *IFCC-EFLM EuroMedLab Congress* Rome (Italy) 2023, *Labquality Days – International Congress on Quality in Laboratory Medicine and Health Technology* Helsinki (Finland) 2022, *International Congress of Clinical Chemistry and Laboratory Medicine (IFCC WorldLab)* Seoul (Korea Rep) 2022, *IFCC-ICHCLR Workshop on Barriers to Global Standardization of Clinical Laboratory Testing* Seoul (Korea Rep) 2021. **Publications** *IFCC Newsletter* (10 a year); *eJournal of the International Federation of Clinical Chemistry (eJIFCC)* (4 a year); *IFCC Handbook* (every 3 years); *IFCC Milestone 2002-2020* (Anniversary). *e-Academy* (2022) – Webinars. Annual Report; monographs; webinars. News and scientific documents also published in formal collaboration with 'Clinica Chimica Acta'. Relevant publications in the field of laboratory medicine can be published on IFCC website.

Members Full; Corporate; Affiliate. Full: national societies representing about 50,000 individual clinical chemists, in 95 countries and territories:

Albania, Algeria, Argentina, Australia, Austria, Belgium, Bolivia, Bosnia-Herzegovina, Brazil, Bulgaria, Canada, Chile, China, Colombia, Croatia, Cuba, Cyprus, Czechia, Denmark, Dominican Rep, Ecuador, Egypt, Estonia, Ethiopia, Finland, France, Germany, Greece, Guatemala, Hong Kong, Hungary, Iceland, India, Indonesia, Iran Islamic Rep, Iraq, Ireland, Israel, Italy, Japan, Jordan, Kazakhstan, Kenya, Korea Rep, Kosovo, Latvia, Lebanon, Libya, Lithuania, Luxembourg, Malawi, Malaysia, Mexico, Montenegro, Morocco, Myanmar, Nepal, Netherlands, New Zealand, Nigeria, North Macedonia, Norway, Pakistan, Palestine, Panama, Paraguay, Peru, Philippines, Poland, Portugal, Romania, Russia, Saudi Arabia, Serbia, Singapore, Slovakia, Slovenia, South Africa, Spain, Sri Lanka, Sudan, Sweden, Switzerland, Syrian AR, Taiwan, Thailand, Tunisia, Türkiye, UK, Ukraine, Uruguay, USA, Vietnam, Zambia, Zimbabwe.

Corporate: clinical chemists (56) in 19 countries:
Belgium, Canada, China, Denmark, Finland, France, Georgia, Germany, Hungary, India, Italy, Japan, Kazakhstan, Mexico, Norway, Sri Lanka, UK, USA, Venezuela.

Affiliate: clinical chemists in 18 countries:
Botswana, Brazil, China, Egypt, France, India, Iran Islamic Rep, Jordan, Kazakhstan, Mexico, Nepal, Philippines, Romania, Serbia, Spain, Sri Lanka, Türkiye, Ukraine.

Regional societies (6):
African Federation of Clinical Chemistry (AFCC, #00306); Arab Federation of Clinical Biology (AFCB, #00941); Asia Pacific Federation for Clinical Biochemistry and Laboratory Medicine (APFCB, #01896); Confederación Latinoamericana de Bioquimica Clinica (COLABIOCLI, #04454); European Federation of Clinical Chemistry and Laboratory Medicine (EFLM, #07080); North American Federation of Clinical Chemistry and Laboratory Medicine (NAFCC).

Consultative Status Consultative status granted from: *ECOSOC (#05331)* (Ros C); *WHO (#20950)* (Official Relations). **IGO Relations** Accredited by (1): *United Nations Office at Vienna (UNOV, #20604)*. Working relationship with: *Bureau international des poids et mesures (BIPM, #03367); Joint Research Centre (JRC, #16147); Pan American Health Organization (PAHO, #18108)*. Associated with Department of Global Communications of the United Nations. **NGO Relations** Member of (1): *Council for International Organizations of Medical Sciences (CIOMS, #04905)* (as Associate Member). Cooperates with (1): *European Association for the Study of Diabetes (EASD, #06228)*. Affiliated with (1): *International Union of Biochemistry and Molecular Biology (IUBMB, #15759)*. Instrumental in setting up (1): *Joint Committee for Traceability in Laboratory Medicine (JCTLM, #16127)*. [2022.10.18/XC1890/y/**B**]

♦ International Federation of Clinical Neurophysiology (IFCN) 13393

Fédération internationale de neurophysiologie clinique

Main Office 555 E Wells St, Ste 1100, Milwaukee WI 53202, USA. E-mail: info@ifcn.info.
URL: http://www.ifcn.info/

History Sep 1949, Paris (France). Constitution adopted Nov 1951. Absorbed *International Society of Electromyography (inactive)*, 1973. Absorbed *Brainstem Society (BSS, inactive)*, 2018. Former names and other names: *International Federation of Electroencephalography and Clinical Neurophysiology* – former; *Fédération internationale d'électroencéphalographie et de neurophysiologie clinique* – former. **Aims** Ensure that the highest possible standards are reached in all countries in the field of *electroencephalography* and clinical neurophysiology; encourage scientific research; promote effective international collaboration between learned societies, professional associations, institutions and individuals contributing to progress in the field. **Structure** General Assembly (meets at Congresses); Council; Executive Committee; Special Commissions. Regional Chapters (4): Asian-Oceania; Europe, Middle East and Africa; Latin America; North america. Special Interest Groups (4): Advanced EEG-MEG Techniques in Clinical Neurophysiology; Brainstem; Education; Noninvasive Brain Stimulation. **Languages** English, French. **Staff** Voluntary. **Finance** Sources: members' dues. **Activities** Advocacy/lobbying/activism; events/meetings; research and development; standards/guidelines. **Events** *European Congress of Clinical Neurophysiology (ECCN)* Marseille (France) 2023, *International Congress of Clinical Neurophysiology (ICCN)* Geneva (Switzerland) 2022, *International Congress of Clinical Neurophysiology* Geneva (Switzerland) 2022, *International Congress of Clinical Neurophysiology* Melbourne, VIC (Australia) 2022, *Congress* Kuala Lumpur (Malaysia) 2021. **Publications** *Clinical Neurophysiology Practice* (2018); *Clinical Neurophysiology* (2008).

Members National societies or groups of societies in 60 countries and territories:
Argentina, Australia, Austria, Belgium, Bolivia, Brazil, Bulgaria, Canada, Chile, China, Colombia, Croatia, Cuba, Cyprus, Czechia, Denmark, Dominican Rep, Egypt, Estonia, Finland, France, Georgia, Germany, Greece, Guatemala, Hungary, India, Indonesia, Iran Islamic Rep, Iraq, Ireland, Israel, Italy, Japan, Jordan, Korea Rep, Luxembourg, Malaysia, Mexico, Netherlands, Peru, Philippines, Poland, Portugal, Romania, Russia, Serbia, Singapore, Slovakia, Slovenia, South Africa, Spain, Sweden, Switzerland, Taiwan, Thailand, Türkiye, UK, Uruguay, USA.

IGO Relations Collaborates with: *UNESCO (#20322)*. **NGO Relations** European Chapter is member of: *European Brain Council (EBC, #06391)*. Instrumental in setting up: *Latin American Society of Electroencephalography (inactive)*. [2023.02.14/XC2008/**C**]

♦ International Federation of Coalitions for Cultural Diversity (IFCCD) 13394

Fédération internationale des coalitions pour la diversité culturelle (FICDC) – Federación Internacional de Coaliciones para la Diversidad Cultural

SG c/o CDCE, 33 Milton St, Ste 500, Montréal QC H2X 1V1, Canada. E-mail: coalition@cdc-ccd.org.
URL: http://www.ficdc.org/

History 19 Sep 2007, Seville (Spain). Replaces *International Liaison Committee of Coalitions for Cultural Diversity (ILCCCD, inactive)*. **Aims** Protect and promote diversity of cultural expressions worldwide; support development and implementation of national, regional and international policies; support ratification process of UNESCO Convention on the Diversity of Cultural Expressions. **Structure** Secretariat ensured by Canadian Coalition for Cultural Diversity. **Languages** English, French, Spanish. **Finance** Members' dues. Other sources: Canadian Coalition for Cultural Diversity; French Coalition for Cultural Diversity; *Organisation internationale de la Francophonie (OIF, #17809)* finances specific activities of developing member countries. **Activities** Events/meetings. Active in all regions of the world, mainly: Europe; Africa; Latin America; North America; Oceania. **Events** *International Conference on Legislative Reforms around the World to Protect and Promote the Diversity of Cultural Expressions* Montréal, QC (Canada) 2022, *Congress* Lomé (Togo) 2019, *Congress* Montréal, QC (Canada) 2018, *Congress* Mons (Belgium) 2015, *Congress* Bratislava (Slovakia) 2012. **Publications** *Coalition Currents* (4 a year) in Arabic, Chinese, English, French, Spanish – newsletter. *Cultural Dimension of Sustainable Development: Insights into the Current Practices of 'Measuring' Results of Cultural Projects* (2014); *The Trade and Culture Issue, at the Origin of the Convention on the Protection and the Promotion of the Diversity of Cultural Expressions* (2014); *Funding Sources for Cultural Initiatives in ACP Countries* (2013); *Role of the International Federation of Coalitions for Cultural Diversity in Promoting Culture in Sustainable Development* (2013); *The Campaign for Cultural Diversity: Why It Matters to You.*

Members National coalitions in 44 countries:
Argentina, Australia, Austria, Belgium, Benin, Brazil, Burkina Faso, Cameroon, Canada, Chad, Chile, Colombia, Congo DR, Côte d'Ivoire, Ecuador, France, Gabon, Germany, Guinea, Hungary, Ireland, Italy, Korea Rep, Mali, Mauritania, Mauritius, Mexico, Morocco, New Zealand, Niger, Paraguay, Peru, Portugal, Senegal, Slovakia, South Africa, Spain, Sweden, Switzerland, Togo, Tunisia, UK, Uruguay, Venezuela.

Consultative Status Consultative status granted from: *UNESCO (#20322)* (Consultative Status); *ECOSOC (#05331)* (Special). **IGO Relations** Supports ratification of: *Convention on the Protection and Promotion of the Diversity of Cultural Expressions (2005)*. **NGO Relations** Member of: *NGO-UNESCO Liaison Committee (#17127)*. [2021/XM3384/**D**]

- ♦ International Federation of Colonial and Former Colonial Civil Servants (inactive)
- ♦ International Federation of Commerce and Industry (inactive)
- ♦ International Federation of Commercial Arbitration Institutions (internationally oriented national body)
- ♦ International Federation of Commercial, Clerical, Professional and Technical Employees (inactive)
- ♦ International Federation of Commercial Transport by Car (inactive)
- ♦ International Federation of Committees for European Cooperation (inactive)
- ♦ International Federation of Communication Associations (internationally oriented national body)

♦ International Federation of Community Health Centres (IFCHC) 13395

Main Office c/o CACHC, 340 College St, Ste 500, Toronto ON M5T 3A9, Canada.
URL: http://www.ifchc.org/

History 1 Jul 2013, by Canadian Association of Community Health Centres, Community Health Australia, *European Forum for Primary Care (EFPC, #07326)* and US National Association of Community Health Centers. **Aims** Foster global collaboration in community-oriented primary health care; expand access to community health centres as the optimal way to achieve the WHO's vision for equitable access to primary health care for all. **Structure** Directing Council. **Publications** *IFCHC e-Bulletin.*

Members CHC members of founding organizations. Health Community Centres in 44 countries:
Albania, Armenia, Australia, Austria, Belarus, Belgium, Canada, Croatia, Cyprus, Denmark, Egypt, Estonia, Finland, France, Georgia, Germany, Hungary, Iceland, Ireland, Italy, Jordan, Kazakhstan, Korea Rep, Kosovo, Latvia, Malta, Moldova, Netherlands, Nigeria, North Macedonia, Poland, Portugal, Romania, Russia, Serbia, Slovakia, Slovenia, Spain, Sweden, Switzerland, Türkiye, UK, Ukraine, USA. [2020/XJ8508/**C**]

♦ International Federation of Comparative Endocrinological Societies (IFCES) 13396

Sec/Treas Dept of Integrative Biology, Univ of Guelph, 50 Stone Rd E, Guelph ON N1G 2W1, Canada. T. +15198244120ext56093. Fax +15197671656.
URL: https://www.ifces-icce.org/

History 20 May 1989, Malaga (Spain). Founded at 11th International Symposium on Comparative Endocrinology, when statutes were adopted by founding (constituent) societies: *Asia and Oceania Society for Comparative Endocrinology (AOSCE, #01806); European Society for Comparative Endocrinology (ESCE, #08558)*; American, Japanese and Indian national societies. Approved by *International Committee on Comparative Endocrinology*, 17 May 1989. **Aims** Promote and advance research in comparative endocrinology, neuroendocrinology and neurobiology; facilitate collaboration and exchange of ideas among scientists worldwide. **Structure** Council. Organizes *International Congress on Comparative Endocrinology (ICCE)*. **Languages** English. **Finance** Annual dues of constituent societies on a per capita basis. **Activities** Events/meetings; knowledge management/information dissemination. **Events** *International Congress of Comparative Endocrinology (ICCE19)* Sendai (Japan) 2025, *International Congress of Comparative Endocrinology (ICCE19)* Sendai (Japan) 2021, *International Congress of Comparative Endocrinology (ICCE)* Lake Louise, AB (Canada) 2017, *International Congress of Comparative Endocrinology (ICCE)* Barcelona (Spain) 2013, *International Congress of Comparative Endocrinology (ICCE)* Hong Kong (Hong Kong) 2009. **Publications** Congress proceedings. [2021/XD2147/y/**D**]

♦ International Federation for Computational Logic (IFCoLog) 13397

Dir c/o Dept of Philosophy, Univ of Cambridge, Sidgwick Avenue, Cambridge, CB3 9DA, UK. E-mail: mg639@cam.ac.uk – dov.gabbay@kcl.ac.uk.
URL: http://www.ifcolog.net/

History Registered in accordance with Dutch law. Registration: Charity Commission, No/ID: 1112512, England and Wales; Companies House, No/ID: 1112512, UK. **Aims** Advance and promote research and education in all areas of computational logic worldwide. **Structure** General Assembly. Advisory Board. Council comprising President, 5 Vice-Presidents, Executive Board, Founding President, Treasurer, PR Officer, Coordinator, Secretary and technical staff. **Activities** Organizes triennial conference. **Events** *NaBIC : world congress on nature and biologically inspired computing* Salamanca (Spain) 2011.

Members include the following organizations listed in this Yearbook (5):
Association of Logic, Language and Information (FoLLI, #02789); Association of Logic Programming (ALP, #02790); Australasian Association for Logic; European Association for Computer Science Logic (EACSL, #05987); Formal Methods Europe (FME, #09872). [2021/XJ2755/y/**C**]

♦ International Federation of Computer Law Associations (IFCLA) . . . 13398

Fédération internationale des associations nationales de droit de l'informatique

Pres 2A Templar Street, London, SE5 9JB, UK.
Treas Astrea, Av Louise 235, 1050 Brussels, Belgium. E-mail: sds@astrealaw.be.
URL: http://www.ifcla.com/

History Dec 1986, Brussels (Belgium). Registered in accordance with Belgian law. **Aims** Arouse scientific exchanges of opinions on development and juridical, social and economic impact of computer law and juridical informatics. **Structure** General Assembly (annual); Management Board; Executive Committee. **Languages** English, French. **Finance** Members' dues. Other sources: gifts; subsidies. **Activities** Events/meetings. **Events** *Biennial Conference* Helsinki (Finland) 2022, *Biennial Conference* Barcelona (Spain) 2021, *Biennial Conference* Barcelona (Spain) 2020, *Biennial Conference* Paris (France) 2018, *Biennial Conference* London (UK) 2016.

Members National organizations (14) in 14 countries:
Argentina, Australia, Belgium, Brazil, Canada, Denmark, Finland, France, Germany, Netherlands, Norway, Portugal, Sweden, UK.

Consultative Status Consultative status granted from: *World Intellectual Property Organization (WIPO, #21593)* (Permanent Observer Status). **NGO Relations** *Instituto Latinoamericano de Alta Tecnologia, Informatica y Derecho (ILATID, #11341).* [2015/XD2533/**D**]

- ♦ International Federation of Consular Corps and Associations / see World Federation of Consuls (#21422)

♦ International Federation of Consulting Engineers 13399

Fédération internationale des ingénieurs-conseils (FIDIC) – Internationale Vereinigung Beratender Ingenieure – Federación International de Ingenieros Consultores

Main Office World Trade Center II, Geneva Airport, PO Box 311, 1215 Geneva 15, Switzerland. T. +41225680500. E-mail: fidic@fidic.org.
URL: http://www.fidic.org/

History 22 Jul 1913, Ghent (Belgium). Reorganized under new Statutes 29 Jun 1937. Statutes completely revised 3 Jun 1955; amended Sep 2015; revised Sep 2020. Instrumental in setting up: *Asia Pacific Grouping of Consulting Engineers (ASPAC, #01920); FIDIC Group of African Member Associations (GAMA, #09752).* Registration: Swiss Civil Code, Start date: 23 May 1967; Start date: 2007, Switzerland, Geneva. **Aims** As the recognized global voice for the consulting engineering industry, enable development of a sustainable world. **Structure** General Assembly (annual); Board; Specialized Committees; Task Groups; Secretariat in Geneva, headed by CEO; Regional Groups. **Languages** English. **Staff** 20.00 FTE, paid. **Finance** Sources: fees for services; meeting proceeds; members' dues; revenue from activities/projects; sale of publications. **Activities** Awards/prizes/competitions; capacity building; events/meetings; networking/liaising; standards/guidelines; training/education. **Events** *FIDIC International Contract Users' Conference* London (UK) 2023, *Global Infrastructure Conference* Singapore (Singapore) 2023, *ICC – FIDIC Conference on International Construction Contracts and Dispute Resolution* Dubrovnik (Croatia) 2022, *Global Infrastructure Conference* Geneva (Switzerland) 2022, *FIDIC International Contract Users' Conference* London (UK) 2022. **Publications** *CEO's Update* (10 a year); *FIDIC Newsletter.* Annual Report; policy statements; position papers; contracts; guidelines; training manuals and resource kits.

Members National associations and associates in 93 countries and territories:
Albania, Australia, Austria, Bahrain, Bangladesh, Belgium, Bosnia-Herzegovina, Botswana, Brazil, Bulgaria, Canada, China, Colombia, Costa Rica, Côte d'Ivoire, Croatia, Cyprus, Czechia, Denmark, Egypt, Finland, France, Georgia, Germany, Ghana, Greece, Hong Kong, Hungary, Iceland, India, Indonesia, Iran Islamic Rep, Ireland, Israel, Italy, Japan, Jordan, Kazakhstan, Kenya, Korea Rep, Latvia, Lebanon, Lithuania, Luxembourg, Malaysia, Maldives, Mali, Mauritius, Mexico, Moldova, Mongolia, Morocco, Mozambique, Nepal, Netherlands, New Zealand, Nigeria, North Macedonia, Norway, Pakistan, Palestine, Peru, Philippines, Poland, Portugal, Romania, Russia, Saudi Arabia, Serbia, Singapore, Slovakia, Slovenia, South Africa, Spain, Sri Lanka, Sudan, Suriname, Sweden, Switzerland, Taiwan, Tanzania UR, Thailand, Trinidad-Tobago, Türkiye, Uganda, UK, Ukraine, United Arab Emirates, USA, Uzbekistan, Vietnam, Zambia, Zimbabwe.

Affiliate members in 25 countries and territories:
Bahamas, China, France, Germany, India, Indonesia, Iran Islamic Rep, Italy, Kazakhstan, Korea Rep, Kuwait, Lebanon, Libya, Malawi, Peru, Philippines, Qatar, Romania, South Africa, Spain, Sudan, Taiwan, Tanzania UR, UK, United Arab Emirates.

Consultative Status Consultative status granted from: *ECOSOC (#05331)* (Ros C); *UNIDO (#20336)*. **IGO Relations** Memorandum of Understanding with (10): *African Development Bank (ADB, #00283); Asian Development Bank (ADB, #01422); Asian Infrastructure Investment Bank (AIIB, #01512); Caribbean Development Bank (CDB, #03492); European Bank for Reconstruction and Development (EBRD, #06315); European Investment Bank (EIB, #07599); Inter-American Development Bank (IDB, #11427); International Fund for Agricultural Development (IFAD, #13692); Islamic Development Bank (IsDB, #16044); The World Bank Group (#21218).* **NGO Relations** Partner of (1): *World Urban Campaign (WUC, #21893)* (as Associate partner of). Cooperates with (2): *European Federation of Engineering Consultancy Associations (EFCA, #07109); Federación Panamericana de Consultores (FEPAC, #09379).* In liaison with technical committees of: *International Organization for Standardization (ISO, #14473).* [2023.01.02/XC1896/**B**]

- ♦ International Federation of Cooks (inactive)
- ♦ International Federation of Corporate Football (unconfirmed)
- ♦ International Federation of Cotton and Allied Textile Industries / see International Textile Manufacturers Federation (#15679)

♦ International Federation of Culture Collection of Microbic Types (inactive)

♦ **International Federation of Customs Brokers Associations (IFCBA)** . 13400
Sec c/o CSCB, 55 Murray St, Ste 320, Ottawa ON K1N 5M3, Canada. T. +16135623543. Fax +16135623548. E-mail: ifcba@ifcba.org.
URL: http://www.ifcba.org/
History Founded Nov 1990, Singapore (Singapore). **Aims** Encourage and facilitate cooperation and ideas on matters affecting broker associations at international level; facilitate the exchange of information and ideas of matters affecting national customs broker associations; associate, affiliate and federate with any other association, society or organization with the same or similar objects. **Structure** Board of Directors, comprising officers and representatives from all member associations. **Languages** English. **Finance** Members' dues. **Events** *Biennial World Conference* Shanghai (China) 2016, *Biennial World Conference* Seoul (Korea Rep) 2014, *Biennial World Conference* Buenos Aires (Argentina) 2010, *Biennial world conference* Istanbul (Turkey) 2008, *Biennial world conference* Beijing (China) 2006.
Members Associated Businesses in 25 countries:
Angola, Argentina, Australia, Canada, China, Greece, India, Iran Islamic Rep, Italy, Jamaica, Japan, Korea Rep, Liberia, Maldives, Mauritius, Mexico, Mozambique, Myanmar, Nepal, Nigeria, Portugal, Thailand, Türkiye, Uruguay, USA.
IGO Relations Memorandum of Understanding with: *World Customs Organization (WCO, #21350)*. **NGO Relations** Cooperates with: *Confédération internationale des agents en douanes (CONFIAD, #04559)*; *International Chamber of Commerce (ICC, #12534)*; *Professional Customs Brokers Association of the Americas (#18512)*. [2020/XD5679/**D**]

♦ International Federation of Cycle Messengers and Companies / see International Federation of Bike Messenger Associations (#13371)

♦ **International Federation of Daseinsanalysis (IFDA)** 13401
Pres/Treas Rue Leys 18, 1000 Brussels, Belgium. T. +32475714120. E-mail: president@i-f-da.org.
Sec address not obtained.
URL: http://www.i-f-da.org/
History 1990. Founded by Gion Condrau (1919-2006) and the Zurich Daseinsanalytic School. Former names and other names: *International Federation of Daseinsanalytic Psychotherapy (IFDA)* – former. **Aims** Unfold the essence of Daseinsanalysis; promote creation of national associations and provide them with guidelines on necessary steps; federate the Daseinsanalytic national associations into an international association; further the teaching and research in the areas of daseinsanalytic phenomenology, anthropology and Daseinsanalytical therapy; spread out Daseinsanalysis. **Languages** English. **Activities** Research/documentation; events/meetings; knowledge management/information dissemination; networking/liaising. **Events** *What does it mean to be a Daseinsanalyst* Athens (Greece) 2015, *General Assembly* Athens (Greece) / Hydra Is (Greece) 2015, *General assembly* Anhée (Belgium) 2014, *Forum* Budapest (Hungary) 2012.
Members Full in 9 countries:
Austria, Belgium, Brazil, Canada, Czechia, France, Greece, Switzerland, UK. [2018/XJ5253/**D**]

♦ International Federation of Daseinsanalytic Psychotherapy / see International Federation of Daseinsanalysis (#13401)
♦ International Federation of Data Organizations / see International Federation of Data Organizations for the Social Sciences (#13402)

♦ **International Federation of Data Organizations for the Social Sciences (IFDO)** 13402
Fédération internationale des organisations de services des données en sciences sociales
Pres H W Odum Inst for Research in Social Science, Univ of North Carolina at Chapel Hill, 229B Davis Library, Chapel Hill NC 27599-3355, USA. T. +19199620517.
URL: http://www.ifdo.org/
History Founded 22 May 1977, Louvain-la-Neuve (Belgium). Also referred to as *International Federation of Data Organizations – Fédération internationale des organisations de service de données*. **Aims** Facilitate and support research through cooperation between data organizations across countries, regions and continents; promote and work for open access to digital data; advocate the preservation of valuable digital resources; support development of standards, procedures and tools enhancing data usage; promote and support establishment and development of data organizations to further these objectives. **Structure** General Assembly (annual); Board. **Languages** English. **Staff** 7.00 FTE, voluntary. **Finance** Members' dues. Annual budget: euro 4,000. **Activities** Knowledge management/information dissemination; events/meetings; training/education. **Events** *General Assembly* Montréal, QC (Canada) 2018, *General Assembly* Bergen (Norway) 2016, *International Conference* Minneapolis, MN (USA) 2015, *International Conference* Toronto, ON (Canada) 2014, *Meeting* Toronto, ON (Canada) 2014. **Publications** Workbooks; training packages, electronic data catalogues.
Members Social science data organizations (37) in 29 countries and territories:
Australia, Austria, Canada, Czechia, Denmark, Estonia, Finland, France, Germany, Greece, Hungary, India, Israel, Italy, Japan, Luxembourg, Netherlands, New Zealand, Norway, Philippines, Romania, Slovenia, South Africa, Spain, Sweden, Switzerland, Taiwan, UK, USA.
NGO Relations Member of: *International Science Council (ISC, #14796)*. [2017.03.14/XD9517/**D**]

♦ **International Federation of Dental Anesthesiology Societies (IFDAS)** 13403
SG 1-43-9 Komagome TS Building, Komagome, Toshima-ku, Tokyo, 170-003 Japan. T. +81339478891. Fax +81339478341.
URL: http://www.ifdas.org/
History 1982. **Aims** Promote study and practice of improved methods of anaesthesia, analgesia and sedation in dentistry. **Structure** Education Committee. **Languages** English. **Finance** Members' dues. **Events** *Congress* Moscow (Russia) 2021, *Triennial Congress* Nara (Japan) 2018, *Triennial Congress* Berlin (Germany) 2015, *Triennial Congress* Hawaii (USA) 2012, *Triennial Congress* Kohala Coast (USA) 2012. **Publications** *Anesthesia Progress* (4 a year).
Members National societies in 16 countries and territories:
Australia, Germany, Hong Kong, India, Israel, Italy, Japan, Korea Rep, Kuwait, New Zealand, Russia, South Africa, Taiwan, UK, Ukraine, USA.
Affiliated member (1):
European Federation for the Advancement of Anaesthesia in Dentistry (EFAAD, #07040). [2019.10.26/XD5040/**D**]

♦ International Federation of Dental Education Associations / see International Federation of Dental Educators and Associations (#13404)

♦ **International Federation of Dental Educators and Associations (IFDEA)** 13404
Admin Office Dental Univ Hosp, Trinity College, Lincoln Place, Dublin, 2, CO. DUBLIN, Ireland. T. +35316127287. Fax +35316127294. E-mail: administrator@adee.org.
URL: http://www.ifdea.org/
History 1992. Former names and other names: *International Federation of Dental Education Associations* – former. **Aims** Serve as an axis of information, best practices, exchange programmes, news and professional development for regional dental education associations, academic dental institutions and individual dental educators worldwide. **Structure** Council (meets annually); Executive Committee/Board of Directors. **Languages** English. **Staff** 0.10 FTE, paid. **Activities** Events/meetings; guidance/assistance/consulting. **Events** *Global congress on dental education* Dublin (Ireland) 2007, *Annual meeting* Baltimore, MD (USA) 2005, *Annual meeting* Honolulu, HI (USA) 2004, *Annual meeting* Gothenburg (Sweden) 2003, *Annual Meeting* Jerusalem (Israel) 2003.
Members Full in 41 countries and territories:
Argentina, Australia, Austria, Belgium, Brazil, Canada, Chile, Colombia, Costa Rica, Czechia, Denmark, Ecuador, Finland, France, Germany, Greece, Hong Kong, Hungary, India, Indonesia, Ireland, Israel, Italy, Japan, Korea Rep, Malaysia, Mexico, Netherlands, New Zealand, Norway, Portugal, Puerto Rico, Singapore, South Africa, Spain, Sweden, Taiwan, Thailand, UK, USA, Venezuela.
National and international organizations (10); supporting (8), including 4 organizations listed in this Yearbook:
Association for Dental Education in Europe (ADEE, #02467); *Australasian Association of Schools of Dentistry (AASD, #03020)*; *Organización de Facultades, Escuelas y Departamentos de Odontologia de la Unión de Universidades de América Latina (OFEDO/UDUAL, #17837)*; *South East Asian Association for Dental Education (SEAADE, #19757)*.
NGO Relations Member of (1): *FDI – World Dental Federation (#09281)*. Instrumental in setting up (1): *Global Network on Dental Education*. Official relations with: *International Association for Dental Research (IADR, #11838)*. [2023.02.15/XD4721/y/**D**]

♦ **International Federation of Dental Hygienists (IFDH)** 13405
Exec Dir 100 S Washington St, Rockville MD 20850, USA. T. +12407786790. Fax +12407786112. E-mail: director@ifdh.org.
URL: http://www.ifdh.org/
History 1973. Officially set up 28 Jun 1986, Oslo (Norway). Former names and other names: *International Liaison Committee on Dental Hygiene* – former (1973 to 28 Jun 1986); *International Dental Hygienists' Federation* – former (28 Jun 1986 to 1992). **Aims** Unite national dental hygienist organizations by fostering leadership and collaboration; promote excellence in oral health education, research and practice. **Structure** Board of Directors; House of Delegates. **Languages** English. **Staff** 4.00 FTE, paid. **Finance** Sources: members' dues; revenue from activities/projects; sponsorship. **Activities** Awareness raising; events/meetings; knowledge management/information dissemination; projects/programmes. **Events** *International Symposium on Dental Hygiene* Milan (Italy) 2026, *International Symposium on Dental Hygiene* Seoul (Korea Rep) 2024, *International Symposium on Dental Hygiene* Dublin (Ireland) 2022, *International Symposium on Dental Hygiene* Brisbane, QLD (Australia) 2019, *International Symposium on Dental Hygiene* Basel (Switzerland) 2016. **Publications** *International Journal of Dental Hygiene* (4 a year); *CONTACT eNews* (3 a year).
Members Full; Individual; Corporate; Honorary-Life; Student and Allied Supporter. Full member associations in 34 countries:
Australia, Austria, Belgium, Cameroon, Canada, Czechia, Denmark, Finland, Georgia, Germany, India, Ireland, Israel, Italy, Japan, Korea Rep, Latvia, Lithuania, Malta, Nepal, Netherlands, New Zealand, Norway, Portugal, Russia, Singapore, Slovakia, South Africa, Spain, Sweden, Switzerland, UK, United Arab Emirates, USA.
Individuals in 7 countries:
Australia, Canada, Japan, New Zealand, Switzerland, UK, USA.
NGO Relations Also links with national and international oral health organizations. [2021.03.01/XD3489/**D**]

♦ **International Federation of Denturists** 13406
Chief Exec 8150 Metropolitain Bd East, Ste 230, Anjou, Montréal QC H1K 1A1, Canada.
URL: http://international-denturists.org/
History Founded 1964. **Aims** Promote denturists worldwide. **Structure** Committees (3): Education; Eastern and Central Europe; Australasia. **Languages** English. **Staff** 1.00 FTE, paid; 1.00 FTE, voluntary. **Finance** Sources: members' dues. **Events** *Annual General Assembly* Las Vegas, NV (USA) 2021, *World Symposium* Las Vegas, NV (USA) 2021, *Annual General Assembly* Montréal, QC (Canada) 2020, *Annual General Assembly* Brisbane, QLD (Australia) 2019, *World Symposium* Brisbane, QLD (Australia) 2019. **Publications** *IFD Newsletter* (annual).
Members Denturists associations; individuals. Members in 16 countries:
Australia, Belgium, Canada, Cyprus, Denmark, Finland, France, Ireland, Malta, Netherlands, Poland, South Africa, St Kitts-Nevis, Switzerland, UK, USA. [2021/XN8729/**C**]

♦ International Federation for the Development of Herbal, Aromatic and Similar Medicines (inactive)

♦ **International Federation of Digital Seismograph Networks (FDSN)** . 13407
Chairman CSN, FCFM, Univ of Chile, Beauchef 850, Santiago, Santiago Metropolitan, Chile. T. +56229784309. E-mail: sbarrien@dgf.uchile.cl.
Sec Council for Geoscience, Private Bag X112, Pretoria, 0001, South Africa. T. +27128411200.
URL: http://www.fdsn.org/
History 1986, as *Federation of Digital Broadband Seismograph Networks*. Previously also known as *Federation of Digital Seismograph Networks*. A Commission of *International Association of Seismology and Physics of the Earth's Interior (IASPEI, #12157)*, within *International Union of Geodesy and Geophysics (IUGG, #15776)*. **Aims** Coordinate the efforts in seismological instrumentation and distribution of seismic data. **Structure** Steering Committee of 47 members. Executive Committee, including Chair and Secretary. Working Groups (5). **Languages** English. **Staff** None. **Finance** No budget. **Activities** Working Groups (5): Station Siting and Instrumentation; Data Format and Centers; Software Coordination; CTBT Coordination; Portable Instrumentation. **Events** *Annual Meeting* Gothenburg (Sweden) 2013, *Annual Meeting* Melbourne, VIC (Australia) 2011, *Annual Meeting* Cape Town (South Africa) 2009, *Annual Meeting* Perugia (Italy) 2007, *Annual Meeting* Bangkok (Thailand) 2006. **Publications** Annual Report.
Members Organizations (68) in 63 countries and territories:
Albania, Algeria, Argentina, Australia, Austria, Brazil, Bulgaria, Canada, Chile, China, Colombia, Costa Rica, Croatia, Czechia, Denmark, Ecuador, Egypt, Finland, France, Georgia, Germany, Greece, Hungary, Iceland, Indonesia, Iran Islamic Rep, Israel, Italy, Jamaica, Japan, Jordan, Kazakhstan, Kyrgyzstan, Malaysia, Mexico, Netherlands, New Caledonia, New Zealand, Nicaragua, North Macedonia, Norway, Pakistan, Poland, Portugal, Puerto Rico, Romania, Russia, Slovakia, Slovenia, South Africa, Spain, Sweden, Switzerland, Taiwan, Tajikistan, Thailand, Tunisia, Türkiye, UK, United Arab Emirates, USA, Uzbekistan, Vanuatu.
Included in the above, 2 international organizations:
Comprehensive Nuclear-Test-Ban Treaty Organization (CTBTO, #04420); *Observatories and Research Facilities for European Seismology (ORFEUS, #17639)*. [2019/XE1296/y/**E**]

♦ International Federation of Disabled Workers and Civilian Handicapped / see International Federation of Persons with Physical Disability (#13504)
♦ International Federation of Doctors in Engineering and Engineers-Doctors of Science (inactive)
♦ International Federation of Draftsmen's Unions / see International Federation of Professional and Technical Engineers
♦ International Federation of Dramatic and Musical Criticism (inactive)
♦ International Federation of East-Central European Institutes (no recent information)

♦ **International Federation for East Timor (IFET)** 13408
Secretariat 142 Altamont Avenue, Tarrytown NY 10591, USA. T. +19144733185. E-mail: ifet@etan.org.
Contact c/o ETAN, PO Box 1663, New York NY 10035-1663, USA. T. +19176904391.
URL: http://www.etan.org/ifet/
History May 1991, Hiroshima (Japan). **Aims** Contribute to efforts being made to create an environment in which the people of Timor-Leste (East Timor) can freely exercise their right to self-determination; endeavour to guarantee internationally recognized human rights for all involved in the decolonization process of the territory. **Structure** A network with no permanent office; Secretariat. **Languages** English, Tetum. **Staff** No permanent staff. Work carried out by volunteers from member organizations. **Finance** Annual budget: 50 USD. **Activities** Advocacy/lobbying/activism; guidance/assistance/consulting; knowledge management/information dissemination; politics/policy/regulatory. **Publications** Open letters to UN and other officials released for media and public information.
Members Non-governmental organizations (35) in 25 countries and territories:
Australia, Canada, Fiji, Finland, France, Germany, Greece, Hong Kong, India, Indonesia, Ireland, Italy, Japan, Malaysia, Netherlands, New Zealand, Norway, Philippines, Portugal, Scotland, Spain, Sweden, Timor-Leste, UK, USA.
Included in the above, 7 organizations listed in this Yearbook:
Asia Pacific Solidarity Coalition (APSOC, #02050); *Association de solidarité avec Timor oriental (ASTO)*; *East Timor and Indonesia Action Network (ETAN)*; *Instituto de Estudios Politicos para América Latina y Africa (IEPALA)*; *International Platform of Jurists for East Timor (IPJET, #14601)*; *Latin American and Mediterranean Coalition for East Timor (LAMCET, #16348)*; *Pacific Concerns Resource Centre (PCRC)*.
IGO Relations Associated with Department of Global Communications of the United Nations. **NGO Relations** Member of (1): *International Peace Bureau (IPB, #14535)*. [2022.10.18/XE3108/y/**E**]

♦ International Federation of East-West Tai Chi Chuan (inactive)
♦ International Federation for the Economy for the Common Good / see Economy for the Common Good (#05323)
♦ International Federation for Educational Exchanges of Children and Adolescents (no recent information)
♦ International Federation of Educative Communities (#09622)
♦ International Federation of Electroencephalography and Clinical Neurophysiology / see International Federation of Clinical Neurophysiology (#13393)

♦ International Federation for Emergency Medicine (IFEM) 13409

Main Office 34 Jeffcott Street, WEST, Melbourne VIC 3003, Australia. T. +61393200444. Fax +61393200400. E-mail: enquiries@ifem.cc.
URL: http://www.ifem.cc/

History 1991. Founded when charter was signed by Presidents of American College of Emergency Physicians, *Australasian College for Emergency Medicine (ACEM)*, British Association of Emergency Medicine and Canadian Association of Emergency Physicians. **Aims** Promote access to, and lead the development of, the highest quality of emergency medical care for all people. **Structure** Assembly; Board; Regions (6); Standing Committees (8); Special Interest Groups (14); Headquarters, located in Melbourne (Australia). **Languages** English. **Staff** 1.50 FTE, paid. **Finance** Costs borne by individual organizations. **Activities** Events/meetings. **Events** *International Conference on Emergency Medicine* Hamburg (Germany) 2026, *International Conference on Emergency Medicine* Montréal, QC (Canada) 2025, *International Conference on Emergency Medicine* Taipei (Taiwan) 2024, *International Conference on Emergency Medicine* Amsterdam (Netherlands) 2023, *International Conference on Emergency Medicine* Melbourne, VIC (Australia) 2022. **Publications** Annual Reports; policies; guidelines.

Members National and regional organizations: Full; Affiliate; Ex-officio. Members in 54 countries and territories:
Argentina, Australia, Bahrain, Brazil, Canada, Chile, Colombia, Costa Rica, Dominica, Finland, Georgia, Hong Kong, Iceland, India, Iran Islamic Rep, Iraq, Ireland, Israel, Japan, Korea Rep, Libya, Malaysia, Mexico, Nepal, Netherlands, New Zealand, Nigeria, Norway, Oman, Pakistan, Panama, Papua New Guinea, Paraguay, Peru, Philippines, Poland, Saudi Arabia, Singapore, South Africa, Spain, Sri Lanka, Sudan, Sweden, Taiwan, Tanzania UR, Thailand, Trinidad-Tobago, Türkiye, UK, United Arab Emirates, USA, Uzbekistan, Vietnam, Yemen.
Ex-officio members (6):
African Federation for Emergency Medicine (AFEM, #00307); *Asian Society for Emergency Medicine (ASEM, #01718)*; *European Society for Emergency Medicine (EuSEM, #08590)*; *Gulf Federation of Emergency Medicine (GFEM, #10827)*; Latin American Federation of Emergency Medicine (FLAME); Pan American Collaborative Emergency Medicine Development Program. [2023.03.03/XD7226/y/**C**]

♦ International Federation for Employees of Commerce (inactive)

♦ International Federation of Employees in Public Services (INFEDOP) 13410

Fédération internationale du personnel des services publics – Federación Internacional del Personal de los Servicios Públicos – Internationale Föderation der Öffentlich Bediensteten – Internationale Federatie van het Overheidspersoneel

SG c/o EUROFEDOP, Rue Montoyer 39, boîte 20, 1000 Brussels, Belgium. T. +3222303865. E-mail: infedop@infedop.org.
Sec address not obtained.
URL: http://www.infedop.org/

History 27 Aug 1930, Cologne (Germany). Amalgamated, Sep 1950, Innsbruck (Austria), with *International Federation of Christian Postal Workers (inactive)*, set up 3 Aug 1922. One of the *International Trade Federations (ITF, inactive)* (a World Secretariat for Trade Action) of *World Confederation of Labour (WCL, inactive)*. WCL merged with *International Confederation of Free Trade Unions (ICFTU, inactive)* to form *International Trade Union Confederation (ITUC, #15708)*, Nov 2006. Former names and other names: *International Federation of Christian Trade Unions of Public Services* – former; *Fédération internationale des syndicats chrétiens du personnel des services publiques* – former; *International of Functionaries* – former; *Fédération internationale des fonctionnaires des services publiques* – former. **Structure** Congress (every 5 years). Executive Board, constituting the World Council (meeting annually), comprises 10 members including one or more representatives of each affiliated trade union. World Executive Committee, comprising Daily Management Board – Chairman, 1st Vice-Chairman, Secretary-General and Treasurer – together with 4 regional Vice-Chairmen (Europe, Asia, Latin America, Africa). Occupational groups. Special Committees (9). Meetings closed. **Languages** Dutch, English, French, German, Spanish. **Staff** 4.00 FTE, paid. **Finance** Annual dues from affiliated unions: euro 0.75 per member. **Activities** Events/meetings; research/documentation. **Events** *Seminar* Belgrade (Serbia) 2019, *Annual Conference of Ministers* Vilnius (Lithuania) 2014, *Congress* Luxembourg (Luxembourg) 2013, *Congress* Monterrey (Mexico) 2008, *Seminar on leadership in the public sector* Beijing (China) 2005.

Members Trade unions in 67 countries and territories:
Albania, Argentina, Armenia, Aruba, Austria, Benin, Bolivia, Bonaire Is, Brazil, Bulgaria, Burkina Faso, Cameroon, Central African Rep, Chad, Chile, Colombia, Congo Brazzaville, Congo DR, Costa Rica, Côte d'Ivoire, Croatia, Curaçao, Czechia, Denmark, Dominican Rep, Ecuador, El Salvador, France, Gabon, Gambia, Ghana, Guadeloupe, Guatemala, Guinea, Haiti, Honduras, Hungary, Ireland, Italy, Kosovo, Lithuania, Madagascar, Mali, Malta, Mauritania, Mauritius, Mexico, Namibia, Netherlands, Nicaragua, North Macedonia, Panama, Paraguay, Peru, Puerto Rico, Senegal, Sierra Leone, Slovakia, Slovenia, South Africa, Spain, Switzerland, Togo, UK, Uruguay, Venezuela, Zimbabwe.
Regional organizations (5), listed in this Yearbook:
Asia Federation of Employees in Public Service (ASIAFEDOP, no recent information); *Coordinadora Latinoamericana de Trabajadores de los Servicios Públicos (CLATSEP, #04809)*; *European Federation of Employees in Public Services (EUROFEDOP, #07106)*; *Fédération panafricaine des syndicats des services publics (FPSSP, no recent information)*; *Latin American Confederation of Communication Workers (CLTC, no recent information)*.
NGO Relations *Fédération internationale des organisations syndicales du personnel des transports (FIOST, inactive)*. [2020/XC2035/y/**C**]

♦ International Federation of Endodontic Associations (IFEA) 13411

Fédération internationale des associations endodontiques

Sec address not obtained.
URL: http://www.ifeaendo.org/

History 1986. **Aims** Promote endodontics and endodontic education; represent the interests of the profession on a global scale. **Structure** General Assembly; Board of Directors; Executive Committee; Education Committee; Research Committee. **Languages** English. **Staff** Voluntary. **Finance** Members' dues. Other sources: donations; congress proceeds. **Activities** Awards/prizes/competitions; events/meetings; training/education; research/documentation; publishing activities. **Events** *World Congress 2020ONE* Chennai (India) 2020, *World Congress* Chennai (India) 2020, *World Congress* Seoul (Korea Rep) 2018, *World Congress* Cape Town (South Africa) 2016, *World Congress / World Endodontic Congress* Tokyo (Japan) 2013. **Publications** Teaching manual.

Members Endodontic organizations in 41 countries and territories:
Argentina, Australia, Bangladesh, Belgium, Brazil, Canada, Chile, Colombia, Egypt, Finland, France, Germany, Greece, Guatemala, Hong Kong, India, Indonesia, Iran Islamic Rep, Iraq, Israel, Italy, Japan, Jordan, Korea Rep, Kosovo, Lebanon, Lithuania, Mexico, New Zealand, Philippines, Portugal, Russia, Spain, Switzerland, Thailand, Türkiye, UK, Ukraine, United Arab Emirates, USA, Venezuela. [2021/XD1408/**D**]

♦ International Federation of Engineering Education Societies (IFEES) 13412

Secretariat 4400 University Dr, MS 4A3, Fairfax VA 22030, USA. T. +12022994942. E-mail: a.pappas@ifees.net.
URL: http://www.ifees.net/

History 9 Oct 2006, Rio de Janeiro (Brazil). Founded at the American Society for Engineering Education's Global Conference. Registration: 501(c)(3), Start date: 2012, USA. **Aims** Connect the world's engineering education societies to leverage members' collective strengths to improve engineering education worldwide. **Structure** President; Executive Committee; Secretariat. **Languages** Arabic, English, French, German, Greek, Portuguese, Russian, Spanish. **Staff** 2.50 FTE, paid. **Finance** Sources: donations; fees for services; meeting proceeds; members' dues. **Activities** Capacity building; events/meetings; networking/liaising. **Events** *EPOKA IFEES GEDC Regional Conference* Tirana (Albania) 2023, *World Engineering Education Forum* Cape Town (South Africa) 2022, *World Engineering Education Forum* Madrid (Spain) 2021, *World Engineering Education Forum* 2020, *World Engineering Education Forum* Chennai (India) 2019. **Publications** *GlobalEngineer: IFEES-GEDC Quarterly Bulletin*. *Rising to the Top – Women Engineering Leaders Share their Journeys to Professional Success* (2019).

Members Societies in 28 countries and territories:
Argentina, Australia, Austria, Belgium, Brazil, Canada, China, Colombia, France, Germany, India, Iran Islamic Rep, Japan, Kazakhstan, Korea Rep, Malaysia, Mexico, Myanmar, Nigeria, Peru, Russia, South Africa, Spain, Taiwan, Türkiye, UK, United Arab Emirates, USA.

IGO Relations Memorandum of Understanding with (1): *UNESCO (#20322)*. **NGO Relations** Cooperates with (1): *World Federation of Engineering Organizations (WFEO, #21433)*. Instrumental in setting up (2): *International Institute for Developing Engineering Academics (IIDEA, #13873)*; *POLIS (#18419)*. [2022.10.19/XJ1434/y/**C**]

♦ International Federation of Engine Reconditioners / see Fédération internationale des rectifieurs et reconstructeurs de moteurs (#09654)

♦ International Federation for Enteric Phage Typing (IFEPT) 13413

Sec 16 St Peters Way, Chorleywood, WD3 5QE, UK. T. +441923283021.
Co-Chairperson 163 Scotchmer Street, North Fitzroy, Melbourne VIC 3068, Australia. T. +61394814283.
Co-Chairperson Health Protection Agency, Centre for Infections, Lab of Gastrointestinal Pathogens, 61 Colindale Ave, London, NW9 5EQ, UK. T. +442083276114. Fax +442089059929.

History 1947, Copenhagen (Denmark), as *International Committee for Enteric Phage Typing*. Present name adopted 1974. **Aims** Secure international standardization of routine phage typing of typhoid and paratyphoid bacilli as employed in epidemiological investigations directed to the control of the enteric fevers; study development of resistance to antimicrobial drugs in strains of Salmonella typhi; study phage typing S Typhimurum and S Enteritidis, using international schemes developed in the UK. **Structure** Executive Council, comprising 2 joint chairpersons, Secretary and 6 members constituting the Executive Committee and 1 Honorary member. **Languages** English. **Staff** 1.00 FTE, voluntary. **Finance** No outside finance; individual countries finance their representative. **Activities** Meets every 3 years during Congress of *IUMS Division of Bacteriology and Applied Microbiology (BAM, see: #15794)*. **Events** *Meeting* Sapporo (Japan) 2011, *Meeting* Istanbul (Turkey) 2008, *Interim Meeting* Vienna (Austria) 2007, *Meeting / Interim Meeting* Prague (Czech Rep) 2006, *Meeting* San Francisco, CA (USA) 2005. **Publications** Report on the geographical distribution of Salmonella typhi and Salmonella paratyphi A and B (every 3 years).

Members Directors and/or Representatives of National and Regional Reference Laboratories for Enteric Phage Typing in 53 countries and territories:
Algeria, Australia, Austria, Bahrain, Belgium, Brazil, Bulgaria, Canada, Chile, Croatia, Czechia, Denmark, Egypt, Finland, France, Germany, Greece, Hong Kong, Hungary, India, Indonesia, Israel, Italy, Jamaica, Japan, Kenya, Korea Rep, Malaysia, Mexico, Morocco, Netherlands, New Zealand, Norway, Peru, Philippines, Poland, Portugal, Romania, Russia, Singapore, Slovakia, South Africa, Spain, Sri Lanka, Sweden, Switzerland, Thailand, Trinidad-Tobago, Tunisia, UK, USA, Venezuela, Vietnam. [2010.08.12/XD1405/v/**F**]

♦ International Federation of Environmental Health (IFEH) 13414

Sec c/o CIEH, Chadwick Court, 15 Hatfields, London, SE1 8DJ, UK. T. +442078275831. Fax +442079286953.
URL: http://www.ifeh.org/

History 1986, UK. Registration: England and Wales. **Aims** Provide a focal point for those whose concern is *protection* of the environment in the interests of human health. Promote: the *holistic* nature of environmental health; capacity building; networking of members; educational standards; cooperation among countries; interchange of professionals engaged in environmental health work. Disseminate results of research and provide a means of exchanging information. **Structure** Governing Council (meets at least annually). Board of Directors of 4 members. Regional groups (4): Africa; Americas; Asia and the Pacific; Europe. **Languages** English. **Staff** 4.00 FTE, paid. **Finance** Members' dues. Other sources: donations. **Activities** Adopts policies related to specific topics, including: WHO Declaration of Almaty, updating the definition of health; role of public bodies in developing environmental health management systems; regard for environmental health issues in negotiation of trade agreements; realistic and generic approach to environmental health and adequate training for environmental health professionals; smoking; water and sanitation; Declaration on Environmental Health; indicators for sustainable development. **Events** *World Congress on Environmental Health* Kuala Lumpur (Malaysia) 2022, *World Academic Conference on Environmental Health* Tartu (Estonia) 2021, *Biennial World Congress on Environmental Health* Kuala Lumpur (Malaysia) 2020, *Biennial World Congress on Environmental Health* Auckland (New Zealand) 2018, *Biennial World Congress on Environmental Health* Lilongwe (Malawi) 2016. **Publications** *Environment and Health International* (2 a year). Annual report.

Members National associations of environmental health professionals in 39 countries and territories:
Australia, Austria, Botswana, Canada, Cyprus, Denmark, Finland, France, Germany, Hong Kong, Indonesia, Ireland, Jamaica, Kenya, Latvia, Liberia, Lithuania, Malawi, Malaysia, Malta, Mauritius, Netherlands, New Zealand, Nigeria, Norway, Portugal, Rwanda, Scotland, Singapore, South Africa, Spain, Sri Lanka, Sweden, Tanzania UR, Uganda, UK, USA, Zambia, Zimbabwe.
Academic Associate members in 12 countries and territories:
Australia, Botswana, Canada, Hong Kong, Ireland, Kenya, Malawi, Singapore, South Africa, Sweden, UK, USA.
Associate members in 2 countries:
UK, USA.
IGO Relations Working dialogue with: *WHO Regional Office for Europe (#20945)*. [2021/XF2398/**F**]

♦ International Federation of Environmental Journalists (inactive)
♦ International Federation of Equestrian Tourism (#09666)
♦ International Federation of Esperantist Progressionist Teachers (inactive)

♦ International Federation of Esperantist Railwaymen 13415

Fédération internationale des cheminots espérantistes – Internacia Fervojista Esperanto Federacio (IFEF)

Contact address not obtained. E-mail: ifefesperanto@gmail.com.
URL: http://ifef.free.fr/spip/

History 1909. **Aims** Disseminate Esperanto among railwaymen and the railways. **Languages** Esperanto. **Staff** 5.00 FTE, voluntary. **Activities** Events/meetings. **Events** *Annual Congress* Malaga (Spain) 2019, *Annual Congress* Wroclaw (Poland) 2018, *Annual Congress* Colmar (France) 2017, *Annual Congress* Varna (Bulgaria) 2016, *Annual Congress* Kunming (China) 2015. **Publications** *Internacia Fervojisto* (6 a year); *Fervoj Fakaj Kajeroj* (2 a year). Dictionary.

Members National organizations, totalling over 2,300 individual members, in 21 countries:
Austria, Belgium, Bulgaria, China, Croatia, Czechia, Denmark, France, Germany, Hungary, Italy, Japan, Norway, Poland, Romania, Serbia, Slovakia, Slovenia, Spain, Sweden, Switzerland.
NGO Relations Affiliated member of: *Universal Esperanto Association (UEA, #20676)*. [2016.06.01/XD1908/**D**]

♦ The International Federation of Essential Oils and Aroma Trades (IFEAT) 13416

Secretariat c/o TC Group, Level 1, Devonshire House, One Mayfair Place, London, W1J 8AJ, UK. T. +441707245826. E-mail: secretariat@ifeat.org.
URL: http://www.ifeat.org/

History 1977, Kyoto (Japan). Registration: Companies House, Start date: 18 May 1978, UK. **Aims** Represent the interests of companies involved in the production, processing, trading and manufacturing of the ingredients used in flavours, fragrances and aromatherapy. **Languages** English. **Staff** 7.00 FTE, paid; 20.00 FTE, voluntary. **Finance** Sources: members' dues. **Activities** Events/meetings. **Events** *Annual Conference* Berlin (Germany) 2023, *Annual Conference* Vancouver, BC (Canada) 2022, *Virtual Conference* 2021, *Annual Conference* Berlin (Germany) 2021, *Online Conference* London (UK) 2021. **Publications** *IFEATWORLD* (4 a year) – newsletter. Conference proceedings. **Members** Companies (658) from 70 countries directly and indirectly involved in the flavour and fragrance industries. Membership countries not specified. **IGO Relations** Recognized by: *European Commission (EC, #06633)*. **NGO Relations** In liaison with technical committees of: *International Organization for Standardization (ISO, #14473)*. [2022.06.15/XD2619/t/**C**]

♦ International Federation of Esthetic Dentistry (IFED) 13417

Sec 13 Totnes Walk, London, N2 0AD, UK. T. +447590013057. E-mail: infoifed@gmail.com.
URL: http://www.ifed.org/

History 1994. Founded by American Academy of Esthetic Dentistry, European Academy of Esthetic Dentistry and Japanese Academy of Esthetic Dentistry. **Aims** Contribute to the progress and development of education in Esthetic dentistry worldwide. **Structure** General Assembly (annually); Executive Council. **Events** *World Congress of Esthetic Dentistry* Abu Dhabi (United Arab Emirates) 2022, *World Congress of Esthetic Dentistry* Abu Dhabi (United Arab Emirates) 2021, *World Congress* Barcelona (Spain) 2019, *World Congress* Toyama City (Japan) 2017, *World Congress* Munich (Germany) 2015.
Members National academies (23) in 19 countries and territories:

Belgium, Brazil, Canada, China, France, Germany, Greece, India, Italy, Japan, Korea Rep, Poland, Romania, Russia, Taiwan, Türkiye, UK, USA, Venezuela.
Included in the above, 3 organizations listed in this Yearbook:
Asian Academy of Aesthetic Dentistry (#01293); European Academy of Esthetic Dentistry (EAED, #05791); Scandinavian Academy of Esthetic Dentistry (SAED). [2022/XD7954/y/**D**]

♦ International Federation of Eugenics Associations (inactive)

♦ International Federation of Eurhythmics Teachers 13418

Fédération internationale des enseignants de rythmique (FIER)

Pres Sonnenterrasse 48, 6030 Ebikon LU, Switzerland.
URL: http://www.fier.com/

History 1975. Former names and other names: *International Union of Teachers of Jaques-Dalcroze* – former; *Union internationale des professeurs de rythmique Jaques-Dalcroze (UIPD)* – former. **Aims** Promote eurhythmics education based on the method of Jaques-Dalcroze. **Structure** General Assembly; Central Committee. **Languages** English, French, German, Spanish. **Staff** Voluntary. **Finance** Sources: members' dues. **Activities** Events/meetings; financial and/or material support; knowledge management/information dissemination; publishing activities; training/education. **Events** *Quadrennial Congress* Geneva (Switzerland) 2019, *Quadrennial Congress* Remscheid (Germany) 2015, *Quadrennial Congress* Geneva (Switzerland) 2007, *Quadrennial Congress* Geneva (Switzerland) 2003, *Quadrennial Congress* Geneva (Switzerland) 1999. **Publications** *Le Rythme* (every 2 years) – review. *Chemins de Rythmique 1, 2, 3.*
Members National associations in 15 countries and territories:
Argentina, Australia, Austria, Belgium, Canada, France, Germany, Italy, Japan, Poland, Sweden, Switzerland, Taiwan, UK, USA. [2023.03.03/XD4027/**D**]

♦ International Federation of European Contractors of Building and Public Works / see European Construction Industry Federation (#06766)

♦ International Federation for European Law 13419

Fédération internationale pour le droit européen (FIDE) – Internationale Vereinigung für Europarecht

Contact address not obtained.
URL: http://www.fide-europe.eu/

History 12 Oct 1961, Brussels (Belgium). New statutes adopted in 1981. Registered in accordance with Belgian law. **Aims** Bring together lawyers concerned with community law for common studies of questions connected with the development of the structures and institutions of the European Community. **Structure** Managing Board, consisting of members designated by each national association; Bureau. **Languages** English, French, German. **Events** *Biennial Congress* Sofia (Bulgaria) 2023, *Biennial Congress* The Hague (Netherlands) 2021, *Biennial Congress* The Hague (Netherlands) 2020, *Biennial Congress* Budapest (Hungary) 2016, *Biennial Congress* Copenhagen (Denmark) 2014. **Publications** Reports on Congresses.
Members National associations of lawyers in 12 countries:
Belgium, Denmark, France, Germany, Greece, Ireland, Italy, Luxembourg, Netherlands, Portugal, Spain, UK.
Associate members in 5 countries:
Austria, Finland, Norway, Sweden, Switzerland.
IGO Relations Recognized by: *European Commission (EC, #06633).* [2016/XD1825/**D**]

♦ International Federation of Europe Houses (inactive)

♦ International Federation of Exhibition and Event Services (IFES) . . . 13420

Fédération internationale des services d'exposition et d'événement

Exec Dir Comcret, Adenauerallee 9, 61440 Oberursel, Germany. T. +4961719797584. E-mail: info@ifesnet.org.
Registered Office Rue de l'Amazone 2, 1050 Brussels, Belgium. T. +3225884722.
URL: http://www.ifesnet.com/

History 1985, Brussels (Belgium). Founded on the initiative of national associations of Belgium, France, Germany FR, Great Britain, Italy, and the Netherlands. Former names and other names: *International Federation of Exhibition Services* – former (1985); *Fédération internationale des services d'exposition* – former (1985). Registration: Tribunal de l'entreprise Francophone de Bruxelles, No/ID: 0436936993, Belgium. **Aims** Represent, promote and support the commercial, professional, and socio-political business interests of its members by enhancing international collaboration and helping the members to share ideas and knowledge on how to best serve their clients; provide industry professionals with an educational program and a network dedicated to helping them face new challenges and acquire new business opportunities. **Structure** General Assembly; Board of Directors. **Languages** English. **Staff** 3.00 FTE, paid. **Finance** Sources: members' dues. **Activities** Certification/accreditation; events/meetings; guidance/assistance/consulting; knowledge management/information dissemination; monitoring/evaluation; networking/liaising; politics/policy/regulatory; publishing activities; research and development; standards/guidelines; training/education. Active in all member countries. **Events** *Annual World Summit* Amsterdam (Netherlands) 2021, *Annual World Summit* Amsterdam (Netherlands) 2020, *Annual World Summit* Athens (Greece) 2019, *Annual World Summit* Chicago, IL (USA) 2018, *Annual World Summit* Montpellier (France) 2017. **Publications** *IFES Newsletter* (12 a year); *IFES Worldview* (annual).
Members National organizations representing 1,600 companies in 46 countries:
Algeria, Argentina, Australia, Austria, Belgium, Brazil, Bulgaria, Canada, China, Colombia, Czechia, Denmark, Egypt, Finland, France, Germany, Greece, India, Iran Islamic Rep, Israel, Italy, Japan, Korea Rep, Lebanon, Malaysia, Malta, Mexico, Myanmar, Netherlands, Norway, Philippines, Poland, Portugal, Romania, Russia, Saudi Arabia, Singapore, South Africa, Spain, Sweden, Switzerland, Türkiye, UK, Ukraine, United Arab Emirates, USA.
Experiential Designers and Producers Association (EDPA).
More on national members: https://www.ifesnet.com/national-associations/. [2021.02.17/XD1080/**D**]

♦ International Federation of Exhibition Services / see International Federation of Exhibition and Event Services (#13420)

♦ International Federation of Ex-Libris Societies (FISAE) 13421

Fédération internationale des sociétés d'amateurs d'exlibris – Gesellschaften von Exlibris-Freunden

Exec Sec Mikroskooppikuja 4 A 18, FI-00790 Helsinki, Finland.

History Founded 28 Jul 1966, Hamburg (Germany FR), when Charter was adopted; Charter amended 29 Aug 1996, Chrudim (Czech Rep). **Aims** Cultivate and promote an interest in and devotion to *bookplates* and enhance their artistic qualities. **Structure** Assembly of Delegates (every 2 years); Managing Committee. **Languages** English, French, German. **Staff** Voluntary. **Finance** Sources: contributions; gifts, legacies. **Activities** Events/meetings; networking/liaising; publishing activities. **Events** *Congress* Oakland, CA (USA) 2022, *Biennial Congress* Cambridge (UK) 2020, *Biennial Congress* Prague (Czechia) 2018, *Biennial Congress* Vologda (Russia) 2016, *Biennial Congress* Tarragona (Spain) 2014.
Members Member societies; Affiliate societies: various artistic associations. Members in 37 countries:
Argentina, Australia, Austria, Belarus, Belgium, Bulgaria, Canada, China, Czechia, Denmark, Estonia, Finland, France, Germany, Greece, Hungary, Israel, Italy, Japan, Lithuania, Luxembourg, Mexico, Netherlands, Poland, Portugal, Romania, Russia, Serbia, Slovakia, Slovenia, Spain, Sweden, Switzerland, Türkiye, UK, Ukraine, USA. [2020/XD7083/**C**]

♦ International Federation of Experts' Associations (inactive)
♦ International Federation of Eye and Tissue Banks (inactive)
♦ International Federation of Fabric Printers (inactive)

♦ International Federation of Facial Plastic Surgery Societies (IFFPSS) 13422

Contact AAFPRS, 310 South Henry St, Alexandria VA 22314, USA. T. +17032999291 ext 229. E-mail: iffpssinfo@aafprs.org.
URL: http://www.iffpss.org/

History 1998. **Aims** Promote and support the growth of facial plastic surgery worldwide. **Structure** Board of Directors; Executive Committee. **Activities** Training/education; events/meetings. **Events** *Congress* Taipei (Taiwan) 2020, *Congress* Rio de Janeiro (Brazil) 2016, *Congress* Rome (Italy) 2012, *Congress* Venice (Italy) 2012, *Congress* Miami, FL (USA) 2010. **Publications** *IFFPSS Newsletter, JAMA Facial Plastic Surgery.*
Members National organizations in 10 countries and territories:
Brazil, Canada, Colombia, Ecuador, India, Korea Rep, Mexico, Taiwan, USA, Venezuela.
Regional organizations (3):
Australasian Academy of Facial Plastic Surgery (AAFPS); European Academy of Facial Plastic Surgery (EAFPS, #05792); Pan Asia Academy of Facial Plastic and Reconstructive Surgery (PAAFPRS, #18159). [2020/XJ3130/y/**D**]

♦ International Federation of Factory Workers (inactive)
♦ International Federation of Family Associations of Missing Persons from Armed Conflicts / see Families of the Missing

♦ International Federation for Family Development (IFFD) 13423

Federación Internacional para la Orientación Familiar

Secretariat c/ Artistas no 2 – 2o, 28020 Madrid, Spain. T. +34917260293. E-mail: mail@iffd.org.
URL: http://www.iffd.org/

History Jan 1998, Orlando, FL (USA). Founded by *International Family Foundation (IDF, inactive).* **Aims** Support families through training; promote the family perspective in national and international organisms in order to ensure that the repercussions on the family of each recommendation, regulation or law are taken into consideration. **Structure** General Assembly; Board of Directors; Management Team. **Languages** English, Spanish. **Activities** Advocacy/lobbying/activism; events/meetings; training/education. **Events** *Congress* London (UK) 2019, *Family, meeting place for generations* Mexico City (Mexico) 2015, *European Meeting on Confronting Family Poverty and Social Exclusion, Ensuring Work-Family Balance, Advancing Social Integration and Intergenerational Solidarity* Brussels (Belgium) 2012, *Raise Awareness Meeting on Poverty, Work-Family Balance and Intergenerational Solidarity* Brussels (Belgium) 2012, *Congress* Valencia (Spain) 2010. **Publications** *IFFD Papers.*
Members Organizations in 66 countries and territories:
Argentina, Australia, Austria, Belarus, Belgium, Bolivia, Botswana, Brazil, Cameroon, Canada, Chile, Colombia, Congo DR, Costa Rica, Côte d'Ivoire, Croatia, Czechia, Dominican Rep, Ecuador, El Salvador, Estonia, Finland, France, Germany, Guatemala, Honduras, Hong Kong (China), Hungary, India, Ireland, Israel, Italy, Japan, Kazakhstan, Kenya, Korea Rep, Latvia, Lebanon, Lithuania, Mexico, Netherlands, New Zealand, Nicaragua, Nigeria, Panama, Paraguay, Peru, Philippines, Poland, Portugal, Puerto Rico, Romania, Russia, Singapore, Slovakia, Slovenia, South Africa, Spain, Sweden, Switzerland, Trinidad-Tobago, Uganda, UK, Uruguay, USA, Venezuela.
Consultative Status Consultative status granted from: *ECOSOC (#05331)* (General). **IGO Relations** Cooperates with: *European Union Agency for Fundamental Rights (FRA, #08969).* **NGO Relations** Member of: *Vienna NGO Committee on the Family (#20774).* [2020/XD8412/**C**]

♦ International Federation for Family Health (IFFH) 13424

Fédération internationale pour la santé de la famille – Fedevasi Kesehatan Keluarga Internasional

Contact 1127 River Forest Rd, Pittsboro NC 27312, USA. T. +19199422061.
URL: https://iffh.org/

History 1977, Bangkok (Thailand), by a group of representatives of national professional organizations in the developing world, as *International Federation of Family Health Research.* Current name adopted 1979. **Aims** Link professional, non-political, public health individuals and organizations dedicated to research for improvement of reproductive health, family welfare planning and health measures throughout the world; attempt to solve problems of family health and fertility in developing countries. **Structure** General Assembly elects Executive Committee. Standing committees (2): Selection; Scientific. Executive Secretary; Programme Officer. **Languages** English, French. **Staff** 2.50 FTE, voluntary. **Finance** Support from international organizations in the field, including *Church World Service (CWS).* Budget (annual): US$ 200,000. **Activities** Research/documentation; training/education; monitoring/evaluation; guidance/assistance/consulting; events/meetings. **Events** *Symposium* Santiago (Chile) 2003, *Symposium* Washington, DC (USA) 2000, *Symposium* Copenhagen (Denmark) 1997, *Symposium* Bandung (Indonesia) 1991, *General Assembly* Rio de Janeiro (Brazil) 1988. **Publications** *AIDS: Essential Drugs for Primary Health Care* – video series. **Information Services** *Database on the Quinacrine Method of Nonsurgical Female Sterilization.*
Members Organizations in 16 countries:
Bangladesh, Brazil, Colombia, Egypt, India, Indonesia, Korea Rep, Malaysia, Nepal, Pakistan, Singapore, Sri Lanka, Sudan, Thailand, UK, USA.
Associate member (1) included in this Yearbook:
International Islamic Centre for Population Studies and Research (IICPSR, #13956).
NGO Relations UK office is member of: *British Overseas NGO's for Development (BOND).* Cooperates with: *Fédération Internationale de Gynécologie et d'Obstétrique (FIGO, #09638).* [2019/XC5485/y/**D**]

♦ International Federation of Family Health Research / see International Federation for Family Health (#13424)
♦ International Federation for Family Life Promotion (inactive)
♦ International Federation of Farmers' Unions (inactive)

♦ International Federation of Fe y Alegria (FIFyA) 13425

Federación Internacional de Fe y Alegria

Gen Coordinator Carrera 5 No 34-39, Bogota 110311, Bogota DC, Colombia. T. +5717712362. E-mail: fi.coordinador@feyalegria.org – fi.secrejec@feyalegria.org.
URL: http://www.feyalegria.org/

History Founded 1955, Caracas (Venezuela). Also referred to as *Fe y Alegria Movimiento Internacional de Educación Popular Integral y Promoción Social.* Statutes adopted 10 Nov 1986, Caracas. Registered in accordance with Venezuelan law and comprises the different national 'Fe y Alegria' organizations, these organizations keeping their own autonomy. **Aims** Promote a popular, inclusive and quality *education* to build a more equitable, just and sustainable society. **Structure** General Assembly (Asamblea General FIFyA); Board of Directors; Council of National Directors; Federative Priorities (Axes); Coordination Team; General Coordinator. **Languages** English, French, Portuguese, Spanish. **Staff** 10.00 FTE, paid. **Finance** Members' dues. Other sources: contributions and projects; support from Ministries of Education of national governments; private donations; international aid. **Activities** Training/education; advocacy/lobbying/activism; projects/programmes. **Events** *Annual Congress and General Assembly* Madrid (Spain) 2018, *Annual Congress and General Assembly* Sao Paulo (Brazil) 2013, *Annual Congress and General Assembly / Annual Congress* Cochabamba (Bolivia) 2012, *Annual Congress and General Assembly / Annual Congress* Bogota (Colombia) 2011, *Annual Congress and General Assembly / Annual Congress* Quito (Ecuador) 2010. **Publications** *International Memoir of Fe y Alegria* (annual) in English, French, Spanish. Periodicals; guides; manuals; books brochures.
Members National associations in 22 countries:
Argentina, Bolivia, Brazil, Chad, Chile, Colombia, Congo DR, Dominican Rep, Ecuador, El Salvador, Guatemala, Haiti, Honduras, Italy, Madagascar, Nicaragua, Panama, Paraguay, Peru, Spain, Uruguay, Venezuela.
Consultative Status Consultative status granted from: *ECOSOC (#05331)* (Special); *UNICEF (#20332).* **NGO Relations** Member of: *Forum of Catholic Inspired NGOs (#09905); Global Campaign for Education (GCE, #10264); International Catholic Cooperation Centre for UNESCO (CCIC, #12454); NGO Committee on UNICEF (#17120).* Cooperates with: *Entreculturas.* Partner of: *Consejo Latinoamericano de Ciencias Sociales (CLACSO, #04718).* [2020.01.08/XF0424/**F**]

♦ International Federation of Fertility Societies (IFFS) 13426

Fédération internationale des sociétés de fertilité – Federación Internacional de las Sociedades de Fertilidad

Secretariat LLC 10685-B Hazelhurst Dr., Suite 26427, Houston TX 77043, USA. T. +18564230047. E-mail: secretariat@iffsreproduction.org.
Europe Office 20 Harcourt St, Dublin, 2, CO. DUBLIN, D02 H364, Ireland.
URL: http://www.iffs-reproduction.org/

History 18 Oct 1951, Rio de Janeiro (Brazil). Former names and other names: *International Fertility Association (IFA)* – former (18 Oct 1951); *Association internationale de fertilité* – former (18 Oct 1951). **Aims** Stimulate basic and clinical research, disseminate education and encourage superior clinical *care* of patients in infertility and reproductive medicine worldwide. **Structure** Congress (every 3 years). Board of Directors, comprising President, President-Elect, Secretary-General, Assistant Secretary-General, Treasurer, Assistant Treasurer, Past President and Director of Medical Education. Committees (4): Education; Scientific; Standards and

Practice; Surveillance. Meetings open to all interested scientists and physicians. **Languages** English, French, Spanish. **Staff** Voluntary. **Finance** Sources: meeting proceeds; members' dues. **Activities** Events/meetings. **Events** *IFFS World Congress* Athens (Greece) 2023, *IFFS World Congress* 2022, *Triennial Congress* Athens (Greece) 2022, *Triennial Congress* Shanghai (China) 2019, *Triennial Congress* Delhi (India) 2016. **Publications** *IFFS Newsletter* (2 a year). Transactions of Congresses.

Members Affiliated Societies in 64 countries and territories:
Argentina, Australia, Austria, Bangladesh, Belgium, Brazil, Bulgaria, Canada, Chile, China, Colombia, Czechia, Ecuador, Egypt, El Salvador, Finland, France, Georgia, Germany, Ghana, Greece, Guatemala, Hungary, India, Indonesia, Iran Islamic Rep, Iraq, Israel, Italy, Japan, Jordan, Korea Rep, Malaysia, Mexico, Mongolia, Morocco, Myanmar, Nigeria, Pakistan, Paraguay, Peru, Philippines, Poland, Portugal, Romania, Russia, Saudi Arabia, Serbia, Singapore, Slovenia, South Africa, Spain, Sudan, Sweden, Switzerland, Taiwan, Tunisia, Türkiye, Uganda, UK, Uruguay, USA, Venezuela, Vietnam.
Associated societies (4):
Asociación Latinoamericana de Medicina Reproductiva (ALMER, #02240); European Society of Human Reproduction and Embryology (ESHRE, #08625); Groupe Interafricain d'Etudes, de Recherches et d'Application sur la Fertilité (GIERAF, #10747); Middle East Fertility Society (MEFS, #16765); Sociedad Latina de Biologia y Medicina de la Reproducción (SOLAMER, #19387).

Consultative Status Consultative status granted from: *WHO (#20950)* (Official Relations). **NGO Relations** Cooperates with (1): *Fédération Internationale de Gynécologie et d'Obstétrique (FIGO, #09638).* [2023/XD2052/y/**B**]

♦ International Federation of Film Archives 13427

Fédération internationale des archives du film (FIAF) – Federación Internacional de Archivos Filmicos – Internationaler Verband der Filmarchive

Admin Rue Blanche 42, 1060 Brussels, Belgium. T. +3225383065 – +3225346130. Fax +3225344774. E-mail: info@fiafnet.org.
URL: http://www.fiafnet.org/

History Jul 1938, Paris (France), as a federation of international, national and regional film archives and museums, whether official, semi-official or private, devoted to the history, preservation and aesthetics of the cinema, and accessible to the public. Previously also referred to in Spanish as *Federación Internacional de Archivos de Imagenes en Movimiento.* Registered in accordance with Belgian law, 18 Nov 1976. **Aims** Rescue, collect, preserve and screen moving images, which are valued both as works of art and culture and as historical documents. **Structure** General Assembly (annual, at Congress); Executive Committee; Commissions (3); Secretariat in Brussels (Belgium). **Languages** English, French, Spanish. **Staff** 5.00 FTE, paid. **Finance** Sources: members' dues. Other sources: Support from donors. **Activities** Events/meetings; research/documentation; standards/guidelines; training/education. **Events** *Annual Congress* Budapest (Hungary) 2022, *Annual Congress* Dhaka (Bangladesh) 2021, *Annual Congress* Mexico City (Mexico) 2020, *Annual Congress* Lausanne (Switzerland) 2019, *Annual Congress* Prague (Czechia) 2018. **Publications** *Journal of Film Preservation* (2 a year); *FIAF Directory* (annual); *International Index to Film Periodicals* (annual). **Information Services** *FIAF Databases Online.*

Members Leading institutions (85). Affiliates in 57 countries and territories:
Albania, Argentina, Armenia, Australia, Austria, Bangladesh, Belgium, Brazil, Bulgaria, Canada, Chile, China, Colombia, Croatia, Cuba, Czechia, Denmark, Finland, France, Germany, Greece, Holy See, Hong Kong, Hungary, India, Iran Islamic Rep, Ireland, Israel, Italy, Japan, Korea DPR, Korea Rep, Luxembourg, Mexico, Morocco, Netherlands, New Zealand, North Macedonia, Norway, Poland, Portugal, Puerto Rico, Romania, Russia, Serbia, Slovakia, Slovenia, South Africa, Spain, Sweden, Switzerland, Türkiye, UK, Uruguay, USA, Venezuela, Vietnam.
Associate members (56) in 35 countries:
Afghanistan, Algeria, Angola, Argentina, Australia, Bolivia, Bosnia-Herzegovina, Brazil, Burkina Faso, Canada, Colombia, Dominican Rep, Ecuador, Egypt, France, Germany, Iceland, Indonesia, Italy, Japan, Latvia, Luxembourg, Mexico, Mongolia, Netherlands, Nicaragua, Nigeria, Peru, Slovenia, Spain, Switzerland, Thailand, Ukraine, USA, Venezuela.

Consultative Status Consultative status granted from; *ECOSOC (#05331)* (Ros C); *UNESCO (#20322)* (Consultative Status). **IGO Relations** Invited to sessions of Intergovernmental Council of: *International Programme for the Development of Communication (IPDC, #14651).* **NGO Relations** Member of: *Co-ordinating Council of Audiovisual Archives Associations (CCAAA, #04820).* Special cooperative agreement with: *International Association of Sound and Audiovisual Archives (IASA, #12172); International Council on Archives (ICA, #12996); International Federation of Library Associations and Institutions (IFLA, #13470); International Federation of Television Archives (IFTA, #13568).* [2019/XC1912/**C**]

♦ International Federation of Film Critics (#09651)

♦ International Federation of Film Distributors Associations 13428

Fédération internationale des associations de distributeurs de films (FIAD)

SG c/o Europe Analytica, Av des Arts 43, 1040 Brussels, Belgium. T. +3222311299. Fax +3222307658.
Pres 74 av Kléber, 75016 Paris, France.
URL: http://www.fiad.eu/

Aims Group the national associations of film distributors of the major *European* countries. **Structure** General Assembly (meets twice a year); Board; Secretariat. **Languages** English, French. **Activities** Knowledge management/information dissemination; politics/policy/regulatory.

Members National associations in 14 countries:
Austria, Belgium, Denmark, Finland, France, Germany, Malta, Morocco, Netherlands, North Macedonia, Spain, Sweden, Switzerland, UK.

Consultative Status Consultative status granted from: *World Intellectual Property Organization (WIPO, #21593)* (Permanent Observer Status). **IGO Relations** Observer status with (2): *Intergovernmental Committee of the International Convention of Rome for the Protection of Performers, Producers of Phonograms and Broadcasting Organizations (#11474); Union for the International Registration of Audiovisual Works (#20444).* Consultative Status with: *United Nations Commission on International Trade Law (UNCITRAL, #20531).* Member of Advisory Committee of: *European Audiovisual Observatory (#06294).* [2021/XD3624/**D**]

♦ International Federation of Film Producers' Associations 13429

Fédération internationale des associations de producteurs de films (FIAPF) – Federación Internacional de Asociaciones de Productores Cinematograficos – Internationaler Verband der Filmproduzenten-Vereinigungen

Pres Avenue des Arts 41, 1040 Brussels, Belgium. T. +3225028167. Fax +3225033719. E-mail: info@fiapf.org.
URL: http://www.fiapf.org/

History Jan 1933, Paris (France). **Aims** Address international legal, technical, economic and social problems concerning film production; arrange mutual help and exchange of information; encourage friendly relations between film producers in different countries. **Structure** General Assembly; Executive Committee; Bureau. **Languages** English, French. **Finance** Sources: members' dues. **Activities** Knowledge management/information dissemination; networking/liaising. **Publications** Information circulars.

Members Producer organizations (36) in 29 countries:
Argentina, Austria, Belgium, Canada, China, Croatia, Czechia, Denmark, Finland, Germany, Iceland, India, Iran Islamic Rep, Japan, Latvia, Malta, Netherlands, Nigeria, North Macedonia, Norway, Poland, Russia, Slovakia, Sweden, Switzerland, Türkiye, UK, Ukraine, USA.

Consultative Status Consultative status granted from: *World Intellectual Property Organization (WIPO, #21593)* (Permanent Observer Status). **IGO Relations** Observer status with (2): *Intergovernmental Committee of the International Convention of Rome for the Protection of Performers, Producers of Phonograms and Broadcasting Organizations (#11474); Union for the International Registration of Audiovisual Works (#20444).* **NGO Relations** In liaison with technical committees of: *International Organization for Standardization (ISO, #14473).* Together with: *Association for the International Collective Management of Audiovisual Works (AGICOA, #02658)* and *Confédération internationale des sociétés d'auteurs et compositeurs (CISAC, #04563),* set up: *ISAN International Agency (ISAN-IA, #16023).* [2022.06.21/XC1913/**C**]

♦ International Federation of Films on Art (inactive)

♦ International Federation of Film Societies (IFFS) 13430

Fédération internationale des ciné-clubs (FICC)

SG Fed Catalana de Cineclubs, C/Arenys 41, Soterrani 1er 1a, 08035 Barcelona, Spain. T. +34932890562. E-mail: info.ficc.contact@gmail.com.
Pres address not obtained.
URL: https://infoficc.wordpress.com/

History 16 Sep 1947, Cannes (France), at International Film Festival, on the instigation of French and UK film societies. Constitution revised 1957. **Members** Membership countries not specified. [2018/XD1983/**D**]

♦ International Federation of Foot and Ankle Societies (IFFAS) 13431

Pres 9400 West Higgins Road, Suite 220, Rosemont IL 60018-4975, USA. T. +18474305100. Fax +18476923315. E-mail: iffas@iffas.org.
URL: http://www.iffas.org/

History 1965. Constitution adopted 16 Oct 1999; amended 21 Mar 2013. Former names and other names: *International College of Medicine and Surgery of the Foot* – former; *Collège international de médecine et chirurgie du pied (CIP)* – former; *International College of Foot Medicine and Surgery of the Foot* – former. **Aims** Initiate, promote and develop international scientific relations among students of the foot; develop and disseminate knowledge on all aspects of anatomy, physiology and pathology of the foot; represent this branch of the medical science and profession on an international scale. **Structure** Council; Permanent Secretariat. **Languages** English. **Staff** 0.50 FTE, paid. **Activities** Events/meetings. **Events** *Triennial Scientific Meeting* Seattle, WA (USA) 2026, *Triennial Scientific Meeting* Seoul (Korea Rep) 2024, *Triennial Scientific Meeting* Viña del Mar (Chile) 2022, *Triennial Scientific Meeting* Viña del Mar (Chile) 2021, *Triennial Scientific Meeting* Viña del Mar (Chile) 2020.

Members Regional organizations (4) representing national societies:
American Orthopaedic Foot and Ankle Society; *Asian Federation of Foot and Ankle Surgeons (AFFAS, #01460); European Foot and Ankle Society (EFAS, #07290); Federación Latinoamericana de Medicina y Cirugia de la Pierna y Pié (FLAMECIPP, no recent information);* Southern Federation of Foot and Ankle Societiesot. [2022.10.13/XD6203/y/**A**]

♦ International Federation of Football History and Statistics (IFFHS) . 13432

Fédération internationale pour l'histoire et les statistiques du football

Pres Balz-Zimmerman Strasse 7, 8302 Kloten ZH, Switzerland. T. +41582698091. Fax +41582698092. E-mail: awards@iffhs.org.
URL: http://www.iffhs.de/

History 27 Mar 1984, Leipzig (German DR). Registered in accordance with Danish law. **Aims** Ensure chronological documentation of international soccer and of authentic world records achieved in its various aspects. **Structure** Executive Committee. **Languages** English, French, German, Spanish. **Staff** Voluntary. **Finance** No members' dues. **Activities** Events/meetings; research/documentation; monitoring/evaluation. **Events** *Biennial Meeting* Wiesbaden (Germany) 1998, *Biennial meeting* Wiesbaden (Germany) 1996. **Members** Individual experts, either recommended by national committees or other members or applying themselves. Initial provisional membership becomes regular membership on satisfactory completion of assigned tasks. Members in over 120 countries (not specified). **NGO Relations** Cooperates with *International Federation of Association Football (#13360)* and the 5 continental confederations: *Asian Football Confederation (AFC, #01487); Confederación Norte-Centroamericana y del Caribe de Fútbol (CONCACAF, #04465); Confederación Sudamericana de Fútbol (CONMEBOL, #04487); Confédération africaine de football (CAF, #04500); Oceania Football Confederation (OFC, #17662).* [2017.11.29/XD3376/v/**D**]

♦ International Federation of Former Iberoamerican Students of the INAP (internationally oriented national body)
♦ International Federation of Former Political Prisoners of Fascism (inactive)
♦ International Federation of Forwarding Organizations / see Fédération internationale des associations de transitaires et assimilés (#09610)
♦ International Federation of Foundry Workers (inactive)

♦ International Federation of Free Evangelical Churches (IFFEC) 13433

Fédération internationale des Eglises évangéliques libres (FIEEL) – El Federación Internacional de las Iglesias Evangelicas Libres (FIIEL) – Internationaler Bund Freier Evangelischer Gemeinden (IBFEG)

Gen Sec c/o Evangelical Covenant Church, 8303 West Higgins Rd, Chicago IL 60631, USA.
Pres des Bundes Freier evangelischer Gemeinden, Goltenkamp 4, 58452 Witten, Germany.
URL: http://www.iffec.org/

History 1948, Bern (Switzerland). Member churches and the cooperation have a history dating back to mid 19th century. **Aims** Unite Free Evangelical and Covenant Churches in mutual support and mission. **Structure** General Assembly (every 4 years); Executive Committee. Committees (3). **Languages** English, German. **Staff** 0.50 FTE, paid. **Activities** Events/meetings. **Events** *IFFEC Worldwide* 2022, *IFFEC Worldwide* Lake Geneva, WI (USA) 2020, *General Assembly* L'Ametlla del Vallès (Spain) 2018, *General Assembly / Quadrennial General Assembly* Oaxtepec (Mexico) 2014, *Quadrennial theological conference* Athens (Greece) 2012.

Members National federations in 31 countries and territories:
Argentina, Belgium, Brazil, Bulgaria, Canada, Chile, Colombia, Czechia, Denmark, Ecuador, Estonia, Finland, France, Germany, Greece, Hong Kong, India, Lebanon, Mexico, Netherlands, Norway, Philippines, Poland, Slovakia, Spain, Sweden, Switzerland, Syrian AR, Ukraine, USA, Venezuela. [2021/XD1186/**D**]

♦ International Federation of Free Journalists (inactive)
♦ International Federation of Free Teachers' Unions (inactive)
♦ International Federation of Freight Forwarders Associations (#09610)
♦ International Federation of French-Language Writers (no recent information)
♦ International Federation of French-Speaking Accountants (#09630)
♦ International Federation of French-Speaking Scrabble (#09657)
♦ International Federation of Fruit Juice Producers / see International Fruit and Vegetable Juice Association (#13687)
♦ International Federation of Gastronomical, Vinicultural and Touristic Press (inactive)
♦ International Federation of Gestalt Training Organizations (#09646)
♦ International Federation of Glass-Workers (inactive)
♦ International Federation of Global & Green Information Communication Technology (unconfirmed)
♦ International Federation of Glucose Industries (inactive)
♦ International Federation of Goat Breeding (inactive)
♦ International Federation for the Graphical Industries – WCL (inactive)
♦ International Federation of Grocers' Associations (inactive)
♦ International Federation of Grocery Manufacturers Associations / see International Council of Grocery Manufacturers Associations (#13026)
♦ International Federation of Guide Dog Schools for the Blind / see International Guide Dog Federation (#13763)
♦ International Federation of Gynecology and Obstetrics (#09638)

♦ International Federation of Hainan Associations (IFHA) 13434

Address not obtained.
URL: http://www.hainan.com.my/

History 1989, as *World Federation of Hainanese Associations.* **Aims** Promote and strengthen the well-being of the Hainanese worldwide; promote friendly relationship among nations; contribute towards a better understanding in culture, sport and academy; pool Hainanese resources for commercial activities to enhance the economy and social standing of the Hainanese. **Activities** Events/meetings. **Events** *Congress* Hong Kong (Hong Kong) 2017, *Congress* Sydney, NSW (Australia) 2015, *Congress* Medan (Indonesia) 2013, *Welcome to Hong Kong for a better tomorrow* Hong Kong (Hong Kong) 2011, *World forum for hainanese youth* Hong Kong (Hong Kong) 2011. [2017/XJ1284/**E**]

♦ International federation of Hair and Beauty Workers (unconfirmed)
♦ International Federation of the Hard of Hearing / see International Federation of Hard of Hearing People (#13435)

♦ International Federation of Hard of Hearing People (IFHOH) 13435

Fédération internationale des malentendants

Gen Sec address not obtained. E-mail: info@ifhoh.org.
URL: http://www.ifhoh.org/

History 15 Mar 1977. Former names and other names: *International Federation of the Hard of Hearing* – former (1977 to 1988). **Aims** Encourage greater understanding among hard of hearing people; investigate problems of hearing loss; cooperate with organizations and governments in its prevention and cure, in the preservation of hearing and in all services for hard of hearing people; press for increased research into *deafness*, hearing loss and for available facilities; encourage hard of hearing people themselves to take part in such research; collect and distribute information on facilities by and for hard of hearing people. **Structure** General Meeting (every 2 years); Executive Board. *European Federation of Hard of Hearing People (EFHOH, #07136)* comprises European members. **Languages** English. **Staff** Voluntary. **Finance** Sources: members' dues; sponsorship. Annual budget: 15,000 EUR. **Activities** Awareness raising; knowledge management/information dissemination; networking/liaising. **Events** *Quadrennial Congress* Budapest (Hungary) 2022, *Quadrennial Congress* Budapest (Hungary) 2020, *Biennial General Meeting* Ljubljana (Slovenia) 2018, *International Hearing Loops and Accessibility Conference* Berlin (Germany) 2017, *Quadrennial Congress* Washington, DC (USA) 2016. **Publications** *IFHOH Journal* (3 a year). Congress reports.

Members General national organizations of and for hard of hearing people. Associate Organizations; Individuals; Sponsoring Members. Contact Persons. As of Apr 2007, General and Associate members totalling 45 in 33 countries:
Australia, Austria, Belgium, Bosnia-Herzegovina, Canada, China, Croatia, Czechia, Denmark, Estonia, Finland, France, Germany, Hungary, Ireland, Israel, Italy, Japan, Kazakhstan, Kenya, Kuwait, Netherlands, Norway, Pakistan, Slovakia, Slovenia, Sweden, Switzerland, Türkiye, Uganda, UK, USA, Vietnam.

Consultative Status Consultative status granted from: *ECOSOC (#05331)* (Special); *ILO (#11123)* (Special List). **IGO Relations** Informal links with: *WHO (#20950)*. Relevant treaty: *Convention on the Rights of Persons with Disabilities (CRPD, 2006)*. **NGO Relations** Member of: *International Disability Alliance (IDA, #13176)* and IDA CRPD Forum. [2022.06.15/XD9369/y/**C**]

♦ International Federation of Hard-of-Hearing Young People (IFHOHYP) 13436

Fédération internationale pour les jeunes malentendants

President Castberggård – Østerskovvej 1, 8722 Urlev, Denmark. E-mail: info@ifhohyp.org.
Sec address not obtained.
URL: http://www.ifhohyp.org/

History 1968. First Constitution adopted 11 Apr 1980, Berlin West (Germany FR). Current Constitution, adopted 1994, redesigns the Federation. Former names and other names: *International Committee of Hard-of-Hearing Young People* – former; *Comité international pour les jeunes malentendants* – former. **Aims** Improve the quality of life of hearing impaired youth worldwide; promote equal rights for hard of hearing young people at all levels of society. **Structure** General Meeting (annual); Board. **Languages** English. **Staff** Voluntary. **Finance** Sources: fundraising; members' dues; sponsorship. **Activities** Events/meetings; training/education. **Events** *Annual General Meeting* Zurich (Switzerland) 2019, *Annual General Meeting* Istanbul (Turkey) 2018, *Annual General Meeting* Helsinki (Finland) 2017, *Annual General Meeting* Washington, DC (USA) 2016, *Annual General Meeting* Amsterdam (Netherlands) 2015. **Publications** *IFHOHYP E-Newsletter* (12 a year). Annual report.

Members General; Associate; Individual. National hard of hearing youth organizations (21) in 19 countries:
Bangladesh, Canada, Czechia, Denmark, Finland, Georgia, Germany, Israel, Nepal, Netherlands, Norway, Philippines, Poland, Russia, Sweden, Switzerland, Tunisia, Türkiye, Uganda.

NGO Relations Member of (2): *European Disability Forum (EDF, #06929)*; *International Federation of Hard of Hearing People (IFHOH, #13435)*. Cooperates with (1): *European Federation of Hard of Hearing People (EFHOH, #07136)*. [2021.06.28/XD9779/**D**]

♦ International Federation of Hardware and Housewares Associations (IHA) 13437

Contact c/o NRHA, 136 N Delaware St, Suite 200, Indianapolis IN 46204, USA. T. +18007724424.
URL: http://www.ihaworldwide.com/

History 1909, Bournemouth (UK). Statutes adopted 1909; new statutes adopted: 19 Sep 1953, Zurich (Switzerland), 23 Jun 2000, Barcelona (Spain); 2004, Dublin (Ireland); 2010, London (UK). Former names and other names: *International Federation of Ironmongers' and Iron Merchants' Associations (IFIA)* – former (1909); *Fédération internationale des associations de quincailliers et marchands de fer (FIDAQ)* – former (1909); *Internationale Vereinigung der Eisenwaren- und Eisenhändlerverbände (IVE)* – former (1909); *Federación Internacional de Asociaciones de Ferreteros y Almacenistas de Hierros (FIDAF)* – former (1909). Registration: Switzerland. **Aims** Inform, influence and educate: the international prestige of national members; the commercial future of all members; the interests of the consumer, through good trading practices and a policy of corporate social responsibility. **Structure** International Congress (every 2-3 years). Council comprises up to 3 delegates of each national association. Managing Committee (meets annually), comprising President, Chairman, Immediate Past President, Honorary Treasurer, Secretary-General and 5 members. **Languages** English, French, German. **Staff** 1.00 FTE, paid. **Finance** Sources: members' dues. **Activities** Events/meetings. Sub-committees (14): DIY Products; Household Electrical Appliances; Household Articles; Extruded Metal Fittings; Constructional Materials; Self-Service; Packaging; Tools; Fixings; Decorating Materials; Business Management; Training; Garden Products; Pet Products. **Events** *Biennial Congress* Paris (France) 2015, *Biennial Congress* Las Vegas, NV (USA) 2013, *Biennial Congress* Las Vegas, NV (USA) 2011, *Biennial congress* London (UK) 2009, *Biennial Congress* Shanghai (China) 2006.

Members National associations representing some 95,000 retail and wholesale enterprises in 17 countries:
Australia, Austria, Canada, China, Finland, France, Germany, Italy, Japan, Netherlands, Norway, Pakistan, Spain, Sweden, Switzerland, UK, USA.

Associated members manufacturer's associations, manufacturers of the product range and international exhibition organizers (9). Membership countries not specified.

IGO Relations Accredited by (1): *European Commission (EC, #06633)*. [2020/XC1936/**C**]

♦ International Federation of Harmonica Associations (inactive)

♦ International Federation of Head and Neck Oncologic Societies (IFHNOS) 13438

Founder and CEO Memorial Sloan-Kettering Cancer Ctr, 1275 York Ave, New York NY 10065, USA. Fax +12127173302. E-mail: info@ifhnos.net – admin@ifhnos.net.
Dir address not obtained.
URL: http://www.ifhnos.net/

History 1 May 1987, London (UK). Registration: No/ID: 2902242, Start date: 2004, USA, New York State. **Aims** Establish channels of communication to enhance exchange of information an improving knowledge as well as explore new directions in the diagnosis, treatment and rehabilitation of patients with head and neck *cancer*. **Structure** Governing Council; Executive Committee. **Languages** English. **Staff** 3.00 FTE, paid; 6.00 FTE, voluntary. **Finance** Sources: members' dues. **Activities** Events/meetings; networking/liaising; training/education. **Events** *World Congress* Rome (Italy) 2023, *World Congress* Rome (Italy) 2022, *World Congress* Buenos Aires (Argentina) 2018, *World Congress* New York, NY (USA) 2014, *World Congress* Seoul (Korea Rep) 2010. **Publications** *Head and Neck* – official journal.

Members National and regional organizations in 48 countries and territories:
Argentina, Australia, Austria, Bangladesh, Belarus, Belgium, Brazil, Canada, Chile, Colombia, Czechia, Denmark, Egypt, Germany, Greece, Hong Kong, India, Indonesia, Ireland, Israel, Italy, Japan, Kazakhstan, Korea Rep, Malaysia, Mexico, Moldova, Mongolia, Nepal, Netherlands, New Zealand, Pakistan, Peru, Philippines, Poland, Portugal, Russia, Singapore, South Africa, Spain, Taiwan, Thailand, Türkiye, UK, Ukraine, United Arab Emirates, USA, Venezuela.

Included in the above 5 regional organizations:
Asian Society of Head and Neck Oncology (ASHNO, #01722); *European Head and Neck Society (EHNS, #07452)*; *European Laryngological Society (ELS, #07653)*; *European Organisation for Research and Treatment of Cancer (EORTC, #08101)*; *Scandinavian Society for Head and Neck Oncology (SSHNO, #19109)*. [2023.02.14/XD8824/y/**C**]

♦ International Federation of Healthcare Engineering (IFHE) 13439

Fédération internationale d'ingénierie hospitalière (FIIH) – Federación Internacional de Ingenieria y Arquitectura Hospitalaria – Internationaler Verband Krankenhaustechnik – Federazione Internazionale di Ingegneria Ospedaliera

Gen Sec 2 Abingdon House, Cumberland Business Centre, Northumberland Road, Portsmouth, PO5 1DS, UK. T. +442392823186. Fax +442392815927. E-mail: ifhe@iheem.org.uk.
URL: http://www.ifhe.info/

History Founded 1970 as *International Federation of Hospital Engineering (IFHE)*. Statutes most recently amended 25 May 2003; Standing Orders most recently revised 11 Sep 2007. **Aims** Promote, develop and disseminate hospital engineering technology; compare international experience; promote the principle of integrated planning, design and evaluation by improved cooperation among professional institutions and individuals; promote more efficient management of operation, maintenance and safety of hospitals, their engineering installations, equipment and buildings; offer collaboration with other international organizations. **Structure** General Assembly (every 2 years, at International Congress); Council; Executive Committee. **Languages** English. **Staff** 1.00 FTE, paid. **Finance** Sources: donations; meeting proceeds; members' dues; sale of publications. **Activities** Events/meetings; knowledge management/information dissemination; publishing activities. **Events** *Biennial Congress* Toronto, ON (Canada) 2022, *Biennial Congress* Rome (Italy) 2021, *Biennial Congress* Rome (Italy) 2020, *Biennial Congress* Brisbane, QLD (Australia) 2018, *Biennial Congress* The Hague (Netherlands) 2016. **Publications** *Health Estate Journal* (4 a year); *IFHE NEWSletter* (3 a year); *IFHE DIGEST* (annual) – joint publication.

Members 'A' – National National Organizations of Hospital Engineering (32) in 30 countries:
Argentina, Australia, Austria, Belgium, Brazil, Canada, China, Denmark, Finland, France, Germany (2), India, Indonesia, Israel, Italy (2), Japan, Kenya, Korea Rep, Malaysia, Netherlands, New Zealand, Norway, Portugal, South Africa, Spain, Switzerland, Uganda, UK, Uruguay, USA.

'B' – Associate Individuals or small groups interested in promoting aims of IFHE, who either cannot be members of an 'A' member association or are members of an 'A' association but wish to contribute personally. Members in 11 countries and territories:
Botswana, Germany, Honduras, Italy (2), Malawi, Malaysia, Saudi Arabia, Switzerland, Taiwan, UK (2), USA (2).

'C' – Institutional Governmental organizations, health authorities and other bodies directly concerned in the health care field (1) in 1 country:
Malta.

'D' – Affiliate Firms (3) interested in the health-care field in 3 countries:
Austria, India, Malaysia.

'E' – Honorary Members (13) in 9 countries:
France, Italy (2), Japan (1), Norway, Portugal (2), South Africa (2), Spain, UK, USA (2).

Consultative Status Consultative status granted from: *WHO (#20950)* (Official Relations). [2019.12.12/XD4597/**C**]

♦ International Federation of Health Funds / see International Federation of Health Plans (#13442)

♦ International Federation of Health and Human Rights Organisations (IFHHRO) 13440

Address not obtained.
URL: http://www.ifhhro.org/

History 1989, by *Johannes Wier Foundation for Health and Human Rights, Netherlands (JWS)* and *Physicians for Human Rights, USA (PHR-USA)*. Transformed into a federation in 1996. **Aims** Promote international cooperation for protection and promotion of health-related human rights; promote monitoring the right to health by mobilizing expertise and involvement of health professionals worldwide, both using rights-based strategies and responding to violations. **Structure** International Board, comprising 5 representatives of member organizations and a Coordinator. Secretariat, headed by Project Officer. Focal Points (3): Asia (India); Africa (Uganda); Latin America (Peru). **Languages** English. **Staff** 1.50 FTE, voluntary. Interns. **Finance** Budget (annual): about euro 250,000. **Activities** Organizes: Annual Conference; Regional Trainings on Realizing the Right to Health. Provides expertise in: right to health; patient's rights; health and human rights under political violence; human rights and forensic medicine; hunger strikes. Provides solidarity and information exchange between organizations, individuals and professional associations working on issues related to health and human rights; education and networking activities; mobilizes medical expertise in investigation of human rights violations and supports protection of health workers seeking promotion of human rights; helps with the dilemma that medical professionals face when their professional and legal obligations are in conflict; motivates medical associations domestically and abroad to take an active interest in human rights and to develop health and human rights education for health professionals. **Events** *Annual Meeting* Tbilisi (Georgia) 2010, *Annual Meeting* Netherlands 2009, *Annual Conference* Harare (Zimbabwe) 2007, *Annual Meeting* Zimbabwe 2007, *Annual conference / Annual Meeting* Peru 2006. **Publications** Annual Report.

Members Affiliated; Observer national organizations in 14 countries and territories:
Bangladesh, Congo Brazzaville, Congo DR, Denmark, India, Israel, Kenya, Netherlands, Palestine, Peru, Uganda, UK, USA, Zimbabwe.

Included in the above, 2 organizations listed in this Yearbook:
Physicians for Human Rights, Israel (PHR-Israel); *Physicians for Human Rights, USA (PHR-USA)*.

Observers national and international organizations (8), including 5 organizations listed in this Yearbook:
Amnesty International (AI, #00801); *International Council of Nurses (ICN, #13054)*; *International Federation of Medical Students' Associations (IFMSA, #13478)*; *International Rehabilitation Council for Torture Victims (IRCT, #14712)*; *World Medical Association (WMA, #21646)*. [2015/XD9166/y/**D**]

♦ International Federation of Health Information Management Associations (IFHIMA) 13441

Pres Halton Healthcare, 3001 Hospital Gate, Oakville ON L6M 0L8, Canada. T. +19053384634. Fax +19053384639.
URL: http://ifhima.org/

History 1968, Sweden, as *International Federation of Medical Records Organizations*. Subsequently changed title to *International Federation of Health Records Organizations (IFHRO)* – *Fédération internationale des associations du dossier de santé* – *Federación Internacional de Organizaciones de Registros Sanitarios*, 1976. Constitution amended Jan 1979, Apr 1980, Oct 1988, Sep 2000, Oct 2004, May 2007, Nov 2010 and May 2013. Present title adopted, 2010. **Aims** Promote development and use of health records in all countries; advance development and use of international health records standards; provide exchange of information on health record education requirements and training programmes; provide opportunities for communication among persons working in the field in all countries. **Structure** General Assembly (at Triennial Congress); Executive Board; Committees; Task Groups; Projects. **Languages** English. **Staff** Voluntary. **Finance** Sources: members' dues. **Activities** Events/meetings; knowledge management/information dissemination; networking/liaising; projects/programmes; research and development; training/education. **Events** *Triennial Congress* Brisbane, QLD (Australia) 2022, *Triennial Congress* Dubai (United Arab Emirates) 2019, *Triennial Congress* Tokyo (Japan) 2016, *Triennial Congress* Montréal, QC (Canada) 2013, *Triennial Congress* Milan (Italy) 2010. **Publications** *IFHIMA Global News*.

Members National; Associate; Affiliate; Honorary; Corporate; Educational Institutions. National organizations (one per country) in 23 countries:
Australia, Barbados, Botswana, Canada, China, Germany, Ghana, India, Indonesia, Israel, Italy, Jamaica, Japan, Kenya, Korea Rep, Netherlands, Nigeria, Philippines, Saudi Arabia, Spain, Tanzania UR, UK, USA.

Associate: individuals where there is no national association. Affiliate: international organizations which have an alliance or partnership. Corporate: companies. Educational Institutions: involved in the delivery of Health Information Management educational programs. Honorary. Membership bestowed to individuals of esteemed service to IFHIMA (countries not specified).

Consultative Status Consultative status granted from: *ECOSOC (#05331)* (Ros C); *WHO (#20950)* (Official Relations). **NGO Relations** Partnership with: *International Medical Informatics Association (IMIA, #14134)*. [2018.09.19/XC6229/**C**]

♦ International Federation of Health Plans (iFHP) 13442

Association des fonds d'assurance de la santé

Main Office China Works, Black Prince Road, London, SE1 7SJ, UK. E-mail: hello@ifhp.com.
URL: http://www.ifhp.com/

History 1966, Dublin (Ireland). Founded following 1st International Conference of Voluntary Health Insurance. Secretariat transferred to: London (UK), 1979; Reading (UK), 1992. Constitution adopted at 2nd International Conference on Voluntary Health Insurance, 3 May 1968, Sydney (Australia). Former names and other names: *International Federation of Voluntary Health Service Funds (IFVHSF)* – former (1966); *Fédération internationale de caisses d'assurance volontaires* – former (1966); *International Federation of Health Funds (FHF)* – alias (1990); *International Association of Health Insurance Funds* – alias. Registration: Start date: 1971, Ireland. **Aims** Promote: international contact between members by exchanging information and expertise; further advances in health care financing by facilitating international studies and debates. **Structure** General Assembly (every 2 years). Council of Management, consisting of 12 elected members, elects from its members a President and one or more Deputy Presidents. Secretariat, headed by Chief-Executive. **Languages** English. **Staff** 2.00 FTE, paid. **Finance** Members' dues (80%). Other sources: conferences (17%); other (3%). Annual budget: 600,000 USD. **Activities** Events/meetings; projects/programmes. Submits evidence to commissions, enquiries and conferences. Interfund transfer agreement covers subscribers of participating funds who change country of residence. **Events** *Biennial Conference* Vancouver, BC (Canada) 2022, *Biennial Conference* Paris (France) 2020, *Biennial Conference* Lisbon (Portugal) 2018, *Biennial Conference* Berlin (Germany) 2016, *CEO Forum* Zurich (Switzerland) / Davos (Switzerland) 2015. **Publications** *IFHP Newsletter* (4 a year); *IFHP Information* (occasional). Conference proceedings published on website.
Members Full membership: non-governmental health funds and other organisations in 24 countries and territories:
Australia, Belgium, Botswana, Canada, China, Colombia, Denmark, France, Germany, Hong Kong, Ireland, Mauritius, Namibia, Netherlands, New Zealand, Nigeria, Puerto Rico, Rwanda, South Africa, Spain, Thailand, UK, USA, Zimbabwe.
[2021/XF2996/**C**]

♦ International Federation of Health Records Organizations / see International Federation of Health Information Management Associations (#13441)
♦ International Federation for Heat Treatment of Materials / see International Federation for Heat Treatment and Surface Engineering (#13443)

♦ International Federation for Heat Treatment and Surface Engineering (IFHTSE) 13443

Association internationale de traitement thermique et de l'ingénierie des surfaces (AITT) – Internationaler Verband für Die Wärmebehandlung und Randschichttechnik (IVW) – Mezdunarodnoe Obscestvo po Termiceskoj Obrabotke i Tehnologij Obrabotki Poverhnosti (MOTO)
SG c/o Listemann AG, Sulzer Allee 25, Postfach, 8404 Winterthur ZH, Switzerland. E-mail: info@ifhtse.org.
URL: http://www.ifhtse.org/
History 11 Oct 1971, Switzerland. Constitution adopted 17 May 1972, Zurich (Switzerland), at 1st Assembly of the Governing Council; amended, 19 Oct 1986, Budapest (Hungary), at 15th Assembly. Most recently amended 19 May 2015, Venice (Italy). Former names and other names: *International Federation for Heat Treatment of Materials (IFHT)* – former; *Association internationale de traitement thermique des matériaux* – former. Registration: Swiss Civil Code, Switzerland. **Aims** Facilitate and promote international and multidisciplinary exchange of information in the science and technology of heat treatment and surface engineering of materials, in particular of metals, uniting science and industry. **Structure** Governing Council (meets annually); Board of Directors; Executive Committee; Financial Examiners; Technical Committees. **Languages** English, French, German, Italian. **Staff** 2.00 FTE, paid. **Finance** Sources: donations; meeting proceeds; members' dues. **Activities** Events/meetings; knowledge management/information dissemination; projects/programmes; training/education. **Events** *International Congress of Heat Treatment of Materials* Yokohama (Japan) 2023, *International Congress of Heat Treatment of Materials* Moscow (Russia) 2019, *International Congress of Heat Treatment of Materials* Xian (China) 2018, *International Congress of Heat Treatment of Materials* Nice (France) 2017, *International Congress of Heat Treatment of Materials* Savannah, GA (USA) 2016. **Publications** *IFHTSE e-Bulletin.* Congress and seminar proceedings as state-of-the-art books.
Members Scientific and technical societies (22) and companies (5) in 22 countries:
Austria, China, Croatia, Czechia, Estonia, France, Germany, Hungary, India, Italy, Japan, Korea Rep, Malta, Mexico, Poland, Romania, Russia, Slovenia, Sweden, Switzerland, Türkiye, USA.
Consultative Status Consultative status granted from: *ECOSOC (#05331)* (Ros C); *UNIDO (#20336)*. **NGO Relations** In liaison with technical committees of: *International Organization for Standardization (ISO, #14473).*
[2021/XD2410/**C**]

♦ International Federation of Helicopter Associations (IFHA) 13444

Contact 1920 Ballenger Ave, 4th Floor, Alexandria VA 22314-2898, USA. T. +17036834646 ext 1605. E-mail: chris.martino@rotor.org.
URL: https://www.rotor.org/resources/operations/ifha
History 1993. Activated through leadership of: *European Helicopter Association (EHA, #07472)* and *Helicopter Association International (HAI)*. **Aims** Serve as the focal point for civil helicopter interests, worldwide; provide helicopter representation at the International Civil Aviation Organization (ICAO); and work in partnership with fellow member international helicopter associations to bring the expertise and concerns of civil helicopter industries to an international forum. **Languages** English. **Finance** Members' dues. **Events** *Affiliate Meeting* 2021, *European Rotors Conference* Cologne (Germany) 2021, *Affiliate Meeting* Anaheim, CA (USA) 2020, *European Rotors Conference* Cologne (Germany) 2020.
Members Affiliate: national organizations in 8 countries:
Australia, Brazil, Canada, Chile, India, Japan, New Zealand, UK.
Affiliate: regional organizations (3) listed in this Yearbook:
European Helicopter Association (EHA, #07472); Helicopter Association International (HAI); Helicopter Association of Southern Africa (no recent information).
Consultative Status Consultative status granted from: *ECOSOC (#05331)* (Ros C). **IGO Relations** Observer status with: *International Civil Aviation Organization (ICAO, #12581).*
[2020.06.29/XD7077/**D**]

♦ International Federation of Highrise Structures (IFHS) 13445

Pres No 20, 4th Cross, Shankara Puram, Bangalore, Karnataka 560004, Bangalore KARNATAKA 560004, India. T. +918026603857 – +918026614325. Fax +918026603857 – +918026600440.
URL: http://www.ifhsassociation.org/
History Founded 1994. **Aims** Improve every phase of highrise technology and construction and emphasize the interdisciplinary nature of related problems; research new knowledge and assemble known information on highrise structures; develop means for disseminating this information to all concerned. **Structure** Board; Advisory Board; Committees. **Languages** English. **Staff** 10.00 FTE, paid. **Finance** Through international conferences. **Activities** Knowledge management/information dissemination; events/meetings. **Events** *Conference on Multi-Purpose High-Rise Towers and Tall Buildings* Singapore (Singapore) 2019, *Conference on Multi-Purpose High-Rise Towers and Tall Buildings* Madrid (Spain) 2016, *Conference on Multi-Purpose High-Rise Towers and Tall Buildings* Krakow (Poland) 2015, *International Conference on Multi-Purpose High-Rise Towers and other Structures* Munich (Germany) 2010, *Conference on Multi-Purpose High-Rise Towers and Tall Buildings* Abu Dhabi (United Arab Emirates) 2007. **Publications** *IFHS Journal*; *IFHS Newsletter.* Conference proceedings; books.
Members Individuals in 14 countries:
Australia, Canada, China, Germany, India, Italy, Malawi, Malaysia, Singapore, Sweden, Switzerland, Tanzania UR, United Arab Emirates, USA.
[2018.09.07/XD5541/v/**D**]

♦ International Federation for Historical European Martial Arts (IFHEMA) 13446

Contact address not obtained. E-mail: secretary@ifhema.com.
URL: http://ifhema.com/
History Current by-laws adopted Feb 2014, Vienna (Austria). Registered in accordance with Swiss Civil Code. **Aims** Promote and develop historical European martial arts as a sport and as an art at all levels; coordinate and promote research and studies in the field of historical European martial arts. **Structure** General Assembly; Executive Committee. **Languages** English. **Finance** Members' dues. **Publications** *IFHEMA Newsletter.*
Members Full in 14 countries:
Austria, Belgium, France, Germany, Greece, Hungary, Netherlands, Poland, Portugal, Russia, Slovakia, Slovenia, Sweden, Switzerland.
[2021/XM7532/**D**]

♦ International Federation of Historic Motor Vehicle Clubs (#09669)

♦ International Federation for Home Economics (IFHE) 13447

Internationaler Verband für Hauswirtschaft (IVHW)
Exec Dir Kaiser-Friedrich-Str 13, 53113 Bonn, Germany. T. +492289212590. Fax +492289212591. E-mail: office@ifhe.org.
URL: http://www.ifhe.org/
History 1908, Fribourg (Switzerland). Current constitution adopted/amended, 29 Jul 2010, Sligo (Ireland). Former names and other names: *International Federation for the Teaching of Home Economics* – former; *Fédération internationale pour le développement de l'enseignement ménager* – former; *Internationaler Verband für Hauswirtschaftsunterricht* – former; *Fédération internationale pour l'enseignement ménager (FIEM)* – former; *Fédération internationale pour l'économie familiale (FIEF)* – former; *Federación Internacional para la Economia Familiar (FIEF)* – former. Registration: North Rhine-Westphalia District court, No/ID: VR 8050, Start date: 6 Sep 2002, Germany, Bonn; France; Swiss Civil Code, Switzerland. **Aims** Improve the quality of everyday life for individuals, families and households, through promotion of science, in particular of home economics, education, research and communication, and through development and presentation of political statements in national and international context; work to advance protection of families; promote equal rights for men and women; support education of children, popular education and vocational training. **Structure** General Assembly (every 2 years); Delegate Assembly/Council (at least every 2 years); Executive Committee. Regional organizations: *Asian Regional Association for Home Economics (ARAHE, #01682)*; *European Association for Home Economics (EAHE, #06072)*; IFHE US; IFHE Switzerland; IFHE Germany; IFHE Sweden; IFHE UK. **Languages** English. **Staff** None. **Finance** Sources: donations; fundraising; members' dues. **Activities** Advocacy/lobbying/activism; events/meetings. **Events** *Quadrennial World Congress* Atlanta, GA (USA) 2022, *Quadrennial World Congress* Atlanta, GA (USA) 2020, *Annual Meeting* Port-of-Spain (Trinidad-Tobago) 2019, *Quadrennial World Congress* Daejeon (Korea Rep) 2016, *Annual Meeting* Vienna (Austria) 2013. **Publications** *Home Economics* (4 a year) in English – newsletter; *International Journal of Home Economics* (2 a year). Congress reports; reports and accounts of conferences and seminars; statements.
Members Organizations and individuals in 57 countries. Professional associations, university departments and institutions in 22 countries:
Australia, Austria, Barbados, Cameroon, Canada, China, Finland, France, Germany, Greece, Indonesia, Ireland, Japan, Mauritius, New Zealand, Nigeria, Philippines, South Africa, Sweden, Switzerland, Thailand, USA.
Caribbean Association of Home Economists (CAHE, #03446).
Consultative Status Consultative status granted from: *ECOSOC (#05331)* (Special); *UNESCO (#20322)* (Consultative Status); *FAO (#09260)* (Special Status). **IGO Relations** Associated with Department of Global Communications of the United Nations. **NGO Relations** Member of (6): *Conference of Non-Governmental Organizations in Consultative Relationship with the United Nations (CONGO, #04635)*; *International Conference of NGOs (#12883)*; *NGO Committee on Sustainable Development, Vienna (#17119)*; *NGO Committee on UNICEF (#17120)*; *Vienna NGO Committee on the Family (#20774)*; *Vienna NGO Committee on the Status of Women (#20775)*. Cooperates with (4): *Alliance for Health Promotion (A4HP, #00687)*; *Clean Cooking Alliance (#03987)*; Supreme Council for the Environment Ten-Year Framework Program (10YFP); Zero Hunger Challenge.
[2021/XB1929/**B**]

♦ International Federation of Home and School (inactive)

♦ International Federation of Horse Racing Academies (IFHRA) 13448

Headquarters PO Box 113011, Abu Dhabi, United Arab Emirates. T. +97124444055.
Street address HH Sheikh Mansour Festival Lounge, Jannah – Eastern Mangrove, Abu Dhabi, United Arab Emirates.
URL: http://www.ifhra.ae/
History Current statutes affective 2 Jan 2015. **Aims** Develop horse racing academies worldwide by providing scientific, educational curriculum and world class standards of jockey practices to apprentices. **Structure** General Assembly (annual); Board of Directors; Executive Committee; Headquarters. Standing Committees; Tribunal. **Finance** Sources: members' dues.
Members National academies in 33 countries and territories:
Argentina, Australia, Bahrain, Belgium, Brazil, Canada, China, Denmark, France, Germany, Hong Kong, Ireland, Italy, Korea Rep, Malaysia, Morocco, Netherlands, New Zealand, Oman, Poland, Portugal, Puerto Rico, Slovakia, South Africa, Spain, Sweden, Switzerland, Tunisia, Türkiye, UK, United Arab Emirates, Uruguay, USA.
[2019/XM7531/**C**]

♦ International Federation of Horseracing Authorities (IFHA) 13449

Fédération internationale des autorités hippiques de courses au galop
SG 46 place Abel Gance, 92100 Boulogne-Billancourt, France. T. +3318592242741. E-mail: secretarygeneral@ifhaonline.org.
URL: http://www.ifhaonline.org/
History 1993. Founded following coordination of horse racing activities by relevant authorities in France, Ireland, UK and USA which began in 1961 and institution by these authorities of the annual conference held in Paris (France) from 1967. **Aims** Promote horse racing and breeding, and the integrity and prestige thereof, throughout the world; foster and develop exchanges between various racing authorities without discrimination; make recommendations to competent authorities for improvements in laws and regulations; promulgate the International Agreement on Breeding, Racing and Wagering. **Structure** General Assembly; Executive Council; Steering Committee on Wagering; Advisory Council on Prohibited Substances. Committees (5): International Movement of Horses; International Grading and Race Planning Advisory; Technical Advisory; International Classification; International Stud Book. **Events** *Annual International Conference and General Assembly* Paris (France) 2019, *Annual International Conference and General Assembly* Paris (France) 2018, *Annual International Conference and General Assembly* Paris (France) 2017, *Annual International Conference and General Assembly* Paris (France) 2016, *Annual International Conference and General Assembly* Paris (France) 2015.
Members Horseracing authorities in 51 countries and territories:
Algeria, Argentina, Australia, Bahrain, Belgium, Brazil, Canada, Chad, Chile, Cyprus, Czechia, Denmark, France, Germany, Greece, Hong Kong, Hungary, India, Ireland, Italy, Japan, Korea Rep, Lebanon, Macau, Malaysia, Mauritius, Mexico, Morocco, Netherlands, New Zealand, Norway, Pakistan, Peru, Philippines, Qatar, Romania, Russia, Saudi Arabia, Serbia, Slovakia, South Africa, Spain, Sweden, Switzerland, Thailand, Tunisia, Türkiye, UK, United Arab Emirates, USA, Venezuela.
Regional associations (4):
Asian Racing Federation (#01677); *Confederación Hipica del Caribe (#04447)*; *European and Mediterranean Horseracing Federation (EMHF, #07770)*; *Organización Sudamericana de Fomento del Pura Sangre de Carrera (OSAF, #17850)*; *Racing Commissioners International (RCI).*
NGO Relations Member of (1): *Sports Rights Owners Coalition (SROC, #19929).* Instrumental in setting up (1): *International Horse Sports Confederation (IHSC, #13811).*
[2020/XC0097/y/**C**]

♦ International Federation of Hospital Engineering / see International Federation of Healthcare Engineering (#13439)

♦ International Federation for Housing and Planning (IFHP) 13450

Fédération internationale pour l'habitation, l'urbanisme et l'aménagement des territoires (FIHUAT) – Federación Internacional de Vivienda y Urbanismo (FIVU) – Internationaler Verband für Wohnungswesen, Städtebau und Raumordnung (IVWSR)
Main Office Bryghuspladsen 8, Entrance C, 3rd floor, 1473 Copenhagen K, Denmark. E-mail: info@ifhp.org.
URL: http://www.ifhp.org/
History 1913, London (UK). Moved from The Hague (Netherlands) to Copenhagen (Denmark), 2013. Former names and other names: *International Garden Cities and Town Planning Association* – former (1913 to 1926); *Fédération internationale des cités-jardins et de l'urbanisme* – former (1913 to 1926); *International Federation for Housing and Town Planning (IFHP)* – former (1926 to 1958); *Fédération internationale de l'habitation et de l'urbanisme* – former (1926 to 1958); *Internationaler Verband für Wohnungswesen und Städtebau* – former (1926 to 1958). Registration: Denmark. **Aims** As a worldwide network of professional institutions and individuals active in the broad fields of housing, urban development and planning: interact with people who make cities better; seek to understand and act on the most dominant urban challenges of our time. **Structure** Council (meets annually); Board; Secretariat. **Languages** Danish, Dutch, English, German, Portuguese, Spanish. **Finance** Sources: donations; grants; meeting proceeds; members' dues; sponsorship. **Activities**

Events/meetings; guidance/assistance/consulting; training/education. **Events** *Summit* Copenhagen (Denmark) 2020, *Design Declaration Summit* Montréal, QC (Canada) 2017, *International Housing Forum* Singapore (Singapore) 2017, *Summit* Rotterdam (Netherlands) 2016, *Smart Solutions for Innovative Cities Conference* Copenhagen (Denmark) 2015. **Publications** *IFHP Newsletter* (4 a year). Congress, conference and seminar reports; special publications of Working Parties; reports on international student competitions; reports on international student competitions.
Members Corporate local, regional and national authorities; firms, companies, corporations and societies; national associations of professionals, firms or other bodies; universities and their departments, faculties, research institutes and libraries; international non-governmental organizations; all engaged in housing, planning, urban development, environment or related fields. Individual persons professionally or voluntarily engaged in housing, planning, urban development, environment or related fields. Members in 34 countries and territories:
Australia, Austria, Belgium, Brazil, Canada, China, Colombia, Czechia, Denmark, Fiji, Finland, France, Germany, Italy, Japan, Kuwait, Lithuania, Luxembourg, Mexico, Netherlands, Norway, Portugal, Puerto Rico, Qatar, Russia, Saudi Arabia, Singapore, Slovenia, Spain, Sweden, Switzerland, Türkiye, UK, USA.
Consultative Status Consultative status granted from: *ECOSOC (#05331)* (Special); *UNESCO (#20322)* (Consultative Status); *UNEP (#20299)*; *Council of Europe (CE, #04881)* (Participatory Status). **NGO Relations** Associate partner of: *World Urban Campaign (WUC, #21893)*. Cooperates with: *Association of European Schools of Planning (AESOP, #02542)*. Supporter member of: *Global Planners Network (GPN, #10548)*.
[2022/XB1826/y/**B**]

♦ International Federation for Housing and Town Planning / see International Federation for Housing and Planning (#13450)

♦ International Federation of Human Genetics Societies (IFHGS) 13451

Pres IFHGS Secretariat, c/o Vienna Medical Acad, Alserstrasse 4, 1090 Vienna, Austria. T. +431405138322. Fax +4314078274. E-mail: ifhgs@medacad.org.
URL: http://www.ifhgs.org/

History 1996, as a successor to *Permanent Committee of the International Congresses of Human Genetics*. **Aims** Provide a forum for groups dedicated to all aspects of human genetics. **Structure** Executive Committee, consisting of representatives of all full members. **Events** *International Congress of Human Genetics* Cape Town (South Africa) 2023, *International Symposium of Human Genetics* 2022, *International Congress of Human Genetics* Cape Town (South Africa) 2022, *International Symposium of Human Genetics* 2021, *International Congress of Human Genetics* Cape Town (South Africa) 2021.
Members Full; Corresponding; Affiliate. Full (7; " indicates founding):
African Society of Human Genetics (AfSHG, #00462); American Society of Human Genetics (); *Asia Pacific Society of Human Genetics (APSHG, #02038)*; *East Asian Union of Human Genetics Societies (EAUHGS, #05211)*; *European Society of Human Genetics (ESHG, #08624)*; *Human Genetics Society of Australasia (HGSA)*; *Red Latino Americana de Genetica Humana (RELAGH, no recent information)*.
Corresponding National organizations in 42 countries:
Argentina, Austria, Bangladesh, Belgium, Brazil, Canada, Colombia, Croatia, Czechia, Denmark, Ecuador, Finland, France, Germany, Greece, Guatemala, Hungary, India, Ireland, Israel, Italy, Japan, Korea Rep, Latvia, Lithuania, Mexico, Netherlands, Norway, Panama, Portugal, Romania, Russia, Serbia, Slovenia, South Africa, Spain, Sweden, Switzerland, Türkiye, UK, USA, Vietnam.
Affiliates (7):
Canadian Association of Genetic Disorders; *European Cytogeneticists Association (ECA, #06880)*; *Human Genome Organization (HUGO, #10968)*; *Human Genome Variation Society (HGVS, #10969)*; *Ibero-American Society of Human Genetics of North America (IASHGNA)*; *International Genetic Alliance (IGA, #13709)*; *International Genetic Epidemiology Society (IGES, #13710)*. [2018/XD7474/y/**D**]

♦ International Federation of Human Rights / see International Federation for Human Rights (#13452)

♦ International Federation for Human Rights 13452

Fédération Internationale pour les Droits Humains (fidh) – Federación Internacional por los Derechos Humanos

Headquarters 17 Passage de la Main d'Or, 75011 Paris, France. T. +33143552518.
URL: https://www.fidh.org/

History 1922, Paris (France). Since 1926, includes the *Organisation de la paix par la justice internationale*. Proposed in 1927 the *'Déclaration mondiale des droits de l'homme'*. Added in 1936 new chapters to the *'Déclaration mondiale des droits de l'homme'*. Dispersed or underground in occupied Europe, re-established 31 Oct 1948. Has worked for the application of the Universal Declaration of Human Rights since its inception on 10 Dec 1948. Former names and other names: *International Federation of Leagues for the Defence of the Rights of Man and of Citizens* – former; *Fédération internationale des ligues pour la défense des droits de l'homme et du citoyen* – former; *International Federation of Human Rights* – former; *Fédération internationale des droits de l'homme* – former; *International Federation for the Rights of Man* – former; *International Federation of Human Rights Leagues (IFHR)* – legal name; *Fédération internationale des ligues des droits de l'homme (FIDH)* – legal name; *Federación Internacional de las Ligas de los Derechos Humanos* – legal name. Registration: RNA, No/ID: W751104411, France; EU Transparency Register, No/ID: 97628146980-33, Start date: 20 Oct 2011. **Aims** Contribute to the respect of all rights as defined in the Universal Declaration of Human Rights; obtain effective improvement in protection of *victims*, prevention of Human Rights violations and the sanction of their perpetrators; federate human rights organizations and coordinate and support their activities at the local, regional and international level; work in partnership with like-minded organizations so as to raise public awareness of human rights abuse worldwide and to raise funds for activities. **Structure** World Congress (every 3 years); International Board (meets 3 times a year); Executive Board. Units (4): Administrative; Research and Operations; Geographical and Thematic Desks; Communications. Permanent Delegations: UN – Geneva (Switzerland); UN – New York NY (USA); EU – Brussels (Belgium); ICC – The Hague (Netherlands). International Secretariat, headquartered in Paris (France). **Languages** Arabic, English, French, German, Russian, Spanish, Wolof. **Staff** 30.00 FTE, paid; 200.00 FTE, voluntary. **Finance** Sources: international organizations; members' dues. Supported by: *Coalition of the Flemish North South Movement – 11 11 11*; *Comité Catholique contre la Faim et pour le Développement-Terre Solidaire (CCFD-Terre Solidaire)*; *DANIDA*; *Department for International Development (DFID, inactive)*; *European Commission (EC, #06633)*; *Ford Foundation (#09858)*; *Irish Aid*; *Jean-Jaurès Foundation (FJJ)*; *Oxfam Novib*; *Swedish Foundation for Human Rights (SFHR)*; *Swedish International Development Cooperation Agency (Sida)*; *UNESCO (#20322)*; *Westminster Foundation for Democracy (WFD)*.
Activities Advocacy/lobbying/activism; awareness raising; capacity building; capacity building; events/meetings; monitoring/evaluation; standards/guidelines. /Thematic/, as defined by the 35th Congress in Mar 2004, Quito (Ecuador); implemented in the framework of the statutory priorities:
– *'World Order Founded on Law, the Fight Against Terrorism Must Be Founded on Human Rights'* – strives to expose opportunism with which the antiterrorist struggle has been exploited for domestic ends of political repression, restrictions on freedom of information or the right to a private life; advocates instituting international and regional guarantees against arbitrary infringements of fundamental freedoms; carries out actions for the right to an equitable trial before an independent jurisdiction and against the death penalty; campaigns against forced disappearances by supporting such efforts as the *International Convention for the Protection of all Persons from Enforced Disappearance (2006)* of the United Nations.
– *'Right to Defend Endangered Human Rights'* – works towards implementation of the United Nations Declaration on Human Rights Defenders, with special emphasis on the *FIDH/OMCT Observatory for the Protection of Human Rights Defenders* designed to alert and mobilize decision-making bodies – established with *World Organisation Against Torture (OMCT, #21685)*; helps mobilize public opinion world-wide through the social forum process and by other means and pushes for greater involvement of independent human rights defence NGOs in intergovernmental organizations.
– *'Protection of Women's Rights as Fundamental Human Rights'* – Action Group for Women's Rights gives partners renewed incentive and revives alliances between NGOs defending women's rights and human rights; works towards practical implementation of the *Convention on the Elimination of all Forms of Discrimination Against Women (CEDAW, 1979)*.
– *'Economic Globalization Founded on Respect for Human Rights'* – speaks out for pre-eminence of human rights over international trade, for accountability in economic, social and cultural rights and for the legal responsibility of economic bodies, particularly multinationals; continues to support the emergence of legal standards and corresponding inspection mechanisms, which materialize the corporate duty to respect universal standards for protection of human rights; supports efforts to implement the system stemming from the *International Convention on the Protection of the Rights of all Migrant Workers and Members of Their Families (1990)*; works on establishing the right to cultural diversity, promoted through a Convention adopted by UNESCO; advocates reforming public institutions that regulate globalization to introduce greater transparency, responsibility and opportunities for civil society to participate.
– *'Criminal Proceedings Against Perpetrators of International Crimes – No Impunity'* – strives to have the perpetrators of international crimes, whatever their title, position or economic role, brought before a fair court of justice to answer for their crimes.

Works, alongside victims, for the right to effective and enforceable remedy by intervening in both national and international jurisdictions, and first of all at the *International Criminal Court (ICC, #13108)*, through its Legal Action Group (GAJ); Permanent Delegation, opened with the ICC in early 2004, works to strengthen the Court – ratification, passage of domestic incorporation laws and recourse by victims before the ICC.
Events *Triennial Congress* Taipei (Taiwan) 2019, *Triennial Congress* Johannesburg (South Africa) 2016, *Triennial World Congress* Istanbul (Turkey) 2013, *Triennial Congress* Tunis (Tunisia) 2013, *Triennial Congress / Triennial World Congress* Yerevan (Armenia) 2010. **Publications** *La lettre de la FIDH* (6 a year) in French – newsletter; *Annual FIDH/OMCT Observatory Programme for the Protection of Human Rights Defenders* (every 3 years) – report, latest edition covering 2004-2007. Reports of missions and activities, in Arabic, English, French, Spanish; position papers; alternative reports to UN treaty monitoring bodies; press releases.
Members Affiliates; Corresponding – national and regional human rights organizations, commissions and associations (141, with a joint membership of over 500,000) in 102 countries and territories:
Afghanistan, Albania, Algeria, Argentina, Austria, Azerbaijan, Bahrain, Bangladesh, Belarus, Belgium, Benin, Bhutan, Bolivia, Brazil, Burkina Faso, Burundi, Cambodia, Cameroon, Canada, Central African Rep, Chad, Chile, China, Colombia, Congo Brazzaville, Congo DR, Côte d'Ivoire, Croatia, Cuba, Czechia, Djibouti, Ecuador, Egypt, El Salvador, Ethiopia, Finland, France, Georgia, Germany, Greece, Guatemala, Guinea, Guinea-Bissau, Honduras, Iran Islamic Rep, Iraq, Ireland, Israel, Italy, Japan, Jordan, Kenya, Kosovo, Kyrgyzstan, Laos, Latvia, Lebanon, Liberia, Libya, Lithuania, Malaysia, Mali, Malta, Mauritania, Mexico, Moldova, Morocco, Mozambique, Netherlands, New Caledonia, Nicaragua, Niger, Nigeria, Pakistan, Palestine, Panama, Peru, Philippines, Polynesia Fr, Portugal, Romania, Russia, Rwanda, Senegal, Serbia, South Africa, Spain, Sudan, Switzerland, Syrian AR, Tanzania UR, Thailand, Togo, Tunisia, Türkiye, Uganda, UK, USA, Uzbekistan, Vietnam, Yemen, Zimbabwe.
Included in the above, 9 organizations listed in this Yearbook:
Association africaine de défense des droits de l'homme (ASADHO); *European Association for the Defence of Human Rights (AEDH, no recent information)*; *Inter-American Legal Services Association (ILSA, #11439)*; *International Campaign for Tibet (ICT, #12429)*; *International League for Human Rights (ILHR, inactive)* (German Office); *Latvian Human Rights Committee (LHRC)*; *Ligue suisse des droits de l'homme*; *Ligue tunisienne pour la défense des droits de l'homme (LTDH)*; *Österreichische Liga für Menschenrechte (LIGA)*.
Consultative Status Consultative status granted from: *ECOSOC (#05331)* (Special); *UNESCO (#20322)* (Consultative Status); *ILO (#11123)* (Special List); *Council of Europe (CE, #04881)* (Participatory Status); *Organisation internationale de la Francophonie (OIF, #17809)*; *African Commission on Human and Peoples' Rights (ACHPR, #00255)* (Observer). **IGO Relations** Consultative status with: *Commonwealth Secretariat (#04362)*. Associated with Department of Global Communications of the United Nations.
NGO Relations Observer status with (3): *International Committee of the Red Cross (ICRC, #12799)*; *International Federation of Red Cross and Red Crescent Societies (#13526)*; *International Red Cross and Red Crescent Movement (#14707)*.
Member of (22):
– *Coalition for an Effective African Court on Human and Peoples' Rights (African Court Coalition, #04055)*;
– *Coalition for the International Criminal Court (CICC, #04062)*;
– *ETO Consortium (ETOs, #05560)*;
– *EU-LAT Network (#05585)*;
– *EuroMed Non-Governmental Platform (#05730)*;
– *EuroMed Rights (#05733)*;
– *European Coalition for Corporate Justice (ECCJ, #06591)*;
– *European NGO Platform Asylum and Migration (EPAM, #08051)*;
– *Human Rights and Democracy Network (HRDN, #10980)*;
– *International Coalition against Enforced Disappearances (ICAED, #12605)*;
– *International Coalition to Stop Crimes Against Humanity in North Korea (ICNK, #12622)*;
– *International Network for Economic, Social and Cultural Rights (ESCR-Net, #14255)*;
– *International NGO Platform on the Migrant Workers' Convention (IPMWC, #14367)*;
– *NGO Shipbreaking Platform (#17126)*;
– *NGO Working Group on the Security Council (#17128)*;
– *OECD Watch (#17694)*;
– *Permanent Forum of European Civil Society (#18322)*;
– *ProtectDefenders.eu (#18546)*;
– *Sudan Consortium (#20031)*;
– *World Coalition Against the Death Penalty (#21281)*;
– *World Organisation Against Torture (OMCT, #21685)*;
– *World Social Forum (WSF, #21797)*.
Cooperates with (3): *Crisis Action (#04957)*; *Inter-African Committee on Traditional Practices Affecting the Health of Women and Children (IAC, #11384)*; *REDRESS*.
Supports: *International Campaign Against Mass Surveillance (ICAMS, no recent information)*. Instrumental in setting up: *International Federation of Human Rights Archives and Documentation Centers (no recent information)*. Proposed setting up: *Conseil européen des minorités (no recent information)*.
[2022/XD1841/y/**B**]

♦ International Federation of Human Rights Archives and Documentation Centers (no recent information)
♦ International Federation of Human Rights Leagues / see International Federation for Human Rights (#13452)
♦ International Federation for Hydrocephalus and Spina Bifida – Europe (inactive)

♦ International Federation of Hydrographic Societies (IFHS) 13453

Chair Senate Court, Southernhay Gardens, Exeter, EX1 1NT, UK. E-mail: info@hydrographicsociety.org.
URL: http://www.hydrographicsociety.org/

History 1972, London (UK). Former names and other names: *Hydrographic Society, The (THS)* – former. **Aims** Facilitate the coalition of people, resources and information for the active promotion of hydrographic expertise, undersea exploration and associated *maritime* technologies; promote excellence in the application, history, dissemination and technological development of hydrography and related sciences; promote the highest level of accuracy and thoroughness in the application of hydrography and related sciences in accordance with internationally defined standards; promote free exchange of information; encourage the broadest possible inclusion of people and organizations interested in hydrography and related sciences; promote the broadest pursuit of technological innovation in the field; promote the highest possible standards of safety by and for the application of hydrography and related sciences. **Structure** Annual Assembly; Board of Directors. **Languages** English. **Finance** Sources: members' dues. **Activities** Events/meetings. **Events** *Hydro22 Conference* Monaco (Monaco) 2022, *Hydrography Workshop* Marseille (France) 2019, *HYDRO Annual International Conference* Sydney, NSW (Australia) 2018, *HYDRO Annual International Conference* Rotterdam (Netherlands) 2017, *HYDRO Annual International Conference* Warnemünde (Germany) 2016. **Publications** *The Hydrographic Journal* (4 a year); *IFHS Newsletter*. Symposium and workshop proceedings; papers; CD-Roms.
Members Categories Corporate; Associate Corporate; Individual; Student; Retired. Member societies (7) in 9 countries:
Australia, Belgium, Denmark, Germany, Italy, Luxembourg, Netherlands, South Africa, UK.
Included in the above, 2 organizations listed in this Yearbook:
Australasian Hydrographic Society (AHS); *Hydrographic Society Benelux (HSB, #10999)*.
IGO Relations Memorandum of Understanding with (1): *International Hydrographic Organization (IHO, #13825)*. [2021.05.18/XF5481/**F**]

♦ International Federation on Hydrotherapy and Climatotherapy / see Fédération mondiale du thermalisme et du climatisme (#09692)
♦ International Federation for Hygiene, Preventive and Social Medicine (inactive)

♦ International Federation of Icelandic Horse Associations (FEIF) ... 13454

Secretariat Kurzbauergasse 5/11, 1020 Vienna, Austria. T. +436644237870. E-mail: office@feif.org.
Chair Hrisdalur, 311 Borgarnes, Iceland. T. +3548602337. E-mail: president@feif.org.
URL: http://www.feif.org/

History 25 May 1969, Switzerland. Former names and other names: *Internationale Föderation der Islandpferde Vereine* – former; *Föderation Europäischer Islandpferde Freunde (FEIF)* – former (1969). Registration: 94.99.9 non-profit association, No/ID: Kt: 421116-1720, Iceland. **Aims** Connect Icelandic horse culture, riding, lifestyle, enjoyment and passion; continuously improve and unify standards; promote the pure-bred Icelandic horse throughout the world; improve recognition of the Icelandic horse. **Structure** Delegates' Assembly; Board; Committees; Subcommittees; Working Groups; Arbitration Council. **Languages** English. **Staff** 0.50 FTE, paid. **Finance** Sources: members' dues. Other sources: revenue from rankings for sport riders;

registration of events and horses; breeding assessments. **Activities** Awards/prizes/competitions; events/meetings; monitoring/evaluation; sporting activities; training/education. **Events** *Conference* Oslo (Norway) 2022, *Delegates Assembly* Borgarnes (Iceland) 2021, *Conference* Reykjavik (Iceland) 2020, *Conference* Berlin (Germany) 2019, *Conference* Stockholm (Sweden) 2018. **Publications** *FEIF Newsletter* (26 a year). *50 years of FEIF* (1st ed 2019). News articles.
Members Full: national associations in 22 countries and territories:
Australia, Austria, Belgium, Canada, Denmark, Faeroe Is, Finland, France, Germany, Great Britain, Hungary, Iceland, Italy, Liechtenstein, Luxembourg, Netherlands, New Zealand, Norway, Slovenia, Sweden, Switzerland, USA.
Associate in 1 country:
New Zealand.
NGO Relations Member of (1): *European Horse Network (EHN, #07499)* (as founding member of).
[2022.05.11/XD7235/**D**]

♦ International Federation Icestocksport (IFI) 13455
International Föderation Eisstock Sport (IFE)
Registered Address c/o DESV, Haus des Sports DOSB, Otto-Fleck-Schneise 12, 60528 Frankfurt-Main, Germany. E-mail: office@icestocksport.com.
URL: https://www.icestocksport.com/
History 1950, Vienna (Austria). Former names and other names: *International Icing Federation (IIFE)* – former; *Fédération internationale de pétanque sur glace* – former; *Internationale Föderation für Eisstockschiessen (IFE)* – former. **Languages** English, German. **Staff** 2.00 FTE, paid; 8.00 FTE, voluntary. **Activities** Sporting activities. **Events** *Annual congress / Annual International Congress* Kastelruth (Italy) 1991, *Annual congress / Annual International Congress* Schladming (Austria) 1990, *Annual congress / Annual International Congress* Klagenfurt am Wörthersee (Austria) 1989, *Annual congress / Annual International Congress* Budapest (Hungary) 1988, *Annual congress / Annual International Congress* Calgary, AB (Canada) 1987.
Members National organizations in 53 countries and territories:
Argentina, Australia, Austria, Belarus, Brazil, Canada, China, Colombia, Croatia, Czechia, Denmark, Dominican Rep, Egypt, Estonia, Finland, France, Germany, Greece, Guatemala, Hong Kong, Hungary, India, Indonesia, Iran Islamic Rep, Israel, Italy, Japan, Kenya, Liechtenstein, Lithuania, Luxembourg, Malta, Namibia, Netherlands, Nigeria, Norway, Paraguay, Peru, Poland, Russia, Singapore, Slovakia, Slovenia, Spain, Sweden, Switzerland, Tunisia, Türkiye, Uganda, UK, Ukraine, USA, Venezuela.
NGO Relations Member of (3): *Alliance of Independent recognised Members of Sport (AIMS, #00690)* (Associate); *Association of the IOC Recognized International Sports Federations (ARISF, #02767)*; *Olympic Movement (#17719)*. Recognized by: *International Olympic Committee (IOC, #14408)*.
[2022.02.14/XD9640/**D**]

♦ International Federation of Importers and Wholesale Grocers Associations (inactive)
♦ International Federation of Independent Air Transport (inactive)
♦ International Federation of the Independent Shoe Trade (inactive)
♦ International Federation of Industrial Energy Consumers (inactive)

♦ International Federation of Industrial Energy Consumers, Europe (IFIEC – Europe) 13456
Fédération internationale des industries consommatrices d'énergie, Europe
SG Av Louise 250/80, 1050 Brussels, Belgium. T. +3228885269 – +322491722699063. E-mail: ifieceurope@ifieceurope.org.
URL: http://www.ifieceurope.org/
History Oct 1988. Founded as the European branch of *International Federation of Industrial Energy Consumers (IFIEC, inactive)*, taking over the activities of the now dissolved *Fédération européenne des producteurs autonomes et des consommateurs industriels d'énergie (FEPACE, inactive)*. Registration: Banque-Carrefour des Entreprises, Belgium; EU Transparency Register, No/ID: 1978775156-31. **Aims** Represent the interests of industrial energy users in Europe for whom energy is a significant component of production costs and a key factor of competitiveness in their activities. **Structure** General Assembly (annual); Bureau. **Languages** English. **Finance** Sources: members' dues. **Activities** Advocacy/lobbying/activism; politics/policy/regulatory. **Events** *Energy Forum* Brussels (Belgium) 2016, *Energy Forum* Brussels (Belgium) 2015, *Energy Forum* Brussels (Belgium) 2014, *Energy Forum* Brussels (Belgium) 2013.
Members Non-governmental associations representing energy producing and consuming industries in EU, EFTA and United Nations Economic Commission for Europe countries, in 12 countries:
Belgium, Bulgaria, Czechia, Finland, France, Germany, Hungary, Italy, Netherlands, Norway, Portugal, UK.
NGO Relations Member of (2): *European Association for the Streamlining of Energy Exchange-gas (EASEE-gas, #06224)*; *Industry4Europe (#11181)*.
[2021.06.01/XE0916/t/**E**]

♦ International Federation of Industrial Property Attorneys / see Fédération Internationale des Conseils en Propriété Intellectuelle (#09624)
♦ International Federation of Infantile and Juvenile Gynecology / see Fédération internationale de gynécologie infantile et juvénile (#09637)

♦ International Federation of Infection Control (IFIC) 13457
Address not obtained.
URL: http://www.theific.org/
History 1987. Registration: Charity Commission, No/ID: 1072681, England and Wales. **Aims** Facilitate worldwide networking to improve the prevention and control of health care associated infections. **Structure** Board. **Languages** English. **Staff** 3.00 FTE, paid. **Finance** Sources: members' dues. Other sources: Support from corporate partners. **Activities** Awards/prizes/competitions; events/meetings; training/education. **Events** *Congress* Budapest (Hungary) 2023, *Annual Congress* Vienna (Austria) 2016, *Annual Congress* Delhi (India) 2015, *Annual Congress* St Julian's (Malta) 2014, *Annual Congress* Buenos Aires (Argentina) 2013. **Publications** *International Journal of Infection Control* (2 a year); *IFIC Newsletter*.
Members Societies in 41 countries and territories:
Argentina, Australia, Austria, Bolivia, Bosnia-Herzegovina, Brazil, Bulgaria, Canada, China, Croatia, Cyprus, Czechia, Denmark, Egypt, Finland, France, Germany, Greece, Hong Kong, Hungary, India, Indonesia, Italy, Libya, Malaysia, Malta, Netherlands, New Zealand, North Macedonia, Norway, Pakistan, Romania, Saudi Arabia, Serbia, Singapore, Spain, Sweden, Taiwan, UK, Ukraine, USA.
Included in the above, 3 organization listes in this Yearbook:
Association for Professionals in Infection Control and Epidemiology (APIC); *Infection Control Africa Network (ICAN, #11184)*; *International Scientific Forum on Home Hygiene (IFH)*.
IGO Relations *WHO (#20950)*.
[2019/XD9395/y/**C**]

♦ International Federation of Infertility Patient Associations (inactive)
♦ International Federation for Information and Communication Processing (#09667)
♦ International Federation for Information and Documentation (inactive)
♦ International Federation for Information Processing / see Fédération internationale pour le traitement de l'information et de la communication (#09667)

♦ International Federation for Information Processing (IFIP) 13458
Fédération internationale pour le traitement de l'information – Federación Internacional para el Tratamiento de la Información – Internationale Föderation für Datenverarbeitung
Head Hofstrasse 3, 2361 Laxenburg, Austria. T. +43223673616. Fax +432236736169. E-mail: ifip@ifip.org.
URL: http://www.ifip.org/
History Jan 1960. Founded under the auspices of UNESCO, following 1st International Conference on Information Processing, June 1959, Paris (France), also under the sponsorship of UNESCO. **Aims** Provide a meeting place for *IT* societies' members to share experience and discuss challenges and opportunities; contribute to, and often lead, progress in state-of-the-art knowledge and practice. **Structure** General Assembly (annual); Board (meets annually); Executive Board; Technical Assembly; Technical Committees; Standing Committees (10); Technical Committees (14); Working Groups; Special Interest Groups; Secretariat in Laxenburg (Austria). **Languages** English. **Staff** 2.50 FTE, paid. **Activities** Advocacy/lobbying/activism; events/meetings; networking/liaising; research and development; standards/guidelines. **Events** *Network Operations and Management Symposium (NOMS)* Miami, FL (USA) 2023, *International Conference on Advances in Production Management Systems* Gyeongju (Korea Rep) 2022, *Conference on Reliability and Optimization of Structural Systems* Kyoto (Japan) 2022, *Working Conference on the Practice of Enterprise Modeling* London (UK) 2022, *International Conference on Very Large Scale Integration (VLSI-SoC)* Patras (Greece) 2022. **Publications** *IFIP Newsletter* (4 a year); *Computers and Security*; *Education and Computing*; *IFIP Information Bulletin*; *Information and Management*. *Fractals in the Fundamental and Applied Sciences* (1990); *Concepts in User Interfaces: A Reference Model for Command and Response Languages* (1986); *Computerization and Work: A Reader on Social Aspects of Computerization* (1985). Proceedings of congresses and various conferences; proceedings of technical committee and working group conferences, seminars and workshops; scientific papers; state-of-the-art reports; computer graphics series.
Members Professional and technical organizations or national groupings of such organizations. Full members in 38 countries:
Australia, Austria, Brazil, Bulgaria, Canada, China, Croatia, Cyprus, Czechia, Denmark, Finland, France, Germany, India, Iran Islamic Rep, Ireland, Italy, Japan, Korea Rep, Lithuania, Netherlands, New Zealand, Norway, Poland, Portugal, Serbia, Slovakia, Slovenia, South Africa, Sri Lanka, Sweden, Switzerland, Tunisia, UK, Ukraine, United Arab Emirates, Zimbabwe.
Included in the above, 2 organizations listed in this Yearbook:
Association for Computing Machinery (ACM, #02447); *Latin American Center for Studies in Informatics (#16293)*.
Associate members (4):
Council of European Professional Informatics Societies (CEPIS, #04893); *International Medical Informatics Association (IMIA, #14134)*; *South East Asia Regional Computer Confederation (SEARCC, #19794)*; *Very Large Databases Endowment (VLDB)*.
Consultative Status Consultative status granted from: *ECOSOC (#05331)* (Ros); *UNESCO (#20322)* (Consultative Status); *UNIDO (#20336)*. **IGO Relations** Working relations with: *International Telecommunication Union (ITU, #15673)*. Participates in the work of: *United Nations Economic Commission for Europe (UNECE, #20555)*. **NGO Relations** Member of: *International Conference of NGOs (#12883)*; *International Science Council (ISC, #14796)*. Consultative status with: *International Federation of Library Associations and Institutions (IFLA, #13470)*.
[2022.11.30/XC1828/y/**B**]

♦ International Federation for Information Technology in Agriculture / see International Network for Information Technology in Agriculture (#14287)

♦ International Federation of Information Technology and Tourism (IFITT) 13459
Contact c/o MCI Management Center Innsbruck, Universitätsstr 15, 6020 Innsbruck, Austria. E-mail: ifitt@ifitt.org.
URL: http://www.ifitt.org/
History 24 Jan 1997, Edinburgh (UK). Founded at inaugural meeting. **Aims** Share knowledge, experience, and a true passion for *information technology* in travel and tourism, being relevant for the industry and responsible for society at large, as well as ensuring scientific excellence. **Structure** Board of Directors. **Languages** English. **Staff** 0.50 FTE, paid. **Finance** Sources: members' dues. **Activities** Events/meetings; knowledge management/information dissemination; networking/liaising. **Events** *ENTER : International Conference on Information Technology and Travel and Tourism* Izmir (Türkiye) 2024, *ENTER : International Conference on Information Technology and Travel and Tourism* Johannesburg (South Africa) 2023, *ENTER : International Conference on Information Technology and Travel and Tourism* Nicosia (Cyprus) 2019, *ENTER : International Conference on Information Technology and Travel and Tourism* Jönköping (Sweden) 2018, *ENTER : International Conference on Information Technology and Travel and Tourism* Rome (Italy) 2017. **Publications** Conference proceedings; short papers; workshop proceedings.
Members Individual and institutional membership. Members (over 200) in 39 countries and territories:
Australia, Austria, Belgium, Brazil, Bulgaria, Canada, China, Croatia, Denmark, Finland, France, Germany, Hong Kong, Iceland, India, Indonesia, Iran Islamic Rep, Israel, Italy, Japan, Kenya, Korea Rep, Netherlands, New Zealand, Nigeria, Norway, Poland, Portugal, Serbia, Slovenia, South Africa, Spain, Sweden, Switzerland, Taiwan, Türkiye, UK, United Arab Emirates, USA.
[2023.02.23/XD6083/**D**]

♦ International Federation for Inner Mission and Christian Social Work / see European Federation for Diaconia (#07099)
♦ International Federation of Insolvency, Bankruptcy and Turnaround Professionals / see International Federation of Restructuring, Insolvency and Bankruptcy Professionals (#13530)
♦ International Federation of Insolvency Professionals / see International Federation of Restructuring, Insolvency and Bankruptcy Professionals (#13530)
♦ International Federation of Inspection Agencies (inactive)
♦ International Federation of Institutes for Advanced Study (inactive)
♦ International Federation of Institutes for Medieval Studies (#09639)
♦ International Federation of Institutes for Socio-Religious Research (inactive)
♦ International Federation of Institutions for the Teaching of Spanish (inactive)
♦ International Federation of Intellectual Property Attorneys (#09624)
♦ International Federation of Intellectual Unions (inactive)

♦ International Federation of Interior Architects / Designers (IFI) 13460
Fédération internationale des architectes d'intérieur – Internationale Föderation der Innenarchitekten
Secretariat 155 East 44th Street, 6the floor, New York NY 10017, USA. T. +12128846275. Fax +12128846247. E-mail: info@ifiworld.org – staff@ifiworld.org.
Pres c/o Steve Leung Design, 30/F Manhattan Place, 23 Wang Tai Road, Kowloon, Hong Kong. T. +85225271600.
URL: http://www.ifiworld.org/
History 20 Sep 1963, Copenhagen (Denmark). Articles approved by Dutch Royal Decree dated 2 Feb 1970; amendment approved 21 May 1976. Present statutes adopted: 17 May 1978, Washington DC (USA); amended: 2 Aug 1981, Helsinki (Finland); 26 May 1983, Hamburg (Germany FR); 22 May 1989, Bergen (Norway); 9 Jun 1991, Chicago IL (USA). Former names and other names: *International Federation of Interior Designers (IFI)* – former; *Fédération internationale des architectes d'intérieur* – former; *Internationale Föderation der Innenarchitekten* – former. Registration: 501c6, USA, New York. **Aims** Expand, internationally and across all levels of society, the contribution of the interior architecture/design profession through exchange and development of knowledge and experience, in education practice and fellowship. **Structure** General Assembly (every 2 years); Executive Board; Advisory Council; Resources Council; Secretary General. **Languages** English, French. **Staff** 2.00 FTE, paid. **Finance** Sources: members' dues; sponsorship. **Activities** Events/meetings; knowledge management/information dissemination; networking/liaising; publishing activities; research and development; standards/guidelines. **Events** *Biennial General Assembly and Congress* Dubai (United Arab Emirates) 2020, *Busan International Architecture Design Workshop* Busan (Korea Rep) 2019, *Biennial General Assembly and Congress* Lagos (Nigeria) 2017, *Biennial General Assembly and Congress* Gwangju (Korea Rep) 2015, *Biennial General Assembly and Congress* Kuala Lumpur (Malaysia) 2014. **Publications** *IFI Newsletter* (annual); *Internatinal Interiors Annual* (every 2 years); *IFI e-newsletter*. Press releases; conference reports; various other publications.
Members Full national and professional associations, normally one per country; Associate institutes concerned with an aspect of interior design (such as qualifications, education, promotion, research) or associations not falling within full membership category; Affiliate international NGOs in related fields; Correspondent invited individuals representing countries with no full member; Sponsors. Full in 34 countries and territories:
Australia, Austria, Belgium, Brazil, China, Denmark, Estonia, Finland, France, Germany, Hong Kong, Iceland, India, Ireland, Israel, Italy, Japan, Korea Rep, Malaysia, Netherlands, Norway, Philippines, Puerto Rico, Singapore, South Africa, Spain, Sweden, Switzerland, Taiwan, Thailand, UK, Uruguay, USA.
Associates in 21 countries and territories:
Australia, Czechia, Finland, France, Hong Kong, India, Italy, Japan, Korea Rep, Malaysia, Mexico, Northern Cyprus, Norway, Slovakia, South Africa, Spain, Sweden, Switzerland, UK, United Arab Emirates, USA.
Correspondents (4) in 4 countries and territories:
Czechia, Lithuania, Nigeria, Russia.
International affiliates (4), listed in this Yearbook:
International Association of Art (IAA, #11710); *International Council of Design (ICoD, #13013)*; *International Council on Monuments and Sites (ICOMOS, #13049)*; *World Crafts Council AISBL (WCC International, #21342)*.
Consultative Status Consultative status granted from: *World Intellectual Property Organization (WIPO, #21593)* (Permanent Observer Status). **IGO Relations** *UNESCO (#20322)*. **NGO Relations** Together with: *Bureau of European Design Associations (BEDA, #03359)*, took over activities of *Comité européen d'architectes d'intérieurs (inactive)*.
[2018.03.15/XC1935/y/**C**]

♦ International Federation of Interior Designers / see International Federation of Interior Architects / Designers (#13460)
♦ International Federation of International Furniture Removers / see FIDI Global Alliance (#09753)
♦ International Federation for Interuniversity Sport (inactive)

♦ International Federation of Inventors' Associations (IFIA) 13461

Fédération internationale des associations d'inventeurs – Internationale Vereinigung der Erfinder-Verbände

Pres Palexpo, CP 112, Route François-Peyrot 30, Le Grand-Saconne, 1218 Geneva, Switzerland. T. +41227611111. Fax +41227860096. E-mail: info@ifia.com – president@ifia.com.
URL: https://www.ifia.com/

History 12 Jul 1968, London (UK). Registration: Swiss Civil Code, No/ID: 080.335.043, Start date: 2016, Switzerland, Geneva. **Aims** Connect and support inventors internationally and represent their common interests; disseminate the culture of invention and innovation development; protect inventors' rights; raise the status of inventors; promote inventive and entrepreneurial spirit; engage women in innovative activities; promote the culture of invention and innovation in Africa; encourage creativity among kids and youth. **Structure** General Assembly (every 2 years); President; Executive Committee; Directors. **Languages** English, French. **Staff** 30.00 FTE, voluntary. **Finance** Sources: donations; gifts, legacies; members' dues; sponsorship; subsidies. Other resources authorized by law. **Activities** Awards/prizes/competitions; events/meetings; knowledge management/information dissemination; training/education. **Events** *Electronic and Green Materials International Conference* Bandung (Indonesia) 2018, *Electronic and Green Materials International Conference* Krabi (Thailand) 2017, *World Congress* Istanbul (Turkey) 2016, *Extraordinary General Assembly* Nürburg (Germany) 2015, *World Congress* Stockholm (Sweden) 2015. **Publications** *IFIA Magazine* (annual); *IFIA Newsletter* (52 a year). Activity Report; brochures; calendars; reference books; guides; surveyx; studies.
Members Full; Corresponding; Collaborating. Members (185) in 105 countries and territories. Membership countries not specified.
Regional organizations (2):
Asian Alliance of Appropriate Technology Practitioners (APPROTECH ASIA, #01306); *International Energy Foundation (IEF, #13273)*.
Consultative Status Consultative status granted from: *World Intellectual Property Organization (WIPO, #21593)* (Permanent Observer Status); *UNCTAD (#20285)* (Special Category); *ECOSOC (#05331)* (Special). **IGO Relations** Consultative status with: *UNIDO (#20336)*. Member of Standing Advisory Committee of: *European Patent Office (EPO, #08166)*. **NGO Relations** Memorandum of Understanding with: *European Alliance for Innovation (EAI, #05872)*. [2022.06.14/XD3909/y/**C**]

♦ International Federation of Ironmongers' and Iron Merchants' Associations / see International Federation of Hardware and Housewares Associations (#13437)

♦ International Federation of Journalists (IFJ) 13462

Fédération internationale des journalistes (FIJ) – Federación Internacional de Periodistas (FIP) – Internationale Journalisten-Föderation (IJF)

SG IPC-Résidence Palace, Rue de la Loi 155, Bloc C, 1040 Brussels, Belgium. T. +3222352210 – +3222352200. Fax +3222352219. E-mail: ifj@ifj.org.
URL: http://www.ifj.org/

History 7 May 1952, Brussels (Belgium). Founded at 1st World Congress, as a continuation of earlier groups dating as far back as 1892, Antwerp (Belgium), when *International Union of Press Associations (IUPA, inactive)* was set up. A body with the same name as the current organization, *International Federation of Journalists, 1926 (inactive)*, created May 1926, Paris (France), was superseded, Jun 1946, Copenhagen (Denmark), together with *International Federation of Journalists of the Allied and Free Countries (inactive)*, by IOJ (based in Prague); and it was national organizations which had withdrawn from the latter body which were instrumental in setting up the present IFJ, 1952. The Declaration of Principles (Code of Conduct) was adopted at 2nd World Congress, 1954, Bordeaux (France) and amended at 18th World Congress, 1986, Helsinki (Finland); IFJ Mass Media Policies text adopted at 16th World Congress, 17-21 May 1982, Lugano (Switzerland). Current constitution revised, Jun 2016, Angers (France). Registration: Belgium. **Aims** Defend and enhance the working rights and conditions of journalists. **Structure** Congress (every 3 years); Executive Committee (meets at least twice a year); Working parties. European section: *European Federation of Journalists (EFJ, #07152)*. Membership open; congresses closed. **Languages** English, French, Spanish. **Staff** 14.00 FTE, paid. **Finance** Sources: members' dues. **Activities** Advocacy/lobbying/activism; financial and/or material support; research/documentation; training/education. **Events** *Congress* Muscat (Oman) 2022, *Congress* Tunis (Tunisia) 2019, *Congress* Angers (France) 2016, *World Journalists Conference* Seoul (Korea Rep) 2014, *Congress* Dublin (Ireland) 2013. **Publications** *IFJ Online* in English, French, Spanish. *For a Free Press and Free Journalism 1952-1977*. Brochures; manuals; reports.
Members National Unions (179), representing about 600,000 journalists, in 135 countries and territories:
Afghanistan, Albania, Angola, Argentina, Armenia, Australia, Austria, Azerbaijan, Bahrain, Belarus, Belgium, Benin, Bhutan, Bosnia-Herzegovina, Botswana, Brazil, Bulgaria, Burkina Faso, Burundi, Cambodia, Cameroon, Canada, Cape Verde, Chile, Colombia, Congo Brazzaville, Congo DR, Costa Rica, Côte d'Ivoire, Croatia, Cyprus, Czechia, Denmark, Djibouti, Dominican Rep, Ecuador, Estonia, Ethiopia, Faeroe Is, Finland, France, Gabon, Gambia, Georgia, Germany, Ghana, Greece, Guinea, Guinea-Bissau, Haiti, Hong Kong, Hungary, Iceland, India, Indonesia, Iran Islamic Rep, Iraq, Ireland, Italy, Jamaica, Japan, Jordan, Kazakhstan, Kenya, Korea Rep, Kuwait, Latvia, Lesotho, Liberia, Libya, Luxembourg, Malawi, Malaysia, Maldives, Mali, Mauritania, Mexico, Moldova, Monaco, Mongolia, Montenegro, Morocco, Mozambique, Myanmar, Nepal, Netherlands, New Caledonia, New Zealand, Niger, Nigeria, North Macedonia, Norway, Oman, Pakistan, Palestine, Panama, Paraguay, Peru, Philippines, Poland, Portugal, Romania, Russia, Rwanda, Senegal, Serbia, Sierra Leone, Slovakia, Slovenia, Somalia, South Africa, Spain, Sri Lanka, Sudan, Sweden, Switzerland, Taiwan, Tanzania UR, Thailand, Timor-Leste, Togo, Tunisia, Türkiye, Uganda, UK, Ukraine, United Arab Emirates, Uruguay, USA, Vanuatu, Venezuela, Yemen, Zambia, Zimbabwe.
Consultative Status Consultative status granted from: *ECOSOC (#05331)* (Special); *UNESCO (#20322)* (Associate Status); *World Intellectual Property Organization (WIPO, #21593)* (Permanent Observer Status); *Council of Europe (CE, #04881)* (Participatory Status).
NGO Relations Member of:
- *Africa Freedom of Information Centre (AFIC, #00175)*;
- *Culture First Coalition (inactive)*;
- *Federación Latinoamericana de Facultades de Comunicación Social (FELAFACS, #09353)*;
- *Global Forum for Media Development (GFMD, #10375)*;
- *Global Union Federations (GUF, #10638)*;
- *International Federation of Reproduction Rights Organizations (IFRRO, #13527)*;
- *Permanent Conference of Mediterranean Audiovisual Operators (COPEAM, #18320)*;
- *Redes de Comunicación de América Latina y el Caribe para el Desarrollo (G-8, no recent information)*.

Cooperates with: *GRET*; *International Press Institute (IPI, #14636)*; *World Association for Christian Communication (WACC, #21126)*. Supports: *Observatorio Control Interamericano de los Derechos de los Migrantes (OCIM, no recent information)*; *South East European Network for Professionalisation of the Media (SEENPM, #19817)*. Instrumental in setting up: *International News Safety Institute (INSI, #14364)*; *Play the Game (#18404)*. [2022/XC1937/**B**]

♦ International Federation of Journalists, 1926 (inactive)
♦ International Federation of Journalists of the Allied and Free Countries (inactive)
♦ International Federation of Kennel Clubs / see Fédération cynologique internationale (#09477)
♦ International Federation of Kidney Foundations / see International Federation of Kidney Foundations – World Kidney Alliance (#13463)

♦ International Federation of Kidney Foundations – World Kidney Alliance (IFKF-WKA) 13463

Secretariat c/o Tanker Foundation, Abiramee Apartments Flat No 11, 3rd fl, Old No 6 & New No 11 Thirumurthy Street, T Nagar, Chennai, Tamil Nadu 600017, Chennai TAMIL NADU 600017, India. E-mail: info@ifkf.org.
Registered Office Cordillera de los Andes 650 Col Lomas de Chapultepec, 11000 Mexico City CDMX, Mexico.
URL: https://ifkf.org/

History 1999. Previously registered in accordance with Panamanian law. Former names and other names: *International Federation of Kidney Foundations (IFKF)* – former. Registration: Mexico. **Aims** Promote better kidney health with primary, secondary and tertiary preventive measures; promote optimal treatment and care so as to maximize the health, quality of life, and longevity for people with or at high risk for developing Kidney Disease or Kidney Failure. **Structure** Council. Sub-committees. **Activities** Awards/prizes/competitions; events/meetings; research/documentation; training/education. **Events** *Annual Meeting* 2020, *Annual Meeting* Lyon (France) 2014, *Annual Meeting* Budapest (Hungary) 2012, *Annual meeting* Vancouver, BC (Canada) 2011, *Annual meeting* Kuala Lumpur (Malaysia) 2010.
Members Full in 14 countries and territories:
Bhutan, Canada, Egypt, Ghana, Guatemala, Hong Kong, Hungary, Italy, Malaysia, Mexico, Türkiye, USA, Yemen, Zimbabwe.
Associate in 5 countries:
India, Italy, Netherlands, UK, USA. [2022/XM2324/**C**]

♦ International Federation of Kitesports Organizations (IFKO) 13464

Contact Praceta de S Bras No 30, Areia do Guincho, 2750-058 Cascais, Portugal. T. +351214869324. E-mail: kitesports@ifkitesports.org.
URL: http://ifkitesports.org/

History Founded 2015. **Aims** Promote the ideals, principles and objectives behind the Olympic Movement; develop and promote the practice of kitesports worldwide for all categories of the population. **Structure** General Assembly; Executive Council; General Meetings Board; Fiscal Council. Working Committees.
Members Full in 10 countries:
Argentina, Dominican Rep, France, India, Italy, Mauritius, Mexico, Portugal, Spain, Türkiye.
Included in the above, 1 organization listed in this Yearbook:
International Kiteboarding Organization (IKO).
NGO Relations Member of: *The Association for International Sport for All (TAFISA, #02763)*. [2019/XM7399/**D**]

♦ International Federation of Knitting Technologists (IFKT) 13465

Fédération internationale des techniciens de la bonneterie (FITB) – Internationale Föderation von Wirkerei- und Strickerei-Fachleuten (IFWS)

Secretariat Am Bachmannsgraben 65, 41844 Wegberg, Germany. T. +4921611866010. Fax +4921611866013. E-mail: info@knittingfed.com.
Registered Address Hallwylstrasse 71, 8004 Zurich ZH, Switzerland.
URL: http://www.knittingfed.com/

History Founded 1956, Switzerland. **Aims** Bring together experts from knitting industries of different nations through the formation of informal groups in order to promote the interests of the knitting industry and to serve its technical and scientific development. **Structure** International Secretariat. **Languages** English, German. **Staff** Voluntary. **Finance** Members' dues. **Events** *Congress* Belfast (UK) 2022, *Congress* Belfast (UK) 2020, *Congress* Lódz (Poland) 2018, *Congress* Mönchengladbach (Germany) 2016, *Congress* Cesme (Turkey) 2014. **Publications** Meeting reports.
Members Associations in 16 countries:
Austria, Bulgaria, Croatia, Czechia, Germany, Hungary, Israel, Korea Rep, Poland, Romania, Russia, Slovenia, Switzerland, Türkiye, UK, Ukraine.
Individuals in 7 countries and territories:
Canada, Egypt, Finland, Korea Rep, Spain, Sweden, Taiwan. [2016.06.01/XD1941/**D**]

♦ International Federation of the Korean War Veterans' Associations (IFKWVA) 13466

Contact c/o KWVA, 4037 Chelsea Ln, Lakeland FL 33809-4063, USA. E-mail: kwvasec@gmail.com.
Dir Gen International Div of KVA, 7-13 Sincheon-dong, Songpa-gu, Seoul 138-792, Korea Rep.
URL: http://www.kwva.org/p_logo_ifkwva.htm

Aims Serve as an association of the nations which served in the Korean War under UN auspices. **Structure** General assembly. **Events** *General Assembly* Seoul (Korea Rep) 2008, *General Assembly* Seoul (Korea Rep) 2004, *General Assembly* Seoul (Korea Rep) 2000, *General Assembly* Seoul (Korea Rep) 1994, *General Assembly* Seoul (Korea Rep) 1990. **Members** Korean War veterans' associations (21). Membership countries not specified. **NGO Relations** *Association of Nordic War and UN Military Veterans (ANWUNMV, #02834)*. [2013.07.30/XE0905/**F**]

♦ International Federation of Landscape Architects (IFLA) 13467

Fédération internationale des architectes paysagistes – Federación Internacional de Arquitectos Paisajistas – Internationaler Verband der Landschafts-Architekten

Exec Sec Av Louise 149/24 – 12th floor, 1050 Brussels, Belgium. T. +32495568285. E-mail: admin@iflaworld.org – president@iflaworld.org.
URL: https://www.iflaworld.com/

History Sep 1948, Cambridge (UK). Founded following discussions having been held: 1935, Brussels (Belgium); 1937, Paris (France); 1938, Berlin (Germany). **Aims** Develop and promote: the *profession* of landscape architecture, together with its related arts and sciences, throughout the world; the understanding of landscape architecture as physical and cultural phenomena concerned with environmental heritage and ecological and social *sustainability*; the establishment of high standards of professional practice in landscape design, its management, conservation and development. **Structure** World Council (meets annually); Executive Committee; International Committees; Regional Councils (4): Africa; Americas; Asia-Pacific; *IFLA Europe (#11103)*. Committees (9). **Languages** English. **Staff** Part-time, voluntary. **Finance** Sources: donations; gifts, legacies; grants; meeting proceeds; members' dues. **Activities** Awards/prizes/competitions; events/meetings; research/documentation. **Events** *Annual World Congress* Gwangju (Korea Rep) 2022, *Annual World Congress* George Town (Malaysia) 2021, *Annual World Congress* George Town (Malaysia) 2020, *Asia Pacific Regional Congress* Cebu City (Philippines) 2019, *Annual World Congress* Oslo (Norway) 2019. **Publications** *IFLA Newsletter* (4 a year); *Yearbook* in English. Congress reports; working papers; press information; reports on education.
Members National professional associations of landscape architects, each nation being represented by only one association (approved by IFLA), in 71 countries and territories:
Argentina, Australia, Austria, Belgium, Bermuda, Bolivia, Brazil, Bulgaria, Canada, Chile, China, Colombia, Costa Rica, Croatia, Czechia, Denmark, Ecuador, Estonia, Finland, France, Germany, Greece, Hong Kong, Hungary, Iceland, India, Indonesia, Iran Islamic Rep, Ireland, Israel, Italy, Japan, Kenya, Korea Rep, Latvia, Lithuania, Luxembourg, Malawi, Malaysia, Mexico, Morocco, Netherlands, New Zealand, Nigeria, Norway, Panama, Paraguay, Peru, Philippines, Poland, Portugal, Puerto Rico, Romania, Russia, Serbia, Singapore, Slovakia, Slovenia, South Africa, Spain, Sri Lanka, Sweden, Switzerland, Taiwan, Thailand, Türkiye, UK, Ukraine, Uruguay, USA, Venezuela.
Individuals in 11 countries:
Bhutan, Cyprus, Dominican Rep, Egypt, Georgia, Malta, Pakistan, Saudi Arabia, Tunisia, United Arab Emirates, Zambia.
Consultative Status Consultative status granted from: *UNESCO (#20322)* (Consultative Status). **IGO Relations** Accredited by (1): *United Nations Office at Vienna (UNOV, #20604)*. **NGO Relations** Working relations with: *International Council on Monuments and Sites (ICOMOS, #13049)*; *International Council of Museums (ICOM, #13051)*; *World Design Organization (WDO, #21358)*; *Union internationale des architectes (UIA, #20419)*. Associate partner of: *World Urban Campaign (WUC, #21893)*. Memorandum of Understanding with: *World Urban Parks (#21894)*. [2022/XC1942/**B**]

♦ International Federation der Landwirtschaftlichen Geistesarbeiter (inactive)

♦ International Federation of Language Teacher Associations 13468

Fédération internationale des professeurs de langues vivantes (FIPLV) – Federación Internacional de Profesores de Lenguas Vivas

Pres Univ of Westminster, 309 Regent Street, London, W1B 2HW, UK. T. +447779309852.
SG Werther Inst, Avda Barão do Rio Branco 2288/1605, Juiz de Fora MG, 36016-901, Brazil.
URL: http://fiplv.com/

History 4 Apr 1931, Paris (France). Statutes drafted 16 July 1931 and amended: 19 Dec 1959, Amsterdam (Netherlands); Mar 1969; 19 Oct 1973; 22 Mar 1992; 14 Nov 1992; 21 July 2002; 1 July 2003; 1 Sep 2009; 14 Nov 2018. Former names and other names: *World Federation of Foreign-Language Teachers' Associations* – former; *World Federation of Modern Language Associations* – former. **Aims** Support, develop and promote languages, language learning and teaching, and multilingualism through professional associations. **Structure** World Assembly (every 3 years); Executive Committee. **Languages** English, Esperanto, French, German, Italian, Russian, Spanish. **Staff** Voluntary. **Finance** Sources: meeting proceeds; members' dues; revenue from activities/projects. **Activities** Events/meetings; projects/programmes; research/documentation. **Events** *World Congress of Modern Languages* Auckland (New Zealand) 2024, *World Congress of Modern Languages* Warsaw

(Poland) 2022, *World Congress of Modern Languages* Warsaw (Poland) 2021, *Triennial Congress* New Orleans, LA (USA) 2018, *Triennial Congress* Niagara Falls, ON (Canada) 2015. **Publications** *History of the Fédération International des Professeur de Langues Vivantes* (2009); *Languages Teaching: A Worldwide Perspective* (2006); *Linguistic Diversity in the Pacific* (2006) by D Cunningham et al; *An International Perspective on Language Policies, Practices and Proficiencies* (2005); *European Year of Languages 2001* (2002); *Language Teaching and Tolerance – Collection of Materials for Teachers* (1998) in English, French; *Formation Autonome: a European Self-Study Professional Development Project for Language Teachers.* Proceedings of colloquia and workshops; videos; educational materials.
Members Branches of international unilingual associations (6), listed in this Yearbook:
ESPERANTO + EDUKADO (ILEI, #05544); Fédération internationale des professeurs de français (FIPF, #09652); International Association of Teachers of English as a Foreign Language (IATEFL, #12222); Internationale Deutschlehrerverband / Der (IDV, #13228); Mezdunarodnaja Associacija Prepodavatelej Russkogo Jazyka i Literatury (MAPRYAL, #16739); Sociedade Internacional Portugues / Lingua Estrangeira (SIPLE, #19356).
National multilingual associations in 28 countries:
Australia, Bulgaria, Canada, Colombia, Czechia, Estonia, Finland, France, Georgia, Hungary, Iceland, Italy, Latvia, Lithuania, Malaysia, Netherlands, New Zealand, Poland, Russia, Serbia, Slovenia, Somalia, South Africa, Sri Lanka, Sweden, Switzerland, UK, USA.
Consultative Status Consultative status granted from: *Council of Europe (CE, #04881)* (Participatory Status); *ECOSOC (#05331)* (Ros C); *UNESCO (#20322)* (Consultative Status). **IGO Relations** Accredited by (1): *United Nations Office at Vienna (UNOV, #20604).* **NGO Relations** Member of (1): *European Civil Society Platform for Multilingualism (ECSPM, #06569).* Actively participates in initiatives of: *Association internationale de linguistique appliquée (AILA, #02713).* [2022.10.12/XA1959/y/**A**]

♦ International Federation for Latin American and Caribbean Studies (#09338)
♦ International Federation of Law Students (inactive)
♦ International Federation of League of Nations Societies (inactive)
♦ International Federation of Leagues Against Anti-Semitism (inactive)
♦ International Federation of Leagues for the Defence of the Rights of Man and of Citizens / see International Federation for Human Rights (#13452)
♦ International Federation of Leather Guilds (internationally oriented national body)
♦ International Federation of Legal and Fiscal Consultants (inactive)
♦ International Federation of Liberal and Radical Youth / see International Federation of Liberal Youth (#13469)

♦ International Federation of Liberal Youth (IFLRY) 13469

Fédération internationale des jeunesses libérales – Federación Internacional de las Juventudes Liberales – Internationale Federatie van Liberale Jongeren
SG Mulackstrasse 29, 10119 Berlin, Germany. T. +491713780240. E-mail: office@iflry.org.
URL: http://www.iflry.org/
History 26 Aug 1947, Cambridge (UK). Founded 1947, in succession to *International Union of Radical, Liberal and Democratic Youth (inactive)*, set up 1929, Berlin (Germany), as *World Federation of Liberal and Radical Youth (WFLRY) – Fédération mondiale des jeunesses libérales et radicales (FMJLR)*, following decision taken 7 Nov 1945, London (UK). Constitution amended Sep 1965, Bremen (Germany FR). Joined *European Federation of Liberal and Radical Youth (EFLRY, inactive)*, 1979. . Former names and other names: *International Federation of Liberal and Radical Youth (IFLRY)* – former (1979 to 2001); *Fédération internationale des jeunesses libérales et radicales* – former (1979 to 2001); *Federación Internacional de las Juventudes Liberales y Radicales* – former (1979 to 2001); *Internationale Federatie van Liberale en Radicale Jongeren* – former (1979 to 2001). Registration: Belgium. **Aims** Provide means of cooperation between national liberal and radical youth organizations; promote friendship between liberal and radical youth of all countries; encourage young liberals and radicals to form organizations in those countries where such do not exist; cooperate with the Liberal International in the pursuit of common aims; encourage cooperation and interchange of ideas between student organizations of liberal tendency. **Structure** General Assembly (annual); Executive Committee; Bureau; Office based in Berlin, Germany. **Languages** English, French, Spanish. **Staff** 2.00 FTE, paid. Several voluntary. **Finance** Sources: government support; grants; international organizations; members' dues. **Activities** Awareness raising; events/meetings; projects/programmes. **Events** *General Assembly and Conference* Cape Town (South Africa) 2019, *General Assembly and Conference* Vienna (Austria) 2015, *Conference* Budapest (Hungary) 2012, *Conference* Chisinau (Moldova) 2012, *Conference* Istanbul (Turkey) 2011. **Publications** *IFLRY Newsletter* (12 a year). Seminar and delegation reports.
Members Full; Observer; Candidate. Full in 46 countries and territories:
Andorra, Argentina, Armenia, Austria, Azerbaijan, Belarus, Bosnia-Herzegovina, Bulgaria, Canada, Colombia, Costa Rica, Côte d'Ivoire, Croatia, Denmark, Egypt, Estonia, Finland, France, Georgia, Germany, Gibraltar, Honduras, Jordan, Lebanon, Lithuania, Moldova, Montenegro, Morocco, Nepal, Netherlands, North Macedonia, Norway, Paraguay, Peru, Poland, Russia, Senegal, Slovenia, South Africa, Sri Lanka, Sweden, Switzerland, Türkiye, UK, Ukraine, USA.
Observer in 4 countries:
Dominican Rep, Egypt, Ghana, Tanzania UR.
Consultative Status Consultative status granted from: *Council of Europe (CE, #04881)* (Participatory Status); *ECOSOC (#05331)* (Special). **IGO Relations** Cooperates with: *European Parliament (EP, #08146); European Youth Centres (EYCs, #09138); European Youth Foundation (EYF, #09141).* Associated with Department of Global Communications of the United Nations. **NGO Relations** Member of: *Espacio Iberoamericano de Juventud (EIJ, no recent information); European Youth Forum (#09140); Liberal International (LI, #16454); UNITED for Intercultural Action – European Network Against Nationalism, Racism, Fascism and in Support of Migrants and Refugees (UNITED, #20511).* Supports: *European Citizens' Initiative Campaign (ECI Campaign, #06558).* Instrumental in setting up *Juventudes Liberales de las Américas (JuLiA, #16174)* in 2005. [2020.09.07/XC3526/**C**]

♦ International Federation of Library Associations / see International Federation of Library Associations and Institutions (#13470)

♦ International Federation of Library Associations and Institutions (IFLA) 13470

Fédération internationale des associations de bibliothécaires et des bibliothèques – Federación Internacional de Asociaciones de Bibliotecarios y de Bibliotecas – Internationaler Verband der bibliothekarischen Vereine und Institutionen – Mezdunarodnaja Federacija Bibliotecnyh Associacij i Ucrezdenij
Acting SG IFLA Headquarters, Prins Willem-Alexanderhof 5, 2595 BE The Hague, Netherlands. T. +31703140884. E-mail: ifla@ifla.org.
URL: http://www.ifla.org/
History 30 Sep 1927, Edinburgh (UK). Founded at 50th Anniversary Conference of the British Library Association, when representatives of 15 countries signed the resolution. Statutes adopted 1929, Rome (Italy); modified: 1930; 1964; 1967. Statutes changed and present name adopted at 42nd Council meeting, 23 Aug 1976, Lausanne (Switzerland); Statutes amended at the following Council meetings: 49th, 21 and 26 Aug 1983, Munich (Germany FR); 51st, 18 Aug 1985, Chicago IL (USA); 53rd, 16 Aug 1987, Brighton (UK) 1987; 55th, 20 Aug 1989, Paris (France). New Statutes adopted, 14 Aug 2008; Québec QC (Canada). Rules of Procedure adopted by the Council, 27 Aug 1979; amended by the Council in 1983, 1985, 1987, 1989, 1993, 2001. New Statutes and Rules of Procedure adopted, 26 Aug 2021, amended by the Governing Board 2022. Former names and other names: *International Federation of Library Associations* – former; *Fédération internationale des associations de bibliothécaires (FIAB)* – former; *Internationaler Verband der Bibliothekar-Vereine* – former. Registration: Netherlands. **Aims** Promote high standards of delivery of library and *information services*; encourage widespread understanding of the value and importance of high quality library and information services in the private, public and voluntary sectors; represent the interests of members worldwide; encourage appropriate forms of association with IFLA in countries where library associations are non-existent or too weak to take an active part in international activity. **Structure** General Assembly (annual); World Library and Information Congress (annual); Governing Board; Professional Council; Regional Council; Professional Divisions (8) with Sections; Special Interest Groups; Regional Divisions (6); Advisory Committees (4) with Review Groups (4); Regional Offices (3); Language Centres (4). Headquarters in The Hague (Netherlands). **Languages** Arabic, Chinese, English, French, German, Russian, Spanish. **Staff** 20.00 FTE, paid. **Finance** Sources: donations; gifts, legacies; government support; grants; members' dues; sale of publications. **Activities** Advocacy/lobbying/activism; awards/prizes/competitions; awareness raising; capacity building; events/meetings; guidance/assistance/consulting; knowledge management/information dissemination; networking/liaising; projects/programmes; publishing activities; standards/guidelines; training/education. **Events** *World Library and Information Congress (WLIC) : Annual General Conference and Assembly* Rotterdam (Netherlands) 2023, *World Library and Information Congress (WLIC) : Annual General Conference and Assembly* Dublin (Ireland) 2022, *World Library and Information Congress (WLIC) : Annual General Conference and Assembly* The Hague (Netherlands) 2021, *World Library and Information Congress (WLIC) : Annual General Conference and Assembly* Dublin (Ireland) 2020, *Conference on Interlending and Document Supply* Prague (Czechia) 2019. **Publications** *IFLA Journal* (4 a year); *International Cataloguing and Bibliographic Control* (4 a year) – also annual; *IFLA Newsletter* – from Sections and Round Tables. *IFLA Statutes and Rules of Procedure* in English, French, German, Spanish. Annual Report; monograph series; professional reports; brochures. **Information Services** *IFLA-L* – mailing list; *LIBJOBS* – mailing list for job seekers.
Members Total members: over 1,500 in 139 countries and territories:
Albania, Argentina, Armenia, Australia, Austria, Azerbaijan, Bahamas, Bangladesh, Barbados, Belarus, Belgium, Belize, Bhutan, Bolivia, Bosnia-Herzegovina, Botswana, Brazil, Brunei Darussalam, Bulgaria, Canada, Chile, China, Colombia, Costa Rica, Croatia, Curaçao, Cyprus, Czechia, Denmark, Dominican Rep, Ecuador, Egypt, El Salvador, England, England and Wales, Estonia, Eswatini, Ethiopia, Faeroe Is, Fiji, Finland, France, Georgia, Germany, Ghana, Gibraltar, Greece, Guam, Holy See, Honduras, Hong Kong, Hungary, Iceland, India, Indonesia, Iran Islamic Rep, Iraq, Ireland, Israel, Italy, Jamaica, Japan, Jordan, Kazakhstan, Kenya, Korea DPR, Korea Rep, Kosovo, Latvia, Lebanon, Lesotho, Liechtenstein, Lithuania, Luxembourg, Malawi, Malaysia, Maldives, Malta, Mauritius, Mexico, Moldova, Montenegro, Morocco, Myanmar, Namibia, Netherlands, New Zealand, Nigeria, North Macedonia, Norway, Oman, Pakistan, Palau, Palestine, Panama, Paraguay, Peru, Philippines, Poland, Portugal, Puerto Rico, Qatar, Romania, Russia, Samoa, Saudi Arabia, Scotland, Senegal, Serbia, Sierra Leone, Singapore, Slovakia, Slovenia, Somalia, South Africa, Spain, Sri Lanka, Suriname, Sweden, Switzerland, Taiwan, Tanzania UR, Thailand, Trinidad-Tobago, Tunisia, Türkiye, Tuvalu, Uganda, UK, Ukraine, United Arab Emirates, Uruguay, USA, Uzbekistan, Vanuatu, Vietnam, Wales, Zambia, Zimbabwe.
Consultative Status Consultative status granted from: *ECOSOC (#05331)* (Ros C); *UNESCO (#20322)* (Associate Status); *World Intellectual Property Organization (WIPO, #21593)* (Permanent Observer Status). **IGO Relations** Accredited by (1): *United Nations Office at Vienna (UNOV, #20604).* Regular cooperation between Asia regional office and: *UNESCO Asia and Pacific Regional Bureau for Education (#20301).* Associated with Department of Global Communications of the United Nations. **NGO Relations** Member of (5): *Conference of Non-Governmental Organizations in Consultative Relationship with the United Nations (CONGO, #04635); Copyright for Creativity (C4C, #04832); International Council for Scientific and Technical Information (ICSTI, #13070); International Science Council (ISC, #14796); Transparency, Accountability and Participation Network (TAP Network, #20222).* Instrumental in setting up (4): *Association internationale francophone des bibliothécaires et documentalistes (AIFBD, #02703); Blue Shield International (BSI, #03286); International Association of Library Centres (IALC, inactive); International Committee of the Blue Shield (ICBS, inactive).* Asian regional office is member of: *Asian Pacific Regional Coordinating Committee (no recent information).* Proposes setting up: *Association des documentalistes parlementaires francophones africains (no recent information).* [2023.02.14/XA1945/y/**A**]

♦ International Federation for the Lipizzaner Horse / see Lipizzan International Federation (#16487)
♦ International Federation of Lithographers, Process Workers and Kindred Trades (inactive)

♦ International Federation of Little Brothers of the Poor (IFLBP) 13471

Fédération internationale des petits frères des pauvres (FIPFP)
SG 33 av Parmentier, 75011 Paris, France. T. +33149231300. Fax +33147009466.
Pres address not obtained.
URL: http://www.petitsfreres.org/
History 31 Oct 1979, Rolle (Switzerland). Founded by 4 founding members. Statutes adopted by General Assembly, 4 Jun 2004, Montréal (Canada); most recently adopted, Nov 2016, Berlin (Germany). Previously registered in accordance with Swiss Code. Registration: RNA, No/ID: W751208105, Start date: 2011, France. **Aims** Promote expansion of the action of Little Brothers around the world; participate in the network of international organizations through exchange of expertise in the area of *aging* and in problems related to exclusion, loneliness and isolation. **Structure** General Assembly (annual); Board of Directors. **Languages** English, French, Spanish. **Staff** Voluntary. **Finance** Members' dues. Public donations. **Events** *Biennial General Assembly* Philadelphia, PA (USA) 2008, *Biennial General Assembly* Paris (France) 2006, *Biennial General Assembly* Montréal, QC (Canada) 2004, *Biennial General Assembly* Barcelona (Spain) 2001, *Biennial General Assembly* Acapulco (Mexico) 1999.
Members National organizations in 10 countries:
Canada, France, Germany, Ireland, Mexico, Poland, Romania, Spain, Switzerland, USA.
IGO Relations Accredited by: *United Nations Office at Vienna (UNOV, #20604).* **NGO Relations** Member of: *Conference of Non-Governmental Organizations in Consultative Relationship with the United Nations (CONGO, #04635).* [2019/XF0787/**F**]

♦ International Federation of Logistics and SCM Systems (IFLS) 13472

Contact 1-2-1 Izumi-chou, Narashino, Chiba, 275-8575 Japan. T. +81474742633. Fax +81474742633. E-mail: wakabayashi.keizou@nihon-u.ac.jp.
URL: http://ifls-world.jp/
History Mar 2003. **Aims** Enhance logistics and SCM research; exchange technology and science; collaborate research activities concerned; promote and disseminate research results and real cases. **Structure** Board, comprising Chairman, Vice-Chairmen and members. **Events** *International Congress on Logistic and Supply Chain Management Systems* Taipei (Taiwan) 2019, *International Congress on Logistic and Supply Chain Management Systems* Ho Chi Minh City (Vietnam) 2018, *International Congress on Logistic and Supply Chain Management Systems* Beijing (China) 2017, *International Congress on Logistic and Supply Chain Management Systems* Chiang Mai (Thailand) 2015, *International Congress on Logistic and Supply Chain Management Systems* Poznań (Poland) 2014.
Members Full in 8 countries:
Australia, China, Japan, Korea Rep, Netherlands, Singapore, Taiwan, Thailand.
NGO Relations *Asia Pacific Federation of Logistics and SCM Systems (APFLS, #01901).* [2014/XJ7119/**D**]

♦ International Federation of Lusophone Veterinarians (#09285)

♦ International Federation of Magic Societies 13473

Fédération Internationale des Sociétés Magiques (FISM) – Federación Internacional de Sociedades Magicas – Internationaler Verband Magischer Gesellschaften
Pres address not obtained. E-mail: craigmitchell@fism.org – info@fism.org.
Sec address not obtained.
URL: http://www.fism.org/
History 1948, Lausanne (Switzerland). **Aims** Enhance the art of magic. **Structure** General Assembly; Board of Directors; Executive Board. Continental divisions (6): Africa; Asia; Europe; Latin America; North America; Oceania. **Languages** English, French, German, Spanish. **Staff** 3.00 FTE, voluntary. **Finance** Sources: members' dues. **Activities** Championships. **Events** *Triennial Convention* Québec, QC (Canada) 2022, *Triennial Convention* Québec, QC (Canada) 2021, *Triennial Convention* Busan (Korea Rep) 2018, *Triennial Convention* Rimini (Italy) 2015, *Triennial Convention* Blackpool (UK) 2012. **Publications** *FISM Newsletter.*
Members Magicians' societies in 44 countries and territories:
Albania, Argentina, Australia, Austria, Belgium, Brazil, Bulgaria, Canada, Chile, China, Colombia, Czechia, Denmark, Ecuador, Finland, France, Germany, Greece, Guatemala, Hong Kong, Hungary, Israel, Italy, Japan, Korea Rep, Luxembourg, Malaysia, Mexico, Netherlands, Norway, Peru, Philippines, Poland, Portugal, Russia, Singapore, South Africa, Spain, Sweden, Switzerland, Taiwan, Thailand, UK, USA.
Included in the above, 1 organization listed in this Yearbook:
International Brotherhood of Magicians (IBM, #12402). [2022/XD1947/**C**]

♦ International Federation of Mallyuddha (unconfirmed)
♦ International Federation of Mammalogists (see: #15760)
♦ International Federation of Management and Professional Staff in the Chemical and Related Industries / see European Federation of Managerial Staff in the Chemical and Allied Industries (#07160)
♦ International Federation of the Managerial Staff of Agricultural and Alimentary Industry and Commerce (inactive)

- ♦ International Federation of Manual Medicine / see Fédération internationale de médecine manuelle (#09642)
- ♦ International Federation of Manual/Musculoskeletal Medicine (#09642)
- ♦ International Federation of Manufacturers and Converters of Pressure-Sensitive and Heatseals on Paper and Other Base Materials / see FINAT (#09773)
- ♦ International Federation of Manufacturers of Gummed Paper (#09631)
- ♦ International Federation of Marfan Syndrome Organizations / see Marfan World (#16574)
- ♦ International Federation of Margarine Associations (inactive)

♦ International Federation of Maritime Associations and Navy Leagues 13474

Federación Internacional de Ligas y Asociaciones Marítimas y Navales (FIDALMAR)

SG c/o Real Liga Naval Española, C/Mayor no 16, 28013 Madrid, Spain. T. +34913664494. Fax +34913661284.

History 1978. **Structure** General Assembly. **Events** *General Assembly* Valencia (Spain) 2007, *General Assembly* Santo Domingo (Dominican Rep) 2006, *General Assembly* Belém (Brazil) 2003, *General Assembly* Rio de Janeiro (Brazil) 2000.
Members Full in 13 countries:
Argentina, Brazil, Chile, Colombia, Cuba, Curaçao, Dominica, Italy, Mexico, Netherlands, Panama, Peru, Portugal, Spain, USA.
[2015.01.09/XM3671/**D**]

- ♦ International Federation of Maritime Philately (inactive)

♦ International Federation of Marriage Preparation Centres 13475

Fédération internationale des centres de préparation au mariage (FICPM)

Sec Ave du Bouchet 13, 1209 Geneva, Switzerland. T. +41227964923.
URL: http://www.ficpm.org/

History 7 May 1978, Turin (Italy). Founded, on the initiative of Alphonse D'Heily, when statutes were adopted. Statutes most recently modified: 2 May 2003, Lignano Sabbiadoro (Italy); 3 May 2013, Assisi (Italy). Registration: ASBL, Luxembourg. **Aims** Establish and maintain contacts with countries from Central Europe and Mozambique and Cape Verde. **Structure** General Assembly (annual); Board of Directors; Board of Presidency; Consultative Committee. **Languages** English, French. **Staff** 5.00 FTE, voluntary. **Finance** Members' dues. Other sources: subventions from befriended organizations. Budget (2014): euro 6,930. **Events** *International Days / Annual Congress* Valencia (Spain) 2014, *International Days / Annual Congress* Assisi (Italy) 2013, *Annual Congress* Québec, QC (Canada) 2012, *International Days* Québec, QC (Canada) 2012, *Annual Congress* Krk (Croatia) 2011. **Publications** *Les cahiers de la FICPM* (periodical). Congress proceedings.
Members Active national Catholic associations and organizations in 10 countries:
Belgium, Canada, France, Italy, Luxembourg, Madagascar, Portugal, Slovenia, Spain, Switzerland.
Associate in 11 countries and territories:
Croatia, Czechia, Hungary, Madagascar, Malta, Mauritius, Netherlands, Réunion, Rodriguez Is, Seychelles, Slovakia.
[2019/XE1686/**D**]

- ♦ International Federation of Married Catholic Priests (inactive)
- ♦ International Federation of Masons (inactive)
- ♦ International Federation of Master Cotton Spinners' and Manufacturers' Associations / see International Textile Manufacturers Federation (#15679)
- ♦ International Federation of Master Cotton Spinners and Manufacturers' Associations (inactive)
- ♦ International Federation of Master-Craftsmen (inactive)
- ♦ International Federation of Match Poker (unconfirmed)
- ♦ International Federation of Mazdaznan Women (inactive)
- ♦ International Federation of Meat Traders' Associations / see International Butchers' Confederation (#12421)
- ♦ International Federation of Medal Producers / see International Art Medal Federation (#11675)
- ♦ International Federation of Medals / see International Art Medal Federation (#11675)

♦ International Federation of Medical Associations of Neural Therapy (IFMANT) 13476

Internationaler Dachverband der Medizinischen Gesellschaften für Neuraltherapie – Federación Internacional de Asociaciones Médicas de Terapia Neural

Contact Gemeindemattenstr 4, PO Box 659, 3860 Meiringen BE, Switzerland. T. +41339716155. Fax +41339716154. E-mail: info@santh.ch.
Sec Hirschgasslein 11-15, 4051 Basel BS, Switzerland.
URL: https://www.ifmant.at/

Structure Steering Committee.
Members Full in 13 countries:
Austria, Belgium, Brazil, Bulgaria, Colombia, Germany, Greece, Hungary, Italy, Netherlands, Spain, Switzerland, Türkiye.
[2021/AA1883/**D**]

♦ International Federation for Medical and Biological Engineering (IFMBE) 13477

Fédération internationale du génie médical et biologique – Federación Internacional de Ingenieria Médica y Biológica – Internationale Federation für Medizinische und Biologische Technik

SG address not obtained. E-mail: contact@ifmbe.org.
URL: https://www.ifmbe.org/

History 1959, Paris (France). Founded at 2nd International conference. New statutes adopted 1984; most recent statutes adopted 2003. Former names and other names: *International Federation for Medical Electronics* – former; *Fédération internationale d'électronique médicale* – former; *International Federation for Medical Electronics and Biological Engineering* – former. **Aims** Encourage, support, represent and unify the worldwide medical and biological engineering community in order to promote health and quality of life through advancement of research, development, application and management of technology. **Structure** General Assembly (every 3 years, at Congress); Administrative Council. Divisions; Committees; Working Groups. Includes: International Academy of Medical and Biological Engineering (IAMBE). **Languages** English. **Staff** 6.00 FTE, voluntary. **Finance** Sources: meeting proceeds; members' dues; sale of publications. **Activities** Awards/prizes/competitions; events/meetings. **Events** *NBC: Nordic-Baltic Conference on Biomedical Engineering and Medical Physics* Liepaja (Latvia) 2023, *MEDICON: Mediterranean Conference on Medical and Biological Engineering and Computing* Sarajevo (Bosnia-Herzegovina) 2023, *APCMBE: IFMBE Asian Pacific Conference on Medical and Biological Engineering* Suzhou (China) 2023, *IUPESM World Congress on Medical Physics and Biomedical Engineering (IUPESM WC2022)* Singapore (Singapore) 2022, *International Biomedical Engineering Conference* Seoul (Korea Rep) 2021. **Publications** *Journal of Medical and Biological Engineering and Computing (MBEC)* (6 a year); *IFMBE News* (6 a year); *IFMBE Directory* (annual) – online. *IFMBE Proceeding Series. Clinical Engineering Monographs.* Conference Digests.
Members Honorary Life; Affiliated. National Affiliated Organizations in 67 countries and territories:
Argentina, Australia, Austria, Belgium, Benin, Bosnia-Herzegovina, Brazil, Bulgaria, Canada, Chile, China, Colombia, Congo DR, Costa Rica, Croatia, Cuba, Cyprus, Czechia, Denmark, El Salvador, Estonia, Ethiopia, Finland, France, Germany, Ghana, Greece, Hong Kong, Hungary, Iceland, Ireland, Israel, Italy, Japan, Kenya, Korea Rep, Latvia, Lithuania, Macau, Malaysia, Mexico, Moldova, Mongolia, Netherlands, Nigeria, Panama, Peru, Poland, Portugal, Romania, Rwanda, Serbia, Singapore, Slovakia, Slovenia, South Africa, Spain, Sweden, Switzerland, Taiwan, Thailand, Uganda, UK, Ukraine, USA, Venezuela, Vietnam.
Transnational Affiliated organizations (6), include:
Consejo Regional de Ingeniería Biomédica para América Latina (CORAL, #04724); European Alliance for Medical and Biological Engineering and Science (EAMBES, #05873); Institute of Electrical and Electronics Engineers (IEEE, #11259) (EMBS).
Consultative Status Consultative status granted from: *ECOSOC (#05331)* (Ros C); *WHO (#20950)* (Official Relations); *UNIDO (#20336)*. **IGO Relations** Participates in the work of: *United Nations Economic Commission for Europe (UNECE, #20555)*. Accredited by: *United Nations Office at Vienna (UNOV, #20604)*. Associated with Department of Global Communications of the United Nations. **NGO Relations** Instrumental in setting up (2): *European Alliance for Medical and Biological Engineering and Science (EAMBES, #05873); International Union for Physical and Engineering Sciences in Medicine (IUPESM, #15799)*. Conference on Medical and Biological Engineering is held jointly with Conference on Medical Physics of *International Organization for Medical Physics (IOMP, #14453)*.
[2023/XC1829/y/**C**]

- ♦ International Federation for Medical Electronics / see International Federation for Medical and Biological Engineering (#13477)
- ♦ International Federation for Medical Electronics and Biological Engineering / see International Federation for Medical and Biological Engineering (#13477)
- ♦ International Federation for Medical Psychotherapy / see International Federation for Psychotherapy (#13523)
- ♦ International Federation of Medical Records Organizations / see International Federation of Health Information Management Associations (#13441)

♦ International Federation of Medical Students' Associations (IFMSA) 13478

Fédération Internationale des Associations d'Étudiants en Médecine – Federación Internacional de Asociaciones de Estudiantes de Medicina

Head of Secretariat Nørre Allé 14, 2200 Copenhagen N, Denmark. T. +4530117713. E-mail: gs@ifmsa.org.
URL: http://ifmsa.org/

History Leading up to foundation, a Student International Clinical Conference (SICC) was held, 1948, UK, at the initiative of *International Union of Students (IUS, inactive)*. An international congress on the establishment of such a federation was held, Dec 1950, Paris (France), when Denmark was assigned to investigate the possibilities of receiving financial support from the World Health Organization. The rough outline of a constitution was drawn up, 26-28 May 1951, Copenhagen (Denmark), at meeting of representatives of 8 countries (Sweden, Denmark, Norway, Finland, Germany, Netherlands, Switzerland, UK and Austria). A provisional body under British chairmanship was created to investigate establishing a stable federation, and 3 committees were formed: Standing Committee on Medical Exchange (SCOME, under the responsibility of Netherlands), Standing Committee on Professional Exchange (SCOPE, under that of Denmark) and Standing Committee on Students' Health (SCOSH, under Finland). Current constitution adopted, Mar 2000, Kuopio (Finland), at extraordinary General Assembly. General Secretariat originally located in Copenhagen, 1951. Temporarily transferred to Canada, 1962, before returning to Copenhagen, 1963. Moved to London, 1970, Helsinki (Finland), 1971, Vienna (Austria), 1978, L'Aquila (Italy), 1987, and Amsterdam (Netherlands), 1989. In 1999, an agreement was reached with the World Medical Association (WMA) and the General Secretariat was moved to Geneva, in Ferney-Voltaire (France). In 2014, moved back to AMC in Amsterdam; moved back to Copenhagen (Denmark), 2018. Registration: EU Transparency Register, No/ID: 431215415539-52, Start date: 12 Jan 2015; Chamber of Commerce, No/ID: 40538062, Denmark. **Aims** Unite medical students worldwide to lead initiatives that impact positively the communities served. **Structure** General Assembly (twice a year); Executive Board; Supervising Council; Standing Committees; General Secretariat, located in Copenhagen (Denmark). **Languages** English. **Staff** 1.00 FTE, paid. Several voluntary. **Finance** Sources: contributions; grants; members' dues; sale of products. **Activities** Advocacy/lobbying/activism; capacity building; events/meetings; networking/liaising; training/education. Active in all member countries. **Events** *General Assembly* Istanbul (Türkiye) 2022, *Asia-Pacific Regional Meeting* Kuala Lumpur (Malaysia) 2022, *General Assembly* 2021, *General Assembly* Panama (Panama) 2021, *General Assembly* 2020. **Publications** *Medical Student International (MSI)* (2 a year) – thematic magazine. Annual Report; IFMSA Booklet; IFMSA Information Leaflet.
Members Restricted to national organizations of medical students (139) – no personal affiliates except Honorary Life Members. Full; Associate, Candidate: national organizations in 122 countries and territories:
Algeria, Antigua-Barbuda, Argentina, Armenia, Australia, Austria, Azerbaijan, Bangladesh, Belgium, Benin, Bolivia, Bosnia-Herzegovina, Brazil, Bulgaria, Burkina Faso, Burundi, Canada, Chile, China, Colombia, Congo DR, Costa Rica, Croatia, Cyprus, Czech Rep, Denmark, Dominican Rep, Ecuador, Egypt, El Salvador, Estonia, Ethiopia, Fiji, Finland, France, Gambia, Georgia, Germany, Ghana, Greece, Grenada, Guatemala, Guinea, Guyana, Haiti, Honduras, Hungary, Iceland, India, Indonesia, Iraq, Ireland, Israel, Italy, Jamaica, Japan, Jordan, Kazakhstan, Kenya, Korea Rep, Kosovo, Kuwait, Latvia, Lebanon, Lesotho, Libya, Lithuania, Luxembourg, Malawi, Mali, Malta, Mexico, Moldova, Mongolia, Montenegro, Morocco, Namibia, Nepal, Netherlands, Nicaragua, Nigeria, North Macedonia, Norway, Oman, Pakistan, Palestine, Panama, Paraguay, Peru, Philippines, Poland, Portugal, Romania, Russia, Rwanda, Serbia, Sierra Leone, Singapore, Slovakia, Slovenia, South Africa, Spain, Sudan, Sweden, Switzerland, Syrian AR, Taiwan, Tanzania UR, Thailand, Togo, Tunisia, Türkiye, Uganda, UK, Ukraine, United Arab Emirates, Uruguay, USA, Uzbekistan, Venezuela, Zambia, Zimbabwe.
Consultative Status Consultative status granted from: *ECOSOC (#05331)* (Special); *UNESCO (#20322)* (Consultative Status); *WHO (#20950)* (Official Relations); *Council of Europe (CE, #04881)* (Participatory Status). **IGO Relations** Accredited by (1): *United Nations Office at Vienna (UNOV, #20604)*. Cooperates with (6): *Joint United Nations Programme on HIV/AIDS (UNAIDS, #16149); UNICEF (#20332); United Nations Office on Drugs and Crime (UNODC, #20596); United Nations Population Fund (UNFPA, #20612); WHO Regional Office for Europe (#20945); WHO Tobacco Free Initiative (TFI, #20949)*. Associated with Department of Global Communications of the United Nations.
NGO Relations Observer status with (1): *International Federation of Health and Human Rights Organisations (IFHHRO, #13440)*. Member of (13): *Alliance for Health Promotion (A4HP, #00687); European Environment and Health Youth Coalition (EEHYC, #07001); European Public Health Alliance (EPHA, #08297); European Students' Union (ESU, #08848); European Youth Forum (#09140); Framework Convention Alliance (FCA, #09981); International Youth Health Organization (YHO, #15933); Planetary Health Alliance (PHA, #18383); The Network: Towards Unity for Health (The Network: TUFH, #17060); The Right to Research Coalition (no recent information); UHC2030 (#20277); World Federation of Public Health Associations (WFPHA, #21476); World Health Students' Alliance (WHSA, #21559)*.
Cooperates with (21):
- *Association for Medical Education in Europe (AMEE, #02797);*
- *Child Family Health International (CFHI);*
- *Federación Latinoamericana de Sociedades Científicas de Estudiantes de Medicina (FELSOCEM, no recent information);*
- *Federation of African Medical Students' Associations (FAMSA, #09407);*
- *Global Alcohol Policy Alliance (GAPA, #10177);*
- *Global Health Council (GHC, #10402);*
- *HelpAge International (#10904);*
- *International AIDS Society (IAS, #11601);*
- *International AIDS Vaccine Initiative (IAVI, #11602);*
- *International Association of Gerontology and Geriatrics (IAGG, #11920);*
- *International Association of Students in Agricultural and Related Sciences (IAAS, #12191);*
- *International Physicians for the Prevention of Nuclear War (IPPNW, #14578);*
- *Medical Women's International Association (MWIA, #16630);*
- *Rotary International (RI, #18975);*
- *Save the Children International (#19058);*
- *Union for International Cancer Control (UICC, #20415);*
- *WACI Health;*
- *World Federation for Medical Education (WFME, #21454);*
- *World Federation for Mental Health (WFMH, #21455);*
- *World Heart Federation (WHF, #21562);*
- *World Medical Association (WMA, #21646).*

[2022.11.01/XB1956/**B**]

- ♦ International Federation of Merchant-Tailors (inactive)
- ♦ International Federation of Metallurgists (inactive)
- ♦ International Federation of Micromount Societies (no recent information)
- ♦ International Federation of Midwives / see International Confederation of Midwives (#12863)
- ♦ International Federation of Mining and Energy Executives (no recent information)
- ♦ International Federation of Mining and Metallurgical Students (inactive)

♦ International Federation of Model Auto Racing (IFMAR) 13479

Sec Leceage 8 CD, 48002 Bilbao, Biscay, Spain. E-mail: secretary@ifmar.org.
Pres address not obtained.
URL: http://www.ifmar.org/

Aims Promote friendship and cooperation worldwide through and for constructions and operation of Radio Controlled (RC) Automobiles; establish uniform international rules and regulation for the construction and operation of RC Automobiles. **Structure** Officers. **Activities** Awards/prizes/competitions; sporting activities.
Members Blocs (4):
European Federation of Radio Operated Model Automobiles (EFRA, #07204); Far East Model Car Association (FEMCA); Fourth Association of Model Auto Racing (FAMAR); Remotely Operated Auto Racers (ROAR).
[2022/XM5258/y/**C**]

♦ International Federation for Modern Languages and Literatures ... 13480

Fédération internationale des langues et littératures modernes (FILLM) – Internationale Vereinigung für Neuere Sprachen und Literaturen

Pres University of Vienna, African Studies Dept, Spitalgasse 2, Court 5.1, 1090 Vienna, Austria. T. +431427743214.
SG Victoria Univ, College of Arts, PO box 14428, Melbourne VIC 8001, Australia. T. +61399192196. Fax +61399192658.
URL: http://www.fillm.org/

History Aug 1928, Oslo (Norway). Reorganized 1951, Florence (Italy). Constitution adopted at 6th International Congress, 14-15 Sep 1954, Oxford (UK). Statutes modified at 7th Congress, 25 Aug 1957, Heidelberg (Germany FR), and again Oct 2012. Former names and other names: *International Committee on Modern Literary History* – former (Aug 1928 to 1951); *Commission internationale d'histoire des littératures modernes* – former (Aug 1928 to 1951); *Commission internationale d'Histoire littéraire moderne* – former. **Aims** Develop and encourage scholarly study of modern and medieval languages and literatures. **Structure** Congress (every 3 years); Committee. **Languages** English, French. **Staff** Voluntary. **Finance** Sources: members' dues. **Activities** Advocacy/lobbying/activism; awareness raising; events/meetings; publishing activities. **Events** *Triennial Congress* Vienna (Austria) 2021, *Triennial Congress* Vienna (Austria) 2020, *The contribution of learned societies to the humanities* Vienna (Austria) 2018, *Triennial Congress* Delhi (India) 2017, *Triennial Congress* Ningbo (China) 2014. **Publications** *FILLM Newsletter* (4 a year). Book series. Congress proceedings.
Members Affiliated international associations (13):
Asociación de Lingüística y Filología de la América Latina (ALFAL, #02278); *Association for Commonwealth Literature and Language Studies (ACLALS, #02439)*; *Association for Rhetoric and Communication in Southern Africa (ARCSA)*; *Australasian Universities Language and Literature Association (AULLA, #03033)*; *European Society for the Study of English (ESSE, #08743)*; Finnish Literary Research Society (KTS); *Global Rhetoric Society (GRC)*; *International Association for Dialogue Analysis (IADA, #11847)*; *International Association for Scandinavian Studies (IASS, #12145)*; *International Association for the Study of the Italian Language and Literature (AISLLI, #12202)*; *International Association of University Professors of English (IAUPE, #12249)*; *International Comparative Literature Association (ICLA, #12829)*; *International Society for the Oral Literatures of Africa (ISOLA, #15327)*.
NGO Relations Member of (1): *International Council for Philosophy and Human Sciences (CIPSH, #13061)* (as constituent member federation). [2021/XA1831/y/**A**]

♦ International Federation of Modern School Movements (Pedagogy Freinet) 13481

Fédération internationale des mouvements d'école moderne (FIMEM)

Pres 10 chemin de la Roche Montigny, 5 Rue Réaumur, 44000 Nantes, France. E-mail: cafimem@gmail.com.
Sec address not obtained.
URL: http://www.fimem-freinet.org/

History Apr 1957, Nantes (France). Founded at an international congress of ICEM (French Freinet movement). Since 1968, all movements in FIMEM refer to "Charter of Modern School". **Aims** Bring together associations and groups worldwide which adhere to the "Charter of Modern School", Freinet pedagogy. **Structure** General Assembly (every 2 years); Management Board; Specialized Commissions. **Languages** English, French, Spanish. **Staff** 5.00 FTE, voluntary. **Finance** Sources: members' dues. **Activities** Knowledge management/information dissemination; networking/liaising; training/education. **Events** *RIDEF Meeting* Agadir (Morocco) 2022, *RIDEF Meeting* Québec, QC (Canada) 2020, *RIDEF Meeting* Ljungskile (Sweden) 2018, *RIDEF Meeting* Dogbo-Tota (Benin) 2016, *RIDEF Meeting* Reggio Emilia (Italy) 2014. **Publications** *Ne pas se taire.*
Members National associations of practising teachers and individuals. Members in 28 countries:
Austria, Belgium, Benin, Brazil, Bulgaria, Burkina Faso, Cameroon, Canada, Chile, Côte d'Ivoire, Finland, France, Georgia, Germany, Greece, Italy, Japan, Mexico, Morocco, Netherlands, Poland, Russia, Senegal, Spain, Sweden, Switzerland, Togo, Uruguay. [2021/XC1905/**F**]

♦ International Federation of Motorhome Clubs (#09621)
♦ International Federation of Motor Transport and Road Construction Workers' Unions (inactive)

♦ International Federation of Muaythai Associations (IFMA) 13482

Dir 1029 Navamin 14, Navamin Road, Klongjan, Bangkapi, Bangkok, 10240, Thailand. T. +6622582711. Fax +6626620132. E-mail: info@muaythai.sport.
Lausanne Office Manager Maison du Sport International, Av de Rhodanie 54, Bldg B – 2nd Floor, 1007 Lausanne VD, Switzerland.
URL: http://www.muaythai.sport/

History 1993. **Aims** Offer everyone, who chooses to, the possibility of participation without discrimination of any kind, and in the spirit of solidarity, to practice and participate in any form or aspect of the sport. **Languages** English. **Staff** 8.00 FTE, paid. **Finance** Sources: meeting proceeds; members' dues; sponsorship. **Activities** Projects/programmes; sporting activities; training/education. **Events** *Meeting* Bangkok (Thailand) 2018. **Publications** *Muaythai Revealed* (annual). **Members** National federations (147). Membership countries not specified. **IGO Relations** Memorandum of Understanding with (2): *UNESCO (#20322)*; *UN Women (#20724)*. **NGO Relations** Member of (5): *Alliance of Independent recognised Members of Sport (AIMS, #00690)* (Associate); *Association of the IOC Recognized International Sports Federations (ARISF, #02767)*; *International World Games Association (IWGA, #15914)*; *Olympic Movement (#17719)*; *The Association for International Sport for All (TAFISA, #02763)*. Cooperates with (1): *International Testing Agency (ITA, #15678)*. Recognized by: *International Olympic Committee (IOC, #14408)*. [2021.06.15/XM2770/**D**]

♦ International Federation of Multimedia Associations (IFMA) 13483

Fédération internationale des associations de multimedia (FIAM) – Federación Internacional de Asociaciones de Multimedia

CEO/Vice-Pres PO Box 92039, CSP Portobello, Brossard, Brossard QC J4W 3K8, Canada.
Pres 201 rue du Faubourg Saint-Honoré, 75008 Paris, France.
URL: http://www.fiam.org/

History May 1997, Montréal (Canada). **Aims** Promote international cooperation between multimedia associations worldwide. **Structure** Board, comprising President, Vice President, Treasurer, Secretary, General Director and 7 Directors. **Events** *World Summit on Internet and Multimedia* Chongqing (China) 2013, *World Summit on Internet and Multimedia / Summit* Fuzhou (China) 2012, *World Summit on Internet and Multimedia / Summit* Beijing (China) 2011, *World Summit on Internet and Multimedia / Summit* Shenyang (China) 2010, *World Summit on Internet and Multimedia / Summit* Shenyang (China) 2009. **Publications** *FIAM Newsletter* (12 a year). **Consultative Status** Consultative status granted from: *ECOSOC (#05331)* (Special); *UNCTAD (#20285)* (Special). **NGO Relations** Set up: *Multimedia World Watch (M2W, no recent information)*. [2019.06.03/XD7819/**D**]

♦ International Federation of Multiple Sclerosis Societies / see Multiple Sclerosis International Federation (#16899)
♦ International Federation of Municipal Employees / see Public Services International (#18572)

♦ International Federation of Municipal Engineering (IFME) 13484

Fédération internationale d'ingégnierie municipal (FIIM)

SG IPWEA Australasia Office, Level 6, Suite 6/03, 99 Walker Street, Sydney NSW 2060, Australia. T. +61407207934. E-mail: sec-gen@ifmeworld.org.
URL: http://www.ifmeworld.org/

History 29 Apr 1960, Paris (France). Originally registered under French law. Former names and other names: *International Federation of Municipal Engineers (IFME)* – former; *Fédération internationale des ingénieurs municipaux (FIIM)* – former; *Federación Internacional de Ingenieros Municipales* – former. Registration: Netherlands. **Aims** Foster continued improvement in the quality of public works and wider community services. **Structure** General Assembly; Congress (every 3 years); Society to Steering Committee; Executive Committee. **Languages** English. **Staff** Voluntary. **Finance** Sources: members' dues. Annual budget: 15,500 EUR. **Activities** Events/meetings; guidance/assistance/consulting; networking/liaising. **Events** *Triennial Congress* Netherlands 2024, *Triennial Congress* Birmingham (UK) 2023, *Triennial Congress* Kansas City, MO (USA) 2018, *Triennial Congress* Rotorua (New Zealand) 2015, *Triennial Congress* Helsinki (Finland) 2012. **Publications** *IFME Newsletter* (occasional). Technical briefs.
Members National associations; individuals. Members in 17 countries:
Australia, Belgium, Canada, China, Estonia, Finland, France, Iceland, Israel, Italy, Netherlands, New Zealand, Norway, South Africa, Sweden, UK, USA. [2022.05.12/XC1961/**D**]

♦ International Federation of Municipal Engineers / see International Federation of Municipal Engineering (#13484)

♦ International Federation of Musculoskeletal Research Societies (IFMRS) 13485

CEO PO Box 600, Bristol, BS34 9GU, UK. T. +441454610255. E-mail: ifmrs@ifmrs.org.
URL: http://www.ifmrs.org/

History 2012. Registered in accordance with Canadian law, Jul 2016. **Aims** Advance musculoskeletal research globally so as to prevent and treat musculoskeletal *diseases* by collaborating with international societies to share resources, raise public awareness and provide education. **Structure** Officers. **Languages** English. **Staff** 0.50 FTE, paid. **Finance** Sources: members' dues; sponsorship. **Activities** Events/meetings; financial and/or material support; knowledge management/information dissemination; networking/liaising; training/education. **Events** *Herbert Fleisch Workshop* Bruges (Belgium) 2019, *Joint Meeting* Brisbane, QLD (Australia) 2017.
Members National and regional organizations in 4 countries:
Australia, Japan, New Zealand, USA.
Regional societies (3):
European Calcified Tissue Society (ECTS, #06429); *Iberoamerican Society of Osteology and Mineral Metabolism (#11032)*; *International Chinese Musculoskeletal Research Society (ICMRS)*. [2021/XM5345/y/**C**]

♦ International Federation of Musical Youth / see Jeunesses Musicales International (#16110)

♦ International Federation of Musicians 13486

Fédération internationale des musiciens (FIM) – Federación Internacional de Músicos – Internationale Musiker-Föderation

SG 21 bis rue Victor Massé, 75009 Paris, France. T. +33145263123. Fax +33184178572. E-mail: office@fim-musicians.org.
Coodinator address not obtained.
URL: http://www.fim-musicians.org/

History 3 Aug 1948, Zurich (Switzerland). Founded at International Musicians' Congress convened by the Swiss Musicians' Union. Registration: EU Transparency Register, No/ID: 01953872943-65. **Aims** Protect and further the economic, social and artistic interests of musicians. **Structure** Congress; Executive Committee; Presidium; Secretariat. Regional groups (3): Africa – FIM-AF/FIM African Committee; Latin America – *Grupo Latinoamericano de Músicos (GLM)*; Europe – FIM European Group. **Languages** English, French, German, Spanish. **Staff** 3.00 FTE, paid. **Finance** Sources: members' dues. Annual budget: 426,850 EUR. **Activities** Advocacy/lobbying/activism; events/meetings; guidance/assistance/consulting. **Events** *Quadrennial Congress* Yokohama (Japan) 2021, *Quadrennial Congress* Yokohama (Japan) 2020, *International Orchestra Conference* Montréal, QC (Canada) 2017, *Quadrennial Congress* Reykjavik (Iceland) 2016, *Quadrennial Congress* Buenos Aires (Argentina) 2012. **Publications** *FIM Bulletin. FIM CD-ROM.* Information circulars to members. Information Services: Information circulars to members. Information centre; press service.
Members National unions in 61 countries:
Albania, Argentina, Australia, Austria, Belgium, Brazil, Bulgaria, Burkina Faso, Cameroon, Canada, Central African Rep, Chile, Costa Rica, Côte d'Ivoire, Croatia, Cyprus, Denmark, Finland, France, Gambia, Germany, Ghana, Greece, Guinea, Hungary, Iceland, India, Iran Islamic Rep, Ireland, Israel, Italy, Japan, Kenya, Latvia, Liberia, Malawi, Mexico, Morocco, Namibia, Netherlands, New Zealand, Niger, Norway, Panama, Peru, Poland, Romania, Senegal, Serbia, Slovakia, Slovenia, Spain, Sweden, Switzerland, Togo, Uganda, UK, Ukraine, Uruguay, USA, Zimbabwe.
Consultative Status Consultative status granted from: *ECOSOC (#05331)* (Ros C); *UNESCO (#20322)* (Consultative Status); *World Intellectual Property Organization (WIPO, #21593)* (Permanent Observer Status). **IGO Relations** Accredited by (1): *United Nations Office at Vienna (UNOV, #20604)*. Observer status with (2): *Intergovernmental Committee of the International Convention of Rome for the Protection of Performers, Producers of Phonograms and Broadcasting Organizations (#11474)*; *Union for the International Registration of Audiovisual Works (#20444)*. Consultative status with: *ILO (#11123)*. **NGO Relations** Accredited by (2): *Association Européenne des Conservatoires, Académies de Musique et Musikhochschulen (AEC, #02560)*; *International Federation of Coalitions for Cultural Diversity (IFCCD, #13394)*. Member of (7): *Association of European Performers' Organisations (AEPO-ARTIS, #02530)*; *Culture First Coalition (inactive)*; *European Arts and Entertainment Alliance (EAEA, #05918)*; *European Music Council (EMC, #07837)*; *International Arts and Entertainment Alliance (IAEA, #11676)*; *International Music Council (IMC, #14199)*; *Pro-music.* Close working relations with: *International Federation of Actors (#13337)*; *UNI Global Union (#20338)*. Together with FIA and IFPI set up a standing committee on 'neighbouring rights'. [2022/XC1962/**B**]

♦ International Federation "Musique Espérance" 13487

Fédération internationale Musique espérance (FIME)

Gen Sec 22 rue Deparcieux, Boite72, 75014 Paris, France. T. +33153801002.
URL: http://musiqueesperance.org/

History 21 Mar 1988, Switzerland, on the initiative of Miguel Angel Estrella, when Statutes were adopted. Originally registered in accordance with Swiss Civil Code. Subsequently registered in accordance with French law. **Aims** Contribute, by means of music, to the defence of human rights, peace, and the promotion of youth. **Structure** General Assembly. Board of Directors, including Board, comprising President, 2 Vice-Presidents, Secretary General, Deputy Secretary General, Treasurer and Deputy Treasurer. local associations. **Languages** English, French, Spanish. **Staff** Voluntary. **Finance** Members' dues. Other sources: incomes from concerts; subsidies from UNESCO and some Ministries; private sponsors. **Activities** Organizes concerts for the benefit of humanitarian organizations in countries where human rights are flouted. Brings quality music to defavourized sectors: rural zones, old people's homes, hospitals, prisons, Fourth World. Organizes: international music workshops *'Ateliers musicaux internationaux (AMI)'*, opening appreciation of music to children in developing countries through their own traditions; organizes selections of young musicians without aggressive competition; organizes seminars and summer schools for young musicians. Set up *'Orchestre pour la Paix'*. **Publications** Books.
Members Associations in 5 countries:
Argentina, Belgium, France, Italy, Switzerland.
Individuals in 12 countries and territories:
Bolivia, Brazil, Burundi, Chile, Israel, Jordan, Lebanon, Mexico, Morocco, Palestine, Spain, Uruguay.
Consultative Status Consultative status granted from: *UNESCO (#20322)* (Consultative Status). [2018/XD1503/**D**]

♦ International Federation for Mutual Assistance (inactive)
♦ International Federation for Narcotic Education (inactive)
♦ International Federation of National Associations of Engineering Students (inactive)
♦ International Federation of National Associations of Engineers / see Fédération Européenne d'Associations Nationales d'Ingénieurs (#09558)
♦ International Federation of National Associations of Passenger Transport by Rope Railways (#09608)
♦ International Federation of National Associations of Tyre Specialists and Retreaders / see BIPAVER – European Retread Manufacturers Association (#03264)
♦ International Federation of National Canine Organizations / see Fédération cynologique internationale (#09477)
♦ International Federation of National CdLS Support Organizations (unconfirmed)
♦ International Federation of National Standardizing Associations (inactive)
♦ International Federation of National Teaching Fellows (unconfirmed)
♦ International Federation of Naturopaths (inactive)

♦ International Federation of Nematology Societies (IFNS) 13488

Sec UC Riverside Kearney Ctr, 9240 S Riverbend Ave, Parlier CA 93648, USA. T. +15596466555.
Pres Univ of Florida, IFAS – Citrus Research and Education Center, 700 Experiment Station Road, Lake Alfred FL 33850, USA. T. +18639568821. Fax +18639564631.
URL: http://www.ifns.org/

History 10 Jul 1996, Guadeloupe. **Aims** Foster communication among nematologists worldwide. **Structure** Officers: President; Vice-President; Secretary-Treasurer. Committees (4). **Languages** English. **Staff** 3.00 FTE, voluntary. **Finance** Sources: funds; sponsoring. **Activities** Committees (4): Communication and Information Exchange; Congress-Site Selection/Programme; Finance; Constitution-Operations Manual. Organizes congresses. **Events** *International Congress of Nematology* Juan-les-Pins (France) 2022, *International Congress of Nematology* Juan-les-Pins (France) 2021, *International Congress* Antibes (France) 2020, *International Congress of Nematology* Juan-les-Pins (France) 2020, *International Congress of Nematology* Cape Town (South Africa) 2014. **Publications** *IFNS Newspage.* Conference proceedings.
Members Affiliated national and international Nematology Societies (14). National societies in 8 countries:
Brazil, China, Egypt, India, Italy, Japan, Pakistan, Russia.
Regional organizations (6), listed in this Yearbook:
Afro-Asian Society of Nematologists; Australasian Association of Nematologists (AAN); European Society of Nematologists (ESN, #08661); Nematological Society of Southern Africa (NSSA, #16971); Organization of Nematologists of Tropical America (ONTA, #17878); Society of Nematologists (SON, #19604).
[2016/XD6283/y/**D**]

♦ International Federation of Netball Associations / see World Netball (#21668)

♦ International Federation on Neuroendoscopy (IFNE) 13489

Main Office v/o Erasmus Conference, 6 Drosini St, 166 73 Voula, Greece. E-mail: info@ifneuroendoscopy.org.
URL: http://www.ifneuroendoscopy.org/
History Oct 2001, Hyogo (Japan). Former names and other names: *International Study Group on Neuroendoscopy (ISGNE)* – former (2001 to 2007). **Aims** Promote use of neuroendoscopy and other related minimally invasive neurosurgical techniques worldwide by encouraging the ethical transmission and exchange of scientific information and techniques related to neuroendoscopy. **Structure** Executive Board, including President and Secretary. **Events** *World Congress of Neuroendoscopy* Singapore (Singapore) 2023, *Interim Meeting* Hyderabad (India) 2022, *World Congress of Neuroendoscopy* Singapore (Singapore) 2021, *World Congress of Neuroendoscopy* Orlando, FL (USA) 2019, *World Conference* Cape Town (South Africa) 2017.
[2022/XM2521/**E**]

♦ International Federation of NGOs Against Drug Abuse / see International Federation of Non-Government Organizations for the Prevention of Drug and Substance Abuse (#13490)
♦ International Federation of Non-Governmental Organizations / see International Federation of Non-Government Organizations for the Prevention of Drug and Substance Abuse (#13490)

♦ International Federation of Non-Government Organizations for the Prevention of Drug and Substance Abuse (IFNGO) 13490

Hon Sec 8 Jalan Ledang, 50480 Kuala Lumpur, Malaysia. T. +60320941190. Fax +60320943233.
History Founded 1981, Kuala Lumpur (Malaysia), following recommendations of a conference 1979, Jakarta (Indonesia). Also referred to as: *International Federation of NGOs Against Drug Abuse (IFND); International Federation of Non-Governmental Organizations.* **Aims** Attain harmonious and fruitful relations among NGOs in the Asia-Pacific region and internationally in pursuing activities to prevent and control drug abuse; consolidate efforts to achieve a drug-free society; attain a common mechanism for collection and collation of drug abuse data and for rapid dissemination of such data to members; attain concerted action among members within intents and purposes of 'Kuala Lumpur Declaration'. **Structure** General Meeting (every 2 years); Board of Management; Council of Advisors; Standing and Ad hoc Committees; Secretariat. **Languages** English. **Staff** 1.50 FTE, voluntary. **Finance** Members' dues. Other sources: sponsorship by members; sponsorship by Colombo (Sri Lanka) Plan Bureau; donations. Annual budget: US$ 75,428. **Activities** Events/meetings; training/education. **Events** *Conference / World Conference* Putrajaya (Malaysia) 2015, *World Conference* Macau 2013, *Conference* Macau (Macau) 2013, *Conference / World Conference* Kuala Lumpur (Malaysia) 2011, *Conference / World Conference* Bandar Seri Begawan (Brunei Darussalam) 2009. **Publications** *IFNGO Bulletin* (4 a year). Conference proceedings; workshop reports; guides; translations.
Members Founding; Ordinary; Associate. Members in 42 countries and territories:
Australia, Bangladesh, Barbados, Brunei Darussalam, Cambodia, Canada, China, Egypt, Fiji, Germany, Greece, Hong Kong, Hungary, India, Indonesia, Iran Islamic Rep, Italy, Japan, Korea Rep, Macau, Malaysia, Maldives, Malta, Mauritius, Myanmar, Nepal, New Zealand, Pakistan, Philippines, Portugal, Russia, Saudi Arabia, Singapore, South Africa, Spain, Sri Lanka, Sudan, Taiwan, Thailand, United Arab Emirates, USA, Vietnam.
International organizations (13), include 8 organizations listed in this Yearbook:
Arab Federation of NGOs for Drug Abuse Prevention (AFNDA, #00948); Asian Federation of Therapeutic Communities (AFTC, #01476); Colombo Plan for Cooperative Economic and Social Development in Asia and the Pacific (CPS, #04120); International Bodyguard and Security Services Association (IBSSA, #12377); Organization of the Families of Asia and the Pacific (OFAP, #17867); South Asian Federation of NGOs for the Prevention of Drug and Substance Abuse (SAFNGO, no recent information); World Assembly of Muslim Youth (WAMY, #21112); World Islamic Association for Mental Health (WIAMH, no recent information).
Consultative Status Consultative status granted from: *ILO (#11123)* (Special List); *ASEAN (#01141).* **IGO Relations** Cooperates with: *UNESCO (#20322).* Accredited by: *United Nations Office at Vienna (UNOV, #20604).* Associated with Department of Global Communications of the United Nations. **NGO Relations** Member of: *Conference of Non-Governmental Organizations in Consultative Relationship with the United Nations (CONGO, #04635); New York NGO Committee on Drugs (NYNGOC, #17097).* [2018.03.08/XD1631/y/**D**]

♦ International Federation of Nonlinear Analysts (IFNA) 13491

Pres Dept Mathematics and Statistics, Univ South Florida, 1202 Parrilla de Avila, Tampa FL 33613, USA.
Vice-Pres The Pedagogue, 11311 N 50th St – box 2, Tampa FL 33617, USA.
URL: http://ifnaworld.org/
History 12 Aug 1991. Deriving from a loose-knit working group. **Aims** Promote, encourage and sustain interest in theory and application of nonlinear analysis in problems arising in a diversity of disciplines; provide technical solutions to interdisciplinary problems involving nonlinear models governing complex physical, engineering, economic, sociological, biological and ecological phenomena; provide fora for dissemination of information at a level of technical detail appropriate for technical professionals. **Languages** English. **Staff** 1.00 FTE, paid. **Finance** Sources: members' dues. **Activities** Acts as apex organization of regional (national) federations which conduct their own internal affairs, hold professional meetings and publish journals in the following sciences: aerospace; atmospheric; biological; chemical; cosmological; economics; engineering and technological; environmental; geophysical; mathematical; medical and health; numerical and computational; oceanographic; physical; social. **Events** *Quadrennial World Congress* Athens (Greece) 2012, *Quadrennial world congress* Orlando, FL (USA) 2008, *Quadrennial world congress* Orlando, FL (USA) 2004, *Quadrennial world congress* Catania (Italy) 2000, *International conference on nonlinear problems in aviation and aerospace* Daytona Beach, FL (USA) 1998. **Publications** *Nonlinear Analysis Series B: Real World Applications. Nonlinear Analysis A: Theory, Methods and Applications; Nonlinear Studies; Nonlineas Analysis: Hybrid System.* Congress proceedings.
Members Organizations in 25 countries:
Australia, Austria, Belgium, Bulgaria, Canada, China, Finland, France, Germany, Hungary, India, Ireland, Israel, Italy, Korea Rep, Mexico, Philippines, Poland, Russia, Singapore, Spain, Switzerland, Türkiye, UK, USA. [2020/XC0081/**C**]

♦ International Federation of Nurse Anesthetists (IFNA) 13492

Fédération internationale des infirmiers anesthésistes – Federación Internacional de Enfermeros Anestesistas
Exec Dir 56 rue de Verdun, 78200 Mantes-la-Jolie, France. T. +33668128393.
URL: https://ifna.site/
History Jun 1989, Switzerland. Bylaws adopted 10 Jun 1989; revised 10 Jun 1995, 26 Apr 1997, 25 May 1998 and 4 Jun 2010. Registration: Switzerland. **Aims** Promote cooperation between nurse anaesthetists internationally; develop and promote educational standards and standards of practice in the field; provide opportunities for continuing education in anaesthesia; assist nurse anaesthetists' associations to improve standards and competence; promote recognition of nurse anaesthesia; establish and maintain effective cooperation between nurse anaesthetists, anaesthesiologists and other members of the medical profession, nursing profession, hospitals and agencies representing a community of interest in nurse anaesthesia. **Structure** World Congress (every 4 years). Council of National Representatives (CNR) (meeting every 2 years), comprising a representative of each full member association. Executive Committee, consisting of Board of Officers (President, 2 Vice Presidents and Treasurer) and 6 national representatives. Committees (3): Education; Practice; Congress Planning. **Languages** English. **Staff** 0.50 FTE, paid. **Finance** Members' dues. **Activities** Develops standards and guidelines for nurse anaesthesia practice and education. Accreditation of non-physician anaesthesia programmes of education; continuing education. **Events** *World Congress* Sibenik (Croatia) 2022, *Pan African Nurse Anesthetists Conference (PANAC)* Nairobi (Kenya) 2021, *Pan African Nurse Anesthetists Conference (PANAC)* Nairobi (Kenya) 2020, *World Congress* Budapest (Hungary) 2018, *World Congress* Glasgow (UK) 2016.
Members National; Regional or Joint Association. National organizations in 35 countries and territories:
Australia, Austria, Belgium, Benin, Bosnia-Herzegovina, Burundi, Cambodia, Congo DR, Côte d'Ivoire, Croatia, Denmark, Ethiopia, Finland, France, Germany, Ghana, Greece, Hungary, Iceland, Indonesia, Jamaica, Japan, Kenya, Korea Rep, Liberia, Luxembourg, Morocco, Netherlands, Nigeria, Norway, Poland, Serbia, Sierra Leone, Slovenia, Spain, Sweden, Switzerland, Taiwan, Tunisia, Türkiye, Uganda, UK, USA.
IGO Relations Formal relationship with: *WHO (#20950).* **NGO Relations** Member of (3): *European Specialist Nurses Organisation (ESNO, #08808); Global Alliance for Surgical, Obstetric, Trauma and Anaesthesia Care (G4 Alliance, #10229); International Society for Quality in Health Care (ISQua, #15405).* Affiliated with (1): *International Council of Nurses (ICN, #13054).* Acts as advisor to *Health Volunteers Overseas (HVO)* – Nurse Anaesthesia Overseas. [2021/XD5038/**D**]

♦ International Federation of Old Town Areas (inactive)
♦ International Federation of Open Air Journalists and Writers (inactive)

♦ International Federation of Operational Research Societies (IFORS) 13493

Fédération internationale des sociétés de recherche opérationnelle – Federación Internacional de Sociedades de Investigaciones Operacionales – Internationale Föderation der Gesellschaften für Unternehmensforschung
Sec 5521 Research Park Drive, Ste 200, Catonsville MD 21228, USA. T. +14437573534. Fax +14437573535. E-mail: secretary@ifors.org.
URL: http://www.ifors.org/
History Jan 1959. Founded by UK, USA and French national societies. **Aims** Stimulate development of operational research as a unified science and promote its advancement worldwide. **Structure** Board of member societies (meets every 3 years). Administrative Committee, comprising President, Immediate Past-President, Treasurer, Secretary, plus 1 elected and 4 regional Vice-Presidents. Regional Groupings (4): *Association of European Operational Research Societies (EURO, #02528),* set up Jan 1975; *Latin-Iberian-American Association of Operations Research Societies (#16398),* set up 1982; *Association of Asian-Pacific Operational Research Societies within IFORS (APORS, #02381),* set up Mar 1985; *Association of North American Operations Research Societies within IFORS (NORAM),* set up 1987. Coordinators (7): External Affairs; IFORS Publications; Plans and Programmes; Education; Meetings; Scientific Activities; Developing Countries. **Languages** English. **Staff** 1.00 FTE, paid. **Finance** Sources: meeting proceeds; members' dues; sale of publications. **Activities** Events/meetings; knowledge management/information dissemination. **Events** *Triennial Conference* Santiago (Chile) 2023, *Triennial Conference* Seoul (Korea Rep) 2021, *The Corona-Pandemic: Re-shaping the Global Textile Supply Chain* Seoul (Korea Rep) 2020, *Triennial Conference* Seoul (Korea Rep) 2020, *Symposium on Analysis, Design and Evaluation of Human-Machine Systems* Tallinn (Estonia) 2019. **Publications** *International Transactions in Operational Research (ITOR)* (6 a year) – journal, including conference proceedings; *IFORS News. International Abstracts in Operations Research (IAOR).*
Members No individual membership. National societies in 53 countries and territories:
Argentina, Australia, Austria, Belarus, Belgium, Brazil, Bulgaria, Canada, Chile, China, Croatia, Czechia, Denmark, Estonia, Finland, France, Germany, Greece, Hong Kong, Hungary, Iceland, India, Iran Islamic Rep, Ireland, Israel, Italy, Japan, Korea Rep, Lithuania, Malaysia, Mexico, Nepal, Netherlands, New Zealand, Nigeria, Norway, Peru, Philippines, Poland, Portugal, Serbia, Singapore, Slovakia, Slovenia, South Africa, Spain, Sweden, Switzerland, Tunisia, Türkiye, UK, Uruguay, USA.
Included in the above, one organization listed in this Yearbook:
Institute for Operations Research and the Management Sciences (INFORMS, #11286).
Kindred national societies (non-voting) in USA, including one organization listed in this Yearbook:
Airline Group of IFORS (AGIFORS, #00605).
Consultative Status Consultative status granted from: *ECOSOC (#05331)* (Ros A); *UNCTAD (#20285)* (General Category). [2021/XC1966/y/**C**]

♦ International Federation of Ophthalmological Societies (inactive)
♦ International Federation of Oral Medicine / see International Academy of Oral Medicine (#11562)
♦ International Federation of Organic Agriculture Movements / see IFOAM – Organics International (#11105)
♦ International Federation for the Organization of Meetings for the Handicapped (inactive)
♦ International Federation of Organizations for School Correspondence and Exchanges (inactive)

♦ International Federation of Orgonomic Colleges (IFOC) 13494

Sec 9 avenue des Lilas, 44850 Saint-Mars-du-Désert, France. T. +33240774450. Fax +33240774363.
History 1979, as *Scuola Europea di Orgonoterapia (SEOR).* Registered in accordance with Spanish law. **Aims** Promote investigation and encourage better knowledge of the benefits and characteristics of orgonomy, a *psychotherapy* treatment developed by Wilhelm Reich (1897-1957). **Structure** General Meeting; Board.
Members Orgonomic Colleges in 7 countries:
Brazil, Finland, France, Greece, Italy, Mexico, Spain.
NGO Relations *European Association for Psychotherapy (EAP, #06176).* [2013/XG0660/**D**]

♦ International Federation of Orthopaedic Manipulative Physical Therapists (IFOMPT) 13495

Exec Dir PO Box 301 295, Albany, Auckland 0752, New Zealand. T. +64211878753. E-mail: admin@ifompt.org.
Pres address not obtained.
URL: https://www.ifompt.org/
History 1974, Montréal, QC (Canada). Founded on adoption of Constitution and election of officers, the setting up of a *World Confederation of Manipulative Therapists* having been recommended at Conference of *World Confederation for Physical Therapy (WCPT, #21293),* 1970, Amsterdam (Netherlands) and Committee appointed 1973, Gran Canaria (Spain). Since 1978, a subgroup of WCPT. **Aims** Promote international excellence and unity in clinical and academic standards for manual/musculoskeletal physiotherapists. **Structure** Delegate Assembly; Executive Committee; Standards Committee; Office in Auckland (New Zealand). **Languages** English. **Staff** 0.50 FTE, paid. **Finance** Sources: meeting proceeds; members' dues; revenue from activities/projects. **Activities** Events/meetings; networking/liaising; research/documentation; standards/guidelines. **Events** *Quadrennial Congress* Basel (Switzerland) 2024, *Quadrennial Congress* Melbourne, VIC (Australia) 2022, *Quadrennial Congress* Melbourne, VIC (Australia) 2020, *Quadrennial Congress* Glasgow (UK) 2016, *Quadrennial Congress* Québec, QC (Canada) 2012. **Publications** *IFOMPT Release* (4 a year); *Manual Therapy Research Review* (4 a year). *International Framework for Examination of the Cervical Region for Potential of Cervical Arterial Dysfunction (CAD).*
Members Full in 25 countries and territories:
Australia, Austria, Belgium, Canada, Cyprus, Denmark, Finland, France, Germany, Greece, Hong Kong, Ireland, Italy, Japan, Netherlands, New Zealand, Norway, Philippines, Portugal, South Africa, Spain, Sweden, Switzerland, UK, USA.
Associate and Registered Interest Groups in 13 countries:
Australia, Brazil, Chile, Colombia, Egypt, Hungary, Iceland, Korea Rep, Poland, Romania, Saudi Arabia, Slovenia, Spain.
[2022.05.05/XD2071/**E**]

♦ International Federation of Orthopaedic Manipulative Therapists / see International Federation of Orthopaedic Manipulative Physical Therapists (#13495)

♦ International Federation of Oto-Rhino-Laryngological Societies (IFOS) 13496

Fédération internationale des sociétés oto-rhino-laryngologiques
Gen Sec Antolska 11, 851 07 Bratislava, Slovakia. E-mail: secretariat@ifosworld.org – info@ifosworld.org.

URL: http://www.ifosworld.org/
History 1965, Tokyo (Japan). Present Constitution and Bylaws adopted 23 May 1973, Venice (Italy); and revised: 14 Mar 1977, Buenos Aires (Argentina); Jun 1981, Budapest (Hungary); May 1985, Miami FL (USA); 3 Oct 2001, Cairo (Egypt); 2017, Paris (France). Registration: Slovakia. **Aims** Promote the advancement of oto-rhino-laryngology; encourage close international relations among otorhinolaryngologists and coordination among national member societies; represent ORL interests in other international organizations dedicated to prevention and control of diseases and disorders related to ORL or training of otorhinolaryngologists. Mission Statement: Identification of critical, global ORL care needs and communication disorders. Proposing ways to prevent and treat them and setting priorities to their impact on societies. **Structure** General Assembly (every 4 years, at World Congress), consisting of delegates of member countries. Executive Committee, comprising 18 members (of whom at least one must be from each of the following continents: Europe, Africa and Middle East, South and West Asia, East Asia, Oceania, North America and Caribbean, Central and South America), plus President, Vice-President and General Secretary *'ex officio'*. Ad Hoc Committees. Regional Secretaries (6) for: Africa and Middle-East; Central and South America; Europe; North America and Caribbean; South East Asia and Western Pacific/Oceania; South and Western Asia. **Languages** English, French, German, Spanish. **Staff** 0.50 FTE, paid. **Finance** Member societies' dues. Other sources: subsidies, gifts and bequests; contributions from World Congresses; fees collected from exhibitors. **Activities** Ad Hoc Committees: Rhinology and Allergy; Oncology and Head and Neck Surgery; Otology, Neuro-Otology; Neuro-Otology and Skull Base Surgery; Laryngology and Broncho-Oesophology; Phoniatrics and Audiology; Paediatric Otolaryngology; Equilibrium. Instrumental in setting up: *Hearing International (#10895)*; *IFOS Standing Committee for Audiovisual Education (AVEC-IFOS, no recent information)*; *Pan African Federation of Oto-Rhino-Laryngological Societies (PAFOS, #18051)*. **Events** *ENT World Congress* Dubai (United Arab Emirates) 2023, *Quadrennial Congress* Vancouver, BC (Canada) 2022, *Quadrennial Congress* Vancouver, BC (Canada) 2021, *Quadrennial Congress* Paris (France) 2017, *Meeting* Paris (France) 2016. **Publications** *IFOS Newsletter* (2 a year). Directory; programmes; books of abstracts; proceedings or transactions of each Congress.
Members National Societies in 93 countries and territories:
Argentina, Australia, Austria, Belarus, Belgium, Bolivia, Botswana, Brazil, Bulgaria, Canada, Chile, Colombia, Congo DR, Costa Rica, Croatia, Cuba, Czechia, Denmark, Dominican Rep, Ecuador, Egypt, El Salvador, Estonia, Finland, France, Georgia, Germany, Ghana, Greece, Guatemala, Honduras, Hungary, Iceland, Iraq, Ireland, Israel, Italy, Jamaica, Japan, Jordan, Kazakhstan, Kenya, Korea DPR, Korea Rep, Kuwait, Latvia, Lebanon, Lithuania, Luxembourg, Malawi, Malaysia, Maldives, Mexico, Netherlands, New Zealand, Nigeria, Norway, Pakistan, Panama, Peru, Philippines, Poland, Portugal, Puerto Rico, Romania, Russia, Saudi Arabia, Serbia, Singapore, Slovakia, South Africa, Spain, Sri Lanka, Sudan, Suriname, Sweden, Switzerland, Syrian AR, Taiwan, Tanzania UR, Thailand, Trinidad-Tobago, Tunisia, Türkiye, Uganda, UK, Ukraine, United Arab Emirates, Uruguay, USA, Uzbekistan, Venezuela, Vietnam.
Included in the above, 1 organization listed in this Yearbook:
Caribbean Association of Otolaryngologists (CAO, #03457).
Individuals in 7 countries and territories:
Bangladesh, Brunei Darussalam, China, Hong Kong, India, Indonesia, Iran Islamic Rep.
Consultative Status Consultative status granted from: *WHO (#20950)* (Official Relations). **IGO Relations** *FAO (#09260)*. **NGO Relations** Member of: *Council for International Organizations of Medical Sciences (CIOMS, #04905)*. Speciality member of: *International Federation of Surgical Colleges (IFSC, #13560)*.
[2022/XB1970/y/**B**]

♦ International Federation of Oxygen-Ozone Therapy / see International Medical Ozone Federation (#14136)

♦ International Federation of Paediatric and Adolescent Gynaecology (#09637)

♦ International Federation of Paediatric Orthopaedic Societies (IFPOS) 13497

SG Washington Univ School of Medicine and St L Shriners Hospital, Children's Place 1, Suit 4S-60, St Louis MO 63110, USA. T. +13144544814.
URL: http://www.ifpos.org/
History Apr 1998, Madrid (Spain). **Aims** Improve scientific exchange; cooperate to improvement of the care to children in all fields. **Structure** Board, comprising President, President Elect, Vice-President, Secretary, Treasurer, 6 Councillors and 1 Ex Officio member. **Languages** English. **Staff** Voluntary. **Events** *Congress* Seoul (Korea Rep) 2010, *Meeting* Hong Kong (Hong Kong) 2008, *Congress* Sorrento (Italy) 2007, *Meeting* Buenos Aires (Argentina) 2006, *Congress* Salvador (Brazil) 2004. **Publications** *Journal of Pediatric Orthopedic* (6 a year).
Members Organizations in 47 countries and territories:
Argentina, Australia, Austria, Belgium, Bolivia, Brazil, Bulgaria, Canada, Chile, China, Croatia, Czechia, Denmark, Egypt, Finland, France, Germany, Greece, Hungary, India, Ireland, Israel, Italy, Japan, Korea Rep, Mexico, Netherlands, New Zealand, Norway, Poland, Portugal, Romania, Russia, Serbia, Singapore, Slovakia, Slovenia, Spain, Sweden, Switzerland, Taiwan, Thailand, Türkiye, UK, USA, Venezuela, Vietnam.
Regional organizations (4):
Asia Pacific Orthopaedic Association (APOA, #01987) (Pediatric Section); *European Paediatric Orthopaedic Society (EPOS, #08128)*; Pediatric Orthopedic Society of North America; *Sociedad Latinoamericana de Ortopedia y Traumatologia Infantil (SLAOTI, #19419)*.
NGO Relations Affiliated to: *International Society of Orthopaedic Surgery and Traumatology (#15335)*.
[2014/XD6951/y/**D**]

♦ International Federation of Palynological Societies (IFPS) 13498

Sec-Treas British Geological Survey, Keyworth, NG12 5GG, UK. T. +441159363447.
Pres Dept of Botany, Univ of Innsbruck, Sternwartestrasse 15, 6020 Innsbruck, Austria. T. +4351250751058.
URL: https://palyno-ifps.com/
History 1 Sep 1966, Utrecht (Netherlands). Founded at 2nd International Pollen Conference, a 1st Conference having been held 23 – 27 Apr 1962, Tucson AZ (USA). Present federation accepted 23 Aug – 1 Sep 1984, Calgary (Canada). Former names and other names: *International Commission for Palynology (ICP)* – former. **Aims** Promote the interests of palynologists; further the study of pollen, *spores* and other palynomorphs, whether living or *fossil*; secure continuity in international multidisciplinary conferences on palynology. **Structure** Council (meets at quadrennial conference). **Languages** English. **Staff** Voluntary. **Finance** Sources: members' dues. **Events** *Congress* Prague (Czechia) 2024, *Congress* Prague (Czechia) 2021, *Quadrennial Congress* Prague (Czechia) 2020, *Quadrennial Congress* Salvador (Brazil) 2016, *Quadrennial Congress* Tokyo (Japan) 2012. **Publications** *Palynos Newsletter* (2 a year). *World Directory of Palynologists* (2012).
Members Individuals (3,700), through their affiliated societies, in 59 countries and territories:
Algeria, Argentina, Australia, Austria, Belgium, Benin, Bolivia, Brazil, Brunei Darussalam, Cameroon, Canada, Chile, China, Colombia, Congo Brazzaville, Congo DR, Côte d'Ivoire, Czechia, Denmark, Egypt, Finland, France, Gabon, Germany, Greece, Hungary, India, Indonesia, Israel, Italy, Japan, Kenya, Madagascar, Malaysia, Netherlands, New Zealand, Niger, Nigeria, Norway, Peru, Poland, Portugal, Romania, Russia, Singapore, Slovakia, South Africa, Spain, Sri Lanka, Suriname, Sweden, Switzerland, Taiwan, Türkiye, UK, Ukraine, Uruguay, USA, Venezuela.
Constituent organizations (22) in 16 countries and territories:
Australia, Belgium, Brazil, Canada, China, Czechia, Denmark, France, Germany, India, Italy, Japan, Russia, Türkiye, UK, USA.
Included in the above, 5 organizations listed in this Yearbook:
Asociación de Palinólogos de Lengua Española (APLE); *Asociación Latinoamericana de Paleobotanica y Palinologia (ALPP, #02249)*; *Association des palynologues de langue française (APLF, #02849)*; *Collegium Palynologicum Scandinavicum (CPS, #04118)*; *Commission internationale de microflore du paléozoïque (CIMP, #04225)*.
NGO Relations Affiliated member of: *International Association for Aerobiology (IAA, #11691)*; *International Union of Geological Sciences (IUGS, #15777)*. Scientific member of: *International Union of Biological Sciences (IUBS, #15760)* (of which it is a commission).
[2021.02.24/XC1585/y/**C**]

♦ International Federation of Pankration Athlima (inactive)

♦ International Federation for Parent Education (IFPE) 13499

Fédération internationale pour l'éducation des parents (FIEP) – Federación Internacional para Educación de Padres

SG 1 av Léon-Journault, 92318 Sèvres CEDEX, France. T. +33145072164. Fax +33146266927. E-mail: admin@fiep-ifpe.org.
URL: http://www.fiep-ifpe.org/
History 24 Apr 1964, Sèvres (France). International statutes adopted 27 Jun 1965. Former names and other names: *Fédération internationale des écoles de parents et d'éducateurs* – former (24 Apr 1964 to 1978). Registration: France. **Aims** Participate internationally in the continued improvement, evolution and defence of the role of parent; work to establish close ties among parents and assist them in their role of preparing the future of younger generations; in view of the rapid pace of evolution of ideas and living conditions, carry out common studies on challenges encountered by different civilizations in adapting to new *life styles*, relationships and *family* education; assist parents in their educational tasks by adapting proven methods to the needs of different countries; conduct research and encourage discussion of principles and methods of underlying continuing education in relation to children, youth and adults during their training, their personal maturing and the development of their social relationships; channel this education towards development of greater international understanding, cooperation and peace so as to allow constructive utilization of scientific and technological progress in the common interest; coordinate the efforts of parents' schools and similar institutions and of governmental, intergovernmental and nongovernmental organizations. **Structure** General Assembly (annual). Executive Board of 36 members. Board of Directors, comprising: President; 2 Vice-Presidents; 5 Regional Presidents – Latin America, North America, Arab World, Asia Pacific, Africa; Secretary; Treasurer; Delegates to 3 international organizations (UNESCO, Council of Europe, UNOV). Bureau, comprising Honorary President, President, 2 Vice-Presidents and General Delegate. Founding President. **Languages** English, French, Spanish. **Staff** Volunteers. **Finance** Sources: donations; grants; members' dues. **Activities** Events/meetings; knowledge management/information dissemination; research/documentation; training/education. **Events** *Conference* Hammamet (Tunisia) 2015, *General Assembly* Rabat (Morocco) 2013, *Congress* Sao Paulo (Brazil) 2013, *Congress* Porto (Portugal) 2012, *General Assembly and Conference* Sèvres (France) 2011. **Publications** *Lettre de la FIEP* (2 a year) in French. *Bibliothèque de la famille éducatrice*. Conference proceedings.
Members Active associations and institutions. Adhering individuals. Members in 37 countries:
Algeria, Argentina, Australia, Austria, Belgium, Benin, Brazil, Cameroon, Canada, China, Congo Brazzaville, Côte d'Ivoire, Cyprus, Denmark, Finland, France, Gabon, Germany, Greece, Iran Islamic Rep, Israel, Italy, Japan, Madagascar, Mauritania, Mexico, Monaco, New Zealand, Paraguay, Russia, Spain, Sweden, Switzerland, Thailand, Tunisia, Uruguay, USA.
Consultative Status Consultative status granted from: *ECOSOC (#05331)* (Ros C); *UNESCO (#20322)* (Consultative Status); *UNICEF (#20332)*; *Council of Europe (CE, #04881)* (Participatory Status). **IGO Relations** Accredited by: *United Nations Office at Vienna (UNOV, #20604)*. **NGO Relations** Member of: *Conference of INGOs of the Council of Europe (#04607)*; *Fédération africaine des associations nationales de parents d'élèves et étudiants (FAPE, #09398)*; *End Corporal Punishment (#05457)*; *Vienna NGO Committee on the Family (#20774)*.
[2019/XC1833/**B**]

♦ International Federation of Parkinson's Disease Foundations / see Melvin Yahr International Parkinson's Disease Foundation

♦ International Federation of Park and Recreation Administration (inactive)

♦ International Federation for the Pastoral Care to Hearing Impaired Persons 13500

Association internationale d'aide spirituelle aux personnes souffrant de troubles auditifs – Internationaler Verband für Schwerhörigenseelsorge (IVSS-Churchear)

Sec Bekkeliveien 5, 3470 Slemmestad, Norway. E-mail: post@churchear.org.
URL: http://www.churchear.org/
History 27 Sep 1979, Frankfurt-Main (Germany). Former names and other names: *International Society for the Pastoral Care of Persons Hard of Hearing* – former; *Association internationale d'aide spirituelle aux personnes souffrant de troubles auditifs* – former; *International Society for the Pastoral Care of Persons with Defective Hearing* – alias. **Aims** Promote reciprocal knowledge concerning work of pastoral care for disabled persons and implementation of diaconal aid. **Structure** General Assembly (every 2 years). Board of Directors, comprising President, Vice-President, Secretary and 6 other members. Day-to-day business effected by management of the *'Protestant Society for the Pastoral Care of People with Defective Hearing'* within the *'Diakonisches Werk'* of the Protestant Church in Germany. **Languages** English, German. **Staff** 2.00 FTE, paid. **Finance** Sources: members' dues; sponsorship. **Activities** Events/meetings. **Events** *Biennial Conference* Eisenach (Germany) 2021, *Biennial Conference* Løgumkloster (Denmark) 2016, *Biennial Conference* Krakow (Poland) 2014, *Biennial Conference* Freising (Germany) 2012, *Biennial Conference* Hvittorp (Finland) 2008. **Publications** *IVSS Newsletter*. Conference reports.
Members Churches; church institutions; diaconal institutions; working teams and study groups in the field; competent individuals active in the field. Members in 21 countries:
Austria, Chile, Czechia, Denmark, Estonia, Finland, France, Germany, Hungary, Netherlands, Norway, Poland, Romania, Russia, Serbia-Montenegro, Slovakia, Sweden, Switzerland, Thailand, UK, USA.
[2022/XD1177/**F**]

♦ International Federation of Patent Agents / see Fédération Internationale des Conseils en Propriété Intellectuelle (#09624)

♦ International Federation of Patent Attorneys / see Fédération Internationale des Conseils en Propriété Intellectuelle (#09624)

♦ International Federation of Pavers (inactive)

♦ International Federation for Peace and Conciliation (IFPC) 13501

Federacija Mira I Soglacija (FMS)

Pres Prospekt Mira 36, Moscow MOSKVA, Russia, 129090. T. +74956803576 – +74956801275 – +74956809977. Fax +74956889587 – +74956800245.
History Founded as *Federation for Peace and Conciliation (FPC) – Federacija Mira i Soglacija (FMS)*, a signatory of *Soviet Peace Committee (inactive)*. Statutes adopted 4 Feb 1992. Registration: Russia. **Aims** Unite organizations, particularly in CIS and Baltic States, working for civil peace, ethnic and national conciliation, disarmament, economic cooperation, environmental protection and human rights; create and propagate culture of non-violence, tolerance and mutual understanding, thus assisting integration and democratization of society and its development; build democratic civil-military relations and develop democratic and civil control over the security and military sphere. **Structure** Conference (every 5 years); Council; Bureau. **Languages** English, Russian. **Staff** 10.00 FTE, paid; 30.00 FTE, voluntary. **Finance** Sources: voluntary donations; sponsorship; projects proceeds. Set up *'Peace and Conciliation'* (a foreign trade association) to contribute to self-sufficiency. **Activities** Conflict resolution; advocacy/lobbying/activism; guidance/assistance/consulting; events/meetings; networking/liaising. **Events** *International conference on civil military relations in conflict regions* Krasnodar (Russia) 2005, *Annual international session on human rights education* Moscow (Russia) 2005, *International conference on new approaches to peace and stability in the North East Asia* Moscow (Russia) 2005, *International research seminar on security and culture* Moscow (Russia) 2005, *International workshop on prospects for NATO-Russian peace support operations* Moscow (Russia) 2005. **Publications** *Mir i Soglacije – Peace and Conciliation* (4 a year) in English, Russian – scientific magazine. *World War II: Myths, Legends and Reality* (2010) in Russian; *Peace in One's Own Home and All over the World* (2009) in English, Russian. Conference proceedings; brochures; booklets; analytical reports.
Members Peace and conciliation committees, councils and branches and other related organizations in 13 countries:
Armenia, Azerbaijan, Belarus, Germany, Kazakhstan, Kyrgyzstan, Lithuania, Moldova, Russia, Tajikistan, Turkmenistan, Ukraine, Uzbekistan.
Affiliated international or internationally-oriented organizations, including 3 listed in this Yearbook:
Center for Political and International Studies, Moscow (CPIS); *International A S Pushkin Foundation*; *International League of Sobriety and Health (inactive)*.
Consultative Status Consultative status granted from: *ECOSOC (#05331)* (Ros A); *Council of Europe (CE, #04881)* (Participatory Status). **IGO Relations** Cooperates with: *Collective Security Treaty Organization (CSTO, #04103)*. Associated with Department of Global Communications of the United Nations. **NGO Relations** Member of: *Conference of INGOs of the Council of Europe (#04607)*.
[2019.07.08/XD3216/y/**D**]

♦ International Federation for Peace and Sustainable Development (internationally oriented national body)

♦ International Federation of Pedestrians (IFP) 13502

Fédération internationale des piétons (FIP) – Internationale Föderation der Fussgängerverbände

SG c/o Assoc de Cidados Auto-Mobilizados, Av 5 de Outubro, 142-R/C Esquerdo, 1050-061 Lisbon, Portugal. E-mail: secretary@pedestrians-int.org.

Pres address not obtained.
URL: http://www.pedestrians-int.org/
History 30 Mar 1963, The Hague (Netherlands). **Aims** Promote a world that is inviting, safe and comfortable for all to walk. **Structure** General Assembly (annual); Board; Technical Committees. **Languages** English, French, German. **Staff** 1.00 FTE, voluntary. **Finance** Sources: contributions; grants. **Activities** Awareness raising; capacity building; knowledge management/information dissemination; politics/policy/regulatory. **Events** *General Assembly* Rotterdam (Netherlands) 2019, *General Assembly* Bogota (Colombia) 2018, *General Assembly* Calgary, AB (Canada) 2017, *Symposium* London (UK) 2015, *Congress* Delhi (India) 1991.
Members Full – national associations (45); Associate. Full members in 32 countries:
Australia, Austria, Belgium, Brazil, Bulgaria, Canada, Colombia, Czechia, Denmark, Ecuador, Estonia, France, Georgia, Germany, Greece, India, Indonesia, Ireland, Italy, Korea Rep, Mexico, Netherlands, New Zealand, Poland, Portugal, Serbia, Spain, Sweden, Switzerland, Türkiye, UK, USA.
Consultative Status Consultative status granted from: *ECOSOC (#05331)* (Ros A); *UNICEF (#20332)*. **IGO Relations** Cooperates with: *United Nations Economic Commission for Europe (UNECE, #20555)*; Working Party on Road Traffic Safety (WP-1); Inland and Transport Committee. **NGO Relations** Member of: *International Cooperation on Theories and Concepts in Traffic Safety (ICTCT, #12942)*. [2020/XD1973/**C**]

♦ International Federation of Pelota Vasca (#09340)
♦ International Federation of Pension Funds Administrators (#09334)
♦ International Federation of the Periodical Press / see FIPP (#09776)

♦ International Federation of Perioperative Nurses (IFPN) 13503

Headquarters c/o AFPP, Daisy Ayris House, 6 Grove Park Court, Harrogate, HG1 4DP, UK. T. +441423508079. Fax +441423531613. E-mail: secretary@ifpn.world – info@ifpn.world.
URL: https://www.ifpn.world/
History Jul 1999. **Aims** Improve patient care by promoting, preserving and advancing the role of perioperative nurses. **Structure** Board; Executive. **Languages** English. **Staff** Voluntary. **Finance** Sources: members' dues. Sponsorship; sales; educational endorsements. **Activities** Guidance/assistance/consulting; research/documentation; standards/guidelines. **Events** *Conference* Ottawa, ON (Canada) 2013. **Publications** *IFPN Newsletter* (6 a year) – online. Online journal; guidelines.
Members National organizations in 12 countries and territories:
Australia, Brazil, Canada, Japan, Kenya, Korea Rep, New Zealand, Papua New Guinea, South Africa, Thailand, UK, USA.
NGO Relations Affiliated with: *International Council of Nurses (ICN, #13054)*; national organizations. [2020/XD8840/**D**]

♦ International Federation of Permanent Exhibition Committees (inactive)

♦ International Federation of Persons with Physical Disability (FIMITIC) 13504

Fédération internationale des personnes handicapées physiques – Federación Internacional de Personas con Discapacidad Fisica – Internationaler Verband Körperbehinderter Menschen
Pres Camino de Valderribas 115, 28038 Madrid, Spain. T. +34917775544. Fax +34914776182. E-mail: international@medular.org – info@fimitic.org.
Office Rue Antoine Gautier 110, 1040 Brussels, Belgium.
URL: https://www.fimitic.org/
History 4 Oct 1953, Namur (Belgium). Former names and other names: *International Federation of Disabled Workers and Civilian Handicapped* – former; *Fédération internationale des mutilés, des invalides du travail et des invalides civils* – former; *Federación Internacional de Mutilados, de Invalidos de Trabajo y de Invalidos Civiles* – former. **Aims** As an international *humanitarian*, politically and religiously neutral umbrella federation of persons with physical disability under guidance of the disabled themselves, focus activities on insuring the equalization of opportunities and full participation of persons with physical disabilities in society and fight against any kind of discrimination against persons with disabilities. **Structure** Delegates' Conference (every 2 years); Executive Board. Special Commission: Disabled Women. Expert Groups (5): European Projects; Employment; Social Protection; Accessibility; Occupational Risks. **Languages** English, French, German. **Staff** 3.00 FTE, paid. **Finance** Members' dues. **Activities** Advocacy/lobbying/activism; events/meetings. **Events** *Annual General Assembly* Rome (Italy) 2015, *Annual General Assembly* Budapest (Hungary) 2014, *Biennial Delegates Conference* Madrid (Spain) 2011, *Biennial delegates conference / Delegates Conference* Nottwil (Switzerland) 2005, *Equalization Participation Conference* Rome (Italy) 2003. **Publications** *Bulletin NOUVELLES* (4 a year) in English, German. Information sheets; proceedings.
Members National federations in 26 countries:
Albania, Austria, Belarus, Belgium, Bulgaria, Croatia, Cyprus, Czechia, Estonia, Germany, Greece, Hungary, Ireland, Italy, Latvia, Liechtenstein, Lithuania, Moldova, North Macedonia, Poland, Portugal, Romania, Slovakia, Slovenia, Spain, Switzerland.
Consultative Status Consultative status granted from: *ILO (#11123)* (Special List). **IGO Relations** Accredited by: *United Nations Office at Vienna (UNOV, #20604)*. Associated with Department of Global Communications of the United Nations. **NGO Relations** Coordinator for the sector within: *European Disability Forum (EDF, #06929)*. In liaison with technical committees of: *International Organization for Standardization (ISO, #14473)*. [2019/XC1900/**D**]

♦ International Federation of Pétanque and Provençal Game (#09648)
♦ International Federation of Petroleum and Chemical Workers (inactive)

♦ International Federation of Pharmaceutical Manufacturers and Associations (IFPMA) 13505

Pres Chemin des Mines 9, PO BOX 195, 1211 Geneva 20, Switzerland. T. +41223383200. E-mail: info@ifpma.org.
URL: http://www.ifpma.org/
History Aug 1968. Founded following a joint meeting of *Groupement international de l'industrie pharmaceutique des pays de la CEE (GIIP, inactive)* and *Pharmaceutical Industries' Association in the EFTA (PIA, inactive)*, with Pharmaceutical Manufacturers Association (PMA) of the United States and Pharmaceutical Manufacturers Association of Canada (PMAC), Jun 1968, Stockholm (Sweden). Former names and other names: *Fédération internationale de l'industrie du médicament (FIIM)* – former; *Federación Internacional de la Industria del Medicamento (FIIM)* – former. Registration: EU Transparency Register, No/ID: 164230540254-23, Start date: 9 Nov 2020. **Aims** Engage with international organizations to build mutual understanding and find effective and sustainable solutions to major global health issues with a focus on medicines quality, innovation and access. **Structure** General Assembly (every 2 years); Council (meeting biannually); Committees (4). Secretariat in Geneva (Switzerland), headed by Director General. **Languages** English. **Staff** 19.00 FTE, paid. **Finance** Sources: members' dues. **Activities** Advocacy/lobbying/activism; events/meetings; networking/liaising. **Events** *Asia Regulatory Conference* Beijing (China) 2019, *Asia Partnership Conference of Pharmaceutical Associations* Tokyo (Japan) 2019, *Asia Partnership Conference of Pharmaceutical Associations* Tokyo (Japan) 2017, *Asia Regulatory Conference* Tokyo (Japan) 2017, *Biennial General Assembly* Washington, DC (USA) 2016. **Publications** *Biotherapeutic Medicines: Grasping the New Generation of Treatments* (2012); *Delivering the Promise of the Decade of Vaccines* (2012); *Developing World Health Partnership Directory* (2012); *Ending Neglected Tropical Diseases* (2012); *IFPMA Code of Practice* (2012); *Improving Global Health through Pharmaceutical Innovation* (2012); *Mental and Neurological Disorders: Innovative Theories, Innovative Collaborations* (2012); *The Changing Landscape on Access to Medicines* (2012); *The New Frontiers of Biopharmaceutical Innovation* (2012); *The Pharmaceutical Industry and GLobal Health: Facts and Figures* (2012). Reports; surveys.
Members Leading international companies and national and regional industry associations in the research-based pharmaceutical, biotech and vaccine sectors, covering developed and developing countries. Members in 45 countries and territories:
Argentina, Australia, Austria, Bangladesh, Belarus, Belgium, Bosnia-Herzegovina, Brazil, Canada, Chile, China, Colombia, Denmark, Ecuador, Finland, France, Georgia, Germany, Guatemala, Hong Kong, India, Indonesia, Ireland, Italy, Japan, Kenya, Korea Rep, Malaysia, Mexico, Netherlands, Norway, Peru, Philippines, Portugal, Russia, Singapore, South Africa, Spain, Sweden, Switzerland, Taiwan, Thailand, Türkiye, UK, USA.
Consultative Status Consultative status granted from: *ECOSOC (#05331)* (Ros C); *UNCTAD (#20285)* (General Category); *UNICEF (#20332)*; *UNIDO (#20336)*; *WHO (#20950)* (Official Relations); *World Intellectual Property Organization (WIPO, #21593)* (Permanent Observer Status). **IGO Relations** Consultative status with: *International Bank for Reconstruction and Development (IBRD, #12317)* (World Bank); *World Trade Organization (WTO, #21864)*. [2020/XC1976/y/**B**]

♦ International Federation of Pharmaceutical Wholesalers (IFPW) ... 13506

General Manager 10569 Crestwood Dr, Manassas VA 20109, USA. T. +17033313714. E-mail: info@ifpw.com.
URL: http://www.ifpw.com/
History 1977. **Aims** Help members advance health standards worldwide through effective use of pharmaceuticals. **Structure** General Meeting; Board of Directors. **Finance** Sources: members' dues; sponsorship. **Activities** Events/meetings; knowledge management/information dissemination. **Events** *Biennial General Membership Meeting* Tokyo (Japan) 2021, *Biennial General Membership Meeting* Tokyo (Japan) 2020, *Biennial General Membership Meeting* Washington, DC (USA) 2018, *Biennial General Membership Meeting* London (UK) 2016, *Biennial General Membership Meeting* Beijing (China) 2014. **Publications** *Focus* (26 a year) – newsletter. Membership directory.
Members Associations; distributors/wholesaler; manufacturers; service. Associations (5) in 4 countries:
China, Japan, Korea Rep, USA.
Regional association (1):
Groupement International de la Répartition Pharmaceutique (GIRP, #10762).
Distributor/wholesaler members in 14 countries and territories:
Argentina, Australia, Brazil, China, Finland, France, Hong Kong, Japan, Mexico, Norway, Peru, South Africa, Switzerland, USA.
Manufacturer members in 2 countries:
China, USA.
Service members in 3 countries:
Austria, Japan, USA.
NGO Relations Member of: *PMNCH (#18410)*. Partner of: *Every Woman Every Child (EWEC, #09215)*; *Fight the Fakes (#09755)*; *Gavi – The Vaccine Alliance (Gavi, #10077)*. [2016/XD5774/**C**]

♦ International Federation of Philosophical Societies (FISP) 13507

Fédération internationale des sociétés de philosophie (FISP) – Federación Internacional de Sociedades de Filosofia (FISP) – Internationale Vereinigung Philosophischer Gesellschaften (FISP)
Pres Via Lamberto de Bernardi 1, 20129 Milan MI, Italy.
SG Dept of Philosophy, Fac of Arts, Chulalongkorn Univ, Bangkok, Thailand.
URL: http://www.fisp.org/
History Founded at 10th International Philosophical Congress, when statutes were adopted. Superseded *Permanent Committee of the International Congresses of Philosophy (inactive)*, set up in Aug 1900. Statutes adopted at the 10th International Congress of Philosophy, Aug 1948, Amsterdam (Netherlands). Statutes modified: 22 Aug 1953, Brussels (Belgium); 24 Sep 1958, Venice (Italy); 16 Sep 1973, Varna (Bulgaria); 30 Aug 1978, Düsseldorf (Germany FR); 24 Aug 1983, Montréal (Canada); 24 Aug 1988, Brighton (UK); 25 Aug 1993, Moscow (Russia); 13 Aug 1998, Boston MA (USA); 13 Aug 2003, Istanbul (Turkey); 3 Aug 2008, Seoul (Korea Rep); 9 Aug 2013, Athens (Greece); 16 Aug 2018, Beijing (China). **Aims** Contribute to development of professional relations between philosophers; foster contacts between institutions and societies worldwide; collect documentation useful for development of philosophical studies; take action to overcome gender and race inequalities within philosophical communities; organize World Congress of Philosophy (WCP); promote philosophical education; prepare publications of global interest; contribute to impact of philosophical knowledge on global problems. **Structure** General Assembly (every 5 years); Bureau; Steering Committee; Honorary Presidents (3); Committees (9); Secretariat. **Languages** Chinese, English, French, German, Russian, Spanish. **Finance** Sources: members' dues. **Activities** Advocacy/lobbying/activism; events/meetings; guidance/assistance/consulting; knowledge management/information dissemination; networking/liaising; politics/policy/regulatory; publishing activities. Active in all member countries. **Events** *World Congress of Philosophy* Rome (Italy) 2024, *Conference* Seoul (Korea Rep) 2022, *World Congress of Philosophy* Beijing (China) 2018, *World Congress of Philosophy* Athens (Greece) 2013, *World Congress of Philosophy* Seoul (Korea Rep) 2008. **Publications** *FISP Newsletter / Bulletin* (2 a year) in English, French. *A Short History of the International Federation of Philosophical Societies (FISP)* (2003) by Evandro Agazzi; *Enseigner la philosophie aux non-philosophes – Teaching Philosophy to Non-Philosophers* (2003); *Les philosophes et la technique* (2003); *The Idea of Values* (2003); *Teaching Philosophy on the Eve of the Twenty-first Century* (1998); *The Idea and the Documents of Human Rights* (1995); *Philosophy and Cultural Development* (1993); *The Idea of Development: Between its Past and its Future* (1993); *Socrates pour tous – Socrates for Everybody*. Congress proceedings; various other works.
Members National Societies (102) in 68 countries and territories:
Argentina, Australia, Austria, Azerbaijan, Belarus, Belgium, Brazil, Bulgaria, Canada, Chile, China, Colombia, Côte d'Ivoire, Croatia, Cuba, Czechia, Denmark, Finland, France, Germany, Greece, Guatemala, Hungary, Iceland, India, Iran Islamic Rep, Ireland, Israel, Italy, Japan, Kazakhstan, Korea DPR, Korea Rep, Kosovo, Latvia, Luxembourg, Malta, Mexico, Mongolia, Montenegro, Morocco, Nepal, Netherlands, New Zealand, Nigeria, North Macedonia, Pakistan, Philippines, Poland, Portugal, Romania, Russia, Senegal, Singapore, Slovakia, South Africa, Spain, Sweden, Switzerland, Taiwan, Thailand, Türkiye, UK, Ukraine, Uruguay, USA, Uzbekistan, Venezuela.
Included in the above 2 organizations listed in this Yearbook:
Australasian Association of Philosophy (AAP); *Philosophical Society of Southern Africa (PSSA)*.
International societies (42), of which 38 listed in this Yearbook:
- *Asociación de Filosofía y Liberación (AFYL)*;
- *Asociación Latinoamericana de Filosofía Analítica (ALFAn, #02221)*;
- *Association des sociétés de philosophie de langue française (ASPLF, #02918)*;
- *Association for the Philosophy of Mathematical Practice (APMP, #02859)*;
- *Association internationale des professeurs de philosophie (AIPPh, #02732)*;
- *Association of Philosophers from South-Eastern Europe (#02857)*;
- *Conference of Philosophical Societies (CoPS)*;
- *Council for Research in Values and Philosophy (RVP, #04915)*;
- *European Association for Chinese Philosophy (EACP, #05972)*;
- *Friedrich Nietzsche Society (FNS, #09998)*;
- *George Santayana Society (GSS)*;
- *Gottfried-Wilhelm-Leibniz-Gesellschaft (GWLG, #10683)*;
- *Inter-African Council for Philosophy (IACP, no recent information)*;
- *International Academy of Philosophy of Sciences (IAPS, #11570)*;
- *International Association for Aesthetics (IAA, #11692)*;
- *International Association for Greek Philosophy (IAGP, #11925)*;
- *International Association for Japanese Philosophy (IAJP)*;
- *International Association for the Philosophy of Sport (IAPS, #12078)*;
- *International Association for the Study of Controversies (IASC, #12196)*;
- *International Association of Centrers for Peirce Studies (IACPS, #11762)*;
- *International Association of Women Philosophers (#12269)*;
- *Internationale Hegel-Vereinigung (#13247)*;
- *International Hegel Society (#13788)*;
- *International Institute of Philosophy (IIP, #13910)*;
- *International Plato Society (#14603)*;
- *International Society for Chinese Philosophy (ISCP, #15007)*;
- *International Society for Environmental Ethics (ISEE, #15094)*;
- *International Society for Islamic Philosophy (ISIP, #15220)*;
- *International Society for Metaphysics (ISM, #15265)*;
- *International Society for the History of Philosophy of Science (HOPOS, #15174)*;
- *International Society for Universal Dialogue (ISUD, #15529)*;
- *International Society for Value Inquiry (ISVI)*;
- *North American Society for Social Philosophy (NASSP)*;
- *Schopenhauer Society (#19135)*;
- *Sociedade de Filosofia da Educação de Lingua Portuguesa (SOFELP, #19355)*;
- *Société internationale pour l'étude de la philosophie médiévale (SIEPM, #19483)*;
- *Society for Asian and Comparative Philosophy (SACP)*;
- *World Union of Catholic Philosophical Societies (WUCPS, #21875)*.

Friends of FISP (3), listed in this Yearbook:
International Council for Philosophy and Human Sciences (CIPSH, #13061); *International Union of History and Philosophy of Science and Technology (IUHPST, #15779)* (Division of Logic, Methodology and Philosophy of Science DLMPS); *UNESCO (#20322)* (Section Human Security, Democracy and Philosophy, Division of Social and Human Sciences).
NGO Relations Member of (1): *International Council for Philosophy and Human Sciences (CIPSH, #13061)*. [2021.08.30/XA2011/y/**A**]

♦ International Federation of the Phonographic Industry (IFPI) 13508

Fédération internationale de l'industrie phonographique – Federación Internacional de la Industria Fonografica

Chief Exec 7 Air Street, London, W1B 5AD, UK. T. +442078787900. Fax +442078787950. E-mail: info@ifpi.org.

Registered Office c/o Markus Berni, Holbeinstrasse 30, 8008 Zurich ZH, Switzerland. T. +4112546161. Fax +4112546171.

URL: http://www.ifpi.org/

History Nov 1933, Rome (Italy). First statutes adopted at General Meeting, 31 May 1978, Oslo (Norway); amended at General Meetings: 19 Jun 1985, Geneva (Switzerland); 11 Jun 1987, Hamburg (Germany FR); 15 Jun 1989, Athens (Greece). Rules adopted: 31 May 1978, Oslo; amended: 14 Oct 1980, Delhi (India); 3 Jun 1982, Lisbon (Portugal); 19 Jun 1985, Geneva; 13 Mar 1986, London (UK); 11 Jun 1987, Hamburg; 15 Jun 1989, Athens; 11 Jun 1991, Budapest (Hungary). Current statutes adopted at General Meeting, 18 Apr 1996, Washington DC (USA); amended in 1997, 1998, 2000. Former names and other names: *International Federation of Producers of Phonograms and Videograms* – former; *Fédération internationale des producteurs de phonogrammes et vidéogrammes* – former; *Federación Internacional de Productores de Fonogramas y Videogramas* – former. Registration: Swiss Civil Code, Switzerland; EU Transparency Register, No/ID: 60394321918-91, Start date: 29 Jun 2009. **Aims** Promote the value of recorded music; campaign for record producer rights; expand commercial uses of recorded music in all member markets. **Structure** Secretariat, located in London (UK); Regional Offices (3); Representative Office; National Groups. **Languages** English, French. **Staff** None. **Finance** Sources: contributions; members' dues. **Activities** Advocacy/lobbying/activism; politics/policy/regulatory; research/documentation. **Events** *Annual Council Meeting* Stockholm (Sweden) 1994, *Annual Council Meeting* Brussels (Belgium) 1993, *Conference* Vienna (Austria) 1993, *Annual Council Meeting* London (UK) 1992, *Annual Council Meeting* Budapest (Hungary) 1991. **Publications** *IFPI Global Music Report*; *Investing in Music*; *Mastering of a Music City*; *Music Consumer Insight Report*.

Members National groups and affiliated music licensing companies in 57 countries and territories:
Argentina, Australia, Austria, Barbados, Belgium, Brazil, Bulgaria, Canada, Chile, Colombia, Costa Rica, Croatia, Czechia, Denmark, Dominican Rep, Ecuador, El Salvador, Finland, France, Germany, Greece, Guatemala, Hong Kong, Hungary, Iceland, India, Indonesia, Ireland, Israel, Italy, Jamaica, Japan, Korea Rep, Malaysia, Mexico, Netherlands, New Zealand, Norway, Panama, Paraguay, Peru, Poland, Portugal, Romania, Serbia, Singapore, South Africa, Spain, Sweden, Switzerland, Taiwan, Thailand, Türkiye, UK, Uruguay, USA, Venezuela.

Member companies (about 1,300) in 59 countries and territories:
Albania, Argentina, Australia, Austria, Belgium, Brazil, Bulgaria, Canada, Chile, China, Colombia, Congo DR, Costa Rica, Croatia, Czechia, Denmark, Egypt, Finland, France, Germany, Greece, Guatemala, Hong Kong, Hungary, Iceland, India, Indonesia, Iraq, Ireland, Israel, Italy, Japan, Korea Rep, Lebanon, Malaysia, Mexico, Nepal, Netherlands, New Zealand, Nigeria, Norway, Pakistan, Poland, Portugal, Romania, Russia, Serbia, Singapore, South Africa, Spain, Sri Lanka, Sweden, Switzerland, Taiwan, Thailand, Türkiye, UK, USA, Venezuela.

Consultative Status Consultative status granted from: *World Intellectual Property Organization (WIPO, #21593)* (Permanent Observer Status). **NGO Relations** Member of (1): *Creative Media Business Alliance (CMBA, #04947)*. Supports (1): *Music Climate Pact*. Associate expert of: *Business and Industry Advisory Committee to the OECD (BIAC, #03385)*. [2022.02.08/XB2028/t/**B**]

♦ International Federation of Photographic Art 13509

Fédération Internationale de l'Art Photographique (FIAP) – Federación Internacional del Arte Fotografico – Internationaler Verband der Photographischen Kunst

SG BP 19, L-3601 Kayl, Luxembourg. E-mail: info@fiap.net.

Headquarters 22 rue de Tétange, L-3672 Kayl, Luxembourg.

URL: http://www.fiap.net/

History 17 Jun 1950, Bern (Switzerland). Charter promulgated 1954, Barcelona (Spain). **Aims** Create links and friendly relations among affiliated federations and ensure defence of their legitimate interests; disseminate photographic knowledge by developing its artistic possibilities, notably by means of exhibitions and circulating portfolios; ensure representation before public authorities and international organizations. **Structure** Congress (every 2 years), consisting of up to 3 delegates per member country. Directory Board, comprising President, 2 Vice-Presidents, Secretary General, Treasurer and 4 members. **Languages** English, French, German, Spanish. **Staff** Voluntary. **Finance** Sources: members' dues. **Activities** Organizes: biennial photographic events for Monochrome Prints, Colour Prints, Projected Images and AV Sequences; international photographic exhibitions; travelling exhibitions. Youth photography. Historical collection. **Events** *Biennial Congress* Jaipur (India) 2020, *Biennial Congress* Durban (South Africa) 2018, *Biennial Congress* Seoul (Korea Rep) 2016, *Biennial Congress* Ankara (Turkey) 2014, *Biennial Congress* Singapore (Singapore) 2012. **Publications** National periodicals in English, French, German, Spanish.

Members National associations in 82 countries and territories:
Andorra, Argentina, Australia, Austria, Bahrain, Bangladesh, Belarus, Belgium, Bosnia-Herzegovina, Brazil, Bulgaria, Cameroon, Canada, Chile, China, Colombia, Croatia, Cuba, Cyprus, Czechia, Denmark, Dominican Rep, Egypt, Finland, France, Germany, Great Britain, Greece, Guatemala, Haiti, Hong Kong, Hungary, India, Indonesia, Iran Islamic Rep, Iraq, Ireland, Israel, Italy, Japan, Jordan, Korea Rep, Kuwait, Latvia, Liechtenstein, Luxembourg, Macau, Malaysia, Malta, Mauritius, Netherlands, New Zealand, North Macedonia, Norway, Oman, Pakistan, Panama, Poland, Qatar, Romania, Russia, San Marino, Saudi Arabia, Scotland, Serbia, Singapore, Slovakia, Slovenia, South Africa, Spain, Sri Lanka, Suriname, Sweden, Switzerland, Thailand, Tunisia, Türkiye, Ukraine, United Arab Emirates, Uruguay, Vietnam, Wales.

Consultative Status Consultative status granted from: *UNESCO (#20322)* (Consultative Status). [2020/XB1977/**B**]

♦ International Federation of Physical Education / see International Federation of Physical and Sport Education (#13510)

♦ International Federation of Physical Medicine and Rehabilitation (inactive)

♦ International Federation of Physical and Sport Education 13510

Fédération internationale d'éducation physique et sportive (FIEPS) – Federación Internacional de Educación Física e Sportiva – Federação Internacional de Educação Física e Sportiva

Pres Caixa Postal 437, CEP 85 857-970 PR, Foz do Iguaçu PR, Brazil. T. +554535230039. Fax +554535250039. E-mail: atendimento@fiep.net – fiep.brasil.fiep@gmail.com.

FIEPS Europe Comenius University in Bratislava, Fac of Physical Education and Sports, L Svobodu 9, 814 69 Bratislava, Slovakia. E-mail: branislav.antala@uniba.sk.

Main: http://www.fieps.net/

History 1923, Brussels (Belgium). *World Manifesto on Physical Education'* adopted by General Assembly, 1971, Lisbon (Portugal). *'World Manifesto 2000'* adopted, Jan 2000, Foz do Iguaçu (Brazil). Former names and other names: *Fédération internationale de gymnastique éducative* – former (1923 to 1930); *Fédération internationale de gymnastique Ling (FIGL)* – former (1930 to 1953); *International Federation of Physical Education* – former (1953 to 2021); *Fédération internationale d'éducation physique (FIEP)* – former (1953 to 2021); *Federación Internacional de Educación Física* – former (1953 to 2021); *Federação Internacional de Educação Física* – former (1953 to 2021). **Aims** Promote development of activities in the fields of education, Sport for All, *recreation* and the outdoors, for people of all ages and in all countries; foster and contribute to international cooperation in these fields; promote pedagogical and technical experience, scientific research and exchange of ideas; find best possible solutions to problems in the field. **Structure** General Assembly (annual, at Congress); Council; Executive Board; International sections. **Languages** English, French, Portuguese, Spanish. **Staff** Voluntary. **Finance** Sources: government support; grants; members' dues. Supported by: *International Olympic Committee (IOC, #14408)*. **Activities** Awards/prizes/competitions; events/meetings; financial and/or material support; research/documentation; training/education. **Events** *World Congress* Foz do Iguaçu (Brazil) 2023, *European Congress* Galati (Romania) 2023, *Asia Conference* Chiba (Japan) 2022, *European Congress* Vierumäki (Finland) 2022, *World Congress* Vierumäki (Finland) 2022. **Publications** *FIEP Bulletin* (3 a year) in English, French, Portuguese, Spanish – journal. Scientific books. Scientific Sessions published in articles and abstracts in FIEP Bulletins.

Members Individual; Collective – Institutions; Collective – National; Honorary; Benefactor; Correspondent. Members in 129 countries and territories:
Algeria, Argentina, Australia, Austria, Bahrain, Bangladesh, Belgium, Benin, Bolivia, Bosnia-Herzegovina, Botswana, Brazil, Bulgaria, Burkina Faso, Cameroon, Canada, Chad, Chile, China, Colombia, Congo Brazzaville, Congo DR, Cook Is, Costa Rica, Croatia, Cuba, Czechia, Denmark, Djibouti, Dominica, Dominican Rep, Ecuador, Egypt, El Salvador, Estonia, Ethiopia, Fiji, Finland, France, Gambia, Germany, Ghana, Greece, Guatemala, Guyana, Haiti, Honduras, Hong Kong, Hungary, India, Indonesia, Iran Islamic Rep, Iraq, Ireland, Israel, Italy, Jamaica, Japan, Jordan, Kenya, Kiribati, Korea Rep, Kuwait, Latvia, Lebanon, Libya, Lithuania, Luxembourg, Madagascar, Malawi, Malaysia, Mali, Malta, Marshall Is, Mauritania, Mexico, Montenegro, Morocco, Netherlands, New Zealand, Niger, Nigeria, North Macedonia, Norway, Oman, Pakistan, Palau, Palestine, Papua New Guinea, Paraguay, Peru, Philippines, Poland, Portugal, Puerto Rico, Qatar, Romania, Russia, Samoa, Saudi Arabia, Senegal, Serbia, Singapore, Slovakia, Slovenia, South Africa, Spain, Sri Lanka, Sudan, Sweden, Switzerland, Taiwan, Tanzania UR, Thailand, Togo, Tonga, Trinidad-Tobago, Tunisia, Uganda, UK, Ukraine, United Arab Emirates, Uruguay, USA, Vanuatu, Venezuela, Yemen, Zambia, Zimbabwe.

NGO Relations Member of (1): *International Council of Sport Science and Physical Education (ICSSPE, #13077)*. [2022.10.11/XB1834/**B**]

♦ International Federation of Physical Therapists working in Occupational Health and Ergonomics (IFPTOHE) 13511

Pres address not obtained.

URL: https://ifptohe.wixsite.com/ifptohe

History May 2019, Geneva (Switzerland). Founded as a subgroup of *World Confederation for Physical Therapy (WCPT, #21293)*. **Aims** Support, develop and promote, the international practice of physiotherapists working in occupational health and ergonomics, so as to improve the health and wellbeing of the global workforce. **Structure** Committee.

Members Full in 22 countries:
Australia, Brazil, Denmark, Estonia, Finland, Greece, Iceland, Ireland, Japan, Kenya, Malta, Netherlands, New Zealand, Norway, Peru, Slovenia, South Africa, Spain, Sweden, Switzerland, Uganda, UK. [2023/AA3137/**E**]

♦ International Federation of Phytosociology (inactive)

♦ International Federation of Pigment Cell Societies (IFPCS) 13512

Main Office address not obtained. E-mail: ifpcs@ifpcs.org.

URL: http://www.ifpcs.org/

History 1977. Former names and other names: *International Pigment Cell Society (IPCS)* – former (1977 to 1990). **Aims** Foster and enhance internationally the study of and research on normal or abnormal pigment cells and pigmentation in humans and other animals; foster scientific collaboration, cooperation and communication among member societies dedicated to research in the field: establish guidelines or mechanisms for interaction of member societies; encourage dissemination of knowledge and results of new investigations in the field. **Structure** Council (meets annually), comprising President, Vice-President, Secretary, Treasurer, Webmaster and 12 members (3 ex-officio). Committees (2): Publications; Women Scientists. Special Committee, comprising one member from each constituent society collects data on resources available to the pigment cell community. Special Interest Groups (7): Genetics of Pigmentation; Biology of Melanoma; Pigment Cell Development; Hypo/Hyperpigmentation; Ocular/Extracutaneous Pigmentation; Vitiligo; InterPig Database. **Languages** English. **Staff** Council, part-time; voluntary. **Finance** Sources: meeting proceeds; members' dues; sale of publications; sponsorship. Budget varies. **Activities** Awards/prizes/competitions; events/meetings; guidance/assistance/consulting; research and development. Offers: Myron Gordon Award at triennial conference; Visiting Scientist Awards. Provides a mechanism for selecting a scientist who has made recent and significant advances in pigment cell research, to present Seiji Lecture at triennial conference; addresses and/or resolves research issues and problems of international concern or which transcend national or regional boundaries; provides consultation and information to groups, nations or international bodies regarding all aspects of pigmentation, pigment cells, tanning and related topics. **Events** *International Pigment Cell Conference (IPCC)* Bilbao (Spain) 2023, *International Pigment Cell Conference (IPCC)* Yamagata (Japan) 2020, *International Pigment Cell Conference (IPCC)* Denver, CO (USA) 2017, *International Pigment Cell Conference (IPCC)* Singapore (Singapore) 2014, *International Pigment Cell Conference (IPCC)* Bordeaux (France) 2011. **Publications** *Pigment Cell and Melanoma Research* (6 a year) – journal. **Information Services** *InterPig DataBase* – lists all reagents, probes and other materials available for research targeted towards pigment cells, including those for chemical, biochemical, immunological, molecular biology and other types of studies; *Mouse Coat Color Genes* – lists all cloned and uncloned mouse pigmentary genes and human orthologues and related diseases.

Members National, regional and international societies. Membership countries not specified. Founding members (3):
Founding members (3):
European Society for Pigment Cell Research (ESPCR, #08707); Japanese Society of Pigment Cell Research; *Pan American Society for Pigment Cell Research (PASPCR, #18132)*.
Other international member:
Asian Society for Pigment Cell Research (ASPCR, #01735). [2023.02.20/XD4683/y/**D**]

♦ International Federation of Placenta Associations (IFPA) 13513

Sec c/o Hudson Inst, 27-31 Wright St, Clayton VIC 3168, Australia. E-mail: info@ifpa.epineux.com.

URL: http://www.ifpa.epineux.com/

History Oct 1994, Sydney (Australia), as *International Federation of Placental Associations (IFPA)*, at 1st International Meeting of World Placental Associations, following suggestion, 1992, of 12th Rochester Trophoblast Conference and 5th Meeting of European Placenta Group, Sep 1993, Manchester (UK). Registered in the state of Delaware (USA). **Aims** Provide official representation of placentology; organize professional interaction; promote excellence in the field of placental research; encourage further development of existing and new regional groups and coordinate their meetings; provide organizational base for association with appropriate publications; forum for information dissemination; facilitate international cooperation. **Structure** General Assembly; Executive Committee. Officers: President; Secretary; Treasurer. **Activities** Events/meetings; training/education. **Events** *Meeting* Erfurt (Germany) 2025, *Meeting* Montréal, QC (Canada) 2024, *Meeting* Rotorua (New Zealand) 2023, *Meeting* Rotorua (New Zealand) 2022, *Meeting* Amsterdam (Netherlands) 2021. **Publications** *Placenta*; *Trophoblast Research*.

Members Corporate national placenta organizations (2) in 2 countries, representing their respective regions:
Australia (for Australia/New Zealand/Southeast Asia), Japan.
Regional organizations (2):
European Placenta Group (EPG, #08209) (for Europe/Middle East); *Placenta Association of the Americas (PAA)* (for North America/Central America/South America).
Individual scientists involved in placental research in 12 countries:
Australia, Austria, Canada, Denmark, France, Germany, Japan, Switzerland, Taiwan, UK, USA, Venezuela. [2019/XD5176/**D**]

♦ International Federation of Placental Associations / see International Federation of Placenta Associations (#13513)

♦ International Federation of Plantation, Agricultural and Allied Workers (inactive)

♦ International Federation of Podiatrists (IFP) 13514

Fédération Internationale des Podologues (FIP)

Hon Pres 57 rue Eugene Carriere, 75018 Paris, France. E-mail: secretariat@fip.global.

URL: http://www.fip.global

History 1947. Reorganized 1979. Former names and other names: *International Federation of Podology* – former (1947 to 1993); *Fédération internationale de podologie* – former (1947 to 1993); *International Federation of Chiropodists and Podiatrists (IFP)* – former (1993 to 2016); *Fédération internationale des podologues et podiatres (FIP)* – former (1993 to 2016); *Federación Internacional de Podologos y Podiatras (FIPP)* – former (1993 to 2016); *Internationalen Podologen- und Podiaterverbands* – former (1993 to 2016); *Federazione Internazionale Podologi e Podiatri* – former (1993 to 2016); *Fédération Internationale des Podiatres et Podologues (FIP)* – former (1993 to 2016); *International Federation of Podiatrists and Podologues* – former (1993 to 2016). Registration: Start date: 27 Jun 1963, France. **Aims** Advance podiatry worldwide through education, advocacy and strategic alliances for the benefit of those with foot and ankle ailments. **Structure** Governing Council; Executive Board; *Academy of International Podiatric Educators*. Committees (6): Articles of Association (AAC); *European Council of Podiatrists (ECP)*; Scientific Committee; International Recruitment (IRC); Special Olympics International (SOI); *World Foot Health Awareness Committee (WFHAMC)*. Commissions (3): *International Humanitarian Aid Commission (IHAC)*; World Congress Advisory Commission (WCAC); *World Diabetes Commission*, International Podiatry Day(IPD). **Languages** English, French. **Staff** Paid; voluntary. **Finance** Sources: members' dues; sponsorship. **Activities** Events/meetings; training/education. **Events** *World Congress of Podiatry* 2024, *Annual General Meeting* Sliema (Malta) 2022, *World Congress of Podiatry* Barcelona (Spain) 2021, *World Congress of Podiatry* Miami, FL (USA) 2019, *World Congress of Podiatry* Montréal, QC (Canada) 2016. **Publications** Newsletter.

Members Active (national associations); Associate (individuals); Honorary. National associations, representing over 80,000 individual podiatrists in 22 countries and territories:
Belgium, Canada, Czechia, Denmark, Finland, France, Germany, Greece, Hong Kong, Iceland, Ireland, Israel, Italy, Malta, Morocco, Netherlands, Norway, Poland, South Africa, Sweden, Switzerland, USA. [2022.12.27/XD5206/**C**]

- ♦ International Federation of Podiatrists and Podologues / see International Federation of Podiatrists (#13514)
- ♦ International Federation of Podology / see International Federation of Podiatrists (#13514)
- ♦ International Federation of Police Officials (inactive)

♦ International Federation of Popular Sports 13515

Fédération internationale des sports populaires – Internationaler Volkssportverband (IVV)
Sec 20 rue des Remparts, L-4303 Esch-sur-Alzette, Luxembourg.
URL: http://www.ivv-web.org/

History 1968, Germany FR. Founded 1968, Lindau/Bodensee (Germany FR), by clubs from Austria, Germany FR, Liechtenstein and Switzerland. Previously also known under the English acronym *IFPS* and the French *FISP*. Registered 20 Jan 1972, Munich (Germany). Current statutes and by-laws adopted 8 Jun 2001. **Aims** Foster public health by encouraging outdoor sports *leisure* activity; promote peace and understanding among peoples through friendship developed among participants from different countries. **Structure** Congress of Delegates; Praesidium. **Languages** English, German. **Staff** Voluntary. **Finance** Self-financed. Annual budget: 100,000 EUR. **Activities** Events/meetings. **Events** *Congress* Ottawa, ON (Canada) 2022, *Congress* Ostend (Belgium) 2020, *Congress* Mazara del Vallo (Italy) 2018, *Congress* Rio de Janeiro (Brazil) 2016, *Congress* Hamburg (Germany) 2014. **Publications** Calendar of events (annual).
Members National organizations and individual sports and walking clubs in countries with no national organization (marked ") totalling 5,500 member clubs in 37 countries and territories:
Australia, Austria, Belgium, Brazil, Canada, China, Croatia, Czechia, Denmark, Estonia, Finland, France, Germany, Greece, Hungary, Iceland, Ireland, Italy, Japan, Korea Rep, Liechtenstein, Luxembourg, Netherlands, New Zealand, Norway, Poland, Portugal, Russia, Slovakia, Slovenia, Spain, Sweden, Switzerland, Taiwan, Türkiye, UK, USA.
IGO Relations Cooperates with: *WHO (#20950)*. **NGO Relations** Member of: *The Association for International Sport for All (TAFISA, #02763)*. [2015.02.02/XD6260/**C**]

- ♦ International Federation of Popular Travel Organizations (inactive)
- ♦ International Federation of Porcelain Manufacturers (inactive)
- ♦ International Federation of Potters (inactive)
- ♦ International Federation of Power Agriculture (inactive)
- ♦ International Federation of Practitioners of Natural Therapeutics (inactive)
- ♦ International Federation of Press Clipping and Media Monitor Bureaux / see Fédération internationale des bureaux d'extraits de presse (#09617)
- ♦ International Federation of Press Cutting Agencies (#09617)

♦ International Federation of Primary Care Research Networks (IFPCRN) 13516

Chair School of Health Sciences, Univ of Crete, PO Box 2208, 710 03 Heraklion, Greece.
URL: http://www.ifpcrn.org/

History 2001, under auspices of the Task Force on Research of *World Organization of Family Doctors (WONCA, #21690)*. **Aims** Support research for primary health care. **Structure** Steering Committee, including Chair and Vice-Chair. **Languages** English. **Finance** On budget of *World Organization of Family Doctors (WONCA, #21690)*. **Activities** Collaborative research; policy and advocacy campaigns; mutual support; capacity building. Formal meetings held during WONCA and affiliated meetings and the meetings of *North American Primary Care Research Group (NAPCRG)*. **Publications** Books. **Members** Individuals (153) representing networks (53) in 45 countries and territories. Membership countries not specified. [2010.06.01/XM8150/**E**]

♦ International Federation of Private Water Operators (AquaFed) 13517

Exec Dir 135 rue Saint Martin, 75004 Paris, France. T. +33153890810. Fax +33153890810. E-mail: info@aquafed.org.
Brussels Office Rond Point Schuman 6, Box 5, 1040 Brussels, Belgium. T. +3222347807. Fax +3222347911. E-mail: thomas@aquafed.org.
URL: http://www.aquafed.org/

History 2005. Registration: Start date: 3 Mar 2005, France; EU Transparency Register, No/ID: 09175433167-27, Start date: 2 Feb 2010. **Aims** Connect international organizations with private sector providers of water and *sanitation* services. **Structure** General Meeting (annual); Executive Committee; Secretariat; Working Groups. **Languages** Dutch, English, French, Spanish. **Activities** Advocacy/lobbying/activism; standards/guidelines.
Members Categories National Industry Associations; Corporate; Associate. National Industry Associations in 7 countries:
Benin, Brazil, Chile, Czechia, France, Uganda, USA.
Corporate members in 132 countries:
Australia, Brazil, China, France, Gabon, Germany, India, Indonesia, Italy, Morocco, Philippines, Spain, USA.
Consultative Status Consultative status granted from: *ECOSOC (#05331)* (Special). **IGO Relations** Registered in the EU Transparency Register. Partner of: *UN-Water (#20723)*. **NGO Relations** Member of: *European PPP Operating Companies in Infrastructure and Services (E3PO, #08266)*; *European Water Partnership (EWP, #09083)*; *Global Water Operators' Partnerships Alliance (GWOPA, #10652)*; *Water Integrity Network (WIN, #20830)*; *World Water Council (WWC, #21908)*. Associate partner of: *Business and Industry Advisory Committee to the OECD (BIAC, #03385)*. Partner of: *Sanitation and Water for All (SWA, #19051)*; *World Business Council for Sustainable Development (WBCSD, #21254)*. [2020/XJ0349/**C**]

- ♦ International Federation for Produce Coding / see International Federation for Produce Standards (#13518)
- ♦ International Federation of Producers of Phonograms and Videograms / see International Federation of the Phonographic Industry (#13508)

♦ International Federation for Produce Standards (IFPS) 13518

Secretariat PO Box 6036, Newark DE 19714-6036, USA. E-mail: info@ifpsglobal.com.
Contact c/o Fresh Produce Consortium, Minerva House, Minerva Business Park, Peterborough, PE2 6FT, UK.
URL: http://www.ifpsglobal.com/

History 2001. Former names and other names: *International Federation for Produce Coding (IFPC)* – former (2001). Registration: England and Wales. **Aims** Improve the supply chain efficiency of the fresh produce industry through developing, implementing and managing harmonized international standards. **Structure** Board of Directors; Secretariat. Committees (4): Food Safety; Product Identification; Chain Information Management; Communications. **Activities** Events/meetings; knowledge management/information dissemination.
Members Full in 8 countries:
Australia, Canada, Chile, Netherlands, New Zealand, Norway, UK, USA.
IGO Relations Observer to: *Codex Alimentarius Commission (CAC, #04081)*. [2021/XM5604/**C**]

- ♦ International Federation of Professional Abortion and Contraception Associates (#09612)
- ♦ International Federation of Professional Aromatherapists (internationally oriented national body)
- ♦ International Federation of Professional Coaches and Mentors (inactive)
- ♦ International Federation of Professional Footballers' Associations (#09633)
- ♦ International Federation of Professional Relief Workers (inactive)
- ♦ International Federation of Professional Speakers / see Global Speakers Federation (#10612)
- ♦ International Federation of Professional and Technical Engineers (internationally oriented national body)
- ♦ International Federation of Progressist Composers and Musicologists (inactive)
- ♦ International Federation for the Promotion of the French Language (inactive)

♦ International Federation for the Promotion of Mechanism and Machine Science (IFToMM) 13519

SG address not obtained.
Pres address not obtained.
URL: https://iftomm-world.org/

History 27 Sep 1969, Zakopane (Poland). Founded at Inaugural Assembly which formally adopted the Constitution, following 2nd International Congress on Theory of Machines and Mechanism. Constitution most recently amended at 12th General Assembly, 2015, Taimei (Taiwan). Former names and other names: *International Federation for the Theory of Machines and Mechanisms* – former (1969). **Aims** Promote developments in the field of machines and mechanisms by theoretical and experimental research and practical application; broaden contacts among persons and organizations engaged in this field; promote exchange of scientific and *engineering* information, experts and students among countries; honour eminent scientists, engineers and organizations in the field; establish necessary relationships with other international organizations. **Structure** General Assembly of members (normally at IFoMM World Congress, at least every 4 years); Executive Council; Committees (3); Permanent Commissions (4); Technical Committees (13). **Languages** English. **Staff** None. **Finance** Members' dues from IFToMM territory members (5 categories of voting members). Other sources: subsidies, donations or grants from organizations or private persons. **Activities** Events/meetings; research and development. **Events** *World Congress* Tokyo (Japan) 2023, *World Congress* Krakow (Poland) 2019, *International Symposium on Robotics and Mechatronics* Taipei (Taiwan) 2019, *International Tribology Symposium* Jeju (Korea Rep) 2017, *International Symposium on Robotics and Mechatronics* Sydney, NSW (Australia) 2017. **Publications** *Chinese Journal of Mechanical Engineering*; *IFToMM Newsletter*; *Journal of Vibration Engineering and Technologies*; *Mechanism and Machine Theory* – journal; *Open-acess Mechanical Sciences*.
Members Voting: (A) national or territorial organizations (one per territory); (B) international organizations (not specified) with allied interests. Non-voting: (C) Honorary. National Committees in 47 countries and territories:
Armenia, Australia, Austria, Azerbaijan, Belarus, Brazil, Bulgaria, Canada, China, Croatia, Czechia, Egypt, Finland, France, Georgia, Germany, Greece, Hungary, India, Israel, Italy, Japan, Kazakhstan, Korea Rep, Lithuania, Mexico, Mongolia, Netherlands, North Macedonia, Peru, Poland, Portugal, Romania, Russia, Serbia, Singapore, Slovakia, Slovenia, Spain, Switzerland, Taiwan, Tunisia, Türkiye, UK, Ukraine, USA, Vietnam. [2022/XC3907/**C**]

- ♦ International Federation of Property Managers and Real Estate Consultants / see Fédération internationale des professions immobilières (#09653)
- ♦ International Federation for Proprioceptive and Biomechanical Therapies (internationally oriented national body)
- ♦ International Federation for the Protection of Indigenous Races Against Alcoholism (inactive)
- ♦ International Federation for the Protection of Populations (inactive)
- ♦ International Federation for the Protection of the Rights of Ethnic, Religious, Linguistic and Other Minorities (inactive)

♦ International Federation of Psoriasis Associations (IFPA) 13520

Exec Dir Gustavslundsvägen 143, SE-167 51 Bromma, Sweden. E-mail: info@ifpa-pso.com.
URL: http://ifpa-pso.com/

History 1973, Umeå (Sweden). **Aims** Unite psoriasis associations so that their global campaign for improved *medical care*, greater public understanding and increased research will improve the lives of people who live with psoriasis and psoriatic arthritis and explore the challenges psoriasis presents to the international psoriasis community. **Structure** General Assembly (at least every third year). Executive Committee, comprising President, Vice-President, Secretary, Treasurer, Member-at-Large and 2 Substitutes. **Languages** English. **Staff** 3.00 FTE, paid. **Finance** Sources: members' dues. **Activities** Advocacy/lobbying/activism; events/meetings; knowledge management/information dissemination; networking/liaising. Events/meetings. *Global Psoriasis Coalition*. **Events** *World Psoriasis and Psoriatic Athritis Conference* Stockholm (Sweden) 2021, *General Assembly* Barcelona (Spain) 2019, *World Psoriasis and Psoriatic Arthritis Conference* Stockholm (Sweden) 2018, *General Assembly* Brussels (Belgium) 2017, *General Assembly* Lisbon (Portugal) 2016. **Publications** *IFPA Newsletter*.
Members National bodies in 47 countries and territories:
Argentina, Australia, Austria, Belgium, Canada, Chile, Colombia, Croatia, Czechia, Denmark, El Salvador, Estonia, Finland, France, Germany, Iceland, Indonesia, Ireland, Israel, Japan, Kenya, Malaysia, Mexico, Netherlands, New Zealand, Norway, Panama, Peru, Philippines, Poland, Portugal, Puerto Rico, Russia, Scotland, Singapore, Slovakia, South Africa, Spain, Sweden, Switzerland, Tanzania UR, Türkiye, UK, Ukraine, USA, Venezuela, Vietnam.
Consultative Status Consultative status granted from: *ECOSOC (#05331)* (Special). **IGO Relations** Cooperates with: *WHO (#20950)*. **NGO Relations** Full member of: *International Alliance of Patients' Organizations (IAPO, #11633)*. [2021/XD9525/**B**]

♦ International Federation of Psychiatric Epidemiology (IFPE) 13521

Fédération internationale d'épidémiologie psychiatrique (FIEP) – Federación Internacional de Epidemiologia Psiquiatrica (FIEP) – Internationaler Verband Psychiatrischer Epidemiologie (IVPE)
SG Dept of Paediatrics, Univ of Melbourne, Parkville VIC 31052, Australia. T. +61393456502.
Pres Med Univ of Vienna, Dept of Psychiatry and Psychotherapy, Währinger Gürtel 18-20, 1090 Vienna, Austria.
URL: http://proj1.sinica.edu.tw/~ifpe/

History 1985. Statutes adopted 1993; revised 1999; 2004. Registered in accordance with Swiss Civil Code. **Aims** Promote the acquisition, dissemination and application of epidemiological knowledge in the fields of psychiatry and mental health. **Structure** General Assembly (during Congress); Committee. **Languages** English. **Staff** None. **Finance** Members' dues. **Events** *Congress* Bergen (Norway) 2015, *The uses of psychiatric epidemiology in improving population mental health* Leipzig (Germany) 2013, *Mental health and global recession – psychiatric illness, violence and substance abuse in populations under stress* Kaohsiung (Taiwan) 2011, *Congress* Vienna (Austria) 2009, *Congress* Gothenburg (Sweden) 2007. **Publications** *IFPE Bulletin* (2 a year).
Members Individuals in 25 countries and territories:
Argentina, Armenia, Australia, Austria, Belgium, Brazil, Canada, China, Cuba, Denmark, France, Germany, India, Israel, Italy, Japan, Malaysia, Netherlands, Norway, Spain, Sweden, Switzerland, Taiwan, UK, USA.
Corporate members in 6 countries:
Canada, France, Italy, Spain, Switzerland, UK.
Regional Corporate member (1):
Nordic Association for Psychiatric Epidemiology (NAPE, #17201). [2014.09.23/XD4876/**D**]

♦ International Federation of Psychoanalytic Societies (IFPS) 13522

Federación Internacional de Sociedades Psicoanaliticas – Internationale Vereinigung Psychoanalytischer Gesellschaften
SG Avda las Condes, 9792D, OF 1203, Las Condes, 755 0000 Santiago, Santiago Metropolitan, Chile. T. +5623713902. E-mail: contact@ifps.info.
Deputy SG address not obtained.
URL: http://www.ifps.info/

History 30 Jul 1962, Amsterdam (Netherlands). **Aims** Create and maintain a space permitting production and reconstruction of psychoanalytic theory and technique. **Structure** Assembly of Delegates; Executive Committee. **Languages** English, German, Spanish. **Staff** 0.50 FTE, voluntary. **Finance** Members' dues. Annual budget: about US$ 30,000. **Events** *Forum* Lisbon (Portugal) 2020, *Forum* Florence (Italy) 2018, *Forum* New York, NY (USA) 2016, *Forum* Kaunas (Lithuania) 2014, *Forum* Mexico City (Mexico) 2012. **Publications** *International Forum of Psychoanalysis* – journal. *International Federation of Psychoanalytic Societies – Membership Directory*.
Members Psychoanalytic societies in 17 countries:
Austria, Brazil, Canada, Chile, Finland, Germany, Greece, Iran Islamic Rep, Italy, Lithuania, Mexico, Norway, Portugal, Spain, Sweden, Switzerland, USA.
Study Groups in 2 countries:
Cuba, Egypt. [2020/XD7361/**D**]

- ♦ International Federation of the Psychological-Medical Organizations (inactive)

♦ International Federation for Psychotherapy (IFP) 13523

Fédération internationale de psychothérapie (FIP) – Federación Internacional de Psicoterapia (FIP) – Internationale Föderation für Psychotherapie (IGP)
Secretariat Zentralstrasse 91, 2503 Biel BE, Switzerland.
URL: https://ifpnet.org/

History 1934, Germany. Founded as *International General Society for Psychotherapy (IGMSP)*. Re-established, 1954, as *International Federation for Medical Psychotherapy (IFMP) – Fédération internationale de psychothérapie médicale (FIPM) – Federación Internacional de Psicoterapia Médica (FIPM) – Internationale Gesellschaft für Ärztliche Psychotherapie (IGAP)*. Statutes modified, 7 Sep 1958, Barcelona (Spain). New statutes adopted Aug 1993; revised 24 Aug 2006, Kuala Lumpur (Malaysia). Originally to promote psychotherapy in the field of medicine, renamed with current title when goals were extended to cover non-medical professions. Registered in accordance with Swiss Civil Code. **Aims** Facilitate and promote international communication among schools, professional groups and cultures within psychotherapy. **Structure** Assembly (convened during Congress); Council; Board; Regional Chapters, including *Asia-Pacific Association of Psychotherapists (APAP, #01852)*. **Languages** English, French, German, Spanish. **Staff** 0.50 FTE, paid. **Finance** Sources: members' dues. **Activities** Events/meetings; knowledge management/information dissemination; research and development; standards/guidelines; training/education. **Events** *World Congress of Psychotherapy* Casablanca (Morocco) 2023, *Congress* Amsterdam (Netherlands) 2018, *Contributing to global health* Shanghai (China) 2014, *Psychotherapy – science and culture* Lucerne (Switzerland) 2010, *Well being across cultures – psychotherapy in a biological era* Kuala Lumpur (Malaysia) 2006. **Publications** *Psychotherapy and Psychosomatics* (6 a year) – official journal; *IFP Newsletter* (2 a year). Congress reports.
Members Societies (30) and individuals in 25 countries:
Australia, Austria, Brazil, Canada, China, Cyprus, Germany, Honduras, India, Indonesia, Israel, Italy, Korea Rep, Mexico, Netherlands, Norway, Poland, Portugal, Singapore, South Africa, Spain, Sweden, Switzerland, UK, USA.
NGO Relations Affiliated with: *Society for the Exploration of Psychotherapy Integration (SEPI, #19557)*; *Society for Psychotherapy Research (SPR, #19626)*; *World Psychiatric Association (WPA, #21741)* (Psychotherapy Section). [2020/XC1830/**C**]

♦ International Federation of PTT Employees (inactive)
♦ International Federation for Public Health (inactive)

♦ International Federation for Public History (IFPH) 13524
Fédération internationale pour l'histoire publique (FIHP)

Pres C2DH, 11 Porte des Sciences, University of Luxembourg, L-4365 Esch-sur-Alzette, Luxembourg. T. +3524666446247.
URL: http://ifph.hypotheses.org/

History 2009. Launched as an NCPH Task force for International Public History. Became an internal commission of *International Committee of Historical Sciences (ICHS, #12777)*, 2010. Transformed into current federation between 2011 and 2012. **Aims** Encourage, promote, and coordinate, at an international level, teaching and research in public history. **Structure** General Assembly; Steering Committee; Committees (3). **Languages** English, French. **Finance** Sources: members' dues. **Events** *World Conference* Berlin (Germany) 2022, *World Conference* Berlin (Germany) 2020, *Annual Conference* Sao Paulo (Brazil) 2018, *Annual Conference* Ravenna (Italy) 2017, *Annual Conference* Bogota (Colombia) 2016. **NGO Relations** Member of (1): *International Committee of Historical Sciences (ICHS, #12777)*. [2020.05.10/XJ5062/**E**]

♦ International Federation of Pueri Cantores (#09649)
♦ International Federation of Purchasing (inactive)
♦ International Federation of Purchasing and Materials Management / see International Federation of Purchasing and Supply Management (#13525)

♦ International Federation of Purchasing and Supply Management (IFPSM) 13525

Registered Office 7 Lynwood Court, Priestlands Place, Lymington, S041 9GA, UK.
Pres address not obtained.
URL: http://www.ifpsm.org/

History 14 May 1974, London (UK), as *International Federation of Purchasing and Materials Management (IFPMM) – Fédération internationale de l'approvisionnement et de l'achat – Internationale Vereinigung für Einkauf und Materialwirtschaft – Federación Internacional de Compras y Dirección de Materiales*, when *International Federation of Purchasing (IFP, inactive)*, set up 15 May 1965, New York NY (USA), in succession to *International Committee of Purchasing (inactive)*, set up 1964, London, merged with *European Federation of Purchasing (EFP, inactive)*, created 18 Oct 1958, Düsseldorf (Germany FR). **Aims** Further the principles and practice of purchasing and materials management as a basic and distinct function of the management structure of industry, *trade* and public undertaking; promote, encourage, undertake and coordinate study of problems affecting purchasing and materials management and further relevant solutions; ensure the highest standards of business ethics of those engaged in the profession; promote and encourage development of personal capabilities of all involved in purchasing and materials management activities; provide a recognized body through which purchasing and materials management can be represented in matters of international interest; encourage and assist development of national associations and national education schemes; assist in founding national associations in countries where such bodies do not as yet exist. **Structure** Congress (every 2 years); Council (meets annually), consisting of 2 representatives from each member association; Executive Committee; Secretary General. **Languages** English. **Staff** 1.00 FTE, paid. **Finance** Contributions of member associations. **Activities** Supports the programmes of national associations and helps in particular those which are developing towards a professional standard. Organizes world congresses and supports regional conferences and congresses sponsored by national associations. World Certification Programme; Eurodiploma Educational Scheme; Certificate of Competence. Acts as a clearing house for information on members' research activities; sustains flexible specialized groups. Annual awards: Garner-Thémoin Medal; Maple Leaf Award to increase the availability of written communication among member associations; Lew Spangler – Purchasing Professional Award; Hans Ovelgönne Purchasing Research Award. Hans Ovelgönne Fund supports important research projects and development programmes. **Events** *World Summit* Bali (Indonesia) 2022, *World Summit* Bali (Indonesia) 2021, *World Summit* Bali (Indonesia) 2020, *World Summit* Mombasa (Kenya) 2019, *Biennial World Summit* Helsinki (Finland) 2018. **Publications** *IFPMM Newsletter* (2 a year). Annual report. Business Briefing; purchasing and materials management journal for Europe and Global Edition; international trade directory.
Members National associations (43), representing more than 200,000 purchasing professionals. Members in 39 countries and territories:
Australia, Austria, Belgium, Chile, China, Denmark, Eswatini, Finland, France, Germany, Greece, Hong Kong, Hungary, Indonesia, Ireland, Italy, Kenya, Korea Rep, Malaysia, Mexico, Monaco, Morocco, Netherlands, New Zealand, Norway, Philippines, Poland, Portugal, Singapore, Slovakia, South Africa, Spain, Sri Lanka, Sweden, Switzerland, Thailand, Türkiye, USA.
Consultative Status Consultative status granted from: *ECOSOC (#05331)* (Ros C); *UNCTAD (#20285)* (General Category). [2018/XC1989/**C**]

♦ International Federation of Radio Officers (inactive)
♦ International Federation of Railway Advertising Companies (inactive)
♦ International Federation of Railwaymen's Art and Intellectual Societies (#09660)
♦ International Federation of Railwaymen's Travel Associations (inactive)
♦ International Federation of Record Libraries (inactive)
♦ International Federation of Recreational Vehicle Users (inactive)

♦ International Federation of Red Cross and Red Crescent Societies . 13526
Fédération internationale des sociétés de la Croix-Rouge et du Croissant-Rouge – Federación Internacional de Sociedades de la Cruz Roja y de la Media Luna Roja

SG IFRC Secretariat, PO Box 303, 1211 Geneva 19, Switzerland. T. +41227304222. Fax +41227304200. E-mail: secretariat@ifrc.org.
Visiting Address Chemin des Crêts 17, Petit-Saconnex, 1211 Geneva 19, Switzerland.
URL: http://www.ifrc.org/

History 5 May 1919, Paris (France). Original title: *League of Red Cross Societies (LORCS) – Ligue des sociétés de la Croix-Rouge (LSCR) – Liga de Sociedades de la Cruz Roja Liga der Rotkreuz-Gesellschaften*, on the initiative of Henry P Davison, one of the leaders of the American Red Cross. Name changed, Oct 1983, to *League of Red Cross and Red Crescent Societies – Ligue des sociétés de la Croix-Rouge et du Croissant-Rouge – Liga de Sociedades de la Cruz Roja y de la Media Luna Roja – Liga der Rotkreuz- und Rothalbmond-Gesellschaften*. Current name adopted Nov 1991, having already been referred to in that way as a supplementary title. The acronym *IFRC* is sometimes used. Together with *International Committee of the Red Cross (ICRC, #12799)* and all officially recognized national Red Cross and Red Crescent societies, a constituent part of the *International Red Cross and Red Crescent Movement (#14707)*. Registration: EU Transparency Register, No/ID: 132236315085-89, Start date: 1 Dec 2014. **Aims** As a volunteer-based humanitarian network, act before, during and after *disasters* and *health* emergencies to meet the needs and improve the lives of *vulnerable* people, impartial to nationality, race, gender, religious beliefs, class and political opinions. **Structure** Governing Bodies: General Assembly (every 2 years); Executive Council. These are assisted by Commissions. Permanent Secretariat in Geneva (Switzerland) comprises divisions and departments dealing with the spheres of activity in which national societies are permanently engaged. Regional delegations (15). Country delegations (43). Reference Centres (12): *Red Cross Red Crescent Climate Centre (Climate Centre)*; Global Disaster Preparedness Center; Red Cross Caribbean Disaster Risk Management Reference Centre; Disaster Preparedness Reference Center; IFRC Global First Aid Reference Centre; Centre for Evidence-Based Practice; Livelihoods Centre; Psychosocial Support Centre; Reference Centre for Community Education on Disaster Preparedness; Reference Centre on Volunteering; Shelter Technical Unit; *Asia Pacific Disaster Resilience Centre (APDRC)*. **Languages** Arabic, English, French, Spanish. **Staff** Worldwide: 2,000, of which 300 based at Geneva Secretariat. *Administrative Tribunal of the International Labour Organization (ILO Tribunal, #00118)* is competent to settle disputes. **Finance** Contributions of member societies on a pro-rata basis. Specific activities (such as in relief operations and development programmes) financed by voluntary contributions of national societies.
Activities *'Disaster Response'*
- Assess, Train and Evaluate Relief Services.
- Emergency Response Units – independent units ready for the field, specialized in basic health care, referral hospitals, water/sanitation, logistics and telecommunications and information/media.
- Relief Health – communicable diseases alleviation and vaccinations; psychological support and stress management; health education; medicines; mobile clinics and nursing care.
- Food Distribution and Nutrition.
- Clothing/Shelter.
- Refugee Camp Management.
- Water/Sanitation – wells; bore holes; pumping; water distribution; latrines and health education.
- Information on Humanitarian Rights – promotion of international humanitarian law and basic standards for humanitarian assistance.

'Development Assistance':
- Capacity Building of National Societies – training and development of staff and volunteers; establishment and strengthening of structures of national societies through resource and institutional development; improving governance and management systems and processes.
- Disaster Preparedness – identifying disaster risks and strengthening local structure of national societies; provision of training, personnel and equipment; building relations with other humanitarian organizations.
- Health – community-based health care; AIDS/substance abuse prevention; first aid in the community; health education, family planning; strengthening existing health services (medicine, equipment and training).
- Youth Activities and Gender Integration.
- *Red Cross and Red Crescent Youth (see: #13526)*.
- Social Welfare – community development; vulnerable and homeless children; the elderly; people with disabilities.
- Promotion of Humanitarian Values – building awareness of the fundamental principles of the Red Cross/Red Crescent Movement (humanity, impartiality, neutrality, independence, voluntary service, unity, universality) and of international humanitarian law.

'Joint Activities with ICRC':
- Joint ICRC/Federation Commission for National Society Statutes;
- Joint ICRC/Federation Meetings (at least 3 times a year), including *European Regional Red Cross and Red Crescent Conference*.

Events *AidEx : Europe's Leading Humanitarian and Development Aid Conference* Brussels (Belgium) 2019, *World Conference on Health and Climate Change* Cannes (France) 2019, *Conference on Histories of the Red Cross Movement since 1919* Geneva (Switzerland) 2019, *General Assembly* Geneva (Switzerland) 2019, *Asia Pacific Regional Conference* Manila (Philippines) 2018. **Publications** *Red Cross/Red Crescent Magazine* (3 a year); *World Disaster Report* (annual). *Code of Conduct for the International Red Cross and Red Crescent Movement and Non-Governmental Organizations (NGOs) in Disaster Relief* (1995); *Improving the Situation of the Most Vulnerable: Strategic Work Plan for the Nineties* (1995); *Codes of Ethics and Fundamentals of Voluntary Service* (1993). Basic and reference texts; training manuals; handbooks; guides; strategic work plans; brochures and surveys on such subjects as AIDS, appeals, arms race, development, development assistance, disasters, environment, first aid, floods, health, human rights, humanitarian assistance, international humanitarian law, management, national societies, organizations, policies, Red Cross movement, refugees, safety measures, social welfare, strategy, violence, volunteers, war, women and youth.
Members Full: national Red Cross and Red Crescent societies, independent and officially recognized, working in accordance with the principles of the Geneva Conventions and those formulated by the International Conference of the Red Cross and the Federation's General Assembly. Societies with full membership in 186 countries:
Afghanistan, Albania, Algeria, Andorra, Angola, Antigua-Barbuda, Argentina, Armenia, Australia, Austria, Azerbaijan, Bahamas, Bahrain, Bangladesh, Barbados, Belarus, Belgium, Belize, Benin, Bolivia, Bosnia-Herzegovina, Botswana, Brazil, Brunei Darussalam, Bulgaria, Burkina Faso, Burundi, Cambodia, Cameroon, Canada, Cape Verde, Central African Rep, Chad, Chile, China, Colombia, Comoros, Congo Brazzaville, Congo DR, Cook Is, Costa Rica, Côte d'Ivoire, Croatia, Cuba, Czechia, Denmark, Djibouti, Dominica, Dominican Rep, Ecuador, Egypt, El Salvador, Equatorial Guinea, Estonia, Eswatini, Ethiopia, Fiji, Finland, France, Gabon, Gambia, Georgia, Germany, Ghana, Greece, Grenada, Guatemala, Guinea, Guinea-Bissau, Guyana, Haiti, Honduras, Hungary, Iceland, India, Indonesia, Iran Islamic Rep, Iraq, Ireland, Israel, Italy, Jamaica, Japan, Jordan, Kazakhstan, Kenya, Kiribati, Korea DPR, Korea Rep, Kuwait, Kyrgyzstan, Laos, Latvia, Lebanon, Lesotho, Liberia, Libya, Liechtenstein, Lithuania, Luxembourg, Madagascar, Malawi, Malaysia, Mali, Malta, Mauritania, Mauritius, Mexico, Micronesia FS, Moldova, Monaco, Mongolia, Montenegro, Morocco, Mozambique, Myanmar, Namibia, Nepal, Netherlands, New Zealand, Nicaragua, Niger, Nigeria, North Macedonia, Norway, Pakistan, Palau, Palestine, Panama, Papua New Guinea, Paraguay, Peru, Philippines, Poland, Portugal, Qatar, Romania, Russia, Rwanda, Samoa, San Marino, Sao Tomé-Principe, Saudi Arabia, Senegal, Serbia, Seychelles, Sierra Leone, Singapore, Slovakia, Slovenia, Solomon Is, Somalia, South Africa, Spain, Sri Lanka, St Kitts-Nevis, St Lucia, St Vincent-Grenadines, Sudan, Suriname, Sweden, Switzerland, Syrian AR, Tajikistan, Tanzania UR, Thailand, Timor-Leste, Togo, Tonga, Trinidad-Tobago, Tunisia, Türkiye, Turkmenistan, Uganda, UK, Ukraine, United Arab Emirates, Uruguay, USA, Uzbekistan, Vanuatu, Venezuela, Vietnam, Yemen, Zambia, Zimbabwe.
National Societies pending recognition and admission in 1 country:
Maldives.
Consultative Status Consultative status granted from: *ILO (#11123)* (Special List); *UNESCO (#20322)* (Consultative Status); *FAO (#09260)*; *UNICEF (#20332)*; *UNEP (#20299)*.
IGO Relations Main United Nations partners: UNICEF; WHO; *World Food Programme (WFP, #21510)*. Recognized by: *European Commission (EC, #06633)*. Guest status with: *Coordinating Bureau of the Non-Aligned Countries (#04815)* and *Non-Aligned Movement (NAM, #17146)* – represented at *Conference of Heads of State or Government of Non-Aligned Countries*. Participates in the work of: *United Nations Economic Commission for Europe (UNECE, #20555)*, and member of Working Party (Prevention Road Traffic Accidents). Accredited to the Conference of the Parties of: *Secretariat of the United Nations Convention to Combat Desertification (Secretariat of the UNCCD, #19208)*. Accredited by: *United Nations Framework Convention on Climate Change – Secretariat (UNFCCC, #20564)*; *United Nations Office at Vienna (UNOV, #20604)*. Permanent Observer to: *ECOSOC (#05331)*. Observer to: *International Organization for Migration (IOM, #14454)*; General Assembly of *United Nations (UN, #20515)*. Member of: *Arctic Council (#01097)*; *Arctic Monitoring and Assessment Programme (AMAP, #01100)*. Associated with Department of Global Communications of the United Nations. Cooperates with:
- *African Centre of Meteorological Applications for Development (ACMAD, #00242)*;
- *African Development Bank (ADB, #00283)*;
- *Center for Information on Migration in Latin America (#03643)*;
- *Economic Community of West African States (ECOWAS, #05312)*;
- *ESCAP/WMO Typhoon Committee (TC, #05534)*;
- *Intergovernmental Panel on Climate Change (IPCC, #11499)*;
- *Joint United Nations Programme on HIV/AIDS (UNAIDS, #16149)*;
- *Organisation of Islamic Cooperation (OIC, #17813)*;
- *PAHO/WHO Health Emergencies Department (PHE, #18023)*;
- *Pan American Health Organization (PAHO, #18108)*;
- *UNDP (#20292)*;
- *UNHCR (#20327)*;
- *United Nations Office on Drugs and Crime (UNODC, #20596)*;
- *United Nations Population Fund (UNFPA, #20612)*;
- *United Nations Volunteers (UNV, #20650)*;
- *WHO Regional Office for Africa (AFRO, #20943)*;

- *WHO Regional Office for the Eastern Mediterranean (EMRO, #20944);*
- *WHO Regional Office for Europe (#20945);*
- *WHO Regional Office for South-East Asia (SEARO, #20946);*
- *WHO Regional Office for the Western Pacific (WPRO, #20947);*
- *World Customs Organization (WCO, #21350);*
- *World Meteorological Organization (WMO, #21649).*

NGO Relations Instrumental in setting up: *Arab Red Crescent and Red Cross Organization (ARCO, #01033); European Network for Psychosocial Support (ENPS, #07978); European Network on Volunteer Development (ENDOV, #08032); Red Cross and Red Crescent Network against Trafficking in Human Beings (no recent information).* Memorandum of Understanding with: *International Amateur Radio Union (IARU, #11646).* British and South African offices receive support from: *Charities Aid Foundation of America (CAF America).* Cooperates with: *Environment Liaison Centre International (ELCI, no recent information); International Life Saving Federation (ILS, #14040); International Olympic Committee (IOC, #14408); PfP Consortium of Defence Academies and Security Studies Institutes (#18345).* Netherlands Society cooperates with: *Unrepresented Nations and Peoples Organization (UNPO, #20714).* Permanent observer of: *International Council of Voluntary Agencies (ICVA, #13092).* Represented on: *Inter-Agency Task Force for Disaster Reduction (IATF, inactive).* In liaison with technical committees of: *International Organization for Standardization (ISO, #14473).* Supports: *Development Training International (DTI); Media for Development International (MFDI); Red Cross EU Office (#18643).* Partner of: *Global Health Cluster (GHC, #10401); International Communications Volunteers (ICVolunteers, #12817); ProVention Consortium (inactive); Stop TB Partnership (#19999).* Represented on the Board of: *The Sphere Project (#19918).* Member of:

- *Active Learning Network for Accountability and Performance in Humanitarian Action (ALNAP, #00101);*
- *Association for Human Resources Management in International Organizations (AHRMIO, #02634);*
- *CHS Alliance (#03911);*
- *EarthAction (EA, #05159);*
- *European Council on Refugees and Exiles (ECRE, #06839);*
- *Fédération des Institutions Internationales établies à Genève (FIIG, #09599);*
- *Global Partnership for the Prevention of Armed Conflict (GPPAC, #10538);*
- *Global Road Safety Partnership (GRSP, #10581);*
- *International Council on Archives (ICA, #12996);*
- *NetHope (#16979);*
- *NGO Committee on the Status of Women, Geneva (#17117);*
- *NGO Committee on UNICEF (#17120);*
- *Steering Committee for Humanitarian Response (SCHR, #19978);*
- *Vereniging voor Personele Samenwerking met Ontwikkelingslanden (PSO, inactive).* [2021/XB2907/**B**]

♦ International Federation of Regional Airlines Associations (inactive)

♦ International Federation of Registered Equine Massage Therapists (unconfirmed)

♦ International Federation of Religions for Eternal Peace of the World / see Office of the World Peace Envoy

♦ International Federation of Renal Registries (no recent information)

♦ International Federation of Reproduction Rights Organizations (IFRRO) 13527

Fédération internationale des organisations défendant les droits de reproduction

Secretariat Rue de Prince Royal 85-87, 1050 Brussels, Belgium. T. +3222346260. Fax +3222346269. E-mail: secretariat@ifrro.org.

URL: http://www.ifrro.org/

History 1980. Founded as a working group of *International Publishers Association (IPA, #14675)* and *International Association of Scientific, Technical and Medical Publishers (STM, #12154).* In May 1984, became a consortium known as *International Forum for Reproduction Rights Organizations (IFRRO) – Forum international des organisations défendant les droits de reproduction*, also referred to as *Forum international des organisations de droit de réprographie* and *Fédération internationale des sociétés d'auteurs.* Current name adopted at 14th IFRRO Meeting, 14-16th Oct 1987, London (UK). Became a formal international federation as of Apr 1988. Current statutes adopted Oct 2006, Auckland (New Zealand). Relevant conventions: *Bern Convention for the Protection of Literary and Artistic Works, 1886 (1886), Universal Copyright Convention, 1971 (1971)* and *WTO Agreement on Trade Related Aspects of Intellectual Property Rights (TRIPS, 1994).* Registration: EU Transparency Register, No/ID: 860729437196-92; Belgium. **Aims** Foster the fundamental international *copyright* principles embodied in the above conventions. **Structure** General Meeting (annual); Board of Directors; Permanent Secretariat in Brussels (Belgium), headed by Chief Executive. **Languages** English. **Staff** 4.50 FTE, paid. **Finance** Sources: members' dues. **Activities** Training/education. **Events** *Annual General Meeting* Reykjavik (Iceland) 2023, *Annual General Meeting* Brussels (Belgium) 2022, *Annual General Meeting* Montréal, QC (Canada) 2021, *Annual General Meeting* Brussels (Belgium) 2020, *World Congress* Singapore (Singapore) 2020. **Publications** *IFRRO Newsletter* (5 a year). *RRO Development Handbook.* Quick Guides; papers; annual brochure.

Members Full RROs; Creator and Publisher Associations. Members in 72 countries and territories:
Andorra, Argentina, Australia, Austria, Azerbaijan, Barbados, Belgium, Belize, Brazil, Bulgaria, Burkina Faso, Cameroon, Canada, Chile, China, Colombia, Côte d'Ivoire, Croatia, Czechia, Denmark, Faeroe Is, Finland, France, Georgia, Germany, Ghana, Greece, Hong Kong, Hungary, Iceland, India, Indonesia, Ireland, Italy, Jamaica, Japan, Kazakhstan, Kenya, Korea Rep, Lithuania, Luxembourg, Malawi, Mauritius, Mexico, Netherlands, New Zealand, Nigeria, Norway, Panama, Philippines, Portugal, Romania, Russia, Serbia, Singapore, Slovakia, Slovenia, South Africa, Spain, St Lucia, Sweden, Switzerland, Taiwan, Tanzania UR, Trinidad-Tobago, Türkiye, Uganda, UK, Uruguay, USA, Zambia, Zimbabwe.

International organizations (12):
European Magazine Media Association (EMMA, #07723); European Newspaper Publishers' Association (ENPA, #08048); European Visual Artists (EVA, #09071); European Writers' Council (EWC-FAAE, #09123); Federation of European Publishers (FEP, #09536); FIPP (#09776); International Association of Scientific, Technical and Medical Publishers (STM, #12154); International Council of Design (ICoD, #13013); International Federation of Journalists (IFJ, #13462); International Publishers Association (IPA, #14675); Press Database Licensing Network (PDLN, #18487); Pyramide Europe (#18585).

Observer in 1 country:
Poland.

Consultative Status Consultative status granted from: *World Intellectual Property Organization (WIPO, #21593)* (Permanent Observer Status); *UNESCO (#20322)* (Consultative Status). **NGO Relations** Member of: *EDItEUR (#05361); European Policy Centre (EPC, #08240); International DOI Foundation (IDF, #13188).* Supports: *PLR International (#18407).* [2020/XD1501/y/**C**]

♦ International Federation for Research in Women's History (IFRWH) . 13528

Fédération internationale pour la recherche en histoire des femmes (FIRHF)

Vice-Pres Dept of History, Univ of Oulu, PO Box 1000, FI-90014 Oulu, Finland.

URL: http://www.ifrwh.com/

History Apr 1987. **Aims** Encourage and promote research in all aspects of women's and gender history at international level. **Structure** Board; Committees (4). **Languages** English, French. **Staff** 8.00 FTE, voluntary. **Finance** Sources: members' dues. **Activities** Events/meetings. **Events** *Conference* Poznań (Poland) 2022, *Conference* Poznań (Poland) 2020, *Transnationalisms, transgressions, translations – conversations and controversies* Vancouver, BC (Canada) 2018, *Women and Modernity* Jinan (China) 2015, *Women's histories – the local and the global* Sheffield (UK) 2013. **Publications** *IFRWH Newsletter* (2 a year). *Women's Activism: Global Perspectives from the 1890s to the Present* (2013); *Women's History Review – vol 20* (2011); *Women's Rights and Human Rights: International Historical Perspectives* (2001); *Nation, Empire, Colony* (1998); *Writing Women's History: International Perspectives* (1991). Conference reports.

Members National committees in 36 countries:
Argentina, Australia, Austria, Bangladesh, Brazil, Bulgaria, Canada, Croatia, Czechia, Denmark, Finland, France, Germany, Greece, Hungary, India, Ireland, Israel, Italy, Japan, Lithuania, Malta, Netherlands, New Zealand, Nigeria, Norway, Pakistan, Poland, Portugal, Russia, Slovakia, Spain, Sweden, Switzerland, UK, USA.

NGO Relations Affiliated to: *International Committee of Historical Sciences (ICHS, #12777).* [2022/XD1850/**C**]

♦ International Federation of Resistance Fighters / see International Federation of Resistance Movements (#13529)

♦ International Federation of Resistance Movements 13529

Fédération internationale des résistants (FIR) – Federación Internacional de Resistentes – Internationale Föderation der Widerstandskämpfer – Mezdunarodnaja Federacija Borcov Soprotivlenija

Gen Sec c/o VVN-BdA, Magdalenenstr 19, 10365 Berlin, Germany. E-mail: office@fir.at.

URL: http://www.fir.at/

History 3 Jul 1951, Vienna (Austria). Founded by *Fédération internationale des anciens prisonniers politiques du fascisme (FIAPP, inactive).* New statutes adopted 16 Dec 1962, Warsaw (Poland); amended: 16 Nov 1969, Venice (Italy); 28 Nov 1973, Paris (France); Nov 2004, Berlin (Germany). Former names and other names: *International Federation of Resistance Movements – Antifascist Association* – former; *Fédération internationale des résistants (FIR – association antifasciste)* – former; *Federación Internacional de Resistentes* – former; *Internationale Föderation der Widerstandskämpfer – Bund der Antifaschisten* – former; *Mezdunarodnaja Federacija Borcov Soprotivlenija* – former; *International Federation of Resistance Fighters* – former. Registration: EU Transparency Register, No/ID: 241644214670-52. **Aims** Act against *neo-fascism* and extreme rightwing, xenophobia and *anti-Semitism*, war and terrorism as well as their social roots; preserve the memories of the victims of Nazism and the women and men who fought against fascist barbarism in the ranks of the Anti-Hitler-Coalition, as partisans and resistance fighters. **Structure** Congress (at least every 3 years); Executive Committee; Secretariat. **Languages** English, French, German, Russian. **Staff** 1.00 FTE, paid. **Finance** Sources: gifts, legacies; members' dues. **Activities** Awareness raising; events/meetings; research/documentation. **Events** *Danger of Extreme Right Wing Policy in Europe* Belgrade (Serbia) 2022, *Congress* Reggio Emilia (Italy) 2019, *Congress* Prague (Czechia) 2016, *Congress* Sofia (Bulgaria) 2013, *Extraordinary Congress* Vienna (Austria) 2011. **Publications** *E-Newsletter* (weekly); *FIR – News* (4 a year) in English, French, German. Conference reports; brochures. **Information Services** *Documentation Centre.*

Members National organizations of ex-resistance fighters for freedom against an occupying power; ex-political prisoners, deportees, internees and all other victims of nazism or their legal representatives (totalling over 5 million members). Affiliated national associations in 30 countries:
Albania, Austria, Belarus, Belgium, Bosnia-Herzegovina, Bulgaria, Chile, Croatia, Cyprus, Czechia, Denmark, Estonia, France, Germany, Greece, Hungary, Israel, Italy, Latvia, Netherlands, North Macedonia, Poland, Portugal, Romania, Russia, Serbia, Slovakia, Slovenia, Spain, Ukraine.

IGO Relations Accredited by (1): *United Nations Office at Vienna (UNOV, #20604).* **NGO Relations** Member of (3): *European Network against Racism (ENAR, #07862); NGO Committee on Disarmament, Peace and Security, New York NY (#17106); United4Rescue.* Together with: *Confédération Européenne des Anciens Combattants (CEAC, #04537); International Confederation of Former Prisoners of War (ICFPW, inactive); The World Veterans Federation (WVF, #21900)*, instrumental in setting up *Coordinating Committee of 4 International Veterans Organizations – Comité de coordination des 4 organisations internationales d'anciens combattants.* [2022.10.11/XD1996/**C**]

♦ International Federation of Resistance Movements – Antifascist Association / see International Federation of Resistance Movements (#13529)

♦ International Federation of Restructuring, Insolvency and Bankruptcy Professionals (INSOL International) 13530

COO 6-7 Queen St, London, EC4N 1SP, UK. T. +442072483333. Fax +442072483384. E-mail: heather@insol.ision.co.uk – info@insol.ision.co.uk.

URL: http://www.insol.org/

History Founded 1982, as *International Federation of Insolvency Professionals (INSOL International).* Subsequently named *International Federation of Insolvency, Bankruptcy and Turnaround Professionals.* **Aims** Seek international *professional* recognition of insolvency practitioners; improve their knowledge and communications with each other. **Structure** Board of Directors. **Finance** Members' dues. **Activities** Events/meetings. **Events** *INSOL Conference* London (UK) 2022, *Quadrennial Conference* San Diego, CA (USA) 2021, *Regional Conference* Singapore (Singapore) 2019, *Regional Conference* New York, NY (USA) 2018, *Quadrennial Conference* Sydney, NSW (Australia) 2017. **Publications** *INSOL World* (4 a year) – journal; *INSOL International Insolvency Review* (3 a year).

Members National associations of accountants and lawyers who specialize in the insolvency area ('member professionals'), representing 10,000 insolvency practitioners and individual practitioners in 73 countries and territories:
Argentina, Australia, Austria, Bahamas, Bahrain, Belgium, Bermuda, Brazil, Bulgaria, Canada, Cayman Is, Chile, China, Croatia, Cyprus, Czechia, Denmark, Estonia, Finland, France, Germany, Ghana, Greece, Hong Kong, Hungary, Iceland, India, Indonesia, Ireland, Israel, Italy, Japan, Jordan, Kuwait, Latvia, Lithuania, Luxembourg, Malaysia, Mauritius, Mexico, Moldova, Nepal, Netherlands, New Zealand, Nigeria, North Macedonia, Norway, Peru, Philippines, Poland, Portugal, Qatar, Romania, Russia, Serbia, Singapore, Slovakia, Slovenia, South Africa, Spain, Sri Lanka, Sweden, Switzerland, Türkiye, UK, Ukraine, United Arab Emirates, Uruguay, USA, Venezuela, Virgin Is UK, Zambia, Zimbabwe.

Included in the above, 2 organizations listed in this Yearbook:
INSOL Europe (#11231); International Women's Insolvency and Restructuring Confederation (IWIRC). [2019.04.24/XF0553/ty/**F**]

♦ International Federation of Retail Jewellers, Watchmakers and Goldsmiths (inactive)

♦ International Federation for the Rights of Man / see International Federation for Human Rights (#13452)

♦ International Federation of Risk and Insurance Management Associations (IFRIMA) 13531

Pres c/o Companhia Siderúrgica Nacional, Av Brigadeiro Faria Lima 3400, 20 Andar, Itaim Bibi, Sao Paulo SP, 04538-132, Brazil.

Sec c/o FERMA, Av de Tervuren 273, 1150 Brussels, Belgium.

URL: http://www.ifrima.org/

History 1984, Paris (France). **Aims** Provide a forum for interaction and communications among risk management associations and their members. **Structure** Board of Directors, comprising one representative of each member association, is chaired by immediate Past-President and also includes President, Executive Vice-President, Vice-President, Secretary and Treasurer. **Languages** English. **Staff** 0.50 FTE, paid. **Finance** Members are assessed to cover specific costs incurred. **Activities** Events/meetings. **Events** *Conference* Geneva (Switzerland) 2007, *Europe, the world and the future – opportunities for risk management* Lisbon (Portugal) 2005, *Risk management evolution or extinction* Johannesburg (South Africa) 2002.

Members National risk and insurance management associations (23) in 16 countries:
Argentina, Australia, Belgium, Brazil, Canada, France, Italy, Japan, Malaysia, Mexico, Russia, Singapore, South Africa, Spain, UK, USA.

Regional associations (2):
Asociación Latinoamericano de Administradores de Riesgos y Seguros (ALARYS, #02275); Federation of European Risk Management Associations (FERMA, #09539). [2022.10.25/XD1960/y/**C**]

♦ International Federation of Robotics (IFR) 13532

Gen Sec c/o VDMA Robotics and Automation, Lyoner Str 18, 60528 Frankfurt-Main, Germany. T. +496966031502. E-mail: secretariat@ifr.org.

URL: https://ifr.org/

History 1987. Founded in connection with the 17th International Symposium on Robotics (ISR), by robotics organizations from over 15 countries. **Aims** Promote research, development, use and international cooperation in the entire field of robotics; act as focal point for organizations, governmental representatives and robotics manufacturing companies in related activities. **Structure** General Assembly; Executive Board; Robot Suppliers Committee; Research Committee; Service Robot Group; Working Groups. **Languages** English. **Staff** 3.00 FTE, paid. **Finance** Sources: members' dues. **Activities** Events/meetings; guidance/assistance/consulting; knowledge management/information dissemination; networking/liaising; publishing activities; research and development. **Events** *International Symposium on Robotics (ISR Europe)* Munich (Germany) 2022, *ISR : International Symposium on Robotics* Yekaterinburg (Russia) 2021, *ISR : International Symposium on Robotics* Munich (Germany) 2020, *ISR : International Symposium on Robotics* Chicago, IL (USA) 2019, *ISR : International Symposium on Robotics* Munich (Germany) 2018. **Publications** *World Robotics – Service Robots, Statistics* (annual); *World Robotics – Industrial Robots, Statistics* (annual); *IFR Robotics Newsletter.*

Members Full; Supporting; Affiliate. Member associations in 26 countries and territories:
Austria, Canada, China, Denmark, France, Germany, India, Israel, Italy, Japan, Korea Rep, Luxembourg, Malaysia, Netherlands, Norway, Romania, Russia, Slovakia, Slovenia, Spain, Sweden, Switzerland, Taiwan, Türkiye, UK, USA.

Included in the above, one international organization listed in this Yearbook:
Institute of Electrical and Electronics Engineers (IEEE, #11259).
Consultative Status Consultative status granted from: *ECOSOC (#05331)* (Ros A). **NGO Relations** Cooperates with (1): *International Organization for Standardization (ISO, #14473).* [2022.06.14/XD1851/C]

♦ International Federation of Rock Art Organizations (IFRAO) 13533

Convenor PO Box 216, Caulfield VIC SOUTH 3162, Australia. Fax +61395230549. E-mail: auraweb@hotmail.com.
URL: http://www.ifrao.com/

History 1988, Darwin, NT (Australia). Constitution approved at Meeting, 1 Sep 1995, Turin (Italy). **Aims** Promote high scholarly standards of rock art research and publications by providing guidelines for global standards of rock art study, *conservation*, recording and classifying; serve as a clearing house for the dissemination of rock art data; ensure maximum appreciation and protection of rock art resources. **Structure** Authorized Meeting (usually every 2 years). **Languages** English. **Staff** 60.00 FTE, voluntary. **Finance** Sources: donations; grants. **Activities** Events/meetings; training/education. **Events** *Congress* Perth, WA (Australia) 2024, *Congress* Darfo Boario Terme (Italy) 2018, *Symbols in the landscape – rock art and its context* Caceres (Spain) 2015, *Congress* Guiyang (China) 2014, *Congress* Albuquerque, NM (USA) 2013. **Publications** *IFRAO Report in Rock Art Research.*
Members Organizations in 34 countries:
Argentina, Australia, Austria, Bolivia, Brazil, China, Colombia, Cuba, Finland, France, Georgia, Germany, Greece, India, Indonesia, Israel, Italy, Japan, Kenya, Korea Rep, Mexico, Morocco, Mozambique, Peru, Portugal, Russia, South Africa, Spain, Tanzania UR, UK, Uruguay, USA, Venezuela, Zimbabwe.
Included in the above, 2 organizations listed in this Yearbook:
Association pour le rayonnement de l'art pariétal européen (ARAPE, #02886); East African Rock Art Research Association (EARARA, no recent information). [2022.06.14/XD5154/y/C]

♦ International Federation of Roller-Skating / see World Skate (#21786)
♦ International Federation of Roofing Contractors / see International Federation for the Roofing Trade (#13534)

♦ International Federation for the Roofing Trade 13534

Fédération internationale du métier de couvreur – Internationale Föderation des Dachdeckerhandwerks (IFD)
SG Lohnerhofstrasse 2, 78467 Konstanz, Germany. T. +41762314257. E-mail: info@ifd-roof.com.
URL: http://www.ifd-roof.com/

History 1952, Germany FR. Statutes adopted 12 Sep 1953, Lucerne (Switzerland); amended Nov 1976, Scheveningen (Netherlands); Oct 1986, Lucerne (Switzerland); Oct 1999, Zurich (Switzerland) 1999. New name adopted, 2001, when Statutes were also renewed; amended 2005 and 2006. Statutes and structure renewed, Nov 2014, Bucharest (Romania). Former names and other names: *International Federation of Roofing Contractors* – former (1952 to 2001); *Fédération internationale des entreprises de couverture* – former (1952 to 2001). **Aims** Constitute a permanent bond between member organizations; study professional problems of common interest as they arise in individual organizations; centralize professional documentation; organize international conventions and world championships. **Structure** Congress (annual); General Assembly (annual). Management Board; Steering Committee. Technical Commissions (3): Pitched Roof; Waterproofing; Façade/Wall Cladding. Working Groups (3): Marketing; Training and Education; Finances, Economy and Statistics. **Languages** English, German. **Staff** 1.00 FTE, paid. **Finance** Sources: members' dues. **Activities** Awards/prizes/competitions; events/meetings; knowledge management/information dissemination; training/education. **Events** *Annual Congress* St Gallen (Switzerland) 2022, *Annual Congress* Marburg (Germany) 2021, *Annual Congress* Marburg (Germany) 2020, *Annual Congress* Edinburgh (UK) 2019, *Annual Congress* Riga (Latvia) 2018. **Publications** Handbooks; recommendations; guidelines.
Members Full – national professional organizations (19) of the roofing trade, in 19 countries:
Austria, Belgium, Croatia, Czechia, Estonia, France, Germany, Hungary, Ireland, Latvia, Luxembourg, Netherlands, Poland, Romania, Russia, Slovakia, Slovenia, Switzerland, UK.
Partner members (24) – manufacturers from industry and commerce – in 9 countries:
Austria, Belgium, Denmark, Finland, Germany, Liechtenstein, Poland, Russia, South Africa.
Cooperative Partners (7) in 6 countries:
Belgium, China, Germany, Poland, Türkiye, USA.
IGO Relations Recognized by: *European Commission (EC, #06633).* **NGO Relations** Member of (1): *Small Business Standards (SBS, #19311).* In liaison with technical committees of: *European Organisation for Technical Assessment (EOTA, #08103).* Sectoral member of: *SMEunited (#19327).* [2022/XD1998/t/D]

♦ International Federation of Ropemakers (inactive)

♦ International Federation of Rural Adult Catholic Movements 13535

Fédération internationale des mouvements d'adultes ruraux catholiques (FIMARC) – Federación Internacional de Movimientos de Adultos Rurales Católicos – Federação Internacional dos Movimentos de Adultos Rurais Católicos
SG FIMARC Secretariat, Rue Maurice Jaumain 15, 5330 Assesse, Belgium. T. +3283656236. Fax +3283656236. E-mail: fimarc@skynet.be.
Pres address not obtained.
URL: http://www.fimarc.org/

History 1964, Fatima (Portugal). Registered in accordance with Belgian law, 10 Jul 1975. **Aims** Promote an integral *development* based on *Christian* values through educational process of rural populations in the various countries of the world, in cooperation with the other organizations, at all levels, working for similar objectives. **Structure** General Assembly (at least every 4 years); Executive Committee; Bureau. **Languages** English, French, Portuguese, Spanish. **Staff** 1.00 FTE, paid. **Finance** Sources: donations; grants; members' dues. **Activities** Events/meetings; training/education. **Events** *Quadrennial General Assembly* Bad Brückenau (Germany) 2014, *Quadrennial general assembly* Atyra (Paraguay) 2010, *Quadrennial General Assembly* Daejeon (Korea Rep) 2006, *Quadrennial General Assembly* Cotonou (Benin) 2002, *Quadrennial general assembly* Miajadas (Spain) 1998. **Publications** *Voix du monde rural* (4 a year) in English, French, Portuguese, Spanish; *Cahiers du monde rural* in English, French, Portuguese, Spanish.
Members Affiliated, Associated movements and Individuals. Members in 58 countries:
Algeria, Argentina, Bangladesh, Belgium, Benin, Bolivia, Brazil, Bulgaria, Burkina Faso, Cameroon, Canada, Central African Rep, Chad, Chile, Colombia, Congo DR, Costa Rica, Côte d'Ivoire, Croatia, Cuba, Dominican Rep, Ecuador, Egypt, El Salvador, Estonia, France, Germany, Guatemala, Honduras, India, Indonesia, Italy, Korea Rep, Madagascar, Malaysia, Mali, Mexico, Nepal, Nicaragua, Niger, Pakistan, Paraguay, Peru, Philippines, Poland, Portugal, Romania, Rwanda, Senegal, South Africa, Spain, Sri Lanka, Switzerland, Thailand, Togo, Uganda, USA, Zambia.
Consultative Status Consultative status granted from: *ECOSOC (#05331)* (Ros A); *UNESCO (#20322)* (Consultative Status). **IGO Relations** Accredited by: *United Nations Office at Vienna (UNOV, #20604).* Formal relations with: *FAO (#09260).* Participates in: *Committee on World Food Security (CFS, see: #09260).* **NGO Relations** Member of: *Forum of Catholic Inspired NGOs (#09905); International NGO/CSO Planning Committee for Food Sovereignty (IPC, #14365); More and Better (#16855).* [2018/XC1845/C]

♦ International Federation for the Safety of Electricity Users (#09658)

♦ International Federation of Scholarly Associations of Management (IFSAM) 13536

Sec address not obtained.
Pres address not obtained.
URL: http://www.ifsam.org/

History Jun 1990, Frankfurt-Main (Germany FR). Current statutes approved 10 Jul 1995; revised 2005. **Aims** Promote the development of management research and teaching, and encourage the development of new fields; establish and maintain standards of competence in management research and teaching; provide other means for information exchange on management research and teaching among associations of scholars throughout the world; encourage the establishment of national associations of scholars of management. **Structure** Council, comprising Executive Committee (President, Past-President, President-Elect, Secretary, Honorary Assistant-Secretary and Treasurer) and 2 representatives from each member association. Committees (8): Nominating; Communications; Membership; Conference Site; Journal; Finance; Research; Business. **Languages** English. **Finance** Sources: members' dues. **Activities** Organizes conference (every 2 years); sponsors international conferences. **Events** *Biennial Conference* Porto Alegre (Brazil) 2020, *World Congress / World Conference* Shanghai (China) 2018, *New World Equilibrium* Mérida (Mexico) 2016, *World Congress* Tokyo (Japan) 2014, *World Congress/World Conference* Limerick (Ireland) 2012. **Publications** Newsletter.
Members Full; Associate; Institutional. Associations in 13 countries:
Australia, Brazil, Canada, China, France, Germany, Ireland, Italy, Japan, Netherlands, New Zealand, Spain, USA.
Regional organization:
Nordisk Företagsekonomiska Förening (NFF, #17510). [2020/XD9046/C]

♦ International Federation of Schools of Family History (no recent information)
♦ International Federation of Scientific Editors (no recent information)
♦ International Federation of Scoliosis Associations (inactive)

♦ International Federation of Scout and Guide Stamp Collecting Organizations (IFSCO) 13537

Pres Folemarksvej 6, 2605 Brøndby, Denmark.
URL: http://www.ifsco.org/

History 23 Sep 2000, Comacchio (Italy). **Aims** Compile information on Scout Stamp issues and forgeries; exchange literature. **Structure** General Meeting (every 2 years, usually during EUROSCOUT); President (elected for 2-year term); Secretary. **Languages** English. **Finance** Members bear their own expenses. **Activities** Events/meetings. **Events** *Euroscout Meeting* Vienna (Austria) 2016, *Euroscout Meeting / EUROSCOUT* Taastrup (Denmark) 2014, *EUROSCOUT* Rothenburg-Tauber (Germany) 2012, *Annual Congress* Sibenik (Croatia) 2012, *Euroscout meeting / EUROSCOUT / EUROSCOUT* Chelmsford (UK) 2010.
Members Philatelic clubs, societies (over 3000) and individuals. Members in 32 countries:
Argentina, Australia, Austria, Belgium, Brazil, Canada, Czechia, Denmark, France, Germany, Greece, Hong Kong, Hungary, India, Indonesia, Italy, Japan, Mexico, Netherlands, New Zealand, Norway, Philippines, Poland, Portugal, Singapore, Slovenia, South Africa, Spain, Sweden, Switzerland, UK, USA.
Included in the above, 1 organization listed in this Yearbook:
Scouts on Stamps Society International (SOSSI). [2015.01.24/XD8782/y/D]

♦ International Federation of Screen and Television Writers' Associations (inactive)
♦ International Federation of Secondary Teachers (inactive)
♦ International Federation for Secular and Humanistic Judaism (inactive)
♦ International Federation of the Seed Trade (inactive)
♦ International Federation of Senior Police Officers (no recent information)
♦ International Federation of Settlements Eurogroup (see: #13538)

♦ International Federation of Settlements and Neighbourhood Centres (IFS) 13538

Fédération internationale des centres sociaux et communautaires – Federación Internacional de Centros Sociales y Centros Vécinales – Internationale Föderation der Sozial-Kulturellen Nachbarschaftszentren
Contact c/o Finnish Federation, Sturenkatu 11, FI-00510 Helsinki, Finland. E-mail: info@ifsnetwork.org.
URL: http://www.ifsnetwork.org/

History 1926, London (UK). Founded, the first conference having been held in 1922, London. **Aims** Stimulate development of community work in all countries, with a basic concern for community action and development at all levels of society, from local to international by: supporting international projects; coordinating the work of federations in different countries; acting as a documentation centre; encouraging international exchange of community workers and development of national federations; promoting training of volunteers and professional workers. **Structure** Membership Meeting (every 2 years); Board of Directors; Secretariat. **Languages** English, French, German. **Staff** 0.50 FTE, paid. **Finance** Sources: donations; members' dues. Other sources: Transnational projects; Fondations. **Activities** Programmes. Includes: *International Federation of Settlements Eurogroup (IFS-Eurogroup, see: #13538).* **Events** *Social justice – the unfinished journey* Sydney, NSW (Australia) 2021, *Europe Network Meeting* Rotterdam (Netherlands) 2020, *Social justice – the unfinished journey* Sydney, NSW (Australia) 2020, *Conference* Helsinki (Finland) 2018, *Conference* Berlin (Germany) 2016. **Publications** *IFS East-West News* (2 a year); *IFS Newsletter* (2 a year); *IFS Handbook* (annual). Conference reports; occasional papers.
Members Full national, regional and local federations and associations of settlements, neighbourhood centres and similar bodies, each nominating 2 representatives to Membership Meetings. Affiliate single settlements, neighbourhood centres and similar bodies, each nominating 1 representative. Corporate Associates other organizations supporting IFS' work. Individual Associates individual persons supporting IFS' work. Full members (19) in 11 countries and territories:
Full members (19) in 11 countries and territories:
Canada, Finland, France, Germany, Israel, Netherlands, Sweden, UK, USA, Venezuela.
Included in the above, 1 confederation listed in this Yearbook:
Confederación Latinoamericana de Pobladores en la Marginación Social (COLAPOM, #04461).
Affiliates (34) in 15 countries:
Austria, Bangladesh, Canada, Czechia, Denmark, Germany, Hungary, India, Lithuania, Netherlands, Russia, Spain, Sweden, UK, USA.
Corporate Associates (4) in 4 countries:
Egypt, Liberia, Netherlands, UK.
Individual Associates (36) in 11 countries:
Canada, Finland, Germany, Greece, Hong Kong, Japan, Lithuania, Netherlands, Poland, UK, USA.
Consultative Status Consultative status granted from: *ECOSOC (#05331)* (General); *UNICEF (#20332).* **IGO Relations** Accredited by: *United Nations Office at Vienna (UNOV, #20604).* Associated with Department of Global Communications of the United Nations. **NGO Relations** Member of (2): *NGO Committee on the Status of Women, Geneva (#17117); NGO Committee on UNICEF (#17120).* Board member of: *Conference of Non-Governmental Organizations in Consultative Relationship with the United Nations (CONGO, #04635).* [2021/XD2002/C]

♦ International Federation of Sewing Thread Manufacturers (inactive)
♦ International Federation for a Shared Development (inactive)
♦ International Federation of Ship, Dock and River Workers / see International Transport Workers' Federation (#15726)

♦ International Federation of Shipmasters Associations (IFSMA) 13539

Fédération internationale des associations de patrons de navires
SG 202 Lambeth Road, London, SE1 7JY, UK. T. +442072610450. Fax +4434682134. E-mail: hq@ifsma.org.
URL: http://www.ifsma.org/

History 1974. Founded by 8 international shipmasters' associations. **Aims** Uphold international standards of professional competence for *seafarers* commensurate with the need to ensure safe operational practices, preservation from human injury, protection of the *marine* environment and safety of life and property at *sea*. **Structure** General Assembly (biennial); Executive Council. **Languages** English. **Staff** 1.50 FTE, paid. **Finance** Sources: members' dues. **Activities** Guidance/assistance/consulting; knowledge management/information dissemination. **Events** *Biennial General Assembly* London (UK) 2021, *Annual General Assembly* Helsinki (Finland) 2019, *Annual General Assembly* Buenos Aires (Argentina) 2018, *Annual General Assembly* Baltimore, MD (USA) 2017, *Annual General Assembly* Istanbul (Turkey) 2016. **Publications** *IFSMA Newsletter.* Annual Report; papers.
Members Affiliated trade unions, national associations, professional institutes and learned societies. National associations (34) and individuals (200) in 58 countries and territories:
Algeria, Argentina, Australia, Belgium, Bulgaria, Canada, Chile, Croatia, Cyprus, Denmark, Estonia, Finland, France, Gabon, Georgia, Germany, Ghana, Greece, Hong Kong, India, Indonesia, Iran Islamic Rep, Ireland, Italy, Jamaica, Japan, Korea Rep, Latvia, Libya, Lithuania, Madagascar, Malaysia, Maldives, Malta, Mauritius, Netherlands, New Zealand, Nigeria, Norway, Oman, Pakistan, Panama, Peru, Philippines, Poland, Portugal, Romania, Russia, Serbia, Slovenia, Spain, Sweden, Switzerland, Thailand, Türkiye, UK, Ukraine, USA.

Consultative Status Consultative status granted from: *ECOSOC (#05331)* (Ros C); *International Maritime Organization (IMO, #14102)*; *ILO (#11123)* (Special List). **IGO Relations** *International Convention on Standards of Training, Certification and Watchkeeping for Fishing Vessel Personnel (STCW-F, 1995)*. *International Convention on Standards of Training, Certification and Watchkeeping for Seafarers (STCW, 1978)*. **NGO Relations** Member of: *Maritime Piracy Humanitarian Response Programme (MPHRP, #16583)*. [2022/XD1260/**C**]

♦ International Federation of Shock Societies 13540

Sec Concincnati Children's Hosp Medical Center, Univ of Cincinnati, 2600 Clifton Ave, Cincinnati OH 45220, USA.
URL: http://www.europeanshocksociety.org/IFSS

History 1993. Registration: Start date: 2017, Austria. **Aims** Promote cooperation between societies for research in the areas of shock, *trauma*, sepsis or other relevant fields and clinically oriented societies. **Structure** Assembly; Presiding Committee; Executive Committee; Conciliation Board. **Languages** English. **Staff** 6.00 FTE, voluntary. **Finance** Members' dues. Other sources: donations; funding by sponsors; conference benefits. **Activities** Events/meetings. **Events** *International Shock Congress* Chania (Greece) 2019, *International Shock Congress* Tokyo (Japan) 2016, *International shock congress* Miami, FL (USA) 2012, *International congress* Cologne (Germany) 2008, *International Shock Congress* Munich (Germany) 2004. **Publications** *SHOCK Injury, Inflammation, and Sepsis: Laboratory and Clinical Approaches* (12 a year) – journal.
Members National organizations in 5 countries:
Brazil, China, Japan, Russia, USA.
Regional organization: [2019/XD4692/y/**D**]

♦ International Federation of Sleddog Sports (IFSS) 13541

Office Avenue Louise 149/24, 1050 Brussels, Belgium. E-mail: info@sleddogsport.net.
Exec Dir PO Box 474, Seward AK 99664, USA. T. +19074910393. E-mail: executivedirector@sleddogsport.net.
URL: http://www.sleddogsport.net/

History 1985. Founded by *European Sled Dog Racing Association (ESDRA, inactive)* and *International Sled Dog Racing Association (ISDRA)*. Previously incorporated in the State of Idaho (USA), Oct 1992. **Aims** Promote comprehensive development, expansion, and participation in sleddog sports in all their diverse aspects; foster understanding and appreciation of the history and traditions of the use of sled dogs. **Structure** General Assembly (every 2 years); Council. Committees (12): Disciplinary; Anti-Doping; World Cup-Accreditation; World Championships; Race Judges and Race Regulations; Animal Health and Welfare; 1-2 Dog; Development; Inclusive Global Access; Youth; Nordic Breed; Membership; Sport Discipline Development. Commissions (3): Athletes; Legal; Nominating. **Languages** English. **Staff** Voluntary. **Finance** Sources: meeting proceeds; members' dues; sponsorship. Other sources: licensing. **Activities** Awards/prizes/competitions; sporting activities. **Events** *General Assembly* Brussels (Belgium) 2022, *Biennial general assembly* Stockholm (Sweden) 2018, *Biennial General Assembly* Oslo (Norway) 2012, *Biennial General Assembly* Ashford (Ireland) 2010, *Biennial General Assembly* Vancouver, BC (Canada) 2008.
Members National federations in 27 countries:
Australia, Austria, Belgium, Canada, Chile, Czechia, Denmark, Finland, France, Germany, Great Britain, Hungary, Ireland, Italy, Korea Rep, Latvia, Lithuania, Netherlands, New Zealand, Norway, Poland, Russia, Slovakia, Spain, Sweden, Switzerland, USA.
Provisioan national federations in 10 countries:
Andorra, Argentina, Belarus, Brazil, Estonia, Iceland, Kazakhstan, Mongolia, Slovenia, Ukraine.
Honorary member:
International Sled Dog Racing Association (ISDRA).
Associate in 3 countries:
Germany, Italy, USA.
Included in the above, 2 organizations listed in this Yearbook:
International Sled Dog Veterinary Medical Association (ISDVMA, #14874); *World Sleddog Association (WSA, #21792)*.
NGO Relations Member of (3): *Alliance of Independent recognised Members of Sport (AIMS, #00690)*; *International Masters Games Association (IMGA, #14117)*; *Olympic Movement (#17719)*. Recognized by: *International Olympic Committee (IOC, #14408)*. [2018/XD0659/y/**C**]

♦ International Federation of Small and Medium-Sized Commercial Enterprises (inactive)
♦ International Federation of Small and Medium-Sized Industrial Enterprises (inactive)

♦ International Federation of Snowsport Instructors (IFSI) 13542

Fédération internationale des instructeurs de sport de neige (FISI) – Internationalen Verband der Schneesportinstruktoren (IVSI)

Secretariat Toisenweg 7, 4040 Linz, Austria. T. +43732246369. Fax +43732246369. E-mail: office@ivsi.info.
Pres Pfaffenbachweg 10, 73527 Schwäbisch Gmünd, Germany.
URL: http://www.ivsi.info/

History Former names and other names: *Internationalen Verbandes der Ski-Instruktoren (IVSI)* – former (2005). **Aims** Promote snow sports. **Structure** Delegates Assembly. A working body of: *Interski International (INTERSKI, #15975)*. **Languages** English, French, German. **Staff** 0.50 FTE, voluntary. **Finance** Members' dues. Budget (annual): euro 5,000. **Activities** Events/meetings. **Events** *Congress* Hakuba (Japan) 2017, *Congress* Alpe d'Huez (France) 2013, *Congress* Matraszentistvan (Hungary) 2009, *Congress* Lech am Arlberg (Austria) 2005, *Congress* Zakopane (Poland) 2001.
Members Full in 21 countries:
Austria, Belgium, Croatia, Czechia, Denmark, France, Germany, Hungary, Ireland, Japan, Korea Rep, Liechtenstein, Montenegro, Netherlands, Norway, Poland, Serbia, Slovenia, Sweden, Switzerland, UK.
NGO Relations Member of (1): *Interski International (INTERSKI, #15975)*. [2017/XJ8165/**D**]

♦ International Federation of the Socialist and Democratic Press (no recent information)
♦ International Federation of Socialist Physicians (inactive)

♦ International Federation of Social Science Organizations (IFSSO) . . 13543

Fédération internationale des organisations de sciences sociales (FIOSS)

Pres Room 3055 – Fac Center, Univ of the Philippines, Diliman, 1101 Quezon City, Philippines. T. +6324261454.
SG Instanbul Univ, Beyazit, Fatih, 34452 Istanbul/Istanbul, Türkiye.
URL: http://ifsso.net/

History Nov 1979, having previously functioned as *Standing Committee for Cooperation with National Social Science Councils and Analogous Bodies – Comité permanent pour la coopération avec les conseils nationaux de sciences sociales et organismes similaires (CPCCN)*, within *International Social Science Council (ISSC, inactive)*; and subsequently, 1975, as a membership organization (Regular Member) still within the framework of ISSC, with the title *Conference of National Social Science Councils and Analogous Bodies (CNSSC) – Conférence des conseils nationaux de sciences sociales et organismes similaires (CCNSS)*. **Aims** Contribute to and strengthen international cooperation in the field of social sciences; further and support social sciences in general; in particular contribute to their development in developing countries; stimulate and facilitate exchange of ideas and experience among members; disseminate information on national, regional and international levels; provide an international forum for cooperation and communication among councils, academies and other bodies responsible for developing and funding social science research and research training, social science policy issues and similar. **Structure** General Assembly (every 2 years, at General Conference) comprises one delegate from each member. Executive Board (meets prior to General Conference), consisting of President, 1st Vice-President, 2 Vice-Presidents, Secretary-General, Treasurer and 7 members, elected so as to give fair representation to all 3 membership groupings (I, II and II world). Secretariat. **Languages** English, French. **Staff** 1.00 FTE, paid. **Finance** Sources: members' dues. Scientific activities financed through special funding. **Activities** Organizes General Conference; stimulates and sponsors international and regional workshops and seminars, giving high priority to participation of Third World organizations and supporting their structures. Fellowship programme, mainly for Third World members, allows officers of member organizations to visit those of other members, study relevant procedures and aspects of programme administration and policy implementation. **Events** *Biennial Conference* Sanliurfa (Turkey) 2019, *Biennial General Conference* Denpasar (Indonesia) 2017, *Biennial General Conference* Tokyo (Japan) 2015, *Biennial General Conference* Istanbul (Turkey) 2013, *Biennial General Conference* Batangas City (Philippines) 2011. **Publications** *IFSSO Newsletter* (4 a year). *1990-1991 International Directory of Social Science Organizations*. Proceedings of General Conference; occasional papers.
Members National councils or academies and individuals. Members in 24 countries:
Argentina, Australia, Bangladesh, Belgium, Brazil, Burkina Faso, Canada, China, Czechia, Denmark, Egypt, Ghana, Hungary, India, Indonesia, Japan, Korea Rep, New Zealand, Nigeria, Philippines, Sri Lanka, Thailand, Türkiye, USA.
Regional bodies (5):
Centre for the Coordination of Research and Documentation in Social Science for Sub-Saharan Africa (no recent information); *Consejo Latinoamericano de Ciencias Sociales (CLACSO, #04718)*; *Council for the Development of Social Science Research in Africa (CODESRIA, #04879)*; *Federation of Arab Scientific Research Councils (FASRC, no recent information)*; *Latin American Faculty of Social Sciences (#16316)*.
IGO Relations *UNICEF (#20332)*; *OECD Development Centre (#17692)*; *OECD (#17693)*; *United Nations University (UNU, #20642)*; *UNICEF/UNDP/World Bank/WHO Special Programme for Research and Training in Tropical Diseases (TDR, #20331)*; *UNESCO (#20322)*. **NGO Relations** Member of ISSC. Communication and cooperation with: *Association of Development Research and Training Institutes of Asia and the Pacific (ADIPA, inactive)*; *European Association of Development Research and Training Institutes (EADI, #06012)*; *European Science Foundation (ESF, #08441)*; *International Association for Social Science Information Service and Technology (IASSIST, #12169)*; *International Committee for Social Science Information and Documentation (ICSSD, no recent information)*; *International Council for Science (ICSU, inactive)*; *International Federation of Data Organizations for the Social Sciences (IFDO, #13402)*; *World Association for Public Opinion Research (WAPOR, #21180)*. Formalized cooperation with 5 member organizations. [2020/XC2333/y/**C**]

♦ International Federation of Social Workers (IFSW) 13544

Fédération internationale des travailleurs sociaux – Federación Internacional de Trabajadores Sociales

SG Maiengässli 4, 4310 Rheinfelden AG, Switzerland. E-mail: global@ifsw.org.
URL: http://www.ifsw.org/

History 1928, Paris (France). Reconstituted 1956, Munich (Germany FR), at International Conference on Social Welfare, following preliminary work inaugurated at earlier Conference, 1950, Paris. Former names and other names: *International Permanent Secretariat of Social Workers* – former; *Secrétariat permanent international des travailleurs sociaux* – former; *Internationales Ständiges Sekretariat der Sozialarbeiter* – former; *Fédération internationale des assistants sociaux et des assistantes sociales* – former. Registration: Swiss Civil Code, No/ID: CHE-109.240.290, Switzerland. **Aims** Promote social work as a *profession* through international cooperation and action, especially as regards professional standards, training, ethics and working conditions; promote establishment of national associations of social workers where they do not yet exist; support national associations in promoting participation of social workers in social planning and formulation of social *policies*, nationally and internationally; encourage and facilitate contacts among social workers of all countries and provide media for discussion and exchange of ideas; present the point of view of the profession on an international level by establishing relations with international governmental or voluntary organizations operating in, or interested in, the social *welfare* field; assist in carrying out social planning, social action and welfare programmes sponsored by such organizations. **Structure** General Meeting (at least every 2 years), consisting of representatives of member organizations (3 from each country), elects Executive Committee (meets at least annually), comprising up to 12 members (2-year terms), including the Officers – President, 5 Vice-Presidents (according to geographical regions – Africa, Asia and Pacific, Europe, Latin America and Caribbean, North America) and Treasurer. European organization: *IFSW Europe (#11106)*. **Languages** English, French, Spanish. **Staff** 3.00 FTE, paid. **Finance** Sources: donations; fees for services; gifts, legacies; members' dues; sale of publications. **Activities** Events/meetings. **Events** *European Social Work Conference* Prague (Czechia) 2023, *People's Global Online Summit* Geneva (Switzerland) 2022, *APASWE : Asia-Pacific Social Work Conference* Brisbane, QLD (Australia) 2021, *Africa Regional Conference* Kigali (Rwanda) 2021, *European Conference on Social Work* Zagreb (Croatia) 2021. **Publications** *IFSW Update* (6 a year); *International Social Work* (6 a year). Policy statements.
Members National associations (one per country) in 81 countries and territories:
Argentina, Armenia, Australia, Austria, Azerbaijan, Bangladesh, Barbados, Belgium, Benin, Bolivia, Brazil, Bulgaria, Cameroon, Canada, Chile, China, Colombia, Costa Rica, Croatia, Cuba, Czechia, Denmark, Dominican Rep, Faeroe Is, Finland, France, Gambia, Georgia, Germany, Ghana, Greece, Grenada, Hong Kong, Iceland, Indonesia, Ireland, Israel, Italy, Japan, Kenya, Korea Rep, Kosovo, Kuwait, Kyrgyzstan, Lebanon, Lesotho, Luxembourg, Macau, Malaysia, Malta, Mauritius, Morocco, New Zealand, Nicaragua, Niger, Nigeria, Norway, Palestine, Papua New Guinea, Peru, Philippines, Portugal, Puerto Rico, Russia, Singapore, Spain, Sri Lanka, Suriname, Sweden, Switzerland, Tajikistan, Tanzania UR, Togo, Türkiye, Uganda, UK, Ukraine, Uruguay, USA, Vietnam, Zimbabwe.
Consultative Status Consultative status granted from: *ECOSOC (#05331)* (Special); *ILO (#11123)* (Special List); *UNICEF (#20332)*; *Council of Europe (CE, #04881)* (Participatory Status). **IGO Relations** Accredited by: *United Nations Office at Vienna (UNOV, #20604)*. Participant in Fundamental Rights Platform of: *European Union Agency for Fundamental Rights (FRA, #08969)*. *Council of Arab Ministers for Social and Economic Affairs (#04864)*; Proclaimed a Peace Messenger by the United Nations Secretary General in Sep 1987. Designated Patron of the International Year of the Family by the United Nations 1994. Associated with Department of Global Communications of the United Nations. **NGO Relations** Member of (16): *Child Rights Connect (#03884)*; *Child Rights International Network (CRIN, #03885)*; *Committee of NGOs on Human Rights, Geneva (#04275)*; *Conference of Non-Governmental Organizations in Consultative Relationship with the United Nations (CONGO, #04635)*; *European Anti-Poverty Network (EAPN, #05908)*; *European Network for Social Action (ENSACT, #08003)*; *European Social Action Network (ESAN, #08499)*; *Geneva Global Health Hub (G2H2, #10122)*; *Global Call for Climate Action (GCCA, inactive)*; *International Council on Social Welfare (ICSW, #13076)*; *NGO Committee on Sustainable Development, Vienna (#17119)*; *NGO Committee on UNICEF (#17120)*; *NGO/UNICEF Regional Network for Children in CEE, CIS and Baltic States (RNC, inactive)*; *Social Platform (#19344)*; *Vienna NGO Committee on Drugs (VNGOC, #20773)*; *Vienna NGO Committee on the Status of Women (#20775)*. Cooperates with (1): *Formation d'éducateurs sociaux européens (FESET, #09873)*. [2022.02.02/XB2007/**B**]

♦ International Federation of the Societies of Classical Studies (#09607)

♦ International Federation of Societies of Cosmetic Chemists (IFSCC) 13545

Fédération internationale des sociétés des chimistes cosméticiens – Internationale Föderation der Gesellschaften der Kosmetik-Chemiker

SG 14 Wall St, Suite 1620, New York NY 10005, USA. T. +12126681503. E-mail: secretary@ifscc.org.
Registered Address Grafenauweg 6, P.O. Box 7243, 6302 Zug, Switzerland.
URL: http://www.ifscc.org/

History 8 Sep 1959, Brussels (Belgium). Founded following activities initiated in 1956 in Paris (France). Amended Constitution approved: 1 Sep 1961, Copenhagen (Denmark); 26 Sep 1970, Barcelona (Spain). **Aims** Advance cosmetic science. **Structure** Annual Council; Praesidium. **Languages** English. **Staff** 1.00 FTE, paid. **Finance** Sources: members' dues. **Activities** Awards/prizes/competitions; events/meetings; training/education. **Events** *Congress* Las Vegas, NV (USA) 2028, *Congress* Switzerland 2027, *Congress* Adelaide, SA (Australia) 2026, *Congress* France 2025, *Congress* Foz do Iguaçu (Brazil) 2024. **Publications** *IFSCC Magazine* (4 a year). Monographs.
Members Societies of cosmetic chemists (49) in 58 countries and territories:
Argentina, Australia, Austria, Belgium, Brazil, Bulgaria, Chile, China, Colombia, Costa Rica, Croatia, Czechia, Denmark, Ecuador, El Salvador, Finland, France, Germany, Greece, Guatemala, Honduras, Hong Kong, Hungary, India, Indonesia, Iran Islamic Rep, Israel, Italy, Japan, Korea Rep, Malaysia, Mexico, Netherlands, New Zealand, Nicaragua, Norway, Panama, Peru, Philippines, Poland, Portugal, Romania, Russia, Senegal, Singapore, Slovakia, South Africa, Spain, Sweden, Switzerland, Taiwan, Thailand, Türkiye, UK, United Arab Emirates, Uruguay, USA, Venezuela.
Included in the above, 1 organization listed in this Yearbook:
Scandinavian Society of Cosmetic Chemists (SCANCOS, #19105). [2022/XC2010/y/**C**]

♦ International Federation of Societies for Electron Microscopy / see International Federation of Societies for Microscopy (#13550)

♦ International Federation of Societies of Endoscopic Surgeons (IFSES) 13546

Sec-Treas NUS Yong Loo Lin School of Medicine, 1E Kent Ridge Road, NUHS Tower Block, Level 11, Singapore 119228, Singapore.
URL: http://www.ifses.org/

History Proposed 1992, Bordeaux (France), at 3rd World Congress of Endoscopic Surgery. Set up 1992. **Aims** Enhance and promote endoscopic surgery and *Minimal Access Techniques* (MAS). **Structure** Advisory Board. **Languages** English. **Staff** None. **Finance** Budget (2014): US$ 28,000. **Activities** Knowledge management/ information dissemination; events/meetings. **Events** *World Congress of Endoscopic Surgery* Kolkata (India) 2024, *WCES : Biennial World Congress of Endoscopic Surgery* Busan (Korea Rep) 2022, *WCES : Biennial World Congress of Endoscopic Surgery* Barcelona (Spain) 2021, *WCES : Biennial World Congress of Endoscopic Surgery* Yokohama (Japan) 2020, *WCES : Biennial World Congress of Endoscopic Surgery* Seattle, WA (USA) 2018. **Publications** *Surgical Endoscopy.*
Members Societies of endoscopic surgeons (9). National societies in 5 countries:
Canada, China, India, Japan, USA.
Regional organizations (4):
Endoscopic and Laparoscopic Surgeons of Asia (ELSA, #05462); European Association for Endoscopic Surgery and Other Interventional Techniques (EAES, #06026); Federación Latinoamericana de Cirurgia (FELAC, #09349); Latin American Association of Endoscopic Surgeons (#16239). [2018/XD3538/y/**D**]

♦ International Federation of Societies of Hand Therapists / see International Federation of Societies for Hand Therapy (#13547)

♦ International Federation of Societies for Hand Therapy (IFSHT) 13547

Fédération internationale des sociétés de rééducation de la main

SG address not obtained. T. +16012597802. E-mail: secretarygeneral@ifsht.org.
Pres address not obtained. T. +61414564187. E-mail: president@ifsht.org.
URL: http://www.ifsht.org/

History Dec 1985, France, as *International Federation of Societies of Hand Therapists*, at meeting of *'Société française de chirurgie de la main'*. Registered in accordance with French law, 10 Dec 1987, Paris (France). Re-registered in accordance with Swiss Civil Code, 12 Jun 2006, Winterthur (Switzerland). **Aims** Promote the principles and practice of hand therapy internationally, thereby increasing the number of patients with hand injuries who receive *rehabilitation.* **Structure** Council; Executive Committee; Committees (5). **Languages** English. **Staff** Voluntary. **Finance** Sources: grants; members' dues. Other sources: bequests. **Activities** Events/meetings; knowledge management/information dissemination; networking/liaising; training/education. **Events** *Triennial Congress* Washington, DC (USA) 2025, *Triennial Congress* London (UK) 2022, *Triennial Congress* Berlin (Germany) 2019, *Triennial Congress* Buenos Aires (Argentina) 2016, *Triennial Congress* Delhi (India) 2013. **Publications** *IFSHT Update* (4 a year). Online newsflashes; membership directory.
Members Full in 35 countries and territories:
Argentina, Australia, Austria, Belgium, Brazil, Canada, Colombia, Czechia, Denmark, Finland, France, Germany, Greece, Hong Kong, India, Ireland, Israel, Italy, Japan, Kenya, Korea Rep, Netherlands, New Zealand, Norway, Portugal, Slovenia, South Africa, Spain, Sweden, Switzerland, Türkiye, UK, Uruguay, USA, Venezuela.
Corresponding in 10 countries and territories:
Bahrain, Barbados, Iran Islamic Rep, Nepal, Qatar, Romania, Saudi Arabia, Sri Lanka, United Arab Emirates, West Bank-Gaza.
Associate in 3 countries:
Bangladesh, Mexico, Singapore. [2019/XD7990/**C**]

♦ International Federation of Societies for Histochemistry and Cytochemistry (IFSHC) 13548

Fédération internationale des sociétés d'histochimie et de cytochimie

SG Dep Histology, Medical Univ of Gdansk, ul Debinki 1, 80-210 Gdansk, Poland.
Pres Copenhagen Biocentre – BRIC, Univ of Copenhagen, Ole Maalies Vej 5, 2200 Copenhagen, Denmark. E-mail: hmu.ifshc@gmail.com.
URL: http://ifshc.com/

History 3 Sep 1960, Paris (France). Statutes adopted 16 Aug 1964, Frankfurt-Main (Germany FR); amended Aug 1980, Brighton (UK); Aug 1988, Washington DC (USA). **Aims** Organize international coordinate national symposia and promote scientific cooperation in the widest sense; establish histochemistry and cytochemistry institutes; promote histochemistry and cytochemistry as independent basic sciences and their teaching in universities. **Structure** Congress (every 4 years). Committee of Delegates (meets at least at or prior to Congress), consisting of the Executive Committee (President, Secretary-General, Treasurer and member) and 2 delegates from each of the national societies. Local Organizing Committee, comprising members of that national society hosting the next international congress. **Languages** English. **Staff** Voluntary. **Finance** Sources: members' dues. **Activities** Awards/prizes/competitions; events/meetings; training/education. **Events** *International Congress of Histochemistry and Cytochemistry* Prague (Czechia) 2022, *International Congress of Histochemistry and Cytochemistry* Prague (Czechia) 2021, *International Congress of Histochemistry and Cytochemistry* Prague (Czechia) 2020, *Quadrennial Congress* Istanbul (Turkey) 2016, *Quadrennial Congress* Kyoto (Japan) 2012. **Publications** *Acta Histochemica et Cytochemica*; *Basic and Applied Histochemistry*; *Cellular and Molecular Biology*; *Cytometry*; *Folia Histochemica et Cytochemica*; *Histochemical Journal*; *Histochemistry*; *IFSHC Newsletter*; *Journal of Histochemistry and Cytochemistry*; *Progress in Histochemistry and Cytochemistry.*
Members National Societies in 20 countries:
Austria, Belgium, Bulgaria, China, Croatia, Czechia, Denmark, Finland, France, Germany, Hungary, Japan, Netherlands, Poland, Russia, Slovakia, Switzerland, Türkiye, UK, USA.
NGO Relations Commission of Division of Cellular, Molecular and Developmental Biology of: *International Union of Biological Sciences (IUBS, #15760).* [2019/XC1581/**C**]

♦ International Federation of Societies and Institutes for the Study of the Renaissance 13549

Fédération internationale des sociétés et instituts pour l'étude de la Renaissance (FISIER) – Federación Internacional de Sociedades e Institutos del Renacimiento

Sec c/o Renaissance Cente, Rm H448b 4th fl ext, Humanities Bldg, Univ Warwick, Coventry, CV4 7AL, UK.
URL: https://warwick.ac.uk/fac/arts/ren/fisier/

History 1 Apr 1957. **Aims** Encourage, promote and coordinate on an international scale the scholarly study and investigation of the Renaissance period in all its phases and aspects; encourage the publication of the results of such study and investigation. **Structure** Council (meets annually), composed of a delegate from each member body. Bureau, comprising President, Secretary, Assistant Secretary, Treasurer/Bibliography Commissioner and 4 members. **Languages** Latin. **Staff** None. **Finance** Members' dues. Budget (annual): Swiss Fr 3,600. **Events** *Colloquium / Congress* Brussels (Belgium) / Liège (Belgium) 2007, *Congress* Italy 2006, *Congress* Geneva (Switzerland) 2001, *Session / Congress* Paris (France) 1999, *Session / Congress* Montréal, QC (Canada) 1995. **Publications** *Bibliographie internationale de l'humanisme et de la Renaissance* (annual). *Les études sur la Renaissance aujourd'hui: actualité et perspectives d'avenir* (2003); *Le contrôle des idées à la Renaissance* (1996).
Members National societies or institutes substantially concerned with Renaissance studies (52) in 16 countries:
Belgium (4), Canada (5), Denmark, France (13), Germany (5), Hungary, Israel, Italy (7), Japan, Netherlands (2), Poland, Russia, Spain, Switzerland (3), UK, USA (5).
Included in the above, 3 organizations listed in this Yearbook:
International Association for Neo-Latin Studies (IANLS, #12048); International Council for the Publication of the Opera Omnia of Erasmus (#13066); Société internationale des amis de Montaigne (SIAM).
NGO Relations Affiliated to: *International Committee of Historical Sciences (ICHS, #12777)*, organizing sessions at this organization's congress. [2018/XD1995/y/**D**]

♦ International Federation of Societies of Mechanical Reproduction Rights / see International Bureau of the Societies Administering the Rights of Mechanical Recording and Reproduction (#12416)

♦ International Federation of Societies for Microscopy (IFSM) 13550

Fédération internationale des sociétés de microscopie électronique – Federación Internacional de Sociedades de Microscopia Electrónica – Internationaler Verband der Gesellschaften für Elektronenmikroskopie

Pres Materials Dept – Oxford, 16 Parks Road, Oxford, OX1 3PH, UK. E-mail: info@ifsm.com.
URL: http://ifsm.info/

History Oct 1951. Founded as Joint Commission for Electron Microscopy of *International Council for Science (ICSU, inactive).* Became independent federation July 1955. Former names and other names: *International Federation of Societies for Electron Microscopy (IFSEM)* – former. **Aims** Foster international cooperation between *electron* microscopists. **Structure** Assembly (every 4 years); Executive Board; Regional Committees (3): *Comité Interamericano de Sociedades de Microscopia Electrónica (CIASEM, #04171); Committee of Asia/Pacific Societies for Microscopy (CAPSM, #04244); European Microscopy Society (EMS, #07795).* **Languages** English. **Staff** 1.00 FTE, voluntary. **Finance** Sources: members' dues. **Activities** Events/meetings. **Events** *International Microscopy Congress* Busan (Korea Rep) 2022, *East-Asia Microscopy Conference (EAMC)* Taipei (Taiwan) 2021, *East-Asia Microscopy Conference (EAMC)* Taipei (Taiwan) 2020, *Quadrennial Conference* Sydney, NSW (Australia) 2018, *Young Scientists Assembly* Sydney, NSW (Australia) 2018.
Members National societies in 34 countries:
Armenia, Australia, Austria, Belgium, Brazil, Canada, China, Croatia, Cuba, Czechia, France, Germany, Hungary, India, Ireland, Israel, Italy, Japan, Korea Rep, Mexico, Netherlands, New Zealand, Poland, Portugal, Russia, Singapore, South Africa, Spain, Switzerland, Thailand, Türkiye, UK, USA, Venezuela.
Also in Scandinavia.
Associate members in 8 countries:
Bulgaria, Cuba, Ecuador, Egypt, Latvia, Moldova, Romania, Slovenia.
Included in the above, 1 organization listed in the Yearbook:
Microscopy Society of Southern Africa (MSSA).
NGO Relations Member of (1): *International Science Council (ISC, #14796).* [2022.06.20/XC2009/**C**]

♦ International Federation of Societies on Skeletal Diseases (inactive)

♦ International Federation of Societies for Surgery of the Hand (IFSSH) 13551

Fédération internationale des sociétés de chirurgie de la main

Admin Officer Dept Hand Surgery, Royal North Shore Hosp, St Leonards NSW 2065, Australia. T. +61294631820. E-mail: secretary@ifssh.info – administration@ifssh.info.
SG Room 8629, Dept of Orthopedic Surgery, Seoul Natl Univ Hosp, 101 Daehak-ro, Jongno-gu, Seoul 03080, Korea Rep. E-mail: secretary@ifssh.info.
URL: http://www.ifssh.info/

History 20 Jan 1966, Chicago IL (USA), at annual convention of the American Society for Surgery of the Hand, when Charter was developed. Charter amended: 1972; 1983; 16 Feb 1986; 10 Apr 1989, Tel Aviv; 26 May 1992, Paris (France); 19 Jun 2008, Lausanne (Switzerland). **Aims** Coordinate activities of societies for surgery of the hand by: maintaining liaison; promoting exchange of knowledge; increasing opportunities for study; establishing standards of nomenclature, classification, evaluation and treatment; collecting and disseminating information; improving education and research; studying socio-economic impact of disorders of the hand; furthering availability of hand surgery and cooperation among hand surgeons. **Structure** Council (meets annually); Executive Committee. Scientific Committees. **Languages** English. **Staff** 0.50 FTE, paid. **Finance** Members' dues: US$ 100 per society plus US$ 10 per member of that society; Reduced dues – US$ 50 per society plus US$ per member of that society for low income countries. Donations. **Activities** Events/meetings; research/documentation; training/education. **Events** *Triennial Congress* Singapore (Singapore) 2028, *Triennial Congress* Washington, DC (USA) 2025, *Triennial Congress* London (UK) 2022, *Triennial Congress* Berlin (Germany) 2019, *Triennial Congress* Buenos Aires (Argentina) 2016. **Publications** *Journal of Hand Surgery* (12 a year) – in UK, USA; *IFSSH Ezine* – digital.
Members Societies or clubs for surgery of the hand in 58 countries and territories:
Argentina, Australia, Austria, Bangladesh, Belgium, Bolivia, Brazil, Bulgaria, Canada, Chile, China, Colombia, Czechia, Denmark, Dominican Rep, Ecuador, Egypt, Finland, France, Georgia, Germany, Greece, Guatemala, Hong Kong, Hungary, India, Indonesia, Iran Islamic Rep, Israel, Italy, Japan, Korea Rep, Kuwait, Lithuania, Malaysia, Mexico, Netherlands, New Zealand, Norway, Philippines, Poland, Portugal, Puerto Rico, Romania, Russia, Singapore, Slovakia, South Africa, Spain, Sweden, Switzerland, Taiwan, Thailand, Türkiye, UK, Uruguay, USA, Venezuela.
NGO Relations Affiliated with (1): *Hand and Wrist Biomechanics International (HWBI, #10859).* [2020/XD6041/y/**C**]

♦ International Federation of Societies of Toxicologic Pathologists (no recent information)
♦ International Federation of Sound Hunters (inactive)

♦ International Federation for Spina Bifida and Hydrocephalus (IF SBH) 13552

Fédération internationale des personnes atteintes de spina-bifida et d'hydrocéphalie – Internationale Vereniging voor Spina Bifida en Hydrocephalus

SG Rue des Alexiens 16, 1000 Brussels, Belgium. T. +32471844154. E-mail: info@ifglobal.org.
Main Website: https://www.ifglobal.org/

History 1981. Former names and other names: *IF* – alias. Registration: Banque-Carrefour des Entreprises, No/ID: 0473.326.247, Start date: 29 Apr 2000, Belgium; European Commission Disability Platform, No/ID: E03820, Start date: 1 Jan 2022; EU Transparency Register, No/ID: 718277924839-56, Start date: 19 Dec 2016. **Aims** Improve the quality of life of people with Spina Bifida and/or Hydrocephalus throughout the world; decrease the prevalence of Spina Bifida and Hydrocephalus by primary prevention. **Structure** General Assembly (including subdivision Chapters); Election Committee; Board of Directors; Secretariat, headed by Secretary General. **Languages** English. **Staff** 6.00 FTE, paid; 15.00 FTE, voluntary. **Finance** Sources: fundraising; members' dues; sponsorship. **Activities** Advocacy/lobbying/activism; awareness raising; networking/liaising; research/documentation; training/education. **Events** *International Conference on Spina Bifida and Hydrocephalus* 2022, *Conference on Multidisciplinary care* Brussels (Belgium) 2021, *European Workshop* Belgrade (Serbia) 2019, *Congress* Delhi (India) 2018, *European Workshop* Madrid (Spain) 2018. **Publications** *IF Newsletter* – electronic. **Information Services** *E-Library.*
Members National organizations and individuals. Members in 85 countries and territories:
Algeria, Argentina, Australia, Austria, Bangladesh, Belgium, Brazil, Bulgaria, Canada, Chile, China, Colombia, Costa Rica, Croatia, Cyprus, Denmark, Dominican Rep, Egypt, Estonia, Finland, France, Germany, Ghana, Greece, Guatemala, Honduras, Hong Kong, Hungary, Iceland, India, Indonesia, Iran Islamic Rep, Ireland, Israel, Italy, Japan, Kazakhstan, Kenya, Korea Rep, Kosovo, Latvia, Lithuania, Luxembourg, Madagascar, Malawi, Malaysia, Mexico, Mongolia, Montenegro, Morocco, Nepal, Netherlands, New Zealand, Nigeria, Norway, Pakistan, Paraguay, Peru, Philippines, Poland, Portugal, Puerto Rico, Romania, Russia, Saudi Arabia, Scotland, Serbia, Singapore, Slovakia, Slovenia, South Africa, Spain, Sudan, Sweden, Switzerland, Taiwan, Tanzania UR, Türkiye, Uganda, UK, Ukraine, USA, Venezuela, Zambia, Zimbabwe.
Consultative Status Consultative status granted from: *ECOSOC (#05331)* (Special). **IGO Relations** Accredited by (7): *ECOSOC (#05331)*; European Commission Disability Platform; *UNICEF (#20332)*; *United Nations Office at Vienna (UNOV, #20604)*; *UN Women (#20724)* (Disability Inclusion); *WHO (#20950)* (Collaborative Global Network for Rare Diseases); *World Food Programme (WFP, #21510).* Associated with Department of Global Communications of the United Nations. **NGO Relations** Member of (8): ERN-ITHACA; *European Disability Forum (EDF, #06929)*; *European Patients' Forum (EPF, #08172)*; *EURORDIS – Rare Diseases Europe (#09175)*; *International Disability and Development Consortium (IDDC, #13177)*; *Platform Handicap en Ontwikkelingssamenwerking (PHOS)*; *PMNCH (#18410)*; *Rare Diseases International (RDI, #18621).* Cooperates with (8): CDC's National Center on Birth Defects and Developmental Disabilities; *European Association of Urology (EAU, #06264)*; *Food Fortification Initiative (FFI, #09844)*; *Global Alliance for Improved Nutrition (GAIN, #10202)*; Governor Kremers Centre-Maastricht University Medical Centre (GKC); *International Association of Operative Millers (IAOM)*; *International Children's Continence Society (ICCS, #12552)*; *Micronutrient Forum (#16748).* In liaison with technical committees of: *International Organization for Standardization (ISO, #14473).* Participates in: European Reference Networks; *Global Partnership on Children with Disabilities (GPcwd, #10529).* Close links with: EUROlinkCAT; International Neuro-Urology Society; *Society for Research into Hydrocephalus and Spina Bifida (SRHSB, #19634)*; World Federation of Neurosurgical Societies. [2023.02.28/XD7460/**C**]

♦ International Federation of Spirits Producers / see Alliance Against Counterfeit Spirits (#00654)
♦ International Federation of Sport in Catholic Education / see International Sporting Federation of Catholic Schools (#15589)

♦ International Federation of Sport Climbing (IFSC) 13553

Administration Corso Vinzaglio 12, 10121 Turin TO, Italy. T. +39113853995. E-mail: administration@ifsc-climbing.org – office@ifsc-climbing.org – communications@ifsc-climbing.org.
Legal Seat Effingerstr 1, 3001 Bern, Switzerland.
URL: http://www.ifsc-climbing.org/

History 27 Jan 2007. Takes over activities of *International Council for Competition Climbing (UIAA Climbing, inactive)*. Current statutes approved 27 Feb 2010. Registration: Switzerland. **Aims** Direct, regulate, promote, develop and further the sport of competition climbing worldwide. **Structure** Plenary Assembly (annual); Executive Board; Continental Councils (5); Commissions. **Languages** English. **Staff** 7.00 FTE, paid. **Finance** Members' dues. Other sources: events fees; sponsorship agreements; broadcasting and TV rights. **Activities** Sporting activities; events/meetings. **Events** *Plenary Assembly* Tokyo (Japan) 2019, *Plenary Assembly* Rome (Italy) 2011.
Members National federations (87) in 84 countries and territories:
Algeria, Andorra, Argentina, Armenia, Australia, Austria, Azerbaijan, Belarus, Belgium, Bolivia, Bosnia-Herzegovina, Botswana, Brazil, Bulgaria, Cameroon, Canada, Chile, China, Colombia, Costa Rica, Croatia, Cyprus, Czechia, Denmark, Ecuador, El Salvador, Estonia, Finland, France, Georgia, Germany, Greece, Guatemala, Honduras, Hong Kong, Hungary, India, Indonesia, Iran Islamic Rep, Ireland, Israel, Italy, Japan, Jordan, Kazakhstan, Korea Rep, Kyrgyzstan, Latvia, Lithuania, Luxembourg, Malaysia, Mexico, Mongolia, Nepal, Netherlands, New Caledonia, New Zealand, North Macedonia, Norway, Pakistan, Peru, Philippines, Poland, Portugal, Romania, Russia, Rwanda, Senegal, Serbia, Singapore, Slovakia, Slovenia, South Africa, Spain, Sweden, Switzerland, Taiwan, Thailand, Türkiye, UK, Ukraine, USA, Uzbekistan, Venezuela.
NGO Relations Member of (5): *Association of Summer Olympic International Federations (ASOIF, #02943)* (Associate); *Association of the IOC Recognized International Sports Federations (ARISF, #02767)*; *International Paralympic Committee (IPC, #14512)*; *International World Games Association (IWGA, #15914)*; *Olympic Movement (#17719)*. Cooperates with (1): *International Testing Agency (ITA, #15678)*. Recognized by: *International Olympic Committee (IOC, #14408)*. [2022/XM3326/**D**]

♦ International Federation of Sport Fly Fishing (see: #04562)
♦ International Federation of Sportive Walking (inactive)
♦ International Federation of Sports Acrobatics (inactive)
♦ International Federation of Sports Chiropractic (#09620)

♦ International Federation of Sports Medicine 13554

Fédération internationale de médecine sportive (FIMS)

Headquarters Maison du Sport Intl, Av de Rhodanie 54, 1007 Lausanne VD, Switzerland. E-mail: headquarters-ch@fims.org.
Pres Dept of Health Sciences, Univ of Rome "Foro Italico", Piazza Lauro de Bosis 15, 00135 Rome RM, Italy. T. +39636733569. Fax +3963613065. E-mail: president@fims.org.
SG Auf der Schmelz 6A, 1150 Vienna, Austria.
URL: http://www.fims.org/

History 1928, St Moritz (Switzerland). Former names and other names: *Aassociation internationale médico-sportive (AIMS)* – former. **Aims** Promote the study and development of sports medicine worldwide; preserve and improve health of mankind through *physical fitness* and sports participation; study scientifically the natural and pathological implications of physical training and sports participation. **Structure** General Meeting (every 4 years); Council of Delegates; Executive Committee; Commissions (4). **Languages** English, French, Spanish. **Staff** 3.00 FTE, paid; 34.00 FTE, voluntary. **Finance** Sources: grants; members' dues; sale of publications. **Activities** Events/meetings; training/education. **Events** *World Congress of Sports Medicine* Kazan (Russia) 2024, *World Congress of Sports Medicine* Guadalajara (Mexico) 2022, *World Congress of Sports Medicine* Athens (Greece) 2021, *World Congress of Sports Medicine* Athens (Greece) 2020, *Biennial World Congress* Rio de Janeiro (Brazil) 2018. **Publications** *FIMS Newsletter* (4 a year); *The World of Sports Medicine. FIMS Directory.* Books; congress reports.
Members National Associations in 139 countries and territories:
Albania, Algeria, Andorra, Antigua-Barbuda, Argentina, Aruba, Australia, Austria, Bahamas, Bahrain, Bangladesh, Barbados, Belarus, Belgium, Benin, Bermuda, Bolivia, Bosnia-Herzegovina, Brazil, Brunei Darussalam, Bulgaria, Burkina Faso, Burundi, Cameroon, Canada, Chad, Chile, China, Colombia, Comoros, Congo DR, Costa Rica, Côte d'Ivoire, Croatia, Cuba, Curaçao, Cyprus, Czechia, Denmark, Dominican Rep, Ecuador, Egypt, El Salvador, Estonia, Eswatini, Ethiopia, Finland, France, Gabon, Georgia, Germany, Ghana, Greece, Grenada, Guatemala, Guinea-Bissau, Haiti, Honduras, Hong Kong, Hungary, India, Indonesia, Iran Islamic Rep, Iraq, Ireland, Israel, Italy, Jamaica, Japan, Jordan, Kazakhstan, Kenya, Korea Rep, Kuwait, Latvia, Lithuania, Luxembourg, Macau, Madagascar, Malaysia, Mali, Malta, Mauritania, Mexico, Moldova, Mongolia, Morocco, Mozambique, Nepal, Netherlands, New Zealand, Nicaragua, Nigeria, North Macedonia, Norway, Oman, Pakistan, Palestine, Panama, Paraguay, Peru, Philippines, Poland, Portugal, Puerto Rico, Qatar, Romania, Russia, San Marino, Saudi Arabia, Senegal, Serbia, Singapore, Slovakia, Slovenia, South Africa, Spain, Sri Lanka, St Lucia, St Vincent-Grenadines, Sweden, Switzerland, Syrian AR, Taiwan, Tanzania UR, Thailand, Togo, Trinidad-Tobago, Tunisia, Türkiye, Uganda, UK, Ukraine, United Arab Emirates, Uruguay, USA, Venezuela, Virgin Is UK, Zimbabwe.
Multinational groups (4):
Asian Federation of Sports Medicine (AFSM, #01475); *European Federation of Sports Medicine Associations (EFSMA, #07219)*; *Pan American Confederation of Sports Medicine (COPAMEDE, no recent information)*; *Union africaine de médecine du sport (UAMS, no recent information).*
NGO Relations Member of (1): *Olympic Movement (#17719)*. Recognized Organization by: *International Olympic Committee (IOC, #14408)*. Coordination Commission with: *International Council for Health, Physical Education, Recreation, Sport and Dance (ICHPER-SD, #13028)*. [2021/XD2013/y/**B**]

♦ International Federation for Sports Officials (IFSO) 13555

SG Prinses Margrietplnts 33, 2595 AM The Hague, Netherlands. E-mail: info@ifso.sport.
URL: https://www.ifso.sport/

History Mar 2019, The Hague (Netherlands). **Aims** Enhance sports officiating across all sports.
Members National and International organizations in 7 countries:
Belgium, Djibouti, France, Hungary, Netherlands, UK, Vanuatu.
Confédération mondiale des sports de boules (CMSB, inactive); *European Hockey Federation (EHF, #07494)*; *Fédération internationale de basketball (FIBA, #09614)*; *Fédération internationale de SAMBO (FIAS, #09655)*; *Fédération Internationale de Savate (FISav, #09656)*; *International Bobsleigh and Skeleton Federation (IBSF, #12375)*; *International Federation of American Football (IFAF, #13354)*; *International Powerlifting Federation (IPF, #14630)*; *International Rafting Federation (IRF, #14691)*; *International School Sport Federation (ISF, #14792)*; *International University Sports Federation (FISU, #15830)*; *International Wushu Federation (IWUF, #15918)*; *Union Cycliste Internationale (UCI, #20375)*; *World Rowing (#21756)*; *World Squash Federation (WSF, #21826)*.
Associated organizations (2):
International Committee for Fair Play (#12769); *United Paintball Federation (UPBF, #20654)*.
[2021/AA1938/**D**]

♦ International Federation of Sports Physical Therapy (IFSPT) 13556

Pres address not obtained. E-mail: president@ifspt.org.
Sec address not obtained. E-mail: secretary@ifspt.org.
Registered Office c/o Sportfisio Switzerland, Feithierestr 140, 3952 Susten, Switzerland.
URL: http://www.ifspt.org/

History 8 Dec 2000. Since 2003, a subgroup of *World Confederation for Physical Therapy (WCPT, #21293)*. Former names and other names: *International Federation of Sports Physiotherapy (IFSP)* – former. Registration: Switzerland. **Aims** Promote sports physiotherapy worldwide; advance professional interest and stature of sports physiotherapy; improve quality of sports physiotherapy on the level of knowledge, skills and professional responsibility; facilitate efforts to conduct research in order to promote evidence based sports physiotherapy; encourage communication and exchange of educational and professional information. **Structure** General Meeting (at least every 4 years, in conjunction with Congress); Board; Committees. **Languages** English, French, Spanish. **Staff** None. **Finance** Members' dues. Funding from Dutch government. **Activities** Awards/prizes/competitions; events/meetings; knowledge management/information dissemination; research/documentation; training/education. **Events** *World Congress of Sports Physical Therapy* Oslo (Norway) 2024, *World Congress* Nyborg (Denmark) 2022, *World Congress* Vancouver, BC (Canada) 2019, *World Congress* Belfast (UK) 2017, *World Congress* Bern (Switzerland) 2015. **Publications** Congress book (annual).
Members Members in 38 countries and territories:
Argentina, Australia, Austria, Brazil, Bulgaria, Cameroon, Canada, Chile, Cyprus, Denmark, Finland, France, Germany, Greece, Hong Kong, Indonesia, Ireland, Israel, Italy, Japan, Korea Rep, Luxembourg, Netherlands, New Zealand, Nigeria, Norway, Poland, Portugal, Saudi Arabia, Slovenia, South Africa, Spain, Sweden, Switzerland, Thailand, Türkiye, UK, Zambia.
NGO Relations *International Acupuncture Association of Physical Therapists (IAAPT, #11587)*; *International Federation of Orthopaedic Manipulative Physical Therapists (IFOMPT, #13495)*; *International Federation of Sports Medicine (#13554)*; *International Organization of Physical Therapists in Pelvic and Women's Health (IOPTPWH, #14462)*; *International Private Physical Therapy Association (IPPTA, #14644)*; *International Olympic Committee (IOC, #14408)*; *World Federation of Athletic Training and Therapy (WFATT, #21413)*.
[2023/XD9009/**D**]

♦ International Federation of Sports Physiotherapy / see International Federation of Sports Physical Therapy (#13556)
♦ International Federation for Sports Shooting (#09665)

♦ International Federation of Stamp Dealers' Associations (IFSDA) .. 13557

Fédération Internationale des Chambres Syndicales de Négociants en Timbres-Poste – Federación Internacional de Asociaciones de Filatélicos – Internationaler Dachverband der Briefmarkenhändelverbände

Sec Postnet Suite 11, Private Bag X0002, The Fig Tree, Charlo, 6033, South Africa. E-mail: info@stampsfriend.com.
Pres c/o PostBeeld, Kloosterstraat 17, 2021 VJ Haarlem, Netherlands. E-mail: info@postbeeld.com.
URL: http://www.ifsda.org/

History 8 May 1952, London (UK). Former names and other names: *Internationale Vereinigung der Nationalen Briefmarkenhändelverbände* – former. **Aims** Promote and maintain a high standard of professional integrity among stamp dealers throughout the world; promote the interchange between member organizations of all information and literature likely to be of service to the stamp trade; endeavour in all possible ways to reduce the barriers to international trade in stamps; promote the interchange of information regarding the marketing of forged, faked, repaired or otherwise unsatisfactory stamps. **Structure** General Assembly (annual); Board. **Languages** English. **Staff** 1.00 FTE, voluntary. **Finance** Sources: donations; fees for services; members' dues; sale of products. **Activities** Events/meetings. **Events** *Annual General Assembly / Annual Meeting* Melbourne, VIC (Australia) 2013, *Annual General Assembly / Annual Meeting* Vaduz (Liechtenstein) 2012, *Annual General Assembly* Monte Carlo (Monaco) 2011, *Annual Meeting* Monte Carlo (Monaco) 2011, *Annual general assembly / Annual Meeting* Antwerp (Belgium) 2010. **Publications** *IFSDA Magazine. IFSDA Handbook.*
Members National organizations in 22 countries:
Argentina, Australia, Austria, Belgium, Brazil, Denmark, Finland, France, Germany, Greece, India, Ireland, Israel, Italy, Netherlands, Norway, Russia, South Africa, Spain, Sweden, Switzerland, USA.
NGO Relations Partner of (1): *World Association for the Development of Philately (WADP, #21132)*.
[2021.08.31/XC2015/**C**]

♦ International Federation of Standards Users (IFAN) 13558

Assistant Sec c/o ISO Central Sec, BIBC II, Chemin de Blandonnet 8, CP 401, 1214 Geneva, Switzerland. T. +41227490111. E-mail: ifan@ifan.org.
URL: http://www.ifan.org/

History 1974, Paris (France), on occasion of 1st International Conference, as *International Federation for the Application of Standards – Fédération internationale des associations pour la pratique des normes – Internationale Föderation der Ausschüsse Normenpraxis (IFAN)*. Present name adopted, 1999. **Aims** Promote cooperation among organizations dealing with application of standards, by exchange of experience and coordination of work and training; promote uniform implementation of international standards. **Structure** Members' Assembly (annual); Board, consisting of President, Immediate Past President, 2 Vice-Presidents, Treasurer and 4 additional elected members and the Secretary; Working and Project Groups; Secretariat. **Languages** English. **Activities** Carries out studies at international level; organizes symposia, conferences, seminars and meetings. **Events** *Members Assembly* Berlin (Germany) 2020, *International Conference* Chicago, IL (USA) 2017, *Members Assembly* London (UK) 2013, *Triennial Conference* London (UK) 2013, *Members Assembly* Geneva (Switzerland) 2012.
Members National members in 12 countries:
Canada, China, France, Germany, Israel, Luxembourg, Netherlands, Norway, Slovenia, Switzerland, UK, USA.
Included in the above, one regional member (covers Canada and USA):
Society for Standards Professionals (SES).
Corporate members (11). Membership countries not specified. [2021/XD6102/**D**]

♦ International Federation of State and Public Employees (no recent information)
♦ International Federation of Stationery, Office Machines and Furniture Associations (inactive)
♦ International Federation for Stenography and Typewriting / see Fédération internationale pour le traitement de l'information et de la communication (#09667)
♦ International Federation for Sterile Supply (inactive)
♦ International Federation of Stock Exchanges / see World Federation of Exchanges (#21434)
♦ International Federation for Structural Concrete (#09615)
♦ International Federation of Students in Political Sciences (inactive)
♦ International Federation of Super-8 Cinema (inactive)
♦ International Federation for the Surgery of Obesity / see International Federation for the Surgery of Obesity and Metabolic Disorders (#13559)

♦ International Federation for the Surgery of Obesity and Metabolic Disorders (IFSO) 13559

Exec Dir Rione Sirignano 5, 80121 Naples NA, Italy. T. +39817611085. Fax +3981664372. E-mail: secretariat@ifso.com – info@ifso.com.
URL: http://www.ifso.com/

History 1995, Stockholm (Sweden). Former names and other names: *International Federation for the Surgery of Obesity* – former. **Aims** Unify global scientific, surgical and integrated health communities for the purpose of dissemination of knowledge, collaboration and establishing universal standards of care for the treatment of individuals with adiposity-based chronic disease. **Structure** General Council; Board of Trustees; Executive Board. **Languages** English, German, Italian. **Staff** 2.00 FTE, paid. **Finance** Sources: donations; meeting proceeds; members' dues. **Activities** Advocacy/lobbying/activism; events/meetings; knowledge management/information dissemination; networking/liaising; standards/guidelines. **Events** *World Congress* Toronto, ON (Canada) 2026, *World Congress* Santiago (Chile) 2025, *World Congress* Melbourne, VIC (Australia) 2024, *World Congress* Naples (Italy) 2023, *World Congress* Miami, FL (USA) 2022. **Publications** *Obesity Surgery* (12 a year) – official journal.
Members Full: national societies. Affiliate: individuals in countries where no national society exists. Members in 71 countries and territories:
Argentina, Australia, Austria, Azerbaijan, Belgium, Bolivia, Brazil, Bulgaria, Canada, Chile, China, Colombia, Costa Rica, Czechia, Dominican Rep, Ecuador, Egypt, El Salvador, Finland, France, Germany, Greece, Guatemala, Honduras, Hong Kong, Hungary, Iceland, India, Indonesia, Iran Islamic Rep, Israel, Italy, Japan, Jordan, Kazakhstan, Korea Rep, Kuwait, Lebanon, Lithuania, Malaysia, Mexico, Netherlands, New Zealand, Norway, Pakistan, Panama, Paraguay, Peru, Philippines, Poland, Portugal, Romania, Russia, Saudi Arabia, Serbia, Singapore, Slovenia, South Africa, Spain, Sri Lanka, Sweden, Switzerland, Taiwan, Thailand, Türkiye, UK, Ukraine, United Arab Emirates, Uruguay, USA, Venezuela. [2022.02.15/XD7432/y/**D**]

♦ International Federation of Surgical Colleges (IFSC) 13560

Fédération internationale des collèges de chirurgie – Federación Internacional de Colegios de Cirurgia – Internationale Vereinigung von Gesellschaften für Chirurgie

Main Office Temple Usk, 95 Main Road, Colden Common, Winchester, SO21 1TB, UK. T. +441962712383. E-mail: admin@theifsc.org.
URL: http://www.theifsc.org/

History 4 Jul 1958, Stockholm (Sweden). Founded by representatives of national surgical institutions. Constitution revised: 1963, Rome (Italy); 1992, New Orleans LA (USA); 2006, Heidelberg (Germany). Registration: Chairy Commission, No/ID: 1144865, England and Wales; USA. **Aims** Raise awareness of global surgery and in particular the need to improve emergency surgical and anaesthesia care in low and middle-income countries (LMICs). **Structure** General Meeting (annual); Council; Executive Committee. **Languages** English. **Staff** 0.50 FTE, paid. **Finance** Sources: members' dues. Contributions for special purposes from foundations and individuals. **Activities** Events/meetings; financial and/or material support; training/education. **Events** *Annual General Meeting* Winchester (UK) 2022, *Annual General Meeting* Winchester (UK) 2021, *Annual General Meeting* Kampala (Uganda) 2019, *Annual General Meeting* Mombasa (Kenya) 2016, *Annual General Meeting* Blantyre (Malawi) 2015. **Publications** *International Federation of Surgical Colleges Newsletter. IFSC Collected Papers. Dictionary of Disaster Medicine and Humanitarian Relief, Teaching Manual for District Hospitals.* Reports of Symposia.

Members Individual associates (630); national colleges or associations of surgeons. Members in 66 countries and territories:
Argentina, Armenia, Australia, Austria, Bahrain, Bangladesh, Brazil, Bulgaria, Canada, Chile, China, Colombia, Costa Rica, Côte d'Ivoire, Czechia, Denmark, Egypt, Ethiopia, Finland, France, Germany, Greece, Guatemala, Hong Kong, Hungary, India, Indonesia, Ireland, Israel, Italy, Jamaica, Japan, Kazakhstan, Kenya, Korea Rep, Lebanon, Malawi, Malaysia, Malta, Mongolia, Netherlands, Nigeria, Norway, Pakistan, Papua New Guinea, Philippines, Poland, Romania, Russia, Saudi Arabia, Scotland, Singapore, South Africa, Spain, Sri Lanka, Sudan, Sweden, Switzerland, Thailand, Tunisia, Türkiye, UK, USA, Vietnam, Zambia, Zimbabwe.
Included in the above, 6 organizations listed in this Yearbook:
Baltic Association of Surgeons (BAS, #03102); College of Surgeons of East, Central and Southern Africa (COSECSA, #04110); International Association for Humanitarian Medicine Chisholm-Gunn (IAHM, #11946); International Society of Surgery (ISS, #15496); Royal Australasian College of Surgeons (RACS); West African College of Surgeons (WACS, #20876).
Speciality members, including the following 8 organizations listed in this Yearbook:
Baltic Association of Burns and Fire Disasters (BABFD, no recent information); Euro-Mediterranean Council for Burns and Fire Disaster (MBC, #05719); International Federation of Oto-Rhino-Laryngological Societies (IFOS, #13496); International Society for Burn Injuries (ISBI, #14986); International Society for Digestive Surgery (ISDS, #15060); World Federation of Associations of Pediatric Surgeons (WOFAPS, #21411); World Federation of Surgical Oncology Societies (WFSOS, #21488).
Consultative Status Consultative status granted from: *ECOSOC (#05331)* (Ros C); *WHO (#20950)* (Official Relations). **IGO Relations** Accredited by: *United Nations Office at Geneva (UNOG, #20597); United Nations Office at Vienna (UNOV, #20604).* Associated with Department of Global Communications of the United Nations. **NGO Relations** Member of: *Global Alliance for Surgical, Obstetric, Trauma and Anaesthesia Care (G4 Alliance, #10229).* [2022/XC2019/y/**B**]

♦ International Federation of Surveyors (FIG) 13561

Fédération internationale des géomètres (FIG) – Internationale Vereinigung der Vermessungsingenieure

Dir Kalvebod Brygge 31-33, 1780 Copenhagen V, Denmark. T. +4538861081. E-mail: fig@fig.net.
Events Manager address not obtained.
URL: https://www.fig.net/

History 18 Jul 1878, Paris (France). **Aims** Provide an international forum for discussion and development aiming to promote professional practice and standards. **Structure** General Assembly (annual); Council; Commissions; Inter Commission; Advisory Committee; Ad hoc Task Forces. Permanent institutions: *International Office of Cadastre and Land Records (#14398); International Institution for the History of Surveying and Measurement (#13936); 'FIG Foundation'.* **Languages** English. **Staff** 2.50 FTE, paid. **Finance** Sources: members' dues. **Activities** Events/meetings; knowledge management/information dissemination; publishing activities; standards/guidelines; training/education. **Events** *Congress* Cape Town (South Africa) 2026, *Congress* Warsaw (Poland) 2022, *Working Week* Utrecht (Netherlands) 2021, *Working Week* Amsterdam (Netherlands) 2020, *South East Asia Survey Congress* Darwin, NT (Australia) 2019. **Publications** *e-Newsletter* (12 a year); *FIG Annual Review. FIG Publications.* Congress proceedings.
Members National associations or organizations (105) in 89 countries and territories:
Albania, Algeria, Argentina, Australia, Austria, Belarus, Belgium, Benin, Bosnia-Herzegovina, Botswana, Brazil, Brunei Darussalam, Bulgaria, Cameroon, Canada, China, Congo DR, Costa Rica, Croatia, Cyprus, Czechia, Denmark, Egypt, Estonia, Ethiopia, Fiji, Finland, France, Georgia, Germany, Ghana, Greece, Hong Kong, Hungary, Indonesia, Iran Islamic Rep, Ireland, Israel, Italy, Jamaica, Japan, Kenya, Korea Rep, Kosovo, Latvia, Lebanon, Liberia, Lithuania, Luxembourg, Malaysia, Mali, Malta, Mongolia, Morocco, Nepal, Netherlands, New Zealand, Niger, Nigeria, Norway, Palestine, Papua New Guinea, Philippines, Poland, Portugal, Puerto Rico, Romania, Russia, Senegal, Serbia, Slovakia, Slovenia, South Africa, Spain, Sri Lanka, Sweden, Switzerland, Syrian AR, Tanzania UR, Togo, Trinidad-Tobago, Tunisia, Türkiye, UK, Ukraine, Uruguay, USA, Vietnam, Zimbabwe.
Affiliates: groups of surveyors or surveying organizations (41) in 38 countries:
Afghanistan, Argentina, Australia, Belgium, Brunei Darussalam, Cambodia, Chile, China, Colombia, Croatia, Cyprus, Denmark, Fiji, Finland, Hungary, Iceland, Iran Islamic Rep, Iraq, Israel, Italy, Jordan, Laos, Mexico, Moldova, Mongolia, Namibia, Nepal, Netherlands, North Macedonia, Norway, Romania, Russia, Rwanda, Saudi Arabia, Sri Lanka, Sweden, Switzerland, USA.
Corporate (21): organizations, institutions and agencies which provide commercial services to the profession of surveyor, in 17 countries:
Cameroon, China, Denmark, Germany, India, Italy, Morocco, Netherlands, Portugal, Qatar, Russia, Saudi Arabia, Spain, Switzerland, Türkiye, UK, USA.
Academic (92): organizations, institutions and agencies which promote education or research in one or more of the disciplines of surveying, in 56 countries and territories:
Australia, Austria, Belgium, Botswana, Brazil, Canada, China, Colombia, Croatia, Cyprus, Czechia, Denmark, Ethiopia, Fiji, Finland, France, Gabon, Germany, Ghana, Greece, Hong Kong, Hungary, Ireland, Israel, Jamaica, Kazakhstan, Kosovo, Latvia, Lebanon, Malaysia, Mexico, Morocco, Nepal, Netherlands, New Zealand, Nigeria, Norway, Palestine, Poland, Puerto Rico, Romania, Russia, Rwanda, Saudi Arabia, Serbia, Singapore, Slovenia, South Africa, Spain, Sweden, Switzerland, Trinidad-Tobago, Türkiye, Uganda, UK, USA.
Correspondents (12): individuals in 12 countries:
Bhutan, Gabon, India, Lesotho, Madagascar, Peru, Senegal, St Lucia, Tanzania UR, Thailand, Tonga, Tuvalu.
Consultative Status Consultative status granted from: *ECOSOC (#05331)* (Ros A); *UNEP (#20299).* **IGO Relations** Accredited by (1): *United Nations Office at Vienna (UNOV, #20604).* Member of (1): *International Committee on Global Navigation Satellite Systems (ICG, #12775).* Cooperates with (1): *International Hydrographic Organization (IHO, #13825).* Associated with Department of Global Communications of the United Nations. **NGO Relations** Member of (4): *International Cost Management Standard Coalition (ICMS Coalition, #12978); International Property Measurement Standards Coalition (IPMSC, #14656); International Science Council (ISC, #14796); UN-GGO: Geospatial Societies (UN-GGIM GS, #20324).* Cooperates with (1): *International Council for Research and Innovation in Building and Construction (CIB, #13069).* Scientific associate of: *International Cost Engineering Council (ICEC, #12976); International Society for Mine Surveying (ISM, #15272).* In liaison with technical committees of: *International Organization for Standardization (ISO, #14473).* Partner of: *Appraisal Institute (AI).* [2023/XB2020/**B**]

♦ International Federation for Sustainable Development and Fight to Poverty in the Mediterranean-Black Sea (FISPMED) 13562

Sviluppo Sostenibile e Lotta alla Povertà nel Mediterraneo e nel Mal Nero

Contact Casella Postale 10, San Marco 1, 30124 Venice VE, Italy. T. +393455370728. E-mail: fispmed@gmail.com.
URL: http://fispmed.wordpress.com/

History 2004, developing out of the experiences from the SeaM project. Registered in accordance with Italian law. **Aims** Contribute to the social and civil increase, sustainable development of the Mediterranean and Black Sea; strengthen the critical ability to stimulate the planning and intellectual autonomy of the persons, so as to increase the knowledge of the exercise of their rights, the responsibility and the solidarity. **Structure** Assembly (at least annually); Scientific Committee. Presidency, comprising President and Vice-President. Auditors Board.
Members Associate partners in 39 countries and territories:
Albania, Algeria, Armenia, Belgium, Bosnia-Herzegovina, Brazil, Bulgaria, Cyprus, Egypt, France, Georgia, Germany, Greece, Ireland, Israel, Italy, Jordan, Latvia, Lebanon, Libya, Luxembourg, Malta, Mauritania, Moldova, Morocco, North Macedonia, Palestine, Portugal, Romania, Russia, Slovenia, Spain, Sweden, Syrian AR, Tunisia, Türkiye, UK, Ukraine, USA.
Included in the above, 20 organizations listed in in this Yearbook:
Agency for the Promotion of European Research, Rome (APRE); BirdLife International (#03266); Black Sea NGO Network (BSNN, #03276); Center of Arab Women for Training and Research, Tunis (CAWTAR, #03637); EUROPARC Federation (#05768); European Institute of Cultural Routes (EICR); European University Centre for Cultural Heritage, Ravello (CUEBC); International Centre for Black Sea Studies (ICBSS, #12478); International Ocean Institute (IOI, #14394); International Telematic University UNINETTUNO; Istituto di Studi sul Mediterraneo (ISMed); MEDCITIES Network (#16610); Mediterranean Agronomic Institute of Chania (MAICh, #16642); Mediterranean Association to Save the Sea Turtles (MEDASSET, #16647); Mediterranean Coastal Foundation (MEDCOAST, #16649); Mediterranean Network of Basin Organisations (MENBO, #16664); MEDITERRANEAN SOS Network (MEDSOS); South East European Environmental NGOs Network (SEEENN, no recent information); The Mediterranean Wetlands Initiative (MedWet, #16688); Union of Black Sea and Caspian Business (BCB, #20369).
NGO Relations Member of: *International Ocean Institute (IOI, #14394); Sustainable Development Solutions Network (SDSN, #20054).* [2016/XJ1148/**E**]

♦ International Federation of Swimming Teachers' Association, UK (IFSTA) 13563

CEO STA, Anchor House, Birch Street, Walsall, WS2 8HZ, UK. T. +441922645097. Fax +441922720628. E-mail: info@ifsta.co.uk.
URL: http://www.ifsta.co.uk/

History Founded 1977. **Aims** Represent and unite the world's swimming teaching bodies in the common goal of reducing deaths by drowning, by improving standards in teaching swimming and other survival techniques. **Structure** Council. **Languages** English. **Finance** Members' dues. **Activities** Training/education; projects/programmes; events/meetings. **Events** *Conference* Incheon (Korea Rep) 2016, *Conference* Taiwan 2008, *Conference* Fareham (UK) 2006, *Conference* Hong Kong (Hong Kong) 2004, *Conference* Singapore (Singapore) 2002. **Publications** *Aquatic Survival Programme Manual; International Swimming Standards Teaching Manual; International Swimming Standards Teaching Portfolio.*
Members Organizations (24) in 21 countries and territories:
Antigua-Barbuda, Australia, Cameroon, Finland, Germany, Hong Kong, India, Ireland, Italy, Kenya, Korea Rep, Malaysia, Netherlands, New Zealand, Papua New Guinea, Singapore, Sri Lanka, Taiwan, UK, USA, Vietnam.
NGO Relations Cooperates with: *International Life Saving Federation of Europe (ILSE, #14043).* [2019.04.25/XD8966/**D**]

♦ International Federation for Systems Research (IFSR) 13564

Fédération internationale de recherches sur les systèmes

SG Paulanergasse 13, 1040 Vienna, Austria. T. +4316766914488. E-mail: office@ifsr.org.
Pres address not obtained.
URL: http://www.ifsr.org/

History 1981. Registered in accordance with Austrian law. **Aims** Stimulate and promote all activities associated with scientific study of systems; coordinate and support such activities at international level; strengthen programmes of member societies; promote international publications in the area of systems research; promote systems education. **Structure** General Assembly (every 2 years); Executive Committee (annual). **Languages** English. **Staff** None. **Finance** Members' dues. Other sources: license fees from publications; events proceeds. **Activities** Research/documentation; knowledge management/information dissemination; events/meetings. **Events** *Meeting* Linz (Austria) 2018, *Bienial European meeting* Linz (Austria) 2012, *Fuschl conversation* Fuschl (Austria) 2006, *Biennial European meeting on cybernetics and systems research* Vienna (Austria) 2006, *Biennial European meeting on cybernetics and systems research* Vienna (Austria) 2004. **Publications** *Systems Research and Behavioural Science* (6 a year) – journal; *IFSR Newsletter* (1-2 a year). *IFSR International Series on Systems Science and Engineering* – book series. Proceedings of ISFR Conversations (every 2 years).
Members Full; Affiliate; Fellows; Supporting. Organizations (45) in 25 countries:
Argentina, Australia, Austria, Belgium, Bulgaria, China, Croatia, France, Germany, Greece, India, Ireland, Italy, Japan, Mexico, Netherlands, New Zealand, Peru, Poland, Portugal, Slovenia, Spain, Switzerland, UK, USA.
Included in the above, 6 organizations listed in this Yearbook:
Global Institute of Flexible Systems Management (GIFT); Instituto Andino de Sistemas (IAS); International Council on Systems Engineering (INCOSE, #13083); International Institute of Informatics and Systemics (IIIS, #13889); International Society for Knowledge and Systems Sciences (ISKSS); International Society for the Systems Sciences (ISSS, #15500).
NGO Relations Cooperates with: *International Academy for Systems and Cybernetic Sciences (IASCYS, #11578).* Affiliated with: *World Organisation of Systems and Cybernetics (WOSC, #21686).* [2022/XD5599/y/**D**]

♦ International Federation of Teachers' Associations (inactive)
♦ International Federation of Teachers of French (#09652)
♦ International Federation for Teaching the Art of Drawing (inactive)

♦ International Federation for the Teaching of English (IFTE) 13565

Pres address not obtained.

History 1983. Founded following activities of the 'International Steering Committee (ISC)' founded in 1967 following the international conference held, Dartmouth NH (USA), in 1966. **Aims** Promote exchange of thinking and research about the teaching of English. **Structure** Steering Committee. **Events** *IF Conference* Sydney, NSW (Australia) 2020, *Quadrennial conference / Conference* Auckland (New Zealand) 2011, *Interim meeting* Auckland (New Zealand) 2009, *Quadrennial conference / Conference* Winnipeg, MB (Canada) 2007, *Interim meeting* Vancouver, BC (Canada) 2005. **Publications** *International Digest.*
Members Full in 6 countries:
Australia, Barbados, Canada, New Zealand, UK, USA. [2020/XD0953/**D**]

♦ International Federation for the Teaching of Home Economics / see International Federation for Home Economics (#13447)

♦ International Federation of Technical Analysts (IFTA) 13566

Office 1300 Piccard Drive, LL-14, Rockville MD 20850, USA. T. +12404046508. Fax +12409909771. E-mail: admin@ifta.org.
URL: http://www.ifta.org/

History 1986. **Aims** Promote exchange of information related to technical analysis. **Structure** Board, comprising Chairpersons, 3 Vice-Chairpersons, Treasurer, Secretary, Committee Chairs and Members-at-Large. **Languages** English. **Finance** Sources: members' dues. **Events** *Annual Conference* Melbourne, VIC (Australia) 2022, *Annual Conference* Philadelphia, PA (USA) 2021, *Annual Conference* Rockville, MD (USA) 2020, *Annual Conference* Cairo (Egypt) 2019, *Annual Conference* Kuala Lumpur (Malaysia) 2018. **Publications** *IFTA Newsletter* (4 a year); *IFTA Journal* (annual).
Members Individuals and federations in 23 countries and territories:
Argentina, Australia, Belgium, Canada, Czechia, Egypt, France, Germany, Hong Kong, Indonesia, Italy, Japan, Jordan, Netherlands, New Zealand, Pakistan, Russia, Singapore, South Africa, Spain, Switzerland, UK, USA.
Included in the above, 1 organization listed in this Yearbook:
Scandinavian Technical Analysts Federation (STAF, #19123). [2021.02.17/XD6677/**D**]

♦ International Federation of Technical Engineers, Architects, and Draftsman's Union / see International Federation of Professional and Technical Engineers
♦ International Federation of the Technical and Trade Press (inactive)

♦ International Federation of Telephone Emergency Services (IFOTES) 13567

Fédération internationale des services de secours par téléphone – Federación Internacional de Servicios Telefónicos de Emergencia – Internationaler Verband für Telefonseelsorge – Federazione Internazionale dei Centri di Aiuto per Telefono

Mailing address c/o ARTESS, Via Trento 45, 33100 Udine UD, Italy. T. +39432202076. E-mail: secretariat@ifotes.org.
Registered Office Rue du Nord 6, 1180 Rolle VD, Switzerland.
URL: http://www.ifotes.org/

History 1967, Bossey (Switzerland). Founded during 1st Congress. Legal seat in Geneva (Switzerland) since 1967. Former names and other names: *International Centre of Information for Telephonic Help* – former; *Centre international d'information des secours par téléphone* – former; *International Federation of Telephonic Emergency Services (IFOTES)* – former. Registration: Swiss Civil Code, Switzerland, Geneva. **Aims** Coordinate and disseminate information concerning telephonic *help* services; support efforts to create telephone emergency services centres and national associations worldwide; promote exchange of experience among national members; organize international congresses and seminars on emotional health and emotional health support. **Structure** General Assembly (every 3 years, at International Congress); International Committee (IC); Executive Committee; Standing Working Committee; Secretariat, based in Switzerland. **Languages** English, French, German, Italian, Spanish. **Staff** 3.00 FTE, paid; 20.00 FTE, voluntary. **Finance** Sources: contributions; gifts, legacies; grants; members' dues; revenue from activities/projects; sponsorship. **Activities** Events/meetings; healthcare; humanitarian/emergency aid; knowledge management/information dissemination; networking/liaising; projects/programmes; training/education. **Events** *Triennial Congress* Udine (Italy) 2019, *Triennial Congress* Aachen (Germany) 2016, *Triennial Congress* Gothenburg (Sweden) 2013, *Triennial congress* Vienna (Austria) 2010, *Triennial Congress* Prato, RN (Italy) 2007. **Publications** *IFOTES Newsletter* (2 a year) in English, French, German, Italian, Spanish. Reports.

Members Full national federations in 13 countries:
Austria, Belgium, Denmark, Finland, France, Germany, Hungary, Italy, Norway, Singapore, Slovenia, Spain, Switzerland.
Associated members in 11 countries:
Czechia, Ecuador, Estonia, Israel, Italy, Latvia, Luxembourg, Peru, Portugal, Sweden, Ukraine.
IGO Relations Working relations with: *WHO (#20950)*. **NGO Relations** Member of: *International Association for Suicide Prevention and Crisis Intervention (IASP, #12213)*; *World Federation for Mental Health (WFMH, #21455)*. Working relations with: *Child Helpline International (CHI, #03870)*; *LifeLine International (LLI, #16465)*; *Befrienders Worldwide (#03192)*. [2022.06.15/XC1485/**C**]

♦ International Federation of Telephonic Emergency Services / see International Federation of Telephone Emergency Services (#13567)

♦ International Federation of Television Archives (IFTA) 13568

Fédération Internationale des Archives de Télévision (FIAT)
Gen Sec RTE Archives, Donnybrook, Dublin, CO. DUBLIN, D6W F8HK, Ireland. E-mail: office@fiatifta.org – generalsecretary@fiatifta.org.
Pres address not obtained.
URL: http://www.fiatifta.org/

History 13 Jun 1977, Rome (Italy). Current Statutes in force since 1981; modified (Article 4) at 5th General Assembly, Oct 1984, Madrid (Spain); revised at 11th General Assembly, Sep 1996, Paris (France). Former names and other names: *Federación Internacional de Archivos de Televisión* – former; *Federação Internacional dos Arquios de Televisão* – former. Registration: Start date: 7 Oct 1977, France. **Aims** Promote cooperation among radio and television archives, *multimedia* and *audiovisual* archives and libraries, and all those engaged in preservation and exploitation of moving image and recorded sound materials and associated documentation. **Structure** General Assembly (at least every 2 years); Executive Council. **Languages** English, French. **Staff** 1.00 FTE, paid; 10.00 FTE, voluntary. **Finance** Sources: meeting proceeds; members' dues; sponsorship. **Activities** Events/meetings; knowledge management/information dissemination; networking/liaising. **Events** *World Conference* Cape Town (South Africa) 2022, *World Conference* 2021, *World Conference* Dublin (Ireland) 2020, *World Conference* Dubrovnik (Croatia) 2019, *World Conference* Venice (Italy) 2018. **Publications** Conference papers; resources; guidelines; standards documents. **Members** Public Service Broadcasters and National Audio Visual Archives; individual and organizational members (120) in 50 countries. Membership countries not specified. **Consultative Status** Consultative status granted from: *UNESCO (#20322)* (Consultative Status). **NGO Relations** Cooperates with: *Asia-Pacific Broadcasting Union (ABU, #01863)*; (US) Association of Moving Image Archivists; *European Broadcasting Union (EBU, #06404)*; *ICOM International Committee for Audiovisual and New Technologies of Image and Sound (AVICOM, see: #13051)*; *International Association of Sound and Audiovisual Archives (IASA, #12172)*; *International Council on Archives (ICA, #12996)*; *International Federation of Film Archives (#13427)*. Member of: *Co-ordinating Council of Audiovisual Archives Associations (CCAAA, #04820)*. Participant in: *Europeana Foundation (#05839)*. [2022.07.05/XD7875/**C**]

♦ International Federation of the Temperance Blue Cross Societies / see International Blue Cross (#12364)
♦ International Federation of Teqball (#09663)
♦ International Federation of Teratology Societies (inactive)
♦ International Federation of Terminology Banks (inactive)
♦ International Federation Terre des Hommes / see Terre des Hommes International Federation (#20133)
♦ International Federation Textile and Clothing (inactive)
♦ International Federation of Textile Workers' Associations (inactive)

♦ International Federation of Thanatologists Associations (IFTA) 13569

Fédération internationale des associations de thanatologues (FIAT)
Exec Sec Apolloweg 325, 8239 DC Lelystad, Netherlands. T. +31320322110. E-mail: info@thanos.org.
URL: https://www.thanos.org

History 14 Apr 1970, Monaco. Former names and other names: *International Federation of Undertakers' Associations* – former; *World Organization of Funeral Operatives* – alias. Registration: Handelsregister, No/ID: KVK 34391917, Netherlands, Amsterdam metropolitan area. **Aims** Promote international understanding and goodwill among funeral service professionals worldwide to offer a platform for the exchange of professional views and information and to achieve uniformed standards, rules, regulations and treaties for the cost efficient international repatriation of deceased individuals; research and study legal, moral, social and scientific issues relating to funeral services and thanatological activities; encourage and develop education for funeral services and embalming or thanatopraxy throughout the world and achieve uniform standards and regulations; improve the quality of services; increase the level of professional knowledge; promote and represent the funeral industry. **Structure** General Meeting (every 2 years). International Council of Direction (ICD) (annual); International Board; International Executive Committee; Permanent Executive Secretariat. Includes: FIAT IFTA Heritage Committee; *International Association of Funeral Museums (IAFM)*. **Languages** English. **Staff** 1.50 FTE, paid. **Finance** Sources: members' dues. **Activities** Events/meetings; knowledge management/information dissemination; standards/guidelines. Operates *European Centre of Teaching of Thanatopractic (inactive)*. **Events** *Annual Meeting* Varna (Bulgaria) 2023, *Annual Meeting* Budapest (Hungary) 2022, *Convention* Yokohama (Japan) 2021, *Convention* Yokohama (Japan) 2020, *Convention* Santa Cruz (Bolivia) 2018. **Publications** *THANOS Magazine* (3 a year) in English, French, Spanish.
Members Associate; National; Honorary; Other. National in 45 countries:
Australia, Austria, Belgium, Bolivia, Brazil, Bulgaria, Canada, China, Colombia, Croatia, Estonia, France, Germany, Greece, Hungary, Iceland, India, Ireland, Israel, Italy, Japan, Latvia, Malaysia, Malta, Mexico, Monaco, Mongolia, Netherlands, Nigeria, Norway, Poland, Portugal, Russia, Sierra Leone, Singapore, Slovakia, Slovenia, South Africa, Spain, Sweden, Thailand, Uganda, UK, Ukraine, USA.
Membership in 84 countries and territories:
Andorra, Argentina, Australia, Austria, Belarus, Belgium, Bolivia, Brazil, Bulgaria, Cameroon, Canada, Chile, China, Colombia, Congo DR, Croatia, Cyprus, Czechia, Denmark, Dominican Rep, Ecuador, Egypt, El Salvador, England, Estonia, Finland, France, Germany, Ghana, Greece, Guatemala, Honduras, Hungary, Iceland, India, Indonesia, Ireland, Israel, Italy, Japan, Korea Rep, Latvia, Lithuania, Luxembourg, Malaysia, Malta, Mauritania, Mexico, Monaco, Mongolia, Morocco, Nepal, Netherlands, New Zealand, Nicaragua, Nigeria, Norway, Pakistan, Panama, Peru, Philippines, Poland, Portugal, Romania, Russia, Scotland, Sierra Leone, Singapore, Slovakia, Slovenia, South Africa, Spain, Sweden, Switzerland, Thailand, Tunisia, Türkiye, Uganda, UK, Ukraine, Uruguay, USA, Venezuela, Vietnam.
Consultative Status Consultative status granted from: *ECOSOC (#05331)* (Special). [2023.02.16/XD3981/**B**]

♦ International Federation for Theatre Research (IFTR) 13570

Fédération internationale pour la recherche théâtrale (FIRT)
Joint SG Stockholm Univ, Dept of Culture and Aesthetics, SE-106 91 Stockholm, Sweden. T. +468164190.
Joint SG Room B77 Trent Building, University Park, Nottingham, NG7 2RD, UK. T. +441157486363. Fax +441159515924.
URL: http://www.firt-iftr.org/

History Founded Jul 1957, Venice (Italy), at 2nd Conference on the History of the Theatre, following a proposal made at 1st Conference, 1955, London (UK). Constitution adopted Jul 1957, most recently amended 2014. Registered in accordance with Swiss Civil Code. **Aims** Promote collaboration and exchange of information between individuals and organizations concerned with theatre research. **Structure** General Assembly (every 4 years); Executive Committee. **Languages** English. **Staff** None. **Finance** Sources: members' dues. **Activities** Events/meetings; guidance/assistance/consulting; research/documentation. **Events** *Annual Conference* Galway (Ireland) 2021, *Annual Conference* Galway (Ireland) 2020, *Annual Conference* Shanghai (China) 2019, *Quadrennial World Congress and General Assembly* Belgrade (Serbia) 2018, *Annual Conference* Sao Paulo (Brazil) 2017. **Publications** *Theatre Research International* (3 a year).
Members Life (4); Individual (over 600); Student (over 150). Members in 53 countries and territories:
Argentina, Australia, Austria, Bangladesh, Belgium, Brazil, Bulgaria, Canada, China, Croatia, Czechia, Denmark, Ecuador, Estonia, Finland, France, Germany, Ghana, Greece, Hong Kong, Hungary, India, Indonesia, Ireland, Israel, Italy, Japan, Korea Rep, Latvia, Lithuania, Mexico, Netherlands, New Zealand, Nigeria, Norway, Pakistan, Paraguay, Philippines, Poland, Portugal, Russia, Saudi Arabia, Serbia, Slovakia, Slovenia, South Africa, Spain, Sweden, Switzerland, Türkiye, UK, Ukraine, USA.
NGO Relations Affiliated to: *International Theatre Institute (ITI, #15683)*. Cooperates with: *Société internationale des bibliothèques et des musées des arts du spectacle (SIBMAS, #19475)*, having right of membership and one vote in General Assembly and Executive Committee. [2018.06.01/XC1842/**C**]

♦ International Federation for the Theory of Machines and Mechanisms / see International Federation for the Promotion of Mechanism and Machine Science (#13519)
♦ International Federation for Therapy and Assistance through Mediation (#09664)
♦ International Federation of Thermalism and Climatism / see Fédération mondiale du thermalisme et du climatisme (#09692)
♦ International Federation of Tiddlywinks / see International Federation of Tiddlywinks Associations
♦ International Federation of Tiddlywinks Associations (internationally oriented national body)
♦ International Federation of Tobacco Workers (inactive)
♦ International Federation of Tourist Centres (inactive)

♦ International Federation of Tour Operators (IFTO) 13571

Fédération internationale des opérateurs de tours
Secretariat c/o FTO, 30 Park Street, London, SE1 9EQ, UK. T. +442031170590. Fax +442031170581.

History Jun 1970, London (UK). **Aims** Deal with problems faced by tour operator associations with particular reference to holiday destination countries and aviation matters; discuss with national and international bodies, matters relating to: facilities, air licensing, airport and route charges, flying curfews, tourist and hotel legislation. **Structure** Officers: President, 4 Vice-Presidents, Director General. **Languages** English. **Staff** 1.00 FTE, paid. **Finance** Members' contributions. **Activities** Organizes quarterly meetings open to tour operator members of national organizations. Specific concerns: environment; safety standards; infrastructure (airports, roads, water and sewage systems); charter regulations; taxation; airport scheduling; customer care at airports; legislation.
Members National associations, each composed of operators representing 70% of the national international tour market, in 14 countries:
Belgium, Croatia, Denmark, Finland, France, Germany, Italy, Netherlands, Norway, Slovenia, Spain, Sweden, Türkiye, UK.
IGO Relations Affiliate member of: *World Tourism Organization (UNWTO, #21861)*. [2011/XD4852/**D**]

♦ International Federation for Toys and Childhood (inactive)
♦ International Federation of Trade Unions (inactive)
♦ International Federation of Trade Unions (inactive)
♦ International Federation of Trade Unions of Audio-Visual Workers (inactive)
♦ International Federation of Trade Unions of Transport Workers (inactive)

♦ International Federation of Training Centres for the Promotion of Progressive Education 13572

Fédération internationale des centres d'entraînement aux méthodes d'éducation active (FICEMEA)
Secretariat 24 rue Marc Séguin, 75883 Paris CEDEX 18, France. T. +33153262461. Fax +33153262419. E-mail: secretariat@ficemea.org.
Registered Office Hallepoortlaan 39, boîte 3, 1060 Brussels, Belgium.
URL: http://www.ficemea.org/

History 13 Dec 1954, Paris (France). Statutes adopted 2 Apr 1971; revised Marly-le-Roi (France) 1982, Paris (France) 2013. Former names and other names: *CEMEA* – former alias. Registration: Start date: 2 Apr 1971, Belgium. **Aims** Organize and promote new methods in global adult and child education; encourage the formation of new national federations; ensure uniformity of teaching methods; promote projects for educators and teacher trainers; encourage social awareness in education; promote development and scientific cultural education, supporting local environments and techniques. **Structure** General Assembly (every 4 years). Administrative Council (meets annually), consisting of 4 representatives of each effective member. Executive Committee of 4 members. Bureau, consisting of President, Secretary-General, Treasurer and a number of Vice-Presidents. Regional Groups (4): Africa; Europe; Indian Ocean; America. **Languages** English, French, Spanish. **Staff** 1.50 FTE, paid; 5.00 FTE, voluntary. **Finance** Sources: members' dues. **Activities** Organizes: short courses; international symposia; workshops; study days; information exchange. Regional Groups organize their own programmes as well as participating in the international programme. **Events** *International Meeting* Budapest (Hungary) 2012, *International Meeting* Paris (France) 2012, *International Meeting* Amiens (France) 2011, *International Meeting* Amiens (France) 2011, *International Meeting* Paris (France) 2011. **Publications** *FICEMEA Bulletin* (periodical). Journals published by national federations; books on education.
Members National federations or associations in 36 countries and territories:
Algeria, Argentina, Austria, Belgium, Benin, Burkina Faso, Cameroon, Colombia, Congo DR, Côte d'Ivoire, Czechia, France, Gabon, Germany, Greece, Hungary, Italy, Lebanon, Madagascar, Mali, Mauritius, Niger, Palestine, Peru, Poland, Portugal, Romania, Russia, Senegal, Seychelles, Spain, Switzerland, Togo, UK, Ukraine, Uruguay.
Individuals in 23 countries:
Belarus, Brazil, Burundi, Cambodia, Central African Rep, Chad, Chile, Comoros, Croatia, Cuba, Denmark, Egypt, Haiti, Luxembourg, Mauritania, Mexico, Moldova, Netherlands, Slovakia, South Africa, Sweden, Tunisia, Vietnam.
Consultative Status Consultative status granted from: *UNESCO (#20322)* (Consultative Status); *Council of Europe (CE, #04881)* (Participatory Status); *Organisation internationale de la Francophonie (OIF, #17809)*. **NGO Relations** Member of: *Lifelong Learning Platform – European Civil Society for Education (LLLP, #16466)*; *International Movement for Leisure Activities in Science and Technology (IMLAST)*; *SOLIDAR (#19680)*. Observer member of: *European Youth Forum (#09140)*. [2019/XC4231/**C**]

♦ International Federation of Training and Development Organizations (IFTDO) 13573

SG S 50, Greater Kailash I, Delhi NEW 110048, DELHI NEW 110048, India. T. +911141619842. Fax +911126451604. E-mail: sgiftdo@gmail.com – sg@iftdo.net – amira@iftdo.net.
URL: http://www.iftdo.net/

History Founded Oct 1973, Bath (UK), at 2nd International Conference on Training and Development, following resolution of 1st international conference, 1972, Geneva (Switzerland). Incorporated 3 Jul 1984. Registered in accordance with UK and USA laws. **Aims** Be a unique and effective resource to the Human Resources Development (HRD) profession globally; promote the concept of HRD as an effective tool, across all sectors of society, in order to increase personal and organizational effectiveness. **Structure** World Conference (annual); General Body; Executive Board. **Languages** English. **Staff** 2.00 FTE, paid. **Finance** Sources: donations; meeting proceeds; meeting proceeds; members' dues; revenue from activities/projects; sponsorship. Members' dues. Other sources: conference surplus; projects; donations/sponsorships. **Activities** Events/meetings; guidance/assistance/consulting; knowledge management/information dissemination. **Events** *World Conference* Cairo (Egypt) 2023, *World Conference and Exhibition* New Delhi (India) 2022, *Annual World Conference* Sarajevo (Bosnia-Herzegovina) 2019, *Annual World Conference* Dubai (United Arab Emirates) 2018, *Annual Conference of Human Capital Development in Africa* Addis Ababa (Ethiopia) 2017. **Publications** *International Journal of HRD Practice, Policy and Research* (2 a year); *IFTDO News* (2-3 a year).
Members Full: professional membership HR societies with at least 50 members, multi-national and large corporations; government organizations; academic/training bodies. Associate: business organizations (public and private companies); training providers; consultancies; NGOs/non-profit organizations. Reciprocal: federations with similar objectives. Members in 23 countries and territories:
Bahrain, Bangladesh, Botswana, Canada, Cyprus, Egypt, Ethiopia, Finland, Germany, India, Ireland, Jordan, Kuwait, Malaysia, Mauritius, Nigeria, Oman, Poland, Saudi Arabia, Sudan, Taiwan, United Arab Emirates, USA.
Consultative Status Consultative status granted from: *ILO (#11123)* (Special List); *ECOSOC (#05331)* (Special). **IGO Relations** Formal links with Department of Global Communications of the United Nations. **NGO Relations** Member of: *Conference of Non-Governmental Organizations in Consultative Relationship with the United Nations (CONGO, #04635)*. Participant of: *United Nations Global Compact (#20567)*. [2022/XC8505/y/**C**]

♦ International Federation of Translators 13574

Fédération internationale des traducteurs (FIT)
SG c/o REGUS, 57 rue d'Amsterdam, 75008 Paris, France. E-mail: secretariat@fit-ift.org.
URL: http://www.fit-ift.org/

History Dec 1953, Paris (France). Statutes amended: 1977, Montréal QC (Canada); 1981, Warsaw (Poland); 1984, Vienna (Austria); 1990, Belgrade (Yugoslavia); 1993, Brighton (UK); 1999, Mons (Belgium); 2002, Vancouver BC (Canada); 2005, Tampere (Finland); 2008, Shanghai (China); 2011, San Francisco CA (USA); 2014, Berlin (Germany). Registered in accordance with French law. **Aims** As a federation of associations of translators, *interpreters* and *terminologists*: promote *professionalism* in represented disciplines; work on conditions of professional practice in various countries; defend translators' *rights* in particular and freedom of expression in general. **Structure** Congress (every 3 years); Council; Executive Committee; FIT Regional Centres (3). Membership open only to non-commercial organizations. **Languages** English, French. **Staff** Voluntary. **Finance** Sources: grants; members' dues. **Activities** Events/meetings; research/documentation; training/education. **Events** *FIT World Congress* Costa Rica 2025, *FIT World Congress* Varadero (Cuba) 2022, *FIT World Congress* Varadero (Cuba) 2021, *FIT World Congress* Varadero (Cuba) 2020, *Asia Pacific Translation and Interpreting Forum* Seoul (Korea Rep) 2019. **Publications** *Translatio* (4 a year) in English, French; *Babel – International Journal of Translation* (occasional) in English, French, French, German, Russian, Spanish.
Members Regular; Associate; Observer. Groups (120) of various categories of translators in 55 countries:
Argentina, Australia, Austria, Belgium, Brazil, Bulgaria, Canada, Chile, China, Colombia, Congo DR, Costa Rica, Croatia, Cuba, Cyprus, Czechia, Denmark, Ecuador, Egypt, Finland, France, Germany, Greece, Guatemala, India, Indonesia, Iran Islamic Rep, Iraq, Ireland, Italy, Japan, Korea Rep, Lebanon, Macau, Malaysia, Mexico, Netherlands, New Zealand, Norway, Panama, Peru, Poland, Romania, Russia, Slovakia, Slovenia, South Africa, Spain, Sweden, Switzerland, Türkiye, UK, Uruguay, USA, Venezuela.
Consultative Status Consultative status granted from: *ECOSOC (#05331)* (Special); *UNESCO (#20322)* (Consultative Status); *World Intellectual Property Organization (WIPO, #21593)* (Permanent Observer Status). **IGO Relations** Accredited by (1): *United Nations Office at Vienna (UNOV, #20604)*. Associated with Department of Global Communications of the United Nations. **NGO Relations** Member of: *International Information Centre for Terminology (INFOTERM, #13846)*. Memorandum of Understanding with: *European Legal Interpreters and Translators Association (EULITA, #07678)*; *European Society for Translation Studies (EST, #08766)*; *International PEN (#14552)*. In liaison with technical committees of: *International Organization for Standardization (ISO, #14473)*. [2022/XC2036/**B**]

♦ International Federation of Travel Agencies (inactive)
♦ International Federation of Travel Journalists and Writers / see World Federation of Travel Journalists and Writers (#21494)

♦ International Federation for Tropical Medicine (IFTM) 13575

Gen Sec LIPMC, IMR-MD3, Inst of Research for Development, 911 av Agropolis, BP 64501, 34394 Montpellier CEDEX 5, France.
URL: http://iftm-hp.org/

History Founded 1984, Calgary (Canada), during 11th *International Congress for Tropical Medicine and Malaria (ICTMM)*, to act as interim committee, the Congress having been created 1913, London (UK), and amalgamated, 1939, Amsterdam (Netherlands), with *International Society for Tropical Medicine (inactive)*, set up in 1908, London, and *International Congress on Malaria (inactive)*, held since 1925, Rome (Italy). **Aims** Promote periodic international congresses on tropical medicine and other appropriate meetings. **Structure** General Assembly (annual or biannual, at Congress); Council; Executive Committee; National Organizing Committee (of the Congress). **Languages** English. **Staff** 5.00 FTE, voluntary. **Events** *International Congress for Tropical Medicine and Malaria* Bangkok (Thailand) 2022, *International Congress for Tropical Medicine and Malaria* Bangkok (Thailand) 2020, *International Congress for Tropical Medicine and Malaria* Brisbane, QLD (Australia) 2016, *International Congress for Tropical Medicine and Malaria* Rio de Janeiro (Brazil) 2012, *International Congress for Tropical Medicine and Malaria* Jeju (Korea Rep) 2008. **Publications** Congress proceedings.
Members Societies of tropical medicine and parasitology and allied health fields, in 59 countries and territories:
Algeria, Australia, Austria, Belgium, Brazil, Bulgaria, Canada, Chile, China, Colombia, Costa Rica, Cuba, Czechia, Denmark, Ecuador, Estonia, Finland, France, Georgia, Germany, Greece, Guatemala, Hungary, India, Iran Islamic Rep, Ireland, Israel, Italy, Japan, Korea Rep, Lithuania, Malaysia, Mali, Mexico, Morocco, Netherlands, New Zealand, Nigeria, Norway, Pakistan, Peru, Philippines, Poland, Portugal, Romania, Russia, Slovakia, South Africa, Spain, Sweden, Switzerland, Taiwan, Tanzania UR, Thailand, Türkiye, UK, USA, Uzbekistan, Venezuela.
Included in the above, 8 organizations listed in this Yearbook:
American Society of Tropical Medicine and Hygiene (ASTMH); *Australasian College of Tropical Medicine (ACTM, #03022)*; *East African Society for Parasitology*; *Federation of European Societies for Tropical Medicine and International Health (FESTMIH, #09551)*; *German Society of Tropical Medicine and International Health (DTG)*; *Parasitological Society of Southern Africa (PARSA)*; *Scandinavian-Baltic Society for Parasitology (SBSP, #19081)*; *SEAMEO TROPMED Regional Centre for Tropical Medicine (#19187)*. [2017.10.04/XD1509/y/**B**]

♦ International Federation Una Voce (#09668)
♦ International Federation of Undertakers' Associations / see International Federation of Thanatologists Associations (#13569)
♦ International Federation of Unions of Employees in Public and Civil Services / see Public Services International (#18572)
♦ International Federation of University Women / see Graduate Women International (#10688)
♦ International Federation of Vexillological Associations (#09611)
♦ International Federation of Voluntary Health Service Funds / see International Federation of Health Plans (#13442)

♦ International Federation Vo Vietnam 13576

Fédération internationale de Vo Viêtnam
Pres Avenue de Sévelin 58, 1004 Lausanne VD, Switzerland. T. +41216262623.
URL: http://www.vo-vietnam.org/

History Founded 1987, having existed as a French body since 1957. Registered in accordance with French law. **Aims** Develop the *Vietnamese style* of *martial arts*. **Languages** French, Vietnamese. **Staff** 1.00 FTE, paid. Voluntary staff. **Finance** Members' dues.
Members National federations in 11 countries:
Algeria, Austria, Belgium, Burkina Faso, Canada, France, Morocco, Poland, Switzerland, USA, Vietnam. [2019.10.16/XF1659/**F**]

♦ International Federation of Warehousing and Logistics Associations (inactive)
♦ International Federation of War Veterans' Organizations / see The World Veterans Federation (#21900)
♦ International Federation for Weeks of Art (inactive)
♦ International Federation of Wholesalers and Importers in Automobile Fittings / see Fédération internationale des grossistes importateurs et exportateurs en fournitures automobiles (#09635)
♦ International Federation of Widows' and Widowers' Organizations (inactive)
♦ International Federation of Wildlife Photography (inactive)
♦ International Federation of Wine Brotherhoods (#09623)

♦ International Federation of Wine and Spirits Journalists and Writers 13577

Fédération internationale des journalistes et écrivains des vins et spiritueux (FIJEV)
SG Via Calatafimi 26, 42123 Reggio Emilia RE, Italy. E-mail: secgen@fijev.org.
Chairman address not obtained.
URL: http://www.fijev.org/

History 1987, Paris (France). Registration: France. **Aims** Promote contacts between wine journalists and writers; defend the profession internationally. **Structure** General Assembly (annual); Council. **Languages** English, French. **Finance** Sources: donations; members' dues. **Activities** Events/meetings. **Members** Professional wine and spirits journalists and authors in over 60 countries. Membership countries not specified. [2020.06.22/XD9241/**D**]

♦ International Federation of Wines and Spirits / see FIVS (#09789)

♦ International Federation of Women Lawyers (FIDA) 13578

Fédération Internationale Des Femmes Juristes (FIDA) – Federación Internacional de Abogadas (FIDA)
Int Office 185 Madison Ave, 6th Floor, New York NY 10016, USA. T. +12126866608. Fax +12123627952.
URL: http://www.fidafederation.org/

History 4 Aug 1944, Mexico City (Mexico). Founded during 3rd Conference of *Inter-American Bar Association (IABA, #11401)*. Former names and other names: *IFWL* – alias. **Aims** Establish friendly international relations on a basis of equality and mutual respect of all peoples; promote the study of comparative law; promote the principles and aims of the United Nations in their *legal* and social aspects; enhance and promote the welfare of women and children realizing that on their wellbeing depends the happiness of the home and the strength of society. **Structure** Plenary Convention (normally every 2 years). Executive Council (meeting twice a year), comprising President, Vice-President, Secretary, Treasurer, 6 Directores, 8 Regional Vice-Presidents, UN Representative, Editor-in-Chief, Historian and Parliamentarian. Regional Meeting (once a year). Meetings closed. **Languages** English, French, Spanish. **Staff** Voluntary. **Finance** Sources: members' dues. Other sources: gifts and assessments; contributions from affiliated organizations. **Activities** Standing Committees (21) on: Administrative Law; Comparative Civil and Commercial Law; Constitution and By Laws; Convention; Domestic Relations; Immigration, Nationality and Naturalization; International Hospitality; International Law; Juvenile Law; Labour Legislation; Legal Education; Legal Status of Women; Legislation; Membership; Aero Space Law; Penal Law; and Procedure; Public Relations; Scholarship Facilitation; Unesco; United Nations. **Events** *International Convention* New York, NY (USA) 2021, *International Convention* Freeport (Bahamas) 2017, *International Convention* Bangalore (India) 2014, *International Convention* Lagos (Nigeria) 2011, *Biennial international convention* Milan (Italy) 2008. **Publications** *La Abogada Newsletter* (4 a year) in English, Spanish – for members only; *La Abogada Internacional* (every 2 years) in English, French, Spanish.
Members Affiliated organizations; Individuals. Members in 73 countries and territories:
Argentina, Australia, Bangladesh, Belgium, Bermuda, Bolivia, Brazil, Cameroon, Canada, Chile, Colombia, Congo DR, Costa Rica, Cyprus, Denmark, Dominica, Dominican Rep, Ecuador, Egypt, Finland, France, Germany, Ghana, Greece, Guatemala, Guyana, Honduras, Hong Kong, India, Indonesia, Iran Islamic Rep, Ireland, Israel, Italy, Jamaica, Japan, Kenya, Korea Rep, Lebanon, Lesotho, Liberia, Luxembourg, Malaysia, Mexico, Netherlands, New Zealand, Nigeria, Norway, Pakistan, Panama, Paraguay, Peru, Philippines, Portugal, Senegal, Sierra Leone, Singapore, South Africa, Spain, Sri Lanka, Sudan, Sweden, Switzerland, Taiwan, Thailand, Togo, Trinidad-Tobago, Türkiye, UK, Uruguay, USA, Venezuela.
Consultative Status Consultative status granted from: *ECOSOC (#05331)* (Special); *UNESCO (#20322)* (Consultative Status); *ILO (#11123)* (Special List); *UNEP (#20299)*. **IGO Relations** Kenyan Chapter has observer status with: *African Commission on Human and Peoples' Rights (ACHPR, #00255)*. Accredited by: *United Nations Office at Vienna (UNOV, #20604)*. Partner of: *UNHCR (#20327)*. Associated with Department of Global Communications of the United Nations. **NGO Relations** Associate member of: *International Bar Association (IBA, #12320)*. Member of: *CIVICUS: World Alliance for Citizen Participation (#03962)*; *Conference of Non-Governmental Organizations in Consultative Relationship with the United Nations (CONGO, #04635)*; *EarthAction (EA, #05159)*. [2020/XB2042/**C**]

♦ International Federation of Women in Legal Careers (IFWLC) 13579

Fédération internationale des femmes des carrières juridiques – magistrats, avocats, avoués, notaires, professeurs de droit ou exerçant une autre carrière juridique (FIFCJ) – Federación Internacional de Mujeres Juristas
Contact Rua Atletico Clube n 27, Maputo, Cidade de Maputo, Mozambique. E-mail: infopresident.fifcj@gmail.com – ammcjm@gmail.com.
URL: http://www.fifcj-ifwlc.org/index_ingles.html

History 3 Nov 1929, Paris (France). Founded after a preliminary meeting, 12 Jul 1928, Paris. Former names and other names: *International Federation of Women Magistrates, Barristers and Members of other Branches of the Legal Profession* – former; *Fédération internationale des femmes magistrats et avocats ou qui exercent une autre carrière juridique* – former. **Aims** Fight for eradication of all forms of discrimination against women and promote their *human rights*; promote and divulge knowledge of the above mentioned fundamental principles; encourage and help members in their activities with parliaments, governments or any other competent authority, as well as public opinion in order to get the above mentioned principles embodied in national legislation and applied at a practical level in the judicial system and in social administration; assemble information about the juridical, social and economical status of women worldwide and study all laws affecting that status; promote establishment of bonds of friendship and unity between members as well as with other international women's organizations and international jurists associations; contribute to promotion of peace in the world, as an indispensable support to obtain an equal and conscientious progress of humanity. **Structure** Congress; Council; Bureau; Commissions (3). **Languages** English, French, Portuguese, Spanish. **Staff** Voluntary. **Finance** Sources: members' dues. Annual budget: 10,670 EUR. **Activities** Events/meetings. **Events** *The construction of gender equality and women's rights* Goiânia (Brazil) 2019, *Triennial Congress* Lisbon (Portugal) 2018, *Meeting* Palermo (Italy) 2016, *Triennial Congress* Barcelona (Spain) 2015, *Triennial Congress* Dakar (Senegal) 2012. **Publications** Conference proceedings.
Members National Associations in 32 countries and territories:
Angola, Argentina, Azerbaijan, Benin, Brazil, Burundi, Cameroon, Cape Verde, Chile, Congo Brazzaville, Congo DR, Côte d'Ivoire, France, Greece, Guinea-Bissau, Israel, Italy, Mali, Mexico, Moldova, Mozambique, Paraguay, Peru, Portugal, Romania, Russia, Sao Tomé-Principe, Senegal, Spain, Türkiye, USA.
ational Associations also in Guinea Conackry.
Individuals in 21 countries and territories:
Algeria, Angola, Belgium, China, Colombia, Cyprus, Denmark, Finland, Gabon, Germany, Honduras, Hong Kong, Israel, Lebanon, Malaysia, Netherlands, Nicaragua, Nigeria, Spain, Timor-Leste, USA.
Consultative Status Consultative status granted from: *ECOSOC (#05331)* (Special); *UNESCO (#20322)* (Consultative Status); *ILO (#11123)* (Special List); *FAO (#09260)* (Liaison Status); *UNICEF (#20332)*. **IGO Relations** Accredited by (1): *United Nations Office at Vienna (UNOV, #20604)*. Associated with Department of Global Communications of the United Nations. **NGO Relations** Member of (4): *Conference of Non-Governmental Organizations in Consultative Relationship with the United Nations (CONGO, #04635)*; *European Women's Lobby (EWL, #09102)*; *NGO Committee on the Status of Women, Geneva (#17117)*; *NGO Committee on UNICEF (#17120)*. [2021/XB2041/**B**]

♦ International Federation of Women Magistrates, Barristers and Members of other Branches of the Legal Profession / see International Federation of Women in Legal Careers (#13579)
♦ International Federation of Women's Basketball and Netball Associations / see World Netball (#21668)
♦ International Federation of Women's Football (inactive)
♦ International Federation of Women's Hockey Associations (inactive)
♦ International Federation of Women's Lacrosse Associations (inactive)
♦ International Federation of Women's Travel Organizations (inactive)

♦ International Federation of Workers' Education Associations (IFWEA) 13580

Fédération internationale des associations pour l'éducation des travailleurs (FIAET) – Federación Internacional de Asociaciones para la Educación de los Trabajadores (FIAET) – Internationaler Verband für Arbeiterbildung (IVA)
SG c/o Labour Research Service, PO Box 376, Woodstock, Cape Town, 7915, South Africa. T. +27214861118. E-mail: ifweasecretariat@lrs.org.za.
URL: http://www.ifwea.org/

History Oct 1947, London (UK). Founded at 1st General Conference, following preparatory meeting, Oct 1945, London, called by the United Kingdom Workers' Educational Association. A Statement of Policy which outlined the objects and functions of the Federation was adopted at 3rd General Conference, 1953, London. *International Charter of Workers' Education – Charte internationale de l'éducation des travailleurs*, a statement of IFWEA principles and policies as well as a programme of action in the 1980's, was adopted at 12th General Conference, June 1980, Oslo (Norway). Most recent Charter and Constitution approved 16 Sep 1992, Port Elgin (Canada) and adopted Jan 1993, Brussels (Belgium); amended 1996, 2000. Former names and other names: *Fédération internationale des sociétés de l'éducation ouvrière* – former. **Aims** On the basis of the *democratic* labour movement, promote free and voluntary educational work, according to the principles of solidarity and cooperation, justice and equality, democracy and freedom. **Structure** General Conference (from 1992, every 4 years); Executive Committee; Regional organization: *Comunidade Sindical dos Paises de Lingua Portuguesa (CSPLP, #04431)*. Secretariat hosted by the Labour Research Service, Cape Town (South Africa). Membership open; meetings closed. **Languages** Arabic, English, French, Portuguese, Spanish. **Staff** 6.00 FTE, paid. **Finance** Sources: members' dues. Solidarity Fund for special projects. Annual budget: 49,840 GBP. **Activities** Events/meetings; guidance/assistance/consulting; knowledge management/information dissemination; projects/programmes; research/documentation; training/education. **Events** *General Conference*

Cape Town (South Africa) 2019, *General Conference* Lima (Peru) 2015, *General Conference* Cape Town (South Africa) 2011, *General Conference* Ahmedabad (India) 2007, *General Conference* Albufeira (Portugal) 2003. **Publications** *E-Bulletin* (12 a year); *Workers' Education* (4 a year) in English – formerly 'International Bulletin of Workers' Education'. *Blue Pamphlet Series* – political freedom and democracy; *Red Pamphlet Series* – social and economic issues; *White Pamphlet Series* – technical concerns of the Movement. *Content and Methods of Education in Dealing with Race Discrimination* (1964) by Ulf Himmelstr; *Workers' Education-Sudan* (1962) by W E Styler; *Independent Voluntarism in Workers' Education* (1953) by G D H Cole; *The Story of IFWEA* in English, French, German. *Mundo Sindical* in Spanish – mailing list. General Conference proceedings; seminar reports; leaflets.
Members Workers' education organizations; foundations in the framework of the labour movement and workers' education; educational organizations of trade unions; institutes and organizations for vocational education. Organizations in 50 countries and territories:
Angola, Australia, Austria, Bangladesh, Belgium, Bolivia, Bulgaria, Cape Verde, Chile, Denmark, Egypt, Finland, Germany, Ghana, Hong Kong, Hungary, Iceland, India, Iraq, Ireland, Jordan, Korea Rep, Lebanon, Malta, Mauritania, Mauritius, Morocco, Mozambique, Namibia, Nepal, New Zealand, Norway, Pakistan, Palestine, Peru, Philippines, Portugal, Sao Tomé-Principe, South Africa, Spain, Sri Lanka, Sweden, Switzerland, Thailand, Tunisia, Uganda, UK, USA, Zambia, Zimbabwe.
Included in the above, 7 organizations listed in this Yearbook:
Education International (EI, #05371); *International Labour Research and Information Group (ILRIG)*; *International Transport Workers' Federation (ITF, #15726)*; *SOLIDAR (#19680)*; StreetNet Association; *UNI Global Union (#20338)*; *Women Working Worldwide (WWW)*.
Consultative Status Consultative status granted from: *ECOSOC (#05331)* (Ros C); *UNESCO (#20322)* (Consultative Status); *ILO (#11123)* (Special List). **IGO Relations** Associated with Department of Global Communications of the United Nations. **NGO Relations** Cooperates with (1): *Socialist International (SI, #19340)*. Cooperates in related fields of interest with: *International Trade Union Confederation (ITUC, #15708)* and its *International Council for Adult Education (ICAE, #12983)*. [2023.02.15/XC2044/y/**B**]

- ♦ International Federation of Workers Employed in the Construction of Roads (inactive)
- ♦ International Federation of Working Women (inactive)
- ♦ International Federation of Wrestling on Belts "Alysh" (unconfirmed)
- ♦ International Federation of Young Singers / see Fédération internationale des petits chanteurs (#09649)
- ♦ International Federation of Youth Hostel Wardens Associations (inactive)
- ♦ International Feed Association / see International Feed Industry Federation (#13581)
- ♦ International Feed Conference (meeting series)

♦ International Feed Industry Federation (IFIF) 13581

Association internationale d'alimentation animale

Exec Dir PO Box 1340, 51657 Wiehl, Germany. T. +4922628059572. E-mail: info@ifif.org.
Registered Address Rue Alcide de Gasperi 7, L-1013 Luxembourg, Luxembourg.
URL: http://www.ifif.org/

History 1 Dec 1987. Former names and other names: *International Feed Association* – former. Registration: Luxembourg. **Aims** Promote a unified voice and leadership to represent and promote the global feed industry as an essential participant in the food chain that provides sustainable, safe, nutritious and affordable food for a growing world population. **Structure** General Assembly; Board of Directors; Executive Committee. **Languages** English. **Staff** 2.00 FTE, paid. **Activities** Capacity building; events/meetings; knowledge management/information dissemination; networking/liaising; politics/policy/regulatory; standards/guidelines. **Events** *Global Feed and Food Congress* Bangkok (Thailand) 2024, *International Feed Regulators Meeting* Atlanta, GA (USA) 2023, *International Feed Regulators Meeting (IFRM)* Wiehl (Germany) 2021, *International Feed Regulators Meeting* Atlanta, GA (USA) 2020, *Global Feed and Food Congress* Bangkok (Thailand) 2019. **Publications** *IFIF Newsletter*. *IFIF FAO Manual – Good Practices for the Feed Sector: Implementing the Codex Alimentarius Code of Practice on Good Animal Feeding* (2nd 2020) in English, Mandarin Chinese, Vietnamese; *Comparison of Regulatory Management of Authorized Ingredients, Approval Processes, and Risk-Assessment Procedures for Feed Ingredients* (2013) – report; *IFIF FAO Feed Manual of Good Practices for the Feed Industry* (2010) in Arabic, Chinese, English, French, Spanish. IFIF Annual Report.
Members National and regional feed associations, as well as feed-related organizations and corporate members, representing over 80% of total compound animal feed production worldwide. National associations in 10 countries:
Australia, Brazil, Canada, China, India, Iran Islamic Rep, Japan, New Zealand, South Africa, USA.
Regional associations (3):
Asociación de la Industrias de Alimentación Animal de América Latina y Caribe (FEEDLATINA, #02158); *Fédération européenne des fabricants d'aliments composés pour animaux (FEFAC, #09566)*; *FEFANA – EU Association of Specialty Feed Ingredients and their Mixtures (#09720)*.
IGO Relations Observer status with (1): *Codex Alimentarius Commission (CAC, #04081)*. Cooperates with (3): *FAO (#09260)*; *OIE – World Organisation for Animal Health (#17703)*; *WHO (#20950)*. **NGO Relations** Through membership in the Livestock Sector Consortium (Private Sector Steering Committee – PSSC Livestock), cooperates with: *International Dairy Federation (IDF, #13128)*; *International Egg Commission (IEC, #13245)*; *International Meat Secretariat (IMS, #14125)*; *International Poultry Council (IPC, #14628)*. Partner of: *Livestock Environmental Assessment and Performance Partnership (LEAP, #16500)*. [2022.11.07/XD1504/ty/**B**]

♦ International Feldenkrais Federation (IFF) 13582

Contact 8 rue du General Renault, Boîte 100, 75011 Paris, France. E-mail: iffadmin@feldenkrais-method.org – iffsecretary@feldenkrais-method.org.
URL: http://www.feldenkrais-method.org/

History 1992, Paris (France), to honour the work of Dr Moshé Feldenkrais (1904-1984). **Aims** Promote cooperation and communication in the spirit of the Feldenkrais method, an *educational* system that develops a functional awareness of the self in the environment. **Structure** General Assembly (annual); Board of Directors; administrative staff. Training and Accreditation Boards (3): Australia; Europe; North America. **Events** *Annual General Assembly* High Wycombe (UK) 2019, *Biennial Conference* Madrid (Spain) 2018, *Annual general assembly* Soesterberg (Netherlands) 2006, *Annual General Assembly* Soesterberg (Netherlands) 2003.
Members National organizations (17) in 17 countries:
Argentina, Australia, Austria, Belgium, Canada, France, Germany, Israel, Italy, Mexico, Netherlands, New Zealand, Norway, Sweden, Switzerland, UK, USA. [2008/XE4692/**E**]

- ♦ International Fellowship of Chaplains (internationally oriented national body)
- ♦ International Fellowship of Christian Churches / see International Federation of Christian Churches (#13389)
- ♦ International Fellowship for Christian Revival (inactive)
- ♦ International Fellowship of Christians and Jews (internationally oriented national body)
- ♦ International Fellowship of Evangelical Mission Theologians / see International Fellowship for Mission as Transformation (#13584)

♦ International Fellowship of Evangelical Students (IFES) 13583

Union internationale des groupes bibliques universitaires

SG 5 Blue Boar Street, Oxford, OX1 4EE, UK. T. +441865263777. E-mail: info@ifesworld.org.
USA Office PO Box 436, Platteville WI 53818, USA. E-mail: office.usa@ifesworld.org.
Registered Office Rue du Simplon 37, 1006 Lausanne VD, Switzerland.
URL: http://www.ifesworld.org/

History 1947. Founded by delegates of 10 national student movements, international conferences having been held from 1934 to 1946. Registration: Switzerland, Lausanne; Chaity Commission, No/ID: 247919, England and Wales; Companies House, No/ID: 876229, England and Wales; 501(c)3, USA. **Aims** Work and pray for a vibrant gospel witness to *Christ* in every university in the world. **Structure** General Committee (meets at quadrennial World Assembly). Officers: Chairman; Treasurer; General Secretary. Regional Secretaries. **Finance** Donations and grants from national mouvements, individuals and Christian agencies. **Events** *World Assembly* Durban (South Africa) 2019, *East Asia Regional Graduate Conference* Tokyo (Japan) 2019, *Quadrennial world assembly* Canada 2007, *Quadrennial world assembly* Dalfsen (Netherlands) 2003, *Quadrennial World Assembly* Netherlands 2003. **Publications** *Praise and Prayer* (4 a year) – newsletter.
Members National student mouvements (118), associated mouvements (32) and students (about 300,000) actively involved in member mouvements in 101 countries and territories:
Angola, Antigua-Barbuda, Argentina, Australia, Austria, Bangladesh, Barbados, Belgium, Benin, Bolivia, Brazil, Burkina Faso, Burundi, Cameroon, Canada, Central African Rep, Chad, Chile, Colombia, Congo Brazzaville, Congo DR, Costa Rica, Côte d'Ivoire, Croatia, Cuba, Czechia, Denmark, Dominican Rep, Ecuador, Eswatini, Ethiopia, Fiji, Finland, France, Germany, Ghana, Guatemala, Guinea, Guinea-Bissau, Guyana, Honduras, Hong Kong, Hungary, Iceland, India, Indonesia, Ireland, Israel, Italy, Jamaica, Japan, Kenya, Korea Rep, Lebanon, Liberia, Madagascar, Malawi, Malaysia, Mali, Mexico, Nepal, Netherlands, New Zealand, Niger, Nigeria, Norway, Pakistan, Panama, Papua New Guinea, Paraguay, Peru, Philippines, Poland, Portugal, Puerto Rico, Russia, Rwanda, Senegal, Serbia, Sierra Leone, Singapore, Slovakia, South Africa, Spain, Sri Lanka, St Lucia, Suriname, Sweden, Switzerland, Tanzania UR, Thailand, Togo, Trinidad-Tobago, Uganda, UK, Ukraine, Uruguay, USA, Venezuela, Zambia, Zimbabwe.
NGO Relations Member of: *European Evangelical Alliance (EEA, #07010)*; *Global Connections*. [2021/XF2048/**F**]

- ♦ International Fellowship of Former Scouts and Guides / see International Scout and Guide Fellowship (#14812)

♦ International Fellowship for Mission as Transformation (INFEMIT) . 13584

Registered Address 108 W. High St, Lexington KY 40507, USA. E-mail: admin@infemit.org.
URL: https://infemit.org/

History 1987. Early beginnings traced back to 1980, Pattaya (Thailand). Former names and other names: *International Fellowship of Evangelical Mission Theologians (INFEMIT)* – former. Registration: Section 501 (c)(3), No/ID: 46-3781676, Start date: 15 Oct 2013, USA. **Aims** Serve local churches and other Christian communities to embody the Kingdom of God through transformational engagement, both locally and globally. **Structure** Networking Team; Regional Fellowships. **Activities** Events/meetings; guidance/assistance/consulting; knowledge management/information dissemination; networking/liaising; publishing activities; religious activities. **Events** *Stott-Bediako Forum* 2020. **NGO Relations** Cooperates with (2): *Fraternidad Teológica Latinoamericana (FTL)*; *Micah Global (#16741)*. Instrumental in setting up (1): *Oxford Centre for Mission Studies (OCMS)*. [2021.05.18/XM0459/**F**]

♦ International Fellowship of Paediatric and Adolescent Gynaecology (IFEPAG) 13585

Examen Internacional de Ginecólogia Pediatrica y de la Adolescencia

Chairman Hospital de Clinicas de la Univ de BsAs, Sección Ginecológica Infanto Juvenil, Córdoba 2351, Buenos Aires, Argentina. E-mail: mr@consultoriointegral.com.ar.
URL: http://www.cemera.cl/ifepag/

History Founded 1997, by *Fédération internationale de gynécologie infantile et juvénile (FIGIJ, #09637)*. **Aims** Stimulate the interest of obstetricians/gynaecologists, paediatricians, endocrine surgeons, paediatric surgeons, specialists in adolescence and family physicians to work and develop research in this area of the medicine. **Languages** English, Spanish. **Activities** Examinations held at congresses of FIGIJ. [2013.10.10/XF6141/**F**]

♦ International Fellowship of Reconciliation (IFOR) 13586

Mouvement international de la réconciliation (MIR) – Movimiento Internacional de Reconciliación – Internationaler Versöhnungsbund

Intl Coordinator Postbus 1528, 3500 BM Utrecht, Netherlands. T. +31303039930. Fax +31305151102. E-mail: office@ifor.org.
Street address Joseph Haydnlaan 2a, 3533 AE Utrecht, Netherlands.
URL: http://www.ifor.org/

History Oct 1919, Bilthoven (Netherlands). Founded uniting groups set up following an ecumenical conference of Christians, 1914, Switzerland, interrupted by the outbreak of World War I, and following the founding of *Fellowship of Reconciliation (FOR)*, Dec 1914. In 1922, absorbed *Movement towards a Christian International (inactive)*, also set up Oct 1919. IFOR subsequently developed from a Christian to an interfaith mouvement including Jews, Christians, Buddhists, Muslims and people of other faith traditions, including those with no formal religious affiliation at all but who can subscribe to IFOR's spiritual basis. Registration: ANBI, No/ID: 8103.27.144, Netherlands. **Aims** Promote *spiritually* based active nonviolence both as a way of life and as a means of personal, social and political transformation; resolve conflict in a nonviolent way and develop resources for active nonviolent intervention; work to abolish war, refuse to participate in it or to sanction military preparations; strive to build a social order which utilizes human ingenuity and wisdom for the benefit of all and in which no individual or group is exploited or oppressed for the profit or pleasure of others. **Structure** Council (meeting every 4 years); Board; International Representatives; International Secretariat. **Languages** English, French, Spanish. **Staff** 1.50 FTE, paid; 1.00 FTE, voluntary. Staff of national branches may be paid or voluntary. **Finance** Contributions from national branches; voluntary contributions; bequests and legacies; grants for programme and project work. **Activities** Advocacy/lobbying/activism; projects/programmes. **Events** *Council Meeting* Baarlo (Netherlands) 2010, *Meeting / Council Meeting* Tokyo (Japan) 2006, *Consultation on interfaith education for a global society* Barcelona (Spain) 2004, *Consultation on interfaith education for a global society* New York, NY (USA) 2004, *Consultation on interfaith education for a global society* New York, NY (USA) 2003. **Publications** *YO (IFOR Youth Opportunities)* (12 a year) – newsletter; *IFOR in Action* (4 a year) in English, French – electronic newsletter; *International Reconciliation* (4 a year) in English, French, German – magazine. *Patterns in Reconciliation* in English – occasional paper series. *Violence Prevention in the Educational Institution Kindergarten* (2008). Annual Report, in English, French. Information Services: Resource Centre includes library and data base.
Members Branches, groups and affiliates (71). Branches in 28 countries and territories:
Austria, Bangladesh, Belgium, Benin, Chad, Congo Brazzaville, Congo DR, France, Germany, Hungary, India, Italy, Japan, Madagascar, Nepal, Netherlands, Norway, Palestine, Philippines, South Sudan, Sudan, Sweden, Switzerland, Uganda, UK, USA, Zambia, Zimbabwe.
Included in the above, 1 regional organization:
Affiliates in 12 countries:
Bangladesh, Belgium, Burundi, Cameroon, China, Finland, India, Ireland, Pakistan, Thailand, Uganda, UK.
Included in the above, 1 organization listed in this Yearbook:
Consultative Status Consultative status granted from: *ECOSOC (#05331)* (Special); *UNESCO (#20322)* (Consultative Status). **NGO Relations** Member of (8): *Conference of Non-Governmental Organizations in Consultative Relationship with the United Nations (CONGO, #04635)*; *Global Partnership for the Prevention of Armed Conflict (GPPAC, #10538)*; *ILGA World (International Lesbian, Gay, Bisexual, Trans and Intersex Association, #11120)*; *International Network – Education for Democracy, Human Rights and Tolerance (no recent information)*; *International Network for a Culture of Nonviolence and Peace (#14247)*; *International Peace Bureau (IPB, #14535)*; *NGO Committee on Disarmament, Peace and Security, New York NY (#17106)*; *UNITED for Intercultural Action – European Network Against Nationalism, Racism, Fascism and in Support of Migrants and Refugees (UNITED, #20511)*. Partner of (1): *International Campaign to Abolish Nuclear Weapons (ICAN, #12426)*. Instrumental in setting up (3): *Church and Peace (#03916)*; *International Christian Peace Service (EIRENE, #12564)*; *International Service for Peace (SIPAZ)*. Represented on the Organizing Committee of: *Nonviolent Peaceforce (NP, #17153)*. [2021/XC2050/y/**F**]

- ♦ International Fencing Federation (#09629)

♦ International Ferrocement Society (IFS) 13587

Sociedad Internacional del Ferrocemento (SIF)

Sec c/o CBA Associates, 601 Lake Dora Dr, Tavares FL 32778, USA. E-mail: ifs.contact2@gmail.com.
URL: https://www.ferrocement-ifs.com/

History 1991, Bangkok (Thailand). Founded at and initially within *Asian Institute of Technology (AIT, #01519)*. 2016, operations moved to USA. Registration: USA, Florida. **Aims** Coordinate and cater to the needs of practitioners, engineers and researchers on application, development and research on ferrocement and other related materials; foster joint research activities between faculty members and/or researchers; provide a forum for the exchange of ideas, enhance collaboration and cooperation; promote utilization of ferrocement as a *construction material*. **Structure** General Committee. Technical Committees (2): research and development; international coordination. International Panel of Assessors (for membership applications). **Languages** English. **Activities** Organizes: annual training course; triennial symposium; seminars. **Events** *International Symposium on Ferrocement and Thin Fiber Reinforced Inorganic Matrices (FERRO 13)* Lyon (France) 2021, *International Symposium on Ferrocement and Thin Fiber Reinforced Cement Composites (FERRO12)* Belo Horizonte (Brazil) 2018, *International Symposium on Ferrocement (FERRO11)* Aachen

(Germany) 2015, *International Symposium on Ferrocement and Thing Reinforced Cement Composites / Simposio Internacional del Ferrocemento y Compuestos Delgados de Cemento Reforzado* Havana (Cuba) 2012, *International symposium on ferrocement and thin reinforced cement composites* Bali (Indonesia) 2009. **Publications** *Journal of Ferrocement* (4 a year). Information Services: Access to: IFIC/AIT reference collection; electronic network, databases and CD-ROMs; IFIC networks of experts and organizations.
Members Regular; Professional; Fellow, in 72 countries:
Algeria, Argentina, Australia, Bangladesh, Barbados, Belgium, Bhutan, Bolivia, Botswana, Brazil, Brunei Darussalam, Cambodia, Canada, Chile, China, Colombia, Costa Rica, Cuba, Cyprus, Denmark, Dominican Rep, Egypt, Ethiopia, Fiji, Finland, France, Germany, Ghana, Guatemala, Hong Kong, Hungary, India, Indonesia, Iraq, Ireland, Israel, Italy, Japan, Korea Rep, Kuwait, Malaysia, Mexico, Nepal, Netherlands, New Zealand, Nigeria, Norway, Oman, Pakistan, Panama, Papua New Guinea, Peru, Philippines, Poland, Romania, Samoa, Saudi Arabia, Sierra Leone, Singapore, South Africa, Spain, Sri Lanka, Sweden, Switzerland, Taiwan, Tanzania UR, Thailand, Trinidad-Tobago, Türkiye, UK, USA, Venezuela.
NGO Relations Asian Institute of Technology; *International Ferrocement Information Centre (IFIC, inactive).*
[2021/XD3702/**C**]

♦ International Fertiliser Society (IFS) 13588

Secretariat PO Box 12220, Colchester, CO1 9PR, UK. T. +441206851819. Fax +441206851819. E-mail: secretary@fertiliser-society.org.
URL: http://www.fertiliser-society.org/
History 1947. **Aims** Provide an international forum for discussion and dissemination of knowledge of scientific, technical, environmental, economic and safety aspects of the production, marketing, use and application of fertilisers. **Structure** Society Meeting; Council. **Languages** English. **Staff** 1.00 FTE, paid. **Finance** Sources: members' dues. **Activities** Events/meetings. **Events** *IFS Agronomic Conference* Cambridge (UK) 2021, *Agronomic Conference* Cambridge (UK) 2018, *Agronomic Conference* Cambridge (UK) 2017, *Agronomic Conference* Cambridge (UK) 2016, *Agronomic Conference* Cambridge (UK) 2015. **Publications** Booklets; PDFs.
Members Individuals in 50 countries:
Algeria, Argentina, Australia, Austria, Belgium, Brazil, Bulgaria, Canada, Colombia, Czechia, Denmark, Egypt, Estonia, Finland, France, Germany, Greece, Hungary, Iceland, India, Ireland, Israel, Italy, Latvia, Libya, Lithuania, Malaysia, Morocco, Netherlands, New Zealand, Norway, Pakistan, Poland, Portugal, Qatar, Russia, Serbia, Singapore, Slovenia, South Africa, Spain, Sweden, Switzerland, Syrian AR, Tunisia, Türkiye, UK, Ukraine, USA, Zimbabwe. [2021.09.01/XD7787/**D**]

♦ International Fertility Association / see World Foundation for Medical Studies in Female Health
♦ International Fertility Association / see International Federation of Fertility Societies (#13426)
♦ International Fertility Research Program / see FHI 360

♦ International Fertilizer Association (IFA) 13589

Sec 49 av d'Iéna, 75116 Paris, France. T. +33153930500. E-mail: ifa@fertilizer.org.
URL: http://www.fertilizer.org/
History Jan 1927, London (UK). Manufacturers of other fertilizers were admitted as ordinary members from 1962. Rules amended, 1979, to admit nitrogen and potash producers as ordinary members (phosphate rock producers are also ordinary members). Sulphur producers admitted as ordinary members in 1989. Secretariat and offices in Paris (France). Former names and other names: *International Superphosphate Manufacturers' Association (ISMA)* – former (Jan 1927 to 1975); *International Phosphate Industry Association* – former (14 Nov 1975 to 1982); *International Fertilizer Industry Association (IFA)* – former (May 1982 to 2016); *Association internationale de l'industrie des fertilisants* – former (May 1982 to 2016); *Association internationale de l'industrie des engrais* – former; *Asociación Internacional de la Industria de los Fertilizantes* – former; *Internationale Vereinigung der Superphosphat-Fabrikanten* – former. Registration: Companies House, No/ID: 00718812, Start date: 22 Mar 1962, England. **Aims** Promote the global fertilizer industry through research and outreach initiatives. **Structure** General Assembly (annual); Council; Executive Committee; General Standing Committees; Executive Management Group (EMG); Committees; Secretariat, headed by Director General. **Languages** English, French. **Staff** 31.00 FTE, paid. **Finance** Sources: members' dues. **Activities** Events/meetings; knowledge management/information dissemination. **Events** *Annual Conference* Vienna (Austria) 2022, *Strategic Forum* Dubai (United Arab Emirates) 2021, *Annual Conference* Lisbon (Portugal) 2021, *Annual Conference* New Delhi (India) 2021, *Annual Conference* New Delhi (India) 2020. **Publications** *Fertilizers and Agriculture* (periodical). Statistics; proceedings of conferences and scientific and technical reports (available to members and cooperating organizations).
Members Ordinary; Affiliate; Associate; Corresponding. Members (about 545) in 87 countries and territories:
Algeria, Argentina, Australia, Austria, Bahrain, Bangladesh, Belarus, Belgium, Benin, Brazil, Bulgaria, Canada, Chile, China, Colombia, Côte d'Ivoire, Croatia, Cuba, Cyprus, Ecuador, Egypt, Estonia, Ethiopia, Finland, France, Germany, Greece, Hong Kong, India, Indonesia, Iran Islamic Rep, Iraq, Ireland, Israel, Italy, Japan, Jordan, Kazakhstan, Kenya, Korea Rep, Kuwait, Latvia, Lebanon, Lithuania, Malaysia, Mauritius, Mexico, Mongolia, Morocco, Namibia, Nepal, Netherlands, New Zealand, Norway, Pakistan, Peru, Philippines, Poland, Portugal, Qatar, Romania, Russia, Saudi Arabia, Senegal, Serbia, Singapore, Slovakia, South Africa, Spain, Sri Lanka, Sweden, Switzerland, Syrian AR, Taiwan, Tanzania UR, Thailand, Togo, Tunisia, Türkiye, UK, Ukraine, United Arab Emirates, USA, Uzbekistan, Venezuela, Vietnam, Zimbabwe.
Consultative Status Consultative status granted from: *ECOSOC (#05331)* (Ros C); *FAO (#09260)* (Liaison Status); *UNCTAD (#20285)* (General Category); *UNIDO (#20336)*; *UNEP (#20299)*. **IGO Relations** Accredited by (1): *United Nations Framework Convention on Climate Change – Secretariat (UNFCCC, #20564)*. Founder member of *'FAO Fertilizer Industry Advisory Committee'*. Working relationships with *'FAO/UNIDO/World Bank Fertilizer Working Group'*. **NGO Relations** Member of (2): *Global Alliance for Climate-Smart Agriculture (GACSA, #10189)*; *International Agri-Food Network (IAFN, #11599)*. Cooperates with (1): *International Fertilizer Development Center (IFDC, #13590)*. Supports (1): *Farming First*. In liaison with technical committees of: *International Organization for Standardization (ISO, #14473)*. Associate expert of: *Business and Industry Advisory Committee to the OECD (BIAC, #03385)*. [2022.10.18/XB2609/**B**]

♦ International Fertilizer Development Center / see International Fertilizer Development Center (#13590)

♦ International Fertilizer Development Center (IFDC) 13590

Headquarters PO Box 2040, Muscle Shoals AL 35662, USA. T. +12563816600. Fax +12563817408.
URL: http://www.ifdc.org/
History 7 Oct 1974, Muscle Shoals, AL (USA). Founded as a centre of excellence with expertise in fertilizers to service the needs of developing countries. Designated a public international organization by US President Jimmy Carter, 14 Mar 1977. Former names and other names: *International Fertilizer Development Center* – former (7 Oct 1974); *Centre international de développement des engrais* – former (7 Oct 1974). **Aims** Increase *agricultural productivity* in a *sustainable* manner through development and transfer of effective, *environmentally* sound *plant nutrient* technology and agricultural marketing expertise, focusing primarily on *developing nations*; advance fertilizer research and technology through worldwide scientific collaboration. **Structure** Board (meets annually). Divisions (4): East and Southern Africa (ESAFD); North and West Africa (NWAFD); Asia (EAD); Office of Programs. **Languages** Bengali, English, French, Portuguese. **Staff** 1000.00 FTE, paid. **Finance** Supported by various bilateral and multilateral aid agencies, private foundations and national governments. **Activities** Training/education; research/documentation; capacity building; research and development; advocacy/lobbying/activism. **Events** *Phosphate Fertilizer Production Technology Workshop* Bangkok (Thailand) 2013, *Nitrogen Fertilizer Production Technology Workshop* Sanya (China) 2013, *Phosphate fertilizer production technology workshop* Marrakech (Morocco) 2009, *Nitrogen fertilizer production technology workshop* Penang (Malaysia) 2009, *Phosphate fertilizer production technology workshop* Brussels (Belgium) 2007. **Publications** *Perspectives* (2 a year) in English, French. Annual Report; reference manuals; technical papers; books; training manuals; research papers; videos.
IGO Relations Cooperates with:
- *Africa Rice Center (AfricaRice, #00518)*;
- *African Development Bank (ADB, #00283)*;
- *African Union (AU, #00488)*;
- *Banque ouest africaine de développement (BOAD, #03170)*;
- *CABI (#03393)*;
- *Common Fund for Commodities (CFC, #04293)*;
- *Common Market for Eastern and Southern Africa (COMESA, #04296)*;
- *Department for International Development (DFID, inactive)*;
- *East African Community (EAC, #05181)*;
- *Economic Community of West African States (ECOWAS, #05312)*;
- *ECOWAS Bank for Investment and Development (EBID, #05334)*;
- *European Union (EU, #08967)*;
- *FAO (#09260)*;
- *Global Agriculture and Food Security Program (GAFSP, #10174)*;
- *International Crops Research Institute for the Semi-Arid Tropics (ICRISAT, #13116)*;
- *International Fund for Agricultural Development (IFAD, #13692)*;
- *New Partnership for Africa's Development (NEPAD, #17091)* through Comprehensive Africa Agriculture Development Programme (CAADP);
- *Southern African Development Community (SADC, #19843)*;
- *Swiss Agency for Development and Cooperation (SDC)*;
- *Union économique et monétaire Ouest africaine (UEMOA, #20377)*;
- *United States Agency for International Development (USAID)*.

NGO Relations Cooperates with:
- *ACDI/VOCA*;
- *Netherlands Food Partnership (NFP)*;
- *Agriterra*;
- *Alliance for a Green Revolution in Africa (AGRA, #00685)*;
- *Bill and Melinda Gates Foundation (BMGF)*;
- *CropLife Africa Middle East (CLAME, #04963)*;
- *DANIDA*;
- *Farming First*;
- *Forum for Agricultural Research in Africa (FARA, #09897)*;
- *The William and Flora Hewlett Foundation*;
- *International Centre for Development Oriented Research in Agriculture (ICRA)*;
- *International Fertilizer Association (IFA, #13589)*;
- *International Food Policy Research Institute (IFPRI, #13622)*;
- *International Institute of Tropical Agriculture (IITA, #13933)*;
- *International Potash Institute (IPI, #14626)*;
- national organizations;
- *SNV Netherlands Development Organisation (SNV)*;
- *The Rockefeller Foundation (#18966)*;
- *Royal Tropical Institute (KIT)*;
- *Sulphur Institute, The (TSI, #20034)*;
- *West and Central African Council for Agricultural Research and Development (WECARD, #20907)*. [2021/XE3975/**E**]

♦ International Fertilizer Industry Association / see International Fertilizer Association (#13589)
♦ International FES Society / see International Functional Electrical Stimulation Society (#13690)
♦ International Festivals and Events Association (internationally oriented national body)

♦ International Festivals and Events Association Europe (IFEA-E) ... 13591

Treas/Office Manager AOIFE, Town Hall Theatre, Society Street, Ballinasloe, Galway, CO. GALWAY, Ireland. T. +353909643779. E-mail: info@aoifeonline.com – ifea@aoifeonline.com.
Chairman – Europe Gentoftegade 76, 2820 Gentofte, Denmark. T. +4540969484. E-mail: ag.tcm@cbs.dk.
URL: http://ifeaeuropeblog.wordpress.com
History Founded 1992, as the European affiliate of *International Festivals and Events Association (IFEA)*. Previously registered in accordance with Dutch law; currently registered in accordance with Irish law. **Aims** Serve the needs of the industry which produces support quality celebrations for the benefit of their respective communities and all those who share the core values of the association. **Structure** Executive Board, comprising Chairman, Vice Chairman, Treasurer and 6 members. Programme Committee; Secretariat. **Staff** Works with Contract Service Provider which has 3 part-time, paid staff working for IFEA-E; Business Development Manager works free-lance; usually one intern/trainee, voluntary. **Finance** Members' dues. Conference fees. **Activities** Organizes conferences and seminars. Provides: professional education; programming; products and resources; networking opportunities; representation. Core values: excellence and quality; sharing of experience, knowledge, creativity and best practices; importance of community building both locally and globally. **Events** *Annual Conference* Nice (France) 2014, *Annual Conference* Rotterdam (Netherlands) 2013, *Annual conference* Copenhagen (Denmark) 2010, *Annual Conference* Bratislava (Slovakia) 2009, *Annual conference* Reykjavik (Iceland) 2008. **Publications** *International Events* (4 a year) – magazine; *IFEA Newsletter*. *Who's Who* – membership directory. Maintains a library, an onlin member area with resources and a forum on website.
Members Festival organizers, policy makers (including governments), tourism agencies, cultural services and companies. Over 3,500 members in 22 countries:
Austria, Belgium, Croatia, Denmark, Estonia, Germany, Greece, Hungary, Iceland, Ireland, Italy, Netherlands, Norway, Poland, Portugal, Romania, Russia, Slovenia, Spain, Sweden, Türkiye, UK.
Included in the above, one organization listed in this Yearbook:
Art Cities in Europe.
NGO Relations *Audiences Europe Network (AEN, #03013)*. [2019/XE3799/**E**]

♦ International Fetal Medicine and Surgery Society 13592

Contact address not obtained.
URL: https://ifmss.org/
History 1983. Founded following activities begun in 1981. Former names and other names: *International Foetal Medicine and Surgery Society* – alias. **Events** *Annual Meeting* Los Cabos (Mexico) 2022, *Annual Meeting* Bali (Indonesia) 2018, *Annual Meeting* USA 2017, *Annual Meeting* Kasane (Botswana) 2016, *Annual Meeting* Greece 2015. **Publications** *Fetal Diagnosis and Therapy* – journal, jointly with International Society 'The Foetus as a Patient'. **Members** Membership countries not specified. **NGO Relations** Joint publication with: *International Society – The Fetus as a Patient (#15118)*. [2022/XD4406/**D**]

♦ International Feuchtwanger Society (IFS) 13593

Sec Doheny Memorial Library, Univ of Southern California, Los Angeles CA 90089-0189, USA. E-mail: schuetze@usc.edu.
URL: http://www.usc.edu/libraries/feuchtwanger/ifs/
History 11 Jul 2001, Pacific Palisades CA (USA). **Aims** Promote interest in the life and work Lion and Marta Feuchtwanger and other German *émigrés* who settled in Southern California during the Nazi period. **Events** *Conference* Los Angeles, CA (USA) 2015, *Conference* Los Angeles, CA (USA) 2011, *Conference* Vienna (Austria) 2009, *Conference* Los Angeles, CA (USA) 2007, *Conference* Sanary sur Mer (France) 2005. **Publications** *IFS Newsletter* – online.
Members Individuals in 10 countries:
Austria, Belgium, France, Germany, Ireland, Israel, Portugal, Switzerland, UK, USA. [2011.07.15/XE4247/**E**]

♦ International Fibre Drum Institute (internationally oriented national body)

♦ International Fibrinogen Research Society (IFRS) 13594

Pres Univ of Maryland, School of Medicine – CVID, 800 West Baltimore St, Baltimore MD 21201, USA. T. +14107068065. Fax +14107068121.
Sec-Treas Erasmus Univ Med Centre, Hematology, Mathenesserlaan 249, 3021 HD Rotterdam, Netherlands. T. +31107033442. Fax +31107035814.
URL: http://www.fibrinogen.org/
History 1990, Rouen (France). **Aims** Promote scientific knowledge on fibrinogen. **Structure** Board of Councillors; Executive Committee. **Languages** English. **Finance** Members' dues. **Events** *International Fibrinogen Workshop* Jongny (Switzerland) 2022, *International Fibrinogen Workshop* Winston-Salem, NC (USA) 2018, *Biennial International Fibrinogen Workshop* Skukuza (South Africa) 2016, *Biennial Workshop* Marseille (France) 2014, *Biennial Workshop* Brighton (UK) 2012.
Members Full in 16 countries:
Australia, Austria, Belgium, Canada, France, Germany, Hungary, Italy, Japan, Netherlands, New Zealand, South Africa, Sweden, Switzerland, UK, USA. [2015.06.25/XD7068/**D**]

♦ International Fibrodysplasia Ossificans Progressiva Association (internationally oriented national body)

♦ International Field Archery Association (IFAA) 13595

Pres PO Box 67109, Highveld Park, Pretoria, 0169, South Africa. E-mail: socialmedia@ifaa.news.
URL: http://www.ifaa-archery.org/

History 1969. Founded involving *Archery Association of Europe (AAE)*, England, Sweden and Germany FR. Registration: No/ID: CH-501.6.008.204-9, Switzerland, Lugano. **Aims** Promote the sport of field archery at an international level, allowing for both elite and mass participation. **Structure** Committee, comprising President, Vice-President, Secretary, Treasurer and one representative of each member country. **Languages** English. **Staff** None. **Finance** Sources through hosting of regional and world tournaments. **Activities** Organizes – in even years: IFAA World Field Archery Championship; IFAA 3D World Championship; in odd years: World Bow Hunter Championship; World Indoor Championship; Australasia Region Field Championship; annually: European Field Archery Championship; European Bow Hunter Championship; African Region Field Archery Championship; North American Field Archery Championships; World Field Mail Match; world Indoor Mail Match. **Publications** *US and International Archery Magazine.*
Members National organizations in 25 countries and territories:
Argentina, Australia, Austria, Belgium, Botswana, Canada, England, Finland, France, Germany, Hong Kong, Ireland, Italy, Namibia, New Zealand, Portugal, San Marino, Scotland, Singapore, South Africa, Sweden, Switzerland, USA, Wales, Zambia.
Regional organization (1) Archery Association of Europe (AAE).
NGO Relations Member of: *The Association for International Sport for All (TAFISA, #02763).*
[2021/XD7192/**D**]

♦ International Field Emission Society (IFES) 13596

Sec c/o Dept of Metallurgical and Materials Engineering, Univ of Alabama, Box 870202, 245 7th Avenue, 360 HM Comer Hall, Tuscaloosa AL 35487-0202, USA.
URL: http://www.fieldemission.org/

History 1985, Wheeling WV (USA), during the 33rd Field Emission Symposium. Statutes amended 1992; 1996; 2004; 2006. **Aims** Promote progress in the science, education and technology of field emission and related phenomena, including atom-probe *tomography.* **Structure** International Steering Committee of 12 members, comprising President, Vice-President, Treasurer, Secretary and 8 members. Society consists of 2 groups, specializing in Atom Probe Tomography and in High-Field Surface Science and Technology. **Languages** English. **Staff** Voluntary. **Finance** Members' dues. **Events** *Biennial Symposium* Oxford (UK) 2020, *Biennial Symposium* Gaithersburg, MD (USA) 2018, *Microscopy and Microanalysis Annual Congress* St Louis, MO (USA) 2017, *Biennial Symposium* Gyeongju (Korea Rep) 2016, *Biennial Symposium* Stuttgart (Germany) 2014. **Publications** None.
Members Individuals in 16 countries and territories:
Austria, Canada, China, France, Germany, Greece, India, Japan, Jordan, Russia, Sweden, Switzerland, Taiwan, UK, Ukraine, USA. [2017/XD3120/v/**D**]

♦ International Field Hockey Federation / see International Hockey Federation (#13802)
♦ International Fight Kickboxing Federation (unconfirmed)
♦ International Filariasis Association (inactive)
♦ International Film Chamber (inactive)
♦ International Film Conciliation Group (inactive)
♦ International Film and Television Council / see International Council for Film, Television and Audiovisual Communication (#13022)
♦ International Film-Writers' Federation (inactive)
♦ International Finance and Banking Society (internationally oriented national body)
♦ International Finance and Commodities Institute / see International Financial Risk Institute

♦ International Finance Corporation (IFC) 13597

Société financière internationale (SFI) – Corporación Financiera Internacional (CFI)
Exec Vice-Pres/CEO 2121 Pennsylvania Avenue NW, Washington DC 20433, USA. T. +12024737711 – +12024733800. Fax +12029744384. E-mail: ifc-newsroom@ifc.org.
Vice-Pres/Treas address not obtained.
URL: http://www.ifc.org/

History 24 Jul 1956, Washington DC (USA), by international agreement among member countries. Although closely affiliated with *International Bank for Reconstruction and Development (IBRD, #12317)* (popularly known as 'World Bank'), IFC is a separate legal entity comprising, with IBRD and its other affiliates, *International Development Association (IDA, #13155)* and *Multilateral Investment Guarantee Agency (MIGA, #16888)*, the umbrella organization *The World Bank Group (#21218).* Through the World Bank Group, IFC is a specialized agency of *United Nations (UN, #20515)* since 1957, within *United Nations System (#20635)* and linked to *ECOSOC (#05331).* World Bank organizations are part of what are often referred to as *Bretton Woods Institutions (BWIs, #03322).* Previously also referred to in French and Spanish as *Société Financière Internationale – Corporación Financiera Internacional.* **Aims** In order for people to escape poverty and improve their lives: promote open and competitive markets in developing countries; support companies and other private sector partners where there is a gap; help generate productive jobs and deliver essential services to the underserved; catalyze and mobilize other sources of finance for private enterprise development.
Structure Board of Governors consists of IBRD Governors and Alternates who represent countries which are also IFC members. Board of Directors comprises, ex officio, IBRD Executive Directors representing IFC member countries, chaired by IBRD President.
/Management/ -
President; Executive Vice President/CEO; Compliance Advisor/Ombudsman; CEO of IFC Management Company; 12 Vice-Presidents, each responsible for a specific area:
- Human Resources, Communications, and Administration;
- Financial and Private Sector Development (FPD);
- Asia-Pacific;
- Treasury and Information Technology;
- Global Industries;
- Risk Management, Financial Reporting, and Corporate Strategy;
- Special Advisor to the Executive Vice-President and CEO;
- General Counsel;
- Business Advisory Services;
- Sub-Saharan Africa, Latin America and the Caribbean, and Western Europe;
- Eastern and Southern Europe, Central Asia, Middle East and North Africa;
- CEO, IFC Asset Management Company;

Departments (33):
- Corporate Advice;
- Business Risk;
- Corporate Portfolio Management;
- Corporate Relations;
- Corporate Risk Management;
- Corporate Strategy;
- Credit Review;
- East Asia and the Pacific;
- Environment and Social Development;
- Equity;
- Europe and Central Asia;
- Financial Operations;
- Global Capital Markets;
- Global Financial Markets;
- Global Manufacturing and Services;
- Human Resources and Administration;
- Independent Evaluation Group;
- Global Infrastructure and Natural Resources;
- Public Private Partnerships;
- Short-Term Finance;
- Latin American and the Caribbean;
- Legal;
- Middle East and North Africa;
- Oil, Gas, Mining and Chemicals;
- Partnerships and Advisory Services Operations;
- Resource Mobilization;
- South Asia;
- Southern Europea and Central Asia;
- Special Operations.
- Structured and Securitized Products;
- Sub-Saharan Africa;
- Syndicated Loans and Management;
- Treasurer.

Departments (16):
- Controller's and Budgeting;
- Corporate Business Technologies;
- Corporate Portfolio Management;
- Corporate Relations;
- Corporate Risk Management and Financial Policy;
- Credit Review;
- Environment, Social, and Governance;
- Financial Operations;
- Human Resources and Administration;
- Legal;
- Operations Evaluation Group;
- Climate Business Solutions;
- Inclusive Business;
- Investment Operations;
- Global Knowledge Office;
- Treasury.

Committees: Audit; Budget; Development Effectiveness; Personnel.
Languages English. **Staff** IFC draws on IBRD for administrative and other services but has its own operating and legal staff. Staff negotiations through *World Bank Group Staff Association (#21219).* **Finance** Share capital provided by member countries. Net income for the fiscal year 2010: over US$ 1,700 million (after a US$ 200 million transfer to IDA).
Activities Combines the characteristics of a multilateral development bank and a private merchant bank. Main activities are: project financing, including long-term loans, equity investments, quasi-equity instruments (subordinated loans, preferred stock, income notes), guarantees and standby financing, risk management (intermediation of currency and interest rate swaps, provision of hedging facilities); mobilization by syndicating loans with international commercial banks and underwriting investment funds and corporate securities issues; advice and technical assistance to businesses and governments. For fiscal year 2011, new investment commitments totalled US$ 18,700 million, with US$ 12,200 million for IFC's own account and US$ 6,500 million mobilized from others.
Investment Services: Equity; Short-term Liquidity; Loans and Intermediary Services; Syndicated Loans; Structured Finance; Risk Management Products; Trade Finance; Subnational Finance; Treasury Operations. Advisory Services: Access to Finance; Investment Climate; Sustainable Business; Public-Private Partnerships. **Events** *Scaling Up Sustainable Investing in Emerging Market* Seoul (Korea Rep) 2021, *Infrastructure Workshop* Seoul (Korea Rep) 2020, *Global SME Finance Forum* Amsterdam (Netherlands) 2019, *Innovation Day Meeting* Seoul (Korea Rep) 2019, *Investing in Women along Agribusiness Value Chains Seminar* Singapore (Singapore) 2019. **Publications** *Doing Business 2009 – How to Reform.* Annual report in 2 vols; statistical reports. **Information Services** *Africa Business Network (ABN)* – electronic information clearinghouse for international investors and African entrepreneurs; *Emerging Markets Data Base (EMDB)* – statistics and indexes on developing countries' stock markets, currently owned by a commercial company but maintains relations with IFC.
Members Members must first be members of IBRD. As of 2011, governments of 178 countries and territories (" indicates one or more national offices, including HQ in USA):
Afghanistan, Albania (*), Algeria, Angola, Antigua-Barbuda, Argentina (*), Armenia, Australia (*), Austria, Azerbaijan, Bahamas, Bahrain, Bangladesh (*), Barbados, Belarus, Belgium, Belize, Benin, Bhutan, Bolivia, Bosnia-Herzegovina (*), Botswana, Brazil (*), Bulgaria, Burkina Faso, Burundi, Cambodia (*), Cameroon, Canada, Cape Verde, Central African Rep, Chad, Chile, China (*), Colombia, Comoros, Congo Brazzaville, Congo DR, Costa Rica (*), Côte d'Ivoire, Croatia, Cyprus, Czechia (*), Denmark, Djibouti, Dominica, Dominican Rep, Ecuador, Egypt (*), El Salvador, Equatorial Guinea, Eritrea, Estonia, Eswatini, Ethiopia, Fiji, Finland, France (*), Gabon, Gambia, Georgia, Germany (*), Ghana, Greece, Grenada, Guatemala, Guinea, Guinea-Bissau, Guyana, Haiti, Honduras, Hungary (*), Iceland, India (*), Indonesia (*), Iran Islamic Rep, Iraq, Ireland, Israel, Italy, Jamaica, Japan (*), Jordan, Kazakhstan (*), Kenya, Kiribati, Korea Rep, Kuwait, Kyrgyzstan, Laos, Latvia, Lebanon, Lesotho, Liberia, Libya, Lithuania, Luxembourg, Madagascar, Malawi, Malaysia, Maldives, Mali, Malta, Marshall Is, Mauritania, Mauritius, Mexico (*), Micronesia FS, Moldova, Mongolia, Montenegro, Morocco (*), Mozambique, Myanmar, Namibia, Nepal, Netherlands, New Zealand, Nicaragua, Niger, Nigeria, North Macedonia (*), Norway, Oman, Pakistan (*), Palau, Panama, Papua New Guinea, Paraguay, Peru, Philippines (*), Poland (*), Portugal, Qatar, Romania (*), Russia (*), Rwanda, Samoa, Sao Tomé-Principe, Saudi Arabia, Senegal, Serbia, Seychelles, Sierra Leone, Singapore, Slovakia, Slovenia, Solomon Is, Somalia, South Africa, Spain, Sri Lanka, St Kitts-Nevis, St Lucia, Sudan, Sweden, Switzerland, Syrian AR, Tajikistan, Tanzania UR, Thailand (*), Timor-Leste, Togo, Tonga, Trinidad-Tobago (*), Tunisia, Türkiye (*), Turkmenistan, Uganda, UK (*), Ukraine (*), United Arab Emirates, Uruguay, USA (*), Uzbekistan (*), Vanuatu, Venezuela, Vietnam (*), Yemen, Zambia, Zimbabwe.
Consultative Status Consultative status granted from: *World Intellectual Property Organization (WIPO, #21593)* (Permanent Observer Status). **IGO Relations** Relationship with the United Nations authorized by the Board of Directors and governed by provisions of an agreement between the UN and IBRD. Working relations with: *Intergovernmental Oceanographic Commission (IOC, #11496).* Memorandum of Understanding with: *Nordic Investment Bank (NIB, #17327).* Observer to: *Global Forum on Transparency and Exchange of Information for Tax Purposes (#10379).* Special links with: *UNDP (#20292).* Cooperates with: *International Telecommunication Union (ITU, #15673).* Member of: *African Management Services Company (AMSCO, #00367)*; *Consultative Group to Assist the Poor (CGAP, #04768).* Partner of: *Global Green Growth Forum (3GF).* Supports: *Public-Private Infrastructure Advisory Facility (PPIAF, #18569).* **NGO Relations** Co-founder of: *SIFIDA Investment Company (inactive).* Hosts Secretariat of: *Global Banking Alliance for Women (GBA, #10248).* Founding partner of: *Water Footprint Network (WFN, #20829).* Member of *Aspen Network of Development Entrepreneurs (ANDE, #02310)*; *Consultative Group to Assist the Poor (CGAP, #04768)*; *World Benchmarking Alliance (WBA, #21228).* [2020/XF2057/e/**F***]

♦ International Finance Facility for Immunisation (IFFIm) 13598

Contact c/o Gavi Alliance, Global Health Campus, Chemin du Pommier 40, 1218 Le Grand-Saconnex GE, Switzerland.
Registered Office 2 Lambs Passage, London, EC1Y 8BB, UK.
URL: http://www.iffim.org/

History Nov 2006. Founded as a development financing institution to raise funds for *Gavi – The Vaccine Alliance (Gavi, #10077).* Registration: Companies House, No/ID: 05857343, Start date: 26 Jun 2006, England; Charity Commission, No/ID: 1115413, England and Wales. **Aims** Raise money in capital markets through issuance of *Vaccine* Bonds to support the GAVI Alliance mission of immunizing *children* in the world's poorest countries. **Structure** Board of Directors. Administrative support functions outsourced to *Gavi – The Vaccine Alliance (Gavi, #10077)*; treasury functions and related accounting services outsources to *International Bank for Reconstruction and Development (IBRD, #12317)* (World Bank). **Finance** Supported by the governments of Australia, France, Italy, Netherlands, Norway, South Africa, Spain, Sweden and the UK. **Activities** Financial and/or humanitarian aid. **Publications** *IFFIm Newsletter.* [2020/XM1814/**F**]

♦ International Finance Forum (IFF) 13599

Contact Mingzhu Development Bldg, No1 Mingzhu One Street, Mingzhu Bay District, Nansha District, Guangzhou, 511466 Guangdong, China. E-mail: iff@iff.org.cn.
URL: http://www.iff.org.cn/

History 2003, Beijing (China). **Aims** Promote sustainable development of China and the world economy. **Structure** General Assembly; Board of Directors; Executive Committee; Advisory Committee; Academic Committee; Specialists Committee; other Committees; Working Group. **Languages** English; Chinese. **Activities** Awards/prizes/competitions; events/meetings; guidance/assistance/consulting; knowledge management/information dissemination; networking/liaising; publishing activities; research/documentation. **Events** *International Finance Forum 2021 Annual Meeting (F20 Summit)* Guangzhou (China) 2021. **Publications** *Global Finance and Development Report* (2021); *Global Green Finance Award Case Collection*; *IFF China Report.*
[2022.10.26/AA2980/**F**]

♦ International Finance and Leasing Association (IFLA) 13600

Pres address not obtained.
SG address not obtained.
URL: http://www.ifla.com/

History 1965. **Aims** Provide a forum for members to exchange ideas, knowledge, experience and information. **Structure** Advisory Committee. **Languages** English. **Events** *Annual General Meeting* Bergen (Norway) 2023, *Annual General Meeting* 2022, *Autumn Meeting* Stockholm (Sweden) 2022, *Annual General Meeting* 2021, *Annual General Meeting* 2020.
Members Leasing companies in 15 countries:
Belgium, Croatia, Denmark, Iceland, India, Iran Islamic Rep, Ireland, Italy, Jordan, Netherlands, Norway, Spain, Sweden, Tunisia, UK. [2022.10.25/XD9435/**D**]

♦ International Financial Commission (inactive)
♦ International Financial Consumer Protection Organisation (unconfirmed)

♦ International Financial Cryptography Association (IFCA) 13601

Sec Prinsengracht 748, 1017 LC Amsterdam, Netherlands. E-mail: secretary@ifca.ai – info@ifca.ai.
Pres address not obtained. E-mail: president@ifca.ai.
URL: http://www.ifca.ai/
History Feb 1998, Anguilla. **Aims** Advance theory and practice of financial cryptography and related fields. **Structure** Board of Directors. **Events** *International Conference – Financial Cryptography and Data Security* Grenada 2022, *Annual Conference* Nago (Japan) 2013, *Annual Conference* Gros-Islet (St Lucia) 2011, *Annual Conference* Santa Cruz de Tenerife (Spain) 2010, *Annual Conference* Barbados 2009. **Publications** Conference proceedings. [2021/XF4808/**F**]

♦ International Financial Litigation Network (IFLN) 13602

Contact Jorge Juan 30 – 6th Floor, 28001 Madrid, Spain. T. +34914264050. Fax +34914264052. E-mail: dsolana@cremadescalvosotelo.com.
URL: http://www.ifln-network.com/
History Launched, when constitution was adopted, 22 May 2013, New York NY (USA) and 23 May 2013, Washington DC (USA). Registered in accordance with Spanish law. **Aims** Disseminate communication; enhance members' capabilities to serve the needs of clients in financial litigation. **Structure** General Assembly; Board of Directors; Central Administrative Office. **Events** *Congress* Madrid (Spain) 2016, *Congress* Madrid (Spain) 2015.
Members Full in 24 countries and territories:
Austria, Belgium, Brazil, Canada, Colombia, Ecuador, Finland, Greece, India, Ireland, Israel, Italy, Japan, Lebanon, Luxembourg, Macau, Morocco, Netherlands, Pakistan, Slovenia, Spain, Türkiye, UK, USA.
NGO Relations Cooperates with: *World Federation of Investors (WFI, #21447).* [2015/XM4254/**F**]

♦ International Financial Reporting Standards Foundation (IFRS Foundation) 13603

Headquarters Columbus Bldg, 7 Westferry Circus, Canary Wharf, London, E14 4HD, UK. T. +442072466410. E-mail: info@ifrs.org.
Asia-Oceania Office Financial City, South Tower 5F, 1-9-7 Otemachi, Chiyoda-ku, Tokyo, 100-0004 Japan.
URL: https://www.ifrs.org/
History Re-organized, 6 Feb 2001. Former names and other names: *International Accounting Standards Committee Foundation (IASC Foundation)* – former. Registration: Companies House, No/ID: BR012252, Start date: 1 Oct 2009, England and Wales; Companies House, No/ID: FC023235, Start date: 2 May 2001, England and Wales; USA, State of Delaware. **Aims** Develop IFRS Standards that bring transparency, accountability and efficiency to financial markets around the world; serve the public interest by fostering trust, growth and long-term financial stability in the global economy. **Structure** IFRS Monitoring Board; Trustees; *International Accounting Standards Board (IASB, #11583)*; *International Sustainability Standards Board (ISSB, #15634)*; IFRS Advisory Council; Interpretations Committee. Also includes Integrated Reported Framework. **Languages** English. **Staff** 150.00 FTE, paid. **Finance** Sources: voluntary contributions from jurisdictions around the world (54%); voluntary contributions from international accounting firms (17%); self-generated income from sale of subscription services, publications and licensing of intellectual property (29%). Annual budget: 30,500,000 GBP. **Activities** Events/meetings; standards/guidelines. **Events** *World Standard Setters Conference* London (UK) 2022, *Forum on General Insurance* Singapore (Singapore) 2020, *World Standard Setters Conference* London (UK) 2019, *Conference* Amsterdam (Netherlands) 2017, *Conference* Paris (France) 2015. **Publications** Volumes of IFRS Standards. **IGO Relations** Memorandum of Understanding with (1): *International Bank for Reconstruction and Development (IBRD, #12317)* (World Bank). **NGO Relations** Memorandum of Understanding with (1): *Basel Committee on Banking Supervision (BCBS, #03183).* [2023.02.14/XJ9011/f/**F**]

♦ International Financial Risk Institute (internationally oriented national body)
♦ International Fine Art and Specie Insurance Conference (unconfirmed)

♦ International Fine Particle Research Institute (IFPRI) 13604

Main Office 2045 Wooddale Dr, Woodbury MN 55125, USA.
URL: http://www.ifpri.net/
History 1979. **Aims** Fund research in particle technology. **Structure** Board of Directors; Technical Advisory Committee. Technical Committee; Executive Committee. Programmes (5): Wet Systems Flow / Separations; Dry Powder Flow; Characterization and Measurement; Particle Formation; Size Reduction. **Finance** Members' dues. Research budget (annual): over US$ 750,000. **Events** *General Meeting* Woodbury, MN (USA) 2020, *General Meeting* Burlington, VT (USA) 2019, *Annual General Meeting / Annual Meeting* Ithaca, NY (USA) 2015, *Annual General Meeting / Annual Meeting* Edinburgh (UK) 2014, *Annual general meeting / Annual Meeting* Philadelphia, PA (USA) 2004. **Publications** Books; proceedings.
Members Organizations and individuals in 11 countries:
Australia, Belgium, Canada, France, Germany, Japan, Netherlands, Poland, UK, USA, Venezuela. [2020/XE2627/j/**E**]

♦ International Finn Association (see: #21760)
♦ International Finno-Ugric Students' Conference (meeting series)
♦ International Fireball Class Association / see Fireball International (#09777)

♦ International Fire Chiefs' Association of Asia (IFCAA) 13605

Association internationale des chefs pompiers d'Asie
Secretariat Kojimachi 1-6-2, Chiyoda-Ku, Tokyo, 102-8199 Japan. T. +81332341321. Fax +81332341847.
URL: http://www.fcaj.gr.jp/ifcaa/en/
History 26 May 1960. **Aims** Maintain friendly relations among fire chiefs in Asia and Oceania; promote study of techniques and measures for protecting human lives and property from fire; exchange knowledge and information on the fire service, contributing to development of fire services in Asia and Oceania. **Structure** General Conference (every 2 years); Board of Directors; Head Office, headed by Secretary General. **Languages** English, Japanese. **Staff** 2.00 FTE, paid. **Finance** Sources: contributions; members' dues. **Activities** Events/meetings; knowledge management/information dissemination; networking/liaising; projects/programmes; publishing activities; research and development. **Events** *General Conference* Kuala Lumpur (Malaysia) 2024, *General Conference* Yokohama (Japan) 2022, *General Conference* Tokyo (Japan) 2020, *General Conference* Tokyo (Japan) 2018, *General Conference* Osaka (Japan) 2016. **Publications** *IFCAA* (annual) – magazine; *IFCAA Fire Statistics* (every 2 years).
Members Active; Associate; Assisting; Honorary. Individuals (about 800) in 22 countries and territories:
Australia, Bahrain, Bangladesh, Brunei Darussalam, Guam, Hong Kong, India, Indonesia, Iran Islamic Rep, Israel, Japan, Korea Rep, Kuwait, Malaysia, Mongolia, New Zealand, Papua New Guinea, Philippines, Singapore, Taiwan, Thailand, Vietnam. [2022.10.19/XD2641/v/**D**]

♦ International Firemen's Council (inactive)

♦ International Fire Safety Standards Coalition (IFSS Coalition) 13606

Chair c/o RICS, Parliament Square, London, SW1P 3AD, UK. T. +447837303926.
Contact address not obtained.
URL: https://ifss-coalition.org/
History 9 Jul 2018, Geneva (Switzerland). Launched at *United Nations (UN, #20515).* **Aims** Develop consistent global fire safety standards in the public interest; improve global knowledge of fire safety, best practice, research and guidance; increase awareness of fire safety; uphold the highest ethical practice in design, construction and management of buildings and infrastructure regarding fire safety. **Structure** Consists of a broad range of representatives from professional bodies globally. **Languages** English. IFSS Common Principles standard also available in Chinese. **Staff** 2.00 FTE, voluntary. **Finance** No budget required, entirely voluntary. **Activities** Standards/guidelines. Active in all member countries. **Publications** *Decade of Action for Fire Safety 2022-2032 plan* (October 2021) – The launch of the Decade of Action for Fire Safety 2022-2032 (see url) will ensure improvements in fire safety across the world are made in education, training, research, public awareness, firefighting infrastructure, standards, and guidance. It is a monumental shift in the importance of fire safety as the global population increases, and fires, fatalities and injuries inevitably increase. Our aim is to decrease the incidence of fire, fatalities and injuries over the Decade, working with Governments, NGOs, the UN, and World Bank together with experts from over 100 bodies.; *International Fire Safety Standards: Common Principles* (1st ed 2020-10-05).
Members Organizations – national and regional. National in 14 countries and territories:
Australia, France, Hong Kong, India, Kenya, Kuwait, Malaysia, New Zealand, Philippines, Singapore, South Africa, UK, United Arab Emirates, USA.
Regional organizations or organizations listed in this Yearbook (14):
Association of European Experts in Building and Construction (The) (AEEBC, #02510); *Commonwealth Association of Surveying and Land Economy (CASLE, #04313)*; Confederation of Fire Protection Associations Asia (CFPA-A); *Consortium of European Building Control (CEBC, #04739)*; *CTIF International Association of Fire and Rescue Services (#04979)*; *European Fire Safety Alliance (EuroFSA, #07258)*; *Fire Safe Europe (FSEU, #09780)*; *Institution of Fire Engineers (IFE, #11321)*; *International Code Council (ICC)*; *International Federation of Surveyors (FIG, #13561)*; *Royal Institution of Chartered Surveyors (RICS, #18991)*; *Society of Fire Protection Engineers (SFPE)*; *The World Bank Group (#21218)*; *United Nations Economic Commission for Europe (UNECE, #20555).*
For a full list of members: https://ifss-coalition.org/coalition-organisations/. [2022.06.23/XM6740/y/**C**]

♦ International Fire Sprinkler Association / see International Fire Suppression Alliance (#13607)

♦ International Fire Suppression Alliance (IFSA) 13607

Dir 132 South Franklin St, Chagrin Falls OH 44022, USA. E-mail: ifsa@firesprinkler.global.
URL: https://www.firesprinkler.global/
History Former names and other names: *International Fire Sprinkler Association (IFSA)* – former (1999 to 2017); *International Fire Suppression Association (IFSA)* – former. **Aims** Globally promote use of effective water-based fire protection systems. **Structure** Board of Directors; Managing Director. **Languages** English. **Staff** 0.30 FTE, paid. **Finance** Members' dues. Annual budget: about US$ 400,000. **Activities** Financial and/or material support; events/meetings. **Events** *Americas Conference / International Conference* Panama (Panama) 2014, *Annual Meeting* Long Beach, CA (USA) 2012, *International Conference / Annual Meeting* Paris (France) 2012, *Conference on Inertial Fusion Sciences and Applications* Bordeaux (France) 2011, *Annual Meeting* Seattle, WA (USA) 2011. **Publications** *International Sprinkler Scene* (4 a year) – newsletter.
Members Governing; Manufacturer; Distributor; Contractor; Professional; Association. Membership countries not specified. [2023/XD8556/**D**]

♦ International Fire Suppression Association / see International Fire Suppression Alliance (#13607)

♦ International Fiscal Association (IFA) 13608

Association fiscale internationale – Asociación Fiscal Internacional – Internationale Vereinigung für Steuerrecht – Internationale Vereniging voor Belastingrecht
Contact PO Box 30215, 3001 DE Rotterdam, Netherlands. T. +31104052990. Fax +31104055031. E-mail: congress@ifa.nl.
URL: http://www.ifa.nl/
History 12 Feb 1938, The Hague (Netherlands). Statutes revised Nov 1992; Jan 1999; Oct 2010. Former names and other names: *International Association for Public Finance and Fiscal Law* – former (12 Feb 1938 to 1949); *Association internationale pour le droit financier et fiscal* – former (12 Feb 1938 to 1949); *Internationale Vereeniging voor Financieel en Fiscal Recht* – former (12 Feb 1938 to 1949). Registration: Netherlands. **Aims** Study and advance international and comparative *law* with regard to *public finance*, especially international and comparative fiscal law and financial and economic aspects of taxation. **Structure** General Assembly (annual); General Council (meets during congress); Executive Committee; Permanent Scientific Committee. **Languages** English. **Staff** 5.00 FTE, paid. **Finance** Members' dues: Individuals euro 70; Corporations euro 160. Other sources: donations; legacies; occasional gifts. **Activities** Awards/prizes/competitions; events/meetings; research/documentation. **Events** *Annual Congress* Stockholm (Sweden) 2027, *Annual Congress* Melbourne, VIC (Australia) 2026, *Annual Congress* Lisbon (Portugal) 2025, *Annual Congress* Cape Town (South Africa) 2024, *Annual Congress* Cancún (Mexico) 2023. **Publications** *Cahiers de droit fiscal international* (annual). *IFA Congress Seminar Series.* Congress report.
Members IFA Branches (refers to Aruba and Curaçao which form one branch); Individuals and Corporate members. IFA Branches in 72 countries and territories:
Argentina, Aruba (*), Australia, Austria, Belgium, Bolivia, Bosnia-Herzegovina, Brazil, Bulgaria, Canada, Chile, China, Colombia, Congo DR, Costa Rica, Curaçao (*), Cyprus, Czechia, Denmark, Dominican Rep, Ecuador, Egypt, Estonia, Finland, France, Germany, Greece, Guatemala, Honduras, Hong Kong, Hungary, India, Indonesia, Ireland, Israel, Italy, Japan, Korea Rep, Liechtenstein, Luxembourg, Malaysia, Malta, Mauritius, Mexico, Morocco, Netherlands, New Zealand, Nigeria, Norway, Panama, Peru, Poland, Portugal, Romania, Russia, Serbia, Singapore, Slovakia, Slovenia, South Africa, Spain, Sri Lanka, Sweden, Switzerland, Taiwan, Türkiye, UK, Ukraine, United Arab Emirates, Uruguay, USA, Venezuela.
Individuals (about 13,500). Membership countries not specified.
Consultative Status Consultative status granted from: *ECOSOC (#05331)* (Ros A). **IGO Relations** Liaison officers with: *European Commission (EC, #06633)*; *OECD (#17693).* Accredited by: *United Nations Office at Vienna (UNOV, #20604).* **NGO Relations** Liaison officers with: *BUSINESSEUROPE (#03381)*; *Inter-American Centre for Tax Administrations (#11405)*; *International Chamber of Commerce (ICC, #12534).* [2020.02.10/XB2059/**B**]

♦ International Fisheries Commission / see International Pacific Halibut Commission
♦ International Fishing Association (inactive)
♦ International Fishmeal and Fish Oil Organisation / see The Marine Ingredients Organisation (#16579)
♦ International Fish Meal and Oil Manufacturers Association / see The Marine Ingredients Organisation (#16579)
♦ International Fission Yeast Meeting (meeting series)

♦ International Fistball Association (IFA) 13609

Pres Hölderlinstrasse 26, 4040 Linz, Austria. T. +436765648146. E-mail: office@ifa-fistball.com.
SG address not obtained.
Main Website: http://www.ifa-fistball.com/
History 30 Jan 1960, Frankfurt-Main (Germany). Original statutes adopted 12 Nov 1960, Frankfurt-Main (Germany FR). Statutes altered and supplemented: 27 Nov 1964, Schaffhausen (Switzerland); 21 Jun 1969, Pfungstadt (Germany FR); 19-20 Sep 1990, Kirchdorf (Austria), 25 Nov 1992, Llanquihue (Chile), 27 Aug 1995, Windhoek (Namibia), 24 Aug 1999, Olten (Switzerland); 20 Nov 2003, Porto Alegre (Brazil). Former names and other names: *International Fistball Federation* – former (1960 to 2003); *Internationaler Faustball-Verband (IFV)* – former (1960 to 2003). **Aims** Promote, encourage and develop the game of fistball (indoor and outdoor; male and female) and other related sports. **Structure** Congress (at least every 4 years); Board of Directors; Executive Committee; Commissions. **Languages** English, German. **Activities** Events/meetings; sporting activities. **Events** *Extraordinary Congress* 2022, *Congress* Winterthur (Switzerland) 2019, *Youth Congress* Roxbury, MA (USA) 2018, *Congress* Linz (Austria) 2011, *Congress* Oldenburg (Germany) 2007.
Members National fistball associations in 67 countries and territories:
Afghanistan, Albania, Argentina, Australia, Austria, Belgium, Benin, Bolivia, Brazil, Burkina Faso, Cameroon, Canada, Central African Rep, Chile, China, Colombia, Cook Is, Côte d'Ivoire, Cyprus, Czechia, Denmark, Dominican Rep, Eswatini, Fiji, Germany, Greece, Haiti, Hong Kong, Hungary, Iceland, India, Iran Islamic Rep, Italy, Japan, Kenya, Korea Rep, Kuwait, Malta, Mongolia, Morocco, Namibia, Nepal, Netherlands, New Zealand, Nigeria, North Macedonia, Pakistan, Poland, Russia, Samoa, Serbia, Sierra Leone, South Africa, Spain, Sri Lanka, Sweden, Switzerland, Taipei, Taiwan, Togo, Trinidad-Tobago, Uganda, UK, Ukraine, Uruguay, USA, Venezuela.
NGO Relations Member of (5): *Alliance of Independent recognised Members of Sport (AIMS, #00690)*; *International World Games Association (IWGA, #15914)*; *Olympic Movement (#17719)*; *The Association for International Sport for All (TAFISA, #02763)*; *World Anti-Doping Agency (WADA, #21096).* Cooperates with (1): *International Testing Agency (ITA, #15678).* Recognized by: *International Olympic Committee (IOC, #14408).* [2022.02.15/XD1524/**D**]

♦ International Fistball Federation / see International Fistball Association (#13609)

♦ **International Fitness and Bodybuilding Federation (IFBB)** **13610**

Pres c/ Dublin 39-I, Europolis, Las Rozas, 28232 Madrid, Spain. T. +34915352819. Fax +34915361518. E-mail: contact@ifbb.com – info@ifbb.com.
URL: http://www.ifbb.com/

History 1946, Montréal, QC (Canada). Reconstituted 1970, Belgrade (Yugoslavia). Constitution and Rules approved by Congress, 26 Oct 1986, Tokyo (Japan); amended 1987, Madrid (Spain); 1989, Paris (France); 1995, Guam; Nov 2010. Former names and other names: *International Federation of Body-Builders (IFBB)* – former (1946); *Fédération internationale de culture physique* – former; *International Federation of Bodybuilding and Fitness (IFBB)* – former. **Aims** Promote, control and develop bodybuilding and physical culture on an international scale; promote interest in, and dedication to, better fitness and health through physical culture, proper nutrition and *weight training*; conduct drug testing at all international competitions; ensure that drug testing is carried out in the countries of all affiliated nations by enforcing rules and regulations for drug testing on national federations; conduct research into the benefits of bodybuilding and nutrition in relation to strength conditioning, as a basis for peak performance in sport and to improve the general health of populations at large; distribute without charge such information to National Olympic Committees and international sports federations worldwide; develop and intensify friendship and cooperation amongst national federations and bodybuilders from all countries; coordinate and supervise activities of national federations practising bodybuilding, fitness and physical culture. **Structure** International Congress and meetings of the Executive Council and Committees (annual, at site of the annual Men's World Championships). Special Congress (every 4 years): Executive Council. Committees: Judges Committee; Medical and Doping Commission; Technical Committee; Women's Committee; Exercise and Education Committee. Congresses open. **Languages** English. **Staff** 2.00 FTE, paid; 2.00 FTE, voluntary. **Finance** Sources: members' dues. Other sources: sale of publications and badges; fees for contests; income from television; sponsors. **Activities** Awards/prizes/competitions; events/meetings; sporting activities. **Events** *Annual Congress* Benidorm (Spain) 2020, *Annual Congress* Fujairah (United Arab Emirates) 2019, *Annual Congress* Benidorm (Spain) 2018, *Annual Congress* Benidorm (Spain) 2017, *Annual Congress* Benidorm (Spain) 2016. **Publications** *IFBB Universe* (6 a year) – magazine; *Newlsetter* (bi-weekly) – online, in 9 languages; *E-Body Code* – online. Technical reports issued by Technical and Medical Committee.

Members National federations and observers in 176 countries and territories:
Afghanistan, Albania, Algeria, Andorra, Angola, Antigua-Barbuda, Argentina, Armenia, Aruba, Australia, Austria, Azerbaijan, Bahamas, Bahrain, Bangladesh, Barbados, Belarus, Belgium, Belize, Bermuda, Bhutan, Bolivia, Brazil, Brunei Darussalam, Bulgaria, Cambodia, Canada, Cayman Is, Chile, China, Colombia, Congo Brazzaville, Congo DR, Cook Is, Costa Rica, Côte d'Ivoire, Croatia, Cuba, Curaçao, Czechia, Denmark, Dominica, Dominican Rep, Ecuador, Egypt, El Salvador, Estonia, Eswatini, Ethiopia, Fiji, Finland, France, Georgia, Germany, Greece, Grenada, Guam, Guatemala, Guyana, Haiti, Honduras, Hong Kong, Hungary, Iceland, India, Indonesia, Iran Islamic Rep, Iraq, Ireland, Israel, Italy, Jamaica, Japan, Jordan, Kazakhstan, Kenya, Kiribati, Korea Rep, Kuwait, Kyrgyzstan, Laos, Latvia, Lebanon, Libya, Liechtenstein, Lithuania, Luxembourg, Macau, Malaysia, Maldives, Malta, Mauritius, Mexico, Moldova, Mongolia, Montenegro, Montserrat, Morocco, Mozambique, Myanmar, Namibia, Nepal, Netherlands, New Caledonia, New Zealand, Nicaragua, Nigeria, Niue, Norfolk Is, North Macedonia, Northern Mariana Is, Norway, Oman, Pakistan, Palau, Palestine, Panama, Papua New Guinea, Paraguay, Peru, Philippines, Poland, Polynesia Fr, Portugal, Puerto Rico, Qatar, Romania, Russia, Samoa USA, San Marino, Saudi Arabia, Senegal, Serbia, Seychelles, Singapore, Slovakia, Slovenia, Solomon Is, South Africa, Spain, Sri Lanka, St Kitts-Nevis, St Lucia, St Maarten, St Vincent-Grenadines, Sudan, Suriname, Sweden, Switzerland, Syrian AR, Tahiti Is, Taiwan, Taiwan, Tanzania UR, Thailand, Tonga, Tortola Is, Trinidad-Tobago, Tunisia, Türkiye, Turkmenistan, Uganda, UK, Ukraine, United Arab Emirates, Uruguay, USA, Vanuatu, Venezuela, Vietnam, Virgin Is UK, Virgin Is USA, Yemen, Zambia, Zimbabwe.
Also in Bonaire Is.

IGO Relations *UNESCO (#20322)*. **NGO Relations** Member of (6): *Alliance of Independent recognised Members of Sport (AIMS, #00690)*; *Asociación de Confederaciones Deportivas Panamericanas (ACODEPA, #02119)*; *International Council for Coaching Excellence (ICCE, #13008)*; *International Council of Sport Science and Physical Education (ICSSPE, #13077)*; *International World Games Association (IWGA, #15914)*; *Olympic Movement (#17719)*. Recognized by: *International Olympic Committee (IOC, #14408)*. [2022/XB3908/**B**]

- ♦ International Fixed Calendar League (inactive)
- ♦ International Flame Radiation Association / see International Flame Research Foundation (#13611)

♦ **International Flame Research Foundation (IFRF)** **13611**

Contact Translational Energy Research Centre, Sheffield Business Park, Europa Avenue, Sheffield, S9 1ZA, UK. E-mail: administration@ifrf.net.
URL: http://www.ifrf.net/

History 1948. Current title and structure adopted in 1955, to reflect growth in scope of work and size of the organization. Former names and other names: *International Flame Radiation Association* – former (1948 to 1955). Registration: Italy. **Aims** Advance applied research for safe, clean and efficient combustion; facilitate cooperation, information sharing and research capacity development throughout the international combustion community. **Structure** Council; National Committees (8). **Languages** English. **Staff** 1.50 FTE, paid. **Finance** Sources: members' dues. Other sources: private research contracts; participation in European Union projects. **Activities** Capacity building; events/meetings; knowledge management/information dissemination; research/documentation. **Events** *Hydrogen for decarbonisation* Paris (France) 2022, *Nordic Flame Days* Turku (Finland) 2019, *Triennial Conference* Sheffield (UK) 2018, *Triennial Conference* Freising (Germany) 2015, *Triennial Conference* Munich (Germany) 2015. **Publications** *The Monday Night Mail* (bi-weekly) – newsletter; *Industrial Combustion* – online peer reviewed journal. *Spirit of Ijmuiden: Fifty years of the IFRF 1948-1998* (1998) by Roman Weber. Technical reports related to current research; conference proceedings.

Members Full; Associate. Industrial companies and academic institutes in 21 countries:
Australia, Belgium, Brazil, Canada, China, Denmark, Finland, France, Germany, India, Italy, Japan, Luxembourg, Mexico, Netherlands, Poland, South Africa, Spain, Sweden, UK, USA.

NGO Relations Memorandum of Understanding with (1): *International Electrical Research Exchange (IERE, #13254)*. [2022.10.20/XF1231/f/**F**]

- ♦ International Flight Engineers' Organization (inactive)
- ♦ International In-Flight Food Service Association / see International Flight Services Association

♦ **International Flight Information Service Association (IFISA)** **13612**

Administrator address not obtained.
Sec address not obtained. E-mail: secretary@ifisa.info.
URL: http://ifisa.info/

Aims Further the professional status of Flight Information Services; enhance its stature; promote aviation safety both nationally and internationally. **Structure** Executive Board. **Activities** Events/meetings. **Events** *International Seminar* Budapest (Hungary) 2019, *International Seminar* Bodø (Norway) 2018, *International Seminar* Warsaw (Poland) 2017, *International Seminar* Manchester (UK) 2016.

Members Full; Associate; Honorary; Corporate. Full in 14 countries and territories:
Angola, Canada, Chile, Denmark, Germany, Greece, Greenland, Indonesia, Norway, Peru, Poland, Switzerland, UK, USA.
Associate in 1 country:
Greece.
Corporate in 8 countries:
Canada, Denmark, France, Germany, Poland, Sweden, Thailand, UK.

NGO Relations *International Federation of Air Traffic Safety Electronic Associations (IFATSEA, #13351)*. [2018/XM7324/**C**]

- ♦ International Flight Inspection Symposium (meeting series)
- ♦ International Flight Services Association (internationally oriented national body)
- ♦ International FLINS Conference on Robotics and Artificial Intelligence (meeting series)

♦ **International Flood Initiative (IFI)** **13613**

Secretariat ICHARM, Public Works Research Inst, 1-6 Minamihara, Tsukuba IBARAKI, 305-8516 Japan. T. +81298796815. Fax +81298796709. E-mail: icharm@pwri.go.jp.
URL: http://www.ifi-home.info/

History 19 Jan 2005, Kobe (Japan), during World Conference on Disaster Reduction, by *UNESCO (#20322)* and *World Meteorological Organization (WMO, #21649)*. Also referred to as *Joint UNESCO/WMO Flood Initiative (JUWFI)*. **Aims** Promote an integrated approach to flood management to take advantage of floods and use of flood plains while reducing the social, environmental and economic risks. **Structure** Joint Committee, comprising Advisory Committee and Management Committee. Secretariat. **Activities** Projects. **Events** *World landslide forum* Rome (Italy) 2011, *International Conference on Flood Management* Tsukuba (Japan) 2011, *Meeting on the resolution of conflicts on shared waters* Oslo (Norway) 2005.

Members Collaborating partners (7):
Institute for Catastrophic Loss Reduction (ICLR); *International Association for Hydro-Environment Engineering and Research (IAHR, #11950)*; *International Association of Hydrological Sciences (IAHS, #11954)*; *UNESCO (#20322)*; *United Nations Office for Disaster Risk Reduction (UNDRR, #20595)*; *United Nations University (UNU, #20642)*; *World Meteorological Organization (WMO, #21649)*.

IGO Relations *International Centre for Water Hazard and Risk Management (ICHARM)*. **NGO Relations** *International Conference on Flood Management (ICFM)*. [2017/XJ4336/y/**E**]

♦ **International Flood Network (IFNet)** **13614**

Contact Infrastructure Development Inst, Suido-cho Bldg 6F 3-1, Suido-Cho, Shinjuku-ku, Tokyo, 162-0811 Japan. T. +81352274102. Fax +81352274109. E-mail: info@internationalfloodnetwork.org.
URL: http://internationalfloodnetwork.org/

History 19 Mar 2003, Kyoto (Japan), during the 3rd World Water Forum, organized by *World Water Council (WWC, #21908)*. **Aims** Facilitate international cooperation in flood management; promote flooding as a priority international policy issue to be addressed by both governments and institutions; provide technology and knowledge related to floods. **Publications** *IFNet Newsletter*. **Members** Membership countries not specified. [2014.06.24/XF6918/**F**]

♦ **International Floorball Federation (IFF)** **13615**

SG Alakiventie 2, FI-00920 Helsinki, Finland. T. +358945421425. E-mail: office@floorball.sport.
URL: http://www.floorball.sport/

History 1986, Huskvarna (Sweden). **Aims** Be the internationally recognized sole owner of the *sport* of floorball; promote all its different forms and identities (innebandy, salibandy, unihockey); serve as an attractive competition and sport for all. **Structure** General Assembly; Association Meeting; Committees (8); Functions (7); Permanent Working Groups (3). **Languages** English. **Staff** 8.25 FTE, paid. **Finance** Sources: fees for services; members' dues; sponsorship. Other sources: material approval; advertisement; transfers; television agreements. Annual budget: 1,987,000 CHF (2021). **Activities** Events/meetings; projects/programmes; sporting activities; training/education. **Events** *Biennial General Assembly* Helsinki (Finland) 2020, *Biennial General Assembly and Congress* Prague (Czechia) 2018, *Biennial General Assembly and Congress* Zurich (Switzerland) 2012, *Biennial general assembly and congress* Helsinki (Finland) 2010, *Biennial general assembly and congress* Prague (Czech Rep) 2008. **Publications** *IFF School Curriculum, an Introduction to Floorball in Schools* (2017); *Urban Floorball Guide* (2017); *Learn – Start – Play* (2013).

Members Associations in 74 countries and territories:
Argentina, Armenia, Australia, Austria, Belarus, Belgium, Brazil, Burkina Faso, Cameroon, Canada, Central African Rep, China, Côte d'Ivoire, Croatia, Czechia, Denmark, Estonia, Finland, France, Georgia, Germany, Haiti, Hong Kong, Hungary, Iceland, India, Indonesia, Iran Islamic Rep, Ireland, Israel, Italy, Jamaica, Japan, Kenya, Kiribati, Korea Rep, Kuwait, Latvia, Liechtenstein, Lithuania, Malaysia, Malta, Moldova, Mongolia, Mozambique, Netherlands, New Zealand, Nigeria, Norway, Pakistan, Philippines, Poland, Portugal, Romania, Russia, Rwanda, Serbia, Sierra Leone, Singapore, Slovakia, Slovenia, Somalia, South Africa, Spain, Sweden, Switzerland, Thailand, Togo, Türkiye, Uganda, UK, Ukraine, USA, Venezuela.

NGO Relations Member of (3): *Association of the IOC Recognized International Sports Federations (ARISF, #02767)*; *International World Games Association (IWGA, #15914)*; *Olympic Movement (#17719)*. Recognized by: *International Olympic Committee (IOC, #14408)*. [2022/XD3678/**D**]

♦ **International Florist Organisation (FLORINT)** **13616**

Head Office Horaplantsoen 20, 6717 LT Ede, Netherlands. T. +31641618140. E-mail: info@florint.org.
URL: http://www.florint.org/

History 9 Nov 1958, Strasbourg (France). Since 1994, a grouping of the type *European Economic Interest Grouping (EEIG, #06960)*. Former names and other names: *European Federation of Professional Florists Associations* – former (1958); *Federation of European Florists Groups* – former; *Fédération européenne des unions professionelles de fleuristes (FEUPF)* – former; *Vereinigung der Europäischen Fachverbände der Floristen* – former. **Aims** Facilitate or develop economic activities of members and those involved, whether individuals or federations of *professionals*; improve or increase results of the activities to which the EEIG is related; develop and keep brotherly relations among members; maintain the dignity and protect the interests of the profession; participate in elaborating both social and financial regulations concerning the profession; contribute to professional education and training of personnel; represent members' interests with international organizations, particularly those of the *European Union*; arbitrate in cases of unexpected differences. **Structure** General Meeting (annual, at Congress); Board of Directors (meeting twice a year). Taskforces (4): Education; Competitions; Commercial Development; European Affairs. **Languages** English, French, German. **Staff** Voluntary. **Finance** Sources: members' dues. Members' dues related to number of members of each organization. European funding for projects. **Activities** Awards/prizes/competitions; certification/accreditation; events/meetings; knowledge management/information dissemination; networking/liaising. **Events** *General Assembly* Amsterdam (Netherlands) 2016, *General Assembly* Brussels (Belgium) 2014, *General Assembly* Split (Croatia) 2013, *General Assembly* Brussels (Belgium) 2012, *General assembly / Annual Congress* Havirov (Czech Rep) 2011.

Members National florist associations in 19 countries:
Austria, Belgium, Croatia, Czechia, Denmark, Finland, France, Germany, Greece, Hungary, Italy, Netherlands, Norway, Poland, Russia, Slovenia, Spain, Switzerland, UK.
Pre-accession countries (10):
Armenia, Azerbaijan, Estonia, Latvia, Lithuania, Portugal, Romania, Serbia, Slovakia, Türkiye.

NGO Relations Cooperates with (2): *FLORNET (#09799)*; *WorldSkills Europe (#21790)*. [2022.05.07/XD0748/**F**]

- ♦ International Flow Battery Forum (meeting series)
- ♦ International Flower Trade Association / see UNION FLEURS (#20408)
- ♦ International Flow Visualization Society (inactive)
- ♦ International Flue-Cured Tobacco Growers' Association / see International Tobacco Growers' Association (#15694)

♦ **International Fluency Association (IFA)** **13617**

Pres address not obtained.
Treas address not obtained.
URL: http://www.theifa.org/

History Founding articles adopted 1990; revised 1992 and 1994. Bylaws adopted 1994; revised 2013. Registration: No/ID: 63-1128766, USA. **Aims** Promote the understanding of fluency, understanding and management of fluency disorders; improve the quality of life for persons with fluency disorders. **Structure** Board of Directors; Executive Board. Committees (9): Membership; Nominations, Elections and Awards; Finance; Meetings and Conferences; Professional Liaisons; Research and Publications; Self-Help and Consumer Affairs; Website and Technology; Instruction and Training. **Languages** English. **Finance** Sources: members' dues. **Events** *Joint World Congress on Stuttering and Cluttering* Montréal, QC (Canada) 2022, *Joint World Congress on Stuttering and Cluttering* Montréal, QC (Canada) 2021, *Joint World Congress on Stuttering and Cluttering* Hiroshima (Japan) 2018, *World Congress on Fluency Disorders* Lisbon (Portugal) 2015, *World Congress on Fluency Disorders* Tours (France) 2012. **Publications** *Journal of Fluency Disorders*. **Members** Individuals. Membership countries not specified. **NGO Relations** Cooperates with (2): *International Cluttering Association (ICA, #12603)*; *International Stuttering Association (ISA, #15621)*. *European League of Stuttering Associations (ELSA, #07673)*. [2022/XG6395/**C**]

- ♦ International Fluid Academy (internationally oriented national body)
- ♦ International Fluid Power Conference (meeting series)
- ♦ International Fluoridation Society (no recent information)
- ♦ International Flying Dutchman Class Organization (see: #21760)
- ♦ International Flying Fifteen Class Association (see: #21760)
- ♦ International Flying Junior Organization (see: #21760)
- ♦ International Flying Saucer Bureau (inactive)
- ♦ International Föderation Eisstock Sport (#13455)
- ♦ International Föderation der Kosmetikerinnen (#13344)
- ♦ International Foetal Medicine and Surgery Society / see International Fetal Medicine and Surgery Society (#13592)

♦ International Fog and Dew Association (IFDA) 13618

Pres Westfälische Wilhelms-Uni Münster, Klimatologie, Heisenbergstr 2, 48149 Münster, Germany. T. +492518333921.
URL: http://fogdew.org/

History 29 Jul 2016, Wroclaw (Poland). Founded at the 7th International Conference on Fog, Fog Collection, and Dew; took over conference series organizing from *FogQuest: sustainable water solutions.* **Structure** General Assembly; Board. **Activities** Events/meetings. **Events** *International Conference on Fog, Fog Collection and Dew* Fort Collins, CO (USA) 2023, *International Conference on Fog, Fog Collection and Dew* Taipei (Taiwan) 2019. **NGO Relations** *FogQuest: sustainable water solutions.* [2019/XM8647/c/**E**]

- ♦ International Folk Music Council / see International Council for Traditional Music (#13087)
- ♦ International Font Technology Association (inactive)
- ♦ International Food Additives Council (internationally oriented national body)

♦ International Food and Agribusiness Management Association (IFAMA) 13619

Exec Dir 922 NW Circle Blvd, Ste 160, 234, Corvallis OR 97330, USA. T. +15413685545. E-mail: ifama@ifama.org.
URL: http://www.ifama.org/

History 1993. Bylaws revised: July 2020. Former names and other names: *International Agribusiness Management Association (IAMA)* – former (1993). Registration: Charitable Organization 501(c)(3), No/ID: EIN: 74-2585021, Start date: 1992, USA. **Languages** English. **Staff** 3.00 FTE, paid. **Finance** Budget: US$ 500,000. **Activities** *World Food and Agribusiness Forum*; organizaes symposia. **Events** *World Congress* Alajuela (Costa Rica) 2022, *World Conference* Corvallis, OR (USA) 2021, *World Conference* Rotterdam (Netherlands) 2020, *World Conference* Rotterdam (Netherlands) 2020, *World Congress* Hangzhou (China) 2019. **Publications** *International Food and Agribusiness Management Review* (periodical). **Members** Individuals (approx 700) in 50 countries. Membership countries not specified. [2021/XD5867/**D**]

- ♦ International Food Aid Information System (inactive)
- ♦ International Food Authenticity Assurance Organization (unconfirmed)

♦ International Food and Beverage Alliance (IFBA) 13620

SG c/o Landmark Europe, Rue du Collège 27, 1050 Brussels, Belgium. T. +3228080644. Fax +3225028870. E-mail: secretariat@ifballiance.org.
Registered Office c/o WEALTHINGS SA, Chemin Frank-Thomas 34, 1208 Geneva, Switzerland.
URL: http://ifballiance.org/

History 2008. Registered in accordance with Swiss Civil Code. **Aims** Bring together global, regional and national food and non-alcoholic beverages companies around a common goal of helping consumers around the world to achieve balanced *diets* and healthy, active lifestyles. **Structure** General Assembly (annual); Executive Committee. **Publications** *IFBA Newsletter.*
Members Full – companies; Observer – companies; Associate – associations and organizations. Associate members in 7 countries:
Australia, Belgium, Brazil, Canada, Mexico, Singapore, USA.
Included in the above, 3 organizations listed in this Yearbook:
FoodDrinkEurope (#09841); Food Industry Asia (FIA); World Federation of Advertisers (WFA, #21407).
Consultative Status Consultative status granted from: *ECOSOC (#05331)* (Special). [2020/XJ9922/**C**]

♦ International Food and Beverage Association (IFBA) 13621

Sec 1 Choa Chu Kang Grove, ITE College West, Singapore 688236, Singapore. E-mail: ifbaworld@gmail.com.
URL: http://www.ifba-world.com/

History Registered 8 Feb 2012, Singapore: T12SS0023H. **Aims** Enhance the image of the industry and professionalism level; promote educational interests relating to hospitality; strengthen knowledge and professionalism in food and beverage industry; improve work environment and processes; create career progression; increase overall job satisfaction and lifelong employability; develop industry communication. **Structure** Annual General Meeting; Executive Committee. **Languages** English. **Activities** Advocacy/lobbying/activism; networking/liaising.
Members Full; Honorary; Associate. Members in 10 countries and territories:
Cambodia, China, Germany, Greece, Indonesia, Malaysia, Singapore, Switzerland, Taiwan, UK. [2016/XM7624/**C**]

- ♦ International Food Information Council (internationally oriented national body)
- ♦ International Food Information Service / see IFIS (#11101)
- ♦ International Food Institute (inactive)

♦ International Food Policy Research Institute (IFPRI) 13622

Institut international de recherche sur les politiques alimentaires – Instituto Internacional de Investigaciones sobre Politicas Alimentarias

Headquarters 1201 Eye St NW, 12th Fl, Washington DC 20005, USA. T. +12028625600. Fax +12024674439. E-mail: ifpri@cgiar.org.
URL: http://www.ifpri.org/

History Mar 1975. Founded following a recommendation of the *CGIAR System Organization (CGIAR, #03843).* Formally accepted as a member by CGIAR in 1979. **Aims** Provide research-based policy solutions that sustainably reduce poverty and end *hunger* and *malnutrition.* **Structure** Board of Trustees; Research and Outreach Divisions: (6); Regional Offices (4): East and Southern Africa – Addis Ababa (Ethiopia); West and Central Africa – Dakar (Senegal); East and Central Asia – Beijing (China); Middle East and North Africa – Cairo (Egypt). **Languages** English. **Staff** US based – 324; overseas – 257.
Finance Donors: governments of Bangladesh, Belgium, Finland, Japan, Malawi, Mali, Netherlands, Peru, Russia, and Yemen; agencies, foundations and other organizations, including the following listed in this Yearbook:
- *African Development Bank (ADB, #00283);*
- *Asian Development Bank (ADB, #01422);*
- *Australian Centre for International Agricultural Research (ACIAR);*
- *Bill and Melinda Gates Foundation (BMGF);*
- UK
- *Department for International Development (DFID, inactive);*
- *Deutsche Gesellschaft für Internationale Zusammenarbeit (GIZ);*
- *FAO (#09260);*
- *Ford Foundation (#09858);*
- *Inter-American Development Bank (IDB, #11427);*
- *Irish Aid;*
- *Swedish International Development Cooperation Agency (Sida);*
- *Swiss Agency for Development and Cooperation (SDC);*
- *UNDP (#20292);*
- *UNICEF (#20332);*
- *United Nations Foundation (UNF, #20563);*
- *United Nations University (UNU, #20642);*
- *United States Agency for International Development (USAID).*

Activities Politics/policy/regulatory; capacity building; knowledge management/information dissemination; research/documentation. **Events** *Conference on Accelerating the End of Hunger and Malnutrition* Bangkok (Thailand) 2018, *ReSAKSS-Asia Conference on Agriculture and Rural Transformation in Asia* Bangkok (Thailand) 2017, *Conference on Quantitative Methods for Integrated Food and Nutrition Security Measurements* Brussels (Belgium) 2017, *2020 Conference on Building Resilience for Food and Nutrition Security* Addis Ababa (Ethiopia) 2014, *International groundwater conference* Coimbatore (India) 2007. **Publications** Annual Report; books; book chapters; briefs; datasets; discussion papers; impact assessment; journal articles; reports; tools.
Members Board of Trustees: individuals in 13 countries:
Australia, Brazil, Canada, China, Hungary, India, Malawi, Morocco, Norway, Romania, Thailand, UK, USA.
Consultative Status Consultative status granted from: *ECOSOC (#05331)* (Ros C); *FAO (#09260)* (Liaison Status); *UNCTAD (#20285)* (Special Category); *WHO (#20950)* (Official).
IGO Relations Collaborates with:
- *African Union (AU, #00488);*
- *Association of Agricultural Research Institutions in the Near East and North Africa (AARINENA, #02364);*
- *Codex Alimentarius Commission (CAC, #04081);*
- *FAO (#09260);*
- *Institute of Nutrition of Central America and Panama (INCAP, #11285);*
- *Inter-American Institute for Cooperation on Agriculture (IICA, #11434);*
- *International Bank for Reconstruction and Development (IBRD, #12317)* (World Bank);
- *International Development Research Centre (IDRC, #13162);*
- *International Fund for Agricultural Development (IFAD, #13692);*
- *New Partnership for Africa's Development (NEPAD, #17091);*
- *United Nations Economic Commission for Africa (ECA, #20554);*
- *United Nations Framework Convention on Climate Change – Secretariat (UNFCCC, #20564);*
- *World Food Programme (WFP, #21510).*

Cooperates with the other CGIAR supported centres: *Africa Rice Center (AfricaRice, #00518); Bioversity International (#03262); International Center for Agricultural Research in the Dry Areas (ICARDA, #12466); International Crops Research Institute for the Semi-Arid Tropics (ICRISAT, #13116); International Livestock Research Institute (ILRI, #14062); International Rice Research Institute (IRRI, #14754).*
NGO Relations Cooperates with the other CGIAR supported centres: *Center for International Forestry Research (CIFOR, #03646); International Centre for Tropical Agriculture (#12527); International Institute of Tropical Agriculture (IITA, #13933); International Maize and Wheat Improvement Center (#14077); International Potato Center (#14627); International Water Management Institute (IWMI, #15867); World Agroforestry Centre (ICRAF, #21072); WorldFish (#21507).*
Also collaborates with more than 200 institutions, including the following listed in this Yearbook:
- *ACDI/VOCA;*
- *ActionAid (#00087);*
- *Association for Strengthening Agricultural Research in Eastern and Central Africa (ASARECA, #02933);*
- *CARE International (CI, #03429);*
- *Catholic Relief Services (CRS, #03608);*
- *Centre for Research on Sustainable Agriculture and Rural Development (Swaminathan Research Foundation);*
- *Global Alliance for Climate-Smart Agriculture (GACSA, #10189);*
- *Helen Keller International (HKI, #10902);*
- *Oxfam International (#17922);*
- *World Vision International (WVI, #21904).* [2019/XE6331/jv/**E**]

♦ International Food Security Network (IFSN) 13623

Global Coordinator c/o ActionAid International, House-08, Road-136, Gulshan 1, Dhaka 1212, Bangladesh. T. +88029894331. Fax +88028815087.
URL: http://www.ifsn.info/

Aims Strengthen regional food security networks to ensure food and nutritional security in southern countries. **Structure** International Secretariat.
Members Civil society organizations (over 1100) in 31 countries:
Angola, Bangladesh, Bolivia, Burkina Faso, Cambodia, Cape Verde, Colombia, Ecuador, El Salvador, Ethiopia, France, Gambia, Germany, Ghana, Guatemala, Guinea-Bissau, Honduras, India, Malawi, Mozambique, Nicaragua, Pakistan, Paraguay, Peru, Portugal, Sao Tomé-Principe, Senegal, Spain, Uganda, UK, Vietnam.
Sub-regional and Regional Networks (6):
Alianza por la Soberania, Autonomia y Seguridad Alimentaria y Nutricional (ASASAN); Asia Food Security Network (AFSN); ESA Food Security Network; Red Centroamericana de Seguridad y Soberania Alimentaria (REDCASSAN); *Rede Regional da Sociedade Civil para a Segurança Alimentar e Nutricional na CPLP (REDSAN-CPLP, #18648);* West Africa Food Security Network (WAFSN).
IGO Relations *European Commission (EC, #06633).* **NGO Relations** Core partners include: *ActionAid (#00087).* [2014/XJ0633/**F**]

- ♦ International Food Security and Nutrition Civil Society Mechanism / see Civil Society and Indigenous Peoples' Mechanism for Relations with the UN Committee on World Food Security (#03969)
- ♦ International Foodservice Manufacturers Association (internationally oriented national body)

♦ International Foot and Ankle Biomechanics Community (i-FAB) . . . 13624

Contact School of Health/Sport/Rehabilitation Sciences, Brian Blatchford Bldg – Rm P032, Univ of Salford, Salford, M5 4WT, UK.
URL: http://www.i-fab.org/

History 2 Jul 2007, Taipei (Taiwan), at a meeting of *International Society of Biomechanics (ISB, #14966).* **Aims** Improve understanding of foot and ankle biomechanics as it applies to health, disease, and the design, development and evaluation of foot and ankle surgery, and interventions such as footwear, insoles and surfaces. **Structure** Steering Group of 5 members. **Events** *Congress* Sao Paulo (Brazil) 2021, *Congress* New York, NY (USA) 2018, *Foot International Congress* Berlin (Germany) 2016, *Congress* Busan (Korea Rep) 2014, *Congress* Sydney, NSW (Australia) 2012. [2015/XJ1285/**C**]

- ♦ International Football Association Board (see: #13360)
- ♦ International Footwear and Leather Bureau (inactive)
- ♦ International FOP Association / see International Fibrodysplasia Ossificans Progressiva Association

♦ International Forecourt Standards Forum (IFSF) 13625

Administration Peershaws, Berewyk Hall Court, White Colne, Colchester, C06 2QB, UK. T. +441787221025. Fax +448707418774. E-mail: admin.manager@ifsf.org.
Chair address not obtained.
URL: http://www.ifsf.org/

History 1991. Registration: Companies House, No/ID: 4866237, Start date: 14 Aug 2003, England and Wales. **Aims** Enable technology standards for the benefit of retailers of *automotive fuel* and *energy.* **Structure** Forum of international petroleum retailers, suppliers and others. Working Groups; Branch Office in China. **Languages** English. **Staff** 1.00 FTE, paid. **Finance** Sources: members' dues; sale of products. **Activities** Events/meetings; standards/guidelines. **Events** *Conference* Prague (Czechia) 2022, *Conference* 2021, *Conference* 2020, *Conference* Budapest (Hungary) 2019, *Conference* Hamburg (Germany) 2018. **Publications** *IFSF Newsletter.* **Members** Petroleum and energy retailers and suppliers of equipment, systems and services to the retail petroleum and convenience sector. Membership countries not specified. [2022/XF4845/**F**]

- ♦ International Forening af Forhenvaerende EU-Medarbejdere (#02667)
- ♦ International Forensic Centre of Excellence for the Investigation of Genocide (internationally oriented national body)
- ♦ International Forensic Medicine Association (unconfirmed)

♦ International Forensic Strategic Alliance (IFSA) 13626

Pres Forensic Science South Australia, GPO Box 464, Adelaide SA 5001, Australia.
URL: https://www.ifsa-forensics.org/

History 2010. **Aims** Represent the global operational forensic science community dedicated to improvement of forensic science in all jurisdictions. **Structure** Rotating Presidency (every 2 years). **Activities** Events/meetings. **Events** *Annual Meeting* Seoul (Korea Rep) 2014, *Annual Meeting* Lyon (France) 2013, *Annual Meeting* Hobart, TAS (Australia) 2012, *Annual Meeting* Vienna (Austria) 2012, *Annual Meeting* Madeira (Portugal) 2011.
Members Regional networks (6):
Academia Iberoamericana de Criminalistica y Estudios Forenses (AICEF, #00012); American Society of Crime Laboratory Directors (ASCLD); *Asian Forensic Sciences Network (AFSN, #01488); European Network of Forensic Science Institutes (ENFSI, #07910);* National Institute of Forensic Science Australia New Zealand; Southern Africa Regional Forensic Science Network. [2021/XJ4589/y/**C**]

♦ International Forest Products Transport Association (IFPTA) 13627

Contact c/o Quint Strategies, 511 Avenue of the Americas, Ste 368, New York NY 10011, USA. T. +12125379130. Fax +18146909063. E-mail: info@ifpta.org.
URL: http://www.ifpta.org/

History Founded Oct 1982. **Aims** Establish a permanent framework to ensure continued vitality, within which experience and information can be shared in a professional and timely manner. **Structure** Board of Directors. **Languages** English. **Staff** Voluntary. **Activities** Events/meetings; networking/liaising. **Events** *PPI Transport Symposium / Symposium* Bremen (Germany) 2015, *PPI transport symposium / Symposium* Amsterdam (Netherlands) 2011, *Biennial international forestry, wood resources and technology conference for China* Beijing (China) 1993, *International symposium on transport, handling and distribution of pulp, paper and their raw materials* New Orleans, LA (USA) 1987. **Publications** *IFPTA Journal* (4 a year) – members only. **Members** Professional involved in transport, handling, warehousing and distribution of forest products. Membership countries not specified. [2015.02.11/XG8403/**D**]

♦ International Forestry Institute, Russia (unconfirmed)
♦ International Forestry and Resources Institutions (internationally oriented national body)

♦ International Forestry Students' Association (IFSA) 13628

Secretariat Tennenbacher Strasse 4, 79106 Freiburg, Germany. E-mail: info@ifsa.net.
URL: http://www.ifsa.net/

History 1990, Lisbon (Portugal). Founded during the International Forestry Students Symposium (IFSS). First IFSS held in 1973, London (UK), and resulting from this and subsequent Symposia *INFOCENTER* was created, an office established to coordinate exchange of information among forestry students. During 18th IFSS, 1988, Lisbon (Portugal), it was decided to expand cooperation beyond the Symposium by founding the IFSA. INFOCENTER took on official role as IFSA's communicative and informational organ. Became a truly worldwide organization when new statutes approved at 5th General Assembly and 22nd IFSS, 1994, Switzerland. Registration: Germany. **Aims** Enrich the formal education of forestry students through extracurricular activities; create cultural understanding through international meetings; enable students to take part in international policy events. **Structure** General Assembly; Board; Commissions; Regional Representatives. **Languages** English. **Staff** Voluntary. **Finance** Sources: grants; members' dues; sponsorship. **Activities** Awards/prizes/competitions; events/meetings; knowledge management/information dissemination; networking/liaising. **Events** *Asia Pacific Regional Meeting* Daejeon (Korea Rep) 2019, *International Forestry Students Symposium* Tartu (Estonia) 2019, *International Forestry Students Symposium* Mexico 2018, *International Forestry Students Symposium* South Africa 2017, *International Forestry Students Symposium* Vienna (Austria) 2016. **Publications** *IFSA News*; *IFSA Online Editorial*.
Members Ordinary in 43 countries and territories:
Australia, Austria, Belgium, Belize, Brazil, Bulgaria, Canada, Colombia, Croatia, Czechia, Denmark, Estonia, Finland, France, Germany, Ghana, Hungary, India, Indonesia, Iran Islamic Rep, Italy, Japan, Korea Rep, Latvia, Mexico, Netherlands, Nigeria, Philippines, Poland, Russia, Serbia, Slovakia, Slovenia, South Africa, Spain, Sweden, Switzerland, Taiwan, Türkiye, UK, Ukraine, USA, Zimbabwe.
Supporting members (individuals) in 11 countries:
Denmark, Finland, France, Germany, Greece, Ireland, Italy, Netherlands, Spain, Sweden, UK.
Consultative Status Consultative status granted from: *ECOSOC (#05331)* (Special); *UNEP (#20299)*. **IGO Relations** Observer status with (1): *Ministerial Conference on the Protection of Forests in Europe (FOREST EUROPE, #16817)*. Member of (1): *European Forest Institute (EFI, #07297)*. Cooperates with (1): *United Nations Forum on Forests (UNFF, #20562)*. **NGO Relations** Member of (1): *Global Youth Biodiversity Network (GYBN, #10664)*. Cooperates with (3): *European Forest Science Academic Network (Silva Network, #07300)*; *Informal Forum of International Student Organizations (IFISO, #11193)*; *International Union of Forest Research Organizations (IUFRO, #15774)*. [2021.09.02/XD6648/**D**]

♦ International Forfaiting Association / see International Trade and Forfaiting Association (#15705)
♦ International Formula 18 Class Association (see: #21760)
♦ International Formula Windsurfing Class (see: #21760)
♦ International Fortification Council / see International Fortress Council (#13629)

♦ International Fortress Council (IFC) 13629

SG Mariaplaats 51, 2511 LM Utrecht, Netherlands. E-mail: info@coehoorn.nl – secretariat@internationalfortresscouncil.org.
URL: http://www.internationalfortresscouncil.org/

History Oct 1989, The Hague (Netherlands), as *International Fortification Council (IFC)*. Registered in accordance with Dutch law. **Aims** Promote study and *preservation* of *fortifications*. **Structure** Assembly (annual); Executive Committee. **Languages** English. **Staff** None. **Finance** Members' dues. Annual budget: about euro 1,500. **Publications** *Multilingual Fortification Dictionary (MFD)* – online.
Members Organizations (" indicates founding members) in 11 countries:
Austria, Belgium (*), Croatia, Czechia, France, Germany (*), Luxembourg, Netherlands (*), Switzerland, UK (*), USA.
Included in the above, 1 organization listed in this Yearbook: [2017.12.08/XJ1165/**D**]

♦ International Forum (internationally oriented national body)
♦ International Forum of Accounting Standard Setters (unconfirmed)

♦ International Forum for Acute Care Trialists (InFACT) 13630

Contact address not obtained. E-mail: marshallj@smh.ca – gomersall@cuhk.edu.hk.
URL: http://www.infactglobal.org/

History 2008. **Aims** Improve the care of acutely ill patients around the world through high quality clinical research into the causes, prevention, and management of acute, life-threatening illness. **Structure** Steering Committee. **Events** *Annual Meeting* Whistler, BC (Canada) 2017. **Publications** *InFACT Newsletter*.
Members Full in 12 countries:
Australia, Brazil, Canada, China, Germany, Greece, Ireland, Italy, Netherlands, New Zealand, UK, USA.
Also members in the Scandinavian region.
Included in the above, 2 organizations listed in this Yearbook:
European Society of Intensive Care Medicine (ESICM, #08632); *Latin American Sepsis Institute (ILAS)*.
NGO Relations Member of: *Global Sepsis Alliance (GSA, #10590)*. [2018/XJ4701/y/**F**]

♦ International Forum for Back and Neck Pain Research in Primary Care (meeting series)
♦ International Forum of Bible Agencies / see Forum of Bible Agencies International (#09903)

♦ International Forum on Business Ethical Conduct (IFBEC) 13631

Exec Sec address not obtained. T. +17033581064.
URL: https://ifbec.info/

History Founded 2010, by members of the (US) Aerospace Industries Association and *Aerospace and Defence Industries Association of Europe (ASD, #00146)*. Full title: *International Forum on Business Ethical Conduct for the Aerospace and Defense Industry (IFBEC)*. **Aims** Exchange information on best practices in the area of ethical business practices and global trends among industry participants. **Structure** Steering Committee. **Languages** English. **Finance** Members' dues. **Activities** Events/meetings. **Events** *Annual Conference* Washington, DC (USA) 2019, *Annual Conference* Paris (France) 2018, *Annual Conference* Washington, DC (USA) 2017, *Annual Conference* London (UK) 2016, *Annual Conference* Boston, MA (USA) 2015. [2020.03.11/XM8442/**F**]

♦ International Forum on Business Ethical Conduct for the Aerospace and Defense Industry / see International Forum on Business Ethical Conduct (#13631)
♦ International Forum of Catholic Action (#09919)

♦ International Forum for the Challenges of Peace Operations (Challenges Forum) 13632

Dir c/o Folke Bernadotte Ac, Drottning Kristinas väg 37, SE-114 28 Stockholm, Sweden. T. +46104562300. E-mail: info@challengesforum.org.
URL: http://www.challengesforum.org/

History 1996. **Aims** Shape the debate on peace operations by identifying critical challenges facing military, police and civilian operations; promote awareness of emerging issues and generate recommendations for solutions for the consideration of the broader international peace operations community. **Structure** Partners' Meeting; Partners' Organizations Advisory Committee; International Secretariat. **Events** *Forum* Delhi (India) 2022, *Forum* Berlin (Germany) 2021, *Politics, peacebuilding, transition, and leadership* Montréal, QC (Canada) 2019, *Forum* Stockholm (Sweden) 2018. **Publications** Annual Forum Report; policy briefs.
Members Partner organizations in 24 countries:
Argentina, Armenia, Australia, Canada, China, Egypt, Ethiopia, France, Germany, India, Indonesia, Japan, Jordan, Nigeria, Norway, Pakistan, Russia, South Africa, Sweden, Switzerland, Türkiye, UK, Uruguay, USA.
International organization:
World Federation of United Nations Associations (WFUNA, #21499).
IGO Relations Housed at: *Folke Bernadotte Academy (FBA)*. [2022.11.07/XM8331/**F**]

♦ International Forum for Child Welfare (IFCW) 13633

Forum international pour la protection de l'enfance (FIPE) – Foro Internacional para el Bienestar de la Infancia

Sec Indonesian Child Welfare Foundation, Jl Penghulu no 18 Bidaracina, Jakarta 1330, Indonesia. T. +62218190451. E-mail: icwfhq@yahoo.com.
Pres Cape Town Child Welfare, PO Box 374, Gtesville, Cape Town, 7766, South Africa. T. +27216383127. Fax +27216384193.
URL: http://www.ifcw.org/

History 26 Jun 1989, Haikko (Finland). Registered in accordance with Swiss Civil Code. **Aims** Work for *children* worldwide to improve the quality of their lives and to enhance the opportunities for the development of their full potential; strengthen non-governmental organizations worldwide in their direct and indirect service to children and *families*; organize and improve information exchange and cooperation between members; educate world opinion on the interests and overall well being of children everywhere. **Structure** General Assembly (annual). Executive Committee, consisting of President and Treasurer, Vice President, Deputy President, Secretary, Assistant Secretary, Special Advisor and Members. Regional Offices (2): *African Forum for Child Welfare (AFCW, no recent information)*; *Asia-Pacific Forum for Child Welfare (APFCW, no recent information)*. **Finance** Members' dues. Start-up fees. **Activities** Events/meetings. **Events** *Annual World Forum* Santa Fe, NM (USA) 2016, *Annual World Forum / Annual Worldforum for Child Welfare* Helsinki (Finland) 2014, *Annual World Forum / Annual Worldforum for Child Welfare* Naples (Italy) 2012, *Annual world forum / Annual Worldforum for Child Welfare* Melbourne, VIC (Australia) 2011, *Annual world forum / Annual Worldforum for Child Welfare* New York, NY (USA) 2010. **Publications** *IFCW Newsletter*. Conference proceedings.
Members National and international voluntary child welfare organizations; foundations; governmental and intergovernmental agencies; representatives of the media and academia; individual specialists. Members (102) in 43 countries and territories:
Argentina, Australia, Bangladesh, Belgium, Canada, Chile, Colombia, Costa Rica, Ecuador, Estonia, Finland, France, Gambia, Germany, Ghana, India, Indonesia, Ireland, Israel, Italy, Kenya, Latvia, Luxembourg, Mauritius, Mexico, Morocco, Netherlands, New Zealand, Philippines, Portugal, Russia, Senegal, Slovenia, South Africa, Spain, Sweden, Taiwan, Thailand, Uganda, UK, USA, Venezuela, Zambia.
Consultative Status Consultative status granted from: *ECOSOC (#05331)* (Special). **IGO Relations** Associated with Department of Global Communications of the United Nations. **NGO Relations** Member of: *Fédération internationale des communautés éducatives (FICE-International, #09622)*. [2014/XF1302/**F**]

♦ International Forum of Culture and Literature for Paving Peace / see IFLAC – International Forum for the Literature and Culture of Peace (#11102)
♦ International Forum for the Culture of World Peace / see IFLAC – International Forum for the Literature and Culture of Peace (#11102)
♦ International Forum for Democratic Studies (internationally oriented national body)
♦ International FORUM on Development Service / see International Forum for Volunteering in Development (#13659)

♦ International Forum on Diplomatic Training (IFDT) 13634

Contact Diplomatische Akad Wien, Favoritenstrasse 15a, 1040 Vienna, Austria.
URL: http://forum.diplomacy.edu/

History 1972, Vienna (Austria), as an annual Meeting of Deans and Directors of Diplomatic Academies and Institutes of International Relations. **Aims** Discuss issues of modern diplomacy and trends in diplomatic education. **Activities** Networking/liaising; events/meetings.
Members Full in 53 countries:
Angola, Argentina, Armenia, Australia, Austria, Azerbaijan, Bahrain, Belgium, Brazil, Bulgaria, Canada, Chile, China, Congo DR, Croatia, Czechia, Estonia, Ethiopia, Georgia, Germany, Guatemala, Haiti, Hungary, India, Indonesia, Israel, Italy, Japan, Korea Rep, Kosovo, Lithuania, Malaysia, Montenegro, Netherlands, Nicaragua, North Macedonia, Peru, Philippines, Poland, Qatar, Romania, Russia, Serbia, Singapore, South Africa, Spain, Sri Lanka, Switzerland, Thailand, UK, Ukraine, United Arab Emirates, USA.
Included in the above, 11 organizations listed in this Yearbook:
Asia-Pacific College of Diplomacy (APCD); *Centre for International Studies and Diplomacy (CISD)*; *College of Europe (#04105)*; *Diplo Foundation*; *European Academy of Diplomacy (EAD)*; *Fletcher School of Law and Diplomacy*; *Geneva Centre for Security Policy (GCSP)*; *Institute for the Study of Diplomacy (ISD)*; *Moskovskij Gosudarstvennyj Institut Mezdunarodnyh Otnosenij (MGIMO)*; *Netherlands Institute of International Relations – Clingendael*; *Società Italiana per l'Organizzazione Internazionale (SIOI)*. [2019.02.12/XM5609/y/**F**]

♦ International Forum for Drug and Alcohol Testing (unconfirmed)

♦ International Forum on Engineering Decision Making (IFED) 13635

Chairman Dept of Civil Engineering, Univ of Calgary, 2500 University Drive NW, Calgary AB T2N 1N4, Canada. T. +14032207400. Fax +14032827026.
URL: http://www.ifed.byg.dtu.dk/

History Set up by Five-University Consortium on Uncertainty, Risk and Decision Making in Engineering. **Aims** Stimulate new initiatives in engineering decision making and risk analysis for engineering systems. **Structure** 'IFED Consortium' comprising Chairman, 2 Vice-Chairmen and 2 further members. Advisory Council. **Events** *Forum* Manly, NSW (Australia) 2019, *Forum* Lake Louise, AB (Canada) 2012, *Forum* Stoos (Switzerland) 2010, *Forum* Hakone (Japan) 2009, *Optimal strategies for disaster and hazard mitigation* Port Stephens, NSW (Australia) 2007. [2013/XM1744/**F**]

♦ International FORUM of Fire Research Directors 13636

Chair c/o VTT, PO Box 1000, FI-02044 Espoo, Finland.
URL: https://www.fireforum.org/

History 1991. **Aims** Reduce the burden of fire (including the loss of life and property, and effects of fire on the environment and heritage). **Activities** Awards/prizes/competitions; events/meetings; networking/liaising.
Members Individuals in 7 countries:
Canada, China, Finland, France, Japan, Norway, USA.
NGO Relations Cooperates with (4): *European Group of Organisations for Fire Testing, Inspection and Certification (EGOLF, #07427)*; *International Association for Fire Safety Science (IAFSS, #11892)*; *International Council for Research and Innovation in Building and Construction (CIB, #13069)*; *International Organization for Standardization (ISO, #14473)*. [2023/AA3065/v/**F**]

♦ International Forum on Globalization (IFG) 13637

Contact 1009 General Kennedy Ave, Suite 2, San Francisco CA 94129, USA. T. +14155617650. Fax +14155617651. E-mail: ifg@ifg.org.
URL: http://www.ifg.org/

History Jan 1994, San Francisco CA (USA). **Aims** Expose multiple effects of economic globalization in order to stimulate debate; seek to reverse the globalization process by encouraging ideas and activities which revitalize local economies and communities and ensure long term *ecological* stability; educate activists, policy makers, the general public and the media about the negative effects of economic globalization; advocate policies that are more equitable, democratic and ecologically sustainable. **Structure** Board of Directors of 16 members. **Finance** Members' dues. Budget (annual): US$ 1.2 million. **Activities** Developing comprehensive website that documents alternatives models and visions with an aim to: document "living" alternatives – existing alternative models now in action such as renewable energy initiatives, Slow Food mouvements, seed saving practices, fair trade co-ops and participatory budget practices; catalyze a global alternatives mouvement by providing contact information of groups focusing on this work; demonstrate that their are civil society mouvements and governments which have positive, intelligent inputs. Committees (3): Globalization of Water; Global Finance; Corporations. Forest and Globalization Working Group. Programmes: Food and Agriculture; Alternatives to Globalization; Environmental Impacts of Economic Globalization; Technology and Globalization; Indigenous Peoples and Globalization. Organizes *'Teach Ins'*. **Events** *Economic globalization and the role of the world trade organization* Seattle, WA (USA) 1999, *Meeting* Ulm (Germany) 1997. **Publications** *IFG Bulletin*.

Paradigm Wars: Indigenous Peoples' Resistance to Globalization (2nd ed 2006); *Alternatives to Economic Globalization* (2nd ed); *Fatal Harvest: The Tragedy of Industrial Agriculture*. Reports; documents; booklets. **Members** Associates (individuals representing over 60 organizations) in 25 countries. Membership countries not specified. **NGO Relations** Member of: *Climate Justice Now ! (CJN!, inactive)*; *World Social Forum (WSF, #21797)*. [2016/XF4220/F]

- ♦ International Forum for Hypertension Control in Africa / see International Forum for Hypertension Control and Prevention in Africa (#13638)
- ♦ International Forum for Hypertension Control and CVD Prevention in Africa / see International Forum for Hypertension Control and Prevention in Africa (#13638)

♦ International Forum for Hypertension Control and Prevention in Africa (IFHA) 13638

Exec Pres ULB – Erasme Hosp, Lennik Road 808, 1070 Brussels, Belgium. T. +3225553907. Fax +3225556713.
Gen Sec Cardiology – Dept of Medicine, Univ of Nigeria Teaching Hospital, Enugu 40001, Nigeria.
History 2003, Brussels (Belgium). Also referred to as *International Forum for Hypertension Control in Africa* and *International Forum for Hypertension Control and CVD Prevention in Africa*. **NGO Relations** Associate member of: *World Heart Federation (WHF, #21562)*. Member of: *The NCD Alliance (NCDA, #16963)*. [2008/XM0007/F]

- ♦ International Forum of Immunonutrition for Education and Research / see International Society for Immunonutrition (#15194)

♦ International Forum of Independent Audit Regulators (IFIAR) 13639

Exec Dir 18F Otemachi Financial City Grand Cube, 1-9-2 Otemachi, Chiyoda-ku, Tokyo, 100-0004 Japan. T. +81345103495. Fax +81345103499. E-mail: secretariat@ifiar.org.
URL: http://www.ifiar.org/
History 15 Sep 2006. **Aims** Serve the public interest, including investors, by enhancing audit oversight globally. **Structure** Plenary Meeting (annual); Board; Working Groups (6). **Languages** English. **Finance** Members' dues. **Activities** Knowledge management/information dissemination; monitoring/evaluation. **Events** *Plenary Meeting* Tokyo (Japan) 2022, *Plenary Meeting* Tokyo (Japan) 2021, *Plenary Meeting* Zurich (Switzerland) 2020, *Inspection Workshop* Paris (France) 2019, *Plenary Meeting* Tokyo (Japan) 2017. **Publications** Annual Report; Inspection Findings Survey Reports; press releases; announcements.
Members Independent audit oversight authorities in 53 countries and territories:
Albania, Australia, Austria, Belgium, Botswana, Brazil, Bulgaria, Canada, Cayman Is, Croatia, Cyprus, Czechia, Denmark, Egypt, Finland, France, Georgia, Germany, Gibraltar, Greece, Hungary, Indonesia, Ireland, Italy, Japan, Korea Rep, Liechtenstein, Lithuania, Luxembourg, Malaysia, Mauritius, Netherlands, New Zealand, Norway, Philippines, Poland, Portugal, Russia, Saudi Arabia, Singapore, Slovakia, Slovenia, South Africa, Spain, Sri Lanka, Sweden, Switzerland, Taiwan, Thailand, Türkiye, UK, United Arab Emirates, USA.
Observers (7):
Basel Committee on Banking Supervision (BCBS, #03183); *European Commission (EC, #06633)*; *Financial Stability Board (FSB, #09770)*; *International Association of Insurance Supervisors (IAIS, #11966)*; *International Bank for Reconstruction and Development (IBRD, #12317)* (World Bank); *International Organization of Securities Commissions (IOSCO, #14470)*; Public Interest Oversight Board (PIOB). [2020/XM3705/y/F]

♦ International Forum on Industrial Bioprocesses (IFIBiop) 13640

Administrator c/o Polytech Clermont Ferrand, Univ Blasie Pascal, 63174 Aubière, France. E-mail: ifibiop@gmail.com.
Chief Exec Biotechnology Div, CSIR-Natl Inst for Interdisciplinary Science and Technology, Industrial Estate, Thiruvananthapuram, Kerala 695019, Thiruvananthapuram KERALA 695019, India.
URL: http://www.ifibiop.org/
History Set up following International Congress in Bioprocesses in Food industries (ICBF), 2004, Clermont-Ferrand (France). Former names and other names: *International Bioprocessing Association – An International Forum on Industrial Bioprocesses (IBA-IFIBiop)* – full title; *IBA Forum* – alias. **Aims** Organize an efficient and structured networking in the field of industrial biotechnology and biological engineering, food engineering, biofuels and biorefineries. **Structure** Central Council. **Languages** English. **Staff** 0.50 FTE, paid; 3.00 FTE, voluntary. **Finance** Sources: donations; in-kind support; members' dues; sponsorship. **Activities** Awards/prizes/competitions; events/meetings. **Events** *International Conference on Bioprocessing (IBA-IFIBiop 2022)* Kaohsiung (Taiwan) 2022, *International Forum on Industrial Bioprocesses* Miri (Malaysia) 2019, *SWTM : International Conference on Sustainable Solid Waste Treatments and Management* Yangling (China) 2019, *International Forum on Industrial Bioprocesses* Wuxi (China) 2017, *International Forum on Industrial Bioprocesses* Lille (France) 2014. **Publications** Books; articles.
Members Individuals in 32 countries and territories:
Argentina, Australia, Austria, Belgium, Brazil, Canada, China, Cyprus, Finland, France, Germany, Greece, Hong Kong, India, Indonesia, Japan, Korea Rep, Malaysia, Mexico, Netherlands, Nigeria, Norway, Portugal, Singapore, Spain, Sweden, Taiwan, Thailand, Türkiye, UK, USA, Vietnam.
IGO Relations None. **NGO Relations** None. [2022.10.16/XJ9075/t/F]

- ♦ International Forum for Innovative Northeast Asia Strategy (internationally oriented national body)

♦ International Forum of Insurance Guarantee Schemes (IFIGS) 13641

Contact 300 North Meridian Street, Suite 2500, Indianapolis IN 46204, USA. T. +13172371201. E-mail: sara.powell@faegredrinker.com.
URL: http://www.ifigs.org/
History May 2013. Registration: EU Transparency Register, No/ID: 228119235464-27, Start date: 17 Jul 2019. **Aims** Facilitate and promote international cooperation between insurance guarantee schemes, and other stakeholder organizations with an interest in policy holder protection. **Structure** Management Committee; Working Groups (4). **Events** *General Meeting* 2020, *Business Unusual – Normal, Disrupted* Malaysia 2020, *General Meeting* Washington, DC (USA) 2019, *General Meeting* Bucharest (Romania) 2018, *General Meeting* Bangkok (Thailand) 2017.
Members Full; Associate; Observer. Full in 20 countries and territories:
Australia, Canada, Denmark, Ecuador, France, Germany, Greece, Isle of Man, Kenya, Korea Rep, Malaysia, Norway, Poland, Romania, Singapore, Spain, Taiwan, Thailand, UK, USA.
Associate in 2 countries and territories:
Egypt, Hong Kong.
Observer in 1 country:
Indonesia. [2021.06.02/XM8501/F]

- ♦ International Forum – International Forum on Quality and Safety in Healthcare (meeting series)

♦ International Forum for Investor Education (IFIE) 13642

Sec/Treas c/o ANBIMA, Av República do Chile 230, andar 13, Centro, Rio de Janeiro RJ, 20031-919, Brazil. T. +552138143800. Fax +552134714230.
URL: http://www.ifie.org/
History Early 2003, deriving from *Working Group on Investor Education* of *International Council of Securities Associations (ICSA, #13071)*. Set up as an independent organization, early 2005. **Aims** Improve investor education on a worldwide basis so that consumers in all jurisdictions are able to make informed choices about financial products and investments. **Events** *Global Investor Education Conference* Tokyo (Japan) 2018, *Investor Education Conference* Toronto, ON (Canada) 2013, *Investor Education Conference* Seoul (Korea Rep) 2012, *Global investor education conference* Cairo (Egypt) 2010, *Joint seminar on investor education* Osaka (Japan) 2009. **Publications** *IFIE Newsletter*. Clearinghouse.
Members Full in 10 countries and territories:
Brazil, Canada, Egypt, India, Japan, Korea Rep, Malaysia, Switzerland, Taiwan, USA.
NGO Relations Cooperates with: *International Organization of Securities Commissions (IOSCO, #14470)*. [2017/XM3655/y/F]

♦ International Forum of Jewish Scouts (IFJS) 13643

Forum international des scouts juifs
Contact address not obtained. E-mail: info@jewishscoutsforum.org.
URL: http://www.jewishscoutsforum.org/
Aims Strengthen and enrich the Jewish identity of young Jews around the world by encouraging them to join Jewish Scouts organization. **Languages** English, French, Hebrew, Portuguese, Spanish. **Staff** 1.00 FTE, paid. [2017.03.28/XJ0769/E]

- ♦ International Forum for the Literature and Culture of Peace / see IFLAC – International Forum for the Literature and Culture of Peace (#11102)
- ♦ International Forum of Liver Surgery (meeting series)

♦ International Forum of Meteorological Societies (IFMS) 13644

Pres 1755 St-Regis, Suite 100, Dollard-des-Ormeaux QC H9B 2M9, Canada. E-mail: ha@info-electronics.com.
URL: http://www.ifms.org/
History 13 Jan 2009, Phoenix AZ (USA). Granted status as 501(c)(3) USA nonprofit organization, 2018. **Aims** Facilitate exchange of knowledge, experience and information among the world's national and regional meteorological societies. **Structure** Council. **Languages** English. **Staff** 0.25 FTE, voluntary. **Finance** No operating budget. **Events** *Global Meeting* Xiamen (China) 2011, *Global Meeting* Atlanta, GA (USA) 2010.
Members National and regional organizations in 27 countries and territories:
Argentina, Australia, Canada, China, Cuba, Czechia, Ethiopia, Finland, Hong Kong, Hungary, India, Italy, Japan, Kenya, Korea Rep, Mexico, Nepal, New Zealand, Philippines, Portugal, South Africa, Spain, Sudan, Taiwan, Tanzania UR, UK, USA.
Included in the above, 8 organizations listed in this Yearbook:
East African Meteorological Society (EAMS, #05187); *European Meteorological Society (EMS, #07786)*; *Federación Latinoamericana e Ibérica de Sociedades de Meteorologia (FLISMET, #09354)*; *International Association for Urban Climate (IAUC, #12251)*; *International Association of Broadcast Meteorology (IABM, #11740)*; *International Association of Meteorology and Atmospheric Sciences (IAMAS, #12031)*; *International Society of Biometeorology (ISB, #14969)*; *World Meteorological Organization (WMO, #21649)*. [2019.06.05/XJ5014/y/F]

♦ International Forum for Minisurgery of Varicose Veins 13645

Internationales Forum für Minichirurgie der Varizen
Contact Rossmarkt 23, 60311 Frankfurt-Main, Germany. T. +4969284044.
URL: http://www.phlebo-varady.de/sites/en-forum.html
History 20 Mar 1993, Frankfurt-Main (Germany). **Aims** Acquire the approporate appreciation for the minisurgery method. **Structure** Board; Advisory Committee. **Activities** Training/education; events/meetings; knowledge management/information dissemination. **Events** *Workshop for Phlebology, Lymphology and Angiology* Riga (Latvia) 2023, *Workshop for Phlebology, Lymphology and Angiology* St Petersburg (Russia) 2022, *Workshop for Phlebology, Lymphology and Angiology* Bratislava (Slovakia) 2021, *Workshop for Phlebology, Lymphology and Angiology* Vienna (Austria) 2021, *Workshop for Phlebology, Lymphology and Angiology* Vienna (Austria) 2020. **NGO Relations** *Baltic Society of Phlebology (BSP, #03153)*. [2015/XJ9979/F]

♦ International Forum on Mood and Anxiety Disorders (IFMAD) 13646

Main Office c/o Publi Creations, 74 blvd d'Italie, 98000 Monte Carlo, Monaco. T. +37797973554. Fax +37797973550. E-mail: ifmad@publicreations.com.
URL: http://www.ifmad.org/
History 2000. Founded by Prof Siegfried Kasper and Prof Stuart Montgomery, supported by a scientific committee consisting of leading figures in mood and anxiety disorders worldwide. **Aims** Raise awareness of the latest international thinking and innovations in mood and anxiety disorders; promote exchange of ideas across the global psychiatric community. **Structure** Committee, comprising Chairman, Co-Chairman and 32 Scientific Advisers. **Languages** English. **Activities** Events/meetings; training/education. **Events** *Congress* 2021, *Congress* Vienna (Austria) 2019, *Congress* Madrid (Spain) 2017, *Congress* Rome (Italy) 2016, *Congress* Prague (Czech Rep) 2015. **Publications** Scientific Programme; abstract book. **IGO Relations** None. **NGO Relations** Cooperates with (2): *Association Internationale pour la promotion de Formations Spécialisées en Médecine et en Sciences Biologiques (AFISM, #02733)*; *International Society for Affective Disorders (ISAD, #14910)*. [2020/XM3976/F]

- ♦ International Forum of National NGO Platforms / see Forus (#09934)
- ♦ International Forum of Oceanic Races (no recent information)
- ♦ International Forum for Peace (inactive)
- ♦ International Forum of the Person Centered Approach (meeting series)

♦ International Forum of Psychosis and Bipolarity (IFPB) 13647

Contact address not obtained. T. +442088788289. Fax +442083380714.
URL: http://www.ifpb.info/
History Set up at *International Review of Bipolar Disorders (IRBD)*. Original title: *European Bipolar Forum (EBF)*. Current title adopted when IRBD merged with Winter Workshop on Psychosis to become *International Review of Psychosis and Bipolarity*. **Aims** Broaden the understanding of psychosis and *bipolar disorders* and the relationship between the two, on an international basis; raise public and political awareness about the importance of the understanding and treatment of psychosis and bipolar disorders internationally; strengthen the standard, availability and uniformity of psychosis and bipolar disorder *treatments*; create and maintain continuing medical education accreditation. **Structure** Committee, comprising President, Secretary and 2 members. Scientific Secretariat. **Languages** English. **Staff** 2.50 FTE, paid. **Finance** Members' dues. Other sources: Delegate fees; sponsorship. **Events** *Annual Conference* Lisbon (Portugal) 2015, *Annual Conference / Annual Meeting* Athens (Greece) 2014, *Annual Conference / Annual Meeting* Seville (Spain) 2013, *Annual Conference / Annual Meeting* Nice (France) 2012, *Annual Conference* Rome (Italy) 2011. **Publications** *Verba Mentis* – electronic newsletter. [2013.09.10/XJ1368/F]

- ♦ International Forum for Public Health (unconfirmed)

♦ International Forum of Public Universities (IFPU) 13648

Forum international des universités publiques (FIUP)
SG Nankai Univ, Room 201, Aichi Guest-house, Wenjin Road 94, Nankai District, 30071 Tianjin, China. T. +862223503481. Fax +862223503481. E-mail: ifpunankai@gmail.com.
URL: http://www.ifpu-fiup.org/
History 11 Oct 2007, following meetings held in Montréal (Canada) in 2004 and Brussels (Belgium) in 2005. **Aims** Enhance mutual understanding among IFPU professors, integrating possible resources for supporting teachers among members, and facilitating the application of joint research projects in accordance with international influential events or organizations. **Structure** Annual General Meeting. **Languages** Chinese, English. Also members' languages. **Staff** 2.00 FTE, paid. **Finance** Members' dues. **Activities** Research/documentation; networking/liaising; training/education; events/meetings. **Events** *Annual General Meeting* Tianjin (China) 2016, *Deans and Experts Meeting* Tianjin (China) 2016.
Members Universities (8) in 7 countries:
Canada, China, Czechia, Morocco, Poland, Spain, Switzerland. [2017.07.19/XM4644/F]

- ♦ International Forum on Quality and Safety in Healthcare (meeting series)
- ♦ International Forum for Reproduction Rights Organizations / see International Federation of Reproduction Rights Organizations (#13527)

♦ International Forum for Road Transport Technology (IFRTT) 13649

Sec c/o Advantia Transport Consulting, PO Box 145, Diamond Creek, Melbourne VIC 3089, Australia.
URL: http://www.road-transport-technology.org/
History 1986, Canada. after 1st Heavy Vehicle Weights and Dimensions Symposium. **Aims** Provide a forum for discussion of issues related to the weights and dimensions of heavy vehicles. **Structure** Board of Trustees. **Activities** *Heavy Vehicle Transport Technology Symposium (HVTT)*. **Events** *Biennial International Symposium on Heavy Vehicle Transport Technology* Rotterdam (Netherlands) 2018, *Biennial International Symposium on Heavy Vehicle Transport Technology* Rotorua (New Zealand) 2016, *Biennial International Symposium on Heavy Vehicle Transport Technology* Stockholm (Sweden) 2012, *Biennial international symposium on heavy vehicle transport technology / Symposium* Melbourne, VIC (Australia) 2010, *Biennial international symposium on heavy vehicle transport technology* Paris (France) 2008. **NGO Relations** *International Society for Weigh-In-Motion (ISWIM, #15548)*. [2018/XJ3334/F]

♦ International Forum for Rural Transport and Development (IFRTD) . 13650

Forum international pour le transport rural et le développement – Foro Internacional para el Transporte Rural y el Desarrollo

Exec Dir PO Box 314, Karen, Nairobi, 00502, Kenya. T. +25420883323.
URL: http://www.ifrtd.org/

History 1992. Registered in accordance with UK law: 6835743. **Aims** Overcome the physical, economic and social isolation of the rural poor in developing countries; improve accessibility of rural communities by developing rural transport systems which respond to their needs and potential. Promote a broader approach to meeting transport needs of rural people by: introducing and disseminating intermediate means of transport, e g bicycles, pack animals, wheelbarrows and low-cost motor vehicles; addressing gender issues in rural transport; improving local transport infrastructure; expanding appropriate rural transport services; increasing the use of an integrated planning approach to rural transport problems. **Structure** Executive Committee. Officers: Executive Secretary; Regional Coordinators; Executive Secretary; Communications Coordinator. Project/Office Coordinator; Finance Officer. **Languages** English, French, Spanish. **Finance** Supported by: *Swedish International Development Cooperation Agency (Sida); Swiss Agency for Development and Cooperation (SDC).* **Events** *Workshop on Understanding and Improving Rural Transport Services* Bagamoyo (Tanzania UR) 2015. **Publications** *Forum News* (3 a year). *Balancing the Load* (2002); *Networking for Development* (1998) by Paul Starkey in English, French, Spanish; *An Annotated Bibliography on Rural Transport* (1997) by Niklas Sieber; *IFRTD Networked Research Manual.* Report.

Members Full (about 3,500) in 83 countries (indicates National Forum Groups):
Argentina, Australia, Bangladesh (*), Belgium, Benin, Bhutan, Bolivia, Botswana, Brazil (*), Burkina Faso (*), Burundi, Cambodia (*), Cameroon, Canada, Cape Verde, Central African Rep, Chad, Chile, China, Colombia (*), Congo Brazzaville, Congo DR (*), Côte d'Ivoire (*), Cuba (*), Denmark, Djibouti, Ecuador, El Salvador, Ethiopia (*), Finland, France, Gabon, Germany (*), Ghana, Guatemala, Guinea (*), Guinea-Bissau, Honduras, India (*), Indonesia (*), Ireland, Japan, Kenya (*), Korea Rep, Kuwait, Lesotho, Luxembourg, Madagascar, Malawi, Malaysia, Mali, Mauritius, Mexico, Mozambique, Namibia, Nepal (*), Netherlands, New Zealand, Nicaragua, Niger, Nigeria, Norway, Pakistan (*), Papua New Guinea, Peru, Philippines (*), Rwanda (*), Senegal (*), Sierra Leone, South Africa (*), Sri Lanka (*), Sudan, Sweden, Switzerland, Tanzania UR, Thailand, Togo, Uganda (*), UK, Uruguay, USA, Zambia, Zimbabwe (*). [2015/XF4275/**F**]

♦ International Forum of Sciences, Bonn (internationally oriented national body)

♦ International Forum for Social Innovation (IFSI) 13651

Forum international de l'innovation sociale (FIIS)

Secretariat 60 rue de Bellechasse, 75007 Paris, France. T. +33145513949 – +33145517933. Fax +33145513942. E-mail: ifsi.fiis@wanadoo.fr.
URL: http://www.ifsi-fiis-conferences.com/

History Feb 1976, as *International Foundation for Social Innovation – Fondation internationale de l'innovation sociale*, by *Mankind 2000 (inactive)* and *'Centre d'études des conséquences générales des grandes techniques nouvelles (CTN)'.* Current name adopted 1993. Registered in accordance with French law. **Aims** Promote social innovation and institutional transformation in an international perspective by encouraging meetings, studies and exchange of information; participate in implementing such projects and disseminate information relating to them. **Structure** General Assembly (annual). Board. **Languages** English, French. **Finance** Members' dues. Other sources: donations; the fruit of its activities. Annual budget: euro 152,450. **Activities** Projects/programmes; training/education; events/meetings; knowledge management/information dissemination. **Events** *Annual international working conference* Giens (France) 2011, *General Assembly* Paris (France) 2010, *Annual international working conference* Dourdan (France) 2003, *Annual international working conference* Dourdan (France) 2002, *Annual international working conference* Dourdan (France) 2001. **Publications** *FIIS Bulletin* (irregular).

Members Associations in 9 countries:
Australia, Belgium, Denmark, Finland, France, India, Israel, Sweden, USA.
Individuals in 20 countries and territories:
Australia, Belgium, Cuba, Denmark, Finland, France, Guyana, India, Israel, Italy, Jamaica, Netherlands, Norway, Palestine, Peru, Spain, Sweden, Switzerland, Trinidad-Tobago, USA. [2017.06.01/XF4645/**F**]

♦ International Forum of Sovereign Wealth Funds (IFSWF) 13652

Secretariat St Clements House, 27/28 Clements Lane, London, EC4N 7AE, UK. T. +442039067321. E-mail: secretariat@ifswf.org.
URL: http://www.ifswf.org/

History Apr 2009, Kuwait, by *International Working Group of Sovereign Wealth Funds (IWG)*, through 'Kuwait Declaration', as a voluntary group of Sovereign Wealth Funds (SWFs). Inaugural meeting, Oct 2009, Baku (Azerbaijan). **Aims** Enhance collaboration, promote a deeper understanding of SWF activity and raise the industry standard for best practice and governance. **Structure** Board; Secretariat. **Languages** English. **Staff** 4.00 FTE, paid. **Finance** Members' dues. **Activities** Networking/liaising; standards/guidelines; awareness raising. **Events** *Meeting* Auckland (New Zealand) 2016, *Annual Meeting / Meeting* Milan (Italy) 2015, *Annual Meeting / Meeting* Doha (Qatar) 2014, *Meeting* Norway 2013, *Annual Meeting* Oslo (Norway) 2013. **Publications** *Case Studies*; *Santiago Principles.*

Members Sovereign Wealth Funds of 29 countries:
Angola, Australia, Azerbaijan, Bahrain, Botswana, Canada, Chile, China, Iran Islamic Rep, Ireland, Italy, Kazakhstan, Korea Rep, Kuwait, Libya, Malaysia, Mexico, New Zealand, Nigeria, Norway, Oman, Palestine, Qatar, Russia, Singapore, Timor-Leste, Trinidad-Tobago, United Arab Emirates, USA.

IGO Relations *International Monetary Fund (IMF, #14180)* is founding sponsor. [2019/XJ4487/**F***]

♦ International of Forums – School of Psychoanalysis of the Forums of the Lacanian Field (#13234)

♦ International Forum for Steiner/Waldorf-Education (Hague Circle) . 13653

International Konferenz der Waldorf/Steiner Pädagogik (Haager Kreis)

Contact c/o Henning Kullak-Ublick, Bogt-Bornkast-Weg 14 B, 22457 Hamburg, Germany. T. +4940341076995. E-mail: info@haager-kreis.org.
Contact Goetheanum, c/o Pädagogische Sektion, Postfach, 4143 Dornach SO 1, Switzerland.
URL: http://www.haager-kreis.org/

History 1970, The Hague (Netherlands). **Structure** Assembly. Executive Board. **Languages** English, German. **Staff** 3.00 FTE, voluntary. **Finance** Members' dues. **Activities** Training/education; meeting activities.

Members Full in 27 countries and territories:
Argentina, Australia, Austria, Belgium, Brazil, Czechia, Denmark, Finland, France, Germany, Hungary, India, Italy, Japan, Kenya, Netherlands, New Zealand, Norway, Peru, South Africa, Spain, Sweden, Switzerland, Taiwan, UK, Ukraine, USA.

NGO Relations Partner of (1): *International Association for Steiner/Waldorf Early Childhood Education (IASWECE, #12185).* [2021/XJ8283/c/**F**]

♦ International Forum for Sustainable Underwater Activities (IFSUA) . 13654

Contact Aragón 517 5o 1o, 08013 Barcelona, Spain. E-mail: ifsua@ifsua.net.
URL: http://www.ifsua.net/

Aims Defend members' interests promoting, defending and spreading a responsible practice of underwater activities. **Finance** Members' dues. **Members** Federations; companies; associations. Membership countries not specified. **IGO Relations** *European Commission (EC, #06633); General Fisheries Commission for the Mediterranean (GFCM, #10112); International Council for the Exploration of the Sea (ICES, #13021).* **NGO Relations** Member of: *Mediterranean Advisory Council (MEDAC, #16639).* [2020.03.11/XJ9737/**F**]

♦ International Forum on Sustainable Value Chains (ISVC) 13655

Pres Seegartenstr 61, 8810 Horgen ZH, Switzerland. E-mail: isvc@unisg.ch.
URL: http://susvc.org/

History 2013. Registered in accordance with Swiss Civil Code. **Aims** Develop and apply science-based capabilities that help companies in implementing and ensuring long-term environmental, social and economic performance in their value chains to transition into a circular economy. **Structure** General Assembly; Council. **Languages** English, German. **Staff** None paid. **Finance** Members' dues. Sponsorship; donations. **Activities** Research/documentation; events/meetings. **Events** *Annual Meeting* Frankfurt-Main (Germany) 2018, *Annual Meeting* Frankfurt-Main (Germany) 2015, *Annual Meeting* Paris (France) 2014.

Members Full in 15 countries:
Australia, Brazil, Canada, China, Costa Rica, Finland, France, Germany, India, Ireland, Italy, Spain, Switzerland, UK, USA. [2019.12.11/XM4901/**F**]

♦ International Forum for System Constellations in Organisations . . . 13656

Internationales Forum für System-Aufstellungen in Organisationen und Arbeitskontexten (infosyon) – Foro Internacional de Constalaciones Sistémicas en Organizaciones

Main Office Leinenweberstr 1, 36251 Bad Hersfeld, Germany. T. +4966211723148. Fax +4966219662349. E-mail: office@infosyon.de.
URL: http://infosyon.com/

History 27 Nov 2003, Kassel (Germany). Registered in accordance with German law, 4 Jul 2004. **Aims** Support and bring together people working with system constellations professionally on a national and international basis. **Structure** Board. **Languages** English, German, Spanish. **Staff** 0.50 FTE, paid. **Finance** Members' dues. **Activities** Events/meetings; research and development. **Events** *Conference* Vienna (Austria) 2015, *Workshop on Innovative Fields of Use in Organisations* Bremen (Germany) 2014, *Conference* Salzburg (Austria) 2014, *Conference* Amsterdam (Netherlands) 2013. **Publications** *infosyon Newsletter* (4 a year).

Members Full in 19 countries:
Argentina, Australia, Austria, Belgium, Brazil, China, Colombia, Denmark, France, Italy, Mexico, Netherlands, Peru, Portugal, Spain, Switzerland, UK, Uruguay, USA. [2020/XJ7099/**F**]

♦ International Forum of Towns and Villages in Graz (internationally oriented national body)

♦ International Forum of Travel and Tourism Advocates (IFTTA) 13657

Coordinator Schenge 7, 2134 WA Hoofddorp, Netherlands. E-mail: hello@iftta.org – webmaster@iftta.org.
Pres address not obtained. E-mail: president@iftta.org.
Sec address not obtained. E-mail: secretary@iftta.org.
URL: https://www.iftta.org/

History Nov 1983, Jerusalem (Israel). Former names and other names: *Forum international des avocats des voyages et du tourisme* – former. Registration: Dutch Trade Register, No/ID: 40539082, Start date: 12 Feb 1996, Netherlands. **Aims** Provide a forum for information exchange on the legal aspects of travel and tourism *law*; provide a resource of travel and tourism law legal materials from around the world; encourage the establishment of common legal standards for the industry; promote the highest ethical standards for the industry and for the *lawyers* that advise it; work with educational institutes in developing courses and fostering research on legal aspects. **Structure** Board of Directors. **Languages** English, Spanish. **Staff** 0.00 FTE, paid. Voluntary. **Finance** Sources: contributions; donations; gifts, legacies; grants; subscriptions; subsidies. **Activities** Events/meetings; knowledge management/information dissemination. Active in all member countries. **Events** *World Conference* Uruguay 2023, *World Conference* Valletta (Malta) 2022, *World Conference* Cancún (Mexico) 2018, *World Conference* Brussels (Belgium) 2017, *World Conference* Buenos Aires (Argentina) 2015. **Publications** *IFTTA Law Review* (3 a year). Information Services: Maintains a Glossary of legal terms in travel and tourism. **Information Services** *UNWTO Online Multilingual Terminology TourisTerm.*

Members Travel and tourism attorneys, legal advisors, law professors and travel executives in 40 countries and territories:
Albania, Argentina, Australia, Austria, Belgium, Brazil, Canada, Cyprus, Denmark, Ecuador, Egypt, Finland, France, Germany, Greece, Hong Kong, Hungary, India, Ireland, Israel, Italy, Japan, Malta, Mexico, Netherlands, Nigeria, Paraguay, Peru, Poland, Portugal, Singapore, Slovenia, South Africa, Spain, Sweden, Switzerland, Türkiye, UK, Uruguay, USA. [2023.01.27/XF2181/v/**F**]

♦ International Forum on Urbanism (IFoU) 13658

Central Office Architecture – TU Delft, Julianalaan 134, 2628 BL Delft, Netherlands. T. +31152784254. Fax +31152784162. E-mail: info@ifou.org.
URL: http://ifou.org/

Aims Strengthen international collaboration in the field of urbanism. **Structure** Scientific Board; Board of Supervisors. Executive Team, headed by Executive Director. **Activities** Organizes: Annual Conference; Summer School; Training courses. **Events** *Conference* Jakarta (Indonesia) 2019, *Conference* Barcelona (Spain) 2018, *Conference* Incheon (Korea Rep) 2015, *Conference* Barcelona (Spain) 2012, *Global visions – risks and opportunities for the urban planet* Singapore (Singapore) 2011.

Members Institutions in 12 countries and territories:
Argentina, China, Hong Kong, Indonesia, Italy, Japan, Korea Rep, Netherlands, Singapore, Spain, Switzerland, Taiwan.
Associated partner institutions (3) in 2 countries and territories:
Netherlands, Taiwan. [2019/XJ5073/**F**]

♦ International Forum for Volunteering in Development (Forum) 13659

Forum International du Volontariat pour le Développement (Forum) – FORUM Internacional de Voluntariado para el Desarrollo – Internationales FORUM für den Entwicklungsdienst

Exec Dir c/o WUSC, 1404 Scott Street, Ottawa ON K1Y 4M8, Canada. E-mail: info@forum-ids.org.
URL: http://www.forum-ids.org/

History 1964. Former names and other names: *Regional Conference on International Voluntary Service (RCIVS)* – former (1964 to 1989); *Conférence régionale du Service volontaire international (CRSVI)* – former (1964 to 1989); *European FORUM on Development Service (FORUM)* – former (1989 to 2000); *FORUM européen du volontariat pour le développement (FORUM)* – former (1989 to 2000); *FORUM Europeo de Voluntariado para el Desarrollo* – former (1989 to 2000); *Europäisches FORUM für den Entwicklungsdienst* – former (1989 to 2000); *FEVP* – former; *International FORUM on Development Service (FORUM)* – former (2000). Registration: Corporations Canada, No/ID: 836646-2, Start date: 22 Apr 2013, Canada. **Aims** Share information, develop good practice and enhance cooperation across international volunteering and development sectors. **Structure** Members' Meeting (annual); Board of Directors; Executive Coordinator; Working Groups. **Languages** English, French. **Staff** 0.80 FTE, paid. **Finance** Sources: contributions; grants; international organizations; meeting proceeds; members' dues. **Activities** Events/meetings; knowledge management/information dissemination; networking/liaising; research and development. **Events** *Annual Conference of International Volunteer Cooperation Organisations* Saly (Senegal) 2022, *Annual Conference of International Volunteer Cooperation Organisations* Thessaloniki (Greece) 2021, *Annual Conference of International Volunteer Cooperation Organizations* Suva (Fiji) 2020, *Annual Conference of International Volunteer Cooperation Organizations* Kigali (Rwanda) 2019, *Annual Conference of International Volunteer Cooperation Organizations* Montréal, QC (Canada) 2018. **Publications** Research, position and discussion papers.

Members Non-profit organizations, NGOs and state bodies actively engaged in one or more aspects of development service. Included in the above, 20 organizations listed in this Yearbook:
AKLHÜ – Netzwerk und Fachstelle für internationale Personelle Zusammenarbeit; AVI; Canadian Centre for International Studies and Cooperation (CECI); Canadian Crossroads International (CCI); Canadian Executive Service Organization (CESO); Comhlamh; Deutsche Gesellschaft für Internationale Zusammenarbeit (GIZ); Federazione Organismi Cristiani Servizio Internazionale Volontario (Volontari nel Mondo – FOCSIV); International Service (inactive); Japan International Cooperation Agency (JICA); Korea International Cooperation Agency (KOICA); Norwegian Agency for Exchange Cooperation (NOREC); Peace Corps; Singapore International Foundation (SIF); Swiss Association for the Exchange of Personnel in Development Cooperation (Unité); United Nations Volunteers (UNV, #20650); Vereniging voor Personele Samenwerking met Ontwikkelingslanden (PSO, inactive); Voluntary Service Overseas (VSO); Volunteer Service Abroad (VSA); World University Service (WUS, #21892) (of Canada). [2022/XD3152/y/**F**]

♦ International Forum for Young Choir Music (internationally oriented national body)

♦ International Forwarding Association (IFA) 13660

Contact Coöperatie UA, Postbus 414, 5900 AK Venlo, Netherlands. T. +31773246007. E-mail: ifa@ifa-forwarding.net – pr@ifa-forwarding.net.
URL: http://www.ifa-forwarding.net/

History 1992. **Events** *Meeting* Vienna (Austria) 2012, *Meeting* Athens (Greece) 2011, *Meeting* Palma (Spain) 2011, *Congress* Lisbon (Portugal) 2010, *Congress* Palma (Spain) 2009.

Members Companies (35) in 21 countries:
Austria, Belgium, Czechia, Denmark, Estonia, Finland, France, Germany, Greece, Hungary, Ireland, Italy, Netherlands, Norway, Poland, Slovakia, Spain, Sweden, Switzerland, Türkiye, UK. [2014/XD9074/**D**]

♦ **International Forward Osmosis Association (IFOA)** **13661**

Contact address not obtained. E-mail: info@forwardosmosis.biz.
URL: http://forwardosmosis.biz/

Aims Commercialize forward osmosis technology. **Structure** Board of Directors. Committees (4): Membership; Technical Standards; Events; Public Relations and Advocacy. **Finance** Members' dues. **Activities** Events/meetings. **Events** *World Summit* Sydney, NSW (Australia) 2016, *World Summit* Vancouver, BC (Canada) 2015, *World Summit* Lisbon (Portugal) 2014. **Members** Private companies; industry professionals; research and academic organizations. Membership countries not specified. [2017/XM5496/**D**]

♦ **International Fossil Algae Association (IFAA)** **13662**

Contact Dept of Earth/Planetary Sciences, Univ of Tennessee, Knoxville TN 37996-1410, USA. Fax +18659742368.

History 1974. **Aims** Promote international research and collaboration on fossil algae, with particular reference to calcareous algae, their systematics, geological history, palaeoecology and sedimentology. **Structure** International Symposium (every 2 years) designates the country for the next Symposium and new President. **Languages** English, French. **Staff** Voluntary. **Finance** Symposium usually supported by registration fees and by host-institute of the country in which it is held. **Activities** Assembles research on fossil algae, particularly calcified algae and bacteria and their associated sediments, and their geological significance and applications. **Events** *International Symposium on Fossil Algae* Milan (Italy) 2023, *International Symposium on Fossil Algae* Lucknow (India) 2019, *International Symposium on Fossil Algae* Okinawa (Japan) 2015, *Regional Symposium on Fossil Algae* Schladming (Austria) 2013, *International Symposium on Fossil Algae* Cluj-Napoca (Romania) 2011. **Publications** Symposium proceedings.

Members Individuals in 35 countries:
Australia, Austria, Belgium, Brazil, Bulgaria, Canada, China, Croatia, Czechia, Denmark, Estonia, France, Germany, Greece, Hungary, India, Israel, Italy, Japan, Netherlands, Norway, Poland, Portugal, Romania, Russia, Serbia, Slovakia, Slovenia, Spain, Sweden, Tunisia, Türkiye, UK, Ukraine, USA. [2013.09.30/XD1820/v/**C**]

♦ **International Foster Care Organization (IFCO)** **13663**

Organisation internationale de placement familial (OIPF)

Contact 10 Queen Street Place, London, EC4R 1AG, UK. E-mail: info@ifco.info.
URL: http://www.ifco.info/

History 1981, Oxford (UK). UK Registered Charity: 1081324. **Aims** Provide family-based care for all children in alternative care across the world. **Structure** Board; Secretariat. **Languages** English, French, Hindi, Maltese, Spanish. **Finance** Sources: fundraising; members' dues. **Activities** Events/meetings; guidance/assistance/consulting; knowledge management/information dissemination; projects/programmes; publishing activities; training/education. **Events** *Biennial Conference* Montréal, QC (Canada) 2020, *Biennial Conference* Valletta (Malta) 2017, *European Conference* Sheffield (UK) 2016, *Biennial Conference* Sydney, NSW (Australia) 2015, *European Conference* Waterford (Ireland) 2014. **Publications** *IFCO Newsletter* (regular). Conference proceedings; recorded plenaries; lectures; powerpoints.

Members Individual; Lifetime; Youth; Organizations. Organizations in 15 countries:
Albania, Australia, Belgium, Bulgaria, Canada, India, Malta, New Zealand, Norway, Sierra Leone, Sweden, Tanzania UR, UK, Ukraine, USA.

Individuals in 27 countries:
Australia, Belgium, Canada, Czechia, Finland, Germany, Greece, Guinea, Hong Kong, India, Ireland, Italy, Japan, Lithuania, Malta, Netherlands, New Zealand, Norway, Philippines, Portugal, Russia, Sweden, Switzerland, Türkiye, UK, Ukraine, USA.

IGO Relations Partners and contacts include: *Committee on the Rights of the Child (#04283)*; *European Commission (EC, #06633)*; *European Union (EU, #08967)*; *UNICEF (#20332)*. **NGO Relations** Member of: *Eurochild (#05657)*; *Child Rights Connect (#03884)*; *End Corporal Punishment (#05457)*; *International Coalition for the Optional Protocol to the Convention on the Rights of the Child on a Communications Procedure (Ratify OP3CRC, #12617)*; Opening Doors for Europe's Children. Partners and contacts include: *Bernard van Leer Foundation (BvLF)*; *Defence for Children International (DCI, #05025)*; *EveryChild*; *International Child Development Initiatives (ICDI)*; *Fédération internationale des communautés éducatives (FICE-International, #09622)*; *Red Latinoamericana de Acogimiento Familiar (RELAF, #18700)*; *Save the Children International (#19058)*; *SOS-Kinderdorf International (#19693)*. [2022/XD1718/**B**]

♦ International Foundation for African Children (unconfirmed)
♦ International Foundation for Art Research (internationally oriented national body)
♦ International Foundation for Autoimmune & Autoinflammatory Arthritis (internationally oriented national body)

♦ **International Foundation for Autonomous Agents and Multiagent Systems (IFAAMAS)** **13664**

Sec Cheriton School U-Waterloo, 200 University Ave West, Waterloo ON N2L 3G1, Canada. E-mail: info@ifaamas.org.
URL: http://www.ifaamas.org/

Aims Promote science and technology in the areas of *artificial intelligence*, autonomous agents and multi-agent systems. **Structure** Board of Directors of 27 members, including President, Past-President, Secretary and Treasurer. **Events** *Conference* 2021, *Conference* 2020, *Conference* Montréal, QC (Canada) 2019, *Conference* Stockholm (Sweden) 2018, *Conference* Sao Paulo (Brazil) 2017. [2020/XJ1253/f/**F**]

♦ **International Foundation for Biosynthesis (IFB)** **13665**

Pres IIBS, Benzenrüti 6, 9410 Heiden AR, Switzerland. T. +41718916855. Fax +41718915855. E-mail: info@biosynthesis.org – ifb@baer-und-krieger.de.
URL: http://www.biosynthesis.org/

History 7 Oct 2001, Zurich (Switzerland). **Structure** Consists of: *International Institute for Biosynthesis (IIBS)*; *European Association for Biosynthesis (EABS)*; *Overseas Association for Biosynthesis (OABS)*; *National Professional Associations for Biosynthesis*. Board; Executive Office. **Events** *Biosynthesis conference / International Congress* Zurich (Switzerland) 2010, *International biosynthesis congress / International Congress* Lisbon (Portugal) 2006, *Congress on body experience and expression of the soul* Zurich (Switzerland) 2001. **NGO Relations** Member of: *World Council for Psychotherapy (WCP, #21337)*. [2016.06.01/XG8604/f/**F**]

♦ International Foundation For Biotechnology Research and Early Stimulation in the Culture of Health, Nutrition, Sport, Art, Science, Technology and Society (internationally oriented national body)
♦ International Foundation for CDKL5 Research (internationally oriented national body)

♦ **International Foundation for Computer Assisted Radiology and Surgery (IFCARS)** **13666**

Office Im Gut 15, 79790 Küssaberg, Germany. T. +497742922436. Fax +497742922438. E-mail: office@ifcars.org.
URL: http://www.ifcars.org/

Aims Support all measures promoting development of computer assisted radiology and surgery (CARS), in particular, the creation and communication of information in the field of computer assisted medicine and the study of its medical, social and ethical effects on our society. **Structure** Board. **Events** *CARS : International Congress on Computer Assisted Radiology and Surgery* Tokyo (Japan) 2022, *CARS : International Congress on Computer Assisted Radiology and Surgery* Munich (Germany) 2021, *CARS : International Congress on Computer Assisted Radiology and Surgery* Munich (Germany) 2020, *CARS : International Congress on Computer Assisted Radiology and Surgery* Rennes (France) 2019, *CARS : International Congress on Computer Assisted Radiology and Surgery* Berlin (Germany) 2018. **Publications** *International Journal for Computer Assisted Radiology and Surgery (IJCARS)*. [2020/XJ6468/f/**F**]

♦ International Foundation for the Conservation of Game / see International Foundation for the Conservation of Wildlife (#13667)

♦ **International Foundation for the Conservation of Wildlife (IGF)** **13667**

Fondation internationale pour la sauvegarde de la faune – Internationale Stiftung Zur Erhaltung der Fauna

Contact address not obtained. T. +33156597755. Fax +33156597756.
URL: http://www.wildlife-conservation.org/

History 1976, under the name *International Foundation for the Conservation of Game – Fondation internationale pour la sauvegarde du gibier – Internationale Stiftung zur Erhaltung des Wildes*, as two sister foundations in France and Switzerland having the same title. Present name adopted 1990. **Aims** Contribute throughout the world towards conservation of wildlife and of *nature* in all its forms and aspects; help to promote the rational and reasonable harvesting of national and international *game* populations in order to ensure their perennity and their development for the benefit of humanity. **Structure** Board of Directors. **Finance** Donations. Budget (annual): about French Fr 2 million. **Activities** Informs and educates the public. Encourages the progress of scientific knowledge concerning wildlife, its utilization and its ecology. Promotes the creation of reserves for certain endangered species and generally restores game and wildlife to their rightful place in nature, for the enjoyment of the hunting and non-hunting public. **Events** *Symposium* Harare (Zimbabwe) 1987, *General Assembly* Paris (France) 1986. **Publications** *Faune Sauvage Africaine: la ressource oubliée* (1996).

Members Board of Directors of 20 individuals in 6 countries:
Belgium, France, Poland, Portugal, Spain, Switzerland.

IGO Relations *European Commission (EC, #06633)*. **NGO Relations** Member of: *International Union for Conservation of Nature and Natural Resources (IUCN, #15766)*. Instrumental in setting up: *Association des chasseurs professionnels d'Afrique francophone (ACP, inactive)*; *Institute for World Conservation and Development (no recent information)*; *International Association for Falconry and Conservation of Birds of Prey (IAF, #11888)*. [2016/XF9979/f/**F**]

♦ International Foundation for Crime Prevention and Victim Care (internationally oriented national body)
♦ International Foundation for Cultural Cooperation in the Mountains (#09813)
♦ International Foundation Dedicated to the Prevention of Drug Abuse Among Children and Adolescents / see Mentor International (#16716)

♦ **International Foundation for Dermatology (IFD)** **13668**

Exec Dir Willan House, 4 Fitzroy Square, London, W1P 5HG, UK. E-mail: info@ilds.org.
URL: http://www.ifd.org/

History 1987, Berlin (Germany). Serving under the aegis of the *'International Committee of Dermatology'*, the executive Committee of *International League of Dermatological Societies (ILDS, #14018)*. **Aims** Improve dermatologic *care* of patients in underserved areas of the world. **Structure** Sub-committee of *International League of Dermatological Societies (ILDS, #14018)*. Leading partner in running *Regional Dermatology Training Centre (RDTC)*. **Languages** English. **Staff** None. **Finance** Supported by *International League of Dermatological Societies (ILDS, #14018)*. **Activities** Awareness raising; financial and/or material support. **Events** *Annual symposium on dermatology* Moshi (Tanzania UR) 2003, *World congress* Paris (France) 2002, *Meeting* Sydney, NSW (Australia) 1997, *Meeting* New York, NY (USA) 1992. **Publications** *Community Dermatology Journal* (2 a year). **Members** ILDS Membership. **NGO Relations** Member of (1): *Neglected Tropical Diseased NGO Network (NNN, #16969)*. [2022/XF2216/f/**F**]

♦ International Foundation for Development Alternatives (inactive)
♦ International Foundation for Dharma Nature Time (internationally oriented national body)
♦ International Foundation for Economic and Social Development (internationally oriented national body)
♦ International Foundation for Education and Self-Help (internationally oriented national body)
♦ International Foundation for Election Systems / see International Foundation for Electoral Systems (#13669)

♦ **International Foundation for Electoral Systems (IFES)** **13669**

Fondation internationale des systèmes électoraux

Main Office 2011 Crystal Dr, 10th Fl, Arlington VA 22202, USA. T. +12023506700. E-mail: media@ifes.org.
URL: http://www.ifes.org/

History 1987. Former names and other names: *International Foundation for Election Systems* – former (1987). **Aims** Provide professional support to electoral *democracy* through field work, applied research and advocacy; promote citizen participation, transparency and accountability in *political* life and civil society. **Structure** Board of Directors; Headquarters in Arlington VA (USA); Field Offices (about 30). **Languages** Arabic, English, French, Spanish, Ukrainian. **Staff** 130 domestic; 43 international. **Finance** Funding from bilateral and multilateral development agencies, private corporations, individuals and foundations. **Activities** Advocacy/lobbying/activism; politics/policy/regulatory; projects/programmes; research and development. Active in: Afghanistan, Albania, Belarus, Bosnia-Herzegovina, Brazil, Bulgaria, Cambodia, Jamaica, Kosovo, Lebanon, Montenegro, Myanmar, Nicaragua, Peru, Romania, Syrian AR, Timor-Leste. **Events** *Annual international judicial conference* Bucharest (Romania) 2004, *Annual conference* Bratislava (Slovakia) 1999, *Campaign and election financing – community involvement in financing votes information programs* Manila (Philippines) 1998, *Meeting* Ottawa, ON (Canada) 1998, *Conference on promoting disabled citizens access to the political process* San Juan (Puerto Rico) 1998. **Publications** White papers; books; reports; manuals. **Information Services** *ACE Electoral Knowledge Network*.

Members Offices in 35 countries:
Armenia, Bangladesh, Burkina Faso, Congo DR, Czechia, Ecuador, El Salvador, Ethiopia, Georgia, Guatemala, Guinea, Guyana, Haiti, Honduras, Indonesia, Iraq, Kenya, Kyrgyzstan, Libya, Maldives, Mali, Nepal, Niger, Nigeria, North Macedonia, Pakistan, Papua New Guinea, Senegal, Serbia, Sri Lanka, Sudan, Tanzania UR, Tunisia, Ukraine, Uzbekistan.

Consultative Status Consultative status granted from: *ECOSOC (#05331)* (Special). **IGO Relations** Ongoing Memorandum of Understanding with: *OAS (#17629)*; *OSCE – Office for Democratic Institutions and Human Rights (OSCE/ODIHR, #17902)*; *UNDP (#20292)*. Bi-lateral agreements with: *Canadian International Development Agency (CIDA, inactive)*; *Department for International Development (DFID, inactive)*; *Department for International Development Cooperation*; *Swedish International Development Cooperation Agency (Sida)*; *United States Agency for International Development (USAID)*. Cooperation agreement with: *International Institute for Democracy and Electoral Assistance (International IDEA, #13872)*. Formal partnership agreement with: *United Nations Democracy Fund (UNDEF, #20551)*. **NGO Relations** Special links with: *Association of African Election Authorities (AAEA, #02355)*; *Association of Asian Election Authorities (AAEA, #02379)*; *Association of Caribbean Electoral Organizations (ACEO, #02405)*; *Association of European Election Officials (ACEEEO, #02508)*; *Centre for Development and Population Activities (CEDPA, inactive)*; *International Association of Clerks, Recorders, Election Officials and Treasurers (IACREOT)*; *International Institute of Municipal Clerks (IIMC)*; *International Republican Institute (IRI)*; *The Carter Center*. Member of: *InsideNGO (inactive)*. [2023.02.17/XF4147/f/**F**]

♦ International Foundation of Employee Benefit Plans (internationally oriented national body)
♦ International Foundation for Environment and Nature / see Global Nature Fund (#10479)
♦ International Foundation for Fair Trade and Development (internationally oriented national body)

♦ **International Foundation of Fashion Technology Institutes (IFFTI)** .. **13670**

Secretariat c/o Pearl Academy, B-66 Slotco Bldg, Naraina Industrial Area Phase II, Delhi 110028, DELHI 110028, India. T. +911141418789 – +911141418790. Fax +911141418790. E-mail: secretariat@iffti.org.
URL: http://www.iffti.org/

History Nov 1998. Registered in accordance with Indian law. **Aims** Advance education and research in fashion design, technology, and business and related industries; serve as an international forum for exchange of ideas and collaborative research and development in these fields; promote the interests of students of member institutions; foster development of fashion and related industries internationally. **Structure** General Council. **Languages** English. **Staff** 3.00 FTE, paid. **Finance** Members' dues. **Activities** Knowledge management/information dissemination; networking/liaising; research/documentation; events/meetings. **Events** *Annual Conference* Dunedin (New Zealand) 2023, *Annual Conference* Nottingham (UK) 2022, *Annual Conference* Delhi (India) 2021, *Annual Conference* Kent, OH (USA) 2020, *Annual Conference* Manchester (UK) 2019. **Publications** *IFFTI Journal* (annual).

Members Full in 25 countries and territories:
Australia, Bangladesh, Belgium, Canada, China, Denmark, France, Germany, Hong Kong, India, Italy, Japan, Korea Rep, Mauritius, Netherlands, New Zealand, Peru, Russia, Singapore, Spain, Sweden, Taiwan, Türkiye, UK, USA. [2019.10.22/XJ0015/f/**F**]

♦ International Foundation for Global Economic Development (#10029)

♦ International Foundation of the High Altitude Research Stations Jungfraujoch and Gornergrat (HFSJG) 13671

Fondation internationale des stations scientifiques à haute altitude de Jungfraujoch et du Gornergrat – Internationale Stiftung Hochalpine Forschungsstationen Jungfraujoch und Gornergrat (HFSJG)

Dir Sidlerstrasse 5, 3012 Bern, Switzerland. T. +41316314052 – +41316314056. Fax +41316314405.

URL: http://www.ifjungo.ch/

History 1930, Bern (Switzerland), by Austria, France, Germany, Switzerland and UK, as *Jungfraujoch Scientific Station, International Foundation – Station scientifique du Jungfraujoch, fondation internationale,* under supervision of Swiss Federal Council. Originated from 1894 concession given to the Jungfrau Railway Company, stipulating the building of an Observatory on the Jungfraujoch; and formation, 1922, of Swiss Jungfraujoch Commission. Commenced activities 4 Jul 1931. **Aims** Enable scientific research work to be carried out at altitudes above 3,500 m or which require an *Alpine climate.* **Structure** Council, which is also Administrative Council of Research Station, consisting of representatives of each adhering organization and the President of the Foundation. **Finance** Budget: US$ 610,000. **Activities** Research work in solar astronomy, astrophysics, environmental research, atmospheric physics, atmospheric chemistry, geology, glaciology, medicine, meteorology and physics, at an altitude of 3,500 metres. Machine shop, laboratories, library. **Events** *Biennial council meeting* Interlaken (Switzerland) 1999, *Biennial council meeting* Zermatt (Switzerland) 1997, *Biennial council meeting* Interlaken (Switzerland) 1995, *Biennial meeting / Biennial Council Meeting* Interlaken (Switzerland) 1993, *Biennial meeting / Biennial Council Meeting* Zermatt (Switzerland) 1991.

Members Principal scientific institutions of 6 countries:
Austria, Belgium, Germany, Italy, Switzerland, UK. [2012/XF2852/f/F]

- ♦ International Foundation for a History of European Civilization (#09822)
- ♦ International Foundation for Human Progress / see Fondation Charles Léopold Mayer pour le progrès de l'homme (#09815)
- ♦ International Foundation for Human Rights and Tolerance (internationally oriented national body)
- ♦ International Foundation for Industrial Ergonomics and Safety Research / see International Society of Occupational Ergonomics and Safety Research

♦ International Foundation for Integrated Care (IFIC) 13672

Admin c/o Wolfson College, Annexe Offices, Linton Rd, Oxford, OX2 6UD, UK. T. +447455723372. E-mail: info@integratedcarefoundation.org.

URL: http://integratedcarefoundation.org/

History 2004. Restructured under current title, Oct 2011. Former names and other names: *International Network on Integrated Care (INIC)* – former (2004 to 2011). Registration: Netherlands, Utrecht. **Aims** Bring people together to advance the science, knowledge and adoption of integrated care policy and practice. **Structure** Board; Executive Committee. **Activities** Publishing activities; research/documentation; networking/liaising; events/meetings; training/education; knowledge management/information dissemination. **Events** *International Conference on Integrated Care (ICIC)* Antwerp (Belgium) 2023, *International Conference on Integrated Care (ICIC)* Odense (Denmark) 2022, *International Conference on Integrated Care (ICIC)* 2021, *North American Conference* Toronto, ON (Canada) 2021, *North American Conference* Toronto, ON (Canada) 2020. **Publications** *International Journal of Integrated Care (IJIC).* **NGO Relations** Associated member of: *European Forum for Primary Care (EFPC, #07326).* [2020/XJ1559/f/F]

♦ International Foundation Manifesta 13673

Main Office Herengracht 474, 1017 CA Amsterdam, Netherlands. T. +31206721435. Fax +31204700073. E-mail: office@manifesta.org.

URL: http://www.manifesta.org/

History 1993, as *Foundation European Art Manifestation.* Current title adopted, 1999. **Aims** Provide a dynamic platform to support a growing network of *visual arts* professionals throughout Europe, contributing to advancement and enhancement of a dialogue in the field of *contemporary art.* **Structure** International Board; Honorary Board Members; Director; Financial Controller; External Relations and Education Coordinator; Liaisons Officer; Office Manager; Public Programs Officer. **Staff** 6.00 FTE, paid. **Activities** Responsible for: *Manifesta: European Biennial of Contemporary Art*; Manifesta Coffee Break (public meeting). **Events** *European Biennial of Contemporary Art* St Petersburg (Russia) 2014, *European Biennial of Contemporary Art* Genk (Belgium) 2012, *European Biennial of Contemporary Art* Murcia (Spain) 2010, *European Biennial of Contemporary Art* Trento (Italy) 2008, *European Biennial of Contemporary Art* San Sebastian (Spain) 2004. **Publications** *Manifesta Biennial Catalogue. Manifesta Journal* – series. *The Manifesta Workbook.* [2017/XF6380/f/F]

- ♦ International Foundation for Mother and Child Health (internationally oriented national body)
- ♦ International Foundation for Political and Legal Research / see International Public Foundation (#14667)

♦ International Foundation for Population and Development (IFPD) 13674

Fondation internationale pour la population et le développement

Exec Assistant Cours des Bastions 5, 1205 Geneva, Switzerland. E-mail: info@ifpd.org.

URL: http://www.ifpd.org/

History 1999, Lausanne (Switzerland). **Aims** Promote micro-businesses to foster sustainable social and economic integration; address social marginalization; contribute to the autonomy of vulnerable people through implementation of vocational training and entrepreneurship programmes. **Structure** Board of Trustees. **Languages** English, French. **Staff** 8.00 FTE, paid. Several voluntary. **Finance** Sources: donations. **Activities** Projects/programmes. Active in: Brazil, India, Nepal, Switzerland. **NGO Relations** Member of (2): *Girls not Brides (#10154); Global Health Workforce Alliance (GHWA, inactive).* [2022.05.22/XG9205/f/F]

♦ International Foundation for Production Research (IFPR) 13675

SG Fraunhofer Inst for Industrial Engineering, Nobelstrasse 12, 70569 Stuttgart, Germany. T. +497119702001.

URL: http://www.ifpr-icpr.net/

History 1970. **Aims** Encourage communication among researchers of production systems and processes around the world. **Structure** Board; Committees (4); Regional Committees (3). **Activities** Events/meetings. **Events** *Conference* Manila (Philippines) 2015, *Asia Pacific Meeting* Jeju (Korea Rep) 2014, *Conference* Foz do Iguaçu (Brazil) 2013, *Biennial conference / Conference* Stuttgart (Germany) 2011, *Biennial conference / Conference* Shanghai (China) 2009. **Publications** *International Journal of Production Economics* (24 a year). **NGO Relations** Member of: *Asia Pacific Industrial Engineering and Management Society (APIEMS, #01930).* [2014.10.31/XF5474/f/F]

- ♦ International Foundation for the Protection of Drinking Water (internationally oriented national body)
- ♦ International Foundation for Protection of Freedom of Speech – Adil Soz (internationally oriented national body)
- ♦ International Foundation for the Protection of Human Rights Defenders / see Front Line Defenders (#10008)

♦ International Foundation of Robotics Research (IFRR) 13676

Pres Computer Science Dept, Stanford Univ, 353 Serra Mall, Stanford CA 94305-9025, USA. T. +16507239753. Fax +16507251449.

URL: http://www.ifrr.org/

History 1986, following a series of symposia. **Aims** Promote the development of robotics research as a scientific field establishing the theoretical foundations and technology basis for its ever expanding applications, with emphasis on its potential role to benefit humans. **Structure** Board. **Languages** English. **Staff** 1.50 FTE, voluntary. **Finance** Organization of scientific meetings; private donations. **Activities** Organizes symposia and workshops; cosponsors international robotics summer school. Sponsors: Field and Service Robotics (FSR); Robotics Science and Systems (RSS). **Events** *International Symposium on Robotics Research* Switzerland 2021, *International Symposium on Experimental Robotics* Valletta (Malta) 2021, *International Symposium on Experimental Robotics* Valletta (Malta) 2020, *International Symposium on Experimental Robotics* Tokyo (Japan) 2016, *International Symposium on Robotics Research* Singapore (Singapore) 2013.

Members in 8 countries:
Australia, Belgium, France, Germany, Italy, Japan, Switzerland, USA.

NGO Relations Memorandum of Understanding with: Robotics and Automation Society of *Institute of Electrical and Electronics Engineers (IEEE, #11259).* [2020/XF7108/f/F]

- ♦ International Foundation for the Rule of Law and the Independence of Lawyers and Judges (internationally oriented national body)

♦ International Foundation for Science (IFS) 13677

Fondation internationale pour la science

Dir Karlavägen 108, 8th floor, SE-115 26 Stockholm, Sweden. T. +46854581800. Fax +46854581801. E-mail: info@ifs.se.

URL: http://www.ifs.se/

History 26 May 1972, Stockholm (Sweden). Statutes adopted Sep 1975, Stockholm. Registered according to Swedish law. **Aims** Contribute towards strengthening the capacity of *developing countries* to conduct relevant and high quality research on the sustainable management of biological resources, including the study of physical, chemical and biological processes, as well as relevant social and economic aspects, important in the conservation, production and renewable utilization of the natural resources base. **Structure** Board of Trustees; Executive Committee; Scientific and Grants Committee; Nominations and Membership Committee. Donors Group. Scientific Advisory Committees. Secretariat located in Stockholm (Sweden). **Languages** English, French. **Staff** 22.00 FTE, paid. **Finance** Contributions from: governmental sources; member organizations; international development agencies, including: *Department for International Development (DFID, inactive); Norwegian Agency for Development Cooperation (Norad); Organisation for the Prohibition of Chemical Weapons (OPCW, #17823); OIC Ministerial Standing Committee on Scientific and Technological Cooperation (COMSTECH, #17702); United Nations University (UNU, #20642); Swedish International Development Cooperation Agency (Sida).* **Activities** Awards/prizes/competitions. **Events** *Regional assembly* Kuala Lumpur (Malaysia) 2005, *Governance meeting* Vienna (Austria) 2004, *Workshop on off forest tree resources of Africa* Arusha (Tanzania UR) 1999, *Triennial general assembly / General Assembly* Rio de Janeiro (Brazil) 1997, *Asian symposium on medicinal plants, spices and other natural products / Annual Meeting / Workshop / Asian Symposium on Medicinal Plants, Spices and Other Natural Products – ASOMPS* Melaka (Malaysia) 1994. **Publications** *IFS E-News. Monitoring and Evaluation System for Impact Assessments (MESIA) Reports.* Annual Report.

Members Scientific academies, research councils and other broadly representative scientific societies from both developing and industrialized parts of the world. National, regional and international organizations (126) in 82 countries:
Argentina, Australia, Austria, Bangladesh, Belgium, Bolivia, Brazil, Burkina Faso, Cameroon, Central African Rep, Chad, Chile, China, Colombia, Congo Brazzaville, Costa Rica, Côte d'Ivoire, Cuba, Denmark, Ecuador, Egypt, El Salvador, Ethiopia, Finland, France, Germany, Ghana, Guinea, Guinea-Bissau, Guyana, Honduras, India, Indonesia, Israel, Jamaica, Jordan, Kenya, Korea DPR, Korea Rep, Kuwait, Latvia, Lesotho, Liberia, Madagascar, Malawi, Malaysia, Mali, Mexico, Mongolia, Morocco, Mozambique, Nepal, Netherlands, Niger, Nigeria, Norway, Pakistan, Panama, Papua New Guinea, Peru, Philippines, Poland, Saudi Arabia, Senegal, Seychelles, Sierra Leone, South Africa, Sri Lanka, Sudan, Sweden, Switzerland, Tanzania UR, Thailand, Tunisia, Uganda, UK, Uruguay, USA, Venezuela, Vietnam, Zambia, Zimbabwe.

Included in the above-mentioned bodies, 3 organizations listed in this Yearbook:
Centre de coopération internationale en recherche agronomique pour le développement (CIRAD, #03733); Institut de recherche pour le développement (IRD); Royal Academy of Overseas Sciences (RAOS).

Regional and International Organizations (20):
African Academy of Sciences (AAS, #00193); Association of African Universities (AAU, #02361); BioNET INTERNATIONAL – Global Network for Taxonomy (BI, #03253); Bioversity International (#03262); Caribbean Academy of Sciences (CAS); Caribbean Agricultural Research and Development Institute (CARDI, #03436); Center for International Forestry Research (CIFOR, #03646); CGIAR System Organization (CGIAR, #03843); Institut du Sahel (INSAH, #11357); International Center for Agricultural Research in the Dry Areas (ICARDA, #12466); International Centre for Tropical Agriculture (#12527); International Organization for Chemical Sciences in Development (IOCD, #14440); International Union of Forest Research Organizations (IUFRO, #15774); International Water Management Institute (IWMI, #15867); Tropical Agriculture Research and Higher Education Center (#20246); TWAS (#20270); West and Central African Council for Agricultural Research and Development (WECARD, #20907); Western Indian Ocean Marine Science Association (WIOMSA, #20916); World Agroforestry Centre (ICRAF, #21072); WorldFish (#21507).

Consultative Status Consultative status granted from: *ECOSOC (#05331)* (Ros C); *FAO (#09260)* (Special Status). **IGO Relations** Memorandum of Understanding and Partnership Agreements with: *African Development Bank Group (ADB Group, #00284); DANIDA;* FAO; *Institut de recherche pour le développement (IRD); International Atomic Energy Agency (IAEA, #12294); OIC Ministerial Standing Committee on Scientific and Technological Cooperation (COMSTECH, #17702); Organisation for the Prohibition of Chemical Weapons (OPCW, #17823); Southeast Asian Regional Center for Graduate Study and Research in Agriculture (SEARCA, #19781); Tropical Agriculture Research and Higher Education Center (#20246).*

NGO Relations Member of: *Asian Coordinating Group for Chemistry (ACGC, no recent information); International Science Council (ISC, #14796).* Instrumental in setting up: *Network of Users of Scientific Equipment in Southern Africa (NUSESA, no recent information).*

Memorandum of Understanding and Partnership Agreements with:
- *African Academy of Sciences (AAS, #00193);*
- *Biosciences Eastern and Central Africa (BecA, #03259);*
- *Council for the Development of Social Science Research in Africa (CODESRIA, #04879);*
- *International Union for Conservation of Nature and Natural Resources (IUCN, #15766);*
- *International Water Management Institute (IWMI, #15867);*
- *Organization for Women in Science for the Developing World (OWSD, #17890);*
- *UNLEASH;*
- *UNU Institute for Natural Resources in Africa (UNU-INRA, #20718);*
- *Water and Sanitation for Africa (WSA, #20836);*
- *West and Central African Council for Agricultural Research and Development (WECARD, #20907);*
- *Western Indian Ocean Marine Science Association (WIOMSA, #20916).* [2019/XF4243/fy/F]

- ♦ International Foundation of the Scientific Miracle in the Holy Quran and Sunna (unconfirmed)
- ♦ International Foundation of Security and Safety Sciences (internationally oriented national body)
- ♦ International Foundation for Social Innovation / see International Forum for Social Innovation (#13651)
- ♦ International Foundation of Socio-Economic and Political Studies (internationally oriented national body)
- ♦ International Foundation for the Support of Local Social Development (internationally oriented national body)

♦ International Foundation for Sustainable Peace and Development (IFSPD) 13678

Coordinator ul "Pozitano" 9, Floor 6, Office 19A, 1000 Sofia, Bulgaria. T. +35924440033. Fax +35924440033. E-mail: secretariat@ifspd.org.

URL: https://ifspd.org/

History 4 Mar 2009. Former names and other names: *Black Sea – Caspian Sea International Fund* – alias; *International Fund for Cooperation and Partnership of the Black Sea and the Caspian Sea (BSCSIF)* – former. Registration: Romania. **Aims** Promote dialogue, mutual understanding, people diplomacy, values of multiculturalism, analysis of challenges and threats to regional and international security, contributing to international efforts in prevention and settlement of conflicts, development of cooperation in the sphere of democratization, justice, and human rights, economy, scientific research, education, culture and environment, development of competence, human resource development, poverty reduction, fight against terrorism, organized crime, illegal drug trafficking and fight against addictions. **Structure** General Assembly. Board of Directors. Branches (8): Brussels (Belgium); Moscow (Russia); Istanbul (Turkey); Varna (Bulgaria); Belgrade (Serbia), Bangalore (India), Minsk (Belarus), Sandton (South Africa). **Languages** English, Russian. **Staff** 5.00 FTE, paid; 20.00 FTE, voluntary. **Finance** Sources: members' dues; sponsorship. Annual budget: 200,000 EUR. **Activities** Advocacy/lobbying/activism. **Events** *General Assembly* Turkey 2019, *General Assembly* Turkey 2017, *General Assembly* Bucharest (Romania) 2016, *General Assembly* Baku (Azerbaijan) 2015, *General Assembly* Istanbul (Turkey) 2014. **Publications** *Dialogue of the Seas* – magazine. **Members** Full in 40 countries. Membership countries not specified. **Consultative Status** Consultative status granted from: *ECOSOC (#05331)* (Special). [2022.05.04/XJ8571/f/F]

♦ International Foundation for Telemetering (internationally oriented national body)

♦ International Foundation for Women Artists (IFWA) 13679

Co-founder 325 West 38th St, Ste 510, New York NY 10018, USA.
URL: http://www.ifwartists.org/
History 2013, New York NY (USA). Registered in the USA. **Aims** Support, promote, educate, and unite women artists internationally. **Languages** English, French. **Staff** 2.00 FTE, voluntary. **Activities** Meeting activities; guidance/assistance/consulting; training/education. [2021/XJ7948/f/F]

♦ International FOXG1 Foundation (internationally oriented national body)

♦ International Fragrance Association (IFRA) 13680

Head Office Rue de la Croix d'Or 3, 1204 Geneva, Switzerland. T. +41227163060. E-mail: info@ifrafragrance.org.
Operations Office Av des Arts 6, 1210 Brussels, Belgium. T. +3222142060. Fax +3222142069.
URL: https://ifrafragrance.org/
History 1973, Geneva (Switzerland). Former names and other names: *Association internationale des matières premières pour la parfumerie* – former. Registration: Switzerland; EU Transparency Register, No/ID: 14130436110-87. **Aims** Develop and advance the fragrance industry; collect and study scientific data, regulations and other relevant documents, with special reference to biological effects; promote self-regulatory disciplines in the industry; disseminate timely information to membership on matters of relevance to the industry. **Structure** General Assembly (annual); Board of Directors; Committees; Working Groups. Regional Committees (4): IFRA Europe; Fragrance Creators Association; IFRA Latin America; IFRA Asia-Pacific. **Languages** English. **Staff** 5.00 FTE, paid. **Finance** Members' dues. **Activities** Maintains a Code of Practice and guidelines for the use of fragrance ingredients. **Events** *Global Fragrance Summit* Sao Paulo (Brazil) 2022, *Global Fragrance Summit* Singapore (Singapore) 2021, *Workshop* Singapore (Singapore) 2019, *Annual Meeting* Paris (France) 2018, *International conference on occupational environmental exposure of skin to chemicals* Edinburgh (UK) 2009. **Publications** *Code of Practice for the Fragrance Industry* – defining good manufacturing practices for the use of fragrance ingredients.
Members National associations of fragrance manufacturers in 16 countries (" grouped within IFRA Europe):
Australia, Brazil, Colombia, France (*), Germany (*), Indonesia, Italy (*), Japan, Mexico, Netherlands (*), Singapore, Spain (*), Switzerland (*), Türkiye (*), UK (*), USA.
NGO Relations Member of (3): *Conseil européen de l'industrie chimique (CEFIC, #04687)*; *Downstream Users of Chemicals Co-ordination group (DUCC, #05127)*; *European Partnership for Alternative Approaches to Animal Testing (EPAA, #08155)*. In liaison with technical committees of: *International Organization for Standardization (ISO, #14473)*. Associate Expert Group of *Business and Industry Advisory Committee to the OECD (BIAC, #03385)*. [2022/XD9729/t/D]

♦ International Framework for Nuclear Energy Cooperation (IFNEC) . . 13681

Contact address not obtained. E-mail: ifnec@nuclear.energy.gov.
URL: http://www.ifnec.org/
History 16 Sep 2007, on signing of Statement of Principles, as *Global Nuclear Energy Partnership (GNEP)*. Jun 2010, present name and structure adopted. **Aims** Provide a forum for cooperation among participant states to explore mutually beneficial approaches to ensure that the use of nuclear energy for peaceful purposes proceeds in a manner that is efficient and meets the highest standards of safety, security and non-proliferation. **Structure** Executive Committee. Steering Group. Working Groups (2). **Activities** Working Groups (2): Reliable Nuclear Fuel Services; Infrastructure Development. **Events** *Meeting* Paris (France) 2015, *Steering Group Meeting* Paris (France) 2015, *Steering Group Meeting* Seoul (Korea Rep) 2014, *Steering Group Meeting* Jeju (Korea Rep) 2011, *Meeting* Tokyo (Japan) 2010. **Members** Participants (31); Observers (30); International Organizations (3). Membership countries not specified. [2015/XM3757/F*]

♦ International Franchise Association (internationally oriented national body)

♦ International Francophone Institute (IFI) 13682

Institut Francophone International
Dir C3 – 2ème Etage, 144 Xuan Thuy, Cau Ciay, Hanoi, Vietnam. T. +842437450173 ext 368.
Deputy Dir address not obtained.
URL: http://www.ifi.vnu.edu.vn/
History 1994, Vietnam. Founded by *Université des réseaux d'expression française (UREF, inactive)*, following recommendations, 1991, Chaillot (France), of *Conférence au sommet des chefs d'Etat et de gouvernement des pays ayant le français en partage (Sommet de la Francophonie, #04648)*. First students accepted Dec 1995. Implemented by UREF within *Agence universitaire de La Francophonie (AUF, #00548)*, as an international francophone training and research institute. Former names and other names: *Institut de la Francophonie pour l'Informatique (IFI)* – former; *Institut de la Francophonie pour l'Innovation (IFI)* – former. **Aims** Organize and develop high quality international and interdisciplinary research and educational activities, specializing in IT and business. **Structure** Large support network of universities, public research labs and private companies in French-speaking European countries and in French Canada. **Languages** English, French, Vietnamese. **Staff** 25.50 FTE, paid. **Finance** Main funding provided by AUF; also funding from Vietnam National University, Hanoi; indirect contribution from Vietnam which donates building space; some contributions for student scholarships from private companies; funding within the framework of bilateral cooperation between IFI and various francophone countries. Annual budget: 800,000 EUR (2020). **Activities** Events/meetings; training/education. **Events** *RIVF : conférence internationale de recherche en informatique vietnamienne et francophone* Paris (France) 2004, *RIVF : conférence internationale de recherche en informatique vietnamienne et francophone* Paris (France) 2003. **Publications** *Le journal des étudiants de l'IFI*; *Revue Scientifique La Francophonie en Asie-Pacifique (FAP)*. [2021.05.27/XE1952/j/E]

♦ International Frankenstein Society (internationally oriented national body)
♦ International Franz Lehar Society (#13235)
♦ International Freedom Alliance (unconfirmed)
♦ International Freedom of Expression Exchange / see IFEX (#11100)
♦ International Free Economy Union (inactive)
♦ International Free Press Society (inactive)

♦ International Freight Association (IFA) 13683

Exec Officer PO Box 655, Lane Cove NSW 2066, Australia. T. +61297151715. Fax +61297151617. E-mail: ifaheadoffice@iinet.net.au.
Street Address Suite 2D, 9 Burwood Road, Burwood NSW 2134, Australia.
URL: http://www.ifa-online.com/
History 1985. **Events** *Annual General Meeting* San Francisco, CA (USA) 2019, *Annual General Meeting* Athens (Greece) 2018, *Annual General Meeting* Seoul (Korea Rep) 2017, *Annual General Meeting* New York, NY (USA) 2016, *Annual General Meeting* Amsterdam (Netherlands) 2015. [2018/XD5187/D]

♦ International Freight and Logistics Network (IFLN) 13684

Pres 14950 Heathrow Forest Pkwy, Ste 180, Houston TX 77032, USA. T. +12812276600. Fax +12812276606. E-mail: inquiries@ifln.net.
URL: http://www.ifln.net/
History May 2000. **Aims** Promote provision of logistics services by enabling members to cooperate with like-minded logistics companies worldwide and in turn offer a global service to their customers. **Structure** Includes: *IFLN Healthcare & Pharma* network; *IFLN Global Projects* network. **Languages** English. **Activities** Events/meetings; knowledge management/information dissemination. **Events** *Annual Conference* Bangkok (Thailand) 2023, *Annual Conference* Las Vegas, NV (USA) 2022, *Virtual Annual Conference* 2021, *Annual Conference* Las Vegas, NV (USA) 2020, *Annual Conference* Vienna (Austria) 2019. **Members** Companies (300) in 100 countries. Membership countries not specified. [2021.08.31/XF7172/F]

♦ International Freight Pipeline Society (inactive)
♦ International French-Language Congress of Forensic and Social Medicine (#04674)
♦ International French-Speaking Association for Odontological Research (no recent information)
♦ International Frequency Registration Board (inactive)
♦ International Frequency Sensor Association (internationally oriented national body)
♦ International Friends of the Cello Association / see International Friends of Music Association
♦ International Friendship Development Organization (internationally oriented national body)
♦ International Friendship Evangelism (internationally oriented national body)

♦ International Friendship League (IFL) 13685

Intl Sec IFL Worldwide Office, PO Box 217, Ross-on-Wye, HR9 9FD, UK. E-mail: info@iflworld.org.
Treasurer address not obtained.
URL: http://www.iflworld.org/
History 1926, UK. Revised international Constitution adopted at International Assembly, May 2009, Malaga (Spain); Mar 2018, Dakar (Senegal). Former names and other names: *Ligue d'amitié internationale* – former; *Liga de Amistad Internacional* – former; *Internationale Freundschaftsliga* – former. **Aims** Promote a spirit of peace, friendship and mutual respect among the people of the world with a view to peaceful *cooperation* in *international affairs*. **Structure** International Assembly (annual); International Committee; National and Local Groups. **Languages** English, French, Portuguese. **Staff** Voluntary. **Finance** Sources: donations; members' dues. **Activities** Awards/prizes/competitions; awareness raising; events/meetings; networking/liaising; publishing activities. **Events** *International Assembly* Mzuzu (Malawi) 2024, *Assembly* St John's, NL (Canada) 2023, *Assembly* Le Plessis-Robinson (France) 2020, *Assembly* Malaga (Spain) 2019, *Assembly* Dakar (Senegal) 2018. **Publications** *Courier* (4 a year) – journal. British group publishes a quarterly magazine.
Members Groups in 15 countries:
Burundi, France, Germany, Kenya, Netherlands, Portugal, Rwanda, Senegal, Seychelles, Sweden, Tanzania UR, Togo, Uganda, UK, Zambia.
Individuals in 19 countries:
Belarus, Belgium, China, Cuba, Ethiopia, Finland, Greece, Indonesia, Iran Islamic Rep, New Zealand, Norway, Poland, Russia, Spain, Switzerland, Tanzania UR, Tunisia, Ukraine, USA. [2022.11.07/XC2069/y/F]

♦ International Friends of Music Association (internationally oriented national body)
♦ International Friends of Nature / see Internationals amis de la nature (#14780)
♦ International Friends of the Spiritual Order (inactive)
♦ International Front Runners (internationally oriented national body)

♦ International Frozen Food Association (IFFA) 13686

Association internationale des denrées congelées
Contact address not obtained. T. +17038210770. Fax +17038211350. E-mail: info@affi.com.
History 1974, Washington DC (USA). **Aims** Advance interests of frozen food *industry* worldwide. **Events** *Frozen food summit of the Americas / Congress* Mexico City (Mexico) 1998, *Conference* Hong Kong (Hong Kong) 1995, *The emerging Mexican frozen food market* Mexico City (Mexico) 1993, *Conference* Honolulu, HI (USA) 1989, *World frozen food congress* Lausanne (Switzerland) 1986.
Members Frozen food processing companies, associations, individuals and suppliers in 9 countries and territories:
Canada, Hong Kong, Italy, Japan, Netherlands, Norway, Spain, Sweden, Taiwan.
IGO Relations Participates as observer in the activities of: *Codex Alimentarius Commission (CAC, #04081)*. [2009.08.01/XF1344/F]

♦ International Frozen Food Press Organization (no recent information)
♦ International Fructose Association (inactive)

♦ International Fruit and Vegetable Juice Association (IFU) 13687

Exec Dir 23 boulevard des Capucines, 75002 Paris, France. T. +441934627844. E-mail: john@ifu-fruitjuice.com – ifu@ifu-fruitjuice.com.
URL: http://www.ifu-fruitjuice.com/
History 25 Jan 1949, Paris (France). Founded following 1st International Congress, Apr 1948. Former names and other names: *International Federation of Fruit Juice Producers (IFJU)* – former; *Fédération internationale des producteurs de jus de fruits (FIJU)* – former; *Federación Internacional de los Productores de Jugos de Frutas (FIJUG)* – former; *Internationale Früchtsaft Union (IFU)* – former. Registration: France. **Aims** Represent the worldwide juice interests as an NGO at governmental and international organizations; act as an information and communication centre/facilitator; harmonize standards and practices for juice products and producers; coordinate scientific activities to benefit the juice industry. **Structure** General Assembly of Delegates; Executive Committee. Commissions (4): Science and Technology; Methods of Analysis; Legislation; Marketing. **Languages** English. **Staff** 3.50 FTE, paid. **Finance** Sources: members' dues. **Activities** Events/meetings; knowledge management/information dissemination. **Events** *Annual Juice Summit* Antwerp (Belgium) 2019, *Annual Juice Summit* Antwerp (Belgium) 2018, *Annual Juice Summit* Antwerp (Belgium) 2017, *General Assembly of Delegates* Antwerp (Belgium) 2017, *Asia Seminar* Dubai (United Arab Emirates) 2017. **Publications** *IFU Newsletter* in English, French. Congress reports; scientific brochures; IFU Analytical Methods.
Members National organizations in 21 countries:
Australia, Austria, Brazil, China, Colombia, France, Germany, Hungary, Israel, Italy, Netherlands, New Zealand, Poland, Russia, South Africa, Spain, Switzerland, Thailand, Türkiye, UK, USA.
Individuals in 17 countries:
Algeria, Argentina, Belgium, China, Cuba, Germany, Greece, Ireland, Italy, Malta, Mexico, Morocco, Netherlands, Russia, South Africa, Switzerland, UK.
Associated members in 11 countries:
Argentina, Belgium, Ecuador, France, Germany, Israel, Italy, Norway, Sweden, Switzerland, USA.
Consultative Status Consultative status granted from: *ECOSOC (#05331)* (Ros C); *FAO (#09260)* (Liaison Status). **IGO Relations** Participates as observer in the activities of: *Codex Alimentarius Commission (CAC, #04081)*. **NGO Relations** In liaison with technical committees of: *International Organization for Standardization (ISO, #14473)*. [2021.03.02/XC1921/C]

♦ **International FTTs** Fair Trade Towns International (#09241)

♦ International Fuel and Power Association (IFPA) 13688

Association internationale de combustible et énergie – Mezdunarodnaja Toplivno-Energeticheskaja Associacija (MTEA)
Contact Vernadsky, Ave 94 – Bldg 1 of 6-7-9, Moscow MOSKVA, Russia, 119571. T. +74995039393 – +74995039383. Fax +74995039393 – +74995039383. E-mail: ec@ecifpa.ru.
History Founded 27 Nov 1989, Moscow (USSR), by large coal, oil and gas recovering and processing enterprises. Re-registered, 3 Jun 1992, as an international non-governmental public organization. Re-registered in the Ministry of Justice of Russia, 1999. **Aims** Promote comprehensive development of international ties so as to concentrate scientific and technical potential of scientists and scientific organizations on the settlement of problems in the sphere of production, development and rational utilization and saving of fuel and energy resources, and improvement of the ecological situation in different regions of the world. **Structure** Congress; Board; Bureau of the Board; Scientific and Expert Council. Branches in Yerevan (Armenia) and Moscow (Russia); Science and Technology Centres in Moscow and St Petersburg (Russia); Energy-Society Institute. **Languages** English, Russian. **Staff** 15.00 FTE, paid. **Finance** Members' dues. Other sources: receipts from newly founded enterprises. **Activities** Networking/liaising; research and development; events/meetings. **Events** *International forum on energy and society* Moscow (Russia) 2000, *International scientific and practice-oriented conference* Moscow (Russia) 1998, *International conference* Khabarovsk (Russia) 1997, *Use of natural gas as a motor fuel – gas into engines* Moscow (Russia) 1996. **Publications** Monographs; research and project reports; proceedings.
Members National organizations and enterprises (over 200) in 10 countries:
Armenia, Austria, Azerbaijan, Belgium, Bulgaria, Kazakhstan, Netherlands, Russia, Ukraine, Uzbekistan.
NGO Relations Links with a number of natural gas vehicle associations (not specified). [2016/XD3128/D]

♦ International Fuel Quality Center (IFQC) 13689

Exec Dir 1616 S Voss, Ste 1000, Houston TX 77057-2627, USA. T. +17132606474. Fax +17138408585. E-mail: ifqc@hartenergy.com.
URL: http://www.ifqc.org/
History 1998. **Aims** Bring together leading refining, automotive and engine manufacturers, technology and government stakeholders, facilitating and improving their understanding of fuel quality issues. **Structure** Offices in: Houston TX (USA); Washington DC (USA); Singapore (Singapore); Brussels (Belgium); London (UK). **Languages** English. **Staff** 10.00 FTE, paid. **Activities** Meeting activities. **Events** *Biofuels markets Asia conference* Bangkok (Thailand) 2006, *Hart world refining and fuels conference* Beijing (China) 2006. **Publications** *Worldwide Fuel Specificiations*. Reports; dabatases.

Members Full in 34 countries:
Australia, Austria, Brazil, Canada, China, Colombia, Finland, France, Germany, Hong Kong, Hungary, India, Italy, Jamaica, Japan, Jordan, Korea Rep, Kuwait, Malaysia, Netherlands, North Macedonia, Poland, Russia, Saudi Arabia, Singapore, Slovenia, South Africa, Sweden, Taiwan, Thailand, Türkiye, UK, USA, Venezuela.
NGO Relations Member of: *Partnership for Clean Fuels and Vehicles (PCFV, #18231).* [2014/XJ7830/**F**]

♦ International Funboard Class Association (see: #21760)

♦ International Functional Electrical Stimulation Society (IFESS) 13690

Main Office c/o Inst Health Care Engineering, TUG, Stremayrgasse 16, 8010 Graz, Austria. E-mail: office@ifess.org.
Sec address not obtained.
URL: http://www.ifess.org/
History 19 Aug 1995, Vienna (Austria). Founded following discussions held at the 1993 FES Conference in Slovenia. Former names and other names: *International FES Society* – alias. **Aims** Promote research, application and understanding of electrical stimulation as utilized in the field of medicine. **Structure** Board of Directors, including President, Vice-President, Secretary and Treasurer. **Languages** English. **Staff** Voluntary. **Finance** Members' dues. **Events** *RehabWeek* Rotterdam (Netherlands) 2022, *Annual Conference* Toronto, ON (Canada) 2019, *Annual IFESS Conference* Nottwil (Switzerland) 2018, *Annual Conference* La Grande Motte (France) 2016, *Annual Conference* Chicago, IL (USA) 2015.
Members Full in 41 countries and territories:
Argentina, Australia, Austria, Belarus, Belgium, Brazil, Canada, Croatia, Denmark, Finland, France, Germany, Greece, Hong Kong, Hungary, Iceland, India, Indonesia, Iran Islamic Rep, Ireland, Israel, Italy, Japan, Korea Rep, Lithuania, Netherlands, Nigeria, Norway, Poland, Portugal, Russia, Saudi Arabia, Serbia, Slovenia, Spain, Sweden, Switzerland, Taiwan, Thailand, UK, USA.
NGO Relations Member of (2): *International Consortium for Rehabilitation Technology (ICRT, #12921); International Industry Society in Advanced Rehabilitation Technology (IISART, #13840)* (Associate).
[2021/XD7487/**D**]

♦ International Functional Fitness Federation (iF3) 13691

SG address not obtained.
URL: https://functionalfitness.sport/
History Registration: 501(c)(3), Start date: Oct 2016, USA. **Aims** Promote and grow competitive functional fitness worldwide. **Structure** General Asembly; Executive Board. Committees (7): Technical; Programming; Adaptive; Medical; Gender Equality; Athletes'; Ethics. **Activities** Standards/guidelines; training/education.
Members National federations in 54 countries and territories:
Andorra, Argentina, Aruba, Australia, Austria, Barbados, Belgium, Brazil, Canada, Central African Rep, Chile, China, Czechia, Denmark, Ecuador, Egypt, El Salvador, Finland, France, Germany, Greece, Guatemala, Hong Kong, Hungary, Iceland, India, Ireland, Italy, Japan, Jersey, Kazakhstan, Korea Rep, Latvia, Lebanon, Libya, Lithuania, Mauritius, Mexico, Netherlands, Norway, Pakistan, Panama, Portugal, Puerto Rico, Russia, Serbia, Spain, Sri Lanka, Sweden, Switzerland, UK, USA, Uzbekistan, Venezuela.
NGO Relations Member of (1): *The Association for International Sport for All (TAFISA, #02763).* Cooperates with (1): *International Testing Agency (ITA, #15678).* [2022/AA3051/**C**]

♦ International of Functionaries / see International Federation of Employees in Public Services (#13410)

♦ International Fund for Agricultural Development (IFAD) 13692

Fonds international de développement agricole (FIDA) – Fondo Internacional de Desarrollo Agrícola (FIDA)

Pres Via Paolo di Dono 44, 00142 Rome RM, Italy. T. +39654591. Fax +3965043463. E-mail: ifad@ifad.org.
URL: http://www.ifad.org/
History Following resolution adopted by World Food Conference, Nov 1974, establishment agreement adopted by *'United Nations Conference on the Establishment of an International Fund for Agricultural Development',* 13 Jun 1976, Rome (Italy). Opened for signature, in accordance with Article 13.1 (a), on 20 Dec 1976, New York NY (USA). Entered into force 30 Nov 1977. Amendment of Article 6.8, 11 Dec 1986, entered into force 11 Mar 1987. Articles 3.3, 3.4, 4.2, 4.5, 5.2, 6.2, 6.4, 6.5, 6.6, 12 (a), 11.3 and schedules I, II and III amended, in accordance with Article 12, by Resolution 86/XVIII of the Governing Council on 26 Jan 1995. Amendments entered into force 20 Feb 1997. Article 4.1 amended, by Resolution 100/XX of Governing Council, 21 Feb 1997. Articles 7.2 (a) and (b) amended by Resolution 124/XXIV of the Governing Council, 21 Feb 2001 and again by Resolution 124/XXIV, 16 Feb 2006 as revised by Resolution 141/XXIX/Rev.1, amendments entered into force, 22 Dec 2006; Article 7.2 (g) amended by Resolution 143/XXIX, 16 Feb 2006 – amendments entered into force, 16 Aug 2006. A specialized agency of the United Nations within *United Nations System (#20635),* linked to *ECOSOC (#05331).* Although not one of the financial institutions set up following the Bretton Woods Conference, 22 Jul 1944, Bretton Woods NH (USA), IFAD is nevertheless sometimes included when referring to the *Bretton Woods Institutions (BWIs, #03322).* Statutes registered in *'UNTS 1/16041'.* **Aims** Focus on agriculture and reduce poverty in rural areas of developing countries, by helping poor rural people to increase their food production and incomes, through investment in 6 main areas: Natural resources, especially land and water; Improved agricultural technologies and production services; Rural financial services; Transparent and competitive markets for agricultural inputs and products; Opportunities for rural off-farm employment and enterprise development; Local and national policy and programming processes, with emphasis on seeing smallholder farmers as business people and entrepreneurs. **Structure** Governing Council (meets annually), in which all members are represented. Votes are based on membership and on share of their paid contributions within replenishments. Executive Board, comprising 18 members (8 from List A, 4 from List B, 6 from List C) and 18 alternates, elected by Council for 3-year term, headed by President. Houses: *International Land Coalition (ILC, #13999).* **Languages** Arabic, English, French, Spanish. **Staff** As of 31 Dec 2017: 608 staff members, including the independent Office of Evaluation, consisting of 327 Professionals and higher-category staff (excluding President and Vice-President), 51 National Officers and 230 General service staff. Staff negotiations through *IFAD Staff Association (#11099). Administrative Tribunal of the International Labour Organization (ILO Tribunal, #00118)* is competent to settle disputes. **Finance** Sources: contributions of member/participating states. Other sources: special contributions from non-member states and other sources. **Activities** Events/meetings; projects/programmes. Financed 1,069 projects and programmes in 125 countries and territories since 1978, committing US$ 2,100,000,000 in investment projects. **Events** *Meeting* Incheon (Korea Rep) 2019, *Session* Rome (Italy) 2019, *Session* Rome (Italy) 2018, *Session* Rome (Italy) 2017, *Session* Rome (Italy) 2016. **Publications** Annual Report. Rural Poverty Report; technical working papers; special studies; descriptive materials; policy papers; corporate public relations and advocacy materials.
Members Open to any UN member state or of any of its specialized agencies or of IAEA. Member states (173) are classified as follows: List A (primarily OECD members); List B (primarily OPEC members); List C (developing countries), further divided into sub-list C1 (countries in Africa), sub-list C2 (countries in Europe, Asia and the Pacific), and sub-list C3 (countries in Latin America and the Caribbean). List A: 25 countries:
List A: 25 countries:
Canada, Cyprus, Denmark, Estonia, Finland, France, Germany, Greece, Hungary, Iceland, Ireland, Israel, Italy, Japan, Luxembourg, Netherlands, New Zealand, Norway, Portugal, Russia, Spain, Sweden, Switzerland, UK, USA.
List B: 12 countries:
Algeria, Gabon, Indonesia, Iran Islamic Rep, Iraq, Kuwait, Libya, Nigeria, Qatar, Saudi Arabia, United Arab Emirates, Venezuela.
List C: 139 countries:
Afghanistan, Albania, Angola, Antigua-Barbuda, Argentina, Armenia, Azerbaijan, Bahamas, Bangladesh, Barbados, Belize, Benin, Bhutan, Bolivia, Bosnia-Herzegovina, Botswana, Brazil, Burkina Faso, Burundi, Cambodia, Cameroon, Cape Verde, Central African Rep, Chad, Chile, China, Colombia, Comoros, Congo Brazzaville, Congo DR, Cook Is, Costa Rica, Côte d'Ivoire, Croatia, Cuba, Cyprus, Djibouti, Dominica, Dominican Rep, Ecuador, Egypt, El Salvador, Equatorial Guinea, Eritrea, Eswatini, Ethiopia, Fiji, Gambia, Georgia, Ghana, Grenada, Guatemala, Guinea, Guinea-Bissau, Guyana, Haiti, Honduras, India, Israel, Jamaica, Jordan, Kazakhstan, Kenya, Kiribati, Korea DPR, Korea Rep, Kyrgyzstan, Laos, Lebanon, Lesotho, Liberia, Madagascar, Malawi, Malaysia, Maldives, Mali, Malta, Marshall Is, Mauritania, Mauritius, Mexico, Micronesia FS, Moldova, Mongolia, Montenegro, Morocco, Mozambique, Myanmar, Namibia, Nauru, Nepal, Nicaragua, Niger, Niue, North Macedonia, Oman, Pakistan, Palau, Panama, Papua New Guinea, Paraguay, Peru, Philippines, Romania, Rwanda, Samoa, Sao Tomé-Principe, Senegal, Seychelles, Sierra Leone, Solomon Is, Somalia, South Africa, South Sudan, Sri Lanka, St Kitts-Nevis, St Lucia, St Vincent-Grenadines, Sudan, Suriname, Syrian AR, Tajikistan, Tanzania UR, Thailand, Timor-Leste, Togo, Tonga, Trinidad-Tobago, Tunisia, Türkiye, Tuvalu, Uganda, Uruguay, Uzbekistan, Vanuatu, Vietnam, Yemen, Zambia, Zimbabwe.
IGO Relations Cooperating international organizations and institutions invited as observers pursuant to Rule 42 of the Rules of Procedure of the Governing Council:
- *African Development Bank (ADB, #00283);*
- *African Union (AU, #00488);*
- *Arab Authority for Agricultural Investment and Development (AAAID, #00902);*
- *Arab Bank for Economic Development in Africa (#00904);*
- *Arab Centre for the Studies of Arid Zones and Dry Lands (ACSAD, #00918);*
- *Arab Fund for Economic and Social Development (AFESD, #00965);*
- *Arab Gulf Programme for United Nations Development Organizations (AGFUND, #00971);*
- *Arab Organization for Agricultural Development (AOAD, #01018);*
- *Asian Development Bank (ADB, #01422);*
- *Banque ouest africaine de développement (BOAD, #03170);*
- *Caribbean Agricultural Research and Development Institute (CARDI, #03436);*
- *Caribbean Development Bank (CDB, #03492);*
- *Central American Bank for Economic Integration (CABEI, #03658);*
- *CGIAR System Organization (CGIAR, #03843);*
- *Comité permanent inter-Etats de lutte contre la sécheresse dans le Sahel (CILSS, #04195);*
- *Commonwealth Secretariat (#04362);*
- *Comunidade dos Paises de Lingua Portuguesa (CPLP, #04430);*
- *Development Bank of Latin America (CAF, #05055);*
- *European Bank for Reconstruction and Development (EBRD, #06315);*
- *European Union (EU, #08967);*
- *FAO (#09260);*
- *Fondo Financiero para el Desarrollo de la Cuenca del Plata (FONPLATA, #09833);*
- *Global Environment Facility (GEF, #10346);*
- *Gulf Cooperation Council (GCC, #10826);*
- *ILO (#11123);*
- *Inter-American Development Bank (IDB, #11427);*
- *Inter-American Institute for Cooperation on Agriculture (IICA, #11434);*
- *Intergovernmental Authority on Development (IGAD, #11472);*
- *International Atomic Energy Agency (IAEA, #12294);*
- *International Bank for Reconstruction and Development (IBRD, #12317)* (World Bank);
- *International Center for Agricultural Research in the Dry Areas (ICARDA, #12466);*
- *International Civil Aviation Organization (ICAO, #12581);*
- *International Crops Research Institute for the Semi-Arid Tropics (ICRISAT, #13116);*
- *International Development Association (IDA, #13155);*
- *International Grains Council (IGC, #13731);*
- *International Livestock Research Institute (ILRI, #14062);*
- *International Maritime Organization (IMO, #14102);*
- *International Monetary Fund (IMF, #14180);*
- *International Organization for Migration (IOM, #14454);*
- *International Rice Research Institute (IRRI, #14754);*
- *International Telecommunication Union (ITU, #15673);*
- *Islamic Development Bank (IsDB, #16044);*
- *Islamic World Educational, Scientific and Cultural Organization (ICESCO, #16058);*
- *Joint United Nations Programme on HIV/AIDS (UNAIDS, #16149);*
- *League of Arab States (LAS, #16420);*
- *New Partnership for Africa's Development (NEPAD, #17091);*
- *OAS (#17629);*
- *OECD (#17693);*
- *OECD Development Assistance Committee (DAC, see: #17693);*
- *OPEC Fund for International Development (OFID, #17745);*
- *Organisation of Islamic Cooperation (OIC, #17813);*
- *Regional Centre on Agrarian Reform and Rural Development for the Near East (#18755);*
- *Sistema Económico Latinoamericano (SELA, #19294);*
- *Southern African Development Community (SADC, #19843);*
- *Tropical Agriculture Research and Higher Education Center (#20246);*
- *UNEP (#20299);*
- *UNCTAD (#20285);*
- *UNDP (#20292);*
- *UNESCO (#20322);*
- *UNHCR (#20327);*
- *UNICEF (#20332);*
- *UNIDO (#20336);*
- *United Nations (UN, #20515);*
- *United Nations Convention to Combat Desertification (UNCCD, 1994);*
- *United Nations Economic Commission for Africa (ECA, #20554);*
- *United Nations Economic Commission for Europe (UNECE, #20555);*
- *United Nations Economic Commission for Latin America and the Caribbean (ECLAC, #20556);*
- *United Nations Economic and Social Commission for Asia and the Pacific (ESCAP, #20557);*
- *United Nations Economic and Social Commission for Western Asia (ESCWA, #20558);*
- *United Nations Human Settlements Programme (UN-Habitat, #20572);*
- *United Nations Institute for Training and Research (UNITAR, #20576);*
- *United Nations Joint Staff Pension Fund (UNJSPF, #20581);*
- *United Nations Office for the Coordination of Humanitarian Affairs (OCHA, #20593);*
- *United Nations Office on Drugs and Crime (UNODC, #20596);*
- *United Nations Population Fund (UNFPA, #20612);*
- *World Trade Organization (WTO, #21864).*

Observer organizations:
- *African-Asian Rural Development Organization (AARDO, #00203);*
- *African Development Bank Group (ADB Group, #00284);*
- *Centre for Environment and Development for the Arab Region and Europe (CEDARE, #03738);*
- *International Development Research Centre (IDRC, #13162);*
- *United Nations Office for Project Services (UNOPS, #20602);*
- *United Nations Research Institute for Social Development (UNRISD, #20623);*
- *United Nations University (UNU, #20642);*
- *United Nations Volunteers (UNV, #20650);*
- *Universal Postal Union (UPU, #20682);*
- *WHO (#20950);*
- *World Food Programme (WFP, #21510);*
- *World Intellectual Property Organization (WIPO, #21593);*
- *World Meteorological Organization (WMO, #21649).*

Cooperation Agreements with:
- AAAID;
- Accord entre le gouvernement belge et le FIDA agissant en qualité decoordinateur pour un programme conjoint FIDA/OMS/FISE/PNUD s'inscrivant dansles actions du fonds de survie belge;
- AfDB;
- AFESD;
- *African Export-Import Bank (Afreximbank, #00305);*
- *African Regional Centre of Technology (ARCT, #00432);*
- *African Union Scientific Technical Research Commission (AU STRC, #00493);*
- AGFUND;
- AOAD;
- AsDB;
- BADEA;
- BCIE;
- BOAD;
- CAF;
- CDB;
- CILSS;
- Comité français pour le FIDA (Comifad);
- *Common Fund for Commodities (CFC, #04293);*
- Commonwealth Secretariat (Memorandum of Understanding);
- CPLP;
- *ECOWAS Bank for Investment and Development (EBID, #05334);*
- European Community (Financial and Administrative Framework Agreement);
- FAO, IBRD and IDA (Working Arrangements);
- FAO, WFP and Italy (Protocol Agreement);
- FONPLATA;
- GCC Secretariat;
- IDB;
- IDRC (Memorandum of Understanding);

- IICA;
- ILO;
- International Development Association (Letter of Agreement);
- ISESCO;
- Italy and IDB (Memorandum of Understanding);
- Joint Food Security Theme Group at Country Level for FAO, WFP and IFAD;
- LAS;
- NEPAD (Memorandum of Understanding);
- OECD;
- OIC;
- ONU (Memorandum of Understanding regarding use of premises in permanentheadquarters seat building of the UNU;
- Rome based agencies (FAO, WFP and IFAD) for Global operations, regional and at country level;
- UNAIDS (Memorandum of Understanding);
- UNCCD Implementation in Central Asia Republics (Strategic PartnershipAgreement);
- UNCHS (Memorandum of Understanding);
- UNCTAD (exchange of letters);
- UNDP;
- UNDTCD;
- UNFPA;
- UNHCR;
- UNICEF;
- UNICEF in Burkina Faso (Protocol Agreement);
- UNIDO (Letter of Agreement);
- *Union économique et monétaire Ouest africaine (UEMOA, #20377)*;
- United Nations through Dag Hammarskjöld Library for consortium-basedpurchasing of electronic information services (Memorandum of Agreement);
- *United Nations Fund for International Partnerships (UNFIP, #20565)* (Basic Implementation Agreement);
- UNOPS;
- Venenzuelan Banc (Inter Institutional Cooperation framework Agreement);
- WFP (Memorandum of Understanding for Operational Partnership in the AsiaRegion;
- WFP China Office and IFAD Asia and Pacific Division Relating to cost-sharingarrangement for using the service of one WFP national professional staff asIFAD Program Liaison Officer (Letter of Understanding);
- WFP – Cost-Sharing Arrangement for Support to IFAD Consultants (Letter ofAgreement);
- WHO;
- WHO concerning the Second Phase of the Belgian Survival Fund for the ThirdWorld (Supplementary Arrangement);
- WHO concerning the Third Phase of the BSF-JP (Supplementary Agreement);
- WHO, UNICEF and UNDP (Memorandum of Understanding);
- WHO/UNICEF/UNDP (Memorandum of Understanding);
- WMO (Working Arrangements);
- World Bank;
- World Bank concerning Financing for Completion of the Farmod Project (Letterof Agreement);
- World Bank concerning Financing for the Consultative Group to Assist thePoorest (Letter of Agreement);
- World Bank concerning Financing of SDA Activities in Sub-Saharan Africa(Letter of Agreement);
- World Bank concerning Financing to Support New Phase of Regional Project ofTechnial Assistance for Agricultural Development of Central America (Letter ofAgreement);
- World Bank Concerning Multi-Donor Secretariat (Letter of Agreement).

Represented on: *United Nations System Chief Executives Board for Coordination (CEB, #20636)*. Cooperates with governments and international agencies in: *Consultative Group to Assist the Poor (CGAP, #04768)*. Member of: *Inter-Agency Working Group on Desertification (IAWGD, inactive)*; *UN-Water (#20723)*. Partner of: *UN System Network on Rural Development and Food Security (no recent information)*. Strategic partner of: *International Centre for Integrated Mountain Development (ICIMOD, #12500)*. Collaborates with: *African Development Institute (ADI, #00286)*. Supports: *Africa Rice Center (AfricaRice, #00518)*; *CABI (#03393)*. Instrumental in setting up: *Inter-Agency Task Force on Employment and Sustainable Livelihoods for All (inactive)*; *Joint Consultative Group on Policies (JCGP, no recent information)*; *Regional Animal Disease Surveillance and Control Network (RADISCON, inactive)*. Adheres to: *Global Partnership for Effective Development Co-operation (GPEDC, #10532)*.

NGO Relations Works directly with NGOs under grant-funded programme and indirectly through loan-fund programmes implemented by borrowing member governments. With emphasis on a particular development process, considers NGOs as natural partners. Collaborates with several types of NGO, including operational cooperation with many organizations at project level. The following list is indicative:

- *ACORD – Agency for Cooperation and Research in Development (#00073)*;
- *ActionAid (#00087)*;
- *American Near East Refugee Aid (ANERA)*;
- *CARE International (CI, #03429)*;
- *Centre international du crédit mutuel (CICM)*;
- *Global Forum on Agricultural Research (GFAR, #10370)*;
- *Institut Africain pour le Développement Economique et Social – Centre Africain de Formation (INADES-Formation, #11233)*;
- *International Development Enterprises (IDE, #13156)*;
- *International Fertilizer Development Center (IFDC, #13590)*;
- *International NGO Network on Desertification (inactive)*;
- *Kenya Women Finance Trust (KWFT)*;
- MYRADA – India;
- *SNV Netherlands Development Organisation (SNV)*;
- *One UN Climate Change Learning Partnership (UN CC:Learn, #17735)*;
- *Palestine Agricultural Relief Committee (PARC)*.

Cooperation agreements with: *Alliance for a Green Revolution in Africa (AGRA, #00685)* (joint cooperation agreement through a Memorandum of Understanding); *International Food Policy Research Institute (IFPRI, #13622)*; *Former FAO and Other United Nations Staff Association (FFOA)*; *IPS – Inter Press Service International Association (#16013)* (Letter of cooperation); *Worldview International Foundation (WIF, #21903)* (Letter of understanding).

Invited as observers to Governing Council sessions:

- *ACDI/VOCA*;
- *Africare (#00516)*;
- *Aga Khan Foundation (AKF, #00545)*;
- *American Council for Voluntary International Action (InterAction)*;
- *Association for Promotion of International Cooperation (APIC)*;
- *Associazione per la Cooperazione Internazionale e l'Aiuto Umanitario (ALISEI)*;
- *Brot für die Welt*;
- *Cooperation Canada*;
- CARE International;
- *Caritas Internationalis (CI, #03580)*;
- *Catholic Relief Services (CRS, #03608)*;
- *Club of Rome (COR, #04038)*;
- *Coalition of the Flemish North South Movement – 11 11 11*;
- *Comitato Internazionale per lo Sviluppo dei Popoli (CISP)*;
- *Confédération européenne des ong d'urgence et de développement (CONCORD, #04547)*;
- *Council of Non-Governmental Organizations for Development Support (#04911)*;
- *Counterpart International (FSP)*;
- *Environment Liaison Centre International (ELCI, no recent information)*;
- *Ingénieurs du monde (IdM)*;
- *FINCA International*;
- *Friends of the Islands of Peace (Islands of Peace)*;
- *Global Justice Now*;
- *Green Belt Movement (#10713)*;
- *Heifer International*;
- *Human Appeal (#10961)*;
- *Hunger Project (#10994)*;
- *IFOAM – Organics International (IFOAM, #11105)*;
- *International Catholic Organizations Information Center (ICO Center)*;
- *International Center for Biosaline Agriculture (ICBA, #12468)*;
- *International Centre of Insect Physiology and Ecology (ICIPE, #12499)*;
- *International Coalition for Development Action (ICDA, inactive)*;
- *International Commission on Irrigation and Drainage (ICID, #12694)*;
- *International Council of Voluntary Agencies (ICVA, #13092)*;
- *International Council of Women (ICW, #13093)*;
- *International Federation of Business and Professional Women (BPW International, #13376)*;
- *International Institute for Environment and Development (IIED, #13877)*;
- *International Institute of Tropical Agriculture (IITA, #13933)*;
- *International Juridical Organization for Environment and Development (IJO, no recent information)*;
- *International Potato Center (#14627)*;
- *International Union of Nutritional Sciences (IUNS, #15796)*;
- *Lutheran World Relief (LWR)*;
- *Mani Tese (MT)*;
- *MOVIMONDO (no recent information)*;
- Order of Malta;
- *Oxfam International (#17922)*;
- *Oxfam Novib*;
- *Ricerca e Cooperazione (RC)*;
- *Rotary International (RI, #18975)*;
- *Save the Children Federation (SCF)*;
- *Society for International Development (SID, #19581)*;
- *Strømme Foundation (SF)*;
- *Trickle Up Program (TUP, #20236)*;
- *Winrock International*;
- *World Council of Credit Unions (WOCCU, #21324)*;
- *World Council of Independent Christian Churches (WCICC, #21330)*;
- *World Neighbors (WN)*;
- *World Resources Institute (WRI, #21753)*;
- *World Wide Fund for Nature (WWF, #21922)*;
- *WorldFish (#21507)*.

Formal links with:

- *Band Aid Charitable Trust*;
- *France Volontaires*;
- *Oxfam Australia*;
- *Plenty International (#18405)* (Canada);
- *SOS SAHEL (#19695)*;
- *'Swedish Community for Afghanistan'*.

NGOs receiving grants under the IFAD/NGO Extended Cooperation Programme (some already listed under other categories):

- *Canadian Centre for International Studies and Cooperation (CECI)*;
- *Caribbean Network for Integrated Rural Development (CNIRD, #03528)*;
- CARITAS Senegal;
- *Centre for Research on Sustainable Agriculture and Rural Development (Swaminathan Research Foundation)*;
- *Centro Andino de Investigación Pedagógica (CAIP, no recent information)*;
- ELC International;
- *Entreprise Works / VITA*;
- *Freedom from Hunger (inactive)*;
- *International Forum for Development of Sustainable Land Use Systems (INFORUM, no recent information)*;
- *Near East Foundation (NEF)*;
- SOS Sahel, UK;
- TWIN – Eritrea.

Member of: *Association for Women's Rights in Development (AWID, #02980)*; *Better Than Cash Alliance (#03220)*; *International Council on Archives (ICA, #12996)*; *Permanent Conference of Mediterranean Audiovisual Operators (COPEAM, #18320)*. Instrumental in setting up: *Global Youth Innovation Network (GYIN)*; *World Peace Bell Association (WPBA, #21716)*. Representatives invited from: *Association internationale des traducteurs de conférence (AITC, #02748)*. Contact with: *Mouvement international de la jeunesse agricole et rurale catholique (MIJARC, #16865)*; *World Forum of Fisher Peoples (WFFP, #21517)*. Signatory to: *International Aid Transparency Initiative (IATI, #11604)*. Supports: *Africa Microfinance Network (AFMIN, #00189)*; *Asia Network for Sustainable Agriculture and Bioresources (ANSAB, #01445)*; *Asian NGO Coalition for Agrarian Reform and Rural Development (ANGOC, #01566)*; *Coconut Genetic Resources Network (COGENT, #04080)*; *International Centre for Trade and Sustainable Development, Geneva (ICTSD, #12524)*; *International Centre for Tropical Agriculture (#12527)*; *International Water Management Institute (IWMI, #15867)*; *PROLINNOVA (#18537)*; *Tropical Soil Biology and Fertility Institute (TSBF-CIAT, inactive)*.

In addition, links also with:

- *African Association of Insect Scientists (AAIS, #00207)*;
- *African Forest Research Network (AFORNET, inactive)*;
- *African Rural and Agricultural Credit Association (AFRACA, #00446)*;
- *Agricultural Libraries Network (AGLINET, #00571)*;
- *Air Serv International*;
- *Alley Farming Network for Tropical Africa (AFNETA, no recent information)*;
- *Alliance Against Hunger and Malnutrition (AAHM, no recent information)*;
- *Amref Health Africa (#00806)*;
- *APT Action on Poverty*;
- *Asia-Pacific Islands Rural Advisory Services Network (APIRAS, #01937)*;
- *Asia Pacific Rural and Agricultural Credit Association (APRACA, #02019)*;
- *Asian Farmers'Association for Sustainable Rural Development (AFA, #01450)*;
- *Asian Partnership for the Development of Human Resources in Rural Asia (AsiaDHRRA, #01654)*;
- *Association coopérative financière des fonctionnaires internationaux (AMFIE, #02455)*;
- *Bread for the World Institute (BFW Institute)*;
- *Centre for Applied Studies in International Negotiations (CASIN, no recent information)*;
- *Centro Latinoamericano para el Desarrollo Rural (RIMISP, #03813)*;
- *Coordination of Nongovernmental Organizations for International Development Cooperation (COCIS)*;
- *Diobass, écologie et société (DES)*;
- *Federation of International Civil Servants' Associations (FICSA, #09603)*;
- *Food and Disarmament International (FDI, no recent information)*;
- *Global Forum on Agricultural Research (GFAR, #10370)*;
- *Global Knowledge Partnership Foundation (GKPF, #10443)*;
- *Global Land Tool Network (GLTN, #10452)*;
- *Global Meeting of Generations (GMG)*;
- *Institut international d'appui au développement (AGRISUD)*;
- *Institute of Tropical Medicine Antwerp (IMT)*;
- *Inter-Parliamentary Union (IPU, #15961)*;
- *International Association of Students in Agricultural and Related Sciences (IAAS, #12191)*;
- *International Council for Science (ICSU, inactive)*;
- *International Forum for Rural Transport and Development (IFRTD, #13650)*;
- *International Forum for Rural Transport and Development (IFRTD, #13650)*;
- *International Institute of Social Studies, The Hague (ISS)*;
- *International Islamic Charitable Organization (IICO, #13957)*;
- *International Program for Technology and Research in Irrigation and Drainage (IPTRID, inactive)*;
- *International Service for National Agricultural Research (ISNAR, inactive)*;
- *International Steering Committee for the Economic Advancement of Rural Women (ISC, no recent information)*;
- *International Work Group for Indigenous Affairs (IWGIA, #15907)*;
- *Inter Press Service (IPS, #15964)*;
- *ISRIC – World Soil Information (#16068)*;
- *Mediterranean Information Office for Environment, Culture and Sustainable Development (MIO-ECSDE, #16657)*;
- *Mediterranean NGO Network for Ecology and Sustainable Development (MED Forum, no recent information)*;
- *Middle East Centre for the Transfer of Appropriate Technology (MECTAT, no recent information)*;
- *Mountain Forum (MF, #16861)*;
- *MOVIMONDO Molisv*;
- *Near East and North Africa Regional Agricultural Credit Association (NENARACA, inactive)*;
- *Network of IFAD Supported Projects in Latin America and the Caribbean (FIDAMERICA, #17035)*;
- *Network for International Policies and Cooperation in Education and Training (NORRAG, #17043)*;
- *Organisation internationale des experts (ORDINEX, #17808)*;
- *Pan African Institute for Development (PAID, #18053)*;
- *Pan African Organization for Sustainable Development (POSDEV, #18057)*;
- *Positive Planet International (#18465)*;
- *RECOFTC – The Center for People and Forests (RECOFTC, #18628)*;
- *Réseau de prévention des crises alimentaires (RPCA, #18905)*;
- *Rikolto*;
- *Sahel défis – développement et environnement, formation et insertion sociale (inactive)*;
- *Sahel and West Africa Club (SWAC, #19034)*;
- *Save the Children UK (SC UK)*;
- *South Research*;
- *TerrAfrica (#20127)*;
- *Third World Information Network (TWIN)*;

- *World Agroforestry Centre (ICRAF, #21072)*;
- *World Fair Trade Organization (WFTO, #21396)*. [2020/XF1721/f/**F***]

♦ International Fund for Agricultural Research (internationally oriented national body)

♦ International Fund for Animal Welfare (IFAW) 13693

Pres/CEO 290 Summer St, Yarmouth Port MA 02675, USA. T. +15087442000. E-mail: info@ifaw.org.
URL: http://www.ifaw.org/

History 1969. Founded by a small group of citizens to stop Canada's commercial seal hunt. Former names and other names: *Fonds international pour le bien-être des animaux* – former. Registration: EU Transparency Register, No/ID: 22644632329-52. **Aims** Improve the welfare of wild and domestic animals throughout the world, by reducing commercial exploitation of animals, protecting wildlife habitats and assisting animals in distress; motivate the public to prevent cruelty to animals; promote animal welfare and conservation policies that advance the well-being of both animals and people. **Structure** Headquarters in USA. Regional offices and presence worldwide. **Languages** Arabic, Chinese, Dutch, English, French, German, Russian, Spanish. **Staff** 200.00 FTE, paid; 250.00 FTE, voluntary. **Finance** Funded primarily by individual donations. Budget (2015): US$ 108 million. **Activities** Advocacy/lobbying/activism; projects/programmes; training/education. Teaching guides, lessons, worksheets, videos and interactive activities aligned with core curricula in over 40 countries and 12 languages plus Braille. **Publications** *World of Animals Magazine* (3 a year). Annual Report; periodic campaign reports and scientific papers. **Members** Active national branches (13) working in over 40 countries; individuals worldwide; supporters (2 million) worldwide. Membership countries not specified. **Consultative Status** Consultative status granted from: *ECOSOC (#05331)* (Special); *UNEP (#20299)*. **IGO Relations** Observer status with: *International Whaling Commission (IWC, #15879)*. Consultative status with: *International Maritime Organization (IMO, #14102)*. Signatory to: *Memorandum of Understanding for the Conservation of Cetaceans and Their Habitats in the Pacific Islands Region (2006)*. Member of: *Global Tiger Forum (GTF, #10628)*; *Standing Committee to the Bern Convention on the Conservation of European Wildlife and Natural Habitats (#19949)*. **NGO Relations** Member of: *Antarctic and Southern Ocean Coalition (ASOC, #00849)*; *Ape Alliance (#00871)*; *Deep Sea Conservation Coalition (DSCC, #05024)*; *Extractive Industries Transparency Initiative (EITI, #09229)*; *GEF CSO Network (GCN, #10087)*; *International Coalition for Animal Welfare (ICFAW, #12607)*; *International Tiger Coalition (ITC)*; *International Union for Conservation of Nature and Natural Resources (IUCN, #15766)*. Cooperates with: *Global Tiger Initiative (GTI, #10629)*. Supports: *Wildcare Africa Trust*. Partner of: *Elephant Protection Initiative Foundation (EPI Foundation, #05429)*. [2021/XF6032/f/**F**]

♦ International Fund for Cooperation and Partnership of the Black Sea and the Caspian Sea / see International Foundation for Sustainable Peace and Development (#13678)
♦ International Fund for the Development of Physical Education and Sport (no recent information)
♦ International Funders for Indigenous Peoples (internationally oriented national body)
♦ International Fund for Ireland (internationally oriented national body)
♦ International Fund for the Manufacturing of Equipment for Sports Training (see: #04634)
♦ International Fund for Monuments / see World Monuments Fund (#21657)
♦ International Fund for the Promotion of Culture (inactive)
♦ International Fund Raising Group / see Resource Alliance (#18914)

♦ International Fund for Saving the Aral Sea (IFAS) 13694

Mezdunarodnyj Fond Spasenija Arala (MFSA)

Contact Aini Str 48, 734000 Dushanbe, Tajikistan. T. +992433770000. E-mail: info@ecifas-tj.org.
URL: https://ecifas-tj.org/en/main/

History 26 Mar 1993, Kzyl-Orda (Kazakhstan). Established, taking over activities of *Interstate Council of the Central Asia States on the Aral Sea Basin Problems (inactive)*, following decision of Heads of State of 5 Central Asian nations, Mar 1993, Tashkent (Uzbekistan). Former names and other names: *International Aral Sea Rehabilitation Fund* – alias. **Aims** Overcome the *ecological* crisis and improve the socio-economic situation in the Aral Sea basin. **Structure** Council of the Heads of Central Asia States Board, comprising Deputy Prime Minister of each State. Executive Committee, with branches in all Central Asian States. Inspection Commission. Subordinate bodies: *Inter-State Commission for Water Coordination of Central Asia (ICWC, #15979)* and its *Scientific Information Centre of Interstate Coordination Water Commission of Central Asia (SIC ICWC, #19152)*; Interstate Sustainable Development Commission and its Scientific Information Centre (SIC ISDC). **Finance** Sources: contributions; contributions of member/participating states; international organizations. Other sources: contributions from companies and national organizations. **Activities** Finances and credits joint interstate ecological and scientific-practical programmes and projects, focused on saving the Aral Sea and improving the ecological and sanitary conditions in the whole area. Finances joint fundamental and applied research activities and technological development for restoration of ecological balance, rational use of natural resources and environmental protection. Organizes workshops and other meetings. Includes: *'Executing Agency of the International Fund for Saving the Aral Sea for Implementation of the GEF and ASBP Projects'*, which runs the *'Water and Environmental Management in the Aral Sea Basin'*, consisting of 5 components: Water and Salt Management, with the Subcomponent Water Conservation Competition; Public Awareness; Dam and Reservoir Management; Transboundary Water Monitoring; Wetlands Restoration. **Events** *Workshop on Water-Energy-Food Security Nexus in Central Asia* Vienna (Austria) 2019, *International conference on regional cooperation in transboundary river basins* Dushanbe (Tajikistan) 2005, *Annual State Presidents Meeting* Almaty (Kazakhstan) 1997, *Annual State Presidents Meeting* Dashkhovus (Turkmenistan) 1995, *Annual state presidents meeting* Nukus (Uzbekistan) 1994. **Publications** *Novyj Den* (12 a year) in Russian; *Vestnik Arala* (4 a year) in English, Russian.

Members Governments of 5 countries:
Kazakhstan, Kyrgyzstan, Tajikistan, Turkmenistan, Uzbekistan.

IGO Relations Observer status with (1): *United Nations (UN, #20515)* (General Assembly). Partner of (7): *Asian Development Bank (ADB, #01422)*; *International Bank for Reconstruction and Development (IBRD, #12317)*; *International Network of Basin Organizations (INBO, #14235)*; *Swiss Agency for Development and Cooperation (SDC)*; *UNDP (#20292)*; *UNEP (#20299)*; *United States Agency for International Development (USAID)*. Formal contacts with: *European Bank for Reconstruction and Development (EBRD, #06315)*; *European Commission (EC, #06633)*; *Global Environment Facility (GEF, #10346)*; *Kuwait Fund for Arab Economic Development (KFAED)*; *Swedish International Development Cooperation Agency (Sida)*; *UNESCO (#20322)*; *UNICEF (#20332)*; *WHO (#20950)*. **NGO Relations** Partner of (1): *International Water Management Institute (IWMI, #15867)*. [2022/XF4413/f/**F***]

♦ International Fur Animal Scientific Association (IFASA) 13695

Treas PO Box 14, 8830 Tjele, Denmark. E-mail: ifasa@anis.au.dk.
URL: http://www.ifasanet.org/

History 1988, Toronto ON (Canada), at 4th International Scientific Congress on Fur Animal Production. Current constitution adopted 13 Aug 1992; revised 20 Aug 1996, 17 Sep 2004 and 25 Aug 2016. **Aims** Promote the advancement of knowledge of all aspects of fur animal science and the fur industry; act as a formal link between scientists, fur breeder associations and governmental agencies on an international level. **Languages** English. **Activities** Events/meetings; networking/liaising. **Events** *Congress* Warsaw (Poland) 2021, *Congress* Warsaw (Poland) 2020, *Congress* Helsinki (Finland) 2016, *Congress* Copenhagen (Denmark) 2012, *Congress* Halifax, NS (Canada) 2008. **Publications** *Scientifur* – journal. [2020.02.10/XJ7091/**C**]

♦ International Fur Federation / see International Fur Federation (#13696)

♦ International Fur Federation (IFF) 13696

Contact 153 Wandsworth Road, Unit 401 Sky Gardens, London, SW8 2GB, UK. T. +442039290100. E-mail: info@wearefur.com – info@iftf.com.
URL: http://www.wearefur.com/

History 30 Apr 1949, London (UK). Former names and other names: *International Fur Trade Federation (IFTF)* – former; *Fédération internationale du commerce de la fourrure* – former; *International Fur Federation (IFF)* – former. Registration: EU Transparency Register, No/ID: 647352441013-57, Start date: 20 Jan 2021. **Aims** Promote, develop and protect trade in furskins; secure mutual support and cooperation; maintain concern with *conservation* of fur-bearing animals and work in close cooperation with reputable conservation organizations; collect and disseminate statistics and other information. **Structure** Annual General Meeting; General Council; Board. Meetings closed. **Languages** English. **Staff** 10.00 FTE, paid. **Finance** Members' dues; entrance fees. **Publications** Research reports.

Members Associations (55) in 44 countries and territories:
Afghanistan, Argentina, Austria, Belarus, Belgium, Brazil, Canada, China, Czechia, Denmark, Estonia, Finland, France, Germany, Greece, Hong Kong, Hungary, Iceland, Ireland, Italy, Japan, Kazakhstan, Korea Rep, Malaysia, Namibia, Netherlands, New Zealand, Norway, Poland, Portugal, Romania, Russia, Slovakia, Slovenia, Spain, Sweden, Switzerland, Taiwan, Türkiye, UK, Ukraine, United Arab Emirates, USA, Uzbekistan.

NGO Relations Member of: *European Policy Centre (EPC, #08240)*; *International Union for Conservation of Nature and Natural Resources (IUCN, #15766)*. In liaison with technical committees of: *International Organization for Standardization (ISO, #14473)*. [2021/XC2070/**C**]

♦ International Furriers Federation (inactive)
♦ International Fur Trade Federation / see International Fur Federation (#13696)
♦ International Fusion Research Council (see: #12294)
♦ International Future Research Committee / see World Futures Studies Federation (#21535)
♦ International Futures Library, Salzburg – Robert-Jungk Foundation (internationally oriented national body)

♦ International Fuzzy Systems Association (IFSA) 13697

Pres Dept of Electrical Engineering, National Chung Hsing University, 145 Xingda Rd, South Dist., Taichung 402, Taiwan. T. +886422851549 ext 222. E-mail: president@fuzzysystems.org.
Sec Sustainable System Sciences, Osaka Prefecture Univ, 1-1 Gakuen-cho, Naka-ku, Sakai, Osaka, 599-8531 Japan. T. +81722549351.
Events – Vice-Pres Conferences Dept of Statistics, Univ of Oviedo, Fac of Sciences, Capus Llamaquique, c/ Federico Garcia Lorca 18, 33007 Oviedo, Asturias, Spain. T. +34985103349.
URL: http://fuzzysystems.org/

History 1984. **Aims** Communicate and promote worldwide knowledge of the theory of fuzzy sets and related areas and of their applications; establish cooperation and mutual exchange of information between national and international scientific societies; promote the formation of national research communities, especially in developing countries; promote and harmonize relevant educational training standards on fuzzy sets. **Structure** General Business Meeting (every 2 years, at World Congress); Council. **Languages** English. **Staff** 4.00 FTE, voluntary. **Finance** Sources: members' dues. **Activities** Events/meetings; research/documentation. **Events** *World Congress* Daegu (Korea Rep) 2023, *International Conference on Soft Computing and Intelligent Systems* Ise (Japan) 2022, *World Congress* Bratislava (Slovakia) 2021, *International Symposium on Advanced Intelligent Systems* Edmonton, AB (Canada) 2020, *International Conference on Soft Computing and Intelligent Systems* Tokyo (Japan) 2020. **Publications** *Bulletin for Studies and Exchanges on Fuzziness and its Applications*; *International Journal of Approximate Reasoning*; *International Journal of Fuzzy Sets and Systems* – official journal; *International Journal of Uncertainty, Fuzziness and Konwledge-Based Systems*.

Members Societies in 15 countries and territories:
Brazil, China, Finland, Hungary, Indonesia, Iran Islamic Rep, Japan, Korea Rep, Mexico, Russia, Spain, Taiwan, Türkiye, USA, Vietnam.

Included in the above, 2 organizations listed in this Yearbook:
European Society for Fuzzy Logic and Technology (EUSFLAT, #08603); *Sociedad Internacional de Gestión y Economia Fuzzy (SIGEF, #19386)*. [2022.10.13/XD0301/y/**C**]

♦ International Game Developers Association (internationally oriented national body)
♦ International Game Fish Association (internationally oriented national body)

♦ International Garden Centre Association (IGCA) 13698

Office c/o South African Nursery Association, PO Box 514, Halfway House, 1685, South Africa. T. +27879454621. Fax +27867187269. E-mail: igca1960@gmail.com.
Pres Rivers of Yarrambat 28 Kurrak Road, Yarrambat VIC 3091, Australia. T. +6194363239. Fax +6194363239.
URL: http://www.intgardencentre.org/

History 1960. **Aims** Provide a forum for the mutual exchange of information and benefit of similar minded independent garden retailers on a worldwide basis. **Structure** General Meeting (annual, at Congress), comprising 2 representatives of each national association. Board (meets twice a year). Officers: President; Vice-President; General Secretary; Treasurer. **Languages** English. **Staff** 1.00 FTE, paid. **Finance** Members' dues: Canadian $ 2,050 per national association. **Activities** Annual congress; study visits. **Events** *Annual Congress* Italy 2023, *Annual Congress* Amsterdam (Netherlands) 2022, *Annual Congress* Johannesburg (South Africa) / Cape Town (South Africa) 2020, *Annual Congress* Windsor (UK) 2019, *Annual Congress* Prague (Czechia) 2018. **Publications** *IGC Newsletter*. Membership lists; meetings reports.

Members National associations in 17 countries:
Australia, Canada, Czechia, Denmark, France, Germany, Hungary, Ireland, Italy, Japan, Netherlands, Poland, South Africa, Spain, Switzerland, UK, USA.

NGO Relations Corresponding member of: *International Association of Horticultural Producers (#11940)*. [2022/XD1369/**D**]

♦ International Garden Cities and Town Planning Association / see International Federation for Housing and Planning (#13450)
♦ International Garment Workers Federation (inactive)
♦ International Gas Research Conference (meeting series)

♦ International Gastric Cancer Association (IGCA) 13699

IGCA Office c/o Cancer Institute Hospital, 3-8-31 Ariake, Koto-ku, Tokyo, 135-8550 Japan. T. +81335200111. Fax +81335700343. E-mail: igca@jfcr.or.jp.
URL: http://www.igca.info/

History 1995. **Aims** Provide an international forum for advancement of research into prevention, diagnosis and treatment of gastric cancer; facilitate eradication of gastric cancer worldwide. **Languages** English. **Finance** Members' dues. **Events** *International Gastric Cancer Congress* Yokohama (Japan) 2023, *International Gastric Cancer Congress* Houston, TX (USA) 2022, *International Gastric Cancer Congress* Houston, TX (USA) 2021, *International Gastric Cancer Congress* Prague (Czechia) 2019, *Biennial Congress* Beijing (China) 2017. **Publications** *Gastric Cancer* – journal.

Members Individuals in 53 countries and territories:
Argentina, Australia, Austria, Belgium, Brazil, Bulgaria, Canada, Chile, China, Colombia, Costa Rica, Croatia, Denmark, Finland, France, Germany, Greece, Hong Kong, Hungary, India, Israel, Italy, Japan, Korea Rep, Lebanon, Malaysia, Mexico, Nepal, Netherlands, New Zealand, North Macedonia, Norway, Peru, Philippines, Poland, Portugal, Romania, Russia, San Marino, Serbia, Singapore, Slovenia, Spain, Sweden, Switzerland, Taiwan, Tajikistan, Thailand, Türkiye, UK, Ukraine, USA, Venezuela. [2018/XD5646/v/**D**]

♦ International Gastro-Surgical Club / see International Association of Surgeons, Gastroenterologists and Oncologists (#12216)

♦ International Gas Union (IGU) 13700

Union Internationale du Gaz (UIG)

SG 44 Southampton Buildings, London, WC2A 1AP, UK. E-mail: info@igu.org.
URL: http://www.igu.org/

History 2 Jun 1931, London (UK). Constitution approved 2 Oct 1996, Edinburgh (UK) and last amended 2012. Former names and other names: *Union internationale de l'industrie du gaz (UIIG)* – former. Registration: Switzerland, Vevey. **Aims** Advocate gas as an integral part of a sustainable global energy system; promote the political, technical and economic progress of the gas industry. **Structure** Membership based organisation, consisting of: Charter members; Premium Associate members; Associate members. Secretariat located in London (UK). **Languages** English. **Staff** 7.50 FTE, paid. **Finance** Sources: members' dues. **Activities** Advocacy/lobbying/activism; capacity building; events/meetings; knowledge management/information dissemination; networking/liaising; research and development. **Events** *World Gas Conference (WGC)* 2027, *World Gas Conference (WGC 2025)* Beijing (China) 2025, *International Conference on Liquefied Natural Gas* Vancouver, BC (Canada) 2023, *World Gas Conference* Daegu (Korea Rep) 2022, *LNG : Triennial International Conference on Liquefied Natural Gas* St Petersburg (Russia) 2022. **Publications** *Global Voice of Gas* (4 a year) in English – IGU magazine; *Global Gas Report* (annual) in English; *Global Renewable and Low-Carbon Gases Report* (annual) in English; *Global Wholesale Gas Price Survey* (annual) in English; *World LNG Report* (annual) in English. *International Gas Union 1931-2012: Commemorating more than 80 years of service to the global gas industry and 25 World Gas Conferences*. Surveys; reports; strategic statements; booklets.

Members Charter Members (91) in 91 countries and territories:

Albania, Algeria, Angola, Argentina, Armenia, Australia, Austria, Azerbaijan, Bahrain, Belarus, Belgium, Bolivia, Bosnia-Herzegovina, Brazil, Brunei Darussalam, Bulgaria, Cameroon, Canada, Chile, China, Colombia, Côte d'Ivoire, Croatia, Cyprus, Czechia, Denmark, Egypt, Equatorial Guinea, Estonia, Finland, France, Germany, Greece, Hong Kong, Hungary, India, Indonesia, Iran Islamic Rep, Iraq, Ireland, Israel, Italy, Japan, Kazakhstan, Korea Rep, Kuwait, Latvia, Lebanon, Libya, Lithuania, Malaysia, Mexico, Monaco, Mongolia, Morocco, Mozambique, Netherlands, Nigeria, North Macedonia, Norway, Oman, Pakistan, Peru, Poland, Portugal, Qatar, Romania, Russia, Saudi Arabia, Serbia, Singapore, Slovakia, Slovenia, South Africa, Spain, Sweden, Switzerland, Taiwan, Thailand, Timor-Leste, Trinidad-Tobago, Tunisia, Türkiye, UK, Ukraine, United Arab Emirates, USA, Uzbekistan, Venezuela, Vietnam, Yemen.
Associate Members (51) in 27 countries:
Australia, Austria, Belgium, Brazil, China, Egypt, France, Germany, India, Indonesia, Ireland, Italy, Japan, Korea Rep, Mongolia, Netherlands, Norway, Peru, Portugal, Qatar, Russia, Spain, Switzerland, Türkiye, UK, United Arab Emirates, USA.
NGO Relations Accredited by (8): *European Gas Research Group (#07380)*; *Gas Technology Institute (GTI)*; *NGV Global (#17131)*; *Oil and Gas Industry Energy Access Platform (EAP, #17710)*; Russian National Gas-Vehicle Association (NGVRUS); *Sustainable Energy for All (SEforALL, #20056)*; *World LPG Association (WLPGA, #21629)*; *World Petroleum Council (WPC, #21722)*. Affiliated with (10): *Asociación Regional de Empresas del Sector Petróleo, Gas y Biocombustibles en Latinoamérica y el Caribe (ARPEL, #02296)*; *Energy Delta Institute (EDI)*; *Gas Infrastructure Europe (GIE, #10073)*; *GasNaturally (#10074)*; *Groupe international des importateurs de gaz naturel liquefié (GIIGNL, #10750)*; *International Petroleum Industry Environmental Conservation Association (IPIECA, #14562)*; *International Pipe Line and Offshore Contractors Association (IPLOCA, #14586)*; *MARCOGAZ – Technical Association of the European Natural Gas Industry (#16572)*; *NGVA Europe (#17130)*; *Pipeline Research Council International (PRCI)*. [2022.06.18/XC2074/y/**C**]

♦ International Gaucher Alliance (IGA) 13701

Contact 8 Silver Street, Dursley, GL11 4ND, UK. T. +441453796402. Fax +441453796402. E-mail: admin@gaucheralliance.org.
URL: http://www.gaucheralliance.org/

History Set up within *European Working Group on Gaucher Disease (EWGGD, #09112)*. Became an independent organization, Jun 2008, Budapest (Hungary). Original title: *European Gaucher Alliance (EGA)*. Current title adopted Oct 2018, Riga (Latvia). **Aims** Be the global voice for Gaucher patients and their families. **Structure** Board of Directors. **Staff** 2.00 FTE, paid. **Finance** Grants from pharmaceutical companies. **Activities** Events/meetings; awareness raising. **Events** *Members Meeting* Leiden (Netherlands) 2020. **Publications** *IGA Newsletter*.
Members Patient associations in 51 countries:
Australia, Austria, Belgium, Bosnia-Herzegovina, Botswana, Bulgaria, Canada, China, Croatia, Czechia, Denmark, Estonia, Finland, France, Germany, Greece, Guatemala, India, Ireland, Israel, Italy, Japan, Jordan, Kazakhstan, Latvia, Lithuania, Luxembourg, Mexico, Moldova, Mongolia, Morocco, Netherlands, New Zealand, North Macedonia, Norway, Pakistan, Paraguay, Poland, Romania, Russia, Serbia, Slovakia, Slovenia, South Africa, Spain, Sweden, Switzerland, Türkiye, UK, Ukraine, USA.
NGO Relations Member of: *EGAN – Patients Network for Medical Research and Health (EGAN, #05394)*; *Rare Diseases International (RDI, #18621)*. [2021/XJ8148/**E**]

♦ International Gay Association / see ILGA World (#11120)
♦ International Gay Bowling Organization (internationally oriented national body)

♦ International Gay and Lesbian Aquatics (IGLA) 13702

Contact address not obtained. E-mail: secretary@igla.org.
URL: http://www.igla.org/

History Founded 1987. Statutes adopted 1990. **Aims** Promote participation in aquatic *sports* among lesbians and gay men. **Structure** Board of Directors. **Languages** English. **Staff** 4.50 FTE, voluntary. **Finance** Members' dues. **Activities** Sporting activities. **Events** *Championship* Stockholm (Sweden) 2015, *Championship* Seattle, WA (USA) 2013, *Championship* Reykjavik (Iceland) 2012, *Championship* Honolulu, HI (USA) 2011, *Championship* Copenhagen (Denmark) 2009. **Publications** *Wetnotes* (4 a year) – newsletter.
Members Full in 11 countries:
Australia, Belgium, Canada, France, Germany, Italy, Netherlands, New Zealand, South Africa, UK, USA.
NGO Relations Member of: *Federation of Gay Games (#09589)*. [2022/XD6143/**D**]

♦ International Gay and Lesbian Chamber of Commerce (no recent information)

♦ International Gay and Lesbian Football Association (IGLFA) 13703

Sec address not obtained. E-mail: info@iglfa.org.
URL: http://www.iglfa.org/

History 1992. **Aims** Foster and augment the self respect of gay women and men throughout the world and engender respect and understanding from the non-gay world through the medium of organized football. **Structure** Board of Directors. **Activities** Organizes championships. **Publications** *Kick International* (4 a year) in English, German, Spanish. **Members** Membership countries not specified. **NGO Relations** Member of: *Federation of Gay Games (#09589)*; *Gay and Lesbian International Sport Association (GLISA, #10078)*. [2011/XD9060/**D**]

♦ International Gay and Lesbian Human Rights Commission / see OutRight Action International
♦ International Gay and Lesbian Travel Association (internationally oriented national body)
♦ International Gay and Lesbian Youth Organization / see International Lesbian, Gay, Bisexual, Transgender, Queer and Intersex Youth and Student Organization (#14032)
♦ International Gay Press Association (inactive)
♦ International Gay Travel Association / see International Gay and Lesbian Travel Association

♦ International Gemmological Conference (IGC) 13704

Exec Sec address not obtained.
URL: https://www.igc-gemmology.org/

History Oct 1952, Lugano (Switzerland). Inaugural meeting held at a Technical Conference, at the initiative of Prof K Schlossmacher and Dr E Gubelin, when the creation of a "Committee of an International Gemmological Association" was proposed. Owes much of its origin to BIBOA – the current *CIBJO – The World Jewellery Confederation (CIBJO, #03923)*. **Structure** Executive Committee. **Events** *International Gemmological Conference* Tokyo (Japan) 2023, *International Gemmological Conference* 2021, *International Gemmological Conference* Nantes (France) 2019, *International Gemmological Conference* Windhoek (Namibia) 2017, *International Gemmological Conference* Vilnius (Lithuania) 2015. [2022/AA2413/c/**F**]

♦ International Gender Champions (IGC) 13705

Contact address not obtained. E-mail: admin@genderchampions.com.
URL: https://genderchampions.com/

History Jul 2015, Geneva (Switzerland). **Aims** Bring together female and male decision-makers determined to break down gender barriers and make gender equality a working reality in their spheres of influence. **Structure** Global Advisory Board. **Activities** Advocacy/lobbying/activism; events/meetings. **Publications** Toolkits; information packs. **Members** Heads of international organizations, permanent missions, civil society or private sector organizations. Membership countries not specified. [2020.11.24/XM8505/v/**E**]

♦ International Gender and Language Association (IGALA) 13706

Sec Room 311 – Colin Clark Bldg, St Lucia Campus, Univ of Queensland, St Lucia QLD 4072, Australia. T. +61733469989.
Pres Ho Sin Hang Bldg HSH321, Lingnan Univ, 8 Castle Peak Road, Tuen Mun, New Territories, Hong Kong, Central and Western, Hong Kong. T. +85226167799.
URL: http://igalaweb.wixsite.com/igala/

History 1999, evolving from the 'Women and Language' group at the University of California, Berkeley CA (USA). **Aims** Promote and support research on language, gender and sexuality. **Structure** Executive Council; Advisory Council; Board. **Activities** Events/meetings. **Events** *Biennial Conference* Gaborone (Botswana) 2018, *Biennial Conference* Hong Kong (Hong Kong) 2016, *Biennial Conference* Tokyo (Japan) 2010, *Biennial conference / Conference* Wellington (New Zealand) 2008, *Biennial conference / Conference* Valencia (Spain) 2006. **Publications** *Gender and Language* – journal. Conference proceedings. [2018/XQ0017/**D**]

♦ International Gender Studies Centre, Oxford (internationally oriented national body)

♦ International Gender and Trade Network (IGTN) 13707

Red Internacional de Género y Comercio

SG Instituto EQUIT, REBRIP, FASE, Rua das Palmeiras 90, Botafogo, Rio de Janeiro RJ, 22270-070, Brazil. T. +552125367350. Fax +552125367379. E-mail: enlace@generoycomercio.org.
Latin America Contact c/o CIEDUR, 18 de Julio 1645/7, CP 11200 Montevideo, Uruguay. Fax +59824084520.
URL: http://www.generoycomercio.org/

History Dec 1999, Granada (Spain). Dec 1999, Grenada (Spain). **Structure** Steering Committee of 11 members. Regional networks (7): Africa; Asia; Caribbean; Europe; Latin America; North America; Pacific. **NGO Relations** Member of: *Alianza Social Continental (ASC, #00635)*; *Alliance for Lobbying Transparency and Ethics Regulation (ALTER-EU, #00705)*; *Climate Justice Now ! (CJN!, inactive)*; *Feminist Articulation Marcosur (FAM, #09730)*; *Our World is Not for Sale (OWINFS, #17917)*; *Women's Working Group on Financing for Development (WWG on FfD, #21036)*; *World Social Forum (WSF, #21797)*. Close cooperation with: *Caribbean Association for Feminist Research and Action (CAFRA, #03445)*. Supports: *Global Call for Action Against Poverty (GCAP, #10263)*. [2019/XF5871/t/**F**]

♦ International General Medical Society for Psychotherapy (inactive)
♦ International General Society for Psychotherapy / see International Federation for Psychotherapy (#13523)

♦ International Generic and Biosimilar Medicines Association (IGBA) 13708

SG Rue de Cornavin 11, c/o INTEREXPERTS SA, 1201 Geneva, Switzerland. E-mail: info@igbamedicines.org.
URL: http://www.igbamedicines.org/

History Mar 1997. Former names and other names: *International Generic Pharmaceutical Alliance (IGPA)* – former. **Aims** Ensure *affordable* pharmaceutical *health care* for patients worldwide; promote international pharmaceutical harmonization and regulatory decisions. **Structure** Management Committee. Committees (4): Science; International Trade; Intellectual Property; Biosimilars. **Events** *Annual Conference* Orlando, FL (USA) 2023, *Annual Conference* Kuala Lumpur (Malaysia) 2022, *Annual Conference* Athens (Greece) 2021, *Annual Conference* Warsaw (Poland) 2019, *Annual Conference* Budapest (Hungary) 2018.
Members Full in 6 countries:
Canada, Japan, Jordan, South Africa, Taiwan, USA.
Generic and Biosimilar Medicines of Southern Africa (GBM); *Medicines for Europe (#16633)*.
Associate members in 6 countries:
Argentina, Australia, Brazil, Malaysia, Mexico, Saudi Arabia.
Observer in 1 country:
Bangladesh.
Consultative Status Consultative status granted from: *World Intellectual Property Organization (WIPO, #21593)* (Observer Status). **IGO Relations** Memorandum of Understanding with (1): *WHO (#20950)*. **NGO Relations** Member of (1): *International Council on Harmonisation of Technical Requirements for Registration of Pharmaceuticals for Human Use (ICH, #13027)*. [2021/XF4734/**F**]

♦ International Generic Horse Association (no recent information)
♦ International Generic Pharmaceutical Alliance / see International Generic and Biosimilar Medicines Association (#13708)

♦ International Genetic Alliance (IGA) 13709

Contact Helios, Gerstkamp 130, 2592 CV The Hague, Netherlands. T. +31356831920. Fax +31356831891.

History 10 Apr 2003, Lyon (France). Former names and other names: *International Genetic Alliance of Parent and Patient Organizations* – alias. **Aims** Serve and voice the interests of families involved in genetic and congenital conditions. **Structure** General Meeting. Board of 12 members. Executive Committee, comprising President, Secretary-General and Treasurer. Central Office; 5 Regional Secretariats: Washington DC (USA); Sao Paulo (Brazil); Sydney (Australia); Johannesburg (South Africa); London (UK). **Events** *International conference on birth defects and disabilities in the developing world* Delhi (India) 2009.
Members Full; Affiliate; Observer. Organizations in 13 countries:
Australia, Belgium, Brazil, India, Iran Islamic Rep, Ireland, Netherlands, New Zealand, South Africa, Switzerland, UK, Ukraine, USA.
Included in the above, 1 organization listed in this Yearbook:
EGAN – Patients Network for Medical Research and Health (EGAN, #05394).
IGO Relations *WHO (#20950)*. **NGO Relations** Member of: *International Alliance of Patients' Organizations (IAPO, #11633)*; *International Federation of Human Genetics Societies (IFHGS, #13451)*. [2020/XF7027/y/**F**]

♦ International Genetic Alliance of Parent and Patient Organizations / see International Genetic Alliance (#13709)

♦ International Genetic Epidemiology Society (IGES) 13710

Sec-Treas c/o Mayo Clinic, 200 First St SW, Harwick 7, Rochester MN 55905, USA. E-mail: iges@geneticepi.org.
URL: http://www.geneticepi.org/

Aims Promote the study of genetic epidemiology and statistical genetics. **Structure** Board of Directors, comprising President, President-Elect, Past President, Secretary-Treasurer, Editor and Directors. Committees (6): Scientific Program; Local Organizing; Publications; ELSI; Membership; Educational. **Finance** Members' dues. **Activities** Organizes annual scientific meetings. **Events** *Annual Meeting* Paris (France) 2022, *Annual Scientific Meeting* Vienna (Austria) 2014, *Annual Scientific Meeting* Chicago, IL (USA) 2013, *Annual Scientific Meeting* Heidelberg (Germany) 2011, *Annual Scientific Meeting* Boston, MA (USA) 2010. **Publications** *Genetic Epidemiology* – journal.
Members Full in 25 countries and territories:
Australia, Austria, Belgium, Brazil, Canada, Chile, China, Croatia, Denmark, France, Gambia, Germany, India, Ireland, Israel, Italy, Japan, Korea Rep, Netherlands, Russia, Spain, Sweden, Switzerland, Taiwan, UK.
NGO Relations Affiliate member of: *International Federation of Human Genetics Societies (IFHGS, #13451)*. [2018/XD9481/**D**]

♦ International Genetic Resources Programme / see Action Group on Erosion, Technology and Concentration (#00091)
♦ International Genetics of Ankylosing Spondylitis Conference (meeting series)

♦ International Genetics Federation (IGF) 13711

Fédération internationale de génétique

Sec c/o Bio21 Institute, 30 Flemington Rd, Parkville VIC 3010, Australia. E-mail: intlgeneticsfederation@gmail.com.
URL: https://www.geneticsfederation.com/

History 23 Sep 1911, Paris (France). Former names and other names: *Comité permanent des conférences internationales de génétique et de l'hybridation* – former (23 Sep 1911); *Permanent International Committee for Genetic Congresses (PICGC)* – former (28 Aug 1968); *Comité international permanent des congrès de génétique* – former (28 Aug 1968). **Aims** Promote the science of genetics at the international level. **Structure** Congress (every 5 years). Executive Board, comprising President, Secretary General, Treasurer and 3 members at large. **Languages** English. **Staff** 3.00 FTE, voluntary. **Finance** Sources: members' dues. **Activities** Organizes international congresses of genetics. **Events** *International Congress of Genetics* Melbourne, VIC (Australia) 2023, *International Congress of Genetics* Vancouver, BC (Canada) 2018, *International Congress of Genetics* Singapore (Singapore) 2013, *International Congress of Genetics* Berlin (Germany) 2008, *International Congress of Genetics* Melbourne, VIC (Australia) 2003. **Publications** Congress proceedings.
Members National societies of genetics in 37 countries and territories:
Argentina, Australia, Brazil, Bulgaria, Canada, Chile, China, Croatia, Cuba, Denmark, Egypt, Finland, France, Germany, Hungary, India, Iran Islamic Rep, Israel, Italy, Japan, Korea Rep, Malaysia, Mexico, New Zealand, Nigeria, Norway, Poland, Portugal, Romania, Russia, Sweden, Switzerland, Taiwan, Thailand, USA, Venezuela, Vietnam.
Regional and international organizations (5):
Association of Maize Researchers in Africa (AMRA, no recent information); *International Society for Oil Palm Breeders (ISOPB, #15320)*; *International Union of Microbiological Societies (IUMS, #15794)* (Genetics Section); *Scandinavian Association of Geneticists (no recent information)*; *Society for the Advancement of Breeding Research in Asia and Oceania (SABRAO, #19515)*.
NGO Relations Constitutes the Genetics Section of: *International Union of Biological Sciences (IUBS, #15760)*. [2022/XC2076/y/**C**]

♦ International Geneva Association of Hotel and Restaurant Employees (inactive)
♦ International Geodetic Association / see International Association of Geodesy (#11914)
♦ International Geodetic Student Organization / see International Geodetic Students Organization (#13712)

♦ International Geodetic Students Organization (IGSO) 13712

Internationale Geodätische Studentenorganisation

Address not obtained.
URL: http://igso.info/

History 10 May 1991, Graz (Austria). Founded during 4th International Geodetic Students Meeting. Statutory seat is in Delft (Netherlands). Former names and other names: *International Geodetic Student Organization* – alias. Registration: Switzerland. **Aims** Unite students studying all disciplines of geodesy. **Structure** General Assembly (annual). *International Geodetic Student Agency (IGSA)*. **Languages** English. **Activities** International Geodetic Student Meetings (IGSM), held annually. **Events** *International Geodetic Student Meetings (IGSM)* Hannover (Germany) 2021, *International Geodetic Student Meetings (IGSM)* Thessaloniki (Greece) 2020, *Meeting* Munich (Germany) 2016, *Meeting* Espoo (Finland) 2015, *Meeting* Jaén (Spain) 2012. **Members** Schools (99) in 35 countries. Membership countries not specified. **NGO Relations** *International Association of Geodesy (IAG, #11914)*; *International Federation of Surveyors (FIG, #13561)*. [2022/XD3096/**D**]

♦ International Geographical Association (inactive)
♦ International Geographical Institute (inactive)

♦ International Geographical Union (IGU) 13713

Union géographique internationale (UGI) – Unión Geografica Internacional

Sec-Treas Geography Dept, Delhi School of Economics, University of Delhi, Delhi 110007, DELHI 110007, India. E-mail: rbsgeo@hotmail.com.
URL: http://www.igu-online.org/

History 27 Jul 1922, Brussels (Belgium), international congresses having been held since 1871, Antwerp (Belgium). Current statutes adopted: Aug 1988; revised: Aug 1992, Washington DC (USA); 1996, The Hague (Netherlands); Aug 2000; Aug 2002, Durban; Aug 2004; 2008, Tunis (Tunisia). **Aims** Promote geography through initiating and coordinating geographical research and teaching in all countries of the world. **Structure** General Assembly (every 4 years, at International Geographical Congress); Executive Committee; Commissions and Task Forces. **Languages** English, French. **Staff** None. **Finance** Sources: donations; members' dues; sponsorship. Annual budget: 150,000 USD. **Activities** Events/meetings. **Events** *International Geographical Congress* Melbourne, VIC (Australia) 2028, *International Geographical Congress* Dublin (Ireland) 2024, *Centennial Congress* Paris (France) 2022, *WMESS : World Multidisciplinary Earth Sciences Symposium* Prague (Czechia) 2022, *Quadrennial Geographical Congress and General Assembly* Istanbul (Turkey) 2021. **Publications** *IGU eNewsletter* (4 a year); *IGU Bulletin/Bulletin de l'UGI* (annual). Congress, conference and commission reports; bibliographies; catalogues; directories.

Members National Committees in 66 countries and territories:
Argentina, Armenia, Australia, Austria, Azerbaijan, Belgium, Brazil, Canada, Chile, China, Colombia, Croatia, Czechia, Denmark, Ecuador, Egypt, Estonia, Finland, France, Germany, Ghana, Greece, Hong Kong, Hungary, Iceland, India, Ireland, Israel, Italy, Japan, Kenya, Korea Rep, Kuwait, Luxembourg, Macau, Mexico, Netherlands, New Zealand, Nigeria, Norway, Oman, Pakistan, Peru, Poland, Portugal, Romania, Russia, Samoa, Saudi Arabia, Serbia, Singapore, Slovakia, Slovenia, South Africa, Spain, Sweden, Switzerland, Taiwan, Türkiye, Uganda, UK, Ukraine, USA, Venezuela, Vietnam, Zimbabwe.
Affiliated international associations (3):
International Association of Geomorphologists (IAG, #11917); *International Permafrost Association (IPA, #14558)*; *International Union of Speleology (#15818)*.

Consultative Status Consultative status granted from: *ECOSOC (#05331)* (Ros C); *FAO (#09260)* (Liaison Status). **IGO Relations** Cooperates with: *United Nations University (UNU, #20642)*; *WHO (#20950)*; *World Meteorological Organization (WMO, #21649)*. Accredited by: *International Hydrographic Organization (IHO, #13825)*. Partner of: *United Nations Committee of Experts on Global Geospatial Information Management (UN-GGIM, #20540)*. Member of: *International Council for Philosophy and Human Sciences (CIPSH, #13061)*. Observer to: *United Nations Group of Experts on Geographical Names (UNGEGN, #20569)*.
NGO Relations Represented in: *Committee on Data for Science and Technology (CODATA, #04247)*; *Scientific Committee on Antarctic Research (SCAR, #19147)*. Member of: *International Science Council (ISC, #14796)*; *UN-GGO: Geospatial Societies (UN-GGIM GS, #20324)*. Appointed observer of: *Committee on Space Research (COSPAR, #04287)*. Spatial Data Handling cooperates with: *International Society for Photogrammetry and Remote Sensing (ISPRS, #15362)*.
Various levels of official liaison with: *International Mountain Society (IMS, #14190)*; *International Union for Conservation of Nature and Natural Resources (IUCN, #15766)*; *International Union of History and Philosophy of Science and Technology (IUHPST, #15779)*; *International Union for Quaternary Research (INQUA, #15811)*; *Scientific Committee on Problems of the Environment (SCOPE, #19150)*. [2020/XB2079/y/**B**]

♦ International Geological Congress (meeting series)
♦ International Geological Correlation Programme / see International Geoscience Programme (#13715)
♦ The International Georgist Union / see International Union for Land Value Taxation and Free Trade (#15787)

♦ International Geoscience Education Organization (IGEO) 13714

Chair address not obtained.
Sec address not obtained.
URL: http://www.igeoscied.org/

History 18 Jan 2000, Sydney, NSW (Australia). **Aims** Promote geoscience education internationally at all levels; work for enhancement of the quality of geoscience education internationally; encourage developments raising public awareness of geoscience, particularly amongst younger people. **Structure** General Meeting (in conjunction with Conference); Council. **Languages** English. **Staff** None. **Finance** No budget. Limited funding from donation of: *International Union of Geological Sciences (IUGS, #15777)*. **Activities** Monitoring/evaluation; networking/liaising; research/documentation; events/meetings. **Events** *GeoSciEd Conference* Matsue (Japan) 2022, *GeoSciEd Conference* Campinas (Brazil) 2018, *GeoSciEd Conference* Hyderabad (India) 2014, *GeoSciEd Conference* Johannesburg (South Africa) 2010, *International conference on geoscience for global development* Dhaka (Bangladesh) 2009. **Publications** *IGEO Newsletter* in English. Conference proceedings.

Members Full in 22 countries and territories:
Argentina, Australia, Bangladesh, Brazil, Canada, France, Germany, India, Indonesia, Israel, Japan, Korea Rep, Mozambique, New Zealand, Norway, Philippines, Portugal, South Africa, Spain, Taiwan, UK, USA.

NGO Relations Cooperates with (2): *International Association for Geoethics (IAGETH, #11915)*; *International Association for Promoting Geoethics (IAPG, #12107)*. Affiliated with (1): *International Union of Geological Sciences (IUGS, #15777)*. [2022/XJ3073/**D**]

♦ International Geoscience Programme (IGCP) 13715

Programme international de géoscience (PICG) – Programa Internacional de Ciencias de la Tierra (PICG)

Sec UNESCO, Earth Sciences and Geo-hazards Risk Reduction Sect, Div of Ecological and Earth Sciences, Natural Sciences Sector, 7 place de Fontenoy, 75352 Paris 07 SP, France. T. +33145681433 – +33145680784.
URL: http://www.unesco.org/new/en/natural-sciences/environment/earth-sciences /inter national-geoscience-programme/

History Founded Nov 1972, Paris (France), *International Geological Correlation Programme – Programme international de corrélation géologique – Programa Internacional de Correlación Geológica*, as a joint IUGS/UNESCO programme, on acceptance as an approved programme of *UNESCO (#20322)* at at 17th session of UNESCO General Conference, following approval by General Assembly of *International Union of Geological Sciences (IUGS, #15777)*, Aug 1972, Montréal (Canada). A joint initiative of: *International Council for Science (ICSU, inactive)*. **Aims** Provide scientists with a multi-discipline platform to exchange knowledge and methodology on geological problems of global importance with special focus on projects related to a safer environment, the relationship between natural geological factors and health problems, biodiversity, climate change, and mineral and groundwater resources extraction. **Structure** Scientific Board (meets annually), appointed jointly by UNESCO and IUGS. Scientific Working Groups (5): Earth Resources – Sustaining our Society; Global Change and Evolution of Life – Evidence from Geological Record; Geohazards – Mitigating the Risks; Geoscience of the Water Cycle; Deep Earth – How it Controls our Environment. Secretariat at UNESCO Headquarters in Paris (France). **Languages** English, French. **Staff** 4.00 FTE, paid. **Finance** Funded jointly by UNESCO and IUGS. Budget (annual): US$ 170,000. **Activities** Projects/programmes; capacity building. **Events** *Asia-Pacific Cretaceous Ecosystems Symposium* Jeju (Korea Rep) 2017, *Session* Paris (France) 2015, *Session* Paris (France) 2014, *International Symposium on Cretaceous Ecosystems and their Responses to Paleoenvironmental Changes in Asia and the Western Pacific* Tokyo (Japan) 2014, *Annual Symposium* Sapporo (Japan) 2011.

Members National Committees in 45 countries:
Argentina, Australia, Austria, Bangladesh, Belarus, Belgium, Benin, Brazil, Bulgaria, Canada, China, Congo DR, Croatia, Cyprus, Czechia, Finland, France, Germany, Greece, Hungary, Indonesia, Iran Islamic Rep, Ireland, Italy, Japan, Korea Rep, Malaysia, Nepal, New Zealand, Poland, Portugal, Russia, Saudi Arabia, Slovakia, Slovenia, Spain, Sweden, Switzerland, Tanzania UR, Thailand, Türkiye, UK, Ukraine, USA, Vietnam.

NGO Relations Cooperates with: *Commission mondiale d'éthique des connaissances scientifiques et des technologies de l'UNESCO (COMEST, #04235)*. Instrumental in setting up: *International Medical Geology Association (IMGA, #14133)*. [2018/XF5114/**F***]

♦ International Geosciences Student Conference (meeting series)
♦ International Geostatistical Congress (meeting series)

♦ International Geosynthetics Society (IGS) 13716

Secretariat Manager 9225 Bee Caves Rd, Bldg B Ste 206, Austin TX 78733, USA. T. +15617689489. E-mail: igssec@geosyntheticssociety.org.
URL: http://www.geosyntheticssociety.org/

History 10 Nov 1983, Paris (France). Former names and other names: *International Geotextile Society* – former. **Aims** Promote scientific and *engineering* development of geotextiles, geomembranes, related products and associated technologies. **Structure** General Assembly; Council; Committees; National and Regional Chapters (34). **Languages** English. **Staff** 1.00 FTE, paid. **Finance** Sources: members' dues. **Activities** Knowledge management/information dissemination; events/meetings; awards/prizes/competitions. **Events** *International Conference on Geosynthetics* Montréal, QC (Canada) 2026, *International Conference on Geosynthetics* Rome (Italy) 2023, *Geosynthetics Asia : Asian Regional Conference on Geosynthetics* Taipei (Taiwan) 2022, *European Geosynthetics Conference (EuroGeo)* Warsaw (Poland) 2022, *European Geosynthetics Congress (EuroGeo)* Warsaw (Poland) 2021. **Publications** *IGS News* (3 a year); *Geosynthetics International* – journal; *Geotextiles and Geomembranes* – journal. *IGS Directory* – online. Educational leaflets – online.

Members Chapters (35) in 32 countries and territories:
Argentina, Belgium, Brazil, Chile, China, Czechia, Finland, France, Germany, Greece, India, Indonesia, Italy, Japan, Kazakhstan, Korea Rep, Mexico, Netherlands, Norway, Pakistan, Peru, Philippines, Poland, Portugal, Romania, Russia, Slovakia, South Africa, Spain, Thailand, Türkiye, UK.
Also Chapters in Australasia, North America and West Pacific (not specified).
Individuals (about 2,900) in 64 countries and territories:
Argentina, Australia, Austria, Bangladesh, Belgium, Brazil, Canada, Chile, China, Colombia, Croatia, Czechia, Denmark, Dominican Rep, Ecuador, Egypt, Finland, France, Germany, Greece, Guatemala, Hong Kong, Hungary, Iceland, India, Indonesia, Iran Islamic Rep, Ireland, Israel, Italy, Japan, Korea Rep, Luxembourg, Macau, Malaysia, Mexico, Netherlands, New Zealand, Norway, Pakistan, Panama, Peru, Philippines, Poland, Portugal, Romania, Russia, Saudi Arabia, Singapore, Slovakia, South Africa, Spain, Sri Lanka, Sweden, Switzerland, Taiwan, Thailand, Trinidad-Tobago, Türkiye, UK, Ukraine, United Arab Emirates, Venezuela, Vietnam.
Corporate (138) in 43 countries and territories:
Argentina, Austria, Belgium, Brazil, Canada, Chile, China, Colombia, Costa Rica, Croatia, France, Germany, Greece, Hong Kong, Hungary, India, Indonesia, Iran Islamic Rep, Ireland, Italy, Japan, Korea Rep, Luxembourg, Malaysia, Mexico, Netherlands, New Zealand, Norway, Panama, Peru, Portugal, Russia, Saudi Arabia, South Africa, Spain, Switzerland, Taiwan, Türkiye, UK, Ukraine, United Arab Emirates, USA, Venezuela.

NGO Relations Member of (1): *Federation of International Geo-Engineering Societies (FedIGS, #09673)*. [2022/XD1216/v/**D**]

♦ International Geotextile Society / see International Geosynthetics Society (#13716)

♦ International Geothermal Association (IGA) 13717

Europe HQ Charles-de-Gaulle-Str 5, 53113 Bonn, Germany. E-mail: iga@lovegeothermal.org.
URL: http://www.lovegeothermal.org/

History 6 Jul 1988, Auckland (New Zealand). First considered Sep 1970, Pisa (Italy) at UN Symposium of Geothermal Energy; initiative relaunched Jan 1986, USA, which led to the founding. **Aims** Promote coordination of activities related to geothermal research, development and utilization. **Structure** General Meeting (annual); Board of Directors; Permanent Committees (8). **Languages** English. **Staff** 3.00 FTE, paid. **Finance** Sources: donations; members' dues; revenue from activities/projects. **Activities** Events/meetings; guidance/assistance/consulting; knowledge management/information dissemination; networking/liaising; training/education. **Events** *World Geothermal Congress* 2026, *World Geothermal Congress* Beijing (China) 2023, *World Geothermal Congress* Reykjavik (Iceland) 2021, *World Geothermal Congress* Reykjavik (Iceland) 2020, *World geothermal congress* Melbourne, VIC (Australia) 2015. **Publications** *IGA News* (12 a year). *Geothermal Exploration – Global Strategies and Applications*. **Information Services** *IGA Geothermal Power Database*.

Members Members (4,600) and affiliated organizations (35) in 53 countries:
Albania, Algeria, Argentina, Australia, Austria, Belarus, Belgium, Bulgaria, Canada, Chile, Colombia, Costa Rica, Croatia, Denmark, Djibouti, Ecuador, El Salvador, Ethiopia, France, Georgia, Germany, Greece, Guatemala, Hungary, Iceland, India, Indonesia, Italy, Japan, Kenya, Korea Rep, Lithuania, Mexico, Netherlands, New Zealand, North Macedonia, Norway, Peru, Philippines, Poland, Portugal, Romania, Russia, Singapore, Slovakia, Slovenia, Spain, Switzerland, Tanzania UR, Thailand, Türkiye, UK, USA.

Consultative Status Consultative status granted from: *ECOSOC (#05331)* (Special). **IGO Relations** Accredited by (1): *Green Climate Fund (GCF, #10714)*. Partner of (1): *International Renewable Energy Agency (IRENA, #14715)*. **NGO Relations** Memorandum of Understanding with (1): *World Wind Energy Association (WWEA, #21937)*. Member of (1): *International Renewable Energy Alliance (Ren Alliance, #14716)*. Partner of (2): *European Forum for Renewable Energy Sources (EUFORES, #07329)*; *International Hydropower Association (IHA, #13828)*. Supports (1): *Global 100% RE (#10160)*. [2021.09.06/XD0240/**C**]

♦ International Geranium Society (internationally oriented national body)
♦ International Gerbil Federation (no recent information)
♦ International Geriatric Fracture Society (internationally oriented national body)
♦ International Gesellschaft Christlicher Künstler (#15009)
♦ International Gesellschaft für Endoskopie / see World Endoscopy Organization (#21380)
♦ International Gesellschaft für Psychotronische Forschung (no recent information)
♦ International Gesellschaft für Verkehrsmedizin (#15713)
♦ International Ginseng Symposium (meeting series)

♦ International Glaciological Society (IGS) 13718

SG High Cross, Madingley Road, Cambridge, CB3 0ET, UK. T. +441223355974. E-mail: igsoc@igsoc.org.
URL: https://www.igsoc.org/

History 1936, London (UK). Former names and other names: *Association for the Study of Snow and Ice* – former (1936 to 16 Jul 1945); *British Glaciological Society (BGS)* – former (16 Jul 1945 to 12 Jun 1961); *Glaciological Society* – former (12 Jun 1961 to 1 Jan 1972). Registration: Charity Commission, No/ID: 231043, England and Wales. **Aims** Stimulate research and interest in the practical and scientific problems of *snow* and *ice* in all countries. **Structure** General Meeting (annual); Council; Committees (4). **Languages** English. **Staff** 1.00 FTE, paid. **Finance** Sources: members' dues; revenue from activities/projects; sale of publications. **Activities** Events/meetings; knowledge management/information dissemination. **Events** *International Symposium on Maritime Glaciers* Juneau, AK (USA) 2022, *International Symposium on Ice, Snow and Water in a Warming World* Reykjavik (Iceland) 2022, *Nordic Branch Meeting* Oslo (Norway) 2021, *International Symposium on Ice, Snow and Water in a Warming World* Reykjavik (Iceland) 2021, *International Symposium on Southern Hemisphere Glaciers under Pressure* Valdivia (Chile) 2021. **Publications** *Journal of Glaciology* (6 a year); *ICE Newsletter* (3 a year); *Annals of Glaciology* (2-4 a year).

Members Individuals (about 750) in 32 countries:

Argentina, Australia, Austria, Belgium, Brazil, Canada, Chile, China, Denmark, Estonia, Finland, France, Germany, Iceland, India, Ireland, Italy, Japan, Korea Rep, Netherlands, New Zealand, Norway, Pakistan, Peru, Poland, Portugal, Russia, Spain, Sweden, Switzerland, UK, USA.
NGO Relations Member of (1): *Association of Learned and Professional Society Publishers (ALPSP, #02786).* [2023.02.14/XC0999/v/**C**]

♦ International Glassfibre Reinforced Concrete Association (internationally oriented national body)

♦ International Glaucoma Association (IGA) 13719

Registered Office Woodcote House, 15 Highpoint Business Village, Henwood, Ashford, TN24 8DH, UK. T. +441233648164. E-mail: info@iga.org.uk.
URL: http://www.glaucoma-association.com/

History 1974, as *Glaucoma Association.* Registered as a charity in England and Wales: 274681; registered as as charity in Scotland: SC041550. **Aims** Raise awareness of glaucoma; promote research related to early diagnosis and treatment; provide support to patients and all those who care for them. **Structure** General Meeting (annual); Council; Officers. **Languages** English. **Staff** 12.00 FTE, paid. **Finance** Sources: donations; members' dues. Other sources: bequests. **Activities** Advocacy/lobbying/activism; events/meetings; guidance/assistance/consulting. **Events** *Summer meeting* Bristol (UK) 1993, *Autumn meeting and annual general meeting* London (UK) 1992, *Summer meeting* Newcastle upon Tyne (UK) 1992. **Publications** *IGA Newsletter* (4 a year). Booklets; leaflets; posters. **Members** Patients, ophthalmologists, optometrists and opticians, doctors and all those interested in preventing loss of sight from glaucoma (8,000) – mostly in UK. Membership countries not specified. **NGO Relations** Representative Member of: *International Agency for the Prevention of Blindness (IAPB, #11597).* Member of: *European Coalition for Vision (ECV).* [2018.06.01/XD2822/v/**C**]

♦ International Glaucoma Congress (meeting series)

♦ International Glima Association (IGA) 13720

Contact Engjavegi 6, Laugardal, 104 Reykjavik, Iceland.
URL: http://internationalglima.com/

History Autumn 2007. **Aims** Promote the ancient sport of ethnic grips *wrestling.*
Members Full in 5 countries:
Denmark, Germany, Iceland, Netherlands, Sweden. [2010/XJ1051/**D**]

♦ International Global Atmospheric Chemistry Project (IGAC) 13721

Exec Officer Univ of Colorado, CIRES, Box 216 UCB, Boulder CO 80309, USA. E-mail: megan@igacproject.org – info@igacproject.org.
URL: http://www.igacproject.org/

History Set up as a component project of *International Geosphere-Biosphere Programme (IGBP, inactive).* Set up by *International Commission on Atmospheric Chemistry and Global Pollution (ICACGP, #12664).* Currently operates under the umbrella of *Future Earth (#10048).* **Aims** Facilitate atmospheric chemistry research towards a sustainable world. **Structure** Scientific Steering Committee. **Finance** Funded by national organizations in USA, Italy and Taiwan. **Activities** Events/meetings; research and development; capacity building. **Events** *Conference* Oslo (Norway) 2019, *Conference* Takamatsu (Japan) 2018, *Conference* Breckenridge, CO (USA) 2016, *International Workshop on Heterogeneous Kinetics Related to Atmospheric Aerosols* Tsukuba (Japan) 2016, *Conference* Natal (Brazil) 2014. **Publications** *IGACnews.* Occasional reports. **NGO Relations** Closely linked to: *World Climate Research Programme (WCRP, #21279) – 'Stratospheric Processes and their Role in the Climate (SPARC)'* project. [2017/XK0378/**E**]

♦ International Global Change Institute, Hamilton (internationally oriented national body)
♦ International Glove Association (internationally oriented national body)
♦ International Glovers Federation (inactive)

♦ International Glutamate Technical Committee (IGTC) 13722

Comité Technique International du Glutamate

Contact address not obtained. E-mail: igtc@kelleneurope.com.

History 1971, Washington, DC (USA). Registration: Start date: 18 Feb 2011, Belgium. **Aims** Study, assemble and disseminate scientific data and information related to all aspects of the safety, quality and use of glutamate and its salts, particularly monosodium glutamate with a particular emphasis on their use in *foods* for human beings; promote the uses of glutamates as food *ingredients* especially on an international level. **Languages** English. **Staff** 1.50 FTE, paid. **Finance** Members' dues (annual): euro 3,000 per association. **Activities** Carries out research; disseminates technical information; organizes scientific meeting (as of 2010, every 2 years). **Events** *Meeting* Malta 2012, *Meeting* Manila (Philippines) 2010, *Meeting* Sao Paulo (Brazil) 2009, *Meeting* Hakodate (Japan) 2008, *Meeting* Hualien (Taiwan) 2007.
Members Associations (6), each consisting of MSG manufacturers in their respective regions, representing 11 countries and territories:
Brazil, Indonesia, Japan, Korea Rep, Malaysia, Peru, Philippines, Taiwan, Thailand, USA (2), Vietnam (3).
Also one association representing Europe.
IGO Relations Participates as observer in the activities of: *Codex Alimentarius Commission (CAC, #04081).*
NGO Relations Informal cooperation with: *International Council on Amino Acid Science (ICAAS, #12991); International Life Sciences Institute (ILSI, #14044).* [2012.06.09/XD3223/**D**]

♦ International Glycoconjugate Organization (IGO) 13723

Sec Univ of Milan, School of Medicine, Dept Medical Biotechnology and Translational Medicine, Polo LITA-Segrate, Via F Cervi 93, 20090 Segrate MI, Italy. T. +39250330360. Fax +39250330365.
URL: https://intl-glyco.org/

History 1989. Founded following an event series; the first symposium having taken place in 1964, and became a biennial event in 1973. **Aims** Further international collaboration for the study of glycoconjugates. **Structure** Board. **Languages** English. **Staff** None. **Finance** Symposia are responsibility of National Representative hosting the meeting. **Activities** Events/meetings; awards/prizes/competitions. **Events** *International Symposium on Glyconjugates* Chiba (Japan) 2027, *International Symposium on Glyconjugates* Vancouver, BC (Canada) 2025, *International Symposium on Glyconjugates* Taipei (Taiwan) 2023, *International Symposium on Glycoconjugates* Milan (Italy) 2019, *International Symposium on Glyconjugates* Jeju (Korea Rep) 2017. **Publications** *Glycoconjugate Journal.*
Members National Representatives in 30 countries and territories:
Argentina, Australia, Austria, Belgium, Brazil, Canada, China, Croatia, Czechia, Denmark, Finland, France, Germany, India, Israel, Italy, Japan, Korea Rep, Netherlands, Norway, Poland, Portugal, Russia, Slovakia, Spain, Sweden, Switzerland, Taiwan, UK, USA. [2022/XD9324/**D**]

♦ International GNSS Service (IGS) 13724

Service GNSS international – Servicio Internacional GNSS

Central Bureau c/o Jet Propulsion Lab, Mail Stop 238-600, 4800 Oak Grove Dr, Pasadena CA 91109, USA. T. +18183544260. E-mail: cb@igs.org.
URL: http://igs.org/

History 1993. Founded within the framework of *International Association of Geodesy (IAG, #11914).* Began formal operation, 1 Jan 1994, following 1-year pilot phase. Responsible union: *International Union of Geodesy and Geophysics (IUGG, #15776).* Former names and other names: *International GPS Service for Geodynamics (IGS)* – former (1993); *Service GPS international pour la géodynamique* – former (1993); *Servicio Internacional GPS para Geodinamica* – former (1993); *International GPS Service (IGS)* – alias; *Service GPS international* – alias; *Servicio Internacional GPS* – alias. **Aims** Provide the highest quality data and products as the standard for global *navigation satellite* systems (GNSS) in support of earth science research, multidisciplinary applications and education; advance scientific understanding of the earth system components and their interactions; facilitate other applications benefiting society. **Structure** International Governing Board, comprising Chair, Director of Central Bureau and 14 members (elected and appointed representatives of Analysis Centers, Data Centers and Networks; Analysis Coordinator; representatives of IAG and IERS; appointed members at large). Working Group. Central Bureau based at Jet Propulsion Laboratory, Pasadena CA (USA). **Activities** Foundation of IGS is a global network over over 350 permanent, continuously operating geodetic-quality Global Positioning System (GPS) and GPS/GLONASS sites. Analysis centers (10) regularly process the data and contribute products to the analysis center coordinator, who produces the official IGS combined products. IGS classic product set consists of: satellite orbits; clocks; earth rotation parameters; station positions. Newer products include: GLONASS satellite ephemerides; tropospheric zenith path delay; ionospheric total electron content grid products. Contributes to the *International Terrestrial Reference Frame (ITRF).* **Events** *Workshop* Paris (France) 2017, *Annual Multi-GNSS Asia Conference* Bandar Seri Begawan (Brunei Darussalam) 2015, *Asia Oceania Regional Workshop on Global Navigation Satellite Systems* Phuket (Thailand) 2014, *Workshop and symposium* Bern (Switzerland) 2004. **Publications** Information Services: Tracking data are available at distributed, hierarchical data centres via FTP and HTTP. **Information Services** *Central Bureau Information System (CBIS)* – maintains and provides historical configuration data for the tracking network, and documentation.
Members Contributing national agencies, universities and research institutions (over 200) in 90 countries and territories:
Argentina, Armenia, Australia, Austria, Bahrain, Barbados, Belgium, Bermuda, Brazil, Bulgaria, Canada, Chile, China, Colombia, Côte d'Ivoire, Croatia, Cuba, Cyprus, Czechia, Denmark, Ecuador, El Salvador, Fiji, Finland, France, Gabon, Germany, Greece, Greenland, Guam, Guatemala, Guiana Fr, Honduras, Hungary, Iceland, India, Indonesia, Iran Islamic Rep, Israel, Italy, Jamaica, Japan, Jordan, Kazakhstan, Kenya, Korea Rep, Kyrgyzstan, Latvia, Malaysia, Mexico, Mongolia, Morocco, Namibia, Netherlands, New Caledonia, New Zealand, Nicaragua, North Macedonia, Norway, Oman, Papua New Guinea, Peru, Philippines, Poland, Portugal, Romania, Russia, Samoa USA, Saudi Arabia, Senegal, Seychelles, Singapore, Slovakia, Slovenia, South Africa, Spain, Sweden, Switzerland, Tahiti Is, Taiwan, Türkiye, Uganda, UK, Ukraine, Uruguay, USA, Uzbekistan, Vietnam, Virgin Is USA, Zambia.
IGO Relations *European Space Agency (ESA, #08798) – European Space Operations Centre (ESOC, #08800)* is an Analysis Centre. Member of: *International Committee on Global Navigation Satellite Systems (ICG, #12775).*
NGO Relations Member of: *Global Geodetic Observing System (GGOS, see: #11914); ISC World Data System (ISC-WDS, #16024).* [2021/XK0951/**E**]

♦ International Goat Association (IGA) 13725

Association internationale caprine – Asociación Internacional de Cabras – Associação Internacional de Caprinos (AIC) – Associazione Internazionale della Capra

Exec Dir 12709 Grassy Dr, Little Rock AR 72210, USA. E-mail: admin@iga-goatworld.com.
URL: http://www.iga-goatworld.com/

History 12 Jan 1982, Tucson AZ (USA), during Third International Conference on Goats. Registered in the USA. **Aims** Foster the use of goats to provide for the needs of humankind; encourage research with and development of goats to increase their productivity and usefulness throughout the world; perpetuate the international conferences on goats. **Structure** Board of Directors; Advisory Board. Committees. **Languages** English. **Staff** 0.50 FTE, voluntary. **Finance** Members' dues: US$ 35. **Activities** Events/meetings. **Events** *International Conference on Goats* Eger (Hungary) 2022, *Virtual Conference* Budapest (Hungary) 2021, *International Conference on Goats* Eger (Hungary) 2021, *International Conference on Goats* Eger (Hungary) 2020, *International Conference on Goats* Antalya (Turkey) 2016. **Publications** *Small Ruminant Research Journal* (12 a year) – official journal; *IGA Newsletter* (3 a year).
Members Individuals in 70 countries and territories:
Albania, Argentina, Australia, Barbados, Belgium, Belize, Benin, Bolivia, Bosnia-Herzegovina, Brazil, Cambodia, Cameroon, Canada, Chad, Chile, China, Congo DR, Costa Rica, Côte d'Ivoire, Cyprus, Czechia, Djibouti, Dominican Rep, Ecuador, Egypt, Ethiopia, Fiji, France, Germany, Ghana, Greece, Guatemala, Honduras, India, Indonesia, Iran Islamic Rep, Iraq, Israel, Italy, Jordan, Kenya, Lebanon, Liberia, Mexico, Morocco, Mozambique, Netherlands, New Zealand, Nigeria, Oman, Pakistan, Peru, Philippines, Poland, Puerto Rico, Romania, Saudi Arabia, Sierra Leone, Singapore, South Africa, Spain, Taiwan, Tanzania UR, Thailand, Uganda, UK, USA, Vietnam, Zambia, Zimbabwe. [2019/XD1379/v/**C**]

♦ International Go Federation (IGF) 13726

SG 4th Floor, Nihon Ki-in Kaikan, 7-2 Gobancho, Chiyoda-ku, Tokyo, 102-0076 Japan. T. +81332888727. Fax +81332390899. E-mail: office@intergofed.org.
URL: http://www.intergofed.org/

History Founded 18 Mar 1982, Tokyo (Japan), with 29 founding members. **Aims** Advance the skills and spirit of Go around the world; promote amicable relations among members; support development of regional and national Go associations. **Structure** General Meeting (annual); Board of Directors; Secretariat. **Languages** English. **Activities** Events/meetings. **Events** *World Amateur Go Championship* Gyeongju (Korea Rep) 2014, *World Amateur Go Championship* Sendai (Japan) 2013, *World Amateur Go Championship* Guangzhou (China) 2012, *World Amateur Go Championship* Matsue (Japan) 2011, *World Amateur Go Championship* Hangzhou (China) 2010.
Members Organizations in 77 countries and territories:
Argentina, Armenia, Australia, Austria, Azerbaijan, Belarus, Belgium, Bosnia-Herzegovina, Brazil, Brunei Darussalam, Bulgaria, Canada, Chile, China, Colombia, Costa Rica, Croatia, Cuba, Cyprus, Czechia, Denmark, Ecuador, Finland, France, Georgia, Germany, Guatemala, Hong Kong, Hungary, Iceland, India, Indonesia, Iran Islamic Rep, Ireland, Israel, Italy, Japan, Kazakhstan, Korea DPR, Korea Rep, Latvia, Lithuania, Luxembourg, Macau, Madagascar, Malaysia, Mexico, Mongolia, Morocco, Nepal, Netherlands, New Zealand, Norway, Panama, Peru, Philippines, Poland, Portugal, Romania, Russia, Serbia, Singapore, Slovakia, Slovenia, South Africa, Spain, Sweden, Switzerland, Taiwan, Thailand, Türkiye, UK, Ukraine, Uruguay, USA, Venezuela, Vietnam.
NGO Relations Member of (2): *Alliance of Independent recognised Members of Sport (AIMS, #00690); Olympic Movement (#17719).* Instrumental in setting up (1): *International Mind Sports Association (IMSA, #14164).* Recognized by: *International Olympic Committee (IOC, #14408).* [2018.07.25/XD0609/**D**]

♦ International Golden Oldies (internationally oriented national body)

♦ International Golf Federation (IGF) 13727

Exec Dir Maison du Sport Intl, Av de Rhodanie 54, 1007 Lausanne VD, Switzerland. T. +41216231212. Fax +4121016477. E-mail: info@igfmail.org.
URL: http://www.igfgolf.org/

History 2 May 1958, Washington, DC (USA). Founded during meeting hosted by the USGA attended by representatives from 35 countries. Statutes amended: 6 Oct 1964; 26 Oct 1966; 8 Oct 1968; 22 Sep 1970; 29 Oct 1974; Nov 1984; Oct 1986; Sep 1988; Oct 1990; Oct 2004; Oct 2010. Former names and other names: *World Amateur Golf Council (WAGC)* – former. **Aims** Foster international development of the *sport* of golf. **Structure** Federation Meeting (every 2 years); Board; Administrative Committee; Executive Committee. **Languages** English, French. **Staff** 6.00 FTE, paid. **Finance** No members' dues. **Activities** Events/meetings; sporting activities. **Events** *Biennial Meeting* Lausanne (Switzerland) 2020, *Biennial Meeting* Dublin (Ireland) 2018, *Biennial Meeting* Cancún (Mexico) 2016, *Biennial Meeting* Karuizawa (Japan) 2014, *Biennial Meeting* Antalya (Turkey) 2012. **Publications** *IGF Record Book* (every 2 years).
Members National Federations (152) in 142 countries and territories:
Afghanistan, Algeria, Argentina, Armenia, Australia, Austria, Azerbaijan, Bahamas, Bahrain, Bangladesh, Barbados, Belarus, Belgium, Benin, Bermuda, Bolivia, Bosnia-Herzegovina, Botswana, Brazil, Bulgaria, Cambodia, Canada, Cayman Is, Chile, China, Colombia, Congo DR, Cook Is, Costa Rica, Côte d'Ivoire, Croatia, Cyprus, Czechia, Denmark, Dominican Rep, Ecuador, Egypt, El Salvador, England, Estonia, Eswatini, Fiji, Finland, France, Gabon, Gambia, Germany, Ghana, Greece, Guam, Guatemala, Haiti, Honduras, Hong Kong, Hungary, Iceland, India, Indonesia, Iran Islamic Rep, Ireland, Israel, Italy, Jamaica, Japan, Kazakhstan, Kenya, Korea Rep, Kuwait, Kyrgyzstan, Latvia, Lebanon, Libya, Liechtenstein, Lithuania, Luxembourg, Madagascar, Malawi, Malaysia, Malta, Mauritius, Mexico, Moldova, Monaco, Mongolia, Morocco, Myanmar, Namibia, Netherlands, New Zealand, Nicaragua, Nigeria, North Macedonia, Norway, Oman, Pakistan, Panama, Papua New Guinea, Paraguay, Peru, Philippines, Poland, Portugal, Puerto Rico, Qatar, Romania, Russia, Samoa, San Marino, Saudi Arabia, Scotland, Senegal, Serbia, Singapore, Slovakia, Slovenia, Solomon Is, South Africa, Spain, Sri Lanka, St Lucia, Sweden, Switzerland, Taiwan, Tanzania UR, Thailand, Trinidad-Tobago, Tunisia, Türkiye, Turks-Caicos, Uganda, Ukraine, United Arab Emirates, Uruguay, USA, Uzbekistan, Vanuatu, Venezuela, Vietnam, Virgin Is USA, Wales, Zambia, Zimbabwe.
Professional Federations (22) in 9 countries and territories:
Australia, Canada, England, India, Japan, Scotland, Singapore, South Africa, USA.
NGO Relations Member of (2): *Association of Summer Olympic International Federations (ASOIF, #02943); Olympic Movement (#17719).* Cooperates with (1): *International Testing Agency (ITA, #15678).* Recognized by: *International Olympic Committee (IOC, #14408).* [2023.02.16/XB4626/**B**]

♦ International Good Neighbour Council (IGNC) 13728

Conseil international du bon voisinage – Consejo Internacional de Buena Vecindad (CIBV)

Exec Dir Juan Ignacio Ramon 506 Ote, Edificio Latino Desp 513, 64000 Monterrey NL, Mexico. T. +528183427633. Fax +528183427634.
Pres Diego Diaz de Berlanga 1107, Col Jardines de Anahuac, San Nicolas de los Garza NL, Mexico. Fax +528183427634.
URL: http://www.cibv-ignc.org/

History 1954. **Aims** Promote *understanding* and *goodwill* among the peoples of the *Western hemisphere*; facilitate cooperation between countries, agencies and organizations with common interests; promote and encourage actions aimed at establishing security and furthering the cause of peace in the region. **Activities** Bestows 'Good Neighbour Award'. **Publications** *IGNC Newsletter* (12 a year) in English, Spanish; *IGNC Bulletin* (6 a year); *IGNC Directory* (annual); *IGNC Executive Directory* (annual).

Members Organizations and enterprises in 3 countries:
Canada, Mexico, USA. [2013/XF1412/**F**]

♦ International Good Templar Youth Federation (inactive)
♦ International Gorilla Conservation Programme (internationally oriented national body)
♦ International Gorilla Consortium Programme / see International Gorilla Conservation Programme
♦ International Gorilla Consortium Project / see International Gorilla Conservation Programme

♦ International Gothic Association (IGA) 13729

Contact Dep English, Univ Westminster, 32-38 Wells Street, London, W1T 3UW, UK.
URL: http://www.iga.stir.ac.uk/

Aims Promote the study and dissemination of information on gothic *culture*. **Events** *Biennial Conference* Paris (France) 2015, *Biennial Conference* Guildford (UK) 2013, *Biennial Conference* Heidelberg (Germany) 2011, *Biennial Conference* Lancaster (UK) 2009, *Biennial conference* Aix-en-Provence (France) 2007. **Publications** *Gothic Studies* – journal. [2013/XM1673/**E**]

♦ International Gottfried-Wilhelm-Leibniz Society (#10683)

♦ International Governance Forum Support Association (IGFSA) 13730

Sec World Trade Ctr II, CP 228, AIRPORT, 1215 Geneva, Switzerland. E-mail: info@igfsa.org.
URL: http://igfsa.org/

History Set up in support of *Internet Governance Forum (IGF, #15950)*. Registered in accordance with Swiss Civil Code. **Aims** Promote and support the global International Governance Forum and National and Regional IGF Initiatives (NRIs). **Structure** General Assembly; Executive Committee; Secretariat. **Finance** Members' dues. **Activities** Financial and/or material support; awareness raising.
Members Individuals; organizations; companies. Membership countries not specified. Included in the above, 5 organizations listed in this Yearbook:
Included in the above, 5 organizations listed in this Yearbook:
Arab World Internet Institute (AW2I, #01079); *Internet Corporation for Assigned Names and Numbers (ICANN, #15949)*; *Internet Society (ISOC, #15952)*; *Latin American and Caribbean Top Level Domains (LACTLD, #16287)*; *Number Resource Organization (NRO, #17625)*. [2018/XM6650/y/**E**]

♦ International GPS Service / see International GNSS Service (#13724)
♦ International GPS Service for Geodynamics / see International GNSS Service (#13724)
♦ International Graduate Centre for Hebrew and Jewish Studies (internationally oriented national body)
♦ International Graduate School of Management, University of Navarre / see IESE Business School, University of Navarra
♦ International Grail Movement / see The Grail – International Movement of Christian Women (#10689)
♦ International Grains Agreement (treaty)
♦ International Grains Arrangement 1967 (1967 treaty)

♦ International Grains Council (IGC) 13731

Conseil international des céréales – Consejo Internacional de Cereales – Mezdunarodnyj Sovet po Zernu

Exec Dir 1 Canada Square, Canary Wharf, London, E14 5AE, UK. T. +442075131122. Fax +442075130630. E-mail: igc@igc.int.
URL: http://www.igc.int/

History 1 Jul 1949, as *International Wheat Council (IWC) – Conseil international du blé (CIB) – Consejo Internacional del Trigo (CIT) – Mezdunarodnyj Sovet po Psenice*, under provisions of International Wheat Agreement, 1949, and continued in being under the Agreements of 1953, 1956, 1959 and 1962 and the Wheat Trade Conventions of 1967, 1971 and 1986 – *International Wheat Convention (1986)*. These conventions comprise, with the relevant Food Aid Conventions, the *International Grains Arrangement 1967 (1967)*, *International Wheat Agreement, 1971 (IWA)* and *International Wheat Agreement, 1986 (IWA, 1986)*. Currently administers the *Grains Trade Convention (GTC, 1994)*, 1995 of the *International Grains Agreement (IGA)*. **Aims** Administer the 1995 Grains Trade Convention, which is designed to meet more effectively the needs and aspirations of member countries, especially developing countries, and to reinforce international cooperation between grain exporting and importing members, through exchange of views on matters of mutual concern. Coverage under the GTC includes *wheat*, *barley*, *maize* (corn), *sorghum*, other coarse grains, rice and oilseeds and their products. As an instrument of international cooperation, the Convention does not attempt to influence the market through price ranges or a reserve/buffer stock mechanism but aims to contribute to transparency of the market through the collection and dissemination of reliable information and through regular consultations. Its objectives include: furthering international cooperation in all aspects of trade in grains; promoting expansion of international trade in grains, securing its freest possible flow in the interests of members, particularly developing members, contributing to stability of international grain markets and enhancing world food security; providing a forum for exchange of information and discussion of members' concerns. **Structure** Council (meeting twice in each crop-year). Administrative Committee (meeting as required) comprises up to 16 members. Market Conditions Committee (usually meeting twice a year), open to all Council members. Meetings normally closed. **Languages** English, French, Russian, Spanish. **Staff** 17.00 FTE, paid. **Finance** Member countries' contributions in proportion to the number of votes under the Convention. **Activities** Council and Market Conditions Committee provide a forum where issues may be debated in a constructive manner. **Events** *Conference* London (UK) 2022, *Conference* London (UK) 2021, *Conference* London (UK) 2020, *US Corn Quality Seminar* Busan (Korea Rep) 2019, *Conference* London (UK) 2019. **Publications** *Grain Market Indicators* (weekly); *Report for the Fiscal Year* (annual); *Wheat and Coarse Grains Shipments* (annual); *World Grain Statistics* (annual); *Grain Market Reports* (11 a year). *Ocean Freight Rates*.
Members Importing members, 18 countries:
Algeria, Côte d'Ivoire, Cuba, Egypt, Holy See, Iran Islamic Rep, Iraq, Japan, Kenya, Korea Rep, Morocco, Norway, Oman, Pakistan, Saudi Arabia, South Africa, Switzerland, Tunisia.
Exporting members, 9 countries:
Argentina, Australia, Canada, India, Kazakhstan, Russia, Türkiye, Ukraine, USA.
Regional EU integration entity (exporting member as such):
IGO Relations *World Trade Organization (WTO, #21864)* (Observer Status). Member of Secretariat of: *Agricultural Market Information System (AMIS, #00573)*. Observer to: *International Fund for Agricultural Development (IFAD, #13692)*. Relationship agreement with: *FAO (#09260)*. Participates in the activities of: *UNCTAD (#20285)*. Designed International Commodity Body of: *Common Fund for Commodities (CFC, #04293)*. [2020.02.05/XB2812/**B***]

♦ International Grain Trade Coalition (IGTC) 13732

Secretariat Avenue Krieg 40, 1208 Geneva, Switzerland. T. +41789329618.
URL: http://igtcglobal.org/

History 21 Oct 2014, Geneva (Switzerland). Statement of Organization adopted 6 Apr 2011. Articles of Association adopted 21 Oct 2014, updated 28 Nov 2018; 3 Nov 2020. Registration: Swiss Civil Code, Switzerland. **Aims** Provide representation and share expertise on the commercial requirements and economics of the world's food, feed and processing industries. **Structure** General Assembly; Management Council; Secretariat. **Finance** Sources: donations; members' dues; sponsorship. **Activities** Events/meetings; knowledge management/information dissemination.
Members National associations in 21 countries:
Argentina, Australia, Brazil, Burundi, Canada, China, Congo DR, Ethiopia, India, Kenya, Malawi, Mexico, Paraguay, Rwanda, South Africa, South Sudan, Tanzania UR, Uganda, Ukraine, USA, Zambia.
International organizations (3):
Committee of the Trade in Cereals, Oilseeds, Pulses, Olive Oil, Oils and Fats, Animal Feed and Agrosupply of the EU (COCERAL, #04289); *Eastern Africa Grain Council (EAGC, #05222)*; *Grain and Feed Trade Association (GAFTA, #10692)*. [2021.09.02/XM6366/ty/**C**]

♦ International Gramsci Society (IGS) 13733

Sec PCC Social Sci Div C-321, 1570 E Colorado Blvd, Pasadena CA 91106, USA. E-mail: marcus@internationalgramscisociety.org.
URL: http://www.internationalgramscisociety.org/

History 1989, Formia (Italy), during the international conference 'Gramsci nel mondo'. **Aims** Facilitate communication and exchange of information among individuals worldwide who are interested in the life and work of Antonio Gramsci (1891-1937), Italian socialist, *political theorist* and *activist*. **Events** *Conference* Italy 2007, *Conference* Rio de Janeiro (Brazil) 2001, *Conference* Naples (Italy) 1997. **Publications** *IGS Newsletter* (annual).
Members Societies and individuals. Members in 33 countries:
Argentina, Australia, Austria, Brazil, Canada, China, Colombia, Cuba, Cyprus, Denmark, Ecuador, Finland, France, Germany, Greece, Hungary, India, Israel, Italy, Japan, Korea Rep, Malta, Mexico, New Zealand, Puerto Rico, Romania, Russia, South Africa, Spain, Switzerland, Tunisia, UK, USA. [2019/XN8651/**E**]

♦ International Grand Lodge of Druidism (religious order)
♦ International Graphical Federation (inactive)
♦ International Graphic Arts Education Association / see Graphic Communications Education Association
♦ International Graphic Arts Society (inactive)

♦ International Graphonomics Society (IGS) 13734

Pres Dept of Electrical and Computer Engineering, W310 Engineering Bldg 1, Univ of Houston, Houston TX 77004-4005, USA. T. +17137434429. Fax +17137434444.
Sec School of Kinesiology, Louisiana State Univ, 112 HP Long Fieldhouse, Baton Rouge LA 70803-7101, USA. T. +12255789142. Fax +12255783680.
URL: http://www.graphonomics.org/

History Founded 11 Jul 1985, Hong Kong, during 2nd International Graphonomics Conference. Legally established: 30 Jan 1987, Nijmegen (Netherlands); 14 Aug 2014, State of Nevada (USA). Subtitle: *Society for the Science and Technology of Handwriting and Other Graphic Skills*. **Aims** Study handwriting and graphic skills with a multidisciplinary approach involving motor control, computer science, pattern recognition and neuroscience; foster the application of those studies to handwriting and drawing recognition, human-computer interaction, forensic science, education, physical rehabilitation, medicine and paleography. **Structure** Governing Board, acting as Executive Committee; Advisory Council of Members. **Languages** English. **Staff** 4.00 FTE, voluntary. **Finance** Members' dues (every 2 years). Conference fees. Annual budget: 2,500 USD. **Activities** Events/meetings; financial and/or material support; financial and/or material support; knowledge management/information dissemination; networking/liaising; research/documentation. **Events** *Biennial Conference* Cancún (Mexico) 2019, *Biennial Conference* Gaeta (Italy) 2017, *Biennial Conference* Pointe-à-Pitre (Guadeloupe) 2015, *Biennial Conference* Nara (Japan) 2013, *Biennial Conference* Cancún (Mexico) 2011. **Publications** Conference proceedings; pamphlets; graphonomics research directory. **Information Services** *Forum*.
Members Individuals in 30 countries and territories:
Australia, Belgium, Brazil, Canada, China, France, Germany, Greece, Guadeloupe, Hong Kong, India, Ireland, Israel, Italy, Japan, Mexico, Morocco, Netherlands, Norway, Pakistan, Russia, Singapore, Spain, Sweden, Switzerland, Taiwan, Tunisia, Türkiye, UK, USA. [2015.06.24/XD0630/v/**C**]

♦ International Grassland Congress (meeting series)
♦ International Grass Ski Association (inactive)
♦ International Gravimetric Bureau (#03361)

♦ International Gravity Sports Association (IGSA) 13735

Pres 638 N Crestview Drive, Glendora CA 91741, USA. T. +16269635304. Fax +16269631185. E-mail: igsainfo@verizon.net.
URL: http://www.igsaworldcup.com/

History 1996. **Aims** Foster strong and fair competition; provide reasonable rules; administer the competition program with impartiality; reduce the hazards associated with the sport. **Activities** Sporting activities. [2018/XQ2976/**C**]

♦ International Green Automotive Lightweight Technology Alliance (unconfirmed)

♦ International Green Purchasing Network (IGPN) 13736

Secretariat 9F Bakurocho Daiichi Bldg, 1-4-16 Nihonbashi Bakurocho, Chuo-ku, Tokyo, 103-0002 Japan. E-mail: igpn.secretariat@igpn.org.
URL: http://www.igpn.org/

History 25 Apr 2005, Tokyo (Japan), following 1st International Conference on Green Purchasing, 2004, Sendai (Japan). **Aims** Promote the spread of *environmentally friendly* product, service development and green purchasing activities globally. **Structure** Council; Advisory Board; Green Purchasing Networks; Secretariat. **Languages** English. **Activities** Events/meetings; knowledge management/information dissemination. **Events** *Sapporo Forum* Sapporo (Japan) 2014, *International Conference on Green Purchasing* Subang Jaya (Malaysia) 2013, *Low Carbon Green Growth Conference* Seoul (Korea Rep) 2011, *International Conference of Design for Sustainability, Destination 2011-2021* Tokyo (Japan) 2011, *International green technology and purchasing conference* Kuala Lumpur (Malaysia) 2010. **Publications** *IPGN Newsletter*. *Green Purchasing and Green Public Procurement Starter Kit*; *Green Purchasing: The New Growth Frontier*. **Members** Corporate; Individual. Membership countries not specified. **IGO Relations** *Asian Productivity Organization (APO, #01674)*; Japan Environmental Association (JEA); UN Department of Economic and Social Affairs; *UNEP (#20299)*. **NGO Relations** *Global Ecolabelling Network (GEN, #10328)*; *Local Governments for Sustainability (ICLEI, #16507)*. [2017/XM0865/**F**]

♦ International Green Roof Association (inactive)

♦ International Greeter Association (IGA) 13737

Chair Avenue d'Auderghem 63, 1040 Brussels, Belgium. E-mail: chair@internationalgreeter.org.
Sec address not obtained. E-mail: secretary@internationalgreeter.org.
URL: https://internationalgreeter.org/

History Originated 2005. Founded as *Global Greeter Network Foundation (GGN)*, 2012, from which IGA split 2016. Legally founded under current title Mar 2019, Brussels (Belgium). **Aims** Promote and develop the founding values of the Greeter movement. **Structure** General Assembly; Board of Directors. **Activities** Advocacy/lobbying/activism; events/meetings; networking/liaising. [2021/XM8420/**C**]

♦ International Grid Trust Federation (IGTF) 13738

Contact address not obtained. E-mail: info@igtf.net.
URL: http://www.igtf.net/

Aims Establish common policies and guidelines among member Policy *Management* Authorities (PMAs) covering large scale distributed *computing* grids on a production scale, across organizations, countries and continents, for the advancement of science and engineering.
Members Policy Management Authorities (3):
Americas Grid PMA; *Asia Pacific Grid Policy Management Authority (APGrid PMA, no recent information)*; *European Policy Management Authority for Grid Authentication in e-Science (EUGridPMA, #08244)*. [2011/XJ3972/y/**F**]

♦ International Groundfish Forum (meeting series)
♦ International Ground Water Modelling Center (internationally oriented national body)

♦ International Groundwater Resources Assessment Centre (IGRAC) . 13739

Contact Westvest 7, 2611 AX Delft, Netherlands. T. +31152152310. E-mail: info@un-igrac.org.
URL: http://www.un-igrac.org/

History Proposed by *UNESCO (#20322)* and *World Meteorological Organization (WMO, #21649)*, 1999. Launched Mar 2003, Kyoto (Japan) during 3rd World Water Forum, hosted by Netherlands Organization for Applied Scientific Research (TNO). Registered in accordance with Dutch law, Jun 2011. Since Oct 2012, serves as UNESCO *Global Groundwater Centre*, under the auspices of WMO. Previously also known under the acronym *INGRACE*. **Aims** Contribute to world-wide availability of relevant information and knowledge on groundwater resources, with particular emphasis on developing countries, in order to support sustainable utilization and management; promote the role of groundwater in integrated water resources planning and elucidate the impact of groundwater on ecosystems of the Earth. **Languages** English. **Staff** 6.00 FTE, paid. **Finance** Financed by Dutch government through Partners for Water Programme. **Activities** Monitoring/evaluation; knowledge management/information dissemination; training/education; capacity building. **Events** *Symposium on groundwater* Amsterdam (Netherlands) 2008, *International symposium on transboundary* *waters management* Thessaloniki (Greece) 2008. **Publications** *Transboundary Aquifers of the World: map* (2015). Reports; papers; maps; brochures; flyers. **Information Services** *Global Groundwater Information System (GGIS); Global Groundwater Monitoring Network (GGMN).* **IGO Relations** Network member of: *Global Terrestrial Network – Hydrology (GTN-H, #10624).* **NGO Relations** Cooperates with: *International Association of Hydrogeologists (IAH, #11953).* Maintains: *Internationally Shared Aquifer Resources Management (ISARM, #14071).* [2017.10.30/XG9069/**E**]

♦ International Group for Advancement in Spinal Science (IGASS) . . . 13740

Administration 47 rue du Bas Huet, 78100 Saint-Germain-en-Laye, France. T. +33139163386 – +331(33683648808. Fax +33960106155.
URL: http://igass-spine.org/

Aims Provide top level case based education in spine surgery. **Structure** Executive Committee; Scientific Committee. **Activities** Events/meetings. **Events** *Forum* Helsinki (Finland) 2019, *Spine surgery in the over 80 year old patients* Berlin (Germany) 2016, *Forum* Copenhagen (Denmark) 2015, *Forum* Lyon (France) 2014, *Forum* Liverpool (UK) 2013.
Members Individuals in 13 countries:
Austria, Brazil, Czechia, Ecuador, France, Germany, India, Libya, Netherlands, South Africa, Switzerland, UK, United Arab Emirates.
NGO Relations *European Accreditation Council for Continuing Medical Education (EACCME, #05823); EUROSPINE – Spine Society of Europe (EUROSPINE, #09185).* [2016/XJ9473/v/**D**]

- ♦ International Group of Agencies and Bureaus / see International Association of Speakers Bureaus
- ♦ International Group for Agricultural and Home Economics Extension Officers / see Internationale Akademie land- und hauswirtschaftlicher Beraterinnen und Berater (#13212)
- ♦ International Group of Associations for French Language and Culture / see Union culturelle et technique de langue française (#20374)

♦ International Group on Aviation and Multimodal Transport Research (IGAMT) 13741

Scientific Coordinator Europe address not obtained.
URL: https://www.igamt.eu/

History Registration: No/ID: KVK 88270947, Netherlands, Amsterdam. **Activities** Knowledge management/ information dissemination; research/documentation.
Members Individuals in 10 countries:
Argentina, Australia, Canada, France, Germany, Mexico, Netherlands, Singapore, Spain, Türkiye. [2023/AA1840/jv/**C**]

♦ International Group of Controlling (IGC) 13742

Chairman c/o FH Steyr, Wehrgrabengasse 1-3, 4400 Steyr, Austria. T. +435080433710.
URL: http://www.igc-controlling.org/

History 1995. **Aims** Promote function and role of controllers; certify controller education programmes; serve as a forum for the exchange of ideas and experience in the field. **Structure** General Assembly (annual); Management Committee; Working Groups. **Languages** Czech, English, French, German, Italian, Polish, Russian. **Finance** Members' dues. Budget (annual): euro 40,000. **Events** *General Assembly* Budapest (Hungary) 2015, *General Assembly* Split (Croatia) 2014, *General Assembly* Bucharest (Romania) 2013, *Congress* Munich (Germany) 2004, *Congress* Munich (Germany) 2003.
Members Full in 13 countries:
Austria, Belarus, Croatia, Czechia, Germany, Hungary, Italy, Poland, Romania, Russia, Serbia, Slovenia, Switzerland.
Includes:
Internationaler Controller Verein (ICV, #13292). [2014.06.05/XJ3368/y/**E**]

- ♦ International Group for Cooperation and Research on Documentation: Territorial Planning Housing Information (inactive)

♦ International Group of Educational Publishers (IGEP) 13743

Contact Menntamalastofnun, Vikurhvarf 3, 203 Kópavogur, Iceland. T. +3545147500.
URL: http://igep.education/

History 1963. **Aims** Share information on educational publishing; stay informed of developments in the field, both technological and content-wise; establish contacts across countries and cultures. **Languages** English. **Activities** Events/meetings; standards/guidelines. **Events** *Annual Meeting* Stockholm (Sweden) 2018, *Annual Meeting* Cambridge (UK) 2017, *Annual Meeting* Madrid (Spain) 2016, *Annual Meeting* Helsinki (Finland) 2015, *Annual Meeting* Paris (France) 2014.
Members Full in 11 countries:
Denmark, Finland, France, Germany, Iceland, Italy, Norway, Poland, Portugal, Sweden, UK. [2019.10.28/XF2878/**E**]

♦ International Group for Equestrian Qualifications (IGEQ) 13744

Sec address not obtained.
URL: http://www.igeq.org/

History 1992. **Aims** Develop, promote and maintaining equestrian qualifications. **Structure** Executive Committee. **Activities** Certification/accreditation; training/education. **Events** *Conference* Durban (South Africa) 2022, *Conference* 2021, *Conference* 2020, *Conference* Warendorf (Germany) 2019, *Conference* Budapest (Hungary) 2018.
Members Full in 36 countries:
Australia, Austria, Bermuda, Canada, China, Czechia, Denmark, Estonia, Finland, France, Germany, Greece, Hungary, Ireland, Israel, Italy, Latvia, Lithuania, Malawi, Malaysia, Mauritius, Mexico, Netherlands, New Zealand, Norway, Palestine, Poland, Portugal, Romania, San Marino, Slovenia, South Africa, Spain, Sweden, Switzerland, UK.
Associated organizations (5):
Equestrian Educational Network (EEN, #05522); European Equestrian Federation (EEF, #07005); Fédération Équestre Internationale (FEI, #09484); Federation of Horses in Education and Therapy International (HETI, #09593); International Federation of Icelandic Horse Associations (FEIF, #13454). [2022/XJ9444/y/**C**]

♦ International Group of Ex Libris Users (IGeLU) 13745

Secretariat Univ of Siena, Via Banchi di Sotto 55, 53100 Siena SI, Italy. T. +39577235170. E-mail: secretariat@igelu.org – secretariat@new.igelu.org.
Chair c/o State Library of Queensland, PO Box 3488, Brisbane QLD 4101, Australia.
URL: http://igelu.org/

History 30 Apr 2006, Stockholm (Sweden). Successor organization of *International Consortium of ALEPH Users (ICAU, inactive)* and *SFX – MetaLib Users Group (SMUG, inactive).* Registration: Italy. **Aims** Promote information exchange between institutions that use Ex Libris products in order to enhance their library services. **Structure** General Assembly (annual); Steering Committee; Working Groups. **Languages** English. **Finance** Members' dues. **Activities** Events/meetings. **Events** *Annual Conference* Cardiff (UK) 2022, *Annual Conference / Digital Conference* 2021, *Annual Conference* 2020, *Annual Conference* Singapore (Singapore) 2019, *Annual Conference* Prague (Czechia) 2018.
Members Libraries (340) in 41 countries and territories:
Australia, Austria, Belgium, Brazil, Canada, Chile, China, Croatia, Cyprus, Czechia, Denmark, Estonia, Finland, France, Germany, Greece, Hungary, Iceland, Ireland, Israel, Italy, Japan, Korea Rep, Latvia, Liechtenstein, Luxembourg, Netherlands, New Zealand, Norway, Poland, Portugal, Romania, Singapore, Slovenia, South Africa, Spain, Sweden, Switzerland, Taiwan, UK, USA. [2021/XM2655/**F**]

♦ International Group of Experts on the Explosion Risks of Unstable Substances (IGUS) 13746

Sec TNO, Process Safety Solutions, PO Box 45, 2280 AA Rijswijk, Netherlands. T. +31888861265.
URL: http://www.igus-experts.org/

History 1962, Paris (France), under the sponsorship of *OECD (#17693)*, to promote safety matters in fire and explosion hazards of energetic chemicals. Previously known as *OECD-IGUS.* **Aims** Exchange information and thoughts on phenomenology of *explosions*, the thermodynamics and kinetics of explosive reactions, testing of unstable substances with regard to explosion hazards, analysis of accident case histories and prediction of explosive properties; improve safe manufacture, handling, transport and storage of various kinds of *hazardous* materials and so facilitate international trade as well as promote the *safety* of people. **Structure** Plenary Meeting (every 4 years); Management Board; Steering Committee; Working Groups (2); Ad-hoc Sub-groups as needed. **Languages** English. **Staff** 4.00 FTE, paid. **Finance** Members and officers cover their own costs. **Activities** Knowledge management/information dissemination. **Events** *Plenary Meeting* Berlin (Germany) 2012, *Plenary Meeting* St Petersburg (Russia) 2009, *Plenary Meeting* Rijswijk (Netherlands) 2007, *Biennial plenary meeting* Verneuil-en-Halatte (France) 2007, *Biennial plenary meeting / Plenary Meeting* Buxton (UK) 2005.
Members Expert representatives from OECD countries insofar as they are members of National Laboratories or scientists who are involved in research and who are permanent government consultants not in the employ of private commercial enterprise (experts from non-OECD countries may join as independents). Members and independents in 21 countries and territories:
Australia, Belgium, Canada, China, Finland, France, Germany, Hong Kong, Ireland, Japan, Korea Rep, Netherlands, Norway, Poland, Portugal, Spain, Sweden, Switzerland, Taiwan, UK, USA. [2018.03.08/XE0679/v/**E**]

♦ International Group for Eye Movement Research 13747

Chairman SCIANS Ltd, Moosgasse 16, Iffwil, 3305 Bern, Switzerland. T. +41317610035.
Main: http://www.eyemovement.org/

History 1979, Heidelberg (Germany FR), as *European Group for Eye Movement Research.* **Aims** Disseminate information on current research and equipment. **Structure** Open access group. **Languages** English. **Staff** 5.00 FTE, paid. **Finance** External support; publication fees. **Activities** Knowledge management/information dissemination; events/meetings; publishing activities. **Events** *European Conference on Eye Movements* Leicester (UK) 2022, *European Conference on Eye Movements* Alicante (Spain) 2019, *Biennial Conference* Wuppertal (Germany) 2017, *Biennial Conference* Vienna (Austria) 2015, *Biennial Conference* Lund (Sweden) 2013. **Publications** *Journal of Eye Movement Research.* **Members** Individuals. Membership countries not specified. [2017.10.25/XF0095/v/**E**]

- ♦ International Group for High Pressure Biology / see International High Pressure Biology Group (#13796)

♦ International Group for Hydraulic Efficiency Measurement (IGHEM) 13748

Sec Etaeval GmbH, Altsagenstrasse 3, 6048 Horw LU, Switzerland. T. +41792552350.
URL: http://www.ighem.org/

History 31 Jan 1995, Zurich (Switzerland), by merger of Groupe des Practiciens de la Méthode Thermodynamique (GPMT) and *International Current Meter Group (inactive).* **Aims** Support specialists in the field of Hydraulic Efficiency Measurement through: a networking platform to exchange knowledge and know-how; improvement of measuring accuracy (especially for refurbishment projects); technical support of standardization groups. **Structure** Officers: President; 2 Vice-Presidents; Secretary. **Activities** Events/meetings. **Events** *Biennial Conference* Grenoble (France) 2020, *Biennial Conference* Beijing (China) 2018, *Biennial Conference* Linz (Austria) 2016, *Biennial Conference* Itajuba (Brazil) 2014, *Biennial Conference* Trondheim (Norway) 2012. **Members** Individuals involved in hydraulic power plant efficiency measurements. Membership countries not specified. [2019.12.12/XE4639/**E**]

♦ International Group for Lean Construction (IGLC) 13749

SG Technion Civil and Env Eng, Rabin Bldg, 3200003 Haifa, Israel.
URL: http://www.iglc.net/

History Founded 1993. **Aims** Improve *architecture*, engineering and construction processes and products. **Structure** Includes *European Group for Lean Construction.* **Languages** English. **Staff** None. **Finance** No financing or budget. **Activities** Awards/prizes/competition; research and development. **Events** *Annual Conference* Perth, WA (Australia) 2015, *Annual Conference* Oslo (Norway) 2014, *Annual Conference* Fortaleza (Brazil) 2013, *Annual Conference* San Diego, CA (USA) 2012, *Annual Conference* Lima (Peru) 2011.
Members Individuals in 35 countries and territories:
Australia, Brazil, Canada, Chile, China, Colombia, Denmark, Ecuador, Egypt, Finland, France, Germany, Hong Kong, Indonesia, Israel, Italy, Japan, Korea Rep, Malaysia, Mexico, Netherlands, New Zealand, Nigeria, Norway, Peru, Portugal, Russia, Singapore, South Africa, Spain, Sweden, Taiwan, Türkiye, UK, USA. [2019.02.12/XD7809/v/**E**]

- ♦ International Group of the Library Association / see International Library and Information Group (#14037)
- ♦ International Group of Liquefied Natural Gas Importers (#10750)
- ♦ International Group of National Associations of Manufacturers of Agrochemical Products / see CropLife International (#04966)
- ♦ International Group of National Pesticide Manufacturers' Associations / see CropLife International (#04966)
- ♦ International Group of National Textile Care Labelling Committees / see Groupement International de l'Etiquetage pour l'Entretien des Textiles (#10761)

♦ International Group for Paper Distribution Quality (IGP) 13750

Sec Innventia, Box 5604, SE-114 86 Stockholm, Sweden. T. +4686767050.

History 1999. A trade and industry group within Innventia AB. **Aims** Reduce damage and damage risks in all parts of the distribution chain of paper reels and paper sheets on pallets. **Structure** Steering Committee. **Events** *Annual Meeting* Gävle (Sweden) 2011, *Annual meeting* Halden (Norway) 2006, *Annual Meeting* Norway 2006. **Members** Companies (approx 40). Membership companies not specified. [2011/XM0826/**D**]

- ♦ International Group of Pastors for Circus and Showmen of All Confessions / see International Group of Priests for Circus and Showmen of All Confessions (#13752)
- ♦ International Group for Pharmaceutical Distribution in the Countries of the European Community / see Groupement International de la Répartition Pharmaceutique (#10762)
- ♦ International Group for Pharmaceutical Distribution in the Countries of the European Community and other Countries in Europe / see Groupement International de la Répartition Pharmaceutique (#10762)
- ♦ International Group for Pharmaceutical Distribution in Europe / see Groupement International de la Répartition Pharmaceutique (#10762)

♦ International Group of P and I Clubs 13751

Main Office 3rd floor, 78/79 Leadenhall Street, London, EC3A 3DH, UK. T. +442079293544. Fax +442076210675. E-mail: secretariat@internationalgroup.org.uk.
URL: http://www.igpandi.org/

History 1982. Former names and other names: *International Group of Protection and Indemnity Associations (P and I)* – alias; *International Group of Protection and Indemnity Clubs (P and I Clubs)* – alias. **Events** *Correspondents Conference* London (UK) 2022, *Asia Pacific Regional Seminar* Singapore (Singapore) 2019, *Quadrennial Correspondents Conference* London (UK) 2017. **Consultative Status** Consultative status granted from: *ECOSOC (#05331)* (Ros C); *UNCTAD (#20285)* (Special Category); *International Maritime Organization (IMO, #14102).* **IGO Relations** Observer status at: *International Oil Pollution Compensation Funds (IOPC Funds, #14402).* **NGO Relations** Member of: *Maritime Piracy Humanitarian Response Programme (MPHRP, #16583).* Consultative member of: *Comité maritime international (CMI, #04192).* [2022/XF0592/**F**]

♦ International Group of Priests for Circus and Showmen of All Confessions 13752

Internationale Arbeitsgemeinschaft der Circus-und Schausteller-Seelsorger
Address not obtained.

History 1979, Berlin West (Germany FR), within the framework of *European Showmen's Union (ESU, #08483).* Also referred to as *Group for Pastoral Work for Circus and Showmen of All Confessions – Europäische Arbeitsgemeinschaft der Circus- und Schausteller-Seelsorger aller Konfessionen* and *International Group of Pastors for Circus and Showmen of All Confessions.* **Structure** Divisions (3): Circusmen and variety artists, their employees and families; Showmen, their employees and families; Fun-park enterprises, their employees and families. **Activities** Provides care for members of the travelling community, including religious services at festivals, circuses and fun parks; gives advice on the family, pension and education; provides accommodation in own school boarding houses and for old people; work with children including baptism, communion, confirmation; youth work. **Events** *Meeting* Berlin (Germany) 1999, *Meeting* Budapest (Hungary) 1999, *Meeting* Athens (Greece) 1998, *Meeting* Nürburg (Germany) 1998, *Meeting* Brussels (Belgium) 1997.
Members Covers 24 countries:
Austria, Belgium, Canada, Denmark, Finland, France, Germany, Greece, Holy See, Hungary, Ireland, Italy, Luxembourg, Mexico, Monaco, Netherlands, Norway, Poland, Portugal, Spain, Sweden, Switzerland, UK, USA. [2010/XF2024/**F**]

♦ International Group of Protection and Indemnity Associations / see International Group of P and I Clubs (#13751)
♦ International Group of Protection and Indemnity Clubs / see International Group of P and I Clubs (#13751)

♦ International Group for the Psychology of Mathematics Education (PME) 13753

Admin Manager address not obtained. E-mail: info@igpme.org.
Pres address not obtained.
URL: http://igpme.org/

History 1976, Karlsruhe (Germany). Former names and other names: *IGPME* – alias. **Aims** Promote international contacts and exchange of *scientific* information in the field of mathematics education; promote and stimulate interdisciplinary research in the aforesaid area; further a deeper understanding of the psychological and other aspects of teaching and learning mathematics and the implications thereof. **Structure** Annual General Meeting; International Committee. **Languages** English. **Staff** 0.50 FTE, paid. **Finance** Members' dues. Donations. **Activities** Events/meetings. **Events** *Conference* Alicante (Spain) 2022, *Conference* Pretoria (South Africa) 2019, *Annual Conference* Umeå (Sweden) 2018, *Annual Conference* Singapore (Singapore) 2017, *Annual Conference* Szeged (Hungary) 2016. **Publications** *PME Newsletter* (2 a year). *Mathematics and Cognition: A Research Synthesis by the International Group for the Psychology of Mathematics Education Cognition* – study series. *Handbook of Research on the Psychology of Mathematics Education* (2016); *Mathematics Teacher Development: International Perspectives* (1999); *Mathematics Teacher Education: Critical International Perspectives* (1999); *Developing Practice: Teachers Inquiry and Educational Change* (1997); *Significant Influences on Children's Learning of Mathematics* (1993) by Alan J Bishop et al. Journal articles. **Members** Full (700-800) in about 60 countries. Membership countries not specified. **NGO Relations** An affiliated international study group of: *International Commission on Mathematical Instruction (ICMI, #12700).* [2018.06.01/XF1687/v/**F**]

♦ International Group on Radiation Damage Mechanisms (meeting series)
♦ International Group for Research on Pathogenic Actinomycetes (#10807)

♦ International Group of Research Reactors (IGORR) 13754

Chairman CEA, Cadarache Research Centre, 13108 Saint-Paul-lez-Durance, France.
URL: http://www.igorr.com/

History Founded 1989. **Aims** As a scientific forum: increase exchanges between research reactors community; optimize and harmonize practice, efficiency and safety. **Structure** Steering Committee. **Languages** English. **Staff** None. Hosting country of each conference takes charge of logistical aspects. **Finance** Conference fees. **Activities** Events/meetings; research/documentation. **Events** *Meeting* Berlin (Germany) 2016, *Meeting* Bariloche (Argentina) 2014, *Meeting* Daejeon (Korea Rep) 2013, *Meeting* Prague (Czech Rep) 2012, *Meeting* Knoxville, TN (USA) 2010. **Publications** Conference proceedings. **IGO Relations** Close links with Research Reactor Section of: *International Atomic Energy Agency (IAEA, #12294).* [2014.11.03/XE2726/**E**]

♦ International Group for Research in the Teaching of Physics / see International Research Group on Physics Teaching (#14731)
♦ International Group for Scientific Research in Stomatology / see International Group for Scientific Research on Stomato-Odontology (#13755)

♦ International Group for Scientific Research on Stomato-Odontology 13755

Groupement international pour la recherche scientifique en stomatologie et odontologie (GIRSO)
Sec c/o Instituto Superior de ciências da saúde – Norte, Rua Central de Gandra 1317, PRD, 4585-116 Gandra, Portugal. T. +351224157151 – +351224157129.

History 25 Sep 1957, Paris (France), as *International Group for Scientific Research in Stomatology – Groupe international de recherche scientifique en stomatologie.* Constitution amended and name changed to *European Group for Scientific Research on Stomato-Odontology – Groupement européen de recherche scientifique en stomato-odontologie (GERSO)*, 1974, Giessen (Germany FR). Present name adopted 25 Sep 1977, Paris. **Aims** Encourage collaboration between research workers in the fields of odonto-stomatology; facilitate exchange of material, documentation and visits; contribute to improving methods of preventing oral diseases. **Structure** Annual Meeting. Executive Committee, consisting of President, Vice-Presidents (3), Secretary, Treasurer. **Languages** English, French. **Staff** Voluntary. **Finance** Members' dues: euro 85. **Events** *Annual Congress* Barcelona (Spain) 2013, *Annual Congress* Lille (France) 2011, *Annual Congress* Andorra 2009, *Annual Congress* Palermo (Italy) 2006, *Annual Congress* Barcelona (Spain) 2005. **Publications** *Bulletin du GIRSO* (4 a year) in French.
Members Individuals (200) in 17 countries:
Austria, Belgium, Brazil, Canada, Denmark, France, Germany, Greece, Italy, Japan, Netherlands, Norway, Portugal, Spain, Switzerland, UK, USA. [2013/XC2089/**D**]

♦ International Group of Scientific, Technical and Medical Publishers / see International Association of Scientific, Technical and Medical Publishers (#12154)
♦ International Group on Sheltered and Special Employment / see Workability International (#21049)

♦ International Group of Specialist Racing Veterinarians (IGSRV) 13756

Editor address not obtained.
URL: http://www.igsrv.org/

Aims Unite regulatory racing veterinarians; advise authorities; encourage research on drugs, health and welfare of the horse. **Structure** Executive Committee. **Finance** Sources: members' dues. **Activities** Advocacy/lobbying/activism; awards/prizes/competitions; events/meetings. **Events** *ICRAV : Biennial International Conference of Racing Analysts and Veterinarians* Hong Kong (Hong Kong) 2022, *ICRAV : Biennial International Conference of Racing Analysts and Veterinarians* Hong Kong (Hong Kong) 2021, *ICRAV : Biennial International Conference of Racing Analysts and Veterinarians* Hong Kong (Hong Kong) 2020, *ICRAV : Biennial International Conference of Racing Analysts and Veterinarians* Dubai (United Arab Emirates) 2018, *ICRAV : Biennial International Conference of Racing Analysts and Veterinarians* Montevideo (Uruguay) 2016. **Publications** *IGSRV Newsletter.* Conference Proceedings. **Members** Regulatory racing veterinarians (about 85) in 32 countries. Membership countries not specified. [2022/XM6284/v/**C**]

♦ International Group for the Study of Gastrointestinal Motility (no recent information)
♦ International Group for Study of Intervertebral Disks Approaches / see International Group for Study of Intervertebral Spine Approaches (#13757)

♦ International Group for Study of Intervertebral Spine Approaches . . 13757

Groupe international d'étude des approches intervertébrales du rachis (GIEDA INTER RACHIS)
SG Clinique St Charles, 25 rue de Flesselles, 69001 Lyon, France. T. +33472102637. Fax +33472102693.
URL: http://www.gieda.com/

History Founded 1988, Blois (France). Also referred to in French as *Groupe international d'étude des approches des disques intervertébraux (GIEDA)* and in English as *International Group for Study of Intervertebral Disks Approaches.* **Aims** Promote scientific multidisciplinary exchanges on spine *disease.* **Structure** Bureau; Scientific Committee (meets annually). **Languages** English, French. **Staff** 20.00 FTE, voluntary. **Finance** Members' dues. Budget (annual): about euro 40,000. **Events** *Annual Meeting* Paris (France) 2019, *Annual Meeting* Paris (France) 2018, *Annual Meeting* Paris (France) 2014, *Annual Meeting* Nice (France) 2013, *Annual Meeting* Paris (France) 2012. **Publications** *European Journal of Orthopaedic Surgery and Traumatology*; *Rachis* – review. *Classifications et Scores en Chirurgie Orthopedique et en Traumatologie* (2007) by Emmanuel Favreul; *Instabilités vertébrales lombaires* (1995) by D Gastambide et al. Congress summaries.
Members Organizations and individuals in 10 countries:
Egypt, France, Germany, Italy, Luxembourg, Monaco, Morocco, Spain, Switzerland, USA. [2014.11.04/XF2892/y/**F**]

♦ International Group for the Study of Neurogastroenterology and Motility 13758

Address not obtained.

History 1991. **Aims** Organize symposia on neurogastroenterology and motility in relation to both clinical and basic studies; encourage exchange of information in the field. **Structure** Steering Committee of 12 members. **Events** *Meeting* Phuket (Thailand) 2013, *Joint Meeting* Boston, MA (USA) 2010, *Joint International Neurogastroenterology and Mobility Meeting* Chicago, IL (USA) 2009, *Joint international neurogastroenterology and motility meeting* Lucerne (Switzerland) 2008, *Biennial Symposium* Jeju (Korea Rep) 2007. [2010/XM2388/**F**]

♦ International Group for the Study and Utilization of Railway Sleeping-Cars in Europe (inactive)
♦ International Group for Textile Care Labelling / see Groupement International de l'Etiquetage pour l'Entretien des Textiles (#10761)

♦ International Group of Treasury Associations (IGTA) 13759

Chair c/o EACT, 3 rue d'Edimbourg, 75008 Paris, France. T. +33142815398. E-mail: secretary@eact.eu.
URL: http://www.igta.org/

History Sep 1996, Toronto, ON (Canada). Founded during 1st meeting following inaugural talks held 1995, Boston MA (USA). Memorandum of Understanding signed between national associations in Dublin (Ireland), Oct 1996. Registration: Belgium. **Aims** Share views and information on issues that impact the treasury and finance profession and association management; agree on priorities and coordinate resources on projects that advance the profession. **Structure** Board of Directors (meets annually). **Languages** English. **Staff** Voluntary. **Finance** No members' dues. **Activities** Events/meetings. **Events** *Annual conference / Meeting* Dublin (Ireland) 2006, *Annual conference / Meeting* San Francisco, CA (USA) 2005, *Annual conference / Meeting* Sydney, NSW (Australia) 2004, *Annual conference / Meeting* Strbské Pleso (Slovakia) 2003, *Annual Conference* Johannesburg (South Africa) 2002. **Publications** *IGTA e-Journal* (4 a year).
Members Organizations in 27 countries and territories:
Austria, Belgium, China, Côte d'Ivoire, Croatia, Czechia, Finland, France, Germany, Hong Kong, Hungary, Ireland, Japan, Luxembourg, Malaysia, Netherlands, New Zealand, Poland, Russia, Singapore, Slovakia, Slovenia, South Africa, Spain, Switzerland, UK, USA.
Observers in 2 countries:
Australia, Korea Rep.
Observers include one organization listed in this Yearbook:
European Association of Corporate Treasurers (EACT, #05992).
NGO Relations *International Swaps and Derivatives Association (ISDA, #15638).* [2021/XD6218/y/**D**]

♦ International Group for Wind-Related Disaster Risk Reduction (IG-WRDRR) 13760

Secretariat State Key Lab for Disaster Reduction in Civil Engineering, Tongji Univ, Siping Road 1239, 200032 Shanghai, China. E-mail: shuyang@tongji.edu.cn.
URL: http://www.iawe.org/WRDRR/

History Jun 2009, Geneva (Switzerland), by *International Association of Wind Engineering (IAWE, #12266), United Nations Office for Disaster Risk Reduction (UNDRR, #20595)* Secretariat, *United Nations University (UNU, #20642)*, TPU Global COE, *Asian Disaster Reduction Center (ADRC, #01427)* and *SEEDS Asia (#19216).* **Aims** Establish linkages and coordinate various communities to serve as inter-agency coordinators. **Structure** Chairman; Vice-Chairman; Secretariat. **Languages** English. **Staff** All voluntary. **Finance** Voluntary contributions. **Activities** Projects/programmes; events/meetings. Active in: Bangladesh, China, Japan, USA. **Publications** Proceedings.
Members Organizations (12):
Asian Disaster Reduction and Response Network (ADRRN, #01428); Asian Disaster Reduction Center (ADRC, #01427); Bangladesh Disaster Preparedness Centre; *International Association of Wind Engineering (IAWE, #12266); International Centre for Water Hazard and Risk Management (ICHARM); International Federation of Red Cross and Red Crescent Societies (#13526); SEEDS Asia (#19216); United Nations Economic and Social Commission for Asia and the Pacific (ESCAP, #20557); United Nations Human Settlements Programme (UN-Habitat, #20572); United Nations Office for Disaster Risk Reduction (UNDRR, #20595); United Nations University (UNU, #20642); World Meteorological Organization (WMO, #21649).*
NGO Relations *World Wind Energy Institute (WWEI, #21938).* [2015.07.10/XJ9779/y/**E**]

♦ International Guarantee Fund (IGF) 13761

Fonds international de garantie (FIG)
Secretariat RAFAD Foundation, Rue de Varembé 1, CP 117, 1211 Geneva 20, Switzerland. T. +41227335073. Fax +41227347083. E-mail: info@fig-igf.org.
URL: http://www.fig-igf.org/

History Dec 1996, Geneva (Switzerland), originally with the help of *One Percent for Development Fund (1% for Development Fund, #17733).* **Aims** Help microfinance institutions (MFIs) and agriculture cooperatives in the developing world obtain local currency loans from local commercial lenders by providing bank guarantees to MFIs. **Structure** General Assembly; Board of Directors. **Languages** English, French, Spanish. **Staff** 1.00 FTE, paid; 2.00 FTE, voluntary. **Finance** Subscription shares. Supported by: Michelham Foundation; *Inter-American Foundation (IAF, #11431); Agencia Española de Cooperación Internacional para el Desarrollo (AECID).* Annual budget: US$ 300,000. **Activities** Financial and/or material support; events/meetings. **Publications** Annual Report; newsletter.
Members Full: organizations in 12 countries:
Benin, Burkina Faso, Burundi, Chile, Ecuador, El Salvador, Guatemala, Honduras, Nicaragua, Peru, Senegal, Togo.
Included in the above, 1 organization listed in this Yearbook: [2018.01.29/XF5798/fy/**F**]

♦ International Guardianship Network (IGN) 13762

Chairman Schneewittchenstr 26, 12555 Berlin, Germany. T. +493053637315. Fax +493065499835.
URL: http://www.international-guardianship.com/

History Dec 2001, Berlin (Germany). Registered in accordance with German law. **Aims** Provide support, information and networking opportunities for guardians worldwide; put the legal proceedings of the UN Convention on the Rights of Persons with *Disabilities* into practice. **Activities** Events/meetings. **Events** *World Congress on Adult Capacity* Galway (Ireland) 2028, *World Congress on Adult Capacity* Amsterdam (Netherlands) 2026, *World Congress on Adult Capacity* Edinburgh (UK) 2022, *World Congress* Buenos Aires (Argentina) 2021, *World Congress on Adult Guardianship Law* Buenos Aires (Argentina) 2020.
Members Individuals in 37 countries and territories:
Andorra, Argentina, Australia, Austria, Belgium, Brazil, Canada, China, Czechia, Denmark, Finland, France, Germany, Greece, India, Ireland, Israel, Italy, Japan, Korea Rep, Liechtenstein, Luxembourg, Malta, Netherlands, New Zealand, Norway, Poland, Romania, Samoa, Singapore, Slovenia, Spain, Sweden, Switzerland, Taiwan, UK, USA.
IGO Relations *Convention on the Rights of Persons with Disabilities (CRPD, 2006).* [2020/XJ6526/**F**]

♦ International Guide Dog Federation (IGDF) 13763

Company Sec Hillfields, Burghfield Common, Reading, RG7 3YG, UK. T. +441189838356. E-mail: enquiries@igdf.org.uk.
URL: http://www.igdf.org.uk/

History 26 Apr 1989. Founded following conference activities in: 1973, 1976, 1983; 1986. Former names and other names: *International Federation of Guide Dog Schools for the Blind* – former; *Fédération internationale des écoles de chiens guides d'aveugles* – former; *Internationale Bund der Blindenführhundeschulen* – former. Registration: Companies House, No/ID: 02376162, Start date: 26 Apr 1989, UK; Charities Commission, No/ID: 1062441, Start date: May 1997, England and Wales. **Aims** Build a world where people who are blind or have low vision can access quality guide dogs and associated services so that they can live life on their terms. **Structure** General Meeting (annual); Board; Standing Committees; Company Secretary. **Languages** English. **Staff** 1.80 FTE, paid. **Finance** Sources: donations; members' dues; sponsorship. **Activities** Certification/accreditation; events/meetings; training/education. **Events** *Conference* Vancouver, BC (Canada) 2023, *Seminar* Sydney, NSW (Australia) 2018, *Biennial Conference* Tokyo (Japan) 2014, *Biennial Conference* Paris (France) 2012, *Biennial Conference* Ottawa, ON (Canada) 2010. **Publications** *The Visionary.*
Members Organizations (99) in 33 countries and territories:

Australia, Austria, Belgium, Brazil, Bulgaria, Canada, China, Croatia, Czechia, Finland, France, Germany, Hong Kong, Hungary, Ireland, Israel, Italy, Japan, Korea Rep, Netherlands, New Zealand, Norway, Poland, Portugal, Russia, Slovakia, Slovenia, South Africa, Spain, Switzerland, Taiwan, UK, USA.
NGO Relations Memorandum of Understanding with (1): *European Guide Dog Federation (EGDF, #07440).* Member of (1): *World Blind Union (WBU, #21234).* [2021.06.14/XD2362/**D**]

♦ International Guides' Club (inactive)
♦ International Guild of Dispensing Opticians / see International Opticians Association (#14415)

♦ International Guild of Musicians in Dance 13764

Contact address not obtained. E-mail: dancemusiciansguild@gmail.com.
URL: http://igomid.camp9.org/

History Founded 1991, Brockport NY (USA). **Aims** Foster collaborative relationships between dancers and musicians. **Finance** Members' dues. Conference revenue. **Activities** Events/meetings. **Events** *European Conference* Phoenix, AZ (USA) 2015, *European Conference* Brockport, NY (USA) 2013, *European Conference* Los Angeles, CA (USA) 2012, *European Conference* Minneapolis, MN (USA) 2011, *European Conference* Tucson, AZ (USA) 2010.
Members Full in 22 countries and territories:
Austria, Brazil, Colombia, Czechia, Finland, France, Greece, Hong Kong, Hungary, Ireland, Israel, Italy, Netherlands, Norway, Portugal, Russia, Singapore, Spain, Sweden, Taiwan, UK, USA. [2019.02.18/XF4130/**F**]

♦ International Guild of Opticians / see International Opticians Association (#14415)
♦ International Guild of Sorcery (inactive)

♦ International Gustav Mahler Society (IGMS) 13765

Société internationale Gustav Mahler – Internationale Gustav Mahler Gesellschaft (IGMG)
Secretariat Wiedner Gürtel 6/2, 1040 Vienna, Austria. T. +4315057330. Fax +4315057330. E-mail: office@gustav-mahler.org – info@gustav-mahler.org.
URL: https://www.gustav-mahler.org/

History 11 Nov 1955, Vienna (Austria). **Aims** Edit the New Critical Edition of the Complete Works; organize and contribute to exhibitions and symposia; maintain a library and archive publications, manuscripts and media. **Structure** Annual Meeting, always in Vienna (Austria), in the Society library; Board of Directors; Main office in Vienna (Austria). **Languages** English, German. **Staff** 3.00 FTE, paid. **Finance** Sources: donations; members' dues. **Activities** Awards/prizes/competitions. **Events** *Annual meeting* Vienna (Austria) 2006, *Annual meeting* Vienna (Austria) 2005, *Annual meeting* Vienna (Austria) 2004, *Annual meeting* Rotterdam (Netherlands) 1992, *Annual meeting* Rotterdam (Netherlands) 1990. **Publications** *News about Mahler Research* (annual). *Kritische Gesamtausgabe der Werke Gustav Mahlers* – Complete Critical Edition. Annual Report; books.
Members Regular (389); Organizations (11); Supporting (29); Sponsors (11); Founding (22); Honorary (35). Members in 37 countries and territories:
Australia, Austria, Belgium, Canada, China, Croatia, Cyprus, Czechia, Denmark, Finland, France, Germany, Greece, Hungary, Iceland, Israel, Italy, Japan, Luxembourg, Mexico, Monaco, Netherlands, New Zealand, Norway, Poland, Portugal, Russia, Singapore, Slovenia, Spain, Sweden, Switzerland, Taiwan, Türkiye, UK, USA, Vietnam. [2021.05.26/XE2610/v/**E**]

♦ International Gutenberg Society 13766

Société internationale de Gutenberg – Internationale Gutenberg-Gesellschaft in Mainz
SG Liebfrauenplatz 5, 55116 Mainz, Germany. T. +4961226420. Fax +4961233530. E-mail: info@gutenberg-gesellschaft.de.
URL: http://www.gutenberg-gesellschaft.de/

History 1900, Mainz (Germany). Founded together with the Mainz Gutenberg Museum, also known as *World Museum of Printing – Weltmuseum der Druckkunst.* Opened its doors, 23 Jun 1901. Former names and other names: *Gutenberg Society – International Association for Past and Present History of the Art of Printing* – former; *Société Gutenberg – Association internationale pour l'histoire et le développement contemporain de l'imprimerie et du livre* – former; *Gutenberg-Gesellschaft – Internationale Vereinigung für Geschichte und Gegenwart der Druckkunst* – former. Registration: Germany. **Aims** Provide moral and material support for the Gutenberg Museum in Mainz; promote research on the past and present history of printing and *books* in all countries of the world and disseminate the results in the Gutenberg Yearbook. **Structure** General Assembly (annual, in Mainz); Governing Board; Executive Committee. **Languages** English, German. **Finance** Sources: members' dues. **Activities** Awards/prizes/competitions; events/meetings; financial and/or material support; knowledge management/information dissemination. **Events** *Annual General Meeting* Mainz (Germany) 2005, *Annual General Meeting* Mainz (Germany) 2004, *Annual General Meeting* Mainz (Germany) 2003, *Annual General Meeting* Mainz (Germany) 2000, *Annual General Meeting* Mainz (Germany) 1999. **Publications** *Gutenberg Jahrbuch*; *Kleine Drucke der Gutenberg-Gesellschaft.*
Members Corporate institutes, firms; Individual. Members in 37 countries:
Austria, Belgium, Brazil, Bulgaria, Canada, Czechia, Denmark, Finland, France, Germany, Greece, Hungary, Iceland, Ireland, Italy, Japan, Korea Rep, Lebanon, Lithuania, Luxembourg, Malta, Netherlands, Norway, Pakistan, Poland, Portugal, Romania, Russia, Slovakia, Slovenia, South Africa, Spain, Sweden, Switzerland, Türkiye, UK, USA. [2022.02.15/XE4939/**E**]

♦ International Gut Microbiology Symposium (meeting series)
♦ International Gymnastic Federation (#09636)

♦ International Gynecologic Cancer Society (IGCS) 13767

CEO PO Box 170645, Austin TX 78717, USA. T. +17077324427. E-mail: igcs@igcs.org.
URL: https://igcs.org/

History 3 May 1986, San Francisco, CA (USA). Proposals for the setting up of the society having been made at previous meetings: Jun 1985, London (UK); Oct 1985, Berlin West (Germany FR). **Aims** Contribute to the prevention, treatment and study of gynecologic cancer and improve the quality of life of women suffering from gynecologic cancer; promote and facilitate the enrichment and dissemination of knowledge and skills of its members in the areas of prevention, treatment and study of gynecologic cancer. **Structure** Executive Committee; Council. Committees (5): Development; Education; Finance; Membership; Nominating. **Languages** English. **Staff** 2.00 FTE, paid. **Activities** Advocacy/lobbying/activism; events/meetings; research/documentation; training/education. **Events** *Annual Global Meeting* New York, NY (USA) 2022, *Annual Global Meeting* Rome (Italy) 2021, *Annual Global Meeting* Austin, TX (USA) 2020, *Annual Global Meeting* Rio de Janeiro (Brazil) 2019, *Biennial Meeting* Kyoto (Japan) 2018. **Publications** *IGCS Newsletter*, *International Journal of Gynecologic Cancer.*
Members Individuals (about 1,900) with a professional interest in prevention, treatment or study of gynecologic cancer. Members in 84 countries and territories:
Argentina, Armenia, Australia, Austria, Bahamas, Bangladesh, Belgium, Brazil, Bulgaria, Cameroon, Canada, Chile, China, Colombia, Costa Rica, Croatia, Cyprus, Czechia, Denmark, Dominican Rep, Egypt, El Salvador, Finland, France, Germany, Ghana, Greece, Haiti, Honduras, Hong Kong, Hungary, Iceland, India, Indonesia, Iran Islamic Rep, Ireland, Israel, Italy, Japan, Jordan, Kenya, Korea Rep, Lebanon, Malaysia, Mexico, Netherlands, New Zealand, Nicaragua, Nigeria, North Macedonia, Norway, Panama, Peru, Philippines, Poland, Portugal, Puerto Rico, Qatar, Romania, Russia, Saudi Arabia, Serbia, Singapore, Slovakia, Slovenia, South Africa, Spain, Sri Lanka, Sudan, Sweden, Switzerland, Taiwan, Thailand, Trinidad-Tobago, Türkiye, Uganda, UK, Ukraine, United Arab Emirates, Uruguay, USA, Venezuela, Vietnam, Zimbabwe. [2021/XD2927/v/**C**]

♦ International Hadith Study Association Network (internationally oriented national body)

♦ International Haemovigilance Network (IHN) 13768

Pres TRIP Nationaal bureau voor hemo- en biovigilantie, Schuttersveld 2 (5de etage), 2316 ZA Leiden, Netherlands. T. +31713031540. E-mail: secretariat@ihn-org.com.
URL: http://www.ihn-org.com/

History 1998. Former names and other names: *European Haemovigilance Network (EHN)* – former (1989 to 2009). Registration: Netherlands. **Aims** Develop and maintain a common structure with regard to safety of blood and blood products and haemovigilance in *blood* transfusion and transfusion medicine in Europe. **Structure** General Meeting (annual); Board. **Activities** Events/meetings. International Surveillance of Transfusion-Associated Reactions and Events (ISTARE). **Events** *Annual Symposium* Brighton (UK) 2022, *International Haemovigilance Seminar* Leiden (Netherlands) 2022, *International Haemovigilance Seminar* Leiden (Netherlands) 2021, *International Haemovigilance Seminar* Leiden (Netherlands) 2021, *Annual Symposium* Oslo (Norway) 2020.
Members Full in 38 countries:
Australia, Austria, Belgium, Brazil, Canada, China, Croatia, Cyprus, Denmark, Finland, France, Germany, Greece, Iceland, India, Iran Islamic Rep, Ireland, Italy, Japan, Korea Rep, Luxembourg, Malta, Namibia, Netherlands, New Zealand, Norway, Pakistan, Portugal, Serbia, Singapore, Slovenia, South Africa, Spain, Sri Lanka, Sweden, Switzerland, UK, USA. [2021/XM3341/**F**]

♦ International Hahnemannian Association (inactive)
♦ International Hairdressers' Federation (inactive)

♦ International Halal Accreditation Forum (IHAF) 13769

Contact Office 514, Business Avenue Bldg, Port Saeed Area, Dubai, United Arab Emirates. E-mail: info@ihaf.org.ae.
URL: http://ihaf.org.ae/

History Set up 2016. **Aims** Protect halal consumers; facilitate international trade. **Structure** General Assembly; Board of Directors; General Secretariat. Committees (3): Multilateral Recognition Agreement; Technical Affairs; Marketing and Media. **Languages** Arabic, English. **Finance** Funded by government of United Arab Emirates. **Activities** Certification/accreditation; advocacy/lobbying/activism; awareness raising; events/meetings. **Events** *General Assembly* Singapore (Singapore) 2018, *General Assembly* Vancouver, BC (Canada) 2017, *General Assembly* Dubai (United Arab Emirates) 2016.
Members Full in 24 countries:
Argentina, Australia, Brazil, Egypt, Hungary, India, Italy, Jamaica, Jordan, Kazakhstan, Kuwait, Libya, Mexico, Morocco, New Zealand, Nigeria, Pakistan, Philippines, Saudi Arabia, Spain, Thailand, UK, United Arab Emirates, USA.
Included in the above, 1 organization listed in this Yearbook:
GCC Accreditation Center (GAC, #10082).
IGO Relations *Arab Accreditation Cooperation (ARAC, #00892)*; Dubai Islamic Economic Development Center (DIEDC). [2018.09.28/XM6809/**F**]

♦ International Halal Authority Board (unconfirmed)
♦ International Halfway House Association / see International Community Corrections Association (#12822)

♦ International Halliwick Association (IHA) 13770

Sec address not obtained. E-mail: ihasecretary@hotmail.com.
URL: http://halliwick.org/

History 1994, Bad Ragaz (Switzerland). **Aims** Maintain the Halliwick Concept of *swimming* for *disabled* people; develop the concept and teaching and treatment method in accordance with new experiences and scientific advances. **Structure** General Meeting; Executive Committee; Education and Research Committee. **Finance** Sources: members' dues. **Activities** Events/meetings; training/education. **Events** *Conference* Poland 2011, *Conference* Austria 2009.
Members National associations in 7 countries:
Brazil, Denmark, Greece, Ireland, Japan, Slovakia, UK.
Individuals in 8 countries:
Belgium, Croatia, Germany, Israel, Italy, Malta, Poland, Spain. [2015/XJ9728/**C**]

♦ International Handball Federation (IHF) 13771

Fédération Internationale de Handball – Internationale Handball Federation
Head Office Peter Merian-Strasse 23, 4002 Basel BS, Switzerland. T. +41612289040. Fax +41612289055. E-mail: ihf.office@ihf.info.
Pres address not obtained.
URL: http://www.ihf.info/

History 12 Jul 1946, Copenhagen (Denmark). Founded by member organizations of *International Amateur Handball Federation (IAHF, inactive).* Statutes changed Jul 1988, Jul 1992; Sept 1994; Jul 1996. **Aims** Develop and encourage the games of handball, mini handball, beach handball, outdoor handball and indoor handball (7 a side). **Structure** Congress (every 2 years); Council; Executive Committee; Commissions (6); Arbitration Commission; Arbitration Tribunal; Ethics Commission; Head Office, headed by General Director. **Languages** English, French, German. **Staff** 17.00 FTE, paid. **Activities** Events/meetings; sporting activities. **Events** *Ordinary Congress* Katowice (Poland) 2023, *Ordinary Congress* 2021, *Biennial Congress* Gothenburg (Sweden) 2019, *Biennial Congress* Antalya (Turkey) 2017, *Congress on Sports Medicine and Handball* Paris (France) 2017. **Publications** *World Handball Magazine* (3 a year). *50 Year IHF – 100 Years Handball* in English, French, German; *IHF Handbook.* Reports; series of booklets.
Members National Federations in 209 countries and territories:
Afghanistan, Albania, Algeria, Andorra, Angola, Antigua-Barbuda, Argentina, Armenia, Australia, Austria, Azerbaijan, Bahamas, Bahrain, Bangladesh, Barbados, Belarus, Belgium, Belize, Benin, Bhutan, Bolivia, Bosnia-Herzegovina, Botswana, Brazil, Brunei Darussalam, Bulgaria, Burkina Faso, Burundi, Cambodia, Cameroon, Canada, Cape Verde, Cayman Is, Central African Rep, Chad, Chile, China, Colombia, Comoros, Congo Brazzaville, Congo DR, Cook Is, Costa Rica, Côte d'Ivoire, Croatia, Cuba, Cyprus, Czechia, Denmark, Djibouti, Dominica, Dominican Rep, Ecuador, Egypt, El Salvador, England, Equatorial Guinea, Estonia, Eswatini, Ethiopia, Faeroe Is, Fiji, Finland, France, Gabon, Gambia, Georgia, Germany, Ghana, Great Britain, Greece, Greenland, Grenada, Guadeloupe, Guam, Guatemala, Guiana Fr, Guinea, Guinea-Bissau, Guyana, Haiti, Honduras, Hong Kong, Hungary, Iceland, India, Indonesia, Iran Islamic Rep, Iraq, Ireland, Israel, Italy, Jamaica, Japan, Jordan, Kazakhstan, Kenya, Kiribati, Korea DPR, Korea Rep, Kosovo, Kuwait, Kyrgyzstan, Laos, Latvia, Lebanon, Lesotho, Liberia, Libya, Liechtenstein, Lithuania, Luxembourg, Macau, Madagascar, Malawi, Malaysia, Maldives, Mali, Malta, Marshall Is, Martinique, Mauritania, Mauritius, Mexico, Micronesia FS, Moldova, Monaco, Mongolia, Montenegro, Morocco, Mozambique, Namibia, Nauru, Nepal, Netherlands, New Caledonia, New Zealand, Nicaragua, Niger, Nigeria, North Macedonia, Northern Mariana Is, Norway, Oman, Pakistan, Palau, Palestine, Panama, Papua New Guinea, Paraguay, Peru, Philippines, Poland, Polynesia Fr, Portugal, Puerto Rico, Qatar, Romania, Russia, Rwanda, Samoa, Samoa USA, Sao Tomé-Principe, Saudi Arabia, Scotland, Senegal, Serbia, Seychelles, Sierra Leone, Singapore, Slovakia, Slovenia, Solomon Is, Somalia, South Africa, South Sudan, Spain, Sri Lanka, St Kitts-Nevis, St Lucia, Sudan, Sweden, Switzerland, Syrian AR, Taiwan, Tajikistan, Tanzania UR, Thailand, Timor-Leste, Togo, Tonga, Trinidad-Tobago, Tunisia, Türkiye, Turkmenistan, Tuvalu, Uganda, Ukraine, United Arab Emirates, Uruguay, USA, Uzbekistan, Vanuatu, Venezuela, Vietnam, Virgin Is UK, Yemen, Zambia, Zimbabwe.
Asian Handball Federation (AHF, #01500); *Confederación de Sur y Centro America de Balonmano (Coscabal, #04443)*; *Confédération Africaine de Handball (CAHB, #04501)*; *European Handball Federation (EHF, #07446)*; *North America and the Caribbean Handball Confederation (NACHC, #17557)*; *Oceania Continent Handball Federation (OCHF, #17657).*
NGO Relations Member of (5): *Association of Summer Olympic International Federations (ASOIF, #02943)*; *International Committee for Fair Play (#12769)*; *International Paralympic Committee (IPC, #14512)*; *International World Games Association (IWGA, #15914)*; *Olympic Movement (#17719).* Recognized by (1): *International Olympic Committee (IOC, #14408).* Cooperates with (1): *International Testing Agency (ITA, #15678).* [2023.03.03/XB2098/y/**B**]

♦ International Handbell Committee 13772

Past Chair Box 5555 Mail Centre, Mackay QLD 4741, Australia. E-mail: president@handbells.org.au.
Chair address not obtained.
URL: http://www.internationalhandbells.org/

History 1990. **Aims** Promote the art of handbell ringing; promote recognition of handbells as a musical art; set standards and goals for the International Handbell Symposium. **Structure** World Symposium; Executive Director. **Staff** Voluntary. **Finance** Sources: meeting proceeds. **Activities** Awareness raising; capacity building; events/meetings; knowledge management/information dissemination; networking/liaising. **Events** *Biennial Symposium* Japan 2024, *Biennial Symposium* Nashville, TN (USA) 2022, *Biennial Symposium* Hong Kong (Hong Kong) 2020, *Biennial Symposium* Cairns, QLD (Australia) 2018, *Biennial Symposium* Vancouver, BC (Canada) 2016.
Members Presidents and representatives of member guilds in 10 countries and territories:
Australia, Canada, Great Britain, Hong Kong, Japan, Korea Rep, New Zealand, Singapore, UK, USA.
Included in the above, 1 regional organization listed in this Yearbook:
Handbell Society of Australasia (HSA). [2022/XG7455/y/**E**]

♦ International Handicap Sailing Committee / see International Association for Disabled Sailing (#11849)
♦ International Handwriting Psychology Society / see International Society of Psychology of Handwriting (#15398)

♦ International Hansa Class Association (IHCA) 13773

Contact address not obtained. E-mail: president@hansaclass.org.
URL: http://hansaclass.org/

History Founded as *International Access 23 Class Association.* A sailing Class association for Hansa 2.3, Hansa 303, Liberty, and SKUD18 class boats. **NGO Relations** International Class Association of: *World Sailing (#21760).* [2017/XM2792/**E**]

♦ International Hapkido Federation (internationally oriented national body)

♦ **International Harbour Masters' Association (IHMA)** **13774**

Sec PO Box 3111, Lancing, BN15 5BQ, UK. T. +441903218269. E-mail: secretary.ihma@harbourmaster.org.
URL: http://www.harbourmaster.org/

History Inaugurated 21 Jun 1996, Reykjavik (Iceland), at Ordinary General Meeting of *European Harbour Masters' Association (EHMA)*, following study by *'International Harbour Masters' Association Founding Group Committee (IHMAFG Committee)'*. EHMA became an integral part of IHMA on IHMA's foundation and, since May 2004, exists as *European Harbour Masters' Committee (EHMC, #07449)*. **Aims** Unite those responsible for, and promote the safe, secure, efficient and environmentally sound conduct of marine operations in port waters; develop collaboration, sharing of good practice and good relations among harbour masters; represent the role of the harbour master; promote the professional standing and interests of harbour masters. **Structure** Council; Executive Committee (ExCo). **Languages** English. **Staff** 0.50 FTE, paid. **Finance** Sources: members' dues. **Activities** Events/meetings; guidance/assistance/consulting; knowledge management/information dissemination; networking/liaising. **Events** *International Biennial Congress* Tangiers (Morocco) 2024, *International Biennial Congress* Kuala Lumpur (Malaysia) 2022, *Biennial Congress* Lancing (UK) 2020, *Biennial Congress* London (UK) 2018, *Biennial Congress* Vancouver, BC (Canada) 2016. **Members** Full; Associate; Senior; Commercial; Honorary. Members in over 50 countries. Membership countries not specified.
Consultative Status Consultative status granted from: *International Maritime Organization (IMO, #14102)*.
IGO Relations Observer status with: *International Hydrographic Organization (IHO, #13825)*. Working relations with: *European Commission (EC, #06633)*, specifically with Directorate General – Mobility and Transport (DG-MOVE). **NGO Relations** Working relations with: *BIMCO (#03236)*; *International Association of Marine Aids to Navigation and Lighthouse Authorities (IALA, #12013)*; *International Association of Ports and Harbors (IAPH, #12096)*; *International Federation of Shipmasters Associations (IFSMA, #13539)*; *International Maritime Pilots' Association (IMPA, #14103)*; *Nautical Institute*; *PIANC (#18371)*. [2018.06.01/XC0057/**C**]

♦ International Hardwood Products Association / see International Wood Products Association
♦ International Hardy Plant Union (#13277)

♦ **International Harmonization Council (IHC)** **13775**

Contact Compressed Gas Assn, 8484 Westpark Drive, Ste 220, McLean VA 22102, USA. E-mail: cga@cganet.com.

History 2001. **Aims** Develop international standards for industrial and medical gases. **Activities** Standards/guidelines. **Events** *Meeting* 2019, *Meeting* Montréal, QC (Canada) 2019.
Members Organizations (4):
Asia Industrial Gases Association (AIGA, #01283); Compressed Gas Association; *European Industrial Gases Association (EIGA, #07525)*; Japan Industrial and Medical Gases Association. [2019/AA2019/y/**C**]

♦ International Harm Reduction Association / see Harm Reduction International (#10861)
♦ International Harm Reduction Network / see Harm Reduction International (#10861)
♦ International Harp Centre (internationally oriented national body)
♦ International Havundersøgelsesråd (#13021)
♦ International H-Boat Class Association (see: #21760)

♦ **International HCH and Pesticides Association (IHPA)** **13776**

Dir Elmevej 14, 2840 Holte, Denmark. T. +4545410321.
Contact Handelskade 11, 7417 DE Deventer, Netherlands.
URL: http://www.ihpa.info/

History Founded Aug 1998. Registered in accordance with Dutch law, 26 Sep 2002. EU Transparency Register: 147211221858-48. **Aims** Facilitate and promote international cooperation and the exchange of experiences within management of *pollution* problems stemming from the production and use of HCH and other unwanted pesticides worldwide. **Structure** Board. **Languages** English. **Staff** 1.00 FTE, paid. **Finance** Budget (anual): US$ 25,000. **Activities** Awareness raising; knowledge management/information dissemination; training/education; events/meetings. **Events** *International HCH and Pesticides Forum* Saragossa (Spain) 2023, *International HCH and Pesticides Forum* Saragossa (Spain) 2021, *International HCH and Pesticides Forum* Astana (Kazakhstan) 2017, *International HCH and Pesticides Forum* Saragossa (Spain) 2015, *International HCH and Pesticides Forum* Kiev (Ukraine) 2013. **Publications** *POPs Newsletter* (2 a year). Forum proceedings; reports; other documents.
Members Not a membership organization. Nominated/inscribed ambassadors (about 150) in 46 countries and territories:
Albania, Armenia, Austria, Azerbaijan, Bangladesh, Belarus, Belgium, Bolivia, Brazil, Bulgaria, Canada, Czechia, Denmark, Egypt, Estonia, Georgia, Germany, India, Iran Islamic Rep, Italy, Jordan, Kyrgyzstan, Moldova, Netherlands, New Zealand, North Macedonia, Norway, Pakistan, Palestine, Poland, Romania, Russia, Serbia, Slovakia, Slovenia, South Africa, Spain, Sudan, Switzerland, Tajikistan, Türkiye, UK, Ukraine, United Arab Emirates, USA, Uzbekistan.
NGO Relations Member of: *GEF CSO Network (GCN, #10087)*. [2014.06.18/XJ7899/**D**]

♦ **International Headache Society (IHS)** **13777**

Secretariat 6th Floor, 2 London Wall Place, London, EC2Y 5AU, UK. T. +441629733406. E-mail: ihsoffice@i-h-s.org.
Gen Sec address not obtained.
URL: http://www.ihs-headache.org/

History 1982, London (UK). Registration: Charity Commission, No/ID: 1042574, England and Wales. **Aims** Relieve sickness and protect and preserve health by promoting research into the causes, mechanisms, diagnosis, treatment and other aspects of headache and by disseminating results of such research; provide a forum for the exchange of medical data and belief related to headache; educate physicians, other health workers and the general public in the diagnosis, treatment and management of headache; encourage the management of headache in a scientific and ethical manner. **Structure** Board of Trustees; Advisory Council; Standing Committees (10); Special Interest Groups (4). **Languages** English. **Staff** 0.50 FTE, paid. **Finance** Sources: meeting proceeds; members' dues; sale of publications; sponsorship. **Activities** Awards/prizes/competitions; events/meetings; knowledge management/information dissemination; research/documentation; training/education. **Events** *International Headache Congress* Vienna (Austria) 2022, *International Headache Congress* 2021, *Biennial Congress* Helsinki (Finland) 2021, *Biennial Congress* Dublin (Ireland) 2019, *Biennial Congress* Vancouver, BC (Canada) 2017. **Publications** *IHS Newsletter* (3 a year); *Cephalalgia* (14 a year) – journal. Reports.
Members National societies in 50 countries and territories:
Argentina, Australia, Austria, Azerbaijan, Belgium, Brazil, Bulgaria, Canada, China, Colombia, Czechia, Denmark, Egypt, Estonia, France, Georgia, Germany, Greece, Hungary, India, Iran Islamic Rep, Israel, Italy, Japan, Korea Rep, Kyrgyzstan, Latvia, Lithuania, Malaysia, Moldova, Netherlands, Norway, Pakistan, Peru, Philippines, Portugal, Romania, Russia, Serbia, Slovakia, Slovenia, South Africa, Spain, Sweden, Switzerland, Taiwan, Türkiye, UK, Ukraine, USA.
Individuals in 60 countries and territories:
Argentina, Australia, Austria, Azerbaijan, Belgium, Brazil, Canada, Chile, China, Colombia, Costa Rica, Croatia, Czechia, Denmark, Egypt, Finland, France, Georgia, Germany, Greece, Hong Kong, India, Indonesia, Ireland, Israel, Italy, Japan, Korea Rep, Kyrgyzstan, Latvia, Lithuania, Luxembourg, Malaysia, Mexico, Moldova, Morocco, Netherlands, Norway, Pakistan, Peru, Philippines, Poland, Portugal, Romania, Russia, Serbia, Singapore, Slovakia, South Africa, Spain, Sweden, Switzerland, Taiwan, Thailand, Türkiye, UK, Ukraine, United Arab Emirates, USA, Venezuela. [2022.10.12/XD1512/**C**]

♦ International Health Academy (internationally oriented national body)

♦ **International Health Awareness Network (IHAN)** **13778**

Founder/Pres 160 W 66th St, Ste 57B, New York NY 10023, USA. T. +13476704426. E-mail: info@ihan.org.
URL: http://www.ihan.org/

History 1986. Re-established and present name adopted in 1990. Former names and other names: *International Health Network for Women and Children (IHNW)* – former (1986 to 1990). Registration: 501(c)3, USA. **Aims** Improve health and welfare of women and children, at local, national and international levels, particularly among the poor and underprivileged and in developing countries, through education and empowerment; promote primary care and awareness of human rights. **Structure** Advisory Board of 25 members. Board of Directors, consisting of President, 3 Vice-Presidents, Treasurer, Secretary, Executive Director and Program Coordinator. **Finance** Donations and contributions by medical and health professionals worldwide. **Activities** Training/education; events/meetings. **Events** *Conference on the Culture of Peace and Women's Contribution in Building Global Peace and Reducing Violence* New York, NY (USA) 2014, *Annual conference* Izmir (Turkey) 1997. **Publications** *IHAN Newsletter* (4 a year). Conference proceedings.
Members Full in 17 countries:
Australia, Bangladesh, China, Egypt, India, Iran Islamic Rep, Japan, Jordan, Kenya, Niger, Pakistan, Philippines, South Africa, Switzerland, Türkiye, UK, USA.
International member (1):
International Council of Women (ICW, #13093).
Consultative Status Consultative status granted from: *ECOSOC (#05331)* (General). **IGO Relations** Associated with Department of Global Communications of the United Nations. **NGO Relations** Member of: *Global Movement for the Culture of Peace (GMCOP)*; *New York NGO Committee on Drugs (NYNGOC, #17097)*. [2020/XF0981/y/**F**]

♦ International Health Care Foundation / see IHCF African Christian Hospitals (#11109)
♦ International Health Care Worker Safety Center (internationally oriented national body)

♦ **International Health Cooperative Organization (IHCO)** **13779**

SG c/o Fundación Espriu, Av Josep Tarradellas 123 4a, 08029 Barcelona, Spain. T. +349349544590.
Main Website: https://health.coop/

History Nov 1996, Costa Rica. Founded as a sectoral organization of *International Co-operative Alliance (ICA, #12944)*. **Aims** Showcase cooperatives as an alternative to private and public healthcare, which combines economic goals with social values; highlight the global scale of the cooperative business model in the health sector; raise awareness about added value as people-oriented companies. **Structure** Annual General Assembly; Board of Directors. **Languages** English. **Activities** Events/meetings; guidance/assistance/consulting. **Events** *General Meeting* Kuala Lumpur (Malaysia) 2017, *General Meeting* Antalya (Turkey) 2015, *General Meeting* Cape Town (South Africa) 2013, *Conference on Cooperatives and Development* Cancún (Mexico) 2011, *General Meeting* Cancún (Mexico) 2011. **Publications** *Cooperatives in the health sector* (2022); *The Cooperative Health Report*. Surveys.
Members Health cooperatives in 18 countries:
Argentina, Australia, Brazil, Cameroon, Canada, Colombia, Greece, India, Italy, Japan, Malaysia, Panama, Philippines, Poland, Russia, Spain, UK, Uruguay. [2023.02.14/XE3699/**E**]

♦ International Health Council (internationally oriented national body)
♦ International Health Data Linkage Network / see International Population Data Linkage Network (#14620)

♦ **International Health Economics Association (iHEA)** **13780**

Exec Dir address not obtained.
CEO and Pres 411 Richmond Street East, Suite 200, Toronto ON M5A 3S5, Canada. E-mail: ihea@healtheconomics.org.
URL: http://www.healtheconomics.org/

History 10 May 1994. **Aims** Increase communication among health economists; foster a higher standard of debate in the application of economics to health and health care systems; assist young researchers. **Structure** Board of Directors, including Executive Director, President, President-Elect and Secretary/Treasurer. **Activities** Events/meetings; awards/prizes/competitions. **Events** *World Congress* Basel (Switzerland) 2019, *World Congress* Boston, MA (USA) 2017, *World Congress* Milan (Italy) 2015, *World Congress* Dublin (Ireland) 2014, *World Congress* Sydney, NSW (Australia) 2013. **Information Services** *iHEA News* – (12 a year) – electronic newsletter. **Members** Mainly North American membership. [2019/XN1444/**D**]

♦ International Health Economics and Management Institute / see International Health Policy and Management Institute (#13782)
♦ International Health Evaluation Association / see International Health Evaluation and Promotion Association (#13781)

♦ **International Health Evaluation and Promotion Association (IHEPA)** **13781**

Association internationale pour le contrôle et la promotion de la santé

Contact 960 E 3rd St, Ste 100, Chattanooga TN 37403, USA.
URL: http://www.ihepa-region3.org/

History 29 Jan 1971, Honolulu HI (USA), as *International Health Evaluation Association (IHEA)*. Present name adopted, 2002. **Aims** Improve *health care* through advancement of computer-based health testing and evaluation techniques, refinement of associated data-processing systems and *biomedical* devices; acquaint physicians, health care planners and other health professionals with the benefits of computer aided health evaluation, health risk appraisal and associated techniques; act as a forum to discuss ongoing applications and research programs to refine the practice and establish the value of *preventive* medicine techniques. **Structure** Board of Directors, including: President; President Elect; Executive Vice President; Vice Presidents and Chairs, Regions I, II and III; Secretary; Treasurer; Directors-at-Large. Regions: I – North, Central and South America, Caribbean; II – Europe and Africa; III – Asia, Australia, islands of the Pacific and Hawaii. Central Office located in Region I. **Activities** Organizes: international symposia; regional conferences; worldwide exchange of information. Standardizes programs and techniques in health evaluation. **Events** *International Symposium* Yokohama (Japan) 2020, *International Symposium* Tokyo (Japan) 2016, *International Symposium* Taipei (Taiwan) 2014, *International Symposium* Tokyo (Japan) 2012, *International Symposium* Honolulu, HI (USA) 2011. **Publications** Symposium proceedings. Information Services: Provides information on progress and problems of health evaluation worldwide.
Members Health-testing centers; individual physicians and other professionals involved in health evaluation; developers, manufacturers and suppliers of computer-based systems and biomedical instrumentation used in health evaluation. Members in 9 countries and territories:
Canada, India, Israel, Japan, Korea Rep, Sweden, Taiwan, UK, USA. [2020/XD5763/**D**]

♦ International Health Exchange (internationally oriented national body)
♦ International Health and Fitness Association (unconfirmed)
♦ International Health Food Association / see Adventist Health Food Association (#00132)
♦ International Health Food Ministry / see Adventist Health Food Association (#00132)
♦ International Health Network for Women and Children / see International Health Awareness Network (#13778)
♦ International Health Partners (internationally oriented national body)
♦ International Health Partnership / see UHC2030 (#20277)
♦ International Health Partnership for UHC 2030 / see UHC2030 (#20277)

♦ **International Health Policy and Management Institute (IHPMI)** **13782**

Pres 5325 MacArthur Blvd NW, Washington DC 20016-2521, USA. T. +12029666251. Fax +12023648397.

History Mar 1983, Paris (France), as *International Health Economics and Management Institute (IHEMI)*. Present name adopted 8 Apr 1988. **Aims** Improve and expand knowledge in health policy, economics and management systems; provide a mechanism for health care professionals, educators, government officials and business leaders to gain a better understanding of health policy issues around the world. **Structure** International Conference (annual). Board of Directors, consisting of President, Vice-President, Chief Executive Officer, Executive Administrator and 4 members. **Languages** English. **Staff** 2.00 FTE, voluntary. **Finance** Members' dues. Other sources: conferences; sale of publications; grants from official and private bodies. **Activities** Research; demonstration projects. Organizes annual professional meetings. **Events** *Annual Conference* Edinburgh (UK) 1996, *Annual conference* Amsterdam (Netherlands) 1993, *Annual Conference* Budapest (Hungary) 1992, *Annual Conference* Vienna (Austria) 1991, *Annual conference* Berlin (Germany FR) 1990. **Publications** *International Perspectives* (4 a year). *Restructuring Health Policy: An International Challenge* (1986); *Exploring New Vistas in Health Care* (1985); *Health Care: An International Perspective* (1984).
Members Class A (general members); Class B (distinguished associates); Class C (organizations). Members in 16 countries:
Australia, Austria, Belgium, Canada, Czechoslovakia, France, Germany, Israel, Italy, Netherlands, Russia, Saudi Arabia, Sweden, UK, United Arab Emirates, USA. [2012.07.10/XF0457/j/**F**]

♦ International Health Professions Association (inactive)

♦ International Health, Racquet and Sportsclub Association (IHRSA) . 13783

Headquarters 70 Fargo St, Boston MA 02210, USA. T. +16179510055. Fax +16179510056.
URL: http://www.ihrsa.org/

History 13 Mar 1981, Chicago, IL (USA). Former names and other names: *International Racquet Sports Association (IRSA)* – former (1981 to 1988); *IRSA – Association of Quality Clubs* – former (1988 to 1994). **Aims** Grow, protect and promote the health and fitness industry. **Structure** Board of Directors. **Events** *Annual International Convention* Dallas, TX (USA) 2021, *Annual European Congress* 2020, *Annual International Convention* San Diego, CA (USA) 2020, *Annual European Congress* Dublin (Ireland) 2019, *Annual International Convention* San Diego, CA (USA) 2019. **Members** Primarily North American membership but member clubs (over 10,000) in 70 countries. Membership countries not specified. **NGO Relations** Cooperates with (1): *World Wellness Weekend (WWW)*. Associate expert of: *Business and Industry Advisory Committee to the OECD (BIAC, #03385)*. [2020/XN1091/**C**]

- ♦ International Health Regulations, 1969 (1969 treaty)
- ♦ International Health and Safety Association for Radio and Television (no recent information)
- ♦ International Health Services / see IHS Global

♦ international HealthTechScan (i-HTS) 13784

SG c/o bkm consultants, Weinsbergstr 190 c/o dhHealth, 50825 Cologne, Germany. E-mail: secretariat@euroscan-network.global – secretariat@i-hts.org.
URL: https://www.i-hts.org/

History 1996. Former names and other names: *European Information Network on New and Emerging Health Technologies* – former (2006); *EuroScan international network* – legal name; *International Information Network on New and Emerging Health Technologies (EuroScan)* – former (2006); *EuroScan (i-HTS)* – former. Registration: North Rhine-Westphalia District court, No/ID: VR 19436, Start date: 5 Oct 2017, Germany, Cologne; EU Transparency Register, No/ID: 120625842850-13, Start date: 20 May 2021. **Aims** Promote information exchange on important emerging new drugs, devices, procedures, programmes and settings in *health care*. **Structure** Executive Committee; Secretariat. **Languages** English. **Staff** 2.00 FTE, paid. **Finance** Members' dues. **Activities** Awareness raising; capacity building. **Publications** *EuroScan Newsletter*. *EuroScan Methods Toolkit*. Articles.
Members Full (18) in 15 countries:
Australia, Brazil, Canada, France, Germany, Israel, Italy, Korea Rep, Netherlands, New Zealand, Norway, Spain, Sweden, Switzerland, UK.
NGO Relations Cooperates with: *European Network for Health Technology Assessment (EUnetHTA, #07921)*. [2020/XJ0101/**F**]

- ♦ International Health and Temperance Association (internationally oriented national body)
- ♦ International Health Terminology Standards Development Organization / see SNOMED International (#19330)

♦ The International Hearing Voices Network (Intervoice) 13785

Contact c/o Mind in Camden, Barnes House, 9-15 Camden House, London, NW1 9LQ, UK. E-mail: info@intervoiceonline.org.
URL: http://www.intervoiceonline.org/

History Former names and other names: *International Hearing Voices Projects* – former. Registration: Charity Commission, No/ID: 1148779, England and Wales. **Aims** Support the International Hearing Voices Movement by connecting people, sharing ideas, distributing information, highlighting innovative initiatives, encouraging high quality respectful research and promoting its values across the world. **Structure** Annual General Meeting; Board. **Activities** Awards/prizes/competitions; events/meetings. **Events** *World Hearing Voices Congress* Montréal, QC (Canada) 2019, *World Hearing Voices Congress* The Hague (Netherlands) 2018, *World Hearing Voices Congress* Madrid (Spain) 2015.
Members National networks in 27 countries and territories:
Australia, Austria, Belgium, Canada, Denmark, England, Finland, France, Germany, Greece, Ireland, Italy, Japan, Malta, Netherlands, New Zealand, Norway, Palestine, Portugal, Scotland, Slovenia, Spain, Sweden, Switzerland, Uganda, USA, Wales. [2022.05.10/XM7845/**F**]

- ♦ International Hearing Voices Projects / see The International Hearing Voices Network (#13785)
- ♦ International Heart Network / see European Heart Network (#07467)

♦ International Heat Flow Commission (IHFC) 13786

Chairman University of Genoa, Experimental Geophysics and Radiometrics Lab, 16132 Genoa GE, Italy. E-mail: chair@ihfc-iugg.org.
Sec address not obtained. E-mail: secretary@ihfc-iugg.org.
URL: http://ihfc-iugg.org/

History Aug 1963, Berkeley, CA (USA). Founded at General Assembly of *International Union of Geodesy and Geophysics (IUGG, #15776)*. IHFC is a Commission of, and operates generally under guidelines set by *International Association of Seismology and Physics of the Earth's Interior (IASPEI, #12157)*. The *International Association for the Physical Sciences of the Oceans (IAPSO, #12082)* and *International Association of Volcanology and Chemistry of the Earth's Interior (IAVCEI, #12259)* are co-sponsors of and participate in the activities of the Commission. **Aims** Promote either alone or in co-operation with other international scientific organizations all aspects of geothermal research as they pertain to the missions of the parent and co-sponsoring associations. **Structure** Bureau; Working Groups (5). **Finance** Source: allocation from mother organization IASPEI. **Activities** Events/meetings; knowledge management/information dissemination; monitoring/evaluation; publishing activities; research and development; standards/guidelines. **Events** *CERMAK : International Meeting on Heat Flow and the Thermal Structure of the Lithosphere* Potsdam (Germany) 2022, *Meeting* Hyderabad (India) 2021, *Meeting* Montréal, QC (Canada) 2019, *Meeting* Kobe (Japan) 2017, *Meeting* Prague (Czech Rep) 2015. **Publications** *Thermal Regimes in the Continental and Oceanic Lithosphere* (1999); *Terrestrial Heat Flow and Geothermal Energy in Asia* (1995); *Heat Flow Density Global Database* (1993); *Geothermal Atlas of Europe* (1991); *Heat Flow and the Lithosphere Structure* (1991); *Handbook on Heat Flow Density Determinations* (1988); *Bibliography of Heat and Mass Transfer in Porous Media* (1987); *Paleogeothermics* (1986); *World Heat Flow Data Collection* (1986).
Members Individuals (16) in 13 countries:
Australia, Brazil, Canada, China, Estonia, Germany, India, Italy, Romania, Russia, South Africa, Switzerland, USA. [2022.05.17/XE2180/v/**E**]

♦ International Heavy Haul Association (IHHA) 13787

CEO 2808 Forest Hills Court, Virginia Beach VA 23454-1236, USA. T. +17574969384. Fax +17574962622.
URL: http://www.ihha.net/

History 1978. 1986, registered in the state of Missouri (USA). **Aims** Provide railway engineering conferences on heavy haul operations of trains. **Languages** English. **Staff** 2.00 FTE, paid. **Finance** Members' dues. **Events** *Conference* Narvik (Norway) 2019, *Quadrennial Conference* Cape Town (South Africa) 2017, *Operational excellence* Perth, WA (Australia) 2015, *Quadrennial Conference* Delhi (India) 2013, *Conference* Calgary, AB (Canada) 2011.
Members Full in 8 countries:
Australia, Brazil, Canada, China, France, South Africa, Sweden, USA. [2014/XD5781/**D**]

- ♦ International Hebrew Christian Alliance / see International Messianic Jewish Alliance (#14148)
- ♦ International Hegel Association / see International Hegel Society (#13788)

♦ International Hegel Society 13788

Société internationale pour la promotion des études hégéliennes – Sociedad Hegel Internacional – Internationale Hegel-Gesellschaft

Contact Carl-von-Ossietzky Univ Oldenburg, Inst für Philosophie, Ammerländer Heerstr 114-118, 26129 Oldenburg, Germany.
URL: https://www.hegel-gesellschaft.org/

History 1953, Nuremberg (Germany). Became an international association under the present name at 2nd Congress, 1958, Frankfurt-Main (Germany FR). Former names and other names: *Deutsche Hegel-Gesellschaft* – former (1953 to 1958); *International Hegel Association* – alias; *Association internationale pour la promotion des études hégéliennes* – alias. Registration: Germany. **Aims** Promote the study and comprehension of the *philosophy* of Georg Wilhelm Friedrich Hegel (1770-1831) and its effects. **Languages** English, French, German. **Staff** Voluntary. **Finance** Members' dues. Sponsors. **Activities** Organizes International Hegel Congress. **Events** *International Congress* Warsaw (Poland) 2021, *International Congress* Warsaw (Poland) 2020, *Hegel International Congress / Internationaler Hegel-Kongress* Vienna (Austria) 2014, *International Congress* Istanbul (Turkey) 2012, *International Congress* Sarajevo (Bosnia-Herzegovina) 2010. **Publications** *Hegel-Jahrbuch* (annual).
Members Individuals (250) in 36 countries:
Argentina, Australia, Austria, Belgium, Brazil, Bulgaria, Canada, China, Croatia, Czechia, Denmark, Finland, France, Germany, Greece, Hungary, Iran Islamic Rep, Israel, Italy, Japan, Korea Rep, Liechtenstein, Mexico, Montenegro, Netherlands, New Zealand, Poland, Portugal, Romania, Serbia, Slovenia, South Africa, Spain, Switzerland, Türkiye, UK, USA.
NGO Relations Member society of: *International Federation of Philosophical Societies (FISP, #13507)*. [2021/XE5434/v/**E**]

- ♦ International Heinrich Schütz Society (#13248)
- ♦ International Hemipteran-Plant Interactions Symposium (meeting series)
- ♦ International Hemp Association (no recent information)

♦ International Hemp Building Association (IHBA) 13789

Dir Rusheens, Kenmare, CO. KERRY, Ireland. E-mail: news@internationalhempbuilding.org.
URL: http://internationalhempbuilding.org/

History 20 Nov 2009, Ireland. Registration: No/ID: 477769, Ireland. **Aims** Develop, promote and support the production and use of all hemp based construction materials and their by-products in a sustainable and bio-regional manner for the benefit of the ecology and communities of all regions of the world. **Languages** English. **Staff** 7.00 FTE, paid. **Finance** Sources: members' dues. **Activities** Events/meetings. **Events** *Symposium* Bolton Percy (UK) 2020, *Symposium* Brussels (Belgium) 2018. **Publications** *Best Practice Guide*. Information leaflets. **Members** Full (over 200) in 25 countries. Membership countries not specified. **NGO Relations** Partner of (2): *European Industrial Hemp Association (EIHA, #07526)*; Hemp Industries Association. [2021.06.08/XM6607/**D**]

- ♦ International Hepato-Biliary-Pancreato Association / see International Hepato-Pancreato-Biliary Association (#13790)

♦ International Hepato-Pancreato-Biliary Association (IHPBA) 13790

Exec Dir 14 Laurel Park Gardens, Glasgow, G13 1RA, UK. T. +441415301687. E-mail: info@ihpba.org.
USA Office 21 First St SW, Suite 300, Rochester MN 55902, USA.
URL: http://www.ihpba.org/

History 15 Oct 1978, San Francisco, CA (USA). Decision taken, 11 Aug 1990, Paris (France), at joint meeting of *World Association of Hepato-Pancreato-Biliary Surgery (WAHPBS)*, inaugurated 8 Jun 1986, Lund (Sweden), and IHBPA to amalgamate the two associations using the current title of the Association; formally inaugurated at 1st General Assembly on 31 May 1994, Boston MA (USA). Former names and other names: *International Biliary Association* – former (15 Oct 1978 to 11 Sep 1988); *International Hepato-Biliary-Pancreato Association (IHBPA)* – former (11 Sep 1988 to 11 Aug 1990). Registration: 501(c)(3) organization, No/ID: EIN: 39-2036877, Start date: 2002, USA, Minnesota. **Aims** Improve evidence-based care and optimize the outcomes of patients with HPB disorders, by: disseminating research findings and best treatment practices throughout the world; advancing HPB specific training; fostering research and innovation; encouraging multidisciplinary international collaboration. **Structure** General Assembly (previously annual, every 2 years since 1994, in conjunction with World Congress); Executive Council; Executive Committee. Committees (6); HPB Editorial Board. Regional societies (3): Americas Hepato-Pancreato-Biliary Association (AHPBA); *Asian-Pacific Hepato-Pancreato-Biliary Association (A-PHPBA, #01616)*; *European-African Hepato-Pancreato-Biliary Association (E-AHPBA, #05840)*. **Languages** English. **Staff** 3.00 FTE, paid. **Finance** Sources: members' dues. **Activities** Awards/prizes/competitions; events/meetings; knowledge management/information dissemination; networking/liaising; research/documentation. **Events** *World Congress* Vancouver, BC (Canada) 2028, *World Congress* Singapore (Singapore) 2026, *World Congress* Cape Town (South Africa) 2024, *World Congress* New York, NY (USA) 2022, *World Congress* Melbourne, VIC (Australia) 2020. **Publications** *IHPBA Newsletter* (4 a year); *HPB Journal*. Technical guidelines; other guidelines.
Members Active Specialists in the field; Senior retired active members; Honorary. Members (1,044) in 81 countries and territories:
Argentina, Australia, Austria, Bahrain, Belgium, Brazil, Bulgaria, Canada, Chile, China, Colombia, Czechia, Denmark, Ecuador, Egypt, El Salvador, France, Germany, Ghana, Greece, Hungary, India, Indonesia, Iraq, Ireland, Israel, Italy, Jamaica, Japan, Jordan, Kenya, Korea Rep, Kuwait, Latvia, Lebanon, Libya, Lithuania, Luxembourg, Malaysia, Malta, Mexico, Mongolia, Netherlands, New Zealand, Nicaragua, Nigeria, Norway, Oman, Pakistan, Panama, Paraguay, Peru, Philippines, Poland, Portugal, Puerto Rico, Qatar, Romania, Russia, Saudi Arabia, Singapore, Slovakia, Slovenia, South Africa, Spain, Sudan, Sweden, Switzerland, Taiwan, Thailand, Tunisia, Türkiye, Uganda, UK, Ukraine, United Arab Emirates, Uruguay, USA, Venezuela, Vietnam, Zimbabwe. [2022/XD2458/v/**C**]

♦ International Herbage Seed Group (IHSG) 13791

Pres Dept of Agroecology – Crop Health, Aarhus University, Forsøgsvej 1, 4200 Slagelse, Denmark.
Contact SEGES, Agro Food Park 15, 8200 Aarhus, Denmark.
URL: http://www.ihsg.org/

History 1978. Current name adopted at International Grassland Congress, Brazil. Former names and other names: *International Herbage Seed Production Research Group (IHSPRG)* – former (1978 to 2001). **Aims** Encourage cooperation and communication between workers actively engaged in herbage seed production research. **Structure** Executive Committee. **Languages** English. **Staff** 2.00 FTE, voluntary. **Finance** Funds for Newsletter obtained through donations and sponsorships. **Activities** Events/meetings; publishing activities. **Events** *International Herbage Seed Conference* Novi Sad (Serbia) 2021, *International Herbage Seed Conference* Corvallis, OR (USA) 2019, *International Herbage Seed Conference* Pergamino (Argentina) 2017, *International Herbage Seed Conference* Lanzhou (China) 2015, *International Herbage Seed Conference* Dallas, TX (USA) 2010. **Publications** *IHSG Newsletter* (2 a year).
Members Full in 40 countries:
Argentina, Australia, Brazil, Cameroon, Canada, Chile, China, Costa Rica, Cuba, Czechia, Denmark, Egypt, Ethiopia, Finland, France, Germany, India, Iran Islamic Rep, Italy, Japan, Lithuania, Myanmar, Netherlands, New Zealand, Norway, Pakistan, Poland, Russia, Serbia, South Africa, Sudan, Sweden, Syrian AR, Thailand, Tunisia, Türkiye, UK, Uruguay, USA, Zimbabwe.
IGO Relations *CABI (#03393)*. [2021/XD1189/**F**]

- ♦ International Herbage Seed Production Research Group / see International Herbage Seed Group (#13791)
- ♦ International Hereditary Cancer Center (internationally oriented national body)

♦ International Heteropterists' Society 13792

Treas Dept Entomology, Plant Pathology, Weed Science, New Mexico State Univ, 945 College Avenue, Las Cruces NM 88003, USA.
URL: http://heteroptera.org/

History 29 Dec 1997, Washington DC (USA). **Aims** Promote systematic, biogeographic and biological studies of Heteroptera; cultivate cooperative research among heteropterists throughout the world. **Structure** General Business Meeting and Conference (every 4 years); Committees (3). **Languages** English. **Finance** Members' dues. **Events** *Quadrennial Meeting* Bangkok (Thailand) 2026, *Quadrennial Meeting* Barcelona (Spain) 2022, *Quadrennial Meeting* La Plata (Argentina) 2018, *Quadrennial Meeting* Washington, DC (USA) 2014, *Quadrennial meeting* Tianjin (China) 2010.
Members Regular; Life; Sustaining; Emeritus; Honorary. Individuals (236) in 47 countries and territories:
Argentina, Australia, Austria, Belarus, Belgium, Brazil, Bulgaria, Canada, China, Colombia, Czechia, Denmark, Finland, France, Georgia, Germany, Greece, Guiana Fr, Hungary, India, Iran Islamic Rep, Italy, Japan, Korea Rep, Mexico, Moldova, Nepal, Netherlands, New Zealand, Nigeria, Pakistan, Poland, Portugal, Russia, Serbia, Slovakia, Slovenia, South Africa, Spain, Sweden, Switzerland, Taiwan, Tajikistan, Türkiye, UK, Ukraine, USA. [2023/XD7869/**D**]

♦ **International Hibernation Society** **13793**
Chairman Science and Engineering Bldg 3168, School of Life Sciences, Univ of Nevada, 4505 Marlyland Parkway, Las Vegas NV 89154, USA. T. +17028953956.
History Founded 1996, following a series of symposia being organized since 1959. **Aims** Exchange information on hibernation, temperature acclimatization and bioenergetics. **Languages** English. **Staff** None. **Finance** No budget. **Activities** Organizes symposia. **Events** *Symposium* Las Vegas, NV (USA) 2016, *Symposium* Semmering (Austria) 2012, *Symposium* Swakopmund (Namibia) 2008, *Symposium* Vancouver, BC (Canada) 2004, *Symposium* Jungholz (Austria) 2000. **Publications** Symposium proceedings published in a special edition of *Journal of Comparative Physiology B*. **NGO Relations** Links with organizations supporting basic research, including: *European Science Foundation (ESF, #08441)*. [2013.09.18/XD5873/**D**]

♦ International Hibernation Society (inactive)
♦ International Hide and Allied Trades Improvement Society (inactive)

♦ **International Higher Education Foundation** **13794**
Fundación para la Educación Superior Internacional (FESI)
Pres Moctezuma 65, Col Centro, Xalapa, 91000 Veracruz CHIS, Mexico. T. +522288124470. Fax +522288124470.
URL: http://www.fesi.org.mx/
History 1998. **Aims** Take any action oriented to improve higher education worldwide; identify, cultivate and develop collaboration networks with all nations so as to increase academic and cultural exchange, in order to achieve a better understanding within global society; promote scientific and technological innovation in developing countries to raise living standards. **Structure** Board of Directors; International Advisory Council. **Languages** English, French, Italian, Portuguese, Spanish. **Staff** Voluntary. **Finance** Members' dues. Income from: consulting; contributions; events; publications. **Events** *International conference on education and development / Conference* Veracruz, CHIS (Mexico) 2013, *BIOPMAT : international conference on biopolymeric materials engineering / Conference* Mexico City (Mexico) 2012, *BIOPMAT : international conference on biopolymeric materials engineering / Conference* Puebla (Mexico) 2010, *International conference* Veracruz, CHIS (Mexico) 2008, *Conference* Veracruz, CHIS (Mexico) 2007. **Publications** Books (paper and electronic).
Members in 26 countries and territories:
Argentina, Australia, Bolivia, Brazil, Canada, Chile, Colombia, Cuba, Ecuador, El Salvador, France, Germany, Italy, Korea Rep, Mexico, Netherlands, Peru, Poland, Puerto Rico, Russia, South Africa, Spain, Taiwan, Uruguay, USA, Venezuela. [2020/XM1157/f/**D**]

♦ **International Higher Education Teaching and Learning Association (HETL)** **13795**
Exec Dir 13844 Queens Blvd, Unit 105, Briarwood NY 11435, USA. E-mail: support@hetl.org.
URL: http://www.hetl.org/
History 2010. Registration: USA, New York State. **Aims** Bring together higher education professionals and thought leaders from around the world to dialogue, network, and collaborate on issues relevant to teaching and learning in higher education. **Structure** Board of Directors. **Events** *Conference* Aberdeen (UK) 2023, *Conference* Istanbul (Türkiye) 2022, *Conference* Paisley (UK) 2017, *Conference* Orem, UT (USA) 2015, *Innovative learning-scapes – e-scapes, play-scapes* Anchorage, AK (USA) 2014. **Publications** *International HETL Review*. Books. **Consultative Status** Consultative status granted from: *ECOSOC (#05331)* (Special). **NGO Relations** Member of: *EDEN Digital Learning Europe (EDEN, #05356)*. [2020/XJ6795/**C**]

♦ International Higher Institute of Tourism (internationally oriented national body)

♦ **International High Pressure Biology Group** **13796**
Pres 12901 Bruce B Downs Blvd, MDC 7 – USF, Tampa FL 33612, USA.
History 1988. Also referred to as *International Group for High Pressure Biology*. **Aims** Promote research on the effects of high pressure and *inert gases* on living organisms. **Structure** 2 Co-Presidents. **Staff** 2.00 FTE, paid. **Events** *Conference* Eilat (Israel) 2012, *Effects of pressure at cellular and molecular levels, effects of pressure and inert gases on physiological system and whole organisms, basic mechanisms of hyperbaric oxygen and hyperoxia* Brest (France) 2009, *Conference* Sharm el Sheikh (Egypt) 2007, *Conference* Barcelona (Spain) 2005, *Conference* Moscow (Russia) 2003. **Members** 250 in 20 countries and territories. Member countries not specified. [2012/XF2414/**F**]

♦ International High-Speed Rail Association (internationally oriented national body)
♦ International Highway Project (unconfirmed)

♦ **International Hip Society (IHS)** **13797**
Administrator SHPR, Registercentrum VG, SE-413 45 Gothenburg, Sweden.
URL: http://www.ihshome.org/
History 1966, Paris (France). **Activities** Open meeting takes place during triennal event of *International Society of Orthopaedic Surgery and Traumatology (#15335)*. **Events** *Meeting* Zurich (Switzerland) 2012, *Meeting* Prague (Czech Rep) 2011, *Meeting* Paris (France) 2008, *Meeting* Vienna (Austria) 2005, *Meeting* Vienna (Austria) 2005. **Members** Individuals. Membership countries not specified. [2015/XU1977/**D**]

♦ **International Histocompatibility Working Group (IHWG)** **13798**
Contact c/o Fred Hutchinson Cancer Research Ctr, 1100 Fairview Ave North, PO Box 19024, Seattle WA 98109-1024, USA. T. +12066675000. E-mail: communications@fredhutch.org.
URL: https://www.fredhutch.org/en/research/institutes-networks-ircs/international-h istocompatibility-working-group.html/
History Following a series of histocompatibility workshops organized since 1964. **Activities** *International Histocompatibility and Immunogenetics Workshop and Congress*. **Events** *International histocompatibility workshop* Liverpool (UK) 2012, *International Histocompatibility Workshop and Conference* London (UK) 2012, *International Histocompatibility Workshop and Conference* Armação de Búzios (Brazil) 2008, *International histocompatibility and immunogenetics workshop* Rio de Janeiro (Brazil) 2008, *International HLA and immunogenetics workshop* Melbourne, VIC (Australia) 2005. **Publications** *IHWG Newsletter*. [2020/XE4334/**E**]

♦ **International History, Philosophy, and Science Teaching Group (IHPST)** **13799**
Sec 73 Sioux Drive, Millsboro DE 19966, USA. E-mail: secretary@ihpst.net – president@ihpst.net.
URL: http://ihpst.org/
History 1989. **Aims** Promote the betterment of school and university science and mathematics education by making them informed by the history, philosophy, and sociology of science and mathematics. **Structure** Council. **Activities** Events/meetings. **Events** *Biennial Conference* Calgary, AB (Canada) 2022, *Biennial Conference* Busan (Korea Rep) 2016, *Biennial Conference* Pavia (Italy) / Como (Italy) 1999. **Publications** *Science & Education*. [2022/AA2755/**C**]

♦ International HIV/AIDS Alliance / see Frontline AIDS (#10007)
♦ International HIV Fund (internationally oriented national body)

♦ **International Hobbes Association (IHA)** **13800**
Presiding Officer Dept of Philosophy, Kent State Univ, PO Box 5190, Kent OH 44242-0001, USA. T. +13306722315. Fax +13306724867.
Editor Dept Political Science, Univ of Oregon, Eugene OR 97403, USA. T. +15413464884.
URL: https://hobbesassoc.org/
Aims Promote research and discussion of *philosophical, political*, historical, literary and scientific matters related to Thomas Hobbes' thought; encourage comparison of Hobbes' views to those of other important thinkers from the beginning of the modern state and the rise of science to the present; encourage application of Hobbes' thought to contemporary issues that can be informed by his thinking. **Structure** Steering Committee; Honorary Board; Editorial Board. **Languages** English. **Activities** Events/meetings. **Events** *Annual Meeting* Denver, CO (USA) 2023, *Conference* San Francisco, CA (USA) 2003, *The possibility of justifying world government on hobbesean principles* Helsinki (Finland) 1987. **Publications** *Hobbes Studies* (2 a year) – journal. [2023.02.13/XE4664/**E**]

♦ International Hobie 14 Class Association (see: #21760)
♦ International Hobie 16 Class Association (see: #21760)
♦ International Hobie Cat Class Association / see International Hobie Class Association (#13801)

♦ **International Hobie Class Association (IHCA)** **13801**
Exec Dir 18 Arafura Crescent, Tingalpa QLD 4173, Australia. T. +61738905224. Fax +61733489923.
URL: http://www.hobieclass.com/
History 1982, as *World Hobie Class Association (WHCA)*. Present name adopted 1989. Sometimes referred to as *International Hobie Cat Class Association*. Constitution and world-class events cleared through and approved by: *World Sailing (#21760)*. **Aims** Promote one-design *racing*, specifically Hobie Cat racing. **Structure** Officers. Classes: *International Hobie 14 Class Association (see: #21760)*; *International Hobie 16 Class Association (see: #21760)*; *International Hobie Tiger Class Association (see: #21760)*. **Finance** Members' dues. Sponsoring. **Activities** Events/meetings. **Events** *Meeting* Suva (Fiji) 1986. **Publications** *Hobie Hotline* (6 a year).
Members Fleets (524) world-wide in 34 countries and territories:
Antigua-Barbuda, Australia, Austria, Bahamas, Belgium, Bermuda, Brazil, Canada, Chile, Costa Rica, Denmark, Finland, France, Germany, Hong Kong, Italy, Japan, Mauritius, Mexico, Netherlands, New Zealand, Norway, Papua New Guinea, Philippines, Puerto Rico, Seychelles, Singapore, South Africa, Spain, Switzerland, Thailand, USA, Venezuela. [2016/XE9686/**E**]

♦ International Hobie Tiger Class Association (see: #21760)

♦ **International Hockey Federation** **13802**
Fédération internationale de hockey (FIH)
CEO Rue du Valentin 61, 1004 Lausanne VD, Switzerland. T. +41216410606. Fax +41216410607. E-mail: info@fih.ch.
Pres address not obtained.
URL: http://fih.ch/
History Founded 7 Jan 1924, Paris (France), by representatives of 7 European countries. *International Federation of Women's Hockey Associations (IFWHA, inactive)*, formed in 1927, merged with IHF in 1983. Previous statutes adopted 3 Oct 1992; current statutes adopted 1 Jan 2013. Registered in accordance with Swiss Civil Code. Also referred to as *International Field Hockey Federation*. Previously also known under the English acronym *IHF*. **Aims** Serve as the world governing body for hockey, as recognized by the International Olympic Committee. **Structure** Congress (meets every 2 years); Executive Board; Board Committees/Panels (5); Operational Committees/Panels (9). **Languages** English. **Staff** 41.00 FTE, paid. **Finance** Affiliation fees. Other sources: royalties; sponsorship; TV rights. **Activities** Knowledge management/information dissemination; monitoring/evaluation; sporting activities. **Events** *Congress* Lausanne (Switzerland) 2021, *Congress* Delhi (India) 2018, *Congress* Dubai (United Arab Emirates) 2016, *Congress* Marrakech (Morocco) 2014, *Congress* Kuala Lumpur (Malaysia) 2012. **Publications** Guidelines; rules.
Members National Associations in 136 countries and territories:
Afghanistan, Algeria, Argentina, Armenia, Australia, Austria, Azerbaijan, Bahamas, Bangladesh, Barbados, Belarus, Belgium, Bermuda, Bolivia, Botswana, Brazil, Brunei Darussalam, Bulgaria, Burkina Faso, Burundi, Cambodia, Cameroon, Canada, Cayman Is, Chile, China, Colombia, Costa Rica, Croatia, Cuba, Cyprus, Czechia, Denmark, Dominican Rep, Ecuador, Egypt, El Salvador, England, Estonia, Eswatini, Fiji, Finland, France, Georgia, Germany, Ghana, Gibraltar, Greece, Guatemala, Guyana, Haiti, Honduras, Hong Kong, Hungary, India, Indonesia, Iran Islamic Rep, Ireland, Israel, Italy, Jamaica, Japan, Kazakhstan, Kenya, Korea DPR, Korea Rep, Libya, Lithuania, Luxembourg, Macau, Malawi, Malaysia, Malta, Mauritius, Mexico, Moldova, Mongolia, Morocco, Myanmar, Namibia, Nepal, Netherlands, New Zealand, Nicaragua, Nigeria, North Macedonia, Norway, Oman, Pakistan, Panama, Papua New Guinea, Paraguay, Peru, Philippines, Poland, Portugal, Puerto Rico, Qatar, Romania, Russia, Samoa, Scotland, Serbia, Seychelles, Sierra Leone, Singapore, Slovakia, Slovenia, Solomon Is, South Africa, Spain, Sri Lanka, Sudan, Sweden, Switzerland, Taiwan, Tajikistan, Tanzania UR, Thailand, Togo, Tonga, Trinidad-Tobago, Türkiye, Turkmenistan, Uganda, Ukraine, United Arab Emirates, Uruguay, USA, Uzbekistan, Vanuatu, Venezuela, Vietnam, Wales, Zambia, Zimbabwe.
Adherent member in 1 country:
UK.
NGO Relations Member of (6): *Association of Summer Olympic International Federations (ASOIF, #02943)*; *International Committee for Fair Play (#12769)*; *International Council for Coaching Excellence (ICCE, #13008)*; *International Masters Games Association (IMGA, #14117)* (Full); *International World Games Association (IWGA, #15914)*; *Olympic Movement (#17719)*. Cooperates with (1): *International Testing Agency (ITA, #15678)*. Affiliated with (1): *EMEA Synthetic Turf Council (ESTC, #05436)*. Recognized by: *International Olympic Committee (IOC, #14408)*. Continental federations under the authority of FIH: *African Hockey Federation (AfHF, #00338)*; *Asian Hockey Federation (AHF, #01505)*; *European Hockey Federation (EHF, #07494)*; *Oceania Hockey Federation (#17664)*; *Pan American Hockey Federation (PAHF, #18110)*. [2019.03.06/XB2103/**B**]

♦ International Holiday Service Home Exchange / see INTERVac – International Home Exchange Holiday Service (#15989)
♦ International Holistic University, Brasilia / see Universidade Internacional da Paz (#20689)

♦ **International Holocaust Remembrance Alliance (IHRA)** **13803**
SG Friedrichstr 200, 10117 Berlin, Germany. E-mail: info@holocaustremembrance.com.
Communication Officer address not obtained.
Main Website: http://www.holocaustremembrance.com/
History May 1998, Stockholm (Sweden). Founded on the initiative of former Swedish Prime Minister Göran Persson. Officially launched 26-28 Jan 2000, at the Stockholm International Forum on the Holocaust. Commitments reaffirmed through 2020 IHRA Ministerial Declaration, adopted in Brussels (Belgium). Former names and other names: *Task Force for International Cooperation on Holocaust Education, Remembrance and Research (ITF)* – former. **Aims** Unite governments and experts to strengthen, advance and promote Holocaust education, remembrance and research, and uphold the commitments of the 2000 Stockholm Declaration and the 2020 IHRA Ministerial Declaration. **Structure** Plenary Session (maximum 2 a year); Chair rotates annually between countries; Working Groups (3); Committees (3); Secretariat. **Languages** English. **Staff** 9.00 FTE, paid. **Finance** Sources: members' dues. **Activities** Awareness raising; events/meetings; financial and/or material support; networking/liaising; politics/policy/regulatory; projects/programmes; research/documentation; standards/guidelines. **Events** *Plenary Meeting* Stockholm (Sweden) 2022, *Ministerial Meeting* Brussels (Belgium) 2020, *Symposium on Holocaust and Genocide Education* Salzburg (Austria) 2014, *Conference* Toronto, ON (Canada) 2013, *Plenary Meeting* The Hague (Netherlands) 2011. **Publications** *Recognizing and Countering Holocaust Distortion: Recommendations for Policy and Decision Makers* (2021); *Mass Murder of People with Disabilities and the Holocaust* (2019); *Recommendations for Teaching and Learning about the Holocaust* (2019); *Refugee Policies from 1933 until Today: Challenges and Responsibilities* (2018); *Research in Teaching and Learning about the Holocaust: A Dialogue Beyond Borders* (2017); *Killing Sites – Research and Remembrance*. *Bystanders, Rescuers or Perpetrators? The Neutral Countries and the Shoah* (2016); *The Genocide and Persecution of Roma and Sinti. Bibliography and Historiographical Review* (2016).
Members States committed to the Declaration of the Stockholm International Forum on the Holocaust and to implementation of national policies and programmes in support of Holocaust education, remembrance and research. The IHRA consists of representatives of governments. Delegations are chaired by ambassadors or officials of a senior rank. Non-governmental organizations are formally affiliated through national delegations and nominated by respective governments to participate in the working groups. Member States (35):
Argentina, Australia, Austria, Belgium, Bulgaria, Canada, Croatia, Czechia, Denmark, Estonia, Finland, France, Germany, Greece, Hungary, Ireland, Israel, Italy, Latvia, Lithuania, Luxembourg, Netherlands, North Macedonia, Norway, Poland, Portugal, Romania, Serbia, Slovakia, Slovenia, Spain, Sweden, Switzerland, UK, USA.
Observer countries (10):
Albania, Bosnia-Herzegovina, Brazil, Cyprus, El Salvador, Moldova, Monaco, New Zealand, Türkiye, Uruguay.
IGO Relations Cooperates with (7): *Arolsen Archives – International Center on Nazi Persecution (#01112)*; *Council of Europe (CE, #04881)*; *European Union Agency for Fundamental Rights (FRA, #08969)*; *European Union (EU, #08967)*; *OSCE – Office for Democratic Institutions and Human Rights (OSCE/ODIHR, #17902)*; *UNESCO (#20322)*; *United Nations (UN, #20515)*. **NGO Relations** Member of (1): *Association of Holocaust Organizations (AHO)*. Cooperates with (1): *Conference on Jewish Material Claims Against Germany (Claims Conference, #04624)*. Instrumental in setting up (1): *Vienna Wiestenthal Institute for Holocaust Studies (VWI)*. [2023.02.14/XE3844/**E***]

♦ **International Hologram Manufacturers Association (IHMA)** **13804**
SG 4 Windmill Business Village, Brooklands Close, Sunbury-on-Thames, TW16 7DY, UK. T. +441932785680. Fax +441932780790. E-mail: info@ihma.org.
URL: http://www.ihma.org/

History 1993. Registered in accordance with UK law. **Aims** Advance understanding, use and development of holograms and holographic technology, particularly in authentication of products and documents, decoration and illustration, display systems, energy and environmental improvements. **Structure** Board. **Languages** English. **Staff** 1.50 FTE, paid. **Finance** Members' dues. **Activities** Monitoring/evaluation; knowledge management/information dissemination; awards/prizes/competitions; events/meetings. **Events** *Holo-pack and Holo-print conference* New Orleans, LA (USA) 1995. **Publications** *Holography News* (12 a year); *IHMA Patent Bulletin* (12 a year).
Members Companies (90) in 31 countries and territories:
Armenia, Austria, Bangladesh, Belarus, Bulgaria, China, Colombia, Czechia, France, Germany, Hungary, India, Indonesia, Italy, Japan, Korea Rep, Mexico, Poland, Portugal, Romania, Russia, Serbia, Singapore, Spain, Switzerland, Taiwan, Türkiye, UK, Ukraine, USA, Vietnam.
NGO Relations Member of: *International Currency Association (ICA, #13123)*. [2019.04.25/XF5682/**F**]

♦ International Home Care Nurses Organization (IHCNO) 13805

Contact address not obtained. E-mail: ihcnorg@gmail.com.
URL: https://ihcno.org/
History 2009. Registration: 501(c)(3) non-profit, Start date: 2017, USA. **Aims** Develop and support a vibrant worldwide network of nurses who promote excellence in providing optimal health and well-being to patients living in their homes. **Structure** Board; Advisory Council. **Events** *Conference* Chicago, IL (USA) 2015, *Conference* Singapore (Singapore) 2014, *Conference* Cleveland, OH (USA) 2013. [2021/AA1863/**C**]

♦ International Homeopathic Council (inactive)
♦ International Homeopathic Medical League (#16471)
♦ International Homeopathic Medical Organization (no recent information)
♦ International Homeopathic Medical Organization (no recent information)
♦ International Homework Office (inactive)

♦ International Honey Export Organization (IHEO) 13806

Sec Bee Maid Honey Ltd, 625 Roseberry Street, Winnipeg MB R3H 0T4, Canada. T. +12047868977. Fax +12047838468.
Pres address not obtained.
History 2 May 1984, Mexico City (Mexico). Proposed 1983, during Congress of *International Federation of Beekeepers' Associations (APIMONDIA, #13370)*. Launched at 1st meeting by 3 individuals from Australia, Cuba and Mexico. Registration: No/ID: A1013195B, Start date: Apr 2007, Australia. **Aims** Keep exporters informed of the honey situation and prices in the main exporting countries. **Structure** Committee of Management. **Activities** Events/meetings. **Events** *Meeting* Buenos Aires (Argentina) 2011, *Meeting* Montpellier (France) 2009, *Meeting* Melbourne, VIC (Australia) 2007, *Meeting* Dublin (Ireland) 2005, *Meeting* Ljubljana (Slovenia) 2003.
Members Individuals in 13 countries:
Argentina, Australia, Brazil, Bulgaria, Canada, Chile, China, India, Mexico, New Zealand, Türkiye, Uruguay, Vietnam.
NGO Relations Member of (1): *International Federation of Beekeepers' Associations (APIMONDIA, #13370)*. [2015/XM4235/v/**C**]

♦ International Hop Growers' Convention (IHGC) 13807

Comité international de la culture du houblon (CICH) – Internationales Hopfenbaubüro (IHB)
SG Malgajeva 18, 3000 Celje, Slovenia. T. +38641766544.
Registered Office 22 rue des Roses, BP 81, 67173 Brumath, France.
URL: http://www.ihgc.org/
History Founded 19 Aug 1950, Strasbourg (France), as *European Hop Growers Convention – Comité européen de la culture du houblon*. Statutes adopted 18 Aug 1951; modified: 1964; 1970; 1993; 1998; 2001; 2003; 2013. Registered in accordance with French law. **Aims** Safeguard the common interests of hop growers and hop merchants worldwide. **Structure** General Assembly (biennial); Executive Committee; Commissions (3); Secretariat. **Languages** English, French, German. **Staff** No permanent staff. **Finance** Members' dues. Annual budget: euro 17,500. **Activities** Knowledge management/information dissemination; research/documentation. **Events** *Congress* Prague (Czechia) 2022, *Congress* Ljubljana (Slovenia) / Zalec (Slovenia) 2019, *Congress* Yakima, WA (USA) 2017, *Congress* Bad Gögging (Germany) 2015, *Meeting* Linz (Austria) 2014. **Publications** *Economic Commission Reports* (3 a year). *Hop Dictionary* (2015) in Czech, English, French, German, Slovene. Scientific Technical Commission Meeting proceedings (every 2 years).
Members National organizations and individual members where no national organization exists. National associations and hop industry companies (34) in 20 countries:
Argentina, Australia, Austria, Belgium, Canada, China, Czechia, France, Germany, New Zealand, Poland, Romania, Russia, Slovakia, Slovenia, South Africa, Spain, UK, Ukraine, USA. [2018.06.01/XD0781/**D**]

♦ International HO-RE-CA – International Organization of Hotel and Restaurant Associations (inactive)

♦ International Horizon Scanning Initiative (IHSI) 13808

General Manager Dutch National Health Care Inst, Willem Dudokhof 1, 1112 ZA Diemen, Netherlands. E-mail: info@ihsi-health.org.
Registered Address Tervurenlaan 211, 1150 Brussels, Belgium. E-mail: info@ihsi-health.org.
URL: https://ihsi-health.org/
History A member-state driven organization in which participating countries retain control over the functioning and operations of the initiative. Registration: Banque-Carrefour des Entreprises, No/ID: 0735.645.228, Start date: 3 Oct 2019, Belgium; EU Transparency Register, No/ID: 568636644283-67, Start date: 5 Oct 2021. **Aims** Empower political decision-makers and payer organization negotiators to drive for better pricing in medicinal products. **Structure** Board of Directors; Executive Committee; Secretariat. **Activities** Events/meetings; knowledge management/information dissemination. **Events** *Symposium* Belgium 2021.
Members Full; Affiliate; Joined. Full in 8 countries:
Belgium, Denmark, Ireland, Netherlands, Norway, Portugal, Sweden, Switzerland.
Affiliate in 5 countries:
Belgium, Denmark, Ireland, Norway, Sweden. [2021/AA2104/**F**]

♦ International Hormone Society (IHS) 13809

Pres Av Van Bever 7-9, 1180 Brussels, Belgium. T. +3223793442. Fax +3227325743. E-mail: ihs@intlhormonesociety.org.
History Registration: Banque-Carrefour des Entreprises, No/ID: 0820.591.096, Start date: 17 Nov 2009. **Aims** Provide medical professionals with information about advance hormone therapies. **Structure** Board of Directors. **Events** *Evidence-Based Hormone Lectures* Kuala Lumpur (Malaysia) 2021, *Conference* Paris (France) 2008, *Asia Pacific conference on anti-aging medicine* Nusa Dua (Indonesia) 2006, *Australasia conference on anti-aging medicine* Nusa Dua (Indonesia) 2006, *International conference on wellness and anti-aging medicine* Nusa Dua (Indonesia) 2006. [2022/XM0173/**C**]

♦ International Horn Society (IHS) 13810

Société internationale des cornistes – Sociedad Internacional de Trompas – Internationale Horngesellschaft
Exec Dir PO Box 5486, Toledo OH 43613, USA.
URL: http://www.hornsociety.org/
History Jun 1970. **Aims** Work on the performance, teaching, composition, research, and the preservation and promotion of the horn as a *musical* instrument. **Structure** Officers: President; Vice-President; Secretary/Treasurer; Executive Director. **Staff** 2.00 FTE, paid. **Events** *Annual Symposium* Kingsville, TX (USA) 2022, *Annual Symposium* Montréal, QC (Canada) 2021, *Annual Symposium* Eugene, OR (USA) 2020, *Annual Symposium* Ghent (Belgium) 2019, *Annual Symposium* Muncie, IN (USA) 2018. **Publications** *E-Newsletter* (6 a year); *The Horn Call* (3 a year). **Members** Individuals (about 3,000). Membership countries not specified. [2020/XN2727/**C**]

♦ International Horse Association (inactive)

♦ International Horse Sports Confederation (IHSC) 13811

Contact Chemin de la Joliette 8, 1006 Lausanne VD, Switzerland. T. +41213104747. E-mail: info@fei.org.
URL: https://horsesport.org/
History 2013. Founded by *Fédération Équestre Internationale (FEI, #09484)* and *International Federation of Horseracing Authorities (IFHA, #13449)*. Registration: Swiss Civil Code, Switzerland. **Aims** Encourage cooperation and information exchange on all matters of mutual interest between the IFHA and the FEI. **Structure** Secretariat based at *Fédération Équestre Internationale (FEI, #09484)*. **Events** *Inaugural Meeting* Lausanne (Switzerland) 2014. [AA1864/**E**]

♦ International Horticultural Congress (meeting series)
♦ International Hospital Association (inactive)
♦ International Hospital Christian Fellowship / see Healthcare Christian Fellowship International (#10873)
♦ International Hospital Committee (inactive)

♦ International Hospital Federation (IHF) 13812

CEO c/o Hôpital de Loëx, Route de Loëx 151, 1233 Bernex GE, Switzerland. T. +41228509420. Fax +41228509427. E-mail: ihf.secretariat@ihf-fih.org.
URL: http://www.ihf-fih.org/
History 27 May 1947, Lucerne (Switzerland). Founded as successor to *International Hospital Association (inactive)*, formed in 1931, but which had ceased to function during World War II. The Association was itself preceded by *International Hospital Committee (inactive)*, set up at 1st International Hospital Congress, 1929, New York NY (USA). Former names and other names: *Fédération internationale des hôpitaux (FIH)* – alias; *Federación Internacional de Hospitales (FIH)* – alias. Registration: Swiss Civil Code, Switzerland. **Aims** Bring together leaders and organizations to share knowledge, to help strengthen the work of members; provide opportunities for exchange, development and collaboration; shape the future of healthcare around the world. **Structure** General Assembly; Governing Council; Executive Committee; Audit and Finance Committee; Secretariat headed by CEO. **Languages** English, French, German, Italian, Portuguese, Spanish. **Staff** 5.00 FTE, paid. **Finance** Sources: fees for services; grants; members' dues; sponsorship. **Activities** Events/meetings; knowledge management/information dissemination; networking/liaising; training/education. **Events** *World Hospital Congress* Lisbon (Portugal) 2023, *World Hospital Congress* Dubai (United Arab Emirates) 2022, *World Hospital Congress* Barcelona (Spain) 2021, *COVID-19 Safe Hospital Seminar* Incheon (Korea Rep) 2021, *Learning from COVID-19 – Transforming Health Services* 2020. **Publications** *IHF Newsletter* (12 a year) in English. Recommendations; white papers; reports.
Members Categories: Full – associations and bodies representing hospitals and healthcare organizations; Associate (Premier, group, or standalone) – hospitals, healthcare organizations and other healthcare services not eligible for full membership.
Full (43) in 37 countries and territories:
Argentina, Australia, Austria, Belgium, Brazil, Canada, Colombia, Egypt, Finland, France, Germany, Guinea, Hong Kong, Indonesia, Japan, Jordan, Korea Rep, Lebanon, Luxembourg, Morocco, Nigeria, Norway, Oman, Philippines, Poland, Portugal, Rwanda, Saudi Arabia, South Africa, Spain, Switzerland, Taiwan, Tunisia, UK, United Arab Emirates, USA, Zambia.
Premier Associate (29) in 11 countries and territories:
Belgium, Georgia, India, Israel, Kazakhstan, Portugal, Qatar, Saudi Arabia, Tanzania UR, United Arab Emirates, USA.
Group and Standalone Associate (68) in 39 countries and territories:
Afghanistan, Australia, Austria, Belgium, Bosnia-Herzegovina, Brazil, Canada, Croatia, Egypt, Finland, France, Greece, Hungary, India, Indonesia, Iraq, Italy, Jordan, Kenya, Korea Rep, Malaysia, Myanmar, Nigeria, Northern Mariana Is, Pakistan, Palestine, Philippines, Portugal, Sierra Leone, Singapore, Spain, Sweden, Switzerland, Taiwan, United Arab Emirates, USA, Vietnam, Zambia, Zimbabwe.
Consultative Status Consultative status granted from: *ECOSOC (#05331)* (Ros C); *WHO (#20950)* (Official Relations). **IGO Relations** Cooperates with (8): *Comunidade dos Paises de Lingua Portuguesa (CPLP, #04430)*; *International Finance Corporation (IFC, #13597)*; *OECD (#17693)*; *WHO (#20950)*; *WHO Patient Safety (#20940)*; *WHO Regional Office for Europe (#20945)*; *WHO Regional Office for the Eastern Mediterranean (EMRO, #20944)*; World Bank. **NGO Relations** Partner of (16): *European Association of Hospital Managers (EAHM, #06073)*; *European Health Management Association (EHMA, #07458)*; *Geneva Health Forum – Towards Global Access to Health*; Hospital Management Asia; *International Alliance of Patients' Organizations (IAPO, #11633)*; *International Committee of the Red Cross (ICRC, #12799)*; *International Council of Nurses (ICN, #13054)*; *International Federation of Pharmaceutical Manufacturers and Associations (IFPMA, #13505)*; *International Network of Health Promoting Hospitals and Health Services (HPH, #14277)*; *International Society for Quality in Health Care (ISQua, #15405)*; *Union for International Cancer Control (UICC, #20415)*; *Union internationale des architectes (UIA, #20419)* (Public Health Group); *World Federation of Public Health Associations (WFPHA, #21476)*; *World Health Professions Alliance (WHPA, #21557)*; *World Medical Association (WMA, #21646)*; *World Organization of Family Doctors (WONCA, #21690)*. [2023.03.01/XB2109/**B**]

♦ International Hospitality and Conference Service Association (internationally oriented national body)
♦ International Hospitality Information Technology Association (internationally oriented national body)
♦ International Hot Atom Chemistry Symposium (meeting series)
♦ International Hotel Alliance (inactive)
♦ International Hotel Association / see International Hotel and Restaurant Association (#13813)
♦ International Hotelmen's Association (inactive)

♦ International Hotel and Restaurant Association (IH&RA) 13813

Association internationale de l'hôtellerie et de la restauration (IH&RA)
Headquarters Ave Theodore Flournoy 5, 1207 Geneva, Switzerland. T. +41225948145. E-mail: admin@ih-ra.org – president@ih-ra.org.
URL: http://www.ih-ra.org/
History 18 Mar 1946, Paris (France). Replaces *Union internationale des hôteliers (UIH, inactive)*, set up Jun 1869, Koblenz (Germany), and *'International Hotel Mens Alliance'*, formed Apr 1921, later known as *International Hotel Alliance (inactive)*. Bylaws created and Association recognized by UN as the representative of the private industry worldwide. New constitution and statutes came into force 1 Jan 1978. Current statutes entered into force 1 Nov 1997, when adopted present name. Moved to Lausanne (Switzerland) in 2008 when new statutes and bylaws were adopted. Former names and other names: *International Hotel Association (IHA)* – former (1946 to 1997); *Association internationale de l'hôtellerie (AIH)* – former (1946 to 1997); *Asociación Internacional de Hosteleria (AIH)* – former (1946 to 1997); *Internationaler Hotelverband* – former (1946 to 1997). Registration: RNA, No/ID: W751235588, Start date: Sep 2016, France; Start date: 23 Sep 1949, France. **Aims** Promote and defend the interests of the hotel and restaurant industry worldwide. **Structure** General Assembly (annual, at Congress); Board; Executive Committee; Chains Council; National Association Chief Executive (NACE) Council (meets at least twice a year); Finance Committee. Members can participate or appoint representatives to serve on Global Councils. **Languages** English, French. **Staff** 6.00 FTE, paid. Several voluntary. **Finance** Sources: members' dues. **Activities** Advocacy/lobbying/activism; awards/prizes/competitions; standards/guidelines. **Events** *Annual Congress* Hangzhou (China) 2017, *AHIC : Annual Arabian Hotel Investment Conference* Dubai (United Arab Emirates) 2016, *Annual Congress* Barcelona (Spain) 2015, *Annual Congress* Interlaken (Switzerland) 2014, *Annual Congress* Istanbul (Turkey) 2013. **Publications** *Hotels* (12 a year); *Members' Yearbook* (annual); *Industry Watch* – electronic newsletter. *Horwath Worldwide Hotel Study* (1999); *Into the Millennium* (1996); *IH and RA/WTO Report on Hotel Classification*. Studies, surveys, guides, papers, guidelines, toolkits in hotel management, environment, technology and automation and human resources; online members directory. Information Services: Website provides members with information on the industry worldwide.
Members National hotel and restaurant associations; international, national and regional/local hotel and restaurant chains; individual hotels and restaurants; Worldwide Partners; Industry Supporters. Members in 142 countries and territories:
Algeria, Andorra, Anguilla, Antigua-Barbuda, Argentina, Aruba, Australia, Austria, Bahamas, Bahrain, Bangladesh, Barbados, Belarus, Belgium, Belize, Benin, Bermuda, Botswana, Brazil, Bulgaria, Burkina Faso, Cambodia, Cameroon, Canada, Cayman Is, Channel Is, Chile, China, Colombia, Congo DR, Costa Rica, Côte d'Ivoire, Croatia, Cuba, Curaçao, Cyprus, Czechia, Denmark, Djibouti, Dominica, Dominican Rep, Ecuador, Egypt, Estonia, Fiji, Finland, France, Germany, Gibraltar, Greece, Grenada, Guadeloupe, Guam, Guyana, Haiti, Honduras, Hong Kong, Hungary, Iceland, India, Indonesia, Iraq, Ireland, Italy, Jamaica, Japan, Jordan, Kenya, Korea DPR, Korea Rep, Kuwait, Laos, Latvia, Lebanon, Lesotho, Libya, Liechtenstein, Lithuania, Luxembourg, Macau, Madagascar, Malaysia, Maldives, Martinique, Mexico, Montenegro, Myanmar, Nepal, Netherlands, New Caledonia, New Zealand, Nicaragua, Nigeria, Norway, Oman, Pakistan, Palau, Panama, Paraguay, Peru, Philippines, Poland,

Portugal, Puerto Rico, Réunion, Romania, Russia, Rwanda, Senegal, Singapore, Slovakia, Slovenia, South Africa, Spain, Sri Lanka, St Barthélemy, St Kitts-Nevis, St Lucia, St Martin, St Vincent-Grenadines, Sweden, Switzerland, Taiwan, Tanzania UR, Thailand, Trinidad-Tobago, Tunisia, Türkiye, Turks-Caicos, Uganda, UK, Ukraine, United Arab Emirates, Uruguay, USA, Venezuela, Vietnam, Virgin Is UK, Virgin Is USA, Zambia, Zimbabwe.

Consultative Status Consultative status granted from: *UNCTAD (#20285)* (General Category); *World Intellectual Property Organization (WIPO, #21593)* (Permanent Observer Status); *OAS (#17629)*. **IGO Relations** Observer status with: *ILO (#11123)*. Affiliate member of: *World Tourism Organization (UNWTO, #21861)*. Accredited by: *United Nations Office at Vienna (UNOV, #20604)*. Associated with Department of Global Communications of the United Nations. Observer to: *Intergovernmental Committee of the International Convention of Rome for the Protection of Performers, Producers of Phonograms and Broadcasting Organizations (#11474)*. Monitors and lobbies the United Nations, its agencies and other IGOs whose work directly or indirectly impacts the industry, including: ILO; *OECD (#17693)*. *UNEP (#20299)*; *UNESCO (#20322)*; UNWTO; *WHO (#20950)*; *The World Bank Group (#21218)*; *World Intellectual Property Organization (WIPO, #21593)*; *World Trade Organization (WTO, #21864)*. **NGO Relations** Board member of: *European Foundation for the Accreditation of Hotel School Programmes (EFAP, #07341)*. Member of: *Hotel Technology Next Generation (HTNG, #10952)*. In liaison with technical committees of: *International Organization for Standardization (ISO, #14473)*. Instrumental in setting up: *IHRA Foundation for the Future (FFF, #11113)*, 1989. Regional hotel associations: *Caribbean Hotel and Tourism Association (CHTA, #03516)*; *Inter-American Hotel Association (IAHA, no recent information)*; *Nordic Union Hotels, Restaurants, Catering and Tourism (NU HRCT, #17454)*.
[2021/XB2110/**B**]

- ♦ International Hotel Sales Management Association / see Hospitality Sales and Marketing Association International (#10948)
- ♦ International Hotels Environment Initiative / see Sustainable Hospitality Alliance (#20061)
- ♦ International Hot Rod Association (internationally oriented national body)
- ♦ International House Association (inactive)
- ♦ International House of Japan (internationally oriented national body)
- ♦ International House, New York (internationally oriented national body)
- ♦ International House Sonnenberg (internationally oriented national body)

♦ International House World Organization (IHWO) 13814

Main Office Unity Wharf, 13 Mill St, London, SE1 2BH, UK. T. +442073946580. Fax +442073942149. E-mail: info@ihworld.com.
URL: http://www.ihworld.com/

History 1953, by John and Brita Haycraft. Teacher training courses commenced in 1962. Registration: Companies House, No/ID: 04423501, England and Wales. **Aims** As a network of *schools* and institutions in *language teaching* and ancillary services: promote high standards in education and business by raising teaching standards; develop communication and *international understanding* through language-learning within and outside the classroom. **Structure** International House Affiliate Network (executive body) provides central coordination for affiliated schools and is part of the charitable trust that runs International House London (UK). **Activities** Human resources recruits staff on behalf of affiliates and coordinates movement of staff within International House schools. Affiliate Network organizes annually: Directors' Conference; Directors of Studies' Conference; several educational conferences. Makes regular visits to affiliates for communication, exchange of ideas and information, provision of in-service development opportunities for staff and ensuring that the spirit and terms of the affiliation agreement are being honoured. Sanctions use of the internationally known name 'International House'. Provides advice and support through network of accumulated knowledge and experience. Develops teacher training methods which are now the model for the Cambridge/RSA Certificate. **Events** *International House Directors Conference and AGM* London (UK) 2021, *International House Directors Conference* Sydney, NSW (Australia) 2020, *International House Directors Conference* Catania (Italy) 2019, *International House Directors Conference* Sofia (Bulgaria) 2018, *International House Directors Conference* Dubai (United Arab Emirates) 2014. **Publications** Newsletters; handbooks; educational materials. **Members** Member schools (over 100), affiliated to IHWO under the terms of an affiliation agreement, in 34 countries:
Argentina, Armenia, Australia, Belarus, Brazil, Czechia, Egypt, Estonia, Finland, France, Georgia, Germany, Hungary, Ireland, Italy, Lithuania, Malaysia, Mexico, Mongolia, New Zealand, North Macedonia, Poland, Portugal, Romania, Russia, Singapore, South Africa, Spain, Switzerland, Türkiye, UK, Ukraine, Uruguay, USA.
NGO Relations Member of: *Global Alliance of Education and Language Associations (GAELA)*.
[2021/XE3905/**E**]

♦ International Housing Association (IHA) 13815

Contact c/o Natl Assn of Home Builders, 1201 15th St NW, Washington DC 20005, USA. T. +12022668182. E-mail: ihasecretariat@nahb.org.
URL: http://www.internationalhousingassociation.org/

History 1984. **Aims** Provide an international forum for the world's housing industry leaders to allow them to explore and address common issues related to housing and home building. **Languages** English, Spanish. **Staff** 2.00 FTE, paid. **Activities** Events/meetings. **Events** *Annual Meeting* Orlando, FL (USA) 2012, *Annual Meeting* Orlando, FL (USA) 2011.
Members Organizations in 12 countries and territories:
Australia, Canada, France, Japan, Malaysia, Mexico, Myanmar, Norway, Peru, South Africa, Taiwan, USA.
Included in the above, 1 organization listed in this Yearbook:
NGO Relations Member of: *International Housing and Home Warranty Association (IHHWA, #13816)*.
[2018.02.16/XJ6373/**C**]

- ♦ International Housing Association (inactive)
- ♦ International Housing Coalition (internationally oriented national body)

♦ International Housing and Home Warranty Association (IHHWA) . . . 13816

Chairman NHBC – 6th floor, 1 Minster Court, Mincing Lane, London, EC3R 7AA, UK. T. +442076484077.
URL: http://www.ihhwa.com/

History Set up 1993, as *Association of European Home Warranty Organisations (AEHWO, see: #13816)*. Expanded Oct 2010, when set up under current title with AEHWO as a body within IHHWA. **Aims** Promote the benefits of construction guarantees and warranties at international level. **Structure** Includes *Association of European Home Warranty Organisations (AEHWO, see: #13816)*. **Events** *Conference* Dublin (Ireland) 2020, *Conference* Tokyo (Japan) 2017, *Conference* Vancouver, BC (Canada) 2014, *International Seminar on Development of Housing Finance and Guarantee Scheme* Seoul (Korea Rep) 2013, *Conference* Cape Town (South Africa) 2011.
Members Full in 9 countries:
Canada, France, Ireland, Japan, Korea Rep, Namibia, Netherlands, South Africa, Sweden, UK, USA.
Included in the above, 1 organization listed in this Yearbook:
[2018/XJ6372/y/**C**]

♦ International Humana People to People Movement (HPP) 13817

Contact Av Louis-Casaï 18, 1209 Geneva, Switzerland. T. +41227477540. Fax +41227477616.
Headquarters Murgwi Estate, Shamva, PO Box 6345, Harare, HARARE, Zimbabwe. T. +2634717811. Fax +2634716427. E-mail: hqchair@humana.org.
URL: http://www.humana.org/

History Grew out of anti-apartheid movement in Europe and Southern Africa during 1970s. Sometimes referred to simply as *Humana*. **Aims** Contribute to development worldwide. **Structure** Includes: *Federation for Associations Connected to the International Humana People to People Movement (see: #13817)*. Headquarters in Zimbabwe. **Languages** English, French, Portuguese. **Staff** 1000.00 FTE, paid. **Activities** Projects.
Members in 34 countries:
Angola, Austria, Belize, Botswana, Brazil, Bulgaria, China, Congo DR, Denmark, Ecuador, Estonia, Finland, Germany, Guinea-Bissau, India, Italy, Laos, Latvia, Lithuania, Malawi, Mozambique, Namibia, Netherlands, Norway, Poland, Portugal, Romania, South Africa, Spain, Sweden, UK, USA, Zambia, Zimbabwe.
[2013.07.23/XF4933/s/**F**]

- ♦ International Human Development Project (internationally oriented national body)

♦ International Human Epigenome Consortium (IHEC) 13818

Chair Executive Committee Canadian Inst of Health Research, 160 Elgin Street, 9th Floor, Address Locator 4809A, Ottawa ON K1A 0W9, Canada. E-mail: info@ihec-epigenomes.org.
URL: http://ihec-epigenomes.org/

History 2010. **Aims** Provide free access to high-resolution reference human epigenome maps for normal and disease *cell* types. **Structure** Executive Committee; International Scientific Steering Committee. Working Groups (5). **Languages** English. **Staff** Voluntary. **Finance** National and regional scientific funding agencies. **Activities** Events/meetings; knowledge management/information dissemination; research and development; research/documentation. **Events** *Annual Meeting* Banff, AB (Canada) 2019, *Annual Meeting* Hong Kong (Hong Kong) 2018, *Annual Meeting* Berlin (Germany) 2017, *Annual Meeting* Brussels (Belgium) 2016, *Annual Meeting* Tokyo (Japan) 2015. **Publications** Manuscripts; papers. **Information Services** *IHEC Data Portal*.
Members Countries and agencies contributing reference epigenomes (7):
Canada, Germany, Hong Kong, Japan, Korea Rep, Singapore, USA.
Included in the above, 1 organization listed in this Yearbook:
Countries and agencies supportive if IHEC goals (4):
Australia, France, Italy, UK.
Included in the above, 1 organization listed in this Yearbook:
[2018/XM4695/**C**]

♦ International Human Frontier Science Program Organization (HFSPO) 13819

SG 12 quai Saint-Jean, BP 10034, 67080 Strasbourg CEDEX, France. T. +33388215123. Fax +33388328897. E-mail: communications@hfsp.org.
URL: http://www.hfsp.org/

History Oct 1989, Strasbourg (France). Registration: France. **Aims** Promote basic *research* on the elucidation of the sophisticated and complex mechanisms of living *organisms*. **Structure** Board of Trustees; Council of Scientists; Secretariat. **Languages** English. **Staff** 16.00 FTE, paid. **Finance** Funded by voluntary contributions of Management Supporting Parties. **Activities** Financial and/or material support. **Events** *Annual Awardees Meeting* Leuven (Belgium) 2020, *Annual Awardees Meeting* Tokyo (Japan) 2019, *Annual Awardees Meeting* Toronto, ON (Canada) 2018, *Annual Awardees Meeting* Lisbon (Portugal) 2017, *Annual Awardees Meeting* Singapore (Singapore) 2016. **Publications** Reports; articles; position papers.
Members in 14 countries:
Australia, Canada, France, Germany, India, Israel, Italy, Japan, Korea Rep, New Zealand, Singapore, Switzerland, UK, USA.
Regional member (1):
European Commission (EC, #06633).
[2022/XM2677/y/**D**]

- ♦ International Human Genetics Society (no recent information)
- ♦ International Humanist and Ethical Union / see Humanists International (#10972)
- ♦ International Humanist and Ethical Youth Organization / see Young Humanists International (#21993)
- ♦ International Humanistic Management Association (unconfirmed)
- ♦ International Humanistic Psychology Association (internationally oriented national body)
- ♦ International Humanitarian Aid Organization of Orthodox Christians in the United States and Canada / see International Orthodox Christian Charities
- ♦ International Humanitarian Centre for Rehabilitation of Survivors after Chernobyl Disaster (internationally oriented national body)

♦ International Humanitarian Fact-Finding Commission (IHFFC) 13820

Commission internationale humanitaire d'établissement des faits (CIHEF)

Contact Kochergasse 10, 3003 Bern, Switzerland. T. +41584654200. Fax +41584650767. E-mail: info@ihffc.org.
Contact address not obtained.
URL: http://www.ihffc.org/

History 8 Jun 1977. Established by Article 90 of Protocol I Additional to the Geneva Conventions. Full title of Treaty: *Protocol Additional to the Geneva Conventions of 12 August 1949 and Relating to the Protection of Victims of International Armed Conflicts (Protocol I, 1977)*. First meeting (when the Commission became operational): 12-13 Mar 1992, Bern (Switzerland). Election / re-election of the 15 members of the Commission by Diplomatic Conference: 29 Oct 1996, Bern; 9 Nov 2001, Bern; 7 Dec 2006, Bern; 9 Dec 2011, Bern; 8 Dec 2016, Bern; 19 Nov 2021, Bern. **Aims** Inquire into any facts alleged to be a grave breach as defined in the four 1949 *Geneva Conventions* and their Protocol I, or other serious *violation* of the Conventions or of Protocol I, concerning protection of *victims* of international *armed conflict*; inquire into other violations of humanitarian *law*, including those arising in non-international armed conflicts, provided all parties to the conflict agree; through good offices, facilitate restoration of respect for the Conventions and Protocol I. **Structure** Commission, consisting of 1 President, 4 Vice-Presidents and 10 members, all serving in their personal capacity, not as representatives of their countries of origin. Secretariat, headed by General Secretary. **Languages** English, French. **Staff** 3.00 FTE, paid. **Finance** State Parties pay a proportion of administrative expenses. **Events** *Annual Meeting – 2nd Part* Geneva (Switzerland) 2022, *Annual Meeting – 1st Part* Geneva (Switzerland) 2022, *Annual Meeting* Switzerland 2021, *Meeting* Geneva (Switzerland) 2013, *Meeting* Geneva (Switzerland) 2012. **Publications** Reports.
Members States accepting the competence of IHFFC based on Protocol I (76):
Algeria, Argentina, Australia, Austria, Belarus, Belgium, Bolivia, Bosnia-Herzegovina, Brazil, Bulgaria, Burkina Faso, Canada, Cape Verde, Chile, Colombia, Congo DR, Cook Is, Costa Rica, Croatia, Cyprus, Czechia, Denmark, Estonia, Finland, Germany, Greece, Guinea, Hungary, Iceland, Ireland, Italy, Japan, Korea Rep, Kuwait, Laos, Lesotho, Liechtenstein, Lithuania, Luxembourg, Madagascar, Malawi, Mali, Malta, Monaco, Mongolia, Montenegro, Namibia, Netherlands, New Zealand, North Macedonia, Norway, Palestine, Panama, Paraguay, Poland, Portugal, Qatar, Romania, Rwanda, Serbia, Seychelles, Slovakia, Slovenia, Spain, St Kitts-Nevis, St Vincent-Grenadines, Sweden, Switzerland, Tajikistan, Togo, Tonga, Trinidad-Tobago, UK, Ukraine, United Arab Emirates, Uruguay.
IGO Relations Observer status with (1): *United Nations (UN, #20515)* (General Assembly). *European Commission (EC, #06633)*; *International Criminal Court (ICC, #13108)*. Relevant treaties: *Geneva Convention for the Amelioration of the Condition of the Wounded and Sick in Armed Forces in the Field, 1949 (1949)*; *Geneva Convention for the Amelioration of the Condition of Wounded, Sick and Shipwrecked Members of Armed Forces at Sea (1949)*; *Geneva Convention Relative to the Treatment of Prisoners of War (1949)*; *Geneva Convention on Torture (1949)*. Additional protocol: *Protocol II Additional to the Four 1949 Geneva Conventions Relating to the Protection of Victims of Non-international Armed Conflicts (1977)*. Earlier related treaties: *Convention for the Amelioration of the Condition of the Wounded in Armies in the Field, 1864 (Geneva convention, 1864)*; *Convention de Genève pour la Protection des Blessés dans les Armées en Campagne, 1906 (Convention de Genève, 1906)*; *Convention for the Adaptation of the Principles of the Geneva Convention to Maritime War (1907)*; *Geneva Convention for the Amelioration of the Condition of the Wounded and Sick in Armies in the Field, 1929 (1929)*.
[2021.09.02/XE1668/**E***]

♦ International Humanitarian Studies Association (IHSA) 13821

Interim Pres International Institute of Social Sciences, Kortenaerkade 12, 2518 AX The Hague, Netherlands. E-mail: info@ihsa.info.
URL: http://www.ihsa.info/

History Feb 2009, Groningen (Netherlands). Founded at 1st World Conference of Humanitarian Studies. **Aims** Strengthen and advance a global network of universities, specialized research centres, intergovernmental and non-governmental organizations in order to enhance a better alignment between knowledge, policy and practice in resolving humanitarian crises. **Structure** Board, comprising President, General Secretary and 8 members. **Activities** Events/meetings. **Events** *World conference* Paris (France) 2021, *World conference* The Hague (Netherlands) 2018, *World conference* Addis Ababa (Ethiopia) 2016, *World conference* Istanbul (Turkey) 2013, *World conference* Boston, MA (USA) 2011. **Members** Individuals. Membership countries not specified.
NGO Relations Member of (1): *Active Learning Network for Accountability and Performance in Humanitarian Action (ALNAP, #00101)*.
[2021/XJ2810/v/**C**]

- ♦ International Humanitarian Zoophile Office (inactive)
- ♦ International Humanify Foundation (internationally oriented national body)
- ♦ International Human Microbiome Consortium (unconfirmed)
- ♦ International Human Motricity Network (unconfirmed)

♦ International Human-Powered Vehicle Association (IHPVA) 13822

Association internationale pour les véhicules à traction humaine

Treas PO Box 357, Cutten CA 95534-0357, USA. Fax +18773331029.
Sec address not obtained.
Pres address not obtained.
URL: http://www.ihpva.org/

History 1975. **Aims** Promote improvement, innovation and creativity in the design and development of human-powered transportation; sanction records and racing of non-traditional HP vehicles. **Structure** Board, including officers. **Languages** English. **Staff** Voluntary. **Finance** Members' dues. **Activities** Provides a forum where inventors may test and evaluate new machines through races, symposia and contest. Organizes annual World Human Powered Speed Challenge. Keeps and sanctions records. **Events** *Annual membership meeting* Battle Mountain, NV (USA) 2007, *Meeting* Adrian, MI (USA) 1989. **Publications** *HPV News* (2-4 a year) – newsletter; *Human Power* (1-4 a year) – journal.

Members Individuals in 37 countries:
Argentina, Australia, Austria, Belgium, Brazil, Bulgaria, Canada, Chile, China, Czechia, Denmark, Finland, France, Germany, Greece, Hungary, Iceland, Iran Islamic Rep, Ireland, Italy, Japan, Mexico, Netherlands, New Zealand, Norway, Poland, Portugal, Slovenia, South Africa, Spain, Sri Lanka, Sweden, Switzerland, Thailand, Türkiye, UK, USA. [2016/XD8066/**D**]

♦ International Human Resource Management Conference (meeting series)
♦ International Human Rights and Anti-Corruption Society (internationally oriented national body)
♦ International Human Rights Association of American Minorities (internationally oriented national body)
♦ International Human Rights Clinic / see International Human Rights Law Clinic
♦ International Human Rights Committee for Protection (internationally oriented national body)
♦ International Human Rights Council (internationally oriented national body)
♦ International Human Rights Funders Group / see Human Rights Funders Network
♦ International Human Rights Law Clinic (internationally oriented national body)
♦ International Human Rights Law Group / see Global Rights
♦ International Human Rights Law Institute (internationally oriented national body)
♦ International Human Rights Observer (internationally oriented national body)
♦ International Human Rights Protector's Group (internationally oriented national body)
♦ International Human Science Research Conference (meeting series)
♦ International Human Unity Conference (meeting series)

♦ International Humic Substances Society (IHSS) 13823

Sec Inst de Recursos Naturales y Agrobiologia Sevilla, Consejo Superior de Investigaciones Cientificas (IRNAS-CSIC), Avenida Reina Mercedes 10, 41012 Seville, Sevilla, Spain. T. +34954624711.
Pres Univ di Bari, Dipto Biologia e Chimica e Agro-Forestale e Ambientale, Via G Amendola 165/A, 70126 Bari BA, Italy. T. +39805442857.
URL: http://humic-substances.org/

History 11 Sep 1981, Denver CO (USA), to bring together scientists in the coal, soil and water sciences with interest in humic substances and to provide opportunities for them to exchange ideas. **Aims** Advance the knowledge and research of natural organic matter in soil and water. **Structure** Board of Directors, including Past President, President, Vice President, Secretary, Treasurer and 2 members. **Languages** English. **Staff** Voluntary. **Finance** Sources: members' dues. **Activities** Collects standard samples of humic and fulvic acids from lignite, fresh water, a mineral soil and an organic soil, and assembles characterization data. Has added reference samples that are a source of humic materials for research. Convenes biennial international conference, which bring together scientists from the soil, coal, freshwater and marine sciences, convened by leading scientists in collaboration with the IHSS Board. Provides limited support for travel and training through travel support awards and training awards. **Events** *Conference* Estes Park, CO (USA) 2021, *Conference* Varna (Bulgaria) 2018, *Biennial Conference* Kanazawa (Japan) 2016, *Biennial Conference / Meeting* Hangzhou (China) 2012, *Nordic-Baltic symposium* Drøbak (Norway) 2011. **Publications** *Humic Substances* – 3 vols.

Members Full in 50 countries and territories:
Argentina, Australia, Austria, Belgium, Brazil, Bulgaria, Canada, China, Colombia, Costa Rica, Czechia, Denmark, Egypt, Estonia, Finland, France, Germany, Greece, Hungary, India, Indonesia, Iran Islamic Rep, Ireland, Israel, Italy, Japan, Jordan, Kazakhstan, Latvia, Lithuania, Malaysia, Mexico, Monaco, Morocco, Netherlands, Norway, Poland, Portugal, Romania, Russia, Slovakia, South Africa, Spain, Sweden, Switzerland, Taiwan, Türkiye, UK, USA, Venezuela. [2012.07.04/XD5829/**C**]

♦ International Hunting Council / see International Council for Game and Wildlife Conservation (#13024)
♦ International Hunting and Shooting Council / see International Council for Game and Wildlife Conservation (#13024)

♦ International Huntington Association (IHA) 13824

Pres Vognsneset 30, 4643 Søgne, Norway.
URL: https://huntington-disease.org/

History Founded 1979, Oxford (UK), first international meeting having been held in 1974. Also referred to as *International Huntington's Disease Association.* **Aims** Promote international collaboration in the search for a cure for Huntington's Disease (HD); assist in organizing and developing new and existing national HD organizations; cooperate with other voluntary *health* agencies and international health organizations. **Structure** Executive Committee; European sub-organization: *European Huntington Association (EHA, #07509).* **Languages** English. **Staff** 1.00 FTE, voluntary. **Finance** Members' dues. Donations. **Activities** Events/meetings; standards/guidelines; research and development. **Events** *Biennial Conference* Rio de Janeiro (Brazil) 2013, *Biennial Conference* Melbourne, VIC (Australia) 2011, *Biennial Conference* Vancouver, BC (Canada) 2009, *Biennial Conference* Dresden (Germany) 2007, *World congress on Huntington's disease* Dresden (Germany) 2007. **Publications** Information material; video tapes.

Members Full national voluntary societies legally registered in their particular countries. Associate Huntington societies under formation and individuals. Members in 56 countries and territories:
Argentina, Australia, Austria, Belgium, Brazil, Bulgaria, Canada, Chile, China, Colombia, Cuba, Cyprus, Czechia, Denmark, Egypt, Finland, France, Germany, Greece, Hungary, India, Iran Islamic Rep, Ireland, Israel, Italy, Japan, Korea Rep, Lithuania, Malta, Mexico, Netherlands, New Zealand, Northern Ireland, Norway, Oman, Pakistan, Peru, Poland, Portugal, Romania, Russia, Slovakia, Slovenia, South Africa, Spain, Sri Lanka, Sweden, Switzerland, Taiwan, Thailand, Türkiye, UK, Uruguay, USA, Venezuela, Zimbabwe.

NGO Relations Member of: *European Federation of Neurological Societies (EFNS, inactive).* Associate member of: *EURORDIS – Rare Diseases Europe (#09175).* [2022/XE2572/**E**]

♦ International Huntington's Disease Association / see International Huntington Association (#13824)
♦ International Hurricane Center / see International Hurricane Research Center
♦ International Hurricane Research Center (internationally oriented national body)
♦ International Husserl and Phenomenological Research Society (see: #21725)
♦ International Hydatidological Association / see International Association of Hydatidology (#11949)
♦ International Hydatidology Association / see International Association of Hydatidology (#11949)
♦ International Hydrodynamics Committee (see: #15318)
♦ International Hydrographic Bureau / see International Hydrographic Organization (#13825)

♦ International Hydrographic Organization (IHO) 13825

Organisation hydrographique internationale (OHI) – Organización Hidrografica Internacional

SG 4b quai Antoine 1er, BP445, 98011 Monte Carlo, Monaco. T. +37793108100. Fax +37793108140. E-mail: info@iho.int.
URL: http://www.iho.int/

History Established Jun 1919, London (UK), as *International Hydrographic Bureau (IHB) – Bureau hydrographique international,* at International Hydrographic Conference, following conferences held in 1899, Washington DC (USA), and 1908 and 1912, St Petersburg (Russia). Activities commenced in Jun 1921. Current legal status and name adopted 22 Sep 1970, on entry into force of an intergovernmental convention whose official custodian is the Government of the Principality of Monaco. Statutes registered in *'UNTS 1/10764'.* **Aims** Ensure that all the world's seas, oceans and navigable waters are surveyed and charted. **Structure** *International Hydrographic Conference – Conférence hydrographique internationale* (every 5 years, in Monaco); *International Hydrographic Bureau (IHB) – Bureau hydrographique international (BHI)*; Directing Committee; Permanent headquarters in Monaco. Meetings open to observers by invitation only. Committees and Working Groups, including: *Joint IOC/IHO Guiding Committee for the General Bathymetric Chart of the Oceans (GEBCO, #16137).* Regional Hydrographic Commissions (16):
- *Arctic Regional Hydrographic Commission (ARHC, #01101);*
- *Baltic Sea Hydrographic Commission (BSHC, see: #13825);*
- *East Asia Hydrographic Commission (EAHC, see: #13825);*
- *Eastern Atlantic Hydrographic Commission (EAtHC, see: #13825);*
- *Hydrographic Commission on Antarctica (HCA, see: #13825);*
- *Mediterranean and Black Seas Hydrographic Commission (MBSHC, see: #13825);*
- *Meso-American-Caribbean Sea Hydrographic Commission (MACHC, see: #13825);*
- *North Sea Hydrographic Commission (NSHC, see: #13825);*
- *Nordic Hydrographic Commission (NHC, see: #13825);*
- *North Indian Ocean Hydrographic Commission (NIOHC, see: #13825);*
- *ROPME Sea Area Hydrographic Commission (RSAHC, #18971);*
- *South East Pacific Hydrographic Commission (SEPHC, see: #13825);*
- *Southern African and Islands Hydrographic Commission (SAIHC, see: #13825);*
- *South West Atlantic Hydrographic Commission (SWAtHC, see: #13825);*
- *South West Pacific Hydrographic Commission (SWPHC, see: #13825);*
- *US/Canada Hydrographic Commission (US/CHC, see: #13825).*

Languages English, French. **Staff** 19.00 FTE, paid. The *Administrative Tribunal of the International Labour Organization (ILO Tribunal, #00118)* is competent to settle disputes. **Finance** Members' dues (based on declared national tonnage). Budget (annual): about euro 2.7 million. **Activities** Capacity building; knowledge management/information dissemination; networking/liaising; research and development; standards/guidelines; training/education. Participates in ICO Sponsored Regional International Bathymetric Chart Projects. **Events** *Conference* Cape Verde 2022, *Conference* Lisbon (Portugal) 2021, *Session* Busan (Korea Rep) 2019, *Tides, Water Level and Currents Working group Meeting* Busan (Korea Rep) 2019, *Meeting* Cape Town (South Africa) 2019. **Publications** *IHO Yearbook*; *International Hydrographic Review* – online and electronic. Annual Report. Guidelines; manuals; regulations; conference proceedings. **Information Services** *Electronic Chart Display and Information Systems (ECDIS).*

Members Governments of 85 states (rights of membership suspended):
Algeria, Argentina, Australia, Bahrain, Bangladesh, Belgium, Brazil, Brunei Darussalam, Cameroon, Canada, Chile, China, Colombia, Congo DR (*), Croatia, Cuba, Cyprus, Denmark, Dominican Rep (*), Ecuador, Egypt, Estonia, Fiji, Finland, France, Georgia, Germany, Greece, Guatemala, Iceland, India, Indonesia, Iran Islamic Rep, Ireland, Italy, Jamaica, Japan, Korea DPR, Korea Rep, Kuwait, Latvia, Malaysia, Mauritius, Mexico, Monaco, Montenegro, Morocco, Mozambique, Myanmar, Netherlands, New Zealand, Nigeria, Norway, Oman, Pakistan, Papua New Guinea, Peru, Philippines, Poland, Portugal, Qatar, Romania, Russia, Saudi Arabia, Serbia, Singapore, Slovenia, South Africa, Spain, Sri Lanka, Suriname, Sweden, Syrian AR, Thailand, Tonga, Trinidad-Tobago, Tunisia, Türkiye, UK, Ukraine, United Arab Emirates, Uruguay, USA, Venezuela, Vietnam.

IGO Relations
- *Antarctic Treaty (AT, #00850);*
- *Association of Caribbean States (ACS, #02411);*
- *FAO (#09260);*
- *Group on Earth Observations (GEO, #10735);*
- *Intergovernmental Oceanographic Commission (IOC, #11496);*
- *International Civil Aviation Organization (ICAO, #12581);*
- *International Maritime Organization (IMO, #14102);*
- *International Mobile Satellite Organization (IMSO, #14174);*
- *International Seabed Authority (ISBA, #14813);*
- *International Tribunal for the Law of the Sea (ITLOS, #15731);*
- *Joint WMO-IOC Technical Commission for Oceanography and Marine Meteorology (JCOMM, #16151);*
- *Maritime Organization of West and Central Africa (MOWCA, #16582);*
- *The Mediterranean Science Commission (CIESM, #16674);*
- *Pacific Community (SPC, #17942);*
- *Pan American Institute of Geography and History (PAIGH, #18113);*
- *Port Management Association of West and Central Africa (PMAWCA, #18463);*
- *Regional Committee of United Nations Global Geospatial Information Management for Asia and the Pacific (UN-GGIM-AP, #18766);*
- *Regional Organization for the Protection of the Marine Environment (ROPME, #18805);*
- *UNDP (#20292);*
- *UNESCO (#20322);*
- *United Nations (UN, #20515);*
- *United Nations Committee of Experts on Global Geospatial Information Management (UN-GGIM, #20540);*
- *United Nations Economic Commission for Africa (ECA, #20554);*
- *United Nations Group of Experts on Geographical Names (UNGEGN, #20569);*
- *World Meteorological Organization (WMO, #21649).*

NGO Relations
- *Asia-Pacific Heads of Maritime Safety Agencies (APHoMSA, #01922);*
- *Chart and Nautical Instrument Trade Association (CNITA);*
- *Comité International Radio-Maritime (CIRM, #04186);*
- *Commonwealth Association of Surveying and Land Economy (CASLE, #04313);*
- *Cruise Lines International Association (CLIA, #04973);*
- *European Federation of Marine Science and Technology Societies (EFMS, inactive);*
- *European Harbour Masters' Committee (EHMC, #07449);*
- *European Umbrella Organization for Geographical Information (EUROGI, #08964);*
- *International Federation of Surveyors (FIG, #13561);*
- *International Association of Antarctica Tour Operators (IAATO, #11702);*
- *International Association of Geodesy (IAG, #11914);*
- *International Association of Institutes of Navigation (IAIN, #11965);*
- *International Association of Marine Aids to Navigation and Lighthouse Authorities (IALA, #12013);*
- *International Association of Ports and Harbors (IAPH, #12096);*
- *International Cartographic Association (ICA, #12446);*
- *International Chamber of Shipping (ICS, #12535);*
- *International Council for Science (ICSU, inactive);*
- *International Electrotechnical Commission (IEC, #13255);*
- *International Federation of Hydrographic Societies (IFHS, #13453);*
- *International Geographical Union (IGU, #13713);*
- *International Harbour Masters' Association (IHMA, #13774);*
- *International Maritime Pilots' Association (IMPA, #14103);*
- *International Organization for Standardization (ISO, #14473);*
- *International Society for Mine Surveying (ISM, #15272);*
- *International Society for Photogrammetry and Remote Sensing (ISPRS, #15362);*
- *UN-GGO: Geospatial Societies (UN-GGIM GS, #20324);*
- *Radio Technical Commission for Aeronautics (RTCA);*
- *Radio Technical Commission for Maritime Services (RTCM);*
- *Scientific Committee on Antarctic Research (SCAR, #19147).*

[2019/XB2115/**B***]

♦ International Hydrological Programme (IHP) 13826

Programme hydrologique international (PHI) – Programa Hidrológico Internacional (PHI)

Dir Water Sciences Div – UNESCO, 1 rue Miollis, 75732 Paris CEDEX 15, France. T. +33145684001. Fax +33145685811. E-mail: ihp@unesco.org.
SG Dept of Irrigation and Drainage, Jalan Sultan Salahuddin, 50626 Kuala Lumpur, Malaysia. T. +60326982618 – +60378740188. Fax +60326914282.
URL: http://www.unesco.org/water/ihp/

History 1 Jan 1975, within the framework of *UNESCO (#20322),* by decision of 17th and 18th sessions of UNESCO General Conference, to take over activities of the Coordinating Council of *International Hydrological Decade (IHD)* (1965-1975). Regional network of *UNESCO Office, Jakarta – Regional Bureau for Sciences in Asia and the Pacific (#20313).* **Aims** Improve *living conditions* of populations through scientific and technological development of water sciences using holistic, multi-objective and multi-dimensional approaches, based on Dublin (Ireland) guiding principles, Agenda 21, Science for the 21st Century (Budapest) and the Santa Cruz de la Sierra Declaration. **Structure** *Intergovernmental Council of the International Hydrological Programme – Conseil intergouvernemental du Programme hydrologique international – Consejo Intergubernamental del Programa Hidrológico Internacional* comprises representatives of member countries elected at UNESCO General Conference. Geographical regions have their own programmes. **Activities** Assessment, management and conservation of water resources; support to scientific research in specific areas; training of specialists; strengthening networks of hydraulics, hydrology and water resource research centres; support for publication and dissemination of scientific, technical and popularized documentation on hydrology and water resources via the Internet; assistance to countries in formulating, preparing and negotiating extrabudgetary projects. **Events** *International Symposium on Land Subsidence* Delft (Netherlands) 2021, *International Symposium on Land Subsidence* Delft (Netherlands) 2020, *NOVATECH : International Conference on Sustainable Techniques* *and Strategies in Urban Water Management* Lyon (France) 2019, *Colloque international sur les sécheresses, les étiages et les déficits en eau* Paris (France) 2019, *Water Science/Policy Interface Colloquium* Paris (France) 2018. **Publications** Studies; reports; technical documents. Information Services: *Flow Regimes from International Experimental and Network Data (FRIEND, see: #13826).* FRIEND regional flow regimes: *FRIEND – West and Central Africa (no recent information); FRIEND/Nile Basin (see: #13826); FRIEND/Alpine and Mediterranean Hydrology (FRIEND/AMHY, see: #13826); FRIEND / Hindu Kush-Himalayan (HKH-FRIEND, see: #13826); FRIEND/Northern European (see: #13826); Caribbean Mesoamerica FRIEND (AMIGO FRIEND, see: #13826); Asian Pacific FRIEND (FRIEND/APF, no recent information); FRIEND/Southern Africa (no recent information).* Also includes: *European Regional Centre for Ecohydrology of the Polish Academy of Sciences, Lodz (ERCE PAS, #08341).* **Information Services** *IHP Publications Database.*

Members Council members (for 2002-2003), governments of 36 countries:
Angola, Argentina, Azerbaijan, Cameroon, Canada, China, Colombia, Costa Rica, Cuba, Egypt, El Salvador, Ethiopia, France, Germany, Hungary, India, Iran Islamic Rep, Italy, Japan, Jordan, Korea Rep, Libya, Malawi, Malaysia, Netherlands, Nigeria, Panama, Romania, Saudi Arabia, South Africa, Sri Lanka, Sweden, Switzerland, Tunisia, Ukraine, Yemen.

IGO Relations Works in conjunction with: *UNESCO Office, Cairo – Regional Bureau for Sciences in the Arab States (ROSTAS, #20312); UNESCO Asia-Pacific Regional Bureau for Communication and Information (#20300); UNESCO Office, Montevideo – Regional Bureau for Sciences in Latin America and the Caribbean (#20314).* Special links with: *Programme on Man and the Biosphere (MAB, #18526).* Member of: *International Commission for the Protection of the Danube River (ICPDR, #12720).* Cooperates with: *Regional Humid Tropics Hydrology and Water Resources Centre for South East Asia and the Pacific (HTC, #18787); Water Center for the Humid Tropics of Latin America and the Caribbean (#20824).* **NGO Relations** Invited to participate in the work of: *Commission mondiale d'éthique des connaissances scientifiques et des technologies de l'UNESCO (COMEST, #04235).* Observer to: *International Water-Related Associations' Liaison Committee (IWALC, #15869).* Instrumental in setting up: *Centre international de l'UNESCO pour la recherche et la formation en écohydrologie (UICERT, no recent information); International Sediment Initiative (ISI, #14827); Megacities Alliance for Water and Climate (MAWAC, #16697); UNESCO Centre for Water Law, Policy and Science.* Supports: *International Consortium on Landslides (ICL, #12917); Water and Development Information for Arid Lands Global Network (G-WADI, #20826).* [2016/XE0426/**F***]

♦ International Hydrologic Environment Society (IHES) 13827

Contact c/o Water Resources Research Ctr, School of Civil and Environmental Engineering Yeungnam Univ, 214-1 Daedong, Gyeongsan NORTH GYEONGSANG 712-749, Korea Rep. T. +82538101791. Fax +82538125048.
URL: http://www.ihes.org/

Aims Promote the study and development of the science of hydrologic environment interpreted in its widest sense; foster the application and dissemination of knowledge of the hydrologic environment. **Structure** Honorary President; President; 5 Vice-Presidents; Executive Director; 12 Directors. Council. International Advisory Committee of 11 members. Auditors (2).
Activities Furthers the progress of the understanding and application of the hydrologic environmental science through international contacts among scientists, engineers, organizations, institutions and governments; works to build capacity; organizes symposia and conferences.
Research fields:
- Hydrologic Cycle Environment – Global Environmental Hydrologic Cycle; Small Watershed Hydrologic Cycle; Large Watershed Hydrologic Cycle; Urban Watershed Hydrologic Cycle.
- River Hydrologic Environment – Surface Water Hydrologic Environment; Groundwater Hydrologic Environment; River Channel Hydrologic Environment.
- River Ecohydrology – River Ecohydrologic Environment; River Basin Vegetation Environment.
- Environmental Hydraulics and Hydrology – Ecohydraulic Environment; River Channel Hydraulic-Hydrologic Environment.
- Total Pollution Load Management and Its Hydrologic Environment – Change of Flow Regime and Pollution Load Management; Hydrologic Environment by Total Pollution Load Management; River Basin Hydrologic Environment Management.
- International Hydrological Programme (IHP) and related programmes – IHP-FRIEND Research Project; IHP-HELP Research Project; IHP Research Projects; PUB Research Projects; International Projects and Technical Development of Hydrologic Environment.

Events *International Symposium on Restoring and Managing Rivers for Future* Daegu (Korea Rep) 2011, *International symposium on hydrological environment* Daegu (Korea Rep) 2008. **Publications** Journal; other publications. [2012.07.27/XJ0589/**D**]

♦ International Hydrolyzed Protein Council (internationally oriented national body)

♦ International Hydropower Association (IHA) 13828

Main Office One Canada Square, London, E14 5AA, UK. E-mail: iha@hydropower.org.
URL: http://www.hydropower.org/

History 16 Nov 1995. Founded under the auspices of *International Hydrological Programme (IHP, #13826)* of *UNESCO (#20322).* Registration: UK. **Aims** Advance the role of sustainable hydropower in providing solutions for *renewable energy, freshwater management* and *climate change.* **Structure** Board; Central Office; Regional Offices (2); Ad-hoc Sub-Committees and Working Groups. **Languages** Chinese, English, French, Portuguese, Russian, Spanish. **Staff** 18.00 FTE, paid. **Finance** Sources: members' dues. **Activities** Advocacy/lobbying/activism; politics/policy/regulatory. **Events** *World Hydropower Congress* San José (Costa Rica) 2021, *Biennial Congress* Paris (France) 2019, *Biennial Congress* Addis Ababa (Ethiopia) 2017, *Biennial Congress* Beijing (China) 2015, *Biennial Congress* Kuching (Malaysia) 2013. **Publications** *Hydropower Today e-newsletter.* **Members** Corporate (82) and Individual (55), including 8 platinum sponsors. Members in over 80 countries. Membership countries not specified. **Consultative Status** Consultative status granted from: *UNEP (#20299).* **IGO Relations** Accredited by (1): *Green Climate Fund (GCF, #10714).* Partner of (1): *UN-Water (#20723).* **NGO Relations** Member of (2): *International Water-Related Associations' Liaison Committee (IWALC, #15869); World Water Council (WWC, #21908).* Cooperates with (3): *International Commission on Irrigation and Drainage (ICID, #12694); International Commission on Large Dams (ICOLD, #12696); World Energy Council (WEC, #21381).* In liaison with technical committees of: *International Chamber of Commerce (ICC, #12534); International Organization for Standardization (ISO, #14473).* Together with: *International Geothermal Association (IGA, #13717), International Solar Energy Society (ISES, #15564), World Bioenergy Association (WBA, #21231)* and *World Wind Energy Association (WWEA, #21937),* instrumental in setting up: *International Renewable Energy Alliance (Ren Alliance, #14716).* [2022.02.15/XD5652/**C**]

♦ International Hyperhidrosis Society (IHhS) 13829

Exec Dir 348 Cafferty Rd, Pipersville PA 18947, USA. E-mail: info@sweathelp.org.
URL: http://www.sweathelp.org/

History 2003. **Aims** Improve the quality of life of those affected by excessive *sweating.* **Structure** Board of Directors. **Languages** English, French, German, Portuguese, Spanish. **Finance** Corporate and individual donations. **Activities** Research and development; training/education; awareness raising; advocacy/lobbying/activism. **Events** *Symposium* Anaheim, CA (USA) 2005, *Symposium* Boston, MA (USA) 2005, *Symposium* London (UK) 2005, *Symposium* New York, NY (USA) 2005. **Publications** *Sweat Solutions.* **Members** Individuals worldwide. Membership countries not specified. **NGO Relations** *European Academy of Dermatology and Venereology (EADV, #05788); International League of Dermatological Societies (ILDS, #14018);* national organizations. [2021/XM0689/**D**]

♦ International Hypothermia and Temperature Management Symposium (meeting series)
♦ International Iberian Nanotechnology Laboratory (internationally oriented national body)
♦ International and Ibero-American Foundation for Administration and Public Affairs (#10030)

♦ International Ice Charting Working Group (IICWG) 13830

SG 120 Sherway Dr, Ottawa ON K1A 1P1, Canada.
URL: http://nsidc.org/noaa/iicwg/

History Oct 1999. Founded same date when charter was signed. Charter most recently updated Nov 2016. **Aims** Promote coordination of operational sea ice and iceberg information services to better meet the needs of national and international maritime clients; enhance the *safety* of *maritime* operations in ice-covered waters. **Structure** Meeting; 2 Co-Chairs; Task Teams; Secretariat. **Languages** English. **Finance** Sources: contributions of member/participating states. **Activities** Knowledge management/information dissemination; research/documentation; standards/guidelines; training/education. **Events** *Meeting* Buenos Aires (Argentina) 2022, *Meeting* 2021, *Meeting* 2020, *Meeting* Copenhagen (Denmark) 2019, *Ice information for navigating the Sub-Polar seas* Helsinki (Finland) 2018.
Members Participating agencies in 16 countries:
Argentina, Australia, Canada, Chile, Denmark, Finland, Germany, Iceland, Japan, Norway, Poland, Russia, South Africa, Sweden, UK, USA. [2021.05.19/XM7151/**F**]

♦ International Ice Cream Association (internationally oriented national body)

♦ International Ice Hockey Federation (IIHF) 13831

Fédération internationale de hockey sur glace – Internationaler Eishockey Verband

SG Brandschenkestrasse 50, Postfach 1817, 8027 Zurich ZH, Switzerland. T. +41445622200. Fax +41445622239. E-mail: office@iihf.com.
URL: http://www.iihf.com/

History 1908, Paris (France). Statutes amended: 1963, Montana (Switzerland); 1982, Nice (France); 1986, Colorado Springs CO (USA); 1990, Aosta (Italy); 1994, Venice (Italy); 1998, Lausanne (Switzerland); 2003, Marbella (Spain); 2008, Montréal QC (Canada); 2012, Tokyo (Japan); 2016, Moscow (Russia). **Aims** Encourage the playing of ice hockey; draw up uniform rules and establish a central control; promote formation of new national associations; organize regular international *competitions,* world and European championships; settle disputes between affiliated organizations. **Structure** Congress (annual and semi-annual); Council; Executive Committee; General Secretariat. Committees (14); Departments (5). Headquarters located in Zurich (Switzerland). **Languages** English. **Staff** 33.00 FTE, paid. **Activities** Awards/prizes/competitions. **Events** *General Congress* Tampere (Finland) 2022, *Half-Yearly Congress* St Petersburg (Russia) 2021, *Half-Yearly Congress* St Petersburg (Russia) 2020, *General Congress* Zurich (Switzerland) 2020, *General Congress* Zurich (Switzerland) 2020. **Publications** *Ice Times.* Annual Report; address directory; arena guide; record book.
Members National federations: Full; Associate; Affiliate. Full in 54 countries and territories:
Australia, Austria, Azerbaijan, Belarus, Belgium, Bosnia-Herzegovina, Bulgaria, Canada, China, Croatia, Czechia, Denmark, Estonia, Finland, France, Georgia, Germany, Hong Kong, Hungary, Iceland, India, Ireland, Israel, Italy, Japan, Kazakhstan, Korea DPR, Korea Rep, Latvia, Lithuania, Luxembourg, Mexico, Mongolia, Netherlands, New Zealand, Norway, Poland, Qatar, Romania, Russia, Serbia, Slovakia, Slovenia, South Africa, Spain, Sweden, Switzerland, Taiwan, Thailand, Türkiye, UK, Ukraine, United Arab Emirates, USA.
Associate in 21 countries and territories:
Andorra, Argentina, Armenia, Brazil, Greece, Indonesia, Jamaica, Kuwait, Kyrgyzstan, Liechtenstein, Macau, Malaysia, Moldova, Morocco, Nepal, North Macedonia, Oman, Philippines, Portugal, Singapore, Turkmenistan.
NGO Relations Member of (5): *Association of European Team Sports (ETS, #02546); Association of the International Olympic Winter Sports Federations (AIOWF, #02757); International Council for Coaching Excellence (ICCE, #13008); International Masters Games Association (IMGA, #14117); Olympic Movement (#17719).* Recognized by: *International Olympic Committee (IOC, #14408).* [2020/XC2116/**B**]

♦ International Ice Patrol (IIP) 13832

Patrouille internationale des glaces

Contact 4231 Suitland Rd, Suitland MD 20746, USA. T. +18602358171. E-mail: iipcomms@uscg.mil.
URL: http://www.navcen.uscg.gov/iip/

History 1914. Founded following sinking of the RMS Titanic on 15 Apr 1912. With the agreement of then 13 nations, under the provisions of Title 46, US Code, Section 738a and the *International Convention for the Safety of Life at Sea, 1974 (SOLAS, 1974),* regulations 6, the US Coast Guard conducts the International Ice Patrol. Former names and other names: *International Ice Patrol in the North Atlantic* – alias; *International Ice Patrol Service in the North Atlantic* – alias; *North Atlantic Ice Patrol* – alias; *United States Ice Patrol* – alias. **Aims** Monitor iceberg danger in the North Atlantic Ocean and provide relevant iceberg warning products to the *maritime* community. **Structure** Administered and operated by the US Coast Guard. **Languages** English. **Staff** 16.00 FTE, paid. **Finance** Costs of IIP services are financed by SOLAS member governments, with shares computed based on the tonnage of shipping passing through the patrol region. **Activities** Knowledge management/information dissemination; monitoring/evaluation. **Publications** Season bulletin; reports; daily ice bulletins; facsimile charts.
Members Governments of 17 countries:
Belgium, Canada, Denmark, Finland, France, Germany, Greece, Italy, Japan, Netherlands, Norway, Panama, Poland, Spain, Sweden, UK, USA.
NGO Relations Links with national organizations. [2021.10.25/XF0257/**F***]

♦ International Ice Patrol in the North Atlantic / see International Ice Patrol (#13832)
♦ International Ice Patrol Service in the North Atlantic / see International Ice Patrol (#13832)
♦ International Icing Federation / see International Federation Icestocksport (#13455)
♦ **International IDEA** International Institute for Democracy and Electoral Assistance (#13872)

♦ International IgA Nephropathy Network (IIgANN) 13833

Admin Officer LGH John Walls Renal Unit, Gwendolen Road, Leicester, LE5 4PW, UK.

History 1987, as *IgA Club.* Present name adopted 2000. **Aims** Provide clinicians, research students, patients and their families with information about IgA nephropathy; promote international research collaborations. **Structure** Steering Committee. **Languages** English. **Finance** Symposium revenue; charitable donations; unrestricted educational grants from industry partners. **Activities** Organizes international symposia (every 2-3 years). **Events** *Symposium* Buenos Aires (Argentina) 2018, *Symposium* Tours (France) 2016, *Symposium* Nanjing (China) 2013, *Symposium* Stresa (Italy) 2009, *Symposium* Turin (Italy) 2008. **Members** Full (350) in 50 countries. Membership countries not specified. [2014/XJ3316/**F**]

♦ International IGF Research Society / see International Society for IGF Research (#15191)
♦ International Iguana Foundation (internationally oriented national body)

♦ International Image Sensor Society (IISS) 13834

Treas Thayer School of Eng, 14 Engineering Dr, Hanover NH 03755, USA.
Pres address not obtained.
URL: http://imagesensors.org/

Structure Board of Directors. **Activities** Awards/prizes/competitions; events/meetings. **Events** *Workshop* 2021, *Workshop* Snowbird, UT (USA) 2019, *Workshop* Hiroshima (Japan) 2017, *Workshop* Vaals (Netherlands) 2015. [2019/XM5058/**C**]

♦ International Immigrants Foundation (internationally oriented national body)

♦ International Immunocompromised Host Society (ICHS) 13835

Exec Dir address not obtained.
Pres Dept of Biomedicine, University Hospital of Basel, Hebelstrasse 20, 4031 Basel BS, Switzerland.
URL: http://www.ichs.org/

History 1980. Former names and other names: *Immunocompromised Host Society (IHS)* – former. **Aims** Provide education on management and treatment of *infections* in immuno-compromised patients. **Structure** Council of 13 members. Executive Committee, comprising President, President-Elect, Vice President, 1 Past President and Executive Director. **Languages** English. **Staff** 1.00 FTE, paid. **Finance** Sources: grants. **Events** *Symposium on Infections in the Immunocompromised Host* Basel (Switzerland) 2022, *Symposium on Infections in the Immunocompromised Host* Melbourne, VIC (Australia) 2021, *Symposium on Infections in the Immunocompromised Host* Melbourne, VIC (Australia) 2020, *Symposium on Infections in the Immunocompromised Host* Athens (Greece) 2018, *Symposium on Infections in the Immunocompromised Host* Santiago (Chile) 2016. **Publications** *ICHS Informer* (4 a year) – e-newsletter. **Members** Individual; Corporate. Individual clinicians and researchers (over 600) in over 60 countries. Membership countries not specified. [2021/XD7521/**D**]

♦ International immunosuppression & Transplant Skin Cancer Collaborative (internationally oriented national body)
♦ International Inbound Services Forum (unconfirmed)
♦ International Independent Authors and Artists Consortium (unconfirmed)
♦ International Independent Christian Youth (no recent information)
♦ International Independent Ecologo-Politological University, Moscow / see International Independent University of Environmental and Political Sciences, Moscow
♦ International Independent University of Ecology and Political Sciences, Moscow / see International Independent University of Environmental and Political Sciences, Moscow
♦ International Independent University of Environmental and Political Sciences, Moscow (internationally oriented national body)

♦ International Indian Press Agency, Mexico (internationally oriented national body)

♦ International Indian Treaty Council (IITC) 13836

Conseil international des traités indiens – Consejo Internacional de los Tratados Indios (CITI)

Exec Dir 100 E Ajo Way, Tucson AZ 85713, USA. T. +15208339797. Fax +15208339799.
Office Manager The Redstone Bldg, 2940 16th St, Suite 305, San Francisco CA 94103-3664, USA. T. +14156414482.
URL: http://www.iitc.org/

History 1974, Standing Rock, SD (USA). Founded at a gathering called by the American Indian Movement and attended by over 5,000 representatives of 98 indigenous nations. Reorganized in 1977. **Aims** Seek, promote and build official participation of indigenous peoples in the United Nations and its specialized agencies and in other international fora; seek international recognition for agreements between indigenous peoples and nation-states; support the human rights, self-determination and sovereignty of indigenous peoples; oppose colonialism and its effect on indigenous peoples; build solidarity and mutual support among indigenous peoples worldwide; disseminate information about indigenous peoples, human rights issues, struggles, concerns and perspectives. **Structure** Board of Directors. Executive Director. **Languages** English, Spanish. **Activities** Awareness raising; events/meetings; guidance/assistance/consulting; knowledge management/information dissemination; networking/liaising; training/education. In particular: disseminates information about the United Nations and opportunities for involvement of grassroots indigenous communities; works to educate and build awareness about indigenous struggles among non-indigenous peoples and organizations. Setting up organizational offices to carry out information dissemination, networking and human rights programs. **Events** *Annual conference* Ustupo (Panama) 2009, *Annual Conference* Chimaltenango (Guatemala) 2008, *Annual Conference* Ft Drum, FL (USA) 2006, *Annual Conference* Canada 2005, *Annual Conference* Fall River Mills, CA (USA) 2004. **Publications** *Treaty Council News* (4 a year). Handbooks; position papers. **Members** Indigenous peoples from North, Central, South America and the Pacific. Membership countries not specified. **Consultative Status** Consultative status granted from: *ECOSOC (#05331)* (General). **IGO Relations** Accredited by (1): *United Nations Office at Vienna (UNOV, #20604).* **NGO Relations** Member of (2): *International NGO/CSO Planning Committee for Food Sovereignty (IPC, #14365); Right to Food and Nutrition Watch Consortium (#18943).* Instrumental in setting up (1): *International Committee for the Indigenous Peoples of the Americas (Incomindios).* [2023.02.20/XF5418/F]

♦ International Indigenous Council for Healing Our Spirit Worldwide (unconfirmed)

♦ International Indigenous Forum on Biodiversity (IIFB) 13837

Forum international des autochtones sur la biodiversité (FIAB) – Foro Internacional Indigena por la Biodiversidad (FIIB)

Coordinator c/o LAMA, 2515 Dole St, Room 207, Honolulu HI 96822, USA.
URL: http://iifb.indigenousportal.com/

History Nov 1996, Buenos Aires (Argentina), during 3rd Conference of the Parties to *Convention on Biological Diversity (Biodiversity convention, 1992).* **Structure** Ad Hoc Coordinating Committee; Working Groups. **Events** *Forum* Curitiba (Brazil) 2008, *Forum* Nairobi (Kenya) 2005, *Forum* Kuala Lumpur (Malaysia) 2004, *Forum* Bonn (Germany) 2001. **IGO Relations** *United Nations (UN, #20515); UNEP (#20299).* **NGO Relations** Affiliate partner of: *Biodiversity Indicators Partnership (BIP, #03242). International Alliance of the Indigenous Tribal Peoples of the Tropical Forests (IAITPTF, #11629)* is a member. Member of: *Forest Peoples Programme (FPP, #09865).* [2012/XM2684/c/F]

♦ International Indigenous Forum on Climate Change (unconfirmed)

♦ International Indigenous Women's Forum (IIWF) 13838

Foro Internacional de Mujeres Indigenas (FIMI)

Main Office Av Horacio Urteaga 534-602, Jesús Maria, 11, Lima, Peru. E-mail: info@iiwf.org.
URL: http://www.fimi-iiwf.org/

History 2000, following discussions initiated during UN Fourth World Conference on Women and the Beijing+5 meetings. **Structure** Includes *Indigenous Women's Fund – Fondo de Mujeres Indigenas.* **Members** Membership countries not specified. **NGO Relations** Member of: *Prospera – International Network of Women's Funds (INWF, #18545).* [2015/XJ8039/F]

♦ International Indigenous Working Group on HIV and AIDS (unconfirmed)
♦ International Indology Graduate Research Symposium (meeting series)

♦ International Indoor Bowls Council (IIBC) 13839

Sec/Treas c/o BIIBC, 50 Penryheol Road, Gorseinon, Swansea, SA4 4GA, UK.
URL: http://iibc.org.uk/

History 1979, as *World Indoor Bowls Council (WIBC).* Since 1999, one organization for both women and men. Current title adopted 2018. **Aims** Promote, foster and safeguard the game of indoor bowls throughout the world; encourage the growth of the *sport* on a worldwide basis; formulate the rules and regulations of indoor bowls which will apply to all *games* played under the auspices of the Council and add or revise these rules as and when required. **Structure** General Meeting (annual); Council. Executive Committee; Tournament Committee. Rotating Presidency. **Languages** English. **Staff** 2.00 FTE, paid. **Finance** Members' dues. Sponsorship. **Activities** Sporting activities. **Events** *Annual meeting* Belfast (UK) 2005, *Annual meeting* Belfast (UK) 2004, *Annual meeting* Belfast (UK) 2003.
Members Full; Associate; Affiliate. Member nations (8):
Canada, England, Guernsey, Ireland, Isle of Man, Netherlands, Scotland, Wales.
NGO Relations Member of (1): *World Bowls (WB, #21240).* [2018/XD5376/D]

♦ International Industrial Relations Association / see International Labour and Employment Relations Association (#13997)
♦ International Industrial Relations Institute (inactive)

♦ International Industry Society in Advanced Rehabilitation Technology (IISART) 13840

Sec c/o Thouvenin Anwälte, Klaussstr 33, 8034 Zurich ZH, Switzerland.
URL: https://iisart.org/

History 2011, Switzerland. **Aims** Advance and promote modern *healthcare* technology in rehabilitation for the benefit of the patient and society at large. **Structure** General Assembly; Steering Committee; Working Groups (5). **Languages** English. **Staff** Voluntary. **Finance** Sources: members' dues. **Activities** Events/meetings. **Events** *RehabWeek* Rotterdam (Netherlands) 2022, *General Assembly* Düsseldorf (Germany) 2015.
Members Company (20); Associate (5), listed in this Yearbook:
International Consortium on Rehabilitation Robotics (ICORR); International Functional Electrical Stimulation Society (IFESS, #13690); International Society for Virtual Rehabilitation (ISVR, #15543); International Society of Physical and Rehabilitation Medicine (ISPRM, #15366); World Federation for NeuroRehabilitation (WFNR, #21464).
NGO Relations Member of (1): *International Consortium for Rehabilitation Technology (ICRT, #12921).* Affiliated with (1): *International Society for Virtual Rehabilitation (ISVR, #15543).* [2022/XM4426/t/C]

♦ International Industry Working Group (IIWG) 13841

Contact c/o IATA, Route de l'Aeroport 33, PO Box 16 AIRPORT, 1215 Geneva 15, Switzerland. T. +41227702525. E-mail: lanuzam@iata.org.
URL: http://www.iata.org/whatwedo/workgroups/Pages/iiwg.aspx

History Sep 1970, under the sponsorship of: *Airport Associations Coordinating Council (AACC, inactive)* – currently *Airports Council International (ACI, #00611); International Air Transport Association (IATA, #11614); International Coordinating Council of Aerospace Industry Associations (ICCAIA, #12956);* Air Transport Association of America (ATA) – currently Airlines for America (A4A). **Aims** Promote and develop open exchange of information between airlines, aircraft manufacturers and airports with a view to minimizing interface problems through well-informed design, development and operation of both *aircraft* and *airports;* study jointly possible solutions to major problems which appear to impede or are likely to impede the development of air *transport* system; share information with a view to establishing a unified industry position on matters of common interest to two or more of the three parties; assist in developing and keeping up date standard formats and content specifications for documents specifying aircraft characteristics, airport characteristics and future trends in aircraft and airport design. **Activities** Exchanges reports and other information between airlines, airports and craft manufacturers. Evaluates reported new types of aircraft and related propulsion equipment in terms of compatibility with existing airport facilities. Conducts trade-off studies of cost-effective alternatives for future aircraft/airport compatibility. Reviews regularly basic documentation illustrating aircraft characteristics for airport planning. Produces periodically projections in respect of new trends in aircraft, airports and traffic growth. Organizes meetings (every 8-9 months). **Events** *Meeting* Toulouse (France) 2006, *Meeting* Cape Town (South Africa) 2004, *Meeting* Miami, FL (USA) 2002, *Annual meeting* New York, NY (USA) 1987, *Annual meeting* Paris (France) 1986.
Members Aircraft and aeroengine manufacturers, airlines and airport authorities in 21 countries:
Australia, Austria, Bahrain, Belgium, Canada, France, Germany, Hong Kong, India, Italy, Japan, Netherlands, New Zealand, Russia, Singapore, Sweden, Switzerland, Taiwan, Thailand, UK, USA.
IGO Relations *International Civil Aviation Organization (ICAO, #12581)* represented in an observer capacity. [2019/XE2399/t/E]

♦ International Infection Control Council (IICC) 13842

Contact APIC, 1400 Crystal Drive, Ste 900, Arlington VA 22202, USA. T. +12027891890. Fax +12027891899. E-mail: info@apic.org.

History 2000. **Aims** Encourage collaborative activities to enhance the practice of infection control and epidemiology.
Members in 3 countries:
Canada, UK, USA. [2008/XE4719/E]

♦ International Infertility Counseling Organization (IICO) 13843

Chair Univ of Minnesota, Reproductive Med Ctr, 606 24th Ave S, Ste 500, Minneapolis MN 55454, USA. Fax +16126274888.
Sec Leuven Univ Fertility Ctr, Herestraat 49, 3000 Leuven, Belgium. T. +3216342860.
URL: http://www.iico-infertilitycounseling.org/

Aims Bring together professional organizations in infertility counselling worldwide. **Structure** Board, comprising Chair, Vice-Chair, Secretary, Past Secretary, Treasurer and Past Treasurer. **Activities** Organizes courses.
Members Organizations in 17 countries:
Australia, Belgium, Canada, Czechia, Finland, France, Germany, Greece, Ireland, Japan, Netherlands, New Zealand, Portugal, Spain, Switzerland, UK, USA.
Also members in South America. Membership countries not specified.
Included in the above, 1 organization listed in this Yearbook:
European Society of Human Reproduction and Embryology (ESHRE, #08625). [2017/XJ2064/C]

♦ International Inflammatory Neuropathy Consortium (see: #18314)
♦ International Inflight Food Service Association / see International Flight Services Association
♦ International Information Bureau (inactive)
♦ International Information Bureau of Commerce, Office and Shop Workers (inactive)
♦ International Information Bureau for the Use of Modern Language Teachers (inactive)

♦ International Information Centre for Balkan Studies (CIBAL) 13844

SG 45 Moskovska St, 1000 Sofia, Bulgaria. T. +3592431512. Fax +3592431512. E-mail: info@cibal.eu.
URL: http://www.cibal.eu/

History 13 Sep 1976, Sofia (Bulgaria). 13-15 Sep 1976, Sofia (Bulgaria), at Constituent Assembly, when statutes were adopted, as *International Information Centre on the Sources of Balkan and Mediterranean History – Centre international d'information sur les sources de l'histoire balkanique et méditerranéenne (CIBAL).* Recognized by resolution of 18th General Assembly of UNESCO, 1978, Paris (France). **Aims** Promote research into the history, economy, politics and *culture* of the Balkan countries in libraries, archives and databases; disseminate the results of this research. **Structure** International Council; International Bureau. International Commissions (4). **Languages** Bulgarian, English, French, German, Irish Gaelic, Italian, Romanian, Russian, Serbian, Turkish. **Staff** 4.00 FTE, paid. **Finance** Sources: subsidies, donations and grants from international institutions and organizations and private persons; contracts for carrying out projects; sale of publications; subsidies from Unesco. **Activities** Knowledge management/information dissemination. **Events** *International Seminar* Sofia (Bulgaria) 1998, *International Seminar* Belgrade (Yugoslavia) 1997, *International Seminar* Sofia (Bulgaria) 1996, *International Seminar* Sofia (Bulgaria) 1994, *International Seminar* Venice (Italy) 1990. **Publications** *CIBAL Information Bulletin* (annual). Specialized: catalogues; inventories; bibliographies; monographs. Automated databases in the following fields: politics; economy; defence; foreign affairs; law and society; civilization of Balkan countries.
Members Represented countries (25):
Albania, Austria, Bosnia-Herzegovina, Bulgaria, Croatia, France, Germany, Greece, Holy See, Hungary, Israel, Italy, Netherlands, North Macedonia, Poland, Romania, Russia, Serbia, Slovakia, Slovenia, Spain, Tunisia, Türkiye, UK, USA.
Individuals in 17 countries:
Algeria, Armenia, Australia, Belgium, Canada, Cyprus, Czechia, Denmark, Egypt, India, Korea Rep, Luxembourg, Malta, Moldova, Sweden, Switzerland, Ukraine.
NGO Relations Member of: *International Council on Archives (ICA, #12996).* [2017.02.27/XE0520/E]

♦ International Information Centre for Local Credit / see International Centre for Local Credit (#12501)

♦ International Information Centre for Natural Gas and Gaseous Hydrocarbons 13845

Centre international d'information sur le gaz naturel et tous hydrocarbures gazeux (CEDIGAZ)

Contact 1-4 av de Bois-Préau, 92852 Rueil-Malmaison, France. T. +33147526720.
URL: http://www.cedigaz.org/

History 1961. Former names and other names: *Centre européen d'information sur la production, le traitement, le transport et le stockage du gaz naturel et autres hydrocarbures gazeux, Reuil Malmaison* – former. **Aims** Gather, compile, analyse and diffuse information on natural gas, LNG, LPG and SNG; promote cooperation between members. **Structure** General Meeting; Board. **Activities** Knowledge management/information dissemination. **Events** *Asia Pacific Oil and Gas Security Forum* Bangkok (Thailand) 2015. **Members** in 40 countries. Membership countries not specified. [2021/XU3683/E]

♦ International Information Centre on the Sources of Balkan and Mediterranean History / see International Information Centre for Balkan Studies (#13844)

♦ International Information Centre for Terminology (INFOTERM) 13846

Centre international d'information pour la terminologie – Internationales Informationszentrum für Terminologie

Dir Gumpendorfer Strassse 65/1, 1060 Vienna, Austria. T. +4366473131771. Fax +436645876990. E-mail: terminfo@infoterm.org.
URL: http://www.infoterm.info/

History 1971, Vienna (Austria), under the sponsorship of *UNESCO (#20322).* EU Transparency Register: 97653128762-13. **Aims** Promote and support cooperation of existing and establishment of new terminology centres and networks with the general aim to improve specialist *communication,* knowledge transfer and provision of content with a view to facilitate participation of all in the global *multilingual* knowledge society. **Structure** General Assembly (annual); Executive Board; Secretariat, headed by Director. **Languages** English, French, German, Spanish. **Staff** 1.50 FTE, paid. **Finance** Funded through joint projects at international or European level. **Activities** Networking/liaising; training/education; events/meetings; standards/guidelines; guidance/assistance/consulting. **Events** *International Conference on Computers Helping People with Special Needs* Vienna (Austria) 2010, *International conference on terminology, standardization and technology transfer* Beijing (China) 2006, *International conference on terminology and knowledge engineering* Frederiksberg (Denmark) 2005, *Meeting / Congress* Cologne (Germany) 2004, *International congress on terminology and knowledge engineering* Nancy (France) 2002. **Publications** *Infoterm Newsletter (INL).* Annual Report; documents and reports; proceedings.
Members Organizations with an official or de-facto mandate for terminological activities in 31 countries:
Argentina, Austria, Belgium, Canada, China, Colombia, Croatia, Denmark, Finland, France, Germany, Greece, Hungary, Iceland, Iran Islamic Rep, Ireland, Italy, Korea Rep, Lithuania, Luxembourg, Netherlands, Norway, Poland, Russia, South Africa, Spain, Sweden, Switzerland, Tanzania UR, Tunisia, Ukraine.

Included in the above, and in addition to organizations it co-founded, 1 organization listed in this Yearbook:
Consultative Status Consultative status granted from: *ECOSOC (#05331)* (Ros A); *UNESCO (#20322)* (Consultative Status). **IGO Relations** Associated with Department of Global Communications of the United Nations. **NGO Relations** Operates Technical Committee 37 (ISO/TC 37) of: *International Organization for Standardization (ISO, #14473)*. Member of: *International Network for Terminology (TermNet, #14332)*. Instrumental in setting up: *International Institute for Terminology Research (#13932)*; *International Network for Terminology (TermNet, #14332)*; *Red Iberoamericana de Terminologia (RITerm, #18685)*. [2017.12.25/XE4583/**E**]

♦ International Information and Ecology Parliament (internationally oriented national body)
♦ International Information Management Congress (inactive)

♦ International Information and Networking Centre for Intangible Cultural Heritage in the Asia-Pacific Region under the auspices of UNESCO (ICHCAP) 13847

Dir 132 Munji-ro, Yuseong-gu, Daejeon 305-380, Korea Rep. T. +824282035358203508. Fax +82428203500. E-mail: ichcap@ichcap.org.
URL: http://www.ichcap.org/

History Officially announced Oct 2005, during the inauguration of the Establishment Initiative for the Intangible Cultural Heritage Centre for the Asia-Pacific (EIICHCAP). Establishment approved of a *UNESCO (#20322)* Category 2 Centre. Official establishment, Jul 2011. **Aims** Promote the UNESCO Convention for the Safeguarding of the Intangible Cultural Heritage and contribute to its implementation in the Asia-Pacific region; increase the participation of communities, groups and individuals in safeguarding ICH, and raise awareness of and ensure respect of ICH in the region; enhance the capacity for safeguarding ICH in the region through coordination and dissemination of information; foster regional and international cooperation for the safeguarding of ICH. **Structure** Governing Board; Executive Committee; Secretariat. Sections (5): Information and Research; Cooperation and Networking; Knowledge and Publication; Information Management; Planning and Management. **Languages** English, Korean. **Activities** Knowledge management/information dissemination; guidance/assistance/consulting; research/documentation; events/meetings; awareness raising. **Events** *World Intangible Culture Heritage Forum* Daejeon (Korea Rep) 2021, *Conference on Exploring and Safeguarding Shared Intangible Culture Heritage in East Asia* Jeonju (Korea Rep) 2021, *Meeting on Silk Roads ICH Networks* Jeonju (Korea Rep) 2020, *World Intangible Culture Heritage Forum* Jeonju (Korea Rep) 2020, *International Seminar on Protecting the Past for the Future* Seoul (Korea Rep) 2019. **Publications** *ICH Courier* (4 a year) – newsletter. *Promotion of Intellectual Property Rights Related to Informational Materials and Documentation: Public Events on ICH*. ICH Archives. [2014.01.15/XJ5243/**E***]

♦ International Information Network on New and Emerging Health Technologies / see international HealthTechScan (#13784)
♦ International Information Service on Mental Retardation / see SIIS Social Information and Research Centre (#19275)

♦ International Information System for the Agricultural Sciences and Technology (AGRIS) 13848

Système international d'information pour les sciences et la technologie agricoles – Sistema Internacional de Información para las Ciencias y la Tecnologia Agricolas

Contact Food and Agriculture Organization of the United Nations, Viale delle Terme di Caracalla, 00150 Rome RM, Italy. E-mail: agris@fao.org.
URL: http://www.fao.org/agris/

History Established 1974, by *FAO (#09260)*. **Aims** Facilitate access to publications, journal articles, monographs, book chapters and grey literature, including unpublished science and technical reports, theses, dissertations and conference papers in the area of agriculture and related sciences. **Structure** A collaborative network of over 400 institutions from 141 countries, maintained by: *FAO (#09260)*. **Languages** Arabic, Chinese, English, French, German, Italian, Japanese, Korean, Portuguese, Russian, Spanish, Thai. All languages available to AGROVOC. **Finance** Financed by: *FAO (#09260)*. **Activities** Knowledge management/information dissemination; events/meetings. **Events** *Biennial consultation on agricultural information management* Rome (Italy) 2000, *Joint technical consultation* Rome (Italy) 1998, *Joint technical consultation* Rome (Italy) 1992, *Arab technical consultation* Cairo (Egypt) 1989, *Technical consultation of Arab AGRIS and CARIS centres* Baghdad (Iraq) 1987. **Publications** Conference papers.
Members Data providers (over 400) in 144 countries. Membership countries not specified. Included in the above, 12 organizations listed in this Yearbook:
Included in the above, 12 organizations listed in this Yearbook:
Bioversity International (#03262); *Center for International Forestry Research (CIFOR, #03646)*; *European Food Safety Authority (EFSA, #07287)*; *Global Forum on Agricultural Research (GFAR, #10370)*; *International Bank for Reconstruction and Development (IBRD, #12317)*; *International Centre for Tropical Agriculture (#12527)*; *International Potato Center (#14627)*; *International Rice Research Institute (IRRI, #14754)*; *International Water Management Institute (IWMI, #15867)*; *Mediterranean Agronomic Institute of Chania (MAICh, #16642)*; *Mediterranean Agronomic Institute of Zaragoza (MAIZ, #16644)*; *WorldFish (#21507)*. [2019.12.20/XF6349/y/**F***]

♦ International Information System Security Certification Consortium / see International Information Systems Security Certification Consortium (#13849)

♦ International Information Systems Security Certification Consortium (ISC2) 13849

Exec Dir 1650 King St, Ste 200, Alexandria VA 22314, USA. E-mail: connect@isc2.org.
EMEA Office One Mayfair Place, London, W1J 8AJ, UK. E-mail: info-emea@isc2.org.
Asia Operations 25 Canton Road, Tsim Sha Tsui Unit 807, 8th Floor, Tower 1, The Gateway, Harbour City, Kowloon, Hong Kong. T. +85228506951. Fax +85228506959. E-mail: isc2asia@isc2.org.
URL: http://www.isc2.org/

History 1989. Former names and other names: *International Information System Security Certification Consortium* – former (1989). **Aims** Develop a certification programme for information systems security practitioners. **Structure** Board, comprising President, Vice President, Treasurer, Secretary and 6 Directors. **Activities** Organizes annual meeting. Grants the 'Certified Information Systems Security Practitioner' designation. **Events** *Security Congress* Las Vegas, NV (USA) 2022, *Cybersecurity Management for Startups* Singapore (Singapore) 2020, *Secure Singapore Conference* Singapore (Singapore) 2020, *Seminar on Cyber Leadership and Strategies for Effective CISOs* Singapore (Singapore) 2020, *Seminar on Resource Lifeline in Uncertain Times* Singapore (Singapore) 2020. **Members** Not a membership organization. **IGO Relations** Cooperates with: *International Multilateral Partnership Against Cyber Threats (IMPACT, #14196)*. [2022/XF5989/**F**]

♦ International Informatization Academy 13850

Académie internationale d'informatisation

Montréal Headquarters address not obtained. T. +15148074794. E-mail: info@iia.ca.
Southern Headquarters IIA lane Dolomanovsky d 104/109 of 213, Rostov on Don ROSTOV, Russia, 344065. T. +79169996799. E-mail: south.hg.iia@gmail.com.
URL: http://www.iia.ca/

History 1990. **Aims** Operate in the fields of information, knowledge and consensus needed to solve problems of ecology, cities, economy, status of women, standardization, establish information and communication infrastructures, ensure international collaboration and shape the global culture of development. **Structure** Offices in: Geneva (Switzerland); Kazan (Russia); Montréal QC (Canada); Moscow (Russia); New York NY (USA); St Petersburg (Russia); Vienna (Austria); San Diego CA (USA). **Staff** 6.00 FTE, paid. **Activities** Events/meetings; publishing activities.
Members Branches (over 600) in 15 countries:
Armenia, Belgium, Canada, China, Finland, France, Germany, Italy, Kazakhstan, Moldova, Netherlands, Russia, Switzerland, Ukraine, USA.
Consultative Status Consultative status granted from: *ECOSOC (#05331)* (General). **IGO Relations** Associated with Department of Global Communications of the United Nations. [2019.07.05/XG4719/**F**]

♦ International Initiative for Impact Evaluation (3ie) 13851

Main Office 1020 19th St, NW, Suite 400, Washington DC 20036, USA. T. +12026293939. E-mail: info@3ieimpact.org.
URL: http://www.3ieimpact.org/

History 25 Jun 2006, Bellagio (Italy). Founded following Working Group recommendations of *Center for Global Development (CGD)*. Registration: USA. **Aims** Promote evidence-informed equitable, inclusive and sustainable development. **Structure** Members Conference; Board of Commissioners; Executive Director. Offices in London (UK), Delhi (India) and Washington DC (USA). **Languages** English. **Staff** 57.00 FTE, paid. **Events** *Conference on Impact Evaluation* Washington, DC (USA) 2020, *Mind the gap conference on impact evaluation* Cuernavaca (Mexico) 2011. **Members** Bill & Melinda Gates Foundation; William and Flora Hewlett Foundation; Mastercard Foundation; Department for International Development, UK; Global Affairs Canada; International Fund for Agricultural Development; Asian Development Bank; CAF-Development Bank for Latin America; Queen Rania Foundation; Sightsavers; American Institutes for Research; KDI School of Public Policy & Management; Hand in Hand India; Population Foundation of India; BRAC Institute of Governance and Development; National Council for the Evaluation of Social Development Policy (CONEVAL); Office of the Prime Minister, Uganda; National Planning Department, Colombia; Department for Planning, Monitoring and Evaluation, The Presidency, Government of South Africa; Public Policies Evaluation Bureau, Office of the Prime Minister, Benin; National Social Protection Agency, Maldives; Ministry of Public Health, Cameroon; National Economic and Development Authority, Philippines; General Directorate of Planning and Poverty Alleviation, Ministry of Planning and Development, Côte d'Ivoire; General Directorate of Planning, Ministry of Economy and Finance, Guinea-Bissau; High Commission for State Modernisation, Niger; Secretary of Planning, Evaluation, and Coordination, Autonomous City of Buenos Aires; Ministry of Development Planning, Togo; Ministry of Economy and Finance, Mali; Department of the Premier of the Government of the Province of Western Cape, South Africa; West African Development Bank (BOAD); Centre de Connaissances en Santé en RD. Congo (CCSC); M. S. Swaminathan Research Foundation (MSSRF); SDPI Pakistan; Ministry of Economy, Finance and Planning, Senegal; The Directorate General of the Economy and Planning (DGEP) of the Ministry of the Economy, Finance and Development, Burkina Faso. [2021.09.02/XJ8245/y/**F**]

♦ International Initiative for Mental Health Leadership (IIMHL) 13852

Pres/CEO PO Box 189, Keene NH 03431, USA.
URL: http://www.iimhl.com/

History as a government-to-government initiative of 7 governments: England, USA, New Zealand, Scotland, Ireland, Australia and Canada. **Aims** Provide a single international point of reference of for key mental health leaders; strengthen workforce development and mentoring of mental health leaders; identify and disseminate best management and operation practices; foster innovation and creativity; expand the knowledge of building community capacity, implementing best practices for consumer recovery and expanding methodologies for integration with other health and social systems; promote international collaboration and research; provide assistance to international organizations and sponsoring countries to build low and middle income countries to increase their ability to operate community based recovery systems. **Structure** Sponsoring Country Leadership Group (SCLG), comprising representatives from each country as well as IIMHL Director and President/CEO and Board Chair of Mental Health Corporations of America (MHCA). **Activities** Organizes: Leadership Exchange. **Events** *Leadership Exchange Meeting* 2022, *Leadership Exchange Meeting* Washington, DC (USA) 2019, *Leadership Exchange Meeting* Stockholm (Sweden) 2018, *Leadership Exchange Meeting* Sydney, NSW (Australia) 2017, *Network Meeting* San Francisco, CA (USA) 2011. **Publications** *IIMHL Update* (6 a year). Annual Report.
Members From supporting countries through CEO of mental health, substance abuse provider organizations. Leaders from non-supporting countries can also join. Members (about 2000). Membership countries not specified. Supporting countries (7):
Supporting countries (7):
Australia, Canada, England, Ireland, New Zealand, Scotland, USA. [2012.08.12/XJ3935/**C**]

♦ International Initiative for Peace (internationally oriented national body)

♦ International Initiative for Promoting Political Economy (IIPPE) 13853

Gen Sec 65 Thrale Road, London, SW6 1NU, UK. E-mail: iippe@soas.ac.uk.
URL: http://iippe.org/wp/

History 2006. **Aims** Promote engagement with Marxist political economy; welcome participation of and critical engagement with other political economy and heterodox schools in economics; command and criticize mainstream economics; assess and advance political economy across other social sciences; engage with activism through formulation of progressive policy and support for progressive movements. **Structure** Council; Executive Committee; Working Groups. **Languages** English. **Staff** 6.00 FTE, voluntary. **Finance** Members' dues. **Activities** Events/meetings; training/education. **Events** *Annual Conference* London (UK) 2021, *Annual Conference* Ferrara (Italy) 2020, *Annual Conference* Lille (France) 2019, *Annual Conference* Pula (Croatia) 2018, *Annual Conference* Berlin (Germany) 2017. **Publications** *IIPPE Newsletter* (regular). Working Papers.
Members Individuals. Membership countries not specified. [2021/XJ6878/**F**]

♦ International Initiative for a Sustainable Built Environment (iiSBE) 13854

Exec Dir 40 The Driveway, Ste 1803, Ottawa ON K2P 2C9, Canada.
Pres Civil Engineering Dept, Univ of Minho, 4800-058 Guimarães, Portugal. T. +351253510241.
URL: http://www.iisbe.org/

History Founded 2001. **Aims** Facilitate and promote the adoption of policies, methods and tools to accelerate the movement towards a global sustainable built environment. **Structure** General Meeting (annual); Board of Directors; Regional Directors; Secretariat in Ottawa (Canada). **Languages** Czech, English, French, Italian, Polish, Spanish, Swedish. **Staff** Voluntary. **Finance** Members' dues. Consulting income. Annual budget: about euro 25,000. **Activities** Guidance/assistance/consulting; events/meetings; training/education; research and development. **Events** *World Sustainable Built Environment (WSBE) Conference* Montréal, QC (Canada) 2023, *World Sustainable Built Environment (WSBE) Conference* Gothenburg (Sweden) 2020, *SBE19 SEOUL : Sustainable Built Environment Seoul Conference* Seoul (Korea Rep) 2019, *SBE19 Tokyo : Sustainable Built Environment Tokyo Conference* Tokyo (Japan) 2019, *World Sustainable Built Environment (WSBE) Conference* Hong Kong (Hong Kong) 2017. **Publications** Newseltter (irregular).
Members (about 400) in 20 countries (not specified). Chapters in 9 countries and territories:
Austria, Canada, Czechia, Italy, Korea Rep, Malta, Portugal, Spain, Taiwan.
IGO Relations Cooperates with: *UNEP (#20299)* Sustainable Building and Climate Initiative. **NGO Relations** Member of: *Global Alliance for Buildings and Construction (GlobalABC, #10187)*. Cooperates with: *International Organization for Standardization (ISO, #14473)* TC59/SC17. [2017.12.07/XJ3767/**F**]

♦ International Inner Wheel (IIW) 13855

Secretariat 20 Market Street, Altrincham, WA14 1PF, UK. T. +441619273116. E-mail: admin@internationalinnerwheel.org.
URL: http://www.internationalinnerwheel.org/

History 1934, London (UK), as *Association of Inner Wheel Clubs*, the first clubs having been started in 1923 by the wives of Rotarians. New constitution and present name adopted 1967. **Aims** Promote true *friendship*; encourage the ideals of personal *service*; foster *international understanding*. **Structure** Governing Body (elected annually); Board of Directors. **Languages** English. **Staff** 1.00 FTE, paid. **Finance** Members' dues. **Activities** Projects/programmes. Organizes an International Triennial Convention. **Events** *International Convention* New Delhi (India) 2021, *Triennial Convention* Melbourne, VIC (Australia) 2018, *Triennial Convention* Copenhagen (Denmark) 2015, *Conference* Espoo (Finland) 2014, *Triennial Convention* Istanbul (Turkey) 2012. **Publications** *IIW Magazine* (annual). **Members** Clubs, totalling 104,000 individual women in about 100 countries. Membership countries not specified. **Consultative Status** Consultative status granted from: *ECOSOC (#05331)* (Ros A). **IGO Relations** Accredited by: *United Nations Office at Vienna (UNOV, #20604)*. Associated with Department of Global Communications of the United Nations. **NGO Relations** Member of: *Conference of Non-Governmental Organizations in Consultative Relationship with the United Nations (CONGO, #04635)*; *NGO Committee on the Status of Women, Geneva (#17117)*; *Child Rights Connect (#03884)*; *NGO Committee on UNICEF (#17120)*; *Committee of NGOs on Human Rights, Geneva (#04275)*; *Vienna NGO Committee on the Family (#20774)*; *Vienna NGO Committee on Drugs (VNGOC, #20773)*; *Vienna NGO Committee on the Status of Women (#20775)*. [2018/XE2122/**E**]

♦ **International Input-Output Association (IIOA)** **13856**

Sec Urbangasse 16/19, 1170 Vienna, Austria. T. +4317982601261. Fax +4317989386. E-mail: office@iioa.org.
URL: http://www.iioa.org/

History Apr 1988, Vienna (Austria). **Aims** Advance knowledge in the field of input-output data and analysis, including: improvements in compilation of supply-use data and symmetrical input-output tables; greater theoretical and practical insights into input-output modelling, and its diverse applications; expansion of the knowledge and teaching of both traditional and novel input-output analysis techniques. **Structure** Council. **Languages** English. **Staff** 2.00 FTE, voluntary. **Activities** Events/meetings. **Events** *Conference* Kuah (Malaysia) 2022, *Conference* Glasgow (UK) 2019, *Conference* Juiz de Fora (Brazil) 2018, *Conference* Atlantic City, NJ (USA) 2017, *Conference* Seoul (Korea Rep) 2016. **Publications** *Economic Systems Research* (4 a year) – journal.

Members Organizations in 16 countries:
Australia, Canada, Denmark, Finland, Iran Islamic Rep, Japan, Korea Rep, Kuwait, Latvia, Luxembourg, Netherlands, New Zealand, Norway, Switzerland, UK, USA.
Individuals in 54 countries and territories:
Argentina, Australia, Austria, Belgium, Brazil, Bulgaria, Canada, China, Croatia, Czechia, Denmark, Ethiopia, Finland, France, Georgia, Germany, Greece, Guatemala, Hungary, India, Indonesia, Iran Islamic Rep, Ireland, Israel, Italy, Japan, Korea Rep, Kuwait, Latvia, Lesotho, Luxembourg, Malaysia, Mexico, Netherlands, New Zealand, Nicaragua, Norway, Pakistan, Philippines, Poland, Portugal, Russia, Singapore, Slovakia, Slovenia, South Africa, Spain, Sweden, Switzerland, Tunisia, Türkiye, UK, Ukraine, USA.

NGO Relations *Pan Pacific Association of Input-Output Studies (PAPAIOS).* [2017.12.12/XD9478/**D**]

♦ **International Insolvency Institute (III GLOBAL)** **13857**

Exec Dir PO Box 249, Stanardsville VA 22973, USA. T. +14349396003. Fax +14349396030.
Communications Dir address not obtained.
URL: http://www.iiiglobal.org/

History 2000. **Aims** Improve international cooperation in insolvency; promote greater cooperation and coordination through improvements in law and legal procedures; study, analyse and provide solutions to problems in cross-border insolvencies and reorganizations. **Structure** Board of Directors; Board of Governors; Committees. **Languages** English. **Staff** 1.00 FTE, paid. **Activities** Awards/prizes/competitions; events/meetings. **Events** *Annual Conference* Hong Kong (Hong Kong) 2022, *Annual Conference* Sao Paulo (Brazil) 2021, *Annual Conference* New York, NY (USA) 2020, *Annual Conference* Barcelona (Spain) 2019, *Annual Conference* New York, NY (USA) 2018.

Members Individuals in 44 countries and territories:
Argentina, Australia, Austria, Belgium, Brazil, Canada, Chile, China, Colombia, Croatia, Czechia, Denmark, Estonia, Finland, France, Germany, Greece, Hong Kong, Hungary, Indonesia, Ireland, Israel, Italy, Jamaica, Japan, Korea Rep, Malaysia, Mexico, Netherlands, Nigeria, Norway, Peru, Poland, Portugal, Russia, Serbia, Singapore, Slovenia, South Africa, Spain, Sweden, Switzerland, UK, USA.

IGO Relations *United Nations Commission on International Trade Law (UNCITRAL, #20531).* [2021/XM2104/j/**C**]

♦ **International Institute of Acoustics and Vibration (IIAV)** **13858**

Exec Dir Mechanical Engineering, 1418 Wiggins Hall, Auburn Univ, Auburn AL 36849-5341, USA. T. +13348443310. Fax +13348443307.
Pres Institute of Automatic Control, Silesian University of Tech, Akademicka 16, 44-100 Gliwice, Poland.
URL: http://www.iiav.org/

History 1995. **Aims** Advance the sciences of acoustics and vibration through an international organization responsive to the needs of scientists and engineers concerned with acoustics and vibration problems all around the world. **Structure** Board of Directors; Executive Committee; Standing Committees (5). **Finance** Members' dues. **Activities** Events/meetings; liaising/networking; publishing activities. **Events** *International Congress on Sound and Vibration* Prague (Czechia) 2023, *International Congress on Sound and Vibration* Singapore (Singapore) 2022, *International Congress on Sound and Vibration* Prague (Czechia) 2021, *International Congress on Sound and Vibration* Prague (Czechia) 2020, *International Congress on Sound and Vibration* Montréal, QC (Canada) 2019. **Publications** *ISVD Digest* (6 a year); *International Journal of Acoustics and Vibration* (4 a year). Congress proceedings.

Members Fellow; Member; Associate; Student; Emeritus; Honorary Fellow. Individuals in 63 countries and territories:
Algeria, Argentina, Australia, Austria, Bangladesh, Belarus, Belgium, Brazil, Bulgaria, Canada, Chile, China, Croatia, Czechia, Denmark, Ecuador, Egypt, Estonia, Finland, France, Germany, Greece, Hong Kong, Hungary, India, Indonesia, Iran Islamic Rep, Israel, Italy, Japan, Jordan, Korea Rep, Kuwait, Latvia, Lithuania, Malaysia, Mexico, Morocco, Netherlands, New Zealand, Norway, Pakistan, Panama, Peru, Poland, Portugal, Romania, Russia, Serbia, Singapore, Slovakia, Slovenia, South Africa, Spain, Sweden, Switzerland, Taiwan, Thailand, Trinidad-Tobago, Türkiye, UK, Ukraine, USA.

NGO Relations Affiliate member of: *International Commission for Acoustics (ICA, #12658).* Affiliated with: *International Union of Theoretical and Applied Mechanics (IUTAM, #15823).* [2021/XE3468/j/**E**]

♦ **International Institute of Administrative Sciences (IIAS)** **13859**
Institut international des Sciences administratives (IISA)

Dir Gen Rue du Commerce 96, 6th floor – bloc C, 1040 Brussels, Belgium. T. +3225360880. Fax +3225379702. E-mail: info@iias-iisa.org.
Operational Assistant address not obtained.
Communications Officer address not obtained.
URL: http://www.iias-iisa.org/

History Oct 1930, Madrid (Spain). Founded to replace *Standing International Committee of International Congresses on Administrative Sciences (inactive)*, set up 1910. Statutes modified: 1953; 1961; 1968; 1971; 1974; 1980; 1983; 1985; 1989; 1997. New statutes adopted 13 July 2010. Current Statutes adopted June 2013 and modified Mar 2017. Registration: Banque-Carrefour des Entreprises, No/ID: 0407.572.125, Start date: 6 Feb 1932. **Aims** Produce and disseminate scientific knowledge on public governance; organize high-impact events that engage both public service and academia; enable collaborative and strategic projects with members and partners; accredit academic and professional training programmes that align with best practices in public governance; produce, promote and support development of comprehensive content on public governance research and practice to diverse audiences. **Structure** Governance: Council of Administration (CA); Programme and Research Advisory Committee (PRAC); Finance Committee; IASIA Board of Management (IASIA BoM); ICAPA Steering Committee; ICAPA Accreditation Committee; EGPA Steering Committee; LAGPA Steering Committee; AGPA Steering Committee. Entities: International Institute of Administrative Sciences (IIAS); International Association of Schools and Institutes of Administration (IASIA); European Group for Public Administration (EGPA); Latin American Group for Public Administration (LAGPA); Asian Group for Public Administration (AGPA). **Languages** English, French. **Staff** 7.00 FTE, paid. **Finance** Sources: contributions of member/participating states; fees for services; revenue from activities/projects; sale of publications. Annual budget: 900,000 EUR (2022). **Activities** Advocacy/lobbying/activism; certification/accreditation; events/meetings; guidance/assistance/consulting; knowledge management/information dissemination; networking/liaising; projects/programmes; publishing activities; research and development; standards/guidelines; training/education. **Events** *IIAS-SEAPP Doha Conference* Doha (Qatar) 2023, *IASIA Conference* Manila (Philippines) 2023, *IASIA Conference* Rabat (Morocco) 2022, *IIAS-EUROMENA Conference* Rome (Italy) 2022, *Conference* Bela-Bela (South Africa) 2021. **Publications** *International Review of Administrative Sciences (IRAS)* (4 a year) in English, French, Mandarin Chinese, Spanish – The International Review of Administrative Sciences (IRAS) is an international peer-reviewed journal devoted to academic and professional public administration. Founded in 1927 it is the oldest scholarly public administration journal specifically focused on comparative and international topics. IRAS seeks to shape the future agenda of public administration around the world by encouraging reflection on international comparisons, new techniques and approaches, the dialogue between academics and practitioners, and debates about the future of the field itself. IRAS is the official journal of the International Institute of Administrative Sciences (IIAS), the European Group of Public Administration (EGPA) and the International Association of Schools and Institutes of Administration (IASIA). IRAS is published in four different language editions – English, French, Spanish and Chinese.; *Developments in Administration (DinA)* (2 a year) in English – Developments in Administration (DinA) is the international, open access, and double-blind peer-reviewed online scientific journal of the International Institute of Administrative Sciences (IIAS) and the International Association of Schools and Institutes of Administration (IASIA). It provides a scientific contribution in the fields of Public Administration, Development Studies, and Area Studies.. *IIAS Public Governance Series* – The Public Governance Series of the International Institute of Administrative Sciences aims at widely diffusing the original scientific content it produces. Its volumes are available for free as e-book and on sale as paperback.; *Larcier/Bruylant Public Administration Today Series* – Le monde juridique et fiscal évolue rapidement. La digitalisation, l'augmentation de la réglementation et l'amélioration de l'information des clients, qui deviennent de plus en plus exigeants, vous posent d'importants défis. Pour mieux vous accompagner, Larcier, Indicator, Intersentia et Bruylant unissent leurs forces. Ces éditeurs sont des références absolues dans tous les domaines juridiques et fiscaux : chacun d'entre eux s'adresse à son propre groupe cible, qu'il s'agisse d'universitaires, de juristes, de fiscalistes, de comptables, de chefs d'entreprise ou d'indépendants. À présent, nous formons ensemble une entreprise et un partenaire de connaissances pour vous soutenir dans votre pratique quotidienne, aujourd'hui et demain.; *Palgrave Governance and Public Management Series* – The Governance and Public Management series, published in conjunction with Palgrave, brings the best research in public administration and management to a global audience. Encouraging a diversity of approach and perspective, the series reflects the Institute's conviction for a neutral and objective voice, grounded in the exigency of fact. How is governance conducted now? How could it be done better? What defines the law of administration and the management of public affairs, and can their implementation be enhanced? Such questions lie behind the Institute's core value of accountability: those who exercise authority must account for its use to those on whose behalf they act..

Members Member States (28):
Austria, Bahrain, Belgium, Brazil, Cameroon, China, Cyprus, Germany, Greece, Holy See, Hungary, India, Indonesia, Italy, Japan, Korea Rep, Luxembourg, Malta, Morocco, Namibia, Poland, Qatar, San Marino, Saudi Arabia, South Africa, Spain, Switzerland, Tunisia.
National sections (16):
Austria, Belgium, China, Ethiopia, Finland, Germany, Greece, Hungary, Ireland, Italy, Japan, Portugal, San Marino, Saudi Arabia, Spain, Switzerland.
International organizations (2):
National Interdisciplinary Institute on Ageing (NIIA); *United Cities and Local Governments of Africa (UCLG Africa, #20500).*
Corporate members in 75 countries and territories:
Albania, Armenia, Australia, Austria, Azerbaijan, Bahrain, Belgium, Brazil, Bulgaria, Cameroon, Canada, Chile, China, Colombia, Costa Rica, Croatia, Cyprus, Czechia, Denmark, Ecuador, Egypt, Estonia, Ethiopia, Finland, France, Germany, Greece, Holy See, Hungary, India, Indonesia, Ireland, Italy, Japan, Kazakhstan, Kenya, Korea Rep, Kosovo, Lebanon, Lithuania, Luxembourg, Malaysia, Malta, Morocco, Myanmar, Namibia, Netherlands, Norway, Oman, Palestine, Peru, Philippines, Poland, Portugal, Qatar, Romania, Russia, San Marino, Saudi Arabia, Singapore, Slovakia, Slovenia, South Africa, Spain, Sweden, Switzerland, Taiwan, Tanzania UR, Thailand, Tunisia, Uganda, UK, Ukraine, USA, Vietnam.
International and regional bodies in the field, founded by and/or within the Institute (4):
Asian Group for Public Administration (AGPA, #01498); European Group for Public Administration (EGPA, #07430); International Association of Schools and Institutes of Administration (IASIA, #12147); Latin American Group for Public Administration (LAGPA/IIAS, #16337).

Consultative Status Consultative status granted from: *ECOSOC (#05331)* (General); *ILO (#11123)* (Special List). **IGO Relations** Cooperates with: *United Nations Public Administration Network (UNPAN, #20615).* Consultative Status with: *United Nations Committee of Experts on Public Administration (CEPA, #20542).* Associated with Department of Global Communications of the United Nations. **NGO Relations** Member of: *Federation of European and International Associations Established in Belgium (FAIB, #09508).* [2023.03.01/XB2138/jy/**B**]

♦ International Institute for Adult Education Methods (no recent information)
♦ International Institute for Advanced Asian Studies (internationally oriented national body)
♦ International Institute of Advanced Islamic Studies, Malaysia (internationally oriented national body)
♦ International Institute for Advanced Purchasing and Supply (internationally oriented national body)
♦ International Institute of Advanced Studies, Caracas (internationally oriented national body)
♦ International Institute for Advanced Studies in Systems Research and Cybernetics (internationally oriented national body)
♦ International Institute of African Languages and Cultures / see International African Institute (#11596)
♦ International Institute of Afro-American Studies (inactive)

♦ **International Institute on Ageing, United Nations – Malta (INIA)** . . . **13860**
Institut international sur le vieillissement, Nations Unies -Malte

Sec 117 St Paul Street, Valletta, VLT1216, Malta. T. +35621243044 – +35621243045 – +35621243046. E-mail: tarcisio.zammit@inia.org.mt – info@inia.org.mt.
Dir address not obtained.
URL: http://www.inia.org.mt/

History Established by resolution 1987/41 of *ECOSOC (#05331).* Established as an autonomous body under the auspices of the *United Nations (UN, #20515)* on signature of official agreement, 9 Oct 1987, by the United Nations and the Government of Malta. Inaugurated, 15 Apr 1988, by the United Nations Secretary-General. Former names and other names: *United Nations International Institute on Ageing* – alias; *Institut international sur le vieillissement des Nations Unies* – alias. **Aims** Facilitate, in a practical way, the implementation of the Vienna International Plan of Action on Aging adopted by the United Nations in 1982, and of the Madrid International Plan of Action on Ageing, 2002. **Structure** Board of Governors; Director; Satellite Centres (5). **Languages** English. **Staff** 8.00 FTE, paid. **Finance** Yearly grant for local expenses by Government of Malta and donations from a number of national and international organizations, including: UNFPA. **Activities** Research/documentation; publishing activities; guidance/assistance/consulting; training/education; events/meetings. **Events** *Meeting* Valletta (Malta) 2015, *Seminar on medicines management in older persons* Malta 2004, *World Assembly on Ageing* Madrid (Spain) 2002, *Meeting on ageing as a global development* Joensuu (Finland) 1998, *Growing old in the XXIst century* Valletta (Malta) 1998. **Publications** *International Journal on Ageing in Developing Countries (IJADC).*

Members Network members active in 47 countries:
Argentina, Australia, Austria, Azerbaijan, Barbados, Belarus, Brazil, Canada, China, Czechia, Egypt, France, Gambia, Germany, Ghana, Hungary, India, Israel, Italy, Japan, Kazakhstan, Korea Rep, Malaysia, Malta, Mauritius, Moldova, Montenegro, Netherlands, Nigeria, Panama, Philippines, Romania, Russia, Serbia, Singapore, Slovakia, South Africa, Sri Lanka, Switzerland, Thailand, Trinidad-Tobago, Tunisia, Türkiye, UK, Ukraine, USA, Vietnam.
International organizations (8), listed in this Yearbook:
American Association for International Aging (AAIA, no recent information); Centre of West African Studies, Birmingham (CWAS); EURAG – European Federation of Older Persons (#05597); HelpAge International (#10904); International Council of Women (ICW, #13093); International Federation on Ageing (IFA, #13345); International Social Security Association (ISSA, #14885); World Confederation for Physical Therapy (WCPT, #21293).

IGO Relations Collaborative agreements with: *ILO (#11123); UNDP (#20292); UNESCO (#20322); United Nations Economic Commission for Europe (UNECE, #20555); United Nations Economic and Social Commission for Western Asia (ESCWA, #20558); United Nations Population Fund (UNFPA, #20612); WHO (#20950).* **NGO Relations** Collaborative agreements with over 30 international and national non-governmental organizations, agencies and institutions, some of which are international, internationally-oriented or regional bodies, including with: Ageconcern UK; *EURAG – European Federation of Older Persons (#05597); HelpAge International (#10904); International Federation on Ageing (IFA, #13345)* (these 4 also being members); *International Association of Gerontology and Geriatrics (IAGG, #11920).* [2020/XE1501/jy/**E**]

♦ International Institute of Agriculture (inactive)
♦ International Institute of Ammonia Refrigeration (internationally oriented national body)
♦ International Institute, Ann Arbor MI (internationally oriented national body)
♦ International Institute of Anticancer Research (internationally oriented national body)
♦ International Institute of Applied Aesthetics (internationally oriented national body)

♦ **International Institute for Applied Systems Analysis (IIASA)** **13861**
Internationales Institut für Angewandte Systemanalyse (IIASA)

Dir Gen Schlossplatz 1, 2361 Laxenburg, Austria. T. +432236807525. Fax +43223671313. E-mail: info@iiasa.ac.at.
URL: http://www.iiasa.ac.at/

History 4 Oct 1972, London (UK). Founded on signature of Charter by representatives of USA, USSR and 10 countries from Eastern and Western blocs. Charter revised 1979, 2008, 2022. Former names and other names: *Institut international pour l'analyse des systèmes appliqués* – former; *Mezdunarodnyj Institut Prikladnogo Sistemnogo Analiza* – former. Registration: Zentrales Vereinsregister (ZVR), No/ID: 524808900, Start date: 15 Nov 1972, Austria, Bezirkshauptmannschaft Mödling; EU Transparency Register, No/ID: 011033140197-04, Start date: 5 Nov 2020. **Aims** Advance systems analysis and applies its research methods to identify policy solutions to reduce human footprints, enhance resilience of natural and socioeconomic systems, and help achieve the Sustainable Development Goals. **Structure** Council (meets twice a year); Research Programs; Scientific (Advisory) Committees. **Languages** English. **Staff** 275.00 FTE, paid. **Finance** Sources: contributions of member/participating states; grants; members' dues. Annual budget: 22,800,000 EUR (2021). **Activities** Events/meetings; research/documentation. Consultative Science platform: online consultative meetings, organized in collaboration with the International Science Council (ISC), to design systemic and sustainable pathways and inform policy choices for a post COVI-19 recovery period. Platform under the patronage of the former Secretary General of the United Nations, HE. Ban Ki-moon. Main research activities carried out at the Institute in Austria, events/workshops, guest seminars, lectures etc. in several member countries. In addition, the annual Young Scientists Summer Program (YSSP) brings students from all member countries to IAISA for 3 months working on aspects of their PhD research. **Events** *International Seminar* Hayama (Japan) 2022, *Workshop on User and Policy Needs of the European Biodiversity Observation Network* Laxenburg (Austria) 2021, *Systems Analysis in Eurasia* Moscow (Russia) 2021, *Resilience and Networks – Principles for resetting a post-Corona world* Vienna (Austria) 2021, *VEF : Biennial Vienna Energy Forum* Vienna (Austria) 2021. **Publications** *Options Magazine* (2 a year) in English – Options magazine showcases the complex interdisciplinary research carried out at IIASA by highlighting the latest research news and bringing together different strands of work from across the institute to show how they fit together to inform policy and solve the interconnected global problems that society face today.. Annual Report; books; journal articles; reports; working papers; conference proceedings.
Members National member organizations (MOs) in 21 countries:
Austria, Brazil, China, Egypt, Finland, Germany, India, Indonesia, Iran Islamic Rep, Israel, Japan, Jordan, Korea Rep, Norway, Russia, Slovakia, Sweden, UK, Ukraine, USA, Vietnam.
Regional organization:
Sub-Saharan African Regional Member Organization (SSARMO).
Consultative Status Consultative status granted from: *ECOSOC (#05331)* (General); *FAO (#09260)* (Liaison Status); *UNEP (#20299)*. **IGO Relations** Accredited by (1): *United Nations Framework Convention on Climate Change – Secretariat (UNFCCC, #20564)*. Observer status with (1): *Committee on the Peaceful Uses of Outer Space (COPUOS, #04277)*. Member of (2): *Abdus Salam International Centre for Theoretical Physics (ICTP, #00005)*; *International Nuclear Information System (INIS, #14378)*. Affiliated with (1): *International Atomic Energy Agency (IAEA, #12294)*. Working arrangements with: *World Meteorological Organization (WMO, #21649)*. Participates in the work of: *United Nations Economic Commission for Europe (UNECE, #20555)*. Participates in: *Group on Earth Observations (GEO, #10735)*. Observer to: *Ministerial Conference on the Protection of Forests in Europe (FOREST EUROPE, #16817)*. Accredited to the Conference of the Parties of: *Secretariat of the United Nations Convention to Combat Desertification (Secretariat of the UNCCD, #19208)*. **NGO Relations** Member of (9): *Council for Global Problem-Solving (CGP, #04898)*; *European Forum on Integrated Environmental Assessment (EFIEA, no recent information)*; *European Rural Development Network (ERDN, #08413)*; *Global Alliance of Disaster Research Institutes (GADRI, #10194)*; *Global Commons Alliance*; *Integrated Assessment Modeling Consortium (IAMC, #11366)*; *International Science Council (ISC, #14796)*; *Science Based Targets Network*; *Scientific Committee on Problems of the Environment (SCOPE, #19150)*. Partner of (3): *Food and Land Use Coalition (FOLU)*; *International Institute for Sustainability Analysis and Strategy (#13929)*; *Sustainable Energy for All (SEforALL, #20056)*. Collaboration with: *INSEAD (#11228)*; *ISRIC – World Soil Information (#16068)*. Together with: *Asia Research Institute (ARI)*, set up: *Asian MetaCentre for Population and Sustainable Development Analysis*. Signatory to Charter of: *Institute for Global Environmental Strategies (IGES, #11266)*. [2023.02.14/XC4518/j/**D**]

♦ International Institute for Archival Science Maribor / see International Institute for Archival Science of Trieste and Maribor (#13862)

♦ International Institute for Archival Science of Trieste and Maribor (IIAS) 13862

Istituto Internazionale per le Scienze Archivistiche di Trieste e Maribor – Mednarodni Institut za Arhivsko Znanost Trst – Maribor

Deputy Dir Archivio di Stato di Trieste, Via A La Marmora 17, 34139 Trieste TS, Italy. T. +39400647921. Fax +39409880033. E-mail: info@iias-trieste-maribor.eu.
Dir CIMRS/Univ v Mariboru, Krekova ulica 2, 2000 Maribor, Slovenia. T. +38622355430. Fax +38622355431. E-mail: info@iias-trieste-maribor.eu.
URL: http://www.iias-trieste-maribor.eu/

History 1986, as *'Centre for Technical and Professional Problems in Archives'*. Changed name to *International Institute for Archival Science Maribor – Mednarodni Institut Arhivskih Znanosti Maribor*, 1992. Subsequently changed title to *International Institute for Archival Science, University of Maribor – Mednarodni Institut Arhivskih Znanosti, Univerze v Maribor (MIAZ)*. Became part of the University of Maribor (Slovenia), 2000. When headquarters were transferred to the State Archive of Trieste (Italy), adopted current title. Previously also referred to in Italian as *Istituto Internazionale per le Scienza Archivistica*. **Aims** Deal with technical and professional problems linked to archival matters, taking in special consideration the *Balkan-Danube* area; improve services and take advantage of contributions from more advanced countries in the field of archival science. **Structure** Assembly; Executive Board. **Languages** English, Italian, Slovene. **Staff** 11.00 FTE, paid. **Finance** Public and private sponsorship. **Activities** Events/meetings; training/education. **Events** *Archival Day / Annual Conference* Trieste (Italy) 2014, *Archival Day / Annual Conference* Trieste (Italy) 2013, *Archival Day / Annual Conference* Trieste (Italy) 2012, *Archival Day / Annual Conference* Trieste (Italy) 2011, *Archival Day / Annual Conference* Trieste (Italy) 2010. **Publications** *Atlanti* (annual) – review; *Modern Archives* – 25 issues to date. *IIAS Dictionary of Archival Terminology* – online.
Members Full in 21 countries:
Austria, Belarus, Bosnia-Herzegovina, Canada, Croatia, Czechia, Estonia, France, Germany, Greece, Israel, Italy, Montenegro, North Macedonia, Oman, Poland, Russia, Slovakia, Slovenia, Spain, Ukraine.
NGO Relations Member of: *Foundation for East European Family History Societies (FEEFHS)*; *International Council on Archives (ICA, #12996)*. [2021/XE2145/j/**E**]

♦ International Institute for Archival Science, University of Maribor / see International Institute for Archival Science of Trieste and Maribor (#13862)
♦ International Institute of Arts and Letters (inactive)
♦ International Institute for Asian Studies, Leiden (internationally oriented national body)
♦ International Institute of Association and Foundation Lawyers (internationally oriented national body)
♦ International Institute for Beet Research / see International Institute of Sugar Beet Research (#13928)

♦ International Institute for Bioenergetic Analysis (IIBA) 13863

Exec Administrator C/ dels Ametllers, 6, 08670 Barcelona, Spain. T. +3462356347. E-mail: info@bioenergeticanalysis.com.
Main Website: https://www.bioenergetic-therapy.com

History 1956, New York, NY (USA). Initially founded by Alexander Lowen and two other students of Wilhelm Reich (John Pierrakos and William Walling). Former names and other names: *Institute for Bioenergetic Analysis (IBA)* – former (1956 to 1976). Registration: Start date: 2011, Spain. **Aims** Promote understanding of *biological energy* processes important in the fields of physical and mental *health*; support and encourage members in their work as bioenergetic therapists. **Structure** Board of Trustees. **Languages** Chinese, English, French, German, Italian, Portuguese, Russian, Spanish. **Staff** No full-time staff. **Finance** Sources: members' dues. **Activities** Events/meetings; training/education. **Events** *Conference* 2021, *Biennial Conference* Vimeiro (Portugal) 2019, *Biennial Conference* Toronto, ON (Canada) 2017, *Biennial Conference* Porto de Galinhas (Brazil) 2015, *Biennial Conference / Biennial International Conference* Palermo (Italy) 2013. **Publications** *Bioenergetic Analysis: The Clinical Journal of the International Institute for Bioenergetic Analysis* (annual) – Free.
Members Active (1,400); Affiliated local societies and institutes (50) in 32 countries and territories:
Argentina, Australia, Austria, Belgium, Brazil, Bulgaria, Canada, China, Colombia, Denmark, France, Germany, Greece, Israel, Italy, Lithuania, Mexico, Netherlands, New Zealand, Norway, Poland, Portugal, Réunion, Russia, Singapore, Slovenia, Spain, Sweden, Switzerland, UK, Uruguay, USA. [2022.05.04/XF0380/j/**E**]

♦ International Institute of Biomedical Engineering (inactive)
♦ International Institute of Business (internationally oriented national body)

♦ International Institute of Business Analysis (IIBA) 13864

Main Office 115 George Street, Ste 509, Oakville ON L6J 0A2, Canada. E-mail: info@iiba.org.
URL: http://www.iiba.org/

History 2003, Canada. **Aims** Help members identify education providers that offer courses on business analysis that are aligned with the IIBAT Business Analysis Body of Knowledge (BABOK). **Structure** Annual General Meeting. Board of Directors, comprising President, Secretary, Treasurer, Executive Vice-President and Chief Operations Officer, 4 Vice-Presidents, 2 Directors at Large and Chief Information Officer (ex-officio). Committees (9): Executive; Body of Knowledge; Communications; Education and Certification; Corporate Sponsorship; Governance; Membership Services; IIBA Special Events; Technology. **Finance** Members' dues (annual): US$ 95. **Events** *Building Business Capacity Conference* Sydney, NSW (Australia) 2013. **Publications** Newsletter.
Members Chapters in 16 countries:
Australia, Bangladesh, Brazil, Canada, China, Egypt, India, Italy, New Zealand, Nigeria, Poland, Singapore, South Africa, Türkiye, UK, USA. [2020/XM3482/j/**E**]

♦ International Institute of Business Management, Bilbao (internationally oriented national body)
♦ International Institute of Business Technologies (internationally oriented national body)

♦ International Institute for Cannabinoids (ICANNA) 13865

Dir Kodeljevo Castle, Koblarjeva 34, 1000 Ljubljana, Slovenia. E-mail: info@institut-icanna.com.
URL: https://www.institut-icanna.com/

History Registered in accordance with Slovenian law: 7027338000. **Aims** Cooperate in the field of cannabinoid research. **Structure** Governing Board; Expert Council; Managing Director. **Activities** Research and development; research/documentation; training/education; guidance/assistance/consulting; knowledge management/information dissemination; awareness raising. **NGO Relations** *International Cannabis and Cannabinoids Institute (ICCI)*. [2019/XM8644/**D**]

♦ International Institute Canon Triest 13866

Institut international Chanoine Triest – Internationaal Instituut Kanunnik Triest

Gen Sec Jozef Guislainstraat 43, 9000 Ghent, Belgium. T. +3292163550. Fax +3292163551.
URL: http://www.iictriest.org/

History 5 Sep 2000. Founded as a training centre of *Brothers of Charity (FC)*. Named in honour of Petrus Jozef Triest (1760-1836). Registration: Belgium. **Aims** Serve as a training center of the Congregation Brothers of Charity. **Structure** General Assembly (annual); Executive Committee. Departments (5): Mental Health Care; Special Education; Management; Spirituality; Research. Associated Department: Distance Education. **Activities** Training/education; events/meetings; certification/accreditation. **Publications** *Proceedings of the International Institute Canon Triest*. Newsletter in English.
Members Founding members in 4 countries:
Belgium, Ireland, Italy, Netherlands. [2018/XE4296/j/**E**]

♦ International Institute for Carbon-Neutral Energy Research (internationally oriented national body)

♦ International Institute of Catechetics and Pastoral Studies 13867

Institut international de catéchèse et de pastorale

Contact c/o Lumen Vitae, Rue Joseph Grafé 4 – bte 2, 5000 Namur, Belgium. T. +3281826255. E-mail: international@lumenvitae.be.
URL: http://www.lumenvitae.be/

History An international institute of *International Centre for Studies in Religious Education (LUMEN VITAE, #12519)*. Affiliated to the Theology Faculty of the Catholic University of Louvain (Belgium) which confers the degrees. **Aims** Promote *religious* training on an international level by means of *education*. **Activities** Offers to catechists, religious educators and community workers from all over the world university level courses and seminars based on research, leading to: Master's Degree in Catechetics and Pastoral Theology (2 years); Diploma in Catechetics and Pastoral Studies (2 years); Postgraduate Diploma in Catechetics and Pastoral Theology (one year); Certificate of Catechetics and Pastoral Studies (one year); Certificate of Training in Pastoral Ministry and Social Development (one year). A 3-month renewal course is offered (Sep-Dec). **Publications** *Revue Lumen Vitae* (4 a year). Books; handbooks. [2019/XE2469/j/**E**]

♦ International Institute for Central Asian Studies (IICAS) 13868

Institut International d'Etudes d'Asie Centrale (IIEAC)

Dir University Boulevard 19, Samarkand, Uzbekistan, 140129. T. +998662391540. Fax +998662391540. E-mail: iicasunesco@gmail.com – info@unesco-iicas.org.
URL: http://www.unesco-iicas.org/

History 5 Jul 1995, Samarkand (Uzbekistan). Founded as a direct outcome of *UNESCO (#20322)* Silk Road Expeditions. Institute inaugurated 27 Aug 1995. Former names and other names: *Institute for Central Asian Studies* – alias. **Aims** Bring to the attention of the international community historical and cultural issues on Central Asia; strengthen collaboration between local scholars and their colleagues abroad through a multidisciplinary study of the region. **Structure** General Assembly; Academic Council; Secretariat. **Languages** English, Russian. **Staff** 7.00 FTE, paid. **Finance** Membership contributions from founding Member States, based on their 1% membership dues (or according to the possibilities of each member state) to *UNESCO (#20322)* regular budget. **Activities** Events/meetings; networking/liaising; knowledge management/information dissemination. **Events** *Meeting on Silk Roads ICH Networks* Jeonju (Korea Rep) 2020, *Arts and Humanities Conference of the Silk Road* Daegu (Korea Rep) 2015, *General Assembly* Paris (France) 2001. **Publications** *IICAS Bulletin*. *Atlas of Central Asian Artistic Crafts and Trades* – 4 vols. Books; documents; proceedings; other publications.
Members Full in 10 countries (" indicates founding):
Azerbaijan, China (*), Iran Islamic Rep (*), Kazakhstan (*), Korea Rep, Kyrgyzstan, Pakistan (*), Tajikistan (*), Türkiye, Uzbekistan (*). [2021/XE3598/j/**E**]

♦ International Institute of Chemical, Biological and Environmental Engineering (unconfirmed)
♦ International Institute for Children's, Juvenile and Popular Literature / see International Institute for Children's Literature and Reading Research (#13869)
♦ International Institute for Children's Literature, Osaka (internationally oriented national body)

♦ International Institute for Children's Literature and Reading Research 13869

Institut international pour la littérature juvénile et de la recherche sur la lecture – Internationales Institut für Jugendliteratur und Leseforschung (Institut für Jugendliteratur)

Dir-Gen Mayerhofgasse 6, 1040 Vienna, Austria. T. +4315050359. E-mail: office@jugendliteratur.at.
Sec address not obtained.
URL: http://www.jugendliteratur.at/

History 7 Apr 1965, Vienna (Austria). Former names and other names: *International Institute for Children's, Juvenile and Popular Literature* – former; *Institut international pour la littérature enfantine, juvénile et populaire* – former. **Aims** Promote and coordinate national and international research in the field of juvenile literature, reading education and reading research. **Structure** General Assembly; Committee. **Languages** English, French, German. **Staff** 8.00 FTE, paid. **Finance** Sources: members' dues; subsidies. **Activities** Events/meetings; knowledge management/information dissemination; networking/liaising; research/documentation. **Events** *Biennial Conference* Vienna (Austria) 2012, *Biennial Conference* Wels (Austria) 2010, *Biennial Conference* Wels (Austria) 2008, *Biennial Conference* Hall (Austria) 2006, *Biennial Conference* Hall (Austria) 2004. **Publications** *1001 Buch* (4 a year) in German. Occasional lists of recommended juvenile books. Conference proceedings.
Members Individuals librarians, teachers, authors; Group members institutions, associations, publishing houses, book-shops, etc. Members in 32 countries:
Argentina, Australia, Austria, Belgium, Canada, Croatia, Finland, France, Germany, Greece, Hungary, Iceland, India, Indonesia, Israel, Italy, Japan, Liechtenstein, Luxembourg, Namibia, Netherlands, Norway, Poland, Russia, Slovenia, South Africa, Spain, Sweden, Switzerland, Türkiye, UK, USA. [2022.06.29/XC2123/j/**C**]

- ♦ International Institute for Child Rights and Development (internationally oriented national body)
- ♦ International Institute of Chocolate and Cacao Tasting (unconfirmed)
- ♦ International Institute for Christian Studies / see Global Scholars
- ♦ International Institute of Civil Procedural Law / see International Association for Procedural Law (#12102)
- ♦ International Institute of Commerce (inactive)
- ♦ International Institute for Commercial Competition (inactive)

♦ International Institute of Communications (IIC) 13870

Institut international des communications

Dir Gen Highlands House, 165 The Broadway, London, SW19 1NE, UK. T. +442085448076. Fax +442085448077.
Events and Membership Secretary address not obtained.
URL: http://www.iicom.org/

History Jun 1967, Ditchley Park (UK). Established and chartered in Rome (Italy), 25 Sep 1968. Transferred to London (UK), Sep 1971. Former names and other names: *International Broadcast Institute (IBI)* – former; *Institut international de radiotélédiffusion* – former. Registration: Charity Commission, No/ID: 996225, Start date: 1971, England and Wales. **Aims** Further international cooperation in the field of communication; promote and disseminate research and policy studies concerned with the impact of *broadcast media* and *telecommunications* on society and systematic analysis of economic, cultural, social, legal and political implications of contemporary communications technology; define and seek programme quality and professional competence; eliminate barriers to free flow of communication and its wider use for informational, cultural and educational purposes. **Structure** Members' Meeting (at least annual); Board of Trustees; Executive Committee. **Languages** English. **Staff** 4.00 FTE, paid. **Finance** Sources: contributions; grants; members' dues; private foundations. **Activities** Events/meetings; monitoring/evaluation; research/documentation. **Events** *Telecommunications and Media Forum* Brussels (Belgium) 2022, *Annual Conference* Ottawa, ON (Canada) 2022, *Annual Conference* 2021, *Annual Conference* 2020, *Regulation in Times of Pandemic and Lessons for the Future: A European view* Riga (Latvia) 2020. **Publications** *Intermedia* (4 a year); *Communications Technology Decisions*. Conference and seminar reports and papers.

Members Corporate; Institutional; Individual; National Associations. Members in 67 countries and territories:
Argentina, Australia, Austria, Bangladesh, Belgium, Bolivia, Brazil, Bulgaria, Canada, Chile, Colombia, Costa Rica, Cyprus, Denmark, Egypt, Finland, France, Germany, Greece, Guyana, Hong Kong, Hungary, India, Indonesia, Ireland, Israel, Italy, Jamaica, Japan, Jordan, Kenya, Korea Rep, Kuwait, Kyrgyzstan, Luxembourg, Malaysia, Malta, Mexico, Morocco, Namibia, Netherlands, New Zealand, Nigeria, Norway, Pakistan, Peru, Philippines, Poland, Portugal, Saudi Arabia, Sierra Leone, Singapore, Slovenia, South Africa, Spain, Sri Lanka, Sweden, Switzerland, Syrian AR, Taiwan, Tanzania UR, Thailand, Trinidad-Tobago, UK, USA, Venezuela.

Consultative Status Consultative status granted from: *World Intellectual Property Organization (WIPO, #21593)* (Permanent Observer Status). **IGO Relations** Observer status with: *Intergovernmental Committee of the International Convention of Rome for the Protection of Performers, Producers of Phonograms and Broadcasting Organizations (#11474)*. **NGO Relations** Consultative status with: *International Federation of Library Associations and Institutions (IFLA, #13470)*. Member of: *International Association for Media and Communication Research (IAMCR, #12022)*. Cooperates with: *International Council for Adult Education (ICAE, #12983)*. [2020.09.01/XB1408/j/**B**]

- ♦ International Institute of Comparative Linguistic Law / see International Academy of Linguistic Law (#11556)
- ♦ International Institute of Concurrent Engineering (internationally oriented national body)
- ♦ International Institute of Conference Management / see Connected International Meeting Professionals Association
- ♦ International Institute for Conflict Prevention and Resolution (internationally oriented national body)

♦ International Institute for Conservation of Historic and Artistic Works (IIC) 13871

Institut international pour la conservation des objets d'art et d'histoire

Exec Sec 3 Birdcage Walk, London, SW1H 9JJ, UK. T. +442077595500. Fax +442077994961. E-mail: iic@iiconservation.org.
URL: http://www.iiconservation.org/

History 1950, London (UK). Founded as *International Institute for the Conservation of Museum Objects – Institut international pour la conservation des objets de musée*. Present name adopted 5 May 1959. Articles modified several times. Registration: Companies House, No/ID: 481522, Start date: 27 Apr 1950, England and Wales; Charity Commission, No/ID: 209677, Start date: 22 Sep 1962, England and Wales. **Aims** Serve as a forum for communication among professionals with responsibility for the preservation of *cultural heritage*; advance knowledge, practice and standards for the conservation of historic and artistic works; promote professional excellence and public awareness. **Structure** General Meeting (annual); Council (meets 3 times a year); Sub-committees; Regional Groups (8), including: *Nordic Association of Conservators – Restorers (#17188)*. **Languages** English, French. **Staff** 4.00 FTE, paid. Voluntary. **Finance** Sources: members' dues. **Activities** Awards/prizes/competitions; awareness raising; events/meetings; knowledge management/information dissemination; publishing activities; standards/guidelines. **Events** *Biennial Conference* Wellington (New Zealand) 2022, *Biennial Conference* Edinburgh (UK) 2020, *Student and Emerging Conservator Conference* Cologne (Germany) 2019, *Biennial Conference* Turin (Italy) 2018, *Student and Emerging Conservator Conference* Bern (Switzerland) 2017. **Publications** *News in Conservation* (6 a year) in English; *Congress Preprints* (every 2 years); *Studies in Conservation* (8 a year) in English – additional occasional supplementary issues.

Members Honorary Fellows; Fellows; Individuals; Students; Institutional. Members in 71 countries and territories:
Argentina, Australia, Austria, Belgium, Bermuda, Bosnia-Herzegovina, Brazil, Bulgaria, Canada, Chile, China, Colombia, Croatia, Cuba, Cyprus, Czechia, Denmark, Dominican Rep, Ecuador, Egypt, Faeroe Is, Fiji, Finland, France, Germany, Greece, Holy See, Hong Kong, Hungary, Iceland, India, Iran Islamic Rep, Ireland, Israel, Italy, Jamaica, Japan, Korea Rep, Latvia, Lebanon, Lithuania, Luxembourg, Malta, Mexico, Monaco, Netherlands, New Zealand, Norway, Pakistan, Peru, Philippines, Poland, Portugal, Romania, Russia, Singapore, Slovenia, South Africa, Spain, Sweden, Switzerland, Taiwan, Thailand, Türkiye, UK, United Arab Emirates, Uruguay, USA, Venezuela, Vietnam, Zimbabwe.

NGO Relations Partner of (1): *European Network for Conservation/Restoration Education (ENCoRE, #07883)*. [2023/XB2125/j/**B**]

- ♦ International Institute for the Conservation of Museum Objects / see International Institute for Conservation of Historic and Artistic Works (#13871)
- ♦ International Institute of Convention Management / see Connected International Meeting Professionals Association
- ♦ International Institute of Costs / see International Cost Institute (#12977)
- ♦ International Institute for Cotton (inactive)
- ♦ International Institute for Counter-Terrorism (internationally oriented national body)
- ♦ International Institute of Creative Design and Media (unconfirmed)
- ♦ International Institute for Democracy (inactive)

♦ International Institute for Democracy and Electoral Assistance (International IDEA) 13872

Institut international pour la démocratie et l'assistance électorale – Instituto Internacional para la Democracia y la Asistencia Electoral (IDEA Internacional)

Headquarters Strömsborg, SE-103 34 Stockholm, Sweden. T. +4686983700. Fax +468202422. E-mail: info@idea.int.
URL: http://www.idea.int/

History 27 Feb 1995, Stockholm (Sweden). Established on adoption of a declaration by 14 states. **Aims** Promote *sustainable democracy* worldwide; bring together those who analyse and monitor trend in democracy and those who engage in *political reform*; strengthen the institutions and culture of democracy in both new and long-established democratic states; assist countries in developing and strengthening democratic institutions; offer researchers, policy makers, activists and professionals a forum to discuss democratic principles; blend research and field experience and develop practical tools to improve democratic processes; promote transparency, accountability and efficiency in managing elections; help local citizens evaluate, monitor and promote democracy. **Structure** Council; Board of Advisors. Headquarters headquarters located in Stockholm (Sweden). **Finance** Budget (2015): nearly euro 22 million. **Activities** Politics/policy/regulatory; guidance/assistance/consulting; knowledge management/information. **Events** *Round Table on Inter-Agency Collaboration on Cyber Security Elections* The Hague (Netherlands) 2018, *Annual Democracy Forum* Bern (Switzerland) 2015, *Anniversary Meeting* Stockholm (Sweden) 2015, *Annual Democracy Forum* Gaborone (Botswana) 2014, *Annual Democracy Forum* Santiago (Chile) 2013. **Publications** *IDEA Newsletter* (4 a year) in English – electronic. Annual Report; handbooks; reports; leaflets.

Members Governments of 29 states:
Australia, Barbados, Belgium, Botswana, Canada, Cape Verde, Chile, Costa Rica, Denmark, Dominican Rep, Finland, Germany, Ghana, India, Indonesia, Mauritius, Mexico, Mongolia, Namibia, Netherlands, Norway, Peru, Philippines, Portugal, South Africa, Spain, Sweden, Switzerland, Uruguay.
Observer in 1 country:
Japan.

IGO Relations Observer status with: *United Nations (UN, #20515)*. Cooperates with: *Economic Community of West African States (ECOWAS, #05312)*; *Inter-American Development Bank (IDB, #11427)*; *OAS (#17629)*; *Organisation internationale de la Francophonie (OIF, #17809)*; *Parlamento Latinoamericano (PARLATINO, #18203)*; *UNDP (#20292)*; *United Nations Economic Commission for Africa (ECA, #20554)*; *University for Peace (UPEACE, #20702)*. **NGO Relations** Cooperates with: *Arab NGO Network for Development (ANND, #01016)*; *Association of European Election Officials (ACEEEO, #02508)*; *Ibero-American Foundations Confederation (CIF, no recent information)*; *Instituto Interamericano de Derechos Humanos (IIDH, #11334)*; Inter-American Institute of Human Rights (IIDH); *Inter-Parliamentary Union (IPU, #15961)*; *International Commission of Jurists (ICJ, #12695)*; *International Foundation for Electoral Systems (IFES, #13669)*; *International Press Institute (IPI, #14636)*; *Parliamentarians for Global Action (PGA, #18208)*. [2021/XE2404/j/**E***]

- ♦ International Institute of Dental Ergonomics and Technology (inactive)

♦ International Institute for Developing Engineering Academics (IIDEA) 13873

Co-Dir c/o SEFI, Rue des Deux Eglises 39, 1000 Brussels, Belgium. T. +3225023609. Fax +3225029611.
Co-Dir address not obtained.
URL: http://www.sefi.be/iidea/

History Set up 2011, by *Société européenne pour la formation des ingénieurs (SEFI, #19462)* and *International Federation of Engineering Education Societies (IFEES, #13412)*. **Aims** Provide engineering education associations, institutions and other stakeholders with a clearing house. **Structure** Directors (2). Advisory Board. **Activities** Events/meetings; training/education. **Events** *World Engineering Education Forum* Florence (Italy) 2015, *World Engineering Education Forum* Dubai (United Arab Emirates) 2014. [2016/XJ6307/j/**E**]

- ♦ International Institute for the Development of the Citizenship (internationally oriented national body)
- ♦ International Institute for Dialogue among Cultures and Civilizations (internationally oriented national body)
- ♦ International Institute of Differing Civilizations (inactive)
- ♦ International Institute for Digital Humanities (internationally oriented national body)
- ♦ International Institute of Earthquake Engineering and Seismology (internationally oriented national body)
- ♦ International Institute for Ecological Agriculture (internationally oriented national body)

♦ International Institute for Educational Planning (IIEP) 13874

Institut international de planification de l'éducation (IIPE) – Instituto Internacional de Planeamiento de la Educación (IIPE)

Dir 7-9 rue Eugène-Delacroix, 75116 Paris, France. T. +33145037700. Fax +33140728366. E-mail: director@iiep.unesco.org – info@iiep.unesco.org – documentationcentre@iiep.unesco.org.
Info Services address not obtained.
URL: http://www.iiep.unesco.org/

History Jul 1963, Paris (France), within the framework of *UNESCO (#20322)*, following a resolution of General Conference, Dec 1962. 1st meeting of Governing Board: 18-22 Jul 1963, Paris. **Aims** Support governments in planning and managing their education systems to achieve national objectives and internationally agreed development goals; focus on gender equality, quality of education, education financing, governance and management, education in crisis and conflict, with an overall geographic focus on Africa; develop sustainable educational capacity. **Structure** Legally and administratively a part of UNESCO but enjoys intellectual autonomy. Governing Board (meeting annually). Headquarters in Paris (France); regional offices in Buenos Aires (Argentina) and Dakar (Senegal). **Languages** English, French. **Staff** and fellows: 112. **Finance** Cash contributions from UNESCO; UNESCO member states' voluntary contributions; contract resources from national and international agencies; miscellaneous income. **Activities** Capacity building; training/education; monitoring/evaluation; knowledge management/information dissemination. **Events** *Policy Forum* Paris (France) 2012, *Workshop on educational planning and management in a world with AIDS* Accra (Ghana) 2009, *Workshop on education for the world of work and fight against poverty* Buenos Aires (Argentina) 1995. **Publications** *IIEP Letter* (2 a year). *Expert Directory*. Books; manuals; policy briefs. **Information Services** *Etico*; *Plan4Learning*; *Planipolis*; *UNESCO HIV and Health Clearing House* – databases. **Members** UNESCO member states and associate members. **IGO Relations** UNESCO Institutes/Regional Offices for Education: *International Bureau of Education (IBE, #12413)*; *UNESCO Asia and Pacific Regional Bureau for Education (#20301)*; *UNESCO Institute for Information Technologies in Education (IITE, #20304)*; *UNESCO Institute for Lifelong Learning (UIL, #20305)*; *UNESCO Institute for Statistics (UIS, #20306)*; *UNESCO – International Institute for Capacity Building in Africa (IICBA, #20308)*; *UNESCO Regional Office for Education in the Arab States (UNEDBAS, #20320)*. Regular relations with other organizations of the UN system: *ILO (#11123)*; *International Bank for Reconstruction and Development (IBRD, #12317)*; *UNDP (#20292)*; *UNICEF (#20332)*; *WHO (#20950)*. **NGO Relations** Provides secretariat for: *International Working Group on Education (IWGE, #15909)*. [2016.10.19/XE3384/j/**E***]

- ♦ International Institute for Education Studies (inactive)
- ♦ International Institute of Embryology / see International Society of Developmental Biologists (#15052)
- ♦ International Institute of Embryology (inactive)

♦ International Institute for Energy Conservation (IIEC) 13875

Main Office 1068 King Way, Breinigsville PA 18031, USA. E-mail: iiecus@iiec.org.
URL: https://www.iiec.org/

History 1984, Washington, DC (USA). **Aims** Promote sustainable energy policies and practices in developing countries and economies in transition; work out solutions in the areas of sustainable energy, including energy efficiency, renewable energy and integrated transport planning. **Structure** Board of Directors. Offices: IIEC Africa; IIEC Asia; *International Institute for Energy Conservation – Europe (IIEC-Europe, see: #13875)* (separately listed in this Yearbook); IIEC North America. Project offices in: China, India, Philippines. **Staff** 35.00 FTE, paid. **Finance** Annual budget: 3,500,000 USD. **Activities** Advocacy/lobbying/activism; financial and/or material support; networking/liaising; training/education. **Events** *International conference on practical applications for environmental and energy efficiency management* Bangkok (Thailand) 1990. **Publications** *E-notes* (4 a year) – newsletter. **IGO Relations** Accredited by: *United Nations Framework Convention on Climate Change – Secretariat (UNFCCC, #20564)*. **NGO Relations** Member of (3): *Asia Pacific Urban Energy Association (APUEA, #02073)*; *Climate Action Network (CAN, #03999)*; *Climate Technology Centre and Network (CTCN, #04023)*. Partner of (1): *Global Alliance for Energy Productivity (#10196)*. Instrumental in setting up (1): *CLASP (#03979)*. Provides secretariat for: *Global Energy Efficiency Initiative (GEEI, no recent information)*. [2023/XF4163/j/**F**]

- ♦ International Institute for Energy Conservation – Europe (see: #13875)
- ♦ International Institute for Environmental Affairs / see International Institute for Environment and Development (#13877)

♦ **International Institute for Environmental Studies (IIES)** **13876**

Dir c/o Trent Univ, 1600 West Bank Drive, Peterborough ON K9L 0G2, Canada. T. +17057481011.
URL: https://ii-es.com/

Aims Support the mobility of student and faculty researchers working on environmental problems that cross international boundaries. **Structure** Board of Directors. **Languages** English, Mandarin Chinese. **Activities** Events/meetings; research and development; training/education. **Events** *IIES-ICED Workshop on Circular Economy* 2021, *Annual IIES Science & Policy Workshop* Peterborough, ON (Canada) 2021, *IIES Science and Policy Workshop* Seoul (Korea Rep) 2019.
Members University and research institutes in 8 countries and territories:
Canada, China, Finland, Hong Kong, Korea Rep, Taiwan, UK, USA. [2022.02.07/AA0231/**C**]

♦ **International Institute for Environment and Development (IIED)** **13877**

Institut international pour l'environnement et le développement – Instituto Internacional de Medio Ambiente y Desarrollo

Main Office 235 High Holborn, Holborn, London, WC1V 7LE, UK. E-mail: inforequests@iied.org.
URL: http://www.iied.org/

History Jan 1971. Founded in London (UK) and Washington DC (USA) simultaneously, by Barbara Ward. Washington DC office became part of *World Resources Institute (WRI, #21753)* in 1988. Former names and other names: *International Institute for Environmental Affairs* – former (Jan 1971 to 1973). Registration: Companies House, No/ID: 2188452, England and Wales; Charity Commission, No/ID: 800066, England and Wales; Charity Commission, No/ID: 039864, Scotland. **Aims** Make the world a fairer and more *sustainable* place, in alliance with like-minded partners; acting as a catalyst, broker and facilitator, add voice to *poorer* and more *vulnerable* groups to ensure their interests are heard in decision-making and can bring about progressive change; stress the importance of sustainable development and the principles on which it is built as lying at the heart of all hopes for a secure future for our world. **Structure** International Board of Trustees, nominated by IIED Programmes and Board members; Director; Regional Advisory Panels. *International Institute for Environment and Development – Europe (IIED Europe, #13878).* **Staff** 100.00 FTE, paid. **Finance** Sources: private foundations; UN agencies; certain governments; the corporate sector. **Activities** Advocacy/lobbying/activism; events/meetings; research and development. **Events** *International Conference on Community-based Adaptation to Climate Change (CBA14)* London (UK) 2020, *Community Based Adaptation International Conference* Vietnam 2012, *Social embeddedness of rights and public policy* Montpellier (France) 2006, *International workshop on research partnerships for sustainable development* Cambridge (UK) 2002, *Workshop on urban poverty* Bergen (Norway) 1994. **Publications** *Environment and Urbanization* (2 a year) – journal; *Gatekeeper* – journal. Annual Report; briefing and opinion papers; reports. **Members** Not a membership organization. **Consultative Status** Consultative status granted from: *ECOSOC (#05331)* (Ros B); *UNEP (#20299).* **IGO Relations** Observer at: *OECD (#17693)* – Working Party of Development Assistance and Environment, plus cooperation with *OECD Development Assistance Committee (DAC, see: #17693); United Nations Framework Convention on Climate Change (UNFCCC, 1992).* Invited to Governing Council sessions of: *International Fund for Agricultural Development (IFAD, #13692).* Accredited by: *Green Climate Fund (GCF, #10714); International Whaling Commission (IWC, #15879); United Nations Office at Vienna (UNOV, #20604).* Special relationship with: *Committee of International Development Institutions on the Environment (CIDIE, no recent information).* **NGO Relations** Member of (13): *Active Learning Network for Accountability and Performance in Humanitarian Action (ALNAP, #00101); British Overseas NGO's for Development (BOND)* (Full); *Coalition of European Lobbies on Eastern African Pastoralism (CELEP, #04059); Council for Education in the Commonwealth (CEC); Environment Liaison Centre International (ELCI, no recent information); European Association of Development Research and Training Institutes (EADI, #06012); European Tropical Forest Research Network (ETFRN, #08950); Habitat International Coalition (HIC, #10845); International Centre for Earth Simulation (ICES Foundation); International Union for Conservation of Nature and Natural Resources (IUCN, #15766); Jubilee Research (#16158); National Council for Voluntary Organizations (NCVO); World Benchmarking Alliance (WBA, #21228).* Partner of (7): *Blue Finance (#03283); Fauna & Flora International (FFI, #09277); Global Battery Alliance (GBA, #10249); Global Call for Climate Action (GCCA, inactive); Global Resilience Partnership (GRP, #10577); Green Economy Coalition (GEC, #10717); World Business Council for Sustainable Development (WBCSD, #21254).* Cooperates with (1): *GRET.* Supports (2): *Asia Network for Sustainable Agriculture and Bioresources (ANSAB, #01445); Many Strong Voices (MSV, #16568).* Instrumental in setting up (1): *Innovations, environnement, développement Afrique (IED).* [2022/XE4305/j/**E**]

♦ **International Institute for Environment and Development – Europe (IIED Europe)** **13878**

Treas Plantage Middenlaan 2K, 1018 DD Amsterdam, Netherlands. E-mail: director@iied-europe.org.
URL: https://www.iied.org/iied-europe

History 2021. Set up by *International Institute for Environment and Development (IIED, #13877).* Former names and other names: *Stichting International Institute for Environment and Development Europe* – legal name. Registration: Handelsregister, No/ID: KvK 81230710, Netherlands; RSIN, No/ID: 862003234, Netherlands; EU Transparency Register, No/ID: 338805547817-77, Start date: 3 Oct 2022. **Aims** Advance the education of the public by all charitable means; promote sustainable development for the public benefit by the preservation, conservation and protection of the environment and the prudent use of natural resources, the relief of poverty and the improvement of the conditions of life in socially and economically disadvantaged communities and the promotion of sustainable means for achieving economic growth and regeneration. **Structure** Supervisory Board; Management Board. [2022/AA2941/f/**F**]

♦ International Institute for Environment and Development – Latin America / see IIED América-Latina (#11114)
♦ International Institute for Ethnic Group Rights and Regionalism (#13300)

♦ **International Institute for Ethnomethodology and Conversation Analysis (IIEMCA)** **13879**

Contact c/o UB Französisches Seminar, Maiengasse 51, 4056 Basel BS, Switzerland. E-mail: krimo@sdu.dk.
URL: https://iiemca.org/

History 1989. **Aims** Advance the theory and methodology of ethnomethodology and conservation analytic studies. **Structure** Honorary President; Board; Steering Committee. **Finance** Conference and publication proceeds. **Activities** Events/meetings. **Events** *Conference* Seoul (Korea Rep) 2021, *Practices* Mannheim (Germany) 2019, *Conference* Westerville, OH (USA) 2017, *Living the material world* Kolding (Denmark) 2015, *Conference* Waterloo, ON (Canada) 2013. **Publications** Books.
Members Individuals and institutions working in the fields of ethnomethodology, conversation analysis or doing work associated with the field. Members in 6 countries:
Canada, France, Germany, Netherlands, UK, USA.
NGO Relations *Australasian Institute for Ethnomethodology and Conversation Analysis (AIEMCA).*
[2021/XN8112/j/**C**]

♦ International Institute for European Studies Antonio Rosmini (internationally oriented national body)
♦ International Institute of Family Pedagogics (inactive)
♦ International Institute of Films on Art (inactive)

♦ **International Institute of Fisheries Economics & Trade (IIFET)** **13880**

Exec Dir Dept of Applied Economics, Oregon State University, 226A Ballard Hall, Corvallis OR 97331, USA. T. +15417375354.
URL: https://iifet.oregonstate.edu/

History 1982. Registration: Oregon Secretary of State, USA; System for Award Management, USA. **Aims** Promote interaction and exchange between people from all countries and professional disciplines about marines resource economics and trade issues. **Structure** Executive Committee; Secretariat, headed by Executive Director. **Languages** English. **Finance** Sources: meeting proceeds; members' dues. **Activities** Events/meetings; humanitarian/emergency aid; knowledge management/information dissemination. **Events** *Biennial Conference* Vigo (Spain) 2022, *Biennial Conference* Vigo (Spain) 2020, *Biennial Conference* Seattle, WA (USA) 2018, *Biennial Conference* Aberdeen (UK) 2016, *Biennial Conference* Brisbane, QLD (Australia) 2014. **Publications** *IIFET Newsletter* (annual).
Members Institutional; Individual. Individuals (500) in 61 countries and territories:
Argentina, Australia, Bangladesh, Belgium, Belize, Benin, Brazil, Bulgaria, Cameroon, Canada, Cape Verde, Chile, China, Côte d'Ivoire, Denmark, Estonia, Fiji, Finland, France, Germany, Ghana, Guam, Hong Kong, Iceland, India, Ireland, Italy, Japan, Korea Rep, Madagascar, Malawi, Malaysia, Mauritania, Mauritius, Mexico, Morocco, Mozambique, Netherlands, New Zealand, Nigeria, Norway, Philippines, Poland, Portugal, Romania, Russia, Senegal, Seychelles, South Africa, Spain, Sri Lanka, Sweden, Taiwan, Tanzania UR, Togo, Türkiye, UK, Uruguay, USA, Vietnam, Yemen.
Institutions (24) in 12 countries and territories:
Chile, Denmark, France, Ireland, Japan, Morocco, Netherlands, New Zealand, Norway, Taiwan, UK, USA.
Included in the above, one organization listed in this Yearbook:
International Organisation for the Development of Fisheries and Aquaculture in Europe (EUROFISH, #14427).
NGO Relations Provides secretariat for: *North American Association of Fisheries Economists (NAAFE, #17559).* [2023.02.15/XF8601/j/**F**]

♦ **International Institute of Forecasters (IIF)** **13881**

Business Manager 53 Tesla Ave, Medford MA 02155, USA. T. +17812344077. Fax +15093575530. E-mail: forecasters@forecasters.org.
URL: http://www.forecasters.org/

History 1981. **Aims** Stimulate the generation, distribution, and use of knowledge on forecasting. **Structure** Board of Directors, consisting of President, Secretary, Treasurer and 10 other members. **Languages** English. **Staff** 1.00 FTE, paid. **Finance** Members' dues. **Activities** Research – develops and unifies forecasting as a multidisciplinary field of research drawing on management, behavioural, social engineering, and other sciences. Practice – contributes to the professional development of analysts, managers, and policy makers with responsibilities for making and using forecasting in business and government. Theory and practice – bridges the gap between theory and practice, the latter helping to set the research agenda and research providing useful results. International scope – brings decision makers, forecasters, and researchers from all nations together to improve the quality and usefulness of forecasting. **Events** *Annual Symposium* 2021, *Annual Symposium* 2020, *Annual Symposium* Thessaloniki (Greece) 2019, *Annual Symposium* Boulder, CO (USA) 2018, *Annual Symposium* Cairns, QLD (Australia) 2017. **Publications** *Foresight: International Journal for Practitioners* (4 a year); *International Journal of Forecasting (IJF)* (4 a year); *The Oracle* (4 a year) – newsletter.
Members Individuals in 42 countries and territories:
Argentina, Australia, Austria, Barbados, Belgium, Brazil, Canada, China, Colombia, Cyprus, Czechia, Finland, France, Germany, Hungary, India, Indonesia, Ireland, Italy, Japan, Korea Rep, Malaysia, Mexico, Netherlands, New Zealand, Norway, Pakistan, Portugal, Singapore, South Africa, Spain, St Kitts-Nevis, Sweden, Switzerland, Taiwan, Thailand, Trinidad-Tobago, Türkiye, UK, United Arab Emirates, USA, Venezuela. [2020/XE2587/jv/**E**]

♦ International Institute of Forensic Engineering Sciences / see International Board of Forensic Engineering Sciences
♦ International Institute for Franchise Education (internationally oriented national body)

♦ **International Institute for FRP in Construction (IIFC)** **13882**

Admin Ctr c/o Queen's Univ, Dept of Civil Engineering, Ellis Hall, 58 Univ Ave, Kingston ON K7L 3N6, Canada. E-mail: iifc@iifc.org.
Pres Floor/Room 1 56, Engineering North, North Terrace, School of Civil, Environmental and Mining Engineering, University of Adelaide, Adelaide SA 5005, Australia.
URL: http://www.iifc.org/

History Mar 2003. **Aims** Advance understanding and application of fibre-reinforced polymer (FRP) *composites* in the civil infrastructure, in the service of the engineering profession and society. **Structure** Council (meets every 2 years); Executive Committee; Advisory Committee. Working Groups (4). **Languages** English. **Finance** Members' dues. **Activities** Events/meetings; awards/prizes/competitions. **Events** *CICE : International Conference on Fibre-Reinforced Polymer (FRP) Composites in Civil Engineering* Istanbul (Turkey) 2021, *CICE : International Conference on Fibre-Reinforced Polymer (FRP) Composites in Civil Engineering* Istanbul (Turkey) 2020, *International Symposium on Fiber-Reinforced Polymer Reinforcement of Concrete Structures (FRPRCS)* Belfast (UK) 2019, *APFIS Asia-Pacific Conference on Fibre-Reinforced Polymer (FRP) in Structures* Gold Coast, QLD (Australia) 2019, *CICE : International Conference on Fibre-Reinforced Polymer (FRP) Composites in Civil Engineering* Champs-sur-Marne (France) 2018. **Publications** *FRP International Newsletter.* Proceedings; books; journals; reports. [2021/XM0158/j/**E**]

♦ **International Institute of Gastronomy, Culture, Arts and Tourism (IGCAT)** **13883**

Registered Address Carrer Mas Morell 12 – 2a2a, Sant Pol de mar, 08395 Barcelona, Spain. T. +34937601472. E-mail: info@igcat.org.
URL: https://igcat.org/

History 2010. Originally an informal gathering. Former names and other names: *ARTIDEA* – former. Registration: Start date: 2012. **Aims** Empower local communities by raising awareness of the importance to safeguard and promote distinct food, culture, arts and sustainable tourism assets. **Structure** Board. **Activities** Advocacy/lobbying/activism; awards/prizes/competitions; awareness raising; events/meetings; guidance/assistance/consulting. **Events** *Annual Meeting* Kuopio (Finland) 2020, *Annual Meeting* Barcelona (Spain) 2019, *Annual Meeting* Braga (Portugal) 2018, *Annual Meeting* Barcelona (Spain) 2017, *Annual Meeting* Barcelona (Spain) 2016. **Publications** *IGCAT Newsletter* (4 a year). **NGO Relations** Member of (1): *European Tourism Manifesto (#08921).* [2020/AA0965/**C**]

♦ International Institute for Global Leadership (internationally oriented national body)
♦ International Institute for Global Peace / see Institute for International Policy Studies, Tokyo
♦ International Institute for Health Care Professionals (internationally oriented national body)

♦ **International Institute for Hermeneutics (IIH)** **13884**

Pres address not obtained.
URL: https://www.iih-hermeneutics.org/

History 2001. **Aims** Foster and articulate a general hermeneutics. **Activities** Events/meetings. **Events** *International Congress on the Polyphony of Text and Life* Krakow (Poland) 2015, *Congress* St Bonaventure, NY (USA) 2002. **Publications** *Analecta Hermeneutica* – journal. **Members** Individuals. Membership countries not specified. [2023.02.14/XJ9803/**C**]

♦ International Institute for Higher Education in Latin America and the Caribbean / see UNESCO International Institute for Higher Education in Latin America and the Caribbean (#20309)
♦ International Institute of Higher Studies in Criminal Sciences / see Siracusa International Institute for Criminal Justice and Human Rights (#19289)
♦ International Institute of History of the French Revolution (inactive)
♦ International Institute of Holistic Medicine (internationally oriented national body)
♦ International Institute for Holocaust Research (internationally oriented national body)
♦ International Institute for Housing and Building / see International Association for Housing Science (#11943)
♦ International Institute of Human Economy (inactive)

♦ **International Institute of Humanitarian Law (IIHL)** **13885**

Institut international de droit humanitaire (IIDH) – Istituto Internazionale di Diritto Umanitario (IIDU)

SG Villa Ormond, Corso Cavallotti 113, 18038 San Remo IM, Italy. T. +39184541848. Fax +39184541600. E-mail: sanremo@iihl.org.
Liaison Office Av de la Paix 7bis, 1211 Geneva, Switzerland. T. +41229073671. Fax +41229197933. E-mail: geneve@iihl.org.
URL: http://www.iihl.org/

History 26 Sep 1970, San Remo (Italy). Founded at a meeting of 150 lawyers, academics and other experts. Statutes last amended by General Assembly, Sep 2009. Registration: Italy. **Aims** Disseminate, reaffirm and develop humanitarian law at the national and international level, encouraging and developing all initiatives for its effective implementation; provide armed forces of all countries with knowledge of humanitarian principles contained in existing instruments of international law, such as The Hague and Geneva conventions; promote and disseminate knowledge of existing norms in the field of refugee protection, human rights and migration law, and improve and harmonize their practical application at national and international levels.

Structure General Assembly (annual, always in San Remo – Italy); Council; Executive Board. **Languages** Arabic, Chinese, English, French, Italian, Russian, Spanish. **Staff** 8.00 FTE, paid. **Finance** Members' dues. Contributions of governments and of other international institutions or organizations; course fees. **Activities** Awards/prizes/competitions; knowledge management/information dissemination; research/documentation; training/education. **Events** *Round Table on Current Issues of International Humanitarian Law* San Remo (Italy) 2019, *Round Table on Current Issues of International Humanitarian Law* San Remo (Italy) 2014, *Round table on current problems of international humanitarian law* San Remo (Italy) 2007, *Oslo seminar on current international humanitarian law and human rights issues* Oslo (Norway) 2006, *Round table on current problems of international humanitarian law* San Remo (Italy) 2006. **Publications** *IIHL Newsletter* (6 a year). Books; proceedings of round tables, congresses and seminars; material for courses; reports.
Members Individuals (266) in 52 countries:
Afghanistan, Algeria, Argentina, Australia, Austria, Belgium, Brazil, Canada, China, Costa Rica, Denmark, Egypt, Finland, France, Georgia, Germany, Greece, India, Indonesia, Iran Islamic Rep, Iraq, Ireland, Israel, Italy, Japan, Jordan, Korea Rep, Lebanon, Libya, Netherlands, North Macedonia, Norway, Palestine, Poland, Portugal, Romania, Saudi Arabia, Senegal, Serbia, Sierra Leone, Singapore, South Africa, Spain, Sudan, Sweden, Switzerland, Togo, Tunisia, UK, USA, Venezuela, Zambia.
Honorary members (16). Membership countries not specified. Institutions (8) in 4 countries:
Institutions (8) in 4 countries:
France, Italy (5), Libya, Switzerland.
Associated members (29) in 15 countries:
Afghanistan, Australia, Austria, Belgium, Greece, Indonesia, Italy, Jordan, Lebanon, Malawi, Netherlands, North Macedonia, Saudi Arabia, Switzerland, UK.
Consultative Status Consultative status granted from: *ECOSOC (#05331)* (Special); *Council of Europe (CE, #04881)* (Participatory Status); *UNESCO (#20322)* (Consultative Status). **IGO Relations** Permanent observer: *UNHCR (#20327)*. Close links with: *European Commission (EC, #06633)*; *International Organization for Migration (IOM, #14454)*; *NATO (#16945)*; *United Nations System Staff College (UNSSC, #20637)*. Accredited by: *United Nations Office at Vienna (UNOV, #20604)*. Informal contacts with: *Inter-American Commission on Human Rights (IACHR, #11411)*; *League of Arab States (LAS, #16420)*. Associated with Department of Global Communications of the United Nations. **NGO Relations** Permanent observers: *International Committee of the Red Cross (ICRC, #12799)*; *International Federation of Red Cross and Red Crescent Societies (#13526)*; *International Institute of Human Rights – Fondation René Cassin (IIHR, #13887)*; *Sovereign Military Hospitaller Order of St John of Jerusalem, of Rhodes and of Malta (SMOM)*. Special links with: *Italian Institute for International Political Studies (ISPI)*; *International Commission of Jurists (ICJ, #12695)*; *International Society for Military Law and the Law of War (#15270)*. Observer to: *International Red Cross and Red Crescent Movement (#14707)*. [2022/XC4269/j/**C**]

♦ International Institute for Human Labour Problems (inactive)
♦ International Institute of Human Rights / see International Institute of Human Rights – Fondation René Cassin (#13887)

♦ International Institute for Human Rights, Environment and Development (INHURED International) 13886

Contact GPO Box 12684, Kathmandu, Nepal. T. +97715010536. Fax +97715010616. E-mail: info@inhuredinternational.org.
URL: http://www.inhuredinternational.org/

History 1987. A *Human Rights Information and Documentation Service (HURIDS)* having existed previously. Former names and other names: *Institute for Human Rights, Environment and Development (INHURED)* – former (1990 to 1991). **Aims** Advance: human and peoples' rights; genuine and participatory *democracy*; environmental conservation; people-centred development. Monitor policies and programmes of international financial and trade institutions, including opposing destructive mega-dams and promoting international instruments on human rights, environment and development; help establish and strengthen national and regional human rights instruments and mechanisms in *Asia-Pacific*; provide advocacy for women, children, refugees, *racial discrimination* such as untouchability and indigenous peoples. **Structure** General Assembly (every 3 years). International Executive Committee. Board of Directors. Advisory Council, comprising 15 members. International Secretariat, headed by Executive Director. National Committees; Regional Representatives; Local Affiliates and Networks. **Languages** English, French, Hindi, Nepali. **Staff** 6.50 FTE, paid; 15.00 FTE, voluntary. **Finance** Sources: donations; grants; members' dues; sale of publications. No governmental or foreign funding from 1997-1999. **Activities** Advocacy/lobbying/activism; events/meetings; knowledge management/information dissemination; monitoring/evaluation; research/documentation; training/education. Acts as host secretariat for various Nepalese organizations and networks. **Events** *Global conference on buddhism, peace and human rights* Lumbini (Nepal) 2000, *International conference on destructive dams and human rights* Kathmandu (Nepal) 1998, *South Asia regional conference on social action litigation* Kathmandu (Nepal) 1997. **Publications** *Adhikar* (6 a year) – in Nepalese; *Liberty* (6 a year) in English. Occasional publications. Information Services: Human rights database.
Members Organizations and individuals. Representatives in 19 countries:
Australia, Bhutan, Brazil, Canada, Chile, France, India, Japan, Netherlands, Norway, Pakistan, Philippines, South Africa, Sri Lanka, Sweden, Switzerland, Thailand, UK, USA.
Consultative Status Consultative status granted from: *ECOSOC (#05331)* (Special). **NGO Relations** Working relations with: *Amnesty International (AI, #00801)*; *Women's International League for Peace and Freedom (WILPF, #21024)*. Member of: *EarthAction (EA, #05159)*; *International Action Network on Small Arms (IANSA, #11585)*; *World Organisation Against Torture (OMCT, #21685)*. [2020/XE2287/j/**E**]

♦ International Institute of Human Rights – Fondation René Cassin (IIHR) 13887

Institut international des droits de l'homme – Fondation René Cassin (IIDH) – Instituto Internacional de Derechos Humanos – Fondation René Cassin
Dir 2 allée René Cassin, 67000 Strasbourg, France. T. +33388458445. Fax +33388458450. E-mail: administration@iidh.org.
URL: http://www.iidh.org/

History Dec 1969, Strasbourg (France). Founded by René Cassin (1887-1976), name later changed in his honour. Former names and other names: *International Institute of Human Rights (IIHR)* – former (1969); *Institut international des droits de l'homme (IIDH)* – former (1969); *Instituto Internacional de Derechos Humanos* – former (1969). Registration: France. **Aims** Promote fundamental *protection* and development of human rights, through education and research; encourage development of human rights *teaching* in universities, law and political science faculties and all other institutes and university centres. **Structure** Board; Administrative Board; President; Director. **Languages** English, French. **Finance** Financed by: contributions and grants from international and regional organizations, specialized institutes, NGOs, state and local authorities; private legacies. **Activities** Training/education; research/documentation; knowledge management/information dissemination. **Events** *Annual Session* Strasbourg (France) 2018, *Colloquium on Comparative Human Rights* Strasbourg (France) 2018, *Annual Session* Strasbourg (France) 2017, *Annual Session* Strasbourg (France) 2016, *Annual Session* Strasbourg (France) 2015. **Publications** *Dossier documentaire – Documentary File*. Proceedings; books. **Consultative Status** Consultative status granted from: *African Commission on Human and Peoples' Rights (ACHPR, #00255)* (Observer). **NGO Relations** Permanent observer to: *International Institute of Humanitarian Law (IIHL, #13885)*. Associate member of: *International Association for Media and Communication Research (IAMCR, #12022)*. [2021/XF3831/j/**F**]

♦ International Institute for Human Rights and Peace (internationally oriented national body)
♦ International Institute for Human Rights Studies, Trieste (internationally oriented national body)
♦ International Institute for Hydraulic and Environmental Engineering / see IHE Delft Institute for Water Education (#11110)
♦ International Institute of the Hylean Amazon (inactive)

♦ International Institute of Ibero-American Literature 13888

Institut international de littérature ibéroaméricaine – Instituto Internacional de Literatura Iberoamericana (IILI)
Dir of Publications 1312 Cathedral of Learning, Univ of Pittsburgh, Pittsburgh PA 15260, USA. T. +14126245246. Fax +14126240829. E-mail: iiilisus@pitt.edu – iili@pitt.edu.
URL: http://www.iilionline.org/

History 15 Aug 1938, Mexico City (Mexico). Founded at 1st Congress of Teachers of Latin American Literature. Constitution adopted 22 Aug 1938, Mexico City; amended at 1st Congress of the Institute, 12-17 Aug 1940, Los Angeles CA (USA). **Aims** Promote study of Ibero-American literature; strengthen cultural relations among the peoples of the Americas; coordinate linguistic and literary research; establish chairs of Ibero-American literature in USA and chairs of American literature in the South American countries; publish the works of the principal Ibero-American authors in the original and in English translation. **Structure** Congress (every 2 years); Administrative Council; Editorial Committee. **Languages** Portuguese, Spanish. **Staff** 2.00 FTE, paid. **Finance** Sources: donations; members' dues; sale of publications. **Events** *Congress* Athens (Greece) 2023, *Congress* Reims (France) 2021, *Congress* Reims (France) 2020, *Congress* Bogota (Colombia) 2018, *Congress* Jena (Germany) 2016. **Publications** *Revista Ibero-Americana* (4 a year). *Antonio Cornejo Polar*; *Nueva América*; *Nuevo Siglo*. Congress proceedings.
Members Individuals (over 1,500) and institutions (over 1,000) in 54 countries and territories:
Argentina, Australia, Austria, Belgium, Bolivia, Brazil, Canada, Chile, China, Colombia, Costa Rica, Czechia, Denmark, Dominican Rep, Ecuador, El Salvador, France, Germany, Greece, Guatemala, Honduras, Hong Kong, Hungary, Iceland, India, Ireland, Israel, Italy, Jamaica, Japan, Korea DPR, Korea Rep, Mexico, Netherlands, New Zealand, Nicaragua, North Macedonia (former Yugoslav Rep of), Norway, Panama, Peru, Poland, Portugal, Puerto Rico, Romania, Russia, South Africa, Spain, Sweden, Switzerland, Taiwan, UK, Uruguay, USA, Venezuela. [2021.06.15/XC2148/j/**C**]

♦ International Institute of Industrial Ecology and Green Economy (internationally oriented national body)
♦ International Institute for Industrial Environmental Economics (internationally oriented national body)

♦ International Institute of Informatics and Systemics (IIIS) 13889

Instituto Internacional sobre Informatica y Sistemas
USA Office 13750 West Colonial Dr, Ste 350-408, Winter Garden FL 34787, USA. E-mail: contact-us@iiis.org.
Secretariat Torre Profesional La California, Suite PH-4, Av Francisco de Miranda, La California Norte, Caracas, Miranda 1071 CA, Venezuela.
URL: http://www.iiis.org/

Aims Contribute to the identification of synergetic relationships among the areas of The Systems Approach, Cybernetics and Informatics, as well as between them and society; foster, promote and stimulate anything that can provide support and catalyze post-modernist methods in the post-industrial information society, especially regarding the emerging and growing plurality of conceptions of what is and/or should be Science, Technology and Engineering; foster, promote and stimulate the tolerance required for the emergence of plural reasoning, alternative methods and diversity of rigour in thought; foster, promote, and stimulate the tolerance required for the integration of knowledge and solutions in (a) the different fields of science and technology, with the spirit that has given rise to the Systems Movement (systems theory and methodology), and (b) the different cultural, epistemological, ethical, praxiological and aesthetic realities, within the context of the post-modernist phenomenon. **Activities** Organizes international conferences. **Events** *CISCI : Conferencia Iberoamericana en Sistemas, Cibernética e Informatica* Orlando, FL (USA) 2015, *EISTA : International Conference on Education and Information Systems, Technologies and Applications* Orlando, FL (USA) 2015, *IMSCI : International Multi-Conference on Society, Cybernetics and Informatics* Orlando, FL (USA) 2015, *SIECI : Simposio Iberoamericano de Educacion, Cibernética e Informatica* Orlando, FL (USA) 2015, *World Multi-Conference on Systemics, Cybernetics and Informatics* Orlando, FL (USA) 2015. **Publications** *Journal on Systemics, Cybernetics and Informatics*; *Revista de Sistemas, Cibernetica e Informatica*.
Members Individuals in 102 countries and territories:
Algeria, Argentina, Armenia, Australia, Austria, Bangladesh, Barbados, Belarus, Belgium, Bolivia, Bosnia-Herzegovina, Botswana, Brazil, Brunei Darussalam, Bulgaria, Cameroon, Canada, Chile, China, Colombia, Costa Rica, Croatia, Cuba, Cyprus, Czechia, Denmark, Dominica, Ecuador, Egypt, El Salvador, Estonia, Finland, France, Germany, Greece, Honduras, Hong Kong, Hungary, Iceland, India, Indonesia, Iran Islamic Rep, Iraq, Ireland, Israel, Italy, Japan, Jordan, Kenya, Korea Rep, Kuwait, Latvia, Lebanon, Libya, Lithuania, Luxembourg, Macau, Malaysia, Malta, Mexico, Morocco, Netherlands, New Zealand, Nicaragua, Nigeria, Norfolk Is, Norway, Oman, Pakistan, Panama, Paraguay, Peru, Philippines, Poland, Portugal, Puerto Rico, Qatar, Romania, Russia, Rwanda, Saudi Arabia, Serbia, Singapore, Slovakia, Slovenia, South Africa, Spain, Sweden, Switzerland, Taiwan, Thailand, Trinidad-Tobago, Tunisia, Türkiye, Uganda, UK, Ukraine, United Arab Emirates, USA, Venezuela, Vietnam, Virgin Is UK.
NGO Relations Member of: *International Federation for Systems Research (IFSR, #13564)*. Cooperates with: *Informing Science Institute (ISI, #11201)*. [2016/XN7612/j/**F**]

♦ International Institute for Information Design (internationally oriented national body)
♦ International Institute for Infrastructural, Hydraulic and Environmental Engineering / see IHE Delft Institute for Water Education (#11110)
♦ International Institute for Infrastructure Renewal and Reconstruction / see International Institute for Infrastructure Resilience and Reconstruction (#13890)

♦ International Institute for Infrastructure Resilience and Reconstruction (IIIRR) 13890

Convener Canada Research Chair in Project Management Systems, Ctr for Project Management Excellence, Schulich School of Engineering, Univ of Calgary – ENF 232, University Dr NW, Calgary AB T2N 1N4, Canada. T. +14032206892. Fax +14032827026. E-mail: janaka@ucalgary.ca.
Dep Convener Strcutures Lab – Dept of Civil Engineering, Univ of Peradeniya, Peradeniya, 20400, Sri Lanka. T. +94812393502 – +9481(974777809895. E-mail: ranjith@fulbrightmail.org.
URL: http://www.iiirr.ucalgary.ca/

History Original name: *International Institute for Infrastructure Renewal and Reconstruction*. **Aims** Provide overall leadership in research, education, planning, design and implementation for *natural disaster* related mitigation, resilience enhancement, and reconstruction projects. **Structure** Founder; 2 Co-Convenors; Immediate Part Convenor; 2 Co-Chairs. **Languages** English. **Staff** 3.00 FTE, paid. **Finance** Sponsorship; conference registration fees; research grants. **Activities** Events/meetings; research/documentation. **Events** *Annual International Conference* Kandy (Sri Lanka) 2016, *Annual International Conference* Seoul (Korea Rep) 2015, *Annual International Conference* West Lafayette, IN (USA) 2014, *Annual International Conference* Brisbane, QLD (Australia) 2013, *Annual International Conference* Kumamoto (Japan) 2012. **Publications** Conference proceedings.
Members Universities (18) in 6 countries:
Australia, Canada, Germany, Sri Lanka, UK, USA. [2018/XM4200/**D**]

♦ International Institute of Innovation and Technology (unconfirmed)

♦ International Institute of Innovative Acoustic Emission (I3AE) 13891

Contact C3-b4S15, Katsura Campubs, Kyoto Univ, Nishikyoo-Ku, Kyoto, 615-8540 Japan. T. +81753833495. Fax +81753833495. E-mail: info@iiiae.org.
URL: http://iiiae.org/

History Founded by Acoustic Emission Working Group (AEWG), Acoustic Emission Division of Japanese Society of Non-Destructive Inspection, aka, Japanese Committee on Acoustic Emission (JCAE), and *European Working Group on Acoustic Emission (EWGAE, #09108)*. **Activities** Advocacy/lobbying/activism; events/meetings. **Events** *International Conference on Acoustic Emission* Ljubljana (Slovenia) 2022, *International Conference on Acoustic Emission* Kyoto (Japan) 2016. **Publications** *Journal of Acoustic Emission (JAE)*.
Members Charters groups (3):
Acoustic Emission Division of Japanese Society of Non-Destructive Inspection; Acoustic Emission Working Group (AEWG); *European Working Group on Acoustic Emission (EWGAE, #09108)*. [2017/XM5679/j/**C**]

♦ International Institute of Inspiration Economy (IIIE) 13892

Contact 3661 – Road 456, Block 1204, Hamad Town, Bahrain. E-mail: buhejim@gmail.com – inspirationeconomy@gmail.com.
URL: http://www.inspirationeconomy.org/

History Aug 2015, Slovenia. **Aims** Develop and accelerate best practices of Inspiration Economy; establish unique inspiration currency models worldwide. **Structure** Council. **Languages** Arabic, English. **Staff** 4.00 FTE, paid. **Finance** Self-financing. **Activities** Awards/prizes/competitions; awareness raising; capacity building; certification/accreditation; events/meetings; guidance/assistance/consulting; humanitarian/emergency aid; monitoring/evaluation; projects/programmes; publishing activities; research and development; training/education. Active in all member countries. **Publications** *IIIE Newsletter*, *International Journal of Inspiration and Resilience Economy*; *International Journal of Youth Economy*. Books.
Members Collective (companies and institutions); Individual. Members in 11 countries:
Algeria, Bahrain, Bangladesh, Bosnia-Herzegovina, China, Egypt, India, Mauritania, Morocco, Slovenia, Tanzania UR.
NGO Relations Universities; organizations; societies. [2020.06.22/XM6029/j/**D**]

♦ International Institute of Insurance, Yaoundé (#11309)
♦ International Institute of Integral Human Sciences (internationally oriented national body)
♦ International Institute of Intellectual Cooperation (inactive)

♦ International Institute for Intellectual Property Management (I3PM) 13893

Contact Friedtalweg 5, 9500 Wil SG, Switzerland.
URL: http://www.i3pm.org/

Aims Promote the field of IP Management; enhance the emergence of a dynamic IP-driven economy. **Structure** Bureau; Advisory Board. **Finance** Members' dues. **Activities** Knowledge management/information dissemination; research/documentation; events/meetings. **Publications** *I3PM Newsletter*. **Consultative Status** Consultative status granted from: *World Intellectual Property Organization (WIPO, #21593)* (Observer Status). [2019/XJ8412/j/**D**]

♦ International Institute of Interpreters (inactive)
♦ International Institute of Islamic Economics (internationally oriented national body)
♦ International Institute of Islamic Medicine (internationally oriented national body)

♦ International Institute of Islamic Thought (IIIT) 13894

Headquarters 500 Grove St, Suite 200, Herndon VA 20170-4735, USA. T. +17034711133. Fax +17034713922. E-mail: iiit@iiit.org.
URL: http://www.iiit.org/

History 1981. Former names and other names: *Institut Internationale de la pensée Islamique* – alias. Registration: USA. **Aims** Advance knowledge and education in Muslim societies worldwide. **Structure** Departments (5): Research; Publications; Human Resources Development; Academic Outreach; Continuing Education. **Languages** Arabic, English. **Finance** Public trust fund. **Publications** *American Journal of Islam and Society (AJIS)* (2 a year); *al Fikr al islami al Mu'asir*. Books.
Members Affiliates in 19 countries and territories:
Azerbaijan, Bangladesh, Belgium, Bosnia-Herzegovina, Egypt, Hong Kong, India, Indonesia, Iraq, Japan, Jordan, Kenya, Korea Rep, Malaysia, Morocco, Nigeria, South Africa, Sri Lanka, UK.
IGO Relations Cooperates with: *Islamic World Educational, Scientific and Cultural Organization (ICESCO, #16058)*. **NGO Relations** Joint publication: *Association of Muslim Social Scientists, UK (AMSS UK)*. [2020.04.29/XF0641/j/**F**]

♦ International Institute of Islamic Thought and Civilization (internationally oriented national body)
♦ International Institute of Journalism, Berlin – Brandenburg (internationally oriented national body)
♦ International Institute of Journalism, College of Solidarity / see International Institute of Journalism, Berlin – Brandenburg
♦ International Institute of Journalism and Communication (internationally oriented national body)

♦ International Institute for Justice Excellence (IIJE) 13895

Contact WTC The Hague Business Ctr, Prinses Margrietplantsoen 33, 2595 AM The Hague, Netherlands.
URL: https://www.iije.nl/

History EU Transparency Register: 687723337469-12. **Aims** Develop a collaborative approach to improving, globally, the administration of justice more uniformly and efficiently. **Structure** Board of Directors. **Activities** Knowledge management/information dissemination; research/documentation; training/education. [2020/XM8922/**C**]

♦ International Institute for Justice and the Rule of Law (IIJ) 13896

Institut International pour La Justice et l'Etat de Droit

Contact Old University Bldg, St Paul Street, Valletta, VLT-1216, Malta. T. +35621226148. E-mail: info@theiij.org.
URL: http://theiij.org/

History Proposed Jun 2012, at Ministerial meeting of *Global Counterterrorism Forum (GCTF, #10311)*, and with support of *Group of Eight (G-8, #10745)*. Inaugurated 18 Jun 2014, Malta. Registered as foundation in accordance with Maltese law. **Aims** Enhance and strengthen the competencies of criminal justice practitioners and other stakeholders to address terrorism and related transnational criminal activities within a rule of law framework; promote cooperation and information exchange on national, regional and international basis. **Structure** Governing Board of Administrators (GBA); Advisory Board; Executive Secretariat. **Languages** Arabic, English, French. **Staff** 25-30. **Finance** Grants from: *European Union (EU, #08967)*; governments of Australia, Canada, Germany, Malta, Spain, Switzerland, Netherlands, Turkey, UK and USA; in-kind, programmatic and administrative support from donors and secondments of criminal justice practitioners. **Activities** Training/education; capacity building; events/meetings. **Publications** Annual Report; practitioner tools and resources; factsheets.
Members Governments of 13 countries represented on IIJ Governing Board of Administrators:
Algeria, France, Italy, Jordan, Kuwait, Malta, Morocco, Netherlands, Nigeria, Tunisia, Türkiye, UK, USA.
Regional entity:
European Union (EU, #08967).
IGO Relations *African Center for the Study and Research on Terrorism (ACSRT, #00236)*; *European Judicial Training Network (EJTN, #07617)*; *Global Counterterrorism Forum (GCTF, #10311)*; *Organization for Security and Cooperation in Europe (OSCE, #17887)*; *United Nations (UN, #20515)* Counter-Terrorism Committee Executive Directorate (CTED) and Office of Counter-Terrorism (OCT); *United Nations Interregional Crime and Justice Research Institute (UNICRI, #20580)*; *United Nations Office on Drugs and Crime (UNODC, #20596)*. **NGO Relations** *Central and Eastern European Law Initiative (CEELI, #03693)*; *Global Center on Cooperative Security (GCCS)*; *Global Community Engagement and Resilience Fund (GCERF, #10303)*; *Institute for Security Studies (ISS)*; *International Centre for Counter-Terrorism – The Hague (ICCT)*; *Siracusa International Institute for Criminal Justice and Human Rights (SII, #19289)*; *United States Institute of Peace (USIP)*; University of Malta; national institutions. [2020.01.07/XM4681/**F***]

♦ International Institute of Labour and Social Relations (internationally oriented national body)

♦ International Institute for Labour Studies (IILS) 13897

Institut international d'études sociales (IIES) – Instituto Internacional de Estudios Laborales (IIEL)

Contact address not obtained. T. +41227997908 – +41227996128. Fax +41227998542.
URL: http://www.ilo.org/inst/

History Mar 1960, Geneva (Switzerland), by the Governing Body of *ILO (#11123)*, as an autonomous centre. **Aims** Undertake leading-edge research on policies for a sustainable world economy. **Structure** Board of 12 members, appointed by ILO Governing Body, and comprising ILO members as well as independent individuals. Chairman is ILO Director-General. **Staff** Core staff: international specialists and experts associated with particular projects. **Finance** Resources are drawn from: ILO; grants and contributions from governments and organizations of employers and workers; other funding agencies; sales of publications. **Activities** Major areas (2): *'International Research'* programme aims to shed light on the interactions between global trends and the world of work, and examine key policy dilemmas in achieving a more sustainable world economy; *'Educational Programmes'* assist labour administrations, employers' organizations and trade unions in developing their institutional capacity for research, analysis and policy formulation in the economic and social fields. **Events** *Conference on labour in the international economy* Geneva (Switzerland) 1996, *Social policy forum on social exclusion* Geneva (Switzerland) 1996, *Workshop on global commodity chains* Geneva (Switzerland) 1996, *Social policy forum on social exclusion* New York, NY (USA) 1996, *International forum on equality for women workers in the context of global change* 1994. **Publications** *International Labour Review* (4 a year); *World of Work Report* (annual). *Studies on Growth with Equity* – series. *The Global Crisis: Causes, Responses and Challenges*; *Towards a Greener Economy: The Social Dimensions Recovery*. Books; discussion papers; policy briefs; special publications. **Members** Not a membership organization. **NGO Relations** Cooperates with various academic and public policy institutions and networks, including: *European Trade Union Institute (ETUI, inactive)*; *International Labour and Employment Relations Association (ILERA, #13997)*. [2017/XE5485/j/**E***]

♦ International Institute of Law Association Chief Executives (IILACE) 13898

Sec Gen c/o Relationships are Everything Inc, 190 O'Connor Street – 7th Floor, Ottawa ON K2P 2R3, Canada. T. +16137993856. E-mail: info@iilace.org.
Pres c/o Law Society of Namibia, 333 Independence Ave – 1st floor, PO Box 714, Windhoek, Namibia. T. +26461230263. Fax +26461230223.
URL: http://www.iilace.org/

History Founded in Jul 1999, Edinburgh (UK). **Aims** Provide professional development for chief executives on association law/society issues; enable mutual assistance in dealing with challenges of law association management; facilitate exchange of views and information among members. **Structure** Officers: President; Past President; Vice-President; Officers-at-Large (3); Secretary-Treasurer. **Staff** 0.50 FTE, paid. **Finance** Members' dues. Sponsorship. **Activities** Organizes an Annual Conference, webinars and internet exchanges. **Events** *Annual Conference* Ottawa, ON (Canada) 2018, *Annual Conference* London (UK) 2017, *Annual Conference* Wellington (New Zealand) 2016, *Annual Conference* Washington, DC (USA) 2015, *Annual Conference* Cape Town (South Africa) 2014.
Members Full bar associations and law societies (over 50) in 22 countries and territories:
Australia, Botswana, Canada, China, Cyprus, England, Estonia, Germany, Hong Kong, Ireland, Kenya, Macau, Netherlands, New Zealand, Nigeria, Norway, Scotland, Singapore, South Africa, Sweden, Uganda, USA. [2019/XE4299/j/**E**]

♦ International Institute for Law and the Environment (internationally oriented national body)
♦ International Institute of Law of the French-Speaking Countries (#11310)
♦ International Institute for Ligurian Studies (#11311)
♦ International Institute of Linguistics and Law / see Kyiv International University
♦ International Institute for Management Development (internationally oriented national body)
♦ International Institute of Management LINK (internationally oriented national body)

♦ International Institute for the Management of Logistics and Supply Chain (IML) 13899

Exec Dir EPFL-CDM-IML, Odyssea Building, Station 5, 1015 Lausanne VD, Switzerland.
URL: http://iml.epfl.ch/

History 1990, Lausanne (Switzerland). **Aims** Promote development and use of supply chain organization methods through education and research; participate in development of procedures concerning international *trade*; train high level managers in the field and introduce young people to the foundations of the field. **Structure** General Meeting (annual); Management Board; Chairman's Committee; Steering Committee; Supervisory Board. **Languages** English, French. **Finance** Members' dues. Admission fee: Swiss Fr 50,000. Grants; donations; other sources. **Activities** Organizes seminars, Executive Master courses (MAS) and continuing education programme (CAS). Annual meeting in Lausanne (Switzerland) and Paris (France). **Events** *Seminar on supply chain and E logistics* Geneva (Switzerland) 2000, *Seminar on logistics and total quality management* Lausanne (Switzerland) 1996, *New OR technologies for transportation and facility location international conference* Thun (Switzerland) 1995, *CALS seminar* Lausanne (Switzerland) 1994, *Séminaire sur la logistique de distribution européenne* Paris (France) 1994. **Publications** *CDM* – newsletter. Documentation of postgraduate studies in the management of logistics systems (annual). Annual report.
Members Institute; Associate; Benefactor; Honorary. Members (60) in 8 countries:
Belgium, Canada, France, Germany, Italy, Netherlands, Switzerland, UK.
Included in the above, 4 organizations listed in this Yearbook:
European University Research and Operations Network in Logistics (EURONIL, no recent information); *International Committee of the Red Cross (ICRC, #12799)*; *International MultiModal Transport Association (IMMTA, inactive)*; *UNCTAD (#20285)*.
NGO Relations Member of: *European Logistics Association (ELA, #07710)*. [2021/XE2102/jy/**E**]

♦ International Institute of Management in Technology (internationally oriented national body)

♦ International Institute of Marine Surveyors (IIMS) 13900

Institut international des experts maritimes

CEO Murrills House, 48 East St, Portchester, Fareham, PO16 9XS, UK. T. +442392385223. Fax +442392385224. E-mail: info@iims.org.uk.
URL: http://www.iims.org.uk/

History UK Registered Company: 4742692. **Aims** Promote professionalism and the advancement of knowledge in the profession of marine surveying. **Structure** General Meeting (annual). Management Board of 23, with 10 members based in UK. Officers: President; Vice-President. Management headed by CEO. Branches in: Australia; India; New Zealand; United Arab Emirates. **Finance** Members' dues. **Activities** Organizes: annual meeting, always in London (UK); conferences adn seminars; training courses; education programmes; setting standards; meetings and working groups. Acts umbrella organization for marine surveying organizations worldwide. **Events** *Conference* Singapore (Singapore) 2019, *Annual General Meeting* London (UK) 2003, *Annual General Meeting* London (UK) 2001. **Members** Founder; Full; Fellow; Honorary; Associate; Supporting; Graduate; Student; Corporate; Corporate Supporting; Allied. Members in 98 countries. Membership countries not specified. [2011.12.09/XE4221/j/**E**]

♦ International Institute of Mediterranean Theatre (internationally oriented national body)

♦ International Institute for Middle East and Balkan Studies (IFIMES) 13901

Mednarodni Inštitut za Bližnjevzhodne in Balkanske Študije

Dir Vošnjakova ulica 1, PO Box 2795, 1001 Ljubljana, Slovenia.

Structure Advisory Board; Special Departments (5). **Activities** Events/meetings; knowledge management/information dissemination; networking/liaising; research/documentation. **Events** *Europe Future Neighbourhood* Vienna (Austria) 2021, *75 Years of Europe's Collective Security and Human Rights System* Vienna (Austria) 2020. **Publications** *European Perspectives* (2 a year). **Consultative Status** Consultative status granted from: *ECOSOC (#05331)* (Special). **IGO Relations** Partner of (2): *EDU (#05363)*; *International Anti-Corruption Academy (IACA, #11654)*. **NGO Relations** Partner of (2): *Geneva International Peace Research Institute (GIPRI)*; *Research Institute for European and American Studies (RIEAS)*. [2021/AA1457/**F**]

♦ International Institute of Molecular and Cell Biology, Warsaw (internationally oriented national body)

♦ International Institute of Monitoring Democracy Development, Parliamentarianism and Suffrage Protection for the Citizens of the IPA CIS Member Nations (IIMDP) 13902

Dir Shpalernaya Str 47, Tavrichesky Palace, St Petersburg SANKT-PETERBURG, Russia, 193015. T. +78123266926 – +78123266982. Fax +78122722248. E-mail: kanz@iacis.ru.
URL: http://www.iacis.ru/html/index-eng.php?id=84/

History 10 Feb 2006, Kiev (Ukraine), by *Interparliamentary Assembly of Member Nations of the Commonwealth of Independent States (IPA CIS, #15958)* through *Convention on Standards of Democratic Elections, Electoral Rights and Freedoms in Member Nations of the Commonwealth of Independent States (2002)*. **Aims** Monitor elections in the Nations of the Commonwealth and beyond; draft recommendations on the results of monitoring; train international observers. [2011/XJ3774/j/**E***]

♦ International Institute of Municipal Clerks (internationally oriented national body)
♦ International Institute for Nationality Rights and Regionalism / see Internationales Institut für Nationalitätenrecht und Regionalismus (#13300)
♦ International Institute for Natural Resources in Africa / see UNU Institute for Natural Resources in Africa (#20718)

♦ International Institute of Noise Control Engineering (IINCE) 13903

Institut international de la technologie de contrôle du bruit

SG Univ of Zagreb, Fac of EE and Computing, Unska 3, HR-10000 Zagreb, Croatia. T. +38516129833. E-mail: secretarygeneral@i-ince.org.
URL: http://www.i-ince.org/

History 1974, Zurich (Switzerland). Founded as international association, following an American (USA) organization, formed 1971. **Aims** Promote international cooperation in research, application of engineering techniques for the control of environmental noise and vibration and the exchange of technical information. **Structure** General Assembly; Board of Directors. **Finance** Sources: members' dues. **Activities** Events/meetings; training/education. **Events** *International Congress on Noise Control Engineering* Chiba (Japan) 2023, *International Congress on Noise Control Engineering* Glasgow (UK) 2022, *International Congress on Noise Control Engineering* Washington, DC (USA) 2021, *International Congress on Noise Control Engineering* Seoul (Korea Rep) 2020, *International Congress on Noise Control Engineering* Madrid (Spain) 2019. **Publications** *Noise News International* (4 a year). Conference Proceedings.

Members Full; sustaining; institutional. Member societies in 45 countries and territories:
Argentina, Australia, Austria, Belgium, Brazil, Canada, Chile, China, Croatia, Czechia, Denmark, Egypt, Finland, France, Germany, Greece, Hong Kong, Hungary, India, Iran Islamic Rep, Italy, Japan, Korea Rep, Lithuania, Mexico, Netherlands, New Zealand, Nigeria, Norway, Poland, Portugal, Romania, Russia, Serbia, Singapore, Slovakia, Slovenia, South Africa, Spain, Sweden, Switzerland, Tunisia, Türkiye, UK, USA.
Included in the above, 3 organizations listed in this Yearbook:
East European Acoustical Association (EEAA); *Ibero-American Federation of Acoustics (#11021)*; *INCE Europe*.
International Sustaining members in 6 countries:
Belgium, Denmark, Japan, Liechtenstein, Norway, Sweden.
International Institutional member in 1 country:
Sweden.

NGO Relations In liaison with technical committees of: *International Organization for Standardization (ISO, #14473)*. Affiliate member of: *International Commission for Acoustics (ICA, #12658)*.
[2022.02.02/XE3614/j/C]

♦ International Institute for Non-Aligned Studies (IINS) 13904

Head Office A-2/59, Safdarjung Enclave, Delhi 110029, DELHI 110029, India. T. +911126102520. Fax +911126196294. E-mail: iins@iins.org.
URL: http://www.iins.org/

History 19 Sep 1980, by Dr Govind Narain Srivastava. **Aims** Promote the role of non-alignment in guiding and leading all other countries of the world in finding solutions to global/regional problems. **Structure** Executive Committee (Governing Body) is elected from among members and comprises President, 3 Vice-Presidents, Director General (chief executive), 3 Directors and Treasurer. International Executive/Steering Committee of internationally-known personalities. Based in Delhi (India), with offices in Geneva (Switzerland), Vienna (Austria) and New York NY (USA) and regional offices in 5 other countries. *IINS Centre for Human Rights (CHR)* with 5 divisions: Rights of Minorities and Ethnic Groups; Rights of Women and Children; Right to Sustainable Development (Economic): Right to Life, Democracy and Human Rights; Human Rights – Specific Violations; A Principled Fight against Terrorism. **Finance** Sales of publications; advertisements; donations; endowments; subscriptions; grants. **Activities** Organizes national and international conferences, seminars, colloquia, symposia and workshops; conducts studies and research concerning different aspects and issues of, and trends in, the Non-Aligned Movement and other areas related to Non-Aligned; trains workers for dissemination of ideas, philosophy and movement of the Non-Aligned and sends them to various countries for carry out work among the people and their government; offers consultancy services and research facilities; serves as a focal point for coordinating public, academic and research activities among the non-aligned countries; maintains a reference library and documentation centre. Major areas: peace; security; human rights; human resource development; advancement of science education and culture. Provides a platform *'NGOs Forum for Nam'* to various non-governmental organizations in NAM countries. **Publications** *News Bulletin* (12 a year) – of the Coordinating Committee; *Non-Aligned World* (4 a year) – journal; *News from the Non-Aligned World* (2 a month) in English, Hindi. *Towards a more Dynamic and Cohesive NAM: Challenges of the 21st Century* (2006); *Child Labour in India* (2006); *Women Empowerment* (2006); *Magazine on 50 Years of Bandung Anniversary* (2005) by Pramila Srivastava; *Terrorism the Global Perspective* (2001) by Pramila Srivastava; *NAM Extending Frontiers* (2000) by Pramila Srivastava; *Hotbed of Repression and Conflicts: A Threat to Peace* (1998) by Refaqat Ali Khan; *Socialism and Non-Alignment* (1998) by Govind Srivastava; *Democracy and Terrorism* (1997) by Govind Srivastava; *Non-Aligned Movement* (1997) by Reena Marwah. Research papers; conference publications. Information Services: Maintains reference library and documentation centre. **Members** Individuals – academicians, scholars, retired diplomats, present and past parliamentarians, people in the media and educators; organizations – organizations, associations, institutions and corporate bodies with similar aims and objectives. Members drawn from NAM member countries and other developing countries in Asia, Africa, North America, South America, Europe and Australia. Membership countries not specified. **Consultative Status** Consultative status granted from: *ECOSOC (#05331)* (General). **IGO Relations** Accredited by: *United Nations Office at Vienna (UNOV, #20604)*. Participates in meetings of: ECOSOC; *United Nations Commission on Human Rights (inactive)*. Guest of: *Non-Aligned Movement (NAM, #17146)*. Participates as guest in: *Conference of Heads of State or Government of Non-Aligned Countries*; *Conference of Foreign Ministers of Non-Aligned Countries*; ministerial meetings of *Coordinating Bureau of the Non-Aligned Countries (#04815)*. Associated with Department of Global Communications of the United Nations. **NGO Relations** Member of: *Afro-Asian Peoples' Solidarity Organization (AAPSO, #00537)*; *Conference of Non-Governmental Organizations in Consultative Relationship with the United Nations (CONGO, #04635)*. Instrumental in setting up: *CONGO Committee on Human Rights (#04663)*. [2008.06.01/XE3325/j/E]

♦ International Institute of Obsolescence Management (IIOM) 13905

Office Unit 3 Curo Park, Frogmore, St Albans, AL2 2DD, UK. T. +441727876029. E-mail: admin@theiiom.org.
URL: http://www.theiiom.org/

History 1997. Former names and other names: *Component Obsolescence Group* – former. **Aims** Advance the science and practice of obsolescence management; promote and recognize high standards of practice and professional competence; open opportunities for development and career paths for practitioners of obsolescence management; generate widespread awareness and understanding of the discipline. **Structure** Board of Management; Chapters in UK and Benelux; Sub group in Germany. **Languages** English. **Staff** Voluntary. **Finance** Sources: members' dues. **Activities** Events/meetings. **Events** *International Conference* Munich (Germany) 2022, *International Conference* St Albans (UK) 2021, *International Conference* London (UK) 2019, *Members Meeting* Basingstoke (UK) 2017, *International Conference* Bristol (UK) 2017. **Publications** *IIOM Newsletter*. **Members** Individual (Student; Affiliate; Associate; Member; Fellow); Corporate. Membership countries not specified. [2023.02.14/XM6112/j/D]

♦ International Institute for the Organisation of Intellectual Work, Die Brücke (inactive)

♦ International Institute for the Pastoral Theology of Health Care . . . 13906

Institut international de théologie pour la pastorale de la santé – Instituto Internacional de Teología Pastoral Sanitaria – Istituto Internazionale di Teologia Pastorale Sanitaria (CAMILLIANUM)

Secretariat CAMILLIANUM, Largo Ottorino Respighi 6, 00135 Rome RM, Italy. T. +3963297495. Fax +3963296950.
URL: http://www.camillianum.it/

History 28 Apr 1987, when approved and erected by the Holy See. Under the care of *Order of the Servants of the Sick (Camillians)*. Incorporated into 'Teresianum' Pontifical Theological Faculty as a course of specialization in the second and third cycle. **Aims** Prepare teachers in pastoral care theology, social welfare experts and representatives for diocesan pastoral care. **Activities** Knowledge management/information dissemination; publishing activities; events/meetings; training/education. [2016.02.16/XF0866/j/F]

♦ International Institute for Peace (IIP) 13907

Internationales Institut für den Frieden (IIF)

Dir Möllwaldplatz 5/7, 1040 Vienna, Austria. T. +4315046437. E-mail: office@iip.at.
URL: http://www.iipvienna.com/

History Jul 1957, Vienna (Austria). Refounded 1989, by former president Erwin Lanc. Former names and other names: *Institut international de la paix* – former; *Instituto Internacional pro Paz* – former; *Mezdunarodnyj Institut Mira* – former. Registration: Austria. **Aims** Promote peace and non-violent conflict resolution across the world; promote dialogue, public engagement and a common understanding to ensure a holistic approach to conflict resolution and durable peace. **Structure** General Assembly (at least every 4 years); Executive Board; Advisory Board; Court of Arbitration. **Languages** English, German. **Activities** Events/meetings; knowledge management/information dissemination; networking/liaising; politics/policy/regulatory; publishing activities; training/education. **Events** *Thirty Years On – Is There Still a Post-Soviet Space?* Vienna (Austria) 2021, *Vienna Peace and Security Talks Conference* Vienna (Austria) 2021, *Friends with Enemies: Neutrality and Nonalignment Then and Now* Vienna (Austria) 2020, *International Peace Studies Conference* Vienna (Austria) 2018, *International symposium* Vienna (Austria) 2008. **Publications** *Iran in the International System: Between Great Powers and Great Ideas* (2020) by Prof Heinz Gärtner and Mitra Shahmoradi; *Gerechte Intervention? Zwischen Gewaltverbot und Schutzverantwortung* (2017) by Stephanie Fenkart and Dr Hannes Swoboda et al in English, German. Annual Report: https://www.iipvienna.com/annual-report

Members Individuals and corporate bodies in East and West on invitation of the Executive Board in 44 countries:
Argentina, Australia, Austria, Belgium, Bulgaria, Canada, Chile, Costa Rica, Croatia, Cuba, Czechoslovakia, Denmark, Egypt, Finland, France, Germany, Greece, Hungary, India, Ireland, Italy, Japan, Mexico, Netherlands, New Zealand, Nicaragua, Nigeria, Norway, Pakistan, Panama, Poland, Portugal, Romania, Russia, Serbia, Slovenia, Spain, Sweden, Switzerland, Türkiye, UK, USA, Venezuela, Vietnam.

Consultative Status Consultative status granted from: *ECOSOC (#05331)* (Ros C); *UNESCO (#20322)* (Consultative Status). **IGO Relations** Accredited by (2): *Organization for Security and Cooperation in Europe (OSCE, #17887)*; *United Nations Office at Vienna (UNOV, #20604)*. **NGO Relations** Accredited by (1): *European Network of Independent Non-Proliferation Think Tanks (EU Non-Proliferation Network, #07930)*. Member of: Forum Außenpolitische Think Tanks (FATT); Network of Think Tanks on Eastern Partnership; Netzwerk für Friedens- und Konfliktforschung Österreich (NEFKÖ). [2022.05.10/XE2128/j/E]

♦ International Institute for Peace (internationally oriented national body)
♦ International Institute for Peace and Conflict Research / see Stockholm International Peace Research Institute (#19994)

♦ International Institute of Peace and Development Studies (IIPDS) . . 13908

Contact 12/8 M 14 S 4, Suwinthawong 51, Soi Rom Yen, Kratumrai Amhoe Nong Chok, Bangkok, Thailand. T. +6620515578. E-mail: iipds@arf-int.org.
URL: http://www.arf-int.org/about-us-iipds/

History Co-hosted by *Asian Muslim Action Network (AMAN, #01544)* and *Asian Resource Foundation (ARF)*. **Aims** Facilitate collective learning process about understanding of the causes of conflict, ways and means to transform conflict and build sustainable peace; develop critical awareness about realities and challenges, and engage participants in social actions for peace, justice and development; strengthen "Peace Network" across the globe. **Languages** English. **Staff** 5-7. **Activities** Training/education; events/meetings. **NGO Relations** Collaborates with national organizations. [2019.03.04/XM6289/j/E]

♦ International Institute on Peace Education (internationally oriented national body)
♦ International Institute for Peace, Monaco (inactive)
♦ International Institute of Peace Studies (internationally oriented national body)

♦ International Institute of Peace Studies and Global Philosophy (IIPSGP) 13909

Dir c/o European Peace Museum, 13 Grande rue, 23270 Bétête, France. E-mail: iipsgp@educationaid.net.
Media Coordinator 213 Ham Road, Worthing, BN11 2QB, UK.
URL: http://www.educationaid.net/

History Founded 1990, arising out of a feasibility study investigating the possibility of creating a Peace Studies Institute in the University of London, and subsequent years of active educational research, networking and consultancy, when everyone interested in advancing peace research in London (UK) and internationally were invited to join. Took over activities of *International Institute for Peace and Global Responsibility (inactive)* and *International Philosophers for Peace and Global Responsibility (inactive)*. Has built on the work of *European Philosophers for Peace*. **Aims** Advance comprehensive study and research into the possibilities for *conflict resolution* and transformation; focus in particular on linking practical work in *mediation* and conflict resolution with philosophical and theoretical research, with special attention to the diversity of philosophical and *spiritual traditions*; provide access to a network of research and information on peace and global education activities worldwide; act as support structure and information clearinghouse to empower individuals to develop their own research and action projects in the field of peace and global *ethics*. **Structure** Advisory Council; Secretariat. Includes: *Association of Spiritual Academies International (ASAI)*; *Balkan Centre for Peace and Culture*; Centre for Peace Policy Research (CEPPR); Centre for the Periodic Table of the World's Religious and Philosophical Traditions; Centre for Transpersonal History; Commonwealth Interfaith Network; Ecumenical School of Peace Theology; *European Philosophers for Peace*; European Union Mediation Service (EUMS); Forest Garden; *Global Green University (GGU)*; Historians for Peace and Justice; Multifaith and Multicultural Education and Mediation Services; Order of Wandering Poets for Peace; Pagan Academic Network; School of Nonviolence; Truth and Reconciliation Commission for Britain and Ireland; Truth and Reconciliation Commission for the Middle East. **Languages** English, French, German, Hebrew, Hindi, Italian, Russian, Sanskrit. **Staff** Voluntary. **Finance** Members' dues. Donations. **Activities** Conflict resolution; training/education; knowledge management/information dissemination; events/meetings; guidance/assistance/consulting. **Events** *Israeli-Palestinian peace symposium on ending the wars, making the peace* Bethlehem (Palestine) 2008. **Publications** *IIPSGP Newsletter*; *The Muses Love Journal – the International Journal of Peace and Global Philosophy*. **Members** Members in over 53 countries. Membership countries not specified. **NGO Relations** Instrumental in setting up: *Islamic and Interfaith Middle Eastern Peace Studies Association (IIMEPSA)*. [2017.12.19/XG3620/j/F]

♦ International Institute for Peace through Tourism (internationally oriented national body)

♦ International Institute of Philosophy (IIP) 13910

Institut international de philosophie (IIP) – Instituto Internacional de Filosofia – Internationales Institut für Philosophie

Gen Sec 96 bd Raspail, 75006 Paris, France. T. +33143363911. E-mail: inst.intern.philo@wanadoo.fr.
URL: http://www.i-i-p.org/

History Founded 6 Aug 1937, Paris (France), at the Descartes Congress, under the patronage of *International Institute of Intellectual Cooperation (IICI, inactive)*, formed 9 Aug 1925, and amalgamated, 1945, with UNESCO, on the initiative of Ake Petzäll (Sweden) and Raymond Bayer (France). Formerly named *Institut international de collaboration philosophique*. Had been under the auspices of *Permanent Committee of the International Congresses of Philosophy (inactive)*, set up in Aug 1900, until Aug 1948 when the latter was superseded by *International Federation of Philosophical Societies (FISP, #13507)*. Present name adopted 1942. Statutes changed: 1952, 1954, 1957, 1959, 1967, 1969, 1983, 2011, 2014. Registered by French Ministerial Decree, 11 Oct 1955. **Aims** Serve as a scientific and spiritual link between philosophers from different countries; establish regular working relations between them; encourage exchange of professors and lecturers. **Structure** General Assembly (annual); Managing Committee. Participation at congresses on invitation only. **Languages** English, French. **Staff** 1.00 FTE, paid. **Finance** Grants from: Centre national de la recherche scientifique (France). **Activities** Meeting activities. **Events** *Congress* Helsinki (Finland) 2019, *Congress* Istanbul (Turkey) 2016, *Congress* Beijing (China) 2015, *The relationships of philosophy with its history* Rome (Italy) 2014, *Congress* Athens (Greece) 2013. **Publications** *Bibliographie de la philosophie. Philosophy and World Community* in Czech, English, French, German, Hebrew, Hungarian, Italian – series. *Vivre en philosophe* (2016); *Cause, connaissance et responsabilité – Cause, Knowledge and Responsibility* (2015); *Nature in Education* (2015); *Philosophy of Justice* (2014); *Chroniques de philosophie/Philosophical Surveys: Ethics and Moral Philosophy* (2013); *Politics in Education* (2012); *Idées sans frontières: Histoire et structures de l'Institut international de philosophie* (2005); *Controverses philosophiques*; *L'origine de l'Institut international de philosophie* by Ake Petzäll; *Philosophes critiques d'eux-mêmes*; *Problèmes philosophiques d'aujourd'hui*. Proceedings of meetings.

Members Titular (66); Emeritus (41). Members in 45 countries:
Argentina, Austria, Belgium, Bosnia-Herzegovina, Brazil, Cameroon, Canada, Chile, China, Côte d'Ivoire, Croatia, Czechia, Denmark, Ecuador, Egypt, Finland, France, Germany, Greece, Iceland, India, Iran Islamic Rep, Ireland, Israel, Italy, Japan, Korea Rep, Luxembourg, Mexico, Morocco, Netherlands, Norway, Peru, Poland, Portugal, Romania, Russia, Senegal, Spain, Sweden, Switzerland, Tunisia, Türkiye, UK, USA. [2017.10.11/XE2152/jv/E]

♦ International Institute of the Philosophy of Law and Judicial Sociology (inactive)
♦ International Institute of Photography (inactive)
♦ International Institute of Plasmology (inactive)
♦ International Institute of Pneumiatrics (see: #21330)
♦ International Institute of Political Sciences (internationally oriented national body)
♦ International Institute for Popular Culture (internationally oriented national body)

♦ International Institute for Population Sciences (IIPS) 13911

Dir International Institute for Population Sciences, Govandi Station Road, Opposite Sanjona Chamber,, B.S. Devashi Marg, Deonar, Mumbai, Maharashtra 400088, Mumbai MAHARASHTRA 400088, India. T. +912225562062 – +9122225574943. Fax +912225563257. E-mail: director@iipsindia.ac.in.
URL: https://iipsindia.ac.in/

History 1956. Founded by *United Nations Economic and Social Commission for Asia and the Pacific (ESCAP, #20557)* and the Government of India. Former names and other names: *Demographic Training and Research Centre (DTRC)* – former (1956 to 1971); *International Institute for Population Studies (IIPS)* – former (Apr 1971 to Mar 1984). **Aims** Serve as a research and training institution in population and *demographic* studies for *Asia* and *Pacific* (ESCAP) region. **Structure** General Council, chaired by the Union Minister of Health and Family Welfare (India). Executive Council, consisting of educationists and administrators and chaired by Secretary to the Government of India in the Ministry of Health and Family Welfare. Director, assisted by Registrar. Academic Departments (7): Mathematical Demography and Statistics; Fertility Studies; Public Health and Mortality Studies; Migration and Urban Studies; Population Policies and Programmes; Development Studies; Extra Mural Studies. **Finance** Main source: Ministry of Health and Family Welfare – Government of India. **Activities** Events/meetings; projects/programmes; research/documentation; training/education. **Events** *Indo Swedish international seminar on affordable housing problems and perspectives* Mumbai (India) 1993. **Publications** *IIPS Newsletter* (4 a year); *IIPS Information Bulletin* (annual). Annual Report. Research brief; working paper series. Information Services: computer centre; library. Provides bibliographic and reference services. **Information Services** *Data Centre on Population.*
Members Individuals in 46 countries and territories:
Australia, Austria, Belgium, Bulgaria, Canada, China, Croatia, Czechia, Denmark, Estonia, Finland, France, Germany, Greece, Hungary, Iceland, India, Indonesia, Ireland, Israel, Italy, Japan, Jordan, Kuwait, Mexico, Montenegro, Morocco, Netherlands, New Zealand, Norway, Poland, Portugal, Russia, Saudi Arabia, Serbia, Slovenia, South Africa, Spain, Sweden, Switzerland, Taiwan, Thailand, Türkiye, UK, USA, Venezuela.
Consultative Status Consultative status granted from: *United Nations Population Fund (UNFPA, #20612).*
NGO Relations Member of (2): *PMNCH (#18410); United Nations Academic Impact (UNAI, #20516).*
[2022.02.02/XE2637/j/**E**]

♦ International Institute for Population Studies / see International Institute for Population Sciences (#13911)
♦ International Institute of Projectiology / see International Institute of Projectiology and Conscientiology (#13912)

♦ International Institute of Projectiology and Conscientiology (IIPC) . 13912

Instituto Internacional de Proyecciologia y Conscientiologia – Instituto Internacional de Projeciologia e Conscienciologia
Administrative Seat Av Felipe Wandscheer No 6200, sala 103, Bairro Cognópolis, Foz do Iguaçu PR, 85856-530, Brazil. T. +554521021448. Fax +554521021443.
URL: http://www.iipc.org/

History 1988, Rio de Janeiro (Brazil), as *International Institute of Projectiology (IIP) – Instituto Internacional de Proyecciología – Instituto Internacional de Projeciologia.* **Aims** Study *human consciousness*; develop methods and techniques for the study and research of the *out-of-body experience*; develop *bioenergetic* technology; disseminate the results of projectiology and conscientiology research experiments; train teachers and prepare researchers of conscientiology and projectiology. **Structure** General Assembly. Executive Committee; Consultative Committee. **Finance** Sources: income from courses; sales of publications. **Activities** Educational activities, conferences, fora, courses and lectures at IIPC laboratory-schools throughout Brazil and at IIPC international offices. Offers the Consciousness Development Program (CDP), consisting of systematic experiential training in developing and controlling one's capacity to work with bioenergy and consciousness projection – the out-of-body experience (OBE). Research Groups (91) in 7 areas: Computer Science; Conscientiological Intraphysical Society; Conscientiotherapy; Existential Inversion; Existential Recycling; Leading-edge Research; Personal Energetic Task. **Events** *International Congress of Projectiology* Belo Horizonte (Brazil) 2008, *Congress / International Congress of Projectiology* New York, NY (USA) 2002, *Forum on paranormal phenomena* Coral Gables, FL (USA) 2001, *International forum on consciousness research* Barcelona (Spain) 1999, *International congress on existential inversion* Florianópolis (Brazil) 1998. **Publications** *BIPRO* (12 a year) in Portuguese – bulletin; *CPQ Noticias* (12 a year) in Portuguese – bulletin; *Informativo do CEAEC* (12 a year) in Portuguese – bulletin; *Jornal da Invéxis* (12 a year) in Portuguese – bulletin; *Recéxis* (12 a year) in Portuguese – magazine; *Journal of Conscientiology* (4 a year) in English, Spanish. Books. Annals.
Members Full in 8 countries:
Argentina, China, Italy, Netherlands, Portugal, Spain, UK, USA.
NGO Relations Instrumental in setting up: *International Academy of Consciousness (IAC).*
[2017/XF4165/j/**F**]

♦ International Institute for Promotion and Prestige (#11315)
♦ International Institute of Psychagogy / see International Institute of Psychoanalysis and Psychotherapy Charles Baudouin (#13913)
♦ International Institute of Psychagogy and Psychotherapy: Charles Baudouin / see International Institute of Psychoanalysis and Psychotherapy Charles Baudouin (#13913)

♦ International Institute of Psychoanalysis and Psychotherapy Charles Baudouin 13913

Institut international de psychanalyse et de psychothérapie Charles Baudouin
Contact address not obtained. E-mail: secretariat.iipb@gmail.com.
URL: http://institut-baudouin.com/

History 1924, Geneva (Switzerland), on the initiative of Charles Baudouin (1893-1963), as *International Institute of Psychagogy.* Reorganized 1951 and 1975, Geneva, when the name was changed to *International Institute of Psychagogy and Psychotherapy: Charles Baudouin – Institut international de psychagogie et de psychothérapie: Charles Baudouin*, in honour Charles Baudouin (1893-1963). Current title adopted 10 Nov 1990. Current statutes adopted by Extraordinary General Assembly, 7 Nov 1998. **Aims** Apply *psychology* to the conduct of life and to *therapeutics*, in accordance with the spirit of synthesis defined in its founder's works, Charles Baudouin. **Structure** General Assembly (annual); Executive Board; 'Conseil des didacticiens'. **Languages** French. **Staff** 3.00 FTE, voluntary. **Finance** Members' dues. **Activities** Research; training; seminars; workshops; publications. **Events** *Annual Symposium* Geneva (Switzerland) 2015, *Annual Symposium* Brussels (Belgium) 2014, *Annual Symposium* Lyon (France) 2013, *Annual Symposium* Geneva (Switzerland) 2006, *Annual Symposium* Brussels (Belgium) 2005. **Publications** *Action et pensée* – magazine. *Charles Baudoin: Pyschanalyse du Symbole Religieux* (2006); *Charles Baudouin – L'Ame et l'action – Prémisses d'une philosophie de la psychanalyse* (2006); *Charles Baudouin (1893-1963) – Je suis celui qu'on ne connaît pas et qui passe* (2005).
Members Categories (4) Active members; 'candidats en contrôle' (members under supervision); 'candidats en didactique' (members in training analysis); associate members. National organizations in 3 countries:
Belgium, France, Switzerland.
Individuals in 5 countries:
Belgium, France, Italy, Spain, Switzerland.
NGO Relations Member of: *Fédération des Institutions Internationales établies à Genève (FIIG, #09599).*
[2019.02.12/XE3005/j/**E**]

♦ International Institute of Public Art (inactive)

♦ International Institute for Public Ethics (IIPE) 13914

Pres c/o IEGL, Key Centre, Mt Gravatt Campus, Mt Gravatt, Griffith Univ, 176 Messines Ridge Road, Mount Gravatt QLD 4122, Australia. T. +61731381101. Fax +61737356985.
URL: http://www.iipe.org/

History Aug 1998, France. Aug 1998, Brittany (France). Inaugural conference 24-28 Sep 2000, Ottawa (Canada). Registered in accordance with Australian law. **Aims** Develop an international and professional community of public sector ethicists; offer support for scholars and practitioners in the field. **Structure** Board of Directors of 5 members. **Languages** English. **Staff** Voluntary. **Finance** Members' dues. **Activities** Conducts research; provides advice and counsel; provides training; develops exchanges programmes; organizes conferences and seminars. **Events** *Biennial Conference* Oxford (UK) 2006, *World ethics forum* Oxford (UK) 2006, *Biennial conference* Brisbane, QLD (Australia) 2002, *Biennial conference* Ottawa, ON (Canada) 2000. **Publications** *IIPE Newsletter.*
Members Founding members in 3 countries:
Australia, Canada, USA.
Currently members in 25 countries. Membership countries not specified.
IGO Relations Strong relations with: *International Bank for Reconstruction and Development (IBRD, #12317); United Nations University (UNU, #20642).*
[2017/XE4096/j/**E**]

♦ International Institute of Public Finance (IIPF) 13915

Institut international de finances publiques (IIFP) – Instituto Internacional de Hacienda Pública
Office Manager Poschingerstr. 5, 81679 Munich, Germany. T. +498992241281. Fax +49899077952281. E-mail: info@iipf.org.
URL: http://www.iipf.org/

History 1937, Paris (France). Founded on the initiative of Dean Edgard Allix. Registration: Germany. **Aims** Study public finance and public *economics*; promote research and publications in these areas; establish scientific contacts and exchange of knowledge and experience among persons of all nationalities; generate intellectual interchanges among all who research, teach or practice in the fields of Public Economics, at universities and in the civil Service, in industrialized and developing countries alike. **Structure** General Assembly (annual, at Congress); Board of Management; Executive Committee; Treasurer; Scientific Committee. **Languages** English, French, German. **Staff** 3.00 FTE, paid. **Finance** Sources: gifts, legacies; members' dues. **Activities** Awards/prizes/competitions; events/meetings; knowledge management/information dissemination. **Events** *Annual Congress* Logan, UT (USA) 2023, *Annual Congress* Linz (Austria) 2022, *Annual Congress* 2021, *Annual Congress* Reykjavik (Iceland) 2020, *Annual Conference* Glasgow (UK) 2019. **Publications** Selected IIPF congress papers published in International Tax and Public Finance (ITAX).
Members Individuals (700-800) in 62 countries and territories:
Angola, Argentina, Australia, Austria, Bahrain, Bangladesh, Belgium, Benin, Brazil, Bulgaria, Cameroon, Canada, China, Colombia, Croatia, Cyprus, Czechia, Denmark, Egypt, Finland, France, Germany, Greece, Hong Kong, India, Indonesia, Ireland, Israel, Italy, Japan, Korea Rep, Lebanon, Luxembourg, Nepal, Netherlands, New Zealand, Nigeria, North Macedonia, Norway, Pakistan, Palestine, Poland, Portugal, Qatar, Romania, Russia, Saudi Arabia, Serbia, Slovakia, Slovenia, South Africa, Spain, Sri Lanka, Suriname, Sweden, Switzerland, Taiwan, Trinidad-Tobago, Türkiye, UK, USA, Venezuela.
Institutions (8) in 6 countries:
Belgium, China, France, Germany, Hungary, Spain.
Consultative Status Consultative status granted from: *ECOSOC (#05331)* (Ros A). **IGO Relations** *UNESCO (#20322); United Nations Economic Commission for Latin America and the Caribbean (ECLAC, #20556).* **NGO Relations** *International Social Security Association (ISSA, #14885).*
[2022.10.12/XB2158/jv/**B**]

♦ International Institute of Public Law (inactive)
♦ International Institute of Puppetry / see Institut international de la marionnette (#11314)

♦ International Institute for Qualitative Methodology (IIQM) 13916

Dir Faculty of Arts, Univ of Alberta, Edmonton AB T6G 2E5, Canada. T. +17804922787. Fax +17804927251. E-mail: iiqm@ualberta.ca.
URL: http://www.iiqm.ualberta.ca/

History 1998, Edmonton, AB (Canada). Founded at the University of Alberta. **Aims** Provide leadership to address issues in qualitative enquiry and facilitate development of qualitative methods; promote excellence in qualitative research through education and research; provide a forum for collaboration among international experts. **Structure** Advisory Board. **Staff** 3.00 FTE, paid. **Activities** Events/meetings; projects/programmes; research and development. **Events** *Thinking Qualitatively Conference* 2023, *Thinking Qualitatively Virtual Conference* Edmonton, AB (Canada) 2021, *Annual Qualitative Health Research Conference* Victoria, BC (Canada) 2014, *Annual Qualitative Health Research Conference* Montréal, QC (Canada) 2012, *Qualitative Health Research Conference* Montréal, QC (Canada) 2012. **Publications** *International Journal of Qualitative Methods* (4 a year). *Qual Institute Press Series.*
Members Past and current affiliations (over 25) including 8 countries:
Australia, Brazil, Canada, Israel, Korea Rep, Mexico, Netherlands, South Africa.
[2023.02.14/XE3467/j/**E**]

♦ International Institute on Race, Equality, and Human Rights (unconfirmed)

♦ International Institute for Race Medicine (IIRM) 13917

Exec Dir 41 Lafayete Lane, Norfolk MA 02056, USA. T. +17817103301. E-mail: troyanos@racemedicine.org.
URL: http://www.racemedicine.org/

History Set up Oct 2003, as 'American Road Racing Medical Society (ARRMS)'. **Aims** Ensure that event and medical staff have accurate medical information and guidelines that will improve the *athlete's* experience; further research, education and practice in *marathons* and other endurance road races worldwide. **Structure** Board; Advisory Board; Research Board. **Activities** Advocacy/lobbying/activism; training/education. **NGO Relations** *Association of International Marathons and Distance Races (AIMS, #02756).*
[2017/XM5685/j/**C**]

♦ International Institute of Reflexology, Walkley (internationally oriented national body)

♦ International Institute of Refrigeration (IIR) 13918

Institut international du froid (IIF)
Dir Gen 177 bvd Malesherbes, 75017 Paris, France. T. +33142273235. Fax +33147631798. E-mail: iif-iir@iifiir.org.
URL: http://www.iifiir.org/

History 5 Oct 1908, Paris (France). Established on signature of a Convention, replacing *International Association of Refrigeration (inactive)*, set up in 1908, Paris. Convention modified 31 May 1937, then replaced by an International Agreement, 1 Dec 1954, which was subsequently modified on 2 Sep 1967 and 28 Aug 1971. Statutes registered in *'LNTS 207'* and *'LNTS 4394'.* Former names and other names: *Instituto Internacional del Frio* – former. **Aims** Promote knowledge of refrigeration and associated technologies and applications on a global scale that improve quality of life in a cost effective and environmentally sustainable manner. **Structure** General Conference (every 4 years); Executive Committee; Management Committee; Science and Technology Council; Commissions (10); Sections (5). **Languages** English, French. **Staff** 12.00 FTE, paid. **Finance** Sources: members' dues. **Activities** Events/meetings; monitoring/evaluation; projects/programmes; research/documentation; standards/guidelines. **Events** *Conference on Thermophysical Properties and Transfer Processes of Refrigerants* College Park, MD (USA) 2025, *Conference on Caloric Cooling and Applications of Caloric Materials* Baotou (China) 2024, *Conference on Compressors and Refrigerants* Bratislava (Slovakia) 2024, *Gustav Lorentzen Conference on Naturals Refrigerants* College Park, MD (USA) 2024, *Conference on Sustainability and the Cold Chain* Tokyo (Japan) 2024. **Publications** *IIR Newsletter* (12 a year); *International Journal of Refrigeration (IJR)* (12 a year). Informatory notes; congress and conference proceedings; books; files on regulations; thematic files; news; directories. **Information Services** *FRIDOC* – comprehensive database dedicated to refrigeration information; *International Dictionary of Refrigeration.*
Members Governments of 59 countries (each country chooses its own category out of 6 categories of membership):
Algeria, Australia, Austria, Belgium, Benin, Bulgaria, Burkina Faso, Cameroon, Canada, Chad, China, Congo DR, Côte d'Ivoire, Croatia, Cuba, Czechia, Egypt, Finland, France, Gabon, Germany, Guinea, Hungary, India, Ireland, Israel, Italy, Japan, Jordan, Korea Rep, Lebanon, Madagascar, Malaysia, Mali, Morocco, Netherlands, New Zealand, Niger, North Macedonia, Norway, Poland, Qatar, Romania, Russia, Saudi Arabia, Serbia, Slovakia, Slovenia, Spain, Sudan, Sweden, Togo, Tunisia, Türkiye, UK, United Arab Emirates, USA, Uzbekistan, Vietnam.

Private and Corporate members, including, but not limited to: public agencies; educational and research institutions; manufacturers; professional organizations and associations; research and development companies; refrigeration professionals. Membership countries not specified.
IGO Relations Observer status with (1): *Codex Alimentarius Commission (CAC, #04081)*. Cooperates with (3): *CIHEAM – International Centre for Advanced Mediterranean Agronomic Studies (CIHEAM, #03927)*; *FAO (#09260)*; *UNIDO (#20336)*. **NGO Relations** Cooperates with (2): *Comité européen de normalisation (CEN, #04162)*; *International Organization for Standardization (ISO, #14473)*. Supports (1): *Farming First*. Links with national organizations. [2022.10.11/XB2159/j/**B***]

♦ International Institute for Religious Freedom (IIRF) 13919

Dir Friedrichstr 38, 2nd Floor, 53111 Bonn, Germany.
URL: http://iirf.eu/

History Functions under *World Evangelical Alliance (WEA, #21393)*. **Aims** Establish reliable data on the violation of religious freedom worldwide and implement this topic in college and university programs and curricula, especially in the areas of law, sociology, religious studies and theological programs. **Structure** Board of 5 Supervisors. Executive Directors (Germany; South Africa; Sri Lanka). Academic Council. Editorial Board. Offices (8): Bonn (Germany); Brasília (Brazil); Brussels (Belgium); Cape Town (South Africa); Colombo (Sri Lanka); Delhi (India); Tübingen (Germany); Vancouver (Canada). **Languages** Arabic, English, French, German, Spanish. **Activities** Knowledge management/information dissemination; networking/liaising. **Events** *International Consultation on Religious Freedom Research* Istanbul (Turkey) 2013. **Publications** *IIRF Bulletin* in German; *IIRF Reports* in English; *International Journal of Religious Freedom (IJRF)*. *Studies in Religious Freedom* – book series; *WEA Global Issues Series* – book series. **Members** Individuals. Membership countries not specified. **IGO Relations** *European Commission (EC, #06633)*; *Organization for Security and Cooperation in Europe (OSCE, #17887)*; *UNHCR (#20327)*; *United Nations Human Rights Council (HRC, #20571)*. **NGO Relations** *Asia Evangelical Alliance (AEA, #01275)*. [2021/XJ6475/jv/**E**]

♦ International Institute for Research and Education (internationally oriented national body)
♦ International Institute for the Rights of the Child (internationally oriented national body)
♦ International Institute for Rights and Development-Geneva (unconfirmed)

♦ International Institute of Risk and Safety Management (IIRSM) ... 13920

Chief Exec 4th Fl – No 1 Farrier's Yard, 77-85 Fulham Palace Road, London, W6 8AH, UK. T. +442087419100. E-mail: info@iirsm.org.
URL: http://www.iirsm.org/

History Founded 1975. UK Registered Charity: 1107666. **Aims** Transform decision-making through collective risk management capability. **Structure** Council; Chief Executive; Committees (5). **Languages** English. **Staff** 12.00 FTE, paid. **Finance** Member's dues. Corporate sponsorship. **Activities** Events/meetings; training/education. **Events** *KIHSSE : Kuwait International Health, Safety, Security and Environment Conference* Kuwait (Kuwait) 2019, *Annual Conference* London (UK) 2019, *Annual Conference* London (UK) 2018, *Annual General Meeting* London (UK) 2018, *Extrarordinary General Meeting* London (UK) 2018. **Publications** *Bi-Monthly Member Magazine*; *IIRSM e-newsletter*. Bulletins; handbooks.
Members Individual membership: Student; Affiliate; Associate (AIIRSM); Member (MIIRSM); Fellow (FIIRSM). Members (mostly in UK) in 92 countries and territories:
Albania, Algeria, Argentina, Australia, Austria, Azerbaijan, Bahrain, Bangladesh, Barbados, Belgium, Belize, Botswana, Brazil, Brunei Darussalam, Burundi, Canada, Cayman Is, Chad, China, Colombia, Croatia, Cyprus, Egypt, Falklands/Malvinas, France, Germany, Ghana, Gibraltar, Greece, Guernsey, Guyana, Hong Kong, India, Indonesia, Iran Islamic Rep, Ireland, Israel, Italy, Jamaica, Japan, Jersey, Jordan, Kazakhstan, Kenya, Korea Rep, Kuwait, Latvia, Lebanon, Libya, Lithuania, Malaysia, Mali, Malta, Mauritius, Mexico, Morocco, Mozambique, Nepal, Netherlands, New Zealand, Nigeria, North Macedonia, Oman, Pakistan, Philippines, Poland, Portugal, Qatar, Romania, Russia, Saudi Arabia, Serbia, Singapore, South Africa, Spain, Sri Lanka, Sudan, Sweden, Switzerland, Syrian AR, Tanzania UR, Thailand, Trinidad-Tobago, Tunisia, Türkiye, Uganda, UK, United Arab Emirates, USA, Vietnam, Zambia, Zimbabwe.
NGO Relations Sustaining member of: *International Commission on Occupational Health (ICOH, #12709)*. Active in: *International Federation of Associations of Specialists in Occupational Safety and Industrial Hygiene (IFAS, no recent information)*. [2020.03.04/XF5533/jv/**F**]

♦ International Institute of Rural Reconstruction (IIRR) 13921

Institut international pour la reconstruction rurale – Instituto Internacional de Reconstrucción Rural

Pres 99 Wall Street, Suite 1258, New York NY 10005, USA. T. +19174107886. E-mail: us.office@iirr.org.
Dir Y C James Yen Center, Km 39 Aguinaldo Highway, Biga 2, 4118 Silang CAV, Philippines. T. +63464198600. E-mail: information@iirr.org.
URL: http://www.iirr.org/

History 1960, USA. Founded, Delaware (USA), as successor to 'Chinese National Association of the Mass Education Movement', set up Aug 1923, Beijing (China). Incorporated in USA as private non-profit educational institution. **Aims** Enable communities and those who work with them to develop innovative yet practical solutions to poverty through a community-led development approach and widely share these lessons to encourage replication. **Structure** International Board of Trustees; Regional Centres and Offices (3). **Languages** English. **Staff** 70.00 FTE, paid. **Finance** Sources: grants. **Activities** Guidance/assistance/consulting; research/documentation; training/education. Active in: Cambodia, Ethiopia, Kenya, Myanmar, Philippines, South Sudan, Uganda, USA, Zimbabwe. **Events** *Innovation Africa symposium* Kampala (Uganda) 2006, *International conference on participatory spatial information management and communication* Nairobi (Kenya) 2005, *Going to the scale meeting* Cavite (Philippines) 2000, *Workshop* Cavite (Philippines) 2000, *Workshop on reproductive health* Bangalore (India) 1995. **Publications** *50th Year Souvenier Magazine*; *International SHARING* – newsletter. Annual Report; books; monographs; workshop proceedings; manuals.
Members National rural reconstruction movements and alumni associations in 10 countries:
Bangladesh, Colombia, Ghana, Guatemala, Honduras, India, Kenya, Nepal, Philippines, Thailand.
Consultative Status Consultative status granted from: *ECOSOC (#05331)* (Ros A); *UNICEF (#20332)*. **IGO Relations** Associated with Department of Global Communications of the United Nations. **NGO Relations** Member of (2): *Conference of Non-Governmental Organizations in Consultative Relationship with the United Nations (CONGO, #04635)*; *NGO Committee on UNICEF (#17120)*. Partner of (1): *Development Innovations and Networks (#05057)*. Supports (2): *Asia South Pacific Association for Basic and Adult Education (ASPBAE, #02098)*; *PROLINNOVA (#18537)*. [2021.05.28/XE0639/j/**E**]

♦ International Institute of Science Ivo Lapenna / see Internacia Scienca Instituto Ivo Lapenna (#11525)

♦ International Institute for the Science of Sintering (IISS) 13922

Institut international pour la science de frittage

Sec Knez Mihailova 35, PO Box 334, Belgrade, 11001, Serbia. T. +3811126373767. Fax +381112185263. E-mail: iiss@iiss-sci.org – scisint@sanu.ac.rs.
URL: https://www.iiss-sci.org/

History 1969. Constitution amended and present name adopted Sep 1973, Herceg-Novi (Yugoslavia). Currently a unit of the Institute of Topical Associations within *World Academy of Ceramics (WAC, #21067)*. Former names and other names: *International Team for Studying Sintering (ITS)* – former. **Aims** Promote fundamental achievements in theory, science and technology of sintering and related fields. **Structure** Council; Managing Board Committees (2); Executive Secretariat. Patron: Serbian Academy of Sciences and Arts. **Languages** English, Russian. **Staff** 7.00 FTE, paid. **Finance** Sources: grants. **Activities** Awards/prizes/competitions; events/meetings; knowledge management/information dissemination; networking/liaising. **Events** *World Round Table Conference on Sintering* Herceg Novi (Montenegro) 2022, *World round table conference* Belgrade (Serbia) 2007, *Summer School* Novosibirsk (Russia) 2004, *World round table conference / Round Table* Belgrade (Yugoslavia) 2002, *Summer School* Delhi (India) 2000. **Publications** *Science of Sintering* (3 a year) in English – with abstracts in Serbian. Books, in English, Russian, Serbian; reports.
Members Honorary (9); Full (57); Corresponding (27), in 23 countries:
Australia, Brazil, Canada, China, Egypt, France, Germany, India, Israel, Italy, Japan, Korea Rep, Mexico, North Macedonia, Poland, Russia, Serbia, Slovakia, Slovenia, Sweden, UK, Ukraine, USA. [2022.10.25/XC4452/jv/**E**]

♦ International Institute for Secular Humanistic Judaism (IISHJ) 13923

Dean North America 175 Olde Half Day Rd, Ste 124, Lincolnshire IL 60069, USA. T. +18473836330. E-mail: info@iishj.org.
Michigan Campus c/o Ben and Lorraine Pivnick Center for Humanistic Judaism, 28611 West Twelve Mile Road, Farmington Hills MI 48334, USA.
URL: http://www.iishj.org/

History Founded 1985, within the framework of *International Federation for Secular and Humanistic Judaism (IFSHJ, inactive)*. **Aims** Offer professional training for Secular Humanistic Rabbis, Leaders and Officiants. **Structure** Board of Governors (meets twice a year); Administrative Center in Lincolnshire IL (USA). **Languages** English. **Staff** 2.75 FTE, paid. **Finance** Board of Governors; public donations; publication sales; endowment and investment returns. **Activities** Training/education; publishing activities; events/meetings. **Events** *Biennial Colloquium* Farmington Hills, MI (USA) 2013, *Biennial Colloquium* Evanston, IL (USA) 2012, *Biennial colloquium / Colloquium* Farmington Hills, MI (USA) 2009, *Biennial colloquium / Colloquium* Detroit, MI (USA) 2005, *Biennial meeting / Biennial Conference* San Francisco, CA (USA) 2004. **Publications** Books; colloquium proceedings.
Members Individuals in 13 countries:
Argentina, Australia, Belgium, Canada, France, Germany, Israel, Italy, Mexico, Russia, UK, Uruguay, USA. [2018.08.15/XE1899/j/**E**]

♦ International Institute of Security and Safety Management (internationally oriented national body)
♦ International Institute of Social Bibliography (inactive)
♦ International Institute of Social Christianity (inactive)
♦ International Institute of Social Economics (inactive)

♦ International Institute of Social and Economic Sciences (IISES) ... 13924

Dir Trebesovska 14/2038, 193 00 Prague 9, Czechia. T. +420602393619. E-mail: iises@iises.net – info@iises.net.
URL: http://www.iises.net/

History Founded 2011, Prague (Czech Rep). **Aims** Facilitate communication and open discussion between scholars, researchers and practitioners interested in social and economic sciences. **Structure** Academic Board; Scientific Committees. **Languages** English. **Staff** 5.00 FTE, paid; 3.00 FTE, voluntary. **Finance** Members' dues. **Activities** Knowledge management/information dissemination; events/meetings; publishing activity. **Events** *International Academic Conference* London (UK) 2019, *Teaching and Education Conference* Vienna (Austria) 2019, *Arts and Humanities Conference* Stockholm (Sweden) 2018, *Teaching and Education Conference* Vienna (Austria) 2018, *International Law and Political Science Conference* Vienna (Austria) 2017. **Publications** *Journal of Business and Management*; *Journal of Economic Sciences*; *Journal of Social Sciences*; *Journal of Teaching and Education*. Conference proceedings. **Members** Individual; Institutional. Membership countries not specified. [2018.09.06/XJ6363/j/**D**]

♦ International Institute of Social History (internationally oriented national body)
♦ International Institute of Social Studies, The Hague (internationally oriented national body)
♦ International Institute for Socio-Informatics (internationally oriented national body)

♦ International Institute of Sociology (IIS) 13925

Institut international de sociologie – Instituto Internacional de Sociologia – Internationales Institut für Soziologie

Secretariat c/o The Swedish Collegium for Advanced Study, Linneanum, Thunbergsvägen 2, SE-752 38 Uppsala, Sweden. T. +4618557085. E-mail: info@iisoc.org.
URL: http://www.iisoc.org/

History 1893, Paris (France). Founded on the initiative of Prof René Worms; now constituted as a professional association. **Aims** Develop, stimulate and facilitate the study of sociology in *universities* throughout the world; bring together sociologists in different countries with a view to scientific research on sociological questions; foster cross-national and multi-disciplinary research and theoretical development. **Structure** General Assembly; Bureau (4-year term), comprising Officers: President; 3 Vice-Presidents; Secretary General/Treasurer; 5 Council Members; Auditor. Congress Organizing Committee. **Languages** English, French, German, Italian, Spanish. **Finance** Sources: meeting proceeds; members' dues; sale of publications. **Activities** Events/meetings; knowledge management/information dissemination; publishing activities. **Events** *Congress / Biennial Congress* Uppsala (Sweden) 2013, *After Western hegemony – social science and its publics* Delhi (India) 2012, *Congress / Biennial Congress* Yerevan (Armenia) 2009, *Congress / Biennial Congress* Budapest (Hungary) 2008, *Congress / Biennial Congress* Stockholm (Sweden) 2005. **Publications** *Annals of the International Institute of Sociology* – journal. Congress proceedings in English, French.
Members Individuals in 47 countries and territories:
Albania, Angola, Australia, Belgium, Brazil, Canada, China, Czechia, Denmark, Finland, France, Germany, Greece, Holy See, Hungary, India, Israel, Italy, Japan, Korea Rep, Latvia, Lithuania, Luxembourg, Malaysia, Mexico, Morocco, Netherlands, New Zealand, Nigeria, Norway, Poland, Portugal, Romania, Russia, Serbia, Slovenia, South Africa, Spain, Sweden, Switzerland, Taiwan, Thailand, Tunisia, Türkiye, UK, USA, Zimbabwe. [2013/XE2162/jv/**E**]

♦ International Institute for the Sociology of Law / see Oñati International Institute for the Sociology of Law (#17725)
♦ International Institute of Sociology and Political and Social Reform (inactive)
♦ International Institute of Sound (inactive)

♦ International Institute of Space Law (IISL) 13926

Institut international de droit spatial

Exec Sec 94 bis av de Suffren, 75015 Paris, France. T. +33145674260. Fax +33142732120. E-mail: secretary@iisl.space.
Main Website: https://iisl.space/

History 1960, Paris (France). Founded as a subsidiary body of *International Astronautical Federation (IAF, #12286)*, replacing the Permanent Committee on Space Law, created by IAF in 1958. Statutes adopted 1961; amended 2013. Registration: Netherlands. **Aims** Promote development of *legal* and 'social science' aspects of *astronautics*, space *navigation* and *exploration*. **Structure** General Meeting of Members (annual, during the Colloquium); Board of Directors; Secretariat, located at IAF headquarters in Paris (France); ad hoc Committees. **Languages** English, French. **Staff** Voluntary. **Finance** Sources: contributions; donations; grants; meeting proceeds; members' dues. **Activities** Awards/prizes/competitions; events/meetings; research and development; research/documentation. **Events** *Colloquium on the Law of Outer Space* Paris (France) 2022, *Colloquium on the Law of Outer Space* Dubai (United Arab Emirates) 2021, *Colloquium on the Law of Outer Space* 2020, *Symposium on the Moon Agreement Revisited* Vienna (Austria) 2019, *Colloquium on the Law of Outer Space* Washington, DC (USA) 2019. **Publications** *International Institute of Space Law Newsletter* (periodical). *History of the International Institute of Space Law*. Studies; reports; proceedings.
Members Individuals (about 350) and institutional (20), elected for life, in 43 countries and territories:
Argentina, Austria, Belgium, Brazil, Bulgaria, Canada, Chile, China, Colombia, Croatia, Czechia, Finland, France, Germany, Greece, Hong Kong, Hungary, India, Indonesia, Iran Islamic Rep, Italy, Japan, Korea Rep, Luxembourg, Malaysia, Mexico, Montenegro, Netherlands, Norway, Pakistan, Paraguay, Poland, Romania, Russia, Serbia, Singapore, Spain, Switzerland, Taiwan, Thailand, Uruguay, USA, Venezuela.
Consultative Status Consultative status granted from: *ECOSOC (#05331)* (Special). **IGO Relations** Observer status with (1): *Committee on the Peaceful Uses of Outer Space (COPUOS, #04277)*. [2022.10.31/XE2163/j/**E**]

♦ International Institute for Special Education (internationally oriented national body)
♦ International Institute for the Spreading of Social Experiments (inactive)
♦ International Institute of Stenography (inactive)
♦ International Institute of Stochastic Optimization (inactive)

♦ International Institute for Strategic Studies (IISS) 13927

Institut international d'études stratégiques

Dir-Gen and Chief Exec Arundel House, 6 Temple Place, London, WC2R 2PG, UK. T. +442073797676. E-mail: iiss@iiss.org.
URL: http://www.iiss.org/

History 1958, London (UK). Former names and other names: *Institute for Strategic Studies* – former (1958 to 1972); *Institut d'études stratégiques* – former (1958 to 1972). Registration: Charity Commission, No/ID: 206504, England and Wales. **Aims** Promote adoption of sound policies to further global peace and security and maintain civilized international relations. **Structure** Board of Trustees; Council; Director-General; Chief Executive; Headquarters in London (UK); Offices in: Berlin (Germany); Manama (Bahrain); Singapore (Singapore); Washington DC (USA). **Languages** English. **Staff** 160.00 FTE, paid. **Finance** Sources: donations; grants; meeting proceeds; members' dues; sale of publications. **Activities** Events/meetings; knowledge management/information dissemination; networking/liaising; research/documentation. **Events** *Seminar on the Military Balance in Europe* Brussels (Belgium) 2022, *IISS Manama Dialogue* Manama (Bahrain) 2022, *Shangri-La Dialogue* Singapore (Singapore) 2022, *Annual Fullerton Forum* Singapore (Singapore) 2021, *Shangri-La Dialogue* Singapore (Singapore) 2021. **Publications** *Survival* (6 a year); *Military Balance* (annual); *Strategic Survey* (annual); *Strategic Comments* (50 a year). *Adelphi Books* – (8 a year) monograph series. **Information Services** *Armed Conflict Database*; *Military Balance Plus Database*.
Members (about 2,500). Politicians, scholars, military personnel, officials, corporate representatives and journalists, in 83 countries and territories:
Afghanistan, Argentina, Australia, Austria, Bahrain, Bangladesh, Belgium, Brazil, Brunei Darussalam, Bulgaria, Canada, Chile, China, Congo DR, Costa Rica, Cyprus, Czechia, Denmark, Dubai, Egypt, Finland, France, Germany, Ghana, Greece, Guyana, Hungary, Iceland, India, Indonesia, Iran Islamic Rep, Iraq, Ireland, Israel, Italy, Japan, Jordan, Kenya, Korea Rep, Kuwait, Lebanon, Libya, Luxembourg, Malaysia, Malta, Mexico, Morocco, Myanmar, Nepal, Netherlands, New Zealand, Nigeria, Norway, Oman, Pakistan, Peru, Philippines, Poland, Portugal, Romania, Saudi Arabia, Senegal, Serbia, Singapore, South Africa, Spain, Sri Lanka, Sudan, Sweden, Switzerland, Syrian AR, Taiwan, Thailand, Trinidad-Tobago, Tunisia, Türkiye, Uganda, UK, United Arab Emirates, USA, Venezuela, Yemen, Zimbabwe.
IGO Relations Relations with all major IGOs active in the field of security studies and international relations, including with: United Nations; *European Commission (EC, #06633)*; *Geneva Centre for Security Sector Governance (DCAF, #10121)*; *NATO (#16945)*; *Russia's Institute for Strategic Studies (RISS)*; *United Nations Institute for Disarmament Research (UNIDIR, #20575)*; *Western European Union (WEU, inactive)*. **NGO Relations** Member of: *Council for Asia Europe Cooperation (CAEC, no recent information)*; *European Information Network on International Relations and Area Studies (EINIRAS, #07534)*. Jointly manages: *European Network of Independent Non-Proliferation Think Tanks (EU Non-Proliferation Network, #07930)*. Relations with all major NGOs active in the field of security studies and international relations, including with: *Centre for Defence and International Security Studies (CDISS)*; *Ford Foundation (#09858)*; *Institut français des relations internationales (IFRI)*; *Norwegian Atlantic Committee (DNAK)*. [2020.02.06/XC1026/y/**B**]

♦ International Institute for the Studies of Social Defence / see International Society of Social Defence and Humane Criminal Policy (#15447)
♦ International Institute for the Study of Causes and Prevention of Mental Illness (inactive)
♦ International Institute for the Study of Nomadic Civilizations (internationally oriented national body)
♦ International Institute for the Study of Religions (internationally oriented national body)

♦ International Institute of Sugar Beet Research (IIRB) 13928

SG Holtenser Landstr 77, 37079 Göttingen, Germany. T. +495515006584. E-mail: mail@iirb.org.
Registered Office Rue Washington 40, 1050 Brussels, Belgium.
URL: http://www.iirb.org/

History Founded 1931, Brussels (Belgium)/Prague (Czechoslovakia). Statutes adopted 1953; revised 1993; 2011; 2018. Former names and other names: *International Institute for Beet Research (IIRB)* – former; *Institut International de Recherches Betteravières (IIRB)* – former; *Internationales Institut für Rübenforschung (IIRB)* – former. Registration: Banque-Carrefour des Entreprises, No/ID: 0408.293.091, Start date: 11 Jul 1963, Belgium. **Aims** Advance *sugar beet* production by promoting knowledge transfer and cooperation between specialists interested in improving beet growing techniques as well as research in these fields. **Structure** General Assembly; Administrative Council; Scientific Advisory Committee; Study Groups. **Languages** English. **Staff** 1.00 FTE, paid. **Finance** Sources: contributions. **Activities** Events/meetings; knowledge management/information dissemination. **Events** *Congress* Brussels (Belgium) 2024, *Congress* Mons (Belgium) 2022, *Congress* Brussels (Belgium) 2020, *Congress* Deauville (France) 2018, *Congress* Brussels (Belgium) 2016. **Publications** *IIRB Journal* – 1965-1975; *IIRB newsletter*. *Advances in Sugar Beet Research*; *Azote et betterave sucrière*; *Ecologie de la betterave à sucre dans la Région méditerranéenne*; *Fifty Years of Sugar Beet Research*; *Sugar Beet Dictionary*; *Virus Yellows Monograph*. Congress proceedings.
Members Individuals (350) and national organizations in 23 countries:
Austria, Belarus, Belgium, Chile, Czechia, Denmark, Finland, France, Germany, Hungary, Iran Islamic Rep, Italy, Japan, Netherlands, Poland, Romania, Serbia, Slovakia, Spain, Sweden, Switzerland, UK, USA.
NGO Relations Member of (1): *Federation of European and International Associations Established in Belgium (FAIB, #09508)*. [2022.10.12/XC2132/j/**C**]

♦ International Institute for Sustainability Analysis and Strategy 13929

Internationales Institut für Nachhaltigkeitsanalysen und -strategien (IINAS)
Office Heidelberger Str 129 1/2, 64285 Darmstadt, Germany. T. +4961518506077. Fax +4961518506080. E-mail: info@iinas.org.
URL: http://iinas.org/

History Operations started Apr 2012, Darmstadt (Germany). Registered in accordance with German law: HRB 90827. **Aims** Provide integrated research, analyses and consultancy services in the sustainability domain. **Structure** Scientific Advisory Board. **Languages** English, German, Spanish. **Finance** Donors include: national government agencies in Germany and other European countries; *European Commission (EC, #06633)*; *European Parliament (EP, #08146)*; *FAO (#09260)*; *Global Environment Facility (GEF, #10346)*; *International Energy Agency (IEA, #13270)*; *UNEP (#20299)*. **Activities** Research/documentation; knowledge management/information dissemination; guidance/assistance/consulting. **IGO Relations** Accredited to the Conference of the Parties of: *Secretariat of the United Nations Convention to Combat Desertification (Secretariat of the UNCCD, #19208)*. **NGO Relations** Partners include: *Ecologic Institut (#05303)*; *International Institute for Applied Systems Analysis (IIASA, #13861)*; *Tellus Institute*. [2018.01.22/XM5974/j/**D**]

♦ International Institute for Sustainable Development (IISD) 13930

Institut international du développement durable (IIDD)
CEO 111 Lombard Avenue, Ste 325, Winnipeg MB R3B 0T4, Canada. T. +12049587700. Fax +12049587710. E-mail: info@iisd.org.
Geneva Office Int Enviro House 2, 9 chemin de Balexert, Châtelaine, 1219 Geneva, Switzerland. T. +41229178683. Fax +41229178054. E-mail: geneva@iisd.org.
URL: https://www.iisd.org/

History 19 Mar 1990, Winnipeg, MB (Canada). Follows on from the *World Commission on Environment and Development (WCED, inactive)*. **Aims** Advance and promote sustainable development in decision making at international, national and local levels by conducting policy and action research and undertaking communications initiatives. **Structure** Board of Directors (about half the members are from outside of Canada); President/Chief Executive Officer. Official Observers (7), all Canada-based institutions, including: *Canadian International Development Agency (CIDA, inactive)*. **Finance** Funded by Government of Canada (20%) and Internationally (80%). Grants from private sector, philanthropic foundations, UN agencies and international organizations, including the following bodies listed in this Yearbook: *Australian Aid (inactive)*; *Charles Stewart Mott Foundation*; *Department for International Development (DFID, inactive)*; *International Union for Conservation of Nature and Natural Resources (IUCN, #15766)*; *UNEP (#20299)*; *UNDP (#20292)*; *United States Agency for International Development (USAID)*; *Wallace Global Fund*. **Activities** Knowledge management/information dissemination; advocacy/lobbying/activism; capacity building; research/documentation; training/education. **Events** *African Great Lakes Stakeholder Network Annual Meeting* Ann Arbor, MI (USA) 2020, *Sustainable Development Transition Forum* Incheon (Korea Rep) 2017, *Workshop on Hydrofluorocarbon Management* Paris (France) 2014, *Joint conference on increasing the Momentum of fossil-fuel subsidy reform* Geneva (Switzerland) 2010, *International conference on environment, security and sustainable development* The Hague (Netherlands) 2004. **Publications** *Sustainable Developments* (periodical); *Earth Negotiations Bulletin*; *Linkages Journal* – electronic publication. Annual Report; books.
Members Board members in 9 countries:
Canada, Denmark, France, Ghana, India, Pakistan, Switzerland, Trinidad-Tobago, USA.
Organizations cooperating belonging to the 3 Networks in 21 countries:
Argentina, Brazil, China, Ecuador, El Salvador, Hungary, India, Japan, Kenya, Netherlands, Norway, Pakistan, Poland, Puerto Rico, Senegal, South Africa, Sweden, Ukraine, USA, Vietnam, Zimbabwe.

Consultative Status Consultative status granted from: *ECOSOC (#05331)* (Ros A); *UNCTAD (#20285)* (General Category); *UNEP (#20299)*. **IGO Relations** Associate member of: *NDC Partnership (#16964)*. Partner of: *Group on Earth Observations (GEO, #10735)*. Accredited by: *United Nations Framework Convention on Climate Change – Secretariat (UNFCCC, #20564)*; *United Nations Office at Vienna (UNOV, #20604)*. **NGO Relations** In liaison with technical committees of: *International Organization for Standardization (ISO, #14473)*. Founding member of: *International Centre for Trade and Sustainable Development, Geneva (ICTSD, #12524)*. Member of: *Climate and Clean Air Coalition (CCAC, #04010)*; *Climate Knowledge Brokers (CKB, #04016)*; *Finance Alliance for Sustainable Trade (FAST, #09763)*; *GEF CSO Network (GCN, #10087)*; *Global Partnership for Sustainable Development Data (Data4SDGS, #10542)*; IUCN; *LEDS Global Partnership (LEDS GP, #16435)*; *Manitoba Council for International Cooperation (MCIC)*. Located at: *International Environment House (IEH)*. Partner of: *Green Economy Coalition (GEC, #10717)*; *Green Growth Knowledge Platform (GGKP, #10719)*. Signatory to charter of: *Institute for Global Environmental Strategies (IGES, #11266)*. Provides secretariat for: *Intergovernmental Forum on Mining, Minerals, Metals and Sustainable Development (IGF, #11484)*. [2022/XF0930/j/**F**]

♦ International Institute for Sustainable Transportation (internationally oriented national body)

♦ International Institute of Synthetic Rubber Producers (IISRP) 13931

Institut international de producteurs de caoutchouc synthétique – Instituto Internacional de Productores de Caucho Sintético
Dir 3535 Briarpark Dr, Ste 250, Houston TX 77042-5241, USA. T. +17137837511. Fax +17137837253. E-mail: info@iisrp.com.
URL: http://www.iisrp.com/

History 1960, New York, NY (USA). Registration: 501(c)(6) organization, No/ID: EIN: 13-1929277, Start date: 1961, USA. **Aims** Further long-term growth of the synthetic rubber industry worldwide to benefit producers, customers and ultimate users. **Structure** General Meeting (annual); Board and Directors; Executive Committee; Standing Committees; Operating Committees; Sections (3): Americas; European; Far East; Headquarters in Houston TX (USA). Regional offices (3): Beijing (China); Milan (Italy); Tokyo (Japan). **Languages** English. **Staff** 4.00 FTE, paid. **Finance** Sources: members' dues; sale of publications. Other sources: webinars. **Activities** Events/meetings; projects/programmes; research/documentation. **Events** *Annual General Meeting* Estoril (Portugal) 2022, *Annual General Meeting* St Petersburg (Russia) 2022, *Annual General Meeting* 2021, *Annual General Meeting* St Petersburg (Russia) 2021, *Annual General Meeting* Bangkok (Thailand) 2020. **Publications** *Butadiene Popcorn Polymer Source Book*; *Synthetic Rubber Manual*; *Worldwide Rubber Statistics*. Proceedings of Annual Meeting. **Members** Companies in 22 countries and territories. Membership countries not specified. **IGO Relations** *International Agency for Research on Cancer (IARC, #11598)*; *International Rubber Study Group (IRSG, #14772)*. **NGO Relations** Cooperates with: *International Organization for Standardization (ISO, #14473)*. [2023/XC2166/j/**C**]

♦ International Institute of Systems Automation / see International Institute of Concurrent Engineering
♦ International Institute of Techno-Bibliography (inactive)
♦ International Institute of Technology and Economy in Apiculture (internationally oriented national body)

♦ International Institute for Terminology Research 13932

Institut international des recherches sur la terminologie – Internationales Institut für Terminologieforschung (IITF)
Pres Univ of Bergen, Postboks 7800, 5020 Bergen, Norway.
Treas Univ of Vaasa, Dept of Scandinavian Languages, PO Box 700, FI-65101 Vaasa, Finland.
URL: http://www.iitf.fi/

History 25 Jan 1989, Vienna (Austria), by *International Information Centre for Terminology (INFOTERM, #13846)*. **Aims** Promote and coordinate basic research in terminology; advance terminology training; provide those actively engaged in terminology research, especially academics, with a professional platform for exchange of experience and information and for joint research and training projects. **Structure** Annual General Meeting; International Board. **Finance** Members' dues. Annual budget: about US$ 2,000. **Activities** Holds training courses; acts as co-organizer of scientific symposia and conferences. **Events** *Colloquium* Vienna (Austria) 2015, *Colloquium* Vienna (Austria) 2013, *Colloquium* Perm (Russia) 2011, *Seminar on methods of terminology management* Vienna (Austria) 1996, *International workshop on theoretical issues of terminology science* Jurmala (Latvia) 1992. **Publications** *Terminology Science and Research* (2 a year) – journal. *IITF Series* – 10 vols since 1990. **Members** Membership countries not specified. **NGO Relations** Member of: *International Network for Terminology (TermNet, #14332)*. [2016/XE1348/j/**E**]

♦ International Institute for Textbook Improvement / see Georg Eckert Institute for International Textbook Research
♦ International Institute for Theoretical Sciences (internationally oriented national body)
♦ International Institute for Trade and Development (internationally oriented national body)
♦ International Institute for Traditional Music (inactive)
♦ International Institute of Transportation Engineers (internationally oriented national body)

♦ International Institute of Tropical Agriculture (IITA) 13933

Institut international d'agriculture tropicale – Instituto Internacional de Agricultura Tropical
Main Office Oyo Road, PMB 5320, Ibadan, Oyo, Nigeria. T. +23422412626. Fax +23422412221. E-mail: iita@cgiar.org.
URL: http://www.iita.org/

History 24 Jul 1967, Ibadan, by Ford Foundation and Rockefeller Foundation, as one of 15 international agricultural research centres organized under the auspices of *CGIAR System Organization (CGIAR, #03843)*. Registered in accordance with Nigerian law. **Aims** Fight hunger and *poverty* in the poor world, with a special focus on sub-Saharan Africa. **Structure** International Board of Trustees of 14 members. IITA-East based in Tanzania UR; IITA-West based in Nigeria; IITA-South based in Zambia. **Languages** English. **Staff** International: 105; local: 928. **Finance** Central budget funded through *OECD (#17693)* countries, including: Austria, Belgium, Canada, China, Denmark, Germany, Ireland, Korea Rep, Netherlands, Nigeria, Norway, South Africa, Sweden, UK and USA. **Activities** Research-for-development (R4D) programmes (7): Agriculture and Health; Agrobiodiversity; Banana and Plantain Systems; Cereals and Legumes System; Horticulture and Tree Systems; Roots and Tubers Systems; Opportunities and Threats. Coordinates CGIAR System-wide Program on Integrated Pest Management (SP-IPM). Conducts research, germplasm conservation, training and information exchange activities in partnership with regional bodies and national programmes including universities, NGOs and the private sector. Research addresses crop improvement, plant health and resource and crop management within a food systems framework, targeted at the identified needs of 4 major agroecological zones: dry savanna; moist savanna; humid forests; mid-altitude savanna. Research focuses on smallholder cropping and postharvest systems and on the following food crops; cassava; cowpea; maize; plantain and banana; soybean; yam. Organizes conferences and symposia. Includes: *Biological Control Center for Africa (see: #13933)*. **Events** *AYA : African Youth Agripreneurs Forum* Ibadan (Nigeria) 2017, *Seminar* Cotonou (Benin) 2003, *International nematology workshop* Ibadan (Nigeria) 2003, *Workshop on commercialization and impact on gender* Ibadan (Nigeria) 2003, *Technical workshop* Lusaka (Zambia) 2003. **Publications** *IITA Annual Report*; *R4D Review*. Technical and information papers; research monographs; manuals; training guides; networking newsletters. Information Services: IITA Library Service; database.
Members Full, including Regional Offices (9) in 65 countries:
Angola, Australia, Austria, Belgium, Benin (*), Botswana, Brazil, Burkina Faso, Burundi, Cameroon (*), Canada, Cape Verde, Central African Rep, Chad, China, Colombia, Congo DR, Côte d'Ivoire (*), Denmark, Djibouti, Ethiopia, Gabon, Gambia, Georgia, Germany, Ghana, Guinea, Guinea-Bissau, India, Indonesia, Ireland, Italy, Japan, Kenya, Korea Rep, Liberia, Madagascar, Malawi (*), Malaysia, Mali, Mexico, Mozambique (*), Namibia, Netherlands, Nigeria (*), Norway, Peru, Philippines, Rwanda, Sao Tomé-Principe, Senegal, Sierra Leone, Somalia, Sri Lanka, Sudan, Sweden, Switzerland, Syrian AR, Tanzania UR (*), Togo, Uganda (*), UK, USA, Zambia, Zimbabwe (*).
IGO Relations Partner of: *Global Soil Partnership (GSP, #10608)*. Cooperates with: *African Union (AU, #00488)*; *Common Market for Eastern and Southern Africa (COMESA, #04296)*; *Economic Community of West African States (ECOWAS, #05312)*; *Southern African Development Community (SADC, #19843)*. **NGO Relations** Cooperates with other CGIAR supported centres: *Center for International Forestry Research (CIFOR, #03646)*; *International Centre for Tropical Agriculture (#12527)*; *International Food Policy Research Institute (IFPRI, #13622)*; *International Maize and Wheat Improvement Center (#14077)*; *International Potato Center (#14627)*; *International Water Management Institute (IWMI, #15867)*; *World Agroforestry Centre (ICRAF, #21072)*;

WorldFish (#21507). Participates in: *Agricultural Libraries Network (AGLINET, #00571)*; *International Union of Soil Sciences (IUSS, #15817)*; *USAID/SADC/IITA/CIP Southern Africa Root Crops Research Network (SARRNET, #20734)*; *West African Farming Systems Research Network (WAFSRN, #20880)*. Cooperates with: *International Fertilizer Development Center (IFDC, #13590)*. Supporting organization of: *Scaling Up Nutrition Movement (SUN Movement, #19064)*. Instrumental in setting up: *Africa Regional Centre for Information Science (ARCIS, #00517)*; *International Soil Conservation Organization (ISCO, #15560)*. [2018/XE4109/j/E]

♦ International Institute of Tropical Forestry (internationally oriented national body)

♦ International Institute for the Unification of Private Law (UNIDROIT) 13934

Institut international pour l'unification du droit privé – Instituto Internacional para la Unificación del Derecho Privado – Internationales Institut für die Vereinheitlichung des Privatrechts – Istituto Internazionale per l'Unificazione del Diritto Privato

SG Via Panisperna 28, 00184 Rome RM, Italy. T. +396696211. Fax +39669941394. E-mail: info@unidroit.org.
URL: http://www.unidroit.org/

History 20 Apr 1926, Rome (Italy). Founded by agreement between the Government of Italy and the Council of *League of Nations (SDN, inactive)*, of which it was an auxiliary organ. Inaugurated 30 May 1928. Re-constituted by multilateral agreement ("Statut Organique"), 21 Apr 1940, Rome, with statutes adopted on 15 Mar 1940, Rome. Statutes modified: Jun 1957; Jul 1958; Dec 1963; 1976; Jan 1986; Mar 1993. **Aims** Study needs and methods for modernizing, harmonizing and coordinating private and in particular commercial law as between States and groups of States; formulate uniform law instruments, principles and rules to achieve those objectives. **Structure** General Assembly (at least annual); Governing Council; Permanent Committee; Finance Committee; Secretariat, headed by Secretary-General. **Languages** English, French, German, Italian, Spanish. **Staff** 20.00 FTE, paid. Staff matters dealt with by *Administrative Tribunal of UNIDROIT (see: #13934)*, consisting of 3 full members and one substitute, chosen by General Assembly for five years from outside the Institute and being preferably of different nationalities. **Finance** Sources: contributions of member/participating states. Annual budget: 2,700,000 USD.

Activities Prepares the following instruments addressed to states: international conventions; uniform laws; model laws; sets of principles; recommendations. Instruments concluded under UNIDROIT auspices, include:
- *Convention Relating to a Uniform Law on the Formation of Contracts for the International Sale of Goods (ULFIS, 1964)*;
- *Convention Relating to a Uniform Law on the International Sale of Goods (ULIS, 1964)*;
- *Convention Internationale Relative au Contrat de Voyage (CCV, 1970)*;
- *Convention Providing a Uniform Law on the Form of an International Will (1973)*;
- *Convention on Agency in the International Sale of Goods (1983)*;
- *Convention on International Factoring (1988)*;
- *Convention on International Financial Leasing (1988)*;
- *Convention on Stolen or Illegally Exported Cultural Objects (1995)*;
- *UNIDROIT Convention on International Interests in Mobile Equipment (Cape Town convention, 2001)* and its protocols *Protocol to the Convention on International Interests in Mobile Equipment on Matters Specific to Aircraft Equipment (2001)*, *Luxembourg Protocol to the Convention on International Interests in Mobile Equipment on Matters Specific to Railway Rolling Stock (Luxembourg Protocol, 2007)*,*Protocol to the Convention on International Interests in Mobile Equipment on Matters Specific to Space Assets (2012)*; and Protocol to the Convention on International Interests in Mobile Equipment on Matters Specific to Mining, Agricultural and Construction Equipment (Pretoria).
- *UNIDROIT Convention on Substantive Rules for Intermediated Securities (Geneva Securities Convention, 2009)* (2009);
- background work for *Convention on the Contract for the International Carriage of Goods by Road (CMR, 1956)* and *Protocol to the Convention on the Contract for the International Carriage of Goods by Road (CMR, 1978)*, as adopted by the UNECE.

Prepares sets of Principles addressed to arbitrators and directly to professional circles and legal Guides addressed to professional circles.
Meeting activities.

Events *Conference for the Adoption of the Draft Protocol on Matters Specific to Mining, Agricultural and Construction Equipment* Pretoria (South Africa) 2019, *Session* Rome (Italy) 2019, *Session* Rome (Italy) 2018, *Session* Rome (Italy) 2017, *Session* Rome (Italy) 2016. **Publications** *Uniform Law Review* (4 a year). Convention texts; commentaries; studies; acts and proceedings; texts; guides. Information Services: Specialized library functions as a major European resource for books, legal periodicals, documents and other publications on commercial, comparative and private international law.

Members Governments of 63 countries:
Argentina, Australia, Austria, Belgium, Bolivia, Brazil, Bulgaria, Canada, Chile, China, Colombia, Croatia, Cuba, Cyprus, Czechia, Denmark, Egypt, Estonia, Finland, France, Germany, Greece, Holy See, Hungary, India, Indonesia, Iran Islamic Rep, Iraq, Ireland, Israel, Italy, Japan, Korea Rep, Latvia, Lithuania, Luxembourg, Malta, Mexico, Netherlands, Nicaragua, Nigeria, Norway, Pakistan, Paraguay, Poland, Portugal, Romania, Russia, San Marino, Saudi Arabia, Serbia, Slovakia, Slovenia, South Africa, Spain, Sweden, Switzerland, Tunisia, Türkiye, UK, Uruguay, USA, Venezuela.

IGO Relations Observer status with (1): *United Nations (UN, #20515)* (General Assembly). Member of (1): *European Committee on Legal Cooperation (#06655)*. Partner of (1): *Organisation pour l'Harmonisation en Afrique du Droit des Affaires (OHADA, #17806)*. Relationship agreement with: *Asian-African Legal Consultative Organization (AALCO, #01303)*; *Parlamento Centroamericano (PARLACEN, #18201)*; *Commonwealth Secretariat (#04362)*; *Council of Europe (CE, #04881)*; *European Commission (EC, #06633)*; *FAO (#09260)*; *ILO (#11123)*; *International Maritime Organization (IMO, #14102)*; *OAS (#17629)*; *UNCTAD (#20285)*; *UNESCO (#20322)*; United Nations. Permanent observer status with: *World Intellectual Property Organization (WIPO, #21593)*. Observer to: *Intergovernmental Committee of the International Convention of Rome for the Protection of Performers, Producers of Phonograms and Broadcasting Organizations (#11474)*; *International Oil Pollution Compensation Funds (IOPC Funds, #14402)*. **NGO Relations** Instrumental in setting up (1): *Rail Working Group (RWG, #18610)*. Agreements with: *European Centre for Peace and Development (ECPD, #06496)*; *International Union of Notaries (#15795)*; *Union Internationale des Avocats (UIA, #20422)*; national organizations. [2022.02.15/XB2136/j/B*]

♦ International Institute for the Urban Environment (internationally oriented national body)
♦ International Institute for Visually Impaired / see Blind Children's Fund (#03280)
♦ International Institute for Water Administration (see: #14399)
♦ International Institute for Water and Environmental Engineering (#11313)

♦ International Institute of Welding (IIW) 13935

CEO Via Lungobisagno Istria 15A, 16141 Genoa GE, Italy. T. +393357626643 – +390108341320. E-mail: iiw@iiwelding.org.
Communication address not obtained.
URL: https://iiwelding.org/

History Jun 1948, Brussels (Belgium). **Aims** Promote and encourage development of welding, as regards both equipment and raw materials, and welding applications; provide exchange of scientific and technical information relating to welding research and education; assist in formulating international standards for welding. **Structure** General Assembly (annual); Board of Directors. **Languages** English. **Staff** Secretariat work is carried out by staff employed by the Italian Institute of Welding, which receives grants from IIW for salaries and facilities. **Finance** Sources: meeting proceeds; members' dues; sale of publications. Annual budget: 550,000 EUR (2020). **Activities** Knowledge management/information dissemination; networking/liaising; research and development; standards/guidelines. **Events** *Annual Assembly* Singapore (Singapore) 2023, *Annual Assembly* Tokyo (Japan) 2022, *Annual Assembly* Genoa (Italy) 2021, *Annual Assembly* Genoa (Italy) 2020, *International Congress* Mumbai (India) 2020. **Publications** *Welding in the World* (6 a year). Books; reference radiographs; films.

Members Non-profit making bodies, wholly or partly connected with scientific and technical aspects of welding, in 50 countries:
Australia, Austria, Belgium, Bulgaria, Cameroon, Canada, China, Croatia, Cyprus, Czechia, Denmark, Finland, France, Germany, Greece, Hungary, India, Indonesia, Israel, Italy, Japan, Kazakhstan, Korea Rep, Lithuania, Malaysia, Morocco, Netherlands, New Zealand, Nigeria, Norway, Pakistan, Poland, Portugal, Romania, Russia, Serbia, Singapore, Slovakia, Slovenia, South Africa, Spain, Sweden, Switzerland, Thailand, Tunisia, Türkiye, UK, Ukraine, USA, Vietnam.

Consultative Status Consultative status granted from: *ECOSOC (#05331)* (Ros C); *UNIDO (#20336)*. **IGO Relations** Cooperates with (2): *UNESCO (#20322)*; *United Nations Economic Commission for Europe (UNECE, #20555)*. **NGO Relations** Cooperates with (1): *International Organization for Standardization (ISO, #14473)*. [2021.03.19/XC2170/j/C]

♦ International Institution for the History of Surveying and Measurement 13936

Sec 24 Woodbury Avenue, Petersfield, GU32 2EE, UK. T. +441730262619.
Dir Av de Meysse 5, 1020 Brussels, Belgium. T. +3222681025. Fax +3222621033.
URL: http://www.fig.net/hsm/index.htm

History 1998, as an organ of *International Federation of Surveyors (FIG, #13561)*, following the activities of an ad hoc committee. Officially known as *International Institution for the History of Surveying and Measurement – A Permanent Institution of FIG*. **Aims** Bring together interested people who are keen to preserve the heritage and history of surveying and measurement. **Structure** Officers: Directory; Deputy Director; Treasurer; Honorary Secretary. **Languages** English. **Activities** Research/documentation; knowledge management/information dissemination; events/meetings; networking/liaising. **Events** *Charting and Mapping the Pacific Paradise of the Pitcairners* Kingston, ACT (Australia) 2014, *Working Week Conference* Rome (Italy) 2012, *Working Week Conference* Marrakech (Morocco) 2011, *Working Week Conference* Sydney, NSW (Australia) 2010, *Working Week Conference* Eilat (Israel) 2009. [2016.06.01/XE3747/j/E]

♦ International Institution for the History of Surveying and Measurement – A Permanent Institution of FIG / see International Institution for the History of Surveying and Measurement (#13936)
♦ International Institution for Physical Education (inactive)
♦ International Institution for Production Engineering Research / see CIRP – The International Academy for Production Engineering (#03945)
♦ International Instrument Users' Association / see Evaluation International
♦ International Instrument Users' Association – WIB (internationally oriented national body)

♦ International Insulin Foundation (IIF) 13937

Chair Liverpool School of Tropical Medicine, Pembroke Place, Liverpool, L3 5QA, UK.
URL: http://www.access2insulin.org/

History Nov 2002. Registration: Charity Commission, No/ID: 1099032, England and Wales. **Aims** Create sustainable nation-wide access to affordable and reliable sources of insulin through projects that improve distribution and educated use of insulin by people with Type 1 diabetes currently unable to obtain it. **Structure** Trustees; Steering Group. **Consultative Status** Consultative status granted from: *WHO (#20950)* (Official Relations). [2016.07.12/XJ1808/f/F]

♦ International Insurance Law Association (#02684)
♦ International Insurance Library, Leuven (internationally oriented national body)

♦ International Insurance Press 13938

Presse internationale des assurances (PIA) – Prensa Internacional de Seguros

Pres Str Horei no 15-17 sector 2, 021377 Bucharest, Romania. T. +40212524671.
URL: http://www.piassurance.eu/

History 1954, Paris (France). **Aims** Act as an international organization of the insurance press for exchange of information, articles and documents and of relevant facts and occurrences emerging in national insurance industries of member magazines. **Structure** General Assembly (annual). President; Vice-President; Administrative Secretariat. **Languages** English. **Staff** 2.00 FTE, voluntary. **Finance** Financed by the company of the president in charge. **Events** *General Meeting* Sofia (Bulgaria) 2010, *General Meeting* Warsaw (Poland) 2008, *Annual general meeting / General Meeting* Madrid (Spain) 2007, *Annual general meeting / General Meeting* Amsterdam (Netherlands) 2006, *Annual general meeting / General Meeting* Athens (Greece) 2005.

Members Organizations and firms publishing insurance magazines in 20 countries:
Austria, Belgium, Bulgaria, Croatia, Czechia, Germany, Greece, Hungary, Mexico, Netherlands, Poland, Portugal, Romania, Russia, Serbia, Slovakia, Spain, Switzerland, UK, USA. [2011.10.18/XD3110/D]

♦ International Insurance Seminars / see International Insurance Society (#13939)

♦ International Insurance Society (IIS) 13939

Address not obtained.
URL: https://www.internationalinsurance.org/

History 1965, USA, as *International Insurance Seminars*, at 1st Worldwide Seminar, having begun as a series of invitational seminars at Ohio State University (USA) and University of Texas (USA) from 1959 to 1964. **Aims** Facilitate international understanding, transfer of ideas and innovations and the development of personal networks across insurance markets through a joint effort of leading executives and academics on a worldwide basis. **Structure** Board of Directors. **Languages** English. **Staff** 5.00 FTE, paid. **Activities** Knowledge management/information dissemination; networking/liaising; events/meetings; awards/prizes/competitions. **Events** *Annual Global Forum* New York, NY (USA) 2021, *Annual Global Forum* New York, NY (USA) 2020, *Annual Global Forum* Singapore (Singapore) 2019, *Annual Global Forum* Berlin (Germany) 2018, *Insurance Summit on Industrial Revolution 4.0* Seoul (Korea Rep) 2018. **Publications** *Special Competition Edition – Geneva Papers on Risk and Insurance*.

Members Corporate; Individual. Members (900) in 86 countries and territories:
Antigua-Barbuda, Argentina, Australia, Austria, Bahrain, Bangladesh, Barbados, Belgium, Belize, Bermuda, Brazil, Cameroon, Canada, Chile, China, Colombia, Costa Rica, Cyprus, Czechia, Denmark, Dominican Rep, Ecuador, Egypt, El Salvador, Finland, France, Gambia, Germany, Ghana, Greece, Guatemala, Haiti, Hong Kong, Hungary, Iceland, India, Indonesia, Ireland, Israel, Italy, Jamaica, Japan, Jordan, Kazakhstan, Kenya, Korea Rep, Kuwait, Lebanon, Luxembourg, Macau, Malaysia, Malta, Mexico, Morocco, Myanmar, Netherlands, New Zealand, Nigeria, Norway, Oman, Pakistan, Panama, Papua New Guinea, Paraguay, Peru, Philippines, Poland, Portugal, Puerto Rico, Qatar, Russia, Saudi Arabia, Singapore, South Africa, Spain, Switzerland, Taiwan, Thailand, Trinidad-Tobago, Tunisia, Uganda, UK, United Arab Emirates, USA, Venezuela.

NGO Relations Administers: *Insurance Hall of Fame*. [2020/XF1105/F]

♦ International Integrated Yoga Association (no recent information)

♦ International Integration Institute of the Andrés Bello Convention 13940

Institut international d'intégration de la Convention Andrés Bello – Instituto Internacional de Integración del Convenio Andrés Bello (III-CAB)

Exec Dir Av Sanchez Lima Nro 2146, Sopocachi, Casilla 7796, La Paz, Bolivia. T. +59122410401 – +59122411041. Fax +59122411741. E-mail: iiicab@iiicab.org.bo.
URL: http://www.iiicab.org.bo/

History 10 Apr 1975, Viña del Mar (Chile), following Resolution No 24, 10 Apr 1975, during the 6th Meeting of Ministers of Education of signatory countries to the *Convenio Andrés Bello de integración educativa, cientifica y cultural de América Latina y España (Convenio Andrés Bello, #04785)*, of which it is a specialized entity. **Aims** Serve as a specialized organization of educational, cultural, scientific and technological integration in areas bordering on the signatory countries to the Andrés Bello Convention; promote integration through education and human resources capacity building; develop renewed ideas on integration based on universal human values; develop activities oriented to this field. **Structure** Executive Committee. General coordination: Integrated Centre of Documentation and Information; Communication; Informatics. Juridical Legal Advisors; Administration and Finances Unit. Secretariat in La Paz (Bolivia). **Languages** Spanish. **Staff** 35.00 FTE, paid. **Finance** Resources granted by the Andrés Bello Convention for development of projects; funds from the government of Bolivia. **Activities** Work programme realized in collaboration with the Executive Secretary in agreement with the lines of Cross-Sectional Programming of the Andrés Bello Convention. Projects: Training for Educators and Other Social Actors – promotes capacity building of actors working in the area of education; *'Network of Advanced Studies on Integration'* – aims to attain convergence of theoretical actions and practices destined to deepen the process of regional integration, articulating through the Network to actors in the academic world, the public sector, enterprises agents and civil society. *Information Network of the Andrés Bello Convention (RICAB)* – built within the framework of lines of management drafted by the Andrés Bello Convention, with the aim of reaching coordinated action on integration; *Integrated Centre of Documentation and Information (CIDI)* – specializes in economic, social and cultural integration bodies and functions as a node of RICAB. Cooperates and collaborates with: embassies of CAB countries members accredited in Bolivia; Education Ministry of Bolivia and other CAB countries; indigenous intercultural universities (UNIBOL) of Bolivia; universities in Bolivia and other CAB countries, including through joint post-graduate programmes. Initiated interdisciplinary, international PhD Programme in Humanities and Sciences with the National University "Siglo XX", 2010. Offers post-graduate courses in education, culture and methodology, and a country-wide Master's programme in collaboration with Education Ministry on Productive Community Education. Supports and evaluates impact of the literacy and post-literacy programmes in Bolivia and other CAB countries. Organizes:

Scientific Event (annual), in cooperation with other organizations; monthly academic seminars; international conferences. **Publications** *Boletin Internacional* (3 a year); *Entegra Educativa* (3 a year) – journal, free PDF version online; *Informe sobre el Estado de la Integracion – Report on the State of Integration* (annual) – proceedings of Scientific Event. Over 60 book titles since 2007 on education, cultures, society, politics.
Members Governments of 12 countries:
Bolivia, Chile, Colombia, Cuba, Dominican Rep, Ecuador, Mexico, Panama, Paraguay, Peru, Spain, Venezuela.
NGO Relations Cooperates with: *Centro Latinoamericano para les Relaciones con Europa (CELARE)*. Member of: *Red de Centros Culturales de América y Europa (RCCAE, #18639).* [2011.10.22/XE6768/j/**E***]

♦ International Intellectual Property Alliance (internationally oriented national body)
♦ International Intellectual Property Institute (internationally oriented national body)

♦ International Intellectual Property Law Association (IIPLA) 13941

Founder/Exec Dir 589 South 22nd street, San Jose CA 95116, USA. Fax +14086681000. E-mail: mail@iipla.org – events@iipla.org.
URL: http://www.iipla.org/
History Proposed 2012. Launched 3 Mar 2014. **Aims** Unify the global IP laws and bridge the gap in IP fraternity; Provide a platform to bring together everyone who deals with IP and its challenges around the world. **Structure** Board of Managers. **Languages** English. **Staff** 18.00 FTE, paid; 13.00 FTE, voluntary. **Finance** Sources: members' dues. **Activities** Events/meetings. **Events** *Dubai IP Congress* Dubai (United Arab Emirates) 2023, *Dubai IP Congress* Dubai (United Arab Emirates) 2018, *Dubai IP Congress* Dubai (United Arab Emirates) 2017, *Annual Congress* Washington, DC (USA) 2017, *Annual Meeting* San Jose, CA (USA) 2016. **Publications** *IIPLA Journal*.
Members Full in 22 countries:
Algeria, Australia, Bangladesh, Cyprus, Denmark, Dominican Rep, Egypt, Guatemala, India, Iran Islamic Rep, Korea Rep, Malaysia, Nigeria, North Macedonia, Pakistan, Philippines, Qatar, Singapore, Trinidad-Tobago, UK, United Arab Emirates, USA. [2018/XJ8670/**C**]

♦ International Intelligence History Association (IIHA) 13942

Arbeitskreis Geschichte der Nachrichtendienste (AGN)
Exec Dir PO Box 11 02 05, 97029 Würzburg, Germany.
Registered Office Fürstenrieder Str 143, 80686 Munich, Germany.
URL: http://intelligence-history.org/
History 1993. Registration: No/ID: VR 14101, Start date: 21 Jun 1994, Germany. **Aims** Promote scholarly research on intelligence organizations and their impact on historical development and international relations. **Structure** General Assembly; Board. **Finance** Sources: members' dues. **Activities** Events/meetings. **Events** *Conference* Tutzing (Germany) 2021, *Conference* Tutzing (Germany) 2020, *Conference* Berlin (Germany) 2019, *Conference* Graz (Austria) 2018. **Publications** *Journal of Intelligence History.* [2020/AA0736/**D**]

♦ International Interchurch Film Organization (INTERFILM) 13943

Internationale Kirchliche Filmorganisation
Pres Teichhöfe 4, 30659 Hannover, Germany. E-mail: president.interfilm@gmx.net.
Exec Dir c/o GEP, Filmkulturelles Zentrum, Emil-von Behringstrasse 3, Postfach 500 550, 60394 Frankfurt-Main, Germany. T. +496958098155. Fax +496958098274.
URL: http://www.inter-film.org/
History 1955, Paris (France). Founded on the initiative of representatives of protestant film and media institutions in France, Germany, Netherlands and Switzerland. An affiliate of *World Council of Churches (WCC, #21320)*. Self-understanding is defined with reference to WCC aims, included in revision of statuts, 17 Nov 1993, Arnoldshain (Germany). Latest revision of statutes, 11 Jun 2016. Former names and other names: *International Church Film Organization* – alias; *Organisation Protestante orthodoxe de film* – alias. Registration: Switzerland. **Aims** Promote appreciation of cinema's artistic, spiritual and social significance in the church; call attention to the relevance of church, theology and religion for cinema. **Structure** General Assembly (every 3 years); Board; Praesidium; Juries: Festival, Ecumenical. **Languages** English, French, German. **Finance** Sources: members' dues. **Activities** Awards/prizes/competitions; events/meetings; research/documentation; training/education. **Events** *Conference* Erlangen (Germany) 2019, *General Assembly* Erlangen (Germany) 2019, *The Future of INTERFILM: Confessional, Ecumenical, and Interreligious Perspectives* Uppsala (Sweden) 2016, *Triennial General Assembly* Uppsala (Sweden) 2016, *International Film Meeting* Hannover (Germany) 2013. **Publications** *INTERFILM Newsletter*. *Church and Film in Dialogue: 50 Years of INTERFILM 1955-2005* (2005) by Julia Helmke and Hans Hodel et al.
Members Corporate and individual concerned with film and theology, church and cinema. Associations in 10 countries:
Denmark, Finland, France, Germany, Hungary, Italy, Netherlands, Sweden, Switzerland, UK.
Individuals in 31 countries:
Argentina, Austria, Belgium, Brazil, Bulgaria, Canada, Croatia, Czechia, Denmark, Egypt, Estonia, Finland, France, Germany, Greece, Hungary, Iceland, India, Italy, Latvia, Netherlands, Norway, Poland, Romania, Serbia, Slovakia, Sweden, Switzerland, UK, Ukraine, USA.
NGO Relations Cooperates with (3): *Conference of European Churches (CEC, #04593)*; *World Association for Christian Communication (WACC, #21126)*; *World Catholic Association for Communication (SIGNIS, #21264).* [2022.02.01/XE0729/**E**]

♦ International and Interdisciplinary Association on the Pharmaceutical Life Cycle (#02707)
♦ International and Interdisciplinary Conference on Emotional Geographies (meeting series)
♦ International Interdisciplinary Conference on Land Use and Water Quality (meeting series)
♦ International Interdisciplinary Congress on Women (meeting series)
♦ International Interfaith Centre, Oxford (internationally oriented national body)

♦ International Interfaith Investment Group (3iG) 13944

Contact Rambla del Poblenou 26 1-2, 08005 Barcelona, Spain. T. +34655131325.
URL: http://www.3ignet.org/
History Apr 2005, at the initiative of *Alliance of Religions and Conservation (ARC, inactive)*. **Aims** Contribute to a just and sustainable society through promoting responsible investment in a spirit of inter-faith and international dialogue and cooperation. **NGO Relations** Founding members and partners include: *Benedictine Confederation*; *Catholic Foreign Missionary Society of America (Maryknoll Fathers)*; *Charles Stewart Mott Foundation*; *Foundation for the Preservation of the Mahayana Tradition (FPMT, #09970)*; *Missionary Oblates of Mary Immaculate (OMI)*; *Oikocredit International (Oikocredit, #17704)*; *World Council of Churches (WCC, #21320).* [2010/XM1401/**F**]

♦ International Interfaith Organizations Network (IION) 13945

Contact address not obtained. T. +441865202745. Fax +441865202746.
URL: http://interfaithorganisations.net/
History Mar 2001, Oxford (UK). Also referred to as *Network of International Interfaith Organizations*. **Aims** Promote effective communication and cooperation between interfaith organizations. **Events** *Annual Meeting* Kochi (India) 2008, *Annual Meeting* Kochi (India) 2008, *Annual Meeting* Oxford (UK) 2003, *Annual Meeting* Budapest (Hungary) 2002.
Members International organizations (12):
International Association for Religious Freedom (IARF, #12130); International Interfaith Centre, Oxford (IIC); *Minorities of Europe (MOE, #16818)*; *Parliament of the World's Religions (PoWR, #18222)*; *Project Towards the Creation of a Spiritual Forum for World Peace at the United Nations*; *Religions for Peace (RfP, #18831)*; *Temple of Understanding (ToU, #20124)*; *United Religions Initiative (URI, #20658)*; *World Congress of Faiths (WCF, #21304)*; *World Council of Religious Leaders (WCRL, #21339)*; *World Faiths Development Dialogue (WFDD)*; *World Fellowship of Inter-Religious Councils (WFIRC)*.
NGO Relations Coordinated by: *International Interfaith Centre, Oxford (IIC).* [2011/XM0250/y/**F**]

♦ International Interfaith Peace Corps (internationally oriented national body)

♦ International Interior Design Association (IIDA) 13946

Headquarters 111 E Wacker Dr, Suite 22, Chicago IL 60654, USA. T. +13124671950. E-mail: iidahq@iida.org.
URL: http://www.iida.org/
History 1963. Name changed 1994 when it merged with 2 USA organizations (*Institute of Business Designers (IBD)* and the *Council of Federal Interior Designers (CFID)*). UK Chapter merged with *Interior Decorators and Designers Association (IDDA, inactive)* to form *British Interior Design Association*. Former names and other names: *International Society of Interior Designers (ISID)* – former (1963 to 1994). **Aims** Support design professionals, industry affiliates, educators, students, firms and their clients. **Structure** International Board of Directors; Headquarters in Chicago IL (USA). **Languages** English. **Staff** 30.00 FTE, paid. **Activities** Events/meetings. **Publications** *Perspective* – journal. Reports. **Members** Individuals (over 15,000) in 58 countries. Membership countries not specified. [2020/XD9039/**D**]

♦ International Intermediary Institute (inactive)
♦ International Internet Leathercrafter's Guild (internationally oriented national body)

♦ International Internet Preservation Consortium (IIPC) 13947

Senior Program Officer address not obtained.
URL: http://netpreserve.org/
History Jul 2003, France. **Aims** Acquire, preserve and make accessible knowledge and information from the Internet for future generations everywhere, promoting global exchange and international relations by: enabling the collection of a rich body of Internet content from around the world to be preserved in a way that it can be archived, secured and accessed over time; fostering development and use of common tools, techniques and standards that enable the creation of international archives; encouraging and supporting national libraries, archives and research organizations everywhere to address Internet archiving and preservation. **Structure** General Assembly; Steering Committee of 15 members (2015), elected by the General Assembly for 3-year terms. Officers voted on by Steering Committee (3-year terms). Working Groups (4): Harvesting; Access; Preservation; Collection Development. **Staff** 2.00 FTE, paid. **Finance** Sources: members' dues. **Activities** Knowledge management/information dissemination; projects/programmes. **Events** *General Assembly* USA 2022, *General Assembly* Luxembourg 2021, *General Assembly* Texas (USA) 2020, *General Assembly* Wellington (New Zealand) 2018, *General Assembly* Ottawa, ON (Canada) 2017.
Members Regional or national libraries, non profit foundations; university libraries, service providers and national archives in 30 countries:
Australia, Austria, Canada, Chile, China, Croatia, Czechia, Denmark, Egypt, Estonia, Finland, France, Germany, Iceland, Israel, Japan, Korea Rep, Latvia, Netherlands, New Zealand, Norway, Poland, Portugal, Singapore, Slovenia, Spain, Sweden, Switzerland, UK, USA. [2022/XJ9139/**C**]

♦ International Interplanetary Space Travel Research Association (inactive)
♦ International Intervisitation Programme (meeting series)
♦ International Intradiscal Therapy Society / see International Intradiscal and Transforaminal Therapy Society
♦ International Intradiscal and Transforaminal Therapy Society (internationally oriented national body)

♦ International Intra-Ocular Implant Club (IIIC) 13948

Club international d'implants oculaires
Exec Dir FreeVis LASIK Zentrum, Theodor Kutzer Ufer 1-3, 68167 Mannheim, Germany. T. +496213833410. Fax +496213831984. E-mail: info@iiiclub.org.
Executive Office 1 Green Street, Mayfair, London, W1K 6RG, UK.
URL: http://www.iiiclub.org/
History 1966, London (UK), as *Intraocular Implant Club*. **Aims** Further knowledge in the field of intraocular lens implantation. **Structure** Board, consisting of President, President-Elect, Secretary, Treasurer, Immediate Past President and Executive Director. **Languages** English. **Staff** Voluntary. **Finance** Sources: members' dues. **Events** *Meeting* Amsterdam (Netherlands) 2013, *Meeting* Québec, QC (Canada) 2013, *Meeting* Milan (Italy) 2012, *Meeting* Bali (Indonesia) 2011, *Meeting* New Zealand 2009. **Publications** Newsletter – members only.
Members Membership limited to 250 surgeons interested and active in the field, elected by existing members. Individuals in 37 countries and territories:
Argentina, Australia, Austria, Belgium, Brazil, Canada, China, Czechia, Denmark, Finland, France, Germany, Greece, Hong Kong, Hungary, India, Indonesia, Ireland, Israel, Italy, Japan, Korea Rep, Malaysia, Mexico, Netherlands, Pakistan, Panama, Philippines, Portugal, Saudi Arabia, Singapore, Slovakia, South Africa, Spain, Sweden, Switzerland, UK.
NGO Relations Affiliated to: *International Congress of Ophthalmology.* [2014/XD6005/v/**C**]

♦ International Inventory of Musical Iconography / see Répertoire international d'iconographie musicale (#18844)
♦ International Inventory of the Musical Press (internationally oriented national body)

♦ International Inventory of Musical Sources 13949

Répertoire international des sources musicales (RISM) – Internationales Quellenlexikon der Musik
Main Office c/o Goethe Univ, Senckenberganlage 31-33, 60325 Frankfurt-Main, Germany. T. +4969706231. Fax +4969706026. E-mail: contact@rism.info.
URL: http://www.rism.info/
History 1952, Paris (France). Founded by *International Musicological Society (IMS, #14201)* and the then *'International Association of Music Libraries'*, since Aug 1980, *International Association of Music Libraries, Archives and Documentation Centres (IAML, #12042)*. **Aims** Describe and document musical sources worldwide. **Structure** Commission internationale mixte (CM); Internationales Quellenlexikon der Music eV, Frankfurt (Germany); Editing Head Office; national groups; specialists; authors. **Languages** English, French, German. **Staff** 6.00 FTE, paid. **Finance** Supported by German government, through Union der Deutschen Akademien der Wissenschaften, Mainz (Germany). **Activities** Knowledge management/information dissemination. **Events** *Conference* Mainz (Germany) 2019, *International Conference* Korea Rep 2016, *Conference* Mainz (Germany) 2016, *Colloquium* Frankfurt-Main (Germany) 2015, *Conference* Mainz (Germany) 2012. **Publications** *RISM Online Catalog* – Series A/I, A/II, and years 1500-1550 and 1601-1610 of B/I. Catalogues.
Members National groups, collaborating via Internet directly using our program Muscat or by exchanging data concerning music manuscripts or prints, in 39 countries:
Australia, Austria, Belgium, Brazil, Canada, Colombia, Croatia, Czechia, Denmark, Estonia, Finland, France, Germany, Guatemala, Hungary, Ireland, Israel, Italy, Japan, Korea Rep, Mexico, Netherlands, New Zealand, Norway, Poland, Portugal, Romania, Russia, Serbia, Slovakia, Slovenia, Spain, Sweden, Switzerland, UK, Ukraine, Uruguay, USA, Venezuela. [2020.05.22/XF1983/**F**]

♦ International Investigative Interviewing Research Group (iIIRG) 13950

Co-Chair address not obtained.
Co-Chair address not obtained.
Registered Office 31 High Street, Stokesley, TS9 5AD, UK.
URL: http://www.iiirg.org/
History 2007. Registration: Companies House, No/ID: 07320417, Start date: 2010, England and Wales. **Aims** Work with national and international bodies to improve investigative interviewing and ensure all improvements are underpinned by a robust evidence base. **Structure** Executive Committee; Scientific Committee. **Languages** English, French, Spanish. **Finance** Sources: fees for services. **Activities** Awards/prizes/competitions; events/meetings; research/documentation; training/education. **Events** *Annual Conference* Winchester (UK) 2022, *Conference* Stokesley (UK) 2021, *Conference* Winchester (UK) 2020, *Annual Conference* Stavern (Norway) 2019, *Annual Conference* London (UK) 2016. **Publications** *Investigative Interviewing: Research and Practice* – Open access journal. [2022.12.30/XJ1169/**E**]

♦ International Investment Bank (IIB) 13951

Banque internationale d'investissements – Internationale Investitionsbank – Mezdunarodnyj Investicionnyj Bank (MIB)
Chairman 7 Mashi Poryvayeva Str, Moscow MOSKVA, Russia, 107078. T. +74956047300. Fax +74959752070. E-mail: soe@iibbank.com – mail@iibbank.com.
Deputy Chairman address not obtained.
URL: http://www.iibbank.org/
History 10 Jul 1970, Moscow (USSR). Commenced activities on 1 Jan 1971. Membership of the German Democratic Republic lost validity from 3 Oct 1990, due to discontinuance of its existence as a subject of international law. Maintained regular relations in related fields of interest with *Council for Mutual Economic Assistance (CMEA, inactive)* until dissolution of the Council in 1991, when mass default on debt meant the Bank effectively ceased operations. By decision of the Supervisory Board, limited operations recommenced in 1996, so as to cover operating costs. Following decision by the Russian government, summer 2002, to

make good on its debt, IIB is expected to recommence full operations during 2004. **Aims** Support economies of member states through direct project financing as well as through financial intermediaries. **Structure** Council; Board. **Languages** English, Russian. **Finance** Plans to tap international capital markets for funds. Following international standard audit is to seek a rating from one of the big agencies. Authorized capital: euro 1,300,000,000. Paid-in capital: euro 313 million. **Activities** Financial and/or material support. **Publications** Annual report in Russian/English.

Members Member countries (9):
Bulgaria, Cuba, Czechia, Hungary, Mongolia, Romania, Russia, Slovakia, Vietnam.

IGO Relations Cooperation agreements (over 70) with various entities. Observer or special guest at annual meetings of: *Asian Development Bank (ADB, #01422)*; *Asian Infrastructure Investment Bank (AIIB, #01512)*; *Black Sea Trade and Development Bank (BSTDB, #03278)*; *European Bank for Reconstruction and Development (EBRD, #06315)*; *Inter-American Development Bank (IDB, #11427)*; *International Bank for Reconstruction and Development (IBRD, #12317)* (World Bank); *International Monetary Fund (IMF, #14180)*. Agreement with: *International Finance Corporation (IFC, #13597)*. Memorandum of Understanding with: *Development Bank of Latin America (CAF, #05055)*; *Eurasian Development Bank (EDB, #05605)*. [2017.03.09/XF3912/**F***]

♦ International Investment Centre (internationally oriented national body)
♦ International Investment and Development Company / see International Solidarity for Development and Investment

♦ International Investment Funds Association (IIFA) 13952

Association internationale des fonds d'investissement

Main Office 333 Bay St, Ste 2601, Toronto ON M5H 2R2, Canada. E-mail: info@iifa.ca.
URL: http://www.iifa.ca/

Aims Promote protection of investment fund investors; facilitate growth of the investment funds industry internationally; act as a medium for the advancement of understanding of the investment fund business worldwide; encourage adherence to high ethical standards by all participants in the industry. **Structure** Board; Board Committees; Working Committees. **Events** *Annual Conference* Cyprus 2023, *Annual Conference* London (UK) 2022, *Annual Conference* Toronto, ON (Canada) 2020, *Annual Conference* Buenos Aires (Argentina) 2019, *Annual Meetng* Beijing (China) 2018.

Members Full in 38 countries and territories:
Argentina, Australia, Austria, Brazil, Canada, Chile, China, Cyprus, Denmark, Finland, France, Germany, Greece, Hong Kong, India, Ireland, Italy, Japan, Korea Rep, Liechtenstein, Luxembourg, Malaysia, Mexico, Netherlands, Norway, Pakistan, Poland, Portugal, Singapore, Slovakia, South Africa, Spain, Sweden, Switzerland, Taiwan, Türkiye, UK, USA.

International organizations (2):
European Fund and Asset Management Association (EFAMA, #07365); *Federación Iberoamericana de Fondos de Inversión (FIAFIN, #09309)*. [2022/XM3466/**C**]

♦ International Investor Relations Federation (inactive)
♦ International Ion Voicu Foundation (internationally oriented national body)
♦ International IP ADR Center (unconfirmed)
♦ International IP Commercialization Council (unconfirmed)
♦ International Iron Lung Polio Assistance / see Post-Polio Health International

♦ International Iron Metallics Association (IIMA) 13953

SG Oaklands, 99 Woodfoot Road, Moorgate, Rotherham, S60 3EH, UK. T. +441709375064. Fax +441709910525. E-mail: info@metallics.org.uk.
Chairman Rue Vallin 2, 1201 Geneva, Switzerland. T. +41227151770. Fax +41227151780.
URL: http://www.metallics.org.uk/

History Founded 1 Jan 2011, London (UK), on merger of *Hot Briquetted Iron Association (HBIA, inactive)* and *International Pig Iron Association (IPIA, inactive)*. Registered as a not for profit company, incorporated in England. **Aims** Promote use of *ore*-based metallics as *value-adding raw materials* for the iron and *steel* and ferrous *casting* industries; represent collective interests of members in international industry, trade and maritime forums. **Structure** Board of Directors; Committees; Working Groups. **Languages** English. **Staff** 2.00 FTE, paid. **Finance** Sources: members' dues. Annual budget: 625,000 USD. **Activities** Events/meetings; knowledge management/information dissemination; networking/liaising. **Events** *General Meeting* Vienna (Austria) 2015, *Spring Meeting* Barcelona (Spain) 2014, *General Meeting* Montréal, QC (Canada) 2014, *General Meeting* Lisbon (Portugal) 2012. **Publications** Guides; fact sheets.

Members Member companies (100) in 36 countries:
Argentina, Australia, Austria, Barbados, Belgium, Brazil, Canada, China, Cyprus, Czechia, France, Germany, India, Italy, Japan, Luxembourg, Malaysia, Mexico, Netherlands, Norway, Oman, Russia, Singapore, Slovakia, South Africa, Spain, Sweden, Switzerland, Trinidad-Tobago, Türkiye, UK, Ukraine, United Arab Emirates, Uruguay, USA, Venezuela.

Consultative Status Consultative status granted from: *International Maritime Organization (IMO, #14102)*. **NGO Relations** Affiliate member of: *South East Asia Iron and Steel Institute (SEAISI, #19756)*; *World Steel Association (worldsteel, #21829)*. Member of: *International Council on Mining and Metals (ICMM, #13048)*. Working relationship with: *Arab Iron and Steel Union (AISU, #00998)*; Steel Manufacturers Association (SMA). Memorandum of Understanding with: International Bulk Terminals Association. [2018.06.01/XJ2653/**C**]

♦ International Iron and Steel Institute / see World Steel Association (#21829)

♦ International Irradiation Association (iiA) 13954

Gen Manager 5 Eco Park Rd, Ludlow, SY8 1FD, UK. E-mail: info@iiaglobal.com.
URL: https://iiaglobal.com/

History 30 Nov 2004. Replaced *Association of International Industrial Irradiation (AIII, inactive)*. Registration: Companies House, No/ID: 05106505, Start date: 20 Apr 2004, England and Wales. **Aims** Provide leadership and support membership in advancing the safe and beneficial use of irradiation technology. **Structure** Board. **Activities** Events/meetings. **Events** *International Meeting on Radiation Processing* Bangkok (Thailand) 2022, *Conference* Ludlow (UK) 2021, *International Meeting on Radiation Processing* Strasbourg (France) 2019, *International Meeting on Radiation Processing* Vancouver, BC (Canada) 2016, *International Meeting on Radiation Processing* Shanghai (China) 2013. **IGO Relations** Affiliated with (1): *International Atomic Energy Agency (IAEA, #12294)*. **NGO Relations** Instrumental in setting up (1): *Society for Sterility Assurance Professionals (SfSAP)*. [2023/XJ3963/**C**]

♦ International Irrigation Management Institute / see International Water Management Institute (#15867)

♦ International ISBN Agency 13955

Agence internationale ISBN – Agencia Internacional ISBN – Internationale ISBN-Agentur – Mezdunarodnoe Agenstvo MSKN

Exec Dir 48-49 Russell Square, London, WC1B 4JP, UK. E-mail: info@isbn-international.org.
URL: http://www.isbn-international.org/

History 1970. Founded to internationalize the book numbering system introduced in UK in 1967. Former names and other names: *International Standard Book Number (ISBN)* – former; *Numéro normalisé international du livre* – former; *Internationale Standard-Buchnummer* – former; *Número Internacional Normalizado para Libros* – former; *Internationaal Standaard Boeknummer* – former; *Mezdunarodnyj Standartnyj Kniznyj Nomer* – former. **Aims** Promote, coordinate and supervise worldwide use of the ISBN system. **Structure** General Meeting (annual, normally in September). **Languages** English, French, Spanish. **Staff** 2.00 FTE, paid. **Finance** Sources: members' dues. **Activities** Guidance/assistance/consulting; knowledge management/information dissemination. **Events** *Annual General Meeting* Rabat (Morocco) 2023, *Annual General Meeting* Oslo (Norway) 2022, *Annual General Meeting* 2021, *Annual General Meeting* 2020, *Annual General Meeting* Santiago (Chile) 2019. **Publications** *ISBN Users' Manual* (7th ed 2017); *Global Register of Publishers*.

Members Participants in the ISBN scheme in 178 countries and territories, in a total of 151 ISBN group agencies, with groups of countries of the Caribbean Community (CARICOM) marked 'C' – the South Pacific Region marked 'P' – and the UK and Ireland agency covering those territories marked 'U' – each counting as one member:
Albania, Algeria, Andorra, Anguilla (U), Antigua-Barbuda (C), Argentina, Armenia, Aruba, Australia, Austria, Azerbaijan, Bahamas (C), Bahrain, Bangladesh, Barbados (C), Belgium (Flemish-speaking/French-speaking/German-speaking), Belize (C), Benin, Bermuda, Bhutan, Bolivia, Bosnia-Herzegovina, Botswana, Brazil, Brunei Darussalam, Bulgaria, Cambodia, Cameroon, Canada (English-speaking/French-speaking), Cayman Is (U), Chile, China, Colombia, Cook Is (P), Costa Rica, Croatia, Cuba, Curaçao, Cyprus, Czechia, Denmark, Dominica (C), Dominican Rep, Ecuador, Egypt, El Salvador, Eritrea, Estonia, Eswatini, Ethiopia, Faeroe Is, Fiji (P), Finland, France, Gambia, Georgia, Germany, Ghana, Gibraltar, Greece, Grenada (C), Guatemala, Guyana (C), Haiti, Honduras, Hong Kong, Hungary, Iceland, India, Indonesia, Iran Islamic Rep, Iraq, Ireland (U), Israel, Italy, Jamaica (C), Japan, Jordan, Kazakhstan, Kenya, Kiribati (P), Korea DPR, Korea Rep, Kosovo, Kuwait, Kyrgyzstan, Laos, Latvia, Lebanon, Lesotho, Libya, Liechtenstein, Lithuania, Luxembourg, Macau, Malawi, Malaysia, Maldives, Mali, Malta, Marshall Is (P), Mauritius, Mexico, Micronesia FS (P), Moldova, Mongolia, Montenegro, Montserrat (U), Morocco, Myanmar, Namibia, Nauru (P), Nepal, Netherlands, New Zealand, Nicaragua, Nigeria, Niue (P), North Macedonia, Norway, Oman, Pakistan, Palau (P), Palestine, Panama, Papua New Guinea, Paraguay, Peru, Philippines, Poland, Portugal, Puerto Rico, Qatar, Romania, Rwanda, Samoa (P), Saudi Arabia, Serbia, Seychelles, Sierra Leone, Singapore, Slovakia, Slovenia, Solomon Is (P), South Africa, Spain, Sri Lanka, St Kitts-Nevis (C), St Lucia (C), St Vincent-Grenadines (C), Sudan, Sweden, Switzerland (French-speaking/German-speaking/Italian-speaking), Syrian AR, Taiwan, Tajikistan, Tanzania UR, Thailand, Tokelau (P), Tonga (P), Trinidad-Tobago (C), Tunisia, Türkiye, Turks-Caicos (U), Tuvalu (P), Uganda, UK (U), Ukraine, United Arab Emirates, Uruguay, USA, Uzbekistan, Vanuatu (P), Venezuela, Vietnam, Virgin Is UK (U), Zambia, Zimbabwe.

NGO Relations Member of (1): *Linked Content Coalition (LCC)*. [2022.10.11/XC4391/**B**]

♦ International Islamic Centre for Population Studies and Research (IICPSR) 13956

Centre islamique international des études et recherches démographiques

Dir Al Azhar University, PO Box 1894, Cairo, 11651, Egypt. E-mail: iicpsr_azhar2@hotmail.com.
URL: http://alazhar-iicpsr.org/

History 1975, by Al-Azhar University (Cairo). **Aims** Promote an awareness and understanding of population issues vital to all *Muslim* countries. **Structure** Governing Council, consisting of President of Al-Azhar University (head), members from theological and scientific faculties and population experts from outside Al-Azhar. Director, assisted by Deputy Director, UN advisor and national advisors. **Finance** Most of activities supported from *United Nations Population Fund (UNFPA, #20612)* funding (main cash source). In-kind support from Al-Azhar University. **Activities** Seminars, workshops and conferences; training programmes; research; documentation, translation, publication and dissemination of material in the field of Islam and population; advisory assistance. **Events** *International conference on population issues in the context of Islam* Cairo (Egypt) 2007, *International workshop on research methodology in human reproduction* Cairo (Egypt) 1990, *International conference on Islam and population policies* Jakarta (Indonesia) 1990.

Members Governing Council members from 6 countries:
Egypt, Jordan, Pakistan, Saudi Arabia, Sudan, USA.

IGO Relations Cooperation agreement with: *Islamic World Educational, Scientific and Cultural Organization (ICESCO, #16058)*. **NGO Relations** Member of: *International Federation for Family Health (IFFH, #13424)*. [2013/XE3947/**E**]

♦ International Islamic Charitable Organization (IICO) 13957

Main Office PO Box 3434, Safaa, 13035 Kuwait, Kuwait. T. +96522274000. Fax +96522274003. E-mail: info@iico.org.
URL: http://www.iico.org/

History 1984. **Aims** Help the poor; present Islamic culture; provide the basic humanitarian needs: health, education, vocational training, work opportunities, social and economic needs, relief work. **Structure** General Assembly; Board of Directors; Executive Committee. Regional offices (12): Benin; Burkina Faso; Niger; Nigeria; Sudan; Uganda; Jordan; Kazakhstan; Kyrgyzstan; Uzbekistan; Azerbaijan; Russia. **Languages** Arabic, English. **Staff** 219.00 FTE, paid. **Finance** Donations. **Activities** Financial and/or material support. **Events** *General Assembly* Kuwait 2008, *International conference on wadi hydrology* Sanaa (Yemen) 2005, *General Assembly* Kuwait 1989. **Publications** Brochures; books.

Members Active members in 39 countries and territories:
Afghanistan, Algeria, Bahrain, Bangladesh, Brazil, Brunei Darussalam, Egypt, France, Germany, Hong Kong, India, Indonesia, Italy, Japan, Kenya, Kuwait, Lebanon, Libya, Malawi, Malaysia, Mali, Mauritania, Mauritius, Morocco, Nigeria, Pakistan, Qatar, Saudi Arabia, Senegal, South Africa, Spain, Sri Lanka, Switzerland, Tanzania UR, Tunisia, Türkiye, United Arab Emirates, USA, Yemen.

NGO Relations Member of: *CIVICUS: World Alliance for Citizen Participation (#03962)*; *International Partnership on Religion and Sustainable Development (PaRD, #14524)*. [2019/XD2418/**D**]

♦ International Islamic Court of Justice 13958

Contact c/o OIC, Intersection of Madina Road and King Abdullah Road, PO Box 178, Jeddah 21411, Saudi Arabia. T. +96626515222. Fax +96626512288. E-mail: info@oic-oci.org.
URL: http://www.oic-oci.org/

History Upon entry into force of Statute, will be the principal judicial organ of *Organisation of Islamic Cooperation (OIC, #17813)*. Set up following decision of the 5th *Islamic Summit of Kings and Heads of States and Governments (#16053)*, 1987, Kuwait. Statute: 29 Jan 1987. Seat in Kuwait. **Aims** Cover all cases whose reference to it is agreed by Member States and all special cases stipulated in OIC Charter or in the treaties and conventions in force and: (a) examine disputes that may arise among Member States if the parties concerned agree to submit it to the Court or if any treaty or agreement so decides; (b) examine facts which constitute breaches to international law as well as the nature and extent of legislation due to breaches of international law; (c) provide interpretation of the Charter, Treaties or agreements; (d) provide advisory legal opinion upon demand of any organ and endorsement of the Council of Foreign Ministers; (e) undertake mediation, conciliation or arbitration in disputes upon request of the concerned parties, the Summit or the Council of Foreign Ministers. **Structure** Court will comprise a panel of 7 members elected by *Council of Foreign Ministers (CFM, see: #17813)*. It will elect President and Vice-President from among its members. Registrar and other personnel as necessary. To be in permanent session except for vacations. **Languages** Arabic, English, French. **Finance** Member states of OIC. **Members** Member states of OIC. **IGO Relations** *United Nations (UN, #20515)*. [2014.01.05/XF0962/p/**F***]

♦ International Islamic Economic Organization (inactive)
♦ International Islamic Federation of Student Organizations (inactive)

♦ International Islamic Financial Market (IIFM) 13959

Contact 7th Floor Zamil Tower, Government Avenue, PO Box 11454, Manama, Bahrain. T. +97317500161. E-mail: info@iifm.ne.
URL: http://www.iifm.net/

History by *Islamic Development Bank (IsDB, #16044)* and national banks of Bahrain, Brunei, Indonesia, Malaysia and Sudan. **Aims** Take part in the establishment, development, self-regulation and promotion of Islamic *capital* and *money* market. **Structure** Board of Directors; Executive Committee; Management Team; Advisory Panel. **Events** *Annual World Islamic Banking Conference* Singapore (Singapore) 2013, *Meeting on Islamic Hedging and Liquidity Management Instruments* Singapore (Singapore) 2012, *Islamic master agreement conference* Hong Kong (Hong Kong) 2010, *Islamic master agreement conference* Kuala Lumpur (Malaysia) 2010, *Islamic master agreement conference* Singapore (Singapore) 2010. **Publications** *IIFM Sukuk Report* (annual).

Members National organizations of 14 countries:
Bahrain, Bangladesh, Brunei Darussalam, Indonesia, Jordan, Kuwait, Malaysia, Pakistan, Qatar, Saudi Arabia, Sudan, UK, United Arab Emirates, USA.

Institutional member:
Islamic Development Bank (IsDB, #16044). [2022/XM3784/**E***]

♦ International Islamic Fiqh Academy (IIFA) 13960

Académie internationale du Fiqh islamique (AIFI) – majmae alfiqh al'iislamii aldawli

Head of International Cooperation and External Relations PO Box 13719, Jeddah 21414, Saudi Arabia. T. +966122575662 – +966126900346 – +966126900347. Fax +966122575661. E-mail: info@iifa-aifi.org.
URL: https://www.iifa-aifi.org/en

History 28 Jan 1981, Makkah (Saudi Arabia). As a subsidiary organ of the Organization of Islamic Cooperation (OIC), established following a resolution at the Third Islamic Summit of the Organization (N.8/3-T/S-I), 25-28 Jan 1981. Former names and other names: *Académie islamique du Fiqh (AIF)* – former; *Islamic Fiqh Academy (IFA)* – former. **Aims** Achieve intellectual harmony and integration between jurists from recognized schools of Islamic jurisprudence and experts in the field of human, social, natural, and applied sciences to elucidate the positions of Shariah towards contemporary life issues; promote collective Ijtihad (Ijtihad jama'e) on contemporary life questions and issues, in order to elaborate Shariah-based solutions, and clarify valid preferences among several legal opinions on the same issue, in accordance with the interests of Muslims -whether individuals, communities, or States- and in full harmony with the legal arguments and ultimate

purposes of Shariah; coordinate between authorities of Ifta and institutions of jurisprudence inside and outside the Muslim world to avoid contradictions and hostilities between opinions on the same issue, especially on general issues that may cause conflicts; reject denominational intolerance, religious fanaticism, and excommunication of Islamic doctrines and their followers through spreading the spirit moderation, openness, and tolerance among the followers of different schools of law and sects; issue fatwas to Muslim communities and organizations outside the Muslim world in a way that would preserve the values of Islam, its culture and traditions; conduct constructive interreligious and intercultural dialogue, in order to cooperate for the benefit of humanity, in coordination with the Secretariat General of the OIC. **Structure** Council, composed of the representatives of 56 Members states; Bureau, composed of both appointed members and representative members. General Secretariat, composed of 9 Departments: Cabinet of the Secretary General of the Academy; Cabinet, Protocols and Legal Affairs; Planning, Development, International Cooperation, Archives and Follow-up; Family, Woman, Childhood and Elderly; Administrative and Financial Affairs; Media, Public Relations, Information and Communication Technology; Funding, Investment and Projects; Research, Studies, Fatwa, Encyclopedias, Translation and Printing; Sessions, Conferences and Seminars. **Languages** Arabic, English, French. Three official languages of the OIC and its subsidiary agencies such as IIFA. **Finance** Sources: contributions of member/participating states; donations; grants. Mandatory contributions of OIC Member States; IIFA Waqf (Endowment) Fund. **Activities** Awareness raising; capacity building; events/meetings; guidance/assistance/consulting; knowledge management/information dissemination; monitoring/evaluation; networking/liaising; politics/policy/regulatory; projects/programmes; publishing activities; religious activities; research and development; research/documentation; standards/guidelines; training/education. Active in OIC Member States and Muslim communities outside OIC. **Events** *Session* Dubai (United Arab Emirates) 2019, *Session* Makkah (Saudi Arabia) 2003, *Session* Qatar 2003, *Session* Kuwait 2001, *Session* Doha (Qatar) 1998. **Publications** *Newsletter* (12 a year) – in three languages.. Journal; Books of Resolutions and Recommendations in different languages; other publications.
Members Muslim jurists, scholars, researchers, and intellectuals who specialize in jurisprudential, cultural, educational, scientific, economic, and social fields of knowledge from different parts of the Muslim world. States (56):
Afghanistan, Albania, Algeria, Azerbaijan, Bahrain, Bangladesh, Benin, Brunei Darussalam, Burkina Faso, Cameroon, Chad, Comoros, Côte d'Ivoire, Djibouti, Egypt, Gabon, Gambia, Guinea, Guinea-Bissau, Guyana, Indonesia, Iran Islamic Rep, Iraq, Jordan, Kazakhstan, Kuwait, Kyrgyzstan, Lebanon, Libya, Malaysia, Maldives, Mali, Mauritania, Morocco, Mozambique, Niger, Nigeria, Oman, Pakistan, Palestine, Saudi Arabia, Senegal, Sierra Leone, Somalia, Sudan, Suriname, Syrian AR, Tajikistan, Togo, Tunisia, Türkiye, Turkmenistan, Uganda, United Arab Emirates, Uzbekistan, Yemen. [2022.10.19/XE5955/**E***]

♦ International Islamic Front for Jihad Against the Jews and Crusaders (#00748)
♦ International Islamic News Agency / see Union of OIC News AGencies (#20467)
♦ International Islamic Organization (no recent information)
♦ International Islamic Relief Organization (internationally oriented national body)
♦ International Islamic Relief Organization in the Kingdom of Saudi Arabia / see International Islamic Relief Organization
♦ International Islamic University / see International Islamic University Malaysia (#13961)
♦ International Islamic University, Islamabad (internationally oriented national body)

♦ International Islamic University Malaysia (IIUM) 13961

Université internationale islamique Malaisie – Universiti Islam Antarabangsa Malaysia
Mailing Address PO Box 10, 50728 Kuala Lumpur, Malaysia. T. +60361964000. Fax +60361964053.
URL: http://www.iium.edu.my/
History 10 May 1983, Kuala Lumpur (Malaysia). Founded following a treaty between the Government of Malaysia, a number of other Muslim Governments and the *Organisation of Islamic Cooperation (OIC, #17813)*. Former names and other names: *International Islamic University (IIU)* – alias. **Aims** Cater for *students* from any part of the world who wish to pursue a university *education* in law, economics, accounting, business administration, education, engineering, social sciences and humanities; ensure that Islamic values and principles are integrated in all programmes. **Structure** Board of Governors; University Council (Majlis); University Senate. Includes *International Institute of Islamic Thought and Civilization (ISTAC)*. **Finance** Co-sponsored by the Malaysian Government, OIC, and the Governments of: Bangladesh, Egypt, Libyan Arab Jamahiriya, Maldives, Pakistan, Saudi Arabia, Turkey. **Events** *ASAIHL Conference* Japan 2023, *International Conference on Law and Society* Kota Kinabalu (Malaysia) 2018, *World Prosumer Convention* Kuala Lumpur (Malaysia) 2017, *Engineering Congress* Kuala Lumpur (Malaysia) 2014, *Engineering Congress* Kuala Lumpur (Malaysia) 2013. **Publications** *IIUM Newsletter* (12 a year); *IIUM News Bulletin* (4 a year).
Members Co-sponsored by OIC and the governments of 8 countries:
Bangladesh, Egypt, Libya, Malaysia, Maldives, Pakistan, Saudi Arabia, Türkiye.
NGO Relations Member of: *Asia-Pacific Research and Training Network on Trade (ARTNeT, #02014)* through the Department of Economics; *Association of Universities of Asia and the Pacific (AUAP, #02968)*; *European Network for Social Intelligence (ENSA, #08010)*; *Federation of the Universities of the Islamic World (FUIW, #09710)*; *League of Islamic Universities (#16425)*. Partner of: *Global Land Tool Network (GLTN, #10452)*. [2021/XF0283/**F***]

♦ International Islamic Youth League – African Youth Development Centre (unconfirmed)

♦ International Island Games Association (IIGA) 13962

Address not obtained.
URL: http://www.iiga.org/
History 1985, Isle of Man. Previously also known under the acronym *IGA*. **Aims** Foster and encourage friendship through sporting activities between Island communities; provide opportunities for sportsmen and sportswomen to participate in international *sport*; promote and establish rules and regulations for the NatWest International Island Games. **Structure** General Meeting (annual); Executive Committee. **Languages** English. **Staff** 0.50 FTE, paid. **Finance** Subscriptions; sponsorship. **Activities** Events/meetings; sporting activities. **Events** *Annual General Meeting* Guernsey (UK) 2003, *Annual General Meeting* Guernsey (UK) 2002, *Annual General Meeting* Isle of Man 2000.
Members Island organizations (24) in 24 self-governing states and dependencies:
Åland, Alderney, Bermuda, Cayman Is, Faeroe Is, Falklands/Malvinas, Gibraltar, Gotland, Greenland, Guernsey (Sark), Isle of Man, Isle of Wight, Jersey, Norway (Frøya, Hitra), Orkney Is, Rhodes Is, Saaremaa, Scotland, Shetland Is, Spain (Menorca), St Helena, Wales (Anglesey), Western Isles. [2020/XJ3614/**D**]

♦ International ISMN Agency 13963

Internationale ISMN-Agentur
Exec Dir Hardenbergstr 9a, 10623 Berlin, Germany. E-mail: ismn@ismn-international.org.
URL: http://ismn-international.org/
History 1994. Registration: No/ID: VR 26007 B, Germany, Charlottenburg. **Aims** Promote, coordinate and supervise the International *Standard* Music Number (ISMN) system for editions of notated *music*. **Languages** English, German. **Activities** Certification/accreditation; guidance/assistance/consulting; standards/guidelines. **Events** *Panel Meeting* Santiago (Chile) 2019, *Panel Meeting* Sliema (Malta) 2018, *Panel Meeting* Ottawa, ON (Canada) 2017, *Panel Meeting* Vienna (Austria) 2016, *Panel Meeting* Bali (Indonesia) 2015. **Publications** *ISMN Newsletter* (annual).
Members National and regional agencies in 63 countries:
Argentina, Armenia, Australia, Austria, Azerbaijan, Belgium, Bosnia-Herzegovina, Botswana, Bulgaria, Canada, Colombia, Croatia, Cyprus, Czechia, Denmark, Estonia, Finland, France, Georgia, Germany, Ghana, Greece, Hungary, Iceland, Indonesia, Iran Islamic Rep, Ireland, Israel, Italy, Kazakhstan, Kenya, Kosovo, Kyrgyzstan, Latvia, Lithuania, Luxembourg, Malta, Moldova, Montenegro, Morocco, Myanmar, New Zealand, North Macedonia, Norway, Philippines, Poland, Portugal, Romania, Russia, Serbia, Singapore, Slovakia, Slovenia, South Africa, Spain, Sri Lanka, Srpska, Sweden, Switzerland, Türkiye, UK, Ukraine, USA.
NGO Relations Member of: *Linked Content Coalition (LCC)*. Cooperates with: *International Organization for Standardization (ISO, #14473)*. [2020/XJ3228/**E**]

♦ International Isocyanate Institute, New York (internationally oriented national body)
♦ International Isoptera Society (no recent information)

♦ International Isotope Society (IIS) 13964

Exec Sec Merck Research Labs, 126 East Lincoln Ave, RY 80R, Rahway NJ 07065-0900, USA. T. +17325940724. Fax +17325946921.
URL: http://iis-ced.de/
History 1986. Current Statutes adopted 2011. **Aims** Encourage throughout the scientific community advancement in knowledge of the synthesis, measurement and applications of isotopes and isotopically labelled compounds. **Structure** Council; Board of Trustees; Board of Representatives. **Languages** English. **Staff** 0.50 FTE, paid; 8.00 FTE, voluntary. **Finance** Subscription fees. **Activities** Events/meetings; knowledge management/information dissemination. **Events** *Workshop* Bad Soden am Taunus (Germany) 2019, *Meeting* Morristown, NJ (USA) 2019, *Triennial International Symposium* Prague (Czechia) 2018, *Workshop* Bad Soden am Taunus (Germany) 2017, *Meeting* Princeton, NJ (USA) 2017. **Publications** *Journal of Labelled Compounds and Radiopharmaceuticals* (14 a year).
Members Full in 17 countries:
Austria, Belgium, Canada, China, Denmark, Finland, France, Germany, Japan, Korea Rep, Poland, Romania, Russia, Sweden, Switzerland, UK, USA.
NGO Relations *World Council of Isotopes (WCI, #21331)*. [2018/XE4752/**E**]

♦ Internationalis Societas Dacryologiae / see International Society of Dacryology and Dry Eye (#15045)
♦ International Issues Study Centre, Milan (internationally oriented national body)

♦ Internationalist Communist Union (ICU) 13965

Union communiste internationaliste – Unión Comunista Internacionalista – Unione Comunista Internazionalista
Main Address Lutte ouvrière, BP 233, 75865 Paris CEDEX 18, France. T. +33148108620. Fax +33148108626. E-mail: contact-fr@union-communiste.org.
Contact Workers' Fight, BM ICLC, London, WC1N 3XX, UK. E-mail: contact-en@union-communiste.org.
URL: http://www.union-communiste.org/
Aims Promote revolutionary communist (Trotskyist) ideas. **Languages** Arabic, English, French, German, Irish Gaelic, Italian, Russian, Spanish, Turkish. **Activities** Advocacy/lobbying/activism; politics/policy/regulatory; events/meetings. **Events** *Meeting* Presles (France) 2010, *Meeting* Presles (France) 2008, *Meeting* Presles (France) 2007, *Meeting* Presles (France) 2006, *Meeting* Presles (France) 2005. **Publications** *Lutte Ouvrière* (weekly) in French; *Workers' Fight* (12 a year) in English; *Class Struggle* in English – journal; *Lutte de Classe* in French – journal.
Members Full in 11 countries and territories:
Belgium, Côte d'Ivoire, France, Germany, Guadeloupe, Haiti, Italy, Martinique, Spain, Türkiye, UK. [2020/XD6728/**D**]

♦ Internationalis Veterinariorum Zootechnicorum (inactive)
♦ Internationalizing Entrepreneurship Education and Training – Conference (meeting series)
♦ International J/22 Class Association (see: #21760)
♦ International J/24 Class Association (see: #21760)

♦ International Jack-Up Barge Operators' Association (IJUBOA) 13966

Office Lower Key House, Dorchester Road, Yeovil, BA22 9RD, UK. T. +441935471892. E-mail: info@ijuboa.com.
Registered Office Francis Clark, North Quay House, Sutton Harbour, Plymouth, PL4 0RA, UK.
URL: http://www.ijuboa.com/
History 2008. Registered in accordance with UK law. **Aims** Set, sustain and promote standards for the safe and effective operation of Jack-Up barges and self elevating platforms throughout the world. **Structure** Executive Committee. **Languages** English. **Finance** Members' dues. **Activities** Training/education; certification/accreditation; events/meetings. **Members** Companies. Membership countries not specified. [2020.03.10/XJ9866/**D**]

♦ International Jacques Ellul Society (internationally oriented national body)

♦ International Jacques Maritain Institute 13967

Institut international Jacques Maritain – Instituto Internacional Jacques Maritain – Istituto Internazionale Jacques Maritain (IIJM)
Pres Via Napoleone III 10/A, 00185 Rome RM, Italy. T. +39064874336. E-mail: segreteria@maritain.net – istituto.maritain@gmail.com.
URL: https://istituto.maritain.net/
History 1974, Gallarate (Italy). Registration: Start date: 1992, Italy. **Aims** Study and propagate the thinking of Jacques Maritain; promote study and research on problems of *humankind*, culture and *contemporary society*; use findings to operate in the *cultural, social* and *educational* fields. **Structure** General Assembly; Board of Directors; Scientific Council; Secretariat in Rome (Italy). **Languages** English, French, Italian, Spanish. **Staff** 2.00 FTE, paid; 3.00 FTE, voluntary. **Finance** Sources: grants; members' dues. Grants from Italian Ministries of Education and Cultural Heritage; public and private bodies. **Activities** Events/meetings; publishing activities; research/documentation; training/education. **Events** *Mediterranean – Economy and Educational Poverty in the Mediterranean Countries* Matera (Italy) 2021, *Educating for peace – Beyond the Emergency the Challenges of Peace* Rome (Italy) 2021, *The Future of the Planet – Ethics and Sustainable Development* Rome (Italy) 2021, *70 years after "Man and the State"* Rome (Italy) / Potenza (Italy) 2021, *What kind of globalization for peace conference* Treviso (Italy) 2001. **Publications** *Notes et Documents* (4 a year) in English, French, Italian, Spanish. *Giorgio la Pira: diplomazia, politica e pace nel Mediterraneo* (2021) by Prof Gennaro Giuseppe Curcio and Prof Jean-Dominique Durand; *Il viaggio: inizio e fine dell'avventura cristiana. In ricordo di Eleonora Mauri* (2021) by Prof Samuele Pinna; *Roberto Papini e l'Istituto Internazionale Jacques Maritain* (2021) by Dr Maria Silvia Pacetti Serafini. Monographs in main European languages, over 200 volumes since 1974. **Information Services** *Library of the Person* – collection of literature on personalism, open to the public; *Newspaper and Periodical Library*.
Members Full (64); Associate (210). National institutes and associations in 16 countries:
Argentina, Bolivia, Brazil, Canada, Chile, Cuba, Dominican Rep, Guatemala, Hungary, Italy, Netherlands, Romania, Senegal, Spain, USA, Venezuela.
Individuals in 37 countries:
Argentina, Belgium, Bolivia, Brazil, Cameroon, Canada, Chile, Colombia, Côte d'Ivoire, Croatia, Dominican Rep, El Salvador, France, Germany, Guatemala, Holy See, Hungary, India, Indonesia, Italy, Japan, Kenya, Korea Rep, Netherlands, Philippines, Poland, Portugal, Romania, Senegal, Serbia, Spain, Sri Lanka, Switzerland, Thailand, Uruguay, USA, Venezuela.
Consultative Status Consultative status granted from: *ECOSOC (#05331)* (Ros C); *UNESCO (#20322)* (Consultative Status); *FAO (#09260)* (Liaison Status).
NGO Relations Links with numerous international and internationally-oriented national bodies, including the following organizations listed in this Yearbook:
- *African Centre for Development and Strategic Studies (ACDESS)*;
- *Bischöfliche Aktion ADVENIAT*;
- *Calouste Gulbenkian Foundation*;
- *Centre international LEBRET-IRFED*;
- *Center of Research and Action for Peace (CERAP, #03651)*;
- *Centro de Investigación y Promoción Iberoamérica-Europa (CIPIE, no recent information)*;
- *Fondazione Lelio e Lisli Basso – ISSOCO*;
- *Institute for Strategic and International Studies, Lisbon (IEEI)*;
- *Instituto Latinoamericano de Doctrinas y Estudios Sociales (ILADES, #11345)*;
- *International Catholic Cooperation Centre for UNESCO (CCIC, #12454)*;
- *International Centre for Study and Documentation – Istituto Paolo VI*;
- *Konrad Adenauer Foundation (KAF)*;
- *Pontifical Council for Culture (#18443)*;
- *Pontifical Council for Justice and Peace (inactive)*;
- *Trans European Policy Studies Association (TEPSA, #20209)*;
- *Universidad de los Trabajadores de América Latina (UTAL, no recent information)*. [2022.02.03/XE2496/j/**E**]

♦ International Jazz Federation (inactive)

♦ International Jendo Federation (IJF) 13968

Contact 16 Mariveles Street, 80 Gabriel Ext, 5th Street, Road 2, Pasig City RIZ, Philippines. T. +6327940260. E-mail: philjendo@yahoo.com.
URL: http://internationaljendo.blogspot.com/

History 1973. Formally launched in 1994. **Aims** Serve as the official international sports governing body of Jendo and traditional Arnis martial arts; promote and advance these arts, and elevate them to Olympic sports standard; foster unity, cooperation and service among members and practitioners. **Languages** English. **Finance** Sources: donations; members' dues; revenue from activities/projects; sponsorship. **Activities** Sporting activities.
Members Full in 15 countries and territories:
Bangladesh, Egypt, Georgia, Hong Kong, India, Iran Islamic Rep, Italy, Japan, Morocco, Nepal, Pakistan, Philippines, Trinidad-Tobago, UK, USA.
NGO Relations Member of (1): *International Martial Art Games Committee (IMGC, #14107).*
[2021.09.07/XJ0433/**C**]

♦ International Jet Ski Boating Association / see International Jet Sports Boating Association (#13969)

♦ International Jet Sports Boating Association (IJSBA) 13969

Headquarters 330 Purissima St, Ste C, Half Moon Bay CA 94019, USA. T. +17147518695. Fax +17147518609. E-mail: info@ijsba.com.
URL: http://www.ijsba.com/

History 24 Feb 1982, Newport Beach, CA (USA). Former names and other names: *International Jet Ski Boating Association (IJSBA)* – former (1982). **Aims** Further the interest of membership by providing a wide range of quality personal *watercraft* activities, services and benefits; act as an international governing and sanctioning body for personal watercraft *racing*; foster fair competition by formulating and promoting uniform rules and safety *standards*; promote the positive image of personal watercraft by communicating with and educating members and other users on the fun, safe and responsible usage of personal watercraft; be an effective, unified voice for the sport. **Structure** Annual Members' Meeting. Board of Directors (meets annually) of a minimum of 7 members, including Chairman, Vice-Chairman and Secretary-Treasurer. Committees (6): Technical/Rules; Advisory; Racer; Affiliate; Manufacturer; Associate/After Market. **Languages** English, French, German, Italian, Norwegian, Spanish, Swedish. **Staff** 15.00 FTE, paid. **Finance** Members' dues. **Activities** Promotes, organizes and supervises personal watercraft events; supervises and grants affiliation to international organizations with similar purposes and cooperates with such organizations; collects and disseminates information relating to the sport; undertakes activities aimed at advancing the sport. Organizes local and national championships and world finals. Racing categories: Closed Course; Slalom; Freestyle; Endurance/Offshore; Drag Racing. **Publications** *Jet Sports* (9 a year).
Members Categories Manufacturer; International Affiliate; Associate; Managing Director; Rider. Affiliate members in 45 countries and territories:
Argentina, Australia, Austria, Belgium, Bermuda, Brazil, Canada, Costa Rica, Croatia, Denmark, England, Estonia, Finland, France, Germany, Greece, Guam, Hungary, Indonesia, Ireland, Israel, Italy, Japan, Korea Rep, Kuwait, Malaysia, Mexico, Netherlands, New Zealand, Nigeria, Norway, Paraguay, Peru, Philippines, Poland, Portugal, Qatar, Serbia, Slovenia, South Africa, Spain, Tahiti Is, Thailand, Uruguay, USA.
Associate members in 2 countries:
Belgium, USA. [2022/XE2316/**E**]

♦ International Jewish Anti-Zionist Network (unconfirmed)
♦ International Jewish-Catholic Liaison Committee / see International Catholic-Jewish Liaison Committee (#12458)

♦ International Jewish Committee on Interreligious Consultations (IJCIC) 13970

Comité juif international pour les consultations interreligieuses
Contact c/o AJC, 165 East 56th St, New York NY 10022, USA. T. +12128916768.
URL: http://ijcic.org

History 1967. Also referred to by initials *IJCIR*. **Activities** Liaises with international Catholic and Protestant organizations, including: *International Catholic-Jewish Liaison Committee (ILC, #12458)*; *Lutheran European Commission on the Church and the Jewish People (#16528)*. **Events** *New electricity 21 conference* Paris (France) 1995. [2020/XD5314/**E**]

♦ International Jewish Defence League (inactive)

♦ International Jewish Vegetarian and Ecological Society (IJVS) 13971

Contact 855 Finchley Road, London, NW11 8LX, UK. T. +442084550692. E-mail: info@jvs.org.uk.
URL: http://www.jvs.org.uk/

History 1966, London (UK). Former names and other names: *International Jewish Vegetarian Society* – former. Registration: Charity Commission, No/ID: 258581, Start date: 29 May 1969, England and Wales. **Aims** Advocate a vegetarian world which conserves natural resources, promotes human health and protects the environment. **Languages** English. **Staff** 1.00 FTE, paid. **Finance** Sources: donations; members' dues. **Publications** *The Jewish Vegetarian* (4 a year).
Members Full practising vegetarians; Associate non-vegetarians in sympathy with the movement. Individuals in 30 countries:
Australia, Bahamas, Barbados, Belgium, Bermuda, Canada, Finland, France, Germany, Ghana, Greece, India, Ireland, Israel, Italy, Jamaica, Luxembourg, Malta, Netherlands, New Zealand, Nigeria, Norway, Poland, Romania, Russia, South Africa, Sweden, Switzerland, UK, USA. [2022/XF1405/v/**F**]

♦ International Jewish Vegetarian Society / see International Jewish Vegetarian and Ecological Society (#13971)
♦ International Joint Commission (internationally oriented national body)
♦ International Joint Commission of Canada and the United States / see International Joint Commission

♦ International Joint Commission for Dialogue between the World Methodist Council and the Vatican 13972

Gen Sec P O Box 518, Lake Junaluska NC 28745, USA. T. +18284569432. Fax +18284569433. E-mail: georgefreeman@mindspring.com.
Catholic Co-Sec c/o PCPCU, 00120 Vatican City, Vatican. T. +39669884552. Fax +39669885365.
URL: http://www.worldmethodistcouncil.org/

History 1967, as an international theological dialogue and study commission sponsored by *Pontifical Council for Promoting Christian Unity (PCPCU, #18446)* and *World Methodist Council (WMC, #21650)*. Also referred to as: *Joint Commission for Dialogue between the Representatives of the Vatican and the the World Methodist Council*; *Roman Catholic / World Methodist International Commission*. **Aims** Become familiar with traits and characteristics of Methodism and Catholicism; study general and specific topics of common interest; discuss the church in relation to historical and theological background. **Activities** Commission has met regularly since 1967 and reports at 5-year intervals to the Council and to the Vatican. **Events** *Quinquennial ecumenical conference* Brighton (UK) 2001, *Quinquennial ecumenical conference* Rio de Janeiro (Brazil) 1996, *Joint meeting* Lisbon (Portugal) 1988. [2012.07.08/XE4059/**E**]

♦ International Joint Committee of Associations of Adoptive Parents (inactive)
♦ International Joint Conference on Automated Reasoning (meeting series)
♦ International Joint Conference on Industrial Engineering and Operations Management (meeting series)
♦ International Joint Conference on Rules and Reasoning (meeting series)

♦ International Joint Conferences on Artificial Intelligence (IJCAI) . . . 13973

Sec-Treas Informatik Inst ALU-F, Georges-Koehler-Allee Geb 052, 79110 Freiburg, Germany. T. +497612038221. Fax +497612038222.
Exec Sec TUWien IDMG E104, Wiedner Hauptstr 8-10, 1040 Vienna, Austria. E-mail: vsfritz@ijcai.org.
URL: http://ijcai.org/

History Founded in 1969, USA. Also referred to as *International Joint Conferences on Artificial Intelligence Organization (IJCAI)*. Registered in accordance with USA law. **Aims** Disseminate information on Artificial Intelligence. **Structure** Board of Trustees; Secretariat. **Activities** Events/meetings; knowledge management/information dissemination; awards/prizes/competitions. **Events** *Conference* Vienna (Austria) 2022, *Conference* Montréal, QC (Canada) 2021, *Conference* Yokohama (Japan) 2021, *Conference* Yokohama (Japan) 2020, *Conference* Macau (Macau) 2019. **Publications** *AI Journal*. Conference proceedings. **Members** Not a membership organization. [2020/XF1031/c/**F**]

♦ International Joint Conferences on Artificial Intelligence Organization / see International Joint Conferences on Artificial Intelligence (#13973)
♦ International Joint Policy Committee of the Societies of Epidemiology / see International Network for Epidemiology in Policy (#14264)
♦ International Joseph A Schumpeter Society / see International J A Schumpeter Society (#13974)

♦ International J A Schumpeter Society (ISS) 13974

Internationale J A Schumpeter Gesellschaft
SG Friedrich-Schiller-Univ, Wirtschaftswissenschaftliche Fak, Carl-Zeiss-Str 3, 07743 Jena, Germany.
URL: https://www.issevec.uni-jena.de/

History 1986, Augsburg (Germany FR). Previously also referred to as *International Joseph A Schumpeter Society*. Current statutes modified Jun 2004. Registered in accordance with German law. **Aims** Promote scientific study of economic development in industrialized and developing countries. **Structure** General Assembly; Executive Committee; Board of Management. **Languages** English, German. **Staff** 0.50 FTE, paid. **Finance** Members' dues. Donations. **Activities** Awards/prizes/competitions; events/meetings. *European Meeting on Applied Evolutionary Economics (EMAEE)*. **Events** *Biennial Conference* Rome (Italy) 2021, *Biennial Conference* Seoul (Korea Rep) 2018, *Biennial Conference* Montréal, QC (Canada) 2016, *Biennial Conference* Jena (Germany) 2014, *Biennial conference* Brisbane, QLD (Australia) 2012. **Publications** *Journal of Evolutionary Economics* (5 a year). Conference proceedings.
Members Individuals (364) in 46 countries and territories:
Argentina, Australia, Austria, Belgium, Brazil, Canada, Chile, China, Colombia, Costa Rica, Czechia, Denmark, Estonia, Finland, France, Georgia, Germany, Greece, Hungary, India, Ireland, Israel, Italy, Japan, Korea Rep, Lithuania, Mexico, Netherlands, New Zealand, Norway, Philippines, Poland, Portugal, Puerto Rico, Romania, Russia, Singapore, Spain, Sweden, Switzerland, Taiwan, Türkiye, UK, Ukraine, Uruguay, USA. [2019/XE3617/v/**E**]

♦ International Judicial Academy (internationally oriented national body)
♦ International Judicial Committee on Aviation (inactive)

♦ International Judo Federation (IJF) 13975

Fédération internationale de judo (FIJ) – Federación Internacional de Judo – Internationale Judo-Föderation – Kokusai Judo Remnei
Gen Sec FFJDA, 21-25 avenue de la Porte de Châtillon, 75014 Paris, France. T. +33140521635. Fax +33140521670. E-mail: gs@ijf.org – media@ijf.org.
Pres Jozsef Attila Str 1, Budapest 1051, Hungary. T. +3613027270. Fax +3613027271. E-mail: president@ijf.org.
URL: http://www.ijf.org/

History 1951, Paris (France). **Aims** Promote the sport of judo throughout the world. **Structure** Congress (every 2 years); Executive Committee; Continental Unions (5); Commissions (15). **Languages** Arabic, English, French, Russian, Spanish. **Finance** Sources: donations; members' dues. Other sources: remittances from other sources. **Activities** Events/meetings. **Events** *Congress* Tokyo (Japan) 2019, *Congress* Rio de Janeiro (Brazil) 2013, *Congress* Paris (France) 2011, *Congress* Rotterdam (Netherlands) 2009, *Congress* Bangkok (Thailand) 2008. **Publications** Newsletter diffused during each IJF event.
Members National Federations grouped into Continental Unions. National Federations (Israel being member of European Judo Federation) in 198 countries and territories:
Afghanistan, Albania, Algeria, Andorra, Angola, Argentina, Armenia, Aruba, Australia, Austria, Azerbaijan, Bahamas, Bahrain, Bangladesh, Barbados, Belarus, Belgium, Belize, Benin, Bhutan, Bolivia, Bosnia-Herzegovina, Botswana, Brazil, Brunei Darussalam, Bulgaria, Burkina Faso, Burundi, Cameroon, Canada, Cape Verde, Central African Rep, Chad, Chile, China, Colombia, Comoros, Congo Brazzaville, Congo DR, Cook Is, Costa Rica, Côte d'Ivoire, Croatia, Cuba, Curaçao, Cyprus, Czechia, Denmark, Djibouti, Dominican Rep, Ecuador, Egypt, El Salvador, Equatorial Guinea, Estonia, Eswatini, Ethiopia, Faeroe Is, Fiji, Finland, France, Gabon, Gambia, Georgia, Germany, Ghana, Greece, Guadeloupe, Guam, Guatemala, Guinea, Guinea-Bissau, Guyana, Haiti, Honduras, Hong Kong, Hungary, Iceland, India, Indonesia, Iran Islamic Rep, Iraq, Ireland, Israel, Italy, Jamaica, Japan, Jordan, Kazakhstan, Kenya, Kiribati, Korea DPR, Korea Rep, Kosovo, Kuwait, Kyrgyzstan, Laos, Latvia, Lebanon, Liberia, Libya, Liechtenstein, Lithuania, Luxembourg, Macau, Madagascar, Malawi, Malaysia, Mali, Malta, Marshall Is, Mauritania, Mauritius, Mexico, Moldova, Monaco, Mongolia, Montenegro, Morocco, Mozambique, Myanmar, Namibia, Nauru, Nepal, Netherlands, New Caledonia, New Zealand, Nicaragua, Niger, Nigeria, Niue, Norfolk Is, North Macedonia, Northern Mariana Is, Norway, Pakistan, Palau, Palestine, Panama, Papua New Guinea, Paraguay, Peru, Philippines, Poland, Polynesia Fr, Portugal, Puerto Rico, Qatar, Romania, Russia, Rwanda, Samoa, San Marino, Saudi Arabia, Senegal, Serbia, Seychelles, Sierra Leone, Singapore, Slovakia, Slovenia, Solomon Is, Somalia, South Africa, South Sudan, Spain, Sri Lanka, St Lucia, St Martin, Sudan, Suriname, Sweden, Switzerland, Syrian AR, Taiwan, Tajikistan, Tanzania UR, Thailand, Togo, Tonga, Trinidad-Tobago, Tunisia, Türkiye, Turkmenistan, Uganda, UK, Ukraine, United Arab Emirates, Uruguay, USA, Uzbekistan, Vanuatu, Venezuela, Vietnam, Yemen, Zambia, Zimbabwe.
Continental Unions (5):
African Judo Union (AJU, #00350); *Confederación Panamericana de Judo (CPJ, #04476)*; *Judo Union of Asia (JUA, #16162)*; *Oceania Judo Union (OJU, #17665)*; *Union européenne de judo (UEJ, #20399)*.
NGO Relations Member of (2): *Association of Summer Olympic International Federations (ASOIF, #02943)*; *Olympic Movement (#17719)*. Partner of (1): *General Association of Asia Pacific Sports Federations (GAAPSF, #10106)*. Cooperates with (1): *International Testing Agency (ITA, #15678)*. Recognized by: *International Olympic Committee (IOC, #14408)*. [2022/XB2178/y/**B**]

♦ International Ju-Jitsu Federation / see Ju-Jitsu International Federation (#16164)
♦ International Jukskei Federation (unconfirmed)

♦ International Jumping Officials Club (IJOC) 13976

Contact Kennels Cottage, Solsgirth, Dollar, FK14 7NZ, UK. T. +447778063382. E-mail: isjclub@gmail.com.
URL: http://www.ijoclub.com/

History Founded 1998, as *International Show Jumping Officials Club (ISJC)*. **Aims** Bring together all international judges, course designers and chief stewards in the *equestrian* sport of show jumping. **Structure** Annual General Assembly; Board. **Languages** English. **Staff** Voluntary. **Finance** Members' dues. **Activities** Events/meetings; training/education. **Events** *General Assembly* Leipzig (Germany) 2017, *General Assembly* Madrid (Spain) 2016, *General Assembly* Basel (Switzerland) 2014. **Members** Full in 63 countries. Membership countries not specified. **NGO Relations** *European Equestrian Federation (EEF, #07005)*; *Fédération Équestre Internationale (FEI, #09484)*. [2017.03.13/XJ5792/**D**]

♦ International Jumping Riders Club (IJRC) 13977

Club international des cavaliers de saut d'obstacle
Dir Via al Forte 3, 6900 Lugano TI, Switzerland. E-mail: ijrc1977@gmail.com.
URL: https://www.ijrc.org/

History Apr 1977. Founded by a group of international riders. Set up in Vienna (Austria), 24 Jun 1977. **Aims** Represent the riders opinions and interests, and promote the image of show jumping; stay current and cooperate with competent federal authorities concerning new norms and regulations; promote the ideals of sportsmanship and fair play; support national and international associations, as well as international show jumping organisers in all their efforts; put the riders views in matters of rules and regulations before the governing body. **Structure** Board. **Languages** English, French, German, Italian. **Activities** Events/meetings; sporting events. **Events** *General Assembly* Madrid (Spain) 2011. **Publications** *A Book to Celebrate the 15th Anniversary of the Rolex IJRC Top 10 Final*; *A Special Book to Celebrate the 40th IJRC Birthday*; *Dossier Argo*; *Know more about the International Jumping Riders Club*; *Know the Rules for a Proper Sport: Awareness and Ride Fair*. **Members** Membership open to first 250 riders of the world ranking list; riders having taken part in World Championships, Olympics or 5 Nations' Cups; riders ranked in the first 3,000 of world ranking list; fans and supporters. Membership countries not specified. **NGO Relations** Member of: *European Equestrian Federation (EEF, #07005)*. [2022/XF1688/**F**]

♦ International Jump Rope Union (IJRU) 13978

Exec Vice-Pres address not obtained. E-mail: info@ijru.org.
Co-SG address not obtained.
URL: http://www.ijru.org/

History 2018. Founded on merger of *World Jump Rope Federation (WJRF, inactive)* and *International Rope Skipping Federation (IRSF, inactive)*. Until first championship is organized by IJRU, both organizations continued to organize their own championships. Constitution approved 10 Jul 2019, Oslofjord (Norway). Registration: USA. **Aims** Spread the sport of jump rope/rope *skipping*, and with it the joy, physical strength, and connectedness jumping rope provides. **Structure** General Congress; Board of Directors; Executive. Technical

Committees; Specialized Committees; Judicial Panel; Commissions. **Languages** English. **Finance** Sources: members' dues. **Events** *General Congress* 2022, *General Congress* 2021, *General Congress* 2020, *General Congress* Melsomvik (Norway) 2019.
Members National Rope Skipping Organizations (41):
Antigua-Barbuda, Australia, Bermuda, Brazil, Canada, China, Colombia, Denmark, France, Germany, Guyana, Hungary, India, Iran Islamic Rep, Japan, Kazakhstan, Kenya, Korea Rep, Kyrgyzstan, Macau, Malaysia, Mexico, Mozambique, Nepal, Nigeria, Pakistan, Portugal, Puerto Rico, Russia, Singapore, South Africa, Spain, Sweden, Switzerland, Tanzania UR, Thailand, Trinidad-Tobago, Uganda, USA, Uzbekistan, Zambia.
NGO Relations Member of (2): *Alliance of Independent recognised Members of Sport (AIMS, #00690)* (Observer); *The Association for International Sport for All (TAFISA, #02763)*. [2021/XM7395/**B**]

♦ International Junior Brangus Breeders Association (internationally oriented national body)
♦ International Juridical Organization for Environment and Development (no recent information)

♦ International Jurist Organization (IJO) 13979

Chairman 67 Lawyers Chambers, Supreme Court Compound, Tilak Marg, Delhi 110001, DELHI 110001, India. T. +91113387522. Fax +91113383473.
URL: http://www.ijo.org.in/
History Dec 1987, after a number of meetings and deliberations in Lima (Peru), New York NY (USA), Paris (France) and Delhi (India). Original title: *International Jurists Organization – Asia (IJO Asia)*. **Aims** Stand for a more active role of the United Nations for peace, development and international order; bring together members of the legal community from different countries in one international forum; encourage awareness and research in all branches of law including international law; cooperate, coordinate and channel the work of various international and regional organizations and institutions having similar objects. **Structure** Board of Governors; Praesidium; Executive Committee; Advisory Committee. **Languages** English. **Staff** 1.00 FTE, paid. **Finance** Members' dues. **Activities** Focused on UN programmes, global law system, international law, international problems of human rights, environmental law and international trade and business law. Organization of seminars and conventions of lawyers, judges, social action groups, legislators and law implementing authorities. Research projects centred on social objectives. **Events** *Anniversary Meeting* Delhi (India) 2012, *Annual meeting* Delhi (India) 2001, *Asia regional conference on social development* Delhi (India) 1995. **Publications** *Asia Law Review* (annual); *IJO Newsletter*.
Members Lawyers, law officers, judges, law teachers and jurists in 38 countries:
Austria, Bangladesh, Benin, China, Colombia, Cuba, Egypt, Fiji, Germany, Ghana, Hungary, India, Israel, Japan, Jordan, Lesotho, Mauritius, Mexico, Namibia, Nepal, Netherlands, Nigeria, Norway, Pakistan, Papua New Guinea, Peru, Philippines, Poland, Serbia, Seychelles, South Africa, Sri Lanka, Sweden, Switzerland, UK, USA, Venezuela, Zambia.
Consultative Status Consultative status granted from: *ECOSOC (#05331)* (Special). **NGO Relations** Member of: *Academic Council on the United Nations System (ACUNS, #00020)*. [2018/XD5792/v/**D**]

♦ International Jurists Organization – Asia / see International Jurist Organization (#13979)
♦ International Justice Analysis Forum (internationally oriented national body)
♦ International Justice Cooperation (internationally oriented national body)
♦ International Justice Group / see Al-Jihad (#00637)
♦ International Justice Mission (internationally oriented national body)
♦ International Justice Project (internationally oriented national body)
♦ International Justice Resource Center (internationally oriented national body)
♦ International Jute Organization (inactive)
♦ International Jute Study Group (no recent information)
♦ International Juvenile Justice Observatory (internationally oriented national body)

♦ International Karate Do and Martial Arts Union (IKUMA) 13980

Gen Sec address not obtained. T. +393480040835. E-mail: info@ikuma.it.
Pres address not obtained.
History Sep 1993. **Aims** Organize and disseminate Japanese Martial Arts and oriental sports. **Languages** English, Italian. **Staff** All voluntary. **Finance** Members' dues. Other sources: internships; sponsorship. **Activities** Awards/prizes/competitions; training/education.
Members in 3 countries:
Germany, Italy, Japan. [2015.02.25/XM3339/**D**]

♦ International Kawasaki Disease Symposium (meeting series)

♦ International Kempo Federation (IKF) 13981

SG 237ter avenue Sainte Marguerite, 06200 Nice, France. E-mail: ikfkempo@yahoo.com – office@kempoikf.com.
URL: http://www.kempoikf.com/
History Registration: No/ID: 0062027610, Start date: 22 Dec 2006, France. **Structure** Executive Committee. **Activities** Sporting activities.
Members Federations in 63 countries and territories:
Afghanistan, Algeria, Argentina, Armenia, Australia, Azerbaijan, Bangladesh, Belarus, Belgium, Bolivia, Bosnia-Herzegovina, Brazil, Bulgaria, Cameroon, Canada, China, Colombia, Congo Brazzaville, Croatia, Dominican Rep, Egypt, Estonia, France, Georgia, Germany, Hungary, India, Indonesia, Iran Islamic Rep, Iraq, Italy, Japan, Kazakhstan, Kuwait, Kyrgyzstan, Latvia, Lithuania, Mexico, Moldova, Mongolia, Montenegro, Morocco, Nepal, Netherlands, Nigeria, Northern Cyprus, Pakistan, Poland, Portugal, Romania, Russia, Serbia, Slovakia, Spain, Sweden, Syrian AR, Tunisia, Türkiye, UK, Ukraine, USA, Venezuela, Yemen.
NGO Relations Member of (2): *General Association of Asia Pacific Sports Federations (GAAPSF, #10106)*; *International Sport Network Organization (ISNO, #15592)*. Partner of (1): *European Esports Observatory (EEO)*. [2020/AA1079/**C**]

♦ International Kenaf Development Board (unconfirmed)

♦ International Kendo Federation (FIK) 13982

Pres 2F Yasukuni-Kudan-Minami Bldg, 2-3-14 Kudan-Minami, Chiyoda-ku, Tokyo, 102-0074 Japan. T. +81332346271. Fax +81332346007. E-mail: kendo-fik@kendo.or.jp.
URL: http://www.kendo-fik.org/
History Founded 1970. Previously also known under the acronym *IKF*. **Aims** Foster international propagation and development of Kendo, including Iai-do and Jo-do, and mutual trust and friendship among members. **Structure** General Assembly (every 3 years, at World Championship); Board of Directors (meets annually). **Languages** English, Japanese. **Staff** 3.00 FTE, paid. **Finance** Sources: members' dues. **Activities** Events/meetings; sporting activities; standards/guidelines. **Events** *General Assembly* Tokyo (Japan) 2015, *American Referee Seminar* Montréal, QC (Canada) 2012, *General Assembly* Novara (Italy) 2012, *General Assembly* Sao Paulo (Brazil) 2009, *Referee seminar* Brussels (Belgium) 2007.
Members Full in 57 countries and territories:
Andorra, Argentina, Aruba, Australia, Austria, Belgium, Brazil, Bulgaria, Canada, Chile, China, Croatia, Czechia, Denmark, Dominican Rep, Ecuador, Finland, France, Germany, Greece, Hawaii, Hong Kong, Hungary, Indonesia, Ireland, Israel, Italy, Japan, Korea Rep, Latvia, Lithuania, Luxembourg, Macau, Malaysia, Mexico, Mongolia, Montenegro, Netherlands, New Zealand, Norway, Poland, Portugal, Romania, Russia, Serbia, Singapore, Slovenia, South Africa, Spain, Sweden, Switzerland, Taiwan, Thailand, Türkiye, UK, USA, Venezuela.
NGO Relations Member of (2): *Alliance of Independent recognised Members of Sport (AIMS, #00690)*; *Olympic Movement (#17719)*. Recognized by: *International Olympic Committee (IOC, #14408)*. [2018/XD2759/**C**]

♦ International Kidney Cancer Coalition (IKCC) 13983

Manager 't Ven 30, 1115 HB Duivendrecht, Netherlands. T. +447973777202. E-mail: info@ikcc.org.
URL: https://ikcc.org/
History 2009. Founded by 10 national organizations. Former names and other names: *Stichting International Kidney Cancer Coalition* – legal name. Registration: No/ID: KvK 62070665, Start date: Dec 2014, Netherlands. **Aims** Empower and represent the kidney cancer community through advocacy, awareness, information and research. **Structure** Board of Directors. **Languages** Dutch, English, German. **Activities** Advocacy/lobbying/activism; awareness raising; knowledge management/information dissemination; research/documentation. **Events** *Global Kidney Cancer Summit* Milan (Italy) 2022, *Conference* Duivendrecht (Netherlands) 2021, *Conference* Duivendrecht (Netherlands) 2020, *Conference* Lisbon (Portugal) 2019, *Conference* Chantilly (France) 2016. **Publications** Brochure.
Members Founding members in 5 countries:
Canada, Germany, India, UK, USA.
NGO Relations Member of (4): *European Cancer Organisation (ECO, #06432)* (Patient Advisory Committee); *Global Cancer Coalitions Network (GCCN, #10270)*; *Rare Cancers Europe (RCE, #18620)*; *Workgroup of European Cancer Patient Advocacy Networks (WECAN, #21054)*. [2023.02.15/XJ6442/**C**]

♦ International Kidney & Monoclonal Gammopathy Research Group (IKMG) 13984

Sec address not obtained.
URL: https://www.ikmgresearchgroup.com/
History Oct 2010, Bath (UK). **Aims** Specifically bring together the world's experts in kidney disease caused by monoclonal proteins. **Structure** Board of Directors. **Finance** Sources: members' dues. **Activities** Events/meetings; research/documentation; training/education. **Events** *International Meeting* Montréal, QC (Canada) 2019. [2020/AA0011/**F**]

♦ International Kierkegaard Society (IKS) 13985

Dir Søren Kierkegaard Research Ctr, Karen Blixen Plads 16, 2300 Copenhagen, Denmark. T. +4533766900. Fax +4533766910. E-mail: sec@sk.ku.dk.
URL: http://teol.ku.dk/skc/english/
Aims Facilitate the globalization of Kierkegaard studies by serving as a forum of communication and exchange for the different national and local groups of scholars around the world. **Structure** Board of Directors, including President. Advisory Board. **Events** *Annual Conference* Copenhagen (Denmark) 2018, *Annual Conference* Copenhagen (Denmark) 2017, *Annual Conference* Copenhagen (Denmark) 2016, *Annual Conference* Copenhagen (Denmark) 2015.
Members National Societies in 19 countries:
Argentina, Australia, Belgium, Brazil, Canada, Denmark, France, Germany, Hungary, Italy, Japan, Korea Rep, Mexico, Norway, Russia, Slovakia, Spain, UK, USA.
Included in the above, 1 organization listed in this Yearbook:
Sociedad Iberoamericana de Estudios Kierkegaardianos (SIEK). [2020/XJ6791/y/**E**]

♦ International Kindergarten Union / see Childhood Education International

♦ International Kinesiology College (IKC) 13986

Contact address not obtained. T. +610478244744. Fax +61753026452. E-mail: registrar@ikc.global.
URL: http://www.ikc.global
History 1990. Established with the seat of the foundation in Zurich (Switzerland). Reformed with new office in (Australia), 2004. Registration: ASIC, No/ID: ACN 108 817 830, Start date: 22 Apr 2004, Australia, QLD. **Aims** Provide certified training. **Structure** Executive Board. **Events** *International Kinesiology Conference* 2023, *Annual Conference* Budapest (Hungary) 2022, *Annual Conference* Budapest (Hungary) 2021, *Annual Conference* Bali (Indonesia) 2019, *Annual conference* Kirchzarten (Germany) 2017. [2022/XM0355/**E**]

♦ International Kiteboarding Association / see International Kiteboarding Class Association (#13987)

♦ International Kiteboarding Class Association (IKA) 13987

Exec Sec 137 chemin des Crets, 01280 Prévessin-Moëns, France. T. +447418418308.
URL: http://www.internationalkiteboarding.org/
History within *World Sailing (#21760)*. Also referred to as *International Kiteboarding Association*. **Aims** Coordinate and manage the affairs of the class; make recommendations on the control of the class to the International Sailing Federation (ISAF); encourage and coordinate national and international competitions in the class. **Structure** Annual General Meeting; Executive Committee. Sub-Committees (2): Audit; National Kite Associations. **Languages** English. **Finance** Members' dues. **Activities** Organizes world continental and national championships in the class. **Members** Full; Corporate; Associate; Supporting. Membership countries not specified. [2017/XM3821/**E**]

♦ International Kiteboarding Organization (unconfirmed)

♦ International Kiwifruit Organization (IKO) 13988

Contact address not obtained. E-mail: ixisk@aphorticultura.pt – mantunes@ualg.pt.
URL: http://www.ikiwifruit.org/
Activities Events/meetings. **Events** *Annual Conference* New Zealand 2020, *Annual Conference* Turin (Italy) 2019, *Annual Conference* Bordeaux (France) 2018, *Annual Conference* Porto (Portugal) 2017, *Annual Conference* Greece 2015. [2017/XN3169/**C**]

♦ International Knowledge Centre of Brown Bears / see Bear Information Centre
♦ International Knowledge Centre for Engineering Sciences and Technology under the Auspices of UNESCO (unconfirmed)

♦ International Knowledge Network of Women in Politics (iKNOW Politics) 13989

Contact address not obtained. E-mail: connect@iknowpolitics.org.
URL: http://iknowpolitics.org/en/
History Launched 2007, as a joint project of *International Institute for Democracy and Electoral Assistance (International IDEA, #13872)*, *Inter-Parliamentary Union (IPU, #15961)*, *UNDP (#20292)* and *UN Women (#20724)*. **Aims** Increase participation and effectiveness of women in political life. **Languages** Arabic, English, French, Spanish. **Activities** Knowledge management/information dissemination; networking/liaising; advocacy/lobbying/activism. **Publications** iKNOW Politics e-Discussion summaries. [2019.12.12/XM6726/**F**]

♦ International Kodaly Society (IKS) 13990

Société internationale Kodaly
Exec Sec PO Box 67, Budapest 1364, Hungary. T. +3613434503. Fax +3614130138. E-mail: office@iks.hu.
Street Address Róna utca 120-122, Budapest 1149, Hungary.
URL: http://www.iks.hu/
History Founded 1975, Kecskemét (Hungary), Kodaly's birthplace. **Aims** Encourage, assist and promote the musical, educational and cultural concepts associated with Zoltan Kodaly for the benefit of *music* in general, and in particular for the *educational* advancement of *youth* in the service of mutual understanding and friendship among nations. **Structure** General Assembly (in conjunction with Symposium); Board of Directors. **Languages** English. **Staff** 1.00 FTE, paid. Occasional voluntary. **Finance** Members' dues. Donations. **Activities** Knowledge management/information dissemination; financial and/or material support; events/meetings. **Events** *Biennial Symposium* Kuching (Malaysia) 2019, *Biennial Symposium* Camrose, AB (Canada) 2017, *Biennial Symposium* Edinburgh (UK) 2015, *Biennial Symposium* Kecskemét (Hungary) 2013, *Biennial symposium* Brisbane, QLD (Australia) 2011. **Publications** *Bulletin of the International Kodaly Society* (2 a year). *Music – a Universal Language* (2006); *An Ode for Music – 11 analyses of choral compositions of Zoltan Kodaly* (2002); *Music Should Belong to Everyone – 120 quotes from Kodaly's writings and speeches* (2002); *The Legacy of Kodaly – An Oral History Perspective* (1992) by Sr Mary Alice Hein; *Reflections on Kodaly* by Laszló Vikar.
Members Honorary; Individual; Institutional; Supporting; Affiliated National Bodies. Members in 35 countries and territories:
Argentina, Australia, Austria, Belgium, Brazil, Canada, China, Cyprus, Denmark, Egypt, Finland, France, Germany, Greece, Hungary, Ireland, Israel, Italy, Japan, Korea Rep, Lebanon, Malaysia, Norway, Philippines, Poland, Portugal, Russia, Spain, Sweden, Switzerland, Taiwan, Thailand, Trinidad-Tobago, UK, USA. [2014.12.02/XE0292/**E**]

♦ International Kolping Society / see KOLPING INTERNATIONAL (#16203)
♦ International Kommission für Strahlenschutz (#12724)
♦ International Konferenz der Waldorf/Steiner Pädagogik (#13653)

♦ International Korean Adoptee Associations (IKAA) 13991

Contact 1920 Fourth Ave, Ste 1405, Seattle WA 98101-5114, USA. E-mail: info@ikaa.org – europe@ikaa.org.
URL: http://ikaa.org/en/
History 2004, as *IKAA Europe*. Registered in accordance with US law. **Aims** Enrich the global adoption community; promote sharing of information and resources between adult adoptee associations; strengthen cross-cultural relations and post-adoption services for the broader international adoptee community. **Structure** International Committee; Executive Board; Advisory Committee. **Events** *Gathering* Seoul (Korea Rep) 2019, *Gathering* Seoul (Korea Rep) 2016, *Gathering* Seoul (Korea Rep) 2013, *European Gathering* Paris (France) 2012, *Gathering* Stockholm (Sweden) 2011. **Publications** *IKAA e-zine*; *IKAA Newsletter*.
Members Associations in 6 countries:
Denmark, France, Netherlands, Norway, Sweden, USA. [2022/XJ5022/**E**]

♦ International Korfball Federation (IKF) 13992

Main Office Orteliuslaan 1041, 3528 BE Utrecht, Netherlands. T. +31614033775. E-mail: office@ikf.org.
URL: http://www.korfball.sport

History 11 Jun 1933, Antwerp (Belgium). Founded by Dutch and Belgian korfball associations, as a continuation of *International Korfball Bureau (inactive)*, started by both associations in 1924. From 1946 became more international. Former names and other names: *Fédération internationale de korfbal* – former (1933 to 1982). Registration: Handelsregister, No/ID: 40479755, Netherlands. **Aims** Encourage, promote, develop and control korfball at all levels throughout the world; increase the level of play worldwide; support and maintain the ideals and objectives of the Olympic movement and in particular the fight against doping by means of appropriate tests; exercise jurisdiction over and determine disputes or disagreements between members, between continental confederations, between members and continental confederations, between athletes or officials and IKF and between athletes or officials and a continental confederation; establish and maintain an efficient administration. **Structure** General Meeting; Council; Executive Committee. Continental Federations (5): Africa; Americas; Asia; Europe; Oceania. **Languages** Dutch, English. **Finance** Sources: donations; members' dues; sponsorship. Other sources: fees; levies; royalties. **Activities** Events/meetings; sporting activities; standards/guidelines; training/education. **Events** *Congress* Antwerp (Belgium) 2021, *General Meeting* Antwerp (Belgium) 2021, *General Meeting* Durban (South Africa) 2019, *Biennial General Meeting* Lisbon (Portugal) 2013, *Biennial General Meeting* Shaoxing (China) 2011. **Publications** *IKF Directory* (annual); *IKF Technical Bulletin* – online. Annual Report.

Members National korfball organizations in 69 countries and territories:
Argentina, Armenia, Aruba, Australia, Belgium, Bosnia-Herzegovina, Botswana, Brazil, Bulgaria, Cameroon, Canada, Catalunya, China, Colombia, Costa Rica, Côte d'Ivoire, Croatia, Curaçao, Cyprus, Czechia, Dominican Rep, England, Finland, France, Georgia, Germany, Ghana, Greece, Hong Kong, Hungary, India, Indonesia, Ireland, Italy, Japan, Kenya, Korea Rep, Luxembourg, Macau, Malawi, Malaysia, Morocco, Nepal, Netherlands, New Zealand, Pakistan, Peru, Philippines, Poland, Portugal, Romania, Russia, Scotland, Serbia, Singapore, Slovakia, South Africa, Sri Lanka, Suriname, Sweden, Switzerland, Taiwan, Thailand, Türkiye, Ukraine, USA, Wales, Zambia, Zimbabwe.

NGO Relations Member of (3): *Association of the IOC Recognized International Sports Federations (ARISF, #02767)*; *International World Games Association (IWGA, #15914)*; *Olympic Movement (#17719)*. Recognized International Federation of: *International Olympic Committee (IOC, #14408)*. [2022.02.02/XD9162/**B**]

♦ International Krav Maga Federation (unconfirmed)
♦ International Kundalini Yoga Teachers Association (see: #22046)

♦ International Kurash Association (IKA) 13993

Gen Sec 70 A Usmon Yusupov Street, Tashkent, Uzbekistan, 100128. T. +998712447198. Fax +998712447197. E-mail: info@kurash-ika.org.
Pres address not obtained.
URL: http://www.kurash-ika.org/

History 6 Sep 1998, Tashkent (Uzbekistan). **Aims** Promote and protect the interests of the *sport* of Kurash. **Structure** Congress; Directing Committee. **Languages** English, French, Russian, Spanish, Uzbek. **Staff** 30.00 FTE, paid. **Finance** Members' dues. **Activities** Events/meetings; training/education. **Events** *Congress and World Senior Kurash Championships* Bournemouth (UK) 2012, *Congress and World Senior Kurash Championships* Termez (Uzbekistan) 2011, *Congress and World Senior Kurash Championships* Delhi (India) 2010, *Congress and World Senior Kurash Championships* Alushta (Ukraine) 2009, *Congress and World Senior Kurash Championships* Istanbul (Turkey) 2008.

Members National federations in 105 countries and territories:
Afghanistan, Angola, Argentina, Armenia, Austria, Azerbaijan, Bahamas, Barbados, Belarus, Bolivia, Botswana, Brazil, Bulgaria, Canada, Chile, Colombia, Congo Brazzaville, Congo DR, Costa Rica, Côte d'Ivoire, Cyprus, Czechia, Dominican Rep, Ecuador, Egypt, Eswatini, Fiji, France, Georgia, Germany, Great Britain, Greece, Haiti, Hong Kong, Hungary, India, Iran Islamic Rep, Iraq, Ireland, Israel, Italy, Japan, Jordan, Kazakhstan, Korea Rep, Kyrgyzstan, Latvia, Lebanon, Libya, Lithuania, Macau, Madagascar, Malaysia, Mali, Mauritius, Moldova, Monaco, Mongolia, Morocco, Mozambique, Namibia, Nepal, Netherlands, New Caledonia, New Zealand, Nicaragua, Niger, Nigeria, North Macedonia, Northern Mariana Is, Pakistan, Panama, Papua New Guinea, Paraguay, Peru, Philippines, Poland, Polynesia Fr, Puerto Rico, Russia, Samoa, Samoa USA, Senegal, Serbia, Singapore, South Africa, Sri Lanka, Suriname, Syrian AR, Taiwan, Tajikistan, Thailand, Tonga, Trinidad-Tobago, Türkiye, Turkmenistan, Ukraine, Uruguay, USA, Uzbekistan, Venezuela, Vietnam, Yemen, Zambia, Zimbabwe.

Continental federations (4):
African Kurash Union (AKU, #00352); *European Kurash Confederation (EKC, #07631)*; *Kurash Confederation of Asia-Oceania (KCAO, #16211)*; *Pan American Kurash Union (#18116)*. [2022/XD8749/y/**D**]

♦ International Kyudo Federation (IKYF) 13994

Office Kishi Memorial hall, 1-1-1 Jinnan, Shibuya-Ku, Tokyo, 150-8050 Japan. T. +81334812387. Fax +81334812398. E-mail: mailto@kyudo.jp.
URL: http://www.ikyf.org/

History 2 May 2006. **Aims** Promote the art and spirit of Kyudo – traditional Japanese *archery* – worldwide. **Languages** English, Japanese.

Members Organizations in 18 countries:
Austria, Belgium, Canada, Finland, France, Germany, Iceland, Italy, Japan, Luxembourg, Netherlands, Norway, Portugal, Spain, Sweden, Switzerland, UK, USA.

NGO Relations *European Kyudo Federation (EKF, #07633)*. [2013/XJ6750/**C**]

♦ International Label Conference (meeting series)
♦ International Labelling Centre (inactive)
♦ International Laboratory Accreditation Conference / see International Laboratory Accreditation Cooperation (#13995)

♦ International Laboratory Accreditation Cooperation (ILAC) 13995

Secretariat 7 Leeds Street, Rhodes NSW 2138, Australia. T. +61297368374. Fax +61297368373. E-mail: ilac@nata.com.au.
URL: http://www.ilac.org/

History 1977. ILAC was formalized, 1996, as a cooperation between 44 national bodies which signed a Memorandum of Understanding (MOU) in Amsterdam (Netherlands). ILAC Arrangement came into effect in 2001. Former names and other names: *International Laboratory Accreditation Conference* – former (1977 to 1996). **Aims** Enhance and facilitate international acceptance of laboratory test and *calibration* data; eliminate technical barriers to *trade*; provide advice and assistance to countries in the process of developing their own accreditation systems. **Structure** General Assembly; Executive Committee; Committees (7); Groups (2); Secretariat held by NATA, Australia. **Languages** English. **Staff** 6.00 FTE, paid. **Finance** Sources: members' dues. **Events** *General Assembly* 2022, *Joint Midterm Meeting* Montréal, QC (Canada) 2022, *Joint Midterm Meeting* Rhodes, NSW (Australia) 2021, *Joint Midterm Meeting* Beijing (China) 2020, *Joint Midterm Meeting* Montréal, QC (Canada) 2020. **Publications** *ILAC Newsletter* (2 a year). *Guidance Series (G Series)*; *ILAC-IAF Joint Publications (A Series)*; *Procedure and Policy Series (P Series)*; *Rules Series (R Series)*. Brochures.

Members Full (Accreditation bodies that meet the requirements for Associates and have also been accepted as signatories to the ILAC Mutual Recognition Arrangement); Associate (Accreditation bodies that are not yet signatories to the ILAC Arrangement); Affiliate; Regional Cooperation Bodies; Stakeholders. Members (155) cover about 68,000 laboratories and over 10,000 inspection bodies.

Recognized Regional Cooperation Bodies (6):
African Accreditation Cooperation (AFRAC, #00196); *Arab Accreditation Cooperation (ARAC, #00892)*; *Asia Pacific Laboratory Accreditation Cooperation (APLAC, inactive)* (Asia Pacific Accreditation Cooperation Incorporated (APAC)); *European Cooperation for Accreditation (EA, #06782)*; *Inter-American Accreditation Cooperation (IAAC, #11396)*; Southern African Development Community Cooperation in Accreditation (SADCA).

Full in 103 countries and territories:
Albania, Algeria, Angola, Argentina, Australia, Austria, Bahrain, Bangladesh, Belarus, Belgium, Bosnia-Herzegovina, Botswana, Brazil, Bulgaria, Canada, Chile, China, Colombia, Comoros, Congo DR, Costa Rica, Croatia, Cuba, Cyprus, Czechia, Denmark, Ecuador, Egypt, El Salvador, Eswatini, Ethiopia, Finland, France, Germany, Greece, Guatemala, Hong Kong, Hungary, India, Indonesia, Ireland, Israel, Italy, Jamaica, Japan, Jordan, Kazakhstan, Kenya, Korea Rep, Kuwait, Kyrgyzstan, Lesotho, Lithuania, Luxembourg, Madagascar, Malawi, Malaysia, Mauritania, Mauritius, Mexico, Moldova, Mongolia, Mozambique, Namibia, Netherlands, New Zealand, Nicaragua, North Macedonia, Norway, Oman, Pakistan, Paraguay, Peru, Philippines, Poland, Portugal, Qatar, Romania, Russia, Saudi Arabia, Serbia, Seychelles, Singapore, Slovakia, Slovenia, South Africa, Spain, Sri Lanka, Sweden, Switzerland, Taiwan, Tanzania UR, Thailand, Tunisia, Türkiye, UK, Ukraine, United Arab Emirates, Uruguay, USA, Vietnam, Yemen, Zambia, Zimbabwe.

Associate in 20 countries:
Azerbaijan, Benin, Burkina Faso, Côte d'Ivoire, Dominican Rep, Guinea-Bissau, India, Iran Islamic Rep, Iraq, Kosovo, Mali, Montenegro, Morocco, Nepal, Niger, Nigeria, Papua New Guinea, Senegal, Togo, Uzbekistan.

Affiliate in 13 countries:
Benin, Cameroon, Côte d'Ivoire, Gabon, Georgia, Ghana, Kuwait, Nigeria, Russia, Saudi Arabia, Senegal, Trinidad-Tobago, USA.

Stakeholders in 16 countries and territories:
Australia, Belgium, Brazil, Congo DR, Croatia, Germany, Hong Kong, India, Italy, Japan, Lebanon, Netherlands, South Africa, Switzerland, UK, USA. [2020.09.07/XF4579/y/**F**]

♦ International Laboratory of High Magnetic Fields and Low Temperatures (ILHMFLT) 13996

Dir ul Gajowicka 95, 53-421 Wroclaw, Poland. T. +48713610681 – +48713907114. Fax +48713612721.
URL: http://www.ml.pan.wroc.pl/

History Established 11 May 1968, Wroclaw (Poland), on signature of an agreement between the Academies of Science of Bulgaria, German DR, Poland and USSR. **Aims** Conduct investigations of properties of materials and novel phenomena in high stationary (up to 15T), quasistationary (up to 36T) and pulsed (up to 42T) magnetic fields in wide temperature range (from 1.5 to 320K). **Structure** Scientific Council (meetings annually); Sections (3): Scientific; Technical; Administrative-financial. Meetings (annual) closed. **Staff** 7.00 FTE, paid. **Finance** Members' annual contributions. **Activities** Research priorities: physical properties of nano-sized materials; investigation of materials with important effects driven by magnetic field; critical phenomena in superconductors. **Events** *Seminar* Wroclaw (Poland) 1998, *Meeting* Wroclaw (Poland) 1988. **Publications** Annual periodic transactions.

Members Ordinary (who, according to international agreements, are obliged to maintain the International Laboratory) Academies of Science of 4 countries:
Bulgaria, Poland, Russia, Ukraine.

Associate in 3 countries:
Germany, Moldova, UK (2). [2013.12.05/XF7502/**F***]

♦ International Laboratory of Marine Radioactivity / see IAEA Environment Laboratories (#11004)
♦ International Labor Communications Association (internationally oriented national body)
♦ International Labor Press Association / see International Labor Communications Association
♦ International Labor Rights Education and Research Fund / see Global Labor Justice-International Labor Rights Forum
♦ International Labor Rights Forum / see Global Labor Justice-International Labor Rights Forum
♦ International Labor Rights Fund / see Global Labor Justice-International Labor Rights Forum
♦ International Labor and Working Class History Study Group / see Study Group on International Labor and Working Class History

♦ International Labour and Employment Relations Association (ILERA) 13997

Sec Research Dept, Intl Labour Office, 1211 Geneva 22, Switzerland. T. +41227997954. Fax +41227998542. E-mail: ilera@ilo.org.
URL: https://ilo-ilera.org/

History 30 Jun 1966. Founding members: *International Institute for Labour Studies (IILS, #13897)* of the ILO; British Universities Industrial Relations Association (BUIRA, UK); Industrial Relations Research Association (now called Labour Employment Relations Association, LERA, USA); Japan Institute of Labour (JIL). Former names and other names: *International Industrial Relations Association (IIRA)* – former; *Association internationale de relations professionnelles (AIRP)* – former; *Asociación Internacional de Relaciones de Trabajo (AIRT)* – former. **Aims** Promote study of labour and employment relations worldwide in relevant academic disciplines by: encouraging establishment and development of national associations of labour and employment relations specialists; facilitating spread of information on significant developments in research and education in the field; organizing worldwide and regional congresses; promoting internationally planned research, by organising study groups on particular topics. **Structure** Council (meeting every 3 years at World Congress); Executive Committee. Administrative support from *ILO (#11123)*. **Languages** English, French, Spanish. **Staff** 1.00 FTE, paid. **Finance** Sources: gifts, legacies; grants; investments; members' dues. **Activities** Awards/prizes/competitions; events/meetings; publishing activities; training/education. **Events** *Triennial World Congress* New York, NY (USA) 2024, *European Regional Congress* Barcelona (Spain) 2022, *Triennial World Congress* Lund (Sweden) 2021, *Asian Regional Congress* Quezon City (Philippines) 2020, *Regional Congress for the Americas* Toronto, ON (Canada) 2020. **Publications** *IIRA Membership Directory* – online; *IIRA Newsletter*.

Members Full – national industrial relations associations in 38 countries and territories:
Argentina, Australia, Bangladesh, Belgium, Benin, Brazil, Canada, Chile, China, Colombia, Congo DR, Cyprus, Denmark, Finland, France, Germany, India, Indonesia, Ireland, Israel, Italy, Japan, Korea Rep, Mexico, Netherlands, New Zealand, Nigeria, Norway, Peru, Philippines, Slovakia, South Africa, Sri Lanka, Sweden, UK, Uruguay, USA, Venezuela. [2022.10.30/XB2117/**B**]

♦ International Labour Film Institute (inactive)
♦ International Labour Network of Solidarity and Struggles (unconfirmed)
♦ International Labour Organization (#11123)
♦ International Labour Organization – International Programme on the Elimination of Child Labour / see International Programme on the Elimination of Child Labour and Forced Labour (#14652)
♦ International Labour Process Conference (meeting series)
♦ International Labour Research and Information Group (internationally oriented national body)
♦ International Labour Sports Confederation / see International Workers and Amateurs in Sports Confederation (#15905)
♦ International Lacrosse Federation (inactive)
♦ International Lactation Consultant Association (internationally oriented national body)
♦ International Laity and Christian Community Group (inactive)
♦ International Lake Constance Conference (#13217)
♦ International Lake Environment Committee / see International Lake Environment Committee Foundation (#13998)

♦ International Lake Environment Committee Foundation (ILEC) 13998

SG 1091 Oroshimo-cho, Kusatsu SHIGA, 525-0001 Japan. T. +81775684567. Fax +81775684568. E-mail: infoilec@ilec.or.jp.
Dir Support and Training Div address not obtained.
URL: https://www.ilec.or.jp/

History 1986. Reorganized 1987, when became a foundation. A supporting foundation of *International Environmental Technology Centre (IETC, #13282)* (1994-2011). Former names and other names: *International Lake Environment Committee* – former (1986 to 1987). **Aims** Promote environmentally sound management of natural and man-made lakes and their environment, consistent with *sustainable development* policies. **Structure** Board of Directors; Board of Trustees; Scientific Committee; Secretariat. **Languages** English, Japanese. **Staff** 10.00 FTE, paid. **Finance** Sources: donations; fees for services; gifts, legacies. Annual budget: 912,000 USD. **Activities** Knowledge management/information dissemination; training/education. **Events** *Workshop on Fostering the Value of Lakes for Future Generations* Kusatsu (Japan) 2022, *World Lake Conference* Guanajuato (Mexico) 2021, *World Lake Conference* Guanajuato (Mexico) 2020, *World Lake Conference* Tsukuba (Japan) 2018, *African Great Lakes Conference* Entebbe (Uganda) 2017. **Publications** *Lakes and Reservoirs: Research and Management* (4 a year); *ILEC Newsletter* (annual) in English, Japanese. *Data-Book of World Lake Environments*; *World Lake Vision*. **Consultative Status** Consultative status granted from: *UNEP (#20299)*. **IGO Relations** Involved with the following convention secretariats: *Secretariat of the Convention of Wetlands (#19200)* for *Convention on Wetlands of International Importance Especially as Waterfowl Habitat (Convention on Wetlands, 1971)*. Accredited by: *United Nations Framework Convention on Climate Change – Secretariat (UNFCCC, #20564)* for *United Nations Framework Convention on Climate Change (UNFCCC, 1992)*. Also cooperates with: *GEMS/Water (see: #20299)*; *Global Environment Facility (GEF, #10346)*; *International Bank for Reconstruction and Development (IBRD, #12317)* (World Bank); *International Data Centre on Hydrology of Lakes and Reservoirs (HYDROLARE, #13137)*; *UNESCO (#20322)*; *United Nations University (UNU, #20642)*; *WHO (#20950)*; *World Meteorological Organization (WMO, #21649)*. **NGO Relations**

Member of: *International Partnership for the Satoyama Initiative (IPSI, #14525)*. Close cooperation with: *Global Environment Centre (GEC)*. Also cooperates with: *Global Water Partnership (GWP, #10653)* and its Forum; *International Society of Limnology (#15232)*; *International Water Association (IWA, #15865)*; *World Water Council (WWC, #21908)*. [2020.09.03/XE1042/fv/**F**]

♦ International Land Coalition (ILC) 13999

Coalition internationale pour l'accès à la terre – Coalición internacional para el acceso a la tierra

Dir c/o IFAD, Via Paolo di Dono 44, 00142 Rome RM, Italy. T. +39654592445. Fax +39654593113. E-mail: info@landcoalition.org.

URL: http://www.landcoalition.org/

History Jan 1996. Founded as a follow-up to the Conference on Hunger and Poverty, Nov 1995, Brussels (Belgium), sponsored by *International Fund for Agricultural Development (IFAD, #13692)*. Former names and other names: *Popular Coalition to Eradicate Hunger and Poverty* – former (1996 to 2003). **Aims** As a global alliance of civil society and intergovernmental organizations, work to put people at the centre of land governance with a vision of achieving a just, equitable and inclusive world in which land rights are secure and poverty is eradicated. **Structure** Assembly of Members; Council; Regional Committees (Africa; Asia; LAC); Secretariat; Regional Coordination Units. Coordinated by IFAD. **Languages** English, French, Spanish. **Staff** 20.00 FTE, paid. **Activities** Advocacy/lobbying/activism; projects/programmes. The Assembly of Members / General Assembly usually takes place during the larger Global Land Forum event. **Events** *Global Land Forum* Sweimeh (Jordan) 2022, *Global Land Forum* Bandung (Indonesia) 2018, *Global Land Forum* Dakar (Senegal) 2015, *Global Land Forum* Antigua (Guatemala) 2013, *Assembly* Tirana (Albania) 2011. **Publications** *Advancing Together* – newsletter.

Members National and international organizations (36), including the following listed in this Yearbook:

Asian NGO Coalition for Agrarian Reform and Rural Development (ANGOC, #01566); *Asociación Latinoamericana de Organizaciones de Promoción (ALOP, inactive)*; *Bread for the World, USA (BFW)*; *Caribbean Network for Integrated Rural Development (CNIRD, #03528)*; *Environment Liaison Centre International (ELCI, no recent information)*; *European Commission (EC, #06633)*; *FAO (#09260)*; IFAD; *Inter-American Development Bank (IDB, #11427)*; *International Bank for Reconstruction and Development (IBRD, #12317)*; *International Food Policy Research Institute (IFPRI, #13622)*; *International Union of Food, Agricultural, Hotel, Restaurant, Catering, Tobacco and Allied Workers Associations (IUF, #15772)*; *UNEP (#20299)*; *World Agroforestry Centre (ICRAF, #21072)*; *World Food Programme (WFP, #21510)*.

Partner organizations in 43 countries and territories:

Albania, Argentina, Bangladesh, Belgium, Benin, Bolivia, Brazil, Burkina Faso, Cambodia, Cameroon, Canada, Chile, Costa Rica, Ecuador, Egypt, France, Georgia, Germany, Ghana, Guatemala, Guyana, Honduras, India, Indonesia, Italy, Kenya, Madagascar, Malawi, Mali, Nepal, Netherlands, Nicaragua, Niger, Palestine, Peru, Philippines, South Africa, Switzerland, Trinidad-Tobago, Uganda, USA, Zambia, Zimbabwe.

BirdLife International (#03266); *South Asia Rural Reconstruction Association (SARRA, #19748)*; *Women's Environment and Development Organization (WEDO, #21016)*.

IGO Relations *FAO (#09260)*; *International Bank for Reconstruction and Development (IBRD, #12317)* (World Bank); *International Fund for Agricultural Development (IFAD, #13692)*; *Secretariat of the United Nations Convention to Combat Desertification (Secretariat of the UNCCD, #19208)*; *UNEP (#20299)*; *World Food Programme (WFP, #21510)*. **NGO Relations** Supports: *Asian NGO Coalition for Agrarian Reform and Rural Development (ANGOC, #01566)*; *Women in Law and Development in Africa-Afrique de l'Ouest (WiLDAF-AO, #21005)*. [2021/XF5729/y/**F**]

- ♦ International Landslide Research Group (internationally oriented national body)
- ♦ International Language and Law Association (internationally oriented national body)
- ♦ International Language Network / see ICC – the international language association (#11050)

♦ International Language Testing Association (ILTA) 14000

Office 1827 Powers Ferry Rd, Bldg 14 Ste 100, Atlanta GA 30339, USA. T. +16782292702. E-mail: info@iltaonline.com.

URL: http://www.iltaonline.com/

History 1992, Vancouver BC (Canada), formally consituted during the *Language Testing Research Colloquium (LTRC)*, following informal networking initiated in the 1970s. **Events** *Annual Language Testing Research Colloquium* Tokyo (Japan) 2022, *Annual Language Testing Research Colloquium* Hammamet (Tunisia) 2021, *Annual Language Testing Research Colloquium* Hammamet (Tunisia) 2020, *Annual Language Testing Research Colloquium* Atlanta, GA (USA) 2019, *Annual Language Testing Research Colloquium* Auckland (New Zealand) 2018. **Publications** *Language Testing Bibliography 1991-1999*. Code of Ethics. **Members** Membership countries not specified. **NGO Relations** Associate member of: *Association internationale de linguistique appliquée (AILA, #02713)*. [2018/XD4716/**D**]

♦ International Laparoscopic Liver Society (ILLS) 14001

Admin Office Chez Hopscotch Congrès, 23-25 rue Notre Dame des Victoires, 75002 Paris, France. E-mail: ills@lp-etc.com.

URL: http://www.lap-liver.com/

History 2015. **Aims** Promote the skills and techniques of laparoscopic liver resection. **Structure** Officers. **Activities** Events/meetings. **Events** *World Congress* Rome (Italy) 2023, *World Congress* 2021, *World Congress* Tokyo (Japan) 2019, *World Congress* Paris (France) 2017.

Members Individuals in 26 countries and territories:

Argentina, Australia, Belgium, Brazil, Bulgaria, Canada, Chile, China, Colombia, France, Hong Kong, India, Italy, Japan, Korea Rep, Lebanon, Netherlands, Norway, Philippines, Russia, Singapore, Slovenia, Spain, Taiwan, UK, USA. [2018/XM6466/v/**C**]

- ♦ International Laser Class Association (see: #21760)

♦ International Laser Display Association (ILDA) 14002

Exec Dir 7602 Edgeworth Dr, Orlando FL 32819, USA. T. +14077977654. E-mail: mail@ilda.com.

URL: http://www.ilda.com

History Aug 1986. Registration: USA, State of Florida. **Aims** Advance and promote professional application of laser display by: maintaining standards of safety; promoting better understanding between professionals, FDA, FAA and other regulatory agencies; fostering development of new technology; promoting advancement of laser artistry; providing information for the public and increasing public awareness; promoting cooperation within the industry. **Structure** General Meeting (annual); Board of Directors; Committees (7). **Languages** English. **Staff** 0.50 FTE, paid. **Finance** Annual budget: 35,000 USD (2022). **Events** *Annual Conference* Dartford (UK) 2022, *Annual Conference* Orlando, FL (USA) 2021, *Annual Conference* Orlando, FL (USA) 2020, *Annual Conference* Orlando, FL (USA) 2019, *Annual Conference* Montréal, QC (Canada) 2018. **Publications** *Laserist* – magazine. Membership directory; handbook; technical standards.

Members Producers of laser entertainment devices, vendors, not-for-profit organizations, individuals and students, agreeing to abide by ILDA Code of Ethics. Members (150), mainly in the USA (40), but in a total of 35 countries and territories:

Argentina, Australia, Austria, Belgium, Brazil, Bulgaria, Canada, China, Egypt, France, Germany, Greece, Hungary, Italy, Japan, Korea Rep, Mexico, Netherlands, Pakistan, Poland, Portugal, Romania, Russia, Saudi Arabia, Slovakia, South Africa, Spain, Sweden, Taiwan, Türkiye, UK, Ukraine, United Arab Emirates, USA, Venezuela. [2022.05.10/XD3613/**D**]

- ♦ International Laser II Class Association (see: #21760)
- ♦ International Laser Physics Workshop (meeting series)
- ♦ International Laser Ranging Service (see: #11914)
- ♦ International Latin Federation of Barristers and Lawyers (inactive)

♦ International Law Association (ILA) 14003

Association de droit international – Asociación de Derecho Internacional

SG Charles Clore House, 17 Russell Square, London, WC1B 5DR, UK. T. +442073232978. Fax +442075806344. E-mail: info@ila-hq.org.

URL: http://www.ila-hq.org/

History 11 Oct 1873, Brussels (Belgium). Former names and other names: *Association for the Reform and Codification of the Law of Nations* – former (1873 to 1895); *Association pour la réforme et la codification du droit des nations* – former (1873 to 1895). Registration: Charity Commission, No/ID: 249637, Start date: 11 Oct 1966, England and Wales. **Aims** Study, clarify and develop international law, both public and private; further international understanding and respect for international law. **Structure** International Conference (every 2 years), hosted by a Member Branch; Executive Council (meets twice a year); Committees; Study Groups. **Languages** English, French. **Staff** 1.00 FTE, paid. **Finance** Sources: grants; members' dues; sale of publications. **Events** *Biennial Conference* Lisbon (Portugal) 2022, *Biennial Conference* Kyoto (Japan) 2020, *Seminar on Data Privacy and Protection in International Law* Singapore (Singapore) 2020, *Seminar on Informers, Collaborators and the Laws of Armed Conflict* Singapore (Singapore) 2019, *Seminar on International Human Rights in a Time of Populism* Singapore (Singapore) 2019. **Publications** *ILA Newsletter / ADI-Actualités* in English, French. *Extraterritorial Application of Laws and Responses Thereto* (2nd ed 1989 1985); *Index of Conference Reports 1873-1972* (1975); *The Present State of International Law* (1973) – a collection of essays published for the Association's Centenary; *The Effect of Independence on Treaties* (1965). Biennial Conference Reports; special reports.

Members Regional branches in 51 countries and territories:

Albania, Argentina, Australia, Austria, Bangladesh, Belgium, Brazil, Bulgaria, Canada, Chile, Colombia, Croatia, Czechia, Denmark, Egypt, Finland, France, Germany, Greece, Hong Kong, Hungary, India, Ireland, Israel, Italy, Japan, Jordan, Kenya, Korea Rep, Mexico, Nepal, Netherlands, New Zealand, Nigeria, Norway, Poland, Portugal, Qatar, Romania, Russia, Slovenia, South Africa, Spain, Sweden, Switzerland, Taiwan, Türkiye, Uganda, UK, Ukraine, USA.

Members also in Caribbean. Membership countries not specified.

Consultative Status Consultative status granted from: *ECOSOC (#05331)* (Special); *FAO (#09260)* (Liaison Status); *World Intellectual Property Organization (WIPO, #21593)* (Permanent Observer Status); *UNCTAD (#20285)* (General Category); *UNEP (#20299)*; *International Civil Aviation Organization (ICAO, #12581)*. **IGO Relations** Observer status with: *Committee on the Peaceful Uses of Outer Space (COPUOS, #04277)*; *Intergovernmental Committee of the International Convention of Rome for the Protection of Performers, Producers of Phonograms and Broadcasting Organizations (#11474)*. [2022/XB2189/**B**]

- ♦ International Law Book Facility (internationally oriented national body)

♦ International Law Commission (ILC) 14004

Commission du droit international (CDI)

Sec 2 United Nations Plaza, 323 E 44th St, Room DC2-0566, New York NY 10017, USA. T. +12129635331. Fax +12129631963.

URL: https://legal.un.org/ilc/

History 21 Nov 1947. Established as a Commission of *United Nations (UN, #20515)*, by resolution 174 (II) of the General Assembly. 1st annual session: 12 Apr 1949. **Aims** Promote the progressive development of international law and its codification in accordance with Article 13-1-a of the Charter of the United Nations. **Structure** Commission (meetings annually in Geneva – Switzerland), comprising 34 members elected for 5-year terms in their personal capacity. Enlarged Bureau comprises Officers, previous Chairman of the Commission and Special Rapporteurs. Planning Group. Drafting Committee. Geographical distribution of Commission members: 8 from African states; 7 from Asian states; 3 from Eastern European states; 6 from Latin American states; 8 from Western European and other states; plus one from African or Eastern European states in rotation and one from Asian or Latin American states in rotation. Secretariat. **Languages** Arabic, Chinese, English, French, Russian, Spanish. **Staff** Serviced by the Codification Division of the Office of Legal Affairs of the United Nations Secretariat. **Finance** Regular budget of the United Nations. **Activities** Research/documentation; knowledge management/information dissemination; events/meetings; training/education. Worked on the setting up of: *International Criminal Court (ICC, #13108)*. **Events** *International law seminar* Geneva (Switzerland) 2011, *Second part* Geneva (Switzerland) 2011, *First part* Geneva (Switzerland) 2010, *Second part* Geneva (Switzerland) 2010, *International law seminar* Geneva (Switzerland) 2009. **Publications** *Yearbook of the International Law Commission* (annual). *The Work of the International Law Commission* (2017); *International Law Commission Fifty Years After: An Evaluation* (2000); *Analytical Guide to the Work of the International Law Commission, 1949-1997* (1998); *Making Better International Law: the International Law Commission at 50 – Proceedings of the United Nations Colloquium on Progressive Development and Codification of International Law* (1998); *International Law on the Eve of the Twenty-first Century: Views from the International Law Commission* (1997).

Members Individuals, being experts in international law, from 34 countries (2017-2021):

Algeria, Austria, Brazil, Chile, China, Colombia, Côte d'Ivoire, Czechia, Ecuador, Egypt, Finland, Germany, India, Japan, Jordan, Kenya, Korea Rep, Mexico, Morocco, Nicaragua, Peru, Portugal, Qatar, Romania, Russia, Sierra Leone, Slovenia, South Africa, Spain, Tanzania UR, Türkiye, UK, USA, Vietnam.

IGO Relations Observer to: *European Committee on Legal Cooperation (#06655)*. [2021/XE0223/**E***]

♦ International Law Institute – African Centre for Legal Excellence (ILI – ACLE) 14005

Contact Third Floor Block B, Nakawa Business Park, PO Box 23933, Kampala, Uganda. T. +256414347523. E-mail: administrator@ili.or.ug – lawexecediliacle@georgetown.edu.

URL: http://www.iliacle.org/

History 1997, Kampala (Uganda). Founded by *International Law Institute, Washington DC (ILI)*. Former names and other names: *International Law Institute – Uganda (ILI)* – former. Registration: Uganda. **Aims** Build Africa's legal infrastructure and engage in rule of law reform towards economic development; provide post-professional training and technical support in law, *finance*, project management and *governance* to institutions and professionals, particularly in the Sub-Saharan region, so that they can have the knowledge and experience to achieve practical solutions to their problems in ways that fit their own needs. **Structure** Board of Directors, headed by Chairman; Departments (3). **Languages** English, French. **Staff** 5.00 FTE, paid. **Finance** Sources: donations; meeting proceeds; revenue from activities/projects. **Activities** Capacity building; certification/accreditation; events/meetings; guidance/assistance/consulting; projects/programmes; training/education. Active in: Kenya, Nigeria, South Africa, Uganda. **Publications** Annual calendar brochure.

Members Affiliate in 3 countries:

South Africa, Türkiye, USA.

IGO Relations Cooperates with (1): *International Centre for Settlement of Investment Disputes (ICSID, #12515)*. **NGO Relations** Partner of (1): *Global Forum on Law, Justice and Development (GFLJD, #10373)*. [2022/XG9252/j/**E**]

- ♦ International Law Institute – Uganda / see International Law Institute – African Centre for Legal Excellence (#14005)
- ♦ International Law Institute, Washington DC (internationally oriented national body)
- ♦ International Lawn Tennis Federation / see International Tennis Federation (#15676)
- ♦ International Law Students Association (internationally oriented national body)
- ♦ International Lawyers for Africa (internationally oriented national body)
- ♦ International Lawyers in Alcoholics Anonymous (internationally oriented national body)

♦ International Lawyers and Economists Against Poverty (ILEAP) . . . 14006

Juristes et économistes internationaux contre la pauvreté (JEICP)

Administration/Finance Officer 260 Salem Avenue, Toronto ON M6H 3C7, Canada. T. +14168759498.

History May 2002, Nairobi (Kenya). **Aims** Promote pro-development outcomes in international negotiations; provides professional backstopping capacity and support in trade negotiations to a variety of beneficiaries in Africa and the Caribbean. **Finance** Donations from governments and private sector. **Events** *Workshop on trade in services negotiations and the private sector* Nairobi (Kenya) 2009. **Publications** *Background Briefs*; *Negotiation Advisory Briefs*. Annual Report; papers; workshop proceedings. **NGO Relations** *African Economic Research Consortium (AERC, #00292)*. [2017/XF6653/**F**]

♦ International Lawyers Network (ILN) 14007

Exec Dir 11B Opal Court, Barnegat NJ 08005, USA.

URL: http://www.ilntoday.com/

History 1988. **Aims** Increase cooperation and information exchange between the members. **Structure** Board of Directors; Chairperson; Specialty Groups (14). **Languages** English. **Staff** 1.00 FTE, paid. **Finance** Sources: meeting proceeds; members' dues. **Activities** Events/meetings. **Events** *Asia Pacific Regional Conference* Bangkok (Thailand) 2019, *Americas Regional Meeting* Laguna Beach, CA (USA) 2019, *Annual Meeting* Milan (Italy) 2019, *European Regional Meeting* Paris (France) 2019, *Americas Regional Meeting* Las Vegas, NV (USA) 2018. **Publications** *Firm of the Month* (12 a year) – membership e-mail; *ILN Estates International* (4 a year) – e-mail newsletter; *ILNQuarterly* (4 a year) – membership newsletter; *ILN Tax Plus* (4 a year) – e-mail newsletter; *This Quarter in ILN Labor and Employment News* (4 a year) – e-mail newsletter; *ILN-ergy* (2 a year) – e-mail newsletter. *ILN IP Insider* – blog; *Zen Legal Networking* – blog. Website functions as a daily publication platform where substantive member content is shared and can be subscribed to by RSS feed.
Members Law firms (74) in 59 countries and territories:
Argentina, Austria, Bahamas, Belarus, Belize, Brazil, Bulgaria, Canada, Chile, China, Colombia, Costa Rica, Cyprus, Czechia, Denmark, Ecuador, England, Estonia, Finland, France, Germany, Greece, Hungary, India, Ireland, Israel, Italy, Japan, Latvia, Lebanon, Liechtenstein, Lithuania, Luxembourg, Malaysia, Malta, Mexico, Mozambique, Netherlands, New Zealand, Norway, Panama, Philippines, Poland, Portugal, Romania, Russia, Scotland, Seychelles, Singapore, Slovakia, Spain, Sweden, Switzerland, Thailand, Türkiye, Ukraine, United Arab Emirates, USA, Virgin Is UK. [2020.07.01/XG4778/**F**]

♦ International-Lawyers.Org (INTLawyers) 14008

Contact Rue Cramer 4, 1202 Geneva, Switzerland. Fax +12069844734. E-mail: intlawyers2010@gmail.com.
URL: http://intlawyers.org/

History 10 Dec 2010, Geneva (Switzerland). Current statutes adopted, 5 Dec 2010; amended 4 Dec 2018 and 2020. Former names and other names: *Nord-Sud XXI (NSXXI)* – full title. Registration: Swiss Civil Code, No/ID: 080.502.093, Start date: 6 Dec 2016, Switzerland, Geneva. **Aims** Promote global justice, which is understood as including human rights, development, rights of peoples, self-determination, mediation, disarmament, health, information technology, labour, education and training, peace, economic justice, climate justice, environmental justice and rights of Mother Earth. **Structure** General Assembly; Management Board; Advisory Board. **Languages** Arabic, Dutch, English, French, Italian, Spanish. **Staff** No full-time staff. **Finance** Sources: donations; members' dues. INTLawyers receives support from its members and independent non-profit, non-governmental organizations. Annual budget: 15,000 CHF (2020). **Activities** Events/meetings; guidance/assistance/consulting; knowledge management/information dissemination; publishing activities; training/education. **Events** *Human Rights and Climate Change* Geneva (Switzerland) 2022, *Session* Geneva (Switzerland) 2020. **Publications** Annual Report; annual accounts; working papers; written and oral statements.
Members Full in 13 countries and territories:
Egypt, Gambia, Italy, Netherlands, Nigeria, Palestine, Sierra Leone, Spain, Switzerland, UK, United Arab Emirates, USA, Vanuatu.
Consultative Status Consultative status granted from: *ECOSOC (#05331)* (Special); *United Nations Framework Convention on Climate Change – Secretariat (UNFCCC, #20564)*. **IGO Relations** Accredited by (2): *ECOSOC (#05331)*; *United Nations Human Rights Council (HRC, #20571)*. **NGO Relations** Member of (1): *Conference of Non-Governmental Organizations in Consultative Relationship with the United Nations (CONGO, #04635)*. Cooperates with numerous NGOs. [2022.10.19/XM6049/**F**]

♦ International Lay Buddhist Forum / see Bodhimitra – International Lay Buddhist Forum (#03298)

♦ International Lead Association (ILA) 14009

Managing Dir 120 New Cavendish Street, London, W1W 6XX, UK. T. +442078338090. E-mail: enq@ila-lead.org.
URL: http://www.ila-lead.org/

History 1946, London (UK). Former names and other names: *Lead Development Association (LDA)* – former; *Lead Development Association International (LDA International)* – former. **Aims** Represent the lead *industry* at national and international levels; promote the use of lead. **Languages** English. **Staff** 11.00 FTE, paid. **Activities** Events/meetings; guidance/assistance/consulting; knowledge management/information dissemination. **Events** *European Lead Battery Conference* Lyon (France) 2022, *European Lead Battery Conference* London (UK) 2020, *Biennial International Lead Conference* Madrid (Spain) 2019, *European Lead Battery Conference* Vienna (Austria) 2018, *Biennial International Lead Conference* Berlin (Germany) 2017.
Members Mining companies, metal producers and some users of lead in 17 countries:
Australia, Belgium, China, Czechia, France, Germany, India, Ireland, Israel, Italy, Netherlands, Slovakia, Slovenia, Spain, Sweden, UK, USA.
NGO Relations Member of (2): *Association européenne des métaux (EUROMETAUX, #02578)*; *International Council on Mining and Metals (ICMM, #13048)*. Partner of (1): *Global Battery Alliance (GBA, #10249)*. [2022.10.18/XD5150/**D**]

♦ International Leadership Association (ILA) 14010

Pres/CEO 8601 Georgia Ave, Ste 1010, Silver Spring MD 20910-3440, USA. T. +12024704818. Fax +12024702724. E-mail: ila@theila.org.
URL: https://ilaglobalnetwork.org/

History Developed out of the 4-year *Kellogg Leadership Studies Project (KLSP)* and with support of *W K Kellogg Foundation (WKKF)*, 1st international conference resulting in ILA organized 1999. Registration: USA. **Aims** Promotes a deeper understanding of leadership knowledge and practices for the greater good of individuals and communities worldwide. **Structure** Board of Directors of up to 18 members. Executive Committee. **Languages** English. **Staff** 6.50 FTE, paid. **Finance** Members'dues, based on sliding income scale. **Events** *Global Conference* Washington, DC (USA) 2022, *Annual Conference* Geneva (Switzerland) 2021, *Annual Conference* San Francisco, CA (USA) 2020, *Annual Conference* Ottawa, ON (Canada) 2019, *Annual Conference* Palm Beach, FL (USA) 2018. **Publications** *The Member Connector* (12 a year) – bulletin. *Building Leadership Bridge Series*. Conference proceedings. **Members** Individuals in over 100 countries and territories. Membership countries not specified. **NGO Relations** Member of: *EFMD – The Management Development Network (#05387)*. [2021/XD8433/**D**]

♦ International Leading Association / see International Lodging Association (#14063)
♦ International Lead Management Center (internationally oriented national body)

♦ International Lead Zinc Research Organization (ILZRO) 14011

Contact 2530 Meridian Pkwy, Ste 115, Durham NC 27713, USA. T. +19193614647. Fax +19193611957.
URL: http://www.ilzro.org/

History Sep 1958, as *'Expanded Research Program (AZI-LIA)'*. Present name adopted Jul 1963 when the organization became international in character. Incorporated in: New York State (USA), Nov 1965; North Carolina (USA), Apr 1988. **Aims** Promote welfare of lead and zinc *industries* through cooperative research on present and potential uses of lead and zinc, thereby contributing to the retention of existing *markets* and developing new markets for lead and zinc, their compounds and by-products. **Structure** Meeting (annual); Board of Directors. **Languages** English, French, Japanese. **Staff** 13.00 FTE, paid. **Finance** Supported by: *International Lead Association (ILA, #14009)*. Programme support of steel and battery industries. **Activities** Operates a program of research and development activities via contracts with other bodies and individuals and disseminates results of these activities. Major effort is through technical committees (both in Lead and in Zinc/Cadmium) for product technology and environmental health. Cooperates closely in exchange of publications and other data with other market development associations worldwide. **Events** *International Lead and Zinc Conference* Singapore (Singapore) 2012, *GALVATECH : triennial international conference on zinc and zinc alloy coated steel sheet* Osaka (Japan) 2007, *Annual meeting* London (UK) 2003, *Annual meeting* London (UK) 2002, *Annual meeting* London (UK) 2001. **Publications** Contractors' research reports. **NGO Relations** In liaison with technical committees of: *International Organization for Standardization (ISO, #14473)*. [2017/XF2192/**F**]

♦ International Lead and Zinc Study Group (ILZSG) 14012

Groupe d'étude international du plomb et du zinc – Grupo Internacional de Estudio sobre el Plomo y el Zinc – Mezdunarodnaja Issledovatelskaja Gruppa po Svincu i Cinku

SG Rua Almirante Barroso 38 – 5th Floor, 1000-013 Lisbon, Portugal. T. +351213592420. Fax +351213592429. E-mail: sales@ilzsg.org.
URL: http://www.ilzsg.org/

History May 1959, New York NY (USA), following resolution of United Nations Conference on Lead and Zinc, 1958, Geneva (Switzerland), as successor body to 'Lead and Zinc Committee', set up Sep 1958, London (UK). First session Jan 1960, Geneva. From inception until 1 Apr 1977, located in United Nations Headquarters, New York NY, later in London and since in Lisbon (Portugal). **Aims** Provide opportunities for regular intergovernmental consultations on international *trade* in lead and zinc; provide continuous information regarding *supply* and demand and its probable development; improve transparency in global lead and zinc markets; make special studies of the world situation in lead and zinc; consider possible solutions to special problems or difficulties unlikely to be resolved in the ordinary development of world trade. **Structure** Group meets in full session once a year. Officers: Chairman and 2 Vice-Chairmen. Secretariat, headed by Secretary-General. Committees on which all members are represented (4): Standing; Statistical and Forecasting; Mine and Smelter Projects; Economic and Environment. Sub-committees under the Economic Committee (3): Economic; Environment; Recycling. Industry Advisory Panel. Membership open to member countries of the United Nations or of its specialized agencies or of WTO which are substantially interested in production or consumption of or trade in lead and/or zinc. Membership currently represents about 90% of production and consumption of lead and zinc. **Languages** Chinese, English, French, Russian, Spanish. **Staff** 7.00 FTE, paid. **Finance** Sources: contributions of member/participating states. **Activities** Events/meetings; monitoring/evaluation; research/documentation. **Events** *Annual session / Annual Conference* Lisbon (Portugal) 2010, *Annual Session* Lisbon (Portugal) 2009, *Annual Session* Lisbon (Portugal) 2008, *Annual Session* 2007, *Annual Session* Lisbon (Portugal) 2006. **Publications** *Lead and Zinc Statistics* (12 a year) – bulletin; *Principal Uses of Lead and Zinc* (annual). *Lead and Zinc New Mine and Smelter Projects* (2005); *The Use of Zinc in Construction and Public Infrastructure* (2002); *Lead and Zinc New Mine and Smelter Projects 2002* (2002); *World Directory: Lead and Zinc Mines* (2001); *Environmental and Health Controls on Lead* (2000); *Economic and Environmental Role of Zinc: 2000* (2000); *Environmental and Health Controls on Zinc* (2000); *Environment and Health Controls on Lead* (2000); *Study on the Image of Lead* (1999); *World Lead Sheet Supply and Demand 1999* (1999); *Zinc Usage by the Automotive Industry 1999* (1999); *The Market Situation for Zinc* (1997); *World Directory: Continuous Galvanizing Lines* (1997); *World Directory: Primary and Secondary Lead Plants* (1997); *World Directory: Primary and Secondary Zinc Plants* (1997); *Lead in Batteries* (1996); *Trends in Production of Lead and Zinc* (1996); *Zinc Die Casting and Zinc Hot Dip Galvanising in Selected Developing Countries* (1995). Conference proceedings; production and market surveys; reviews of current trends. **Information Services** *Lead and Zinc Statistics: 1960-1988* – database.
Members Governments of 27 countries:
Australia, Belgium, Brazil, Bulgaria, China, Finland, France, Germany, India, Iran Islamic Rep, Ireland, Italy, Japan, Korea Rep, Mexico, Morocco, Namibia, Netherlands, Norway, Peru, Poland, Portugal, Russia, Serbia, Spain, Sweden, USA.
Regional organization (1):
European Union (EU, #08967).
IGO Relations Participates in activities of: *UNCTAD (#20285)*. Permanent observers: *European Commission (EC, #06633)*; *OECD (#17693)*; UNCTAD; *UNEP (#20299)*; *UNIDO (#20336)*. Designed International Commodity Body of: *Common Fund for Commodities (CFC, #04293)*. **NGO Relations** Permanent observers: *Association européenne des métaux (EUROMETAUX, #02578)*; *Battery Council International (BCI)*; *European General Galvanizers Association (EGGA, #07383)*; *International Lead Association (ILA, #14009)*; *International Lead Zinc Research Organization (ILZRO, #14011)*; *International Zinc Association (IZA, #15942)*. [2018.06.19/XC2191/**C***]

♦ International League for the Abolition of the Death Penalty by the Year 2000 / see Hands Off Cain – Citizens' and Parliamentarians' League for the Abolition of the Death Penalty Worldwide (#10857)
♦ International League Against the Abuse of Alcoholic Liquor (inactive)
♦ International League Against Antisemitism / see International League Against Racism and Antisemitism (#14014)

♦ International League Against Epilepsy (ILAE) 14013

Ligue internationale contre l'épilepsie

Admin Dir 2221 Justin Rd, Ste 119-352, Flower Mound TX 75028, USA. T. +18605867547. Fax +18602011111. E-mail: info@ilae.org.
Europe Office Suite 105, The Crescent Building, Northwood, Dublin, CO. DUBLIN, D09 C6X8, Ireland. E-mail: info@epilepsycongress.org.
URL: http://www.ilae.org/

History 1909, Budapest (Hungary). Reorganized and new constitution adopted, 9 Sep 1973; latest revision Sep 1985, Hamburg (Germany FR). **Aims** Act as parent organization for individual national associations; advance and disseminate knowledge concerning epilepsy; maintain effective cooperation with international institutions active in the field of public health and social care; promote research and education in the field and application of fruits of research. **Structure** General Assembly of national chapters (at least every 2 years). Council, comprising one delegate from each national chapter and the Executive Committee, consisting of President, Past-President, 1st and 2nd Vice-Presidents, Secretary-General, Treasurer, Editor, and President and Secretary-General of *International Bureau for Epilepsy (IBE, #12414)* – this organization serving for social aspects of epilepsy and as medium of contact with lay organizations in the field. Regional Commissions (5): Asian and Oceanian; Easter Mediterranean; European; Latin America; North American. **Languages** Dutch, English, French, German, Spanish. **Staff** 3.00 FTE, paid. **Finance** Sources: members' dues. Other sources: Journal revenue. **Activities** Events/meetings; research and development; training/education. Events series include: *Workshop on Neurobiology of the Epilepsies (WONOEP)*. **Events** *European Epilepsy Congress* Rome (Italy) 2024, *International Epilepsy Congress* Dublin (Ireland) 2023, *Asian & Oceanian Epilepsy Congress* 2022, *Latin American Epilepsy Congress (LAEC)* Medellin (Colombia) 2022, *Eastern Mediterranean Epilepsy Congress* Riyadh (Saudi Arabia) 2022. **Publications** *Epilepsia* (12 a year); *Epigraph* (3 a year) – newsletter. *Advances in Epileptology* – conference proceedings. **Members** National chapters (123), representing national organizations, in 123 countries and territories. Membership countries not specified. **Consultative Status** Consultative status granted from: *WHO (#20950)* (Official Relations). **NGO Relations** Member of (2): *Council for International Organizations of Medical Sciences (CIOMS, #04905)*; *International Brain Research Organization (IBRO, #12392)*. Instrumental in setting up (2): *Asian Epilepsy Academy (ASEPA, #01439)*; *Epilepsy Alliance Europe (EAE, #05512)*. Corporate member of: *World Federation of Neurology (WFN, #21461)*. European Commission is member of: *European Brain Council (EBC, #06391)*. [2022/XC2193/**C**]

♦ International League Against Racism and Antisemitism 14014

Ligue internationale contre le racisme et l'antisémitisme (LICRA)

Secretariat 42 rue du Louvre, 75001 Paris, France. T. +33145080808. Fax +33145081818. E-mail: licra@licra.org.
URL: http://www.licra.org/

History Founded Mar 1927, Paris (France). *World Assembly Against Racism – Rassemblement mondial contre le racisme*, set up in 1929, with member sections in 12 countries. Originally called *Ligue internationale contre les pogromes*, name changed to *International League Against Antisemitism – Ligue internationale contre l'antisémitisme (LICA)*, 1928, when merged with *International Federation of Leagues Against Anti-Semitism (inactive)*. Current title adopted, 1979. Registration: Association régie par la loi du 1er juillet 1901, No/ID: 78445168400020, France. **Aims** Fight racism and anti-Semitism in all its forms and expressions through all possible means, such as defence of victims, legal actions, education against racism, lobbying and public information. **Structure** Director Committee. **Languages** English, French, German. **Finance** Members' dues. Donations. **Activities** Advocacy/lobbying/activism; awareness raising. **Events** *Geneva Summit for Human Rights, Tolerance and Democracy* Geneva (Switzerland) 2010, *Geneva Summit for Human Rights, Tolerance and Democracy* Geneva (Switzerland) 2009, *Congress* Paris (France) 2007, *Congress* Paris (France) 2004, *Congress* Paris (France) 1999. **Publications** *Le droit de vivre* (6 a year) – magazine. *Contre le racisme – les combats de la LICRA*. Brochures; videos; CD-ROMs; conference reports.
Members Individual Full; Honorary; Supporting, in 7 countries:
Austria, Belgium, Cameroon, France, Luxembourg, Switzerland, USA.
International member (1):
International Network Against Cyber Hate (INACH, #14229).
Consultative Status Consultative status granted from: *ECOSOC (#05331)* (Special); *Council of Europe (CE, #04881)* (Participatory Status). **NGO Relations** Member of: *European Network against Racism (ENAR, #07862)*; *Football Against Racism in Europe (FARE Network, #09853)*; *UNITED for Intercultural Action – European Network Against Nationalism, Racism, Fascism and in Support of Migrants and Refugees (UNITED, #20511)*. [2020/XF2194/y/**F**]

♦ International League Against Rheumatism / see International League of Associations for Rheumatology (#14016)
♦ International League Against Unfair Competition / see Ligue internationale du droit de la concurrence (#16478)
♦ International League of Agricultural Specialists-Esperantists (inactive)
♦ International League of Anti-Prohibitionists (inactive)

♦ International League of Antiquarian Booksellers (ILAB) 14015

Ligue internationale de la librairie ancienne (LILA)

Exec Sec address not obtained.
Registered Address c/o Venthams Ltd, 51 Lincoln's Inn Fields, London, WC2A 3NA, UK.
URL: http://www.ilab.org/

History 3 Sep 1947, Amsterdam (Netherlands). Registration: Companies House, No/ID: 11841023, England and Wales; Switzerland. **Aims** Coordinate efforts and ideas for development and good of the trade of antiquarian bookselling, thereby creating friendly relations among individuals, associations and firms actively engaged in buying and selling old, rare and second-hand *books*, manuscripts, autographs and related material, including prints and drawings, throughout the world. **Structure** Congress and General Assembly. Executive Committee, comprising President, Vice-President, Treasurer, General-Secretary and 4 members. Meetings closed. **Languages** English, French. **Staff** None. **Finance** Sources: members' dues. **Activities** Maintains world card index; awards quadrennial ILAB-Breslauer Prize for Bibliography; organizes international book fair (every 2 years). **Events** *Congress* Oxford (UK) 2022, *Congress* Amsterdam (Netherlands) 2020, *Congress* Pasadena, CA (USA) 2018, *Congress* Paris (France) 2014, *Congress* Lucerne (Switzerland) / Zurich (Switzerland) 2012. **Publications** *International Directory of Antiquarian Booksellers* in English, French. *Compendium of Usage and Customs*; *Dictionary for the Antiquarian Booktrade*. Newsletters.

Members National associations in 24 countries:
Australia, Austria, Belgium, Brazil, Canada, China, Czechia, Denmark, Finland, France, Germany, Hungary, Italy, Japan, Korea Rep, Netherlands, New Zealand, Norway, Russia, Spain, Sweden, Switzerland, UK, USA.
Individuals in 9 countries:
Argentina, Greece, Ireland, Israel, Liechtenstein, Monaco, Portugal, Singapore, South Africa. [2021/XC2208/**C**]

♦ International League of Associations for Rheumatology (ILAR) 14016

Ligue internationale d'associations pour la rhumatologie – Liga Internacional de Asociaciones para la Reumatologia

Exec Dir American College of Rheumatology, 2200 Lake Boulevard NE, Atlanta GA 30319, USA. E-mail: ilar@rheumatology.org.
Chair Institute of Infection, Immunity and Inflammation, Univ of Glasgow, B4/13 Iii – Gbrc, University Place, Glasgow, G12 8TA, UK.
URL: http://www.ilar.org/

History Oct 1928, Paris (France), as *International Committee Against Rheumatism – Comité international contre le rhumatisme*. Reorganized, 1949, New York NY (USA), and name changed to *International League Against Rheumatism – Ligue internationale contre le rhumatisme – Liga Internacional contra el Reumatismo*. Registration: USA, Illinois. **Aims** Stimulate and promote development of awareness, knowledge and the means of prevention, treatment, *rehabilitation* and relief of *musculoskeletal* diseases; advance rheumatology in developing countries. **Structure** General Assembly (every 4 years). Council. Executive Committee, consisting of the Presidents and Presidents-Elect of ACR, AFLAR, APLAR, EULAR and PANLAR. Standing Committees, consisting of representatives of the 4 regional leagues. **Languages** English, French, Spanish. **Staff** Voluntary. **Finance** Sources: members' dues. **Activities** Projects/programmes. **Events** *European congress on clinical and economic aspects of osteoporosis and osteoarthritis* Nice (France) 2003, *Quadrennial congress* Edmonton, AB (Canada) 2001, *Quadrennial congress* Singapore (Singapore) 1997, *Quadrennial Congress* Barcelona (Spain) 1993, *Quadrennial Congress* Rio de Janeiro (Brazil) 1989. **Publications** *Clinical Rheumatology* – journal. *Up and about with arthritis* (1997) by Jane Hampton.

Members National organizations, affiliated through regional leagues against rheumatism, in 92 countries and territories:
Algeria, Argentina, Australia, Austria, Belgium, Bolivia, Brazil, Bulgaria, Canada, Chile, China, Colombia, Congo Brazzaville, Congo DR, Costa Rica, Côte d'Ivoire, Croatia, Cuba, Cyprus, Czechia, Denmark, Dominican Rep, Ecuador, Egypt, El Salvador, Estonia, Finland, France, Gabon, Georgia, Germany, Greece, Guatemala, Honduras, Hong Kong, Hungary, Iceland, India, Indonesia, Iran Islamic Rep, Ireland, Israel, Italy, Jamaica, Japan, Jordan, Kenya, Korea Rep, Kuwait, Latvia, Lebanon, Lithuania, Luxembourg, Malaysia, Mexico, Moldova, Morocco, Netherlands, New Zealand, Nicaragua, Nigeria, North Macedonia, Norway, Pakistan, Panama, Paraguay, Peru, Philippines, Poland, Portugal, Romania, Russia, Saudi Arabia, Senegal, Singapore, Slovakia, Slovenia, South Africa, Spain, Sweden, Switzerland, Taiwan, Thailand, Togo, Tunisia, Türkiye, UK, Ukraine, Uruguay, USA, Venezuela, Vietnam.
Regional leagues (5):
African League of Associations for Rheumatology (AFLAR, #00360); American College of Rheumatology (ACR); *Asia Pacific League of Associations for Rheumatology (APLAR, #01945)*; *European Alliance of Associations for Rheumatology (EULAR, #05862)*; *Pan American League of Associations for Rheumatology (PANLAR, #18118)*.
Consultative Status Consultative status granted from: *ECOSOC (#05331)* (Ros C); *UNICEF (#20332)*. **NGO Relations** Member of: *NGO Committee on UNICEF (#17120)*. [2019/XB2195/y/**B**]

♦ International League of Aviators (inactive)

♦ International League of Blind Esperantists 14017

Ligue internationale des aveugles espérantistes – Ligo Internacia de Blindaj Esperantistoj (LIBE)

Sec Velika Dijivska 22-226, Dnipro, Dnipropetrovsk, 49068, Ukraine. T. +38050679578645. E-mail: amatalena@ukr.net.
URL: http://www.libe.slikom.info/

History 1951, Munich (Germany FR). **Aims** Promote the use of the international language Esperanto among the blind and *visually impaired* in their associations, institutes, libraries, printing offices, conferences, etc; enable them to study and practice through publications in braille and on cd; unite all blind and visually impaired esperantists for friendly relations; represent blind esperantists in contacts with official institutes. **Structure** Board. **Languages** Esperanto. **Staff** 7.00 FTE, voluntary. **Finance** Members' dues. Donations. **Activities** Events/meetings; training/education. **Events** *Annual Congress* Belgrade (Serbia-Montenegro) 2004, *Annual Congress* Gothenburg (Sweden) 2003, *Annual Congress* Balatonlelle (Hungary) 2002, *Annual Congress* Kraljevica (Croatia) 2001, *Annual Congress* Plovdiv (Bulgaria) 2000. **Publications** *Esperanta Ligilo* (10 a year) – in Esperanto-braille and on cd.

Members in 50 countries:
Argentina, Australia, Austria, Belarus, Belgium, Bosnia-Herzegovina, Brazil, Bulgaria, Canada, Chile, China, Croatia, Cuba, Czechia, Denmark, Estonia, Finland, France, Georgia, Germany, Hungary, India, Iran Islamic Rep, Israel, Italy, Japan, Kazakhstan, Lithuania, Luxembourg, Mexico, Moldova, Netherlands, Nicaragua, North Macedonia, Norway, Poland, Portugal, Romania, Russia, Serbia, Slovakia, Spain, Sweden, Switzerland, Tajikistan, Togo, UK, Ukraine, USA, Uzbekistan, Vietnam.
NGO Relations Affiliated member of: *Universal Esperanto Association (UEA, #20676)*. Associate member of: *European Blind Union (EBU, #06350)*. [2018.10.17/XC2210/v/**D**]

♦ International League for the Campaign Against Trachoma / see International Organization Against Trachoma (#14436)
♦ International League of Catholic Pacifists (inactive)
♦ International League for Child and Adult Education / see International League for Teaching, Education and Popular Culture (#14023)
♦ International League of Commercial Travellers and Agents (inactive)
♦ International League of Competition Law (#16478)
♦ International League of Conservation Photographers (internationally oriented national body)
♦ International League of Culture (inactive)
♦ International League for the Defence and Development of Protestantism (inactive)
♦ International League for the Defence of the Soldier (inactive)
♦ International League of Democracy Cities (unconfirmed)

♦ International League of Dermatological Societies (ILDS) 14018

Ligue internationale des sociétés dermatologiques – Liga Internacional de Sociedades Dermatológicas – Internationale Liga der Dermatologischen Gesellschaften

Exec Dir Willan House, 4 Fitzroy Square, London, W1T 5HQ, UK. Fax +442073886515. E-mail: info@ilds.org.
URL: http://web.ilds.org/

History 31 Jul 1957, Stockholm (Sweden). Founded in succession to *Permanent Committee of the International League / of Dermatological Societies / – Comité permanent de la Ligue internationale / des sociétés dermatologiques/*, set up 1935, Budapest (Hungary), the first Congress having been held 1889, Paris (France). Rules and Regulations adopted at 11th Congress, 1957, Stockholm, and revised at each subsequent Congress. New Bylaws adopted at 17th Congress, 1987, Berlin West (Germany FR) and at 18th Congress, 1992, New York NY (USA). Bylaws revised 2 Jul 2002, Paris. Registration: Companies House, No/ID: 05466148, Start date: 27 May 2005, England and Wales; Charity Commission, No/ID: 1111469, England and Wales. **Aims** Encourage worldwide advancement of dermatological education, care and science; stimulate cooperation among societies of dermatology and societies interested in all fields of cutaneous medicine and biology worldwide; promote personal and professional relations among dermatologists; represent dermatology in commissions and international health organizations. **Structure** Assembly of National Delegates elects 12 members of *International Committee of Dermatology (ICD)*, which functions as Executive Committee, comprises President, Secretary-General, Treasurer, 7 additional members and 4 ex-officio members. Organizing Committee (responsible for the organization of the next Congress). Includes *International Foundation for Dermatology (IFD, #13668)*, which is responsible for *Regional Dermatology Training Centre (RDTC)*. **Languages** English, French, German, Spanish. **Staff** 0.50 FTE, paid. **Finance** Contributions from national societies pro rata to membership. **Activities** Awards/prizes/competitions; awareness raising; events/meetings; financial and/or material support; projects/programmes. **Events** *World Congress* Singapore (Singapore) 2023, *World Congress* Milan (Italy) 2019, *Quadrennial Congress* Vancouver, BC (Canada) 2015, *Quadrennial congress / World Congress* Seoul (Korea Rep) 2011, *Quinquennial congress / World Congress* Buenos Aires (Argentina) 2007. **Publications** *International League of Dermatological Societies Newsletter* (annual); *Dermatology International* – jointly with IFD; *News from the International Committee for Dermatology*. *Manual of the International League of Dermatological Societies*. Congress proceedings.

Members Regular; Affiliated Societies. Members in 90 countries and territories:
Algeria, Angola, Argentina, Australia, Austria, Bangladesh, Belarus, Belgium, Bolivia, Brazil, Bulgaria, Canada, Chile, China, Colombia, Congo Brazzaville, Croatia, Cyprus, Czechia, Denmark, Dominican Rep, Ecuador, Egypt, El Salvador, Finland, France, Georgia, Germany, Greece, Guatemala, Honduras, Hong Kong, Hungary, Iceland, India, Indonesia, Iran Islamic Rep, Ireland, Israel, Italy, Japan, Jordan, Kazakhstan, Korea Rep, Kuwait, Latvia, Lebanon, Libya, Malaysia, Malta, Mauritania, Mauritius, Mexico, Morocco, Netherlands, New Zealand, Nigeria, Norway, Pakistan, Palestine, Panama, Paraguay, Peru, Philippines, Poland, Portugal, Romania, Russia, Saudi Arabia, Serbia, Singapore, Slovakia, South Africa, Spain, Sri Lanka, Sudan, Sweden, Switzerland, Syrian AR, Taiwan, Tanzania UR, Thailand, Tunisia, Türkiye, UK, Ukraine, Uruguay, USA, Uzbekistan, Venezuela.

- *African Association of Dermatology (AFRAD, no recent information)*;
- *African Dermatovenereology Officers Association (ADVOA)*;
- *African Society of Dermatology and Venerology (ASDV, #00460)*;
- *Arab Academy of Dermatology and Aesthetics (AADA)*;
- *Asian Academy of Dermatology and Venereology (AADV)*;
- *Asian Dermatological Association (ADA, #01421)*;
- *Asian Society of Dermatopathology (ASD, #01717)*;
- *Association des dermatologistes francophones (#02469)*;
- *Australasian College of Dermatologists*;
- *Caribbean Dermatology Association (CDA, #03490)*;
- *Colegio Ibero-Latinoamericano de Dermatologia (CILAD, #04093)*;
- *Dermatology, Aesthetics, and Surgery International League (DASIL, #05040)*;
- *European Academy of Dermatology and Venereology (EADV, #05788)*;
- *European Board of Dermatology and Venereology (EBDV, #06358)*;
- *European Dermatology Forum (EDF, #06907)*;
- *European Hidradenitis Suppurativa Foundation (EHSF, #07482)*;
- *European Society for Cosmetic and Aesthetic Dermatology (ESCAD, #08570)*;
- *European Society for Dermatological Research (ESDR, #08578)*;
- *European Society for Dermatology and Psychiatry (ESDaP, #08579)*;
- *European Society for Lasers and Energy Based Devices (ESLD, #08640)*;
- *European Society for Pediatric Dermatology (ESPD, #08691)*;
- *European Society for Photodermatology (ESPD, #08703)*;
- *European Society of Contact Dermatitis (ESCD, #08567)*;
- *International Academy of Cosmetic Dermatology (IACD, #11542)*;
- *International Committee for Dermatopathology (ICDP, #12762)*;
- *International Dermoscopy Society (IDS, #13151)*;
- *International Eczema Council (IEC, #13227)*;
- *International immunosuppression & Transplant Skin Cancer Collaborative (ITSCC)*;
- *International Peeling Society (IPS, #14550)*;
- *International Psoriasis Council (IPC, #14661)*;
- *International Society for Biophysics and Imaging of Skin (ISBS, #14971)*;
- *International Society for Cutaneous Lymphomas (ISCL, #15044)*;
- *International Society for Dermatologic Surgery (ISDS, #15047)*;
- *International Society for the Study of Itch (IFSI, #15478)*;
- *International Society of Dermatology (ISD, #15048)*;
- *International Society of Dermatopathology (ISDP, #15049)*;
- *International Society of Pediatric Dermatology (ISPD, #15345)*;
- *International Society of Teledermatology (ISTD, #15503)*;
- *International Trichoscopy Society (#15732)*;
- *International Union against Sexually Transmitted Infections (IUSTI, #15751)*;
- *League of Dermatologists in the GCC States (#16422)*;
- *Nordic Dermatology Association (NDA, #17269)*;
- *Pan Arab League of Dermatology (#18148)*;
- *Sociedad Latinoamericana de Dermatologia Pediátrica (SLADP, inactive)*;
- *Société francophone de dermatologie psychosomatique (SFDPS, #19467)*;
- *Society for Cutaneous Ultrastructure Research (SCUR, #19540)*;
- *South Asian Regional Association of Dermatologists, Venereologists and Leprologists (SARAD, #19739)*.

[2021/XB2213/y/**B**]

♦ International League of Dermatopathology Societies / see International Committee for Dermatopathology (#12762)
♦ International League of Doctors for the Abolition of Vivisection / see International Doctors – ILDAV (#13186)
♦ International League of Esperantist Cooperators (inactive)
♦ International League for Esperantist Post-Office Workers (inactive)
♦ International League of Esperantist Radio Amateurs (#11524)
♦ International League of Esperantist Teachers / see ESPERANTO + EDUKADO (#05544)
♦ International League of Esperanto Instructors / see ESPERANTO + EDUKADO (#05544)
♦ International League for Family Life (inactive)

♦ International League of Humanists for Peace and Tolerance (ILH) .. 14019

Internacionalna Liga Humanista za Mir i Toleranciju

Contact address not obtained. T. +38733230825 – +38733277280. Fax +38733277285.
URL: http://www.intlh.com/

History 1974, Dubrovnik (Yugoslavia). **Aims** Resolve numerous problems related to the establishment of peace through a humanistic approach and strict respect for humanistic principles and tenets in the entire world. **Structure** General Assembly; Permanent Standing Committee of 17 up to 21 members. Officers: President; Honorary Life-Time President; Secretary General. Sub-Committees (10). **Finance** Donations; income from projects. **Activities** Sub-Committees (10): Moral; Humanism Research; Education; Technological Development and Co-existence with Natural Environment; Business-Economic Cooperation; Humanism and Order; Congresses and Conferences; Promotion of the Idea of Peace and Humanism; Protection of Children against Abuse and Violence; Protection of Health. **Events** *Conference* Hungary 2005, *Annual conference* Dubrovnik (Croatia) 1999, *Conference on protection of children from abuse and violence / Conference* Dubrovnik (Croatia) 1999, *Strategy of pharmacy industry for 21st century* Sarajevo (Bosnia-Herzegovina) 1999, *International congress of humanist unity / World Congress* Sarajevo (Bosnia-Herzegovina) 1998. **NGO Relations** Set up: *International Peace Centre, Sarajevo (IPC)*. [2008/XF5805/**F**]

♦ International League for Modern Gymnastics (inactive)
♦ International League of Mothers and Women Teachers for the Promotion of Peace (inactive)

♦ International League of Non-Believers and Atheists / see International League of Non-Religious and Atheists (#14020)

♦ International League of Non-Religious and Atheists (ILNA) 14020

Ligue internationale des non-religieux et des athées – Internationaler Bund der Konfessionslosen und Atheisten (IBKA)

Secretariat Tilsiter Strasse 3, 51491 Overath, Germany. T. +4922068673261. E-mail: info@ibka.org.
General: http://www.ibka.org/

History 1972, as Bund der Konfessionslosen Berlin (Germany). Also referred to as *International League of Non-Believers and Atheists*. Statutes most recently amended, 1999. Registered in accordance with German law. **Aims** Assert universal human rights – in particular the freedom of thought and religion, and separation of religion and state; advocate for individual self-determination; promote rational thinking; inform about the social role of religion. **Structure** Annual Meeting; Board; Scientific Advisory Board; Council. **Languages** English, German. **Staff** 6.00 FTE, voluntary. **Finance** Members' dues. Donations. **Activities** Projects/programmes; awards/prizes/competitions; advocacy/lobbying/activism. **Events** *Annual Congress* Bad Homburg (Germany) 2015, *Annual Congress* Oberwesel (Germany) 2014, *Annual Congress* Cologne (Germany) 2013, *Annual Congress* Hannover (Germany) 2012, *Annual Congress* Cologne (Germany) 2011. **Publications** *Materialien und Informationen zur Zeit (MIZ)* (4 a year) in German – magazine; *IBKA Rundbrief* (2 a year). *Politischer Leitfaden* (2005) – charter statement. Books; brochures.

Members Individuals in 14 countries:
Austria, Brazil, Germany, Hungary, India, Israel, Italy, Luxembourg, Netherlands, South Africa, Sweden, Switzerland, Türkiye, USA.

NGO Relations Member of: *Atheist Alliance International (AAI, #03003)*; national organizations.
[2018.10.05/XD1645/v/**D**]

♦ International League of Peace and Liberty (inactive)

♦ International League of Peoples' Struggle (ILPS) 14021

Ligue internationale de luttes des peuples – Liga Internacional de Lucha de los Pueblos – Internationale Bund des Kampfes der Völker

Chairman P.O. Box 23402, Docklands, Melbourne VIC 8012, Australia. E-mail: officeofthechair@ilps.info – gensec@ilps.info.
URL: http://ilps.info/

History 27 May 2001, Zutphen (Netherlands). Officially launched at founding Assembly. **Aims** As an anti-imperialist and democratic formation, promote, support and develop the anti-imperialist and democratic struggles of the people of the world. **Structure** International Assembly (every 3 years); International Coordinating Committee; International Coordinating Group; General Secretariat; Global Regional Committees; National Chapters. **Languages** English, French, Spanish. **Staff** 4.00 FTE, paid. **Finance** Sources: contributions; meeting proceeds; members' dues; sale of publications. **Activities** Events/meetings; projects/programmes. **Events** *International Meeting of Native Indigenous Peoples of Guatemala and Latin America* Cobán (Guatemala) 2019, *Assembly* Hong Kong (Hong Kong) 2019, *Assembly* Quezon City (Philippines) 2015, *Assembly* Manila (Philippines) 2011, *Assembly* Hong Kong (Hong Kong) 2008. **Publications** *Documents of the International Assembly* (6th ed). Reports; speeches; general declaration and resolutions; articles; press statements.

Members Organizations (over 350) in 45 countries and territories:
Argentina, Australia, Austria, Bangladesh, Belgium, Canada, Denmark, Dominican Rep, Ecuador, France, Germany, Greece, Guatemala, Hong Kong, India, Indonesia, Italy, Japan, Kenya, Korea Rep, Kurdish area, Luxembourg, Macau, Malaysia, Mexico, Nepal, Netherlands, New Zealand, Norway, Pakistan, Palestine, Peru, Philippines, Senegal, Spain, Sri Lanka, Switzerland, Taiwan, Tanzania UR, Thailand, Türkiye, UK, United Arab Emirates, USA, Venezuela. [2020.05.04/XF6404/**F**]

♦ International League for the Protection of the Hand (inactive)
♦ International League for the Protection of Horses / see World Horse Welfare
♦ International League for the Protection of Native Races-Coloured Races (inactive)
♦ International League for the Rational Education of Children (inactive)

♦ International League of Religious Socialists (ILRS) 14022

Fédération internationale des socialistes religieux – Liga Internacional de Socialistas Religiosos – Internationaler Bund Religiöser Sozialisten

Pres c/o Partido Socialista Obrero Español – PSOE, Calle de Ferraz, 70, 28008 Madrid, Spain. E-mail: ilrs@ilrs.net.
URL: https://ilrs.net/

History 1922, Switzerland. 1922, Bad Eptingen (Switzerland), as *International Union of Religious Socialists – Union internationale des socialistes religieux*. Reorganized 1938. **Aims** Represent over 200,000 socialists of different faiths in the world's socialist, social democratic and labour parties. **Structure** Representative Assembly (every 3 years); Executive Committee. Meetings closed. **Languages** English, French, German, Spanish. **Staff** 1.00 FTE, paid. **Finance** Members' dues. **Activities** Events/meetings; politics/policy/regulatory. **Events** *Congress* Helsinki (Finland) 2022, *Congress* Utrecht (Netherlands) 2018, *Congress* Córdoba (Spain) 2009, *Social globalisation* Oslo (Norway) 2006, *Congress* Lucerne (Switzerland) 2003. **Publications** *Faith* (4 a year) – newsletter.

Members National associations representing 217,500 members in 21 countries:
Australia, Austria, Denmark, Dominican Rep, Estonia, Finland, Germany, Hungary, Italy, Latvia, Lithuania, Netherlands, Norway, Philippines, South Africa, Spain, Sri Lanka, Sweden, Switzerland, UK, USA.

NGO Relations Associate member of: *Socialist International (SI, #19340)*; *Socialist International Women (SIW, #19341)*. [2022/XD2220/**D**]

♦ International League of Societies for the Mentally Handicapped / see Inclusion International (#11145)
♦ International League of Societies for Persons with Mental Handicap / see Inclusion International (#11145)
♦ International League of Stamp Dealers (inactive)

♦ International League for Teaching, Education and Popular Culture (ILFCAAE) 14023

Ligue internationale de l'enseignement, de l'éducation et de la culture populaire (LIEECP) – Liga Internacional de la Enseñanza, de la Educación y de la Cultura Popular – Internationale Liga für Unterricht, Erziehung und Volksbildung – Lega Internazionale dell'Insegnamento, dell'Educazione e della Cultura Popolare – Liga Internacionais do Ensino e da Educação Permanente

Contact c/o Ligue française, Centre Confédéral, 3 rue Récamier, 75007 Paris CEDEX 07, France. T. +33143589500. E-mail: informations@laligue.org.
Admin Office 21 rue Saint-Fargeau, 75989 Paris CEDEX 20, France.
URL: http://laligue.org/

History 1947, Paris (France). Founded following a French national organization having been founded, 1889, in response to the centenary of the French Revolution.Statutes modified: 1957; 1985. Former names and other names: *International League for Child and Adult Education* – alias. Registration: Start date: 19 Mar 1948, France. **Aims** In a spirit of secular *humanism*, opposed to clericalism, and with a view to developing the individual's humanity and citizenship: promote continuing public education in every country; bring together national organizations whose object is respect of freedom of conscience, the principle of free discussion and the democratic ideal; assist in the foundation, development and expansion of institutions and groups which pursue the same ideal through teaching, education and cultural activities. **Structure** General Assembly (annual). Executive Committee, consisting of President, 3 Regional Vice-Presidents, Secretary General, Assistant Secretary General, Treasurer, Assistant Treasurer and other officers as necessary. Meetings closed. International Office. **Languages** English, French. **Staff** Voluntary. **Finance** Members' dues (graded). Other sources: subventions from public and intergovernmental organizations. **Activities** Advocacy/lobbying/activism; research/documentation; training/education. **Events** *Meeting* Paris (France) 2007, *Meeting* Luxembourg (Luxembourg) 2005, *Meeting* Lyon (France) 2004, *Meeting* Bordeaux (France) 2001, *Seminar* Nancy (France) 1998. **Publications** Information brochures in French, English, German, Spanish.

Members National associations in 21 countries and territories:
Austria, Belgium, Benin, Bolivia, Burkina Faso, Cameroon, Côte d'Ivoire, France, Germany, India, Luxembourg, Mexico, Niger, Poland, Québec, Romania, Rwanda, Senegal, Spain, Togo, Uruguay.

Individuals in 20 countries:
Argentina, Austria, Brazil, Central African Rep, Colombia, Congo Brazzaville, Congo DR, Ecuador, Equatorial Guinea, Hungary, Italy, Netherlands, Peru, Portugal, Russia, Sierra Leone, Tunisia, Türkiye, USA, Venezuela.

Consultative Status Consultative status granted from: *Council of Europe (CE, #04881)* (Participatory Status). **IGO Relations** *OECD (#17693)*. **NGO Relations** Member of: *Union des organisations internationales non-gouvernementales établies en France (UOIF, inactive)*. [2018/XC2198/**C**]

♦ International League of Tenants / see International Union of Tenants (#15822)
♦ International League of Women Composers (inactive)
♦ International League of Youth (inactive)
♦ International Learning Cooperative / see Stiftelsen IMTEC (#19988)
♦ International Learning Exchange in Social Education (internationally oriented national body)
♦ International Learning Exchange in Social Pedagogy / see International Learning Exchange in Social Education
♦ International Learning Styles Center (internationally oriented national body)
♦ International Learning Styles Network (internationally oriented national body)
♦ International LED-UV Association (unconfirmed)
♦ International Legal Aid Association (inactive)

♦ International Legal Aid Group (ILAG) 14024

Chair Law School – Univ of Strathclyde, Level 7 – Graham Hills Bldg, 50 George Street, Glasgow, G1 1BA, UK. T. +441415483341.
Events – Conference Coordinator address not obtained.
URL: http://internationallegalaidgroup.org/

Aims Improve evidence-based policy-making in the field of *poverty* legal services through discussion and dialogue relating to international developments in policy and research. **Structure** International Steering Committee. **Activities** Events/meetings. **Events** *New approaches to legal services – technology, innovation and self help and cooperation* Edinburgh (UK) 2015, *Conference* The Hague (Netherlands) 2013, *Conference* The Hague (Netherlands) 2013, *Conference* Helsinki (Finland) 2011, *Conference* Wellington (New Zealand) 2009. **Publications** *ILAG/JUSTICE Newsletter*. [2017/XJ5390/**F**]

♦ International Legal Assistance Consortium (ILAC) 14025

Exec Dir Signalistgatan 9, SE-169 72 Solna, Sweden. T. +46854571423 – +46854571420. E-mail: info@ilac.se.
URL: http://www.ilacnet.org/

History Dec 2000, Stockholm (Sweden), as an umbrella organization. **Aims** Facilitate and assist efforts to improve access to quality justice institutions when a country is either post-conflict, in conflict, or in transition toward peace and democracy. **Structure** Board; Permanant Headquarters in Stockholm (Sweden); Branch Office in Tunis (Tunisia). **Languages** English. **Staff** 15.00 FTE, paid. **Finance** Funding from: Government of Sweden; other governments; foundations. **Activities** Guidance/assistance/consulting; capacity building; projects/programmes; awards/prizes/competitions; events/meetings. Active in: Central African Rep, Guatemala, Libya, Syrian AR, Tunisia. **Events** *Annual General Meeting* Stockholm (Sweden) 2018, *Annual General Meeting* Stockholm (Sweden) 2012.

Members Organizations in 29 countries and territories:
Belgium, Botswana, Canada, Czechia, Denmark, Egypt, England, Finland, France, Germany, Grenada, Hong Kong, India, Ireland, Italy, Japan, Malaysia, Nepal, Netherlands, North Macedonia, Norway, Palestine, Scotland, South Africa, Sweden, Switzerland, Tanzania UR, Tunisia, USA.

Included in the above, 23 organizations listed in this Yearbook:
- *Arab Lawyers' Union (ALU, #01002)*;
- *Arab Organization for Human Rights (AOHR, #01020)*;
- *Central and Eastern European Law Initiative (CEELI, #03693)*;
- *Commonwealth Lawyers Association (CLA, #04345)*;
- *Council of Bars and Law Societies of Europe (CCBE, #04871)*;
- *Inter-American Bar Association (IABA, #11401)*;
- *International Association for Court Administration (IACA)*;
- *International Association of Prosecutors (IAP, #12111)*;
- *International Association of Women Judges (IAWJ, #12267)*;
- *International Association of Young Lawyers (#12282)*;
- *International Bar Association (IBA, #12320)*;
- *International Bridges to Justice*;
- *International Commission of Jurists (ICJ, #12695)*;
- *International Criminal Court Bar Association (ICCBA, #13109)*;
- *International Foundation for the Rule of Law and the Independence of Lawyers and Judges (FIDIAM)*;
- *International Human Rights Law Institute (IHRLI)*;
- *International Judicial Academy (IJA)*;
- *International Legal Foundation (ILF, #14026)*;
- *International Senior Lawyers Project (ISLP)*;
- *Pan-African Lawyers Union (PALU, #18054)*;
- *Public International Law and Policy Group (PILPG)*;
- *Raoul Wallenberg Institute of Human Rights and Humanitarian Law (RWI)*;
- *Union Internationale des Avocats (UIA, #20422)*.

NGO Relations Partner of: *International Bar Association's Human Rights Institute (IBAHRI, #12322)*. [2018/XF6212/y/**F**]

♦ International Legal Association for Conflict Prevention (no recent information)
♦ International Legal Center / see International Center for Law in Development
♦ International Legal Defense Counsel (internationally oriented national body)
♦ International Legal Forum (internationally oriented national body)

♦ International Legal Foundation (ILF) 14026

Contact 111 John St, Ste 1040, New York NY 10038, USA. T. +12126081188. E-mail: info@theilf.org.
URL: http://theilf.org/

History 2001. **Aims** Assist post-*conflict* and transitional countries to establish public defender systems that provide effective, quality criminal defence services for the *poor*. **Structure** Board of Directors; Advisory Board. **Activities** Advocacy/lobbying/activism; capacity building; politics/policy/regulatory; projects/programmes; publishing activities; research/documentation; training/education. **Consultative Status** Consultative status granted from: *ECOSOC (#05331)* (Special). **NGO Relations** Partner of: *Global Forum on Law, Justice and Development (GFLJD, #10373)*. Member of: *International Legal Assistance Consortium (ILAC, #14025)*. [2016.06.01/XJ9781/f/**F**]

♦ International Legal Fraternity Phi Delta Phi / see Phi Delta Phi International Legal Fraternity
♦ International Legal Institute for the Protection of Animals (inactive)
♦ International Legal Union (inactive)
♦ International Legislative Support Services Association (no recent information)

♦ International Legume Society (ILS) 14027

Pres address not obtained.
Treas address not obtained.
URL: https://www.legumesociety.org/

History 2011. **Aims** Become the main hub of information and exchange on legume research and exploitation worldwide, linking together different aspects of agricultural research on the genetic improvement, agronomy and utilization of grain and forage legumes from the Old World and the Americas. **Structure** Scientific Committee; Executive Committee. **Activities** Events/meetings; publishing activities. **Events** *Conference* Granada (Spain) 2023, *Conference* Granada (Spain) 2022, *Conference* Poznań (Poland) 2019, *Conference* Troia (Portugal) 2016, *Conference* Novi Sad (Serbia) 2013. **Publications** *Legume Perspectives* (4 a year). Webinars [2023.02.14/XM5562/**D**]

♦ International Leksell Gamma Knife Society 14028

Chairman PO Box 7572, SE-103 93 Stockholm, Sweden. T. +46858725797. Fax +46858725500. E-mail: dl@lgksociety.com – info@lgksociety.com.
URL: http://www.lgksociety.com/

History Founded 1989, by Dr Dan Leksell, son of the inventor of non-invasive stereotactic radiosurgery. Registered in accordance with Swedish law. **Aims** Foster international collaboration and learning; increase scientific foundation of radiosurgery; further define and expand the role of radiosurgery in the treatment of *intracranial* disorders; make radiosurgery available to more patients worldwide. **Structure** Board. **Staff** 4.00 FTE, paid. **Activities** Training/education; events/meetings; financial and/or material support. **Events** *Asian Meeting* Sendai (Japan) 2019, *Meeting* Dubai (United Arab Emirates) 2018, *Asian Meeting* Jeju (Korea Rep) 2017, *Meeting* Amsterdam (Netherlands) 2016, *Giving it your best shot* New York, NY (USA) 2014. **Members** About 2,000 neuroscientists, neurosurgeons, radiation oncologists, medical physicists as well as several other specialties worldwide. Membership countries not specified. [2018/XM3136/**E**]

♦ International Leprosy Association (ILA) 14029

Association internationale contre la lèpre – Asociación Internacional de la Lepra

Pres 03 BP 1463, Cotonou, Benin. T. +22921307843. E-mail: ila@ilsl.com.
Sec/Treas address not obtained.
URL: http://www.leprosy-ila.org/

History Jan 1931, Manila (Philippines). Founded following 3 congresses in 1897, 1909, 1923, organized by *International Committee of Leprologists*. Constitution and By-Laws revised: 1932; 1935; 1948; 1953; 1963; 1978; 1988; 2002. **Aims** Encourage collaboration between persons of all nationalities concerned in leprosy work; facilitate dissemination of knowledge of leprosy and its control; help in any other practicable manner the anti-leprosy campaign throughout the world; cooperate with any other institution or organization concerned with leprosy. **Structure** Officers: President; Immediate Past President; Secretary; Treasurer; Vice-Presidents (4), one each from Africa, Americas, Asia and Europe; Editor of the Journal. Council, consisting of Officers and 15 elected Members selected on the basis of geographic representation. Officers and Council members elected for 5 years. **Languages** English, French, Spanish. **Finance** Sources: donations; members' dues; sale of publications. **Activities** Holds frequent international meetings of experts; representatives participate in regional leprosy campaigns; organizes world congresses. **Events** *International Leprosy Congress* Hyderabad (India) 2022, *International Leprosy Congress* Pasay City (Philippines) 2019, *Triennial Congress* Beijing (China) 2016, *Quinquennial Congress* Brussels (Belgium) 2013, *Quinquennial Congress* Hyderabad (India) 2008. **Publications** *ILA Forum* (4 a year) in English; *International Journal of Leprosy and Other Mycobacterial Diseases* (4 a year) in English, French, Spanish – ILA official organ.
Members Regular; Sustaining; Grantors; Honorary. Individuals in 59 countries and territories:
Argentina, Armenia, Australia, Bangladesh, Belgium, Benin, Brazil, Cambodia, Canada, Central African Rep, China, Comoros, Congo DR, Egypt, Ethiopia, France, Germany, India, Indonesia, Iran Islamic Rep, Ireland, Israel, Japan, Kenya, Korea Rep, Laos, Malawi, Mali, Mexico, Morocco, Mozambique, Myanmar, Nepal, Netherlands, Nigeria, Norway, Pakistan, Paraguay, Philippines, Poland, Russia, Sao Tomé-Principe, Singapore, South Africa, Spain, Sudan, Suriname, Sweden, Switzerland, Taiwan, Tanzania UR, Türkiye, Uganda, UK, United Arab Emirates, USA, Vietnam, Yemen, Zimbabwe.
Consultative Status Consultative status granted from: *ECOSOC (#05331)* (Ros C); *WHO (#20950)* (Official Relations). **IGO Relations** Accredited by: *United Nations Office at Vienna (UNOV, #20604)*. **NGO Relations** Founder member of: *Council for International Organizations of Medical Sciences (CIOMS, #04905)*. Member of: *International Union Against Tuberculosis and Lung Disease (The Union, #15752)*. [2019/XB2224/v/**B**]

♦ International Leprosy Union (ILU) 14030

Main Office c/o CASP Bhavan, Sr No 132/2, Plot No 3, Pashan-Baner Link Road, Pune, Maharashtra 411 021, Pune MAHARASHTRA 411 021, India. T. +912032317932 – +9120(919823196070. E-mail: ilupune@gmail.com.
URL: http://ilu.org.in/

History Sep 1986. Registered in accordance with Indian law. **Aims** Highlight issues such as *prevention of disability, integrated rehabilitation*, full coverage by *multi-drug therapy* (MDT), provision of *corrective surgery* and vocational training. **Structure** General Body (meets annually). Officers: President, Chairman, 6 Vice Presidents, 2 Secretaries and Honorary Secretary/Executive Director. Managing Committee. **Finance** Members' dues. Other sources: donations. **Activities** Training and exchange programmes; meetings; seminars and workshops at national and international levels in various countries. Research activities. Special programmes to: teach patients to avoid deformity and disability; educate them to take special care of their hands, feet and eyes; develop integrated rehabilitation, both physical and economic on CBR principles, without uprooting the patients from their social and family life; solve the special problem of children in the shadow of leprosy, though supportive services and provision of rehabilitation services. Awards the *'International Leprosy Awards'*. **Publications** *ILU Newsletter* (periodical). Country reports; technical papers; books.
Members Voluntary agencies; Government agencies; International agencies; Individuals. Organizations in 9 countries:
Belgium, Brazil, Canada, Eswatini, Germany, India, Japan, Malaysia, Sri Lanka.
Individuals in 22 countries:
Argentina, Australia, Belgium, Brazil, Canada, China, Congo DR, Eswatini, Germany, Ghana, Indonesia, Japan, Korea Rep, Malaysia, Nepal, Pakistan, Sri Lanka, Tanzania UR, Thailand, Türkiye, UK, Vietnam. [2014/XF4202/**F**]

♦ International Leptospirosis Society (ILS) 14031

Adjunct Sec School of Veterinary Science, Massey Univ, Priv Bag 11222, Palmerston North 4442, New Zealand. T. +6469518143. E-mail: leptosociety@gmail.com.
Pres address not obtained.
URL: https://leptosociety.org/

History 1994. **Aims** Promote knowledge on leptospirosis through the organization of regional and global leptospirosis meetings. **Structure** Executive, comprising President, Secretary, Adjunct Secretary and 8 members. **Events** *Scientific Meeting* Bangkok (Thailand) 2022, *Scientific Meeting* Bangkok (Thailand) 2021, *Scientific Meeting* Vancouver, BC (Canada) 2019, *Scientific Meeting* Palmerston North (New Zealand) 2017, *Scientific Meeting* Semarang (Indonesia) 2015. **Members** Over 700 worldwide. Membership countries not specified. **NGO Relations** *European Leptospirosis Society (ELS, #07682)*. [2022/XJ4544/**C**]

♦ International Lesbian and Gay Association / see ILGA World (#11120)

♦ International Lesbian, Gay, Bisexual, Transgender, Queer and Intersex Youth and Student Organization (IGLYO) 14032

Organisation internationale de jeunes et étudiants LGBTQI

Communications Officer IGLYO Secretariat, Chaussée de Boondael 6, 1050 Brussels, Belgium. E-mail: managers@iglyo.com.
Exec Dir address not obtained.
URL: http://www.iglyo.com/

History 1986, Oslo (Norway). Founded at 3rd International Gay Youth Congress, a 1st Congress having been held 1984, Amsterdam (Netherlands), and an *International Gay Youth Information Pool (IGYIP)* having been organized following 2nd Congress, 1985, Dublin (Ireland). Former names and other names: *International Gay and Lesbian Youth Organization* – former (1986); *International Lesbian and Gay Youth Organization (IGLYO)* – former; *Organisation internationale de la jeunesse homosexuelle et lesbienne* – former; *International Lesbian, Gay, Bisexual, Transgender and Queer Youth and Student Organization (IGLYO)* – former; *Organisation internationale de jeunes et étudiants LGBTQ* – former; *International LGBTQI Youth and Student Organisation (IGLYO)* – alias. Registration: Banque-Carrefour des Enterprises, No/ID: 0808.808.665, Start date: 21 Nov 2008, Belgium; EU Transparency Register, No/ID: 394013515467-95, Start date: 28 Jan 2015. **Aims** Combat discrimination against lesbian, gay, bisexual, transgender, queer and intersex youth and students; promote and support their emancipation; support partnership, cooperation and joint strategies on regional, national and international levels. **Structure** Annual Members' Conference; Executive Board; Secretariat. **Languages** English. **Staff** 9.00 FTE, paid. **Finance** Supported by: Dutch Ministry for Education; *European Commission (EC, #06633)*; *European Youth Foundation (EYF, #09141)*; *UNESCO (#20322)*. **Activities** Advocacy/lobbying/activism; events/meetings; knowledge management/information dissemination; networking/liaising; politics/policy/regulatory; research/documentation; training/education. **Events** *Conference* Brussels (Belgium) 2020, *Conference* Helsinki (Finland) 2019, *Conference* Copenhagen (Denmark) 2013, *General Assembly* Copenhagen (Denmark) 2013, *General Assembly* Mykolayiv, Mykolaiv (Ukraine) 2012. **Publications** *LGBTQI Inclusive Education Index* (2017). Toolkits; guidelines; guides; analyses.
Members Lesbian, gay, bisexual, transgender, queer and intersex youth and/or student groups (over 95) in 41 countries:
Albania, Armenia, Austria, Azerbaijan, Belgium, Bosnia-Herzegovina, Bulgaria, Croatia, Cyprus, Czechia, Denmark, Estonia, Finland, France, Georgia, Germany, Greece, Hungary, Iceland, Ireland, Italy, Latvia, Lithuania, Malta, Moldova, Montenegro, Netherlands, Norway, Poland, Portugal, Romania, Russia, Serbia, Slovakia, Slovenia, Spain, Sweden, Switzerland, Türkiye, UK, Ukraine.
Consultative Status Consultative status granted from: *UNESCO (#20322)* (Consultative Status). **IGO Relations** Cooperates with (1): *Council of Europe (CE, #04881)* (Directorate of Youth and Sport). Participant in Fundamental Rights Platform of: *European Union Agency for Fundamental Rights (FRA, #08969)*. **NGO Relations** Member of (5): *European Students' Union (ESU, #08848)* (Associate); *European Youth Forum (#09140)* (Full); *ILGA-Europe (#11118)* (Full); *ILGA World (International Lesbian, Gay, Bisexual, Trans and Intersex Association, #11120)* (Full); *Social Platform (#19344)*. Participates in: *HIV Young Leaders Fund (HYLF, no recent information)*. Cooperates with: *Organising Bureau of European School Student Unions (OBESSU, #17829)*. [2021.06.16/XD1099/**C**]

♦ International Lesbian, Gay, Bisexual, Transgender and Queer Youth and Student Organization / see International Lesbian, Gay, Bisexual, Transgender, Queer and Intersex Youth and Student Organization (#14032)
♦ **International Lesbian, Gay, Bisexual, Trans and Intersex Association** ILGA World (#11120)
♦ International Lesbian and Gay Youth Organization / see International Lesbian, Gay, Bisexual, Transgender, Queer and Intersex Youth and Student Organization (#14032)
♦ International Leucocyte Culture Conference (meeting series)

♦ International Lexical Functional Grammar Association (ILFGA) 14033

Sec-Treas The Oriental Institute, University of Oxford, Pusey Lane, Oxford, OX1 2LE, UK.
URL: https://ling.sprachwiss.uni-konstanz.de/pages/home/lfg/ilfga/index.html

History 1997. Registration: USA. **Aims** Advance lexical-functional grammar-based (LFG) approaches for scientific study of language. **Structure** Executive Committee. **Activities** Events/meetings. **Events** *International Lexical Functional Grammar Conference (LFG22)* Groningen (Netherlands) 2022, *International Lexical-Functional Grammar Conference* 2021, *Annual Conference* Oslo (Norway) 2020, *Annual Conference* Canberra, ACT (Australia) 2019, *Annual Conference* Vienna (Austria) 2018. **Publications** *LFG Bulletin* (4 a year) – electronic. *LFG Online Proceedings*. **Members** Full in 41 countries. Membership countries not specified. [2021/XN9260/**D**]

♦ International LGBTQI Youth and Student Organisation / see International Lesbian, Gay, Bisexual, Transgender, Queer and Intersex Youth and Student Organization (#14032)

♦ International Liaison Centre for Agricultural Machinery Distributors and Maintenance 14034

Centre de Liaison International des Marchands de Machines Agricoles et des Réparateurs (CLIMMAR)

SG p/a FEDECOM, Einsteinbaan 1, 3439 NJ Nieuwegein, Netherlands. T. +31306049111. Fax +31306053208. E-mail: info@climmar.com.
URL: http://www.climmar.com/

History 28 Nov 1953, Paris (France). **Aims** Cover common interests and exchange information in the field of agricultural machinery distribution and maintenance. **Structure** General Assembly; Presidency; Secretary General. Working Groups. **Languages** English. **Staff** 1.00 FTE, paid. **Finance** Members' dues. **Activities** Events/meetings; knowledge management/information dissemination; publishing activities; monitoring/evaluation; advocacy/lobbying/activism. **Events** *Annual Spring Meeting* Brussels (Belgium) 2022, *Congress* Budapest (Hungary) 2022, *Annual Spring Meeting* Nieuwegein (Netherlands) 2021, *Annual Spring Meeting* Gdansk (Poland) 2020, *Congress* Thun (Switzerland) 2019. **Publications** *CLIMMAR Index* (2 a year); *CLIMMAR Branch Reports* (annual); *Dealer Satisfaction Index (DSI)* (annual); *Annual CLIMMAR Magazine/Report of Activities*; *CLIMMAR Newsletter*.
Members Associations in 16 countries:
Austria, Belgium, Czechia, Denmark, France, Germany, Hungary, Italy, Latvia, Luxembourg, Netherlands, Portugal, Slovakia, Sweden, Switzerland, UK.
NGO Relations Associate member of: *WorldSkills Europe (#21790)*. [2019.10.17/XD2225/**E**]

♦ International Liaison Centre for Film and Television Schools / see International Association of Cinema, Audiovisual and Media Schools (#11771)
♦ International Liaison Centre for Institutes and Associations for African Studies (inactive)
♦ International Liaison Committee on Dental Hygiene / see International Federation of Dental Hygienists (#13405)
♦ International Liaison Committee for Embroideries, Curtains and Laces (inactive)

♦ International Liaison Committee for Microcirculation 14035

Chairman Dalton Cardiovascular Research Ctr, Dept Medical Pharmacology and Physiology, Univ of Missouri-Columbia, 134 Research Park Drive, Columbia MO 65211, USA. T. +15738829662. Fax +15738844232.

History 1979. Founded as a semi-official body. Former names and other names: *International Liaison Committee for Microcirculation* – former. **Aims** Choose the sites of World Congress for Microcirculation and develop guidelines for their structure and content; stimulate cooperation among international microcirculation and allied societies. **Structure** Committee. **Languages** English. **Staff** None. **Finance** No budget. **Events** *World Congress of Microcirculation* Beijing (China) 2023, *World Congress for Microcirculation* Beijing (China) 2022, *World Congress for Microcirculation* Vancouver, BC (Canada) 2018, *World Congress for Microcirculation* Kyoto (Japan) 2015, *World Congress for Microcirculation* Paris (France) 2010.
Members Individuals (11) in 10 countries:
Australia, China, France, Hungary, Japan, Netherlands, New Zealand, Thailand, UK, USA. [2023/XF1128/cv/**E**]

♦ International Liaison Committee of Organizations for Peace / see International Peace Bureau (#14535)
♦ International Liaison Committee for Peace Foundation (see: #14535)
♦ International Liaison Committee of Peace Societies / see International Peace Bureau (#14535)
♦ International Liaison Committee of Professional Organizations of Gynaecologists and Obstetricians / see Union professionnelle internationale des gynécologues et obstétriciens (#20473)

♦ International Liaison Committee on Resuscitation (ILCOR) 14036

Consejo mundial de Enlace sobre Resucitación

Sec address not obtained.
Registered Address Emile Vanderveldelaan 35, 2845 Niel, Belgium.
URL: http://www.ilcor.org/

History 1992. By-laws updated: 2005; 2018. Registration: Belgium. **Aims** Provide a forum for liaison between principal resuscitation organizations worldwide. **Structure** General Assembly. Executive Committee, including Executive Officers (2 Co-Chairs, Honorary Secretary and Honorary Treasurer). Task Forces. **Events** *International Resuscitation Science Symposium* Singapore (Singapore) 2016, *International Consensus Conference* Dallas, TX (USA) 2015, *Meeting* Vienna (Austria) 2012, *Meeting* Orlando, FL (USA) 2011, *International consensus conference* Dallas, TX (USA) 2010.
Members Organizations (8) in 5 countries:
Australia, Canada, New Zealand, South Africa, USA.
Member organizations include the following 4 listed in this Yearbook:
European Resuscitation Council (ERC, #08385); *InterAmerican Heart Foundation (IAHF, #11432)*; *Resuscitation Council of Asia (RCA, #18924)*; *Resuscitation Council of Southern Africa (RCSA)*. [2021/XE2986/y/**E**]

♦ International Liaison Committee of Women's Associations (internationally oriented national body)
♦ International Liaison Conference for Producers of Electrical Energy (inactive)
♦ International Liaison for the Food Industries (inactive)
♦ International Liaison Group on Tobacco and Health (internationally oriented national body)
♦ International Library of African Music (internationally oriented national body)
♦ International Library on Earthen Architecture (internationally oriented national body)
♦ International Library and Information Group / see International Library and Information Group (#14037)

♦ **International Library and Information Group (CILIP ILIG)** **14037**
Contact 12 Ridgmount Street, London, WC1E 7AE, UK. E-mail: secretary.ilig@cilip.org.uk.
URL: http://www.cilip.org.uk/ilig/
History 1968, London (UK). One of 25 Special Interest Groups of the (UK) *Chartered Institute of Library and Information Professionals (CILIP)*. Former names and other names: *International and Comparative Librarianship Group of the Library Association (ICLG – Groupe de bibliothéconomie internationale et comparée)* – former (1968 to 1991); *International Group of the Library Association (IGLA)* – former (1991 to Apr 2002); *International Library and Information Group (ILIG)* – former (Apr 2002 to 2017). Registration: Charities Commission, No/ID: 313014, England and Wales. **Aims** Unite Chartered Institute of Library and Information Professionals (CILIP) members both in the UK and abroad who have a strong interest in international work; foster international relations within the profession; lessen professional isolation; encourage closer international understanding and contribute to the development of library and information services globally. **Structure** Committee, headed by Chair, and including Secretary and Treasurer. **Languages** English. **Staff** 12.50 FTE, voluntary. **Finance** Sources: meeting proceeds. Capitation allowance from CILIP. **Activities** Awards/prizes/competitions; events/meetings. **Events** *EIFL Power – Electronic Information for Libraries* UK 2021, *Decolonising Libray Collections and Practices – From Understanging to Impact* Cardiff (UK) 2019, *Emerging democracies and freedom of information* Oxford (UK) 1994, *Nothing to read? The crisis of document provision in the Third World* Birmingham (UK) 1989. **Publications** *Focus on International Library and Information Work* (3 a year).
Members Individual; organizational. Organizational in 25 countries and territories:
Australia, Belgium, Canada, Cayman Is, China, Cuba, Denmark, France, Germany, Hong Kong, India, Ireland, Israel, Japan, Netherlands, New Zealand, Poland, Puerto Rico, Russia, Spain, Sweden, Switzerland, Taiwan, UK, USA.
Individual in 73 countries and territories:
Antigua-Barbuda, Australia, Austria, Bahamas, Bahrain, Bangladesh, Barbados, Belgium, Botswana, Brazil, Brunei Darussalam, Cambodia, Canada, Chad, Colombia, Curaçao, Cyprus, Denmark, Egypt, Ethiopia, Finland, France, Gambia, Germany, Ghana, Greece, Honduras, Hong Kong, Iceland, India, Indonesia, Ireland, Italy, Jamaica, Japan, Jordan, Kenya, Lebanon, Luxembourg, Malaysia, Malta, Mauritius, Monaco, Namibia, Netherlands, New Caledonia, New Zealand, Nigeria, Norway, Oman, Papua New Guinea, Puerto Rico, Romania, Russia, Sierra Leone, Singapore, South Africa, Spain, Sri Lanka, Sweden, Switzerland, Taiwan, Tanzania UR, Thailand, Trinidad-Tobago, Türkiye, Uganda, UK, United Arab Emirates, USA, Virgin Is UK, Zambia, Zimbabwe.
[2020.11.18/XE2855/E]

♦ **International Library and Information Science Society (I-LISS)** **14038**
Contact Central Library, SRM Inst of Science and Technology, Kattankulathur, Kancheepuram, Tamil Nadu 603 203, Kancheepuram TAMIL NADU 603 203, India. T. +914427456274. E-mail: ilisssociety@gmail.com.
URL: http://i-liss.org/
History Founded Jun 2015, Tamil Nadu (India), *Library and Information Science Society for Asia and the Pacific (LISSAPAC)*. Current title adopted 2019. Registered in accordance with Indian law: 13 May 2016. **Aims** Promote international level library and information professional network; understand the value and services of Library and information services. **Structure** Governing Board; Executive Committee. **Finance** Members' dues. **Activities** Events/meetings. **Events** *Conference* Taipei (Taiwan) 2019, *Conference* Nonthaburi (Thailand) 2018. **Members** Full; Associate; Corporate. Membership countries not specified. [2019/XM8067/D]

♦ International Licensing, Innovation and Technology Consultants' Association (inactive)
♦ International Licensing Platform Vegetable (internationally oriented national body)
♦ International Lifeboat Federation / see International Maritime Rescue Federation (#14104)

♦ **International Lifesaving Appliance Manufacturers Association (ILAMA)** **14039**
Association internationale de fabricants d'équipements de sauvetage
Managing Exec PO Box 952, Shoreham, BN43 9EJ, UK. T. +441273454187. Fax +441273454260. E-mail: admin@ilama.org.
URL: http://www.ilama.org/
History prior to 1975. **Aims** Promote *safety* standards worldwide. **Structure** General Meeting; Technical Committees. **Languages** English. **Events** *SASMEX : safety at sea and marine electronics conference* Brighton (UK) 1996, *SASMEX : international safety at sea and marine electronics conference* London (UK) 1990.
Members Full Manufacturing companies whose products are subject to International Convention for the Safety of Life at Sea, 1974. Associate organizations; associations; other companies who meet membership criteria. Full in 18 countries:
Austria, Canada, China, Denmark, Finland, France, Germany, Greece, Italy, Japan, Korea Rep, Netherlands, Norway, Singapore, Sweden, Türkiye, UK, USA.
Consultative Status Consultative status granted from: *International Maritime Organization (IMO, #14102)*. **NGO Relations** *International Organization for Standardization (ISO, #14473)* (Category 'A' Liaison).
[2019.06.10/XD5327/D]

♦ **International Life Saving Federation (ILS)** **14040**
SG Gemeenteplein 26, 3010 Leuven, Belgium. T. +3216896060. E-mail: info@ilsf.org – hq@ilsf.org.
Events Dir address not obtained.
URL: http://www.ilsf.org/
History 24 Feb 1993, Leuven (Belgium). Founded on official signing of merger agreement between *World Life Saving (WLS, inactive)*, which had been set up 24 Mar 1971, Sydney (Australia), with *International Life-Saving Federation (FIS, inactive)*, formed 1910, Paris (France). ILS was officially constituted 3 Sep 1994, Cardiff (UK). Registration: Banque-Carrefour des Entreprises, No/ID: 0461.424.545, Start date: 18 Sep 1997. **Aims** Lead, support and collaborate with national and international organizations engaged in drowning prevention, water safety, water rescue, lifesaving, lifeguarding and lifesaving sport. **Structure** Annual General Assembly; Elective General Assembly (every 4 years); Board of Directors. Regional branches (4): African branch; *International Life Saving Federation – Americas (#14041)*; *International Life Saving Federation – Asia/Pacific (ILSAP, #14042)*; *International Life Saving Federation of Europe (ILSE, #14043)*. **Languages** English. **Staff** 2.00 FTE, paid. **Finance** Sources: international organizations; members' dues; sponsorship. Supported by: *International Olympic Committee (IOC, #14408)*. **Activities** Events/meetings; projects/programmes; sporting activities. **Events** *World Conference on Drowning Prevention* Marrakech (Morocco) 2025, *World Conference on Drowning Prevention* Colombo (Sri Lanka) 2023, *World Conference on Drowning Prevention* Durban (South Africa) 2019, *World Conference on Drowning Prevention* Vancouver, BC (Canada) 2017, *General Assembly* Eindhoven (Netherlands) 2016. **Publications** *World Drowning Report*. **Members** National lifesaving organizations (137). Membership countries not specified. **Consultative Status** Consultative status granted from: *WHO (#20950)* (Official Relations). **NGO Relations** Member of (4): *Association of the IOC Recognized International Sports Federations (ARISF, #02767)*; *Federation of European and International Associations Established in Belgium (FAIB, #09508)*; *International World Games Association (IWGA, #15914)*; *Olympic Movement (#17719)*. Cooperates with (1): *International Testing Agency (ITA, #15678)*. Recognized by: *International Federation of Red Cross and Red Crescent Societies (#13526)*; *Conseil international du sport militaire (CISM, #04695)*; *International Olympic Committee (IOC, #14408)*. Observer to the Board of Directors: *Royal Life Saving Society (RLSS, #18992)*. [2022/XC0121/y/B]

♦ International Life-Saving Federation (inactive)
♦ International Life Saving Federation of the Americas / see International Life Saving Federation – Americas (#14041)

♦ **International Life Saving Federation – Americas** **14041**
Federación Internacional de Salvamento Acuatico – Región de las Américas
SG c/o Galveston Beach Patrol, 601 Tremont St, Ste 200, Galveston TX 77550, USA.
URL: http://www.ilsamericas.org/
History 24 Feb 1993, as one of 4 world regions of *International Life Saving Federation (ILS, #14040)*. Also referred to as *International Life Saving Federation of the Americas (ILSAM)*. **Aims** Link together and support national federations of the Americas which are concerned with *safety* and the preservation of human life in the *aquatic* environment. **Structure** Regional Board, comprising President, Vice-President and Secretary. **Activities** Training/education; networking/liaising; advocacy/lobbying/activism; meeting activities. **Events** *International medical rescue conference / Conference* San Diego, CA (USA) 1997.
Members Full in 16 countries and territories:
Argentina, Bahamas, Barbados, Bermuda, Brazil, Canada, Cayman Is, Dominican Rep, Jamaica, Mexico, Peru, St Kitts-Nevis, St Lucia, Suriname, Trinidad-Tobago, Venezuela. [2016/XE2464/E]

♦ International Life Saving Federation of Asia/Oceania / see International Life Saving Federation – Asia/Pacific (#14042)

♦ **International Life Saving Federation – Asia/Pacific (ILSAP)** **14042**
Contact c/o ILS Headquarters, Gemeenteplein 26, 3010 Leuven, Belgium. T. +3216896060. E-mail: info@ilsf.org.
URL: http://www.ilsf.org/
History as a regional branch of *International Life Saving Federation (ILS, #14040)*. Previously referred to as *International Life Saving Federation of Asia/Oceania*. **Structure** Regional Board, comprising President, Secretary, and 11 members.
Members Full; Associate; Corresponding. National life saving associations in 22 countries and territories:
Australia, Bangladesh, China, Hong Kong, India, Indonesia, Iran Islamic Rep, Japan, Jordan, Korea Rep, Kuwait, Malaysia, New Zealand, Pakistan, Palestine, Philippines, Qatar, Saudi Arabia, Singapore, Sri Lanka, Taiwan, Thailand. [2016/XE2465/E]

♦ **International Life Saving Federation of Europe (ILSE)** **14043**
Secretariat Im Niedernfeld 1-3, 31542 Bad Nenndorf, Germany. T. +495723955500. Fax +495723955509. E-mail: secretariat@ilseurope.org.
Pres Rosenweg 6, 14476 Potsdam, Germany. E-mail: president@ilseurope.org.
URL: http://europe.ilsf.org/
History 2 Sep 1994, Cardiff (UK). Founded as a regional branch of *International Life Saving Federation (ILS, #14040)*. **Aims** Create, develop and support life-saving activities in and at *water*; disseminate the concept of socially useful activities aimed at strengthening every person in psycho-physical aptitude for life saving; support training of voluntary life-savers; practice life-saving in water and ashore; improve life-saving devices; popularize new methods, disaster operation/management and civil protection. **Structure** General Assembly; Regional Board. **Languages** English. **Staff** 1.00 FTE, paid; 15.00 FTE, voluntary. **Finance** Sources: members' dues. Supported by: German National Lifesaving Society. **Activities** Events/meetings; financial and/or material support; monitoring/evaluation; training/education. **Events** *General Assembly* 2021, *General Assembly* Riccione (Italy) 2020, *General Assembly* Oropesa del Mar (Spain) 2016, *Conference on Physical Culture and Sports* Bydgoszcz (Poland) 2015, *Extraordinary General Assembly* Dublin (Ireland) 2015. **Publications** *ILSE Circulars*.
Members Full: associations in 38 countries:
Albania, Austria, Belgium, Bosnia-Herzegovina, Bulgaria, Croatia, Cyprus, Czechia, Denmark, Estonia, Finland, France, Germany, Greece, Hungary, Ireland, Israel, Italy, Latvia, Lithuania, Malta, Montenegro, Netherlands, North Macedonia, Norway, Poland, Portugal, Romania, Russia, San Marino, Serbia, Slovakia, Slovenia, Spain, Sweden, Switzerland, Türkiye, UK.
Corresponding: associations in 7 countries and territories:
Faeroe Is, Great Britain, Greece, Israel, Netherlands, Romania, Ukraine.
Associate: associations in 5 countries:
Denmark, Germany, Malta, Portugal, UK.
NGO Relations Member of (2): *Global Association of International Sport Federations (GAISF, inactive)*; *International Masters Games Association (IMGA, #14117)*. [2022.11.25/XE2466/E]

♦ **International Life Sciences Institute (ILSI)** **14044**
Global Office 740 15th St NW, Ste 600, Washington DC 20005, USA. T. +12026590074. Fax +12026593859. E-mail: info@ilsi.org.
ILSI Europe Ave E Mounier 83, Box 6, 1200 Brussels, Belgium. E-mail: info@ilsieurope.be.
URL: http://www.ilsi.org/
History 1978. *ISLI Europe* founded in 1986 and registered in accordance with Belgian law. Former names and other names: *ILSI Global* – alias. Registration: 501(c)3, USA. **Aims** Advance the understanding of scientific issues relating to nutrition, food safety, toxicology, risk assessment, and the environment; provide the scientific basis for regulatory harmonization in these areas; bring together scientists from academia, government and industry to give a balanced approach to solving problems with broad implications for the wellbeing of the general public. **Structure** Board of Trustees. Branches: Global; Argentina; Brazil; Europe; Focal Point China; HESI; India; Japan; Korea; Mesoamerica; Mexico; Middle East; North America; North Andean; South Africa; South Andean; Southeast Asian Region; Taiwan. **Finance** Supported by: corporate contributions; foundation grants; government grants and contracts; cooperative agreements. **Activities** Supports scientific research, conferences, workshops and publications through its worldwide network of branches; 'ILSI Research Foundation'; 'ILSI Health and Environmental Sciences Institute'. **Events** *International Symposium on Food Packaging* Barcelona (Spain) 2022, *Annual Meeting and Science Symposium* Brussels (Belgium) 2022, *ILSI SEA Region Annual Meeting* Singapore (Singapore) 2022, *International Symposium on Food Packaging* Barcelona (Spain) 2021, *Southeast Asia Region Meeting* Singapore (Singapore) 2021. **Publications** *ILSI News* (6 a year); *Nutrition Reviews* – scientific review journal. *Monographs on Pathology of Laboratory Animals (MOPLA)*; *Present Knowledge in Nutrition* (9th ed). Monographs; reports; journal supplements.
Members Companies (400) in 35 countries:
Argentina, Australia, Austria, Belgium, Brazil, Chile, China, Colombia, Ecuador, Egypt, Finland, France, Germany, Hong Kong, India, Indonesia, Italy, Japan, Korea Rep, Malaysia, Mexico, Netherlands, New Zealand, Peru, Philippines, Singapore, South Africa, Sweden, Switzerland, Taiwan, Thailand, UK, United Arab Emirates, USA, Venezuela.
Consultative Status Consultative status granted from: *ECOSOC (#05331)* (Ros C); *FAO (#09260)* (Special Status). **IGO Relations** Participates as observer in the activities of: *Codex Alimentarius Commission (CAC, #04081)*. **NGO Relations** Serves as secretariat for: *Micronutrient Forum (#16748)*. Supports: *HarvestPlus (#10862)*. [2020/XF1551/jt/F]

♦ **International Light Association (ILA)** **14045**
Pres Rue Washington 40, 1050 Brussels, Belgium. E-mail: info@ilacolor.org.
URL: http://www.international-light-association.org/
History Nov 2003, Antwerp (Belgium). Registration: Banque-Carrefour des Entreprises, No/ID: 0588.974.595, Start date: 13 Jan 2015, Belgium. **Aims** Serve as a network for people focused on *therapeutic* use of light, colour and sound; determine professional standards and develop a code of ethics in the field of light and its applications for *health* and wellbeing. **Structure** General Assembly (annual); Council; Board. **Languages** English. **Staff** None. **Finance** Sources: meeting proceeds; members' dues; sponsorship. **Activities** Events/meetings; knowledge management/information dissemination. **Events** *Annual Conference* Pula (Croatia) 2019, *Annual Conference* Oslo (Norway) 2018, *Annual Conference* Fort Lauderdale, FL (USA) 2017, *Annual Conference* Vienna (Austria) 2016, *Annual Conference* Tallinn (Estonia) 2015. **Publications** *ILA Newsletter*, *Journal of Light* – in 3 vols. *The Power of Light, Colour and Sound for Health and Wellbeing* (1st 2022) by Thelma van der Werff and Rasmus Gaupp-Berghausen; *The Power of Light, colour and Sound for Health and Wellness* (1st ed 2019) by Thelma van der Werff and Rasmus Gaupp-Berghausen; *Light Therapy Case Studies Report* (2013).
Members Professional (practitioners, educators, researchers, commercial, designers, manufacturers, artists, consultants); Associate; Affiliate; Student; Lifetime; Honorary. Members in 36 countries and territories:
Argentina, Australia, Austria, Belgium, Canada, Croatia, Denmark, Egypt, Estonia, France, Germany, Greece, Hungary, India, Ireland, Israel, Japan, Korea Rep, Malta, Mexico, Netherlands, New Zealand, Nicaragua, Norway, Panama, Peru, Poland, Portugal, Romania, South Africa, Spain, Sweden, Switzerland, Taiwan, UK, USA.
NGO Relations Member of (1): *Federation of European and International Associations Established in Belgium (FAIB, #09508)*. [2023.02.19/XM1936/D]

♦ International Light Committee / see International Union of Photobiology (#15798)

♦ **International Light-Cone Advisory Committee (ILCAC)** **14046**
Sec Southeastern Univ Research Assoc, 1201 New York Ave NW, Ste 430, Washington DC 20005, USA. T. +12024087872. Fax +12024088250.
Pres Dept of Physics, North Carolina State Univ, Raleigh NC 27695-8202, USA. T. +19195153478. Fax +19195156538.
URL: http://www.ilcacinc.org/
History Founded 2008, under the auspices of the (USA) Southeastern Universities Research Association (SURA). **Aims** Advance research in *quantum* field theory, particularly light-cone quantization methods applicable to the solution of physical problems. **Structure** Committee; Sub-Committees (3). **Activities** Events/meetings. **Events** *Light Cone Conference* Jeju (Korea Rep) 2021, *Light Cone Conference* Suwon (Korea Rep) 2020, *Light Cone Conference* Palaiseau (France) 2019, *Light Cone Conference* Mumbai (India) 2017, *Light Cone Conference* Lisbon (Portugal) 2016.
Members Individuals in 8 countries:
Australia, Brazil, Germany, Italy, Korea Rep, Netherlands, Poland, USA. [2018/XE4724/E]

♦ International Light Metal Congress (meeting series)
♦ International Lightning Class Association (see: #21760)

♦ **International Lignin Institute (ILI)** **14047**
Main Office Zone Industrielle Les Ducats, Chemin des Ducats 40B, 1350 Orbe VD, Switzerland. T. +41217291234. Fax +41213187511. E-mail: admin@ili-lignin.com.
URL: http://www.ili-lignin.com/
History 1991, Switzerland. 1991, Plaffeien (Switzerland), with full title *'International Lignin Institute of Schwarzsee'*. Statutes adopted 13 Jul 1992, Bourgillon (Switzerland). Registered in accordance with the Swiss Civil Code. **Aims** Promote use of *renewable resources* and low *polluting processes*; in particular, enhance the technical and economic possibilities of using lignin as a renewable resource. **Structure** General Assembly (annual); Executive Committee. **Languages** English, French, German, Spanish. **Finance** Members' dues. **Activities** Events/meetings; knowledge management/information dissemination. **Events** *Forum* Stockholm (Sweden) 2011, *Forum* Zurich (Switzerland) 2008, *Forum* Rome (Italy) 2007, *Forum* Rome (Italy) 2007, *Bringing lignin back to the headlines – priority research and new approaches* Barcelona (Spain) 2005. **Publications** *ILI-Series* – reports, surveys, proceedings. Public (information) activities: patents; studies; addresses; literature; references; meetings; workshops; database.
Members Individual and collective, in 18 countries:
Canada, Denmark, Finland, France, Germany, Hungary, Italy, Japan, Latvia, Netherlands, Norway, Romania, Slovakia, South Africa, Spain, Sweden, Switzerland, USA. [2018.06.01/XE2656/j/**E**]

♦ International Lignin Institute of Schwarzsee / see International Lignin Institute (#14047)

♦ **International Lilac Society (ILS)** **14048**
Treas 325 W 82nd St, Chaska MN 55318, USA. T. +19524433703.
Exec Vice Pres 13902 E Placita Ocho Puntas, Vail AZ 85641, USA. E-mail: execvp@internationallilacsociety.org.
URL: http://www.internationallilacsociety.org/
History May 1971, Long Island NY (USA). Primarily a US organization. **Aims** Stimulate interest in the genus *Syringa*; promote its use in public and private *landscaping*; unite gardeners, nursery owners and employees, geneticists, researchers, arboretum staff, taxonomists and *botanists* working in the field. **Languages** English, French, Russian. **Activities** Events/meetings. **Events** *Annual Convention* Saint-Georges, QC (Canada) 2020, *Annual Convention* Des Moines, IA (USA) 2019, *Annual Convention* Riverside, CA (USA) 2018, *Annual Convention* Boston, MA (USA) 2017, *Annual Convention* Philadelphia, PA (USA) 2016. **Publications** *LILACS* (4 a year); *Lilacs* (annual) – convention proceedings; *Quarterly Journal of the International Lilac Society*. Handbook on lilac culture; list of plant sources.
Members Individuals/Families; Sustaining; Institutional/Commercial; Lifetime. Members in 19 countries:
Australia, Belgium, Canada, China, Croatia, Denmark, France, Germany, Hungary, Italy, Kazakhstan, Netherlands, New Zealand, Poland, Russia, Switzerland, UK, Ukraine, USA. [2019.06.18/XN2798/**E**]

♦ **International Lime Association (ILA)** **14049**
Association internationale de la chaux – Internationaler Kalkverband
SG Annastrasse 67-71, 50968 Cologne, Germany. T. +4922193467440. Fax +4922193467410. E-mail: post.ila@kalk.de.
URL: http://www.internationallime.org/
History 27 Nov 1970, Paris (France). **Aims** Promote exchange of information and experiences on all subjects that are of interest to the lime industry worldwide. **Structure** General Assembly (annual); Board of Directors; Committees; Permanent Secretariat, based in Cologne (Germany). **Languages** English, French, German. **Finance** Members' dues. **Events** *General Assembly and Symposium* Paris (France) 2022, *General Assembly and Symposium* Paris (France) 2021, *General Assembly and Symposium* Paris (France) 2020, *General Assembly and Information Exchange Forum* Buenos Aires (Argentina) 2019, *General Assembly and Information Exchange Forum* Cape Town (South Africa) 2018.
Members National associations and individual companies concerned with the production of burnt and hydrated limes, in 33 countries:
Austria, Belgium, Bulgaria, Canada, Czechia, Estonia, Finland, France, Germany, Hungary, India, Indonesia, Iran Islamic Rep, Ireland, Italy, Japan, Malaysia, Mexico, New Zealand, Norway, Poland, Portugal, Saudi Arabia, Slovakia, South Africa, Spain, Sweden, Switzerland, Thailand, Türkiye, UK, Ukraine, USA.
Regional organization (1), listed in this Yearbook: [2022/XF5673/**F**]

♦ International Limnological Society / see International Society of Limnology (#15232)

♦ **International Limousin Council (ILC)** **14050**
Pres Home Farm, Cilycwm, Llandovery, SA20 0TG, UK. T. +441550720464.
URL: http://www.limousin-international.com/
Aims Promote and represent the Limousin *cattle* breed internationally. **Structure** Executive Committee. **Languages** English, French, Spanish. **Activities** Organizes International Limousin Conference (every 2 years) by on of the member associations. **Events** *Congress* Ireland 2016, *Congress* Argentina 2014, *Congress* Buenos Aires (Argentina) 2014, *Congress* Aarhus (Denmark) 2012, *Congress* Denmark 2012. [2013.11.18/XN3167/**E**]

♦ **International Linear Algebra Society (ILAS)** **14051**
Pres Mathematics – Univ Ljubljana, Jadranska 19, 1000 Ljubljana, Slovenia. Fax +38612517281.
URL: http://www.ilasic.org/
History 1989, as successor to *International Matrix Group*. Registered in accordance with Florida (USA) law. **Aims** Encourage activities in linear algebra; promote education and research in pure and applied linear algebra and matrix theory. **Structure** Board of Directors of 10 members; Executive Board, consisting of President, Vice-President, Secretary/Treasurer. Committees (4): Advisory; Education; Institution Membership; Journals. **Finance** Sources: members' dues. **Activities** Awards/prizes/competitions; events/meetings; knowledge management/information dissemination; training/education. **Events** *Classical connections* Galway (Ireland) 2020, *Conference* Rio de Janeiro (Brazil) 2019, *Conference* Ames, IA (USA) 2017, *Conference* Leuven (Belgium) 2016, *Conference* Seoul (Korea Rep) 2014. **Publications** *IMAGE* (2 a year) – bulletin; *Electronic Journal of Linear Algebra (ELA)*.
Members Mathematicians in 51 countries:
Argentina, Australia, Austria, Belgium, Brazil, Canada, Chile, China, Colombia, Croatia, Cuba, Czechia, Egypt, Finland, France, Germany, Greece, Hong Kong, Hungary, India, Indonesia, Ireland, Israel, Italy, Jamaica, Japan, Korea Rep, Kuwait, Malaysia, Mexico, Netherlands, New Zealand, Norway, Poland, Portugal, Qatar, Russia, Saudi Arabia, Singapore, Slovenia, South Africa, Spain, Sweden, Switzerland, Taiwan, Türkiye, UK, Ukraine, USA, Venezuela, Vietnam. [2019/XN5626/v/**C**]

♦ **International Linear Collider (ILC)** **14052**
Contact DESY, Notkestr 85, 22607 Hamburg, Germany. T. +494089981847. Fax +494089981812.
Contact c/o Fermilab WH 13X, PO Box 500, Batavia IL 60510-5011, USA.
URL: http://www.linearcollider.org/
History A project involving 300 laboratories worldwide. **Aims** Complement the Large Hadron Collider, based at CERN. **Structure** Global Design Effort (GDE) Executive Committee. **Events** *International Symposium on ILC Promotion* Tokyo (Japan) 2018, *Tokyo Symposium* Tokyo (Japan) 2015. **IGO Relations** *European Organization for Nuclear Research (CERN, #08108)*. **NGO Relations** *International Committee for Future Accelerators (ICFA, #12774)*. [2013/XM3929/**E**]

♦ International Linen and Hemp Confederation / see Confédération européenne du lin et du chanvre (#04546)
♦ International Linguapax Committee / see Linguapax International (#16482)

♦ **International Linguistic Association** **14053**
Treas Calkins Hall 322, Hofstra Univ, Hempstead NY 11549-1000, USA. T. +15164636552. Fax +15164637082.
URL: http://www.ilaword.org/
History Founded 1945, New York NY (USA). **Aims** Promote study of *language*. **Structure** Executive Committee. **Staff** Voluntary. **Finance** Members' dues. **Events** *Annual Conference* Hempstead, NY (USA) 2016, *Annual Conference* Paris (France) 2014, *Annual Conference* New York, NY (USA) 2009, *International conference on linguistic interfaces* Seoul (Korea Rep) 2009, *Annual conference* New York, NY (USA) 2007. **Publications** *Word* (3 a year).
Members Individuals in 20 countries and territories:
Argentina, Australia, Canada, Finland, Georgia, Germany, Hong Kong, Italy, Japan, Mexico, Netherlands, New Zealand, Puerto Rico, Russia, Spain, Switzerland, Tahiti Is, UK, USA. [2016/XD1305/v/**F**]

♦ International Linguistics Center, Dallas (internationally oriented national body)

♦ **International Link of Orthodox Christian Scouts (DESMOS)** **14054**
Pres 17 E Kairi str, 112 55 Athens, Greece. T. +302102234887. E-mail: mmpbgd@gmail.com – office@desmos.info.
URL: http://www.desmos.info/en
History 7 Jun 1997, Athens (Greece). **Aims** Develop and promote the spirit of brotherhood and understanding among Scouts of the Orthodox Christian Faith; motivate and promote Scouting to Orthodox boys and girls on global basis. **Structure** Conference; Executive Committee; Secretary General; Honorary President. **Languages** English, French. **Staff** 7.00 FTE, voluntary. **Finance** Sources: contributions; donations; members' dues. **Activities** Events/meetings; religious activities. **Events** *Conference* Ljubljana (Slovenia) 2014, *Conference* Belgrade (Serbia) 2011, *Conference* Jeju (Korea Rep) 2008, *Conference* Tunis (Tunisia) 2005, *Conference* Thessaloniki (Greece) 2002.
Members Founding members: Scout organizations (9) in 9 countries and territories:
Armenia, Cyprus, Greece, Lebanon, Palestine, Poland, Romania, Serbia, USA.
Regular members in 14 countries:
Albania, Belarus, Bosnia-Herzegovina, Bulgaria, Finland, Georgia, Israel, Jordan, Moldova, Montenegro, North Macedonia, Russia, Uganda, Ukraine.
NGO Relations Consultative status with: *World Organization of the Scout Movement (WOSM, #21693)*. Member of: *European Interreligious Forum for Religious Freedom (EIFRF, #07596)*; *World Scout Interreligious Forum (see: #21693)*. [2020.08.28/XF5720/**F**]

♦ International Links and Services for Local Economic Development Agencies (unconfirmed)

♦ **International Liquid Crystal Society (ILCS)** **14055**
Pres PO Box 5190, Kent OH 44242-0001, USA. E-mail: hyokoyam@kent.edu.
URL: http://www.ilcsoc.org/
History 1990. **Structure** Executive Committee, comprising President, Past-President, Vice-President, Secretary, Treasurer and Membership Secretary. **Languages** English. **Staff** 1.50 FTE, voluntary. **Finance** Sources: members' dues. **Events** *Biennial International Liquid Crystal Conference* Lisbon (Portugal) 2022, *Biennial International Liquid Crystal Conference* Lisbon (Portugal) 2020, *Biennial International Liquid Crystal Conference* Kyoto (Japan) 2018, *Biennial International Liquid Crystal Conference* Kent, OH (USA) 2016, *Biennial International Liquid Crystal Conference* Dublin (Ireland) 2014. **Publications** *Liquid Crystals Today*.
Members Individuals and organizations in 53 countries and territories:
Argentina, Armenia, Barbados, Belarus, Belgium, Brazil, Bulgaria, Canada, Chile, China, Croatia, Czechia, Egypt, France, Georgia, Germany, Greece, Hong Kong, Hungary, India, Iran Islamic Rep, Ireland, Israel, Italy, Japan, Jordan, Kazakhstan, Korea Rep, Malaysia, Mauritania, Mexico, Mongolia, Netherlands, Nigeria, North Macedonia, Norway, Oman, Philippines, Poland, Portugal, Romania, Russia, Saudi Arabia, Singapore, Slovenia, Spain, Sweden, Switzerland, Taiwan, Türkiye, UK, Ukraine, USA. [2020/XC0079/**C**]

♦ International Liquid Terminals Association (internationally oriented national body)
♦ International Listening Association (internationally oriented national body)

♦ **International Liszt Association (ILA)** **14056**
Coordination Hungarian Liszt Society, Vörösmarty utca 32, Budapest 1061, Hungary. T. +3613421573. E-mail: lisztferenctarsasag@lft.t-online.hu.
URL: http://liszt-international.org/
History 2009. **Structure** Board, comprising President, Vice-Presidents, Secretary-General and members. **Publications** *ILA Newsletter*.
Members Institutions in 11 countries:
Austria, France, Germany, Hungary, Indonesia, Italy, Japan, Lithuania, Netherlands, UK, USA. [2011.06.01/XJ1884/**E**]

♦ **International Literacy Association (ILA)** **14057**
Exec Dir PO Box 8139, Newark DE 19714-8139, USA. Fax +13027311057. E-mail: customerservice@reading.org.
URL: http://www.literacyworldwide.org/
History 1956, USA. Founded on merger of *International Council for the Improvement of Reading Instruction (ICIRI)* and (US) National Association for Remedial Teaching (NART). Commenced operations as an incorporated non-profit professional organization, 1 Jan 1956. Former names and other names: *International Reading Association (IRA)* – former; *Association internationale pour la lecture (AIL)* – former; *Asociación Internacional de Lectura* – former; *Internationale Lesegesellschaft* – former. **Aims** Promote reading by continuously advancing the quality of *literature* instruction and research worldwide. **Structure** Board of Directors; Standing Committees; Task Forces. **Languages** English. **Staff** 100.00 FTE, paid. **Finance** Sources: members' dues. **Activities** Acts as an umbrella organization to a network of over 1,250 councils and works with 45 special interest groups that promote understanding of a broad range of issues; presents annually more than 26 awards recognizing outstanding achievement in research, teaching, writing, and professional and community service. Networking with professionals. Organizes conventions. Publishing activity. **Events** *Biennial Pan African Literacy for All Conference* Kampala (Uganda) 2019, *Annual Convention* New Orleans, LA (USA) 2019, *Annual Convention* Austin, TX (USA) 2018, *Biennial Pan African Literacy for All Conference* Abuja (Nigeria) 2017, *Annual Convention* Orlando, FL (USA) 2017. **Publications** *Journal of Adolescent and Adult Literacy* (6 a year); *Reading Today* (6 a year); *The Reading Teacher* (6 a year); *Reading Research Quarterly* – with abstracts in English, French, German, Spanish; *Reading Today Online*. Other publications (6-8 a year).
Members Individuals (about 70,000) in 122 countries and territories:
Albania, Antigua-Barbuda, Argentina, Armenia, Australia, Austria, Bahamas, Bahrain, Bangladesh, Barbados, Belgium, Belize, Bermuda, Bolivia, Botswana, Brazil, Bulgaria, Cameroon, Canada, Cayman Is, Chile, China, Colombia, Cook Is, Costa Rica, Croatia, Cyprus, Czechia, Denmark, Dominica, Dominican Rep, Ecuador, Egypt, El Salvador, Estonia, Eswatini, Ethiopia, Finland, France, Gambia, Georgia, Germany, Ghana, Greece, Grenada, Guatemala, Guyana, Honduras, Hong Kong, Hungary, Iceland, India, Indonesia, Iraq, Ireland, Israel, Italy, Jamaica, Japan, Jordan, Kazakhstan, Kenya, Korea Rep, Kuwait, Latvia, Lithuania, Luxembourg, Malawi, Malaysia, Malta, Mauritius, Mexico, Moldova, Mongolia, Montenegro, Morocco, Mozambique, Namibia, Nepal, Netherlands, New Zealand, Nigeria, North Macedonia, Norway, Pakistan, Panama, Papua New Guinea, Peru, Philippines, Poland, Portugal, Qatar, Romania, Russia, Saudi Arabia, Senegal, Serbia, Singapore, Slovenia, South Africa, Spain, Sri Lanka, St Kitts-Nevis, St Lucia, St Vincent-Grenadines, Sweden, Switzerland, Taiwan, Tanzania UR, Thailand, Trinidad-Tobago, Türkiye, Uganda, UK, United Arab Emirates, Uruguay, USA, Vanuatu, Venezuela, Virgin Is UK, Zimbabwe.
Consultative Status Consultative status granted from: *UNESCO (#20322)* (Consultative Status); *OAS (#17629)*. **NGO Relations** Member of: *International Board on Books for Young People (IBBY, #12366)*; *International Council of Psychologists (ICP, #13065)*; *International Federation of Library Associations and Institutions (IFLA, #13470)*; *International Literacy Network (ILN, no recent information)*. [2021/XB2401/v/**B**]

♦ International Literacy and Education Research Network / see Learner Research Network (#16428)
♦ International Literacy Institute (internationally oriented national body)

♦ **International Literary and Artistic Association** **14058**
Association littéraire et artistique internationale (ALAI) – Asociación Literaria y Artistica Internacional – Internationale Vereinigung für Literatur und Kunst
SG Hoyng Rokh Monegier LLP, Av des Nerviens 9-31, 1040 Brussels, Belgium. T. +3227400005. Fax +3227400001.
URL: http://www.alai.org/
History 29 Jun 1878, Paris (France), at international literary congress chaired by Victor Hugo. Registered in accordance with French law. **Aims** Safeguard and extend legal principles ensuring international protection of the *authors'* rights; study national legislation on authors' rights and proposals to perfect and harmonize such legislation; improve, revise and extend international conventions. **Structure** General Assembly (annual); Executive Committee; Bureau. Membership subject to approval by Executive Committee. Meetings closed. **Languages** English, French, Spanish. **Staff** None. **Finance** Sources: members' dues. **Activities** Events/meetings; networking/liaising; research/documentation. **Events** *Annual Congress* Madrid (Spain) 2020, *Annual Congress* Prague (Czechia) 2019, *Annual Congress* Montréal, QC (Canada) 2018, *Annual Congress* Copenhagen (Denmark) 2017, *Annual Congress* Bonn (Germany) 2015. **Publications** Congress reports and proceedings in English, French; main reports also in Spanish; opinions in English, French, Spanish.
Members National groups in 33 countries:
Argentina, Austria, Belgium, Brazil, Canada, Chile, Colombia, Croatia, Cyprus, Czechia, Denmark, Finland, France, Germany, Greece, Hungary, Iceland, Israel, Italy, Japan, Korea Rep, Mexico, Netherlands, Norway, Paraguay, Portugal, South Africa, Spain, Sweden, Switzerland, UK, Uruguay, USA.

Individuals in 9 countries:
Australia, Cameroon, Egypt, Lebanon, New Zealand, Slovakia, Trinidad-Tobago, Türkiye, United Arab Emirates.
Consultative Status Consultative status granted from: *World Intellectual Property Organization (WIPO, #21593)* (Permanent Observer Status). **IGO Relations** Observer to: *European Commission (EC, #06633)*; *Intergovernmental Committee of the International Convention of Rome for the Protection of Performers, Producers of Phonograms and Broadcasting Organizations (#11474)*; *Union for the International Registration of Audiovisual Works (#20444).* [2018.09.20/XC2235/**C**]

♦ International Lithosphere Program / see International Lithosphere Program (#14059)

♦ International Lithosphere Program (ILP) 14059

SG 101 Geology Bldg, Univ of Missouri, Columbia MO 65211, USA. T. +15738823784. Fax +15738825458. E-mail: ilp@nju.edu.cn.
President Eurasia Inst of Earth Sciences, Istanbul Technical Univ, Maslak, 34469 Istanbul/Istanbul, Türkiye.
URL: https://ilp.nju.edu.cn

History 1980. Founded as successor to *International Geodynamics Project* by *International Council for Science (ICSU, inactive)* at the request of *International Union of Geological Sciences (IUGS, #15777)* and *International Union of Geodesy and Geophysics (IUGG, #15776)*. Originally functioning within *Scientific Committee on the Lithosphere (SCL)*, but currently functioning under proper title. Former names and other names: *International Program on Dynamics and Evolution of the Lithosphere – the Framework for Earth Resources and Reduction of Hazards* – full title; *Inter-Union Commission on the Lithosphere (ICL)* – former (Sep 1980); *Scientific Committee on the Lithosphere (SCL)* – former; *International Lithosphere Program (ILP)* – former. **Aims** Elucidate the nature, dynamics, origin and evolution of the lithosphere through international, multidisciplinary geoscience research projects and coordinating committees. **Structure** Bureau; Committee of National Representatives; Task Forces (9); Coordinating Committees. **Languages** English. **Staff** No permanent staff. **Finance** Sources: contributions of member/participating states; international organizations. Supported by: *International Union of Geodesy and Geophysics (IUGG, #15776)*; *International Union of Geological Sciences (IUGS, #15777).* **Activities** Awards/prizes/competitions; events/meetings; research/documentation; training/education. **Events** *Geosynthesis conference* Cape Town (South Africa) 2011, *Workshop on lithosphere dynamics and sedimentary basins* Abu Dhabi (United Arab Emirates) 2009, *GeoMod : international geological modelling conference* Florence (Italy) 2008, *Symposium on terrestrial heat flow, hot spots, mantle plumes and thermal structure of the lithosphere* Beijing (China) 1996, *International workshop on heat flow and the thermal structure of the lithosphere* Trest (Czech Rep) 1996. **Publications** Annual Report; directory.
Members National members and individual contributors in 49 countries and territories:
Argentina, Australia, Botswana, Brazil, Cameroon, Canada, Chile, China, Colombia, Congo DR, Costa Rica, Cyprus, Denmark, Ecuador, Finland, France, Georgia, Germany, Hungary, India, Indonesia, Iran Islamic Rep, Israel, Italy, Japan, Mexico, Morocco, Netherlands, New Zealand, Norway, Pakistan, Papua New Guinea, Peru, Philippines, Puerto Rico, Romania, Russia, South Africa, Spain, Sweden, Switzerland, Taiwan, Türkiye, UK, USA, Venezuela, Vietnam, Zambia, Zimbabwe. [2022.05.19/XK0370/**F**]

♦ International Live Events Association (internationally oriented national body)

♦ International Liver Cancer Association (ILCA) 14060

Main Office Bvd du Souverain 280, 1160 Brussels, Belgium. T. +3223202531. E-mail: info@ilca-online.org.
URL: http://www.ilca-online.org/

History Registered in accordance with Swiss law. **Aims** Advance research in the pathogenesis, prevention and treatment of liver cancer; promote novel pathogenic, diagnostic and therapeutic interventions for liver cancer by taking a transversal approach to research and bringing together scientists, physicians and allied professionals from all interrelated fields. **Structure** Council; Executive Committee. **Finance** Sources: members' dues. **Activities** Annual conference; ILCA School of Liver Cancer. **Events** *Annual Conference* Brussels (Belgium) 2021, *Annual Conference* Brussels (Belgium) 2020, *Annual Conference* Chicago, IL (USA) 2019, *Annual Conference* London (UK) 2018, *Annual Conference* Seoul (Korea Rep) 2017. [2018/XM2738/**C**]

♦ International Liver Transplantation Society (ILTS) 14061

Secretariat c/o KIT Group, Kurfurstendamm 71, 10709 Berlin, Germany. E-mail: ilts@ilts.org.
URL: http://www.ilts.org/

History 1992, Pittsburgh, PA (USA). Registration: 501(c)(3) organization, No/ID: EIN: 54-1624149, Start date: 1996, USA, Fredericksburg VA. **Aims** Promote advancement of the science and practice of liver transplantation. **Structure** Council; Committees (11); Special Interest Groups (8); Secretariat. **Languages** English. **Activities** Awards/prizes/competitions; events/meetings; publishing activities; training/education. **Events** *Joint International Congress* Rotterdam (Netherlands) 2023, *Joint International Congress* Istanbul (Turkey) 2022, *Joint International Congress* Florence (Italy) 2021, *Joint International Congress* Istanbul (Turkey) 2020, *Liver Transplant Symposium* Singapore (Singapore) 2019. **Publications** *Transplantion* (12 a year) – official journal; *ILTS eNewsletter* (11 a year). **Members** Full (1,600). Membership countries not specified. [2022.10.12/XD8112/**C**]

♦ International Livestock Research Institute (ILRI) 14062

Mailing Address PO Box 30709, Nairobi, 00100, Kenya. T. +254204223000. Fax +254204223001. E-mail: ilri-kenya@cgiar.org.
URL: http://www.ilri.org/

History 1 Jan 1995. Founded as a single institute deriving from *International Laboratory for Research on Animal Diseases (ILRAD, inactive)* and *International Livestock Centre for Africa (ILCA, inactive).* **Aims** Increase *animal health, nutrition* and productivity; tailor long-term sustainable production systems and develop technologies to protect environment supporting animal production; characterize and conserve the *genetic diversity* of indigenous *tropical forage* species and livestock *breeds*; promote equitable and sustainable national policies for animal agriculture and related *natural resource* management. **Structure** Board; Director General. **Languages** English. **Staff** Internationally recruited staff (IRS) – 92; Nationally Recruited Staff (NRS) Nairobi (Kenya) – 252. **Finance** Sources: over 60 private, public and government organizations of both North and South. Government sources include: Australia, Belgium, Canada, China, Denmark, Finland, France, Germany, India, Ireland, Italy, Japan, Korea Rep, Netherlands, Norway, Philippines, South Africa, Sweden, Switzerland, UK, USA; *International Bank for Reconstruction and Development (IBRD, #12317).* **Activities** Research/documentation. **Events** *GEOGLAM RAPP and SDG Workshop and Regional Open Data Cube Workshop* Nairobi (Kenya) 2018, *International Congress on Pathogens at the Human-Animal Interface* Chiang Mai (Thailand) 2015, *Innovation Africa symposium* Kampala (Uganda) 2006, *International workshop on grasspea as a food/feed crop in drought-prone areas in Africa and Asia* Aleppo (Syrian AR) 2004, *Seminar on sustainable crop livestock production for improved livelihoods and natural resources management in West Africa* Nigeria 2001. **Publications** Annual Report. Research reports; briefing papers.
IGO Relations Partners include the following organizations listed in this Yearbook:
- *African Development Bank (ADB, #00283)*;
- *African Union (AU, #00488)*;
- *Asian Development Bank (ADB, #01422)*;
- *Belgian Fund for Food Security (BFFS)*;
- *Bernhard Nocht Institut für Tropenmedizin (BNITM)*;
- *Bioversity International (#03262)*;
- *CIHEAM – International Centre for Advanced Mediterranean Agronomic Studies (CIHEAM, #03927)*;
- *CGIAR System Organization (CGIAR, #03843)*;
- *Comité permanent inter-Etats de lutte contre la sécheresse dans le Sahel (CILSS, #04195)*;
- *Common Fund for Commodities (CFC, #04293)*;
- *Commonwealth Secretariat (#04362)*;
- *DANIDA*;
- *Department for International Development (DFID, inactive)*;
- *Deutsche Gesellschaft für Technische Zusammenarbeit (GTZ, inactive)*;
- *European Commission (EC, #06633)*;
- *FAO (#09260)*;
- *Global Environment Facility (GEF, #10346)*;
- *Inter-American Institute for Cooperation on Agriculture (IICA, #11434)*;
- *Interafrican Bureau for Animal Resources (AU-IBAR, #11382)*;
- *International Atomic Energy Agency (IAEA, #12294)*;
- *International Center for Agricultural Research in the Dry Areas (ICARDA, #12466)*;
- *International Crops Research Institute for the Semi-Arid Tropics (ICRISAT, #13116)*;
- *International Development Research Centre (IDRC, #13162)*;
- *International Fund for Agricultural Development (IFAD, #13692)*;
- *International Rice Research Institute (IRRI, #14754)*;
- *Southern African Development Community (SADC, #19843)*;
- *UNEP (#20299)*;
- *UNDP (#20292)*;
- *United States Agency for International Development (USAID)*;
- *WHO (#20950).*

NGO Relations Partners include the following organizations listed in this Yearbook:
- *African Agricultural Technology Foundation (AATF, #00199)*;
- *African Centre for Technology Studies (ACTS, #00243)*;
- *African Conservation Centre (ACC)*;
- *African Wildlife Foundation (AWF, #00498)*;
- *Association for Strengthening Agricultural Research in Eastern and Central Africa (ASARECA, #02933)*;
- *CARE International (CI, #03429)*;
- *Cattle Research Network (CARNET, inactive)*;
- *Center for Development Research, Bonn (ZEF)*;
- *Centre international de recherche-développement sur l'élevage en zone subhumide (CIRDES, #03760)*;
- *Centre for Tropical Veterinary Medicine, Edinburgh (CTVM)*;
- *Consortium for the Sustainable Development of the Andean Ecoregion (#04758)*;
- *Eastern and Central Africa Programme for Agricultural Policy Analysis (ECAPAPA, inactive)*;
- *Forum for Agricultural Research in Africa (FARA, #09897)*;
- *Foundation for Advanced Studies on International Development (FASID)*;
- *Institute of Development Studies, Brighton (IDS)*;
- *Institute of Tropical Medicine Antwerp (IMT)*;
- *International Centre of Insect Physiology and Ecology (ICIPE, #12499)*;
- *International Centre for Tropical Agriculture (#12527)*;
- *International Fertilizer Development Center (IFDC, #13590)*;
- *International Food Policy Research Institute (IFPRI, #13622)*;
- *International Foundation for Science (IFS, #13677)*;
- *International Institute for Environment and Development (IIED, #13877)*;
- *International Institute of Tropical Agriculture (IITA, #13933)*;
- *International Maize and Wheat Improvement Center (#14077)*;
- *International Potato Center (#14627)*;
- *International Trypanotolerance Centre (ITC, #15739)*;
- *International Water Management Institute (IWMI, #15867)*;
- *Japan International Research Centre for Agricultural Sciences (JIRCAS)*;
- *Natural Resources Institute (NRI)*;
- *SNV Netherlands Development Organisation (SNV)*;
- *Nile Basin Society (NBS, inactive)*;
- *Overseas Development Institute (ODI)*;
- *The Rockefeller Foundation (#18966)*;
- *Swiss Tropical and Public Health Institute (Swiss TPH)*;
- *TechnoServe (#20120)*;
- *Université de la Méditerranée, Marseille*;
- *Vétérinaires Sans Frontières International (VSF International, #20760)*;
- *West and Central African Council for Agricultural Research and Development (WECARD, #20907)*;
- *World Agroforestry Centre (ICRAF, #21072)*;
- *World Resources Institute (WRI, #21753).* [2021/XE2297/j/**E***]

♦ International Living Future Institute (internationally oriented national body)
♦ International Load Line Convention (1930 treaty)
♦ International Loans Tribunal (inactive)

♦ International Lodging Association (ILA) 14063

Châteaux et hôtels de charme
CEO – Pres Av de la Terre Franche 25, 1325 Chaumont-Gistoux, Belgium. T. +3210680300.
URL: http://www.ila-chateau.com/

History 1986, under the name *International Leading Association (ILA)*, as an organization of deluxe hotels. Previously referred to in English as *Châteaux and Hotels – ILA.* **Aims** Present a guide of hotel-keepers and restaurateurs throughout the world who are eager to provide their guests with the highest possible standards of professionalism, service, accommodation and cuisine in attractive surroundings. **Publications** *The International Travellers Guide to Special Places* (8th ed 1995-1996).
Members Hotels (over 200) in 18 countries:
Austria, Belgium, Canada, Congo DR, France, Germany, Greece, Ireland, Italy, Luxembourg, Netherlands, Portugal, Seychelles, South Africa, Spain, Switzerland, UK, USA. [2017.03.09/XF0771/e/**F**]

♦ International Longevity Centre Global Alliance (ILC Global Alliance) . 14064

Exec Dir Columbia Mailman School, 722 West 168th St, 14th Floor, New York NY 10032, USA. T. +12123050424. Fax +12123046677. E-mail: contact@ilc-alliance.org.
URL: http://www.ilc-alliance.org/

History 1990, by US and Japanese centers. **Aims** Help societies to address longevity and population *ageing* in positive and productive ways, typically using a life course approach, highlighting older people's productivity and contributions to family and society as a whole. **Events** *Annual Meeting* UK 2014, *Annual Meeting* Singapore (Singapore) 2013, *Symposium* Singapore (Singapore) 2013, *Annual Meeting* Prague (Czech Rep) 2012, *Annual Meeting* Netherlands 2011. **Publications** Reports.
Members National centres in 17 countries:
Argentina, Australia, Brazil, Canada, China, Czechia, Dominican Rep, France, Germany, India, Israel, Japan, Netherlands, Singapore, South Africa, UK, USA.
Consultative Status Consultative status granted from: *ECOSOC (#05331)* (Special). **NGO Relations** Member of: *Global Alliance for the Rights of Older People (#10226).* Partner of: *International Federation on Ageing (IFA, #13345).* [2020/XJ7484/**C**]

♦ International Longshoremen's Association (internationally oriented national body)
♦ International Longshore and Warehouse Union (internationally oriented national body)

♦ International Long-Term Ecological Research Network (ILTER) 14065

Contact c/o Environment Agency Austria, Spittelauer Lände 5, 1090 Vienna, Austria. E-mail: ilter.network@gmail.com.
URL: http://www.ilternet.edu/

History 1993, at a meeting of the US Long-Term Ecological Research Network (LTER). **Aims** Improve understanding of global ecosystems; inform solutions to current and future environmental problems. **Structure** Coordinating Committee; Executive Committee; Chair. *European Long-Term Ecosystem Research Network (LTER-Europe, #07712).* **Activities** Training/education; events/meetings; research and development; knowledge management/information dissemination. **Events** *Annual Meeting* Rome (Italy) 2015, *Annual Meeting* Rome (Italy) 2015, *Annual Europe Conference* Vienna (Austria) 2015, *Annual Meeting* Chiloe Is (Chile) 2014, *All-Scientists Meeting of the Americas* Valdivia (Chile) 2014.
Members Sections in 40 countries and territories:
Australia, Austria, Brazil, Bulgaria, Canada, Chile, China, Costa Rica, Czechia, Finland, France, Germany, Hungary, Israel, Italy, Japan, Korea Rep, Latvia, Lithuania, Malawi, Mexico, Mongolia, Mozambique, Namibia, Philippines, Poland, Portugal, Romania, Serbia, Slovakia, Slovenia, South Africa, Spain, Sweden, Switzerland, Taiwan, Thailand, UK, USA, Venezuela.
IGO Relations Member of: *Global Biodiversity Information Facility (GBIF, #10250).* Partner of: *Group on Earth Observations (GEO, #10735).* [2014/XN8691/**F**]

♦ International Luge Federation (FIL) 14066

Fédération Internationale de Luge (FIL) – Internationaler Rodelverband (FIL)
Headquarters Nonntal 10, 83471 Berchtesgaden, Germany. T. +498652975770. Fax +4986529757755. E-mail: office@fil-luge.org.
Registered Office Oberst-Lepperdinger-Straße 21, 5071 Wals-Siezenheim, Austria.
URL: http://www.fil-luge.org/

History 1913, Dresden (Germany). Re-founded, 1927, Dresden. In 1935, became 'Section de Luge' of *International Bobsleigh and Skeleton Federation (IBSF, #12375).* Became an autonomous organization, 25 Jan 1957, Davos (Switzerland). Former names and other names: *International Sled Sport Federation* – former (1913 to 1935); *Internationaler Schlittensportverband* – former (1913 to 1935); *Internationaler Rodelsportverband* – former (1935 to 1957); *Fédération Internationale de Luge de Course (FIL)* – former

(1935 to 1957); *Internationaler Rennrodelverband* – former (1935 to 1957). **Aims** Develop the sport of luge worldwide, supervise it, promote it, and direct it; represent the sport of luge in the Olympic Movement. **Structure** Congress (annual); Executive Board. **Languages** English, German. **Staff** 7.00 FTE, paid. **Finance** Sources: members' dues. Television and marketing rights. **Activities** Sporting activities; training/education. **Events** *Annual Congress* Hall in Tirol (Austria) 2022, *Annual Congress* Salzburg (Austria) 2021, *Annual Congress* Grossgmain (Austria) 2020, *Annual Congress* Ljubljana (Slovenia) 2019, *Annual Congress* Bratislava (Slovakia) 2018. **Publications** *FIL Magazine* (periodical). *International Luge Regulations* (2022) – revised; *FIL Media Guide*.
Members National Federations and individuals in 52 countries and territories:
Argentina, Australia, Austria, Belgium, Bermuda, Bosnia-Herzegovina, Brazil, Bulgaria, Canada, China, Croatia, Czechia, Dominican Rep, Estonia, Finland, France, Georgia, Germany, Great Britain, Greece, Hungary, India, Ireland, Italy, Japan, Kazakhstan, Korea Rep, Kuwait, Latvia, Liechtenstein, Moldova, Netherlands, New Zealand, Norway, Poland, Portugal, Puerto Rico, Romania, Russia, Serbia, Slovakia, Slovenia, Spain, Sweden, Switzerland, Taipei, Thailand, Tonga, Türkiye, Ukraine, USA, Virgin Is USA.
NGO Relations Member of (4): *Association of the International Olympic Winter Sports Federations (AIOWF, #02757); International Committee for Fair Play (#12769); International Council of Sport Science and Physical Education (ICSSPE, #13077); Olympic Movement (#17719)*. Recognized by: *International Olympic Committee (IOC, #14408)*. [2023.03.06/XC2236/**C**]

♦ International Lunar Observatory Association (ILOA) 14067

Dir 65-1230 Mamalahoa Highway, D20, Kamuela HI 96743, USA. T. +18088853474. Fax +18088853475.
URL: http://www.iloa.org/
History 2007. Registration: 501(c)(3), USA, Hawaii. **Aims** Advance human knowledge of the Cosmos through observation from the Moon; participate in lunar base build-out. **Structure** Board of Directors. **Staff** 1.00 FTE, paid. **Activities** Events/meetings; networking/liaising; research and development; training/education. **Publications** *ILOA News*. **NGO Relations** Member of (1): *International Astronautical Federation (IAF, #12286)*. [2022/XJ8715/**C**]

♦ International Lupin Association (ILA) 14068

Pres Campex Semillas Baer, Casilla 87, Temuco, Araucanía, Chile.
History Apr 1980, Lima (Peru). Statutes adopted 6 May 1982, Torremolinos (Spain). Statutes modified May 1996, Asilomar CA (USA) and March 2019, Cochabamba (Bolivia). Sometimes also referred to in Spanish as *Asociación Internacional del Lupino*. **Aims** Promote and develop lupin research projects in distinct areas by means of encouraging international cooperation in the study of agronomic, technological, chemical, economic and nutritional aspects of lupin; coordinate extension activities at international level; provide members with updated information on new research findings; facilitate communication among them and with other institutions. **Structure** General Assembly; Executive Committee; Advisory Board; Audit Board; Honorary Board; Conference Organizing Committee. **Languages** English. **Finance** Sources: members' dues. Other sources: donations from national and international institutions; sale of conference proceedings and other items related to conference activities. **Activities** Events/meetings; research and development. **Events** *Conference* Rostock (Germany) 2023, *Conference* Cochabamba (Bolivia) 2019, *Conference* Milan (Italy) 2015, *Conference* Poznań (Poland) 2011, *Conference* Fremantle, WA (Australia) 2008. **Publications** *Advances in Lupin Science* – open access journal. Conference proceedings.
Members Associate organizations in 6 countries:
Bolivia, Chile, Germany, Mexico, Peru, Poland.
Individuals in 22 countries:
Argentina, Australia, Belarus, Belgium, Bolivia, Chile, Czechia, Denmark, Ecuador, Finland, France, Germany, Italy, Mexico, Netherlands, New Zealand, Peru, Poland, Portugal, Russia, Sweden, UK.
IGO Relations *FAO (#09260); European Commission (EC, #06633)* through DGVI and DGXII. [2019.08.13/XD1376/**C**]

♦ International Lutheran Council (ILC) 14069

Gen Sec PO Box 18775, St Louis MO 63118, USA. T. +13148000310. Fax +13148148062. E-mail: info@ilcouncil.org.
URL: http://www.ilc-online.org/
History 1993, Antigua (Guatemala), following informal meetings since 1952. **Aims** Encourage, strengthen and promote confessional Lutheran theology and practice centering in Jesus Christ, both among member churches and throughout the world. **Structure** Council (meets every 3 years). Executive Committee. Officers: Chairman; Vice-Chairman; Secretary. Executive Secretary. **Languages** English, Spanish. **Staff** 0.50 FTE, voluntary. **Finance** Members' dues. **Events** *Biennial Conference* Niagara Falls, ON (Canada) 2012, *Conference* Korea Rep 2009, *Biennial Conference* Seoul (Korea Rep) 2009, *Biennial conference / Conference* Accra (Ghana) 2007, *Biennial conference / Conference* Berlin (Germany) 2005. **Publications** *ILC News* (4 a year).
Members Confessional Lutheran Churches in 32 countries and territories:
Argentina, Australia, Belgium, Bolivia, Brazil, Canada, Chile, Denmark, France, Germany, Ghana, Guatemala, Haiti, Hong Kong, India, Japan, Kenya, Korea Rep, Mexico, Nigeria, Papua New Guinea, Paraguay, Peru, Philippines, Portugal, Russia, South Africa, Sri Lanka, Taiwan, UK, USA, Venezuela. [2020/XG7916/**E**]

- ♦ International Lutheran Hour Ministries (internationally oriented national body)
- ♦ International Lutheran Layman's League (internationally oriented national body)
- ♦ International Lutheran Women's Missionary League (internationally oriented national body)
- ♦ International Lyme and Associated Diseases Society (internationally oriented national body)

♦ International Lymphoedema Framework (ILF) 14070

Secretariat CAP Partner, Nordre Fasanvej 113, 2000 Frederiksberg, Denmark. E-mail: aw@cap-partner.eu – info@lympho.org.
URL: http://www.lympho.org/
History Registration: Companies House, No/ID: 06792587, Start date: 15 Jan 2009, UK; Charity Commission, No/ID: 1134989, Start date: 17 Mar 2010, UK, England and Wales. **Aims** Develop and evaluate appropriate *health care* services worldwide for patients with all forms of lymphoedema. **Structure** Board of Trustees; Secretariat. **Languages** English. **Staff** 4.00 FTE, paid. **Activities** Projects/programmes; research/documentation; training/education. **Events** *Annual Conference* Copenhagen (Denmark) 2021, *Annual Conference* Copenhagen (Denmark) 2020, *Annual Conference* Chicago, IL (USA) 2019, *Annual Conference* Rotterdam (Netherlands) 2018, *Annual Conference* Kanazawa (Japan) 2017. **Publications** *Lymphoedema Journal*.
Members National frameworks in 16 countries and territories:
Australia, Belgium, Canada, Denmark, England, France, Greece, Ireland, Italy, Japan, Netherlands, Saudi Arabia, South Africa, Switzerland, USA, Wales.
NGO Relations Member of (1): *World Alliance for Wound and Lymphedema Care (WAWLC, #21089)*. [2022.05.10/XM2972/**F**]

♦ Internationally Shared Aquifer Resources Management (ISARM) . . 14071

Contact c/o IGRAC, Westvest 7, 2611 AX Delft, Netherlands. E-mail: info@un-igrac.org.
Contact c/o IHP, Div of Water Services, Groundwater Systems and Settlements Section, 7 place de Fontenoy – 1095, 75007 Paris, France. E-mail: ihp@unesco.org.
URL: http://isarm.org/
History Launched Jun 2000, at 14th Session of the Intergovernmental Council of *International Hydrological Programme (IHP, #13826)* of *UNESCO (#20322)*. **Aims** Contribute to the multifaceted efforts in global cooperation through providing for the planets' needs in sustainable environments, economy, social and political security on internationally shared aquifers. **Structure** Maintained by *International Groundwater Resources Assessment Centre (IGRAC, #13739)*. **Finance** Sponsored by: *International Hydrological Programme (IHP, #13826)*. **Activities** Research/documentation; knowledge management/information dissemination. **IGO Relations** Partners include: *FAO (#09260); OAS (#17629); Observatoire du Sahara et du Sahel (OSS, #17636); Organization for Security and Cooperation in Europe (OSCE, #17887); United Nations Economic Commission for Europe (UNECE, #20555); United Nations Economic and Social Commission for Western Asia (ESCWA, #20558)*. **NGO Relations** Partners include: *International Association of Hydrogeologists (IAH, #11953); International Groundwater Resources Assessment Centre (IGRAC, #13739)*. [2017/XM5999/**E**]

♦ Internationally United Commercial Agents and Brokers (IUCAB) . . . 14072

SG Wiedner Hauptstrasse 57, 1040 Vienna, Austria. T. +435909003379. Fax +43590900233. E-mail: info@iucab.com.
Pres address not obtained.
URL: https://iucab.com/
History 21 Sep 1953, Amsterdam (Netherlands). Founded upon agreement of a charter between societies of commercial agents and brokers. Revised charter agreed 7 Oct 1988, Trento (Italy), 4 June 1999, Dublin (Ireland), 21 May 2010, Athens (Greece), 19 May 2016, Malaga (Spain) and 9 Oct 2020 (virtual). Former names and other names: *International Union of Commercial Agents and Brokers (IUCAB)* – former; *Union internationale des agents commerciaux et des courtiers* – former; *Internationale Union der Handelsvertreter und Handelsmakler* – former. Registration: EU Transparency Register, No/ID: 119913534218-35, Start date: 11 Mar 2019. **Aims** Uphold freedom and sound development of international trade; protect and promote common interests of commercial agents and brokers of all countries and strengthen the position of commercial agents and brokers as independent businessmen. **Structure** Conference of Delegates (annual, including every 3 to 4 years with Congress); Executive Committee; Praesidium; Secretarial Working Group; Legal Working Group. **Languages** English, French, German, Italian, Spanish. **Staff** 3.00 FTE, paid. **Finance** Sources: members' dues. **Activities** Guidance/assistance/consulting; networking/liaising. **Events** *Annual Delegates Meeting* Berlin (Germany) 2023, *Annual Delegates Meeting* Limassol (Cyprus) 2022, *Annual Delegates Meeting* Vienna (Austria) 2021, *Annual Delegates Meeting* 2020, *Annual Delegates Meeting* Valencia (Spain) 2019. **Publications** *IUCAB Newsletter* (10 a year). Articles; social media updates.
Members National associations in 23 countries:
Austria, Belgium, Canada, Congo Brazzaville, Cyprus, Denmark, Finland, France, Germany, Greece, Ireland, Italy, Mexico, Netherlands, Norway, Peru, Russia, Slovenia, Spain, Sweden, Switzerland, UK, USA.
IGO Relations Recognized by: *European Commission (EC, #06633)*. **NGO Relations** Recognized by: *International Chamber of Commerce (ICC, #12534)*. [2022.05.10/XD2706/y/**D**]

- ♦ International Machiavelli Society (unconfirmed)
- ♦ International Machine Learning Society (internationally oriented national body)
- ♦ International Machinery Insurers' Association / see International Association of Engineering Insurers, The (#11874)
- ♦ International Magic Congress (inactive)

♦ International Magnesium Association (IMA) 14073

Exec Vice-Pres 1000 Westgate Drive, Ste 252, Minneapolis MN 55114, USA. T. +18474471702 – +1847(16513797305. Fax +18472902266. E-mail: info@intlmag.org.
URL: http://www.intlmag.org/
History Founded 1943, as *Magnesium Association*, with international membership. Present name adopted 1973. **Aims** Promote general welfare of the magnesium industry by collecting and disseminating information, encouraging research and publicizing innovative uses of the *metal*; improve the image of the magnesium producer, processor, supplier and user; encourage greater use of magnesium metal. **Structure** Board of Directors, comprising member representatives from throughout the world, elected for 3-year terms. **Languages** English. **Staff** 4.00 FTE, paid. **Activities** Knowledge management/information dissemination; events/meetings; awards/prizes/competitions. **Events** *Annual Conference* Minneapolis, MN (USA) 2021, *Annual Conference* Fukuoka (Japan) 2020, *Annual Conference* Budapest (Hungary) 2019, *Annual Conference* New Orleans, LA (USA) 2018, *Annual Conference* Singapore (Singapore) 2017. **Publications** *Magnesium Buyer's Guide* (every 2 years); *Magnesium Newsletter* (9 a year). *Desulfurization of Hot Metal by Magnesium* by N A Voronova; *Electrolytic Production of Magnesium* by Kh L Strelets; *Magnesium Products Design* by Robert S Busk; *Safe Handling of Magnesium*. World Conference proceedings; brochures; technical papers; video tapes.
Members Regular corporate members in 25 countries:
Australia, Austria, Bahrain, Belgium, Brazil, China, Denmark, Finland, France, Germany, Hungary, Iceland, Israel, Italy, Japan, Netherlands, New Zealand, Norway, Poland, Russia, Spain, Sweden, Switzerland, UK, Ukraine.
NGO Relations Member of: *Critical Raw Materials Alliance (CRM Alliance, #04959); Minor Metals Trade Association (MMTA, #16821)*. [2018/XD3556/**D**]

- ♦ International Magnetic Sign Association Inc / see International Sign Association
- ♦ International Mahavira Jain Mission (internationally oriented national body)

♦ International Mahayana Institute (IMI) 14074

Institut international Mahayana – Istituto Mahayana Internazionale
Dir Nalanda Monastery, Lieu dit Rouzegas, 81500 Labastide-Saint-Georges, France. E-mail: director@imisangha.org – office@imisangha.org.
URL: https://imisangha.org/
History 1973, Kathmandu (Nepal). Founded as the association of monks and nuns of the *Foundation for the Preservation of the Mahayana Tradition (FPMT, #09970)*. **Aims** Provide an environment conducive to development of higher *moral conduct* and service to others, and for intensive study and practice of *Buddhist philosophy* and *meditation*. **Structure** Includes: Nalanda Monastery, Lavaur (France); Thubten Shedrup Ling Monastery (Australia); Chenrezig Nuns Community (Australia); Lhungtok Choekhorling (Italy); Dorje Pamo Nunnery (France); Sera IMI House/Shedrup Sungdrel Ling (India). **Languages** English. **Staff** Voluntary. **Finance** Sources: donations. **Publications** *IMI e-newsheet*.
Members Monks and nuns (321), in 31 countries:
Argentina, Australia, Brazil, Canada, China, Denmark, France, Germany, Hong Kong, India, Ireland, Israel, Italy, Japan, Malaysia, Mexico, Mongolia, Nepal, Netherlands, New Zealand, Norway, Poland, Russia, Singapore, South Africa, Spain, Sweden, Switzerland, Taiwan, UK, Vietnam. [2022/XE3995/jv/**E**]

♦ International Maillard Reaction Society (imars) 14075

Sec-Treas Case Western Reserve Univ, Dept of Pathology, Cleveland OH 44106, USA.
Pres Food Science and Agricultural Chemistry, McGill Univ, 845 Rue Sherbrooke O, Montréal QC H3A 0G4, Canada. E-mail: foodscience.macdonald@mcgill.ca.
URL: http://www.imars.org/
History 2005. **Aims** Foster a balanced approach to understanding both the advantageous and deleterious properties of *carbonyl* compounds and their end products in *food science*, technology and medicine. **Structure** Council. Committees (5): Finance and Future Meetings; Journal; Website and Education; Nominating; Membership. **Languages** English. **Staff** 1.00 FTE, paid. **Activities** Events/meetings; training/education. **Events** *International Symposium* Montréal, QC (Canada) 2018, *International Symposium* Tokyo (Japan) 2015, *International Symposium* Nancy (France) 2012, *International Symposium* Cairns, QLD (Australia) 2009, *International Symposium* Munich (Germany) 2007. **Publications** *IMARS Highlights* (6 a year).
Members Full in 22 countries and territories:
Australia, Belgium, Canada, Chile, Czechia, Denmark, France, Germany, Italy, Japan, Korea Rep, Mexico, Netherlands, Russia, Slovakia, Spain, Sweden, Switzerland, Taiwan, Türkiye, UK, USA.
IGO Relations None. [2015.11.30/XM4288/**E**]

♦ International Maintenance Association (IMA) 14076

Main Office Via delle Scuole 13, Paradiso, 6900 Lugano TI, Switzerland. T. +41912258713. E-mail: info@ima-world.org.
URL: https://www.ima-world.org/
History 2013, Lugano (Switzerland). Founded following the "Lugano Declaration" issued at the World Maintenance Forum. Registration: No/ID: CH-501.6.014.973-0, Start date: 17 Jan 2014, Switzerland. **Aims** Enhance physical assets maintenance management. **Structure** Advisory Board; Committees. **Languages** Arabic, English. **Activities** Certification/accreditation; events/meetings; networking/liaising; research and development; training/education. Africa; Americas; Europe; Far East; Middle East. **Events** *World Maintenance Forum* Riyadh (Saudi Arabia) 2022, *World Maintenance Forum* Lugano (Switzerland) 2019. **Members** Organizations and agencies; professionals and students. Membership countries not specified. **NGO Relations** Partner of (1): *Arab Council of Operations and Maintenance (OMAINTEC, #00931)*. [2020.10.21/XM8590/**D**]

♦ International Maize and Wheat Improvement Center 14077

Centre international d'amélioration du maïs et du blé – Centro Internacional de Mejoramiento de Maiz y Trigo (CIMMYT)
Dir Gen Apdo Postal 041, CAP Plaza Galerías, Col Verónica Anzures, 11305 Mexico City CDMX, Mexico. T. +525558042004. Fax +525558047558 – +525558047559. E-mail: cimmyt@cgiar.org.

URL: http://www.cimmyt.org/

History 1966, Mexico City (Mexico). Founded as an international agricultural research centre. CIMMYT grew out of a pilot programme sponsored by the Mexican government and the Rockefeller Foundation in the 1940s and 1950s aimed at raising farm productivity in Mexico. **Aims** Improve livelihoods and foster more productive, sustainable maize and wheat *farming* throughout the *developing world*, specifically targeting food insecurity and malnutrition, climate change and environmental degradation. **Structure** Board of Trustees; Management Team; Director General; Headquarters in Mexico City (Mexico). **Languages** English. **Staff** 1250.00 FTE, paid. 570 in Headquarters; 510 working in 18 countries throughout Africa, Asia and Latin America. **Finance** Support through: *Bill and Melinda Gates Foundation (BMGF)*; *CGIAR System Organization (CGIAR, #03843)*; development banks; public and private agencies, including *Australian Centre for International Agricultural Research (ACIAR)*; *Department for International Development (DFID, inactive)*; *Deutsche Gesellschaft für Internationale Zusammenarbeit (GIZ)*; *United States Agency for International Development (USAID)*. Annual budget: US$ 150,000,000. **Activities** Research/documentation; training/education; networking/liaising; capacity building; events/meetings. **Events** *CIMMYT50* Mexico City (Mexico) 2016, *Turning research into impact* Mexico City (Mexico) 2016, *Asian Maize Conference* Bangkok (Thailand) 2015, *Asian maize conference* Nanning (China) 2010, *International wheat conference* St Petersburg (Russia) 2010. **Publications** Annual Report; monographs; conference proceedings; manuals. **Information Services** *CIMMYT Dataverse Network*; *International Wheat Information System (IWIS)* – data management system handling and integrating information on bread, durum wheat and triticale. **Members** Not a membership organization. **IGO Relations** Member of: *Intergovernmental Organizations Conference (IGO Conference, #11498)*; *International Information System for the Agricultural Sciences and Technology (AGRIS, #13848)*. Part of CGIAR consortium of 15 agricultural research centres, including: *Africa Rice Center (AfricaRice, #00518)*, Bouak (Cte d'Ivoire); *Bioversity International (#03262)*, Rome (Italy); *International Center for Agricultural Research in the Dry Areas (ICARDA, #12466)*; *International Livestock Research Institute (ILRI, #14062)*, Nairobi (Kenya); *International Rice Research Institute (IRRI, #14754)*, Manila (Philippines). **NGO Relations** Member of (4): *Extractive Industries Transparency Initiative (EITI, #09229)*; *UNESCO Network of Associated Libraries (UNAL, #20311)*; *Whole Grain Initiative (WGI, #20939)*; *World Association of Agronomists (WAA, #21115)* (Associate). Participates in: *Agricultural Libraries Network (AGLINET, #00571)*; *International Plant Phenotyping Network (IPPN, #14593)*. Cooperates with the other CGIAR supported centres: *Center for International Forestry Research (CIFOR, #03646)*, Bogor (Indonesia); *International Centre for Tropical Agriculture (#12527)*, Cali (Colombia); *International Food Policy Research Institute (IFPRI, #13622)*, Washington DC (USA); *International Institute of Tropical Agriculture (IITA, #13933)*, Ibadan (Nigeria); *International Potato Center (#14627)*, Lima (Peru); *International Water Management Institute (IWMI, #15867)*, Rajagiriya (Sri Lanka); *World Agroforestry Centre (ICRAF, #21072)*, Nairobi (Kenya); *WorldFish (#21507)*, Manila (Philippines). Instrumental in setting up: *Association of Maize Researchers in Africa (AMRA, no recent information)*; *Eastern and Central Africa Maize and Wheat Network (ECAMAW, inactive)*.
[2021/XE0270/**E**]

♦ International Making Cities Livable Council (IMCL Council) 14078

Contact 1209 SW 6th Ave, Ste 404, Portland OR 97204, USA.
URL: http://www.livablecities.org/

History 1985. **Aims** Enhance the *well-being* of inhabitants of cities and towns; strengthen community; improve social and physical health increase civic engagement by reshaping the built environment of cities, suburbs and towns. **Structure** Board. **Activities** Through conferences, brings together officials, practitioners and scholars in planning, public health, urban design, transportation planning, land development, landscape architecture, architecture, pediatrics, social sciences, child development and the arts, from around the world. **Events** *Conference* Charleston, SC (USA) 2010, *Conference* Portland, OR (USA) 2009, *Conference* Santa Fe, NM (USA) 2008, *Conference* Portland, OR (USA) 2007, *Conference* Santa Fe, NM (USA) 2006. **Publications** Proceedings; books.
Members Organizations and individuals in 48 countries and territories:
Australia, Austria, Belgium, Bosnia-Herzegovina, Brazil, Canada, China, Colombia, Croatia, Czechia, Denmark, Finland, France, Germany, Greece, Hong Kong, Hungary, India, Indonesia, Ireland, Israel, Italy, Japan, Korea Rep, Lebanon, Luxembourg, Malaysia, Mexico, Netherlands, New Zealand, Norway, Papua New Guinea, Poland, Portugal, Romania, Russia, Singapore, Slovakia, Slovenia, South Africa, Spain, Sweden, Switzerland, Taiwan, Türkiye, UK, USA, Venezuela. [2018/XE3918/**E**]

♦ International Malnutrition Task Force (IMTF) 14079

Contact Inst of Human Nutrition, Univ of Southampton, Southampton General Hosp (MP 113), Tremonar Rd, Southampton, SO16 6YD, UK.
URL: http://imtf.org/

History Sep 2005, Durban (South Africa), by *International Union of Nutritional Sciences (IUNS, #15796)*, at 18th International Congress of Nutrition. **Aims** Raise the profile of malnutrition; build capacity to prevent and treat malnutrition. **Structure** Group of Governors of 7. Steering Committee. Regional focal points (3): South/Southeast Asia; Sub-Saharan Africa; Latin America. **IGO Relations** *International Atomic Energy Agency (IAEA, #12294)*; *UNICEF (#20332)*; *WHO (#20950)*. **NGO Relations** Partners include: *International Pediatric Association (IPA, #14541)*; *Valid International*; *Regional Centre for Quality of Health Care (RCQHC, inactive)*.
[2011/XJ2257/**F**]

♦ International Mammalian Genome Society 14080

Pres McLaughlin Research Inst for Biomedical Sciences, 1520 23rd St South, Great Falls MT 59405, USA.
URL: http://www.imgs.org/

History Founded 1991. **Aims** Foster and stimulate research in mammalian genetics from sequencing and functional genomics to mutagenesis and mutant analysis; represent the concerns of members in their professional activities. **Finance** Members' dues. **Events** *Annual Conference* Tsukuba (Japan) 2023, *Annual Conference* Vancouver, BC (Canada) 2022, *Annual Conference* Washington, DC (USA) 2020, *Annual Conference* Yokohama (Japan) 2015, *Annual Conference* St Petersburg, FL (USA) 2012. **Publications** *Mammalian Genome* – journal.
Members Individuals in 20 countries:
Australia, Canada, China, Czechia, France, Germany, Israel, Italy, Japan, Korea Rep, Netherlands, Poland, Russia, Slovenia, Spain, Switzerland, Taiwan, Türkiye, UK, USA. [2015/XM3485/v/**D**]

♦ International Management Assistants (IMA) 14081

Exec Sec address not obtained. E-mail: associationsecretary@ima-network.org – executivechairman@ima-network.org.
URL: http://www.ima-network.org/

History 1974. Former names and other names: *European Association of Professional Secretaries (EAPS)* – former (1974 to 1 Jan 1999); *European Management Assistants (EUMA)* – former (1 Jan 1999 to Feb 2017). Registration: France. **Aims** Be the leading international network of Management Support Professionals; connect and engage peers within and across borders and empower members to excel. **Structure** Annual General Meeting; Council; Executive Committee. **Languages** English. **Staff** Voluntary. **Finance** Sources: meeting proceeds; members' dues. **Activities** Events/meetings; knowledge management/information dissemination; monitoring/evaluation; networking/liaising; training/education. **Events** *Annual Conference* Berlin (Germany) 2026, *Annual Conference* Ghent (Belgium) 2025, *Annual Conference* Stockholm (Sweden) 2024, *Annual Conference* Cape Town (South Africa) 2023, *Annual Conference* Helsinki (Finland) 2022.
Members National groups in 20 countries:
Belgium, Cyprus, Denmark, Finland, France, Germany, Greece, Hungary, Iceland, India, Italy, Luxembourg, Netherlands, Norway, South Africa, Spain, Sweden, Switzerland, Türkiye, UK.
Individual membership where no national group exists in 17 countries:
Bosnia-Herzegovina, Botswana, Canada, Croatia, Ireland, Lithuania, Nigeria, Poland, Portugal, Russia, Saudi Arabia, Slovenia, South Africa, Türkiye, Ukraine, United Arab Emirates, USA. [2022.05.22/XD0118/v/**D**]

- ♦ International Management Centre, Budapest / see CEU Business School
- ♦ International Management Centres Association (inactive)

♦ International Management Development Association (IMDA) 14082

Contact 548 Springbrook Drive, Palmyra PA 17078, USA. T. +17175666586. Fax +17175661191. E-mail: k9x@psu.edu.
URL: http://www.imda-usa.org/

History 1987, Pennsylvania (USA). **Aims** Provide an interdisciplinary and global platform for the exchange of ideas in the pursuit of professional growth and opportunities for academics, practitioners and public policy-makers at all levels. **Structure** Executive Board; Board of Country Directors. **Languages** English. **Staff** 1.00 FTE, paid. **Finance** Sources: donations; meeting proceeds; members' dues. Annual budget: 50,000 USD (2022). **Activities** Publishing activities; training/education. **Events** *Annual World Business Congress* Jyväskylä (Finland) 2022, *Annual World Business Congress* Nicosia (Cyprus) 2019, *Annual World Business Congress* Hong Kong (Hong Kong) 2018, *Annual World Business Congress* Bishkek (Kyrgyzstan) 2017, *Annual World Business Congress* London (UK) 2016. **Publications** *Journal of Euromarketing* (4 a year); *IMDA Newsletter* (4 a year); *Journal of Transnational Management* (4 a year); *Advances in Global Business* – journal. Books; monographs; proceedings; reports.
Members Institutional; Individual; Student. Members in 78 countries and territories:
Albania, Argentina, Australia, Austria, Bangladesh, Belgium, Bosnia-Herzegovina, Botswana, Brazil, Brunei Darussalam, Bulgaria, Canada, Chile, China, Colombia, Croatia, Czechia, Denmark, Dominican Rep, Egypt, Estonia, Fiji, Finland, France, Germany, Greece, Hong Kong, Hungary, Iceland, India, Indonesia, Ireland, Israel, Italy, Japan, Jordan, Kenya, Korea Rep, Kuwait, Kyrgyzstan, Macau, Malaysia, Malta, Mexico, Montenegro, Morocco, Netherlands, New Zealand, Nigeria, Northern Cyprus, Norway, Pakistan, Peru, Philippines, Poland, Portugal, Romania, Russia, Saudi Arabia, Serbia, Singapore, South Africa, Spain, Sudan, Suriname, Sweden, Switzerland, Taiwan, Tanzania UR, Thailand, Türkiye, UK, Ukraine, United Arab Emirates, Uruguay, USA, Venezuela, Zimbabwe. [2022.02.08/XF3519/**F**]

- ♦ International Management Institute, Kiev (internationally oriented national body)
- ♦ International Management Institute, St Petersburg (internationally oriented national body)
- ♦ International Management Systems Association / see International Project Management Association (#14655)

♦ International Manganese Institute (IMnI) 14083

Institut international du manganèse

Exec Dir 56 rue de Londres, 75008 Paris, France. T. +33145630634. Fax +33142894292. E-mail: imni@manganese.org.
URL: http://www.manganese.org/

History 5 May 1975, Paris (France). Bylaws adopted: Dec 2008; Jun 2013. Former names and other names: *Manganese Centre* – former; *Centre du manganèse* – former. **Aims** Provide vision and guidance to the manganese industry by promoting economic, social and environmental responsibility and sustainability for all stakeholders, based on independent studies and sound science. **Structure** General Assembly (annual); Supervisory Board; Executive Board; Committees (2); Sub-Committee; Division (1). **Languages** English, French. **Staff** 4.00 FTE, paid. **Finance** Sources: members' dues. **Activities** Research/documentation; standards/guidelines; advocacy/lobbying/activism; events/meetings. **Events** *Annual Conference and General Assembly* Cape Town (South Africa) 2021, *Annual Conference and General Assembly* Cape Town (South Africa) 2020, *Annual Conference and General Assembly* Vienna (Austria) 2019, *Annual Conference and General Assembly* Kuala Lumpur (Malaysia) 2018, *Annual Conference and General Assembly* Miami, FL (USA) 2017. **Publications** *IMnI China Weekly*; *IMnI ROW Weekly*. Annual reviews; regulatory reports. **Members** Ordinary; Affiliate; EPD Members; Chemical Products. Members in over 30 countries. Membership countries not specified. **NGO Relations** Member of (2): *International Council on Mining and Metals (ICMM, #13048)*; *ResponsibleSteel (#18921)* (associate). [2020/XD4437/j/**D**]

♦ International Map Collectors' Society (IMCoS) 14084

Vice Chairperson address not obtained.
URL: http://www.imcos.org/

History 1980, London (UK). Founded by a group lead by Yasha Beresiner and Malcolm Young. **Aims** Promote and encourage map collecting, the study of *cartography* and its history; encourage preservation of maps for future generations and provide practical information to assist this. **Structure** Advisory Council; Executive Committee; President; National Representatives. **Languages** English. **Staff** Part-time, paid. **Finance** Members' dues. Advertising revenue. **Activities** Awards/prizes/competitions; events/meetings; networking/liaising. **Events** *IMCoS International Symposium* Arlington, TX (USA) 2022, *Mapping the Pacific Conference* Sydney, NSW (Australia) 2022, *International Symposium* Brussels (Belgium) 2021, *International Symposium* Sydney, NSW (Australia) 2020, *International Symposium* Manila (Philippines) / Hong Kong (Hong Kong) 2018. **Publications** *IMCoS Journal* (4 a year).
Members Individuals in 51 countries and territories:
Andorra, Argentina, Australia, Austria, Belgium, Bulgaria, Canada, China, Croatia, Cyprus, Czechia, Finland, France, Georgia, Germany, Greece, Guatemala, Hong Kong, Hungary, Iceland, India, Indonesia, Ireland, Israel, Italy, Japan, Korea Rep, Latvia, Luxembourg, Malta, Mexico, Netherlands, New Zealand, Norway, Pakistan, Philippines, Portugal, Romania, Russia, Saudi Arabia, Singapore, South Africa, Spain, Sweden, Switzerland, Thailand, Türkiye, UK, United Arab Emirates, USA, Zimbabwe.
[2022/XD0082/v/**C**]

- ♦ International Map Dealers Association / see International Map Industry Association (#14085)

♦ International Map Industry Association (IMIA) 14086

Contact 7467 Ridge Rd, Ste 220, Hanover MD 21043, USA. E-mail: info@imiamaps.org.
URL: https://imiamaps.org/

Aims Represent the world of maps. **Structure** Board of Directors. **Activities** Events/meetings. **Publications** *IMIA e-newsletter* (regular). **NGO Relations** Affiliated organizations: *International Cartographic Association (ICA, #12446)*; *UN-GGO: Geospatial Societies (UN-GGIM GS, #20324)*; *Royal Institution of Chartered Surveyors (RICS, #18991)*; national organizations. [2023/XJ7866/t/**C**]

♦ International Map Industry Association (IMIA) 14085

Exec Dir 7467 Ridge Rd, Ste 220, Hanover MD 21043, USA. E-mail: info@imiamaps.org.
URL: https://imiamaps.org/

History 1981. Former names and other names: *International Map Dealers Association (IMDA)* – former; *International Map Traders Association* – former; *International Map Trade Association (IMTA)* – former. **Aims** Represent the world of maps. **Structure** Board of Directors. **Events** *Asia Pacific Conference* Sydney, NSW (Australia) 2013, *Asia Pacific global conference* Bangkok (Thailand) 2011, *Annual European conference* Novara (Italy) 2011, *Annual European conference* Bayonne (France) 2010, *Asia Pacific global conference* Melbourne, VIC (Australia) 2010. **Publications** *IMIA e-newsletter*. Membership Directory. **NGO Relations** Member of (1): *UN-GGO: Geospatial Societies (UN-GGIM GS, #20324)*. Cooperates with (1): *Geo-Information for Disaster Management (Gi4DM)*. [2023/XN1649/t/**C**]

- ♦ International Map Trade Association / see International Map Industry Association (#14085)
- ♦ International Map Traders Association / see International Map Industry Association (#14085)

♦ International Marangoni Association (IMA) 14087

Contact Inst of Fluid Mechanics and Heat Transfer, Vienna Univ of Technology, Getreidemarkt 9, 1060 Vienna, Austria. T. +4315880132212. Fax +4315880132298.
URL: http://marangoniassociation.com/

History Sep 2001, Rauischholzhausen (Germany). **Aims** Expose young scientists to research themes and applications of interfacial *fluid mechanics*, network among researchers from academia and industry, and promote new collaborations. **Structure** Steering Committee. **Languages** English. **Staff** None permanent. **Finance** Organizational support for conference organization. **Activities** Events/meetings. **Events** *Biennial Conference* Iasi (Romania) 2022, *Biennial Conference* Iasi (Romania) 2020, *Biennial Conference* Guilin (China) 2018, *Biennial Conference* Bad Honnef (Germany) 2016, *Biennial Conference* Vienna (Austria) 2014. **Publications** Conference proceedings. **Members** Full. Membership countries not specified.
[2019.02.12/XJ7393/c/**E**]

♦ International Marathon Medical Directors Association (IMMDA) . . . 14088

Chair 24 West 57th St, Ste 605, New York NY 10019, USA. T. +12127655763. E-mail: immdanyc@aol.com.
URL: http://immda.org/

History 1982, by medical directors of 3 international marathons (London, Madrid (Spain) and New York City). **Aims** Study the health of long-distance *runners*; promote knowledge of the best methods in prevention and treatment of injuries; offer guidelines that may provide standardization in the medical support of marathon races throughout the world. **Structure** Board of Governors. **Activities** Organizes annual Scientific and Business Meetings; Autumn event held in USA city and Spring event held outside USA. **Events** *Meeting*

Barcelona (Spain) 2010, *Scientific meeting* Barcelona (Spain) 2007, *Annual General Meeting* New York, NY (USA) 2007. **Members** Marathon Medical Directors (43). Membership countries not specified. [2019/XD8480/**D**]

♦ International Marcé Society for Perinatal Mental Health (Marcé Society) 14089

Office 5034-A Thoroughbred Lane, Brentwood TN 37027, USA. T. +16153242362. E-mail: info@marcesociety.com.
URL: http://www.marcesociety.com/

History 1980. Named after French psychiatrist Louis Victor Marcé (1828-1864). Former names and other names: *International Society for Psychiatric Disorders of Childbearing* – alias; *International Association for the Study of Psychiatric Disorders of Childbearing* – former; *International Society for the Understanding, Prevention and Treatment of Mental Illness Relating to Child Bearing* – former. **Aims** Improve understanding, prevention and treatment of *mental* illness related to childbearing. **Structure** Executive Committee; Board of Directors. Nordic branch: *Nordic Marcé Society (#17341)*. **Events** *Biennial International Conference* London (UK) 2022, *Biennial International Conference* Iowa City, IA (USA) 2020, *Biennial International Conference* Bangalore (India) 2018, *Conference* Stockholm (Sweden) 2017, *Biennial International Conference* Melbourne, VIC (Australia) 2016. **Publications** *Marcé Society Newsletter*.
Members Full in 18 countries:
Australia, Belgium, Canada, Finland, France, Germany, Iceland, India, Ireland, Israel, Italy, Japan, New Zealand, South Africa, Sweden, Switzerland, UK, USA.
NGO Relations Member of: *Global Alliance for Maternal Mental Health (GAMMH, #10208)*. [2021/XE4749/**E**]

♦ International Marching League / see IML Walking Association (#11130)
♦ International Margaret Cavendish Society (unconfirmed)
♦ International Margarine Association of the Countries of Europe / see European Margarine Association (#07736)
♦ International Marie de France Society (internationally oriented national body)
♦ International Marine Animal Trainers Association (internationally oriented national body)

♦ International Marine Biotechnology Association (IMBA) 14090

Sec-Treas Inst of Marine and Environmental Technology, 701 E Pratt St, Baltimore MD 21202, USA. T. +14102348883.
URL: http://www.theimba.org/

History Founded 1989, Tokyo (Japan), at the 1st International Marine Biotechnology Conference. **Aims** Promote marine biotechnology for the benefit of humanity and natural ecosystems; work to benefit and inform students, scientists and technologists, decision-makers and industry leaders, industries and governments of the world; facilitate communication among and between practising experts and the various affiliated marine biotechnology societies and associations. **Structure** Board, comprising President, Vice-President, Secretary-Treasurer, Immediate Past President, Conference Director, Chair Nominating Committee and 11 members. **Activities** Events/meetings. **Events** *International Marine Biotechnology Conference* Shizuoka (Japan) 2019, *International Marine Biotechnology Conference* Baltimore, MD (USA) 2016, *International Marine Biotechnology Conference / International Marine Biotechnology Conference – IMBC* Brisbane, QLD (Australia) 2013, *International Marine Biotechnology Conference – IMBC* Qingdao (China) 2010, *International conference on marine biotechnology* Tromsø (Norway) 2009. [2014.12.08/XJ6459/**E**]

♦ International Marine Centre (internationally oriented national body)

♦ International Marine Certification Institute (IMCI) 14091

CEO Rue Abbé Cuypers 3, 1040 Brussels, Belgium. T. +3227416836. Fax +3227412418. E-mail: info@imci.org.
URL: http://www.imci.org/

History 10 Nov 1992, Zaventem (Belgium). Founded on the initiative of Lars Erik Granholm. Registration: Start date: 24 Jun 1993, Belgium. **Aims** Serve the interests of the European and international *recreational boating* (boats and yachts) industry through provision of a valuable certification service, recognized by the European Commission. **Structure** International Board of 34 Directors. **Languages** English, French, German, Italian. **Activities** Certification/accreditation; events/meetings. **Publications** Articles.
Members Full in 19 countries and territories:
Belgium, Canada, Croatia, Denmark, Estonia, Finland, Germany, Greece, Italy, Malta, Netherlands, New Zealand, Portugal, Russia, Spain, Sweden, Türkiye, UK, USA.
IGO Relations Recognized by: *European Commission (EC, #06633)*. [2021/XE2119/j/**E**]

♦ International Marine Design Conference (meeting series)
♦ International Marine Electronics Alliance (unconfirmed)

♦ International Marine Environment Protection Association (INTERMEPA) 14092

Office c/o HELMEPA, Pergamou Str 5, Nea Smirni, 171 21 Athens, Greece. E-mail: helmepa@helmepa.gr.
URL: http://www.intermepa.org/

History 6 Jun 2006. Registered in accordance with Greek law. **Structure** Steering Committee.
Members Full in 7 countries:
Australia, Cyprus, Greece, Türkiye, Ukraine, Uruguay, USA.
IGO Relations *International Maritime Organization (IMO, #14102)*. [2019.06.11/XJ5966/**C**]

♦ International Marinelife Alliance (IMA) 14093

Contact address not obtained. T. +6326378860.

History 1985, USA. National branches set up: Philippines, 1986; Canada, 1987 – became *Ocean Voice International (no recent information)*; Indonesia, 1998; Hong Kong, 1999; Guam. Currently based in the Philippines. **Aims** As a nongovernmental marine conservation organization, help conserve marine biodiversity and eliminate human-induced stresses on the marine environment through programs and initiatives that promote sustainable use of living marine resources, conserve biodiversity and protect marine habitat for the benefit of local people; advocate judicious utilization of marine resources and conservation of coral reefs in underdeveloped countries; combat destructive fishing practices; advocate defence of the environment and nurture environmental activism; popularize alternative livelihoods for surplus fisherfolk; promote "clean" harvesting technology. **Activities** Works to elevate the predominantly extractive orientation of Philippine fisheries into the realm of sustainable management. Participates in initiatives in the Indo-Pacific region to combat cyanide fishing. **Events** *Annual General Meeting* Megisti (Greece) 2015, *Annual General Meeting* Sant'Antioco (Italy) 2014. **NGO Relations** Partner of: *WorldFish (#21507)*. [2021/XF6171/**F**]

♦ International Marine Minerals Society (internationally oriented national body)

♦ International Marine Purchasing Association (IMPA) 14094

Secretariat East Bridge House, East Street, Colchester, CO1 2TX, UK. T. +441206798900. Fax +441206798909. E-mail: enquiries@impa.net.
CEO and Chair Dannebrog Rederi, 113 Rungsted Strandvej, 2960 Rungsted, Denmark. T. +4545177734. Fax +4545177737. E-mail: swk@dannebrog.com.
URL: http://www.impa.net/

History 1978. **Aims** Promote and facilitate cooperation and understanding between purchasers and suppliers in the global maritime business; create, develop and support standards within the industry; enhance and promote the art and science of marine purchasing in all applied forms. **Structure** General Council (meets 3 times a year). **Finance** Sources: members' dues. **Activities** Events/meetings; networking/liaising; standards/guidelines. **Events** *Annual Conference* London (UK) 2019, *Conference* Singapore (Singapore) 2019, *Annual Conference* London (UK) 2018, *Conference* Singapore (Singapore) 2018, *Annual Conference* London (UK) 2017. **Publications** *Marine Trader* – journal. *IMPA Marine Stores Guide* (4th ed).
Members Honorary; Purchaser; Supplier; Student. Companies and individuals in 83 countries and territories:
Algeria, Argentina, Australia, Bahrain, Bangladesh, Belgium, Brazil, Bulgaria, Cameroon, Canada, Chile, China, Colombia, Congo Brazzaville, Côte d'Ivoire, Cyprus, Denmark, Djibouti, Egypt, Faeroe Is, Fiji, Finland, France, Germany, Ghana, Greece, Hong Kong, India, Indonesia, Isle of Man, Italy, Japan, Jordan, Kenya, Korea Rep, Kuwait, Latvia, Lebanon, Libya, Lithuania, Malaysia, Malta, Mexico, Morocco, Mozambique, Namibia, Netherlands, Nigeria, Norway, Oman, Pakistan, Panama, Peru, Philippines, Poland, Portugal, Qatar, Russia, Saudi Arabia, Senegal, Singapore, South Africa, Spain, Sri Lanka, Sudan, Sweden, Switzerland, Syrian AR, Taiwan, Tanzania UR, Thailand, Togo, Trinidad-Tobago, Tunisia, Türkiye, UK, Ukraine, United Arab Emirates, Uruguay, USA, Venezuela, Vietnam, Yemen. [2020/XG0297/v/**C**]

♦ International Marine Simulator Forum (IMSF) 14095

Chair address not obtained. T. +31653590001.
URL: http://www.imsf.org/

History 1978. Current constitution revised 26 Sep 1993. **Aims** Advance maritime education, training and research through the use of simulation. **Structure** General Meeting (annual); Executive. **Languages** English. **Staff** 4.00 FTE, voluntary. **Finance** Members' dues. **Activities** Knowledge management/information dissemination; guidance/assistance/consulting; publishing activities; events/meetings. **Events** *Annual General Assembly / Annual General Meeting Workshop Seminar* Dalian (China) 2014, *Annual General Assembly / Annual General Meeting Workshop Seminar* Turku (Finland) 2013, *MARSIM : International Conference on Marine Simulation and Ship Maneuverability* Singapore (Singapore) 2012, *MARTECH : Biennial International Conference on Maritime Training Communication and Technology / Triennial MARSIM Conference* Singapore (Singapore) 2012, *Annual General Assembly / Annual General Meeting Workshop Seminar* Haugesund (Norway) 2011. **Publications** Conference proceedings.
Members Organizations (85) in 35 countries and territories:
Australia, Belgium, Brazil, Canada, China, Croatia, Denmark, Finland, Germany, India, Ireland, Italy, Japan, Korea Rep, Latvia, Lithuania, Malaysia, Netherlands, New Zealand, Norway, Panama, Philippines, Poland, Romania, Russia, Singapore, South Africa, Spain, Sri Lanka, Sweden, Taiwan, Türkiye, UK, USA, Vietnam. [2019.02.14/XF5061/**F**]

♦ International Marine Transit Association / see INTERFERRY (#11470)
♦ International Maritime Association (inactive)
♦ International Maritime Association of the Eastern Mediterranean / see International Maritime Association of the Mediterranean (#14096)

♦ International Maritime Association of the Mediterranean (IMAM) . . 14096

Pres address not obtained. E-mail: jasnapo@riteh.hr.
URL: http://www.imamhomepage.org/

History 1977, as *International Maritime Association of the Eastern Mediterranean (IMAEM)*. Current constitution approved Sep 2015. Registered in accordance with Greek law. **Aims** Promote international cooperation among researchers and engineers in the fields of naval architecture and *marine engineering*. **Structure** Executive Committee; Secretariat (rotates with congresses). Technical Committees. **Languages** English. **Activities** Events/meetings; knowledge management/information dissemination. **Events** *International Congress* Lisbon (Portugal) 2017. **Publications** *IMAM Newsletter*.
Members Senior; Ordinary; Associate. Senior (11) in 7 countries:
Bulgaria, Croatia, Greece, Italy, Portugal, Spain, Türkiye.
Ordinary (21) in 14 countries:
Albania, Bulgaria, Croatia, Egypt, France, Greece, Italy, Malta, Morocco, Portugal, Romania, Spain, Türkiye, Ukraine.
Associate (2) in 2 countries:
Iran Islamic Rep, Japan. [2018/XM6440/**C**]

♦ International Maritime Bureau (IMB) 14097

Bureau maritime international (BMI)

Dir ICC Commercial Crime Services, Cinnabar Wharf, 26 Wapping High St, London, E1W 1NG, UK. T. +442074236960. Fax +442074236961. E-mail: imb@icc-ccs.org.
URL: https://www.icc-ccs.org/index.php/icc/imb

History Jan 1981. Founded within the framework of *International Chamber of Commerce (ICC, #12534)*, following decision of ICC Council, Nov 1980. One of 3 units comprising *ICC Commercial Crime Services (CCS, see: #12534)*. Former names and other names: *ICC International Maritime Bureau* – former. **Aims** Prevent and contain fraud and suspect practices in international *transportation* systems; provide information on potential trading partners, investigations, negotiations, authentication of documents, special reports, seminars, advice on claims and recoveries; design and provide educational services; assist injured parties to effect financial recovery. **Structure** Board of Directors; Director/CEO. Head office in UK; Regional Office in Kuala Lumpur (Malaysia), including piracy reporting centre. **Languages** English. **Staff** 80.00 FTE, paid. **Finance** Sources: fees for services; members' dues. **Activities** Events/meetings; guidance/assistance/consulting; knowledge management/information dissemination. **Events** *International Meeting on Global Piracy Armed Robbery and Maritime Security / International Meeting on Piracy* Kuala Lumpur (Malaysia) 2015, *Annual Workshop* Liphook (UK) 2015, *Triennial meeting on piracy and maritime security* Kuala Lumpur (Malaysia) 2007, *Annual Workshop* UK 2004, *Annual Workshop* UK 2003. **Publications** *IMB Confidential Bulletin* (bi-weekly); *Commercial Crime International* (12 a year). Information Services: Confidential databases on all aspects of trading fraud.
Members Corporations; banks; underwriters; shipping owners and traders in 51 countries. Membership countries not specified. [2020.11.16/XE0237/**E**]

♦ International Maritime Bureau of Zanzibar Against the Slave Trade (inactive)
♦ International Maritime Committee / see Comité maritime international (#04192)
♦ International Maritime Economic History Association / see International Maritime History Association (#14100)
♦ International Maritime Employers Committee / see International Maritime Employers' Council (#14098)

♦ International Maritime Employers' Council (IMEC) 14098

CEO 2 Turnberry House, The Links, Solent Business Park, Whiteley, Fareham, PO15 7FJ, UK. T. +442077029138. E-mail: info@imec.org.uk.
URL: http://www.imec.org.uk/

History Former names and other names: *International Maritime Employers Committee (IMEC)* – former. Registration: Companies House, Start date: 2006, UK. **Aims** Provide a forum for employers to exchange views and information on seafarers' wages and conditions worldwide. **Structure** Executive Committee; Secretariat.
Members Companies in 38 countries and territories:
Bahamas, Bangladesh, Belgium, Bermuda, Canada, Chile, China, Cyprus, Denmark, Estonia, France, Germany, Greece, Hong Kong, India, Iran Islamic Rep, Italy, Kuwait, Latvia, Luxembourg, Monaco, Netherlands, Norway, Philippines, Poland, Portugal, Romania, Russia, Singapore, Slovenia, Spain, Sri Lanka, Switzerland, Taiwan, Türkiye, UK, United Arab Emirates, USA.
NGO Relations Member of (1): *Maritime Piracy Humanitarian Response Programme (MPHRP, #16583)*. Cooperates with (1): *International Transport Workers' Federation (ITF, #15726)*. [2022.02.10/XJ5075/**F**]

♦ International Maritime Health Association (IMHA) 14099

Association internationale de médecine maritime – Internationale Vereniging voor Maritieme Geneeskunde

Secretariat Italiëlei 51, 2000 Antwerp, Belgium. T. +3232290776. Fax +3232252038. E-mail: imha@online.be.
URL: http://www.imha.net/

History 22 Jun 1997. Registration: Banque-Carrefour des Entreprises, No/ID: 0464.811.231, Start date: 24 Dec 1998, Belgium. **Aims** Promote and advance scientific research and the quality of maritime medicine worldwide; create a forum where people, ideas, data, efforts, research and questions regarding maritime health can meet. **Structure** General Assembly (every 2 years); Council. **Languages** English. **Staff** 0.50 FTE, paid. **Finance** Members' dues. **Activities** Knowledge management/information dissemination. **Events** *Biennial Symposium* Hamburg (Germany) 2019, *Biennial Symposium* Manila (Philippines) 2017, *Biennial Symposium* Bergen (Norway) 2015, *Biennial Symposium* Brest (France) 2013, *Biennial Symposium* Odessa (Ukraine) 2011. **Publications** *International Maritime Health* (4 a year) – newsletter.
Members Individuals (200) in 37 countries:
Australia, Belgium, Brazil, Bulgaria, Canada, China, Côte d'Ivoire, Croatia, Denmark, Estonia, Finland, France, Germany, Greece, Hungary, India, Indonesia, Italy, Jamaica, Japan, Kuwait, Latvia, Netherlands, Norway, Pakistan, Panama, Philippines, Poland, Russia, Saudi Arabia, Singapore, Spain, Sweden, Thailand, UK, USA, Vietnam.
Consultative Status Consultative status granted from: *International Maritime Organization (IMO, #14102)* (provisional). **NGO Relations** Member of (1): *Maritime Piracy Humanitarian Response Programme (MPHRP, #16583)*. [2019/XD6702/v/**D**]

♦ International Maritime History Association (IMHA) 14100

Sec Dept of History, Old Dominion Univ, 8047 Batten Arts and Letters Lldg, Norfolk VA 23529, USA. E-mail: iheidbri@odu.edu.
Pres School of Business and Governance, Murdoch Univ, South Str, Murdoch WA 6150, Australia.
URL: https://imha.info/

History Aug 1990, Leuven (Belgium), but tracing back to 1986. Original title: *International Maritime Economic History Association (IMEHA)*. Current title adopted Jul 2016, when merged with *International Commission of Maritime History (ICMH, inactive)*. **Aims** Promote maritime history globally; facilitate collaboration between maritime researchers. **Structure** General Assembly (every 4 years); Executive Group. **Languages** English. **Staff** Part-time, voluntary. **Finance** Members' dues. **Activities** Events/meetings. **Events** *Congress* Porto (Portugal) 2022, *Quadrennial Congress* Perth, WA (Australia) 2016, *Quadrennial Congress* Ghent (Belgium) 2012, *Quadrennial Congress* Greenwich (UK) 2008, *Meeting on historical perspectives on port economics* Kotka (Finland) 2006. **Publications** *IMHA Newsletter* (4 a year); *International Journal of Maritime History* (4 a year); *Research in Maritime History* (2 a year). [2018.09.10/XD2742/**D**]

♦ International Maritime Industries Forum (inactive)

♦ International Maritime Lecturers' Association (IMLA) 14101

Hon Pres c/o Maritime Academy, Noordkasteel Oost 6, 2030 Antwerp, Belgium.
URL: http://imla.co/

History Constitution adopted Jun 1980. Constitution amended: May 1984; Sep 1996; Oct 2010. **Aims** Promote contact and cooperation among lecturers of all disciplines; develop a body of professional expertise; provide a forum for discussion of common problems and exchange of information, experience, views and ideas. **Structure** Committee of 12, including Honorary Officers (Chairman, Secretary, Treasurer), Steering Committee Chairmen of ICERS, INSLC and IMEC, and those responsible for industry relations. **Languages** English. **Staff** Voluntary. **Finance** Sources: members' dues. **Activities** Events/meetings. **Events** *Conference* Odessa (Ukraine) 2023, *International Maritime English Conference (IMEC)* Novorossiisk (Russia) 2022, *Conference* Odessa (Ukraine) 2022, *Seas of Transition: Setting a Course for the Future* Malmö (Sweden) 2021, *IMEC : International Maritime English Conference* Mariehamn (Finland) 2019.

Members Colleges and individuals in 49 countries and territories:
Algeria, Argentina, Australia, Belgium, Bulgaria, Canada, China, Croatia, Denmark, Egypt, Estonia, Finland, France, Germany, Ghana, Greece, Hong Kong, India, Indonesia, Iran Islamic Rep, Italy, Japan, Korea Rep, Kuwait, Latvia, Malaysia, Maldives, Mexico, Mozambique, Myanmar, Netherlands, Nigeria, Norway, Panama, Philippines, Poland, Portugal, Romania, Russia, Singapore, Slovenia, Spain, Sri Lanka, Sweden, Trinidad-Tobago, Türkiye, UK, USA, Vietnam.

Consultative Status Consultative status granted from: *International Maritime Organization (IMO, #14102)*.
NGO Relations Located at: *World Maritime University (WMU, #21633)*. [2022/XC0118/v/**C**]

♦ International Maritime Organization (IMO) 14102

Organisation maritime internationale (OMI) – Organización Marítima Internacional (OMI)

SG 4 Albert Embankment, London, SE1 7SR, UK. T. +442077357611. Fax +442075873210. E-mail: info@imo.org.
Media enquiries address not obtained. E-mail: media@imo.org.
URL: https://www.imo.org/

History 6 Mar 1948, Geneva (Switzerland). Founded during Maritime Conference of the United Nations, on conclusion of a Convention which came into force 17 Mar 1958, after acceptance by 21 states (7 having a minimum tonnage of 1 million gross tons). Current title adopted 22 May 1982, on entry into force of amendments to the Convention passed at Assembly in Nov 1975. On the basis of a relationship agreement concluded on 13 Jan 1959, recognized as the specialized agency of *United Nations (UN, #20515)* in the field of shipping, coming within *United Nations System (#20635)* and linked to *ECOSOC (#05331)*. Former names and other names: *Inter-Governmental Maritime Consultative Organization (IMCO)* – former; *Organisation intergouvernementale consultative de la navigation maritime (OMCI)* – former; *Organización Consultiva Marítima Intergubernamental (OCMI)* – former. **Aims** Provide machinery for *cooperation* among governments on technical matters affecting international *merchant shipping* and, having special responsibility for *safety* and security of life at sea, ensure achievement of the highest possible standards of safety at sea and of efficient *navigation*; prevent *pollution* caused by ships and other craft operating in the marine environment (both sea and atmosphere). **Structure** Assembly (every 2 years in regular session). Council of 40 member States serving 2-year terms: 10 States with the largest interest in providing international shipping services; 10 other States with the largest interest in international seaborne trade; 20 other States with special interests in maritime transport or navigation, and whose election will ensure representation of all major geographic areas worldwide. Committees (5): Maritime Safety (MSC); Marine Environment Protection (MEPC); Legal; Technical Cooperation; Facilitation. Sub-Committees (7). Secretariat, headed by Secretary-General, based in London (UK). Regional coordinators/advisors: Côte d'Ivoire; Ghana; Kenya; Philippines; Trinidad-Tobago. Non-governmental organizations in consultative status and inter-governmental organizations which have signed an agreement of cooperation with IMO may send observers to IMO meetings and conferences. **Languages** Arabic, Chinese, English, French, Russian, Spanish. **Staff** 30.00 FTE, paid. Personnel negotiations through *IMO Staff Association (#11135)*. **Finance** Sources: contributions of member/participating states. Members' contributions based primarily on gross tonnage of merchant fleet. Annual budget: 67,007,000 GBP (2021).

Activities Management of treaties and agreements; politics/policy/regulatory. Management of treaties and agreements:

/On maritime safety/:
- *International Convention for the Safety of Life at Sea, 1948 (1948)*;
- *International Convention for the Safety of Life at Sea, 1974 (SOLAS, 1974)* with the *Protocol of 1978 Relating to the International Convention for the Safety of Life at Sea, 1974 (1978)* and the *Protocol of 1988 Relating to the International Convention for the Safety of Life at Sea (SOLAS PROT 1988, 1988)*;
- *International Convention on Load Lines (LL, 1966)* and the *Protocol Relating to the International Convention on Load Lines (1988)* (1988);
- *Special Trade Passenger Ships Agreement, 1971 (STP, 1971)* and the *Protocol on Space Requirements for Special Trade Passenger Ships (1973)* (1973);
- *Convention on the International Regulations for Preventing Collisions at Sea (COLREG, 1972)* (1972);
- *International Convention for Safe Containers (CSC, 1972)* (1972);
- Convention on the International Maritime Satellite Organization (INMARSAT) and Operating Agreement (1976), setting up Inmarsat;
- The Torremolinos *International Convention for the Safety of Fishing Vessels (SFV, 1977)* and the *Torremolinos Protocol of 1993 Relating to the Torremolinos International Convention for the SAfety of Fishing Vessels (SFV PROT 1993, 1993)* relating to SFV and absorbing parent convention;
- Cape Town Agreement of 2012 on the Implementation of the Provisions of the 1993 Protocol relating to the Torremolinos International Convention for the Safety of Fishing Vessels, 1977;
- *International Convention on Standards of Training, Certification and Watchkeeping for Seafarers (STCW, 1978)* (1978);
- *International Convention on Standards of Training, Certification and Watchkeeping for Fishing Vessel Personnel (STCW-F, 1995)* (1995);
- *International Convention on Maritime Search and Rescue (SAR, 1979)* (1979).

/On marine pollution/:
- *International Convention for the Prevention of Pollution from Ships (MARPOL, 1973)* (1973/1978), with protocols:
  - *International Convention for the Prevention of Pollution from Ships as Modified by the Protocol of 1978 (1978)*;
  - *Protocol of 1997 to Amend the International Convention for the Prevention of Pollution from Ships, 1973, as Modified by the Protocol of 1978 Relating Thereto (MARPOL PROT 1997, 1997)*;
- *International Convention Relating to Intervention on the High Seas in Cases of Oil Pollution Casualties (INTERVENTION, 1969)*, with protocols:
  - *Protocol of 1973 to the International Convention Relating to Intervention of the High Seas in Cases of Oil Pollution Casualties (1973)*;
  - *Protocol Relating to Intervention on the High Seas in Cases of Marine Pollution by Substances other Than Oil (INTERVENTION PROT 1973, 1973)*;
  - *Convention on the Prevention of Marine Pollution by Dumping of Wastes and other Matter (LDC, 1972)* (1972) and the *1996 Protocol to the Convention on the Prevention of Marine Pollution by Dumping of Wastes and other Matter (LC Prot 1996, 1996)*;
  - *International Convention on Oil Pollution Preparedness Response and Cooperation (OPRC, 1990)* and the *Protocol on Preparedness, Response and Cooperation to Pollution Incidents by Hazardous and Noxious Substances (OPRC-HNS 2000, 2000)*;
  - *International Convention on the Control of Harmful Anti-fouling Systems on Ships (2001)* (2001);
  - *International Convention for the Control and Management of Ships' Ballast Water and Sediments (BWM 2004, 2004)*;
  - *Hong Kong International Convention for the Safe and Environmentally Sound Recycling of Ships*.

/On liability and compensation/:
- *International Convention on Civil Liability for Oil Pollution Damage (CLC, 1969)* with protocols:
  - *Protocol to the International Convention on Civil Liability for Oil Pollution Damage, 1976 (1976)*;
  - *Protocol to Amend the International Convention on Civil Liability for Oil Pollution Damage, 1984 (1984)*;
  - *Protocol to the International Convention on Civil Liability for Oil Pollution Damage, 1992 (1992)*;
  - *'International Convention on Establishment of an International Fund for Compensation for Oil Pollution Damage (1971)'*, setting up IOPC Fund and the *'Protocol of 1992 relating to the International convention on the establishment of an International Fund for Compensation for Oil Pollution Damage'* and the Protocol of 2003;
  - *Convention Relating to Civil Liability in the Field of Maritime Carriage of Nuclear Material (NUCLEAR, 1971)* (1971);
- *Athens Convention Relating to the Carriage of Passengers and Their Luggage by Sea (PAL, 1974)* (1974) with protocols:
  - *Protocol to the Athens Convention Relating to the Carriage of Passengers and Their Luggage by Sea, 1976 (1976)*;
  - *Protocol to the Athens Convention Relating to the Carriage of Passengers and Their Luggage by Sea, 1990 (1990)*;
  - *Protocol to the Athens Convention Relating to the Carriage of Passengers and Their Luggage by Sea, 2002 (2002)*;
  - *Convention on Limitation of Liability for Maritime Claims (LLMC, 1976)* (1976) and the *Protocol of 1996 to the Convention on Limitation of Liability for Maritime Claims (1996)*;
  - *International Convention on Liability and Compensation for Damage in Connection with the Carriage of Hazardous and Noxious Substances by Sea (HNS, 1996)* (1996) and *Protocol of 2010 to Amend the International Convention of Liability and Compensation for Damage in Connection with the Carriage of Hazardous and Noxious Substances by Sea (HNS PROT 2010, 2010)*;
  - *International Convention on Civil Liability for Bunker Oil Pollution Damage (BUNKERS, 2001)* (2001);
  - *Nairobi International Convention on the Removal of Wrecks, 2007 (Nairobi WRC 2007, 2007)*;
  - *Hong Kong International Convention for the Safe and Environmentally Sound Recycling of Ships, 2009 (Hong Kong Convention, 2009)*.

/On other subjects/:
- *Convention on Facilitation of International Maritime Traffic (FAL, 1965)* (1965);
- *International Convention on Tonnage Measurement of Ships (TONNAGE, 1969)* (1969);
- *Convention for the Suppression of Unlawful Acts Against the Safety of Maritime Navigation (SUA, 1988)*,
- *Protocol for the Suppression of Unlawful Acts Against the Safety of Fixed Platforms Located on the Continental Shelf (SUA PROT, 1988)* with *Protocol of 2005 to the Protocol for the Suppression of Unlawful Acts against the Safety of Fixed Platforms Located on the Continental Shelf (SUA PROT 2005, 2005)*, and *Protocol of 2005 to the Convention for the Suppression of Unlawful Acts against the Safety of Maritime Navigation (SUA 2005, 2005)*;
- *International Convention on Salvage (1989)* (1989).

/Other IMO Agreements/:
- *Agreement Concerning Specific Stability Requirements for Ro-ro Passenger Ships Undertaking Regular Scheduled International Voyages Between, to or from Designated Ports in North West Europe and the Baltic Sea (SOLAS AGR 1996, 1996)*.

/Conventions adopted in cooperation with other bodies/:
- *International Convention for the Unification of Certain Rules Relating to Arrest of Sea-going Ships (1952)* (1952);
- *International Convention on Maritime Liens and Mortgages (1993)* (1993);
- *International Convention on Arrest of Ships (1999)* (1999).

IMO also maintains the secretariat of *Consultative Meeting of Contracting Parties to the London Convention/ Meeting of Contracting Parties to the London Protocol (#04769)*.

Covers many issues previously handled through *Diplomatic Conference of International Maritime Law (inactive)* and works with *OSPAR Commission for the Protection of the Marine Environment of the North-East Atlantic (OSPAR Commission, #17905)*. A partner with UNEP in organizing *Regional Seas Programme (#18814)*. With INMARSAT and ITU, developed *Global Maritime Distress and Safety System (GMDSS / SMDSM)*, which came into force on 1 Feb 1992 and, since 1 Feb 1999, with which all ships must comply. With FAO, UNESCO and WMO, set up what is now *Joint Group of Experts on the Scientific Aspects of Marine Environmental Protection (GESAMP, #16131)*. IMO was also instrumental in setting up: *Red Operativa de Cooperación Regional de Autoridades Marítimas de Sudamérica, México, Panama y Cuba (ROCRAM, #18725)*; *Regional Marine Pollution Emergency Information and Training Centre – Wider Caribbean (REMPEITC-Carib, #18794)*; *Regional Marine Pollution Emergency Response Centre for the Mediterranean Sea (REMPEC, #18795)*; *World Maritime University (WMU, #21633)*, Malmö (Sweden). As of 2008, *International Conference on Coastal and Port Engineering in Developing Countries (COPEDEC)* is organized under the aegis of IMO.

Events *IOSC : Triennial International Oil Spill Conference* New Orleans, LA (USA) 2024, *World Maritime Conference* Durban (South Africa) 2022, *Marine Environment Protection of the South East Asian Seas High Level Regional Meeting* Ha Long City (Vietnam) 2022, *IMO-WMU Joint International Conference* Malmö (Sweden) 2022, *Marine Environment Protection of the South East Asian Seas Conference* Singapore (Singapore) 2022.

Publications *IMO News* (4 a year) – magazine. International conventions and other documents concluded at conferences sponsored by IMO; technical publications relating to maritime safety, marine pollution and other aspects of IMO's work; codes of practice. **Information Services** *Global Integrated Shipping Information System (GISIS)*; *IMO Resolutions Database* in English, French, Spanish – on CD-ROM.

Members Full: governments of 175 countries and territories (shown with year of joining):
Albania (1993), Algeria (1963), Angola (1977), Antigua-Barbuda (1986), Argentina (1953), Armenia (2018), Australia (1952), Austria (1975), Azerbaijan (1995), Bahamas (1976), Bahrain (1976), Bangladesh (1976), Barbados (1970), Belarus (2016), Belgium (1951), Belize (1990), Benin (1980), Bolivia (1987), Bosnia-Herzegovina (1993), Botswana (2021), Brazil (1963), Brunei Darussalam (1984), Bulgaria (1960), Cambodia (1961), Cameroon (1961), Canada (1948), Cape Verde (1976), Chile (1972), China (1973), Colombia (1974), Comoros (2001), Congo Brazzaville (1975), Congo DR (1973), Cook Is (2008), Costa Rica (1981), Côte d'Ivoire (1960), Croatia (1992), Cuba (1966), Cyprus (1973), Czechia (1993), Denmark (1959), Djibouti (1979), Dominica (1979), Dominican Rep (1953), Ecuador (1956), Egypt (1958), El Salvador (1981), Equatorial Guinea (1972), Eritrea (1993), Estonia (1992), Ethiopia (1975), Fiji (1983), Finland (1959), France (1952), Gabon (1976), Gambia (1979), Georgia (1993), Germany (1959), Ghana (1959), Greece (1958), Grenada (1998), Guatemala (1983), Guinea (1975), Guinea-Bissau (1977), Guyana (1980), Haiti (1953), Honduras (1954), Hungary (1970), Iceland (1960), India (1959), Indonesia (1961), Iran Islamic Rep (1958), Iraq (1973), Ireland (1951), Israel (1952), Italy (1957), Jamaica (1976), Japan (1958), Jordan (1973), Kazakhstan (1994), Kenya (1973), Kiribati (2003), Korea DPR (1986), Korea Rep (1962), Kuwait (1960), Latvia (1993), Lebanon (1966), Liberia (1959), Libya (1970), Lithuania (1995), Luxembourg (1991), Madagascar (1961), Malawi (1989), Malaysia (1971), Maldives (1967), Malta (1966), Marshall Is (1998), Mauritania (1961), Mauritius (1978), Mexico (1954), Moldova (2001), Monaco (1989), Mongolia (1996), Montenegro (2006), Morocco (1962), Mozambique (1979), Myanmar (1951), Namibia (1994), Nauru (2018), Nepal (1979), Netherlands (1949), New Zealand (1960), Nicaragua (1982), Nigeria (1962), North Macedonia (1993), Norway (1958), Oman (1974), Pakistan (1958), Palau (2011), Panama (1958), Papua New Guinea (1976), Paraguay (1993), Peru (1968), Philippines (1964), Poland (1960), Portugal (1976), Qatar (1977), Romania (1965), Russia (1958), Samoa (1996), San Marino (2002), Sao Tomé-Principe (1990), Saudi Arabia (1969), Senegal (1960), Serbia (2000), Seychelles (1978), Sierra Leone (1973), Singapore (1966), Slovakia (1993), Slovenia (1993), Solomon Is (1988), Somalia (1978), South Africa (1995), Spain (1962), Sri Lanka (1972), St Kitts-Nevis (2001), St Lucia (1980), St Vincent-Grenadines (1981), Sudan (1974), Suriname (1976), Sweden (1959), Switzerland (1955), Syrian AR (1963), Tanzania UR (1974), Thailand (1973), Timor-Leste (2005), Togo (1983), Tonga (2000), Trinidad-Tobago (1965), Tunisia (1963), Türkiye (1958), Turkmenistan (1993), Tuvalu (2004), Uganda (2009), UK (1949), Ukraine (1994), United Arab Emirates (1980), Uruguay (1968), USA (1950), Vanuatu (1986), Venezuela (1975), Vietnam (1984), Yemen (1979), Zambia (2014), Zimbabwe (2005).

Associate: governments of 3 territories:
Faeroe Is (2002), Hong Kong (1967), Macau (1990).

IGO Relations Agreements of cooperation with:
- *Action Plan for Protection, Development and Management of the Marine Environment of the Northwest Pacific Region (NOWPAP, #00092)*;
- *African Union (AU, #00488)*;
- *Agreement on the Conservation of Cetaceans of the Black Sea, Mediterranean Sea and contiguous Atlantic Area (ACCOBAMS, 1996)*;
- *Arab Federation of Shipping (AFS, #00953)*;
- *Asian-African Legal Consultative Organization (AALCO, #01303)*;
- *Association of Caribbean States (ACS, #02411)*;
- *Baltic Marine Environment Protection Commission – Helsinki Commission (HELCOM, #03126)*;
- *Caribbean Community (CARICOM, #03476)*;
- *Caribbean Memorandum of Understanding on Port State Control (Caribbean MOU, 1996)*;
- *Comisión Centroamericana de Transporte Marítimo (COCATRAM, #04131)*;
- *Comisión Permanente del Pacífico Sur (CPPS, #04141)*;
- *Commission du Danube (CD, #04210)*;
- *Commission on the Protection of the Black Sea Against Pollution (Black Sea Commission, #04237)*;
- *Commonwealth Secretariat (#04362)*;
- *Commonwealth Telecommunications Organisation (CTO, #04365)*;
- *Conférence européenne des administrations des postes et des télécommunications (CEPT, #04602)*;
- *Council of Europe (CE, #04881)*;
- *European Commission (EC, #06633)*;
- *European Space Agency (ESA, #08798)*;
- *Commission de l'Océan Indien (COI, #04236)*;
- *Organisation intergouvernementale pour les transports internationaux ferroviaires (OTIF, #17807)*;
- *Inter-Governmental Standing Committee on Shipping (ISCOS, #11501)*;
- *International Cospas-Sarsat Programme (#12975)* Agreement;
- *International Council for the Exploration of the Sea (ICES, #13021)*;
- *International Criminal Police Organization – INTERPOL (ICPO-INTERPOL, #13110)*;
- *International Hydrographic Organization (IHO, #13825)*;
- *International Institute for the Unification of Private Law (UNIDROIT, #13934)*;
- *International Mobile Satellite Organization (IMSO, #14174)*;
- *International Oil Pollution Compensation Funds (IOPC Funds, #14402)* (1971 and 1992 Funds and IOPCSF);

- *International Organization for Migration (IOM, #14454)*;
- *International Seabed Authority (ISBA, #14813)*;
- *International Telecommunications Satellite Organization (ITSO, #15670)*;
- *International Transport Forum (ITF, #15725)*;
- *International Whaling Commission (IWC, #15879)*;
- *Latin American Agreement on Port State Control of Vessels (Viña del Mar agreement, 1992)*;
- *Latin American Integration Association (LAIA, #16343)*;
- *League of Arab States (LAS, #16420)*;
- *Marine Accident Investigators' International Forum (MAIIF, #16577)*;
- *Maritime Organization of West and Central Africa (MOWCA, #16582)*;
- *Memorandum of Understanding on Port State Control in the Arab States of the Gulf (Riyadh MOU, 2004)*;
- *Memorandum of Understanding on Port State Control in the Asia-Pacific Region (Tokyo MOU, #16709)*;
- *Memorandum of Understanding on Port State Control in the Black Sea (Black Sea MOU, 2000)*;
- *Memorandum of Understanding on Port State Control in the Indian Ocean (Indian Ocean MOU, 1998)*;
- *Memorandum of Understanding on Port State Control in the Mediterranean (Mediterranean MOU, 1997)*;
- *Memorandum of Understanding on Port State Control in West and Central Africa (Abuja MOU, 1999)*;
- *North-East Atlantic Fisheries Commission (NEAFC, #17581)*;
- *OAS (#17629)*;
- *OECD (#17693)*;
- *Organization of Arab Petroleum Exporting Countries (OAPEC, #17854)*;
- *OSPAR Commission for the Protection of the Marine Environment of the North-East Atlantic (OSPAR Commission, #17905)*;
- *Pacific Community (SPC, #17942)*;
- *Paris Memorandum of Understanding on Port State Control (Paris MOU, 1982)*;
- *Port Management Association of Eastern and Southern Africa (PMAESA, #18462)*;
- *Port Management Association of West and Central Africa (PMAWCA, #18463)*;
- *Regional Cooperation Agreement on Combating Piracy and Armed Robbery against Ships in Asia – Information Sharing Centre (ReCAAP ISC, #18771)*;
- *Regional Organization for the Conservation of the Environment of the Red Sea and Gulf of Aden (PERSGA, #18804)*;
- *Regional Organization for the Protection of the Marine Environment (ROPME, #18805)*;
- *Secretariat of the Pacific Regional Environment Programme (SPREP, #19205)*;
- *South Asia Cooperative Environment Programme (SACEP, #19714)*;
- *Sub-Regional Fisheries Commission (SRFC, #20026)*;
- *World Customs Organization (WCO, #21350)*;
- *World Tourism Organization (UNWTO, #21861)*.

Member of: *UN-OCEANS (#20711)*. Permanent observer status with: *World Intellectual Property Organization (WIPO, #21593)*. Observer status with: *Arctic Council (#01097)*. Formal relations with: *International Civil Aviation Organization (ICAO, #12581)*; *International Telecommunication Union (ITU, #15673)*; *UNIDO (#20336)*. Close links with: *UNEP (#20299)*. Represented on: *United Nations System Chief Executives Board for Coordination (CEB, #20636)*. Has been represented in meetings of: *Round Table on Sustainable Development at the OECD (see: #17693)*.

NGO Relations Agreement of cooperation with: *International Committee of the Red Cross (ICRC, #12799)*. Rules Governing Relationship with Non-Governmental Organizations adopted by Council in Mar 1960 and approved by 2nd Session of the Assembly, Apr 1961; Guidelines on the Grant of Consultative Status adopted by Council in May 1978 and endorsed by 11th Session of the Assembly in Nov 1979. Rules amended by Council Nov 1984 and endorsed 1985. Both Rules and Guidelines amended Jun 2001 by Council endorsed 2001. As of 2018 the following non-governmental organizations enjoy consultative status with IMO:

- *Active Shipbuilding Experts' Federation (ASEF, #00103)*;
- *Advisory Committee on Protection of the Sea (ACOPS, #00139)*;
- *BIMCO (#03236)*;
- *Bureau international des containers et du transport intermodal (BIC, #03364)*;
- *Clean Shipping Coalition (CSC, #03989)*;
- *Comité International Radio-Maritime (CIRM, #04186)*;
- *Comité maritime international (CMI, #04192)*;
- *Conseil européen de l'industrie chimique (CEFIC, #04687)*;
- *Cruise Lines International Association (CLIA, #04973)*;
- *Dangerous Goods Advisory Council (DGAC, #05001)*;
- *European Association of Internal Combustion Engine Manufacturers (EUROMOT, #06090)*;
- *Federation of National Associations of Shipbrokers and Agents (FONASBA, #09694)*;
- *Friends of the Earth International (FoEI, #10002)*;
- *Global Maritime Education and Training Association (GlobalMET, #10464)*;
- *Greenpeace International (#10727)*;
- *ICHCA International Limited (IIL, #11053)*;
- *IMCA International Marine Contractors Association (IMCA, #11127)*;
- *Institute of International Container Lessors (IICL, #11273)*;
- *Institute of Marine Engineering, Science and Technology (IMarEST, #11280)*;
- *Instituto Iberoamericano de Derecho Maritimo (IIDM)*;
- *INTERFERRY (#11470)*;
- *InterManager (#11520)*;
- *International Association of Classification Societies (IACS, #11778)*;
- *International Association of Drilling Contractors (IADC)*;
- *International Association of Dry Cargo Shipowners (INTERCARGO, #11853)*;
- *International Association of Independent Tanker Owners (INTERTANKO, #11959)*;
- *International Association of Institutes of Navigation (IAIN, #11965)*;
- *International Association of Marine Aids to Navigation and Lighthouse Authorities (IALA, #12013)*;
- *International Association of Maritime Universities (IAMU, #12016)*;
- *International Association of Oil and Gas Producers (IOGP, #12053)*;
- *International Association of Ports and Harbors (IAPH, #12096)*;
- *International Bunker Industry Association (IBIA, #12411)*;
- *International Chamber of Commerce (ICC, #12534)*;
- *International Chamber of Shipping (ICS, #12535)*;
- *International Christian Maritime Association (ICMA, #12561)*;
- *International Council of Marine Industry Associations (ICOMIA, #13044)*;
- *International Dry Bulk Terminals Group (DBTG, #13206)*;
- *International Electrotechnical Commission (IEC, #13255)*;
- *International Federation of Shipmasters Associations (IFSMA, #13539)*;
- *International Fund for Animal Welfare (IFAW, #13693)*;
- *International Group of P and I Clubs (#13751)*;
- *International Harbour Masters' Association (IHMA, #13774)*;
- *International Iron Metallics Association (IIMA, #13953)*;
- *International Lifesaving Appliance Manufacturers Association (ILAMA, #14039)*;
- *International Maritime Health Association (IMHA, #14099)*;
- *International Maritime Lecturers' Association (IMLA, #14101)*;
- *International Maritime Pilots' Association (IMPA, #14103)*;
- *International Maritime Rescue Federation (IMRF, #14104)*;
- *International Ocean Institute (IOI, #14394)*;
- *International Organization for Standardization (ISO, #14473)*;
- *International Parcel Tankers Association (IPTA)*;
- *International Petroleum Industry Environmental Conservation Association (IPIECA, #14562)*;
- *International Port Community Systems Association (IPCSA, #14623)*;
- *International Road Transport Union (IRU, #14761)*;
- *International Salvage Union (ISU, #14779)*;
- *International Ship Suppliers and Services Association (ISSA, #14850)*;
- *International Spill Control Organization (ISCO, #15580)*;
- *ITOPF Ltd (#16073)*;
- *International Towing Tank Conference (ITTC, #15698)*;
- *International Transport Workers' Federation (ITF, #15726)*;
- *International Union for Conservation of Nature and Natural Resources (IUCN, #15766)*;
- *International Union of Marine Insurance (IUMI, #15789)*;
- *International Vessel Operators Dangerous Goods Association (IVODGA)*;
- *International Water Mist Association (IWMA, #15868)*;
- *InterPortPolice (#15963)*;
- *NACE International – The Corrosion Society (#16925)*;
- *Nautical Institute*;
- *Oil Companies International Marine Forum (OCIMF, #17709)*;
- *Pacific Environment*;
- *Pew Charitable Trusts*;
- Royal Institution of Naval Architects (RINA);
- *Society of International Gas Tanker and Terminal Operators (SIGTTO, #19582)*;
- *Superyacht Builders Association (SYBAss, #20037)*;
- *World Coatings Council (#21283)*;
- *World Nuclear Transport Institute (WNTI, #21676)*;
- *World Sailing (#21760)*;
- *World Shipping Council (WSC, #21781)*;
- *World Wide Fund for Nature (WWF, #21922)*. [2023/XB1117/**B***]

♦ International Maritime Pilots' Association (IMPA) 14103

Association internationale des pilotes maritimes – Asociación de Pilotos Maritimos Internacionales

SG HQS Wellington, Temple Stairs, Victoria Embankment, London, WC2R 2PN, UK. T. +442072403973. Fax +442072403518. E-mail: office@impahq.org – secgen@impahq.org.
Executive Assistant address not obtained.
URL: http://www.impahq.org/

History Jun 1970, Germany FR. Jun 1970, Kiel (Germany FR). Officially launched May 1971, Amsterdam (Netherlands). **Aims** Promote professional standards of pilotage worldwide in the interests of pilots' safety. **Structure** General Meeting (every 2 years); Executive Committee (meets twice a year); Secretariat; Advisory Committee. **Languages** English. **Staff** 3.00 FTE, paid. **Finance** Sources: members' dues. **Activities** Guidance/assistance/consulting; knowledge management/information dissemination. **Events** *Biennial Congress* Cancún (Mexico) 2022, *Biennial Congress* Cancún (Mexico) 2021, *Biennial Congress* Cancún (Mexico) 2020, *Biennial Congress* Dakar (Senegal) 2018, *Biennial Congress* Seoul (Korea Rep) 2016. **Publications** *IMPA Newsletter*; *IMPA Notices*; *IMPA Safety Campaign*; *International Pilot* – magazine. Working Group Reports; guidelines; recommendations; briefings; brochures; poster.

Members Pilots' associations in 50 countries and territories:
Argentina, Aruba, Australia, Belgium, Bermuda, Brazil, Canada, Chile, China, Colombia, Cuba, Curaçao, Cyprus, Denmark, Ecuador, France, Germany, Guatemala, Hong Kong, Ireland, Italy, Jamaica, Japan, Korea Rep, Malaysia, Malta, Mexico, Montenegro, Morocco, Namibia, Netherlands, New Zealand, Norway, Panama, Philippines, Portugal, Saudi Arabia, Senegal, Serbia, Slovenia, Spain, Sri Lanka, St Kitts-Nevis, Suriname, Thailand, Trinidad-Tobago, Türkiye, UK, Uruguay, USA.

Consultative Status Consultative status granted from: *ECOSOC (#05331)* (Ros C); *International Maritime Organization (IMO, #14102)*. **IGO Relations** Accredited by: *International Hydrographic Organization (IHO, #13825)*. **NGO Relations** In liaison with technical committees of: *International Organization for Standardization (ISO, #14473)*. [2020/XC4551/**C**]

♦ International Maritime and Port Technology and Development Conference (meeting series)

♦ International Maritime Rescue Federation (IMRF) 14104

Fédération internationale de sauvetage en mer – Federación Internacional para Salvamento Maritimo

CEO PO Box 1389, Enfield, EN1 9GF, UK. T. +441569767405. E-mail: info@imrf.org.uk.
Main Website: http://www.international-maritime-rescue.org/

History 1924, London (UK). Founded at 1st International Lifeboat Conference (ILC). Former names and other names: *International Lifeboat Federation (ILF)* – former (1924 to 2006); *Fédération internationale pour les bateaux de sauvetage* – former (1924 to 2006); *Federación Internacional para los Barcos de Salvamento* – former (1924 to 2006). Registration: Charity Commission, No/ID: 1100883, England and Wales. **Aims** Promote international cooperation to prevent loss of life on the world's waters by: working to improve global maritime search and rescue (SAR) capability, supporting SAR organisations with advice and training and raising awareness of issues associated with maritime SAR. **Structure** Quadrennial General Meeting (QGM); Board of Trustees; Chief Executive Officer (CEO). **Languages** English. **Staff** 2.40 FTE, paid. **Finance** Sources: donations; members' dues. Other sources: funding from international maritime and non-maritime trusts. **Activities** Advocacy/lobbying/activism; events/meetings; knowledge management/information dissemination. **Events** *WMRC : Quadrennial World Maritime Rescue Congress* Rotterdam (Netherlands) 2023, *WMRC : Quadrennial World Maritime Rescue Congress* Rotterdam (Netherlands) 2023, *International Maritime Rescue Federation – Forward Look 2022* Enfield (UK) 2022, *Specialist SAR Operations: Dealing with Potential Contamination at the Rescue Site* Enfield (UK) 2022, *International Mass Rescue Conference* Gothenburg (Sweden) 2022. **Publications** *IMRF Bookshop Newsletter* (12 a year) in English; *SAR HUB Bulletin* (10 a year) in English – For Members Only; *General News E-mails* in English – General news about events and news articles. *Mass Rescue Operations Guidance* (4th ed). Conference/meeting/event reports.

Members Full; Affiliate; Associate. Full in 40 countries and territories:
Australia, Belgium, Brazil, Canada, Cape Verde, Chile, China, Côte d'Ivoire, Croatia, Curaçao, Denmark, Estonia, Finland, France, Georgia, Germany, Ghana, Greece, Iceland, Ireland, Italy, Liberia, Malta, Morocco, Netherlands, New Zealand, Nigeria, Norway, Poland, Portugal, Seychelles, South Africa, Spain, St Maarten, Sweden, UK, United Arab Emirates, Uruguay, USA, Venezuela.
Affiliate in 26 countries and territories:
Antigua-Barbuda, Bangladesh, Bulgaria, Canada, China, Côte d'Ivoire, France, Germany, Italy, Japan, Kenya, Latvia, Malta, New Zealand, Polynesia Fr, Russia, Sierra Leone, Spain, Sweden, Switzerland, Tonga, Türkiye, Uganda, UK, USA, Virgin Is UK.
Associate in 13 countries:
Australia, China, Cyprus, Denmark, Finland, Germany, India, Ireland, New Zealand, Norway, Portugal, Sweden, UK.

Consultative Status Consultative status granted from: *International Maritime Organization (IMO, #14102)*. **IGO Relations** Represented at: *International Civil Aviation Organization (ICAO, #12581)* / IMO Joint Working Group of Search and Rescue (SAR). **NGO Relations** Member of (3): *International Association for Safety and Survival Training (IASST, #12141)*; *International Life Saving Federation (ILS, #14040)*; The Nautical Institute. [2022.10.12/XC2232/y/**C**]

♦ International Maritime Satellite Organization / see International Mobile Satellite Organization (#14174)

♦ International Maritime Statistics Forum (IMSF) 14105

Program Organiser address not obtained. T. +442075467053.
URL: http://www.imsf.info/

History Early 1970s. Current constitution adopted Apr 2007. **Aims** Promote harmonization and improvement in quality and scope of statistics within the international maritime industries, by means of ongoing work programmes and by affiliation with prominent national and international maritime institutions. **Structure** Officers: Chairman; Secretary; Program Organizer; 2 Steering Committee members. Regional Representatives (3): Europe; North America; Australasia. **Events** *Annual meeting* 2011, *Annual Meeting* Lisbon (Portugal) 2010, *Annual meeting* New Orleans, LA (USA) 2009, *Annual meeting* Gdansk (Poland) 2008, *Annual Meeting* Singapore (Singapore) 2007.

Members Full in 22 countries:
Australia, Belgium, Canada, Chile, China, Denmark, Finland, France, Germany, Greece, Luxembourg, Netherlands, Norway, Poland, Portugal, Singapore, South Africa, Spain, Sweden, Switzerland, UK, USA.
Included in the above, 7 organizations listed in this Yearbook:
BIMCO (#03236); *European Commission (EC, #06633)* (DG TREN); *European Community Shipowners' Associations (ECSA, #06683)*; *European Maritime Safety Agency (EMSA, #07744)*; *International Union of Marine Insurance (IUMI, #15789)*; *Nordic Association of Marine Insurers (Cefor, #17198)*; *Statistical Office of the European Union (Eurostat, #19974)*. [2019.06.03/XJ2341/y/**F**]

♦ International Marketing Commission (#04224)

♦ International Marketing Federation (IMF) 14106

Fédération internationale du marketing – Federación Internacional de Marketing

Address not obtained.

History May 1967, Rome (Italy). Organized as a free association in Zurich (Switzerland), 1967. Revised 1982, 1996. **Aims** Foster application of *scientific* methods and principles in the study and practice of marketing; encourage application of those principles of integrity, ethics, objectivity and thoroughness which mark *professional* activities in other scientific fields; aid international exchange of knowledge and experience and contribute to the improvement of education in marketing. **Languages** English. **Events** *International marketing research seminar / Seminar* London (UK) 1998, *How to market meetings* St Petersburg, FL (USA) 1990, *How to market meetings* St Petersburg, FL (USA) 1989. **Publications** *Journal of International Selling and Sales Management*.

Members Professional associations in 30 countries:
Argentina, Australia, Belgium, Chile, China, Croatia, Czechia, Denmark, Finland, France, Germany, India, Iran Islamic Rep, Italy, Japan, Mexico, Netherlands, New Zealand, Norway, Peru, Poland, Romania, Russia, Singapore, Spain, Sweden, Switzerland, UK, Ukraine, USA.

NGO Relations Member of: *Commission internationale de marketing (#04224)*. [2010.06.01/XF2244/**F**]

♦ International Marketing Supervision Network / see International Consumer Protection and Enforcement Network (#12930)

♦ International Martial Art Games Committee (IMGC) 14107

Pres Draugasse 3, 1210 Vienna, Austria. T. +4312928467. Fax +4312925509. E-mail: president@itfhq.org.
SG Chukjon-dong, Mangyongdae Dist, PO Box 700, Pyongyang, Korea DPR. T. +850218111. Fax +85023814410. E-mail: imgc@silibank.net.kp.
URL: http://www.imgc-99.org/

History 2 Sep 1999, Buenos Aires (Argentina). **Aims** Preserve and develop all martial arts sports as a common asset of humankind along with social progress. **Structure** Congress (every 2 years); Executive Board; Commissions (4). **Languages** English. **Staff** 21.00 FTE, paid. **Finance** Members' dues. Other sources: donations; subsidies; operational income. **Activities** Sporting activities. **Events** *Congress* Delhi (India) 2015, *Congress* Melbourne, VIC (Australia) 2013, *Congress* Tallinn (Estonia) 2011, *Congress* Bangkok (Thailand) 2008, *Congress* Pyongyang (Korea DPR) 2006. **Publications** *World Martial Arts* (4 a year).
Members National federations in 34 countries and territories:
Australia, Azerbaijan, Bulgaria, Chile, Colombia, Dominica, England, Estonia, Germany, Greece, Haiti, Honduras, India, Iran Islamic Rep, Italy, Jamaica, Kazakhstan, Korea Rep, Latvia, Madagascar, Mongolia, Morocco, New Zealand, Northern Ireland, Paraguay, Philippines, Puerto Rico, Scotland, Spain, Sweden, Tajikistan, United Arab Emirates, USA, Uzbekistan.
International organizations. Full (10):
International Jendo Federation (IJF, #13968); International Taekwon-Do Federation (ITF, #15652); International Tai Chi Federation (ITCF); World Federation of Kowat Alrami and Self Defense (WFKA, #21450); World Jiu Jitsu Confederation (WJJC); World Judo Federation (WJF, #21603); World Karate Confederation (WKC, #21607); World Muay Federation (WMF, #21662); World Pangration Athlima Federation (WPAF, #21709); World Union of TOA Associations (WUTA).
Associate (6) including the following 3 organizations listed in this Yearbook:
Sports Jiu-Jitsu African Federation (SJJAF, #19927); World Pahuyuth Federation (WPF, #21706); World Pan Amateur Kickboxing Association (WPKA, #21707). [2019.12.25/XM2808/y/E]

♦ International Martial Arts Federation (IMAF) 14108

Fédération internationale des arts martiaux – Kokusai Budoin

Pres Prof Shizuya Sato, 3-24-1, Shinbori, Higashi-Yamato-Shi, Tokyo, 207-0012 Japan. T. +81425659146. Fax +81425664452. E-mail: international@imaf.com.
European Chairman PO Box 5464, 79021 Freiburg, Germany. T. +4976616730. Fax +49766199132.
URL: http://www.imaf.com/

History 1979. **Aims** Promote the practice of martial arts – Aikido, Bo Jutsu, laido, Jodo, Judo, Jujitsu, Karate, Kendo, Kobudo – in their traditional Japanese style. **Events** *European congress / Congress* Munich (Germany) 1992, *Congress* Paris (France) 1988, *European congress* Rueil-Malmaison (France) 1988, *Congress* Tokyo (Japan) 1985, *Congress* Scarborough (UK) 1982. **Members** Individuals (over 80,000). Membership countries not specified. [2016/XD2624/D]

♦ International Martial Arts Federation of the Deaf (IMAFD) 14109

Pres address not obtained.
Vice-Pres address not obtained.
URL: https://www.imafd.com/

History 1978, Tokyo (Japan), as *International Silent Martial Arts Federation (ISMAF)*. Present name adopted, 1995. [2020/XF5850/F]

♦ International Martial Arts Union (IMAU) 14110

Pres Str Mahdieh, Qorveh KORDESTAN, 6661853418, Iran Islamic Rep. E-mail: officeimau@yahoo.com.
URL: http://www.imau.org/

History Registration: Iran. **Aims** Develop and research martial arts; administer scientific and training courses; issues educationaland technical certificates. **Structure** Founder; Board of Directors; Central Council; Secretary General. **Languages** English, Persian. **Staff** Voluntary. **Finance** Sources: members' dues; revenue from activities/projects; sponsorship. Other sources: proceeds from training courses; competitions. **Activities** Advocacy/lobbying/activism; training/education. **Members** Full in 60 countries. Membership countries not specified. **IGO Relations** *UNDP (#20292).* **NGO Relations** Member of (1): *International Science, Technology and Skill Union (ISTSU).* [2021/XJ6381/C]

♦ International Martin Buber Society (internationally oriented national body)

♦ International Mask Arts and Culture Organization (IMACO) 14111

Contact 36709-239 – Yuksa-ro, 300-15 Unheung-dong, Andong NORTH GYEONGSANG, Korea Rep. T. +82548536397. Fax +82548536398. E-mail: worldmask@gmail.com.

History Set up 29 Sep 2006. **Aims** Build a network for international mask arts and culture; heighten the culture of masks. **Structure** General Assembly; International Board of Directors; Secretariat. Teams (2): Cultural Contents; International Cooperation. **Languages** English, Korean. **Finance** Members' dues. **Activities** Events/meetings. **Events** *IMACO International Conference* Andong (Korea Rep) 2021, *IMACO International Conference* Bacolod (Philippines) 2019, *Symposium* Andong (Korea Rep) 2018, *Symposium* Andong (Korea Rep) 2018, *Symposium* Andong (Korea Rep) 2018.
Members Individuals; organizations. Members in 62 countries:
Australia, Bahrain, Bangladesh, Belgium, Bhutan, Bolivia, Brazil, Brunei Darussalam, Bulgaria, Burkina Faso, Cambodia, Canada, China, Colombia, Costa Rica, Côte d'Ivoire, El Salvador, Finland, France, Gabon, Germany, Greece, Guatemala, India, Indonesia, Iran Islamic Rep, Japan, Kenya, Kuwait, Laos, Latvia, Liberia, Malaysia, Mali, Mauritius, Mexico, Mongolia, Myanmar, Netherlands, New Zealand, Nigeria, Pakistan, Peru, Philippines, Poland, Russia, Saudi Arabia, Sierra Leone, Singapore, Slovakia, Spain, Sri Lanka, Sudan, Taiwan, Thailand, Türkiye, Turkmenistan, UK, USA, Uzbekistan, Vietnam, Zambia.
NGO Relations *European Association of Folklore Festivals (EAFF, #06043).* [2019/XJ4892/D]

♦ International Masonic Association (inactive)

♦ International Masonic Order 'DELPHI' 14112

Ordre Maçonnique International 'DELPHI'

Contact 49 Epindamnou and Skiathou St, 112 54 Athens, Greece. T. +302102111505 – +302102111509. Fax +302102066417. E-mail: secretariat@delphiorder.org.
URL: http://www.delphiorder.org/

History 1926, within the framework of *Masonic Movement (#16593).* 1996, reconstituted under current name. EU Transparency Register: 47099812316-80. **Aims** Preserve International Freemasonic tradition as cultural heritage and a field for application of high moral values and promotion of Humanistic principles. **Structure** Supreme Council, functions as International Grand Lodge; Symbolic and Philosophical Lodges in Brazil, Bulgaria, Greece and USA. **Languages** English, French, Irish Gaelic. **Finance** Members' dues. **Publications** *CORYMB (Knotted Rope)* (annual); *DIONE* (annual). Commemorative Editions.
Members Individuals (about 1,000) in 4 countries:
Brazil, Greece, Romania, USA.
NGO Relations Member of: *European Political Strategy Centre (EPSC, #08248); Centre de liaison et d'information des puissances maçonniques signataires de l'Appel de Strasbourg (CLIPSAS, #03770);* national and regional masonic organizations. [2019/XE4417/E]

♦ International Masonic Union (CATENA) 14113

Internationale Vrijmetselaars Unie

Contact Lindenstr 3, 84428 Buchbach, Germany.
URL: http://www.catena.org/

History Jul 1961. Registered in accordance with German law. **Aims** Increase friendship and cooperation between member lodges. **Structure** Curatorium; Executive Committee. **Languages** English. **Finance** Members' dues. **Activities** Events/meetings.
Members Lodges in 9 countries:
Austria, Czechia, France, Germany, Greece, Italy, Romania, Spain, UK. [2020.03.04/XJ4408/D]

♦ International Masonry Apprenticeship Trust / see International Masonry Institute
♦ International Masonry Institute (internationally oriented national body)
♦ International Masonry Institute Apprenticeship and Training / see International Masonry Institute

♦ International Masonry Society (IMS) 14114

Sec Shermanbury, 6 Church Road, Whyteleafe, CR3 0AR, UK. T. +442086603633. Fax +442086602799. E-mail: secretary@masonry.org.uk.
Registered Address Lucideon Limited, Queens Rd, Penkhull, Stoke-on-Trent, ST4 7LQ, UK.
URL: http://www.masonry.org.uk/

History 1986. Former names and other names: *British Masonry Society (BMS)* – former (1986 to 1 Jan 2008). **Aims** Promote discussion and advancement of the science and practice of masonry as allied to its constituent materials and to all aspects of the design and use of masonry and the construction process. **Structure** Council. **Languages** English. **Staff** Voluntary. **Finance** Sources: members' dues. **Activities** Events/meetings. **Events** *International Masonry Conference* Leeds (UK) 2022, *International Masonry Conference* Milan (Italy) 2018, *International Masonry Conference* Guimarães (Portugal) 2014, *International Masonry Conference* Dresden (Germany) 2010. **Publications** *Masonry International* (3 a year) – journal. Conference proceedings.
Members in 5 countries:
Australia, Canada, China, UK, USA.
Members also in South America. Membership countries not specified. [2021.06.21/XJ0023/C]

♦ International Mass Marketing Fraud Working Group (IMMFWG) . . . 14115

Address not obtained.

History Founded Sep 2007. **Aims** Exchange intelligence; coordinate cross-border operations to disrupt and apprehend mass-marketing fraudsters; develop strategic projects; discuss awareness, education, and prevention campaigns for the public.
Members Law enforcement, regulatory and consumer protection agencies in 7 countries:
Australia, Belgium, Canada, Netherlands, Nigeria, UK, USA.
Regional entity:
European Police Office (Europol, #08239). [2018/XM7774/F]

♦ International Mass Retail Association / see Retail Industry Leaders Association

♦ International Mass Spectrometry Foundation (IMSF) 14116

Sec School of Chemistry, University of Southampton, Southampton, SO17 1BJ, UK. T. +442380592182. Fax +442380592182. E-mail: gjl@soton.ac.uk.
Pres Institute of Chemistry, State University of Campinas, Campinas SP, SP 13083-970, Brazil. T. +551935213073. Fax +551935213073.
Office Montanalaan 8, 7313 CJ Apeldoorn, Netherlands.
URL: http://www.imss.nl/

History 29 Aug 1997, Tampere (Finland). Founded during the 14th International Mass Spectrometry Conference. Former names and other names: *International Mass Spectrometry Society (IMSS)* – former (29 Aug 1997 to 2006). **Aims** Advance the science and practice of mass spectrometry worldwide by promotion and dissemination of knowledge. **Structure** Executive Board, comprising President, Past-President, Vice-President (Society), Vice-President (Conference), Treasurer, Secretary and 3 Regional Representatives. **Languages** English. **Staff** None. **Finance** Dues from national societies and personal memberships. **Activities** Organizes triennial conference; awards programme. **Events** *International Mass Spectrometry Conference* Melbourne, VIC (Australia) 2024, *International Mass Spectrometry Conference* Maastricht (Netherlands) 2022, *International Mass Spectrometry Conference* Rio de Janeiro (Brazil) 2021, *International Mass Spectrometry Conference* Rio de Janeiro (Brazil) 2020, *International Mass Spectrometry Conference* Florence (Italy) 2018. **Publications** Conference proceedings.
Members National Affiliates in 35 countries and territories:
Australia, Austria, Belgium, Brazil, Canada, China, Croatia, Czechia, Finland, France, Germany, Hong Kong, Hungary, India, Ireland, Israel, Italy, Japan, Korea Rep, Netherlands, New Zealand, Norway, Poland, Portugal, Romania, Russia, Slovenia, South Africa, Spain, Sweden, Switzerland, Taiwan, UK, Ukraine, USA.
NGO Relations Links with national mass spectrometry societies. [2014/XD7834/f/F]

♦ International Mass Spectrometry Society / see International Mass Spectrometry Foundation (#14116)
♦ International Master Printers Association / see Intergraf (#11505)

♦ International Masters Games Association (IMGA) 14117

CEO Maison du Sport International, Av de Rhodanie 54, 1007 Lausanne VD, Switzerland. T. +41216018171. Fax +41216018173. E-mail: info@imga.ch.
URL: http://www.imga.ch/

History Founded as *Masters Games International (MGI)*. Has also been referred to as *World Masters Games Association (WMGA)*. Registered in accordance with Swiss Civil Code. **Aims** Promote and encourage mature individuals of any age from all over the world to practise sport and especially to participate in the World Master Games, with the awareness that competitive sport can continue throughout life; establish quadrennially an international multisport festival for mature people of any age, condition or standard called the "World Masters Games"; promote, through these games, friendship and understanding among mature sportspeople, regardless of age, gender, race, religion or sport status. **Structure** General Assembly (annual) comprises member international federations (IFs). International Board of Governors (meets annually). **Languages** English. **Staff** 2.00 FTE, paid. **Finance** Funded through rights fees from organizing cities. Annual budget: 500,000 USD. **Activities** Organizes *World Masters Games* (every 4 years), a multisport games held at a venue previously decided and presented at the GAISF Congress which precedes the Games by 5 years. /Core Sports/ are all popular masters sports, most having been strongly developed through respective member federations, and all must be offered at each Games: athletics (track and field); archery; badminton; basketball; canoe-kayak; cycling; field hockey; football; golf; orienteering; rowing; shooting; softball; squash; swimming; table tennis; tennis; triathlon; weightlifting. /Optional Sports/, of which between 5 and 10 optional sports are offered at each World Masters Games from 1998 onwards, are selected by the host city, with approval from the IMGA and the relevant international federation, which then becomes an associate member for the 4 year cycle up to and including the Games. Typical optional sports are: baseball; bowls (lawn and tenpin); cricket; indoor cricket; fencing; handball; ice hockey; judo; netball; powerlifting; racquetball; rugby; sailing; surf lifesaving; touch rugby; volleyball; water polo; water skiing; windsurfing.
Members Full: international federations (20), listed in this Yearbook:
Badminton World Federation (BWF, #03060); Fédération internationale de basketball (FIBA, #09614); Fédération Internationale de Ski (FIS, #09659); International Biathlon Union (IBU, #12336); International Canoe Federation (ICF, #12437); International Federation of Association Football (#13360); International Hockey Federation (#13802); International Ice Hockey Federation (IIHF, #13831); International Life Saving Federation of Europe (ILSE, #14043); International Orienteering Federation (IOF, #14485); International Shooting Sport Federation (ISSF, #14852); International Table Tennis Federation (ITTF, #15650); International Weightlifting Federation (IWF, #15876); Union Cycliste Internationale (UCI, #20375); World Archery (#21105); World Athletics (#21209); World Curling Federation (WCF, #21348); World Rowing (#21756); World Skating Federation (WSF, no recent information); World Squash Federation (WSF, #21826).
Associate: 4-year temporary membership up to and including the Games in which they are represented. 4 organizations:
Fédération internationale de volleyball (FIVB, #09670); International Bowling Federation (IBF, #12384); World Rugby (#21757).
NGO Relations Member of (1): *Olympic Movement (#17719).* Recognized by: *International Olympic Committee (IOC, #14408).* [2016/XE0222/y/C]

♦ International Masters of Gaming Law (IMGL) 14118

Main Office PO Box 27106, Las Vegas NV 89126, USA.
URL: http://www.imgl.org/

Aims Promote education and the exchange of professional information concerning all aspects of gaming law. **Structure** Officers: President; Vice-President; Secretary; Treasurer; Vice-President Affiliated Members; Vice-President Affiliates. Committees (26): Casino Industry Executives; Conference Partnerships; Cooley Law School Directed Study; Gaming Executive of the Year; Gaming Law Educator Forum; Gaming Regulator of the Year – Americas; Gaming Regulator of the Year – Europe; Gaming Regulator of the Year – Evolving Jurisdictions; Gaming Regulator of the Year – Indian Country; Gaming Regulators; Indian Gaming; Interactive/Internet Gaming; Member Services; Membership; Membership Recruitment; Pari-Mutual Wagering; Program – Spring

Conference; Program – Autumn Conference; Program – North American Gaming Regulators Association; Program – Southern Gaming Summit; Publications; Regulatory Enhancement; Responsible Gaming; Strategic Planning; Website; Young Lawyers. **Events** *Autumn Conference* London (UK) 2022, *Autumn Conference* Boston, MA (USA) 2021, *Autumn Conference* Boston, MA (USA) 2020, *Autumn Conference* Munich (Germany) 2019, *Autumn Conference* Prague (Czechia) 2018. **Publications** *Canadian Gaming Lawyer* – magazine; *Casino Lawyer* – magazine; *European Gaming Lawyer* – magazine; *La Ley del Juego* – magazine.
Members Individuals in 32 countries and territories:
Antigua-Barbuda, Argentina, Australia, Austria, Belgium, Canada, China, Costa Rica, Curaçao, Denmark, Finland, France, Germany, Greece, Ireland, Israel, Italy, Jamaica, Malta, Mexico, Netherlands, Panama, Peru, Philippines, Slovenia, South Africa, Spain, Sweden, Switzerland, UK, USA, Virgin Is USA. [2017/XJ2367/v/C]

♦ International Mastic Asphalt Association (IMAA) 14119

Association internationale de l'asphalte (AIA) – Internationale Gussasphalt-Vereinigung (IGV)
Sec Seilerstr 22, Box 5853, 3001 Bern, Switzerland. T. +41313102032. Fax +41313102035. E-mail: info@mastic-asphalt.eu.
URL: http://www.mastic-asphalt.eu/
History 1972, Paris (France), as *European Mastic Asphalt Association (EMAA) – Association européenne de l'asphalte (AEA) – Europäische Gussasphalt-Vereinigung (EGV)*. **Aims** Promote the use of mastic asphalt. **Structure** Management Board; Commissions (2). **Languages** English, French, German. **Finance** Members' dues. **Events** *Annual Congress* Cologne (Germany) 2019, *Annual Congress* Chongqing (China) 2018, *Annual Congress* Stockholm (Sweden) 2017, *Annual Congress* Paris (France) 2015, *Annual Congress* St Petersburg (Russia) 2014. **Publications** *IMAA Technical Bulletin* (annual). Congress reports.
Members Mastic asphalt councils and employers' federations in 12 countries:
Austria, Belgium, China, France, Germany, Italy, Netherlands, Russia, Spain, Sweden, Switzerland, UK.
[2018.07.24/XD0562/D]

♦ International Materials Conference (inactive)
♦ International Maternal and Child Health Foundation Canada (unconfirmed)

♦ International Mathematical Olympiad Foundation (IMOF) 14120

Sec c/o Australian Mathematics Trust, Univ of Canberra, Locked Bag 1, Canberra ACT 2601, Australia. T. +61262012440.
Dir address not obtained.
URL: https://imof.co/
History 2011, Amsterdam (Netherlands). Olympiads organized since 1959. Registration: Handelsregister, No/ID: KVK 53195949, Netherlands. **Aims** Bring young people together from all over the world to enjoy the challenges of mathematics in a spirit of friendly competition. **Structure** Council. **Finance** Sources: donations. **Activities** Awards/prizes/competitions. **Events** *International Mathematical Olympiad* Chiba (Japan) 2023. **IGO Relations** Affiliated with (1): *UNESCO (#20322)*. [2021/AA2232/f/F]

♦ International Mathematical Union (IMU) 14121

Union mathématique internationale (UMI)
Head of Secretariat/Treas Hausvogteiplatz 11A, 10117 Berlin, Germany. T. +493020372430. Fax +493020372439. E-mail: office@mathunion.org – secretary@mathunion.org.
URL: http://www.mathunion.org/
History 1920. Founded, superseding *International Congresses of Mathematicians (inactive)*, set up 9 Aug 1897, Zurich (Switzerland). Dissolved in 1932. Following World War 2 efforts to re-establish the IMU began. 10 Sep 1951, the modern IMU came into being *de jure*. **Aims** Promote international cooperation in mathematics; support and assist the International Congress of Mathematicians and other scientific meetings or conferences; encourage and support other international mathematical activities considered likely to contribute to the development of mathematical science in any of its aspects – pure, applied or educational; encourage and support mathematical activities in the developing countries. **Structure** General Assembly (every 4 years, at Congress); Executive Committee; Secretariat. Committee for Mathematics comprises representatives of national committees or individuals representing member countries. **Languages** English. **Staff** 0.50 FTE, paid. **Finance** Sources: members' dues. Annual budget: 400,000 CHF. **Activities** Awards/prizes/competitions; events/meetings; financial and/or material support; training/education. Commissions (4): *International Commission on Mathematical Instruction (ICMI, #12700)* – including *International Study Group for the Relations between the History and Pedagogy of Mathematics (ISGHPM, see: #14121)*; *Commission on Development and Exchanges (CDE, see: #14121)*; *International Commission on the History of Mathematics (ICHM, #12686)* (with International Union of the History and Philosophy of Science); *International Committee on Electronic Information and Communication (CEIC, #12766)*. **Events** *International Congress of Mathematicians* Philadelphia, PA (USA) 2026, *International Congress of Mathematicians* Berlin (Germany) 2022, *General Assembly* Helsinki (Finland) 2022, *General Assembly* Rio de Janeiro (Brazil) 2018, *International Congress of Mathematicians* Rio de Janeiro (Brazil) 2018. **Publications** *Bulletin of the International Mathematical Union*; *IMU-Net* – electronic newsletter.
Members Full mathematics associations in 85 countries and territories:
Algeria, Argentina, Armenia, Australia, Austria, Bangladesh, Belarus, Belgium, Bosnia-Herzegovina, Brazil, Bulgaria, Cameroon, Canada, Chile, China, Colombia, Côte d'Ivoire, Croatia, Cuba, Cyprus, Czechia, Denmark, Ecuador, Egypt, Estonia, Finland, France, Gabon, Georgia, Germany, Greece, Hong Kong, Hungary, Iceland, India, Indonesia, Iran Islamic Rep, Ireland, Israel, Italy, Japan, Kazakhstan, Kenya, Korea Rep, Kyrgyzstan, Latvia, Lithuania, Luxembourg, Malaysia, Mexico, Mongolia, Netherlands, New Zealand, Nigeria, Norway, Oman, Pakistan, Papua New Guinea, Peru, Philippines, Poland, Portugal, Romania, Russia, Saudi Arabia, Senegal, Serbia, Singapore, Slovakia, Slovenia, South Africa, Spain, Sweden, Switzerland, Thailand, Tunisia, Türkiye, UK, Ukraine, Uruguay, USA, Uzbekistan, Venezuela, Vietnam.
Associate members in 6 countries:
Bangladesh, Gabon, Mongolia, Papua New Guinea, Paraguay, Uzbekistan.
Affiliate members (5):
African Mathematical Union (AMU, #00370); *European Mathematical Society (EMS, #07755)*; *Mathematical Council of the Americas (MCofA, #16600)*; *Southeast Asian Mathematical Society (SEAMS, #19773)*; *Unión Matematica de América Latina y el Caribe (UMALCA, #20456)*.
IGO Relations *Abdus Salam International Centre for Theoretical Physics (ICTP, #00005)*. **NGO Relations** Member of (1): *International Science Council (ISC, #14796)*. Represented in: *Committee on Space Research (COSPAR, #04287)*. [2022/XC2247/B]

♦ International Mauthausen Committee (#04179)

♦ International Maxi Association (IMA) 14122

Contact c/o BfB Gestion, Corraterie 26, 1211 Geneva 11, Switzerland. T. +393334858385. E-mail: info@internationalmaxiassociation.com.
URL: http://www.internationalmaxiassociation.com/
History 1980, Geneva (Switzerland), as *International Class 'A' Yacht Association*. Current title adopted, 2 Mar 2001. Previously an Affiliated Offshore Class Association within *World Sailing (#21760)*. Registered in accordance with Swiss Civil Code. **Aims** Encourage amateur *yacht racing*; organize Corinthian sailing, match races, regattas and *competitions* for the sailing yachts of the Categories indicated in Appendix ALPHA. **Structure** General Meeting. Officers; Secretary General. Operational Office in Porto Cervo (Italy); Technical Office in USA. **Languages** English. **NGO Relations** Recognized by: *World Sailing (#21760)*.
[2012/XE2118/E]

♦ International Maxibasketball Federation (#09339)

♦ International Max Scheler Society 14123

Internationale Max Scheler Gesellschaft
Dir Europa-Universität Viadrina, Fak der Kulturwissenschaften, Lehrstuhl für Sozialphilosophie, Grosse Scharrnstrasse 59, 15230 Frankfurt-Oder, Germany.
URL: https://maxscheler2.wordpress.com/
History 2 Jun 1993, Cologne (Germany). **Aims** Promote the work of *philosopher* Max Scheler. **Activities** Events/meetings. Biennial Colloquium in Germany. **Events** *Congress* 2022.
Members Individuals (about 100) in 14 countries:
Belgium, Croatia, France, Germany, Hungary, Italy, Japan, Liechtenstein, Netherlands, Romania, Russia, Serbia, Spain, USA.
[2022/XE3776/E]

♦ International Mayors Communication Centre / see Global Mayors' Forum (#10467)

♦ International Mazdayasnan Order (religious order)
♦ International Mazdaznan Youth Movement (inactive)
♦ International MBA Network / see International Network for the MBA in Agribusiness and Commerce (#14295)
♦ International Measurement Association (unconfirmed)

♦ International Measurement Confederation (IMEKO) 14124

Confédération internationale de la mesure – Confederación Internacional de la Medida – Internationale Messtechnische Konföderation (IMEKO) – Mezdunarodnaja Konfederacija po Izmeritelnoj Tehnike i Priborostroeniju
Secretariat address not obtained. E-mail: imeko@hunmeko.org.
SG PTP-BEV, Arltgasse 35, 1160 Vienna, Austria. T. +431211106607. Fax +431211106000.
URL: http://www.imeko.org/
History 1 Jul 1961, Budapest (Hungary). Preparatory Committee having been set up 1958, Budapest, at 1st International Measurement Conference. Charter, Constitution and By-Laws adopted Jun 1965, Warsaw (Poland), when present name was adopted. Constitution amended 1972, 1979, 1986, 1988, 1994, 2000, 2004, 2005, 2009, 2014. **Aims** Promote international exchange of scientific and technical information relating to developments in measuring techniques, instrument design and manufacture, and application of *instrumentation* in scientific research and in industry; facilitate cooperation among scientists and engineers in studying problems in this field. **Structure** General Council (annual session); Advisory Board; Technical Board; Drafting Committee; Credentials and Membership Committee; Technical Committees (24); Secretariat. **Languages** English. **Staff** 1.00 FTE, paid; 1.00 FTE, voluntary. **Finance** Sources: members' dues; revenue from activities/projects. **Activities** Awards/prizes/competitions; events/meetings. **Events** *World Congress* Hamburg (Germany) 2024, *World Congress* Yokohama (Japan) 2021, *Conference* Brussels (Belgium) 2019, *International Flow Measurement Conference* Lisbon (Portugal) 2019, *World Congress* Belfast (UK) 2018. **Publications** *Measurement* (10 a year) – scientific journal; *Acta IMEKO* (4 a year) – e-journal; *IMEKO* (2-3 a year) – e-Bulletin Newsletter. *IMEKO TC*. Congress, symposica, conference and colloquia proceedings (held by Technical Committees). **Information Services** *IMEKO Measurement Information Service*; *IMEKO Scientific Expertise System*.
Members National scientific and technical societies concerned with measurement science, technology and instrumentation, in 42 countries:
Albania, Austria, Belgium, Brazil, Bulgaria, Canada, China, Congo DR, Croatia, Czechia, Egypt, Finland, France, Germany, Greece, Hungary, India, Italy, Jamaica, Japan, Kazakhstan, Kenya, Korea Rep, Nigeria, Poland, Portugal, Romania, Russia, Rwanda, Serbia, Slovakia, Slovenia, South Africa, Spain, Sweden, Switzerland, Thailand, Türkiye, Uganda, UK, Ukraine, USA.
Supporting member in 1 country:
Germany.
Consultative Status Consultative status granted from: *ECOSOC (#05331)* (Ros C); *UNIDO (#20336)*.
[2022/XC2250/C]

♦ International Measurement Conference / see International Measurement Confederation (#14124)

♦ International Meat Secretariat (IMS) 14125

Office international de la viande (OIV) – Oficina Permanente Internacional de la Carne (OPIC)
SG 5 rue Lespagnol, 75020 Paris, France. T. +33144936020. Fax +33144936001.
URL: http://www.meat-ims.org/
History 26 Nov 1974, Madrid (Spain). Founded at 'Jornadas Internacionales de Carne', simultaneously with the creation of *Federación Ganadera Internacional (inactive)*. Statutes modified: 29 May 1981; 18 Sep 2000. Former names and other names: *Permanent International Meat Office* – former (26 Nov 1974); *Bureau international permanent de la viande* – former (26 Nov 1974). **Aims** Represent the global meat and *livestock* sector as a vital motor of growth and prosperity to meet future demands for sustainable, high-quality, nutritious and safe animal protein. **Structure** General Meeting (every 2 years, preceding Congress); Board of Directors; Executive Council; General Secretariat in Paris (France), headed by Secretary-General. **Languages** English, French, Spanish. **Staff** 2.00 FTE, paid. **Finance** Sources: members' dues. **Activities** Events/meetings; knowledge management/information dissemination. **Events** *World Meat Congress* Cancún (Mexico) 2022, *World Meat Congress* Cancún (Mexico) 2021, *World Meat Congress* Cancún (Mexico) 2020, *Economics Workshop* Buenos Aires (Argentina) 2019, *World Pork Conference* Chengdu (China) 2019. **Publications** *IMS Newsletter* (12 a year) in English, French, Spanish; *IMS-GIRA World Meat Facts Book* (annual). Occasional publications on aspects of the meat industry (scientific, economic, etc).
Members Organizations in 26 countries:
Argentina, Australia, Austria, Belgium, Brazil, Canada, China, Denmark, Egypt, France, Germany, India, Ireland, Italy, Japan, Mexico, Namibia, Netherlands, New Zealand, Norway, Paraguay, Spain, Switzerland, UK, Uruguay, USA.
Consultative Status Consultative status granted from: *ECOSOC (#05331)* (Ros C); *FAO (#09260)* (Liaison Status). **IGO Relations** Observer status with: *Codex Alimentarius Commission (CAC, #04081)*. Cooperation agreement with: *OIE – World Organisation for Animal Health (#17703)*. **NGO Relations** Instrumental in setting up: *International Meat Research and Technology Institute (no recent information)*. Partner of: *Livestock Environmental Assessment and Performance Partnership (LEAP, #16500)*. Cooperates with: *International Feed Industry Federation (IFIF, #13581)* through Livestock Sector Consortium (Private Sector Steering Committee – PSSC Livestock). [2021/XC6198/C]

♦ International Mechanical Pulping Conference (meeting series)
♦ International Mechanism of Scientific Expertise on Biodiversity (unconfirmed)

♦ International Mechanochemical Association (IMA) 14126

Pres Inst of Nanotechnology, Nanostructured Materials Unit, Room 0-404, Campus North – Bldg 640, Karlsruhe Inst of Technology, PO Box 3640, 76021 Karlsruhe, Germany.
History Founded Aug 1989. **Aims** Promote studies in the field of mechanochemistry; provide scientific exchange among scientists engaged in this branch of science. **Structure** Council. **Languages** English. **Staff** 3.00 FTE, voluntary. **Finance** Members' dues. **Activities** Events/meetings. **Events** *Mechanochemistry and mechanical alloying* Cagliari (Italy) 2021, *Mechanochemistry and mechanical alloying* Cagliari (Italy) 2020, *Mechanochemistry and mechanical alloying* Košice (Slovakia) 2017, *Conference* Krakow (Poland) 2014, *Conference* Herceg Novi (Montenegro) 2011. **Publications** *Bibliography of the Literature on Mechanical Activation of Inorganic Solids*. Newsletters; circulars.
Members Scientists; scientific institutions; national and regional societies. Organizations and individuals in 24 countries and territories:
Armenia, Australia, Belarus, Belgium, Bulgaria, China, Czechia, France, Germany, Hungary, India, Israel, Italy, Japan, Korea Rep, Mongolia, Netherlands, Poland, Portugal, Russia, Slovakia, Spain, Taiwan, USA. [2016.10.21/XD4253/D]

♦ International Media Help (internationally oriented national body)

♦ International Media Lawyers Association (IMLA) 14127

Contact c/o IMLA, Progr in Comparative Media Law and Policy, Ctr for Socio-Legal Studies, Univ of Oxford, Manor Road, Oxford, OX1 3UQ, UK. T. +441865284252. Fax +441865284253.
URL: http://www.internationalmedialawyers.org/
History 23 Feb 2004, Tbilisi (Georgia). **Aims** Serve as a forum for the exchange of information, ideas and strategies on critical issues in media law and policy; provide support in addressing issues related to freedom of expression and media law. **Structure** Steering Committee; Interim Steering Committee; Coordinator. **Members** Membership countries not specified. [2009/XM0356/D]

♦ International Media Ministries (see: #10110)

♦ International Media Support (IMS) 14128

Exec Dir Nørregade 18, 1165 Copenhagen K, Denmark. T. +4532698989. Fax +4532698994. E-mail: info@mediasupport.org.
URL: https://www.mediasupport.org/
History 2001, Denmark. **Aims** Enhance peace, stability, democracy, freedom of expression and pluralism of the press in conflict and conflict threatened areas through rapid assistance to media practitioners and media institutions. **Structure** Board. **Events** *Meeting* Copenhagen (Denmark) 2004, *Workshop on media and Indonesian conflicts* Bandung (Indonesia) 2003. **Consultative Status** Consultative status granted from: *Council of Europe (CE, #04881)* (Participatory Status). **NGO Relations** Member of (5): *Communicating*

with Disaster Affected Communities Network (CDAC Network, #04379); *Ethical Journalism Network (EJN, #05554)*; *Global Forum for Media Development (GFMD, #10375)*; *Global Investigative Journalism Network (GIJN, #10433)*; *Global Network Initiative (GNI)*. Partner of (1): *CartONG (#03591)*. Supports (2): *ARTICLE 19 (#01121)*; *International News Safety Institute (INSI, #14364)*. Instrumental in setting up (1): *Arab Reporters for Investigative Journalism (ARIJ, #01036)*. [2021/XG9638/**F**]

♦ International Mediation Institute (IMI) 14129

Exec Dir Bertha von Suttner Bldg, Laan van Meerdervoort 70, 2517 AN The Hague, Netherlands. E-mail: imisupport@imimediation.org.
URL: https://www.imimediation.org/

History 2007. Registration: Charitable foundation, Netherlands. **Aims** Develop global, professional standards for experienced mediators, advocates and others involved in collaborative dispute resolution and negotiation processes; promote understanding; disseminate skills. **Structure** Board of Directors; Independent Advisory Committee; Advisory Council. **Languages** English. **Staff** 1.00 FTE, paid. several voluntary. **Finance** Sources: donations; grants. Annual budget: 35,000 EUR. **Activities** Certification/accreditation; conflict resolution; events/meetings. **Events** *Global Pound Conference* Johannesburg (South Africa) 2017, *Global Pound Conference* London (UK) 2017, *Summit* Madrid (Spain) 2017, *Global Pound Conference* Moscow (Russia) 2017, *Global Pound Conference* Paris (France) 2017. **Publications** *7-Year Anniversary Review for IMI*. *Global Pound* – report. **Members** Not a membership organization. **Consultative Status** Consultative status granted from: *ECOSOC (#05331)* (Special). **IGO Relations** *Commission européenne pour l'efficacité de la justice (CEPEJ, #04213)*; *United Nations Commission on International Trade Law (UNCITRAL, #20531)*. **NGO Relations** *Mediators Beyond Borders International (MBB)*. [2020.05.06/XJ6546/j/**F**]

♦ International Medical Alliance (inactive)
♦ International Medical Assistance Foundation (internationally oriented national body)
♦ International Medical Association for the Study of Living Conditions and Health (inactive)

♦ International Medical Cannabis Patients Coalition (IMCPC) 14130

Contact address not obtained.
Contact address not obtained.
URL: http://imcpc.org/

History Founded 2015, Prague (Czech Rep). **Aims** Organize safe and legal access to medical cannabis worldwide; change the UN Single Treaty to recognize medical cannabis; help patient advocates in the world create patient organizations; serve as resource for patient organizations worldwide. **Languages** English. **Staff** 4.00 FTE, paid. **Finance** Funded by Americans for Safe Access. **Activities** Events/meetings; guidance/assistance/consulting; knowledge management/information dissemination.
Members Governing organizations in 11 countries:
Australia, Austria, Czechia, Estonia, France, Israel, Philippines, Slovenia, Spain, UK, USA.
Supporting organizations in 12 countries:
Australia, Bulgaria, Canada, Czechia, France, Greece, Hungary, Italy, Mexico, Netherlands, Serbia, Spain.
NGO Relations *International Cannabis and Cannabinoids Institute (ICCI)*. [2020.03.13/XM8643/**C**]

♦ International Medical Centre of Japan / see Nation Center for Global Health and Medicine
♦ International Medical Children's Aid (internationally oriented national body)
♦ International Medical College / see International Medical University, Malaysia
♦ International Medical Congress of Malady and Invalidity Insurance (inactive)

♦ International Medical Contact Lens Council (IMCLC) 14131

Scientific Vice-Pres 1 av Jean-Daniel Maillard, 1247 Meyrin GE, Switzerland. T. +41227831090. Fax +41227831099.
URL: http://www.imclc.com/

History Founded 1994, as *International Contact Lens Society of Ophthalmologists (ICLSO)*. Registered according to the law of Colorado (USA). **Aims** Contribute to the dissemination of knowledge about eye health, and, in particular, for the correct use of contact lenses. **Structure** Council of the Regional Societies of Contact Lenses. **Languages** English. **Staff** 5.00 FTE, paid. **Finance** Members' dues. **Activities** Events/meetings. **Events** *World Ophthalmology Congress* Tokyo (Japan) 2014, *World Ophthalmology Congress* Dubai (United Arab Emirates) 2012, *World Ophthalmology Congress* Berlin (Germany) 2010, *World Ophthalmology Congress* Hong Kong (Hong Kong) 2008.
Members National associations in 4 countries:
Brazil, China, Japan, USA.
Regional member:
European Contact Lens Society of Ophthalmologists (ECLSO, #06775).
NGO Relations Member of: *International Council of Ophthalmology (ICO, #13057)*. [2018.07.20/XD5275/y/**D**]

♦ International Medical Cooperation / see Artsen Zonder Vakantie
♦ International Medical Cooperation – Africa / see Artsen Zonder Vakantie
♦ International Medical Cooperation Committee (internationally oriented national body)
♦ International Medical Corps (internationally oriented national body)

♦ International Medical Device Regulators Forum (IMDRF) 14132

Secretariat address not obtained. E-mail: imdrfsecretariat@ccfdie.org.
URL: http://www.imdrf.org/

History Oct 2011, Ottawa ON (Canada). **Aims** Accelerate international medical device regulatory harmonization and convergence. **Structure** Management Committee, composed of regulatory officials, with *WHO (#20950)* as observer. Rotating Chair and Secretariat. **Events** *Meeting* Beijing (China) 2018, *Meeting* Shanghai (China) 2018, *Meeting* Ottawa, ON (Canada) 2017, *Meeting* Vancouver, BC (Canada) 2017, *Meeting* Florianópolis (Brazil) 2016.
Members Government agencies of 6 countries:
Australia, Brazil, Canada, Japan, USA.
Regional entity:
European Commission (EC, #06633) (DG Health and Consumers).
IGO Relations Affiliated with: APEC Regulatory Harmonization Steering Committee. **NGO Relations** Affiliate organization: *Global Harmonization Working Party (GHWP, #10399)*. [2018/XJ7278/**F***]

♦ International Medical Education Trust 2000 (internationally oriented national body)
♦ International Medical Equipment Collaborative (internationally oriented national body)

♦ International Medical Geology Association (IMGA) 14133

Co-Chair Geological Sciences Geoscience Dept, Univ of Aveiro, Campus de Santiago, 3810-193 Aveiro, Portugal. E-mail: secretary@medicalgeology.org.
Chair Fundación Centro de Estudios Infectológicos, French 30185, C1425AWK, Buenos Aires, Argentina.
URL: http://www.medicalgeology.org/

History 1990. Founded under *International Union of Geological Sciences (IUGS, #15777)*, under COGEOENVIRONMENT – then *IUGS Commission on Geoscience for Environmental Management (IUGS-GEM, inactive)* – as *International Working Group on Medical Geology*. Subsequently became a special initiative, under IUGS, 1997, and also an *International Geoscience Programme (IGCP, #13715)*, with funding from *International Council for Science (ICSU, inactive)*. Founded as a permanent organization building on all previous activities, 2006, when constitution and by-laws were adopted. **Aims** Facilitate interactions between geoscientists and biomedical / public health researchers in addressing human and animal health problems caused by geologic materials or geologic processes. **Structure** General Assembly; Executive Committee; Supervisor Board; Regional Divisions and Chapters. **Languages** English, Portuguese, Spanish. **Staff** Voluntary. **Finance** Sources: members' dues. **Activities** Events/meetings; training/education. **Events** *WMESS : World Multidisciplinary Earth Sciences Symposium* Prague (Czechia) 2022, *WMESS : World Multidisciplinary Earth Sciences Symposium* Prague (Czechia) 2019, *WMESS : World Multidisciplinary Earth Sciences Symposium* Prague (Czechia) 2018, *MEDGEO : International Conference on Medical Geology* Moscow (Russia) 2017, *MEDGEO : International Conference on Medical Geology* Moscow (Russia) 2017. **Publications** *IMGA Newsletter* (2 a year). Books.
Members Individuals (180) in 70 countries and territories:
Argentina, Australia, Austria, Belarus, Belgium, Bolivia, Botswana, Brazil, Bulgaria, Cameroon, Canada, Chile, China, Colombia, Czechia, Denmark, Egypt, Estonia, Finland, France, Georgia, Germany, Ghana, Greece, Hungary, India, Indonesia, Iran Islamic Rep, Iraq, Ireland, Italy, Jamaica, Japan, Jordan, Kenya, Latvia, Lebanon, Lithuania, Malaysia, Mexico, Mongolia, Morocco, Namibia, Netherlands, New Zealand, Nigeria, Norway, Pakistan, Peru, Philippines, Poland, Puerto Rico, Russia, Saudi Arabia, Serbia, Slovakia, Somalia, South Africa, Spain, Sri Lanka, Sweden, Switzerland, Taiwan, Türkiye, UK, Ukraine, USA, Venezuela, Zambia, Zimbabwe.
NGO Relations *Global Science and Technology Forum (GSTF)*. [2022/XJ2484/v/**C**]

♦ International Medical Health Organization (internationally oriented national body)

♦ International Medical Informatics Association (IMIA) 14134

Association internationale d'informatique médicale

CEO address not obtained. E-mail: imia@imia-services.org.
URL: http://www.imia-medinfo.org/

History May 1979. Founded by *International Federation for Information Processing (IFIP, #13458)*, as a Special Interest Group replacing the former IFIP Technical Committee 4 'Information Processing in Health Care and Biomedical Research'. Statutes most recently updated, 12 Sep 2010, Cape Town (South Africa). Registration: Swiss Civil Code, Switzerland. **Aims** Promote informatics in health care and biomedical research; move theory into practice by linking academic and research informaticians with care givers, consultants, vendors and vendor-based researchers; promote cross fertilization of health informatics information across geographical and professional boundaries; serve as a catalyst for worldwide health information infrastructures for patient care and health research; monitor the range of special interest areas and focus support on new developments; minimize fragmentation between scientific and operational medical informaticians; harmonize competing organizations that emerge to address informatics issues; adapt to changes in the medical informatics marketplace and discipline. **Structure** General Meeting (annual, in Congress years held at Congress); Board; Executive Committee; Secretariat. Standing and Ad Hoc Advisory Committees (5); Special Interest Groups. Includes: *International Academy of Health Sciences Informatics (IAHSI)*. **Languages** English. **Staff** 0.50 FTE, paid. Several voluntary. **Finance** Sources: contributions; donations; investments; meeting proceeds; members' dues; sale of publications. **Activities** Events/meetings; research/documentation; training/education. **Events** *MedInfo : World Congress on Medical and Health Informatics* 2027, *MedInfo : World Congress on Medical and Health Informatics* Taiwan 2025, *MedInfo : World Congress on Medical and Health Informatics* Sydney, NSW (Australia) 2023, *International Congress on Nursing Informatics* 2021, *MedInfo : World Congress on Medical and Health Informatics* 2021. **Publications** *Yearbook of Medical Informatics*. MEDINFO proceedings; Working Conference proceedings.
Members National institutions and representatives in 56 countries and territories:
Argentina, Australia, Austria, Belgium, Bosnia-Herzegovina, Brazil, Cameroon, Canada, China, Côte d'Ivoire, Croatia, Cuba, Czechia, Denmark, Ethiopia, Finland, France, Germany, Greece, Hong Kong, Hungary, India, Iran Islamic Rep, Ireland, Israel, Italy, Japan, Kazakhstan, Korea Rep, Malawi, Malaysia, Mali, Netherlands, New Zealand, Nigeria, Norway, Philippines, Poland, Romania, Saudi Arabia, Singapore, Slovakia, Slovenia, South Africa, Spain, Sweden, Switzerland, Taiwan, Thailand, Togo, Türkiye, UK, Ukraine, Uruguay, USA, Venezuela.
Regional Affiliates (6):
Asian Pacific Association for Medical Informatics (APAMI, #01600); *European Federation for Medical Informatics (EFMI, #07164)*; *Health Informatics in Africa (HELINA, #10884)*; *International Medical Informatics Association for Latin America and the Caribbean (IMIA-LAC, #14135)*; Middle East and North African Health Informatics Association (MENAHIA); North American Medical Informatics (NAMI).
Consultative Status Consultative status granted from: *WHO (#20950)* (Official Relations). **NGO Relations** In liaison with technical committees of: *International Organization for Standardization (ISO, #14473)*. [2022.10.12/XC9451/y/**C**]

♦ International Medical Informatics Association for Latin America and the Caribbean (IMIA-LAC) 14135

Association internationale d'informatique médicale pour l'Amérique latine et les Caraïbes – Asociación Internacional de Informatica Médica para Latino América y Caribe

Pres Medisist, Lopez Mateos 2077 L-28, 44510 Guadalajara JAL, Mexico. T. +523330307030.
URL: http://www.imia-medinfo.org/

History 21 Aug 1983, Amsterdam (Netherlands), within the framework of *International Medical Informatics Association (IMIA, #14134)*. Also referred to as *Federation of Health Societies in Latin America*. Previously also known as *Regional Federation of Health Informatics Societies in Latin America and the Caribbean – Federación Regional de Informatica de la Salud para América Latina y el Caribe*. **Aims** Develop health informatics within the region; strengthen regional ties. **Structure** Council; Executive Committee. **Languages** English, Spanish. **Staff** 2.00 FTE, paid. **Finance** Members' dues. Other sources: fund raising; course fees. **Activities** Networking/liaising; events/meetings; training/education; projects/programmes. **Events** *Latin American Conference* Montevideo (Uruguay) 2014, *Regional Conference* Guadalajara (Mexico) 2011, *Regional congress* Havana (Cuba) 1992, *International Symposium on Health Informatics* Havana (Cuba) 1991, *Regional Conference* Brasilia (Brazil) 1990. **Publications** *IMIA-LAC Newsletter*.
Members Full in 5 countries:
Argentina, Brazil, Chile, Cuba, Mexico.
Associate member in 1 country:
Uruguay.
Observer in 9 countries:
Bolivia, Colombia, Costa Rica, Dominican Rep, Ecuador, El Salvador, Guatemala, Paraguay, Peru. [2017.06.01/XE1149/**E**]

♦ International Medical Interpreters Association (unconfirmed)

♦ International Medical Ozone Federation (IMEOF) 14136

Federación Internacional Médica de Ozono

Pres Avda Juan Andrés 60, local 1 bajo, 28032 Madrid, Spain. T. +34913515175. Fax +34913515175. E-mail: info@aepromo.org – info@imeof.org.
URL: http://www.imeof.org/

History 2008, Mexico City (Mexico) as *International Federation of Oxygen-Ozone Therapy (FIOOT)*. Present title adopted 4 Jan 2011. Registered in accordance with Spanish law. **Aims** Actively work to obtain official recognition of ozone therapy by member countries' authorities. **Structure** Governing Board. **Languages** English, Spanish. **Staff** Voluntary. **Finance** Sources: members' dues. **Activities** Awards/prizes/competitions; events/meetings; knowledge management/information dissemination; networking/liaising. **Events** *Congress* Nizhniy Novgorod (Russia) 2018, *Congress* Madrid (Spain) 2017, *Congress* Moscow (Russia) 2016, *Congress* Havana (Cuba) 2015, *Congress* Madrid (Spain) 2014. **Publications** *Legal Situation of Ozone Therapy in Brazil* (2018).
Members National associations (22) in 20 countries:
Argentina, Chile, Colombia, Cuba, Dominican Rep, Ecuador, Egypt, Guatemala, Honduras, Japan, Mexico, Pakistan, Peru, Romania, Russia, Spain, Türkiye, Ukraine, USA, Venezuela.
Regional association: Latin American Ozone Therapists Dental Association.
Latin American Ozone Therapists Dental Association.
NGO Relations *International Scientific Committee on Ozone Therapy (ISCO3, #14803)*. [2020.03.03/XJ9455/y/**C**]

♦ International Medical Parliamentarians Organization (IMPO) 14137

SG c/o AFPPD, Phayathai Plaza Bldg, Ste 9-C, Phayathai Road, Ratchathewi, Bangkok, 10400, Thailand. T. +6622192903 – +6622192904. Fax +6622192905.

History 1989. Current constitution adopted Feb 1994, Bangkok (Thailand). Former names and other names: *International Organization of Parliamentarians for Health* – former (1989); *Organisation internationale de parlementaires pour la santé* – former (1989). **Aims** Promote: cooperation in law and policy making and parliamentary activities on issues of concern to world health and medical care; the highest standards of ethics in medical and health care; better global understanding of health and medical care issues; improved ecological environment and stable, environmentally sound economic development; international exchange of experience, information and opinion. Mobilize parliamentarians with medical background to achieve the above aims. **Structure** General Assembly (at least every 3 years). Executive Committee of up to 15 full members, including ex-officio President, the 4 Regional Vice-Presidents, Secretary-General and Treasurer. Regions (4): Africa; Americas; Asia-Pacific; Europe. Secretariat, headed by Secretary-General. Setting up a

task force of women medical parliamentarians. **Languages** English. **Staff** 2.00 FTE, paid. **Finance** Support from WHO and its regional offices; *United Nations Population Fund (UNFPA, #20612)*. **Activities** Training courses; conferences; study visits. **Events** *Asian medical parliamentarians conference* Bangkok (Thailand) 2009, *European conference* Dublin (Ireland) 2005, *Conference* Bangkok (Thailand) 2004, *Conference on family health* Bangkok (Thailand) 2003, *International conference* Bangkok (Thailand) 1999. **Publications** *IMPO Information* – newsletter. *International Directory of Medical Parliamentarians* (1998). Conference reports.
Members Parliamentarians with medical qualifications in 88 countries:
Albania, Algeria, Antigua-Barbuda, Argentina, Armenia, Australia, Austria, Bangladesh, Belarus, Belgium, Belize, Benin, Bolivia, Botswana, Bulgaria, Burkina Faso, Cambodia, Colombia, Côte d'Ivoire, Denmark, Djibouti, Dominican Rep, Equatorial Guinea, Estonia, Ethiopia, Fiji, Finland, France, Gabon, Georgia, Germany, Guatemala, India, Indonesia, Iran Islamic Rep, Ireland, Jamaica, Japan, Jordan, Kiribati, Korea Rep, Kyrgyzstan, Laos, Latvia, Lesotho, Lithuania, Malawi, Malaysia, Maldives, Malta, Monaco, Mongolia, Nepal, New Zealand, North Macedonia, Norway, Pakistan, Panama, Peru, Poland, Portugal, Romania, Russia, Seychelles, Singapore, Slovakia, Slovenia, Solomon Is, South Africa, Spain, Sri Lanka, St Kitts-Nevis, St Vincent-Grenadines, Suriname, Sweden, Switzerland, Syrian AR, Thailand, Togo, Trinidad-Tobago, Türkiye, Uganda, UK, Ukraine, Uruguay, Uzbekistan, Zambia, Zimbabwe.
IGO Relations *United Nations Population Fund (UNFPA, #20612)*; *WHO Regional Office for South-East Asia (SEARO, #20946)*. **NGO Relations** *Asian Forum of Parliamentarians on Population and Development (AFPPD, #01493)*; *Inter-American Parliamentary Group on Population and Development (IAPG, inactive)*.
[2014/XD4346/v/**C**]

♦ International Medical Rehabilitation Center (internationally oriented national body)

♦ International Medical Research Association (IMRA) 14138

Chairman Yeungnam Univ, 280 Daehak-Ro, Gyeongsan NORTH GYEONGSANG 712-749, Korea Rep. T. +82536204342. E-mail: eunoung@korea.kr.
URL: http://imra2013.com/

History 10 Feb 2010. **Aims** Facilitate interactions and collaborations among research institutes for research and development of advanced medical science and technologies; train human resources that can contribute to the prosperity of the nations and the international community. **Structure** General Assembly. Committee, headed by Chairman. **Finance** Members' dues. **Events** *Conference* Taiwan 2013, *Conference* Kobe (Japan) 2012, *Conference* Daegu (Korea Rep) 2011, *Conference* Barcelona (Spain) 2010.
Members Institutes (11) in 4 countries and territories:
Japan, Korea Rep, Spain, Taiwan. [2013/XJ6743/**D**]

♦ International Medical Research Centre, Franceville (internationally oriented national body)
♦ International Medical Sciences Academy (internationally oriented national body)
♦ International Medical Services for Health / see INMED Partnerships for Children

♦ International Medical Society for Applied Kinesiology (IMAK) 14139

Internationale Ärztegesellschaft für Applied Kinesiology

Sec Postfach 38, 9330 Althofen, Austria. T. +43426229098. Fax +43426229107.
URL: http://www.funktionelle-myodiagnostik.com/

History 1993. Registered in accordance with Austrian law. **Aims** Further research, doctrine and distribution of applied kinesiology. **Structure** General Assembly. Board, including President, Secretary and Treasurer. Auditors; Arbitration Board. **Finance** Members' dues. **Events** *Meeting on applied kinesiology* Vienna (Austria) 2006. **NGO Relations** *International College of Applied Kinesiology (ICAK, #12641)*. [2011/XM2740/**D**]

♦ International Medical Society for Energy Medicine (no recent information)
♦ International Medical Society of Paraplegia / see International Spinal Cord Society (#15581)
♦ International Medical Sports Federation for Aid to Cancer Research (inactive)
♦ International Medical Students' Organization on Population (inactive)
♦ International Medical Symposium on Soft Lenses (meeting series)
♦ International Medical Travel Association (inactive)
♦ International Medical University, Malaysia (internationally oriented national body)

♦ International Medieval Latin Committee (IMLC) 14140

Pres Dept of the Classics, 206 Boylston Hall, Harvard Univ, Cambridge MA 02138, USA. T. +16174966062.
URL: http://imlc.huygens.knaw.nl/

History 1988. **Aims** Organize international congresses so as to further, expand and promote the study of Medieval Latin around the world. **Structure** Board. **Languages** English, French, German, Italian, Spanish. **Finance** Various sources, including governmental and university. **Activities** Events/meetings. **Events** *Nostalgia and/in the Latin Middle Ages* Prague (Czechia) 2022, *Mittellatein Vernetzt/Medieval Latin Networks* Vienna (Austria) 2017, *Le Sens du Temps* Lyon (France) 2014, *Auctor et Auctoritas in Latinis Medii Aevi Litteris* Benevento (Italy) / Naples (Italy) 2010, *Interpreting Latin Texts in the Middle Ages* Toronto, ON (Canada) 2006. **Publications** Congress proceedings.
Members Full in 11 countries:
Austria, Belgium, Canada, France, Italy, Netherlands, Portugal, Spain, Switzerland, UK, USA. [2022.10.18/XJ9088/c/**E**]

♦ International Medieval Sermon Studies Society (IMSSS) 14141

Pres Dipto Studi Storici, Univ Torino, Via Sant'Ottavio 20, 10124 Turin TO, Italy.
Sec 2005 Lee Hall, English Dept, PO Box E, Starkville MS 39762, USA. E-mail: hj71@msstate.edu.
URL: http://imsss.net/

History Founded Jul 1988, Dijon (France), during the 6th *International Symposium on Medieval Sermon Studies*, following activities initiated by Gloria Cigman and other scholars, 1979. **Aims** Promote and foster the study of medieval sermons, and preaching in Latin and vernacular languages within their social, literary, religious, intellectual, theological, catechetical, political and historical contexts. **Structure** Council. **Languages** English, French. **Staff** Voluntary. **Finance** Sources: members' dues; subscriptions. **Activities** Events/meetings; knowledge management/information dissemination. **Events** *Symposium* León (Spain) 2021, *Symposium* León (Spain) 2020, *Symposium* Bristol (UK) 2018, *Symposium* St Augustine, FL (USA) 2016, *Symposium* Krakow (Poland) 2014. **Publications** *Medieval Sermon Studies* – official journal.
[2018.08.02/XN8684/**C**]

♦ International Medieval Society, Paris (IMS) 14142

Société Internationale des Médiévistes, Paris

Main Office 110 quai Louis Blériot, 75016 Paris, France. E-mail: communications.ims.paris@gmail.com.
Contact c/o LAMOP, 1 rue Victor Cousin, Bureau G670-esc R – 3e étage, 75232 Paris CEDEX 05, France.
URL: http://www.ims-paris.org/

History 2003. 2009, officially affiliated to *Laboratoire de médiévistique occidentale de Paris (LAMOP)*. Registration: 501c3 Nonprofit, USA; Loi du 1er juillet 1901, France. **Structure** Board of Directors, comprising President, Treasurer and 7 Directors. **Events** *Annual Symposium* Paris (France) 2019, *Annual Symposium* Paris (France) 2018, *Annual Symposium* Paris (France) 2017, *Annual Symposium* Paris (France) 2016, *Annual Symposium* Paris (France) 2015.
Members Individuals in 6 countries:
Belgium, Canada, France, Switzerland, UK, USA. [2019/XJ6540/**E**]

♦ International Mediterranean Society of Orthopedic Surgery (unconfirmed)

♦ International Mediterranean Women's Forum (IMWF) 14143

Forum international des femmes de la méditerranée (FIFM) – Fórum Internacional de las Mujeres del Mediterraneo (FIMM) – Forum Internazionale delle Donne del Mediterraneo (FIDM)

Contact Centro UNESCO di Torino, Viale Maestri del Lavoro 10, 10127 Turin TO, Italy. T. +39116965476 – +39116936425. Fax +39116936425. E-mail: segreteria@centrounesco.to.it.
URL: http://www.centrounesco.to.it/

History Founded 1992, Valencia (Spain), within *UNESCO Mediterranean Programme (inactive)* as component of *Network of Mediterranean Women for Cooperation and Parity (no recent information)*, by the Instituto de la Mujer de Valencia and *UNESCO (#20322)*. Original title: *Mediterranean Women's Forum – Forum des femmes de la méditerranée (FFM) – Fórum de las Mujeres del Mediterraneo – Forum delle Donne del Mediterraneo*. Transferred in 1997 to Turin (Italy). Original focus was on the Mediterranean; remit expanded in 1997 to include the Balkans. **Aims** Further cooperation and interchange of experiences between women of Mediterranean countries in order to propose and carry out sustainable solutions for effective improvement of women's condition throughout the Mediterranean and globally. **Structure** Permanent Committee; Presidency; International Secretariat; Office of the President located in Turin (Italy). **Languages** English, French, Italian, Spanish. **Staff** 10.00 FTE, voluntary. **Finance** Members' dues. Other sources: private contributions; donations. **Activities** Events/meetings; networking/liaising; knowledge management/information dissemination; training/education. **Events** *International Meeting on Global Ethics and Equal Opportunities* Turin (Italy) 2014, *Biennial International Conference* Turin (Italy) 2005, *Biennial International Conference* Athens (Greece) 2003, *Biennial International Conference* Dubrovnik (Croatia) 2001, *What stakes for women?* Paris (France) 2001. **Publications** Books; booklets; CD-ROMs; DVDs.
Members National institutions and NGOs in 16 countries and territories:
Albania, Algeria, Croatia, Egypt, France, Greece, Israel, Italy, Jordan, Lebanon, Morocco, Palestine, Slovenia, Spain, Tunisia, Türkiye.
Consultative Status Consultative status granted from: *UNESCO (#20322)* (Consultative Status). **NGO Relations** Founding member of: *Euro-Mediterranean Women's Foundation (#05729)*. [2018.09.18/XK1406/**E**]

♦ International Meeting on Antimicrobial Peptides (meeting series)
♦ International Meeting on Atomic and Molecular Physics and Chemistry (meeting series)
♦ International Meeting of Carbonate Sedimentologists (meeting series)
♦ International Meeting on Chemical Engineering and Biotechnology (meeting series)
♦ International Meeting on Chemical Sensors (meeting series)
♦ International Meeting on Cognitive Neuropsychology (meeting series)
♦ International Meeting in Community Service (internationally oriented national body)
♦ International Meeting on Experimental and Behavioral Social Sciences (meeting series)
♦ International Meeting on Fundamental Physics (meeting series)
♦ International Meeting of Hepatocellular Carcinoma – Eastern and Western Experiences (meeting series)
♦ International Meeting on High Performance Computing for Computational Science (meeting series)
♦ International Meeting on Human Ecology (meeting series)
♦ International Meeting – Integrated Management of Acute and Chronic Coronary Artery Disease (meeting series)
♦ International Meeting on Lithium Batteries (meeting series)
♦ International Meetings of Architects (inactive)
♦ International Meetings on Nature and the Environment (meeting series)
♦ International Meeting on Thermodiffusion (meeting series)
♦ International Megaprojects Workshop (meeting series)
♦ International Melges 24 Class Association (see: #21760)
♦ International Membrane Research Forum (meeting series)
♦ International Memorialization Supply Association (internationally oriented national body)
♦ International Menarini Foundation (internationally oriented national body)
♦ International Ménière Federation (inactive)

♦ International Meningioma Society (IMS) 14144

Exec Dir PO Box 5564, San Mateo CA 94402, USA. T. +16502885339. E-mail: meningiomasociety@gmail.com.
Sec Dept of Neurosurgery, Univ of Utah, Health Science Ctr, Bldg 550 – 5th Floor, 175 N Medical Drive East, Salt Lake City UT 84132, USA. T. +18015816908. Fax +18015814385.
URL: http://www.meningiomasociety.org/

History 2008. **Aims** Advance clinical care and research in meningiomas and thereby promote the best possible care for patients suffering from meningiomas. **Structure** Board of Directors. **Events** *International Congress on the Cerebral Venous System and Meningiomas* Prague (Czechia) 2018, *Meningioma Meeting* Beijing (China) 2017, *International Congress on the Cerebral Venous System and Meningiomas* Osaka (Japan) 2016, *International Congress on the Cerebral Venous System and Meningiomas* Napa, CA (USA) 2014, *International Congress on the Cerebral Venous System and Meningiomas* Little Rock, AR (USA) 2012.
[2017/XJ9952/**C**]

♦ International Menopause Society (IMS) 14145

CEO 13 Leechwell St, Totnes, TQ9 5SX, UK.
URL: http://www.imsociety.org/

History 25 Nov 1978, Jerusalem (Israel). Founded at 2nd *International Congress on the Menopause*. Statutes adopted 1979, Geneva (Switzerland). Registration: Charity Commission, Start date: 2014, England and Wales; Start date: 1979, Switzerland. **Aims** Promote knowledge, study and research on all aspects of aging in women. **Structure** General Assembly (at least every 2 years); Executive Committee; Sub-organs: *Council of Affiliated Menopause Societies (CAMS)*, *World School for the Study of Menopause (WSSM)*. **Languages** English. **Staff** 2.00 FTE, paid. **Finance** Sources: members' dues. **Activities** Events/meetings; knowledge management/information dissemination. **Events** *World Congress on Menopause* Melbourne, VIC (Australia) 2024, *World Congress on Menopause* Lisbon (Portugal) 2022, *Biennial Congress* Melbourne, VIC (Australia) 2021, *Biennial Congress* Melbourne, VIC (Australia) 2020, *Congress on Menopause, Andropause and Anti-Aging* Vienna (Austria) 2020. **Publications** *Our Menopause World* (12 a year) – newsletter; *Climacteric* (6 a year) – journal.
Members National societies and individuals in 64 countries and territories:
Argentina, Australia, Austria, Bangladesh, Belgium, Bolivia, Brazil, Canada, Chile, China, Colombia, Costa Rica, Croatia, Czechia, Denmark, Dominican Rep, Ecuador, Finland, France, Germany, Greece, Guatemala, Hong Kong, Hungary, India, Indonesia, Israel, Italy, Japan, Korea Rep, Luxembourg, Malaysia, Mexico, Mongolia, Netherlands, New Zealand, Nicaragua, Norway, Pakistan, Panama, Paraguay, Peru, Philippines, Poland, Portugal, Puerto Rico, Romania, Russia, Saudi Arabia, Serbia, Singapore, South Africa, Spain, Sweden, Switzerland, Taiwan, Thailand, Türkiye, UK, United Arab Emirates, Uruguay, USA, Venezuela, Vietnam.
IGO Relations *WHO (#20950)*. [2021/XC9480/**C**]

♦ International Mentoring Association (internationally oriented national body)
♦ International Menuhin Association / see International Yehudi Menuhin Foundation (#15922)
♦ International Menuhin Music Academy (internationally oriented national body)
♦ International Mercantile Marine Officers' Association (inactive)

♦ International Mesostructured Materials Association (IMMA) 14146

Sec c/o Shanghai Normal Univ, College of Chemistry, 200234 Shanghai, China.
URL: http://mesostructured.org/

History 2000, Québec, QC (Canada). Founded by International Advisory Board of 2nd International Symposium on Mesoporous Molecular Sieves (ISMMS2000). Registration: Canada. **Activities** Organizes 'International Mesostructured Materials Symposium (IMMS)'. **Events** *International Mesostructured Materials Symposium* 2024, *International Mesostructured Materials Symposium* Dalian (China) 2021, *International Mesostructured Materials Symposium (IMMS)* Los Angeles, CA (USA) 2018, *Symposium* Brisbane, QLD (Australia) 2015, *Symposium* Awaji (Japan) 2013. [2021/XJ5510/c/**E**]

♦ International Mesothelioma Interest Group (IMIG) 14147

Pres Dept of Radiology, Univ of Chicago, 5801 S Ellis Ave, Chicago IL 60637, USA. E-mail: info@imig.org.
URL: http://imig.org/

History 1991, Paris, at International Conference on mesothelioma. **Aims** Promote research, treatment and education of and for mesothelioma. **Structure** Board. **Events** *Meeting* Chicago, IL (USA) 2021, *Meeting* Brisbane, QLD (Australia) 2020, *Meeting* Ottawa, ON (Canada) 2018, *Meeting* Birmingham (UK) 2016, *Meeting* Cape Town (South Africa) 2014. **Members** Full in 35 countries. Membership countries not specified.
[2019.12.11/XJ4675/**F**]

♦ International Messianic Jewish Alliance (IMJA) 14148

Exec Dir address not obtained.
Treas address not obtained.
URL: http://www.imja.org/

History 8 Sep 1925, London (UK), as *International Hebrew Christian Alliance (IHCA) – Alliance internationale des juifs chrétiens.* **Aims** Unite and provide pastoral care and material support (where necessary) to Jewish believers in Jesus as Messiah, who are members of a recognized fellowship. **Structure** International Legislative Conference (every 5 years). Executive Committee, comprising Office Bearers (President, up to 4 Vice-Presidents, Treasurer and Executive Secretary), Presidents of affiliated national alliances, up to 12 members elected by the Conference and up 5 members coopted by the Executive Committee. Standing Committees. **Languages** English, French, German, Russian, Spanish. **Staff** 35.00 FTE, paid. **Finance** Members' dues. Donations. **Activities** Education and relief funds. Conferences. **Events** *Meeting* Berlin (Germany) 2011, *Meeting* Israel 2007, *Meeting* USA 2002, *Conference / Meeting* Paris (France) 2001, *Meeting* USA 1999. **Publications** *IMJA Newsletter* (12 a year).
Members Affiliated national alliances in 17 countries:
Argentina, Australia, Brazil, Canada, Colombia, France, Germany, Israel, Mexico, Netherlands, New Zealand, Russia, South Africa, UK, Ukraine, Uruguay, USA. [2015/XC2099/**F**]

♦ International Metabolic Engineering Society (IMES) 14149

Headquarters 120 Wall St, Fl 23, New York NY 10005-4020, USA. Fax +12037755177. E-mail: imes@aiche.org.
URL: https://www.aiche.org/imes

History Metabolic Engineering Conferences have been running since 1998 with IMES being set up afterwards. A Technical Group of American Institute of Chemical Engineers (AIChE). **Aims** Promote and advance metabolic engineering as an enabling science for bio-based production of materials, pharmaceuticals, food ingredients, chemicals and fuels. **Structure** Board of Directors. **Events** *Conference* Awaji (Japan) 2016, *Conference* Vancouver, BC (Canada) 2014, *Conference / Metabolic Engineering* Biarritz (France) 2012. **Members** Individuals. Membership countries not specified. [2015/XJ9966/v/**E**]

♦ International Metallic Silhouette Shooting Union (IMSSU) 14150

Pres address not obtained. E-mail: president@imssu.org.
URL: http://www.imssu.org/

History 7 Nov 1992. Registered in accordance with French law. **Aims** Promote development of amateur metallic silhouette shooting sports; promote friendship between metallic silhouette associations worldwide. **Structure** General Assembly (annual); Council. **Languages** English. **Staff** 10.00 FTE, voluntary. **Finance** Members' dues. **Activities** Sporting activities.
Members National organizations in 25 countries:
Australia, Austria, Brazil, Czechia, Denmark, Finland, France, Germany, Hungary, Ireland, Italy, Lithuania, Malta, Namibia, Netherlands, New Zealand, Norway, Philippines, Russia, South Africa, Sri Lanka, Sweden, Switzerland, USA, Zimbabwe. [2020/XD9199/**D**]

♦ International Metallographic Society (IMS) 14151

Société métallographique internationale

Dir – Affiliate Societies c/o ASM International, 9639 Kinsman Rd, Materials Park OH 44073-0002, USA. T. +14403385151. E-mail: memberservicecenter@asminternational.org.
URL: http://www.asminternational.org/web/ims/

History Sep 1967, USA. 1992, became an Affiliate Society of *ASM International (ASM).* Former names and other names: *International Microstructural Analysis Society* – alias. Registration: Start date: Sep 1967, USA, New Mexico. **Aims** Benefit the art and science of, and stimulate interest in, characterization of materials and their structures; raise professional standards of light and electron microscopy, quantitative/computer-aided microstructural analysis, metallography, ceramography, petrography, and allied sciences. **Structure** Board of Directors; Committees (7). **Languages** English. **Staff** 2.00 FTE, paid. **Finance** Members' dues. Annual budget: US$ 100,000 – 125,000. **Activities** Events/meetings; training/education; awards/prizes/competitions. **Events** *Microscopy and Microanalysis Annual Congress* Columbus, OH (USA) 2016, *Microscopy and Microanalysis Annual Congress* Portland, OR (USA) 2015, *Annual Technical Meeting* Hartford, CT (USA) 2014, *Microscopy and microanalysis annual congress* Indianapolis, IN (USA) 2013, *Microscopy and Microanalysis Annual Congress* Phoenix, AZ (USA) 2012. **Publications** *Metallography, Microstructure, and Analysis Journal* (4 a year); *Sliplines* (4 a year) – newsletter.
Members Institutional; Individual; Sustaining. Members in 17 countries and territories:
Australia, Brazil, Canada, Chile, Denmark, France, Germany, India, Ireland, Israel, Italy, Japan, Mexico, Norway, Taiwan, UK, USA. [2019.06.25/XD2654/**D**]

♦ International Metallurgy and Materials Congress (meeting series)
♦ International Metal Union / see European Metal Union (#07785)
♦ International Metalworkers' Federation (inactive)
♦ International Meteorological Organization (inactive)

♦ International Meteor Organization (IMO) 14152

SG 1828 Cobblecreek St, Chula Vista CA 91913-3917, USA. E-mail: lunro.imo.usa@cox.net.
Contact Mattheessensstraat 60, 2540 Hove, Belgium. E-mail: secretary@imo.net.
URL: http://www.imo.net/

History Founded 1 May 1988. Founding General Assembly, 3 Oct 1989, Balatonföldvar (Hungary). Registered in accordance with Belgian law. **Aims** Affirm the need to study meteors and related phenomena; promote a global perspective by striving towards common standards and research programmes and by developing the international spirit among meteor workers; encourage theoretical and practical study by amateurs and professionals and international cooperation among them; centralize and distribute scientific data. **Structure** General Assembly (at least twice every 2 years). Council, consisting of 5 to 20 members. Officers: President and Secretary General. Commissions (5): Photographic; Radio; Telescopic; Visual; *Fireball Data Centre (FIDAC).* **Languages** English, French. **Staff** 2.00 FTE, voluntary. **Finance** Members' dues: DM35. Other sources: gifts; sale of publications. Budget (annual): euro 18,000. **Activities** Global coverage of meteor appearances in the Earth's atmosphere by instructing volunteers worldwide (amateur astronomers, students) on observation and reporting. *'Visual studies'* round-the-clock studies of meteor stream appearances; *'Radio studies'* detection of sudden, unpredicted meteor activity during clouded periods or in daylight. Data also collected on fireballs, bolides and meteorite impacts. Proposes international standards for observing and reporting data; collects and distributes observational data; organizes conferences, lectures, introductory camps, observations, exhibitions. **Events** *International Meteor Conference* Libin (Belgium) 2023, *International Meteor Conference* Poroszló (Hungary) 2022, *International Meteor Conference* Poroszló (Hungary) 2021, *International Meteor Conference* Budapest (Hungary) 2020, *International Meteor Conference* Bollmannsruh (Germany) 2019. **Publications** *FIDAC News* (6 a year) in English; *WGN Journal* (6 a year) in English. *WGN Observational Report Series* (annual). Handbooks; conference proceedings. **Information Services** *BMDB* – bibliographic catalogue; *FIDAC Database* – database of the Fireball Data Centre; *Photographic Meteor Data Base (PMDB)*; *PosDat* – positional database; *VMDB* – visual observational data.
Members Full; Associate; Adherent; Honorary. Full (individuals) in 43 countries and territories:
Argentina, Australia, Austria, Belgium, Bolivia, Brazil, Bulgaria, Canada, China, Croatia, Czechia, Denmark, Finland, France, Germany, Hungary, Ireland, Italy, Japan, Jordan, Korea Rep, Malta, Netherlands, New Caledonia, New Zealand, Norway, Pakistan, Poland, Portugal, Romania, Russia, Serbia, Slovakia, Slovenia, South Africa, Spain, Sweden, Switzerland, Taiwan, Tajikistan, UK, Ukraine, USA.
NGO Relations *International Astronomical Union (IAU, #12287)* – Commission on Meteors, Meteorites and Interplanetary Dust. [2018/XD2620/**C**]

♦ International Methane Emission Observatory (unconfirmed)

♦ International Methanol Producers and Consumers Association (IMPCA) 14153

Association internationale des producteurs et consommateurs de méthanol

Sec ad interim Avenue de Tervuren 270, 1150 Brussels, Belgium. T. +3227418683. Fax +3227418684. E-mail: info@impca.eu.
URL: http://www.impca.eu/

History 1987, Brussels (Belgium). Registration: Belgium. **Aims** Represent, promote and study problems of common interest to the worldwide methanol industry. **Structure** Board of Directors; Executive Committee; Technical Committee; Methanol Sampling Methods Committee (IMPCA MSMC). **Languages** English. **Staff** 0.50 FTE, paid. **Finance** Sources: members' dues. **Activities** Events/meetings; knowledge management/information dissemination. **Events** *Mini Promoting America Conference* Miami, FL (USA) 2020, *Annual European Mini-Conference* Porto (Portugal) 2020, *Mini Promoting America Conference* Miami, FL (USA) 2019, *Annual European Mini-Conference* Wiesbaden (Germany) 2019, *Annual European Mini-Conference* Como (Italy) 2018. **Publications** *IMPCA Methanol Reference Specifications*; *IMPCA Methanol Sampling Methods.*
Members Companies in 24 countries and territories:
Austria, Belgium, Cyprus, Denmark, France, Germany, Israel, Italy, Japan, Malaysia, Netherlands, Norway, Poland, Qatar, Russia, Slovenia, Spain, Sweden, Switzerland, Taiwan, Trinidad-Tobago, UK, USA, Venezuela. [2020.07.24/XD1009/**D**]

♦ International Methodist Historical Society / see World Methodist Historical Society (#21651)

♦ International Methods Time-Measurement Directorate (IMD) 14154

Exec Dir c/o Fondazione Ergo-MTM Italia, Via Procaccini 10, 21100 Varese MB, Italy. T. +39332239979. E-mail: office@mtm-international.org.
Legal Seat 218 East State St, Columbus OH 43215, USA.
URL: http://www.mtm-international.org/

History 25 Jun 1957, Paris (France). Current objectives and purposes confirmed 1969, London (UK), at General Assembly. Also referred to as *International MTM Directorate.* **Aims** Develop, spread and employ knowledge concerning man at work so as to improve his *productivity*, his *job* satisfaction and his *working conditions*; encourage close cooperation among all those interested in the study of man at work whether it be in research, training or field of application. **Structure** Board, consisting of Officers (President, Vice-President, Executive Secretary) and members, normally one from each national association. **Activities** Major areas of activity: research; standards and practice; membership development; communication. Projects include studies and researches to apply MTM techniques to ergonomic principle. **Events** *General Assembly* Wroclaw (Poland) 2006, *Musculo-skeletal disorders and MTM* Paris (France) 2005, *Advanced industrial engineering – productivitiy improvement through methods management in production systems* Stuttgart (Germany) 2005, *Work scientific organization and lean manufacturing* Turin (Italy) 2005, *MTM in Polish industry* Wroclaw (Poland) 2005.
Members National Methods-Time-Measurement (MTM) associations in 17 countries (Canada and USA share one association):
Austria, Belgium, Brazil, Canada, Czechia, France, Germany, Italy, Japan, Montenegro, Poland, Serbia, South Africa, Spain, Switzerland, UK, USA.
Also members in Scandinavian countries. Membership countries not specified.
Membership in development in 12 countries and territories:
Australia, China, Greece, Hong Kong, Korea Rep, Malaysia, New Zealand, Philippines, Portugal, Russia, Singapore, Türkiye. [2016/XF0282/**F**]

♦ International Metropolis Project 14155

Exec Head Metropolis Project, Carleton University, Dunton Tower, 1125 Colonel By Drive, Ottawa ON K1S 5B6, Canada. T. +16135202600.
URL: http://international.metropolis.net/

History Founded 1995. **Aims** Strengthen *migration* and ethnic diversity policy by means of applied academic research. **Structure** International Steering Committee; Offices in Ottawa ON (Canada), Amsterdam (Netherlands), Seoul (Korea Rep)/Manila (Philippines), Beijing (China). **Languages** English. **Staff** 10.00 FTE, paid. **Finance** Activities financed by members. **Activities** Research/documentation; networking/liaising; events/meetings. **Events** *International Metropolis Conference* Berlin (Germany) 2022, *International Metropolis Conference* Ottawa, ON (Canada) 2019, *International Metropolis Conference* Sydney, NSW (Australia) 2018, *International Metropolis Conference* The Hague (Netherlands) 2017, *International Metropolis Conference* Nagoya (Japan) 2016. **Publications** *Journal of International Migration and Integration.*
Members Representatives of 33 countries and territories:
Argentina, Australia, Austria, Belgium, Canada, China, Denmark, Finland, France, Germany, Greece, Hong Kong, India, Israel, Italy, Japan, Korea Rep, Malaysia, Mexico, Netherlands, New Zealand, Norway, Philippines, Portugal, Singapore, South Africa, Spain, Sweden, Switzerland, Thailand, Türkiye, UK, USA.
Included in the above, 7 international organizations listed in this Yearbook:
European Commission (EC, #06633); *International Centre for Migration Policy Development (ICMPD, #12503)*; *International Organization for Migration (IOM, #14454)*; *Local Urban Development European Network (LUDEN, #16508)*; *Migration Policy Group (MPG, #16801)*; *OECD (#17693)*; *UNESCO (#20322).*
IGO Relations *European Commission (EC, #06633)*; *International Bank for Reconstruction and Development (IBRD, #12317)* (World Bank); *International Centre for Migration Policy Development (ICMPD, #12503)*; *International Organization for Migration (IOM, #14454)*; *UNHCR (#20327).* **NGO Relations** *Migration Policy Group (MPG, #16801)*; *Migration Policy Institute (MPI)*; *Southern African Migration Programme (SAMP, #19850)*; national organizations. [2017.10.10/XF6230/y/**F**]

♦ International Micro Air Vehicle Conference (meeting series)

♦ International Microelectronics Assembly and Packaging Society (IMAPS) 14156

Exec Dir PO Box 14727, Pittsburgh PA 15234, USA. E-mail: info@imaps.org.
URL: http://www.imaps.org/

History 1 Nov 1996. Founded on merger of *International Electronics Packaging Society (IEPS, inactive)* and *International Society for Hybrid Microelectronics (ISHM, inactive).* **Aims** Advance and expand the use of microelectronics and microelectronic packaging. **Structure** Officers: President; President-Elect; 1st Past President; Secretary; Treasurer; Regional Directors. Advisory Council. **Languages** English. **Staff** 8.00 FTE, paid. **Finance** Budget (annual): US$ 2.5 million. **Activities** Standing Committees (8): Budget; Executive; Finance; Foundation Trustees; Nominating; Publications; Technical; Symposium. Organizes conferences and symposia. **Events** *Annual Conference* Toyama City (Japan) 2024, *Annual Conference* Kumamoto (Japan) 2023, *International Symposium on Microelectronics* Boston, MA (USA) 2022, *Annual Conference* Sapporo (Japan) 2022, *Annual Conference* Tokyo (Japan) 2021. **Publications** *International Journal of Microcircuits and Electronic Packaging.* **Members** Individuals in over 50 countries. Membership countries not specified. [2022/XD6297/**D**]

♦ International Microencapsulation Society (inactive)

♦ International Microgravity Strategic Planning Group (IMSPG) 14157

Groupe international de planification stratégique en microgravité

Contact CSA Headquarters, John H Chapman Space Centre, 6767 Route de l'Aéroport, Longueuil QC J3Y 8Y9, Canada. T. +14509264800. Fax +14509264352.

History 6 May 1995. **Aims** Coordinate development and use of research apparatus among microgravity research programmes in ares of common interest to maximize the productivity of microgravity research internationally. **Activities** *International Symposium on Physical Sciences in Space (ISPS).* **Events** *Symposium* Bonn (Germany) 2011, *International symposium on physical sciences in space / Symposium* Nara (Japan) 2007, *International symposium on physical sciences in space / Symposium* Toronto, ON (Canada) 2004, *Symposium* Sorrento (Italy) 2000.
Members Partners (8) in 6 countries:
Canada, France, Germany, Italy, Japan, USA.
Included in the above, 1 organization listed in this Yearbook:
European Space Agency (ESA, #08798). [2010/XM3241/**E**]

♦ international MicroNano Conference (meeting series)
♦ International Micropatrological Society (inactive)

♦ International Microsimulation Association (IMA) 14158

Registered Address 11 Porte Des Sciences, L-4366 Esch-sur-Alzette, Luxembourg. E-mail: contact@jinjingli.com.
URL: http://www.microsimulation.org/

History Oct 2005. Registration: Luxembourg. **Aims** Promote free inter-change of experience and ideas between practitioners of microsimulation worldwide. **Events** *World Congress* Los Angeles, CA (USA) 2021, *European Meeting* Nuremberg (Germany) 2020, *World Congress* Galway (Ireland) 2019, *Asia-Pacific Regional Conference* Narita (Japan) 2018, *European Meeting* Maastricht (Netherlands) 2014. [2020/XM3629/**D**]

♦ International Microstructural Analysis Society / see International Metallographic Society (#14151)

♦ **International Microsurgery Simulation Society (IMSS)** **14159**
Contact c/o Barts and the London School of Medicine and Dentistry, Dept for Cutaneous Research, 4 Newark Str, London, E1 2AT, UK.
Facebook: https://www.facebook.com/internationalmicrosurgery
History UK Registered Charity. **Aims** Promote excellence in microsurgery education and training worldwide. **Structure** Scientific Committee. **Events** *Annual Meeting* Antalya (Turkey) 2016, *Annual Meeting* Mumbai (India) 2015, *Annual Meeting* Naples (Italy) 2014, *Annual Meeting* New York, NY (USA) 2013, *Annual Meeting* London (UK) 2012.
Members Full in 10 countries:
Austria, France, Italy, Japan, Korea Rep, Romania, Singapore, Türkiye, UK, USA. [2022/XJ7578/**C**]

♦ International Microsurgical Society (inactive)

♦ **International Microwave Power Institute (IMPI)** **14160**
Institut international d'énergie par les micro-ondes
Exec Dir PO Box 1140, Mechanicsville VA 23111, USA. T. +18045596667. E-mail: info@impi.org.
URL: http://www.impi.org/
History 28 Apr 1965, Edmonton (Canada). **Aims** Further the use and understanding of microwave *energy* by bringing together scientists, engineers and individuals interested in the technology and applications of microwave energy, and by encouraging industrial and university research and development into microwave energy applications. **Structure** Board of Governors; Officers. **Languages** English. **Staff** 1.50 FTE, paid. **Finance** Members' dues. **Activities** Sections (2): Microwave Food Technology and Applications (MFTA); Scientific, Industrial, Medical and Instrumentation (ISMI). Symposia; courses; library; scientific and technical information. **Events** *Annual Symposium* San Diego, CA (USA) 2015, *Annual Symposium* New Orleans, LA (USA) 2014, *Annual Symposium* Providence, RI (USA) 2013, *Annual Symposium* Las Vegas, NV (USA) 2012, *Annual Symposium* New Orleans, LA (USA) 2011. **Publications** *Journal of Microwave Power* (4 a year); *Microwave World* (4 a year). Symposium proceedings and transactions.
Members Qualified individuals in 24 countries and territories:
Australia, Austria, Belgium, Canada, China, Czechia, Denmark, Finland, France, Germany, Hong Kong, Italy, Mexico, Monaco, Netherlands, Norway, Poland, Portugal, Spain, Sweden, Switzerland, Taiwan, UK, USA.
NGO Relations Founding member of: *International Federation of Associations in the Field of Microwave and RF Power Engineering (MAJIC, #13362).* [2011.07.14/XC4420/jv/**F**]

♦ International Midwives Union / see International Confederation of Midwives (#12863)

♦ **International Migrants Alliance (IMA)** **14161**
Chair c/o APMM, G/F, No 2 Jordan Road, Kowloon, Hong Kong. T. +85227237536. Fax +85227354559. E-mail: ima.sect@gmail.com.
URL: http://wearemigrants.net/
History Founding assembly held Jun 2008, Hong Kong. **Aims** Deepen the perspective and understanding through the root causes of migration, its direct consequences and other related issues and problems, and the role of imperialism and governments and international institutions in the process of labour-export and forced migration, support struggles for fundamental change and genuine development in labour exporting countries. **Structure** General Assembly. International Coordinating Body, including Chairperson, Vice Chairperson, Secretary General, Deputy Secretary and Treasurer. **Languages** English. **Staff** 1.00 FTE, paid; 2.00 FTE, voluntary. **Finance** Sources: members' dues. Annual budget: 50,000 USD. **Activities** Organizes campaigns; strengthens cooperation; encourages coordination and cooperation at national and regional levels. **Events** *International Assembly of Migrants and Refugees – IAMR* New York, NY (USA) 2015, *International Assembly of Migrants and Refugees / International Assembly of Migrants and Refugees – IAMR* New York, NY (USA) 2013, *Triennial General Assembly* Manila (Philippines) 2011, *International Assembly of Migrants and Refugees / International Assembly of Migrants and Refugees – IAMR* Mexico City (Mexico) 2010, *International Assembly of Migrants and Refugees / International Assembly of Migrants and Refugees – IAMR* Athens (Greece) 2009.
Members Organizations in 16 countries and territories:
Argentina, Australia, Austria, Canada, Hong Kong, Italy, Japan, Korea Rep, Mexico, Nepal, Netherlands, New Zealand, Philippines, Switzerland, Taiwan, USA. [2016/XJ4899/**C**]

♦ International Migrants Rights Watch Committee / see Migrants Rights International (#16799)
♦ International Migration and Gender Research Institute (unconfirmed)
♦ International Migration Institute (unconfirmed)
♦ International Migration, Integration and Social Cohesion in Europe / see IMISCOE Research Network (#11129)
♦ International Migration, Integration and Social Cohesion Europe / see IMISCOE Research Network (#11129)
♦ International Migration Service / see International Social Service (#14886)
♦ International Military Apostolate (religious order)

♦ **International Military Music Society (IMMS)** **14162**
Société de la musique militaire internationale – Sociedad de Música Militar internacional – Internationale Militärmusik-Gesellschaft – Società Internazionale di Musica Militare
Pres address not obtained.
Public Relations address not obtained.
URL: https://www.immsociety.com/
History 1 Jan 1977, London (UK). **Aims** Encourage interest in all aspects of military, brass, concert, symphonic, percussion, pipe, choir, youth bands and wind ensembles of the world, as well as interest in wind music, including published music, recordings (sound and visual), instrumentation, history, traditions and uniforms; provide a worldwide means of communication between members. **Structure** International Committee (governing body); Executive Officers, comprising Chairman, Treasurer, Distribution Secretary, Editor, Promotion Officer and Webmaster; Honorary President. Chairmanship rotates every 2 years. **Languages** English. **Staff** 5.00 FTE, voluntary. **Finance** Sources: members' dues. **Activities** Events/meetings; projects/programmes. **Publications** *Band International* (3 a year). Music recordings.
Members National branches in 12 countries:
Australia, Belgium, Canada, Denmark, France, Japan, Netherlands, New Zealand, Norway, Portugal, UK, USA.
National representatives in 15 countries and territories:
Austria, Finland, Germany, Hong Kong, Hungary, Italy, Korea Rep, Luxembourg, Pakistan, Poland, Samoa, South Africa, Sweden, Switzerland, Tonga. [2022.11.10/XD7516/**D**]

♦ International Military Sports Council (#04695)

♦ **International Military Testing Association (IMTA)** **14163**
Communications Behavioral Sciences Dept, Belgian Royal Military Ac, Renaissancelaan 30, 1000 Brussels, Belgium. E-mail: imta@imta.info.
URL: http://www.IMTA.info/
History USA, as (US) Military Testing Association. Present name adopted 1993. Registered under Belgian law. **Aims** Promote research on military testing, assessment and psychometrics, as well as most facets of behavioural sciences as applied in the military setting, such as selection and classification, training, morale, mental health, leadership, family issues, security, human resources and human factors. **Structure** Steering Committee; Management Board. **Languages** English. **Staff** No permanent staff. **Finance** Conference registration fees; subsidies; donations; other revenues. **Activities** Events/meetings; awards/prizes/competitions. **Events** *Annual Conference* Raleigh, NC (USA) 2022, *Annual Conference* Tallinn (Estonia) 2019, *Annual Conference* Kingston, ON (Canada) 2018, *Annual Conference* Bern (Switzerland) 2017, *Annual Conference* Delhi (India) 2016. **Publications** *International Military Leadership Association Workshop* (annual). Conference proceedings; academic publications.
Members Organizations in 20 countries:
Australia, Austria, Belgium, Canada, Croatia, Denmark, Estonia, Germany, India, Indonesia, Korea Rep, Netherlands, Norway, Singapore, South Africa, Sweden, Switzerland, Türkiye, UK, USA.
IGO Relations *NATO (#16945).* [2017.06.01/XJ3163/**D**]

♦ International Milling Association (inactive)

♦ **International Mind Sports Association (IMSA)** **14164**
Exec Dir MSI Av de Rhodanie 54, 1007 Lausanne VD, Switzerland.
URL: http://www.imsaworld.com/
History 19 Apr 2005, Berlin (Germany). Founded by *World Bridge Federation (WBF, #21246), Fédération internationale des échecs (FIDE, #09627), Fédération Mondiale du Jeu de Dames (FMJD, #09690)* and *International Go Federation (IGF, #13726).* **Aims** Engage in a dialogue with the International Olympic Committee for the organization of the World Mind Games to be held in the Olympic cities following the Winter or Summer games. **Structure** Executive Committee, comprising President, Deputy President, General Secretary, Treasurer and Honorary Secretary. **Languages** English. **Finance** Members' dues. Sponsorship. **Events** *World Mind Sports Games* Beijing (China) 2008. **NGO Relations** Member of (2): *Olympic Movement (#17719); The Association for International Sport for All (TAFISA, #02763).* Partner of (1): *General Association of Asia Pacific Sports Federations (GAAPSF, #10106).* [2022/XM1258/**E**]

♦ International Mine Initiative (internationally oriented national body)

♦ **International Mineralogical Association (IMA)** **14165**
Sec Geosciences Montpellier CNRS & Université de Montpellier, Place Eugène Bataillon, 34095 Montpellier, France. T. +33467144942.
Pres School of Earth and Space Science, Peking University, 100871 Beijing, China. T. +8601062753555.
URL: http://www.ima-mineralogy.org/
History 8 Apr 1958, Madrid (Spain). Statutes drafted at International Congress of Crystallography, Jul 1957, Montréal (Canada). Statutes modified: 5 Sep 2002; 27 Jul 2006; 26 Aug 2010; 3 Sep 2014. **Aims** Further international cooperation in the mineralogical sciences and include: (I) The promotion of intercourse among mineralogists of all nations by organizing meetings and field excursions and by sponsoring publications of mineralogical interest; (II) the maintenance of Commissions to examine and report on certain aspects of mineralogical practice and of committees to expedite other matters; (III) the participation in action with other international groups having mineralogical interests. **Structure** General Meeting (every 4 years); Business Meeting (every 2 years); Council (meeting annually); Executive Committee; Commissions (6); Working Groups (1). **Languages** English. **Staff** Voluntary. **Finance** Sources: members' dues. Annual budget: 8,300 USD. **Activities** Events/meetings. **Events** *General Meeting and Congress* China 2026, *General Meeting and Congress* Lyon (France) 2022, *International Conference on Mineralogy and Museums* Sofia (Bulgaria) 2021, *Quadrennial General Meeting and Congress* Melbourne, VIC (Australia) 2018, *Quadrennial General Meeting and Congress* Johannesburg (South Africa) 2014. **Publications** *Elements*; *IMA News*; *Secretary Bulletin.*
Members National societies and individuals in 39 countries:
Argentina, Australia, Austria, Belgium, Brazil, Bulgaria, Canada, China, Croatia, Czechia, Denmark, Egypt, Finland, France, Georgia, Germany, Greece, Hungary, India, Italy, Japan, Korea Rep, Netherlands, New Zealand, Norway, Poland, Portugal, Romania, Russia, Slovakia, Slovenia, South Africa, Spain, Sweden, Switzerland, UK, Ukraine, USA, Uzbekistan.
NGO Relations Member of (1): *International Union of Geological Sciences (IUGS, #15777).* [2021.02.25/XD2264/**C**]

♦ **International Mineral Processing Council (IMPC)** **14166**
Sec c/o Ausimm, PO Box 600, Carlton VIC 3053, Australia.
URL: http://impc-council.com/
History 1968. Founded following conference activities initiated in 1952. Constitution adopted, 2003, Cape Town (South Africa); amended 2008, Beijing (China). **Structure** Council, comprising Chair, Vice-Chair/Chair of future Congress, Vice-Chair designate/Chair of next but one Congress, Immediate Past Chair, Presidents of last 6 Congresses, Commission Chairs (Sustainability; Education; Mineral Processing), plus members. International Advisory Committee. **Activities** Organizes *'International Mineral Processing Congress'.* Grants the 'Lifetime Achievement Award'. **Events** *International Mineral Processing Congress (IMPC 2022)* Melbourne, VIC (Australia) 2022, *International Mineral Processing Congress* Cape Town (South Africa) 2020, *International Mineral Processing Congress* Moscow (Russia) 2018, *International Mineral Processing Congress* Québec, QC (Canada) 2016, *International mineral processing congress / Congress* Santiago (Chile) 2014. [2020/XJ2976/**E**]

♦ **International Mine Rescue Body (IMRB)** **14167**
Manager Mines and Aggregates Safety and Health Ass, 760 Notre Dame Avenue, Unit M, Sudbury ON P3A 2T4, Canada. T. +17056705709. Fax +17056716398.
URL: http://www.minerescue.org/
History 2001, Ustron (Poland). **Events** *Conference* Beijing (China) 2011, *Conference* Prague (Czech Rep) / Ostrava (Czech Rep) 2009, *Conference* Nashville, TN (USA) 2007, *Conference* Sydney, NSW (Australia) 2005, *Conference* Johannesburg (South Africa) 2003.
Members Full (" indicates founding) in 16 countries:
Australia (*), Canada, China, Czechia (*), France (*), Germany, India, New Zealand, Norway, Poland (*), Romania (*), Slovakia (*), South Africa (*), UK (*), Ukraine, USA (*). [2010/XJ1986/**F**]

♦ International Miners' Mission (internationally oriented national body)
♦ International Miners' Organization (no recent information)

♦ **International Mine Water Association (IMWA)** **14168**
Association internationale d'étude sur les eaux dans des mines
Gen Sec Ginsterweg 4, 90530 Wendelstein, Germany. T. +4932121058369. E-mail: c.wolke@imwa.info – generalsecretary@imwa.info.
URL: http://www.imwa.info/
History 1979. **Aims** Cover the needs of solving water problems related to mining during exploration, planning, construction and operation of mines; provide guidance on: improved exploitation of *mineral deposits* consistent with the desirable standards of safety against water hazards, increased protection of environment against the impact of mine drainage and related activities, improved utilization of mine waters, improved technology and economy of mine drainage operations, pollution and restoration of abandoned mine sites, as well as geothermal applications. **Structure** General Assembly. Executive Council, consisting of President, Vice-President, Secretary-General, Treasurer and 8 Councillors. Includes: *Partnership for Acid Drainage Remediation in Europe (PADRE, see: #14168).* **Languages** English. **Staff** Voluntary. **Finance** Sources: gifts, legacies; grants; members' dues; sale of publications; subsidies. **Activities** Sponsors congresses and symposia. **Events** *Reconnect* Christchurch (New Zealand) 2022, *Mine Water Management for Future Generations* Cardiff (UK) 2021, *Congress* Christchurch (New Zealand) 2020, *Mine water – technological and ecological challenges* Perm (Russia) 2019, *Mine water and circular economy – a green congress* Lappeenranta (Finland) 2017. **Publications** *Mine Water and the Environment* (4 a year); *Mine Water* (annual). Bibliography of published literature in the field of mining and environmental hydrology. Congress and symposia proceedings.
Members Voting Individual; Corporate. Non-voting Student; Honorary; International Organizations. Members in 44 countries:
Argentina, Australia, Austria, Belgium, Bosnia-Herzegovina, Brazil, Canada, Chile, China, Croatia, Czechia, Denmark, Finland, France, Germany, Ghana, Greece, Hungary, India, Indonesia, Iran Islamic Rep, Ireland, Italy, Netherlands, New Zealand, Nigeria, Peru, Philippines, Poland, Portugal, Romania, Russia, Slovakia, Slovenia, South Africa, Spain, Sweden, Switzerland, Türkiye, UK, Ukraine, USA, Venezuela, Zambia. [2013.06.01/XD5219/**C**]

♦ International Miniature Aerobatic Club (internationally oriented national body)
♦ International Mini-Football Federation (inactive)
♦ International Minigolf Federation / see World Minigolf Sport Federation (#21653)
♦ International Mining for Development Centre (internationally oriented national body)
♦ International Mint Directors Conference / see Mint Directors Conference (#16822)

♦ **International Mire Conservation Group (IMCG)** **14169**
SG Inst of Botany and Landscape Ecology, Soldmannstrasse 15, 17487 Greifswald, Germany. T. +4938344204177. Fax +4938344204114. E-mail: info@imcg.net.
General: http://www.imcg.net/
History 1984, Klagenfurt am Wörthersee (Austria). Founded following meeting at conference of *International Peatland Society (IPS, #14538)*, 1983, Finland. Registration: Start date: 1 Jun 2001, France; EU Transparency Register, No/ID: 453186645428-48, Start date: 7 Feb 2022. **Aims** Highlight problems facing peatlands on a worldwide basis; promote and support peatland conservation efforts; stimulate international exchange of ideas, scientific information and experience in the area of mire conservation and research. **Structure**

Main Board; Executive Committee. **Languages** English. **Staff** 3.50 FTE, voluntary. **Finance** Sources: donations; revenue from activities/projects. **Activities** Events/meetings. **Events** *Biennial Symposium* South Africa 2022, *Biennial Symposium* South Africa 2020, *Biennial Symposium* Amsterdam (Netherlands) 2018, *Biennial Symposium* Kuching (Malaysia) / Malaysia 2016, *Biennial Symposium* Berezinsky (Belarus) 2014. **Publications** *IMCG Bulletin*; *IMCG Newsletter*; *Mires and Peat* – journal. *The Wise Use of Mires and Peatlands – Background and Principles* (2002) by Hans Joosten and Donald Clarke; *Mires and Peatlands of Europe*. Symposium proceedings.
Members Individuals in 69 countries:
Albania, Argentina, Armenia, Australia, Austria, Belarus, Belgium, Botswana, Canada, Chile, China, Colombia, Croatia, Cuba, Czechia, Denmark, Ecuador, Egypt, Estonia, Ethiopia, Finland, France, Georgia, Germany, Ghana, Greece, Hungary, Iceland, India, Indonesia, Iran Islamic Rep, Ireland, Italy, Japan, Kenya, Latvia, Lesotho, Lithuania, Luxembourg, Malaysia, Malta, Moldova, Mongolia, Mozambique, Namibia, Netherlands, New Zealand, Norway, Pakistan, Peru, Poland, Portugal, Romania, Russia, Rwanda, Serbia, Slovakia, Slovenia, South Africa, Spain, Sri Lanka, Sweden, Switzerland, Tanzania UR, Türkiye, UK, Ukraine, USA, Zimbabwe.
NGO Relations Member of (1): *European Habitats Forum (EHF, #07443)*. Partner of (1): *Wetlands International (#20928)*. [2023.02.13/XF3210/v/**F**]

♦ International Mirror Class Association (see: #21760)

♦ International Missionary Benefit Society 14170

Entraide missionnaire internationale (EMI) – Internationales Hilfswerk für Missions Personal – Opera Internazionale per il Personale Missionario

Admin Office 3 Rue Duguay-Trouin, 75280 Paris CEDEX 06, France. T. +33142220777. Fax +33145485390. E-mail: emi@entraide-missionnaire.com.
URL: http://www.entraide-missionnaire.com/

History 30 Jun 1965, Geneva (Switzerland). Registered according to the Swiss Civil Code. **Aims** Provide *health insurance* to *missionaries* worldwide. **Structure** General Assembly (every 3 years). Steering Committee of 14 members. **Languages** English, French, Portuguese, Spanish. **Publications** Guides. **Members** Individuals (over 23,000) in 147 countries. Membership countries not specified. [2009.12.02/XR6874/**F**]

♦ International Missionary Council (inactive)
♦ International Mission Board (internationally oriented national body)
♦ International Mission Study Council (inactive)

♦ International Mito Patients (IMP) 14171

Chair PO Box 664, 8000 AR Zwolle, Netherlands. T. +31384201764. E-mail: info@mitopatients.org.
URL: http://www.mitopatients.org/

History Aug 2011. Registered in accordance with Dutch law: 850872236. **Aims** Increase quality of life for people with *mitochondrial* disease by facilitating cross-border cooperation and collaborating among national patients' organizations. **Structure** General Assembly. Board, comprising Chair, Vice-Chair, Secretary and Treasurer. **Languages** English. **Staff** All voluntary. **Finance** Members' dues. Special funding for projects. **Events** *Meeting / International Meeting* Netherlands 2013, *Meeting / International Meeting* Paris (France) 2012, *Meeting / International Meeting* Seville (Spain) 2011.
Members Patient organizations in 9 countries:
Australia, Belgium, France, Germany, Italy, Netherlands, Spain, UK, USA.
NGO Relations Member of: *EURORDIS – Rare Diseases Europe (#09175)*. [2013.02.28/XJ6568/**D**]

♦ International Mixed Martial Arts Association (IMMAA) 14172

Contact c/o IMMAA President, 51 Elizabeth St, St Thomas ON N5R 2X2, Canada. T. +15196331379.
History 2002, Clinton, ON (Canada). **Aims** As the world's parent umbrella organization, foster international and inter-stylistic cooperation; provide a community promoting the benefits of martial arts training, embracing similarities amongst martial arts styles, researching ideas such as ethics, non-violence, self-protection and individual excellence in the context of martial arts study, educating members and the public, creating an egalitarian community of like-minded organizations and individuals so as to promote virtues of martial arts training. **Structure** General Assembly; Board; Advisory Board. **Languages** English, French, German, Italian. **Staff** Voluntary. **Finance** Members' dues. Other sources: entry fees; limited corporate sponsorship. **Activities** Meetings/events; training/education. **Events** *International Mixed Martial Arts Conference* London, ON (Canada) 2012, *International Mixed Martial Arts Conference* Jersey City, NJ (USA) 2011, *International Mixed Martial Arts Conference* London, ON (Canada) 2010, *International Mixed Martial Arts Conference* London, ON (Canada) 2009, *International Mixed Martial Arts Conference* London, ON (Canada) 2008. **Members** Full Pledge; Associate; Affiliate; NGO; Chartered Schools. Membership countries not specified. [2014.08.19/XM3835/**D**]

♦ International Mixed Martial Arts Federation (IMMAF) 14173

CEO address not obtained. E-mail: info@immaf.org.
URL: https://immaf.org/

History Founded 29 Feb 2012, Stockholm (Sweden). *World MMA Association (WMMAA, inactive)* merged into IMMAF, 2018. Registered in accordance with Swedish law. **Aims** Further the development, recognition and regulation of the sport of MMA, enabling international amateur competition through the organization of national MMA federations worldwide. **Structure** General Assembly; Board of Directors; Technical Committees. **Activities** Sporting activities.
Members Full in 92 countries and territories:
Afghanistan, Albania, Algeria, Armenia, Australia, Austria, Azerbaijan, Bahamas, Bahrain, Belarus, Belgium, Brazil, Bulgaria, Cameroon, Canada, China, Colombia, Congo DR, Croatia, Cyprus, Czechia, Denmark, Egypt, El Salvador, England, Estonia, Finland, France, Georgia, Germany, Ghana, Greece, Guinea, Hong Kong, Hungary, Iceland, India, Indonesia, Iran Islamic Rep, Iraq, Ireland, Italy, Jamaica, Japan, Jordan, Kazakhstan, Korea Rep, Kyrgyzstan, Latvia, Lebanon, Lithuania, Luxembourg, Malaysia, Mauritius, Mexico, Moldova, Morocco, Namibia, Nepal, New Zealand, Nigeria, Northern Ireland, Norway, Pakistan, Panama, Paraguay, Philippines, Poland, Portugal, Romania, Russia, Saudi Arabia, Serbia, Seychelles, Singapore, Slovakia, South Africa, Spain, Sweden, Switzerland, Taiwan, Tajikistan, Thailand, Trinidad-Tobago, Tunisia, Türkiye, Ukraine, United Arab Emirates, USA, Uzbekistan, Venezuela, Wales.
NGO Relations Founding member of: *Sport Integrity Global Alliance (SIGA, #19925)*. Member of: *International Council for Coaching Excellence (ICCE, #13008)*. [2020/XM8838/**B**]

♦ International Mobile Satellite Organization (IMSO) 14174

Organisation internationale de télécommunications mobiles par satellite – Organización Internacional de Telecomunicaciones Móviles por Satélite

Dir Gen 4 Albert Embankment, London, SE1 7SR, UK. T. +442039701060. E-mail: info@imso.org.
URL: http://www.imso.org/

History 16 Jul 1979, as an intergovernmental organization with the title *International Maritime Satellite Organization (Inmarsat) – Organisation internationale de télécommunications maritimes par satellites – Organización Internacional de Telecomunicaciones Marítimas por Satélite*, pursuant to the signing, 1976, by 28 Member States and Signatories of a Convention and Operating Agreement. Establishment followed an initiative in 1973 by the then 'Inter-Governmental Maritime Consultative Organization (IMCO)', currently, since 22 May 1982, *International Maritime Organization (IMO, #14102)*. Provision of maritime services commenced 1 Feb 1982. Amendments to Inmarsat Convention approved, Oct 1985, by Inmarsat Assembly of Parties – at which all member countries were entitled to be represented – to permit the offering of aeronautical satellite communication services; in Jan 1989, further amendments enabled provision of land-mobile satellite services. Amendments to Convention approved Sep 1998 to provide for restructuring of Inmarsat and retaining governmental oversight by the organization (IMSO) of public services obligations; entered into force on the basis of provisional application 15 Apr 1999; amendments entered formally into force 31 Jul 2001. Amendments to Convention approved Oct 2008 to provide for extending governmental oversight to other potential *Global Maritime Distress and Safety System (GMDSS / SMDSM)* providers and for IMSO's functions as coordinator of Long Range Identification and Tracking of Ships (LRIT); amendments entered into force on the basis of provisional application 6 Oct 2008, pending their formal entry into force. Current title adopted 9 Dec 1994, together with abbreviation *Inmarsat Mobile*. **Aims** Ensure the provision, by each Provider, of maritime mobile satellite communications services for the GMDSS according to the legal framework set up by IMO. **Structure** Assembly of Parties (every 2 years); Advisory Committee, headed by Director General. **Languages** English, French, Russian, Spanish. **Staff** 7.00 FTE, paid. **Finance** Finance'd by GMDSS providers (currently only Inmarsat) and LRIT Data Centres.
Activities Provides mobile satellite communications worldwide through the Inmarsat-3 and Inmarsat-2 series of satellites. Customers include: merchant shipping; fisheries; airlines and corporate jets; land transport; oil and gas; news media; business executives travelling out of reach of conventional communication. Services (including distress and safety services) are: direct dial telephone, telex, data, facsimile and data connections for maritime applications; flight-deck voice and data, automatic position and status reporting and direct-dial passenger telephone for aircraft; two-way data communications, position reporting and fleet management for land transport. Two-way data messaging services using low cost mobile terminals have been introduced. Possibilities are being explored for position determination and navigation applications.
Satellite space segment, operational since 1 Feb 1982, provides coverage of the Atlantic Ocean-East, and Atlantic Ocean-West, Pacific and Indian Ocean areas, by means of geostationary satellites in orbit at a height of some 36,000 km. Five new third generation satellites have been launched. Land Earth Stations are owned and operated by Inmarsat signatories around the world and interface with international public switched networks. 39 land earth stations operate within the Inmarsat system as of Nov 1997, providing access to the space segment; other stations are planned or under construction. As of 24 Sep 1998, over 125,000 mobile terminals on ships, oil rigs, in aircraft, on trucks in use on land were commissioned for use in the system. The satellite communication network is controlled from an Operational Control Centre at Inmarsat's headquarters in London (UK) on a 24-hour, 7 days per week, basis.
Inmarsat Systems:
– *'Inmarsat Mini-M'* – a digital phone, fax and data system, working with compact terminals;
– *'Inmarsat-B'* – (successor of Inmarsat-A) based on digital telecommunications technology, supports high-quality, direct-dial phone, telex, fax and data at low cost;
– *'Inmarsat-C'* – provides data messaging communications through small, lightweight terminals and supports 2-way text and data messaging, data-reporting and fleet broadcast communications at 600 bits/sec.

Services available, or in development, for aircraft (4):
– *'Aero-C'* – allows text and data messages (except flight safety communications) to be sent and received by aircraft operating anywhere in the world;
– *'Aero-L'* – low speed (600 bits/sec) real-time data communications mainly for airline operational and administrative purposes;
– *'Aero-I'* – multichannel passenger and operational voice and data services for domestic and regional routes, introduced in 1998;
– *'Aero-H'* – high-speed (up to 10.5 k bit/sec) service supporting multichannel voice, fax and data communications for passengers and administrative applications for large, intercontinental aircraft.

Service available for land mobile customers:
– *'Inmarsat-D Plus'* – 2-way data messaging system using equipment the size of a personal CD.

Inmarsat is a major shareholder in 'ICO Global Communications', set up in 1995 to develop and implement a new satellite system supplying a global service to hand-held phones. It will use 12 satellites (10 operational and 2 spare) and is expected to be operational in the year 2000, supplying services to dual-mode handsets operating with cellular systems (where available) and via satellite.
Events *Advisory Committee Meeting* London (UK) 2020, *Annual international satellite and communications conference* Long Beach, CA (USA) 2004, *Aeronautical users conference* London (UK) 1998, *Annual marketing conference* London (UK) 1998, *International conference on mobile satellite communications* Paris (France) 1993. **Publications** *Ocean Voice* (4 a year); *Via INMARSAT* (4 a year); *INMARSAT Review* (annual); *Inside Track to INMARSAT Partnership* – newsletter. Corporate brochures; news releases; fact sheets; marketing brochures.
Members Signatory States (103):
Algeria, Antigua-Barbuda, Argentina, Australia, Bahamas, Bahrain, Bangladesh, Belarus, Belgium, Bolivia, Bosnia-Herzegovina, Brazil, Brunei Darussalam, Bulgaria, Cameroon, Canada, Chile, China, Colombia, Comoros, Cook Is, Costa Rica, Croatia, Cuba, Cyprus, Czechia, Denmark, Egypt, Fiji, Finland, France, Gabon, Georgia, Germany, Ghana, Greece, Honduras, Hungary, Iceland, India, Indonesia, Iran Islamic Rep, Iraq, Israel, Italy, Japan, Jordan, Kenya, Korea DPR, Korea Rep, Kuwait, Latvia, Lebanon, Liberia, Libya, Malaysia, Malta, Marshall Is, Mauritius, Mexico, Monaco, Mongolia, Montenegro, Morocco, Mozambique, Netherlands, New Zealand, Nigeria, Norway, Oman, Pakistan, Palau, Panama, Peru, Philippines, Poland, Portugal, Qatar, Romania, Russia, Saudi Arabia, Senegal, Serbia, Singapore, Slovakia, South Africa, Spain, Sri Lanka, Sweden, Switzerland, Tanzania UR, Thailand, Tonga, Tunisia, Türkiye, UK, Ukraine, United Arab Emirates, USA, Vanuatu, Venezuela, Vietnam, Yemen.
IGO Relations Maintains relations with the United Nations and Specialized Agencies. Relations with: *European Commission (EC, #06633)*; *European Telecommunications Satellite Organization (EUTELSAT IGO, #08896)*; *International Civil Aviation Organization (ICAO, #12581)*; *International Hydrographic Organization (IHO, #13825)*; *International Maritime Organization (IMO, #14102)*; *International Telecommunication Union (ITU, #15673)*; *International Telecommunications Satellite Organization (ITSO, #15670)*; UN Office for Outer Space Affairs. **NGO Relations** Full member of: *GVF (#10842)*. Member of: *European Telecommunications Standards Institute (ETSI, #08897)*. Relations with: *Comité International Radio-Maritime (CIRM, #04186)*; *International Association of Marine Aids to Navigation and Lighthouse Authorities (IALA, #12013)*; *International Chamber of Shipping (ICS, #12535)*; *International Organization for Standardization (ISO, #14473)*. Instrumental in setting up: *Piracy Reporting Centre, Kuala Lumpur (#18373)*. [2019/XC4643/**F***]

♦ International Mobility Alliance (unconfirmed)

♦ International Model Forest Network (IMFN) 14175

Réseau international de Forêts Modèles (RIFM) – Red Internacional de Bosques Modelo (RIBM)

Head of Secretariat 580 Booth Street, Ottawa ON K1A 0E4, Canada. T. +16139477350. Fax +16139477399. E-mail: imfn@imfn.net.
URL: http://www.imfn.net/

History 1994. Secretariat abbreviated as *IMFNS*. **Aims** Foster cooperation and collaboration in advancing management, conservation and *sustainable development* of forest resources worldwide through the model forest approach, central concept being people working in voluntary partnership on landscape scale. **Structure** Regional networks (6): Canadian Model Forest Network (CMFN); *African Model Forest Network (AMFN, #00377)*; *Mediterranean Model Forest Network (MMFN, #16662)*; *Red Iberoamericana de Bosques Modelo (RLABM, #18659)*; Northern Europe and Russia; *Regional Model Forest Network – Asia (RMFN-Asia, #18797)*. **Languages** English, French, Spanish. **Staff** 3.00 FTE, paid. **Finance** Sources: government support; in-kind support. Secretariat funded by Canadian Government. Model forests receive national and local level support. **Events** *Global forum* Burgos (Spain) 2011, *Global Forum* Spain 2011, *Global Forum* Hinton, AB (Canada) 2008, *Global forum* Hinton, AB (Canada) 2008. **Publications** *The International Model Forest Recipe Book* (2012); *International Model Forest Network: A Global Approach to Ecosystem Sustainability* (2011); *Partnerships to Success in Sustainable Forest Management* (2005). Annual Report.
Members Model forests in 31 countries:
Algeria, Argentina, Bolivia, Brazil, Cameroon, Canada, Chile, China, Colombia, Costa Rica, Croatia, Cuba, Dominican Rep, Finland, France, Guatemala, Honduras, India, Indonesia, Italy, Japan, Morocco, Peru, Philippines, Poland, Puerto Rico, Russia, Spain, Sweden, Thailand, Türkiye.
IGO Relations Also links with national programmes. **NGO Relations** Partner of (1): *Global Partnership on Forest and Landscape Restoration (GPFLR, #10535)*. [2020.10.13/XF6819/**F**]

♦ International Model United Nations Association (internationally oriented national body)
♦ International Modern Pentathlon and Biathlon Union / see World Penthathlon (#21720)
♦ International Modern Pentathlon Union / see World Penthathlon (#21720)
♦ International Mohair Association (inactive)

♦ International Molecular Moss Science Society (iMOSS) 14176

Pres Heuweilerweg 33, 79194 Gundelfingen, Germany. E-mail: info@imoss.org.
URL: https://imoss.org/

History 3 Sep 2016, Leeds (UK). Registration: Non-profit, No/ID: VR 701733, Start date: 23 Nov 2016, Germany. **Aims** Foster research on and scientific exchange about non-seed plants. **Structure** Board. **Activities** Awards/prizes/competitions; events/meetings. **Events** *Conference* Madrid (Spain) 2019. [2020/AA0545/**C**]

♦ The International Molinological Society (TIMS) 14177

Sec Aegidiusstraat 218, 3061 XT Rotterdam, Netherlands. T. +31615256442.
Pres Eichendorffstr 45, 71665 Vaihingen-Enz, Germany. T. +497042288180. E-mail: wdvb@gmx.de – tims-president@molinology.org.
URL: http://www.molinology.org/

History 1973. Founded during International Mill Symposium and by agreement of the General Meeting. First Symposium of what became TIMS held in 1965 on invitation of Mr Sao Miguel dos Santos Simoes. **Aims** Foster worldwide interest and understanding of wind, water, animal and human-driven *mills.* **Structure** General Meeting (every 4 years, at Symposium); TIMS Council. **Languages** English. **Staff** Voluntary. **Finance** Sources: members' dues. **Activities** Events/meetings; guidance/assistance/consulting; knowledge management/ information dissemination. **Events** *Quadrennial Symposium* Berlin (Germany) 2019, *Quadrennial Symposium* Sibiu (Romania) 2015, *Quadrennial Symposium* Aalborg (Denmark) 2011, *Quadrennial symposium* Aalborg (Denmark) 2011, *Quadrennial Symposium* Putten (Netherlands) 2007. **Publications** *International Molinology* (2 a year) – journal; *TIMS E-news* (2 a year). *Bibliotheca Molinologica* – series. *Symposium Transactions.*
Members National societies organizations; individuals. Members in 36 countries and territories:
Australia, Austria, Belgium, Bulgaria, Canada, Colombia, Cyprus, Czechia, Denmark, Estonia, Finland, France, Germany, Greece, Hungary, Iran Islamic Rep, Ireland, Italy, Japan, Lithuania, Luxembourg, Mexico, Moldova, Netherlands, Poland, Portugal, Romania, South Africa, Spain, Sweden, Switzerland, Türkiye, UK, Ukraine, USA, Virgin Is USA. [2023.02.14/XD4552/**D**]

♦ International Molybdenum Association (IMOA) 14178

Association internationale du molybdène

SG 454-458 Chiswick High Road, London, W4 5TT, UK. T. +442087476120. Fax +442087420128. E-mail: info@imoa.info.
URL: http://www.imoa.info/

History Mar 1989. Registration: Banque-Carrefour des Entreprises, No/ID: 0441.894.485, Start date: 8 Nov 1990, Belgium. **Aims** Promote the use of molybdenum; monitor health and environmental issues; maintain a historical record of production and use of molybdenum. **Structure** Executive Committee; Health, Safety and Environment Committee; Market Development Committee. **Languages** English. **Staff** 4.00 FTE, paid. **Activities** Advocacy/lobbying/activism; events/meetings; guidance/assistance/consulting; research/ documentation. **Events** *Annual General Meeting* Vail, CO (USA) 2019, *Annual General Meeting* Seoul (Korea Rep) 2018, *Annual General Meeting* Vienna (Austria) 2016, *Annual General Meeting* Hangzhou (China) 2014, *International Symposium on Nb and Mo Alloying in High Performance Steels* Jeju (Korea Rep) 2013. **Publications** *MolyReview* (2 a year). Statistical information; case studies; presentations; guide; fabrication guidelines; brochures.
Members Full (66) in 21 countries:
Australia, Austria, Belgium, Chile, China, Denmark, Finland, France, Germany, Israel, Japan, Kazakhstan, Korea Rep, Luxembourg, Mexico, Peru, Russia, Sweden, Switzerland, UK, USA.
NGO Relations Associate member of: *Association européenne des métaux (EUROMETAUX, #02578).* Member of: *International Council on Mining and Metals (ICMM, #13048); TEAM STAINLESS (#20113).*
[2022/XD2376/**D**]

♦ International Monarchist League / see Monarchist League (#16848)
♦ International Monarchist Union (no recent information)
♦ International Monetary Conference (meeting series)

♦ International Monetary and Financial Committee (IMFC) 14179

Comité monétaire et financier international (CMFI)

Main Office c/o IMF, 700 Nineteenth St NW, Washington DC 20431, USA. T. +12026237000.
Chairman address not obtained.
URL: http://www.imf.org/

History 2 Oct 1974, within the framework of *International Monetary Fund (IMF, #14180)*, succeeding *Committee on Reform of the International Monetary System and Related Issues*, subsequently known as *Committee of 20* – or *Committee of Twenty* – set up 26 Jul 1972, following adoption of resolution by IMF Board of Governors. Original title: *Interim Committee of the Board of Governors of the International Monetary Fund on the International Monetary System (Interim Committee) – Comité intérimaire du Conseil des gouverneurs du Fonds monétaire international sur le système monétaire international (Comité intérimaire)*, also referred to as *International Monetary Fund's Interim Committee.* Current title adopted on approval by IMF Board of Governors, 30 Sep 1999. **Aims** Provide ministerial guidance to IMF Executive Board; advise and report to IMF Board of Governors on issues regarding management and adaptation of the international monetary and financial system, including sudden disturbances that might threaten the international monetary system, and on proposals to amend IMF's Articles of Agreement. **Structure** Committee comprises 24 members – IMF Governors, Ministers of Finance of Central Bank Governors – with the same constituencies as IMF's Executive Board. *Intergovernmental Group of Twenty-Four on International Monetary Affairs (Group of Twenty-Four, #11495)* makes reports and recommendations. **Activities** Reviews developments in global liquidity and in transfer of real resources to developing countries. Reports to the Board of Governors on any other matter on which the Board seeks advice. Usually meets twice a year, once at IMF's Annual Meeting (Autumn) and once in Washington DC (USA) (Spring). *Joint Ministerial Committee of the Boards of Governors of the Bank and the Fund on the Transfer of Real Resources to Developing Countries (Development Committee, #16141)* normally meets the day after IMFC meetings. **Events** *Meeting* Washington, DC (USA) 2010, *Autumn meeting* Dubai (United Arab Emirates) 2003, *Spring meeting* Washington, DC (USA) 2003, *Autumn meeting* Washington, DC (USA) 2002, *Spring meeting* Washington, DC (USA) 2002.
Members IMF Governors of 25 countries:
Algeria, Austria, Brazil, Canada, Chile, China, Finland, France, Gabon, Germany, India, Italy, Japan, Korea Rep, Mexico, Netherlands, Russia, Saudi Arabia, Singapore, South Africa, Switzerland, Thailand, UK, United Arab Emirates, USA.
IGO Relations Observers include: *Bank for International Settlements (BIS, #03165); International Bank for Reconstruction and Development (IBRD, #12317)* (World Bank). [2014/XE8249/**E***]

♦ International Monetary Fund (IMF) 14180

Fonds monétaire international (FMI) – Fondo Monetario Internacional (FMI)

Managing Dir 700 19th St NW, Washington DC 20431, USA. T. +12026237000. Fax +12026234661. E-mail: publicaffairs@imf.org.
Headquarters 2 1900 Pennsylvania Ave NW, Washington DC 20431, USA.
Paris Office 64-66 av d'Iena, 75116 Paris, France. T. +33140693070.
Brussels Office 8 bv de Berlaimont, 1000 Brussels, Belgium. T. +3222215130.
URL: http://www.imf.org/

History Establishted 22 Jul 1944, Bretton Woods NH (USA), by representatives of the 45 countries which negotiated details of the Articles of Agreement/Charter. Came into being on 27 Dec 1945, with a membership of 29 of these countries, after acceptance of the Charter for ratification. Commercial operations commenced 1 Mar 1947. **Aims** Promote international monetary cooperation, the expansion of international trade and exchange rate stability; assist in the removal of exchange restrictions and the establishment of a multilateral system of payments; alleviate any serious disequilibrium in members' international balance of payments by making the financial resources of the IMF available to them, usually subject to economic policy conditions to ensure the revolving nature of IMF resources. **Structure** Board of Governors (meets annually, jointly with Board of Governors of the 'World Bank') is the highest authority, in which each member country is represented by one Governor and an Alternate Governor. Governors may take votes by mail or other means between meetings. The Board is responsible for conditions governing admission of new members, adjustment of quotas, election of Directors and certain other important matters. Other responsibilities are delegated to the Board of Executive Directors (meeting several times a week), which comprises 24 Executive Directors, chaired by the Managing Director, who is also the head of IMF staff. Officers: Managing Director; 1st Deputy Managing Director; 2 Deputy Managing Directors; 2 Counsellors; Directors of Departments (17) – African, Asia and Pacific, European, External Relations, Finance, Fiscal Affairs, Human Resources, IMF Institute, Legal, Middle East and Central Asia, Monetary and Capital Markets, Strategy, Policy and Review, Research, Secretary's, Statistics, Technology and General Services, Western Hemisphere; Directors of the Office of Budget and Planning, Office of Internal Audit and Inspection, Regional Office for Asia and the Pacific, Office in Europe (Paris) and Office at the United Nations (New York NY). *International Monetary and Financial Committee (IMFC, #14179)* (meets twice a year) advises the Board of Governors on supervising the management and adaptation of the international monetary system. **Languages** English. **Staff** 2400.00 FTE, paid. Staff from 141 countries. Staff negotiations through *IMF Staff Association (#11128).* **Finance** IMF accounts are denominated in terms of the *'SDR'* an interest-bearing international reserve asset, which was created by the IMF in 1969, pursuant to the First Amendment to the Fund's Articles of Agreement. It is now the Fund's unit of account. Members may keep their SDRs on reserve in the IMF, use them to acquire foreign exchange, or transfer them to other members through a variety of transactions. The value of the unit is determined daily on the basis of a basket of 4 currencies: the US dollar, the euro, the Japanese yen, and the pound sterling. The SDR interest rate is determined weekly by reference to specified short-term obligations in the money markets of the countries whose currencies constitute the SDRs. As of 15 Dec 2009, SDR 1 equals US$ 1.58081.
Activities Original impetus was to combat conditions contributing to and prolonging the depression of the 1930s. Functions have evolved in response to changing needs of members and of the international monetary system. Currency inconvertibility and lack of a standard for determining the value of national currencies (owing to the collapse of the gold standard) were identified by British economist John Maynard Keynes and US Treasury official Harry Dexter White as the major issues to address. Prospective members had therefore to set down a par value (ie a value in terms of a certain weight of gold) for their currencies and make every effort to eliminate restrictions on the conversion of their currencies into other currencies. Par values were finally established by the 1960s and most major currencies had become convertible. SDR, created in 1969, added necessary liquidity to the international monetary system. In 1971 the USA suspended convertibility of the dollar for gold and several other countries allowed their currencies to float away from par value. Attempts to re-establish the par value system failed; but IMF charter was amended in 1978 and a revised monetary system put in place. Under this present system, members are still obliged to strive for convertibility; but, since par values have been abolished, members can choose any exchange regime they wish (eg floating rates, rates tied to other currencies or to a standard such as the SDR), except to value their currencies in terms of gold. IMF is no longer monitoring a system of par values but is authorized to exercise firm surveillance over exchange rate policies of members.
Current activities emphasize strengthening global growth through: surveillance and crisis prevention; crisis resolution; lending policies and practices; combating poverty in low-income countries; technical assistance and training; transparency. *IMF Institute (see: #14180)*, set up 1964, provides training in economic management to officials of member countries. *Joint Vienna Institute (JVI, #16150)* trains officials from formerly centrally planned economies in various aspects of public administration and economic management. *Independent Evaluation Office (IEO)*, set up Jul 2001, conducts objective and independent assessment of issues related to IMF's mandate.
'Quotas' IMF's main financial role is to provide temporary credits to members experiencing balance-of-payments difficulties. In return, members borrowing from IMF agree to undertake policy reforms to correct problems underlying these difficulties. Amounts that members may borrow are limited to their quotas, assigned on joining the Fund and based on economic strength. Members pay a subscription equal to their quota into a common pool of currencies from which, with the approval of the Executive Board, they and other members may draw during periods of balance-of-payment difficulty. The size of the quota determines:
– The cumulative amount of loan a member country can have outstanding from IMF at any one time;
– The member's voting power over IMF policies – each member country has 250 votes plus one additional vote for each SDR 100,000 of its quota;
– How many SDRs the member receives whenever a distribution of SDRs is made.

Quotas are reviewed every 5 years and may be adjusted to reflect expansion in the world economy or changes in the economies of individual member countries.
Following a 45% quota increase effective 22 Jan 1999, under the 11th General Review of Quotas, total quotas in the Fund are SDR 212,000 million (almost US$ 270,000 million). As of 2010, the IMF Executive Board approved a set of measures to transform the IMF over time into a more effective and legitimate multilateral institution. The Board agreed to a significant shift of quota share toward countries that have been under-represented in the governance of the institution, especially those countries that have grown rapidly and taken on a central role in the global economy over the past decade.
'Borrowing' If resources seem likely to fall short of members' needs then they may be supplemented through borrowing. Temporary supplements include bilateral loan agreements, issuing notes to the official sector and enlarging existing borrowing arrangements. *General Arrangements to Borrow (GAB)*, adopted 5 Jan 1962, under *Revised General Arrangements to Borrow (1962)*, enables IMF to borrow specified amounts of currencies from 11 industrial countries (or their central banks), under certain circumstances, at market-related rates of interest. Potential amount of credit available to IMF under GAB total SDR 17,000 million, with an additional SDR 1,500 million available under an associated arrangement with Saudi Arabia. *New Arrangements to Borrow (NAB)*, approved 27 Jan 1997 and in effect in 1998, is is the facility of first and principal recourse vis-à-vis GAB and comprises a set of credit arrangements between IMF and 26 member countries and institutions Maximum amount of resources available to the IMF under the NAB and GAB is SDR 34,000 million. These credit arrangements provide supplementary resources to the IMF to forestall or cope with an impairment of the international monetary system or to deal with an exceptional situation that poses a threat to the stability of that system. In Apr 2009, *Group of Twenty (G20, #10793)* agreed to increase lending resources available to IMF by up to US$ 500,000 million, in 2 steps: immediate bilateral financing from IMF member countries; incorporating this financing into an expanded and more flexible NAB increased by up to US$ 500,000 million. This objective was achieved by Sep 2009.
'Bilateral loans' – a member normally commits to allow the Fund to make drawings up to a specified ceiling during the period for which drawings can be made.
'IMF notes' – a framework for issuing notes to the official sector, approved 2009, enabling members to invest in IMF paper while providing an immediate supplement to IMF resources for financial assistance to members.
Main IMF Facilities:
'Stand-By Arrangements (SBAs)' – provide short-term balance-of-payments assistance for deficits of a temporary or cyclical nature. These must be repaid within 3.25-5 years – or 2.25-4 years if the country's external position allows these shorter repayment terms. Interest surcharge on high levels of credit outstanding: 100-200 basis points. The *'Flexible Credit Line (FCL)'*, introduced in 2009, for country with strong fundamentals, policies and track records of policy implementation. Disbursements under FCL would not be phased or subject to conditionality.
'Extended Fund Facility (EFF)' – supports medium-term programmes aimed at overcoming balance-of-payments difficulties due to macroeconomic or structural problems. Such financial assistance must be repaid within 4.5-10 years, which may be shortened to 7 years if the country's external position allows these shorter repayment terms. Interest surcharge on high levels of credit outstanding: 100-200 basis points.
Poverty Reduction and Growth Facility (PRGF) – a concessional facility to assist low-income member countries with loans carrying an annual interest of 0.5%, repayments half-yearly from 5.5 to 10 years after disbursement. PRGF makes poverty reduction a more explicit element of the growth strategy for low-income countries than did the previous *Enhanced Structural Adjustment Facility (ESAF).* Members qualifying for PRGF funding may borrow up to 140% (under exceptional circumstances, 185%) of their quota under a 3-year PRGF arrangement.
'Compensatory Financing Facility' – timely financing for members experiencing temporary export shortfalls or excesses in cereal import costs.
'Supplementary Reserve Facility (SRF)' – provides financial assistance for exceptional balance-of-payments difficulties due to sudden and disruptive loss of market confidence in financial crises. Repayments normally in 1-1.5 years but may be extended to 2-2.5 years. Early repayment encouraged through interest surcharge of 200-500 basis points.
Enhanced Heavily Indebted Poor Countries Initiative (HIPC Initiative, #05483) – a comprehensive approach to debt relief, assisting heavily indebted poor countries (HIPCs) with sound financial policies by providing exceptional assistance for eligible countries to reduce external debts to sustainable levels. Involves multilateral, *Paris Club of Industrial Country Creditors (#18199)* and other official bilateral and commercial creditors.
Africa Capacity-Building Initiative (no recent information) aims to enable African countries to design and implement poverty-reducing strategies and to improve coordination of capacity-building technical assistance in the Poverty Reduction Strategy Paper (PRSP) process. It includes *African Regional Technical Assistance Centres (AFRITACs)* in Dar es Salaam and Abidjan (Côte d'Ivoire), IMF's contribution to *New Partnership for Africa's Development (NEPAD, #17091).*
'Surveillance of Exchange Rate Policies' – conducts comprehensive analysis and assessment of the general economic situation and policies of each member through annual consultations with individual countries and through twice-yearly multilateral surveillance through discussions with regional groupings in the context of the *World Economic Outlook* exercise. IMF also provides precautionary arrangements, enhanced surveillance and programme monitoring.
'Technical Assistance' – supports the development of the productive resources of member countries by helping them to manage their economic policy and financial affairs more effectively. Provides technical assistance in its areas of core expertise: macroeconomic policy, tax policy and revenue administration,

expenditure management, monetary policy, exchange rate system, financial sector sustainability, amd macroeconomic and financial statistics. About 90% goes to low and lower-middle income countries. Operates 7 regional technical assistance centres: Pacific (Fiji); Caribbean (Barbados); Africa (Gabon, Mali, Tanzania UR); Middle East (Lebanon); Central America (Guatemala).

As a cooperative monetary institution, IMF is neither primarily a lending institution nor a multilateral development institution, the latter role having been assigned to its sister institution, *International Bank for Reconstruction and Development (IBRD, #12317)*, unofficially referred to as *'World Bank'*, in the international economic order established at Bretton Woods. The two are often referred to collectively as *Bretton Woods Institutions (BWIs, #03322)*. Executive Directors, Alternate Directors, and Governors of the Fund in some cases also serve in the same capacity for the Bank. The annual meeting of the Board of Governors jointly with the Board of Governors of the 'World Bank' constitutes a meeting of the important financial officials of member countries. Management and staff of the IMF collaborate with opposite numbers in the 'World Bank'. To be eligible to apply for membership of the Bank a country must first be a member of IMF. However, while the Bank may lend only to poor countries, the IMF may lend to any member country lacking sufficient foreign currency to cover short-term obligations to creditors in other countries. *Joint Ministerial Committee of the Boards of Governors of the Bank and the Fund on the Transfer of Real Resources to Developing Countries (Development Committee, #16141)* was set up on 2 Oct 1974 and, from 1 Apr 1989, the 'World Bank' requires IMF approval for some of its loans to developing countries. The Joint Committee normally meets the day after the International Monetary and Financial Committee.

Events *25th Anniversary Conference of the OAP* Tokyo (Japan) 2022, *Conference on IMF's World Economic Outlook and Wage-Price Spiral Risks* Tokyo (Japan) 2022, *Joint Policy Conference on Managing Financial Risks in a Shock Prone World* Tokyo (Japan) 2022, *Seminar on Current Fiscal Developments and Issues* Tokyo (Japan) 2022, *Tokyo Fiscal Forum* Tokyo (Japan) 2022. **Publications** *International Financial Statistics* (12 a year); *Annual Report of the Executive Board*; *Annual Report on Exchange Arrangements and Exchange Restrictions*; *Finance and Development*; *Global Financial Stability Report*; *IMF Economic Review*; *IMF Survey* – online; *World Economic Outlook*.

Members Board of Governors admits new members on terms and conditions set by the Fund. Membership in the Fund is a prerequisite for membership in the IBRD. As of 2009, governments of 186 countries:
Afghanistan, Albania, Algeria, Angola, Antigua-Barbuda, Argentina, Armenia, Australia, Austria, Azerbaijan, Bahamas, Bahrain, Bangladesh, Barbados, Belarus, Belgium, Belize, Benin, Bhutan, Bolivia, Bosnia-Herzegovina, Botswana, Brazil, Brunei Darussalam, Bulgaria, Burkina Faso, Burundi, Cambodia, Cameroon, Canada, Cape Verde, Central African Rep, Chad, Chile, China, Colombia, Comoros, Congo Brazzaville, Congo DR, Costa Rica, Côte d'Ivoire, Croatia, Cyprus, Czechia, Denmark, Djibouti, Dominica, Dominican Rep, Ecuador, Egypt, El Salvador, Equatorial Guinea, Eritrea, Estonia, Eswatini, Ethiopia, Fiji, Finland, France, Gabon, Gambia, Georgia, Germany, Ghana, Greece, Grenada, Guatemala, Guinea, Guinea-Bissau, Guyana, Haiti, Honduras, Hungary, Iceland, India, Indonesia, Iran Islamic Rep, Iraq, Ireland, Israel, Italy, Jamaica, Japan, Jordan, Kazakhstan, Kenya, Kiribati, Korea Rep, Kosovo, Kuwait, Kyrgyzstan, Laos, Latvia, Lebanon, Lesotho, Liberia, Libya, Lithuania, Luxembourg, Madagascar, Malawi, Malaysia, Maldives, Mali, Malta, Marshall Is, Mauritania, Mauritius, Mexico, Micronesia FS, Moldova, Mongolia, Montenegro, Morocco, Mozambique, Myanmar, Namibia, Nepal, Netherlands, New Zealand, Nicaragua, Niger, Nigeria, North Macedonia, Norway, Oman, Pakistan, Palau, Panama, Papua New Guinea, Paraguay, Peru, Philippines, Poland, Portugal, Qatar, Romania, Russia, Rwanda, Samoa, San Marino, Sao Tomé-Principe, Saudi Arabia, Senegal, Serbia, Seychelles, Sierra Leone, Singapore, Slovakia, Slovenia, Solomon Is, Somalia, South Africa, Spain, Sri Lanka, St Kitts-Nevis, St Lucia, St Vincent-Grenadines, Sudan, Suriname, Sweden, Switzerland, Syrian AR, Tajikistan, Tanzania UR, Thailand, Timor-Leste, Togo, Tonga, Trinidad-Tobago, Tunisia, Türkiye, Turkmenistan, Uganda, UK, Ukraine, United Arab Emirates, Uruguay, USA, Uzbekistan, Vanuatu, Venezuela, Vietnam, Yemen, Zambia, Zimbabwe.

IGO Relations IMF's Articles call for cooperation with other international agencies. This involves frequent contact with agencies dealing with problems that have significance for the Fund. An agreement of relationship concluded with the United Nations outlines a programme of mutual assistance between the UN and the Fund, as an independent international organization. The Fund comes within: *United Nations System (#20635)*. In this context, it cooperates particularly in the work of: the Secretariat of *United Nations (UN, #20515)*; *ECOSOC (#05331)*; *United Nations Economic Commission for Africa (ECA, #20554)*; *United Nations Economic Commission for Europe (UNECE, #20555)*; *United Nations Economic Commission for Latin America and the Caribbean (ECLAC, #20556)*; *United Nations Economic and Social Commission for Asia and the Pacific (ESCAP, #20557)*. It participates in their meetings and in joint working parties, missions and study groups. Represented on: *United Nations System Chief Executives Board for Coordination (CEB, #20636)*. Continuous coordination with: *World Trade Organization (WTO, #21864)*. Permanent observer status with: *World Intellectual Property Organization (WIPO, #21593)*. Observer: *European Central Bank (ECB, #06466)*. Cooperates with international and regional organizations having related responsibilities or interests:
- *Bank for International Settlements (BIS, #03165)*;
- *Central American Monetary Council (#03672)*;
- *Egmont Group of Financial Intelligence Units (#05396)*;
- *European Commission (EC, #06633)*;
- *Financial Stability Board (FSB, #09770)*;
- *OAS (#17629)*;
- *OECD (#17693)*;
- *OECD Development Assistance Committee (DAC, see: #17693)*;
- *Sistema Económico Latinoamericano (SELA, #19294)*;
- *South East Asian Central Banks Research and Training Centre (SEACEN Centre, #19760)*.

NGO Relations Maintains dialogue with a wide range of international development-oriented NGOs and other civil society organizations (not specified). Contacts take place between IMF staff and management and NGOs through regular meetings at IMF headquarters, at conferences on issues of mutual concern and through IMF field offices in developing countries. IMF increasingly solicits input from national NGOs for development of policies vis-à-vis developing countries. Instrumental in setting up: *Financial Sector Reform and Strengthening Initiative (FIRST Initiative, #09769)*. [2020/XF2266/f/**F***]

♦ International Monetary Fund's Interim Committee / see International Monetary and Financial Committee (#14179)

♦ International Money Laundering Information Network (IMoLIN) . . . 14181

Réseau international d'information sur le blanchiment de l'argent – Red Informatica Internacional sobre Blanqueo de Dinero

Secretariat c/o UNODC – GPML, PO Box 500, 1400 Vienna, Austria. T. +431260604269. Fax +431260606878. E-mail: gpml@unodc.org.
URL: http://www.imolin.org/

History Established as an Internet-based network administered by *United Nations Global Programme Against Money Laundering, Proceeds of Crime and the Financing of Terrorism (GPML, #20568)* within *United Nations Office on Drugs and Crime (UNODC, #20596)*. **Aims** Provide a readily searchable database of information on national money laundering laws and regulations, and contacts for inter-country assistance, for the benefit of *law enforcement*, prosecution and related personnel in countries worldwide. **Structure** Secretariat maintained by GPML, based at *Vienna International Centre (VIC)*. **Languages** English, French. **Finance** Extra-budgetary funding; donor funding. **Activities** Knowledge management/information dissemination. **Information Services** *Anti-Money Laundering International Database (AMLID)*. **Members** UN Membership. **IGO Relations** Partner organizations: *Caribbean Financial Action Task Force (CFATF, #03505)*; *Commonwealth Secretariat (#04362)*; *Council of Europe (CE, #04881) Committee of Experts on the Evaluation of Anti-Money Laundering Measures and the Financing of Terrorism (MONEYVAL, #04257)*; *Eastern and Southern African Anti-Money Laundering Group (ESAAMLG, #05252)*; *Eurasian Group on Combating Money Laundering and Financing of Terrorism (EAG, #05608)*; *Financial Action Task Force (FATF, #09765)*; *Grupo de Acción Financiera de Latinoamérica (GAFILAT, #10799)*; *Intergovernmental Action Group against Money Laundering in West Africa (#11471)*; *International Criminal Police Organization – INTERPOL (ICPO-INTERPOL, #13110)*; *OAS (#17629)*. **NGO Relations** Participating organizations: *Group of International Finance Centre Supervisors (GIFCS, #10782)*. [2020/XF5568/**F***]

♦ International Money Transfer and Payments Conferences (meeting series)
♦ International Monohull Open Classes Association (see: #21760)

♦ International Monorail Association (IMA) 14182

Office Schützenstr 19, PO Box 269, 3627 Heimberg BE, Switzerland. T. +41334398085. Fax +41334398081.
Contact c/o Innova Technologies Inc, 1432 South Jones Blvd, Las Vegas NV 89146, USA. T. +17022206640. Fax +17022207740.
URL: http://monorailex.com/

History Originally incorporated 19 May 2010, Netherlands. Liquidated 19 Sep 2014. Re-established, when registered in accordance with Swiss Civil Code, 7 Feb 2015. **Aims** Organize the global monorail sector; promote the application of monorail; initiate and support standardization processes of monorail for public mass transport infrastructure. **Structure** Executive Council. **Finance** Sources: members' dues. **Activities** Events/meetings. **Events** *Workshop* Heimberg (Switzerland) 2020, *Annual Conference* Chiba (Japan) 2019, *Annual Conference* Berlin (Germany) 2018, *Annual Conference* Beijing (China) 2017, *Annual Conference* Las Vegas, NV (USA) 2015. **Publications** *IMA Newsletter*. [2019/XM8373/**C**]

♦ International Montessori Association (#02812)
♦ International Moral Education Congress (inactive)
♦ International Morphology Meeting (meeting series)

♦ International Mortgage Broker Federation (IMBF) 14183

Chair c/o FBAA, PO Box 4792, Eight Mile Plains QLD 4113, Australia. E-mail: info@fbaa.com.au.
Contact c/o NAMB, 601 Pennsylvania Ave NW, South Blg, Washington DC 20004, USA. E-mail: membership@namb.org.
URL: http://www.imbf.co/

History Launched Oct 2018. **Aims** Bring the international mortgage brokering community and its suppliers together to collaborate on shaping market practices; influence regulation and legislation through global advocacy; develop and adapt new and existing standards that enhance the industry; promote strong ethical practices.
Members Full in 5 countries:
Australia, Canada, Ireland, UK, USA. [2022/XM7476/**C**]

♦ International Mosaic Down Syndrome Association (IMDSA) 14184

Exec Dir PO Box 321, Grand Haven MI MI 49417, USA. E-mail: president@imdsa.org.
URL: http://www.imdsa.org/

History Apr 2002. **Aims** Assist families and individuals affected by Mosaic Down Syndrome. **Finance** Members' dues. **Activities** Organizes conferences. **Events** *Convention* Orlando, FL (USA) 2003.
Members Individuals in 13 countries:
Argentina, Australia, Belgium, Canada, France, Indonesia, Iraq, Mexico, Netherlands, Romania, Sweden, UK, USA. [2022/XD8631/**D**]

♦ International Moselle Commission / see Moselle Commission (#16857)
♦ International Moselle Company (#13263)
♦ International Moslem Brotherhood / see Muslim Brotherhood (#16915)

♦ International MotherBaby Childbirth Organization (IMBCO) 14185

Admin Dir address not obtained. T. +19048135822.
URL: http://www.imbci.org/

History Registration: 501(c)(3) non-profit, USA. **Aims** Improve maternity care in both developed and developing countries. **Structure** Board of Directors; Advisory Council. **Consultative Status** Consultative status granted from: *ECOSOC (#05331)* (Special). **NGO Relations** Instrumental in setting up (1): *International Childbirth Initiative (ICI, #12547)*. *1,000 Days*. [2020/XJ9926/**F**]

♦ International Motorcycle Manufacturers Association (IMMA) 14186

Association internationale des constructeurs de motocycles

Contact Route de Pré-Bois 20, CP 1838, 1215 Geneva 15, Switzerland. T. +41229202123. Fax +41229202121. E-mail: info@immamotorcycles.org.
URL: http://www.immamotorcycles.org/

History Founded 1947, as *International Permanent Bureau of Motor Cycle Manufacturers – Bureau permanent international des constructeurs de motocycles (BPICM)*. Current name adopted 1987. Registered in accordance with Swiss Civil Code, 12 Mar 1996. **Aims** Work in collaboration with governments on legislation, environmental questions and road safety for the mutual benefit of industry and customers. **Structure** General Assembly (annual); Technical Committee; Specialist Groups. **Languages** English. **Staff** 3.00 FTE, paid. **Finance** Members' dues. **Activities** Events/meetings. **Events** *Annual General Assembly / General Assembly* Bangalore (India) 2014, *Annual General Assembly / General Assembly* Washington, DC (USA) 2013, *Annual General Assembly / General Assembly* Madrid (Spain) 2012, *Annual General Assembly* Sepang (Malaysia) 2011, *Annual general assembly / General Assembly* San Antonio, TX (USA) 2002. **Publications** *The Shared Road to Safety* (2014); *Motorcycle Safety: IMMA's contribution to the Decade of Action for Road Safety 2011-20* (2010).
Members National associations (), Associate members () and other members in 21 countries and territories:
Australia (*), Austria, Belgium, Canada (**), Czechia, France, Germany, India, Indonesia, Italy, Japan, Malaysia, Netherlands, Philippines, Singapore, Spain, Sweden, Taiwan, Thailand, UK, USA (*).
Regional organizations (2):
Association des constructeurs européens de motocycles (ACEM, #02450); *Federation of Asian Motorcycle Industries (FAMI, #09435)*.
Consultative Status Consultative status granted from: *ECOSOC (#05331)* (Ros A). **NGO Relations** Cooperates with: *International Organization for Standardization (ISO, #14473)*. [2018.06.01/XD5058/y/**D**]

♦ International Motor Impairment Meeting (meeting series)

♦ International Motor Vehicle Inspection Committee (CITA) 14187

Comité international de l'inspection technique automobile

Exec Dir Rue du Commerce 123, 1000 Brussels, Belgium. T. +3224690670. E-mail: secretariat@citainsp.org.
Pres address not obtained.
URL: http://citainsp.org/

History 24 Sep 1969, Ostend (Belgium). Articles of Corporation modified Apr 1999; Apr 2015; May 2021. Former names and other names: *Internationale Vereinigung für die technische Prüfung von Kraftfahrzeugen* – former. Registration: Banque-Carrefour des Entreprises, Belgium. **Aims** Enable programmes and policies for safe and clean vehicles. **Structure** General Assembly; Permanent Bureau; Regional Advisory Groups; Topic Areas; Task Forces; Secretariat. **Languages** English, French, Italian, Spanish. **Staff** 4.00 FTE, paid. **Finance** Sources: members' dues. **Activities** Events/meetings; knowledge management/information dissemination; research/documentation; standards/guidelines; training/education. **Events** *General Assembly and Conference* Rotterdam (Netherlands) 2023, *General Assembly* Brussels (Belgium) 2022, *International Conference* Brussels (Belgium) 2022, *Regional Advisory Group RAG EUROPE Conference* Brussels (Belgium) 2022, *General Assembly and Conference* Seoul (Korea Rep) 2019. **Publications** *CITA NewsRelease* (2 a year). Annual Report; studies; position papers; recommendations; news.
Members Full; Corporate; Provisional; Affiliate Association; Affiliate Non-Association. Members (153) in 56 countries and territories:
Andorra, Argentina, Austria, Belgium, Bosnia-Herzegovina, Burkina Faso, Chile, China, Costa Rica, Côte d'Ivoire, Croatia, Denmark, Estonia, Finland, France, Georgia, Germany, Hungary, Ireland, Israel, Italy, Japan, Korea Rep, Kosovo, Kurdish area, Latvia, Lebanon, Lithuania, Luxembourg, Malaysia, Mongolia, Netherlands, New Zealand, Nigeria, North Macedonia, Panama, Poland, Portugal, Qatar, Romania, Russia, Saudi Arabia, Serbia, Singapore, Slovakia, Slovenia, South Africa, Spain, Sweden, Switzerland, Tunisia, Türkiye, UK, United Arab Emirates, USA, Vietnam.
Consultative Status Consultative status granted from: *ECOSOC (#05331)* (Special). **IGO Relations** Accredited by (1): *United Nations Office at Vienna (UNOV, #20604)*. **NGO Relations** Member of: *Global Alliance of NGOs for Road Safety (#10216)*. Sponsor of: *European Transport Safety Council (ETSC, #08940)* – Road Safety Performance Index. [2023.02.14/XD7840/**E**]

♦ International Motor Yachting Union / see Union internationale Motonautique (#20431)

♦ International Mountain Bicycling Association (IMBA) 14188

Headquarters PO Box 20280, Boulder CO 80308, USA. T. +13035459011. Fax +13035459026.
URL: http://www.imba.com/

History 1988. **Aims** Promote mountain bicycling opportunities, that are environmentally and socially responsible, through education in *environmentally* sound and socially riding practices and *land management* policies. **Activities** Events/meetings; training/education. **Publications** *IMBA TRAIL NEWS* (6 a year) – newsletter. **Members** Individuals (35,000); bicly clubs (over 750); corporate partners (over 200); retailer shops (about 600). Membership countries not specified. **NGO Relations** Partner of (1): *1% for the Planet*. [2021/XN5019/**C**]

♦ International Mountain Bicycling Association Europe (IMBA Europe) 14189

Contact Deventerweg 2a, 3843 GD Harderwijk, Netherlands. T. +31318581306. E-mail: info@imba-europe.com.
URL: http://www.imba-europe.org/

History Registered in accordance with Dutch law, 2012. Registration: Handelsregister, No/ID: KVK 55346847, Netherlands. **Aims** Secure sustainable access for mountain *bikers*; unlock opportunities for train development at regional, national, European Union, local and/or community level by integrating mouting biking into landscapes, habitats and communities. **Structure** Board. **Events** *Summit* Ramatuelle (France) 2015.
Members National associations in 22 countries:
Austria, Bulgaria, Czechia, Denmark, Finland, France, Germany, Greece, Italy, Latvia, Netherlands, North Macedonia, Norway, Poland, Portugal, Romania, Slovakia, Slovenia, Spain, Sweden, Switzerland, UK.
NGO Relations Member of (1): *European Network of Outdoor Sports (ENOS, #07961)*. Cooperates with (1): *Cycling Industries Europe (CIE, #04988)*. [2021/XJ9405/**D**]

♦ International Mountaineering and Climbing Federation (#20420)
♦ International Mountain Explorers Connection (internationally oriented national body)

♦ International Mountain Society (IMS) 14190

Associate Editor Centre for Development and Environment, Univ of Bern, Mittelstr 43, 3012 Bern, Switzerland. T. +41316313822.
Managing Dir address not obtained.
URL: http://www.mrd-journal.org/

History 1981, Boulder, CO (USA). Founded following meetings, 1974, Munich (Germany FR) and 1976, Cambridge (UK), of *IGU Commission on Mountain Geoecology and Sustainable Development (inactive)*. Instigated among others by *International Geographical Union (IGU, #13713)* and *United Nations University (UNU, #20642)*. Re-established, 2000, Bern (Switzerland). Registration: Swiss Civil Code, Switzerland. **Aims** Advance knowledge and disseminate information about mountain research and mountain development worldwide; promote *sustainable development* through improved communication among institutions and individuals, with a particular focus on mountains in the developing world. **Structure** General Assembly; Board of Directors. **Languages** English. **Staff** None. **Finance** Sources: grants; international organizations; members' dues. Other sources: author's fees. Supported by: *Austrian Development Agency (ADA)* (grant); *Centre for Development and Environment, Bern (CDE)* (grant); *International Centre for Integrated Mountain Development (ICIMOD, #12500)* (grant). Annual budget: 220,000 CHF. **Events** *International conference on transformation of mountain environment* Tsaghkadzor (USSR) 1989, *Joint international workshop on African mountains and highlands* Addis Ababa (Ethiopia) 1986. **Publications** *Mountain Research and Development (MRD)* (4 a year) – open access, international peer reviewed journal.
Members Institutional membership (13) of which 4 are listed in this Yearbook:
Centre for Development and Environment, Bern (CDE); Consortium for the Sustainable Development of the Andean Ecoregion (#04758); International Centre for Integrated Mountain Development (ICIMOD, #12500); Mountain Research Initiative (MRI, #16863). [2023.02.20/XC0370/y/**C**]

♦ International Movement (inactive)
♦ International Movement for Advancement of Education Culture Social and Economic Development (internationally oriented national body)

♦ The International Movement Against All Forms of Discrimination and Racism (IMADR) 14191

Mouvement international contre toutes les formes de discriminations et le racisme
Contact 6F 1-7-1 Irifune, Chuo-ku, Tokyo, 106-0042 Japan. T. +81362803101. Fax +81362803102. E-mail: imadr@imadr.org.
Geneva Office Route de Ferney 150, CP2100, 1211 Geneva 2, Switzerland. T. +41227916263. Fax +41227916480. E-mail: geneva@imadr.org.
URL: http://imadr.org/

History 25 Jan 1988, Tokyo (Japan), when Articles came into effect. Articles partially revised: 18 Mar 1990; Nov 1992; 13 Nov 1995; 22 Nov 1998; 23 Nov 2002; 13 Sep 2011; 8 Jun 2015. **Aims** Eliminate discrimination and racism, forge international *solidarity* among discriminated *minorities* and improve the international *human rights* system. **Structure** General Assembly; Board of Directors; Secretariat. **Languages** English, Japanese. **Staff** 4.00 FTE, paid. **Finance** Members' dues. Other sources: fund-raising through campaigns and grant applications; public contributions. **Activities** Advocacy/lobbying/activism; awareness raising; research/documentation; events/meetings. **Events** *International Symposium on UN Guidance Tool on Descent-Based Discrimination* Tokyo (Japan) 2018, *Seminar on the use of international conventions to protect the rights of migrants and ethnic minorities* Strasbourg (France) 1993, *Symposium – Indigenous peoples and development* Quezon City (Philippines) 1992. **Publications** *IMADR Info* (weekly) – magazine; *E-CONNECT* (4 a year) – newsletter. Booklets.
Members Group; Individual. Members in 12 countries:
Argentina, Bangladesh, France, Germany, India, Japan, Korea Rep, Nepal, Netherlands, Senegal, Sri Lanka, USA.
Consultative Status Consultative status granted from: *ECOSOC (#05331)* (Special and Ros A). **IGO Relations** Campaigns for: *International Convention on the Elimination of all Forms of Racial Discrimination (1965)*. Accredited by: *United Nations Office at Vienna (UNOV, #20604)*, Geneva and New York NY. **NGO Relations** Member of: *International Dalit Solidarity Network (IDSN, #13129)*; NGO Network on UN Treaty Bodies (TB-Net). [2019.02.12/XF0708/**F**]

♦ International Movement of Apostolate of Children (IMAC) 14192

Mouvement international d'apostolat des enfants (MIDADE) – Movimiento Internacional de Apostolado de los Niños (MIDADEN)
SG 7 av de la Marne, 92120 Montrouge, France. T. +33175325060.
Pres address not obtained.
URL: http://www.midade.org/

History Jul 1962, Paris (France), following 30 years work in different parts of the world. Previously known as *International Commission CV-AV Apostolic Movement for Children*. Registered in accordance with French law. **Aims** Promote and uphold throughout the world the human and *Christian* development of children, and their capacity of apostolic action. **Structure** General Assembly (every 4 years). International Bureau, comprising President, 4 Vice-Presidents, 2 Secretaries General and International Chaplain. **Languages** English, French, Portuguese, Spanish. **Staff** 7.00 FTE, paid. **Finance** Sources: grants; members' dues. **Activities** Coordinating work includes: personal contacts; sessions; circulars and newsletters. **Events** *Quadrennial general assembly* Santiago (Chile) 2008, *Quadrennial General Assembly* Damascus (Syrian AR) 2003, *Latin American regional meeting* Lima (Peru) 2000, *European regional meeting* Lyon (France) 2000, *Quadrennial general assembly* Dakar (Senegal) 1998. **Publications** *Enfants en Mouvement* (2 a year) in English, French – journal. Working papers; reports.
Members Full in 45 countries and territories:
Benin, Bolivia, Brazil, Burkina Faso, Cameroon, Canada, Central African Rep, Chad, Chile, Colombia, Congo Brazzaville, Côte d'Ivoire, Egypt, France, Gabon, Guadeloupe, Guinea, Haiti, Italy, Japan, Jordan, Korea Rep, Lebanon, Madagascar, Malaysia, Mali, Mauritius, Mexico, Peru, Portugal, Réunion, Rodriguez Is, Romania, Senegal, Seychelles, Singapore, Slovakia, Spain, Sri Lanka, Switzerland, Syrian AR, Thailand, Togo, Venezuela, Zambia.
Consultative Status Consultative status granted from: *ECOSOC (#05331)* (Ros A); *ILO (#11123)* (Special List); *UNICEF (#20332)*. **IGO Relations** Accredited by (1): *United Nations Office at Vienna (UNOV, #20604)*. Associated with Department of Global Communications of the United Nations. **NGO Relations** Member of: *Forum of Catholic Inspired NGOs (#09905)*. [2019/XB2273/**B**]

♦ International Movement for the Apostolate in the Independent Social Milieux (#16864)

♦ International Movement ATD Fourth World 14193

Mouvement international ATD Quart Monde – Movimiento Internacional ATD Cuarto Mundo
Secretariat 12 rue Pasteur, 95480 Pierrelaye, France. T. +33134304610. Fax +33134304621. E-mail: atdint@atd-quartmonde.org – secretariat.amis@atd-quartmonde.org – intl.comms@atd-fourthworld.org.
URL: https://www.atd-fourthworld.org/

History 1958. Founded by Joseph Wresinski (1917-1988), following establishment of the association *'Aide à toute détresse'* in 1957, Noisy-le-Grand (France). The Movement extended through France, Europe and eventually throughout the world. Statutes adopted 6 Sep 1973, when registered according to French law. Since 29 Apr 2009, ATD stands for *All Together in Dignity – Agir tous pour la dignité – Actuar Todos por la Dignidad*. Statutes modified 18 Jan 2002. Former names and other names: *International Movement for Science and Service for a Just and Free World* – former (1973). Registration: No/ID: SIREN 442029146, France; No/ID: RNA W953001514, France; EU Transparency Register, No/ID: 14200875377-44, Start date: 24 Feb 2011. **Aims** Break the vicious circle of extreme *poverty*; eliminate *social exclusion*; through practical action and scientific research, promote free and full participation of the most *underprivileged* individuals, groups and social strata in the socio-economic, cultural and political life of the society surrounding them; pursue reappraisal of policies and programmes on the basis of their achievements on behalf of those who remain at the bottom of the social scale and have been most and longest deprived; provide means of enabling Fourth World families to think and speak out for themselves. **Structure** General Assembly; Board of Directors; Office of the Board of Directors. **Languages** English, French, Spanish. **Finance** Sources: grants; members' dues. Annual budget: 16,326,000 EUR. **Activities** Grassroots projects; representation and participation of people in poverty in national and international institutions; public debate projects; street libraries and educational outreach. Organizes: International Forum on the Eradication of Poverty; International Day for the Eradication of Poverty (17 Oct); seminars; training sessions. Developed the *'Street Library Project'*. Contributed to creation of, and serves as permanent contributor to: *'Fourth World Study Group'* within the Parliamentary Assembly of the Council of Europe; *'Fourth World Committee'* within the European Parliament. Constituent bodies: *'Tapori Movement Network'* for children; *Fourth World Youth (no recent information)*; *'Université populaire Quart Monde'*; *'Institut de recherche du Mouvement ATD'*; *'Joseph Wresinski Reflection Groups – Cercles de pensées Joseph Wresinski'*; Fourth World *'Crossroads of Knowledge'* project and *'Crossroads of Practice'*; *Permanent Forum Extreme Poverty in the World (see: #14193)*. **Events** *Meeting* Washington, DC (USA) 2010, *Meeting* Geneva (Switzerland) 2009, *Meeting* Port-au-Prince (Haiti) 2008, *Meeting* Montréal, QC (Canada) 2006, *International forum on the eradication of poverty* New York, NY (USA) 2006. **Publications** *Feuille de Route* (12 a year); *Revue Quart Monde* (4 a year); *International Movement Triennial Report*; *Letter to Friends around the World* in English, French, Portuguese, Spanish; *Tapori Newsletter*. National annual reports and newsletters; books; reports; studies; post cards; videos and DVDs.
Members Families and individuals with direct experience of poverty and people from diverse social, ideological, ethnic and geographical backgrounds committed to a world without extreme poverty or exclusion; no religious or political affiliation. Individuals (about 100,000; over 12,000 active), grouped into national branches and national secretariats, in 33 countries:
Belgium, Benin, Bolivia, Burkina Faso, Cameroon, Canada, Central African Rep, Congo DR, Côte d'Ivoire, France, Germany, Guatemala, Haiti, Honduras, Ireland, Italy, Luxembourg, Madagascar, Mali, Mauritius, Netherlands, Peru, Philippines, Poland, Portugal, Rwanda, Senegal, Spain, Switzerland, Tanzania UR, Thailand, UK, USA.
Correspondents individual members and organizations working at grassroot level, all members of the "Permanent Forum on Extreme Poverty in the World" – a network open to people and small organizations committed to the very poor, in 106 countries and territories:
Algeria, Argentina, Australia, Austria, Bangladesh, Belgium, Benin, Bolivia, Brazil, Burkina Faso, Burundi, Cambodia, Cameroon, Canada, Central African Rep, Chad, Chile, China, Colombia, Congo Brazzaville, Congo DR, Costa Rica, Côte d'Ivoire, Cyprus, Czechia, Denmark, Ecuador, Egypt, Ethiopia, Fiji, Finland, France, Gabon, Germany, Ghana, Greece, Guatemala, Guinea, Guyana, Haiti, Holy See, Honduras, Hong Kong, Hungary, India, Indonesia, Iran Islamic Rep, Ireland, Israel, Italy, Japan, Jordan, Korea Rep, Lebanon, Lesotho, Liberia, Luxembourg, Madagascar, Malawi, Malaysia, Mali, Mauritania, Mauritius, Mexico, Morocco, Mozambique, Nepal, Netherlands, New Zealand, Niger, Nigeria, Norway, Pakistan, Palestine, Paraguay, Peru, Philippines, Poland, Portugal, Russia, Rwanda, Samoa, Senegal, Sierra Leone, Singapore, Slovakia, Slovenia, South Africa, Spain, Sri Lanka, Sudan, Sweden, Switzerland, Syrian AR, Tanzania UR, Thailand, Togo, Tunisia, Türkiye, UK, Ukraine, Uruguay, USA, Venezuela, Zambia, Zimbabwe.
Consultative Status Consultative status granted from: *ECOSOC (#05331)* (General); *UNESCO (#20322)* (Associate Status); *ILO (#11123)* (Special List); *UNICEF (#20332)*; *Council of Europe (CE, #04881)* (Participatory Status). **IGO Relations** Contacts with: *European Commission (EC, #06633)* (Directorates for Employment, Social Affairs and Education; Development; Information, Communication and Culture). Accredited by: *United Nations Office at Vienna (UNOV, #20604)*. Member of: *European Youth Centres (EYCs, #09138)*. Participant in Fundamental Rights Platform of: *European Union Agency for Fundamental Rights (FRA, #08969)*. Associated with Department of Global Communications of the United Nations.
NGO Relations Supports: *Global Call for Action Against Poverty (GCAP, #10263)*. Cooperates with: *Association internationale des femmes francophones (AIFF, no recent information)*. Member of:
- *Child Rights Connect (#03884)*;
- *Conference of Non-Governmental Organizations in Consultative Relationship with the United Nations (CONGO, #04635)*;
- *Coordination SUD*;
- *Council for Education in the Commonwealth (CEC)*;
- *Council of Non-Governmental Organizations for Development Support (#04911)*;
- *European Anti-Poverty Network (EAPN, #05908)*;
- *European Youth Forum (#09140)*;
- *Forum of Catholic Inspired NGOs (#09905)*;
- *Global Coalition to End Child Poverty (#10292)*;
- *International Catholic Child Bureau (#12450)*;
- *International Coalition for the Optional Protocol to the Convention on the Rights of the Child on a Communications Procedure (Ratify OP3CRC, #12617)*;
- *National Council for Voluntary Organizations (NCVO)*;
- *NGO Committee on UNICEF (#17120)*;
- *Permanent Forum of European Civil Society (#18322)*;
- *Social Platform (#19344)*;
- *Union des organisations internationales non-gouvernementales établies en France (UOIF, inactive)*.

Observer to: *International Committee of the Red Cross (ICRC, #12799)*; *International Federation of Red Cross and Red Crescent Societies (#13526)*; *International Red Cross and Red Crescent Movement (#14707)*. [2023/XF4639/**F**]

♦ International Movement for Atlantic Union (inactive)
♦ International Movement of Catholic Agricultural and Rural Youth (#16865)
♦ International Movement of Catholic Lawyers (inactive)
♦ International Movement for Child Welfare (internationally oriented national body)
♦ International Movement of Christian Women – The Grail / see The Grail – International Movement of Christian Women (#10689)

♦ International Movement for the Defence of and the Right to Pleasure (Slow Food) 14194

Internationale Beweging voor de Verdediging van het Recht op het Genot
Pres Piazza XX Settembre 5, 12042 Bra CN, Italy. T. +39172419611. Fax +39172421293. E-mail: international@slowfood.com – communication@slowfood.it.
URL: http://www.slowfood.com/

History 9 Nov 1989, Paris (France). Former names and other names: *International Slow Food Movement* – alias; *Slow Food International* – alias. Registration: EU Transparency Register, No/ID: 01936914624-97, Start date: 29 Nov 2010. **Aims** Prevent the disappearance of local food cultures and *traditions*; counteract the rise of fast life; combat people's dwindling interest in the food they eat. **Structure** International Council; Executive Committee. National Ruling Committee. Regional offices (3): Münster (Germany); New York NY (USA); Switzerland. Includes: *Slow Food Foundation for Biodiversity*. **Activities** Advocacy/lobbying/activism; training/education; events/meetings; networking/liaising. **Events** *International Slow Food Congress* Pollenzo (Italy) 2022, *International Slow Food Congress* Turin (Italy) 2020, *International Slow Food Congress* Chengdu (China) 2017, *International Slow Food Congress* Turin (Italy) 2012, *International slow food congress* Puebla (Mexico) 2007.
Members Individuals (about 80,000) in 60 countries and territories:
Andorra, Argentina, Armenia, Australia, Austria, Belarus, Belgium, Brazil, Bulgaria, Canada, Cayman Is, Chile, China, Colombia, Croatia, Cyprus, Czechia, Denmark, Dominican Rep, Estonia, Finland, France, Georgia, Ghana, Greece, Hungary, Iceland, India, Ireland, Israel, Japan, Kenya, Korea Rep, Latvia, Lebanon, Luxembourg, Mexico, Monaco, Nepal, Netherlands, New Zealand, Norway, Philippines, Poland, Portugal, Russia, Singapore, Slovenia, South Africa, Spain, Sweden, Switzerland, Taiwan, Thailand, Türkiye, UK, Ukraine, Uruguay, Uzbekistan, Venezuela.
Consultative Status Consultative status granted from: *FAO (#09260)* (Liaison Status). **NGO Relations** Declaration with: *Arco Latino (#01094)*. Instrumental in setting up: *Terra Madre Foundation (#20130)*. [2022/XF6271/**F**]

♦ International Movement for Fraternal Union among Races and Peoples / see Unis pour l'Équite et la Fin du Racisme (#20490)
♦ International Movement for the Global Ban of Weapons which Manipulate the Human Nervous System (unconfirmed)
♦ International Movement for a Just World (internationally oriented national body)
♦ International Movement for Leisure Activities in Science and Technology (internationally oriented national body)
♦ International Movement for a New Museology (#16866)
♦ International Movement of Parliamentarians for Democracy (see: #21661)
♦ International Movement for Peace Action (inactive)
♦ International Movement for the Promotion and Realization of Human Rights and Responsibilities / see Rights and Humanity (#18946)
♦ International Movement of the Red Cross and Red Crescent / see International Red Cross and Red Crescent Movement (#14707)
♦ International Movement for Science and Service for a Just and Free World / see International Movement ATD Fourth World (#14193)
♦ International Movement We Are Church / see We Are Church International (#20841)
♦ International Mozart Society (inactive)

♦ International MPS Network 14195

Secretariat c/o MPS Society, MPS House, Repton Place, White Lion Road, Amersham, HP7 9LP, UK. T. +448453899901. Fax +448453899902. E-mail: info@impsnetwork.org.
URL: https://impsnetwork.org/

History Memorandum of Understanding approved 25 Jun 2008, Vancouver BC (Canada), at International Symposium of Mucopolysaccharide Diseases. **Aims** Act as an independent forum for MPS societies and relevant *patient* association at European and global levels; promote the well-being of those affected by *Mucopolysaccharide* and related *Lysosomal* diseases. **Languages** English. **Staff** 2.00 FTE, voluntary. **Finance** Members' dues. **Activities** Events/meetings; awards/prizes/competitions. **Events** *International Symposium on MPS and Related Diseases* Lucerne (Switzerland) 2023, *International Symposium of MPS and Related Diseases* Barcelona (Spain) 2021, *International Symposium of MPS and Related Diseases* Barcelona (Spain) 2020, *International Symposium on MPS and Related Diseases* San Diego, CA (USA) 2018, *International Symposium on MPS and Related Diseases* Bonn (Germany) 2016. **Publications** None.
Members Full in 35 countries and territories:
Australia, Austria, Belgium, Brazil, Canada, China, Croatia, Czechia, Denmark, France, Germany, Greece, Hong Kong, Hungary, India, Indonesia, Ireland, Italy, Japan, Korea Rep, Malaysia, Netherlands, New Zealand, Norway, Poland, Romania, Russia, Serbia, Spain, Sweden, Switzerland, Taiwan, Türkiye, UK, USA.
IGO Relations *European Medicines Agency (EMA, #07767).* [2021/XJ9951/**F**]

♦ International MS Cognition Society / see International Multiple Sclerosis Cognition Society (#14197)
♦ International MTM Directorate / see International Methods Time-Measurement Directorate (#14154)
♦ International Multidisciplinary Modelling & Simulation Multiconference (meeting series)
♦ International Multidisciplinary Neuroscience Research Centre (internationally oriented national body)
♦ International Multihull Society (inactive)

♦ International Multilateral Partnership Against Cyber Threats (IMPACT) 14196

Global HQ Jalan IMPACT, 63000 Cyberjaya, Selangor, Malaysia. T. +60383132020. Fax +60383192020.
URL: http://www.impact-alliance.org/

History Through a Memorandum of Understanding, signed 3 Sep 2008, serves as executing arm of *International Telecommunication Union (ITU, #15673)* and as operational home of ITU's *Global Cybersecurity Agenda (GCA)*. **Aims** Bring together governments, industry and academia against cyber threats. **Structure** International Advisory Board; Management Board. Centres (4): Global Response; Security Assurance and Research; Policy and International Cooperation; Training and Skills Development. Divisions (2): Infrastructure Services; Administration.
Members ITU Member States that are receiving cybersecurity services from IMPACT (146):
Afghanistan, Albania, Algeria, Andorra, Angola, Antigua-Barbuda, Armenia, Austria, Azerbaijan, Bangladesh, Barbados, Belarus, Belize, Benin, Bhutan, Bosnia-Herzegovina, Botswana, Brazil, Brunei Darussalam, Bulgaria, Burkina Faso, Burundi, Cambodia, Cameroon, Cape Verde, Chad, China, Comoros, Congo Brazzaville, Congo DR, Costa Rica, Côte d'Ivoire, Croatia, Cuba, Cyprus, Djibouti, Dominican Rep, Ecuador, Egypt, Eritrea, Eswatini, Ethiopia, Fiji, Gabon, Gambia, Georgia, Ghana, Grenada, Guatemala, Guinea, Guinea-Bissau, Guyana, Haiti, Holy See, Honduras, India, Indonesia, Iran Islamic Rep, Iraq, Israel, Italy, Jamaica, Jordan, Kenya, Kiribati, Kyrgyzstan, Laos, Lebanon, Lesotho, Liberia, Lithuania, Madagascar, Malawi, Malaysia, Maldives, Mali, Malta, Marshall Is, Mauritania, Mauritius, Micronesia FS, Moldova, Monaco, Mongolia, Montenegro, Morocco, Mozambique, Myanmar, Namibia, Nauru, Nepal, Niger, Nigeria, Oman, Pakistan, Panama, Papua New Guinea, Paraguay, Peru, Philippines, Poland, Qatar, Romania, Rwanda, Samoa, San Marino, Sao Tomé-Principe, Saudi Arabia, Senegal, Serbia, Seychelles, Sierra Leone, Slovakia, Slovenia, Solomon Is, Somalia, South Africa, South Sudan, Spain, Sri Lanka, St Kitts-Nevis, St Lucia, St Vincent-Grenadines, Sudan, Suriname, Switzerland, Syrian AR, Tanzania UR, Thailand, Timor-Leste, Togo, Tonga, Trinidad-Tobago, Tunisia, Türkiye, Tuvalu, Uganda, Ukraine, United Arab Emirates, Uruguay, Vanuatu, Venezuela, Vietnam, Yemen, Zambia, Zimbabwe.
IGO Relations Cooperates with: *Commonwealth Telecommunications Organisation (CTO, #04365)*; *International Criminal Police Organization – INTERPOL (ICPO-INTERPOL, #13110)*. **NGO Relations** Partners include: *Association of African Universities (AAU, #02361)*; *International Information Systems Security Certification Consortium (ISC2, #13849).* [2015/XJ6946/**E***]

♦ International Multilateral Trade Cooperation Organization (unconfirmed)
♦ International MultiMedia Modeling Conference (meeting series)
♦ International MultiModal Transport Association (inactive)

♦ International Multiple Sclerosis Cognition Society (IMSCOGS) 14197

Sec INSERM U 1215, Univ de Bordeaux, 33076 Bordeaux CEDEX, France. E-mail: info@imscogs.com.
URL: http://www.imscogs.com/

History 2011. Also referred to as *International MS Cognition Society*. **Aims** Bring together researchers and health professionals with an interest in cognition in MS and all related areas. **Structure** Executive Committee. **Events** *Annual Conference* Bordeaux (France) 2020, *Annual Conference* Amsterdam (Netherlands) 2019, *Annual Conference* Berlin (Germany) 2018, *Annual Conference* Düsseldorf (Germany) 2017, *Annual Conference* New York, NY (USA) 2016. **NGO Relations** *European Committee for Treatment and Research in Multiple Sclerosis (ECTRIMS, #06673).* [2017.10.31/XJ9640/**C**]

♦ International Multiracial Shared Cultural Organization (internationally oriented national body)

♦ International Multisensory Research Forum (IMRF) 14198

Contact The City College of New York, 160 Convent Avenue, North Academic Center 7/120, New York NY 10031, USA.
URL: http://www.imrf.info/

Aims Facilitate communication among scientists working with sensory systems in which more than one sense modality plays a role. **Events** *Annual Meeting* Ulm (Germany) 2021, *Annual Meeting* Ulm (Germany) 2020, *Annual Meeting* Chicago, IL (USA) 2019, *Annual Meeting* Toronto, ON (Canada) 2018, *Annual Meeting* Nashville, TN (USA) 2017. **Publications** *Crossmodal Space and Crossmodal Attention*; *Handbook of Multisensory Processes.* [2017/XM3467/**F**]

♦ International Musculoskeletal Laser Society (no recent information)
♦ International Museum Membership Conference (meeting series)
♦ International Museums Office (inactive)
♦ International Museum Theatre Alliance (internationally oriented national body)
♦ International Museum Theatre Alliance Asia Pacific (internationally oriented national body)
♦ International Museum Theatre Alliance for Europe (internationally oriented national body)
♦ International Mushroom Dye Institute (unconfirmed)
♦ International Mushroom Society for the Tropics (inactive)
♦ International Music Centre / see IMZ International Music + Media Centre (#11139)

♦ International Music Council (IMC) 14199

Conseil international de la musique (CIM) – Consejo Internacional de la Música (CIM) – Internationaler Musikrat

SG IMC General Secretariat, Maison de l'UNESCO, 1 rue Miollis, 75732 Paris CEDEX 15, France. T. +33145684850. Fax +33145684866. E-mail: info@imc-cim.org.
Pres address not obtained.
URL: http://www.imc-cim.org/

History 28 Jan 1949, Paris (France). Founded at the request of the Director-General of UNESCO. Statutes ratified 1950. Statutes revised: 2009, Tunis (Tunisia); 2013, Brisbane (Australia). **Aims** Promote access to music for all and the value of music in the lives of all peoples. **Structure** General Assembly (every 2 years); Executive Board; Permanent Secretariat in Paris (France). Regional Councils (3): *African Music Council (AMC, #00379)*; *European Music Council (EMC, #07837)*; *Consejo de le Música de las Tres Américas (COMTA, #04723).* **Languages** English, French, Spanish. **Finance** Sources: donations; fees for services; grants; members' dues; sponsorship. **Activities** Advocacy/lobbying/activism; awards/prizes/competitions; capacity building; events/meetings; knowledge management/information dissemination; politics/policy/regulatory; projects/programmes; research/documentation. **Events** *Biennial General Assembly* Paris (France) 2019, *World Forum on Music* Paris (France) 2019, *Biennial General Assembly* Paphos (Cyprus) 2017, *Biennial General Assembly* Rabat (Morocco) 2015, *International Rostrum of Composers* Tallinn (Estonia) 2015. **Publications** *IMC Music World News* (bi-weekly) – online newsletter; *IMC Newsflashes*; *President's Letter*.
Members National Music Councils; international and regional music organizations; national and specialized organizations; honorary (a total of 130 members worldwide). National Music Councils in 33 countries and territories:
Albania, Algeria, Argentina, Australia, Austria, Azerbaijan, Benin, Cameroon, China, Congo DR, Côte d'Ivoire, Czechia, Egypt, Estonia, Finland, Germany, Ghana, Hungary, Iraq, Israel, Italy, Jordan, Latvia, Monaco, Morocco, Palestine, Philippines, Poland, Russia, Switzerland, Ukraine, Uruguay, USA.
Organizations include the following 36 listed in this Yearbook:
- *Arab Academy of Music (AAM, #00890)*;
- *Arthur Rubinstein International Music Society (#01120)*;
- *Asia-Pacific Society for Ethnomusicology (APSE, #02036)*;
- *Asociación Latinoamericana de Conservatorios y Escuelas de Música (ALCEM, #02197)*;
- *Association Européenne des Conservatoires, Académies de Musique et Musikhochschulen (AEC, #02560)*;
- *Europäische Musikschul-Union (EMU, #05756)*;
- *European Association for Music in Schools (EAS, #06127)*;
- *European Choral Association – Europa Cantat (#06541)*;
- *European Composer and Songwriter Alliance (ECSA, #06691)*;
- *European Conference of Promoters of New Music (ECPNM, #06736)*;
- *European Early Music Network (EEMN, #06953)*;
- *European Federation of National Youth Orchestras (EFNYO, #07176)*;
- *European Festivals Association (EFA, #07242)*;
- *European Modern Music Education Network (EMMEN, #07811)*;
- *European Orchestra Federation (EOFed, #08092)*;
- *European Society for Ethnomusicology (#08598)*;
- *European String Teachers Association (ESTA, #08842)*;
- *European Union of Music Competitions for Youth (EMCY, #09003)*;
- *Europe Jazz Network (EJN, #09160)*;
- *IMZ International Music + Media Centre (#11139)*;
- *International Adkins Chiti: Women in Music Foundation (FACDIM)*;
- *International Association of Music Information Centres (IAMIC, #12041)*;
- *International Association of Music Libraries, Archives and Documentation Centres (IAML, #12042)*;
- *International Association of Schools of Jazz (IASJ, #12148)*;
- *International Confederation for Electroacoustic Music (ICEM, #12858)*;
- *International Confederation of Accordionists (ICA, #12841)*;
- *International Council of Organizations for Folklore Festivals and Folk Art (#13058)*;
- *International Federation for Choral Music (IFCM, #13388)*;
- *International Federation of Chopin Societies (IFCS, #13387)*;
- *International Federation of Musicians (#13486)*;
- *International Music Managers' Forum (IMMF, #14200)*;
- *International Music Products Association (NAMM)*;
- *International Society for Contemporary Music (ISCM, #15035)*;
- *International Society for Music Education (ISME, #15287)*;
- *Jeunesses Musicales International (JMI, #16110)*;
- *World Federation of International Music Competitions (WFIMC, #21445)*.

Consultative Status Consultative status granted from: *ECOSOC (#05331)* (Ros C); *UNESCO (#20322)* (Associate Status). **IGO Relations** Observer status with (1): *Convention on the Protection and Promotion of the Diversity of Cultural Expressions (2005).* [2022.10.13/XA2277/**y**/**A**]

♦ International Music Critics (#18488)
♦ International Music Institute, Darmstadt (internationally oriented national body)

♦ International Music Managers' Forum (IMMF) 14200

Exec Dir Val Ste Croix 3A, L-1371 Luxembourg, Luxembourg. E-mail: info@immf.com.
URL: http://www.immf.com/

History 1991. Registered in accordance with Luxembourg law. **Aims** Raise professional standards in management; help members develop management skills and knowledge of the music industry; provide networking and advocacy opportunities throughout the world. **Structure** Board, including Executive Officers. **Finance** Members' dues. Other sources: government grant; sponsorship. **Activities** Events/meetings; networking/liaising; training/education; advocacy/lobbying/activism. **Publications** *IMMF Newsletter*.
Members Full in 59 countries:
Angola, Argentina, Armenia, Australia, Austria, Belgium, Botswana, Brazil, Bulgaria, Canada, Chile, China, Colombia, Costa Rica, Croatia, Cuba, Czechia, Denmark, Ecuador, El Salvador, Estonia, Finland, France, Germany, Greece, Guatemala, Honduras, Hungary, India, Indonesia, Ireland, Italy, Japan, Latvia, Luxembourg, Malawi, Mexico, Namibia, Netherlands, New Zealand, Nicaragua, Nigeria, Norway, Panama, Paraguay, Peru, Poland, Portugal, Romania, Slovakia, South Africa, Spain, Sweden, Switzerland, Uganda, USA, Venezuela, Zambia, Zimbabwe.
Included in the above, 1 regional entity:
Asociación Latinoamericana de Managers Musicales (MMF Latam).
Consultative Status Consultative status granted from: *World Intellectual Property Organization (WIPO, #21593)* (Permanent Observer Status). **NGO Relations** Member of: *Copyright for Creativity (C4C, #04832)*; *European Music Council (EMC, #07837)*; *International Music Council (IMC, #14199)*; *Pro-music.* [2018/XF1131/**F**]

♦ International Musicological Society (IMS) 14201

Contact PO Box 1561, 4001 Basel BS, Switzerland. E-mail: office@musicology.org.
URL: http://www.musicology.org

History Sep 1927, Basel (Switzerland). 1st Congress: 1-6 Sep 1930, Liège (Belgium). Former names and other names: *Société internationale de musicologie (SIM)* – former; *Sociedad Internacional de Musicologia (SIM)* – former; *Internationale Gesellschaft für Musikwissenschaft (IGMW)* – former; *Società Internazionale di Musicologia (SIM)* – former. **Aims** Connect every musicologist to the world community of musicology by embracing the study of music in all its diversity; advance musicological research across the globe in a spirit of cooperation and collaboration. **Structure** General Assembly; Bureau; Directorium. **Languages** English. **Activities** Events/meetings. **Events** *Quinquennial Congress (IMS2027)* 2027, *Quinquennial Congress* Athens (Greece) 2022, *Biennial Conference of the IMS Regional Association for East Asia (IMSEA)* Daegu (Korea Rep) 2022, *Meeting* Daegu (Korea Rep) 2021, *Intercongressional Symposium* Lucerne (Switzerland) 2019. **Publications** *Acta Musicologica* (2 a year); *IMS Newsletter* in English. *IMS Musicological Brainfood* in English. **NGO Relations** Together with *International Association of Music Libraries, Archives and Documentation Centres (IAML, #12042)*, instrumental in setting up: *Répertoire international d'iconographie musicale (RIdIM, #18844)*; *Répertoire International de Littérature Musicale (RILM, #18845)*; *International Inventory of the Musical Press (RIPM)*; *International Inventory of Musical Sources (#13949).* [2022.06.14/XC2278/**C**]

♦ International Music Products Association (internationally oriented national body)
♦ International Music Publishers Association (inactive)

♦ International Music Therapy Assessment Consortium (IMTAC) 14202

Contact address not obtained.
Contact address not obtained.
URL: https://www.musictherapy.aau.dk/imtac/

Aims Develop, standardize and increase the implementation of assessment in music therapy. **Structure** Rotating Coordinating period. **Activities** Awareness raising; events/meetings; guidance/assistance/consulting; networking/liaising; research/documentation; standards/guidelines; training/education.
Members Full in 6 countries and territories:
Denmark, Faeroe Is, Finland, Germany, UK, USA. [2022/AA2684/**C**]

- ♦ International Muslim Association for Animals and Nature (inactive)
- ♦ International Muslim Organization for Woman and Family (unconfirmed)
- ♦ International Muslim Union (inactive)

♦ International Mycological Association (IMA) 14203

Association internationale de mycologie – Asociación Internacional Micológica – Internationale Mykologische Gesellschaft

Pres Curtin Medical School, Curtin Univ, Molecular Mycology Research Laboratory, Brand Drive, Bldg 308, Room 227, Bentley, WA 6102, Australia.
SG BIOTEC NSTDA, 113 Thailand Science Park, Phahonyothin Rd, Khlong Nueng Khlong Luang, Pathum Thani, 12120, Thailand.
Main: http://www.ima-mycology.org/

History 14 Sep 1971, Exeter (UK). Founded at 1st International Mycological Congress. Constitutes the Section for General Microbiology of *International Union of Biological Sciences (IUBS, #15760)*. Current statutes adopted 6 Aug 2010, Edinburgh (UK). Former names and other names: *International Mycological Society* – former. **Aims** Encourage all branches of mycology, in particular international aspects; represent mycological interests at international level; encourage liaison among national, regional and international bodies with mycological interests. **Structure** General Assembly (at International Mycological Congress); Executive Committee. *International Commission on the Taxonomy of Fungi (ICTF, #12734)*, founded 1982, is a joint commission of IMA and IUMS Division of Mycology. **Languages** English, French, German, Spanish. **Staff** Honorary. **Finance** Sources: contributions; donations; investments; members' dues; revenue from activities/projects. **Activities** Events/meetings; knowledge management/information dissemination. **Events** *International Mycological Congress* Maastricht (Netherlands) 2024, *International Mycological Congress* Amsterdam (Netherlands) 2022, *International Mycological Congress* San Juan (Puerto Rico) 2018, *International Mycological Congress* Bangkok (Thailand) 2014, *International Mycological Congress* Edinburgh (UK) 2010. **Publications** *IMA Fungus*; *IMA News*; *International Mycological Directory*. **Information Services** *MycoBank* – online database service to mycological and scientific society, documents mycological nomenclatural novelties (new names and combinations) and associated data.
Members Sustaining Member Mycological Organizations (SMMOs); Member Mycological Organizations (MMOs) – active affiliates, including national and international mycological organizations (13); Regional Member Mycological Organizations (RMMOs) for Africa, Asia, Europe, North America, Latin America and Australasia; individuals (mycologists). SMMOs and MMOs in 110 countries and territories:
Algeria, Argentina, Armenia, Australia, Austria, Azerbaijan, Bangladesh, Belgium, Bolivia, Botswana, Brazil, Bulgaria, Burundi, Cameroon, Canada, Chile, China, Colombia, Congo DR, Costa Rica, Croatia, Cuba, Czechia, Denmark, Djibouti, Egypt, Estonia, Ethiopia, Finland, France, Gabon, Germany, Ghana, Greece, Guatemala, Guinea, Honduras, Hong Kong, Hungary, Iceland, India, Indonesia, Iran Islamic Rep, Iraq, Ireland, Israel, Italy, Japan, Jordan, Kazakhstan, Kenya, Korea Rep, Kuwait, Latvia, Lesotho, Libya, Lithuania, Luxembourg, Malaysia, Mauritania, Mauritius, Mexico, Montenegro, Morocco, Nepal, Netherlands, New Zealand, Nicaragua, Nigeria, Norway, Pakistan, Papua New Guinea, Paraguay, Philippines, Poland, Portugal, Puerto Rico, Romania, Russia, Saudi Arabia, Senegal, Serbia, Sierra Leone, Singapore, Slovakia, Slovenia, Solomon Is, South Africa, Spain, Sri Lanka, Sudan, Sweden, Switzerland, Syrian AR, Taiwan, Thailand, Togo, Türkiye, Turkmenistan, Tuvalu, Uganda, UK, Ukraine, Uruguay, USA, Uzbekistan, Venezuela, Vietnam, Zambia, Zimbabwe.
Of the 6 affiliated societies, 1 international body listed in this Yearbook:
International Society for Mushroom Science (ISMS, #15286).
RMMOs in 6 countries:
Australia, Brazil, China, South Africa, Spain, UK.
NGO Relations Member of (2): *International Association of Botanical and Mycological Societies (IABMS, #11730)*; *International Society for Fungal Conservation (ISFC, #15134)* (as Council member). Cooperates with (1): *European Mycological Association (EMA, #07845)*. Affiliated with (1): *International Society for Plant Pathology (ISPP, #15371)*. [2023/XD4105/**B**]

- ♦ International Mycological Association Committee for Asia / see Asian Mycological Association (#01545)
- ♦ International Mycological Society / see International Mycological Association (#14203)

♦ International Myeloma Foundation (IMF) 14204

Pres/CEO 12650 Riverside Drive, Ste 206, Hollywood CA NORTH 91607-3421, USA. T. +18184877455. Fax +18184877454. E-mail: theimf@myeloma.org.
URL: http://www.myeloma.org/

History 1990, Los Angeles CA (USA). **Aims** Promote research in multiple myeloma; provide a broad spectrum of services for patients, physicians, nurses and family members and other concerned individuals regarding myeloma *treatment* and management. **Structure** Scientific Advisory Board of 76 members. Board of Directors of 15 members, including Chairman. **Languages** Arabic, Chinese, Czech, English, French, German, Hebrew, Italian, Japanese, Polish, Portuguese, Russian, Spanish, Turkish. **Finance** Donations. **Activities** Organizes educational seminars and congresses worldwide. Set up *'Nurse Leadership Board'*, 2006. **Events** *Annual Summit* Amsterdam (Netherlands) 2019, *Annual Summit* Stockholm (Sweden) 2018, *Annual Summit* Madrid (Spain) 2017, *Summit* Seoul (Korea Rep) 2017, *Annual Summit* Copenhagen (Denmark) 2016. **Publications** *Myeloma Today* (4 a year). *Understanding Series*. *Concise Review of the Disease and Treatment Options* by Brian G M Durie; *Patient Handbook*. Brochures; tip cards. Information Services: Internet Discussion Group. **Members** Full (over 185,000) in 113 countries. Membership countries not specified. **NGO Relations** *International Myeloma Society (IMS, #14205)*. [2018/XF2995/f/**F**]

♦ International Myeloma Society (IMS) 14205

Contact address not obtained. E-mail: adminassistant@myelomasociety.org.
URL: https://www.myelomasociety.org/

History 2010. **Aims** Bring together clinical and experimental scientists involved in the study of myeloma. **Structure** Board of Directors. **Languages** English. **Staff** 1.00 FTE, voluntary. **Finance** Sources: members' dues. **Events** *International Myeloma Workshop* Vienna (Austria) 2021, *International Myeloma Workshop* Boston, MA (USA) 2019, *International Myeloma Workshop* Delhi (India) 2017, *International Myeloma Workshop* Rome (Italy) 2015, *International Myeloma Workshop* Kyoto (Japan) 2013.
Members Members in 29 countries and territories:
Argentina, Australia, Austria, Belgium, Brazil, Canada, Chile, China, Czechia, Denmark, France, Germany, Greece, Iceland, India, Ireland, Israel, Italy, Japan, Korea Rep, Netherlands, New Zealand, Norway, Spain, Sweden, Switzerland, Taiwan, UK, USA.
NGO Relations Affiliates include: *International Myeloma Foundation (IMF, #14204)*; national societies and foundations. [2021/XJ6327/**C**]

♦ International MYOPAIN Society (IMS) 14206

Contact 1722 Venus Avenue, Arden Hills MN 55112, USA. T. +16128609661. E-mail: info@myopain.org.
URL: http://www.myopain.org/

History Aug 1995, San Antonio, TX (USA). Aug 1995, San Antonia TX (USA). **Aims** Promote communication, education and research regarding soft tissue *pain* syndromes, fibromyalgia syndrome and myofacial pain syndrome. **Structure** Board of Directors, including President, Vice-President, Secretary-Treasurer and Chairman. **Languages** English. **Staff** 2.00 FTE, paid. **Finance** Members' dues. **Events** *Symposium* Padua (Italy) 2023, *Symposium* Padua (Italy) 2022, *World Congress on Myofacial Pain and Fibromyalgia* Bangalore (India) 2017, *World Congress on Myofacial Pain and Fibromyalgia* Seattle, WA (USA) 2013, *World Congress on Myofacial Pain and Fibromyalgia* Toledo (Spain) 2010. **Publications** *Journal of Musculoskeletal Pain*.
Members Regular; sponsor. Members in 40 countries and territories:
Argentina, Australia, Austria, Belgium, Brazil, Canada, China, Colombia, Denmark, Finland, France, Germany, Greece, Hong Kong, India, Ireland, Israel, Italy, Japan, Korea Rep, Mexico, Netherlands, New Zealand, Northern Mariana Is, Norway, Peru, Portugal, Russia, Saudi Arabia, Singapore, South Africa, Spain, Sweden, Switzerland, Taiwan, Türkiye, UK, USA, Venezuela, Virgin Is UK. [2022/XD9379/**D**]

- ♦ International Myopia Conference (meeting series)
- ♦ International Myopia Institute (unconfirmed)
- ♦ International Myositis Assessment & Clinical Studies Group (unconfirmed)
- ♦ International NaB Golf Association (internationally oriented national body)
- ♦ International Nacra Class Racing Association / see International Nacra F18 Class Association
- ♦ International Nacra F18 Class Association (internationally oriented national body)

♦ International Naikan Association (INA) 14207

Exec Chair Europe c/o Neue Welt Institut, Breitergasse 6, 2620 Neunkirchen, Austria. E-mail: nwi@naikan.com – ina@naikan.com.
URL: http://www.naikan-association.org/

History 1991. **Aims** Promote the Naikan method of *psychotherapy* and *self-development* through observation of the inner *self* to discover own possibilities and inner potentials, expressed via increased intelligence, flexibility and *joy* of living, to discover meaning of living and to reestablish the base for *motivation*. **Languages** English, German, Japanese. **Activities** Events/meetings. **Events** *Congress* Sankt Oswald (Germany) 2016, *Congress* Dresden (Germany) 2014, *Congress* Tokyo (Japan) 2013, *Congress* Shanghai (China) 2010, *Congress* Dresden (Germany) 2009. [2017.03.13/XE2245/**E**]

♦ International Nannoplankton Association (INA) 14208

Membership Sec-Treas Inst für Geowissenschaften, Christian-Albrechts-Uni, Ludewig-Meyn-Str 10, 24118 Kiel, Germany. T. +491781422010.
URL: http://ina.tmsoc.org/

History 1977. **Aims** Enhance communication between academic and industrial scientists working on calcareous nannofossils and living coccolithophores. **Structure** Council. **Languages** English. **Staff** Voluntary. **Finance** Members' dues. Budget (annual): US$ 6,000. **Events** *Conference* Bohol (Philippines) 2015, *International Conference* Porto (Portugal) 2013, *Biennial Conference / Conference* Reston, VA (USA) 2013, *Biennial conference / Conference* Yamagata (Japan) 2010, *Biennial conference / Conference* Lyon (France) 2008. **Publications** *Journal of Nannoplankton Research* (2 a year). Conference proceedings.
Members Organizations in 13 countries:
Australia, Austria, Croatia, France, Germany, Hungary, India, Indonesia, Nigeria, Slovakia, Switzerland, UK, USA.
Individuals in 46 countries:
Argentina, Australia, Austria, Belgium, Brazil, Brunei Darussalam, Bulgaria, Canada, China, Czechia, Denmark, Egypt, France, Georgia, Germany, Ghana, Greece, Hungary, India, Iran Islamic Rep, Israel, Italy, Japan, Lebanon, Libya, Mexico, Netherlands, New Zealand, Nigeria, Norway, Pakistan, Philippines, Portugal, Romania, Russia, Slovakia, Slovenia, Spain, Sweden, Switzerland, Tunisia, UK, Ukraine, USA, Venezuela, Vietnam.
NGO Relations Affiliated with: *Micropalaeontology Society, The (TMS, #16749)*. [2015/XD4985/**D**]

♦ The International NanoScience Community (TINC) 14209

Creator address not obtained. E-mail: editor@nanopaprika.eu.
URL: http://www.nanopaprika.eu/

History 2007. An online social networking community. **Structure** Science and Advisory Board. **Events** *International conference of nanotechology in medicine and biology* Krems (Austria) 2009.
Members Individuals (over 6,000) in 66 countries and territories:
Argentina, Australia, Austria, Azerbaijan, Bangladesh, Belgium, Brazil, Canada, Chile, China, Colombia, Costa Rica, Czechia, Denmark, Ecuador, Egypt, Estonia, Ethiopia, France, Germany, Greece, Hong Kong, Hungary, India, Indonesia, Iran Islamic Rep, Iraq, Ireland, Israel, Italy, Kazakhstan, Korea Rep, Luxembourg, Malaysia, Mexico, Morocco, Namibia, Nepal, Netherlands, Nigeria, Pakistan, Palestine, Peru, Philippines, Poland, Portugal, Romania, Russia, Saudi Arabia, Serbia, Singapore, Slovenia, South Africa, Spain, Sudan, Sweden, Switzerland, Syrian AR, Taiwan, Tunisia, Türkiye, UK, Ukraine, United Arab Emirates, USA, Vietnam. [2013/XJ1461/**F**]

- ♦ International Nanoscience Student Conference (meeting series)

♦ International NanoSPD Steering Committee 14210

Chair Inst of Physics of Advanced Materials, Ufa State Aviation Technical Univ, 12 K Marx St, Ufa BASHKORTOSTAN, Russia, 450008. T. +73472733422.
URL: http://www.NanoSPD.org/

History Set up Dec 2002, Vienna (Austria), at 2nd International Conference on Nanomaterials by Severe Plastic Deformation (NanoSPD2). **Aims** Coordinate research efforts in NanoSPD; provide a platform for the exchange of ideas and information relating to all aspects of the nanoSPD field; introduce and discuss the terminology applied in this field of science and *engineering*. **Structure** Committee. **Languages** English. **Staff** No official staff. **Finance** No financing. **Events** *International Conference on Nanomaterials by Severe Plastic Deformation* Sydney, NSW (Australia) 2017, *International Conference on Nanomaterials by Severe Plastic Deformation* Metz (France) 2014, *Conference* Nanjing (China) 2011, *Conference* Goslar (Germany) 2008, *Conference* Fukuoka (Japan) 2005. **Publications** Conference proceedings.
Members Individuals in 10 countries:
Australia, Austria, Brazil, China, Germany, Japan, Korea Rep, Russia, UK, USA. [2018.08.29/XJ6971/**E**]

♦ International Napoleonic Society (INS) 14211

Société napoléonnienne internationale

Admin Dir 2875 Chemin Bates, Montréal QC H3S 1B7, Canada. E-mail: ins@napoleonicsociety.com.
Pres 81 Navy Wharf Court, Ste 3315, Toronto ON M5V 3S2, Canada.
URL: http://www.napoleonicsociety.com/

History 1995, Canada. Founded on the initiative of Ben Weider (1924-2008). **Aims** Promote better understanding of the Napoleonic Era (1769 – 1821). **Structure** President; Committees. **Languages** English, French. **Finance** Private funds. **Events** *International Napoleonic Congress* Cork (Ireland) 2022, *International Napoleonic Congress* Warsaw (Poland) 2020, *International Napoleonic Congress* Grenoble (France) 2019, *International Napoleonic Congress* Vienna (Austria) 2018, *International Napoleonic Congress* Dublin (Ireland) 2016. **Publications** *Napoleonic Scholarship* – online.
Members Fellows in 43 countries:
Australia, Austria, Belarus, Belgium, Bulgaria, Canada, Chile, Colombia, Cuba, Czechia, Egypt, Finland, France, Georgia, Germany, Hungary, India, Ireland, Israel, Italy, Kazakhstan, Lebanon, Luxembourg, Malta, Mexico, Monaco, Mongolia, Netherlands, Pakistan, Palestine, Panama, Poland, Portugal, Romania, Russia, Slovakia, South Africa, Spain, Sweden, Switzerland, Syrian AR, UK, USA. [2022/XN8843/v/**E**]

- ♦ International Narcotic and Antiterrorist Enforcement Officers Association (internationally oriented national body)
- ♦ International Narcotic Enforcement Officers Association (internationally oriented national body)

♦ International Narcotics Control Board (INCB) 14212

Organe international de contrôle des stupéfiants (OICS) – Junta Internacional de Fiscalización de Estupefacientes (JIFE)

Sec Vienna International Centre, PO Box 500, 1400 Vienna, Austria. T. +431260600. Fax +431260605867 – +431260605868. E-mail: incb.secretariat@un.org.
URL: http://www.incb.org/

History 1968. Established under *Single Convention on Narcotic Drugs, 1961 (1961)*, which entered into force 13 Dec 1964, in accordance with resolution 1106 (XL) of ECOSOC, enacted under the authority of Article 45 of the Convention. Replaced the *Permanent Central Narcotics Board* and *Drug Supervisory Body* created by *International Opium Convention, 1925 (1925)*, and *Convention for Limiting the Manufacture and Regulating the Distribution of Narcotic Drugs (1931)* of 1931, respectively. Exercised the functions of these bodies in respect of countries party to the earlier narcotics treaties and not yet party to the Single Convention. As between Parties, the Single Convention replaces other multilateral treaties concerning narcotic drugs except the *Convention for the Suppression of the Illicit Traffic in Dangerous Drugs, 1936 (1936)*. The Single Convention on Narcotic Drugs, 1961, as amended by *Protocol Amending the Single Convention on Narcotic Drugs (1972)* 1961, entered into force on 8 Aug 1975. The *Convention on Psychotropic Substances (1971)*, signed 21 Feb 1971, Vienna (Austria), entered into force 16 Aug 1976, ensures the international control of this type of drug. The *United Nations Convention against Illicit Traffic in Narcotic Drugs and Psychotropic Substances (1988)*, 1988, entered into force 11 Nov 1990, entrusted the Board with new functions in the control of precursor chemicals used in the illicit manufacture of narcotic drugs and psychotropic substances. **Aims** Monitor and promote the implementation of the international drug control conventions; monitor global licit production, manufacture, trade in and use of narcotic drugs and psychotropic substances; monitor

precursor chemicals and assess substances for possible modification of the scope of control of Tables I and II of the 1988 Convention. **Structure** Board (meeting as often as necessary, usually 3 times a year, in Vienna, Austria) comprises 13 individuals elected in their personal capacity by ECOSOC, 3 from candidates nominated by WHO and 10 from a list of persons nominated by UN member states or states party to the Single Convention. Secretariat is administratively part of *United Nations Office on Drugs and Crime (UNODC, #20596)* and structured into 5 sections: Office of the Secretary; Convention Evaluation; Narcotics Control and Estimates; Psychotropics Control; Precursors Control. Based at: *Vienna International Centre (VIC)*. **Languages** Arabic, Chinese, English, French, Russian, Spanish. **Staff** Secretariat is an administrative entity of UNODC. **Finance** Regular budget of the United Nations. **Activities** Events/meetings; management of treaties and agreements; monitoring/evaluation; politics/policy/regulatory. Manages the following treaties/agreements: *Convention on Psychotropic Substances (1971)*; *Single Convention on Narcotic Drugs, 1961 (1961)*; *United Nations Convention against Illicit Traffic in Narcotic Drugs and Psychotropic Substances (1988)*. **Events** *Session* Vienna (Austria) 2022, *Session* Vienna (Austria) 2022, *Session* Vienna (Austria) 2021, *Session* Vienna (Austria) 2021, *Session* Vienna (Austria) 2021. **Publications** *Precursors and Chemicals Frequently Used in the Illicit Manufacture of Narcotic Drugs and Psychotropic Substances* (annual) – report; *Narcotic Drugs: Estimated World Requirements and Statistics* (annual) – report; *Psychotropic Substances: Statistics and Assessments of Medical and Scientific Requirements* (annual) – report; *Report of the International Narcotics Control Board* (annual); *Availability of Internationally Controlled Drugs* – theological journal.
Members As of 2022, members in 12 countries serving in their personal capacities. Term expiry date, eve of the May session of the year in parentheses:
Australia (2027), China (2027), France (2025), India (2025), Madagascar (2027), Morocco (2025), Netherlands (2027), Paraguay (2025), Russia (2027), South Africa (2025), Türkiye (2027), USA (2027).
IGO Relations Cooperates with (2): *United Nations Office on Drugs and Crime (UNODC, #20596)*; *WHO (#20950)*. Administrative and functional relationship with: Secretary-General of *ECOSOC (#05331)* and its Commission on Narcotic Drugs; *United Nations (UN, #20515)*; UN General Assembly.
[2022.11.10/XE2279/**E***]

♦ International Narcotics Research Conference (INRC) 14213

Information Officer OSU-Ctr for Health Sci, 1111 W 17th St, Tulsa OK 74107-1898, USA. T. +19185618234. Fax +19185618276.
URL: http://www.inrcworld.org/
Aims Advance science relating to all aspects of opioid research primarily by providing an international forum where there can be exchanges of information among interested scientists from different disciplines. **Structure** Board of Trustees. **Activities** Events/meetings. **Events** *Meeting* New York, NY (USA) 2019, *Meeting* San Diego, CA (USA) 2018, *Meeting* Chicago, IL (USA) 2017, *Meeting* Bath (UK) 2016. [2017/XM5397/cv/**E**]

♦ International National Trusts Organisation (INTO) 14214

Secretariat 20 Grosvenor Gardens, London, SW1W 0DH, UK. T. +442078247157. E-mail: info@into.org.
URL: https://www.into.org/
History Registration: Charity, No/ID: 1175994, England and Wales. **Aims** Promote the conservation and enhancement of the heritage of all nations for the benefit of the people of the world and future generations. **Structure** Board of Trustees; Secretariat. **Activities** Awards/prizes/competitions; events/meetings; projects/programmes; training/education. **Events** *INTO Dundee Conference* Dundee (UK) 2022, *Conference* 2021, *Conference* Hamilton (Bermuda) 2019, *Conference* Cambridge (UK) 2015, *Conference* Entebbe (Uganda) 2013.
Members Full in 33 countries and territories:
Australia, Barbados, Belgium, Bermuda, Canada, Cayman Is, China, Falklands/Malvinas, Fiji, Grenada, Guernsey, India, Indonesia, Ireland, Jersey, Kenya, Korea Rep, Malaysia, Malta, Montserrat, Netherlands, Russia, Slovakia, Sri Lanka, St Helena, St Lucia, Taiwan, Tanzania UR, Thailand, Uganda, UK, USA, Zimbabwe.
Associate in 16 countries and territories:
Bahrain, Czechia, Ethiopia, France, India, Italy, Japan, Kenya, Korea Rep, Malta, New Zealand, Russia, Senegal, South Africa, Taiwan, Uganda.
Regional Associate member:
Europa Nostra (#05767).
NGO Relations Member of (2): *Building Understanding through International Links for Development (BUILD)*; *European Heritage Alliance 3.3 (#07477)*. Partner of (1): *Global Call for Climate Action (GCCA, inactive)*.
[2022.10.19/XJ1047/**C**]

♦ International Natural Fiber Organization (INFO) 14215

Contact Alexanderstr 6, 2713 AT Zoetermeer, Netherlands. T. +31793169531. E-mail: info@naturalfibersinfo.org.
URL: http://www.naturalfibersinfo.org/
Aims Reduce *poverty* through *livelihood* development; develop the fiber value chain; build awareness; contribute to sustainability. **Structure** Officers. **Activities** Advocacy/lobbying/activism; awareness raising.
Members Active in 7 countries:
Bangladesh, Brazil, India, Malaysia, Philippines, Sri Lanka, Tanzania UR. [2017/XM5726/**C**]

♦ International Natural Gums Association for Research (inactive)
♦ International Natural Hazards Society / see International Society for the Prevention and Mitigation of Natural Hazards (#15386)
♦ International Natural Rubber Agreement (1979 treaty)
♦ International Natural Rubber Agreement, 1995 (1995 treaty)
♦ International Natural Rubber Agreement on Price Stabilisation (1976 treaty)
♦ International Natural Rubber Organization (inactive)

♦ International Natural Sausage Casing Association (INSCA) 14216

Exec Dir 136 Galal El Dessouky St. – Suite 703, Waboor El Maya, Alexandria, 21500, Egypt. T. +201223173612. Fax +2035414158. E-mail: insca@insca.org.
URL: http://www.insca.org/
History 1965. **Structure** Board of Directors, comprising Chairman, Vice Chairman, 9 Directors, Treasurer, Secretary, Legal Counselor, Vice Presidents/Committee Chairs and Accountant. **Finance** Members' dues. **Activities** Organizes annual and semi-annual meetings. **Events** *Annual Meeting* Berlin (Germany) 2019, *Annual Meeting* Madrid (Spain) 2016, *Meeting* Dublin (Ireland) 2013, *Annual meeting* Frankfurt-Main (Germany) 2013, *Meeting* San Diego, CA (USA) 2012. **Publications** *Natural Link Newsletter* (4 a year); *Members Directory* (annual); *Yearbook* (annual).
Members Regular; Associate associations (over 200) in 34 countries:
Argentina, Australia, Austria, Belgium, Brazil, Canada, China, Croatia, Denmark, Egypt, Finland, France, Germany, Hungary, Ireland, Italy, Japan, Mongolia, Netherlands, New Zealand, Norway, Pakistan, Poland, Romania, Russia, South Africa, Spain, Sweden, Switzerland, Türkiye, UK, Ukraine, Uruguay, USA.
NGO Relations Associate member of: *European Natural Sausage Casings Association (ENSCA, #07854)*.
[2008.09.29/XD7626/**D**]

♦ International Natural Textile Association 14217

Association international du textile naturel – Internationaler Verband der Naturtextilwirtschaft (IVN) – Associazione Internazionale del Tessile Naturale
Contact Chemnitzer Strasse 229, 12621 Berlin, Germany. T. +493055616075. Fax +493055648081. E-mail: info@naturtextil.com.
URL: http://www.naturtextil.org/
History Founded Jan 1999, Wiesbaden (Germany). Also referred to in English a *International Association for Natural Textile Industry*. **Events** *Far beyond organic symposium* Berlin (Germany) 2010, *International conference on organic textiles* Düsseldorf (Germany) 2002. **NGO Relations** Member of: *Global Organic Textile Standard International Working Group (GOTS, #10515)*. [2015/XD8187/**D**]

♦ International Natural Zeolite Association (INZA) 14218

Sec/Treas Indiana Univ Molecular Structure Center, Chemistry Bldg A421, 800 E Kirkwood Ave, Bloomington IN 47405-7102, USA. T. +18128552039.
URL: https://www.inza.it/
History 2005. Founded evolving from the ad hoc *International Committee on Natural Zeolites (ICNZ)*, set up Jun 1976, Tucson AZ (USA). Current by-laws adopted Jul 2006. **Aims** Promote and encourage interest in natural zeolite materials throughout the scientific and technical community. **Structure** Executive Committee; Standing Committees. **Languages** English. **Staff** Voluntary. **Finance** Sources: donations; revenue from activities/projects; sale of publications. **Activities** Awards/prizes/competitions; events/meetings; publishing activities; research and development. **Events** *International Conference on the Occurence, Properties and Utilization of Natural Zeolites* Ischia (Italy) 2022, *International Conference on the Occurence, Properties and Utilization of Natural Zeolites* Krakow (Poland) 2018, *EUROCLAY : International Conference on Clay Science and Technology* Edinburgh (UK) 2015, *Quadrennial International Conference on the Occurence, Properties and Utilization of Natural Zeolites* Belgrade (Serbia) 2014, *Quadrennial international conference on the occurence, properties and utilization of natural zeolites* Sofia (Bulgaria) 2010.
Members Individuals and companies in 39 countries:
Armenia, Australia, Austria, Belgium, Brazil, Bulgaria, Canada, China, Croatia, Cuba, Ecuador, Ethiopia, Finland, France, Germany, Greece, Hungary, India, Iran Islamic Rep, Italy, Japan, Kazakhstan, Korea Rep, Mexico, Mongolia, Nigeria, Philippines, Poland, Portugal, Romania, Russia, Saudi Arabia, Serbia, Slovakia, Spain, Sweden, Türkiye, UK, USA.
IGO Relations None. [2022.10.17/XJ0877/**D**]

♦ International Nature Farming Research Center (internationally oriented national body)

♦ International Naturist Federation (INF) 14219

Fédération naturiste internationale (FNI) – Internationale Naturisten-Föderation
Pres Eduard Nittnerstrasse 14/6, 4063 Hörsching, Austria. E-mail: president@inf-fni.org – naturism@inf-fni.org.
Vice-Pres/Sec Bd Robert Schuman 68, OLM, L-8340 Luxembourg, Luxembourg. T. +352309893. E-mail: vicepresident@inf-fni.org.
URL: http://www.inf-fni.org/
History 22 Aug 1953, Montalivet-les-Bains (France). Statutes amended: 1954, 1956, 1964, 1980, 1984, 1986, 2004, 2008, 2012, 2014, 2016. Registration: No/ID: 334261452, Austria, Linz-Land. **Aims** Facilitate mutual relations and afford a medium for study of all questions affecting the naturist movement; aid in development of friendly contact between naturists of all countries; promote mental and physical health. **Structure** Congress (every 2 years); Central Committee; Executive Committee. **Languages** English, French, German. **Staff** 2.00 FTE, paid. Voluntary. **Finance** Sources: members' dues. **Activities** Events/meetings; knowledge management/information dissemination; networking/liaising. **Events** *Biennial World Congress* Luxembourg (Luxembourg) 2022, *Biennial World Congress* Banovci (Slovenia) 2021, *Biennial World Congress* Banovci (Slovenia) 2020, *Biennial World Congress* Lisbon (Portugal) 2018, *Biennial World Congress* Upper Hutt (New Zealand) 2016. **Publications** *Focus*; *INF World Handbook of Naturism*. Booklets based on an international experience in various naturist subjects.
Members Federations in 38 countries:
Argentina, Australia, Austria, Belgium, Brazil, Bulgaria, Canada, Congo Brazzaville, Croatia, Czechia, Denmark, Dominican Rep, Finland, France, Germany, Hungary, Ireland, Israel, Italy, Liechtenstein, Luxembourg, Malaysia, Mexico, Netherlands, Norway, Poland, Portugal, Romania, Russia, Serbia, Slovakia, Slovenia, South Africa, Spain, Sweden, Switzerland, Thailand, UK.
[2021.06.18/XC2280/y/**C**]

♦ International Naturist Organization for Esperanto (INOE) 14220

Organisation naturiste espérantiste internationale – Internacia Naturista Organizo Esperantista (INOE)
Treas Fő u 41/5, Ihasz 8531, Hungary. T. +36205183169.
Pres Viking Photography Inc, PO Box 22159, San Francisco CA 94122, USA.
URL: http://www.esperanto-naturismo.org/
History 1961. Reorganized 1978. **Aims** Disseminate ideas of naturists in Esperantist circles and promote use of Esperanto in naturist circles. **Structure** Principal Convention elects: Committee (Estraro), comprising President, Vice-President, Secretary and Treasurer, Journal Editor and Members; Larger Committee (Komitato), comprising Committee and helpers. Sections (2): Fakoj (neutral); Frakcioj (non-neutral). National representatives. **Languages** Esperanto. **Staff** 2.00 FTE, voluntary. **Finance** Sources: members' dues. **Activities** Principal Convention within the framework of the Universal Congress of Esperanto organized by UEA; non-official meetings. **Events** *Annual Convention* Adelaide, SA (Australia) 1997, *Annual Convention* Prague (Czech Rep) 1996, *Annual Convention* Tampere (Finland) 1995, *Annual Convention* Seoul (Korea Rep) 1994, *Annual Convention* Valencia (Spain) 1993. **Publications** *Naturista Vivo* (4 a year).
Members Individuals in 24 countries:
Austria, Belgium, Brazil, Croatia, Czechia, Denmark, Estonia, France, Germany, Greece, Hungary, Italy, Japan, Korea Rep, Lithuania, Netherlands, Norway, Poland, Russia, Spain, Sweden, Switzerland, UK, USA.
NGO Relations Member of: *Universal Esperanto Association (UEA, #20676)*. [2020/XD1809/v/**C**]

♦ International Naval Research Organization (INRO) 14221

Organisation internationale de recherches navales
Main Office PO Box 48, Holden MA 01520-0048, USA. T. +15088866025. E-mail: warshipinternational@gmail.com.
URL: http://www.warship.org/
History 1963, as *'Naval Records Club'*. Present name adopted 1976. **Aims** Provide information and a means of contact for those interested in *warships*. **Staff** Voluntary. **Finance** Members' dues. Donations. **Activities** Encourages the study of naval vessels and their histories, principally in the era of iron and steel warships (about 1860 to date). **Publications** *Warship International* (4 a year).
Members Organizations and individuals (more than 3,000) – mostly in USA – in 53 countries and territories:
Australia, Austria, Barbados, Belgium, Brazil, Canada, Chile, Colombia, Czechia, Denmark, Ecuador, Finland, France, Germany, Greece, Guatemala, Hong Kong, Hungary, India, Ireland, Israel, Italy, Japan, Latvia, Malaysia, Malta, Mexico, Monaco, Montenegro, Netherlands, New Zealand, Norway, Philippines, Poland, Portugal, Puerto Rico, Russia, Saudi Arabia, Serbia, Singapore, South Africa, Spain, Sweden, Switzerland, Taiwan, Thailand, Türkiye, UK, Ukraine, United Arab Emirates, Uruguay, USA, Venezuela. [2020/XF5503/**F**]

♦ International Navigation Association / see PIANC (#18371)

♦ International Needs (IN) 14222

Contact Unit 210, 4031 Fairview St, Burlington ON L7L 2A4, Canada. T. +19056379411. E-mail: office@innetwork.org – info@internationalneeds.ca.
Contact PO Box 1165, Tauranga 3140, New Zealand. T. +6475786198. E-mail: director@internationalneeds.org.nz.
URL: http://www.innetwork.org/
History 1974. Former names and other names: *Council of International Needs* – former; *Council of International Needs Network* – former; *IN Network (IN)* – alias. Registration: Charitable Society, New Zealand. **Aims** Connect Christian partners in effective evangelism, discipleship and community development. **Finance** Annual budget: 3,000,000 USD. **Activities** Church planting and evangelism; discipleship and leadership training; community development. **Events** *Quadrennial convocation* Kampala (Uganda) 2006, *Quadrennial convocation* Prague (Czech Rep) 2002, *Quadrennial convocation* Jerusalem (Israel) 1998. **Publications** *IN Global Update* (4 a year).
Members Global Partners in 17 countries:
Bangladesh, Canada, Colombia, Czechia, Egypt, Ghana, India, Nepal, New Zealand, Philippines, Romania, Slovakia, Sri Lanka, Uganda, UK, USA, Zambia.
Associate in 11 countries:
Australia, Congo DR, Dominican Rep, Ethiopia, Kenya, Mali, Netherlands, Papua New Guinea, Switzerland, Türkiye, Vietnam.
NGO Relations Associate Member of: *World Evangelical Alliance (WEA, #21393)*. [2010.06.01/XG6144/**F**]

♦ International Neo-Malthusian Correspondence and Resistance Bureau (inactive)

♦ International Neonatal Consortium (INC) 14223

Project Manager C-Path Main Office, 1730 E River Rd, Tucson AZ 85718, USA. T. +15205473440. Fax +15205473456. E-mail: info@c-path.org.
URL: http://c-path.org/programs/inc/
History 19 May 2015. Founded as a consortium of *Critical Path Institute*. **Aims** Accelerate the development of safe and effective therapies for neonates. **Events** *Scientific Meeting* Washington, DC (USA) 2022. **Publications** *INC News*.
Members Academic Institutions in 13 countries:
Belgium, Canada, Estonia, France, Germany, Ireland, Italy, Japan, Korea Rep, Latvia, Netherlands, UK, USA.

Government and regulatory agencies in 8 countries:
Australia, Canada, France, Japan, Korea Rep, New Zealand, Norway, USA.
Included in the above, 1 organization listed in this Yearbook:
Patient and nurse advocacy organizations include 1 organization listed in this Yearbook:
Pharmaceutical industry. Membership countries not specified. [2022/XM6223/E]

♦ International Neonatology Association (INA) 14224

Main Office c/o Paragon Group, Av Louis-Casai 18, 5th Floor, 1209 Geneva, Switzerland. T. +41225330948. Fax +41225802953. E-mail: secretariat@worldneonatology.com – info@worldneonatology.org.
URL: http://worldneonatology.com/

Aims Promote high quality care for neonates and their families; decrease health disparities; improve neonatal outcomes globally. **Structure** Governing Board; Standing Committee. **Languages** English. **Activities** Events/meetings; knowledge management/information dissemination. **Events** *Conference (INAC)* Dublin (Ireland) 2023, *Conference (INAC)* Dubai (United Arab Emirates) 2022, *Dubai International Pediatric Conference* Dubai (United Arab Emirates) 2019, *Conference* Tijuana (Mexico) 2019, *Conference* Ghent (Belgium) 2018. **Publications** *INA Newsletter* (4 a year). **Members** National societies; individuals (where no national societies exist). Membership countries not specified. [2022/XJ7429/C]

♦ International Nepal Fellowship (internationally oriented national body)
♦ International Netball Federation / see World Netball (#21668)

♦ International Network for the Abolition of Foreign Military Bases (No Bases) 14225

Address not obtained.

History Mar 2007, Quito (Ecuador). **Aims** Close foreign military bases around the world; help local groups share experiences; provide support to local efforts; conduct research in the field. [2010/XM2833/F]

♦ International Network for Academic Steiner Teacher Education (INASTE) 14226

Contact Zentrum für Kultur und Pädagogik, Tilgnstr 3, 1040 Vienna, Austria. T. +4315048483. E-mail: office@inaste-network.com.
URL: https://www.inaste-network.com/

History Originating from a symposium, held 2007, Vienna (Austria), with subsequent symposiums held 2008, Vienna and 2009, Krems (Austria), when Krems Declaration was reached. Krems Protocol signed Jan 2010, Krems (Austria). Current title adopted when membership expanded beyond Europe. Former names and other names: *European Network for Academic Steiner Teacher Education (ENASTE)* – former (2011 to 2017); *Europäische Hochschulkonferenz für Waldorfpädagogik* – former (2010 to 2011). **Aims** Promote cooperation among universities and educational institutes offering academic accreditation for Waldorf teacher education programmes to strengthen their position in educational policy making; support other Waldorf education programs which are working to achieve academic accreditation. **Languages** English, German. **Activities** Research/documentation; events/meetings. **Events** *Realizing Humanity* Vienna (Austria) 2021, *Congress* Vienna (Austria) 2020, *Congress* Vienna (Austria) 2015, *Congress* Vienna (Austria) 2013, *Congress* Vienna (Austria) 2011. **Publications** *RoSE – Research on Steiner Education* – special issues. Congress papers; studies.
Members Schools in 13 countries and territories:
Austria, Brazil, France, Germany, Hungary, Israel, Netherlands, New Zealand, Norway, Sweden, Switzerland, Taiwan, USA.
Associated organizations (2) listed in this Yearbook:
European Council for Steiner Waldorf Education (ECSWE, #06844). [2021/XJ8282/y/F]

♦ International Network of Accountants and Auditors / see INAA Group (#11140)

♦ International Network for Acid Prevention (INAP) 14227

Admin 2105 Oneida St, Salt Lake City UT 84109, USA. T. +18014852279.
URL: http://www.inap.com.au/

History Apr 1998. Launched Oct 1998. **Aims** Work towards reducing liabilities associated with sulphide mine materials. **Structure** Board of Directors; Operating Committee. **Finance** Members' dues. **Activities** Provides central coordination for the *International Conference on Acid Rock Drainage (ICARD)*. *Global Alliance* organized on a Statement of Mutual Intent provides cooperation and information sharing opportunities for partner organizations. **Events** *ICARD : Triennial International Conference on Acid Rock Drainage / ICARD* Ottawa, ON (Canada) 2012, *ICARD : triennial international conference on acid rock drainage / ICARD* Skellefteå (Sweden) 2009, *ICARD : triennial international conference on acid rock drainage* St Louis, MO (USA) 2006, *ICARD : triennial international conference on acid rock drainage / ICARD* Cairns, QLD (Australia) 2003, *ICARD : triennial international conference on acid rock drainage / ICARD* Denver, CO (USA) 2000. **Publications** *INAP Newsletter* (4 a year). **Members** Mining companies (7). Membership countries not specified. **NGO Relations** Partners: *Partnership for Acid Drainage Remediation in Europe (PADRE, see: #14168)*; national organizations. [2014/XJ3607/F]

♦ International Network of Address Research (unconfirmed)
♦ International Network of Administrations and Research Organisms Involved in the Plant Conservation in Europe / see Planta Europa (#18388)

♦ International Network of Affiliated Ports (INAP) 14228

Contact Kochi Prefectural Govt, Port Promotion Div, 1-2-20 Marunouchi, Kochi, 780-8570 Japan. T. +81888239888. Fax +81888239657. E-mail: 175201@ken.pref.kochi.lg.jp.
URL: http://www.pref.kochi.lg.jp/soshiki/175201/inap50.html

Aims Promote consultation, cooperation and exchange of information on expertise, know-how and marketing, planning, technology, technical skills and overall developments of ports and any other matters of mutual interest to ports. **Events** *General Assembly* Mokpo (Korea Rep) 2015, *Meeting* Kochi (Japan) 2013, *General Assembly* Mokpo (Korea Rep) 2009, *General assembly and symposium* Kochi (Japan) 2007. [2013.07.19/XJ0126/F]

♦ International Network Against Cyber Hate (INACH) 14229

Address not obtained.
URL: http://www.inach.net/

History 4 Oct 2002. Registration: Handelsregister, No/ID: KVK 34183849, Netherlands; EU Transparency Register, No/ID: 725884747931-95, Start date: 21 Oct 2022. **Aims** Combat *discrimination* on the *Internet*. **Structure** Council; Board; Secretary-General. **Activities** Advocacy/lobbying/activism; awareness raising; events/meetings; knowledge management/information dissemination. **Events** *Annual Conference* Amsterdam (Netherlands) 2022, *Conference* Vienna (Austria) 2017, *Conference* Brussels (Belgium) 2016, *Annual Conference* Brussels (Belgium) 2014, *Annual Conference* Uppsala (Sweden) 2013.
Members Full (32) in 27 countries:
Argentina, Austria, Belgium, Bulgaria, Cameroon, Congo Brazzaville, Croatia, Czechia, Estonia, France, Germany, Greece, Hungary, Israel, Italy, Latvia, Lithuania, Netherlands, North Macedonia, Poland, Romania, Russia, Slovakia, Spain, Switzerland, UK, USA.
Included in the above, 6 organizations listed in this Yearbook:
Anti-Defamation League of B'nai B'rith (ADL); CEJI (#03628); CESIE; Global Project Against Hate and Extremism (GPAHE); International League Against Racism and Antisemitism (#14014); Simon Wiesenthal Centre-Europe (CSWE). [2022/XJ5971/y/F]

♦ International Network of Agencies for Health Technology Assessment (INAHTA) 14230

Secretariat c/o Inst of Health Economics, 10405 Jasper Ave, Ste 1200, Edmonton AB T5J 3N4, Canada. T. +17804484881ext245. Fax +17804480018. E-mail: inahta@ihe.ca.
URL: http://www.inahta.org/

History 1 Oct 1993. **Aims** Promote global networking for effective healthcare; accelerate exchange and collaboration among agencies; promote information sharing and comparison; prevent unnecessary duplication of activities. **Structure** Board, comprising Executive Committee (Chair, Vice-Chair and Secretary/Treasurer), 3-5 Directors and immediate past Chair. Secretariat. **Languages** English. **Staff** 1.50 FTE, paid. **Finance** Members' dues. **Activities** Organizes annual exhibition. **Events** *Congress* Utrecht (Netherlands) 2022, *Annual meeting* Singapore (Singapore) 2009, *Annual meeting* Montréal, QC (Canada) 2008, *Annual meeting* Barcelona (Spain) 2007, *Annual meeting* Adelaide, SA (Australia) 2006. **Publications** *INAHTA Newsletter* (4 a year) in English, French, Spanish; *INAHTA Brief Compilation* (annual) in English, Spanish. *INAHTA Briefs* – series. Occational papers; reports; checklists of reports. **Information Services** *HTA Database*.
Members Agencies in 27 countries:
Argentina, Australia, Austria, Belgium, Brazil, Canada, China, Denmark, Finland, France, Germany, Israel, Italy, Korea Rep, Lithuania, Malaysia, Mexico, Netherlands, New Zealand, Norway, Poland, Spain, Sweden, Switzerland, Taiwan, UK, USA.
NGO Relations Partner of: *European Network for Health Technology Assessment (EUnetHTA, #07921); Guidelines International Network (GIN, #10817).* [2022/XF6641/F]

♦ International Network for Aid Relief and Assistance (internationally oriented national body)

♦ International Network of Analytical Sociologists (INAS) 14231

Pres address not obtained.
URL: https://analyticalsociology.com/

History 2008. Former names and other names: *European Network of Analytical Sociologists* – former. **Structure** Council. **Activities** Awards/prizes/competitions; events/meetings. **Events** *Conference* Princeton, NJ (USA) 2023, *Conference* San Domenico di Fiesole (Italy) 2022, *Conference* Tokyo (Japan) 2021, *Conference* Tokyo (Japan) 2020, *Conference* St Petersburg (Russia) 2019. **NGO Relations** *European Group for Organizational Studies (EGOS, #07428); European Network for the Philosophy of the Social Sciences (ENPOSS, #07966).* [2023/XJ9537/C]

♦ International Network of AtmoDust Scientists (unconfirmed)

♦ International Network for Autonomous Ships (INAS) 14232

Secretariat SINTEF Ocean, Torgardsveien 12, 7092 Trondheim, Norway. T. +4793094401.
URL: http://autonomous-ship.org/

History 30 Oct 2017, Oslo (Norway). Founded as in informal group. **Aims** Exchange information about technology, use and approval of autonomous surface ships (MASS) on an international level. **Structure** International Contact Points; Secretariat. **Languages** English. **Finance** Supported by: Norwegian Forum for Autonomous Ships (NFAS). **Activities** Events/meetings. **Events** *International Conference on Maritime Autonomous Surface Ships (ICMASS)* Singapore (Singapore) 2022, *International Conference on Maritime Autonomous Surface Ships (ICMASS)* Ulsan (Korea Rep) 2020, *Workshop on Development of Autonomous Ships* London (UK) 2019, *International Conference on Maritime Autonomous Surface Ships (ICMASS)* Trondheim (Norway) 2019, *Seminar* Busan (Korea Rep) 2018.
Members Participants in 16 countries:
Australia, Belgium, Canada, China, Denmark, Estonia, Finland, Germany, Japan, Korea Rep, Netherlands, Norway, Singapore, Sweden, UK, USA.
Regional members (2):
European Maritime Safety Agency (EMSA, #07744); European Space Agency (ESA, #08798) (Satellite for 5G Initiative). [2022.10.21/XM8307/F]

♦ International Network for the Availability of Scientific Publications (INASP) 14233

Réseau international d'accès aux publications scientifiques

Exec Dir 2-3 Cambridge Terrace, Oxford, OX1 1RR, UK. T. +441865249909. Fax +441865251060. E-mail: inasp@inasp.info.
URL: http://www.inasp.info/

History 1992, by *International Council for Science (ICSU, inactive) – ICSU Committee on the Dissemination of Scientific Information (CDSI, inactive), American Association for the Advancement of Science (AAAS)*, in collaboration with *European Commission (EC, #06633), TWAS (#20270)* and *UNESCO (#20322)*. UK Registered Charity, 2004: 1106349. **Aims** Support Southern individuals and institutions to produce, share and use research and knowledge which can transform lives. **Structure** Board of Trustees. **Languages** English. **Staff** 21.00 FTE, paid. **Finance** Current funders include: *Department for International Development (DFID, inactive); Swedish International Development Cooperation Agency (Sida)*. **Activities** Knowledge management/information dissemination; research/documentation; training/education; publishing activities; capacity building. **Events** *Publishers for Development Conference* London (UK) 2013, *Publishers for Development Conference* Oxford (UK) 2012, *Seminar on scholarly publishing and the developing world* London (UK) 2002. **Publications** *INASP Newsletter* (3 a year). Leaflets; books. Information Services: Database containing details of development, aid, philanthropic, governmental and non-governmental organizations and over 2,000 institutions. Advisory and liaison services.
Members Covers 101 countries:
Afghanistan, Albania, Algeria, Angola, Armenia, Azerbaijan, Bangladesh, Belarus, Belgium, Belize, Benin, Bhutan, Bolivia, Botswana, Burkina Faso, Burundi, Cambodia, Cameroon, Canada, Central African Rep, Chad, China, Colombia, Comoros, Congo Brazzaville, Congo DR, Côte d'Ivoire, Cuba, Denmark, Djibouti, Dominican Rep, Ecuador, Egypt, El Salvador, Equatorial Guinea, Eritrea, Eswatini, Ethiopia, Fiji, Gabon, Gambia, Georgia, Ghana, Grenada, Guatemala, Guinea, Guinea-Bissau, Guyana, Haiti, Honduras, India, Indonesia, Iran Islamic Rep, Iraq, Jamaica, Kazakhstan, Kenya, Kiribati, Korea DPR, Kyrgyzstan, Laos, Latvia, Lebanon, Malawi, Mali, Mauritius, Moldova, Mongolia, Mozambique, Myanmar, Namibia, Nepal, Netherlands, Nicaragua, Niger, Nigeria, North Macedonia, Pakistan, Papua New Guinea, Paraguay, Peru, Philippines, Rwanda, Senegal, Solomon Is, South Africa, Sri Lanka, Sudan, Suriname, Tajikistan, Tanzania UR, Thailand, Tonga, Turkmenistan, Uganda, Uzbekistan, Vanuatu, Vietnam, Yemen, Zambia, Zimbabwe. [2022/XF5351/F]

♦ International Network for Bamboo and Rattan (INBAR) 14234

Organisation Internationale pour le Bambou et le Rotin – Organización Internacional del Bambú y el Ratán

Dir Gen PO Box 100102 86, 100102 Beijing, China. T. +861064706161. Fax +861064702166. E-mail: info@inbar.int.
Street address No 8, Fu Tong Dong Da Jie, Wang Jing Area, Chaoyang District, 100102 Beijing, China.
URL: http://www.inbar.int/

History 6 Nov 1997. Established on signature of an agreement by 9 countries in Asia, Africa, North America and Latin America, following work of a Task Force, set up Mar 1995. Formalizes a network first set up in 1993, by *International Development Research Centre (IDRC, #13162)*, consolidating an informal research network which had operated for over 10 years. **Aims** Work with countries to focus use of bamboo and rattan as strategic resources that support sustainable development and green economy action plans. **Structure** Council; Board of Trustees; Secretariat in Beijing (China), headed by Director General; Programme Advisors; Network Partners. **Languages** Chinese, English, French, Spanish. **Staff** 57.00 FTE, paid. **Finance** Members' dues. Support from: *Common Fund for Commodities (CFC, #04293); European Commission (EC, #06633); Blue Moon Fund; International Fund for Agricultural Development (IFAD, #13692)*; governments of the Netherlands and China. **Activities** Research and development; advocacy/lobbying/activism; ppolitics/policy/regulatory; knowledge management/information dissemination; projects/programmes. **Events** *Global Bamboo and Rattan Congress (BARC)* Beijing (China) 2022, *Global Bamboo and Rattan Congress* Beijing (China) 2018, *International Symposium on Bamboo and Guadua* Bogota (Colombia) 2017, *World Bamboo Congress* Korea Rep 2015, *World bamboo congress* Bangkok (Thailand) 2009. **Publications** *INBAR Newsletter* (2 a year). Annual Report; general information material; guidelines; manuals; policy reports; proceedings; technical advisory notes; technical reports; working papers. Information Services: publications center.
Members Governments of 43 countries:
Argentina, Bangladesh, Benin, Bhutan, Brazil, Burundi, Cameroon, Canada, Chile, China, Colombia, Cuba, Ecuador, Eritrea, Ethiopia, Ghana, India, Indonesia, Jamaica, Kenya, Liberia, Madagascar, Malawi, Malaysia, Mozambique, Myanmar, Nepal, Nigeria, Panama, Peru, Philippines, Rwanda, Senegal, Sierra Leone, Sri Lanka, Suriname, Tanzania UR, Thailand, Togo, Tonga, Uganda, Venezuela, Vietnam.
IGO Relations Observer status with (1): *United Nations (UN, #20515)* (General Assembly).
Designed International Commodity Body of: *Common Fund for Commodities (CFC, #04293)*. Accredited by: *Secretariat of the United Nations Convention to Combat Desertification (Secretariat of the UNCCD, #19208)*.
Partners include:

- *Bioversity International (#03262)*;
- *CABI (#03393)*;
- *Canadian International Development Agency (CIDA, inactive)*;
- *Centre de coopération internationale en recherche agronomique pour le développement (CIRAD, #03733)*;
- *CGIAR System Organization (CGIAR, #03843)*;
- *Commonwealth of Learning (COL, #04346)*;
- *Department for International Development (DFID, inactive)*;
- *Deutsche Gesellschaft für Internationale Zusammenarbeit (GIZ)*;
- *European Commission (EC, #06633)*;
- *FAO (#09260)*;
- *Global Environment Facility (GEF, #10346)*;
- *International Cocoa Organization (ICCO, #12627)*;
- *International Coffee Organization (ICO, #12630)*;
- *International Rubber Study Group (IRSG, #14772)*;
- *International Sugar Organization (ISO, #15623)*;
- *International Trade Centre (ITC, #15703)*;
- *International Tropical Timber Organization (ITTO, #15737)*;
- *UN Environment Programme World Conservation Monitoring Centre (UNEP-WCMC, #20295)*;
- *UNDP (#20292)*;
- *UNIDO (#20336)*;
- *United Nations Forum on Forests (UNFF, #20562)*.

NGO Relations Member of: *Asia-Pacific Association of Forestry Research Institutions (APAFRI, #01841); Association of International Research and Development Centers for Agriculture (AIRCA, #02760); Global Open Data for Agriculture and Nutrition (GODAN, #10514); International Partnership for the Satoyama Initiative (IPSI, #14525); International Society of Tropical Foresters (ISTF, #15522); International Union of Forest Research Organizations (IUFRO, #15774)*. Charter member of: *Global Landscapes Forum (GLF, #10451)*. In liaison with technical committees of: *International Organization for Standardization (ISO, #14473)*. Partners include:
- *Center for International Forestry Research (CIFOR, #03646)*;
- *Crops For the Future (CFF, #04968)*;
- *European Bamboo Society (EBS, #06309)*;
- *Ford Foundation (#09858)*;
- *Global Network for Sustainable Housing (GNSH, #10502)*;
- *International Centre for Bamboo and Rattan (ICBR)*;
- *International Centre for Integrated Mountain Development (ICIMOD, #12500)*;
- *International Cotton Association (ICA, #12980)*;
- *International Model Forest Network (IMFN, #14175)*;
- *The Nature Conservancy (TNC)*;
- *SNV Netherlands Development Organisation (SNV)*;
- *Opportunities Industrialization Centers International (OICI, #17775)*;
- *World Agroforestry Centre (ICRAF, #21072)*;
- *World Bamboo Organization (WBO, #21214)*;
- *World Forestry Center, Portland (WFC)*;
- *World Wide Fund for Nature (WWF, #21922)*. [2023/XF4527/**F***]

♦ International Network of Basin Organizations (INBO) 14235

Réseau international des organismes de bassin (RIOB) – Red Internacional de Organismos de Cuenca

SG c/o OIE, 21 rue de Madrid, 75008 Paris, France. T. +33144908860. Fax +33140080145. E-mail: secretariat@inbo-news.org.
Pres address not obtained.
URL: http://www.riob.org/

History 6 May 1994, Aix-les-Bains (France). Established following a proposal by the French government. Current statutes adopted Oct 2000, Zakopane (Poland). Registration: EU Transparency Register, No/ID: 840971822618-68, Start date: 7 Jul 2016. **Aims** Promote integrated water resources management at the level of river basins as an essential tool for sustainable development. **Structure** General Assembly (currently every 3 years); Liaison Bureau; Permanent Technical Secretariat at *International Office for Water (IOW, #14399)*. Regional networks (7): *African Network for Basin Organizations (ANBO, #00381)*; Brazilian Network of Basin Organizations (REBOB); *Group of European Basin Organizations for the Implementation of the Water Framework Directive (EURO-INBO, #10771); Latin American Network of Basin Organizations (LANBO, #16351); Mediterranean Network of Basin Organisations (MENBO, #16664); Network of Asian River Basin Organizations (NARBO, #16993); North American Network of Basin Organizations (NANBO); Regional Network of Water-Basin – Organizations from Eastern Europe, Caucasus and Central Asia (NWO EECCA, #18803)*. **Languages** English, French, Russian, Spanish. **Staff** 4.50 FTE, paid. **Finance** Secretariat financed by bi- and multilateral cooperation agencies (not specified). **Activities** Events/meetings; guidance/assistance/consulting; knowledge management/information dissemination; projects/programmes; research/documentation; training/education. **Events** *Europe-INBO Conference* Annecy (France) 2022, *Europe-INBO Conference* Mellieha (Malta) 2021, *European River Symposium* Vienna (Austria) 2021, *Europe-INBO Conference* Paris (France) 2020, *World General assembly* Marrakech (Morocco) 2019. **Publications** *Network Newsletter* (2 a year) in English, French, Russian, Spanish; *Inbo Magazine* (annual). **Information Services** *AQUADOC-INTER* – database. **Members** Governmental administrations in charge of water management, basin organizations and permanent observers (over 100) in 71 countries. Membership countries not specified. **Consultative Status** Consultative status granted from: *ECOSOC (#05331)* (Special). **IGO Relations** Provides secretariat for: *Global Alliances for Water and Climate (GAfWaC, #10230)*. **NGO Relations** Memorandum of Understanding with (1): *World Council of Civil Engineers (WCCE, #21321)*. Member of (1): *European Centre for River Restoration (ECRR, #06499)*. Partner of (1): *Africa-EU Innovation Alliance for Water and Climate (AfriAlliance, #00169)*. Cooperates with (1): *Global Water Partnership (GWP, #10653)*. [2022.11.29/XF3178/**F***]

♦ International Network on Brief Interventions for Alcohol and Other Drugs (INEBRIA) 14236

Contact Progr on Substance Abuse, Public Health Agency of Catalonia, Roc Boronat 81-95, 08005 Barcelona, Spain. T. +34935513610. E-mail: inebria@gencat.cat.
URL: http://www.inebria.net/

History 2004. Set up following end of *WHO (#20950)* Collaborative Project on Identification and Management of Alcohol-related Problems in Primary Health Care. Network activities expanded 2011. **Aims** Provide global leadership in development, evaluation and implementation of evidence-based practice in the area of early identification and brief intervention for hazardous and harmful *substance use*. **Structure** Assembly (annual); Coordinating Committee; Secretariat. Semi-autonomous branch, supported by *Pan American Health Organization (PAHO, #18108)*, based in Mexico: *INEBRIA-Latina*. **Languages** English, Spanish. **Staff** 3.00 FTE, paid. Voluntary. **Finance** Sources: contributions. Supported by: Program on Substance Abuse, Barcelona (Spain). **Activities** Events/meetings; knowledge management/information dissemination. **Events** *Conference* Goa (India) 2021, *International Meeting* Barcelona (Spain) 2020, *Seminar* Washington, DC (USA) 2020, *Conference* Lübeck (Germany) 2019, *Conference* Santiago (Chile) 2018. **Publications** *Inebria Bulletin*; *Inebria Latina Bulletin*.
Members Full in 58 countries and territories:
Afghanistan, Argentina, Australia, Austria, Bangladesh, Belgium, Belize, Bolivia, Brazil, Bulgaria, Canada, Chile, Colombia, Costa Rica, Côte d'Ivoire, Czechia, Denmark, Dominican Rep, Ecuador, Estonia, Ethiopia, Finland, France, Germany, Ghana, Guatemala, Iceland, India, Ireland, Italy, Japan, Korea Rep, Malawi, Mexico, Montserrat, Netherlands, New Zealand, Nigeria, Norway, Panama, Paraguay, Peru, Poland, Portugal, Romania, Russia, Slovenia, South Africa, Spain, Sri Lanka, Sweden, Switzerland, Tanzania UR, Thailand, Trinidad-Tobago, UK, Uruguay, USA.
IGO Relations None. [2021/XJ8727/**F**]

♦ International Network of Business Advertising Agencies (inactive)

♦ International Network of Business and Management Journal Editors (INBAM) 14237

Treas Tremain House, 8 Maple Drive, Kings Worthy, Winchester, SO23 7NG, UK. T. +441962790607. E-mail: admin@inbam-editors.org.
URL: https://www.inbam-editors.org/

History 2009, Spain. Reformed Feb 2017. Former names and other names: *International Network of Business and Management Journals (INBAM)* – former (2009 to 2017). Registration: Registered Charity, No/ID: 1171512, England and Wales. **Aims** Advance the education of the public in general (and particularly amongst researchers) on the subject of publishing research in journals of business, management and associated social sciences, and to promote that research where possible for the public benefit; support and encourage the education of young researchers, early and later career academics wherever they may live or work, in the development, composition and publishing of their research papers in reputable journals. **Structure** Executive Team; Trustees. **Activities** Events/meetings; guidance/assistance/consulting. **Events** *Conference* Utrecht (Netherlands) 2015, *Conference* Barcelona (Spain) 2014, *Conference* Lisbon (Portugal) 2013, *Brokering knowledge* Valencia (Spain) 2012, *Conference* Valencia (Spain) 2010. **NGO Relations** Member of (1): *Global Labor Organization (GLO, #10445)*. [2020/XJ2453/**F**]

♦ International Network of Business and Management Journals / see International Network of Business and Management Journal Editors (#14237)

♦ International Network for Cancer Treatment and Research (INCTR) 14238

Sec c/o Institut Pasteur, Rue Engeland 642, 1180 Brussels, Belgium. T. +3223739323. Fax +3223739313. E-mail: info@inctr.be.
Pres address not obtained.
URL: http://www.inctr.org/

History 1998, by *Union for International Cancer Control (UICC, #20415)* and *Pasteur Institute*. Inaugural meeting Nov 1999, Antwerp (Belgium). **Aims** Assist in controlling cancer in *developing countries* through the development of infrastructure for cancer treatment and research and through collaboration with physicians and scientists in such countries; take advantage of unique opportunities to improve our understanding of factors (genetic and environmental) that predispose to various types of cancer. **Structure** General Meeting (every 18 months). Council of 18 members. Officers: President; 2 Vice-Presidents; Secretary/Treasurer. Committees (4): Ethical Review; Disease-Specific Strategy Groups; Information Technology; Funding. Offices and Branches: Alliance Mondial Contre le Cancer, France; INCTR Brazil; INCTR Canada; INCTR Egypt; INCTR India; INCTR Tanzania; INCTR UK; INCTR USA; NNCTR/INCTR Nepal. **Languages** English, French. **Staff** 4.00 FTE, paid. 6-7 voluntary (Palliative Programme). Offices and branches: 7 full-time; 7 part-time; 40 voluntary. **Finance** Members' dues. Other sources: US National Cancer Institute (NCI); grants and donations.
Activities Conducts research in collaboration with developing countries, initial emphasis being on potentially curable cancers, haematological malignancies (leukaemias and lymphomas), cancers occurring in women and children and cancers associated with infectious diseases. Organizes international meetings and workshops on cancer in countries with limited resources.
Programmes:
- Cancer Registration;
- Clinical Research, including projects on coordination of disease-specific Strategy Groups; management of clinical research studies; administration of the INCTR Ethical Review Committee; education and training;
- Oncology Nursing;
- Palliative Access (PAX);
- Pathology, including projects on central pathology review and implementation of iPath, a web-based programme for pathology training, histopathology review and consultation;
- Paediatric Oncology.
- Foundation Programmes and Projects: thematic workshops; cataloguing the evidence base and undertaking systematic review; training professionals and providing educational tools; building infrastructure for clinical trials; catalyzing and coordinating partnerships; community health centers.

Events *Meeting on Cancer in Countries with Limited Resources / Annual Meeting* Brussels (Belgium) 2011, *Meeting* Paris (France) 2011, *Meeting on Cancer in Countries with Limited Resources / Annual Meeting* Antalya (Turkey) 2009, *Global insight conference on leukaemia* Mumbai (India) 2007, *Annual meeting* Sao Paulo (Brazil) 2007. **Publications** *Network* (4 a year) – including special issues; *INCTR Report*. *INCTR Palliative Care Handbook*. President's message; reports; reviews; case report.
Members Associate corporations and institutions in 41 countries:
Afghanistan, Belgium, Bolivia, Brazil, Cameroon, Canada, China, Colombia, Egypt, France, Germany, India, Iran Islamic Rep, Iraq, Israel, Italy, Jordan, Kenya, Kuwait, Lebanon, Mexico, Morocco, Nepal, Netherlands, Nigeria, Oman, Pakistan, Peru, Philippines, Saudi Arabia, Singapore, South Africa, Sri Lanka, Sudan, Tanzania UR, Türkiye, Uganda, UK, USA, Vietnam, Yemen.
Associate individuals in 54 countries and territories:
Afghanistan, Argentina, Bangladesh, Bolivia, Brazil, Cameroon, Canada, China, Colombia, Cuba, Egypt, France, Germany, Ghana, Hong Kong, India, Iran Islamic Rep, Iraq, Israel, Italy, Jordan, Kenya, Kuwait, Lebanon, Malaysia, Mexico, Morocco, Nepal, Netherlands, Nigeria, Oman, Pakistan, Peru, Philippines, Saudi Arabia, Senegal, Singapore, South Africa, Sri Lanka, Sudan, Sweden, Switzerland, Tanzania UR, Türkiye, Uganda, UK, Ukraine, USA, Uzbekistan, Venezuela, Vietnam, Yemen, Zambia, Zimbabwe.
Consultative Status Consultative status granted from: *WHO (#20950)* (Official Relations). **NGO Relations** Affiliated with: *Global Knowledge Initiative*. [2019/XF4071/**F**]

♦ International Network for Caregiving Children (unconfirmed)

♦ International Network of Centres for Computer Applications (INCCA) 14239

Contact c/o CIMNE, Edifici C1, Campus Norte UPC, Gran Capita s/n, 08034 Barcelona, Spain. T. +34932057016. Fax +34934016517. E-mail: cimne@cimne.upc.edu.
Journal: https://www.inderscience.com/browse/index.php?journalID=5

History Founded 1985, Barcelona (Spain), operating under the auspices of *UNESCO (#20322)*, as an international association of centres of excellence in the field of engineering applications of computers. **Aims** Promote international scientific cooperation and technology transfer in computer applications in engineering, with particular emphasis on the needs of developing countries. **Structure** President; Vice-President. Scientific Council, consisting 8 members. Secretariat. **Activities** Operates mainly by organizing postgraduate training and research; providing specialized computing services through the participating centres, carrying out joint training and research projects; exchanging computer programmes, software and training curricula among members; organizing exchange of specialists; disseminating information on computer applications in engineering sciences. **Events** *COMPLAS : international conference on computational plasticity* Barcelona (Spain) 1997, *COMPLAS : international conference on computational plasticity* Barcelona (Spain) 1995, *COMPLAS : international conference on computational plasticity* Barcelona (Spain) 1992, *PACTA : international conference on parallel computing and transputers applications* Barcelona (Spain) 1992, *International conference on computer modelling in ocean engineering* Venice (Italy) 1988. **Publications** *International Journal of Computer Applications in Technology* (12 a year). **Members** Participating centres scientific and educational institutions (112) in Africa, America, Europe and the Pacific. Membership countries not specified.
[2011.08.03/XF0549/**F**]

♦ International Network for Chemical Information / see International Chemical Information Network (#12542)

♦ International Network on Children's Health, Environment and Safety (INCHES) 14240

Contact Kastanjelaan 5, 6955 AM Ellecom, Netherlands. T. +31313413534. E-mail: info@inchesnetwork.net.
URL: http://www.inchesnetwork.net/

History Aug 1998. Initiated by the Dutch branch of *International Society of Doctors for the Environment (ISDE, #15065)*. Former names and other names: *International Children's Health and Environment Network (ICEH)* – former (1998 to 1999). **Aims** Promote healthy and supportive environments that protect the foetus and child from environmental and safety hazards. **Structure** Elected Board. **Languages** English. **Staff** Voluntary. **Finance** Sources: none. **Activities** Events/meetings; training/education. **Events** *International Conference on Children's Environment and Health* Tashkent (Uzbekistan) 2023, *International Conference on Children's Health, Environment and Safety* Amsterdam (Netherlands) 2020, *International Conference on Children's Health, Environment and Safety* Seoul (Korea Rep) 2018, *International Conference on Children's Health, Environment and Safety* Barcelona (Spain) 2016, *Triennial Prenatal Programming and Toxicity International Conference* Boston, MA (USA) 2014. **Publications** Training modules.
Members Organizations in 45 countries and territories:

Albania, Argentina, Australia, Austria, Bangladesh, Belarus, Bulgaria, Canada, China, Croatia, Denmark, Ecuador, Finland, France, Georgia, Germany, Hungary, India, Indonesia, Ireland, Italy, Kazakhstan, Kenya, Lebanon, Mauritius, Nepal, Netherlands, Norway, Pakistan, Poland, Russia, Serbia, Slovakia, South Africa, Sri Lanka, Sweden, Switzerland, Taiwan, Thailand, UK, Ukraine, Uruguay, USA, Uzbekistan, Venezuela.
Consultative Status Consultative status granted from: *WHO (#20950)* (Official Relations). **NGO Relations** Member of (2): *Global Climate and Health Alliance (GCHA, #10288)*; *Health and Environment Alliance (HEAL, #10879)*. [2023.02.19/XF5701/**F**]

♦ International Network for Christian Higher Education (INCHE) 14241

Exec Dir Youngsma Center, 3201 Burton St SE, Grand Rapids MI 49546, USA. T. +16165267906. E-mail: office@inche.one – director@inche.one.
URL: http://www.inche.one/

History 1975, South Africa. Former names and other names: *International Conference of Institutions for Christian Higher Education (ICICHE)* – former (1975 to 1981); *International Council for the Promotion of Christian Higher Education (ICPCHE)* – former (1981 to 2019); *International Association for the Promotion of Christian Higher Education (IAPCHE)* – former (1981 to 2019). **Aims** Advance Christian higher education. **Structure** Board; Executive Director. **Languages** English, Spanish. **Staff** 0.70 FTE, paid; 0.50 FTE, voluntary. **Finance** Sources: donations; grants; members' dues. Annual budget: 80,000 USD. **Activities** Capacity building; events/meetings; networking/liaising; training/education. **Events** *INCHE Europe Conference* Budapest (Hungary) 2022, *INCHE North America Conference* Grand Rapids, MI (USA) 2022, *INCHE Europe Conference* Budapest (Hungary) 2021, *INCHE Latin America conference* San José (Costa Rica) 2020, *IAPCHE Biennial North America Conference* Grand Rapids, MI (USA) 2019. **Publications** *Contact* (4 a year) – newsletter. Books; conference proceedings.
Members National and international organizations include 1 organization listed in this Yearbook:
Global Scholars. [2022.10.11/XD8668/y/**C**]

♦ International Network for Circumpolar Health Research (inactive)
♦ International Network of Cities where living is easy / see Cittaslow (#03958)

♦ International Network of Civil Liberties Organizations (INCLO) 14242

Contact Avenue Blanc 49, c/o Allina Family Office Sàrl, 1202 Geneva, Switzerland. E-mail: info@inclo.net.
Contact Piedras 547 1o, C1070AAK, Buenos Aires, Argentina.
URL: https://www.inclo.net/

Aims Advance four key principles around the world: protest rights, privacy, religious freedom and equal treatment, and the protection of civic space. **Structure** General Meeting; Board.
Members Organizations (15) in 15 countries:
Argentina, Australia, Canada, Colombia, Egypt, Hungary, India, Indonesia, Ireland, Israel, Kenya, Russia, South Africa, UK, USA.
Consultative Status Consultative status granted from: *Council of Europe (CE, #04881)* (Participatory Status). [2019/XM8866/**F**]

♦ International Network of Civil Society Organizations on Competition (INCSOC) 14243

Co-Chairman CUTS Ctre for Competition, D-217, Bhaskar Marg, Bani Park, Jaipur, Rajasthan 302 016, Jaipur RAJASTHAN 302 016, India. T. +911412282821. Fax +911412282733 – +911412282485. E-mail: c-cier@cuts.org.
Co-Chairman address not obtained.
URL: http://www.incsoc.net/

History 20 Feb 2003, Geneva (Switzerland), during 1st General Meeting, as an offshoot of a project of *Consumer Unity and Trust Society (CUTS)*. **Aims** Promote and maintain a healthy competition culture around the world by coalition building among civil society and other organizations. **Structure** A virtual network. General Meeting. Steering Committee of 24. Working Groups. Headquarters at *Consumer Unity and Trust Society (CUTS)*. **Activities** Working Groups (3): Capacity Building; Advocacy; WCR 2005. INCSOC Forum. **Events** *General Meeting* Bangkok (Thailand) 2006, *General Meeting* Geneva (Switzerland) 2005, *General Meeting* Geneva (Switzerland) 2003. **Publications** *Competition Regimes in the World – A Civil Society Report.* **Members** Primary; Associate. Membership countries not specified. **IGO Relations** Close contacts with: *International Bank for Reconstruction and Development (IBRD, #12317)* (World Bank); *OECD (#17693)*; *UNCTAD (#20285)*; *World Trade Organization (WTO, #21864)*. **NGO Relations** Close contacts with: *International Competition Network (ICN, #12832)*. *International Resources for Fairer Trade, India (IRFT)* is a member. [2010/XM2523/**F**]

♦ International Network for Climate and Health for Africa (Clim-HEALTH Africa) 14244

Contact c/o WHO Africa regional office, Cité du Djoué, PO Box 06, Brazzaville, Congo Brazzaville.
URL: http://www.climhealthafrica.org/

Aims Predict, prevent and manage acute public health effects for *climate change* in Africa. **Structure** Scientific Advisory Committee. **Activities** Research and development; knowledge management/information dissemination; training/education; advocacy/lobbying/activism. **Events** *Annual Meeting* Johannesburg (South Africa) 2015.
Members Institutions in 7 countries:
Cameroon, Ghana, Kenya, Mali, South Africa, Tanzania UR, USA.
Included in the above, 6 organizations listed in this Yearbook:
African Centre of Meteorological Applications for Development (ACMAD, #00242); *INDEPTH Network (#11156)*; *International Research Institute for Climate and Society (IRI)*; *UNEP (#20299)*; *WHO (#20950)*; *World Meteorological Organization (WMO, #21649)*.
IGO Relations *UNEP (#20299)*; *WHO (#20950)*. [2015/XM4302/y/**F**]

♦ International Network for Community Supported Agriculture / see International Network URGENCI (#14339)

♦ International Network for the Conservation of Contemporary Art (INCCA) 14245

Coordinator c/o RCE – Conservation and Restoration Dept, PO Box 1600, 3800 BP Amersfoort, Netherlands. T. +31611195340. E-mail: info@incca.org.
Street address Smallepad 5, 3811 MG Amersfoort, Netherlands.
URL: http://www.incca.org/

History 1999. **Structure** Steering Committee. Regional Groups (4): Asia Pacific; CEE – Central and Eastern Europe; f – French language, Italia. **Activities** Training/education; knowledge management/information dissemination. **Publications** *INCCA Update.* **Members** Full (over 1,500) in around 70 countries. Membership countries not specified. **NGO Relations** *International Institute for Conservation of Historic and Artistic Works (IIC, #13871)*. [2018/XM5117/**F**]

♦ International Network on Cultural Policy (INCP) 14246

Réseau international sur la politique culturelle (RIPC) – Red Internacional de Politicas Culturales

Contact address not obtained. T. +18199535327. Fax +18199538439.

History 1998, Ottawa (Canada). **Aims** Strengthen cultural policies so that governments, together with civil society, can create an international environment that values diversity, creativity, accessibility and freedom; serve as an informal international venue where national ministers responsible for culture can explore and exchange views on new and emerging cultural policy issues and develop strategies to promote cultural diversity. **Structure** Ministerial Meeting (annual); Contact Group; Working Groups; Special Policy Research Teams. **Languages** English, French, Spanish. **Staff** 3.00 FTE, paid. **Finance** Members' voluntary contributions; each member country responsible for costs of participation in meetings and activities; Liaison Bureau housed within and financed by the Department of Canadian Heritage. **Activities** Offers a means through which countries can share their expertise, exchange views and information and strengthen domestic and international partnerships; raises awareness of the importance of cultural diversity and identity to social and economic development; demonstrates the links between national cultural objectives and international development; advances dialogue on cultural policy issues by ensuring that culture is on the table in international, national and local fora; examines the importance of cultural diversity and identity in an increasingly globalized world relating to such issues as increasing mobility of people, trade liberalization, new communication technologies and industry consolidation; explores how diversity can be integrated into a common approach to global development. **Events** *Annual Meeting* Seville (Spain) 2007, *Annual Meeting* Rio de Janeiro (Brazil) 2006, *Annual ministerial meeting / Annual Meeting* Dakar (Senegal) 2005, *Annual ministerial meeting / Annual Meeting* Shanghai (China) 2004, *Annual all officials meeting* Stockholm (Sweden) 2004.
Members Open to UNESCO member countries having a national minister of culture or the equivalent. Observer status granted to other international or regional organizations on ad hoc basis. Governments of 69 countries:
Angola, Argentina, Armenia, Austria, Bahamas, Barbados, Belgium, Botswana, Brazil, Burkina Faso, Cameroon, Canada, Central African Rep, Chile, China, Colombia, Côte d'Ivoire, Croatia, Cuba, Denmark, El Salvador, Estonia, Finland, France, Georgia, Germany, Greece, Guyana, Haiti, Hungary, Iceland, Iran Islamic Rep, Italy, Jamaica, Jordan, Korea Rep, Latvia, Lebanon, Lesotho, Luxembourg, Malaysia, Mauritius, Mexico, Morocco, Mozambique, Netherlands, New Zealand, Nigeria, Norway, Philippines, Poland, Portugal, Romania, Russia, Senegal, Slovakia, Slovenia, South Africa, Spain, St Lucia, Sweden, Switzerland, Trinidad-Tobago, Tunisia, UK, Ukraine, Venezuela, Vietnam, Zimbabwe. [2009/XF6704/**F***]

♦ International Network for a Culture of Nonviolence and Peace 14247

Coordination internationale pour une culture de non-violence et de paix

Secretariat 148 rue du Faubourg Saint-Denis, 75010 Paris, France. T. +33140360660. E-mail: secretariat@nvpnetwork.net.
URL: http://www.nvpnetwork.net/

History Founded 2003, as *International Coalition for the Decade for the Promotion of a Culture of Peace and Non-violence for the Children of the World.* Current name adopted, 2011. Registered in accordance with French law. **Aims** Promote a culture of non-violence and peace through education. **Structure** General Assembly; International Committee. **Languages** English, French, German, Italian, Spanish. **Finance** Members' dues. Private donations. **Activities** Advocacy/lobbying/activism; events/meetings. **Publications** *Newsletter* in English, French.
Members Active – national coalitions and international organizations; Observing; Individuals; Honorary. National coalitions (14) in 14 countries:
Benin, Canada, Congo Brazzaville, Congo DR, France, Germany, Guinea, Italy, Mali, Morocco, Netherlands, Niger, Senegal, Togo.
International organizations (12):
Association Montessori Internationale (AMI, #02812); *Church and Peace (#03916)*; *Franciscans International (FI, #09982)*; *Friends World Committee for Consultation (FWCC, #10004)*; *Initiatives of Change International – Caux (IofC, #11213)*; *International Fellowship of Reconciliation (IFOR, #13586)*; *Pax Christi – International Catholic Peace Movement (#18266)*; *Pax Romana, International Catholic Movement for Intellectual and Cultural Affairs (ICMICA, #18267)*; *Pontifical Council for Justice and Peace (inactive)*; Réseau Foi, Culture et Education – Central Africa; *Servicio Paz y Justicia en América Latina (SERPAJ-AL, #19247)*; *World Catholic Association for Communication (SIGNIS, #21264)*.
Observers (4):
Everest Range Network; *Gandhi International*; International Network Youth and Non-Violence; *World Council of Churches (WCC, #21320)*. [2016.12.14/XM0389/y/**E**]

♦ International Network of Customs Universities (INCU) 14248

Secretariat Locked Bag 119, Kingston ACT 2604, Australia. T. +61262726300. E-mail: info@incu.org.
Street Aadress Level 1, 10-12 Brisbane Avenue, Barton ACT 2601, Australia.
URL: https://incu.org/

History 2005. Current constitution adopted 2012; amended May 2014. Registered in accordance with Australian law. **Aims** Promote the academic standing of the customs profession and academic excellence in customs matters; support research; generate greater public awareness of the profession; represent the collective interests of members; provide a global resource for governments and the private sector, and an educational source for students; organize academic conferences. **Structure** General Meeting; Management Committee; Subcommittees; Advisory Board; Secretariat. **Languages** English. **Staff** Part-time. **Finance** Sources: members' dues. **Activities** Awareness raising; events/meetings; guidance/assistance/consulting; publishing activities; research/documentation. **Publications** *INCU Newsflash*; *World Customs Journal.* Conference proceedings. **Members** Institutional (26); Honorary Fellows (3); Individuals (132); Young/Student (14); Affiliate Academic Institutions (150); Affiliate Non-academic Institutions (3). Membership countries not specified. **IGO Relations** *United Nations Office for the Coordination of Humanitarian Assistance to Afghanistan (UNOCHA, inactive)*; *United Nations Office on Drugs and Crime (UNODC, #20596)*; *World Customs Organization (WCO, #21350)*; *World Trade Organization (WTO, #21864)*. **NGO Relations** Associate member of: *International Port Community Systems Association (IPCSA, #14623)*. [2019.12.17/XM6511/**C**]

♦ International Network for the Dances of Universal Peace / see Dances of Universal Peace International (#05000)

♦ International Network on the Definition of Death 14249

Coordinator Inst de Neurologia y Neurocirurgia, 29 y D Vedado, Ciudad de La Havana, Apt Postal 4268, 10400 Havana, Cuba. T. +537327501. Fax +537336321. E-mail: braind@infomed.sld.cu.
URL: http://www.komabraindeathcuba.com/

History 1995. **Activities** Organizes symposia. **Events** *Symposium* Varadero (Cuba) 2008, *Coma and death* Havana (Cuba) 2004, *Coma and death* Havana (Cuba) 2000, *Symposium* Havana (Cuba) 1996, *Symposium* San Francisco, CA (USA) 1996. **NGO Relations** Affiliated with: *International Association of Bioethics (IAB, #11725)*. [2008/XF4918/**F**]

♦ International Network for Didactic Research in University Mathematics (INDRUM) 14250

Address not obtained.

History Conferences organized since 2016. **Aims** Contribute to the development of research in didactics of mathematics at all levels of tertiary education, with a particular concern for the development of young researchers in the field and for dialogue with mathematicians. **Structure** Scientific Committee. **Activities** Events/meetings. **Events** *Conference* Hannover (Germany) 2022. [2019/XM8059/**F**]

♦ International Network on Displacement and Resettlement (INDR) .. 14251

Pres 1402 E Kleindale Rd, Tucson AZ 85719, USA.
URL: http://indr.org/

History 2000. **Structure** Officers: President; Secretary/Treasurer. Advisory Board. **Publications** *Resettlement News.* [2013/XJ7197/**F**]

♦ International Network for Doctoral Education in Nursing (INDEN) .. 14252

Pres Univ of Michigan, School of Nursing, 400 North Ingalls, Ann Arbor MI 48109, USA. T. +17347647188. Fax +17347639357. E-mail: rwr@umich.edu.
URL: http://www.umich.edu/~inden/

History Jun 1999, London (UK), after conference 17 Jun 1997, Vancouver (Canada). **Aims** Advance and promote high quality doctoral education in nursing worldwide through international collaboration and cooperation. **Structure** General Meeting (every 2 years). Board of Directors, comprising President, Treasurer, Secretary and Members at large. **Languages** English. **Staff** Voluntary. **Finance** Members' dues. Budget (annual): US$ 5,000. **Activities** Facilitates: (post) doctoral student exchange, workshops and networking; exchange of faculty across nursing doctoral programmes; international research collaboration. Maintains a website and database. **Events** *Biennial conference / Meeting* Valletta (Malta) 2011, *Biennial conference / Meeting* Durban (South Africa) 2009, *Biennial conference / Meeting* Yokohama (Japan) 2007, *Biennial conference / Meeting* Taipei (Taiwan) 2005, *Biennial conference / Meeting* Toronto, ON (Canada) 2003. **Publications** *Doctoral Education in Nursing: International Perspectives* (2005).
Members Individuals in 32 countries and territories:
Argentina, Australia, Belgium, Brazil, Canada, Chile, China, Colombia, Czechia, Egypt, Finland, Germany, Greece, Hong Kong, Ireland, Japan, Korea Rep, Mexico, Namibia, Netherlands, New Zealand, Norway, Philippines, Poland, South Africa, Sweden, Taiwan, Thailand, Türkiye, UK, USA, Venezuela.
NGO Relations Contacts with: *International Council of Nurses (ICN, #13054)*; *Sigma Theta Tau International.* [2011.06.01/XF5781/v/**F**]

♦ International Network For Early Mobilization Of Mechanically Ventilated Intensive Care Patients (unconfirmed)

♦ International Network of Ecoclubs (Ecoclubes International) 14253

Contact Fundacion Ecoclubes, Florida 253, 3o C, 1005 Buenos Aires, Argentina.

History 1992, Argentina, by Ricardo Bertolino. Also referred to as *ECOCLUBES*. **Aims** As an international movement of *young* people, construct *sustainable* communities.

Members Full in 30 countries:
Argentina, Bolivia, Brazil, Chile, Colombia, Costa Rica, Dominican Rep, Ecuador, El Salvador, Germany, Ghana, Guatemala, Guinea, Guyana, Haiti, Honduras, Mexico, Morocco, Nicaragua, Nigeria, Panama, Paraguay, Peru, Poland, Portugal, Russia, Spain, Ukraine, Uruguay, Venezuela.

NGO Relations Member of: *Espacio Iberoamericano de Juventud (EIJ, no recent information).* [2010/XJ1720/F]

♦ International Network for Economic Method (INEM) 14254

Pres c/o ASU Sustainability, MC 5502, PO Box 875502, Tempe AZ 85287-5502, USA.
Twitter: https://twitter.com/econmethodology

History Founded 1989, Hong Kong. **Aims** Promote links among economic *methodologists*, economists and scholars. **Structure** Executive Board. **Languages** English. **Staff** None. **Finance** Members' dues. **Events** *Conference* Helsinki (Finland) 2019, *Conference* Cape Town (South Africa) 2015, *Conference* Rotterdam (Netherlands) 2013, *Conference* St Petersburg (Russia) 2012, *Conference* Helsinki (Finland) 2011. **Publications** *Journal of Economic Methodology* (4 a year). *Advances in Economic Methodology* – series.

Members Individuals in 25 countries and territories:
Argentina, Australia, Austria, Belgium, Brazil, Canada, Costa Rica, Finland, France, Germany, Greece, Hong Kong, Ireland, Italy, Japan, Mexico, Netherlands, Norway, Portugal, South Africa, Spain, Sweden, Switzerland, UK, USA. [2020/XF5845/F]

♦ International Network for Economic, Social and Cultural Rights (ESCR-Net) 14255

Réseau international pour les droits économiques, sociaux et culturels (Réseau-DESC) – Red Internacional para los Derechos Económicos, Sociales y Culturales (Red-DESC)

Dir 370 Lexington Ave, Ste 700, New York NY 10017, USA. T. +12126811236. E-mail: info@escr-net.org.
URL: http://www.escr-net.org/

History Jun 2003, Chiang Mai (Thailand). Founded at inaugural conference. **Aims** Facilitate strategic exchange and collective advocacy to build a global movement to make human rights and social justice a reality for all. **Structure** Board; Membership; Secretariat; Working Groups. **Languages** English, French, Spanish. **Staff** 8.50 FTE, paid. Voluntary. **Finance** Supported by: *American Jewish World Service (AJWS)*; *Ford Foundation (#09858)*; *Sigrid Rausing Trust.* Donations. **Activities** Advocacy/lobbying/activism; education/training; knowledge management/information dissemination; events/meetings. **Events** *General Assembly* Nairobi (Kenya) 2008, *Creating new paths towards social justice* Chiang Mai (Thailand) 2003. **Publications** *ESCR-Justice* (12 a year) – caselaw update. Manuals; factsheets; statements; guidelines; assessments. **Information Services** *ESCR-Net Caselaw Database.*

Members Organizations (over 230); individuals (about 50). Members in 69 countries and territories:
Angola, Argentina, Australia, Belgium, Benin, Bolivia, Brazil, Bulgaria, Cambodia, Cameroon, Canada, Chile, China, Colombia, Congo Brazzaville, Congo DR, Côte d'Ivoire, Dominican Rep, Ecuador, Egypt, El Salvador, Eswatini, France, Gambia, Germany, Ghana, Guatemala, Guinea, Honduras, Hong Kong, Hungary, India, Indonesia, Ireland, Italy, Kenya, Korea Rep, Lebanon, Liberia, Malaysia, Mali, Mauritania, Mauritius, Mexico, Mongolia, Myanmar, Nepal, Netherlands, Niger, Nigeria, Pakistan, Palestine, Paraguay, Peru, Philippines, Sierra Leone, Slovakia, South Africa, Spain, Switzerland, Tanzania UR, Thailand, Trinidad-Tobago, Uganda, UK, Uruguay, USA, Venezuela, Zimbabwe.

IGO Relations Active in consultations with: *Office of the United Nations High Commissioner for Human Rights (OHCHR, #17697)*; UN and regional human rights bodies. **NGO Relations** Member of (3): *ETO Consortium (ETOs, #05560)*; NGO Coalition for the Optional Protocol to the ICESCR; *ProtectDefenders.eu (#18546).* Works actively with a wide range of human rights, development and grassroots organizations (not specified). [2022/XF6849/y/F]

♦ International Network of Editors of Diplomatic Documents / see International Committee of Editors of Diplomatic Documents (#12765)
♦ International Network for Educational Exchange (internationally oriented national body)

♦ International Network of Education Institutes (INEI) 14256

Contact WISCAPE, School of Education, UW-Madison, 353 Education Bldg, 1000 Bascom Mall, Madison WI 53706-1326, USA. T. +16082653047.
URL: http://internationaleducationnet.org/

History Memorandum of Understanding signed by 8 founding members, 21 Aug 2007, Singapore (Singapore), as *International Alliance of Leading Education Institutes (IALEI).* Current title adopted 2014. **Aims** Make an impact on policy decisions; influence funding; inspire research and interventions that have a meaningful impact on education locally and globally. **Events** *Conference* London (UK) 2015, *Conference* Sao Paulo (Brazil) 2014, *Conference* Beijing (China) 2013, *Annual Conference* Melbourne, VIC (Australia) 2012. **Publications** *INEI E-Newsletter*, *INEI Magazine.*

Members Institutions (9) in 9 countries:
Australia, Brazil, Canada, China, Korea Rep, Singapore, South Africa, UK, USA. [2015/XJ6536/F]

♦ International Network of Employers and University Careers Services (INEUCS) 14257

Contact address not obtained. E-mail: info@ineucs.org.
URL: https://ineucs.org/

Members Associations in countries:
Australia, Canada, Ireland, South Africa, UK, USA.
Global Career Services Summit; *South East Asian Association of Graduate Employers (SEAAGE).* [2022/AA2779/y/F]

♦ International Network to End Violence Against Women and Girls (INEVAWG) 14258

Contact address not obtained. E-mail: anusha@masimanyane.co.za.
URL: https://www.masimanyane.org.za/inevaw/

History Founded 2014, South Africa, by *Masimanyane Women's Rights International (Masimanyane).* **Aims** Create a world where all women and girls live without violence and enjoy equality, autonomy, freedom and justice. [2018/XM8538/F]

♦ International Network of Engaged Buddhists (INEB) 14259

Exec Sec 666 Charoen Nakorn Road, Klong San, Bangkok, 10600, Thailand. T. +6628602194. Fax +6628601277. E-mail: secretariat@inebnetwork.org.
URL: http://www.inebnetwork.org/

History Feb 1989, Thailand, at a conference of 36 concerned clergy and lay persons from 11 countries. **Aims** Bring together *socially engaged* Buddhists and other religious activists to encourage them to work on issues such as human rights, environment, gender, Buddhist education, sustainable development and the integration of *spirituality* and *action.* **Structure** Executive Committee, comprising Chairperson, Vice-Chairperson and members. Advisory Board. Executive Secretary. **Finance** Programmes funded by outside donors and foundations. **Activities** Events/meetings; training/education; knowledge management/information dissemination. **Events** *Conference* Bir (India) 2019, *General Conference* Taoyuan (Taiwan) 2017, *Biennial Conference* Colombo (Sri Lanka) / Anuradhapura (Sri Lanka) 2016, *Inter-Religious Dialogue on Climate Change* Anuradhapura (Sri Lanka) 2012, *International Conference* Bodhgaya (India) 2011. **Publications** *Seeds of Peace* (3 a year); *INEB Reader* – newsletter. Pamphlets; essays. Information Services: Collects and distributes information on areas of concern: alternative education; human rights; environment; women's issues; alternative development; integration of spirituality and activism.

Members Partner organizations (55) in 21 countries and territories:
Australia, Bangladesh, Belgium, Bhutan, Brazil, Cambodia, Costa Rica, India, Indonesia, Japan, Korea Rep, Laos, Malaysia, Myanmar, Nepal, Netherlands, South Africa, Sri Lanka, Taiwan, Thailand, USA.
Individuals in 2 countries:
Singapore, Vietnam.

NGO Relations Member of: *International Union for Conservation of Nature and Natural Resources (IUCN, #15766).* [2019/XF5237/F]

♦ International Network of Engineers and Scientists Against Proliferation (see: #14260)

♦ International Network of Engineers and Scientists for Global Responsibility (INES) 14260

Program Dir Marienstr 19-20, 10117 Berlin, Germany. T. +493031996686. Fax +493031996689.
URL: http://inesglobal.net/

History 29 Nov 1991, Berlin (Germany), during the Congress 'CHALLENGES – Science and Peace in a Rapidly Changing Environment'. **Aims** Encourage and facilitate international communication among scientists and engineers seeking to promote international peace and security, justice and *sustainable development*; work for responsible use of *science* and *technology*; work for reduction in military spending and for transfer of resources thus liberated for the satisfaction of basic needs; promote environmentally sound technologies, taking into account long-term effects; enhance awareness of ethical principles among engineers and scientists and support those victimized for acting upon such principles; promote collaborative research relating to these issues; publicize relevant research; contribute to education and scientific training; inform the public and professional colleagues; facilitate and undertake expert and responsible contributions to relevant policy debates; advocate change in national and international policies. **Structure** Council, comprising representatives of member organizations. Executive Committee, consisting of Chairperson, Deputy Chairperson, Treasurer and up to 6 members. INES Advisory Council. Executive Secretary and Central Network Office. Includes: *International Network of Engineers and Scientists Against Proliferation (INESAP, see: #14260)*; *International Network of Engineers and Scientists' Projects on Ethics (INESPE, see: #14260).* **Languages** English. **Staff** 1.00 FTE, paid. **Finance** Members' dues. Other sources: donations; grants. **Activities** Meeting activities; advocacy/lobbying/activism. **Events** *Conference* Vienna (Austria) 2012, *Conference* Braunschweig (Germany) 2011, *Conference* Nagpur (India) 2010, *Workshop on science and sustainability / Conference* Mexico City (Mexico) / Oaxtepec (Mexico) 2008, *Conference* Nagpur (India) 2008. **Publications** *Global Responsibility* – open access journal; *What's New in INES (WNII)* – e-mail bulletin. Annual report.

Members Academies and peace organizations (75) and individual engineers and scientists in 31 countries:
Argentina, Australia, Austria, Belgium, Canada, Cuba, Denmark, Egypt, El Salvador, Finland, France, Germany, India, Italy, Japan, Mexico, Nepal, Netherlands, New Zealand, Nigeria, Pakistan, Philippines, Russia, Serbia, South Africa, Spain, Sweden, Türkiye, UK, Ukraine, USA.
Included in the above, 5 listed in this Yearbook:
Global Resource Action Center for the Environment (GRACE); *Institute for Peace and International Security (IPIS, no recent information)*; *Nuclear Age Peace Foundation*; *Science for Peace (SFP)*; *Scientists for Global Responsibility (SGR).*

NGO Relations A founding organization of: *International Coalition for Nuclear Non-Proliferation and Disarmament (inactive).* Represented on the Organizing Committee of: *Hague Appeal for Peace (HAP, #10848).* Member of: *International Campaign to Abolish Nuclear Weapons (ICAN, #12426)*; *International Peace Bureau (IPB, #14535)*; *Middle Powers Initiative (MPI, #16795)*; *NGO Committee on Disarmament, Peace and Security, New York NY (#17106).* [2020/XF2341/y/F]

♦ International Network of Engineers and Scientists' Projects on Ethics (see: #14260)

♦ International Network for Environmental Compliance and Enforcement (INECE) 14261

Contact c/o Environmental Law Inst, 1730 M St NW, Ste 700, Washington DC 20036, USA. T. +12029393800. Fax +12029399202. E-mail: info@inece.org.
Contact address not obtained.
URL: http://www.inece.org/

History 1989. Founded as a bilateral exchange between the US Environmental Protection Agency and the Dutch Environment Ministry. Inaugural international Enforcement Workshop held in Utrecht (Netherlands), 1990. Expanded into a partnership of governmental officials around the globe, NGOs and international organizations, in particular *UNEP (#20299)*, *International Bank for Reconstruction and Development (IBRD, #12317)* (World Bank) and *European Commission (EC, #06633).* **Aims** Facilitate enforcement and compliance cooperation; strengthen capacity throughout the regulatory cycle to implement and secure compliance with environmental requirements; raise awareness of the importance of environmental compliance and enforcement to *sustainable development.* **Structure** Executive Committee; Global Council; Regional Networks; Staff Group; Correspondents; Secretariat located in Washington DC (USA), set up May 2001. **Languages** Chinese, English, French, Spanish. **Staff** None. **Finance** Sources: government support; members' dues. Funding from Netherlands Inspectorate for Human Environment and Transport, and US Environmental Protection Agency and Environment Agency of England, with additional support from national governments, international organizations and others. **Activities** Awareness raising; capacity building; events/meetings; monitoring/evaluation; training/education. **Events** *Joint Conference AELERT-INECE* Adelaide, SA (Australia) 2020, *Conference* Canada 2011, *Linking concepts to action – sucessful strategies for environmental compliance and enforcement* Cape Town (South Africa) 2008, *Conference* Morocco 2005, *Enforcement and compliance issues associated with emissions trading schemes* Oxford (UK) 2004. **Publications** *INECE Newsletter* (weekly). *Principles of Environmental Compliance and Enforcement Handbook.* Conference proceedings; training manuals; workshop proceedings.

Members Attorneys, judges, government officials, academic experts and individuals (over 2,100) in over 150 countries. Membership countries not specified.
Included in the above, 26 organizations listed in this Yearbook:
- *African Development Bank (ADB, #00283)*;
- *ASEAN (#01141)*;
- *Asian Development Bank (ADB, #01422)*;
- *Asia-Pacific Centre for Environmental Law, Singapore (APCEL)*;
- *Center for International Environmental Law (CIEL)*;
- *Centre for Environment and Development for the Arab Region and Europe (CEDARE, #03738)*;
- *Comisión Centroamericana de Ambiente y Desarrollo (CCAD, #04129)*;
- *Commission for Environmental Cooperation (CEC, #04211)*;
- *Commonwealth Secretariat (#04362)*;
- *Environmental Investigation Agency (EIA)*;
- *European Commission (EC, #06633)*;
- *European Union Network for the Implementation and Enforcement of Environmental Law (IMPEL, #09005)*;
- *Inter-American Development Bank (IDB, #11427)*;
- *International Bank for Reconstruction and Development (IBRD, #12317)* (World Bank);
- *International Criminal Police Organization – INTERPOL (ICPO-INTERPOL, #13110)*;
- *International Union for Conservation of Nature and Natural Resources (IUCN, #15766)*;
- *Mediterranean Action Plan (MAP, #16638)*;
- *OAS (#17629)*;
- *OECD (#17693)*;
- *Regional Environmental Centre for Central and Eastern Europe (REC, #18782)*;
- *Secretariat of the Pacific Regional Environment Programme (SPREP, #19205)*;
- *South Asia Cooperative Environment Programme (SACEP, #19714)*;
- *UNDP (#20292)*;
- *UNEP (#20299)*;
- *World Customs Organization (WCO, #21350)*;
- *World Wide Fund for Nature (WWF, #21922).*

NGO Relations Observer status with (1): *European Union Network for the Implementation and Enforcement of Environmental Law (IMPEL, #09005).* Cooperates with (1): *Asian Environmental Compliance and Enforcement Network (AECEN, #01437).* [2022.02.11/XF6598/y/F]

♦ International Network of Environmental Forensics (INEF) 14262

Sec address not obtained.
URL: http://www.rsc-inef.net/

History 2008. A non-profit interest group within *Royal Society of Chemistry (RSC)*. **Aims** Provide a forum for scientists, environmental consultants, regulators and lawyers to share information regarding the use of environmental forensics. **Structure** Committee. **Activities** Events/meetings. **Events** *Annual Conference* Copenhagen (Denmark) 2020, *Annual Conference* Honolulu, HI (USA) 2019, *Annual Conference* Salt Lake City, UT (USA) 2018, *Annual Conference* Beijing (China) 2017, *Annual Conference* Örebro (Sweden) 2016. **Publications** Conference proceedings. [2021/AA1378/c/F]

♦ International Network for Environmental Management (INEM) 14263

Chairman Osterstrasse 58, 20259 Hamburg, Germany. T. +494049071600. Fax +494049071601. E-mail: info@inem.org.
URL: http://www.inem.org/

History 19 Feb 1991. Registration: Germany. **Aims** Protect the environment, especially water, soil and air, as well as animals and plants from ecological damage; protect human health; promote science and scientific research in the field of environmental protection. **Structure** Board of Directors. **Languages** English. **Finance** Members' dues. Other sources: corporate contributions; public funding; foundations. **Activities** Guidance/assistance/consulting; standards/guidelines; events/meetings. **Events** *ERSCP : European round table on sustainable consumption and production* Bilbao (Spain) 2004, *Annual conference / Conference* Stuttgart (Germany) 2003, *Conference* Berlin (Germany) 2001, *International Industry Conference for Sustainable Development – IICSD* Berlin (Germany) 2001, *Conference* Shefayim (Israel) 1999. **Publications** *Case Studies in Environmental Management in Small and Medium-sized Enterprises*; *Experiences of European Companies in Implementing Environmental Management*. Guides; guidelines; reports.

Members Full members in 13 countries:
Austria, Belarus, Belgium, Brazil, Czechia, Germany, Hungary, Latvia, Lithuania, Malaysia, Poland, Sweden, Switzerland.
Affiliated associations in 15 countries:
Denmark, Estonia, France, Greece, Ireland, Jordan, Romania, Russia, Slovakia, Spain, Taiwan, Tanzania UR, Tunisia, UK, Vietnam.

Consultative Status Consultative status granted from: *ECOSOC (#05331)* (Ros A); *UNIDO (#20336)*. **NGO Relations** In liaison with technical committees of: *International Organization for Standardization (ISO, #14473)*. [2018.06.22/XF5458/F]

♦ International Network for Epidemiology in Policy (INEP) 14264

Sec c/o College of Epidemiology, 230 Washington Ave Ext, Ste 101, Albany NY 12203-5319, USA. E-mail: info@epipolicy.org.
URL: http://www.epidemiologyinpolicy.org/

History Jun 2006, Seattle, WA (USA). Current title adopted 2018. Current Founding Bylaws approved 13 May 2014. Former names and other names: *Joint Policy Committee of the Societies of Epidemiology (JPC-SE)* – former (Jun 2006 to Dec 2013); *International Joint Policy Committee of the Societies of Epidemiology (IJPC-SE)* – former (Dec 2013 to 2018). Registration: 501(c)3, USA. **Aims** Promote integrity, equity and evidence in policies impacting health in order to inform rational policy development by governments and NGOs. **Structure** Board; Executive Committee; Expert Advisors. **Languages** English. **Staff** Voluntary. **Finance** In-kind contributions; direct and indirect solicitation. Annual budget: about US$ 25,000. **Activities** Politics/policy/regulatory; knowledge management/information dissemination; research and development. **Events** *Quinquennial Epidemiology Congress of the Americas* Miami, FL (USA) 2016. **Publications** Policy briefs; positions statements.

Members Organizations: Full (17); Associate (6). Full in 7 countries:
Cameroon, Canada, Germany, Romania, Spain, UK, USA.
Included in the above, Included in the above, 5 organizations listed in this Yearbook:
Australasian Epidemiological Association (AEA); *International Epidemiological Association (IEA, #13287)*; *International Society for Children's Health and the Environment (ISCHE)*; *International Society for Environmental Epidemiology (ISEE, #15092)*; *International Society for Pharmacoepidemiology (ISPE, #15355)*.
Associate in 5 countries:
Brazil, Italy, Japan, South Africa, USA.
Included in the above, 1 organization listed in this Yearbook:
European Society for Environmental and Occupational Medicine (EOM, #08597).

IGO Relations None. [2020/XM3913/y/E]

♦ International Network of Esophageal Atresia (INoEA) 14265

Pres address not obtained.
URL: http://www.inoea.org/

History Feb 2013. Set up following 2nd meeting on Esopahgeal Atresia, Oct 2012, Montréal QC (Canada). **Aims** Promote scientific knowledge and better care in the field of Esophageal Atresia. **Structure** Board. **Languages** English. **Events** *International Conference on Oesophageal Atresia* Istanbul (Türkiye) 2025, *International Conference on Oesophageal Atresia* Cincinnati, OH (USA) 2022, *International Conference on Esophageal Atresia* Rome (Italy) 2019, *International Conference on Oesophageal Atresia* Sydney, NSW (Australia) 2016, *International Conference on Oesophageal Atresia* Rotterdam (Netherlands) 2014. **Publications** Guidelines; position papers; e-book; articles. [2022.02.08/AA2327/F]

♦ International Network for the Exchange of Experiences and Reflections Useful for Action / see Dialogues, propositions, histoires pour une citoyenneté mondiale (#05067)
♦ International Network of Expertise on Landscapes / see LANDSCAPE EUROPE (#16229)

♦ International Network on Explosive Weapons (INEW) 14266

Coordinator c/o Article 36, 81 Rivington Street, London, EC2A 3AY, UK.
URL: http://www.inew.org/

History 29 Mar 2011, Geneva (Switzerland). **Aims** Call for immediate action to prevent human suffering from the use of explosive weapons in populated areas. **Structure** Steering Committee. **Publications** *INEW Bulletin*.

Members Full in 14 countries:
Canada, Colombia, Denmark, Netherlands, New Zealand, Nigeria, Norway, Pakistan, Spain, Sweden, Thailand, UK, USA, Zambia.
Included in the above, 15 organizations listed in this Yearbook:
Action on Armed Violence (AOAV); *Arab Human Security Network (AHSN)*; *Article 36*; *Center for Civilians in Conflict (CIVIC)*; *Danish Refugee Council (DRC)*; *Humanity and Inclusion (HI, #10975)*; *Human Rights Watch (HRW, #10990)*; *Medact*; *Norwegian People's Aid (NPA)*; *Oxfam International (#17922)*; *PAX*; *Save the Children UK (SC UK)*; *Seguridad Humana en América Latina y el Caribe (SEHLAC, #19218)*; *Swedish Peace and Arbitration Society (SPAS)*; *Women's International League for Peace and Freedom (WILPF, #21024)*. [2022/XM4891/y/F]

♦ International Network on Family Poultry Development (INFPD) 14267

Réseau internationale pour le développement de l'aviculture familiale (RIDAF) – Red Internacional para el Desarrollo Aves Caseras de Familia (RIDAF)

Contact Senegalese Inst of Agricultural Research, BP 2057, Dakar, Senegal. T. +221772823000 – +221(22373064000.

History Nov 1989, Ile Ife (Nigeria), as *African Network on Rural Poultry Development – Réseau africain pour le développement de l'aviculture en milieu rurale*. Relaunched in 1990, Thessaloniki (Greece), after a seminar of *Centre technique de coopération agricole et rurale (CTA, inactive)*. Subsequently changed to: *Afro-Asian Network on Rural Poultry Development (ANRPD) – Réseau afro-asiatique pour le développement de l'aviculture en milieu rurale (RADAR)*. Current title adopted Dec 1997, M'Bour (Senegal). 2002, became a Working Group within *World's Poultry Science Association (WPSA, #21825)*. **Aims** Consolidate knowledge of family poultry production and coordinate efforts to develop it. **Structure** Steering Committee, with a regional representation; Coordinator/Chairman; Secretary; Treasurer; Editor-in-Chief. **Languages** English, French, Spanish. **Staff** 5.00 FTE, voluntary. **Finance** Members' dues. Other sources: publication grant from *FAO (#09260)*; conference grants from various sources, principally FAO. Annual budget: about US$ 50,000. **Activities** Projects/programmes; training/education. **Events** *Conference* Salvador (Brazil) 2012, *Conference* Dhaka (Bangladesh) 2011, *Conference* Tours (France) 2010, *Conference* Brisbane, QLD (Australia) 2008, *Conference* Istanbul (Turkey) 2004. **Publications** *Family Poultry Communications* (2 a year) in English, French, Spanish – newsletter; *Family Poultry Development Directory* (annual). *Small-scale Poultry Production* (2004) in Arabic, English, French; *Sustainable Rural Poultry Development in Africa* (1997); *Rural Poultry in Africa* (1990).

Members Individual research and development workers (945) in 104 countries and territories:
Afghanistan, Algeria, Angola, Argentina, Australia, Bangladesh, Belgium, Benin, Bhutan, Bolivia, Botswana, Brazil, Burkina Faso, Burundi, Cameroon, Canada, Cape Verde, Central African Rep, Chad, Chile, China, Colombia, Comoros, Congo Brazzaville, Congo DR, Côte d'Ivoire, Cuba, Czechia, Denmark, Dominican Rep, Ecuador, Egypt, Eswatini, Ethiopia, Fiji, France, Gabon, Gambia, Germany, Ghana, Guatemala, Guinea, Guinea-Bissau, Haiti, Hungary, India, Indonesia, Iran Islamic Rep, Iraq, Israel, Italy, Japan, Kenya, Lesotho, Liberia, Madagascar, Malawi, Malaysia, Mali, Mauritania, Mauritius, Mexico, Mongolia, Morocco, Mozambique, Myanmar, Namibia, Netherlands, New Zealand, Nicaragua, Niger, Nigeria, Norway, Pakistan, Papua New Guinea, Peru, Philippines, Portugal, Rwanda, Samoa, Senegal, Sierra Leone, South Africa, Spain, Sri Lanka, Sudan, Sweden, Switzerland, Syrian AR, Taiwan, Tanzania UR, Thailand, Togo, Tunisia, Türkiye, Uganda, UK, United Arab Emirates, Uruguay, USA, Venezuela, Vietnam, Zambia, Zimbabwe.

IGO Relations FAO; *European Commission (EC, #06633)*. [2020.01.02/XF2805/v/F]

♦ International Network on Family Violence (INFV) 14268

Contact c/o NCCAFV, 1025 Connecticut Ave NW, Ste 1000, Washington DC 20036, USA. T. +12024296695. Fax +12025213479.
URL: http://www.nccafv.org/international.htm

History Sep 1998, Singapore (Singapore). Founded during the World Congress on Family Violence. **Aims** Strengthen the international network of advocates, prevention specialists and protective service workers addressing family violence in all its forms including child *abuse*, spouse/partner abuse (domestic violence) and elder abuse. **Languages** English. **Staff** 4.50 FTE, paid. **Finance** Private and corporate contributions. **Events** *World congress on family violence* Montréal, QC (Canada) 2005, *World congress on family violence / World Congress* Prague (Czech Rep) 2003, *World congress on family violence* Singapore (Singapore) 1998. **IGO Relations** *UNESCO (#20322)*; *UNICEF (#20332)*. [2015.01.27/XF6864/F]

♦ International Network for Farming Systems Research Methodology / see Centro Latinoamericano para el Desarrollo Rural (#03813)

♦ International Network for Fatty Acid Oxidation Research and Management (INFORM) 14269

Coordinator Medical Genetics, Faculty Pavilion, 4401 Penn Ave, Pittsburgh PA 15224, USA. T. +14126925099.
URL: https://informnetwork.org/

History Founded 2013. **Aims** bring together genetic researchers and clinicians worldwide, working to discover treatments and cures for fatty acid oxidation disorders (FAODs) to improve the lives of *patients* and their families. **Structure** Committee. **Activities** Events/meetings. **Events** *Annual Conference* Amsterdam (Netherlands) 2019, *Annual Conference* Athens (Greece) 2018, *Annual Conference* Rio de Janeiro (Brazil) 2017, *Annual Conference* Boston, MA (USA) 2016. [2019/XM8588/F]

♦ International Network on Feminist Approaches to Bioethics (FAB) . 14270

Coordinator PO Box 1712, Dearborn MI 48121-1712, USA. E-mail: jlnelson@msu.edu.
URL: http://www.fabnet.org/

History 1992. Founded at inaugural congress of *International Association of Bioethics (IAB, #11725)*. **Aims** Develop a more inclusive theory of bioethics encompassing the standpoints and experiences of *women* and other *marginalized* social groups; examine presuppositions embedded in the bioethical discourse; create new methodologies and strategies responsive to the disparate conditions of women's lives worldwide. **Structure** Meeting (every 2 years, in conjunction with FAB and IAB Congresses). Officers: 2 Coordinators; Archivist; Country Representatives Coordinator; Grants Coordinator; IJFAB Editor; Liaison with IAB; Listserv Facilitator; Membership Secretary; Treasurer; Website Facilitator; 2 Co-Chairs of Congress Coordinating Committee. Advisory Board, comprising FAB Officers and 7 elected members. Most terms of Officers and Advisory Board members have 2-year renewable appointments. **Languages** English, Spanish. **Staff** Voluntary. **Finance** Sources: donations; grants; members' dues. **Activities** Events/meetings. **Events** *Conference* Edinburgh (UK) 2016, *Congress* Mexico 2014, *Health care ethics – local, global, universal* Mexico City (Mexico) 2014, *Conference / Congress* Rotterdam (Netherlands) 2012, *Conference* Singapore (Singapore) 2010. **Publications** *International Journal of Feminist Approaches to Bioethics* (2 a year) – sponsor. Newsletter (1993-2007); themed anthologies from conferences with related papers.

Members Individuals (about 150) in 27 countries and territories:
Argentina, Australia, Belgium, Brazil, Canada, Chile, Colombia, Germany, Greece, Hong Kong, India, Ireland, Israel, Italy, Korea Rep, Mexico, Netherlands, New Zealand, Panama, Peru, Saudi Arabia, Singapore, Switzerland, Taiwan, Türkiye, UK, USA. [2022/XF4752/v/F]

♦ International Network of Food Data Systems (INFOODS) 14271

Réseau international de systèmes de données sur l'alimentation

Coordinator c/o Nutrition Division – ESN, FAO, Viale delle Terme di Caracalla, 00153 Rome RM, Italy. T. +39657056134.
URL: http://www.fao.org/infoods/

History 1984. Founded on recommendations of an international group of 30 experts in nutrition convened in Bellagio (Italy) in 1983, under the auspices of *United Nations University (UNU, #20642)*, with active engagement of *Nevin Scrimshaw International Nutrition Foundation (INF)*. *FAO (#09260)* has taken an active role in the Network since 1990; since 1999 serves as the global coordinator. A Task Force of *International Union of Nutritional Sciences (IUNS, #15796)*. **Aims** Promote international participation and cooperation in the acquisition and dissemination of complete and accurate data on the composition of foods, beverages and their ingredients, in forms appropriate to meet the needs of various users, government agencies, *nutrition* scientists and educators, *health* and *agriculture* professionals, policy makers and planners, food producers/processors/retailers and consumers; develop international criteria for judging the quality of data on food composition; identify existing sources of useful data on food composition; promote generation, acquisition and dissemination of new data on the composition of foods, beverages and their ingredients that meet the criteria developed; facilitate, on a world-wide basis, access, retrieval, interchange and general harmonization of food composition data. **Structure** Organized into Regional Data Centres, each with a regional coordinator and national members. A Global Coordinator oversees activities. Regional and Subregional Data Centres (18): *African Food Network of Food Data Systems (AFROFOODS, #00317)*; *Red Latinoamericana de Composición de Alimentos (LATINFOODS, #18708)*; *MEFOODS and GULFOODS* – parts of Middle Eastern and Northern Africa; *OCEANIAFOODS*; *Association of Southeast Asian Networks of Food Data Systems (ASEANFOODS, #02921)*; *NORAMFOODS* – Mexico, Canada, USA, the Caribbean; *SAARCFOODS* – South Asia; *NEASIAFOODS* – China, Korea Rep, Japan; *GULFOODS* – Persian Gulf countries; *EUROFOODS* – Western Europe; *CEECFOODS* – Central and Eastern Europe; *CARKFOODS* – Central Asia and Kazakhstan. **Languages** English, French, Spanish. **Staff** Not paid by INFOODS: coordinators and contact points from organizations into which INFOODS' activities have been integrated and mandated. **Finance** Main source: FAO. Governmental and regional funding for regional affiliates; support from organizations and private industry for some specific projects. **Activities** Provides: international guidelines and standards; food composition database management system; pool of experts in generation and compilation of food composition data; professionals with the means to generate, compile and use food composition data, according to international guidelines and standards; information and data on food biodiversity and for nutrition labelling; a forum for information exchange. Assists countries to compile and publish a food composition database and tables according to international standards; shares food composition data; increases knowledge of professionals regarding food composition and biodiversity; incorporates food composition into formal education curricula of schools and universities; strengthen collaboration with other national and international bodies, organizations and projects working in the field; raises awareness for the importance of high-quality food composition data for all applications. Organizes International Food Data Conference (every 2 years). **Events** *International Food Data Conference* Lisbon (Portugal) 2019, *International Food Data Conference* Hyderabad (India) 2015, *International Food Data Conference / International Conference* Granada (Spain) 2013, *International food data conference / Conference / International Conference* Norwich (UK) 2011, *International food data conference / International Conference* Bangkok (Thailand) 2009. **Publications** Guidelines; standards; tools; capacity development tools; courses; databases.

Members Regional affiliates in Europe, Latin America, Asia, Africa and Oceania. Individual correspondents in 122 countries and territories:

Algeria, Angola, Argentina, Australia, Austria, Bahrain, Belgium, Benin, Bolivia, Botswana, Brazil, Bulgaria, Burkina Faso, Burundi, Cameroon, Canada, Cape Verde, Central African Rep, Chad, Chile, China, Colombia, Comoros, Congo Brazzaville, Congo DR, Côte d'Ivoire, Denmark, Djibouti, Ecuador, Egypt, Equatorial Guinea, Eritrea, Eswatini, Ethiopia, Fiji, Finland, France, Gabon, Gambia, Germany, Ghana, Greece, Guatemala, Guinea, Guinea-Bissau, Hong Kong, Hungary, Iceland, Indonesia, Ireland, Italy, Jamaica, Kenya, Kiribati, Korea Rep, Lesotho, Liberia, Libya, Luxembourg, Madagascar, Malawi, Malaysia, Mali, Marshall Is, Mauritania, Mauritius, Mexico, Micronesia FS, Montenegro, Morocco, Mozambique, Myanmar, Namibia, Nauru, Netherlands, New Zealand, Niger, Nigeria, Norway, Oman, Pakistan, Palau, Papua New Guinea, Paraguay, Peru, Philippines, Poland, Portugal, Qatar, Romania, Rwanda, Samoa, Sao Tomé-Principe, Senegal, Serbia, Seychelles, Sierra Leone, Solomon Is, Somalia, South Africa, Spain, Sudan, Sweden, Switzerland, Taiwan, Tanzania UR, Thailand, Togo, Tonga, Tunisia, Türkiye, Tuvalu, Uganda, UK, United Arab Emirates, Uruguay, USA, Vanuatu, Venezuela, Vietnam, Zambia, Zimbabwe. [2021/XF0546/F]

♦ International Network on Gender and Sustainable Energy (ENERGIA) 14272

Secretariat c/o HIVOS, People Unlimited, Grote Marktstraat 47a, 2511 BH The Hague, Netherlands. T. +31703765500. E-mail: energia@hivos.org.
URL: http://www.energia.org/

History 1995. **Aims** Contribute to the empowerment of rural and urban poor women through a specific focus on energy issues. **Structure** Advisory Group; Secretariat; National/Regional Focal Points; Regional Network Coordinators for Asia and Africa. **Languages** English. **Finance** Core funding from: *Directorate-General for Development Cooperation (DGDC)*; *Swedish International Development Cooperation Agency (Sida)*; *European Commission (EC, #06633)*. **Activities** include: regionalization; advocacy; capacity building through, gender and energy training workshops, international and regional advocacy, support to emerging national and regional networks in the South, development of gender and energy knowledge resources and research and case study development on gender and energy, gender, energy and climate change, and gender, energy and biofuels. **Publications** *ENERGIA News* (3 a year) – newsletter; *ENERGIANet* – electronic newsletter. *Gender and Energy Training Pack*. Toolkits; bibliographies; databases.

Members National focal points in 22 countries:
Bangladesh, Botswana, Eswatini, Ghana, India, Indonesia, Kenya, Laos, Lesotho, Mali, Nepal, Nigeria, Pakistan, Philippines, Senegal, South Africa, Sri Lanka, Tanzania UR, Uganda, Vietnam, Zambia, Zimbabwe.

IGO Relations Cooperates with: *International Bank for Reconstruction and Development (IBRD, #12317)* (World Bank); *UNDP (#20292)*. **NGO Relations** Member of: *Global Gender and Climate Alliance (GGCA, no recent information)*; *International Network for Sustainable Energy (INFORSE, #14331)*. Cooperates with: *All India Women's Conference (AIWC, #00737)*; *Asian Alliance of Appropriate Technology Practitioners (APPROTECH ASIA, #01306)*; *Environnement et développement du Tiers-monde (enda, #05510)*; *Friends of the Earth International (FoEI, #10002)*; *Regional Information Service Centre for Southeast Asia on Appropriate Technology (RISE-AT)*; *Winrock International*; national organizations. [2020/XF1670/F]

♦ International Network for Genetic Evaluation of Rice (see: #14754)
♦ International Network on Genetics in Aquaculture (see: #21507)
♦ International Network of Geoparks / see Global Geoparks Network (#10389)

♦ International Network for Girls (INfG) 14273

Contact UNICEF House, 3 UN Plaza, H-10F, New York NY 10017, USA. T. +12128246394. Fax +12128246482.
URL: http://www.girlsrights.org/

History 1995, by NGO Working Group on Girls of *NGO Committee on UNICEF (#17120)*. **Aims** Advance the rights and status of girls worldwide; links grassroots organizations to each other, to the international community and UN system and strengthen their capacity to advocate collectively and effectively with their own governments on behalf of girls; promote active participation of girls as leaders, decision makers and agents of change in their own lives and in their families, communities and societies; focus on implementation of government commitments made at Beijing (China) as a goal in itself and as a mobilizing tool. **Activities** Organizes workshops. Lobbies government delegates. **Publications** Position papers; other advocacy materials.

Members Organizations and individuals in 80 countries:
Afghanistan, Argentina, Armenia, Australia, Austria, Bangladesh, Belgium, Belize, Benin, Bolivia, Brazil, Burkina Faso, Cambodia, Cameroon, Canada, Chile, China, Colombia, Costa Rica, Côte d'Ivoire, Czechia, Ecuador, Egypt, Eswatini, Ethiopia, France, Gambia, Germany, Ghana, Greece, Guatemala, Honduras, India, Iraq, Ireland, Israel, Jamaica, Japan, Jordan, Kenya, Korea DPR, Korea Rep, Laos, Lebanon, Lithuania, Malawi, Mali, Mexico, Mozambique, Nepal, Netherlands, New Zealand, Nicaragua, Niger, Nigeria, North Macedonia, Norway, Pakistan, Panama, Papua New Guinea, Peru, Philippines, Portugal, Russia, Senegal, Sierra Leone, Somalia, South Africa, Spain, Sri Lanka, Sweden, Switzerland, Thailand, Türkiye, Uganda, Uruguay, USA, Vietnam, Zambia, Zimbabwe.

IGO Relations *UNICEF (#20332)*. [2008/XF4449/F]

♦ International Network for Government Science Advice (INGSA) 14274

Contact address not obtained. E-mail: info@ingsa.org.
URL: http://www.ingsa.org/

History 2014. Operates under the auspices of *International Science Council (ISC, #14796)*. **Aims** Provide a forum for policy makers, practitioners, national academies, and academics to share experience, build capacity and develop theoretical and practical approaches to the use of scientific evidence in informing policy at all levels of government. **Structure** Executive Group; Regional Chapters; Special Interest Divisions; Secretariat. **Activities** Capacity building; events/meetings; knowledge management/information dissemination; networking/liaising; research/documentation. **Events** *Conference* Montréal, QC (Canada) 2021, *Conference* Montréal, QC (Canada) 2020, *Biosecurity and Science Advice Workshop* Warsaw (Poland) 2019, *Conference* Tokyo (Japan) 2018, *SFSA : Science Forum South Africa* Pretoria (South Africa) 2017. **Publications** *INGSA Report: Digital Well-being – Understanding well-being in the context of rapid digital and associated transformations. Implications for research policy and measurement.* (2018). Case studies. **Members** Individuals (about 5,000) from over 100 countries. Membership countries not specified. **NGO Relations** Partner of (3): *International Science Council (ISC, #14796)*; Royal Society; *Wellcome Trust*. [2020.05.20/XM5532/F]

♦ International Network of Graduate Surveys (unconfirmed)
♦ International Network for Harmonized and Recognized Measurements in Wind Energy / see Measuring Network of Wind Energy Institutes (#16609)

♦ International Network for Hate Studies (INHS) 14275

Acting Dir address not obtained.
URL: http://www.internationalhatestudies.com/

History Founded 2013, following a seminar organized Apr 2012, Cardiff (UK). **Aims** Provide an accessible forum through which individuals and groups can engage with the study of hate and hate crime in a manner which is both scholarly and accessible to all; promote understanding about the root causes of hate and hate crime; understand ways in which it can be combatted in society. **Structure** 2 Co-Directors; Advisory Board. **Languages** English. **Staff** Voluntary. **Finance** No funding. **Activities** Events/meetings; knowledge management/information dissemination; research/documentation. **Events** *Biennial Conference* Oshawa, ON (Canada) 2018, *Biennial Conference* Limerick (Ireland) 2016, *Biennial Conference* Brighton (UK) 2014. **Publications** *INHS Newsletter* (12 a year). **IGO Relations** *OSCE – Office for Democratic Institutions and Human Rights (OSCE/ODIHR, #17902)*. [2019.06.12/XM8030/F]

♦ International Network on Health and Hepatitis in Substance Users (INHSU) 14276

Exec Dir c/o Arud Centres, Schützengasse 31, 8001 Zurich ZH, Switzerland. E-mail: info@inhsu.org.
Contact c/o ASHM, Level 3, 160 Clarence St, Sydney NSW 2000, Australia.
URL: https://www.inhsu.org

History 2009, Switzerland. Former names and other names: *International Network on Hepatitis in Substance Users (INHSU)* – former (2009). **Aims** Advance research of pathogenesis, prevention, and treatment of hepatitis among substance users. **Structure** General Assembly; Board of Directors; Secretariat. **Activities** Advocacy/lobbying/activism; events/meetings; knowledge management/information dissemination; training/education. **Events** *International Conference on Health and Hepatitis Care in Substance Users* Glasgow (UK) 2022, *International Conference on Health and Hepatitis Care in Substance Users* Sydney, NSW (Australia) 2021, *International Conference on Health and Hepatitis Care in Substance Users* Glasgow (UK) 2020, *International Conference on Health and Hepatitis Care in Substance Users* Montréal, QC (Canada) 2019, *International Symposium on Hepatitis Care in Substance Users* Cascais (Portugal) 2018. **Publications** *INSHU Newsletter*. **NGO Relations** Partner of (1): *Australasian Society for HIV, Viral Hepatitis and Sexual Health Medicine (ASHM)*. Joint meetings with: *European Association for the Study of the Liver (EASL, #06233)*. [2021/XJ7897/F]

♦ International Network of Health Promoting Hospitals / see International Network of Health Promoting Hospitals and Health Services (#14277)

♦ International Network of Health Promoting Hospitals and Health Services (HPH) 14277

CEO Burchardstrasse 17, 20095 Hamburg, Germany. T. +494022621149 ext 0. E-mail: info@hphnet.org.
URL: http://www.hphnet.org/

History as *European Network of Health Promoting Hospitals (HPH)*, by *WHO Regional Office for Europe (#20945)*. Subsequently changed title to *International Network of Health Promoting Hospitals*. **Aims** Facilitate and encourage cooperation and exchange of experience between hospitals of a region or country, including identification of areas of common interest, sharing of resources and development of common evaluation systems; implement health promotion into the culture of hospitals and health services; broaden the focus of hospital management and structures to include health care and to develop documented and evaluated examples of good practice for the use of other institutions. **Structure** General Assembly; Governance Board. Secretariat in Hamburg (Germany). International Conferences coordinated by WHO CC Vienna (Austria). Task Forces; Working Groups; Regional/National Networks. **Languages** English. **Finance** Members' dues. **Activities** Events/meetings. **Events** *Annual International Conference on Health Promoting Hospitals and Health Services* Seoul (Korea Rep) 2020, *Annual International Conference on Health Promoting Hospitals and Health Services* Warsaw (Poland) 2019, *Annual International Conference on Health Promoting Hospitals and Health Services* Bologna (Italy) 2018, *Annual International Conference on Health Promoting Hospitals and Health Services* Vienna (Austria) 2017, *Annual International Conference on Health Promoting Hospitals and Health Services* Derby, CT (USA) 2016. **Publications** *Implementing Health Promotion in Hospitals: Manual and Self-Assessment Forms* (2006); *Health Promotion in Hospitals: Evidence and Quality Management* (2005); *Standards for Health Promotion in Hospitals* (2004).

Members Hospitals (682). National/Regional Networks in 23 countries:
Austria, Belgium, Bulgaria, Canada, Czechia, Estonia, Finland, France, Germany, Greece, Ireland, Italy, Lithuania, Norway, Poland, Russia, Slovakia, Spain, Sweden, Switzerland, Taiwan, UK, USA.
Individual Hospitals/Health Services in 12 countries:
Australia, Brazil, Denmark, Japan, Saudi Arabia, Serbia, Singapore, Slovenia, South Africa, Spain, UK, USA.
[2020.01.02/XF3661/F]

♦ International Network of Health Promotion Foundations (INHPF) . . . 14278

Secretariat c/o Thai Health Promotion Foundation, 99/8 Soi Ngamduplee, Thung Maha Mek, Sathorn, Bangkok, 10120, Thailand.

History 1999. **Aims** Enhance performance of existing health promotion foundations or similar organizations which are members; provide information, advice and support to members; support establishment and build capacity of new health promotion foundations to apply innovative financing mechanisms. **Languages** English. **Activities** Knowledge sharing. **Events** *Annual Meeting* Thailand 2013, *Conference / Annual Meeting* Seoul (Korea Rep) 2012, *Conference / Annual Meeting* Kuala Lumpur (Malaysia) 2011, *Conference / Annual Meeting* Geneva (Switzerland) 2010, *Conference / Annual Meeting* Austria 2009. **Publications** *Health Promotion Fund: Sustainable Financing and Governance* (2013).

Members Full in 6 countries and territories:
Australia, Korea Rep, Malaysia, Taiwan, Thailand, Tonga.

IGO Relations Partner organization: *WHO (#20950)*. **NGO Relations** Partner organizations: *International Union for Health Promotion and Education (IUHPE, #15778)*; *The NCD Alliance (NCDA, #16963)*; *Nossal Institute for Global Health*; *Southeast Asian Tobacco Control Alliance (SEATCA, #19785)*. [2013.09.03/XJ5054/F]

♦ International Network for Health Workforce Education (INHWE) . . . 14279

Dir address not obtained.
URL: https://inhwe.org/

Aims Bridge the gap between health workforce educators, researchers and policy makers so as to improve education and training provided to health professionals internationally. **Structure** Advisory Board; Secretariat. **Finance** Members' dues. **Activities** Networking/liaising; knowledge management/information dissemination; advocacy/lobbying/activism; events/meetings. **Events** *European Conference of Health Workforce Education and Research* Dublin (Ireland) 2021, *Congress of Health Workforce Education and Research* Barcelona (Spain) 2020, *European Conference of Health Workforce Education and Research* Dublin (Ireland) 2019, *Congress of Health Workforce Education and Research* Nicosia (Cyprus) 2019, *European Conference of Health Workforce Education and Research* Athens (Greece) 2018. **Publications** *INHWE Newsletter*. **IGO Relations** *European Commission (EC, #06633)*. **NGO Relations** Associated member of: *European Forum for Primary Care (EFPC, #07326)*. [2020/XM8917/F]

♦ International Network on Hepatitis in Substance Users / see International Network on Health and Hepatitis in Substance Users (#14276)

♦ international network of Historians without Borders 14280

Contact Post Box 54, Univ of Helsinki, FI-00014 Helsinki, Finland. E-mail: info@hwb.fi.
URL: https://historianswithoutborders.fi/

History 20 May 2016, Helsinki (Finland). Registration: No/ID: 215.568, Finland. **Aims** Promote and deepen general and comprehensive knowledge and understanding of history; promote open and free access to historical material and archives; promote interactive dialogue between different views and interpretations of history; contribute to the use of history in defusing and resolving conflicts. **Structure** Coordinating Committee. **Activities** Events/meetings.

Members Signatories of the Historians without Borders Declaration in 49 countries:
Albania, Argentina, Armenia, Australia, Austria, Belarus, Bosnia-Herzegovina, Brazil, Canada, Croatia, Cyprus, Czechia, Denmark, Egypt, Estonia, Finland, France, Germany, Greece, Hungary, India, Ireland, Israel, Italy, Korea Rep, Kosovo, Lithuania, Mexico, Mozambique, Namibia, Netherlands, Nigeria, North Macedonia, Norway, Pakistan, Poland, Portugal, Russia, Serbia, South Africa, Spain, Sri Lanka, Sweden, Switzerland, Trinidad-Tobago, Türkiye, UK, Ukraine, USA. [2023/AA2189/v/F]

♦ International Network for the History of Homeopathy 14281

Contact Inst für Geschichte der Medizin, Robert Bosch Stiftung, Straussweg 17, 70184 Stuttgart, Germany. T. +49711460841167. Fax +4971146084181. E-mail: info@igm-bosch.de.
URL: http://www.igm-bosch.de/

History 1994, Stuttgart (Germany). **Aims** Encourage comparative research in the international history of homeopathy. **Languages** English, German. **Staff** 1.00 FTE, paid. **Finance** Supported by: *European Association for the History of Medicine and Health (EAHMH, #06070)*; *Robert Bosch Foundation*. **Events** *International Conference* 2019, *International Conference* Stuttgart (Germany) 2011, *International Conference* Stuttgart (Germany) 2007, *International conference* Stuttgart (Germany) 2006, *International conference* Budapest (Hungary) 2003. **Publications** *Patients in the History of Homeopathy* (2002); *Patients in the History of Homeopathy* (2001); *Historical Aspects of Unconventional Medicine: Approaches, Concepts, Case Studies* (2001); *Culture, Knowledge and Healing: Historical Perspectives of Homeopathic Medicine in Europe and North America* (1998); *Weltgeschichte der Homöopathie, Länder – Schulen – Heilkundige* (1996). Conference proceedings.

Members Full in 24 countries:
Australia, Austria, Bangladesh, Belgium, Brazil, Canada, France, Germany, Greece, Hungary, India, Israel, Italy, Japan, Mexico, Netherlands, Poland, Russia, Slovenia, Spain, Sweden, Switzerland, UK, USA. [2022.02.09/XF6041/F]

♦ International Network for the History of Hospitals (INHH) 14282

Founder Member University of East Anglia, Norwich Research Park, Norwich, NR4 7TJ, UK. T. +441603592872.
URL: https://inhh.org/

History 1995, UK. **Aims** Promote studies related to the historical evolution of hospitals from their beginnings to the present day. **Structure** Advisory Board. **Activities** Organizes conferences, seminars and workshops. **Events** *Conference* 2021, *Conference* Barcelona (Spain) 2019, *Segregation and integration in the history of the hospital* Dubrovnik (Croatia) 2015, *Conference* Brussels (Belgium) 2013, *Conference* Lisbon (Portugal) 2011. **Publications** *INHH Newsletter* (annual).

Members Full in 26 countries:
Algeria, Australia, Belgium, Bosnia-Herzegovina, Brazil, Canada, Croatia, Czechia, Denmark, France, Germany, Greece, Ireland, Israel, Italy, Korea Rep, Mexico, Netherlands, New Zealand, Peru, Russia, Spain, Sweden, Switzerland, UK, USA.

NGO Relations Supported by: *European Association for the History of Medicine and Health (EAHMH, #06070).* [2021/XF6040/F]

♦ International Network for the History of Neuropsychopharmacology (INHN) 14283

Central Administrative Unit Av Sagrada Familia Esq Nazaret, X5009 Córdoba, Argentina. T. +543514818335. E-mail: inhn.org@gmail.com.
URL: http://inhn.org/

History Founded 2012. Commenced activities May 2013. **Aims** Document, preserve and disseminate all contributions relevant to the history of neuropsychopharmacology. **Structure** Coordinating Committee; Central Administrative Unit. **Languages** English. **Staff** Voluntary. **Finance** No financial support. **Activities** Training/education; research/documentation.
Members Individuals in 31 countries:
Argentina, Australia, Austria, Bosnia-Herzegovina, Brazil, Canada, Czechia, Denmark, Estonia, France, Germany, Greece, Hungary, India, Ireland, Israel, Italy, Japan, Korea Rep, Mexico, Morocco, Netherlands, Pakistan, Peru, Poland, Spain, Sweden, Switzerland, Türkiye, UK, Uruguay, USA.
IGO Relations None. [2016.11.14/XM5211/F]

♦ International Network for the History of Public Health (INHPH) 14284

Editor-in-Chief Dept for Studies of Social Change and Culture, Linköping Univ, SE-581 83 Linköping, Sweden. T. +4613282940.
URL: http://www.ep.liu.se/ej/hygiea/

History 1993. **Aims** Promote the study of the history of collective efforts for the improvement of the health of populations from antiquity to modernity. **Finance** No funding for organization; some funding for the journal. **Activities** Current topics of interest include: summarizing the state of the art; investigating the social and cultural constructions of disease – disease visibility; analysing public health campaigns; interpreting social and demographic data related to public health activities. **Events** *Conference* London (UK) 2007, *Conference* Paris (France) 2005, *Health between the private and the public – shifting approaches* Oslo (Norway) 2003, *Occupational health and public health, lessons from the past – challenges for the future* Norrköping (Sweden) 2001, *Biennial conference* Almuñécar (Spain) 1999. **Publications** *INHPH Newsletter* (2 a year); *Hygiea Internationalis – an Interdisciplinary Journal for the History of Public Health.*
Members Individuals (388) in 47 countries and territories:
Algeria, Argentina, Australia, Bangladesh, Belgium, Bhutan, Brazil, Canada, Croatia, Denmark, Finland, France, Germany, Ghana, Greece, Iceland, India, Ireland, Israel, Italy, Jamaica, Japan, Kenya, Korea Rep, Kuwait, Malawi, Mauritius, Mexico, Namibia, Netherlands, New Caledonia, New Zealand, Norway, Pakistan, Peru, Philippines, Poland, Russia, South Africa, Spain, Switzerland, Taiwan, Tanzania UR, Trinidad-Tobago, Türkiye, UK, USA. [2016/XF4284/v/F]

♦ International Network for Humane Education (InterNICHE) 14285

Coordinator 98 Clarendon Park Rd, Leicester, LE2 3AE, UK. T. +441162109652. Fax +441162109652. E-mail: coordinator@interniche.org.
URL: http://www.interniche.org/

History 1988, as *European Network of Individuals and Campaigns for Humane Education (EuroNICHE).* Present name adopted 2000. **Aims** Promote and implement humane alternatives to *animal experiments* in education in biological science, veterinary and human medicine. **Structure** Network comprises students, teachers and animal campaigners. Decision-making for international issues and project work is democratic and by consensus, usually resting with a Committee of National Contacts. Activity performed by the Coordinator at the international level and by national contacts within their countries. A Core Group supports the Coordinator in guiding and maintaining the network. **Finance** Donations; grants. **Activities** Carries out national and international projects; organizes conferences; also organizes local and regional outreach tours; grants the 'Humane Education Award'. Set up an international loan system (library) of alternatives. Setting up several regional loan systems. **Events** *Conference* Oslo (Norway) 2005, *Conference* Brussels (Belgium) 2001, *Conference* Netherlands 1997. **Publications** *From Guinea Pig to Computer Mouse* (2nd ed 2003). Video, available in almost 20 languages. **Information Services** *Alternative Loans System* – library of products, literature, support and advice for teachers and students.
Members No a membership organization. National contacts in 31 countries:
Argentina, Australia, Belgium, Bosnia-Herzegovina, Brazil, Canada, Cuba, Czechia, Denmark, Estonia, Finland, Georgia, Germany, Hungary, Iran Islamic Rep, Israel, Japan, Korea Rep, Mexico, Netherlands, New Zealand, Norway, Romania, Russia, Serbia, Singapore, Slovenia, South Africa, Spain, Sweden, Ukraine. [2018/XF3733/F]

♦ International Network of Human Rights (#18891)

♦ International Network of Human Rights I Europe (RIDHE) 14286

Réseau International des Droits Humains I Europe (RIDHE) – Red Internacional de Derechos Humanos I Europa

Dir Bureau Mundo-B, Rue d'Edimbourg 26, 1050 Brussels, Belgium. T. +3228930980. E-mail: info@ridheuropa.org.
URL: https://ridheuropa.org/

History 2019, Brussels (Belgium). Registration: Banque-Carrefour des Entreprises, No/ID: 0730.618.747, Start date: 11 Jul 2019, Belgium; EU Transparency Register, No/ID: 259152048349-92, Start date: 9 Dec 2022. **Aims** Protect and promote human rights through capacity-building skills and international cooperation projects. **Languages** Dutch, English, French, Portuguese, Spanish. **Staff** 11.00 FTE, paid. **Activities** Advocacy/lobbying/activism; capacity building; events/meetings; guidance/assistance/consulting; humanitarian/emergency aid; projects/programmes; training/education. Active in: Belgium, Brazil, Colombia, Costa Rica, El Salvador, Guatemala, Honduras, Nicaragua, Peru, Venezuela. [2023.02.17/AA3173/F]

♦ International Network of Independent Law Firms / see ADVOC (#00141)
♦ International Network for Information in Science and Technology Education (inactive)

♦ International Network for Information Technology in Agriculture (INFITA) 14287

Contact International Center for Food Chain and Network Research, Meckenheimer Allee 174, 53115 Bonn, Germany.

History Former names and other names: *World Federation for Information Technology in Agriculture (WFITA)* – former; *International Federation for Information Technology in Agriculture (IFITA)* – former. **Aims** Advance and promote information technology in agriculture by: improving quality of food and fiber; improving competitiveness and productivity of agricultural producers; promoting sustainable practice; reducing environmental impacts. **Events** *World Congress on Computers in Agriculture* Rhodes Is (Greece) 2019, *Meeting* Taichung (Taiwan) 2019, *World Congress on Computers in Agriculture* Mumbai (India) 2018, *World Congress on Computers in Agriculture* Montpellier (France) 2017, *World Congress on Computers in Agriculture* Suncheon (Korea Rep) 2016. **Publications** *Journal of Information Technology in Agriculture.*
Members Regional organizations (3):
Asia-Pacific Federation for Information Technology in Agriculture (APFITA, #01900); European Federation for Information Technology in Agriculture (EFITA, #07143); Pan-American Federation for Information Technology in Agriculture (PanAFITA, #18102). [2019/XM0126/y/D]

♦ International Network for Information on Ventilation / see International Network for Information on Ventilation and Energy Performance (#14288)

♦ International Network for Information on Ventilation and Energy Performance (INIVE) 14288

Mailing Address Lozenberg 7, 1932 Sint-Stevens-Woluwe, Belgium. Fax +3225298110. E-mail: info@inive.org – info@aivc.org.
Secretariat Boulevard Poincaré 79, 1060 Brussels, Belgium.
URL: http://www.inive.org/

History 23 May 2001. A grouping of the type *European Economic Interest Grouping (EEIG, #06960).* Also referred to as *International Network for Information on Ventilation.* **Events** *European conference on Building Information Modelling and Energy Performance of Buildings* Brussels (Belgium) 2018, *Workshop on High Performance Buildings* Brussels (Belgium) 2013, *International Symposium on Superinsulating Materials* Brussels (Belgium) 2012, *International Workshop on Achieving Relevant and Durable Airtightness Levels* Brussels (Belgium) 2012, *International symposium on building and ductwork air tightness* Berlin (Germany) 2009.
Members Institutes (5) in 4 countries:
Belgium, France, Greece, Norway.
NGO Relations Operates: *Air Infiltration and Ventilation Centre (AIVC, #00603).* [2020/XF6338/F]

♦ International Networking for Educational Transformation (iNET) . . . 14289

Operational Dir c/o SSAT, 5th Floor, Central House, 142 Central Street, London, EC1V 8AR, UK. E-mail: inet@ssatrust.org.uk.
URL: http://www.ssatuk.co.uk/

History 2004, as an initiative of *'Specialist Schools and Academies Trust (SSAT)'.* **Aims** Create powerful and innovative networks of schools – nationally and internationally – that are committed to the sharing of transformational practice; develop leadership expertise that provides the capacity to lead and manage educational transformation; create international development and research networks that bring together leading academics and practitioners to investigate, develop, disseminate and share knowledge and practice that leads to educational transformation; develop an international network of students and to provide them with opportunities to develop as global citizens; explore new and emerging technologies with a range of partners and develop new ways of communication and sharing knowledge; bring together internationally known education thinkers with innovative practitioners to share and develop the transformation journey of education in to the 21st century. **Activities** Organizes: workshops; study tours; conferences; online fora. Publishing activity. **Events** *International conference* Schiphol (Netherlands) 2005.
Members Schools, organizations and individuals in 14 countries and territories:
Australia, Canada, Chile, China, Gambia, Hong Kong, Mauritius, Netherlands, New Zealand, South Africa, Sweden, UK, United Arab Emirates, USA. [2015/XJ0547/E]

♦ International Network on Integrated Care / see International Foundation for Integrated Care (#13672)

♦ International Network for Interreligious Research and Education (INIRE) 14290

Contact address not obtained. E-mail: religion.authority@gmail.com.
URL: https://sites.duke.edu/inire/

Aims Study from an interdisciplinary and inter-religious perspective, various, past and present religious issues; promote inter-religious knowledge among undergraduate and graduate students; implement research in contemporary social issues; encourage inter-religious dialogue among scholars, students and the public. **Activities** Events/meetings; research/documentation; training/education. **Events** *International Conference on Religious Heritage in a Diverse Europe* Groningen (Netherlands) 2019.
Members Universities (7) in 4 countries:
Germany, Netherlands, UK, USA. [2021/AA0482/F]

♦ International Network in Kangaroo Mother Care (INK) 14291

Address not obtained.
URL: https://kangaroomothercare.org/

History 1996, Trieste (Italy). Founded by participants at a meeting to discuss the potential of 'Kangaroo Mother Care'. **Structure** Steering Committee; Scientific Committee. **Activities** Advocacy/lobbying/activism; events/meetings; knowledge management/information dissemination; training/education. **Events** *International Kangaroo Mother Care Congress* Madrid (Spain) 2022, *International Meeting / Encuentro Internacional en Método Madre Canguro* Bogota (Colombia) 2018, *Congress* Trieste (Italy) 2016, *Congress* Kigali (Rwanda) 2014, *International Conference on Kangaroo Mother Care* Ahmedabad (India) 2012. [2022/AA3142/C]

♦ International Network of Laboratories Researching Retrovirus and AIDS (see: #05781)

♦ International Network of Law Firms (LEGUS) 14292

Pres 2232 S Main St, Ste 472, Ann Arbor MI 48103, USA. T. +17349772185.
URL: http://www.legusLaw.com/

History Founded 1995. **Aims** Help small to mid-sized law firms compete more effectively in the global market; build close relationships between members through referrals, legal and educational programming held at meetings, and an exchange of information focusing on member law firm business operations. **Events** *Annual Meeting* London (UK) 2022, *Spring Meeting* Copenhagen (Denmark) 2018, *Fall Meeting* Chicago, IL (USA) 2016, *Annual Meeting* St Petersburg (Russia) 2016, *Spring Meeting* Vienna (Austria) 2016.
Members Law firms in 35 countries and territories:
Argentina, Australia, Austria, Belgium, Brazil, Canada, Cyprus, Denmark, Dominican Rep, England, Germany, Ghana, Greece, Hungary, Israel, Italy, Japan, Luxembourg, Mauritius, Mexico, Netherlands, Nigeria, Peru, Philippines, Poland, Portugal, Scotland, Singapore, South Africa, Spain, Sweden, Switzerland, Taiwan, USA, Virgin Is UK. [2017.10.11/XJ1909/F]

♦ International Network on Leave Policies and Research (LP&R) 14293

Editor address not obtained. E-mail: lprcoordinators@gmail.com.
URL: https://www.leavenetwork.org/

History 2004. **Aims** Provide a forum for exchange, dialogue and collaboration on issues of care, employment and gender. **Structure** Coordinators. **Activities** Events/meetings. **Events** *Annual Seminar* Helsinki (Finland) 2021, *Annual Seminar* 2020, *Annual Seminar* Hamburg (Germany) 2019. **Publications** *International Review on Leave Policies and Related Research* (annual).
Members Individuals (over 60). Full in 46 countries:
Argentina, Australia, Austria, Belgium, Brazil, Bulgaria, Canada, Chile, China, Croatia, Cyprus, Czechia, Denmark, Estonia, Finland, France, Germany, Greece, Hungary, Iceland, Ireland, Israel, Italy, Japan, Korea Rep, Latvia, Lithuania, Luxembourg, Malta, Mexico, Netherlands, New Zealand, Norway, Poland, Portugal, Romania, Russia, Slovakia, Slovenia, South Africa, Spain, Sweden, Switzerland, UK, Uruguay, USA.
Associate in 8 countries:
Canada, Iceland, Ireland, Korea Rep, Poland, Russia, Serbia, Slovakia.
Junior affiliates in 11 countries:
Argentina, Georgia, Germany, Korea Rep, Poland, Qatar, Slovakia, Switzerland, Türkiye, UK, USA. [2022/AA2609/F]

♦ International Network for Lesbian, Gay and Bisexual Concerns and Gender Identity Issues in Psychology / see International Network for Lesbian, Gay and Bisexual Concerns and Transgender Issues in Psychology
♦ International Network for Lesbian, Gay and Bisexual Concerns and Transgender Issues in Psychology (internationally oriented national body)

♦ International Network of Liberal Women (INLW) 14294

Pres c/o Wittenburgerweg 124, 2244 CH Wassenaar, Netherlands. T. +31705178929. E-mail: inlw@inlw.org.
Official Seat c/o Liberal International, 1 Whitehall Place, London, SW1A 2HD, UK. T. +442078395905. Fax +79252685315588.
URL: http://www.inlw.org/

History 1990, Helsinki (Finland), within *Liberal International (LI, #16454).* Also referred to as *International Network of Women Liberals.* Now an independent partner organization of IL. **Aims** Raise liberal women's awareness of their *political* rights and responsibilities; expand participation of liberal women in politics at local, national and international levels and within liberal parties worldwide; strengthen relationships and exchange information; encourage liberal women to promote values of liberalism and spread liberal ideas; advance *empowerment* of all women worldwide. **Structure** General Meeting. Management Board. Patrons. Working Parties. **Languages** English. **Finance** Members' dues. Donations. **Activities** Organizes: workshops; round tables; panel and dinner discussions. **Events** *General Meeting* Dakar (Senegal) 2018, *General Meeting* Escaldes-Engordany (Andorra) 2017, *General Meeting* Mexico City (Mexico) 2015, *General Meeting* Rotterdam (Netherlands) 2014, *General Meeting* Abidjan (Côte d'Ivoire) 2012. **Publications** *Newsline* (6 a year).
Members Groups; individual. Group members in 31 countries:
Andorra, Angola, Belgium, Burundi, Cambodia, Canada, Costa Rica, Côte d'Ivoire, Croatia, Egypt, Estonia, Finland, Guatemala, Iceland, Israel, Lebanon, Malaysia, Moldova, Morocco, Netherlands, Nicaragua, Philippines, Russia, Senegal, Singapore, Sri Lanka, Sweden, Taiwan, Tanzania UR, Tunisia, UK.
Consultative Status Consultative status granted from: *ECOSOC (#05331)* (Special). **NGO Relations** Full member of Liberal International. [2018/XF8600/F]

♦ **International Network for the MBA in Agribusiness and Commerce (AGRIMBA)** 14295

Coordinator Warsaw Agricultural Univ, Fac of Agriculture and Biology – Bldg 37, 159 Nowoursynowska Str, 02-776 Warsaw, Poland.
Secretariat Wageningen Univ – Bldg 201/2115L, Postbus 8130, 6700 EW Wageningen, Netherlands.
URL: http://agrimba.sggw.waw.pl/

History 1995, Warsaw (Poland), with the support of Leonardo Da Vinci Programme of *European Commission (EC, #06633)*. Since 2003, functions as a Standing Committee of *Association for European Life Science Universities (ICA, #02519)*. Also referred to as *International MBA Network*. **Aims** Set standards for the programmes overseen by the network based on the best practices and accredit them on the basis of these standards. **Structure** General Board (meets annually), consisting of all members. Executive Committee, comprising Chair and 3 members. Secretariat. **Activities** Organizes the biennial AVA Congress. **Events** *Biennial Congress* Porec (Croatia) 2015, *Biennial Congress* Budva (Montenegro) 2013, *Biennial Congress / Congress* Wageningen (Netherlands) 2011, *Biennial Congress / Congress* Debrecen (Hungary) 2009. **Publications** *Apstract* – journal.
Members Universities and educational institutions in 13 countries and territories:
Croatia, Czechia, England, Germany, Hungary, Ireland, Netherlands, Poland, Russia, Scotland, Serbia, Ukraine, USA.
[2011/XJ5289/F]

♦ International Network of Mechatronics Universities (unconfirmed)

♦ **International Network on Migration and Development (INMD)** 14296

Exec Dir address not obtained.
URL: http://rimd.reduaz.mx/pagina/indexing

History 2002. Set up as a non-profit, 2003. **Aims** Contribute to the global debate on the complex links between development and international migration aiming at enhancing civil society organizations capacities and affecting public policies at different levels. **Structure** Board of Directors. **Staff** 7.00 FTE, paid. **Events** *Congress* Quito (Ecuador) 2011, *Congress* Morelos, PUE (Mexico) 2006, *Congress* Zacatecas (Mexico) 2003. **Publications** *Migration and Development* (2 a year) – journal. Books; technical reports.
Members Institutional; Individual. Organizations in 17 countries:
Argentina, Canada, Costa Rica, Ecuador, El Salvador, Germany, Ghana, Guatemala, India, Italy, Mexico, Philippines, South Africa, Spain, Sweden, Uruguay, USA.
Included in the above, 4 organizations listed in this Yearbook:
African Centre for Migration and Society (ACMS); *Centro de Estudios Migratorios Latinoamericanos (CEMLA)*; *Scalabrini International Migration Institute (SIMI, #19062)*; *Scalabrini Migration Centre, Manila (SMC)*.
NGO Relations Member of: *Global Coalition on Migration (GCM, #10293)*. [2014/XJ8935/y/F]

♦ **International Network of Museums for Peace (INMP)** 14297

Secretariat c/o Kyoto Museum for World Peace, 56-1 Kitamachi, Toji-in, Kita-ku, Kyoto, 603-8577 Japan. E-mail: inmp.coordinators@gmail.com.
URL: https://sites.google.com/view/inmp-museums-for-peace/

History Sep 1992, Bradford (UK). Founded at International Conference, called jointly by Bradford University Department of Peace Studies and *Give Peace a Chance Trust (GPAC Trust)*. Up until 2005, largely an informal and loose network. Former names and other names: *International Network of Peace Museums* – former (1992 to 2005). Registration: Handelsregister, Start date: 2009, Netherlands. **Aims** Provide information exchange for peace museums; facilitate their cooperation, including exchange or coproduction of exhibitions; provide a resource for individuals, groups and organizations intending to establish a peace museum, or produce peace exhibitions; assist museums in becoming more professional and effective; promote peace museums as effective instruments of peace education and for developing a culture of peace. **Structure** General Meeting (at international conference); Senior Board; Advisory Board; Executive Board; General Coordinators. **Languages** English. **Staff** Voluntary. **Finance** Sources: donations; fundraising; members' dues. **Activities** Capacity building; events/meetings; knowledge management/information dissemination; networking/liaising; publishing activities; training/education. **Events** *International Conference* Uppsala (Sweden) 2023, *International Conference* Kyoto (Japan) 2020, *International Conference* Belfast (UK) 2017, *International Conference* No Gun Ri (Korea Rep) 2014, *Celebrating peace philanthropy* The Hague (Netherlands) 2013. **Publications** *Museums for Peace: Transforming Cultures* (2012); *Museums for Peace: Past, Present and Future* (2008); *Museums for Peace Worldwide* (2008). Conference proceedings.
Members Peace museums and related institutions in 27 countries and territories:
Austria, Belgium, Canada, China, Germany, Guatemala, India, Iran Islamic Rep, Iraq, Italy, Japan, Kenya, Korea Rep, Netherlands, North Macedonia, Norway, Pakistan, Rwanda, South Africa, Spain, Sweden, Switzerland, Taiwan, UK, Ukraine, USA, Uzbekistan.
Consultative Status Consultative status granted from: *ECOSOC (#05331)* (Special). **IGO Relations** Associated with Department of Global Communications of the United Nations. **NGO Relations** Member of (1): *International Peace Bureau (IPB, #14535)*. [2022.02.10/XF3794/y/F]

♦ International Network of Next-Generation Ecologists (unconfirmed)

♦ **International Network of Nicotine Consumer Organisations (INNCO)** 14298

Registered Address Quai de l'Ile 13, 1204 Geneva, Switzerland. E-mail: info@innco.org.
Dir address not obtained.
COO address not obtained.
URL: https://innco.org/

History Jun 2017. Statutes most recently revisedJune 2019. Registration: Swiss Civil Code, Switzerland; EU Transparency Register, No/ID: 657522841173-59, Start date: 1 Feb 2021. **Aims** As a non-profit alliance, support the rights of adult ex-smokers who use safer nicotine to avoid toxic forms of tobacco; promote Tobacco Harm Reduction (THR) on the global stage. **Structure** General Assembly; Governing Board; General Secretariat. **Languages** English. **Staff** Voluntary. **Finance** Sources: contributions. Secretariat supported by a grant from *Foundation for a Smoke-Free World (FSFW)*
Members Full: Organizations in 32 countries:
Austria, Belgium, Brazil, Canada, Chile, Colombia, Costa Rica, Cyprus, Denmark, Estonia, Finland, France, Germany, Greece, Hungary, Iceland, India, Kenya, Malawi, Mexico, Netherlands, Nigeria, Norway, Peru, Philippines, Slovenia, Spain, Sweden, Switzerland, Thailand, Tunisia, USA.
ARDT Iberoamérica; *Campaign For Safer Alternatives (CASA, #03404)*; EU for SNUS; Medical Organisations Supporting Vaping and E-Cigarettes (MOVE).
Affiliate organizations in 3 countries and territories:
Malaysia, Taiwan, UK. [2023/AA1324/y/F]

♦ **International Network of Observatories in Cultural Policies** 14299

Contact UNESCO Headquarters, 7 place de Fontenoy, 75352 Paris 07SP, France. T. +33145681000. Fax +33145671690.

Aims Promote networking between organizations worldwide that analyze, collect and disseminate policy-relevant knowledge and information.
Members National observatories (14) and organizations (5) in 14 countries:
Argentina, Australia, Brazil, Cuba, Germany, Italy, Netherlands, Portugal, Russia, Senegal, Sweden, Tunisia, UK, Uruguay.
International organizations (5):
Asia-Europe Foundation (ASEF, #01270); *European Institute for Comparative Cultural Research (ERICarts, #07547)*; *INTERARTS Foundation*; *Organisation internationale de la Francophonie (OIF, #17809)*; *Southern African Cultural Information System (SACIS)*.
IGO Relations *European Network of National Observatories on Childhood (ChildONEurope, #07951)*; *UNESCO (#20322)*. [2007/XM2621/y/F]

♦ **International Network of Paediatric Surveillance Units (INoPSU)** ... 14300

Contact British Paediatric Surveillance Unit, 5-11 Theobalds Road, London, WC1X 8SH, UK. E-mail: bpsu@rcpch.ac.uk.
URL: http://www.inopsu.com/

History Aug 1998, Amsterdam (Netherlands). **Aims** Advance knowledge of uncommon *childhood infections and disorders*; increase participation of paediatricians in surveillance on a national and international basis. **Structure** Executive Committee, comprising Convenor, Vice-Convenor and Liaison Officer. **Languages** English. **Staff** 0.50 FTE, paid. **Finance** No budget. Costs for activities picked up by individual units. **Activities** Facilitates communication and cooperation between existing national paediatric surveillance units; assists in development of new units; facilitates sharing information and collaboration between researchers; shares information on current, past and anticipated studies and their protocols and on conditions that have been nominated for surveillance but are not selected; encourages use of identical protocols to potentially enable simultaneous or sequential collection of data on rare paediatric disorders in 2 or more countries; shares and distributes information of educational benefit to constituent units, notably on study and surveillance methodologies; shares school techniques and models of evaluation for units; conducts peer reviews and evaluates existing and proposed units; identifies rare disorders of mutual interest and public health importance for cooperative surveys through each national unit; collaborates with, and provides information to, other groups interested in rare childhood diseases; responds to international emergencies relating to rare childhood conditions where national and international studies can make a contribution to science or public health. **Events** *Conference* Melbourne, VIC (Australia) 2013, *Conference* Montreux (Switzerland) 2011, *Conference* Dublin (Ireland) 2010, *Conference* Munich (Germany) 2008, *Conference* London (UK) 2006. **Publications** *INoPSU Progress Report* (occasional). *Beyond Counting Numbers – Public Health Impact of Studies Conducted through National Paediatric Surveillance Units* (2006). Conference reports.
Members Full; Associate paediatric surveillance units (13) in 12 countries:
Australia, Belgium, Canada, Germany, Greece, Ireland, Latvia, Netherlands, New Zealand, Portugal, Switzerland, UK.
NGO Relations Member of: *International Pediatric Association (IPA, #14541)*. [2012.07.06/XF7101/F]

♦ International Network of Pasteur Institutes / see Pasteur Network (#18256)
♦ International Network of Pasteur Institutes and Associate Institutes / see Pasteur Network (#18256)
♦ International Network for Patient-Centered Care (internationally oriented national body)
♦ International Network of Peace Museums / see International Network of Museums for Peace (#14297)
♦ International Network for Pensions, Aging, and Retirement Research / see International Pension Research Association (#14556)

♦ **International Network of People who Use Drugs (INPUD)** 14301

Secretariat Unit 2B15, South Bank Technopark, 90 London Road, London, SE1 6LN, UK.
URL: http://www.inpud.net/

History Registered in accordance with UK law. **Aims** Promote the health and defend the rights of people who use drugs. **Structure** Board. Subsidiary Group: *International Network of Women who Use Drugs (INWUD)*. **NGO Relations** Member of: *Civil Society Forum on Drugs (CSFD, #03968)*; *International Drug Policy Consortium (IDPC, #13205)*. Cooperates with: *Asian Network of People Who Use Drugs (ANPUD, #01553)*; *Eurasian Harm Reduction Association (EHRA, #05609)*; *Eurasian Network of People Who Use Drugs (ENPUD)*; *MPact Global Action for Gay Men's Health and Rights (MPact, #16875)*; *Global Network of People Living with HIV/AIDS (GNP+, #10494)*; *Global Network of Sex Work Projects (NSWP, #10498)*; *ICASO (#11040)*. [2018/XJ8263/F]

♦ International Network of Performing and Visual Arts Schools / see Arts Schools Network (#01127)
♦ International Network on Personal Meaning (internationally oriented national body)
♦ International Network on Person-Centered Medicine / see International College of Person-Centered Medicine (#12647)

♦ **International Network of Philosophers of Education (INPE)** 14302

Pres c/o KU Leuven Kulak – PPW, Gebouw A – lokaal A 103, Etienne Sabbelaan 53, 8500 Kortrijk, Belgium. E-mail: stefan.ramaekers@ppw.kuleuven.be.
URL: http://www.ucm.es/info/inpe/

History 24 Aug 1988, Pécs (Hungary). Formally structured 17-20 Aug 1992, Varna (Bulgaria). **Aims** Foster dialogue among philosophers of education globally; facilitate better understanding between thinkers of different schools of thought; exchange information; encourage joint and comparative research; organize conferences for in-depth discussions and development of new initiatives and perspectives. **Structure** Steering Committee; Programme Committee. **Finance** Members' dues. **Events** *Biennial Conference* Warsaw (Poland) 2016, *Biennial Conference* Cosenza (Italy) 2014, *Biennial Conference* Addis Ababa (Ethiopia) 2012, *Biennial Conference* Bogota (Colombia) 2010, *Biennial conference* Kyoto (Japan) 2008. **Publications** *Studies in Philosophy and Education* (6 a year) – journal.
Members Individuals in 28 countries and territories:
Australia, Belgium, Brazil, Bulgaria, Canada, Czechia, Denmark, France, Germany, Greece, Hong Kong, Hungary, Ireland, Israel, Korea Rep, Malta, New Zealand, Norway, Poland, Portugal, Russia, South Africa, Spain, Sweden, Taiwan, Türkiye, UK, USA.
[2016/XF5428/v/F]

♦ **International Network for Philosophy and Psychiatry (INPP)** 14303

Sec c/o Univ of Oxford, Fac of Philosophy, Radcliffe Humanities, Radcliffe Observatory Quarter, Woodstock Road, Oxford, OX2 6GG, UK.
URL: http://www.inpponline.com/

History Registration: Charity Commission, No/ID: 1101747, UK. **Events** *Conference* Warsaw (Poland) 2019, *Conference* Hong Kong (Hong Kong) 2018, *Conference* Madrid (Spain) 2017, *Conference* Venice (Italy) 2015, *Neuroscience, logics, mental development* Varna (Bulgaria) 2014. **Publications** *International Perspectives in Philosophy and Psychiatry* – book series. [2021/XJ3351/F]

♦ **International Network for Planning and Improving Quality and Safety in Health Systems in Africa (INPIQS)** 14304

Réseau International pour la Planification et l'Amélioration de la Qualité et la Sécurité dans les systèmes de santé en Afrique (RIPAQS)

Head Office Université Bordeaux 2 Victor Segalen (ISPED), 146 rue Léo-Saignat, 33076 Bordeaux CEDEX, France. T. +33557571465. Fax +33556240081.
URL: http://www.ripaqs.net/

History 2006. **Aims** Reform national health policies in sub-Saharan Africa to harmonize professional practices of care, and assist professionals in developing technical standards of health care. **Events** *International Conference on Blood Safety and Haemovigilance in Africa* Abidjan (Côte d'Ivoire) 2013, *International Congress* Abidjan (Côte d'Ivoire) 2013, *International Conference on Blood Safety and Safety Surveillance* Abidjan (Côte d'Ivoire) 2012. [2012/XJ5633/F]

♦ **International Network of Political Leaders Promoting Democracy in Burma (PD Burma)** 14305

Address not obtained.

History Apr 1996, Geneva (Switzerland). A project of: *Worldview Rights* now known as *Point of Peace Foundation*. **Aims** Improve freedom of speech, respect for human rights; promote democratization process in Burma. **Structure** Officers: Chair and Co-Chair. Administrative Office in Oslo (Norway); regional offices in Japan. **Activities** Engages in lobby work, communication. Organizes workshops and conferences. **Events** *Meeting* Bangkok (Thailand) 1999, *Meeting* Bangkok (Thailand) 1998, *Meeting* Tokyo (Japan) 1997. **Publications** *Burma Today* (52 a year) – newsletter.
Members Individuals (31) in 18 countries:
Australia, Belgium, Canada, Denmark, Finland, France, India, Japan, Korea Rep, Malaysia, Netherlands, New Zealand, Northern Ireland, Norway, Philippines, Sri Lanka, Sweden, UK. [2008/XF3931/v/F]

♦ **International Network on the Prevention of Accidents and Trauma at Work (Workingonsafety.net)** 14306

Contact KTH Royal Inst of Technology, SE-100 44 Stockholm, Sweden. E-mail: torel@kth.se.
URL: http://www.workingonsafety.net/

History Sep 2002, Helsingør (Denmark). Sep 2002, Helsingír (Denmark). **Aims** Facilitate exchange of information and experience between accident prevention experts. **Structure** International Scientific Committee; informal network of professionals. **Languages** English. **Staff** None. **Finance** Supported by: *European Agency for Safety and Health at Work (EU-OSHA, #05843)*; national agencies and local industries in relation to conferences. **Activities** Events/meetings. **Events** *Conference* Vienna (Austria) 2019, *Conference* Prague (Czechia) 2017, *Conference* Portugal 2015, *Conference* Glasgow (UK) 2014, *Biennial Conference / Conference* Sopot (Poland) 2012. **Publications** *Safety Science Monitor* – newsletter. **IGO Relations** *European Agency for Safety and Health at Work (EU-OSHA, #05843)*. [2017.10.11/XF6713/F]

♦ **International Network for the Prevention of Elder Abuse (INPEA)** . . **14307**

Pres Somers Law Firm, PO Box 368, Nassau NY 12123, USA. T. +15184026782. Fax +15184748572. E-mail: sailesh2000@gmail.com.
SG address not obtained.
URL: http://www.inpea.net/

History Founded 1997, Adelaide (Australia). Since 2002, a Standing Committee of *International Association of Gerontology and Geriatrics (IAGG, #11920)*. Incorporated, 1999, as a Not for Profit Corporation in the Commonwealth of Massachusetts (USA). **Aims** Increase public awareness in recognizing and responding to the mistreatment of older people; promote education and training of professionals and paraprofessionals in identification, treatment and prevention; further advocacy on behalf of abused and neglected elders; stimulate research into the causes, consequences, prevalence, treatment and prevention of elder abuse and neglect. **Structure** Executive of 4 members. Regional Representatives for Africa, Asia, Latin America and Caribbean, Middle East and North Africa, North America, and Oceania. National Representatives. **Languages** English. **Staff** Voluntary. **Finance** Members' dues. Other sources: donations; conference revenue. **Activities** Events/meetings; research/documentation; training/education; advocacy/lobbying/activism. **Events** *World Congress* Prague (Czech Rep) 2012, *World Congress* London (UK) 2011. **Publications** *INPEA Newsletter* (4 a year).
Members Individuals and organizations in 50 countries and territories:
Argentina, Aruba, Australia, Austria, Belgium, Brazil, Cameroon, Canada, China, Czechia, Dominican Rep, Finland, France, Germany, Ghana, Greece, Hong Kong, Hungary, India, Ireland, Israel, Italy, Japan, Kenya, Korea Rep, Lebanon, Liberia, Malta, Mexico, Mongolia, Nepal, Netherlands, New Zealand, Nigeria, Pakistan, Panama, Portugal, Romania, Slovenia, South Africa, Spain, St Martin, Switzerland, Syrian AR, Türkiye, Uganda, UK, United Arab Emirates, USA, Zambia.
Consultative Status Consultative status granted from: *ECOSOC (#05331)* (Special). **NGO Relations** Member of: *Conference of Non-Governmental Organizations in Consultative Relationship with the United Nations (CONGO, #04635)*; *Global Alliance for the Rights of Older People (#10226)*; *NGO Alliance on Global Concerns and Values (NGO Alliance, #17102)*; *NGO Committee on Ageing, Geneva (see: #04635)*; *NGO Committee on Ageing, New York (#17103)*; *NGO Committee on Social Development (#17115)*; *NGO Committee on the Status of Women, New York NY (see: #04635)* [2022/XF6643/F]

♦ International Network of Private Business Organizations / see International Counterparts Network (#13095)

♦ **International Network of Productive Learning Projects and Schools (INEPS)** **14308**

Internationale Netz Produktiver Bildungsprojekte und Schulen

Pres IPLE, Innsbrucker Str 37, 10825 Berlin, Germany. T. +493021792123.
Vice-Pres PROTASI, Sarantaporou 20, 262 23 Patras, Greece. T. +302610451790. Fax +302610451790. E-mail: protasi@pat.forthnet.gr.
URL: http://www.ineps.org/

History 1990, Berlin (German DR), as an international network of *International Community Education Association (ICEA, inactive)* set up by *Institute for Productive Learning in Europe (IPLE)*. **Aims** Promote the idea of "Productive Learning" – learning through activity and experience. **Structure** General Assembly; Administration Council. **Languages** English. **Staff** Voluntary. **Activities** Events/meetings; knowledge management/ information dissemination; projects/programmes; training/education. **Events** *Congress* Tampere (Finland) 2016, *The pedagogical concept of productive learning – in dialogue with students, parents and companies* Hilversum (Netherlands) 2015, *Students in focus – individual education in productive learning* Berlin (Germany) 2014, *Educating for the 21st century – connecting school and community through experiential learning* New York, NY (USA) 2013, *Congress* Vilnius (Lithuania) 2012.
Members in 12 countries:
Bulgaria, Finland, France, Germany, Greece, Hungary, Lithuania, Netherlands, Russia, Spain, Sweden, USA.
[2018.09.05/XK2055/E]

♦ International Network for Progressive Governance / see Policy Network (#18417)

♦ **International Network to Promote Household Water Treatment and Safe Storage (INHWTS)** **14309**

Main Office WHO Public Health-Env, Avenue Appia 20, 1211 Geneva 27, Switzerland. T. +41227912111. Fax +41227913111. E-mail: hhwater@who.int – info@who.int.
URL: http://www.who.int/household_water/en/

History 2003, by *WHO (#20950)*. 2011, *UNICEF (#20332)* became a co-host of the network. **Aims** Promote household water treatment and safe storage. **Events** *Meeting* Accra (Ghana) 2008, *Meeting* Bangkok (Thailand) 2005. [2011/XM0982/F]

♦ **International Network to Promote the Rule of Law (INPROL)** **14310**

Dir c/o United States Inst of Peace, 2301 Constitution Ave NW, Washington DC 20037, USA.
Twitter: https://twitter.com/INPROL/

History 2007. Set up as a global, online community of practice, by *United States Institute of Peace (USIP)*, in partnership with US Department of State's Bureau of International Narcotics and Law Enforcement, *Organization for Security and Cooperation in Europe (OSCE, #17887)*, Center of Excellence for Police Stability Unit, William and Mary School of Law and *International Human Rights Law Institute (IHRLI)*. **Aims** Help rule of law practitioners solve problems they face in the field; promote professional development and learning. **Structure** Advisory Council; Council of Experts. Director. **Languages** English. **Staff** 4.00 FTE, paid. **Finance** Support from: *United States Institute of Peace (USIP)*; US Department of State International Narcotics and Law Enforcement Bureau (INL). **Publications** Research memoranda; practitioners guides. **Members** Rule of law practitioners (about 2,300) from 300 organizations and 120 countries and territories. Membership countries not specified. [2019/XM2994/F]

♦ International Network Promoting Volunteer Action Across Europe / see Volonteurope (#20807)
♦ International Network for Psychological Perspectives on Same-Gender Sexual Orientation and Transgender Diversity / see International Network for Lesbian, Gay and Bisexual Concerns and Transgender Issues in Psychology
♦ International Network of Psychology and the Developing World (see: #15807)

♦ **International Network on Public Communication of Science and Technology (PCST)** **14311**

Sec Leverhulme Research Centre for Forensic Science, Univ of Dundee – Ewing Bldg, Nethergate, Dundee, DD1 4HN, UK. E-mail: admin@pcst.co.
URL: https://pcst.co/

History Founded as a loose network with 1st conference in 1989, Poitiers (France). Inaugural President elected in 2006. Former names and other names: *The Network for the Public Communication of Science and Technology Incorporated (PCST Network)* – legal name. Registration: No/ID: A05352, Australia. **Aims** Foster public communication of science and technology; encourage discussion of practices, methods, ethical issues, policies, conceptual frameworks, economic and social concerns related to public communication of science and technology; link researchers and practitioners. **Structure** Executive Committee, comprising President, Vice-President and 3 Sub-Committee Chairs. Scientific Committee. **Languages** English. **Staff** None. **Finance** No budget. Conferences and activities largely self-financed, with additional support from hosting organizations and governments. **Events** *International Conference on Public Communication, Science and Technology* Aberdeen (UK) 2025, *International Public Communication of Science and Technology Conference* Rotterdam (Netherlands) 2023, *International Public Communication of Science and Technology Conference* Aberdeen (UK) 2021, *International Public Communication of Science and Technology Conference* Aberdeen (UK) 2020, *International Public Communication of Science and Technology Conference* Dunedin (New Zealand) 2018. **Publications** Books. **Members** Individual membership. Membership countries not specified.
[2022/XF6645/F]

♦ **International Network of Quality Assurance Agencies in Higher Education (INQAAHE)** **14312**

Réseau international des organismes de promotion de la qualité en enseignement supérieur

Pres AQU Catalunya, Carrer d'Enric Granados 33, 08007 Barcelona, Spain. T. +34932688950. E-mail: secretariat@inqaahe.org – president@inqaahe.org.
URL: http://www.inqaahe.org/

History 1991. **Aims** Promote and advance excellence in higher education through support of an active international community of quality assurance agencies. **Structure** General Assembly (annual, at INQAAHE events); Board of Directors. **Languages** English. **Activities** Events/meetings; standards/guidelines. **Events** *Biennial Members Forum* Bucharest (Romania) 2024, *Biennial Conference* Astana (Kazakhstan) 2023, *Biennial Members Forum* Mexico City (Mexico) 2022, *Biennial Conference* Glasgow (UK) 2021, *Biennial Conference* Colombo (Sri Lanka) 2019. **Publications** *INQAAHE Bulletin* (4 a year); *Quality in Higher Education* (3 a year).
Members Centres, institutes and organizations in 77 countries and territories:
Albania, Argentina, Australia, Austria, Bahamas, Barbados, Belgium, Botswana, Canada, Chile, China, Colombia, Costa Rica, Croatia, Cyprus, Czechia, Denmark, Egypt, Estonia, Ethiopia, Fiji, Finland, France, Germany, Ghana, Hungary, Iceland, India, Indonesia, Ireland, Israel, Italy, Jamaica, Japan, Jordan, Kazakhstan, Kenya, Kuwait, Latvia, Lithuania, Malaysia, Maldives, Mauritius, Mexico, Mongolia, Namibia, Netherlands, New Zealand, Nigeria, Norway, Oman, Pakistan, Palestine, Peru, Philippines, Poland, Portugal, Romania, Russia, Rwanda, Samoa, Saudi Arabia, Serbia, Singapore, Slovakia, South Africa, Spain, Sri Lanka, Sweden, Switzerland, Taiwan, Thailand, Trinidad-Tobago, UK, United Arab Emirates, USA, Vietnam.
Included in the above, 4 organizations listed in this Yearbook:
Agencia Centroamericana de Acreditación de Programas de Arquitectura y de Ingenieria (ACAAI, #00549); *European Council for Theological Education (ECTE, #06846)*; *European Network for Accreditation of Engineering Education (ENAEE, #07859)*; *Foundation for International Business Administration Accreditation (FIBAA, #09961)*.
Consultative Status Consultative status granted from: *UNESCO (#20322)* (Consultative Status).
[2023.02.14/XF6637/y/F]

♦ **International Network for Rational Use of Drugs (INRUD)** **14313**

Réseau international pour l'usage rationnel des médicaments

Coordinator c/o Management Sciences for Health, Ctr for Pharmaceutical Management, 4301 North Fairfax Drive, Ste 400, Arlington VA 22203, USA. T. +17035246575. Fax +17035247898.
URL: http://www.inrud.org/

History Founded 1989. **Aims** Promote safer, more effective and more economically efficient use of *medicines*. **Structure** Board; Secretariat, based at *Management Sciences for Health (MSH)*. **Languages** English. **Staff** None. **Finance** Currently no funding. **Activities** Research/documentation; capacity building; training/education. **Events** *International conference on improving use of medicines / Conference* Antalya (Turkey) 2011, *International conference on improving use of medicines / Conference* Chiang Mai (Thailand) 2004, *International conference on improving use of medicines / Conference* Chiang Mai (Thailand) 1997. **Publications** *INRUD Group updates* – online. Conference proceedings. **Information Services** *Bibliography on Improving Adherence to Antiretrovirals in Sub-Saharan Africa* – database; *INRUD Bibliography on Improving Use of Medicines* – database.
Members Groups in 25 countries:
Bangladesh, Cambodia, China, Ethiopia, Ghana, India, Indonesia, Iran Islamic Rep, Jordan, Kenya, Kyrgyzstan, Malaysia, Moldova, Nepal, Nigeria, Peru, Philippines, Sweden, Switzerland, Tanzania UR, Thailand, Uganda, USA, Vietnam, Zimbabwe.
[2015.08.27/XF4197/F]

♦ **International Network on Regional Economics, Mobility and Tourism (INRouTe)** **14314**

Vice-Pres Nicolás Alcorta 2, 48003 Bilbao, Biscay, Spain. T. +34644746087. E-mail: technicalsecretariat@inroutenetwork.org.
URL: http://www.inroutenetwork.org/

History Set up as a project of the *World Tourism Organization (UNWTO, #21861)* Department of Statistics and Tourism Satellite Account (TSA). Properly set up 7 Jul 2009; officially presented Oct 2009, Donostia-San Sebastian (Spain). Moved from a project to a non-profit International Association, 2010. **Aims** Provide guidance to entities involved with sub-national and local tourism destinations so as to develop policy-oriented measurement and analysis of tourism according to the conceptual framework for statistical purposes established by the UN. **Structure** Chair; Founding Partners; Associate Partners; Scientific Committee. **Languages** English. **Staff** 5.00 FTE, voluntary. **Finance** Financed by Founding Partners. **Activities** Events/ meetings; knowledge management/information dissemination; research/documentation. **Events** *International Conference on Sub-national Measurement and Economic Analysis of Tourism (MOVE)* Bogota (Colombia) 2021, *International Conference on Sub-national Measurement and Economic Analysis of Tourism (MOVE)* Pamplona (Spain) 2017, *International Conference on Sub-national Measurement and Economic Analysis of Tourism (MOVE)* San Juan (Puerto Rico) 2015, *Seminar* Venice (Italy) 2014, *International Conference on Sub-national Measurement and Economic Analysis of Tourism (MOVE)* Medellin (Colombia) 2013. **Publications** *INRouTe Newsletter* (2 a year).
Members Founding partners (2) in one country:
Spain.
Institutional Associate Partners (9) in 7 countries:
Austria, Brazil, Denmark, Italy, Mexico, Norway, Spain.
Individual Associate Partners (70) in 24 countries and territories:
Argentina, Austria, Brazil, Colombia, Czechia, Denmark, Ecuador, France, Germany, Hong Kong, Iceland, India, Ireland, Italy, Japan, Mexico, New Zealand, Romania, South Africa, Spain, Switzerland, UK, Uruguay, USA. [2021.05.26/XJ8883/E]

♦ International Network of Religious Against Trafficking in Persons (unconfirmed)

♦ **International Network of Religious Leaders Living with or Personally Affected by HIV and AIDS (INERELA+)** **14315**

Exec Dir Corner Rabie St and 4th Avenue North, Fontainebleau, Randburg, Johannesburg, 2032, South Africa. T. +27117927029. E-mail: info@inerela.org.
URL: http://www.inerela.org/

History 2002. Former names and other names: *African Network of Religious Leaders Living with or Personally Affected by HIV and AIDS (ANERELA+)* – former.
Members Individuals in 52 countries and territories:
Angola, Argentina, Benin, Bolivia, Botswana, Brazil, Burkina Faso, Burundi, Central African Rep, Chad, Congo DR, Côte d'Ivoire, Djibouti, Equatorial Guinea, Eritrea, Eswatini, Ethiopia, Gabon, Gambia, Ghana, Guinea, Guinea-Bissau, India, Indonesia, Jamaica, Kenya, Lesotho, Liberia, Madagascar, Malawi, Mali, Mozambique, Namibia, Netherlands, Niger, Nigeria, Russia, Rwanda, Senegal, Sierra Leone, Somalia, South Africa, Sudan, Sweden, Tanzania UR, Thailand, Uganda, UK, Ukraine, USA, Zambia, Zimbabwe.
NGO Relations Member of (2): *Ecumenical Advocacy Alliance (EAA, inactive)*; *Robert Carr civil society Networks Fund (RCNF, #18956)*. [2021.09.02/XM4655/F]

♦ International Network on Renewable Energy Sources / see Inter-Islamic Network on Renewable Energy Sources (#11510)

♦ **International Network for Research on Inequalities in Child Health (INRICH)** **14316**

Coordinator address not obtained. E-mail: info@inrichnetwork.org.
URL: https://inrichnetwork.org/

History 2008, Montréal, QC (Canada). **Aims** Share and advance knowledge and research into: inequalities in child health and well-being; social equity in child health and well-being; child policy for child health and well-being. **Activities** Events/meetings; research/documentation. **Events** *Annual Workshop* Rotterdam (Netherlands) 2021, *Annual Workshop* Rotterdam (Netherlands) 2020, *Annual Workshop* Toronto, ON (Canada) 2019, *Annual Workshop* Bradford (UK) 2018, *Annual Workshop* Ithaca, NY (USA) 2017. [2020/AA0289/bv/F]

♦ **International Network of Research Management Societies (INORMS)** **14317**

Contact c/o ARMA, Holyrood Park House, 106 Holyrood Road, Edinburgh, EH8 8AS, UK. T. +441313579851. E-mail: inorms.secretariat@gmail.com.
URL: https://inorms.net/

History 2001. **Aims** Internationalize the body of knowledge on research management; exchange best practice; develop international approaches to supporting the research enterprise. **Languages** English. **Activities** Events/meetings. **Events** *Congress* Durban (South Africa) 2023, *Congress* Hiroshima (Japan) 2021, *Congress* Hiroshima (Japan) 2020, *Congress* Edinburgh (UK) 2018, *Research management in a connected world* Melbourne, VIC (Australia) 2016.

Members National societies in 4 countries:
Canada, Denmark, UK, USA.
Regional organizations (6) listed in this Yearbook:
Association of Commonwealth Universities, The (ACU, #02440); Australasian Research Management Society (ARMS, #03027); European Association of Research Managers and Administrators (EARMA, #06195); Society of Research Administrators International (SRA); Southern African Research and Innovation Management Association (SARIMA); West African Research and Innovation Management Association (WARIMA, #20895).
[2022/XJ0174/y/F]

♦ International Network of Research into Tourism, Cooperation and Development (COODTUR) 14318

Red Internacional de Investigadores en Turismo, Cooperación y Desarrollo – Xarxa Internacional d'Investigadors en Turisme, Cooperació i Desenvolupament
Technical Secretariat Centre de Cooperació per al Desenvolupament Rural, Univ de Lleida, c/Jaume II 67 bis, 25001 Lleida, Spain. T. +34973003537.
Instagram: https://www.instagram.com/coodtur/
History Nov 2008. **Aims** Create knowledge about cooperation; centralize, share and transfer information relevant to cooperation agencies. **Structure** Secretariat. **Activities** Organizes congresses and seminars. **Events** *Congress* Temuco (Chile) 2019, *Congress* Tarragona (Spain) 2009, *Congress* Vila-seca (Spain) 2009. **Members** Membership countries not specified. [2019/XJ0587/F]

♦ International Network of Resource Centers on Urban Agriculture and Food Security (RUAF Foundation) 14319

Senior Programme Officer Postbus 357, 5, 3830 AK Leusden, Netherlands. T. +31334343003. E-mail: info@ruaf.org.
URL: http://www.ruaf.org/
History 1999, as *Resource Centre on Urban Agriculture and Forestry (RUAF)*, on the initiative of ETC Foundation. The project developed into an international network of 1 global and 7 regional organizations jointly implementing the programme and obtained independent legal status under the listed title in Mar 2005. Registered in accordance with Dutch law. **Aims** Contribute to development of sustainable cities for resilient and equitable urban food systems. **Structure** Executive Board; Programme Coordination Team; International Advisory Panel; International Secretariat. **Languages** Arabic, Chinese, English, French, Portuguese, Spanish. **Staff** 4.00 FTE, paid. **Finance** Main support from: Ministry of Foreign Affairs, Netherlands; *Deutsche Gesellschaft für Internationale Zusammenarbeit (GIZ); European Union (EU, #08967); FAO (#09260); International Bank for Reconstruction and Development (IBRD, #12317)*, Canada; *Swiss Agency for Development and Cooperation (SDC); UNEP (#20299); United Nations Human Settlements Programme (UN-Habitat, #20572)*, Norway; *Welthungerhilfe*; various others. **Activities** Advocacy/lobbying/activism; capacity building; knowledge management/information dissemination; training/education. **Publications** *Urban Agriculture Magazine* (annual) – in 5 languages; *RUAF Update* – newsletter. Books; articles; research reports; policy briefs; practitioner briefs.
Members Municipalities, research institutes and NGOs in 7 countries:
Belgium, Canada, China, Ecuador, Italy, Kenya, Sri Lanka.
Included in the above, 1 organization listed in this Yearbook:
International Water Management Institute (IWMI, #15867).
IGO Relations Cooperates with: *Centre de coopération internationale en recherche agronomique pour le développement (CIRAD, #03733); CGIAR System Organization (CGIAR, #03843)*, especially with Urban Harvest Programme; *FAO (#09260)*; Food for the Cities Initiative; *United Nations Human Settlements Programme (UN-Habitat, #20572)*; Urban Development Programme of the World Bank.
NGO Relations Partner of: *WASH Alliance International (WAI)*. Cooperates with:
- *ActionAid (#00087);*
- *CARE International (CI, #03429);*
- *Catholic Organization for Relief and Development (Cordaid);*
- Development of Humane Action (DHAN) Foundation (India);
- *German Catholic Bishops' Organisation for Development Cooperation (MISEREOR);*
- *Heifer International;*
- *ICCO – Interchurch Organization for Development Cooperation;*
- *Local Governments for Sustainability (ICLEI, #16507);*
- *SNV Netherlands Development Organisation (SNV);*
- other NGOs in specific activities at global or local level;
- *Oxfam Novib;*
- *Practical Action (#18475);*
- *Rainwater Harvesting Implementation Network (RAIN);*
- *Royal Tropical Institute (KIT);*
- *SIMAVI;*
- Support Group on Urban Agriculture (SGUA);
- *WASTE;*
- *Welthungerhilfe;*
- *World Vision International (WVI, #21904).* [2016.12.14/XG9829/y/E]

♦ International Network of Resource Information Centers (INRIC) 14320

Admin Coordinator 719 Town House Rd, Cornish NH 03745, USA.
URL: http://www.balatongroup.org/
History 1982, by Donella Meadows (died 2001) and Dennis Meadows. Also known as *Balaton Group*. **Aims** Accelerate and deepen general understanding of systems orientation, long-term perspective and unshakable personal commitment to achieving positive change for sustainable development. **Structure** Officers. **Finance** Contributions; grants.
Members Centers in 20 countries:
Austria, Canada, China, Costa Rica, Denmark, France, Germany, Hungary, India, Indonesia, Netherlands, Norway, Poland, Portugal, Sweden, Switzerland, Tanzania UR, Thailand, UK, USA.
Members also in the former USSR; countries not specified. [2014.06.24/XF6474/F]

♦ International Network for Safety Assurance of Fuel Cycle Industries (unconfirmed)

♦ International Network of Safety and Health Practitioner Organisations (INSHPO) 14321

Secretariat c/o ASSE, 1800 E Oakton St, Des Plaines IL 60018, USA. E-mail: copa@asse.org.
URL: http://www.inshpo.org/
History 2001, by American Society of Safety Engineers (ASSE), Canadian Society of Safety Engineering (CSSE), and *Institution of Occupational Safety and Health (IOSH)*. **Aims** Advance the occupational safety and health (OSH) profession through development and promotion of professional standards and exchange of evidence-based practices. **Structure** Board of Directors, consisting Executive Committee, Member Organization Representatives and Affiliate Organization Representatives.
Members Organizations. Full in 10 countries:
Australia, Canada, Italy, Korea Rep, Mauritius, New Zealand, Russia, Singapore, UK, USA.
Included in the above, 1 organization listed in this Yearbook:
Institution of Occupational Safety and Health (IOSH).
Affiliate in 3 countries:
Canada, UK, USA. [2014/XJ7932/F]

♦ International Network for School Attendance (INSA) 14322

Pres address not obtained. E-mail: info@insa.network.
URL: https://www.insa.network/
History 16 Mar 2018, Leiden (Netherlands). **Aims** Promote school attendance; respond to school attendance problems. **Structure** Executive Committee. **Activities** Events/meetings; research/documentation; training/education. **Events** *Conference* Egmond aan Zee (Netherlands) 2022, *Conference* 2021, *Conference* Melbourne, VIC (Australia) 2020, *Conference* Oslo (Norway) 2019. [2020/AA0703/C]

♦ International Network of Schools for the Advancement of Arts Education / see Arts Schools Network (#01127)

♦ International Network for School Social Work 14323

Contact address not obtained.
URL: http://internationalnetwork-schoolsocialwork.htmlplanet.com/
History Founded 1990. **Aims** Gather and disseminate information about school social work around the world; maintain a network of social workers who work in schools in order to facilitate international communication and cooperation between national school social work associations and school social workers around the world. **Structure** No formal structure. **Languages** English. **Staff** 1.00 FTE, paid. **Activities** Knowledge management/information dissemination; guidance/assistance/consulting; events/meetings. **Events** *Conference / International Conference* Ulaanbaatar (Mongolia) 2015, *International Conference* Accra (Ghana) 2012, *International Conference* New Zealand 2009, *International conference* Busan (Korea Rep) 2006, *International conference* Stockholm (Sweden) 2003. **Publications** Newsletter (12 a year).
Members No formal membership. National school social work organizations and school social workers in 53 countries and territories:
Argentina, Australia, Austria, Bahamas, Botswana, Bulgaria, Canada, China, Croatia, Curaçao, Cyprus, Denmark, Estonia, Finland, France, Germany, Ghana, Hong Kong, Hungary, Iceland, India, Jamaica, Japan, Korea Rep, Laos, Latvia, Liechtenstein, Lithuania, Luxembourg, Malta, Mauritius, Mongolia, Netherlands, New Zealand, Nigeria, North Macedonia, Norway, Pakistan, Poland, Russia, Saudi Arabia, Singapore, Slovakia, South Africa, Sri Lanka, Sweden, Switzerland, Taiwan, Trinidad-Tobago, UK, United Arab Emirates, USA, Vietnam. [2015.06.01/XF7186/F]

♦ International Network of Science and Technology Centres of Excellence for Sustainable Development in the South / see Network of International Science and Technology Centers (#17044)

♦ International Network of Sex Work Projects / see Global Network of Sex Work Projects (#10498)

♦ International Network on Small Hydro Power (IN-SHP) 14324

Dir 136 Nanshan Road, PO Box 202, Hangzhou, 310002 Zhejiang, China. T. +8657187023380. Fax +8657187023353. E-mail: secretariat@inshp.org.
URL: http://www.inshp.org/
History following a meeting, 12 Dec 1994, Hangzhou (China), where foundation was announced. International legal status acknowledged, 14 Feb 1999. Formally founded 5 Dec 2000, Hangzhou, under the auspices of *UNIDO (#20336)* and under close cooperation with the Chinese government. Originally referred to as *Asia Development and Training Centre for Small Hydro-Power Generation*. Pilot activity phase started 2002. **Aims** Promote small hydropower (SHP) development globally through the concept of triangular cooperation, which involves technical and economic cooperation among development countries, developed countries and international organizations, so as to supply rural areas in developing countries with *environmentally-friendly*, affordable and sufficient *energy*, which will lead to increases in employment opportunities, economic development, improvements in the ecological environment, poverty alleviation and more generally substantial and spiritual improvements in local living standards. **Structure** Coordinating Committee. *International Centre on Small Hydro-Power (IC-SHP)* serves as headquarters. **Finance** Sponsored by: *UNDP (#20292)*; UNIDO; Chinese Ministries of Water Resources (MRW) and of Foreign Trade and Economic Cooperation (MOFTEC). **Activities** Guidance/assistance/consulting; training/education; financial and/or material support.
Members Organizations (about 400) in 63 countries. Membership countries not specified. Founding members (10):
Founding members (10):
Global Sustainable Electricity Partnership (#10617); HPPEA, Egypt; *International Centre for Hydropower (ICH)*; IT Power, UK; *Latin American Energy Organization (#16313)*; Ministry of Commerce, China; Ministry of Water Resources, China; *Pacific Islands Applied Geoscience Commission (SOPAC, inactive); UNDP (#20292); UNIDO (#20336).*
Regional Focal Points (4):
AFREPREN/FWD (#00153); CANMET, Canada; *European Small Hydropower Association (ESHA, #08495)*; OLADE, Ecuador.
NGO Relations Member of: *International Network for Sustainable Energy (INFORSE, #14331); World Water Council (WWC, #21908).* [2014/XK1602/y/E]

♦ International Network for Small and Medium Sized Enterprises (INSME) 14325

Réseau international pour les petites et moyennes entreprises – Red Internacional para las Pequeñas y Medianas Empresas – Rede Internacional para as Pequeñas e Médias Empresas – Rete internazionale per le Piccole e Medie Imprese
SG Via Giosué Carducci 4, 3rd floor, 00187 Rome RM, Italy. T. +39668806803. E-mail: secretariat@insme.org.
URL: http://www.insme.org/
History 18 Feb 2004, Rome (Italy). Founded as an initiative promoted by the Italian Government within the *OECD (#17693)* Bologna Process on SMEs. Originally an informal multi-stakeholder community. Evolved into an independent legal entity, Feb 2004. Registration: EU Transparency Register, No/ID: 669977544298-19, Start date: 11 Oct 2021. **Aims** Strengthen international cooperation, exchange of know-how, best practice approaches and expertise in the field of innovation and technology transfer among economic players and intermediaries. **Structure** General Assembly; Board; Secretariat; Auditors Committee. **Languages** English. **Staff** 2.50 FTE, paid. **Finance** Sources: fees for services; members' dues. **Activities** Capacity building; events/meetings; knowledge management/information dissemination; projects/programmes; training/education. **Events** *Annual Meeting* Sofia (Bulgaria) 2021, *Annual Meeting* Naples (Italy) 2019, *Annual Meeting* Brussels (Belgium) 2018, *Annual Meeting* Doha (Qatar) 2016, *Annual Meeting* Johannesburg (South Africa) 2015. **Publications** *INSME Members Compendium* (annual); *INSME Newsletter* (11 a year) in English, Spanish.
Members For profit and non profit organizations; public bodies. Members in 40 countries:
Austria, Azerbaijan, Belgium, Brazil, Bulgaria, Canada, China, Colombia, Finland, France, Germany, Iran Islamic Rep, Italy, Japan, Jordan, Korea Rep, Kuwait, Lebanon, Luxembourg, Malaysia, Mexico, Nigeria, Oman, Pakistan, Peru, Philippines, Poland, Qatar, Romania, Russia, Saudi Arabia, Slovenia, South Africa, Switzerland, Tunisia, UK, United Arab Emirates, Uruguay, USA, Venezuela.
Included in the above, 21 organizations listed in this Yearbook:
- *African Development Bank Group (ADB Group, #00284);*
- *APEC SME Innovation Center (SMEIC, #00873);*
- *Asian Development Bank (ADB, #01422);*
- *Central European Initiative (CEI, #03708);*
- *Commission on Science and Technology for Sustainable Development in the South (COMSATS, #04239);*
- *EU-Japan Centre for Industrial Cooperation;*
- *European Investment Fund (EIF, #07601);*
- *Inter-American Investment Corporation (IIC, #11438);*
- *International Society for Professional Innovation Management (ISPIM, #15389);*
- *International Trade Centre (ITC, #15703);*
- *Latin American Integration Association (LAIA, #16343);*
- *Organization for Security and Cooperation in Europe (OSCE, #17887);*
- *Red de Información Tecnológica Latinoamericana (RITLA, see: #19294);*
- *Sistema Económico Latinoamericano (SELA, #19294);*
- *UNCTAD (#20285);*
- *UNDP (#20292)* (Mexico Office);
- *UNESCO (#20322);*
- *UNIDO (#20336);*
- *United Nations Economic Commission for Europe (UNECE, #20555);*
- *World Business Angels Association (WBAA, no recent information);*
- *World Intellectual Property Organization (WIPO, #21593).*

Consultative Status Consultative status granted from: *ECOSOC (#05331)* (Special); *UNIDO (#20336)*. **IGO Relations** Cooperates with (1): *OECD (#17693)*. **NGO Relations** Member of (2): *ANIMA Investment Network (#00833); European Alliance for Innovation (EAI, #05872)*. Cooperates with (2): *European Association of Regional Development Agencies (EURADA, #06187); European Trade Association for Business Angels, Seed Funds, and other Early Stage Market Players (EBAN, #08923)*. Partnerships with national organizations. [2021.01.14/XJ3395/y/F]

♦ International Network for Social Network Analysis (INSNA) 14326

Réseau international pour l'analyse des réseaux sociaux
Sr Assn Manager 2900 Delk Road, Suite 700, PMB 321, Marietta GA 30067, USA. E-mail: insna@insna.org.

URL: http://www.insna.org/
History 1977, Toronto, ON (Canada). Founded as the network linking network analysts. Registration: USA, State of Delaware. **Aims** Facilitate exchange of information among social network analysts. **Structure** Board of Directors. **Languages** English. **Staff** 10.00 FTE, voluntary. **Finance** Sources: members' dues. **Activities** Events/meetings; financial and/or material support; knowledge management/information dissemination. **Events** *Sunbelt : Annual International Social Network Conference* Cairns, QLD (Australia) 2022, *Networks Conference* Washington, DC (USA) 2021, *Sunbelt : Annual International Social Network Conference* 2020, *Sunbelt : Annual International Social Network Conference* Montréal, QC (Canada) 2019, *Sunbelt : Annual International Social Network Conference* Utrecht (Netherlands) 2018. **Publications** *Social Networks* (4 a year); *Connections* (2 a year) – bulletin; *Journal of Social Structure* (4-6 a year) – journal. **Information Services** *SOCNET* – ListServ electronic discussion forum.
Members Full; Student; Institutional. Individual scholars (1,194) in 73 countries and territories:
Afghanistan, Argentina, Australia, Austria, Azerbaijan, Bangladesh, Belgium, Bolivia, Bosnia-Herzegovina, Brazil, Bulgaria, Cameroon, Canada, Chile, China, Colombia, Costa Rica, Croatia, Cyprus, Czechia, Denmark, Dominica, Egypt, Estonia, Eswatini, Ethiopia, Finland, France, Germany, Ghana, Greece, Hong Kong, Hungary, India, Indonesia, Ireland, Israel, Italy, Jamaica, Japan, Kenya, Korea Rep, Kuwait, Latvia, Lithuania, Luxembourg, Malaysia, Mexico, Netherlands, New Zealand, Nigeria, Norway, Peru, Philippines, Poland, Portugal, Puerto Rico, Romania, Russia, Singapore, Slovenia, South Africa, Spain, Sweden, Switzerland, Taiwan, Thailand, Tunisia, Türkiye, UK, United Arab Emirates, Uruguay, USA. [2022.02.09/XF5132/v/**F**]

♦ International Network of Social Work in Health and Mental Health . . 14327

Address not obtained.
URL: http://icsw2016singapore.org/
History A virtual network. **Aims** Promote the development of social work in health and mental health, encourage information sharing on education, research and practice of social work in health and mental health. **Structure** No formal structure. **Languages** English. **Events** *Enhancing the human condition – negotiating and creating change* Singapore (Singapore) 2016, *Conference* Los Angeles, CA (USA) 2013, *Changing health – acting and reacting, challenges for social work theory and practice* Dublin (Ireland) 2010, *Living in harmony – promoting creative synergy in a stressful world* Hong Kong (Hong Kong) 2006, *Sharing experiences and knowledge – how social work can contribute to building a compassionate* Québec, QC (Canada) 2004. [2013/XJ4285/**F**]

♦ International Network of Societies for Catholic Theology (INSeCT) . 14328

Internationales Netzwerk der Gesellschaften für Katholische Theologie
Pres address not obtained.
URL: https://www.insecttheology.org/
History 4 Aug 1996. **Aims** Foster academic theology and theological research through communication. **Structure** Council (meets every 3 years); Steering Committee (meets annually). **Languages** English, French, Spanish. **Finance** Members' dues. Other sources: contributions; sponsors. **Activities** Projects: African Catholic Theology; Catholic Theology Worldwide – Regional Reports; International Colloquium (every 3 years). **Events** *INSeCT Twin Conference* Leuven (Belgium) / Manila (Philippines) 2023, *Symposium* Vienna (Austria) 2020, *Meeting* Graz (Austria) 2001. **Publications** Minutes and papers from international colloquia.
Members Organizations (16) in 13 countries:
Argentina, Australia, Belgium, Brazil, Canada, Chile, Colombia, Mexico, Nigeria, Philippines, South Africa, Uruguay, USA.
Included in the above, 2 organizations listed in this Yearbook:
Catholic Theological Society of Southern Africa (CTSSA); European Society for Catholic Theology (ET, #08540).
Affiliate Groups (6) in 5 countries:
Benin, Cameroon, Sri Lanka, Switzerland, USA.
Included in the above, 4 organizations listed in this Yearbook:
Association oecuménique des théologiens africains (AOTA, no recent information); Circle of Concerned African Women Theologians (CAWT, #03931); Conference of Catholic Theological Institutions (COCTI, see: #13381); Theological Advisory Commission of . [2022/XF5978/y/**F**]

♦ International Network of Sport and Health Science (unconfirmed)

♦ International Network for Standardization of Higher Education Degrees (INSHED) 14329

Contact Rue Gutenberg 5, 1201 Geneva, Switzerland.
URL: http://www.inshed.eu/
History Registered in accordance with Swiss Civil Code. **Structure** General Assembly; Executive Committee. **Activities** Training/education. **Consultative Status** Consultative status granted from: *ECOSOC (#05331)* (Special); *UNCTAD (#20285)* (General Category); *World Intellectual Property Organization (WIPO, #21593)* (Observer Status). [2020/XJ6086/**F**]

♦ International Network of Steiner Waldorf Parents / see European Network of Steiner Waldorf Parents (#08014)
♦ International Network of Street Newspapers / see International Network of Street Papers (#14330)

♦ International Network of Street Papers (INSP) 14330

CEO 43 Bath Street, Glasgow, G2 1HW, UK. T. +441413026552. E-mail: info@insp.ngo.
URL: https://insp.ngo/
History Jul 1994. Former names and other names: *International Network of Street Newspapers (INSP)* – former; *Réseau international des journaux de rue* – former; *Internationales Netz der Strassenzeitungen* – former; *Rete Internazionale di Giornali di Strada* – former. Registration: OSCR, No/ID: SC036369, Start date: 18 Feb 2002, UK, Scotland; Companies House, No/ID: SC280250, Start date: 18 Feb 2005, UK, Scotland. **Aims** Support development and sustainability of street paper organizations and add value to their work so that thousands of homeless vendors – 250,000 so far – can earn a living and improve their lives. **Structure** Board. **Finance** Members' dues. Funds raised through grant making bodies. **Activities** Financial and/or material support. **Events** *Global Street Paper Summit* Milan (Italy) 2022, *Annual international conference* Melbourne, VIC (Australia) 2010, *Annual International Conference* Bergen (Norway) 2009, *Annual International Conference* Prague (Czech Rep) 2003, *Annual International Conference* Madrid (Spain) 2002. **Publications** *INSP Newsletter* (4 a year). Annual Report. Conference reports.
Members Street newspapers (106) in 35 countries:
Argentina, Australia, Austria, Brazil, Burundi, Canada, Colombia, Croatia, Czechia, Denmark, France, Germany, Hungary, Ireland, Italy, Japan, Kenya, Korea Rep, Malawi, Netherlands, North Macedonia, Philippines, Poland, Portugal, Russia, Slovakia, Slovenia, South Africa, Sweden, Switzerland, UK, Ukraine, Uruguay, USA, Zambia.
Consultative Status Consultative status granted from: *ECOSOC (#05331)* (Ros A). **IGO Relations** *Council of Europe (CE, #04881); Swedish International Development Cooperation Agency (Sida).* **NGO Relations** Member of (2): *European Federation of National Organisations Working with the Homeless (#07174); Scotland's International Development Alliance (the Alliance).* Partner of (1): *Homeless World Cup Foundation (HWC, #10939).* Supports (1): *Global Call for Action Against Poverty (GCAP, #10263).* Delegate to the International Council of *World Social Forum (WSF, #21797).* [2023/XJ4136/**F**]

♦ International Network for Sustainable Design / see 02 Global Network (#17628)

♦ International Network for Sustainable Energy (INFORSE) 14331

Secretariat Klosterport 4F, 1 floor, 8000 Aarhus C, Denmark. T. +4586227000. Fax +4586227096. E-mail: inforse@inforse.org – ove@inforse.org.
URL: http://www.inforse.org/
History 4 Jun 1992, Rio de Janeiro (Brazil). Founded at Global Forum, on the basis of NGO energy strategy "Sustainable Energy Development – towards a world strategy". INFORSE-Europe is on EU Transparency Register: 1651695283-80. **Aims** Encourage and support sound energy strategies for sustainable *development* at all levels. **Structure** Regional Networks (7); Regional Coordinators (8); Coordinators Meeting; Secretariat hosted by INFORSE-Europe/OVE Denmark. **Languages** English. **Staff** 2-5 (project dependent). **Finance** No membership fee. **Activities** Advocacy/lobbying/activism; awareness raising; events/meetings; knowledge management/information dissemination. **Events** *European sustainable energy policy seminar* Samso Is (Denmark) 2007, *International Central Asian conference on renewable energy* Karaganda (Kazakhstan) 2005, *Seminar on sustainable energies and social change* Pola de Lena (Spain) 2004, *Pan-European sustainable energy seminar* Machynlleth (UK) 2003, *Workshop on media and environment* Ebeltoft (Denmark) 1998. **Publications** *Sustainable Energy News.* **Information Services** *EU Policy Update; INFORSE Database* – about 1,000 contacts online.

Members NGOs (about 160) in 69 countries:
Albania, Argentina, Armenia, Belarus, Belgium, Belize, Brazil, Bulgaria, Burkina Faso, Burundi, Canada, Chile, Congo Brazzaville, Croatia, Czechia, Denmark, Estonia, Finland, France, Gambia, Georgia, Germany, Ghana, Greece, Guinea, Guinea-Bissau, Hungary, India, Indonesia, Japan, Kazakhstan, Kenya, Korea Rep, Kyrgyzstan, Latvia, Lithuania, Malaysia, Mali, Malta, Mauritania, Moldova, Namibia, Nepal, Netherlands, Nigeria, North Macedonia, Norway, Pakistan, Philippines, Poland, Portugal, Romania, Russia, Senegal, Serbia, Sierra Leone, Slovakia, Slovenia, Spain, Sri Lanka, Switzerland, Thailand, Uganda, UK, Ukraine, Uruguay, USA, Venezuela, Zimbabwe.
Included in the above, 16 organizations listed in this Yearbook:
Artefact – Centre for Energy, Appropriate Technology and International Development Cooperation; Asian Alliance of Appropriate Technology Practitioners (APPROTECH ASIA, #01306); Centre for Alternative Technology (CAT); Climate and Development Initiative (CDI); *Danube Delta Friends – Foundation Sulina (no recent information); Environmental Defense Fund (EDF); Environnement et développement du Tiers-monde (enda, #05510); Fondation internationale pour le développement (FID, no recent information); Friends of the Earth International (FoEI, #10002)* (national members); *International Network on Gender and Sustainable Energy (ENERGIA, #14272); International Solar Energy Society (ISES, #15564)* (UK); *NOAH International* (Denmark); *Nordic Folkecenter for Renewable Energy; Ryan Foundation International; Society for Development Alternatives; Technology and Action for Rural Advancement (TARA).*
Consultative Status Consultative status granted from: *ECOSOC (#05331)* (Special). **IGO Relations** *Centre for Science and Technology of the Non-Aligned and Other Developing Countries (NAM S and T Centre, #03784); European Commission (EC, #06633); International Energy Agency (IEA, #13270); Regional Environmental Centre for Central and Eastern Europe (REC, #18782); United Nations Commission on Sustainable Development (CSD, inactive); United Nations Framework Convention on Climate Change – Secretariat (UNFCCC, #20564).* **NGO Relations** Member of: *GEF CSO Network (GCN, #10087).* [2020/XF5422/y/**F**]

♦ International Network for Terminology (TermNet) 14332

Réseau international de terminologie – Internationales Terminologienetz
Dir Mooslackengasse 17, 1190 Vienna, Austria. T. +431230603965. Fax +431230603966. E-mail: termnet@termnet.org.
URL: http://www.termnet.org/
History 12 Dec 1988, as the commercial but not-for-profit spin-off from *International Information Centre for Terminology (INFOTERM, #13846)*, having previously functioned since 1979 as an informal network. Currently a fully independent association. **Aims** Serve as international cooperation forum to develop services and tools in the field of terminology and its applications; facilitate and promote members' services engaging in further development of the global terminology market and collaboration; promote quality in the field of terminology through partnerships, training and capacity building, certification and standards, and innovation; work specifically in the areas of: *information* and *communication; classification* and *categorization; translation* and localization. **Structure** Assembly (annual); Board; Executive Committee; Secretariat, headed by Director. **Languages** English, French, German. **Staff** 2.00 FTE, paid. External consultants and trainers. **Finance** Members' dues. Income from projects, courses and certification, meetings and publications. **Activities** Events/meetings; training/education; certification/accreditation; publishing activities. *International Terminology Summer School (TSS).* **Events** *International conference* Dublin (Ireland) 2010, *International conference* Ankara (Turkey) 2009, *TAMA – Terminology in Advanced Management Applications* Gatineau, QC (Canada) 2008, *General Assembly* Copenhagen (Denmark) 2005, *TAMA – Terminology in Advanced Management Applications* Wiesbaden (Germany) 2005. **Publications** *TermNet Publisher* – proceedings, monographs, reports, studies, booklets.
Members Regular Members (TermNet Partners) corporate bodies that participate actively in the work of TermNet. Sponsors individuals or corporate bodies that support the objectives of TermNet through financial means or services in kind. Members in 19 countries:
Australia, Austria, Belgium, Canada, China, Denmark, Finland, France, Germany, Iran Islamic Rep, Ireland, Italy, Korea Rep, Malaysia, South Africa, Spain, Switzerland, Türkiye, USA.
Included in the above, 2 organizations listed in this Yearbook:
International Information Centre for Terminology (INFOTERM, #13846); International Institute for Terminology Research (#13932).
NGO Relations Member of: *European Certification and Qualification Association (ECQA, #06511).* Liaison Status with: *International Organization for Standardization (ISO, #14473)* / TC 37. [2021/XF0510/y/**F**]

♦ International Network Theatre in Prison (INTiP) 14333

Contact Teatro Aenigma, Via G De Carlo 5, 61029 Urbino FM, Italy.
URL: https://www.theatreinprison.org/
Aims Support theatre projects for planning, relationship-building, debate and qualification in prison institutions around the world. **Publications** *INTiP Newsletter.* **NGO Relations** Partner of: *International Theatre Institute (ITI, #15683).* [2019/XM8955/**F**]

♦ International Network of Theological Associations / see World Conference of Associations of Theological Institutions (#21296)
♦ International Network for Theory of History (unconfirmed)
♦ International Network of Tibet Support Groups (meeting series)
♦ International Network Towards Smokefree Hospitals / see Anti-Smoking International Alliance (#00861)

♦ International Network for Traditional Building, Architecture and Urbanism (INTBAU) 14334

Main Office 19-22 Charlotte Road, London, EC2A 3SG, UK. T. +442076138530. Fax +442076138599. E-mail: info@intbau.org.
URL: http://www.intbau.org/
History 2001, Rome (Italy). Registration: Charity Commission, No/ID: 1132362, England and Wales, 2009. **Aims** Promote support of traditional building, maintenance of local character and the creation of better places to live. **Structure** Board; College of Chapters; INTBAU College of Traditional Practitioners (ICTP). **Languages** English. **Staff** 1.00 FTE, paid. **Finance** Members' dues. Private charitable donations; project-specific grants; event attendance fees; training course fees. **Activities** Events/meetings. **Events** *World Congress* London (UK) 2022, *Congress* Norway 2020, *World Congress* Paris (France) 2018, *Conference on relevance of traditional architecture* Kano (Nigeria) 2008, *Swedish grace – the forgotten modern* Stockholm (Sweden) 2005. **Publications** *Venice Charter Revisited: Modernism and Conservation in the Postwar Word* (2009); *Tradition Today: Continuity in Architecture and Society* (2008).
Members Full (4,150) in 101 countries. Membership countries not specified. Chapters in 21 countries:
Chapters in 21 countries:
Australia, Canada, Cuba, Cyprus, Estonia, Germany, India, Iran Islamic Rep, Ireland, Italy, Netherlands, Nigeria, Norway, Philippines, Poland, Portugal, Romania, Russia, Spain, UK, USA.
Chapters in formation in 2 countries:
Brazil, Mexico. [2014.06.01/XM1684/**F**]

♦ International Network of Translation and Interpreting Studies Associations (INTISA) 14335

Contact address not obtained. E-mail: intisa00@gmail.com.
URL: http://usuaris.tinet.cat/intisa/
History 15 Sep 2016, Aarhus (Denmark), by representatives of 11 associations. **Aims** Promote translation and interpreting studies in all its forms; mutually enhance the status and public recognition of member associations; ensure efficient and widespread distribution of information on translation and interpreting studies evens and activities.
Members National and regional associations (12). National in 7 countries:
Brazil, Canada, Germany, Greece, Japan, Korea Rep, USA.
International organizations (5):
Asociación Ibérica de Estudios de Traducción e Interpretación (AIETI); European Association for Studies in Screen Translation (ESIST, #06227); European Society for Translation Studies (EST, #08766); International Association for Translation and Intercultural Studies (IATIS, #12236); Red Latinoamericana de Estudios de Traducción e Interpretación (RELAETI). [2017.06.01/XM5584/y/**F**]

♦ International Network of Tropical Architecture (iNTA) 14336

Contact Dept of Architecture, School of Design and Environment, NUS, 4 Architecture Drive, Singapore 117566, Singapore.
Contact address not obtained.

History 2004, Singapore. **Aims** Bring together international researchers and practitioners to collaborate and learn from each other about problems and solutions pertaining to architecture and urban design in the tropical (and sub-tropical) regions and brought together by the shared climatic imperatives and opportunities of these regions. **Activities** Events/meetings. **Events** *Conference* Brisbane, QLD (Australia) 2019, *Conference* Gainesville, FL (USA) 2017, *Conference* Johor Bahru (Malaysia) 2015, *Conference* Singapore (Singapore) 2012, *Conference* Bangkok (Thailand) 2009. [2019/AA1189/c/**F**]

♦ International Network of Universities (INU) 14337

Contact Kingston Univ, Study Abroad & International Learning Office, Yorkon bldg, Kingston Hill campus, Kingston upon Thames, KT2 7LB, UK. T. +442084173256. E-mail: inu@kingston.ac.uk.
URL: http://www.inunis.net/

History 1999. Current constitution amended Nov 2010. **Aims** Advance internationalization of member institutions through cooperation in university management, research collaboration and student and staff mobility. **Structure** Council (meets twice a year); Executive Committee. **Languages** English. **Staff** 1.00 FTE, paid. **Finance** Sources: members' dues. **Activities** Events/meetings; networking/liaising; projects/programmes; training/education. **Events** *Council Meeting* 2021, *Council Meeting* 2020, *Council Meeting* Tarragona (Spain) 2020, *Council Meeting* Bandung (Indonesia) 2019, *Council Meeting* Malmö (Sweden) 2019. **Publications** *INU Newsletter*.
Members Institutions (10) in 9 countries:
Argentina, Germany, Indonesia, Japan, South Africa, Spain, Sweden, UK, USA. [2021.06.16/XJ6742/**C**]

♦ International Network of Universities Forum UNESCO – University and Heritage / see Forum UNESCO – University and Heritage (#09931)

♦ International Network for Urban Development / see International Urban Development Association (#15832)

♦ International Network for Urban Research and Action (INURA) 14338

Common Office Hardturmstrasse 261, 8005 Zurich ZH, Switzerland. T. +41445638692. Fax +41445638686. E-mail: contact@inura.org.
URL: https://www.inura.org/

History 18 May 1991, Maloja (Switzerland). Founded at Salecina House in Maloja (Switzerland)/Zurich (Switzerland), simultaneously. **Aims** Develop and promote interaction, exchange and mutual learning of *social* and *environmental* urban movements with urban research and theoretical analysis. **Structure** Common Office; City Contact Points (18). **Languages** English. **Staff** 0.50 FTE, paid. **Finance** Sources: members' dues. **Activities** Events/meetings. **Events** *Conference* Zurich (Switzerland) 2023, *Annual Conference* Luxembourg (Luxembourg) 2022, *Annual Conference* Luxembourg (Luxembourg) 2021, *Annual Conference* Luxembourg (Luxembourg) 2020, *Annual Conference* Zagreb (Croatia) 2019. **Publications** *The Contested Metropolis: Six Cities at the Beginning of the 21st Century* (2004); *Possible Urban Worlds: Urban Strategies at the End of the 20th Century* (1999).
Members Individuals in 47 countries and territories:
Angola, Australia, Austria, Belgium, Brazil, Canada, Chile, Colombia, Croatia, Cuba, Czechia, Denmark, Ecuador, Estonia, Finland, France, Germany, Greece, Hong Kong, Hungary, India, Ireland, Italy, Japan, Kenya, Latvia, Lithuania, Luxembourg, Malaysia, Mexico, Netherlands, Nigeria, Norway, Poland, Portugal, Romania, Russia, Serbia, Singapore, South Africa, Spain, Sweden, Switzerland, Türkiye, UK, Ukraine, USA.
NGO Relations Member of (2): *From the Sea to the City*; *Habitat International Coalition (HIC, #10845)*. [2023/XF6020/v/**F**]

♦ International Network URGENCI 14339

Treas c/o Maison de la vie Associative, 140 Allée Robert Govi, 13400 Aubagne, France. T. +33687044930. E-mail: contact@urgenci.net.
URL: http://www.urgenci.net/

History Also referred to as *International Network for Community Supported Agriculture*. **Aims** Maintain and expand *peasant agriculture*; implement *food* sovereignty in all regions and communities of the world; improve health through food and combat *hunger* and *malnutrition*; develop citizenship in the economic sphere and social networks of solidarity between producers and consumers and between people in urban and rural communities; educate people on the environment and citizenship; combat exclusion and poverty. **Structure** General Assembly (every 2 years); International Committee; Executive Bureau. Permanent Urgenci Office, Aubagne (France). **Languages** English, French. **Finance** Members' dues. **Events** *International Symposium* Beijing (China) 2015, *International Symposium* China 2015, *International Symposium* Monterey, CA (USA) 2013, *International Symposium* Japan 2010, *International Symposium* Aubagne (France) 2008. **Publications** *URGENCI Newsletter*. **NGO Relations** Member of: *Intercontinental Network for the Promotion of the Social Solidarity Economy (INPSSE, #11463)*. [2016/XJ8664/**F**]

♦ International Network for Water and Ecosystem in Paddy Fields (INWEPF) 14340

Secretariat Min Agriculture/Forestry/ Fisheries, Rural Dvlpt Bureau, Design Div, Overseas Land Improvement Cooperation Office, 1-2-1 Kasumigaseki, Chiyoda-ku, Tokyo, 100-8950 Japan. T. +81335956339. Fax +81335921481.
URL: http://www.maff.go.jp/e/nousin/kaigai/inwepf/

History 2004, Japan, following 3rd World Water Forum. **Aims** Work towards food security and poverty alleviation, sustainable water use and partnership; provide a framework for promoting better management of water for paddy fields toward rural development with due consideration for the environment. **Activities** Events/meetings. **Events** *International Conference* Seoul (Korea Rep) 2019, *International Conference* Nara (Japan) 2018, *Joint symposium* Jeju (Korea Rep) 2010, *Meeting* Seoul (Korea Rep) 2007. **IGO Relations** *African Union (AU, #00488)*. [2018/XM3662/**F**]

♦ International Network of Water Training Centres (INWTC) 14341

Réseau international des centres de formations aux métiers de l'eau (RICFME) – Red Internacional de Centros de Capacitación en Agua (RICCA)

Secretariat c/o Office international de l'eau, 21 rue de Madrid, 75008 Paris, France. T. +33144908860. Fax +33140080145. E-mail: contact@inwtc.org – contact@ricfme.org.
Africa Office c/o 2iE Foundation, 01 BP 594, Ouagadougou 01, Burkina Faso. T. +22625492800. Fax +22625492801. E-mail: 2ie@2ie-edu.org.
URL: http://www.inwtc.org/

History Nov 2008, Paris (France), upon signature of Charter. **Aims** Develop relations between interested institutions; increase awareness on the significance of professional training on water; promote account taking by concerned authorities; strengthen cooperation with institutions involved in development of the water sector; encourage good practices and innovation in vocational training; promote innovative training; facilitate development of common tools and training materials support development of new water training centres; develop a platform for competencies and human resources in the field of water and sanitation services; evaluate undertaken actions. **Languages** English, French, Spanish. **Activities** Events/meetings. **Events** *Session sur la formation professionnelle technique aux métiers de l'eau et de l'assainissement* Kampala (Uganda) 2010. **IGO Relations** *Global Alliances for Water and Climate (GAfWaC, #10230)*; *Institut International d'Ingénierie de l'Eau et de l'Environnement (2iE, #11313)*; *Scientific Information Centre of Interstate Coordination Water Commission of Central Asia (SIC ICWC, #19152)*. **NGO Relations** *African Water Association (AfWA, #00497)*; *International Office for Water (IOW, #14399)*; *Tunis International Centre for Environmental Technologies (CITET)*; national water institutes. [2019.12.12/XJ8271/**D**]

♦ International Network for Whaling Research (INWR) 14342

Contact History Dept, 225 McKee Bldg, Western Carolina Univ, Cullowhee NC 28723, USA.
URL: http://www.ualberta.ca/~inwr/

History Sep 1991, Winnipeg (Canada), at annual meeting of *International Association for the Study of the Commons (IASC, #12195)*. Previously also referred to as *Network for Whaling Research*. **Aims** Maintain communication among researchers and others interested in current research being conducted on whaling societies and management, throughout the world. **Structure** An informal network; a number of 'correspondents' in different countries send reports of relevant happenings in their geographic/personal network area to the editor. **Activities** Maintains website posting news on whaling publications and developments. **Events** *International conference on community-based whaling / Whaling Symposium* Berkeley, CA (USA) 1996, *Symposium / Whaling Symposium* Bodø (Norway) 1995, *Sustainable and equitable use of marine mammal resources* Halifax, NS (Canada) 1994, *Whaling Symposium* Halifax, NS (Canada) 1994, *Whaling Symposium* Québec, QC (Canada) 1992. **Publications** *INWR Digest* (1-2 a year) – online. [2013.11.01/XF1758/v/**F**]

♦ International Network of Women Against Tobacco (INWAT) 14343

Red Internacional de Mujeres contra el Tabaco

Pres address not obtained.
URL: http://www.inwat.org/

History 1990, Perth (Australia). **Aims** Contribute to the reduction and prevention of tobacco use among girls and women worldwide; develop women's leadership in tobacco control; promote communication and exchange of information; develop research and policy advice on women-centred tobacco control; raise awareness of women's tobacco control issues. **Structure** Includes: *International Network of Women Against Tobacco – Europe (INWAT Europe, #14344)*; *Red Latinoamericana y del Caribe de Mujeres para el Control del Tabaco (INWAT-LAC)*. **Activities** Provides contacts, who are primarily women, to individuals and organizations working in tobacco control. Collects and distributes information regarding global women and tobacco issues. Shares strategies to counter tobacco advertising and promotion. Supports the development of women-centred tobacco use prevention and cessation programs. Assists in the organization and planning of conferences on tobacco control. Collaborates on the development of publications regarding women and tobacco issues. Promotes female leadership. Promotes and carries out research on women and tobacco. **Events** *WATCH : world assembly on tobacco counters health* Delhi (India) 2004, *Conference* Paris (France) 1998.
Members Active in 50 countries and territories:
Argentina, Australia, Belgium, Bolivia, Brazil, Canada, Chile, China, Colombia, Costa Rica, Czechia, Denmark, Finland, France, Germany, Greece, Honduras, Hong Kong, Hungary, Iceland, India, Indonesia, Ireland, Italy, Japan, Kenya, Lithuania, Malaysia, Mexico, Netherlands, New Zealand, Nigeria, Norway, Panama, Paraguay, Peru, Philippines, Poland, Portugal, Singapore, Spain, Sweden, Switzerland, Taiwan, Tanzania UR, Thailand, UK, Uruguay, USA, Zambia.
Consultative Status Consultative status granted from: *WHO (#20950)* (Official Relations). **NGO Relations** Member of: *Framework Convention Alliance (FCA, #09981)*. [2018/XF2311/**F**]

♦ International Network of Women Against Tobacco – Europe (INWAT Europe) 14344

Réseau international des femmes contre le tabac

Contact Ctr for Population Health Sciences, Medical School – Edinburgh Univ, Teviot Place, Edinburgh, EH8 9AG, UK.
URL: http://www.inwat.org/

History Aug 1997, within *International Network of Women Against Tobacco (INWAT, #14343)*. **Aims** Contribute to reduction and prevention of tobacco use among girls and women in Europe; develop women's leadership in tobacco control; promote communication and exchange of information; develop research and policy advice on women-centred tobacco control; raise awareness of women's tobacco control issues. **Structure** Advisory Board. **Languages** English. **Publications** *Network Europe – Réseau Europe* (2 a year) in English, French.
Members Full in 20 countries:
Austria, Belgium, Bulgaria, Czechia, Denmark, Finland, France, Germany, Greece, Hungary, Ireland, Israel, Italy, Malta, Netherlands, Poland, Spain, Sweden, Switzerland, UK.
IGO Relations *WHO (#20950)*. [2014.10.28/XE3396/**E**]

♦ International Network of Women Engineers and Scientists (INWES) 14345

Contact 65 University Street, Univ of Ottawa, Ottawa ON K1N 6N5, Canada. E-mail: info@inwes.org.
SG c/o African Women in Science and Engineering, Dept of Chemistry, Kenyatta Univ, PO Box 43844, Nairobi, Kenya. E-mail: secretariat@inwes.org.
URL: http://www.inwes.org/

History Founded 31 Jul 2002, Ottawa (Canada), following a founding meeting, 29 May 2001, Merrickville (Canada). Took over activities of *International Conference of Women Engineers and Scientists (ICWES, inactive)*. **Aims** Strengthen the capacity of individuals, organizations, university/institute and corporations to influence policies in STEM (science, technology, engineering, mathematics) worldwide; encourage education, recruitment, retention, support and advancement of professional women and students through an international network of organizations and experts. **Structure** General Meeting; Board of Directors; Committees (10). **Languages** English. **Staff** 1.00 FTE, paid. **Finance** Members' dues. Funding. **Activities** Networking/liaising; knowledge management/information dissemination; advocacy/lobbying/activism; projects/programmes; training/education. **Events** *Triennial Conference* Coventry (UK) 2021, *Triennial Conference* Coventry (UK) 2020, *Triennial Conference* Delhi (India) 2017, *Asia and Pacific Nation Network Meeting* Yokohama (Japan) 2017, *Global Women in Science and Technology Conference* Yokohama (Japan) 2017. **Publications** *INWES Newsletter* (3-4 a year). Annual Report; Triennial Report.
Members Individual; Corporate; Organizational. Members in 14 countries and territories:
Australia, Brazil, Canada, India, Kenya, Korea Rep, Malawi, Malaysia, Nigeria, Norway, Serbia, Taiwan, UK, Zambia.
Consultative Status Consultative status granted from: *UNESCO (#20322)* (Consultative Status); *ECOSOC (#05331)* (Special). **IGO Relations** Contacts with: *OECD (#17693)*. **NGO Relations** Official relations with: *World Federation of Engineering Organizations (WFEO, #21433)*. [2020/XJ4188/**F**]

♦ International Network of Women Liberals / see International Network of Liberal Women (#14294)

♦ International Network of Young Journalists 14346

Réseau international de jeunes journalistes – Red Internacional de Jóvenes Perodistas – Internationales Kontaktnetz Junger Journalisten

Contact c/o ICOM, CP 197, 1211 Geneva 20, Switzerland. E-mail: icom@bluewin.ch.
URL: http://www.icomworld.info/yj/aae.htm

History Oct 1987, under the auspices of *International Christian Organisation of the Media (ICOM, #12563)*. **Aims** Unite young journalists (less than 35 years old) worldwide, with a view of good journalism; function as a meeting point for discussing journalistic *ethics* and *standards*, *policies* and initiatives, problems and solutions, approaches and results. **Languages** English, French, German, Spanish. **Finance** Contributions. **Activities** Events/meetings; awards/prizes/competitions; projects/programmes; training/education. **Events** *Triennial World Convention* Panama (Panama) 2013, *Triennial World Convention* Ouagadougou (Burkina Faso) 2010, *Triennial World Convention* Sherbrooke, QC (Canada) 2007, *Triennial world convention* Sherbrooke, QC (Canada) 2007, *Triennial world convention* Bangkok (Thailand) 2004. **Publications** *ICOM Information*.
Members Individual: professional journalists less than 35 years old (over 1,700); Collective. Members in 98 countries and territories:
Angola, Argentina, Australia, Austria, Bangladesh, Belgium, Benin, Bolivia, Bosnia-Herzegovina, Brazil, Burkina Faso, Burundi, Cameroon, Canada, Central African Rep, Chad, Chechnya, Chile, China, Colombia, Congo Brazzaville, Congo DR, Cook Is, Costa Rica, Côte d'Ivoire, Croatia, Cuba, Czechia, Dominican Rep, Ecuador, Egypt, Eswatini, Fiji, Finland, France, Germany, Ghana, Grenada, Guatemala, Haiti, Hong Kong, Hungary, India, Indonesia, Ireland, Italy, Japan, Kenya, Kiribati, Korea Rep, Lebanon, Lesotho, Liberia, Luxembourg, Madagascar, Malawi, Malaysia, Mauritius, Mexico, Namibia, Nepal, Netherlands, New Zealand, Nicaragua, Nigeria, North Macedonia, Pakistan, Panama, Papua New Guinea, Paraguay, Peru, Philippines, Poland, Portugal, Rwanda, Senegal, Serbia, Singapore, Slovakia, Slovenia, Solomon Is, South Africa, Spain, Sri Lanka, Sudan, Sweden, Switzerland, Taiwan, Tanzania UR, Thailand, Trinidad-Tobago, Uganda, UK, Uruguay, USA, Venezuela, Zambia, Zimbabwe.
IGO Relations Through ICOM, consultative status with: *ECOSOC (#05331)*; *UNESCO (#20322)*. [2013.06.01/XF0907/**F**]

♦ International Network for Young Researchers in Male Fertility / see Network for Young Researchers in Andrology (#17067)

♦ International Neuengamme Committee 14347

Amicale internationale de Neuengamme (AIN) – Internationales Neuengamme-Komitee – Mezdunarodnyj Komitet Byvshih Uznikov Nojergamme (MKN)

Contact c/o KZ-Gedenkstätte Neuengamme, Jean-Dolidier-Weg 75, 21039 Hamburg, Germany.

URL: http://www.ag-neuengamme.de/
History 1956. Also referred to as *Amicale Internationale KZ Neuengamme – Internationalen Lagergemeinschaft des KZ Neuengamme*. **Aims** Commemorate the experience and honour the *victims* of the Neuengamme *concentration camp*. [2019/XE5081/E]

♦ International Neural Network Society (internationally oriented national body)

♦ International Neuroendocrine Cancer Alliance (INCA) 14348

Exec Dir 1150 Walnut Street, Newton, Boston MA 02461, USA. E-mail: post@incalliance.org.
URL: https://incalliance.org/
History Registered in the State of Delaware (USA). Registration: 501(c)3 non-profit organization, Start date: 1 May 2013, USA. **Aims** Raise awareness about all types of neuroendocrine cancer and genetic neuroendocrine tumors (NETs); push for scientific advancements with a focus on identified unmet needs; provide a platform for global collaboration to address the many challenges NET patients and the medical community face, in securing a timely diagnosis and accessing optimal treatment, support and care. **Structure** Board of Directors. **Languages** English. Information about neuroendocrine cancer in 10 languages. **Activities** Advocacy/lobbying/activism; awareness raising; networking/liaising; publishing activities; research and development. Active in all member countries. **Information Services** *Global NET Patient Information Pack* in Arabic, Chinese, English, French, German, Hindi, Italian, Japanese, Russian, Spanish; *NET Abstracts and Articles*; *Survey of Challenges in Access to Diagnostics and Treatment for NET Patients (SCAN)* in Arabic, Chinese, English, French, German, Hindi, Italian, Japanese, Russian, Spanish.
Members National and multinational registered NET organizations or cancer groups in 26 countries and territories:
Argentina, Australia, Belgium, Bulgaria, Canada, Denmark, France, Germany, India, Ireland, Israel, Italy, Japan, Kenya, Netherlands, New Zealand, Norway, Portugal, Singapore, South Africa, Spain, Sweden, Switzerland, Taiwan, UK, USA.
NGO Relations Member of (4): *European Cancer Organisation (ECO, #06432)* (Patient Advisory Committee); *Health Technology Assessment International (HTAi, #10889)*; *Union for International Cancer Control (UICC, #20415)*; *Workgroup of European Cancer Patient Advocacy Networks (WECAN, #21054)*.
[2022.06.30/AA0351/C]

♦ International Neuroendocrine Federation (INF) 14349

Pres Univ of Edinburgh, Ctr for Integrative Physiology, Hugh Robson Bldg, 15 George Square, Edinburgh, EH8 9XD, UK. T. +441316502869. Fax +441316511691.
SG Fac de Odontologia de Ribeirão Preto, Univ de Sao Paulo, Av Café s/n, Ribeirão Preto, Sao Paulo SP, 14040 904, Brazil. T. +551663024032. Fax +5536024102.
URL: http://www.isneuro.org/
History 22 Jun 2000, Toronto ON (Canada), replacing *International Society of Neuroendocrinology (ISN, inactive)*. **Aims** Promote development of research and education in basic and clinical neuroendocrinology; disseminate scientific information in the field. **Structure** Council (meets every 2 years); Executive Committee. **Languages** English. **Staff** 6.00 FTE, voluntary. **Finance** Members' dues. **Activities** Training/education; events/meetings; knowledge management/information dissemination; research and development. **Events** *Congress* Glasgow (UK) 2022, *Congress* Toronto, ON (Canada) 2018, *Congress / Quadrennial Conference* Sydney, NSW (Australia) 2014, *Congress / Quadrennial Conference* Rouen (France) 2010, *Congress / Quadrennial Conference* Pittsburgh, PA (USA) 2006. **Publications** *Masterclass* – e-books series.
Members Individuals in 27 countries:
Australia, Austria, Belgium, Brazil, Canada, Chile, China, Denmark, Finland, France, Germany, Hungary, India, Ireland, Israel, Italy, Japan, Mexico, Netherlands, New Zealand, Portugal, Russia, Spain, Sweden, Switzerland, UK, USA.
[2014.10.06/XD7926/v/D]

♦ International Neuroethics Society (INS) 14350

Exec dir 4938 Hampden Ln, Ste 553, Bethesda MD 20814, USA. T. +13012291660.
URL: http://www.neuroethicssociety.org/
History May 2006. **Aims** Encourage and inspire research and dialogue on the responsible use of advances in *brain* science. **Structure** Board of Directors. Committees Program; Communication, Outreach and Membership; Governance; Nominating; Student/Postdoc. **Activities** Knowledge management/information dissemination; networking/liaising; training/education; events/meetings. **Events** *Annual Meeting* Montréal, QC (Canada) 2022, *Annual Meeting* 2021, *Annual Meeting* 2020, *Annual Meeting* Chicago, IL (USA) 2019, *Annual Meeting* San Diego, CA (USA) 2018. **Publications** *INS Newsletter*. **NGO Relations** Member of (1): *International Brain Research Organization (IBRO, #12392)*. [2022/XM7480/D]

♦ International Neuroinformatics Coordinating Facility (INCF) 14351

Secretariat Karolinski Inst, Nobels väg 15-A, SE-171 77 Stockholm, Sweden. T. +46852489093. Fax +46852487094. E-mail: info@incf.org.
URL: http://www.incf.org/
History 2005, through *OECD (#17693)* Global Science Forum. **Aims** Foster international activities in neuroinformatics and related fields. **Structure** Governing Board. Secretariat. National Nodes. **Activities** Annual conference series. **Events** *Congress* Montréal, QC (Canada) 2018, *Nodes Workshop* Montréal, QC (Canada) 2018, *Congress* Kuala Lumpur (Malaysia) 2017, *Nodes Workshop* Oslo (Norway) 2017, *Congress* Reading (UK) 2016. **Publications** Annual Report. Platform documents; technical publications; reports.
Members National Nodes in 14 countries:
Belgium, Czechia, Finland, France, Germany, Italy, Japan, Netherlands, Norway, Poland, Sweden, Switzerland, UK, USA.
NGO Relations Member of: *International Brain Research Organization (IBRO, #12392)*. [2018/XJ1408/E*]

♦ International Neuro-Linguistic Programming Trainer's Association (INLPTA) 14352

Intl Coordinator address not obtained.
INLPTA Europe Herzogstr 83, 80796 Munich, Germany.
INLPTA Asia/Australia address not obtained.
URL: http://www.inlpta.org/
History 1993. By Wyatt Woodsmall, Bert Feustel, and Marvin Oka. **Aims** Facilitate alignment of professional neuro-linguistic programming (NLP) trainers worldwide in the ethical and professional use of NLP through the standardization and continual improvement of the NLP accreditation process. **Structure** Directors (3). **Activities** Advocacy/lobbying/activism; certification/accreditation; standards/guidelines; training/education. **Publications** *NLP News* (6 a year).
Members Representatives in 9 countries and territories:
Australia, Austria, France, Germany, Slovenia, Sweden, Türkiye, UK, USA. [2020/XD9284/D]

♦ International Neurological Congress / see World Federation of Neurology (#21461)

♦ International Neurological Physical Therapy Association (INPA) 14353

Pres c/o Independent Living Teams, Somerset Partnership NHS Foundation Trust, Glanville House, Church Street, Bridgwater, TA6 5AT, UK.
URL: https://www.inpaneuropt.org/
History 2007. Since 2011, a subgroup of *World Confederation for Physical Therapy (WCPT, #21293)*. **Aims** Connect neuro physiotherapists globally, advancing practice to maximize activity, participation, health and wellbeing. **Structure** Executive Committee. **Languages** English. **Activities** Events/meetings; guidance/assistance/consulting; research/documentation. **Events** *General Meeting* Dubai (United Arab Emirates) 2023. **Publications** *Journal of Neurologic Physical Therapy*.
Members Full in countries:
Australia, Brazil, Canada, Denmark, Finland, Israel, Italy, Japan, Netherlands, New Zealand, Nigeria, South Africa, Sweden, Türkiye, UK, USA, Zambia.
Associate in 10 countries:
Benin, Eswatini, Ghana, Malawi, Namibia, Nepal, Niger, Tanzania UR, Togo, Uganda. [2023/XJ5280/E]

♦ International Neuromodulation Society (INS) 14354

Exec Dir 2000 Van Ness Ave, Ste 414, San Francisco CA 94109, USA. T. +14516833237. Fax +14516833218. E-mail: ins@neuromodulation.com.
URL: http://www.neuromodulation.com/
History 1989, Groningen (Netherlands). Registration: 501(c)3, USA. **Aims** Foster scientific development and awareness of neuromodulation – the alteration of nerve activity through delivery of electrical stimulation or agents to targeted sites of the body. **Structure** International Board representing various disciplines. Regional chapters include: *Nordic Neuromodulation Society (NNS, #17366)*. **Languages** English. **Staff** 4.00 FTE, paid. **Activities** Training/education; events/meetings. **Events** *World Congress* Vancouver, BC (Canada) 2024, *Joint Congress of the INS European Chapters* Hamburg (Germany) 2023, *World Congress* Barcelona (Spain) 2022, *World Congress* Barcelona (Spain) 2021, *Joint Congress of the INS European Chapters* Paris (France) 2021. **Publications** *Neuromodulation* – journal. **Members** Neurologists, cardiologists, neurosurgeons, vascular surgeons, angiologists, anaesthesiologists and neurophysiologists. Membership countries not specified.
[2022/XD3676/D]

♦ International Neuro Ophthalmology Society (inactive)
♦ International Neuropalliative Care Society (internationally oriented national body)
♦ International Neuropeptide Y, Peptide YY, Pancreatic Polypeptide Meeting (meeting series)

♦ International Neuropeptide Society (INPS) 14355

Sec Fonds de Recherche du Québec, Bureau 800, 500 Sherbrooke St West, Montréal QC H3A 3C6, Canada. T. +15148732114.
Pres Pennington Biomedical Research Center, 6400 Perkins Road, Baton Rouge LA 70808-4124, USA. T. +12257630266. Fax +12257630265.
History 1964. **Aims** Bring together scientists working in the field of neuropeptides; distribute information of interest to these scientists and have scientific meetings in which these scientists can confer and plan cooperative research projects. **Structure** Board, including President, Secretary and Treasurer. Groups and societies: (7): Winter Neuropeptide Society; Summer Neuropeptide Society; European Neuropeptide Club; Invertebrate Neuropeptide Society; Bacterial/Antibiotic Peptide Group; Venom Peptide Group; Plant Peptide Group. Branches (12): Africa; Asia Minor; Australia; Canada; China; Indian Subcontinent; Japan; Korea Rep; Latin America; Middle East; Singapore; Taiwan. **Activities** Events/meetings. **Events** *Regional conference* Japan 2014, *Africa conference* Cape Town (South Africa) 2013, *Regional Conference* Singapore (Singapore) 2012, *Regional conference* Australia 2011, *Annual winter neuropeptide conference* Liverpool (UK) 2011. **Publications** *International Neuropeptide Society Newsletter*. **NGO Relations** Member of (1): *European Neuropeptide Club (ENC, #08044)*. [2018.06.01/XG9730/C]

♦ International Neuropsychiatric Association (INA) 14356

Secretariat 3121 CABA, C1426DBG Buenos Aires, Argentina. E-mail: secretary.ina@gmail.com.
Pres address not obtained.
URL: http://www.inawebsite.org/
History Founded 30 May 1998, Toronto (Canada). **Aims** Prevent or reduce the suffering of people with brain behaviour disorders by increasing, integrating and disseminating knowledge and understanding about the relationships between brain function and human behaviour; provide a forum for interaction and exchange of ideas among a variety of professionals with an interest in neuropsychiatric issues; publicize and disseminate both clinical and academic advances in the field to bring about improved health for people throughout the world; strive to preserve the humanistic values of medicine; raise awareness of neuropsychiatry, particularly in those countries where it is not well known or recognized. **Structure** Advisory Council; Executive Committee. **Languages** English. **Activities** Events/meetings; training/education. **Events** *International Congress of Neuropsychiatry* Bangalore (India) 2018, *International Congress of Neuropsychiatry* Jerusalem (Israel) 2015, *International Congress of Neuropsychiatry* Athens (Greece) 2014, *Latinamerican Congress of Neuropsychiatry* Buenos Aires (Argentina) 2014, *Congress* Chicago, IL (USA) 2013. **Publications** *Brain and Mind Matters Newsletter*. **Members** Membership countries not specified. [2015.02.09/XD9405/C]

♦ International Neuropsychoanalysis Society 14357

Sec 13 Prowse Place, London, NW1 9PN, UK. T. +442074826999. Fax +442072844030. E-mail: society@npsa-association.org.
URL: http://npsa-association.org/
History Jul 2000, London (UK). Registration: USA, Delaware. **Aims** Promote inter-disciplinary work between the fields of psychoanalysis and *neuroscience*. **Structure** Co-Chairs (2). **Languages** English. **Staff** 1.50 FTE, paid. **Finance** Sources: donations; members' dues. **Activities** Events/meetings. **Events** *Congress* San Juan (Puerto Rico) 2021, *Congress* San Juan (Puerto Rico) 2020, *Satisfaction at last – neuropsychoanalysis on sex, drive and enjoyment* Brussels (Belgium) 2019, *Repression and defence* Mexico City (Mexico) 2018, *Compulsion to predict – the development of the self and its disorders* London (UK) 2017. **Publications** *Neurpsychoanalysis* (2 a year). **Members** Individuals (about 400). Membership countries not specified.
[2020/XD8876/C]

♦ International Neuropsychological Society (INS) 14358

Exec Sec 2319 S Foothill Dr, Ste 260, Salt Lake City UT 84109, USA. T. +18014870475. E-mail: ins@the-ins.org.
URL: http://www.the-ins.org/
History 1967. Previously also known as *European International Neuropsychology Society*. Title changed to *International Neuropsychology Society (INS)*, 1973. **Aims** Promote research, service and education in neuropsychology; enhance communication among scientific disciplines which can contribute to understanding brain-behaviour relationships, in particular neuropsychological disorders. **Activities** Organizes: Annual North American Meeting (February), including Herbert Birch Lecture and Philip M Rennick Award; Annual European Conference (summer). Awards 'Benton Prize Lectureship' (periodically) for outstanding contributions to neuropsychology by mid-career scientists and clinicians. **Events** *Annual Mid-Year Meeting* Osaka (Japan) 2023, *Annual Mid-Year Meeting* Barcelona (Spain) 2022, *Annual Meeting* San Diego, CA (USA) 2021, *Annual Meeting* Denver, CO (USA) 2020, *Annual Mid-Year Meeting* Salt Lake City, UT (USA) 2020. **Publications** *Journal of the International Neuropsychology Society (JINS)* (7 a year).
Members Individuals regular membership; associate membership. Members in 74 countries and territories:
Albania, Algeria, Argentina, Australia, Austria, Bahamas, Belgium, Bermuda, Bolivia, Brazil, Canada, Chile, China, Colombia, Costa Rica, Czechia, Denmark, Egypt, El Salvador, Finland, France, Germany, Greece, Guatemala, Honduras, Hong Kong, Hungary, Iceland, India, Indonesia, Iran Islamic Rep, Iraq, Ireland, Israel, Italy, Jamaica, Japan, Jordan, Kenya, Korea Rep, Lebanon, Luxembourg, Malaysia, Mexico, Morocco, Mozambique, Myanmar, Netherlands, Norway, Pakistan, Panama, Peru, Philippines, Poland, Portugal, Puerto Rico, Romania, Saudi Arabia, Serbia, Singapore, South Africa, Spain, Suriname, Sweden, Switzerland, Taiwan, Thailand, Türkiye, UK, United Arab Emirates, Uruguay, USA, Venezuela, Zimbabwe.
NGO Relations Member of: *International Union of Psychological Science (IUPsyS, #15807)*.
[2020/XF0762/v/C]

♦ International Neuropsychological Symposium (meeting series)
♦ International Neuropsychology Society / see International Neuropsychological Society (#14358)

♦ International Neurotoxicology Association (INA) 14359

Sec Regulatory Science Associates, Kip Marina, Inverkip, PA16 0AS, UK.
Pres Inst for Risk Assessment Sciences, Utrecht Univ, PO Box 80 177, 3508 TD Utrecht, Netherlands.
URL: http://www.neurotoxicology.org/
History Founded 1984. Current title adopted, 1985. **Aims** Promote scientific knowledge regarding the action of toxic agents on the nervous system and information exchange in the field among members as well as with scientists of other disciplines. **Structure** Executive Committee. **Languages** English. **Staff** Voluntary. **Finance** Members' dues. **Activities** Events/meetings. **Events** *Biennial Conference* Düsseldorf (Germany) 2019, *Biennial Conference* Florianópolis (Brazil) 2017, *Biennial Conference* Montréal, QC (Canada) 2015, *Biennial Conference* Egmond aan Zee (Netherlands) 2013, *Biennial Conference* Xian (China) 2011. **Publications** *INA Newsletter* (2 a year).
Members Full (104); Student (9). Members in 20 countries:
Australia, Brazil, Canada, China, France, Germany, Hungary, Iraq, Israel, Italy, Japan, Netherlands, Norway, Portugal, Russia, Spain, Sweden, Switzerland, UK, USA.
NGO Relations Member of: *International Union of Toxicology (IUTOX, #15824)*. [2018.06.01/XD7663/D]

♦ International Neurotoxin Association (INA) 14360

Secretariat 48 Wall St, 11th Fl, New York NY 10005, USA. T. +12125004672. Fax +12124611011.
URL: http://www.neurotoxins.org/

History Registration: USA, Delaware. **Aims** Advance scientific research, support education and foster understanding about botulinum and other neurotoxins. **Structure** Board of Directors. **Activities** Events/ meetings; knowledge management/information dissemination. **Events** *North American Regional Conference* New Orleans, LA (USA) 2022, *Conference* New York, NY (USA) 2021, *Conference* Copenhagen (Denmark) 2019, *Basic science and clinical aspects of botulinum and other neurotoxins* Madrid (Spain) 2017, *Conference* Lisbon (Portugal) 2015. [2021/XM7666/**C**]

♦ International Neurotrauma Research Organization (inactive)

♦ International Neurotrauma Society (INTS) 14361

Chair Reagan UCLA Med Ctr, Neurosurgery Dept – Geffen School, 10833 Le Conte Ave, 18-228 Semel, Box 957039, Los Angeles CA 90095-7039, USA.
URL: http://www.ints2014.com/

History 1995, Toronto (Canada), during 3rd International Neurotrauma Symposium. **Aims** Support the International Neurotrauma Symposium. **Events** *Symposium* Melbourne, VIC (Australia) 2021, *Symposium* Melbourne, VIC (Australia) 2020, *Joint Symposium* Toronto, ON (Canada) 2018, *Symposium* Toronto, ON (Canada) 2018, *Symposium* Cape Town (South Africa) 2016. **Members** Membership countries not specified. [2014/XF7135/**F**]

♦ International Neutrino Commission 14362

Address not obtained.
URL: http://neutrino2016.iopconfs.org/home

Structure Commission, consisting of organizers of past conferences. **Events** *International Conference on Neutrino Physics and Astrophysics* London (UK) 2016, *International Conference on Neutrino Physics and Astrophysics / International Conference on Neutrino Physics and Astrophysics – NEUTRINO* Boston, MA (USA) 2014, *International Conference on Neutrino Physics and Astrophysics – NEUTRINO* Kyoto (Japan) 2012, *International Conference on Neutrino Physics and Astrophysics – NEUTRINO* Athens (Greece) 2010, *International Conference on Neutrino Physics and Astrophysics – NEUTRINO* Christchurch (New Zealand) 2008. [2016/XJ9049/c/**E**]

♦ International News Media Association (INMA) 14363

Association internationale de marketing de journaux – Asociación Internacional de Marketing de Periódicos – Internationaler Zeitungs Marketing-Verband

Exec Dir PO Box 740186, Dallas TX 75374, USA. T. +12143739111. Fax +12143739112.
Europe Office Minderbroedersrui 9, Bus 9, 2000 Antwerp, Belgium. T. +3222886946. Fax +3222886947.
Asia Office First Floor, B-5 Kailash Colony, Delhi 110048, DELHI 110048, India.
URL: http://www.inma.org/

History 1930. Former names and other names: *National Newspaper Promotion Association* – former (1930 to 1969); *International Newspaper Promotion Association* – former (1969 to 1987); *International Newspaper Marketing Association (INMA)* – former (1987 to 2008); *International Newsmedia Marketing Association (INMA)* – former (2008 to 2012). **Aims** Serve as a provider of global best practices for news media companies looking to grow revenue, audience and brand amid profound market change through sharing global best practices, spotting of trends, commonalities and outliers, identifying new business model opportunities, and rewarding new ways of building brand and corporate value. **Structure** Board of Directors; Regional Boards. **Activities** Awards/prizes/competitions; events/meetings; guidance/assistance/consulting; knowledge management/ information dissemination; networking/liaising; training/education. **Events** *World Congress of News Media* Dallas, TX (USA) 2021, *World Congress* Paris (France) 2020, *World Congress* New York, NY (USA) 2019, *World Congress* Washington, DC (USA) 2018, *European Conference* Oslo (Norway) 2017. **Members** Individuals (over 16000) in 72 countries. Membership countries not specified. [2021/XD7024/v/**C**]

♦ International Newsmedia Marketing Association / see International News Media Association (#14363)
♦ International Newspaper Marketing Association / see International News Media Association (#14363)
♦ International Newspaper Promotion Association / see International News Media Association (#14363)
♦ International Newsreel and News Film Association (no recent information)
♦ International News-Reel Union (inactive)

♦ International News Safety Institute (INSI) 14364

Dir c/o Thomson Reuters Foundation, 5 Canada Square, Canary Wharf, London, E14 5AQ, UK. E-mail: info@newssafety.org.
URL: http://www.newssafety.org/

History 3 May 2003, Brussels (Belgium). Founded by *International Federation of Journalists (IFJ, #13462)* and *International Press Institute (IPI, #14636)*, to mark the World Press Freedom Day. Registration: Charity Commission, No/ID: 1144296, England and Wales. **Aims** Promote safety training and awareness programmes in all regions of the world, particularly those where media staff face human rights abuses on a routine and daily basis. **Languages** English, French. **Activities** Events/meetings; guidance/assistance/consulting; knowledge management/information dissemination; research/documentation; training/education. **Publications** *Under Threat: The Changing State of Media Safety* (2015); *No Woman's Land – On the Frontlines with Female Reporters* (2012). Reports; survival guides.
Members Full in 16 countries:
Belgium, Brazil, Canada, Denmark, Finland, France, Germany, Japan, Kenya, Netherlands, Norway, Pakistan, Sweden, Switzerland, UK, USA. [2022.05.05/XE4606/j/**E**]

♦ International New Towns Association / see International Urban Development Association (#15832)
♦ International NF Association (inactive)
♦ International NGO Charter of Accountability / see Accountable Now (#00060)

♦ International NGO/CSO Planning Committee for Food Sovereignty (IPC) 14365

Comité international de planification pour la souveraineté alimentaire (CIP) – Comité Internacional de Planificación para la Soberanía Alimentaria (CIP)

Contact CIC, Via Tuscolana 1111, 00173 Rome RM, Italy. T. +39672902263. Fax +39672907846. E-mail: fc@foodsovereignty.org – ipc-cip@foodsovereignty.org.
URL: http://www.foodsovereignty.org/

Aims Serve as a forum for diffusion of information and training on issues regarding food sovereignty. **Structure** General Meeting; Facilitating Committee; Secretariat. Working Groups; IPC4CMS Group. **Events** *Forum* Sélingué (Mali) 2007. **Publications** *IPC Newsletter*.
Members National and international organizations. Membership countries not specified. Included in the above, 15 organizations listed in this Yearbook:
Arab Group for the Protection of Nature (APN, #00970); *Asian NGO Coalition for Agrarian Reform and Rural Development (ANGOC, #01566)*; Centro Internazionale Crocevia (CIC); *Collectif Stratégies Alimentaires (CSA)*; *FIAN International (#09743)*; *Institute for Agriculture and Trade Policy (IATP)*; *International Collective in Support of Fishworkers (ICSF, #12639)*; *International Federation of Rural Adult Catholic Movements (#13535)*; *International Indian Treaty Council (IITC, #13836)*; *International Union of Food, Agricultural, Hotel, Restaurant, Catering, Tobacco and Allied Workers Associations (IUF, #15772)*; *Mouvement international de la jeunesse agricole et rurale catholique (MIJARC, #16865)*; *Movimiento Agroecológico para Latinoamérica y El Caribe (MAELA, #16872)*; *Pesticide Action Network (PAN, #18336)*; *Practical Action (#18475)*; *World Forum of Fisher Peoples (WFFP, #21517)*.
NGO Relations *Centro Internazionale Crocevia (CIC)* serves as secretariat. Close cooperation with: *Alliance Against Hunger and Malnutrition (AAHM, no recent information)*. Partner of: *Livestock Environmental Assessment and Performance Partnership (LEAP, #16500)*. [2021/XJ3950/y/**E**]

♦ International NGO Forum on Indonesian Development (INFID) 14366

Forum international des ONG pour le développement en Indonésie

Exec Dir Jl Jatipadang Raya Kav 3 No 105, Pasar Minggu, Jakarta 12540, Indonesia. T. +62217819734 – +62217919735. Fax +622178844703. E-mail: info@infid.org.
URL: http://www.infid.org/

History Jun 1985, as *International NGO Group on Indonesia (INGI)*. New name adopted 1993. **Aims** Endeavour to ensure that formulation and implementation of national and international policies on development in Indonesia, including those related to *lending* that creates *debt* dependency, *investment* and *trade*, are in the interests of the *poor* and *disadvantaged*, and are based on principles of peace and justice; create conditions to allow strengthening of democratic life through broadening people's participation in, access to, and control of development in Indonesia. **Structure** General Assembly (annual); Conference (every 2 years); Board (meets twice a year); International Secretariat; 1 Liaison Office. **Languages** English, Indonesian. **Staff** 19.00 FTE, paid. **Finance** Annual budget: about US$ 919,000. **Activities** Projects/programmes; advocacy/lobbying/ activism; research/documentation; networking/liaising; knowledge management/information dissemination; publishing activities; events/meetings. **Events** *Biennial Conference* Jakarta (Indonesia) 2005, *International conference on Indonesia's debt* Paris (France) 2002, *Biennial Conference* Yogyakarta (Indonesia) 2002, *Biennial Conference* Bali (Indonesia) 1999, *Biennial Conference* Bonn (Germany) 1998. **Publications** Statements; position papers; books; leaflets; news digests.
Members Not a membership body. Participating NGOs (over 100) in 13 countries:
Australia, Belgium, Canada, France, Germany, Indonesia, Italy, Japan, Netherlands, Philippines, Switzerland, UK, USA.
Consultative Status Consultative status granted from: *ECOSOC (#05331)* (Special). **NGO Relations** Member of: *Asia Civil Society Forum (ACSF, no recent information)*; *Asia-Pacific Research Network (APRN, #02013)*; *Financial Transparency Coalition (FTC, #09772)*; *Climate Justice Now ! (CJN!, inactive)*; *Forus (#09934)*; *National Platforms' Coalition of Asia (NPCOA, #16939)*; *NGO Forum on ADB (#17123)*; *The Reality Of Aid (ROA, #18626)*; *Transparency, Accountability and Participation Network (TAP Network, #20222)*. [2018.06.01/XE0440/**E**]

♦ International NGO Group on Indonesia / see International NGO Forum on Indonesian Development (#14366)
♦ International NGO History Forum / see History NGO Forum for Peace in East Asia
♦ International NGO History Forum for Peace in East Asia / see History NGO Forum for Peace in East Asia

♦ International NGO Platform on the Migrant Workers' Convention (IPMWC) 14367

Plate-forme internationale des ong sur la Convention pour les travailleurs migrants – Plataforma Internacional ONG para la Convención sobre Trabajadores Migratorios

Secretariat c/o ICMC, PO Box 96, 1211 Geneva 20, Switzerland. T. +41229191025. Fax +41229191048.
URL: http://www.december18.net/

Aims Facilitate promotion, implementation and monitoring of International convention on the protection of the rights of all migrant workers and members of their families, approved 18 Dec 1990. **Structure** Advisory Committee. **Finance** Supported by: *Inter Pares*; *Oxfam Novib*; *UNESCO (#20322)*.
Members National organizations (3) in 3 countries:
Belgium, Indonesia, Israel.
International organizations (11):
Amnesty International (AI, #00801); *Anti-Slavery International (#00860)*; *Franciscans International (FI, #09982)*; *Human Rights Watch (HRW, #10990)*; *International Catholic Migration Commission (ICMC, #12459)*; *International Federation for Human Rights (#13452)*; *Jesuit Refugee Service (JRS, #16106)*; *Migrants Rights International (MRI, #16799)*; *Public Services International (PSI, #18572)*; *World Council of Churches (WCC, #21320)*; *World Organisation Against Torture (OMCT, #21685)*. [2011/XM1259/y/**F**]

♦ International NGO Safety and Security Association (INSSA) 14368

Contact 52-55 Lower Camden Str, Dublin, CO. DUBLIN, Ireland. T. +35314177749. E-mail: info@ ingossa.org.
URL: http://ingossa.org/

History Set up with the help of *American Council for Voluntary International Action (InterAction)*, at the instigation of *United States Agency for International Development (USAID)* – Office of Foreign Disaster Assistance (OFDA). Incorporated 12 May 2010. Granted non-profit status in the US, Feb 2011. **Aims** Enhance the professional development; build the safety and security capacity of those working in the humanitarian aid and development sector. **Structure** Board of Directors; Executive Committee. **Finance** Donors: *United States Agency for International Development (USAID)*; *Save the Children International (#19058)*; *Habitat for Humanity International (HFHI)*; Clements Worldwide. Supporters include: *Concern Worldwide*; *Blumont International*; *Search for Common Ground (SFCG)*; *Centre for Safety and Development (CSD)*. **Members** Individuals; organizations. Membership countries not specified. [2014/XJ8592/**C**]

♦ International NGO Task Group on Legal and Institutional Matters (INTGLIM) 14369

Groupe de travail international des ONG sur les questions légales et institutionnelles – Organización No Gubernamental Internacional – Grupo de Trabajo en Cuestiones Legales e Institucionales

Contact c/o CDIL, PO Box 2022, Grand Central Station, New York NY 10163, USA. T. +16464658512. Fax +16465991332. E-mail: cdilnyc@gmail.com.

History 1991, at the end of the 2nd Preparatory Committee for the *United Nations Conference on Environment and Development (UNCED)*. **Aims** Establish more effective communications between NGOs from all regions. **Structure** Informal network. **Activities** Coordinates dialogues and sessions; convenes meetings and briefings. **IGO Relations** Instrumental in setting up: *United Nations Commission on Sustainable Development (CSD, inactive)*. **NGO Relations** *Center for Development of International Law, New York (CDIL)*; *World Federalist Movement – Movement for a Just World Order through a Strengthened United Nations (WFM, #21404)*. [2018/XF0638/j/**F**]

♦ International NGO Training and Development Centre, Oxford / see International NGO Training and Research Centre, Oxford
♦ International NGO Training and Research Centre, Oxford (internationally oriented national body)

♦ International Nickel Study Group (INSG) 14370

Groupe d'étude international du nickel

SG Rua Almirante Barroso 38-5, 1000-013 Lisbon, Portugal. T. +351213567030. Fax +351213567039. E-mail: insg@insg.org.
URL: http://www.insg.org/

History 28 Jun 1990, The Hague (Netherlands), the Terms of Reference having been negotiated in 1985-1986 by the UN Conference on Nickel. Secretariat established in early 1991. **Aims** Promote international cooperation on issues concerning nickel, especially by improving statistics and other information on the nickel market and by providing a forum for members to discuss nickel issues of common interest and concern. **Structure** General Session (annual); Standing Committee; Statistics Committee; Environmental and Economics Committee; Industry Advisory Panel; Secretariat. **Languages** English, French, Russian, Spanish. **Staff** 5.00 FTE, paid. **Finance** Annual budget: about euro 400,000. **Activities** Knowledge management/information dissemination; networking/liaising. **Events** *Meeting* Lisbon (Portugal) 2019, *Meeting* Lisbon (Portugal) 2017, *Meeting* The Hague (Netherlands) 1993, *Meeting* The Hague (Netherlands) 1993. **Publications** *World Nickel Statistics* (12 a year); *World Directory of Nickel Production Facilities* (annual).
Members Governments of 14 countries:
Australia, Brazil, Cuba, Finland, France, Germany, Greece, Italy, Japan, Norway, Portugal, Russia, Sweden, UK.
IGO Relations Designed International Commodity Body of: *Common Fund for Commodities (CFC, #04293)*. **NGO Relations** Relations with industry associations representing nickel and specialty steel industries, environmental and occupational health concerns, and the like, including: *Nickel Institute (#17133)*. Member of: *TEAM STAINLESS (#20113)*. [2018.06.01/XF2757/**F***]

♦ International Niemann-Pick Disease Alliance (INPDA) 14371

Contact address not obtained. E-mail: info@inpda.org.
URL: http://www.inpda.org/

History 2009. Registration: No/ID: 1150256, UK. **Aims** Relieve sickness and distress amongst families affected by Niemann Pick Diseases worldwide; provide a forum for *patient* groups and professionals working in the field of NPD. **Structure** General Meeting; Governing Council; Executive Committee. **Languages** Chinese, English, French, German, Italian, Norwegian, Portuguese, Spanish. **Activities** Knowledge management/ information dissemination.
Members Members (22) in 17 countries:
Argentina, Australia, Brazil, Canada, China, France, Germany, Italy, Netherlands, Norway, Pakistan, Spain, Switzerland, Taiwan, Tunisia, UK, USA.
NGO Relations Member of (2): *EURORDIS – Rare Diseases Europe (#09175)*; *Rare Diseases International (RDI, #18621)*. [2021.02.24/XM7437/**C**]

♦ International Nightlife Association (unconfirmed)

♦ International Nitrogen Initiative (INI) 14372

Chair IRI 117 Monell Bldg, 61 Route 9W, Palisades NY 10964, USA. Fax +18456804864.
URL: http://www.initrogen.org/
History Feb 2003, Denver CO (USA), following a proposal made during 1st International Nitrogen Conference, The Netherlands, 1998. **Aims** Optimize nitrogen's beneficial role in sustainable food production; minimize nitrogen's negative effects on human health and the environment resulting from food and energy production. **Structure** Steering Committee comprising Chairman, representative from *International Geosphere-Biosphere Programme (IGBP, inactive)* and *Scientific Committee on Problems of the Environment (SCOPE, #19150)* and representatives of regional centres. Regional centres (5): African; Asian; European; Latin American; North American. **Finance** Supported by the Dutch Ministry and the following international organizations: *International Geosphere-Biosphere Programme (IGBP, inactive)*; *Scientific Committee on Problems of the Environment (SCOPE, #19150)*. **Events** *International Nitrogen Conference* Berlin (Germany) 2021, *International Nitrogen Conference* Berlin (Germany) 2020, *Towards the Establishment of an International Nitrogen Management System (INMS) Project General Assembly* Nairobi (Kenya) 2019, *International Nitrogen Conference* Melbourne, VIC (Australia) 2016, *International Nitrogen Conference* Kampala (Uganda) 2013. **Publications** *INI News*. [2014/XM3157/**F**]

♦ International Nobel Peace Prize Recommendation Forum (INPRRF) . 14373

SG 3/106 – 1st Floor, Vivek Khand-3, Gomti Nagar, Lucknow, Uttar Pradesh 226010, Lucknow UTTAR PRADESH 226010, India. T. +915222303663 – +915222303664. Fax +915222397710. E-mail: mseransi786@gmail.com – info@nobelpeaceforum.org.
URL: http://www.nobelpeaceforum.org/
History 8 Jun 2004, Lucknow (India), by Mohd Seraj Ansari, Secretary-General of *International Non-Olympic Committee (INOC, #14374)*. Registered in accordance with Indian law. **Aims** Promote and create awareness about the Nobel Peace Prize Awards internationally; increase tolerance, understanding, solidarity and cooperation worldwide; promote friendship between world peace movements, international sports organizations and national Nobel Peace Prize recommendation forums. **Structure** Delegate's Conference. Executive Committee, including President, Vice-President, Secretary-General, Director General, 7 Directors and Treasurer. **Members** National Peace Movement/National Sports Organizations. Membership countries not specified. **NGO Relations** *World Council for Regular and Distance Education (WCRDE, #21338)*. [2014/XM0692/**F**]

♦ International Noma Federation / see Fédération Internationale No-Noma (#09645)
♦ International Nomenclature Committee for Paediatric and Congenital Heart Disease / see International Society for Nomenclature of Paediatric and Congenital Heart Disease (#15306)
♦ International Non-Governmental Organization – INCORVUZ Corporation / see International Coordination Council of Educational Institutions Alumni (#12959)
♦ International Non-governmental Organizations Committee on Human Rights / see CONGO Committee on Human Rights (#04663)
♦ International Non-Ionizing Radiation Committee / see International Commission on Non-Ionizing Radiation Protection (#12707)

♦ International Non-Olympic Committee (INOC) 14374

Gen Sec / Founder 3/106 – 1st Floor, Vivek Khand-3, Gomti Nagar, Lucknow, Uttar Pradesh 226010 UP, Lucknow UTTAR PRADESH 226010 UP, India. T. +915222303663. Fax +915222397710. E-mail: press@non-olympic.org.
URL: http://non-olympic.org/
History Founded 25 Mar 1997, India, as an International Charter for the World Non-Olympic Sports. Registered in accordance with Indian law, Indian Trusts Act of 1882. **Aims** Support all sport affiliated member organizations of the Non-Olympic Mouvement and encourage all members to promote Non-Olympic principles; promote Non-Olympic Games internationally; represent the interests of members at international level with regard to the authorities, other sports committees, the mass media and the public; promote sporting contact between all international sports federations and national Non-Olympic Committee sports, games and players; monitor and ensure the keeping of the existing system-specific rules, develop a set of standard rules; fight against doping in the sense of the INOC-Charter, and support all measures for stopping the use of all forbidden stimulating means. **Structure** Delegates' Conference; Executive Committee; Technical Commission; Legal Committee. Includes *International Non-Olympic University (INOU)*. **Languages** English. **Staff** 8.00 FTE, paid. Voluntary. **Finance** Members' dues. **Activities** Research and Development; training; education; championships.
Members Full membership open to International Sports Federations who are not members of the International Olympic Committee (IOC). National organizations; individuals. National organizations (10) in 10 countries and territories:
Afghanistan, China, Hong Kong, India, Iran Islamic Rep, Iraq, Malaysia, Pakistan, Sri Lanka, Taiwan.
Individuals (10,000) in 45 countries and territories:
Afghanistan, Bahrain, Bangladesh, Bhutan, Brunei Darussalam, Cambodia, China, Hong Kong, India, Indonesia, Iran Islamic Rep, Iraq, Israel, Japan, Jordan, Kazakhstan, Korea DPR, Korea Rep, Kuwait, Kyrgyzstan, Laos, Lebanon, Malaysia, Maldives, Mongolia, Myanmar, Nepal, Oman, Pakistan, Palestine, Philippines, Qatar, Saudi Arabia, Singapore, Sri Lanka, Syrian AR, Taiwan, Tajikistan, Thailand, Timor-Leste, Turkmenistan, United Arab Emirates, Uzbekistan, Vietnam, Yemen.
IGO Relations *UNESCO (#20322)*; sports ministries in many countries worldwide. **NGO Relations** *International Nobel Peace Prize Recommendation Forum (INPRRF, #14373)*; *International Super-Cricket Committee (ISCC, #15626)*; *World Council for Regular and Distance Education (WCRDE, #21338)*; *World Sports Karate Federation (WSKF, #21824)*. [2014.03.08/XE4151/**E**]

♦ International Non-Olympic University (internationally oriented national body)
♦ International NoNoma Federation (#09645)
♦ International Non-Party Organization Europe 2000 (inactive)
♦ International Nonviolence Training Fund (internationally oriented national body)
♦ International Nonviolent Initiatives (internationally oriented national body)
♦ International NORCOFEL Association (inactive)

♦ International Nordic Walking Federation (INWA) 14375

Pres Jollaksentie 27-A, FI-00850 Helsinki, Finland. E-mail: info@inwa-nordicwalking.com.
URL: http://www.inwa-nordicwalking.com/
History 2000, Finland. **Aims** Promote Nordic walking; train internationally; create a global network for Nordic walkers, instructors, national coaches, associations and health, fitness and sport organizations. **Structure** Board. Executive, comprising President, 2 Vice-Presidents and Committee Chairmen (Membership; Education; Science). **Activities** Organizes: World Nordic Walking Day; International Convention; Instructors and Coach courses. **Events** *Convention* Barcelona (Spain) 2015, *Convention* Barcelona (Spain) 2014, *Convention* Otepää (Estonia) 2010. **Publications** *INWA e-Newsletter* (6 a year).
Members Full in 22 countries:
Australia, Belgium, Canada, China, Croatia, Estonia, France, Germany, Hungary, India, Italy, Japan, Korea Rep, Latvia, Netherlands, New Zealand, Poland, Russia, Slovenia, Spain, UK, USA.
NGO Relations Member of: *The Association for International Sport for All (TAFISA, #02763)*. [2018/XJ6356/**C**]

♦ International North Pacific Fisheries Commission (inactive)

♦ International Nosocomial Infection Control Consortium (INICC) 14376

Comunidad Científica Internacional de Control de Infecciones Nosocomiales
Dir 11 de Septiembre No 4567, Floor 12 – Apt 1201, 1429 Buenos Aires, Argentina. T. +541147047227.
URL: http://www.inicc.org/
History Founded 2002, evolving from itinerant information work and training that started in the 90's by Dr Victor D Rosenthal which led to implementation of Process Surveillance and Outcome Surveillance methodologies and the concept of Cost-effectiveness of Nosocomial Infection Control. **Aims** Work interactively through a network aimed at reducing *healthcare*-associated infection rates. **Structure** Headquarters Team in Buenos Aires (Argentina); Country Directors and Secretaries; Researchers; Principle Investigators; Advisory Board. **Languages** Chinese, English, Portuguese, Spanish, Turkish. **Staff** 15.00 FTE, paid; 2000.00 FTE, voluntary. **Finance** From 1998-2007: funds from donations by Dr Rosenthal. Since 2007, funding through INICC Research Foundation, established under the laws of Argentina. **Activities** Research/documentation; training/education; publishing activities. **Publications** Papers; reports; studies; abstracts.
Members Medical centres (463) in 69 countries and territories:
Argentina, Bahrain, Bolivia, Botswana, Brazil, Bulgaria, Chile, China, Colombia, Costa Rica, Croatia, Cuba, Cyprus, Dominican Rep, Ecuador, Egypt, El Salvador, Georgia, Germany, Greece, Guatemala, Honduras, India, Indonesia, Iran Islamic Rep, Italy, Jordan, Kenya, Kosovo, Kuwait, Lebanon, Libya, Lithuania, Malaysia, Mexico, Mongolia, Morocco, Nepal, Nicaragua, Nigeria, North Macedonia, Oman, Pakistan, Palestine, Panama, Papua New Guinea, Paraguay, Peru, Philippines, Poland, Puerto Rico, Qatar, Romania, Russia, Saudi Arabia, Serbia, Singapore, Slovakia, Sri Lanka, Sudan, Thailand, Tunisia, Türkiye, Ukraine, United Arab Emirates, Uruguay, Venezuela, Vietnam, Yemen.
NGO Relations Cooperates with: Blacksea Society of Clinical Microbiology and Infectious Diseases (BSCMID); *European Network of Laboratories for Sequence Based Typing of Microbial Pathogens (SEQNET, #07936)*; national organizations. [2018/XM1951/**F**]

♦ International Novialist Union (inactive)
♦ International Nuclear Chemistry Society (inactive)

♦ International Nuclear Energy Academy 14377

Sec 1414 Epping Forest Dr, Atlanta GA 30319, USA. T. +14043886588. Fax +14042540160.
URL: http://www.ineacademy.com/
History Founded 22 Jun 1993, as society to honour nuclear scientists and engineers. **Aims** Promote discussion of, and issue occasional authoritative papers on nuclear energy, especially topical issues. **Structure** General Meeting (annual), in Vienna (Austria); Executive Committee. **Languages** English. **Staff** 1.00 FTE, voluntary. **Finance** Members' dues. **Activities** Research/documentation. **Events** *Annual General Meeting* Vienna (Austria) 2007, *Annual General Meeting* Vienna (Austria) 2006, *Annual General Meeting* Vienna (Austria) 2005, *Annual General Meeting* Vienna (Austria) 2004, *Annual General Meeting* New Orleans, LA (USA) 2003.
Members Individuals in 28 countries and territories:
Argentina, Australia, Austria, Belgium, Brazil, Bulgaria, Canada, Chile, China, Egypt, France, Germany, India, Israel, Italy, Japan, Korea Rep, Mexico, Pakistan, Russia, South Africa, Spain, Sweden, Switzerland, Taiwan, UK, Ukraine, USA.
NGO Relations Cooperates with: *International Nuclear Societies Council (INSC, #14382)*. [2018/XD7006/v/**F**]

♦ International Nuclear Fuel Cycle Evaluation (inactive)
♦ International Nuclear Graphite Specialist Meeting (meeting series)

♦ International Nuclear Information System (INIS) 14378

Système international d'information nucléaire
Secretariat c/o IAEA, Wagramer Strasse 5, PO Box 100, 1400 Vienna, Austria. T. +431260022842. Fax +431260072842. E-mail: inis.feedback@iaea.org.
URL: http://www.iaea.org/inis/
History 1970, Vienna (Austria). Established by *International Atomic Energy Agency (IAEA, #12294)*. **Aims** Provide access to qualified nuclear information published worldwide; provide mechanisms to access other types of nuclear information. **Structure** Not an organization, but an international cooperative system operated by the IAEA on behalf of members. **Languages** Arabic, Chinese, English, French, Russian, Spanish. **Staff** 50.00 FTE, paid.
Activities Subject scope is developed to respond to information needs of the international community in areas of IAEA interests and activities. System currently comprises 3 million records, bibliographic descriptions of literature published by INIS members on all aspects of the peaceful use of nuclear science and technology and covers:
- Nuclear power, including nuclear engineering and instrumentation, fission reactors and nuclear fuel cycle;
- Nuclear safety;
- Material of nuclear interest;
- Environmental aspects of nuclear and non-nuclear energy sources;
- Safeguards and non-proliferation;
- Nuclear applications, including production of isotopes and radiation sources, industrial applications of isotopes and radiation sources, radioisotopes and radiation in earth sciences and radioisotopes and radiation in agriculture, biology and medicine;
- Radiation protection;
- Nuclear aspects of physics, including plasma physics and nuclear fusion, condensed matter, atomic and molecular physics, nuclear physics, elementary particle physics and classical and quantum mechanics;
- Nuclear aspects of chemistry, including radio chemistry, radiation chemistry, nuclear chemistry and nuclear analytical methods;
- Legal aspects.

Each participant country is individually responsible for: collecting, scanning, selecting and, where necessary, abstracting all literature published within its boundaries and coming within the scope of the System; preparing input on this literature consistent with the established set of rules. INIS Centres, directed by Liaison Officers, organize: collection of information; preparation of input; setting up and maintaining information services using INIS products; encouraging use of these products. INIS Secretariat at IAEA in Vienna (Austria): merges information prepared by national participants, controls quality and uniformity of data and makes output products of the system available in each country; provides training on database production and utilization to members.
Events *Consultative meeting of INIS liaison officers* Vienna (Austria) 2006, *Consultative meeting of liaison officers* Vienna (Austria) 2005, *Biennial Seminar* Vienna (Austria) 1989, *Biennial Seminar* Vienna (Austria) 1987. **Publications** *ETDE/INIS Joint Reference Series*; *INIS Reference Series*. Annual Report. Information Services: Database may also be accessed through STN International, ESA-IRS and Fachinformationszentrum (FIZ), Karlsruhe (Germany). Cooperative arrangement with Nuclear Energy Agency (NEA) allows for operation of a computer programme service for IAEA member states which are not members of OECD. **Information Services** *Database may also be accessed through STN International, ESA-IRS and Fachinformationszentrum (FIZ), Karlsruhe (Germany)*; *INIS Bibliographic Database* – online and CD-ROM; *INIS Non-Conventional Literature on CD-ROM*; *Internet Directory of Nuclear Resources* – online.
Members INIS Liaison Officers in 130 IAEA member states:
Afghanistan, Albania, Algeria, Argentina, Armenia, Australia, Austria, Azerbaijan, Bangladesh, Belarus, Belgium, Benin, Bolivia, Bosnia-Herzegovina, Botswana, Brazil, Bulgaria, Burkina Faso, Burundi, Canada, Central African Rep, Chad, Chile, China, Colombia, Congo DR, Costa Rica, Côte d'Ivoire, Croatia, Cuba, Cyprus, Czechia, Denmark, Ecuador, Egypt, El Salvador, Estonia, Ethiopia, Finland, France, Gabon, Georgia, Germany, Ghana, Greece, Guatemala, Haiti, Hungary, India, Indonesia, Iran Islamic Rep, Iraq, Ireland, Israel, Italy, Jamaica, Japan, Jordan, Kazakhstan, Kenya, Korea Rep, Kuwait, Kyrgyzstan, Latvia, Lebanon, Lesotho, Libya, Lithuania, Luxembourg, Madagascar, Malaysia, Mali, Mauritania, Mauritius, Mexico, Moldova, Mongolia, Morocco, Mozambique, Myanmar, Namibia, New Zealand, Nicaragua, Niger, Nigeria, North Macedonia, Norway, Oman, Pakistan, Panama, Paraguay, Peru, Philippines, Poland, Portugal, Qatar, Romania, Russia, Saudi Arabia, Senegal, Serbia, Seychelles, Sierra Leone, Singapore, Slovakia, Slovenia, South Africa, Spain, Sri Lanka, Sudan, Sweden, Switzerland, Syrian AR, Tajikistan, Tanzania UR, Thailand, Tunisia, Türkiye, Uganda, UK, Ukraine, United Arab Emirates, Uruguay, USA, Uzbekistan, Venezuela, Vietnam, Yemen, Zambia, Zimbabwe.
Organizations (11):
Arab Atomic Energy Agency (AAEA, #00901); *European Commission (EC, #06633)*; *European Organization for Nuclear Research (CERN, #08108)*; *FAO (#09260)*; *International Atomic Energy Agency (IAEA, #12294)*; *International Institute for Applied Systems Analysis (IIASA, #13861)*; *International Organization for Standardization (ISO, #14473)*; *Joint Institute for Nuclear Research (JINR, #16134)*; *Nuclear Energy Agency (NEA, #17615)*; *Synchrotron-light for Experimental Science and Applications in the Middle East (SESAME, #20078)*; *World Nuclear Association (WNA, #21674)*.
NGO Relations Member of: *International Council for Scientific and Technical Information (ICSTI, #13070)*. [2009.10.27/XF5816/y/**F***]

♦ International Nuclear Law Association (INLA) 14379

Association internationale du droit nucléaire (AIDN)
SG Square de Meeûs 29, 1000 Brussels, Belgium. T. +3225475841. Fax +3225030440.
URL: http://aidn-inla.be/

History 8 Dec 1970. Statutes amended: 6 Dec 1972, Brussels (Belgium); Feb 1973, when present name adopted; 5 Oct 1977, Brussels; 25 Oct 1979, Buenos Aires (Argentina); 24 Sep 1987, Antwerp (Belgium); 28 Oct 1999 Washington DC (USA); 5 Oct 2007, Brussels (Belgium); 5 Oct 2009, Toronto ON (Canada); 8 Oct 2012, Manchester (UK); 20 Oct 2014, Buenos Aires (Argentina); 7 Nov 2016, Delhi (India). Former names and other names: *International Association for Nuclear Law and Economics* – former (8 Dec 1970 to 1973). Registration: Start date: 12 Aug 1971, Belgium. **Aims** Promote and pursue, on an international level, studies and knowledge of legal issues related to peaceful utilization of nuclear energy, with a focus on protecting persons, property and the environment, information exchange between members, and scientific cooperation with other organizations having similar objectives. **Structure** General Assembly (every 2 years at Congress); Administrative Council; Secretary-General. **Languages** English, French. **Staff** Voluntary. **Finance** Sources: members' dues. **Activities** Events/meetings. **Events** *Biennial Congress* Washington, DC (USA) 2022, *Virtual Congress* 2021, *Biennial Congress* Washington, DC (USA) 2020, *Biennial Congress* Abu Dhabi (United Arab Emirates) 2018, *Biennial Congress* Delhi (India) 2016. **Publications** Conference proceedings.

Members Qualified legal experts in 48 countries and territories:
Argentina, Australia, Austria, Belgium, Brazil, Bulgaria, Canada, China, Croatia, Czechia, Finland, France, Germany, Ghana, Hungary, India, Indonesia, Ireland, Israel, Italy, Japan, Korea Rep, Lithuania, Luxembourg, Malawi, Mali, Mexico, Morocco, Netherlands, Niger, Nigeria, Norway, Poland, Portugal, Romania, Russia, Slovakia, Slovenia, South Africa, Spain, Sweden, Switzerland, Taiwan, Türkiye, UK, United Arab Emirates, Uruguay, USA.

IGO Relations Affiliated with (1): *International Atomic Energy Agency (IAEA, #12294).* [2020/XC4313/v/**C**]

♦ International Nuclear Non-proliferation and Security Academy (internationally oriented national body)

♦ International Nuclear Regulators Association (INRA) 14380

Address not obtained.

Activities Biannual meeting. **Events** *Meeting* Jeju (Korea Rep) 2009.

Members Senior nuclear regulatory staff in 8 countries:
Canada, France, Germany, Japan, Spain, Sweden, UK, USA. [2015/XD8209/**D**]

♦ International Nuclear Safety Advisory Group / see International Nuclear Safety Group (#14381)

♦ International Nuclear Safety Group (INSAG) 14381

Secretariat IAEA Dept of Nuclear Safety and Security, Wagramerstrasse 5, PO Box 100, 1400 Vienna, Austria. T. +43126000. Fax +43126007. E-mail: official.mail@iaea.org.
URL: http://www-ns.iaea.org/committees/insag.asp

History Founded 1985, as *International Nuclear Safety Advisory Group (INSAG).* Current title adopted in 2003, to expand charter to communicate beyond IAEA to the nuclear community and public. Currently in its 8th term. **Aims** Provide recommendations and opinions on current and emerging nuclear safety issues to the IAEA, the nuclear community and the public. **Structure** *International Atomic Energy Agency (IAEA, #12294)* serves as Secretariat for the group. Department of Nuclear Safety and Security serves as support organization and provides Scientific Secretary. **Languages** English. **Staff** Staff from IAEA Secretariat. **Finance** Expenses of members are preferably borne by their respective organizations. Some members are supported by IAEA. **Activities** Knowledge management/information dissemination; events/meetings. **Events** *Meeting* Vienna (Austria) 2017, *Meeting* Vienna (Austria) 2017. **Publications** *INSAG* – report series.

Members Individuals, independent of their respective country of origin, in 17 countries:
Argentina, Belgium, Canada, China, France, Germany, India, Japan, Korea Rep, Malaysia, Norway, Russia, Slovakia, South Africa, Türkiye, UK, USA.
One representative from:
Nuclear Energy Agency (NEA, #17615).

IGO Relations *Nuclear Energy Agency (NEA, #17615); OECD (#17693).* [2016/XJ3262/**E**]

♦ International Nuclear Societies Council (INSC) 14382

Contact address not obtained.
URL: http://insc.ans.org/

History 11 Nov 1990, by the *International Nuclear Societies Group (INSG).* **Aims** Act as a global forum for nuclear societies and as a global NGO in nuclear matters of international nature; represent the views and positions of professionals and workers; value the work and achievements of the nuclear community; increase the operational efficiency of nuclear societies by establishing means for cooperation and complementation in the execution of their programmes. **Structure** Council with 6 seats per geographical region. Geographical regions (5): Asia-Pacific; Europe; Latin America; North America; At Large (representing the other regions of the world). Officers: Chairman; 1st Vice-Chairman; 2nd Vice-Chairman; Secretary/Treasurer. **Languages** English. **Staff** None; all voluntary. **Finance** None. **Events** *Half-Yearly Meeting* Anaheim, CA (USA) 2014, *Half-Yearly Meeting* Busan (Korea Rep) 2014, *Half-Yearly Meeting* Buenos Aires (Argentina) 2013, *Half-Yearly Meeting* Washington, DC (USA) 2013, *Half-Yearly Meeting* San Diego, CA (USA) 2012.

Members National societies in 15 countries and territories:
Argentina, Australia, Brazil, Canada, China, Egypt, India, Israel, Japan, Korea Rep, Mexico, Pakistan, Taiwan, Thailand, USA.
Also members in Latin-America. Membership countries not specified.
Regional Society (1), listed in this Yearbook:
European Nuclear Society (ENS, #08059).

Consultative Status Consultative status granted from: *UNEP (#20299).* **IGO Relations** Affiliated with: *International Atomic Energy Agency (IAEA, #12294).* **NGO Relations** Cooperation agreement with: *International Nuclear Energy Academy (#14377).* [2019/XE2395/**F**]

♦ International Nuclear Target Development Society (INTDS) 14383

Corresponding Sec-Treas c/o NIST, 100 Bureau Dr, Stop 8463, Gaithersburg MD 20899-8463, USA.
URL: http://www.intds.org/

History Founded 1976, Menlo Park CA (USA). **Aims** Encourage sharing of techniques to provide research-quality targets and reference samples, mostly for basic research in *physics, chemistry* and related sciences; publish technique developments in easily accessed scientific venues; mentor people new to target and sample preparation. **Structure** Conference (every 2 years); Board of Directors. **Languages** English. **Staff** None. **Finance** Members' dues. **Events** *World Conference* Stellenbosch (South Africa) 2016, *World Conference / Biennial World Conference* Tokyo (Japan) 2014, *World Conference / Biennial World Conference* Mainz (Germany) 2012, *Biennial World Conference* Vancouver, BC (Canada) 2010, *Biennial world conference* Vancouver, BC (Canada) 2010. **Publications** *INTDS Newsletter* (irregular). Conference proceedings, published in the journals. **Information Services** *INTDS Publication Index* – INTDS mail list enables members to post questions and correspond with other list subscribers.

Members Individuals in 19 countries:
Algeria, Belgium, Canada, China, Finland, France, Germany, Hungary, India, Ireland, Israel, Italy, Japan, Netherlands, Poland, Russia, South Africa, Switzerland, USA. [2018.06.26/XF5549/v/**F**]

♦ International Nuclear Track Society (INTS) 14384

Sec Lab Microanalyses Nucléaires, EA-473 – LRC CEA M07 – UFR St, La Bouloie, 16 route de Gray, 25030 Besançon CEDEX, France. T. +33381666560. Fax +33381666522.
URL: http://www.fisica.unam.mx/ints/25thICNTS-2011/

History 1983, Acapulco (Mexico). Constitution adopted in 1985, Rome (Italy). **Aims** Promote development of scientific knowledge of tracks of nuclear particles in solid materials and application of this knowledge for human benefit. **Structure** Regular Meeting (at International Conference). Executive Committee, consisting of Officers – President, Executive Vice-President, Secretary and Treasurer – and up to 6 additional members. Regional Representatives. **Languages** English. **Staff** 2.00 FTE, voluntary. **Finance** Sources: members' dues. Annual budget: 1,300 USD. **Activities** Carries out international standardization of neutron and charged particle measurements using solid state nuclear track detectors. Holds scientific meetings. **Events** *International Conference on Nuclear Tracks in Solids* Kobe (Japan) 2014, *International conference on nuclear tracks in solids* Puebla (Mexico) 2011, *International conference on nuclear tracks in solids* Bologna (Italy) 2008, *International conference on nuclear tracks in solids* Beijing (China) 2006, *International conference on nuclear tracks in solids* Barcelona (Spain) 2004. **Publications** *INTS Newsletter* (3 a year). Conference proceedings.

Members Individuals and groups in 56 countries and territories:
Algeria, Argentina, Australia, Austria, Belarus, Belgium, Bolivia, Bosnia-Herzegovina, Brazil, Bulgaria, Canada, China, Croatia, Czechia, Egypt, France, Georgia, Germany, Greece, Hong Kong, Hungary, India, Iran Islamic Rep, Ireland, Israel, Italy, Japan, Jordan, Korea Rep, Kuwait, Luxembourg, Malaysia, Mexico, Morocco, Pakistan, Poland, Romania, Russia, Saudi Arabia, Singapore, Slovenia, Spain, Sweden, Switzerland, Syrian AR, Taiwan, Tajikistan, Thailand, Türkiye, UK, Ukraine, USA, Uzbekistan, Venezuela, Vietnam, Yemen.

NGO Relations Member of: *International Confederation of Associations for Pluralism in Economics (ICAPE, #12849).* [2012.07.30/XD2135/**C**]

♦ International Numismatic Commission / see International Numismatic Council (#14385)

♦ International Numismatic Council (INC) 14385

Conseil international de numismatique (CIN) – Consejo Internacional de Numismatica – Consiglio Internazionale di Numismatica – Internationaler Numismatischer Rat
Sec Royal Library of Belgium, Mont-des-Arts, Bd de l'Empereur 4, 1000 Brussels, Belgium.
Pres Kunsthistorisches Museum Wien, Burgring 5, 1010 Vienna, Austria.
URL: http://www.inc-cin.org/

History 1927, Vienna (Austria). Re-constituted, 1934, Paris (France); reorganized, 1953, Paris. Current constitution adopted 14 Sep 2003, Madrid (Spain). Former names and other names: *International Numismatic Commission (INC)* – former; *Commission internationale de numismatique (CIN)* – former; *Comisión Internacional de Numismatica* – former; *Commissione Internazionale di Numismatica* – former; *Internationale Numismatische Kommission* – former. **Aims** Promote numismatics and related disciplines by facilitating cooperation among individuals and institutions in the field. **Structure** General Meeting (every 6 years, at Congress); Bureau; Seat in Winterthur (Switzerland). **Languages** English, French, German, Italian, Spanish. **Staff** None. **Finance** Sources: gifts, legacies; grants; members' dues. **Activities** Events/meetings; financial and/or material support; knowledge management/information dissemination. **Events** *Congress* Melbourne, VIC (Australia) 2027, *Congress* Warsaw (Poland) 2021, *Congress / International Numismatic Congress* Taormina (Italy) 2015, *Congress / International Numismatic Congress* Glasgow (UK) 2009, *Congress / International Numismatic Congress* Madrid (Spain) 2003. **Publications** *Compte rendu* (annual) in English, French, German, Italian, Spanish. Congress proceedings.

Members Public numismatic collections; universities; non-commercial organizations, institutions and societies (local, national or international); national mints; individuals (elected honorary members). Numismatic institutions in 35 countries and territories:
Austria, Belgium, Brazil, Canada, China, Croatia, Cyprus, Czechia, Denmark, Estonia, Finland, France, Germany, Greece, Holy See, Hungary, Israel, Italy, Japan, Latvia, Lithuania, Luxembourg, Netherlands, Norway, Peru, Poland, Romania, Russia, Slovenia, Spain, Sweden, Switzerland, Taiwan, UK, USA.
Included in the above, 6 organizations listed in this Yearbook:
Association of Baltic Numismatists (ABN, #02394); Centro Internazionale di Studi Numismatici, Napoli (no recent information); Federation of European Numismatic Trade Associations (FENAP, #09523); International Association of Professional Numismatists (IAPN, #12104); Oriental Numismatic Society (ONS, #17893); Sociedad Iberoamericana de Estudios Numismaticos (SIAEN, #19367).
Honorary in 18 countries:
Cyprus, Denmark, France, Germany, Greece, Hungary, India, Italy, Luxembourg, Norway, Poland, Romania, Russia, Spain, Sweden, Switzerland, UK, USA. [2020.03.03/XD2286/y/**C**]

♦ International Nuremberg Principles Academy (internationally oriented national body)
♦ International Nurse Education Conference (meeting series)
♦ International Nurses Society on Addictions (internationally oriented national body)
♦ International Nursing Association for Clinical Simulation and Learning (internationally oriented national body)

♦ International Nursing Group for Immunodeficiencies (INGID) 14386

Pres c/o Dept of Allergy-Immunology, Children's Hospital JFMC, 601 5th St South, St Petersburg FL 33701, USA. E-mail: president@ingid.org – secretary@ingid.org.
URL: http://www.ingid.org/

Finance Members' dues. **Events** *Biennial Meeting* Prague (Czech Rep) 2014, *Biennial Meeting* Florence (Italy) 2012, *Biennial Meeting* Istanbul (Turkey) 2010, *Meeting* 's Hertogenbosch (Netherlands) 2008, *Meeting* Budapest (Hungary) 2006. **Publications** *INGID Journal.* **NGO Relations** Joint meetings with: *European Society for Immunodeficiencies (ESID, #08630); International Patient Organization for Primary Immunodeficiencies (IPOPI, #14533).* [2016/XJ4440/**D**]

♦ International Nursing Services Association / see Global Health Action
♦ International Nut Council / see International Nut and Dried Fruit Council Foundation (#14387)
♦ International Nut and Dried Fruit Council / see International Nut and Dried Fruit Council Foundation (#14387)

♦ International Nut and Dried Fruit Council Foundation (INC) 14387

Main Office Carrer de la Fruita Seca 4, Poligon Tecnoparc, 43204 Reus, Tarragona, Spain. T. +34977331416. E-mail: inc@nutfruit.org.
URL: http://www.nutfruit.org/

History Jun 1983, Reus (Spain). Statutes approved 17 Aug 1983. Former names and other names: *International Tree Nut Council (INC)* – former (Jun 1983); *Conseil international de fruits secs (CIFS)* – former (Jun 1983); *Consejo Internacional de los Frutos Secos* – former (Jun 1983); *Internationale Mandel- und Nussvereinigung* – former (Jun 1983); *Consiglio Internazionale della Frutta Secca* – former (Jun 1983); *Uluslararasi Sert Meyveler Komitesi* – former (Jun 1983); *International Nut and Dried Fruit Foundation* – former; *International Nut Council* – former; *International Nut and Dried Fruit Council* – former. Registration: EU Transparency Register, No/ID: 87904443479-87. **Aims** Represent the interests of the global nut and dried fruit industry. **Structure** General Assembly (annual); Executive Committee; Board of Trustees; Senators; Ambassadors; Observers. **Languages** English, Spanish. **Staff** 11.00 FTE, paid. **Finance** Members' dues. Donations. **Activities** Events/meetings; politics/policy/regulatory; standards/guidelines; projects/programmes; research/documentation; training/education; awareness raising. **Events** *World Nut and Dried Fruit Congress* Dubai (United Arab Emirates) 2022, *World Nut and Dried Fruit Congress* Dubai (United Arab Emirates) 2021, *World Nut and Dried Fruit Congress* Boca Raton, FL (USA) 2019, *World Nut and Dried Fruit Congress* San Diego, CA (USA) 2016, *World Nut and Dried Fruit Congress* Antalya (Turkey) 2015. **Publications** *Nutfruit* (3 a year) – magazine. *Go Nuts Go Health* – in 12 languages; *Nut and Dried Fuit Recipes*; *Nutrition in Every Handful.* Information Services: Online database.

Members Founder; Associate; Numerary; of Honour. Members (481) in 49 countries and territories:
Algeria, Argentina, Australia, Austria, Belgium, Bolivia, Brazil, Canada, Chile, China, Colombia, Costa Rica, Czechia, Denmark, Egypt, Finland, France, Georgia, Germany, Ghana, Greece, Hong Kong, India, Iraq, Ireland, Israel, Italy, Japan, Kenya, Lebanon, Luxembourg, Morocco, Netherlands, New Zealand, Norway, Portugal, Russia, Saudi Arabia, Singapore, South Africa, Spain, Sri Lanka, Sweden, Switzerland, Tunisia, Türkiye, UK, United Arab Emirates, USA.

IGO Relations Recognized by: *United Nations Economic Commission for Europe (UNECE, #20555).* Participates as observer in the activities of: *Codex Alimentarius Commission (CAC, #04081).* [2022/XD7310/f/**F**]

♦ International Nut and Dried Fruit Foundation / see International Nut and Dried Fruit Council Foundation (#14387)
♦ International Nutrition Foundation / see Nevin Scrimshaw International Nutrition Foundation
♦ International Nutrition Foundation for Developing Countries / see Nevin Scrimshaw International Nutrition Foundation

♦ International Oak Society (IOS) 14388

Vice President Starhill Forest Arboretum of Illinois College, 12000 Boy Scout Trail, Petersburg IL 62675, USA. E-mail: postmaster@internationaloaksociety.org – roderickcameron66@gmail.com.
URL: http://www.internationaloaksociety.org/

History 1985. Current bylaws adopted, 2010. Registration: USA, State of Illinois. **Aims** Further study, sustainable management, preservation, appreciation and dissemination of knowledge about oak *trees* and their ecosystems. **Structure** Board of Directors. **Languages** English. **Staff** Voluntary. **Finance** Sources: donations; members' dues. **Activities** Events/meetings. **Events** *Triennial Conference* Las Cruces, NM (USA) 2022, *Triennial Conference* Taiwan 2021, *Triennial Conference* Davis, CA (USA) 2018, *Triennial Conference* Lisle, IL (USA) 2015, *Triennial Conference* Bordeaux (France) 2012. **Publications** *The Cupule* (4 a year) – e-bulletin; *Oak News and Notes* (2 a year); *International Oaks* (annual). Conference proceedings.

Members Individuals (about 500) in 35 countries and territories:
Argentina, Australia, Austria, Belgium, Brazil, Canada, China, Costa Rica, Czechia, Denmark, Estonia, Finland, France, Germany, Ireland, Israel, Italy, Japan, Lebanon, Luxembourg, Mexico, Netherlands, New Zealand, Poland, Portugal, Romania, Spain, Sweden, Switzerland, Taiwan, Türkiye, UK, Uruguay, USA, Vietnam. [2021.08.31/XD6886/v/**D**]

- ♦ International Oat Conference (meeting series)
- ♦ International Observatory of Organization and Globalization (internationally oriented national body)
- ♦ International Observatory of Participatory Democracy (#17640)
- ♦ International Observatory on Statelessness (internationally oriented national body)
- ♦ International Observatory of Violence in School / see International Observatory of Violence in the School Environment (#14389)

♦ International Observatory of Violence in the School Environment (IOVS) 14389

Observatoire International de la Violence a l'Ecole (OIVE)

Contact Univ Nice Sophia Antipolis, Ecole Supérieure du Professorat, 89 Ave George V, 06046 Nice CEDEX 1, France.

History Sep 1998, Bordeaux (France), as *Observatoire Européen de la Violence en Milieu Scolaire*. Subsequently referred to as *European Observatory of Violence in Schools (EOVS) – Observatoire européen de la violence scolaire (OEVS) – Observatorio Europeo de la Violencia Escolar*. Current title adopted to reflect worldwide nature of the organization. Registered in accordance with French law. **Aims** Collect, promote and disseminate around the world inter-disciplinary studies of the phenomenon of violence in the school environment; conduct scientific evaluation of the studies and analyses published on the subject; conduct scientific evaluation of public programmes and policies to combat this phenomenon; make an ongoing assessment of violence in the school environment around the world; draw up and disseminate around the world concrete proposals for action in the field based on the results of scientific studies; assist in the training of teachers and professionals; provide training in research on violence in the school environment and support young researchers in the field. **Structure** General Meeting. Board of Directors of 25 members, including Executive Committee, comprising President, Vice-President, Secretary General, Deputy Secretary General, Treasurer and Deputy Treasurer. **Activities** Conducts research. **Events** *World Conference* Québec, QC (Canada) 2018, *Conference* Lima (Peru) 2015, *International conference on violence in schools, public policies and social inclusion of young people / Conference* Ottawa, ON (Canada) 2009, *International conference on violence in schools, public policies and social inclusion of young people / Conference* London (UK) 2007, *Conference* Bordeaux (France) 2006. **Publications** *International Journal on Violence and Schools*.

Members Partners in 10 countries:
Australia, Brazil, Canada, France, Germany, Italy, Japan, Mexico, Spain, UK. [2014/XF7081/**F**]

♦ International Occultation Timing Association (IOTA) 14390

Exec Sec PO Box 446 78620, Dripping Springs TX 78620, USA.
Sec/Treas PO Box 20313, Fountain Hills AZ 85268, USA. E-mail: business@occultations.org.
URL: http://www.occultations.org/

History 26 Jul 1975, Highland Park, IL (USA). As of Apr 2009, took over activities of *International Lunar Occultation Centre (ILOC, inactive)*. **Aims** Predict, observe and devise techniques to analyse *lunar* and *asteroid* occultations; carry out long range studies into the solar diameter from observation of *solar eclipses*. **Structure** Annual Meeting, in close proximity to spectacular occultation events. *International Occultation Timing Association / European Section (IOTA/ES)* functions as a separate organization but shares publication distribution. **Languages** English. **Staff** Voluntary. **Finance** Sources: members' dues. **Activities** Events/meetings; research/documentation. **Events** *Annual Meeting* 2021, *Annual Meeting* Greenbelt, MD (USA) 2020, *European Symposium* Barcelona (Spain) 2013, *Meeting* Frederick, MD (USA) 2001, *Meeting* Kansas City, KS (USA) 2000. **Publications** *Journal of Occultation Astronomy (JOA)* (4 a year). Manual; handbook.

Members Members worldwide, including 3 countries listed below and South/Central America and Europe:
Australia, Japan, USA. [2022.05.10/XF0247/v/**F**]

- ♦ International Occultation Timing Association / European Section (unconfirmed)

♦ International Occupational Hygiene Association (IOHA) 14391

Secretariat 5/6 Melbourne Business Court, Millennium Way, Pride Park, Derby, DE24 8LZ, UK. T. +441332298101. Fax +441332298099. E-mail: admin@ioha.net.
URL: http://www.ioha.net/

History 1987, Montréal (Canada), during the American Industrial Hygiene Conference. Registered in accordance with UK law. **Structure** Executive Committee, comprising President, Immediate Past President, President-Elect and Secretary/Treasurer. Secretariat. **Languages** English. **Events** *Vision Zero Summit* Tokyo (Japan) 2022, *Conference* Daegu (Korea Rep) 2021, *Conference* Daegu (Korea Rep) 2020, *Conference* Washington, DC (USA) 2018, *Conference* London (UK) 2015. **Publications** Newletter; conference abstracts.

Members Associations in 25 countries:
Australia, Belgium, Brazil, Canada, Colombia, Finland, France, Germany, Hong Kong, Ireland, Italy, Japan, Korea Rep, Malaysia, Mexico, Netherlands, New Zealand, Norway, Poland, South Africa, Sweden, Switzerland, Taiwan, UK, USA.

Consultative Status Consultative status granted from: *WHO (#20950)* (Official Relations); *ILO (#11123)* (Special List). **IGO Relations** Member of: *European Agency for Safety and Health at Work (EU-OSHA, #05843)*. [2018/XD3318/**D**]

- ♦ International Occupational Safety and Health Hazard Alert System (inactive)
- ♦ International Occupational Safety and Health Knowledge Network (no recent information)

♦ International Ocean Colour Coordinating Group (IOCCG) 14392

Address not obtained.
URL: http://www.ioccg.org/

History 1996, under the auspices of *Intergovernmental Oceanographic Commission (IOC, #11496)*. Affiliated programme of *Scientific Committee on Oceanic Research (SCOR, #19149)*. **Aims** Promote international cooperation and coordination in the acquisition, calibration, validation, distribution and utilization of ocean-colour *data*. **Structure** Committee, headed by Chair. **Languages** English. **Staff** 1.00 FTE, paid. **Finance** Supported by: national space agencies of USA, Canada, France, Korea Rep and India; *European Space Agency (ESA, #08798)*; *Joint Research Centre (JRC, #16147)*. **Activities** Organizes training courses. Commissions scientific working groups to investigate relevant topics and write reports. **Events** *Ocean Colour Science Meeting* Busan (Korea Rep) 2019, *Meeting* Hanoi (Vietnam) 2019, *Meeting* Rome (Italy) 2018, *Ocean Colour Science Meeting* Lisbon (Portugal) 2017, *Meeting* Perth, WA (Australia) 2017. **Publications** Reports (7 to date).

Members Organizations in 7 countries:
Canada, France, India, Italy, Japan, Korea Rep, USA.
Individuals in 13 countries (3 year rotating membership):
Australia, Brazil, Canada, China, France, Germany, India, Italy, Japan, Korea Rep, South Africa, UK, USA.

NGO Relations Associate member of: *Committee on Earth Observation Satellites (CEOS, #04249)*. [2017/XE4158/v/**E**]

♦ International Ocean Discovery Program (IODP) 14393

Exec Dir Scripps Inst of Oceanography, Univ of California San Diego, 9500 Gilman Drive, La Jolla CA 92093, USA. T. +18588224260.
Chair Univ of Edinburgh, Old College, South Bridge, Edinburgh, EH8 9YL, UK.
URL: http://www.iodp.org/

History Oct 2013. *'Deep Sea Drilling Project (DSDP)'*, ran 1966-1983. Succeeded by *International Ocean Drilling Program (ODP, inactive)*, 1983-2003. *Integrated Ocean Drilling Program (IODP)* built upon ODP and ran 2003-2013. Current phase started 2013. **Aims** Explore Earth's history and dynamics using ocean-going research platforms to recover data recorded in seafloor *sediments* and rocks; monitor subseafloor environments in the broad areas of *climate* and ocean change, biosphere frontiers, deep earth connections and natural hazards. **Structure** Facility Boards; Advisory Panels; Science Operators; IODP Forum; Science Support Office; Program Member Offices. **Languages** English. **Staff** 200.00 FTE, paid; 40.00 FTE, voluntary. **Finance** Funding partners include: agencies/ministries in USA, Japan, China, Korea Rep, Australia/New Zealand, India and Brazil; *European Consortium for Ocean Research Drilling (ECORD, #06758)*. **Activities** Research and development; publishing activities; projects/programmes; training/education. **Events** *Colloquium* Trondheim (Norway) 2018, *Forum* Busan (Korea Rep) 2014, *Meeting* Amsterdam (Netherlands) 2011, *Board of Governors meeting* Kyoto (Japan) 2010, *Meeting* Kyoto (Japan) 2010. **Publications** *Scientific Drilling* (2 a year). Prospectus; reports; proceedings. **Information Services** *Scientific Ocean Drilling Bibliographic Database*.

Members Participants in 22 countries:
Australia, Austria, Brazil, Canada, China, Denmark, Finland, France, Germany, India, Ireland, Italy, Japan, Korea Rep, Netherlands, New Zealand, Norway, Portugal, Spain, Sweden, Switzerland, UK, USA.

NGO Relations Participants include: *European Consortium for Ocean Research Drilling (ECORD, #06758)*. Member of: *Partnership for Observation of the Global Oceans (POGO, #18239)*. [2018.09.07/XF6727/**F**]

♦ International Ocean Institute (IOI) 14394

Institut international de l'océan – Instituto Oceanico Internacional

Managing Director International Ocean Institute Headquarters, University of Malta, P. O. Box 3, Tal-Qroqq, Msida, MSD 2080, Malta. T. +35621346528 – +35621346529. E-mail: ioihq@ioihq.org.mt.
Street address International Ocean Institute Headquarters, University of Malta, Blk4,, Tal-Qroqq, Msida, MSD 2080, Malta.
URL: https://www.ioinst.org/

History 10 Jun 1972, Valletta (Malta). Founded by a committee set up for the purpose, with the assistance of *UNDP (#20292)*. Foundation followed annual conferences organized in Malta by 'Center for the Study of Democratic Institutes', Santa Barbara CA (USA). Headquarters agreement with Government of Malta. Former names and other names: *Pacem in Maribus (PIM)* – former; *Peace in the Oceans* – former. Registration: No/ID: KVK 41132402, Netherlands. **Aims** Ensure sustainability of the oceans as "a source of life"; uphold and expand the principle of the common heritage of mankind as enshrined in the United Nations Convention on the Law of the Sea (UNCLOS); train future ocean leaders in ocean governance. **Structure** Governing Board (meeting annually); Network of Centres and Focal Points (31) in 30 countries, administered through Headquarters based in Malta; Secretariat, hosted by Headquarters, Malta. **Languages** English. **Staff** 4.00 FTE, paid; 200.00 FTE, voluntary. **Finance** Sources: grants; private foundations; subscriptions. Other sources: support from UN agencies and governments, on a project basis. Annual budget: 700,000 USD. **Activities** Capacity building; events/meetings; guidance/assistance/consulting; knowledge management/information dissemination; research and development; training/education. Active in all member countries. **Events** *Triennial Pacem in Maribus Conference / Pacem in Maribus Conference* Bangkok (Thailand) 2013, *Coastal Cities Summit* St Petersburg, FL (USA) 2012, *Triennial pacem in maribus conference / Pacem in Maribus Conference* Beijing (China) 2010, *Joint conference* Busan (Korea Rep) 2010, *Joint conference* Busan (Korea Rep) 2010. **Publications** *Annual Report* (annual); *IOInforma*; *Ocean Yearbook. The World Ocean Review (WOR)*. Convocation proceedings. **Information Services** *Databank of IOI courses alumni.*; *Information system on marine affair*.

Members IOI Training Centres in 5 countries:
Canada, China, Malta, South Africa, Thailand.
IOI Centres in 6 countries:
Costa Rica, Cuba, Egypt, Germany, Iran Islamic Rep, Nigeria.
20 IOI Focal Points:
Astrakhan, Chile, China, Cyprus, Egypt, India, Indonesia, Japan, Kazakhstan, Kenya, Lebanon, Malaysia, Pakistan, Philippines, Russia, Singapore, Slovenia, Türkiye, Ukraine, USA.
Included in the above, 1 organization listed in this Yearbook:
International Federation for Sustainable Development and Fight to Poverty in the Mediterranean-Black Sea (FISPMED, #13562).

Consultative Status Consultative status granted from: *ECOSOC (#05331)* (Special); *UNESCO (#20322)* (Consultative Status); *UNCTAD (#20285)* (Special Category); *International Maritime Organization (IMO, #14102)*. **IGO Relations** Cooperates with (5): *Intergovernmental Oceanographic Commission (IOC, #11496)*; *UNCTAD (#20285)*; *UNEP (#20299)*; *United Nations Institute for Training and Research (UNITAR, #20576)*; *United Nations Office for Disaster Risk Reduction (UNDRR, #20595)*. Cooperates with: UNDP Special Unit for South-south Cooperation (UNDP SUSSC); United Nations Office of Legal Affairs / Division for Ocean Affairs and the Law of the Sea (UN DOALOS). Associated with Department of Global Communications of the United Nations. **NGO Relations** Member of (4): *European Centre for Information on Marine Science and Technology (EurOcean)*; *High Seas Alliance (HSA, #10918)*; *International Federation for Sustainable Development and Fight to Poverty in the Mediterranean-Black Sea (FISPMED, #13562)*; *Pacific Islands GOOS (PI-GOOS, #17971)*. Cooperates with (1): *International Council for Adult Education (ICAE, #12983)*. [2023.02.14/XC3987/j/**E**]

- ♦ International Ocean Institute – Pacific Islands (see: #14394)

♦ International Ocean Noise Coalition (IONC) 14395

Contact c/o OceanCare, Oberdorfstrasse 16, PO Box 372, 8820 Wädenswil ZH, Switzerland. T. +41447806688. E-mail: slueber@oceancare.org.
URL: http://www.oceannoisecoalition.org/

History 2002, as a project of *OceanCare*, *Ocean Mammal Institute (OMI)* and Animal Welfare Institute. **Aims** Promote awareness of the issue of ocean noise pollution in various international fora with the aim of helping states work to address its negative impacts through regulation of noise intensive activities, mitigation measures, Environmental Impact Assessment and the application of the precautionary principle. **Structure** Representatives from 4 areas: Europe; Latin America; North America; Pacific Region. **Languages** English, French, German, Spanish. **Staff** 5.00 FTE, paid. **Finance** Financed by: Animal Welfare Institute (AWI); *OceanCare*; *Ocean Mammal Institute (OMI)*. **Activities** Events/meetings; networking/liaising; knowledge management/information dissemination; advocacy/lobbying/activism. **Publications** *Drowning in Sound* – brochure. Scientific studies; legal analysis.

Members Partners (over 150) worldwide, including 14 organizations listed in this Yearbook:
Animals Asia Foundation (AAF, #00842); *Cetacean Society International (CSI)*; *Eurogroup for Animals (#05690)*; *European Cetacean Bycatch Campaign*; *Greenpeace International (#10727)*; *Humane Society International (HSI, #10966)*; *International Fund for Animal Welfare (IFAW, #13693)*; *International Wildlife Coalition (IWC, inactive)*; *OceanCare*; *Ocean Defense International (no recent information)*; *Oceanomare-Delphis*; *Pacific Whale Foundation*; *Save Our Seas (SOS)*; *Stop LFAS Worldwide*.

IGO Relations Cooperates with: *Agreement on the Conservation of Cetaceans of the Black Sea, Mediterranean Sea and contiguous Atlantic Area (ACCOBAMS, 1996)*; *Agreement on the Conservation of Small Cetaceans of the Baltic, North East Atlantic, Irish and North Seas (ASCOBANS, 1992)*; *Convention on Biological Diversity (Biodiversity convention, 1992)*; *Convention on International Trade in Endangered Species of Wild Fauna and Flora (CITES, 1973)*; *European Union (EU, #08967)*; *International Maritime Organization (IMO, #14102)*; *International Whaling Commission (IWC, #15879)*; *Secretariat of the Convention on the Conservation of Migratory Species of Wild Animals (UNEP/CMS, #19198)*. [2015.06.01/XM3142/y/**F**]

♦ International Oceanographic Data and Information Exchange (IODE) 14396

Echange international des données et de l'information océanographique – Sistema de Intercambio Internacional de Datos y Información Oceanograficos

Head Project Office InnovOcean Campus, Jacobsenstraat 1, 8400 Ostend, Belgium. T. +33145682411. E-mail: info@iode.org.
URL: http://www.iode.org/

History 1961. Established as a Working Group on Oceanographic Data Exchange, within the framework of *Intergovernmental Oceanographic Commission (IOC, #11496)*. Became a Working Committee, 1973. **Aims** Enhance *marine* research, exploitation and development by facilitating exchange of oceanographic data and information among participating member states and by meeting needs of data and information product users; ensure active and full participation of developing countries, especially through establishing, maintaining and strengthening cooperation with ocean research and monitoring programmes. **Structure** Committee (meets every 2-3 years), including 2 Co-Chairs, directors of IODE data centres, directors of WDCs-Oceanography and WDCs-Marine Geology and Geophysics. Officers: 2 Co-Chairs; Chair Group of Experts on Biological and Chemical Data Management and Exchange Practices (GEBICH); Chair Group of Experts on Marine Information Management (GEMIM). Other Expert Group: Joint JCOMM/IODE Expert Team on Data Management Practices (ETDMP). **Languages** English, French, Russian, Spanish. **Staff** 8.00 FTE, paid. **Finance** Supported by: *UNESCO (#20322)*. Annual budget: 1,000,000 EUR. **Activities** Awards/prizes/competitions; events/meetings; monitoring/evaluation; research/documentation; training/education. **Events** *International Ocean Data Conference* Sopot (Poland) 2022, *Scientific conference* Liège (Belgium) 2011, *Session* Liège (Belgium) 2011, *COASTGIS : international symposium on GIS and computer cartography for coastal zone management* Ostend (Belgium) 2011, *Session* Tianjin (China) 2009. **Publications** Session reports; IOC Circular Letters; Session working documents; manuals and guides; books; information documents; brochures; training course reports; workshops reports; Groups of Experts reports.

Members 80 Oceanographic Data Centres (NODCs) Designated National Agencies; National Oceanographic Data Centres; Responsible National Oceanographic Data Centres; World Data Centres – Oceanography. NODCs (80) in 75 countries:
Angola, Argentina, Australia, Austria, Barbados, Belgium, Benin, Brazil, Bulgaria, Cameroon, Canada, Chile, China, Colombia, Comoros, Congo DR, Côte d'Ivoire, Croatia, Cuba, Cyprus, Denmark, Ecuador, Egypt, El Salvador, Eritrea, Estonia, Finland, France, Georgia, Germany, Ghana, Greece, Guinea, Iceland, India, Indonesia, Iran Islamic Rep, Iraq, Israel, Italy, Japan, Kazakhstan, Kenya, Korea Rep, Madagascar, Malaysia, Mauritania, Mauritius, Mexico, Morocco, Mozambique, Netherlands, New Zealand, Norway, Oman, Panama, Peru, Poland, Romania, Russia, Senegal, Slovenia, South Africa, Spain, Sri Lanka, Sweden, Tanzania UR, Thailand, Togo, Tunisia, Türkiye, UK, Ukraine, USA, Vietnam.
NGO Relations Member of (1): *ISC World Data System (ISC-WDS, #16024)* (Network member). Formal contact with: *European Association of Aquatic Sciences Libraries and Information Centres (EURASLIC, #05939); International Association of Aquatic and Marine Science Libraries and Information Centers (IAMSLIC, #11707).* [2022.10.11/XE6957/**F***]

♦ International Ocular Inflammation Society (IOIS) 14397

Main Office Rue de l'Industry 24, 1040 Brussels, Belgium. E-mail: office@iois.info.
URL: http://www.iois.info/

History 1992, Jerusalem (Israel). Founded at 2nd *International Symposium on Ocular Immunology and Inflammation*, on the initiative of Jorge L Alío y Sanz. Registration: No/ID: 0677.418.405, Start date: 5 Apr 2017, Belgium. **Aims** Promote the study of ocular inflammatory diseases. **Structure** Executive International Council; Executive Board; Committees (2). **Languages** English. **Finance** Members' dues. Other sources: endowments; government grants; commercial contributions. **Activities** Events/meetings; research and development; knowledge management/information dissemination; standards/guidelines. **Events** *Congress* Berlin (Germany) 2023, *Congress* 2021, *Congress* Kaohsiung (Taiwan) 2019, *Congress* Lausanne (Switzerland) 2017, *Congress* San Francisco, CA (USA) 2015. **Publications** *IOIS Newsletter* (4 a year). *Blepharitis and Conjunctivitis: Guidelines for Diagnosis and Treatment* (2006); *Ocular Surface Inflammation Guideliness* (2003) – guidelines; *Cornea and Sclera* (2002) – guidelines; *Anterior Segment Intraocular Inflammation* (2000) – guidelines; *Posterior Segment Intraocular Inflammation* (1998) – guideliness; *Conjunctivitis* (1996) – guidelines; *Uveitis Guidelines Clinical Images* – CD-ROM.
Members Individuals in 40 countries:
Argentina, Australia, Austria, Belgium, Brazil, Bulgaria, Canada, Chile, Colombia, Croatia, Cyprus, Czechia, Denmark, Dominican Rep, Egypt, France, Germany, Greece, Hungary, India, Ireland, Israel, Italy, Japan, Mexico, Netherlands, Norway, Peru, Philippines, Poland, Portugal, Saudi Arabia, South Africa, Spain, Sweden, Switzerland, Türkiye, UK, USA, Venezuela.
[2022/XD7448/v/**D**]

- ♦ International Oculoplastic Society (no recent information)
- ♦ International Odonata Research Institute (internationally oriented national body)
- ♦ International Odonatological Foundation (#19445)
- ♦ International Office of Allotment Gardens Leagues / see Fédération Internationale des Jardins Familiaux (#09641)
- ♦ International Office of Allotment and Leisure Garden Societies / see Fédération Internationale des Jardins Familiaux (#09641)
- ♦ International Office for Audiophonology (#03362)

♦ International Office of Cadastre and Land Records 14398

Office international du cadastre et du régime foncier (OICRF) – Internationales Amt für Kataster und Grundbuchwesen

Dir Hofstraat 110, 7311 KZ Apeldoorn, Netherlands. T. +31881833110. Fax +31883557362. E-mail: info@oicrf.org.
URL: http://www.oicrf.org/

History 1958, as an organ of *International Federation of Surveyors (FIG, #13561)*, with the title of *International Office of Cadastre and Land Registry.* **Aims** Collect and systematically file and index all documentary material relating to existing cadastres and land registration systems; make comparative studies of that material, followed by publication of the results; give information and advice on all cadastres and land registration systems to all interested persons and institutions, whether for the purpose of study or to help countries wishing either to introduce a cadastre or a land registration system or improve the existing system. **Structure** Bureau/documentation centre in Apeldoorn (Netherlands). A global network of experts who are correspondents to OICRF. **Activities** Knowledge management/information dissemination. [2016.02.15/XE3510/**E**]

- ♦ International Office of Cadastre and Land Registry / see International Office of Cadastre and Land Records (#14398)
- ♦ International Office for Catholic Scouting (inactive)
- ♦ International Office of Chocolate and Cocoa Manufacturers / see International Confectionery Association (#12840)
- ♦ International Office of Cocoa and Chocolate (inactive)
- ♦ International Office of Cocoa, Chocolate and Sugar Confectionery / see International Confectionery Association (#12840)
- ♦ International Office of Commercial Statistics (inactive)
- ♦ International Office of Consumers Unions / see Consumers International (#04773)
- ♦ International Office of Documentation on Military Medicine (inactive)
- ♦ International Office of Epizootics / see OIE – World Organisation for Animal Health (#17703)
- ♦ International Office of Fishing Documentation (inactive)
- ♦ International Office of Hunting Documentation (inactive)
- ♦ International Office of Legal Translations (inactive)
- ♦ International Office for Mechanical Cultivation (inactive)
- ♦ International Office of Musicians (inactive)
- ♦ International Office for People's Education (inactive)
- ♦ International Office of People's Houses (inactive)
- ♦ International Office for the Protection of Nature (inactive)
- ♦ International Office for Public Health (inactive)

♦ International Office for Water (IOW) 14399

Office international de l'eau (OIEau) – Oficina Internacional del Agua – Internationales Wasseramt

Dir Gen 21 rue de Madrid, 75008 Paris, France. T. +33144908860. Fax +33140080145. E-mail: dg@oieau.fr.
Secretariat General 22 rue Edouard Chamberland, 87065 Limoges CEDEX, France. T. +335114770. Fax +33555114737. E-mail: secretariat.general@oieau.fr.
URL: http://www.oieau.fr/

History Founded Sep 1991, on the initiative of the French Government, with support from *Deutsche Gesellschaft für Technische Zusammenarbeit (GTZ, inactive), European Commission (EC, #06633)* and *UNEP (#20299).* Also referred to as *IOWater.* Registered in accordance with French law. **Aims** Provide training for *sustainable development* and sound management of *water resources* respecting the *environment*; contribute to building up local capacity in the water and environment sector by developing ideas and sectoral strategies, especially with regard to development of human resources; within the *European Union* and the main developed countries, develop exchanges and services to improve water resources management, *ecological* quality of surroundings, *waste water* treatment and prevention of diffused *pollution* by a more integrated approach among users within EU; participate in joint efforts to support Central and Eastern European countries, Africa, Latin America, Mediterranean and developing countries. **Structure** Board of Directors; International Steering Committee; Scientific and Technical Council; International Orientation Council (CIO); Orientation Committee for African and Mediterranean Countries; Network of Experts; *International Institute for Water Administration (see: #14399).* **Languages** English, French, German, Portuguese, Russian, Spanish. **Staff** 110.00 FTE, paid. **Finance** Annual budget: euro 10,000,000. **Events** *NOVATECH : International Conference on Sustainable Techniques and Strategies in Urban Water Management* Lyon (France) 2019, *Colloque international sur les sécheresses, les étiages et les déficits en eau* Paris (France) 2019, *Journée sur les Dispositifs en Assainissement non Collectifs* Paris (France) 2019, *Journée sur la prise en compte du changement climatique pour les projets des services d'eau et d'assainissement* Paris (France) 2018, *Journée sur le Transfert des Compétences Eau et Assainissement* Paris (France) 2018. **Consultative Status** Consultative status granted from: *UNEP (#20299).* **IGO Relations** Member of: *European Environment Information and Observation Network (EIONET, #07002)* European Topic Centre on Water. **NGO Relations** Founding member of: *Global Water Solidarity (GWS, #10655).* Member of: *Mediterranean Network of Water Training Centers (AquaForMed, #16666); Regional Institute of Environmental Technology (RIET, no recent information).* Partner in: *Africa-EU Innovation Alliance for Water and Climate (AfriAlliance, #00169).* [2020.02.06/XE3163/**E**]

- ♦ International Officials Motoring Association (#02454)

♦ International Offshore Helicopter Association (HeliOffshore) 14400

CEO 10 Greycoat Place, London, SW1P 1SB, UK. T. +442079606341. E-mail: info@helioffshore.org.
URL: http://helioffshore.org/

History Launched 21 Oct 2014, by 5 helicopter operators. **Aims** Improve flight safety and advance technical competence globally. **Events** *Annual Conference* Cascais (Portugal) 2022, *Annual Conference* London (UK) 2021, *Annual Conference* London (UK) 2020, *Annual Conference* Athens (Greece) 2019, *Annual Conference* Baveno (Italy) 2018. **Members** Operational; Client; Alliance; Public Sector. Membership countries not specified. **NGO Relations** *European Helicopter Association (EHA, #07472).* [2015/XJ9988/**C**]

♦ International Offshore Petroleum Environmental Regulators (IOPER) 14401

Address not obtained.
URL: http://www.ioper.org/

History 2013. **Aims** Focus and drive improvements to environmental performance in the global offshore petroleum exploration and production industry. **Structure** Plenary Meeting. **Activities** Events/meetings. **Events** *Annual General Meeting* Dublin (Ireland) 2016, *Annual General Meeting* Washington, DC (USA) 2015, *Annual General Meeting* Cancún (Mexico) 2014.
Members Full in 8 countries:
Australia, Brazil, Canada, Mexico, New Zealand, Norway, UK, USA. [2016/XM5251/**F**]

♦ International Oil Pollution Compensation Funds (IOPC Funds) 14402

Fonds internationaux d'indemnisation pour les dommages dus à la pollution par les hydrocarbures (FIPOL) – Fondos Internacionales de Indemnización de Daños Debidos a la Contaminación por Hidrocarburos (FIDAC)

Dir 4 Albert Embankment, London, SE1 7SR, UK. T. +442075927100. Fax +442075927111.
Main: http://www.iopcfunds.org/

History Established 16 Oct 1978, London (UK), by *'International Convention on the Establishment of an International Fund for Compensation for Oil Pollution Damage, 1971'*, adopted at a conference convened by the then *'Inter-Governmental Maritime Consultative Organization (IMCO)'*, since 22 May 1982, *International Maritime Organization (IMO, #14102).* This Convention supplemented *International Convention on Civil Liability for Oil Pollution Damage (CLC, 1969)*, and created the International Oil Pollution Compensation Fund 1971 (1971 Fund). The 1971 Fund Convention ceased to be in force, 24 May 2002 and consequently does not apply to incidents occurring after that date; ceased to exist 31 Dec 2014.
Both the 1969 CLC and the 1971 Fund Convention were amended by Protocols in 1976 (essentially formal amendments), 1984 (never entered into force), 1992 (in force 30 May 1996), 2000 (in force 27 Jun 2001) and 2003 (in force 3 Mar 2005). *Protocol to the International Convention on Civil Liability for Oil Pollution Damage, 1992 (1992)* provided for higher limits of compensation and a wider scope of application than the original versions, and led to the establishment of the *International Oil Pollution Compensation Fund 1992 (IOPC Fund 1992)* on 30 May 1996. A further protocol providing an even higher limit of compensation was adopted in 2003 and led to the establishment of the Supplementary Fund, Mar 2005. Together, the 1992 and Supplementary Funds form the IOPC Funds. Previously also known as: *Internationale Entschädigunsfonds für Ölverschmutzungsschäden – Fondi Internazionali di Indennizzo per i Danni Dovut All'Inquinamento Mediante Idrocarburi.*
Aims Provide compensation for oil pollution damage resulting from spills of persistent oil from *tankers.* **Structure** Composed of 2 inter-governmental organizations, namely: *'1992 Fund'*, which has an Assembly comprising 115 Member States as of 1 Jul 2019, and Executive Committee of 15 elected Member States; *'Supplementary Fund'*, which has an Assembly, comprising 32 Member States as of 1 Jul 2019. Administered by Secretariat, comprising Director's Office and 3 Departments: Claims; External Relations and Conference; Finance and Administration. **Languages** English, French, Spanish. **Staff** 27.00 FTE, paid. **Finance** Contributions from oil companies (annual). **Events** *Extraordinary Session* London (UK) 2021, *Session* London (UK) 2021, *Session* London (UK) 2021, *Session* London (UK) 2021, *Session* London (UK) 2021. **Publications** Annual Report; booklet; brochures; manuals; guidelines.
Members Contracting Parties to both the 1992 Protocol to the Civil Liability Convention and the 1992 Protocol to the Fund Convention as of 1 Jul 2019 (110):
Albania, Algeria, Angola, Antigua-Barbuda, Argentina, Australia, Bahamas, Bahrain, Barbados, Belgium, Belize, Benin, Brunei Darussalam, Bulgaria, Cambodia, Cameroon, Canada, Cape Verde, Colombia, Comoros, Congo Brazzaville, Cook Is, Côte d'Ivoire, Croatia, Cyprus, Denmark, Djibouti, Dominica, Dominican Rep, Ecuador, Estonia, Fiji, Finland, France, Gabon, Georgia, Germany, Ghana, Greece, Grenada, Guinea, Hong Kong, Hungary, Iceland, India, Iran Islamic Rep, Ireland, Israel, Italy, Jamaica, Japan, Kenya, Kiribati, Korea Rep, Latvia, Liberia, Lithuania, Luxembourg, Madagascar, Malaysia, Maldives, Malta, Marshall Is, Mauritania, Mauritius, Mexico, Monaco, Montenegro, Morocco, Mozambique, Namibia, Netherlands, New Zealand, Nicaragua, Nigeria, Niue, Norway, Oman, Palau, Panama, Papua New Guinea, Philippines, Poland, Portugal, Qatar, Russia, Samoa, Senegal, Serbia, Seychelles, Sierra Leone, Slovakia, Slovenia, South Africa, Spain, St Kitts-Nevis, St Lucia, St Vincent-Grenadines, Sweden, Switzerland, Tanzania UR, Tonga, Trinidad-Tobago, Tunisia, Türkiye, Tuvalu, UK, Uruguay, Vanuatu, Venezuela.
State Parties to the Supplementary Fund Protocol as of 1 Jul 2019 (30):
Barbados, Belgium, Canada, Congo Brazzaville, Croatia, Denmark, Estonia, Finland, France, Germany, Greece, Hungary, Ireland, Italy, Japan, Korea Rep, Latvia, Lithuania, Montenegro, Morocco, Netherlands, Norway, Poland, Portugal, Slovakia, Slovenia, Spain, Sweden, Türkiye, UK.
IGO Relations Organizations having observer status: *Baltic Marine Environment Protection Commission – Helsinki Commission (HELCOM, #03126); Central Commission for the Navigation of the Rhine (CCNR, #03687); European Commission (EC, #06633); International Institute for the Unification of Private Law (UNIDROIT, #13934); International Maritime Organization (IMO, #14102); Maritime Organization of West and Central Africa (MOWCA, #16582); Regional Marine Pollution Emergency Response Centre for the Mediterranean Sea (REMPEC, #18795); UNEP (#20299); United Nations (UN, #20515).* **NGO Relations** Organizations having observer status: *BIMCO (#03236); Comité maritime international (CMI, #04192); Conference of Peripheral Maritime Regions of Europe (CPMR, #04638); Conseil européen de l'industrie chimique (CEFIC, #04687); International Association of Classification Societies (IACS, #11778); International Association of Independent Tanker Owners (INTERTANKO, #11959); International Chamber of Shipping (ICS, #12535); International Group of P and I Clubs (#13751); International Salvage Union (ISU, #14779); International Spill Control Organization (ISCO, #15580); International Union of Marine Insurance (IUMI, #15789); Oil Companies International Marine Forum (OCIMF, #17709); World LPG Association (WLPGA, #21629).* [2019.07.01/XF7953/f/**F***]

- ♦ International Oil Spill Conference (meeting series)
- ♦ International Oil Union (inactive)

♦ International Old Catholic Bishops' Conference (IBC) 14403

Conférence internationale des évêques vieux-catholiques – Internationalen Altkatholischen Bischofskonferenz (IBK)

Pres Kon Wilhelminalaan 3, 3818 HN Amersfoort, Netherlands. T. +31334620875.
URL: http://www.utrechter-union.org/pagina/140/ibc/

History Founded 24 Sep 1889, Utrecht (Netherlands), by those Catholic bishops who gave their assent to the Declaration of Utrecht of that date, as *Old Catholic Church Association.* This became the *Union of Utrecht – Union d'Utrecht*, 5 Aug 1902, a title by which IBC is also known. Separation from the Roman Catholic had begun in the 18th century, Netherlands, on issues of authority and leadership. Latest Agreement between the Old Catholic Bishops, 12 Sep 1974; new Statute of the Old Catholic Bishops United in the Union of Utrecht, 2001. **Aims** Link national churches which at various times have separated from the Church of Rome, particularly those which refused in 1870 to accept doctrine of the infallibility of the Pope and his primacy of jurisdiction at the time of 1st Vatican Council. **Structure** Conference. **Languages** English, German. **Staff** 1.00 FTE, paid. **Finance** Contributions from member Churches. **Activities** Guidance/assistance/consulting; networking/liaising. **Events** *Congress* Bonn (Germany) 2022, *Meeting* Lublin (Poland) 2019, *International Congress* Vienna (Austria) 2018, *International Congress* Vienna (Austria) 2017, *International Congress* Cologne (Germany) 2016. **Publications** *Internationale Kirchliche Zeitschrift.*
Members The Old Catholic Churches in 6 countries:
Austria, Czechia, Germany, Netherlands, Poland, Switzerland. [2015.11.10/XD5295/**D**]

♦ International Old Catholic Theologians Conference (meeting series)

♦ International Oleander Society 14404

Main Office PO Box 3431, Galveston TX 77552-0431, USA.
URL: http://www.oleander.org/

History 1967, Galveston TX (USA). **Aims** Promote, carry on and aid in every way the development, improvement and preservation of oleander (Nerium) of all kinds, including importation and improvement by *cultivation* and *hybridization* of oleander; extend knowledge, *production*, use and appreciation of oleander. **Structure** Board, comprising President, Executive Vice-President, 3 Vice-Presidents, Treasurer, Recording Secretary, Corresponding Secretary, Historian, Webmaster, Immediate Past President, 4 Trustees and one Trustee Emeritus. **Finance** Members' dues. Other sources: grants; sales. **Activities** Conducts scientific research or causes research projects to be carried out for the improvement, development or preservation of oleander and for promotion of a higher degree of efficiency in growing; collects information relating to growing and development of oleander by means of exhibitions, lectures, publications or otherwise; assists others engaged in the growing of oleander in research and dissemination of information; makes awards in the form of certificates and medals for excellence in development or culture of oleander; encourages roadside beautification and other civic plantings with oleander; organizes Annual Oleander Festival and special events; develops an Oleander Garden Park, Galveston TX (USA); organizes annual meeting in Oct, always in Galveston TX. **Publications** *Nerium News* (4 a year); *Oleanders – Guide to Culture and Selected Varieties on Galveston Island.* Videos.

Members Societies and individuals in 17 countries:
Australia, Bulgaria, Canada, France, Germany, Greece, Grenada, Hungary, India, Indonesia, Israel, Italy, Japan, Netherlands, St Kitts-Nevis, UK, USA.
[2015/XF1314/**F**]

♦ International Olive Council (IOC) 14405

Conseil oléicole international (COI) – Consejo Oleicola Internacional (COI) – Consiglio Oleicolo Internazionale (COI)

Exec Dir Principe de Vergara 154, 28002 Madrid, Spain. T. +34915903638. Fax +34915631263. E-mail: iooc@internationaloliveoil.org.
URL: https://www.internationaloliveoil.org/

History 1959. Founded as *International Olive Oil Council*, to administer the International Olive Oil Agreement, which has its roots in the provisions of Chapter VI of the Charter drawn up Mar 1948, Havana (Cuba), by the United Nations Conference on Trade and Employment. Although this Charter was never ratified, its provisions were recommended by *ECOSOC (#05331)* as enshrining the principles which would underline international agreements on commodities and they were observed by governments when such agreements were being negotiated. Such negotiations took place in Geneva (Switzerland) during United Nations International Conferences on Olive Oil which led to: (i) the initial *International Olive Oil Agreement, 1956 (1956)* – also called the *'1956 Agreement, amended in 1958'* – which expired on 31 Sep 1963; (ii) the second *International Olive Oil Agreement, 1963 (1963)* – also called the *'1963 Agreement'* – which came into force on 1 Oct 1963, was successively extended by the Protocols of 30 Mar 1967, 7 Mar 1969, 23 Mar 1973 and 7 Apr 1978 and expired on 31 Dec 1979; (iii) a third *International Olive Oil Agreement, 1979 (1979)* – also called the *'1979 Agreement'*, following negotiations 20-30 Mar 1979, Geneva, during a further United Nations Conference on Olive Oil convened by the Secretary General of *UNCTAD (#20285)*. The third Agreement took into account provisions embodied by UNCTAD in Resolution 93 (IV) and mentioned basic factors brought out by Resolution 1 (III), adopted on 19 Mar 1979 by the United Nations Conference concerning a Common Fund, under the Integrated Programme for Commodities (among which olive oil). The *'1979 Agreement'* came into force provisionally on 1 Jan 1980 and definitively on 1 Jan 1981, for a duration of 5 years; it was extended in 1984 and 1985, and expired 31 Dec 1986. Negotiations at the UNCTAD international conference, 16 June-1 Jul 1986, Geneva, culminated in *International Agreement on Olive Oil and Tables Olives, 1986 (1986)*, which entered into force 1 Jan 1987. Its lifetime has been prolonged twice, ending on 31 Dec 1993. A Protocol adopted Mar 1993, Geneva, extended the Agreement, with amendments, until 31 Dec 1998, after which date the Council could decide to prolong it for successive 2 year periods, re-negotiate it or terminate it in advance. Agreement was prolonged, 4 Jun 1998, Budva (Yugoslavia), until 31 Dec 2000, again, 16 Nov 2000, Madrid (Spain), until 31 Dec 2002, again, 20 Dec 2002, Madrid, until 30 Jun 2003, and again, 25 Jun 2003, until 31 Dec 2004. *International Agreement on Olive Oil and Table Olives, 2005 (2005)* was adopted 29 Apr 2005. Negotion for successor to 2005 agreement ongoing in 2015. Statutes registered in: *'UNTS 1/43557'*; *'UNTS 1/4806'*; *'UNTS 1/7239'*. **Aims** Basic objectives of the International Agreement: put into operation or facilitate application of measures calculated to extend *production* and *consumption* of, and international *trade* in, olive products; ensure fair competition among countries exporting olive oil and table olives, whether producers or not, and ensure to importing countries delivery of a commodity conforming to all specifications of the contracts concluded; strive to obtain a balance between production and consumption; encourage fair competition and abate drawbacks of fluctuating market supplies; improve oil and table olive production; conduct research programmes and undertake any activity and measures to highlight the biological value of olive oil and table olives with particular reference to their nutritional qualities and therapeutic properties; carry out technical cooperation and transfer technology; improve production and raise *productivity* through programmes and action plans for the sustainable development of olive farming and better product quality. **Structure** Council, meeting annually, comprises delegates of both mainly producing members and mainly importing members and elects Chairman and Vice-Chairman; Committees (5); International Arbitration Board; Executive Secretariat including Units (5) and Departments (10); Directorate, covering external relations and reporting directly to the Executive Director; Other Departments (3). **Languages** Arabic, English, French, Italian, Spanish. **Staff** 31.00 FTE, paid. **Finance** Contribution from Members. **Activities** Awards/prizes/competitions; events/meetings; knowledge management/information dissemination; monitoring/evaluation; projects/programmes; publishing activities; research and development; standards/guidelines; training/education. **Events** *Session* Amman (Jordan) 2022, *Session* Madrid (Spain) 2021, *Session* Tbilisi (Georgia) 2021, *Session* Madrid (Spain) 2020, *Session* Madrid (Spain) 2020. **Publications** *IOC Newsletter* (12 a year) in English, French, Spanish; *Olivae* (2 a year) in Arabic, English, French, Italian, Spanish; *National Policies in the Olive Sector* (every 2 years). *Following Olive Footprints*; *World Catalogue of Olive Varieties*; *World Olive Encyclopaedia*. Cookbooks; technical guides; monographs; congress reports; brochures.

Members Governments of 15 countries:
Albania, Algeria, Argentina, Egypt, Iran Islamic Rep, Iraq, Israel, Jordan, Lebanon, Libya, Montenegro, Morocco, Tunisia, Türkiye, Uruguay.
Regional integration EU body (1):
European Union (EU, #08967).

IGO Relations Member of: *Intergovernmental Organizations Conference (IGO Conference, #11498)*. Relationship agreement with: *FAO (#09260)*. Designed International Commodity Body of: *Common Fund for Commodities (CFC, #04293)*. Cooperative and working links established with the following organizations and Specialized Agencies:
- *Administrative Tribunal of the International Labour Organization (ILO Tribunal, #00118)*;
- *Arab Industrial Development, Standardization and Mining Organization (AIDSMO, #00981)*;
- *CIHEAM – International Centre for Advanced Mediterranean Agronomic Studies (CIHEAM, #03927)*;
- *Codex Alimentarius Commission (CAC, #04081)*;
- *International Bank for Reconstruction and Development (IBRD, #12317)*;
- *International Development Association (IDA, #13155)*;
- *International Monetary Fund (IMF, #14180)*;
- *International Trade Centre (ITC, #15703)*;
- *International Union for the Protection of Industrial Property (Paris Union, #15805)*;
- *OECD (#17693)*;
- UNCTAD;
- *UNDP (#20292)*;
- *UNIDO (#20336)*;
- United Nations;
- *WHO (#20950)*;
- *World Customs Organization (WCO, #21350)*;
- *World Intellectual Property Organization (WIPO, #21593)* (Permanent observer status).

NGO Relations Cooperative and working links established with: *Arab Federation for Food Industries (AFFI, #00946)*; Federation of the Olive Oil Industry of the EEC; *International Chamber of Commerce (ICC, #12534)*; *Inter-Regional Cooperative Research Network on Olives (#15969)*. In liaison with technical committees of: *International Organization for Standardization (ISO, #14473)*. Member of: *Federation of International Civil Servants' Associations (FICSA, #09603)*.
[2022/XC2302/**C***]

♦ International Olive Oil Agreement, 1956 (1956 treaty)
♦ International Olive Oil Agreement, 1963 (1963 treaty)
♦ International Olive Oil Agreement, 1979 (1979 treaty)
♦ International Olive Oil Council / see International Olive Council (#14405)
♦ International Olive Oil Federation (inactive)
♦ International Olive-Tree Committee (inactive)

♦ International Olympic Academy (IOA) 14406

Académie internationale olympique (AIO)

Dean 52 Dimitrios Vikelas Avenue, Halandri, 152 33 Athens, Greece. T. +302106878809 – +302106878810 – +302106878813. E-mail: ioa@ioa.org.gr.
URL: http://www.ioa.org.gr/

History 28 Apr 1949, Athens (Greece). Founded by *International Olympic Committee (IOC, #14408)*, following first official submission of a proposal at 26th Plenary Session of the Hellenic Olympic Committee, 3 Feb 1939. Commenced operations in Jun 1961, when the ancient Olympic stadium was handed over to the Greek government. Autonomous since 2003. **Aims** Create an international educational, cultural institute in Olympia. **Structure** 'Ephoria' (Board of Trustees) – elected by Hellenic Olympic Committee (HOC) for a 4-year period. The HOC has the control and responsibility for the overall organization of the IOA which is also under the auspices of the IOC. Includes: *International Research Centre for Advanced Olympic Studies (no recent information)*. **Languages** English, French, Irish Gaelic. **Finance** Funded by the Sport Ministry – IOC. **Activities** Events/meetings; knowledge management/information dissemination; networking/liaising; training/education. **Events** *Session* Athens (Greece) 2015, *Session* Olympia (Greece) 2014, *Annual General Session* Olympia (Greece) 2011, *International session for directors of national olympic academies* Athens (Greece) 2005, *Session* Athens (Greece) 2005. **Publications** Proceedings of: Annual General Sessions; Special Sessions for Educators; Special Sessions for National Olympic Academies and International Federations. Information leaflets. **Members** Organizations involved with Olympic and sports matters. Membership countries not specified. **NGO Relations** IOC Recognized Organization. Cooperates with: *Olympic Solidarity (OS, #17721)*.
[2022/XD7008/**E**]

♦ International Olympic Academy Participants' Association (IOAPA) . 14407

Sec 4 Botasi Street, 106 82 Athens, Greece. E-mail: info@ioapa.org.
URL: https://ioapa.org/

History Jul 1989, Olympia (Greece). Founded by participants of the 1985 General Session of *International Olympic Academy (IOA, #14406)*. Registration: Greek Civil Code, Greece. **Aims** Foster an international and multicultural Olympic fellowship of IOA past participants, providing tools and resources to facilitate Olympic education and support Olympism worldwide. **Structure** General Assembly; Executive Committee. **Publications** *Arete Newsletter* (3 a year). **Members** Individuals (over 1100) in over 125 countries. Membership countries not specified.
[2022/AA2614/v/**E**]

♦ International Olympic Association (inactive)
♦ International Olympic Association for Medical-Sports Research (no recent information)
♦ International Olympic Collectors Association (#02677)

♦ International Olympic Committee (IOC) 14408

Comité international olympique (CIO) – Comité Olimpico Internacional – Internationaal Olympisch Komitee (IOK)

Address not obtained.
URL: http://www.olympic.org/

History 23 Jun 1894, Paris (France). Founded at Congress for the Revival of the Olympic Games, convened by Baron Pierre de Coubertin. Headquarters moved from Paris to Lausanne (Switzerland) in 1915. In 1968, the administration moved to Château de Vidy, offered by Lausanne city authorities. A modern administration centre was built next to the Château in 1986. Recognized by the Swiss Federal Council in 1981. Former names and other names: *Comité Olimpico Internacional* – former; *Internationaal Olympisch Komitee (IOK)* – former. **Aims** Raise awareness of and spread the Olympic values of excellence, friendship and respect; encourage coordination, organization and development of *sport* and sports *competitions*; cooperate with competent public and private organizations and authorities in endeavouring to place sport at the service of humanity; ensure regular celebration of the Olympic Games; combat any form of discrimination affecting the Olympic Movement; support and encourage promotion of sports *ethics*; ensure that the spirit of fair play prevails in sport and that violence is banned; combat doping in sport; take measures to protect the health of clean *athletes*; oppose any political or commercial abuse of sport or athletes; encourage development of sport for all as part of the foundation of high-level sport, which in turn contributes to development of sport for all; ensure that Olympic Games are held in conditions demonstrating responsible concern for environmental issues; support the International Olympic Academy (IOA) and other institutions devoted to Olympic education.

Structure The Session (usually once a year) – supreme IOC body – adopts, modifies and interprets Olympic Charter and elects IOC members on proposal by the Executive Board. IOC is the supreme authority of the *Olympic Movement (#17719)*, which comprises IOC, International Federations (IFs), National Olympic Committees (NOCs), Organizing Committees for the Olympic Games (OCOGs), national associations, clubs and athletes. IOC chooses and elects its members (at Dec 2022 – 101) from persons it considers qualified, who must be nationals of, and be domiciled or have their main centre of interest in, a country with a recognized NOC. Members are its representatives in their respective countries, not delegates of their country within the IOC. Executive Board; President sets up permanent or ad hoc commissions and working groups. Administration, headed by Director General, includes 14 Directors in charge of key sectors: International Cooperation and Development; Sports; Olympic Games; NOC Relations; Television and Marketing Services; Legal Affairs; Technology; Finance and Administration; Communications; Medical and Scientific; Information Management; Culture and Heritage; Olympic Solidarity; Olympic Broadcast Services (OBS); Olympic Archives Television Bureau (OTAB).
Commissions:
- Athletes';
- Athletes' Entourage;
- Audit Committee;
- Coordination;
- Culture and Olympic Heritage;
- Digital engagement and marketing communications;
- Disciplinary;
- Ethics;
- Finance;
- Future Host for the Games of the Olympiad;
- Future Host for the Olympic Winter Games;
- Gender Equality, Diversity and Inclusion;
- Human Resources Committee;
- IOC Members Election;
- IOC Television and Marketing Services – Board of Directors;
- Legal Affairs;
- Medical and Scientific;
- Olympic Broadcasting Services – Boards Of Directors;
- Olympic Channel – Boards of Directors;
- Olympic Education;
- Olympic Programme;
- *Olympic Solidarity (OS, #17721)*;
- Olympism 365;
- Public Affairs and Corporate Communications;
- Revenues and Commercial Partnerships;
- Sustainability and Legacy;
- Technology and Technical Innovation.

Languages English, French. **Staff** 450.00 FTE, paid. **Finance** Sources: fees for services; revenue from activities/projects; sponsorship. **Activities** Sporting activities. **Events** *Session* Paris (France) 2024, *Session* Mumbai (India) 2023, *Session* Beijing (China) 2022, *Session* Athens (Greece) 2021, *Session* Tokyo (Japan) 2021. **Publications** *Olympic Review* (4 a year); *Olympic Charter* (annual); *Olympic Directory* (annual). *Bibliography of the Works of Pierre de Coubertin*; *IOC Medical Controls*; *Olympic Biographies*; *Olympic Hymn*; *The Administration of an Olympic Games*; *The Speeches of Avery Brundage*; *The Speeches of Lord Killanin*. Official reports of Olympic Congresses.

Members Individuals (101) from 71 countries and a refugee recognized by UNHCR:
Afghanistan, Algeria, Argentina, Aruba, Australia, Austria, Belgium, Bhutan, Brazil, Burundi, Cameroon, Canada, Cape Verde, Chile, China, Colombia, Costa Rica, Côte d'Ivoire, Croatia, Cuba, Czechia, Djibouti, Dominican Rep, Ethiopia, Fiji, Finland, France, Germany, Great Britain, Greece, Hungary, India, Italy, Japan, Jordan, Kenya, Korea Rep, Kuwait, Lesotho, Liechtenstein, Lithuania, Luxembourg, Monaco, Mongolia, Morocco, New Zealand, Norway, Pakistan, Palau, Papua New Guinea, Paraguay, Philippines, Qatar, Romania, Russia, Rwanda, Saudi Arabia, Senegal, Serbia, Singapore, Slovakia, South Africa, Spain, Sweden, Switzerland, Thailand, Türkiye, Uganda, Ukraine, USA, Zimbabwe.
IGO Relations Cooperation agreements with: *FAO (#09260)*; *International Bank for Reconstruction and Development (IBRD, #12317)* (World Bank); *UNEP (#20299)*; *UNDP (#20292)*; *UNESCO (#20322)*; *UNHCR (#20327)*; *UNICEF (#20332)*; *WHO (#20950)*; *World Meteorological Organization (WMO, #21649)*.
NGO Relations Instrumental in setting up (3): *International Academy of Sport Science and Technology (AISTS)*; *International Olympic Truce Centre (IOTC, #14409)*; *World Anti-Doping Agency (WADA, #21096)*.
Organizations recognized by IOC are subdivided into the following categories:
1/ International Sports Federations (IFs) (40):
– *Badminton World Federation (BWF, #03060)*
– *Fédération Équestre Internationale (FEI, #09484)*
– *Fédération internationale d'escrime (FIE, #09629)*
– *Fédération internationale de basketball (FIBA, #09614)*
– *Fédération internationale de gymnastique (FIG, #09636)*
– *Fédération Internationale de Ski (FIS, #09659)*
– *Fédération internationale de volleyball (FIVB, #09670)*
– *International Biathlon Union (IBU, #12336)*
– *International Bobsleigh and Skeleton Federation (IBSF, #12375)*
– *International Boxing Association (IBA, #12385)*
– *International Canoe Federation (ICF, #12437)*
– *International Federation of Association Football (#13360)*
– *International Federation of Sport Climbing (IFSC, #13553)*
– *International Golf Federation (IGF, #13727)*
– *International Handball Federation (IHF, #13771)*
– *International Hockey Federation (#13802)*
– *International Ice Hockey Federation (IIHF, #13831)*
– *International Judo Federation (IJF, #13975)*
– *International Luge Federation (FIL, #14066)*
– *International Shooting Sport Federation (ISSF, #14852)*
– *International Skating Union (ISU, #14865)*
– *International Ski Mountaineering Federation (ISMF, #14871)*
– *International Surfing Association (ISA, #15630)*
– *International Table Tennis Federation (ITTF, #15650)*
– *International Tennis Federation (ITF, #15676)*
– *International Weightlifting Federation (IWF, #15876)*
– *Union Cycliste Internationale (UCI, #20375)*
– *United World Wrestling (UWW, #20665)*
– *World Aquatics (#21100)*
– *World Archery (#21105)*
– *World Athletics (#21209)*
– *World Curling Federation (WCF, #21348)*
– *World DanceSport Federation (WDSF, #21354)*
– *World Penthathlon (UIPM, #21720)*
– *World Rowing (#21756)*
– *World Rugby (#21757)*
– *World Sailing (#21760)*
– *World Skate (#21786)*
– *World Taekwondo (#21844)*
– *World Triathlon (#21872)*
2/ Recognized federations (35):
– *Federación Internacional de Pelota Vasca (FIPV, #09340)*
– *Fédération aéronautique internationale (FAI, #09397)*
– *Fédération Internationale de l'Automobile (FIA, #09613)*
– *Fédération internationale de Motocyclisme (FIM, #09643)*
– *Fédération internationale de SAMBO (FIAS, #09655)*
– *Fédération internationale des échecs (FIDE, #09627)*
– *Federation of International Bandy (FIB, #09601)*
– *Federation of International Polo (FIP, #09675)*
– *International Bowling Federation (IBF, #12384)*
– *International Cheer Union (ICU, #12539)*
– *International Cricket Council (ICC, #13105)*
– *International Federation Icestocksport (IFI, #13455)*
– *International Federation of American Football (IFAF, #13354)* (provisional)
– *International Federation of Muaythai Associations (IFMA, #13482)*
– *International Floorball Federation (IFF, #13615)*
– *International Korfball Federation (IKF, #13992)*
– *International Life Saving Federation (ILS, #14040)*
– *International Orienteering Federation (IOF, #14485)*
– *International Racquetball Federation (IRF, #14683)*
– *International Sumo Federation (IFS, #15624)*
– *International Waterski and Wakeboard Federation (IWWF, #15872)*
– *International Wushu Federation (IWUF, #15918)*
– *Tug of War International Federation (TWIF, #20259)*
– *Union internationale des associations d'alpinisme (UIAA, #20420)*
– *Union internationale Motonautique (UIM, #20431)*
– *World Association of Kickboxing Organizations (WAKO, #21151)*
– *World Baseball Softball Confederation (WBSC, #21222)*
– *World Bridge Federation (WBF, #21246)*
– *World Confederation of Billiards Sports (WCBS, #21291)*
– *World Flying Disc Federation (WFDF, #21509)*
– *World Karate Federation (WKF, #21608)*
– *World Lacrosse (#21616)*
– *World Netball (WN, #21668)*
– *World Squash Federation (WSF, #21826)*
– *World Underwater Federation (#21873)*
3/ Sports on the Paris 2024 Olympic Games programme (4):
– *International Federation of Sport Climbing (IFSC, #13553)*
– *International Surfing Association (ISA, #15630)*
– *World Skate (#21786)*
– World DanceSport Federation
4/ Governing Bodies (6):
– *Court of Arbitration for Sport (CAS, #04933)*
– *International Committee for Fair Play (#12769)*
– *International Paralympic Committee (IPC, #14512)*
– *International Testing Agency (ITA, #15678)*
– *World Anti-Doping Agency (WADA, #21096)*
– *World Olympians Association (WOA, #21682)*
5/ IF Associations (4):
– *Alliance of Independent recognised Members of Sport (AIMS, #00690)*
– *Association of Summer Olympic International Federations (ASOIF, #02943)*
– *Association of the International Olympic Winter Sports Federations (AIOWF, #02757)*
– *Association of the IOC Recognized International Sports Federations (ARISF, #02767)*
6/ NOC Associations (8):
– *Association of National Olympic Committees (ANOC, #02819)*
– *Association of National Olympic Committees of Africa (ANOCA, #02820)*
– *Central American and Caribbean Sports Organization (CACSO, #03665)*
– *European Olympic Committees (EOC, #08083)*
– *Oceania National Olympic Committees (ONOC, #17667)*
– *Olympic Council of Asia (OCA, #17718)*
– *Panam Sports Organization (Panam Sports, #18138)*
– *South American Sports Organization (SASO, #19708)*
7/ Recognized bodies in the field of education/dissemination of the Olympic ideal/Fair Play (6):
– *Comité international Pierre de Coubertin (CIPC, #04184)*
– *International Committee for Fair Play (#12769)*
– *International Council for Health, Physical Education, Recreation, Sport and Dance (ICHPER-SD, #13028)*
– *International Olympic Academy (IOA, #14406)*
– *Panathlon International (PI, #18170)*
– *Pan-Iberican Association of Olympic Academies (#18181)*
8/ Recognized multi-sports organizations and events / Sport for all (15):
– *Committee of the International Children's Games (CICG, #04264)*
– *Commonwealth Games Federation (CGF, #04332)*
– *Conseil international du sport militaire (CISM, #04695)*
– *Fédération internationale Sport pour tous (FISpT, #09661)*
– *International Committee of the Mediterranean Games (ICMG, #12783)*
– *International Federation of Physical and Sport Education (#13510)*
– *International Masters Games Association (IMGA, #14117)*
– *International Police Sports Union (#14614)*
– *International School Sport Federation (ISF, #14792)*
– *International Sporting Federation of Catholic Schools (#15589)*
– *International University Sports Federation (FISU, #15830)*
– *International Workers and Amateurs in Sports Confederation (#15905)*
– *International World Games Association (IWGA, #15914)*
– *The Association for International Sport for All (TAFISA, #02763)*
– *World Transplant Games Federation (WTGF, #21868)*
9/ Recognized organizations in the field of disabled sport (3):
– *International Committee of Sports for the Deaf (ICSD, #12805)*
– *International Paralympic Committee (IPC, #14512)*
– *Special Olympics International (SOI, #19910)*
10/ Recognized organizations in the field of sports medicine and scienceees (4):
– *European College of Sport Science (ECSS, #06616)*
– *International Association for Non-Violent Sport (IANVS, no recent information)*
– *International Council of Sport Science and Physical Education (ICSSPE, #13077)*
– *International Federation of Sports Medicine (#13554)*
11/ Recognized organizations in the field of sports equipment and facilities (2):
– *Internationale Vereinigung Sport- und Freizeiteinrichtungen (IAKS, #13319)*
– *World Federation of the Sporting Goods Industry (WFSGI, #21487)*
12/ Recognized organizations in the field of Media – Information (6):
– Agence France Presse
– *Association internationale de la presse sportive (AIPS, #02729)*
– *International Association for Sports Information (IASI, #12179)*
– *International Sporting Cinema and Television Federation (FICTS, #15588)*
– The Associated Press
– Thomson Reuters
13/ Other Recognized Organizations (12):
– *Association Internationale des Collectionneurs Olympiques (AICO, #02677)*
– *European Non-Governmental Sports Organization (ENGSO, #08054)*
– *Federazione Internazionale Cronometristi (FIC, #09717)*
– *Fondation internationale Olympafrica (FINO, #09823)*
– *Generations for Peace (GFP, no recent information)*
– *International Olympic Truce Centre (IOTC, #14409)*
– *International Society of Olympic Historians (ISOH, #15322)*
– Office of the Permanent Observer for the International Committee to the United Nations
– *Olympic Refuge Foundation (ORF, #17720)*
– *Right to Play International (#18945)*
– *World Olympians Association (WOA, #21682)*
– *World Union of Olympic Cities (#21881)* [2023/XA2303/v/**B**]

♦ International Olympic Institute (inactive)
♦ International Olympic Numismatic Federation (inactive)

♦ International Olympic Truce Centre (IOTC) 14409

Main Office 1A Likavittou St, 106 72 Athens, Greece. T. +302103611023. Fax +302103611024. E-mail: about@olympictruce.org.
Chairman c/o IOC, Château de Vidy, 1007 Lausanne VD, Switzerland. T. +41216216111. Fax +41216216354.
URL: http://www.olympictruce.org/
History 24 Jul 2000, Athens (Greece), by *International Olympic Committee (IOC, #14408)* and the Greek Government. Operates under the auspices of *International Olympic Truce Foundation (IOTF, #14410)*. **Aims** Implement projects related to the global promotion of a culture of *peace* through sport and the Olympic ideal, in accordance with the principles and policies established by the IOTF. **Structure** Board of Directors, including Chairman and Vice-Chairman. Headquarters in Athens (Greece); symbolic office in Olympia (Greece). [2015/XJ3006/**E**]

♦ International Olympic Truce Foundation (IOTF) 14410

Fondation internationale pour la trêve olympique (FITO)
Chairperson c/o IOC, Château de Vidy, 1007 Lausanne VD, Switzerland. T. +41216216111. Fax +41216216354.
URL: http://www.olympictruce.org/index.php?lang=en/
History 24 Jul 2000, by *International Olympic Committee (IOC, #14408)*. **Aims** Promote the Olympic ideals to serve peace, friendship and understanding and, in particular, the ancient Greek tradition of the Olympic truce; initiate *conflict prevention* and resolution through sport, culture and the Olympic ideals. **Activities** Operates *International Olympic Truce Centre (IOTC, #14409)*. [2018/XJ3005/f/**F**]

♦ International Ombudsman Association (internationally oriented national body)

♦ International Ombudsman Institute (IOI) 14411

Institut international de l'Ombudsman – Instituto Internacional del Ombudsman – Internationales Ombudsman Institut
SG c/o Austrian Ombudsman Board, Singerstrasse 17, 1015 Vienna, Austria. T. +4315129388. Fax +4315129388200. E-mail: ioi@volksanw.gv.at.
URL: http://www.theioi.com/
History Apr 1978, Edmonton AB (Canada), as a result of 1st International Ombudsman Conference, 1976, Edmonton AB (Canada), which set up *International Ombudsman Steering Committee*. At 2nd Conference, 1980, Jerusalem (Israel), this Committee was replaced by *International Ombudsman Consultative Committee* which is representative of world Ombudsmen. Also referred to as *Institut international du médiateur*. **Aims** Promote the concept of ombudsmanship; encourage and support research on ombudsmanship, civil and *human rights* and *privacy*; secure development of educational programmes; provide a resource centre for storage and dissemination of information. **Structure** Board of Directors. **Finance** Members' dues. Sales of publications. **Activities** Events/meetings; research/documentation; knowledge management/information dissemination. **Events** *Quadrennial Conference* Bangkok (Thailand) 2016, *Workshop on Human Rights Challenges* Barcelona (Spain) 2016, *Annual Meeting* Vienna (Austria) 2014, *Quadrennial Conference / Quadrennial International Ombudsman Conference* Wellington (New Zealand) 2012, *European region conference* Barcelona (Spain) 2010. **Publications** *International Ombudsman Institute Newsletter* (4 a year); *Ombudsman Journal* (annual); *Court Cases of Interest to the Institution of Ombudsman*; *Ombudsman Office Profiles*. *Occasional Paper Series* – about 4 a year. *Ombudsman Readings* by Stanley V Anderson; *Readings on Ombudsmanship* by Randall E Ivany; *The International Ombudsman Institute Bibliography*; *The International Ombudsman Institute Directory of Ombudsmen and Other Complaint-Handlers*; *The Ombudsmen in the Provinces of Canada* by Ulf Lundvik. Series; conference proceedings. Publications in English, French, Spanish, German.
Members Ombudsman offices, complaint-handling organizations, institutions, libraries and individuals in 58 countries and territories:
Argentina, Australia, Austria, Bahamas, Barbados, Belgium, Botswana, Canada, Chile, Costa Rica, Croatia, Cyprus, Denmark, Fiji, Finland, France, Germany, Ghana, Guatemala, Guyana, Hong Kong, Iceland, India, Ireland, Israel, Italy, Japan, Liechtenstein, Malta, Mauritius, Mexico, Namibia, Netherlands, New Zealand, Nigeria, Norway, Pakistan, Papua New Guinea, Philippines, Poland, Portugal, Puerto Rico, Samoa, Senegal, Seychelles, Solomon Is, South Africa, Spain, Sri Lanka, Sudan, Sweden, Switzerland, Taiwan, Tanzania UR, Uganda, USA, Zambia, Zimbabwe. [2016.03.04/XF8952/j/**F**]

♦ **International One Design World Class Association (IOD World Class Association)** **14412**

Sec address not obtained.
Pres address not obtained.
URL: http://www.internationalonedesign.org/

History Set up, originally as a Classic Yacht Class of *World Sailing (#21760)*, but now independent. Current constitution effective, 1 Jan 2015. **Aims** Promote racing of IOD class yachts; maintain one-design principles in hull construction and sail plan; adopt and enforce rules to ensure equality in racing competition. **Structure** Executive Committee. **Languages** English. **Staff** None paid. **Finance** Members' dues. **Activities** Sporting activities; events/meetings. **Events** *Annual General Meeting* San Francisco, CA (USA) 2016, *Annual Meeting* Tønsberg (Norway) 2014, *Annual Meeting* Bermuda 2012, *Annual Meeting* Northeast Harbor, ME (USA) 2011, *Annual Meeting* Sweden 2009. **Publications** *The Saga of the International One Design A Celebration of 75 Years.* **Members** Full (over 175) in 7 countries. Membership countries not specified. [2016.12.14/XK2114/**E**]

♦ International One Metre International Class Association (see: #14687)
♦ International Online Information Meeting (meeting series)
♦ International Onto-Psychology Association (internationally oriented national body)

♦ **International Open Source Network (IOSN)** **14413**

Contact National Telehealth Center Univ of the Philippines Taft Avenue, 1000 Manila, Philippines. T. +6325256501. E-mail: asean3@iosnasean.net.

History at the initiative of the Asia-Pacific Information Development Programme of *UNDP (#20292)*. **Aims** Promote the adoption of free and open source *software* (FOSS), open standards and open content for sustainable human development in the Asia-Pacific region. **Structure** Secretariat. Centres of excellence (3): IOSN ASEAN+3, based in Manila (Philippines); IOSN PIC (Pacific Island Countries), based in Suva (Fiji); IOSN South Asia, based in Chennai (India). **Finance** Supported by: *International Development Research Centre (IDRC, #13162)*. **Activities** Centres provide policy and technical advice on FOSS, Open Standards and Open Content to governments, civil society, academies and the private sector. Produces training and training materials and distributes them under content licenses. Organizes awareness raising, training, research and networking initiatives to assist countries in developing a pool of human resources skilled in the use and development of FOSS, Open Standards and Open Content. **Publications** *FOSS in Asia-Pacific* – newsletter. Books; videos; country profiles; case studies. [2008/XJ3596/**F**]

♦ International Operational Modal Analysis Conference (meeting series)
♦ International Operations Association / see ISITC
♦ International Ophthalmic Exchange Society (inactive)

♦ **International Ophthalmic Nurses Association (IONA)** **14414**

Sec address not obtained. E-mail: iona1955@hotmail.co.uk.
URL: https://ionalive.wordpress.com/

History 1955. **Aims** Provide an opportunity for ophthalmic nurses worldwide to share knowledge and experience. **Structure** Council, including President, Vice President, Honorary Secretary, Treasurer, Conference Organiser, Newsletter Editor and Overseas Liaison Officer. **Languages** English. **Staff** None. **Finance** Members' dues. Others sources: donations; surpluses from conferences. **Events** *Annual Conference* Guildford (UK) 2019, *Annual General Meeting and Conference* Manchester (UK) 2018, *Annual General Meeting and Conference* Leeds (UK) 2009, *Annual general meeting and conference* Leeds (UK) 2008, *Annual general meeting and conference* Swansea (UK) 2007. **Publications** *IONA Newsletter* (2 a year).
Members Full in 12 countries:
Australia, Cameroon, Denmark, Ireland, Malaysia, Netherlands, New Zealand, Portugal, Sweden, Tanzania UR, UK, USA.
[2020/XF1620/**F**]

♦ International Ophthalmology Teacher Training Council (internationally oriented national body)
♦ International Opium Convention, 1912 (1912 treaty)
♦ International Opium Convention, 1925 (1925 treaty)
♦ International Opium Convention, 1946 (1946 treaty)
♦ International Optical League / see World Council of Optometry (#21335)

♦ **International Opticians Association (IOA)** **14415**
Association internationale des opticiens

Sec 199 Gloucester Terrace, London, W2 6LD, UK. T. +442072985100. Fax +442072985111.

History 1951, Cincinnati OH (USA), as *International Guild of Dispensing Opticians (IGDO) – Guilde internationale de maîtres-opticiens.* Subsequently became *International Guild of Opticians (IGO) – Guilde internationale des opticiens.* Listed name adopted 1994, Christchurch (New zealand). **Aims** Encourage, promote and extend the science of ophthalmic dispensing through an intercontinental relationship; maintain, disseminate and advance ethical concepts and standards of knowledge and training; promote cooperation between representative groups. **Structure** Council, composed of 4 members, appointed by each national organization; Central Secretariat. **Languages** English. **Staff** 4.00 FTE, paid. **Finance** Members' dues. Budget: US$ 5,000. **Events** *Biennial Convention* Kuala Lumpur (Malaysia) 2014, *Biennial Convention* Perth, WA (Australia) 2012, *Biennial Convention* Gatineau, QC (Canada) 2010, *Biennial Convention* Gatineau, QC (Canada) 2010, *Biennial Convention* Manchester (UK) 2008.
Members Individuals and organizations in 8 countries:
Australia, Canada, Ireland, Malaysia, New Zealand, South Africa, UK, USA. [2012.08.07/XD2092/**D**]

♦ International Optimist Club / see Optimist International (#17778)
♦ International Optimist Dinghy Association (see: #21760)
♦ International Options Markets Association (inactive)
♦ International Optoelectronics Association (inactive)
♦ International Optometric and Optical League / see World Council of Optometry (#21335)
♦ International Oracle User Council / see International Oracle Users Community (#14416)

♦ **International Oracle Users Community (IOUC)** **14416**

Contact Oracle Corporation, 500 Oracle Parkway, Redwood City CA 94065, USA. T. +16505067000.
URL: http://www.oracle.com/

History 1994, Maastricht (Netherlands), as *International Oracle User Council (IOUC)* by *European, Middle East and Africa ORACLE User Group (EOUG)*. **Structure** Represented by President and Vice-President of the continental user groups and Oracle Applications User Group (OAUG). **Events** *Meeting* Amsterdam (Netherlands) 1996, *Meeting* Sydney, NSW (Australia) 1995. [2017/XD7844/y/**E**]

♦ International Oral Health Association (unconfirmed)

♦ **International Oral History Association (IOHA)** **14417**
Asociación Internacional de Historia Oral

Sec-Treas c/o Inst für Geschichte, Fernuniversitat Hagen, Feithstr 152, 58097 Hagen, Germany.
URL: https://www.ioha.org/

History Jun 1996, Gothenburg (Sweden). Founded during the 9th Oral History Conference. **Aims** Provide a forum for oral historians around the world, and a means for cooperation among those concerned with the documentation of human experience. **Structure** Council. **Languages** English, Spanish. **Staff** 15.00 FTE, voluntary. **Finance** Sources: members' dues. **Activities** Events/meetings; publishing activities. **Events** *International Oral History Conference* Rio de Janeiro (Brazil) 2023, *International Oral History Conference* Singapore (Singapore) 2021, *Biennial Conference* Singapore (Singapore) 2020, *Biennial Conference* Jyväskylä (Finland) 2018, *Biennial Conference* Bangalore (India) 2016. **Publications** *Palabras y Silencios/Words and Silences* (annual) in English, Spanish.
Members Full in 41 countries and territories:
Australia, Austria, Belgium, Brazil, Canada, China, Colombia, Congo DR, Czechia, Denmark, Egypt, Estonia, Finland, France, Germany, Greece, Hungary, India, Ireland, Italy, Japan, Malta, Mexico, Netherlands, New Zealand, Panama, Peru, Portugal, Puerto Rico, Romania, Russia, Saudi Arabia, Singapore, South Africa, Spain, Sweden, Türkiye, UK, United Arab Emirates, Uruguay, USA. [2022.10.21/XD3796/**D**]

♦ **International Orality Network (ION)** **14418**

Exec Dir PO Box 23027, Richmond VA 23223, USA. E-mail: info@orality.net.
URL: http://orality.net/

History 2004, as part of *Lausanne Committee for World Evangelization (LCWE, #16405)*. **Aims** Radically influence the way oral preference learners are *evangelized* and discipled in every people group. **Structure** Global Executive Team; International Advisory Team. **Members** Organizations (over 2,000). Membership countries not specified. [2016/XM4817/**E**]

♦ International Order for Ethics and Morals (inactive)
♦ International Order of Experts and Consultants / see Organisation internationale des experts (#17808)
♦ International Order of Good Templars / see Movendi International (#16871)
♦ International Order of Job's Daughters, Supreme Guardian Council (internationally oriented national body)
♦ International Order of Kabbalists (religious order)
♦ International Order of the King's Daughters and Sons (internationally oriented national body)
♦ International Order of Old Bastards (internationally oriented national body)
♦ International Order of the Rainbow for Girls (internationally oriented national body)

♦ **International Order of Saint Hubertus (IOSH)** **14419**

Contact 2021 L Street NW, Suite 101-288, Washington DC 20036, USA.
URL: https://www.iosh-usa.com/

History 1695. Founded by Count Franz Anton von Sporck, as a knightly organization of sportsmen, hunters and anglers. **Aims** Promote sportsmanline conduct in hunting and fishing; foster good fellowship among sportsmen worldwide; teach and preserve sound traditional hunting and fishing customs; encourage wildlife conservation and help protect endangered species from extinction; promote the concept of hunting and fishing as an intangible cultural heritage of humanity; endeavour to ensure that the economic benefits derived from sports hunting and fishing support the regions where these activities are carried out; enhance respect for responsible hunters and fishermen. **Structure** Grand Master; Grand Chapter.
Members Ordensbrothers and Squires (about 700), by invitation only. Membership countries not specified.
Chapters in 13 countries and territories:
Argentina, Belgium, Canada, Czechia, England, Italy, Luxembourg, Mexico, Netherlands, Portugal, Scotland, Spain, USA.
[2015/AA2227/v/**F**]

♦ International Order of Saint Luke the Physician (religious order)
♦ International Orders Research Society (inactive)

♦ **International Orem Society for Nursing Science and Scholarship (IOS)** **14420**

Treas 323 School of Nursing Bldg, 3525 Caroline Mall, St Louis MO 63104-1099, USA. T. +13149778938.
Co-Editor address not obtained.
URL: http://oreminternationalsociety.org/

History Incorporated in the State of Missouri (USA), 1991. **Aims** Promote Self-Care Deficit Nursing Theory (SCDNT) as developed by Dorothea E Orem (1914-2007). **Activities** World conference. **Events** *World Congress / Conference* Luxembourg (Luxembourg) 2012, *International conference on prevention and management of chronic conditions* Bangkok (Thailand) 2011, *World congress on self-care deficit nursing theory* Bangkok (Thailand) 2011, *Conference* Bangkok (Thailand) 2010, *Conference* Vancouver, BC (Canada) 2008. **Publications** *Self-Care and Dependent-Care Nursing* – official journal. [2016/XJ2740/**E**]

♦ International Organic Accreditation Service / see IOAS (#16001)

♦ **International Organic Inspectors Association (IOIA)** **14421**
Association des inspecteurs organiques internationals – Asociación de Inspectores Organicos Internationales

Exec Dir PO Box 6, Broadus MT 59317, USA. T. +14064362031. Fax +14064362031. E-mail: ioia@ioia.net.
URL: http://www.ioia.net/

History 1991, as *Independent Organic Inspectors Association (IOIA) – Association des inspecteurs organiques indépendants – Asociación de Inspectores Organicos Independientes.* Registered in the State of Minnesota (USA). **Aims** Train organic inspectors all over the world; address organic inspectors' issues and concerns; promote integrity and consistency in the organic certification process. **Structure** Board of Directors of 5 to 12 members. Executive Committee, including Chair, Vice-Chair, Secretary, Treasurer, 1 non-officer. Committees (5): Accreditation; Canadian; Financial; Latin American; Membership. **Finance** Members' dues. Training fees. **Activities** Conducts inspector training courses; develops inspector training curriculum, resource materials and policy proposals; assists regional inspector programmes; participates in organic trade fairs and conferences. **Publications** *The Inspectors' Report* (4 a year). *IFOAM/IOIA International Inspection Manual* (2000).
Members Inspector; Accredited Inspector; Supporting. Organizations in 5 countries:
Australia, Canada, Germany, Japan, USA.
Individuals in 14 countries and territories:
Canada, Chile, Costa Rica, Ecuador, Guatemala, India, Japan, Korea Rep, Mexico, Nepal, Peru, Sweden, Taiwan, USA.
[2018/XG6355/**F**]

♦ **International Organisation of Agro-Industrial Trade Unions** **14422**

Contact 42 Leninsky Prospekt, Moscow MOSKVA, Russia, 119119. T. +7959387735. Fax +7959306827.
URL: http://en.vkp.ru/

Members Trade unions in the CIS region (membership countries not specified). **IGO Relations** *Commonwealth of Independent States (CIS, #04341)*. **NGO Relations** Affiliated with: *General Confederation of Trade Unions (GCTU, #10108)*. [2020/XM2455/t/**D**]

♦ **International Organisation of Aquatic Physical Therapists (IOAPT)** . **14423**

Pres address not obtained. E-mail: ioapt.wcpt@gmail.com.
URL: https://world.physio/subgroups/aquatic

History Since 2019, a subgroup of *World Confederation for Physical Therapy (WCPT, #21293)*. **Aims** Advance aquatic physiotherapy worldwide.
Members Full in 20 countries and territories:
Argentina, Australia, Brazil, Chile, Costa Rica, Denmark, Georgia, Greece, Hong Kong, Ireland, Jordan, Malaysia, Mexico, Peru, Portugal, Puerto Rico, South Africa, Spain, UK, USA. [2023/AA3138/**E**]

♦ **International Organisation for Biological Control (IOBC)** **14424**
Organisation internationale de lutte biologique (OILB) – Organización Internacional de Lucha Biológica – Internationale Organisation für Biologische Bekämpfung

SG Wageningen Univ, Dept of Plant Sciences – Laboratory of Entomology, Droevendaalsesteeg 1, 6708 PB Wageningen, Netherlands. T. +31317484652. E-mail: secretary-general@iobc-global.org.
Pres address not obtained.
URL: http://www.iobc-global.org/

History 1956, France. Founded after ratification of statutes which had been drawn up by provisional committee appointed in 1953, by 12th General Assembly of *International Union of Biological Sciences (IUBS, #15760)*. First steps had been taken at International Entomological Congress, 1948, Stockholm (Sweden). Restructured, and present statutes adopted, 30-31 Mar 1971, Rome (Italy). Scientific Member of IUBS, acting as its Section of Biological Control. Former names and other names: *International Commission for Biological Control* – former; *Commission internationale de lutte biologique contre les ennemis des cultures (CILB)* – former; *International Organization for Biological Control of Noxious Animals and Plants (IOBC)* – former; *Organisation internationale de lutte biologique contre les animaux et les plantes nuisibles (OILB)* – former. Registration: Swiss Civil Code, Switzerland. **Aims** Promote development of biological control and its application in integrated control programmes, and international cooperation to these ends. **Structure** General Assembly (every 4 years); Executive Council; Executive Committee; Autonomous Regional Sections (6); Working Groups (9); Commissions (1). **Languages** English, French, German, Russian, Spanish. **Staff**

50.00 FTE, voluntary. **Finance** Sources: contributions; members' dues; revenue from activities/projects; sale of publications. Regional Sections request additional funds from members. Annual budget: 60,000 USD. **Activities** Advocacy/lobbying/activism; awareness raising; events/meetings; knowledge management/ information dissemination; publishing activities; research/documentation; training/education. **Events** *IOBC Global Working Group on Mass Rearing & Quality Assurance (MRQA)* Bologna (Italy) 2022, *Access and Benefit Sharing and Biological Control Genetic Resources* Helsinki (Finland) 2022, *Omnivorous Predators in Augmentative Biological Control – Blessing or Nightmare?* Helsinki (Finland) 2022, *Global Working Group Ecology of Aphidophaga Meeting* Lleida (Spain) 2022, *IOBC Global Cactus Working Group Meeting* Windhoek (Namibia) 2022. **Publications** *BioControl* (6 a year) – journal; *IOBC Newsletter* (2 a year). Scientific Bulletins; Working Group reports; books.
Members Individual; Institutional; Supporting; Honorary public and private institutions and individuals, including government departments, universities and academies. Members in 97 countries and territories:
Algeria, Argentina, Australia, Austria, Bahrain, Bangladesh, Barbados, Belgium, Benin, Bolivia, Bosnia-Herzegovina, Brazil, Bulgaria, Burkina Faso, Cameroon, Canada, Chile, China, Colombia, Congo Brazzaville, Congo DR, Costa Rica, Côte d'Ivoire, Croatia, Cuba, Cyprus, Czechia, Denmark, Egypt, Estonia, Ethiopia, Fiji, Finland, France, Gabon, Gambia, Germany, Ghana, Greece, Guatemala, Guinea, Hungary, India, Indonesia, Iran Islamic Rep, Ireland, Israel, Italy, Japan, Kenya, Korea Rep, Lebanon, Madagascar, Malaysia, Mexico, Moldova, Morocco, Netherlands, New Zealand, Nicaragua, Niger, Nigeria, Norway, Pakistan, Papua New Guinea, Paraguay, Peru, Philippines, Poland, Portugal, Romania, Russia, Saudi Arabia, Senegal, Serbia, Sierra Leone, Slovakia, Slovenia, South Africa, Spain, Sudan, Sweden, Switzerland, Syrian AR, Taiwan, Thailand, Tonga, Trinidad-Tobago, Tunisia, Türkiye, UK, Ukraine, United Arab Emirates, Uruguay, USA, Venezuela, Vietnam.
Consultative Status Consultative status granted from: *ECOSOC (#05331)* (Ros C); *FAO (#09260)* (Liaison Status). **NGO Relations** Consultative status with: *International Union of Biological Sciences (IUBS, #15760).*
[2022.10.25/XD2309/**B**]

♦ International Organisation of Communications Workers' Unions . . . 14425

Pres 42 Leninsky Prospekt, Moscow MOSKVA, Russia, 119119. T. +74959387782 – +74959388306. Fax +74959302286.
Members Trade unions in the CIS region (membership countries not specified). **NGO Relations** Affiliated with: *General Confederation of Trade Unions (GCTU, #10108).* [2014/XM2471/**D**]

♦ International Organisation for Cooperation in Evaluation (IOCE) . . . 14426

Organisation internationale de coopération en évaluation – Organización Internacional para la Cooperación en Evaluación

Sec Megram Consulting, 3 – 247 Barr St, Renfrew ON K7V 1J6, Canada. T. +16134329491. Fax +16134326840.
Coordinator 451 Rugh Ridge Way, Sevierville TN 37876-1393, USA.
URL: http://ioce.net/
History Launched at inaugural meeting, Mar 2003, Lima (Peru). Registered in accordance with Canadian law. **Aims** Provide leadership in evaluation worldwide by strengthening skills of evaluators, encouraging demand for evaluation, and supporting organizational capacity for Voluntary Organizations for Professional Evaluation (VOPEs); facilitate sharing ideas across the global evaluation community; champion the recognition of the value and contributions of evaluation to improve the lives of people. **Structure** General Meeting (annual); Executive Committee; Board of Trustees. Executive Coordinator; Co-Coordinator; Secretariat. **Languages** English. **Staff** 3.00 FTE, paid. **Finance** Members' dues. Also grants from bilateral and multilateral agencies. Annual budget: 681,395 USD. **Activities** Events/meetings; networking/liaising. **Publications** *IOCE Newsletter.*
Members Organizations: national (124); sub-national (9); regional (19); international (13). National associations in 101 countries:
Afghanistan, Albania, Argentina, Armenia, Australia, Austria, Azerbaijan, Bangladesh, Belgium, Benin, Bhutan, Bolivia, Bosnia-Herzegovina, Botswana, Brazil, Burkina Faso, Cambodia, Cameroon, Canada, Chile, Burkina Faso, China, Colombia, Comoros, Congo DR, Costa Rica, Côte d'Ivoire, Czechia, Denmark, Dominican Rep, Ecuador, Egypt, El Salvador, Ethiopia, Finland, France, Gabon, Georgia, Germany, Ghana, Guatemala, Guinea, Haiti, Honduras, Hungary, Iceland, India, Indonesia, Ireland, Israel, Italy, Japan, Jordan, Kenya, Kyrgyzstan, Luxembourg, Madagascar, Malaysia, Mauritania, Mexico, Morocco, Nepal, Netherlands, New Zealand, Nicaragua, Niger, Nigeria, North Macedonia, Norway, Pakistan, Palestine, Papua New Guinea, Paraguay, Peru, Philippines, Poland, Romania, Russia, Senegal, Serbia, Slovakia, Slovenia, Somalia, South Africa, Spain, Sri Lanka, Sweden, Switzerland, Tajikistan, Tanzania UR, Thailand, Tunisia, Türkiye, Uganda, UK, Ukraine, Uruguay, USA, Venezuela, Vietnam, Yemen, Zambia.
International organizations include 12 organizations listed in this Yearbook:
Active Learning Network for Accountability and Performance in Humanitarian Action (ALNAP, #00101); African Evaluation Association (AfrEA, #00304); Asia-Pacific Evaluation Association (APEA, #01894); Caribbean Evaluators International (CEI, #03498); Community of Evaluators in South Asia (COE, #04398); Environmental Evaluators Network (EEN, #05502); European Evaluation Society (EES, #07009); International Development Evaluation Association (IDEAS, #13158); Organisation internationale de la Francophonie (OIF, #17809); Red de Mujeres Latinoamericanas y del Caribe en Gestion de Organizaciones (Women in Management, #18723); Red de Seguimiento, Evaluación y Sistematización de América Latine y el Caribe (ReLAC); United Nations Evaluation Group (UNEG, #20560).
IGO Relations *UN Women (#20724); UNDP (#20292); UNICEF (#20332); United States Agency for International Development (USAID).* **NGO Relations** Partner of: *EvalPartners (#09208).* [2017/XJ6578/y/**C**]

♦ International Organisation for the Development of Fisheries and Aquaculture in Europe (EUROFISH) 14427

Dir HC Andersens Blvd 44-46, 1553 Copenhagen V, Denmark. T. +4533377755. Fax +4533377756. E-mail: info@eurofish.dk.
URL: http://www.eurofish.dk/
History 31 Oct 2001, Rome (Italy), within the framework of *FAO (#09260)*, having been launched in 1996 as the FAO EASTFISH project; agreement establishing *International Organisation for the Development of Fisheries in Eastern and Central Europe (EUROFISH)* adopted 23 May 2000, Copenhagen (Denmark). Took over activities of *EASTFISH (inactive)*, Jun 2003. Current title adopted 2018. **Aims** Contribute to sustainable development of the *fisheries* and *aquaculture* sector; promote trade of high quality, value-added fishery products; facilitate transfer of information and knowledge. **Structure** Governing Council. Coordinated by *FAO GLOBEFISH (#09261)*, Rome. *Administrative Tribunal of the International Labour Organization (ILO Tribunal, #00118)* is competent to settle disputes. **Activities** Organizes conferences, workshops, seminars, business-to-business meetings; implements projects in the fields of post-harvest fisheries, aquaculture, processing, and trade and marketing. **Events** *Conference on Nordic fisheries and globalisation* Aarhus (Denmark) 2005, *World conference on the shrimp industry and trade* Hong Kong (Hong Kong) 1992. **Publications** *EUROFISH Magazine* (6 a year).
Members Participating countries (13):
Albania, Croatia, Denmark, Estonia, Hungary, Italy, Latvia, Lithuania, Norway, Poland, Romania, Spain, Türkiye.
IGO Relations Cooperation agreement with FAO. A joint work within FAO GLOBEFISH, which also includes: *Centre for Marketing Information and Advisory Services for Fishery Products in the Arab Region (INFOSAMAK, #03772); INFOPECHE (#11191)* (Africa); *INFOPESCA (#11192)* (Latin America and the Caribbean); *INFOSA (#11203)* (Southern Africa); *'INFOYU'* (China); *Intergovernmental Organization for Marketing Information and Technical Advisory Services for Fishery Products in the Asia and Pacific Region (INFOFISH, #11497).* **NGO Relations** Member of: *European Aquaculture Technology and Innovation Platform (EATiP, #05910); International Institute of Fisheries Economics & Trade (IIFET, #13880).* [2019/XF6276/**F***]

♦ International Organisation of Employers (IOE) 14428

Organisation internationale des employeurs (OIE) – Organización Internacional de Empleadores (OIE)

SG Av Louis-Casaï 71, Cointrin, 1216 Geneva, Switzerland. T. +41229290000. Fax +41229290001. E-mail: ioe@ioe-emp.com.
URL: http://www.ioe-emp.org/
History Founded Mar 1920, London (UK) following 1st International Labour Conference, Oct 1919, Washington DC (USA), as *International Organization of Industrial Employers – Organisation internationale des employeurs industriels*. Present name adopted 16 Jun 1938, as the organization defending the interests of all employers, not merely industrial employers. Statutes most recently amended and adopted by General Council 2019. **Aims** Promote the economic, employment and social policy environment necessary to sustain and develop free enterprise and the market economy. **Structure** General Council (meets annually); Management Board; Secretariat. Meetings closed. **Languages** English, French, Spanish. **Staff** 28.00 FTE, paid. **Finance** Members' contributions. **Activities** Awareness raising; capacity building; events/meetings; guidance/assistance/ consulting; knowledge management/information dissemination; networking/liaising. **Events** *Meeting of the Presidents of the Iberoamerican Business Organizations* Geneva (Switzerland) 2019, *Meeting of the Presidents of the Iberoamerican Business Organizations* Antigua (Guatemala) 2018, *Meeting of the Presidents of the Iberoamerican Business Organizations* Madrid (Spain) 2017, *International Business and Human Rights Conference* Berlin (Germany) 2015, *TGAIS : The Global African Investment Summit* London (UK) 2015. **Publications** *IOE net* (6 a year).
Members National business employers' organizations (156) in 149 countries and territories:
Albania, Andorra, Angola, Antigua-Barbuda, Argentina, Armenia, Aruba, Australia, Austria, Azerbaijan, Bahamas, Bahrain, Bangladesh, Barbados, Belgium, Benin, Bermuda, Bolivia, Botswana, Brazil, Bulgaria, Burkina Faso, Cambodia, Cameroon, Canada, Chad, Chile, China, Colombia, Congo Brazzaville, Congo DR, Costa Rica, Côte d'Ivoire, Croatia, Cyprus, Czechia, Denmark, Djibouti, Dominica, Dominican Rep, Ecuador, Egypt, El Salvador, Estonia, Eswatini, Ethiopia, Fiji, Finland, France, Gabon, Gambia, Georgia, Germany, Ghana, Greece, Guatemala, Guinea, Haiti, Honduras, Hungary, Iceland, India, Indonesia, Iran Islamic Rep, Iraq, Ireland, Israel, Italy, Jamaica, Japan, Jordan, Kenya, Korea Rep, Kuwait, Kyrgyzstan, Latvia, Lebanon, Lesotho, Luxembourg, Madagascar, Malawi, Malaysia, Mali, Malta, Mauritania, Mauritius, Mexico, Moldova, Mongolia, Montenegro, Morocco, Mozambique, Myanmar, Namibia, Nepal, Netherlands, New Zealand, Nicaragua, Niger, Nigeria, North Macedonia, Norway, Oman, Pakistan, Panama, Papua New Guinea, Paraguay, Peru, Philippines, Poland, Portugal, Qatar, Romania, Russia, Rwanda, San Marino, Sao Tomé-Principe, Saudi Arabia, Senegal, Serbia, Singapore, Slovakia, Slovenia, South Africa, Spain, Sri Lanka, St Lucia, St Martin, Sudan, Suriname, Sweden, Switzerland, Taiwan, Tanzania UR, Thailand, Togo, Trinidad-Tobago, Tunisia, Türkiye, Uganda, Ukraine, United Arab Emirates, Uruguay, USA, Uzbekistan, Venezuela, Vietnam, Zambia, Zimbabwe.
Consultative Status Consultative status granted from: *ECOSOC (#05331)* (General); *ILO (#11123)* (General); *UNIDO (#20336); UNCTAD (#20285)* (General Category); *UNEP (#20299).*
NGO Relations Member of: *Conference of Non-Governmental Organizations in Consultative Relationship with the United Nations (CONGO, #04635); Fédération des Institutions Internationales établies à Genève (FIIG, #09599).* Working relations with:
- *ASEAN Confederation of Employers (ACE, #01158);*
- *Business Africa (BUSINESSAFRICA, #03377);*
- *Business and Industry Advisory Committee to the OECD (BIAC, #03385);*
- *BUSINESSEUROPE (#03381);*
- *Caribbean Employers' Confederation (CEC, #03495);*
- *Confederation of Asia-Pacific Employers (CAPE, #04513);*
- *Conseil européen de l'industrie chimique (CEFIC, #04687);*
- *European Construction Industry Federation (#06766);*
- *International Chamber of Commerce (ICC, #12534);*
- *International Chemical Employers Labour Relations Committee (LRC, #12541);*
- *International Hotel and Restaurant Association (IH&RA, #13813);*
- *International Labour and Employment Relations Association (ILERA, #13997);*
- *World Business Council for Sustainable Development (WBCSD, #21254);*
- *World Employment Confederation (WEC, #21376).* [2019.08.21/XB2322/**B**]

♦ International Organisation of Great Al-Fateh Births League (unconfirmed)

♦ International Organisation of Industrial and Service Cooperatives (CICOPA) 14429

Organisation internationale des coopératives industrielles et de services – Organización Internacional de las Cooperativas en la Industria y los Servicios

Gen Sec c/o European Cooperative House, Av Milcamps 105, 1030 Brussels, Belgium. T. +3225431033. E-mail: cicopa@cicopa.coop.
URL: http://www.cicopa.coop/
History 1932. Reconstituted in 1947. A specialized body of *International Co-operative Alliance (ICA, #12944).* Former names and other names: *Comité international des coopératives de production et de service industrielles et artisanales (CICOPA)* – former; *Organisation Internationale des Coopératives de Production Industrielles, d'Artisanat et de Services (CICOPA)* – former; *International Organization of Industrial, Artisanal and Service Producers' Cooperatives (CICOPA)* – former. **Aims** Promote and represent workers', social and producers' cooperatives at world level. **Structure** General Assembly; Board. Regional organizations: *CICOPA-Américas (#03925); Confédération européenne des coopératives de travail associé, des coopératives sociales et des entreprises sociales et participatives (CECOP, #04541).* **Languages** English, French, Spanish. **Finance** Sources: members' dues; sale of publications. **Activities** Events/meetings; politics/policy/regulatory; research and development; training/education. **Events** *Asia-Pacific Conference* Seoul (Korea Rep) 2021, *Annual Meeting* Cape Town (South Africa) 2013, *Conference on Cooperatives and Development* Cancún (Mexico) 2011, *General assembly / Annual Meeting* Geneva (Switzerland) 2009, *Annual Meeting* Singapore (Singapore) 2007. **Publications** *CICOPA Link; CICOPA Rules.* Standards; policy recomendations; action plans; reports.
Members Full: Representative organizations of worker, industrial, artisan, service or social cooperatives, at supra-national, national or sub-national level. Associate: organizations promoting or willing to promote such cooperatives. Full in 26 countries:
Argentina, Brazil, Bulgaria, Canada, China, Czechia, Denmark, Finland, France, Italy, Japan, Korea Rep, Malta, Mexico, Poland, Portugal, Puerto Rico, Romania, Slovakia, Spain, Tanzania UR, Uganda, UK, Uruguay, USA, Vietnam.
Associate in 31 countries and territories:
Australia, Belgium, Bulgaria, Cameroon, Canada, China, Colombia, Czechia, Denmark, France, India, Iran Islamic Rep, Italy, Japan, Korea Rep, Malta, Mexico, Paraguay, Philippines, Poland, Portugal, Puerto Rico, Romania, Spain, Sweden, Tanzania UR, Uganda, UK, Uruguay, USA, Vietnam.
Included in the above, 1 organization listed in this Yearbook:
European Research and Development Service for the Social Economy (DIESIS, #08365).
IGO Relations *European Commission (EC, #06633); ILO (#11123); UNDP (#20292); UNIDO (#20336);* think tanks; research institutes. [2023.02.24/XE4541/t/**E**]

♦ International Organisation for Knowledge Economy and Enterprise Development (internationally oriented national body)

♦ International Organisation for the Least Developed Countries / see International Organisation for Least Developed Countries (#14430)

♦ International Organisation for Least Developed Countries (IOLDCs) . 14430

Organisation Internationale pour les Pays les Moins Avancés (OIPMAs)

Pres Maison International de l'Environnement (MIE 2), Chemin de Balexert 7-9, Châtelaine, 1219 Geneva, Switzerland. T. +41223030502. E-mail: info@ioldcs.org – info@oipma.org.
URL: http://ioldcs.org/
History 1996, Geneva (Switzerland). Former names and other names: *International Organisation for the Least Developed Countries* – full title; *Organisation Internationale pour les Pays les Moins Avancés* – full title. **Aims** Defend and promote human *rights* and development in least developed countries, as well as conflict prevention and *peace-building.* **Activities** Advocacy/lobbying/activism; awareness raising; events/meetings; networking/ liaising; research/documentation; training/education. Afghanistan, South Sudan, Sudan, the horn of Africa and the Sahel region. **Publications** *IOLDCs Newsletter.* **Consultative Status** Consultative status granted from: *ECOSOC (#05331)* (Special). [2022.07.15/XJ9933/**C**]

♦ International Organisation of Metalworkers' Unions 14431

Pres 42 Leninsky Prospekt, Moscow MOSKVA, Russia, 119119. T. +74959388710. Fax +74959388158.
Vice-Pres address not obtained.
URL: http://en.vkp.ru/
Languages Russian. **Publications** Information bulletin (12 a year) in Russian.
Members Trade unions in 8 countries:
Armenia, Azerbaijan, Belarus, Kazakhstan, Moldova, Russia, Ukraine, Uzbekistan. [2015.11.17/XM2465/**D**]

♦ International Organisation of Pension Supervisors (IOPS) 14432

SG OECD, 2 rue André Pascal, 75775 Paris CEDEX 16, France. T. +33145249127.
Pres Australian Prudential Regulation Authority, GPO Box 9836, Sydney NSW 2001, Australia. T. +61292103000. Fax +61292103411.
URL: http://www.iopsweb.org/

History 12 Jul 2004, Paris (France). Took over pensions supervision work of *International Network of Pensions Regulators and Supervisors (INPRS, inactive)*, 2005. **Aims** Serve as the standard-setting body on pension supervisory matters and regulating issues related to pension supervision, taking into account the variety of different private pension systems; promote international cooperation on pension supervision and facilitating contact between pension supervisors and other relevant parties, including policy makers, researchers and the private sector; provide a worldwide forum for policy dialogue and information exchange on pension supervision; participate in the work of relevant international bodies in the field, including joint activities to improve statistical collection and analysis; promote, conduct and facilitate the distribution and communication of research, and the collecting of information in cooperation with relevant international bodies. **Structure** General Meeting (annual); Executive Committee; Technical Committee. **Languages** English. **Staff** 2.50 FTE, paid. **Finance** Sources: members' dues. Annual budget: 500,000 EUR (2022). **Activities** Events/meetings; knowledge management/information dissemination; politics/policy/regulatory; research/documentation; standards/guidelines; training/education. **Events** *Global Forum on Private Pensions* Bratislava (Slovakia) 2022, *Workshop on Risk-Based Supervision* Paris (France) 2022, *Workshop on the Implementation of IOPS Supervisory ESG Guidelines and Sustainability Disclosure* 2021, *Workshop on Risk-Based Supervision* Paris (France) 2021, *Annual General Meeting* 2020. **Publications** *IOPS Working Paper*. **Members** Full; Observer. Individuals (90) in 78 countries and territories. Membership countries not specified. **IGO Relations** Member of (1): *International Bank for Reconstruction and Development (IBRD, #12317)* (World Bank). Cooperates with (2): *European Insurance and Occupational Pensions Authority (EIOPA, #07578)*; *OECD (#17693)*. **NGO Relations** Cooperates with (5): *Asociación Internacional de Organismos de Supervisión de Fondos de Pensiones (AIOS, #02167)*; *Insurance Europe (#11362)*; *International Actuarial Association (IAA, #11586)*; *International Association of Insurance Supervisors (IAIS, #11966)*; *International Social Security Association (ISSA, #14885)*. [2022.10.19/XJ3104/**D**]

♦ International Organisation of Physical Therapists in Paediatrics (IOPTP) 14433

Pres 1549 James Hill Way, Hoover AL 35226, USA. E-mail: president.ioptp@gmail.com.
URL: https://www.ioptp.org/

History 2 Jun 2007, Vancouver, BC (Canada). A subgroup of *World Confederation for Physical Therapy (WCPT, #21293)*. Former names and other names: *International Organisation of Physiotherapists in Paediatrics* – alias. **Aims** Foster cooperation between physical therapists practising in paediatrics throughout the world; encourage improved standards and consistency of practice in paediatrics care by physical therapists. **Structure** Board of Directors; Committees. **Languages** English. **Staff** Voluntary. **Finance** Sources: members' dues. **Activities** Knowledge management/information dissemination; research/documentation. **Events** *World Physiotherapy Congress* Dubai (United Arab Emirates) 2023, *World Physiotherapy Congress* Geneva (Switzerland) 2019, *Meeting* Singapore (Singapore) 2015, *Meeting* Anaheim, CA (USA) 2013, *Meeting* Amsterdam (Netherlands) 2011. **Publications** *IOPTP Newsletter* (2 a year).
Members Individuals (about 15,000 in 32 countries and territories:
Australia, Austria, Belgium, Canada, Colombia, Costa Rica, Cyprus, Denmark, Ethiopia, Finland, Germany, Ghana, Greece, Hong Kong, Ireland, Israel, Italy, Japan, Korea Rep, Netherlands, New Zealand, Nigeria, Norway, Portugal, Saudi Arabia, South Africa, Spain, Sweden, Switzerland, Taiwan, UK, USA. [2022.10.25/XM3781/**E**]

- ♦ International Organisation of Physiotherapists in Paediatrics / see International Organisation of Physical Therapists in Paediatrics (#14433)
- ♦ International Organisation to Preserve Human Rights (unconfirmed)
- ♦ International Organisation of Scenographers, Theatre Architects and Technicians (#17811)
- ♦ International Organisation of Social Tourism / see International Social Tourism Organisation (#14889)

♦ International Organisation of Trade Unions of Educational and Scientific Workers (IOTU Education and Science) 14434

Pres 42 Leninsky Prospekt, Moscow MOSKVA, Russia, 119119. T. +74959388777. Fax +74959306815. E-mail: mopobraz@yandex.ru.

Members Trade unions in the CIS region (membership countries not specified). **NGO Relations** Affiliated with: *General Confederation of Trade Unions (GCTU, #10108)*. [2014/XM2468/t/**D**]

♦ International Organisation of Vine and Wine (OIV) 14435

Organisation Internationale de la Vigne et du Vin (OIV)

Dir-Gen 35 rue de Monceau, 75008 Paris, France. T. +33144948080 – +33144948081. Fax +33142669063. E-mail: contact@oiv.int – dgeneral@oiv.int – secretariat@oiv.int.
Sec address not obtained.
URL: https://oiv.int/

History 29 Nov 1924, Paris (France). Ratified by French Law of 15 Apr 1927. New International Agreement, signed 3 Apr 2001, entered into force 1 Jan 2004. Former names and other names: *International Wine Office* – former (1924 to 1958); *Office international du vin* – former (1924 to 1958); *International Vine and Wine Office* – former (4 Sep 1958 to 2004); *Office international de la vigne et du vin (OIV)* – former (4 Sep 1958 to 2004). **Aims** Inform members of measures whereby the concerns of producers, consumers and other players in the vine and wine products sector may be taken into consideration; assist other international organizations, both intergovernmental and non-governmental, especially those which carry out standardization activities; contribute to international harmonization of existing practices and standards, as necessary, to the preparation of new international standards in order to improve the conditions for producing and marketing vine and wine products and to help ensure that the interests of consumers are taken into account. **Structure** General Assembly (annual); Executive Committee; Scientific and Technical Committee; Commissions (4); Secretariat, headed by Director General. Conferences open; other meetings closed. **Languages** English, French, German, Italian, Russian, Spanish. **Staff** 15.00 FTE, paid. **Finance** Sources: contributions of member/participating states; sale of publications. **Activities** Awards/prizes/competitions; events/meetings; knowledge management/information dissemination; research and development; standards/guidelines. **Events** *World Congress* Samarkand (Uzbekistan) 2021, *World Congress* Santiago (Chile) 2020, *World Congress* Geneva (Switzerland) 2019, *World Congress* Punta del Este (Uruguay) 2018, *World Congress* Sofia (Bulgaria) 2017. **Publications** *World Vitivinicultural Statistics* (annual) in English, French, German, Italian, Spanish; *Proceedings of the World Congress of Vine and Wine*. *Code of Descriptive Characteristics of Vitis Varieties and Species* in English, French, German, Italian, Spanish; *Compendium of International Methods of Analysis of Wine and Musts* in English, French – 2 vols; *Description of Wine and Grape Varieties throughout the World* in English, French, German, Spanish; *International Code of Oenological Practices* in English, French, Italian, Spanish; *International List of Vine Varieties and their Synonyms* in English, French, German, Italian, Spanish; *International Oenological Codex* in English, French, Italian, Spanish.
Members Governments that have signed the International Agreement as of Oct 2016 (48):
Algeria, Argentina, Armenia, Australia, Austria, Azerbaijan, Belgium, Bosnia-Herzegovina, Brazil, Bulgaria, Chile, Croatia, Cyprus, Czechia, France, Georgia, Germany, Greece, Hungary, India, Israel, Italy, Lebanon, Luxembourg, Malta, Mexico, Moldova, Montenegro, Morocco, Netherlands, New Zealand, North Macedonia, Norway, Peru, Portugal, Romania, Russia, Serbia, Slovakia, Slovenia, South Africa, Spain, Sweden, Switzerland, Türkiye, UK, Uruguay, Uzbekistan.
International and Regional Organization Observers (15):
Amorim Academy; *Assembly of European Wine Regions (AREV, #02317)*; *Association de la sommellerie internationale (ASI)*; *Association Universitaire Internationale du Vin et des Produits de la Vigne (AUIV)*; *Centro di Ricerche, Studi e Valorizzazione per la Viticoltura Montana (CERVIM, #03819)*; *European Union (EU, #08967)*; *FIVS (#09789)*; Great Wine Capitals (The Great Wine Capitals is a network of major global cities); *International Wine Law Association (IWLA, #15891)*; Ningxia Hui (China); *Oenological Products and Practices (OEnoppia, #17695)*; *Union internationale des oenologues (UIOE, #20432)*; *Wine in Moderation (WIM, #20967)*; *World Federation of Major International Wine and Spirits Competitions (VinoFed, #21452)*; Yantad' Province (China). **IGO Relations** Relationship agreement with: *FAO (#09260)*. Permanent observer status with: *World Intellectual Property Organization (WIPO, #21593)*. Participates as observer in the activities of: *Codex Alimentarius Commission (CAC, #04081)*. **NGO Relations** Observer status with (1): *African Law Foundation (AFRILAW)*. In liaison with technical committees of: *Comité européen de normalisation (CEN, #04162)*; *International Organization for Standardization (ISO, #14473)*. [2021.10.26/XC2803/y/**C***]

- ♦ International Organization for the Advancement of Africa Policy (unconfirmed)
- ♦ International Organization for the Advancement of High Pressure Research / see International Association for the Advancement of High Pressure Science and Technology (#11686)
- ♦ International Organization of Advertisement Administrations (inactive)
- ♦ International Organization Against Modern Slavery (unconfirmed)

♦ International Organization Against Trachoma (IOAT) 14436

Organisation internationale pour la lutte contre le trachome – Organización Internacional contra el Tracoma

Pres Univ Paris-Val-de-Marne, Centre Hosp Intercommunal – Clinique Ophtalmologique de Créteil, 40 avenue Verdun, 94010 Créteil, France. T. +33145175225. Fax +33145175227.

History 1929, Amsterdam (Netherlands), at 13th International Ophthalmological Congress. Statutes adopted 1930, Geneva (Switzerland). Formerly: *International Organization for the Campaign Against Trachoma – Organisation internationale pour la lutte contre le trachoma*. Previously also known as *International Organization for the Prevention of Trachoma* and *International League for the Campaign Against Trachoma*. In French also referred to as *Ligue contre le trachome (LCT)*. **Aims** Promote research, diagnosis and prevention of trachoma; provide a scientific basis for the fight against trachoma by circulating information on current trachoma research and supplying the latest information on etiology, diagnosis, epidemiology, prevention and treatment; facilitate adoption of sanitary and other regulations aimed at implementing the fight against trachoma; promote the SAFE Strategy (developed by WHO) by promoting individual and environmental changes. **Structure** General Assembly; Management Board. Organizes: Scientific Conferences annually in conjunction with: *International Congress of Ophthalmology*. **Languages** English, French. **Staff** 2.50 FTE, paid. Voluntary. **Finance** Sources: donations. **Activities** Events/meetings. **Events** *Annual General Assembly* Paris (France) 2013, *Annual General Assembly / Annual General Assembly and Scientific Meeting* Paris (France) 2012, *Annual General Assembly and Scientific Meeting* Paris (France) 2011, *Biennial scientific conference* Berlin (Germany) 2010, *Annual meeting* Paris (France) 2010. **Publications** *International Review of Trachoma* (annual) in English, French. Annual scientific or research report on trachoma and/or tropical eye diseases.
Members National ophthalmological societies; individuals. Members in 112 countries and territories:
Afghanistan, Algeria, Argentina, Australia, Austria, Belgium, Benin, Bolivia, Bosnia-Herzegovina, Botswana, Brazil, Bulgaria, Burkina Faso, Cambodia, Cameroon, Canada, Central African Rep, Chad, Chile, China, Colombia, Comoros, Congo Brazzaville, Congo DR, Côte d'Ivoire, Croatia, Czechia, Denmark, Djibouti, Egypt, Equatorial Guinea, Ethiopia, Finland, France, Gabon, Gambia, Germany, Ghana, Greece, Guatemala, Guinea, Guinea-Bissau, Hong Kong, India, Indonesia, Iran Islamic Rep, Ireland, Israel, Italy, Japan, Jordan, Kazakhstan, Kenya, Kuwait, Laos, Lebanon, Libya, Luxembourg, Madagascar, Malawi, Malaysia, Mali, Malta, Mauritania, Mexico, Moldova, Morocco, Mozambique, Myanmar, Namibia, Nepal, Netherlands, New Caledonia, Niger, Nigeria, North Macedonia, Oman, Pakistan, Panama, Paraguay, Peru, Philippines, Poland, Portugal, Réunion, Romania, Russia, Saudi Arabia, Senegal, Serbia, Singapore, Slovakia, Solomon Is, South Africa, Spain, Sudan, Sweden, Switzerland, Syrian AR, Tanzania UR, Thailand, Togo, Tunisia, Türkiye, UK, Ukraine, Uruguay, USA, Vietnam, Yemen, Zambia, Zimbabwe.
Consultative Status Consultative status granted from: *ECOSOC (#05331)* (Ros C). **NGO Relations** Official section of: *International Council of Ophthalmology (ICO, #13057)*. [2017.03.08/XB2308/**B**]

- ♦ International Organization for Aid to Revolutionaries (inactive)

♦ International Organization of Aluminium Aerosol Container Manufacturers (AEROBAL) 14437

Internationale Vereinigung der Hersteller von Aluminium-Aerosoldosen

Sec Haus der Metalle, 2nd floor – rooms 213/214, Am Bonneshof 5, 40474 Düsseldorf, Germany. T. +492114796144. Fax +492114796408 – +49211479625144. E-mail: aerobal@aluinfo.de.
URL: http://www.aerobal.org/

History 1976, as *European Association of Aluminium Aerosol Container Manufacturers – Association européenne des fabricants de boîtes en aluminium pour aérosol (AEROBAL) – Europäische Vereinigung der Hersteller von Aluminium-Aerosoldosen*. Current title adopted, 1 Jan 2006. **Aims** Enter into an open dialogue with public and other stakeholders so as to promote aluminium as *packaging* material and the products of its members. **Languages** English. **Staff** 3.00 FTE, paid. **Activities** Events/meetings; awards/prizes/competitions. **Events** *Meeting* Bangkok (Thailand) 2012, *Meeting* Monte Carlo (Monaco) 2011, *Meeting* Zhongshan (China) 2010, *Meeting* Istanbul (Turkey) 2009, *Meeting* New York, NY (USA) 2008.
Members Aluminium aerosol can producers (25) in 19 countries:
Argentina, Canada, China, Czechia, Finland, France, Germany, Italy, Mexico, Netherlands, Russia, Slovenia, South Africa, Spain, Switzerland, Thailand, Türkiye, UK, USA.
IGO Relations Recognized by: *European Commission (EC, #06633)*. **NGO Relations** In liaison with technical committees of: *International Organization for Standardization (ISO, #14473)*. [2018.06.22/XD2598/**D**]

- ♦ International Organization for Animal Protection (#17810)
- ♦ International Organization for Biological Control of Noxious Animals and Plants / see International Organisation for Biological Control (#14424)

♦ International Organization for Biological Crystallization (IOBCr) ... 14438

Sec Institut für Biochemie, Universität zu Lübeck, Ratzeburger Allee 160, 23538 Lübeck, Germany. T. +494515004065.
URL: http://www.iobcr.org/index.html

History Founded 28 Mar 2002, Jena (Germany), during 9th International Conference on the Crystallization of Biological Macromolecules. **Aims** Promote research and practical applications in biological crystallization. **Structure** Council; Executive Committee, including 3 officers. **Activities** Events/meetings; training/education. **Events** *International Conference on the Crystallization of Biological Macromolecules* Prague (Czechia) 2016, *International Conference on the Crystallization of Biological Macromolecules / Biennial Conference* Hamburg (Germany) 2014, *International Conference on the Crystallization of Biological Macromolecules* Huntsville, TX (USA) 2012, *International conference on the crystallization of biological macromolecules / Biennial Conference* Dublin (Ireland) 2010, *International conference on the crystallization of biomacromolecules / Biennial Conference* Cancún (Mexico) 2008. [2022/XM2258/**D**]

- ♦ International Organization of Biosystematics / see International Organization of Plant Biosystematists (#14463)
- ♦ International Organization for Biotechnology and Bioengineering (no recent information)
- ♦ International Organization for the Campaign Against Trachoma / see International Organization Against Trachoma (#14436)
- ♦ International Organization Center of Academic Research (internationally oriented national body)

♦ International Organization of Ceremonial and Protocol 14439

Organización Internacional de Ceremonial Protocolo (OICP)

Pres address not obtained. E-mail: oicppresidencia@gmail.com.

History 14 Nov 2001. **Structure** Assembly. Board of Directors, comprising President, 5 Vice Presidents and Secretary-General. **Events** *Congress* Granada (Spain) 2022, *Ordinary General Assembly* 2020, *Congress* Santo Domingo (Dominican Rep) 2018, *Congress* Valladolid (Spain) 2017, *Congress* Manaus (Brazil) 2016.
Members Associations in 8 countries:
Argentina, Brazil, Hungary, Paraguay, Portugal, Romania, Spain, Venezuela. [2016/XJ0966/**C**]

♦ International Organization for Chemical Sciences in Development (IOCD) 14440

Organisation internationale des sciences chimiques pour le développement – Organización Internacional de las Ciencias Quimicas para el Desarrollo

Exec Dir Dept de Chimie, Univ of Namur, Rue de Bruxelles 61, 5000 Namur, Belgium. T. +32474318181.
URL: http://www.iocd.org/

History 1 Jul 1981, Paris (France), at constitutive meeting held under the auspices of *UNESCO (#20322)*, following consultative meeting, Sep 1979, Tenerife (Spain) and a series of initiatives by different scientists. Also referred to in English as *International Organization for Chemistry in Development*. Registered in accordance with Belgian law, 29 Mar 1983. **Aims** Promote chemical sciences for sustainable, equitable human development and economic growth, especially in low- and middle-income countries (LMICs); collaborate with chemists in LMICs to help them build capacity in chemical sciences and serve their communities in practical ways, while advancing their own careers with originality, entrepreneurship and practicality. **Structure** General Assembly; Executive Committee; US Affiliate 'Organization for Chemical Sciences in Development (OCDI)', led by Board; Scientific and Technical Advisory Committee (STAC); Working Groups (4); Secretariat,

based in Namur (Belgium), led by Executive Director. **Languages** English, French, Spanish. **Staff** 1.00 FTE, paid. Voluntary. **Finance** Grants from individual donors, agencies such as: *UNESCO (#20322)*; US National Academy of Sciences; American Chemical Society; *International Union of Pure and Applied Chemistry (IUPAC, #15809)*; foundations, including Aventis and *MacArthur Foundation*; Royal Society of Chemistry (Belgium); Gesellschaft Deutscher Chemiker. **Activities** Capacity building; events/meetings; knowledge management/information dissemination; projects/programmes; training/education. **Events** *Symposium* Namur (Belgium) 2014, *Symposium* Viña del Mar (Chile) 2009, *International symposium on natural products / Symposium* Kasane (Botswana) 2008, *International symposium on biology, chemistry, pharmacology and clinical studies of asian plants / Symposium* Surabaya (Indonesia) 2007, *Joint symposium on chemistry, biological and pharmacological properties of medicinal plants from the Americas* São Pedro (Brazil) 2004. **Publications** Articles; papers; reports; brochures.
Members Individuals (10) in 9 countries:
Belgium, Canada, China, France, Germany, India, Mexico, UK, USA.
Consultative Status Consultative status granted from: *UNESCO (#20322)* (Consultative Status). **NGO Relations** Member of (1): *International Foundation for Science (IFS, #13677)*. Instrumental in setting up (1): *Network for Analytical and Bioassay Services in Africa (NABSA, no recent information)*. Affiliated with: *International Union of Pure and Applied Chemistry (IUPAC, #15809)*. [2019.12.23/XD5099/v/**C**]

♦ International Organization for Chemistry in Development / see International Organization for Chemical Sciences in Development (#14440)
♦ International Organization for Christian Cooperation (internationally oriented national body)

♦ International Organization of Citrus Virologists (IOCV) 14441

Union internationale des virologistes des agrumes
Sec UC-R Plant Pathology, 900 University Ave, Riverside CA 92521, USA. T. +19518271012.
Chair address not obtained.
URL: http://iocv.org/
History Proposed during International Conference, 18 Nov 1957, Riverside CA (USA). **Aims** Promote cooperative international study of citrus diseases caused by virus and other graft-transmissable agents; disseminate knowledge concerning their identity and relationships, effects and importance, means of spread, control and/or prevent; encourage personal contacts and information exchange; develop mutual understanding among individuals, institutions and agencies concerned with citrus production and encourage their participation in and support of research on graft-transmissible diseases of citrus. **Structure** Advisory Council, comprising Chairperson, Chairperson-elect, Secretary, Treasurer and 5 members. **Languages** English. **Staff** Voluntary. **Finance** Sources: members' dues. Registration fees. **Events** *Conference* Riverside, CA (USA) 2019, *Conference* Chongqing (China) 2016, *Conference* South Africa 2013, *Conference* Brazil 2010, *Conference* Adana (Turkey) 2007. **Publications** *Bibliography on Citrus Viruses* (irregular); *IOCV Newsletter*. *FAO/IOCV Handbook of Detection of Graft Transmissable Pathogens of Citrus* (1991); *Description and Illustration of Graft-transmissible Diseases of Citrus: an IOCV Presentation*. Conference proceedings; slide sets and descriptions of virus and virus-like diseases (4 vols).
Members Individuals in 33 countries and territories:
Argentina, Australia, Belize, Brazil, Chile, Costa Rica, Egypt, Eswatini, France, Germany, Israel, Italy, Japan, Mexico, Mozambique, New Zealand, Oman, Pakistan, Paraguay, Peru, Philippines, Portugal, Saudi Arabia, South Africa, Spain, Taiwan, Thailand, Trinidad-Tobago, Türkiye, United Arab Emirates, Uruguay, USA, Venezuela.
IGO Relations *FAO (#09260)*. [2020/XD2320/v/**C**]

♦ International Organization for Collaborative Outcome Management (IOCOM) 14442

SG 10 Lillico Drive, Ottawa ON K1V 0G5, Canada.
Pres address not obtained.
URL: http://www.iocomsa.org/
History Original title: *International Organization for Collaborative Outcome Management South Asia (IOC-OMSA)*. Current title adopted Sep 2011. **Aims** Invite professionals and academics to create a forum for the exchange of useful and high quality theories, *methodologies* and effective practice in outcome management and development. **Structure** Board of Management. **Languages** English. **Staff** Voluntary. **Finance** Sources: donations; grants. **Activities** Events/meetings; training/education. **Publications** *IOCOM Digest and Dialogue (IDD)* (4 a year) – electronic journal. **Members** Full (over 760) in 83 countries. Membership countries not specified. **IGO Relations** None. **NGO Relations** Ad hoc collaborations with various NGOs. [2017.10.29/XJ8541/**C**]

♦ International Organization for Collaborative Outcome Management South Asia / see International Organization for Collaborative Outcome Management (#14442)
♦ International Organization for Commerce (inactive)
♦ International Organization on Computer Evidence (inactive)
♦ International Organization for Consultation-Liaison Psychiatry (inactive)
♦ International Organization of Consumers Unions / see Consumers International (#04773)
♦ International Organization for Cooperation in Health Care / see Medicus Mundi International – Network Health for All (#16636)
♦ International Organization for Cooperation in Small Volume Chemicals Production (inactive)

♦ International Organization for Crystal Growth (IOCG) 14443

Sec Inst of High Pressure Physics PAS, Sokolowska 29/37, 01-142 Warsaw, Poland. T. +48228880244. Fax +48226324218. E-mail: stach@unipress.waw.pl.
Pres Research Inst for Applied Mechanics, Kyushu Univ, 6-1 Kasuga-koen, Kasuga, Fukuoka, 816-8580 Japan. T. +81925837741. Fax +81925837743.
URL: http://www.iocg.org/
History 1970, Boston, MA (USA). Former names and other names: *International Association for Crystal Growth* – former. **Languages** English. **Events** *International Conference on Crystal Growth and Epitaxy (ICCGE)* Naples (Italy) 2023, *International Conference on Crystal Growth and Epitaxy (ICCGE)* Naples (Italy) 2022, *International Conference on Crystal Growth and Epitaxy* Keystone, CO (USA) 2019, *International Triennial Conference on Crystal Growth and Epitaxy* Nagoya (Japan) 2016, *International triennial conference on crystal growth and epitaxy* Beijing (China) 2010.
Members Associations in 29 countries and territories:
Argentina, Australia, Austria, Belgium, Brazil, Bulgaria, Canada, Czechia, Denmark, Finland, France, Germany, India, Israel, Italy, Japan, Korea Rep, Mexico, Netherlands, New Zealand, Norway, Poland, Puerto Rico, Singapore, South Africa, Switzerland, Taiwan, UK, USA.
Individuals in 8 countries and territories:
China, Georgia, Hong Kong, Ireland, Portugal, Romania, Russia, Spain.
NGO Relations Scientific Associate of: *International Union of Crystallography (IUCr, #15768)*. Associated organization of: *International Union of Pure and Applied Chemistry (IUPAC, #15809)*. Joint activities with: *International Union of Pure and Applied Physics (IUPAP, #15810)*. [2021/XD9377/**C**]

♦ International Organization for Cultivating Human Spirit / see Organization for Industrial, Spiritual and Cultural Advancement International (#17872)
♦ International Organization for Cultural Exchanges (inactive)

♦ International Organization Development Association (IODA) 14444

Association internationale pour le développement organisationnel – Internationale Gesellschaft für Organisationsentwicklung – Asociación Internacional para el Desarrollo Organizacional
Pres address not obtained. E-mail: info@iodanet.org.
URL: http://www.iodanet.org/
History 1986. Founded by a group of committed OD professionals from over 13 countries who saw a need for a network that was truly global in nature, outlook and values. They helped establish an inclusive, decentralized and participative association which is committed to the expansion of OD practices in countries around the globe. **Aims** Support and strengthen the work and vision of organization development practitioners through shared learning, networking and common experience. **Structure** Executive Committee; International Volunteering Teams. **Languages** English. **Staff** 1.00 FTE, paid. **Finance** Sources: members' dues. **Activities** Events/meetings. **Events** *Organization Development World Summit* Bangkok (Thailand) 2021, *Annual World Conference* Viña del Mar (Chile) 2019, *Annual World Conference* Istanbul (Turkey) 2018, *Annual World Conference* Stellenbosch (South Africa) 2017, *Annual World Conference* Mysore (India) 2016. **Publications** *IODA Listens* – newsletter.

Members in 41 countries:
Austria, Belgium, Benin, Burkina Faso, Canada, Chile, Colombia, Czechia, Denmark, Finland, France, Germany, Ghana, Hungary, India, Ireland, Israel, Italy, Kenya, Mali, Mexico, Mozambique, Myanmar, Netherlands, Norway, Peru, Philippines, Poland, Russia, Senegal, Singapore, South Africa, Spain, Sweden, Switzerland, Thailand, Uganda, UK, USA, Venezuela, Zimbabwe. [2020.05.18/XF4584/**F**]

♦ International Organization for the Development of Freedom of Education / see International Organization for the Right to Education and Freedom of Education (#14468)
♦ International Organization for Economic and Scientific Technical Cooperation for Electrical Engineering (inactive)
♦ International Organization for Educational Development (internationally oriented national body)

♦ International Organization for the Elimination of All Forms of Racial Discrimination (EAFORD) 14445

Organisation internationale pour l'élimination de toute forme de discrimination raciale
Secretariat Rue Lissignol 5, 1201 Geneva, Switzerland. T. +41227886233. Fax +41227886245. E-mail: info@eaford.org.
URL: http://eaford.org/
History 1976, Tripoli (Libyan AJ), at international symposium. International Secretariat established in London (UK), 1979, transferred to Geneva (Switzerland), 1986, when also set up EAFORD USA to coordinate with UN activities there. Registered in the District of Columbia (USA). **Aims** Advance the work of the United Nations, which seeks to eliminate racism and racial discrimination as an essential step toward achieving world order and peace. **Structure** Executive Council; Consultative Council; International Secretariat in Geneva (Switzerland); Office in Washington DC (USA). **Finance** Sources: donations. **Activities** Awards/prizes/competitions; events/meetings; knowledge management/information dissemination; research/documentation. **Publications** *Without Prejudice* (2 a year) – journal. Books; analytical papers; videos; reports. Information Services: Provides information to and disseminates information produced by NGOs and UN bodies; surveys current research and publications; monitors and acquires available works; acts as a repository of information in the field. **Members** Not a membership organization. **Consultative Status** Consultative status granted from: *African Commission on Human and Peoples' Rights (ACHPR, #00255)* (Observer); *ECOSOC (#05331)* (Special). **NGO Relations** Observer to: *International Committee of the Red Cross (ICRC, #12799)*; *International Federation of Red Cross and Red Crescent Societies (#13526)*; *International Red Cross and Red Crescent Movement (#14707)*. Member of: Committee of NGOs on the Middle East; *Conference of Non-Governmental Organizations in Consultative Relationship with the United Nations (CONGO, #04635)* and its *Committee of NGOs on Human Rights, Geneva (#04275)*, Sub-Committee on Racism, Racial Discrimination, Apartheid and Decolonization; Coordinating Committee of NGOs on the Question of Palestine; NGO Working Group on Human Rights Education and Learning; *UNITED for Intercultural Action – European Network Against Nationalism, Racism, Fascism and in Support of Migrants and Refugees (UNITED, #20511)*; *World Against Racism Network (WARN)*. [2018.09.05/XC6735/**C**]

♦ International Organization of Emergency Medical Technicians (unconfirmed)
♦ International Organization of Experts (#17808)
♦ International Organization of Financial Regulators (unconfirmed)

♦ International Organization of the Flavor Industry (IOFI) 14446

Operations Office Av des Arts 6, 1210 Brussels, Belgium. T. +3222142050. Fax +3222142069. E-mail: secretariat@iofi.org.
Headquarters Rue de la Fontaine 15, 1204 Geneva, Switzerland.
Scientific Office 1101 17th St NW, Ste 700, Washington DC 20036, USA.
URL: http://www.iofi.org/
History 1969, Geneva (Switzerland). Former names and other names: *Organisation internationale de l'industrie des arômes alimentaires* – former. Registration: Switzerland; EU Transparency Register, No/ID: 730122140412-58, Start date: 23 Nov 2020. **Aims** Study scientific data regarding flavouring materials, particularly their effect on human health; study flavour regulations worldwide; disseminate timely information to membership on matters of relevance to the industry. **Structure** General Assembly (annual); Board of Directors; Working Groups; Committees. **Languages** English. **Staff** 5.00 FTE, paid. **Finance** Sources: members' dues. **Events** *International congress on flavours, fragrances and essential oils* London (UK) 1998, *International congress on flavours, fragrances and essential oils* Istanbul (Turkey) 1995, *International congress on flavours, fragrances and essential oils* Vienna (Austria) 1992, *International congress on flavours, fragrances and essential oils* Delhi (India) 1989. **Publications** Code of Practice.
Members Ordinary; Corresponding; Regional Associations. Members in 29 countries:
Argentina, Australia, Austria, Belgium, Brazil, Canada, Chile, China, Colombia, Denmark, France, Germany, Indonesia, Italy, Japan, Korea Rep, Mexico, Netherlands, New Zealand, Peru, Singapore, South Africa, Spain, Sweden, Switzerland, Thailand, Türkiye, UK, USA.
IGO Relations Observer status with (1): *Codex Alimentarius Commission (CAC, #04081)*. **NGO Relations** In liaison with technical committees of: *International Organization for Standardization (ISO, #14473)*. Works with: *International Chewing Gum Association (ICGA, #12545)*. [2021.02.17/XD2330/t/**D**]

♦ International Organization of Folk Art (IOV World) 14447

Comité international des arts et traditions populaires – Organización Internacional del Arte Popular – Internationale Organisation für Volkskunst (IOV) – Mezdunarodnaja Organizacija po Narodnomu Tvorcestvu
SG Via Spino Pietro 102, 24126 Bergamo BG, Italy. T. +3935315998. Fax +3935313687. E-mail: secretarygeneral@iov.world – info@iov.world.
URL: https://www.iov.world/
History 1979, Oostrozebeke (Belgium). Former names and other names: *IOFA* – former. **Aims** Promote worldwide folk art and folk *culture* in the field of organizing and science, cultivate it purely, maintain and sensibly pass it on, thus contributing to international understanding and to world peace. **Structure** General Assembly (every 4 years); Board of Directors; Executive Committee; Commissions (5); Regions (6); Committees (4). **Languages** English. **Staff** 2.00 FTE, paid. Voluntary. **Finance** Sources: members' dues; sponsorship. **Activities** Events/meetings; training/education. **Events** *World General Assembly* Sharjah (United Arab Emirates) 2023, *World General Assembly and International Conference* Sharjah (United Arab Emirates) 2019, *European Conference* Andorf (Austria) 2017, *General Assembly* Bergamo (Italy) 2016, *European Conference* Sevastopol (Ukraine) 2013. **Publications** *Cultural Heritage of All Nations of the World* (2 a year). Series of videos on authentic folk dancing in all the world's nations /4 cassettes per year/; series of music cassettes on folk songs and folk music of all countries of the world; proceedings.
Members Individual and corporate members in 122 countries and territories:
Afghanistan, Algeria, Angola, Antigua-Barbuda, Argentina, Australia, Austria, Bahrain, Belgium, Belize, Benin, Bolivia, Brazil, Bulgaria, Burkina Faso, Burundi, Cameroon, Canada, Cape Verde, Central African Rep, Chile, China, Colombia, Congo Brazzaville, Costa Rica, Côte d'Ivoire, Cuba, Cyprus, Czechia, Denmark, Ecuador, Egypt, El Salvador, Ethiopia, Faeroe Is, Fiji, Finland, France, Germany, Ghana, Greece, Grenada, Guadeloupe, Guatemala, Guinea, Guinea-Bissau, Honduras, Hungary, India, Indonesia, Iran Islamic Rep, Iraq, Ireland, Israel, Italy, Jamaica, Japan, Jordan, Kenya, Korea Rep, Kuwait, Lebanon, Libya, Liechtenstein, Luxembourg, Malaysia, Maldives, Mauritius, Mexico, Micronesia FS, Morocco, Mozambique, Nepal, Netherlands, New Caledonia, New Zealand, Nicaragua, Nigeria, Northern Mariana Is, Norway, Pakistan, Palau, Panama, Papua New Guinea, Paraguay, Peru, Philippines, Poland, Polynesia Fr, Portugal, Qatar, Romania, Rwanda, Samoa, Sao Tomé-Principe, Saudi Arabia, Senegal, Serbia, Sierra Leone, Solomon Is, South Africa, Spain, Sri Lanka, St Lucia, Suriname, Sweden, Switzerland, Syrian AR, Tanzania UR, Thailand, Timor-Leste, Togo, Trinidad-Tobago, Tunisia, Türkiye, Uganda, UK, United Arab Emirates, USA, Venezuela, Wallis-Futuna, Zambia.
Members also in the former USSR; countries not specified.
Consultative Status Consultative status granted from: *ECOSOC (#05331)* (Special); *UNESCO (#20322)* (Consultative Status). **NGO Relations** Formal cooperative links with: *International Council of Organizations for Folklore Festivals and Folk Art (#13058)*. [2023/XE1723/**B**]

♦ International Organization for Forensic Odonto-Stomatology (IOFOS) 14448

Organisation internationale d'odonto-stomatologie légale
Pres Univ Zagreb School of Dental Medicine, Dept Dental Anthropology, Gunduliceva 5, HR-10000 Zagreb, Croatia.
Sec address not obtained.

URL: http://www.iofos.eu/
History 1973, France. Former names and other names: *International Society of Forensic Odonto-Stomatology (ISFOS)* – former; *Société internationale d'odonto-stomatologie légale* – former. **Aims** Provide a liaison between societies of *legal* forensic *odontology* on a global basis; promote goodwill, advancement and research in forensic odontology. **Structure** General Assembly. **Languages** English. **Staff** Voluntary. **Finance** Sources: members' dues. **Activities** Events/meetings. **Events** *Triennial Conference* Dubrovnik (Croatia) 2021, *Triennial Conference* Dubrovnik (Croatia) 2020, *Triennial Conference* Leuven (Belgium) 2017, *IALM Intersocietal Symposium* Venice (Italy) 2016, *Triennial Conference* Florence (Italy) 2013. **Publications** *JFOS – Journal of Forensic Odonto-Stomatology* (3 a year); *IOFOS Newsletter* (2 a year).
Members National societies in 30 countries:
Australia, Austria, Belgium, Brazil, Canada, Croatia, Denmark, Finland, Germany, Iceland, India, Israel, Italy, Japan, Korea Rep, Netherlands, New Zealand, Nigeria, Norway, Philippines, Poland, South Africa, Sweden, Switzerland, Thailand, Türkiye, UK, Ukraine, United Arab Emirates, USA. [2022.02.09/XD6763/**C**]

♦ International Organization of Good Templars / see Movendi International (#16871)
♦ International Organization of Homeopathic Dispensing Chemists / see Comité international des pharmaciens homéopathes (#04183)
♦ International Organization of Hotel and Restaurant Associations (inactive)
♦ International Organization for Housing Finance Institutions / see International Union for Housing Finance (#15780)
♦ International Organization for Human Ecology (inactive)
♦ International Organization of Indigenous Resource Development (no recent information)
♦ International Organization of Industrial, Artisanal and Service Producers' Cooperatives / see International Organisation of Industrial and Service Cooperatives (#14429)
♦ International Organization of Industrial Employers / see International Organisation of Employers (#14428)

♦ International Organization for Information Integration and Web-Based Applications and Services ('at'WAS) 14449

Gen Sec Co/ Permata Senayan blok C-28, Patal Senayan, Jl Tentara Pelajar 1 no 5, Jakarta 12210, Indonesia. T. +62217196178. Fax +62217196178.
Pres Johannes Kepler Univ of Linz, Dept of Telecooperation, Altenberger Strasse 69, 4040 Linz, Austria. T. +4373224689888. Fax +4373224689829.
URL: http://www.iiwas.org/
History 2003. **Aims** Foster collaborations and exchanges of ideas and information among students, professionals and researchers interested in the field of information integration and web applications and services. **Structure** Steering Committee. **Events** *International Conference* Italy 2022, *International Conference* Linz (Austria) 2021, *International Conference* Chiang Mai (Thailand) 2020, *Intrnational Conference* Munich (Germany) 2019, *International Conference* Yogyakarta (Indonesia) 2018. [2022/XM0204/**D**]

♦ International Organization for Intellectual Cooperation (inactive)
♦ International Organization of Journalists (inactive)

♦ International Organization for Judicial Training (IOJT) 14450

SG c/o NCSC, 300 Newport Ave, Williamsburg VA 23185, USA.
Secretariat The Supreme Court, Sha'arei Mishpat Street, 91950 Jerusalem, Israel. T. +97226759792. Fax +97226527118.
URL: http://www.iojt.org/
History Founded Mar 2002, Jerusalem (Israel). **Aims** Encourage establishment of judicial training institutes; promote the rule of law; consider common issues for training and education of judges; develop platforms for exchange of judges. **Structure** General Assembly (every 2 years); Executive Committee; Board of Governors. **Languages** English. **Activities** Guidance/assistance/consulting; networking/liaising; training/education. Active internationally. **Events** *Conference* Ottawa, ON (Canada) 2022, *Conference* Cape Town (South Africa) 2019, *Conference* Manila (Philippines) 2017, *Conference* Recife (Brazil) 2015, *Conference* Washington, DC (USA) 2013. **Publications** *IOJT Journal*; *IOJT Newsletter*. **Members** Institutes (122) in 73 countries. Membership countries not specified. [2016/XM3664/**C**]

♦ International Organization of Legal Metrology 14451

Organisation internationale de métrologie légale (OIML) – Organización Internacional de Metrologia Legal
Dir 11 rue Turgot, 75009 Paris, France. T. +33148781282. Fax +33142821727.
URL: https://www.oiml.org/
History 12 Oct 1955, Paris (France). Established on signature of an international convention. 1963 amendments in force 18 Jan 1968. **Aims** Serve as information and documentation centre both on the different national departments (agencies) concerned with approval, verification and regular checking of measuring *instruments* subjected or likely to be subjected to legal regulations, and on the conception, construction and use of such instruments; collect legal texts on measuring instruments and their use in force in member states; determine the general principles of legal metrology; study means of harmonizing regulations and of type testing and verification methods on measuring instruments; establish model draft laws and regulations for measuring instruments and their use; determine characteristics and *standards* necessary for their recommended use internationally; manage certification system; assist developing countries. **Structure** Conference (every 4 years), consisting of delegates of member states. Committee (CIML, annually), composed of one official from each member state. Bureau (BIML). Meetings closed. Technical Committees and Subcommittees (65). **Languages** English, French. **Staff** 9.00 FTE, paid. **Finance** Sources: contributions of member/participating states. **Activities** Events/meetings; projects/programmes. **Events** *International Conference of Weighing* Berlin (Germany) 2023, *Annual Meeting* Chiang Mai (Thailand) 2023, *Annual Meeting* Paris (France) 2022, *Quadrennial Conference* Paris (France) 2021, *Annual Meeting* Paris (France) 2020. **Publications** *OIML Bulletin* (4 a year). Documents; recommendations; vocabularies; guides; basic publications.
Members Governments of 61 countries:
Albania, Algeria, Australia, Austria, Belarus, Belgium, Brazil, Bulgaria, Cambodia, Canada, China, Colombia, Croatia, Cuba, Cyprus, Czechia, Denmark, Egypt, Finland, France, Germany, Greece, Hungary, India, Indonesia, Iran Islamic Rep, Ireland, Israel, Italy, Japan, Kazakhstan, Kenya, Korea Rep, Monaco, Morocco, Netherlands, New Zealand, North Macedonia, Norway, Pakistan, Poland, Portugal, Romania, Russia, Saudi Arabia, Serbia, Slovakia, Slovenia, South Africa, Spain, Sri Lanka, Sweden, Switzerland, Tanzania UR, Thailand, Tunisia, Türkiye, UK, USA, Vietnam, Zambia.
Corresponding members in 61 countries and territories:
Angola, Argentina, Azerbaijan, Bahrain, Bangladesh, Barbados, Bolivia, Bosnia-Herzegovina, Botswana, Costa Rica, Dominican Rep, Ecuador, Estonia, Fiji, Georgia, Ghana, Guatemala, Guinea, Hong Kong, Iceland, Iraq, Jordan, Kiribati, Kuwait, Kyrgyzstan, Latvia, Lithuania, Luxembourg, Madagascar, Malawi, Malaysia, Malta, Mauritius, Mexico, Moldova, Mongolia, Montenegro, Mozambique, Namibia, Nepal, Nigeria, Oman, Panama, Papua New Guinea, Paraguay, Peru, Philippines, Qatar, Rwanda, Seychelles, Sierra Leone, Singapore, Sudan, Taiwan, Trinidad-Tobago, Uganda, Ukraine, United Arab Emirates, Uruguay, Uzbekistan, Zimbabwe.
IGO Relations Cooperates with (1): *Bureau international des poids et mesures (BIPM, #03367)*. Instrumental in setting up (1): *Euro-Mediterranean Legal Metrology Forum (EMLMF, no recent information)*. *World Trade Organization (WTO, #21864)* (Observer Status). **NGO Relations** Cooperation agreement with: *European Committee for Electrotechnical Standardization (CENELEC, #06647)*; *International Electrotechnical Commission (IEC, #13255)*. In liaison with technical committees of: *Comité européen de normalisation (CEN, #04162)*; *International Organization for Standardization (ISO, #14473)*. Special links with: *International Laboratory Accreditation Cooperation (ILAC, #13995)*. [2023/XC2326/**B***]

♦ International Organization for Marine Geology (inactive)

♦ International Organization for Masoretic Studies (IOMS) 14452

Pres Cymbalista Jewish Heritage Centre, Tel Aviv Univ, 69978 Tel Aviv, Israel.
URL: http://masoreticstudies.org/
History Founded 5 Sep 1972, Los Angeles CA (USA), during 1st International Congress of Learned Societies in the Field of Religion. **Aims** Promote study and research of the fields of Masora, *Hebrew bible* manuscripts, vocalization and accentuation in all systems and everything connected with Hebrew biblical text *philology*. **Structure** Steering Committee. **Languages** English, French, Hebrew, Spanish. **Staff** None. **Finance** No budget. **Activities** Organizes conferences and congresses. **Events** *Congress* Jerusalem (Israel) 2013, *Congress* Munich (Germany) 2013, *Congress* Chicago, IL (USA) 2012, *Congress* Helsinki (Finland) 2010, *Congress* Jerusalem (Israel) 2009. **Publications** *Masoretic Studies* – series. **NGO Relations** *International Organization for the Study of the Old Testament (IOSOT, #14476)*; *Society of Biblical Literature (SBL)*; *World Union of Jewish Students (WUJS, #21878)*. [2015.01.17/XM1948/**D**]

♦ International Organization of Masters, Mates and Pilots (internationally oriented national body)
♦ International Organization of Materials, Metals and Minerals Societies (no recent information)

♦ International Organization for Medical Physics (IOMP) 14453

Organisation internationale de physique médicale – Organización Internacional de Fisica Medica – Internationale Organisation für Medizinische Physik
SG Fairmount House, 230 Tadcaster Road, York, Y23 1ES, UK. T. +441904610821. E-mail: info@iomp.org.
President University of Crete, 700 13 Heraklion, Greece.
URL: http://www.iomp.org/
History Jan 1963. Present statutes and Bylaws approved by Council, 9 Sep 2009, Munich (Germany). Statutes amended May 2012, Beijing (China); Jun 2015, Toronto ON (Canada). Minor updates June 2018, Prague (Hungary). Registration: Companies House, No/ID: 11119605, England and Wales. **Aims** Contribute to advancement of medical physics in all its aspects. **Structure** Council; Committees (8); Sub-Committees (3). Includes *International Commission on Medical Physics (IComMP)*. **Languages** English. **Staff** 0.50 FTE, paid. **Finance** Sources: meeting proceeds; members' dues; sponsorship. Annual budget: 70,000 USD (2020). **Activities** Events/meetings; knowledge management/information dissemination; research/documentation; training/education. **Events** *International Conference on Medical Physics (ICMP)* Mumbai (India) 2023, *IUPESM World Congress on Medical Physics and Biomedical Engineering (IUPESM WC2022)* Singapore (Singapore) 2022, *World Congress on Medical Physics and Biomedical Engineering* Singapore (Singapore) 2021, *International Conference on Medical Physics* Santiago (Chile) 2019, *World Congress on Medical Physics and Biomedical Engineering* Prague (Czechia) 2018. **Publications** *e-Medical Physics World* (6 a year); *IOMP Newsletter* (6 a year); *Medical Physics International* (2 a year).
Members National organizations in 87 countries and territories:
Algeria, Argentina, Australia, Austria, Bangladesh, Belgium, Brazil, Bulgaria, Cameroon, Canada, Chile, China, Colombia, Croatia, Cuba, Cyprus, Czechia, Denmark, Ecuador, Egypt, Estonia, Finland, France, Georgia, Germany, Ghana, Greece, Hong Kong, Hungary, India, Indonesia, Iran Islamic Rep, Iraq, Ireland, Israel, Italy, Japan, Jordan, Korea Rep, Kuwait, Lebanon, Lithuania, Malaysia, Mexico, Moldova, Mongolia, Morocco, Myanmar, Nepal, Netherlands, New Zealand, Nigeria, North Macedonia, Norway, Pakistan, Panama, Paraguay, Peru, Philippines, Poland, Portugal, Qatar, Romania, Russia, Saudi Arabia, Singapore, Slovenia, South Africa, Spain, Sri Lanka, Sudan, Sweden, Switzerland, Taiwan, Tanzania UR, Thailand, Trinidad-Tobago, Türkiye, Uganda, UK, Ukraine, United Arab Emirates, USA, Venezuela, Vietnam, Zambia, Zimbabwe.
Regional organizations (6), listed in this Yearbook:
Asia-Oceania Federation of Organizations for Medical Physics (AFOMP, #01797); *European Federation of Organisations for Medical Physics (EFOMP, #07183)*; *Federation of African Medical Physics Organizations (FAMPO, #09406)*; *Latin American Association of Medical Physics (#16246)*; *Middle East Federation of Organizations of Medical Physics (MEFOMP, #16764)*; *Southeast Asian Federation of Organizations for Medical Physics (SEAFOMP, #19766)*.
Consultative Status Consultative status granted from: *WHO (#20950)* (Official). **IGO Relations** Affiliated with (1): *International Atomic Energy Agency (IAEA, #12294)*. **NGO Relations** Cooperates with (2): *International Council for Science (ICSU, inactive)*; *International Federation for Medical and Biological Engineering (IFMBE, #13477)*. Instrumental in setting up (1): *International Union for Physical and Engineering Sciences in Medicine (IUPESM, #15799)*. [2022.10.11/XC2311/y/**B**]

♦ International Organization of Memorizing the Holy Quran / see Holy Qu'ran Memorization International Organization (#10938)

♦ International Organization for Migration (IOM) 14454

Organisation internationale pour les migrations (OIM) – Organización Internacional para las Migraciones (OIM)
Dir Gen Route des Morillons 17, PO Box 17, 1211 Geneva 19, Switzerland. T. +41227179111. Fax +41227986150. E-mail: hq@iom.int – info@iom.int.
Street Address Route des Morillons 17, Grand-Saconnex, 1218 Le Grand-Saconnex GE, Switzerland.
URL: http://www.iom.int/
History 5 Dec 1951, Brussels (Belgium). Founded in Brussels (Belgium), following International Migration Conference attended by 16 governments. Constitution came into force 30 Nov 1954. Full juridical personality in each member country. New constitution, including a change in name, approved 20 May 1987; entered into force and current name adopted, 14 Nov 1989, when two thirds of member states formally notified their acceptance; amendments adopted 24 Nov 1998, which entered into force 21 Nov 2013. Former names and other names: *Provisional Intergovernmental Committee for the Movement of Migrants from Europe* – former (5 Dec 1951 to 15 Nov 1952); *Comité intergouvernemental provisoire pour les mouvements migratoires d'Europe* – former (5 Dec 1951 to 15 Nov 1952); *Intergovernmental Committee for European Migration (ICEM)* – former (15 Nov 1952 to 1980); *Comité intergouvernemental pour les migrations européennes (CIME)* – former (15 Nov 1952 to 1980); *Comité Intergubernamental para las Migraciones Europeas* – former (15 Nov 1952 to 1980); *Intergovernmental Committee for Migration (ICM)* – former (1980 to 14 Nov 1989); *Comité intergouvernemental pour les migrations (CIM)* – former (1980 to 14 Nov 1989); *Comité Intergubernamental para las Migraciones (CIM)* – former (1980 to 14 Nov 1989). Registration: EU Transparency Register, No/ID: 14074813668-09. **Aims** Promote humane and orderly migration for the benefit of all by providing services and advice to governments and migrants; promote international *cooperation* on migration issues; aid in the search for practical solutions to migration problems; provide *humanitarian* assistance to migrants in need, whether *refugees*, *displaced persons* or other uprooted people. **Structure** Council (at least annually), decision-making body, comprises representatives of all member governments. Administration, comprising Director General, Deputy Director General and staff. Standing Committee on Programmes and Finances (usually meets twice a year). Offices in over 150 countries; field locations (over 400). Regional offices (9): Dakar (Senegal); Nairobi (Kenya); Cairo (Egypt); Pretoria (South Africa); San José (Costa Rica); Buenos Aires (Argentina); Bangkok (Thailand); Brussels (Belgium); Vienna (Austria). Special Liaison Offices (2): New York NY (USA); Addis Ababa (Ethiopia). Administrative Centres (2): Panama (Panama); Manila (Philippines). Country Offices with Coordinating Functions (5): Canberra (Australia); Rome (Italy); Astana (Kazakhstan); Georgetown (Guyana); Bangkok (Thailand). Country Offices and sub-offices. *African Capacity Building Centre (ACBC)*; *IOM Global Migration Data Analysis Centre (GMDAC, #16007)*. Departments (3): Operations and Emergencies; Migration Management; International Cooperation and Partnerships. **Languages** English, French, Spanish. **Staff** 9000.00 FTE, paid. Personnel negotiations through *IOM Global Staff Association Committee (GSAC, #16008)*. The *Administrative Tribunal of the International Labour Organization (ILO Tribunal, #00118)* is competent to settle disputes. **Finance** *'Administrative Budget'*: mandatory contributions from all member governments according to an agreed percentage scale. *'Operational Budget'*: main source is voluntary contributions from government sources – per capita contributions, paid by emigration and/or immigration countries, based on the number of migrant or refugee movements, and lump sum contributions not necessarily related to the number of movements; other sources include the migrants themselves, their sponsors and voluntary agencies dealing with migration and refugee matters. Member governments may contribute funds for specific programmes or purposes. Total expenditure (2014): US$ 1,400,000,000. **Activities** Advocacy/lobbying/activism; guidance/assistance/consulting; politics/policy/regulatory; research/documentation. **Events** *Regional Meeting on Migration Statistics in the Western Balkans* Belgrade (Serbia) 2021, *AU-ILO-IOM-ECA Steering Committee Meeting on Labour Migration Governance for Development and Integration* Addis Ababa (Ethiopia) 2019, *International Solidarity Conference on the Venezuelan Refugee and Migrant Crisis* Brussels (Belgium) 2019, *International Forum on the Humanitarian-Development-Peace Nexus* Seoul (Korea Rep) 2019, *Round Table on Refugee and Migration Challenges in Rohingya Crisis and Potential of Global Compact* Tokyo (Japan) 2018. **Publications** *International Migration* (5 a year) – journal; *IOM News* (4 a year) in English, French, Spanish; *Migration and Health Newsletter* in English. *Migration Research Series*. Books; brochures; study reports.
Members There is no statutory limit on the number of members – any government with a demonstrated interest in free movement of persons, which undertakes to make a financial contribution at least to administrative requirements (the amount being agreed by Council and the government concerned) and which accepts the Constitution, may be admitted by a two-thirds majority vote of the Council. Current membership comprises governments of 166 countries:

Afghanistan, Albania, Algeria, Angola, Antigua-Barbuda, Argentina, Armenia, Australia, Austria, Azerbaijan, Bahamas, Bangladesh, Belarus, Belgium, Belize, Benin, Bolivia, Bosnia-Herzegovina, Botswana, Brazil, Bulgaria, Burkina Faso, Burundi, Cambodia, Cameroon, Canada, Cape Verde, Central African Rep, Chad, Chile, China, Colombia, Comoros, Congo Brazzaville, Congo DR, Costa Rica, Côte d'Ivoire, Croatia, Cyprus, Czechia, Denmark, Djibouti, Dominican Rep, Ecuador, Egypt, El Salvador, Eritrea, Estonia, Eswatini, Ethiopia, Fiji, Finland, France, Gabon, Gambia, Georgia, Germany, Ghana, Greece, Guatemala, Guinea, Guinea-Bissau, Guyana, Haiti, Holy See, Honduras, Hungary, Iceland, India, Iran Islamic Rep, Ireland, Israel, Italy, Jamaica, Japan, Jordan, Kazakhstan, Kenya, Kiribati, Korea Rep, Kyrgyzstan, Latvia, Lesotho, Liberia, Libya, Lithuania, Luxembourg, Madagascar, Malawi, Maldives, Mali, Malta, Marshall Is, Mauritania, Mauritius, Mexico, Micronesia FS, Moldova, Mongolia, Montenegro, Morocco, Mozambique, Myanmar, Namibia, Nauru, Nepal, Netherlands, New Zealand, Nicaragua, Niger, Nigeria, North Macedonia, Norway, Pakistan, Panama, Papua New Guinea, Paraguay, Peru, Philippines, Poland, Portugal, Romania, Rwanda, Samoa, Sao Tomé-Principe, Senegal, Serbia, Seychelles, Sierra Leone, Slovakia, Slovenia, Solomon Is, Somalia, South Africa, South Sudan, Spain, Sri Lanka, St Kitts-Nevis, St Lucia, St Vincent-Grenadines, Sudan, Suriname, Sweden, Switzerland, Tajikistan, Tanzania UR, Thailand, Timor-Leste, Togo, Tonga, Trinidad-Tobago, Tunisia, Türkiye, Turkmenistan, Tuvalu, Uganda, UK, Ukraine, Uruguay, USA, Vanuatu, Venezuela, Vietnam, Yemen, Zambia, Zimbabwe.

Observers – governments of 8 countries:
Bahrain, Bhutan, Cuba, Indonesia, Qatar, Russia, San Marino, Saudi Arabia.

IGO Relations Cooperation agreements with: *Commonwealth of Independent States (CIS, #04341).* Accredited to the Conference of the Parties of: *Secretariat of the United Nations Convention to Combat Desertification (Secretariat of the UNCCD, #19208).* Accredited by: *United Nations Framework Convention on Climate Change – Secretariat (UNFCCC, #20564).* Signatory to: *International Anti-Corruption Academy (IACA, #11654).* Memorandum of Understanding with: *Economic Cooperation Organization (ECO, #05313); Migration, Asylum, Refugees Regional Initiative (MARRI, #16800).* Member of: *Northern Dimension Partnership in Public Health and Social Well-being (NDPHS, #17587); Regional Cooperation Council (RCC, #18773); Southeast European Law Enforcement Center (SELEC, #19815); Inter-Agency Standing Committee (IASC, #11393).* Cooperates in: *Budapest Process (#03344).* Cooperates with: *United Nations Institute for Training and Research (UNITAR, #20576).* Serves as Secretariat for: *United Nations Network on Migration (#20590).* Observer to: *International Fund for Agricultural Development (IFAD, #13692).* Member of: *United Nations Joint Staff Pension Fund (UNJSPF, #20581).* Support from: *United Nations Central Emergency Response Fund (CERF, #20525); United Nations Peacebuilding Fund (PBF, #20607).*

Organizations holding observer status with IOM:
- *Organisation of African, Caribbean and Pacific States (OACPS, #17796);*
- *African Union (AU, #00488);*
- *Arab Maghreb Union (AMU, #01004);*
- *Asian-African Legal Consultative Organization (AALCO, #01303);*
- *Comunidade dos Paises de Lingua Portuguesa (CPLP, #04430);*
- *Community of Sahel-Saharan States (CEN-SAD, #04406);*
- *Council of Europe (CE, #04881);*
- *European Commission (EC, #06633);*
- *FAO (#09260);*
- *Ibero-American General Secretariat (#11024);*
- *ILO (#11123);*
- *Inter-American Development Bank (IDB, #11427);*
- *International Bank for Reconstruction and Development (IBRD, #12317);*
- *International Centre for Migration Policy Development (ICMPD, #12503);*
- *International Maritime Organization (IMO, #14102);*
- *Islamic World Educational, Scientific and Cultural Organization (ICESCO, #16058);*
- *Italian-Latin American Institute (ILAI, #16071);*
- *League of Arab States (LAS, #16420);*
- *OAS (#17629);*
- *OECD (#17693);*
- *Office of the United Nations High Commissioner for Human Rights (OHCHR, #17697);*
- *Organisation internationale de la Francophonie (OIF, #17809);*
- *Organisation of Islamic Cooperation (OIC, #17813);*
- *Parliamentary Assembly – Union for the Mediterranean (PA – UfM, #18216);*
- *Southeast European Cooperative Initiative (SECI, #19812);*
- *UNCTAD (#20285);*
- *UNDP (#20292);*
- *UNESCO (#20322);*
- *UNHCR (#20327);*
- *UNIDO (#20336);*
- *United Nations (UN, #20515);*
- *United Nations Commission on Human Rights (inactive),* replaced by *United Nations Human Rights Council (HRC, #20571);*
- *United Nations Economic Commission for Africa (ECA, #20554);*
- *United Nations Economic Commission for Latin America and the Caribbean (ECLAC, #20556);*
- *United Nations Economic and Social Commission for Asia and the Pacific (ESCAP, #20557);*
- *United Nations Office for the Coordination of Humanitarian Affairs (OCHA, #20593);*
- *United Nations Population Fund (UNFPA, #20612);*
- *United Nations Research Institute for Social Development (UNRISD, #20623);*
- *Universal Postal Union (UPU, #20682);*
- *WHO (#20950).*

Cooperates closely with international organizations working in the field of refugee assistance or dealing with social, economic and demographic aspects of international migration:
- *Andean Community (#00817);*
- *Comisión Centroamericana de Directores de Migración (OCAM, no recent information);*
- *ECOSOC (#05331);*
- *European Centre for Social Welfare Policy and Research (European Centre, #06500);*
- *Interparliamentary Assembly of Member Nations of the Commonwealth of Independent States (IPA CIS, #15958);*
- *Latin American Fisheries Development Organization (#16335);*
- *OSCE – Office for Democratic Institutions and Human Rights (OSCE/ODIHR, #17902);*
- *Parliamentary Assembly of the Council of Europe (PACE, #18211);*
- *Regional Conference on Women in Latin America and the Caribbean (#18770);*
- *Sistema Económico Latinoamericano (SELA, #19294);*
- *United Nations Commission on Crime Prevention and Criminal Justice (CCPCJ, #20530);*
- *United Nations Volunteers (UNV, #20650);*
- *WHO Regional Office for Europe (#20945);*
- *World Food Programme (WFP, #21510).*

NGO Relations Agreements with a number of voluntary agencies ensure emigration of individuals sponsored by people in countries overseas. Cooperation includes not only procedural and transport matters but also the financing of movements by means of Joint Revolving Funds, to which both the Committee and voluntary agencies contribute.

Organizations holding observer status:
- *Africa Humanitarian Action (AHA);*
- *American Jewish Joint Distribution Committee (JDC, #00785);*
- *Amnesty International (AI, #00801);*
- *Australian Catholic Migrant and Refugee Office (ACMRO);*
- *CARE International (CI, #03429);*
- *Caritas Internationalis (CI, #03580);*
- *Catholic Relief Services (CRS, #03608);*
- *Center for Migration Studies, New York (CMS);*
- *Episcopal Migration Ministries (EMM);*
- *Federation of Ethnic Communities' Councils of Australia;*
- *Femmes Africa solidarité (FAS, #09732);*
- *Food for the Hungry (fh, #09845);*
- *Friends World Committee for Consultation (FWCC, #10004);*
- *The Hague Institute for Global Justice (The Hague Institute);*
- *HIAS;*
- *Human Rights Watch (HRW, #10990);*
- *International Catholic Migration Commission (ICMC, #12459);*
- *International Committee of the Red Cross (ICRC, #12799);*
- *International Council on Social Welfare (ICSW, #13076);*
- *International Council of Voluntary Agencies (ICVA, #13092);*
- *International Federation of Red Cross and Red Crescent Societies (#13526);*
- *International Islamic Relief Organization (IIRO);*
- *International Organisation of Employers (IOE, #14428);*
- *International Rescue Committee (IRC, #14717);*
- *International Social Service (ISS, #14886);*
- *International Trade Union Confederation (ITUC, #15708);*
- *Japan International Friendship and Welfare Foundation (JIFF, no recent information);*
- *Jesuit Refugee Service (JRS, #16106);*
- *The Lutheran World Federation (LWF, #16532);*
- *Migrants Rights International (MRI, #16799);*
- *Niwano Peace Foundation;*
- *Norwegian Refugee Council (NRC);*
- 'Paulino Torras Domènech Foundation';
- *Refugee Council of Australia (RCOA);*
- *Sasakawa Peace Foundation (SPF);*
- *Scalabrini International Migration Network (SIMN, #19063);*
- *Partage – avec les enfants du monde (Partage);*
- *SOLIDAR (#19680);*
- *Sovereign Military Hospitaller Order of St John of Jerusalem, of Rhodes and of Malta (SMOM);*
- *Tolstoy Foundation (TF);*
- *United Ukrainian American Relief Committee (no recent information);*
- *World Council of Churches (WCC, #21320).*

Member of: *Association for Human Resources Management in International Organizations (AHRMIO, #02634); Communicating with Disaster Affected Communities Network (CDAC Network, #04379); European Policy Centre (EPC, #08240); Global Gender and Climate Alliance (GGCA, no recent information); learn4dev (#16427).* Associate member of: *Federation of International Civil Servants' Associations (FICSA, #09603).* Institutional member of: *Centre for European Policy Studies (CEPS, #03741).* Observer to: ICRC; International Federation of Red Cross and Red Crescent Societies; *International Red Cross and Red Crescent Movement (#14707).* Instrumental in setting up: *International Centre for Migration, Health and Development (ICMHD, #12502).* Participates in: *Encuentro Latinoamericano de Informatica e Industrias de Información (ELAII).* Partner of: *Adventist Development and Relief Agency International (ADRA, #00131); AIDS and Mobility Europe (A and M, inactive); Global Health Cluster (GHC, #10401).* Cooperates with: *Fundación Henry Dunant América Latina (FuHD – AL, #10024).* Supports: *Ockenden International.* [2020/XB1112/**B***]

♦ International Organization for Motor Trades and Repairs (inactive)

♦ International Organization of Motor Vehicle Manufacturers 14455

Organisation internationale des constructeurs d'automobiles (OICA)

SG 4 rue de Berri, 75008 Paris, France. T. +33143590013. Fax +33145638441. E-mail: oica@oica.net.
URL: https://www.oica.net/

History 1919, Paris (France). Succeeded *International Union of Motor Manufacturers (inactive)*, which had been set up in 1911 but dissolved 1914-1918. Present title adopted at General Assembly, 28 May 1986, Vienna (Austria). Former names and other names: *International Bureau of Automobile Manufacturers* – former; *Bureau permanent international des constructeurs d'automobiles (BPICA)* – former; *Oficina Permanente Internacional de Constructores de Automóviles* – former; *Internationales Ständiges Büro der Automobilhersteller* – former. Registration: France. **Aims** Defend the interests of vehicle manufacturers, assemblers and importers grouped within national federations. **Structure** General Assembly (annually); Council; Secretariat. **Languages** English, French. **Staff** 5.00 FTE, paid. **Finance** Sources: members' dues. **Events** *General Assembly* Paris (France) 2019, *General Assembly* Bangkok (Thailand) 2015, *Half-Yearly General Assembly* Seoul (Korea Rep) 2014, *Conference* Tokyo (Japan) 2013, *Half-Yearly General Assembly / Half-Yearly General Assembly and Meeting* Bucharest (Romania) 2011.

Members National Associations (39). Full in 29 countries:
Argentina, Australia, Austria, Belgium, Brazil, China, Egypt, France, Germany, India, Indonesia, Iran Islamic Rep, Italy, Japan, Kazakhstan, Korea Rep, Netherlands, Portugal, Romania, Russia, Serbia, South Africa, Spain, Sweden, Switzerland, Thailand, Türkiye, UK, USA.

Associate in 7 countries:
Bulgaria, Croatia, Denmark, Finland, Greece, Norway, USA.

Regional Associate members (2), including 1 organization listed in this Yearbook:
European Automobile Manufacturers' Association (ACEA, #06300).

IGO Relations Accredited by (1): *United Nations Framework Convention on Climate Change – Secretariat (UNFCCC, #20564).* Cooperates with (2): *Committee on Inland Transport (#04262); United Nations Economic Commission for Europe (UNECE, #20555).* **NGO Relations** Member of (1): *Partnership for Clean Fuels and Vehicles (PCFV, #18231). Fédération Internationale de l'Automobile (FIA, #09613).* In liaison with technical committees of: *International Organization for Standardization (ISO, #14473).* [2023/XD1109/**C**]

♦ International Organization of MS Nurses / see International Organization of Multiple Sclerosis Nurses
♦ International Organization of Multiple Sclerosis Nurses (internationally oriented national body)

♦ International Organization for Mycoplasmology (IOM) 14456

Organisation internationale de mycoplasmologie

SG Cardiff Univ, School of Medicine, Dept of Child Health, University Hospital of Wales, Cardiff, CF14 4XN, UK. T. +442920742394. Fax +442920744283.
Chairman ithree Inst, Univ of Technology – Sydney, PO Box 123, 15 Broadway, Ultimo NSW 2007, Australia. T. +6129514412.
URL: http://iom-online.org/

History Sep 1976, Glasgow (UK). **Aims** Promote cooperative international study of all mollicutes, mycoplasmas and mycoplasmal diseases and dissemination of knowledge concerning their identity and relationships, effects and importance, means of spread, control and/or prevention; encourage personal contacts and information exchange; foster educational programmes and prepare and distribute educational materials useful in the study of mollicutes and mycoplasmal diseases; encourage participation in and support of mollicute and mycoplasmal research. **Structure** Board of Directors; Standing Committees; Working Teams (9). **Languages** English. **Staff** 10.00 FTE, voluntary. **Finance** Sources: members' dues. **Activities** Awards/prizes/competitions; events/meetings; research/documentation. **Events** *Biennial Congress* Osaka (Japan) 2023, *Biennial Congress* Tel Aviv (Israel) 2020, *Biennial Congress* Portsmouth, NH (USA) 2018, *Biennial Congress* Brisbane, QLD (Australia) 2016, *Biennial Congress* Blumenau (Brazil) 2014. **Publications** *IOM Newsletter* (at least 2 a year). Congress proceedings.

Members Active; Student; Sustaining; Honorary. Individuals in 44 countries and territories:
Australia, Austria, Belgium, Brazil, Canada, China, Colombia, Croatia, Cuba, Czechia, Denmark, Egypt, France, Germany, Hungary, India, Ireland, Israel, Italy, Japan, Kenya, Korea Rep, Malaysia, Mexico, Namibia, Netherlands, New Zealand, Pakistan, Panama, Peru, Portugal, Puerto Rico, Russia, Slovenia, South Africa, Spain, Sri Lanka, Sudan, Sweden, Switzerland, Taiwan, Türkiye, UK, USA.

NGO Relations Member of: *International Committee on Systematics of Prokaryotes (ICSP, #12807); International Society for Plant Pathology (ISPP, #15371).* [2020/XC8890/v/**C**]

♦ International Organization for Natural Bathing Waters 14457

Internationale Organisation für naturnahe Badegewässer (IOB)

CEO Überseetor 14, 28217 Bremen, Germany. T. +4942117876279. E-mail: office@iob-ev.com.
URL: https://iob-ev.com/

History 29 Sep 2009, Merano (Italy). Registration: Bremen District Court, No/ID: VR 7404 HB, Start date: 21 Apr 2010, Germany, Bremen. **Structure** Board. **Finance** Sources: members' dues. **Activities** Events/meetings. **Events** *International Swimming Pond Congress* Warsaw (Poland) 2019, *Congress* Leeuwarden (Netherlands) 2017, *Congress* Cologne (Germany) 2015, *Congress* Bregenz (Austria) 2013, *Congress* Vienna (Austria) 2013. **Publications** *IOB Newsletter.*

Members Organizations and individuals in 25 countries:
Argentina, Australia, Austria, Belgium, Brazil, Chile, Czechia, Denmark, France, Germany, Greece, Israel, Italy, Netherlands, New Zealand, Poland, Portugal, Slovakia, Slovenia, South Africa, Spain, Switzerland, Türkiye, UK, USA. [2020/XJ8316/**D**]

♦ International Organization New Acropolis (IONA) 14458

Organisation internationale Nouvelle Acropole (OINA) – Organización Internacional Nueva Acrópolis (IONA)

Institutional Relations Advisor Rue Emile François 18, 1474 Ways, Belgium. E-mail: rrii@acropolis.org.
Pres address not obtained.
URL: http://www.acropolis.org/

History 1957, Argentina. Founded by historian and philosopher Jorge Ángel Livraga Rizzi (1930-1991). Former names and other names: *New Acropolis International* – former. Registration: Banque-Carrefour des Entreprises, No/ID: 0440.029.711, Start date: 12 Feb 1990, Belgium. **Aims** Promote an Ideal of international fraternity based on respect for human dignity beyond racial, sexual, cultural, religious, social or other differences. **Structure** Annual Assembly; Governing Board; Executive Council; Secretary General heads Secretariat, based in Madrid (Spain); Regional Coordination Offices in Canada, Czechia, France, Guatemala and Israel; national chapters. **Languages** English, French, Spanish. **Finance** Sources: contributions; fees for services; members' dues; revenue from activities/projects; sale of products; sponsorship. **Activities** Awards/prizes/competitions; capacity building; events/meetings; knowledge management/information dissemination; projects/programmes; publishing activities; training/education. **Events** *Congress* Lima (Peru) 1998, *Congress* Brussels (Belgium) 1996, *Congress* Chinchilla (Spain) 1994, *Congrès international des comités nationaux pour la réhabilitation de Giordano Bruno et sur la liberté de pensée* Vienna (Austria) 1994, *International congress on philosophy and anthropology* Rio de Janeiro (Brazil) 1993. **Publications** Articles; stories; videos.
Members Individuals (about 18,000) in 54 countries and territories:
Albania, Argentina, Australia, Austria, Belgium, Bolivia, Bosnia-Herzegovina, Brazil, Bulgaria, Canada, Chile, Colombia, Costa Rica, Croatia, Cyprus, Czechia, Denmark, Dominican Rep, Ecuador, El Salvador, France, Germany, Greece, Guatemala, Honduras, Hungary, India, Ireland, Israel, Italy, Japan, Kazakhstan, Korea Rep, Mexico, Moldova, Panama, Paraguay, Peru, Poland, Portugal, Romania, Russia, Serbia, Slovakia, Slovenia, South Africa, Spain, Switzerland, Taiwan, UK, Ukraine, Uruguay, USA, Venezuela.
IGO Relations Accredited by (3): *ECOSOC (#05331)*; *OAS (#17629)*; *United Nations (UN, #20515)*.
[2023.02.12/XD9073/**F**]

♦ International Organization of Palaeobotany (IOP) 14459

Organisation internationale de la paléobotanique (OIP) – Organización Internacional de Paleobotanica – Internationale Organisation für Palaeobotanik

Sec-Treas Senckenberg Natural History Collections Dresden, Koenigsbruecker Landstr 159, 01109 Dresden, Germany. T. +493517958414406. Fax +493517958414404.
URL: http://www.palaeobotany.org/

History Jul 1954, Paris (France), during 8th International Botanical Congress of *International Union of Biological Sciences (IUBS, #15760)*. Statutes approved Apr 1955, Rome (Italy). **Aims** Promote international cooperation in the study of palaeobotany including palaeo-palynology. **Structure** General Assembly (every 4 years during quadrennial Congress); Executive Committee; Regional Representatives; Student Regional Representatives; Social Media Facilitators. **Languages** English. **Staff** None. **Finance** Members' dues. **Activities** Knowledge management/information dissemination; Awards/prizes/competitions; financial and/or material support; events/meetings. **Events** *Conference* Prague (Czechia) 2024, *Conference* Prague (Czechia) 2021, *Conference* Prague (Czechia) 2020, *Quadrennial Conference* Salvador (Brazil) 2016, *Quadrennial Conference* Tokyo (Japan) 2012. **Publications** *IOP Newsletter*. Circulars. **Members** Individuals. Membership countries not specified. **NGO Relations** Scientific member of IUBS. Member of: *International Association of Botanical and Mycological Societies (IABMS, #11730)*. Subsidiary of: *International Association for Plant Taxonomy (IAPT, #12092)*. [2019.12.20/XE2327/v/**E**]

♦ International Organization of Parliamentarians for Health / see International Medical Parliamentarians Organization (#14137)

♦ International Organization for a Participatory Society (IOPS) 14460

Contact address not obtained. E-mail: info@iopsociety.org.
URL: http://www.iopsociety.org/

History 6 Jan 2012. **Aims** Win a better world through flexibly exploring and advocating long term vision, building the seeds of the *future* in the present, empowering members' lives, organizing in an internally classless and self-managing way, and winning changes in society that better the situations of suffering constituencies while also laying the ground work for more changes, and construction, to come. **Structure** Self-managed through member participation. **Members** Individuals (3,742) in 109 countries. Membership countries not specified. [2017.09.19/XJ5505/**B**]

♦ International Organization for Peace, Care and Relief (internationally oriented national body)
♦ International Organization of Performing Artists (inactive)

♦ International Organization of Physical Therapists in Mental Health (IOPTMH) 14461

Pres KUL Rehab Sciences, O and N IV Herestraat 49, Box 1510, 3000 Leuven, Belgium. E-mail: info@ioptmh.org.
Vice-Pres Dept of Physiotherapy, Fac of Health and Social Sciences, Bergen Univ College, Millendalsvei 6, 5006 Bergen, Norway.
URL: https://www.ioptmh.org/

History Bergen (Norway). Current title adopted when became a subgroup of *World Confederation for Physical Therapy (WCPT, #21293)*, Jun 2011, Amsterdam (Netherlands). Former names and other names: *International Council of Physiotherapy in Psychiatry and Mental Health (IC-PPMH)* – former. **Aims** Foster cooperation between physical therapists practising in mental health throughout the world; encourage improved standards and consistency of practice in mental health care by physical therapists; advance practice by communication and exchange of information; encourage scientific research and promote opportunities for the spread of knowledge of new developments in the field of mental health; assist WCPT member organizations in the development of recognized sub-sections in mental health. **Structure** Board; Executive Committee. **Activities** Events/meetings. **Events** *International Organisation of Physical Therapy in Mental Health Conference* Athens (Greece) 2022, *International Conference of Physiotherapy in Psychiatry and Mental Health* Helsinki (Finland) 2021, *International Conference of Physiotherapy in Psychiatry and Mental Health* Helsinki (Finland) 2020, *International Conference of Physical Therapy in Psychiatry and Mental Health* Reykjavik (Iceland) 2018, *International Conference of Physical Therapy in Psychiatry and Mental Health* Madrid (Spain) 2016.
Members Individuals in 26 countries:
Argentina, Australia, Austria, Belgium, Brazil, Chile, Colombia, Denmark, Estonia, Ethiopia, Finland, Greece, Iceland, Japan, Latvia, Mexico, Netherlands, New Zealand, Norway, Portugal, South Africa, Spain, Sweden, Switzerland, Türkiye, UK.
[2023/XJ5281/v/**E**]

♦ International Organization of Physical Therapists in Pelvic and Women's Health (IOPTPWH) 14462

Sec address not obtained. E-mail: ioptpwh.secretary@gmail.com.
Pres address not obtained. E-mail: ioptpwh.president@gmail.com.
URL: https://world.physio/subgroups/pelvic-womens-health

History Since 1999, a subgroup within *World Confederation for Physical Therapy (WCPT, #21293)*. Former names and other names: *International Organization of Physical Therapists in Women's Health (IOPTWH)* – former. **Aims** Provide an international support network for member countries of World Physiotherapy to improve health and wellbeing in pelvic and women's health. **Structure** Executive Committee. **Languages** English. **Staff** Voluntary. **Finance** Sources: members' dues; sponsorship. **Activities** Events/meetings. **Events** *Sharing Experiences in MPA management Workshop* Suncheon (Korea Rep) 2016, *International Conference* Singapore (Singapore) 2015, *International Conference* Boston, MA (USA) 2013, *International conference* Amsterdam (Netherlands) 2011, *Biennial conference / International Conference* Oeiras (Portugal) 2009. **Publications** *IOPTWH Newsletter* (2 a year). Documents; position statements.
Members Full in 30 countries and territories:
Australia, Belgium, Bermuda, Brazil, Canada, Chile, Croatia, Denmark, Finland, Germany, Greece, Hong Kong, Ireland, Israel, Japan, Kuwait, Netherlands, New Zealand, Nigeria, Norway, Portugal, Saudi Arabia, Singapore, Slovenia, South Africa, Spain, Sweden, Türkiye, UK, USA.
IGO Relations *WHO (#20950)*. [2022/XE4137/**E**]

♦ International Organization of Physical Therapists in Women's Health / see International Organization of Physical Therapists in Pelvic and Women's Health (#14462)

♦ International Organization of Plant Biosystematists (IOPB) 14463

Organisation internationale de biosystématique des plantes

Pres Inst of Botany, Slovak Ac of Sciences, Dúbravska cesta 9, 845 23 Bratislava, Slovakia. T. +421910128891. Fax +421254771948. E-mail: matus.kempa@gmail.com.
URL: http://www.iopb.org/

History 1960, Copenhagen (Denmark), as *International Organization of Biosystematics*, at meeting of *International Committee for Biosystematic Terminology*. Originally a Committee on Biosystematic Terminology of *International Association for Plant Taxonomy (IAPT, #12092)*, but became autonomous under current title, within IAPT, 1961. Became fully independent, 1983. Following symposium, 2004, Valencia (Spain), became interest group of IAPT. **Aims** Promote international cooperation in the study of biosystematics, which applies methods beyond comparative morphology to analyse taxon boundaries and taxon relationships. **Structure** Council. President; Past President; President Elect. **Languages** English. **Staff** None. **Events** *Triennial Symposium* Washington, DC (USA) 2015, *Triennial Symposium* Lincoln (New Zealand) 2013, *Triennial Symposium* Aurangabad (India) 2010, *Triennial Symposium* Vysoké Tatry (Slovakia) 2008, *Triennial Symposium* Slovakia 2007. **Publications** *IOBP Newsletter* (2 a year); *IOPB Chromosome Number Reports*; *Plant Species Biology* – journal, with Japanese national society. *Experimental and Molecular Approaches to Plant Systematics* (1995); *Biological Approaches and Evolutionary Trends in Plants* (1990); *Differentiation Patterns in Higher Plants* (1987); *Plant Biosystematics* (1984). **Members** Individuals (627). Membership countries not specified.
[2015/XC2328/v/**E**]

♦ International Organization for Plant Information (no recent information)
♦ International Organization for Political and Economic Cooperation (inactive)
♦ International Organization for the Prevention of Trachoma / see International Organization Against Trachoma (#14436)
♦ International Organization of Private and Independent Doctors (inactive)

♦ International Organization for Promoting Public Diplomacy, Science, Education and Youth Cooperation (Eurasian Commonwealth) 14464

Exec Sec Vorobyovy Gory 1, MSU – A-1021, Moscow MOSKVA, Russia, 119991. T. +74959394323. Fax +74959326147. E-mail: dekanat@fgp.msu.ru.
Facebook: https://www.facebook.com/eurasia174/

History 1994. Former names and other names: *Eurasian Student Association* – former. Registration: 1077799008715, No/ID: 0012010830, Start date: 25 Apr 2007, Russia. **Aims** Further consolidation of the youth, promotion of public diplomacy, scientific, educational and youth collaboration, andconsolidation of the specialists and organizations working in the field of youth collaboration. **Structure** Congress; Council; Executive Committee; Council of Trustees. **Languages** Armenian, Azerbaijani, Belarusian, Chinese, English, Italian, Kazakh, Kirghiz, Latvian, Lithuanian, Romanian, Russian, Tajik, Turkish, Ukrainian. **Staff** 1.00 FTE, paid. **Finance** Sources: grants. **Activities** Events/meetings; training/education. **Publications** Books; articles. **Members** Full (over 1,000) in 32 countries. Membership countries not specified. **Consultative Status** Consultative status granted from: *ECOSOC (#05331)* (Special). **IGO Relations** *BRICS (#03325)*; *Commonwealth of Independent States (CIS, #04341)*; *Eurasian Economic Union (EAEU, #05607)*. **NGO Relations** Cooperation agreements with national organizations. [2020.06.25/XM6311/**D**]

♦ International Organization for the Protection of Works of Art (inactive)
♦ International Organization for the Provision of Work for Persons with Disabilities and Who are Occupationally Handicapped / see Workability International (#21049)
♦ International Organization of Psychomotricity / see International Organization of Psychomotricity and Relaxation (#14465)

♦ International Organization of Psychomotricity and Relaxation 14465

Organisation internationale de psychomotricité et de relaxation (OIPR)

SG Pôle Euro Universitaire de Santé, 19-25 Rue Gallieni, 92100 Boulogne-Billancourt, France. T. +33158171850. Fax +33158171851. E-mail: uefp@isrp.fr.
URL: http://www.psychomotricite.com/

History Founded 1979 to organize conference series *International Congress of Psychomotricity – Congrès international de psychomotricité (CIP)*. Former names and other names: *Comité international de psychomotricité (CIP)* – former (1979); *International Organization of Psychomotricity* – former; *Organisation internationale de psychomotricité (OIP)* – former. **Aims** Contribute to the development and the publishing of research in psychomotor therapy and body sciences and techniques. **Structure** International Scientific Committee; Executive Committee. **Languages** Chinese, English, French, Italian, Portuguese, Spanish. **Activities** Events/meetings; training/education. **Events** *International Congress of Psychomotricity* Montevideo (Uruguay) 2008, *Congrès mondial de psychomotricité / International Congress of Psychomotricity* Foz do Iguaçu (Brazil) 2007, *Colloque* Paris (France) 2006, *Congress* Mexico 2005, *International Congress of Psychomotricity* Strasbourg (France) 2005. **Publications** *Evolutions psychomotrices*; *Revue internationale de psychomotricité*.
Members Individuals in 22 countries:
Argentina, Belgium, Bolivia, Brazil, Cameroon, Canada, Chile, Colombia, Cuba, Denmark, Ecuador, France, Germany, Italy, Lebanon, Luxembourg, Mexico, Paraguay, Portugal, Spain, Switzerland, Uruguay.
NGO Relations Member of: Forteneza Red Ibero-Americana de Universidades con Formación de Psicomotricidad; *International Association of Social Educators (#12167)*. [2015.02.13/XF5653/v/**C**]

♦ International Organization of Psychophysiology (IOP) 14466

Organisation internationale de psychophysiologie (OIP) – Organización Internacional de Psicofisiologia (OIP)

Sec Graduate School of Human Sciences, Osaka Univ, 1-2 Yamadaoka – Suita, Osaka, 565-0871 Japan. E-mail: secretary@iopworld.org – contact@iopworld.org.
Pres CIDAAI, Via dei Tigli 30, 20125 Milan MI, Italy. E-mail: president@iopworld.org.
URL: https://iopworld.org/

History May 1978. Constitution, By-Laws, present title and structure adopted 1982. Fully renewed, 2010. Former names and other names: *Committee for the Foundation of the International Organization of Psychophysiology (CFIOP)* – former (1978 to 1982); *Comité pour la fondation de l'Organisation internationale de psychophysiologie* – former (1978 to 1982). **Aims** Disseminate information regarding psychophysiological research, teaching and applications world-wide; establish and stimulate psychophysiological research, teaching and applications; develop and promote international collaboration and discussion in the field of psychophysiology. **Structure** Board of Directors; Officers; Standing and Special Committees. **Languages** English. **Staff** Part-time. **Finance** Sources: members' dues; sale of publications. **Activities** Awards/prizes/competitions; events/meetings; knowledge management/information dissemination; research/documentation; training/education. **Events** *World Congress of Psychophysiology* Geneva (Switzerland) 2023, *World Congress of Psychophysiology* Chengdu (China) 2021, *World Congress of Psychophysiology* Chengdu (China) 2020, *World Congress of Psychophysiology* Lucca (Italy) 2018, *World Congress of Psychophysiology* Havana (Cuba) 2016. **Publications** *International Journal of Psychophysiology*.
Members Full; Associate. Individuals in 31 countries:
Australia, Austria, Belgium, Brazil, Bulgaria, Canada, China, Cuba, Denmark, Finland, France, Germany, Hungary, Indonesia, Ireland, Israel, Italy, Japan, Korea Rep, Mexico, Netherlands, North Macedonia, Poland, Romania, Russia, Singapore, South Africa, Switzerland, Türkiye, UK, USA. [2022.06.15/XC6402/**C**]

♦ International Organization for Qumrân Studies (IOQS) 14467

Contact Fac Theology, KU Leuven, Sint-Michielsstraat 4 bus 3101, 3000 Leuven, Belgium.

History 1989, Groningen (Netherlands). **Aims** Facilitate the international study of the *manuscripts* found since 1947 close to Qumrân. **Events** *Meeting* Munich (Germany) 2013, *Meeting* Helsinki (Finland) 2010, *Meeting* Ljubljana (Slovenia) 2007, *Meeting* Groningen (Netherlands) 2004, *Meeting* Basel (Switzerland) 2001.
[2013/XM1947/**E**]

♦ International Organization of Radio and Television Workers of the Americas (inactive)

♦ International Organization for the Right to Education and Freedom of Education 14468

Organisation internationale pour le droit à l'éducation et la liberté d'enseignement (OIDEL) – Organización Internacional para el Derecho a la Educación y la Libertad de Enseñanza

Pres Rue le Corbusier 8 – Rez supérieur, 1208 Geneva, Switzerland. T. +41227892949. Fax +41227892922. E-mail: oidel@oidel.org.
URL: http://www.oidel.org/

History 1985. Founded by 40 statesmen, educators and parents of school children. Former names and other names: *International Organization for the Development of Freedom of Education* – former; *Organisation internationale pour le développement de la liberté d'enseignement (OIDEL)* – former; *Organización Internacional para el Desarrollo de la Libertad de Enseñanza* – former; *OIDEL* – former. Registration: Swiss Civil Code, Switzerland. **Aims** Promote the right to education as a fundamental human right. **Structure** General Assembly; Executive Committee of 15 members; General Management. **Languages** English, French, Spanish. **Staff** 4.00 FTE, paid. **Finance** Sources: members' dues; revenue from activities/projects; subsidies. **Activities** Events/meetings; training/education. **Events** *A common good approach to COVID-19* Geneva (Switzerland) 2020, *The right to education – Towards a Renewed Commitment to Education* Geneva (Switzerland) 2019, *Education as a Cultural Right* Paris (France) 2019, *Right to Education and New Technologies – A Necessary Dialogue* Geneva (Switzerland) 2018, *Presentation of "Essential content on the right to education" and " International code on the right to education"* Switzerland 2017. **Publications** *OIDEL Newsletter* (3 a year); *Working Paper* (annual).
Members Individual and corporate in 53 countries and territories:
Angola, Argentina, Australia, Austria, Belgium, Bolivia, Brazil, Brunei Darussalam, Bulgaria, Cameroon, Canada, Chile, China, Colombia, Congo Brazzaville, Congo DR, Côte d'Ivoire, Czechia, Ecuador, El Salvador, Finland, France, Germany, Ghana, Greece, Guatemala, India, Ireland, Italy, Japan, Kenya, Lithuania, Luxembourg, Mexico, Netherlands, New Zealand, Nigeria, Pakistan, Peru, Philippines, Poland, Portugal, Russia, Sierra Leone, Slovakia, Spain, Sweden, Switzerland, Türkiye, UK, Uruguay, USA, Venezuela.
Consultative Status Consultative status granted from: *ECOSOC (#05331)* (Special); *UNESCO (#20322)* (Consultative Status); *Council of Europe (CE, #04881)* (Participatory Status). **IGO Relations** Relevant treaties: *International Covenant on Economic, Social and Cultural Rights (ICESCR, 1966)*; *Universal Declaration of Human Rights (UDHR, 1948)*. Accredited by: *United Nations Office at Vienna (UNOV, #20604)*. **NGO Relations** Member of: *Forum of Catholic Inspired NGOs (#09905)*. [2021.03.08/XC0074/**C**]

♦ International Organization for Rural Development (inactive)
♦ International Organization for Safety in Skiing / see International Society for Skiing Safety (#15443)
♦ International Organization of Scenographers and Theatre Technicians / see Organisation Internationale des Scénographes, Techniciens et Architectes de Théâtre (#17811)

♦ International Organization for Science and Technology Education (IOSTE) 14469

Organisation internationale pour l'éducation scientifique et technique (IOSTE) – Organización Internacional para la Educación Científica y Tecnológica (IOSTE)

Founder Fac de Educaçao, Univ de Sao Paulo, Av de Universidade 308, bloco A sala 109, Sao Paulo SP, 05508-040, Brazil. T. +551130913099.
Chairperson address not obtained.
Acting Sec address not obtained.
URL: http://www.ioste.org/

History Aug 1979, Halifax, NS (Canada). Formally organized under present title at 3rd Symposium, 1984, Brisbane (Australia). Former names and other names: *Symposium on World Trends in Science Education* – former (Aug 1979 to 1984). **Aims** Identify Science and Technology education with the changing needs of humankind and with specific needs of its component communities and nations. **Structure** Plenary Session (at Symposium); International Board; Executive. **Languages** English. **Staff** 15.00 FTE, voluntary. **Finance** Sources: members' dues; subscriptions. **Activities** Events/meetings. Active in all member countries. **Events** *International Symposium* Durban (South Africa) 2024, *International Symposium* Recife (Brazil) 2022, *International Symposium* Daegu (Korea Rep) 2021, *International Symposium* Daegu (Korea Rep) 2020, *International Symposium* Malmö (Sweden) 2018. **Publications** *IOSTE Newsletter.* Symposium proceedings; brochure.
Members Leading science and technical educators in 76 countries:
Algeria, Argentina, Australia, Austria, Bangladesh, Belgium, Botswana, Brazil, Bulgaria, Canada, Chile, China, Colombia, Cook Is, Cuba, Cyprus, Czechia, Denmark, Egypt, Estonia, Eswatini, Finland, France, Germany, Ghana, Greece, Honduras, Iceland, India, Indonesia, Ireland, Israel, Italy, Jamaica, Japan, Kenya, Korea Rep, Latvia, Lesotho, Lithuania, Malaysia, Malta, Mauritius, Mexico, Morocco, Namibia, Nepal, Netherlands, New Zealand, Nigeria, Norway, Pakistan, Palestine, Papua New Guinea, Philippines, Poland, Portugal, Russia, Serbia, Singapore, Slovakia, South Africa, Spain, Sri Lanka, Sweden, Switzerland, Tanzania UR, Thailand, Trinidad-Tobago, Uganda, UK, Ukraine, Uruguay, USA, Venezuela, Zambia.
NGO Relations Also links with national organizations. [2022.11.06/XC0073/v/**C**]

♦ International Organization of Securities Commissions (IOSCO) 14470

Organisation internationale des commissions de valeurs (OICV) – Organización Internacional de Comisiones de Valores – Organização Internacional das Comissões de Valores

SG Calle Oquendo 12, 28006 Madrid, Spain. T. +34914175549. Fax +34915559368. E-mail: info@iosco.org.
Communication Manager address not obtained.
URL: http://www.iosco.org/

History 1983, deriving from *Inter-American Association of Securities Commissions (inactive)*. **Aims** Cooperate in developing, implementing and promoting adherence to internationally recognized and consistent standards of regulation, oversight and enforcement so as to protect investors, maintain fair, efficient and transparent markets, and seek to address systemic risks; enhance investor protection and promote investor confidence in the integrity of securities markets, through strengthened information exchange and cooperation in enforcement against misconduct and in supervision of markets and market intermediaries; facilitate exchange of information among security regulators at both global and regional levels in order to help develop global capital markets, strengthen market infrastructure and implement appropriate regulation. **Structure** Annual Conference; Presidents Committee as plenary body (meets annually at Conference); Board; Policy Committees (8); Headquarters currently located in Madrid (Spain). **Languages** Arabic, English, French, Portuguese, Spanish. **Staff** 31.00 FTE, paid. **Finance** Sources: members' dues. **Activities** Capacity building; guidance/assistance/consulting; monitoring/evaluation; networking/liaising; research/documentation; standards/guidelines; training/education. **Events** *Annual Conference* Marrakech (Morocco) 2022, *Annual Conference* Lisbon (Portugal) 2021, *Annual Conference* Dubai (United Arab Emirates) 2020, *Meeting* Tokyo (Japan) 2020, *Meeting* Tokyo (Japan) 2019. **Publications** Annual Report; risk outlook and staff research papers; stock takes on securities markets and regulation; consultation and final reports; media releases; principles; standards; guidelines; recommendations; codes of conduct; speeches.
Members totalling 203. Ordinary (voting) 126 securities regulators. Associate (non-voting) – 23 public regulatory bodies with jurisdiction in the subdivisions of that country, and other eligible body with an appropriate responsibility for securities regulation. Affiliate (on-voting) – 64 SROs and international bodies having a mission related to the development or regulation of securities markets. Membership countries not specified. Included in the above, 9 organizations listed in this Yearbook:
Included in the above, 9 organizations listed in this Yearbook:
Asian Development Bank (ADB, #01422); *European Commission (EC, #06633)*; *EuropeanIssuers (#07605)*; *European Securities and Markets Authority (ESMA, #08457)*; *International Bank for Reconstruction and Development (IBRD, #12317)*; *International Monetary Fund (IMF, #14180)*; *North American Securities Administrators Association (NASAA)*; *OECD (#17693)*; *Union économique et monétaire Ouest africaine (UEMOA, #20377)*.
IGO Relations Participates in working groups of: *Group of Twenty (G20, #10793)*. Member of: *Financial Stability Board (FSB, #09770)*. **NGO Relations** Observer to: *International Forum of Independent Audit Regulators (IFIAR, #13639)*. Cooperates with: *International Association of Insurance Supervisors (IAIS, #11966)*; *International Forum for Investor Education (IFIE, #13642)*. Founder member of: *Joint Forum (#16130)*. [2022/XC0067/y/**B**]

♦ International Organization for Self-Determination and Equality (unconfirmed)

♦ International Organization for Septuagint and Cognate Studies (IOSCS) 14471

Sec Ak der Wissenschaften zu Göttingen, Friedländer Weg 11, 37085 Göttingen, Germany.
Pres Trinity Western Univ, 7600 Glover Road, Langley BC V2Y 1Y1, Canada. T. +16048887511 ext 3842.
URL: http://ccat.sas.upenn.edu/ioscs/

History 1968. **Aims** Carry out critical study of *Jewish Greek scriptures* and related subjects. **Structure** Annual Meeting. **Languages** English, French, German. **Staff** Voluntary. **Activities** Events/meetings. **Events** *Congress* Aberdeen (UK) 2019, *Congress* Boston, MA (USA) 2017, *Congress* Stellenbosch (South Africa) 2016, *Congress* Atlanta, GA (USA) 2015, *Congress* San Diego, CA (USA) 2014. **Publications** *Journal of Septuagint and Cognate Studies (JSCS)*. *Septuagint and Cognate Studies Series*. Monograph series.
Members Individuals: college and university teachers, students and clergy (290); Libraries (135). Members in 29 countries:
Australia, Austria, Belgium, Brazil, Canada, Denmark, Finland, France, Germany, Greece, Iceland, India, Ireland, Israel, Italy, Japan, Korea Rep, Mexico, Netherlands, New Zealand, Norway, Russia, South Africa, Spain, Sweden, Switzerland, Uganda, UK, USA. [2020.08.19/XD7509/**C**]

♦ International Organization on Shape Memory and Superelastic Technologies (internationally oriented national body)

♦ International Organization of Societies for Electrophysiological Technology (OSET) 14472

Pres c/o RSC CLTM Dept, 331 Melrose Dr, Ste 145, Richardson TX 75080, USA.
URL: http://www.oset.org/

History 8 Sep 1977, Amsterdam (Netherlands). Registration: End date: 2015, Switzerland; Start date: 2015, Australia, Camberra. **Aims** Promote education and strive for attainment of the highest level of knowledge and understanding in the field of electrophysiology (neurophysiology or neurodiagnostics) in all modalities including electroencephalography, evoked potentials, nerve conduction studies, polysomnography, long term monitoring for epilepsy, ICU monitoring, magnetoencephalography and intraoperative neuromonitoring during surgical procedures. **Structure** General Assembly; Council; Executive Committee. **Languages** English. **Staff** 5.00 FTE, voluntary. **Finance** Members' dues. **Activities** Training/education; standards/guidelines. **Events** *Quadrennial Congress* Porto (Portugal) 2019, *Quadrennial Congress* Turku (Finland) 2015, *Quadrennial Congress* Bielefeld (Germany) 2011, *Quadrennial congress* Montecatini Terme (Italy) 2007, *Quadrennial Congress* Egmond aan Zee (Netherlands) 2003. **Publications** Information Services: Online education courses.
Members Full organizations in 16 countries:
Australia, Canada, Denmark, Finland, France, Germany, Ireland, Italy, New Zealand, Nigeria, Portugal, South Africa, Sweden, Switzerland, UK, USA. [2019/XD6316/**D**]

♦ International Organization for Spice Trade Associations (internationally oriented national body)

♦ International Organization for Standardization (ISO) 14473

Organisation internationale de normalisation – Organización Internacional de Normalización – Internationale Organisation für Normung – Mezdunarodnaja Organizacija po Standartizacii

Secretariat BIBC II, Chemin de Blandonnet 8, CP 401, Vernier, 1214 Geneva, Switzerland. T. +41227490111. E-mail: central@iso.org.
URL: http://www.iso.org/

History Feb 1947, Geneva (Switzerland). Established to follow up the work of *International Federation of National Standardizing Associations (ISA, inactive)*, 1926-1942, and of *United Nations Standards Coordinating Committee (inactive)*, 1944-1946. Registration: Swiss Civil Code, Switzerland. **Aims** Promote development of standardization and related activities worldwide with a view to facilitating international exchange of goods and services and to developing cooperation in the sphere of intellectual, scientific, technological and economic activity. **Structure** General Assembly (annual). Council, consisting of ISO officers (President, 2 Vice-Presidents, Treasurer and Secretary-General) and 18 elected Member Bodies. Technical Management Board, comprising Chairman and 12 elected Member Bodies. Technical Committees (TCs) for each domain dealt with (190 TCs), including ISO/IEC Joint Technical Committee on Information Technology (JTC 1). Central Secretariat, headed by Secretary- General. Membership limited to one member per country. **Languages** English, French, Russian. **Staff** 154.00 FTE, paid. **Finance** Sources: members' dues; sale of publications. **Activities** International Standards prepared by about 3,000 technical bodies covering virtually all areas of technology, with participation of national delegations and some 580 international organizations in liaison. Develops policies through, inter alia, 3 policy development committees covering: developing country matters; conformity assessment; consumer issues. ISO technical committees organize regular meetings. Together with IEC and *International Telecommunication Union (ITU, #15673)* member of *'World Standards Cooperation (WSC)'*, whose primary function is to strengthen and advance the voluntary consensus-based international standards system. **Events** *Technical Committee Meeting on Rubber and Rubber Products* Nara (Japan) 2024, *ISO Annual Meeting* Brisbane, QLD (Australia) 2023, *Subcommittee on Interoperability, Integration, and Architectures for Enterprise Systems and Automation Applications Meeting* Jeju (Korea Rep) 2022, *Plenary meeting* Osaka (Japan) 2022, *Technical Committee on Cold Chain Logistics Meeting* Tokyo (Japan) 2022. **Publications** *ISO Focus+* (11 a year) in English, French. *ISO/IEC Guides*; *ISO International Standards* – about 19,500 published to date; *ISO Standards Handbooks and Compendia*. *International Classification for Standards (ICS)* (2005); *ISO Code of Ethics*; *ISO Five-Year Action Plan for Developing Countries 2011-2015*; *ISO Strategic Plan 2011-2015*. Annual report. **Information Services** *ISO/IEC Information Centre* – based at ISO Central Secretariat; *ISO Information Network (ISONET)* – coordinates and systematizes international and national exchange of information on standards and standards-type documents by linking ISO members' information centres and ISO/IEC Information Centre into a coherent information system.
Members Members bodies: National standards bodies (119) in 119 countries:
Afghanistan, Algeria, Argentina, Armenia, Australia, Austria, Azerbaijan, Bahrain, Bangladesh, Barbados, Belarus, Belgium, Benin, Bosnia-Herzegovina, Botswana, Brazil, Bulgaria, Burkina Faso, Cameroon, Canada, Chile, China, Colombia, Congo DR, Costa Rica, Côte d'Ivoire, Croatia, Cuba, Cyprus, Czechia, Denmark, Ecuador, Egypt, El Salvador, Estonia, Ethiopia, Fiji, Finland, France, Gabon, Germany, Ghana, Greece, Hungary, Iceland, India, Indonesia, Iran Islamic Rep, Iraq, Ireland, Israel, Italy, Jamaica, Japan, Jordan, Kazakhstan, Kenya, Korea DPR, Korea Rep, Kuwait, Latvia, Lebanon, Libya, Lithuania, Luxembourg, Malawi, Malaysia, Mali, Malta, Mauritius, Mexico, Mongolia, Morocco, Namibia, Nepal, Netherlands, New Zealand, Nigeria, North Macedonia, Norway, Oman, Pakistan, Panama, Peru, Philippines, Poland, Portugal, Qatar, Romania, Russia, Rwanda, Saudi Arabia, Senegal, Serbia, Singapore, Slovakia, Slovenia, South Africa, Spain, Sri Lanka, St Lucia, Sudan, Sweden, Switzerland, Tanzania UR, Thailand, Trinidad-Tobago, Tunisia, Türkiye, Uganda, UK, Ukraine, United Arab Emirates, Uruguay, USA, Uzbekistan, Vietnam, Yemen, Zimbabwe.
Correspondent members in 38 countries and territories:
Albania, Angola, Bahamas, Bhutan, Bolivia, Brunei Darussalam, Burundi, Cambodia, Dominica, Dominican Rep, Eritrea, Eswatini, Gambia, Georgia, Guatemala, Guyana, Haiti, Hong Kong, Kyrgyzstan, Lesotho, Macau, Madagascar, Mauritania, Moldova, Montenegro, Mozambique, Myanmar, Nicaragua, Niger, Palestine, Papua New Guinea, Paraguay, Seychelles, Sierra Leone, Suriname, Tajikistan, Turkmenistan, Zambia.
Subscriber members in 7 countries:
Antigua-Barbuda, Belize, Honduras, Laos, St Vincent-Grenadines.
Consultative Status Consultative status granted from: *ECOSOC (#05331)* (General); *FAO (#09260)* (Special Status); *ILO (#11123)* (Special List); *International Atomic Energy Agency (IAEA, #12294)*; *International Civil Aviation Organization (ICAO, #12581)*; *International Maritime Organization (IMO, #14102)*; *UNCTAD (#20285)* (General Category); *UNESCO (#20322)* (Consultative Status); *UNIDO (#20336)*; *WHO (#20950)* (Official Relations); *World Intellectual Property Organization (WIPO, #21593)* (Permanent Observer Status); *World Meteorological Organization (WMO, #21649)*.
IGO Relations Close working relations with the following United Nations bodies which do not have special provision for consultative status: *Codex Alimentarius Commission (CAC, #04081)*; *UNEP (#20299)*; *Universal Postal Union (UPU, #20682)*. Special links with: *World Trade Organization (WTO, #21864)*. Accredited by: *United Nations Framework Convention on Climate Change – Secretariat (UNFCCC, #20564)*. Observer Status granted by: *Committee on the Peaceful Uses of Outer Space (COPUOS, #04277)*.
Working contacts also with:
- *International Monetary Fund (IMF, #14180)*;
- *United Nations Economic Commission for Africa (ECA, #20554)*;
- *United Nations Economic Commission for Europe (UNECE, #20555)*, especially *'Working Party on Facilitation of International Trade Procedures'*;
- *United Nations Economic Commission for Latin America and the Caribbean (ECLAC, #20556)*;
- *United Nations Economic and Social Commission for Asia and the Pacific (ESCAP, #20557)*;
- *United Nations Economic and Social Commission for Western Asia (ESCWA, #20558)*;
- *United Nations Human Settlements Programme (UN-Habitat, #20572)*.

Liaison with a total of some 50 intergovernmental organizations which contribute to the preparation of International Standards (not specified).
NGO Relations Special relationship with sister organization: *International Electrotechnical Commission (IEC, #13255)*, which handles all international standardization in the electrical and electronic fields. Special links with: *International Laboratory Accreditation Cooperation (ILAC, #13995)*. Liaison with some 560 organizations (not specified). Input or influence on aspects of development or regulation of: *Internet (#15948)*. [2021.03.03/XB2314/**B**]

♦ International Organization for Statistical Studies on Diseases of the Esophagus / see Organisation mondiale d'études spécialisées sur les maladies de l'oesophage (#17818)

♦ International Organization for the Study of Ancient Languages by Computer (inactive)

♦ International Organization for the Study of the Endurance of Wire Ropes 14474

Organisation internationale pour l'étude de l'endurance des cables (OIPEEC) – Internationale Organisation zum Studium der Ermüdungsfestigkeit von Drahtseile – Organizzazione Internazionale per lo Studio della Fatica delle Funi

Address not obtained.
URL: http://www.oipeec.org/

History 7 Sep 1961, Turin (Italy). Founded following decision of participants at the International Colloquium on the Fatigue of Ropes. **Aims** Investigate and promote all forms of research on wire ropes, in particular problems of *fatigue*; collect and disseminate the results obtained. **Structure** Management Committee, consisting of President, Secretary, Editor and Treasurer. **Languages** English, French, German, Italian. **Staff** 2.00 FTE, voluntary. **Finance** Members' dues. **Activities** Gives out awards to young researchers. Organizes international conferences. **Publications** *OIPEEC Bulletin* (2 a year); *Bibliographic Review 1963-1995*. proceedings of roundtables.
Members Individuals (101) in 25 countries:
Australia, Austria, Belgium, Canada, Finland, France, Germany, Hong Kong, India, Israel, Italy, Japan, Korea Rep, Netherlands, Poland, Portugal, Romania, Slovenia, South Africa, Spain, Switzerland, UK, Ukraine, USA, Venezuela.
NGO Relations *European Federation of Steel Wire Rope Industries (EWRIS, #07221).* In liaison with technical committees of: *International Organization for Standardization (ISO, #14473).* [2020/XD5453/v/**D**]

♦ International Organization for the Study of Group Tensions (inactive)
♦ International Organization for the Study of Human Development (inactive)

♦ International Organization for the Study of Inflammatory Bowel Disease (IOIBD) 14475

Admin Dir c/o MK Producties, Javalaan 9a, 3742 CN Baarn, Netherlands. T. +31355426745. E-mail: ioibd@mkproducties.nl.
Treas Dept Gastroenterology, Fac Medicine and Health, Campus USÖ, Örebro Univ, SE-701 82 Örebro, Sweden. T. +31355426745.
URL: http://www.ioibd.org/

History 1981, Lyon (France). Foundation for Research and Education set up, 1997, Stockholm (Sweden). Former names and other names: *Stiftelsen för Utbildning och Forskning Avseende Inflammatoriska Tarmsjukdom (SUFIT)* – alias. Registration: No/ID: 802404-9960, Start date: 11 Jan 1997, Sweden. **Aims** Promote the health of people with IBD by setting the direction for patient care, education and research. **Structure** Annual General Meeting; Executive Committee; Thematic Clusters; Publication Committee; Grant Review Committee. **Languages** English. **Activities** Events/meetings; financial and/or material support; knowledge management/information dissemination; research/documentation. **Events** *Annual General Meeting* Cambridge (UK) 2023, *Annual General Meeting* Napa, CA (USA) 2022, *Annual General Meeting* Bordeaux (France) 2021, *Around Covid-19 and IBD* 2020, *Annual General Meeting* Bordeaux (France) 2020.
Members IBD Centres in 27 countries:
Australia, Austria, Belgium, Brazil, Canada, China, Czechia, Denmark, France, Germany, Greece, Hungary, India, Ireland, Israel, Italy, Japan, Mexico, Netherlands, New Zealand, Norway, Portugal, Spain, Sweden, Switzerland, UK, USA. [2022.02.15/XM3609/**D**]

♦ International Organization for the Study of the Old Testament (IOSOT) 14476

Admin and Logistics University of Zurich, Main Bldg, Rämistrasse 71, KOL-E-21, 8001 Zurich ZH, Switzerland. T. +441224272840. E-mail: iosot2022@theol.uzh.ch.
URL: https://www.iosot2022.uzh.ch/en.html

History Sep 1950, Leiden (Netherlands). **Aims** Further scientific study of the Old Testament and international cooperation in that study. **Structure** Congress (every 3 years); Executive Committee. **Languages** English, French, German. **Finance** Financial arrangements for each Congress made by local organizing committee. **Events** *Triennial Congress* Zurich (Switzerland) 2022, *Triennial Congress* Aberdeen (UK) 2019, *Triennial Congress* Stellenbosch (South Africa) 2016, *Triennial Congress* Munich (Germany) 2013, *Triennial Congress* Helsinki (Finland) 2010. **Publications** *Vetus Testamentum* (4 a year) in English, French, German – with supplements, learned articles, notes, reviews and book lists. *Concordance to the Peshitta* – in preparation; *Peshitta* – (in preparation) Syriac version of the Old Testament. **Members** No formal individual or group membership. Attendance at congresses open to Old Testament scholars from any country. **NGO Relations** Cooperates with (4): *International Organization for Masoretic Studies (IOMS, #14452)*; *International Organization for Qumrân Studies (IOQS, #14467)*; *International Organization for Septuagint and Cognate Studies (IOSCS, #14471)*; *International Organization for Targumic Studies (IOTS, #14480).* [2019/XF2318/**F**]

♦ International Organization for Succulent Plant Study (IOS) 14477

Organisation internationale de recherche sur les plantes succulentes – Organización Internacional para el Estudio de Plantas Suculentas – Internationale Organisation für Sukkulentenforschung

Pres Inst Biologia UNAM, Ciudad Universitaria, Aptdo Postal 70-233, 04510 Mexico City CDMX, Mexico. E-mail: hmhm@ib.unam.mx.
URL: http://succulentresearch.org/

History 1950, Zurich (Switzerland). **Aims** Promote study of succulent and allied plants; encourage international cooperation among those interested in them. **Structure** Executive Board. **Languages** English, French, German, Spanish. **Staff** None. **Finance** Sources: donations. **Events** *Biennial Congress* Ica (Peru) 2019, *Biennial Congress* Cadereyta de Montes (Mexico) 2017, *Biennial Congress* Phoenix, AZ (USA) 2014, *Biennial Congress* Havana (Cuba) 2012, *Inter-congress* Monte Carlo (Monaco) 2011. **Publications** *IOS Bulletin* (annual); *Repertorium Plantarum Succulentarum* (annual).
Members Active; Ordinary; Honorary; Emeritus; Student; Institutional. Individuals (about 100) in 32 countries:
Argentina, Australia, Austria, Belgium, Bolivia, Brazil, Canada, Chile, Czechia, France, Germany, Italy, Kenya, Malta, Mexico, Monaco, Netherlands, New Zealand, Norway, Peru, Poland, Portugal, Russia, South Africa, Spain, Sweden, Switzerland, UK, Ukraine, USA, Venezuela, Zimbabwe.
NGO Relations Scientific member of: *International Union of Biological Sciences (IUBS, #15760).* [2018.06.01/XC2315/v/**C**]

♦ International Organization of Supreme Audit Institutions (INTOSAI) 14478

Organisation internationale des institutions supérieures de contrôle des finances publiques – Organización Internacional de las Entidades Fiscalizadoras Superiores – Internationale Organisation der Obersten Rechnungskontrollbehörden

SG c/o Rechnungshof, Dampfschiffstrasse 1, 1030 Vienna, Austria. T. +431711718905. Fax +4317180969. E-mail: intosai@rechnungshof.gv.at.
URL: http://www.intosai.org/

History 1953, Havana (Cuba). Founded in 1953 at 1st International Congress (INCOSAI). Lima Declaration of Guidelines on Auditing Precepts, adopted at INCOSAI IX; 1977, Lima (Peru), determined the principle of independence of government auditing in methodological and professional terms. First Strategic Plan adopted, 2004; current strategic plan for 2017-2022. Mexico Declaration, adopted at INCOSAI XIX, 2007, defined requirements stated in 1977 Lima Declaration in more concrete terms and identified 8 pillars for the independence of external government auditing. First complete set of ISSAIs (International Standards of Supreme Audit Institutions) presented and endorsed, 2010, Johannesburg (South Africa), INCOSAI XX. UN General Assembly approved Resolution A/66/209 on strengthening independence of Supreme Audit Institutions, 2011. Beijing Declaration adopted at XXI INCOSAI, 2013, China. UN General Assembly approved Resolutions A 66/209, 2011 and A/69/228, 2014. INTOSAI Framework for Professional Pronouncements (IFPP) endorsed, 2016, Abu Dhabi (United Arab Emirates), INCOSAI XXII, replacing ISSAI Framework. INTOSAI Standard Setting body created: Forum for INTOSAI Professional Pronouncements (FIPP). **Aims** Promote exchange of ideas, knowledge and experience between members, the Supreme Audit Institutions (SAIs) of countries around the globe, with other international organizations and stakeholders in the field of government auditing; elaborate, maintain and update auditing standards and guidelines; facilitate initiatives in support of SAIs and regions to build and develop their capacities and enhance their capabilities. **Structure** Congress (every 3 years); Governing Board; General Secretariat; Goal Committees (4). Regional Organizations (7): *African Organization of Supreme Audit Institutions (AFROSAI, #00406)*, set up 1976; *Arab Organization of Supreme Audit Institutions (ARABOSAI, #01021)*, set up 1976; *Asian Organization of Supreme Audit Institutions (ASOSAI, #01594)*, set up 1978; *Caribbean Organization of Supreme Audit Institutions (CAROSAI, #03536)*, set up 1988; *European Organization of Supreme Audit Institutions (EUROSAI, #08115)*, set up 1990; *Organization of Latin American and Caribbean Supreme Audit Institutions (OLACEFS, #17877)*, set up 1965; *Pacific Association of Supreme Audit Institutions (PASAI, #17935)*, set up 1987. **Languages** Arabic, English, French, German, Spanish. **Staff** 8.00 FTE, paid. **Finance** Sources: contributions; in-kind support; members' dues. **Activities** Awareness raising; capacity building; events/meetings; guidance/assistance/consulting; monitoring/evaluation; standards/guidelines. **Events** *Working Group on Impact of Science and Technology (WGISTA) Annual Meeting* Abu Dhabi (United Arab Emirates) 2022, *Triennial INTOSAI Congress* Rio de Janeiro (Brazil) 2022, *Triennial INCOSAI Congress* Moscow (Russia) 2019, *Meeting* Oslo (Norway) 2019, *Capacity Building Committee Meeting* Tokyo (Japan) 2019. **Publications** *International Journal of Government Auditing.* Booklets; books; standards; guides.
Members Full membership open to Supreme Audit Institutions of all countries which are members to the United Nations or any of its Specialized Agencies and the Supreme Audit Institutions of supranational organizations which are a subject under international law and are endowed with a legal status and an appropriate degree of economic, technical/organizational or financial integration. Supreme Audit Institutions in 196 countries and territories:
Afghanistan, Albania, Algeria, Andorra, Angola, Antigua-Barbuda, Argentina, Armenia, Australia, Austria, Azerbaijan, Bahamas, Bahrain, Bangladesh, Barbados, Belarus, Belgium, Belize, Benin, Bhutan, Bolivia, Bosnia-Herzegovina, Botswana, Brazil, Brunei Darussalam, Bulgaria, Burkina Faso, Burundi, Cambodia, Cameroon, Canada, Cape Verde, Central African Rep, Chad, Chile, China, Colombia, Congo Brazzaville, Congo DR, Cook Is, Costa Rica, Côte d'Ivoire, Croatia, Cuba, Cyprus, Czechia, Denmark, Djibouti, Dominica, Dominican Rep, Ecuador, Egypt, El Salvador, Equatorial Guinea, Eritrea, Estonia, Eswatini, Ethiopia, Fiji, Finland, France, Gabon, Gambia, Georgia, Germany, Ghana, Greece, Grenada, Guam, Guatemala, Guinea, Guinea-Bissau, Guyana, Haiti, Holy See, Honduras, Hungary, Iceland, India, Indonesia, Iran Islamic Rep, Iraq, Ireland, Israel, Italy, Jamaica, Japan, Jordan, Kazakhstan, Kenya, Kiribati, Korea Rep, Kosovo, Kuwait, Kyrgyzstan, Laos, Latvia, Lebanon, Lesotho, Liberia, Libya, Liechtenstein, Lithuania, Luxembourg, Madagascar, Malawi, Malaysia, Maldives, Mali, Malta, Marshall Is, Mauritania, Mauritius, Mexico, Micronesia FS, Moldova, Monaco, Mongolia, Montenegro, Morocco, Mozambique, Myanmar, Namibia, Nauru, Nepal, Netherlands, New Zealand, Nicaragua, Niger, Nigeria, North Macedonia, Northern Mariana Is, Norway, Oman, Pakistan, Palau, Palestine, Panama, Papua New Guinea, Paraguay, Peru, Philippines, Poland, Portugal, Puerto Rico, Qatar, Romania, Russia, Rwanda, Samoa, Sao Tomé-Principe, Saudi Arabia, Senegal, Serbia, Seychelles, Sierra Leone, Singapore, Slovakia, Slovenia, Solomon Is, Somalia, South Africa, South Sudan, Spain, Sri Lanka, St Kitts-Nevis, St Lucia, St Vincent-Grenadines, Sudan, Suriname, Sweden, Switzerland, Syrian AR, Tajikistan, Tanzania UR, Thailand, Timor-Leste, Togo, Tonga, Trinidad-Tobago, Tunisia, Türkiye, Tuvalu, Uganda, UK, Ukraine, United Arab Emirates, Uruguay, USA, Uzbekistan, Vanuatu, Venezuela, Vietnam, Yemen, Zambia, Zimbabwe.
SAIs through supranational organizations:
European Court of Auditors (#06854).
Associate members (5):
Association des institutions supérieures de contrôle ayant en commun l'usage du français (AISCCUF, #02647); *Comunidade dos Paises de Lingua Portuguesa (CPLP, #04430)*; *Cour des comptes de l'UEMOA (see: #20377)*; *Institute of Internal Auditors (IIA, #11272)*; *International Bank for Reconstruction and Development (IBRD, #12317)* (World Bank).
Affiliate – overseas or dependent territories, with a certain level of autonomy for their regional and international relations activities:
Guam, Northern Mariana Is.
Consultative Status Consultative status granted from: *ECOSOC (#05331)* (Special). **IGO Relations** Accredited by (1): *United Nations Office at Vienna (UNOV, #20604).* Partner of (8): *ECOSOC (#05331)*; *International Bank for Reconstruction and Development (IBRD, #12317)* (World Bank); *OECD (#17693)*; *UNDP (#20292)*; *United Nations Committee of Experts on Public Administration (CEPA, #20542)*; United Nations Department of Economic and Social Affairs (UNDESA); *United Nations Office on Drugs and Crime (UNODC, #20596)*; *UN Women (#20724).* [2022.10.21/XB2329/y/**B**]

♦ International Organization for Sustainable Development (internationally oriented national body)

♦ International Organization for Systematic and Evolutionary Biology (IOSEB) 14479

Pres FUB-Botanischer, Königin-Luise-Strasse 6-8, 14195 Berlin, Germany.
URL: http://bionomenclature.net/ioseb/

History 1996, Budapest (Hungary). Founded during *International Congress of Systematic and Evolutionary Biology (ICSEB, inactive).* Registration: Switzerland. **Aims** Facilitate the international cooperation among *systematists* and *evolutionalists*. **Activities** *International Congress of Systematic and Evolutionary Biology (ICSEB)*, formerly *International Congress of Systematic and Evolutionary Biology (ICSEB, inactive).* **Events** *International Congress of Systematic and Evolutionary Biology* Seoul (Korea Rep) 2015, *International Congress of Systematic and Evolutionary Biology* Berlin (Germany) 2011, *Biodiversity in the information age* Patras (Greece) 2002, *International congress of systematic and evolutionary biology / Congress* Budapest (Hungary) 1996, *Congress* College Park, MD (USA) 1990. **NGO Relations** Scientific member of: *International Union of Biological Sciences (IUBS, #15760).* [2013/XD8623/**D**]

♦ International Organization for Targumic Studies (IOTS) 14480

Pres Univ College London, Dept of Hebrew Jewish Studies, Foster Court, Gower Street, London, WC1E 6BT, UK.
URL: http://targum.info/

History 1995, Cambridge (UK). **Aims** Study the *Targumim*, the ancient Jewish *translations* of Hebrew bible into *Aramaic*, from any academic approach, methodology or purpose; study subjects related to research into the Targumim. **Structure** Executive Committee of 9 members, including President, Vice-President and Secretary-Treasurer. **Finance** Members' dues. **Activities** Projects/programmes; Knowledge management/information dissemination. **Events** *Triennial Congress* Stellenbosch (South Africa) 2016, *Triennial Congress* Munich (Germany) 2013, *Triennial Congress* Helsinki (Finland) 2010, *Triennial Congress* Ljubljana (Slovenia) 2007, *Triennial Congress* Leiden (Netherlands) 2004. **Publications** *Newsletter for Targumic and Cognate Studies.* **NGO Relations** Joint congress with: *International Organization for the Study of the Old Testament (IOSOT, #14476).* [2015.11.03/XM1946/**E**]

♦ International Organization for Technical Cooperation in Geology (inactive)
♦ International Organization for Timber Technology Transfer / see Combois (#04122)
♦ International Organization for the Transition of Professional Dancer (no recent information)

♦ International Organization for Transportation by Rope 14481

Organisation internationale des transports à câble – Organización Internacional de Transportes por Cable – Internationale Organisation für das Seilbahnwesen – Organizzazione Internazionale dei Trasporti a Fune (OITAF)

Gen Sec Ufficio Trasporti Funiviari, Piazza Silvius Magnago 3, 39100 Bolzano, Italy. T. +39471414600. E-mail: info@oitaf.org.
Pres Bundesministerium für Verkehr, Innovation und Technologie, Sektion IV, Abt. Sch 3 – Seilbahnen u. Schlepplifte, Radetzkystr. 2, 1030 Vienna, Austria.
URL: http://www.oitaf.org/

History 20 Jan 1959, Milan (Italy). Founded following resolutions passed at 1st International Congress of Ropeway Transport, May 1957, Rome (Italy). Registration: Atti Publici, No/ID: 28695 Vol III, Start date: 5 Feb 1959, Italy, Milan. **Aims** Ensure progress and extension of transport by rope; promote research and experimental work to develop and progress rope transportation and harmonize national regulations in the field; propose unified international *standards* for planning, construction, operation, maintenance and supervision of transport by rope. **Structure** General Assembly (at least every 3 years); Management Committee; Executive Committee; other Committees (4); North American Continental Section (OITAF/NACS). **Languages** English, French, German, Italian, Spanish. **Staff** 4.00 FTE, voluntary. **Finance** Sources: members' dues. **Activities** Guidance/assistance/consulting; research and development; research/documentation; standards/guidelines. **Events** *Cableways – Top Level of Safety* Grenoble (France) 2022, *Seminar* Grenoble (France) 2020, *Seminar* Innsbruck (Austria) 2019, *Seminar* Grenoble (France) 2018, *Congress* Bolzano (Italy) 2017. **Publications** *OITAF Information Bulletin* (2 a year). Committee reports; statistical data; technical research; technical recommendations; congress proceedings.

Members Administrations, associations, institutions and individuals interested in technical, juridical, administrative and economic problems of transport by rope, including ski-lifts, in 35 countries and territories:
Andorra, Argentina, Austria, Belgium, Bolivia, Brazil, Chile, China, Colombia, Czechia, Finland, France, Georgia, Germany, Hong Kong, Hungary, Iceland, India, Italy, Japan, Korea Rep, Malaysia, Norway, Poland, Portugal, Romania, Russia, Singapore, Slovenia, Spain, Sweden, Switzerland, Türkiye, UK, USA. [2022.06.15/XC2319/**C**]

♦ International Organization of Turkic Culture (TURKSOY) 14482

Uluslararasy Türk Kültürü Tetkilaty

SG Ferit Recai Ertugrul Cad No 8, Or-An, 06450 Ankara/Ankara, Türkiye. T. +903124910100. Fax +903124910111. E-mail: turksoy@turksoy.org.
URL: http://www.turksoy.org/

History 12 Jul 1993, Almaty (Kazakhstan). Founded when Agreement was signed. Former names and other names: *Joint Administration of the Turkic Arts and Culture* – former (12 Jul 1993); *Türk Kültür ve Sanatlari Ortak Yönetimi (TÜRKSOY)* – former (12 Jul 1993); *Administration conjointe de la culture et des arts turcs* – alias; *Administración Conjunta de la Cultura y las Artes Turcas* – alias. **Aims** Promote development of cultural and artistic relations among Turkic language speaking countries and communities. **Structure** Permanent Council of Ministers of Culture of Turkish Speaking Countries; Team Coordinator; Secretary General; Deputy Secretary General; Head of Department; Representatives; Experts; Secretary. **Languages** English, Russian, Turkish. **Staff** 20.00 FTE, paid. **Finance** Members' dues. **Activities** Events/meetings. **Publications** *Türksoy* (4 a year) – journal. Books; catalogues; brochures; activity reports.
Members Principal members: governments of 6 countries:
Azerbaijan, Kazakhstan, Kyrgyzstan, Türkiye, Turkmenistan, Uzbekistan.
Observers: governments of 8 countries and territories:
Bashkortostan, Gagauzia, Khakassia, Northern Cyprus, Russia (Altai), Sakha-Yakutia, Tatarstan, Tuva.
IGO Relations Cooperation agreement with: *UNESCO (#20322)* (8 Jun 1996). Memorandum of Understanding with: *Intergovernmental Foundation for Educational, Scientific and Cultural Cooperation (IFESCCO, #11485)* (2009). Affiliated to: *Cooperation Council of Turkic Speaking States (Turkic Council, #04793).* **NGO Relations** Formal agreement with: *International Humanitarian Academy Europe-Asia, Ankara (IHA Europe-Asia, no recent information)* (1 Dec 1999). [2020/XD6105/**D***]

- ♦ International Organization of Universities for Sustainable Development and Environmental Conservation (#17843)
- ♦ International Organization for Vacuum Science and Technology / see International Union for Vacuum Science, Technique and Applications (#15826)
- ♦ International Organization for Victim Assistance (internationally oriented national body)
- ♦ International Organization for Water Operators Partnerships (unconfirmed)

♦ International Organization of Women and Mathematics Education (IOWME) 14483

Convenor Stockholm Univ, SE-106 91 Stockholm, Sweden.
Convenor Monash Univ, Wellington Rd, Clayton VIC 3800, Australia.
URL: http://www.mathunion.org/icmi/iowme/

History Founded 1980, Berkeley CA (USA), at Fourth International Congress on Mathematical Education (ICME-4). **Aims** Provide a forum for those interested in the relationship between gender and the learning and teaching of mathematics. **Structure** Study Group (meets every 4 years at ICME). **Languages** English. **Staff** 2.00 FTE, voluntary. **Events** *Quadrennial meeting* Hamburg (Germany) 2016, *International Congress on Mathematical Education* Hamburg (Germany) 2015, *Quadrennial Meeting / International Congress on Mathematical Education* Seoul (Korea Rep) 2012, *Quadrennial meeting / International Congress on Mathematical Education* Monterrey (Mexico) 2008, *Quadrennial meeting / International Congress on Mathematical Education* Copenhagen (Denmark) 2004. **Publications** *IOWME Newsletter* (3 a year).
Members Individuals and groups in 45 countries:
Argentina, Australia, Austria, Belgium, Botswana, Brazil, Burkina Faso, Cameroon, Canada, Côte d'Ivoire, Cyprus, Czechia, Denmark, Dominican Rep, Finland, Germany, Hungary, Iceland, India, Israel, Italy, Japan, Jordan, Kenya, Korea Rep, Malaysia, Mexico, Morocco, Netherlands, New Zealand, Nigeria, Northern Ireland, Norway, Pakistan, Papua New Guinea, Russia, South Africa, Spain, Sweden, Switzerland, Trinidad-Tobago, UK, Ukraine, USA, Zimbabwe.
NGO Relations An affiliated international study group of: *International Commission on Mathematical Instruction (ICMI, #12700).* [2018.09.05/XD2192/**C**]

- ♦ International Organization of Youth with Rheumatism (inactive)

♦ International Organizing Committee for European Conferences on Thermophysical Properties (ECTP) 14484

Conférence européenne sur les propriétés thermophysiques

Contact Thermophysical Properties Lab, Chemical Engineering Dept Aristotle Univ, 541 24 Thessaloniki, Greece.
URL: http://www.thermophysicalpropertiesconferences.com/european-conference -on-ther mophysical-properties/ioc/

History 1968, Baden Baden (Germany). 1968, Baden-Baden (Germany FR). **Aims** Promote information exchange in the field of thermophysics between researchers, university laboratories and industrial partners. **Structure** Chairmanship rotates every 3 years. International Scientific Committee; Local Organizing Committee. **Languages** English. **Staff** Voluntary. **Finance** Conference fee; sponsorship; grants. **Events** *Triennial Conference* Venice (Italy) 2023, *Triennial Conference* Venice (Italy) 2020, *Triennial Conference* Graz (Austria) 2017, *Triennial conference* Thessaloniki (Greece) 2011, *Triennial conference* Pau (France) 2008. **Publications** Conference contributions abstracts. [2009/XF5598/**E**]

- ♦ International Oriental Medicine Society / see International Society of Oriental Medicine (#15332)

♦ International Orienteering Federation (IOF) 14485

Fédération internationale de course d'orientation – Internationale Orientierungslauf Föderation (IOF) – Federación Internacional de Orientación

Main Office Drottninggatan 47 3 1/2 tr, SE-652 25 Karlstad, Sweden. T. +46703147433. E-mail: iof@orienteering.org.
URL: http://www.orienteering.sport/

History 21 May 1961, Copenhagen (Denmark). **Aims** Promote and develop the outdoor *sport* of orienteering, ski orienteering, mountain bike orienteering and trail orienteering. **Structure** General Assembly (every 2 years); Council; Secretary General. **Languages** English. **Staff** 4.00 FTE, paid. **Finance** Sources: international organizations; members' dues; sponsorship. **Activities** Awareness raising; events/meetings; publishing activities; sporting activities; standards/guidelines. **Events** *Biennial Congress* Vejle (Denmark) / Kolding (Denmark) / Fredericia (Denmark) 2022, *Biennial Congress* Vejle (Denmark) / Kolding (Denmark) / Fredericia (Denmark) 2020, *Biennial Congress* Prague (Czechia) 2018, *Biennial Congress* Strömstad (Sweden) 2016, *Biennial Congress* Lavarone (Italy) 2014. **Publications** *IOF Newsletter* (10 a year); *Orienteering World* (annual); *Scientific Journal of Orienteering* (annual). Biennial reports.
Members Full: National associations in 76 countries and territories:
Argentina, Australia, Austria, Azerbaijan, Barbados, Belarus, Belgium, Brazil, Bulgaria, Cameroon, Canada, Chile, China, Colombia, Costa Rica, Croatia, Cuba, Cyprus, Czechia, Denmark, Dominican Rep, Ecuador, Egypt, Estonia, Finland, France, Georgia, Germany, Greece, Hong Kong, Hungary, India, Indonesia, Iran Islamic Rep, Ireland, Israel, Italy, Japan, Kazakhstan, Korea DPR, Korea Rep, Kyrgyzstan, Latvia, Liechtenstein, Lithuania, Malaysia, Moldova, Montenegro, Mozambique, Nepal, Netherlands, New Zealand, North Macedonia, Norway, Philippines, Poland, Portugal, Romania, Russia, Serbia, Singapore, Slovakia, Slovenia, South Africa, Spain, Sweden, Switzerland, Taiwan, Thailand, Türkiye, Uganda, UK, Ukraine, Uruguay, USA, Venezuela.
NGO Relations Member of (4): *Association of the IOC Recognized International Sports Federations (ARISF, #02767); International Masters Games Association (IMGA, #14117); International World Games Association (IWGA, #15914); Olympic Movement (#17719).* Cooperates with (1): *International Testing Agency (ITA, #15678).* Recognized by: *International Olympic Committee (IOC, #14408).* [2022.02.15/XC1969/**C**]

- ♦ International Ornithological Committee / see International Ornithologists' Union (#14487)

♦ International Ornithological Congress (IOC) 14486

Congrès ornithologique international – Congreso Internacional Ornitológico – Internationaler Ornithologenkongress – Congressus Internationalis Ornithologicus

Contact c/o Ornithological Inst, Seerose 1, 6204 Sempach LU, Switzerland.
URL: http://ioc26.jp/

History 10 Apr 1884, Vienna (Austria), at 1st International Ornithological Congress. **Aims** Organize international congresses and promote ornithological research in different countries. **Structure** Congress (every 4 years); *International Ornithologists' Union (IOU, #14487)*, set up at first Congress, elects President, Vice President and Secretary of next Congress and elects 10 members of Executive Committee. **Languages** English. **Finance** Registration fees. **Events** *International Ornithological Congress* Durban (South Africa) 2022, *International Ornithological Congress* Vancouver, BC (Canada) 2018, *International Ornithological Congress* Tokyo (Japan) 2014, *International Ornithological Congress* Campos do Jordão (Brazil) 2010, *International Ornithological Congress* Hamburg (Germany) 2006. **Publications** Congress proceedings/acta.
Members Individual ornithologists (about 200) from 58 countries:
Argentina, Australia, Austria, Belarus, Belgium, Brazil, Bulgaria, Canada, Chile, China, Colombia, Cuba, Czechia, Denmark, Ecuador, Estonia, Finland, France, Georgia, Germany, Ghana, Hungary, Iceland, India, Indonesia, Ireland, Israel, Italy, Japan, Kenya, Korea Rep, Latvia, Lithuania, Mexico, Mongolia, Namibia, Netherlands, New Zealand, Norway, Panama, Peru, Poland, Romania, Russia, Singapore, Slovakia, South Africa, Spain, Sweden, Switzerland, Thailand, Uganda, UK, Ukraine, Uruguay, USA, Venezuela, Zimbabwe.
NGO Relations Scientific member of: *International Union of Biological Sciences (IUBS, #15760).* [2019/XF2332/cv/**F**]

♦ International Ornithologists' Union (IOU) 14487

Union international des ornithologues

Pres Dept of Biological Sciences, 202 Life Sciences Bldg, Louisiana State Univ, Baton Rouge LA 70803-1715, USA. T. +12255781747. Fax +12255782597. E-mail: ioupresident@internationalornithology.org – info@internationalornithology.org.
URL: http://www.internationalornithology.org/

History 10 Apr 1884, Vienna (Austria). Founded at 1st Ornithological Congress. Functions as the Section of Ornithology of the IUBS. Former names and other names: *International Ornithological Committee (IOC)* – former; *Comité ornithologique international* – former. Registration: Section 501 (c) (3), USA. **Aims** Support, promote and advance *avian biology.* **Languages** English. **Staff** 1.00 FTE, paid. **Finance** Sources: none. **Activities** Awards/prizes/competitions; awareness raising; capacity building; events/meetings; financial and/or material support; guidance/assistance/consulting; knowledge management/information dissemination; networking/liaising; projects/programmes; publishing activities; research and development; research/documentation; standards/guidelines. **Events** *International Ornithological Congress* Durban (South Africa) 2022, *International Ornithological Congress* Vancouver, BC (Canada) 2018, *International Ornithological Congress* Tokyo (Japan) 2014, *International Ornithological Congress* Campos do Jordão (Brazil) 2010, *International Ornithological Congress* Hamburg (Germany) 2006. **Publications** Congress proceedings.
Members Fellows (276) in 67 countries and territories:
Algeria, Argentina, Australia, Austria, Belarus, Belgium, Brazil, Bulgaria, Canada, Chile, China, Colombia, Cuba, Czechia, Denmark, Ecuador, Estonia, Finland, France, Germany, Ghana, Hungary, Iceland, India, Indonesia, Israel, Italy, Japan, Kazakhstan, Kenya, Korea Rep, Latvia, Lithuania, Malaysia, Mexico, Morocco, Namibia, Netherlands, New Caledonia, New Zealand, Nigeria, Norway, Palestine, Panama, Peru, Poland, Romania, Russia, Saudi Arabia, Singapore, Slovakia, South Africa, Spain, Sweden, Switzerland, Taiwan, Tanzania UR, Thailand, Tunisia, Türkiye, Uganda, UK, Ukraine, Uruguay, USA, Venezuela, Zimbabwe.
NGO Relations Cooperates with (3): *BirdLife International (#03266); International Ornithological Congress (IOC, #14486); International Union of Biological Sciences (IUBS, #15760).* Also links with national ornithological societies. [2021.05.25/XE0754/v/**E**]

- ♦ International Orthodox Christian Charities (internationally oriented national body)
- ♦ International Orthodox Theological Association (internationally oriented national body)

♦ International Orthopaedic Trauma Association (IOTA) 14488

Contact c/o OTA, 9400 W Higgings Rd, Ste 305, Rosemont IL 60018-4975, USA.
URL: https://ota.org/membership/international-ota

History 11 Oct 2017, Vancouver, BC (Canada). Founded following the activities of the (USA) *Orthopaedic Trauma Association (OTA).* **Aims** Promote international orthopaedic and musculoskeletal trauma care, including patient care, education, and research. **Structure** Steering Committee. **Activities** Events/meetings; guidance/assistance/consulting; networking/liaising. **Events** *Triennial Conference* Amsterdam (Netherlands) 2021, *Triennial Conference* Amsterdam (Netherlands) 2020. **Publications** *IOTA Newsletter.*
Members Full in 20 countries:
Argentina, Australia, Belgium, Brazil, Canada, China, Colombia, Germany, India, Israel, Italy, Japan, Korea Rep, Mexico, Netherlands, South Africa, Spain, Switzerland, UK, USA. [2020/AA1140/**C**]

♦ International Orthoptic Association (IOA) 14489

Association internationale des orthoptistes

Registered Office c/o RPG Crouch Chapman, 14-16 Dowgate Hill, London, EC4R 2SU, UK. E-mail: secretary@internationalorthoptics.org.
URL: http://www.internationalorthoptics.org/

History 1967, London (UK). Registration: Charity Commission, No/ID: 1122060, England and Wales. **Aims** Promote the science of orthoptics; provide information and assistance to national authorities and individual orthoptists; maintain and improve standards of education, training and orthoptic practice. **Structure** General Meeting (annual). Council of Management (meets annually), comprising one representative from each member country. Officers: President; Secretary; Treasurer. Standing committees (7): Finance; International Relations; Website; Membership; Scientific; Terminology; Public Relations. Networks (4): Orthoptic Education and Training; Low Vision; Vision Screening; Neuro-orthoptics. Special committees (2): Congress Scientific Programme; Congress Organizing. **Languages** English. **Staff** None. **Finance** Members' dues from national associations, depending on number of members. Proceeds from International Congresses. **Events** *Quadrennial Congress* 2022, *Quadrennial Congress* Liverpool (UK) 2020, *Quadrennial Congress* Rotterdam (Netherlands) 2016, *Quadrennial congress* Toronto, ON (Canada) 2012, *Quadrennial Congress* Antwerp (Belgium) 2008. **Publications** *IOA News* – online.
Members Full; Individual; Associate; Affiliate. Orthoptists and National Associations in 21 countries. Membership countries not specified. Associated members in 6 countries and territories:
Associated members in 6 countries and territories:
Brazil, Czechia, Hong Kong, New Zealand, Singapore, South Africa.
NGO Relations Member of: *International Pediatric Ophthalmology and Strabismus Council (IPOSC, #14544); Open Access Scholarly Publishers Association (OASPA, #17747).* [2022/XD2696/**C**]

- ♦ The International Osprey Foundation (internationally oriented national body)

♦ International Osteoporosis Foundation (IOF) 14490

Main Office Rue Juste-Olivier 9, 1260 Nyon VD, Switzerland. T. +41229940100. Fax +41229940101. E-mail: info@iofbonehealth.org – info@osteoporosis.foundation.
URL: https://www.osteoporosis.foundation/

History 1987, Bern (Switzerland). Current title adopted when the Foundation joined forces with *International Federation of Societies on Skeletal Diseases (inactive).* Former names and other names: *European Foundation for Osteoporosis and Bone Disease (EFFO)* – former (1987 to 1998). Registration: Swiss Civil Code, Start date: 1987, Switzerland. **Aims** Promote maintenance of *bone* and *musculoskeletal health* as a worldwide priority. **Structure** Board of Governance; Executive Committee; Committees (3). **Languages** English, French, Spanish. **Staff** 10.00 FTE, paid. **Finance** Sources: donations; meeting proceeds; members' dues; sale of publications; sponsorship. **Activities** Awards/prizes/competitions; awareness raising; events/meetings; publishing activities; research/documentation; training/education. **Events** *World Congress on Osteoporosis, Osteoarthritis and Musculoskeletal Diseases* London (UK) 2024, *World Congress on Osteoporosis, Osteoarthritis and Musculoskeletal Diseases* Barcelona (Spain) 2023, *World Congress on Osteoporosis, Osteoarthritis and Musculoskeletal Diseases* 2022, *World Congress on Osteoporosis, Osteoarthritis and Musculoskeletal Diseases* 2022, *Asia-Pacific Osteoporosis Conference* 2021. **Publications** *Osteoporosis International* (12 a year) – journal; *Calcified Tissue International* (12 a year); *Archives of Osteoporosis* (6 a year). *IOF Compendium of Osteoporosis.* Annual Report; articles; scientific and clinical documents; fact sheets; reports.
Members Full; Associate. Regional and national societies (268) in 98 countries and territories:

Albania, Algeria, Argentina, Armenia, Australia, Austria, Bahrain, Belarus, Belgium, Bolivia, Bosnia-Herzegovina, Brazil, Bulgaria, Cameroon, Canada, Chile, China, Colombia, Costa Rica, Croatia, Cuba, Cyprus, Czechia, Denmark, Dominican Rep, Ecuador, Egypt, Estonia, Finland, France, Georgia, Germany, Greece, Guatemala, Hong Kong, Hungary, Iceland, India, Indonesia, Iran Islamic Rep, Iraq, Ireland, Israel, Italy, Jamaica, Japan, Jordan, Kazakhstan, Kenya, Korea Rep, Kuwait, Latvia, Lebanon, Libya, Lithuania, Luxembourg, Malaysia, Malta, Mexico, Moldova, Morocco, Netherlands, New Zealand, North Macedonia, Norway, Pakistan, Palestine, Panama, Peru, Philippines, Poland, Portugal, Puerto Rico, Romania, Russia, Saudi Arabia, Serbia, Singapore, Slovakia, Slovenia, South Africa, Spain, Sri Lanka, Sweden, Switzerland, Syrian AR, Taiwan, Thailand, Tunisia, Türkiye, UK, Ukraine, United Arab Emirates, Uruguay, USA, Uzbekistan, Venezuela, Yemen.
Included in the above, 4 organizations listed in this Yearbook:
European Society for Clinical and Economic Aspects of Osteoporosis, Osteoarthritis and Musculoskeletal Diseases (ESCEO, #08545); Ibero-American College of Rheumatology (#11020); International Society for Clinical Densitometry (ISCD, #15015); Pan-Arab Osteoporosis Society (PAOS, #18153).
Consultative Status Consultative status granted from: *ECOSOC (#05331)* (Ros A). **NGO Relations** Member of (1): *European Patients' Forum (EPF, #08172).* [2021.05.18/XD5988/fy/**F**]

♦ International Ostomy Association (IOA) 14491

Association internationale des stomisés
Chair Coordination Committee IOA Office, PO Box 525, Kennebunk ME 04043-0525, USA. E-mail: chairperson@ostomyinternational.org – ioa@ostomyinternational.org.
URL: http://www.ostomyinternational.org/
History 1975, Weesp (Netherlands). New Constitution approved by delegates during Council Meeting, Frankfurt (Germany), Nov 2010, which changed the organization from a country member association led by elected officers to a regional structure led by a Coordination Committee. **Aims** Improve the quality of life of ostomates and those with related surgeries worldwide; encourage the highest possible standards of surgery, medical attention and patient after-care; assist member associations to help rehabilitate ostomates. **Structure** Coordination Committee, consisting of representatives of each affiliated region. Regional Affiliate Associations (3): *Asian and South Pacific Ostomy Association (ASPOA, #01756); European Ostomy Association (EOA, #08120); Ostomy Association of the Americas (OAA, #17912).* **Languages** English. **Staff** Voluntary. **Finance** Sources: members' dues. **Activities** Events/meetings; guidance/assistance/consulting; networking/liaising. **Events** *World congress* Bangkok (Thailand) 2010, *World Council Meeting* Frankfurt-Main (Germany) 2010, *Meeting* Ljubljana (Slovenia) 2008, *Meeting* Tokyo (Japan) 2008, *World congress* Puerto Real (Puerto Rico) 2007. **Publications** *IOA Today* – archived on website. *World Ostomy Data Survey Report* (2007) – archived on website. [2018.09.18/XC0150/y/**C**]

♦ International Ostrich Association (no recent information)

♦ International Otter Survival Fund (IOSF) 14492

Head of Operations 7 Black Park, Broadford, IV49 9DE, UK. T. +441471822487. Fax +441471822487. E-mail: paul@otter.org.
URL: http://www.otter.org/
History 16 Nov 1993. Registration: OSCR, No/ID: SC003875, Start date: 21 Dec 1989, Scotland. **Aims** Conserve, protect and care for otters in the UK and abroad. **Structure** Co-Directors. **Languages** English, German, Spanish. **Staff** 5.00 FTE, paid; 130.00 FTE, voluntary. **Finance** Sources: grants; sale of products. Other sources: animal adoptions; research. **Activities** Advocacy/lobbying/activism; events/meetings; financial and/or material support; research/documentation; training/education. **Events** *Wild Care Conference* Teangue (UK) 2012, *Conference / Wild Care Conference* Teangue (UK) 2006, *The return of the otter in Europe – where and how?* Broadford (UK) 2003, *Wild Care Conference* Teangue (UK) 2003, *Wild Care Conference* Teangue (UK) 2003. **Publications** *Otter Journal* (annual). *Otters of the World* (2017). Annual Report; reports. **Members** Over 50,000 in about 36 countries. Membership countries not specified. **IGO Relations** Links with many IGOs, including: Department of Natural Resource Environment and Wildlife Management, Laos; Ministry of Forestry, Indonesia. **NGO Relations** Links with many NGOs, not specified; universities; national organizations. [2022.05.04/XF3892/f/**F**]

♦ International Oxygen Manufacturers Association (IOMA) 14493

Association internationale des fabricants d'oxygène
Contact RR 1 Box 562, Roseland VA 22967, USA. T. +17035018581.
URL: http://www.iomaweb.org/
History 1943. Former names and other names: *Independent Oxygen Manufacturers Association* – former (1943 to 1966). Registration: Nonprofit 501(c)(6) organization, No/ID: EIN: 34-1654997, Start date: 1990, USA. **Aims** Support the growth and safety of the global industrial and medical gases industry. **Structure** Meeting (annual); Board of Directors. **Finance** Sources: members' dues. **Activities** Awareness raising; events/meetings; knowledge management/information dissemination; standards/guidelines. **Events** *Annual Meeting* Washington, DC (USA) 2021, *Annual Meeting* 2020, *Annual Meeting* Bangkok (Thailand) 2019, *Annual Meeting* Vienna (Austria) 2018, *Annual Meeting* Dubai (United Arab Emirates) 2017.
Members Voting companies manufacturing any gas qualifying for membership (51); Associate companies manufacturing equipment used by the industry (34). Member companies (42 in North America; rest elsewhere) in 39 countries:
Argentina, Australia, Bahamas, Belgium, Brazil, Chile, China, Denmark, Finland, France, Germany, India, Indonesia, Ireland, Israel, Italy, Jamaica, Japan, Jordan, Kuwait, Lebanon, Malta, Mexico, Mozambique, Netherlands, Norway, Saudi Arabia, Singapore, South Africa, Spain, Switzerland, Taiwan, Thailand, Trinidad-Tobago, Türkiye, UK, United Arab Emirates, USA, Venezuela. [2023.02.14/XD4912/**D**]

♦ International Ozone Association (IOA) 14494

Association internationale de l'ozone – Internationale Ozon-Vereinigung
European-African-Asian-Australian Group 7 rue Marcel Doré, Bât B16, 86000 Poitiers, France. T. +33549454454. Fax +33549454060. E-mail: ioa@esip.univ-poitiers.fr.
Nippon Islands Group Japan Ozone Assc, Suite 301, Nihonbashi-Tomizawa-cho 10-10, Chuo-ku, Tokyo, 103-0006 Japan. T. +81366611622. Fax +81366611623.
Pan American Group address not obtained.
URL: http://www.ioa-ea3g.org/
History 30 Nov 1973, Washington, DC (USA). Current bylaws adopted 8 Sep 1985, Tokyo (Japan). Incorporated under the laws of the State of Ohio (USA). Former names and other names: *International Ozone Institute (IOI)* – former (30 Nov 1973 to 1978). **Aims** Further the science, technology and applications of ozone, particularly treatment and disinfection of drinking water and wastewater as well as in the treatment of air and in medicine. **Structure** General Assembly (every 2 years, at Congress); International Board of Directors; Groups (4); Standing Committees (5); Special or Sub-Committees (4). **Languages** English. **Staff** 1.00 FTE, paid. **Finance** Sources: members' dues. **Activities** Events/meetings; knowledge management/information dissemination; networking/liaising; research/documentation. **Events** *Annual Pan American Conference* Las Vegas, NV (USA) 2022, *Biennial World Ozone Congress* Windsor, ON (Canada) 2021, *Annual Pan American Conference* Las Vegas, NV (USA) 2020, *Annual Pan American Conference* Atlanta, GA (USA) 2019, *Biennial World Ozone Congress* Nice (France) 2019. **Publications** *Ozone News* (6 a year); *Ozone: Science and Engineering* (6 a year). *Medical Applications of Ozone* (1983); *Aquatic Applications of Ozone; Design Guidance Manual for Ozone Systems; Forum on Ozone Disinfection; Handbook of Ozone Technology and Applications; Measuring Methods of Ozone Concentration; Ozone: Analytical Aspects and Odor Control; Ozone/Chlorine Dioxide Oxidation Products of Organic Materials; The Use of Ozone in the Treatment of Swimming Pool Water; Who's Who in the World of Ozone.* Manuals; World Congress and other meeting proceedings.
Members Manufacturers and individuals in 53 countries and territories:
Algeria, Argentina, Australia, Austria, Belgium, Brazil, Brunei Darussalam, Canada, Chile, China, Cuba, Cyprus, Czechia, Denmark, Ecuador, El Salvador, Estonia, Finland, France, Germany, Greece, Hong Kong, Hungary, India, Indonesia, Ireland, Israel, Italy, Japan, Korea Rep, Lebanon, Mexico, Netherlands, New Zealand, Norway, Philippines, Poland, Portugal, Romania, Russia, Serbia, Singapore, South Africa, Spain, Sweden, Switzerland, Taiwan, Thailand, Tunisia, UK, United Arab Emirates, Uruguay, USA. [2021/XC4570/**C**]

♦ International Ozone Commission (IO3C) 14495

Commission internationale de l'ozone
Pres Observatoire de Versailles Saint-Quentin-en-Yvelines, 11 bd d'Alembert, 78280 Guyancourt CEDEX, France. T. +33180285499. Fax +33677183864.
Sec NOAA ESRL Global Monitoring Div, 325 Broadway R/GMD, Boulder CO 80305-3328, USA. T. +13034976279. Fax +12024975590.
URL: https://ioc.atmos.illinois.edu/
History 1948, Oslo (Norway), as a Commission of *International Association of Meteorology and Atmospheric Sciences (IAMAS, #12031).* Also referred to as *IAMAS International Ozone Commission – Commission internationale de l'ozone de l'AIMSA.* **Aims** Stimulate improvements in the measurements and analysis of *atmospheric* ozone; advise other scientific and/or intergovernmental bodies on matters relevant to atmospheric ozone including possible effects of human activities. **Languages** English. **Staff** 1.00 FTE, voluntary. **Activities** Research/documents; events/meetings; knowledge management/information dissemination. **Events** *Quadrennial Ozone Symposium* Daejeon (Korea Rep) 2021, *Quadrennial Ozone Symposium* Seoul (Korea Rep) 2020, *Quadrennial Ozone Symposium* Edinburgh (UK) 2016, *Quadrennial Symposium / Quadrennial Ozone Symposium* Toronto, ON (Canada) 2012, *Quadrennial symposium / Quadrennial Ozone Symposium* Tromsø (Norway) 2008. **Publications** Proceedings of quadrennial Ozone Symposia; reports of scientific workshops – usually as WMO Ozone Reports. Information Services: Provides guidance for the collection and quality control of all atmospheric ozone data collected on regular bases by *WMO World Ozone and Ultra-Violet Data Centre (WOUDC, see: #21649).*
Members Individuals (distinguished scientists in their individual capacity for up to 8-year terms) in 18 countries:
Belgium, Bulgaria, Canada, Czechia, France, Germany, Greece, Italy, Japan, Netherlands, New Zealand, Norway, Russia, South Africa, Spain, Switzerland, UK, USA.
IGO Relations *Group on Earth Observations (GEO, #10735); World Meteorological Organization (WMO, #21649).* **NGO Relations** Part of: *International Council for Science (ICSU, inactive); International Union of Geodesy and Geophysics (IUGG, #15776).* [2017.06.01/XE3836/v/**E**]

♦ International Ozone Institute / see International Ozone Association (#14494)
♦ International Pacific Halibut Commission (internationally oriented national body)
♦ International Pacific Marine Educators Network (unconfirmed)
♦ International Pacific Salmon Fisheries Commission (inactive)
♦ International Pacific Sports Federation (unconfirmed)
♦ International Pacifist Association (inactive)
♦ International Pacifist Party (inactive)
♦ International Packaged Ice Association (internationally oriented national body)
♦ International Packaging Institute (internationally oriented national body)
♦ International Packet Communications Consortium / see IP Multimedia Subsystems Forum

♦ International Padel Federation (FIP) 14496

Federación Internacional de Pádel (FIP)
Gen Sec Calle Ayala n 158 bajo D, 28009 Madrid, Spain. E-mail: secretaria@padelfip.com – hello@padelfip.com.
Registered Address Rue de l'Aurore 1, 1005 Lausanne VD, Switzerland.
URL: https://www.padelfip.com/
History 12 Jul 1991, Madrid (Spain). **Aims** Promote all forms of Padel around the world. **Structure** Board. **Activities** Certification/accreditation; sporting activities; training/education.
Members Federations in 41 countries and territories:
Argentina, Armenia, Australia, Austria, Belgium, Brazil, Canada, Chile, China, Czechia, Denmark, Dominican Rep, Estonia, Finland, France, Germany, Great Britain, Guatemala, Hungary, India, Iran Islamic Rep, Ireland, Italy, Japan, Lithuania, Mexico, Monaco, Netherlands, Norway, Paraguay, Poland, Portugal, Russia, Senegal, Spain, Sweden, Switzerland, Thailand, United Arab Emirates, Uruguay, USA.
NGO Relations Member of (1): *Alliance of Independent recognised Members of Sport (AIMS, #00690)* (Observer). [2021/AA1360/**C**]

♦ International Paediatric Brain Injury Society (IPBIS) 14497

Sec-Treas address not obtained. E-mail: hello@ipbis.org.
URL: http://www.ipbis.org/
Aims Disseminate knowledge by developing and sharing best practices, mentoring colleagues, advancing research and promoting prevention for the benefit of children, adolescents and young adults with ABI and their families. **Structure** Board. **Activities** Events/meetings. **Events** *World Congress on Brain Injury* 2021, *International Conference on Paediatric Acquired Brain Injury* New York, NY (USA) 2021, *International Conference on Paediatric Acquired Brain Injury* New York, NY (USA) 2020, *International Conference on Paediatric Acquired Brain Injury* Belfast (UK) 2018, *International Conference on Paediatric Acquired Brain Injury* Rome (Italy) 2017. **NGO Relations** Cooperates with (1): *International Brain Injury Association (IBIA, #12391).* [2021/XJ9279/**C**]

♦ International Paediatric Pathology Association (IPPA) 14498

Sec B260 Main Hosp, Pathology CHP UPMC, 4401 Penn Ave, Pittsburgh PA 15224, USA.
URL: http://www.ippa-association.com/
History 19 Oct 1976, Washington DC (USA), at 11th Congress of *International Academy of Pathology (IAP, #11567).* Constitution formally adopted, 10-15 Sep 1978, Jerusalem (Israel), at 12th Congress. Constitution amended Sep 1984, Miami Beach FL (USA); Sep 1990, Buenos Aires (Argentina); Oct 1998, Nice (France); Sep 2006, Montréal QC (Canada); Oct 2008, Athens (Greece); 26 Sep 2016, Cologne (Germany). **Aims** Facilitate worldwide increased knowledge of diseases of embryo, foetus, infant and child and its application to health needs of children of all countries. **Structure** General Meeting (at least every 2 years, normally at biennial meeting of IAP); Council; Executive Committee. Course Committee. Constituent societies (4): *Paediatric Pathology Society (PPS, #18018); Society for Pediatric Pathology (SPP); 'Australia and New Zealand Paediatric Pathology Group'; Sociedad Latinoamericana de Patologia Pediatrica (SLAPPE, #19421).* **Languages** English. **Staff** Voluntary. **Finance** Sources: per capita contributions (US$ 3) of constituent societies; course fees. **Activities** Training/education. **Events** *Annual Advanced Course* Segovia (Spain) 2012, *Annual Advanced Course* Cambridge (UK) 2010, *IPPA Update Course* Venice (Italy) 2010, *Annual Advanced Course* Corfu (Greece) 2009, *Annual Advanced Course* Tallinn (Estonia) 2008. **Publications** *Paediatric and Developmental Pathology Journal* – jointly with Society of Paediatric Pathology.
Members Individuals in 50 countries and territories:
Argentina, Australia, Austria, Belgium, Brazil, Cameroon, Canada, Chile, China, Colombia, Costa Rica, Cuba, Czechia, Denmark, Finland, France, Germany, Greece, Hong Kong, Iceland, India, Indonesia, Ireland, Israel, Italy, Japan, Korea Rep, Mexico, Montenegro, Netherlands, New Zealand, Norway, Pakistan, Peru, Philippines, Poland, Puerto Rico, Saudi Arabia, Serbia, Singapore, South Africa, Spain, Sweden, Switzerland, Tunisia, Türkiye, UK, Uruguay, USA, Venezuela. [2020/XC0071/v/**C**]

♦ International Pain Foundation (internationally oriented national body)

♦ International Painful Bladder Foundation (IPBF) 14499

Chairman Mahlerlaan 4, 1411 HW Naarden, Netherlands. T. +31358879516. E-mail: info@painful-bladder.org.
URL: https://www.painful-bladder.org/
History 2 Sep 2005. Officially launched on 1 Jan 2006. Registration: Handelsregister, No/ID: 24382693, Start date: 2 Sep 2005, Netherlands, Rotterdam. **Aims** Increase awareness and knowledge of interstitial *cystitis*/bladder pain syndrome, hypersensitive bladder, chronic pelvic pain and associated *disorders* among patients and health professionals; facilitate and assist new national patient support groups worldwide; promote international cooperation and collaboration in the field; stimulate and participate in research in the field. **Structure** Executive Board; Medical Advisory Board; Central Office in Naarden (Netherlands). **Languages** English. **Staff** None. **Finance** Sources: donations; sponsorship. **Activities** Advocacy/lobbying/activism; awareness raising; capacity building; knowledge management/information dissemination; networking/liaising; projects/programmes; publishing activities; research and development. Active worldwide. **Publications** *IPBF e-Newsletter. IPBF Research Update.* Brochures; leaflets; articles; toilet cards. **Members** Not a membership organization. **NGO Relations** Member of (6): *EURORDIS – Rare Diseases Europe (#09175); International Alliance of Patients' Organizations (IAPO, #11633);* International Pain Management Network; International Pelvic Pain Partnership; *Pain Alliance Europe (PAE, #18026); World Patients Alliance (WPA).* [2023.02.13/XJ3911/f/**F**]

♦ International Paint and Printing Ink Council / see World Coatings Council (#21283)

♦ International Au Pair Association (IAPA) 14500

Managing Dir Oetztalerstr 1, 81373 Munich, Germany. T. +498920189550. E-mail: info@iapa.org.
Chair address not obtained.
URL: http://www.iapa.org/

History 1994, Vancouver, BC (Canada). Founded at 'World Youth and Student Travel Conference', Vancouver BC (Canada). Previously a founding and sector association within *World Youth Student and Educational Travel Confederation (WYSE Travel Confederation, #21959).* An independent organization since 2016. Registration: Danish Chamber of Commerce, No/ID: 29342199, Denmark. **Aims** As a membership trade association, promote cultural exchange and au pair programmes in order to assist in development of friendly relations and strengthen cultural ties between nations. **Structure** General Meeting (annual); Executive Board. **Languages** English. **Staff** 1.00 FTE, paid. **Activities** Advocacy/lobbying/activism; awareness raising; events/meetings; networking/liaising; research and development; standards/guidelines. **Events** *WETM-IAC : Joint Work Experience Travel Market and IAPA Annual Conference* St Julian's (Malta) 2022, *WETM-IAC : Joint Work Experience Travel Market and IAPA Annual Conference* Amsterdam (Netherlands) 2021, *Annual General Meeting* Munich (Germany) 2020, *WETM-IAC : Joint Work Experience Travel Market and IAPA Annual Conference* St Julian's (Malta) 2020, *WETM-IAC : Joint Work Experience Travel Market and IAPA Annual Conference* Luxembourg (Luxembourg) 2019. **Members** Organizations (about 145) in over 40 countries. Membership countries not specified. [2022.10.11/XD5104/E]

♦ International Palaeontological Association (IPA) 14501

Association paléontologique internationale

SG address not obtained.
Pres Inst Vertebrate Paleontology and Paleoanthropology, Academia Sinica, PO Box 643, 100044 Beijing, China. Fax +861068337001.
Treas 81 Beaumont Drive, Hendersonville NC 28739, USA. T. +18286928406.
URL: http://www.ipa-assoc.com/

History Jul 1933, Washington, DC (USA). Constitution changed: Jul 1957, London (UK); Aug 1972; new statutes 1984 and 2006. Former names and other names: *International Palaeontological Union* – former (Jul 1933 to Aug 1972); *Union paléontologique internationale* – former (Jul 1933 to Aug 1972). **Aims** Serve palaeontologists and their science by promoting and coordinating international cooperation in palaeontology; encourage integration and synthesis of all palaeontological knowledge. **Structure** General Assembly; Council; Executive Committee. International Research Groups (affiliated groups): Graptolite Working Group; Association of North American Paleontological Societies (ANAPS); Palaeozoic Microvertebrates; *International Research Group on Ostracoda (IRGO, #14730)*; International Research Group on Charophytes; Chitinozoa Subcommission (CIMP); British Joint Committee for Palaeontology (JCP). **Languages** English, French. **Staff** 0.50 FTE, paid. **Finance** Sources: members' dues. **Activities** Events/meetings; financial and/or material support; knowledge management/information dissemination; research/documentation. **Events** *International Palaeontological Congress* Khon Kaen (Thailand) 2022, *International Palaeontological Congress* Paris (France) 2018, *International Palaeontological Congress* Mendoza (Argentina) 2014, *International Palaeontological Congress* London (UK) 2010, *Meeting* Tsukuba (Japan) 2010. **Publications** *Lethaia* (4 a year) – journal. Annual Report – online. **Information Services** *Directory of Paleontologists of the World* – database; *Fossil Collections of the World: An International Guide* – database; *IPA PaleoParks Database* – with conservation status.
Members National societies and Council delegates in 18 countries:
Argentina, Belgium, Canada, China, Czechia, Denmark, France, Germany, India, Italy, Japan, New Zealand, Poland, Russia, Spain, Switzerland, UK, USA.
Individuals in 33 countries:
Argentina, Australia, Austria, Belgium, Brazil, Canada, China, Croatia, Czechia, Denmark, Finland, France, Germany, Hungary, India, Ireland, Italy, Japan, Korea Rep, Latvia, Malaysia, Mexico, Netherlands, New Zealand, Norway, Russia, South Africa, Spain, Sweden, Switzerland, UK, Uruguay, USA. [2019/XC2337/v/C]

♦ International Palaeontological Union / see International Palaeontological Association (#14501)

♦ International Paleolimnology Association (IPA) 14502

Contact address not obtained. E-mail: fhchen-ips2015@lzu.edu.cn.
URL: http://paleolim.org/

History Constitution adopted 29 Jul 2006, Duluth MN (USA). **Aims** Promote and advance the science of paleolimnology and its applications. **Structure** Executive Board; International Advisory Committee. **Finance** Members' dues. **Activities** Events/meetings. **Events** *IPA-IAL Joint Meeting* Bariloche (Argentina) 2022, *IPA-IAL Joint Meeting* Stockholm (Sweden) 2018, *Symposium* Lanzhou (China) 2015, *Symposium* Glasgow (UK) 2012, *Symposium* Guadalajara (Mexico) 2009. **Publications** *Journal of Paleolimnology*. **NGO Relations** *Federation of European Phycological Societies (FEPS, #09529).* [2014/XJ8712/E]

♦ International Palm Society (internationally oriented national body)

♦ International Pan-Arab Critical Care Medicine Society (IPACCMS) 14503

Address not obtained.

Aims Enhance knowledge in critical care medicine; promote relations between members; provide medical care to those in need in the Arab world. **Structure** Board of Directors (meets twice a year). Executive Committee (meets twice a year), comprising President, Vice President, Secretary-General, Chairman, Treasurer, Secretary-Treasurer and 2 further members. Committees (4). **Finance** Members' dues. **Activities** Committees: Continuing Medical Education; Nominations and Elections; Judicial; Membership. **Events** *Conference* Dubai (United Arab Emirates) 2019, *Conference* Dubai (United Arab Emirates) 2018, *Conference* Dubai (United Arab Emirates) 2017, *Middle East Surviving Sepsis Campaign Meeting* Dubai (United Arab Emirates) 2017, *Conference* Dubai (United Arab Emirates) 2016. **NGO Relations** *World Federation of Intensive and Critical Care (WFICC, #21444).* Member of: *Global Sepsis Alliance (GSA, #10590).* [2016/XM2385/D]

♦ International Pancreas and Islet Transplant Association (IPITA) 14504

Address not obtained.
URL: http://www.ipita.org/

History 27 Jun 1993, Amsterdam (Netherlands). Section of *The Transplantation Society (TTS, #20224).* **Aims** Serve the pancreas and islet transplant scientific community in providing a forum for the open exchange of knowledge and expertise so as to facilitate the advancement of the clinical practice of pancreas and islet transplantation for the treatment of human diabetes. **Structure** General Assembly; Council. **Languages** English. **Finance** Sources: members' dues. **Activities** Awards/prizes/competitions; events/meetings; training/education. **Events** *Biennial Congress* 2021, *Joint Congress* San Diego, CA (USA) 2021, *Biennial Congress* Lyon (France) 2019, *Biennial Congress* Oxford (UK) 2017, *Joint Meeting* Melbourne, VIC (Australia) 2015. **Publications** *IPITA Newsletter* (2 a year) – online. [2021/XD6761/E]

♦ International Panel Data Conference (meeting series)

♦ International Panel of Experts on Sustainable Food Systems (IPES-Food) 14505

Dir Mundo-J, Rue de la Industrie 10, 1000 Brussels, Belgium.
URL: http://www.ipes-food.org/

History 2015. Registration: Belgium. **Aims** Promote transition to sustainable food systems around the world. **Structure** General Assembly; General Council; Secretariat. **Languages** English, French. **Staff** 5.00 FTE, paid. **Finance** Funded by: Daniel and Nina Carasso Foundation; Open Societies Foundation; *Fondation Charles Léopold Mayer pour le progrès de l'homme (FPH, #09815)*; 11th Hour Foundation; Rosa Luxemburg Stiftung. **Activities** Awareness raising; knowledge management/information dissemination; research/documentation. **Events** *Extinction or Regeneration Conference* London (UK) 2023. **Publications** Reports: https://ipes-food.org/reports/ **Members** Individuals (15 to 25 maximum). Membership countries not specified. [2022.10.20/XM8664/v/F]

♦ International Panel of Parliamentarians for Freedom of Religion or Belief (IPPFoRB) 14506

Contact c/o Norwegian Helsinki Committee Office, Kirkegata 5, 0153 Oslo, Norway. E-mail: contact@ippforb.com.
URL: http://www.ippforb.com/

History 8 Nov 2014, Oslo (Norway). Launched when Oslo Charter was signed. **Aims** Advance freedom of religion or belief, as defined in Article 18 of the UN Universal Declaration of Human Rights. **Structure** Steering Committee; Secretariat. **Languages** English. **Finance** Sources: donations. **Activities** Advocacy/lobbying/activism; capacity building; networking/liaising; research/documentation. **Events** *Triennial Conference* Singapore (Singapore) 2019, *Workshop for Parliamentarians from the Balkans and South Caucasus* Bucharest (Romania) 2018, *Inter-Parliamentarian Consultation on Freedom of Religion or Belief in Latin America* Rio de Janeiro (Brazil) 2017, *Meeting* New York, NY (USA) 2015. [2020.10.13/XM6214/F]

♦ International Panel Physicians Association (IPPA) 14507

Exec Dir 123 W Mills Ave, Ste 530, El Paso TX 79901, USA. T. +19152013181. E-mail: info@panelphysician.org.
URL: https://panelphysician.org/

History Founded 2009. **Aims** Improve the capacity of Panel Physicians and healthcare workers who conduct immigration medical evaluations worldwide through professional affiliation, training and education. **Structure** Board of Directors. **Activities** Events/meetings; training/education. **Events** *Summit* Accra (Ghana) 2019, *Summit* Kuala Lumpur (Malaysia) 2018. [2019/XM8342/C]

♦ International Panel on Social Progress (IPSP) 14508

Secretariat Woodrow Wilson School, Princeton Univ, Princeton NJ 08544, USA. E-mail: info@ipsp.org.
URL: http://www.ipsp.org/

History 2014, Paris (France). Registered under French law. **Aims** Harness the competence of experts about social issues; deliver a report addressed to social actors, movements, organizations, politicians and decision-makers, so as to provide them with expertise on questions relating to social change and improvement of the main institutions of modern societies. **Structure** Steering Committee; Scientific Council; Honorary Advisory Committee; Secretariat. **Languages** English. **Staff** 3.00 FTE, paid. 3-4 voluntary. **Finance** Research grants; donations from foundations; copyright fees. **Activities** Awareness raising; events/meetings; guidance/assistance/consulting; knowledge management/information dissemination; networking/liaising; publishing activities; research/documentation; training/education. **Events** *Meeting of the Lead Authors* Lisbon (Portugal) 2017. **Publications** *Rethinking Society for the 21st Century* (2018) – report, in 3 vols, accompanied by A Manifesto for Social Progress. **Members** Individuals (270) in 42 countries. Membership countries not specified. **IGO Relations** *ILO (#11123)*; *International Bank for Reconstruction and Development (IBRD, #12317)* (World Bank); *OECD (#17693)*. **NGO Relations** Member of: *Council for Global Problem-Solving (CGP, #04898).* [2019.12.20/XM6337/F]

♦ International Paneuropean Union 14509

Union paneuropéenne internationale – Internationale Paneuropa Union

Pres 1 rue Saint Léon, 67000 Strasbourg, France. T. +33388234454. E-mail: paneurope.international@gmail.com.
SG address not obtained.
URL: http://www.paneuropa.org/

History 1 Oct 1923, Vienna (Austria), by Count Richard Coudenhove-Kalergi, as *Pan European Union – Union paneuropéenne – Unión Paneuropea – Paneuropa Union – Unione Paneuropea.* New Statutes adopted 9 Dec 1995, Strasbourg (France). **Aims** On the basis of freedom and responsibility of the individual and the Christian view of humanity, promote: rapid further development of the *European Community* into political and economic union respecting the principles of *subsidiarity*; common European foreign policy and security, economic, currency, environment and social policies; increased competence of the European Parliament and creation of a *democratic* European government; total elimination of border controls within the EU; a European charter establishing *rights* of ethnic groups; enlargement of the EU; development of European Union's defence identity as the European pillar of NATO; common European technological research and development programme; assimilation of educational curricula and diplomas; European studies in schools; constructive EU aid for Central and Eastern European countries as long as needed. **Structure** General Assembly; Presidency; Enlarged Presidency; Intergroup in the European Parliament in Strasbourg (France); International General Secretariat. **Languages** Bulgarian, Croatian, Czech, Danish, Dutch, English, French, German, Irish Gaelic, Italian, Norwegian, Polish, Portuguese, Slovakian, Slovene, Spanish, Swedish, Ukrainian. **Staff** Voluntary. **Finance** Members' dues. Donations. **Activities** Advocacy/lobbying/activism; events/meetings. **Events** *Pan European Congress* Vienna (Austria) 2016, *Meeting* Vienna (Austria) 2012, *General Assembly* Strasbourg (France) 2009, *International conference on European identity, culture and globalization* Rome (Italy) 2007, *General Assembly* Strasbourg (France) 2006. **Publications** Magazines and bulletins of national member organizations.
Members National member organizations in 34 countries:
Albania, Andorra, Austria, Belgium, Bosnia-Herzegovina, Bulgaria, Croatia, Czechia, Denmark, Estonia, Finland, France, Germany, Greece, Hungary, Italy, Kosovo, Latvia, Lithuania, Luxembourg, Montenegro, North Macedonia, Poland, Portugal, Romania, San Marino, Serbia, Slovakia, Slovenia, Spain, Sweden, Switzerland, UK, Ukraine.
NGO Relations Instrumental in setting up: *European Society Coudenhove-Kalergi (ES-CK, #08573).* [2019.02.19/XD3079/D]

♦ International Pan Ocean Remote Sensing Conference Association (International PORSEC Association) 14510

Pres North West Research Associates, 4118 148 Ave NE, Redmond WA 98052, USA. T. +14255569099ext324.
URL: http://porsec.nwra.com/

History Founded 1990, as *Pacific Ocean Remote Sensing Society.* **Aims** Promote study of oceans and related atmospheric sciences using satellite remote sensing, concentrating on environmental processes such as ocean primary production, hazards, pollution, greenhouse effect and sea level rise. **Structure** General Assembly; Scientific Organizing Committee; Board. **Languages** English. **Staff** Voluntary. **Activities** Events/meetings; training/education. **Events** *Conference* Johor Bahru (Malaysia) 2021, *Conference* Johor Bahru (Malaysia) 2020, *Conference* Jeju (Korea Rep) 2018, *Conference* Fortaleza (Brazil) 2016, *Conference* Bali (Indonesia) 2014. **Publications** *Bulletin of the PORSEC Association* (3 a year); *PORSEC Newsletter* (irregular). Special issues of the 'International Journal of Remote Sensing'. Conference proceedings.
Members International (mostly Asian) in 21 countries and territories:
Australia, Bangladesh, Canada, China, France, Germany, India, Indonesia, Israel, Italy, Japan, Korea Rep, Malaysia, Norway, Philippines, Russia, Sweden, Taiwan, Thailand, UK, USA. [2018.08.08/XM2874/D]

♦ International Papillomavirus Society (IPVS) 14511

Sociedad Internacional para el Estudio de los Virus del Papiloma

Contact c/o Kenes, 7 rue François-Versonnex, PO BOX 6053, 1211 Geneva 6, Switzerland. E-mail: ipvsoffice@kenes.com.
URL: http://www.ipvsoc.org/

History Registered in the State of Delaware (USA). Former names and other names: *IPV Society* – alias. **Aims** Promote and stimulate exchange of ideas, knowledge and research materials among basic, clinical, and *public health* research workers throughout the world who are concerned with human and animal papillomaviruses, their infections and associated *diseases*. **Structure** Board of Directors; Executive Committee; Committees (5). **Staff** Voluntary. **Finance** Members' dues. **Activities** Training/education; events/meetings; knowledge management/information dissemination. **Events** *Conference* Washington, DC (USA) 2023, *Conference* Geneva (Switzerland) 2021, *Conference* Geneva (Switzerland) 2020, *Conference* Sydney, NSW (Australia) 2018, *Basic Science To global health impact* Cape Town (South Africa) 2017. **Members** Regular; Supporting. Biomedical scientists. Membership countries not specified. **NGO Relations** Member of (1): *European Cancer Organisation (ECO, #06432).* [2021/XD2580/D]

♦ International Paralympic Committee (IPC) 14512

Comité international paralympique (CIP) – Comité Internacional Paralimpico (CIP)

CEO Adenauerallee 212-214, 53113 Bonn, Germany. T. +492282097200. Fax +492282097209. E-mail: info@paralympic.org.
URL: http://www.paralympic.org/

History 22 Sep 1989, Düsseldorf (Germany). **Aims** Enable paralympic *athletes* to achieve sporting excellence and inspire and excite the world. **Structure** General Assembly (at least every 2 years); Governing Board; Management Team; Honorary Board. Standing Committees. Councils (4): Athletes'; IOSDs; Regions; Sports. Standing Committees (11): Anti-Doping; Audit and Finance; Athletes with High Support Needs; Classification; Development; Education; Legal and Ethics; Paralympic Games; Sports Science; Medical; Women in Sport. Sports Technical Committees (8): Para Athletics; Para Swimming; Shooting Para Sport; Powerlifting Sport; Para Dance Sport; Para Alpine Skiing and Snowboard Sports; Para Nordic Skiing; Para Ice Hockey Sport. **Languages** English. **Staff** 70.00 FTE, paid. **Finance** Sources: members' dues; sponsorship. Other sources: revenue from Paralympic Games and other events. **Activities** Advocacy/lobbying/activism; awards/prizes/competitions; sporting activities. **Events** *VISTA Conference* Japan 2021, *VISTA Conference* Amsterdam (Netherlands) 2019, *General Assembly and Conference* Bonn (Germany) 2019, *Project Review Meeting* Tokyo (Japan) 2018, *Project Review Meeting* Tokyo (Japan) 2018. **Publications** *Athletes' Bulletin*; *IPC Bulletin*; *News Flash*; *The Paralympian* – magazine; *TV Newsletter*. *IPC Handbook*. Brochures; press releases.
Members Full: National Paralympic Committees (" suspended nation) in 178 countries and territories:
Afghanistan, Algeria, Andorra, Angola, Antigua-Barbuda, Argentina, Armenia, Aruba, Australia, Austria, Azerbaijan, Bahrain, Barbados, Belarus, Belgium, Benin, Bermuda, Bosnia-Herzegovina, Botswana, Brazil, Brunei Darussalam, Bulgaria, Burkina Faso, Burundi, Cambodia, Cameroon, Canada, Cape Verde, Central African Rep, Chile, China, Colombia, Comoros, Congo Brazzaville, Congo DR, Costa Rica, Côte d'Ivoire, Croatia, Cuba, Cyprus, Czechia, Denmark, Djibouti, Dominican Rep, Ecuador, Egypt, El Salvador, Estonia, Ethiopia, Faeroe Is, Fiji, Finland, France, Gabon, Gambia, Georgia, Germany, Ghana, Great Britain, Greece, Grenada, Guatemala, Guinea, Guinea-Bissau, Haiti, Honduras, Hong Kong, Hungary, Iceland, India, Indonesia, Iran Islamic Rep, Iraq, Ireland, Israel, Italy, Jamaica, Japan, Jordan, Kazakhstan, Kenya, Korea DPR, Korea Rep, Kuwait, Kyrgyzstan, Laos, Latvia, Lebanon, Lesotho, Liberia, Libya, Liechtenstein, Lithuania, Luxembourg, Macau, Madagascar, Malawi, Malaysia, Mali, Malta, Mauritania (*), Mauritius, Mexico, Moldova, Mongolia, Montenegro, Morocco, Mozambique, Myanmar, Namibia, Nepal, Netherlands, New Zealand, Nicaragua, Niger, Nigeria, North Macedonia, Norway, Oman, Pakistan, Palestine, Panama, Papua New Guinea, Peru, Philippines, Poland, Portugal, Puerto Rico, Qatar, Romania, Russia (*), Rwanda, Samoa, San Marino, Sao Tomé-Principe, Saudi Arabia, Senegal, Serbia, Seychelles, Sierra Leone, Singapore, Slovakia, Slovenia, Solomon Is, Somalia, South Africa, Spain, Sri Lanka, St Vincent-Grenadines, Sudan, Suriname, Sweden, Switzerland, Syrian AR, Taiwan, Tajikistan, Tanzania UR, Thailand, Timor-Leste, Togo, Tonga, Trinidad-Tobago, Tunisia, Türkiye, Turkmenistan, Uganda, Ukraine, United Arab Emirates, Uruguay, USA, Uzbekistan, Vanuatu, Venezuela, Vietnam, Virgin Is USA, Yemen, Zambia, Zimbabwe.
Recognized international sports federations (18):
Badminton World Federation (BWF, #03060); *Fédération Équestre Internationale (FEI, #09484)*; *International Canoe Federation (ICF, #12437)*; *International Federation of Sport Climbing (IFSC, #13553)*; *International Handball Federation (IHF, #13771)*; *International Table Tennis Federation (ITTF, #15650)*; *International Tennis Federation (ITF, #15676)*; *International Wheelchair Basketball Federation (IWBF, #15882)*; *International Wheelchair Rugby Federation (IWRF, #15883)*; *Union Cycliste Internationale (UCI, #20375)*; *World Archery (#21105)*; *World Boccia (#21236)*; *World Curling Federation (WCF, #21348)*; *World ParaVolley (#21710)*; *World Penthathlon (UIPM, #21720)*; *World Rowing (#21756)*; *World Taekwondo (#21844)*; *World Triathlon (#21872)*.
Regional Organizations (4):
African Paralympic Committee (APC, #00410) (also known as African Paralympic Committee); *Asian Paralympic Committee (APC, #01652)*; *European Paralympic Committee (EPC, #08140)*; Oceania Paralympic Committee.
NGO Relations Member of (2): *International Council of Sport Science and Physical Education (ICSSPE, #13077)*; *Olympic Movement (#17719)*. Recognized by: *International Olympic Committee (IOC, #14408)*; *World Anti-Doping Agency (WADA, #21096)*. [2020/XE1373/y/**B**]

♦ International Paralympic Equestrian Committee / see Para Equestrian (#05521)

♦ International Parasitic Plant Society (IPPS) 14513

Sec 132 Lanhei Road, Kunming, 650201 Yunnan, China. E-mail: secretary@parasiticplants.org.
Pres address not obtained.
URL: http://www.parasiticplants.org/

History 2001, Nantes (France). Founded following the work of the International Parasitic Weed Symposium initiated in 1973. Registration: Netherlands. **Aims** Promote study and understanding of parasitic plants; increase exchange of information in the field. **Structure** Board of Directors. **Languages** English. **Staff** 5.00 FTE, voluntary. **Finance** Sources: members' dues. **Activities** Awards/prizes/competitions; events/meetings. **Events** *World Congress on Parasitic Plants* Nairobi (Kenya) 2022, *World Congress* Amsterdam (Netherlands) 2019, *World Congress* Pacific Grove, CA (USA) 2017, *World Congress* Kunming (China) 2015, *World Congress* Sheffield (UK) 2013. **Publications** *Haustorium: Parasitic Plants Newsletter* (2 a year). [2021/XM0339/**C**]

♦ International Parcel Tankers Association (internationally oriented national body)

♦ International Parkinson Disease Genomics Consortium (IPDGC) . . . 14514

Contact address not obtained. E-mail: ipdgc.contact@gmail.com.
URL: https://pdgenetics.org/

History Founded by participants at the June 2009 *International Parkinson and Movement Disorder Society (MDS, #14515)* meeting in Paris. **Events** *Meeting* 2020, *Meeting* Lisbon (Portugal) 2019, *Meeting* London (UK) 2019, *Meeting* Reykjavik (Iceland) 2018, *Meeting* Vienna (Austria) 2017.
Members Individuals in 15 countries:
Austria, Canada, Estonia, Finland, France, Germany, Israel, Kazakhstan, Netherlands, Nigeria, Norway, Spain, Sweden, UK, USA.
NGO Relations Cooperates with (1): *Latin American Research consortium on the GEnetics of Parkinson's Disease (LARGE-PD)*. [2021/AA1642/v/**C**]

♦ International Parkinson and Movement Disorder Society (MDS) . . . 14515

Exec Dir 555 East Wells St, Ste 1100, Milwaukee WI 53202-3823, USA. T. +14142762145. Fax +14142763349. E-mail: info@movementdisorders.org.
URL: http://www.movementdisorders.org/

History 1985. Merged with *International Medical Society for Motor Disturbances (ISMD, inactive)*, 1988. Former names and other names: *Movement Disorder Society (MDS)* – former (1985 to 2013). **Aims** Disseminate knowledge about movement disorders; promote research into causes, prevention and treatment of movement disorders; formulate and promote public policy that will affect the care of patients. **Structure** International Executive Committee; Secretariat. Sections (2): Asian and Oceanian; European. **Finance** Sources: members' dues. **Activities** Events/meetings; training/education. **Events** *International Congress of Parkinson's Disease and Movement Disorders* Philadelphia, PA (USA) 2024, *International Congress of Parkinson's Disease and Movement Disorders* Copenhagen (Denmark) 2023, *Asian and Oceanian Parkinson's Disease and Movement Disorders Congress* Kolkata (India) 2023, *International Congress of Parkinson's Disease and Movement Disorders* Madrid (Spain) 2022, *International Congress of Parkinson's Disease and Movement Disorders* Milwaukee, WI (USA) 2021. **Publications** *Movement Disorders* – journal. **Members** Membership countries not specified. **NGO Relations** Member of (1): *European Parkinson's Disease Association (EPDA, #08145)*. [2023.02.14/XJ3071/**F**]

♦ International Parkour Federation (IPF) 14516

SG address not obtained.
URL: https://internationalparkourfederation.org/

History 2014. Founded by founders of *World Freerunning Parkour Federation (WFPF)*. Current constitution adopted Sep 2017. Registration: 501(c)(3) non-profit, USA. **Aims** Promote the practice of Parkour and related disciplines. **Structure** General Assembly; Board of Directors. **Activities** Capacity building; events/meetings; sporting activities.
Members National bodies in 42 countries:
Afghanistan, Bahrain, Bhutan, Bolivia, Burkina Faso, Cameroon, Costa Rica, Côte d'Ivoire, Cuba, Egypt, Ghana, Guinea, Guinea-Bissau, India, Iran Islamic Rep, Italy, Kenya, Kosovo, Kuwait, Libya, Malaysia, Maldives, Mali, Malta, Morocco, Nepal, Nigeria, Pakistan, Palestine, Peru, Portugal, Rwanda, Saudi Arabia, Senegal, Sierra Leone, Syrian AR, Tajikistan, Togo, Uganda, Ukraine, USA, Yemen.
NGO Relations Member of (2): *General Association of Asia Pacific Sports Federations (GAAPSF, #10106)*; *International Sport Network Organization (ISNO, #15592)*. [2020/AA1078/**C**]

♦ International Parliamentarians' Association for Information Technology (inactive)

♦ International Parliamentary Alliance for the Recognition of Ecocide (Ecocide Alliance) 14517

Contact address not obtained. E-mail: contact@ecocidealliance.org.
URL: https://www.ecocidealliance.org/

History Initiated by Marie Toussaint, a member of *Group of the Greens – European Free Alliance (Greens/EFA, #10781)* of *European Parliament (EP, #08146)*. **Aims** Constitute a network of elected representatives willing to work together towards the recognition of ecocide from regional to international level.
Members Parliamentarians in 17 countries:
Australia, Belgium, Brazil, Canada, Cyprus, Finland, France, Iceland, Italy, Netherlands, Philippines, Spain, Sweden, Switzerland, UK, USA, Venezuela.
NGO Relations Partner of (3): *ASEAN Parliamentarians for Human Rights (APHR, #01219)*; *Group of the Greens – European Free Alliance (Greens/EFA, #10781)*; *Stop Ecocide International (SEI, #19998)*. [2021/AA2674/v/**C**]

♦ International Parliamentary Network for Education (IPNEd) 14518

Exec Dir 31-33 Bondway, London, SW8 1SJ, UK. E-mail: info@ipned.org – director@ipned.org.
URL: https://www.ipned.org/

History Sep 2020. Registration: EU Transparency Register, No/ID: 210457245130-10, Start date: 12 Jan 2022. **Aims** Mobilize political leadership to accelerate quality education for all. **Structure** Global Executive Committee; Member Parliamentarians; Secretariat. **Activities** Advocacy/lobbying/activism.
Members Parliamentarians in 54 countries and territories:
Afghanistan, Algeria, Andorra, Argentina, Armenia, Australia, Austria, Bangladesh, Burkina Faso, Cameroon, Canada, Chad, Colombia, Croatia, Czechia, Denmark, Egypt, Finland, France, Georgia, Germany, Ghana, Honduras, Ireland, Isle of Man, Italy, Japan, Kenya, Korea Rep, Lebanon, Luxembourg, Malawi, Maldives, Mexico, Morocco, Nepal, New Zealand, Nigeria, Pakistan, Philippines, Romania, Senegal, Sierra Leone, South Africa, Spain, Sweden, Switzerland, Tanzania UR, Tunisia, Türkiye, UK, USA, Zambia, Zimbabwe.
European Parliament (EP, #08146).
Associate members in 9 countries:
Australia, Canada, Germany, Ghana, Morocco, Norway, Spain, Tanzania UR, Zimbabwe. [2022.02.01/AA2333/v/**F**]

♦ International Parliament for Safety and Peace (internationally oriented national body)
♦ International Particle Accelerator Conference (meeting series)
♦ International Particle Toxicology Conference (meeting series)

♦ International Partnership for Dogs (IPFD) 14519

Contact c/o Svenska Kennelklubben, Box 771, SE-191 27 Sollentuna, Sweden. E-mail: info@ipfdogs.com.
URL: https://dogwellnet.com/

History Launched Aug 2014. Registered in accordance with Swedish law. **Aims** Facilitate collaboration and sharing of resources to enhance the health, well-being and welfare of pedigreed dogs and all dogs worldwide; provide information and support to the global dog community. **Structure** Board. **Activities** Events/meetings; guidance/assistance/consulting; projects/programmes. **Events** *Workshop* Windsor (UK) 2019, *International Dog Health Workshop* Paris (France) 2017, *International Dog Health Workshop* Dortmund (Germany) 2015, *International Dog Health Workshop* Sollentuna (Sweden) 2012.
Members National kennel clubs, industry and non-profit organizations in 8 countries:
Finland, France, Germany, Ireland, Norway, Sweden, UK, USA. [2018.09.17/XM6476/**C**]

♦ International Partnership for Energy Efficiency Cooperation (IPEEC) 14520

Exec Dir c/o IEA, 9 rue de la Fédération, 75739 Paris CEDEX 15, France. T. +33140576524. Fax +33140576509.
URL: http://www.ipeec.org/

History Established 2009, L'Aquila (Italy), at the *Group of Eight (G-8, #10745)* Summit. Proposed during G8 Summit, Jun 2007, Heiligendamm (Germany). **Aims** Facilitate actions that yield high energy efficiency gains. **Structure** Policy Committee, consisting of a high-level representative of each Member. Executive Committee, consisting of a mid-level representative of each Member. Secretariat at *International Energy Agency (IEA, #13270)*. Task Groups include: Assessment of Energy Efficiency Financing Mechanism (AEEFM); Energy Management Action Network for Industrial Efficiency (EMAK); *Global Superior Energy Performance Partnership (GSEP, #10615)*; Improving Policies through Energy Efficiency Indicators (IPEEI); Policies for Energy Provider Delivery of Energy Efficiency (PEPDEE); Super-efficient Equipment and Appliance Deployment Initiative (SEAD); Sustainable Buildings Network (SBN); Worldwide Energy Efficiency Action through Capacity Building and Training (WEACT); National and International Action Plans. **Finance** Voluntary contributions. **Events** *Workshop* Seoul (Korea Rep) 2013, *Energy Management Action Network Workshop* Tokyo (Japan) 2013.
Members Governments of 15 countries:
Australia, Brazil, Canada, China, France, Germany, India, Italy, Japan, Korea Rep, Mexico, Russia, South Africa, UK, USA.
Regional entity:
European Union (EU, #08967).
NGO Relations Member of: *Global Alliance for Buildings and Construction (GlobalABC, #10187)*. [2015/XJ1026/**E***]

♦ International Partnership for Human Development (internationally oriented national body)
♦ International Partnership for Human Rights (internationally oriented national body)
♦ International Partnership for the Hydrogen Economy / see International Partnership for Hydrogen and Fuel Cells in the Economy (#14521)

♦ International Partnership for Hydrogen and Fuel Cells in the Economy (IPHE) 14521

Secretariat c/o NOW GmbH, Fasanenstrasse 5, 10623 Berlin, Germany. E-mail: secretariat@iphe.net.
URL: http://www.iphe.net/

History 2003, as *International Partnership for the Hydrogen Economy*, on the initiative of the USA Departments of Energy and Transportation. Present name adopted, Dec 2009. **Aims** Advance development and implementation of hydrogen and fuel cell technologies and economies. **Structure** Steering Committee; Implementation-Liaison Committee; Secretariat; Working Groups. **Activities** Events/meetings. **Events** *International Hydrogen Economy Forum* Seoul (Korea Rep) 2019, *Meeting* Seoul (Korea Rep) 2019, *Meeting* Kobe (Japan) 2018, *Towards a Clean and Sustainable Hydrogen Supply Chain Workshop* Kōriyama (Japan) 2018, *Forum on Increasing Role of Hydrogen in the Economy* Yokohama (Japan) 2018. **Publications** Newsletter. Educational materials; conference reports. **Members** Membership countries not specified. [2014.11.03/XJ8196/**F**]

♦ International Partnership on Mitigation and MRV 14522

Contact address not obtained. E-mail: info@mitigationpartnership.net.
URL: http://mitigationpartnership.net/

History May 2010, Bonn (Germany), by governments of South Africa, Korea Rep and Germany. Partnership without formal character. **Aims** Support a practical exchange on mitigation-related activities and MRV between developing and developed countries in order to help close the global ambition gap. **Activities** Events/meetings; networking/liaising; capacity building; knowledge management/information dissemination. **Publications** *Mitigation Newsletter*. **IGO Relations** *Deutsche Gesellschaft für Internationale Zusammenarbeit (GIZ)*; *UNDP (#20292)*. **NGO Relations** Member of: *LEDS Global Partnership (LEDS GP, #16435)*. Partners: *Center for Clean Air Policy (CCAP)* *World Resources Institute (WRI, #21753)*. [2016/XM4408/**F***]

♦ International Partnership Network (IPN) 14523

Dir PO Box 741, Harvard MA 01451, USA. T. +19784568823. Fax +19784563288. E-mail: wsouthport@msn.com.
URL: http://www.iebpn.net/

History Jun 1992, Birmingham (UK), during 1st International Partnership Conference. April 1999, registered in accordance with USA law. **Aims** Improve: the quality of learning for children and adults; economic development and workforce preparedness world-wide by the concerted commitment of education, business and community partners; promote the exchange of experience between partnership practitioners and *policymakers* internationally; establish and maintain a network through which *education- industry* collaboration can be disseminated. **Structure** Chairman. **Finance** Members' dues. Other sources: corporate and government funding through donations. **Activities** Case-writing and research programme; international conferences and seminars. **Events** *Conference* Oslo (Norway) / Lillestrøm (Norway) 2016, *Conference* Espoo (Finland) 2008, *Conference* Italy 2006, *Conference* London (UK) 2004, *Conference* Washington, DC (USA) 2002. **Publications** *Circuit: The International Partnership Network Bulletin* (2 a year). Reports and case studies. Information Services: Database; library; information service.

Members Individuals and organizations in 28 countries:
Australia, Belgium, Canada, Czechia, Denmark, Djibouti, Finland, France, Germany, Greece, Hungary, Iceland, India, Ireland, Italy, Luxembourg, Netherlands, New Zealand, Norway, Poland, Portugal, Slovakia, South Africa, Spain, Sweden, Trinidad-Tobago, UK, USA. [2014/XF3546/**F**]

♦ International Partnership for Nuclear Disarmament Verification (unconfirmed)

♦ International Partnership on Religion and Sustainable Development (PaRD) 14524

Secretariat c/o GIZ, Friedrich-Ebert-Allee 36-40, 53113 Bonn, Germany.
URL: http://www.partner-religion-development.org/

History Feb 2016. **Aims** Bring together governmental and intergovernmental entities with diverse civil society organizations (CSOs) and faith-based organizations (FBOs), to engage the social capital and capacities vested in diverse faith communities for sustainable development and humanitarian assistance in the spirit of the 2030 Agenda for Sustainable Development. **Structure** General Assembly; Steering Group; Secretariat, located at *Deutsche Gesellschaft für Internationale Zusammenarbeit (GIZ)*. **Finance** Financed by: German Federal Ministry for Economic Cooperation and Development (BMZ). **Activities** Knowledge management/information dissemination; capacity building; advocacy/lobbying/activism.
Members Organizations include 67 listed in this Yearbook:
- *ACT Alliance (#00081)*;
- *Adventist Development and Relief Agency International (ADRA, #00131)*;
- *African Union (AU, #00488)* (Citizens and Diaspora Directorate AU CIDO);
- African Union – Economic, Social and Cultural Council (AU ECOSOCC);
- *Ahimsa Fund (#00586)*;
- *Arigatou International*;
- *Association des ombudsmans et médiateurs africains (AOMA, #02838)*;
- *Baha'i International Community (#03062)*;
- *Buddhist Global Relief (BGR)*;
- *Catholic Relief Services (CRS, #03608)* (US Conference of Catholic Bishops);
- *Catholic Youth Network for Environmental Sustainability in Africa (CYNESA, #03611)*;
- *Christian AIDS Bureau for Southern Africa (CABSA)*;
- *Community of Sant'Egidio*;
- *Danmission*;
- *Digni*;
- *Episcopal Relief and Development*;
- *European Association of Development Research and Training Institutes (EADI, #06012)*;
- *European Christian Organisations in Relief and Development (EU-CORD, #06545)*;
- *Faith in Water*;
- *Finn Church Aid (FCA)*;
- *German Catholic Bishops' Organisation for Development Cooperation (MISEREOR)*;
- *GHR Foundation*;
- *Global Fund to Fight AIDS, Tuberculosis and Malaria (Global Fund, #10383)*;
- *Global Interfaith WASH Alliance (GIWA)*;
- *Global One*;
- *Globethics.net Foundation (#10669)*;
- *International Center for Religion and Diplomacy (ICRD)*;
- *International Interfaith Peace Corps (IIPC)*;
- *International Islamic Charitable Organization (IICO, #13957)*;
- *Islamic Relief Worldwide (IRWW, #16048)*;
- *Islamic Research and Training Institute, Jeddah (IRTI, #16050)*;
- *Jacob Soetendorp Institute for Human Values*;
- *Joint Learning Initiative on Faith and Local Communities (JLI, #16139)*;
- *King Abdullah Bin Abdulaziz International Centre for Interreligious and Intercultural Dialogue (KAICIID, #16193)*;
- *KOLPING INTERNATIONAL (#16203)*;
- *Maktab Tarighat Oveyssi Shahmaghsoudi (MTO Shahmaghsoudi, #16556)*;
- *Minority Rights Group International (MRG, #16820)*;
- *MISSIO (#16827)*;
- *Muslim Hands*;
- *Network for Religious and Traditional Peacemakers (#17054)*;
- *Norwegian Agency for Development Cooperation (Norad)*;
- *Order of St Augustine (Augustinians International)* (Curia Generalizia Agostiniana);
- *Penny Appeal*;
- *Regional Centre on Small Arms and Light Weapons in the Great Lakes Region, the Horn of Africa and Bordering States (RECSA, #18760)*;
- *Religions for Peace (RfP, #18831)*;
- *Salam Institute for Peace and Justice*;
- *Salvation Army (#19041)*;
- *Search for Common Ground (SFCG)*;
- *Side by Side (#19265)*;
- *Sonke Gender Justice Network*;
- *Tearfund, UK*;
- *The Lutheran World Federation (LWF, #16532)*;
- *The World Bank Group (#21218)*;
- *United Religions Initiative (URI, #20658)*;
- *United States Agency for International Development (USAID)*;
- *United States Institute of Peace (USIP)*;
- *USPG (#20736)*;
- *Woodenfish Foundation*;
- *World Association for Christian Communication (WACC, #21126)*;
- *World Council of Churches (WCC, #21320)*;
- *World Evangelical Alliance (WEA, #21393)*;
- *World Faiths Development Dialogue (WFDD)*;
- *World Food Programme (WFP, #21510)*;
- *World Human Accountability Organization (WHAO)*;
- *World Relief*;
- *World Vision International (WVI, #21904)*;
- *World Young Women's Christian Association (World YWCA, #21947)*.

NGO Relations Cooperates with (1): *G20 Interfaith Forum Association (IF20, #10055)*. [2019.07.30/XM7711/y/**F**]

♦ International Partnership for the Satoyama Initiative (IPSI) 14525

Dir 5-53-70 Jingumae, Shibuya-ku, Tokyo, 150-8925 Japan. T. +81354671212. Fax +81334992828. E-mail: isi@unu.edu.
URL: https://satoyama-initiative.org/

History Initiated by Ministry of the Environment of Japan and *United Nations University Institute for the Advanced Study of Sustainability (UNU-IAS, #20643)*. Launched during 10th Meeting of Conference of the Parties of *Convention on Biological Diversity (Biodiversity convention, 1992)*, Oct 2010, Nagoya (Japan). **Aims** Realize societies in harmony with nature through *conservation* and advancement of socio-ecological production *landscapes* and seascapes (SEPLS) that secure *ecosystem* services and conserve *biodiversity* to support and enhance human *well-being*. **Structure** Assembly; Public Forum; Steering Committee; Secretariat. **Languages** English. **Staff** 8.00 FTE, paid. **Finance** Contribution of the Ministry of the Environment (Japan). **Activities** Awareness raising; capacity building; events/meetings; knowledge management/information dissemination; research/documentation. **Events** *Making OECMs Work Production Landscapes for Effective Area-Based Conservation* Tokyo (Japan) 2022, *Seminar on Community-based Activities and Governance for Seascape Restoration* Tokyo (Japan) 2022, *Strengthening Interlinkages Amongst Biodiversity, Health, and Well-being in SEPLS* Tokyo (Japan) 2022, *Symposium on the International Day for Biological Diversity – Building a Shared Future for All Life* Tokyo (Japan) 2022, *IPSI Case Study Workshop* Tokyo (Japan) 2020. **Publications** *Satoyama Initiative Thematic Review* (annual).
Members Organizations (over 270). Included, 27 organizations listed in this Yearbook:
- *Bioversity International (#03262)*;
- *BirdLife International (#03266)*;
- *Conservation International (CI)*;
- *Critical Ecosystem Partnership Fund (CEPF, #04958)*;
- *Energy and Resources Institute (TERI)*;
- *Forest Peoples Programme (FPP, #09865)*;
- *Global Environment Facility (GEF, #10346)*;
- *Indigenous Peoples' International Centre for Policy Research and Education (Tebtebba Foundation)*;
- *Institute for Global Environmental Strategies (IGES, #11266)*;
- *International Centre for Integrated Mountain Development (ICIMOD, #12500)*;
- *International Council for Game and Wildlife Conservation (#13024)*;
- *International Lake Environment Committee Foundation (ILEC, #13998)*;
- *International Network for Bamboo and Rattan (INBAR, #14234)*;
- *International Tropical Timber Organization (ITTO, #15737)*;
- *International Union for Conservation of Nature and Natural Resources (IUCN, #15766)*;
- *Japan International Cooperation Agency (JICA)*;
- *Landcare International (LI, #16226)*;
- *Secretariat of the Convention on Biological Diversity (SCBD, #19197)*;
- *Secretariat of the Pacific Regional Environment Programme (SPREP, #19205)*;
- *South Asian Forum for Environment (SAFE)*;
- *The Nature Conservancy (TNC)*;
- *Tropical Science Centre, San José (TSC)*;
- *UNDP (#20292)*;
- *UN Environment Programme World Conservation Monitoring Centre (UNEP-WCMC, #20295)*;
- *United Nations Centre for Regional Development (UNCRD, #20526)*;
- *United Nations University (UNU, #20642)*;
- *World Agroforestry Centre (ICRAF, #21072)*.

IGO Relations Partnerships with several organizations, including: *Global Environment Facility (GEF, #10346)*; *International Tropical Timber Organization (ITTO, #15737)*; *Secretariat of the Convention on Biological Diversity (SCBD, #19197)*; *Secretariat of the Pacific Regional Environment Programme (SPREP, #19205)*; *UNDP (#20292)*; *UNESCO (#20322)*; *UNEP (#20299)*. Contributes to: *Intergovernmental Science-Policy Platform on Biodiversity and Ecosystem Services (IPBES, #11500)*. **NGO Relations** Secretariat hosted by: *United Nations University Institute for the Advanced Study of Sustainability (UNU-IAS, #20643)*. Partnerships with several organizations, including: *International Union for Conservation of Nature and Natural Resources (IUCN, #15766)*. [2021/XM7878/y/**E**]

♦ International Partners in Mission (IPM) 14526

CEO 3091 Mayfield Rd, Ste 320, Cleveland Heights OH 44118, USA. T. +12169324082.
Executive Office 67 main St, 3rd Floor, Bar Harbor ME 04609, USA. T. +12078019020.
URL: http://www.ipmconnect.org/

History 1974. Former names and other names: *Partners in Mission (PIM)* – former (2002); *Christians Linked in Mission (CLM)* – former (1988 to 2002). **Aims** Work across borders of faith, culture, and economic circumstance with children, women, and youth to create partnerships that build justice, peace, and hope. **Structure** General Assembly; International Executive Board; Honorary Board; Advisory Councils. **Activities** Programmes/projects. [2021/XJ9784/**F**]

♦ International Passive House Association (iPHA) 14527

Contact Rheinstr 44-46, 64283 Darmstadt, Germany. T. +4961518269955. Fax +4961518269934. E-mail: info@passivehouse-international.org.
URL: http://www.passivehouse-international.org/

History 2010. Former names and other names: *Passive House Institute* – former. **Aims** Serve as a platform of exchange, facilitating international collaboration on energy efficiency in construction; drive uptake of the Passive House Standard worldwide. **Structure** An international membership network. **Languages** Chinese, English, French, German, Italian, Spanish. **Staff** 3.00 FTE, paid. **Activities** Advocacy/lobbying/activism; awareness raising; capacity building; events/meetings; guidance/assistance/consulting; knowledge management/information dissemination; networking/liaising; politics/policy/regulatory; projects/programmes; publishing activities; research/documentation; standards/guidelines; training/education. **Events** *International Passive House Conference* Darmstadt (Germany) 2020, *International Passive House Conference* Gaobeidian (China) 2019, *International Passive House Conference* Munich (Germany) 2018, *International Passive House Conference* Vienna (Austria) 2017, *International Passive House Conference* Leipzig (Germany) 2015. **Publications** *Passive House: Building a sustainable future* in English. *iPHA Blog* in English; *iPHA on BuildUP* in English.
Members Individuals; organizations. Membership countries not specified. **IGO Relations** Cooperates with (1): *Committee on Housing and Land Management (#04259)*. **NGO Relations** Member of (1): *Global Alliance for Buildings and Construction (GlobalABC, #10187)*. [2020.08.18/XM5752/**C**]

♦ International Pasta Organisation (IPO) 14528

SG Viale del Poggio Fiorito 61, 00144 Rome RM, Italy. T. +3968091071. Fax +3968073186. E-mail: ipo@internationalpasta.org.
URL: http://www.internationalpasta.org/

History 25 Oct 2005. Statutes adopted 25 Oct 2006, Rome (Italy). **Aims** Increase pasta consumption and awareness, by advancing consumers' understanding of the nutritional value and health benefits of pasta; promote common business interests. **Structure** General Assembly; Board; Scientific Advisory Committee. **Finance** Sources: members' dues. **Events** *Meeting* Dubai (United Arab Emirates) 2018, *World Pasta Congress* Rio de Janeiro (Brazil) 2010, *World Pasta Congress* Barcelona (Spain) 2005, *World Pasta Congress* Porlamar (Venezuela) 2000.
Members Active; Supporting. Active in 14 countries:
Brazil, Colombia, Costa Rica, France, Guatemala, Iran Islamic Rep, Italy, Mexico, Portugal, Spain, Tunisia, Türkiye, USA, Venezuela.
Supporting in 5 countries:
Belgium, Chile, Italy, Mexico, USA.
Supporting members included in this Yearbook (2):
Union of Organizations of manufacturers of Pasta Products of the EU (#20468); *Union of the Associations of Semolina Manufacturers of the EU (Semouliers, #20363)*. [2019.02.14/XJ2829/y/**C**]

♦ International Patellofemoral Study Group (IPSG) 14529

Sec 2195 Cheat Rd, Ste 2, Morgantown WV 26505, USA. T. +13045990050. Fax +13045990070.
URL: http://www.ipsg.org/

History 1995. **Aims** Advance knowledge of the patellofemoral joint. **Events** *Annual Meeting* Big Sky, MT (USA) 2024, *Annual Meeting* Helsinki (Finland) 2022, *Annual Meeting* Banff, AB (Canada) 2019, *Annual Meeting* Munich (Germany) 2017, *Annual Meeting* Chicago, IL (USA) 2015. [2015/XE4456/**E**]

♦ International Patent Cooperation Union (PCT Union) 14530

Union internationale de coopération en matière de brevets

Address not obtained.
URL: http://www.wipo.org/

History 24 Jan 1978, on the entry into force of the *Patent Cooperation Treaty (PCT, 1970)*, signed 19 Jun 1970, Washington DC (USA). Treaty amended 1979, and modified 1984. A union administered by *World Intellectual Property Organization (WIPO, #21593)*. **Aims** Simplify and render more economical – in the interests of the users of the patent system and the offices which have responsibility for administering it – the previously established means of applying for patent *protection* for *inventions* where such protection is required in several countries. **Structure** Assembly; Committee for Administrative and Legal Matters; Committee for Technical Cooperation. **Finance** The PCT system is self-supporting since the fees paid by the applicants cover the costs incurred by WIPO in administering the system. The (budgeted) income of the PTC Union for 1993 amounts to Swiss Fr 35 million. **Activities** Establishes a system of cooperation that facilitates the application for patent protection for inventions where such protection is desired in several countries. The Treaty provides for the filing of a single international application, which has the effect of a national patent application in those contracting States which the applicant designates. The Treaty also provides for an international search report and for an international preliminary examination report. **Events** *Meeting of International Authorities under the Patent Cooperation Treaty* Madrid (Spain) 2018, *Meeting of International Authorities under the Patent Cooperation Treaty* Tokyo (Japan) 2015, *Biennial Session* 1993. **Publications** *PCT Gazette* (bi-weekly). *PCT Applicant's Guide*.
Members Open to States party to the Patent Cooperation Treaty. State members as of Feb 2014 (148):
Albania, Algeria, Angola, Antigua-Barbuda, Armenia, Australia, Austria, Azerbaijan, Bahrain, Barbados, Belarus, Belgium, Belize, Benin, Bosnia-Herzegovina, Botswana, Brazil, Brunei Darussalam, Bulgaria, Burkina Faso, Cameroon, Canada, Central African Rep, Chad, Chile, China, Colombia, Comoros, Congo Brazzaville, Costa Rica, Côte d'Ivoire, Croatia, Cuba, Cyprus, Czechia, Denmark, Dominica, Dominican Rep, Ecuador, Egypt, El Salvador, Equatorial Guinea, Estonia, Eswatini, Finland, France, Gabon, Gambia, Georgia, Germany, Ghana, Greece, Grenada, Guatemala, Guinea, Guinea-Bissau, Honduras, Hungary, Iceland, India,

Indonesia, Iran Islamic Rep, Ireland, Israel, Italy, Japan, Kazakhstan, Kenya, Korea DPR, Korea Rep, Kyrgyzstan, Laos, Latvia, Lesotho, Liberia, Libya, Liechtenstein, Lithuania, Luxembourg, Madagascar, Malawi, Malaysia, Mali, Malta, Mauritania, Mexico, Moldova, Monaco, Mongolia, Montenegro, Morocco, Mozambique, Namibia, Netherlands, New Zealand, Nicaragua, Niger, Nigeria, North Macedonia, Norway, Oman, Panama, Papua New Guinea, Peru, Philippines, Poland, Portugal, Qatar, Romania, Russia, Rwanda, San Marino, Sao Tomé-Principe, Saudi Arabia, Senegal, Serbia, Seychelles, Sierra Leone, Singapore, Slovakia, Slovenia, South Africa, Spain, Sri Lanka, St Kitts-Nevis, St Lucia, St Vincent-Grenadines, Sudan, Sweden, Switzerland, Syrian AR, Tajikistan, Tanzania UR, Thailand, Togo, Trinidad-Tobago, Tunisia, Türkiye, Turkmenistan, Uganda, UK, Ukraine, United Arab Emirates, USA, Uzbekistan, Vietnam, Zambia, Zimbabwe.

IGO Relations *European Patent Office (EPO, #08166)* acts as an international searching and examining authority. Applicants who are nationals of or resident in a contracting State party to the European Patent Convention may also file the international application with EPO. Applicants who are nationals of or resident in Barbados, Sri Lanka or a contracting State which is a member of: *African Intellectual Property Organization (#00344)* file the international application with WIPO. [2014/XF4432/**F***]

♦ International Patent Institute (inactive)

♦ International Pathwork Foundation 14531

Contact PO Box 725, Madison VA 22727, USA. T. +15409485558. E-mail: pathworkfoundation@pathwork.org.

URL: http://www.pathwork.org/

History 1987, USA, transcription of the teachings of Eva Pierrakos having begun in 1957, New York NY (USA), and the first Pathwork Centre having been set up in 1972, Phoenicia NY (USA). **Aims** Promote *'The Pathwork'*, a body of practical wisdom that lays out a a contemporary *spiritual* discipline comprising a step-by-step journey into personal transformation and wholeness, a voyage of discovery to the Real Self through layers of defence, denial and fear; increase and disseminate Pathwork consciousness worldwide; promote self-responsibility, self-knowledge and self-acceptance. **Finance** Members' dues. Other sources: members' contributions; programme tuition; support from like-minded organizations. **Activities** Edits, translates and disseminates Pathwork material, Pathwork teachings derived from it and other resources. Provides spiritual transformation and growth through work with 258 Guide Lectures channelled by Eva Pierrakos. Programmes include spiritual retreats; intensives; work with individual helpers; extensive training; resident programmes; work exchange programmes. Supports and promotes methods for teaching the concepts in the lectures; authorizes and endorses operation of Pathwork communities worldwide. *'Lecture Study Groups'* study the lectures in depth and apply them to their individual lives. *'Pathwork Process Groups'* provide a dynamic format for applying the Pathwork teachings in the framework of group interaction. **Publications** *In Connection* – newsletter. *Through Pathwork Press: Pathwork Guide Lectures* by Eva Pierrakos. *Complete Lectures of the Pathwork* – CD-ROM. Pathwork books; audiotapes; related materials. **Members** Individuals in all countries. [2019/XF0069/f/**F**]

♦ International Patient Information Board on Tick-Borne Encephalitis (IPI-TBE) 14532

Address not obtained.

URL: http://www.tick-victims.info/

History Apr 2006, by members of *International Scientific Working Group on TBE.* **Aims** Continue the research of the Austrian group on tick-borne Encephalitis (TBE) into all other European countries similarly affected. **Events** *Annual Conference* Vienna (Austria) 2017, *Annual Conference* Vienna (Austria) 2013, *Annual Conference* Vienna (Austria) 2010, *Annual Conference* Vienna (Austria) 2009. [2013/XJ1310/**E**]

♦ International Patient Organization for Primary Immunodeficiencies (IPOPI) 14533

Exec Dir Rocky Bottom, Trerieve Estate, Downderry, PL11 3LY, UK. T. +441503250668. E-mail: info@ipopi.org.

Office – Belgium Avenue Louise 367, 1050 Brussels, Belgium.

URL: http://www.ipopi.org/

History 3 Oct 1992, Lugano (Switzerland). Founded at meeting in which charter was adopted, having been planned over 2 years by an interim organizing committee set up Sep 1990, Oxford (UK). Registration: Charity Commission, No/ID: 1058005, Start date: 12 Sep 1996, England and Wales; Banque-Carrefour des Entreprises, No/ID: 0761.784.055, Start date: 19 Jan 2021, Belgium; EU Transparency Register, No/ID: 379847424451-15, Start date: 11 Nov 2016. **Aims** Promote international cooperation among patient organizations concerned with primary immunodeficiencies, so as to bring together experience, expertise, resources and influence of members in achieving moral comfort and practical assistance in improving care and treatment worldwide. **Structure** General Assembly (every 2 years); Executive Committee; Medical Advisory Panel. **Languages** English. **Staff** 1.50 FTE, paid; 12.00 FTE, voluntary. **Finance** Contributions from member organizations and others. **Activities** Networking/liaising; awareness raising. **Events** *International Primary Immunodeficiencies Congress (IPIC)* Rotterdam (Netherlands) 2023, *International Primary Immunodeficiencies Congress (IPIC)* Vilamoura (Portugal) 2022, *International Primary Immunodeficiencies Congress (IPIC)* Berlin (Germany) 2021, *International Primary Immunodeficiencies Congress* Madrid (Spain) 2019, *Biennial Meeting* Lisbon (Portugal) 2018. **Publications** *Update* (4 a year) – e-newsletter.

Members National organizations in 41 countries:
Argentina, Australia, Austria, Belarus, Belgium, Brazil, Canada, Chile, Colombia, Cyprus, Denmark, Estonia, Finland, France, Germany, Greece, Hungary, Iceland, India, Iran Islamic Rep, Ireland, Italy, Japan, Mexico, Morocco, Netherlands, New Zealand, Norway, Poland, Portugal, Romania, Russia, Serbia, South Africa, Spain, Sweden, Switzerland, Türkiye, Uruguay, USA, Venezuela.

Associate members in 7 countries:
Bosnia-Herzegovina, Bulgaria, Egypt, Peru, Slovenia, Uganda, UK.

NGO Relations Member of (6): *EU Health Coalition*; *European Patients' Forum (EPF, #08172)*; *EURORDIS – Rare Diseases Europe (#09175)*; *Health First Europe (HFE, #10881)*; *International Alliance of Patients' Organizations (IAPO, #11633)*; *Rare Diseases International (RDI, #18621)*. Joint meetings with: *International Nursing Group for Immunodeficiencies (INGID, #14386)*. Cooperates with: *European Foundation for the Care of Newborn Infants (EFCNI, #07344)*; *European Hematology Association (EHA, #07473)*. [2022/XD5101/**D**]

♦ International Payments Framework Association (IPFA) 14534

Address not obtained.

URL: http://www.ipf-a.org/

History Feb 2010. **Aims** Promote the acceptance and use of a global operating framework for cross-border payments. **Structure** Board of Directors; CEO. **Events** *Annual General Meeting* Boston, MA (USA) 2014, *Annual General Meeting* Utrecht (Netherlands) 2014, *Annual General Meeting* New York, NY (USA) 2013, *Annual General Meeting* Vienna (Austria) 2013, *Global Payments Forum / Annual General Meeting* Vienna (Austria) 2013.

Members Primary (17); Affiliate (10). Membership countries not specified. Affiliate members include 3 organizations listed in this Yearbook:
Affiliate members include 3 organizations listed in this Yearbook:
SADC Banking Association (#19022); *Society for Worldwide Interbank Financial Telecommunication (SWIFT, #19661)*; *World Savings Banks Institute (WSBI, #21764)*.

IGO Relations Observers include: *International Bank for Reconstruction and Development (IBRD, #12317)* (World Bank). **NGO Relations** Observers include: *European Payments Council (EPC, #08175)*. [2019/XJ7972/y/**C**]

♦ International Peace Academy / see International Peace Institute (#14536)
♦ International Peacebuilding Alliance / see Interpeace (#15962)
♦ International Peace Bureau / see International Peace Bureau (#14535)

♦ International Peace Bureau (IPB) 14535

Bureau international de la paix – Oficina Internacional de la Paz – Internationales Friedensbüro

Co-Pres Marienstr 19/20, 10117 Berlin, Germany. T. +493012084549. E-mail: info@ipb-office.berlin.

Co-Pres address not obtained.

URL: http://www.ipb.org/

History 13 Nov 1891, Rome (Italy). Founded by 3rd World Peace Congress, with the title *Bureau international permanent de la paix (BIPP)*, as central office and executive organ of *Union internationale des sociétés de la paix (UISP, inactive)*, which was set up at the same time. Commenced activities provisionally on 1 Dec 1891, Bern (Switzerland). Statutes adopted at 4th World Peace Congress, 23 Aug 1892, Bern; registered in accordance with Swiss Civil Code, 22 Sep 1893. UISP ceased to exist during World War I. IPB office transferred to Geneva (Switzerland) in 1924. Activities suspended during World War II. Reconstituted 1949, after re-establishment efforts from 1946, as *International Liaison Committee of Organizations for Peace (ILCOP)* which was recognized by the Swiss Federal Council, 20 Jan 1961, Geneva, as legal successor to UISP. ILCOP has also been referred to as *International Liaison Committee of Peace Societies.* Subsequently ILCOP re-adopted the name *'International Peace Bureau'*, representing both the international organization UISP and its secretariat (the previous BIPP) in Geneva. In 1983, IPB took over activities of *International Confederation for Disarmament and Peace (ICDP, inactive)*, which had been set up, 11 Jan 1964, Tyringe (Sweden), on adoption of a Constitution prepared by a Continuing Committee elected Jan 1963, Oxford (UK). Received the Nobel Peace Prize, 1910. Registration: Switzerland. **Aims** Facilitate channels of communications and sharing of resources, informations and ideas on the international level between organizations and individuals working for peace; campaign on diverse peace issues and especially on *disarmament* and the link between militarization and climate change; support the maintenance of NGO networks and joint platforms. **Structure** General Assembly (every 3 years); Council (annual); Board; Headquarters, located in Berlin (Germany). **Languages** English. **Finance** Sources: donations; gifts, legacies; members' dues. **Activities** Advocacy/lobbying/activism; awards/prizes/competitions; awareness raising; capacity building; events/meetings; guidance/assistance/consulting; knowledge management/information dissemination; networking/liaising; politics/policy/regulatory; projects/programmes; publishing activities; research/documentation; training/education. In 1996 initiated *Hague Appeal for Peace (HAP, #10848)* and subsequent *Global Campaign for Peace Education (#10266)*, together with International Physicians for the Prevention of Nuclear War, International Association of Lawyers Against Nuclear Arms (IALANA) and World Federalist Movement. One of the largest campaigns is the Global Campaign on Military Spending (GCOMS), including Global Day of Action on Military Spending (GDAMS) and nuclear disarmament. **Events** *World Peace Congress* Barcelona (Spain) 2021, *World Peace Conference* New York, NY (USA) 2020, *Workshop ON Challenges of a Common Security Policy in Eurasia* Berlin (Germany) 2019, *World Youth Summit* Berlin (Germany) 2019, *Triennial Conference and Assembly* London (UK) 2019. **Publications** *IPB Newsletter* (12 a year); *IPB Annual Activities Report. Disarmament, Peace and Development – vol 27* (2018); *The Treaty On The Prohibition Of Nuclear Weapons: Analysis and Perspectives* (2018); *Demilitarization for Deep Decarbonization: Reducing Militarism and Military Expenditures to Invest in the UN Green Climate Fund and to Create Low-Carbon Economies and Resilient Communities* (2014); *Opportunity Costs: Military Spending and the UN Development Agenda* (2012); *Whose Priorities ? A Guide for Campaigners on Military and Social Spending* (2007); *Warfare or Welfare?* (2005); *From War to Peace* (2002); *Peace is Possible* (2000). Information papers; conference and symposium reports and proceedings.

Members Full: (i) international peace organizations; (ii) national peace federations; (iii) national peace organizations; (iv) local/area peace organizations. Associate: (v) general organizations having peace as one of several aims; (vi) individuals. National/local members in 73 countries:
Algeria, Argentina, Armenia, Australia, Azerbaijan, Bangladesh, Belgium, Benin, Bermuda, Bolivia, Burundi, Cameroon, Canada, Chad, Colombia, Congo Brazzaville, Congo DR, Côte d'Ivoire, Denmark, Egypt, Finland, France, Gambia, Georgia, Germany, Ghana, Greece, Guatemala, Guinea, Guyana, Haiti, India, Iran Islamic Rep, Iraq, Ireland, Israel, Italy, Japan, Kenya, Korea Rep, Liberia, Malaysia, Mauritius, Mongolia, Nepal, Netherlands, New Zealand, Nicaragua, Nigeria, Norway, Pakistan, Philippines, Portugal, Romania, Russia, Rwanda, Senegal, Serbia, Sierra Leone, South Africa, Spain, Sri Lanka, Sweden, Switzerland, Tanzania UR, Thailand, Togo, Türkiye, Uganda, UK, United Arab Emirates, USA, Uzbekistan.

Included in the above, 84 organizations listed in this Yearbook:
- *Abolition des armes nucléaires – Maison de Vigilance*;
- *Afri – Action from Ireland*;
- *African Centre for Peace Education and Training (ACPET)*;
- *African Peace Network (APNET)*;
- *Anuvrat Global Organization (ANUVIBHA)*;
- *Association for Peace, Rome*;
- *Basel Peace Office*;
- *Bike for Peace*;
- *Buddhist Peace Fellowship (BPF)*;
- *Campaign Against Arms Trade (CAAT)*;
- *Canadian Peace Alliance (CPA)*;
- *Canadian Voice of Women for Peace (VOW)*;
- *Center for War Peace Studies (CW/PS)*;
- *Centre for Peace and Arms Control Studies and Documentation – Archivio Disarmo*;
- *Centre for Peacemaking and Community Development (CPCD, no recent information)*;
- *Deutsche Friedensgesellschaft-Vereinigte Kriegsdienstgegnerinnen (DFG-VK)*;
- *Finnish Peace Committee – Peace Fund*;
- *Foundation for Peace*;
- *Foundation for Peace Studies Aotearoa/New Zealand*;
- *Gandhi Centre for the Service of Life and Humanity*;
- *Gernika Gogoratuz – Peace Research Center*;
- *Global Security Institute (GSI)*;
- *Green Earth Organization (GEO, inactive)*;
- *Indian Institute for Peace, Disarmament and Environmental Protection (IIPDEP)*;
- *Information Workers for Peace*;
- *Initiatives for International Dialogue*;
- *Institute for Law and Peace, London (INLAP)*;
- *International Eurasia-Press Fund (IEPF, #13309)*;
- *International Observatory of Organization and Globalization (PADOP)*;
- *International Relations and Peace Research Institute (IRIPAZ)*;
- *International Teacher Association (ITA, #15662)*;
- *International Voluntary Organisation for Women, Education and Development (IVOWED)*;
- *Islamic Society for International Unity and Peace (ISIUP, no recent information)*;
- *Japan Council against A and H Bombs*;
- *Korea International Volunteer Organization (KVO International)*;
- *Labour Action for Peace (LAP)*;
- *Latin American Council for Peace Research (#16310)*;
- *Lumbini World Peace Forum*;
- *Medact*;
- *Middle Powers Initiative (MPI, #16795)*;
- *Mouvement de la paix (#16867)*;
- *Movement for Disarmament, Peace and Liberty (MDPL)*;
- *Movement for Peace, Human Rights and National Independence (KEADEA, no recent information)*;
- *Movement for the Abolition of War (WAR)*;
- *Movimiento por la Vida y la Paz (MOVIP, no recent information)*;
- *Musicians Against Nuclear Arms (MANA)*;
- *Narvik Peace Centre*;
- *Norwegian Peace Association (NPA)*;
- *Norwegian Peace Council*;
- *Nuclear Age Peace Foundation*;
- *Pan-African Reconciliation Council (PARC, #18063)*;
- *Peace Action Network (PAN)*;
- *Peace Depot*;
- *Peace for All (PFA, no recent information)*;
- *Peace Office, Tokyo (no recent information)*;
- *Peace Union of Finland*;
- *Physicians for Global Survival, Canada (PGS)*;
- *Project Ploughshares*;
- *Repositioning Peace in Africa (REPEAF)*;
- *Science for Peace (SFP)*;
- *Stockholm Peace Association (no recent information)*;
- *Swedish Peace and Arbitration Society (SPAS)*;
- *Swedish Peace Council (no recent information)*;
- *Swiss Peace Council (SFR)*;
- *Uniting for Peace*;
- *Veterans for Peace (VFP)*;
- *War Resisters League (WRL)*;
- *Women for Peace, Switzerland*;

- *Women's International League for Peace and Freedom (WILPF, #21024)*;
- *Women's Network for Peace (FNF)*;
- *Women's World Summit Foundation (WWSF, #21038)*;
- *World BEYOND War (#21229)*;
- *World Peace Organization.*

International members (26):
- Africa Interfaith Youth Network;
- *Anglican Pacifist Fellowship (APF, #00830)*;
- *Corporate Accountability International*;
- *EarthAction (EA, #05159)*;
- *Global Initiatives for Sustainable Development and Humanitarian Action (GI)*;
- *Global Network Against Weapons and Nuclear Power in Space*;
- *Global Network of Women Peacebuilders (GNWP, #10503)*;
- *International Association of Educators for Peace (IAEP)*;
- *International Association of Lawyers Against Nuclear Arms (IALANA, #11994)*;
- International Buddhist Council;
- *International Community of Women Living with HIV/AIDS (ICW, #12826)*;
- *International Federation for East Timor (IFET, #13408)*;
- *International Fellowship of Reconciliation (IFOR, #13586)*;
- *International Network of Engineers and Scientists Against Proliferation (INESAP, see: #14260)*;
- *International Network of Engineers and Scientists for Global Responsibility (INES, #14260)*;
- *International Network of Museums for Peace (INMP, #14297)*;
- *International Philosophers for Peace and the Elimination of Nuclear and Other Threats to Global Existence (IPPNO, #14571)*;
- *Mas Paz Menos SIDA Fundación (+ Paz – sida Fundación, #16594)*;
- *Nonviolence International (NI, #17152)*;
- *Pax Christi – International Catholic Peace Movement (#18266)*;
- *Paz y Cooperación*;
- *Peace Boat*;
- *Religions for Peace (RfP, #18831)*;
- *Ribbon International*;
- *Sovereign Military Order of the Temple of Jerusalem (SMOTJ)*;
- *UNI Global Union (#20338).*

Consultative Status Consultative status granted from: *ECOSOC (#05331)* (Ros A). **IGO Relations** Associated with Department of Global Communications of the United Nations.
NGO Relations Member of:
- *Campaign to Stop Killer Robots (#03405)*;
- *Conference of Non-Governmental Organizations in Consultative Relationship with the United Nations (CONGO, #04635)*;
- *Control Arms (#04782)*;
- *Fédération des Institutions Internationales établies à Genève (FIIG, #09599)*;
- *International Action Network on Small Arms (IANSA, #11585)*;
- *International Campaign to Ban Landmines – Cluster Munition Coalition (ICBL-CMC, #12427)*;
- *International Coalition to Ban Uranium Weapons (ICBUW, #12609)*;
- *Middle Powers Initiative (MPI, #16795)*;
- *NGO Committee for Disarmament, Geneva (#17105)*;
- *Nonviolent Peaceforce (NP, #17153)*;
- *World Social Forum (WSF, #21797).*

Instrumental in setting up: *Abolition 2000 – Global Network to Eliminate Nuclear Weapons (Abolition 2000, #00006)*; *European Network Against the Arms Trade (ENAAT, #07861)*; *International Liaison Committee for Peace Foundation (Foundation ILCOP, see: #14535).*
Links with a large number of organizations, including:
- *Fördergemeinschaft zur Gründung einer Friedensuniversität (FGF, no recent information)*;
- *Helsinki Citizens' Assembly (hCa, #10905)*;
- *HURPEC International Network*;
- *International Physicians for the Prevention of Nuclear War (IPPNW, #14578)*;
- *Mayors for Peace (#16605)*;
- *Parliamentarians for Global Action (PGA, #18208)*;
- *Permanent Secretariat of the World Summit of Nobel Peace Laureates (#18332)*;
- *Uniting for Peace*;
- *World Federalist Movement – Movement for a Just World Order through a Strengthened United Nations (WFM, #21404)*;
- *World Peace Association, Mumbai (WPA, no recent information).* [2020.02.18/XD2340/y/**B**]

♦ International Peace Centre, Sarajevo (internationally oriented national body)
♦ International Peace Commission (internationally oriented national body)
♦ International Peace Information Service (internationally oriented national body)

♦ International Peace Institute (IPI) 14536

Pres 777 UN Plaza, New York NY 10017-3521, USA. T. +12126874300. Fax +12129838246. E-mail: ipi@ipinst.org.
IPI Vienna Freyung 3, 1010 Vienna, Austria. T. +4315338881.
URL: http://www.ipinst.org/

History 1970, as *International Peace Academy (IPA) – Académie mondiale pour la paix – Academia Internacional de la Paz*, a tax-exempt, non-for-profit educational organization. First set up in the State of Minnesota (USA); further developed through preliminary studies and planning conferences in Oslo (Norway), London (UK) and Brattleboro VT (USA). Now the Academy, an independent, non-partisan, international institution devoted to promotion of peace and multilateral approaches to the resolution of international as well as internal conflicts, is wholly transnational in its Board of Directors, programme, staff, administration and publications. Present name adopted, 24 Mar 2008. **Aims** Manage risk and build resilience to promote peace, security and sustainable development. **Structure** Board of Directors; President; International Advisory Council; MENA Advisory Council. **Languages** Arabic, English, French, Spanish. **Staff** 40.00 FTE, paid. **Finance** Financial support provided by governments, multilateral organizations, foundations and individuals. **Activities** Research and development; publishing activities; events/meetings. **Events** *Seminar* Salzburg (Austria) 2016, *Meeting on Lessons from the Past, Visions for the Future* Salzburg (Austria) 2014, *International Conference on War and Peace in a Digital Age* Vienna (Austria) 2014, *War and peace in a digital age* Vienna (Austria) 2014, *Paris seminar* Paris (France) 1996. **Publications** Annual Report; books; policy papers; issue briefs; meeting notes. **Members** Not a membership organization. **Consultative Status** Consultative status granted from: *ECOSOC (#05331)* (Ros A). [2018.08.02/XB2339/j/**F**]

♦ International Peace Operations Association / see International Stability Operations Association
♦ International Peace Press Bureau (inactive)

♦ International Peace Research Association (IPRA) 14537

Association internationale de recherche sur la paix – Asociación Internacional de Investigación para la Paz – Internationale Vereinigung für Friedensforschung – Associação Internacional de Pesquisa da Paz

Co-SG 309 Park Place, Brooklyn NY 11238, USA. E-mail: info@iprapeace.org.
Co-SG address not obtained.
URL: http://www.iprapeace.org/

History 3 Dec 1964, London (UK), following preliminary meetings organized by *Continuing Committee of the Conferences on Research on International Peace and Security – Comité permanent des conférences pour la recherche de la paix et de la sécurité internationales.* Developed from a group of scholars interested in holding research conferences on the topic of international peace and security. **Aims** Increase quantity of research focused on world peace and ensure scientific quality and advance interdisciplinary research into the conditions for sustainable peace and the causes of war and other forms of violence and conflict; promote national and international studies and teaching related to the pursuit of peace; facilitate contacts among scholars and educators worldwide; encourage exchange of information on results of research in the field and on significant developments in peace research. **Structure** General Conference (every 2 years); Council; Executive Committee; 2 Co-Secretaries General. Regional Associations (5): *Africa Peace Research and Education Association (AFPREA, #00511)*; *Asia Pacific Peace Research Association (APPRA, #01991)*; *European Peace Research Association (EUPRA, #08177)*; *Latin American Council for Peace Research (#16310)*; *Peace and Justice Studies Association (PJSA).* Commissions (25). **Languages** English, French, Spanish. **Staff** Voluntary. **Finance** Sources: donations; fees for services; grants; members' dues; subsidies. **Activities** Awards/prizes/competitions; events/meetings; networking/liaising; research/documentation. **Events** *Biennial General Conference* Nairobi (Kenya) 2021, *Biennial General Conference* Ahmedabad (India) 2018, *Biennial General Conference* Freetown (Sierra Leone) 2016, *Biennial General Conference* Istanbul (Turkey) 2014, *Biennial General Conference* Tsu (Japan) 2012. **Publications** *International Journal of Peace Studies (IJPS)*; *Journal of Peace Education.*
Members Individual; Scientific institutions; Scientific associations. Members (about 1,500) in 111 countries and territories:
Albania, Algeria, Argentina, Armenia, Australia, Austria, Azerbaijan, Bangladesh, Belgium, Bolivia, Bosnia-Herzegovina, Brazil, Brunei Darussalam, Bulgaria, Burundi, Cambodia, Cameroon, Canada, Chile, China, Colombia, Congo Brazzaville, Congo DR, Costa Rica, Croatia, Czechia, Denmark, Egypt, El Salvador, Eritrea, Estonia, Eswatini, Ethiopia, Fiji, Finland, France, Georgia, Germany, Ghana, Greece, Guatemala, Hungary, Iceland, India, Indonesia, Iran Islamic Rep, Ireland, Israel, Italy, Japan, Jordan, Kazakhstan, Kenya, Korea Rep, Kosovo, Lebanon, Liberia, Libya, Liechtenstein, Lithuania, Malaysia, Mexico, Montenegro, Myanmar, Nepal, Netherlands, New Zealand, Nicaragua, Nigeria, North Macedonia, Northern Cyprus, Norway, Pakistan, Palestine, Papua New Guinea, Peru, Philippines, Poland, Portugal, Qatar, Romania, Russia, Rwanda, Samoa, Serbia, Sierra Leone, Singapore, Slovakia, South Africa, South Sudan, Spain, Sri Lanka, Sudan, Sweden, Switzerland, Syrian AR, Taiwan, Tajikistan, Tanzania UR, Thailand, Togo, Türkiye, Uganda, UK, Ukraine, United Arab Emirates, USA, Uzbekistan, Venezuela, Vietnam, Zimbabwe.

Included in the above, 30 organizations listed in this Yearbook:
- *Austrian Study Centre for Peace and Conflict Resolution (ASPR)*;
- *Center for Peace and Conflict Studies, Detroit (CPCS)*;
- *Center for Security Studies (CSS)*;
- *Center for War Peace Studies (CW/PS)*;
- *Centre for International Studies, Managua (CEI)*;
- *Centre for Research on Peace and Development (CRPD)*;
- *Danish Institute for International Studies (DIIS)*;
- *Forum per i Problemi della Pace e della Guerra (FPPG)*;
- *Groupe de recherche et d'information sur la paix et la sécurité (GRIP)*;
- *Indian Institute for Peace, Disarmament and Environmental Protection (IIPDEP)*;
- *Institute of Peace Studies, Tokyo (no recent information)*;
- *Institut Henry-Dunant (IHD, inactive)*;
- *International Institute for Peace (IIP, #13907)*;
- *Irish Peace Institute*;
- *Kroc Institute for International Peace Studies*;
- *Mershon Center for International Security Studies*;
- *Peace History Society (PHS)*;
- *Peace Research and European Security Studies (AFES-PRESS)*;
- *Peace Research Institute Frankfurt (PRIF)*;
- *Peace Research Institute of Nigeria (PRIN, no recent information)*;
- *Peace Research Institute Oslo (PRIO)*;
- *Richardson Institute for Peace and Conflict Studies*;
- *Stockholm International Peace Research Institute (SIPRI, #19994)*;
- *Suomen Rauhantutkimusyhdistys Ry (SRTY)*;
- *Swisspeace*;
- *Tami Steinmetz Centre for Peace Research, Tel Aviv*;
- *Tampere Peace Research Institute (TAPRI)*;
- *Technical Peace Research Group, Göteborg (inactive)*;
- *Toda Institute for Global Peace and Policy Research*;
- *Transnational Foundation for Peace and Future Research (TFF, #20217).*

Consultative Status Consultative status granted from: *ECOSOC (#05331)* (Ros C); *UNCTAD (#20285)* (General Category). **IGO Relations** Accredited by (1): *United Nations Framework Convention on Climate Change – Secretariat (UNFCCC, #20564).* Associated with Department of Global Communications of the United Nations. **NGO Relations** Member of (2): *Conference of Non-Governmental Organizations in Consultative Relationship with the United Nations (CONGO, #04635)*; *International Science Council (ISC, #14796).* [2022.02.04/XB2341/y/**B**]

♦ International Peace Research Institute, Meiji Gakuin University (internationally oriented national body)
♦ International Peace Research Institute, Oslo / see Peace Research Institute Oslo
♦ International PEACESAT Consortium / see Consortium for International Pacific Education and Communication Experiments by Satellite (#04750)
♦ International Peace and Security Institute (internationally oriented national body)
♦ International Peace Support Training Centre (unconfirmed)
♦ International Peace Youth Group (unconfirmed)
♦ International Peanut Research and Development Association (no recent information)

♦ International Peatland Society (IPS) 14538

Internationale Gesellschaft für Moor- und Torfkunde (IMTG) – Kansainvälinen Suoyhdistys

SG Nisulankatu 78 B 6, FI-40720 Jyväskylä, Finland. T. +358404184075. E-mail: ips@peatlands.org.
URL: http://www.peatlands.org

History 1968, Québec, QC (Canada). Incorporated *Internationale Gesellschaft für Moorforschung (IGM, inactive)* in 1970. Former names and other names: *International Peat Society (IPS)* – former; *Société internationale de la tourbe* – former; *Mezdunarodnoe Obscestvo po Torfu (MTO)* – former; *Kansainvälinen Turveyhdistys* – former. Registration: PRH, Finland. **Aims** Promote responsible management and wise use of peatlands and peat. **Structure** Assembly of national representatives (annual); Executive Board; Scientific Advisory Board; Commissions (3); National Committees (17). Scientific, industrial and regulatory stakeholders of all areas related to peat and peatlands represented on Commissions, National Committees and other bodies. **Languages** English, Finnish. **Staff** 1.00 FTE, paid. **Finance** Sources: meeting proceeds; members' dues; sale of publications. Annual budget: 200,000 EUR. **Activities** Events/meetings; knowledge management/information dissemination; networking/liaising. **Events** *Quadrennial Congress* Changchun (China) 2024, *Quadrennial Congress* Tallinn (Estonia) 2021, *Quadrennial Congress* Tallinn (Estonia) 2020, *Quadrennial Congress* Kuching (Malaysia) 2016, *SusGro : International Symposium on Growing Media, Composting and Substrate Analysis* Vienna (Austria) 2015. **Publications** *Peatland Snippets* (12 a year); *Peatlands International* (4 a year); *Mires and Peat* – journal. *Global Peat Resources*; *Peatlands and Climate Change*; *Russian-English-German-Finnish-Swedish Peat Dictionary. Mires and Peat* is published jointly with *International Mire Conservation Group (IMCG, #14169).* Congress and symposium proceedings.
Members Total membership comprises about 1,600 members. National Committees, comprising individuals, student and industrial corporate members, research institutes and universities, governmental institutes, NGOs and honorary members, in 47 countries:
Australia, Austria, Belarus, Belgium, Bosnia-Herzegovina, Brunei Darussalam, Bulgaria, Burundi, Canada, Chile, China, Czechia, Denmark, Estonia, Finland, France, Germany, Greece, Hungary, India, Indonesia, Ireland, Israel, Italy, Japan, Latvia, Lithuania, Malaysia, Netherlands, Norway, Peru, Philippines, Poland, Romania, Russia, Rwanda, Singapore, Slovakia, South Africa, Spain, Sweden, Switzerland, Turkey, Uganda, UK, Ukraine, USA.
Consultative Status Consultative status granted from: *FAO (#09260)* (Liaison Status). **NGO Relations** Partner of (1): *Wetlands International (#20928).* Cooperates with (8): *Growing Media Europe (#10796)*; *International Mire Conservation Group (IMCG, #14169)*; *International Society for Horticultural Science (ISHS, #15180)*; *International Union for Conservation of Nature and Natural Resources (IUCN, #15766)*; *International Union of Forest Research Organizations (IUFRO, #15774)*; *International Union of Soil Sciences (IUSS, #15817)*; *Society of Wetland Scientists (SWS)*; *World Energy Council (WEC, #21381).* [2022.10.21/XC4448/**C**]

♦ International Peat Society / see International Peatland Society (#14538)

♦ International Pectin Producers' Association (IPPA) 14539

Association internationale des producteurs de pectine – Internationaler Verband der Pektinproduzenten

SG Turnstrasse 37, 75305 Neuenbürg, Germany. T. +4970827913700. Fax +4970827913701. E-mail: secretary-general@ippa.info.
Exec Sec Nebbegaardsbakken 50, 2400 Copenhagen NV, Denmark. T. +4540288004. E-mail: executive-secretary@ippa.info.
URL: http://www.ippa.info/

History 1969. **Aims** Protect the interests of pectin industries when dealing with national and international authorities and organizations; examine the situation of pectin in comparison with other *hydrocolloids*; collect scientific studies pertaining to pectin research and to pectin uses; agree on technical standards and methods for quality and regulatory control of pectins. **Structure** General Assembly (annual); Board; Technical and Regulatory Working Group; Communication Working Group. **Languages** English, French, German. **Staff** 0.50 FTE, paid. **Finance** Sources: members' dues. **Activities** Knowledge management/information dissemination. **Events** *Meeting* 1994.

Members Pectin manufacturers in 11 countries:
Brazil, China, Czechia, Denmark, France, Germany, Italy, Mexico, Poland, Spain, Switzerland.
IGO Relations Observer status with (1): *Codex Alimentarius Commission (CAC, #04081).* **NGO Relations** Member of (1): *EU Specialty Food Ingredients (#09200).* [2021.06.09/XD8221/**D**]

♦ International Pediatric Academic Leaders Association (IPALA) 14540

Pres Paediatrics and Child Health, Flinders Medical Centre, Bedford Park SA 5042, Australia. T. +61882045259 – +61880244459. Fax +61882043945.
URL: http://www.ipala.org/

History by Dr Alan Gruskin (1938-2003), as *International Pediatric Chairs Association (IPCA).* **Aims** Promote international collaboration in paediatrics and child health; foster excellence in education, research and clinical practice in the fields of paediatrics and child health. **Structure** Meeting (during IPA Triennial Congress and every 18 months). Executive Committee including President, Deputy President and Secretary-Treasurer. **Languages** English. **Activities** Acts as senior integrating organization optimizing communication and collaboration between medical school paediatric departments; promotes academic paediatrics and child health globally; advocates that adequate standards in education and training in paediatrics are promoted, maintained and enhanced; fosters excellence in paediatric and child health related research topics; promotes high quality clinical practice in paediatrics and child health; develops cooperative strategies for undergraduate (medical student) training, including sharing of resources and assessments where possible; develops cooperative strategies for postgraduate training; functions collaboratively with appropriate other international child health organizations such as children's hospitals associations, child health research groups, learned colleges, etc. **Events** *Meeting* Melbourne, VIC (Australia) 2013, *Meeting* Johannesburg (South Africa) 2010, *Meeting* Shanghai (China) 2009, *Meeting* Athens (Greece) 2007, *Meeting* Cancún (Mexico) 2004. **Members** Individuals with senior roles in academic paediatrics and child health. Membership countries not specified. **NGO Relations** Member of: *International Pediatric Association (IPA, #14541).* [2013.09.19/XD9322/**D**]

♦ International Pediatric Association (IPA) 14541

Association internationale de pédiatrie (AIP) – Asociación Internacional de Pediatría (AIP)

Exec Dir 9804 Voss Road, Marengo IL 60152, USA. E-mail: adminoffice@ipa-world.org – membersupport@ipa-world.org.
Hon Dir of Public Relations address not obtained.
URL: http://ipa-world.org/

History 28 Jul 1910, Paris (France). First Congress: Oct 1912, Paris. Current constitution adopted 8 Oct 1974; amended 9 Sep 1980, 8 Nov 1983, Sep 1992, Sep 1995, 11 Aug 1998, 18 Aug 2004. Registration: Switzerland. **Aims** Improve the health and *welfare* of *children* worldwide; bring together paediatricians of all countries for the benefit of children everywhere; encourage research in all aspects of paediatrics; promote dissemination of paediatric knowledge. **Structure** Council of Delegates (meeting every 3 years, at Congress); Executive Committee; Standing Committee. **Languages** English, French, Spanish. **Staff** Voluntary. **Finance** Sources: donations; meeting proceeds; members' dues. **Activities** Advocacy/lobbying/activism; events/meetings. **Events** *Triennial Congress* Gandhinagar (India) 2023, *Triennial Congress* Glasgow (UK) 2021, *Triennial Congress* Panama (Panama) 2019, *Triennial Congress* Vancouver, BC (Canada) 2016, *Triennial Congress* Melbourne, VIC (Australia) 2013.
Members National Societies (147) in 143 countries and territories:
Afghanistan, Albania, Algeria, Angola, Argentina, Armenia, Australia, Austria, Azerbaijan, Bahrain, Bangladesh, Belgium, Benin, Bolivia, Bosnia-Herzegovina, Botswana, Brazil, Bulgaria, Burkina Faso, Cambodia, Cameroon, Canada, Chile, China, Colombia, Congo DR, Costa Rica, Côte d'Ivoire, Croatia, Cuba, Cyprus, Czechia, Denmark, Dominica, Dominican Rep, Ecuador, Egypt, El Salvador, Ethiopia, Finland, France, Gabon, Gambia, Georgia, Germany, Ghana, Greece, Guatemala, Guinea, Guinea-Bissau, Haiti, Honduras, Hong Kong, Hungary, Iceland, India, Indonesia, Iran Islamic Rep, Iraq, Ireland, Israel, Italy, Jamaica, Japan, Jordan, Kazakhstan, Kenya, Korea Rep, Kosovo, Kuwait, Kyrgyzstan, Laos, Latvia, Lebanon, Liberia, Libya, Lithuania, Luxembourg, Madagascar, Malawi, Malaysia, Mali, Mexico, Moldova, Mongolia, Montenegro, Morocco, Myanmar, Nepal, Netherlands, New Zealand, Nicaragua, Niger, Nigeria, Norway, Pakistan, Palestine, Panama, Papua New Guinea, Paraguay, Peru, Philippines, Poland, Portugal, Puerto Rico, Romania, Russia, Rwanda, Saudi Arabia, Senegal, Serbia, Sierra Leone, Singapore, Slovakia, Slovenia, Somalia, South Africa, Spain, Sri Lanka, Sudan, Sweden, Syrian AR, Taiwan, Tanzania UR, Thailand, Togo, Trinidad-Tobago, Tunisia, Türkiye, Turkmenistan, Uganda, UK, Ukraine, United Arab Emirates, Uruguay, USA, Uzbekistan, Venezuela, Vietnam, Yemen, Zambia, Zimbabwe.
Regional and linguistic societies (7):
Asia Pacific Pediatric Association (APPA, #01992); European Academy of Paediatrics (EAP, #05811); European Paediatric Association (EPA/UNEPSA, #08124); Latin American Pediatric Association (#16360); Union of Arab Paediatric Societies (UAPS, #20355); Union of National African Paediatric Societies and Associations (UNAPSA, #20465); Union of National Pediatric Societies of Turkic Republics (UNPSTR, #20466).
International paediatric specialty societies (11):
Federation of International Societies for Pediatric Gastroenterology, Hepatology and Nutrition (FISPGHAN, #09678); International Association for Adolescent Health (IAAH, #11683); International Network of Paediatric Surveillance Units (INoPSU, #14300); International Pediatric Academic Leaders Association (IPALA, #14540); International Society for Pediatric and Adolescent Diabetes (ISPAD, #15344); International Society for Social Pediatrics and Child Health (ISSOP, #15448); International Society of Paediatric Oncology (#15339); International Society of Tropical Pediatrics (ISTP, #15523); World Federation of Associations of Pediatric Surgeons (WOFAPS, #21411); World Federation of Pediatric Intensive and Critical Care Societies (WFPICCS, #21473); World Society of Pediatric Infectious Diseases (WSPID, #21810).
Consultative Status Consultative status granted from: *ECOSOC (#05331)* (Ros C); *WHO (#20950)* (Official Relations); *UNICEF (#20332).* **NGO Relations** Member of (5): *End Corporal Punishment (#05457); Global Coalition Against Child Pneumonia (#10290); Global Health Workforce Alliance (GHWA, inactive); International Childbirth Initiative (ICI, #12547); PMNCH (#18410).* Consultative Status with: *Fédération Internationale de Gynécologie et d'Obstétrique (FIGO, #09638).* Member of Executive Committee of: *Global Alliance for the Prevention of Obesity and Related Chronic Disease (#10219).* [2023/XA2336/y/**A**]

♦ International Pediatric Chairs Association / see International Pediatric Academic Leaders Association (#14540)

♦ International Pediatric Endosurgery Group (IPEG) 14542

Main Office 11300 W Olympic Blvd, Ste 600, Los Angeles CA 90064, USA. T. +13104370553. Fax +13103140585.
URL: http://www.ipeg.org/

Aims Assure that all *surgeons* who treat *children* have access to current information defining the best, least invasive surgical treatment; encourage development and evaluation of those treatments through peer-to-peer communication, education and research. **Structure** Executive Committee, comprising President, President Elect, 2 Vice-Presidents, Secretary and Treasurer, Editor, 4 Regional Representatives and Immediate Past-President. **Languages** English. **Finance** Members' dues (annual): Active Surgeon, US$ 200; Surgeon-In-Training, US$ 125; Allied Health, US$ 125. **Events** *Annual Congress* Sorrento (Italy) 2023, *Annual Congress* Miami, FL (USA) 2022, *Annual Congress* 2020, *Annual Congress* Vienna (Austria) 2020, *Annual Congress* Santiago (Chile) 2019. **Publications** *Journal of Lapaeroendoscopic and Advanced Surgical Techniques* (10 a year) – official journal. Videos.
Members Individuals in 53 countries and territories:
Argentina, Armenia, Australia, Austria, Azerbaijan, Bangladesh, Belgium, Bolivia, Brazil, Canada, Chile, China, Colombia, Ecuador, Egypt, Finland, France, Germany, Greece, India, Ireland, Israel, Italy, Japan, Kazakhstan, Korea Rep, Kuwait, Latvia, Luxembourg, Mexico, Netherlands, New Zealand, Panama, Peru, Poland, Portugal, Qatar, Romania, Russia, Saudi Arabia, Serbia, Singapore, South Africa, Spain, Sudan, Sweden, Switzerland, Taiwan, Türkiye, UK, United Arab Emirates, Uruguay, USA. [2020/XF6095/v/**F**]

♦ International Pediatric Nephrology Association (IPNA) 14543

Association internationale de néphrologie infantile

Headquarters IPNA C/O Divi of Pediatric Nephrology, 2POB.17A, 2401 Gillham Road, Children's Mercy Kansas City, Kansas City KS 64108, USA. E-mail: office@theipna.org.
Secretariat 5. května 65, 140 21 Prague, Czechia.
URL: http://www.theipna.org

History 1974, Washington, DC (USA). **Aims** Promote communication among those interested in *kidney* disease of infants, children, adolescents and young adults. **Structure** Council of 37 members, chaired by Secretary General. **Languages** English. **Staff** 2.00 FTE, paid. **Finance** Sources: contributions; members' dues; sale of publications; sponsorship. Annual budget: 350,000 USD. **Activities** Events/meetings; knowledge management/information dissemination; research and development; training/education. **Events** *IPNA Congress* Calgary, AB (Canada) 2022, *Workshop* Taipei (Taiwan) 2021, *Triennial Congress* Venice (Italy) 2019, *Triennial Congress* Foz do Iguaçu (Brazil) 2016, *Triennial Congress* Shanghai (China) 2013. **Publications** *Pediatric Nephrology* (12 a year) – journal. Congress proceedings.
Members Individuals (about 1,500) in 108 countries and territories:
Albania, Algeria, Argentina, Armenia, Australia, Austria, Bangladesh, Belarus, Belgium, Belize, Benin, Bolivia, Bosnia-Herzegovina, Brazil, Brunei Darussalam, Bulgaria, Cameroon, Canada, Chile, China, Colombia, Costa Rica, Croatia, Cuba, Cyprus, Czechia, Denmark, Dominican Rep, Ecuador, Egypt, El Salvador, Estonia, Ethiopia, Finland, France, Germany, Greece, Guatemala, Haiti, Hong Kong, Hungary, India, Indonesia, Iran Islamic Rep, Iraq, Ireland, Israel, Italy, Jamaica, Japan, Jordan, Kazakhstan, Kenya, Korea DPR, Korea Rep, Kuwait, Latvia, Lebanon, Libya, Lithuania, Luxembourg, Malaysia, Mexico, Mongolia, Morocco, Myanmar, Nepal, Netherlands, New Zealand, Nicaragua, Nigeria, North Macedonia, Norway, Oman, Pakistan, Panama, Paraguay, Peru, Philippines, Poland, Portugal, Puerto Rico, Romania, Russia, Saudi Arabia, Serbia, Singapore, Slovakia, Slovenia, South Africa, Spain, Sri Lanka, Sudan, Sweden, Switzerland, Taiwan, Thailand, Tunisia, Türkiye, UK, Ukraine, United Arab Emirates, Uruguay, USA, Uzbekistan, Venezuela, Vietnam, Yemen.
NGO Relations Links with national societies worldwide. [2021.09.07/XC6187/v/**B**]

♦ International Pediatric Ophthalmology and Strabismus Council (IPOSC) 14544

Main Office 1935 County Rd B2 W, Ste 165, Roseville MN 55113, USA. E-mail: infoiposc@aapos.org.
URL: http://www.iposc.org/

Aims Work together to preserve and restore *eye* health and enhance visual function in children, and ocular alignment and binocularity in children and adults throughout the world. **Structure** Board. Committees: Advocacy and Outreach; Childhood Visual Impairment; Communications; Ethics; Research; Training and Education; Vision Screening. **Activities** Training/education.
Members Organizations in 50 countries and territories:
Argentina, Australia, Azerbaijan, Bangladesh, Brazil, Canada, Chile, China, Colombia, Costa Rica, Denmark, Ecuador, Egypt, France, Germany, Greece, Guatemala, Hong Kong, India, Indonesia, Iran Islamic Rep, Ireland, Israel, Italy, Japan, Jordan, Korea Rep, Lebanon, Malaysia, Mexico, Myanmar, Nepal, New Zealand, Nigeria, Peru, Philippines, Poland, Portugal, Romania, Russia, Saudi Arabia, South Africa, Spain, Sri Lanka, Sudan, Taiwan, Thailand, Türkiye, UK, USA.
Included in the above, 11 organizations listed in this Yearbook:
Asia-Pacific Strabismus and Paediatric Ophthalmology Society (APSPOS, #02055); Consejo Latinoamericano de Estrabismo (CLADE, #04720); European Paediatric Ophthalmological Society (EPOS, #08127); European Strabismological Association (ESA, #08840); International Orthoptic Association (IOA, #14489); International Society for Genetic Eye Diseases and Retinoblastoma (ISGEDR, #15139); International Strabismological Association (ISA, #15609); Middle East Africa Pediatric Ophthalmology and Strabismus Society (MEAPOSS, see: #16752); Orthoptistes de la Communauté européenne (OCE, #17900); Sociedad de Oftalmologia Pediatrica Latinoamericana (SOPLA, #19430); Società Mediterranea di Ortottica (SMO).
NGO Relations Member of: *International Council of Ophthalmology (ICO, #13057).* [2022/XM5913/y/**C**]

♦ International Pediatric Outreach Project / see Global Strategies
♦ International Pediatric PD Network / see International Pediatric Peritoneal Dialysis Network (#14545)

♦ International Pediatric Peritoneal Dialysis Network (IPPN) 14545

Contact address not obtained. E-mail: contact@pedpd.org.
URL: http://www.pedpd.org/

History Also referred to as *International Pediatric PD Network.* **Aims** Improve the quality of paediatric PD care worldwide; collect basic information regarding practices and outcomes; provide tools and management algorithms for daily PD practice; provide global benchmarking of paediatric PD outcomes; perform prospective observational studies on important clinical studies in paediatric PD.
Members Institutions (143); individuals (354). Institutions in 42 countries and territories:
Argentina, Belgium, Brazil, Canada, Chile, China, Colombia, Cuba, Czechia, Denmark, Egypt, Finland, France, Germany, Guatemala, Hong Kong, Hungary, India, Israel, Italy, Korea Rep, Lebanon, Mexico, Netherlands, New Zealand, Nicaragua, North Macedonia, Peru, Poland, Romania, Saudi Arabia, Singapore, South Africa, Spain, Sweden, Thailand, Türkiye, UK, United Arab Emirates, USA, Venezuela, Vietnam. [2012/XM3947/**C**]

♦ International Pediatric Respiratory, Allergy and Immunology Society (no recent information)

♦ International Pediatric Simulation Society (IPSS) 14546

Exec Dir 7309 W 80th St, Suite 300, Overland Park KS 66204, USA. T. +19132021781. E-mail: info@ipssglobal.org.
URL: http://ipssglobal.org/

History 2008. **Aims** Inspire, grow and lead the global Pediatric Simulation community. **Structure** Board of Directors; Executive Committee; Committees (9). **Finance** Sources: members' dues. **Activities** Events/meetings; knowledge management/information dissemination; networking/liaising. **Events** *Symposium* Lisbon (Portugal) 2023, *Symposium* St Petersburg, FL (USA) 2022, *Symposium* 2021, *Symposium* St Petersburg, FL (USA) 2020, *Symposium* Toronto, ON (Canada) 2019. **Publications** *IPSS Newsletter.* **Members** Full; Honorary; Life. Membership countries not specified. **NGO Relations** Member of (1): *World Federation of Pediatric Intensive and Critical Care Societies (WFPICCS, #21473).* [2021/XJ9589/**D**]

♦ International Pediatric Sleep Association (IPSA) 14547

Main Office 3270 19th St NW, Ste 109, Rochester MN 55901, USA. E-mail: info@pedsleep.org.
URL: http://www.pedsleep.org/

Aims Promote basic and applied research in all areas of sleep in infants, children and adolescents; promote teaching programmes; provide information; increase knowledge of pediatric sleep problems and their consequences; provide a forum for information exchange relating to research; establish and maintain standards of reporting and classifying data in the field. **Structure** Board, comprising President, Secretary, Vice-President and 7 members. **Finance** Sources: members' dues. **Activities** Organizes scientific meetings. **Events** *Biennial Congress* Brisbane, QLD (Australia) 2021, *Biennial Congress* Brisbane, QLD (Australia) 2020, *Biennial Congress* Paris (France) 2018, *Congress* Taipei (Taiwan) 2016, *Congress* Porto Alegre (Brazil) 2014. **Members** Full; Student; Associate; Corporate; Honorary. Membership countries not specified. **NGO Relations** Associate member of: *World Sleep Society (#21793).* [2022/XJ5970/**C**]

♦ International Pediatric Stroke Organization (IPSO) 14548

Address not obtained.
URL: https://internationalpediatricstroke.org/

History Feb 2019. Evolved out of the International Pediatric Stroke Study (IPSS), an international pediatric stroke registry, set up 2003. Registration: 501(c)(3), Start date: Feb 2019, USA. **Aims** Improve the lives of children worldwide with cerebrovascular disease. **Structure** Board of Directors; Steering Committee. Committees; Working Groups. **Activities** Advocacy/lobbying/activism; events/meetings; healthcare; research/documentation; training/education. **Events** *Conference* USA 2023, *Founding Members Congress* Vienna (Austria) 2022, *Conference* Vienna (Austria) 2021, *Founding Members Congress* Vienna (Austria) 2020. [2021/AA1455/**C**]

♦ International Pediatric Transplant Association / see International Pediatric Transplant Association (#14549)

♦ International Pediatric Transplant Association (IPTA) 14549

Exec Dir c/o The Transplantation Society, International Headquarters, 505 Bvd René-Lévesque Ouest, Ste 1401, Montréal QC H2Z 1Y7, Canada. T. +15148741717. E-mail: info@tts.org.
Sections Manager address not obtained.
URL: https://www.tts.org/ipta/home

History 1999. Also referred to as *International Pediatric Transplant Association.* A section of *The Transplantation Society (TTS, #20224).* **Aims** Advance the science and practice of pediatric transplantation worldwide so as to improve the health of all children who require such treatment. **Structure** Council; Committees (5). **Languages** English. **Staff** 7.00 FTE, paid. **Events** *Biennial Congress* Austin, TX (USA) 2023, *Biennial Congress* Montréal, QC (Canada) 2022, *Biennial Congress* Prague (Czechia) 2021, *Biennial Congress* Vancouver, BC (Canada) 2019, *Biennial Congress* Barcelona (Spain) 2017. **Publications** *Pediatric Transplantation* (8 a year) – journal. *Pediatric Solid Organ Transplantation* (2nd ed). Member listserv.
Members Individuals in 50 countries and territories:

Argentina, Australia, Austria, Belgium, Brazil, Bulgaria, Canada, Chile, China, Colombia, Croatia, Czechia, Finland, France, Germany, Greece, Hungary, India, Iran Islamic Rep, Ireland, Israel, Italy, Japan, Korea Rep, Mexico, Netherlands, New Zealand, North Macedonia, Norway, Pakistan, Peru, Philippines, Poland, Portugal, Saudi Arabia, Serbia, Singapore, Slovenia, South Africa, Spain, Sri Lanka, Sudan, Sweden, Switzerland, Taiwan, Türkiye, UK, USA, Venezuela, Vietnam.
NGO Relations Affiliated societies: *International Transplant Nurses Society (ITNS)*; *The Transplantation Society (TTS, #20224)*. [2019/XD7740/v/**E**]

♦ International Peeling Society (IPS) 14550

Sec Industriestr 11, 27211 Bassum, Germany. T. +494241933260. E-mail: contact@peelingsociety.com.
Registered Address Praxis Methininserhof, Baselstrasse 9, 4132 Muttenz BL, Switzerland.
URL: https://www.peelingsociety.com/
History 2012. **Aims** Teach and promote the art, science and techniques of chemical peels for both therapeutic and aesthetic medical purposes to core specialists around the globe, notably dermatologists, plastic surgeons, facial plastic surgeons and ophthalmic plastic surgeons. **Structure** Board of Directors; Executive Committee. **Activities** Events/meetings; training/education. **NGO Relations** Member of (1): *International League of Dermatological Societies (ILDS, #14018)*. Partner of (1): *European Society for Cosmetic and Aesthetic Dermatology (ESCAD, #08570)*. [AA2129/**C**]

♦ International Pelvic Floor Dysfunction Society (IPFDS) 14551

Sec Dept of Coloproctology, European Hospital, Via Portuense 700, 00149 Rome RM, Italy. T. +396659751 – +39665975188. Fax +39665975188.
History 1996. **Aims** Unite the experts of such discipline; promote the knowledge and the development of pelvic floor *pathology*. **Structure** Assembly; Directory Board, composed of President, Vice-President and Secretary; Advisory Committee; Scientific Committee. **Languages** English. **Finance** Members' dues. Other sources: donations, gifts. **Events** *Congress* Lódz (Poland) 2011, *Congress* Palermo (Italy) 2010, *Congress* Buenos Aires (Argentina) 2005, *Congress* Taormina (Italy) 2002, *Pelvic floor disorders* Cairo (Egypt) 2001. **Publications** *International Journal of Proctological and Perineal Diseases* (3 a year).
Members Founder; Honorary; Ordinary; Adherent. Members in 51 countries:
Argentina, Australia, Austria, Belgium, Brazil, Canada, Chile, China, Colombia, Croatia, Czechia, Denmark, Egypt, Finland, France, Georgia, Germany, Greece, Hungary, India, Ireland, Israel, Italy, Japan, Jordan, Korea Rep, Liechtenstein, Luxembourg, Mexico, Morocco, Netherlands, New Zealand, Norway, Paraguay, Peru, Poland, Portugal, Russia, Serbia, Slovakia, Slovenia, South Africa, Spain, Sweden, Switzerland, Türkiye, UK, Ukraine, Uruguay, USA, Venezuela. [2010/XD6409/**D**]

♦ International Pelvic Pain Society (internationally oriented national body)
♦ International Pemphigus and Pemphigoid Foundation (internationally oriented national body)

♦ International PEN 14552

PEN International – PEN Internacional
Exec Dir Unit A Koops Mill Mews, 162-164 Abbey Street, London, SE1 2AN, UK. T. +442074050338. E-mail: info@pen-international.org.
URL: http://www.pen-international.org/
History Oct 1921, London (UK). Founded by Mrs C A Dawson Scott, under presidency of John Galsworthy. Most recent constitution passed Jul 1979, Rio de Janeiro (Brazil). Amended 1988 Cambridge; 1998 Helsinki (Finland). Initials *'PEN'* originally stood for poets, playwrights, essayists, editors and novelists; but radio and television scriptwriters, translators, historians and other writers engaged in any branch of literature and who accept the PEN Charter are currently eligible for membership. Former names and other names: *Fédération internationale des PEN clubs (PEN)* – former; *Federación Internacional de PEN Clubs* – former; *Internationaler Verband der PEN Klubs* – former; *PEN* – former. Registration: Charity Commission, No/ID: 1117088, England and Wales. **Aims** As a world association of *writers*, editors and translators in all branches and classes of literature, journalism, poetry, drama, fiction, history, biography, science, translation and philosophy, promote and maintain friendship and intellectual cooperation among writers and readers in all countries in the interests of literature, freedom of expression and international goodwill; enable the unhampered transmission of thought within and among nations. PEN's Charter affirms that literature should remain common currency in spite of political or international upheavals and that works of art are the property of humanity at large. **Structure** Assembly of Delegates (annual); Executive Board. Committees (4): Writers in Prison; Translations and Linguistic Rights; Writers for Peace; Women Writers. **Languages** English, French, Spanish. **Staff** 5.00 FTE, paid. **Finance** International membership dues (each Centre also has its own dues, payable autonomously). Other sources: subventions from UNESCO; donations; foundations; trusts; statutory funders. **Activities** Advocacy/lobbying/activism; events/meetings. **Events** *Congress* Uppsala (Sweden) 2022, *Congress* London (UK) 2021, *Congress* London (UK) 2020, *Congress* Manila (Philippines) 2019, *Joint Conference* Rotterdam (Netherlands) 2019. **Publications** *PEN International* (2 a year) in English, French. Annual Report; Congress reports.
Members Autonomous centres in 102 countries and territories:
Afghanistan, Albania, Algeria, Argentina, Armenia, Australia, Austria, Azerbaijan, Bangladesh, Belarus, Belgium, Benin, Bolivia, Bosnia-Herzegovina, Brazil, Bulgaria, Cambodia, Cameroon, Canada, Chile, China, Colombia, Côte d'Ivoire, Croatia, Cyprus, Czechia, Denmark, Egypt, Ethiopia, Finland, France, Georgia, Germany, Greece, Guatemala, Guinea, Haiti, Hong Kong, Hungary, Iceland, India, Iraq, Ireland, Israel, Italy, Jamaica, Japan, Jordan, Kazakhstan, Kenya, Korea Rep, Kosovo, Kyrgyzstan, Latvia, Liechtenstein, Lithuania, Malawi, Mexico, Moldova, Monaco, Mongolia, Montenegro, Morocco, Nepal, Netherlands, New Zealand, Nicaragua, North Macedonia, Norway, Pakistan, Palestine, Panama, Peru, Philippines, Poland, Portugal, Puerto Rico, Romania, Russia, Scotland, Senegal, Serbia, Sierra Leone, Slovakia, Slovenia, South Africa, Spain, Sweden, Switzerland, Taiwan, Thailand, Tunisia, Türkiye, Uganda, UK, Ukraine, Uruguay, USA, Venezuela, Zambia, Zimbabwe.
As well as the above mentioned national centres, centres (22) for: writers in Catalan, Cuban in exile, Esperanto, Galician, Hungarian Writers in Romania, Kurdish, Languedocian (langue d'oc), Romani, Tartar, Yiddish; Writers from former Yugoslavia, Writers in Exile (London, Germany, USA); African Writers Abroad, Chinese Writers Abroad, German-speaking Writers Abroad, Iranian Writers in Exile, Palestinian Writers, Sardinian, Somali-speaking.
Consultative Status Consultative status granted from: *African Commission on Human and Peoples' Rights (ACHPR, #00255)* (Observer); *ECOSOC (#05331)* (Special); *UNESCO (#20322)* (Associate Status). **IGO Relations** Accredited by (1): *Organisation internationale de la Francophonie (OIF, #17809)*. **NGO Relations** Member of (3): *Global Net Neutrality Coalition (#10480)*; *IFEX (#11100)*; *International Conference of NGOs (#12883)*. Supports (1): *Foundation PEN Emergency Fund*. Advisor to: *International Cities of Refuge Network (ICORN, #12578)*. [2022/XB2343/**B**]

♦ International Penal and Penitentiary Commission (inactive)

♦ International Penal and Penitentiary Foundation (IPPF) 14553

Fondation internationale pénale et pénitentiaire (FIPP)
President address not obtained.
URL: http://www.ru.nl/ippf/
History 5 Jul 1951, Bern (Switzerland). Inherited the funds of *International Penal and Penitentiary Commission (IPPC, inactive)*, set up in 1872, when the latter delegated its functions, 1 Oct 1951, to the United Nations. Statutes modified: 14 Sep 1985; 16 Aug 1965. Registration: Switzerland. **Aims** Promote studies in the field of prevention of *crime*, criminal law and criminal procedure, the penitentiary system, the human rights of prisoners, and treatment of offenders, especially through scientific research, publications and teaching. **Structure** Council (meets annually); Committees. **Languages** English, French. **Staff** 5.00 FTE, paid. **Finance** Income from funds. **Activities** Events/meetings. **Events** *Meeting* Geneva (Switzerland) 2022, *Colloquium* Valparaiso (Chile) 2019, *Meeting* Azores (Portugal) 2017, *Meeting* Helsinki (Finland) 2016, *Meeting* Bangkok (Thailand) 2014. **Publications** Meeting and colloquium proceedings.
Members Full in 42 countries and territories:
Argentina, Australia, Austria, Belgium, Brazil, Canada, Cape Verde, Chile, China, Denmark, Egypt, Finland, France, Germany, Ghana, Greece, Hungary, India, Ireland, Italy, Japan, Luxembourg, Mexico, Moldova, Netherlands, New Zealand, Nigeria, Norway, Peru, Poland, Portugal, Russia, South Africa, Spain, Sweden, Switzerland, Taiwan, Tanzania UR, Thailand, Türkiye, UK, USA.
IGO Relations Special status at the United Nations (Crime Prevention Division). **NGO Relations** Observer status with (1): *Alliance of NGOs on Crime Prevention and Criminal Justice (#00709)*. Partner of (1): *Global Forum on Law, Justice and Development (GFLJD, #10373)*. [2023.02.14/XD2347/f/**F**]

♦ International Pencak Silat Federation (unconfirmed)

♦ International Pen Friends (IPF) 14554

Correspondance internationale
Contact Winterinraitti 10-A-12, FI-33270 Tampere, Finland. E-mail: info@ipfworld.com.
Pres PO Box 430, Paynesville VIC 3880, Australia.
URL: http://www.ipfworld.com/
History 7 Apr 1967, Dublin (Ireland). Also referred to in French as: *Association internationale des amis de plume*; *Correspondants internationaux*. **Aims** Promote peace, harmony and friendship worldwide through sincere personal correspondence. **Structure** Head Office in Australia; agents worldwide. **Languages** English, French, German, Italian, Portuguese, Spanish. **Staff** 2.00 FTE, paid. **Finance** Members' dues. **Activities** Networking/liaising; publishing activities. **Events** *International conference* Australia 2004, *Conference / International Conference* Dublin (Ireland) 1990, *International Conference* Wagga Wagga, NSW (Australia) 1985. **Publications** *People and Places* (annual) – international magazine. Booklet.
Members Club members (over 300,000) in 181 countries and territories:
Abu Dhabi, Albania, Algeria, Angola, Argentina, Australia, Austria, Azores, Bahamas, Bahrain, Balearic Is, Bangladesh, Barbados, Belgium, Belize, Benin, Bermuda, Bolivia, Botswana, Brazil, Brunei Darussalam, Bulgaria, Burkina Faso, Cameroon, Canada, Canaries, Cayman Is, Channel Is, Chile, China, Christmas Is, Colombia, Congo Brazzaville, Congo DR, Corsica, Costa Rica, Côte d'Ivoire, Cuba, Cyprus, Czechia, Denmark, Djibouti, Dominican Rep, Dubai, Ecuador, Egypt, El Salvador, England, Estonia, Eswatini, Ethiopia, Faeroe Is, Falklands/Malvinas, Fiji, Finland, France, Gambia, Germany, Ghana, Gibraltar, Greenland, Grenada, Guadeloupe, Guatemala, Guernsey, Guiana Fr, Guinea, Guyana, Haiti, Honduras, Hong Kong, Hungary, Iceland, India, Indonesia, Iran Islamic Rep, Iraq, Ireland, Isle of Man, Isle of Wight, Israel, Italy, Jamaica, Japan, Jersey, Jordan, Kenya, Korea Rep, Kuwait, Latvia, Lebanon, Lesotho, Liberia, Libya, Liechtenstein, Lithuania, Luxembourg, Macau, Madagascar, Malawi, Malaysia, Maldives, Mali, Malta, Martinique, Mauritania, Mauritius, Mexico, Mongolia, Morocco, Mozambique, Myanmar, Namibia, Nepal, Netherlands, New Zealand, Nicaragua, Niger, Nigeria, Norway, Oman, Pakistan, Panama, Papua New Guinea, Paraguay, Peru, Philippines, Poland, Polynesia Fr, Portugal, Puerto Rico, Qatar, Réunion, Romania, Russia, Samoa, Saudi Arabia, Scotland, Senegal, Serbia, Seychelles, Shetland Is, Sicily, Sierra Leone, Singapore, Slovakia, Solomon Is, Somalia, South Africa, Spain, Sri Lanka, St Helena, Sudan, Suriname, Sweden, Switzerland, Syrian AR, Tahiti Is, Taiwan, Tanzania UR, Thailand, Togo, Trinidad-Tobago, Tunisia, Türkiye, Uganda, UK, Ukraine, United Arab Emirates, Uruguay, USA, Vanuatu, Venezuela, Virgin Is UK, Wales, Windward Is, Yemen, Zambia, Zimbabwe.
Also members in other 29 territories and regions (not specified). [2016.02.12/XF5134/v/**F**]

♦ International Penguin Conference (meeting series)

♦ International Pension and Employee Benefits Lawyers Association (IPEBLA) 14555

Secretariat 150 Elington Ave, Suite 402, Toronto ON M4P 1E8, Canada. T. +14166937775ext502. E-mail: contactipebla@redstoneagency.ca.
URL: http://www.ipebla.org/
History 1987. Registered in accordance with Dutch law. **Aims** Promote greater understanding of the legal aspects of pension and employee benefit plans. **Structure** Steering Committee; Conference Committee; Audit Committee. **Languages** English. **Staff** Voluntary. **Finance** Members' dues. Other sources: donations; teleconference surplus; conference surplus. **Activities** Events/meetings. **Events** *Biennial Conference* Lisbon (Portugal) 2019, *Biennial Conference* Prague (Czechia) 2017, *Joint Colloquium* St John's, NL (Canada) 2016, *Biennial Conference* Brussels (Belgium) 2015, *Joint Conference* Chicago, IL (USA) 2014. **Publications** *International Pension Lawyer* (4 a year) – journal. *Comparative Survey of Pension Law Issues* (4th ed 2017).
Members Individuals in 33 countries. Membership countries not specified. [2019.02.14/XD6695/v/**D**]

♦ International Pension Research Association (IPRA) 14556

Admin Office c/o CEPAR, Level 3, South Entrance, 223 Anzac Pde, Kensington NSW 2033, Australia. E-mail: cepar@unsw.edu.au.
URL: https://www.iprassn.org/
History Former names and other names: *International Network for Pensions, Aging, and Retirement Research (INPARR)* – former. **Aims** Promote and advance high-quality social science research on pensions, ageing, and retirement. **Activities** Events/meetings. **Events** *Conference* Paris (France) 2022, *Annual Conference* 2021, *Annual Conference* 2020, *Annual Conference* Paris (France) 2019, *Annual Conference* Paris (France) 2018.
Members Organizations in 3 countries:
Australia, Netherlands, USA.
IGO Relations *OECD (#17693)*. **NGO Relations** *International Organisation of Pension Supervisors (IOPS, #14432)*. [2022/XM8484/**C**]

♦ International Pentecostal Holiness Church (internationally oriented national body)
♦ International People's College (internationally oriented national body)
♦ International People's Health Council (internationally oriented national body)

♦ International Pepper Community (IPC) 14557

Communauté internationale du poivre
Secretariat BAPPABTI Bldg 8th Floor, Jl Kramat Raya No 172, Jakarta 10430, Indonesia. T. +62213101023 – +62213101024 – +62213100988. Fax +62213100986. E-mail: mail@ipcnet.org.
URL: http://www.ipcnet.org/
History 21 Apr 1971, Bangkok (Thailand). Established during 27th Session of the United Nations Economic Commission for Asia and the Far East (ECAFE), currently *United Nations Economic and Social Commission for Asia and the Pacific (ESCAP, #20557)*, following endorsement of principle by 23rd and 24th sessions of ECAFE, 1967 and 1968. Establishment agreement entered into force on 29 Mar 1972. **Aims** Coordinate, harmonize and promote activities of the pepper industry. **Structure** Regular Session (annual); Chairmanship; Divisions (3); National liaison officers and focal points; Secretariat in Jakarta (Indonesia), headed by Executive Director. **Languages** English. **Staff** 9.00 FTE, paid. **Finance** Sources: contributions of member/participating states. Funding and technical assistance for projects from donor countries and international organizations and institutions. Annual budget: 360,000 USD. **Activities** Events/meetings; knowledge management/information dissemination; research/documentation; training/education. **Events** *Annual Session* Ho Chi Minh City (Vietnam) 2014, *Annual Session* Kuching (Malaysia) 2013, *Annual Session* Colombo (Sri Lanka) 2012, *Annual Session* Senggigi (Indonesia) 2011, *Annual Session* Kochi (India) 2010. **Publications** *Market Review* (12 a year); *Prices Bulletin (PB)* (50-52 a year); *Pepper News*; *Pepper Statistical Yearbook*. Annual Report; abstracts; research findings; standards; guides; brochures; statistics; directories.
Members Governments of 7 pepper producing countries (" indicates Associate):
India, Indonesia, Malaysia, Papua New Guinea (*), Philippines (*), Sri Lanka, Vietnam.
Major pepper importers in 34 countries:
Australia, Austria, Belgium, Canada, Denmark, Egypt, Finland, France, Germany, Greece, Hungary, Italy, Japan, Korea Rep, Kuwait, Morocco, Netherlands, New Zealand, Norway, Pakistan, Poland, Qatar, Romania, Russia, Singapore, South Africa, Spain, Sweden, Switzerland, Tunisia, Türkiye, UK, United Arab Emirates, USA.
IGO Relations Observer status with: *Codex Alimentarius Commission (CAC, #04081)*. [2020.03.03/XD4364/**C***]

♦ International Perimetric Society / see Imaging and Perimetric Society (#11125)
♦ International Perinatal Doppler Society (inactive)
♦ International Peritoneal Dialysis Organization / see International Society for Peritoneal Dialysis (#15352)

♦ International Permafrost Association (IPA) 14558

Association internationale du pergélisol
Exec Dir Carlton University, Dept of Geography and Environmental Studies, Ottawa ON K1S 5B6, Canada. E-mail: contact@ipa-permafrost.org.
URL: http://www.permafrost.org/
History Jul 1983, Fairbanks AK (USA), during 4th International Conference on Permafrost, by representatives from Canada, China, USA and USSR. Constitution and Bylaws approved by Council Meeting, 5 Aug 1987, Ottawa (Canada); last revised Jun 2010. **Aims** Foster dissemination of knowledge concerning permafrost and promote cooperation among persons and national or international organizations engaged in scientific investigations or engineering work on permafrost. **Structure** International Conference on Permafrost (every 4 years); Council; Executive Committee; Standing Committees (2); International Advisory Committee for the International Conference on Permafrost; Action Groups; International Secretariat, led by Executive Director. **Languages** English. **Staff** 1.00 FTE, paid. **Finance** Members' dues. Secretariat supported by host country. **Activities** Knowledge management/information dissemination; research and development; networking/

liaising; projects/programmes; awards/prizes/competitions. **Events** *Quadrennial Conference* Whitehorse, YT (Canada) 2024, *Quadrennial Conference* Lanzhou (China) 2022, *Quadrennial Conference* Lanzhou (China) 2020, *EUCOP : European Conference on Permafrost* Chamonix (France) 2018, *Asian Conference on Permafrost* Sapporo (Japan) 2017. **Publications** *Frozen Ground* (annual) – newsletter. Country reports; PPP reports; conference proceedings; reports and minutes; handbook; glossary; occasional publications. Information Services are produced in conjunction with the International Permafrost Conferences and *ISC World Data System (ISC-WDS, #16024)*. **Information Services** *Permafrost and Frozen Ground: Bibliography 1978 – 2003 – Glaciological Data Report GD-31* – online bibliography of world's literature; *The CAPS: Circumpolar Active-Layer Permafrost System* – CD-ROM, a compilation of global frozen ground data and information.
Members Adhering Bodies (one per country), Associate Members or individuals. Adhering Bodies in 26 countries:
Argentina, Austria, Canada, China, Denmark, Finland, France, Germany, Iceland, Italy, Japan, Korea Rep, Kyrgyzstan, Mongolia, Netherlands, New Zealand, Norway, Poland, Portugal, Romania, Russia, Spain, Sweden, Switzerland, UK, USA.
Associate member in 1 country:
South Africa.
Individuals in 17 countries:
Afghanistan, Australia, Belgium, Brazil, Bulgaria, Chile, Czechia, Egypt, Hungary, India, Kenya, Luxembourg, Malawi, Nepal, Pakistan, Slovenia, Türkiye.
NGO Relations Affiliated member of: *International Geographical Union (IGU, #13713)*; *International Union of Geological Sciences (IUGS, #15777)*. Instrumental in setting up: *Global Terrestrial Network for Permafrost (GTN-P, #10625)*. [2023/XD1235/**D**]

♦ International Permanent Bureau of Motor Cycle Manufacturers / see International Motorcycle Manufacturers Association (#14186)
♦ International Permanent Committee for the Production of a Photographic Map of the Sky (inactive)
♦ International Permanent Secretariat Human Rights and Local Governments (internationally oriented national body)
♦ International Permanent Secretariat of Social Workers / see International Federation of Social Workers (#13544)

♦ International Personal Armour Committee (IPAC) 14559

Vice Chairperson address not obtained.
URL: http://ipac-pass.org/
Structure Committee; Administrative Secretariat. **Activities** Events/meetings. **Events** *PASS – Personal Armour Systems Symposium* Copenhagen (Denmark) 2021, *PASS – Personal Armour Systems Symposium* Copenhagen (Denmark) 2020, *PASS – Personal Armour Systems Symposium* Washington, DC (USA) 2018, *PASS – Personal Armour Systems Symposium* Amsterdam (Netherlands) 2016, *PASS – Personal Armour Systems Symposium* Cambridge (UK) 2014. [2021/AA1401/c/**C**]

♦ International Personnel Certification Association (IPC) 14560

Secretariat 14071 Peyton Dr, Suite 2701, Chino Hills CA 91709, USA. T. +15626501941. E-mail: secretary@ipcaweb.org.
URL: http://www.ipcaweb.org/
History Jul 1995, Cairns (Australia), on signature of a Memorandum of Understanding. Former names and other names: *International Auditor Training Certification Association (IATCA)* – former. Registration: Start date: 3 Jan 2017, USA, State of Wyoming. **Aims** Provide recognition to individuals who, having demonstrated competence to IPC approved schemes, can improve the performance of organizations. **Structure** General Meeting (annual); Board of Directors; Executive Committee. **Languages** English. **Staff** 1.00 FTE, paid. **Finance** Sources: members' dues. **Activities** Certification/accreditation; knowledge management/information dissemination; networking/liaising; standards/guidelines; training/education. **Events** *Annual General Meeting* 2021, *Annual General Meeting* 2020, *Annual General Meeting* Seoul (Korea Rep) 2019, *Meeting* Izmir (Turkey) 2010, *Meeting* Rome (Italy) 2009. **Publications** Annual Report; brochures; criteria.
Members Full; Associate. Accreditation or certification bodies in 23 countries and territories:
Australia, Austria, Belgium, Brazil, Canada, China, France, Germany, Greece, India, Italy, Japan, Korea Rep, Norway, Portugal, Russia, Singapore, Switzerland, Taiwan, Thailand, Türkiye, UK, USA.
NGO Relations In liaison with technical committees of: *International Organization for Standardization (ISO, #14473)*. [2022.02.16/XD7501/**D**]

♦ International Personnel Management Association / see International Public Management Association for Human Resources
♦ International Pest Risk Mapping Workgroup / see International Pest Risk Research Group (#14561)

♦ International Pest Risk Research Group (IPRRG) 14561

Chair address not obtained.
URL: https://pestrisk.org/
History 2007. Constitution ratified, Sep 2015; amended Sep 2017. Former names and other names: *International Pest Risk Mapping Workgroup* – former (2007 to 2015). Registration: ABN, No/ID: 67 115 960 665, Australia. **Aims** Develop enhanced pest risk modelling and mapping methods through rigorous and innovative research focused on key challenges. **Structure** Executive Committee. **Activities** Awards/prizes/competitions; events/meetings. **Events** *Annual Meeting* Athens (Greece) 2022, *Annual Meeting* Poznań (Poland) 2019, *Annual Meeting* Taichung (Taiwan) 2018, *Annual Meeting* Ottawa, ON (Canada) 2017, *Annual Meeting* Parma (Italy) 2016. [2022/AA2910/j/**F**]

♦ International Petroleum Commission (inactive)
♦ International Petroleum Credit Association / see International Energy Credit Association (#13271)

♦ International Petroleum Industry Environmental Conservation Association (IPIECA) 14562

Industrie pétrolière internationale pour la conservation de l'environnement – Industria Petrolera Internacional para la Conservación del Medio Ambiente
Main Office 14th Floor, City Tower, 40 Basinghall Street, London, EC2V 5DE, UK.
URL: http://www.ipieca.org/
History 13 Mar 1974, London (UK), following recommendations of Secretary-General of *United Nations Conference on the Human Environment*, Jun 1972, Stockholm (Sweden). Constitution amended by General Committee, 18 Apr 1978. **Aims** As an oil and gas industry, successfully improve its operations and products to meet society's expectations for environmental and social performance. **Structure** General Committee (meets annually); Executive Committee; Secretariat, headed by Executive Director. **Languages** English. **Staff** 14.00 FTE, paid. **Finance** Members' dues. **Activities** Networking/liaising; standards/guidelines; knowledge management/information dissemination; events/meetings. **Events** *IOSC : Triennial International Oil Spill Conference* New Orleans, LA (USA) 2024, *IOSC : Triennial International Oil Spill Conference* London (UK) 2021, *IOSC : Triennial International Oil Spill Conference* New Orleans, LA (USA) 2020, *Workshop on the Preparedness and Response of a Potential Oil Spill* Abidjan (Côte d'Ivoire) 2019, *Workshop on Improving Practices in Oil Spill Preparedness and Response* Monrovia (Liberia) 2019. **Publications** *IPIECA Newsletter. Management of Oil Spill Response* in English, Spanish; *Oil Spills Chemicals*; *This is IPIECA*. Annual Report.
Members Oil companies (20) in 14 countries:
Bahrain, Canada, Denmark, France, Indonesia, Italy, Japan, Malaysia, Netherlands, Norway, UK, Uruguay, USA, Venezuela.
National petroleum industry associations in 5 countries:
Australia, Canada, France, Japan, USA.
International and regional petroleum industry associations (5):
Asociación Regional de Empresas del Sector Petróleo, Gas y Biocombustibles en Latinoamérica y el Caribe (ARPEL, #02296); *International Association of Oil and Gas Producers (IOGP, #12053)*; *Oil Companies' European Association for Environment, Health and Safety in Refining and Distribution (CONCAWE, #17708)*; *Oil Companies International Marine Forum (OCIMF, #17709)*; *World Petroleum Council (WPC, #21722)*.
Consultative Status Consultative status granted from: *ECOSOC (#05331)* (Special and Ros C); *International Maritime Organization (IMO, #14102)*; *UNEP (#20299)*. **IGO Relations** Accredited by (2): *United Nations Framework Convention on Climate Change – Secretariat (UNFCCC, #20564)*; *United Nations Office at Vienna (UNOV, #20604)*. Partner of (1): *Partnerships in Environmental Management for the Seas of East Asia (PEMSEA, #18242)*. Close contacts with: *WHO (#20950)*. Contacts with: *World Meteorological Organization (WMO, #21649)*. Associated with Department of Global Communications of the United Nations. **NGO Relations** Member of (2): *Conference of Non-Governmental Organizations in Consultative Relationship with the United Nations (CONGO, #04635)*; *Partnership for Clean Fuels and Vehicles (PCFV, #18231)*. Sponsor of: *International Oil Spill Conference (IOSC)*. [2018/XF4629/ty/**F**]

♦ International Petroleum Technology Conference (meeting series)
♦ International Pet Trade Organization (inactive)

♦ International Phalaenopsis Alliance (IPA) 14563

Pres 12661 W State Rd 32, Yorktown IN 47396-9429, USA. Fax +17657495809.
URL: http://www.phal.org/
History 1990. **Aims** Promote the appreciation and conservation of *orchids*. **Activities** Organizes annual meeting. **Events** *Symposium* Taiwan 2007, *Symposium* Sacramento, CA (USA) 2006. **Publications** *Phalaenopsis Newsletter* (4 a year).
Members Full in 26 countries:
Argentina, Australia, Brazil, Canada, Colombia, Czechia, Ecuador, France, Germany, Indonesia, Iran Islamic Rep, Japan, Malaysia, Mexico, Netherlands, New Zealand, Puerto Rico, Russia, South Africa, Spain, Sweden, Taiwan, UK, Uruguay, USA, Zimbabwe. [2010/XF6531/**F**]

♦ International Pharmaceutical Aerosol Consortium (unconfirmed)
♦ International Pharmaceutical Aerosol Consortium on Regulation and Science (internationally oriented national body)
♦ International Pharmaceutical Assistance / see Orbi-Pharma

♦ International Pharmaceutical Congress Advisory Association (IPCAA) 14564

Exec Officer PO Box 182, 4013 Basel BS, Switzerland. T. +41618213133. E-mail: secretariat@ipcaa.org.
URL: http://www.ipcaa.org/
History 1989. Founded as *European Pharmaceutical Congress Advisory Association (EPCAA)*. Present name adopted Dec 1993. 1 Jul 2003, took over activities of *International Exhibitors Association on Radiological Congresses (IEARC, inactive)*. **Aims** Promote the highest possible standards at, and exchange experience, data and documentation on, medical congresses. **Structure** Council. **Languages** English. **Activities** Standards/guidelines; knowledge management/ information dissemination; research/documentation; events/meetings. **Events** *Annual Seminar on Compliance* Basel (Switzerland) 2021, *Annual Seminar on Compliance* Munich (Germany) 2020, *Annual Seminar on Compliance* Berlin (Germany) 2019, *Annual General Assembly* Vienna (Austria) 2019, *Annual Seminar on Compliance* Berlin (Germany) 2018. **Publications** *IPCAA e-News*.
Members Full pharmaceutical companies (21) in 10 countries:
Belgium, Denmark, France, Germany, Netherlands, Norway, Sweden, Switzerland, UK, USA. [2021/XD2262/**D**]

♦ International Pharmaceutical Excipients Certification / see EXCiPACT (#09222)
♦ International Pharmaceutical Excipients Council / see IPEC Federation (#16011)
♦ International Pharmaceutical Excipients Council of the Americas (internationally oriented national body)

♦ International Pharmaceutical Excipients Council Europe (IPEC Europe) 14565

Conseil international des excipients pharmaceutiques
Contact Rue Marie de Bourgogne 52 – 3rd floor, 1000 Brussels, Belgium. T. +3222137440. E-mail: info@ipec-europe.org.
URL: http://www.ipec-europe.org/
History 1992. **Aims** Encourage harmonization of various standards for manufacture and use of pharmaceutical excipients worldwide; ensure and develop better consumer safety in the manufacture and use of pharmaceutical excipients; encourage cooperation in pharmaceuticals and related fields. **Structure** Board of Directors; Committees; Working Groups. **Languages** English, French, Italian. **Staff** 4.00 FTE, paid. **Finance** Sources: members' dues. **Activities** Knowledge management/information dissemination; standards/guidelines. **Events** *Annual Excipients Forum* Brussels (Belgium) 2022, *Annual Excipients Forum* Brussels (Belgium) 2021, *Conference* Frankfurt-Main (Germany) 2021, *Annual Excipients Forum* St Julian's (Malta) 2019, *Conference* Vienna (Austria) 2019. **Publications** *IPEC Europe Newsletter* (10 a year). Guides.
Members Full (74); Associate (2); Co-opted (5) in Europe. Membership countries not specified. **NGO Relations** Member of (2): *European Paediatric Formulation Initiative (EuPFI, #08125)*; *EXCiPACT (#09222)*. Together with *International Pharmaceutical Excipients Council of the Americas (IPEC-Americas)*, is part of the: *IPEC Federation (#16011)*. [2022.05.10/XD6814/**D**]

♦ International Pharmaceutical Federation 14566

Fédération internationale pharmaceutique (FIP) – Federación Internacional Farmacéutica – Internationale Pharmazeutische Föderation
COO and Congress Dir Andries Bickerweg 5, NL-2517 JP, The Hague, Netherlands. E-mail: carola@fip.org.
URL: http://www.fip.org/
History Sep 1912, The Hague (Netherlands), following 10th International Congress of Pharmacy, 1-5 Sep 1910, Brussels (Belgium). Current statutes adopted 4 Sep 2003, Sydney (Australia). **Aims** Represent and serve pharmacy and pharmaceutical science worldwide, principally through education and development of the practice and science of pharmacy. **Structure** Council (meets annually); Bureau; Executive Committee; Board of Pharmaceutical Sciences; Board of Pharmaceutical Practice; FIP Education; Secretariat. **Languages** English, French, German, Spanish. **Staff** 12.00 FTE, paid. **Finance** Sources: donations; meeting proceeds; members' dues. Other sources: voluntary contributions or bequests from individuals, societies, pharmaceutical firms or other institutions. **Activities** Awards/prizes/competitions; events/meetings. **Events** *World Congress of Pharmacy and Pharmaceutical Sciences* Seville (Spain) 2021, *Pharmaceutical Sciences World Congress* Montréal, QC (Canada) 2020, *World Congress of Pharmacy and Pharmaceutical Sciences* Seville (Spain) 2020, *World Congress of Pharmacy and Pharmaceutical Sciences* Abu Dhabi (United Arab Emirates) 2019, *International Symposium on BA/BE of Oral Drug Products* Lisbon (Portugal) 2018. **Publications** *FIP Electronic Newsletter* (12 a year); *Journal of Pharmaceutical Sciences* (12 a year); *International Pharmacy Journal (IPJ)* (2 a year) in English. *World Directory of Pharmacy Schools* (1993); *FIP Facts 2002*. Annual Report; guidelines and statements on pharmaceutical issues; position papers.
Members Organizations; Individuals; Collective (non-commercial organizations or societies); Supporting (commercial companies); Honorary. Ordinary: organizations (137) representing over 3 million pharmacists and pharmaceutical scientists in 100 countries and territories:
Ordinary: organizations (137) representing over 3 million pharmacists and pharmaceutical scientists in 100 countries and territories:
Afghanistan, Albania, Algeria, Argentina, Armenia, Australia, Austria, Bangladesh, Belgium, Bolivia, Bosnia-Herzegovina, Brazil, Burkina Faso, Cameroon, Canada, Chad, China, Colombia, Congo Brazzaville, Congo DR, Costa Rica, Côte d'Ivoire, Croatia, Cuba, Cyprus, Czechia, Denmark, Ecuador, Egypt, El Salvador, Eritrea, Ethiopia, Finland, France, Germany, Ghana, Guinea, Hong Kong, Hungary, Iceland, India, Indonesia, Iran Islamic Rep, Iraq, Ireland, Israel, Italy, Japan, Jordan, Kenya, Korea Rep, Kosovo, Lebanon, Lithuania, Madagascar, Mali, Malta, Mauritius, Mongolia, Montenegro, Morocco, Nepal, Netherlands, Nigeria, North Macedonia, Norway, Pakistan, Panama, Paraguay, Philippines, Poland, Portugal, Romania, Russia, Rwanda, Senegal, Serbia, Sierra Leone, Singapore, Slovenia, South Africa, Spain, Sri Lanka, Sudan, Sweden, Switzerland, Taiwan, Tanzania UR, Thailand, Türkiye, Uganda, UK, Ukraine, United Arab Emirates, Uruguay, USA, Venezuela, Vietnam, Zambia, Zimbabwe.
Included in the above, 3 organizations listed in this Yearbook:
Australasian Pharmaceutical Science Association (APSA); *European Association of Hospital Pharmacists (EAHP, #06074)*; *European Federation for Pharmaceutical Sciences (EUFEPS, #07192)*.
Observer organizations (15), including the following 8 listed in this Yearbook:
Associação de Farmacêuticos dos Paises de Lingua Portuguesa (AFPLP, #02327); *Commonwealth Pharmacists Association (CPA, #04357)*; *Ecumenical Pharmaceutical Network (EPN, #05350)*; *European Association of Employed community Pharmacists in Europe (EPhEU, #06025)*; *Federación Farmacéutica Sudamericana (FEFAS, #09302)*; *Federación Panamericana de Farmacia (FEPAFAR, no recent information)*; *Pharmaceutical Care Network Europe (PCNE, #18349)*; *Pharmaceutical Group of the European Union (PGEU, #18352)*.

Individual: persons wishing to contribute to the development of FIP (4,500) in about 90 countries. Membership countries not specified.
Consultative Status Consultative status granted from: *ECOSOC (#05331)* (Ros C); *WHO (#20950)* (Official Relations). **IGO Relations** Accredited by: *United Nations Office at Vienna (UNOV, #20604)*. Within WHO, contacts with: *Pan American Health Organization (PAHO, #18108)* and *Pan American Sanitary Bureau (PASB, #18129)*; *WHO Regional Office for Africa (AFRO, #20943)*; *WHO Regional Office for the Eastern Mediterranean (EMRO, #20944)*; *WHO Regional Office for Europe (#20945)*; *WHO Regional Office for South-East Asia (SEARO, #20946)*. **NGO Relations** Founding member of: *Associations and Conference Forum (AC Forum, #02909)*. Member of: *Alliance for Health Promotion (A4HP, #00687)*; *Alliance for Safe Online Pharmacies (ASOP Global)*; *Framework Convention Alliance (FCA, #09981)*; *Global Health Workforce Alliance (GHWA, inactive)*; *International Council for Medicinal and Aromatic Plants (ICMAP, #13047)*; *PMNCH (#18410)*; *Pharmaceutical Forum of the Americas (#18351)*; *World Health Professions Alliance (WHPA, #21557)*. Observer of: *Alliance for Safe Online Pharmacy – EU (ASOP EU, #00720)*. Works closely with: *International Federation of Pharmaceutical Manufacturers and Associations (IFPMA, #13505)*; *International Pharmaceutical Students' Federation (IPSF, #14568)*; *Global Self-Care Federation (GSCF, #10588)*. Together with: *International Council of Nurses (ICN, #13054)* and *World Medical Association (WMA, #21646)*, set up: *World Health Professions Alliance (WHPA, #21557)*. [2021/XB2351/y/**B**]

♦ International Pharmaceutical Regulators Programme (IPRP) 14567

Contact ICH Secretariat, Route Pré-Bois 20, 1215 Geneva, Switzerland. E-mail: iprpsecretariat@ich.org.
URL: https://www.iprp.global/

History 1 Jan 2018. Created as a result of the consolidation of International Pharmaceutical Regulators Forum (IPRF) and International Generic Drug Regulators Programme (IGDRP). **Aims** Create an environment for its regulatory members and observers to exchange information on issues of mutual interest, enable cooperation and promote convergence of regulatory approaches for pharmaceutical medicinal products for human use. **Events** *Meeting* Athens (Greece) 2022, *Meeting* 2021, *Meeting* 2021, *Meeting* 2020, *Meeting* 2020.
Members Regulatory authorities of countries and territories:
Argentina, Australia, Brazil, Canada, Colombia, Cuba, Egypt, Indonesia, Iran Islamic Rep, Israel, Japan, Kazakhstan, Korea Rep, Malaysia, Mexico, New Zealand, Russia, Saudi Arabia, Singapore, South Africa, Switzerland, Taiwan, Türkiye, UK, USA.
ASEAN (#01141); *Asia-Pacific Economic Cooperation (APEC, #01887)*; *East African Community (EAC, #05181)*; *European Medicines Agency (EMA, #07767)*; *European Union (EU, #08967)* (DG Health and Consumer Protection); *Gulf Health Council (GHC, #10830)*; *Pan American Network for Drug Regulatory Harmonization (PANDRH, #18121)*; *Southern African Development Community (SADC, #19843)*.
Observers (2):
European Directorate for the Quality of Medicine and Healthcare; *WHO (#20950)*.
NGO Relations Partner of (1): *International Coalition of Medicines Regulatory Authorities (ICMRA, #12616)*. [2022/AA2861/y/**F**]

♦ International Pharmaceuticals, Toiletries and Cosmetics Conference (meeting series)

♦ International Pharmaceutical Students' Federation (IPSF) 14568

Fédération Internationale des Etudiants en Pharmacie – Federación Internacional de Estudiantes de Farmacia

SG Andries Bickerweg 5, 2517 JP The Hague, Netherlands. T. +31703021992. Fax +31703021999. E-mail: secgen@ipsf.org – ipsf@ipsf.org.
Pres address not obtained. E-mail: president@ipsf.org.
URL: https://www.ipsf.org/

History Proposed 1948, during 6th Annual Congress of the British Pharmaceutical Students' Association. Constitution agreed and signed 25 Aug 1949, London (UK) during inaugural conference. Registration: No/ID: KVK 40413709, Netherlands, South Holland; RSIN, No/ID: 808101262, Netherlands. **Aims** Promote improved *public health* through provision of information, education, networking and a range of publications and professional initiatives. **Structure** General Assembly (annual, at World Congress); Executive Committee; Coordinators; Committees; Regional Offices (5); Regional Working Groups; Regional Subcommittees. **Languages** Arabic, English, French, Spanish. **Staff** Voluntary. **Finance** Sources: donations; members' dues; sponsorship. Supported by: *International Pharmaceutical Federation (#14566)*. **Activities** Advocacy/lobbying/activism; events/meetings; financial and/or material support; politics/policy/regulatory; research/documentation; training/education. **Events** *Annual Congress* Seoul (Korea Rep) 2021, *Asia Pacific Symposium* Singapore (Singapore) 2021, *Annual Congress* Seoul (Korea Rep) 2020, *Asia Pacific Symposium* Bandung (Indonesia) 2019, *Annual Congress* Kigali (Rwanda) 2019. **Publications** *ISPF Newsletter*. *Phuture* – supplement. Annual Report; booklets; meeting reports; symposium papers; posters.
Members Full; Associate; Individual; Honorary Life; Friend of the Federation. Full: organizations in 63 countries:
Algeria, Argentina, Australia, Austria, Bangladesh, Bosnia-Herzegovina, Burkina Faso, Canada, Costa Rica, Côte d'Ivoire, Croatia, Czechia, Denmark, Egypt, Estonia, Finland, France, Germany, Ghana, Hungary, India, Indonesia, Iran Islamic Rep, Iraq, Japan, Jordan, Kenya, Korea Rep, Kuwait, Lebanon, Malaysia, Mali, Malta, Morocco, Nepal, Netherlands, New Zealand, Nigeria, Peru, Poland, Portugal, Qatar, Romania, Rwanda, Serbia, Sierra Leone, Singapore, Slovakia, Slovenia, South Africa, Spain, Sudan, Sweden, Switzerland, Tanzania UR, Thailand, Togo, Tunisia, Türkiye, Uganda, UK, USA, Zimbabwe.
Associate: local organizations in 47 countries and territories:
Algeria, Bangladesh, Belize, Benin, Bolivia, Bosnia-Herzegovina, Brazil, Bulgaria, Chile, Colombia, Congo DR, Cyprus, Egypt, El Salvador, Greece, Haiti, Hong Kong, Indonesia, Iraq, Israel, Lebanon, Liberia, Lithuania, Malawi, Mexico, Nepal, Nigeria, Pakistan, Palestine, Papua New Guinea, Peru, Philippines, Poland, Portugal, Russia, Senegal, Spain, Sudan, Taiwan, Türkiye, Uganda, United Arab Emirates, USA, Uzbekistan, Vietnam, Yemen, Zambia.
Consultative Status Consultative status granted from: *ECOSOC (#05331)* (Ros A); *UNESCO (#20322)* (Consultative Status); *WHO (#20950)* (Official Relations). **NGO Relations** Member of (5): *Alliance for Health Promotion (A4HP, #00687)*; *International Pharmaceutical Federation (#14566)*; *PMNCH (#18410)*; *UHC2030 (#20277)*; *World Health Students' Alliance (WHSA, #21559)*. Partner of (2): *Fight the Fakes (#09755)*; *International Student One Health Alliance (ISOHA)*. Cooperates with (1): *Informal Forum of International Student Organizations (IFISO, #11193)*. [2022/XC2353/**C**]

♦ International Pharmaco EEG Society (IPEG) 14569

Sec address not obtained. E-mail: secretary@ipeg-society.org.
Main: http://www.internationalpharmacoeeggroup.org/

History Founded 20 Oct 1980. **Aims** Act as a discussion platform for scientists and clinicians involved in pharmaco-EEG research; promote the use of electroencephalography, electrophysiology and related methods for electrophysiological brain research in preclinical and clinical pharmacology and related fields; put forward recommendations on relevant aspects of pharmaco-EEG studies. **Structure** Executive Board, comprising President, Vice-President, Secretary, Treasurer and 4 members. **Languages** English. **Staff** None. **Finance** Members' dues (every 2 years): Active, US$ 100; Junior, US$ 50. Meetings financed by registration fees. **Activities** Focus groups develop guidelines. Organizes: meeting (every 2 years); training courses. **Events** *Meeting* Nijmegen (Netherlands) 2016, *Meeting* Prague (Czech Rep) 2010, *Biennial meeting / Meeting* Rouffach (France) 2008, *Biennial meeting / Meeting* Awaji (Japan) 2006, *Biennial meeting / Meeting* Antwerp (Belgium) 2004. **Publications** *Neuropsychobiology* – journal. *IPEG Guideline on Statistical Design and Analysis for Pharmacodynamic Trials* (1998); *Standard Operating Procedure for the Registration and Computer-Supported Evaluation of Pharmaco-EEG Data* (1995); *Recommendations for EEG and Evoked Potential Mapping* (1990); *Recommendations for Standardization of Data Acquisition and Signal Analysis in Pharmaco-Electroencephalography* (1987); *Guidelines for Pharmaco-EEG Studies in Man* (1982); *Electroencephalography in Drug Research* (1980); *Electrophysiological Brain Research in Preclinical and Clinical Pharmacology and Related Fields – An Update*; *Pharmaco-EEG and Related Fields: Practical and Theoretical Prospects in Clinical and Preclinical Studies*.
Members Active; Junior; Senior scientists and researchers actively involved in electrophysiological brain research in preclinical and clinical pharmacology, neurotoxicology and related areas of interest. Individuals in 11 countries:
Austria, France, Germany, Italy, Japan, Netherlands, Portugal, Spain, Sweden, Switzerland, USA. [2020/XD8312/**D**]

♦ International Pharmacopuncture Institute (IPI) 14570

Contact AKOM 4F, Korean Pharmacopuncture Inst (KPI), 157-200 4F, 26-27 Gayang-dong, Gangseo-du, Seoul, Korea Rep. T. +82226589020 – +82226589137. Fax +82226589136.
URL: http://pharmacopuncture.net/

History Founded Oct 2005, Korea Rep. **Aims** Work towards unification of terminologies used in various countries; promote academic growth of pharmacopuncture; stimulate information dissemination on pharmacopuncture and herbal goods and exchange of goods/trade; improve human health through instructing advanced techniques to others. **Languages** English, Korean. **Activities** Events/meetings. **Events** *International Scientific Acupuncture and Meridian Studies Symposium* Seoul (Korea Rep) 2019, *Pharmacopuncture Forum* Seoul (Korea Rep) 2017, *iSAMS Symposium* Hong Kong (Hong Kong) 2016, *International Scientific Acupuncture and Meridian Studies Symposium / iSAMS Symposium* Dunedin (New Zealand) 2015, *International Scientific Acupuncture and Meridian Studies Symposium / iSAMS Symposium* Tokyo (Japan) 2014. **Publications** *Journal of Acupuncture and Meridian Studies (JAMS)*; *Journal of Pharmacopuncture (JoP)*. [2018.06.21/XJ4678/j/**E**]

♦ International PhD Student Cancer Conference (meeting series)
♦ International Phenomenological Society (inactive)
♦ International Philatelic Federation (#09650)

♦ International Philosophers for Peace and the Elimination of Nuclear and Other Threats to Global Existence (IPPNO) 14571

Pres Radford Univ, Box 6943, Radford VA 24142, USA.
URL: http://www.philosophersforpeace.org/

History Founded 23 Aug 1983, Montréal (Canada), as *International Philosophers for the Prevention of Nuclear Omnicide*, at 17th World Congress of Philosophy, when Constitution was approved, by John Somerville and other concerned thinkers. The Secretary-General of the United Nations designated IPPNO, 15 Sep 1987, as a Peace Messenger. Subsequently changed title to *International Philosophers for Peace and Prevention of Nuclear Omnicide (IPPNO)*. Registered in accordance with US law. **Aims** Apply the resources of philosophy, in its widest sense of the term, to prevent and eliminate nuclear and other threats to global existence; create an enduring world peace; develop a just social, economic and political basis for peace and *human well-being*. **Structure** President; Executive Secretary. **Languages** English. **Staff** 3.00 FTE, voluntary. **Finance** Members' dues. Donations. **Activities** Research/documentation; networking/liaising; training/education; events/meetings. **Events** *Conference* Sonipat (India) 2019, *International Conference* Kolkata (India) 2015, *International Conference* Kolkata (India) 2012, *International Conference* Kolkata (India) 2010, *International Conference* Nainital (India) 2009. **Publications** *IPPNO Newsletter*.
Members National Section in 1 country:
Canada.
Individuals in 28 countries:
Austria, Bangladesh, Bulgaria, Canada, China, Congo DR, Costa Rica, Croatia, Egypt, Germany, Ghana, India, Israel, Italy, Japan, Kenya, Malta, Mexico, New Zealand, North Macedonia, Poland, Russia, Slovenia, South Africa, Thailand, UK, USA, Zambia.
Regional section in Africa.
NGO Relations Member of: *International Peace Bureau (IPB, #14535)*. [2018.06.01/XF0344/**F**]

♦ International Philosophers for Peace and Prevention of Nuclear Omnicide / see International Philosophers for Peace and the Elimination of Nuclear and Other Threats to Global Existence (#14571)
♦ International Philosophers for the Prevention of Nuclear Omnicide / see International Philosophers for Peace and the Elimination of Nuclear and Other Threats to Global Existence (#14571)

♦ International Philosophy of Nursing Society (IPONS) 14572

Sec Univ of Worcester, Inst of Health and Society, Henwick Grove, St John's, Worcester, WR2 6AJ, UK. T. +441905542778.
URL: https://ipons.online/

History Sep 2003, Stirling (UK), at 7th International Philosophy of Nursing Conference. Constitution adopted Sep 2003; revised Sep 2009 and Sep 2013. Registered in accordance with UK law. **Aims** Bring together individuals from different countries into an international network to promote and support the growing discipline of philosophy of nursing. **Structure** Executive Committee. **Finance** Sources: members' dues. **Events** *Annual International Philosophy of Nursing Conference* Irvine, CA (USA) 2022, *Annual International Philosophy of Nursing Conference* Galway (Ireland) 2018, *Annual International Philosophy of Nursing Conference* Québec, QC (Canada) 2016, *Annual International Philosophy of Nursing Conference* Stockholm (Sweden) 2015, *Annual International Philosophy of Nursing Conference* Nottingham (UK) 2014. **Publications** *Nursing Philosophy* (4 a year) – journal. [2022/XM4213/**C**]

♦ International Philosophy of Religion Association (unconfirmed)

♦ International Phonetic Association (IPA) 14573

Association phonétique internationale – Asociación Fonética Internacional – Weltlautschrift Verein

Sec Arts Education and Law Group, Griffith Univ, Mount Gravatt QLD 4122, Australia. T. +61737351799. E-mail: secretary@internationalphoneticassociation.org.
URL: http://www.internationalphoneticassociation.org/

History Founded May 1886, Paris (France), as *Phonetic Teachers' Association – Association des professeurs de phonétique*. Name changed, 1889, to *Association phonétique des professeurs de langues vivantes*. Present name adopted 1897. **Aims** Promote scientific study of phonetics and various practical applications of that science; provide the academic community world-wide with a notational standard for the phonetic representation of all *languages*. **Structure** Council; Executive. Meetings closed. **Languages** English. **Staff** 1.00 FTE, paid. **Finance** Sources: members' dues. **Activities** Certification/accreditation; events/meetings; knowledge management/information dissemination. **Events** *International Congress of Phonetic Sciences* Melbourne, VIC (Australia) 2019, *International Congress of Phonetic Sciences* Glasgow (UK) 2015, *International Congress of Phonetic Sciences* Hong Kong (Hong Kong) 2011, *International Congress of Phonetic Sciences* Saarbrücken (Germany) 2007, *International Congress of Phonetic Sciences* Barcelona (Spain) 2003. **Publications** *Journal of the International Phonetic Association* (3 a year); *Fonetiks* – newsletter. *Handbook of the International Phonetic Association* (1999). **Information Services** *International Phonetic Alphabet*. **Members** Individuals Full; Student; Life. Subscribing libraries. Members in 51 countries and territories. Membership countries not specified. **NGO Relations** Cooperates with: *International Speech Communication Association (ISCA, #15578)*. [2018.09.16/XB2356/**B**]

♦ International Phosphate Industry Association / see International Fertilizer Association (#13589)
♦ International Photobiology Association / see International Union of Photobiology (#15798)

♦ International Photodynamic Association (IPA) 14574

Pres address not obtained.
Communication and Outreach address not obtained.
URL: http://www.internationalphotodynamic.com/

History 1986, Tokyo (Japan). Founded at 1st meeting. **Aims** Promote study of diagnosis and treatment using light activitated *photosensitisers*; disseminate scientific information to members, the research community and to the community at large. **Structure** Presidential Committee; Board of Directors. **Finance** Sources: members' dues. **Events** *World Congress* Shanghai (China) 2024, *World Congress* Tampere (Finland) 2023, *World Congress* Boston, MA (USA) 2019, *World Congress* Coimbra (Portugal) 2017, *World Congress* Rio de Janeiro (Brazil) 2015.
Members Individuals (about 300) in 25 countries and territories:
Argentina, Australia, Austria, Belgium, Bulgaria, Canada, China, Egypt, France, Germany, Greece, Indonesia, Israel, Italy, Japan, Korea Rep, Malaysia, Netherlands, Norway, Spain, Sweden, Switzerland, Taiwan, UK, USA. [2022/XD1467/v/**C**]

♦ International Photographers Association (inactive)
♦ International Photographic Council (internationally oriented national body)
♦ International Photographic Dealers' Association (inactive)
♦ International Photosynthesis Committee / see International Society of Photosynthesis Research (#15363)

♦ International PhotoTherapy Association (IPTA) 14575

Contact address not obtained. T. +81352691403. Fax +81352691410. E-mail: sec@jmll.co.jp.
URL: http://www.jmll.co.jp/ipta/index.htm

History 2005, Suwa City (Japan). **Structure** General Assembly; Executive Committee. **Events** *LASER FLORENCE : International Congress on Laser Medicine and Surgery* Florence (Italy) 2019, *LASER FLORENCE : International Congress on Laser Medicine and Surgery* Florence (Italy) 2017, *LASER FLORENCE : International Congress on Laser Medicine and Surgery* Florence (Italy) 2015, *Biennial Congress / Congress* Nice (France) 2015, *Biennial Congress / Congress* Vilnius (Lithuania) 2013. **Publications** *Laser Therhas* – journal. [2019/XM2558/D]

♦ International Photovoltaic Equipment Association / see SOLARUNITED (#19677)
♦ International Photovoltaic Science and Engineering Conference (meeting series)

♦ International Phycological Society (IPS) 14576

Société internationale de phycologie

Sec Dept of Botany, Academy of Natural Sciences, 1900 Benjamin Franklin Pkwy, Philadelphia PA 19103, USA.
Registered Address 313 Morning Way, La Jolla CA 92307, USA.
URL: https://intphycsociety.org/

History 15 Sep 1960, Berkeley CA (USA). Incorporated in the State of California (USA). Registration: USA. **Aims** Promote development of phycology; facilitate dissemination of phycological information about *algae*; promote international cooperation among phycologists. **Structure** Board of Directors of 16 members. **Languages** English. **Staff** Voluntary. **Finance** Sources: grants; members' dues. **Activities** Awards/prizes/competitions; events/meetings. *International Phycological Congress (IPC).* **Events** *Quadrennial Congress* Philadelphia, PA (USA) 2021, *Quadrennial Congress* Szczecin (Poland) 2017, *Quadrennial Congress* Orlando, FL (USA) 2013, *Quadrennial congress* Tokyo (Japan) 2009, *Quadrennial congress* Durban (South Africa) 2005. **Publications** *Phycologia* (6 a year) – journal.

Members Institutions; Individuals. Members in 57 countries and territories:
Australia, Austria, Belgium, Brazil, Bulgaria, Canada, Chile, China, Colombia, Croatia, Czechia, Denmark, Egypt, Fiji, Finland, France, Germany, Greece, Hong Kong, Hungary, Iceland, India, Indonesia, Ireland, Israel, Italy, Japan, Korea Rep, Kuwait, Libya, Lithuania, Malaysia, Mexico, Myanmar, Netherlands, New Zealand, Nigeria, Norway, Peru, Philippines, Poland, Portugal, Romania, Russia, Saudi Arabia, Slovenia, South Africa, Spain, Sweden, Switzerland, Taiwan, Thailand, UK, Ukraine, USA, Venezuela, Vietnam.

NGO Relations Member of: *International Association of Botanical and Mycological Societies (IABMS, #11730)*; *International Union of Biological Sciences (IUBS, #15760).* [2018/XD2358/C]

♦ International Physical Culture Union (inactive)
♦ International Physical Internet Conference (meeting series)

♦ International Physically Disabled Chess Association (IPCA) 14577

Pres Lagodna Str 10, 15-757 Bialystok, Poland. T. +48604354530.
Gen Sec address not obtained. T. +381628047002.
URL: http://www.ipca.sweb.cz/

Events *Congress* Bialowieza (Poland) 2003, *Congress* Hrabyne (Czech Rep) 2002, *Congress* Wisla (Poland) 2001. **NGO Relations** *Fédération internationale des échecs (FIDE, #09627).* [2016/XD7224/D]

♦ International Physical Therapists for HOPE / see International Physiotherapists for HIV/AIDS, Oncology, Palliative Care Empowerment (#14580)

♦ International Physicians for the Prevention of Nuclear War (IPPNW) 14578

Association internationale des médecins pour la prévention de la guerre nucléaire – Asociación Internacional de Médicos para la Prevención de la Guerra Nuclear

Exec Dir 339 Pleasant St, Third Floor, Malden MA 02148, USA. E-mail: director@ippnw.org – ippnwbos@ippnw.org.
URL: http://www.ippnw.org/

History 6 Dec 1980, Geneva (Switzerland). Founded during a meeting of physicians from USA and USSR. Received Nobel Peace Prize in 1985. **Aims** Abolish nuclear weapons; focus international attention on the medical consequences of nuclear and conventional war and the nuclear arms race; promote alternative means to conflict resolution and peace through health action. **Structure** Federation of national affiliates. International Council; Board. Representatives of all affiliated groups. Departments: Programs; Administration and Finance; Development. **Staff** 7.50 FTE, paid. **Finance** Sources: contributions; major gifts; funding from private foundations; restricted government project grants. **Activities** Advocacy/lobbying/activism; events/meetings; knowledge management/information dissemination. Received, 30 Oct 1984, UNESCO *'Education for Peace Prize'* and, 1985, *'Nobel Peace Prize'*. Set up: *FHI360-SATELLIFE (inactive)*; *Hague Appeal for Peace (HAP, #10848).* With IPB and IALANA, instrumental in setting up *World Court Project (WCP, inactive)*, full title: *World Court Project on Nuclear Weapons and International Law.* **Events** *World Peace Conference* New York, NY (USA) 2020, *European Students Conference* Berlin (Germany) 2015, *World Congress* Astana (Kazakhstan) 2014, *European Students Conference* Helsinki (Finland) 2014, *Biennial Congress / World Congress* Hiroshima (Japan) 2012. **Publications** *Medicine and Global Survival* (2 a year) – journal; *Vital Signs* (2 a year); *Nuclear Weapons Convention* (annual). *Abolition 2000 Handbook for a World without Nuclear Weapons*; *Bombing Bombay: Effects of Nuclear Weapons and a Case Study of a Hypothetical Explosion*; *Crude Nuclear Weapons: Proliferation and the Terrorist Threat*; *Is Everything Secure: Myths and Realities of Nuclear Disarmament*; *Landmines: A Global Health Crisis*; *Nuclear Wastelands: A Global Guidebook to Nuclear Weapons Production and Its Health and Environmental Effects*; *Plutonium: Deadly Gold of the Nuclear Age*; *Primary Care of Landmine Injuries in Africa*; *Radioactive Heaven and Earth: The Health and the Environmental Effects of Nuclear Weapons Testing in, on, and above the Earth*; *Security and Survival: The Case for a Nuclear Weapons Convention*; *The War in Nicaragua: The Effects of Low-Intensity Conflict on an Underdeveloped Country.* Global Health Watch Information series. Booklets; reports.

Members Groups representing 200,000 doctors. Affiliated groups in 59 countries and territories:
Argentina, Australia, Austria, Bangladesh, Belarus, Belgium, Canada, China, Congo DR, Costa Rica, Cuba, Czechia, Denmark, Egypt, El Salvador, Finland, France, Georgia, Germany, Greece, Guatemala, Hungary, India, Ireland, Israel, Italy, Japan, Kazakhstan, Kenya, Korea DPR, Korea Rep, Malaysia, Mauritius, Mexico, Nepal, Netherlands, New Zealand, Nicaragua, Nigeria, Norway, Pakistan, Palestine, Philippines, Poland, Portugal, Romania, Russia, Serbia, Spain, Sweden, Switzerland, Türkiye, Uganda, UK, Ukraine, Uruguay, USA, Zambia, Zimbabwe.

Included in the above, 2 organizations listed in this Yearbook:
Medact (UK); *Medical Association for the Prevention of War, Australia (MAPW).*

Consultative Status Consultative status granted from: *ECOSOC (#05331)* (Ros C); *WHO (#20950)* (Official Relations). **IGO Relations** Cooperates with: *United Nations Institute for Training and Research (UNITAR, #20576).* Observer to: Meeting of Commonwealth Representatives Prior to the World Health Assembly. Accredited by: *United Nations Office at Vienna (UNOV, #20604).* Associated with Department of Global Communications of the United Nations. **NGO Relations** A founding organization of: *Abolition 2000 – Global Network to Eliminate Nuclear Weapons (Abolition 2000, #00006).* Founding member of: *Basel Peace Office.* Member of: *Consortium for Health and Human Rights (no recent information)*; *Control Arms (#04782)*; *Health Care Without Harm (HCWH, #10875)*; *International Action Network on Small Arms (IANSA, #11585)*; *International Campaign to Abolish Nuclear Weapons (ICAN, #12426)*; *Middle Powers Initiative (MPI, #16795)*; *NGO Committee on Sustainable Development, Vienna (#17119)*; *Violence Prevention Alliance (VPA, #20781).* German, Japanese and Swiss offices are members of: *International Coalition to Ban Uranium Weapons (ICBUW, #12609).* [2020/XF6251/y/F]

♦ International Physics and Control Society (IPACS) 14579

Secretariat Inst of Problems of Mechanical Engineering, 61 Bolshoy Ave VO, St Petersburg SANKT-PETERBURG, Russia, 199178. T. +79213017092. Fax +78123214771. E-mail: ipacs@physcon.ru.
URL: http://physcon.ru/

History Aug 2005, St Petersburg (Russia). Foundation meeting at 2nd PhysCon Conference. **Aims** Unite experts wishing to promote information exchange and interaction between researchers in research areas related to physics and control sciences. **Structure** General Assembly; Board. **Languages** English. **Activities** Awards/prizes/competitions; events/meetings; knowledge management/information dissemination. **Events** *PhysCon : International Conference on Physics and Control* Shanghai (China) 2021, *PhysCon : International Conference on Physics and Control* Innopolis (Russia) 2019, *PhysCon : International Conference on Physics and Control* Florence (Italy) 2017, *PhysCon : International Conference on Physics and Control* Istanbul (Turkey) 2015, *PhysCon : International Conference on Physics and Control* San Luis Potosí, SLP (Mexico) 2013. **Publications** *Cybernetics And Physics (CAP).* **Members** Individuals (about 200). Membership countries not specified. [2022.10.18/XJ8694/E]

♦ International Physiological Laboratories on Monte-Rosa (inactive)

♦ International Physiotherapists for HIV/AIDS, Oncology, Palliative Care Empowerment (IPT-HOPE) 14580

Sec address not obtained. E-mail: secretary.ipthope@gmail.com.
Pres address not obtained. E-mail: president.ipthope@gmail.com.
URL: https://www.ipthope.org/

History Since 2019, a subgroup of *World Confederation for Physical Therapy (WCPT, #21293).* Former names and other names: *International Physical Therapists for HOPE* – alias. **Aims** Advance physical therapy management and prevention of HIV/AIDs, oncologic and palliative care related functional impairments throughout the world and across cultural groups. **Structure** Executive Committee.

Members National organizations in 16 countries:
Australia, Belgium, Canada, Colombia, Denmark, Ireland, Japan, Korea Rep, Netherlands, New Zealand, Nigeria, Portugal, Saudi Arabia, Sweden, UK, USA. [2022/AA3140/E]

♦ International Physiotherapy Group for Cystic Fibrosis (IPG/CF) 14581

Address not obtained.
URL: https://www.ecfs.eu/ipg_cf

History 1986. **Aims** Advance knowledge and understanding of cystic fibrosis (CF); encourage high standards of physiotherapy practice in, promote research in and disseminate information and knowledge of physiotherapy practice in the *treatment* of *patients* with CF. **Structure** General Meeting (annual). Committee, comprising Chairperson, Vice-Chairperson, Secretary and Treasurer. **Finance** Supported by: *Cystic Fibrosis Worldwide (CFW, #04992).* **Events** *Annual General Meeting* Birmingham (UK) 2004, *Annual General Meeting* Belfast (UK) 2003, *Annual General Meeting* Genoa (Italy) 2002, *Annual General Meeting* Vienna (Austria) 2001, *Annual General Meeting* Copenhagen (Denmark) 2000. **Publications** *IPG/CF Newsletter. Physiotherapy in the Treatment of Cystic Fibrosis* (3rd ed 2002) – booklet.

Members Individuals in 50 countries and territories:
Argentina, Australia, Austria, Bangladesh, Belgium, Brazil, Bulgaria, Canada, Cayman Is, Chile, Colombia, Costa Rica, Cuba, Czechia, Denmark, Ecuador, El Salvador, Estonia, Finland, France, Germany, Hong Kong, Hungary, Iceland, Ireland, Israel, Italy, Latvia, Lithuania, Mexico, Netherlands, New Zealand, North Macedonia, Norway, Oman, Panama, Poland, Portugal, Romania, Russia, Saudi Arabia, Slovakia, South Africa, Spain, Sweden, Switzerland, Türkiye, UK, Uruguay, USA. [2013/XF3869/v/F]

♦ International Phytosociological Society / see International Association for Vegetation Science (#12253)

♦ International Phytotechnology Society (IPS) 14582

Pres BP Remediation Management, 150 W Warrenville Rd, Naperville IL 60563, USA. T. +16304205147.
URL: https://phytosociety.org/

Aims Promote research, education, training and application of *technologies* that use plants to deal with problems of environmental contamination, carbon sequestration, alternative fuels and *ecological* restoration. **Structure** Board of Directors. Officers: President; Immediate Past President; Executive Vice President; Vice President. **Finance** Sources: members' dues. **Activities** Awards/prizes/competitions; events/meetings. **Events** *Phytotechnologies for environmental health and food safety* Changsha (China) 2019, *Phytotechnologies and Forestry* Novi Sad (Serbia) 2018, *New sustainable solutions for environmental challenges* Montréal, QC (Canada) 2017, *Conference* Hangzhou (China) 2016, *Phytotechnologies for sustainable development* Manhattan, KS (USA) 2015. **Publications** *International Journal of Phytoremediation.*

Members Full; Student; Emeritus; Limited. Individuals in 13 countries:
Austria, Canada, China, India, Malaysia, Myanmar, Nigeria, Pakistan, Poland, Singapore, Spain, USA, Vietnam. [2021/XJ4933/v/C]

♦ International Pierre de Coubertin Committee (#04184)

♦ International Pierre Gy Sampling Association (IPGSA) 14583

Contact address not obtained. E-mail: intsamp@intsamp.org.
URL: https://intsamp.org/

History 2017. Named after Pierre Gy (1924-2015), founder of the Theory of Sampling (TOS). **Aims** Oversee formal activities of the world sampling community and represent its views. **Structure** Council. **Activities** Awards/prizes/competitions; events/meetings; publishing activities. **Events** *WCSB10 – World Conference on Sampling and Blending* Kristiansand (Norway) 2022, *WCSB10 – World Conference on Sampling and Blending* Kristiansand (Norway) 2021, *WCSB9 – World Conference on Sampling and Blending* Beijing (China) 2019, *WCSB8 – World Conference on Sampling and Blending* Perth, WA (Australia) 2017, *WCSB7 – World Conference on Sampling and Blending* Bordeaux (France) 2015. **Publications** *TOS forum* (2 a year). *Sampling Columns.* [2022.06.14/AA2576/C]

♦ International Piezosurgery Academy (internationally oriented national body)
♦ International Pigeon Fanciers Federation (#09474)
♦ International Pig Iron Association (inactive)
♦ International Pigment Cell Society / see International Federation of Pigment Cell Societies (#13512)

♦ International Pig Veterinary Society (IPVS) 14584

Société internationale de médecine vétérinaire porcine – Sociedad Internacional de Veterinarios Expertos en Cerdos – Internationale Tierärztliche Gesellschaft, Fachgebiet Schweine

Gen Sec PO Box 151, Humansdorp, 6300, South Africa. E-mail: humvet@intekom.co.za.
URL: http://www.theipvs.com/

History 1967. **Aims** Promote the exchange of ideas and information concerning pig health and disease; encourage formation of national pig veterinary societies and co-operation between them. **Structure** General Meeting (every 2 years at Congress); Board. **Languages** English. **Staff** 1.00 FTE, voluntary. **Finance** Sources: meeting proceeds. **Activities** Events/meetings; networking/liaising. **Events** *Biennial Congress* Leipzig (Germany) 2024, *Biennial Congress* Rio de Janeiro (Brazil) 2022, *Biennial Congress* Rio de Janeiro (Brazil) 2020, *Biennial Congress* Chongqing (China) 2018, *Biennial Congress* Dublin (Ireland) 2016. **Publications** Congress proceedings.

Members National organizations of veterinarians in 38 countries and territories:
Australia, Austria, Belgium, Brazil, Bulgaria, Canada, Chile, Czechoslovakia, Denmark, Finland, France, Germany, Greece, Guatemala, Hungary, Ireland, Italy, Japan, Kenya, Luxembourg, Malaysia, Mexico, Netherlands, New Zealand, Norway, Poland, Portugal, Romania, Serbia, Singapore, South Africa, Spain, Sweden, Switzerland, Taiwan, Thailand, UK, USA.

NGO Relations Member of (1): *World Veterinary Association (WVA, #21901)* (as Associate member of). [2021.06.21/XC4260/C]

♦ International Pinzgauer Cattle Breeders Association 14585

Association internationale d'éleveurs de bétail Pinzgauer

Main Office Mayerhoferstrasse 12, 5751 Maishofen, Austria. T. +43654268229. Fax +4365426822981.
Facebook: https://www.facebook.com/Pinzgauercattle

Events *Congress* Maishofen (Austria) 2018, *Congress* Pretoria (South Africa) 2013, *World congress / Congress* Calgary, AB (Canada) 2003, *Congress* Salzburg (Austria) 1982. [2021/XD4739/E]

♦ International Pipe Academy (#00029)
♦ International Pipe Association / see Tube and Pipe Association International

♦ International Pipe Line and Offshore Contractors Association (IPLOCA) 14586

Association internationale des entrepreneurs en pipe lines onshore et offshore

Exec Sec Chemin de Papillons 4, Cointrin, 1216 Geneva, Switzerland. T. +41223060230. Fax +41223060239. E-mail: info@iploca.com.
Events Manager address not obtained.
URL: http://www.iploca.com/

History 21 Jun 1966, Paris (France). Founded by representatives of contracting firms from 5 countries. Registration: France. **Aims** Provide value to members through a forum for sharing ideas, engaging the industry and its stakeholders, facilitating business opportunities and promoting the highest standards in the pipeline industry. **Structure** General Meeting (annual, at Convention); Board of Directors; Secretariat. **Languages** English. **Staff** 5.00 FTE, paid. **Finance** Sources: meeting proceeds; members' dues. **Activities** Awards/prizes/competitions; events/meetings; networking/liaising; research and development; standards/guidelines. **Events** *Annual Convention* Prague (Czechia) 2022, *Annual Convention* Prague (Czechia) 2021, *Annual Convention* Prague (Czechia) 2020, *Annual Convention* Bangkok (Thailand) 2019, *Eastern Europe Regional Meeting* Moscow (Russia) 2019. **Publications** *IPLOCA Newsletter* (4 a year); *HSE Statistics Report* (annual); *IPLOCA Yearbook*. DVD. **Members** Regular; Associate; Corresponding; Academic; Honorary. Members (250) in 40 countries. Membership countries not specified. **NGO Relations** Member of (2): *Fédération des Institutions Internationales établies à Genève (FIIG, #09599)*; *World Federation of Pipe Line Industry Associations (WFPIA, #21475)*. [2022/XC4011/**C**]

♦ International Place Branding Association (IPBA) 14587

Chairman address not obtained. E-mail: info@placebranding.org.
URL: http://placebranding.org/

History 2015. **Aims** Enhance international recognition, visibility and development of place branding and place marketing disciplines among the expert, professional and academic communities as well as among different institutions and public and private organizations involved directly or indirectly in branding and marketing of places by ensuring professional standards in the profession. **Structure** Board. **Languages** English. **Staff** None. **Finance** Sources: meeting proceeds. Annual budget: 3,000 EUR. **Activities** Events/meetings. **Events** *Annual Conference* Aix-en-Provence (France) 2022, *Annual Conference* Barcelona (Spain) 2021, *Annual Conference* Barcelona (Spain) 2020, *Annual Conference* Volos (Greece) 2019, *Annual Conference* Macau (Macau) 2018. **Publications** Conference proceedings.
Members Individuals (100) in 36 countries and territories:
Australia, Belgium, Brazil, Canada, China, Colombia, Cyprus, Czechia, Denmark, Finland, France, Germany, Greece, India, Indonesia, Israel, Italy, Japan, Macau, Netherlands, New Zealand, Norway, Poland, Portugal, Romania, Russia, Saudi Arabia, Slovenia, South Africa, Spain, Sweden, Switzerland, Taiwan, Thailand, UK, USA.
IGO Relations None. **NGO Relations** None. [2023.02.15/XM4858/**D**]

♦ International Planetarium Society (IPS) 14588

Sec Planetarium, Thomas Jefferson High School, 6560 Braddock Rd, Alexandria VA 22312 22312, USA. T. +17037508380. Fax +17037505010.
URL: http://www.ips-planetarium.org/

History 1970, as *International Society of Planetarium Educators*. By-laws most recently revised 2008; Standing Rules most recently revised 2010. **Aims** Exchange information; share professional techniques and expertise; become aware of technological advances by planetarium personnel. **Structure** Regular meeting (every 2 years). Executive Council (meets annually), comprising representatives of regional affiliate organizations plus the Officers (President, President-Elect, Executive Secretary and Treasurer) and the Past President. Standing Committees (6): Awards; Elections; Finance; Membership; Program; Publications. Ad hoc committees (9): Armand Spitz Fund; History; Planetarium Development Group; Portable Planetarium; Public Program/Script Contest; Outreach; Technology; International Relation; Education. **Languages** English. **Staff** None. **Finance** Members' dues: Individual US$ 65 for 1 year, US$ 100 for 2 years; Institutional US$ 250 for first year, US$ 125 thereafter; Corporate US$ 450 a year. **Events** *Conference* Berlin (Germany) / Jena (Germany) 2024, *Conference* St Petersburg (Russia) 2022, *Conference* 2020, *Biennial Conference* Edmonton, AB (Canada) 2020, *Biennial Conference* Toulouse (France) 2018. **Publications** *Planetarian* (4 a year). *IPS Directory of the World's Planetariums* (2000, 2010); *Special Effects Projector Sourcebook* (1998); *IPS Resource Directory* (1997, 2010); *IPS Directory of Planetaria and Planetarians*. Special reports.
Members Individuals and nationals. Planetarians (over 700) representing school, college, university and public facilities in 40 countries and territories:
Argentina, Australia, Belgium, Bolivia, Brazil, Canada, China, Czechia, Denmark, Egypt, Finland, France, Germany, Greece, Hong Kong, India, Israel, Italy, Japan, Korea Rep, Kuwait, Malaysia, Mexico, Netherlands, New Zealand, Nigeria, Norway, Poland, Russia, Slovakia, South Africa, Sri Lanka, Sweden, Switzerland, Thailand, UK, Ukraine, Uruguay, USA, Vietnam.
Regional affiliates (19, 9 of which in North America) in 15 countries:
Australia, Canada, France, Germany, Greece, India, Italy, Japan, Mexico, Russia, Spain, Sweden, UK, Ukraine, USA.
Included in the above affiliates, 4 organizations listed in this Yearbook:
Association des planétariums de langue française (APLF); *Australasian Planetarium Society (APS)*; *European/Mediterranean Planetarium Association (EMPA, #07772)*; *Nordic Planetarium Association (NPA, #17386)*. [2014/XD1420/y/**C**]

♦ International Planned Parenthood Federation (IPPF) 14589

Fédération internationale pour la planification familiale – Federación Internacional de Planificación de la Familia

Dir Gen 4 Newhams Row, London, SE1 3UZ, UK. T. +442079398200. Fax +442079398300. E-mail: web@ippf.org – media@ippf.org.
Europe Office 55 Rue Royale, 1000 Brussels, Belgium. E-mail: info@ippfen.org.
URL: http://www.ippf.org/

History 29 Nov 1952, Mumbai (India). Became a federation under present name at 3rd International Conference of the *International Committee on Planned Parenthood*, set up Sep 1949, following an international conference, Aug 1948, Cheltenham (UK). Incorporated in UK by special Act of UK Parliament with effect from 1 Sep 1977. Regulations most recently amended 1998. Former names and other names: *Fédération internationale pour le planning familial* – alias. Registration: Charity Commission, No/ID: 229476, Start date: 8 Aug 1963, England and Wales. **Aims** Provide global services; advocate sexual and *reproductive* health and rights for all; encourage individuals and women in particular, to take control of their reproductive lives; promote equality between men and women, aiming to eliminate gender biases, especially those that threaten the well-being of *women* and girls. **Structure** Governing Council (meets twice a year); Regional Councils; International Medical Advisory Panel; Youth and Abortion Working Groups; Accreditation Team. Secretariat located in London (UK), divided into Central and Regional functional units. Regional Offices (6): Africa – Nairobi (Kenya); Arab World – Tunis (Tunisia); Europe – Brussels (Belgium); South Asia – Delhi (India); East, South East Asia and Oceania – Kuala Lumpur (Malaysia); Western Hemisphere – New York NY (USA). Regional Executive Committees; Membership and Audit Committees (meet twice a year); Specialist Committees and Panels. Committee meetings closed. **Languages** Arabic, English, French, Spanish. **Staff** 223.00 FTE, paid. **Finance** Sources: donations. Donations from: governments of Australia, Canada, Denmark, Finland, Germany, Japan, Korea Rep, New Zealand, Norway, Spain, Sweden, Switzerland and UK; organizations. Supported by: *Bill and Melinda Gates Foundation (BMGF)*; *Comic Relief*; *Deutsche Gesellschaft für Internationale Zusammenarbeit (GIZ)*; *Elton John AIDS Foundation (EJAF)*; *European Commission (EC, #06633)*; *Ford Foundation (#09858)*; *International Bank for Reconstruction and Development (IBRD, #12317)* (World Bank); *MacArthur Foundation*; *Margaret Sanger Center International (MSCI)*; *PAI (#18025)*; *The Rockefeller Foundation (#18966)*; *The William and Flora Hewlett Foundation*; *United Nations Foundation (UNF, #20563)*; *United Nations Population Fund (UNFPA, #20612)*; *Wallace Global Fund*; *WHO (#20950)*. Annual budget: 120,500,000 USD. **Activities** Provides clinics and facilities to provide counselling, gynaecological care, HIV/AIDS-related activities, diagnosis and treatment of sexually transmitted infections, mother and child health and abortion-related services; sets standards in contraceptive safety, programme management, service provision, working with young people and abortion services. Instrumental in setting up: *European Parliamentary Forum for Sexual & Reproductive Rights (EPF, #08149)*. **Events** *Meeting on the Impact of COVID-19 on Declining Birthrate* Tokyo (Japan) 2021, *European Network Regional Council and Management Meeting* Bruges (Belgium) 2018, *International Conference on Family Planning* Kigali (Rwanda) 2018, *European Network Regional Council and Management Meeting* Copenhagen (Denmark) 2017, *Annual European Regional Management Meeting* Brussels (Belgium) 2016. **Publications** *IPPF Medical Bulletin* (6 a year) in English, French, Spanish; *Africa Link* (2 a year) – from Nairobi; *People and Development Challenges* (2 a year) in English – from Kuala Lumpur; *Real Lives* (2 a year) in English; *X-press* (2 a year) in English, French, Spanish. *Family Planning Handbook for Health Professionals* (1997) in English; *IPPF Directory of Hormonal Contraceptives* (1996) in English, French, Spanish. Annual report in English, French, Spanish, German, Japanese; corporate documetns; toolkits; reports; medical service delivery guidelines; technical documents; articles and papers; newsletters. Information Services: Maintains a resource library.

Members National parent planning associations work in 170 countries. Members in 163 countries and territories:
Afghanistan, Albania, Algeria, Angola, Anguilla, Antigua-Barbuda, Argentina, Armenia, Aruba, Australia, Bahamas, Bahrain, Bangladesh, Barbados, Belgium, Belize, Benin, Bermuda, Bolivia, Bosnia-Herzegovina, Botswana, Brazil, Bulgaria, Burkina Faso, Burundi, Cambodia, Cameroon, Canada, Cape Verde, Central African Rep, Chad, Chile, China, Colombia, Comoros, Congo Brazzaville, Congo DR, Costa Rica, Côte d'Ivoire, Cyprus, Czechia, Denmark, Djibouti, Dominica, Dominican Rep, Ecuador, Egypt, El Salvador, Eritrea, Estonia, Eswatini, Ethiopia, Fiji, Finland, France, Gabon, Gambia, Georgia, Germany, Ghana, Greece, Grenada, Guadeloupe, Guatemala, Guinea, Guinea-Bissau, Guyana, Haiti, Honduras, Hong Kong, Hungary, Iceland, India, Indonesia, Iran Islamic Rep, Iraq, Ireland, Israel, Italy, Japan, Jordan, Kazakhstan, Kenya, Korea DPR, Korea Rep, Kyrgyzstan, Latvia, Lebanon, Lesotho, Liberia, Lithuania, Luxembourg, Madagascar, Malaysia, Maldives, Mali, Martinique, Mauritania, Mauritius, Mexico, Moldova, Mongolia, Montserrat, Morocco, Mozambique, Namibia, Nepal, Netherlands, New Zealand, Nicaragua, Niger, Nigeria, North Macedonia, Norway, Pakistan, Palestine, Panama, Paraguay, Peru, Philippines, Poland, Portugal, Puerto Rico, Romania, Russia, Rwanda, Samoa, Senegal, Serbia, Sierra Leone, Singapore, Slovakia, South Africa, Spain, Sri Lanka, St Kitts-Nevis, St Lucia, St Vincent-Grenadines, Sudan, Suriname, Sweden, Switzerland, Syrian AR, Tajikistan, Tanzania UR, Thailand, Togo, Tonga, Trinidad-Tobago, Tunisia, Türkiye, Uganda, UK, Uruguay, USA, Uzbekistan, Vanuatu, Venezuela, Vietnam, Virgin Is UK, Virgin Is USA, Yemen, Zambia.
Regional affiliation:
Caribbean Family Planning Affiliation (CFPA, #03502).
Consultative Status Consultative status granted from: *ECOSOC (#05331)* (General); *UNESCO (#20322)* (Consultative Status); *FAO (#09260)* (Special Status); *ILO (#11123)* (Special List); *UNICEF (#20332)*; *WHO (#20950)* (Official Relations); *Council of Europe (CE, #04881)* (Participatory Status); *UNEP (#20299)*.
IGO Relations
- *Asia-Pacific Institute for Broadcasting Development (AIBD, #01934)*;
- *Asian and Pacific Development Centre (APDC, #01608)*;
- *Caribbean Centre for Development Administration (CARICAD, #03468)*;
- *Commonwealth Secretariat (#04362)*;
- *Council of Europe (CE, #04881)* (IPPF Europe Region);
- *International Institute for Adult Education Methods (IIAEM, no recent information)*;
- *Pacific Community (SPC, #17942)*;
- *Regional Institute for Population Studies (RIPS, no recent information)*;
- *UNDP (#20292)*;
- *UNHCR (#20327)*;
- *UNICEF (#20332)*;
- *United Nations Economic Commission for Africa (ECA, #20554)*;
- *United Nations Economic and Social Commission for Asia and the Pacific (ESCAP, #20557)*;
- *United Nations Non-Governmental Liaison Service (NGLS, #20591)*;
- *United Nations Population Fund (UNFPA, #20612)*;
- *WHO (#20950)*;
- *WHO Regional Office for Europe (#20945)*.

Associated with Department of Global Communications of the United Nations.
NGO Relations
- *Advocates for Youth, Washington DC* – International Programs Department;
- *Arab Council for Childhood and Development (ACCD, #00929)*;
- *Asian Forum of Parliamentarians on Population and Development (AFPPD, #01493)*;
- *Asian-Pacific Resource and Research Centre for Women (ARROW, #01629)*;
- *Asian Population and Development Association (APDA)*;
- *Centre for African Family Studies (CAFS, #03726)*;
- *Center of Arab Women for Training and Research, Tunis (CAWTAR, #03637)*;
- *Commonwealth HIV and AIDS Action Group (Para55, no recent information)*;
- *Confédération européenne des ong d'urgence et de développement (CONCORD, #04547)*;
- *Environment Liaison Centre International (ELCI, no recent information)*;
- *Equality Now (#05518)*;
- *European Civil Society Forum on HIV/AIDS (CSF, #06568)*;
- *European Parliamentary Forum for Sexual & Reproductive Rights (EPF, #08149)*;
- *Family Care International (FCI, inactive)*;
- *Federation of African Medical Students' Associations (FAMSA, #09407)*;
- *Fédération Internationale de Gynécologie et d'Obstétrique (FIGO, #09638)*;
- *FHI 360*;
- *Girls not Brides (#10154)*;
- *Global Impact*;
- *Independent Commission for Population and Quality of Life (ICPQL, inactive)*;
- *Inter-American Parliamentary Group on Population and Development (IAPG, inactive)*;
- *International Alliance for Planned Parenthood (no recent information)*;
- *International Association of Schools of Social Work (IASSW, #12149)*;
- *International Centre for Conservation Education (ICCE, inactive)*;
- *International Coalition for the Optional Protocol to the Convention on the Rights of the Child on a Communications Procedure (Ratify OP3CRC, #12617)*;
- *International Confederation of Midwives (ICM, #12863)*;
- *International Consortium for Emergency Contraception (ICEC, #12911)*;
- *International Council for Adult Education (ICAE, #12983)*;
- *International Council of Voluntary Agencies (ICVA, #13092)*;
- *International Council of Women (ICW, #13093)*;
- *International Federation of Business and Professional Women (BPW International, #13376)*;
- *International Organization for Standardization (ISO, #14473)*;
- *International Union for Conservation of Nature and Natural Resources (IUCN, #15766)*;
- *International Union for the Scientific Study of Population (IUSSP, #15814)*;
- *IPAS (#16010)*;
- *Latin American Consortium on Emergency Contraception (LACEC, #16306)*;
- *NGO Committee on Sustainable Development, Vienna (#17119)*;
- *NGO Committee on UNICEF (#17120)*;
- *PMNCH (#18410)*;
- *PATH (#18260)*;
- *Abortion and Postabortion Care Consortium (APAC, #00007)*;
- *Refugee Studies Centre, Oxford (RSC)*;
- *Reproductive Health Supplies Coalition (RHSC, #18847)*;
- *Rutgers (#19011)*;
- *SDG Watch Europe (#19162)*;
- *UK Consortium on AIDS and International Development*;
- *United Nations Global Compact (#20567)*. [2023/XB2361/y/**B**]

♦ International Planning History Society 14590

Pres Univ of South Australia, 101 Currie Street, Adelaide SA 5001, Australia. T. +61883020204.
URL: http://www.planninghistory.org/

History Founded Jan 1993, to succeed the 'Planning History Group', founded 1974, UK. **Aims** Advance critical and interdisciplinary studies in history, planning and the environment with reference to the shaping of contemporary urban environments. **Structure** General Meeting; Council; Executive Committee. **Languages** English. **Staff** Voluntary. **Finance** Members' dues. **Activities** Awards/prizes/competitions; events/meetings. **Events** *Biennial Conference* Hong Kong (Hong Kong) 2024, *Biennial Conference* Delft (Netherlands) 2022, *Biennial Conference* Moscow (Russia) 2020, *Biennial Conference* Yokohama (Japan) 2018, *Biennial Conference* Delft (Netherlands) 2016. **Publications** *Planning Perspectives* (6 a year). **Information Services** *IPHS Connect* – electronic discussion board.
Members Institutions and individuals (about 350) from over 30 countries (not specified), drawn from several disciplines (planning, architecture, economic and social history, geography, sociology, politics and related fields). Affiliated associations in 8 countries:
Australia, Brazil, Canada, China, Japan, Spain, UK, USA.
NGO Relations Cooperates with: *Association of European Schools of Planning (AESOP, #02542)*. [2018.12.13/XD6475/**D**]

♦ International Plant and Animal Genome Conference (meeting series)
♦ International Plant Based Foods Working Group (unconfirmed)
♦ International Plant Biomechanics Conference (meeting series)
♦ International Plant Genetic Resources Institute / see Bioversity International (#03262)

♦ International Plant Growth Substances Association (IPGSA) 14591

Association internationale d'étude des substances de croissance de plantes

Sec-Treas address not obtained.

URL: http://pages.wustl.edu/ipgsa
History 1970, Canberra (Australia), following a series of informal meetings. Functions as a section of *International Union of Biological Sciences (IUBS, #15760)*. **Aims** Promote the study of plant growth substances at international level by facilitating exchange of information, particularly through an international conference. **Structure** Council; Standing Committees (4). **Languages** English. **Staff** Voluntary. **Finance** Members' dues. **Activities** Events/meetings; financial and/or material support. **Events** *Conference* Gyeongju (Korea Rep) 2023, *Conference* Paris (France) 2019, *Conference* Toronto, ON (Canada) 2016, *Conference* Shanghai (China) 2013, *Conference* Tarragona (Spain) 2010.
Members Individuals in 31 countries:
Argentina, Australia, Belgium, Brazil, Canada, Chile, China, Czechia, Denmark, Finland, France, Germany, Israel, Italy, Japan, Korea Rep, Lithuania, Mexico, Netherlands, New Zealand, Norway, Poland, Portugal, Russia, Serbia, Spain, Sweden, Switzerland, Taiwan, UK, USA.
NGO Relations Member of: *International Association of Botanical and Mycological Societies (IABMS, #11730)*.
[2017.03.09/XF5270/v/E]

♦ International Plant Nutrition Council (IPNC) 14592

Pres Dept of Crop Science, School of Agronomy, São Paulo State Univ, Av Universitaria 780, Botucatu, Sao Paulo SP, CEP 18610-034, Brazil.
URL: http://www.ipnc2017.org/
History 1954, Paris (France), as *International Committee on Plant Analysis and Fertilizer Problems* with Colloquium as *International Colloquium on Plant Analysis and Fertilizer Problems*. Title changed, 1978, to *International Committee on Plant Nutrition*, followed by first International Colloquium organized 1982, Warwick (UK). Changed title to *International Council of Plant Nutrition (ICPN)*, 1986. Colloquium of *International Association for the Optimization of Plant Nutrition (IAOPN, inactive)* merged into IPNC, 2001. **Aims** Provide an international forum for discussion of advances in *physiological* plant nutrition. **Structure** Council (meets at each Colloquium). **Languages** English. **Events** *Quadrennial Colloquium* Copenhagen (Denmark) 2017, *Quadrennial Colloquium* Istanbul (Turkey) 2013, *Quadrennial colloquium* Sacramento, CA (USA) 2009, *Quadrennial colloquium* Beijing (China) 2005, *International symposium on phytoremediation and ecosystem health* Hangzhou (China) 2005. **Publications** *Plant Nutrition*. Colloquium proceedings.
Members Individuals from 13 countries:
Australia, Brazil, China, Denmark, Germany, Ghana, Japan, Kenya, Mexico, Thailand, Türkiye, UK, USA.
[2019.02.12/XD4686/E]

♦ International Plant Phenotyping Network (IPPN) 14593

Contact c/o Forschungszentrum Juelich, IBG-2, Wilhelm-Johnen Str, 52428 Jülich, Germany. E-mail: ippn@fz-juelich.de – ippn@plant-phenotyping.org.
URL: http://www.plant-phenotyping.org/
History 18 Feb 2016, Düren (Germany). Registration: Amtsgericht Düren, No/ID: VR 2580, Start date: 18 Feb 2016, Germany, NRW. **Aims** Promote science, industry and research in the field of plant phenotyping. **Structure** General Assembly; Executive Board; Coordination Office. **Languages** English, French, German. **Staff** 1.00 FTE, paid. **Finance** Sources: members' dues. **Activities** Awareness raising; events/meetings; networking/liaising; research/documentation; training/education. **Events** *International Plant Phenotyping Symposium (IPPS)* Wageningen (Netherlands) 2022, *International Plant Phenotyping Symposium (IPPS)* Wageningen (Netherlands) 2021, *International Plant Phenotyping Symposium (IPPS2019)* Nanjing (China) 2019, *International Plant Phenotyping Symposium (IPPS)* Adelaide, SA (Australia) 2018, *International Plant Phenotyping Symposium* Texcoco (Mexico) 2016.
Members Participating institutions (44) in 17 countries:
Australia, Belgium, Canada, China, Denmark, Finland, France, Germany, Ireland, Italy, Japan, Mexico, Netherlands, New Zealand, Saudi Arabia, UK, USA.
Included in the above, 2 organizations listed in this Yearbook:
Commonwealth Scientific and Industrial Research Organization (CSIRO); *International Maize and Wheat Improvement Center (#14077)*.
NGO Relations Also links with national and regional phenomics networks. [2020.11.18/XM6699/y/F]

♦ International Plant Propagators' Society (IPPS) 14594

Société internationale des propagateurs de plantes – Internationale Gesellschaft von Pflanzenvermehrern
Sec-Treas 4 Hawthorn Court, Carlisle PA 17015-7930, USA. T. +17172437685. Fax +17172437691. E-mail: secretary@ipps.org.
URL: http://www.ipps.org/
History 1950. **Aims** Further the art and science of plant propagation; promote education in the field. **Structure** International Policy Board. Organized into 9 regions worldwide. **Languages** English. **Staff** 2.00 FTE, paid. **Finance** Members' dues. **Activities** Annual meetings held by regional groups. **Events** *Annual International Tour Conference* Japan 2022, *Annual International Tour Conference* USA 2021, *Meeting* Australia 2019, *Meeting* USA 2018, *Meeting* UK 2017. **Publications** Combined proceedings (annual); regional newsletters – for members only.
Members Regional Chapters; Individuals Active; Associate. Members (mostly in USA) in 31 countries:
Australia, Austria, Belgium, Bulgaria, Canada, Croatia, Czechia, Denmark, Estonia, Finland, France, Germany, Greece, Hungary, Ireland, Italy, Japan, Latvia, Luxembourg, Netherlands, New Zealand, Norway, Poland, Portugal, Romania, South Africa, Spain, Sweden, Switzerland, UK, USA. [2017/XF0410/F]

♦ International Plant Protection Convention, 1951 (1951 treaty)

♦ International Plant Protection Secretariat (IPPC Secretariat) 14595

Sec Viale delle Terme di Caracalla, 00153 Rome RM, Italy. T. +390657054812. E-mail: ippc@fao.org.
URL: https://www.ippc.int/en/about/secretariat/
History Secretariat to *International Plant Protection Convention, 1951 (IPPC, 1951)*. **Aims** Coordinate the core activities of, and provide operational support to, the IPPC work programme. **Structure** Secretary; Standards Setting Unit; Implementation and Facilitation Unit; Integration Support Team; ePhyto Project Group. **Events** *International Plant Health Conference* London (UK) 2022, *Regional Plant Protection Organizations (RPPOs) Annual Technical Consultation* London (UK) 2022, *International Plant Health Conference* Helsinki (Finland) 2021, *Regional Plant Protection Organizations (RPPOs) Annual Technical Consultation* Rome (Italy) 2021, *IPPC Regional Workshop for Caribbean* Rome (Italy) 2020. **IGO Relations** *FAO (#09260)* [2023/AA3279/E*]

♦ International Plasma Chemistry Society (IPCS) 14596

Pres Univ di Bari – Chimica, Via Orabona 4, 70126 Bari BA, Italy. E-mail: info@ispc-conference.org.
URL: http://www.ispc-conference.org/
History 5 Aug 1999, Prague (Czechia). Successor to *Subcommittee on Plasma Chemistry* of *International Union of Pure and Applied Chemistry (IUPAC, #15809)*. Statutes adopted, 2001, Orleans (France). **Aims** Promote excellence in plasma chemistry research. **Structure** General Assembly (every 2 years). Board of Directors of up to 18 members, including President and Vice-President. **Finance** Members' dues. **Activities** General Assembly. Organizes *International Symposium on Plasma Chemistry (SPC)*. **Events** *International Symposium on Plasma Chemistry (ISPC)* Kyoto (Japan) 2023, *Symposium* Naples (Italy) 2019, *Symposium* Montréal, QC (Canada) 2017, *Symposium* Antwerp (Belgium) 2015, *Symposium* Cairns, QLD (Australia) 2013.
[2022/XM1462/D]

♦ International Plasma and Fractionation Association (IPFA) 14597

Exec Dir Plesmanlaan 125, 1066 CX Amsterdam, Netherlands. T. +31205123561. E-mail: info@ipfa.nl.
URL: http://www.ipfa.nl/
History 1990. Former names and other names: *European Plasma Fractionation Association (EPFA)* – former (1990 to 2005). **Aims** Promote the interests and activities of members involved in collection of human blood and plasma from voluntary non-remunerated donors, and on the basis of the not-for-profit business model for manufacture and supply of medicines derived from human plasma. **Structure** General Assembly; Executive Board; Working Groups; Secretariat. **Languages** English. **Staff** 2.00 FTE, paid. **Finance** Sources: members' dues. **Activities** Awareness raising; events/meetings; guidance/assistance/consulting; networking/liaising. **Events** *Workshop on Surveillance and Screening of Blood Borne Pathogens* Bologna (Italy) 2023, *Workshop on Surveillance and Screening of Blood Borne Pathogens* Porto (Portugal) 2022, *Workshop on Surveillance and Screening of Blood Borne Pathogens* Amsterdam (Netherlands) 2021, *Asia Workshop on Plasma Quality and Supply* Chonburi (Thailand) 2020, *Workshop on Surveillance and Screening of Blood Borne Pathogens* Krakow (Poland) 2019. **Publications** Annual Report; reports on special topics; position papers; conference proceedings.
Members Full in 8 countries:
Australia, Canada, France, Japan, Netherlands, New Zealand, South Africa, USA (2). [2021.02.18/XD4931/D]

♦ International Plasma Products Industry Association / see Plasma Protein Therapeutics Association (#18392)
♦ International Plastics Association (inactive)
♦ International Plastic Society / see Society of Plastics Engineers
♦ International Plastic Surgery Residents Group (internationally oriented national body)

♦ International Platform Against Isolation (IPAI) 14598

Plateforme internationale contre l'isolation
Contact address not obtained. E-mail: ipai.symposium2016@gmail.com.
URL: http://www.ipai-isolation.info/
Aims Fight against isolation *imprisonment* worldwide. **Activities** Events/meetings. Has announced 19th to 22nd of December as International Days of Struggle Against Isolation. **Events** *Symposium* Athens (Greece) 2006, *Symposium* Paris (France) 2005, *Symposium* Noordwijk (Netherlands) 2002. **Publications** *Isolation* – magazine. [2015/XM1362/F]

♦ International Platform for Black, Migrant and Refugee Women's Organizations (internationally oriented national body)

♦ International Platform for Citizen Participation (IPCP) 14599

Contact 5 11th August Str, Fl2 – office 7, 4000 Plovdiv, Bulgaria. T. +359887694188. E-mail: info@ipcp.eu.
URL: http://www.ipcp.eu/
History 2002. **Aims** Enhance international understanding and friendship through educational, cultural and humanitarian activities involving the exchange of ideas and experiences directly among peoples of different countries and diverse cultures. **Languages** English. **Staff** 4.00 FTE, paid; 21.00 FTE, voluntary. **Activities** Networking/liaising.
Members Organizations in 21 countries:
Albania, Armenia, Azerbaijan, Bulgaria, Cyprus, Czechia, Denmark, Egypt, France, Georgia, Greece, Italy, Lithuania, Moldova, North Macedonia, Portugal, Romania, Spain, Türkiye, UK, Ukraine.
Included in the above, 1 organization listed in this Yearbook:
European Association of Geographers (EUROGEO, #06054). [2015.06.01/XJ8525/F]

♦ International Platform of Insects for Food and Feed (IPIFF) 14600

SG Rue Joseph Stevens 7, Bte 8, 1000 Brussels, Belgium. E-mail: secretariat@ipiff.org.
URL: http://www.ipiff.org/
History 2012. Registration: Banque-Carrefour des Entreprises, No/ID: 0630.649.755, Start date: 13 Apr 2015; EU Transparency Register, No/ID: 845856417247-32, Start date: 6 May 2015. **Aims** Promote the wider use of insects as an alternative or new source of protein for human consumption and animal feed through continuous dialogue with the European institutions. **Structure** General Assembly; Executive Committee. **Activities** Advocacy/lobbying/activism; events/meetings. **Events** *Annual Conference* Brussels (Belgium) 2022, *Annual Conference* Brussels (Belgium) 2021, *General Assembly* Brussels (Belgium) 2019, *Workshop on Unleashing the Circularity Potential of the European Insect Sector through Research and Innovation* Brussels (Belgium) 2019, *Conference* Brussels (Belgium) 2018. **Publications** *IPIFF Newsletter*. **Members** Ordinary; Associated; Academia; Observer. Members (over 80) in 24 countries. Membership countries not specified.
[2022/XM7793/F]

♦ International Platform of Jurists for East Timor (IPJET) 14601

Sec Gruttohoek 13, 2317 WK Leiden, Netherlands. T. +31715221065 – +351913271527. E-mail: ipjet2@gmail.com.
URL: http://ipjet.org
History 10 Nov 1991. **Aims** Help East Timorese institutions in major legal subject matters; help the people of Western Sahara to exercise their right to self-determination. **Structure** General Assembly; International Council; Secretariat. **Finance** Sources: donations; members' dues. Annual budget: 3,000 USD. **Events** *Conference* The Hague (Netherlands) 2006, *Conference* Lisbon (Portugal) 1999, *Conference* Dublin (Ireland) 1996, *Conference* Iserlohn (Germany) 1994, *Asia-Pacific Conference on East Timor* Manila (Philippines) 1994. **Publications** *Justice on Trial: Law, Politics and Western Sahara* (2022) by Dr Katlyn Thomas and Prof Clive Symmons et al in English; *El Derecho Internacional y la cuestión del Sahara Occidental* (2012); *Le droit international et la question du Sahara occidental* (2009); *International Law and the Question of Western Sahara* (2007); *East Timor Problem and the Role of Europe* (1998); *International Law and the Question of East Timor* (1995).
Members Individuals (650) and organizations (5) in 83 countries and territories:
Algeria, Angola, Argentina, Australia, Austria, Azerbaijan, Belgium, Brazil, Bulgaria, Cameroon, Canada, Cape Verde, China, Colombia, Congo DR, Croatia, Cuba, Czechia, Denmark, Dominican Rep, Egypt, El Salvador, Eritrea, Ethiopia, Fiji, Finland, France, Germany, Greece, Guinea-Bissau, Honduras, Hong Kong, Hungary, India, Indonesia, Ireland, Italy, Jamaica, Japan, Korea Rep, Lithuania, Luxembourg, Macau, Malawi, Malaysia, Mexico, Morocco, Mozambique, Myanmar, Namibia, Nepal, Netherlands, New Zealand, Nigeria, North Macedonia, Norway, Pakistan, Panama, Philippines, Portugal, Puerto Rico, Russia, Sahara West, Sao Tomé-Principe, South Africa, Spain, Sri Lanka, Sudan, Sweden, Switzerland, Taiwan, Thailand, Timor-Leste, Türkiye, Uganda, UK, Ukraine, Uruguay, USA, Vanuatu, Venezuela, Vietnam, Zimbabwe.
NGO Relations Member of (4): *Coalition for the International Criminal Court (CICC, #04062)*; *International Federation for East Timor (IFET, #13408)*; Western Sahara Action Forum (WSAF); Western Sahara Resource Watch (WSRW). [2023.02.15/XF5773/F]

♦ International Platform on Shared Parenting / see International Council on Shared Parenting (#13072)
♦ International Platform on Sport and Development (internationally oriented national body)
♦ International Platinum Association / see International Platinum Group Metals Association (#14602)

♦ International Platinum Group Metals Association (IPA) 14602

Managing Dir Schiess-Staett-Strasse 30, 80339 Munich, Germany. T. +498951996770. Fax +498951996719. E-mail: info@ipa-news.com.
Communications Manager address not obtained.
URL: https://www.ipa-news.com/
History 1987. Former names and other names: *International Platinum Association (IPA)* – former. Registration: Hesse District court, No/ID: VR 9055, Start date: 1 Feb 1988, Germany, Frankfurt-Main; EU Transparency Register, No/ID: 895039148209-70, Start date: 25 Nov 2022. **Aims** Represent the interests of leading mining, production and fabrication companies of the global platinum group metals (PGM's) industry. **Structure** Board; Committees (4). **Finance** Members' dues. **Activities** Monitoring/assessment; knowledge management/information dissemination; research/documentation. **Events** *Seminar on Euro 7 Emissions Standards* Brussels (Belgium) 2022.
Members Full in 8 countries:
Belgium, Canada, Germany, Japan, Russia, South Africa, UK, USA.
NGO Relations In liaison with technical committees of: *International Organization for Standardization (ISO, #14473)*. [2022/XD4960/D]

♦ International Platinum Symposium (meeting series)

♦ International Plato Society 14603

Société Platonicienne Internationale – Sociedad Internacional de Platonistas – Internationale Plato Gesellschaft – Associazione Internazionale dei Platonisti
Pres Univ of Georgia, Dept of Philosophy, 107 Peabody Hall, Athens GA 30602-1627, USA. T. +17065422821.
URL: http://www.platosociety.org/

History 3 Sep 1989, Italy. 3 Sep 1989, Bevagna (Italy), during the 2nd Symposium Platonicum. **Aims** Promote Platonic studies throughout the world and communication among scholars of diverse disciplines working on Plato. **Structure** Officers: President; Co-President; Vice-President; Past-President; Future President; 5 Regional Representatives (2 for Europe; North America; Latin America; Asia, Australia and Africa); Foundation Representative. **Languages** English, French, German, Italian, Spanish. **Activities** Events/meetings. **Events** *Triennial Symposium* Madrid (Spain) 2025, *Triennial Symposium* Athens, GA (USA) 2022, *Triennial Symposium* Paris (France) 2019, *Triennial Symposium* Brasilia (Brazil) 2016, *Regional Meeting on Plato and Rethoric* Yokohama (Japan) 2014. **Publications** *International Plato Studies* – series. *Plato Bibliography*. Symposium proceedings. **Members** Membership countries not specified. **NGO Relations** Member of: *Fédération internationale des associations d'études classiques (FIEC, #09607)*; *International Federation of Philosophical Societies (FISP, #13507)*. [2020.01.01/XE2978/**E**]

♦ International Play Association (IPA) 14604

Association internationale pour le droit au jeu de l'enfant – Asociación Internacional por el Derecho del Niño a Jugar – Internationale Vereinigung für das Recht des Kindes zu Spielen

Contact address not obtained. E-mail: president@ipaworld.org – communications@ipaworld.org.
URL: https://ipaworld.org/

History 12 May 1961, Copenhagen (Denmark). Founded at a conference of European playground experts. Membership subsequently widened to include individuals of all relevant professions, groups, organizations and benefactors, in every continent, endorsing the United Nations Declaration of the Rights of the Child, especially Principle 7, paragraph 3 (on opportunity and right to play) and currently *United Nations Convention on the Rights of the Child (CRC, 1989)*, Article 31. Constitution adopted 25 Aug 1978, Ottawa (Canada); amended: 28 Aug 1981, Rotterdam (Netherlands); 10 Aug 1984, Ljubljana (Yugoslavia); 8 Jun 1990, Tokyo (Japan). Former names and other names: *International Playground Association* – former (12 May 1961); *Association internationale des terrains de jeux* – former (12 May 1961); *Internationale Spielplatzvereinigung* – former; *International Association for the Child's Right to Play* – former; *International Play Association – Promoting the Child's Right to Play (IPA)* – full title. **Aims** Protect, preserve and promote children's play as a fundamental human right of all children, everywhere; provide an international forum to promote and improve the development of play environments, leisure time facilities, for *children* and youth; contribute to a better education including play spaces indoors and outdoors of play-leaders. **Structure** General Meeting (every 3 years), elects Vice-Presidents for the regions and a 5-member Nominations Committee. Council of National Representatives; Board of Directors (meets twice a year). **Languages** English. **Staff** Officers share work on a voluntary basis. **Finance** Sources: members' dues; sale of publications. Annual budget: 20,000 GBP. **Activities** Events/meetings; knowledge management/information dissemination; projects/programmes; research/documentation; standards/guidelines. *'IPA Declaration of the Child's Right to Play'*, produced Nov 1977, Malta; revised Sep 1982, Vienna (Austria) and Sep 1989, Barcelona (Spain). **Events** *World Conference* Glasgow (UK) 2023, *Triennial World Conference* Jaipur (India) 2021, *Triennial World Conference* Jaipur (India) 2020, *Triennial World Conference* Calgary, AB (Canada) 2017, *Triennial world conference* Istanbul (Turkey) 2014. **Publications** *PlayRights* (4 a year) – magazine; *International Play Journal*. *IPA Declaration of the Child's Right to Play*. Conference reports.

Members Organizations; Individuals; Benefactors. Members in 45 countries and territories:
Argentina, Australia, Austria, Belgium, Brazil, Bulgaria, Canada, China, Cyprus, Denmark, Estonia, Finland, France, Germany, Ghana, Greece, Hong Kong, India, Ireland, Israel, Italy, Japan, Kenya, Korea Rep, Malaysia, Malta, Mexico, Netherlands, New Zealand, Nicaragua, Norway, Philippines, Portugal, Russia, Scotland, Singapore, Slovenia, Spain, Sweden, Switzerland, Taiwan, Thailand, Togo, UK (less Scotland), USA.

Consultative Status Consultative status granted from: *ECOSOC (#05331)* (Ros A); *UNICEF (#20332)*. **IGO Relations** Accredited by (1): *United Nations Office at Vienna (UNOV, #20604)*. **NGO Relations** Member of (1): *Child Rights Connect (#03884)*. Affiliated with (4): *European Network Child Friendly Cities (ENCFC, #07877)*; *International Council for Children's Play (ICCP, #13004)*; *International Toy Library Association (ITLA, #15699)*; *World Organization for Early Childhood Education (OMEP, #21689)*. [2023/XC2363/**B**]

♦ International Play Association – Promoting the Child's Right to Play / see International Play Association (#14604)

♦ International Playground Association / see International Play Association (#14604)

♦ International Playing-Card Society (IPCS) 14605

Société internationale de la carte à jouer

Chair 71 Rijndijk, 2394 AD Hazerswoude-Dorp, Netherlands. E-mail: chairman@i-p-c-s.org.
Hon Sec address not obtained. E-mail: secretary@i-p-c-s.org.
URL: http://www.i-p-c-s.org/

History 1972, Norwich (UK), following a meeting of collectors, 1972, Kendal (UK), as 'Playing Card Society'. **Aims** Further the study of the origin and development of playing cards; bring together all people interested in the study and *collecting* of playing cards and *games* played with cards. **Structure** General Meeting (annual); Council. **Languages** English. **Staff** 2.00 FTE, voluntary. **Finance** Members' dues. Annual budget: pounds12,000. **Activities** Events/meetings. **Events** *Annual Convention* Catania (Italy) 2019, *Annual Convention* Leinfelden-Echterdingen (Germany) 2018, *Annual Convention* London (UK) 2017, *Annual Convention* Prague (Czechia) 2016, *Annual Convention* Turnhout (Belgium) 2015. **Publications** *The Playing-Card* (4 a year) – journal. *IPCS Papers* – monographs; *Pattern Sheets*.

Members Individuals Full; Associate. Associations (1, in Switzerland). Members in 29 countries:
Australia, Austria, Belgium, Brazil, Canada, China, Czechia, Denmark, France, Germany, Hungary, India, Ireland, Israel, Italy, Japan, Latvia, Netherlands, New Zealand, Norway, Poland, Portugal, Russia, Singapore, Spain, Sweden, Switzerland, UK, USA. [2017.12.01/XD8106/**D**]

♦ International PLR Network / see PLR International (#18407)

♦ International Plutarch Society 14606

Pres Dept of Philology, Univ of Crete, 741 00 Rethymnon, Greece.
URL: http://www.usu.edu/history/ploutarchos/index.htm

History 1984, Philadelphia PA (USA). **Aims** Further the study of Plutarch and his writings; encourage scholarly communication between those working on Plutarchan studies. **Structure** Officers: President; President-Elect; Editor; Secretary-Treasurer. **Languages** English, French, German, Irish Gaelic, Italian, Latin, Portuguese, Spanish. **Staff** 1.00 FTE, paid. **Finance** Members' dues (annual). **Events** *Congress / Conference* Ravello (Italy) 2011, *Congress / Conference* Coimbra (Portugal) 2008, *Symposium* Göttingen (Germany) 2005, *Congress / Conference* Rethymnon (Greece) 2005, *Congress / Conference* Nijmegen (Netherlands) 2002. **Publications** *Ploutarchos* (annual).

Members Full in 22 countries:
Australia, Belgium, Canada, Cyprus, Denmark, Finland, France, Germany, Greece, Holy See, Ireland, Italy, Mexico, Netherlands, New Zealand, Poland, Portugal, Russia, Spain, Sweden, Switzerland, UK. [2013.06.12/XE3811/**E**]

♦ International PNF Association / see International Proprioceptive Neuromuscular Facilitation Association (#14658)

♦ International Podoconiosis Initiative (Footwork) 14607

Exec Dir Brighton and Sussex Medical School, Univ of Sussex, Falmer, Brighton, BN1 9PX, UK. E-mail: info@podo.org.
URL: http://www.podo.org/

History 2012, UK. Set up as a project of *New Venture Fund (NVF)*. Now a project of US based Social Good Fund. Registration: Section 501(c)(3), USA. **Aims** Enable and champion a world free of podoconiosis (a form of leg swelling found among poor, subsistence farming communities). **Structure** Technical Committee; Advisory Board; Partners. **Languages** English. **Staff** 0.20 FTE, voluntary. **Finance** Sources: international organizations; revenue from activities/projects. Supported by: *Izumi Foundation*. Annual budget: 50,000 USD. **Activities** Advocacy/lobbying/activism; awareness raising; events/meetings; monitoring/evaluation; networking/liaising; projects/programmes; research/documentation; standards/guidelines. Active in: Burundi, Cameroon, Ethiopia, India, Kenya, Rwanda, Uganda. **Events** *Strategy 2021-25 Launch Meeting* Brighton (UK) 2021, *International Podoconiosis Conference* Addis Ababa (Ethiopia) 2018. **Publications** Articles.

Members Full in 4 countries:
Cameroon, Ethiopia, UK, USA.

NGO Relations Member of (1): *Neglected Tropical Diseased NGO Network (NNN, #16969)*. Partners include: *Children Without Worms (CWW, #03881)*; *Global Alliance to Eliminate Lymphatic Filariasis (GAELF, #10195)*; *International Orthodox Christian Charities (IOCC)*; *Liverpool School of Tropical Medicine (LSTM)*; *Tropical Health Alliance Foundation (THAF)*; national organizations and institutions. [2021.09.02/XM5859/**F**]

♦ International Poetry Guild (inactive)

♦ International Polar Commission (inactive)

♦ International Polar Foundation (internationally oriented national body)

♦ International Polar Institute (inactive)

♦ International Polar Motion Service (inactive)

♦ International Polar Tourism Research Network (IPTRN) 14608

Réseau international de recherche en tourisme polaire (RIRTP)

Chair Nipissing University, 100 College Drive, Box 5002, North Bay ON P1B 8L7, Canada. E-mail: iptrnmail@gmail.com.
URL: http://sites.google.com/view/polartourismresearch/

History 2006, Thunder Bay, ON (Canada). **Aims** Generate, share and disseminate knowledge, resources and perspectives on polar tourism; support the development of international collaboration and cooperative relationships between members. **Structure** Steering Committee. **Events** *International conference* Whitehorse, YT (Canada) / Dawson City, YT (Canada) 2018, *International conference* Raufarhöfn (Iceland) 2016, *International Conference* Christchurch (New Zealand) 2014, *From talk to action – how tourism is changing the Polar regions* Nain, NL (Canada) 2012, *International Conference* Nain, NL (Canada) 2012. [2020.04.29/XJ4870/**F**]

♦ International Pole Dance Fitness Association (IPDFA) 14609

Contact address not obtained. T. +61426061976. E-mail: info@ipdfa.com – tracey@ipdfa.com.
Facebook: https://www.facebook.com/ipdfa/

History 2007. **Aims** Serve as the industry's communication network platform. **Finance** Sources: members' dues. **Activities** Awards/prizes/competitions; sporting activities; training/education. **Publications** *IPDFA Newsletter*. **NGO Relations** Member of (2): *General Association of Asia Pacific Sports Federations (GAAPSF, #10106)*; *International Sport Network Organization (ISNO, #15592)*. Partner of (1): *European Esports Observatory (EEO)*. [2022/AA1083/**C**]

♦ International Pole and Line Foundation (IPNLF) 14610

IPNLF Africa NPC (IPNLF Africa) – Stichting International Pole and Line (IPNLF NL) – Yayasan IPNLF Indonesia (YII) – IPNLF Maldives (IPNLF-M)

Managing Dir 1 London Street, Reading, RG1 4QW, UK. E-mail: info@ipnlf.org.
URL: http://ipnlf.org/

History 23 Jan 2012, London (UK). Born out of the need for representation of pole-and-line fishers in the Maldives. Registration: Charity Commission, No/ID: 1145586, Start date: 2012, England and Wales. **Aims** Work to develop, support and promote one-by-one tuna fisheries. **Structure** Board of Trustees; Scientific and Technical Advisory Committee; Market Advisory Group. **Languages** Afrikaans, Dhivehi, Dutch, English, Indonesian, Javanese. **Staff** 18.00 FTE, paid. **Finance** Sources: donations; government support; grants; members' dues; private foundations. Annual budget: 865,235 GBP (2021). URL: https://ipnlf.org/wp-content/uploads/2022/12/IPNLF-Rport-2021-_-2022.pdf **Activities** Advocacy/lobbying/activism; awareness raising; capacity building; events/meetings; financial and/or material support; guidance/assistance/consulting; knowledge management/information dissemination; management of treaties and agreements; networking/liaising; politics/policy/regulatory; projects/programmes; research and development; research/documentation; standards/guidelines. **Publications** *IPNLF Newsletter*. Annual Report. **Consultative Status** Consultative status granted from: *UNCTAD (#20285)* (General Category). **NGO Relations** Member of (1): *High Level Panel for a Sustainable Ocean Economy (Panel, #10917)* (Advisory Network). [2023.02.14/XM8937/t/**F**]

♦ International Pole Sports Federation (IPSF) 14611

Administration address not obtained. T. +442032396974. E-mail: secretary@polesports.org.
URL: http://www.polesports.org/

History 2009. **Aims** Foster the development of the sport of Pole Sports throughout the world. **Structure** Executive Committee; Athletes Commission. **Activities** Sporting activities; training/education.

Members National federations in 31 countries and territories:
Australia, Brazil, Canada, China, Colombia, Czechia, Denmark, Finland, France, Germany, Great Britain, Greece, Hungary, Israel, Italy, Japan, Kazakhstan, Korea Rep, Mexico, Netherlands, Norway, Poland, Portugal, Puerto Rico, Romania, Russia, South Africa, Sweden, Switzerland, Ukraine, USA.

NGO Relations Member of (2): *Alliance of Independent recognised Members of Sport (AIMS, #00690)* (Observer); *The Association for International Sport for All (TAFISA, #02763)*. Signatory to: *World Anti-Doping Agency (WADA, #21096)*. [2020/XM5475/**C**]

♦ International Police Association (IPA) 14612

Association internationale de police – Asociación Internacional de Policia – International Polizei-Assoziation

SG Arthur Troop House, 1 Fox Road, West Bridgford, Nottingham, NG2 6AJ, UK. T. +447459863196. E-mail: iac@ieb-ipa.org – sg@ieb-ipa.org.
URL: https://www.ipa-international.org/

History 1 Jan 1950, UK. 1st Congress held in Sep 1955, Paris (France). Statutes revised at: 8th Congress, 9-14 July 1979, Perugia (Italy); 10th Congress, 21-24 June 1982, Wiesbaden (Germany FR); 12th Congress, Aug 1988, Monte Real (Portugal); 13th Congress, 1991, Wellington (New Zealand); 14th Congress, 1994, Luxembourg; 15th Congress, 1997, Québec (Canada); 16th Congress, 2000, Bournemouth (UK); 17th Congress, 2003, Trondheim (Norway); 18th Congress, 2006, Ljubljana (Slovenia); 19th Congress, 2009, Antalya (Turkey); 20th Congress, 2012, Eilat (Israel); Extraordinary World Congress, 2014, Potsdam (Germany); 21st Congress, 2015, Limassol (Cyprus); 61st Congress, 2016, Auckland (New Zealand); 62nd Congress, 2017, Albena (Bulgaria); 63rd Congress, 2018; 64th Congress, Rotterdam, Netherlands, 2019; 65th Congress, Dubrovnic (Croatia), 2020; 66th Congress, Lloret de Mar (Spain), 2021. Former names and other names: *Associazione Internazionale di Polizia* – former. Registration: Swiss Civil Code, Switzerland; EU Transparency Register, No/ID: 638024732997-86, Start date: 24 Oct 2018. **Aims** Create and strengthen bonds of friendship between members of the police service; promote international cooperation in social, cultural and professional fields; encourage peaceful co-existence and preservation of world peace; improve public image of police service; enhance recognition of the IPA by international bodies. **Structure** International Executive Council (IEC); International Executive Board; International Administration Centre. International Commissions (3): External Relations; Professional; Socio-Cultural. Crisis Committee. Includes *International Conference Centre of the International Police Association (#12877)* – Gimborn (Germany). **Languages** English, French, German, Spanish. **Staff** 2.00 FTE, paid. **Finance** Sources: donations; gifts, legacies; members' dues; subsidies. **Activities** Awards/prizes/competitions; events/meetings; financial and/or material support; humanitarian/emergency aid; networking/liaising; publishing activities; sporting activities; training/education. **Events** *World Congress* Athens (Greece) 2023, *World congress* Lloret de Mar (Spain) 2022, *World congress* Lloret de Mar (Spain) 2021, *World congress* Lloret de Mar (Spain) 2020, *World Congress* Dubrovnik (Croatia) 2019. **Publications** *International Newsletter* (11 a year).

Members National Sections in 69 countries and territories:
Albania, Andorra, Argentina, Armenia, Australia, Austria, Belgium, Bosnia-Herzegovina, Botswana, Brazil, Bulgaria, Canada, Colombia, Croatia, Cyprus, Czechia, Denmark, Estonia, Eswatini, Finland, France, Germany, Gibraltar, Greece, Hong Kong, Hungary, Iceland, Ireland, Israel, Italy, Japan, Kazakhstan, Kenya, Kyrgyzstan, Latvia, Lesotho, Lithuania, Luxembourg, Macau, Malta, Mauritius, Moldova, Monaco, Montenegro, Mozambique, Netherlands, New Zealand, North Macedonia, Norway, Pakistan, Peru, Poland, Portugal, Romania, Russia, San Marino, Serbia, Slovakia, Slovenia, South Africa, Spain, Sri Lanka, Sweden, Switzerland, Türkiye, UK, Ukraine, USA, Uzbekistan.

Associate members in 37 countries and territories:
Angola, Aruba, Bangladesh, Belarus, Benin, Cambodia, Cameroon, China, Costa Rica, Dominican Rep, Fiji, Gambia, Georgia, India, Indonesia, Iraq, Kosovo, Kuwait, Lebanon, Liberia, Liechtenstein, Malaysia, Namibia, Nigeria, Papua New Guinea, Qatar, Saudi Arabia, Singapore, Somalia, South Sudan, Tajikistan, Tanzania UR, Trinidad-Tobago, United Arab Emirates, Uruguay, Vietnam, Zimbabwe.

Consultative Status Consultative status granted from: *ECOSOC (#05331)* (Special); *UNESCO (#20322)* (Consultative Status). **NGO Relations** Member of (2): *Alliance of NGOs on Crime Prevention and Criminal Justice (#00709)*; *Vienna NGO Committee on Drugs (VNGOC, #20773)*. [2023.02.14/XB2366/**B**]

♦ International Police Commission (internationally oriented national body)

♦ International Police Conference (inactive)

♦ International Police Executive Symposium (IPES) 14613

Pres 1 Norwood Dr, Albany NY 12204, USA. T. +15184631938. Fax +15184631858.
Dir address not obtained.
Sec/Treas PO Box 3126, Monroe LA 71294, USA.
Public Relations address not obtained.
URL: http://www.ipes.info/

History 1994. **Aims** Bring police researchers and practitioners together to facilitate cross-cultural, international and interdisciplinary exchanges for enrichment of the policing profession. **Structure** Founding President; Vice President; Treasurer; Directors (10). **Languages** English. **Staff** 1.00 FTE, paid. **Finance** Sources: members' dues; sponsorship. **Activities** Events/meetings; knowledge management/information dissemination; networking/liaising. **Events** *Annual Meeting* Manaus (Brazil) 2023, *Annual Meeting* Callicoon, NY (USA) 2022, *Annual Meeting* Rio de Janeiro (Brazil) 2020, *Annual Meeting* Belgrade (Serbia) 2019, *Annual Meeting* Vienna (Austria) 2018. **Publications** *Police, Practice, and Research – An International Journal. Civilian oversight of police: advancing accountability in law enforcement*; *Policing terrorism: research studies into police counterterrorismo investigations*; *Police reform in China*; *Policing and mentally ill: international perspectives*; *Policing Democracies*; *Policing in France*; *Policing in Hong Kong: history and reform*; *Policing in Israel: studying crime control, community, and counterterrorism*; *Policing of Corruption: An International Comparative Perspective*; *Policing white-collar crime: characteristics of white-collar criminals*; *Police organized crime: intelligence strategy implementation*; *Public Order: A World Perspective*; *Security governance, policing, and local capacity*; *The crime numbers game: management by manipulation*; *The international trafficking of human organs: a multidisciplinary perspective*; *The new khaki: the evolving nature of policing in India*; *Transnational criminology in policing* by David Weisburd; *Women in policing around the world: doing gender and policing in a gendered organization*; *Police performance appraisals: a comparative perspective*; *Police investigative interviews and interpreting: context, challenges and strategies*; *Cold cases: an evaluation model with follow-up strategies for investigators*; *Honor-based violence: policing and prevention*; *Cold cases: evaluation models with follow-up strategies for investigators, second edition*; *Collaborative policing: police, academics, professionals, and communities working together for education, training, and program implementation*; *Community policing and peacekeeping*; *Community policing: international patterns and comparative perspectives*; *Crime linkage: theory, research, and practice*; *Delivering police services effectively*; *Exploring contemporary police challenges: a global perspective*; *International Perspectives on Community Policing and Crime Prevention*; *Police integrity management in Australia: global lessons for combating police misconduct*; *International Police Cooperation: A World Perspective*; *Los Angeles police department meltdown: the fall of the professional-reform model of policing*; *Mission-based policing*; *Organized Crime: World Perspectives*; *Police and society in Brazil*; *Police behavior, hiring, and crime fighting: an international view*; *Police corruption: preventing misconduct and maintaining integrity*; *World Police Encyclopedia*. Official brochures; executive summaries; books; papers; interviews. **Consultative Status** Consultative status granted from: *ECOSOC (#05331)* (Special). [2022.10.21/XM0201/c/**F**]

♦ International Police Sports Union 14614

Union sportive internationale des polices (USIP)

Gen Secretariat PO Box: 159, 3840 AC Harderwijk, Netherlands. E-mail: usiphq@internationalpolicesports.com.
URL: http://www.internationalpolicesports.com/

History 23 May 1990, Paris (France). Registered in accordance with French law. **Aims** Promote sport throughout the police forces from all continents; coordinate the preparation, organization and control of international competitions in all sports' disciplines; build up social, cooperative and professional relations between police forces. **Structure** Congress (every 2 years). Executive Committee, comprising President, 3 Vice-Presidents, Secretary General and Chairman of the Technical Committee. Secretariat General, headed by Secretary General. Presidential Bureau, headed by Assistant Secretary General. Auditing Committee; International Sport Council. **Languages** Arabic, English, French. **Finance** Members' dues. Other sources: registration fees; appeal fees; subsidies; donations; contracts; services rendered. **Activities** Organizes: World Police Championships; World Games of Police Schools; symposia, lectures. Participates in organization of competitions at national or international levels held on the initiative of national police sports organizations; conducts professional training courses for organizers and activists. **Events** *Congress* Kuwait (Kuwait) 2012, *Congress* Kuwait (Kuwait) 2012, *Congress* Kuwait (Kuwait) 2010, *Congress* Kuwait (Kuwait) 2010, *Congress* Prague (Czech Rep) 2007. **Publications** Information magazine.
Members Full in 60 countries:
Albania, Algeria, Argentina, Armenia, Austria, Bahrain, Belarus, Bulgaria, Canada, Chile, China, Croatia, Cyprus, Czechia, Egypt, Estonia, Ethiopia, Finland, France, Gabon, Germany, Greece, Hungary, Iceland, Indonesia, Ireland, Italy, Jordan, Kuwait, Latvia, Lebanon, Libya, Luxembourg, Malaysia, Mauritania, Moldova, Montenegro, Morocco, Netherlands, North Macedonia, Oman, Peru, Poland, Portugal, Qatar, Romania, Russia, Saudi Arabia, Serbia, Slovakia, Slovenia, Somalia, Spain, Syrian AR, Tunisia, Türkiye, Ukraine, United Arab Emirates, USA, Yemen.
NGO Relations Recognized by: *International Olympic Committee (IOC, #14408)*. [2018/XD5724/**D**]

♦ International Police Training Institute (unconfirmed)
♦ International Policewomen's Association / see International Association of Women Police (#12270)
♦ International Policy Institute for Counter-Terrorism / see International Institute for Counter-Terrorism
♦ International Policy Network (internationally oriented national body)
♦ International Poliomyelitis Congress (inactive)

♦ International Political Science Association (IPSA) 14615

Association internationale de science politique (AISP) – Asociación Internacional de Ciencias Politicas – Internationale Vereinigung für Wissenschaft der Politik – Mezdunarodnaja Associacija Politiceskoj Nauki

Exec Dir 1590 Ave Docteur Penfield, Montréal QC H3G 1C5, Canada. T. +15148488717. Fax +15145650529. E-mail: info@ipsa.org.
Administration address not obtained.
URL: http://www.ipsa.org/

History Sep 1949, Paris (France). Founded under the auspices of *UNESCO (#20322)*. Constitution amended at Council Meetings: 19-26 Aug 1955, Stockholm (Sweden); 15-19 Sep 1958, Rome (Italy); 21-25 Sep 1964, Geneva (Switzerland); 31 Aug – 5 Sep 1970, Munich (Germany FR); 12-18 Aug 1979, Moscow (USSR); 9-14 Aug 1982, Rio de Janeiro (Brazil); 21-25 Jul 1991, Buenos Aires (Argentina); 17-21 Aug 1997, Seoul (Korea Rep); 8-12 Jul 2012, Madrid (Spain). Registration: Start date: 1 Jun 1950, France. **Aims** Support development of political science worldwide; create an inclusive and global political science community; promote collaboration between scholars in emerging and established democracies and support academic freedoms needed for social sciences to flourish. **Structure** World Congress (every 2 years); Council; Executive Committee; Research Committees (50); Secretariat, headed by Executive Director. **Languages** English, French. **Staff** 9.00 FTE, paid. **Finance** Sources: meeting proceeds; members' dues; sale of publications. **Activities** Events/meetings; networking/liaising; research/documentation. **Events** *World Congress of Political Science /* Buenos Aires (Argentina) 2023, *Open Access Publishing Conference* Montréal, QC (Canada) 2022, *World Congress of Political Science* Lisbon (Portugal) 2021, *World Congress of Political Science* Lisbon (Portugal) 2020, *Conference* Paris (France) 2019. **Publications** *International Political Science Abstracts* (6 a year); *International Political Science Review/Revue internationale de science politique* (5 a year) – official journal; *Participation: Bulletin of the International Political Science Association* (annual) – newsletter; *Monthly e-Newsletter*. *A History of International Political Science Association* (2009) in English, French. Constitution; rules and procedures; congress and round-table proceedings.
Members Collective (60): national and regional associations. Associate (over 115): associations, organizations; societies and institutions pursuing objectives compatible to those of IPSA in related fields of activity. Individual (more than 3,000): persons suitably qualified by their professional activity or general interest in political science. Members in 106 countries and territories:
Algeria, Angola, Argentina, Australia, Austria, Belgium, Benin, Botswana, Brazil, Bulgaria, Burkina Faso, Burundi, Cameroon, Canada, Cape Verde, Central African Rep, Chad, Chile, China, Colombia, Comoros, Congo Brazzaville, Congo DR, Côte d'Ivoire, Croatia, Czechia, Denmark, Djibouti, Egypt, Equatorial Guinea, Eswatini, Ethiopia, Finland, France, Gabon, Gambia, Georgia, Germany, Ghana, Greece, Guinea, Guinea-Bissau, Hungary, Iceland, India, Ireland, Israel, Italy, Japan, Kazakhstan, Kenya, Korea DPR, Korea Rep, Lebanon, Lesotho, Liberia, Libya, Lithuania, Luxembourg, Madagascar, Malawi, Mali, Mauritania, Mauritius, Mexico, Montenegro, Morocco, Mozambique, Namibia, Nepal, Netherlands, New Zealand, Niger, Nigeria, Norway, Philippines, Poland, Portugal, Romania, Russia, Rwanda, Sao Tomé-Principe, Senegal, Serbia, Seychelles, Sierra Leone, Singapore, Slovakia, Slovenia, Somalia, South Africa, Spain, Sudan, Sweden, Switzerland, Taiwan, Tanzania UR, Thailand, Togo, Tunisia, Türkiye, Uganda, UK, Uruguay, USA, Venezuela, Zambia, Zimbabwe.
Included in the above, 2 regional collective members, listed in this Yearbook:
African Association of Political Science (AAPS); *Central European Political Science Association (CEPSA, #03712)*.
Consultative Status Consultative status granted from: *ECOSOC (#05331)* (Ros C). **IGO Relations** Consultative Status with *UNESCO (#20322)*. Associated with Department of Global Communications of the United Nations. **NGO Relations** Nominates one member of: *Global Development Network (GDN, #10318)*. Member of: *International Science Council (ISC, #14796)*. Affiliated with: *Réseau des associations francophones de science politique*. [2021.03.03/XB2369/**B**]

♦ International Political Science Institute (inactive)
♦ International Polizei-Assoziation (#14612)

♦ International Pollutants Elimination Network (IPEN) 14616

Contact Box 7256, SE-402 35 Gothenburg, Sweden. T. +46317537479. E-mail: ipen@ipen.org.
URL: https://ipen.org/

History Jun 1998. Launched during 1st session of *Intergovernmental Negotiating Committee on Persistent Organic Pollutants (inactive)*, convened by *UNEP (#20299)*. A *United Nations (UN, #20515)* Initiative. Former names and other names: *International POPs Elimination Network* – former. **Aims** Work towards global elimination of persistent *organic pollutants* (POPs), other chemicals of equivalent concern and *toxic* heavy metals. **Structure** General Assembly; Steering Committee; Executive Committee; Regional Hubs; Working Groups (6). **Languages** Arabic, Chinese, English, French, Russian, Spanish. **Activities** Events/meetings; networking/liaising; projects/programmes. **Events** *Global Meeting and Forum* Bishoftu (Ethiopia) 2020, *Global Meeting* San Francisco, CA (USA) 2016, *General Assembly* Kunming (China) 2014, *General Assembly* Petrópolis (Brazil) 2012, *General Assembly* Almaty (Kazakhstan) 2010. **Publications** Reports; guides; brochures; video. **Members** Public interest NGOs (about 600) in 125 countries and territories. Membership countries not specified. **Consultative Status** Consultative status granted from: *ECOSOC (#05331)* (Special); *UNEP (#20299)*. **IGO Relations** Cooperates with (5): *Global Environment Facility (GEF, #10346)*; *Strategic Approach to International Chemicals Management (SAICM, #20005)*; *UNIDO (#20336)*; *United Nations Commission on Sustainable Development (CSD, inactive)*; *United Nations Institute for Training and Research (UNITAR, #20576)*. [2022.05.10/XF4753/**F**]

♦ International Polo Federation / see Federation of International Polo (#09675)

♦ International Polychaetology Association 14617

Contact c/o Invertebrate Biodiversity, National Museum Cardiff, Cathays Park, Cardiff, CF10 3NP, UK. T. +442920573311.
URL: http://www.polychaeteassoc.com/

History 18 Aug 1986, Copenhagen (Denmark). 18-23 Aug 1986, Copenhagen (Denmark), during 2nd international polychaete conference. **Aims** Encourage research on polychaeta and stimulate others to participate and cooperate through informal meetings and correspondence. **Structure** Officers: President, Vice-President, Secretary, Treasurer. Advisory Council, consisting of one member from each of the following countries: Australia, Brazil, Canada, France, Germany, Italy, Japan, Spain, Thailand, USA, USSR. **Languages** English. **Staff** No paid staff members. **Finance** Source: excess funds generated from triennial meetings. Annual budget: 2,000 USD. **Activities** Organizes conferences. **Events** *International Polychaete Conference* Stellenbosch (South Africa) 2023, *International Polychaete Conference* Long Beach, CA (USA) 2019, *International Polychaete Conference* Cardiff (UK) 2016, *Triennial International Polychaete Conference / Triennial Conference* Sydney, NSW (Australia) 2013, *Triennial international polychaete conference / Triennial Conference* Lecce (Italy) 2010. **Publications** Conference proceedings.
Members Individuals in 29 countries and territories:
Argentina, Australia, Brazil, Canada, Chile, China, Colombia, Croatia, Denmark, France, Germany, India, Indonesia, Ireland, Israel, Italy, Japan, Malaysia, Mexico, Netherlands, New Zealand, Norway, Panama, Spain, Sweden, Taiwan, Thailand, UK, USA.
NGO Relations Scientific member of: *International Union of Biological Sciences (IUBS, #15760)*. [2016/XD0989/v/**C**]

♦ International Polymer Characterization Forum (meeting series)
♦ International Polymer Processing Society / see Polymer Processing Society (#18426)

♦ International Pompe Association (IPA) 14618

Address not obtained.
URL: http://www.worldpompe.org/

History 4 Jul 1999, Naarden (Netherlands), at 1st official meeting, following discussion at Dutch Congenital and Metabolic Diagnosis Group, 20 Mar 1998. Registered in accordance with Dutch law. **Aims** Assure early diagnosis, effective, affordable and safe treatment and *therapy*, reliable information and support to all patients with Pompe's disease – an inherited and often fatal disorder caused by *mutations* in a *gene* that makes the *enzyme* alpha-glucosidase (GAA) – and to their families. **Structure** General Assembly (annual); Board. Committees (5): Patient Organization; Scientific; Legal; Website/Internet; Financial. Secretariat. **Finance** Members' dues. **Activities** Knowledge management/information dissemination; research/documentation. **Events** *Conference* USA 2000, *Conference* Naarden (Netherlands) 1999.
Members Full; Associate. Full in 9 countries:
Australia, Germany, Greece, Japan, Mexico, Netherlands, South Africa, UK, USA.
Associate in 3 countries and territories:
Canada, Germany, Taiwan.
NGO Relations Formal contacts with: *European Alliance of Neuromuscular Disorders Associations (EAMDA, #05876)*. [2019/XD7175/**E**]

♦ International Pony Breeders Federation (inactive)

♦ International Poplar Commission (IPC) 14619

Commission internationale du peuplier (CIP) – Comisión Internacional del Alamo – Internationale Pappel-Kommission

Secretariat FAO Forestry Dept, Via delle Terme di Caracalla, 00153 Rome RM, Italy. E-mail: ipc-secretariat@fao.org.
URL: http://www.fao.org/forestry/ipc/en/

History Apr 1947, Paris (France), under the auspices of the Government of France, as a technical statutory body of *FAO (#09260)*, under Article XIV of its Constitution, under Convention approved by Conference of FAO, 19 Nov 1959; came into force 26 Sep 1961. Convention amended by 3rd Special Session of the Commission, 15 Nov 1977, and approved by the 19th Session of FAO Conference, 12 Nov-1 Dec 1977. **Aims** Promote cultivation, conservation and utilization of poplars and *willows* of the *Salicaceae* family. **Structure** Session (every 4 years); Executive Committee; Working Parties (6). **Languages** English, French, Spanish. **Staff** Based at FAO Secretariat, Rome (Italy): 0.5 FTE, paid. **Finance** Secretariat financed through FAO of United Nations budget allocations. National Poplar Commissions, Working Parties and Executive Committee Members are self-financed. **Activities** Knowledge management/information dissemination; research and development; events/meetings. **Events** *Quadrennial Session* Berlin (Germany) 2016, *Quadrennial Session* Dehra Dun (India) 2012, *Quadrennial Session* Beijing (China) 2008, *Quadrennial session* Santiago (Chile) 2004, *Quadrennial session* Portland, OR (USA) 2000. **Publications** Session reports; technical reports. Online publications.
Members FAO Member Nations or Associate Members who accept the Convention. Currently governments of 38 countries:
Argentina, Austria, Belgium, Bulgaria, Canada, Chile, China, Croatia, Czechia, Egypt, Finland, France, Germany, Hungary, India, Iran Islamic Rep, Iraq, Ireland, Italy, Japan, Korea Rep, Lebanon, Morocco, Netherlands, New Zealand, Pakistan, Portugal, Romania, Slovenia, South Africa, Spain, Sweden, Switzerland, Syrian AR, Tunisia, Türkiye, UK, USA.
IGO Relations Comes within the family of statutory bodies of FAO related to the Committee on Forestry, 6 Regional Forestry Commissions and the other 3 technical statutory bodies of FAO. Member of: *Collaborative Partnership on Forests (CPF, #04100)*. [2017/XE2371/**E***]

♦ International POPs Elimination Network / see International Pollutants Elimination Network (#14616)

♦ International Population Data Linkage Network (IPDLN) 14620

Co-Dir c/o ADRUK ESRC, Polaris House, North Star Ave, Swindon, SN2 1UJ, UK. E-mail: info@ipdln.org.
URL: https://www.ipdln.org/

History 2008, UK. Former names and other names: *International Health Data Linkage Network (IHDLN)* – former (2008). **Aims** Specialize communication between centres that specialise in data linkage and users of the linked data. **Structure** Executive Committee. **Activities** Events/meetings; training/education. **Events** *International Population Data Linkage Conference* Chicago, IL (USA) 2024, *International Population Data Linkage Conference* Edinburgh (UK) 2022, *International Population Data Linkage Conference* 2020, *IPDLN Conference* Adelaide, SA (Australia) 2020, *International Population Data Linkage Conference* Banff, AB (Canada) 2018. **Publications** *International Journal of Population Data Science (IJPDS).*
Members Centres in 55 countries and territories:
Algeria, Argentina, Australia, Austria, Bangladesh, Belgium, Brazil, Cameroon, Canada, Central African Rep, Denmark, Estonia, Finland, France, Germany, Ghana, Greece, Iceland, India, Ireland, Italy, Japan, Kenya, Korea Rep, Latvia, Lithuania, Malaysia, Malta, Mexico, Myanmar, Nepal, Netherlands, New Zealand, Nicaragua, Nigeria, Norway, Pakistan, Palestine, Poland, Portugal, Russia, Rwanda, Saudi Arabia, Singapore, South Africa, Spain, Sweden, Switzerland, Taiwan, Tanzania UR, Uganda, UK, United Arab Emirates, USA, Zimbabwe. [2022/AA0480/F]

♦ International Porphyria Patient Network (IPPN) 14621

Contact address not obtained. E-mail: ippn@porphyria.network.
URL: https://porphyria.network/IPPN/
History 6 Sep 2018, Switzerland. **Aims** Offer cross-border support and counselling of patients suffering from porphyria and porphyria patient associations in scientific, medical and healthcare policy matters with special attention to the international promotion; safeguard their interests in regulatory, national and supranational approval processes of related therapies. **Structure** Board of Directors. **Languages** English, French, German, Italian, Swedish. **NGO Relations** Member of (1): *EURORDIS – Rare Diseases Europe (#09175)* (Associate). [2022.10.29/XM7457/F]

♦ **International PORSEC Association** International Pan Ocean Remote Sensing Conference Association (#14510)

♦ International Portable Sanitation Working Group (IPSWG) 14622

Contact c/o PSAI, 2626 E 82nd St, Ste 175, Bloomington MN 55425, USA. T. +19528548300. Fax +19528547560. E-mail: info@psai.org.
History 1996.
Members Organizations, including 2 listed in this Yearbook:
Portable Sanitation Association International (PSAI); Portable Sanitation Europe (PSE).
NGO Relations Secretariat provided by *Portable Sanitation Association International (PSAI).* [2009/XJ8163/E]

♦ International Port Community Systems Association (IPCSA) 14623

SG The Chapel, Maybush Lane, Felixstowe, IP11 7LL, UK. T. +447796334960.
URL: http://www.ipcsa.international/
History Launched Jun 2011, as *European Port Community Systems Association (ECPSA).* Current title adopted Sep 2014. An organization of the type *European Economic Interest Grouping (EEIG, #06960).* Registered in accordance with UK law: GB 135 735606. **Aims** Influence public policy at international level, principally by lobbying, so as to promote the adoption of e-logistics as the key element in the development of international *maritime*, shipping and logistics sectors. **Structure** Executive; Executive Committee; Committees.
Members Full in 18 countries:
Australia, Belgium, Benin, France, Germany, Indonesia, Israel, Italy, Korea Rep, Latvia, Morocco, Netherlands, Portugal, Spain, Togo, UK, Ukraine, United Arab Emirates.
Associate organizations (2):
Federation of National Associations of Shipbrokers and Agents (FONASBA, #09694); International Network of Customs Universities (INCU, #14248).
Consultative Status Consultative status granted from: *International Maritime Organization (IMO, #14102); ECOSOC (#05331)* (Special). [2017/XM6510/D]

♦ International Post Corporation (IPC) 14624

Pres/CEO Avenue du Bourget 44, 1130 Brussels, Belgium. T. +3227247211. Fax +3227260425. E-mail: info@ipc.be.
URL: http://www.ipc.be/
History Founded 1988, as a cooperative holding company registered in the Netherlands. Registered as an operational cooperative subsidiary company in Belgium. **Aims** Set standards for upgrading quality and service performance; develop technology helping members improve service for international letters, parcels, express and e-commerce. **Structure** Board of CEOs. *IPC Technology (inactive).* **Languages** English. **Staff** 60.00 FTE, paid. **Activities** Events/meetings. **Publications** *Market Flash* (bi-weekly) – newsletter; *Regulatory Flash* (10 a year); *Focus on the Future* (annual); *IPC Annual Review.* Reports. **Information Services** *Data Analysis and Control System (DACS)* – analyses UNEX data.
Members Shareholders are national postal services of 24 countries:
Australia, Austria, Belgium, Canada, Cyprus, Denmark, Finland, France, Germany, Greece, Hungary, Iceland, Ireland, Italy, Luxembourg, Netherlands, New Zealand, Norway, Portugal, Spain, Sweden, Switzerland, UK, USA. [2016/XK0281/e/F]

♦ International Postgraduate Organization for Knowledge Transfer Research and Teaching Excellent Students (IPOKRaTES) 14625

Head Office c/o mcon – mannheim:congress GmbH, Rosengartenplatz 2, 68161 Mannheim, Germany. T. +496214106134. Fax +49621410680134. E-mail: lenhart.anja@gmail.com – ipokrates@mcon-mannheim.de.
URL: https://www.ipokrates.org/
History Founded by Dr Georg Simbruner. Registration: Germany. **Aims** Provide the best possible postgraduate education in the field of biomedical sciences; increase transfer and exchange of scientific knowledge worldwide. **Languages** English. **Staff** 0.50 FTE, paid; 20.00 FTE, voluntary. **Finance** Sources: members' dues. Supported by companies. **Activities** Events/meetings; knowledge management/information dissemination; training/education. **Events** *BEST of IPOKRaTES : An Update in Neonatology* Leuven (Belgium) 2023, *Neonatal Hemodynamics* Porto (Portugal) 2023, *Care of the Extremely Low Birth Weight Infant* Yogyakarta (Indonesia) 2023, *Seminar on Protecting and Developing the Brain* Takamatsu (Japan) 2019, *Seminar* Amsterdam (Netherlands) 2017. **NGO Relations** Cooperates with (2): *European Society for Paediatric Research (ESPR, #08687); Union of European Neonatal and Perinatal Societies (UENPS, #20389).* [2023.02.28/XD8932/D]

♦ International Post-Partum Mental Health and Social Support Network / see Postpartum Support, International
♦ International Post and Telecommunications Tourist and Cultural Union (inactive)

♦ International Potash Institute (IPI) 14626

Institut international de la potasse – Instituto Internacional de la Potasa – Internationales Kali-Institut
Dir Industriestr 31, 6300 Zug, Switzerland. T. +41438104922. Fax +41438104925. E-mail: ipi@ipipotash.org.
Registered Office Baumgärtlistrasse 17, 8810 Horgen ZH, Switzerland.
URL: http://www.ipipotash.org/
History 1952, Bern (Switzerland). Founded by German and French potash fertilizer producers. Located in Bern since the foundation of the Institute, the IPI Head Office was transferred to Basel (Switzerland) in 1992 and transferred to Horgen (Switzerland), 2005. Registration: Switzerland. **Aims** Stimulate and coordinate research on *soil fertility* and *fertilizer* use, especially potash *fertilizers* worldwide; publish the results internationally. **Structure** General Assembly (annual). Administrative Board of 9 members. Technical Secretariat of 9 members. **Languages** English. **Staff** 2.00 FTE, paid. **Finance** Members' dues. **Activities** Carries out regional projects to promote balanced fertilization in agriculture; organizes and supports scientific meetings; organizes workshops and seminars; K-documentation; publishing activity. **Events** *Intenational symposium on soil management and potash fertilizer uses in West Asia and North Asia region* Antalya (Turkey) 2010, *International symposium on the importance of soil management and potash for sustainable agricultural development of Central America and Caribbean* San Salvador (El Salvador) 2010, *International conference on nutrient management and nutrient demand of energy plants* Budapest (Hungary) 2009, *Apple fertigation workshop* China 2008, *Joint workshop on balanced fertilization for optimizing plant nutrition* Sharm el Sheikh (Egypt) 2007. **Publications** *International Fertilizer Correspondent (e-ife)* (4 a year) in English – electronic; *IPI Bulletin. IPI Research Topics* – series. *Soil Fertility and Nutritional Status of Alfalfa Growth in Tropical Regions* (2007) in Portuguese; *Training Manual on Role of Balanced Fertilization for Horticultural Crops.* Monographs; brochures; congress and colloquium proceedings.
Members Companies (5) in 4 countries:
Belgium, Germany, Israel, Russia (2).
Consultative Status Consultative status granted from: *ECOSOC (#05331)* (Ros C). **NGO Relations** Cooperates with: *International Fertilizer Development Center (IFDC, #13590).* [2021/XE2373/j/E]

♦ International Potato Center 14627

Centre international de la pomme de terre (CIP) – Centro Internacional de la Papa (CIP)
Acting Gen Dir Apartado Postal 1558, Lima, Peru. E-mail: cip@cgiar.org.
URL: https://cipotato.org/
History 20 Jan 1971, Lima (Peru). Included, 1972, under auspices of the *CGIAR System Organization (CGIAR, #03843).* Registration: Peru. **Aims** Deliver innovative science-based solutions to enhance access to affordable nutritious food, foster inclusive sustainable business and employment growth, and drive the climate resilience of root and tuber agri-food systems. **Structure** Board of Trustees; Regional Offices (4). **Languages** English, French, Spanish. **Finance** Grants through CGIAR. **Activities** Research and development; training/education; knowledge management/information dissemination. **Events** *International late blight conference / Conference* Beijing (China) 2008, *International symposium on potatoes for development* Cusco (Peru) 2005, *NGOs consultation on the mountain agenda* Lima (Peru) 1995, *Workshop on the potato in the Mediterranean region* Saragossa (Spain) 1990, *International symposium on intercropping of potato in the tropics* Kunming (China) 1988. **Publications** Annual report; specialized technical reports and training materials. **Members** Not a membership body. **IGO Relations** Member of: *International Fund for Agricultural Development (IFAD, #13692); International Information System for the Agricultural Sciences and Technology (AGRIS, #13848).* **NGO Relations** Member of: *Extractive Industries Transparency Initiative (EITI, #09229); Mountain Forum (MF, #16861); Mountain Partnership (MP, #16862).* Provides secretariat for: *Consortium for the Sustainable Development of the Andean Ecoregion (#04758).* Instrumental in setting up: *Potato and Sweet Potato Research Network of Eastern and Central Africa (inactive); USAID/SADC/IITA/CIP Southern Africa Root Crops Research Network (SARRNET, #20734).* Cooperates with the other CGIAR supported centres: *Center for International Forestry Research (CIFOR, #03646); International Centre for Tropical Agriculture (#12527); International Food Policy Research Institute (IFPRI, #13622); International Institute of Tropical Agriculture (IITA, #13933); International Maize and Wheat Improvement Center (#14077); International Water Management Institute (IWMI, #15867); World Agroforestry Centre (ICRAF, #21072); WorldFish (#21507).* [2021/XE4103/E]

♦ International Poultry Council (IPC) 14628

SG 2300 West Park Place Blvd, Ste 100, Stone Mountain GA 30087, USA. E-mail: info@internationalpoultrycouncil.org.
URL: http://www.internationalpoultrycouncil.org/
History Founded 7 Oct 2005, Cologne (Germany). **Aims** Strengthen communication between countries; develop and implement policy for international organizations affecting the world's poultry industry; promote a common understanding of, and confidence in, poultry products in the world. **Staff** 1.00 FTE, paid. **Events** *Spring Meeting* Bordeaux (France) 2021, *Spring Meeting* Bordeaux (France) 2020, *Spring Meeting* New Orleans, LA (USA) 2019, *Fall Meeting* Nanjing (China) 2018, *Spring Meeting* Noordwijk (Netherlands) 2018.
Members Country Members (22); Associate (44). Members in 21 countries:
Australia, Brazil, Canada, Chile, China, Colombia, Egypt, Germany, Honduras, Italy, Mexico, New Zealand, Nicaragua, Nigeria, Panama, Russia, South Africa, Thailand, Türkiye, UK, USA.
Included in the above, 2 regional organizations:
Asociación Latinoamericana de Avicultura (ALA, #02185); Association de l'aviculture, de l'industrie et du commerce de volailles dans les pays de l'Union européenne (AVEC, #02390).
IGO Relations Observer status with: *Codex Alimentarius Commission (CAC, #04081); FAO (#09260); OIE – World Organisation for Animal Health (#17703).* **NGO Relations** Memorandum of Understanding with (1): *International Egg Commission (IEC, #13245).* Cooperates with: *International Feed Industry Federation (IFIF, #13581)* through Livestock Sector Consortium (Private Sector Steering Committee – PSSC Livestock). Partner of: *Livestock Environmental Assessment and Performance Partnership (LEAP, #16500).* [2020/XM1298/y/C]

♦ International Poverty Reduction Center in China (unconfirmed)
♦ International Powerball Federation (#13251)
♦ International Powerboating Federation (#20431)

♦ International Powered Access Federation (IPAF) 14629

Dir Moss End Business Village, Crooklands, Milnthorpe, LA7 7NU, UK. T. +441539566700. Fax +441539566084. E-mail: info@ipaf.org.
URL: http://www.ipaf.org/
History 1 Nov 1983, London (UK). Founded on merger of *International Work Platform Association (IWPA, inactive)*, created Sep 1976, and *International Federation of Hydraulic Platform Manufacturers (IFHPM, inactive)*, set up Jan 1977. Registration: No/ID: 30998R, England and Wales. **Aims** Promote and extend the use of members' products; take action on matters of interest to the powered access *equipment industry*; encourage high standards of safety and good trading by members; promote safety training for operators; represent the industry in discussions at government level in user countries; liaise with other trade associations; encourage technical efficiency by cooperation in the establishment of standards and the discussion of common problems. **Structure** General Assembly (annual). Approved Training Centres (over 600 worldwide). **Languages** Dutch, English, French, German, Italian, Portuguese, Spanish. **Staff** 20.00 FTE, paid. **Finance** Members' dues. Proceeds from training programmes. **Activities** Standards/guidelines; training/education. **Events** *Summit* London (UK) 2022, *Asia Conference* Seoul (Korea Rep) 2020, *Summit* Dubai (United Arab Emirates) 2019, *Asia Conference* Hangzhou (China) 2019, *Europlatform Access Rental Conference* Nice (France) 2019. **Publications** *IPAF Bulletin – Access International* (10 a year); *Raising the Standard* (2 a year); *IPAF Elevating Safety* (annual); *IPAF Informazione* (annual) in Italian; *IPAF Journal* (annual) in German; *IPAF Powered Access* (annual). *IPAF MEWPS Operators Safety Guide; IPAF Site Safety Guide for MCWPs.* Annual Report; Powered Access Rental Market Reports for Europe and the USA.
Members Members (over 1,000) in 56 countries and territories:
Argentina, Australia, Austria, Belgium, Brazil, Bulgaria, Canada, Chile, China, Colombia, Czechia, Denmark, Finland, France, Germany, Hong Kong, Hungary, India, Indonesia, Ireland, Italy, Japan, Jordan, Korea Rep, Kuwait, Liechtenstein, Lithuania, Luxembourg, Malaysia, Mexico, Morocco, Netherlands, New Zealand, Norway, Paraguay, Peru, Poland, Portugal, Qatar, Romania, Russia, Saudi Arabia, Singapore, Slovenia, South Africa, Spain, Sweden, Switzerland, Taiwan, Thailand, Tunisia, Türkiye, UK, United Arab Emirates, Uruguay, USA.
NGO Relations Member of: American Rental Association (ARA). [2020/XD4154/D]

♦ International Power Engineering Association (inactive)

♦ International Powerlifting Federation (IPF) 14630

Sec Route d'Arlon 3, L-8009 Strassen, Luxembourg. T. +35226389114. E-mail: office@powerlifting.sport.
URL: https://www.powerlifting.sport/
History 11 Nov 1972, Harrisburg, PA (USA). Former names and other names: *Fédération internationale de powerlifting (FIP)* – former. **Aims** Group all eligible amateur clubs, organizations or other bodies world-wide active in powerlifting; establish and enforce rules which govern international amateur powerlifting; establish and maintain a system for recognizing and approving records. **Structure** General Assembly; Executive Committee; Commissions. **Languages** English. **Staff** 1.00 FTE, paid; 10.00 FTE, voluntary. **Finance** Sources: partnership; sponsorship; TV contracts. **Activities** Projects/programmes; sporting activities. **Events** *Annual Congress* Pilsen (Czech Rep) 2011, *Annual Congress* Potchefstroom (South Africa) 2010, *Annual Congress* Delhi (India) 2009, *Annual Congress* St John's, NL (Canada) 2008, *Annual Congress* Sölden (Austria) 2007. **Publications** *The IPF Magazine.*
Members Full in 136 countries and territories:
Afghanistan, Algeria, Anguilla, Argentina, Armenia, Aruba, Australia, Austria, Bahamas, Bangladesh, Belarus, Belgium, Belize, Benin, Brazil, Brunei Darussalam, Bulgaria, Cameroon, Canada, Cape Verde, Cayman Is, Central African Rep, Chile, China, Colombia, Costa Rica, Côte d'Ivoire, Croatia, Cyprus, Czechia, Denmark, Dominican Rep, Ecuador, Egypt, El Salvador, Estonia, Fiji, Finland, France, Gambia, Georgia, Germany, Ghana, Great Britain, Greece, Guatemala, Guyana, Haiti, Hong Kong, Hungary,

Iceland, India, Indonesia, Iran Islamic Rep, Iraq, Ireland, Israel, Italy, Jamaica, Japan, Jordan, Kazakhstan, Kiribati, Korea Rep, Kuwait, Kyrgyzstan, Latvia, Lebanon, Libya, Lithuania, Luxembourg, Malaysia, Malta, Marshall Is, Mexico, Mongolia, Morocco, Namibia, Nauru, Netherlands, New Caledonia, New Zealand, Nicaragua, Nigeria, Niue, Norway, Oman, Pakistan, Palestine, Panama, Papua New Guinea, Paraguay, Peru, Philippines, Poland, Portugal, Puerto Rico, Romania, Russia, Samoa, Serbia, Sierra Leone, Singapore, Slovakia, Slovenia, Solomon Is, Somalia, South Africa, Spain, Sri Lanka, Suriname, Sweden, Switzerland, Syrian AR, Tahiti Is, Taiwan, Tajikistan, Thailand, Togo, Tonga, Trinidad-Tobago, Tunisia, Türkiye, Turkmenistan, Tuvalu, Uganda, Ukraine, United Arab Emirates, Uruguay, USA, Uzbekistan, Venezuela, Vietnam, Virgin Is UK, Virgin Is USA, Zimbabwe.

Regional federations (6):
African Powerlifting Federation (APF, #00422); Asian Powerlifting Federation (APF, #01671); European Powerlifting Federation (EPF, #08262); Federación Sudamericana de Powerlifting (FESUPO, #09393); North American Powerlifting Federation (NAPF, #17568); Oceania Regional Powerlifting Federation (ORPF, #17671).
NGO Relations Member of (6): *Alliance of Independent recognised Members of Sport (AIMS, #00690); International Masters Games Association (IMGA, #14117); International University Sports Federation (FISU, #15830); International World Games Association (IWGA, #15914); Olympic Movement (#17719); World Anti-Doping Agency (WADA, #21096).* Recognized by: *International Olympic Committee (IOC, #14408).*
[2022/XD4412/y/**B**]

♦ International Poxvirus and Iridovirus Conference (meeting series)
♦ International Practical Scientific Legal Centre (unconfirmed)

♦ International Practical Shooting Confederation (IPSC) 14631

Main Office Carretera Vieja de Bunyola – KM 6,2, 07141 Marratxí, Spain. T. +349058496960. E-mail: info@ipsc.org.
URL: http://www.ipsc.org/

History May 1976, Columbia, MO (USA). **Aims** Promote, maintain, improve and advance practical shooting. **Structure** General Assembly (annual). Executive Council. **Events** *General Assembly* Belgrade (Serbia) 2019, *General Assembly* Lakeland, FL (USA) 2014, *General Assembly* Pattaya (Thailand) 2013, *General Assembly* Asunción (Paraguay) 2012, *General Assembly* Rhodes Is (Greece) 2011.
Members National organizations (11) in 11 countries and territories:
Australia, Brazil, Canada, Denmark, Finland, Hong Kong, Hungary, Netherlands, Norway, Switzerland, USA.
NGO Relations Member of (3): *Alliance of Independent recognised Members of Sport (AIMS, #00690); Olympic Movement (#17719); World Forum on Shooting Activities (WFSA, #21523).* Recognized by: *International Olympic Committee (IOC, #14408).* [2021/XF4560/**C**]

♦ International Practice Group (IPG) 14632

Address not obtained.
URL: http://www.ipg-online.org/

History 1992, UK, as *EU-Lex IPG.* Current title adopted to reflect international status. Merged with *Picatrex*, Jan 2009. Subtitle *Leading International Association of Lawyers, Accountants and Tax Specialists.* **Aims** Provide cooperation on, and referral of, work between members. **Structure** Management Committee; Secretariat. **Events** *Conference* Florence (Italy) 2022, *Conference* Oslo (Norway) 2019, *Conference* Lisbon (Portugal) 2017, *Conference* Paris (France) 2015, *Conference* Dubai (United Arab Emirates) 2014. **NGO Relations** *LEX Africa (#16449).* [2011/XJ2662/**F**]

♦ International Prader-Willi Syndrome Organisation (IPWSO) 14633

Communications Manager Salisbury House, Station Road, Cambridge, CB1 2LA, UK. E-mail: office@ipwso.org.
URL: http://www.ipwso.org/

History 1991, Netherlands. Founded 1991 at 1st International PWS Conference. Registration: No/ID: 1182873, Start date: 2019, England and Wales; Start date: 1993, Sweden. **Aims** Unite the global PWS community to collectively find solutions to the challenges of the syndrome; support and advocate for people with PWS and their families, PWS associations, and professionals who work with people with PWS. **Structure** Board of Trustees. **Languages** English. **Staff** 3.00 FTE, paid. **Finance** Sources: fundraising; grants; members' dues. **Activities** Events/meetings. **Events** *International Conference* Limerick (Ireland) 2022, *International Conference* Havana (Cuba) 2019, *International Conference* Toronto, ON (Canada) 2016, *International Conference* Cambridge (UK) 2013, *International Conference* Taipei (Taiwan) 2010. **Publications** *Medical Alerts* – booklets, translated into several languages.
Members Paid members representing 44 countries. Membership countries not specified.
Associated members representing over 100 countries. Membership countries not specified.
NGO Relations Member of (6): *British Overseas NGO's for Development (BOND); EURORDIS – Rare Diseases Europe (#09175); Global Genes* (RARE Foundation Alliance); *Healthcare Information For All (HIFA, #10878); International Conference on Rare Diseases and Orphan Drugs (ICORD Society, #12886); Rare Diseases International (RDI, #18621).* [2022.10.20/XE1916/**E**]

♦ International Pragmatics Association (IPrA) 14634

Association internationale de pragmatique

Gen Sec Lange Lozanastraat 85 – Box 15, 2018 Antwerp, Belgium. T. +3232301680. E-mail: info@pragmatics.international.
Exec Sec address not obtained.
URL: https://pragmatics.international/

History 1 Jan 1986. Constitution adopted Oct 1987. Registration: Belgium. **Aims** Represent the field of pragmatics in its widest interdisciplinary sense as a functional (cognitive, social and cultural) perspective on language and communication (science of language use). **Structure** Executive Committee; Consultation Board. **Languages** English. **Staff** 1.00 FTE, paid. **Finance** Sources: meeting proceeds; members' dues. **Activities** Events/meetings; research/documentation; training/education. **Events** *International Pragmatics Conference* Brussels (Belgium) 2023, *International Pragmatics Conference* Winterthur (Switzerland) 2021, *International Pragmatics Conference* Hong Kong (Hong Kong) 2019, *International Pragmatics Conference* Belfast (UK) 2017, *International Pragmatics Conference* Antwerp (Belgium) 2015. **Publications** *Pragmatics* (4 a year). *Bibliography of Pragmatics; Handbook of Pragmatics.*
Members Individuals in 73 countries and territories:
Algeria, Argentina, Australia, Austria, Belgium, Bosnia-Herzegovina, Brazil, Brunei Darussalam, Bulgaria, Canada, Chile, China, Colombia, Congo DR, Croatia, Czechia, Denmark, Egypt, Finland, France, Germany, Ghana, Greece, Hong Kong, Hungary, Iceland, Indonesia, Iraq, Ireland, Israel, Italy, Japan, Jordan, Kenya, Korea Rep, Libya, Lithuania, Luxembourg, Mexico, Morocco, Netherlands, New Zealand, Niger, Nigeria, Norway, Palestine, Papua New Guinea, Poland, Portugal, Romania, Russia, Saudi Arabia, Serbia, Singapore, Slovakia, Slovenia, South Africa, Spain, Sweden, Switzerland, Syrian AR, Taiwan, Tanzania UR, Thailand, Tunisia, Türkiye, Uganda, UK, Ukraine, Uruguay, USA, Venezuela, Vietnam. [2022.10.18/XB0053/**B**]

♦ International Precious Metals Institute (internationally oriented national body)

♦ International Presentation Association (IPA) 14635

Contact PBVM, 1011 First Ave, Ste 1313, New York NY 10022, USA. T. +16467943093. E-mail: pbvmipa@msn.com.
IPA Networker PBVM, 2360 Carter Road, Dubuque IA 52001, USA. T. +15635823801. E-mail: imanetworker@gmail.com.
URL: http://internationalpresentationassociation.org/

History As a network of congregations of *Presentation Sisters of the Blessed Virgin Mary (PBVM).* **Aims** Channel resources so as to speak and act in partnership with others for global *justice.* **Structure** General Assembly; Presentation Units (3). **Members** Women (2,200) in 22 countries. Membership countries not specified. **Consultative Status** Consultative status granted from: *ECOSOC (#05331)* (Special). **IGO Relations** Associated with Department of Global Communications of the United Nations. **NGO Relations** Full member of: *NGO Committee on Financing for Development, New York (#17108).* Member of: *Conference of Non-Governmental Organizations in Consultative Relationship with the United Nations (CONGO, #04635); Mining Working Group at the UN (MWG, #16813); NGO Committee to Stop Trafficking in Persons (NGO CSTIP).*
[2016.07.14/XG6249/**F**]

♦ International Press Association (#02868)
♦ International Press Association for Development of Habitat (inactive)
♦ International Press Centre (internationally oriented national body)

♦ International Press Institute (IPI) 14636

Institut international de la presse (IIP) – Instituto Internacional de la Prensa – Internationales Presse Institut – Mezdunarodnyj Institut Pressy

Contact IPI Head Office, Spiegelgasse 2, 1010 Vienna, Austria. T. +4315129011. Fax +4315129014. E-mail: info@ipi.media.
URL: https://ipi.media/

History 1950, New York, NY (USA). First General Assembly: 1952, Paris (France). Amendments to constitution: May 2000, Boston MA (USA); May 2013, Amman (Jordan). Registered in accordance with Swiss law. Subsequently registered in Austria, according to special law on IPI of 26 Jun 1992. Registration: EU Transparency Register, No/ID: 370877536078-58, Start date: 2 Oct 2019. **Aims** Further and safeguard media freedom – free access to news, free expression of views, free publication of newspapers; achieve understanding among journalists and so among peoples; promote free exchange of accurate and balanced news among nations; improve the practice of journalism. **Structure** General Assembly (annual, at World Congress); Executive Board; Secretariat; National Committees. **Languages** English, French, German, Italian, Spanish. **Staff** 9.00 FTE, paid. 1-3 FTE, voluntary. **Finance** Members' dues. Other sources: congress fees; contributions; grants from foundations; project work. **Activities** Knowledge management/information dissemination; research/documentation; events/meetings. **Events** *Annual General Assembly and World Congress* Vienna (Austria) 2021, *Annual General Assembly and World Congress* Vienna (Austria) 2020, *Annual General Assembly and World Congress* Geneva (Switzerland) 2019, *Annual General Assembly and World Congress* Abuja (Nigeria) 2018, *Annual General Assembly and World Congress* Hamburg (Germany) 2017. **Publications** Reports; studies; manuals and trainings; declarations; resolutions; special issue publications.
Members Individual – Full: those responsible for editorial and news policies of newspapers, magazines, broadcasting organizations and news agencies; Associate: those whose work is associated with editorial aspects of journalism. Individual members in 120 countries. Membership countries not specified. National Committees in 19 countries:
National Committees in 19 countries:
Azerbaijan, Bangladesh, Finland, Georgia, Germany, India, Japan, Kazakhstan, Korea Rep, Kyrgyzstan, Nepal, Nigeria, Norway, Pakistan, Slovakia, Taiwan, Türkiye, UK, USA.
Consultative Status Consultative status granted from: *ECOSOC (#05331)* (Special); *UNESCO (#20322)* (Associate Status); *Council of Europe (CE, #04881)* (Participatory Status). **NGO Relations** Accredited by (1): *International News Safety Institute (INSI, #14364).* Member of (3): *Committee of NGOs on Human Rights, Geneva (#04275); Ethical Journalism Network (EJN, #05554); IFEX (#11100).* Cooperates with (2): *Association of Caribbean Media Workers (ACM, #02408); South East Europe Media Organisation (SEEMO, #19823).*
[2020/XB2375/jv/**F**]

♦ International Press Telecommunications Committee / see International Press Telecommunications Council (#14637)

♦ International Press Telecommunications Council (IPTC) 14637

Comité international des télécommunications de presse (CITP) – Consejo Internacional de Telecomunicaciones de Prensa

Managing Dir 25 Southampton Buildings, London, WC2A 1AL, UK. T. +442031784922. E-mail: office@iptc.org.
URL: http://www.iptc.org/

History Founded 22 Sep 1965, London (UK), as *International Press Telecommunications Committee* following consultation between *CPU Media Trust (#04941), World Association of Newspapers (WAN, inactive)* and American Newspaper Publishers Association (ANPA). Present name adopted 1969. Constitution revised, 1978, to allow associations of newspapers, news agencies and news photo agencies, as well as individual newspapers, groups of newspapers, news agencies and news photo agencies to become nominating organizations. Registered in accordance with UK law. **Aims** Simplify distribution of information by developing and promoting efficient technical standards to improve the management and exchange of information between content providers, intermediaries and consumers, thereby enabling an easy, cost-effective and rapid innovation. **Structure** Annual General Meetings; Board of Directors; Committees (2); Working Parties; Office located in London (UK). **Languages** English. **Staff** 1.00 FTE, paid. **Finance** Sources: members' dues. **Activities** Events/meetings; knowledge management/information dissemination. **Events** *Autumn Meeting* London (UK) 2021, *Spring Meeting* Tallinn (Estonia) 2021, *Autumn Meeting* London (UK) 2020, *Spring Meeting* London (UK) 2020, *Photo Metadata Conference* Palma (Spain) 2020. **Publications** Technical specifications and guidelines for implementation.
Members Nominating organizations: news agencies, photo agencies, newspapers and other news providers; Associates (non-voting). Members in 21 countries:
Austria, China, Czechia, Egypt, Finland, France, Germany, Greece, Italy, Korea Rep, Kuwait, Norway, Portugal, Qatar, Russia, Slovenia, Spain, Sweden, Switzerland, UK, USA.
Associated members include 1 organization listed in this Yearbook:
Coordination of European Picture Agencies, Press Stock Heritage (CEPIC, #04825).
Consultative Status Consultative status granted from: *ECOSOC (#05331)* (Ros C). [2021/XC2626/y/**C**]

♦ International Press Union for Peace (inactive)

♦ International Prestressed Hollowcore Association (IPHA) 14638

Exec Dir Rue d'Arlon 55, 6th floor, 1040 Brussels, Belgium. T. +4550512120.
URL: http://www.hollowcore.org/

History 1969. Former names and other names: *International Spiroll Producers Association (ISPA)* – former (1969 to 1986); *International Extruded Concrete Association (IECA)* – former (1986 to 1993). **Aims** Promote exchange of experience among members; promote and fund research and development in the industry; ensure that members' interests are met in the drafting and review of new codes and *standards*; provide links for clients, customs and specifiers; provide a forum for suppliers to the industry to understand current and future trends within the industry and interact with manufacturers. **Structure** General Assembly; Board. Committees (2): Technical; Marketing. Executive Director. **Activities** Events/meetings; awards/prizes/competitions. **Events** *Conference* Leuven (Belgium) 2022, *Conference* Leuven (Belgium) 2021, *Annual Conference* Madrid (Spain) 2017, *IECA Conference* Malta 1993.
Members Full; Associate; Honorary. Full in 31 countries:
Argentina, Australia, Bahrain, Belgium, Czechia, Denmark, Estonia, Finland, France, Germany, Hungary, Israel, Italy, Japan, Jordan, Latvia, Lithuania, Morocco, Netherlands, New Zealand, Nigeria, Norway, Poland, Qatar, Romania, Slovakia, South Africa, Spain, Sweden, UK, United Arab Emirates.
Associate in 13 countries:
Austria, Belgium, Finland, Germany, Ireland, Italy, Netherlands, Russia, Spain, Sweden, Switzerland, UK, USA.
Honorary in 1 country:
UK. [2021/XM6516/**D**]

♦ International Prevention Research Institute (IPRI) 14639

Main Office Le Campus, Bât A l'Américain, 18 chemin des Cuers, 69570 Dardilly, France. T. +33472171199. E-mail: info@i-pri.org.
URL: http://www.i-pri.org/

History Apr 2009. **Aims** Work within defined economic limitations to bring available excellence in scientific method and international expertise to clarify critical issues in *disease* determination and prevention in order to contribute to the improvement of health in populations worldwide. **Structure** Faculty; Senior Faculty. International Governance and Ethics Committee. **Events** *National Cancer Institute Directors Meeting (NCID)* 2021, *National Cancer Institute Directors Meeting (NCID)* 2020, *National Cancer Institute Directors Meeting (NCID)* Lyon (France) 2019. **IGO Relations** Partners include: *European Molecular Biology Laboratory (EMBL, #07813).* **NGO Relations** Partners include various national institutions and *Max Planck Society for the Advancement of Science (MPG).* [2022/XJ5781/j/**D**]

♦ International Primary Aluminium Institute / see International Aluminium Institute (#11643)
♦ International Primary Care Cardiovascular Society foundation (unconfirmed)

♦ International Primary Care Respiratory Group (IPCRG) 14640

Business Manager 19 Armour Mews, Larbert, FK5 4FF, UK. T. +447505954524. E-mail: business-manager@ipcrg.org.
Registered Address 4th Floor, 115 George Street, Edinburgh, EH2 4JN, UK.

URL: http://www.ipcrg.org/
History Jun 2000, Cambridge (UK). Registration: Scottish Charity Regulator, No/ID: SC035056, Start date: 18 Sep 2003, Scotland. **Aims** Work locally in primary care and collaborate globally to improve respiratory health. **Structure** General Meeting (annual); Board of Directors; Senate Subcommittees (5). **Languages** English. **Staff** 1.00 FTE, paid. **Finance** Sources: grants; meeting proceeds; revenue from activities/projects; sponsorship. Annual budget: 200,000 EUR. **Activities** Advocacy/lobbying/activism; awareness raising; capacity building; events/meetings; knowledge management/information dissemination; projects/programmes; research/documentation; training/education. **Events** *World Conference* Malaga (Spain) 2022, *World Conference* Dublin (Ireland) 2021, *International China Conference* Beijing (China) 2020, *Scientific Meeting* Bucharest (Romania) 2019, *World Conference* Porto (Portugal) 2018.
Members Associations in 46 countries and territories:
Argentina, Australia, Bangladesh, Bermuda, Brazil, Bulgaria, Canada, Chile, China, Croatia, Cyprus, Czechia, Finland, France, Georgia, Germany, Greece, India, Ireland, Israel, Italy, Kyrgyzstan, Malaysia, Montenegro, Netherlands, New Zealand, North Macedonia, Norway, Pakistan, Portugal, Romania, Saudi Arabia, Singapore, Slovenia, Spain, Sri Lanka, Sweden, Thailand, Tunisia, Türkiye, Uganda, UK, Ukraine, United Arab Emirates, USA, Vietnam.
NGO Relations Member of (2): *Global Alliance Against Chronic Respiratory Diseases (GARD, #10182); World Organization of Family Doctors (WONCA, #21690).* Endorses: *Steering Group on Influenza Vaccination (#19980).* [2023.02.14/XE4649/**E**]

♦ International Primary Market Association (inactive)

♦ International Primate Protection League (IPPL) 14641
Ligue internationale pour la protection des primates (LIPP)
Office Administrator PO Box 766, Summerville SC 29484, USA. T. +18438712280. Fax +18438717988. E-mail: info@ippl.org.
URL: http://www.ippl.org/
History 1973, Bangkok (Thailand). **Aims** Conserve and protect primates through investigating illegal trade, support rescue centers around the world, running a headquarters sanctuary for gibbons, campaigning against cruelty to laboratory primates and work to end poaching and habitat destruction. **Structure** Board of Directors; Field Representatives; Advisory Board. **Languages** English. **Staff** 9.00 FTE, paid. Many voluntary. **Finance** Members' dues: Regular US$ 20; Sustaining US$ 50; Patron US$ 100. Donations. Budget (annual): about US$ 1 million. **Activities** Awareness raising; events/meetings; monitoring/evaluation. **Events** *Biennial members meeting* Summerville, SC (USA) 2010, *Biennial members meeting* Summerville, SC (USA) 2008, *Biennial members meeting* Summerville, SC (USA) 2006, *Biennial members meeting* Summerville, SC (USA) 2004, *Biennial members meeting* Summerville, SC (USA) 2002. **Publications** *IPPL News* (3 a year).
Members Field Representatives (31), Patron, Regular, Sustaining and Student members in 52 countries and territories:
Argentina, Australia, Austria, Bangladesh, Botswana, Cameroon, Canada, Chile, Congo Brazzaville, Congo DR, Côte d'Ivoire, Denmark, Egypt, Equatorial Guinea, France, Gabon, Gambia, Germany, Guinea, Hong Kong, India, Indonesia, Ireland, Italy, Japan, Kenya, Lesotho, Liberia, Malaysia, Mali, Mexico, Nepal, Netherlands, New Zealand, Nigeria, Peru, Serbia, Sierra Leone, Singapore, South Africa, Spain, Sri Lanka, Switzerland, Taiwan, Tanzania UR, Thailand, Uganda, UK, USA, Vietnam, Zambia, Zimbabwe.
IGO Relations Accredited by: *International Whaling Commission (IWC, #15879).* Observer at: *Secretariat of the Convention on International Trade in Endangered Species of Wild Fauna and Flora (CITES Secretariat, #19199).* **NGO Relations** Member of: *Ape Alliance (#00871); CIVICUS: World Alliance for Citizen Participation (#03962);* Independent Sector (US); *International Union for Conservation of Nature and Natural Resources (IUCN, #15766); Species Survival Network (SSN, #19916).* Partner of: *1% for the Planet.* [2020/XC0374/v/**C**]

♦ International Primatological Society (IPS) 14642
Société internationale de primatologie – Internationale Primatologische Gesellschaft
Gen Sec Pontifícia Univ Católica do Rio Grande do Sul, Escola de Ciências da Saúde e da Vida, Av Ipiranga 6681 Pd. 12A, Porto Alegre RS, 90619-900, Brazil.
Pres address not obtained.
URL: http://internationalprimatologicalsociety.org/
History 6 Nov 1964, Covington, LA (USA). Former names and other names: *Société internationale pour l'étude des primates* – alias; *Internationale Primatologen-Gesellschaft* – alias. **Aims** Encourage all areas of non-human primatological scientific research; facilitate cooperation among scientists of all nationalities engaged in primate research; promote the *conservation* of all primate species. **Structure** Executive Council; Nomination Committees. **Languages** English. **Staff** Voluntary. **Finance** Sources: members' dues. Annual budget: 100,000 USD. **Activities** Awards/prizes/competitions; financial and/or material support. **Events** *Biennial Congress* Antananarivo (Madagascar) 2025, *Biennial Congress* Kuching (Malaysia) 2023, *Biennial Congress* Quito (Ecuador) 2022, *Biennial Congress* Quito (Ecuador) 2020, *Biennial Congress* Nairobi (Kenya) 2018. **Publications** *International Journal of Primatology* (6 a year); *IPS Bulletin* (periodical).
Members Individual and affiliate members. Individuals in 50 countries:
Argentina, Australia, Austria, Bangladesh, Belgium, Benin, Bolivia, Brazil, Cambodia, Cameroon, Canada, China, Colombia, Congo Brazzaville, Congo DR, Costa Rica, Czechia, Denmark, El Salvador, France, Germany, Guatemala, Honduras, India, Indonesia, Italy, Japan, Kenya, Luxembourg, Madagascar, Mauritius, Mexico, Nepal, Netherlands, Nigeria, Panama, Portugal, Rwanda, Sierra Leone, South Africa, Spain, Sri Lanka, Sweden, Switzerland, Tanzania UR, Thailand, Uganda, UK, USA, Vietnam.
Affiliated societies in 21 countries:
Argentina, Australia, Bolivia, Brazil, China, Colombia, Congo Brazzaville, Ecuador, France, Germany, Indonesia, Italy, Japan, Madagascar, Malaysia, Mexico, Portugal, South Africa, Spain, UK, USA.
Regional organizations (2) listed in this Yearbook:
European Federation for Primatology (EFP, #07195); Société francophone de primatologie (SFDP, #19472).
NGO Relations Accredited by (1): *Great Apes Survival Project (GRASP, #10699).* Member of (1): *International Union for Conservation of Nature and Natural Resources (IUCN, #15766).* [2022.07.25/XC2378/**C**]

♦ International Principals Association – International Confederation of School Principals / see International Confederation of Principals (#12868)

♦ International Prison Chaplains' Association (IPCA) 14643
Pres c/o 5 Rue Pierre Varin Brunelière, 35700 Rennes, France.
URL: http://www.ipcaworldwide.org/
History 1985, Bossey (Switzerland). **Aims** Unite, encourage and equip a global network of prison chaplains as they share God's love and restoring justice. **Structure** Worldwide Steering Committee. **Languages** English. **Staff** 2.00 FTE, paid. **Finance** Contributions from: Swedish Correctional Service; Canadian Correctional Service; Church of Sweden. Private donations. Annual budget: 290,000 USD. **Activities** Events/meetings; training/education. **Events** *Quinquennial Conference* Bangkok (Thailand) 2020, *European Conference* Kiev (Ukraine) 2018, *European Conference* Cambridge (UK) 2017, *European Conference* Rome (Italy) 2016, *Quinquennial Conference* Sydney, NSW (Australia) 2015. **Publications** *Justice Reflections* (3-4 a year).
Members in 143 countries and territories:
Albania, Andorra, Antigua-Barbuda, Argentina, Armenia, Australia, Austria, Bahamas, Bangladesh, Belarus, Belgium, Belize, Benin, Bermuda, Bolivia, Botswana, Brazil, Bulgaria, Burkina Faso, Burundi, Cameroon, Canada, Cayman Is, Central African Rep, Chile, China, Colombia, Congo Brazzaville, Congo DR, Cook Is, Costa Rica, Côte d'Ivoire, Cuba, Czechia, Denmark, Djibouti, Dominica, Dominican Rep, Ecuador, Egypt, El Salvador, Estonia, Eswatini, Ethiopia, Fiji, Finland, France, Gambia, Georgia, Germany, Ghana, Greece, Grenada, Guiana Fr, Guinea-Bissau, Guyana, Haiti, Hong Kong, Hungary, Iceland, India, Indonesia, Ireland, Israel, Italy, Jamaica, Japan, Kenya, Kiribati, Korea Rep, Latvia, Lebanon, Lesotho, Liberia, Lithuania, Luxembourg, Madagascar, Malawi, Malaysia, Mali, Malta, Mauritius, Mexico, Moldova, Montserrat, Mozambique, Myanmar, Namibia, Nepal, Netherlands, New Caledonia, New Zealand, Nicaragua, Nigeria, Northern Ireland, Norway, Pakistan, Panama, Papua New Guinea, Paraguay, Peru, Philippines, Poland, Portugal, Puerto Rico, Romania, Russia, Rwanda, Samoa USA, Sierra Leone, Singapore, Slovakia, Slovenia, Solomon Is, South Africa, Spain, Sri Lanka, St Lucia, St Maarten, St Vincent-Grenadines, Sudan, Sweden, Switzerland, Tahiti Is, Taiwan, Tanzania UR, Thailand, Togo, Tonga, Trinidad-Tobago, Tunisia, Türkiye, Tuvalu, Uganda, UK, Ukraine, Uruguay, USA, Vanuatu, Venezuela, Virgin Is UK, Zambia, Zimbabwe.
Consultative Status Consultative status granted from: *ECOSOC (#05331)* (Special). [2021/XD3569/**B**]

♦ International Prisoners' Aid Union (inactive)
♦ International Private Drivers Association (inactive)
♦ International Private Equity and Venture Capital Valuation Association (inactive)
♦ International Private Infrastructure Association (internationally oriented national body)

♦ International Private Physical Therapy Association (IPPTA) 14644
Sec address not obtained. E-mail: ippta.secretary@private.physio.
Pres address not obtained.
URL: https://private.physio/
History Since 1995, a subgroup within *World Confederation for Physical Therapy (WCPT, #21293).* Former names and other names: *International Private Practitioners Association (IPPA)* – former. **Aims** Advance the private *physiotherapy profession* internationally; provide a consultative network for private practitioners around the world; conduct and collate research; develop resources. **Structure** Executive Committee. **Finance** Members' dues. Other sources: in-kind contributions; sales of resources. **Activities** Events/meetings; knowledge management/information dissemination; research/documentation. **Events** *Conference* Singapore (Singapore) 2015, *Conference* Singapore (Singapore) 2015, *Congress / Conference* Melbourne, VIC (Australia) 2005, *Conference* Barcelona (Spain) 2003, *Congress / Conference* Eastbourne (UK) 2001. **Publications** *IPPA World Voice* (2 a year).
Members Organizations in 21 countries:
Australia, Belgium, Canada, Colombia, Denmark, Finland, Germany, Ireland, Lebanon, Malawi, Malta, Namibia, Netherlands, New Zealand, Norway, South Africa, Spain, Sweden, Switzerland, UK, USA.
NGO Relations Formal contacts with: *International Federation of Orthopaedic Manipulative Physical Therapists (IFOMPT, #13495); International Society of Educators in Physiotherapy (ISEP, no recent information).* [2022/XE2583/**E**]

♦ International Private Practitioners Association / see International Private Physical Therapy Association (#14644)
♦ International Prize Court (inactive)
♦ International PR Network / see International Public Relations Network (#14672)
♦ International Probabilistic Workshop (meeting series)

♦ International Probiotics Association (IPA) 14645
Contact 1824 S Robertson Blvd, Los Angeles CA 90035, USA.
Contact 3484 Des Sources, Suite 320, Montréal QC H9B 1Z9, Canada. Fax +15146131472.
Contact Zentralstr 64, 8003 Zurich ZH, Switzerland. T. +18473762750. Fax +41434569715.
URL: http://internationalprobiotics.org/
History 13 Nov 2001. **Aims** Provide a forum for exchange of research and the latest breakthroughs in probiotic technology and new product development. **Structure** Board of Directors; Scientific Board. **Events** *IPA World Congress* Washington, DC (USA) 2022, *Probiota Asia Conference* Singapore (Singapore) 2021, *Probiota Asia Conference* Singapore (Singapore) 2019, *World Congress* Barcelona (Spain) 2018, *Probiota Asia Conference* Singapore (Singapore) 2018.
Members Companies in 14 countries and territories:
Canada, China, Denmark, Germany, Hong Kong, Israel, Italy, Japan, Netherlands, New Zealand, Sweden, Taiwan, UK, USA.
IGO Relations Participates as observer in the activities of: *Codex Alimentarius Commission (CAC, #04081).* [2020/XJ0982/**C**]

♦ International Probiotics Association Europe (IPA Europe) 14646
Exec Dir Ave d'Audergehm 22-28, 1040 Brussels, Belgium. T. +3225495081. E-mail: info@ipaeurope.org.
URL: http://www.ipaeurope.org/
History 2015, Brussels (Belgium). Founded as successor to *Yoghurt and Live Fermented Milk Association (YLFA International, inactive)* and *Global Alliance for Probiotics (GAP, inactive).* Registration: No/ID: 0633.510.166, Start date: 3 Jul 2015, Belgium; EU Transparency Register, No/ID: 294688218286-10, Start date: 27 Jul 2015. **Aims** Serve the general interests of the European probiotic *food* industry in the best possible manner. **Structure** General Assembly; Board; Secretariat. **Members** Active; Associate. Membership countries not specified. **IGO Relations** Registered Stakeholder of: *European Food Safety Authority (EFSA, #07287).* **NGO Relations** *International Probiotics Association (IPA, #14645).* [2020/XM5786/**E**]

♦ International Production Amalgamation for Manufacturing Textile Technological Equipment (inactive)
♦ International Professional Association of Manufactory, Industrial and Handicraft Workers (inactive)
♦ International Professional Association of Medical Ophthalmologists (inactive)
♦ International Professional Association for Transport & Health (internationally oriented national body)
♦ International Professional Horticultural Federation (inactive)

♦ International Professional Hunters Association (IPHA) 14647
Association internationale de chasseurs professionnels
Secretariat 215 W Bandera, Ste 114-175, Boerne TX 78006, USA. E-mail: ipha@gvtc.com.
URL: http://www.internationalprohunters.com/
History 1969. **Aims** Advise, educate and facilitate public enjoyment of the natural world. **Structure** Officers: President; Senior Vice-President; 9 Vice-Presidents. **Members** Individuals (approx 400) in 30 countries. Membership countries not specified. **NGO Relations** *Game Conservation International (GAME COIN, no recent information).* [2010/XD5345/t/**D**]

♦ International Professional Managers Association (internationally oriented national body)

♦ International Professional Pool Players' Association (IPA) 14648
Contact 20 South View, Bamford, Rochdale, OL11 5HU, UK. T. +441706642770.
URL: http://www.propool.org/ [2010/XD6962/**D**]

♦ International Professional Security Association (IPSA) 14649
Association internationale de sécurité professionnelle
Mailing Address PO Box 3413, Littlehampton, BN16 9LD, UK. E-mail: post@ipsa.org.uk.
URL: http://www.ipsa.org.uk/
History 1958, Birmingham (UK). Registration: Companies House, No/ID: 8072214, England and Wales. **Aims** Improve status of individuals employed in the field of security. **Structure** International Council. **Languages** English. **Staff** 2.00 FTE, paid. **Finance** Annual budget: 100,000 GBP. **Activities** Events/meetings; knowledge management/information dissemination; politics/policy/regulatory; standards/guidelines; training/education. **Events** *East-West International Security Conference* Madrid (Spain) 2015. **Publications** *Red Book Security Industry Directory* (annual).
Members Full and associate companies and individuals in 21 countries;:
Albania, Australia, Bangladesh, Barbados, Belgium, Bulgaria, Canada, Cyprus, Germany, Ghana, Ireland, Kenya, Mauritius, Nigeria, Oman, Tanzania UR, UK, United Arab Emirates, USA, Zambia, Zimbabwe.
NGO Relations Member of (1): *Genesis Initiative.* [2022.05.11/XF0108/t/**F**]

♦ International Professional Surfing Federation / see International Surfing League (#15631)
♦ International Professional Tennis Players Association / see ATP World Tour (#03011)
♦ International Professional Union of Gynaecologists and Obstetricians (#20473)
♦ International Program on Dynamics and Evolution of the Lithosphere – the Framework for Earth Resources and Reduction of Hazards / see International Lithosphere Program (#14059)

♦ International Programme on Chemical Safety (IPCS) 14650
Programme international sur la sécurité des substances chimiques (PISC)
Coordinator c/o WHO/IPCS, Av Ammia 20, 1211 Geneva 27, Switzerland. E-mail: ipcsmail@who.int.
Main: http://www.who.int/pcs/
History Founded May 1979, by Resolution WHO 32.31 of the Assembly of *WHO (#20950)*; establishment initially recommended by Resolution WHO 30.47 of WHO 30th Assembly, May 1977. Became a tripartite endeavour, Apr 1980, when Memorandum of Understanding was signed by WHO, *UNEP (#20299)* and *ILO (#11123).* Subsequent WHO Resolution 45.52, May 1992, endorsing an expanded role for IPCS. No longer tripartite following lapse of Memorandum of Understanding. **Aims** Carry out and disseminate evaluations of the risk to human health and the environment from exposure to chemicals and mixtures or combinations of chemicals; promote development, improvement, validation and use of methods for environmental risks and hazards evaluation; promote technical cooperation with WHO Member States, in particular developing countries to facilitate the use of available health and environmental risk (hazard) evaluations, improve capabilities of national authorities in conducting their own assessments when necessary and strengthen infrastructures for safety aspects relating to chemicals – their production, importation, transportation,

storage, use and disposal; develop alert and response mechanisms and promote effective international cooperation with respect to emergencies and accidents involving chemicals; support national programmes for prevention and treatment of poisonings, including establishment of poison centres; promote training of required manpower. **Structure** Programme based at WHO Headquarters. **Languages** Arabic, Chinese, English, French, Russian, Spanish. **Staff** 5.00 FTE, paid. **Finance** Sources: WHO Regular Budget; voluntary contributions of Member States. **Activities** Works primarily through a network of partner institutions and WHO Collaborating Centres, national focal points and with national governments; produces evaluations of the adverse effects of chemicals on human health and environment; prepares guidance on new and harmonized methodologies for assessment of chemicals; undertakes collaborative studies to validate and harmonize test methods for chemicals; produces information on preparedness and response to chemical accidents; produces guidance on the establishment and roles of poisons centres and on prevention and management of poisoning; provides trained manpower and advisory services; carries out chemical risk communication and advocacy for chemical safety; conducts expert workshops and consultative groups to build consensus as part of the work process. **Events** *PAC session* Beijing (China) 2002, *Meeting on chemicals and hormonal interferences* Washington, DC (USA) 1998, *Intergovernmental forum on chemical safety session* Ottawa, ON (Canada) 1997, *International workshop on receptor-mediated mechanisms in chemical carcinogenesis* Lyon (France) 1994, *International symposium on human health and environment* Salsomaggiore Terme (Italy) 1994. **Publications** *Concise International Chemical Assessment Document* – series; *Environmental Health Criteria (EHC)* – series. *International Chemical Safety Cards*. Monographs; technical documents; reports. **Information Services** *INTOX* – computerized poisons information package, in 4 languages; *IPCS INCHEM* – online; *IPCS INTOX* – databank and CD-Rom on chemical safety. **Members** All Member States of WHO and PIs. Membership countries not specified. **IGO Relations** Joint cooperation with: *FAO (#09260)* (for JECFA and JMPR evaluations). Participating organizations: ILO; *OECD (#17693)*; UNEP; *UNIDO (#20336)*; *United Nations Institute for Training and Research (UNITAR, #20576)*; WHO. Observer Organizations: *International Bank for Reconstruction and Development (IBRD, #12317)* (World Bank); *UNDP (#20292)*. Participates in COPs for: *Rotterdam Convention on the Prior Informed Consent Procedure for Certain Hazardous Chemicals and Pesticides in International Trade (Rotterdam convention, 1998)*; *Stockholm Convention on Persistent Organic Pollutants (POP treaty, 2001)*. Also participates in: Sub-Committee of Experts Globally Harmonized System for Classification and Labelling of Chemicals (GHS) of: *United Nations Committee of Experts on the Transport of Dangerous Goods and on the Globally Harmonized System of Classification and Labelling of Chemicals (Committee of Experts on TDG and GHS, #20543)*. [2017.03.16/XF0185/**F***]

♦ International Programme for the Development of Communication (IPDC) 14651

Programme international pour le développement de la communication (PIDC) – Programa Internacional para el Desarrollo de la Comunicación (PIDC)

Deputy Secretary c/o UNESCO, CI, 7 place de Fontenoy, 75007 Paris, France. T. +33145684268. Fax +33145685579.
Dir address not obtained. T. +33145684203. Fax +33145685579.
URL: https://en.unesco.org/programme/ipdc/

History 1980, Belgrade (Serbia). Established by the General Conference of *UNESCO (#20322)*. **Aims** Mobilize the international community to discuss and promote media development in developing countries; provide support for media projects; seek an accord to secure a healthy environment for the growth of free and pluralistic media in developing countries. **Structure** Intergovernmental Council, elected by UNESCO's General Conference, normally meets in a regular plenary session once every two years. Extraordinary sessions may be convened as specified in the Council's Rules of Procedure; Bureau, composed of a Chairman, three Vice-Chairpersons, a Rapporteur and three other members. **Languages** Arabic, Chinese, English, French, Russian, Spanish. **Staff** All full-time. **Finance** Sources: UNESCO; voluntary contributions. Activities financed through IPDC Special Account. **Activities** Monitoring/evaluation; projects/programmes; research and development; training/education. **Events** *Intergovernmental Council Session* Paris (France) 2020, *Intergovernmental Council Session* Paris (France) 2018, *Intergovernmental Council Session* Paris (France) 2016, *Intergovernmental Council Session* Paris (France) 2014, *Intergovernmental Council Session* Paris (France) 2012.
Members Council representatives of governments of 38 states:
Afghanistan, Argentina, Austria, Azerbaijan, Benin, Brazil, Côte d'Ivoire, Cuba, Denmark, Dominican Rep, El Salvador, Finland, Gambia, Honduras, Kazakhstan, Kenya, Kyrgyzstan, Latvia, Lebanon, Libya, Lithuania, Madagascar, Malaysia, Namibia, Netherlands, Nigeria, Pakistan, Palau, Russia, Saudi Arabia, Senegal, St Vincent-Grenadines, Sweden, Thailand, Tunisia, Türkiye, UK, Zambia.
IGO Relations Organizations invited to the sessions of the IPDC Intergovernmental Council:
- *Organisation of African, Caribbean and Pacific States (OACPS, #17796)*;
- *African Development Bank (ADB, #00283)*;
- *African Union (AU, #00488)*;
- *Andean Presidential Council (see: #00817)*;
- *Arab Bureau of Education for the Gulf States (ABEGS, #00910)*;
- *Arab Gulf Programme for United Nations Development Organizations (AGFUND, #00971)*;
- *Arab League Educational, Cultural and Scientific Organization (ALECSO, #01003)*;
- *Arab Satellite Communications Organization (ARABSAT, #01037)*;
- *Arab States Broadcasting Union (ASBU, #01050)*;
- *Arab Telecommunication Union (ATU, inactive)*;
- *Asia-Pacific Institute for Broadcasting Development (AIBD, #01934)*;
- *Asian Development Bank (ADB, #01422)*;
- *Caribbean Community (CARICOM, #03476)*;
- *Comisión Permanente del Pacífico Sur (CPPS, #04141)*;
- *Commonwealth Secretariat (#04362)*;
- *Council of Europe (CE, #04881)*;
- *Economic Community of West African States (ECOWAS, #05312)*;
- *European Commission (EC, #06633)*;
- *European Space Agency (ESA, #08798)*;
- *Instituto Latinoamericano de la Comunicación Educativa (ILCE, #11343)*;
- *Inter-American Development Bank (IDB, #11427)*;
- Intelsat Ltd, replacing *International Telecommunications Satellite Organization (ITSO, #15670)*;
- *Islamic Broadcasting Union (IBU, #16033)*;
- *Islamic World Educational, Scientific and Cultural Organization (ICESCO, #16058)*;
- *League of Arab States (LAS, #16420)*;
- *Non-Aligned News Agency Pool (NANAP, inactive)*;
- *OAS (#17629)*;
- *OECD (#17693)*;
- *Organisation internationale de la Francophonie (OIF, #17809)*;
- *Organisation of Islamic Cooperation (OIC, #17813)*;
- *Organization of Arab Petroleum Exporting Countries (OAPEC, #17854)*;
- *Organization of Ibero-American States for Education, Science and Culture (#17871)*;
- *Pacific Community (SPC, #17942)*;
- *Sistema Económico Latinoamericano (SELA, #19294)*;
- *Southeast Asian Ministers of Education Organization (SEAMEO, #19774)*.

NGO Relations Organizations invited to the sessions of the IPDC Intergovernmental Council:
- *African Union of Broadcasting (AUB, #00490)*;
- *Asia-Pacific Broadcasting Union (ABU, #01863)*;
- *Asian Media Information and Communication Centre (AMIC, #01536)*;
- *Association mondiale des radiodiffuseurs communautaires (AMARC, #02810)*;
- *Conseil international des radios-télévisions d'expression française (CIRTEF, #04694)*;
- *CPU Media Trust (#04941)*;
- *European Broadcasting Union (EBU, #06404)*;
- *FIPP (#09776)*;
- *Inter American Press Association (IAPA, #11444)*;
- *International Advertising Association (IAA, #11590)*;
- *International Association for Cross-Cultural Communication (AIMAV, inactive)*;
- *International Association for Media and Communication Research (IAMCR, #12022)*;
- *International Christian Organisation of the Media (ICOM, #12563)*;
- *International Committee of the Red Cross (ICRC, #12799)*;
- *International Council for Film, Television and Audiovisual Communication (IFTC, #13022)*;
- *International Council for Science (ICSU, inactive)*;
- *International Federation of Film Archives (#13427)*;
- *International Federation of Journalists (IFJ, #13462)*;
- *International Institute of Communications (IIC, #13870)*;
- *International Association of Cinema, Audiovisual and Media Schools (#11771)*;
- *International Press Telecommunications Council (IPTC, #14637)*;
- *International Radio and Television Union (#14689)*;
- *Organización de Telecomunicaciones de Iberoamérica (OTI, #17851)*;
- *Pacific Islands News Association (PINA, #17975)*;
- *Reporters sans frontières (RSF, #18846)*;
- *World Association of Newspapers (WAN, inactive)*;
- *World Catholic Association for Communication (SIGNIS, #21264)*. [2021.10.27/XE2379/**F***]

♦ International Programme on the Elimination of Child Labour and Forced Labour (IPEC+) 14652

Organisation internationale du travail – Programme international pour l'abolition du travail des enfants et du travail forcé – Organización Internacional del Trabajo – Programa Internacional para la Erradicación del Trabajo Infantil y del Travajo Forzoso

Contact c/o International Labour Office, Fundamental Principles and Rights at Work Branch, Route des Morillons 4, 1211 Geneva 22, Switzerland. T. +41227998181. Fax +41227998771. E-mail: fundamentals@ilo.org.
URL: https://www.ilo.org/global/about-the-ilo/how-the-ilo-works/flagships/ipec-plus/lang – en/index.htm

History 1992. Established within the *ILO (#11123)*. Operates according to ILO rules and procedures and is based on Memoranda of Understanding between ILO and participating countries. IPEC+ Flagship Programme brings together the International Programme on the Elimination of Child Labour (IPEC) and the Special Action Programme to Combat Forced Labour (SAP/FL). Former names and other names: *International Labour Organization – International Programme on the Elimination of Child Labour (ILO-IPEC)* – former; *Organisation internationale du travail – Programme international pour l'abolition du travail des enfants (OIT-IPEC)* – former; *Organización Internacional del Trabajo – Programa Internacional para la Erradicación del Trabajo Infantil (OIT-IPEC)* – former. **Aims** Provide ILO leadership in global efforts to eradicate all forms of child labour by 2025 and all forms of contemporary slavery and human trafficking by 2030; ensure that all people are protected from – and can protect themselves against – these gross human rights violations. **Structure** Programme Management Team. **Finance** A multi-donor programme. Current major donor countries: Brazil; Canada; France; Germany; Japan, Netherlands; Norway; Panama; Qatar; Spain; Switzerland; UK, USA. Support from: *European Commission (EC, #06633)*; *FAO (#09260)*; *International Bank for Reconstruction and Development (IBRD, #12317)* (World Bank); *UNICEF (#20332)*. **Activities** Events/meetings; projects/programmes. **Events** *Global Conference on Sustained Eradication of Child Labour* Durban (South Africa) 2022, *Global Conference on Child Labour* Buenos Aires (Argentina) 2017, *Global Conference on Child Labour* Brasilia (Brazil) 2013, *Global Child Labour Conference* The Hague (Netherlands) 2010, *International conference on environmental threats to the health of children* Bangkok (Thailand) 2002. **Publications** *Child Labour: Global estimates 2020, trends and the road forward – Travail des enfants: estimations mondiales 2020, tendances et le chemin à suivre – Trabajo infantil: Estimaciones mundiales 2020, tendencias y el camino a seguir* (1st ed 2021) – ILO-UNICEF joint publication.; *Global Estimates of Child Labour: Results and Trends 2012-2016*; *Global Estimates of Modern Slavery: Forced Labour and Forced Marriage*. IPEC+ Global Flagship Programme Implementation. **Members** 187 ILO Member States. Membership countries not specified. **IGO Relations** *FAO (#09260)*; *International Bank for Reconstruction and Development (IBRD, #12317)*; *International Organization for Migration (IOM, #14454)*; *UNDP (#20292)*; *UNESCO (#20322)*; *UNICEF (#20332)*. **NGO Relations** Cooperates with various international, national and local NGOs in over 80 countries (links not specified). [2021.10.26/XK0996/**F***]

♦ International Programs Center (internationally oriented national body)
♦ International Program Services / see International Branch of the YMCA, New York

♦ International Progress Organization (IPO) 14653

Organisation internationale pour le progrès – Internationale Fortschrittsorganization

Pres Kohlmarkt 4, 1010 Vienna, Austria. T. +4315332877. Fax +4315332962. E-mail: info@i-p-o.org.
URL: http://i-p-o.org/

History Oct 1972, Innsbruck (Austria). **Aims** Encourage cultural exchange between all nations; promote tolerance towards all nationalities and cultures; emphasize human liberties, social and economic development, peace, and the international rule of law. **Structure** General Assembly (at least every 4 years); Executive Board; Arbitration Committee. **Languages** English, French. **Activities** Events/meetings; monitoring/evaluation; networking/liaising; research and development. **Events** *International Round Table* Vienna (Austria) 2023, *International Round Table* Vienna (Austria) 2021, *International Round Table* Rhodes Is (Greece) 2014, *International Round Table* Istanbul (Turkey) 2011, *International Research Seminar* Istanbul (Turkey) / Ankara (Turkey) 2011. **Publications** *Occasional Papers Series*; *Studies in International Relations*. Monographs; abstracts; reports; research papers. **Information Services** *IPO News Releases*.
Members Individuals in 74 countries and territories:
Algeria, Australia, Austria, Bangladesh, Belgium, Brazil, Burkina Faso, Cameroon, Canada, Chad, Congo DR, Croatia, Cyprus, Czechia, Denmark, Dominican Rep, Egypt, Finland, France, Georgia, Germany, Ghana, Greece, Guinea, Guyana, India, Indonesia, Iraq, Italy, Japan, Jordan, Korea DPR, Kuwait, Lebanon, Lesotho, Liberia, Libya, Luxembourg, Maldives, Malta, Mexico, Morocco, Myanmar, Nepal, Nicaragua, Niger, Nigeria, Pakistan, Palestine, Peru, Philippines, Poland, Puerto Rico, Qatar, Romania, Russia, Senegal, Serbia, South Africa, Spain, Sri Lanka, Switzerland, Syrian AR, Tanzania UR, Togo, Tunisia, Türkiye, Uganda, UK, United Arab Emirates, USA, Venezuela, Yemen, Zimbabwe.
Consultative Status Consultative status granted from: *ECOSOC (#05331)* (Ros A). **IGO Relations** Associated with Department of Global Communications of the United Nations. **NGO Relations** Member of (3): *Conference of Non-Governmental Organizations in Consultative Relationship with the United Nations (CONGO, #04635)*; *International Conference of NGOs (#12883)*; International Network of NGOs for the Dialogue of Civilizations. Provides secretariat for: *NGO Committee on Sustainable Development, Vienna (#17119)*. [2022.10.11/XC6078/v/**B**]

♦ International Project of the Association for Voluntary Sterilization / see EngenderHealth

♦ International Project Finance Association (IPFA) 14654

Chairman 38 Chancery Lane, London, WC1A 1EN, UK. E-mail: info@ipfa.org.
URL: http://www.ipfa.org/

History Founded Nov 1998, London (UK). **Aims** Promote and represent the interests of companies involved in *energy* and infrastructure projects. **Structure** Executive Council; Branches (21); Secretariat. **Languages** English. **Staff** 10.00 FTE, paid. **Finance** Subscriptions. Other sources: *European Bank for Reconstruction and Development (EBRD, #06315)*; *European Commission (EC, #06633)*; *European Investment Bank (EIB, #07599)*; *International Bank for Reconstruction and Development (IBRD, #12317)* (World Bank). **Activities** Knowledge management/information dissemination; training/education; events/meetings; networking/liaising. **Events** *Asian Nuclear Power Briefing Meeting* Tokyo (Japan) 2018, *TGAIS : The Global African Investment Summit* London (UK) 2015, *Annual Asia rail congress* Singapore (Singapore) 2010. **Members** Membership countries not specified. [2020/XD8816/**D**]

♦ International Project Management Association (IPMA) 14655

Central Secretariat PO Box 7905, 1008 AC Amsterdam, Netherlands. T. +31332473430. E-mail: info@ipma.world.
URL: http://www.ipma.world/

History 1971. Founded as an association having existed as a discussion group of project managers since 1965. Former names and other names: *International Management Systems Association* – former (1971 to 1982); *INTERNET – International Project Management Association* – former (1982 to 1995). Registration: Switzerland. **Aims** Promote competence through society to enable a world in which all projects succeed. **Structure** Council of Delegates (annual, acts as General Assembly); Executive Board; Management Boards; Working and Projects Groups; Secretariat. **Languages** English. **Staff** 1.00 FTE, paid; 5.00 FTE, voluntary. **Activities** Certification/accreditation; events/meetings; networking/liaising; research/documentation; training/education. Active in all member countries. **Events** *IPMA World Congress* Denmark 2023, *IPMA World Congress* Tokyo (Japan) 2022, *IPMA World Congress* St Petersburg (Russia) 2021, *IPMA World Congress* St Petersburg (Russia) 2020, *Annual World Congress* Mérida (Mexico) 2019. **Publications** *Direct News* (6 a year); *International Journal of Project Management* (6 a year); *IPMA Newsletter* (4 a year); *International Project Management Yearbook* (annual). *Handbook on Management by Projects* (1990). Proceedings of Congresses, Symposia, Expert Seminars.

Members National project management associations. National associations in 71 countries and territories:
Algeria, Argentina, Austria, Azerbaijan, Bolivia, Bosnia-Herzegovina, Brazil, Bulgaria, Canada, Chile, China, Colombia, Costa Rica, Croatia, Cyprus, Czechia, Denmark, Dominican Rep, Ecuador, Egypt, Estonia, Finland, France, Georgia, Germany, Greece, Guatemala, Hungary, Iceland, India, Indonesia, Iran Islamic Rep, Ireland, Italy, Japan, Kazakhstan, Korea Rep, Kosovo, Latvia, Lithuania, Malaysia, Mexico, Montenegro, Morocco, Nepal, Netherlands, Nigeria, Norway, Panama, Paraguay, Peru, Philippines, Poland, Portugal, Romania, Russia, Serbia, Singapore, Slovakia, Slovenia, South Africa, Spain, Sweden, Switzerland, Taiwan, Türkiye, UK, Ukraine, Uruguay, USA, Uzbekistan.
NGO Relations Member of (1): *Global Alliance for the Project Professions (GAPPS, #10220)*. Cooperates with (1): *International Associations of Cost Engineers and Project Management Associations, Australia (no recent information)*. Alliances and agreements with: *Asia Pacific Federation of Project Management (APFPM, #01904)*; *European Construction Institute (ECI, #06767)*; *Green Project Management (GPM)*; *World Commerce and Contracting (WorldCC, #21284)*; *International Cost Engineering Council (ICEC, #12976)*.In liaison with technical committees of: *International Organization for Standardization (ISO, #14473)*.
[2022.06.16/XD1797/**C**]

- ♦ International Projects Assistance Services / see IPAS (#16010)
- ♦ International of Proletarian Freethinkers (inactive)
- ♦ International Promoting Association for Spaceflight Hermann Oberth – Wernher von Braun (internationally oriented national body)
- ♦ International Property Lawyers Association (no recent information)

♦ International Property Measurement Standards Coalition (IPMSC) . 14656

Contact Parliament Square, London, SW1P 3AD, UK. E-mail: standards@rics.org.
URL: http://ipmsc.org/
History May 2013, Washington, DC (USA). Set up during meeting of *International Bank for Reconstruction and Development (IBRD, #12317)*. **Aims** Develop and implement international standards for measuring property. **Structure** Board of Trustees; Standards Setting Committee. **Information Services** *IPMS: All Buildings* in English – Published by a Coalition of more than 80 property organisations representing hundreds of thousands of property professionals globally and drafted by an independent group of 18 experts from 11 countries, the International Property Measurement Standard is a global open-source standard aimed at creating a uniform approach to measuring buildings..
Members Coalition members (over 80) which include 17 organizations listed in this Yearbook:
Asian Association for Investors in Non-Listed Real Estate Vehicles (ANREV, #01327); *ASTM International (#02994)*; *Building Owners and Managers Association International (BOMA)*; *Commonwealth Association of Surveying and Land Economy (CASLE, #04313)*; *Council of European Geodetic Surveyors (#04890)*; *Covered Bond and Mortgage Council (CBMC, #04940)*; *European Association for Investors in Non-listed Real Estate Vehicles (INREV, #06093)*; *Fédération internationale des professions immobilières (FIABCI, #09653)*; *Global Corporate Real Estate Network (CORENET Global, #10308)*; *International Association of Assessing Officers (IAAO)*; *International Consortium of Real Estate Associations (ICREA)*; *International Facility Management Association (IFMA, #13325)*; *International Federation of Surveyors (FIG, #13561)*; *International Monetary Fund (IMF, #14180)*; *International Right of Way Association (IRWA)*; *International Union of Property Owners (#15804)*; *International Union of Tenants (IUT, #15822)*. [2023.02.15/XM4446/**C**]

- ♦ International Property Rights Association (unconfirmed)

♦ International Property Tax Institute (IPTI) 14657

CEO 5 Kodiak Crescent, Unit no 10, Toronto ON M3J 3E5, Canada. T. +14162288874. Fax +14166445152. E-mail: info@ipti.org.
URL: http://www.ipti.org/
History Founded 1992. **Aims** Foster property taxation and assessment ideals on an international level. **Structure** Board of Advisors; Directors. Committees (3): Corporate Advisory; European Corporate Advisory; Editorial and Publication. **Languages** English. **Finance** Sources: meeting proceeds; members' dues. Other sources: training and consultancy fees. **Activities** Events/meetings; guidance/assistance/consulting; knowledge management/information dissemination; research/documentation; training/education. **Events** *Mass Appraisal Valuation Symposium* Calgary, AB (Canada) 2021, *Mass Appraisal Valuation Symposium* Calgary, AB (Canada) 2020, *Mass Appraisal Valuation Symposium* Bled (Slovenia) 2019, *Mass Appraisal Valuation Symposium* Halifax, NS (Canada) 2018, *Mass Appraisal Valuation Symposium* Sydney, NSW (Australia) 2017. **Publications** *Journal of Property Tax Assessment and Administration*. **Members** Corporate/Organization; Professional. Membership countries not specified. **NGO Relations** Cooperates with: *International Association of Assessing Officers (IAAO)*; *Royal Institution of Chartered Surveyors (RICS, #18991)*; national institutes.
[2018.03.01/XM6425/j/**C**]

♦ International Proprioceptive Neuromuscular Facilitation Association (IPNFA) 14658

Sec Shina Rehabilitation Inst, 251-23 Geoyeodong Songpagu, Seoul, Korea Rep. T. +82172530679. E-mail: ipnfa.secretary@gmail.com.
URL: http://www.ipnfa.org/
History Also referred to as *International PNF Association*. Constitution adopted: 1989; updated Oct 1999, Sep 2003, Oct 2005 and Oct 2007. Registered in accordance with Swiss Civil Code. **Structure** General Meeting (annual). Executive Committee, comprising President, Vice-President, Secretary and Treasurer. Committees (3): Nominating; Education; Research. **Languages** English. **Events** *Congress* Seoul (Korea Rep) 2021, *Annual General Meeting* Okinawa (Japan) 2020, *Annual General Meeting* Vallejo, CA (USA) 2019, *Annual General Meeting* Seoul (Korea Rep) 2013, *Annual General Meeting* Budapest (Hungary) 2012. **Members** Individuals Full; Associate; Honorary; Inactive. Membership countries not specified. [2021/XJ6504/**C**]

- ♦ International Prostate Health Council (inactive)
- ♦ International Prostitutes Collective (internationally oriented national body)

♦ International Protea Association (IPA) 14659

Secretariat 258 Main Street, Paarl, 7646, South Africa. T. +27218702900. Fax +27218702915. E-mail: eugenielouw@gmail.com.
URL: http://www.ipa-protea.org/
History 1981, Melbourne (Australia). **Aims** Offer researchers, propagators, farmers, marketers, breeders and educators an open forum of communication and friendship to promote and expand the industry for the benefit of all. **Structure** Board; Council. **Languages** English. **Staff** 2.00 FTE, paid. **Finance** Members' dues. Profits from conference. **Activities** Includes: International Protea Working Group (IPWG). Organizes Biennial Conference; supports research projects. **Events** *International Conference* La Palma Is (Spain) / Santa Cruz de Tenerife (Spain) 2022, *Biennial Conference* Perth, WA (Australia) 2015, *International Conference* Perth, WA (Australia) 2014, *Biennial Conference / International Conference* Santiago (Chile) 2012, *Biennial conference / International Conference* Lisbon (Portugal) 2010. **Publications** *IPA Journal* (2 a year).
Members Full in 12 countries:
Australia, Belgium, Chile, Israel, Japan, Netherlands, New Zealand, Portugal, South Africa, Spain, USA, Zimbabwe.
[2021/XD7106/**D**]

♦ International Proteolysis Society (IPS) 14660

Sec Institute of Organic Chemistry and Biochemistry, Czech Academy of sciences, Flemingovo náměstí 542/2, 160 00 Prague 6, Czechia. T. +13135774451. Fax +13135776739. E-mail: ipssecretary@gmail.com.
URL: http://www.protease.org/
History 28 Sep 1999, Mackinac Island, MI (USA). Founded by *International Committee on Proteolysis (ICOP, inactive)*, whose activities it then took over. **Aims** Increase scientific research relating to fundamental and applied aspects of proteolysis. **Structure** General Meeting (every 2 years). Council, consisting of at least 12 members of whom at least 1 must possess the United States Residency and in which at least 2 different countries from each of the continental blocks must be represented. Each block has at least 3 members on the Council. Continental blocks (3): Europe/Africa; The Americas; Australasia. Officers: Chair; Vice Chair; Secretary; Treasurer. **Finance** Sources: members' dues. **Events** *General Meeting* Singapore (Singapore) 2023, *General Meeting* Singapore (Singapore) 2021, *General Meeting* Penang (Malaysia) 2015, *General Meeting* Cape Town (South Africa) 2013, *General Meeting* San Diego, CA (USA) 2011. **Publications** *Quick Cuts* – newsletter. **Members** Individuals (approx 800). Categories Active; Members in Training; Sponsoring. Membership countries not specified. [2021/XD7818/**D**]

- ♦ International Protestant League (inactive)
- ♦ International Protestant Loan Association (inactive)

♦ International Psoriasis Council (IPC) 14661

CEO 1034 S Brentwood Blvd, Ste 600, St Louis MO 63117, USA. T. +19728610503. Fax +12142423391. E-mail: info@psoriasiscouncil.org.
URL: http://www.psoriasiscouncil.org/
History Founded 2004, USA, on the initiative of Dr Alan Menter. **Aims** Advance psoriasis research and treatment. **Structure** Board of Directors; Committees (5); Working Groups (2); Task Force (1). **Publications** *IPC Psoriasis Review*. Annual Report.
Members General (individuals) in 20 countries:
Argentina, Austria, Brazil, Canada, Denmark, Finland, France, Germany, India, Israel, Italy, Japan, Netherlands, Singapore, South Africa, Spain, Sweden, Switzerland, UK, USA. [2014/XJ2326/**C**]

♦ International Psychoanalytical Association (IPA) 14662

Association psychanalytique internationale – Asociación Psicoanalitica Internacional – Internationale Psychoanalytische Vereinigung
Exec Dir Lexicon – Unit B, Book House, 261a City Road, London, EC1V 1AH, UK. T. +442084468324. Fax +442076813742. E-mail: ipa@ipa.world.
URL: http://www.ipa.world/
History 31 Mar 1910, Nürburg (Germany). Founded 31 Mar 1910, Nuremberg (Germany). Previously also referred to as *International Psychoanalytic Association* and *International Psychoanalytical Association Trust (IPA Trust)*. Constitution revised: 1965, Amsterdam (Netherlands); 1977, Jerusalem (Israel); 1981, Helsinki (Finland); 1983, Madrid (Spain); 1987, Montréal (Canada); 1991, Buenos Aires (Argentina); 1995, San Francisco CA (USA); Mar 2010. **Aims** As an accrediting and regulatory body for psychoanalysis and an umbrella organization for constituent associations: select, supervise and train candidates for the practice of clinical psychoanalysis; assure continued development of psychoanalysis for the benefit of psychoanalytic patients, and encourage its promotion as a method of treatment. **Structure** Congress (every 2 years); Honorary Officers; Board of Representatives. **Languages** English, French, German, Spanish. **Staff** 12.00 FTE, paid. **Finance** Sources: meeting proceeds; members' dues; sale of publications. **Activities** Events/meetings; networking/liaising; politics/policy/regulatory; research/documentation; training/education. **Events** *Biennial Congress* Cartagena de Indias (Colombia) 2023, *Asia-Pacific Conference* New Delhi (India) 2023, *Biennial Congress* Vancouver, BC (Canada) 2021, *Asia-Pacific Conference* Sydney, NSW (Australia) 2020, *Conference on the Feminine withing Revisiting Bisexuality* Lisbon (Portugal) 2019. **Publications** *IPA E-Newsletter*; *IPA Web News*; *Open Door Review*; *PSYCHOANALYSIS today* – e-journal. *IPA Series*. *100 Years of the IPA*; *Roster*.
Members Constituent organizations in 33 countries:
Argentina, Australia, Austria, Belgium, Brazil, Canada, Chile, Colombia, Czechia, Denmark, Finland, France, Germany, Greece, Hungary, India, Israel, Italy, Japan, Mexico, Netherlands, Norway, Peru, Poland, Portugal, Serbia, Spain, Sweden, Switzerland, UK, Uruguay, USA, Venezuela.
Individuals in 48 countries:
Argentina, Australia, Austria, Belgium, Brazil, Bulgaria, Canada, Chile, Colombia, Croatia, Czechia, Denmark, Ecuador, Finland, France, Germany, Greece, Hungary, India, Ireland, Israel, Italy, Jamaica, Japan, Korea Rep, Lebanon, Lithuania, Mexico, Netherlands, New Zealand, Norway, Paraguay, Peru, Poland, Portugal, Romania, Russia, Serbia, Slovakia, South Africa, Spain, Sweden, Switzerland, Türkiye, UK, Uruguay, USA, Venezuela.
Consultative Status Consultative status granted from: *ECOSOC (#05331)* (Special). **NGO Relations** Member of: *Conference of Non-Governmental Organizations in Consultative Relationship with the United Nations (CONGO, #04635)*. Instrumental in setting up: *East European Psychoanalytic Institute (EEPI, see: #14662)*.
[2021/XC2385/v/**C**]

- ♦ International Psychoanalytical Association Trust / see International Psychoanalytical Association (#14662)

♦ International Psychoanalytical Studies Organization (IPSO) 14663

Organisation internationale d'études de la psychoanalyse – Organización Internacional de Estudios de Psicoanalisis – Internationale Psychoanalytische Studienorganization
Pres Broomhills, Woodside Lane, London, N128UD, UK. T. +442084468324. E-mail: ipso-president@ipso-candidates.org.uk – ipso-mail@ipso-candidates.org.uk.
URL: http://www.ipso.world/
History 1971. **Aims** Facilitate communication and free exchange between IPA psychoanalytic candidates and psychoanalytic organizations worldwide; promote scientific events and scientific contributions. **Structure** Business Meeting; Executive Committee. **Languages** English, French, German, Spanish. **Staff** 12.00 FTE, voluntary. **Finance** Sources: members' dues. **Activities** Awards/prizes/competitions; events/meetings; networking/liaising; publishing activities; training/education. **Events** *Congress* Vancouver, BC (Canada) 2021, *The feminine – our frames, fears, focus and fascination* London (UK) 2019, *Intimacy* Buenos Aires (Argentina) 2017, *The aim of all life is death* Vienna (Austria) 2016, *Biennial Congress* Mexico City (Mexico) 2011. **Publications** *IPSO Journal*; *IPSO Newsletter*. Members' scientific publications. **Members** Worldwide membership. Membership countries not specified. [2020.06.26/XD8019/**D**]

- ♦ International Psychoanalytic Association / see International Psychoanalytical Association (#14662)

♦ International Psychogeriatric Association (IPA) 14664

Exec Dir 555 East Wells St, Ste 1100, Milwaukee WI 53202, USA. T. +14149189889. Fax +14142763349. E-mail: ipa@ipa-online.org.
URL: http://www.ipa-online.org/
History Founded 1980, by Imre Fejer and Hans Reichenfeld, following workshop, 1980, Nottingham (UK). Original title: *Psychogeriatrics International*. Official activities commenced, 1982, Cairo (Egypt), at 1st Congress. **Aims** Provide health care professionals and scientists with current, multidisciplinary information regarding behavioural and biological *geriatric mental health*; actively promote basic and applied research in the field and foster cross-cultural research; facilitate consensus/understanding in psychogeriatric issues from an international, cross-cultural perspective; encourage care and research on a multidisciplinary basis, including psychiatry, general medicine, neurology, nursing, social work and psychology. **Structure** Board of 25 Directors (meets twice a year at regional meetings and conferences), plus 4 officers. Secretariat in Northfield IL (USA). Organizational Groups (4): Research; Services; External Affairs; Internal Organization. Committees, task forces and initiatives focus on specific aspects of psychogeriatrics from international, interdisciplinary perspectives. **Languages** English. **Staff** 5.00 FTE, paid. **Finance** Sources: donations; grants; members' dues; sponsorship. **Activities** Awards/prizes/competitions; awareness raising; events/meetings; knowledge management/information dissemination; projects/programmes; training/education. **Events** *International Congress* Milwaukee, WI (USA) 2021, *International Congress* Milwaukee, WI (USA) 2020, *International Congress* Santiago de Compostela (Spain) 2019, *European Regional Meeting* Brussels (Belgium) 2018, *Asian Regional Meeting* Taipei (Taiwan) 2016. **Publications** *International Psychogeriatrics* (6 a year) – journal; *IPA Bulletin* (4 a year). *Delirium: Advances in Research and Clinical Practice* (1991); *Psychogeriatrics: Biomedical and Social Advances* (1991); *Clinical and Scientific Psychogeriatrics: Volume 2, The Interface of Psychiatry and Neurology* (1990); *Clinical and Scientific Psychogeriatrics: Volume I, Holistic Approaches* (1990); *Psychogeriatrics II* (1989); *Psychogeriatrics I* (1987); *Behavioural and Psychological Symptoms of Dementia*. Outsource meeting brochures.
Members Individuals in 72 countries and territories:
Argentina, Armenia, Aruba, Australia, Austria, Bahrain, Belgium, Bosnia-Herzegovina, Brazil, Canada, Chile, China, Colombia, Costa Rica, Croatia, Czechia, Denmark, Dominican Rep, Egypt, Finland, France, Germany, Greece, Hong Kong, Hungary, Iceland, India, Indonesia, Iran Islamic Rep, Ireland, Israel, Italy, Jamaica, Japan, Korea Rep, Latvia, Lithuania, Luxembourg, Malaysia, Mexico, Netherlands, New Zealand, Nigeria, North Macedonia, Norway, Pakistan, Peru, Philippines, Poland, Portugal, Puerto Rico, Romania, Russia, Serbia, Singapore, Slovakia, Slovenia, South Africa, Spain, Sweden, Switzerland, Syrian AR, Taiwan, Thailand, Trinidad-Tobago, Türkiye, Uganda, UK, Ukraine, United Arab Emirates, Uruguay, USA.
NGO Relations Member of: *Standing Committee of Presidents of International NGOs Concerned with Mental Health Issues (no recent information)*. [2020/XC6750/v/**B**]

- ♦ International Psychohistorical Association (internationally oriented national body)
- ♦ International Psychoneuroendocrine Society / see International Society of Psychoneuroendocrinology (#15399)

♦ International Psycho-Oncology Society (IPOS) 14665

Exec Dir 1 – 189 Queen Street East, Toronto ON M5A 1S2, Canada. T. +14169680260. Fax +14169686818. E-mail: info@ipos-society.org.
URL: http://www.ipos-society.org/

History 1984. Current constitutions approved 26 Apr 2003; amended 31 Dec 2003, 1 Aug 2004, 20 Oct 2006, 19 Sep 2007, 13 Nov 2012, 29 May 2015 and 20 Oct 2016. **Aims** Foster training, encourage psychosocial principles and a humanistic approach in cancer care; stimulate research and develop training so psychosocial care may be integrated with all clinical oncologic specialties for optimal patient care. **Structure** Board of Directors; Executive Committee; Executive Director. Committees, including *IPOS Federation of Psycho-Oncology Societies*; Task Forces; Special Interest Groups. **Languages** English. **Staff** Provided by external company. **Finance** Sources: grants; meeting proceeds; members' dues. **Activities** Events/meetings; standards/guidelines; training/education. **Events** *World Congress* Toronto, ON (Canada) 2022, *World Congress* Kyoto (Japan) 2021, *World Congress* Kyoto (Japan) 2020, *World Congress* Banff, AB (Canada) 2019, *World Congress* Hong Kong (Hong Kong) 2018. **Publications** *Psycho-Oncology* (12 a year) – journal. Online web lectures.

Members Active; Early Career; Associate; Members-in-Training; Life; Honoary. National Societies in 53 countries and territories:
Argentina, Australia, Austria, Bangladesh, Belgium, Brazil, Canada, Chile, China, Colombia, Cyprus, Denmark, Ecuador, Finland, France, Germany, Greece, Hong Kong, Hungary, Iceland, India, Indonesia, Iran Islamic Rep, Ireland, Israel, Italy, Japan, Jordan, Korea Rep, Malaysia, Mexico, Nepal, Netherlands, New Zealand, Nigeria, Norway, Pakistan, Paraguay, Peru, Philippines, Poland, Portugal, Russia, South Africa, Spain, Sweden, Switzerland, Taiwan, Thailand, Türkiye, UK, Uruguay, USA.
Included in the above, 2 organizations listed in this Yearbook:
Nordic Society for Pediatric Hematology and Oncology (NOPHO, #17424); Pan African Psycho-Oncology Society (PAPOS, no recent information).
Other Affiliates include:
African Organization for Research and Training in Cancer (AORTIC, #00405); European Association for Palliative Care (EAPC, #06141); International Association for Hospice and Palliative Care (IAHPC, #11941); International Campaign for Establishment and Development of Oncology Centres (ICEDOC, #12428); International Society for Nurses in Cancer Care (ISNCC, #15312).
Full Federation members in 25 countries:
Australia, Austria, Brazil, Canada, France, Germany, Greece, Hungary, Israel, Italy, Japan, Lithuania, Netherlands, New Zealand, Nigeria, Poland, Portugal, Romania, Spain, Sweden, Switzerland, Taiwan, Türkiye, UK, USA.
Affiliate Federation member in 1 country:
India.
Associate Federation members in 2 countries:
India, South Africa.

Consultative Status Consultative status granted from: *WHO (#20950)* (Official). **NGO Relations** Joint activities with: *European School of Oncology (ESO, #08434)*. Member of: *European Cancer Organisation (ECO, #06432); The NCD Alliance (NCDA, #16963); Union for International Cancer Control (UICC, #20415)*. Affiliate member of: *World Psychiatric Association (WPA, #21741)*. [2020/XC0006/y/**C**]

♦ International Public AMC Forum (IPAF) 14666

Coordinator Asian Development Bank, 6 ADB Avenue, 1550 Mandaluyong METRO MANILA, Philippines. T. +636324444.
URL: https://ipaf.adb.org/

History 27 May 2013. Conceptualized 23 Apr 2012, at the conclusion of the Hanoi Conference, co-hosted by *Asian Development Bank (ADB, #01422)*, Vietnam's Finance Ministry and Korea Asset Management Corporation (KAMCO). **Aims** Reinforce the regional asset management companies. **Structure** Coordinating Council; Secretariat. **Activities** Events/meetings; knowledge management/information dissemination; research/documentation; training/education. **Events** *Summit and Conference* Seoul (Korea Rep) 2019, *Summit and Conference* Hanoi (Vietnam) 2018, *Summit and Conference* Beijing (China) 2015, *Summit and Conference* Bangkok (Thailand) 2014, *Summit and Conference* Seoul (Korea Rep) 2013.

Members Founding members (7) in 5 countries:
China, Kazakhstan, Korea Rep, Thailand, Vietnam.
General members in 5 countries:
China, Indonesia, Korea Rep, Thailand, Vietnam.
Associate members in 4 countries:
Kazakhstan, Korea Rep, Malaysia, Thailand. [2019/AA0213/**F**]

♦ International Public Association – Academy of Navigation and Motion Control (internationally oriented national body)

♦ International Public Foundation (INTERLEGAL) 14667

Pres Krupskaya St 19/17, k 126, Moscow MOSKVA, Russia, 117331.

History 1989, Moscow (USSR), as *International Sociological and Legal Research Centre*, as an *European Economic and Social Committee (EESC, #06963)*. Also referred to as *Interlegal Foundation* and as *International Foundation for Political and Legal Research*. Subsequently changed title to *International Charitable Foundation for Political and Legal Research*. Registered in accordance with Russian law. **Aims** Promote *civil society* in *Russia* and the Commonwealth of Independent States – *CIS*; serve as a link between the independent sector of these countries and the rest of the world. **Events** *International conference on NGOs for transparency and against corruption* Amsterdam (Netherlands) 1999. **Publications** *Directory of Classifications of Public Associations.*

Members Branches in 4 countries:
Russia, Ukraine, USA, Uzbekistan.

IGO Relations Associated with Department of Global Communications of the United Nations. [2014/XF5476/f/**F**]

♦ International Public Lending Right Network / see PLR International (#18407)
♦ International Public Management Association for Human Resources (internationally oriented national body)

♦ International Public Management Network (IPMN) 14668

Address not obtained.
URL: https://ipmn.net/

History 1996. A US non-profit of the type 501(c)3. **Aims** Provide a forum for sharing ideas, concepts and results of research and practice in the field of public management; stimulate critical thinking about alternative approaches to problem solving and decision making in the public sector. **Structure** Board of Directors. **Activities** Events/meetings; awards/prizes/competitions. **Events** *Conference* Seoul (Korea Rep) 2021, *Conference* Seoul (Korea Rep) 2020, *Conference* Paris (France) 2019, *Conference* Bergen (Norway) 2018. **Publications** *IPMN Review*; *IPNM Journal*. [2018/XM8046/**F**]

♦ International Public Policy Association (IPPA) 14669

Gen Sec LET-ENTPE, 3 rue Maurice Audin, 69120 Vaulx-en-Velin, France. T. +33472047253. E-mail: icpublicpolicy@gmail.com.
URL: https://www.ippapublicpolicy.org/

History Dec 2014. Founded following the 1st International Conference on Public Policy (ICPP). Registration: No/ID: 809 239 262 000 11, France. **Aims** Promote scientific research in the field of Public Policy and contribute to its international development. **Structure** General Assembly; College; Executive Committee. **Languages** English, French. **Staff** 3.00 FTE, paid. **Finance** Sources: meeting proceeds; members' dues. **Activities** Awards/prizes/competitions; events/meetings; knowledge management/information dissemination; networking/liaising; publishing activities; research and development; training/education. **Events** *International Conference on Public Policy* Toronto, ON (Canada) 2023, *International Conference on Public Policy* Barcelona (Spain) 2021, *International Conference on Public Policy* Montréal, QC (Canada) 2019, *Asia Pacific Public Policy Network Conference* Chiang Mai (Thailand) 2017, *International Conference on Public Policy* Singapore (Singapore) 2017. **Publications** *IPPA Journal* (4 a year). *The International Series on Public Policy*. Teaching resources.

Members Institutional; Individual. Institutional in 19 countries and territories:
Belgium, Brazil, Canada, China, Ecuador, Egypt, Estonia, France, Germany, Hong Kong, India, Italy, Korea Rep, Mexico, Peru, Singapore, Spain, UK, USA.
Included in the above, the following 2 organizations listed in this Yearbook:
Fundació Institut Barcelona d'Estudis Internacionals (IBEI); Graduate School of Public and International Affairs, Pittsburgh (GSPIA).

NGO Relations Memorandum of Understanding with (1): *Asian Association for Public Administration (AAPA, #01334).* [2022.10.12/XM4083/**C**]

♦ International Public Policy Institute (internationally oriented national body)
♦ International Public Procurement Association / see International Public Procurement Conference (#14670)
♦ International Public Procurement Association (inactive)

♦ International Public Procurement Conference (IPPC) 14670

Administration Florida Atlantic Univ, 777 Glades Rd, Boca Raton FL 33431, USA. T. +15612707137.
Contact 4315 Tranquility Dr, Highland Beach FL 33487, USA.
URL: http://ippa.org/

History Founded Aug 2004, Fort Lauderdale FL (USA). Also features under the title: *International Public Procurement Association (IPPA)*. **Aims** Advance and share knowledge and best practices in public procurement. **Structure** Not a formal organization. Voluntary Advisory Council. **Languages** English. **Staff** 1.00 FTE, voluntary. **Finance** operational expenses (minimal) financed by Prof Khi V Thai. Governments sponsor biennial conferences held in their country. No annual budget. **Activities** Events/meetings. Active worldwide. **Events** *Biennial Conference* Arusha (Tanzania UR) 2018, *Biennial Conference* Bali (Indonesia) 2016, *Biennial Conference* Bali (Indonesia) 2016, *Biennial Conference* Dublin (Ireland) 2014, *Biennial Conference* Seattle, WA (USA) 2012. **Publications** Articles; conference papers. **Members** Not a membership organizations. [2018/XJ7520/c/**F**]

♦ International Public Relations Association (IPRA) 14671

Association internationale de relations publiques – Asociación Internacional de Relaciones Públicas

SG Suite 5879, PO Box 6945, London, W1A 6US, UK. T. +441634818308. E-mail: info@ipra.org – secgen@ipra.org.
URL: http://www.ipra.org/

History 1 May 1955, London (UK). Founded 1955, when Constitution was adopted. Current constitution adopted 6 May 2011. Registration: EU Transparency Register, No/ID: 59893117192-26. **Aims** Leading trust and ethics in global communication. **Structure** Board of Directors; Secretariat. **Languages** English. **Staff** 3.00 FTE, paid. **Finance** Sources: members' dues. **Activities** Awards/prizes/competitions; events/meetings; publishing activities; standards/guidelines. **Events** *World Congress* Montréal, QC (Canada) 2018, *Gulf Chapter Public Relations Summit* Dubai (United Arab Emirates) 2016, *World Congress* Johannesburg (South Africa) 2015, *World Congress* Dubai (United Arab Emirates) 2012, *World Congress* Lima (Peru) 2010. **Publications** *IPRA Gold Papers*; *IPRA Thought Leadership Essays*. *Model Code of Conduct*. **Information Services** *IPRA Thought Leadership Webinars*. **Members** Individuals (over 12,000). Membership countries not specified. **Consultative Status** Consultative status granted from: *ECOSOC (#05331)* (Ros A); *UNICEF (#20332)*; *UNEP (#20299)*. **IGO Relations** *ECOSOC (#05331)*. **NGO Relations** Links with national and regional public relations organizations. [2022.10.11/XB2386/v/**B**]

♦ International Public Relations Network (IPRN) 14672

Pres Avda de Europa 9 – Pozuelo, 28224 Madrid, Spain. T. +34629507253.
URL: http://www.iprn.com/

History 1995. Former names and other names: *International PR Network* – former. Registration: No/ID: 617962, Start date: 12 Jul 2019, Spain. **Aims** Provide a network of independent, owner managed PR agencies who are known to each other and trusted to give a thoroughly professional local response to the requirements of any member agencies' clients demanding selective public relations programmes, services and communication activities in any other countries worldwide. **Structure** Annual General Meeting; Board; Executive Council; Chairman; President; CEO; Committees; Administrative Office located in Madrid (Spain). **Languages** Chinese, Dutch, English, French, German, Italian, Polish, Portuguese, Spanish. **Staff** 3.00 FTE, paid; 40.00 FTE, voluntary. **Finance** Sources: members' dues; revenue from activities/projects; sponsorship. **Activities** Events/meetings; guidance/assistance/consulting; knowledge management/information dissemination; networking/liaising. **Events** *Annual General Meeting and Conference* Cartagena de Indias (Colombia) 2022, *Annual General Meeting* Lisbon (Portugal) 2021, *Annual General Meeting and Conference* Porto (Portugal) 2020, *European Regional Meeting* London (UK) 2019, *Annual General Meeting and Conference* Warsaw (Poland) 2019. **Publications** *IPRN Newsletter*. Blog; case studies; white papers; articles; videos; photos.

Members PR agencies (over 50) in 41 countries and territories:
Argentina, Austria, Belgium, Brazil, Canada, Chile, China, Colombia, Czechia, Denmark, Dominican Rep, England, Estonia, Finland, France, Germany, Greece, Hong Kong, India, Ireland, Italy, Japan, Luxembourg, Monaco, Netherlands, Panama, Poland, Portugal, Puerto Rico, Romania, Russia, San Marino, Saudi Arabia, South Africa, Spain, Sweden, Switzerland, UK, United Arab Emirates, USA, Wales.

NGO Relations Also links with local and international public relations associations. [2023/XF6725/**F**]

♦ International Public Safety Consortium (meeting series)

♦ International Public Sector Accounting Standards Board (IPSASB) . 14673

Managing Dir 277 Wellington St West, Toronto ON M5V 3H2, Canada.
Chair address not obtained.
URL: http://www.ipsasb.org/

History 1997. **Aims** Strengthen public financial management and knowledge globally through enhancement of quality and transparency of public sector financial reporting. **Structure** Public Interest Committee (PIC); Chairman; Consultative Advisory Group (CAG). Facilitated by: *International Federation of Accountants (IFAC, #13335)*. **Activities** Standards/guidelines: International Public Sector Accounting Standards (IPSAS). **Events** *Meeting* Toronto, ON (Canada) 2023, *Meeting* Toronto, ON (Canada) 2023, *Meeting* Washington, DC (USA) 2023, *Meeting* Zurich (Switzerland) 2023, *Meeting* Toronto, ON (Canada) 2022.

Members Individuals nominated by stakeholders. Members in 17 countries:
Australia, Austria, Brazil, Canada, China, France, Germany, Italy, Japan, New Zealand, Nigeria, Panama, Romania, South Africa, Switzerland, UK, USA. [2017/XM6030/v/**E**]

♦ International Public Television (INPUT) 14674

SG Prix Europa / RBB, 14046 Berlin, Germany. T. +49309799310910. Fax +49309799310919. E-mail: sec.gen@input-tv.org.
Pres ITVS, 651 Brannan St, Ste 410, San Francisco CA 94107, USA.
URL: http://www.input-tv.org/

History 1978, Bellagio (Italy), by *European Association of Regional Television (CIRCOM Regional, #06189)* and *The Rockefeller Foundation (#18966)*. **Aims** Promote and develop excellence in public *broadcasting*; increase cooperation in the field. **Structure** Board; Officers: President, Vice-President, General Secretary. **Activities** Events/meetings. **Events** *INPUT: International Public Television Screening Conference* Bangkok (Thailand) 2019, *INPUT : International Public Television Screening Conference / Conference* Tokyo (Japan) 2015, *INPUT : International Public Television Screening Conference / Conference* Helsinki (Finland) 2014, *INPUT : International Public Television Screening Conference* San Salvador (El Salvador) 2013, *INPUT : international public television screening conference / Conference* Sydney, NSW (Australia) 2012. **Publications** *INPUT Newsletter*.

Members Associate; Coordinators. Individuals in 28 countries:
Australia, Belgium, Brazil, Canada, Chile, Colombia, Denmark, Finland, France, Germany, Hungary, Ireland, Israel, Italy, Japan, Mexico, Netherlands, Norway, Poland, Russia, South Africa, Spain, Sweden, Switzerland, UK, Uruguay, USA, Venezuela.

Consultative Status Consultative status granted from: *UNESCO (#20322)* (Consultative Status). **NGO Relations** Cooperates with: *European Broadcasting Union (EBU, #06404)*; *Goethe-Institut*. [2018/XD7805/**D**]

♦ International Publishers Advertising Representatives Association (inactive)

♦ International Publishers Association (IPA) 14675

Union internationale des éditeurs (UIE) – Unión Internacional de Editores (UIE) – Internationale Verleger-Union (IVU)

SG 2nd floor, 23 Avenue de France, 1202 Geneva, Switzerland. T. +41227041820. Fax +41227041821. E-mail: secretariat@internationalpublishers.org – info@internationalpublishers.org.

URL: http://www.internationalpublishers.org/
History 1896, Paris (France). Former names and other names: *Congrès international des éditeurs* – former; *International Publishers Congress* – former. Registration: EU Transparency Register, No/ID: 018852925611-63, Start date: 26 Jan 2017. **Aims** Uphold and defend copyright and freedom of publishers to publish and distribute works of the mind; secure international cooperation among members; overcome *illiteracy*, lack of *books* and shortage of educational materials and means. **Structure** General Assembly (annual); Executive Committee; Secretariat; Specialized Sections, Groups and Committees. Meetings closed. **Languages** English, French, German, Spanish. **Staff** 4.00 FTE, paid. **Finance** Sources: members' dues. **Activities** Management of treaties and agreements: *Bern Convention for the Protection of Literary and Artistic Works, 1886 (1886); Universal Copyright Convention, 1952 (1952).* Takes part in revision and drafting of new Copyright Conventions; works to keep the flow of books from one country to another free of tariffs and other obstructions; submits reports to Universal Periodic Review at UN. **Events** *International Publishers Congress* Guadalajara (Mexico) 2024, *International Publishers Congress* Jakarta (Indonesia) 2022, *International Publishers Congress* Lillehammer (Norway) 2020, *Biennial Congress* Delhi (India) 2018, *Biennial Congress* London (UK) 2016. **Publications** *IPA Newsletter*. Reports; congress proceedings.
Members Regular national publisher's organizations in 49 countries:
Argentina, Australia, Belgium, Bosnia-Herzegovina, Brazil, Canada, China, Colombia, Denmark, Egypt, Finland, France, Georgia, Germany, Greece, Hungary, Iceland, India, Indonesia, Ireland, Israel, Italy, Japan, Kenya, Korea Rep, Lebanon, Lithuania, Mexico, Netherlands, New Zealand, Nigeria, Norway, Philippines, Portugal, Russia, Saudi Arabia, South Africa, Spain, Sri Lanka, Sweden, Switzerland, Thailand, Tunisia, Türkiye, UK, Ukraine, United Arab Emirates, USA, Venezuela.
Affiliate members in 3 countries:
Armenia, Serbia, Slovenia.
Associated autonomous groups (4):
African Publishers Network (APNET, #00426); Federation of European Publishers (FEP, #09536); Grupo Iberamericano de Editores (GIE, #10805); International Association of Scientific, Technical and Medical Publishers (STM, #12154).
Consultative Status Consultative status granted from: *ECOSOC (#05331)* (Ros C); *UNESCO (#20322)* (Consultative Status); *World Intellectual Property Organization (WIPO, #21593)* (Permanent Observer Status). **IGO Relations** Observer status with: *Intergovernmental Committee of the International Convention of Rome for the Protection of Performers, Producers of Phonograms and Broadcasting Organizations (#11474).* Accredited by: *United Nations Office at Vienna (UNOV, #20604).* Associated with Department of Global Communications of the United Nations. **NGO Relations** Member of: *EDItEUR (#05361); International Federation of Reproduction Rights Organizations (IFRRO, #13527)* (which was originally a joint working group with STM); *IFEX (#11100).* In liaison with technical committees of: *International Organization for Standardization (ISO, #14473).*
[2023/XB2388/y/**B**]

♦ International Publishers Congress / see International Publishers Association (#14675)
♦ International Publishing Distribution Association (unconfirmed)
♦ International Puijo Symposium (meeting series)
♦ International Pulse Trade and Industry Confederation / see Global Pulse Confederation (#10562)
♦ International Puppeteers Union (#20430)
♦ International Puppet Institute / see Institut international de la marionnette (#11314)
♦ International Purchasing and Supply Education and Research Association (internationally oriented national body)
♦ International A S Pushkin Foundation (internationally oriented national body)
♦ International Puzzle Federation / see World Puzzle Federation (#21743)
♦ International PV Equipment Association / see SOLARUNITED (#19677)

♦ International Pyrotechnics Society (IPS) 14676

Vice-Pres 4458 E Juanita Ave, Gilbert AZ 85234-7461, USA. T. +14803241775. Fax +14803241776.
Pres Weapons/Materials/Research Directorate, US Army Research Lab, Aberdeen Proving Ground, Aberdeen MD 21005, USA.
URL: http://www.intpyro.org/
History May 1980. Founded by Steering Committee of 6th International Pyrotechnics Seminar. **Aims** Promote and facilitate exchange of information concerning the science and technology of *energetic materials.* **Structure** Board of Directors. **Languages** English. **Staff** None. **Activities** Events/meetings. **Events** *Seminar* Colorado Springs, CO (USA) 2022, *Seminar* Tours (France) 2019, *Seminar* Fort Collins, CO (USA) 2018, *Seminar* Grand Junction, CO (USA) 2016, *Seminar* Toulouse (France) 2015. **Publications** *Propellants, Explosives, Pyrotechnics (PEP)* – journal. Seminar proceedings. **Members** Individuals (275) in 30 countries. Membership countries not specified. [2021/XJ3744/**D**]

♦ International Qajar Studies Association (IQSA) 14677

Anjoman-e Beynolmelali-e Ghaadjaarshenassi
Pres PO Box 31107, Santa Barbara CA 93130, USA. T. +18056871148. Fax +18056871148.
URL: https://www.iqsa.ursulinenconvent.com/
History 24 Jul 2000, by Manoutchehr M Eskandari-Qajar. Registered in the State of California (USA), 2001. **Aims** Promote exchange of views among *scholars* on the era of Qajar (Kadjar) *dynasty*, and with the public, so as to ensure survival of the contribution of the Qajars (Kadjars) and their era for future generations. **Structure** Board of Directors. Executive Officers: President; Vice-President; Executive Secretary; Treasurer; Editor-in-Chief; Chair Advisory Board; Regional Vice-Presidents (North America; Europe; Iran and Middle East). **Events** *Doctors and the medicinal arts in Qajar Iran* Vienna (Austria) 2016, *Conference* Maastricht (Netherlands) 2015, *Influences of Persian antiquity on Qajar era culture and thought* Bamberg (Germany) 2014, *Conference* Nijmegen (Netherlands) 2013, *Annual Conference / Conference* Boston, MA (USA) 2012. **Publications** *Qajar Studies* – journal. [2022/XJ1340/v/**C**]

♦ International Quaker Centre / see Quaker United Nations Office (#18588)
♦ International Quality Management and Organisational Development Conference (meeting series)

♦ International Quantitative Linguistics Association (IQLA) 14678

Internationale Gesellschaft für Quantitative Linguistik
Head Office Institut für Slawistic, Spitalgasse 2, Hof 3, 1090 Vienna, Austria. E-mail: office@iqla.org.
URL: http://www.iqla.org/
History Sep 1994, Moscow (Russia), at 2nd International Conference on Quantitative Linguistics (QUALICO-2). **Aims** Promote the development of theoretical and applied quantitative linguistics; stimulate global communication of scientists working in the field. **Structure** Executive Committee. Council comprising President. Vice-President, Treasurer, Secretary-General and 4 Members-at-large. Executive Committee. Other committees: Meeting; Membership and Chapters; Constitution. **Languages** English, French, German. **Staff** None. **Finance** Members' dues. Sales of publications; advertising. **Activities** Holds international conferences, establishes chapters, sponsors other activities. **Events** *International Quantitative Linguistics Conference (QUALICO)* Lausanne (Switzerland) 2023, *International Quantitative Linguistics Conference (QUALICO)* Tokyo (Japan) 2021, *International Quantitative Linguistics Conference (QUALICO)* Tokyo (Japan) 2020, *International Quantitative Linguistics Conference (QUALICO)* Wroclaw (Poland) 2018, *Quantitative Linguistics Conference (QUALICO)* Trier (Germany) 2016. **Publications** *Journal of Quantitative Linguistics.*
Members Individuals in 22 countries:
Austria, Belarus, Belgium, Canada, Czechia, Denmark, Estonia, Finland, France, Germany, Greece, India, Italy, Japan, Korea Rep, Latvia, Netherlands, Russia, Singapore, UK, Ukraine, USA. [2020/XD6483/v/**D**]

♦ International Quantum Electronics Conference (meeting series)
♦ International Quantum Logic Association / see International Quantum Structures Association (#14679)

♦ International Quantum Structures Association (IQSA) 14679

Sec CLEA and FUND, VUB, Dept of Mathematics, Krijgskundestraat 33, 1160 Brussels, Belgium. T. +3226442677. Fax +3226440744.
URL: http://www.vub.ac.be/CLEA/IQSA/
History 3 Mar 1991, when constitution accepted; original title *International Quantum Logic Association*, current name adopted later in 1991. **Aims** Advance and disseminate quantum logic and structures based thereon in their mathematical, philosophical, physical and interdisciplinary aspects. **Activities** Conferences; computer mailing lists. **Events** *Biennial Conference* Tropea (Italy) 2021, *Biennial Conference* Tropea (Italy) 2020, *Biennial Conference* Kazan (Russia) 2018, *Biennial Conference* Leicester (UK) 2016, *Biennial Conference* Olomouc (Czech Rep) 2014.

Members Among others, in 7 countries:
Czechia, France, Germany, Italy, Slovakia, UK, USA. [2013/XD6487/**D**]

♦ International Quorum of Film and Video Producers / see International Quorum of Motion Picture Producers (#14680)
♦ International Quorum of Motion Picture Producers / see International Quorum of Motion Picture Producers (#14680)

♦ International Quorum of Motion Picture Producers (IQ) 14680

Admin Office 810 Dominican Dr, Nashville TN 37228, USA. T. +16152554000. Fax +16152554111. E-mail: info@iqfilm.org.
URL: http://www.iqfilm.org/
History 1966, as *International Quorum of Motion Picture Producers.* Adopted new name *International Quorum of Film and Video Producers (IQ)*, 1982. Currently known under original title. **Aims** Foster exchange of ideas and information on producing high-quality film, video and new media. **Structure** Board of Governors. **Staff** 2.00 FTE, paid. **Finance** Members' dues. **Events** *Annual Conference* Paris (France) 2018, *Annual Conference* Miami, FL (USA) 2016, *Annual Conference* Delhi (India) 2015, *Annual Conference* Reykjavik (Iceland) 2014, *Annual Conference* Montréal, QC (Canada) 2013.
Members Full in 36 countries and territories:
Albania, Argentina, Australia, Austria, Bahamas, Belgium, Brazil, Canada, Chile, China, Costa Rica, Cuba, Czechia, Denmark, Estonia, Finland, France, Germany, Hong Kong, Hungary, Iceland, Italy, Japan, Mexico, Netherlands, New Zealand, Norway, Peru, Romania, Slovenia, South Africa, Spain, Sweden, Switzerland, UK, USA. [2019.02.16/XF0382/**F**]

♦ International Qur'anic Studies Association (IQSA) 14681

Exec Dir c/o The Luce Ctr, 825 Houston Mill Rd Northeast, Atlanta GA 30329, USA. E-mail: contact@iqsaweb.org.
URL: http://iqsaweb.org/
History 2012. **Aims** Be a network for a diverse range of scholars and educators; serve to advocate for the field of Qur'anic studies. **Structure** Board of Directors; Executive Office; Standing Committees. **Activities** Events/meetings; publishing activities; networking/liaising; training/education. **Events** *Annual Meeting* Atlanta, GA (USA) 2015, *Annual Meeting* San Diego, CA (USA) 2014, *Annual Meeting* Baltimore, MD (USA) 2013. **Publications** *Journal of the International Qur'anic Studies Association*; *Review of Qur'anic Research.* Conference papers. [2018.09.05/XJ9717/**D**]

♦ International Qwan Ki Do Federation (IQKDF) 14682

Contact address not obtained. E-mail: info@qwankido.org.
URL: http://qwankido.ca/
Aims Manage all competitions and meetings in Qwan Ki Do – the Vietnamese Traditional *Martial Arts.* **Structure** Office – shared with *World Union of Qwan-Ki-Do (WUQKD, #21884).*
Members Full in 26 countries and territories:
Algeria, Austria, Belgium, Brazil, Burkina Faso, Canada, Central African Rep, Congo Brazzaville, Côte d'Ivoire, Denmark, England, France, Germany, Guinea-Bissau, Hungary, Ireland, Italy, Moldova, Morocco, Norway, Romania, Senegal, Spain, Switzerland, Ukraine, USA.
NGO Relations Member of: *The Association for International Sport for All (TAFISA, #02763).*
[2016/XM5485/**C**]

♦ International Raceboard Class Association (see: #21760)

♦ International Racquetball Federation (IRF) 14683

SG 1631 Mesa Avenue, Colorado Springs CO 80906, USA. T. +17194332017.
Dir address not obtained.
URL: http://www.internationalracquetball.com/
History 1979. Constitution most recently modified 2014. Former names and other names: *International Amateur Racquetball Federation (IARF)* – former. Registration: USA. **Aims** Develop and promote racquetball worldwide by working with countries and organizations to increase participation and competition. **Structure** World Congress; Extra-Ordinary World Congress. Board of Directors; Executive Committee. Standing Committees; Ad-hoc Committees. Regions: South America; Asia; Europe; Central America and Caribbean; North America. **Languages** English. **Activities** Events/meetings. **Events** *Biennial world congress* Phoenix, AZ (USA) 1996, *Congress* 1986. **Publications** *Racquetball Magazine* (2 a month).
Members Full; Developing. National associations and federations in 100 countries and territories:
Antigua, Argentina, Armenia, Aruba, Australia, Austria, Bahamas, Bahrain, Barbados, Belgium, Belize, Bermuda, Bolivia, Brazil, Cameroon, Canada, Cayman Is, Chile, China, Colombia, Cook Is, Costa Rica, Cuba, Czechia, Denmark, Dominican Rep, Ecuador, Egypt, El Salvador, England, Eritrea, Fiji, Finland, France, Germany, Ghana, Greece, Guam, Guatemala, Haiti, Honduras, Hong Kong, Hungary, Iceland, India, Indonesia, Iran Islamic Rep, Iraq, Ireland, Israel, Italy, Jamaica, Japan, Korea Rep, Kuwait, Laos, Lebanon, Lithuania, Luxembourg, Malaysia, Mexico, Moldova, Nepal, Netherlands, New Zealand, Nicaragua, Nigeria, Northern Mariana Is, Norway, Pakistan, Palau, Panama, Paraguay, Peru, Philippines, Poland, Puerto Rico, Samoa, Samoa USA, Saudi Arabia, Singapore, South Africa, Spain, St Kitts Is, Sweden, Switzerland, Taiwan, Tajikistan, Tonga, Trinidad-Tobago, Türkiye, Ukraine, United Arab Emirates, Uruguay, USA, Venezuela, Vietnam, Virgin Is UK, Virgin Is USA, Zimbabwe.
NGO Relations Member of (2): *Association of the IOC Recognized International Sports Federations (ARISF, #02767); Olympic Movement (#17719).* Cooperates with (1): *International Testing Agency (ITA, #15678).* Recognized by: *International Olympic Committee (IOC, #14408).* [2023.02.17/XD7660/**C**]

♦ International Racquet Sports Association / see International Health, Racquet and Sportsclub Association (#13783)

♦ International Radiation Commission (IRC) 14684

Commission internationale des radiations
Sec LASP, Campus Box 311, University of Colorado, Boulder CO 80309-0311, USA. T. +13034925724.
Pres PMOD/WRC, Dorfstrasse 33, 7260 Davos GR, Switzerland. T. +41814175111.
URL: http://www.irc-iamas.org/
History 1924, Madrid (Spain), as Radiation Commission of International Union of Geodesy and Geophysics (IUGG). At IUGG Assembly, 1948, Oslo (Norway), became a commission of the then *'International Association of Meteorology – Association internationale de météorologie'*, currently *International Association of Meteorology and Atmospheric Sciences (IAMAS, #12031).* Also referred to as *IAMAP International Radiation Commission – Commission internationale des radiations de l'AIMPA.* **Aims** Promote research into *atmospheric radiation* as well as application of that research to practical problems, including on the following topics: optical phenomena in the atmosphere; radiative properties of atmospheric constituents and of the earth's surface; radiative properties of planetary atmospheres; radiant energy transfer; radiant energy interaction with other features of the atmosphere; remote sensing of atmosphere and surface. **Structure** Officers: President; Vice-President; Secretary. **Languages** English. **Staff** Voluntary. **Finance** Through IAMAS. **Activities** Research/documentation; awards/prizes/competitions; knowledge management/information dissemination. **Events** *Quadrennial International Radiation Symposium* Auckland (New Zealand) 2016, *International TOVS Study Conference* Jeju (Korea Rep) 2014, *Quadrennial International Radiation Symposium / Quadrennial Symposium* Berlin (Germany) 2012, *Quadrennial international radiation symposium / Quadrennial Symposium* Foz do Iguaçu (Brazil) 2008, *Quadrennial Symposium* Busan (Korea Rep) 2004.
Members Individuals in 17 countries:
Australia, Austria, Belgium, Brazil, Canada, China, France, Germany, India, Italy, Japan, Korea Rep, Russia, South Africa, Switzerland, UK, USA.
IGO Relations Joint Working Group with: *World Meteorological Organization (WMO, #21649).*
[2015/XE3835/v/**E**]

♦ International Radiation Physics Society (IRPS) 14685

Sec Alma Mater Studiorum Univ de Bologna, Labo di Montecuccolino, Dept Industrial Engineering, vi dei Colli 16, 40136 Bologna BO, Italy.
URL: http://www.canberra.edu.au/irps/home/
History 1985, Ferrara (Italy), during the 3rd International Symposium on Radiation Physics. **Aims** Promote global exchange and integration of scientific information pertaining to the interdisciplinary subject of radiation physics, including the promotion of (i) theoretical and experimental research in radiation physics, (ii) investigation of physical aspects of interactions of radiations with living systems, (iii) education in radiation physics and (iv) utilization of radiations for peaceful purposes. **Languages** English. **Activities** Events/

meetings. **Events** *Symposium* Córdoba (Argentina) 2018, *International Forum on Advances in Radiation Physics* Buenos Aires (Argentina) 2017, *International Topical Meeting on Industrial Radiation and Radioisotope Measurement Applications* Chicago, IL (USA) 2017, *Symposium* Beijing (China) 2015, *Symposium* Salvador (Brazil) 2012. **Publications** *IRPS Bulletin* (4 a year).
Members Individuals in 54 countries and territories:
Argentina, Australia, Austria, Belgium, Botswana, Brazil, Canada, China, Croatia, Czechia, Denmark, Ecuador, Egypt, Finland, France, Germany, Ghana, Gibraltar, Greece, Hungary, India, Iran Islamic Rep, Italy, Japan, Jordan, Kenya, Korea Rep, Latvia, Libya, Mexico, Morocco, Namibia, Netherlands, New Zealand, Nigeria, Pakistan, Portugal, Romania, Russia, Saudi Arabia, Serbia, Slovenia, South Africa, Spain, Sweden, Switzerland, Syrian AR, Tanzania UR, Thailand, Togo, Türkiye, UK, Ukraine, USA.
[2017.01.10/XD7627/v/**D**]

♦ International Radiation Protection Association (IRPA) 14686

Association internationale pour la protection contre les radiations
Pres EDF-DPNT/DPN, Cap Ampère, 1 place Pleyel, 93282 St Denis CEDEX, France.
URL: http://www.irpa.net/
History 7 Sep 1966, Rome (Italy). Founded at 1st General Assembly, a preliminary working group having met in 1964, Paris (France), on the initiative of a committee of the *'Health Physics Society'*. Former names and other names: *Association internationale de radioprotection (AIRP)* – alias. **Aims** Provide a medium whereby those engaged in radiation protection activities may communicate more readily with each other; advance radiation protection. **Structure** General Assembly (every 4 years); Executive Council; Committees; Commissions. **Languages** English. **Staff** Voluntary. **Finance** Sources: meeting proceeds; members' dues. **Activities** Awards/prizes/competitions; events/meetings; publishing activities. **Events** *Congress* Orlando, FL (USA) 2024, *European Regional Congress* Budapest (Hungary) 2022, *Congress* Seoul (Korea Rep) 2021, *Congress* Seoul (Korea Rep) 2020, *African Regional Congress* Tunis (Tunisia) 2018. **Publications** *Health Physics Society Journal.* Congress proceedings; brochures.
Members Associate Societies totalling about 20,000 members, in 53 countries:
Argentina, Australia, Austria, Belgium, Brazil, Bulgaria, Canada, China, Colombia, Croatia, Cuba, Cyprus, Czechia, Denmark, Egypt, Finland, France, Germany, Greece, Hungary, India, Iran Islamic Rep, Ireland, Israel, Italy, Japan, Korea Rep, Lithuania, Madagascar, Malaysia, Mexico, Montenegro, Morocco, Netherlands, New Zealand, Norway, Peru, Philippines, Poland, Portugal, Romania, Russia, Serbia, Slovakia, Slovenia, South Africa, Spain, Sweden, Switzerland, UK, Uruguay, USA, Venezuela.
Associate regional societies (2) listed in this Yearbook:
Eastern Africa Association for Radiation Protection (EAARP); Nordic Society for Radiation Protection (#17428).
Consultative Status Consultative status granted from: *ECOSOC (#05331)* (Ros C); *ILO (#11123)* (Special List). **IGO Relations** Affiliated with: *International Atomic Energy Agency (IAEA, #12294).* Accredited by: *United Nations Office at Vienna (UNOV, #20604).* [2022.06.15/XC2390/**C**]

- ♦ International Radiobiological Society (inactive)
- ♦ International Radiocarbon Conference (meeting series)
- ♦ International Radio Consultative Committee (inactive)
- ♦ International Radio-Controlled Models Society (inactive)
- ♦ International Radioecology Laboratory (internationally oriented national body)

♦ International Radio Sailing Association (IRSA) 14687

Sec 1707 Warm Springs, Boise ID 83712, USA. T. +12083673500. E-mail: secretary@radiosailing.org.
URL: http://www.radiosailing.org/
History Original title: ISAF RSD (Radio Sailing Division). Current title adopted 25 Aug 2010. **Aims** Provide technical support for our International Classes and their Class Rules. **Structure** Executive Committee of 11. Includes: *International One Metre International Class Association (IOMICA, see: #14687).* **Activities** Financial and/or material support; sporting activities.
Members National members in 29 countries:
Argentina, Australia, Austria, Barbados, Belgium, Brazil, Canada, Chile, Croatia, Czechia, Denmark, Finland, France, Germany, Ireland, Israel, Italy, Japan, Malta, Netherlands, New Zealand, Norway, Portugal, South Africa, Spain, Switzerland, Türkiye, UK, USA.
NGO Relations Affiliate member of: *World Sailing (#21760).* [2014/XJ6296/**C**]

♦ International Radiostereometry Society (IRSA) 14688

Sec address not obtained.
Pres Albinusdreef 2, 2333 ZA Leiden, Netherlands.
URL: https://radiostereometry.org/
History Apr 2011, Leiden (Netherlands). 1st RSA meeting organized 2009; at 2nd meeting the network was founded; official society founded 2017, Australia. Former names and other names: *Clinical RSA Research Network* – former. Registration: Handelsregister, No/ID: KVK 71384677, Netherlands. **Aims** Promote research and development in radiostereometry (RSA) and related sciences worldwide. **Structure** General Meeting; Board. **Finance** Sources: members' dues. **Activities** Awards/prizes/competitions; events/meetings; knowledge management/information dissemination; networking/liaising; training/education. **Events** *International RSA Meeting* Nijmegen (Netherlands) 2023, *International RSA Meeting* Oslo (Norway) 2021, *International RSA Meeting* Aarhus (Denmark) 2019, *International RSA Meeting* Adelaide, SA (Australia) 2017, *International RSA Meeting* Bologna (Italy) 2015. [2022/AA2799/**C**]

- ♦ International Radiotelegraph Convention (1912 treaty)
- ♦ International Radio and Television Organization (inactive)

♦ International Radio and Television Union 14689

Union radiophonique et télévisuelle internationale (URTI)
Dir Gen 66 Avenue des Champs-Elysées, Bureau 41, 75008 Paris, France. T. +33663894038. E-mail: contact@urti.org.
URL: http://www.urti.org/
History 1947, Nice (France). Founded during an international congress on culture for radio, following resolution of UNESCO General Assembly 1947, Mexico City (Mexico). Present Charter approved by General Assembly, 28 May 1998, Paris (France). Former names and other names: *Université radiophonique internationale (URI)* – former (Feb 1949 to 1961); *International Radio and Television University* – former (1961); *Université radiophonique et télévisuelle internationale (URTI)* – former (1961); *Universidad Internacional de Radio y Televisión* – former (1961); *Internationale Rundfunk- und Fernsehuniversität* – former (1961); *Universidade Radiofónica e Televisiva Internacional* – former (1961); *Unión Internacional de Radio y Televisión* – former; *Unione Radiofónica e Televisiva Internacional* – former. Registration: France. **Aims** Promote international circulation of audiovisual works. **Structure** General Assembly (annual); Bureau/Executive Committee; Radio and Television Programme Commissions. **Languages** Arabic, English, French. **Staff** 5.00 FTE, paid. **Finance** Sources: contributions; donations; grants; in-kind support; members' dues. **Activities** Awards/prizes/competitions; events/meetings; networking/liaising; training/education. **Events** *Annual General Assembly* Paris (France) 2014, *Annual General Assembly* Paris (France) 2006, *Annual General Assembly* Paris (France) 1999, *Annual General Assembly* Paris (France) 1988, *Annual General Assembly* Paris (France) 1986. **Publications** Catalogues; coproduction programmes (CD; DVD); guide of acquisition; flyers.
Members Membership open to: radio or television bodies or groups of bodies; bodies of cultural vocation (universities, museums, research centres); individuals. Members in 50 countries and territories:
Albania, Algeria, Belarus, Belgium, Benin, Bosnia-Herzegovina, Bulgaria, Burkina Faso, Burundi, Cameroon, Canada, Central African Rep, Chad, Comoros, Congo Brazzaville, Côte d'Ivoire, Croatia, Cyprus, Djibouti, Egypt, France, Gabon, Greece, Guinea, Hungary, Iraq, Italy, Jordan, Kosovo, Latvia, Libya, Mali, Mauritania, Moldova, Morocco, Niger, North Macedonia, Palestine, Poland, Portugal, Romania, Russia, Rwanda, Senegal, Syrian AR, Togo, Tunisia, Ukraine, Vietnam, Yemen.
Consultative Status Consultative status granted from: *UNESCO (#20322)* (Associate Status). **IGO Relations** Cooperates with (1): *Arab States Broadcasting Union (ASBU, #01050).* **NGO Relations** Cooperates with (2): *Mediterranean Centre of Audiovisual Communication (#16648); Permanent Conference of Mediterranean Audiovisual Operators (COPEAM, #18320).* [2022/XF2393/**C**]

- ♦ International Radio and Television University / see International Radio and Television Union (#14689)

♦ International Raelian Movement (IRM) 14690

Mouvement raëlien international
Address not obtained.
URL: http://www.rael.org/
History 13 Dec 1973, France, as *Raelian Religion – Religion raëlienne.* **Aims** Establish an embassy for officially receiving *extra-terrestrials*; disseminate the message received by Rael from extra-terrestrials concerning the future of humanity and the value of sensual *meditation* in *personal development.* **Structure** Guide of Guides (Rael); Secretary-Rael's Assistant; Treasurer. Continental Guides (7); Wise Council, consisting of 3 members, including President. **Finance** Members work voluntarily for, and make their own decisions about their level of financial contribution to, the Movement. **Activities** Organizes: international conventions; seminars for training Guides; training in sensual meditation – a set of techniques for awakening the mind. Also organizes annual gatherings: first Sunday of April; 6 August; 7 October; 13 December; dates of transmissions of the cellular plan (Raelian baptême). **Events** *International convention* Geneva (Switzerland) 2000, *International Convention* Clermont-Ferrand (France) 1998, *Convention/seminar* Albi (France) 1991, *Convention/seminar* Montréal, QC (Canada) 1991, *Convention/seminar* Albi (France) 1990. **Publications** *Apocalypse revue.* Books in various languages.
Members National movements in 68 countries and territories:
Angola, Argentina, Australia, Belgium, Benin, Bolivia, Brazil, Burkina Faso, Cameroon, Canada, Chad, Chile, Colombia, Congo Brazzaville, Costa Rica, Côte d'Ivoire, Denmark, Dominican Rep, Ecuador, France, Gabon, Germany, Ghana, Greece, Guadeloupe, Haiti, Hawaii, Hungary, Ireland, Israel, Italy, Japan, Korea Rep, Lithuania, Malaysia, Martinique, Mauritania, Mexico, Nepal, Netherlands, New Zealand, Niger, Nigeria, Panama, Paraguay, Peru, Philippines, Poland, Polynesia Fr, Portugal, Puerto Rico, Réunion, Senegal, Singapore, Slovakia, Slovenia, South Africa, Spain, Sri Lanka, Sweden, Switzerland, Taiwan, Thailand, Togo, UK, Uruguay, USA, Venezuela, Zimbabwe.
Individuals in 11 countries and territories:
China, Denmark, Egypt, Hong Kong, India, Iran Islamic Rep, Mongolia, Morocco, Pakistan, Russia, United Arab Emirates.
[2014/XF4556/**F**]

♦ International Rafting Federation (IRF) 14691

SG 2 Aristea Road, Bergvliet, Cape Town, 7945, South Africa. E-mail: gte@internationalrafting.com – info@internationalrafting.com.
Pres address not obtained.
URL: http://www.internationalrafting.com/
History 1997. Resulting from a growing need and demand for an official body that could represent and unite rafting communities worldwide. **Aims** Promote: development of the rafting *sport*; conservation of river environs; *tourism* through rafting; education and training. Facilitate the growing demands of the rafting fraternity through a unified body that deals exclusively with rafting issues and factors which influence the development of rafting. **Structure** Board of Directors. **Languages** English. **Finance** Sources: fees for services; members' dues. Other sources: guide training and education fees; event hosting fees. **Activities** Capacity building; events/meetings; sporting activities. **Events** *Congress* 2021, *Congress* Tully, QLD (Australia) 2019. **Publications** *IRF Newsletter.*
Members Organizations in 52 countries:
Albania, Argentina, Armenia, Australia, Austria, Belgium, Bosnia-Herzegovina, Brazil, Bulgaria, Canada, Chile, China, Colombia, Costa Rica, Croatia, Czechia, Denmark, Dominican Rep, Ecuador, Finland, France, Georgia, Germany, Hungary, India, Indonesia, Italy, Japan, Kazakhstan, Latvia, Malaysia, Mexico, Mongolia, Montenegro, Nepal, Netherlands, New Zealand, Norway, Portugal, Romania, Russia, Serbia, Slovakia, Slovenia, South Africa, Switzerland, Türkiye, UK, Ukraine, United Arab Emirates, USA, Venezuela.
NGO Relations Member of (1): *Alliance of Independent recognised Members of Sport (AIMS, #00690)* (Observer). [2022/XD5355/**C**]

♦ International Ragweed Society (IRS) 14692

SG Univ of Milano Bicocca, Piazza della Scienza 1, 20126 Milan MI, Italy.
Pres Réseau Natl de Surveillance Aérobilogique, 11 chemin de la Creuzille, 69690 Brussieu, France.
URL: http://www.internationalragweedsociety.org/
History 2 Oct 2009, Nyon (Switzerland). Registration: Switzerland. **Aims** Promote knowledge concerning ragweed (Ambrosia artemisiifolia L) and further its development; facilitate collaboration, research, education, information, technical development, practical applications and laws concerning ragweed and its direct and indirect impacts, as well as fight against that plant. **Structure** General Assembly; Committee. **Languages** English. **Staff** Voluntary. **Finance** Members' dues. **Activities** Events/meetings; awards/prizes/competitions. **Events** *International Ragweed Congress* Budapest (Hungary) 2022, *International Ragweed Congress* Milan (Italy) 2014, *Ambrosia International Colloquium* Lyon (France) 2012, *International Ragweed Congress* Lyon (France) 2012, *International Ragweed Congress* Budapest (Hungary) 2008. **Publications** Conference papers online.
Members Full (40) in 8 countries:
Austria, Canada, Croatia, France, Hungary, Italy, Serbia, Switzerland. [2022/XJ6350/**D**]

- ♦ International Raiffeisen Union (#13291)
- ♦ International Rail Freight Business Association (unconfirmed)
- ♦ International Rail Makers Association (inactive)
- ♦ International Rail Transport Committee (#04188)
- ♦ International Railway Congress Association (inactive)
- ♦ International Railway Strategic Management Institute (internationally oriented national body)
- ♦ International Railway Temperance Union (inactive)

♦ International Rainbowfish Association 14693

Internationale Gesellschaft für Regenbogenfische (IRG)
Pres PO Box 170209, 42624 Solingen, Germany. T. +49212819878. Fax +49212816216.
URL: http://www.irg-online.de/
History 1986. Registration: Germany. **Aims** Propagate the keeping and breeding of and scientific research on rainbowfish – Melanotaeniidae and blue-eyes – Pseudomugilidae. **Languages** Dutch, German. **Staff** 5.00 FTE, voluntary. **Finance** Members' dues. **Activities** Conservation activities. **Events** *Meeting* Mechelen (Belgium) 2008, *Meeting* Harrislee (Germany) 2007, *Meeting* Harrachov (Czech Rep) 2006, *Meeting* Lindau (Germany) 2005, *Meeting* Lindow (Germany) 2005. **Publications** *Rainbowfish* (4 a year).
Members Full in 15 countries:
Australia, Austria, Belgium, Czechia, Denmark, France, Germany, Italy, Luxembourg, Netherlands, Norway, Sweden, Switzerland, UK, USA. [2022/XD7297/**D**]

♦ International Rainwater Catchment Systems Association (IRCSA) . . 14694

Pres address not obtained.
URL: http://ircsa.in/
History Aug 1989, Manila (Philippines), at 4th International Rainwater Cistern Systems Conference. Officially launched, Aug 1991, Taiwan. **Aims** Promote and advance rainwater catchment systems technology with respect to planning, development, management, science, technology, research and education worldwide; establish an international forum for scientists, engineers, educators, administrators and those concerned in this field; draft international guidelines on this technology and update and disseminate information; collaborate with and support international programmes. **Structure** Officers: President; Immediate Past-President; Past-President; 3 Vice-Presidents; Secretary-General; Treasurer. Regional Directors (Africa, Europe, Latin America/Caribbean, North America, South Asia, East Asia, Middle East, Pacific/Australia); 3 Directors (Urban Affairs, Women's Programmes, Special Programmes); Director-at-large. 41 National Representatives. Regional organizations: ARCSA (North America); EARCSA (East Asia); *Latin American and Caribbean Rainwater Harvesting Network (no recent information); Southern and Eastern Africa Rainwater Network (SearNet, #19876).* **Languages** English. **Staff** None. **Finance** Members' dues. **Activities** Organizes *'International Rainwater Catchment Systems Conference'.* **Events** *Conference* Nanjing (China) 2013, *Conference* Taiwan 2011, *Conference* Malaysia 2009, *Conference* Sydney, NSW (Australia) 2007, *Mainstreaming rainwater harvesting* Delhi (India) 2005. **Publications** *Raindrop* (2 a year).
Members Organizational; Individual. Organizations in 22 countries and territories:
Botswana, Brazil, Burundi, China, Ethiopia, Germany, India, Iran Islamic Rep, Japan, Kenya, Malawi, Mexico, Philippines, Rwanda, Somalia, Sri Lanka, Taiwan, Tanzania UR, Uganda, USA, Zambia, Zimbabwe.
Individuals in 51 countries and territories:
Algeria, Argentina, Australia, Austria, Bangladesh, Belgium, Benin, Bolivia, Cameroon, Canada, Chile, Congo DR, Cuba, Denmark, Egypt, Fiji, France, Ghana, Guam, Guinea-Bissau, Haiti, Indonesia, Israel, Kiribati, Korea Rep, Libya, Luxembourg, Malaysia, Morocco, Mozambique, Nepal, Netherlands, New Zealand, Nicaragua, Nigeria, Pakistan, Palestine, Peru, Senegal, Singapore, Slovakia, South Africa, Spain, Sweden, Switzerland, Türkiye, UK, Ukraine, Uzbekistan, Vietnam.
[2014/XD5788/**D**]

♦ International Rainwater Harvesting Alliance (IRHA) 14695

Alliance internationale pour la gestion de l'eau de pluie

Main Office International Environment House 2, Chemin de Balexert 9, Châtelaine, 1219 Geneva, Switzerland. T. +41227974157. E-mail: secretariat@irha-h2o.org.
URL: https://www.irha-h2o.org

History Nov 2002. Founded after World Summit of *United Nations Conference on Environment and Development (UNCED)*, Johannesburg (South Africa). Former names and other names: *Alianza Internacional para la Gestión del Agua de Lluvia* – former. **Aims** Promote rainwater harvesting as an effective and sustainable solution in the face of water shortages and floods, which weaken ecosystems and communities. **Structure** General Assembly; Committee; Secretariat, located in Geneva (Switzerland). **Languages** English, French. **Staff** 1.50 FTE, paid. **Finance** Sources: donations; members' dues; private foundations. Other sources: crowfunding; consultancy fees. **Activities** Advocacy/lobbying/activism; awareness raising; events/meetings; knowledge management/information dissemination; networking/liaising; projects/programmes; training/education. **Publications** *IRHA Newsletter*. Annual Reports; articles. **Members** Individuals; Organizations; Private Sector. Members (150) in 48 countries. Membership countries not specified. **Consultative Status** Consultative status granted from: *ECOSOC (#05331)* (Special). **IGO Relations** Partner of (2): *Swiss Agency for Development and Cooperation (SDC); United Nations Human Settlements Programme (UN-Habitat, #20572)*. **NGO Relations** Member of (4): Aguasan Community of Practice; *International Water Association (IWA, #15865); Sustainable Sanitation Alliance (SuSanA, #20066); World Overview of Conservation Approaches and Technologies (WOCAT, see: #21192)*. [2022.10.19/XM0970/y/**F**]

♦ International Rainwear Council (inactive)
♦ International Ramen Manufacturers Association / see World Instant Noodles Association (#21586)

♦ International Rangeland Congress (IRC) 14696

Address not obtained.
URL: http://www.rangelandcongress.com/

Aims Promote interchange of scientific and technical information on all aspects of rangelands. **Structure** A congress series, not an organization. Continuing Committee, replaces the former *International Rangeland Society*. **Finance** Members' dues. **Events** *International Rangeland Congress (IRC)* Adelaide, SA (Australia) 2025, *International Rangeland Congress (IRC)* Saskatoon, SK (Canada) 2016, *International Rangeland Congress (IRC)* Rosario (Argentina) 2011, *International Rangeland Congress (IRC)* Hohhot (China) 2008, *International Rangeland Congress (IRC)* Durban (South Africa) 2003. **Publications** Proceedings congress.
Members Continuing Committee members (17) in 12 countries:
Algeria, Australia, France, Greece, India, Mexico, Pakistan, South Africa, UK, United Arab Emirates, USA, Zambia.
[2022/XD5701/c/**F**]

♦ International Range Officers Association (internationally oriented national body)

♦ International Ranger Federation (IRF) 14697

Federación Internacional de Guardaparques (FIG)

Sec PO Box 3031, Asquith, Sydney NSW 2077, Australia. E-mail: secretary@internationalrangers.org.
URL: http://internationalrangers.org/

History 1992. **Aims** Further professional standards of *park rangers* and park wardens worldwide; foster communication and professional exchanges among rangers. **Structure** Council. Official charity arm: *Thin Green Line Foundation*. **Languages** English, Spanish. **Staff** 1.00 FTE, paid. **Finance** Donations. **Events** *World Ranger Congress* Sauraha (Nepal) 2019, *World Ranger Congress* Estes Park, CO (USA) 2016, *World Ranger Congress* Arusha (Tanzania UR) 2012, *World Ranger Congress* Santa Cruz (Bolivia) 2009, *World Ranger Congress* Stirling (UK) 2006. **Publications** *Guardeparque* (12 a year) – online; *Thin Green Line* (4 a year).
Members Full national organizations in 35 countries:
Argentina, Australia, Austria, Bolivia, Brazil, Canada, Chile, Costa Rica, Côte d'Ivoire, Czechia, Denmark, Ecuador, Finland, Germany, Guatemala, Iceland, India, Ireland, Italy, Korea Rep, Nepal, Norway, Paraguay, Peru, Poland, Portugal, Romania, Russia, Slovakia, South Africa, Spain, Sweden, UK, Uruguay, USA.
Included in the above, 1 organization listed in this Yearbook:
Game Rangers Association of Africa (GRAA).
Associate national organizations in 9 countries:
Cameroon, China, Dominican Rep, Fiji, Kenya, Malta, Papua New Guinea, Slovenia, Venezuela.
IGO Relations *UNESCO (#20322)*. **NGO Relations** Member of (1): *Species Survival Network (SSN, #19916)*.
[2017/XG7216/**D**]

♦ International Ranking Expert Group / see IREG Observatory on Academic Ranking and Excellence (#16017)

♦ International Raoul Wallenberg Foundation (IRWF) 14698

Fundación Internacional Raoul Wallenberg

Main Office 34 East 67th St, 2nd Floor, New York NY 10065, USA. T. +12127373275. Fax +12125356262. E-mail: board-irwf@irwf.org.
URL: http://www.raoulwallenberg.net/

History Nov 1997, Buenos Aires (Argentina). Founded by Baruch Tenembaum (1933-). **Aims** Spread the message and remember the actions of the saviours who risked their lives – and sometimes lost them – to save *persecuted* people during the Second World *War*, such as Raoul Wallenberg, Nuncio Angelo Roncalli, Aristides de Sousa Mendes, Jan Karski among many others; promote peace among nations and people; develop educational projects based on concepts of solidarity, dialogue and understanding. **Structure** Executive Board. Runs the Wallenberg at School Education Programme. **Activities** Advocacy/lobbying/activism; training/education; awards/prizes/competitions. **Publications** *Interfaith Newsletter*, *IRWF Monthly Newsletter*.
Members Branches in 4 countries:
Argentina, Israel, USA, Venezuela.
Individuals in 18 countries:
Argentina, Australia, Brazil, Canada, Denmark, France, Germany, Hungary, Israel, Italy, Latvia, Mauritius, Sweden, Switzerland, Türkiye, UK, USA, Venezuela. [2019/XE4304/f/**F**]

♦ International Rare Diseases Research Consortium (IRDiRC) 14699

Coordinator Hôpital Charles-Foix, 7 av de la République, 94200 Ivry-sur-Seine, France. E-mail: scisec-irdirc@ejprarediseases.org.
URL: http://www.irdirc.org/

History Officially launched Apr 2011, USA. **Aims** Deliver 200 new *therapies* for rare diseases; diagnose the most rare diseases. **Structure** Consortium Assembly; Operating Committee; Scientific Secretariat. Scientific Committees (3): Diagnostic; Interdisciplinary; Therapeutic. Constituent Committees (3): Funders; Companies; Patient Advocates. Task Forces. **Languages** English. **Activities** Events/meetings; standards/guidelines. **Events** *Conference* Berlin (Germany) 2023, *RE(ACT) International Congress of Research on Rare and Orphan Diseases* Berlin (Germany) 2023, *Conference* 2021, *RE(ACT) International Congress on Research of Rare and Orphan Diseases* 2021, *Conference* Paris (France) 2017. **Publications** Policies; guidelines.
Members Institutions in 18 countries:
Australia, Belgium, Canada, China, Finland, France, Georgia, Germany, Ireland, Italy, Japan, Korea Rep, Netherlands, Saudi Arabia, Spain, Switzerland, UK, USA.
Included in the above, 2 organizations listed in this Yearbook:
European Commission (EC, #06633); European Organisation for Research and Treatment of Cancer (EORTC, #08101).
NGO Relations *EURORDIS – Rare Diseases Europe (#09175); Global Alliance for Genomics and Health (GA4GH, #10199)*; national organizations. [2022/XM5361/y/**C**]

♦ International Raymond Carver Society (IRCS) 14700

Address not obtained.
URL: https://www.raymondcarverreview.org/

History 2005, Boston, MA (USA). **Aims** Encourage worldwide interest in and study of the works and life of American writer Raymond Carver (1938-1988). **Structure** Executive Committee; Advisory Board.
Members Individuals (over 50) in countries:
Bulgaria, Canada, Denmark, France, Ireland, Israel, Italy, Japan, New Zealand, Norway, Philippines, Russia, Spain, Sweden, Switzerland, UK, USA.
NGO Relations Member of (1): *American Literature Association (ALA, #00786)*. [AA1647/v/**E**]

♦ International Rayon and Synthetic Fibres Committee / see CIRFS – European Man-made Fibres Association (#03944)
♦ International Reading Association / see International Literacy Association (#14057)

♦ International Reading Recovery Trainers Organization (IRRTO) 14701

Contact 500 W Wilson Bridge Rd, Ste 250, Worthington OH 43085, USA.
URL: http://www.irrto.org/

History 2001. **Aims** Promote the literacy intervention process developed by Dr Marie M Clay; maintain quality, uphold integrity, improve efficiency and effectiveness, and support change and growth in Reading Recovery through international collaboration, research and resource development. **Structure** Executive Board; Committees. **Languages** English, French, Spanish. **Staff** None paid. **Activities** Events/meetings; training/education. **Events** *Nurturing literate futures* Auckland (New Zealand) 2019, *Seminar* Vancouver, BC (Canada) 2016, *Seminar* Sydney, NSW (Australia) 2013, *Seminar* London (UK) 2010, *Seminar* Baltimore, MD (USA) 2007. **Publications** None.
Members Full in 8 countries:
Australia, Canada, Denmark, Ireland, Malta, New Zealand, UK, USA.
IGO Relations None. **NGO Relations** None. [2023.02.14/XJ7807/**C**]

♦ International Real Estate Federation (#09653)
♦ International Real Estate Institute (internationally oriented national body)

♦ International Real Estate Society (IRES) 14702

Exec Dir Dept of Real Estate, Georgia State Univ, PO Box 3991, Atlanta GA 30302-3991, USA.
URL: http://www.iresnet.net/

History 1994, by members of American Real Estate Society, *European Real Estate Society (ERES, #08332)* and *Pacific Rim Real Estate Society (PRRES, #18001)*. **Aims** Encourage communication, cooperation and coordination regarding real estate research and education worldwide. **Structure** Board. **Languages** English. **Staff** None. **Finance** Members' dues. **Activities** Awards/prizes/competitions. **Events** *World congress* Girdwood, AK (USA) 2001, *PRRES annual conference* Kuala Lumpur (Malaysia) 1999. **Publications** 20-Year Anniversary Monograph.
Members International organizations (6):
African Real Estate Society (AfRES, #00428); American Real Estate Society; *Asian Real Estate Society (AsRES, #01680); European Real Estate Society (ERES, #08332); Latin American Real Estate Society (LARES, #16366); Pacific Rim Real Estate Society (PRRES, #18001)*. [2016.12.14/XE3786/y/**E**]

♦ International Real Property Foundation (internationally oriented national body)
♦ International RECE Conference – International Reconceptualizing Early Childhood Education Conference (meeting series)
♦ International Reclamation Bureau / see Bureau of International Recycling (#03368)
♦ International Reconceptualizing Early Childhood Education Conference (meeting series)
♦ International Recording Media Association / see Content Delivery and Storage Association (#04779)
♦ International Recording Musicians Association (internationally oriented national body)
♦ International Recovering/Recycling Bureau / see Bureau of International Recycling (#03368)
♦ International Recovery Bureau / see Bureau of International Recycling (#03368)

♦ International Recovery Foundation (IRF) 14703

Contact c/o TBF AG, Beckenhofstr 35, 8006 Zurich ZH, Switzerland. T. +41432552300. Fax +41432552399. E-mail: info@ir-foundation.com.
URL: http://www.ir-foundation.com/

Aims Support and promote the transfer of knowledge and experience in the field of *waste* management. **Activities** Events/meetings; knowledge management/information dissemination. **Events** *International IRRC Waste to Energy Conference* Vienna (Austria) 2016.
Members Founding members in 3 countries:
France, Germany, Switzerland. [2017/XM5716/f/**F**]

♦ International Recovery Platform (IRP) 14704

Secretariat DRI East Tower 5F, 1-5-2 Wakinohamakaigan-dori, Chuo-ku, Kobe HYOGO, 651-0073 Japan. T. +81782626041. Fax +81782626046.
URL: https://recovery.preventionweb.net/

History Established following 2nd UN World Conference on Disaster Reduction, 2005, Kobe (Japan), in support of the implementation of the Hyogo Framework for Action (HFA). **Aims** Identify and strengthen knowledge and information on build-back-better in recovery, *rehabilitation*, and *reconstruction*. **Structure** Steering Committee; Secretariat. **Activities** Events/meetings; networking/liaising. **Events** *International Recovery Forum* Kobe (Japan) 2022, *International Recovery Forum* Kobe (Japan) 2021, *International Recovery Forum* Kobe (Japan) 2020, *International Recovery Forum* Kobe (Japan) 2019, *International Recovery Forum* Kobe (Japan) 2018. **Publications** *IRP Herald* – newsletter.
Members Steering Committee Members (17):
Asian Development Bank (ADB, #01422); Asian Disaster Reduction Center (ADRC, #01427); Cabinet Office, Japan; *Centro de Coordinación para la Prevención de los Desastres Naturales en América Central (CEPREDENAC, #03795)*; Hyogo Prefectural Government, Japan; *ILO (#11123); International Bank for Reconstruction and Development (IBRD, #12317)* (World Bank); Ministry of Foreign Affairs, Italy; *Swiss Agency for Development and Cooperation (SDC); UNDP (#20292); UNEP (#20299); UNESCO (#20322); United Nations Centre for Regional Development (UNCRD, #20526); United Nations Human Settlements Programme (UN-Habitat, #20572); United Nations Office for Disaster Risk Reduction (UNDRR, #20595); United Nations Office for Project Services (UNOPS, #20602); WHO (#20950)*. [2022/XM7874/y/**F**]

♦ International Recreation Association / see World Leisure Organization (#21624)

♦ International REC Standard Foundation (I-REC Standard) 14705

Headquarters Achter de Tolbrug 151, 5211 SM 's Hertogenbosch, Netherlands. T. +31203997223. E-mail: secretariat@irecstandard.org.
URL: https://www.irecstandard.org/

History 2015. **Aims** Support standardized Renewable Energy Certificate (REC) ystems. **Structure** Board. **Activities** Events/meetings; standards/guidelines. **Events** *ISC – I-REC Standard Conference* Bangkok (Thailand) 2022. **NGO Relations** Partner of (3): *CDP (#03621); Greenhouse Gas Protocol (GHG Protocol, #10721); RECS International (#18631)*. [2022/AA2823/f/**F**]

♦ International Rectal Microbicide Advocates (unconfirmed)
♦ International Recycling Congress (meeting series)

♦ International Recycling Federation 14706

Fédération internationale de recyclage (FIR)

SG Rue d'Arlon 21, 1050 Brussels, Belgium. T. +3232034426. Fax +3222335301. E-mail: info@fir-recycling.com.
Pres c/o BRB, Haus der Baustoffindustrie Düsseldorfer Str 50, 47051 Duisburg, Germany. T. +4920399239-0. Fax +4920399239-97.
URL: http://www.fir-recycling.net/

History 1990. EU Transparency Register: 563157337033-82. **Aims** Advance recycling of construction and demolition waste. **Events** *Biennial Forum* Spain 2009, *Biennial forum* Amsterdam (Netherlands) 2007, *Biennial Forum* Salzburg (Austria) 2005, *Biennial Forum* Pamplona (Spain) 2003, *Biennial Forum* Prague (Czech Rep) 2001.
Members Individuals and national organizations in 11 countries:
Austria, Belgium, Brazil, Czechia, France, Germany, Greece, Italy, Netherlands, Spain, Switzerland. [2020/XM1397/**D**]

♦ International Recycling Organization / see Bureau of International Recycling (#03368)
♦ International Red Cross / see International Red Cross and Red Crescent Movement (#14707)

♦ International Red Cross and Red Crescent Movement 14707

Mouvement international de la Croix-Rouge et du Croissant-Rouge – Movimiento Internacional de la Cruz Roja y de la Media Luna Roja

Contact c/o CICR, 19 avenue de la Paix, 1202 Geneva, Switzerland. T. +412273020327302063.
URL: http://www.redcross.int/

History 1928, as *International Red Cross – Croix-Rouge internationale (CRI) – Cruz Roja Internacional.* Also referred to as *International Movement of the Red Cross and Red Crescent.* Statutes of the Movement under its current title adopted at 25th International Conference of the Red Cross and Red Crescent, Oct 1986, Geneva (Switzerland). **Aims** In all activities, uphold the Red Cross/Red Crescent principles of humanity, impartiality, neutrality, independence, voluntary service, unity and universality. **Structure** International Conference (every 4 years), comprising ICRC, the International Federation, national Red Cross and Red Crescent societies and representatives of all States party to the Geneva Conventions Council of Delegates (meeting every 2 years) comprises representatives of all components of the Movement: *International Committee of the Red Cross (ICRC, #12799)*, set up in 1863; *International Federation of Red Cross and Red Crescent Societies (#13526)*, set up in 1919; all officially recognized national Red Cross and Red Crescent societies. Standing Commission, the trustee of ICRC. Council of Delegates constitutes the assembly of representatives of ICRC. **Languages** Arabic, Chinese, English, French, Russian, Spanish. **Activities** Awards: Henry Dunant Medal in recognition of outstanding service in the cause of the Movement; Florence (Italy) Nightingale Medal; grants through Empress Shôken Fund; staff assistance through Maurice de Madre French Fund. Instrumental in setting up: *UWC Red Cross Nordic (RCNUWC).* **Events** *International Conference* Geneva (Switzerland) 2019, *Counci of Delegates Meeting* Antalya (Turkey) 2017, *Statutory Meeting* Antalya (Turkey) 2017, *International Conference* Geneva (Switzerland) 2015, *International Conference* Geneva (Switzerland) 2011. **Publications** *Red Cross and Red Crescent Magazine* (4 a year). *Handbook of the International Red Cross and Red Crescent Movement – Manuel du Mouvement international de la Croix-Rouge et du Croissant-Rouge.*

Members National Societies in 185 countries:
Afghanistan, Albania, Algeria, Andorra, Angola, Antigua-Barbuda, Argentina, Armenia, Australia, Austria, Azerbaijan, Bahamas, Bahrain, Bangladesh, Barbados, Belarus, Belgium, Belize, Benin, Bolivia, Bosnia-Herzegovina, Botswana, Brazil, Brunei Darussalam, Bulgaria, Burkina Faso, Burundi, Cambodia, Cameroon, Canada, Cape Verde, Central African Rep, Chad, Chile, China, Colombia, Comoros, Congo Brazzaville, Congo DR, Cook Is, Costa Rica, Côte d'Ivoire, Croatia, Cuba, Czechia, Denmark, Djibouti, Dominica, Dominican Rep, Ecuador, Egypt, El Salvador, Equatorial Guinea, Estonia, Eswatini, Ethiopia, Fiji, Finland, France, Gabon, Gambia, Georgia, Germany, Ghana, Greece, Grenada, Guatemala, Guinea, Guinea-Bissau, Guyana, Haiti, Honduras, Hungary, Iceland, India, Indonesia, Iran Islamic Rep, Iraq, Ireland, Israel, Italy, Jamaica, Japan, Jordan, Kazakhstan, Kenya, Kiribati, Korea DPR, Korea Rep, Kuwait, Kyrgyzstan, Laos, Latvia, Lebanon, Lesotho, Liberia, Libya, Liechtenstein, Lithuania, Luxembourg, Madagascar, Malawi, Malaysia, Mali, Malta, Mauritania, Mauritius, Mexico, Micronesia FS, Moldova, Monaco, Mongolia, Morocco, Mozambique, Myanmar, Namibia, Nepal, Netherlands, New Zealand, Nicaragua, Niger, Nigeria, North Macedonia, Norway, Pakistan, Palau, Palestine, Panama, Papua New Guinea, Paraguay, Peru, Philippines, Poland, Portugal, Qatar, Romania, Russia, Rwanda, Samoa, San Marino, Sao Tomé-Principe, Saudi Arabia, Senegal, Serbia, Seychelles, Sierra Leone, Singapore, Slovakia, Slovenia, Solomon Is, Somalia, South Africa, Spain, Sri Lanka, St Kitts-Nevis, St Lucia, St Vincent-Grenadines, Sudan, Suriname, Sweden, Switzerland, Syrian AR, Tajikistan, Tanzania UR, Thailand, Timor-Leste, Togo, Tonga, Trinidad-Tobago, Tunisia, Türkiye, Turkmenistan, Uganda, UK, Ukraine, United Arab Emirates, Uruguay, USA, Uzbekistan, Vanuatu, Venezuela, Vietnam, Yemen, Zambia, Zimbabwe.

IGO Relations Official relations with: *FAO (#09260); UNDP (#20292); WHO (#20950); World Food Programme (WFP, #21510).* Guest status with: *Coordinating Bureau of the Non-Aligned Countries (#04815).* **NGO Relations** Regional contacts with: *American Society of International Law (ASIL); Instituto Interamericano de Derechos Humanos (IIDH, #11334); International Institute of Human Rights – Fondation René Cassin (IIHR, #13887); International Institute of Humanitarian Law (IIHL, #13885).* Collaborates with: *World Medical Association (WMA, #21646).* [2012/XF2405/**F**]

- ♦ International Red Locust Control Organization for Central and Southern Africa (no recent information)
- ♦ International Red Locust Control Service (inactive)
- ♦ International Redox Network (unconfirmed)
- ♦ International Reefer Transportation Association / see International Refrigerated Transportation Association
- ♦ International Reference Centre for Community Water Supply and Sanitation / see IRC (#16016)
- ♦ International Reference Organization in Forensic Medicine (inactive)
- ♦ International Reformed Agency for Migration (inactive)
- ♦ International Refrigerated Transportation Association (internationally oriented national body)
- ♦ International Refugee Organization (inactive)
- ♦ International Refugee and Relief Program / see International Development and Relief Foundation

♦ International Refugee Rights Initiative (IRRI) 14708

Co-Dir 1483 York Ave, No 20463, New York NY 10021, USA. T. +16468671991. E-mail: info@refugee-rights.org.
Co-Dir Ntinda PO Box 603, Kampala, Uganda.
URL: http://www.refugee-rights.org/

History 2004. Registered in Uganda, UK and USA. **Aims** Advance the protection of refugees in areas of conflict, promote human rights in *Africa.* **Publications** *Refugee Rights News.* **Members** Membership countries not specified. **NGO Relations** Founding member of: *International Coalition for the Responsibility to Protect (ICRtoP, #12620).* Member of: *Coalition for an Effective African Court on Human and Peoples' Rights (African Court Coalition, #04055); Global Campaign for Equal Nationality Rights (#10265); International Council of Voluntary Agencies (ICVA, #13092); Sudan Consortium (#20031).* UK Office is Secretariat for: *Southern Refugee Legal Aid Network (SRLAN, #19879).* [2016/XJ8129/**F**]

- ♦ International Refugee Sport Federation (unconfirmed)
- ♦ International Refugee Trust (internationally oriented national body)
- ♦ International Refugee Year Trust / see International Refugee Trust

♦ International Regions Benchmarking Consortium 14709

Exec Dir Puget Sound Regional Council, 1011 Western Avenue, Ste 500, Seattle WA 98104, USA. T. +12064647515.
URL: http://www.internationalregions.org/

History 2008, by Puget Sound Regional Council and Trade Development Alliance of Greater Seattle. **Aims** Develop a shared set of economic and social *indicators* for each participating region to show evidence of best practice in certain areas; build a learning community sharing such best practice so as to make participating regions more *competitive* in the global economy. **Events** *Members Conference* Stockholm (Sweden) 2016, *Members Conference / Conference* Munich (Germany) 2014, *Members Conference / Conference* Helsinki (Finland) 2012, *Conference* Vancouver, BC (Canada) 2011, *Members Conference* Vancouver, BC (Canada) 2011.

Members Regions (10) in 10 countries:
Australia, Canada, Finland, Germany, Ireland, Japan, Korea Rep, Spain, Sweden, USA. [2016/XJ0681/**F**]

- ♦ International Registry of World Citizens / see Registre des Citoyens du Monde (#18822)
- ♦ International Regulations for Preventing Collisions at Sea, 1960 (1960 treaty)

♦ International Regulators' Forum (IRF) 14710

Contact Natl Offshore Petroleum Safety Authority, GPO Box 2568, Perth WA 6001, Australia. E-mail: information@nopsema.gov.au.
URL: http://www.irfoffshoresafety.com/

Aims Promote best sustainable safety performance globally and the concept that it is inseparable from and interdependent with best sustainable economic performance; enable information exchange; provide a network of offshore *petroleum* health and safety regulators for mutual support and advise when required. **Events** *Conference* Perth, WA (Australia) 2013, *Annual Meeting* Rio de Janeiro (Brazil) 2012, *Safety summit conference* Stavanger (Norway) 2011, *Conference* Vancouver, BC (Canada) 2010, *Annual meeting* Stavanger (Norway) 2009.

Members Full in 8 countries:
Australia, Brazil, Canada, Netherlands, New Zealand, Norway, UK, USA. [2012/XJ1398/**F**]

♦ International Regulatory Peptide Society (REGPEP Society) 14711

Chair Inserm U858 – I2MR, 1 av Jean Poulhès, BP 84225, 31432 Toulouse CEDEX 4, France.
URL: http://www.regulatorypeptide.org/

Aims Promote scientific meetings and exchanges devoted to all aspects of basic and clinical research on regulatory peptides and related topics. **Structure** Steering Committee, comprising Chair, Treasurer and 9 members. Scientific Advisory Board. **Events** *Symposium* Acapulco (Mexico) 2022, *Symposium* Acapulco (Mexico) 2020, *Symposium* Acapulco (Mexico) 2018, *Symposium* Rouen (France) 2016, *Symposium* Kyoto (Japan) 2014. [2014/XJ1798/**C**]

♦ International Rehabilitation Council for Torture Victims (IRCT) 14712

Conseil international de réadaptation pour les victimes de la torture (CIRT)

SG/CEO Copenhagen Europe Center, Vesterbrogade 149, Building 4, 3rd Floor, 1620 Copenhagen V, Denmark. T. +4544401830. Fax +4544401854. E-mail: irct@irct.org.
Brussels Office Rue Belliard 205, 1040 Brussels, Belgium. T. +3222301504. Fax +3222301549.
URL: http://www.irct.org/

History 1985, Copenhagen (Denmark), by *DIGNITY – Danish Institute Against Torture.* Registered in accordance with Danish law. EU Transparency Register: 27797834846-32. **Aims** Promote and support rehabilitation of torture victims; work for prevention of torture worldwide. **Structure** General Assembly; Council; Executive Committee. **Languages** English. **Staff** 26.00 FTE, paid. **Finance** Sources: donations; grants; international organizations. Other sources: Danish, Finnish, Norwegian and Swedish governments. Supported by: *European Commission (EC, #06633).* **Activities** Advocacy/lobbying/activism; events/meetings; financial and/or material support; networking/liaising; research/documentation; training/education. **Events** *Conference* Soesterberg (Netherlands) 2008, *General Assembly* Berlin (Germany) 2006, *International symposium on torture / Symposium* Berlin (Germany) 2006, *International symposium on torture / Symposium* Delhi (India) 1999, *International symposium on torture / Symposium* Cape Town (South Africa) 1995. **Publications** *Torture Journal.* Annual Report; books; articles; teaching material; publications in scientific journals and books.

Members Torture rehabilitation centres (over 160) in 74 countries and territories:
Albania, Argentina, Armenia, Australia, Austria, Bangladesh, Bolivia, Bosnia-Herzegovina, Burundi, Cambodia, Cameroon, Canada, Chad, Chile, Colombia, Congo DR, Croatia, Denmark, Ecuador, Egypt, Finland, France, Georgia, Germany, Guatemala, Honduras, Hong Kong, Hungary, India, Indonesia, Iran Islamic Rep, Iraq, Ireland, Israel, Italy, Jordan, Kenya, Korea Rep, Kosovo, Kyrgyzstan, Lebanon, Liberia, Mexico, Moldova, Morocco, Nepal, Netherlands, New Zealand, Nigeria, Pakistan, Palestine, Peru, Philippines, Poland, Romania, Russia, Rwanda, Senegal, Serbia, Sierra Leone, South Africa, Spain, Sri Lanka, Sudan, Sweden, Switzerland, Tunisia, Türkiye, Uganda, UK, Ukraine, USA, Venezuela, Zimbabwe.

Included in the above, 5 organizations listed in this Yearbook:
African Centre for the Prevention and Resolution of Conflicts (CAPREC); African Centre for Treatment and Rehabilitation of Torture Victims (ACTV); International Medical Rehabilitation Center (IRC); Survivors International (SI); TASSC International.

Consultative Status Consultative status granted from: *African Commission on Human and Peoples' Rights (ACHPR, #00255)* (Observer); *ECOSOC (#05331)* (Special). **IGO Relations** *Committee Against Torture (CAT, #04241).* Participant in Fundamental Rights Platform of: *European Union Agency for Fundamental Rights (FRA, #08969).* Associated with Department of Global Communications of the United Nations. **NGO Relations** Member of: *European Council on Refugees and Exiles (ECRE, #06839); European NGO Platform Asylum and Migration (EPAM, #08051); Human Rights and Democracy Network (HRDN, #10980); International Federation of Health and Human Rights Organisations (IFHHRO, #13440); World Organisation Against Torture (OMCT, #21685).* Links with various relevant organizations, including:
- *Amnesty International (AI, #00801);*
- *Association for the Prevention of Torture (APT, #02869);*
- *Global Campus of Human Rights (#10269);*
- *Human Rights Information and Documentation Systems, International (HURIDOCS, #10985);*
- *Human Rights Watch (HRW, #10990);*
- *International Federation of ACATs – Action by Christians for the Abolition of Torture (#13334);*
- *Physicians for Human Rights, USA (PHR-USA);*
- *REDRESS;*
- *World Confederation for Physical Therapy (WCPT, #21293);*
- *World Medical Association (WMA, #21646).* [2018/XD2692/y/**C**]

- ♦ International Rehabilitation Forum (internationally oriented national body)
- ♦ International Rehabilitation Medicine Association (inactive)
- ♦ International Relations Center (internationally oriented national body)
- ♦ International Relations Institute of Cameroon (internationally oriented national body)
- ♦ International Relations Institute, Rio de Janeiro (internationally oriented national body)
- ♦ International Relations and Peace Research Institute (internationally oriented national body)
- ♦ International Relief Association / see Life for Relief and Development
- ♦ International Relief Committee for Professional Workers (inactive)
- ♦ International Relief and Development / see Blumont International
- ♦ International Relief and Development Fund / see Anglican Overseas Aid

♦ International Relief Friendship Foundation (IRFF) 14713

Fondation mondiale de secours et d'amitié

Vice-Pres 39 N Jefferson Rd, Red Hook NY 12571, USA. T. +19173196206. Fax +18458358214.
URL: https://irff.us/

History 1976. Founded within the framework of *Holy Spirit Association for the Unification of World Christianity (HSA-UWC).* Currently an independent organization. Former names and other names: *World Relief Friendship Foundation* – former. **Aims** Provide immediate humanitarian relief to individuals and families devastated by poverty, illness, natural disasters and conflict while also providing opportunities for long-term sustainable development through educational and economic opportunities. **Structure** Board of Directors; Executive Committee. **Languages** English. **Staff** Voluntary. **Finance** Sources: public contributions; grants. **Activities** Events/meetings; Humanitarian/emergency aid; research and development; projects/programmes; training/education. **Events** *Conference* New York, NY (USA) 2001, *Conference* New York, NY (USA) 2000, *Humanitarian work in the new millennium* Seoul (Korea Rep) 2000.

Members Active in 93 countries:
Albania, Angola, Australia, Austria, Bahamas, Bangladesh, Barbados, Belarus, Bosnia-Herzegovina, Brazil, Bulgaria, Burkina Faso, Cameroon, Canada, Central African Rep, China, Comoros, Congo DR, Côte d'Ivoire, Croatia, Czechia, Denmark, Dominican Rep, Ecuador, Equatorial Guinea, Estonia, Finland, France, Gambia, Germany, Ghana, Guinea-Bissau, Guyana, Haiti, Honduras, Hungary, Iceland, India, Ireland, Italy, Jamaica, Japan, Kazakhstan, Kenya, Korea Rep, Kyrgyzstan, Laos, Liberia, Luxembourg, Mali, Marshall Is, Mexico, Moldova, Mongolia, Nepal, Netherlands, New Zealand, Nigeria, Norway, Panama, Papua New Guinea, Peru, Philippines, Poland, Romania, Russia, Rwanda, Sao Tomé-Principe, Senegal, Serbia, Sierra Leone, Slovakia, Slovenia, South Africa, Spain, Sri Lanka, Sudan, Sweden, Switzerland, Tajikistan, Thailand, Trinidad-Tobago, Türkiye, Uganda, UK, Ukraine, Uruguay, USA, Uzbekistan, Venezuela, Vietnam, Zambia, Zimbabwe.

IGO Relations Associated with Department of Global Communications of the United Nations. **NGO Relations** Full member of: *NGO Committee on Financing for Development, New York (#17108).* Member of: *Council of Non-Governmental Organizations for Development Support (#04911).* Co-sponsors, together with *International Religious Foundation (IRF, no recent information)*, the *Religious Youth Service (RYS).* [2018/XF0561/f/**F**]

- ♦ International Relief and Rescue Committee / see International Rescue Committee (#14717)
- ♦ International Relief Service of Caritas Catholica, Belgium (internationally oriented national body)
- ♦ International Relief Teams (internationally oriented national body)
- ♦ International Relief Union (inactive)
- ♦ International Religious Fellowship (no recent information)
- ♦ International Religious Freedom Alliance (unconfirmed)
- ♦ International Religious Liberty Association (internationally oriented national body)

♦ International REM Sleep Behavior Study Group (IRBDSG) 14714

Sec address not obtained.
URL: https://www.irbdsg.com/

History 29 Sep 2009. **Aims** Promote international scientific research in the field of REM sleep behaviour disorder and associated fields and optimization of medical care for patients by improving diagnostic and therapeutic measures. **Structure** Board; Working Groups. **Finance** Sources: donations; members' dues. **Activities** Events/meetings. **Events** *IRBDSG Meeting* Ravenna (Italy) 2022, *IRBDSG Meeting* Prague (Czechia) 2020, *IRBDSG Meeting* Copenhagen (Denmark) 2019, *IRBDSG Meeting* Prague (Czechia) 2017, *IRBDSG Meeting* Ravenna (Italy) 2016. [2023.02.16/AA2553/**C**]

♦ International Renaissance Foundation (internationally oriented national body)
♦ International Renal Conference (meeting series)

♦ International Renewable Energy Agency (IRENA) 14715

Dir Gen PO Box 236, Masdar City, Abu Dhabi, United Arab Emirates. E-mail: info@irena.org.
URL: http://www.irena.org/

History 26 Jan 2009, Bonn (Germany). Established during the Founding Conference, when 75 States signed the Statutes. Proposed 1990 by *EUROSOLAR – European Association for Renewable Energy (#09183)*. On 10-11 Apr 2008, representatives of 60 countries met in Berlin (Germany) at the invitation of the German Federal Government to attend the Preparatory Conference for the Foundation of the International Renewable Energy Agency. Final preparatory conference held 23-24 Oct 2008, Madrid (Spain). First Interim Director-General elected, 29 Jun 2009, and headquarters established in Abu Dhabi (United Arab Emirates). As of 8 Jul 2010, became a fully fledged international organization. Former names and other names: *International Solar Energy Agency (ISEA)* – former. **Aims** Foster and promote large-scale adoption of renewable energy worldwide, specifically in the following areas: improved *regulatory* frameworks through enhanced policy advice; improvements in transfer *technology*; progress and improvements in skills and know-how; a scientifically sound information basis through applied policy research; better financing. Support renewable energy projects worldwide so as to prove 100% renewable energy supply is feasible. **Structure** Assembly; Council; Secretariat, headed by Director-General. **Languages** English. **Staff** 50.00 FTE, paid. **Finance** Sources: contributions of member/participating states. Annual budget: 13,700,000 USD (2010). **Activities** Advocacy/lobbying/activism; events/meetings. **Events** *General Assembly* Abu Dhabi (United Arab Emirates) 2023, *General Assembly* Abu Dhabi (United Arab Emirates) 2022, *General Assembly* Abu Dhabi (United Arab Emirates) 2021, *General Assembly* Abu Dhabi (United Arab Emirates) 2020, *Round Table* Singapore (Singapore) 2019. **Publications** *IRENA Quarterly* (4 a year). Reports and papers.
Members As of 2022: Signatory States (168):
Afghanistan, Albania, Algeria, Angola, Antigua-Barbuda, Argentina, Armenia, Australia, Austria, Azerbaijan, Bahamas, Bahrain, Bangladesh, Barbados, Belarus, Belgium, Belize, Benin, Bhutan, Bosnia-Herzegovina, Botswana, Brunei Darussalam, Bulgaria, Burkina Faso, Cameroon, Canada, Cape Verde, Central African Rep, Chad, China, Colombia, Comoros, Costa Rica, Côte d'Ivoire, Croatia, Cuba, Cyprus, Czechia, Denmark, Djibouti, Dominica, Dominican Rep, Ecuador, Egypt, El Salvador, Eritrea, Estonia, Eswatini, Ethiopia, Fiji, Finland, France, Gabon, Gambia, Georgia, Germany, Ghana, Greece, Grenada, Guinea, Guyana, Honduras, Hungary, Iceland, India, Indonesia, Iran Islamic Rep, Iraq, Ireland, Israel, Italy, Jamaica, Japan, Jordan, Kazakhstan, Kenya, Kiribati, Korea Rep, Kuwait, Kyrgyzstan, Latvia, Lebanon, Lesotho, Liechtenstein, Lithuania, Luxembourg, Malaysia, Maldives, Mali, Malta, Marshall Is, Mauritania, Mauritius, Mexico, Micronesia FS, Moldova, Monaco, Mongolia, Montenegro, Morocco, Mozambique, Namibia, Nauru, Nepal, Netherlands, New Zealand, Nicaragua, Niger, Nigeria, North Macedonia, Norway, Oman, Pakistan, Palau, Panama, Papua New Guinea, Paraguay, Peru, Philippines, Poland, Portugal, Qatar, Romania, Russia, Rwanda, Samoa, San Marino, Sao Tomé-Principe, Saudi Arabia, Senegal, Serbia, Seychelles, Sierra Leone, Singapore, Slovakia, Slovenia, Solomon Is, Somalia, South Africa, Spain, Sri Lanka, St Kitts-Nevis, St Lucia, St Vincent-Grenadines, Sudan, Sweden, Switzerland, Tajikistan, Thailand, Togo, Tonga, Trinidad-Tobago, Tunisia, Türkiye, Turkmenistan, Tuvalu, Uganda, UK, Ukraine, United Arab Emirates, Uruguay, USA, Uzbekistan, Vanuatu, Yemen, Zambia, Zimbabwe.
European Union (EU, #08967).
IGO Relations Observer status with (1): *United Nations (UN, #20515)* (General Assembly). Memorandum of Understanding with (1): *Regional Center for Renewable Energy and Energy Efficiency (RCREEE, #18754)*. Member of (1): *Global Bioenergy Partnership (GBEP, #10251)*. Partner of (1): *International Solar Alliance (ISA, #15563)*. Signatory to *Global Alliances for Water and Climate (GAfWaC, #10230)*. Agreement with: *Global Green Growth Institute (GGGI, #10392)*. **NGO Relations** Member of (4): *Climate Knowledge Brokers (CKB, #04016)*; *Global Alliance for Buildings and Construction (GlobalABC, #10187)*; *Global Clean Water Desalination Alliance (GCWDA, #10285)*; *LEDS Global Partnership (LEDS GP, #16435)*. Partner of (2): *International Geothermal Association (IGA, #13717)*; *Sustainable Energy for All (SEforALL, #20056)*. Cooperates with (2): *Renewable Energy and Energy Efficiency Partnership (REEEP, #18837)*; *World Wind Energy Association (WWEA, #21937)*. Instrumental in setting up (1): *IRENA Coalition for Action (#16018)*. Organization involved: *World Council for Renewable Energy (WCRE, #21340)*. Involved in: *REN21 (#18836)*. [2023/XJ4129/**B***]

♦ International Renewable Energy Alliance (Ren Alliance) 14716

Contact WWEA, Charles-de-Gaulle-Str 5, 53113 Bonn, Germany. T. +492283694080. Fax +492283694084. E-mail: secretariat@wwindea.org.
URL: http://www.ren-alliance.org/

History Jun 2004, by *International Geothermal Association (IGA, #13717)*, *International Hydropower Association (IHA, #13828)*, *International Solar Energy Society (ISES, #15564)*, *World Wind Energy Association (WWEA, #21937)* and *World Bioenergy Association (WBA, #21231)*. **Aims** Provide a unified voice for the renewable energy sector in the global level. **Languages** English. **Activities** Promotion of renewable energy at global level; Statements on international energy and environment policies; Participation in international events. **Events** *World congress on advancing sustainable hydropower* Antalya (Turkey) 2007.
Members Organizations (5):
International Geothermal Association (IGA, #13717); *International Hydropower Association (IHA, #13828)*; *International Solar Energy Society (ISES, #15564)*; *World Bioenergy Association (WBA, #21231)*; *World Wind Energy Association (WWEA, #21937)*.
NGO Relations Represented at Steering Committee of: *REN21 (#18836)*. [2012.06.01/XM1278/y/**F**]

♦ International Renewable Resources Institute (internationally oriented national body)
♦ International Repertory of Musical Iconography (#18844)
♦ International Repertory of Musical Literature (#18845)
♦ International Republican Institute (internationally oriented national body)

♦ International Rescue Committee (IRC) 14717

Comité international de secours – Comité Internacional de Rescate

Pres 122 East 42nd St, New York NY 10168, USA. T. +12125513000. Fax +12125513180.
European Office IRC-UK, 100 Wood Street, Barbican, London, EC2V 7AN, UK. E-mail: ircuk@rescue-uk.org.
URL: http://www.rescue.org/

History 1933. Founded as American branch of the Europe-based *International Relief Association (IRA)*, originally to aid the democratic opponents of nazism and fascism. In 1942 adopted the name *International Rescue and Relief Committee* or *International Relief and Rescue Committee*, in French *Comité international de sauvetage*, after joining forces with *Emergency Rescue Committee (ERC)*, which had been set up in 1940 to aid European refugees trapped in Vichy France. Name subsequently shortened to listed title. Registered in accordance with US law. Registration: EU Transparency Register, No/ID: 336765244362-96, Start date: 12 Oct 2021. **Aims** Provide *relief*, protection and resettlement for *refugees* and victims of civil unrest, persecution and natural disaster and administer such relief without regard to race, nationality or religion; conduct programs of public education regarding the situation, circumstances, needs and plight of such victims of oppression and civil unrest for the purpose of mobilizing assistance on their behalf. **Structure** Board of Directors; General Counsel; Committees (3). **Finance** Operating expenses (2016): US$ 722,736,000. **Activities** Humanitarian/emergency aid; guidance/assistance/consulting; awards/prizes/competitions. **Publications** *The IRC at Work* (4 a year) – newsletter. Annual Report.
Members Offices in 35 countries:
Bangladesh, Cameroon, Central African Rep, Chad, Colombia, Congo DR, Côte d'Ivoire, El Salvador, Ethiopia, Germany, Greece, Iraq, Italy, Jordan, Kenya, Lebanon, Liberia, Libya, Malaysia, Mali, Niger, Nigeria, Pakistan, Serbia, Sierra Leone, Somalia, South Sudan, Syrian AR, Tanzania UR, Thailand, Uganda, USA, Venezuela, Yemen, Zimbabwe.
Consultative Status Consultative status granted from: *ECOSOC (#05331)* (Special); *WHO (#20950)* (Official Relations). **IGO Relations** Partner of: *UNHCR (#20327)*. Global partner of: *United Nations Girls' Education Initiative (UNGEI, #20566)*. Cooperation and financial support from: *Center for Information on Migration in Latin America (#03643)*; *European Commission (EC, #06633)*; *FAO (#09260)*; *UNDP (#20292)*; *UNICEF (#20332)*; *United States Agency for International Development (USAID)*; *World Food Programme (WFP, #21510)*. Observer to: *International Organization for Migration (IOM, #14454)*. Associated with Department of Global Communications of the United Nations.
NGO Relations Member of:
– *Alliance for Child Protection in Humanitarian Action (The Alliance, #00667)*; *Alliance to End Hunger*; *American Council for Voluntary International Action (InterAction)*; *Better Than Cash Alliance (#03220)*; *Business Humanitarian Forum (BHF, #03383)*; *CHS Alliance (#03911)*; *CORE Group*; *Early Childhood Development Action Network (ECDAN, #05155)*; *European Council on Refugees and Exiles (ECRE, #06839)*; *European NGO Platform Asylum and Migration (EPAM, #08051)*; *European Policy Centre (EPC, #08240)*; *Extractive Industries Transparency Initiative (EITI, #09229)*; *Global Coalition Against Child Pneumonia (#10290)*; *Global Education Cluster (#10333)*; *Global Impact*; *Global WASH Cluster (GWC, #10651)*; *Human Rights and Democracy Network (HRDN, #10980)*; *Inter-agency Network for Education in Emergencies (INEE, #11387)*; *International Childhood and Youth Research Network (ICYRnet, #12549)*; *International Council of Voluntary Agencies (ICVA, #13092)*; *NetHope (#16979)*; *Start Network (#19969)*; *Voluntary Organisations in Cooperation in Emergencies (VOICE, #20809)*.
Supporting organization of: *Scaling Up Nutrition Movement (SUN Movement, #19064)*. Stakeholder in: *Child and Youth Finance International (CYFI, inactive)*. Set up: *FilmAid International (FAI)*; *Women's Refugee Commission (WRC)*. Instrumental in setting up: *ONE (#17728)*. Partner of: *1,000 Days*; *Adventist Development and Relief Agency International (ADRA, #00131)*; *CartONG (#03591)*; *Crisis Action (#04957)*; *Global Health Cluster (GHC, #10401)*; *Global Shelter Cluster (GSC, #10594)*; *Helen Keller International (HKI, #10902)*; *Mastercard Foundation*. [2019.07.09/XF0054/**F**]

♦ International Rescue Corps (internationally oriented national body)
♦ International Rescue and Relief Committee / see International Rescue Committee (#14717)
♦ International Research Association Deinking Technology / see Internationale Forschungsgemeinschaft Deinking-Technik (#13233)

♦ International Research Association for History and Social Sciences Education (IRAHSSE) 14718

Association internationale de recherche en didactique de l'histoire et des sciences sociales

Vice-Pres/Secretariat Chemin Jean-Crotti 16, 1630 Bulle FR, Switzerland. E-mail: irahsse.airdhss@gmail.com.
URL: http://irahsse.org/

History 2009. Statutes adopted Sep 2012, Rome (Italy). Registered in accordance with Swiss Civil Code. **Aims** Promote school construction and the public use of history and the social sciences. **Structure** General Assembly; Board. **Finance** Sources: members' dues. **Events** *International Conference* Trois Rivières, QC (Canada) 2022, *International Conference* Athens (Greece) 2019, *International Conference* Paris (France) 2018, *International Conference* Braga (Portugal) 2016, *Conference / International Conference* Fribourg (Switzerland) 2014. **NGO Relations** *European Association of History Educators (EUROCLIO, #06069)*; *International Committee of Historical Sciences (ICHS, #12777)*; *International Society for History Didactics (ISHD, #15167)*; *International Standing Conference for History of Education (ISCHE, #15599)*. [2018/XJ9476/**C**]

♦ International Research Association for Organic Food Quality and Health (FQH) 14719

Sec c/o KU NEXS, Rolighedsvej 26, 1958 Frederiksberg C, Denmark.
URL: https://www.fqhresearch.org/

History Jan 2003. Founded by 4 European research institutes with the support of stakeholders from the organic food trade and industry. Former names and other names: *Food Quality and Health Association* – alias. **Aims** Establish a network of research institutions that specialize in the background of organic food and its effects on human health; promotes interdisciplinary as well as specialized investigations on organic food quality concepts and novel research methods to study the influence of organic food on human health. **Structure** General Meeting (annual). Board, comprising Chairperson and Treasurer, Vice-Chairperson, Secretary and 2 members. Scientific Advisory Committee. **Languages** English. **Finance** Sources: members' dues. **Activities** Events/meetings; research/documentation. **Events** *General Assembly* Nuremberg (Germany) 2023, *International Conference on Organic Food Quality and Health Research* Warsaw (Poland) 2013, *International Conference on Organic Food Quality and Health Research* Prague (Czech Rep) 2011, *Scientific FQH Conference* Frick (Switzerland) 2005. **Publications** *FQH Newsletter* (3 a year). *Organic, More Healthy? A search for biomarkers of potential health effects induced by organic products, investigated in a chicken model* (2007); *Parameters for Apple Quality 2* (2004); *Growth and Differentiation* (2002); *Parameters for Apple Quality* (2001) – Part 1 – report, Part 2 – annexes. Reports; articles.
Members Research (Ordinary); Supporting; Honorary. Research members in 10 countries:
Austria, Czechia, Denmark, France, Germany, Netherlands, Norway, Poland, Switzerland, UK.
Supporting members in 7 countries:
Denmark, Germany, Netherlands, Spain, Switzerland, UK, USA.
NGO Relations Member of (1): *TP Organics – European Technology Platform (TP Organics, #20180)*. Partner of (1): *IFOAM Organics Europe (#11104)*. [2022.12.08/XJ0894/**E**]

♦ International Research Association for Talent Development and Excellence (IRATDE) 14720

SG Georgskommende 33, 48143 Münster, Germany.
URL: http://www.iratde.org/

History 2008, Regensburg (Germany). **Aims** Initiate, conduct, and support research in the fields of talent development, *creativity*, excellence and innovation; assemble those interested in these fields for exchange of ideas and experience; disseminate research findings; assist development and evaluation of programmes and educational endeavours in these fields. **Structure** Executive Committee. **Activities** Capacity building; events/meetings; knowledge management/information dissemination; networking/liaising. **Events** *Biennial Conference* Taipei (Taiwan) 2019, *Biennial Conference* Dubai (United Arab Emirates) 2017. **Publications** *Talent Development and Excellence* – online journal; *Talent Talks* – newsletter. **NGO Relations** *Stiftung Internationales Centrum für Begabungsforschung (ICBF)*. [2017/XM6614/**C**]

♦ International Research Center for Artificial Intelligence under the auspices of UNESCO (unconfirmed)
♦ International Research Center for Energy and Economic Development (internationally oriented national body)
♦ International Research Centre on Anarchism (internationally oriented national body)
♦ International Research Centre on Environment and Development (internationally oriented national body)

♦ International Research Centre for Intangible Cultural Heritage in the Asia-Pacific Region under the Auspices of UNESCO (IRCI) 14721

Contact Sakai City Museum, 2 Mozusekiun-cho, Sakai-ku, Sakai City, Osaka, Japan. T. +81722758050. Fax +81722758151. E-mail: irci@nich.go.jp.
URL: http://www.irci.jp/

History Approval for establishment of International Research Centre for the safeguarding of Intangible Cultural Heritage (ICH) under the auspices of *UNESCO (#20322)* (UNESCO Category II Centre) granted at General Conference, Oct 2009. Official agreement between UNESCO and Japanese government concluded Aug 2010. Centre opened Oct 2011. Official agreement regarding continuation of IRCI renewed Dec 2018. **Aims** Promote the Convention for the safeguarding of Intangible Cultural Heritage and its implementation; enhance safeguarding of ICH through instigating and coordinating research in the Asia-Pacific region. **Structure** Functions under National Institute for Cultural Heritage. Governing Board. Departments (2): Research; General Affairs. **Languages** English, Japanese. **Staff** 10.00 FTE, paid. **Finance** Funded by Japanese Government. Annual budget: about Yen 100,000,000. **Activities** Research/documentation; networking/liaising. **Events** *Asia-Pacific Regional Workshop on Intangible Cultural Heritage and Natural Disasters* Sendai (Japan) 2018. **Publications** Books. **IGO Relations** *Convention for the Safeguarding of Intangible Cultural Heritage (2003)*; *UNESCO (#20322)*. **NGO Relations** Craft Revival Trust. [2020.01.06/XJ7904/**E***]

♦ International Research Commission on Standardization of Economic Accounting (inactive)

♦ International Research Committee of Oral Implantology (IRCOI) . . . 14722

Pres Via Carducci 2, 80053 Castellammare di Stabia NA, Italy.

History 1976. **Events** *Biennial World Congress* Castellammare di Stabia (Italy) 2012, *Biennial World Congress* Kamen (Germany) 2003, *Biennial world congress* Bucharest (Romania) 2002, *Biennial world congress* Bucharest (Romania) 2000, *World congress / Biennial World Congress* Athens (Greece) 1995. [2013/XE2154/**E**]

♦ International Research Council on the Biokinetics of Impacts / see International Research Council on the Biomechanics of Injury (#14723)
♦ International Research Council on the Biomechanics of Impact / see International Research Council on the Biomechanics of Injury (#14723)

♦ International Research Council on the Biomechanics of Injury (IRCOBI) 14723

Secretariat AGU Zurich, Winkelriedstrasse 27, 8006 Zurich ZH, Switzerland. T. +41442515430. Fax +41442515431. E-mail: secretariat@ircobi.org.
URL: http://www.ircobi.org/

History 7 Apr 1975, Lyon (France). Founded following preliminary discussions with OECD Road Research Secretariat and the setting up of *International Research Committee on the Biokinetics of Impacts*, Sep 1971. Former names and other names: *International Research Council on the Biokinetics of Impacts* – former (1975 to 1992); *Comité international de recherche sur la biocinétique des chocs* – former (1975 to 1992); *International Research Council on the Biomechanics of Impact (IRCOBI)* – former (1992). **Aims** Promote research and training of researchers in the field of biomechanics; encourage studies on the transfer of kinetic energy in and outside the human body; serve as a reference group engaged in epidemiological studies and on studies of motor vehicle design and accident research; collect information on biokinetics of impact. **Structure** Executive Committee of 17. **Languages** English. **Staff** Part-time. **Finance** Members' dues. Secretarial assistance from French national road safety institute. **Activities** Council members engage in research and provide expert advice. Annual conference since 1973, of the form *International Conference of the Biomechanics of Impacts* since 1977. **Events** *European Conference* Porto (Portugal) 2022, *Asia Conference* Beijing (China) 2021, *European Conference* Munich (Germany) 2021, *Asia Conference* Beijing (China) 2020, *European Conference* Munich (Germany) 2020. **Publications** Conference proceedings.
Members Individuals in 15 countries:
Australia, Belgium, Canada, France, Germany, India, Ireland, Italy, Japan, Netherlands, Spain, Sweden, Switzerland, UK, USA.
[2022/XD2786/v/**D**]

- ♦ International Research and Development Actions (internationally oriented national body)
- ♦ International Research and Documentation Centre for War Crimes Trials (internationally oriented national body)
- ♦ International Research in Early Childhood Education Conference (meeting series)
- ♦ International Research and Exchanges Board (internationally oriented national body)
- ♦ International Research Forum on Children and Media (internationally oriented national body)

♦ International Research Foundation for Development (IRFD) 14724

Contact address not obtained. T. +14157293683. Fax +17634452053.
Facebook: https://www.facebook.com/IRFDInc/

History 1993. **Aims** Establish and maintain an integrated global network for scientific policy research and advocacy on contemporary development issues. **Structure** Board of Directors. Regional and Coordinating Directors. **Finance** Members' dues. Donations; grants. **Activities** Events/meetings; training/education. **Events** *World forum on small island developing states* Port Louis (Mauritius) 2005, *World forum on information society* Tunis (Tunisia) 2005, *World forum on information society* Geneva (Switzerland) 2003, *World forum on sustainable development / World Forum* Johannesburg (South Africa) 2002, *World forum on sustainable development / World Forum* New York, NY (USA) 2001. **Publications** *Contemporary Development Analysis* (2 a year); *IRFD Newsletter*. Books; conference proceedings.
Members Individuals and organizations in 64 countries and territories:
Argentina, Australia, Bangladesh, Belize, Botswana, Brazil, Bulgaria, Burkina Faso, Burundi, Cambodia, Cameroon, Canada, Chile, China, Congo Brazzaville, Costa Rica, Cuba, Cyprus, Czechia, Denmark, Dominican Rep, Egypt, Ethiopia, Fiji, France, Gabon, Georgia, Germany, Ghana, Greece, Honduras, Hong Kong, India, Iran Islamic Rep, Italy, Jamaica, Japan, Kenya, Korea Rep, Laos, Malaysia, Maldives, Mozambique, Namibia, Nepal, Netherlands, Nigeria, Pakistan, Peru, Philippines, Poland, Portugal, Puerto Rico, Serbia, South Africa, Sri Lanka, Sudan, Sweden, Taiwan, Thailand, Trinidad-Tobago, Turkmenistan, USA, Vietnam.
IGO Relations Links with a number of organizations active in the field (not specified). **NGO Relations** Member of: *Global Islands Network (GIN, #10437)*. Links with a number of national and international organizations active in the field, including: *Association for Caribbean Transformation (ACT, no recent information)*; *Bangladesh Asiatic Society*; *Bariloche Foundation (FB)*; *Centro para la Investigación y el Desarrollo Económico y Social de Amazonas (CIDESAM, no recent information)*; *International Institute for Environment and Development (IIED, #13877)*; *Plan International (#18386)*. [2013/XF5731/f/**F**]

♦ The International Research Foundation for English Language Education (TIRF) 14725

CEO 177 Webster St, Ste 220, Monterey CA 93940, USA. Fax +18316476650. E-mail: info@tirfonline.org.
URL: http://www.tirfonline.org/

History Feb 1999, Washington, DC (USA). Founded with the support of *TESOL International Association*. Former names and other names: *TESOL International Research Foundation* – alias. **Aims** Support research in the teaching and learning of English. **Activities** Projects/programmes; financial and/or material support. **Publications** *TIRF Today* (12 a year) – newsletter. [2017.08.23/XQ0314/f/**F**]

♦ International Research Group on Biochemistry of Exercise 14726

Chair Place Pierre de Couvertin 1 – L0/10/08, 1348 Louvain-la-Neuve, Belgium.
URL: https://www.biochemistryofexercise.org/

History 1968, Brussels (Belgium), by *International Council of Sport Science and Physical Education (ICSSPE, #13077)*. **Aims** Promote scholarly activity in the broad area of exercise biochemistry. **Structure** Executive Group; Organizing Committee. **Languages** English. **Activities** Events/meetings; awards/prizes/competitions. **Events** *International Biochemistry of Exercise Conference (IBEC)* Toronto, ON (Canada) 2022, *International Biochemistry of Exercise Conference (IBEC)* Beijing (China) 2018, *International Biochemistry of Exercise Conference (IBEC)* Sao Paulo (Brazil) 2015, *International Biochemistry of Exercise Conference (IBEC)* Stockholm (Sweden) 2012, *International Biochemistry of Exercise Conference (IBEC)* Guelph, ON (Canada) 2009. **Members** No formal membership system. [2020.03.04/XE1416/v/**E**]

- ♦ International Research Group for Carcinoembryonic Proteins / see International Society for Oncology and BioMarkers (#15323)

♦ International Research Group on Charophytes (IRGC) 14727

Sec address not obtained.
URL: http://www.sea.ee/irgcharophytes/

History Jul 1989, Montpellier (France). **Aims** Promote and coordinate international cooperation in charophyte research, including living and fossil material of all geological periods; encourage the integration and synthesis of all aspects of botanical and palaeobotanical studies of charophytes, i e molecular studies, Quaternary studies, evolution, inclusion of charophytes in conservation and management of aquatic ecosystems; encourage the exchange of knowledge and discussion between researchers of all disciplines; enhance cooperation with other international organizations interested in phycology and palaeobotany. **Structure** General Assembly; Executive Committee. **Languages** English. **Staff** Voluntary. **Finance** Members' dues: euro 20. **Events** *Quadrennial International Symposium on Extant and Fossil Charophytes* Gammarth (Tunisia) 2020, *Quadrennial International Symposium on Extant and Fossil Charophytes* Astana (Kazakhstan) 2016, *Quadrennial International Symposium on Extant and Fossil Charophytes* Mendoza (Argentina) 2012, *Quadrennial international symposium on extant and fossil charophytes* Rostock (Germany) 2008, *Quadrennial international symposium on extant and fossil charophytes* Robertson, QLD (Australia) 2004. **Publications** *IRGC-News* (annual).
Members Individuals (150) in 41 countries and territories:
Algeria, Argentina, Australia, Austria, Bangladesh, Belgium, Brazil, Canada, China, Denmark, Estonia, Finland, France, Germany, Greece, Hungary, India, Italy, Japan, Kazakhstan, Korea Rep, Latvia, Lithuania, Mongolia, Morocco, Netherlands, New Zealand, North Macedonia, Philippines, Poland, Puerto Rico, Romania, Russia, Serbia, Slovenia, Spain, Switzerland, Taiwan, UK, Ukraine, USA.
NGO Relations Links with *Group of European Charophytologists (#10772)*. [2019/XF3463/**F**]

- ♦ International Research Group on Colour Vision Deficiencies / see International Colour Vision Society (#12656)

♦ International Research Group in Immunoscintigraphy and Immunotherapy (IRIST) 14728

Secretariat Via G Baglivi 12, 00161 Rome RM, Italy. T. +3964402565. Fax +3964402565. E-mail: alberto.signore@uniroma1.it – info@irist.org.
URL: http://www.irist.org/

History Also referred to as *International Research group in Immuno-Scintigraphy and Therapy*. **Events** *Congress* Prague (Czechia) 2018, *Meeting* Bertinoro (Italy) 2012, *Congress* Groningen (Netherlands) 2010, *Congress / Meeting* Krakow (Poland) 2008, *Meeting* London (UK) 2006.
Members Members in 14 countries:
Austria, Belgium, Denmark, France, Germany, Greece, Italy, Netherlands, Norway, Portugal, Spain, Sweden, Switzerland, UK.
[2014/XE3787/**E**]

- ♦ International Research group in Immuno-Scintigraphy and Therapy / see International Research Group in Immunoscintigraphy and Immunotherapy (#14728)

♦ International Research Group on Law and Urban Space (IRGLUS) . . 14729

Contact UNAM, Circuito Mario de la Cueva, Ciudad Universitaria, Coyoacan, 04510 Mexico City CDMX, Mexico.
Contact address not obtained.
URL: http://irglus.wordpress.com/

History 1996, as a working group of the Research Committee on the Sociology of Law, following activities initiated in 1993. Relaunched, 2007, Berlin (Germany). **Events** *Meeting* Oñati (Spain) 2014, *Workshop* Oñati (Spain) 2014, *Meeting* Oñati (Spain) 2009, *Meeting* Milan (Italy) 2008, *Meeting* Berlin (Germany) 2007.
[2014/XE3846/**E**]

♦ International Research Group on Ostracoda (IRGO) 14730

Communication Officer IGAG CNR, Area delle Scienze Roma 1, Montelibretti, Via Salaria KM 29-300, 00015 Monterotondo RM, Italy.
Sec Univ Brasilia, Inst Geosci, Lab Micropaleontol, ICC Ala Cent, Brasilia DF, 70910900, Brazil.
URL: http://www.ostracoda.net/irgo-home/

History Founded 1963, Naples (Italy), at the First International Symposium on Ostracoda, as *Committee on Recent Ostracoda* as a voluntary association. Current title adopted 1977. An official working group of *International Palaeontological Association (IPA, #14501)*, under *International Council for Science (ICSU, inactive)* and *UNESCO (#20322)*. **Aims** Advance knowledge of Ostracoda; facilitate communication among researchers. **Structure** Officers. **Languages** English. **Staff** All voluntary. **Finance** No members' dues. Finances through charitable organization based in Cologne (Germany). **Activities** Training/education; research and development; events/meetings. **Events** *International Symposium on Ostracoda* Lyon (France) 2022, *European Ostracodologists Meeting (EOM)* Gdansk (Poland) 2019, *International Symposium on Ostracoda* Santa Barbara, CA (USA) 2017, *European Ostracodologists Meeting (EOM)* Tartu (Estonia) 2015, *Meeting of Asian Ostracodologists* Seoul (Korea Rep) 2014. **Publications** *CYPRIS* (annual) – newsletter. Symposia proceedings; OSTRACON-Mailing List.
Members Individuals research scientists (about 400) studying living and fossil Ostracoda, in 33 countries:
Argentina, Australia, Austria, Belgium, Brazil, Canada, China, France, Germany, Greece, Iraq, Israel, Italy, Japan, Korea Rep, Luxembourg, Malaysia, Mexico, Morocco, New Zealand, Nigeria, Poland, Portugal, Romania, Russia, Singapore, Slovenia, Spain, Switzerland, Thailand, Türkiye, UK, USA. [2015.09.01/XJ8617/v/**E**]

♦ International Research Group on Physics Teaching 14731

Groupe international de recherche sur l'enseignement de la physique (GIREP) – Internationaler Arbeitskreis zur Förderung des Physikunterrichtes

Sec c/o DCU – Physical Sciences, DCU Glasnevin Campus, Dublin, 9, CO. DUBLIN, D09 W6Y4, Ireland. E-mail: girep.vzw@gmail.com.
Vice-Pres v/o PONTOn vzw, Millegemweg 49, 2531 Boechout, Belgium.
URL: http://www.girep.org/

History 15 Mar 1966. Founded following a series of meetings organized by *Organization for European Economic Cooperation (OEEC, inactive)* and subsequently *OECD (#17693)*. Statutes adopted 17 Mar 1972, Kiel (Germany FR); revised 12 Sep 1989, Balatonfüred (Hungary) and 29 Aug 1995, Trieste (Italy). Former names and other names: *International Group for Research in the Teaching of Physics* – alias. Registration: Belgium. **Aims** Promote and encourage efforts to adapt physics teaching to current knowledge; foster friendly contact, exchange of information and team work among member physics teachers and professors across national barriers and at all levels of education. **Structure** General Assembly. Commission of Representatives, comprising the Committee – President, 2 Vice-Presidents, Secretary and Treasurer – and delegates of the National Sections, meets every 2 years at working seminar. **Languages** English. **Staff** None. **Finance** Members' dues. Sponsorship of: universities; ministries of education; *UNESCO (#20322)*; *European Space Agency (ESA, #08798)*. **Activities** Organizes regular meetings and conferences. **Events** *GIREP Conference 2022* Ljubljana (Slovenia) 2022, *World Conference on Physics Education* Hanoi (Vietnam) 2021, *World Conference on Physics Education* Hanoi (Vietnam) 2020, *Seminar* Msida (Malta) 2020, *Joint Conference* Budapest (Hungary) 2019. **Publications** *GIREP Newsletter*. Meeting proceedings.
Members Individuals (some grouped in national sections), societies and national and international scientific bodies. Members in 41 countries:
Argentina, Armenia, Austria, Belgium, Chile, China, Colombia, Cyprus, Czechia, Denmark, Finland, France, Germany, Greece, Honduras, Hungary, India, Indonesia, Ireland, Israel, Italy, Japan, Korea Rep, Latvia, Malta, Mexico, Netherlands, New Zealand, Norway, Philippines, Portugal, Romania, Slovenia, South Africa, Spain, Sweden, Switzerland, Thailand, Türkiye, UK, USA.
NGO Relations Joint meetings with: *European Physical Society (EPS, #08207)*. [2022/XD5436/**F**]

♦ International Research Group for Psycho-Societal Analysis (IRGFPSA) 14732

Contact Dept of Caring and Ethics, Fac of Health Sciences, Univ of Stavanger, Postboks 8600, 4036 Stavanger, Norway.
URL: http://www.irgfpsa.org/

Aims Promote development and application of psycho-societal approaches to research and methodology. **Structure** Executive Committee. **Activities** Events/meetings; networking/liaising. **Events** *Annual Meeting* Dubrovnik (Croatia) 2016, *Annual Meeting* Dubrovnik (Croatia) 2015, *Annual Meeting* Dubrovnik (Croatia) 2014, *Conference* Dubrovnik (Croatia) 2009, *Conference* Dubrovnik (Croatia) 2006.
Members Full in 4 countries:
Denmark, Germany, Norway, UK. [2019.12.13/XM2123/**D**]

- ♦ International Research Group on Refuse Disposal (inactive)
- ♦ International Research Group on Time Budgets and Social Activities / see International Association for Time Use Research (#12229)
- ♦ International Research Group on Very Low Dose and High Dilution Effects (#10751)
- ♦ International Research Group on Wood Preservation / see International Research Group on Wood Protection (#14733)

♦ International Research Group on Wood Protection (IRG) 14733

Groupe international de recherche sur la protection du bois

Secretariat Drottning Kristinas väg 63B, Box 5604, SE-114 86 Stockholm, Sweden. T. +46105165140. E-mail: irg@ri.se.
URL: http://www.irg-wp.com/

History 25 Jun 1969, Cambridge (UK), as *International Research Group on Wood Preservation – Groupe international de recherche sur la préservation du bois*, after having taken over, 1 Jan 1969, the cooperative research programme of an OECD sponsored group, set up in 1965, and called 'Group of Experts on the Preservation of Wood'. Current Statutes effective 25 May 2007. **Aims** Promote research throughout the world on the subject of wood protection; act as a forum for other international bodies undertaking collaborative research; undertake the early notification and dissemination of research results. **Structure** Executive Council (EC), comprising President, Vice-president, 5 members and 2 ex officio members. Finance Committee (FC); Membership Committee (MC); Ron Cockcroft Award Committee (RCAC); Nominations Sub-Committee (NSC); Scientific Programme Committee (SPC); IRG Travel Awards Committee (TA), Electronic Communications Sub-Committee, comprising Sections (5) with Working Parties. Secretariat. **Languages** English, French,

German, Spanish. **Staff** 1.00 FTE, paid. **Finance** Financed by members and sponsors. Membership fees: Swedish Kr 900; Documents fees for non-member subscribers: Swedish Kr 2,000; Sponsorship subscriptions. Annual budget: 1,200,000 SEK. **Activities** Exchange of technical information on wood protection. Sections (5): Biology; Test Methodology and Assessment; Wood Protecting Chemicals; Processes and properties; Environmental Aspects. **Events** *Scientific Conference* 2021, *Annual Congress* Stockholm (Sweden) 2020, *Annual Congress* Québec, QC (Canada) 2019, *Annual Congress* Johannesburg (South Africa) 2018, *Annual Congress* Ghent (Belgium) 2017. **Publications** *IRG News in brief* – electronic newsletter. *The Compendium* (1969-2010); *International Directory of Members and Sponsors.* Annual Report; Technical documents (about 150 a year).

Members Individuals research workers and others from laboratories, institutes and other organizations; Sponsors (40); Honorary Life-long (9). Members (641) in 56 countries and territories:

Algeria, Argentina, Australia, Austria, Bangladesh, Belgium, Brazil, Burundi, Canada, Chile, China, Colombia, Côte d'Ivoire, Croatia, Denmark, Egypt, Fiji, Finland, France, Germany, Guiana Fr, India, Iran Islamic Rep, Ireland, Italy, Japan, Korea Rep, Latvia, Malaysia, Mauritius, Mexico, Netherlands, New Zealand, Nigeria, Norway, Poland, Portugal, Romania, Russia, Slovakia, Slovenia, South Africa, Spain, Sweden, Switzerland, Taiwan, Thailand, Türkiye, Uganda, UK, Uruguay, USA, Venezuela, Vietnam, Zambia, Zimbabwe.

NGO Relations Regional sponsoring members: *European Institute for Wood Preservation (WEI-IEO, #07575).* [2020/XB5729/v/**B**]

♦ International Research Institute for Climate Prediction / see International Research Institute for Climate and Society

♦ International Research Institute for Climate and Society (internationally oriented national body)

♦ International Research Institute on Jewish Women / see Hadassah-Brandeis Institute

♦ International Research Institutes (Iris) 14734

Central Office c/o DemoSCOPE Research and Marketing, Klusenstrasse 17/18, 6043 Adligenswil LU, Switzerland. T. +41413754000. Fax +41413754001.

URL: http://irisnetwork.org/

History 1986. **Aims** As an association of independent market research agencies, promote full service market research throughout the world. **Structure** Council. **Languages** English. **Staff** None. **Finance** Members' dues. **Activities** Conducts worldwide promotional study every 2 years. **Events** *Meeting* Warsaw (Poland) 2006, *Meeting* Athens (Greece) 2005, *Meeting* Cannes (France) 2005, *Annual meeting / Meeting* Lisbon (Portugal) 2004, *Meeting* London (UK) 2002.

Members Companies in 31 countries and territories:

Argentina, Australia, Belgium, Brazil, Canada, China, Czechia, Denmark, France, Germany, Greece, Hong Kong, Indonesia, Ireland, Italy, Japan, Korea Rep, Mexico, Netherlands, Nigeria, Poland, Portugal, Romania, Russia, Spain, Sweden, Switzerland, Thailand, UK, Uruguay, USA. [2010/XE4348/j/**E**]

♦ International Research Institute of Stavanger (internationally oriented national body)

♦ International Research Network on Interdependent Inequalities in Latin America (internationally oriented national body)

♦ International Research Network for Low Carbon Societies (LCS-RNet) 14735

Secretariat c/o IGES, 2108-11 Kamiyamaguchi, Hayama KANAGAWA, 240-0115 Japan. Fax +81468553809.

URL: http://lcs-rnet.org/

History Founded 2009, on the initiative of Japan as chair of the G8 in 2008, and upon agreement of the G8 countries. The G8 Environmental Ministers Meeting, Apr 2009, Syracuse (Italy), requested the LCS-RNet to report back its outcomes periodically, so knowledge from the network will be reflected at the very top level in environmental policies worldwide. Results have been delivered to the United Nations Framework Convention on Climate Change and other related international institutions. **Aims** As a network established between nations: share scientific knowledge needed to create low-carbon societies; provide an opportunity for researchers and policymakers to converse with each other by supporting timely policy implementation directly linking research and policy. **Structure** Annual Meeting. Secretariat provided by *Institute for Global Environmental Strategies (IGES, #11266).* **Languages** English. **Activities** Politics/policy/regulatory; networking/liaising; events/meetings. **Events** *Annual Meeting* Bogor (Indonesia) 2016, *Annual Meeting* Bogor (Indonesia) 2014, *Annual Meeting* Yokohama (Japan) 2013, *Annual Meeting* Bangkok (Thailand) 2012. **Publications** *Special Issue of Climate Policy* (2013). Newsletters; synthesis reports from annual meetings.

Members Research institutions (16) in 7 countries:

France, Germany, India, Italy, Japan, Korea Rep, UK.

Included in the above, 5 organizations listed in this Yearbook:

Centro Euro-Mediterraneo per i Cambiamenti Climatici (CMCC); Institut du développement durable et des relations internationales (IDDRI); Institute for Global Environmental Strategies (IGES, #11266); International Research Centre on Environment and Development (CIRED); Statistical Services Centre (no recent information).

NGO Relations Member of: *LEDS Global Partnership (LEDS GP, #16435).* [2015.01.06/XJ7844/y/**F**]

♦ International Research Network on Organizing by Projects (IRNOP) 14736

Contact Umeå School of Business, Biblioteksgränd 6, SE-901 87 Umeå, Sweden. E-mail: info@irnop.org.

URL: http://www.irnop.org/

History 1993, as a network of researchers in the field of project management. **Aims** Develop contacts between researchers on projects and temporary organizations around the world; promote advances in this research area. **Structure** Loosely organized network. **Finance** Conference participants take care of costs for arranging and taking part in IRNOP activities. **Activities** Events/meetings. **Events** *Temporary projects in transitional times – moving beyond dichotomous views on projects* Uppsala (Sweden) 2021, *Temporary projects in transitional times – moving beyond dichotomous views on projects* Uppsala (Sweden) 2020, *A skilled hand and a cultivated mind* Melbourne, VIC (Australia) 2018, *Conference* Boston, MA (USA) 2017, *Conference* London (UK) 2015. **Publications** Conference proceedings. **Members** Individuals: scholars with a background of business, economics, engineering and other fields with a common interest in projects, project organizations and temporary systems. Membership countries not specified. [2019.02.11/XF5982/v/**F**]

♦ International Research Network on Time Perspective (Time Perspective Network) 14737

Coordinator address not obtained. E-mail: timeperspectives@gmail.com.

Coordinator address not obtained.

URL: http://www.timeperspective.net/

History 2007. Also known under the acronym *IRN-TP.* **Aims** Enhance and develop research interest and collaborations in the field of the study of temporal dimension of social and psychological phenomena. **Structure** Leading Committee. **Finance** Members' dues. **Activities** Events/meetings; research/documentation. **Events** *International Conference on Time Perspective* Copenhagen (Denmark) 2016.

Members Full in 41 countries:

Albania, Australia, Austria, Belgium, Brazil, Canada, Chile, China, Croatia, Czechia, Denmark, Estonia, France, Germany, Greece, Hungary, India, Ireland, Israel, Italy, Japan, Korea Rep, Latvia, Lithuania, Mexico, Netherlands, New Zealand, Poland, Portugal, Romania, Russia, Serbia, Slovenia, South Africa, Spain, Sweden, Türkiye, UK, Ukraine, Uruguay, USA. [2016/XM5087/**F**]

♦ International Research Network on Transitions to Adulthood from Care (INTRAC) 14738

Contact address not obtained. E-mail: intracexco@gmail.com.

URL: https://globalintrac.com/

History Current constitution adopted 2018. **Aims** Promote national and international research on the transition from care to adulthood (care-leaving). **Structure** Executive Committee. Subgroup: Community of Researchers in Transition (CoRiT). Nordic branch: Nordic Research Network on Care Leavers' Trannsition to Adulthood (NRT). **Events** *Nordic Research Network Meeting* Helsinki (Finland) 2019. [2020/AA0531/v/**F**]

♦ International Research Network of Young Historians of European Integration (RICHIE Association) 14739

Réseau international de jeunes chercheurs en histoire de l'intégration européenne (Association RICHIE)

Pres address not obtained. E-mail: contact@europe-richie.org.

URL: http://www.europe-richie.org/

History Jul 2004. **Aims** Increase cooperation between young researchers in the history of European integration. **Activities** Events/meetings. **Events** *The two Europes* Naples (Italy) 2007, *Annual Conference* Copenhagen (Denmark) 2006, *Annual conference* Paris (France) 2005. **Publications** *Richie Europa Newsletter* (4 a year). **NGO Relations** Partner: *History of European Integration Research Society (HEIRS, #10932).* [2021/XM1661/**F**]

♦ International Research Programme on Health, Solar UV Radiation and Environmental Change (INTERSUN) 14740

Programme international de recherche sur la santé, le rayonnement solaire ultraviolet et les modifications de l'environnement

Contact c/o WHO, Dept of Public Health and Environment, Ave Appia 20, 1211 Geneva 27, Switzerland. T. +41227913427. Fax +41227914123. E-mail: uvinfo@who.int.

URL: http://www.who.int/uv/intersunprogramme/en/

History 1993, by *International Agency for Research on Cancer (IARC, #11598), UNEP (#20299)* and *WHO (#20950),* as a direct response to *United Nations Conference on Environment and Development (UNCED).* **Aims** Promote and undertake research on the effects on human *health* of increasing solar *ultra-violet* radiation reaching the earth's surface as a consequence of depletion of the stratospheric ozone layer; on the basis of the outcome of this research, recommend appropriate remedial measures to mitigate the above mentioned effects on human beings. **Activities** Collaborates with specialist agencies to implement key research needs; develops reliable predictions of health and environmental consequences of changes in UV exposure with stratospheric ozone depletion; develops practical ways of monitoring change in UV-induced health effects over time in relation to environmental and behavioural change; provides practical advice and information to national authorities on health and environmental effects of UV exposure, means of efficiently disseminating this information, and measures to protect the general public, workers and the environment against the adverse effects of increasing UV radiation levels. Priority activities: *'Scientific reviews'*: assesses the global burden of disease attributable to UV radiation; monitors developments in research and publishes up-to-date information through meeting reports, fact sheets, press releases and website. *'Research co-ordination'*: prioritizes research needs and the exchange of information at scientific meetings; facilitates communication between funding agencies and scientists; oversees a network of specialist agencies that facilitate the development of reliable predictions of health and environmental consequences of changes in UV exposure with stratospheric ozone depletion. *'Health risk assessment'*: develops indicators to quantify health effects of UV radiation on the skin, eyes and immune system; monitors these indicators over time and assesses their impact. *'Protection of public and occupational health'*: publications; develops guidelines for public and occupational exposure to UV radiation; promotes use of Global Solar UV Index; develops materials for sun protection in schools; seeks wider, more global representation, especially in developing countries. **Publications** *INTERSUN – The Global UV Project* (2009).

Members Network of national collaborating centres in 8 countries:

Australia, France, Germany, Japan, Mexico, Sweden, UK, USA.

IGO Relations Collaborates with: IARC; UNEP; WHO; *World Meteorological Organization (WMO, #21649).* **NGO Relations** Collaborates with: *European Society of Skin Cancer Prevention (EUROSKIN, #08735).* [2016/XE2183/**E***]

♦ International Research Ship Operators (IRSO) 14741

Chair NIWA Vessel Management Ltd, 301 Evans Bay Parade, Greta Point, Wellington 6021, New Zealand. T. +6443860300.

Vice-Chair National Research Council of Italy, Ple Aldo Moro 7, 00185 Rome RM, Italy. T. +390649932504.

URL: https://irso.info/

History 1986. Former names and other names: *International Ship Operators Meeting (ISOM)* – former. **Aims** Promote the safe, efficient and environmentally responsible operation of research ships in support of the global marine scientific research community. **Structure** Unincorporated association without official headquarters. Chair; Vice-Chair. **Activities** Events/meetings; knowledge management/information dissemination. **Events** *International Marine Technicians Workshop (INMARTECH)* Barcelona (Spain) 2023, *Annual International Research Ship Operators (IRSO) Meeting* Bruges (Belgium) 2023, *Annual International Research Ship Operators (IRSO) Meeting* Honolulu, HI (USA) 2022, *International Marine Technicians Workshop (INMARTECH)* Barcelona (Spain) 2021, *International Marine Technicians Workshop (INMARTECH)* Barcelona (Spain) 2020.

Members National and international organizations in 33 countries:

Argentina, Australia, Belgium, Brazil, Bulgaria, Canada, Chile, China, Denmark, Finland, France, Germany, Greece, Iceland, India, Indonesia, Ireland, Israel, Italy, Japan, Kenya, Korea Rep, Netherlands, New Zealand, Norway, Portugal, Romania, Russia, South Africa, Spain, Sweden, UK, USA.

Arctic and Antarctic Research Institute (AARI); European Centre for Information on Marine Science and Technology (EurOcean); European Commission (EC, #06633) (DG XII D1); *European Science Foundation (ESF, #08441)* (Marine Board); *NATO (#16945)* (Centre for Maritime Research and Exploration); *Royal Netherlands Institute for Sea Research (NIOZ).* [2023.02.14/AA2727/y/**F**]

♦ International Research Society for Children's Literature (IRSCL) ... 14742

Société internationale de recherche en littérature d'enfance et de jeunesse – Asociación Internacional de Investigación de Literatura Infantil y Juvenil – Internationale Forschungsgesellschaft für Kinder- und Jugendliteratur

Pres School of Education, Univ of Glasgow, Glasgow, G12 8QQ, UK. T. +441413301920.

URL: http://www.irscl.com/

History 1970. **Aims** Promote research into literature for children and young people. **Structure** Executive Board. **Languages** English. **Staff** Voluntary. **Finance** Sources: members' dues. **Activities** Events/meetings. **Events** *Biennial Congress* Santa Barbara, CA (USA) 2023, *Biennial Congress* 2021, *Biennial Congress* Stockholm (Sweden) 2019, *Biennial Congress* Toronto, ON (Canada) 2017, *Biennial Congress* Worcester (UK) 2015. **Publications** *International Research in Children's Literature* – journal. Membership directory.

Members Individuals in 45 countries and territories:

Australia, Austria, Belgium, Brazil, Bulgaria, Canada, Chile, China, Croatia, Czechia, Denmark, Faeroe Is, Finland, France, Germany, Greece, Indonesia, Ireland, Israel, Italy, Japan, Korea Rep, Lebanon, Lithuania, Malaysia, Mexico, Namibia, Netherlands, New Zealand, Nigeria, Norway, Poland, Portugal, Romania, Russia, Slovakia, Slovenia, South Africa, Spain, Sweden, Switzerland, Taiwan, UK, USA, Vietnam. [2020.03.03/XD5440/v/**C**]

♦ International Research Society of Orthopaedics and Traumatology (#19495)

♦ International Research Society for Public Management (IRSPM) ... 14743

Communications Sec c/o Univ of Berne, KPM, Schanzeneckstr 1, 3001 Bern, Switzerland. E-mail: info@irspm.org – conference@irspm.org.

Pres Univ of Essex, EBS 3 13 – Colchester Campus, Wivenhoe Park, Colchester, CO4 3SQ, UK. T. +441206872063.

URL: http://www.irspm.org

History 10 May 2006, Glasgow (UK). Founded during 10th International Research Symposium on Public Management. Symposia organized since 1997. **Aims** Foster collaboration in the field of research into and about public management. **Structure** Executive Board. **Languages** English. **Staff** Voluntary. **Finance** Sources: members' dues. **Activities** Events/meetings. **Events** *Annual Conference* Budapest (Hungary) 2023, *Annual Conference* Bern (Switzerland) 2022, *Annual Conference* Bern (Switzerland) 2021, *Annual Conference* Tampere (Finland) 2020, *Annual Conference* Wellington (New Zealand) 2019. **Publications** *Public Management Review.* **Members** From international public management research community around the world. Membership countries not specified. [2023.02.15/XM2260/**D**]

♦ International Research Society of Spinal Deformities (IRSSD) 14744

Contact Prof Dr Carl-Eric Aubin, PO Box 6079, Downtown Station, Montréal QC H3C 3A7, Canada. T. +15143404711ext2836. Fax +15143405867. E-mail: carl-eric.aubin@polymtl.ca.

URL: http://www.liv.ac.uk/HumanAnatomy/phd/irssd/

History 1994. Continues a series of meetings since 1980. **Aims** Provide a forum for the presentation and encouragement of research relating to spinal deformity; disseminate the results of such research. **Structure** Board, including President, President-Elect, Past-President and Secretary-Treasurer. **Events** *Meeting* Milwaukee, WI (USA) 2021, *Meeting* Milwaukee, WI (USA) 2020, *Meeting* Utrecht (Netherlands) 2018, *Meeting* Sapporo (Japan) 2014, *Meeting* Poznań (Poland) 2012. **Publications** *IRSSD Newsletter*. [2010/XM1829/**D**]

♦ International Research Society for Voluntary Associations, Nonprofit Organizations and Philanthropy / see International Society for Third-Sector Research (#15510)

♦ International Research/Study Team on Nonviolent Large Systems Change (internationally oriented national body)

♦ International Research and Training Centre on Erosion and Sedimentation (IRTCES) 14745

Centre international de formation et de recherche sur l'érosion et la sédimentation

SG PO Box 366, 100044 Beijing, China. T. +861068413372. Fax +861068411174. E-mail: liuxy@iwhr.com.

Street Address No 20 Chegongzhuang Road West, 100044 Beijing, China.

URL: http://www.irtces.org/

History Founded 21 Jul 1984, Beijing (China), by the Government of China, under the auspices of, and with support from, *UNESCO (#20322)*. **Aims** Create a mechanism for exchange of scientific and technical information on results of research among specialists in various countries; coordinate cooperative research activities and provide facilities for laboratory and field work for specialists from other countries; promote excellence in scientific research on erosion and sedimentation. **Structure** Officers: Director; Vice-Directors. Advisory Council, comprising representatives of UNESCO, UNDP, UNEP and FAO, representatives of international scientific associations and eminent scientists in the field. Corresponding Advisors (currently 16). Secretariat, composed of Secretary General, Vice Secretary General, Department of Research and Training, Domestic Information Network, Editorial Office, Administrative Office and Jingjiang Experimental Station. **Finance** Financed by Chinese Government and Unesco. Some activities also supported by other organizations such as UNDP and FAO. **Activities** Attention directed to sediment related problems pertaining primarily to rivers, including not only their courses from source to estuary, but also their entire watershed. Priority is given to river regulation, control of soil erosion, rational management and utilization of water and land resources and protection of the environment. Organizes: International Symposia on River Sedimentation; International training courses, symposia and workshops; international study tours; lectures. **Events** *International Symposium on River Sedimentation (ISRS)* 2025, *International Symposium on River Sedimentation* Florence (Italy) 2023, *International Symposium on River Sedimentation* Florence (Italy) 2022, *International Symposium on River Sedimentation* Chengdu (China) 2019, *International Symposium on River Sedimentation* Stuttgart (Germany) 2016. **Publications** *International Journal of Sediment Research* (4 a year) in English; *IRTCES Newsletter* (2 a year). IRTCES Circulars; IRTCES Monographs.

Members Involved countries (14):

Canada, China, France, Germany, India, Japan, Netherlands, New Zealand, Nigeria, Norway, Serbia, Switzerland, UK, USA.

IGO Relations *FAO (#09260)*; *International Bank for Reconstruction and Development (IBRD, #12317)*; *UNDP (#20292)*; *UNEP (#20299)*. **NGO Relations** Instrumental in setting up: *World Association for Sedimentation and Erosion Research (WASER, #21186)*. Member of: *Network of Asian River Basin Organizations (NARBO, #16993)*. Houses technical Secretariat of: *International Sediment Initiative (ISI, #14827)* [2022/XE0619/**E**]

♦ International Research and Training Centre for Information Technologies and Systems (internationally oriented national body)

♦ International Residual Mechanism for Criminal Tribunals (IRMCT) . 14746

Mécanisme international appelé à exercer les fonctions résiduelles des Tribunaux pénaux (MIFRTP)

MICT Registrar Haki Road, Plot No 486 Block A, Lakilaki Area, Arumeru Dist, PO Box 6016, Arusha, Tanzania UR. T. +255272565791. E-mail: mict-registryarusha@un.org.

The Hague branch Churchillplein 1, 2517 JW The Hague, Netherlands. T. +31705125332. E-mail: mict-registrythehague@un.org – mict-press@un.org.

URL: http://www.irmct.org/

History 22 Dec 2010. Established by Resolution 1966 (2010) of *United Nations Security Council (UNSC, #20625)*, as a body to continue the jurisdiction, rights, obligations and essential functions of *International Criminal Tribunal for the former Yugoslavia (ICTY, inactive)* and *International Criminal Tribunal for Rwanda (ICTR, inactive)* following the completion of their respective mandates. Branch covering functions inherited from ICTR is located in Arusha (Tanzania UR) and commenced functioning 1 Jul 2012. Branch covering functions inherited from ICTY is located in The Hague (Netherlands) and commenced functioning 1 Jul 2013. Former names and other names: *Mechanism for International Criminal Tribunals (MICT)* – former. **Aims** Perform essential functions inherited from ICTR and ICTY; locate, arrest and ensure the trial of eight ICTR accused still at large; conduct appeals proceeding originating from ICTR, ICTY and MICT cases; conduct re-trials of ICTR, ICTY and MICT cases; ensure the protection of ICTR, ICTY and MICT victims and witnesses; supervise enforcement of ICTR, ICTY and MICT sentences; provide assistance to national jurisdictions and preserve and manage the ICTR, ICTY and MICT archives. **Structure** Chambers; Office of the Prosecutor; Registry. Branch inherited from ICTY with seat in The Hague (Netherlands); Branch inherited from ICTR with seat in Arusha (Tanzania UR). Common to both branches: President; Prosecutor; Registrar; Independent Judges (25). **Languages** English, French. **Staff** 479.00 FTE, paid. Staff represented through *United Nations Criminal Tribunals Staff Union (UN-CTSU, #20550)*. **Finance** Budget (2016-2017): US$ 137,400,000. **Activities** Guidance/assistance/consulting; politics/policy/regulatory. Active in: Netherlands, Rwanda, Tanzania UR, Yugoslavia. **NGO Relations** *International Commission of Jurists (ICJ, #12695)* – Kenyan Section; *International Committee of the Red Cross (ICRC, #12799)*. [2020/XJ2514/**F***]

♦ International Resource Centre on Utilization of Information in Milk Production of Small Ruminants (internationally oriented national body)

♦ International Resources for Fairer Trade, India (internationally oriented national body)

♦ International Rest Investigators Society (no recent information)

♦ International Restless Legs Syndrome Study Group (unconfirmed)

♦ International Retail Forum / see Federation of International Retail Associations (#09676)

♦ International Retinitis Pigmentosa Association / see Retina International (#18926)

♦ International Retrovirology Association (IRA) 14747

Pres c/o Our GP MC, Level 2, 448 Boundary St, Spring Hill QLD 4000, Australia.

Sec address not obtained.

URL: http://htlv.net/

History 1988. Registration: USA, Maryland. **Aims** Encourage research in HTLV infections and disease; foster collaborations between research groups; provide a platform for critical analysis of new data; contribute to dissemination of knowledge about these infections. **Structure** Executive Committee; Awards Committee; Conference Committee. **Languages** English. **Staff** 4.00 FTE, paid. **Activities** Events/meetings; healthcare; knowledge management/information dissemination; research and development. **Events** *International Conference on Human Retrovirology* Melbourne, VIC (Australia) 2022, *International Conference on Human Retrovirology* Lima (Peru) 2019, *International Conference on Human Retrovirology* Tokyo (Japan) 2017, *International Conference on Human Retrovirology* Les Trois-Îlets (Martinique) 2015, *International Conference on Human Retrovirology* Montréal, QC (Canada) 2013. **Members** Investigators and scientists. Membership countries not specified. [2023/XJ6462/**B**]

♦ International Rett Syndrome Association / see International Rett Syndrome Foundation (#14748)

♦ International Rett Syndrome Foundation (IRSF) 14748

Chairman 4600 Devitt Drive, Cincinnati OH 45246, USA. T. +15138743020. Fax +15138742520. E-mail: admin@rettsyndrome.org.

URL: http://www.rettsyndrome.org/

History Jan 1985, as *International Rett Syndrome Association (IRSA)*. Current title adopted on merger with Rett Syndrome Research Foundation, 1 Jul 2007. **Aims** Fund research on treatment and cure for Rett syndrome; enhance the overall quality of life for those living with Rett syndrome by providing information, programmes and services. **Structure** Board of Trustees; Family Advisory Board. **Activities** Events/meetings. **Events** *Annual International Conference* Itasca, IL (USA) 2016, *Annual Symposium* Chantilly, VA (USA) 2014, *World Rett Syndrome Congress* New Orleans, LA (USA) 2012, *Annual Symposium* Leesburg, VA (USA) 2011, *Annual Symposium* Leesburg, VA (USA) 2010. **Publications** *Rett Syndrome Handbook*.

Members Corresponding; Active; International Organization/Group; Lifetime. Membership mostly in North America (USA and Canada) but in a total of 65 countries and territories:

Argentina, Australia, Austria, Belgium, Brazil, Bulgaria, Canada, Chile, China, Colombia, Costa Rica, Cuba, Czechia, Denmark, Finland, France, Germany, Hong Kong, Hungary, India, Indonesia, Iran Islamic Rep, Ireland, Israel, Italy, Japan, Kuwait, Lebanon, Luxembourg, Malaysia, Malta, Mexico, Montenegro, Nepal, Netherlands, New Zealand, Nicaragua, Nigeria, Norway, Pakistan, Panama, Philippines, Poland, Portugal, Puerto Rico, Russia, Saudi Arabia, Serbia, Singapore, Slovakia, South Africa, Spain, Sri Lanka, Sweden, Switzerland, Taiwan, Thailand, Turkmenistan, UK, Ukraine, United Arab Emirates, USA, Uzbekistan, Venezuela, Zimbabwe. [2017.06.27/XF1422/f/**F**]

♦ International Review of Psychosis and Bipolarity / see International Forum of Psychosis and Bipolarity (#13647)

♦ International Revival Network (IRN) 14749

Contact c/o Armme Resources Inc, 300-1634 Harvey Avenue, Kelowna BC V1Y 6G2, Canada. T. +12507171003. Fax +12507171013.

URL: http://www.revivalnow.com/

History by merger in the cause of unity of several national and international initiatives, including those of REVIVALNOW, TACF, *Global Resource Ministries International (GRMI, no recent information)* and SRN. **Aims** As a network on the *Internet* of *Christian ministries* who share a vision for global revival, seek to be worthy of the calling and use the gifts and ministries each has been given until all come to the unity of the faith and of the knowledge of the Son of God. In this context, function as a communication centre and catalyst for *reconciliation*, unity and the sharing of resources. **Structure** No "authority structure". Managed by Global Resource Ministries (UK) and facilitated by regional coordinators and representatives. **Finance** Voluntary donations, mainly from GRMI. **Activities** Through networks in all 5 continents: processes about 60,000 e-mails a day for member organizations; provides web-space; develops opportunities for raising finance and creating jobs in the developing world through fair-trading practices. Currently setting up a mission agency to reach the poor worldwide. **Publications** *IRN News*. On-line discussion lists.

Members Open to all in agreement with IRN beliefs and objectives, members are simply subscribers to IRN News or discussion lists – membership countries not specified. Coordinators in 5 countries:

Australia, Canada, Ireland, UK, USA. [2017/XF4448/**F**]

♦ International Reynard Society 14750

Société internationale renardienne

Pres Romanisches Seminar, Univ Zürich, Zürichbergstrasse 8, 8032 Zurich ZH, Switzerland.

URL: https://benjamins.com/catalog/rein/

History Founded 1975. **Aims** Study the beast *epic*, with particular reference to the 'Reynard the Fox' corpus, the *fable* and bestiary *tradition* and the short comic narrative genre exemplified by the old French 'fabliau', and with associated fields of art history and iconography and of moral, allegorical, satirical and comic *literature*. **Structure** Business Meeting (every 2 years, at International Colloquium); Committee. **Languages** English, French, German, Italian. **Staff** Voluntary. **Finance** No financing. **Events** *Biennial International Colloquium* Zurich (Switzerland) 2015, *Biennial International Colloquium* Alicante (Spain) 2013, *Biennial International Colloquium* Aix-en-Provence (France) 2011, *Biennial International Colloquium* Utrecht (Netherlands) 2009, *Biennial International Colloquium* Ventimiglia (Italy) 2007. **Publications** *Reinardus* (annual).

Members Teachers, researchers and interested persons. Individuals in 18 countries:

Belgium, Canada, Côte d'Ivoire, Czechia, Finland, France, Germany, Ireland, Israel, Italy, Japan, Netherlands, New Zealand, Russia, Spain, Switzerland, UK, USA. [2019.12.11/XD5865/v/**E**]

♦ International RFID Business Association (RFIDba) 14751

Pres/CEO 900 N Orange St, Ste 195, Media PA 19063, USA. E-mail: stephane@pique.ch.

Registered Address 5 W 37th St and 5th Ave, 9th floor, New York NY 10018, USA. T. +16103570990. Fax +16104978710.

URL: http://www.rfidba.org/

History Dec 2003. RFID stands for: *Radio Frequency Identification*. **Aims** Develop workplace-focused standards for RFID education, training and certification which guide the global business community to effectively implement RFID within the enterprise and across supply chains. **Structure** Executive Committee; Executive Management; Advisory Board. **Events** *Annual world Asia conference* Singapore (Singapore) 2010. **Publications** *RFID Monthly*. **Members** Membership countries not specified. [2013/XJ0134/**E**]

♦ International Rhino Foundation (IRF) 14752

Exec Dir 201 Main St, Ste 2600, Fort Worth TX 76102, USA. T. +15404659595. E-mail: info@rhinos.org.

Pres White Oak Conservation Center, 581705 White Oak Road, Yulee FL 32097, USA. Fax +19042253395.

URL: https://rhinos.org/

History 1989. Former names and other names: *International Black Rhino Foundation (IBRF)* – former. **Aims** Support and operate rhino conservation and research programs both in nature and in managed care with particular emphasis on intensive management and protection. **Structure** Board of Directors. **Events** *Joint Elephant and Rhino Research and Conservation Symposium* Singapore (Singapore) 2016, *Joint annual international elephant research symposium* Vienna (Austria) 2001.

Members Organizations in 11 countries:

Australia, Botswana, Congo DR, Eswatini, Indonesia, Kenya, Malaysia, South Africa, UK, USA, Zimbabwe.

IGO Relations Partners include: *World Heritage Fund (#21568)*. **NGO Relations** Partner of (7): *Gilman International Conservation Foundation (GIC)*; *International Elephant Foundation (IEF)*; *International Union for Conservation of Nature and Natural Resources (IUCN, #15766)*; *Re:wild*; *Save the Tiger Fund (STF)*; *United Nations Foundation (UNF, #20563)*; *World Wide Fund for Nature (WWF, #21922)*. [2021/XG6857/f/**F**]

♦ International Rhino Keeper Association (internationally oriented national body)

♦ International Rhinologic Society (IRS) 14753

Société internationale rhinologique

Gen Sec Hacettepe University, Faculty of Medicine, Sihhiye, 06100 Ankara/Ankara, Türkiye.

Journal: https://www.rhinologyjournal.com/

History 20 Oct 1965, Kyoto (Japan). Founded at a joint meeting of American Rhinologic Society, Japan Rhinologic Society and *European Rhinologic Society (ERS, #08388)*. Former names and other names: *Société internationale de rhinologie* – alias. **Aims** Create a central organization with which all national and regional societies of rhinology may be affiliated; organize international congresses and courses of instruction and stimulate study, research and scientific advancement in the field of rhinology and related basic sciences. **Structure** General Assembly; Board of Directors; Executive Committee. **Languages** English. **Finance** Annual contributions of national and regional societies. **Activities** Events/meetings; research/documentation; training/education. **Events** *Congress* Tokyo (Japan) 2024, *Congress* Sofia (Bulgaria) 2023, *Rhinology World Congress* St Petersburg (Russia) 2022, *The nose across the lifespan* Thessaloniki (Greece) 2021, *The nose across the lifespan* Thessaloniki (Greece) 2020. **Publications** *International Forum of Allergy and Rhinology* (12 a year); *Rhinology* (4 a year).

Members Fellows and Honorary Fellows; National or Regional Societies. Members in 58 countries and territories:

Australia, Austria, Bangladesh, Belgium, Bosnia-Herzegovina, Bulgaria, China, Costa Rica, Croatia, Czechia, Denmark, Egypt, Finland, France, Germany, Greece, Guatemala, Honduras, Hong Kong, Hungary, India, Indonesia, Iran Islamic Rep, Israel, Italy, Japan, Korea Rep, Latvia, Lithuania, Luxembourg, Malaysia, Mexico, Moldova, Montenegro, Netherlands, New Zealand, North Macedonia, Norway, Pakistan, Panama, Philippines, Poland, Portugal, Romania, Russia, Serbia, Singapore, Slovakia, Slovenia, Spain, Sweden, Switzerland, Thailand, Türkiye, UK, Ukraine, Uruguay, USA.

International Organizations (4):

Asia Oceania Rhinologic Society; Australasian Rhinologic Society; Chinese Rhinologic Society; *European Rhinologic Society (ERS, #08388)*; Indian Rhinologic Society; Latin American Rhinologic Society.

NGO Relations Member of: *Council for International Organizations of Medical Sciences (CIOMS, #04905)*; *Global Alliance Against Chronic Respiratory Diseases (GARD, #10182)*. [2021/XC2415/**C**]

♦ International Rhododendron Conference (meeting series)
♦ International Rice Commission (inactive)

♦ International Rice Research Institute (IRRI) 14754

Institut international de recherche sur le riz (IIRR)

Mailing Address 10th Fl Suite 1009, Security Bank Ctr 6776, Ayala Avenue, 1226 Makati, Philippines. T. +6325805600. Fax +6325805699. E-mail: info@irri.org.
URL: http://www.irri.org/

History 8 Mar 1960, Manila (Philippines). Registration: Philippines. **Aims** Improve the wellbeing of present and future generations of rice *farmers* and consumers, particularly those with low income; generate and disseminate rice-related knowledge and technology of short- and long-term *environmental*, social, and economic benefit; help enhance national research systems. **Structure** Board of Trustees. Director General; 3 Deputies Director General (Management Services; Research; Communication and Partnerships). Organizational Units. Country offices (17). Networks, including *International Network for Genetic Evaluation of Rice (INGER, see: #14754)*. **Languages** English. **Staff** 1350.00 FTE, paid. **Finance** Donors: *CGIAR System Organization (CGIAR, #03843)*, include: international aid agencies of the governments of Australia, Bangladesh, Belgium, Brazil, China, Denmark, France, Germany, India, Iran Islamic Rep, Japan, Korea Rep, Mexico, Netherlands, Norway, Philippines, Spain, Sweden, Switzerland, Thailand, UK and USA; international and regional IRRI members; *Deutsche Gesellschaft für Technische Zusammenarbeit (GTZ, inactive)*; *The Rockefeller Foundation (#18966)*. **Activities** Research and development; knowledge management/information dissemination; training/education; events/meetings. **Events** *Annual Meeting* Singapore (Singapore) 2018, *International Rice Congress* Singapore (Singapore) 2018, *Quinquennial International Rice Genetics Symposium* Singapore (Singapore) 2018, *Global Sustainable Rice Conference* Bangkok (Thailand) 2017, *Annual Meeting* Hangzhou (China) 2017. **Publications** *International Rice Research Notes* (3 a year); *Rice Literature Update* (3 a year). Annual Report; specialized technical books; reports; proceedings.

Members National organizations in 43 countries:
Australia, Austria, Bangladesh, Belgium, Brazil, Canada, China, Colombia, Côte d'Ivoire, Denmark, Egypt, Finland, France, Germany, India, Indonesia, Iran Islamic Rep, Ireland, Italy, Japan, Kenya, Korea Rep, Luxembourg, Mexico, Netherlands, New Zealand, Nigeria, Norway, Pakistan, Peru, Philippines, Portugal, Romania, Russia, South Africa, Spain, Sweden, Switzerland, Syrian AR, Thailand, Uganda, UK, USA.

International and regional organizations (12):
African Development Bank (ADB, #00283); *Arab Fund for Economic and Social Development (AFESD, #00965)*; *Asian Development Bank (ADB, #01422)*; *European Commission (EC, #06633)*; *FAO (#09260)*; *Inter-American Development Bank (IDB, #11427)*; *International Bank for Reconstruction and Development (IBRD, #12317)* (World Bank); *International Development Research Centre (IDRC, #13162)*; *International Fund for Agricultural Development (IFAD, #13692)*; *OPEC Fund for International Development (OFID, #17745)*; *UNDP (#20292)*; *UNEP (#20299)*.

IGO Relations Member of: *International Information System for the Agricultural Sciences and Technology (AGRIS, #13848)*. Observer to: *Committee of International Development Institutions on the Environment (CIDIE, no recent information)*. Cooperates with the other CGIAR supported centres:
– *Africa Rice Center (AfricaRice, #00518)*;
– *Bioversity International (#03262)*;
– *International Center for Agricultural Research in the Dry Areas (ICARDA, #12466)*;
– *International Crops Research Institute for the Semi-Arid Tropics (ICRISAT, #13116)*;
– *International Livestock Research Institute (ILRI, #14062)*.

NGO Relations Participates in: *Agricultural Libraries Network (AGLINET, #00571)*. Cooperates with the other CGIAR supported centres:
– *Center for International Forestry Research (CIFOR, #03646)*;
– *International Centre for Tropical Agriculture (#12527)*;
– *International Food Policy Research Institute (IFPRI, #13622)*;
– *International Institute of Tropical Agriculture (IITA, #13933)*;
– *International Maize and Wheat Improvement Center (#14077)*;
– *International Potato Center (#14627)*;
– *International Water Management Institute (IWMI, #15867)*;
– *World Agroforestry Centre (ICRAF, #21072)*;
– *WorldFish (#21507)*.

Member of: *Climate Technology Centre and Network (CTCN, #04023)*; *Consortium of Non-Traditional Security Studies in Asia (NTS-Asia, #04755)*; *Sustainable Development Solutions Network (SDSN, #20054)*. Associate member of: *Asian Venture Philanthropy Network (AVPN, #01778)*. Instrumental in setting up: *Genetic Resources Center (GRC, see: #14754)*; *International Rice Genebank (IRG, inactive)*. Links/cooperates with:
– *Asian Institute of Technology (AIT, #01519)*;
– *Caritas Australia*;
– *Commonwealth Scientific and Industrial Research Organization (CSIRO)*;
– *Ford Foundation (#09858)*;
– *International Centre of Insect Physiology and Ecology (ICIPE, #12499)*;
– *International Fertilizer Development Center (IFDC, #13590)*;
– *International Institute of Rural Reconstruction (IIRR, #13921)*;
– *Japan International Research Centre for Agricultural Sciences (JIRCAS)*;
– *Society for Japanese Arts (no recent information)*;
– *Welthungerhilfe*;
– *Winrock International*;
– *World Vision International (WVI, #21904)*. [2021/XE2417/jy/**E***]

♦ International Right to Life Federation (IRLF) 14755

Fédération internationale du droit à la vie – Federación Internacional del Derecho a la Vida

Pres 1821 W Galbraith Rd, Cincinnati OH 45239, USA. T. +15137293600. E-mail: irtlf@lifeissues.org.

History 1984, Ostend (Belgium). **Aims** Seek equal protection throughout the world for all human life from fertilization until natural death. **Structure** Board. **Languages** English. **Staff** 4.00 FTE, voluntary. **Finance** Voluntary contributions; newsletter subscriptions. **Events** *Euthanasia Conference* Manila (Philippines) 2007, *Euthanasia conference* Toronto, ON (Canada) 2002, *Euthanasia conference* Warsaw (Poland) 2001, *Euthanasia Conference* Warsaw (Poland) 2000, *Euthanasia Conference* Washington, DC (USA) 2000.

Members Delegates representing 12 countries:
Brazil, Canada, Ecuador, India, Italy, Kenya, Netherlands, Nigeria, Philippines, Poland, UK, USA.

Consultative Status Consultative status granted from: *ECOSOC (#05331)* (Ros A). [2017.03.09/XD1192/**D**]

♦ International Right of Way Association (internationally oriented national body)

♦ International Risk Governance Council (IRGC) 14756

Managing Dir c/o EPFL, BAC, Station 5, 1015 Lausanne VD, Switzerland. T. +41216938290. E-mail: info@irgc.org.
URL: http://www.irgc.org/

History 10 Jun 2003, Geneva (Switzerland). Registration: EU Transparency Register, No/ID: 722047014943-13. **Aims** Develop concepts of risk governance, anticipate major risk issues and provide risk governance policy advice for key decision-makers; help improve understanding and management of potentially global risks that have impact on human health and safety, the environment, the economy and society at large. **Structure** Board; Advisory Committee; Secretariat. **Languages** English. **Staff** 0.20 FTE, paid. **Finance** Sources: contributions; government support; private foundations. Contributions from industries, academia. **Activities** Advocacy/lobbying/activism; events/meetings. **Events** *Digital Currencies – Governing Risks and Opportunities* Zurich (Switzerland) 2022, *Governance Of and By Digital Technology Conference* Lausanne (Switzerland) 2020, *From crisis response to learning and innovation* Paris (France) 2014, *From crisis management to risk governance* Beijing (China) 2013, *Symposium on Risk Issues* Lausanne (Switzerland) 2013. **Publications** Concept notes; policy briefs; reports; opinion pieces.

Members Full in 12 countries:
Belgium, Canada, China, France, Germany, India, Japan, Portugal, Sweden, Switzerland, UK, USA.

Consultative Status Consultative status granted from: *ECOSOC (#05331)* (Special); *UNEP (#20299)*. **IGO Relations** Accredited by (2): *ECOSOC (#05331)*; *United Nations Framework Convention on Climate Change – Secretariat (UNFCCC, #20564)*. Memorandum of Understanding with (1): *OECD (#17693)*. Collaborative agreement with: *Joint Research Centre (JRC, #16147)*. **NGO Relations** Member of (1): *Sustainable Development Solutions Network (SDSN, #20054)*. [2023.02.20/XJ3105/**E**]

♦ International RiverFoundation / see International River Foundation
♦ International River Foundation (internationally oriented national body)
♦ International Rivers (internationally oriented national body)
♦ International Rivers Network / see International Rivers

♦ International Road Assessment Programme (iRAP) 14757

Head Office Ocean House, The Ring, Bracknell, RG12 1AX, UK. T. +441256345598.
CEO RACQ House, L12/60 Edward Street, Brisbane QLD 4000, Australia. T. +61733612548.
Registered Address 60 Trafalagar Square, London, WC2N 5DS, UK.
URL: http://www.irap.org

History Registration: Charity Commission, No/ID: 1140357, England and Wales; EU Transparency Register, No/ID: 172833946173-81, Start date: 19 Apr 2022. **Aims** Promote a world free of high-risk roads for road users; prevent road deaths. **Structure** Board of Trustees; Global Policy Advisory Committee; Global Technical Committee. **Staff** 6.00 FTE, paid; 4.00 FTE, voluntary. **Activities** Awards/prizes/competitions; certification/accreditation; monitoring/evaluation; projects/programmes; training/education. Runs Road Assessment Programmes (RAP) in about 70 countries worldwide. Co-chairs *UN Road Safety Collaboration*. Active in: Australia, Brazil, Chile, China, Colombia, Dominica, Ethiopia, Ghana, India, Indonesia, Mexico, Nepal, Pakistan, Philippines, South Africa, Tanzania UR, Thailand, UK, USA, Vietnam. **Events** *Innovation Workshop* Stockholm (Sweden) 2020. **Members** Civil society organizations; Supra-national organizations; Regional RAP Associations; Authorities; Experts. Membership countries not specified. **Consultative Status** Consultative status granted from: *ECOSOC (#05331)* (Special). **NGO Relations** Member of (2): *Fédération Internationale de l'Automobile (FIA, #09613)*; *World Road Association (PIARC, #21754)*. Partner of (2): *International Road Federation (IRF, #14758)*; *Partnership on Sustainable, Low Carbon Transport Foundation (SLoCaT Foundation, #18244)*. [2022/XJ6866/**F**]

♦ International Road Federation (IRF) 14758

Fédération Routière Internationale – Internationaler Strassenverband – Federación Internacional de Carreteras

Dir-Gen Chemin de Blandonnet 2, 1214 Vernier GE, Switzerland. T. +41223060260. Fax +41223060270. E-mail: info@irfnet.ch.
URL: https://irfnet.ch/

History 2 Dec 1964, Switzerland. Unification efforts with *International Road Federation (IRF Global, #14759)*, Washington DC, ended, 2016. Registration: Switzerland, Geneva; EU Transparency Register, No/ID: 94038094048-01, Start date: 23 Aug 2010. **Aims** Support, encourage and promote the development and maintenance of better, safer and sustainable roads and road systems. **Structure** General Assembly; Board of Directors; Executive Committee; Secretariat, headed by Director-General. India Chapter; Africa Board. **Activities** Advocacy/lobbying/activism; events/meetings; knowledge management/information dissemination; networking/liaising; politics/policy/regulatory; research/documentation; training/education. **Events** *World Congress* Istanbul (Türkiye) 2024, *Annual Conference* Marrakech (Morocco) 2022. **Publications** *IRF CROSSROADS*. **Members** Full: stakeholders from private and public sector. Associate: individuals. Membership countries not specified. **Consultative Status** Consultative status granted from: *ECOSOC (#05331)* (Special). **IGO Relations** Partner of (5): *African Union (AU, #00488)*; *Organization of Black Sea Economic Cooperation (BSEC, #17857)*; *The World Bank Group (#21218)*; *United Nations Economic Commission for Africa (ECA, #20554)*; *United Nations Economic Commission for Europe (UNECE, #20555)*. **NGO Relations** Partner of (8): *Association Européenne des Concessionnaires d'Autoroutes et d'Ouvrages à Péage (ASECAP, #02559)*; *EIT Urban Mobility (EIT UM, #05410)*; *ERTICO ITS Europe (#05532)*; *European Union Road Federation (ERF, #09014)*; *Fédération Internationale de l'Automobile (FIA, #09613)*; *International Road Assessment Programme (iRAP, #14757)*; *International Road Transport Union (IRU, #14761)*; *World Road Association (PIARC, #21754)*. [2023/AA3046/**C**]

♦ International Road Federation (IRF Global) 14759

Pres Madison Pl, 500 Montgomery St, Fifth Floor, Alexandria VA 22314, USA. T. +17035351001. Fax +17035351007. E-mail: info@irf.global.
URL: https://www.irf.global/

History 5 May 1948, Washington, DC (USA). Offices subsequently incorporated, 30 Jun 1948, London (UK), and 12 May 1952, Paris (France). Unification efforts with *International Road Federation (IRF, #14758)*, Geneva, ended, 2016. **Aims** Assist countries in progressing towards better, safer and smarter road systems. **Structure** Directors; Executive Committee. **Languages** English, French, German, Spanish. **Staff** 16.00 FTE, paid. **Finance** Subscriptions from sustaining members. **Activities** Advocacy/lobbying/activism; awards/prizes/competitions; events/meetings; knowledge management/information dissemination; training/education. **Events** *IRF World Meeting & Exhibition* 2025, *Africa Regional Congress* Accra (Ghana) 2023, *Regional Conference for Africa* Cape Town (South Africa) 2022, *Asia Pacific Regional Congress* Kuala Lumpur (Malaysia) 2022, *IRF World Meeting & Exhibition* Dubai (United Arab Emirates) 2021. **Publications** *Who's Who* (annual) – membership roster; *World Road Statistics* (annual); *World Highways – Routes du monde* (about 9 a year) – official journal of IRF, published by Route One Publishing Ltd; *IRF Newsletter*. IRF Directories; proceedings of meetings; annual report; technical and statistical reports. Information Services: videotape training programme; databases on European motorways, vertical and horizontal road signing. **Information Services** *IRF Documentation Centre* – at Geneva office.

Members Affiliated national organizations in 33 countries:
Albania, Algeria, Angola, Argentina, Canada, China, Denmark, Egypt, Estonia, Finland, Greece, Hungary, Israel, Japan, Jordan, Kenya, Korea Rep, Kuwait, Latvia, Lithuania, Malaysia, Mexico, New Zealand, North Macedonia, Poland, Romania, Russia, Saudi Arabia, Slovakia, Sweden, Uganda, USA, Yemen.

Sustaining members in 62 countries and territories:
Argentina, Australia, Austria, Belgium, Brazil, Bulgaria, Canada, China, Costa Rica, Croatia, Czechia, Denmark, Egypt, Finland, France, Georgia, Germany, Ghana, Greece, Hong Kong, Hungary, India, Indonesia, Italy, Japan, Jordan, Korea Rep, Kuwait, Kyrgyzstan, Lebanon, Madagascar, Malaysia, Mexico, Morocco, Netherlands, Niger, Nigeria, Norway, Pakistan, Peru, Philippines, Poland, Portugal, Romania, Russia, Saudi Arabia, Serbia-Montenegro, Singapore, Slovenia, South Africa, Spain, Sweden, Switzerland, Thailand, Tunisia, Türkiye, UK, United Arab Emirates, USA, Vietnam, Yemen, Zimbabwe.

Affiliated regional organizations (4):
Arab Urban Development Institute (AUDI, #01071); *International Bridge, Tunnel and Turnpike Association (IBTTA, #12400)*; *Pan American Institute of Highways (PIH, no recent information)*; *Road Engineering Association of Asia and Australasia (REAAA, #18955)*.

Consultative Status Consultative status granted from: *OAS (#17629)*. **IGO Relations** Accredited by (1): *United Nations Office at Vienna (UNOV, #20604)*. Associated with Department of Global Communications of the United Nations. **NGO Relations** Partner of (1): *Partnership on Sustainable, Low Carbon Transport Foundation (SLoCaT Foundation, #18244)*. Cooperates with (3): *European Construction Industry Federation (#06766)*; *Federación Interamericana de la Industria de la Construcción (FIIC, #09333)*; *International Federation of Asian and Western Pacific Contractors' Associations (IFAWPCA, #13359)*. [2023/XB2418/y/**B**]

♦ International Road Racing Press Association (IRRPA) 14760

Pres Via del Fontanile Arenato 288, 00163 Rome RM, Italy. T. +393356217548.

Activities Follows MotoGP World Championship and World Superbike Championship. **Events** *Annual General Assembly* Jarama (Spain) 1993. [2019.12.12/XD0605/**D**]

♦ International Road Racing Teams Association (internationally oriented national body)
♦ International Road Safety Organisation (#18493)
♦ International Road Tar Conference / see International Tar Association (#15655)

♦ International Road Transport Union (IRU) 14761

Union Internationale des Transports Routiers – Unión Internacional de Transportes por Carretera – Internationale Strassentransportunion

SG Chemin de la Voie-Creuse 16, 1211 Geneva 20, Switzerland. T. +41229182700. Fax +41229182741. E-mail: iru@iru.org.
URL: http://www.iru.org/

History 1948, Geneva (Switzerland). Statutes modified: 1956; 1963; 1969; 1995; 1997; 2001, 2020 Former names and other names: *International Bus and Lorry Transport Office* – former (1947 to 1948); *Bureau international de transport par autocar et camion (BITAC)* – former (1947 to 1948). Registration: Civil Code, Switzerland. **Aims** Study, solve, or play a part in solving, questions raised in road transportation; promote harmonization and simplification of regulations and practices relating to such transport; coordinate and support efforts made in different countries with a view to developing transport of passengers and goods by road; improve the safety record and environmental performance of road transport and ensure mobility of people and goods; take the initiative in ensuring that *vehicles* are safe, clean, efficient and economical in fuel consumption; encourage sound fleet management, strict vehicle maintenance and good *working conditions* for *drivers*; help make roads safer and less congested; seek improvements in environmental performance of vehicles; maintain close working relations with competent national, intergovernmental and nongovernmental organizations; strive to lift barriers to international transport and trade. **Structure** General Assembly (meets once or twice a year): Presidential Executive; Secretariat General, headed by Secretary General. Meetings closed. Active members grouped in 2 Transport Councils: Passenger Transport; Goods Transport. Specialized International Commissions (3): Customs; Social affairs and Technical Affairs. Groups of Experts (1): Taxis and Hire Cars with Driver. Liaison bodies (3): *IRU Permanent Delegation to the European Union*; *IRU Permanent Delegation to Eurasia*; *IRU Permanent Delegation to the Middle East Region*. **Languages** English, French. **Staff** 100.00 FTE, paid. **Finance** Sources: members' dues. **Activities** Events/meetings; knowledge management/ information dissemination; networking/liaising; politics/policy/regulatory; training/education. Active in all member countries. **Events** *Biennial World Congress* Berlin (Germany) 2020, *Biennial world congress* Muscat (Oman) 2018, *Road Transport Conference* Brussels (Belgium) 2016, *International IRU Taxi Forum* Cologne (Germany) 2014, *Euro-Asian Road Transport Conference* Amman (Jordan) 2013. **Publications** Studies; practical documents; best practices; guidelines; driver checklists; congress and conference reports; films.

Members Active and Associate (172) in 81 countries:
Afghanistan, Albania, Argentina, Armenia, Australia, Austria, Azerbaijan, Belarus, Belgium, Bosnia-Herzegovina, Brazil, Bulgaria, Canada, Chile, China, Colombia, Croatia, Cyprus, Czechia, Denmark, Egypt, Estonia, Finland, France, Georgia, Germany, Greece, Hungary, India, Iran Islamic Rep, Iraq, Ireland, Israel, Italy, Japan, Jordan, Kazakhstan, Korea Rep, Kosovo, Kuwait, Kyrgyzstan, Latvia, Lebanon, Lithuania, Luxembourg, Malta, Mexico, Moldova, Mongolia, Montenegro, Morocco, Netherlands, New Zealand, North Macedonia, Norway, Pakistan, Poland, Portugal, Qatar, Romania, Russia, Saudi Arabia, Serbia, Singapore, Slovakia, Slovenia, Spain, Sweden, Switzerland, Syrian AR, Tajikistan, Tunisia, Türkiye, Turkmenistan, UK, Ukraine, United Arab Emirates, Uruguay, USA, Uzbekistan, Yemen.
Association of European Vehicle Logistics (ECG, #02551); *European Association of Abnormal Road Transport and Mobile Cranes (ESTA, #05923)*; *European Automobile Manufacturers' Association (ACEA, #06300)*; *European Secure Parking Organisation (ESPORG)*; *Transfrigoroute International (TI, #20213)*.

Consultative Status Consultative status granted from: *ECOSOC (#05331)* (General); *International Maritime Organization (IMO, #14102)*; *UNCTAD (#20285)* (General Category).

IGO Relations Active in drawing up such international conventions as:
- *Agreement on the International Carriage of Passengers by Road by Means of Occasional Coach and Bus Service (ASOR, 1982)*;
- *Agreement on the International Carriage of Perishable Foodstuffs and on the Special Equipment to be Used for Such Carriage (ATP, 1970)*;
- *Convention on the Contract for the International Carriage of Goods by Road (CMR, 1956)*;
- *Convention on the Contract for the International Carriage of Passengers and Luggage by Road (CVR, 1973)*;
- *Convention on Long-range Transboundary Air Pollution (#04787)*;
- *Customs Convention on the International Transport of Goods under Cover of TIR Carnets, 1959 (TIR Convention, 1959)*;
- *European Agreement Concerning the International Carriage of Dangerous Goods by Road (ADR, 1957)*;
- *International Convention on the Harmonization of Frontier Controls of Goods (1982)*;
- *Protocol to the Convention on the Contract for the International Carriage of Goods by Road (CMR, 1978)*;
- *Protocol to the Convention on the Contract for the International Carriage of Passengers and Luggage by Road (CVR, 1978)*.

Memorandum of Understanding with: *Economic Cooperation Organization (ECO, #05313)*; *Organization of Black Sea Economic Cooperation (BSEC, #17857)*; *World Customs Organization (WCO, #21350)*. Affiliate member of: *World Tourism Organization (UNWTO, #21861)*.

NGO Relations Memorandum of Understanding with (1): *Arab Union of Land Transport (AULT, #01069)*. Member of (9): *Bureau international des containers et du transport intermodal (BIC, #03364)*; *Confederation of Organizations in Road Transport Enforcement (CORTE, #04574)*; *Conference of Non-Governmental Organizations in Consultative Relationship with the United Nations (CONGO, #04635)*; *European Logistics Platform (ELP, #07711)*; *European Road Transport Research Advisory Council (ERTRAC, #08396)*; *European Tourism Manifesto (#08921)*; *Fédération des Institutions Internationales établies à Genève (FIIG, #09599)*; *Global Road Safety Partnership (GRSP, #10581)*; *Network for the European Private Sector in Tourism (NET, #17027)*. Partner of (1): *International Road Federation (IRF, #14758)*. In liaison with technical committees of: *International Organization for Standardization (ISO, #14473)*. Close collaboration with: *Association Européenne des Concessionnaires d'Autoroutes et d'Ouvrages à Péage (ASECAP, #02559)*. Participant of: *United Nations Global Compact (#20567)*. Represented in: *European Citizens' Mobility Forum (ECMF, #06559)*.
[2022.11.29/XB2420/y/**B**]

♦ International Robert Musil Society 14762

Société internationale Robert Musil (SIRM) – Internationale Robert-Musil-Gesellschaft (IRMG)
Address not obtained.
URL: http://www.musilgesellschaft.at/

History 1974. **Aims** Facilitate international cooperation in research on Robert Musil; publish his writings. Committee of 14 members. **Languages** English, French, German. **Staff** 2.00 FTE, voluntary. **Finance** Members' dues. Donations from members. **Activities** Maintains archives related to the work and the life of Robert Musil; organizes regular congresses. **Events** *International colloquium* Berlin (Germany) 2005, *International colloquium* Darmstadt (Germany) 2003, *International Colloquium* Saarbrücken (Germany) 2001, *International Colloquium* Strasbourg (France) 1996, *International Colloquium* Saarbrücken (Germany) 1994. **Publications** *Musil Forum* (2 a year) in French, German.

Members Individuals (280, 40 of which are Founder Members) in 29 countries:
Australia, Austria, Belgium, Bulgaria, Canada, China, Czechia, Denmark, Egypt, Finland, Germany, Greece, Hungary, Israel, Italy, Japan, Korea Rep, Luxembourg, Netherlands, Norway, Portugal, Romania, Russia, South Africa, Spain, Sweden, Switzerland, UK, USA.
[2016/XE0148/v/**E**]

♦ International Robot Olympiad Committee (unconfirmed)
♦ International Rock Art Symposium (meeting series)

♦ International Rock Climbing Research Association (IRCRA) 14763

Sec address not obtained.
Pres address not obtained.
URL: http://www.ircra.rocks/

History 2011, Christchurch (New Zealand). **Aims** Bring researchers and climbers together to improve understanding of the sport and assist each other in improving climbing performance, teaching and coaching and interaction with the environments in which climbing takes place. **Structure** Executive Committee. **Events** *International Rock Congress* Tokyo (Japan) 2021, *International Rock Congress* Tokyo (Japan) 2020, *International Rock Congress* Chamonix (France) 2018, *International Rock Congress* Telluride, CO (USA) 2016, *International Rock Congress* Pontresina (Switzerland) 2014.

Members Individuals in 17 countries:
Australia, Austria, Brazil, Canada, Croatia, Czechia, France, Germany, Italy, Netherlands, New Zealand, Slovenia, Spain, Switzerland, Türkiye, UK, USA.
[2015/XJ9479/**C**]

♦ International Rock Garden Plant Conference (meeting series)

♦ International Rogaining Federation (IRF) 14764

Sec Box 3, Central Park VIC 3145, Australia.
URL: http://www.rogaining.org/

History Inaugural meeting 16 Jun 1989, Calgary AB (Canada). Constitution adopted 30 Jun 2000; amended 9 apr 2001, 20 Dec 2003, 31 Dec 2008, 28 Oct 2012 and 1 Jan 2013. **Aims** Promote and develop the sport of rogaining internationally; maintain *rules* and standards of the sport. **Structure** Council; Executive. **Languages** English. **Staff** 8.00 FTE, voluntary. **Finance** Sources: members' dues. **Activities** Events/meetings. **Events** *World Rogaining Championship* USA 2014, *World Rogaining Championship* Pustoshka (Russia) 2013, *World Rogaining Championship* Prebuz (Czech Rep) 2012, *World Rogaining Championship* Cheviot (New Zealand) 2010, *World Rogaining Championship* Estonia 2008.

Members National Associations in 9 countries:
Australia, Czechia, Estonia, Latvia, New Zealand, Russia, Spain, Ukraine, USA.
Observers in 10 countries:
Australia, Brazil, Canada, Finland, Germany, Israel, Lithuania, South Africa, Spain, Sweden.
[2015.02.07/XJ7136/**C**]

♦ International Roller Skating Federation / see World Skate (#21786)
♦ International Roller Skating Trainer Association (no recent information)
♦ International Roller Sports Federation / see World Skate (#21786)

♦ International Romani Union (IRU) 14765

Union internationale des Roms – Romani Unia
Pres ARBICM, Str 376 br 108, 1000 Skopje, North Macedonia. T. +38922656901. Fax +38923216000. E-mail: rbic@t-home.mk – office@iromaniunion.org.
Office Manager Str Dobrimir Hrs No 39, 1000 Skopje, North Macedonia. E-mail: tvbtr@tvbtr.com.mk.
URL: https://www.iromaniunion.org/

History 1971. Former names and other names: *Romani International Union* – former; *International Union of Romani* – alias; *Romani Union* – alias; *Union des Roms* – alias; *Romani Unia* – alias; *Union mondiale des gitans* – alias; *Romani World Union* – alias. **Aims** Bring together groups of gypsies, *romanies*, *sinti*, in the world; foster a sense of reunification among them through language and culture; combat anti gypsy racism in all its forms; provide educational materials about gypsy peoples to non gypsy peoples and monitor media misrepresentation; improve health and employment conditions of the Romanies; seek war crimes reparations, standardization of the Romani language and its orthography; forge stronger ties with India, the ancestral homeland of the Romani people. **Structure** Includes *Romani Congress (no recent information)*, founded 1958. **Events** *Congress* Skopje (Macedonia) 2016, *Congress* Riga (Latvia) 2015, *Congress* Sibiu (Romania) 2013, *Congress* Zagreb (Croatia) 2008, *Congress* Lanciano (Italy) 2004. **Publications** *O Glaso Romano*; *Roma Times News*.

Members National associations (representing 50 million Romanies) and individuals in 54 countries:
Afghanistan, Albania, Argentina, Armenia, Australia, Austria, Belarus, Belgium, Bosnia-Herzegovina, Brazil, Bulgaria, Czechia, Denmark, Egypt, Finland, France, Georgia, Germany, Greece, Hungary, India, Iran Islamic Rep, Ireland, Israel, Italy, Japan, Kyrgyzstan, Latvia, Lithuania, Moldova, Montenegro, Morocco, Netherlands, New Zealand, North Macedonia, Norway, Pakistan, Poland, Portugal, Romania, Russia, Scotland, Serbia, Slovakia, Slovenia, Spain, Sweden, Switzerland, Türkiye, UK, Ukraine, USA, Uzbekistan, Venezuela.

Consultative Status Consultative status granted from: *ECOSOC (#05331)* (Special); *UNICEF (#20332)*. **IGO Relations** Accredited by (1): *United Nations Office at Vienna (UNOV, #20604)*. Associated with Department of Global Communications of the United Nations. **NGO Relations** Observer status with (1): *Unrepresented Nations and Peoples Organization (UNPO, #20714)*. Member of (1): *NGO Committee on UNICEF (#17120)*.
[2022.11.09/XF1359/**F**]

♦ International Roncalli Foundation (internationally oriented national body)
♦ International Rope Skipping Federation (inactive)
♦ International Rorschach Society / see International Society of the Rorschach and Projective Methods (#15430)
♦ International Rosaceae Genomics Conference (meeting series)
♦ International Rossi-Landi Society (internationally oriented national body)

♦ International Rough Set Society (IRSS) 14766

Sec address not obtained.
Pres address not obtained.
URL: http://roughsets.home.pl/

History Reorganized 2005. Most current constitution and bylaws approved 2011. **Structure** Steering Committee; Executive Board; Advisory Board. **Events** *International Joint Conference on Rough Sets* Jeju (Korea Rep) 2015, *International Conference on Rough Sets and Intelligent Systems Paradigms* Madrid (Spain) 2014, *International conference on rough sets and current trends in computing* Madrid (Spain) 2014. **NGO Relations** *European Society for Fuzzy Logic and Technology (EUSFLAT, #08603)*.
[2015/XJ9545/**C**]

♦ International Round Table for the Advancement of Counselling / see International Association for Counselling (#11821)
♦ International Roundtable of Audiovisual Organizations (meeting series)
♦ International Round Table of Audiovisual Records / see Co-ordinating Council of Audiovisual Archives Associations (#04820)
♦ International Round Table of Educational Counselling and Vocational Guidance / see International Association for Counselling (#11821)

♦ International Roundtable for the Semiotics of Law (IRSL) 14767

Address not obtained.
Journal: http://www.springerlink.com/link.asp?id=104162

History 2001, by merger of *International Association for the Semiotics of Law (IASL, inactive)* and Roundtable for the Semiotics of Law. Previously also known under the acronym *IRTSL*. **Aims** Disseminate information on different forms of textual analysis to the discourses of law, including semiotics of Greimas, Perice and Lacan, rhetoric, philosophy of language, pragmatics, sociolinguistics and deconstruction, and on more traditional legal philosophical approaches to the language of the law. **Structure** Advisory/Coordinating Committee of 5 members. President. **Events** *Annual Conference* New York, NY (USA) 2017, *Annual Conference* Poznań (Poland) 2016, *Annual Conference* Hilo, HI (USA) 2015, *Annual Conference* Copenhagen (Denmark) 2014, *Annual Conference* Wollongong, NSW (Australia) 2007. **Publications** *International Journal for the Semiotics of Law* (4 a year). Books.

Members Full in 34 countries:
Argentina, Australia, Austria, Belgium, Brazil, Canada, China, Colombia, Denmark, Finland, France, Germany, Hong Kong, Hungary, India, Iran Islamic Rep, Ireland, Israel, Italy, Mexico, Morocco, Netherlands, Norway, Poland, Portugal, Romania, Russia, Spain, Sweden, Switzerland, Tunisia, UK, USA, Venezuela.
[2016/XJ3852/c/**F**]

♦ International Rowing Federation / see World Rowing (#21756)

♦ International RS Feva Class Association 14768

Secretary address not obtained.
URL: http://www.rsfeva.org/

NGO Relations Recognized Class Association of: *World Sailing (#21760)*.
[2016/XM2793/**E**]

♦ International Rubber Association (IRA) 14769

Exec Sec c/o Thai Rubber Association, 45-47 Chotivithayakun 3 Road, Hatyai, Songkhla, 90110, Thailand. T. +6674429011 – +6674429311. Fax +6674429312. E-mail: ira@csloxinfo.com.
URL: http://www.intlra.org/

History 24 Sep 1971, Ottawa (Canada), by 21 organizations which ratified the Constitution and registered as members. **Aims** Discuss international commercial matters relating to natural rubber and/or related subjects; consider problems related to international rubber trade and submit reports and recommendations on the subject; establish an International Contracts Committee to formulate International Contracts for natural rubber and the interpretation thereof. **Structure** General Meeting (every 2 years); Management Committee. **Languages** English. **Staff** 2.00 FTE, paid. **Finance** Members' dues. **Activities** Networking/ liaising; knowledge management/information dissemination; events/meetings.

Members National and international associations (21) in 14 countries:
Belgium, Cambodia, France, Germany, Indonesia, Japan, Malaysia, Netherlands, Singapore, Sri Lanka, Thailand, UK, USA, Vietnam.
Included in the above, one organization listed in this Yearbook:
Rubber Trade Association of Europe (RTAE, #18995).
[2015.01.12/XD1564/y/**D**]

♦ International Rubber Conference Organisation (IRCO) 14770

SG c/o IOM3, Grantham Ctr – Boilerhouse, Springfield Business Park, Caunt Road, Grantham, NG31 7FZ, UK. E-mail: irco@iom3.org.
URL: http://www.internationalrubberconference.org/

History 13 Oct 1971, Cleveland OH (USA). Current Constitution approved 3 Jun 1982, Paris (France); amended Sep 1999, Orlando FL (USA). **Aims** Increase the *professional* competence of people associated with rubber *industry*; provide a forum for the exchange of information on new developments in the science, technology, *raw materials*, economics, processes, health and safety, and environmental aspects of the industry. **Structure** International Rubber Conference (held annually). *International Rubber Conference Committee (IRCC)*, a permanent body of IRCO, consists of representatives of National and Regional Organizations as agreed from time to time by the Committee. **Languages** English. **Staff** The Institute of Materials, Minerals and Mining provides Secretariat. **Finance** Members' dues. **Activities** International Rubber Conferences (held annually).

Interest focused on current research programmes in various countries. **Events** *IRC : International Rubber Conference* France 2031, *IRC : International Rubber Conference* Malaysia 2030, *IRC : International Rubber Conference* UK 2029, *IRC : International Rubber Conference* Daegu (Korea Rep) 2028, *IRC : International Rubber Conference* USA 2027. **Publications** Proceedings of Conferences.
Members Full in 20 countries:
Australia, Brazil, China, Czechia, Finland, France, Germany, India, Japan, Korea Rep, Malaysia, Netherlands, Norway, Russia, Slovakia, Sweden, Thailand, Türkiye, UK, USA. [2013/XD7358/**F**]

♦ International Rubber Development Committee (inactive)
♦ International Rubber Regulation Scheme / see International Rubber Study Group (#14772)
♦ International Rubber Research Board (inactive)

♦ International Rubber Research and Development Board (IRRDB) .. 14771
Organisation international de recherches et développement sur le caoutchouc
Contact PO Box 10150, 50908 Kuala Lumpur, Malaysia. T. +60342521612. Fax +60342560487. E-mail: sec_gen@theirrdb.org.
Office 260 Jalan Ampang, 50450 Kuala Lumpur, Malaysia.
URL: http://www.theirrdb.org/
History 1960, London (UK), by merger of *International Rubber Development Committee (IRDC, inactive)*, set up 1936, and *International Rubber Research Board (IRRB, inactive)*, formed 1936. Has also been referred to in French as *Conseil international de la recherche et du développement sur le caoutchouc*. **Aims** Foster cooperation between member institutes and provide a forum for concerted action on matters of common interest. **Structure** Meeting (annual); Board, consisting of 29 members; Committee of Directors and Chief Executives; Finance Committee; Secretariat. **Languages** English. **Staff** 2.00 FTE, paid. **Finance** Members' dues, based on volume of rubber production in the country of the member institute. Budget (annual): pounds100,000. **Activities** Events/meetings; training/education; awards/prizes/competitions; research/documentation; research and development. **Events** *Annual Meeting* Manila (Philippines) 2014, *Annual Meeting* London (UK) 2013, *Annual meeting* Siem Reap (Cambodia) 2007, *Annual Meeting* Ho Chi Minh City (Vietnam) 2006, *Annual meeting* Chiang Mai (Thailand) 2003. **Publications** *IRRDB Newsletter* (4 a year) in English; *IRRDB Annual Report* in English, French; *IRRDB Information Quarterly* in English. Symposium proceedings.
Members National organizations (rubber research institutes) in 16 countries:
Brazil, Cameroon, China, Côte d'Ivoire, France, Gabon, India, Indonesia, Malaysia, Mexico, Nigeria, Philippines, Sri Lanka, Thailand, UK, Vietnam.
IGO Relations *Association of Natural Rubber Producing Countries (ANRPC, #02822)*; *International Rubber Study Group (IRSG, #14772)*. **NGO Relations** In liaison with technical committees of: *International Organization for Standardization (ISO, #14473)*. [2016/XD2425/**D**]

♦ International Rubber Study Group (IRSG) 14772
Groupe international d'études du caoutchouc
SG 51 Changi Business Park Central 2, Unit 06 – 04/05 The Signature, Singapore 486066, Singapore. T. +6565880463. Fax +6565880468. E-mail: secgen@rubberstudy.com.
URL: http://www.rubberstudy.com/
History 1944, London (UK), by governments of Netherlands, UK, France and USA, following from *International Rubber Regulation Scheme* which had operated from 1934. First meeting: Jan 1945, Washington DC (USA). Terms of Reference revised: 1947, 1950, 1961, and most recently 14 Feb 1978, London, on signature of Headquarters Agreement with the UK Government. **Aims** Be a source of statistical data and analysis for all aspects of the rubber industry, including production, consumption and trade in rubber and rubber products; prepare current estimates and analyse future supply and demand trends; undertake statistical and economic studies on specific aspects of the industry so as to continually improve its value-added service to stakeholders; be the platform for informal, open, informed and continuing global dialogue among all stakeholders in the natural and synthetic rubber economy. **Structure** Assembly (annual); Subsidiary bodies (4). **Languages** English. **Staff** 5.00 FTE, paid. **Finance** Sources: members' dues. **Activities** Events/meetings; networking/liaising. **Events** *World Rubber Summit* Singapore (Singapore) 2022, *World Rubber Summit* Singapore (Singapore) 2019, *World Rubber Summit* Colombo (Sri Lanka) 2018, *World Rubber Summit* Singapore (Singapore) 2017, *World Rubber Summit* Singapore (Singapore) 2015. **Publications** *Rubber Statistical Bulletin* (4 a year); *Rubber Industry Report* (4 a year); *Outlook for Elastomers* (annual); *Statistical Yearbook* (annual). *IRSG Secretariat Papers*. *Directory of Rubber Organizations* (2000) – also on diskette; *Key Rubber Indicators* (1993); *World Rubber Statistics Handbook – vol 5* (1975-1995) – also on diskette; *World Rubber Statistics Handbook* (1900-1960) – also on diskette; *The World Rubber Economy: Changes and Challenges*. *Rubber Industry Atlas* (2000) – diskette or e-mail. Statistical commentaries; market reports; proceedings of discussion fora; occasional papers.
Members Governments of 8 synthetic/natural rubber producing and/or consuming countries:
Cameroon, Côte d'Ivoire, India, Japan, Nigeria, Russia, Singapore, Sri Lanka.
International organization (1):
European Commission (EC, #06633).
IGO Relations Relationship agreement with: *FAO (#09260)*. Participates in the activities of: *UNCTAD (#20285)*. Designed International Commodity Body of: *Common Fund for Commodities (CFC, #04293)*. [2020/XC2426/**C***]

♦ International Rubiaceae and Gentianales Conference (meeting series)
♦ International Rugby Board / see World Rugby (#21757)
♦ International Rugby Football Board / see World Rugby (#21757)

♦ International Rugby League (IRL) 14773
SG 55 King Street, Manchester, M2 4LQ, UK. E-mail: info@intrl.sport.
URL: https://www.intrl.sport/
History 1998. Registered in accordance with Australian law: 28 091 594 777. **Aims** Foster, develop, extend, govern and administer the Game of Rugby League throughout the world. **Structure** Annual General Meeting; Board. **Events** *Meeting* Sydney, NSW (Australia) 2004.
Members Full; Affiliate. Full in 17 countries and territories:
Australia, Cook Is, England, Fiji, France, Ireland, Jamaica, Lebanon, New Zealand, Papua New Guinea, Russia, Samoa, Scotland, Serbia, South Africa, Ukraine, Wales.
Affiliate in 14 countries:
Brazil, Canada, Chile, Czechia, Germany, Ghana, Greece, Malta, Netherlands, Nigeria, Norway, Spain, Türkiye, USA.
Observer in 21 countries:
Albania, Belgium, Bosnia-Herzegovina, Burundi, Cameroon, Colombia, Congo DR, Denmark, Ethiopia, Georgia, Hungary, Latvia, Libya, Morocco, Palestine, Poland, Saudi Arabia, Solomon Is, Sweden, Trinidad-Tobago, Vanuatu.
NGO Relations Member of (1): *Alliance of Independent recognised Members of Sport (AIMS, #00690)* (Observer). [2021/XM0005/**C**]

♦ International Rugby Union Board / see World Rugby (#21757)
♦ International Ruminant Reproduction Symposium (meeting series)
♦ International Rural Housing Association (inactive)
♦ International Rural Poultry Centre (internationally oriented national body)
♦ International Rural Sociological Association / see International Rural Sociology Association (#14774)

♦ International Rural Sociology Association (IRSA) 14774
Association internationale de sociologie rurale
Sec Dept of Sociology, Michigan State Univ, 506 East Circle Drive, East Lansing MI 48824, USA. T. +15173554640.
URL: http://www.irsa-world.org/
History Aug 1976, Torun (Poland). Founded at 4th World Congress for Rural Sociology, replacing *Committee for International Cooperation in Rural Sociology (inactive)*, set up 1962. Former names and other names: *International Rural Sociological Association* – alias. **Aims** Foster development of the science of rural sociology; further the application of results of sociological inquiry in improving quality of life of rural people; provide a mechanism for rural sociologists to generate dialogue and useful exchange. **Structure** Council. **Languages** English, French, Spanish. **Staff** Voluntary. **Finance** Members' dues of regional rural sociological associations; no dues for individuals. **Activities** Events/meetings; projects/programmes. **Events** *World Congress of Rural Sociology* Cairns, QLD (Australia) 2022, *Quadrennial Congress* Cairns, QLD (Australia) 2021, *Quadrennial Congress* Cairns, QLD (Australia) 2020, *Quadrennial Congress* Toronto, ON (Canada) 2016, *Quadrennial Congress* Lisbon (Portugal) 2012. **Publications** *IRSA Items* (annual).
Members Individual members in 63 countries and territories:
Argentina, Australia, Austria, Bangladesh, Belgium, Brazil, Bulgaria, Burkina Faso, Canada, Chile, Congo DR, Cyprus, Czechia, Denmark, Egypt, Finland, France, Germany, Ghana, Greece, Hungary, India, Indonesia, Iran Islamic Rep, Iraq, Ireland, Israel, Italy, Japan, Jordan, Kenya, Korea Rep, Kuwait, Luxembourg, Malaysia, Mexico, Nepal, Netherlands, New Zealand, Nigeria, Norway, Papua New Guinea, Peru, Philippines, Poland, Portugal, Romania, Russia, Senegal, Serbia, Slovakia, South Africa, Spain, Sri Lanka, Sweden, Switzerland, Taiwan, Tanzania UR, Thailand, Türkiye, UK, USA, Zambia.
Regional rural sociological associations (5):
Asian Rural Sociology Association (ARSA, #01689); *Australia and Oceania Network for Rural Social Research and Community Development (AON, no recent information)* (Oceania); *European Society for Rural Sociology (ESRS, #08731)*; *Latin American Rural Sociological Association (#16368)*; *Rural Sociological Society (RSS)* (North America).
NGO Relations *International Research Centre on Rural Cooperative Communities (CIRCOM, no recent information)*. [2021/XC0293/y/**C**]

♦ International Sacerdotal Brotherhood Saint Pius X / see Priestly Society of Saint Pius X (#18494)
♦ International Sachsenhausen Committee (#04187)
♦ International Sachsensymposion – Research network for the archaeological study of the Saxons and their neighbouring peoples in northwestern Europe (#13305)
♦ International Saddlery Association (inactive)

♦ International Safflower Germplasm Advisory Committee (ISGAC) .. 14775
Contact address not obtained. E-mail: bob.guenthner@ars.usda.gov.
URL: http://safflower.wsu.edu/
History 1992, as an informal network. **Members** Membership countries not specified. **IGO Relations** *Bioversity International (#03262)*. [2009/XJ8032/**E**]

♦ International Sailing Coaches Association (ISCA) 14776
Secretariat 39 rue du Portal d'Amont, 66370 Pezilla-la-Rivière, France. T. +33468926046.
History 2004, France. Registered in accordance with French law. **Aims** Represent the interests and support the work of sailing coaches; improve the sport of sailing. **Structure** Executive Committee of up to 7 members, including President and Honorary Secretary. **Events** *Annual Meeting* Hyères (France) 2004, *Annual Meeting* Cadiz (Spain) 2003, *Annual Meeting* Athens (Greece) 2002. **NGO Relations** Recognized by: *World Sailing (#21760)*. [2010/XM2791/**D**]

♦ International Sailing Craft Association (inactive)
♦ International Sailing Federation / see World Sailing (#21760)

♦ International Sailing Schools Association (ISSA) 14777
Association internationale des écoles de voiles – Asociación Internacional de Escuelas de Vela – Internationale Segelschulen Vereinigung
Contact 22 Lecha Street, 03-610 Warsaw, Poland. T. +48222454978. E-mail: issa@sailingschools.org.
URL: http://www.sailingschools.org/
History 11 Jan 1969, London (UK), following initiatives in 1968. Statutes adopted at 1st Meeting, 11 Jan 1969, London. Statutes amended: 5 Oct 1978, Vienna (Austria); 1 Oct 1981, Palma de Mallorca (Spain); 20 Oct 1982, Tetouan (Morocco); 3 Oct 1985, Tréboul (France); 1976, Helsinki (Finland); 1986, Montréal (Canada) 1987; 1991, Vienna; 1996, Brighton (UK); 2000, Edinburgh (UK). Registered in Lausanne (Switzerland). **Aims** Reinforce internationally all institutions teaching sailing; promote sailing through teaching, initiation, improvement, in collaboration with other international *water sport* associations; encourage more people to take part in sailing; ensure maintenance of high standards of quality and safety. **Structure** General Assembly (annual); Administrative Council; Tellers; Technical Committees. **Languages** English, French, German, Spanish. **Staff** 2.00 FTE, paid. **Finance** Members' dues. Other sources: subsidies; donations; legacies. **Activities** Training/education; knowledge management/information dissemination; events/meetings. **Events** *Annual General Assembly* Phuket (Thailand) 2013, *Annual General Assembly* Lódz (Poland) 2012, *Annual General Assembly* Poznań (Poland) 2011, *Annual General Assembly* Istanbul (Turkey) 2010, *Annual General Assembly* UK 2009. **Publications** *ISSA Bulletin* (4 a year).
Members Honorary; Active; Associate. National sailing schools and centres in 38 countries and territories:
Australia, Austria, Bahrain, Belgium, Brazil, Canada, Cayman Is, Colombia, Croatia, Cyprus, Finland, France, Greece, Grenada, Hong Kong, Iceland, Indonesia, Ireland, Italy, Japan, Jordan, Lebanon, Montenegro, Netherlands, Norway, Pakistan, Poland, Russia, Samoa, Serbia, Spain, Sweden, Switzerland, Thailand, Türkiye, UK, United Arab Emirates, USA. [2014.06.24/XD9163/**D**]

♦ International Sail Training Association (inactive)
♦ International Sakharov Environmental University (internationally oriented national body)
♦ International Sakharov Institute of Radioecology / see International Sakharov Environmental University

♦ International Salivary Gland Society (ISGS) 14778
Pres Cours de Rive 16, 1204 Geneva, Switzerland. T. +41227357240. Fax +41227357058.
URL: http://www.isgs.ch/
History 2003, Geneva (Switzerland), during 1st International Congress on Salivary Gland Diseases. Registered in accordance with Swiss law. **Aims** Increase exchange and dissemination of knowledge and information about basic and clinical science pertinent to saliva, salivary glands and related disorders. **Structure** General Assembly (every 4 years). Steering Committee, including President, President-Elect, Secretary and Treasurer. Branch: *European Salivary Gland Society (ESGS, #08423)*. **Languages** English. **Events** *International congress on salivary gland diseases* Geneva (Switzerland) 2012, *Sialendoscopy conference* Geneva (Switzerland) 2012, *International congress on salivary gland diseases / Congress* Pittsburgh, PA (USA) 2007. [2019/XM3222/**D**]

♦ International Salmon Farmers Association (no recent information)

♦ International Salvage Union (ISU) 14779
SG Holland House, 1-4 Bury Street, London, EC3A 5AW, UK. T. +442072206597.
URL: http://www.marine-salvage.com/
History Founded 1926. **Aims** Foster a wider understanding of the salvage industry's contribution to environmental protection and the salvage of ship casualties, cargoes and other *marine* property. **Structure** Executive Committee; Secretariat. **Languages** English. **Staff** 3.00 FTE, paid. **Finance** Members' dues. Contract levies. **Activities** Events/meetings. **Events** *Annual General Meeting* Rotterdam (Netherlands) 2021, *Annual General Meeting* London (UK) 2020, *Annual Meeting* London (UK) 2019, *Annual Meeting* Cape Town (South Africa) 2018, *Annual Meeting* Singapore (Singapore) 2017. **Publications** *Salvage World* (4 a year) – bulletin; *Annual Review*; *ISU Newsletter*.
Members Full (57) in 32 countries and territories:
Argentina, Belgium, Canada, Chile, China, Colombia, Croatia, Cuba, Curaçao, Denmark, Egypt, Finland, France, Germany, Greece, Hong Kong, India, Ireland, Italy, Japan, Korea Rep, Malta, Netherlands, Norway, Russia, Singapore, South Africa, Spain, Türkiye, UK, United Arab Emirates, USA.
Associate (73) in 15 countries and territories:
Argentina, Bangladesh, Barbados, Belgium, Chile, Denmark, Greece, Hong Kong, India, Japan, Malaysia, Netherlands, Norway, Türkiye, United Arab Emirates.
Affiliate (11):
American Salvage Association; *Association mondiale de dispacheurs (AMD, #02809)*; Baltic Exchange; *BIMCO (#03236)*; China Diving and Salvage Contractors' Association (CDSCA); *European Tugowners Association (ETA, #08956)*; *InterManager (#11520)*; *International Association of Independent Tanker Owners (INTERTANKO, #11959)*; *International Bunker Industry Association (IBIA, #12411)*; *International Union of Marine Insurance (IUMI, #15789)*; London Shipping Law Centre.
Consultative Status Consultative status granted from: *ECOSOC (#05331)* (Ros C); *International Maritime Organization (IMO, #14102)*. **IGO Relations** Observer status with: *International Oil Pollution Compensation Funds (IOPC Funds, #14402)*. **NGO Relations** Consultative member of: *Comité maritime international (CMI, #04192)*. [2021/XD5329/y/**D**]

♦ International SAMBO Federation (#09655)

♦ **Internationals amis de la nature (IAN)** **14780**
Naturefriends International – Naturfreunde Internationale (NFI)
Dir Viktoriagasse 6/1, 1150 Vienna, Austria. T. +4318923877. Fax +4318129789. E-mail: office@nf-int.org.
URL: http://www.nf-int.org/

History 1895, Vienna (Austria). Founded by a group of Austrian social democrats. Reconstituted and new statutes adopted: Jun 1950, Celerina (Switzerland); 1981, Amersfoort (Netherlands); 1987, Brighton (UK); 1990, Königslutter (Germany); 1996, Sévrier (France). An independent international federation since 1975. Former names and other names: *International Friends of Nature (IFN)* – former. Registration: EU Transparency Register, No/ID: 88140777010-24, Start date: 25 Oct 2011. **Aims** Promote *environmental* awareness among members and their cultural activities; encourage mutual understanding, friendship and solidarity, irrespective of religion, nationality, colour, origin or gender; organize environmentally-sound *leisure* activities taking into account social factors; promote *ecological tourism* and sustainable development and foster tourism in social, alpine and associated *sports*; encourage study of natural history and nature conservation; promote transborder protection of the environment; support endeavours for an international language. **Structure** Congress (every 3 years). Presidents' Conference (at least annually), comprising Presidents of member federations and the Executive Committee, which includes the President of *International Young Nature Friends (IYNF, #15929)* – which, although independent since 1975, still functions as NFI Youth Section. Audit and Arbitration Commissions. Special activity groups (6): Mountaineering; Camping; Photography; Environment; Water Sports; Winter Sports. Working Groups and Project Groups (5): Regional Development (Landscape of the Year); Tourism and Climate; Nature and Environment; Europe; Social Movement. General Secretariat. **Languages** English, French, German. **Staff** 3.00 FTE, paid. **Finance** Sources: grants; members' dues. **Activities** Events/meetings; training/education. **Events** *Triennial Congress* Graz (Austria) 2011, *Triennial Congress* Liberec (Czech Rep) 2008, *Forum on the future* Munich (Germany) / Ismaning (Germany) 2005, *Presidents conference* Munich (Germany) / Ismaning (Germany) 2005, *Triennial Congress* Munich (Germany) / Ismaning (Germany) 2005. **Publications** *IAN Newsletter*. Books; brochures.
Members National federations (21) in 19 countries:
Algeria, Austria, Belgium, Czechia, Denmark, Finland, France, Germany, Greece, Italy, Netherlands, Romania, Senegal, Spain, Sweden, Switzerland, Togo, UK, USA.
Partner organizations (19) in 19 countries:
Albania, Benin, Burkina Faso, Cameroon, Canada, Chile, Congo Brazzaville, Egypt, Gambia, Georgia, Guinea, Lithuania, Madagascar, Mali, Morocco, Nepal, Niger, Pakistan, Portugal.
NGO Relations Member of (3): *European Environmental Bureau (EEB, #06996)*; Roundtable Human Rights in Tourism; *The Green 10 (#10711)*. [2023.02.14/XD1920/**D**]

♦ International Sangha Bhiksu Buddhist Association (internationally oriented national body)
♦ International Sanitary Bureau / see Pan American Sanitary Bureau (#18129)
♦ International Sanitary Conference (inactive)
♦ International Sanitary Convention, 1900 (1900 treaty)
♦ International Sanitary Convention, 1912 (1912 treaty)
♦ International Sanitary Convention, 1914 (1914 treaty)
♦ International Sanitary Convention, 1926 (1926 treaty)
♦ International Sanitary Convention, 1944 (1944 treaty)
♦ International Sanitary Convention for Aerial Navigation, 1933 (1933 treaty)
♦ International Sanitary Convention for Aerial Navigation, 1944 (1944 treaty)
♦ International Sanitary Regulations, 1951 (1951 treaty)
♦ International Sanitary Supply Association / see ISSA

♦ **International Sansevieria Society (ISS)** **14781**
Sec 11 Sutherland Avenue, Biggin Hill, Westerham, TN16 3HE, UK.
Communications Dir address not obtained.
Contact PO Box 64759, Tucson AZ 85728-4759, USA.
URL: http://www.sansevieria-international.org/

History 2000, UK. **Aims** Increase knowledge on all aspects of *cultivation*, *ecology* and the correct naming of sansevierias, a genus of plants from Africa and Asia. **Structure** Committee; Overseas Representatives (2): USA/Canada; Indonesia. **Languages** English. **Staff** 7.00 FTE, voluntary. **Finance** Sources: contributions; members' dues. **Activities** Events/meetings. **Publications** *Sansevieria Journal* (2-3 a year).
Members Institutions and individuals in 24 countries and territories:
Australia, Austria, Belgium, Bolivia, Brazil, Czechia, Germany, Hungary, Indonesia, Italy, Japan, Kenya, Mexico, New Zealand, Norway, Poland, Slovakia, South Africa, Spain, Sweden, Switzerland, UK, USA, Zimbabwe. [2022/XD8355/**D**]

♦ International Satellite System for Search and Rescue / see International Cospas-Sarsat Programme (#12975)

♦ **International Sauna Association (ISA)** **14782**
Kansainvälinen Saunaliitto
Pres Vaskiniementie 10, FI-00200 Helsinki, Finland.
URL: https://saunainternational.net/

History 1977. Former names and other names: *International Sauna Society (ISS)* – former; *Internationale Sauna-Gesellschaft* – former. **Aims** Promote research concerning sauna and its health-related benefits; provide correct information on a global scale; promote scientific study on sauna from different viewpoints such as social history, folklore, medicine and technology. **Structure** Board of Directors; President; Vice President. **Languages** English, German. **Finance** Members' dues. **Activities** Awareness raising; research/documentation; knowledge management/information dissemination. **Events** *International Sauna Congress* Stuttgart (Germany) 2022, *International Sauna Congress* Tornio (Finland) / Haparanda (Sweden) 2018, *International Sauna Congress* Vilnius (Lithuania) 2014, *International Sauna Congress* Tokyo (Japan) 2010, *International Sauna Congress* Helsinki (Finland) 2006. **Publications** *Saunaletter* (6 a year). Comics.
Members National associations in 17 countries:
Austria, Belgium, China, Denmark, Finland, Germany, Japan, Kenya, Latvia, Lithuania, Mongolia, Norway, Poland, Russia, Sweden, Ukraine, USA.
NGO Relations Partner of (1): *World Wellness Weekend (WWW)*. [2018.10.23/XD3497/**D**]

♦ International Sauna Society / see International Sauna Association (#14782)

♦ **International Sava River Basin Commission** **14783**
Sec Kneza Branimira 29, HR-10000 Zagreb, Croatia. T. +38514886960. Fax +38514886986. E-mail: isrbc@savacommission.org.
URL: http://www.savacommission.org/

History Established 3 Dec 2002, Kranjska Gora (Slovenia), by signature of the *Framework Agreement on the Sava River Basin (FASRB)*. Agreement entered into force 29 Dec 2004. Constitution officially adopted, 27 Jun 2005. **Aims** Establish an international *navigation* regime on the Sava River and its navigable tributaries; establish *sustainable* water management; undertake measures to prevent and limit *hazards* and reduce and eliminate adverse consequences, including those from floods, ice hazards, droughts and incidents involving substances hazardous to water. **Structure** Sava Commission; Secretariat (functions as Operative body for the Commission); Permanent Experts Groups (PEG); Ad hoc Expert Groups. **Activities** Politics/policy/regulatory; research/documentation. **Events** *Regular Session* Zagreb (Croatia) 2007, *Special Session* Zagreb (Croatia) 2007, *Regular Session* Zagreb (Croatia) 2006, *Regular Session* Zagreb (Croatia) 2005.
Members Governments of 4 countries:
Bosnia-Herzegovina, Croatia, Serbia, Slovenia. [2017.10.11/XM2529/**E***]

♦ International Savate Federation (#09656)
♦ International Save the Children Alliance / see Save the Children International (#19058)
♦ International Savings Agreement (1984 treaty)

♦ **International Saxophone Committee (ISC)** **14784**
Comité International de Saxophone
Headquarters c/o Association A sax, 30 rue de la montoire, 62370 Zutkerque, France. E-mail: contact@asax.fr.
URL: http://www.saxophonecommittee.com/

History Proposed Jul 1979, Evanston IL (USA), at World Saxophone Congress. Statutes adopted Oct 1981, Bordeaux (France); revised Jul 2006 and Sep 2017. **Aims** Elevate the status of the saxophone. **Structure** Committee. **Activities** Events/meetings. Proposes setting up *World Sax Alliance*. **Events** *World Saxophone Congress* Kurashiki (Japan) 2021, *World Saxophone Congress* Zagreb (Croatia) 2018, *World Saxophone Congress* Strasbourg (France) 2015, *World saxophone congress* Nakhon Pathom (Thailand) 2009, *World saxophone congress* Rotterdam (Netherlands) 1995. [2019/XM7073/c/**E**]

♦ International Scholarship Fund Committee (inactive)
♦ International School for Advanced Studies, Trieste (internationally oriented national body)
♦ International School of Ayurveda (internationally oriented national body)
♦ International School of Banking and Finance (internationally oriented national body)

♦ **International School Chess Union (ISCU)** **14785**
Pres Begovaya St 12, Moscow MOSKVA, Russia, 125284. T. +74959461020. Fax +74959457522. E-mail: iscu@mail.ru – iscu1999@gmail.com.
URL: http://www.icce.su/

History Founded 1999. **Aims** Promote university chess education; develop chess in schools. **Structure** Main office located in Moscow (Russia). Branches located in FIDE countries. **Languages** English, Russian. **Staff** Voluntary. **Finance** Donations. **Activities** Events/meetings; training/education. **Members** Membership countries not specified. **NGO Relations** Member of: *European Chess Union (ECU, #06528)*. Cooperates with: *Fédération internationale des échecs (FIDE, #09627)*. [2016.10.18/XD9212/**D**]

♦ International School Choice and Reform Conference (meeting series)

♦ **International School Connection (ISC)** **14786**
Contact address not obtained. T. +18139633899. Fax +18139626598.

History 1994, Berlin (Germany). International Board set up, Oct 2002. Registered in the State of Florida (USA), Nov 2003. **Aims** Foster educational leadership for sustainable school and college development, and for shaping schools and colleges as global learning centers. **Structure** Board of Directors. **Events** *Stockholm Summit for Top Level School Leaders* Stockholm (Sweden) 2012, *Stockholm summit for top level school leaders* Stockholm (Sweden) 2010, *Stockholm summit for top level school leaders* Stockholm (Sweden) 2008, *Annual global summit / Summit* Beijing (China) 2007, *Annual global summit / Summit* Tampa, FL (USA) 2006. [2010/XJ0026/**F**]

♦ International School Counselor Association (internationally oriented national body)
♦ International School on Disarmament and Research on Conflicts (internationally oriented national body)
♦ International School on Environment, Health and Sustainable Development (internationally oriented national body)
♦ International School of French Language and Culture (see: #09814)
♦ International School of the Golden Rosycross (religious order)

♦ **International School Health Network (ISHN)** **14787**
Exec Dir Ctr on Educational Leadership and Policy, Fac Education – Simon Fraser Univ, Office 16655, 64th Avenue, Surrey BC V3S 3V1, Canada. E-mail: info@internationalschoolhealth.org.
URL: http://www.internationalschoolhealth.org/

Structure Steering Committee. **IGO Relations** Recognized by: *WHO (#20950)*. **NGO Relations** *International Union for Health Promotion and Education (IUHPE, #15778)*. [2016/XJ6320/**F**]

♦ International School for Holocaust Studies (internationally oriented national body)
♦ International School of Management (internationally oriented national body)
♦ International School for Molecular Biology and Microbiology / see UNESCO-Hebrew University of Jerusalem International School for Molecular Biology and Microbiology and Science for Peace
♦ International School of Neurological Sciences (internationally oriented national body)
♦ International School of Peace / see World Peace Foundation
♦ International School in Physics and Mathematics (internationally oriented national body)
♦ International School of Protocol and Diplomacy (unconfirmed)

♦ **International School Psychology Association (ISPA)** **14788**
Association internationale de psychologie scolaire
Sec Leidseplein 5, 1017 PR Amsterdam, Netherlands. T. +31206233677. Fax +31206255979. E-mail: ispacentraloffice@ispaweb.org.
URL: http://www.ispaweb.org/

History 1974. Constitution adopted 1986; amended 15 Mar 1990. Current constitution adopted 1999; amended 29 Jul 2002, Nyborg (Denmark) and 30 Nov 2011. Former names and other names: *International School Psychology Committee (ISPC)* – former; *Comité international de psychologie scolaire* – former. **Aims** Promote the use of sound psychological principles within the context of education internationally; promote communication among professionals committed to improvement of mental health of children; encourage training and employment of school psychologists; promote the psychological rights of all children; initiate and promote cooperation with other organizations working for purposes similar to those of ISPA; condemn any discrimination of racial, religious or sexual nature and recommend that members conduct their professional life consistent with this principle. **Structure** General Assembly (annual, during Conference); Executive Committee. Standing Committees (6): Constitution and Bylaws; Nominations and Elections; Membership; Ethics; Communications and Publications; Child Well Being and Advocacy Committee (CWBA), including "Education for All" section. Task Forces (6): Interest Groups (8). **Languages** English. **Staff** 1.00 FTE, paid. **Finance** Sources: contributions; members' dues. **Activities** Awards/prizes/competitions; events/meetings; financial and/or material support; training/education. **Events** *Annual Conference* Leuven (Belgium) 2022, *Annual Conference* Nicosia (Cyprus) 2021, *Annual Conference* Nicosia (Cyprus) 2020, *Annual International Colloquium* Basel (Switzerland) 2019, *Annual International Colloquium* Tokyo (Japan) 2018. **Publications** *International Journal of School and Educational Psychology (IJSEP)* (4 a year); *The World-Go-Round* (4 a year) – newsletter.
Members National and State Associations (Affiliate) of School Psychology in 24 countries:
Australia, Austria, Canada, Czechia, Denmark, Finland, France, Georgia, Germany, Greece, Iceland, India, Ireland, Israel, Italy, Netherlands, Norway, Russia, Slovakia, Sweden, Switzerland, Türkiye, UK, USA.
Psychologist practitioners and scholars in the field of psychology (Full, Honorary Life, Student or Associate) in 55 countries. Membership countries not specified.
Consultative Status Consultative status granted from: *UNESCO (#20322)* (Consultative Status). **NGO Relations** Affiliate of: *International Union of Psychological Science (IUPsyS, #15807)*. [2021/XD0409/**C**]

♦ International School Psychology Committee / see International School Psychology Association (#14788)

♦ **International Schools Association (ISA)** **14789**
Association des écoles internationales – Asociación de Escuelas Internacionales – Verband der Internationalen Schulen
Administration Office 25 rue Schaub, 1202 Geneva, Switzerland. E-mail: administration@isaschools.org – info@isaschools.org.
URL: http://www.isaschools.org/

History Founded 20 Nov 1951, Paris (France), under the auspices of UNESCO. Merged, 1969, with *Conference of Internationally-Minded Schools (CIS, inactive)*, also set up in 1951. The first educational NGO to have consultative status at UNESCO. Established in accordance with Swiss Civil Code. **Aims** Further world peace and international understanding through education. **Structure** General Assembly (annual); Governing Board. **Languages** English, French, Spanish. **Staff** 2.00 FTE, paid. **Finance** Sources: donations; members' dues. **Activities** Events/meetings; networking/liaising; projects/programmes; research/documentation; training/education. **Events** *Youth Leadership Encounter on Global Issues* Lecco (Italy) / Milan (Italy) 2022, *Youth Leadership Encounter on Global Issues* Castellón de la Plana (Spain) 2019, *Youth Leadership Encounter on Global Issues* Jaipur (India) 2018, *Annual Conference* Sidmouth (UK) 2017, *Annual Conference* Valencia (Spain) 2015. **Publications** *ISA Newsletter*. Brochure; guides; self-study guidelines; directory.
Members National and individual schools in 35 countries:

Argentina, Australia, Bahrain, Canada, Chile, Costa Rica, Dominican Rep, Ecuador, El Salvador, Finland, France, Georgia, Germany, Ghana, Hungary, India, Indonesia, Japan, Liberia, Malaysia, Mexico, Netherlands, Nigeria, Pakistan, Panama, Paraguay, Philippines, Russia, Spain, Sri Lanka, Sweden, Switzerland, UK, Uruguay, USA.
Affiliate members in 8 countries and territories:
Argentina, Canaries, France, Haiti, India, Switzerland, UK, USA.
Consultative Status Consultative status granted from: *ECOSOC (#05331)* (Ros A); *UNEP (#20299)* (List). **IGO Relations** Accredited by: *United Nations Office at Vienna (UNOV, #20604)*. Associated with Department of Global Communications of the United Nations. **NGO Relations** Member of: *Environment Liaison Centre International (ELCI, no recent information)*; *Fédération des Institutions Internationales établies à Genève (FIIG, #09599)*. Supports: *Alliance for International Education (AIE)*. [2020/XC2430/**B**]

♦ International Schools of Business Management (ISBM) 14790

Contact Dip di Management, SDA Bocconi Milan, Via Roentgen 1 – 4o piano, 20136 Milan MI, Italy.
URL: http://www.itp-schools.org/
Activities *International Teachers Programme (ITP)*, annual 4-week professional development programme for teachers of management, set up 1968 by Harvard Business School and organized in rotation among ISBM members since 1974. **Events** *Annual International Teachers Programme* Milan (Italy) 2008, *Annual International Teachers Programme* Milan (Italy) 2007, *Annual International Teachers Programme* Stockholm (Sweden) 2006, *Annual International Teachers Programme* Manchester (UK) 2002, *Annual International Teachers Programme* New York, NY (USA) 2001.
Members Business schools (10) in 6 countries:
France, Italy, Sweden, Switzerland, UK, USA. [2008/XF5380/**F**]

♦ International School-to-School Experience (ISSE) 14791

Admin Sec 586 Cleveland Ave, Louisville CO 80027, USA. T. +13036665010. Fax +13034945908.
URL: http://www.isseonline.com/
History 1971, Philadelphia PA (USA). An extension and companion organization of *CISV International (#03949)*, set up in 1951. **Aims** Link *schools* in different countries in order to promote personal friendships among *children* and through these friendships an awareness of the potential wholeness of the world; improve communication and *understanding* around the world, even where no common language exists. **Structure** International Board, consisting of Trustees from each participating national association. **Finance** Members' dues. **Activities** Program partnerships are formed between schools in two different countries, with 3-week exchange and return visits comprising a team of students (plus accompanying adult) visiting the school and living with host families having students of the same age and sex. Visiting delegations share their cultures with each grade level. **Events** *Biennial Conference* Ecuador 2016, *Biennial Conference / Biennial International Meeting* Melbourne, VIC (Australia) 2014, *Biennial Conference / Biennial International Meeting* Cincinnati, OH (USA) 2012, *Biennial Conference / Biennial International Meeting* Tokoname (Japan) 2010, *Biennial conference / Biennial International Meeting* Boulder, CO (USA) 2001.
Members National associations in 12 countries and territories:
Argentina, Australia, Bermuda, Costa Rica, Ecuador, El Salvador, India, Japan, Malaysia, Mexico, Peru, USA.
[2014/XF0142/**F**]

♦ International Schools Examination Syndicate / see International Baccalaureate (#12306)
♦ International School for Social and Business Studies (internationally oriented national body)
♦ International School of Solidarité / see International Institute of Journalism, Berlin – Brandenburg

♦ International School Sport Federation (ISF) 14792

Fédération Internationale du Sport Scolaire – Internationale Schulsport Föderation
SG Rue Archimède 59, 1000 Brussels, Belgium. T. +3227101938. E-mail: admin@isfsports.org.
Deputy SG address not obtained.
URL: http://www.isfsports.org/
History Statutes decided by a Proponent Committee at 1st General Assembly, Jun 1972, Beaufort (Luxembourg); amended by: 2nd General Assembly, Jun 1974, Zrenjanin (Yugoslavia); 4th General Assembly, Jul 1978, Izmir (Turkey); 6th General Assembly, Jun 1982, Lille (France); 10th General Assembly, May 1990, Bruges (Belgium); 12th General Assembly, Sep 1996, Antwerp (Belgium); 14th General Assembly, Nov 2000, Portimão (Portugal) 2000; 15th General Assembly, May 2002, Caen (France); 16th General Assembly, Nov 2004, Cagliari (Italy); 17th General Assembly, Jun 2006, Athens (Greece); 18th General Assembly, Apr 2008, Minorca (Spain); 19th General Assembly, Jun 2010, Villasimius/Sardinia (Italy); 21st General Assembly, Jun 2014, Besançon (France); 22nd General Assembly, May 2016, Marmaris (Turkey). Registration: No/ID: 0476.233.673, Start date: 30 Jun 2000, Belgium; EU Transparency Register, No/ID: 978177636622-02, Start date: 21 Nov 2019. **Aims** Promote among young people: mutual understanding, volunteering empowerment, peace, non-discrimination, healthy lifestyle, social inclusion and gender equality. **Structure** General Assembly (every 2 years); Executive Committee; Management Committee; Advisory Board; Youth Council; Educational Commission; Medical Commission; Continental Presidents (5); Technical Commissions (16). **Languages** English, French, German, Spanish. **Staff** 7.00 FTE, paid. **Finance** Members' dues. Autofinanced and sponsored. **Activities** Events/meetings; networking/liaising; sporting activities. **Events** *ISF General Assembly* Brussels (Belgium) 2021, *ISF General Assembly* Belgrade (Serbia) 2020, *ISF General Assembly* Agadir (Morocco) 2019, *Biennial General Assembly* Rio de Janeiro (Brazil) 2018, *Biennial General Assembly* Trabzon (Turkey) 2016. **Publications** *ISF Magazine*. Symposium/seminar proceedings; minutes.
Members Full in 91 countries and territories:
Afghanistan, Albania, Algeria, Andorra, Armenia, Australia, Austria, Azerbaijan, Belarus, Belgium (French Community of; Ben), Benin, Bolivia, Botswana, Brazil, Bulgaria, Cameroon, Cape Verde, Chile, China, Colombia, Côte d'Ivoire, Croatia, Cuba, Cyprus, Czechia, Denmark, Dominican Rep, England, Equatorial Guinea, Estonia, Finland, France, Gambia, Georgia, Germany, Greece, Guatemala, Haiti, Hong Kong, Hungary, India, Iran Islamic Rep, Ireland, Israel, Italy, Kazakhstan, Kosovo, Kuwait, Latvia, Liechtenstein, Luxembourg, Madagascar, Malta, Montenegro, Morocco, Netherlands, New Zealand, Nicaragua, Nigeria, North Macedonia, Norway, Pakistan, Paraguay, Poland, Polynesia Fr, Portugal, Puerto Rico, Qatar, Romania, Russia, Saudi Arabia, Scotland, Senegal, Serbia, Singapore, Slovakia, Slovenia, South Africa, Spain, Sri Lanka, Srpska, Suriname, Sweden, Switzerland, Taiwan, Thailand, Tunisia, Türkiye, Ukraine, United Arab Emirates, USA.
NGO Relations Memorandum of Understanding with (1): *International Esports Federation (IESF, #13304)*. Member of (2): *International Council of Sport Science and Physical Education (ICSSPE, #13077)*; *Olympic Movement (#17719)*. Recognized by: *International Olympic Committee (IOC, #14408)*. [2020/XD9168/**C**]

♦ International Schools Services (internationally oriented national body)

♦ International Schools Theatre Association (ISTA) 14793

Dir Operations The Old Cattle Market, Coronation Park, Helston, TR13 0SR, UK. E-mail: office@ista.co.uk.
URL: http://www.ista.co.uk/
History 1982, UK. Registration: Companies House, Start date: Oct 1996, UK. **Aims** Bring together people, artists and teachers from different countries in particular settings to experience and learn about theatre, culture and each other. **Structure** Board of Trustees. **Languages** English. **Staff** 8.00 FTE, paid. **Finance** Sources: donations; meeting proceeds; members' dues; sale of products; sale of publications. **Activities** Events/meetings; guidance/assistance/consulting; projects/programmes; training/education. **Events** *Annual general meeting* Shanghai (China) 2006, *Interpreting international education – dimensions of theory and practice* Geneva (Switzerland) 2002, *Annual General Meeting* Stratford-upon-Avon (UK) 2002, *Annual teachers conference* Stratford-upon-Avon (UK) 2000, *Asian teachers conference* Ubud (Indonesia) 2000. **Members** Schools and organisations (240); Individuals (50); Global partners (8). Membership countries not specified. **NGO Relations** Affiliated with (1): *Educational Collaborative for International Schools (ECIS, #05365)*.
[2022.02.02/XD0521/**C**]

♦ International School of Temple Arts (unconfirmed)

♦ International School of Theatre Anthropology (ISTA) 14794

Dir Nordisk Teaterlaboratorium – Odin Teatret, Særkærparken 144, 7500 Holstebro, Denmark. T. +4597424777. Fax +4597410482. E-mail: odin@odinteatret.dk.
URL: http://www.odinteatret.dk/research/ista.aspx
History 1979, Denmark. Founded on the initiative of Eugenio Barba. **Aims** Function as a laboratory of research into the fundamentals of the *performer's* technique from a *transcultural* perspective. **Structure** Director; Advisory Committee; Network of about 50 collaborators from 15 universities (including masters of classical Asian theatre); Permanent Staff. **Activities** Events/meetings; research/documentation. **Events** *Session* Albino (Italy) 2016, *Session* Wroclaw (Poland) 2005, *Session* Seville (Spain) 2004, *Session* Guanajuato (Mexico) 2002, *Odin week* Holstebro (Denmark) 2001. **Publications** *Thinking with the Feet. Actor's techniques and theatre anthropology* (2017) by V A Cremona and F Galli et al – Odin Teatrets Forlag, Holstebro; *A Dictionary of Theatre Anthropology. The Secret Art of the Performer* (2nd ed 2005) by Eugenio Barba and Nicola Savarese – Routledge, Abingdon (UK) – New York (USA); *The Paper Canoe – A Guide to Theatre Anthropology* (1995) by Eugenio Barba – Routledge, Abingdon (UK) – New York (USA). Monographs; articles.
Members Participating Artists in 9 countries:
Brazil, Denmark, India, Indonesia, Italy, Japan, Norway, UK, USA.
NGO Relations Instrumental in setting up (1): *University of Eurasian Theatre* (1990, together with the University of Bologna). [2020.10.14/XF0512/v/**F**]

♦ International School Traditional Aikido (internationally oriented national body)

♦ International Science Academy Comenius 14795

Académie scientifique internationale Coménius – Internacia Scienca Akademio Comenius
SG Uppsala University, Dept of Information Technology, PO Box 337, SE-751 06 Uppsala, Sweden. T. +46184717849.
History 12 Apr 1986, Copenhagen (Denmark), as the academy of sciences of the scientists and scholars who use Esperanto. **Aims** Promote scientific cooperation in all fields of science. **Languages** Esperanto. **Staff** 2.00 FTE, voluntary. **Finance** No budget. **Events** *Meeting* Seoul (Korea Rep) 1994. **Publications** *Aktoj de Akademio Comenius* (irregular) in Esperanto.
Members Individuals in 17 countries:
Belgium, Bulgaria, China, Croatia, Denmark, Germany, Hungary, Italy, Japan, Netherlands, Norway, Romania, Serbia, Spain, Sweden, Tajikistan, UK.
NGO Relations Associated with: *Universal Esperanto Association (UEA, #20676)*. [2017.06.01/XF2041/v/**F**]

♦ International Science Council (ISC) 14796

CEO 5 rue Auguste Vacquerie, 75116 Paris, France. T. +33145250329. Fax +33142889431. E-mail: secretariat@council.science – ceo@council.science.
Communications Dir address not obtained.
URL: http://council.science/
History 2018. Created as result of the merger of *International Council for Science (ICSU, inactive)* and *International Social Science Council (ISSC, inactive)*. Statutes and Rules of Procedure approved by joint meeting of ICSU and ISSC members, Oct 2017, Taipei (Taiwan). **Aims** Advance science as a global public good; act as the global voice for science. **Structure** General Assembly (every 3 years); Governing Board; Executive Board; Advisory Bodies. Global Headquarters: Paris (France). Regional Offices (3): Africa; Latin America and the Caribbean; Asia and the Pacific. Running programmes and entities formerly included in ICSU or ISSC: *International Network for Government Science Advice (INGSA, #14274)*; *Comparative Research Programme on Poverty (CROP, #04412)*; *Committee on Space Research (COSPAR, #04287)*; *Scientific Committee on Antarctic Research (SCAR, #19147)*; *Scientific Committee on Oceanic Research (SCOR, #19149)*; *Scientific Committee on Solar-Terrestrial Physics (SCOSTEP, #19151)*; *Committee on Data for Science and Technology (CODATA, #04247)*; *Scientific Committee on Frequency Allocations for Radio Astronomy and Space Science (IUCAF, #19148)*; *ISC World Data System (ISC-WDS, #16024)*. **Staff** 24.00 FTE, paid. **Activities** Knowledge management/information dissemination; research and development. **Events** *Integrated Research on Disaster Risk International Conference* Japan 2021, *General Assembly* Paris (France) 2021, *Seminar on Future Direction of European Union Defence Research* Brussels (Belgium) 2019, *World Social Science Forum* Fukuoka (Japan) 2018, *General Assembly* Paris (France) 2018.
Members Organizations (141); Unions and Associations (39); Affiliate (31). Member organizations in 118 countries and territories:
Albania, Angola, Argentina, Armenia, Australia, Austria, Azerbaijan, Bangladesh, Belarus, Belgium, Bolivia, Bosnia-Herzegovina, Botswana, Brazil, Bulgaria, Burkina Faso, Cameroon, Canada, Chile, China, Colombia, Costa Rica, Côte d'Ivoire, Cuba, Czechia, Denmark, Dominican Rep, Egypt, El Salvador, Estonia, Eswatini, Ethiopia, Finland, France, Georgia, Germany, Ghana, Greece, Guatemala, Holy See, Honduras, Hungary, India, Indonesia, Iran Islamic Rep, Iraq, Ireland, Israel, Italy, Jamaica, Jordan, Kazakhstan, Kenya, Korea DPR, Korea Rep, Laos, Latvia, Lebanon, Lesotho, Lithuania, Luxembourg, Madagascar, Malawi, Malaysia, Mauritius, Mexico, Moldova, Monaco, Mongolia, Montenegro, Morocco, Mozambique, Namibia, Nepal, Netherlands, New Zealand, Nigeria, North Macedonia, Norway, Oman, Pakistan, Panama, Peru, Philippines, Poland, Portugal, Romania, Russia, Rwanda, Saudi Arabia, Serbia, Seychelles, Singapore, Slovakia, Slovenia, South Africa, Spain, Sri Lanka, Sudan, Sweden, Switzerland, Taiwan, Tajikistan, Tanzania UR, Thailand, Togo, Tunisia, Türkiye, Uganda, UK, Ukraine, Uruguay, USA, Uzbekistan, Venezuela, Vietnam, Zambia, Zimbabwe.
Included in the above, 8 organizations listed in this Yearbook:
Arab Council for the Social Sciences (ACSS, #00932); *Caribbean Academy of Sciences (CAS)*; *Consejo Latinoamericano de Ciencias Sociales (CLACSO, #04718)*; *Council for the Development of Social Science Research in Africa (CODESRIA, #04879)*; *Latin American Faculty of Social Sciences (#16316)*; *Organization for Social Science Research in Eastern and Southern Africa (OSSREA, #17888)*; *Union académique internationale (UAI, #20345)*; *University of the South Pacific (USP, #20703)*.
Unions and Associations (38):
- *International Arctic Social Sciences Association (IASSA, #11669)*;
- *International Association of Legal Science (IALS, #11997)*;
- *International Astronomical Union (IAU, #12287)*;
- *International Cartographic Association (ICA, #12446)*;
- *International Federation of Societies for Microscopy (IFSM, #13550)*;
- *International Geographical Union (IGU, #13713)*;
- *International Mathematical Union (IMU, #14121)*;
- *International Peace Research Association (IPRA, #14537)*;
- *International Political Science Association (IPSA, #14615)*;
- *International Society for Ecological Economics (ISEE, #15069)*;
- *International Society for Photogrammetry and Remote Sensing (ISPRS, #15362)*;
- *International Sociological Association (ISA, #15553)*;
- *International Union for Physical and Engineering Sciences in Medicine (IUPESM, #15799)*;
- *International Union for Pure and Applied Biophysics (IUPAB, #15808)*;
- *International Union for Quaternary Research (INQUA, #15811)*;
- *International Union for the Scientific Study of Population (IUSSP, #15814)*;
- *International Union of Basic and Clinical Pharmacology (IUPHAR, #15758)*;
- *International Union of Biological Sciences (IUBS, #15760)*;
- *International Union of Crystallography (IUCr, #15768)*;
- *International Union of Food Science and Technology (IUFoST, #15773)*;
- *International Union of Forest Research Organizations (IUFRO, #15774)*;
- *International Union of Geodesy and Geophysics (IUGG, #15776)*;
- *International Union of Geological Sciences (IUGS, #15777)*;
- *International Union of History and Philosophy of Science and Technology (IUHPST, #15779)*;
- *International Union of Immunological Societies (IUIS, #15781)*;
- *International Union of Materials Research Societies (IUMRS, #15790)*;
- *International Union of Microbiological Societies (IUMS, #15794)*;
- *International Union of Nutritional Sciences (IUNS, #15796)*;
- *International Union of Physiological Sciences (IUPS, #15800)*;
- *International Union of Psychological Science (IUPsyS, #15807)*;
- *International Union of Pure and Applied Chemistry (IUPAC, #15809)*;
- *International Union of Pure and Applied Physics (IUPAP, #15810)*;
- *International Union of Soil Sciences (IUSS, #15817)*;
- *International Union of Theoretical and Applied Mechanics (IUTAM, #15823)*;
- *International Union of Toxicology (IUTOX, #15824)*;
- *Union radio-scientifique internationale (URSI, #20475)*;
- World Anthropological Union (WAU);
- *World Association for Public Opinion Research (WAPOR, #21180)*.

Affiliate organizations (31):
- Academy of Social Sciences (UK);
- *African Academy of Sciences (AAS, #00193)*;
- *Association of Academies and Societies of Sciences in Asia (AASSA, #02341)*;
- *Commission Internationale de l'Eclairage (CIE, #04219)*;

– *European Association of Development Research and Training Institutes (EADI, #06012);*
– *European Consortium for Political Research (ECPR, #06762);*
– *International Arctic Science Committee (IASC, #11668);*
– *International Association for Hydro-Environment Engineering and Research (IAHR, #11950);*
– *International Association of Applied Psychology (IAAP, #11705);*
– *International Commission for Acoustics (ICA, #12658);*
– *International Commission for Optics (ICO, #12710);*
– *International Council for Industrial and Applied Mathematics (ICIAM, #13032);*
– *International Council for Laboratory Animal Science (ICLAS, #13039);*
– *International Council for Scientific and Technical Information (ICSTI, #13070);*
– *International Federation for Information Processing (IFIP, #13458);*
– *International Federation of Data Organizations for the Social Sciences (IFDO, #13402);*
– *International Federation of Library Associations and Institutions (IFLA, #13470);*
– *International Federation of Surveyors (FIG, #13561);*
– *International Foundation for Science (IFS, #13677);*
– *International Institute for Applied Systems Analysis (IIASA, #13861);*
– *International Society for Digital Earth (ISDE, #15061);*
– *International Studies Association (ISA, #15615);*
– *International Union for Vacuum Science, Technique and Applications (IUVSTA, #15826);*
– *International Union of Speleology (#15818);*
– *International Water Association (IWA, #15865);*
– *Pacific Science Association (PSA, #18003);*
– *Science Council of Asia (SCA, #19137);*
– *Social Science Research Council (SSRC);*
– *Society for Social Studies of Science (4S, #19642);*
– *Transnational Institute (TNI, #20219);*
– *TWAS (#20270).*

Consultative Status Consultative status granted from: *ECOSOC (#05331)* (Special); *UNESCO (#20322)* (Associate Status). **NGO Relations** Member of (2): *Future Earth (#10048); Science and Technology Alliance for Global Sustainability (Alliance, #19143).* Supports (1): *World Climate Research Programme (WCRP, #21279).*
[2021/XM6956/y/**A**]

♦ International Science And Football Association (unconfirmed)

♦ International Science Schools Network (ISSN) 14797

Contact address not obtained. E-mail: ellise@cambornescience.co.uk – peter.corkill@jmss.vic.edu.au – issnwebsite@cambornescience.co.uk.
URL: http://issn21c.org/

History Proposed and agreed 2014, Moscow (Russia), by the Schools involved with International School Science Fair, organized since 2005. **Aims** Engage students in science, mathematics and technologies; establish an identity as a collaborative and influential body of schools that speak clearly to a wide range of audiences about the nature, purpose and significance of the network and its capacity as a forum in promoting leading edge science education on a global scale. **Languages** English. **Activities** Events/meetings. **Events** *Workshop* Busan (Korea Rep) 2017.
Members Schools in 16 countries and territories:
Australia, Canada, China, Indonesia, Iran Islamic Rep, Japan, Kenya, Korea Rep, Macau, Netherlands, Philippines, Russia, Singapore, Thailand, UK, USA.
[2019.03.07/XM6698/c/**F**]

♦ International Science and Technology Center (ISTC) 14798

Centre international pour la science et de technologie (CIST)

Exec Dir Z05T0E9 – 46/1 Turan Avenue, Business Ctr "The Square" – Floor 4, Nur-Sultan, Kazakhstan. T. +77172769534. E-mail: istcinfo@istc.int.
URL: http://www.istc.int/

History Established Nov 1992, Moscow (Russia), by international agreement, as a nonproliferation programme, between *European Union (EU, #08967)*, Japan, Russia and USA. Agreement Continuing the International Science and Technology Center, signed 9 Dec 2015. Became operational Mar 1994. **Aims** Give weapons experts in the CIS the opportunity to redirect their talents to peaceful activities; contribute to the solution of national and international science and technology problems; reinforce the transition of market economies; support basic and applied research; promote integration of CIS scientists into global scientific community. **Structure** Governing Board. Coordination Committee; Scientific Advisory Committee. Secretariat, headed by Executive Director. **Staff** 120.00 FTE, paid. **Finance** Sources: *European Commission (EC, #06633); European Organization for Nuclear Research (CERN, #08108)*; governments of Japan, Korea Rep, Norway and USA. **Activities** Research and development; events/meetings; training/education; knowledge management/information dissemination. **Events** *Korea Workshop* Busan (Korea Rep) 2015, *Korea Workshop* Seoul (Korea Rep) 2015, *International Science Symposium on Combating Radionuclide Contamination in Agro-Soil Environment* Kōriyama (Japan) 2012, *Conference on Spain-ISTC/SCTU cooperation* Madrid (Spain) 2010, *International symposium on environmental conservation of the sea of Okhotsk* Sapporo (Japan) 2009.
Members Governing and other parties (9):
Armenia, Georgia, Japan, Kazakhstan, Korea Rep, Kyrgyzstan, Norway, Tajikistan, USA.
Regional party:
European Union (EU, #08967).
NGO Relations *International Congress of Industrialists and Entrepreneurs (ICIE, #12895).* Member of: *International Federation of Biosafety Associations (IFBA, #13373).*
[2018/XE3252/**E***]

♦ International Science, Technology and Innovation Centre for South-South Cooperation under the auspices of UNESCO (ISTIC) 14799

Dir 902-4 Jalan Tun Ismail, 50480 Kuala Lumpur, Malaysia. T. +60326949898. Fax +60326984549. E-mail: director@istic-unesco.org.
URL: http://www.istic-unesco.org

History 2007. Established under the auspices of *UNESCO (#20322)*. A follow up of the Doha Plan of Action which adopted by the Head of States and Government of *Group of 77 (G-77, #10732)* and China, during meeting of Jun 2005, Doha (Qatar). Constitution adopted 21 Jan 2008. Former names and other names: *International Centre for South-South Cooperation in Science, Technology and Innovation, Kuala Lumpur* – former; *Centre international pour la coopération sud-sud dans le domaine des sciences, de la technologie et de l'innovation, Kuala Lumpur* – former. **Aims** Increase capacity for management of science, technology and innovation throughout developing countries. **Structure** Governing Board; STI Advisory Council; Secretariat. **Languages** English. **Staff** 6.00 FTE, paid. **Finance** Sources: government support. Malaysian Government through Malaysian Ministry of Science, Technology and Innovation (MOSTI). **Activities** Awareness raising; capacity building; certification/accreditation; events/meetings; politics/policy/regulatory; training/education. **Events** *International Conference on Climate Change Education* Kuala Lumpur (Malaysia) 2018, *Conference* Kuala Lumpur (Malaysia) 2013. **Publications** *Discoveries in Islamic Countries*; *Innovations in Science and Technology in Developing Countries* – in 3 vols; *When the Earth Rumbles*. Annual Report.
[2021.09.13/XM3270/**E***]

♦ International Science, Technology and Skill Union (internationally oriented national body)

♦ International Science Writers' Association (ISWA) 14800

Association internationale des écrivains scientifiques

Pres address not obtained. E-mail: president@internationalsciencewriters.org.
URL: http://internationalsciencewriters.org/

History 1967, Montréal, QC (Canada). Former names and other names: *Association internationale des informateurs scientifiques* – former. **Aims** Work to obtain improved science media facilities; get recognition of members on the same basis as local media; maintain and improve standards of science writing generally. **Languages** English. **Staff** 4.00 FTE, voluntary. **Finance** Sources: members' dues. **Activities** Events/meetings; training/education. **Events** *International Science Communication Congress (ISCC-2021)* New Delhi (India) 2021, *Popularization of science and technology, multi-media* Bangalore (India) 1989. **Publications** *ISWA News*. Proceedings.
Members Individuals in 17 countries:
Australia, Brazil, Ecuador, Finland, Germany, Greece, Guatemala, India, Iran Islamic Rep, Japan, Mexico, Morocco, Portugal, Russia, Sri Lanka, UK, USA.
NGO Relations *American Association for the Advancement of Science (AAAS); International Council for Science (ICSU, inactive); World Federation of Science Journalists (WFSJ, #21479)*; national associations.
[2022.06.15/XD3650/v/**C**]

♦ International Scientific Association for Agriculture in Tropical Countries (inactive)
♦ International Scientific Association for Auriculotherapy (inactive)
♦ International Scientific Association of Coffee / see Association for the Science and Information on Coffee (#02905)
♦ International Scientific Association for Micronutrients in Agriculture (inactive)

♦ International Scientific Association for Probiotics and Prebiotics (ISAPP) 14801

Main Office 3230 Arena Blvd, Ste 245-172, Sacramento CA 95834, USA. T. +13037939974. E-mail: info@isappscience.org.
URL: http://www.isapp.net/

History Aug 2002. **Aims** Foster and distribute research regarding probiotics and prebiotics, including that relating to improvements in production, distribution and marketing of *dairy products*; promote scientific investigation and communication in the field of functionality and effect of prebiotics and probiotics; provide an organizational structure and science-based leadership to scientists focused on research and application of probiotics and prebiotics to humans and animals. **Structure** Board of Directors, including President, Vice President, Secretary and Treasurer. **Events** *Annual Meeting* Barcelona (Spain) 2022, *Annual Meeting* Sacramento, CA (USA) 2020, *Annual Meeting* Antwerp (Belgium) 2019, *Annual Meeting* Singapore (Singapore) 2018, *Annual Meeting* Chicago, IL (USA) 2017.
[2021/XM0395/**D**]

♦ International Scientific Centre of Fertilizers (#03767)
♦ International Scientific College (see: #00617)
♦ International Scientific Commission on the Family (inactive)
♦ International Scientific Committee of Asian Congresses of Fluid Mechanics / see Asian Fluid Mechanics Committee (#01484)
♦ International Scientific Committee for Body-Psychotherapy (unconfirmed)
♦ International Scientific Committee for the Drafting of a History of Civilizations of Central Asia (no recent information)

♦ International Scientific Committee of the International Medicinal Mushroom Conference (IMMC) 14802

Contact 4/F – Talent Intl Bldg, No 80 Guangqumennei Street, Dongcheng District, 10062 Beijing, China. T. +861087109860. Fax +861087109861.
URL: http://www.immc7.com/

History Journal launched 1999 and Conference inaugurated 2001. **Structure** Scientific Committee of 32 members. Committees (2): Local Organizing; Publications. **Events** *Conference* Nantong (China) 2019, *Conference* Beijing (China) 2013, *Conference* Zagreb (Croatia) 2011, *Conference* Nantong (China) 2009, *Conference* Ljubljana (Slovenia) 2007. **Publications** *International Journal of Medicinal Mushroom (IJMM).*
[2013/XJ6646/**E**]

♦ **International Scientific Committee for ISPP** International Scientific Committee for the Symposia on Phototrophic Prokaryotes (#14806)

♦ International Scientific Committee on Ozone Therapy (ISCO3) 14803

Scientific Sec Avda Juan Andrés 60, local 1 bajo, 28035 Madrid, Spain. E-mail: secretaria@isco3.org – info@isco3.org.
URL: http://isco3.org

History 2 Jun 2010, Vienna (Austria). Proposed 2 june 2010, Madrid (Spain); founded 8 Oct 2010, Vienna (Austria). **Aims** Become an international scientific and moral authority due to members' composition, whose papers recommendations act as a reference source to all those practising this *medical* therapy. **Structure** Governing Board. **Languages** English. **Staff** Voluntary. **Finance** Sources: members' dues; sale of publications. **Activities** Events/meetings; knowledge management/information dissemination; publishing activities. **Events** *International Meeting* Madrid (Spain) 2015. **Publications** *Madrid Declaration on Ozone Therapy* (3rd ed 2020). Official papers. **Information Services** *ISCO3 Online Ozone Therapy International Library.*
Members Individuals (27) in 11 countries:
Brazil, Canada, Colombia, Italy, Lebanon, Mexico, New Zealand, Peru, Russia, Spain, USA.
Experts (35) in 17 countries:
Argentina, Azerbaijan, Chile, Colombia, Croatia, Cuba, Egypt, Greece, Guatemala, India, Iran Islamic Rep, Italy, Japan, Mexico, Spain, Ukraine, USA.
NGO Relations *International Medical Ozone Federation (IMEOF, #14136)*; national associations.
[2020.03.03/XJ9456/**C**]

♦ International Scientific Committee of Radionuclides in Nephrourology (inactive)

♦ International Scientific Committee on Research in the Alps (ISCAR) 14804

Comité scientifique international de recherche alpine – Internationales Wissenschaftliches Komitee Alpenforschung – Comitato Scientifico Internazionale Ricerca Alpina – Mednarodni Znanstveni Komite za Preucevanje Alp

Secretariat House of Academies, Laupenstr 7, PO Box, 3001 Bern, Switzerland. T. +41313069346. E-mail: iscar@scnat.ch.
URL: http://www.iscar-alpineresearch.org/

History 1999. Established following international cooperation resulting from the organization of *ForumAlpinum*. **Aims** Stimulate scientific research of relevance for the Alps as well as their implementation within international or mountain research programmes; promote interdisciplinary research on the Alps as well as the transfer of scientific knowledge to responsible authorities and to the general public; ensure the continuity and the scientific quality of the ForumAlpinum to promote international co-operation in Alpine research; take up research topics in the interest of the Alpine Convention and advise the responsible authorities for that Convention. **Structure** Rotating Presidency. **Activities** Events/meetings. **Events** *AlpWeek* Brig (Switzerland) 2022, *ForumAlpinum* Brescia (Italy) 2014, *ForumAlpinum* Darfo Boario Terme (Italy) 2014, *AlpWeek* Poschiavo (Switzerland) 2012, *ForumAlpinum* Poschiavo (Switzerland) 2012.
Members Institutions in 6 countries:
Austria, France, Germany, Italy, Slovenia, Switzerland.
NGO Relations Member of (1): *Mountain Partnership (MP, #16862).*
[2022.11.17/XJ0583/**E**]

♦ International Scientific Committee on Shot Peening (ISCSP) 14805

Pres Ecole Polytechnique de Montréal, 2900 Edouard Montpetit Blvd, Montréal QC H3T 1J4, Canada.
URL: http://www.shotpeening.org/

Aims Promote dissemination of knowledge and research activities in the area of shot peening and allied processes. **Events** *Triennial Conference* Milan (Italy) 2022, *Triennial Conference* Milan (Italy) 2020, *Triennial Conference* Montréal, QC (Canada) 2017, *Triennial Conference* Goslar (Germany) 2014, *Triennial Conference* South Bend, IN (USA) 2011.
Members Individuals (26) in 9 countries:
Canada, China, France, Germany, Italy, Japan, Korea Rep, UK, USA.
[2018.09.08/XM3197/**E**]

♦ International Scientific Committee for the Symposia on Phototrophic Prokaryotes (International Scientific Committee for ISPP) 14806

Secretariat Rua do Campo Alegre 823, 4150-180 Porto, Portugal. T. +351226074900. Fax +351226099157. E-mail: anunes@ibmc.up.pt – info@ibmc.up.pt.
URL: http://www.ibmc.up.pt/ispp2012/

Events *International Symposium* Porto (Portugal) 2012, *International Symposium* Montréal, QC (Canada) 2009.
[2013/XJ6463/c/**E**]

♦ International Scientific Committee for Trypanosomiasis Research and Control / see International Scientific Council for Trypanosomiasis Research and Control (#14809)

♦ **International Scientific Committee for Tuna and Tuna-like Species in the North Pacific Ocean (ISC)** 14807

Contact c/o National Research Inst of Far Seas Fisheries, 5-7-1 Orido, Shimizu, Shizuoka, 424-8633 Japan. T. +81543366035. Fax +81543359642.
URL: http://www.isc.fra.go.jp/

History 13 Jan 1995. Founded by the Governments of Japan and USA. Former names and other names: *Interim Scientific Committee for Tuna and Tuna-like Species in the North Pacific Ocean* – former (1995 to 2005). **Aims** Enhance scientific research and cooperation for conservation and rational utilization of the species of tuna and tuna-like fishes in the North Pacific Ocean. **Events** *Plenary Session* Kanazawa (Japan) 2023, *Plenary Session* Kailua-Kona, HI (USA) 2021, *Plenary Session* Shizuoka (Japan) 2020, *Pacific Bluefin Tuna Working Group Workshop* Jeju (Korea Rep) 2019, *Plenary Session* Taipei (Taiwan) 2019.
Members Governments of 7 countries and territories:
Canada, China, Japan, Korea Rep, Mexico, Taiwan, USA.
International observers (5):
FAO (#09260); *Inter-American Tropical Tuna Commission (IATTC, #11454)*; *North Pacific Marine Science Organization (PICES, #17602)*; *Pacific Community (SPC, #17942)*; *Western and Central Pacific Fisheries Commission (WCPFC, #20912)*. [2020/XM3607/y/**E***]

♦ **International Scientific Conference Minorities for Europe of Tomorrow (ISCOMET)** 14808

Mednarodna Znanstvena Konferenca Manjsin za Jutrisnjo Evropo
President Univ of Maribor, Pupinova ulica 6, 2000 Maribor, Slovenia. T. +38622500440.
URL: http://www.iscomet.org/

History 8 Jun 1989, Ljubljana (Slovenia). Founded 8-9 Jun 1989, Ljubljana (Yugoslavia, currently Slovenia), when statutes were adopted. Statutes supplemented and modified at 10th Conference, 22 Aug 1998, Copenhagen (Denmark). Registered in accordance with Slovenian law. Previously also referred to as *Network for Democracy, Human Rights and Protection of Ethnic and Religious Minorities in South Eastern Europe (ISCOMET)*. **Aims** Conduct research, expert and consultancy work in: political, ethnic, cultural and linguistic aspects of the European integration in general; human rights, especially with regard to protection of minorities and vulnerable social groups which are potentially exposed to discrimination on the basis of ethnic origin or religion and belief; respect of the equality principle in securing the development opportunities of each individual and of vulnerable groups; nationalism, racism, xenophobia, ethnic movements, inter-ethnic relations and protection of minorities; prevention and peaceful solution of inter-ethnic conflicts; questions of migrations and issues related to the ethnic identity of migrants and their social integration; the status of an individual in international law with emphasis on international procedures for protection of human rights and rights of members of ethnic minorities; protection and preservation of cultural heritage of ethnic and religious minorities; the role of religious communities in enhancing of democracy, human rights and religious freedoms, protection of minorities and spreading of reconciliation and cooperation between the nations in South East Europe; the role of the civil society in enhancement of democracy and co-operation of citizens in the processes of decision-making; regionalism and European integration, international regional organisations, territorial cooperation, development opportunities of less favoured countries and regions; common foreign and security policy of the EU and especially the implementation of this policy in relation to the South East Europe and European neighbourhood. **Structure** Assembly (every 2 years); Presidency; Scientific Council; Financial Committee. Technical and financial services provided by ISCOMET Institute. **Languages** English, Slovene. **Staff** 1.00 FTE, paid; 250.00 FTE, voluntary. **Finance** Sources: sponsors' donations; grants from *European Commission (EC, #06633)*. Annual budget: about US$ 200,000. **Activities** Networking/liaising; training/education; events/meetings. **Events** *Conference* Ljubljana (Slovenia) 2007, *Conference* Maribor (Slovenia) 2006, *Conference* Rogaska Slatina (Slovenia) 2006, *Conference* Rogaska Slatina (Slovenia) 2005, *Conference* Rogaska Slatina (Slovenia) 2005. **Publications** *Regional Contact* (annual) – journal. *European Union: Decide or Perish – The Major Risks the European Union is Confronted with* (2017); *Tackling Stereotypes and Prejudices Between Roma and Non-Roma in the EU Member States: Bulgaria, Italy, Romania and Slovenia* (2013); *Analyses of EU – Partner Countries' Relations: Reflections from Belarus, Moldova, Russia and Ukraine* (2012); *Cross-border Cooperation as a Tool of Spatial Integration and Cooperation between EU and Eastern Partner Countries* (2012); *EU Migration Policy and its Reflection in Third Countries: Belarus, Moldova, Russia, Ukraine* (2012); *Recommendations for Implementation of Schengen System* (2008); *Discrimination and Rights of a Human in Slovenian Prisons* (2008); *Schengen Border – Challenges and Responsibility* (2008); *The Success Story with the Aftertaste of Bitterness – Discrimination in Slovenia* (2007); *Guide across the Rights of the Victims of Discrimination on Ethnic and Religious Grounds in Slovenia* (2007); *Discrimination on Ethnic and Religious Grounds in Slovenia* (2006); *Religion and Democracy in Moldova* (2005) in English, Romanian; *Legal Position of Churches and Religious Communities in South-Eastern Europe* (2004); *Polozaj posameznika v mednarodnem pravu/The Position of an Individual in International Law* (2003) by Dr Jasna Murgel; *Demographic Changes and the Position of Minorities in Bosnia and Herzegovina* (2001); *Pravica do razlicnosti/The Right to Be Different* (1999) by Prof Dr Silvo Devetak; *Ohraniti sanje/To Preserve the Dreams* (1997); *Small Nations and Ethnic Minorities in Emerging Europe* (1992); *Are You Treated Equally Regardless Your Nationality of Faith?* – in 8 languages; *Present State, Problems and Prospects of Regionalism and Local Development in the Countries of South-East Europe and in Slovenia – Analysis of the relevant information and documents and policy recommendations*. Conference proceedings; syllabuses; didactic manuals.
Members Individual and collective (250) in 35 countries:
Austria, Belarus, Belgium, Bosnia-Herzegovina, Bulgaria, Croatia, Czechia, Denmark, Estonia, Finland, France, Germany, Greece, Hungary, Ireland, Israel, Italy, Latvia, Lithuania, Moldova, Netherlands, North Macedonia, Norway, Poland, Romania, Russia, Serbia, Slovakia, Slovenia, Spain, Sweden, Switzerland, Türkiye, UK, Ukraine.
Consultative Status Consultative status granted from: *Council of Europe (CE, #04881)* (Participatory Status).
NGO Relations Partner of: *Association for Ethnic and Regional Studies (ASER)*; *Centrul Euroregional pentru Democratie (CED)*; *European Centre for Ethnic and Regional Studies – University of Maribor (ECERS)*; *International Centre for Minority Studies and Intercultural Relations (IMIR, #12504)*; International Institute for Legal and Economic Studies for Development (IGES); *Unrepresented Nations and Peoples Organization (UNPO, #20714)*; national universities and institutes of higher education. [2018.09.05/XF2755/**F**]

♦ **International Scientific Council for Trypanosomiasis Research and Control (ISCTRC)** 14809

Comité scientifique international de recherches et de lutte contre la trypanosomiase
Contact AU/IBAR Kenindia Business Park, PO Box 30786-00100, Nairobi, Kenya. T. +254203674000. Fax +254203674341.

History Feb 1949, London (UK), with the assistance of *Organization of African Unity (OAU, inactive)*. An Advisory Committee of *Interafrican Bureau for Animal Resources (AU-IBAR, #11382)*. Also referred to originally as *International Scientific Committee for Trypanosomiasis Research and Control*. **Aims** Serve as the continental structure for the promotion, integration and coordination of activities related to the control of *tsetse* and trypanosomiasis in *Africa*; review work being carried out; stimulate further research and discussion. **Structure** Committee comprises highly qualified experts. **Activities** Coordinates training and information seminars and research programmes. Involved in: preparing and convening meetings on the control of tsetse and trypanosomiasis; preparing joint projects and tsetse distribution maps. **Events** *Biennial Meeting* Abuja (Nigeria) 2019, *Biennial Meeting* Livingstone (Zambia) 2017, *Biennial Meeting* Khartoum (Sudan) 2013, *Biennial Meeting / Conference* Bamako (Mali) 2011, *Biennial Meeting* Entebbe (Uganda) 2009. **Publications** *Trypanosomiasis Information Quarterly (TTIQ)*. Conference proceedings. **IGO Relations** *FAO (#09260)*; *African Union Scientific Technical Research Commission (AU STRC, #00493)*; *WHO (#20950)*. [2012/XE2434/**E**]

♦ International Scientific and Educational 'Znanie' Association / see International Association 'Znanie'
♦ International Scientific Entente for the Adoption of an Auxiliary Language (inactive)
♦ International Scientific Film Association (inactive)
♦ International Scientific Forum 'Danube – River of Cooperation' (internationally oriented national body)
♦ International Scientific Forum on Home Hygiene (internationally oriented national body)
♦ International Scientific Foundation (inactive)

♦ **International Scientific and Professional Advisory Council of the United Nations Crime Prevention and Criminal Justice Programme (ISPAC)** 14810

Conseil consultatif professionnel et scientifique international du Programme des Nations Unies pour la prévention du crime et de la justice (CCPSI)
Chairman c/o CNPDS, Via Palestro 12, 20121 Milan MI, Italy. T. +39286460714. E-mail: cnpds.ispac@cnpds.it.
Deputy Chair and Dir address not obtained.
URL: http://ispac.cnpds.org/

History 21 Sep 1991, Milan (Italy). Founded at constituent assembly, persuant to mandates of the General Assembly of *United Nations (UN, #20515)*. **Aims** Channel professional and scientific input to the United Nations and create a capacity for transfer of knowledge and exchange of information in the field, drawing on contributions of non-governmental organizations, academic institutions and other relevant entities, so as to assist the United Nations in programme formulation and implementation and to provide access to services and expertise of constituent organizations; enhance contribution of NGOs from developing countries. **Structure** General Assembly. Executive Board of 11 members, including one *United Nations Office on Drugs and Crime (UNODC, #20596)* representative, one representative of *United Nations Crime Prevention and Criminal Justice Programme Network (#20549)*, 2 representatives of *'Centro Nazionale di Prevenzione e Difesa Sociale (CNPDS)'*, 1 representative of the Region of Lombardy (Italy), 1 representative of Italy's Permanent Mission to the International Organizations in Vienna (Austria) and 5 representatives elected by the Assembly. UNICRI is ex-officio member. **Languages** English. **Staff** 1.00 FTE, paid. **Finance** Sources: grants. **Activities** Knowledge management/information dissemination. **Events** *Corporate Compliance and Corporate Liability* Milan (Italy) 2022, *Criminal Law Protection of Cultural Heritage in Italy and Ongoing Reform Proposals* Milan (Italy) 2022, *Meeting on Global Enforcement for Cross-Border Corruption* Kyoto (Japan) 2021, *International Economic Sanctions – Risks and Best Practices* Milan (Italy) 2019, *Fake News Flooding Internet – Remedies without Censorship* Milan (Italy) 2017. **Publications** Books; handbooks; proceedings. **Members** Representatives of NGOs and academic institutions and associations. Membership countries not specified. **IGO Relations** Also links with national organizations and institutes. **NGO Relations** Also links with national institutes and organizations. [2022.05.04/XE3165/**E**]

♦ International Scientific Radio Union / see Union radio-scientifique internationale (#20475)
♦ International Scientific and Technical Conference on Mine and Construction / see World Mining Congress (#21654)
♦ International Scientific and Technical Gliding Organization (#17826)
♦ International Scientific Tendinopathy Symposium (meeting series)
♦ International Scientific Working Group on Tick-Borne Encephalitis (unconfirmed)

♦ **International Scientists Association (ISA)** 14811

Pres Smouha, 20 El-Helal El-Ahmar St, Bldg 20, Alexandria, Egypt. T. +2034253874. Fax +2034295336. E-mail: admin@isa-egy.com – pr@isa-egy.com.
URL: http://www.isa-egy.com/

History as *United Scientist for Projects and Development (USPD)*. **Aims** Provide scientific and technical services in the following fields: environmental protection; air pollution; oceanography; food and nutrition; water treatment. **Activities** Organizes conferences and symposia. **Events** *International conference on environmental protection is a must* Alexandria (Egypt) 2010, *International conference on environmental protection is a must* Alexandria (Egypt) 2006, *International conference on environmental protection is a must* Alexandria (Egypt) 2005, *International conference on environmental protection is a must* Alexandria (Egypt) 2004, *International conference on petroleum and the environment* Egypt 2004. [2013/XD9450/**D**]

♦ International Scientists' Peace Congress (meeting series)
♦ International Scout Conference / see World Organization of the Scout Movement (#21693)

♦ **International Scout and Guide Fellowship (ISGF)** 14812

Amitié internationale scoute et guide (AISG)
SG Av de la Porte de Hal 38, 1060 Brussels, Belgium. T. +3225114695. Fax +3225114695. E-mail: worldbureau@isgf.org.
URL: http://www.isgf.org/

History 25 Oct 1953, Lucerne (Switzerland), as *International Fellowship of Former Scouts and Guides (IFOFSAG)* – *Amitié internationale des scouts et guides adultes (AIDSEGA)*. Registered in accordance with Belgian law, 27 Jun 1978. **Aims** Promote the spirit of the Scout and Guide Promise and Law in individual members' daily lives by continuing personal development, serving in the community and actively support the World Association of Girl Guides and Girl Scouts and the World Organisation of the Scout Movement. **Structure** World Conference (every 3 years, formerly every 2 years as General Assembly); World Bureau. Meetings closed. **Languages** English, French. **Staff** 1.00 FTE, paid; 1.00 FTE, voluntary. **Finance** Members' dues. Additional funding. **Activities** Events/meetings; projects/programmes. **Events** *Triennial World Conference* Madrid (Spain) 2022, *Triennial World Conference* Madrid (Spain) 2021, *Triennial World Conference* Madrid (Spain) 2020, *Europe Regional Conference* Bremen (Germany) 2019, *Western Hemisphere Regional Conference* New York, NY (USA) 2019. **Publications** *ISGF Info* (2 a year) in English; *AISG Info*.
Members National organizations in 65 countries and territories:
Algeria, Australia, Austria, Bahrain, Bangladesh, Belgium, Benin, Burkina Faso, Canada, Congo DR, Côte d'Ivoire, Cyprus, Czechia, Denmark, Egypt, Estonia, Finland, France, Gambia, Germany, Ghana, Greece, Haiti, Hungary, Iceland, India, Indonesia, Ireland, Italy, Jordan, Kuwait, Latvia, Lebanon, Libya, Liechtenstein, Lithuania, Luxembourg, Malaysia, Mexico, Morocco, Nepal, New Zealand, Nigeria, Norway, Pakistan, Panama, Poland, Portugal, Qatar, Romania, Saudi Arabia, Senegal, Slovakia, Slovenia, Spain, Sri Lanka, Sweden, Switzerland, Tunisia, Türkiye, Uganda, UK, United Arab Emirates, Zambia.
Members of the Central Branch in 27 countries and territories:
Argentina, Azerbaijan, Brazil, Burundi, Cameroon, Canada, Chile, Congo Brazzaville, Cuba, Ecuador, Iran Islamic Rep, Israel, Japan, Jordan, Kenya, Liberia, Netherlands, Peru, Rwanda, South Africa, Sudan, Taiwan, Tanzania UR, Thailand, Trinidad-Tobago, USA, Zimbabwe.
NGO Relations *World Association of Girl Guides and Girl Scouts (WAGGGS, #21142)* and *World Organization of the Scout Movement (WOSM, #21693)* are represented on Committee with voting rights. [2018.09.07/XC2049/**F**]

♦ International Screen Advertising Services (inactive)
♦ International Screen Publicity Association (inactive)

♦ **International Seabed Authority (ISBA)** 14813

Autorité internationale des fonds marins – Autoridad Internacional de los Fondos Marinos
Contact 14-20 Port Royal Street, 2nd Floor, Kingston, Jamaica. T. +18769229105. Fax +18769220195. E-mail: mbond@isa.org.jm – news@isa.org.jm.
URL: http://www.isa.org.jm/

History 16 Nov 1994, Kingston (Jamaica). Established at first session of Assembly, following activities of *Preparatory Commission for the International Seabed Authority and for the International Tribunal for the Law of the Sea (LOS PrepCom, inactive)* and on entering into force of *United Nations Convention on the Law of the Sea (UNCLOS, 1982)*, one year after Guyana became 60th country to deposit its instrument of ratification. Fully operational since 1996. Also referred to by initials *ISA*. Disputes arising from interpretation or application of the Convention settled via *International Tribunal for the Law of the Sea (ITLOS, #15731)*. **Aims** Organize and control activities on the deep ocean floor in areas beyond the limits of national jurisdiction, particularly with a view to administering the mineral resources of that area, in accordance with the 1982 United Nations Convention on the Law of the Sea, the 1994 Agreement Relating to the Implementation of Part XI of the Convention and the rules, regulations and procedures of the Authority. **Structure** Assembly, consisting of all members. Council, consisting of 36 members, with 5 categories of membership – *'Group A'* 4 members representing States Parties which have, in the last 5 years for which statistics are available, imported or consumed more than 2% in value terms of total world consumption of minerals derived from the international sea-bed Area, provided that the four members include one State from the Eastern European region having the largest economy in that region in terms of gross domestic product, and the State, on the date of entry into force of the Convention, having the largest economy in terms of gross domestic product; *'Group B'* 4 members from the 8 States Parties having the largest investments in preparation for and in the conduct of activities in the Area; *'Group C'* 4 states from among States Parties which are major exporters of the categories of minerals to be derived from the Area, including at least two developing States whose exports of such minerals have a substantial bearing upon their economies; *'Group D'* 6 members from developing State Parties, representing special interests, including those of States with large populations, land-locked or geographically disadvantaged States, island States, States which are major importers of the categories of minerals to be derived from the Area, States which are potential producers of such minerals and least developed States; *'Group E'* 18 members elected to ensure an equitable geographical representation in the Council. Legal and Technical Commission of 25 members. Finance Committee of 15 members. **Languages** Arabic, Chinese, English, French, Russian, Spanish. **Staff** 34.00 FTE, paid. **Finance** Sources: contributions; members' dues. Annual budget: 7,150,000 USD (2014). **Activities** Politics/policy/regulatory; monitoring/evaluation; research/documentation; events/meetings. Management of treaties and agreements: *Protocol on the Privileges and Immunities of the International Seabed Authority (1998).* **Events** *Session* Kingston (Jamaica) 2018, *Joint Workshop* Singapore (Singapore) 2015, *Session* Kingston (Jamaica) 2011, *International workshop on environmental management needs for exploration and exploitation of deep seabed minerals* Nadi (Fiji) 2011, *Session* Kingston (Jamaica) 2010. **Publications** *ISA Handbook* (annual). *International Seabed Authority Basic Texts* (2012) – revised; *Law of the Sea: Compendium of Basic Documents. Law of the Sea Conferences 1968-1994* – 3 CD Pack. Technical reports and studies; proceedings; brochures.

Members States Party to the Convention (167):
Albania, Algeria, Angola, Antigua-Barbuda, Argentina, Armenia, Australia, Austria, Azerbaijan, Bahamas, Bahrain, Bangladesh, Barbados, Belarus, Belgium, Belize, Benin, Bolivia, Bosnia-Herzegovina, Botswana, Brazil, Brunei Darussalam, Bulgaria, Burkina Faso, Cameroon, Canada, Cape Verde, Chad, Chile, China, Comoros, Congo Brazzaville, Congo DR, Cook Is, Costa Rica, Côte d'Ivoire, Croatia, Cuba, Cyprus, Czechia, Denmark, Djibouti, Dominica, Dominican Rep, Ecuador, Egypt, Equatorial Guinea, Estonia, Eswatini, Fiji, Finland, France, Gabon, Gambia, Georgia, Germany, Ghana, Greece, Grenada, Guatemala, Guinea, Guinea-Bissau, Guyana, Haiti, Honduras, Hungary, Iceland, India, Indonesia, Iraq, Ireland, Italy, Jamaica, Japan, Jordan, Kenya, Kiribati, Korea Rep, Kuwait, Laos, Latvia, Lebanon, Lesotho, Liberia, Lithuania, Luxembourg, Madagascar, Malawi, Malaysia, Maldives, Mali, Malta, Marshall Is, Mauritania, Mauritius, Mexico, Micronesia FS, Moldova, Monaco, Mongolia, Montenegro, Morocco, Mozambique, Myanmar, Namibia, Nauru, Nepal, Netherlands, New Zealand, Nicaragua, Niger, Nigeria, Niue, North Macedonia, Norway, Oman, Pakistan, Palau, Palestine, Panama, Papua New Guinea, Paraguay, Philippines, Poland, Portugal, Qatar, Romania, Russia, Samoa, Sao Tomé-Principe, Saudi Arabia, Senegal, Serbia, Seychelles, Sierra Leone, Singapore, Slovakia, Slovenia, Solomon Is, Somalia, South Africa, Spain, Sri Lanka, St Kitts-Nevis, St Lucia, St Vincent-Grenadines, Sudan, Suriname, Sweden, Switzerland, Tanzania UR, Thailand, Timor-Leste, Togo, Tonga, Trinidad-Tobago, Tunisia, Tuvalu, Uganda, UK, Ukraine, Uruguay, Vanuatu, Vietnam, Yemen, Zambia, Zimbabwe.
European Union (EU, #08967).
Observers: States (30); UN and Intergovernmental Organizations (32); Non-Governmental Organizations (30):
Afghanistan, Andorra, Bhutan, Burundi, Cambodia, Central African Rep, Colombia, El Salvador, Eritrea, Ethiopia, Holy See, Iran Islamic Rep, Israel, Kazakhstan, Korea DPR, Kyrgyzstan, Libya, Liechtenstein, Peru, Rwanda, San Marino, South Sudan, Syrian AR, Tajikistan, Türkiye, Turkmenistan, United Arab Emirates, USA, Uzbekistan, Venezuela.
United Nations & Inter-governmental Organizations (32):
- *Comisión Permanente del Pacífico Sur (CPPS, #04141);*
- *Commonwealth Secretariat (#04362);*
- *FAO (#09260);*
- *ILO (#11123);*
- *Inter-American Development Bank (IDB, #11427);*
- *Intergovernmental Oceanographic Commission (IOC, #11496);*
- *International Atomic Energy Agency (IAEA, #12294);*
- *International Bank for Reconstruction and Development (IBRD, #12317)* (World Bank);
- *International Civil Aviation Organization (ICAO, #12581);*
- *International Fund for Agricultural Development (IFAD, #13692);*
- *International Hydrographic Organization (IHO, #13825);*
- *International Maritime Organization (IMO, #14102);*
- *International Monetary Fund (IMF, #14180);*
- *International Oil Pollution Compensation Funds (IOPC Funds, #14402);*
- *International Telecommunication Union (ITU, #15673);*
- *International Union for Conservation of Nature and Natural Resources (IUCN, #15766);*
- *Interoceanmetal Joint Organization (IOM, #15955);*
- *Organization of the Petroleum Exporting Countries (OPEC, #17881);*
- *OSPAR Commission for the Protection of the Marine Environment of the North-East Atlantic (OSPAR Commission, #17905);*
- *Pacific Community (SPC, #17942);*
- *Secretariat of the Convention on Biological Diversity (SCBD, #19197);*
- *Secretariat of the Pacific Regional Environment Programme (SPREP, #19205);*
- *UNDP (#20292);*
- *UNEP (#20299);*
- *UNESCO (#20322);*
- *UNIDO (#20336);*
- *United Nations (UN, #20515);*
- *Universal Postal Union (UPU, #20682);*
- *WHO (#20950);*
- *World Intellectual Property Organization (WIPO, #21593);*
- *World Meteorological Organization (WMO, #21649);*
- *World Trade Organization (WTO, #21864).*

Non-Governmental Organizations (30):
- *Advisory Committee on Protection of the Sea (ACOPS, #00139);*
- *African Minerals Development Centre (AMDC);*
- *Center for Oceans Law and Policy (COLP);*
- Center for Polar and Deep Ocean Development;
- *Committee for Mineral Reserves International Reporting Standards (CRIRSCO, #04272);*
- *Conservation International (CI);*
- *Deep-Ocean Stewardship Initiative (DOSI, #05023);*
- *Deep Sea Conservation Coalition (DSCC, #05024);*
- Durham University's Centre for Borders Research;
- *Earthworks;*
- Fish Reef Project;
- *Greenpeace International (#10727);*
- Institute for Advanced Sustainability Studies;
- *International Association of Drilling Contractors (IADC);*
- *International Cable Protection Committee (ICPC, #12423);*
- *International Dialogue on Underwater Munitions (IDUM, #13169);*
- *International Marine Minerals Society (IMMS);*
- *International Ocean Institute (IOI, #14394);*
- International Policy Laboratory;
- *InterRidge (IR, #15973);*
- Japan Agency for Marine-Earth Science and Technology;
- *Law of the Sea Institute (LOSI);*
- Mining Standards International;
- Ocean Society of India;
- *Pew Charitable Trusts;*
- *RESOLVE;*
- Sargasso Sea Commission;
- Thyssen-Bornemisza Art Contemporary;
- *World Ocean Council (WOC, #21680);*
- *World Wide Fund for Nature (WWF, #21922).*

IGO Relations Member of (2): *United Nations Joint Staff Pension Fund (UNJSPF, #20581); UN-OCEANS (#20711).* Permanent Observer to: UN General Assembly. Observer Status with: *International Maritime Organization (IMO, #14102).* **NGO Relations** Memorandum of Understanding with (1): *International Cable Protection Committee (ICPC, #12423).* [2021/XF2563/**F***]

♦ International Seabuckthorn Association (internationally oriented national body)

♦ International Sea Cadet Association (ISCA) 14814

Exec Dir c/o Navy League of Canada, 66 Lisgar Str, Ottawa ON K2P 0C1, Canada. T. +16139982945. Fax +16139908701.
Facebook: https://www.facebook.com/ISCASeacadets

Aims Encourage *young people* towards high personal standards, teamwork and a sense of responsibility to the community through the medium of disciplined *nautical* training and development of leadership qualities; develop in young people an appreciation of the importance of the sea to international commerce, defence and the protection of the environment. **Events** *Conference* Seoul (Korea Rep) 2020, *Conference* Stockholm (Sweden) 2019, *Conference* Washington, DC (USA) 2010, *Conference* Mumbai (India) 2009, *Conference* Karlskrona (Sweden) 2008.

Members National organizations in 19 countries:
Australia, Austria, Bermuda, Canada, Germany, Hong Kong, India, Japan, Korea Rep, Netherlands, New Zealand, Russia, Singapore, South Africa, Sweden, UK, USA, Zimbabwe. [2020/XD7648/**D**]

♦ International Seafarers Service Study Committee (inactive)

♦ International Seafarers' Welfare and Assistance Network (ISWAN) . 14815

Exec Dir Suffolk House, George Street, Croydon, CR0 1PE, UK. T. +443000124279. Fax +443000124280. E-mail: iswan@iswan.org.uk.
URL: http://www.seafarerswelfare.org/

History Set up on merger of *International Committee on Seafarers' Welfare (ICSW, inactive)* and *International Seafarers Assistance Network (ISAN, inactive).* Registered in England and Wales: 3171109. **Aims** Promote seafarers' welfare worldwide. **Structure** Board. **Languages** English. **Staff** 16.00 FTE, paid. **Events** *Seminar* Helsinki (Finland) 2018.

Members Full in 20 countries:
Australia, Bangladesh, Belgium, Côte d'Ivoire, Denmark, Finland, France, India, Italy, Japan, Netherlands, Nigeria, Norway, Pakistan, Philippines, Poland, Romania, Sweden, UK, USA.
Included in the above, 5 organizations listed in this Yearbook:
International Christian Maritime Association (ICMA, #12561); International Confederation of Water Transport Workers' Unions (ICWTWU, #12873); International Transport Workers' Federation (ITF, #15726); Maritime Piracy Humanitarian Response Programme (MPHRP, #16583); United Seamen's Service (USS, #20661). [2019.12.12/XJ9397/**F**]

♦ International Seafood Sustainability Foundation (internationally oriented national body)
♦ International Sealing Distribution Association (internationally oriented national body)
♦ International Seapower Symposium (meeting series)

♦ International Search and Rescue Advisory Group (INSARAG) 14816

Groupe consultatif international de la recherche et du sauvetage

Sec Emergency Response Support Branch, OCHA, Palais des Nations, 1211 Geneva 10, Switzerland. T. +412291771173. E-mail: insarag@un.org.
URL: http://insarag.org/

History 11 Dec 1991, Beuggen (Germany). Established at meeting convened by *Office of the United Nations Disaster Relief Coordinator (UNDRO, inactive)* under *United Nations (UN, #20515)* General Assembly resolution 57/150 (2002). Currently comes within the framework of the *United Nations Office for the Coordination of Humanitarian Affairs (OCHA, #20593)*, based at *United Nations Office at Geneva (UNOG, #20597).* **Aims** Establish globally accepted international standards for Urban Search and Rescue (USAR) teams and methodology for international coordination in *earthquake* response. **Structure** Steering Group; Regional Groups; Ad-hoc Working Groups; Secretariat. **Languages** Arabic, Chinese, English, French, Spanish. **Finance** Sources: voluntary donor funding; support from UN Member States. **Activities** Events/meetings; knowledge management/information dissemination; training/education. **Events** *Asia-Pacific Group Meeting* Seoul (Korea Rep) 2022, *Global Meeting* Warsaw (Poland) 2021, *Asia-Pacific Group Meeting* 2020, *Asia-Pacific Group Meeting* Tokyo (Japan) 2018, *Team Leaders Meeting* Tokyo (Japan) 2016. **Publications** Guidelines; reference documents. **Members** Membership is open to all countries and/or organizations involved in USAR activities. Membership countries not specified. [2022/XF3440/**F***]

♦ International Search and Rescue Dog Organisation (IRO) 14817

Internationale Rettungshunde Organisation (IRO)

Sec Moosstraße 32, 5020 Salzburg, Austria. T. +4366282652610. Fax +4366282652620. E-mail: office@iro-dogs.org.
URL: http://www.iro-dogs.org/

History 18 May 1993, Stockholm-Rosersberg (Sweden). Founded at Fifth International Search and Rescue Dog Symposium. Current constitution adopted Apr 2007. Registration: Austria. **Aims** Train and certify highly qualified search and rescue dog teams and provide them as supporting units in case of emergency. **Structure** Meeting of Delegates; Executive Board; Executive Committee. **Languages** English, German. **Staff** 5.00 FTE, paid. **Finance** Sources: donations; fundraising; members' dues; revenue from activities/projects; sale of products; sponsorship. **Activities** Awareness raising; certification/accreditation; events/meetings; networking/liaising; standards/guidelines; training/education. **Events** *World conference* Copenhagen (Denmark) 2003, *The rescue dog today* Prague (Czech Rep) 2003, *General assembly / Symposium* Las Palmas de Gran Canaria (Spain) 2001, *General assembly / Symposium* Ig (Slovenia) 1999. **Publications** Annual Report.

Members National rescue dog organizations (123) in 42 countries and territories:
Argentina, Australia, Austria, Belgium, Brazil, Canada, Chile, China, Colombia, Croatia, Czechia, Denmark, Estonia, Finland, France, Germany, Hungary, Italy, Japan, Korea Rep, Malaysia, Mexico, Netherlands, Norway, Poland, Romania, Russia, Saudi Arabia, Slovakia, Slovenia, South Africa, Spain, Sweden, Switzerland, Taiwan, Thailand, Türkiye, UK, Ukraine, United Arab Emirates, USA, Venezuela.
Included in the above, 1 international organization listed in this Yearbook:
Asia Working Dog Support Association (AWDSA). [2022.05.12/XD6705/y/**D**]

♦ International Sea Sportfishing Federation (see: #04562)

♦ International Sea Turtle Society (ISTS) 14818

Sec Marine Turtle Research Program, NOAA-Natl Marine Fisheries Service, Southwest Fisheries Science Ctr, 8604 La Jolla Shores Dr, La Jolla CA 92037, USA.
URL: http://www.seaturtlesociety.org/

History 1981. Feb 1996, registered in accordnace with USA law. **Aims** Promote information exchange so as to advance global knowledge of sea turtle biology and *conservation.* **Structure** Board of Directors; Executive Committee. **Events** *Annual Symposium* Charleston, SC (USA) 2019, *Annual Symposium* Kobe (Japan) 2018, *Annual Symposium* Las Vegas, NV (USA) 2017, *Annual Symposium* Lima (Peru) 2016, *Annual Symposium* San Diego, CA (USA) 2015. **NGO Relations** Partner of: *1% for the Planet.* [2016/XJ0301/**B**]

♦ International Seaweed Association (ISA) 14819

Main Office 631 Moosehead Trail, Waldo ME 04915, USA. E-mail: info@isaseaweed.org.
URL: http://www.isaseaweed.org/

History 1952. **Aims** Promote applied phycology on a global basis; foster interest in academic study of seaweeds and their industrial uses; stimulate interaction among research workers and industrialists. **Structure** *International Seaweed Association Council (ISAC)*, comprising President, President Elect and 10 members. International Advisory Committee. Officers: President; Vice-President/President-Elect; Immediate Past President; Secretary; Treasurer; Editor in Chief. **Languages** English. **Staff** 3.00 FTE, voluntary. **Finance** Industries concerned with seaweeds; governmental and other organizations; fees at international meetings. **Activities** Organizes symposia, workshops and courses, including *International Seaweed Symposium (ISS).* **Events** *International Seaweed Symposium* Victoria, BC (Canada) 2026, *International Seaweed Symposium* Hobart, TAS (Australia) 2023, *International Seaweed Symposium* Jeju (Korea Rep) 2019, *International Seaweed Symposium* Copenhagen (Denmark) 2016, *Triennial Symposium* Bali (Indonesia) 2013. **Publications** Proceedings of ISS symposia and Applied Phycological Forum.

Members Honorary Life, Regular, Student and Institutional members in 62 countries and territories:
Argentina, Australia, Belgium, Brazil, Canada, Chile, China, Colombia, Croatia, Cuba, Denmark, Ecuador, Egypt, Fiji, Finland, France, Germany, Greece, Hong Kong, India, Indonesia, Ireland, Israel, Italy, Japan, Kenya, Kiribati, Korea DPR, Korea Rep, Malaysia, Mexico, Morocco, Namibia, Netherlands, New Zealand, Nigeria, North Macedonia, Norway, Pakistan, Panama, Peru, Philippines, Poland, Portugal, Puerto Rico, Russia, Singapore, Slovenia, Solomon Is, South Africa, Spain, St Lucia, Sweden, Taiwan, Tanzania UR, Thailand, Trinidad-Tobago, UK, Uruguay, USA, Venezuela, Vietnam.

IGO Relations *FAO (#09260).* [2022/XD2439/**D**]

♦ International Seaweed Conference (meeting series)
♦ International Secretariat for Arts, Mass Media and Entertainment Trade Unions (inactive)
♦ International Secretariat for Catholic Engineers, Agronomists and Industry Officials (#19203)
♦ International Secretariat of Catholic Secondary School Teachers / see SIESC – European Federation of Christian Teachers (#19267)
♦ International Secretariat of Catholic Technologists, Agriculturalists and Economists / see Secrétariat international des ingénieurs, des agronomes et des cadres économiques catholiques (#19203)
♦ International Secretariat of Christian Artists / see International Society of Christian Artists (#15009)

♦ International Secretariat Committee of Nuclear Free Zone Local Authorities 14820

Principal Policy Officer c/o Manchester City Council, Town Hall Extension, Level 3, Library Walk, Manchester, M60 2LA, UK. T. +441612343244.
URL: http://www.nuclearpolicy.info/

History Also known as *Nuclear Free Zone Local Authorities International Secretariat.* **Aims** Promote growth of local authority nuclear free movement in order to create a world free of nuclear weapons. **Structure** Steering Group. **Languages** English. **Staff** 2.00 FTE, paid. **Finance** Costs carried by Manchester City Council. **Events** *International Conference on Nuclear Free Zone Local Authorities* The Hague (Netherlands) 1995, *International Conference on Nuclear Free Zone Local Authorities* Manchester (UK) 1994, *International Conference on Nuclear Free Zone Local Authorities* Japan 1993, *International Conference on Nuclear Free Zone Local Authorities* Jerusalem (Israel) 1993, *International Conference on Nuclear Free Zone Local Authorities* Perugia (Italy) 1993.
Members Local authorities in 18 countries and territories:
Argentina, Australia, Finland, France, Germany, Ireland, Italy, Japan, Marshall Is, Netherlands, New Zealand, Portugal, Russia, Spain, Sweden, UK, Ukraine, USA.
IGO Relations Associated with Department of Global Communications of the United Nations. **NGO Relations** Member of: *Abolition 2000 – Global Network to Eliminate Nuclear Weapons (Abolition 2000, #00006).*
[2018/XF0663/F]

- ♦ International Secretariat for the Dietetic Industry / see International Special Dietary Food Industries (#15576)
- ♦ International Secretariat of Glass-Workers (inactive)
- ♦ International Secretariat for Growth and Development (see: #10972)
- ♦ International Secretariat of the Knitting Industries (inactive)
- ♦ International Secretariat of National Societies of Catholic Doctors / see International Federation of Catholic Medical Associations (#13378)
- ♦ International Secretariat of Painters and Similar Professions (inactive)
- ♦ International Secretariat of Radiographers and Radiological Technicians / see International Society of Radiographers and Radiological Technologists (#15410)
- ♦ International Secretariat for Research on the History of Agrarian and Food Technology (inactive)

♦ International Secretariat for Scientific Questions 14821

Secrétariat international des questions scientifiques (SIQS)
Sec Kasteellaan 3, 7004 JK Doetinchem, Netherlands.
URL: http://www.paxromana.org/

History 1951, as a Specialized Secretariat of *Pax Romana, International Catholic Movement for Intellectual and Cultural Affairs (ICMICA, #18267).* Also referred to as *International Secretariat for Scientific Questions of Pax Romana – Secrétariat international des questions scientifiques de Pax Romana.* **Aims** Provide a means of communication between scientists, ie working professionally in the physical, biological and human sciences, applied mathematicians and technologists, theologians and philosophers concerned with the relations between science and the *Catholic* faith. **Structure** Committee. **Languages** English, French. **Activities** Arranges international meetings, called SIQS Days, which take place at intervals of 3 to 5 years and are held in conjunction with Conferences of the European Federations of ICMICA. **Events** *Meeting* London (UK) 1998, *Meeting* Warsaw (Poland) 1996, *Meeting* Fribourg (Switzerland) 1990, *Meeting* Innsbruck (Austria) 1985, *Meeting* Rome (Italy) 1982. **Publications** *Bulletin du SIQS.*
Members Individuals corresponding members in 39 countries and territories:
Australia, Bangladesh, Belgium, Chile, Colombia, Egypt, France, Germany, Ghana, Greece, Holy See, Hungary, India, Indonesia, Italy, Japan, Kenya, Korea Rep, Mexico, Netherlands, Nigeria, Pakistan, Paraguay, Peru, Philippines, Poland, Portugal, Romania, Slovakia, Slovenia, Spain, Sri Lanka, Switzerland, Taiwan, Tanzania UR, Thailand, UK, Uruguay, USA.
[2008.06.01/XE5130/v/E]

- ♦ International Secretariat for Scientific Questions of Pax Romana / see International Secretariat for Scientific Questions (#14821)
- ♦ International Secretariat of Stone Masons (inactive)
- ♦ International Secretariat for Teaching Educational Sciences in Universities / see Association mondiale des sciences de l'éducation (#02811)
- ♦ International Secretariat for the Unification of Pharmacopoeias (inactive)
- ♦ International Secretariat for Volunteer Service (inactive)

♦ International Secretariat for Water (ISW) 14822

Secrétariat international de l'eau (SIE) – Secretariado Internacional del Agua
Exec Dir 911 rue Jean-Talon Est, Suite 205, Montréal QC H2R IV5, Canada. T. +15148494262 – +15148492822. E-mail: info@sie-isw.org.
URL: http://www.sie-isw.org/

History Aug 1991, Montréal, QC (Canada). Incorporated, following meeting in Dec 1989, Sophia-Antipolis (France), of the Water Supply and Sanitation (WSS) Collaborative Council, to facilitate the implementation of the principles laid out in the *Montréal Charter on Drinking Water and Sanitation,* adopted in Jun 1990. **Aims** Take action to promote access to drinking water, hygiene and *sanitation* for the poorest, while contributing to meet their other basic needs; address the impact of climate change; support the capacity of local populations and their partners to choose appropriate solutions; blend "bottom up" and "top down" approaches aiming at application and innovation in the decentralization of political choices and financing mechanisms. **Structure** Board of Trustees. Executive Committee. Organizes: *World Youth Parliament for Water (WYPW, #21958). Solidarity Water Europe (SWE).* **Languages** English, French, Spanish. **Staff** 4.00 FTE, paid. 4 occasional; consultants. **Finance** Funding comes from: national and regional governments; multilateral organizations; private sector; foundations; NGOs; annual contribution from *Canadian International Development Agency (CIDA, inactive).* ISW also depends largely on voluntary efforts and expertise. **Activities** Advocacy/lobbying/activism; events/meetings. **Events** *International Student Summit on Climate (UNIC2020)* Montréal, QC (Canada) 2020, *Global Estuaries Forum* Deauville (France) 2014, *International meeting on governance and social management of water passages* Fez (Morocco) 2002, *World youth parliament for water assembly* Québec, QC (Canada) 2002, *Forum and workshop* Conakry (Guinea) 1997. **Publications** Reports; documents; issue papers. **IGO Relations** Partners: *Global Alliances for Water and Climate (GAfWaC, #10230); International Development Research Centre (IDRC, #13162); International Network of Basin Organizations (INBO, #14235); Niger Basin Authority (NBA, #17134); UNDP (#20292); UNICEF (#20332); United Nations Volunteers (UNV, #20650); Partial Agreement on Youth Mobility Through the Youth Card (#18224).*
NGO Relations Partners listed in this Yearbook:
- *African Network for Integrated Development (ANID, #00390);*
- *The Butterfly Effect (BE, #03389);*
- *Comité Catholique contre la Faim et pour le Développement-Terre Solidaire (CCFD-Terre Solidaire);*
- *Catholic Relief Services (CRS, #03608);*
- *Environment Liaison Centre International (ELCI, no recent information);*
- *Environmental Defense Fund (EDF);*
- *Environnement et développement du Tiers-monde (enda, #05510);*
- *Fondation de France;*
- *Global Water Partnership (GWP, #10653);*
- *Habitat International Coalition (HIC, #10845);*
- *International Council for Adult Education (ICAE, #12983);*
- *International League for the Study and Promotion of Community Health (no recent information);*
- *International Office for Water (IOW, #14399);*
- *International Training Network for Water and Waste Management (ITN, no recent information);*
- *International Union for Conservation of Nature and Natural Resources (IUCN, #15766);*
- *IRC (#16016);*
- *Maghreb-Mashreq Alliance for Water (#16544);*
- *Oxfam Novib;*
- *Programme Solidarité eau (pS-Eau, #18529);*
- *US Council for Human Rights in the Balkans (no recent information);*
- *World Water Council (WWC, #21908).*

Founding member of: *Global Water Solidarity (GWS, #10655).* [2022/XF1436/F]

- ♦ International Secretariat of Women Farmers' Groups (inactive)
- ♦ International Secret Service Association (inactive)

♦ International Secure Information Governance and Management Association (i-SIGMA) 14823

CEO 3030 N 3rd St, Ste 940, Phoenix AZ 85012, USA. T. +16027886243.
URL: https://isigmaonline.org/

History Founded Jun 2018, on merger of National Association for information (NAID) and *PRISM International.* A US non-profit of the type 501(c)6. **Aims** Advance secure data lifecycle management, security, and information governance globally by service providers and their customers through advocacy, education, and standards enforcement. **Structure** Board of Directors; Management Team. International divisions (2): NAID; *PRISM International.* **Activities** Certification/accreditation; events/meetings; training/education.
[2019/XM8572/C]

- ♦ International Securities Association for Institutional Trade Communication / see ISITC
- ♦ International Securities Association for Institutional Trade Communication – International Operations Association / see ISITC Europe (#16032)
- ♦ International Securities Association for Institutional Trade Communications – International Operations Association / see ISITC
- ♦ International Securities Lending Association (internationally oriented national body)

♦ International Securities Services Association (ISSA) 14824

Contact c/o SIX Group Services, Hardturmstrasse 201, 8021 Zurich ZH, Switzerland.
Street address c/o SIX Group Services, West Hard Turm Park, Pfingstweidstrasse 110, 8005 Zurich ZH, Switzerland.
URL: http://www.issanet.org/

History Founded 1988, Zurich (Switzerland), as *International Society of Securities Administrators,* at 4th ISSA Symposium (held since 1979). Present name adopted 1 Sep 1997. **Aims** Contribute to developing and promoting forward-thinking solutions that create efficiencies and mitigate risk within the global securities services industry; foster international coordination and collaboration; facilitate and stimulate active communication among all industry stakeholders. **Structure** General Assembly; Executive Board; Operating Committee; CEO Office and Secretariat. **Languages** English. **Finance** Sources: members' dues; sponsorship. **Activities** Events/meetings. **Events** *Symposium* Wolfsberg (Switzerland) 2022, *Symposium* Zurich (Switzerland) 2020, *Symposium* Zurich (Switzerland) 2018, *Symposium* Ermatingen (Switzerland) 2016, *Conference* London (UK) 2015. **Publications** *ISSA Newsletter* (4 a year). Reports.
Members Institutions and corporations in 50 countries and territories:
Argentina, Australia, Austria, Azerbaijan, Belgium, Brazil, Bulgaria, Canada, Chile, Colombia, Croatia, Czechia, Denmark, Egypt, France, Germany, Ghana, Greece, Hong Kong, Hungary, Iceland, India, Indonesia, Ireland, Italy, Japan, Korea Rep, Liechtenstein, Luxembourg, Mexico, Morocco, Netherlands, Nigeria, Norway, Pakistan, Poland, Romania, Russia, Singapore, Slovenia, South Africa, Spain, Sweden, Switzerland, Taiwan, Thailand, Türkiye, UK, United Arab Emirates, USA. [2019/XD2361/C]

- ♦ International and Security Affairs Centre (internationally oriented national body)
- ♦ International Security Assistance Force (inactive)
- ♦ International Security Association / see ESSA – The International Security Association (#05547)

♦ International Security Association (ISA) 14825

Gen Sec Im Holland 5, 5323 Rietheim AG, Switzerland. T. +41414104008. E-mail: president@isa.us.org.
Main Website: http://www.isa.us.org/

History 1972, Cyprus. Founded 1972, but concept did not proceed then. Another attempt was made early 1980s, but no membership was obtained. Revived 2012 with Presidency in Switzerland. In 2017, converted to a non-profit Scientific Association. Registration: Swiss Civil Code, No/ID: CHE-411 974 865, Start date: 9 Aug 2017, Switzerland. **Aims** Promote science and research in the field of security, safety and *public health.* **Structure** Officers. Includes: *World Bodyguards Association (WBA).* **Languages** English. **Staff** 50.00 FTE, voluntary. **Finance** Sources: donations; international organizations; sponsorship. **Activities** Awareness raising; events/meetings; monitoring/evaluation; research and development; research/documentation; standards/guidelines; training/education. **Members** Mainly individuals. Membership countries not specified. **IGO Relations** Member of (1): United Nations General Marketplace (UNGM). [2022.05.12/XM4983/D]

- ♦ International Security and Development Center (internationally oriented national body)
- ♦ International Security Industry Organization (internationally oriented national body)
- ♦ International Security Information Service (internationally oriented national body)

♦ International Security Ligue 14826

Main Office c/o Securitas AG, Alpenstrasse 20, 3052 Zollikofen BE, Switzerland. T. +41319101680. Fax +41319116334. E-mail: infoliga@security-ligue.org.
URL: http://www.security-ligue.org/

History 2 Jun 1934, Copenhagen (Denmark). Constitution adopted: Nov 2006; 2017. Former names and other names: *Ligue internationale des sociétés de surveillance* – former. Registration: Switzerland. **Aims** Initiate and broaden supranational contacts and exchanges of experience and opinion, thus deepening reciprocal understanding among members and the countries they represent; resolve common problems; develop techniques and organizational methods more effective than those possible to individual initiative and local resources; improve and increase the overall potential of private *security* activity throughout the world. **Structure** General Assembly (every 2 years); Board. **Languages** English. **Staff** None. **Finance** Sources: members' dues. **Events** *Biennial General Assembly* Interlaken (Switzerland) 2015, *Biennial General Assembly* Montréal, QC (Canada) 2012, *Biennial General Assembly* Istanbul (Turkey) 2010, *Biennial General Assembly* Barcelona (Spain) / Seville (Spain) 2008, *Biennial General Assembly* Delhi (India) 2006.
Members Companies (71) in 44 countries:
Argentina, Austria, Bangladesh, Belgium, Brazil, Canada, Chile, Colombia, Czechia, Denmark, Egypt, Finland, France, Germany, Greece, Hungary, India, Ireland, Israel, Italy, Japan, Korea Rep, Luxembourg, Mexico, Netherlands, Norway, Pakistan, Paraguay, Peru, Poland, Portugal, Romania, Singapore, Slovakia, South Africa, Spain, Sweden, Switzerland, Thailand, Türkiye, UK, United Arab Emirates, Uruguay, USA.
Consultative Status Consultative status granted from: *ECOSOC (#05331)* (Ros A). [2017.10.16/XC2219/C]

♦ International Sediment Initiative (ISI) 14827

SG Technical Secretariat, IRTCES, PO Box 366, 20 Chegongzhuang West Road, 100048 Beijing, China. T. +861068786410. Fax +861068411174.
Chairman Inst of Geography, Univ of Bern, Hallerstr 12, 3012 Bern, Switzerland.
URL: http://www.irtces.org/isi/

History 2002, by *UNESCO (#20322)* through *International Hydrological Programme (IHP, #13826).* **Aims** Assess erosion and sediment transport to marines as well as their social, economic and environmental impacts, lake or reservoir environments. **Structure** Advisory Group; Experts Group. Technical Secretariat. **Languages** English. **Activities** Research/documentation; capacity building; training/education; networking/liaising. **Publications** *ISI Newsletter.* Books; reports; proceedings. **Information Services** *ISI Information Service* – database. **NGO Relations** Technical secretariat provided by: *International Research and Training Centre on Erosion and Sedimentation (IRTCES, #14745).* [2017.03.09/XJ2256/E]

♦ International Seed Federation (ISF) 14828

SG ISF Secretariat, Chemin du Reposoir 7, 1260 Nyon VD, Switzerland. T. +41223654420. Fax +41223654421. E-mail: isf@worldseed.org.
Events Assistant address not obtained.
URL: http://www.worldseed.org/

History Jun 2002. Founded on merger of *International Association of Plant Breeders for the Protection of Plant Varieties (ASSINSEL, inactive)* and *International Federation of the Seed Trade (ISF, inactive).* **Aims** Represent the interests of the seed industry at a global level by engaging with public and private institutions to facilitate international seed trade. **Structure** General Assembly; Board of Directors; Executive Committee; Secretariat. **Languages** English. **Staff** 8.00 FTE, paid. **Finance** Sources: members' dues. **Activities** Events/meetings. **Events** *World Seed Congress* Istanbul (Türkiye) 2025, *World Seed Congress* Rotterdam (Netherlands) 2024, *World Seed Congress* Cape Town (South Africa) 2023, *World Seed Congress* Barcelona (Spain) 2022, *World Seed Congress* 2021. **Publications** Newsletter (5 a year). Congress reports; seed trade statistics; leaflets. **Members** Ordinary; Associate; Affiliate; Tree and Shrub Seed Group; Observer. Ordinary national organizations representing seed companies and enterprises within their respective countries, in 42 countries:

Argentina, Australia, Austria, Belgium, Brazil, Canada, Chile, China, Czechia, Denmark, Egypt, Finland, France, Germany, Greece, Hungary, India, Ireland, Israel, Italy, Japan, Kenya, Korea Rep, Mexico, Morocco, Netherlands, New Zealand, Philippines, Poland, Serbia, Slovenia, South Africa, Spain, Sweden, Switzerland, Tanzania UR, Tunisia, Türkiye, UK, Ukraine, Uruguay, USA.
Associate seed companies or enterprises, in 43 countries:
Afghanistan, Algeria, Belarus, China, Colombia, Cyprus, Czechia, Denmark, Ecuador, Egypt, France, Germany, India, Indonesia, Iran Islamic Rep, Japan, Jordan, Lebanon, Libya, Lithuania, Luxembourg, Mongolia, Netherlands, Norway, Pakistan, Peru, Portugal, Romania, Russia, Saudi Arabia, Slovakia, South Sudan, Spain, Switzerland, Syrian AR, Thailand, Tunisia, UK, Ukraine, USA, Yemen, Zambia, Zimbabwe.
Affiliate service providers to the seed industry, in 16 countries and territories:
Australia, Belgium, China, Denmark, France, Germany, Greece, Israel, Italy, Netherlands, Pakistan, Spain, Sweden, Switzerland, Taiwan, UK, USA.
Tree and Shrub Seed Group in 2' countries:
Australia, Belgium, Canada, China, Czechia, Denmark, Finland, France, Germany, Hungary, Ireland, Italy, Japan, Netherlands, New Zealand, Norway, Poland, Romania, Russia, Slovakia, Spain, Sweden, UK, USA.
Observer (seed associations and companies with a time-bound observer status) in 2 countries:
Peru, Somalia.
Consultative Status Consultative status granted from: *FAO (#09260)* (Special Status); *UNEP (#20299).* **IGO Relations** Cooperates in related fields of interest with: *International Plant Protection Convention, 1951 (IPPC, 1951); International Seed Testing Association (ISTA, #14829); International Treaty on Plant Genetic Resources for Food and Agriculture (2001); OECD (#17693); Secretariat of the Convention on Biological Diversity (SCBD, #19197); Union internationale pour la protection des obtentions végétales (UPOV, #20436); World Trade Organization (WTO, #21864); UNEP (#20299).* Supports: *Bioversity International (#03262).* **NGO Relations** Liaises with: *International Chamber of Commerce (ICC, #12534).* Founding member of: *International Agri-Food Network (IAFN, #11599).* Member of: *Business and Industry Advisory Committee to the OECD (BIAC, #03385).* Supports: *Farming First.* [2019/XB0013/t/**B**]

♦ International Seed Testing Association (ISTA) 14829

SG Zurichstrasse 50, 8303 Bassersdorf ZH, Switzerland. T. +41448386000. Fax +41448386001. E-mail: ista.office@ista.ch.
URL: http://www.seedtest.org/
History 1921, Copenhagen (Denmark). Founded at 3rd International Congress, by informal agreement among 16 European countries, as *European Seed Testing Association – Association européenne d'essais de semences.* Previously also known as: *Association internationale d'essais de semences – Internationale Vereinigung für Saatgutprüfung.* Activities extended and the Association reconstituted under present name, Jul 1924, Cambridge (UK). Constitution adopted at the Fourth International Seed Testing Congress, 10 Jul 1924, Cambridge, and subsequently amended at Ordinary Meetings held in: Washington DC (USA) 1950; Dublin (Ireland) 1953; Paris (France) 1956; Lisbon (Portugal) 1962; Washington DC (USA) 1971 (Extra-Ordinary Meeting); Warsaw (Poland) 1974; Brisbane (Australia) 1986; Copenhagen (Denmark) 1995; Angers (France) 2001; Budapest (Hungary) 2004; Bangkok (Thailand) 2005; Zurich (Switzerland) 2006; Iguaçu Falls (Brazil) 2007; Zurich (Switzerland) 2009; Cologne (Germany) 2010; Venlo (Netherlands) 2012; Antalya (Turkey) 2013. **Aims** Develop, adopt and publish standard procedures for *sampling* and seed testing; promote uniform application of these procedures for evaluation of seed moving in international trade with *'ISTA International Seed Lot Certificates'*; promote research in all areas of seed science and technology, including sampling, testing, storing, processing and distributing seeds; encourage variety (cultivar) certification. **Structure** Ordinary General Meeting (annual); Executive Committee; Technical Committees (18). **Languages** English. **Staff** 10.00 FTE, paid. **Finance** Sources: contributions of member/participating states. Annual contributions from member countries. **Activities** Certification/accreditation; events/meetings; research/documentation; standards/guidelines; training/education. **Events** *Annual Meeting* Verona (Italy) 2020, *Triennial Congress* Hyderabad (India) 2019, *Workshop on Seed Health Methods using PCR, ELISA, Dilution Plating and Indexing Methods* Bangalore (India) 2018, *Annual Meeting* Sapporo (Japan) 2018, *Triennial Congress* Tallinn (Estonia) 2016. **Publications** *Seed Science and Technology* (3 a year); *Seed Testing International – ISTA News Bulletin* (2 a year); *ISTA International Rules for Seed Testing* (annual). Technical handbooks; glossaries; directories; surveys; proceedings of symposia and workshops.
Members 'Designated Members' persons and/or laboratories engaged in the science or practice of seed testing or in the technical control of such activities, who are designated by their respective Designated Authority and admitted by the Association to participate in the affairs of the Association. 'Members' persons or seed laboratories who/which support the Association and its objectives and are admitted by the Association. 'Accredited Laboratories' member laboratories accredited by the Executive Committee according to Accreditation Standards approved in the Articles and fulfilling the requirements given in these standards. As of Dec 2012, worldwide membership comprised 202 laboratories and 287 individuals in 79 countries and territories:
Albania, Argentina, Australia, Austria, Bangladesh, Belgium, Bolivia, Bosnia-Herzegovina, Botswana, Brazil, Brunei Darussalam, Bulgaria, Canada, Chile, China, Colombia, Croatia, Cyprus, Czechia, Denmark, Egypt, Estonia, Finland, France, Germany, Ghana, Greece, Hungary, India, Indonesia, Iran Islamic Rep, Iraq, Ireland, Israel, Italy, Japan, Kenya, Korea Rep, Kyrgyzstan, Latvia, Lebanon, Lithuania, Luxembourg, Malawi, Mexico, Moldova, Nepal, Netherlands, New Zealand, Norway, Pakistan, Paraguay, Philippines, Poland, Portugal, Romania, Russia, Serbia, Slovakia, Slovenia, South Africa, Spain, Sri Lanka, Sweden, Switzerland, Syrian AR, Taiwan, Tajikistan, Tanzania UR, Thailand, Tunisia, Türkiye, Uganda, UK, Ukraine, Uruguay, USA, Zambia, Zimbabwe.
IGO Relations Cooperates with: *Bioversity International (#03262); European and Mediterranean Plant Protection Organization (EPPO, #07773); FAO (#09260); International Center for Agricultural Research in the Dry Areas (ICARDA, #12466); International Crops Research Institute for the Semi-Arid Tropics (ICRISAT, #13116); International Rice Research Institute (IRRI, #14754); OECD (#17693); Union internationale pour la protection des obtentions végétales (UPOV, #20436); World Trade Organization (WTO, #21864).* **NGO Relations** Member of: *International Association of Botanical and Mycological Societies (IABMS, #11730); International Union of Biological Sciences (IUBS, #15760).* Cooperates with: *International Organization for Standardization (ISO, #14473).* [2020.02.19/XB2452/**B***]

♦ International Seismological Association (inactive)

♦ International Seismological Centre (ISC) 14830

Centre séismologique international – Centro Internacional de Sismologia – Internationales Seismologisches Zentrum – Mezdunarodnyj Sejsmologiceskij Centr
Dir Pipers Lane, Thatcham, RG19 4NS, UK. T. +441635861022. Fax +441635872351. E-mail: admin@isc.ac.uk.
URL: http://www.isc.ac.uk/
History 1 Jan 1964. Reconstituted 1 Nov 1970. Amendments adopted at Governing Council meetings: 30-31 Jul 1971, Moscow (USSR); 23-24 Aug 1973, Lima (Peru); 21 Aug 1987, Vancouver (Canada); 9 Jan 1994, Wellington (New Zealand); 20 Aug 2001, Hanoi (Vietnam); Gothenburg (Sweden) 2013. Registration: Scotland; Charity Commission, No/ID: 1188971, Start date: 8 Apr 2020, England and Wales. **Aims** Collect, analyse and publish data on terrestrial seismic events for advancement of scientific knowledge of the Earth's structure and regional seismicity. **Structure** Governing Council (meets every 2 years); Executive Committee (meets annually). **Languages** English. **Staff** 15.00 FTE, paid. **Finance** Members' dues: 1 to 80 units (1 unit: pounds2,005 in 2015). Publications; contracts. Budget: pounds800,000. **Activities** Knowledge management/information dissemination. **Events** *Biennial Governing Council Meeting* 2021, *Biennial Governing Council Meeting* 2020, *Biennial Governing Council Meeting* Montréal, QC (Canada) 2019, *Biennial Governing Council Meeting* Kobe (Japan) 2017, *Biennial Governing Council Meeting* Prague (Czech Rep) 2015. **Publications** *Summary of the Bulletin of the ISC* (2 a year). Global and regional maps of seismicity (occasional). Annual CD-ROM of Bulletin data.
Members National academies and agencies in 48 countries and territories:
Algeria, Argentina, Australia, Austria, Belarus, Belgium, Brazil, Canada, Chile, China, Cyprus, Czechia, Denmark, Egypt, Finland, France, Germany, Greece, Hungary, Iceland, India, Iraq, Ireland, Israel, Italy, Jamaica, Japan, Jordan, Korea Rep, Mexico, Netherlands, New Zealand, Norway, Poland, Portugal, Puerto Rico, Romania, Russia, Slovenia, South Africa, Spain, Sweden, Switzerland, Taiwan, Trinidad-Tobago, Türkiye, UK, USA.
Consultative Status Consultative status granted from: *UNESCO (#20322)* (Consultative Status). [2022/XC4603/**C**]

♦ International Self-Care Foundation (internationally oriented national body)

♦ International Self-Monitoring Association of Oral Anticoagulated Patients (ISMAAP) 14831

Address not obtained.
URL: http://www.ismaap.org/
History Jul 2002, Geneva (Switzerland). **Aims** Provide continuing support for patients on oral anticoagulation therapy; motivate them to carry out self-monitoring to reduce potential risks of thrombosis and haemorrhage. **Structure** Executive Committee, comprising President, Vice-President, Treasurer and Secretary. **Languages** English, German. **Activities** Organizes annual Patient/Physician Conference on oral anticoagulant therapy. **Events** *International conference / Conference* Brussels (Belgium) 2009. **Publications** *Anticoagulation News.*
Members National organizations in 10 countries:
Austria, Belgium, Denmark, France, Germany, Italy, Netherlands, Spain, Switzerland, UK.
NGO Relations Associate member of: *World Heart Federation (WHF, #21562).* Member of: *The NCD Alliance (NCDA, #16963).* [2014/XJ4020/**D**]

♦ International Self-Service Organization (no recent information)
♦ International Seminar on Apterygota (meeting series)
♦ International Seminar Earthworks in Europe (meeting series)

♦ International Seminar on Religious Education and Values (ISREV) . 14832

Gen Sec York St John Univ, Lord Mayor's Walk, York, YO31 7EX, UK. T. +441392264983. E-mail: isrevmailing@gmail.com.
URL: http://isrev.org.uk/
History 1978. Former names and other names: *International Standing Seminar on Religious Education and Value Potential* – former. Registration: Charity Commission, No/ID: 1102701, England and Wales. **Aims** Promote high quality research into religious education whether in public or private education systems or within and between religious communities; encourage younger and/or emerging religious educators to undertake such research and disseminate the results; influence the development of religious education in public or private education systems and in religious communities. **Structure** Trustees; Executive Committee. **Activities** Events/meetings. **Events** *International Seminar on Religious Education and Values* 2023, *Seminar* Gothenburg (Sweden) 2021. **Members** Individuals (nearly 300). Membership countries not specified. [2020/AA0670/cv/**F**]

♦ International Seminar on Safety and Security of Autonomous Vessels (meeting series)
♦ International Seminars on Training for Nonviolent Action / see International Nonviolent Initiatives

♦ International Seminar on Urban Form (ISUF) 14833

Séminaire international de la forme urbaine – Seminario Internazionale de la Forma Urbana
SG School of Architecture and Planning, Univ of Auckland, Level 2, Bldg 421, 26 Symonds St, Auckland, New Zealand.
URL: http://www.urbanform.org/
History 1996. **Aims** Promote and develop urban morphology; encourage the dissemination of research on urban form. **Structure** Council (meets once a year), comprising President, Secretary-General, Treasurer, Editor, 6 ordinary members and 2 co-opted members. **Languages** English. **Finance** Proceeds from publications and organizing venues. **Activities** Organizes conferences, seminars and meetings. **Events** *Annual Seminar* Krakow (Poland) / Lódz (Poland) 2022, *Annual Seminar* Rome (Italy) 2015, *Annual Seminar* Porto (Portugal) 2014, *Annual Seminar / Seminar* Brisbane, QLD (Australia) 2013, *Annual Seminar / Seminar* Delft (Netherlands) 2012. **Publications** *Urban Morphology* (2 a year) – journal. [2013/XM1849/c/**F**]

♦ International Semiotics Institute, Imatra (internationally oriented national body)
♦ International Sendo-Ryu Karatedo Federation (internationally oriented national body)
♦ International Senior Citizens Association (inactive)
♦ International Senior Lawyers Project (internationally oriented national body)

♦ International Sentinel Node Society (ISNS) 14834

Contact c/o Office of Dr Faries, Wayne Cancer Inst, 2200 Santa Monica Blvd, Santa Monica CA 90404, USA. T. +1310829-8781.
Treas address not obtained.
Pres address not obtained.
URL: http://isns.online/isns/
History Set up 18 Nov 2002, Yokohama (Japan). **Aims** Encourage collaboration and cooperation among surgeons, pathologists and nuclear medicine physicians in researching the effects of sentinel node *surgery* and *lymphatic* mapping techniques. **Structure** Council. Officers: President; President-Elect; Secretary; Treasurer; Immediate Past President; 2 Past Presidents. **Events** *Exploring the Role of the Sentinel Node in Cancer Care* Houston, TX (USA) 2020, *Biennial Congress* Tokyo (Japan) 2018, *Biennial Congress* Milan (Italy) 2016, *Biennial Congress* San Francisco, CA (USA) 2013, *Biennial Congress* Yokohama (Japan) 2010. **Publications** *ISNS Sentinel.*
Members in 32 countries and territories:
Argentina, Australia, Belgium, Brazil, Canada, Chile, Crete, Denmark, Finland, France, Germany, Hungary, Indonesia, Israel, Italy, Japan, Korea Rep, Lebanon, Montenegro, Netherlands, Poland, Portugal, Puerto Rico, Saudi Arabia, Slovenia, Spain, Sweden, Switzerland, Taiwan, Thailand, UK, USA. [2018/XM2339/**D**]

♦ International Sepak Takraw Federation / see International Sepaktakraw Federation (#14835)

♦ International Sepaktakraw Federation (ISTAF) 14835

SG 63 Market Street No 04-05, Bank of Singapore Ctr, Singapore 048942, Singapore. T. +6565365441. E-mail: sales@asvworld.com – eo@perses.org.
Pres address not obtained.
URL: http://www.sepaktakraw.org/
History 1988. Founded by *Asian Sepak Takraw Federation (ASTAF, inactive).* Former names and other names: *International Sepak Takraw Federation* – alias. **Aims** Control, manage and develop the *sport* of sepaktakraw worldwide. **Structure** Council. **Activities** Sporting activities. **Events** *Congress* Bangkok (Thailand) 2014.
Members Associations and federations in 22 countries:
Australia, Brunei Darussalam, Canada, China, Finland, France, Germany, India, Indonesia, Japan, Korea Rep, Laos, Malaysia, Myanmar, Philippines, Puerto Rico, Singapore, Sri Lanka, Thailand, UK, USA, Vietnam.
NGO Relations Member of (2): *Alliance of Independent recognised Members of Sport (AIMS, #00690); Olympic Movement (#17719).* Recognized by: *International Olympic Committee (IOC, #14408).* [2019/XD6335/**D**]

♦ International Sepsis Forum (ISF) 14836

Contact 7024 Palmetto Pines Ln, Land O' Lakes FL 34637, USA. T. +18132359813. Fax +18132359014. E-mail: elaine@sepsisforum.org.
URL: http://www.sepsisforum.org/
History Mar 1997. US Registered Charity. **Aims** Define severe sepsis and septic shock; create management guidelines for their treatment. **Structure** Council, including Chair. Executive Director. **Languages** English. **Staff** 1.00 FTE, paid. **Finance** Grants; donations. **Activities** Organizes colloquia and symposia. **Events** *Annual Symposium* Bangkok (Thailand) 2018, *Annual Symposium* Paris (France) 2017, *Annual Symposium* Agra (India) 2016, *Annual Symposium* Paris (France) 2016, *Annual Symposium* Paris (France) 2014. **Publications** *ISF Newsletter.* **NGO Relations** Founding member of: *Global Sepsis Alliance (GSA, #10590).* [2012.06.01/XJ4698/**F**]

♦ International Sericultural Commission (ISC) 14837

Commission séricicole internationale (CSI) – Comisión Sericicola Internacional (CSI) – Internationale Seidenbau Kommission (ISK)
SG Central Silk Board Complex, BTM Layout, Madiwala, Bangalore, Karnataka 560068, Bangalore KARNATAKA 560068, India. T. +918026680162 – +918026282189. Fax +918026681511. E-mail: iscbangalore@inserco.in.
URL: http://www.inserco.org/

History 11 Jun 1948, Alès (France). Founded by resolution of 7th International Congress of Sericulture. Present Commission instituted as an intergovernmental organization by international convention of 1 Jul 1957, Paris (France). Registered with United Nations vide Reg No 10418. Former names and other names: *Permanent Commission of the International Sericultural Congresses* – former; *Commission permanente des congrès séricoles internationaux* – former. Registration: Start date: 1 Feb 1962, France. **Aims** Encourage and promote development and improvement in technical, scientific and economic fields of all activities dealing with *silkworm* rearing in general, including *moriculture*, grainage, sericulture and raw silk reeling; develop and coordinate work making the silkworm and related *insects* a biological model. **Structure** Conference (every 3 years); Executive Committee (meets twice a year); Secretariat, headed by Secretary-General. Technical meetings and congresses open; Executive Committees and Conferences open to country delegates. **Languages** English, French. **Staff** 2.50 FTE, paid. **Finance** Sources: donations; members' dues; sale of publications. **Activities** Awards/prizes/competitions; capacity building; events/meetings; knowledge management/information dissemination; networking/liaising; politics/policy/regulatory; projects/programmes; research and development. **Events** *International Congress on Sericulture and Silk Industry* Cluj-Napoca (Romania) 2022, *International Congress on Sericulture and Silk Industry* Tsukuba (Japan) 2019, *International Congress on Sericulture and Silk Industry* Bangkok (Thailand) 2016, *International Congress on Sericulture and Silk Industry* Bangalore (India) 2014, *Triennial Congress* Chiang Mai (Thailand) 2011. **Publications** *Sericologia: Revue des vers à soie/Journal of Silkworms* (4 a year) – scientific journal; *ISC Bulletin* (periodical). Proceedings of congresses, conferences and seminars; books. Information Services: Documentation and Information Centre (1,500 volumes; 20,000 index references).

Members Governments of 21 countries:
Afghanistan, Bangladesh, Brazil, Egypt, France, Ghana, Greece, India, Indonesia, Iran Islamic Rep, Japan, Kenya, Korea Rep, Madagascar, Nepal, Romania, Syrian AR, Thailand, Tunisia, Uganda, Uzbekistan.
Individuals in 26 countries:
Australia, Bulgaria, Canada, China, Czechia, France, Germany, Greece, India, Indonesia, Israel, Italy, Japan, Korea Rep, Lebanon, Peru, Philippines, South Africa, Switzerland, Syrian AR, Taiwan, Thailand, Ukraine, USA, Vietnam, Zimbabwe.

IGO Relations Member of (1): *Intergovernmental Organizations Conference (IGO Conference, #11498).* Relationship agreement with: *African-Asian Rural Development Organization (AARDO, #00203); FAO (#09260); South Asian Association for Regional Cooperation (SAARC, #19721).* Official relations with: *European Union (EU, #08967); ILO (#11123); International Bank for Reconstruction and Development (IBRD, #12317); International Trade Centre (ITC, #15703);* Ministry of External Affairs, India; *OECD (#17693); UNESCO (#20322); United Nations Economic and Social Commission for Asia and the Pacific (ESCAP, #20557).*
[2021.02.25/XC2455/**C***]

♦ International Serum Industry Association (ISIA) 14838

CEO PO Box 926, McHenry MD 21541, USA. E-mail: info@serumindustry.org.
URL: http://www.serumindustry.org/

History Founded Jun 2006. **Aims** Establish, promote and assure compliance with uncompromised standards of excellence and ethics in the business practices of the global animal serum and animal derived products supply industry. **Structure** Board of Directors. **Activities** Advocacy/lobbying/activism; events/meetings; standards/guidelines; training/education. **Events** *Annual Meeting* Denver, CO (USA) 2021, *Annual Meeting* Brisbane, QLD (Australia) 2020, *Annual Meeting* Lisbon (Portugal) 2019. **Members** Companies in 17 countries. Membership countries not specified. **IGO Relations** Governments. [2020.03.11/XM8363/t/**C**]

♦ International Service for the Acquisition of Agri-biotech Applications (ISAAA) 14839

AmeriCenter c/o Global Development, 417 Bradfield Hall, Cornell Univ, Ithaca NY 14853, USA. T. +16072551724. Fax +16072551215. E-mail: americenter@isaaa.org – info@isaaa.org.
SEAsiaCenter Global Coordinator, c/o IRRI, DAPO Box 7777, Manila, Philippines. T. +6328450563 – +6328450569 – +6328450573. Fax +6328450606. E-mail: seasiacenter@isaaa.org.
AfriCenter c/o CIP/ILRI, PO Box 25171, Nairobi, Kenya. T. +2542632054 – +2542632151. Fax +2542631599 – +2542631005. E-mail: africenter@isaaa.org.
URL: http://www.isaaa.org/

History 1 Sep 1991. **Aims** Contribute to poverty alleviation by increasing *crop productivity* and income generation, particularly for resource-poor farmers; bring about a safer environment and more sustainable agricultural development; facilitate acquisition and transfer of agricultural *biotechnology* applications – particularly proprietary technology from the private sector – from industrial countries for the benefit of *developing countries.* **Structure** International Board of Directors, comprising 12 members including Chair, Vice-Chair/Treasurer and Secretary. Regional centres (5): *'AmeriCenter'* for North America, at Cornell University, USA; *'EuroCentre'* at John Innes Centre, UK; *'AsiaCenter'* for the Asian Pacific Rim, in Japan; *'AfriCenter'* at CIP/ILRI, Nairobi (Kenya); *'SEAsiaCenter'* in the Philippines. A *'LatiCenter'* for Latin America is planned. **Languages** English, French, German, Spanish. **Staff** 6.00 FTE, paid. **Finance** Fixed-term commitments through a donor support group composed of public and private sector institutions, including foundations, government agencies, internationally oriented private bodies and companies, including: *DANIDA; Deutsche Gesellschaft für Technische Zusammenarbeit (GTZ, inactive); Hitachi Foundation; International Development Research Centre (IDRC, #13162); McKnight Foundation; The Rockefeller Foundation (#18966); Swedish International Development Cooperation Agency (Sida); Swiss Agency for Development and Cooperation (SDC); United States Agency for International Development (USAID).* **Activities** Pilot programme, focused on Argentina, Brazil, Costa Rica, Egypt, Kenya, Indonesia, Malaysia, Mexico, Philippines, Thailand, Vietnam and Zimbabwe, employs a 5-step strategy to: assist developing countries to identify biotechnology needs and priorities and to assess potential socio-economic impact; monitor and evaluate availability of appropriate proprietary applications in industrialized countries; provide 'honest broker' services matching needs and appropriate proprietary technology; mobilize funding from donor agencies to implement proposals; advise developing countries on safe and responsible testing of recombinant products and assist in implementing regulatory procedures (biosafety, IPR, food safety), in planning commercialization activities and in assessing impact of technology. **Events** *Meeting on worldwide agricultural production and our lives* Sapporo (Japan) 2009, *Biosafety workshop* Bogor (Indonesia) 1993, *Biosafety workshop* Costa Rica 1992. **Publications** *ISAAA Briefs* – series. *Biosafety for Sustainable Agriculture: sharing biotechnology regulatory experiences of the western hemisphere* (1994). Annual Report. Occasional papers.

Members Organizations and/or individuals in 79 countries and territories:
Algeria, Argentina, Australia, Austria, Bahamas, Bangladesh, Barbados, Belgium, Benin, Bolivia, Brazil, Bulgaria, Burkina Faso, Burundi, Cameroon, Canada, Cayman Is, Chile, China, Colombia, Costa Rica, Côte d'Ivoire, Cuba, Czechia, Denmark, Ecuador, Egypt, Finland, France, Gabon, Germany, Ghana, Honduras, Hong Kong, Hungary, India, Indonesia, Ireland, Israel, Italy, Japan, Kenya, Korea Rep, Madagascar, Malawi, Malaysia, Mauritius, Mexico, Morocco, Nepal, Netherlands, New Zealand, Nigeria, Norway, Pakistan, Paraguay, Peru, Philippines, Poland, Portugal, Russia, Senegal, Seychelles, Singapore, South Africa, Spain, Sri Lanka, Sweden, Switzerland, Syrian AR, Taiwan, Thailand, Uganda, UK, Uruguay, USA, Venezuela, Vietnam, Zimbabwe.

NGO Relations Instrumental in setting up: *Papaya Biotechnology Network of Southeast Asia (PBNSEA, no recent information).* [2013/XF5029/**F**]

- ♦ International Service Agencies / see Global Impact
- ♦ International Service Association for Health / see Global Health Action

♦ International Service for Geomagnetic Indices (ISGI) 14840

Service international des indices géomagnétiques

Dir EOST, 5 rue René Descartes, 67084 Strasbourg CEDEX, France. T. +33368850081. Fax +33368850125. E-mail: isgi@unistra.fr.
URL: http://isgi.unistra.fr/

History Founded 1906, as *Central Bureau for Terrestrial Magnetism*, for the calculation of the "International Magnetic Character". Hosted by the *'Koninklijk Nederlands Meteorologisch Instituut'*, De Bilt (Netherlands), until 1987. Moved to France following decision during IUGG meeting, 1987, Vancouver BC (Canada), and hosted by *'Institut de Physique du Globe de Paris'.* Moved, 1990, to *'Centre d'étude des environnements terrestres et planétaires'*, Saint-Maur-des-Fossés (France), which was replaced in 2009 by *'Laboratoire atmosphères, milieux, observations spatiales (LATMOS)'*, Guyancourt (France). Moved to *'EOST'*, 2015. **Aims** Derive, publish and disseminate indices of *International Association of Geomagnetism and Aeronomy (IAGA).* **Structure** Executive Committee; Advisory Board. **Languages** English, French. **Staff** 1.00 FTE, paid. **Finance** Support from French national centres for space (CNES) and scientific research (CNRS). **Activities** Knowledge management/information dissemination; research/documentation. **Publications** *Monthly Bulletin of ISGI* (12 a year). *IAGA Bulletin No 32* (annual).

Members Work carried out by institutes of 6 countries:
Denmark, France, Germany, Japan, Russia, Spain.

NGO Relations A service of: *International Association of Geomagnetism and Aeronomy (IAGA, #11916).* Member of: *ISC World Data System (ISC-WDS, #16024).* [2019.12.11/XF4063/**F**]

♦ International Service for Human Rights (ISHR) 14841

Service international pour les droits de l'homme (SIDH) – Servicio Internacional para los Derechos Humanos (SIDH)

Dir Rue de Varembé 1, 5th Fl, PO Box 16, 1211 Geneva 20 CIC, Switzerland. T. +41229197100. Fax +41229197125. E-mail: information@ishr.ch.
New York Office 777 UN Plaza, New York NY 10017, USA. T. +12124902199. Fax +12124901396. E-mail: ishr@ishrny.org.
URL: http://www.ishr.ch/

History Dec 1984, Geneva (Switzerland). Founded by members of various human rights organizations in Geneva, as an informal network of persons involved in human rights and development work. Registration: 501c3, USA. **Aims** Promote the development, strengthening, effective use and implementation of international and regional standards and mechanisms for protection and promotion of human rights. Provide: analytical and practical information on UN human rights mechanisms; training on how to use international and regional norms and procedures; contributions to standard-setting; logistical support to enable human rights defenders worldwide to take full advantage of international human rights law and procedures. **Structure** General Meeting; Board. **Languages** English, French. **Staff** 16.00 FTE, paid. 6-8 voluntary interns. **Finance** Sources: grants from governments, foundations and non-government development agencies, both religious and secular. Budget (annual): about Swiss Fr 2 million. **Activities** Knowledge management/information dissemination; training/education; guidance/assistance/consulting. **Events** *General Assembly* Geneva (Switzerland) 1995, *Meeting* Geneva (Switzerland) 1989, *Consultation on Timor* Geneva (Switzerland) 1987. **Publications** *Human Rights Monitor* (4 a year). Reports. **Members** Membership countries not specified. **Consultative Status** Consultative status granted from: *African Commission on Human and Peoples' Rights (ACHPR, #00255)* (Observer); *ECOSOC (#05331)* (Special). **IGO Relations** Accredited by (2): *OAS (#17629); Organisation internationale de la Francophonie (OIF, #17809).* **NGO Relations** Observer status with (3): *International Committee of the Red Cross (ICRC, #12799); International Federation of Red Cross and Red Crescent Societies (#13526); International Red Cross and Red Crescent Movement (#14707).* Member of (5): *Coalition for an Effective African Court on Human and Peoples' Rights (African Court Coalition, #04055); Committee of NGOs on Human Rights, Geneva (#04275); Conference of Non-Governmental Organizations in Consultative Relationship with the United Nations (CONGO, #04635); Fédération des Institutions Internationales établies à Genève (FIIG, #09599); NGO Committee on the Status of Women, Geneva (#17117).* Cooperates with (1): *ILGA World (International Lesbian, Gay, Bisexual, Trans and Intersex Association, #11120).* Supports (1): *West African Human Rights Defenders' Network (WAHRDN, #20882).* [2021/XF0356/v/**F**]

- ♦ International Service Innovation Design Association (unconfirmed)

♦ International Service Logistics Association (ISLA) 14842

Contact PO Box 75 04 59, 81334 Munich, Germany. T. +4989749826960. Fax +4989749826696. E-mail: isla@servicelogistics.info.
Street Address Rosenheimer Platz 4, 81669 Munich, Germany.
URL: https://www.servicelogistics.info/

History Nov 2003. Registration: No/ID: VR 18534, Start date: 12 Jul 2004, Germany. **Aims** Act as a networking and training platform for highly skilled and executive personnel in the area of aftersales service, customer support and spare parts logistics. **Structure** General Meeting; Executive Board. **Events** *Service Leaders Summit* Berlin (Germany) 2020, *European Conference on Customer Service and Service Logistics* Rotterdam (Netherlands) 2019, *European Conference on Aftersales Service and Spare Parts Logistics* Vienna (Austria) 2018, *European Conference on Aftersales Service and Spare Parts Logistics* Hamburg (Germany) 2017, *European Conference on Aftersales Service and Spare Parts Logistics* Düsseldorf (Germany) 2016. **Members** Companies. Membership countries not specified. [2020/AA0534/**C**]

- ♦ International Service for Peace (internationally oriented national body)
- ♦ International Services for the Blind / see World Services for the Blind
- ♦ International Service of the Society of Friends (inactive)
- ♦ International Service Volunteers Association / see AVSI Foundation
- ♦ International Shade Tree Conference / see International Society of Arboriculture (#14936)

♦ International Shakespeare Association (ISA) 14843

Exec Sec/Treas c/o The Shakespeare Centre, Henley Street, Stratford-upon-Avon, CV37 6QW, UK. T. +441789201847. Fax +441789296083. E-mail: office@internationalshakespeare.org.uk.
URL: https://internationalshakespeare.org.uk/

History 1974. Registration: Charity Commission, No/ID: 1160312, England and Wales. **Aims** Advance the education of the public by furthering the study of Shakespeare's life and work. **Structure** Executive Committee. **Finance** Sources: members' dues. **Events** *World Shakespeare Congress* Singapore (Singapore) 2021, *World Shakespeare Congress* Stratford-upon-Avon (UK) / London (UK) 2016, *World Shakespeare Congress* Prague (Czech Rep) 2011, *Meeting* Vienna (Austria) 2008, *World Shakespeare Congress* Brisbane, QLD (Australia) 2006. **Publications** *ISA Newsletter.* Occasional papers; conference proceedings.

Members Individual and corporate membership. Individuals in 32 countries:
Australia, Austria, Bangladesh, Belgium, Brazil, Bulgaria, Canada, China, Czechia, Finland, France, Georgia, Germany, Hungary, India, Israel, Italy, Japan, Korea Rep, Netherlands, New Zealand, Poland, Romania, Russia, South Africa, Spain, Sweden, Switzerland, Tunisia, UK, Ukraine, USA. [2021/XE0730/**E**]

- ♦ International Shared Decision Making Conference (meeting series)
- ♦ International Shared Decision Making Society (unconfirmed)

♦ International Shari'ah Council of the AAOIFI 14844

Dir c/o AAOIFI, AL Nakheel Tower, 10Th Fl Off 1001, Building 1074, Road 3622, Manama 436, Bahrain.

History by *Accounting and Auditing Organization for Islamic Financial Institutions (AAOIFI, #00062).* Also referred to as *Islamic Sharia Council* and as *Sharia Council.* **Aims** Supervise and consider proposals made by *Islamic* banking or financial institutions. **Structure** Officers: Chairman; Vice-Chairman. Sub-Committees (3).

Members Individuals (8) in 7 countries:
Egypt, Kuwait, Malaysia, Pakistan, Qatar, Saudi Arabia, Sudan.

IGO Relations Located at: *International Islamic Fiqh Academy (IIFA, #13960).* [2018.06.27/XE2396/**E**]

- ♦ International Shark Class Association (see: #21760)

♦ International Sheep Dog Society 14845

Société internationale du chien de berger

Chief Exec Clifton House, 4a Goldington Road, Bedford, MK40 3NF, UK. T. +441234352672. Fax +441234348214. E-mail: office@isds.org.uk.
URL: http://www.isds.org.uk/

History Founded 1906. Registered UK Charity: 209009. **Activities** Organizes UK, Irish and World Sheep Dog Trials. **Publications** *International Sheepdog News* (6 a year). *The Stud Book – Dog Registration.*

Members Individuals (6,000). Members (" indicates organizational member too) in 20 countries:
Australia, Austria (*), Belgium, Canada, Czechia, Denmark, France, Germany, Ireland, Italy, Japan, Netherlands, New Zealand, Norway, Portugal, South Africa, Spain, Sweden, UK, USA. [2013.11.20/XD8064/**D**]

♦ International Sheep Veterinary Association (ISVA) 14846

Sec Dalvanie Cottage, 2 Douglas Street, Kirriemuir, DD8 4HY, UK. T. +441575572643.
URL: http://www.intsheepvetassoc.org/

Aims Promote and improve the sheep industry; facilitate meetings and other scientific exchanges between members and individuals. **Structure** General Meeting; Executive Committee. **Events** *International Sheep Veterinary Congress* Wollongong, NSW (Australia) 2025, *International Sheep Veterinary Congress* Seville (Spain) 2023, *International Sheep Veterinary Congress* Seville (Spain) 2022, *International Sheep Veterinary Congress* Harrogate (UK) 2017, *International Sheep Veterinary Congress* Rotorua (New Zealand) 2013. **Members** National; Private; Associate; Corporate. Membership countries not specified. [2015/XJ6261/**C**]

♦ International Shelter Conference (meeting series)

♦ International Shiatsu Network (ISN) 14847

Contact Casella postale 239, Tesserete, 6950 Capriasca TI, Switzerland.
URL: http://shiatsunetwork.org/

Aims Be a platform for the exchange of information and cooperation between national federations all over the world.
Members Full in 4 countries:
France, Germany, Italy, Switzerland.
NGO Relations Member of: *Association of Natural Medicine in Europe (ANME).* [2018/XM7764/**F**]

♦ International Shinto Foundation (internationally oriented national body)
♦ International Shinto Studies Association (internationally oriented national body)
♦ International Ship Electrical and Engineering Service Association / see International Ship Engineering Service Association (#14848)
♦ International Ship Electric Service Association / see International Ship Engineering Service Association (#14848)

♦ International Ship Engineering Service Association (ISES) 14848

SG Calle Maria Auxiliadora 22, 4-B, 10002 Caceres, Badajoz, Spain. T. +34627919990. E-mail: secretariat@isesassociation.com.
Registered Office Kemp House, 152-160 City Road, London, EC1V 2NX, UK.
URL: http://www.isesassociation.com/

History 1963, Stockholm (Sweden). Modified bye-laws approved at Annual General Meeting: 13 May 1990; 6 May 1993. Former names and other names: *International Ship Electric Service Association (ISES)* – former (1963 to 1 Mar 1996); *International Ship Electrical and Engineering Service Association (ISES)* – former (1 Mar 1996 to 3 Jun 2016). Registration: UK. **Aims** Unite a quality worldwide service network of companies specializing in repair, service or manufacture of all forms of *marine* related equipment. **Structure** General Meeting (annual); Board. **Languages** English. **Staff** 2.00 FTE, paid. **Finance** Sources: members' dues. **Activities** Guidance/assistance/consulting; knowledge management/information dissemination. **Events** *Annual General Meeting* Athens (Greece) 2022, *Annual General Meeting* Athens (Greece) 2019, *Annual General Meeting* Mumbai (India) 2018, *Annual General Meeting* Singapore (Singapore) 2017, *Annual General Meeting* Rotterdam (Netherlands) 2015. **Publications** *ISES Marine Service Guide* (2 a year); *Marine Service Guide* (annual).
Members Full: marine electrical, electronics, mechanical and engineering companies in 32 countries:
Argentina, Australia, Belgium, Brazil, Canada, China, Colombia, Croatia, Cyprus, France, Germany, Gibraltar, Greece, India, Italy, Japan, Korea Rep, Lithuania, Mexico, Netherlands, Nigeria, Panama, Poland, Romania, Singapore, South Africa, Spain, Sweden, Türkiye, UK, USA, Venezuela. [2023.02.15/XC2456/**C**]

♦ International Ship Managers' Association / see InterManager (#11520)
♦ International Ship Masters' Association (internationally oriented national body)
♦ International Ship Operators Meeting / see International Research Ship Operators (#14741)
♦ International Shipowners' Association (inactive)
♦ International Shipping Conference / see International Chamber of Shipping (#12535)
♦ International Shipping Federation (inactive)

♦ International Ship Recycling Association (ISRA) 14849

SG Scheepmakershaven 59, 3011 VD Rotterdam, Netherlands. E-mail: secretariat@isranetwork.com – natasja.martin@isranetwork.com.
Dir address not obtained.
URL: http://www.isranetwork.com/

History Oct 2007, The Hague (Netherlands). Registration: EU Transparency Register, No/ID: 251468537900-82. **Aims** Promote and facilitate environmentally sound and safe recycling of ships. **Structure** General Meeting; Board. [2020/XM7483/**C**]

♦ International Ship Stability Workshop (meeting series)
♦ International Ship Suppliers Association / see International Ship Suppliers and Services Association (#14850)

♦ International Ship Suppliers and Services Association (ISSA) 14850

Association international d'approvisionneurs de navires – Asociación Internacional de Proveedores de Efectos Navales

Pres The Baltic Exchange, St Mary Axe, London, EC3A 8BH EC3A 8BH, UK. T. +442076266236. Fax +441843609264. E-mail: secretariat@shipsupply.org.
URL: http://www.shipsupply.org/

History 1955. Registered 1963 at the Court of Registry, The Hague (Netherlands), as *International Ship Suppliers Association.* Sometimes referred to unofficially in French as *Association international des approvisionneurs de navires.* **Aims** Promote the economic interests of ship suppliers; promote contacts with and discussion among organizations of ship suppliers concerning questions of common interest; establish contact on an international level with organizations of *shipowners* concerning their relationship with ship suppliers; represent ship suppliers on an international level. **Structure** General Assembly (annual); Board; Executive Committee. Committees include: *European Ship Suppliers Organization (OCEAN, #08478).* **Languages** English. **Staff** 1.00 FTE, paid. **Finance** Sources: members' dues. Other sources: charges for entry in annual Register of Members; catalogue sales; advertising. **Activities** Networking/liaising. **Events** *Annual General Assembly* Busan (Korea Rep) 2019, *Annual General Assembly* Istanbul (Turkey) 2018, *Annual General Assembly* Athens (Greece) 2017, *Annual General Assembly* Dubai (United Arab Emirates) 2016, *Annual General Assembly* Singapore (Singapore) 2015. **Publications** *The Ship Supplier. ISSA Ship Stores Catalogue.* Conditions of sale; code of ethics.
Members National associations in 38 countries:
Argentina, Australia, Belgium, Brazil, Canada, Chile, China, Côte d'Ivoire, Cyprus, Denmark, Estonia, Finland, France, Germany, Greece, Italy, Japan, Kenya, Latvia, Malta, Netherlands, New Zealand, Panama, Peru, Philippines, Poland, Portugal, Singapore, South Africa, Spain, Sri Lanka, Sweden, Türkiye, UK, Ukraine, United Arab Emirates, Uruguay, USA.
Associated members in 49 countries and territories:
Bahrain, Bangladesh, Benin, Cameroon, China, Colombia, Congo DR, Ecuador, Egypt, Fiji, Gabon, Georgia, Ghana, Gibraltar, Hong Kong, India, Indonesia, Ireland, Israel, Jordan, Kuwait, Lithuania, Malaysia, Mauritius, Mexico, Morocco, Nigeria, Oman, Pakistan, Puerto Rico, Qatar, Romania, Russia, Saudi Arabia, Senegal, Serbia, Slovenia, Sudan, Switzerland, Syrian AR, Taiwan, Thailand, Togo, Trinidad-Tobago, Tunisia, Uruguay, Venezuela, Vietnam, Yemen.
Consultative Status Consultative status granted from: *ECOSOC (#05331)* (Ros C); *UNCTAD (#20285)* (Special Category); *International Maritime Organization (IMO, #14102).* **IGO Relations** *United Nations Commission on International Trade Law (UNCITRAL, #20531).* **NGO Relations** *Federation of National Associations of Shipbrokers and Agents (FONASBA, #09694); InterManager (#11520).* [2018.06.01/XC4523/**C**]

♦ International Shock Wave Institute (ISWI) 14851

Main Office Dept of Aerospace Engineering, Nagoya Univ, Furo-cho, Chikusa-ku, Nagoya AICHI, 464-8603 Japan. Fax +81527894402. E-mail: office@iswi.jp.
URL: http://www.iswi.jp/

History 2 Mar 2005, following 24th International Symposium on Shock Wave, 2004, Beijing (China). Former names and other names: *International Association for Shock Wave Research* – alias. Registration: Start date: 24 May 2013, Japan. **Aims** Promote international and interdisciplinary collaboration in all areas of shock wave research; facilitate liaison with other organizations with similar interests and activities. **Structure** General Committee. Executive Committee, comprising President, Vice-President, Treasurer and Webmaster. **Finance** Members' dues. **Activities** Organizes conferences, including *International Symposium on Shock Wave (ISSW); International Shock Interaction Symposium (ISIS).* Grants awards. **Events** *International Symposium on Shock Waves* Daegu (Korea Rep) 2023, *International Symposium on Shock Waves* Brisbane, QLD (Australia) 2021, *International Symposium on Shock Waves* Singapore (Singapore) 2019, *Biennial International Symposium on Shock Waves* Nagoya (Japan) 2017, *Biennial International Symposium on Shock Waves* Tel Aviv (Israel) 2015. **Publications** *Shock Waves* – journal. [2021/XM2061/j/**E**]

♦ International Shoe and Leather Workers' Federation (inactive)
♦ International Shoe-Makers Union (inactive)

♦ International Shooting Sport Federation (ISSF) 14852

Fédération internationale de tir sportif – Federación Internacional de Tiro Deportivo – Internationaler Schiess-Sportverband

Pres Widenmayerstrasse 16, 80538 Munich, Germany. T. +49895443550. Fax +498954435544. E-mail: munich@issf-sports.org.
URL: http://www.issf-sports.org/

History 7 Jul 1907, Zurich (Switzerland). Founded by 8 national shooting federations. Set up following discussions, Jun 1906, Milan (Italy), during a 6-nation shooting competition, when it was agreed to draft a constitution and shooting regulations. Dissolved, 1915, during World War I but reorganized 16 Apr 1921, Paris (France). The initials *'UIT'* had already been used before that date. Activities again suspended during World War II. Reorganized in 1947, with a change from French to English as official language but continuing the use of *'UIT'* as initials. Constitution revised: Oct 1962, Cairo (Egypt); May 1970, Montreux; 15 Jul 1998, Barcelona (Spain); Mar 2000, Sydney (Australia). Former names and other names: *Union internationale des fédérations et associations nationales de tir* – former (1907); *International Union of National Federations and Associations of Shooting* – former (1907); *Union internationale de tir (UIT)* – former (16 Apr 1921); *International Shooting Union* – former (16 Apr 1921); *Unión Internacional de Tiro* – former (16 Apr 1921); *Internationale Schützenunion* – former (16 Apr 1921). Registration: Bavaria District court, No/ID: VR 10152, Start date: 5 Aug 1981, Germany, Munich. **Aims** Promote and manage development of amateur sport shooting; serve as centre for national federations and establish permanent relations among them; organize world *championships*; supervise shooting results within the framework of the Olympic Games and establish technical regulations for all branches of the sport. **Structure** General Assembly; Council; Executive Committee; Committees. Recognized Continental Confederations (5): *African Shooting Sport Federation (#00456); Asian Shooting Confederation (ASC, #01699); European Shooting Confederation (ESC, #08481); Oceania Shooting Federation (OSF, #17674); Confederación Americana de Tiro (CAT, #04439).* **Languages** English. **Finance** Sources: members' dues. **Activities** Research/documentation; sporting activities; standards/guidelines; training/education. **Events** *Biennial General Assembly* Barcelona (Spain) 1998, *Biennial General Assembly* Atlanta, GA (USA) 1996, *Biennial General Assembly* Milan (Italy) 1994, *Biennial General Assembly* Barcelona (Spain) 1992, *Biennial General Assembly* Moscow (USSR) 1990. **Publications** Rules; books; brochures; manuals.
Members National Federations (162) in 149 countries and territories:
Afghanistan, Albania, Algeria, Andorra, Angola, Argentina, Armenia, Aruba, Australia, Austria, Azerbaijan, Bahrain, Bangladesh, Barbados, Belarus, Belgium, Bhutan, Bolivia, Bosnia-Herzegovina, Brazil, Bulgaria, Cambodia, Cameroon, Canada, Cayman Is, Chile, China, Colombia, Costa Rica, Croatia, Cuba, Cyprus, Czechia, Denmark, Dominican Rep, Ecuador, Egypt, El Salvador, Estonia, Faeroe Is, Fiji, Finland, France, Georgia, Germany, Ghana, Great Britain, Greece, Guam, Guatemala, Guyana, Honduras, Hong Kong, Hungary, Iceland, India, Indonesia, Iraq, Ireland, Israel, Italy, Japan, Jordan, Kazakhstan, Kenya, Korea DPR, Korea Rep, Kosovo, Kuwait, Kyrgyzstan, Laos, Latvia, Lebanon, Libya, Liechtenstein, Lithuania, Luxembourg, Macau, Malaysia, Maldives, Malta, Mauritania, Mexico, Moldova, Monaco, Mongolia, Montenegro, Morocco, Myanmar, Namibia, Nepal, Netherlands, New Zealand, Nicaragua, Nigeria, North Macedonia, Norway, Oman, Pakistan, Palestine, Panama, Papua New Guinea, Paraguay, Peru, Philippines, Poland, Portugal, Puerto Rico, Qatar, Romania, Russia, Rwanda, Samoa, San Marino, Saudi Arabia, Senegal, Serbia, Singapore, Slovakia, Slovenia, South Africa, Spain, Sri Lanka, Sudan, Suriname, Sweden, Switzerland, Syrian AR, Taiwan, Tajikistan, Thailand, Timor-Leste, Tonga, Trinidad-Tobago, Tunisia, Türkiye, Turkmenistan, Uganda, Ukraine, United Arab Emirates, Uruguay, USA, Uzbekistan, Venezuela, Vietnam, Virgin Is USA, Yemen, Zimbabwe.
NGO Relations Member of (4): *Association of Summer Olympic International Federations (ASOIF, #02943); International Committee for Fair Play (#12769)* (Full); *International Masters Games Association (IMGA, #14117); Olympic Movement (#17719).* Recognized by: *International Olympic Committee (IOC, #14408).* [2022/XB2460/**B**]

♦ International Shooting Union / see International Shooting Sport Federation (#14852)
♦ International Shopfitting Organisation (inactive)

♦ International Short Break Association (ISBA) 14853

Pres address not obtained.
Conference Team address not obtained.
URL: http://www.isba.me/

History 1995. Founded following 1st International Short Break Conference, Thunder Bay ON (Canada). **Aims** Serve as a forum for the exchange of knowledge, courses of action and working practice with short break *care/respite*, across care provider lines; provide a chance to learn about best practice in supporting families who are caring for individuals with *disabilities* or on-going disabling conditions or impairments. **Structure** Committee. **Activities** Events/meetings; knowledge management/information dissemination. **Events** *Building Better Breaks Together* Wroclaw (Poland) 2023, *Moving respite forward* Madison, WI (USA) 2021, *Moving respite forward* Madison, WI (USA) 2020, *Opportunities and co-creation* Reykjavik (Iceland) 2018, *Conference* Edinburgh (UK) 2016.
Members in 13 countries:
Belgium, Canada, Chile, Denmark, France, Germany, Iceland, Ireland, Poland, Qatar, Sweden, UK, USA. [2023/XM3167/**D**]

♦ International Short Film Conference (ISFC) 14854

Conférence internationale du court métrage

Secretariat c/o Cinema Zed, Naamsestraat 96, 3000 Leuven, Belgium. T. +3216679250. E-mail: info@shortfilmconference.com.
URL: http://shortfilmconference.com/

History 1970, as *International Conference for Short and Documentary Film.* **Aims** Promote the exhibition of short films through all available *media*; foster the role of film *festivals* and monitor their activity as a key to the international distribution of short films; further the exchange of views and information and encourage cooperation between festivals; make recommendations for governmental and non-governmental organizations and festivals according to the media situation in the world; propose standards and guide-lines for all matters concerning the circulation, evaluation or registration of short films. **Structure** An informal body; not an association. Plenary Meeting (annual). Board (meets at least once a year), consisting of 10 members. **Finance** Members' dues. **Events** *General Meeting* Cork (Ireland) 2005, *Plenary Meeting* Montréal, QC (Canada) 1989, *Plenary Meeting* Krakow (Poland) 1988, *Plenary Meeting* Tampere (Finland) 1987, *Plenary Meeting* Nyon (Switzerland) 1985.
Members (a) Delegates or representatives of governmental or national film boards concerned with the production, distribution or promotion of short films; (b) international film organizations or associations concerned with the production, distribution or promotion of short films; (c) organizers of international short film festivals or of feature film festivals presenting short films; (d) persons concerned with producing, distributing, or promoting short films, if invited individually by the Conference. Members in 23 countries:
Argentina, Australia, Belgium, Brazil, Canada, Denmark, Finland, France, Germany, Hungary, Iceland, Ireland, Italy, Netherlands, Norway, Poland, Portugal, Russia, Slovenia, Spain, Sweden, Switzerland, UK. [2014/XF1530/**F**]

♦ International Shoulder Group (ISG) 14855

Chair c/o DIESEL, 200 Univ Ave West, Waterloo ON N2L 3G1, Canada.
URL: https://isbweb.org/isg

History 1989, Los Angeles CA (USA). **Aims** Enhance shoulder research by exchanging ideas, methodologies, data and results. **Structure** Board of 5 members. **Languages** English. **Finance** No expenses. **Events** *Meeting* Delft (Netherlands) 2022, *Meeting* Delft (Netherlands) 2020, *Conference* Rochester, MN (USA) 2018, *Conference* Winterthur (Switzerland) 2016, *Conference* Waterloo, ON (Canada) 2014. **Publications** Congress proceedings; special issues.
Members Individuals in 27 countries and territories:
Argentina, Australia, Austria, Belgium, Brazil, Canada, Chile, Denmark, France, Germany, Greece, India, Ireland, Italy, Netherlands, New Zealand, Poland, Portugal, Slovenia, South Africa, Spain, Sweden, Switzerland, Taiwan, Türkiye, UK, USA.
NGO Relations Technical Group within: *International Society of Biomechanics (ISB, #14966).* [2021/XE3423/v/**E**]

♦ International Shoulder Society / see International Board of Shoulder and Elbow Surgery (#12372)

♦ International Show Caves Association (ISCA) 14856

Association internationale des grottes aménagées

Headquarters Largo Leone XII, 60040 Genga AN, Italy. T. +39732973315. Fax +39732972108. E-mail: renatamarinelli@libero.it.
URL: https://www.i-s-c-a.org/

History Constituent Assembly, 5 Nov 1989, Genga (Italy). Set up, Nov 1990. **Events** *Quadrennial Congress* San Antonio, TX (USA) 2022, *Quadrennial Congress* Genga (Italy) 2018, *Quadrennial Congress* Australia 2014, *Quadrennial Congress* Liptovsky Mikulas (Slovakia) 2010, *Baltic speleological congress* Visby (Sweden) 2007. **Members** Associations and individuals in 20 countries:
Australia, Austria, Belgium, China, Czechia, France, Germany, Hungary, Italy, Korea Rep, Neth Antilles, Russia, Slovakia, Slovenia, South Africa, Spain, Sweden, UK, Ukraine, USA. [2019/XN0107/**D**]

- ♦ International Show Jumping Officials Club / see International Jumping Officials Club (#13976)
- ♦ International Shrimp Council (inactive)
- ♦ International SHRIMP Workshop (meeting series)
- ♦ International Shrine Aviation Association (internationally oriented national body)
- ♦ International Shrine Clown Association (internationally oriented national body)
- ♦ International Shudokan Karate Association (internationally oriented national body)

♦ International Shuffleboard Association (ISA) 14857

Pres address not obtained.
Sec address not obtained.
URL: http://www.world-shuffleboard.org/

History 10 Mar 1979, St Petersburg FL (USA). **Activities** Sporting activities. **Events** *General Meeting* Dieppe, NB (Canada) 2011, *General Meeting* Germany 2010, *General Meeting* USA 2009, *General Meeting* Midland, ON (Canada) 2007, *General Meeting* Lakeside, OH (USA) 2006. [2014/XN3112/**C**]

- ♦ International Side-Saddle Organization (internationally oriented national body)
- ♦ International Sightseeing and Tours Association (inactive)
- ♦ International Sign Association Inc / see International Sign Association
- ♦ International Sign Association (internationally oriented national body)
- ♦ International Sign Language Association (inactive)
- ♦ International Silambam Committee (internationally oriented national body)
- ♦ International Silent Martial Arts Federation / see International Martial Arts Federation of the Deaf (#14109)
- ♦ International Silk Association (inactive)
- ♦ International Silk Federation (inactive)

♦ International Silk Union 14858

Sec Room 1606, Cathaya Mansion, No. 105, Tiyuchang road, Hangzhou, China, 310004 Zhejiang, China. T. +8657185098606. E-mail: isusecretariat@163.com.
URL: http://www.worldsilk.com.cn/

History 23 Oct 2015, Hangzhou (China). Founded following earlier discussions held since Apr 2015. Registration: No/ID: CP/LIC/SO/19/57485, Start date: 19 Sep 2016, Hong Kong; No/ID: G1330000MCW026042N, Start date: 22 Aug 2019, China. **Aims** Promote mutual exchange and cooperation of the silk industry around the world; promote the progress and development in international silk culture, education, scientific research, design, production, standards and testing, trade as well as consumption, and build a good exchange and cooperation platform for the international silk industry. **Structure** General Assembly; Council; Executive Committee. **Languages** Chinese, English. **Staff** 4.00 FTE, paid; 3.00 FTE, voluntary. **Finance** Sources: donations; government support. **Activities** Events/meetings. Active in all member countries. **Publications** *Journal of Silk* (12 a year) in Chinese, English; *ISU NEWS* (4 a year) in Chinese, English.
Members Enterprises and organizations in 27 countries and territories:
Australia, Bangladesh, Brazil, Cambodia, China, France, Hong Kong, India, Indonesia, Iran Islamic Rep, Italy, Japan, Laos, Myanmar, Pakistan, Philippines, Poland, Romania, Singapore, Spain, Switzerland, Thailand, Türkiye, Uganda, USA, Uzbekistan, Vietnam. [2023.01.10/XM8570/**C**]

♦ International Simone de Beauvoir Society 14859

Pres address not obtained.
URL: https://beauvoir.weebly.com/

History Founded Dec 1981. Since May 2018, registered in the US as an organization of the type 501(c)(3). **Aims** Promote the legacy of Simone de Beauvoir. **Structure** Steering Committee. **Finance** Members' dues. **Activities** Events/meetings. **Events** *Conference* Washington, DC (USA) 2019, *Conference* Paris (France) 2018, *Conference* Haifa (Israel) 2017, *Conference* Superior, WI (USA) 2016, *Conference* St Louis, MO (USA) 2014. **Publications** *Simone de Beauvoir Studies* – journal. [2019/XM8438/v/**E**]

♦ International SIMS Society 14860

Contact 209 Chemistry Bldg, Penn State Univ, University Park PA 16802, USA. T. +18148630001. E-mail: nxw@psu.edu.
URL: http://www.simssociety.org/

History SIMS stands for *Secondary Ion Mass Spectrometry*. **Events** *International Conference on Secondary Ion Mass Spectrometry* Kyoto (Japan) 2019, *International Conference on Secondary Ion Mass Spectrometry* Krakow (Poland) 2017, *International Conference on Secondary Ion Mass Spectrometry* Seattle, WA (USA) 2015, *International Conference on Secondary Ion Mass Spectrometry* Jeju (Korea Rep) 2013, *International Conference on Secondary Ion Mass Spectrometry* Riva del Garda (Italy) 2011. [2018/XJ6418/**E**]

♦ International Simulation and Gaming Association (ISAGA) 14861

Association internationale de simulation et de jeux d'entreprises

Chair HIT LAB, University of Canterbury, John Britten Bldg, Level 2, Private Bag 4800, Christchurch 8140, New Zealand. E-mail: info@isaga.net.
Sec KTH Royal Institute of Technology, Division of Health Informatics and Logistics, Hälsovägen 11 C, SE-141 57 Huddinge, Sweden.
URL: https://www.isaga.com/

History 27 Jun 1970, Bonn (Germany). First constitution and bylaws adopted, 7 Jul 1972, Birmingham (UK), at 3rd International Conference on Simulation and Gaming. Registration: Start date: 28 Apr 2010, Netherlands. **Aims** Promote gaming simulation methods, including research, consulting, learning and teaching methods, such as traditional business and management simulation games, policy exercises, computer simulations and computer-supported simulation games, role play, learning games, scenarios, dynamic case studies, experiential learning activities, business-theatre, etc. **Structure** General Assembly (at least annually); Executive Board; Advisory Counsel. **Languages** English. **Staff** None. **Finance** Sources: members' dues. **Activities** Events/meetings. **Events** *Annual Conference* Boston, MA (USA) 2022, *Annual Conference* Indore (India) 2021, *Annual Conference* Stoke-on-Trent (UK) 2020, *Annual Conference* Warsaw (Poland) 2019, *Annual Conference* Nakhon Pathom (Thailand) 2018. **Publications** *ISAGA Newsletter* (periodical) – website; *Simulation and Gaming* – journal. Conference proceedings.
Members Individuals in 29 countries:
Australia, Austria, Brazil, Canada, China, Czechia, Denmark, Estonia, Finland, France, Germany, Israel, Italy, Japan, Latvia, Lithuania, Mexico, Netherlands, Philippines, Poland, Romania, Russia, Singapore, Spain, Sweden, Switzerland, UK, Ukraine, USA. [2022/XC4262/v/**C**]

♦ International Simultaneous Policy Organisation (ISPO) 14862

Trustee PO Box 26547, London, SE3 7YT, UK. T. +442086390121. Fax +442086390123. E-mail: info@simpol.org.
URL: http://www.simpol.org/

History Founded 2000, UK. **Aims** Use the individual right to vote in a way that drives politicians to simultaneously implement global laws, taxes, etc, to solve global problems without any nation, corporation or citizen losing out to any other. **Languages** English, French, German, Spanish. **Staff** 7.00 FTE, voluntary. **Finance** Donations (not from for-profit organizations); book sales. **Publications** *Monetary Reform – Making it Happen* by J Robertson, and J Bunzl; *The Simultaneous Policy: An Insider's Guide to Saving Humanity and the Planet* by John Bunzl.
Members Campaigns in 42 countries:
Argentina, Australia, Bangladesh, Belgium, Brazil, Bulgaria, Cameroon, Canada, Colombia, Congo DR, Denmark, Dominican Rep, Finland, France, Germany, Greece, India, Ireland, Italy, Japan, Kenya, Madagascar, Malaysia, Mali, Montenegro, Nepal, Netherlands, New Zealand, Nigeria, Pakistan, Senegal, Serbia, South Africa, Spain, Suriname, Sweden, Switzerland, UK, United Arab Emirates, Uruguay, USA, Venezuela.
NGO Relations Participates in: *New School of Athens (NSoA, no recent information).* [2016/XD8694/**D**]

- ♦ International Sino-Dance Association (inactive)

♦ International Sivananda Yoga Vedanta Center (ISYVC) 14863

Centre international Sivananda de yoga vedanta – Sivananda Yoga Vedanta Zentrum

Contact Sivananda Yoga Camp, 673 8th Avenue, Val Morin, Québec QC J0T 2R0, Canada. T. +18193223226. Fax +18193225876. E-mail: hq@sivananda.org.
Peace Bank Sivananda Yoga Vedanta Dhanwanthari Ashram, PO Neyyar Dam, Thiruvananthapuram, Kerala 695576, Thiruvananthapuram KERALA 695576, India.
URL: http://www.sivananda.org/

History 1959, Montréal (Canada), by Swami Vishnu Devananda. **Aims** Further the cause of world *peace* through teaching Yoga techniques and *philosophy*. **Activities** Training/education. **Events** *Annual Symposium* Val-Morin, QC (Canada) 1990, *Annual symposium* Val-Morin, QC (Canada) 1989. **Publications** *Yoga Life* (2 a year). Pamphlets.
Members Ashrams – autonomous centers – in 17 countries:
Argentina, Austria, Bahamas, Brazil, Canada, China, France, Germany, India, Israel, Spain, Switzerland, Thailand, UK, Uruguay, USA, Vietnam. [2016.06.22/XF1887/**F**]

- ♦ International Six Metre Class Association (see: #21760)

♦ International Sjögren's Network (ISN) 14864

Contact c/o Sjögren's Syndrome Foundation, 6707 Democracy Blvd, Ste 325, Bethesda MD 20817, USA. T. +13015304420. Fax +13015304415.
URL: http://www.sjogrens.org/

History 2009, Brest (France), by 15 organizations, each representing different countries, meeting at the Xth International Symposium on Sjögren's.
Members Organizations in 18 countries:
Australia, Austria, Canada, Finland, France, Germany, India, Italy, Japan, Korea Rep, Netherlands, New Zealand, Russia, Spain, Sweden, Switzerland, UK, USA. [2010/XJ1842/**E**]

♦ International Skating Union (ISU) 14865

Dir-Gen Av Juste-Olivier 17, 1006 Lausanne VD, Switzerland. T. +41216126666. Fax +41216126677. E-mail: info@isu.ch.
Pres address not obtained.
URL: http://www.isu.org/

History 23 Jul 1892, Scheveningen (Netherlands). Statutes most recently amended, 2016. **Aims** Ensure regulation, control and promotion of skating and its organized development through friendship and mutual understanding among sportsmen and women; improve popularity and quality of and participation in figure and speed skating. **Structure** Congress (every 2 years); Council; Technical Committees; Secretaries. Meetings closed. **Languages** English. **Staff** 16.00 FTE, paid. **Finance** Sources: sponsorship. Other sources: TV rights. Supported by: *International Olympic Committee (IOC, #14408).* **Activities** Sporting activities. **Events** *Biennial Congress* Phuket (Thailand) 2022, *Biennial Congress* Phuket (Thailand) 2021, *Biennial Congress* Phuket (Thailand) 2020, *Biennial Congress* Seville (Spain) 2018, *Meeting* Helsinki (Finland) 2017. **Publications** *Handbook of Competitive Speed Skating* (2000); *Pair Skating as Sport and Art* (1992) – revised; *Figure Skating Book 1891-1967*; *Figure Skating Results Book 1968-1991*; *Olympic Games* – complete results in Figure Skating 1908 and Speed Skating 1924-1994; *Speed Skating Results Book 1968-1991*; *Sprint Speed Skating Results Book 1968-1991.* Judges' handbooks; ISU regulations; congress proceedings; instructional video-films; compact discs.
Members Member Federations (99) and Club Members (2) in 78 countries and territories:
Andorra, Argentina, Armenia, Australia, Austria, Azerbaijan, Belarus, Belgium, Bosnia-Herzegovina, Brazil, Bulgaria, Canada, China, Colombia, Croatia, Cyprus, Czechia, Denmark, Ecuador, Egypt, Estonia, Finland, France, Georgia, Germany, Greece, Hong Kong, Hungary, Iceland, India, Indonesia, Israel, Italy, Japan, Kazakhstan, Korea DPR, Korea Rep, Kuwait, Kyrgyzstan, Latvia, Liechtenstein, Lithuania, Luxembourg, Malaysia, Mexico, Moldova, Monaco, Mongolia, Morocco, Netherlands, New Zealand, North Macedonia, Norway, Peru, Philippines, Poland, Portugal, Qatar, Romania, Russia, Serbia, Singapore, Slovakia, Slovenia, South Africa, Spain, Sweden, Switzerland, Taipei, Thailand, Türkiye, Turkmenistan, UK, Ukraine, United Arab Emirates, USA, Uzbekistan, Vietnam.
NGO Relations Member of (2): *Association of the International Olympic Winter Sports Federations (AIOWF, #02757)*; *Olympic Movement (#17719).* Cooperates with (1): *International Testing Agency (ITA, #15678).* Recognized by: *International Olympic Committee (IOC, #14408).* [2023.02.16/XC2464/**C**]

♦ International Skat Players Association (ISPA) 14866

Weltverband der Skatspieler

Pres Weststr 11, 26931 Elsfleth, Germany. T. +4944049878694. E-mail: info@ispaworld.info.
URL: http://www.ispaworld.org/

History Registered in accordance with German law: 73 VR 17777. **Structure** Executive. **Publications** *Skatmagazin.*
Members Offices in 21 countries:
Argentina, Australia, Austria, Bahamas, Belgium, Bermuda, Brazil, Canada, Chile, Denmark, France, Germany, Namibia, Netherlands, Paraguay, Poland, South Africa, Spain, Switzerland, Thailand, USA. [2020/XN9428/**C**]

- ♦ International Skeletal Dysplasia Society (unconfirmed)

♦ International Skeletal Society (ISS) 14867

Société internationale pour l'étude du squelette

Main Office 1061 E Main St, Ste 300, East Dundee IL 60118, USA. T. +18477526245. E-mail: info@internationalskeletalsociety.com.
URL: http://www.internationalskeletalsociety.com/

History 1973. Current By-laws adopted 30 Sep 2004. **Aims** Promote understanding of musculoskeletal diseases through the unified effort of leaders in radiology, pathology, orthopaedic surgery and other specialities. **Structure** Executive Committee. Standing Committees (18): Audit; Awards; Board of Trustees Endowment Fund; Grants; Convention Planning; Historian; Intersociety Liaison; Liaison; Local Arrangements; Member's Meeting Program; Membership; Nominating; Outreach Program; Prizes; Refresher Course; Refresher Course for Promotion; Rules; Sponsorship. Ah-Hoc Committees. Program; Refresher Course; Auditing; Nominating; Membership; Rules; Editorial; Awards; Liaison-Future Planning; Convention Planning; Promotion of the Refresher Course outside of North America. **Languages** English. **Staff** 0.50 FTE, paid. Voluntary. **Finance** Sources: members' dues. **Activities** Awards/prizes/competitions; events/meetings; training/education. **Events** *Annual Meeting* London (UK) 2023, *Annual Meeting* Barcelona (Spain) 2022, *Annual Meeting* East Dundee, IL (USA) 2021, *Annual Meeting* East Dundee, IL (USA) 2020, *Annual Meeting* Vancouver, BC (Canada) 2019. **Publications** *Skeletal Radiology* (12 a year) – journal; *Bare Bones Newsletter* – online.
Members Individuals in 38 countries:
Argentina, Australia, Austria, Belgium, Brazil, Canada, Chile, China, Czechia, Denmark, Finland, France, Germany, Hungary, India, Israel, Italy, Japan, Korea Rep, Lebanon, Netherlands, New Zealand, North Macedonia, Norway, Poland, Saudi Arabia, Serbia, Singapore, Slovenia, South Africa, Spain, Sweden, Switzerland, Thailand, Türkiye, UK, United Arab Emirates, USA. [2021/XC6208/v/**C**]

♦ International Skibob Federation 14868

Fédération internationale de skibob (FISB)

Pres Landweg 2, 82041 Oberhaching, Germany. T. +498949053265.
Gen Sec address not obtained.
URL: http://www.skibob.org/

History 1963. **Aims** Set policy for the conduct of skibob (snow-bike). **Structure** Executive Committee, comprising President, 2 Vice-Presidents, General Secretary, Treasurer, Sports Director, World Cup Director, Technical Commission Director. Council of Management, comprising Representative for French Speaking Nations, Representative for Recreational Sport, Representative for English speaking Nations, Representative for Eastern European Nations, Representative for Recreational Sport and Representative for Press and Public Relations. Commissions (2): Technical; Doping. **Languages** English, French, German. **Finance** Members' dues. Race fees, sponsorship. **Activities** Coordinates activities of national federations; organizes skibob racing, including World Cup, World Championships and FISB-A races, which includes the following disciplines: Downhill, Super-G, Giant Slalom, Slalom and Parallel Slalom. **Events** *Annual Congress* Grächen (Switzerland) 2005, *Annual Congress* Prague (Czech Rep) 2001, *Annual Congress* Berchtesgaden (Germany) 2000, *Annual Congress* St Johann (Austria) 1999, *Annual Congress* Adelboden (Switzerland) 1998.

Members Full (national federations) and Associate (skibob clubs) members. National federations in 13 countries:
Austria, Czechia, England, Germany, Greece, Ireland, Liechtenstein, Luxembourg, Netherlands, Poland, Scotland, Switzerland, Wales.
Skibob clubs in 11 countries:
Argentina, Australia, Barbados, Brazil, Canada, Chile, Estonia, France, Italy, Jamaica, USA. [2019/XD4940/**D**]

♦ International Ski Club of Journalists 14869
Ski-club international des journalistes (SCIJ)
SG The Claverings, Summer Hill, Canterbury, CT2 8NN, UK.
URL: http://www.scij.info/
History Jan 1955, Méribel-les-Allues (France), by journalists from 8 countries, following initiatives, in 1951, by Gilles de la Rocque. Previously also referred to as *Ski-Club International der Journalisten*. Statutes adopted 24 Sep 1967, Lausanne (Switzerland). **Aims** Sustain and foster friendly links between colleagues of the international *press* within the setting of skis and *mountains*. **Structure** General Assembly (annual); International Committee; Honorary members (10). **Languages** English, French. **Finance** Annual contribution from members who attend an annual meeting. **Events** *Annual Meeting* Pamporovo (Bulgaria) 2018, *Annual Meeting* France 2017, *Annual Meeting* Sestriere (Italy) 2016, *Annual Meeting* Baqueira Beret (Spain) 2015, *Annual Meeting* Champéry (Switzerland) 2014.
Members Individuals. National sections in 39 countries:
Andorra, Argentina, Australia, Austria, Belgium, Bosnia-Herzegovina, Bulgaria, Canada, Croatia, Czechia, Denmark, Estonia, Finland, France, Germany, Hungary, Ireland, Israel, Italy, Kazakhstan, Korea Rep, Latvia, Lithuania, Morocco, Netherlands, North Macedonia, Norway, Poland, Romania, Russia, Serbia, Slovakia, Slovenia, Spain, Sweden, Switzerland, Türkiye, UK, USA.
[2016.06.01/XF7173/v/**F**]

♦ International Ski Federation (#09659)
♦ International Ski Instructors Association / see International Pro Ski Instructors Association

♦ International Ski Instructors Association (ISIA) 14870
Association internationale des moniteurs de ski – Internationaler Skilehrerverband – Associazione Internationale dei Maestri di sci professionisti
Pres An der Kandahar 11, 82491 Grainau, Germany. T. +4988217321444. E-mail: info@isia.ski.
Gen Sec address not obtained.
URL: https://isia.ski/
History 1970. Former names and other names: *International Association for Ski Instruction* – alias. **Aims** Support the professional practice of ski and snow sports teaching in all its forms. **Structure** Assembly of Delegates (at least every 2 years); Executive Committee; Board. **Languages** English, German. **Finance** Annual budget: 60,000 CHF. **Activities** Knowledge management/information dissemination; networking/liaising; training/education. **Events** *Congress and Assembly of Delegates* Budapest (Hungary) 2020, *Delegates Assembly* Switzerland 2016, *Congress* Ushuaia (Argentina) 2015, *Congress* Finland 2014, *Congress* Ushuaia (Argentina) 2013. **Publications** *ISIA News*.
Members National professional snowsports instructor organizations (maximum one per country) in 37 countries and territories:
Andorra, Argentina, Australia, Belgium, Bosnia-Herzegovina, Bulgaria, Canada, Chile, Croatia, Czechia, Denmark, Finland, Germany, Greece, Hungary, Ireland, Israel, Japan, Korea Rep, Montenegro, Netherlands, New Zealand, Norway, Poland, Romania, Russia, San Marino, Serbia, Slovakia, Slovenia, Spain, Sweden, Switzerland, Trentino-South Tyrol, Türkiye, UK, USA.
NGO Relations Associated with: *Interski International (INTERSKI, #15975)*. [2019.02.19/XD4863/**C**]

♦ International Pro Ski Instructors Association (internationally oriented national body)

♦ International Ski Mountaineering Federation (ISMF) 14871
Main Office Piazza Mellano 4B, 12084 Mondovì CN, Italy. T. +39174554755 – +393923566064. E-mail: office@ismf-ski.org.
Gen Manager Av de Rhodanie 54, Case postale 30, 1000 Lausanne VD, Switzerland.
URL: http://www.ismf-ski.org/
History Jan 1999. Founded as an internal body of the *Union internationale des associations d'alpinisme (UIAA, #20420)*, in order to govern and administer the sport of ski mountaineering, replacing the *Comité international du ski alpinisme de compétition (CISAC, inactive)*, set up in 1988, Barcelona (Spain). Became an independent international competition federation with its own legal personality on 6 Oct 2007. Former names and other names: *International Council for Ski Mountaineering Competitions (ISMC)* – former (Jan 1999 to 27 Feb 2008). Registration: Swiss Civil Code, Switzerland. **Aims** Regulate, promote, develop and supervise the sport of ski mountaineering on a worldwide basis. **Structure** Plenary Assembly (annual); Council, consisting of four representatives of the member federations, one representative of male and one representative of female athletes, and one representative of each Continental Council (Asian and North American). Bureau, consisting of President, General Secretary and three representatives of the macro-areas (Sport, Marketing and Communication, Finance). Internal Committees. Legal headquarters, located in Lausanne (Switzerland) and operational headquarters, in Mondovì (Italy). **Languages** English. **Staff** 4.00 FTE, paid. Temporary contracts with external collaborators. **Finance** Sources: donations; fees for services; members' dues; sponsorship. Other sources: athletes licences; competition organiser fees; technical partners fees. Annual budget: 350,000 EUR. **Activities** Awards/prizes/competitions; events/meetings; sporting activities; training/education. **Events** *Extraordinary Plenary Assembly* 2021, *Plenary Assembly* Milan (Italy) 2021, *Plenary Assembly* Mondovì (Italy) 2020, *Plenary Assembly* Antalya (Turkey) 2019, *Plenary Assembly* Zakopane (Poland) 2018.
Members Full; Provisional; Associate. National Federations in 41 countries and territories:
Andorra, Argentina, Austria, Azerbaijan, Belgium, Brazil, Bulgaria, Canada, Catalunya, Chile, China, Czechia, Denmark, France, Germany, Greece, India, Iran Islamic Rep, Ireland, Italy, Japan, Korea Rep, Malta, Mexico, Nepal, Netherlands, Norway, Poland, Portugal, Romania, Russia, Slovakia, Slovenia, Spain, Sweden, Switzerland, Thailand, Türkiye, UK, Ukraine, USA.
NGO Relations Member of (3): *Alliance of Independent recognised Members of Sport (AIMS, #00690)* (Associate); *Association of the IOC Recognized International Sports Federations (ARISF, #02767)*; *Olympic Movement (#17719)*. Cooperates with (1): *International Testing Agency (ITA, #15678)*. Recognized by: *International Olympic Committee (IOC, #14408)*. [2022.06.17/XE3778/**C**]

♦ International Skin-Care Nursing Group (ISNG) 14872
Pres c/o HSH, Klingenbergvegen 8, 5414 Stord, Norway.
Vice-Pres 4 Village on Main, Scott Rd, Hout Bay, 7806, South Africa.
URL: http://www.isng.org/
History 1993, as *International Dermatology Nursing Group (IDNG)*. Previously also known under the acronym *ISCNG*. Inaugural meeting at International Congress of Dermatology, 1998, Egypt. Current title adopted, 1999, Egypt. **Aims** Promote the contribution of dermatology nursing to meeting skin care needs internationally; promote education to develop dermatology nursing in skin care worldwide. **Structure** Advisory Board. Includes: *European Skin-Care Nursing Network (ESNN, no recent information)*. **Languages** English. **Staff** 1.00 FTE, paid. **Finance** Grants; independent sponsorship. Budget (annual): about pounds50,000. **Activities** Events/meetings; research/documentation; training/education. **Events** *Meeting* Vancouver, BC (Canada) 2015, *Meeting* Vancouver, BC (Canada) 2015, *Meeting* Cape Town (South Africa) 2013, *Meeting* Istanbul (Turkey) 2013, *Meeting* Malta 2013. **Publications** *ISNG Bulletin* (3 a year).
Members Individuals in 34 countries:
Australia, Belgium, Brazil, Canada, Denmark, Egypt, Eswatini, Ethiopia, Finland, France, Germany, Ghana, Guatemala, Guyana, Haiti, India, Ireland, Italy, Malta, Namibia, Netherlands, Nigeria, Norway, Sierra Leone, Slovenia, South Africa, Sweden, Switzerland, Tanzania UR, Uganda, UK, USA, Zambia, Zimbabwe.
IGO Relations Partner of: *Global Alliance to Eliminate Lymphatic Filariasis (GAELF, #10195)*.
[2014.07.29/XF6540/v/**F**]

♦ International Skin Pharmacology Society (no recent information)
♦ International Ski Patrol Federation (#09647)
♦ International Skittles Federation / see International Bowling Federation (#12384)

♦ International Skyrunning Federation (ISF) 14873
Main Office Via Mentegazzi 34, 13900 Biella BI, Italy. T. +39152522941. Fax +39152522941. E-mail: info@skyrunning.com.
URL: http://www.skyrunning.com/
History 1995. Present name and structure adopted, 2008. Former names and other names: *Federation for Sport at Altitude (FSA)* – former (1995 to 2008); *Federazione Sport Alta Quota* – former (1995 to 2008). **Aims** Promote, govern and administer the sport of skyrunning and similar multisports activities, including Vertical Running and Skyscraper Racing. **Structure** Plenary Assembly; Management Committee; Executive Board; Continental Councils; Technical Commissions; Appeals Commissions; Athletes' Commission; Auditors. **Languages** English. **Activities** Promotes, regulates and coordinates skyrunning and vertical running and related events. Organizes: Skyrunner World Series; Vertical World Circuit; European Championships; SkyGames; World Championships. **Publications** *Annual Skyrunner World Series Magazine*. Medical scientific publications.
Members National federations in 16 countries and territories:
Andorra, Azerbaijan, Brazil, Bulgaria, Costa Rica, France, Greece, Italy, Kazakhstan, Malaysia, Russia, Spain, Switzerland, UK, USA, Venezuela. [2021/XJ8015/**C**]

♦ International Slavistic Committee (inactive)
♦ International Sled Dog Racing Association (internationally oriented national body)

♦ International Sled Dog Veterinary Medical Association (ISDVMA) . . 14874
Contact PO Box 52, Marlboro VT 05344, USA. E-mail: isdvma@isdvma.org.
URL: http://www.isdvma.org/
History A US organization of the type 501(c)(3). **Aims** Enhance the well-being, welfare and safety of sled dogs through education, research and the collaborative relationship with mushers, veterinary professionals and race organizers. **Structure** Board. **Finance** Sources: members' dues. **Activities** Awards/prizes/competitions; events/meetings; networking/liaising; research/documentation; training/education. **Events** *Biennial Meeting and Symposium* Proctor, MN (USA) 2022, *Biennial Conference* St Augustine, FL (USA) 2021, *Biennial Conference* Montréal, QC (Canada) 2020, *Biennial Conference* Valencia (Spain) 2018, *Biennial Conference* Bloomington, MN (USA) 2016.
Members Individuals in 13 countries:
Australia, Austria, Belgium, Canada, France, Germany, Iceland, Netherlands, New Zealand, Norway, Spain, Sweden, USA.
NGO Relations Associate member of: *International Federation of Sleddog Sports (IFSS, #13541)*.
[2020/XG3454/v/**C**]

♦ International Sled Sport Federation / see International Luge Federation (#14066)
♦ International Slow Food Movement / see International Movement for the Defence of and the Right to Pleasure (#14194)
♦ International Small Angle Scattering Conference (meeting series)
♦ International Small Bowel Transplant Symposium (meeting series)
♦ International Small Business Conference / see International Small Business Congress (#14875)

♦ International Small Business Congress (ISBC) 14875
Contact address not obtained. T. +27117946910 – +27112511789. E-mail: info@isbc2012.org.
History 1973, as *Pan-Pacific Small Business Conference*. Name changed to *International Symposium on Small Business*. Subsequently changed title to *International Small Business Conference*, 1983. **Aims** Exchange views about small and medium-sized business problems, policies and programs. **Structure** Steering Committee. **Events** *Pan Asian Congress / Congress* Macau (Macau) 2013, *Congress* Johannesburg (South Africa) 2012, *Congress* Stockholm (Sweden) 2011, *Congress* Taipei (Taiwan) 2010, *Small business reaching out* Brisbane, QLD (Australia) 2009. [2013/XF6613/c/**F**]

♦ International Small Islands Studies Association (ISISA) 14876
Hon Pres Inst of Island Studies, Univ of Prince Edward Island, 550, University Avenue, Charlottetown PE C1A 4P3, Canada.
Treas Shetland Campus, Univ of the Highlands and Islands, Lerwick, IV3 5SQ, UK.
URL: http://www.isisa.org/
History 25 Jun 1992, Nassau (Bahamas). Founded at 3rd "Islands of the World" Conference. Statutes amended: 28 June 2002, Charlottetown PE (Canada); 13 Dec 2010, Bornholm (Denmark); Nov 2014, Taiwan; May 2016, Lesvos (Greece); July 2017, Kangaroo Island, Australia; June 2018, Terschelling (Netherlands); June 2021, St John's, Newfoundland (Canada); June 2022, Zadar (Croatia). **Aims** Encourage the study of islands on their own terms; encourage free scholarly discussion on small island related matters such as size and scale, islandness, dependency, resource management and environment, and the nature of island life. **Structure** General Meeting (during Conference); Executive Committee. **Languages** English. **Staff** Voluntary. **Finance** Sources: members' dues. **Activities** Events/meetings. **Events** *Islands of the World Conference* St John's, NL (Canada) 2021, *Islands of the World Conference* Terschelling Is (Netherlands) 2018, *Islands of the World Conference* Kangaroo Is (Australia) 2017, *Islands of the World Conference* Mytilene (Greece) 2016, *Islands of the World Conference* Penghu Is (Taiwan) 2014. **Publications** *ISISA Newsletter* (2 a year); *Island Studies Journal* (2 a year).
Members Individuals, entities, organizations and institutes. Full in 39 countries and territories:
Australia, Bahamas, Barbados, Canada, China, Croatia, Cyprus, Denmark, Fiji, Finland, France, Germany, Greece, Grenada, Hong Kong, India, Ireland, Italy, Jamaica, Japan, Kiribati, Korea Rep, Maldives, Malta, Marshall Is, Mauritius, Micronesia FS, New Zealand, Portugal, Réunion, Samoa, Singapore, Solomon Is, Spain, Sri Lanka, Sweden, UK, USA, Vanuatu.
NGO Relations Member of (1): *Global Islands Network (GIN, #10437)*. [2022.06.14/XD4411/**C**]

♦ International Smart Grid Action Network (ISGAN) 14877
Secretariat c/o Austrian Institute of Technology, Giefinggasse 4, 1210 Vienna, Austria. E-mail: isgan@ait.ac.at.
URL: http://www.iea-isgan.org/
History Launched Jul 2010, Washington DC (USA), at first *Clean Energy Ministerial (CEM, #03988)*. Formally established via an Implementing Agreement under the umbrella of *International Energy Agency (IEA, #13270)*. Agreement received initial signatures from interested governments or representatives at 2nd Clean Energy Ministerial, Apr 2011, Abu Dhabi (United Arab Emirates). **Aims** As a mechanism for multilateral collaboration, advance development and deployment of smarter *electric grids* worldwide. **Activities** Foundational projects (4): *'Global Smart Grid Inventory'*; Smart Grid Case Studies; Benefit-Cost Analyses and Toolkits; Synthesis of Insights for Decision Makers. Projects under development: *Smart Grid International Research Facility Network*; Electricity Transmission and Distribution Network project. **Events** *Smart Community Summit* Tokyo (Japan) 2014, *Scandinavian Smart Grid Week* Stavanger (Norway) 2013, *Meeting* Seoul (Korea Rep) 2011, *Korea smart grid week* Jeju (Korea Rep) 2010.
Members Participating governments as of 7 Apr 2011 (19):
Australia, Austria, Belgium, Canada, China, France, Germany, India, Italy, Japan, Korea Rep, Mexico, Netherlands, Norway, Russia, Sweden, Switzerland, UK, USA.
Regional Entity:
European Union (EU, #08967).
NGO Relations Collaborates with: *Global Smart Grid Federation (GSGF, #10601)*. [XJ2649/**E***]

♦ International Smoothed Particle Hydrodynamics European Research Interest Community (SPHERIC) 14878
Chairman School of Mechanical Aerospace and Civil Engineering, Univ of Manchester, Manchester, M13 9PL, UK. T. +441613062615.
URL: http://wiki.manchester.ac.uk/spheric/index.php/Main_Page/
History 2005. Serves as a Special Interest Group of *European Research Community on Flow, Turbulence and Combustion (ERCOFTAC, #08361)*. **Aims** Gather researchers and industrial users of the Smoothed Particle Hydrodynamics (SPH) numerical methods; foster activities linked to this method. **Structure** Steering Committee of 13. **Languages** English. **Staff** None paid. **Finance** No budget. **Activities** Training/education; events/meetings. **Events** *International Workshop* Parma (Italy) 2015, *International Workshop* Paris (France) 2014, *International Workshop* Trondheim (Norway) 2013, *International Workshop* Prato, RN (Italy) 2012, *International Workshop* Hamburg (Germany) 2011. **Publications** *SPHERIC Newsletter* (2 a year).
Members Research and Development; Industry. Members in 23 countries and territories:
Australia, Belgium, Canada, Czechia, France, Germany, Greece, India, Iran Islamic Rep, Ireland, Italy, Japan, Malaysia, Netherlands, New Zealand, Norway, Portugal, Slovenia, Spain, Switzerland, Taiwan, UK, USA.
IGO Relations No relations. **NGO Relations** No official relations. [2014.08.18/XJ8554/**E**]

♦ **International Snoezelen Association** **14879**

Contact Rüdesheimer Strasse 4, 14197 Berlin, Germany.
URL: http://www.isna.de/

Aims Promote the use and development of snoezelen therapies, using light, sound, and scents. **Finance** Members' dues. **Events** *Congress* Buenos Aires (Argentina) 2018, *Congress* Germany 2017, *Congress* Basel (Switzerland) 2016, *Congress* Einbeck (Germany) 2015, *Symposium* Seoul (Korea Rep) 2014. **Members** Individuals. Membership countries not specified. [2014/XM4620/**D**]

♦ International Snowboard Federation (inactive)
♦ International Snow Leopard Trust (internationally oriented national body)
♦ International Snowmobile Industry Association / see International Snowmobile Manufacturers Association
♦ International Snowmobile Manufacturers Association (internationally oriented national body)

♦ **International Snow Science Workshop (ISSW)** **14880**

Contact address not obtained. E-mail: isswsteering@gmail.com.
URL: http://issw.net/

History Originated in meetings held informally in 1950s and early 1960s. **Aims** Facilitate the interdisciplinary exchange of ideas and experiences between snow science researchers and practitioners. Steering Committee set up, 1984, Aspen CO (USA). **Structure** Steering Committee. **Activities** Events/meetings. **Events** *International Snow Science Workshop (ISSW)* Canada 2026, *International Snow Science Workshop (ISSW)* Tromsø (Norway) 2024, *Biennial Workshop* Bend, OR (USA) 2023, *Biennial Workshop* Fernie, BC (Canada) 2021, *Snow Science Workshop* 2020. [2022.03.04/XM4849/c/**E**]

♦ International Social Affiliation of Women Airline Pilots / see International Society of Women Airline Pilots (#15550)

♦ **International Social Democratic Union for Education (ISDUE)** **14881**

Union internationale pour l'education – Union Internacional Socialists de Educación – Internationale Sozialdemokratische Organisation für Bildung – União International Socialista para Educação

Sec Franz-Jonas-Platz 8/2, 1210 Vienna, Austria. T. +4312725975.
Pres Kendermag Utca 29, Budapest 1162, Hungary.
URL: http://www.isdue.org/

History 27 Jul 1951, Versailles (France). New Statutes adopted 2 Aug 1980, Zurich (Switzerland). Former names and other names: *International Union of Social Democratic Teachers (IUSDT)* – former; *Union internationale des enseignants socialistes* – former; *Unión Internacional de Profesores Socialistas Demócratas* – former; *Internationale Union Sozialistischer Demokratischer Erzieher (IUSDE)* – former; *Union internationale universitaire socialiste et démocratique* – alias. **Aims** Unite all socialist educational organizations sharing a political responsibility and an affiliation to a section of the Socialist International. **Structure** General Assembly; Executive Committee. **Languages** English, German. **Finance** Sources: members' dues. **Activities** Advocacy/lobbying/activism; networking/liaising; training/education. **Events** *Annual Congress* Lisbon (Portugal) 2015, *Annual Congress* Brussels (Belgium) 2012, *Annual Congress* Budapest (Hungary) 2012, *Annual Congress* Varna (Bulgaria) 2011, *Annual Congress* Leeds (UK) 2010. **Publications** Conference proceedings; articles; reports.

Members Autonomous national organizations and individuals in 26 countries:
Algeria, Austria, Belgium, Brazil, Bulgaria, Chile, Côte d'Ivoire, Croatia, Czechia, Denmark, Finland, France, Germany, Hungary, Israel, Italy, Luxembourg, Moldova, Portugal, Romania, Senegal, Slovakia, Sweden, Switzerland, Türkiye, UK.

Consultative Status Consultative status granted from: *ECOSOC (#05331)* (Ros A). **NGO Relations** Affiliated with (1): *Socialist International (SI, #19340).* [2020/XD2777/**C**]

♦ International Social and Environmental Accreditation and Labelling Alliance / see ISEAL (#16026)
♦ International Social Environmental Union (internationally oriented national body)
♦ International Social History Association (unconfirmed)
♦ International Social Innovation Research Conference (meeting series)
♦ International Social Insurance Conference / see International Social Security Association (#14885)
♦ International Socialist Advisory Committee (inactive)
♦ International Socialist Committee (inactive)
♦ International Socialist Office (inactive)
♦ International Socialist Women's Secretariat (inactive)
♦ International of the Socialist Youth (inactive)
♦ International Social Law Society (inactive)

♦ **International Social Marketing Association (iSMA)** **14882**

Sec c/o Hager Sharp, 1030 15th St NW, Ste 600E, Washington DC 20005, USA.
URL: https://isocialmarketing.org/

History 2008, Brighton (UK). Founded during the *Global Social Marketing Conference.* **Aims** Advance social marketing practice, research and teaching through collaborative networks of professionals, supporters and enthusiasts. **Structure** Board of Directors. **Finance** Sources: members' dues. **Events** *World Social Marketing Conference* Brighton (UK) 2022, *World Social Marketing Conference* Edinburgh (UK) 2019, *World Social Marketing Conference / World Social Marketing Conference – WMC* Sydney, NSW (Australia) 2015. **NGO Relations** *European Social Marketing Association (ESMA, #08504).* [2022/XJ9233/**C**]

♦ **International Social Media Association (ISMA)** **14883**

Sec Level 4, 9 Barrack Street, Sydney NSW 2000, Australia. T. +61280069964.
Facebook: https://www.facebook.com/ISMAglobal/

History Jan 2014, Sydney, NSW (Australia). **Aims** Facilitate confidential discussions between platforms, government, business and industry groups regarding global developments for a predictive, rather than curative approach to social media law making. **Structure** Board of Directors. **Languages** English. **Finance** Sources: members' dues. **Activities** Conflict resolution; events/meetings; networking/liaising; politics/policy/regulatory; training/education. **Publications** *The Social Media: Global Guides.*

Members Full in 12 counties:
Australia, China, India, Israel, Italy, Malta, New Zealand, Russia, Singapore, South Africa, Thailand, USA. [2021/XM4867/**C**]

♦ **International Social Ontology Society (ISOS)** **14884**

Pres Philosophy Dept – Tufts Univ, Miner Hall, 14 Upper Campus Rd, Medford MA 02155, USA. Fax +16176273899.
URL: https://isosonline.org/

History Registration: Austria. **Aims** Bring together philosophers, social theorists, cognitive scientists, psychologists, economists, political scientists, legal scholars, anthropologists, and other scholars interested in the field of social ontology. **Structure** Steering Committee. **Finance** Sources: members' dues. **Activities** Advocacy/lobbying/activism; awards/prizes/competitions; events/meetings. **Events** *Biennial Collective Intentionality Conference* Vienna (Austria) 2022, *Social Ontology Conference* San Diego, CA (USA) 2021, *Biennial Collective Intentionality Conference* Neuchâtel (Switzerland) 2020, *Biennial ENSO (European Network on Social Ontology) Conference* Tampere (Finland) 2019, *Biennial Collective Intentionality Conference* Medford, MA (USA) 2018. **Publications** *Journal of Social Ontology (JSO).* [2020/AA0436/**C**]

♦ International Social Pharmacy Workshop (meeting series)
♦ International Social Science (unconfirmed)
♦ International Social Science Council (inactive)

♦ **International Social Security Association (ISSA)** **14885**

Association internationale de la sécurité sociale (AISS) – Asociación Internacional de la Seguridad Social (AISS) – Internationale Vereinigung für Soziale Sicherheit (IVSS)

Secretary-General Route des Morillons 4, Case postale 1, 1211 Geneva 22, Switzerland. T. +41227996617. Fax +41227998509. E-mail: issa@ilo.org.
URL: http://www.issa.int/

History 4 Oct 1927, Brussels (Belgium). Founded with the support of the International Labour Organization. New Constitution adopted 1947, Geneva (Switzerland), at 8th General Assembly. Constitution and Financial Regulations revised: 1961; 1977; 1983; 1987; 1992; 1998; 2007; 2013; 2016. Former names and other names: *International Conference of Sickness Insurance Funds and Mutual Benefit Societies* – former (4 Oct 1927 to 1936); *Conférence internationale des unions nationales de sociétés mutuelles et de caisses d'assurance-maladie* – former (4 Oct 1927 to 1936); *International Social Insurance Conference* – former (1936 to 1947); *Conférence internationale de la mutualité et des assurances sociales (CIMAS)* – former (1936 to 1947). **Aims** Promote excellence in social security administration through professional guidelines, expert knowledge, services and support to enable members to develop dynamic social security systems and policy. **Structure** General Assembly (every 3 years); Council; Bureau; Control Commission; Secretariat, headed by Secretary-General, located at International Labour Office, Geneva (Switzerland); Technical Commissions (13); International Prevention Sections (14). **Languages** English, French, German, Spanish. **Staff** 45.00 FTE, paid. Certain services provided by ILO. **Finance** Sources: contributions; members' dues. **Activities** Advocacy/lobbying/activism; events/meetings; knowledge management/information dissemination; networking/liaising; research/documentation; standards/guidelines; training/education. **Events** *Triennial World Congress on Safety and Health at Work* Sydney, NSW (Australia) 2023, *World Social Security Forum* Marrakech (Morocco) 2022, *International Conference on Information and Communication Technology in Social Security* Tallinn (Estonia) 2022, *Regional Social Security Forum for Europe* Tallinn (Estonia) 2022, *Vision Zero Summit* Tokyo (Japan) 2022. **Publications** *International Social Security Review* (4 a year). *10 Global Challenges in Social Security.* Databases available via Web portal. **Members** Affiliate Government ministries and departments, institutions, agencies and other entities and non-international federations of these. Associate non-international organizations with objectives compatible with those of ISSA but not qualified to become affiliate members. As of March 2021, 320 member organizations in 158 countries and territories. Membership countries not specified. **Consultative Status** Consultative status granted from: *ECOSOC (#05331)* (General). **IGO Relations** Cooperates with (1): *Arab Labour Organization (ALO, #01001).* [2022.10.11/XB2468/**B**]

♦ **International Social Service (ISS)** **14886**

Service Social International (SSI) – Servicio Social Internacional (SSI) – Internationaler Sozialdienst

SG and CEO Quai du Seujet 32, 1201 Geneva, Switzerland. T. +41229067700. Fax +41229067701. E-mail: info@iss-ssi.org.
URL: http://www.iss-ssi.org/

History Jan 1921, Geneva (Switzerland). Founded by *World Young Women's Christian Association (World YWCA, #21947)* to deal with social problems resulting from migration (at that time IMS was essentially restricted to Europe and North America). Became an independent organization, Oct 1924, with headquarters in Geneva (Switzerland). Current statutes adopted Apr 2016, Melbourne (Australia). Former names and other names: *International Migration Service (IMS)* – former; *Service international d'aide aux émigrants* – former. Registration: Swiss Civil Code, Switzerland. **Aims** Assist individuals, children and families confronted with social problems as a consequence of *migration.* **Structure** International Council (meets every 2 years), acting as General Assembly; Governing Board; Professional Advisory Committee; General Secretariat, directed by Secretary General, located in Geneva (Switzerland); Regional Office in Senegal. **Languages** English, French, Spanish. **Staff** 15.00 FTE, paid. 600 worldwide. **Finance** Sources: fundraising; government support; international organizations; members' dues. **Activities** Advocacy/lobbying/activism; awareness raising; training/education. **Events** *International Council Meeting* Valletta (Malta) 2018, *International Council Meeting* Melbourne, VIC (Australia) 2016, *International Council Meeting* Cascais (Portugal) 2014, *International Council Meeting* Banff, AB (Canada) 2012, *International Council Meeting* Cape Town (South Africa) 2009. **Publications** *ISS Monthly Review* (12 a year). Thematic fact sheets; statements; guides; guidelines; handbooks; activity report. **Information Services** *Biographical Database.*

Members National members in 26 countries and territories:
Albania, Australia, Belgium, Canada, France, Germany, Greece, Hong Kong, Ireland, Israel, Japan, Lebanon, Malta, Netherlands, New Zealand, Pakistan, Philippines, Poland, Portugal, South Africa, Spain, Switzerland, Türkiye, UK, USA, Venezuela.

National Partners in 90 countries and territories:
Albania, Algeria, Anguilla, Antigua, Argentina, Azerbaijan, Bangladesh, Barbados, Belarus, Belize, Benin, Bermuda, Bolivia, Bosnia-Herzegovina, Botswana, Brazil, Bulgaria, Burkina Faso, Cambodia, Cameroon, Cayman Is, Chile, Colombia, Congo Brazzaville, Costa Rica, Côte d'Ivoire, Croatia, Cuba, Curaçao, Cyprus, Czechia, Dominican Rep, Egypt, El Salvador, Estonia, Finland, France, Gabon, Gambia, Germany, Ghana, Guatemala, Guinea, Guyana, Hungary, India, Indonesia, Jordan, Korea Rep, Kosovo, Latvia, Lithuania, Luxembourg, Malaysia, Malta, Mauritania, Moldova, Monaco, Morocco, Namibia, North Macedonia, Norway, Pakistan, Palestine, Papua New Guinea, Paraguay, Puerto Rico, Romania, Russia, Senegal, Serbia, Seychelles, Singapore, Slovenia, Sri Lanka, St Kitts-Nevis, St Lucia, St Vincent-Grenadines, Syrian AR, Tanzania UR, Thailand, Togo, Trinidad-Tobago, Tunisia, Türkiye, Ukraine, United Arab Emirates, Uruguay, Vietnam, Zambia.

Consultative Status Consultative status granted from: *ECOSOC (#05331)* (Special); *ILO (#11123)* (Special List); *UNICEF (#20332)*; *OAS (#17629)*; *African Committee of Experts on the Rights and Welfare of the Child (ACERWC, #00257)* (Observer Status). **IGO Relations** Observer to: *International Organization for Migration (IOM, #14454).* Accredited by: *United Nations Office at Vienna (UNOV, #20604).* Partner of: *UNHCR (#20327).* Cooperation agreement with: *The Hague Conference on Private International Law (HCCH, #10850)*; *Inter-American Children's Institute (IACI, #11406)*; *UNESCO (#20322).* Associated with Department of Global Communications of the United Nations. **NGO Relations** Member of: *Global Partnership to End Violence Against Children (End Violence Against Children, #10533)*; *Alliance of NGOs on Crime Prevention and Criminal Justice (#00709)*; *Child Rights Connect (#03884)*; *Child Rights International Network (CRIN, #03885)*; *Children and Families Across Borders (CFAB)* serves as UK branch; *Conference of Non-Governmental Organizations in Consultative Relationship with the United Nations (CONGO, #04635)*; *Fédération des Institutions Internationales établies à Genève (FIIG, #09599)*; *International Council on Social Welfare (ICSW, #13076)*; *NGO Committee on UNICEF (#17120).* Working relations with: *International Catholic Child Bureau (#12450)*; *International Committee of the Red Cross (ICRC, #12799)*; *International Federation of Red Cross and Red Crescent Societies (#13526)*; *International Foster Care Organization (IFCO, #13663).* [2021/XC2469/**C**]

♦ International Social Service – Great Britain / see Children and Families Across Borders

♦ **International Social Survey Programme (ISSP)** **14887**

Contact FORS Swiss Centre of Expertise in the Social Sciences, c/o Université de Lausanne, Quartier Mouline, 1015 Lausanne VD, Switzerland. E-mail: issp.sec@gmail.com.
URL: http://www.issp.org/

History 1984, London (UK). Founded as a continuing programme of international collaboration. **Aims** Promote comparative social science and survey research, data and service free of charge for the global scientific community; bring together pre-existing social science projects and coordinate research goals, thereby adding a cross-national, cross-cultural perspective to individual national studies. **Structure** Annual General Meeting; Secretariat; Archive; Methodology Committee; Working Goups. **Languages** English. **Finance** Members meet their own expenses. **Activities** Networking/liaising; projects/programmes; research and development. **Events** *Annual Conference* Lausanne (Switzerland) 2021, *Annual Conference* Jaipur (India) 2019, *Annual Conference* Istanbul (Turkey) 2017, *Annual Conference* Kaunas (Lithuania) 2016, *Annual Conference* Cavtat (Croatia) 2012. **Publications** Journals; books; reports. **Members** Survey organizations and institutes in 44 countries and territories. Membership countries not specified. [2023.02.14/XF5591/**F**]

♦ **International Social Theory Consortium (ISTC)** **14888**

Dir Dept of Sociology, Univ of Tennessee-Knoxville, Knoxville TN 37996, USA. E-mail: istc@socialtheory.org.
URL: http://www.socialtheory.org/

History Inaugural meeting 11 May 2000, Lexington KY (USA). **Activities** Events/meetings. **Events** *Annual Conference* Tampa, FL (USA) 2021, *Annual Conference* Dubrovnik (Croatia) 2019, *Annual Conference* Chicago, IL (USA) 2018, *Annual Conference* Innsbruck (Austria) 2017, *Annual Conference* Ames, IA (USA) 2016.

Members Full in 6 countries:
Australia, Belgium, Bulgaria, Canada, Germany, UK. [2018/XN8992/**C**]

♦ **International Social Tourism Organisation (ISTO)** **14889**

Organisation internationale du tourisme social (OITS) – Organización Internacional de Turismo Social

Dir Rue Watteeu 2-4, 1000 Brussels, Belgium. T. +3222741540. Fax +3225141691. E-mail: info@isto.international.

URL: https://isto.international/
History 7 Jun 1963, Brussels (Belgium). International congresses on social tourism having been held: 1956, Bern (Switzerland); 1959, Vienna (Austria); 1962, Milan (Italy). Former names and other names: *International Bureau of Social Tourism* – former; *Bureau international du tourisme social (BITS)* – former; *Internationales Büro für Sozialtourismus* – former; *Oficina Internacional de Turismo Social* – former; *Buró Internazionale del Turismo Sociale* – former; *International Organisation of Social Tourism (IOST)* – former. Registration: Banque-Carrefour des Entreprises, No/ID: 0408.300.021, Start date: 17 Mar 1965, Belgium. **Aims** Raise awareness among governments, international institutions and local and regional authorities competent for social policies in tourism and best practices which facilitate holidays for all; become a platform for exchanges and services for members by stimulating exchange of experiences, know-how and project development. **Structure** General Meeting (annual); Board of Directors; Executive Committee; General Secretariat; Regional Sections (3); Permanent Commissions (3); Working Groups. **Languages** English, French, Spanish. **Staff** 4.00 FTE, paid. **Finance** Sources: donations; grants; members' dues. **Activities** Events/meetings; knowledge management/ information dissemination; networking/liaising; projects/programmes. **Events** *General Assembly and World Congress* Ponta Delgada (Portugal) 2022, *General Assembly and World Congress* Brussels (Belgium) 2021, *General Assembly and World Congress* Lima (Peru) 2020, *General Assembly and World Congress* Lyon (France) 2018, *Europe General Assembly* La Roche-en-Ardenne (Belgium) 2017. **Publications** *OITS/ISTO Info* (6 a year) in English, French – newsletter; *Social Tourism in the World* (21 a year) in English, French – magazine. *Montréal Declaration – Towards a Humanist, Social Vision of Tourism* (2016). Studies; reports.
Members Active, Associate, Honorary, including: public and private organizations; profit and non-profit organizations such as tourism associations, holiday centres and youth hostels; agencies and operators; trade unions; cooperatives; NGOs; training institutions; official tourism organizations. Members in 35 countries:
Algeria, Belgium, Benin, Brazil, Burkina Faso, Cameroon, Canada, Chile, Colombia, Costa Rica, Dominican Rep, France, Gabon, Germany, Haiti, Italy, Mali, Malta, Mauritania, Mexico, Morocco, Nepal, Paraguay, Portugal, Russia, San Marino, Slovenia, Spain, Switzerland, Togo, Tunisia, Türkiye, UK, USA, Zambia.
International associations (3), included in this Yearbook:
Fédération Internationale de Camping, Caravanning et Autocaravaning (FICC, #09618); *International Co-operative Alliance (ICA, #12944)*; *World Youth Student and Educational Travel Confederation (WYSE Travel Confederation, #21959)*.
Consultative Status Consultative status granted from: *ECOSOC (#05331)* (Ros C); *UNESCO (#20322)* (Consultative Status). **IGO Relations** Affiliate member of: *World Tourism Organization (UNWTO, #21861)*. **NGO Relations** Member of (2): *European Tourism Manifesto (#08921)*; *World Youth Student and Educational Travel Confederation (WYSE Travel Confederation, #21959)*. [2022/XA1434/y/**F**]

♦ International Social Travel Federation (inactive)
♦ International Social Welfare Association of Korea (internationally oriented national body)

♦ International Societies for Investigative Dermatology (ISID) 14890

Contact c/o ESDR, Rue Cingria 7, 1205 Geneva, Switzerland.
URL: http://isiderm.org/
History 9 May 2013. Founded on signing of Memorandum of Understanding by *European Society for Dermatological Research (ESDR, #08578)* Japanese Society for Investigative Dermatology (JSID) and the Society for Investigative Dermatology (SID). **Aims** Unite all organizations of scientists dedicated to investigative dermatology and cutaneous biology so as to encourage and facilitate collaboration and jointly sponsor and support a scientific meeting. **Structure** Board of Directors. **Activities** Events/meetings; networking/liaising. **Events** *Quinquennial Congress* Tokyo (Japan) 2023.
Members Organizations (3). National organizations in 2 countries:
Japan, USA.
Regional organization:
European Society for Dermatological Research (ESDR, #08578). [2018/XM6939/y/**C**]

♦ International Society for the Abolition of Data Processing Machines (inactive)
♦ International Society of Abortion Doctors (inactive)
♦ International Society for Academic Research on Religious Systems / see International Society for Academic Research on Shamanism (#14891)

♦ International Society for Academic Research on Shamanism (ISARS) 14891

Main Office Fotomara 93-95, Neos Kosmos, 117 45 Athens, Greece. E-mail: info@isars.org.
URL: http://www.isars.org/
History 2014. Founded, continuing the work of *International Society for Shamanistic Research (ISSR, inactive)*. Former names and other names: *International Society for Academic Research on Religious Systems (ISARRS)* – legal name. Registration: Greece. **Aims** Promote academic multidisciplinary research of the religious therapeutic systems the world over often described as shamanism. **Structure** Executive Board. **Languages** English. **Events** *Conference* Kuching (Malaysia) 2022, *Conference* Kuching (Malaysia) 2021, *Conference* Santiago (Chile) 2019, *Conference* Hanoi (Vietnam) 2017, *Conference* Delphi (Greece) 2015. **Publications** *SHAMAN* – journal. [2021/XJ9564/**C**]

♦ International Society of Acoustic Remote Sensing of the Atmosphere and Oceans (ISARS) 14892

Contact Inst of Meteorology, Dept Water, Atmosphere and Environment, Peter Jordan Str 82, 1190 Vienna, Austria.
Chairperson c/o Wind Energy Dept, VEA-118, PO Box 49, Frederiksborgvej 399, 4000 Røskilde, Denmark. T. +4546775019.
URL: http://www.boku.ac.at/imp/isars/
History 1981, Calgary (Canada). Former names and other names: *International Society for Acoustic Remote Sensing of the Atmosphere and Oceans and Associated Techniques (ISARS)* – alias. **Structure** Steering Committee of 8 members, including Chairman. **Activities** *International Symposium for the Advancement of Boundary Layer Remote Sensing.* **Events** *International Symposium for the Advancement of Boundary Layer Remote Sensing* Bulgaria 2016, *International Symposium for the Advancement of Boundary Layer Remote Sensing / Symposium* Auckland (New Zealand) 2014, *Symposium* Boulder, CO (USA) 2012, *International symposium for the advancement of boundary layer remote sensing / Symposium* Paris (France) 2010, *International symposium for the advancement of boundary layer remote sensing* Røskilde (Denmark) 2008. **Publications** *ISARS Newsletter.* [2020/XD7458/**D**]

♦ International Society for Acoustic Remote Sensing of the Atmosphere and Oceans and Associated Techniques / see International Society of Acoustic Remote Sensing of the Atmosphere and Oceans (#14892)
♦ International Society of Acrylic Painters (internationally oriented national body)
♦ International Society of Acupuncture (inactive)

♦ International Society for Adaptive Behavior (ISAB) 14893

Pres Maersk Institute, Univ of Southern Denmark, Campussvej 55, 5230 Odense M, Denmark. T. +4565503546. Fax +4566157697.
URL: http://www.isab.org/
Aims Promote education and further research on adaptive behaviour in animals, animats, *software* agents and robots. **Finance** Members' dues. **Events** *Biennial Conference* Aberystwyth (UK) 2016, *Biennial Conference* Castellón de la Plana (Spain) 2014, *Biennial Conference* Odense (Denmark) 2012, *Biennial Conference* Paris (France) 2010, *Biennial Conference* Osaka (Japan) 2008. **Publications** *Adaptive Behavior* (6 a year). Conference proceedings.
Members in 28 countries and territories:
Australia, Austria, Belgium, Brazil, Canada, Denmark, Fiji, Finland, France, Germany, Hong Kong, Ireland, Italy, Japan, Korea Rep, Mexico, Netherlands, New Zealand, Norway, Poland, Portugal, Romania, Spain, Sweden, Switzerland, Thailand, UK, USA. [2015.09.02/XD6657/**D**]

♦ International Society for Adaptive Medicine (ISAM) 14894

Pres Elect Univ of Taipei, No 101 Sec 2 Jhongcheng Rd, Shinlin Dist, Taipei 11153, Taiwan.
Contact Medical Sciences Div, Northern Ontario School of Medicine, Lakehead Univ, 955 Oliver Road, Thunder Bay ON P7B 5E1, Canada.
URL: http://isam2015.umin.jp/index.html/
History 1990, Freiburg (Germany), by scientists from a dozen different countries, during first congress. **Aims** Promote understanding of the basic mechanisms of physiological adaptations at molecular and *cellular* levels as well as at the level of complex interactions responsible for the integrated control of body functions; improve understanding of dismissed adaptations responsible for disease development. **Structure** Board of Directors. **Languages** English. **Staff** 3.00 FTE, paid. **Finance** Self-funded. Government funding for World Congress. **Activities** Organizes triennial meeting. Sponsors regional symposia worldwide. Studies adaptive changes occurring in response to different environmental factors. **Events** *World Congress* Chonburi (Thailand) 2018, *World Congress* Yonago (Japan) 2015, *World congress* Bucharest (Romania) 2012, *World congress* Taipei (Taiwan) 2009, *World congress* Moscow (Russia) 2006. **Publications** *Adaptation Biology and Medicine* – in 8 vols.
Members Clinicians, scientists and engineers in 27 countries and territories:
Argentina, Australia, Austria, Brazil, Canada, China, Cuba, Czechia, Denmark, France, Germany, India, Italy, Japan, Korea Rep, Mexico, Netherlands, Romania, Russia, Singapore, Slovakia, Sweden, Taiwan, Thailand, UK, Ukraine, USA. [2018/XN7416/v/**C**]

♦ International Society of Addiction Journal Editors (ISAJE) 14895

Exec Officer National Addiction Ctr, 4 Windsor Walk, London, SE5 8AF, UK. T. +442078480014. Fax +442078485966.
URL: http://www.isaje.net/
History 2001. **Aims** Promote excellence in communication and dissemination of information on addiction and related sciences within the scientific community and to those who have responsibility for prevention, treatment, cure, professional training and policy formation in this field. **Structure** Management Board; Working Groups. **Staff** 1.00 FTE, paid. **Activities** Training/education; events/meetings. **Events** *Annual Meeting* Helsinki (Finland) 2022, *Annual Meeting* Banff, AB (Canada) 2019, *Annual Meeting* Prague (Czechia) 2018, *Annual Meeting* Boston, MA (USA) 2017, *European Conference on Addictive Behaviours and Dependencies* Lisbon (Portugal) 2017. **Publications** *Publishing Addiction Science: A Guide for the Perplexed* (2nd ed 2008).
Members Full; Associate. Individuals in 15 countries:
Australia, Canada, Denmark, Finland, Germany, Greece, Hungary, Korea Rep, Nigeria, Russia, Spain, Switzerland, Türkiye, UK, USA.
NGO Relations *International Confederation of Alcohol, Tobacco and other Drug Research Associations (ICARA, #12843).* [2016.06.22/XM3073/**D**]

♦ International Society of Addiction Medicine (ISAM) 14896

Contact 47 Tuscany Ridge Terrace NW, Calgary AB T3L 3A5, Canada. T. +14038137217.
URL: http://www.isamweb.org/
History Founded 26 Apr 1999, Palm Springs CA (USA). **Aims** Provide a supportive, educational network to physicians through electronic communication and meetings; develop consensual position papers on issues relevant to the practice of physicians; offer a certification in addiction medicine by examination. **Structure** Governing Board; International Advisory Committee; Board of Directors. **Languages** English. **Staff** 0.50 FTE, paid. **Finance** Sources: members' dues. **Activities** Certification/accreditation; events/meetings; training/ education. **Events** *Annual Meeting* Marrakech (Morocco) 2023, *Annual Meeting* Valletta (Malta) 2022, *Annual Meeting* 2021, *Annual Meeting* Calgary, AB (Canada) 2020, *Annual Meeting* Delhi (India) 2019. **Publications** *International Addiction and Substance Abuse.*
Members Full (physicians practising or involved in Addiction Medicine); Associate (allied health professionals working or interested in the field). Members in 107 countries. Membership countries not specified. Affiliated with national societies in 18 countries:
Affiliated with national societies in 18 countries:
Austria, Canada, Egypt, Finland, Iceland, India, Indonesia, Israel, Italy, Japan, Korea Rep, Netherlands, Norway, Philippines, Switzerland, United Arab Emirates, USA, Vietnam.
Consultative Status Consultative status granted from: *ECOSOC (#05331)* (Ros A). **NGO Relations** Member of: *Vienna NGO Committee on Drugs (VNGOC, #20773).* [2020/XD8117/**C**]

♦ International Society for Adolescent Psychiatry / see International Society for Adolescent Psychiatry and Psychology (#14897)

♦ International Society for Adolescent Psychiatry and Psychology (ISAPP) 14897

Contact PO Box 570218, Dallas TX 75357-0218, USA. E-mail: frda1@airmail.net.
URL: http://www.isapp.org/
History Jul 1985, Paris (France). Former names and other names: *International Society for Adolescent Psychiatry (ISAP)* – former (Jul 1985 to 2003); *Société internationale de psychiatrie de l'adolescence* – former (Jul 1985 to 2003). **Aims** Improve knowledge and scientific researches on adolescence psychiatry and psychopathology; create and develop links between psychiatrists, psychologists and allied professions involved in the field of adolescent psychiatry and psychopathology. **Structure** Board, consisting of President, Secretary and Treasurer. Executive Committee, comprising members of the Board plus President Elect, Honorary President, Regional Vice-Presidents, Assistant Treasurer, Assistant Secretary, "Annals/Newsletter" Editor and Administrative Director. Council of delegates. **Languages** English, French. **Staff** 1.00 FTE, paid. **Finance** Members' dues. Grants and funds from organizations. **Activities** Organizes congresses and symposia. **Events** *Regional Conference* Osaka (Japan) 2018, *International Congress* New York, NY (USA) 2015, *Regional Conference* Ankara (Turkey) 2013, *International Congress* Berlin (Germany) 2011, *International Congress* Montréal, QC (Canada) 2007. **Publications** *International Annals of Adolescence Psychiatry* (annual) in English, French.
Members Full in 20 countries:
Argentina, Belgium, Brazil, Canada, France, Germany, Israel, Italy, Japan, Mexico, Nigeria, Norway, Spain, Sweden, Switzerland, Türkiye, UK, Uruguay, USA, Venezuela. [2020/XD1388/v/**D**]

♦ International Society for Adult Congenital Cardiac Disease / see International Society for Adult Congenital Heart Disease (#14898)

♦ International Society for Adult Congenital Heart Disease (ISACHD) . 14898

Secretariat 1500 Sunday Drive, Ste 102, Raleigh NC 27607, USA. T. +19198615578. Fax +19197874916. E-mail: info@isachd.org.
URL: http://www.isachd.org/
History as *International Society for Adult Congenital Cardiac Disease (ISACCD).* **Aims** Promote, maintain and pursue excellence in the care of adults with congenital cardiac disease. **Structure** Executive Committee, comprising President, President Elect, Past President, Secretary, Treasurer and Regional Directors. **Languages** English. **Staff** 1.00 FTE, paid. **Finance** Members' dues. **Activities** Events/meetings; awards/ prizes/competitions. **Events** *Joint European/North American symposium on congenital heart disease and cardiac surgery in the adult* London (UK) 2004, *Joint European/North American symposium on congenital heart disease and cardiac surgery in the adult* Santorini Is (Greece) 2003. **Publications** *Journal of Cardiology.*
Members Individuals in 19 countries:
Argentina, Australia, Austria, Canada, Colombia, Germany, India, Israel, Italy, Japan, Korea Rep, Pakistan, Sweden, Switzerland, Trinidad-Tobago, UK, United Arab Emirates, USA, Venezuela. [2018/XD7475/**D**]

♦ International Society to Advance Alzheimer's Research and Treatment (internationally oriented national body)
♦ International Society of Advance Care Planning and End of Life Care / see Advance Care Planning International (#00126)
♦ International Society for the Advanced Study of Spacetime (no recent information)

♦ International Society for the Advancement of Clinical Magnetoencephalography (ISACM) 14899

Contact Cognitive Brain Research Unit, Helsinki Univ Central Hosp, Stenbäckinkatu 9, PO Box 100, FI-00029 Helsinki, Finland.

Sec Children's Hosp of Philadelphia, 3401 Civic Center Blvd, Philadelphia PA 19104, USA.
URL: http://www.isacm.info/

History Founded as a nonprofit professional society, incorporated in the state of Pennsylvania (USA). Also referred to as *International Society for the Advancement of Clinical MEG.* **Aims** Promote the use of magnetoencephalography in diagnosis and treatment of *neurologic* and *psychiatric* conditions. **Structure** Executive Committee, comprising President, Vice-President, Secretary, Treasurer and 6 members. **Events** *Biennial Conference* Osaka (Japan) 2023, *Biennial Conference* Toronto, ON (Canada) 2019, *Biennial Conference* Helsinki (Finland) 2015, *Biennial Conference / Conference* Sapporo (Japan) 2013, *Biennial conference / Conference* Athens (Greece) 2009. **Members** Individuals. Membership countries not specified. [2016/XJ8018/**C**]

♦ International Society for the Advancement of Clinical MEG / see International Society for the Advancement of Clinical Magnetoencephalography (#14899)

♦ International Society for Advancement of Cytometry (ISAC) 14900

Main Office 4601 North Fairfax Dr, Ste 1200, Arlington VA 22203, USA. T. +17032878701. E-mail: isac@isac-net.org.
URL: http://www.isac-net.org/

History 1979, USA, as *Society of Analytical Cytology (SAC).* Subsequently changed title to *International Society for Analytical Cytology (ISAC),* 1991. Current title adopted, May 2008. Current constitution revised Sep 2009. **Aims** Promote the development of analytical cytology; transfer methodologies; exchange scientific and technical information. **Structure** Scientific Advisory Committee; Executive Committee, consisting of President, President-Elect, Past President, Secretary and Treasurer; Councillors (10). **Events** *CYTO Virtual 2020* Arlington, VA (USA) 2020, *CYTO Annual Congress* Philadelphia, PA (USA) 2020, *CYTO Annual Congress* Vancouver, BC (Canada) 2019, *CYTO Annual Congress* Prague (Czechia) 2018, *Joint Meeting* Singapore (Singapore) 2017. **Publications** *Cytometry* (12 a year); *Clinical Communication in Cytometry* (6 a year).
Members Individuals in 47 countries and territories:
Argentina, Australia, Austria, Belgium, Brazil, Bulgaria, Canada, Chile, China, Denmark, Egypt, Finland, France, Germany, Greece, Hong Kong, Hungary, India, Israel, Italy, Japan, Kenya, Korea Rep, Malawi, Malaysia, Mexico, Netherlands, New Zealand, Norway, Philippines, Poland, Portugal, Puerto Rico, Romania, Russia, Saudi Arabia, Singapore, Slovakia, South Africa, Spain, Sweden, Switzerland, Taiwan, Thailand, Türkiye, UK, USA.
NGO Relations Member of: *European Society for Clinical Cell Analysis (ESCCA, #08544); Integrating Healthcare Enterprise International (IHE International, #11372).* [2020/XD4590/v/**F**]

♦ International Society for the Advancement of Economic Theory in its Relation to Statistics and Mathematics (inactive)

♦ International Society for the Advancement of Kinanthropometry (ISAK) 14901

SG Univ Católica de Murcia, Catedra Intl de Cineantropometria, Campus de los Jerónimos, Guadalupe, 30107 Murcia, Spain. T. +34968278708. E-mail: info@isak.global.
Pres Colletts Farm, Colletts Road, RD 1, Upper Hutt 5371, New Zealand. T. +6465262330.
URL: http://www.isak.global/

History 20 Jul 1986, Glasgow (UK). Founded during Commonwealth Conference. Statutes modified: 12 Sep 1988, Cheonan (Korea Rep); 29 Jun 2018, Santiago (Chile). Registration: Start date: Oct 2010, New Zealand. **Aims** Provide an international accreditation scheme to train and examine *anthropometrists* worldwide with a focus on the quantitative interface between human structure and function. **Structure** Congress (every 2 years); Executive Council; Working Groups (3). **Languages** English, Spanish. **Finance** Sources: fees for services; members' dues. **Activities** Certification/accreditation; events/meetings; training/education. **Events** *World Congress of Kinanthropometry* Alicante (Spain) 2022, *World Congress on Kinanthropometry* Santiago (Chile) 2018, *World Congress on Kinanthropometry* Mérida (Mexico) 2016, *Biennial Conference* Murcia (Spain) 2014, *Biennial Conference* Glasgow (UK) 2012. **Publications** *ISAK Newsletter* (4 a year) in English, Spanish; *International Journal of Kinanthropometry (IJK)* (2 a year) in English, Spanish.
Members Individuals in 51 countries and territories:
Argentina, Australia, Austria, Belgium, Bolivia, Brazil, Bulgaria, Canada, Colombia, Costa Rica, Croatia, Czechia, Dominican Rep, Ecuador, El Salvador, Estonia, Germany, Greece, Guatemala, Guyana, Hong Kong, India, Iran Islamic Rep, Ireland, Italy, Japan, Korea Rep, Malaysia, Mexico, Nepal, Netherlands, New Zealand, Nigeria, Panama, Paraguay, Peru, Philippines, Poland, Portugal, Puerto Rico, Qatar, Singapore, South Africa, Spain, Suriname, Sweden, Türkiye, UK, Uruguay, USA, Venezuela.
NGO Relations Member of (1): *International Council of Sport Science and Physical Education (ICSSPE, #13077).* [2022.06.15/XD0552/v/**C**]

♦ International Society for the Advancement of Respiratory Psychophysiology (ISARP) 14902

Sec-Treas VCU Psychology Dept, PO Box 842018, Richmond VA 23284, USA.
URL: https://www.isarp.net/

History 1993, during International Symposium on Respiratory Psychophysiology. **Aims** Promote and advance knowledge of relations between psychological and physiological aspects of respiration in research and application. **Structure** Medical/academic and research setting. Board of 6 members. **Languages** English. **Activities** Organizes Annual Conference. **Events** *Annual Meeting* Charlotte, NC (USA) 2022, *Annual Conference* New Brunswick, NJ (USA) 2014, *Annual Conference* Leuven (Belgium) 2013, *Annual Conference* Orlando, FL (USA) 2012, *Annual Conference* Athens (Greece) 2011. **Publications** *ISARP Abstracts.* **Members** in USA and Europe. Membership countries not specified. [2022/XM0081/**D**]

♦ International Society for the Advancement of Spine Surgery (ISASS) 14903

Main Office 301 S County Farm Rd, Suite L, Wheaton IL 60187, USA. T. +16303751432. Fax +16303751437. E-mail: info@isass.org.
URL: http://www.isass.org/

History 1999. Former names and other names: *Spine Arthroplasty Society (SAS)* – former (1999); *ISASS – Society for the Advancement of Spine Surgery* – former. Registration: USA, State of New York. **Aims** Discuss and assess existing strategies and innovative ideas in the clinical and basic sciences related to spine surgery; enhance patient care. **Structure** Board of Directors. Chapters (7): China; India; Korea; Latin America; Middle East; Taiwan; Turkey. **Activities** Events/meetings. **Events** *Annual Conference* San Juan (Puerto Rico) 2020, *Annual Conference* Anaheim, CA (USA) 2019, *Annual Conference* Toronto, ON (Canada) 2018, *Annual Conference* Boca Raton, FL (USA) 2017, *Meeting* Singapore (Singapore) 2016. **Publications** *International Journal of Spine Surgery* – official journal. **Members** Spine surgeons and related professionals (3,122). Membership countries not specified. [2020/XJ5965/**C**]

♦ International Society for the Advancement of Supercritical Fluids (ISASF) 14904

Association internationale pour la promotion des fluids supercritiques (AIPFS)

Sec Univ de Toulouse, Laboratoire de Génie Chimique, 4 allée Emile Monso, 31030 Toulouse CEDEX, France.
URL: http://www.isasf.net/

Aims Promote knowledge and applications of supercritical fluids. **Structure** General Assembly (annual). Board, including President, 2 Vice-Presidents, Secretary, Deputy-Secretary, Treasurer and Deputy-Treasurer. **Staff** 1.00 FTE, voluntary. **Finance** Members' dues. **Activities** Organizes annual meeting and symposia. **Events** *International Symposium on Supercritical Fluids* Montréal, QC (Canada) 2022, *European Meeting on Supercritical Fluids* Toulouse (France) 2021, *European Meeting on Supercritical Fluids* Ciudad Real (Spain) 2019, *International Symposium on Supercritical Fluid* Juan-les-Pins (France) 2018, *European Meeting on Supercritical Fluids* Lisbon (Portugal) 2017.
Members Full in 61 countries and territories:
Algeria, Argentina, Australia, Austria, Azerbaijan, Belgium, Brazil, Bulgaria, Canada, Chile, China, Colombia, Croatia, Czechia, Denmark, Estonia, Finland, France, Germany, Greece, Hungary, India, Indonesia, Iran Islamic Rep, Ireland, Israel, Italy, Japan, Korea Rep, Latvia, Lithuania, Luxembourg, Mexico, Morocco, Netherlands, New Zealand, North Macedonia, Norway, Peru, Poland, Portugal, Qatar, Romania, Russia, Serbia, Slovakia, Slovenia, South Africa, Spain, Sweden, Switzerland, Taiwan, Thailand, Trinidad-Tobago, Tunisia, Türkiye, UK, United Arab Emirates, Uruguay, USA, Venezuela. [2020/XM3072/**D**]

♦ International Society for the Advancement of Writing Research (ISAWR) 14905

Société internationale pour la promotion des recherches sur l'écriture – Sociedad Internacional para el Avance de la Investigación en Escritura

Address not obtained.
URL: http://www.isawr.org/

History Set up following 2 Writing Research Across Borders (WRAB) conferences, 2008, Santa Barbara CA (USA), and 2011, Washington DC (USA). **Aims** Develop interdisciplinary research into the dimensions of writing and learning of writing of people of all ages, languages, and other characteristics. **Structure** General Assembly; Steering Committee. **Languages** English, French, Spanish. **Staff** Voluntary. **Finance** Sources: meeting proceeds. **Events** *Writing Research Across Borders Conference (WRAB)* Trondheim (Norway) 2023, *Writing Research Across Borders Conference (WRAB)* Fairfax, VA (USA) 2021, *Writing Research Across Borders Conference (WRAB)* Xian (China) 2020, *Writing Research Across Borders Conference (WRAB)* Bogota (Colombia) 2017, *Writing Research Across Borders Conference (WRAB)* Paris (France) 2014. **Publications** Conference papers. **Members** Full (about 1,000). Membership countries not specified. [2019/XJ7451/**C**]

♦ International Society for Aeolian Research (ISAR) 14906

Sec-Treas Dept of Geosciences, Texas Tech Univ, Lubbock TX 79409-1053, USA.
URL: https://aeolianresearch.com/

Aims Promote contacts among scientists undertaking research in *wind erosion* processes, *landforms*, and *modelling*; stimulate scientific research in aeolian topics and related fields; further application of results of such research into practical applications. **Activities** *International Conference on Aeolian Research (ICAR).* **Events** *Conference* Las Cruces, NM (USA) 2023, *Conference* Bordeaux (France) 2018, *Conference* Mildura, VIC (Australia) 2016, *Conference* Lanzhou (China) 2014, *Conference* Santa Rosa (Argentina) 2010. **Members** Individuals and institutions. Membership countries not specified. [2022/XJ8101/**D**]

♦ International Society of Aeronautical Telecommunications / see SITA (#19299)

♦ International Society for Aerosols in Medicine (ISAM) 14907

Société internationale pour les aérosols en médecine – Internationale Gesellschaft für Aerosole in der Medizin (IGAeM) – Societas Internationalis pro Aerosolibus in Medicina

Office c/o GS Bio-Inhalation, Wohraer Str 37, 35285 Gemünden am Main, Germany. E-mail: office@isam.org.
URL: http://www.isam.org/

History 14 May 1970, Berlin (Germany). **Aims** Stimulate international cooperation, promote interdisciplinary collaboration, and distribute information on aerosols in medicine; coordinate research, maintain contacts with national societies, institutions and scientists. **Structure** General Assembly (at least every 2 years); Board (at least once a year). **Languages** English, French, German. **Staff** 1.00 FTE, paid. **Finance** Members' dues: Regular – US$ 120; Student – US$ 50; Hardship – US$ 50; Joint Regular with ERS – US$ 102. **Activities** Awards/prizes/competitions; events/meetings; guidance/assistance/consulting; knowledge management/information dissemination; training/education. **Events** *Congress* Saarbrücken (Germany) 2023, *Congress* Boise, ID (USA) 2021, *Congress* Montreux (Switzerland) 2019, *Congress* Santa Fe, NM (USA) 2017, *Congress* Munich (Germany) 2015. **Publications** *Journal of Aerosol Medicine and Pulmonary Drug Delivery* (4 a year).
Members Organizations in 33 countries:
Australia, Austria, Belgium, Brazil, Canada, Chile, China, Czechia, Denmark, Egypt, Finland, France, Germany, Hungary, India, Israel, Italy, Japan, Korea Rep, Mexico, Netherlands, Norway, Peru, Poland, Portugal, Russia, Saudi Arabia, Slovakia, Sweden, Switzerland, Tunisia, UK, USA.
IGO Relations Formal contacts with: *WHO (#20950).* [2021/XD4551/**C**]

♦ International Society of Aesthetic Plastic Surgery (ISAPS) 14908

Société internationale de chirurgie esthétique plastique

Exec Dir 19 Mantua Road, Mount Royal NJ 08061, USA. T. +442070387812. E-mail: isaps@isaps.org.
URL: http://www.isaps.org/

History Feb 1970, New York, NY (USA). Founded at United Nations Headquarters. **Aims** Promote aesthetic plastic surgery education worldwide to improve patient safety. **Structure** Board of Directors; Education Council. **Languages** English. **Staff** 1.00 FTE, paid. **Finance** Sources: donations; meeting proceeds; members' dues; sale of publications. **Activities** Events/meetings; training/education. **Events** *World Congress Olympiad* Athens (Greece) 2023, *World Congress* Istanbul (Türkiye) 2022, *Biennial Congress* Vienna (Austria) 2021, *Biennial Congress* Vienna (Austria) 2020, *Biennial Congress* Miami, FL (USA) 2018. **Publications** *Aesthetic Plastic Surgery* (6 a year) – journal; *ISAPS News* (4 a year).
Members Individuals (over 5,100) in 114 countries and territories:
Afghanistan, Albania, Algeria, Argentina, Armenia, Australia, Austria, Azerbaijan, Bahamas, Bahrain, Bangladesh, Belarus, Belgium, Bolivia, Bosnia-Herzegovina, Brazil, Bulgaria, Canada, Chile, China, Colombia, Costa Rica, Côte d'Ivoire, Croatia, Cuba, Cyprus, Czechia, Denmark, Dominican Rep, Ecuador, Egypt, El Salvador, Estonia, Finland, France, Georgia, Germany, Greece, Guadeloupe, Guatemala, Honduras, Hong Kong, Hungary, Iceland, India, Indonesia, Iran Islamic Rep, Iraq, Ireland, Israel, Italy, Japan, Jordan, Kazakhstan, Kenya, Korea Rep, Kuwait, Latvia, Lebanon, Libya, Lithuania, Luxembourg, Malawi, Malaysia, Mauritius, Mexico, Moldova, Mongolia, Montenegro, Morocco, Netherlands, New Zealand, Nicaragua, Nigeria, North Macedonia, Norway, Oman, Pakistan, Palestine, Panama, Paraguay, Peru, Philippines, Poland, Portugal, Puerto Rico, Qatar, Réunion, Romania, Russia, Saudi Arabia, Serbia, Singapore, Slovakia, Slovenia, South Africa, Spain, St Barthélemy, Sweden, Switzerland, Syrian AR, Taiwan, Thailand, Trinidad-Tobago, Tunisia, Türkiye, UK, Ukraine, United Arab Emirates, Uruguay, USA, Venezuela, Vietnam, Zimbabwe.
NGO Relations Also links with member societies participating in ISAPS Global Alliance. [2022.10.12/XD2298/v/**B**]

♦ International Society of Aesthetics and Mesotherapy (ISAM) 14909

Pres 4 rue de L'Arcade, 75008 Paris, France. T. +33142652747. Fax +33142669515. E-mail: arcademedical@wanadoo.fr.

History by Luc Dewandre and Jean Luc Bachelier. **Members** Membership countries not specified. **NGO Relations** *World College of Aesthetic and Antiageing Medicine (WOCAAM).* [2008/XJ8114/**F**]

♦ International Society for Affective Disorders (ISAD) 14910

Administrator Inst of Psychiatry KCL, PO72 De Crespigny Park, Denmark Hill, London, SE5 8AF, UK. T. +442039253678. E-mail: membership@isad.org.uk.
URL: http://www.isad.org.uk/

History 2001. Founded on the initiative of Prof Chris Thompson. Registration: Charity Commission, No/ID: 1105075, Start date: Feb 2004, England and Wales. **Aims** Promote research into affective disorders through all relevant scientific disciplines, including genetics, neuroscience and social and behavioural sciences. **Structure** General Meeting. Officers: President; Immediate Past President; Treasurer; Company Secretary; Directors/Trustees. **Languages** English. **Staff** 1.00 FTE, paid. Voluntary. **Finance** Sources: fees for services; grants; members' dues. **Activities** Events/meetings; projects/programmes; training/education. **Events** *Conference* London (UK) 2021, *Conference* Milan (Italy) 2020, *Conference* London (UK) 2019, *Biennial Conference* Houston, TX (USA) 2018, *Biennial Conference* Amsterdam (Netherlands) 2016. **Publications** *Journal of Affective Disorders.*
Members Full in 30 countries and territories:
Argentina, Australia, Chile, Denmark, Finland, France, Germany, Greece, Hong Kong, Hungary, India, Ireland, Israel, Italy, Japan, Korea Rep, Kuwait, Mexico, New Zealand, Norway, Portugal, Romania, Serbia, South Africa, Spain, Sweden, Switzerland, Türkiye, UK, USA.
Organizations in 6 countries:
Australia, Brazil, Canada, Ireland, New Zealand, UK.
NGO Relations Cooperates with (1): *International Forum on Mood and Anxiety Disorders (IFMAD, #13646).* [2021/XM0092/**D**]

♦ International Society of Affective Science and Engineering (internationally oriented national body)
♦ International Society for African Jurists / see African Jurists' Association (#00351)
♦ International Society of African Lawyers (inactive)
♦ International Society of African Scientists (internationally oriented national body)
♦ International Society Against Breast Cancer (inactive)

♦ International Society of Agile Manufacturing (ISAM) **14911**

Pres Oakland Univ, 2200 N Squirrel Rd, DHE 105, Rochester MI 48309, USA.
Chairman Dayalbagh Educational Inst, Agra, Uttar Pradesh 282005, Agra UTTAR PRADESH 282005, India.

History 1995. **Aims** Accelerate international exchange of ideas and scientific knowledge without barriers of discipline domain or field of technology application for the welfare of mankind; foster cross-fertilization of technology, strategy and 4M resources (Manpower, Machine, Money and Management) in order to enhance productivity, competitive advantage and improve general quality of life, embracing both traditional and non-traditional fields of engineering. **Structure** Board of Directors; Executive Committee; President; Chairman. **Languages** English. **Staff** None. **Finance** Sales of publications. **Activities** Events/meetings; publishing activities; knowledge management/information dissemination. **Events** *Conference* India 2015, *Conference* Rochester, MI (USA) 2014, *Conference* Varanasi (India) 2012, *Conference* Agra (India) 2011, *Conference* Kalamazoo, MI (USA) 2008. **Publications** *International Journal of Advanced Manufacturing Systems (IJAMS)*; *International Journal of Agile Manufacturing (IJAM).*

Members Individuals (337) in 27 countries and territories:
Austria, Belgium, Bulgaria, Canada, China, Denmark, Finland, France, Germany, Hungary, India, Iran Islamic Rep, Israel, Italy, Japan, Jordan, Kuwait, Mexico, Netherlands, Norway, Portugal, Singapore, Spain, Sweden, Türkiye, UK, USA.
[2016.10.20/XJ4359/v/**D**]

♦ International Society for Aging and Physical Activity / see International Coalition for Aging and Physical Activity (#12606)

♦ International Society for Agricultural Meteorology (INSAM) **14912**

Founding Pres Groenestraat 13, 5314 AJ Bruchem, Netherlands.
URL: http://www.agrometeorology.org/

Structure Web-based organization. Founding President; 6 Vice-Presidents; 3 Correspondents.
Members Founding – organizations, instrument manufacturers. Members (about 2,000) in 125 countries (not specified). Included in the above, 2 organizations listed in this Yearbook:
Included in the above, 2 organizations listed in this Yearbook:
FAO (#09260); World Meteorological Organization (WMO, #21649).
NGO Relations Affiliated with: *International Society of Biometeorology (ISB, #14969).*
[2013.06.27/XJ1927/**C**]

♦ International Society for Agrochemical Adjuvants / see ISAA Agrochemical Network (#16021)
♦ International Society of Airbreathing Engines / see International Society of Air Breathing Engines (#14913)

♦ International Society of Air Breathing Engines (ISABE) **14913**

Exec Sec Aerospace Eng and Eng Mechanics, Univ of Cincinnati, 745 Baldwin Hall, PO Box 210070, Cincinnati OH 45221-0070, USA.
URL: http://www.isabe.org/

History Constitution and bylaws adopted 8 Jun 1983. Also referred to as *International Society of Airbreathing Engines (ISOABE).* Registered in accordance with the law of USA. **Aims** Further the free exchange, on an international level, of knowledge in the field of airbreathing propulsion for flight vehicles. **Structure** Board of Directors, including Steering Committee, comprising President, Vice-President, 2 Joint Secretaries, Secretary Treasurer, Founding President and Immediate Past-President. Plenary Session (Business Meeting, every 2 years at Conference). Executive Committee, comprising: the Executive Officers – President and 2 Joint Secretaries (Executive, Administrative), who together comprise the Steering Sub-Committee, and Vice-President; Immediate Past-President; one Primary Delegate of of each accepted 'member nation'; co-opted members. National Committees and/or National Organizing Sub-Committees. Executive Headquarters in the USA, headed by Executive Secretary; Administrative Headquarters, headed by Administrative Secretary, in the Secretary's nation. **Languages** English. **Finance** Sources: members' dues. **Activities** Organizes symposia; participates in relevant international development projects. Areas of concern: advanced power plant concepts; engine and component design; engine/vehicle integration; design and off-design performance and characteristics; fuels, fuel controls and combustion; fluid mechanics and gas dynamics; advanced materials and manufacturing techniques; engine and integrated flight propulsion controls; advanced diagnostic measurement and health monitoring techniques; economics, operations and life-cycle cost aspects; airworthiness, type certification, test and evaluation techniques; manufacturing, maintenance and reliability aspects of propulsion units. **Events** *Conference* Ottawa, ON (Canada) 2022, *Conference* Canberra, ACT (Australia) 2019, *Conference* Manchester (UK) 2017, *Biennial Conference* Phoenix, AZ (USA) 2015, *Biennial Conference* Busan (Korea Rep) 2013.

Members Full in 29 countries:
Australia, Austria, Belgium, Canada, China, Czechia, Egypt, France, Germany, Greece, India, Israel, Italy, Japan, Korea Rep, Netherlands, Norway, Poland, Portugal, Russia, Slovakia, South Africa, Spain, Sweden, Switzerland, Türkiye, UK, Ukraine, USA.
[2013/XD4401/**C**]

♦ International Society of Air Safety Investigators (ISASI) **14914**

Association internationale des enquêteurs de la sécurité aérienne
Intl Office Manager Park Center, 107 E Holly Avenue, Ste 11, Sterling VA 20164-5405, USA. T. +17034309668. Fax +17034304970. E-mail: isasi@erols.com.
URL: http://www.isasi.org/

History 14 Aug 1964, USA. Former names and other names: *Society of Air Safety Investigators* – former (1964 to 1977). **Aims** Promote air safety investigation by the exchange of ideas, experience and information regarding aircraft accident investigation; promote technical advancement by providing for professional education through lectures, displays and presentations and otherwise aid in the advancement of flight safety; broaden professional relationships among members; maintain and increase the prestige, standing and influence of the Air Safety Investigator in matters of air safety. **Structure** International Council. Regional organization: *European Society of Air Safety Investigators (ESASI, #08516).* Standing Committees (3); Special Objective Committees (6); Technical Working Groups. **Languages** English. **Staff** 1.00 FTE, paid. **Finance** Sources: members' dues. **Activities** Events/meetings; knowledge management/information dissemination; networking/liaising; training/education. **Events** *Annual Seminar* Brisbane, QLD (Australia) 2022, *Annual Seminar* Montréal, QC (Canada) 2021, *Annual Seminar* Montréal, QC (Canada) 2020, *Annual Seminar* Dubai (United Arab Emirates) 2018, *Annual Seminar* San Diego, CA (USA) 2017. **Publications** *ISASI Forum* (4 a year). Seminar papers.

Members Full; Associate; Affiliate; Student; Fellow; Honorary; Charter; Life; Corporate. Individuals and institutions in 69 countries and territories:
Angola, Argentina, Australia, Austria, Bahrain, Belgium, Botswana, Brazil, Bulgaria, Canada, Chile, China, Colombia, Côte d'Ivoire, Cyprus, Czechia, Denmark, Fiji, Finland, France, Germany, Greece, Greenland, Honduras, Hong Kong, Hungary, Iceland, India, Indonesia, Ireland, Israel, Italy, Jamaica, Japan, Kenya, Korea Rep, Kuwait, Lebanon, Libya, Luxembourg, Malaysia, Mexico, Mongolia, Namibia, Netherlands, New Zealand, Nigeria, Norway, Oman, Pakistan, Papua New Guinea, Peru, Philippines, Portugal, Qatar, Russia, Saudi Arabia, Singapore, South Africa, Spain, Sweden, Switzerland, Taiwan, Tanzania UR, Türkiye, UK, United Arab Emirates, USA, Zambia.
[2022.10.18/XD9198/**D**]

♦ International Society for Alström Syndrome Families / see Alström Syndrome International (#00750)
♦ International Society of Amino Acid Research (no recent information)

♦ International Society of Amyloidosis (ISA) **14915**

Sec Boston Univ, Pathology and Lab Medicine, 72 E Concord St, Boston MA 02215, USA. T. +16176384313.
URL: http://www.amyloidosis.nl/

History Officially founded 2002. Registered in the State of Minnesota (USA). **Aims** Promote research, education, clinical studies (including diagnosis and treatment), conferences and symposia on all aspects of amyloidosis worldwide. **Structure** Board of Directors, including President, Vice-President/President-Elect, Secretary and Treasurer. **Finance** Sources: members' dues. **Events** *International Symposium* Tarragona (Spain) 2020, *International Symposium* Kumamoto (Japan) 2018, *International Symposium* Uppsala (Sweden) 2016, *International Symposium* Indianapolis, IN (USA) 2014, *International Symposium* Groningen (Netherlands) 2012. **Publications** *AMYLOID* – journal.
[2015/XJ7346/**C**]

♦ International Society for Anaerobic Bacteria (no recent information)
♦ International Society for Anaesthetic Pharmacology (internationally oriented national body)

♦ International Society for Analysis, its Applications and Computation (ISAAC) **14916**

Sec/Treas Freie Uni Berlin, Fachbereich Mathematik/Informatik, Mathematisches Inst, Arnimallee 3, 14195 Berlin, Germany.
URL: http://www.isaacmath.org

History 1994. Constitution adopted, 1994; renewed 2013. **Aims** Promote and advance analysis, its applications, and its interaction with computation. **Structure** Board; Special Interest Groups. **Languages** English. **Staff** None. **Finance** Members' dues: euro 2,000. **Activities** Events/meetings. **Events** *Congress* Ribeirão Preto (Brazil) 2023, *Congress* Ghent (Belgium) 2021, *Congress* Aveiro (Portugal) 2019, *Congress* Växjö (Sweden) 2017, *Congress* Macau (Macau) 2015. **Publications** *ISAAC Newsletter* (2 a year). *International Society for Analysis, its Applications and Computation: ISAAC* – in 10 vols; *Series on Analysis, Applications and Computation: SAAC.* Congress proceedings.

Members Full in 51 countries and territories:
Algeria, Argentina, Armenia, Australia, Austria, Belarus, Belgium, Canada, China, Cuba, Egypt, Finland, France, Georgia, Germany, Hong Kong, India, Iran Islamic Rep, Israel, Italy, Japan, Kazakhstan, Korea Rep, Kyrgyzstan, Macau, Malaysia, Mexico, Moldova, Montenegro, North Macedonia, Poland, Portugal, Romania, Russia, Saudi Arabia, Serbia, South Africa, Spain, Sweden, Switzerland, Taiwan, Tajikistan, Tanzania UR, Türkiye, UK, Ukraine, United Arab Emirates, USA, Uzbekistan, Venezuela, Vietnam.
Also members in French West Indies. Membership countries not specified.
[2014.06.26/XJ7246/**C**]

♦ International Society for Analytical Cytology / see International Society for Advancement of Cytometry (#14900)

♦ International Society of Analytical Trilogy (ISAT) **14917**

Société internationale de trilogie analytique – Sociedade Internacional de Trilogia Analitica (SITA)
Main Office Avenida Rebouças 3819, Sao Paulo SP, 05401-450, Brazil. T. +551130323616. Fax +551138159920. E-mail: contato@trilogiaanalitica.org.
URL: https://www.trilogiaanalitica.org/

History 1970, Sao Paulo (Brazil), as *Society of Integral Psychoanalysis*, by Norberto R Keppe. **Aims** Improve the quality of life for the individual and society through application of trilogical concepts – psychoanalysis integrating feeling, thought and action – in all spheres of human endeavour. **Languages** English, Finnish, French, German, Italian, Portuguese, Spanish, Swedish. **Finance** Funded by: donations; activities; sale of products. Budget (annual): about US$ 50,000. **Activities** Offers 2 kinds of programme: personal health and development; development of sane socio-economic development. Provides psychoanalytical assistance. Holds meetings and courses; organizes international congresses, lectures and seminars. Runs: *Centre of Integral Psychoanalysis – Analytical Trilogy* – London (UK); centres in Helsinki (Finland), Lisbon (Portugal), London, New York NY (USA), Paris (France), Sao Paulo (Brazil), Stockholm (Sweden) and Vienna (Austria). **Events** *Forum / Meeting* Sao Paulo (Brazil) 1995, *Forum / Meeting* London (UK) 1994, *Forum / Meeting* Moscow (Russia) 1994, *International congress of analytical trilogy* Stockholm (Sweden) / Helsinki (Finland) 1987, *International congress* Tampa, FL (USA) 1986. **Publications** *Savoir c'est pouvoir* – official journal. *Trilogical Metaphysics: The Liberation of Being* (1994) by Norberto R Keppe; *Work and Capital* (1989) by Norberto R Keppe; *The ABC of Analytical Trilogy – Integral Psychoanalysis* (1988) by Claudia B Pacheco; *Women on the Couch – an Analysis of Female Psychopathology* (1987) by Claudia B Pacheco; *Liberation of the People – the Pathology of Power* (1986) by Norberto R Keppe et al. Other books and booklets in English, French, German, Portuguese, Swedish. Conference proceedings.

Members Individuals in 21 countries:
Brazil, Côte d'Ivoire, Denmark, Finland, France, Georgia, Germany, Greece, Honduras, Italy, Japan, Latvia, Nigeria, Poland, Portugal, Russia, Spain, Sri Lanka, Sweden, UK, USA.
NGO Relations *STOP the Destruction of the World (#19997).*
[2008/XF0151/v/**F**]

♦ International Society of Andrology (ISA) **14918**

Contact Domagkstr 11, 48129 Münster, Germany. E-mail: president@andrology.org.
URL: http://www.andrology.org/

History 1981. Also referred to as *International Andrology Society.* Registration: Germany. **Aims** Disseminate knowledge of science and medicine dealing with *male reproductive* organs in animals and in man and with *diseases* of these organs; encourage development of basic and clinical research in andrology; facilitate collaboration and distribution of information among national andrological and other learned societies and qualified persons interested in; encourage and sponsor publications related to the field. **Structure** General Assembly; Executive Council. Officers: President; Secretary; Treasurer. Committees. **Languages** English. **Staff** 3.00 FTE, voluntary. **Finance** Sources: members' dues. **Activities** Events/meetings; training/education. **Events** *Congress* Münster (Germany) 2020, *Lifestyle factors and male reproductive health* Copenhagen (Denmark) 2017, *Global andrology and men's health – present challenges for future generations* Melbourne, VIC (Australia) 2013, *European Workshop on the Molecular and Cellular Endocrinology of the Testis* Stockholm (Sweden) 2012, *Meeting* Stockholm (Sweden) 2012. **Publications** *ISA Newsletter.*

Members Organizations in 18 countries and territories:
Argentina, Australia, Canada, Denmark, Egypt, France, Germany, Greece, Hungary, Indonesia, Italy, Japan, Korea Rep, Poland, Spain, Taiwan, UK, USA.
Regional organizations (3), including the following listed in this Yearbook (2):
European Academy of Andrology (EAA, #05780); Network for Young Researchers in Andrology (NYRA, #17067).
Consultative Status Consultative status granted from: *WHO (#20950)* (Official Relations).
[2021/XD0180/y/**C**]

♦ International Society of Anglo-Saxonists (ISAS) **14919**

Contact c/o School of English, Room A40 Trent, University Park, Nottingham, NG7 2RD, UK.
URL: http://www.isasweb.net/

History 23 Aug 1983, during the first conference held in Belgium. Name change expected in 2019-2020. **Aims** Provide all scholars interested in the languages, literatures, arts, history and material culture of Anglo-Saxon England with support in their research; facilitate the exchange of ideas and materials within and between the disciplines. **Structure** Executive Committee, comprising President, 2 Vice-Presidents, Executive Director, senior members of the Advisory Board. **Finance** Members' dues. **Events** *Biennial Meeting* Albuquerque, NM (USA) 2019, *Biennial Meeting* Honolulu, HI (USA) 2017, *Biennial Meeting* Glasgow (UK) 2015, *Biennial Meeting* Dublin (Ireland) 2013, *Biennial Meeting* Madison, WI (USA) 2011.

Members Individuals in 24 countries:
Australia, Austria, Belgium, Czechia, Denmark, Finland, France, Germany, Hong Kong, Hungary, Ireland, Israel, Italy, Japan, Netherlands, New Zealand, Poland, Romania, Serbia, South Africa, Spain, Switzerland, UK, USA.
[2019/XD6157/v/**D**]

♦ International Society for Animal Blood Group Research / see International Society for Animal Genetics (#14921)
♦ International Society of Animal Clinical Biochemistry / see International Society of Animal Clinical Pathology (#14920)

♦ International Society of Animal Clinical Pathology (ISACP) **14920**

Sec address not obtained. E-mail: info@isacp.org.
URL: http://www.isacp.org/

History 1982, as *International Society of Animal Clinical Biochemistry (ISACB).* **Aims** Advance the science of animal clinical pathology by promoting and encouraging the study and practice of animal pathology and exchange of knowledge within the discipline. **Structure** Officers: President; Vice-President (Next Congress Chair); Secretary; Treasurer; Immediate Past-President; Executive Director. **Languages** English. **Staff** None. **Finance** Members' dues. **Events** *Biennial Congress* Chicago, IL (USA) 2020, *Biennial Congress* Tokyo (Japan) 2018, *Biennial Congress* Cape Town (South Africa) 2016, *Biennial Congress / Scientific Meeting* Copenhagen (Denmark) 2014, *Biennial congress / Scientific Meeting* Ljubljana (Slovenia) 2012.

Members Full in 35 countries:
Argentina, Australia, Austria, Belgium, Brazil, Burkina Faso, Canada, Chile, China, Denmark, Finland, France, Germany, Greece, India, Ireland, Israel, Italy, Japan, Korea Rep, Mexico, Morocco, Netherlands, Norway, Peru, Poland, Russia, Senegal, South Africa, Spain, Sweden, Switzerland, Taiwan, UK, USA.
[2021/XD3843/**D**]

♦ International Society for Animal Genetics (ISAG) **14921**

Société internationale de génétique animale
Sec Box 7023, Ulls väg 26, Dept Animal Breeding, SE-750 07 Uppsala, Sweden. E-mail: isagsecretary@assochq.org.

Exec Assistant 1800 South Oak St, Suite 100, Champaign IL 61820, USA. T. +12173563182. E-mail: isag@assochq.org.
URL: http://www.isag.us/

History 1964, Prague (Czechia). Former names and other names: *European Society for Animal Blood Group Research (ESABR)* – former (1964 to 1972); *Société européenne pour la recherche sur les groupes sanguins des animaux* – former (1964 to 1972); *International Society for Animal Blood Group Research (ISABR)* – former (1972 to 1988); *Sociedad Internacional para la Investigación de los Grupos Sanguineos Animales* – alias. **Aims** Encourage study of genetically influenced characters of animal tissues and fluids; facilitate exchange of ideas and materials between research workers. **Structure** Conference; Executive Committee; Specialist Groups; Standing Committees. **Languages** English. **Staff** None. **Finance** Sources: members' dues. Annual budget: 70,000 USD. **Activities** Events/meetings; research/documentation. **Events** *Conference* Uppsala (Sweden) 2021, *Conference* Lleida (Spain) 2019, *Conference* Dublin (Ireland) 2017, *Biennial Conference* Salt Lake City, UT (USA) 2016, *Biennial Conference* Xian (China) 2014. **Publications** *Animal Genetics* (6 a year) – official journal.

Members Individual (Ordinary), including Honorary members (463); Institutional (145). Members in 57 countries and territories:
Argentina, Australia, Austria, Bangladesh, Belgium, Brazil, Canada, Chile, China, Colombia, Czechia, Denmark, Estonia, Finland, France, Germany, Hungary, India, Iran Islamic Rep, Ireland, Israel, Italy, Japan, Kenya, Korea Rep, Lithuania, Mexico, Mongolia, Morocco, Netherlands, New Zealand, Nigeria, Norway, Peru, Philippines, Poland, Portugal, Puerto Rico, Romania, Russia, Serbia, Slovakia, Slovenia, South Africa, Spain, Sweden, Switzerland, Taiwan, Thailand, Tunisia, Türkiye, UK, Ukraine, United Arab Emirates, Uruguay, USA, Vietnam.

NGO Relations Scientific member of: *International Union of Biological Sciences (IUBS, #15760).*
[2020/XC0850/**C**]

♦ International Society for Animal Hygiene (ISAH) 14922

Société internationale pour l'hygiene animale – Sociedade Internacional de Higiene Animal – Internationale Gesellschaft für Tierhygiene

Pres Inst of Animal Hygiene, Animal Welfare and Farm Animal Behaviour, Univ of Veterinary Medicine, Bünteweg 17 P, 30559 Hannover, Germany.
Sec Research Unit of Epidemiology/Health/Welfare, French Agency for Food, Environmental and Occupational Health and Safety, BP 53, 22440 Ploufragan, France.
URL: http://www.isah-soc.org/

History 1970. **Aims** Promote animal health and welfare, biosecurity, environmental protection and sustainability of animal *husbandry*. **Structure** Executive Board, comprising President, 1st and 2nd Vice-Presidents, Secretary and Treasurer. Country Representatives. **Languages** English. **Staff** Voluntary. **Finance** Members' dues. **Activities** Knowledge management/information dissemination; resesarch/documentation; events/meetings. **Events** *Biennial Congress* Wroclaw (Poland) 2019, *Biennial Congress* Mazatlan, SIN (Mexico) 2017, *Biennial Congress* Košice (Slovakia) 2015, *Biennial Congress / Congress* Nanjing (China) 2013, *Biennial congress / Congress* Vienna (Austria) 2011.

Members Organizations and individuals in 50 countries:
Albania, Algeria, Argentina, Australia, Austria, Belgium, Bosnia-Herzegovina, Brazil, Bulgaria, Canada, Chile, China, Croatia, Cuba, Czechia, Denmark, Egypt, El Salvador, Estonia, Ethiopia, Finland, France, Germany, Greece, Hungary, India, Israel, Italy, Latvia, Lesotho, Lithuania, Mexico, Netherlands, Nigeria, Norway, Pakistan, Philippines, Poland, Romania, Russia, Slovakia, Slovenia, Spain, Sweden, Switzerland, Syrian AR, Tanzania UR, Ukraine, Uruguay, USA, Zimbabwe. [2020.03.03/XD3761/**D**]

♦ International Society for Animal Rights (internationally oriented national body)

♦ International Society for Anthrozoology (ISAZ) 14923

Admin Manager address not obtained. E-mail: adm.manager@isaz.net.
URL: http://www.isaz.net/

History 12 Apr 1991. Registration: Section 501(c)(3), Start date: Feb 2004, USA, State of Pennsylvania. **Aims** Promote study of human-animal interactions and relationships. **Structure** Board of Directors. **Languages** English. **Finance** Sources: meeting proceeds; members' dues; sale of publications. **Activities** Knowledge management/information dissemination; publishing activities; research/documentation. **Events** *Annual Conference* Boise, ID (USA) 2022, *Annual Conference* Buffalo, NY (USA) 2021, *Annual Conference* Liverpool (UK) 2020, *Annual Conference* Orlando, FL (USA) 2019, *Annual Conference* Sydney, NSW (Australia) 2018. **Publications** *Anthrozoos* – journal.

Members Individual; Affiliate; Student; Corporate. Members in 30 countries and territories:
Australia, Austria, Belgium, Brazil, Canada, Denmark, England, Finland, France, Germany, India, Ireland, Israel, Italy, Japan, Korea Rep, Lithuania, Netherlands, Northern Ireland, Norway, Philippines, Poland, Portugal, Scotland, South Africa, Spain, Sweden, Switzerland, USA, Wales. [2022.05.10/XD5536/**D**]

♦ International Society for Anti-Infective Pharmacology (ISAP) 14924

Contact Monash Univ, Wellington Rd, Clayton VIC 3800, Australia.
URL: http://www.isap.org/

History 1991, Berlin (Germany). Established following a series of meetings since 1986. Registration: Australia. **Aims** Study pharmacodynamics and pharmacokinetics; improve dosing anti-infectives; expand basic and applied knowledge in this area of *chemotherapeutics*. **Structure** Committee, including President, Past-President, President-Elect, Secretary and Treasurer. **Languages** English. **Finance** Sources: meeting proceeds; members' dues. **Events** *Annual Meeting* Clayton, VIC (Australia) 2020, *Annual Meeting* Rotterdam (Netherlands) 2019, *Annual Meeting* Madrid (Spain) 2018, *Annual Meeting* Vienna (Austria) 2017, *Annual Meeting* La Jolla, CA (USA) 2015. **Publications** *ISAP Newsletter.* [2020/XD8676/**D**]

♦ International Society for Antimicrobial Activity of Non-Antibiotics / see International Society of Non-Antibiotics (#15307)

♦ International Society of Antimicrobial Chemotherapy (ISAC) 14925

Address not obtained.
URL: https://www.isac.world/

History Sep 1961, Naples (Italy). Founded at 2nd International Symposium of Chemotherapy, the 1st Symposium having been held in 1959, Geneva (Switzerland). Present By-Laws update at 21st International Congress of Chemotherapy, 4 Jul 1999, Birmingham (UK). Previously registered under the number: 1029653. Former names and other names: *International Society of Chemotherapy for Infection and Cancer (ISC)* – former; *International Society of Chemotherapy (ISC)* – former; *Société internationale de chimiothérapie* – former. Registration: Charity Commission, No/ID: 1139367, England and Wales. **Aims** Advance education and science of therapy of infection. **Structure** Council; Executive Committee. **Languages** English. **Staff** 1.00 FTE, voluntary. **Finance** Sources: members' dues. Congress dues. **Activities** Awards/prizes/competitions; events/meetings; training/education. **Events** *International Congress of Antimicrobial Chemotherapy* Perth, WA (Australia) 2022, *International Congress of Antimicrobial Chemotherapy* Perth, WA (Australia) 2021, *Biennial Congress* Dubai (United Arab Emirates) 2019, *Biennial Congress* Taipei (Taiwan) 2017, *Consensus Conference* Palma (Spain) 2016. **Publications** *International Journal of Antimicrobial Agents* (12 a year); *Journal of Global Antimicrobial Resistance (JGAR)* (4 a year) – online; *Antibiotics Chemotherapy* – newsletter. Congress abstracts.

Members National affiliated societies, either individually or through their regional organizations, in 54 countries and territories:
Albania, Argentina, Australia, Austria, Bangladesh, Belarus, Bosnia-Herzegovina, Brazil, Bulgaria, Canada, Chile, China, Colombia, Croatia, Cuba, Cyprus, Czechia, Denmark, Egypt, France, Georgia, Germany, Greece, Hong Kong, Iran Islamic Rep, Israel, Italy, Japan, Korea Rep, Kosovo, Lebanon, Malaysia, New Zealand, North Macedonia, Norway, Pakistan, Philippines, Poland, Portugal, Romania, Russia, Serbia, Singapore, Slovakia, Slovenia, Spain, Switzerland, Taiwan, Thailand, Tunisia, Türkiye, UK, Ukraine, USA.

Included in the above, 11 international and regional affiliated societies listed in this Yearbook:
Arab Society of Chemotherapy, Microbiology and Infectious Diseases (#01043); Asian Association of UTI and STI (AAUS, #01343); Asia-Pacific Society for Medical Virology (APSMV, #01639); Asia-Pacific Society of Clinical Microbiology and Infection (APSCMI, #02032); Asociación Panamericana de Infectologia (API, #02288); Australasian Society for Infectious Diseases (ASID); Federation of European Societies for Chemotherapy and for Infections (FESCI, #09546); Federation of Infectious Diseases Societies of Southern Africa (FIDSSA); International Society of Non-Antibiotics (ISN, #15307); Mediterranean Society of Chemotherapy and Infection (MedSocChemI, #16675); Nordic Society for Clinical Microbiology and Infectious Diseases (NSCMID, #17413).
[2020/XC3915/y/**B**]

♦ International Society of Antioxidant in Nutrition and Health (internationally oriented national body)
♦ International Society of Antioxidants / see International Society of Antioxidant in Nutrition and Health

♦ International Society for Antiviral Research (ISAR) 14926

Sec address not obtained.
URL: http://www.isar-icar.com/

History 14 May 1987. **Aims** Promote and advance scientific knowledge in the field of antiviral research. **Languages** English. **Staff** 11.00 FTE, voluntary. **Finance** Members' dues. Sponsorship. **Activities** Offers career placement service; organizes International Conference on Antiviral Research (annual). **Events** *Conference* Baltimore, MD (USA) 2019, *Conference* Porto (Portugal) 2018, *Conference* Atlanta, GA (USA) 2017, *Conference* La Jolla, CA (USA) 2016, *Conference* Rome (Italy) 2015. **Publications** *ISAR News* (2 a year). Members' directory (members only). **Members** worldwide. Membership countries not specified.
[2014/XD8708/**D**]

♦ International Society for Apheresis (ISFA) 14927

Pres Shiga Univ of Medical Science, Seta-Tsukinowa, Otsu SHIGA, 520-2192 Japan. T. +81775482440. Fax +81775482440. E-mail: isfa@belle.shiga-med.ac.jp.
URL: http://www.e-isfa.org/

History 10 Apr 1996, Kyoto (Japan). Founded at International Conference for Apheresis (ICFA), which became 1st congress of ISFA. **Aims** Disseminate on an international basis the most up-to-date apheresis *technologies* and their *clinical* applications. **Structure** Board of Trustees; Executive Committee; Standing Committees. *European Group – International Society for Apheresis (E-ISFA)*, set up 2016. **Languages** English. **Finance** Members' dues. **Activities** Events/meetings; training/education; standards/guidelines. **Events** *E-ISFA Congress* Berlin (Germany) 2023, *World Congress* Berlin (Germany) 2023, *E-ISFA Congress* Dresden (Germany) 2021, *World Congress* Dresden (Germany) 2021, *World Congress* Kyoto (Japan) 2019. **Publications** *Therapeutic Apheresis and Dialysis (TAD)* (6 a year) in English – journal. *Impact Factor* (2010). Conference proceedings.

Members Regular; Associate. Individuals and corporations in 36 countries and territories:
Argentina, Australia, Austria, Belgium, Brazil, Canada, China, Croatia, Denmark, France, Germany, Greece, Hong Kong, Hungary, India, Italy, Japan, Korea Rep, Lebanon, Malaysia, Mexico, Netherlands, New Zealand, Norway, Portugal, Saudi Arabia, Slovenia, Spain, Sweden, Switzerland, Taiwan, Thailand, Türkiye, UK, Uruguay, USA.

NGO Relations Member of: *World Apheresis Association (WAA, #21097).* [2022/XF4599/**F**]

♦ International Society of the Apocrypha (inactive)

♦ International Society for Applied Biological Sciences (ISABS) 14928

Main Office Ulica kneza Branimira 71E, HR-10000 Zagreb, Croatia. E-mail: info@isabs.hr.
URL: http://www.isabs.hr/

History 2004. Founded at first official Assembly, meetings having taken place since 1997. **Aims** Promote, develop and advance the applied biological sciences, particularly in the areas of clinical medicine, molecular genetics, forensic sciences and biotechnology. **Structure** Members' Assembly; President; Vice President; Secretary. **Languages** Croatian, English. **Staff** Voluntary. **Finance** Members' dues. Other sources: sponsorship; donations. Conferences are supported by the Ministry of Science and Education (Croatia). **Activities** Events/meetings; financial and/or material support. **Events** *Conference* Dubrovnik (Croatia) 2022, *Conference* Dubrovnik (Croatia) 2021, *Conference* Split (Croatia) 2019, *Conference* Dubrovnik (Croatia) 2017, *Conference* Bol (Croatia) 2015. **Publications** *Croatian Medical Journal. Primjena analize DNA u sudskoj medicini i pravosudu* (2001) by D Primorac. ISABS Conference Books of Abstracts. Scientific, education and position papers; books; manuals.

Members Associate; Regular; Student; Collective; Retired; Honorary. Members in 26 countries:
Australia, Azerbaijan, Belgium, Bosnia-Herzegovina, Canada, China, Croatia, Cyprus, Czechia, Germany, Hungary, India, Iran Islamic Rep, Israel, Japan, New Zealand, North Macedonia, Pakistan, Portugal, Romania, Thailand, Türkiye, UK, United Arab Emirates, USA, Vietnam.

NGO Relations Associate member of: American Academy of Forensic Sciences (AAFS). Links with universities and national organizations. [2022/XJ2001/**F**]

♦ International Society for Applied Cardiovascular Biology (ISACB) . . 14929

Contact Office of Research Admin, Summa Health System, 525 E Market St, Akron OH 44304, USA. T. +13303757078. Fax +13303756648.
URL: http://www.isacb.org/

History 1987. **Aims** Improve the quality of basic and applied research in all areas of cardiovascular biology; enhance communication among scientists and clinicians involved in these disciplines throughout the world; provide a forum featuring presentations of original work and topical reviews relevant to basic applied and clinical science of the cardiovascular system in health and disease. **Structure** Biennial Meeting. Executive Council of 15 members. Executive Office, comprising President and Secretary-Treasurer. **Languages** English. **Staff** 0.50 FTE, paid; 0.50 FTE, voluntary. **Finance** Members' dues (annual): Full – US$ 150; Junior – US$ 75; Laboratory Specialist – US$ 50; Institutional – US$ 2,500. Other sources: corporate sponsors; grants. **Events** *Biennial Meeting* Memphis, TN (USA) 2022, *Biennial Meeting* Tokyo (Japan) 2021, *Biennial Meeting* Bordeaux (France) 2018, *Biennial Meeting* Banff, AB (Canada) 2016, *European Meeting* Nuremberg (Germany) 2015. **Publications** *ISACB Circulator* (2 a year) – newsletter.

Members Full individuals with terminal degrees in their fields actively involved in applied cardiovascular biology research; Junior individuals such as resident physicians, graduate students and post-doctoral fellows still involved in the educational process leading toward a terminal degree; Laboratory Specialist research technicians and technologists; Institutional businesses, universities and practice groups. Individuals in 17 countries and territories:
Argentina, Australia, Austria, Canada, Colombia, France, Germany, Ireland, Italy, Japan, Netherlands, New Zealand, South Africa, Sweden, Switzerland, Taiwan, UK. [2013.09.26/XD8077/v/**D**]

♦ International Society for Applied Ethology (ISAE) 14930

Pres Inst of Animal Welfare Science, Univ of Veterinary Medicine, Veterinärplatz 1, 1210 Vienna, Austria.
Contact Animal Biology Div, SRUC, Bush Estate, Penicuik, EH25 0PH, UK. T. +441314454811. E-mail: isaebusiness@hotmail.com.
URL: http://www.applied-ethology.org/

History 1966, Edinburgh (UK). Former names and other names: *Society for Veterinary Ethology (SVE)* – former (1966 to 1991); *Société d'éthologie vétérinaire (SEV)* – former (1966 to 1991). Registration: Scottish Charity Regulator, No/ID: SC047974, Start date: 5 Dec 2017, Scotland. **Aims** Provide a forum for presentation and discussion of advances in *applied animal behaviour science* and education. **Structure** General Meeting (annual); Council; Regional Secretaries. **Languages** English. **Staff** None. **Finance** Sources: members' dues. **Activities** Events/meetings; politics/policy/regulatory. **Events** *Annual Congress* Ohrid (North Macedonia) 2022, *Annual Congress* 2021, *Annual Congress* Bangalore (India) 2020, *Annual Congress* Bergen (Norway) 2019, *Annual Congress* Charlottetown, PE (Canada) 2018. **Publications** *ISAE Newsletter.* Abstracts of congress papers; special editions of Applied Animal Behaviour Science.

Members Individuals involved in the fields of agriculture, veterinary science, zoology and other animal sciences in 54 countries and territories:
Argentina, Australia, Austria, Bangladesh, Belgium, Brazil, Bulgaria, Canada, Chile, China, Colombia, Czechia, Denmark, Ecuador, Egypt, Finland, France, Germany, Hungary, India, Iran Islamic Rep, Ireland, Israel, Italy, Japan, Korea Rep, Lebanon, Lithuania, Malaysia, Mexico, Nepal, Netherlands, New Zealand, Nigeria, North Macedonia, Norway, Pakistan, Poland, Portugal, Russia, Serbia, Slovenia, South Africa, Spain, Sri Lanka, Sweden, Switzerland, Taiwan, Tunisia, Türkiye, UK, Ukraine, USA, Vietnam. [2021.06.16/XD5070/v/**C**]

♦ International Society of Applied Intelligence (ISAI) 14931

Pres TX State San Marcos, Computer Science, 601 University Dr, San Marcos TX 78666-4616, USA. T. +15122458050. Fax +15122458750. E-mail: ma04@txstate.edu.
URL: http://isai.cs.txstate.edu/

History 1988. Registration: USA, State of Texas. **Aims** Disseminate information regarding research and innovative developments related to intelligent systems. **Structure** Board of Directors; Working Groups. **Languages** English. **Finance** Sources: members' dues. **Activities** Events/meetings; publishing activities. **Events** *International Conference on Industrial, Engineering and Other Applications of Applied Intelligent Systems* Kitakyushu (Japan) 2022, *International Conference on Industrial and Engineering Applications of*

Artificial Intelligence and Expert Systems Kuching (Malaysia) 2021, *International Conference on Industrial and Engineering Applications of Artificial Intelligence and Expert Systems* Kitakyushu (Japan) 2020, *International Conference on Industrial and Engineering Applications of Artificial Intelligence and Expert Systems* Graz (Austria) 2019, *International Conference on Industrial and Engineering Applications of Artificial Intelligence and Expert Systems* Montréal, QC (Canada) 2018. **Publications** *International Journal of Applied Intelligence* (12 a year). [2021.02.23/XC0054/**C**]

♦ International Society of Applied Optics, Riga (unconfirmed)

♦ International Society for Applied Phycology (ISAP) 14932

Sec/Treas Inst of Ocean and Earth Sciences, Univ Malaya, 50603 Kuala Lumpur, Malaysia. E-mail: applied.phycologysoc@gmail.com.
Pres Zeestraat 84, 2518 AD The Hague, Netherlands.
URL: http://www.appliedphycologysoc.org/

History 29 Sep 1999. Founded at a special meeting during 8th International Conference on Applied Algology. **Aims** Promote research, preservation of algal genotypes, and dissemination of knowledge concerning utilization of *algae*. **Structure** Executive Committee; Supervisory Board of ISAP Foundation. **Languages** English. **Staff** None paid. **Finance** Sources: members' dues. Annual budget: 5,000 EUR. **Activities** Events/meetings; knowledge management/information dissemination; training/education. **Events** *Congress* Porto (Portugal) 2024, *Congress* 2021, *Congress* Chiba (Japan) 2020, *Congress* Nantes (France) 2017, *Congress* Sydney, NSW (Australia) 2014. **Publications** *ISAP Newsletter*. **Members** Full in over 50 countries. Membership countries not specified. **NGO Relations** Also links with national associations. [2022.06.15/XJ8714/**C**]

♦ International Society of Applied Preventive Medicine (#13236)

♦ International Society of Applied Psycholinguistics (ISAPL) 14933

SG University of Bari, Dept of Psychology, Piazza Umberto I 1, 70121 Bari BA, Italy. T. +39805714551. Fax +39805714606.
Pres Dept of Humanities, Univ of Rome Tor Vergata, Via del Columbia 1, 00133 Rome RM, Italy. E-mail: dpontero@yahoo.com.

History Nov 1982, Milan (Italy), by a committee of 20 founding members, at a conference of the Commission of Psycholinguistics of *Association internationale de linguistique appliquée (AILA, #02713)*. **Aims** Promote the application of psycholinguistic studies, research and theoretical and methodological issues in order to solve problems in various practical fields. **Structure** Committee, comprising President, 2 Honorary Presidents, 4 Vice-Presidents, Secretary-General, Treasurer and 7 members. **Languages** English, French. **Staff** Voluntary. **Finance** Members' dues: US$ 5. Other sources: support from universities and other official institutions; donations. **Activities** Contact, exchange of information and coordination of activities among members; promotes establishment of psycholinguistic courses in universities; organizes congresses, conferences, seminars and symposia. **Events** *Triennial Congress* Rome (Italy) 2021, *Triennial Congress* Rome (Italy) 2020, *Triennial Congress* Tbilisi (Georgia) 2016, *Triennial Congress* Moscow (Russia) 2013, *Triennial Congress* Bari (Italy) 2010. **Publications** *ISAPL Bulletin* (2 a year). *Dynamic Contexts of Language Use* (1994). Congress proceedings. **Members** Individuals. Membership countries not specified. [2019/XC0005/v/**D**]

♦ International Society for Arabic Papyrology (ISAP) 14934

Société internationale pour la papyrologie arabe

Pres Ludwig-Maximilians-Universität München, Institut für den Nahen und Mittleren Osten, Veterinärstr 1, 80539 Munich, Germany.
Sec Auburn University, Dept of History, 310 Thach Hall, Auburn AL 36849, USA.
URL: http://www.naher-osten.uni-muenchen.de/isap/index.html

History 24 Mar 2002, Cairo (Egypt). Registered in the State of New Jersey (USA). **Aims** Encourage scholarship and foster communication about Arabic papyrology and related subjects. **Structure** General Meeting (every 3 years). Board of Directors of 5 members, including President (CEO) and 2 Secretary/Treasurers. **Languages** Arabic, English, French, German. **Staff** 5 part-time, voluntary (Board Members). **Finance** Members' dues. **Activities** Projects: Database of Arabic Documents; Checklist of Arabic Editions. Organizes summer schools. ASEAN plastics industries database. **Events** *Conference* Faiyum (Egypt) 2021, *Conference* Berlin (Germany) 2018, *Conference* Munich (Germany) 2014, *Conference* Carthage (Tunisia) 2012, *Conference* Vienna (Austria) 2009. **Publications** *al-Bardiyyat* – newsletter. Conference proceedings. **Information Services** *Arabic Papryology Database Project*.

Members Regular; Student; Special. Individuals in 20 countries and territories:
Austria, Belgium, Egypt, Finland, France, Germany, Greece, India, Israel, Italy, Japan, Jordan, Lebanon, Netherlands, Palestine, Spain, Switzerland, Tunisia, UK, USA.

NGO Relations Contacts and programmes with universities and libraries in the Middle East, USA, UK and rest of Europe. [2019/XD9196/v/**D**]

♦ International Society of Arachnology (ISA) 14935

Sec Museum für Naturkunde, Leibniz Inst for Evolution and Biodiversity Science, Invalidenstrasse 43, 10115 Berlin, Germany. T. +493020938516. Fax +493020938868.
URL: http://www.arachnology.org/

History 1956, Paris (France), as *International Centre for Arachnological Documentation – Centre international de documentation arachnologique (CIDA)*, as a commission of *International Union of Biological Sciences (IUBS, #15760)*. Current title adopted 1999. **Aims** Promote the study of arachnology (except acarology); coordinate arachnological research; publish arachnological documents; organize congresses and symposia. **Structure** General Meeting (every 3 years); Council. **Languages** English. **Staff** None. **Finance** Sources: members' dues. **Activities** Awards/prizes/competitions; events/meetings; knowledge management/information dissemination. **Events** *Triennial Congress* Maldonado (Uruguay) 2023, *Triennial Congress* Canterbury (New Zealand) 2019, *Triennial Congress* Golden, CO (USA) 2016, *Triennial Congress* Pingtung City (Taiwan) 2013, *Triennial Congress* Siedlce (Poland) 2010.

Members Correspondents in 48 countries:
Albania, Argentina, Austria, Belgium, Brazil, Bulgaria, Canada, China, Colombia, Czechia, Denmark, Egypt, Finland, Georgia, Germany, Greece, Hungary, Iceland, Iran Islamic Rep, Ireland, Israel, Italy, Japan, Kenya, Liechtenstein, Mexico, Morocco, Namibia, Netherlands, New Zealand, Pakistan, Peru, Poland, Portugal, Russia, Singapore, Slovakia, Slovenia, South Africa, Spain, Sri Lanka, Sudan, Sweden, Switzerland, UK, Ukraine, Vietnam, Zimbabwe. [2018.10.04/XE3561/**C**]

♦ International Society of Arboriculture (ISA) 14936

Main Office PO Box 3129, Champaign IL 61826-3129, USA. T. +12173559411. Fax +12173559516. E-mail: isa@isa-arbor.com.
URL: http://www.isa-arbor.com/

History Founded 1924, as (USA) National Shade Tree Conference. Subsequently name changed to *International Shade Tree Conference*. Current name adopted 1975. **Aims** Promote and improve the practice of professional arboriculture; stimulate appreciation of, and interest in planting and preservation of, shade and ornamental *trees*; promote cooperation in the conservation of trees and the beautification of the countryside; initiate and support scientific investigation of related problems and dissemination of the results of such investigations. **Structure** Board of Directors. **Languages** English. **Staff** 48.00 FTE, paid. **Finance** Members' dues. Other sources: certification fees; sales of publications. Budget (annual): US$ 7 million. **Activities** Knowledge management/information dissemination. **Events** *Annual Conference* Albuquerque, NM (USA) 2023, *Annual Conference* Malmö (Sweden) 2022, *Annual Conference* 2021, *Annual Conference* 2020, *Annual Conference* Knoxville, TN (USA) 2019. **Publications** *Arborist News* (6 a year).

Members Categories Professional; Senior; Student; Library; Associate; Affiliate organizations (52). Individual arborists and urban foresters, in 32 countries and territories:
Argentina, Australia, Austria, Bahamas, Belgium, Brazil, Canada, China, Colombia, Denmark, Finland, France, Germany, Hong Kong, Iceland, Ireland, Israel, Italy, Japan, Mexico, Netherlands, New Zealand, Norway, Poland, Puerto Rico, Russia, South Africa, Spain, Sweden, Switzerland, UK, USA.

NGO Relations Member of: *European Arboricultural Council (EAC, #05911)*; US national organizations. [2018/XD6858/v/**F**]

♦ International Society for Archaeoastronomy and Astronomy in Culture (ISAAC) 14937

Pres Dept of Anthropology – MFAC – Rm 377, College of Arts and Sciences, Univ of Buffalo, 380 Fillmore Academic Ctr, Ellicott Complex, Buffalo NY 14261-0026, USA. T. +17166452414ext110.
URL: http://www.archaeoastronomy.org/

History Founded 1996. **Aims** Promote the interdisciplinary study of astronomical practice within the general study of human societies and their relationships to their environments; promote research seeking to develop the understanding of the cultural significance of astronomical knowledge through the integration of techniques and methods within the humanities and social sciences, astronomy and methodological disciplines. **Structure** General Meeting (every 3 years). Council. Executive Committee. Officers: President; Past-President; Vice-President/President-Elect; Secretary; Treasurer. **Languages** English, Spanish. **Staff** Voluntary. **Finance** Members' dues. **Activities** Organizes meetings; sponsors triennial Oxford International Conferences on Archaeoastronomy and Astronomy in Culture. **Events** *Oxford international conference on archaeoastronomy and astronomy in culture* Klaipeda (Lithuania) 2007, *Oxford International Conference on Archaeoastronomy and Astronomy in Culture* Flagstaff, AZ (USA) 2004, *Oxford international conference on archaeoastronomy and astronomy in culture* Santa Cruz de Tenerife (Spain) 1999, *Oxford international conference on archaeoastronomy and astronomy in culture* Mexico / Santa Fe, NM (USA) 1996, *Oxford International Conference on Archaeoastronomy and Astronomy in Culture* Santa Fe, NM (USA) 1996. **Publications** *Archaeoastronomy: The Journal of Astronomy and Culture.*

Members Full in 21 countries:
Australia, Chile, Georgia, Germany, Greece, Hungary, India, Ireland, Italy, Japan, Kazakhstan, Lithuania, Mexico, Netherlands, Peru, Poland, Romania, Slovenia, Spain, UK, USA.

NGO Relations *Société européenne pour l'astronomie dans la culture (SEAC, #19461).* [2015/XM1405/**D**]

♦ International Society for Archaeological Prospection (ISAP) 14938

Treas English Heritage, Fort Cumberland, Eastney, Portsmouth, PO4 9LD, UK.
Chairman address not obtained.
URL: http://www.archprospection.org/

History Inaugural meeting, 13 Sep 2003, Krakow (Poland), during 5th International Conference of Archaeological Prospection. Current constitution adopted 16 Sep 2005. **Aims** Advance education of the public in archaeology (including man-made landscape and built-environment) through promotion of high standards of research, application and communication in the field of archaeological prospection and related studies. **Structure** General Meeting. Management Committee. **Finance** Members' dues. **Events** *International Conference of Archaeological Prospection* Lyon (France) 2021, *Annual General Meeting* Sligo (Ireland) 2019, *International Conference on Archaeological Prospection* Sligo (Ireland) 2019, *Annual General Meeting* Bradford (UK) 2017, *International Conference on Archaeological Prospection* Bradford (UK) 2017. **Publications** *IASP News*. **Members** Corporate and institutional. Membership countries not specified. [2014/XJ7984/**E**]

♦ International Society of Arterial Chemoreception (ISAC) 14939

Contact Johns Hopkins Univ School of Medicine, Johns Hopkins Hospital, 600 N Wolfe St, Baltimore MD 21287, USA.
Hon Sec Dept of Physiology, Univ of Utah, School of Medicine, 410 Chipeta Way, Room 156, Research Park, Salt Lake City UT 84108, USA.
URL: http://www.carotidbody.org/

History Founded 1988. **Aims** Bring together scientists worldwide who are studying chemoreception in the carotid body. **Structure** Scientific Meeting (every 3 years). **Languages** English. **Activities** Research/documentation; events/meetings. **Events** *Symposium* Lisbon (Portugal) 2022, *Kickoff Meeting* Lisbon (Portugal) 2021, *Symposium* Lisbon (Portugal) 2021, *Symposium* Lisbon (Portugal) 2020, *Symposium* Baltimore, MD (USA) 2017. [2021/XD3633/v/**F**]

♦ International Society of Arthroplasty Registries (ISAR) 14940

Admin c/o Höftprotesregistret, Medicinaregatan 18 G, SE-413 45 Gothenburg, Sweden. T. +46702856209. E-mail: info@isarhome.org.
URL: http://www.isarhome.org/

History Feb 2005, Washington, DC (USA). Constitution approved 22 Mar 2006, Chicago IL (USA). **Aims** Improve outcomes of joint replacement surgery. **Structure** General Meeting; Steering Committee; Administrator. **Finance** Sources: members' dues. **Events** *International Congress of Arthroplasty Registries* Copenhagen (Denmark) 2021, *International Congress of Arthroplasty Registries* Adelaide, SA (Australia) 2020, *International Congress* Leiden (Netherlands) 2019, *International Congress* Reykjavik (Iceland) 2018, *International Congress* San Francisco, CA (USA) 2017.

Members Full (National Registries); Associate (National registers in development or regional registries). Full in 8 countries:
Australia, Denmark, Finland, New Zealand, Norway, Slovakia, Sweden, UK.
Associate in 7 countries:
Austria, Canada, France, Italy, Netherlands, Portugal, USA. [2021/XJ5405/**C**]

♦ International Society of Arthroscopy, Knee Surgery and Orthopaedic Sports Medicine (ISAKOS) 14941

Société internationale d'anthroscopie, de la chirurgie du genou et de la médecine orthopédique sportive

Main Office 567 Sycamore Valley Rd W, Danville CA 94526, USA. E-mail: isakos@isakos.com.
URL: http://www.isakos.com/

History 1995. Founded on merger of *International Arthroscopy Association (IAA, inactive)* and *International Society of the Knee (ISK, inactive)*. **Aims** Develop, support and promote charitable, scientific and literary works that disseminate and further the increased knowledge of arthroscopy, knee surgery and orthopaedic sports medicine. **Languages** English. **Staff** 2.00 FTE, paid. **Finance** Sources: members' dues. **Activities** Approves courses and teaching centres. Runs Awards programs: Albert Trillat Young Investigator's Award; Achilles Orthopaedic Sports Medicine Research Award; John J Joyce Award; Richard B Caspari Award. **Events** *Biennial Congress* 2021, *Biennial Congress* Cancún (Mexico) 2019, *Biennial Congress* Shanghai (China) 2017, *Biennial Congress* Lyon (France) 2015, *Biennial Congress* Toronto, ON (Canada) 2013. **Publications** *Arthroscopy: The Journal of Arthroscopic and Related Surgery* (4 a year); *ISAKOS Newsletter* (2 a year).

Members Active; Associate (offered to all members of AOSSM, AANA, APOSSM, APOA, ESSKA and SLARD). Individuals (over 1,500) in 66 countries and territories:
Argentina, Australia, Austria, Belgium, Bolivia, Brazil, Canada, Chile, China, Colombia, Croatia, Denmark, Dominican Rep, Ecuador, Egypt, Estonia, Finland, France, Georgia, Germany, Greece, Guatemala, Honduras, Hong Kong, Hungary, India, Indonesia, Iran Islamic Rep, Ireland, Israel, Italy, Japan, Jordan, Kenya, Korea Rep, Latvia, Lebanon, Liechtenstein, Lithuania, Malaysia, Mexico, Netherlands, New Zealand, Nicaragua, Norway, Oman, Peru, Poland, Portugal, Puerto Rico, Romania, Saudi Arabia, Singapore, Slovakia, Slovenia, South Africa, Spain, Sweden, Switzerland, Taiwan, Thailand, Türkiye, UK, United Arab Emirates, USA, Venezuela.

NGO Relations Associate membership offered to members of: American Orthopaedic Society for Sports Medicine (AOSSM); *Arthroscopy Association of North America (AANA)*; *Asia Pacific Orthopaedic Association (APOA, #01987)*; *Asia-Pacific Knee, Arthroscopy and Sports Medicine Society (APKASS, #01939)*; *European Society of Sports Traumatology, Knee Surgery and Arthroscopy (ESSKA, #08741)*; *Sociedad Latinoamericana de Artroscopia, Rodilla y Traumatologia Deportiva (SLARD, #19390).* [2021/XD0262/v/**C**]

♦ International Society for Artificial Cells, Blood Substitutes and Biotechnology (ISABB) 14942

Coordinator Artificial Cells and Organs Research Cetr, Depts Physiology/Medicine/Biomedical Engineering, Fac of Medicine, McGill Univ, Montréal QC H3G 1Y6, Canada. E-mail: artcell.med@mcgill.ca.
URL: http://www.medicine.mcgill.ca/artcell/

History 1976. Former names and other names: *International Society for Artificial cells, Blood Substitutes and Immobilization Biotechnology (ISABI)* – former (1976). **Aims** Encourage research, development and clinical applications in artificial cells, blood substitutes, nanomedicine, regenerative medicine, tissue engineering, cell/stem therapy, hemoperfusion, bioencapsulation and related areas. **Structure** Executive Committee; Subcommittee: *International Committee on Blood Substitutes*; Scientific Advisory Board. **Languages** English. **Activities** Events/meetings; publishing activities; research/documentation. Active in all member countries. **Publications** *Nanobiotherapeutic based Blood Substitutes* (2021) by TMS Chang and L Buow et al – Free online reading. Online books and papers; videos. [2022.06.24/XM6293/**C**]

♦ International Society for Artificial cells, Blood Substitutes and Immobilization Biotechnology / see International Society for Artificial Cells, Blood Substitutes and Biotechnology (#14942)

♦ International Society for Artificial Internal Organs / see International Federation for Artificial Organs (#13357)

♦ **International Society of Artificial Life (ISAL)** **14943**

Pres Reed College, 3203 SE Woodstock Blvd, Portland OR 97202-8199, USA. T. +15037886697. Fax +15037886643. E-mail: mab@reed.edu – society@alife.org.
URL: http://www.alife.org/

History May 2001, Prague (Czech Rep). **Aims** Promote scientific research and education relating to artificial life. **Structure** Board of Directors, including President, 2 Vice-Presidents, Treasurer and Secretary. **Events** *ALIFE: International Conference on Artificial Life* Sapporo (Japan) 2023, *ALIFE: International Conference on the Synthesis and Simulation of Living Systems* Montréal, QC (Canada) 2020, *ALIFE : International Conference on the Synthesis and Simulation of Living Systems* Tokyo (Japan) 2018, *ECAL : European Conference on Artificial Life* Lyon (France) 2017, *ALIFE : International Conference on the Synthesis and Simulation of Living Systems* Cancún (Mexico) 2016. **Publications** *Artificial Life* – journal. **Members** Regular; student. Membership countries not specified. [2020/XJ3154/**D**]

♦ International Society of Artificial Life and Robotics (internationally oriented national body)
♦ International Society for Artificial Organs / see International Federation for Artificial Organs (#13357)
♦ International Society of Art and Psychopathology / see International Society for Psychopathology of Expression and Art-Therapy (#15400)
♦ International Society of Ascension (no recent information)

♦ **International Society for Asphalt Pavements (ISAP)** **14944**

Secretariat 6776 Lake Drive, Ste 215, Lino Lakes MN 55014, USA. T. +16512939188. Fax +16512939193. E-mail: isapinfo@comcast.net.
URL: http://www.asphalt.org/

History 1987, Ann Arbor MI (USA). **Aims** Promote asphalt pavement technology exchange on a worldwide basis. **Structure** Board of Directors. Executive Committee, comprising Chairman, 2 Vice-Chairmen, Secretary, Treasurer, Executive Manager and 8 members. Standing Committees: Membership; Finance and Audit; Nominations; Information Technology; Editorial Board; Distinguished Lectureship. Ad Hoc Committee for the International Conferences. **Finance** Members' dues. **Activities** Organizes and supports conferences and projects. **Events** *Symposium* Padua (Italy) 2019, *Quadrennial Conference* Fortaleza (Brazil) 2018, *Symposium* Tokyo (Japan) 2017, *Quadrennial Conference* Raleigh, NC (USA) 2014, *Symposium on Heavy Duty Asphalt Pavements and Bridge Deck Pavements* Nanjing (China) 2012. **Publications** Proceedings; lecture series.
Members Associate; Voting; Patron; Corporate. Members in 18 countries:
Australia, Belgium, Canada, China, Croatia, Denmark, France, Italy, Japan, Netherlands, Norway, Portugal, Saudi Arabia, South Africa, Sweden, Trinidad-Tobago, UK, USA.
NGO Relations Member of: *World Road Association (PIARC, #21754).* [2014/XD8142/**D**]

♦ **International Society for Astrological Research (ISAR)** **14945**

Société internationale des recherches astrologiques

Operations Manager PO Box 358945, Gainesville FL 32635-8945, USA.
URL: http://www.isarastrology.com/

History Founded 1969. Incorporated in the State of California (USA), 1979. **Aims** Provide a world-wide forum for reporting current research; encourage responsible astrological studies and research; support high standards of competence within the astrological profession; foster exchange of ideas and information among astrologers around the world; generate goodwill through respect for the ideals of astrology. **Structure** Board of Directors; online astrological groups. **Languages** English. **Staff** Voluntary. **Finance** Members' dues. Other sources: conference proceeds; sale of books. **Activities** Events/meetings; training/education; networking/liaising; certification/accreditation; awareness raising; guidance/assistance/consulting. **Events** *The power of forecasting – meets the consequence of choice* Costa Mesa, CA (USA) 2016, *Conference* Phoenix, AZ (USA) 2014, *United Astrology Congress* New Orleans, LA (USA) 2012, *Conference* Chicago, IL (USA) 2009, *United astrology congress / Conference* Denver, CO (USA) 2008. **Publications** *ISAR Newsletter* (weekly); *International Astrologer* (3 a year). *Astrological Research Methods* – Vol 1. Tapes of past lectures, workshops and seminars. **Information Services** *ISAR Research Data Base.*
Members Individuals in 53 countries:
Argentina, Australia, Austria, Belarus, Belgium, Bosnia-Herzegovina, Brazil, Canada, Chile, China, Colombia, Costa Rica, Croatia, Czechia, Denmark, Finland, France, Germany, Greece, Iceland, India, Ireland, Israel, Italy, Japan, Kenya, Malaysia, Mexico, Mongolia, Montenegro, Netherlands, New Zealand, Nigeria, North Macedonia, Norway, Pakistan, Philippines, Poland, Portugal, Russia, Serbia, Sierra Leone, Singapore, Slovenia, South Africa, Spain, Sweden, Switzerland, Türkiye, UK, Ukraine, Uruguay, USA. [2015.11.09/XD4676/v/**F**]

♦ **International Society for Atmospheric Research Using Remotely Piloted Aircraft (ISARRA)** **14946**

Contact address not obtained. E-mail: info@isarra.org.
URL: http://www.isarra.org/

History 2013. Founded as a result of *European Cooperation in Science and Technology (COST, #06784)* Action ES0802. **Aims** Provide a forum for network and exchange of knowledge within the area of atmospheric and earth sciences when unmanned or remotely piloted aircraft are involved. **Structure** Meeting (annual). **Languages** English. **Staff** All voluntary. **Finance** No budget. **Events** *Conference* Andøya (Norway) 2020, *Conference / Meeting* Odense (Denmark) 2014, *Conference / Meeting* Palma (Spain) 2013.
Members Individuals in 10 countries:
Belgium, Denmark, Germany, Hungary, Iceland, Iran Islamic Rep, Norway, Spain, UK, USA.
NGO Relations No official relations. [2021/XJ7389/v/**D**]

♦ **International Society of Atopic Dermatitis (ISAD)** **14947**

Main Office Hermann Burchardstr 1, Wolfgang, 7265 Davos GR, Switzerland. E-mail: info@isadsociety.org – contact@isadsociety.org.
URL: https://www.isadsociety.org/

History 7 Jun 2012, Verona (Italy). Proposed Jan 2012, Moshi (Tanzania UR), at 7th International Symposium on Atopic Dermatitis, which had been organized since 1979. **Aims** Bring together clinicians and scientists interested in atopic dermatitis in an interdisciplinary atmosphere; provide state-of-the-art updates on clinical and experimental research on this *disease.* **Structure** Board; Executive Committee. **Languages** English. **Activities** Awards/prizes/competitions; events/meetings. **Events** *Georg Rajka International Symposium on Atopic Dermatitis* Melbourne, VIC (Australia) 2025, *Georg Rajka International Symposium on Atopic Dermatitis* Doha (Qatar) 2024, *Georg Rajka International Symposium on Atopic Dermatitis* Gdansk (Poland) 2023, *Georg Rajka International Symposium on Atopic Dermatitis* Montréal, QC (Canada) 2022, *Georg Rajka International Symposium on Atopic Dermatitis* Seoul (Korea Rep) 2021. [2023/XM7804/c/**E**]

♦ **International Society of Audiology (ISA)** **14948**

Société internationale d'audiologie – Sociedad Internacional de Audiologia – Internationale Gesellschaft für Audiologie

Contact address not obtained.
SG Natl Research Centre for Audiology, 3 Romanov per Apt 69, Moscow MOSKVA, Russia, 125009.
URL: http://www.isa-audiology.org/

History 1952, Paris (France). Founded following International Conference on Audiology, 1948, Stockholm (Sweden). Reorganized 30 Sep 1960, Bonn (Germany FR), on merger with other organization that had been founded at 1st International Congress of Audiology, 1953, Leiden (Netherlands). Statutes modified: June1996, Bari (Italy); 1998, Buenos Aires (Argentina); 2000, The Hague (Netherlands). Registration: Handelsregister, No/ID: CH66002909694, Switzerland, Geneva. **Aims** Facilitate knowledge, protection and rehabilitation of human *hearing.* **Structure** General Assembly; Executive Committee; Committees (4). **Languages** English, French, Spanish. **Staff** 2.00 FTE, voluntary. **Finance** Sources: members' dues. **Activities** Events/meetings; guidance/assistance/consulting; knowledge management/information dissemination. **Events** *World Congress of Audiology* Edinburgh (UK) 2028, *World Congress of Audiology* Seoul (Korea Rep) 2026, *World Congress of Audiology* Paris (France) 2024, *World Congress of Audiology* Warsaw (Poland) 2022, *World Congress of Audiology* Warsaw (Poland) 2020. **Publications** *AUDI-news*; *Hearing International Newsletter*, *International Journal of Audiology.*
Members Full and Honorary members in 70 countries and territories. Membership countries not specified.
Affiliate societies in 17 countries and territories:
Argentina, Australia, Brazil, Canada, Colombia, Germany, Hong Kong, Iran Islamic Rep, Israel, Netherlands, New Zealand, Philippines, Russia, South Africa, Spain, UK, USA.
Regional organizations (5):
Bureau international d'audiophonologie (BIAP, #03362); *European Federation of Audiology Societies (EFAS, #07058)*; *Hearing International (#10895)*; *International Collegium of Rehabilitative Audiology (ICRA, #12651)*; *Panamerican Society of Audiology (PASA, no recent information).*
Consultative Status Consultative status granted from: *WHO (#20950)* (Official). **NGO Relations** In liaison with technical committees of: *International Organization for Standardization (ISO, #14473).* [2023.02.16/XC2527/y/**C**]

♦ **International Society for Augmentative and Alternative Communication (ISAAC)** **14949**

Exec Dir 312 Dolomite Drive, Ste 216, Toronto ON M3J 2N2, Canada. T. +19058506848. Fax +19058506852. E-mail: feedback@isaac-online.org.
Pres address not obtained.
URL: http://www.isaac-online.org/

History May 1983, East Lansing MI (USA). **Aims** Advance the transdisciplinary field of augmentative and alternative communication (AAC) by promoting information exchange, advocacy, research and access to communication through AAC approaches and technology; promote the best possible communication for people with complex communications needs. **Structure** Council elects Executive Board, consisting of President, President-Elect, Vice-President Administration and 3 further Vice-Presidents. National/regional chapters (15). **Languages** English. **Staff** 1.00 FTE, paid. **Finance** Sources: donations; members' dues; sale of publications. Other sources: advertising. **Activities** Advocacy/lobbying/activism; awards/prizes/competitions; events/meetings. **Events** *Biennial Conference* Cancún (Mexico) 2022, *Biennial Conference* Cancún (Mexico) 2021, *Biennial Conference* Cancún (Mexico) 2020, *Biennial Conference* Gold Coast, QLD (Australia) 2018, *Biennial Conference* Toronto, ON (Canada) 2016. **Publications** *Augmentative and Alternative Communication* (4 a year); *AGOSCI Newsletter* (3 a year); *Communication Matters* (3 a year); *ISAAC – Israel Journal* (annual); *Unterslutze Kommunikation* (2-3 a year). International membership directory (annual); series of practical books for people who use AAC and practitioners; conference and research proceedings; video. **Members** Professional; Student; Retired; Institutional; Corporate. Members in 60 countries and territories. Membership countries not specified. **Consultative Status** Consultative status granted from: *ECOSOC (#05331)* (Special). **NGO Relations** Member of: *RI Global (#18948).* [2020/XD1389/**C**]

♦ **International Society for Auricular Reconstruction (ISAR)** **14950**

Address not obtained.
URL: http://www.isar.cc/

History Proposed 2012, Sydney (Australia), during 5th Congress on Auricular Reconstruction. Founding meeting held Oct 2012, Malmö (Sweden). **Aims** Promote excellence in all facets of auricular reconstruction; furnish a forum for the best scientific works related to the reconstruction of congenital and acquired auricular deformities; increase knowledge, education and stimulate research on an international level as well as interactions between members. **Structure** General Assembly. Executive Council. **Finance** Sources: members' dues. **Activities** Organizes conferences. **Events** *Congress* 2022, *Congress* Toronto, ON (Canada) 2020, *Congress* Beijing (China) 2017, *Congress* Paris (France) 2014. **Members** Full; Associate; Senior; Honorary. Membership countries not specified. [2019/XJ8506/**C**]

♦ **International Society of Autogenic Training and Psychotherapy (ISATAP)** **14951**

Pres & CEO Avenida de Filipinas 52 -8 b, 28003 Madrid, Spain. T. +34915342941. E-mail: isatapsy@gmail.com.
URL: https://isatapsy.com/

History 20 Sep 2014, Madrid (Spain). Project started May 2012, Madrid (Spain), at meeting of *International Committee for the Coordination of Clinical Application and Teaching of Autogenic Therapy (ICAT, inactive).* **Aims** Further develop the presence of the autogenic approach and the autogenic methods in the world; potentiate synergy among local initiatives and groups working with autogenic methods; reinforce the reality of autogenic psychotherapy in the general scope of current psychotherapies. **Structure** Board. ICAT serves as Scientific Council. **Languages** English, Spanish. **Activities** Events/meetings; training/education. **Events** *Congress* Seville (Spain) 2018, *Congress* Genoa (Italy) 2017, *Congress* Seville (Spain) 2016, *Congress* Las Palmas de Gran Canaria (Spain) 2015, *Congress* Madrid (Spain) 2014. [2022.08.07/XM4422/v/**C**]

♦ International Society for Automatic Image Analysts (inactive)
♦ International Society of Automation (internationally oriented national body)

♦ **International Society for Autonomic Neuroscience (ISAN)** **14952**

International Sec address not obtained. E-mail: int_sec@autonomicneuroscience.info.
URL: http://autonomicneuroscience.info/

History 2 Jul 1994, Melbourne, VIC (Australia). Registration: ASIC, No/ID: A0031130J, Start date: 4 Apr 1995, Australia, Victoria. **Aims** Facilitate communication between those working in, and to raise the profile of, autonomic neuroscience. **Structure** Annual General Meeting; International Executive Committee. **Languages** English. **Finance** Sources: members' dues. **Activities** Awards/prizes/competitions; events/meetings. **Events** *Congress* Birmingham (UK) / Oxford (UK) 2024, *Congress* Cairns, QLD (Australia) 2022, *Congress* Cairns, QLD (Australia) 2021, *Congress* Los Angeles, CA (USA) 2019, *Congress* Nagoya (Japan) 2017. **Publications** *Autonomic Neuroscience: Basic and Clinical* – journal.
Members Individuals in 17 countries and territories:
Australia, Belgium, Brazil, Canada, Chile, France, Germany, Hong Kong, India, Italy, Japan, Saudi Arabia, South Africa, Spain, Sweden, UK, USA. [2021/XD6253/**D**]

♦ International Society of Aviation Writers (inactive)

♦ **International Society for Bayesian Analysis (ISBA)** **14953**

Pres Dept of Applied Mathematics and Statistics, Baskin School of Engineering, Univ of California, 1156 High St, Santa Cruz CA 95064, USA. T. +18314591295. Fax +18314594829.
URL: http://www.bayesian.org/

History 1992. **Aims** Promote the development and application of Bayesian *statistical* theory and methods, useful in the solution of theoretical and applied problems in science, industry and government. **Structure** Board of 12 Directors. Officers: President; President Elect; Past President; Executive Secretary; Treasurer – these 5 comprising the Executive Committee – Vice Programme Chair; Programme Chair; Past Programme Chair. Local chapters in Chile, India and South Africa. **Finance** Members' dues. **Events** *World Meeting* Venice (Italy) 2024, *World Meeting* Montréal, QC (Canada) 2022, *World Meeting* Kunming (China) 2021, *World Meeting* Kunming (China) 2020, *International Workshop on Objective Bayes Methodology* Warwick (UK) 2019. **Publications** *ISBA Newsletter* (4 a year).
Members Full in 30 countries and territories:
Argentina, Australia, Belgium, Brazil, Canada, Chile, China, Denmark, France, Germany, Greece, India, Ireland, Italy, Japan, Korea Rep, Mexico, Netherlands, New Zealand, Poland, Portugal, South Africa, Spain, Sweden, Switzerland, Taiwan, Thailand, UK, USA, Venezuela. [2012/XE4222/**E**]

♦ **International Society for Behavioral Ecology (ISBE)** **14954**

Sec School of Biological Sciences, Monash Univ, Melbourne VIC 3800, Australia. T. +61399055652. Fax +61399055613.
URL: http://www.behavecol.com/

History 1988, following 1st International Behavior Ecology Meeting, Albany NY (USA) in 1986. Previously referred to as *International Behavioral Ecology Association (ISBE).* **Structure** Council. **Finance** Members' dues. **Events** *Congress* Stockholm (Sweden) 2022, *Congress* Minneapolis, MN (USA) 2018, *Congress* Exeter (UK) 2016, *Congress* New York, NY (USA) 2014, *Congress* Lund (Sweden) 2012. **Publications** *ISBE Newsletter* (2 a year); *Behavioral Ecology.* [2016.06.01/XN7026/**D**]

♦ **International Society of Behavioral Medicine (ISBM)** **14955**
Sec c/o International Conference Services Ltd, Suite 6427, 10685-B Hazelhurst Drive, Houston TX 77043, USA. E-mail: admin@isbm.info.
URL: http://www.isbm.info/
History 1990. **Aims** Serve the needs of all health-related disciplines concerned with issues relevant to behavioral medicine. **Structure** Governing Council; Executive Council; Board; President. **Languages** English. **Staff** Voluntary. **Activities** Events/meetings. **Events** *International Congress of Behavioral Medicine* Vancouver, BC (Canada) 2023, *International Congress of Behavioral Medicine* 2021, *International Congress of Behavioral Medicine* Glasgow (UK) 2020, *International Congress of Behavioral Medicine* Santiago (Chile) 2018, *International Congress of Behavioral Medicine* Melbourne, VIC (Australia) 2016. **Publications** *International Journal of Behavioral Medicine (IFBM).*
Members Constituent societies (26) in 25 countries and territories:
Australia, Chile, China, Cuba, Denmark, Finland, Germany, Hong Kong, Hungary, Italy, Japan, Korea Rep, Mexico, Netherlands, Norway, Portugal, Romania, Singapore, Slovakia, Spain, Sweden, Thailand, UK, USA, Venezuela. [2021.11.29/XD1959/**D**]

♦ **International Society of Behavioral Nutrition and Physical Activity (ISBNPA)** **14956**
Exec Dir 1300 S 2nd St, Ste 300, Minneapolis MN 55454, USA. T. +351919659421. E-mail: executivedirector@isbnpa.org.
Pres address not obtained.
URL: http://www.isbnpa.org/
History 2002. **Aims** Stimulate, promote and advocate innovative research and policy in the area of behavioural nutrition and physical activity toward the betterment of human health worldwide. **Structure** Annual Meeting (rotating yearly through every continent); Executive Committee. **Languages** English. **Staff** 0.30 FTE, paid. **Finance** Sources: meeting proceeds; members' dues; sale of publications. **Activities** Events/meetings; knowledge management/information dissemination; training/education. **Events** *Annual Meeting* Uppsala (Sweden) 2023, *Annual Conference* Minneapolis, MN (USA) 2021, *Annual Conference* Minneapolis, MN (USA) 2020, *Annual Conference* Prague (Czechia) 2019, *Annual Conference* Hong Kong (Hong Kong) 2018. **Publications** *International Journal of Behavioral Nutrition and Physical Activity* – scientific journal; *ISBNPA Newsletter.* **Members** Individuals (about 900) in 40 countries. Membership countries not specified.
[2022.10.31/XD9155/v/**D**]

♦ **International Society for Behavioural Neuroscience (ISBN)** **14957**
Contact address not obtained. E-mail: paf22@georgetown.edu.
URL: http://isbngroup.net/
Aims Foster interaction and discussion among people working in the field of behavioural neuroscience, with an emphasis on relative newcomers to the discipline. **Structure** Executive Committee. **Events** *Annual Meeting* Hamburg (Germany) 2023, *Annual Meeting* St John's, NL (Canada) 2022, *Annual Meeting* 2021, *Annual Meeting* Taormina (Italy) 2019, *Annual Meeting* Anchorage, AK (USA) 2018. **Members** Individuals (never over 150). Membership countries not specified. [2016/XM4754/**D**]

♦ **International Society for Behçet's Disease (ISBD)** **14958**
SG Istanbul Fac of Medicine, Istanbul Univ, Kaptani Derya Ibrahim Pasa Sokak, Beyazit, 34116 Istanbul/Istanbul, Türkiye.
URL: http://www.behcet.ws/
History May 2000, Seoul (Korea Rep), during 9th International Conference on Behçet's Disease, organized by International Study Group for Behçet's Disease. **Aims** Advance knowledge of the aetiology, pathogenesis, diagnosis, natural history, clinical features, treatment and management of Behçet's Disease. **Structure** General Assembly (every 2 years). Council. Executive Committee, including President, President-Elect, Past-President, Vice-President, Secretary and Treasurer. **Languages** English. **Events** *Conference* Paris (France) 2014, *Conference* Yokohama (Japan) 2012, *Conference* London (UK) 2010, *Conference* Pörtschach (Austria) 2008, *Conference* Lisbon (Portugal) 2006. **Publications** *BD News.* [2014/XM0087/**D**]

♦ International Society of Beverage Technologists (internationally oriented national body)
♦ International Society of Biocatalysis and Agricultural Biotechnology (unconfirmed)
♦ International Society for Biochemical Systematics (inactive)
♦ International Society of Bioclimatology and Biometeorology / see International Society of Biometeorology (#14969)

♦ **International Society for Biocuration (ISB)** **14959**
Société internationale d'annotation
Registered Office 1 rue Michel Servet, 1211 Geneva, Switzerland. E-mail: intsocbio@gmail.com.
URL: http://www.biocurator.org/
History 2009. Registered in accordance with Swiss law. **Activities** *International Biocurator Conference.* **Events** *Conference* Padua (Italy) 2023, *Conference* Geneva (Switzerland) 2022, *Conference* Geneva (Switzerland) 2021, *Conference* Bar Harbor, ME (USA) 2020, *Conference* Cambridge (UK) 2019. **Members** Individuals. Membership countries not specified. **NGO Relations** Instrumental in setting up: *Global Organisation for Bioinformatics Learning, Education and Training (GOBLET, #10516).* [2018/XJ8099/**D**]

♦ **International Society for Bioelectromagnetism (ISBEM)** **14960**
SG Merituilinkatu 16 A 5, FI-00170 Helsinki, Finland. T. +358400621246.
URL: http://www.isbem.org/
History Founded 16 Aug 1995, Tampere (Finland). **Aims** Facilitate dissemination of knowledge in bioelectromagnetism; encourage new research in bioelectromagnetism. **Structure** General Meeting (annual); Working Groups; Secretariat. **Languages** English. **Finance** Subscription fee. **Events** *Conference* Seoul (Korea Rep) 2022, *Conference* Heiligenstadt (Germany) 2021, *Conference* St Louis, MO (USA) 2020, *Conference* Aachen (Germany) 2018, *Conference* Tallinn (Estonia) 2015. **Publications** *International Journal of Bioelectromagnetism (IJBEM).* **Members** Individuals (about 150). Membership countries not specified.
[2019.02.13/XD8774/**D**]

♦ International Society for Bioengineering and the Skin (inactive)

♦ **International Society of Bioethics (ISB)** **14961**
Société internationale de la bioéthique (SIBI) – Sociedad Internacional de Bioética (SIBI)
Sec Plaza del Humedal 3, 33206 Gijón, Asturias, Spain. T. +34985348185. E-mail: bioetica@sibi.org.
URL: http://www.sibi.org/
History 1996, Gijón (Spain). Founded on the proposal of medical doctor Marcelo Palacios, former member of Spanish Parliament (1982-1996) and member of Parliamentary Assembly of Council of Europe (1986-1996). Formally set up by deed executed 5 Dec 1997 and recorded 18 Jan 1998. Registration: Start date: 18 Jan 1998, Spain, Asturias. **Aims** Attain full application of bioethics in fields such as medical, biological, environmental and food sciences and technologies. **Structure** Scientific Committee (meets at least annually); Latin American Division; Asian Division. **Languages** Arabic, Chinese, English, French, German, Italian, Portuguese, Russian, Spanish. **Staff** 2.00 FTE, voluntary. **Finance** Public and private sources, including: Gijón Town Council; University of Oviedo; Ramón Areces Foundation; Chamber of Commerce, Industry and Navigation of Gijón; House of Representatives of the Principality of Asturias; Pharmaceutical Cooperative of Asturias – COFAS; Medical School of Asturias; and others. **Activities** Awards/prizes/competitions; awareness raising; events/meetings; financial and/or material support; knowledge management/information dissemination; networking/liaising; projects/programmes; training/education. **Events** *World Congress* Gijón (Spain) 2021, *World Conference* Gijón (Spain) 2018, *World Conference* Gijón (Spain) 2016, *World Conference* Gijón (Spain) 2013, *World Conference* Gijón (Spain) 2011. **Publications** *SIBI Journal* (2 a year) in English, Spanish. *Sociedad Internacional de Bioetica – SIBI 1997-2009.* Books; Scientific Committee minutes; conference proceedings.
Members Individuals in 18 countries:
Algeria, Austria, Brazil, Canada, Congo DR, France, Germany, Greece, Ireland, Israel, Italy, Lebanon, Malawi, Portugal, Spain, UK, Ukraine, USA.
Associate: organizations and individuals in 12 countries:
Argentina, Brazil, Chile, Colombia, Costa Rica, Cuba, Ecuador, France, India, Mexico, Peru, Spain. [2021.09.01/XD7993/**D**]

♦ **International Society for Biofabrication (ISBF)** **14962**
SG Otto-Stern-Weg 7, HPL J 22, 8093 Zurich ZH, Switzerland.
URL: http://www.biofabricationsociety.org/
History Current bylaws adopted 6 Oct 2010. **Aims** Promote advances in biofabrication research, development, education, training, and medical and clinical applications. **Structure** General Assembly. Board of Directors of 10. Officers: President; Past-President; Executive Director. **Languages** English. **Finance** Sources: members' dues. **Events** *International Conference on Biofabrication* Montecatini Terme (Italy) 2022, *International Conference on Biofabrication* Columbus, OH (USA) 2019, *International Conference on Biofabrication* Würzburg (Germany) 2018, *International Conference on Biofabrication* Beijing (China) 2017, *Annual Conference* Winston-Salem, NC (USA) 2016. **Members** Regular; Student; Lifetime. Membership countries not specified.
[2021/XJ5484/**C**]

♦ **International Society for Biological Calorimetry (ISBC)** **14963**
No fixed address address not obtained.
URL: http://www.biocalorimetry.ucoz.org/
History 1972, London (UK), as *International Symposium on Microcalorimetric Applications in Biology (ISMAB).* Present name adopted 1990. **Aims** Promote the understanding and application of calorimetry in the study of the physiology or organisms and their resting stages, organs, tissues and cells. **Structure** No formal structure. **Languages** English. **Staff** 3.00 FTE, voluntary. **Finance** Conference subscriptions. **Activities** Organizes workshops, conferences and discussion fora. Provides advice on instruments and methods. **Events** *Conference* Vilnius (Lithuania) 2022, *Conference* Vilnius (Lithuania) 2020, *Conference* Krakow (Poland) 2018, *Conference* Basel (Switzerland) 2016, *Conference* Lund (Sweden) 2014. **Publications** *Thermochimica Acta.* **Members** Full (about 250). Membership countries not specified. [2020/XM1850/**D**]

♦ **International Society for Biological and Environmental Repositories (ISBER)** **14964**
Exec Dir 750 Pender St, Ste 301, Vancouver BC V6C 2T7, Canada. T. +16044845693. Fax +16048744378. E-mail: info@isber.org.
URL: http://www.isber.org/
History 2002. Initially founded as a division of American Society for Investigative Pathology. An independent society since 1 Jun 2013. **Aims** Create opportunities for sharing ideas internationally, and harmonize approaches to evolving challenges in *biobanking* and biological and environmental repository operation. **Structure** Board of Directors, comprising President, President-Elect, Past President, Secretary, Secretary-Elect, Treasurer, Treasurer-Elect, Directors-at-Large, Committee Chairs and Executive Director. **Activities** Events/meetings; training/education. **Events** *Annual Meeting* Atlanta, GA (USA) 2022, *Annual Meeting* 2021, *Annual Meeting* Anaheim, CA (USA) 2020, *Biospecimen Research Symposium* Berlin (Germany) 2019, *Annual Meeting* Shanghai (China) 2019. **Publications** *ISBER Newsletter* (4 a year); *Biopreservation and Biobanking (BIO)* – journal. *ISBER Best Practices and Self-Asessment Tool.* Working group papers. **NGO Relations** Member of: *Global Alliance for Genomics and Health (GA4GH, #10199).* Affiliate partner of: *Asian Network of Research Resource Centers (ANRRC, #01557); Global Genome Biodiversity Network (GGBN, #10388).* Cooperates with: *European, Middle Eastern and African Society for Biopreservation and Biobanking (ESBB, #07798).*
[2018/XM3714/**C**]

♦ **International Society for Bioluminescence and Chemiluminescence (ISBC)** **14965**
Sec address not obtained.
URL: http://www.isbc.unibo.it/
History 1994, following a series of symposia. Registered in the State of Texas. **Aims** Promote fundamental and applied sciences of bioluminescence and chemiluminescence worldwide. **Structure** Executive Committee, including President, Past-President, President-Elect, Secretary, Past-Secretary and Treasurer. Advisory Board. **Finance** Members'dues. **Events** *Symposium* Tsukuba (Japan) 2016, *Symposium* Uppsala (Sweden) 2014, *Symposium* Lyon (France) 2010, *Symposium* Beijing (China) 2008, *Biennial Symposium* Shanghai (China) 2008. **Publications** Symposia proceedings.
Members Individuals in 18 countries:
Austria, Belgium, Brazil, Canada, China, Czechia, Finland, Germany, Italy, Japan, Netherlands, Puerto Rico, Russia, Slovenia, Switzerland, Türkiye, UK, USA. [2014/XD8809/**D**]

♦ **International Society of Biomechanics (ISB)** **14966**
SG c/o Kinesiology Fac, Main Office KNB 135, 376 Collegiate Blvd NW, Calgary AB T2N 1N4, Canada.
Webmaster address not obtained. E-mail: webmaster@isbweb.org.
URL: http://isbweb.org/
History 1973, State College, PA (USA). 1973. **Aims** Promote biomechanics at international level. **Structure** General Assembly (biennial). Executive Council (meets annually). **Languages** English. **Finance** Members' dues. **Activities** Networking/liaising; knowledge management/information dissemination; awards/prizes/competititons; events/meetings. **Events** *Congress* Fukuoka (Japan) 2023, *International Symposium of 3-D Analysis of Human Movement* Tokyo (Japan) 2022, *Congress* Stockholm (Sweden) 2021, *Congress* Calgary, AB (Canada) 2019, *Congress* Brisbane, QLD (Australia) 2017. **Publications** *Journal of Applied Biomechanics* (4 a year); *ISB Newsletter* (4 a year); *Clinical Biomechanics.* Congress proceedings; biomechanics monograph series.
Members National affiliate groups in 13 countries and territories:
Bulgaria, Canada, China, Czechia, France, Japan, Korea Rep, Poland, Romania, Russia, Taiwan, UK, USA.
NGO Relations Cooperates with (1): *International Society for Photogrammetry and Remote Sensing (ISPRS, #15362).* Affiliated with (1): *Hand and Wrist Biomechanics International (HWBI, #10859).* Instrumental in setting up (1): *International Foot and Ankle Biomechanics Community (i-FAB, #13624).* Joint publication with: *International Society of Biomechanics in Sports (ISBS, #14967).* [2021/XD0587/**D**]

♦ **International Society of Biomechanics in Sports (ISBS)** **14967**
SG c/o C42 – Cumberland Campus, Univ of Sydney, Lidcombe NSW 2141, Australia. E-mail: secretary-general@isbs.org.
URL: http://www.isbs.org/
History 27 Aug 1981, San Diego CA (USA). Constitution adopted 7 May 1983. **Aims** Provide a forum for exchange of ideas for sports biomechanics researchers, coaches and teachers; bridge the gap between researchers and practitioners; gather and disseminate information and materials on biomechanics in sports. **Structure** General Meeting (annual); Board of Directors; Executive Council; Standing Committees (9). **Languages** English. **Activities** Awards/prizes/competitions; knowledge management/information dissemination. **Events** *Annual Symposium* Liverpool (UK) 2022, *Annual Symposium* Canberra, ACT (Australia) 2021, *Annual Symposium* Liverpool (UK) 2020, *Annual Symposium* Oxford, OH (USA) 2019, *Annual Symposium* Auckland (New Zealand) 2018. **Publications** *ISBS Newsletter* (4 a year); *Sport Biomechanics* (4 a year). Symposium proceedings.
Members Individuals in 43 countries and territories:
Argentina, Australia, Austria, Belgium, Brazil, Canada, China, Denmark, Egypt, Finland, France, Germany, Greece, Hungary, Iceland, India, Iran Islamic Rep, Ireland, Israel, Italy, Japan, Jordan, Korea Rep, Lithuania, Malaysia, Mexico, Netherlands, New Zealand, Norway, Portugal, Qatar, Romania, Russia, Serbia, Singapore, South Africa, Spain, Sweden, Switzerland, Taiwan, Thailand, UK, USA. [2019.10.23/XD6837/v/**D**]

♦ **International Society for Biomedical Research on Alcoholism (ISBRA)** **14968**
Société internationale de recherches biomédicales sur l'alcoolisme
Manager PO Box 202332, Denver CO 80220-8332, USA. T. +13033556420. Fax +13033551207. E-mail: isbra@isbra.com.
URL: http://www.isbra.com/
History 1982. Registration: USA, Colorado. **Aims** Promote excellence internationally in all aspects of biomedical research on alcoholism and alcohol related biomedical phenomena. **Structure** Board of Directors. Committees (5): Finance; Publication; Membership; Liaison; Education. **Languages** English. **Staff** 0.50 FTE, paid. **Finance** Sources: members' dues. **Activities** Events/meetings. **Events** *Congress* Melbourne, VIC (Australia) 2024, *World Congress on Alcohol and Alcoholism* Krakow (Poland) 2022, *Biennial Congress* Denver, CO (USA) 2021, *Biennial Congress* New Orleans, LA (USA) 2020, *Biennial Congress* Kyoto (Japan) 2018.

Publications *Alcoholism: Clinical and Experimental Research* – official journal. Abstracts; proceedings of meetings.
Members Individuals Regular; Emeritus; Associate; Honorary; Affiliate. Individuals in 38 countries and territories:
Argentina, Australia, Austria, Belarus, Belgium, Brazil, Canada, Chile, Czechia, Denmark, Estonia, Finland, France, Germany, Hungary, India, Ireland, Israel, Italy, Japan, Kenya, Korea Rep, Mexico, Netherlands, Nigeria, Norway, Poland, Portugal, Puerto Rico, Russia, Serbia, Spain, Sweden, Switzerland, Taiwan, Thailand, UK, USA.
Consultative Status Consultative status granted from: *WHO (#20950)* (Official Relations). **NGO Relations** Affiliated regional societies include: *Asia-Pacific Society for Alcohol and Addiction Research (APSAAR, #02028)*; *European Society for Biomedical Research on Alcoholism (ESBRA, #08532)*; *Latin American Society for Biomedical Research on Alcoholism (LASBRA).* [2021/XD2155/**C**]

♦ International Society of Biometeorology (ISB) 14969

Société internationale de biométéorologie (SIB) – Sociedad Internacional de Biometeorologia

Sec Dept of Geography and Environmental Planning, Towson University, 8000 York Rd, Towson MD 21252, USA.
Pres University of Melbourne, School of Ecosystem and Forest Sciences, Baldwin Spencer Bldg 113, Parkville VIC 3010, Australia.
URL: http://www.biometeorology.org/

History 1 Jan 1956, Paris (France). Statutes adopted 29 Aug 1956. Statutes amended: 27 Sep 1957; 10 Sep 1960; 7 Sep 1963; 6 Sep 1969; 12 Nov 1973; 1 Jan 1983; 1 Apr 1996; 4 Apr 2003. Former names and other names: *International Society of Bioclimatology and Biometeorology (ISBB)* – former (1 Jan 1956 to 1963); *Société internationale de bioclimatologie et de biométéorologie* – former (1 Jan 1956 to 1963). **Aims** Provide an international forum to promote interdisciplinary collaboration between meteorologists, health professionals, biologists, *climatologists*, ecologists and other scientists. **Structure** Executive Board, consisting of President, President-Elect, Secretary, Treasurer, 2 Vice-Presidents, Past-President, 3 Councillors, Editor-in-Chief and 3 observers. **Languages** English. **Staff** Voluntary. **Finance** Sources: members' dues. **Activities** Events/meetings. Commissions (5): Phenology; Climate, Tourism and Recreation; Development of a "Universal Thermal Climate Index"; Animal Biometeorology; Climate and Human Health. **Events** *International Congress of Biometeorology* Tempe, AZ (USA) 2023, *International Congress of Biometeorology* 2021, *International Congress of Biometeorology* Jaboticabal (Brazil) 2020, *International Congress of Biometeorology* Durham (UK) 2017, *International Congress of Biometeorology* Cleveland, OH (USA) 2014. **Publications** *International Journal of Biometeorology* (4 a year); *Biometeorology Bulletin* (2 a year). *Biometeorology Book Series*. Congress proceedings; Progress in biometeorology.
Members Affiliate (7); Individual Honorary; Less Developed Country; Life; Regular; Retired; Student. Members in 37 countries:
Argentina, Australia, Austria, Belgium, Brazil, Bulgaria, Canada, China, Croatia, Egypt, Estonia, France, Germany, Hungary, Iceland, India, Israel, Italy, Japan, Kenya, Latvia, Lithuania, Malaysia, Mexico, Netherlands, New Zealand, Norway, Poland, Portugal, Slovenia, Spain, Sweden, Switzerland, Türkiye, UK, Ukraine, USA.
Included in the above, 2 organizations listed in this Yearbook:
International Society of Medical Hydrology and Climatology (ISMH, #15254); *International Society of Zoological Sciences (ISZS, #15552).*
Consultative Status Consultative status granted from: *World Meteorological Organization (WMO, #21649).*
IGO Relations Accredited by (1): *United Nations Framework Convention on Climate Change – Secretariat (UNFCCC, #20564).* Close working relations with: *FAO (#09260)*; *UNEP (#20299)*; *UNESCO (#20322)*; *WHO (#20950)*; *World Meteorological Organization (WMO, #21649).* **NGO Relations** Member of (4): *Council for International Organizations of Medical Sciences (CIOMS, #04905)*; *International Council for Science (ICSU, inactive)*; *International Forum of Meteorological Societies (IFMS, #13644)*; *International Union of Biological Sciences (IUBS, #15760).* Affiliated with (2): *International Association for Urban Climate (IAUC, #12251)*; *International Society for Agricultural Meteorology (INSAM, #14912).* [2023/XB2531/y/**B**]

♦ International Society of Bionic Engineering (ISBE) 14970

Gen Sec C508 Dingxin Bldg, Jilin Univ, 2699 Qianjin Str, Changchun, 130012 Jilin, China. T. +8643185166507. Fax +8643185166507. E-mail: secretariat@isbe-online.org.
URL: http://www.isbe-online.org/

History Founded 2010. **Aims** Foster information exchange on bionic engineering research, development and application. **Structure** Board of Directors. **Activities** Awards/prizes/competitions; events/meetings; research/documentation. **Publications** *ISBE Newsletter*; *Journal of Bionic Engineering*. **Members** Individual; Corporate. Members in 62 countries and territories. Membership countries not specified. **NGO Relations** Partners include: *International Society for Terrain-Vehicle Systems (ISTVS, #15505).* [2020.03.05/XM8428/**C**]

♦ International Society for Biopharmaceutical Statistics (unconfirmed)
♦ International Society of Biophysical Medicine (inactive)

♦ International Society for Biophysics and Imaging of Skin (ISBS) . . . 14971

Sec Unilever R and D, 50 Commerce Drive, Trumbull CT 06615, USA. T. +12033813120.
Pres proDERM Institute for Applied Dermatological Research, Industriestrasse 1, 22869 Schenefeld, Germany. T. +4940839358-17. Fax +4940839358-39. E-mail: kpw@proderm.de.
URL: http://www.i-s-b-s.org/

History 21 Jul 2006, by merger of *International Society for Bioengineering and the Skin (ISBS, inactive)* and *International Society for Skin Imaging (ISSI, inactive).* **Events** *International Meeting* Lisbon (Portugal) 2016, *International Meeting* Vancouver, BC (Canada) 2015, *Meeting* Vancouver, BC (Canada) 2015, *World Congress / Meeting* Mystic, CT (USA) 2014, *Joint International Congress / Meeting* Milan (Italy) 2013. **NGO Relations** Member of: *International League of Dermatological Societies (ILDS, #14018).* [2017/XM1854/**D**]

♦ International Society of Biorheology (ISB) 14972

Société internationale de biorhéologie

SG c/o Lawrence Lab, Box 800759 Health System, Charlottesville VA 22908, USA. T. +14349824269. Fax +14349823870. E-mail: mbl2a@virginia.edu.
URL: http://www.coe.ou.edu/isb/

History 1966, as *International Society of Haemorheology*. Present name adopted 1969. Founder: Prof Alfred L Copley. **Aims** Promote biorheology around the world. **Structure** Council, consisting President, 4 Vice-Presidents, Secretary-General, Treasurer and up to 4 other members. Ex-officio members of the Council: Immediate Past President, Chairman of all Standing Committees, Liaison Officer to IUPAB, representative on the Editorial Board of Biorheology, and next Conference Chairperson designated by the President-Elect. **Finance** Sources: members' dues. **Activities** Organizes *International Congress of Biorheology* at which presents *'Poiseuille Gold Medal Award'*. **Events** *Congress* Seoul (Korea Rep) 2015, *Congress* Istanbul (Turkey) 2012, *Congress* State College, PA (USA) 2008, *Congress* Chongqing (China) 2005, *Congress* Antalya (Turkey) 2002. **Publications** *Biorheology* – official journal; *Clinical Hemorheology* – journal.
Members Regular; Emeritus; Corporate. Individuals in 28 countries:
Argentina, Australia, Austria, Belgium, Canada, China, Czechia, Denmark, Finland, France, Germany, Greece, Hungary, Iceland, India, Indonesia, Israel, Italy, Japan, Mexico, Netherlands, Norway, Spain, Sweden, Switzerland, Türkiye, UK, USA.
NGO Relations *European Conference on Clinical Haemorheology.* Affiliated to: *International Union for Pure and Applied Biophysics (IUPAB, #15808).* [2014/XC9129/v/**C**]

♦ International Society for Biosafety Research (ISBR) 14973

Pres 1010 Vermont Ave. NW, Suite 202, Oxford Mills, Washington DC 20005, USA. E-mail: admin@isbr.info.
URL: http://www.isbr.info/

History Founded following 6th International Symposium on the Biosafety of Genetically Modified Organisms, Jul 2000, Saskatoon SK (Canada). **Aims** Promote the practice and application of science in the fields of *agricultural* biotechnology and environmental risk analysis. **Structure** Executive Committee, including President, Vice-President and Secretary-Treasurer. **Finance** Sources: members' dues. **Activities** Events/meetings. **Events** *Symposium* St Louis, MO (USA) 2023, *Symposium* Tarragona (Spain) 2019, *Symposium* Guadalajara (Mexico) 2017, *Symposium* Cape Town (South Africa) 2014, *Symposium* St Louis, MO (USA) 2012. **Publications** *Environmental Biosafety Research* – journal. **NGO Relations** Member of (1): *International Federation of Biosafety Associations (IFBA, #13373).* [2023/XJ3736/**D**]

♦ International Society for Biosemiotic Studies (ISBS) 14974

Pres address not obtained.
Vice-pres address not obtained.
URL: http://www.biosemiotics.org/

History 12 Jun 2005. Constitution most recently approved, 20 Jul 2012, Tartu (Estonia). **Aims** Constitute an organizational framework for the collaboration among scholars dedicated to biosemiotic studies; propagate knowledge of this field of study to researchers in related areas, as well as to the public in general. **Structure** General Assembly; Executive Committee. **Languages** English. **Staff** None. **Finance** Sources: meeting proceeds; members' dues. **Activities** Events/meetings. **Events** *Conference* Olomouc (Czechia) 2022, *Conference* Stockholm (Sweden) 2021, *Conference* Olomouc (Czechia) 2020, *Conference* Moscow (Russia) 2019, *Conference* Berkeley, CA (USA) 2018. **Publications** *Biosemiotics* (3 a year) – journal.
Members Full in 45 countries and territories:
Argentina, Australia, Austria, Brazil, Canada, Chile, China, Czechia, Denmark, Ecuador, Estonia, Finland, France, Germany, Greece, Hungary, India, Indonesia, Ireland, Israel, Italy, Japan, Korea Rep, Lithuania, Mexico, Morocco, Netherlands, Norway, Poland, Portugal, Romania, Russia, Scotland, Singapore, Slovakia, South Africa, Spain, Sweden, Switzerland, Taiwan, Türkiye, UK, Ukraine, USA, Wales. [2022.02.02/XM3636/**C**]

♦ International Society of Biospeleology 14975

Société internationale de biospéologie (SIBIOS) – Sociedad Internacional de Biospeologia – Internationale Gesellschaft für Biospeologie – Società Internazionale di Biospeologia

Sec address not obtained.
Pres address not obtained.
URL: http://www.sibios-issb.org/

History 1979, Moulis (France), as *Biospeological Society – Société de biospéologie – Sociedad de Biospeología – Gesellschaft für Biospeologie – Società di Biospeologia.* Also referred to as *International Society of Subterranean Biology (ISSB).* **Aims** Promote biological and ecological research in the *hypogean* field; promote the teaching of ecology of karstic, interstitial and superficial underground environment; show the special features of karst in zoology, hydrobiology, ecology, *cave* protection, genetics, evolution and *biodiversity*; carry out research into the biology of cave-dwelling animals; act as a reference for fundamental studies in biochemistry, ethology, physiology and ecology and in modelling. **Structure** General Assembly; Board of up to 20 members. **Languages** English, French. **Staff** Part-time, voluntary. **Finance** Sources: grants; members' dues. **Activities** Events/meetings; research/documentation. **Events** *Symposium / International Conference* Juriquilla (Mexico) 2014, *Symposium* Košice (Slovakia) 2012, *Symposium* 2010, *International Conference* Postojna (Slovenia) 2010, *International Symposium* Fremantle, WA (Australia) 2008. **Publications** *Les mémoires de biospéologie. Encyclopedia Biospeologica.* Abstract books.
Members Individuals and organizations in 28 countries:
Argentina, Australia, Belgium, Brazil, Bulgaria, Croatia, France, Germany, Greece, Hungary, Indonesia, Italy, Japan, Korea Rep, Luxembourg, Mexico, Morocco, Netherlands, Poland, Portugal, Romania, Russia, Serbia, Slovenia, Spain, Switzerland, UK, USA.
NGO Relations *Centre international de myriapodologie (CIM, #03759).* [2018.06.01/XD3438/**C**]

♦ International Society on Biotelemetry (ISOB) 14976

Sec address not obtained.
URL: http://www.biotelemetry.org/

History Founded 1 Jun 1973. **Structure** Council, including President, Vice-President, Secretary and Treasurer. **Activities** Organizes symposia. **Events** *Biennial Symposium* Leuven (Belgium) 2016, *Biennial Symposium* Kyoto (Japan) 2014, *Symposium* Garmisch-Partenkirchen (Germany) 2006, *Biennial Symposium* Knoxville, TN (USA) 2006, *Symposium* Knoxville, TN (USA) 2005. **Publications** *ISOB Bulletin.*
Members Individuals in 26 countries:
Australia, Austria, Belgium, Brazil, Canada, Croatia, Denmark, France, Germany, Greece, Hungary, Ireland, Israel, Italy, Japan, Kenya, Netherlands, Norway, Portugal, South Africa, Spain, Sweden, Switzerland, UK, Ukraine, USA. [2016/XD8617/**D**]

♦ International Society for Bipolar Disorders (ISBD) 14977

Exec Dir PO Box 396, Monroeville PA 15146, USA.
URL: http://www.isbd.org/

History 17 Jun 1999, Pittsburgh, PA (USA). **Aims** Promote of awareness, education and research on all aspects of bipolar disorders. **Structure** Board of Councillors of 15 members. Executive Committee, comprising President, 4 Vice-Presidents (Governance; Research; Education; Global Outreach) and Secretary/Treasurer. Committees (4): Advocacy; Education; Membership and Chapter Development; Research. **Languages** English. **Staff** 2.00 FTE, paid. **Finance** Sources: members' dues. **Events** *ISBD Experience* 2022, *Annual Conference* Chicago, IL (USA) 2020, *Annual Conference* Sydney, NSW (Australia) 2019, *Annual Conference* Mexico City (Mexico) 2018, *Annual Conference* Washington, DC (USA) 2017. **Publications** *Bipolar Disorders* – journal; *ISBD Global* – newsletter.
Members General; Corporate Affiliate; Advocacy Affiliate. Affiliates (3):
Asian Network of Bipolar Disorder (ANBD, #01547); *East Asian Bipolar Forum (EABF, #05200)*; *Iberoamerican Network for Bipolar Disorder (IAN-BD, #11026).*
Chapters in 18 countries and territories:
Argentina, Australia, Brazil, Chile, Colombia, Denmark, France, Hong Kong, India, Japan, Korea Rep, Mexico, Norway, Peru, Portugal, Taiwan, Türkiye, Venezuela.
Included in the above, 1 organization listed in this Yearbook:
Australasian Society for Bipolar and Depressive Disorders (ASBD).
NGO Relations *Global Alliance of Mental Illness Advocacy Networks – Europe (GAMIAN Europe, #10211)* is a member. Affilaite member of: *World Psychiatric Association (WPA, #21741).* [2020/XD9160/y/**C**]

♦ International Society of Blood Purification 14978

Sec Dept of Internal Medicine, Erasmus MC Rotterdam, PO box 2040, 3000 CA Rotterdam, Netherlands. T. +31104639222. Fax +31104366372.
URL: https://intsocbp.wordpress.com/

History Founded 1982, Berlin West (Germany FR), as *International Society of Haemofiltration.* Present name adopted in 1986 to encompass all blood purification techniques. **Aims** Promote science and research concerning problems of organ *prosthesis* for blood cleansing. **Structure** Council; Officers (4). **Languages** English. **Staff** Voluntary. **Finance** Sources: members' dues. Other sources: Funds received from industry. **Events** *Annual Meeting* Yokohama (Japan) 2020, *Annual Meeting* Hyderabad (India) 2019, *Annual Meeting* Skopje (Macedonia) 2018, *Annual Meeting* Hiroshima (Japan) 2016, *Annual Meeting* St Petersburg (Russia) 2015. **Publications** *Journal of Blood Purification.*
Members Individuals in 26 countries:
Australia, Austria, Belgium, China, Czechia, Egypt, France, Germany, Hungary, India, Italy, Japan, Korea Rep, Monaco, Netherlands, Norway, Poland, Romania, Russia, Serbia, Slovenia, Spain, Sweden, Switzerland, UK, USA.
[2014/XD1375/v/**C**]

♦ International Society of Blood Transfusion (ISBT) 14979

Société internationale de transfusion sanguine (SITS) – Sociedad Internacional de Transfusión de Sangre – Internationale Gesellschaft für Blut-Uberleitung

Exec Dir Marnixstraat 317, 1016 TB Amsterdam, Netherlands. T. +31207601760. E-mail: office@isbtweb.org.
Pres address not obtained.
URL: https://www.isbtweb.org/

History 2 Oct 1937, Paris (France). Set up at 2nd Blood Transfusion Congress, following initial steps taken at 1st Congress, 1935, Rome (Italy). Former title in other languages: *Société internationale de transfusion sanguine (SITS) – Sociedad Internacional de Transfusión de Sangre – Internationale Gesellschaft für Blut-Uberleitung.* Statutes renewed Jun 2013. Registration: No/ID: KVK 34205247, Netherlands, Amsterdam. **Aims** Share knowledge to improve the safety of blood transfusion worldwide. **Structure** General Assembly (annually); Board of Directors; Executive Committee; Central Office, based in Amsterdam (Netherlands). **Languages** English. **Staff** 5.00 FTE, paid. **Finance** Sources: members' dues. Other sources: income from congresses; advertisements; corporate partnerships. **Activities** Awards/prizes/competitions; events/meetings; knowledge management/information dissemination; networking/liaising; training/education. **Events** *International Congress* Cape Town (South Africa) 2023, *European Regional Congress* Gothenburg (Sweden) 2023, *International Congress* 2022, *Asian Congress* Brisbane, QLD (Australia) 2021, *European Regional Congress* Milan (Italy) 2021. **Publications** *Transfusion Today* (4 a year); *Vox Sanguinis* – 2 vols a year, 4 issues each. **Members** Corporate; Affiliate; Honorary; Individual. Members (over 2,000) in over 100 countries and territories. Membership countries not specified. **Consultative Status** Consultative status granted from: *WHO (#20950)* (Official Relations). **NGO Relations** *Africa Society for Blood Transfusion (AfSBT, #00519); Alliance for Harmonisation of Cellular Therapy Accreditation (AHCTA, #00686); Arab Transfusion Medicine Forum (ATMF, #01061); European Blood Alliance (EBA, #06351); ICCBBA (#11042); International Federation of Blood Donor Organizations (IFBDO, #13374); International Plasma and Fractionation Association (IPFA, #14597); Thalassaemia International Federation (#20139); Worldwide Network for Blood and Marrow Transplantation (WBMT, #21929).* [2022/XB2532/B]

♦ International Society for Blood and Tumour Diseases (inactive)

♦ International Society for Board Game Studies (BGS) 14980

Contact Museu de Ciênca, Rua da Escola Politécnica 56, 1250-102 Lisbon, Portugal. E-mail: ludus@ludicum.org.
Contact Musée Suisse du Jeu, Au Château, 1814 La Tour de Peilz VD, Switzerland.
URL: http://boardgamestudies.jimdofree.com/

History Founded 1997. **Aims** As an international, interdisciplinary and informal group of academics and field researchers, study the history and development of board games throughout the world. **Structure** Informal structure. **Languages** English. **Staff** None. **Finance** No budget. **Activities** Events/meetings. **Events** *Board Games Studies Colloquium* Selçuk (Türkiye) 2023, *Board Games Studies Colloquium* Leeuwarden (Netherlands) 2022, *Board Games Studies Colloquium* Paris (France) 2021, *Annual Colloquium* Bologna (Italy) 2019, *Annual Colloquium* Athens (Greece) 2018. **Publications** *Board Game Studies Journal (BGSJ)* – online. **Members** Individuals – archaeologists, anthropologists, historians, psychologists, educationalists, linguists, authors, game inventors, collectors and representatives of games and publishers and manufacturers – in 17 countries:
Austria, Belgium, Brazil, France, Germany, India, Israel, Italy, Japan, Mexico, Netherlands, Poland, Portugal, Spain, Switzerland, UK, USA. [2022/XJ4809/C]

♦ International Society for Body Composition Research (ISBCR) 14981

Chair New York Obesity Nutrition Research Ctr, Dept Medicine, Columbia Univ Medical Center, 1150 St Nicholas Ave, 1st Floor Ste 121-AA, New York NY 10032, USA. E-mail: dg108@cumc.columbia.edu.
URL: http://www.isbcr.org/

History 2006, following several years of informal activity. **Aims** Promote research on body composition so as to understand the link between structure and function in health and disease at all stages of life; promote development and application of body composition techniques relevant to public health and clinical practice. **Structure** Executive Committee; International Scientific Committee. **Languages** English. **Activities** Events/meetings. **Events** *International Symposium on In-Vivo Body Composition* New York, NY (USA) 2018, *International Symposium on In-Vivo Body Composition / International Symposium on In-Vivo Body Composition Studies* Cascais (Portugal) 2014, *International symposium on in-vivo body composition / International Symposium on In-Vivo Body Composition Studies* Hangzhou (China) 2011, *International symposium on in-vivo body composition / International Symposium on In-Vivo Body Composition Studies* New York, NY (USA) 2008. **Members** Individuals. Membership countries not specified. [2016.06.01/XJ8063/v/D]

♦ International Society for Bonding Psychotherapy (ISBP) 14982

Vice Pres Rua Sargento José Paulo dos Santos 25, 1880-330 Lisbon, Portugal.
Intl Office Vier Uitersten 2, 8200 Bruges, Belgium.
URL: http://www.bonding-psychotherapy.org/

History Registered in accordance with Belgian law: 0899 608 484. **Aims** Promote and develop bonding psychotherapy worldwide; advance bonding psychotherapy in the areas of practice, theory, research and training. **Events** *Conference* Belluno (Italy) 2021, *Conference* Lisbon (Portugal) 2018, *Attachment, the essence of relationship* Bruges (Belgium) 2013, *Conference* Buenos Aires (Argentina) 2011.
Members Chapters in 11 countries:
Argentina, Belgium, France, Germany, Italy, Netherlands, Portugal, Slovenia, Sweden, Switzerland, USA. [2020/XJ6664/C]

♦ International Society of Bone Morphometry (ISBM) 14983

Treas Univ of Florida, Dept of Physiological Sciences, PO Box 100144, JHMHC, Gainesville FL 32610-0144, USA.
URL: http://www.bonemorphometry.org/

History Registered in the State of Kentucky (USA). **Aims** Establish and promote quality standards and quality assurance control in bone morphometry; promote dissemination of new knowledge, new technology and new approaches to bone morphometry. **Structure** Board of Directors. **Finance** Sources: members' dues. **Events** *Congress* Toronto, ON (Canada) 2024, *Congress* Odense (Denmark) 2022, *Congress* Lake Buena Vista, FL (USA) 2019, *Congress* Tokyo (Japan) 2015, *Congress* Minneapolis, MN (USA) 2012. **NGO Relations** *European Calcified Tissue Society (ECTS, #06429); International Osteoporosis Foundation (IOF, #14490).* [2015/XJ9085/C]

♦ International Society of Bone and Soft Tissue Pathology (internationally oriented national body)
♦ International Society for Boundary Elements (no recent information)
♦ International Society on Brain and Behavior / see International Society on Brain and Behaviour
♦ International Society on Brain and Behaviour (internationally oriented national body)
♦ International Society for Brain Edema (inactive)

♦ International Society for Brain Electromagnetic Topography (ISBET) 14984

Société internationale de la topographie électromagnétique du cerveau

Sec Institute of Physiology, Aulweg 129, 35394 Giesen, Germany. Fax +496419947279.

History Founded 1989. Registered in accordance with Dutch law. **Aims** Advance scientific work on electric and magnetic fields of the brain, from the development of analytical methods for basic research to physiological, psychological and clinical applications. **Structure** Executive Committee, consisting of 2 Co-Chairmen, Secretary, Secretary-Treasurer and 7 further members. Scientific Committee. **Languages** English. **Staff** Voluntary. **Activities** Organizes: international congresses; regional meetings; workshops. **Events** *Joint Annual Meeting* Halifax, NS (Canada) 2022, *BACI : International Conference on Basic and Clinical Multimodal Imaging* Naples (Italy) 2021, *Joint Annual Meeting* Toronto, ON (Canada) 2020, *BACI : International Conference on Basic and Clinical Multimodal Imaging* Chengdu (China) 2019, *BACI : International Conference on Basic and Clinical Multimodal Imaging* Bern (Switzerland) 2017. **Publications** *ISBET Newsletter* (2 a year); *Brain Topography* – journal.
Members Individuals in 29 countries:
Australia, Austria, Belgium, Brazil, Bulgaria, Canada, China, Cuba, Czechia, Denmark, Egypt, France, Germany, Greece, Hungary, Israel, Italy, Japan, Korea Rep, Mexico, Netherlands, New Zealand, Poland, Portugal, Russia, Spain, Sweden, Switzerland, USA.
NGO Relations Joint meetings with: *International Society for Neuroimaging in Psychiatry (ISNIP, #15297); Electroencephalography and Clinical Neuroscience Society (ECNS, #05422).* [2015/XD3897/v/C]

♦ International Society of Breast Pathology (internationally oriented national body)
♦ International Society of Breath Odor Research (inactive)
♦ International Society for British Genealogy and Family History (internationally oriented national body)

♦ International Society of the Built Environment (ISBE) 14985

Sec c/o School of Architecture, Southeast Univ, 2 Si-Pai-Lou, Nanjing, 210096 Jiangsu, China. E-mail: isbe-org@outlook.com.
Registered Address 29 The Nortons, Caldecotte, Milton Keynes, MK7 8HQ, UK. T. +441908370887.
URL: https://www.isbe.uk/

History 1989. Former names and other names: *Indoor Air International (IAI)* – former (1989 to 1995). Registration: Swiss Civil Code, Start date: 1989, Switzerland; Companies House, No/ID: 06956524, Start date: 8 Jul 2009, End date: 22 Nov 2016, England. **Aims** Promote sustainability issues related to indoor and built environment; provide a forum for information transfer and education of architects, building technologists, environmental engineers, environmental health practitioners and indoor air quality scientists; foster international collaboration in research and development, building and environmental design, government policies, regulations and guidelines; promote health and wellbeing for development of built environments for all cultures and nationalities. **Structure** General Assembly (annual); Council. Executive Committee, including President, Past President, Company Secretary, Regional Presidents and Vice-Presidents and Executive Director. **Languages** English. **Staff** 1.00 FTE, paid; 2.00 FTE, voluntary. **Finance** Sources: members' dues; revenue from activities/projects; sale of publications; sponsorship. Other sources: education and research activities; editing services. **Activities** cover the following issues: energy efficiency; infrastructures; acoustics; materials; building services; crime and fire prevention; flood risk management; sustainable urban drainage systems. Particular emphasis on indoor environmental quality concerning health and wellbeing of occupants, such as: noise; lighting; thermal comfort and heating; ventilation; emissions and air pollution; biological effects; moisture and humidity; radon and ingress from contaminated land and living space. Hosts and co-hosts international conferences and seminars. Offers: education; research; editing services. Cooperates with various intergovernmental bodies at the national level, as well as with companies and non-governmental organizations, also at the national level. **Events** *International symposium on sustainability and healthy buildings* Seoul (Korea Rep) 2010, *Conference* Prague (Czech Rep) 2006, *Conference* Birmingham (UK) 2005, *Conference on environmental monitoring of our cultural heritage* London (UK) 2005, *International conference on indoor air quality in hospitals* Prague (Czech Rep) 2005. **Publications** *Indoor and Built Environment* (6 a year).
Members Individuals in 50 countries and territories:
Albania, Argentina, Australia, Austria, Belgium, Brazil, Bulgaria, Canada, Chile, China, Croatia, Czechia, Denmark, Egypt, Estonia, Finland, France, Germany, Greece, Hong Kong, Hungary, India, Indonesia, Iran Islamic Rep, Ireland, Italy, Japan, Korea Rep, Latvia, Lithuania, Morocco, Netherlands, Norway, Philippines, Poland, Portugal, Romania, Russia, Slovenia, South Africa, Spain, Sweden, Switzerland, Taiwan, Thailand, Türkiye, UK, Ukraine, USA, Vietnam. [2021/XD7631/v/D]

♦ International Society for Burn Injuries (ISBI) 14986

Société internationale des brûlures – Sociedad Internacional de Quemaduras

Exec Dir 601 Biscayne Bend Ln, League City TX 77573, USA. E-mail: info@worldburn.org.
URL: https://worldburn.org/

History 24 Sep 1965, Edinburgh (UK). Founded at 2nd International Congress for Research in Burns, the 1st Congress having been held in 1960, Washington DC (USA). **Aims** Promote and coordinate scientific, clinical and social research on burns; promote prevention and education; encourage higher standards of care in all countries and make available active help in developing countries; encourage friendly cooperation in all countries by visits, lectures, scholarships, congresses, symposia. **Structure** Congress (every 2 years); Executive Committee; Regional Representatives (13). **Languages** English. **Staff** Voluntary. **Finance** Sources: members' dues. Other sources: Royalties from publications. **Activities** Awards/prizes/competitions; events/meetings; financial and/or material support; research/documentation. **Events** *Congress* Guadalajara (Mexico) 2022, *Biennial Congress* Birmingham (UK) 2021, *Biennial Congress* Birmingham (UK) 2020, *Biennial Congress* Delhi (India) 2018, *Biennial Congress* Miami, FL (USA) 2016. **Publications** *Burns* (8 a year); *Burns Journal of the International Society for Burn Injuries.*
Members Individuals in 89 countries and territories:
Albania, Algeria, Argentina, Australia, Austria, Azerbaijan, Bangladesh, Belgium, Bolivia, Brazil, Bulgaria, Canada, Chile, China, Colombia, Costa Rica, Côte d'Ivoire, Croatia, Czechia, Dominican Rep, Ecuador, Egypt, El Salvador, Estonia, Finland, France, Germany, Greece, Guatemala, Honduras, Hong Kong, Hungary, India, Iran Islamic Rep, Ireland, Israel, Italy, Jamaica, Japan, Kenya, Korea Rep, Kuwait, Kyrgyzstan, Latvia, Lebanon, Lithuania, Malawi, Malaysia, Mexico, Netherlands, New Zealand, Nicaragua, Nigeria, North Macedonia, Norway, Pakistan, Palestine, Peru, Philippines, Poland, Portugal, Puerto Rico, Qatar, Romania, Russia, Saudi Arabia, Serbia, Singapore, Slovakia, Slovenia, South Africa, Spain, Sri Lanka, Sweden, Switzerland, Taiwan, Tanzania UR, Thailand, Trinidad-Tobago, Tunisia, Türkiye, UK, United Arab Emirates, Uruguay, USA, Venezuela, Vietnam, Zambia, Zimbabwe.
Consultative Status Consultative status granted from: *ECOSOC (#05331)* (Ros C); *WHO (#20950)* (Official Relations). **NGO Relations** Member of: *International Federation of Surgical Colleges (IFSC, #13560); Pan African Burn Society (PABS, #18042).* [2022/XB2474/v/B]

♦ International Society of Business Astrologers 14987

Contact address not obtained. T. +4538287376.

History 10 Mar 1997, Copenhagen (Denmark), by Karen Boesen. **Aims** Increase public awareness of financial and business *astrology*. **Events** *Congress* Amsterdam (Netherlands) 2005. **Publications** *ISBA Monthly Newsletter.* [2010/XM0264/D]

♦ International Society of Business, Economics and Ethics (ISBEE) . . 14988

Société internationale d'éthique, d'économie et de gestion

Secretariat UniSA Business School, 61 North Terrace, City West Campus, Adelaide SA 5000, Australia. T. +161883029309. Fax +161883020512. E-mail: secretariat@isbee.org.
URL: http://isbee.org/

History 1989. **Aims** Provide a forum for exchange of experiences and ideas; enhance cooperation in cross-functional and cross-cultural projects; discuss the ethical dimension of economic, social and environmental issues which affect companies nationally and internationally. **Structure** Executive Committee. **Languages** English, French, German, Portuguese, Spanish. **Finance** Sources: members' dues. **Activities** Events/meetings; knowledge management/information dissemination; networking/liaising; research and development. **Events** *World Congress* Bilbao (Spain) 2022, *World Congress* Bilbao (Spain) 2021, *World Congress* Bilbao (Spain) 2020, *World Congress* Shanghai (China) 2016, *World Congress* Warsaw (Poland) 2012. **Publications** *ISBEE Newsletter* (3 a year). *Developing Business Ethics in China* (2006); *Global Perspectives on Ethics of Corporate Governance* (2006); *Improving Globalization* (2004); *Special Section: Religious Resources for Business Ethics in Latin America* (2003); *Moral Leadership in Action* (2002); *International Business Ethics: Challenges and Approaches* (1999). Proceedings; articles.
Members Individual; Organizational. Members in 56 countries and territories:
Argentina, Australia, Austria, Belgium, Bolivia, Brazil, Bulgaria, Canada, Chile, China, Colombia, Costa Rica, Czechia, Denmark, Ecuador, Finland, France, Germany, Holy See, Hong Kong, Hungary, India, Indonesia, Ireland, Israel, Italy, Japan, Kenya, Korea Rep, Latvia, Luxembourg, Malaysia, Mexico, Moldova, Netherlands, New Zealand, Nigeria, Norway, Pakistan, Palestine, Peru, Philippines, Poland, Russia, Singapore, South Africa, Spain, Sweden, Switzerland, Taiwan, Tanzania UR, Thailand, Uganda, UK, USA, Venezuela.
NGO Relations Partner of: *Globethics.net Foundation (#10669).* [2021/XF3721/C]

♦ International Society for Business Education (#19479)

♦ International Society on Business and Industrial Statistics (ISBIS) . 14989

Vice-Pres/Communications Dept of Mathematics and Statistics – HH 212, McMaster Univ, 1280 Main Street West, Hamilton ON L8S 4M4, Canada. T. +19055259140 ext 23425. E-mail: viveros@math.mcmaster.ca.
Vice-Pres/Membership Dept of Statistics, Univ of California, 1340 Olmsted Hall, Riverside CA 92521, USA. T. +19518273014.
URL: http://www.isbis-isi.org/

History as a Working Group on Industrial Statistics. Transformed into a *Standing Committee on Statistics in Industry*, 1992. Subsequently changed title into *Standing Committee on Statistics in Business and Industry (SBI)*, 1999. Formally founded in its current form, Apr 2005, Sydney (Australia), as a Section of *International Statistical Institute (ISI, #15603)*. **Aims** Promote the advancement and exchange of knowledge in business and industrial statistics; build international cooperation and association among statisticians working in business and industry; foster cooperation at an international level between statistical activities in universities and individuals working in business and industry; increase public awareness of the importance of statistics in business and industry; encourage links between statisticians in developing and developed countries. **Structure** Council of 12 members. Executive, comprising President, President-Elect and 4 Vice-Presidents (Secretariat; Finance; Publications; Membership). **Languages** English. **Events** *Conference* Kuala Lumpur (Malaysia) 2019, *Meeting on Statistics in Business and Industry* Athens (Greece) 2018, *Meeting on Statistics in Business and Industry* New York, NY (USA) 2017, *Meeting on Statistics in Business and Industry* Barcelona (Spain) 2016, *Meeting on Statistics in Business and Industry* Sao Paulo (Brazil) 2015. **Publications** *Applied Statistical Models in Business and Industry* – official journal. **NGO Relations** Sister organization of: *International Association for Official Statistics (IAOS, #12052); International Association for Statistical Computing (IASC, #12183).* [2008/XM0084/t/E]

♦ International Society for Business Innovation and Technology Management (ISBITM) 14990

Exec Sec Fac Environment and Resource Studies, Salaya Campus, Mahidol Univ, 999 Phuttamonthon 4 Road, Salaya, Nakhon Pathom, 73170, Thailand. E-mail: kitikorn.cha@mahidol.ac.th.

URL: http://isbitm.org/

Aims Build a vibrant and supportive community of scholars by markedly expanding opportunities to connect and explore business innovation and technology management. **Structure** Committee; Trustees. Includes: *European Business Innovation and Technology Management Society (EUBITMS); Asia Pacific Business Innovation and Technology Management Society (APBITMS); African Business Innovation and Technology Management Society (AFBITMS)*; American Business Innovation and Technology Management Society (USB-ITMS). **Activities** Events/meetings; awards/prizes/competitions. **Events** *Conference* Bali (Indonesia) 2015, *International Conference on Business Innovation and Technology Management / Conference* Phuket (Thailand) 2014. **Publications** *Progress in Business Innovation and Technology Management.* [2015/XJ9622/**D**]

♦ International Society of Cancer Chemoprevention / see International Society of Cancer Prevention (#14992)

♦ International Society of Cancer Metabolism (ISCaM) 14991

Sec address not obtained. E-mail: info@iscam.net.
URL: https://iscam.net/

History Apr 2009, Madrid (Spain). Former names and other names: *International Society for Proton Dynamics in Cancer (ISPDC)* – former (2009). Registration: Italy. **Aims** Improve communication and foster collaborative activities and research programmes between European and non-European scientists engaged in acidity, proton dynamics, metabolism and microenvironment in cancer research. **Structure** General Assembly; Board; Executive Board; Working Groups. **Languages** English. **Finance** Sources: members' dues. **Activities** Awards/prizes/competitions; awards/prizes/competitions; events/meetings; knowledge management/information dissemination; research/documentation; training/education. **Events** *Annual Meeting* Braga (Portugal) 2019, *Annual Meeting* Bratislava (Slovakia) 2018, *Annual Meeting* Brussels (Belgium) 2016, *Annual Meeting* Smolenice (Slovakia) 2014, *Annual Meeting* Munich (Germany) 2013. [2021/XJ7868/**C**]

♦ International Society of Cancer Prevention (ISCaP) 14992

Exec Gen Sec c/o Tumor and Breast Ctr, ZeTuP, Rorschacherstrasse 150, 9006 St Gallen, Switzerland. T. +41712430043. Fax +41712430044.

History 1995, Naples (Italy), as *International Society of Cancer Chemoprevention (ISCaC)* by 5 organizations, including *European School of Oncology (ESO, #08434)*. Current title adopted 2001. **Aims** Provide an international forum for research and development in cancer chemo- and bio-prevention, as well as related aspects of (secondary) cancer prevention, such as early screening; promote interaction among laboratory, epidemiological and clinical researchers in primary and secondary cancer prevention; enhance professional and public understanding of cancer, including pharmacological interventions to prevent carcinogenesis (chemoprevention). **Structure** General Assembly (every 2 years). Board of Directors, including President, Immediate Past President, Vice-President, Secretary-General and Treasurer. Standing Committees. **Languages** English. **Staff** 2.50 FTE, voluntary. **Finance** Members' dues. Meeting and conference fees; funding from industry and charities. **Activities** Committees (5): Clinical Research; Epidemiology; Laboratory Research; New Agents Development; Membership, Conferences and Publications. **Events** *International Conference on Cancer Prevention* London (UK) 2019, *International Conference on Cancer Prevention* Milan (Italy) 2013, *International conference on cancer prevention* St Gallen (Switzerland) 2010, *International conference on cancer prevention* St Gallen (Switzerland) 2008, *International conference on cancer prevention* St Gallen (Switzerland) 2006. **Publications** *ISCaP Newsletter* (2-3 a year). Abstracts; conference proceedings. **Members** Active; Associate; Honorary. Individuals and organizations in 24 countries and territories:
Algeria, Argentina, Austria, Belgium, Brazil, Canada, China, Croatia, Egypt, France, Germany, Greece, Italy, Japan, Korea Rep, Netherlands, Russia, Singapore, Sweden, Switzerland, Taiwan, UK, Ukraine, USA. [2014/XD7133/**D**]

♦ International Society of Cardiomyopathies (no recent information)
♦ International Society of Cardiomyopathy and Heart Failure / see International Society of Cardiomyopathy, Myocarditis and Heart Failure (#14993)

♦ International Society of Cardiomyopathy, Myocarditis and Heart Failure (ISCMF) 14993

Main Office Bldg 3F – RIPD, 15 Morimoto-cho, Shimogamo, Sakyo-ku, Kyoto, 606-0805 Japan. E-mail: secretariat.iscmf@npo-apacvd.jp.
URL: https://www.iscmf.org/

History 2007, Kyoto (Japan). Former names and other names: *International Society of Cardiomyopathy and Heart Failure (ISCHF)* – former (2007 to 2016). **Structure** Board, comprising President, President-Elect, Vice-President, Secretary and Treasurer. **Events** *Annual Congress* Kyoto (Japan) 2021, *Annual Congress* Kyoto (Japan) 2016, *Annual Congress* Toronto, ON (Canada) 2008, *Annual congress / Congress* Kyoto (Japan) 2007. **Publications** *ISCHF Newsletter.* **NGO Relations** Member of: *The NCD Alliance (NCDA, #16963); World Heart Federation (WHF, #21562).* [2019/XM3628/**C**]

♦ International Society of Cardio-Thoracic Surgeons / see World Society of Cardiovascular & Thoracic Surgeons (#21800)
♦ International Society of Cardio-Thoracic Surgeons – of Japan / see World Society of Cardiovascular & Thoracic Surgeons (#21800)
♦ International Society of Cardiovascular Disease Epidemiology and Prevention (unconfirmed)

♦ International Society for Cardiovascular Disease Prevention (ISCVDP) 14994

Contact PO Box 433, Sarasota FL 34230, USA. T. +18772785300. E-mail: info@iscvdp.org.
URL: http://www.iscvdp.org/

Aims Transform cardiovascular care nationally and internationally by providing guidance and education to medical professionals and the public on early detection and prevention of cardiovascular disease along with recommendations for optimal management of primary and secondary cardio vascular disease. **Structure** Board of Directors; Executive Committee. **Activities** Events/meetings. **Events** *Annual International Cardiology Congress* Cairo (Egypt) / Giza (Egypt) 2022, *International Congress* Japan 2020, *International Congress* Lisbon (Portugal) / Malaga (Spain) 2019, *International Congress* Paris (France) 2018. [2022/XM7526/**C**]

♦ International Society of Cardiovascular Infectious Diseases (ISCVID) 14995

Pres Service Maladies Infectieuses et Tropicales, Dermatologie aet Médecine Interne, CHU de la Guadeloupe, Route de Chauvel, 46597159 CEDEX Pointe-à-Pitre Guadeloupe, France. T. +590891545 – +590891589.
URL: http://www.endocarditis.org/iscvid/

History late 1980s. **Aims** Bring scientific awareness to *endocarditis* and other infections of the cardiovascular system including those involving implanted materials. **Structure** Board. **Languages** English. **Finance** Symposia fees; support from non-restricted grants from industry. **Activities** Events/meetings. **Events** *International Symposium of Cardiovascular Infectious Diseases* Barcelona (Spain) 2022, *International Symposium of Cardiovascular Infectious Diseases (ISCVID)* Barcelona (Spain) 2021, *International Symposium on Modern Concepts in Endocarditis and Cardiovascular Infections* Lausanne (Switzerland) 2019, *International Symposium on Modern Concepts in Endocarditis and Cardiovascular Infections* Dublin (Ireland) 2017, *International Symposium on Modern Concepts in Endocarditis and Cardiovascular Infections* Rio de Janeiro (Brazil) 2015. **Publications** Meeting abstracts; posters. **Members** Individuals attending symposia retain membership for 2 years. Membership countries not specified. [2017.06.01/XJ2161/**F**]

♦ International Society of Cardiovascular Pharmacotherapy (ISCP) . . 14996

Coordinator Via Rotondello 16, 6517 Arbedo TI, Switzerland. T. +44288780308. E-mail: info@iscpcardio.org – begona.lugg@iscpcardio.org.
URL: http://www.iscpcardio.org/

History Comes within the Council on Clinical Cardiology of *World Heart Federation (WHF, #21562).* Registration: Switzerland. **Aims** Promote and facilitate strategies to improve cardiovascular health through cooperation among cardiac physicians and surgeons, pharmacologists, pharmacists, scientists, and medical practitioners worldwide; promotes education, research, and evidence-based clinical management in all areas of cardiovascular pharmacotherapy with the ultimate goal of prevention and improving treatment, outcome and patient well-being. **Structure** Board of Directors; Executive Committee; Governors. **Languages** English, Italian, Spanish. **Staff** 0.50 FTE, paid. **Finance** Sources: meeting proceeds; members' dues; sale of publications. **Activities** Events/meetings. **Events** *Annual Scientific Meeting* Korea Rep 2023, *Annual Scientific Meeting* Bucharest (Romania) 2022, *Congress / Annual Scientific Meeting* Singapore (Singapore) 2021, *Congress* Lugano (Switzerland) 2019, *Congress* Kyoto (Japan) 2018. **Publications** *ISCP Newsletter* (3 a year); *European Cardiology Review.*
Members Full in 44 countries and territories:
Argentina, Armenia, Australia, Brazil, Bulgaria, Chile, China, Colombia, Cuba, Czechia, Denmark, Dominican Rep, France, Georgia, Germany, Greece, Hong Kong, Hungary, India, Israel, Italy, Japan, Korea Rep, Latvia, Lebanon, Lithuania, Mexico, Mozambique, Nigeria, Pakistan, Panama, Peru, Romania, Russia, Singapore, Slovenia, Spain, Sweden, Switzerland, Türkiye, UK, United Arab Emirates, USA, Venezuela.
NGO Relations Member of (2): *The NCD Alliance (NCDA, #16963); World Heart Federation (WHF, #21562).* [2023.02.24/XD6871/**B**]

♦ International Society for Cardiovascular Research / see International Society for Heart Research (#15158)

♦ International Society for Cardiovascular Translational Research (ISCTR) 14997

Contact 3104 E Camelback Rd, Ste 564, Phoenix AZ 85016, USA. T. +14804385015.
URL: http://www.isctr.org/

History 2008. **Aims** Provide an environment for collaboration and guidance among basic and clinical scientists; expedite scientific discoveries into clinical application; disseminate science among the scientific community; promote research, development of guidelines for training and certification in translational research; influence health care policy; educate the public; improve the well being of patients. **Structure** Governing Board; Scientific Advisory Board. Committees (3): Governance/Nominating; Public Awareness and Sustainability; Education and Publications. **Activities** Events/meetings; research/documentation; awards/prizes/competitions. **Events** *Annual Symposium* Chicago, IL (USA) 2012, *Annual Symposium* New Orleans, LA (USA) 2011. **Publications** *Journal of Cardiovascular Translational Research.* **NGO Relations** Memorandum of Understanding with: *International Academy of Cardiovascular Sciences (IACS, #11539).* [2017/XJ5869/**D**]

♦ International Society of Cardiovascular Ultrasound (ISCU) 14998

Pres 4240 Kennesaw Drive, Birmingham AL 35213, USA. T. +12059348256. Fax +12058070731. E-mail: iscuorg@yahoo.com.
URL: http://www.iscu.org/

History 2 Mar 1991, Atlanta, GA (USA). **Aims** Promote exchange of ideas and information in the field and encourage further knowledge of the subject; disseminate recent advances and developments in a rapid manner; promote international exchange of physician and technologist echocardiographers. **Structure** Board of Directors; Scientific Committee. **Languages** English. **Staff** Voluntary. **Finance** Sources: members' dues. **Events** *World Congress of Echocardiography and Allied Techniques* Sofia (Bulgaria) 2023, *World Congress of Echocardiography and Allied Techniques* Adelaide, SA (Australia) 2022, *World Congress of Echocardiography and Allied Techniques* Dubai (United Arab Emirates) 2021, *World Congress of Echocardiography and Allied Techniques* Lima (Peru) 2020, *World Congress of Echocardiography and Allied Techniques* Lódz (Poland) 2019. **Publications** *Echocardiography Journal of Cardiovascular Ultrasound and Allied Techniques.*
Members Regular; Corporate; Honorary. Members in 49 countries and territories:
Australia, Austria, Belgium, Brazil, Canada, Chile, China, Colombia, Côte d'Ivoire, Denmark, Dominican Rep, France, Germany, Greece, Guatemala, Hong Kong, Hungary, India, Indonesia, Ireland, Italy, Japan, Korea Rep, Lithuania, Malaysia, Mexico, Netherlands, New Zealand, Nicaragua, Paraguay, Philippines, Poland, Portugal, Romania, Russia, Saudi Arabia, Serbia, Singapore, Slovakia, Spain, Sri Lanka, Sweden, Switzerland, Taiwan, Türkiye, UK, Uruguay, USA, Venezuela.
NGO Relations Member of: *World Heart Federation (WHF, #21562).* [2022/XD3854/**C**]

♦ International Society of Caricature Artists (internationally oriented national body)
♦ International Society of Caring and Peace (internationally oriented national body)

♦ International Society for Cartilage Repair of the Ankle (ISCRA) 14999

Contact address not obtained. T. +31638522988. E-mail: anklecartilage@gmail.com.
URL: https://anklecartilage.org/

History 2012. **Aims** Ameliorate patient care by uniting worldwide leaders in the field. **Activities** Awards/prizes/competitions; events/meetings. [2020/AA1900/**C**]

♦ International Society of Cell Biology (inactive)

♦ International Society for Cell & Gene Therapy (ISCT) 15000

Exec Dir Ste 325, 744 West Hastings St, Vancouver BC V6C 1A5, Canada. T. +16048744366. Fax +16048744378. E-mail: isct@isctglobal.org.
Events Manager address not obtained.
URL: https://www.isctglobal.org/

History 1992. Former names and other names: *International Society of Haemotherapy and Graft Engineering (ISHAGE)* – former; *International Society for Cellular Therapy (ISCT)* – former. **Aims** Drive the translation of all cellular therapies for the benefit of patients worldwide. **Structure** Board of Directors; Executive Management Committee; Strategic Advisory Council; Regional Executive Committees; Head Office. **Languages** English. **Finance** Sources: meeting proceeds; members' dues. **Activities** Events/meetings; knowledge management/information dissemination. **Events** *Annual Meeting* 2023, *Annual Meeting* San Francisco, CA (USA) 2022, *Annual Meeting* New Orleans, LA (USA) 2021, *Annual Meeting* Paris (France) 2020, *Asia Regional Meeting* Seogwipo (Korea Rep) 2020. **Publications** *Cytotherapy* (12 a year) – journal; *Telegraft* (6 a year) – newsletter.
Members Full in 62 countries and territories:
Argentina, Australia, Austria, Bangladesh, Belgium, Brazil, Canada, Chile, China, Colombia, Czechia, Denmark, Ecuador, Egypt, El Salvador, Finland, France, Germany, Greece, Guatemala, Hong Kong, Hungary, India, Indonesia, Iran Islamic Rep, Ireland, Israel, Italy, Japan, Jordan, Korea Rep, Latvia, Lebanon, Malaysia, Mexico, Netherlands, New Zealand, Norway, Pakistan, Peru, Philippines, Poland, Portugal, Qatar, Russia, Saudi Arabia, Scotland, Senegal, Singapore, Slovenia, Spain, Sweden, Switzerland, Taiwan, Thailand, Türkiye, UK, Ukraine, United Arab Emirates, Uruguay, USA, Vietnam.
NGO Relations Memorandum of Understanding with (2): *Alliance for Regenerative Medicine (ARM); European Infrastructure for Translational Medicine (EATRIS, #07536).* Member of (2): *Alliance for Harmonisation of Cellular Therapy Accreditation (AHCTA, #00686); Worldwide Network for Blood and Marrow Transplantation (WBMT, #21929).* Related organizations: *AABB*; American Society for Blood and Marrow Transplantation (ASBMT). [2021/XD7376/**C**]

♦ International Society of Cellular Oncology (no recent information)
♦ International Society for Cellular Therapy / see International Society for Cell & Gene Therapy (#15000)

♦ International Society for Ceramic Art Education and Exchange (ISCAEE) 15001

Contact Tokyo Natl Univ of Fine Arts and Music, School of Fine Arts, Dept of Crafts Ceramics, Taito-ku, Ueno Koen 12-8, Tokyo, 110-8714 Japan.
URL: http://www.iscaee.org/

History Jan 2006, growing out of the International Ceramic Symposium and Art Education Exchange Program. **Aims** Exchange knowledge of ceramic Art and techniques through education and cultural activities; create worldwide ceramic education through art, technique, and ceramic culture. **Structure** General Assembly; Board of Trustees; Secretariat. **Finance** Members' dues. **Activities** Events/meetings; awards/prizes/competitions. **Events** *Biennial Symposium* Yongin (Korea Rep) 2019, *Biennial Symposium* Beijing (China) 2015, *Biennial Symposium* Antalya (Turkey) 2013, *Biennial Conference* Tokyo (Japan) 2011, *Biennial Symposium* Tokyo (Japan) 2011.
Members Full in 10 countries:
Australia, China, Germany, Japan, Kenya, Korea Rep, Mexico, Türkiye, UK, USA. [2016.07.15/XJ5498/**E**]

♦ International Society for Ceramics in Medicine (ISCM) 15002

Pres Dept of Biomaterials, Fac of Dental Science, Kyushu Univ, 3-1-1 Maidashi, Higashi-ku, Fukuoka, 812-8582 Japan. T. +81926426344.
URL: http://bioceramics.org/

History 1988, Osaka (Japan). **Aims** Advance the science of bioceramics; further their clinical application; promote good fellowship among members. **Structure** President; Executive Committee. **Languages** English. **Activities** Events/meetings; awards/prizes/competitions. **Events** *Bioceramics Symposium and Annual Meeting* Mestre (Italy) 2022, *Bioceramics Symposium and Annual Meeting* Mestre (Italy) 2020, *Bioceramics Symposium and Annual Meeting* New Orleans, LA (USA) 2019, *Bioceramics Symposium and Annual Meeting* Nagoya (Japan) 2018, *Bioceramics Symposium and Annual Meeting* Toulouse (France) 2017. **Members** in Asia, North America, South America, Australia, Europe, Africa (middle West). Membership countries not specified. [2020.03.03/XD8311/**D**]

♦ International Society of Cerebral Blood Flow and Metabolism (ISCBFM) 15003

Main Office 1300 Piccard Dr, Ste LL-14, Rockville MD 20850, USA. E-mail: iscbfm@iscbfm.org.
URL: https://www.iscbfm.org/

Aims Promote advancement of education in the science of cerebral blood flow and metabolism worldwide. **Structure** Board of Directors. **Activities** Events/meetings. **Events** *International Conference on Quantification of Brain Function with PET (BRAIN PET)* Glasgow (UK) 2022, *International Symposium on Cerebral Blood Flow, Metabolism and Function* Glasgow (UK) 2022, *Biennial Symposium* Glasgow (UK) 2021, *International Conference on Quantification of Brain Function with PET* Glasgow (UK) 2021, *Biennial Symposium* Yokohama (Japan) 2019. **Publications** *Journal of Cerebral Blood Flow and Metabolism* (12 a year); *The Complex Heterogeneous Organ* – newsletter.
Members Individuals in 29 countries:
Armenia, Australia, Belgium, Canada, China, Colombia, Denmark, Finland, France, Germany, Greece, Hong Kong, Hungary, India, Israel, Italy, Japan, Korea Rep, Netherlands, New Zealand, Norway, Poland, Portugal, Spain, Sweden, Switzerland, Taiwan, UK, USA. [2023/XD9496/v/**D**]

♦ International Society of Certified Employee Benefit Specialists (internationally oriented national body)

♦ International Society of Chemical Ecology (ISCE) 15004

Sociedad Internacional de Ecologia Quimica

Pres address not obtained. E-mail: president@chemecol.org.
Treas address not obtained. E-mail: treasurer@chemecol.org.
URL: http://www.chemecol.org/

History 12 Sep 1983. **Aims** Promote understanding of the origin, function, and importance of natural chemicals that mediate interactions within and among organisms. **Structure** Council of 16 members. Executive Committee, comprising President, Vice-President, Secretary, Treasurer, Past President and a representative of the Journal of Chemical Ecology. Student Award Committee. **Languages** English. **Staff** 6.00 FTE, voluntary. **Finance** Members' dues. Contributions. **Activities** Carries out research in areas including chemistry, biochemistry and function of natural products, their importance at all levels of ecological organization, their evolutionary origin and their practical application. Presents *'Silver Medal'* and *'Silverstein-Simeone'* awards. Provides student travel awards. **Events** *Annual Meeting* Kuala Lumpur (Malaysia) 2022, *Joint International Chemical Ecology Conference* Kuala Lumpur (Malaysia) 2022, *Annual Meeting* Stellenbosch (South Africa) 2021, *Annual Meeting* Stellenbosch (South Africa) 2020, *Annual Meeting* Atlanta, GA (USA) 2019. **Publications** *Journal of Chemical Ecology* (12 a year); *ISCE Newsletter* (3 a year). Membership Directory.
Members Scientists (600) in 69 countries and territories:
Argentina, Australia, Austria, Bangladesh, Belgium, Brazil, Bulgaria, Canada, Chile, China, Colombia, Costa Rica, Côte d'Ivoire, Cyprus, Czechia, Denmark, Egypt, Estonia, Finland, France, Georgia, Germany, Greece, Hong Kong, Hungary, India, Indonesia, Ireland, Israel, Italy, Jamaica, Japan, Kenya, Korea Rep, Malaysia, Mexico, Morocco, Myanmar, Netherlands, New Zealand, Nigeria, Norway, Pakistan, Papua New Guinea, Paraguay, Peru, Philippines, Poland, Portugal, Puerto Rico, Romania, Russia, Saudi Arabia, Slovakia, South Africa, Spain, Sri Lanka, Sudan, Sweden, Switzerland, Taiwan, Thailand, Türkiye, UK, Ukraine, Uruguay, USA, Venezuela, Zimbabwe.
NGO Relations *International Association for Ecology (INTECOL, #11856); Academia de Ciencias de América Latina (ACAL, #00010).* [2017/XD7290/v/**D**]

♦ International Society of Chemotherapy / see International Society of Antimicrobial Chemotherapy (#14925)
♦ International Society for Chemotherapy and Immunotherapy (inactive)
♦ International Society of Chemotherapy for Infection and Cancer / see International Society of Antimicrobial Chemotherapy (#14925)

♦ International Society for Child and Adolescent Injury Prevention (ISCAIP) 15005

Pres Injury Prevention Research, University of Otago, PO Box 913, Dunedin, New Zealand.
URL: http://iscaip.squarespace.com/

History May 1993, Atlanta GA (USA), during Second World Conference on Injury Control. **Aims** Promote a significant reduction in the number and severity of injuries to children and adolescents through international collaboration. **Structure** Executive Board, comprising Chairman, Secretary, Treasurer, 5 members (one from each continent) and 2 ex-officio members: President and Editor. **Finance** Members' dues. **Events** *Biennial Conference / Meeting* Wellington (New Zealand) 2012, *Meeting* Bristol (UK) 2010, *Biennial conference / Meeting* Durban (South Africa) 2006, *Biennial conference / Meeting* Vienna (Austria) 2004, *Meeting* Montréal, QC (Canada) 2002. **Publications** *Injury Prevention* (4 a year).
Members Full in 6 countries:
Australia, Israel, South Africa, Sweden, UK, USA. [2011/XD6156/**D**]

♦ International Society for Child Ecology (inactive)

♦ International Society for Child Indicators (ISCI) 15006

Co-Chair Paul Baerwald School of Social Work and Social Welfare, Hebrew Univ of Jerusalem, Mount Scopus, 91905 91905 Jerusalem, Israel.
Co-Chair Chapin Hall Ctr for Children, University of Chicago, 1313 East 60th St, Chicago IL 60637, USA. E-mail: bobg@uchicago.edu.
URL: http://www.childindicators.org/

Aims Contribute to the well-being of all children; share knowledge and experience; develop standards; improve data resources; foster collaborative research and projects; foster diversity in methodological approaches; enhance information dissemination on the status of children; help organizations apply the findings to policy and practice; enhance the capacity of the field in countries that are in the initial stages of producing child well-being indicators. **Structure** Standing Committee, comprising 2 Co-Chairs and 11 members. **Finance** Sources: members' dues. **Events** *Conference* Gramado (Brazil) 2022, *Conference* Tartu (Estonia) 2019, *Biennial Conference* Montréal, QC (Canada) 2017, *Biennial Conference* Cape Town (South Africa) 2015, *Biennial Conference* Seoul (Korea Rep) 2013. **Publications** *Child Indicators Research* – journal; *ISCI Newsletter*. [2014/XJ1268/**C**]

♦ International Society for Children's Health and the Environment (internationally oriented national body)
♦ International Society for Chinese Language Teaching (internationally oriented national body)

♦ International Society for Chinese Philosophy (ISCP) 15007

Exec Dir Dept of Philosophy, California State Univ, Fullerton, Fullerton CA 92834, USA. T. +16572787560.
URL: http://www.iscp-online.org/

History Founded 16 Jun 1975, Honolulu HI (USA). Current constitution revised Dec 2007. **Aims** Encourage the continuing evolution of Chinese philosophy; stimulate productive dialogue among prominent scholars in the field. **Structure** Board of Directors; Executive Committee. **Languages** Chinese, English. **Finance** Members' dues. **Activities** Events/meetings; awards/prizes/competitions. **Events** *Biennial Conference* Shanghai (China) 2022, *Biennial Conference* Shanghai (China) 2021, *Biennial Conference* Bern (Switzerland) 2019, *Biennial Conference* Singapore (Singapore) 2017, *Biennial Conference* Hong Kong (Hong Kong) 2015. **Publications** *Journal of Chinese Philosophy*.
Members Individuals in 13 countries:
Canada, China, France, Germany, Hong Kong, Japan, Korea Rep, Nigeria, Philippines, Singapore, Taiwan, UK, USA.
NGO Relations Member of: *International Federation of Philosophical Societies (FISP, #13507).* [2019.10.16/XD0080/**D**]

♦ International Society of Chocolate and Cocoa in Medicine (ISCHOM) 15008

Società Internazionale del Cacao e Cioccolato in Medicina

Contact c/o MCA Scientific Events, Via Ambrogio Binda 34, 20143 Milan MI, Italy. T. +39234934404 ext 203. Fax +39234934397. E-mail: info@mcascientificevents.eu.

History 16 Oct 2010. Registration: Italy. **Aims** Bring together groups and individuals in an interdisciplinary organization so as to promote the science of use of cocoa and chocolate products in the human *diet*, health and medicine for the benefit of the public. **Structure** General Assembly (annual); Executive Committee; Scientific Committee. **Languages** English. **Finance** Sources: members' dues. **Activities** Events/meetings; standards/guidelines; training/education. **Events** *International Congress on Chocolate and Cocoa in Medicine* Modica (Italy) 2019, *International Congress* Barcelona (Spain) 2015, *International Congress on Chocolate and Cocoa in Medicine* Florence (Italy) 2014. **Members** Full; Associate; Honorary. **NGO Relations** Member of: *the Chocolate Way.* [2018/XM4490/v/**C**]

♦ International Society of Christian Artists 15009

Société internationale des artistes chrétiens (SIAC) – Sociedad Internacional de Artistas Cristianos – International Gesellschaft Christlicher Künstler – Società Internazionale degli Artisti Cristiani

Sec 764 Queen Anne Rd, Teaneck NJ 07666, USA.
SG address not obtained.
URL: http://www.s-i-a-c.org/

History 27 Jun 1951, Reims (France), as *International Secretariat of Christian Artists (ISCA) – Secrétariat international des artistes chrétiens – Secretariado Internacional de Artistas Cristianos – Internationales Sekretariat Christlicher Künstler – Segretariato Internazionale degli Artisti Cristiani*, at General Assembly of *Pax Romana, International Catholic Movement for Intellectual and Cultural Affairs (ICMICA, #18267).* Since 1964 the Society is an independent ecumenical Secretariat but remains a member of Pax Romana. **Aims** Coordinate the activities of all societies, groups and individual members with an interest in: (a) employing the artist's imagination for the improvement of environment; (b) bringing together such groups and organizations in order to speak with a unified voice. **Structure** General Assembly and International Congress (every 4 years); International Committee. Regional and national secretaries (7): Austrian, French, German, Netherlands, Swedish, Swiss and of USA; and international (the general) secretary including all other countries like Canada, Czech Rep, Great Britain, Hungary, Ireland, Slovenia. **Languages** English, French, German, Italian, Spanish. **Staff** None; all work done by volunteer officers. **Finance** Sources: donations; members' dues; sponsorship. **Activities** Supplies speakers, tutors and lecturers to any part of the world to confer or teach in specialized aspects of arts and crafts. Organizes conferences; seminars. Exhibitions. Spiritual development. **Events** *Congress* Limerick (Ireland) 2009, *Congress* Reichenau (Germany) 2005, *Prospect 3000* Luxembourg (Luxembourg) 2001, *Quadrennial international assembly / Congress* Schlierbach (Austria) 1998, *Quadrennial international assembly* Munich (Germany) 1994. **Publications** *SIAC Newsletter* (annual) in English, French, German.
Members Specialized societies, groups and individual members active in arts/architecture/environmental study/music/dance/theatre; Individuals. Members in 15 countries:
Austria, Czechia, France, Germany, Hungary, Ireland, Kenya, Luxembourg, Netherlands, Russia, Rwanda, Slovenia, Switzerland, UK, USA. [2013/XD3916/**C**]

♦ International Society for Chronobiology (ISC) 15010

Société internationale de chronobiologie – Sociedad para la Cronobiologia – Gesellschaft für Chronobiologie – Società di Cronobiologia

Sec-Treas Despacho A-504, E I Telecomunicacion, Marcosende, 36310 Vigo, La Coruña, Spain.
URL: http://ischronobiology.org/

History 1937, Ronneby (Sweden). Current constitution adopted 1979, Hannover (Germany FR). Former names and other names: *Society for the Study of Biological Rhythm* – former (1937 to 1971); *Societas pro Studio Rhythmi Biologici* – former (1937 to 1971). **Aims** Further the study of *temporal* changes in living matter, including biological rhythms in development and *ageing* in individuals and populations; study and define mechanisms of these temporal changes; foster application of chronobiological findings in basic and applied *biology, physiology*, work hygiene and the medical sciences; promote education in and wide understanding of chronobiology; further contact among scientists in the field and provide a forum for practitioners. **Structure** General Assembly (usually every 2 years). Officers: President, 1st and 2nd Vice-Presidents, Secretary-Treasurer and President-Elect. Board of Directors, comprising 9 members. **Languages** English. **Staff** Voluntary. **Finance** Members' dues: US$ 86 (includes 1 journal); Student members: US$ 61. Occasional grants. **Activities** Organizes symposia, meetings, conferences, including co-sponsorship on *International Conference of Chronopharmacology and Chronotherapeutics* with *'Federation of American Societies for Experimental Biology (FASEB)'*. **Events** *Conference* Warsaw (Poland) 2019, *Biennial Conference* Suzhou (China) 2016, *Biennial Conference* Bucharest (Romania) 2014, *Biennial Conference* Delhi (India) 2012, *Biennial Conference* Vigo (Spain) 2010. **Publications** *Chronobiology International* (6 a year) – occasional special issues.
Members Regular; Student. Specialists (261) in 37 countries:
Argentina, Australia, Austria, Belgium, Brazil, Bulgaria, Canada, China, Czechia, Denmark, Dominican Rep, France, Germany, India, Ireland, Israel, Italy, Japan, Korea Rep, Kuwait, Mexico, Morocco, Netherlands, New Zealand, Norway, Poland, Portugal, Romania, Russia, Slovakia, Spain, Sweden, Switzerland, Taiwan, Türkiye, UK, USA.
NGO Relations Member of: *World Federation of Societies of Chronobiology (WFSC, #21484).* [2019/XC3226/v/**C**]

♦ International Society of Citriculture (ISC) 15011

Société internationale des travailleurs de l'agrumiculture – Sociedad Internacional de Citricultura

Sec-Treas Botany and Plant Sciences 072, Univ of California, 900 University Ave, Riverside CA 92521-0124, USA. T. +19518274137. Fax +19518274437. E-mail: iscucr@ucr.edu.
Pres Turkish Natl Citrus Council, Limonluk Mah 36, Cad No 4, Yenisehir, Mersin/Van, Türkiye. T. +903243253737. Fax +903243254142.
URL: http://internationalsocietyofcitriculture.org/

History 1970. Incorporated as a non-profit corporation in the State of California (USA), 1976. **Aims** Promote and encourage research and international cooperation in acquisition and exchange of information and education in all aspects of citrus production, handling and distribution of fresh citrus *fruits* and their products. **Structure** Congress; Executive Committee. **Languages** English. **Staff** 1.00 FTE, paid; 1.00 FTE, voluntary. **Finance** Sources: meeting proceeds; members' dues. Other sources: registration fees. **Activities** Events/meetings; knowledge management/information dissemination; training/education. **Events** *Congress* Jeju (Korea Rep) 2024, *Congress* Mersin (Turkey) 2020, *International Symposium on Citrus Biotechnology* Montevideo (Uruguay) 2018, *Sustainable citriculture – the role of applied knowledge* Foz do Iguaçu (Brazil) 2016, *Congress* Valencia (Spain) 2012. **Publications** *ISC Newsletter* (annual). Congress proceedings.
Members Active; Fellow; Honorary. Members in 44 countries:
Argentina, Australia, Belgium, Belize, Bhutan, Brazil, Chile, China, Colombia, Costa Rica, Cuba, Cyprus, Denmark, Ecuador, Egypt, France, India, Iran Islamic Rep, Israel, Italy, Japan, Kenya, Korea Rep, Lebanon, Mexico, Morocco, Mozambique, Netherlands, New Zealand, Nigeria, Oman, Pakistan, Peru, Philippines, Portugal, Saudi Arabia, South Africa, Spain, Thailand, Tunisia, Türkiye, UK, Uruguay, USA.
Consultative Status Consultative status granted from: *ECOSOC (#05331)* (Ros C); *FAO (#09260)* (Special Status); *Codex Alimentarius Commission (CAC, #04081).* [2019/XB4117/v/**B**]

♦ International Society of City and Regional Planners (ISOCARP) 15012

Association internationale des urbanistes (AIU) – Internationale Gesellschaft der Stadt- und Regionalplaner (IGSRP) – Asociación Internacional de Urbanistas (AIU)

Contact Waldorpstraat 17-F, 2521 CA The Hague, Netherlands. T. +31703462654. E-mail: isocarp@isocarp.org.
URL: http://www.isocarp.org/

History 23 Jan 1965, Amsterdam (Netherlands). Registration: Handelsregister, Netherlands. **Aims** Create a platform for exchange between planners from different countries; promote better planning and improvement of planning practice through contacts between planners; promote the profession of city and regional planning in all aspects, notably its identity, the services it can render and the conditions required for it to function; promote planning research; improve theory and practice of planning education and training;

provide information and advice in the field at all levels and contribute to major planning discussions. **Structure** General Assembly; Board; Executive Committee; Secretariat. **Languages** English, French, German, Spanish. **Staff** 6.00 FTE, paid. **Finance** Sources: meeting proceeds; members' dues. **Activities** Events/meetings; knowledge management/information dissemination; networking/liaising; projects/programmes; research/documentation. **Events** *World Planning Congress* Brussels (Belgium) 2022, *Planning Unlocked – New Times, Better Places and Stronger Communities* Doha (Qatar) 2021, *World Planning Congress* The Hague (Netherlands) 2020, *World Planning Congress* Jakarta (Indonesia) 2019, *Annual City Development Conference* Singapore (Singapore) 2019. **Publications** *ISOCARP Review* (annual); *PLAN Magazine*. Manuals; reports; congress reports.

Members Individual; Life; Institutional. Individuals in 89 countries and territories:
Afghanistan, Algeria, Argentina, Australia, Austria, Bangladesh, Barbados, Belarus, Belgium, Bosnia-Herzegovina, Botswana, Brazil, Bulgaria, Burkina Faso, Canada, Chile, China, Colombia, Côte d'Ivoire, Czechia, Denmark, Egypt, Eritrea, Estonia, Finland, France, Georgia, Germany, Greece, Hong Kong, Hungary, India, Indonesia, Iran Islamic Rep, Ireland, Israel, Italy, Jamaica, Japan, Kazakhstan, Kenya, Korea Rep, Lebanon, Liberia, Libya, Lithuania, Luxembourg, Malaysia, Mauritius, Mexico, Montenegro, Morocco, Namibia, Nepal, Netherlands, New Zealand, Nigeria, North Macedonia, Norway, Pakistan, Palestine, Paraguay, Peru, Philippines, Poland, Portugal, Russia, Saudi Arabia, Senegal, Serbia, Seychelles, Singapore, Slovenia, South Africa, Spain, Sudan, Sweden, Switzerland, Thailand, Togo, Trinidad-Tobago, Tunisia, Türkiye, UK, United Arab Emirates, Uruguay, USA, Vietnam, Zambia.

Consultative Status Consultative status granted from: *UNESCO (#20322)* (Consultative Status); *Council of Europe (CE, #04881)* (Participatory Status). **IGO Relations** Associated with Department of Global Communications of the United Nations. **NGO Relations** Member of (1): *European Heritage Alliance 3.3 (#07477)*. Supports (1): *Global Planners Network (GPN, #10548)*. [2022.02.02/XC2534/**B**]

♦ International Society of Classical Bibliography (#19474)
♦ International Society for the Classical Tradition (inactive)

♦ International Society for Clinical Bioethics (ISCB) 15013

Gen Sec Dept of Social Sciences, Univ of Rijeka, School of Medicine, Brace Branchetta 20, HR-51000 Rijeka, Croatia. T. +38551651282. Fax +38551651219.
URL: http://homepage1.nifty.com/awaya/ISCB/

History 17 Jun 2003, Veli Losinj (Croatia). **Aims** Facilitate contacts and information exchange between those working in clinical bioethics and related fields in different parts of the world; encourage the development of research and teaching in clinical bioethics and related fields. **Structure** Board of Directors. **Finance** Sources: members' dues. **Activities** Events/meetings; training/education. **Events** *Annual Conference / Conference* Kazan (Russia) 2014, *Annual Conference* Kushiro (Japan) 2013, *Annual Conference / Conference* Rijeka (Croatia) 2012, *Conference* Moscow (Russia) 2011, *Conference* USA 2010. [2014/XJ8834/**C**]

♦ International Society for Clinical Biostatistics (ISCB) 15014

Office Manager Convin SA, 29 K Varnali Street, Chalandri, 152 33 Athens, Greece. T. +306956665669. E-mail: secretariat@iscb.info.
Legal Seat Chemin du Petit-Bel-Air 115, 1226 Thônex GE, Switzerland.
URL: http://www.iscb.info/

History May 1979, Brussels (Belgium). Set up at 1st International Meeting, following discussions, 1978, Brussels. Society formalized 1980, Exeter (UK); formal Executive Committee formed 14 Sep 1982, Rotterdam (Netherlands). Rules of the Society, adopted 14 Sep 1982, at General Meeting, revised: 11 Sep 1984; 18 Sep 1986; 9 Sep 1987; 1 Sep 1988; 20 Sep 1990; 18 Aug 1992. Rules replaced by a Constitution, 27 Aug 1996, when adopted by General Meeting. Constitution revised 31 Dec 2008 and 31 Dec 2012. Modified Oct 2018, and addition of "Statutes of Association" document compliant with Swiss law. Registration: Répertoire des Entreprises du Canton de Genève, No/ID: CHE-335.703.049, Start date: 1 Jun 2018, Switzerland, Genève. **Aims** Stimulate research into principles and methodology used in design and analysis of clinical research; increase the relevance of *statistical* theory to clinical *medicine*. **Structure** General Meeting (annual, at Scientific Meeting); Executive Committee; Subcommittees (6). **Languages** English. **Staff** None. **Finance** Sources: members' dues. Other sources: private donors; institutional sponsors; surplus from conferences. Annual budget: 100,000 EUR. **Activities** Events/meetings; standards/guidelines. **Events** *Annual Conference* Milan (Italy) 2023, *Annual Conference* Newcastle upon Tyne (UK) 2022, *Annual Conference* Lyon (France) 2021, *Annual Conference* Krakow (Poland) 2020, *Annual Conference* Leuven (Belgium) 2019. **Publications** *ISCB News* (2 a year). Position papers; selected meeting papers in special issue of 'Biometrical Journal'.

Members Individuals in 52 countries and territories:
Australia, Austria, Bangladesh, Belgium, Brazil, Bulgaria, Canada, China, Colombia, Costa Rica, Cyprus, Czechia, Denmark, Finland, France, Germany, Greece, Hungary, India, Indonesia, Iran Islamic Rep, Ireland, Israel, Italy, Japan, Kenya, Korea Rep, Lebanon, Luxembourg, Malaysia, Moldova, Netherlands, New Zealand, Nigeria, Norway, Poland, Portugal, Romania, Russia, Saudi Arabia, Singapore, Slovakia, Slovenia, South Africa, Spain, Sweden, Switzerland, Taiwan, Thailand, Türkiye, UK, USA.

NGO Relations Member of: *International Statistical Institute (ISI, #15603)*. [2021/XD0315/v/**C**]

♦ International Society for Clinical Densitometry (ISCD) 15015

Exec Dir – CEO 955 South Main St, B202, Middletown CT 06457, USA. T. +18602591000. Fax +18602591030. E-mail: moshea@iscd.org – iscd@iscd.org.
URL: http://www.iscd.org/

History 1993. **Aims** Advance high-quality *musculoskeletal health* assessments in the service of superior patient care. **Languages** English. **Staff** 7.00 FTE, paid. **Activities** Certification/accreditation; events/meetings; research/documentation; training/education. **Events** *Position Development Conference* Chicago, IL (USA) 2023, *Annual Meeting* Northbrook, IL (USA) 2023, *Annual Meeting* 2022, *Annual Meeting* 2021, *Annual Meeting* Kuala Lumpur (Malaysia) 2019. **Publications** *Journal of Clinical Densitometry*. **Members** Individuals (1,800) in over 60 countries. Membership countries not specified. [2022.05.10/XD7542/**D**]

♦ International Society for Clinical Electrophysiology of Vision (ISCEV) 15016

Société internationale d'électrophysiologie clinique de la vue

SG c/o Novartis Inst for BioMedical, One Health Plaza, Bldg 438/2421B, East Hanover NJ 07936-1080, USA.
URL: http://www.iscev.org/

History 1958, Brussels (Belgium). Former names and other names: *International Society for Clinical Electroretinography (ISCERG)* – former (1958 to 1979); *Société internationale d'électrorétinographie clinique* – former (1958 to 1979). **Aims** Promote and extend knowledge of clinical electrophysiology of vision; promote cooperation and communication among workers in the field of clinical and basic electrophysiology of vision. **Structure** Board; Extended Board. **Languages** English. **Staff** None. **Finance** Sources: members' dues. **Activities** Awards/prizes/competitions; events/meetings; standards/guidelines; training/education. **Events** *Annual Symposium* Montebello, ON (Canada) 2024, *Annual Symposium* Kyoto (Japan) 2023, *Annual Symposium* Kyoto (Japan) 2022, *Annual Symposium* Liverpool (UK) 2022, *Annual Symposium* Liverpool (UK) 2021. **Publications** *Documenta Ophthalmologica* (6 a year) – journal; *ISCEV Newsletter* (2 a year). Symposia proceedings.

Members Individual physicians, scientists or other professional workers in electrophysiology of vision and allied fields; Institutions; Corporate. Members (328) in 42 countries and territories:
Argentina, Australia, Belgium, Brazil, Canada, Chile, China, Cuba, Czechia, Denmark, Egypt, El Salvador, Estonia, Finland, France, Germany, Greece, Hong Kong, Iceland, India, Indonesia, Israel, Italy, Japan, Korea Rep, Lithuania, Nepal, Netherlands, New Zealand, Nigeria, Poland, Portugal, Romania, Russia, Singapore, Spain, Sri Lanka, Sweden, Switzerland, UK, USA. [2023/XC2479/**C**]

♦ International Society for Clinical Electroretinography / see International Society for Clinical Electrophysiology of Vision (#15016)
♦ International Society for Clinical Enzymology / see International Society for Enzymology (#15098)
♦ International Society for Clinical and Experimental Hypnosis (inactive)

♦ International Society for Clinical Haemorheology (ISCH) 15017

Pres Green Nanotechnology Center, School of Mechanical Engineering, Korea Univ, Seoul, Korea Rep.
URL: http://www.hemorheology.org/

History 1993, Vienna (Austria). **Aims** Advance study of clinical haemorheology. **Activities** Events/meetings. **Events** *International Conference* Seoul (Korea Rep) 2015, *International Conference / Triennial Congress* Istanbul (Turkey) 2012, *International conference / Triennial Congress* State College, PA (USA) 2008, *International conference* Chongqing (China) 2005, *Triennial Congress* Chongqing (China) 2004. **Publications** *Clinical Hemorheology and Microcirculation* – journal; *Handbook of Hemorheology and Hemodynamics* – journal.

Members Societies in 38 countries:
Argentina, Australia, Austria, Belarus, Belgium, Brazil, Canada, China, Croatia, Cyprus, Egypt, Finland, France, Georgia, Germany, Greece, Hungary, India, Israel, Italy, Jamaica, Japan, Jordan, Mexico, Netherlands, Nigeria, Poland, Portugal, Russia, Slovenia, Spain, Sweden, Switzerland, Türkiye, UK, Ukraine, USA, Venezuela. [2016.07.12/XD6833/**D**]

♦ International Society of Clinical Pathology / see World Association of Societies of Pathology and Laboratory Medicine (#21191)
♦ International Society of Clinical Pharmacology (inactive)

♦ International Society for Clinical Spectroscopy (CLIRSPEC) 15018

Contact 32 Bury Avenue, Manchester, M16 0AT, UK. T. +441613064463. E-mail: admin@clirspec.org.
URL: https://clirspec.org/

History 2015. Registration: Companies House, No/ID: 09664461, Start date: 30 Jun 2015, England and Wales. **Aims** Act as a platform for those wishing to promote the translation of spectroscopy into the clinical environment, for the general benefit of patients; for example, to improve patient diagnosis and prognosis. **Structure** Council; Directors. **Activities** Events/meetings; training/education. [2023/AA0267/**C**]

♦ International Society for CNS Clinical Trials and Methodology (internationally oriented national body)

♦ International Society for Coaching Psychology (ISCP) 15019

Contact 2nd Floor, 2 Walsworth Road, Hitchin, SG4 95P, UK. E-mail: office@isfcp.info.
Pres Wales Academy for Professional Practice & Applied Research, UWTSD, Carmarthen Campus, Carmarthen, SA31 3EP, UK.
URL: http://www.isfcp.info/

History Apr 2008. Set up after a meeting was convened at 1st International Coaching Psychology Conference, held at City University, London (UK), 18 Dec 2006. Former names and other names: *Society for Coaching Psychology* – former (2008 to 18 Jul 2011). **Aims** Provide an organizational and practical basis for activities in the field of coaching psychology. **Structure** Board. **Staff** Voluntary. **Activities** Certification/accreditation; events/meetings; knowledge management/information dissemination; networking/liaising; research and development; research/documentation; standards/guidelines; training/education. **Events** *International Congress* UK 2022, *International Congress* Hitchin (UK) 2021, *International Congress* Hitchin (UK) 2020, *International Congress* Aalborg (Denmark) 2019, *International Congress* London (UK) 2018. **Publications** *Coaching Psychology International*.

Members Individuals in 34 countries and territories:
Australia, Brazil, Canada, Chile, China, Cyprus, Denmark, France, Germany, Greece, Hong Kong, Hungary, Ireland, Israel, Italy, Japan, Korea Rep, Luxembourg, Netherlands, New Zealand, Norway, Poland, Portugal, Saudi Arabia, Serbia, Singapore, South Africa, Spain, Sri Lanka, Sweden, Switzerland, UK, United Arab Emirates, USA. [2023.02.15/XM5353/**C**]

♦ International Society of Coating Science and Technology (ISCST) . . 15020

Pres address not obtained.
URL: http://www.iscst.org/

History Founded Dec 1996. **Aims** Provide a forum for presenting advances in the mechanisms and technologies used in preparation, application, solidification and microstructuring of coated films; encourage technology transfer, professional development and networking of scientists active in the field. **Structure** Executive Committee. **Languages** English. **Staff** Voluntary. **Finance** Proceeds from symposia. **Activities** Events/meetings; training/education. **Events** *Biennial Symposium* San Diego, CA (USA) 2014, *Biennial Symposium* Atlanta, GA (USA) 2012, *Biennial Symposium* St Paul, MN (USA) 2010, *Biennial Symposium* Marina del Rey, CA (USA) 2008, *Biennial Symposium* Denver, CO (USA) 2006. **Publications** Symposium abstracts.

Members Individuals in 33 countries and territories:
Australia, Belgium, Brazil, Canada, China, Czechia, Denmark, Egypt, Finland, France, Germany, Greece, Hong Kong, India, Indonesia, Ireland, Israel, Italy, Japan, Korea Rep, Mexico, Netherlands, Norway, Russia, Singapore, Spain, Sweden, Switzerland, Taiwan, Türkiye, UK, Ukraine, USA. [2014.09.23/XD9207/v/**D**]

♦ International Society of Cold Regions Development / see International Association of Cold Regions Development Studies (#11786)
♦ International Society for Communication Science and Medicine (internationally oriented national body)
♦ International Society for Community Development (inactive)

♦ International Society for Companion Animal Infectious Diseases (ISCAID) 15021

Contact UC-Davis Dept of Medicine, 2108 Tupper Hall, One Shields Ave, Davis CA 95616, USA.
URL: http://www.iscaid.org/

History 2006. Constituted Mar 2008, Davis CA (USA). Registration: USA. **Aims** Promote and improve the health of all species by encouraging collaboration between physicians, veterinarians and other scientific health professionals. **Structure** Organizing Committee/Board of Directors. Antimicrobial Guidelines Working Group; Symposium Committee. **Finance** Sources: donations. **Activities** Events/meetings. **Events** *Symposium* Glasgow (UK) 2022, *Symposium* Glasgow (UK) 2021, *Virtual Symposium* Davis, CA (USA) 2020, *Symposium* Glasgow (UK) 2020, *Symposium* Portland, OR (USA) 2018. **Members** Full; Honorary; Training/student. Membership countries not specified. [2020/XM4737/v/**C**]

♦ International Society for Comparative Adult Education (ISCAE) 15022

Pres Univ of Nottingham, School of Education, Faculty of Social Sciences, Room B1 Dearing Building, Jubilee Campus, Wollaton Road, Nottingham, NG8 1BB, UK. T. +441159514486. Fax +441159514436.
Vice-Pres Dept of Human Sciences, Università di Verona, Palazzo di Lettere, floor Terra, room T13, Lungadige Porta Vittoria 17, 37129 Verona BL, Italy. T. +39458028466.
URL: http://www.iscae.org/

History as *Committee for Study and Research in Comparative Adult Education (CSRCAE)*. Present name adopted, 1992. **Aims** Increase awareness, value and quality of adult education studies. **Structure** Board; President; Vice-President. **Languages** English. **Staff** 5.00 FTE, voluntary. **Finance** Budget: none. **Activities** Events/meetings; publishing activities. **Events** *Conference* Las Vegas, NV (USA) 2012, *Conference* Bamberg (Germany) 2006, *Conference* St Louis, MO (USA) 2002, *Conference* Radovljica (Slovenia) 1998, *Conference* Bamberg (Germany) 1995. **Publications** Conference volumes; articles; papers. **Members** Individuals (about 200) in 35 countries. Membership countries not specified. [2019.12.11/XD6651/**D**]

♦ International Society of Comparative Education, Science and Technology (internationally oriented national body)

♦ International Society for Comparative Physical Education and Sport (ISCPES) 15023

Pres address not obtained.
Sec address not obtained.
URL: https://iscpes.pt/

History 1978, Israel. Founded at *First International Seminar on Comparative Physical Education and Sport*. **Aims** Support, encourage and provide assistance to those seeking to initiate and strengthen research and teaching programmes in cross-cultural and comparative physical education and sport. **Structure** General Assembly (every 2 years). Executive Board. Officers: Life President, President, Vice-President, Secretary, Membership Coordinator, Research Coordinator, Treasurer, Conference Director. **Languages** English. **Staff** Voluntary. **Finance** Sources: donations; members' dues. Other sources: sources: conference-related proceeds; book royalties. **Activities** Researches comparative aspects of physical education and sport and competition and sport for all. Distributes research findings and information. Organizes meetings. **Events** *Biennial Conference* 2023, *Biennial Congress* Kerala (India) 2021, *Summit* Porto (Portugal) 2019, *Biennial Congress* Borovets (Bulgaria) 2017, *Board Meeting* Taipa (Macau) 2016. **Publications** *ISCPES Newsletter* (2 a year); *Journal of Comparative Physical Education and Sport* (2 a year). Monograph series; directory; technical reports; conference proceedings; books series.

Members Individuals, mainly social scientists, historians, geographers and educationalists, in 45 countries and territories:
Australia, Austria, Belgium, Brazil, Canada, China, Cuba, Czechia, Egypt, Estonia, Finland, France, Germany, Greece, Hong Kong, Hungary, India, Ireland, Israel, Japan, Kenya, Korea Rep, Kuwait, Latvia, Malawi, Malaysia, Netherlands, New Zealand, Nigeria, Norway, Pakistan, Philippines, Poland, Portugal, Russia, Singapore, Slovakia, South Africa, Spain, Sweden, Switzerland, Taiwan, Thailand, UK, USA.

IGO Relations *UNESCO (#20322)*. **NGO Relations** Member of: *International Council of Sport Science and Physical Education (ICSSPE, #13077)*. [2022/XD0536/v/**C**]

♦ International Society for Comparative Psychology (ISCP) 15024

Société internationale de psychologie comparée – Sociedad Internacional de Psicologia Comparada

Pres address not obtained. E-mail: ijcpmail@gmail.com.
URL: http://www.comparativepsychology.org/

History 15 Jun 1983, Toronto ON (Canada), at 1st international meeting, ad hoc committees having been set up Aug 1980, Montréal ON (Canada). **Aims** Promote the teaching, theoretical development and experimental investigation of comparative psychology; establish worldwide communication among comparative psychologists; encourage the study of the development and evolution of *behaviour.* **Structure** Meeting (every 2 years). Operations Committee, comprising President, President Elect, Secretary and 7 members-at-large. Membership established through participation in the biennial meeting. **Languages** English. **Staff** Voluntary. **Finance** No members' dues. Budget determined by meeting registration fees. **Events** *Biennial Conference* Sydney, NSW (Australia) 2016, *Joint Meeting* Sydney, NSW (Australia) 2016, *Biennial Conference* Bogota (Colombia) 2014, *Biennial Conference* Jaén (Spain) 2012, *Biennial Conference* Awaji (Japan) 2010. **Publications** *International Journal of Comparative Psychology* (4 a year). Conference proceedings.
Members Individuals in 28 countries:
Argentina, Australia, Belgium, Brazil, Canada, Chile, Colombia, Czechia, Finland, France, Germany, Israel, Italy, Japan, Malawi, Mexico, Netherlands, New Zealand, Papua New Guinea, Poland, Portugal, South Africa, Spain, Sweden, UK, USA, Venezuela, Zambia.
NGO Relations Affiliate member of: *International Union of Psychological Science (IUPsyS, #15807).* [2020/XD9550/v/**D**]

♦ International Society for the Comparative Study of Civilizations (internationally oriented national body)

♦ International Society for Complementary Medicine Research (ISCMR) 15025

Main Office 13 – 1201 Lamey's Mill Road, 563 Spadina Crescent, Vancouver BC V6H 3S8, Canada.
URL: http://www.iscmr.org/

History 22 Nov 2003, London (UK). **Aims** Foster cooperative and multidisciplinary research and development in the fields of complementary, traditional and integrative medicine. **Structure** Board of Directors. Executive Committee, comprising President, President Elect, Secretary and Treasurer. International Advisors. **Languages** English. **Staff** 5.00 FTE, voluntary. **Finance** Members' dues: about US$ 90. **Activities** Events/meetings. **Events** *International Congress on Complementary Medicine Research* Florence (Italy) 2021, *International Congress on Complementary Medicine Research* Brisbane, QLD (Australia) 2019, *International Congress on Complementary Medicine Research* Berlin (Germany) 2017, *International Congress on Complementary Medicine Research* Jeju (Korea Rep) 2015, *International Congress on Complementary Medicine Research* Miami, FL (USA) 2014. **Publications** *ISCMR Newsletter.* [2021/XM0077/**D**]

♦ International Society for Complex Environmental Studies (inactive)

♦ International Society for Computational Biology (ISCB) 15026

Admin Office 9650 Rockville Pike, Bethesda MD 20814, USA. T. +18588220852. Fax +16193742894. E-mail: admin@iscb.org.
URL: http://www.iscb.org/

History 1997, as an outgrowth of the *International Conference on Intelligent Systems for Molecular Biology (ISMB).* Registered in the State of California (USA). **Aims** Advance scientific understanding of living systems through computation. **Structure** Board of Directors comprising President, 3 Vice-Presidents, President Elect, Treasurer, Secretary and 22 further members. Executive Director. **Languages** English. **Staff** 5.00 FTE, paid. **Events** *Asia Pacific Bioinformatics Joint Congress* Okinawa (Japan) 2024, *Annual International Conference on Intelligent Systems for Molecular Biology* Lyon (France) 2023, *European Conference on Computational Biology (ECCB)* Lyon (France) 2023, *Annual International Conference on Intelligent Systems for Molecular Biology* Madison, WI (USA) 2022, *European Conference on Computational Biology (ECCB)* Sitges (Spain) 2022. **Publications** *Bioinformatics* – journal; *ISCB Newsletter*; *PLOS Computational Biology* – journal.
Members Full (over 3,000) from nearly 70 countries. Membership countries not specified. Affiliated organizations include 5 organizations listed in this Yearbook:
Affiliated organizations include 5 organizations listed in this Yearbook:
African Society for Bioinformatics and Computational Biology (ASBCB, #00459); Asia Pacific Bioinformatics Network (APBioNet, #01858); European Molecular Biology Network (EMBnet, #07815); Sociedad Iberoamericana de Bioinformatica (SolBio, #19361); Society for Bioinformatics in the Nordic Countries (SocBin, #19526).
NGO Relations Instrumental in setting up: *Global Organisation for Bioinformatics Learning, Education and Training (GOBLET, #10516).* [2020/XD7575/y/**C**]

♦ International Society for Computational Methods in Engineering (inactive)

♦ International Society for Computational Social Science (ISCSS) ... 15027

Sec address not obtained.
URL: https://iscss.org/

History 9 Jul 2021. Founded following a series of conferences initiated in 2015. Registration: 501(c)(3), USA, Pennsylvania. **Aims** Advance path-breaking research at the intersection of the computational, experimental, social, and behavioral sciences. **Structure** Board of Directors. **Activities** Events/meetings; networking/liaising; research/documentation. **Events** *International Conference on Computational Social Science (IC²S²)* Copenhagen (Denmark) 2023, *International Conference on Computational Social Science (IC²S²)* Chicago, IL (USA) 2022, *International Conference on Computational Social Science (IC²S²)* Zurich (Switzerland) 2021, *International Conference on Computational Social Science (IC²S²)* Cambridge, MA (USA) 2020, *International Conference on Computational Social Science (IC²S²)* Amsterdam (Netherlands) 2019. [2023/AA2901/c/**E**]

♦ International Society for Computer Aided Surgery (ISCAS) 15028

SG Dept of Biomedical Engineering, Kate Gleason College of Engineering, RIT, One Lomb Memorial Drive, Rochester NY 14623-5603, USA. T. +15854754926. E-mail: calbme@rit.edu – contact@iscas.co.
URL: http://www.iscas.net/

History Founded 28 Jun 1996, Paris (France). Registered in accordance with French law. **Aims** Encourage scientific and clinical advancement of computer-aided surgery and related medical interventions; promote basic technological and clinical research and technological and related medical interventions developed by the industry; foster a multidisciplinary approach, exchange of information and cooperation among members. **Structure** General Assembly (annual). Administrative Council, with equal representation of the Americas, Asia and Oceania and Europe/Africa. **Languages** English. **Finance** Members' dues. Other sources: grants; donations. **Activities** Events/meetings; awards/prizes/competitions; standards/guidelines; certification/accreditation. **Events** *Annual Conference* Rennes (France) 2019, *Annual Conference* Berlin (Germany) 2018, *Annual Conference* Barcelona (Spain) 2017, *Annual Conference* Heidelberg (Germany) 2016, *Annual Conference* Barcelona (Spain) 2015. **Publications** *International Journal of Computer Assisted Radiology and Surgery*; *Medical Image Analysis* – journal. **Members** Active (individuals); Associate (national or international associations); Honorary (individuals). Membership countries not specified. [2019/XD6189/**D**]

♦ International Society for Computer Assisted Orthopaedic Surgery (CAOS-International) 15029

SG Univ of Bern, Stauffacherstrasse 78, 3014 Bern, Switzerland. T. +41316315959. E-mail: caos@caos-international.org – secretariatcaosinternational@gmail.com.
URL: http://www.caos-international.org/

History 19 Feb 2000, Davos (Switzerland). **Aims** Unite individuals interest in computer assisted orthopaedic surgery; serve as a forum for the exchange of information of an investigative and clinical nature which relates to pre-operative planning, simulation, intraoperative execution and postoperative evaluation of orthopaedic surgical procedures by means of computer assistance; promote cooperation between orthopaedic surgeons and technologists. **Structure** General Meeting. Executive Committee, including President, 2 Past Presidents, 2 Vice-Presidents, Secretary-General and Treasurer. Regional organization: *Asian Society for Computer Assisted Surgery (CAOS Asia, #01713).* **Languages** English. **Finance** Sources: members' dues. **Events** *Annual Meeting* Brest (France) 2020, *Annual Meeting* New York, NY (USA) 2019, *Annual Meeting* Beijing (China) 2018, *Annual Meeting* Aachen (Germany) 2017, *Annual Meeting* Osaka (Japan) 2016. [2014/XD8853/**C**]

♦ International Society of Computerized Dentistry (internationally oriented national body)

♦ International Society for Computing in Civil and Building Engineering (ISCCBE) 15030

Contact Natl Taiwan Univ, No 1 – Section 4, Roosevelt Rd, Da'an District, Taipei 10617, Taiwan.
URL: http://www.isccbe.org/

Aims Encourage international cooperation, collaboration and exchange of ideas and information related to the beneficial use of computers in civil and building engineering. **Structure** General Meeting; Board of Directors; Executive Committee. **Events** *Conference* Osaka (Japan) 2016, *Conference* Orlando, FL (USA) 2014, *Conference* Moscow (Russia) 2012, *Conference* Nottingham (UK) 2010, *Conference* Beijing (China) 2008. **NGO Relations** *European Council of Civil Engineers (ECCE, #06810).* [2015/XD8902/**D**]

♦ International Society for Condensed Matter Nuclear Science (ISCMNS) 15031

Registered Office The Willows, Hobro, Wolverley, Kidderminster, DY11 5ST, UK.
Pres address not obtained. E-mail: info@iscmns.org.
URL: http://www.iscmns.org/

History 2 Jun 2004, following the 10th International Conference on Cold Fusion (ICCF). UK Registered Charity: 1116475. **Aims** Promote science of low energy nuclear reactions in condensed matter, also known as cold fusion. **Structure** General Meeting (annual). Executive Committee, including President, Vice-President, Honorary Treasurer, Treasurer Elect, Honorary Membership Secretary and Honorary Secretary. **Finance** Members' dues. **Events** *International Conference on Cold Fusion* Daejeon (Korea Rep) 2012, *International Conference* Rome (Italy) 2009, *International Conference* Washington, DC (USA) 2008. [2013/XM2116/**D**]

♦ International Society for Construction with Alternative Materials (ISCOWA) 15032

Chair Chem Eng Dept CIT, Willem de Croylaan 46, Box 2423, 3001 Leuven, Belgium. E-mail: secr@iscowa.org.
URL: http://www.iscowa.org/

History 1992, following first WASCON Conference in 1991 where decision was taken to set up the Society. *'International Foundation TTPI (Technology Transfer Promotion ISCOWA)'*, set up in 2004. **Aims** Promote exchange of knowledge and results between (private) international experts, specifically in the field of environmental problems of reuse of *wastes* in building products; be active in the field of technology transfer of reuse and promote low-energy processes and exchange of carbon credits. **Structure** Board, comprising 5 members, including free-lance, private and non-profit. Secretariat based in the Netherlands. Foundation Board, comprising 7 members. Foundation Secretariat. **Languages** English. **Staff** Voluntary board members; 73 experts from 20 countries for Society; 430 private experts from 53 countries for Foundation. **Finance** Members' dues. Sponsoring; workshop or conference proceeds. **Activities** Promotes the organization of triennial WASCON Conference. **Events** *WASCON : International Conference on the Environmental and Technical Implications of Construction with Alternative Materials* Hong Kong (Hong Kong) 2022, *WASCON : International Conference on the Environmental and Technical Implications of Construction with Alternative Materials* Hong Kong (Hong Kong) 2021, *WASCON : International Conference on the Environmental and Technical Implications of Construction with Alternative Materials* Tampere (Finland) 2018, *WASCON : International Conference on the Environmental and Technical Implications of Construction with Alternative Materials* Santander (Spain) 2015, *WASCON : international conference on the environmental and technical implications of construction with alternative materials / Meeting* Gothenburg (Sweden) 2012. **Publications** Conference proceedings, also on CD-Rom. **Members** Governmental and non-governmental officers; officers from educational, training and research institutes, national academics of science, engineering, local and national private sectors. Individuals (73) in 20 countries. Membership countries not specified. [2015/XD3720/v/**D**]

♦ International Society for Contact Lens Research / see International Society of Contact Lens Specialists (#15034)

♦ International Society for Contact Lens Research (ISCLR) 15033

Societas Internationalis Lenti Conformatae Indagandae

Sec c/o Eurolens Research, University of Manchester, Sackville Street, Manchester, M60 1QD, UK. T. +441613064441. Fax +441612004442.
URL: http://www.isclr.org/

History 1978. **Aims** Encourage excellence in contact lens research. **Structure** Executive Committee of about 18 members; Council of 36 members. Overall membership limited to about 100 people. **Languages** English. **Staff** None, organization ran by membership. **Finance** Members' dues. Sponsorship from contact lens industry. **Events** *Biennial Symposium* Kyoto (Japan) 2013, *Biennial Symposium* Napa, CA (USA) 2011, *Biennial Symposium* Napa, CA (USA) 2011, *Biennial Symposium* Crete (Greece) 2009, *Biennial Symposium* Whistler, BC (Canada) 2007. **Publications** *ISCLR Newsletter.*
Members Individuals in 13 countries and territories:
Australia, Canada, Finland, France, Germany, Hong Kong, India, Japan, Spain, Sweden, Switzerland, UK, USA. [2014/XD6868/v/**D**]

♦ International Society of Contact Lens Specialists (ISCLS) 15034

Société internationale de spécialistes de verres de contact

Sec 7 Devonshire Street, London, W1W 5DY, UK.
URL: http://www.iscls.net/

History 1952, Munich (Germany FR). Also referred to as *International Society for Contact Lens Research.* **Aims** Exchange views, experiences and technical information among specialists in many countries of the world; promote educational congresses, scholarships and programmes of research in the furtherance of progressive development of contact lens technique. **Structure** Officers: President, Vice-President, Past President, Secretary, Treasurer and 6 members. Occasional Congresses open to members and invited guests only. **Languages** English. **Staff** No paid officials. **Finance** Subscriptions of members and associates. **Activities** Educational conference (every 18 months). **Events** *Conference* Boston, MA (USA) 2009, *Conference* Buenos Aires (Argentina) 2008, *Conference* Salzburg (Austria) 2006, *Conference* Saint-Paul-de-Vence (France) 2005, *Conference* San Diego, CA (USA) 2003.
Members Full, Associate. Members in 23 countries:
Argentina, Australia, Austria, Belgium, Canada, Colombia, Denmark, Finland, France, Germany, Greece, India, Ireland, Israel, Italy, Japan, Mexico, Netherlands, Norway, South Africa, Switzerland, UK, USA. [2017/XD2535/**D**]

♦ International Society for Contemporary Music (ISCM) 15035

Société internationale pour la musique contemporaine (SIMC) – Sociedad Internacional de Música Contemporanea – Internationale Gesellschaft für Neue Musik (IGNM)

Main Office Stiftgasse 29, 1070 Vienna, Austria.
URL: http://www.iscm.org/

History Founded Aug 1922, Salzburg (Austria). **Aims** Promote contemporary music, irrespective of the aesthetic tendency, nationality, race, religion or political opinions of the composer; help national sections in propagating and developing contemporary music. **Structure** General Assembly (annual), consisting of 1 or 2 Delegates from each national Section, elects Presidential Council. Executive Committee of 8 members. Meetings open. **Languages** English. **Staff** 1.00 FTE, paid. **Finance** Annual dues from Sections. **Activities** Events/meetings. **Events** *Annual General Assembly* Auckland (New Zealand) 2020, *Annual General Assembly* Beijing (China) 2018, *Annual General Assembly* Vancouver, BC (Canada) 2017, *Annual General Assembly* Tongyeong (Korea Rep) 2016, *Annual General Assembly* Ljubljana (Slovenia) 2015. **Publications** *World New Music Magazine* (annual).
Members Sections in 45 countries and territories:
Argentina, Australia, Austria, Belgium, Bulgaria, Canada, Chile, Croatia, Denmark, Estonia, Faeroe Is, Finland, Germany, Greece, Hong Kong, Hungary, Iceland, Ireland, Israel, Italy, Japan, Kazakhstan, Korea Rep, Latvia, Lithuania, Luxembourg, Mexico, Netherlands, New Zealand, Norway, Poland, Portugal, Romania, Russia, Serbia, Slovakia, Slovenia, Spain, Sweden, Switzerland, Taiwan, Türkiye, UK, Ukraine, USA.
NGO Relations Member of: *European Music Council (EMC, #07837); International Music Council (IMC, #14199).* [2020/XB2481/**C**]

♦ International Society of Continuing Education in Dentistry (inactive)

♦ International Society of Corvette Owners (no recent information)

♦ International Society of Cosmetic Dermatology (ISCD) 15036

Executive Office Via Innocenzo XI 41, 00165 Rome RM, Italy. T. +39639378788. Fax +396380839. E-mail: info@iscd.it.
URL: http://www.iscd.it/

History 1982. **Aims** Encourage a more continuous and stable exchange among the medical community, dermatologists, cosmetic chemists, pharmacologists, physiologists, toxicologists and experts of all other disciplines related to cosmetic dermatology. **Structure** Executive Board. **Languages** English. **Staff** Voluntary. **Finance** Associate quotes. **Activities** Organizes: international congress; workshops; scientific conference. **Events** *Congress* Shenyang (China) 2011, *Congress* Rome (Italy) 2009, *Cosmetic dermatology from West to East – the combined reply for a global wellness* Beijing (China) 2007, *Congress* Rome (Italy) 2004, *Congress* Rome (Italy) 2002. **Publications** *Journal of Applied Cosmetology* (4 a year). Congress proceedings.
[2014.06.20/XD7684/**D**]

♦ International Society of Cosmetogynecology (unconfirmed)
♦ International Society of Cranio-Facial Biology (inactive)

♦ International Society of Craniofacial Surgery (ISCFS) 15037

Sec-Treas Eendrachtsweg 57b, 3012 LE Rotterdam, Netherlands. T. +31104636393.
URL: http://www.iscfs.org/

History Jun 1983, Montréal, QC (Canada). Founded, originally as a chapter of *International Confederation for Plastic, Reconstructive and Aesthetic Surgery (IPRAS, inactive)*. Most recent statutes adopted, Oct 1997. Former names and other names: *International Society of Craniomaxillofacial Surgery* – former. **Aims** Furnish leadership and foster advances in craniofacial surgery; provide a forum for exchange of knowledge; stimulate research, investigation and teaching in methods of preventing and correcting *congenital* and acquired craniofacial *deformities*; enhance study and practice. **Structure** Meeting (every 2 years, at Congress); Council; Executive Committee; Committee. Membership by invitation, dependent on sufficient relevant surgical experience in specified categories: cranium; orbit; maxilla; mandible. **Languages** English. **Finance** Sources: members' dues. **Activities** Events/meetings. **Events** *International Congress* Washington, DC (USA) 2023, *International Congress* 2021, *International Congress* 2021, *Biennial Congress* Paris (France) 2019, *Biennial Congress* Cancún (Mexico) 2017. **Publications** *Journal of Craniofacial Surgery*.
Members Founding; Active; Associate; Corresponding; Honorary; Senior; Life. Individuals in 32 countries and territories:
Argentina, Australia, Austria, Belgium, Brazil, Canada, China, Colombia, Cyprus, Ecuador, Finland, France, Germany, Greece, India, Italy, Japan, Korea Rep, Lebanon, Mexico, Netherlands, New Zealand, Singapore, South Africa, Sweden, Switzerland, Taiwan, Thailand, Türkiye, UK, USA, Venezuela.
NGO Relations *European Society of Craniofacial Surgery (ESCFS, #08574)* acts as European branch.
[2022/XD3827/v/**C**]

♦ International Society of Craniomaxillofacial Surgery / see International Society of Craniofacial Surgery (#15037)
♦ International Society for Crime Prevention (inactive)
♦ International Society of Crime Prevention Practitioners (internationally oriented national body)
♦ International Society for Criminology / see International Society of Criminology (#15038)

♦ International Society of Criminology (ISC) 15038

Société internationale de criminologie (SIC) – Sociedad Internacional de Criminologia
SG c/o Law School, University of Buckingham, Hunter Street, Buckingham, MK18 1EG, UK.
Pres c/o AU SPA, 4400 Mass Ave NW, Washington DC 20016, USA.
URL: https://intercrim.com/

History Dec 1934, Paris (France). Founded to group societies for criminology, criminal biology, prophylaxis and anthropology from countries of Europe and South America. The problem of transformation of this Society into an International Society was worked out during preliminary meetings and solved 16 Jul 1937, Rome (Italy). Officially created under the present name at the conclusion of 1st International Congress of Criminology, 1938, Rome. Refounded and Statutes initially adopted Jan 1949, Paris. Statutes modified 1955, London (UK); 2008, Paris (France). Former names and other names: *Society of Criminological Sciences* – former; *Société des sciences criminologiques* – former; *International Society for Criminology* – former. **Aims** Promote activities and research designed to further a better understanding of the crime phenomenon on an international scale; promote crime *prevention*; improve procedures used by the various *criminal justice* systems. **Structure** General Assembly (at least once every 3 years); Board of Directors; Scientific Commission; Secretariat. Honorary Presidents. **Languages** English, French, Spanish. **Staff** None. **Finance** Sources: members' dues. **Activities** Events/meetings; knowledge management/information dissemination; research and development; research/documentation; training/education. **Events** *World Congress (INTERCRIM)* Doha (Qatar) 2019, *World Congress* Delhi (India) 2016, *World Congress* Monterrey (Mexico) 2014, *World Crime Forum* Bologna (Italy) 2013, *World Crime Forum* Canberra, ACT (Australia) 2013. **Publications** *Selected Documentation on Criminology* – published by UNESCO. **Members** Individuals: scholars, judges, criminal justice administrators; associations or groups may acquire Active, Associate or Student membership. Honorary members. Members in 83 countries. Membership countries not specified. **IGO Relations** *UNESCO (#20322)*. Special links with: *Council of Europe (CE, #04881)*. Accredited by: *United Nations Office at Vienna (UNOV, #20604)*. **NGO Relations** Member of: *Alliance of NGOs on Crime Prevention and Criminal Justice (#00709)*. Collective associate member of: *International Social Science Council (ISSC, inactive)*. Instrumental in setting up: *International Centre for Clinical Criminology (ICCC, no recent information)*; *International Centre for Comparative Criminology (ICCC, #12482)*; *International Centre for Research on Delinquency, Marginality and Social Relationships (#12510)*. Partner of: *Global Forum on Law, Justice and Development (GFLJD, #10373)*.
[2019.03.06/XB2537/**B**]

♦ International Society for Crippled Children / see RI Global (#18948)

♦ International Society of Critical Health Psychology (ISCHP) 15039

Chair address not obtained.
URL: http://www.ischp.net/

History Aug 2001, Birmingham (UK), during 2nd International Conference on Critical and Qualitative Approaches to Health Psychology. **Aims** Promote debate about critical ideas, qualitative and participatory research methods as well as social, political and cultural issues within health psychology; facilitate collaboration between critical health psychologists; increase development of resources and training opportunities in critical health psychology. **Structure** Executive Committee, comprising Chair, Past Chair, Treasurer and Secretary. **Languages** English. **Finance** Income from conferences. **Events** *Conference* Boston, MA (USA) 2007, *Conference* Sheffield (UK) 2005, *Conference* Auckland (New Zealand) 2003.
Members Individuals in 29 countries and territories:
Australia, Belgium, Brazil, Bulgaria, Canada, China, Finland, France, Germany, Hong Kong, Hungary, India, Indonesia, Ireland, Italy, Japan, Netherlands, New Zealand, Norway, Palestine, Portugal, Romania, Slovakia, South Africa, Sweden, Switzerland, Türkiye, UK, USA.
[2013/XM0344/**D**]

♦ International Society of Cryosurgery (ISC) 15040

Secretariat Billrothstr 78, 1190 Vienna, Austria. T. +431360365105. Fax +431360365805. E-mail: isc.headquarters@cryosurgery.at.
URL: http://www.isc.cryosurgery.at/

History Separated from *International Society of Cryosurgery (#15041)*, 2011, when new bylaws were adopted. Registered in accordance with Austrian law. **Aims** Promote innovation in *medical* and scientific sectors, especially on the level of cryosurgery, cryomedicine, cryobiology and cryoscience as well as other minor subjects in conjunction with the use of low temperatures; train and further educate young scientists in these areas. **Structure** General Assembly. Board of Governors. **Events** *Congress* Haifa (Israel) 2019, *Congress* Kaunas (Lithuania) 2017, *Congress* Doha (Qatar) 2015, *Congress / World Congress* Bali (Indonesia) 2013, *Congress / World Congress* Vienna (Austria) 2011. **Publications** *ISC Newsletter*. **NGO Relations** Cooperates with: *Asian Society of Cryosurgery (ASC, #01716)*.
[2019/XJ8463/**C**]

♦ International Society of Cryosurgery 15041

Société internationale de cryochirurgie – Società Internazionale di Criochirurgia
Address not obtained.
URL: http://www.societyofcryosurgery.org/

History 1974. *International Society of Cryosurgery (ISC, #15040)* separated, 2011. **Aims** Promote continuing medical education and research in the field of cryosurgery; develop and expand membership of the Society. **Structure** International Meeting (every 2 years in Autumn). Committee, composed of Officers. Board of Directors. **Languages** English. **Staff** 2.00 FTE, paid. **Finance** Members' dues. Meetings funded by registration fees and sponsors. Budget (annual): US$ 50,000. **Activities** Events/meetings. **Events** *World Congress* Madrid (Spain) 2013, *World Congress* Trieste (Italy) 2011, *Congress / Biennial International Meeting* St Petersburg (Russia) 2009, *Congress / Biennial International Meeting* Beijing (China) 2007, *Congress / Biennial International Meeting* Heraklion (Greece) 2005. **Publications** *Cryosurgery* (2 a year). *Cryosurgery for Lung Cancer: Clinical Results and Technical Aspects* (2004) by M O Maiwand and G Asimakopoulos; *Pleural Effusion in Yellow Nail Syndrome: Treatment with Bilateral Pleuro-Peritoneal Shunts* (2004) by M O Maiwand; *The Application of Cryosurgery in the Treatment of Lung Cancer* (2004) by M O Maiwand et al. **Members** Corresponding; Honorary individuals (about 700) with a professional interest in the fields of Cryosurgery, Cryobiology, Cryopreservation and other related disciplines, in 28 countries. Membership countries not specified.
[2013/XD9223/**D**]

♦ International Society of Cryptozoology (inactive)

♦ International Society for Cultural and Activity Research (ISCAR) ... 15042

Pres Dept of Early Childhood Education, School of Education, Univ of Ioannina, 455 00 Ioannina, Greece. T. +306972898463. E-mail: mail@iscar.org – info@iscar.org.
Sec Fed Univ of Rio de Janeiro, Av Horacio Macedo 2151, Cidade Universitaria, Rio de Janeiro RJ, Brazil. T. +5521996895675.
URL: http://www.iscar.org/

History 19 Jun 2002, Amsterdam (Netherlands). Founded by merger of *International Society for Cultural Research and Activity Theory (ISCRAT, inactive)* and Conference for Sociocultural Research. Former names and other names: *International Society for Cultural-historical Activity Research* – alias. **Aims** Develop multidisciplinary theoretical and empirical research on societal, cultural and historical dimensions of human practices; promote mutual scientific communication and research cooperation among members and with other associations. **Structure** Executive Committee; Thematic Sections. **Languages** English. **Staff** 4.00 FTE, paid. **Finance** Sources: members' dues. **Activities** Networking/liaising; research/documentation. **Events** *Nordic Baltic Conference* Helsinki (Finland) 2022, *Triennial Congress* Natal (Brazil) 2021, *Triennial Congress* Natal (Brazil) 2020, *CHACDOC : Cultural-Historical Approaches to Children's Development and Childhood Conference* Bergen (Norway) 2019, *Nordic Conference* Trondheim (Norway) 2019. **Publications** *ISCAR Newsletter* (2 a year).
Members in 45 countries and territories:
Argentina, Australia, Azerbaijan, Belgium, Brazil, Canada, Chile, China, Cuba, Denmark, Finland, France, Germany, Greece, Greenland, India, Indonesia, Ireland, Israel, Italy, Japan, Korea Rep, Luxembourg, Mexico, Montenegro, Netherlands, New Zealand, Norway, Poland, Portugal, Puerto Rico, Russia, Serbia, Singapore, South Africa, Spain, Sweden, Switzerland, Türkiye, UK, Ukraine, Uruguay, USA, Venezuela, Vietnam.
[2022/XD8926/**D**]

♦ International Society for Cultural-historical Activity Research / see International Society for Cultural and Activity Research (#15042)

♦ International Society for Cultural History (ISCH) 15043

Sec address not obtained.
URL: http://www.culthist.org/

History following meeting, Jul 2007, Aberdeen (UK). Founding Meeting, Aug 2008, Ghent (Belgium), when constitution was adopted. **Structure** Committee, comprising President, Chair, Secretary, Treasurer, Past President and members. **Events** *Annual Conference* Tallinn (Estonia) 2019, *Annual Conference* New York, NY (USA) 2018, *Annual conference* Oslo (Norway) 2011, *Annual conference / Annual General Meeting* Turku (Finland) 2010, *Annual conference* Turku (Finland) 2010. **Publications** *Journal of Cultural History*. *Studies in Cultural History* – book series.
Members Individuals in 34 countries:
Australia, Austria, Azerbaijan, Bangladesh, Belgium, Brazil, Canada, Denmark, Estonia, Finland, France, Germany, Greece, Hungary, Iceland, Ireland, Italy, Korea Rep, Mexico, Netherlands, New Zealand, Nigeria, Norway, Portugal, Romania, Russia, South Africa, Spain, St Lucia, Sweden, Switzerland, Türkiye, UK, USA.
[2014/XJ1037/v/**D**]

♦ International Society for Cultural Research and Activity Theory (inactive)

♦ International Society for Cutaneous Lymphomas (ISCL) 15044

Headquarters 303 West State St, Geneva IL 60134, USA. T. +16305783991. Fax +16302621520.
Pres Dept of Dermatology, Stanford University Medical Center, 291 Campus Dr, Stanford CA 94305, USA.
Sec Dept of Dermatology, Leiden University Medical Center, Building 1, 1278, 2300 RC Leiden, Netherlands.
URL: http://www.cutaneouslymphoma.org/

History Founded 1992, during 18th World Congress of Dermatology. **Aims** Increase knowledge of lymphoproliferative and related disorders of the *skin*; foster collaboration among clinicians, scientists and regional or national lymphoma groups; promote dissemination of scientific information. **Structure** Executive Committee, comprising President, Past-President, Secretary-Treasurer and up to 15 additional international members. **Languages** English. **Staff** 0.50 FTE, paid. **Finance** Members' dues: US$ 50. **Activities** Organizes conferences and workshops. **Events** *World Conference of Cutaneous Lymphomas* Barcelona (Spain) 2020, *Conference* Scottsdale, AZ (USA) 2016, *Conference* Atlanta, GA (USA) 2015, *Conference* Albuquerque, NM (USA) 2014, *World Conference of Cutaneous Lymphomas* Berlin (Germany) 2013.
Members Paid members (100); non-paying interested physicians (150). Individuals in 35 countries and territories:
Argentina, Australia, Austria, Belgium, Brazil, Canada, Chile, China, Colombia, Czechia, Denmark, Egypt, Finland, France, Germany, Hungary, India, Iran Islamic Rep, Israel, Italy, Japan, Korea Rep, Lebanon, Netherlands, Philippines, Portugal, Russia, Saudi Arabia, Spain, Sweden, Switzerland, Taiwan, Türkiye, UK, USA.
NGO Relations Member of: *International League of Dermatological Societies (ILDS, #14018)*.
[2013/XC0083/v/**C**]

♦ International Society of Cybernetic Medicine (inactive)
♦ International Society of Dacryology / see International Society of Dacryology and Dry Eye (#15045)

♦ International Society of Dacryology and Dry Eye (ISD and DE) 15045

Sec address not obtained.
URL: http://www.oftalmo.com/isd-de/

History Founded 8 Nov 1982, Lubbock TX (USA), during the International Tear Film Symposium, as an independent international organization. Original title: *International Society of Dacryology – Internationalis Societas Dacryologiae*. **Aims** Join all individuals from all around the world who are interested in or involved in understanding the health and fighting the disease of the *lachrymal* system. **Structure** Executive Board, comprising President, Vice-President, Secretary, Treasurer and 4 Councillors. Officers: President; Vice-President; General Secretary; Treasurer; 2 Advisors. **Languages** English. **Finance** Registration fees. **Activities** Events/meetings; knowledge management/information dissemination; research/documentation. **Events** *Triennial Congress* London (UK) 2020, *Triennial Congress* Athens (Greece) 2017, *Triennial Congress* Naples (Italy) 2014, *Triennial Congress* Manila (Philippines) 2011, *Triennial Congress* Istanbul (Turkey) 2008. **Publications** Congress proceedings – published in a supplement to the journal 'Orbit'.
Members Individuals in 33 countries and territories:
Australia, Austria, Belgium, Bulgaria, Canada, China, Czechia, Denmark, Finland, France, Germany, Greece, Hong Kong, Hungary, India, Ireland, Israel, Italy, Japan, Jordan, Malaysia, Netherlands, New Zealand, Norway, Pakistan, Poland, Portugal, Spain, Sweden, Switzerland, Taiwan, UK, USA.
[2014/XF3462/v/**C**]

♦ International Society of Dental Regulators (ISDR) 15046

Main Office 1619 Duke St, Alexandria VA 22314-3406, USA. E-mail: research@iadr.org.
URL: https://www.iadr.org/

History Current bylaws incorporated Feb 2015. Registered in accordance with Canadian law. **Aims** Support the purposes of dental regulation through scientific, educational and collaborative activities; encourage best practices among dental regulatory authorities worldwide in the achievement of their mandate of protecting, promoting, and maintaining the health and safety of the public by ensuring proper standards for the dental professions. **Structure** General Assembly; Executive Committee. **Languages** English. **Activities** Events/ meetings. **Events** *General Session* Chengdu (China) 2022, *Conference* London (UK) 2017, *Conference* Geneva (Switzerland) 2016, *Conference* Boston, MA (USA) 2015, *Conference* London (UK) 2014.
Members Ordinary; Associate. Founding members in 9 countries:
Australia, Canada, France, Ireland, Korea Rep, New Zealand, Singapore, UK, United Arab Emirates.
NGO Relations *Federation of European Dental Competent Authorities and Regulators (FEDCAR, #09501).*
[2020/XM6237/C]

♦ International Society of Depth Psychology (internationally oriented national body)

♦ International Society for Dermatologic Surgery (ISDS) 15047
Société internationale de chirurgie dermatologique
Main Office c/o CAS GmbH, Donnersbergring 18, 64295 Darmstadt, Germany. T. +4961519518892. Fax +4961519518893. E-mail: info@isdsworld.com.
URL: http://www.isdsworld.com/
History 1976. **Aims** Provide a forum for exchange of ideas and experience; promote high standards in patient care; encourage continuing education and research in dermatologic surgery and related fields. **Structure** Board of Directors. Officers: Founder-President; President; President-Elect; Vice President; Secretary; Treasurer; Historian. **Languages** English. **Staff** 2.00 FTE, paid. **Finance** Annual budget: 250,000 USD. **Events** *Annual Congress* Manila (Philippines) 2019, *Annual Congress* Rome (Italy) 2018, *Annual Congress* Bangkok (Thailand) 2017, *Spring Meeting* Graz (Austria) 2017, *Annual Congress* Amsterdam (Netherlands) 2016. **Publications** *Journal of Dermatologic Surgery and Oncology* (12 a year); *Drugs in Dermatology* (4 a year). **Members** Individual dermatologists, otolaryngologists, plastic surgeons and specialists in skin surgery. Members in 62 countries. Membership countries not specified. **NGO Relations** Member of: *International League of Dermatological Societies (ILDS, #14018).* Supports: *International Foundation for Dermatology (IFD, #13668).* [2017/XD5264/v/C]

♦ International Society of Dermatology (ISD) 15048
Société internationale de dermatologie
Main Office 85 High St, Ste 8, Waldorf MD 20602, USA. T. +13864374405. Fax +13864374427. E-mail: info@intsocderm.org.
URL: http://www.intsocderm.org/
History 1958, Lisbon (Portugal), as *International Society of Tropical Dermatology (ISTD) – Societas Internationalis Dermatologiae Tropicae.* Constituent Assembly 25 Jan 1960, New York NY (USA). Subsequently name change to *International Society of Dermatology: Tropical, Geographical, and Ecological (ISD)*, adopted at 5th World Congress, 20 Oct 1984, Mexico City (Mexico). Incorporated in the State of New York (USA). **Aims** Promote and encourage investigation, and facilitate mutual acquaintance and collaboration between persons of all nationalities, concerning the field of *tropical* dermatology and geographical ecology of global skin diseases. **Structure** Congress (every 4 years); Executive Board; Board of Directors. **Languages** English. **Staff** Editor and staff of journal paid; other staff voluntary. **Finance** Sources: donations; meeting proceeds; members' dues. Annual budget: 250,000 USD. **Events** *Continental Congress of Dermatology* Mexico City (Mexico) 2022, *Quadrennial Congress* Melbourne, VIC (Australia) 2021, *Continental Congress of Dermatology* Mexico City (Mexico) 2020, *Continental Congress of Dermatology* Taipei (Taiwan) 2018, *Quadrennial Congress* Buenos Aires (Argentina) 2017. **Publications** *International Journal of Dermatology* (10 a year) in English.
Members Individuals (approximately 3,000) in 57 countries and territories:
Argentina, Australia, Austria, Bangladesh, Bolivia, Brazil, Canada, Chile, Colombia, Costa Rica, Denmark, Dominica, Dominican Rep, Ecuador, Egypt, El Salvador, France, Germany, Ghana, Greece, Guatemala, Guyana, Honduras, Hong Kong, India, Indonesia, Iran Islamic Rep, Ireland, Israel, Italy, Japan, Kenya, Malaysia, Mexico, New Zealand, Nicaragua, Norway, Pakistan, Panama, Paraguay, Peru, Philippines, Poland, Portugal, Puerto Rico, Saudi Arabia, Singapore, Spain, Sweden, Taiwan, Tanzania UR, Thailand, Türkiye, UK, Uruguay, USA, Venezuela.
NGO Relations Member of (1): *International League of Dermatological Societies (ILDS, #14018).*
[2019/XB2573/v/B]

♦ International Society of Dermatology: Tropical, Geographical, and Ecological / see International Society of Dermatology (#15048)

♦ International Society of Dermatopathology (ISDP) 15049
Société internationale de dermatopathologie
Manager PO Box 2444, Fredericksburg TX 78624, USA. T. +16507291234. E-mail: isdpmanager@gmail.com.
Pres UT MD Anderson Cancer Center, 1515 Holcombe Blvd, Houston TX 77030, USA. T. +17137923187. Fax +17137453740.
URL: http://www.intsocdermpath.org/
History 1979, Amsterdam (Netherlands). Former names and other names: *ISD* – former. **Aims** Increase knowledge of the structure and function of the *skin* and of *diseases* of the skin by *microscopy.* **Structure** Board of Directors (consultative body); Executive Committee/Group; Committees (4). **Languages** English. **Staff** 30.00 FTE, voluntary. **Finance** Sources: members' dues. **Activities** Awards/prizes/competitions; events/ meetings. **Events** *Symposium* Singapore (Singapore) 2026, *Symposium* Cape Town (South Africa) 2025, *Symposium* Milan (Italy) 2024, *Joint Meeting* San Diego, CA (USA) 2024, *Symposium* Dubai (United Arab Emirates) 2023. **Publications** *American Journal of Dermatopathology.* Teaching slides file.
Members Regular; Sponsoring; Patron; Associate; Senior; Residents/Fellows. Individuals (about 800) in 58 countries and territories:
Argentina, Australia, Austria, Belgium, Bolivia, Brazil, Bulgaria, Canada, Chile, China, Colombia, Costa Rica, Czechia, Denmark, Dominican Rep, Ecuador, Egypt, Finland, France, Germany, Greece, Guatemala, Iceland, India, Iran Islamic Rep, Ireland, Israel, Italy, Japan, Kenya, Korea Rep, Kuwait, Lebanon, Mexico, Netherlands, New Zealand, Norway, Philippines, Poland, Portugal, Romania, Russia, Saudi Arabia, Singapore, Slovenia, South Africa, Spain, Sri Lanka, Sweden, Switzerland, Taiwan, Thailand, Türkiye, UK, United Arab Emirates, Uruguay, USA, Venezuela.
NGO Relations Member of (1): *International League of Dermatological Societies (ILDS, #14018).*
[2021.06.18/XC0068/v/C]

♦ International Society for Design and Development in Education (ISDDE) 15050
Sec Shell Ctr, School of Education, Univ of Nottingham, Nottingham, NG8 1BB, UK.
URL: http://www.isdde.org/
History Constitution revised Jan 2012. Registered in accordance with UK law. **Aims** Improve design and development of educational tools and processes; increase impact of good design on educational practice. **Structure** Executive. **Finance** Sources: members' dues. **Activities** Awards/prizes/competitions; events/ meetings. **Events** *Annual Conference* Nottingham (UK) 2021, *Annual Conference* Pittsburg, KS (USA) 2019, *Annual Conference* Galway (Ireland) 2018, *Annual Conference* Berkeley, CA (USA) 2017, *Annual Conference* Utrecht (Netherlands) 2016. **Publications** *Educational Designer* – electronic journal; *ISDDE Newsletter.* **Members** Full; Fellow. Membership countries not specified. [2015/XM4320/C]

♦ International Society for Deuterocanonical and Cognate Literature (ISDCL) 15051
Pres Univ Salzburg, Fachbereich Bibelwissenschaft und Kirchengeschichte, Universitätsplatz 1, 5020 Salzburg, Austria. T. +4366280442923. Fax +4366263892923.
Hon Pres address not obtained.
URL: http://www.uni-salzburg.at/index.php?id=21350
History 2002, Salzburg (Austria). **Aims** Promote academic research into deuterocanonical and cognate literature on an international, interconfessional and interreligious basis, through preparation of scholarly materials. **Structure** Advisory Panel. Officers: President; 3 Vice-Presidents. **Languages** English, German. **Staff** Voluntary. **Finance** Members' dues. **Events** *International Conference* Cambridge (UK) 2016, *International Conference / Conference* Budapest (Hungary) 2015, *International Conference* Haifa (Israel) 2014, *International Conference* Würzburg (Germany) 2014, *International Conference / Conference* Berlin (Germany) 2013. **Publications** *Deuterocanonical and Cognate Literature – Studies* – series; *Deuterocanonical and Cognate Literature – Yearbook* – series.

Members Individuals in 16 countries:
Austria, Belgium, Bolivia, Canada, Denmark, France, Germany, Hungary, Ireland, Israel, Italy, Netherlands, Poland, South Africa, UK, USA. [2020.03.03/XM0556/v/D]

♦ International Society of Developmental Biologists (ISDB) 15052
Société internationale des biologistes du développement
Sec UCL – Biology, 222 Gower Street, London, WC1E 6BT, UK.
URL: http://www.developmental-biology.org/
History Founded 1911, Utrecht (Netherlands), as *International Institute of Embryology (IIE) – Institut international d'embryologie.* Constitution amended, 1968, Paris (France), when changed title to *International Society of Development Biologists.* Also referred to as *International Association of Developmental Biology.* Restructured and constitution amended and adopted 1997. Developmental Biology Section of: *International Union of Biological Sciences (IUBS, #15760).* **Aims** Contribute to international cooperation in study and research on developmental biology. **Structure** General Assembly (every 4 years); Board. **Languages** English. **Staff** 2.00 FTE, voluntary. **Finance** Sources: capitation fees from member societies; royalties from publications. **Activities** Awards/prizes/competitions; events/meetings; training/education. **Events** *International Congress* Albufeira (Portugal) 2022, *Quadrennial Congress* Albufeira (Portugal) 2021, *Quadrennial Congress* Singapore (Singapore) 2017, *Symposium on Complexity of Life* Vienna (Austria) 2014, *Quadrennial Congress* Cancún (Mexico) 2013. **Publications** *Gene Expression Patterns* (10 a year); *Mechanisms of Development* (10 a year).
Members National societies in 16 countries and territories:
Australia, Finland, France, Germany, Hong Kong, India, Israel, Italy, Japan, Korea Rep, New Zealand, Portugal, Spain, Taiwan, UK, USA.
Regional societies (2):
Asia-Pacific Developmental Biology Network (APDBN, #01884); Latin American Society for Developmental Biology (LASDB, #16371).
Individuals in 47 countries and territories:
Argentina, Australia, Austria, Belgium, Brazil, Canada, Chile, China, Croatia, Czechia, Denmark, Ecuador, Egypt, Finland, France, Germany, Greece, Hong Kong, Hungary, India, Iran Islamic Rep, Ireland, Israel, Italy, Japan, Kenya, Korea Rep, Mexico, Netherlands, Norway, Peru, Philippines, Poland, Romania, Russia, Serbia, Singapore, Slovakia, South Africa, Spain, Sweden, Switzerland, Türkiye, Ukraine, Uruguay, USA, Venezuela.
NGO Relations Member of: *International Federation of Associations of Anatomists (IFAA, #13361).* Instrumental in setting up: *Asia-Pacific Developmental Biology Network (APDBN, #01884).* [2018/XC2539/v/C]

♦ International Society of Developmental and Comparative Immunology (ISDCI) 15053
Sec-Treas School of Life Sciences, Heriot Watt Univ, Riccarton, Edinburgh, EH14 4AS, UK. T. +441314518032. E-mail: info@isdci.org.
Pres Dept of Biological Sciences, George Washington Univ, 800 22nd St NW, Washington DC 20052, USA. T. +12029949211.
URL: http://www.isdci.org/
History 1978, Los Angeles, CA (USA). Founded in Los Angeles CA (USA) and Aberdeen (UK) simultaneously. **Aims** Bring together research workers worldwide by fostering and maintaining international scientific cooperation and communication between individual scientists, regional groups and/or national societies interested in the study of developmental and comparative immunology. **Structure** Officers: President; President-Elect; Past President; 3 Vice-Presidents (Americas; Europe and Africa; Asia and Oceania); Secretary-Treasurer; Secretary-Education. **Languages** English. **Staff** None. **Finance** Sources: members' dues. **Activities** Events/ meetings. **Events** *Triennial Congress* Dalian (China) 2023, *Triennial Congress* Dalian (China) 2021, *Triennial Congress* Santa Fe, NM (USA) 2018, *Triennial Congress* Murcia (Spain) 2015, *Triennial Congress* Fukuoka (Japan) 2012. **Publications** *Developmental and Comparitive Immunology* – journal; *eBoard.*
Members Individuals (about 180) in 47 countries and territories:
Argentina, Australia, Austria, Belgium, Brazil, Bulgaria, Canada, Chile, China, Croatia, Cyprus, Czechia, Denmark, Estonia, Finland, France, Georgia, Germany, Greece, Hong Kong, Hungary, Iceland, India, Ireland, Israel, Italy, Japan, Malaysia, Nepal, Netherlands, Norway, Pakistan, Paraguay, Poland, Portugal, Russia, Singapore, South Africa, Spain, Sweden, Switzerland, Taiwan, Thailand, UK, Ukraine, USA, Venezuela.
NGO Relations Affiliated with (1): *International Union of Immunological Societies (IUIS, #15781).*
[2022.06.14/XD2623/v/C]

♦ International Society for Developmental Neuroscience (ISDN) 15054
Société internationale de la neuroscience du développement
SG Montréal Neurological Inst, McGill Univ, 3801 Rue University, Montréal QC H3A 2B4, Canada. T. +15143983946. Fax +15143981319.
URL: http://developmental-neuroscience.org/
History Founded 8 May 1978, Teheran (Iran Islamic Rep). Incorporated in the State of Colorado (USA), 1983. **Aims** Advance research and knowledge concerning development of the *nervous system* and support the effective application of this knowledge for the improvement of human *health.* **Structure** Executive Council; Advisory Council; Standing Committees. **Languages** English. **Staff** Voluntary. **Finance** Royalties from publication of journal. **Activities** Events/meetings; knowledge management/information dissemination; research/documentation. **Events** *Biennial General Meeting* Montréal, QC (Canada) 2021, *Biennial General Meeting* Vancouver, BC (Canada) 2020, *Biennial General Meeting* Nara (Japan) 2018, *Biennial General Meeting* Montréal, QC (Canada) 2014, *Biennial General Meeting* Mumbai (India) 2012. **Publications** *International Journal of Developmental Neuroscience.* **Members** Not a membership organization.
[2014.06.25/XD1799/v/C]

♦ International Society for Developmental Origins of Health and Disease (DOHaD) 15055
Mailing Address KCL Dept Women & Children Health, 10th Floor – North Wing, Westminster Bridge Road, London, SE1 7EH, UK. E-mail: dohadoffice@gmail.com.
URL: https://dohadsoc.org/
History Restructured when current title adopted, 2003, Brighton (UK). Former names and other names: *International Council for Research into the Fetal Origins of Adult Disease* – former (2003). **Aims** Promote research into the fetal and developmental origins of disease. **Structure** Council. **Finance** Sources: members' dues. **Activities** Advocacy/lobbying/activism; events/meetings; knowledge management/information dissemination; networking/liaising; research and development; training/education. **Events** *World Congress on Developmental Origins of Health and Disease* Vancouver, BC (Canada) 2022, *World Congress* Vancouver, BC (Canada) 2021, *World Congress* Melbourne, VIC (Australia) 2019, *World Congress* Rotterdam (Netherlands) 2017, *World Congress* Cape Town (South Africa) 2015. **Publications** *DOHaD Newsletter* (6 a year); *Journal of Developmental Origins of Health and Disease* (6 a year). **Members** Scientists in 55 countries. Membership countries not specified. **NGO Relations** Member of (1): *Global Alliance for Maternal Mental Health (GAMMH, #10208).* [2023.02.20/XE4149/v/E]

♦ International Society for Developmental Psychobiology (internationally oriented national body)
♦ International Society of Development Biologists / see International Society of Developmental Biologists (#15052)
♦ International Society for the Development of Commercial Education (inactive)

♦ International Society for the Development of Intellectual Property . 15056
Association Internationale pour le Développement de la Propriété Intellectuelle (ADALPI)
Chair Rue des Savoises 15, 1205 Geneva, Switzerland. T. +41225181167. E-mail: info@adalpi.org.
URL: https://www.adalpi.org/
History 2 Dec 2010, Bern (Switzerland). Statutes adopted by founding General Assembly. Revised: 16 Sep 2013, London; 27 Nov 2018, Geneva (Switzerland). **Aims** Secure an appropriate working environment in which creators and innovators can flourish by fostering development of Intellectual Property (IP) worldwide in accordance with ethical principles. **Structure** General Assembly; Board; Secretariat. **Languages** English, French, German, Italian. **Finance** Sources: donations; members' dues. **Activities** Awareness raising; capacity building; events/meetings; knowledge management/information dissemination; monitoring/evaluation; projects/programmes; research/documentation; training/education. Active in: Botswana, Malawi, Mexico, Peru, Switzerland.
Members Full in 6 countries:

Canada, Ireland, South Africa, Switzerland, UK, USA.
Consultative Status Consultative status granted from: *World Intellectual Property Organization (WIPO, #21593)* (Observer Status). [2022.05.25/XJ8413/**D**]

- ♦ International Society for the Development of Natural Products (internationally oriented national body)
- ♦ International Society for the Development of Organizations (inactive)
- ♦ International Society of Diabetes and Vascular Disease (inactive)
- ♦ International Society for Diagnostic Quantitative Pathology (inactive)
- ♦ International Society for Dialectology and Geolinguistics (#19477)

♦ International Society for Dialogical Science (ISDS) 15057

Hon Pres address not obtained.
Pres address not obtained.
URL: http://www.dialogicalscience.org/

History Jun 2002. Registration: Start date: Jun 2002. **Aims** Further develop *Dialogical Self Theory* and other theories which deal directly with the relationship between self and dialogue; promote cooperation in the field. **Structure** Executive Committee, including President. **Languages** English. **Staff** Voluntary. **Finance** Sources: sponsorship. **Events** *International Conference on the Dialogical Self* Barcelona (Spain) 2021, *International Conference on the Dialogical Self* Barcelona (Spain) 2020, *Biennial International Conference on the Dialogical Self* Lublin (Poland) 2016, *Biennial Conference* The Hague (Netherlands) 2014, *Biennial International Conference on the Dialogical Self* The Hague (Netherlands) 2014. **Publications** *Journal of Constructivist Psychology*.
Members Individuals in 25 countries:
Australia, Austria, Belgium, Brazil, Canada, Chile, Denmark, Estonia, France, Germany, India, Italy, Japan, Korea Rep, Netherlands, Norway, Philippines, Poland, Portugal, South Africa, Spain, Sweden, Switzerland, UK, USA.
[2022.05.10/XD9380/**D**]

♦ International Society for Diatom Research (ISDR) 15058

Sec address not obtained.
Registered Address 4 Wynwood Close, Toton, Nottingham, NG9 6NA, UK.
URL: http://www.isdr.org/

History 1985, Bristol (UK). Registration: Charity Commission, No/ID: 1054897, England and Wales. **Aims** Promote fundamental diatom research and translation of that research for public benefit throughout the world. **Structure** General Meeting (annual, during International Symposium on Diatom Research); Council; Executive Committee. **Languages** English. **Staff** Voluntary. **Finance** Sources: donations; members' dues. **Events** *Biennial Symposium* Skukuza (South Africa) 2025, *Biennial Symposium* Yamagata (Japan) 2023, *Biennial Symposium* Yamagata (Japan) 2022, *Biennial Symposium* Yamagata (Japan) 2020, *Biennial Symposium* Berlin (Germany) 2018. **Publications** *Diatom Research* – journal. Conference proceedings.
Members Honorary; Ordinary. Individuals in 52 countries and territories:
Argentina, Australia, Austria, Belarus, Belgium, Brazil, Bulgaria, Canada, Chile, China, Costa Rica, Croatia, Denmark, Egypt, Estonia, Finland, France, Germany, Greece, Hungary, India, Indonesia, Iran Islamic Rep, Ireland, Italy, Japan, Korea Rep, Lithuania, Malaysia, Mexico, Netherlands, New Zealand, Norway, Panama, Poland, Portugal, Puerto Rico, Qatar, Romania, Russia, Senegal, Slovenia, South Africa, Spain, Sweden, Switzerland, Taiwan, Thailand, Türkiye, UK, United Arab Emirates, USA. [2020/XD8773/v/**D**]

- ♦ International Society of Dietetic including all Infant and Young Children Food Industry / see International Special Dietary Food Industries (#15576)

♦ International Society of Differentiation (ISD) 15059

Société internationale de différenciation
Admin Officer PO Box 10534, St Paul MN 55110, USA. Fax +18608384242. E-mail: office@isdifferentiation.org.
URL: http://www.isdifferentiation.org/

History 1974, following recommendations 1971, Nice (France), of 1st International Conference. Registered in accordance with French law, 19 Jun 1975. Incorporated in the State of Minnesota (USA), 10 Mar 1986. **Aims** Promote research on *biological* differentiation of normal and *neoplastic* cells and facilitate exchange of information among persons interested in problems of biological differentiation and diversification; stress the importance of interdisciplinary cooperation. **Structure** Conference (every 2 years); Member Business Meeting; Board of Directors. **Languages** English. **Staff** 1.00 FTE, paid. **Finance** Sources: donations; members' dues. Other sources: bequests. Annual budget: 15,000 USD. **Events** *Conference* Valletta (Malta) 2022, *Conference* Valletta (Malta) 2020, *Conference* Sydney, NSW (Australia) 2018, *Conference* Boston, MA (USA) 2016, *Conference* London (UK) 2014. **Publications** *Differentiation* (10 a year). Conference proceedings.
Members Active; Student; Honorary; Emeritus; Individuals in 32 countries:
Argentina, Australia, Austria, Belgium, Canada, China, Finland, France, Germany, Greece, Hungary, India, Israel, Italy, Japan, Korea Rep, Mexico, Netherlands, Nigeria, Norway, Poland, Portugal, Russia, South Africa, Spain, Sweden, Switzerland, Taiwan, Türkiye, UK, United Arab Emirates, USA.
Also in the West Indies (countries not specified). [2018/XD4562/v/**C**]

♦ International Society for Digestive Surgery (ISDS) 15060

Admin Office c/o ISS-SIC, Seltisbergerstrasse 16, 4419 Lupsingen BL, Switzerland. T. +41618159666. Fax +41618114775. E-mail: surgery@iss-sic.com.
SG address not obtained.
Treas Gen address not obtained.
URL: http://www.cicd-isds.org/

History 29 Sep 1969, Rome (Italy), as *Collegium Internationale Chirurgiae Digestivae (CICD)*. Statutes modified 9 Jun 1972, Strasbourg (France); 4 Sep 1986, Jerusalem (Israel); 6 Nov 1990, Delhi (India); 18 Sep 1998, Madrid (Spain); 8 Sep 2000, Hamburg (Germany); 10 Dec 2004, Yokohama (Japan). Present name adopted 1998. Registered in the State of Wisconsin (USA). **Aims** Promote at an international level the study of surgery of the *digestive system*; bring before national and international societies problems of a surgical nature connected with diseases of the digestive system; recommend standards for the education of digestive surgeons. **Structure** General Assembly (at Congress); Executive Committee. **Languages** English. **Finance** Sources: members' dues. **Events** *Asia Pacific Digestive Week* Kuala Lumpur (Malaysia) 2021, *Asia Pacific Digestive Week* Kuala Lumpur (Malaysia) 2020, *Asia Pacific Digestive Week* Kolkata (India) 2019, *Asia Pacific Digestive Week* Seoul (Korea Rep) 2018, *Asia Pacific Digestive Week* Hong Kong (Hong Kong) 2017. **Publications** *World Journal of Surgery* (12 a year); *Digestive Surgery* (6 a year).
Members Individuals: Associate; Corresponding and Honorary, totalling over 2,300 members. Members in 101 countries and territories:
Albania, Algeria, Argentina, Armenia, Australia, Austria, Azerbaijan, Bahrain, Bangladesh, Belgium, Bosnia-Herzegovina, Botswana, Brazil, Bulgaria, Cameroon, Canada, Chile, Colombia, Croatia, Cuba, Cyprus, Czechia, Denmark, Ecuador, Egypt, Estonia, Finland, Georgia, Germany, Ghana, Greece, Guatemala, Hong Kong, Hungary, Iceland, India, Indonesia, Iran Islamic Rep, Iraq, Ireland, Israel, Italy, Japan, Jordan, Kazakhstan, Kenya, Korea Rep, Kuwait, Latvia, Lebanon, Lithuania, Luxembourg, Malaysia, Maldives, Malta, Mexico, Moldova, Mozambique, Myanmar, Namibia, Netherlands, New Zealand, Nigeria, North Macedonia, Norway, Oman, Panama, Peru, Philippines, Poland, Portugal, Qatar, Romania, Russia, Saudi Arabia, Serbia, Singapore, Slovakia, Slovenia, South Africa, Spain, Sri Lanka, Sudan, Sweden, Switzerland, Taiwan, Tajikistan, Thailand, Timor-Leste, Trinidad-Tobago, Tunisia, Türkiye, UK, Ukraine, United Arab Emirates, Uruguay, USA, Uzbekistan, Venezuela, Vietnam, Yemen.
NGO Relations Speciality member of: *International Federation of Surgical Colleges (IFSC, #13560)*. Member of: *Asian Pacific Digestive Week Federation (APDWF, #01609)*. Instrumental in setting up: *European Federation – International Society for Digestive Surgery (EFISDS, #07148)*. [2019.03.05/XC4270/**B**]

♦ International Society for Digital Earth (ISDE) 15061

SG No 9 Dengzhuang South Rd, Haidian District, 100094 Beijing, China. T. +861082178196. Fax +861082178916. E-mail: wcl@aircas.ac.cn.
Exec Dir address not obtained. E-mail: isde@radi.ac.cn.
URL: http://www.digitalearth-isde.org/

History 21 May 2006, Beijing (China). Founded by Chinese Academy of Sciences. Registration: China. **Aims** Provide a platform for understanding evolving society-beneficial Digital Earth technologies, current and newly emerging; revise the Digital Earth Vision in light of new developments. **Structure** Bureau; Council; Secretariat; National and Regional Chapters. **Languages** English. **Staff** 5.00 FTE, paid. **Finance** Sources: meeting proceeds; members' dues; revenue from activities/projects. Supported by: Aerospace Information Research Institute, Chinese Academy of Sciences; Bureau of International Cooperation, Chinese Academy of Sciences. **Activities** Events/meetings; knowledge management/information dissemination; training/education. **Events** *Digital Earth Summit* Chennai (India) 2022, *International Symposium on Digital Earth (ISDE)* Salzburg (Austria) 2021, *Digital Earth Summit* 2020, *Biennial Symposium* Florence (Italy) 2019, *Digital Earth Summit* El Jadida (Morocco) 2018. **Publications** *Big Earth Data*; *International Journal of Digital Earth*. *Manual of Digital Earth* (1st ed 2019) by Prof Huadong Guo and Prof Michael F Goodchild et al in English – Official Publication of the International Society for Digital Earth. **Members** Corporate; Individual. Membership countries not specified.
IGO Relations Member of (3): *Asia-Oceania GEOSS (AOGEOSS, #01800)*; *Group on Earth Observations (GEO, #10735)*; UN-GGIM Geospatial Societies (UN-GGIM GS). **NGO Relations** Member of (1): International Science Council. [2022.05.11/XM2094/**D**]

♦ International Society for Digital Health (ISDH) 15062

Pres c/o School of Public Health, Room 202, Prince of Wales Hospital, Shatin, Hong Kong.
URL: https://www.theisdh.org/

Aims Encourage interdisciplinary research strategies with innovative technology for excellence in healthcare practices. **Structure** Executive Committee; Advisory Committee. **Activities** Events/meetings; research/documentation. **Events** *International Symposium on Digital Health* 2021, *International Symposium on Digital Health* 2020, *International Symposium on Digital Health* Hong Kong (Hong Kong) 2019. **NGO Relations** Partner of: *Worldwide Universities Network (WUN)*. [2021/AA0098/**C**]

♦ International Society for Digital Imaging of the Skin (ISDIS) 15063

Sec-Treas University Dermatology Center PC, 3500 W Purdue Ave, Muncie IN 47304, USA. T. +17657476090.
URL: http://www.isdis.net/index.php/about

History 1992. **Aims** Familiarize members with new and evolving digital skin imaging technologies relevant to clinical practice. **Activities** Events/meetings. **Events** *Annual meeting* San Francisco, CA (USA) 2009, *Annual meeting* San Antonio, TX (USA) 2008, *Joint meeting / Joint Meeting ISDIS-ISBS / Meeting* Seoul (Korea Rep) 2008, *Annual meeting* Washington, DC (USA) 2007, *Annual meeting* San Francisco, CA (USA) 2006. **Publications** *Skin Research and Technology* (periodical). Newsletter. **NGO Relations** *International Confocal Working Group (ICWG)*; *International Society for Biophysics and Imaging of Skin (ISBS, #14971)*. [2016/XD8654/**D**]

- ♦ International Society of Disaster Medicine (inactive)

♦ International Society for Diseases of the Esophagus (ISDE) 15064

Société internationale d'étude des maladies de l'oesophage
Contact Ste 710, 1201 W Pender St, Vancouver BC V6E 2V2, Canada. T. +16046383862. Fax +16046811049. E-mail: info@isde.net.
URL: http://www.isde.net/

History 1979, Tokyo (Japan). Secretariat located in Tokyo (Japan), 1979-2004; relocated to Los Angeles CA (USA), 2004-2010; and since 2010 in Vancouver BC (Canada). **Aims** Promote exchange of scientific and medical knowledge among specialists in the field; maintain interchange with organizations and industries; encourage basic and clinical research in fields related to the esophagus. **Structure** Board of Directors; Executive Committee; Sub-Committees. **Languages** English. **Staff** 1.00 FTE, paid. **Finance** Sources: contributions; members' dues. **Activities** Events/meetings; training/education. **Events** *World Congress* Brisbane, QLD (Australia) 2025, *World Congress* 2024, *World Congress* Toronto, ON (Canada) 2023, *World Congress* Tokyo (Japan) 2022, *World Congress* Vancouver, BC (Canada) 2021. **Publications** *Diseases of the Esophagus* (12 a year) – journal.
Members Medical researchers in 50 countries and territories:
Argentina, Australia, Austria, Belgium, Brazil, Canada, Chile, China, Croatia, Czechia, Denmark, Finland, France, Germany, Greece, Hong Kong, Hungary, India, Indonesia, Iran Islamic Rep, Ireland, Israel, Italy, Japan, Jordan, Korea Rep, Luxembourg, Mexico, Montenegro, Netherlands, New Zealand, Norway, Poland, Portugal, Romania, Russia, Serbia, South Africa, Spain, Sudan, Sweden, Switzerland, Taiwan, Thailand, Türkiye, UK, Ukraine, United Arab Emirates, Uruguay, USA.
[2022.02.07/XD8641/v/**C**]

- ♦ International Society of Divine Love / see Jagadguru Kripalu Parishat (#16086)

♦ International Society of Doctors for the Environment (ISDE) 15065

Internationale Gesellschaft von Ärzten für den Umweltschutz
Pres Ärztinnen une Ärzte für Umweltschutz, Westquai 2, Postfach 620, 4019 Basel BS, Switzerland. T. +41613224949. E-mail: info@isde.org.
URL: http://www.isde.org/

History 25 Nov 1990, Cortona (Italy). Statutes last modified, 12 Sep 2001, Washington DC (USA). **Aims** As a global NGO of medical doctors, scientists and health professionals, focus on the links between human health and environmental factors. **Structure** General Assembly (every 2 years); Directing Board; Executive Committee; Scientific Office; Secretariat. **Languages** English. **Staff** Temporary. **Finance** Sources: grants; members' dues; private foundations; revenue from activities/projects. **Activities** Awareness raising; capacity building; research/documentation; training/education. **Events** *International Conference on Children's Environment and Health* Tashkent (Uzbekistan) 2023, *Biennial General Assembly* Vienna (Austria) 2019, *General Assembly* Geneva (Switzerland) 2017, *General Assembly* Arezzo (Italy) 2015, *Meeting* Arezzo (Italy) 2014. **Publications** *ISDE Newsletter* – electronic.
Members Organizations in 40 countries and territories:
Albania, Algeria, Argentina, Australia, Austria, Belgium, Benin, Canada, Côte d'Ivoire, Croatia, Denmark, Ecuador, Egypt, France, Georgia, Germany, Hong Kong, Hungary, Indonesia, Ireland, Italy, Kenya, Latvia, Madagascar, Malta, Moldova, Montenegro, Netherlands, Nigeria, North Macedonia, Pakistan, Serbia, Slovenia, Sweden, Switzerland, Türkiye, UK, Ukraine, USA, Uzbekistan.
Consultative Status Consultative status granted from: *ECOSOC (#05331)* (Special); *WHO (#20950)* (Official Relations). **IGO Relations** Accredited by (1): *United Nations Framework Convention on Climate Change – Secretariat (UNFCCC, #20564)*. **NGO Relations** Member of (6): *Climate Action Network (CAN, #03999)*; *European ECO Forum (#06955)*; *GEF CSO Network (GCN, #10087)*; *Health and Environment Alliance (HEAL, #10879)*; *Health Care Without Harm (HCWH, #10875)*; *International Court of the Environment Foundation (ICEF, #13097)*. Cooperates with (5): *European Environmental Bureau (EEB, #06996)*; *INTERASMA (#11457)*; *International Physicians for the Prevention of Nuclear War (IPPNW, #14578)*; *World Organization of Family Doctors (WONCA, #21690)*; *World Wide Fund for Nature (WWF, #21922)*. Instrumental in setting up (2): *International Network on Children's Health, Environment and Safety (INCHES, #14240)*; *Scuola Internazionale Ambiente Salute e Sviluppo Sostenibile (SIASS)*. [2022/XC5650/v/**C**]

♦ International Society of Drug Bulletins (ISDB) 15066

Pres Vredenburgplein 40, 3511 WH Utrecht, Netherlands. E-mail: president@isdbweb.org.
URL: http://www.isdbweb.org/

History Aug 1986. Founded with the support of *WHO (#20950)*. **Aims** Encourage and further the development of independent drug bulletins; promote international exchange of good quality information concerning drugs and *therapeutics*; engage in whatever ancillary activities the Committee considers desirable to further these primary purposes. **Structure** General Assembly (every 3 years); Committee; Secretariat. **Languages** English. **Staff** Voluntary. **Finance** Sources: members' dues. Annual budget: 40,000 EUR. **Activities** Knowledge management/information dissemination; research/documentation; standards/guidelines. **Events** *General assembly and workshop* Paris (France) 2019, *General assembly and workshop* Pamplona (Spain) 2015, *General assembly and workshop* Vancouver, BC (Canada) 2012, *General assembly and workshop* Matagalpa (Nicaragua) 2008, *General assembly and workshop* Melbourne, VIC (Australia) 2005. **Publications** *ISDB Newsletter*.
Members Full; Associate. Full in 28 countries:
Australia, Austria, Bangladesh, Belgium, Brazil, Burkina Faso, Canada, Croatia, Czechia, France, Germany, India, Israel, Italy, Japan, Latvia, Moldova, Nepal, Netherlands, New Zealand, Nicaragua, Philippines, Slovenia, Spain, Sri Lanka, Switzerland, UK, USA.
Associate in 20 countries:
Argentina, Armenia, Australia, Colombia, Costa Rica, Cuba, Eritrea, Estonia, France, Georgia, Germany, India, Italy, Madagascar, Malaysia, Nepal, Netherlands, Peru, Spain, Sri Lanka.
Included in the above, 2 organizations listed in this Yearbook:
HAI – Asia-Pacific (HAIAP, #10852); *Health Action International – Europe Association (HAI Europe, #10869)*.
NGO Relations Member of (1): *European Alliance for Responsible R and D and Affordable Medicines (#05879)*.
[2019.02.12/XM6410/**C**]

♦ International Society of Dynamic Games (ISDG) 15067

Pres HEC Montréal, 3000 chemin de la Côte-Sainte-Catherine, Montréal QC H3T 2A7, Canada.
URL: http://www.isdg-site.org/

History 9 Aug 1990, Helsinki (Finland). **Aims** Promote interaction among researchers in the theory and applications of dynamic games; facilitate dissemination of information; enhance the visibility of dynamic games research and its potential applications. **Structure** Executive Board of 12 members. Officers: President; Vice-President; Secretary; Treasurer; Liaison. **Finance** Members' dues. **Activities** Sponsorship of conferences, symposia and workshops; publications. **Events** *Biennial Symposium* Porto (Portugal) 2022, *International Conference on Game Theory and Management* St Petersburg (Russia) 2021, *Biennial Symposium* Porto (Portugal) 2020, *Workshop* St Petersburg (Russia) 2019, *Biennial Symposium* Grenoble (France) 2018. **Publications** *International Game Theory Review. Annals of Dynamic Games.* Electronic newsletter.
[2014/XF3835/F]

♦ International Society for Dynamics of the Upper Urinary Tract (inactive)

♦ International Society on Early Intervention (ISEI) 15068

Contact CHDD, Box 357920, Univ of Washington, Seattle WA 98195-7920, USA. T. +12065432832. Fax +12065433417. E-mail: isei@uw.edu.
URL: https://www.isei.washington.edu/

Aims Provide a framework and forum for professionals worldwide to communicate about advances in the field of early intervention support for *children* with developmental *disabilities* or delays and their *families.* **Structure** Coordinating Committee, comprising Chair and 17 members. **Events** *Joint Conference* Chicago, IL (USA) 2022, *Conference* Sydney, NSW (Australia) 2019, *Children's rights and early intervention* Stockholm (Sweden) 2016, *Early intervention to promote child development and mental health* St Petersburg (Russia) 2013, *Conference* New York, NY (USA) 2011. **Publications** *Brookes Early Intervention Book Series.* Articles.
Members Individuals in 92 countries and territories:
Australia, Austria, Azerbaijan, Bahamas, Bangladesh, Belgium, Bosnia-Herzegovina, Botswana, Brazil, Brunei Darussalam, Bulgaria, Burundi, Canada, Chile, China, Croatia, Cuba, Curaçao, Cyprus, Czechia, Denmark, Ecuador, Egypt, Estonia, Ethiopia, Finland, France, Germany, Ghana, Greece, Hungary, Iceland, India, Indonesia, Iran Islamic Rep, Ireland, Israel, Italy, Jamaica, Japan, Jordan, Kenya, Korea Rep, Laos, Latvia, Lebanon, Lithuania, Luxembourg, Malaysia, Malta, Mauritius, Mexico, Moldova, Mozambique, Nepal, Netherlands, New Zealand, Nigeria, North Macedonia, Norway, Oman, Pakistan, Panama, Peru, Philippines, Poland, Portugal, Puerto Rico, Qatar, Romania, Russia, Saudi Arabia, Serbia, Singapore, Slovakia, Slovenia, South Africa, Spain, Sweden, Switzerland, Syrian AR, Taiwan, Tanzania UR, Thailand, Türkiye, Uganda, UK, Ukraine, United Arab Emirates, USA, Vietnam, Zambia.
[2021/XJ2126/B]

♦ International Society of Ecoacoustics (unconfirmed)

♦ International Society for Ecological Economics (ISEE) 15069

Exec Dir 15 River St, Ste 204, Boston MA 02108, USA. E-mail: secretariat@isecoeco.org.
URL: http://www.isecoeco.org/

History 1988. **Aims** Advance understanding of the relationships among ecological, social and economic systems and the application of this understanding to the mutual *well-being* of *nature* and people, especially that of the most *vulnerable,* including future generations. **Structure** Board of Directors, comprising President, President-Elect, Past President, Secretary-Treasurer and 2 members. Committees (3): Meetings; Education; Publications. **Languages** English. **Staff** 1.00 FTE, paid. **Finance** Sources: grants; members' dues. Other sources: journal royalties. **Activities** Events/meetings; networking/liaising; training/education. **Events** *Biennial Conference* Manchester (UK) 2021, *Biennial Conference* Manchester (UK) 2020, *Biennial Conference* Puebla (Mexico) 2018, *Biennial Conference* Washington, DC (USA) 2016, *Biennial Conference* Reykjavik (Iceland) 2014. **Publications** *Ecological Economics* (12 a year) – journal. *Ecological Economics Working Papers Series. The Local Politics of Global Sustainability* (2000); *Natural Capital and Human Economic Survival* (2nd ed 1999); *An Introduction to Ecological Economics* (1997). Directory of members; conference papers; external working papers.
Members Individual Full; Associate. Institutional. Members (over 1,500) in 63 countries and territories:
Argentina, Australia, Austria, Barbados, Belgium, Belize, Bolivia, Botswana, Brazil, Canada, Chile, China, Colombia, Costa Rica, Croatia, Czechia, Denmark, Ecuador, Finland, France, Georgia, Germany, Greece, Hungary, India, Indonesia, Ireland, Italy, Japan, Kazakhstan, Korea Rep, Lithuania, Malaysia, Mexico, Namibia, Nepal, Netherlands, New Zealand, Norway, Papua New Guinea, Peru, Philippines, Poland, Portugal, Romania, Russia, Singapore, Slovakia, South Africa, Spain, Sri Lanka, Sweden, Switzerland, Taiwan, Tanzania UR, Tunisia, Türkiye, UK, Uruguay, USA, Zambia, Zimbabwe.
Regional societies in 9 countries:
Argentina, Australia, Brazil, India, Korea Rep, New Zealand, Peru, Russia, USA.
Regional society, listed in this Yearbook:
European Society for Ecological Economics (ESEE, #08587).
NGO Relations Member of: *International Science Council (ISC, #14796).* Also links with a number of national organizations active in the field.
[2019/XC0003/y/B]

♦ International Society of Ecological Modelling (ISEM) 15070

Société internationale pour le modèle écologique
SG PMB 255, 550 M Ritchie Highway, Severna Park MD 21146, USA.
Main: http://www.isemworld.org/

History 1975, Copenhagen (Denmark). **Aims** Promote exchange of scientific *knowledge;* enhance creation and application of *ecological* and *environmental* models. **Structure** Regional Chapters (5): North America; Europe; Asia; AustralAsia; Africa. **Languages** English. **Staff** 1.50 FTE, voluntary. **Finance** Annual budget: 5,000 USD. **Activities** Awards/prizes/competitions; events/meetings; knowledge management/information dissemination. **Events** *Global Conference* Scarborough, ON (Canada) 2023, *Global Conference* Scarborough, ON (Canada) 2022, *Global Conference* Salzburg (Austria) 2019, *Global Conference* Jeju (Korea Rep) 2017, *Global Conference* Towson, MD (USA) 2016. **Publications** *ECOMOD* (4 a year) – newsletter; *Ecological Modelling* – journal. Books. **Information Services** *Environmental Data and Ecological Parameters Data Base (ECOBAS).*
Members Institutional; Individuals, in 66 countries and territories:
Algeria, Argentina, Australia, Austria, Bahamas, Bangladesh, Belgium, Brazil, Bulgaria, Canada, Chile, China, Colombia, Czechia, Denmark, Egypt, Finland, France, Germany, Greece, Hong Kong, Hungary, India, Indonesia, Iran Islamic Rep, Iraq, Ireland, Israel, Italy, Jamaica, Japan, Kenya, Korea Rep, Kuwait, Luxembourg, Malaysia, Mexico, Morocco, Netherlands, New Zealand, Nigeria, Norway, Pakistan, Papua New Guinea, Peru, Philippines, Poland, Portugal, Qatar, Romania, Russia, Serbia, Singapore, South Africa, Spain, Sri Lanka, Sweden, Switzerland, Taiwan, Thailand, Türkiye, Uganda, UK, Uruguay, USA, Venezuela.
[2022.04.20/XC5215/F]

♦ International Society for Ecological Psychology (ISEP) 15071

Sec Psychology Dept ASU, PO Box 871104, Tempe AZ 85287-1104, USA.
URL: https://commons.trincoll.edu/isep/

History 1981. **Aims** Promote science of ecological psychology. **Structure** Board of Directors of 15 members. **Languages** English. **Finance** Members' dues. **Activities** Organizes the biennial *International Conference on Perception and Action (ICPA).* **Events** *Biennial Conference* Groningen (Netherlands) 2019, *Biennial Conference* Seoul (Korea Rep) 2017, *Biennial Conference* Minneapolis, MN (USA) 2015, *North American Meeting* Oxford, OH (USA) 2014, *Biennial Conference* Estoril (Portugal) 2013. **Publications** *Ecological Psychology* (4 a year). *Resources for Ecological Psychology.*
Members Individuals in 26 countries:
Australia, Brazil, Canada, China, Denmark, France, Germany, Hong Kong, Hungary, India, Ireland, Israel, Italy, Japan, Korea Rep, Netherlands, New Zealand, Norway, Poland, Portugal, Russia, Serbia, Sweden, Switzerland, UK, USA.
Societies in 2 countries:
Germany, USA.
[2014/XD6622/D]

♦ International Society for Ecology and Culture / see Local Futures (#16506)

♦ International Society for Economics and Social Sciences of Animal Health (ISESSAH) 15072

Contact address not obtained. E-mail: info@isessah.com.
URL: http://www.isessah.com/

History Inaugural meeting Mar 2017, Aviemore (UK). **Aims** Improve animal health and welfare policies, programme and projects through more nuanced use of concepts and tools available in economics and social science disciplines. **Structure** Management Committee; Scientific Committee. **Activities** Events/meetings. **Events** *Conference* Copenhagen (Denmark) 2020, *Conference* Atlanta, GA (USA) 2019, *Conference* Montpellier (France) 2018, *Conference* Aviemore (UK) 2017.
[2020/XM7069/C]

♦ International Society of Ecotoxicology and Environmental Safety (SECOTOX) 15073

Société internationale d'écotoxicologie et de protection de l'environnement
Sec German Research Ctr for Environmental Health, PO Box 1129, 85758 Neuherberg, Germany.
URL: http://www.helmholtz-muenchen.de/secotox/

History 1972, as a subsidiary body associated with *International Academy of Environmental Safety (IAES).* Now a separate organization. Registered in accordance with German law. **Aims** Bring together its members and other interested persons from all aspects of science and the general public and promote a scientific cooperation in order to evaluate the current problems of environmental quality and safety and to investigate solutions to these problems on a national, regional and world-wide basis; elaborate and publish suggestions, including the necessary data, in order to enable the regulatory agencies of various countries to make proper decisions as to evaluation the safety of chemicals, toxic and physical agents in the total environment; make recommendations to ensure environmental safety and quality on a world-wide basis; make recommendations concerning ecotoxicological education and training. **Structure** Assembly (at least annually). Council, comprising President, Past President, First Vice-President (President-Elect), Secretary, Treasurer and at least 4 members. Regional sections (3): Asian Region; Central and Eastern European Region (CEERS-SECOTOX); Mediterranean Region. **Languages** English. **Finance** Members' dues (annual). **Events** *International Conference on Environmental Management, Engineering, Planning and Economics* Mykonos (Greece) 2013, *International conference on environmental management, engineering, planning and economics* Mykonos (Greece) 2009, *International symposium on green chemistry for environment and health* Munich (Germany) 2008, *International conference on environmental management, engineering, planning and economics* Skiathos Is (Greece) 2007, *World congress* Brno (Czech Rep) 2005. **Publications** *Ecotoxicology and Environmental Safety* – journal; *Fresenius Environmental Bulletin* – journal.
Members Full people from science, politics, industry and other scientific disciplines. Sustaining persons; legal entities; industrial firms; public corporations; governmental, academic and international institutions. Honorary. Members in (40) countries:
Australia, Austria, Belgium, Bulgaria, Canada, Croatia, Cyprus, Czechia, Denmark, Estonia, Finland, France, Germany, Greece, Hungary, India, Indonesia, Israel, Italy, Japan, Latvia, Lithuania, Malaysia, Monaco, Morocco, Netherlands, Norway, Poland, Portugal, Russia, Slovakia, South Africa, Spain, Sweden, Switzerland, Türkiye, UK, Ukraine, USA, Vietnam.
[2009.08.06/XD9742/D]

♦ International Society for ECT and Neurostimulation (internationally oriented national body)
♦ International Society for Educational Biography (internationally oriented national body)
♦ International Society of Educational Planners / see International Society for Educational Planning
♦ International Society for Educational Planning (internationally oriented national body)

♦ International Society for Education through Art (INSEA) 15074

Société Internationale pour l'Education à travers l'Art – Sociedad Internacional de la Educación por el Arte
Office Quinta da Cruz, Estrada de São Salvador, 3510-784 Viseu, Portugal. E-mail: secretary.insea@gmail.com – treasurer.insea@gmail.com – president.insea@gmail.com.
URL: http://www.insea.org/

History 1954, Bristol (UK). Founded following a meeting of experts on teaching visual arts in general education, convened by Unesco. Constitution and Rules revised: Aug 1957; Aug 1966; 1982; 1997; 2008; 2014; 2019. Merged in 1966 with *Fédération internationale pour l'éducation artistique (FEA, inactive),* set up in 1900, Paris (France). Former names and other names: *Société internationale pour l'éducation artistique* – former; *Sociedad Internacional para la Educación a través del Arte* – former; *Internationaler Kunsterzieher-Verband* – former. **Aims** Advance education through visual arts. **Structure** General Assembly (every 2 years); World Council; Executive Board; Regional Councils. **Languages** English. **Staff** 6.00 FTE, voluntary. **Finance** Sources: members' dues. **Activities** Events/meetings. **Events** *World Congress* Canakkale (Türkiye) 2023, *INSEA World Forum* 2022, *European Regional Congress* Baeza (Spain) 2021, *World Congress* Vancouver, BC (Canada) 2019, *European Regional Congress* Helsinki (Finland) 2018. **Publications** *INSEA E-Newsletter* (12 a year); *IMAG – ART Education VISUAL Journal* (3 a year); *International Journal of Education Through Art* (3 a year). Books; congress proceedings; occasional papers. **Members** Professional (1,184); Institutional (17); Affiliated (40). Professional members in 72 countries. Membership countries not specified. **Consultative Status** Consultative status granted from: *UNESCO (#20322)* (Consultative Status). **NGO Relations** Member of (1): *World Alliance for Arts Education (WAAE, #21078).* Supports (1): *European Network for Visual Literacy (ENViL, #08031).* Links with national and regional arts education organizations.
[2023/XB2482/v/B]

♦ International Society of Educators in Physiotherapy (no recent information)

♦ International Society for Efficiency and Productivity Analysis (ISEAPA) 15075

Admin Dir 6100 Main St, MS-22, Economics Dept, Houston TX 77005-1892, USA.
URL: https://iseapa.org/

History Registration: 501(c)3, USA. **Aims** Promote the study of productivity and efficiency; enhance the significance of contributions to such study by scholars and practitioners. **Structure** Board; Executive Board. **Finance** Sources: members' dues. **Publications** *Journal of Productivity Analysis (JPA).*
[2023/AA3119/C]

♦ International Society for Eighteenth-Century Studies (ISECS) 15076

Société internationale d'étude du dix-huitième siècle (SIEDS)
Pres IAECS/AIEDS, Centre national de la recherche scientifique, 1 rue Victor Cousin, 75005 Paris, France. E-mail: admin@isecs.org – president@isecs.org.
URL: http://www.isecs.org/

History 1967, St Andrews (UK). Current Constitution adopted 27 Aug 1979, Pisa (Italy). Constitution revised July 1983, Brussels (Belgium); July 1999, Dublin (Ireland); July 2003, Los Angeles CA (USA); July 2007, Montpellier (France). **Aims** Promote growth, development and coordination of studies and research relating to the 18th century in all aspects of its cultural *heritage* – historical, philosophical, ideological, religious, linguistic, literary, scientific, artistic, juridical – in all countries. **Structure** General Meeting and Congress (every 4 years); Executive Committee; Board. Secretariat is managed jointly by the ISECS Communications Secretary and the International Association for Eighteenth-Century Studies (IAECS). **Languages** English, French. **Staff** Voluntary. **Finance** Sources: members' dues. **Activities** Events/meetings; financial and/or material support; knowledge management/information dissemination; networking/liaising. **Events** *Quadrennial Congress* Rome (Italy) 2023, *Quadrennial Congress* Edinburgh (UK) 2019, *Executive Committee Meeting* Rotterdam (Netherlands) 2015, *Quadrennial Congress* Rotterdam (Netherlands) 2015, *Executive Committee Meeting* Rotterdam (Netherlands) 2013. **Publications** *International Studies on the Enlightenment. International Directory of Eighteenth-Century Studies/Répertoire international des dix-huitiémistes* (1983, 1987, 1991, 1995, 1999, 2003) – published by Voltaire Foundation. Online directory.
Members National societies (33) representing 35 countries:
Argentina, Australia, Austria, Belgium, Brazil, Bulgaria, Canada, Czechia, Denmark, Finland, France, Germany, Greece, Hungary, Iceland, India, Ireland, Italy, Japan, Korea Rep, Netherlands, New Zealand, Norway, Poland, Portugal, Romania, Russia, Singapore, Slovenia, Spain, Sweden, Switzerland, Tunisia, UK, USA.
Included in the above, 1 organization listed in this Yearbook:
Australasian and Pacific Society for Eighteenth-Century Studies (APSECS, inactive).
[2021.09.01/XD9928/C]

♦ International Society for Electrical Bio-Impedance (ISEBI) 15077

Pres Dept of Biomedical Engineering, Kyung Hee Univ, 26 Kyungheedae-ro, Seoul 02447, Korea Rep.
Sec address not obtained.
Vice-Pres Universitat Politècnica de Catalunya, Centre de Recerca Enginyeria Biomèdica CREB, Jordi Girona, 1-3 Edifici C4, 08034 Barcelona, Spain.
URL: http://www.isebi.org/

History Sep 2004. Founded by *International Committee for Promotion of Research in Bio-Impedance (ICPRBI, #12797).* **Aims** Promote scientific research on the electrical properties of biomaterials and the development, use and understanding of impedance methods in medicine, biology and biotechnology. **Structure** General Assembly; Executive Committee. **Languages** English. **Events** *International Conference on Biomedical Applications of Electrical Impedance Tomography* Seoul (Korea Rep) 2022, *International Conference on Electrical Bio-Impedance* Seoul (Korea Rep) 2022, *International Conference on Electrical Bio-Impedance* Joinville (Brazil) 2019, *International Conference on Electrical Bio-Impedance* Stockholm (Sweden) 2016. **Publications** *Selected Papers by HP Schwan* (2001); *IFMBE Proceedings.*

Members Members in 33 countries:
Australia, Austria, Belgium, Brazil, China, Colombia, Croatia, Estonia, Finland, France, Germany, India, Iran Islamic Rep, Iraq, Israel, Italy, Japan, Jordan, Korea Rep, Malaysia, Mexico, Netherlands, North Macedonia, Norway, Poland, Romania, Russia, Slovenia, Spain, Sweden, Türkiye, UK, USA. [2020.06.24/XJ0876/**D**]

♦ International Society of Electrocardiology (ISE) 15078

Sec Intl Laser Cntr, Ilkovicova 3, 812 19 Bratislava, Slovakia. T. +421265421575. Fax +421265423244.
URL: http://electrocardiology.org/

History 1966, as *International Council on Electrocardiology.* Reconstituted under present title, 1993. **Aims** Promote advancement of science of electrocardiology. **Structure** General Meeting (annual, at International Congress on Electrocardiology). Council (meets annually) of up to 30 members, including Executive Committee, comprising President, President-Elect, Secretary/Treasurer, Past-President and 3 members of Council. Working Groups (6): Body Surface Potential Mapping; Arrhythmias; Modelling; Electrophysiology; Standards for Core ECG; Laboratories. Secretariat. **Languages** English. **Staff** Voluntary. **Finance** Members' dues (life): US$ 25. **Events** *International Congress of Electrocardiology (ICE)* Zakopane (Poland) 2021, *Annual Congress* Comandatuba Is (Brazil) 2015, *Annual Congress* Bratislava (Slovakia) 2014, *Annual Congress* Kingston, ON (Canada) 2011, *General Meeting* Kingston, ON (Canada) 2011. **Publications** *Journal of Electrocardiology.*
Members Doctors and research workers in the field of cardiovascular physiology and related fields. Members in 33 countries and territories:
Austria, Belgium, Brazil, Canada, China, Cuba, Czechia, Finland, France, Germany, Greece, Hungary, Iran Islamic Rep, Israel, Italy, Japan, Lithuania, Netherlands, New Zealand, Norway, Philippines, Poland, Portugal, Romania, Russia, Slovakia, Spain, Sweden, Switzerland, Taiwan, Türkiye, UK, USA. [2014/XD9383/v/**C**]

♦ International Society of Electrochemistry (ISE) 15079

Main Office Chemin de Closelet 2, 1006 Lausanne VD, Switzerland. Fax +41216483975. E-mail: info@ise-online.org.
URL: http://www.ise-online.org/

History 28 Mar 1949, Brussels (Belgium). Statutes modified: 1955; 1959; 1965; and Oct 1971. Former names and other names: *International Committee of Electro-Chemical Thermodynamics and Kinetics* – former (28 Mar 1949 to Oct 1971); *Comité international de thermodynamique et de cinétique électrochimiques (CITCE)* – former (28 Mar 1949 to Oct 1971). **Aims** Advance electrochemical science and technology; disseminate scientific and technical knowledge; promote international cooperation in electrochemistry; maintain a high professional standard among members. **Structure** General Meeting. Council, comprising National/Regional Secretaries and officers of the 8 Scientific Divisions. Executive Committee. ISE Office in Switzerland. **Languages** English. **Staff** 1.00 FTE, paid. **Finance** Sources: members' dues.
Activities Organizes annual scientific and technological congress and occasional specialised meetings. Scientific and technological activities organized in 8 divisions, each with a chairperson and 2 assistant chairpersons of international repute: Interfacial Electrochemistry; Electronically and Ionically Conducting Phases; Analytical Electrochemistry; Molecular Electrochemistry; Electrochemical Energy Conversion; Corrosion, Electrodeposition and Surface Treatment; Industrial Electrochemistry and Electrochemical Engineering; Bioelectrochemistry.
Makes regular awards for outstanding contributions to electrochemical science and technology: Pergamon Electrochimica Acta Gold Medal; Tajima Prize; Prix Jacques Tacussel; Oronzio de Nora Foundation Young Author Prize; Frumkin Memorial Medal; Hans-Jürgen-Engell Prize; Klaus-Jürgen Vetter Prize for Electrochemical Kinetics; Oronzio de Nora Foundation Prize of ISE on Electrochemical Energy Conversion; Oronzio de Nora Foundation Prize of ISE on Electrochemical Technology and Engineering.
Events *Annual Meeting* Mainz (Germany) 2025, *Meeting* Baveno (Italy) 2024, *Meeting* Manchester (UK) 2024, *Annual Meeting* Montréal, QC (Canada) 2024, *Meeting* Sibenik (Croatia) 2024. **Publications** *Electrochimica Acta* (24 a year).
Members Individual (about 1,400); Corporate (about 75), in 62 countries and territories:
Afghanistan, Argentina, Australia, Austria, Barbados, Belarus, Belgium, Brazil, Bulgaria, Canada, Chile, China, Congo DR, Croatia, Czechia, Denmark, Egypt, Estonia, Ethiopia, Finland, France, Georgia, Germany, Greece, Hungary, India, Ireland, Israel, Italy, Jamaica, Japan, Kazakhstan, Korea Rep, Kuwait, Latvia, Lithuania, Mexico, Netherlands, New Zealand, North Macedonia, Norway, Poland, Portugal, Romania, Russia, Saudi Arabia, Serbia, Singapore, Slovakia, Slovenia, South Africa, Spain, Sweden, Switzerland, Taiwan, Türkiye, UK, Ukraine, United Arab Emirates, Uruguay, USA, Venezuela.
NGO Relations Associated organization of: *European Federation of Corrosion (EFC, #07090); International Union of Pure and Applied Chemistry (IUPAC, #15809).* In liaison with technical committees of: *International Organization for Standardization (ISO, #14473).* [2020/XC1609/**C**]

♦ International Society of Electromyographic Kinesiology / see International Society of Electrophysiology and Kinesiology (#15081)
♦ International Society of Electromyography (inactive)

♦ International Society for Electrophysical Agents in Physical Therapy (ISEAPT) 15080

Pres address not obtained. E-mail: iseapt2011@yahoo.com.
URL: https://www.facebook.com/electrophysicalagents/

History 8 Feb 2009, Las Vegas, NV (USA). Became a subgroup of *World Confederation for Physical Therapy (WCPT, #21293)*, Jun 2011, Amsterdam (Netherlands). **Structure** General Meeting; Executive Committee. **Events** *Summit* Jakarta (Indonesia) 2022.
Members Full in 15 countries and territories:
Argentina, Cambodia, Hong Kong, Indonesia, Japan, Korea Rep, Kuwait, Lithuania, Malaysia, Norway, Singapore, Spain, Taiwan, UK, USA. [2022/XJ5282/**E**]

♦ International Society of Electrophysiological Kinesiology / see International Society of Electrophysiology and Kinesiology (#15081)

♦ International Society of Electrophysiology and Kinesiology (ISEK) . 15081

Société internationale de kinésiologie électrophysiologique

Contact Dept of Bioengineering, Imperial College London, Royal School of Mines, London, SW7 2AZ, UK.
URL: http://www.isek-online.org/

History 1965, as *International Society of Electromyographic Kinesiology – Société internationale de kinésiologie électromyographique.* Previously also referred to in English as *International Society of Electrophysiological Kinesiology.* **Aims** Promote advanced research and teaching in electrophysiology, *kinesiology*, bioengineering. **Structure** Congress (at least every 2 years); Council of 9 members; Officers. **Languages** English. **Staff** 9.00 FTE, voluntary. **Finance** Members' dues. Other sources: congress fees. **Events** *Congress* Nagoya (Japan) 2024, *Congress* Québec, QC (Canada) 2022, *Congress* Nagoya (Japan) 2020, *Congress* Dublin (Ireland) 2018, *Congress* Chicago, IL (USA) 2016. **Publications** *ISER Newsletter* (4 a year); *Journal of Electromyography and Kinesiology.* Books. **Members** Individuals working in the field of biological sciences. Membership countries not specified. [2020/XD4587/v/**D**]

♦ International Society for Electroporation-Based Technologies and Treatments (ISEBTT) 15082

Pres address not obtained. E-mail: isebtt@electroporation.net.
URL: http://www.electroporation.net/

History Registration: USA. **Aims** Promote the advancement of scientific knowledge of the interactions of pulsed electric and electromagnetic fields and ionized gases with biological systems (cells, tissues, organisms, molecules and materials), with an emphasis on electroporation; facilitate the development of applications based on these phenomena in biology, medicine, biotechnology, and food and environmental technologies. **Structure** General Assembly; Council. **Activities** Events/meetings. **Events** *World Congress on Electroporation* Copenhagen (Denmark) 2022, *World Congress on Electroporation* Toulouse (France) 2019, *World Congress on Electroporation* Norfolk, VA (USA) 2017, *World Congress on Electroporation* Portoroz (Slovenia) 2015. [2023.02.15/AA0935/**C**]

♦ International Society for Electrostatic Precipitation (ISESP) 15083

Office 241 Ralph McGill Boulevard, NW BIN 10221, Atlanta GA 30308, USA. T. +12052233985. E-mail: isespwebmaster@gmail.com – isesp2017@gmail.com.
URL: http://www.isesp.org/

History Jun 1986, Abano Terme (Italy). Established at 3rd conference. **Aims** Provide a forum for the exchange of information on research and application of electrostatic precipitation. **Structure** Board, comprising President, Vice-President, Secretary, Treasurer and members. **Activities** Events/meetings; knowledge management/information dissemination; standards/guidelines; training/education. **Events** *Conference* Budapest (Hungary) 2022, *Conference* Charlotte, NC (USA) 2018, *Conference* Wroclaw (Poland) 2016, *Conference* Bangalore (India) 2013, *Conference* Nürburg (Germany) 2011. [2022/XJ6970/**C**]

♦ International Society for Electrostimulation (inactive)

♦ International Society for Empirical Research in Theology (ISERT) .. 15084

Contact address not obtained. E-mail: loviedo@antonianum.eu.
URL: https://isertheology.org/

History 2002, Nijmegen (Netherlands). **Aims** Promote networking and activities to implement the application of empirical methods and approaches in theology and religious studies. **Activities** Events/meetings; research/documentation. **Events** *Conference* Helsinki (Finland) 2018. [2021.02.17/XM7933/**D**]

♦ International Society for the Empirical Study of Literature 15085

Association internationale pour l'étude empirique de la littérature – Internationale Gesellschaft für Empirische Literaturwissenschaft (IGEL)

Sec Modern Lang Dept, Univ of Alberta, Edmonton AB T6G 2E6, Canada.
Pres UU Inst voor Media, Muntstraat 2-a, 3512 EV Utrecht, Netherlands.
URL: http://www.psych.ualberta.ca/IGEL/

History 1987. 2010, registered in accordance with Dutch law. **Aims** Support systematic and empirical literature research projects through information and cooperation; further the application of the framework and methodology of the systematic and empirical approach in the study of literature; support students and junior researchers in the field. **Structure** Executive Committee. **Finance** Sources: members' dues. **Events** *Biennial Conference* Edmonton, AB (Canada) 2021, *Biennial Conference* Liverpool (UK) 2020, *Biennial Conference* Stavanger (Norway) 2018, *Biennial Conference* Turin (Italy) 2014, *Biennial Conference* Montréal, QC (Canada) 2012. **Publications** *IGEL Newsletter* (annual); *Scientific Study of Literature (SSOL)* – journal.
Members in 23 countries:
Australia, Austria, Belgium, Brazil, Bulgaria, Canada, China, Denmark, France, Germany, Hong Kong, Hungary, Italy, Mexico, Netherlands, Portugal, Romania, Russia, Slovenia, Sweden, Taiwan, UK, USA. [2015/XN0983/**C**]

♦ International Society of Endocrinology (ISE) 15086

Exec Dir Rue François-Versonnex 7, PO Box 6053, 1211 Geneva 6, Switzerland. T. +41229069162. E-mail: office@isendo.org.
Sec/Treas address not obtained.
Main Website: http://www.isendo.org/

History 1960. Former names and other names: *Société internationale d'endocrinologie* – alias; *Sociedad Internacional de Endocrinologia* – alias. **Aims** Promote endocrine and metabolic science, education, practice and advocacy worldwide; unite the global endocrinology community. **Structure** General Council; Executive Committee, comprising representatives from Endocrine Society, *European Society of Endocrinology (ESE, #08594), Federação Latino Americana de Endocrinologia (FELAEN, #09286)*, Japan, *ASEAN Federation of Endocrine Societies (AFES, #01175)* and 3 representatives at large. **Languages** English. **Staff** 2.00 FTE, paid; 18.00 FTE, voluntary. **Activities** Advocacy/lobbying/activism; events/meetings; knowledge management/information dissemination; networking/liaising. **Events** *Biennial Congress* Singapore (Singapore) 2022, *Biennial Congress* Buenos Aires (Argentina) 2021, *Biennial Congress* Cape Town (South Africa) 2018, *Biennial Congress* Beijing (China) 2016, *Biennial Congress* Chicago, IL (USA) 2014.
Members Endocrinological societies in 59 countries and territories:
Algeria, Argentina, Australia, Bangladesh, Belarus, Belgium, Benin, Canada, Chile, China, Colombia, Czechia, Denmark, Egypt, Finland, Georgia, Ghana, Greece, Hong Kong, Hungary, Iceland, India, Ireland, Israel, Italy, Japan, Korea Rep, Lebanon, Lithuania, Malaysia, Mexico, Myanmar, Nepal, New Zealand, Nigeria, Norway, Pakistan, Philippines, Portugal, Puerto Rico, Romania, Singapore, Slovakia, Slovenia, South Africa, Spain, Sri Lanka, Sweden, Switzerland, Taiwan, Thailand, Tunisia, Türkiye, Uganda, UK, United Arab Emirates, Uruguay, Uzbekistan, Venezuela. [2022.02.02/XC2541/**B**]

♦ International Society of Endocytobiology (ISE) 15087

Pres FSU Jena, Botanik Inst, Dornburger Str 159, 07743 Jena, Germany. T. +493641949231. Fax +493641949232.
First Sec University of Tsukuba, Tsukuba IBARAKI, 305-8572 Japan. T. +81298537877. Fax +81298536614.
URL: http://www.endocytobiology.org/

History 1983, Germany FR. 1983, Tübingen (Germany FR), during Second International Colloquium on Endocytobiology. Also referred to as *Society for Symbiosis and Cell Research.* **Aims** Promote research of endocytobiology and general (endo) symbiosis; increase understanding of symbiotic interactions and antisymbiotic processes at the cellular level. **Structure** Executive Board, comprising President, 2 Vice-Presidents, 2 Secretaries, Treasurer. Committees (4). **Activities** Committees (4): Education of Endocytobiology; Education in Symbiosis Research; International Colloquia on Endocytobiology and Symbiosis; Statutes Revision. Awards the Miescher-Ishida Prize. **Events** *Triennial Colloquium* Lille (France) 2019, *Triennial Colloquium* Kyoto (Japan) 2016, *Triennial Colloquium* Halifax, NS (Canada) 2013, *Triennial Colloquium* Tromsø (Norway) 2010, *Triennial Colloquium* Gmunden (Austria) 2007. **Publications** *International Journal on Endocytobiosis and Cell Research.* Conference newsletter; conference proceedings. [2016/XD6859/**D**]

♦ International Society for Endomicroscopy (unconfirmed)
♦ International Society for Endoscopy / see World Endoscopy Organization (#21380)
♦ International Society of Endovascular Specialists (internationally oriented national body)
♦ International Society for Endovascular Surgery / see International Society of Endovascular Specialists
♦ International Society of Energy and Built Environment (unconfirmed)

♦ International Society of Engineering Asset Management (ISEAM) .. 15088

Contact c/o Asset Inst, Level 2 – M Block, Queensland Univ of Technology, Gardens Point Campus, 2 George Street, Brisbane QLD 4001, Australia. T. +61731381471. Fax +61731389079.
URL: http://www.iseam.org/

Aims Provide thought-leadership and influence on a global basis to coordinate the discipline's advance with academics, practitioners, and policy makers in the emerging trans-discipline of engineering asset management. **Structure** Board. **Activities** Events/meetings. **Events** *World Congress on Engineering Asset Management* Singapore (Singapore) 2019, *World Congress on Engineering Asset Management* Stavanger (Norway) 2018, *World Congress on Engineering Asset Management* Tampere (Finland) 2015, *World Congress on Engineering Asset Management* Pretoria (South Africa) 2014, *World Congress on Engineering Asset Management* Hong Kong (Hong Kong) 2013.
Members Fellows in 17 countries and territories:
Australia, Canada, China, Finland, Greece, Hong Kong, India, Italy, Korea Rep, Netherlands, Norway, South Africa, Sweden, Switzerland, Taiwan, UK, USA. [2014/XJ8089/**C**]

♦ International Society for Engineering Education / see International Society for Engineering Pedagogy (#15089)

♦ International Society for Engineering Pedagogy 15089

Association internationale pour la formation pédagogique des ingénieurs – Internationale Gesellschaft für Ingenieurpädagogik (IGIP) – Società Internazionale per la Pedagogia dell' Ingegneria

Gen Sec c/o Carinthia Univ, Dept Systems Engineering, Europastrasse 4, 9524 Villach, Austria. E-mail: gs@igip.org – office@igip.org.
Pres c/o TU Dresden, Weberplatz 5, 01217 Dresden, Germany.
URL: http://www.igip.org/

History 1972, Klagenfurt am Wörthersee (Austria). Founded by Prof Adolf Melezinek (died 2015). Former names and other names: *International Society for Engineering Education* – former; *Société internationale d'ingénieurs pédagogues* – former. **Aims** Improve teaching methods in technical subjects; develop practice-oriented curricula; encourage use of media in technical teaching; integrate languages and humanities in engineering education; foster management training for engineers; promote environmental awareness; support development of engineering education in developing countries. **Structure** Assembly (annual); Executive Committee; International Monitoring Committee; National Sections. **Languages** English. **Staff** Voluntary. **Finance** Sources: members' dues. **Activities** Events/meetings; research/documentation. **Events** *Annual Symposium* Vienna (Austria) 2022, *International Conference on Interactive Collaborative Learning* Vienna (Austria) 2022, *Annual Symposium* Dresden (Germany) 2021, *International Conference on Interactive Collaborative Learning* Dresden (Germany) 2021, *Annual Symposium* Tallinn (Estonia) 2020. **Publications** *International Journal of Engineering Pedagogy (iJEP)*. Conference proceedings.
Members Scientists, technical teachers and other educational staff in 37 countries:
Argentina, Austria, Belgium, Bosnia-Herzegovina, Brazil, Canada, Chile, Croatia, Cyprus, Czechia, Estonia, Ethiopia, Finland, Germany, Greece, Hungary, India, Ireland, Italy, Japan, Jordan, Kazakhstan, Lebanon, Netherlands, Poland, Portugal, Puerto Rico, Russia, Serbia, Slovakia, Slovenia, Spain, Switzerland, Thailand, Türkiye, Ukraine, USA.
Consultative Status Consultative status granted from: *ECOSOC (#05331)* (Ros C); *UNIDO (#20336)*. **IGO Relations** Accredited by (1): *United Nations Office at Vienna (UNOV, #20604)*. Consultative Status: *UNESCO (#20322)*. **NGO Relations** Member of (1): *International Federation of Engineering Education Societies (IFEES, #13412)*. Associate member of: *European Network for Accreditation of Engineering Education (ENAEE, #07859)*. [2021.06.15/XC8600/v/**C**]

♦ International Society for Environmental Biogeochemistry (ISEB) . . . 15090

Sec Dept of Earth and Planetary Sciences, 1412 Circle Drive, Univ of Tennessee, Knoxville TN 37996, USA.
URL: http://www.isebiogeochemistry.com/

History 2009, Hamburg (Germany), at 19th biennial symposium, with 1st symposium organized 1973. **Aims** Promote scientific knowledge of biogeochemistry and related fields; stimulate scientific investigations, planning, organization and administration of biennial international symposia on biogeochemistry; improve education in biogeochemistry and related subjects. **Structure** Executive Board, including President, Treasurer, Secretary, Chair and Vice-Chair. **Events** *Biennial Symposium* Australia 2017, *Biennial Symposium* Piran (Slovenia) 2015, *Biennial Symposium* Wuhan (China) 2013, *Biennial Symposium* Istanbul (Turkey) 2011, *Biennial Symposium* Hamburg (Germany) 2009. [2016.06.01/XJ5888/**E**]

♦ International Society of Environmental Bioindicators / see International Society of Environmental Indicators (#15095)

♦ International Society for Environmental Biotechnology (ISEB) 15091

Pres Institute of Ecology, National Council of Science and Technology, Xalapa VER, Mexico.
URL: http://www.environbiotech-iseb.org/

History 1993, Hong Kong. **Structure** Board of Directors, comprising President, 2 Vice-Presidents, Past-President, Secretary-Treasurer. **Events** *Conference* Chania (Greece) 2018, *Conference* Barcelona (Spain) 2016, *Biennial Symposium* Sydney, NSW (Australia) 2008, *Biennial Symposium* Leipzig (Germany) 2006, *Biennial Symposium* Chicago, IL (USA) 2004. **Members** Individuals (400) in 20 countries. Membership countries not specified. [2018/XD5973/**D**]

♦ International Society of Environmental Botanists (internationally oriented national body)
♦ International Society for Environmental Education (inactive)

♦ International Society for Environmental Epidemiology (ISEE) 15092

Secretariat c/o Infinity Conference Group, 1035 Sterling Rd, Ste 202, Herndon VA 20170, USA. T. +17039250178. Fax +17039259453. E-mail: secretariat@iseepi.org.
URL: http://www.iseepi.org/

History 1988. Registration: Start date: 1993, USA. **Aims** Provide a forum for discussion, critical review, collaboration and education on issues of environmental exposure and human health effects. Encourage and support: epidemiological studies of environmental exposure; communication among epidemiologists, *toxicologists*, exposure analysts, other environmental scientists and moral philosophers; innovative approaches to substantive or methodological problems and applications in the field; informing of public policy; involvement of scientists from developing countries; setting up of regional chapters. **Structure** Annual Meeting; Executive Council; Committees; Chapters (4); Secretariat. **Languages** English. **Staff** None. **Finance** Sources: meeting proceeds; members' dues. **Activities** Awards/prizes/competitions; events/meetings; networking/liaising. **Events** *Conference* Athens (Greece) 2022, *Conference* New York, NY (USA) 2021, *Conference* Herndon, VA (USA) 2020, *Asia Chapter Conference* Daegu (Korea Rep) 2019, *Conference* Utrecht (Netherlands) 2019. **Publications** *Environmental Health Perspectives (EHP)* (12 a year) – journal; *Epidemiology* (6 a year) – official journal.
Members Individuals in 57 countries and territories:
Albania, Argentina, Australia, Austria, Azerbaijan, Belgium, Bolivia, Brazil, Bulgaria, Canada, China, Colombia, Czechia, Denmark, Ethiopia, Finland, France, Germany, Greece, Hong Kong, Hungary, India, Indonesia, Ireland, Israel, Italy, Jamaica, Japan, Korea Rep, Kyrgyzstan, Lebanon, Lithuania, Malaysia, Mexico, Netherlands, New Zealand, Nicaragua, Norway, Pakistan, Panama, Peru, Philippines, Portugal, Romania, Russia, Saudi Arabia, Slovakia, South Africa, Spain, Sweden, Switzerland, Taiwan, Thailand, Türkiye, UK, Ukraine, USA.
Consultative Status Consultative status granted from: *WHO (#20950)* (Official Relations). **NGO Relations** Member of: *International Network for Epidemiology in Policy (INEP, #14264)*. [2021/XD3249/v/**C**]

♦ International Society for Environmental Ergonomics 15093

Contact Environmental Ergonomics Research Ctr, Loughborough Univ, Loughborough, LE11 3TU, UK.
URL: http://www.environmental-ergonomics.org/

History 1986, Whistler BC (Canada). **Aims** Promote exchange of scientific information in the area of environmental ergonomics. **Structure** ICEE Executive Committee. **Languages** English. **Staff** None paid. **Finance** Conference proceeds. **Activities** Events/meetings. **Events** *Conference* Amsterdam (Netherlands) 2019, *Conference* Kobe (Japan) 2017, *Conference* Portsmouth (UK) 2015, *Conference* Queenstown (New Zealand) 2013, *Conference* Nafplion (Greece) 2011. **Publications** Conference proceedings. **NGO Relations** *European Society of Protective Clothing (ESPC, #08716)*; *International Union of Physiological Sciences (IUPS, #15800)*. [2019.12.11/XJ6416/c/**E**]

♦ International Society for Environmental Ethics (ISEE) 15094

Pres 1333 Grandview, UCB 0488, Univ of Colorado, Boulder CO 80309, USA. T. +13037353624. Fax +13037351576.
Sec Dept de Philosophie – Univ du Québec, Pavillon Thérèse-Casgrain 455, Bvd René-Lévesque Est – 5e étage, Montréal QC H2L 4Y2, Canada.
URL: http://www.iseethics.org/

History Dec 1989, Atlanta GA (USA). Constitution ratified Dec 1990, Boston MA (USA); revised 2007. **Aims** Promote critical analysis of ethical issues related to the environment. **Structure** Officers: President, Vice-President, Secretary, Treasurer. **Languages** English. **Staff** None. **Finance** Members' dues. **Activities** Events/meetings; financial and/or material support; training/education. **Events** *Annual Joint Conference* New York, NY (USA) 2016, *Joint Annual ISEE IAEP Conference* Boulder, CO (USA) 2010, *Annual joint conference* Allenspark, CO (USA) 2009, *Joint Annual ISEE IAEP Conference* Boulder, CO (USA) 2009, *Annual joint conference* Allenspark, CO (USA) 2008. **Publications** *ISEE Newsletter* (3 a year).
Members Membership largely North American. Members in 35 countries and territories:
Australia, Belarus, Belgium, Bolivia, Canada, China, Czechia, Finland, France, Germany, Hong Kong, India, Italy, Japan, Jordan, Latvia, Malta, Mexico, Netherlands, New Zealand, Nigeria, Norway, Pakistan, Poland, Portugal, Russia, Singapore, South Africa, Spain, Sri Lanka, Sweden, Switzerland, Taiwan, UK, USA.
NGO Relations Member of: *International Federation of Philosophical Societies (FISP, #13507)*. [2016/XF1437/**F**]

♦ International Society for Environmental Geotechnology (no recent information)

♦ International Society of Environmental Indicators (ISEI) 15095

Pres c/o Env Microbiology Lab, Civil & Environmental Eng, Technion, 32000 Haifa, Israel.
Facebook: https://www.facebook.com/ISEIsociety/

History Founded by *International Commission on Bioindicators (#12667)*, on the initiative of Osmo Hänninen (1939-). Former names and other names: *International Society of Environmental Bioindicators (ISEBI)* – former (2009). **Aims** Provide an empirically-derived foundation in the use of indicators to help define environmental health and requisite protection or restoration needs in policy-relevant contexts. **Languages** English. **Finance** Members' dues. **Events** *International Conference on Environmental Indicators* Toledo (Spain) 2022, *International Conference on Environmental Indicators* Haifa (Israel) 2019, *Annual Meeting* Helsinki (Finland) 2017, *Annual Meeting* Windsor, ON (Canada) 2015, *Annual Meeting* Trier (Germany) 2013. **Publications** *Environmental Indicators Journal (JEI)*. [2021/XM1627/**D**]

♦ International Society for Environmental Information Sciences (internationally oriented national body)

♦ International Society of Environmental Micropaleontology, Microbiology and Meiobenthology (ISEMMM) 15096

Pres Dept of Applied Geology, University of Madras, Guindy Campus, A C College Buildings, Chennai, Tamil Nadu 600 025, Chennai TAMIL NADU 600 025, India. T. +914422202725.

History 2001. **Aims** Foster research in the field. **Structure** Council. **Events** *Congress* Erlangen (Germany) 2007, *Congress* Isparta (Turkey) 2004, *Congress* Vienna (Austria) 2002, *Congress* Winnipeg, MB (Canada) 2000, *Congress* Tel Aviv (Israel) 1997. **Publications** *Journal of Environmental Microbiology, Meiobenthology and Micropaleontology* (4 a year); *ISEMMM Newsletter*. [2008/XM0079/**D**]

♦ International Society for Environmental Protection (ISEP) 15097

Société internationale pour la protection de l'environnement – Internationale Gesellschaft für Umweltschutz (IGU)

Chairman Bechardgasse 24/12, 1030 Vienna, Austria. T. +4317152828. Fax +4317134131.
URL: http://www.isep.at/

History Founded 1987, Vienna (Austria). Registered in accordance with Austrian law. **Aims** Initiate, promote and act as a forum for exchange of interdisciplinary environmental knowledge and information among environmental experts, administrators, industry, research and the public so as to support *sustainable development* from an environmental perspective; emphasize equal cooperation among environmental experts and the business world, whether *North-South* or *East-West*; work to avoid *pollution* of the environment; promote cross-border environmental protection, initiate cross-border research projects and encourage, initiate and publish international research programmes; develop integrative strategies; act as a principal organizer of the annual conference series EnviroInfo within the Technical Committee "Environmental Informatics – Informatics for Environmental Protection, Sustainable Development and Risk Management". **Structure** General Assembly; Board; Executive Committee; Council; Scientific Council. **Languages** English, German. **Staff** None. **Finance** Members' dues. Research programmes. **Activities** Events/meetings; knowledge management/information dissemination; networking/liaising. **Events** *EnviroInfo : International Conference on Informatics for Environmental Protection* Hamburg (Germany) 2013, *EnviroInfo : International Conference on Informatics for Environmental Protection* Dessau (Germany) 2012, *EnviroInfo : international conference on informatics for environmental protection* Ispra (Italy) 2011, *EnviroInfo Conference* Bonn (Germany) / Cologne (Germany) 2010, *EnviroInfo : international conference on informatics for environmental protection* Berlin (Germany) 2009. **Publications** Meeting proceedings; conference and workshop documentation. Information Services: *Central European Environmental Data Request Facility (CEDAR, inactive)* – initiated and run by ISEP; Literature database. **Information Services** *Bibliographic Database of Environmental Terminological Resources (ENVBIB)*; *Danube Information System for the International Commission for the Protection of the Danube River (DANUBIS)* – project coordinator for ICPDR; *Environmental Nomenclatures, Coding Lists and Classification Schemes (CODING)* – first draft; *General European Multilingual Environment Thesaurus (GEMET)*; *Information and Communication Technologies for Environmental Sustainability Research (ICT-ENSURE)* – FP7 project; *Multilingual Environmental Terminology Database (ENVIROTERM)* – prototype; *Research Programmes Information System*. **Members** Persons in universities and administration, persons in companies and research institutes, concerned with environmental protection. Membership countries not specified. **NGO Relations** Cooperates with: Gesellschaft für Informatik (Germany); Technical Committee "Environmental Informatics". [2014.07.04/XD5127/**D**]

♦ International Society for Enzymology (ISE) 15098

Exec Sec Univ Medicine Gottingen, Dept Clinical Pharmacology, Kreuzbergring 36, 37075 Göttingen, Germany.
Pres address not obtained.
URL: http://www.isenzymology.org/

History Founded 7 Apr 1976, Venice (Italy), as *International Society for Clinical Enzymology (ISCE)*, when Constitution was adopted. Constitution modified at 7th General Assembly, 24 Apr 1982, Abano Terme (Italy). Present name adopted Jul 1996. **Aims** Encourage and disseminate internationally basic, clinical and applied enzymology research. **Structure** Board, consisting of President, Past President and 6 other members elected by General Meeting; Vice-President, Treasurer and Secretary elected among members of the Board. **Languages** English. **Staff** 7.00 FTE, paid. **Finance** Sources: members' dues. **Activities** Organizes international congresses and symposia; co-sponsors biennial meeting in Italy; awards biennial J Henry Wilkinson Award and John King Memorial Award. **Events** *Annual Conference* Samos (Greece) 2022, *Annual Conference* Chios (Greece) 2019, *International Congress* Crete (Greece) 2010, *Symposium* New York, NY (USA) 2003, *Symposium* Hamamatsu (Japan) 2002. **Publications** *ISCE Newsletter* (4 a year); *Enzyme* – official journal. Proceedings of meetings.
Members Ordinary graduates working in clinical enzymology and other individuals as the Board considers appropriate. Members in 39 countries and territories:
Argentina, Australia, Austria, Belgium, Bulgaria, Canada, Czechia, Denmark, Egypt, Finland, France, Germany, Greece, Hungary, Iceland, Indonesia, Iran Islamic Rep, Ireland, Israel, Italy, Japan, Netherlands, Nigeria, Norway, Pakistan, Poland, Portugal, Romania, Saudi Arabia, Senegal, Serbia, South Africa, Spain, Sweden, Switzerland, Taiwan, Türkiye, UK, USA.
NGO Relations *International Federation of Clinical Chemistry and Laboratory Medicine (IFCC, #13392)*. [2022/XD5404/v/**C**]

♦ International Society for Epidemiology and Economics / see International Society for Veterinary Epidemiology and Economics (#15540)
♦ International Society for Equine Locomotor Pathology (internationally oriented national body)

♦ International Society for Equitation Science (ISES) 15099

Hon Sec ABSc – U Guelph, 50 Stone Road E, Guelph ON N1G 2W1, Canada.
URL: http://www.equitationscience.com/

History Aug 2007, East Lansing, MI (USA). Founded at 3rd Equitation Science Symposium. Constitution most recently updated Oct 2011. Registration: Charity, No/ID: 1176401, England and Wales. **Aims** Promote and encourage the application of objective research and advanced practice to ultimately improve the welfare of *horses* in their associations with humans. **Structure** General Meeting; Council. **Finance** Sources: members' dues. **Activities** Awards/prizes/competitions; events/meetings; research/documentation. **Events** *Conference* Gloucester (UK) 2021, *Conference* Gloucester (UK) 2020, *Conference* Guelph, ON (Canada) 2019, *Equine welfare – good training, good feeding, good housing, good mental state, good health, good behaviour* Rome (Italy) 2018, *Conference* Wagga Wagga, NSW (Australia) 2017. **Publications** Conference proceedings. **Members** Individuals. Membership countries not specified. [2021/XJ8973/**C**]

♦ International Society for Equity in Health (ISEqH) 15100

Sociedad Internacional por la Equidad en Salud

Pres Sanchez de Bustamante 27, CABA, C1173AAA Buenos Aires, Argentina. T. +541148651707.

History 30 Jun 2000, Havana (Cuba). Registered in the State of Maryland (USA). Current constitution adopted 30 Jun 2000. **Aims** Promote equity in health and health services internationally through education, research, publication, communication and charitable support. **Structure** General Assembly (every 2 years). Scientific Advisory Council. Executive Board, comprising President, Past President, Secretary, Treasurer, Executive Secretary and 6 members. Nominating Committee of 4 members. **Languages** English. **Staff** 1.00 FTE, paid. **Finance** Members' dues. **Activities** Organizes scientific meetings. **Events** *Making policy a health equity*

building process Cartagena de Indias (Colombia) 2011, *Conference* Crete (Greece) 2009, *Social and societal influences on equity in health* Hersonissos (Greece) 2009, *Conference* Adelaide, SA (Australia) 2006, *Pathways to equity in health – using research for policy and advocacy* Durban (South Africa) 2004. **Publications** *International Journal for Equity in Health* – electronic; *International Society for Equity in Health Newsletter*.
Members Individuals in 61 countries and territories:
Albania, Argentina, Armenia, Australia, Bangladesh, Belgium, Bolivia, Brazil, Brunei Darussalam, Canada, Chile, China, Colombia, Costa Rica, Cuba, Denmark, Egypt, Finland, France, Georgia, Germany, Ghana, Guatemala, Hong Kong, India, Indonesia, Ireland, Italy, Japan, Kazakhstan, Kenya, Korea Rep, Mexico, Mozambique, Namibia, Netherlands, New Zealand, Nicaragua, Nigeria, Norway, Peru, Philippines, Poland, Portugal, Puerto Rico, Russia, Singapore, South Africa, Spain, Sweden, Switzerland, Taiwan, Tajikistan, Thailand, Uganda, UK, Ukraine, Uruguay, USA, Venezuela, Zimbabwe.
[2011.06.01/XD9051/v/**D**]

♦ International Society of Esperantist Architects and Builders (inactive)
♦ International Society of Esperanto Free-Thinkers (inactive)
♦ International Society for Ethics and Information Technology (internationally oriented national body)

♦ International Society of Ethnobiology (ISE) 15101

Pres Department of Anthropology, Univ of Florida, Turlington Hall – Room 1112, Gainesville FL 32611, USA. T. +13523922253. Fax +13523926929. E-mail: admin@ethnobiology.net.
URL: http://ethnobiology.net/

History Jul 1988, Belém (Brazil). Jul 1988, Belem Para (Brazil). **Aims** Promote and enhance the study and understanding of ethnobiology and ethnoecology throughout the world. **Structure** General Assembly (every 2 years). Board, comprising President, Vice President, Immediate Past President, Secretary, Treasurer, Director and 14 further members. **Languages** English. **Staff** 1.00 FTE, paid. **Finance** Members' dues. **Activities** Global Coalition; Ethics Program; Darrell Posey Fellowship. **Events** *Congress* Belém (Brazil) 2018, *Ethnobiological knowledge for improved human wellbeing and development* Kampala (Uganda) 2016, *Regenerating biocultural ecosystem resilience and traditional knowledge* Thimphu (Bhutan) 2014, *Cultural diversity and biological diversity for sustainable development – exploring the past to build up the future* Montpellier (France) 2012, *Congress* Tofino, BC (Canada) 2010. **Publications** *ISE Newsletter*. **Members** Full in over 50 countries. Membership countries not specified. [2020/XD2043/**D**]

♦ International Society for Ethnology and Folklore (#19481)

♦ International Society for Ethnopharmacology (ISE) 15102

Pres Hirschmann Inst de Quimica de Recursos Naturales, Univ de Talca, Casilla 747, Talca, Maule, Chile.
URL: http://www.ethnopharmacology.org/

History Founded 1990, Strasbourg (France), at 1st International Conference of Ethnopharmacology. **Aims** Promote ethnopharmacology and related transdisciplinary fields as a scientific research discipline for promotion and development of natural products, traditional medicine and medicinal plants. **Structure** Board; Executive. **Languages** English. **Staff** Voluntary. **Finance** Members' dues. Donations. **Activities** Networking/liaising; knowledge management/information dissemination; events/meetings. **Events** *International Congress* Imphal (India) 2023, *International Congress* Taichung (Taiwan) 2022, *International Congress* Thessaloniki (Greece) 2021, *International Congress* Thessaloniki (Greece) 2020, *International Congress* Dresden (Germany) 2019. **Publications** *ISE e-Newsletter*, *Journal of Ethnopharmacology* – official journal.
[2017.10.26/XD8277/**D**]

♦ International Society of European Agricultural Cooperatives / see Intercoop Europe (#11464)

♦ International Society for Evidence-Based Health Care (ISEHC) 15103

Contact CREBP – Health Sciences, Bond University, Robina, Gold Coast QLD 4229, Australia. E-mail: pglaszio@bond.edu.au.
Contact McMaster Univ, 1280 Main St W, Rm 2-C-12, Hamilton ON L8S 4K1, Canada.
URL: http://www.isehc.net/

History Oct 2010. **Aims** Develop, and encourage research in, the appropriate usage of evidence in health care decision making; promote and provide professional and public education in the field. **Structure** Board of 17. Committees (3): Curriculum; Conferences; Policy and Advocacy. **Events** *Conference* 2022, *Conference* Taormina (Italy) 2019, *Best evidence and health care decisions, connecting the dots* Kish (Iran Islamic Rep) 2016, *Conference* Sydney, NSW (Australia) 2015, *International Conference for EBHC Teachers and Developers* Taormina (Italy) 2015. **Publications** *ISEHC Journal*; *ISEHC Newsletter*. [2015/XJ6602/**C**]

♦ International Society for Evolutionary Protistology (ISEP) 15104

Sec Dept Biological Sciences, Mississippi State Univ, PO Box GY, Starkville MS 39762, USA. T. +16623252406.
Pres Dept Biochemistry Molecular Biology, Dalhousie Univ, RM 8B1, 5850 College St, Halifax NS B3H 1X5, Canada. T. +19024942620. Fax +19024941355.
URL: http://www.isepsociety.com/

History 1977. **Aims** Promote study of unicellular Eukaryotes, the taxonomy, phylogeny and evolution of protists. **Structure** Executive Committee, comprising President, President-Elect, Past-President, Secretary, Treasurer, Newsletter Editor, North American Councillor, European Councillor, Councillor-at-large, Membership Director and Office Manager. **Languages** English. **Staff** Voluntary. **Finance** Members' dues. Donations. **Events** *International Congress of Protistology* Seoul (Korea Rep) 2025, *International Congress of Protistology* Seoul (Korea Rep) 2022, *International Congress of Protistology* Seoul (Korea Rep) 2021, *Biennial Meeting* Paphos (Cyprus) 2018, *Biennial Meeting* Moscow (Russia) 2016. **Publications** *ISEP Newsletter* (2 a year). Proceedings.
Members Individuals in 18 countries:
Australia, Belgium, Brazil, Canada, Czechia, Denmark, France, Germany, Japan, Netherlands, Norway, Poland, South Africa, Spain, Switzerland, UK, Ukraine, USA. [2017/XD1280/v/**D**]

♦ International Society for Evolution, Medicine and Public Health (ISEMPH) 15105

Pres address not obtained.
Sec address not obtained.
URL: http://evolutionarymedicine.org/

History 2015, Tempe, AZ (USA). **Aims** Foster communication among scientists, students, clinicians and public health professionals wishing to use evolutionary insights to improve medical research and practice and to use information on human health and disease to advance evolutionary *biology*. **Structure** Council; Executive Committee. Committee (6): Publications; Bylaws; Meetings; Education and Outreach; Williams Prize; Omenn Prize. **Languages** English. **Staff** 0.50 FTE, paid; 1.50 FTE, voluntary. **Finance** Sources: donations; meeting proceeds; members' dues. Annual budget: 75,000 USD. **Activities** Awards/prizes/competitions; events/meetings; knowledge management/information dissemination; networking/liaising; training/education. **Events** *Meeting* Lisbon (Portugal) 2022, *Meeting* 2021, *Meeting* Athens, GA (USA) 2020, *Meeting* Zurich (Switzerland) 2019, *Meeting* Park City, UT (USA) 2018. **Publications** *Evolution, Medicine, and Public Health* – journal; *The Evolution and Medicine Review*.
Members Full in 48 countries and territories:
Argentina, Australia, Austria, Brazil, Canada, Chile, China, Colombia, Costa Rica, Cuba, Denmark, Egypt, Finland, France, Georgia, Germany, Ghana, Hungary, India, Ireland, Italy, Japan, Korea Rep, Malta, Mexico, Namibia, Netherlands, New Zealand, Nigeria, Norway, Pakistan, Poland, Portugal, Romania, Serbia, South Africa, Spain, Sri Lanka, Sweden, Switzerland, Taiwan, Thailand, Türkiye, UK, Ukraine, United Arab Emirates, Uruguay, USA.
IGO Relations None. **NGO Relations** None. [2021/XM6415/**C**]

♦ International Society of Exercise and Immunology (ISEI) 15106

Editor-in-Chief Justus-Liebig-University, Ludwigstrasse 23, 35390 Giessen, Germany.
URL: https://exerciseimmunology.com/

History 1993. **Aims** Foster scientific research and education; disseminate scientific information. **Structure** Board of Directors, comprising President, Vice President, Past-President and Managing Director. **Languages** English. **Activities** Organizes scientific conventions. **Events** *Symposium* Tucson, AZ (USA) 2022, *Symposium* Tucson, AZ (USA) 2021, *Symposium* Shanghai (China) 2019, *Symposium* Coimbra (Portugal) 2017, *Symposium* Vienna (Austria) 2015. **Publications** *Exercise Immunology Review* – journal; *ISEI Newsletter*.
Members Individuals (314) in 27 countries:
Australia, Belgium, Brazil, Canada, China, Denmark, Egypt, France, Germany, Guatemala, Hungary, Ireland, Italy, Japan, Netherlands, Norway, Poland, Portugal, Russia, Singapore, Slovakia, South Africa, Spain, Sweden, Switzerland, UK, USA.
[2021/XD7169/v/**D**]

♦ International Society of Existential Psychology and Psychotherapy (internationally oriented national body)
♦ International Society for Experimental Cytology (inactive)

♦ International Society for Experimental Hematology (ISEH) 15107

Pres 330 North Wabash Ave, Ste 2000, Chicago IL 60611, USA. T. +13123215114. Fax +13126736923. E-mail: info@iseh.org.
URL: http://www.iseh.org/

History Founded 1971, USA. Constitution and by-laws adopted in 1980; amended in 1988, 1989, 1994, 1996, 1997 and 2002. Previously also referred to as *ISEH – Society for Hematology and Stem Cells*. **Aims** Promote scientific knowledge and clinical application of basic haematology, *immunology*, stem cell research, cell and gene therapy and all related aspects through research, publications, discussion, support of young investigators and organization of scientific meetings. **Structure** Board of Trustees; Executive Committee; Ad-hoc and Standing Committees; Headquarters, headed by Executive Director. **Languages** English. **Finance** Sources: members' dues. **Activities** Awards/prizes/competitions; events/meetings; networking/liaising. **Events** *Annual Scientific Meeting* Edinburgh (UK) 2022, *Annual Scientific Meeting* 2021, *Annual Scientific Meeting* 2020, *Annual Scientific Meeting* Brisbane, QLD (Australia) 2019, *Annual Scientific Meeting* Los Angeles, CA (USA) 2018. **Publications** *Experimental Hematology* (12 a year) – journal.
Members Active; Emeriti; Honorary; Associate. Research haematologists (over 1,400) in 32 countries and territories:
Argentina, Australia, Austria, Belgium, Canada, Chile, China, Denmark, France, Germany, Greece, Hungary, India, Ireland, Israel, Italy, Japan, Jordan, Netherlands, New Zealand, Norway, Poland, Portugal, Serbia, South Africa, Spain, Sweden, Switzerland, Taiwan, Thailand, UK, USA.
Members also in the former USSR; countries not specified. [2019/XD0105/v/**C**]

♦ International Society for Experimental Mechanics / see Society for Experimental Mechanics

♦ International Society for Experimental Microsurgery (ISEM) 15108

SG Dept Hepatobiliary/Pancreas/Transplant Surgery, 54 Kawara-cho, Shogoin, Sakyo-ku, Kyoto, Japan. T. +81757513242.
Pres address not obtained.
URL: http://myisem.org/

History Set up by Sun Lee (aka Sil Heung Lee). **Aims** Provide a forum for those interested and engaged in research involving microsurgical techniques; promote the art of microsurgical research activity worldwide; bring scientists up-to-date and familiarize them with current status of experimental microsurgery. **Structure** Society Board; Committees (3). **Languages** English. **Staff** No paid staff. **Finance** Sources: donations; members' dues. **Activities** Events/meetings; knowledge management/information dissemination; research/documentation; training/education. **Events** *Biennial Congress* Genoa (Italy) 2023, *Biennial Congress* Gothenburg (Sweden) 2021, *Biennial Congress* Gothenburg (Sweden) 2020, *Biennial Congress* Debrecen (Hungary) 2018, *Biennial Congress* Tianjin (China) 2016. **Publications** *Microsurgery* – journal.
Members Individuals (about 200) in 24 countries:
Argentina, Australia, Austria, Belgium, Brazil, Canada, China, Denmark, Egypt, France, Germany, Hungary, Italy, Japan, Korea Rep, Netherlands, Romania, South Africa, Spain, Sweden, Türkiye, Uganda, UK, USA. [2020.03.26/XN6162/**C**]

♦ International Society for the Exploration of the Arctic Regions by Means of Aircraft (inactive)
♦ International Society of Explosives Engineers (internationally oriented national body)
♦ International Society of Exposure Analysis / see International Society of Exposure Science
♦ International Society of Exposure Science (internationally oriented national body)
♦ International Society of Extension Education (internationally oriented national body)

♦ International Society for Extracellular Vesicles (ISEV) 15109

Exec Dir 19 Mantua Rd, Mount Royal NJ 08061, USA. T. +18564231621. Fax +18564233420. E-mail: contact@isev.org.
URL: http://www.isev.org/

History 2011, Paris (France). Registration: Start date: 2012, Sweden. **Aims** Promote, foster and encourage basic, translational and clinical research within the field of extracellular vesicles, including microvesicles and *exosomes*; collect, study and disseminate scientific information; encourage and provide opportunities for learning, sharing of research and education in the field so as to advance science and understanding. **Structure** General Assembly; Executive Committee; Board. **Languages** English. **Staff** Voluntary. **Finance** Sources: meeting proceeds; members' dues. **Activities** Events/meetings; training/education. **Events** *Annual Meeting* Melbourne, VIC (Australia) 2024, *Annual Meeting* Seattle, WA (USA) 2023, *EV Blood Workshop* Helsinki (Finland) 2022, *ISEVxTech EV Technology and Methods Summit* Honolulu, HI (USA) 2022, *Annual Meeting* Lyon (France) 2022. **Publications** *Journal of Extracellular Vesicles (JEV)* – official journal. **Members** Membership countries not specified. **IGO Relations** None. **NGO Relations** None. [2021/XJ8666/**C**]

♦ International Society for Extremophiles (ISE) 15110

SG Inst of Technical Microbiology, Hamburg Univ of Technology, Kasernenstr 12, 21073 Hamburg, Germany. T. +4940428783336. Fax +4940428782582.
URL: http://extremophiles.org/

History 2002. **Aims** Serve as a forum for the exchange of information and experience in the field of extremophile *biology*. **Structure** Officers: President; Vice-President; Secretary General; Head of Office. **Languages** English. **Staff** 6.00 FTE, voluntary. **Finance** Members' dues. **Activities** Organizes International Congress on Extremophiles (every 2 years). **Events** *Biennial Conference* Loutraki (Greece) 2022, *Biennial Conference* Loutraki (Greece) 2021, *Biennial Conference* Loutraki (Greece) 2020, *Biennial Conference* Naples (Italy) 2018, *Biennial Conference* Kyoto (Japan) 2016. **Publications** *EXTREMOPHILES* – journal; *ISE Newsletter*.
Members in 20 countries:
Argentina, Australia, Austria, Belgium, Canada, Chile, China, Denmark, France, Germany, India, Israel, Italy, Japan, Korea Rep, Netherlands, Portugal, Spain, UK, USA. [2020/XM0323/**D**]

♦ International Society for Eye Research (ISER) 15111

Secretariat 655 Beach St, San Francisco CA 94109, USA. T. +14155618569. Fax +14155618531. E-mail: mail@iser.org.
Sec School of Medical Sciences, Univ of Sydney, Fac of Medicine and Health, Anderson Stuart Bldg, Eastern Ave, Sydney NSW 2006, Australia.
URL: http://www.iser.org/

History Mar 1969, New York, NY (USA). Initiated Dec 1968, when 14 scientists from 7 countries met in Oxford (UK) and formed a committee to explore the possibility of establishing such a society. May 1974, incorporated in the State of Delaware (USA). Former names and other names: *International Committee for Eye Research (ICER)* – former (1969). **Aims** Provide a unique international platform for discussion and exchange of ideas on contemporary topics in eye and vision research among members and the broader eye/vision research community. **Structure** Officers (8); Councillors (3); Secretariat. **Languages** English. **Staff** 2.00 FTE, paid. **Finance** Sources: meeting proceeds; members' dues; sponsorship. **Activities** Awards/prizes/competitions; events/meetings. **Events** *Biennial Meeting* Buenos Aires (Argentina) 2024, *Biennial Meeting* Gold Coast, QLD (Australia) 2023, *Biennial Meeting* Gold Coast, QLD (Australia) 2022, *Biennial Congress* Buenos Aires (Argentina) 2020, *Biennial Congress* Belfast (UK) 2018. **Publications** *Experimental Eye Research* – journal; *ISER Quarterly Newsletter*.
Members Individuals in 40 countries and territories:
Argentina, Australia, Austria, Belgium, Brazil, Cameroon, Canada, Chile, China, Congo Brazzaville, Czechia, Denmark, Finland, France, Germany, Hong Kong, Hungary, India, Iran Islamic Rep, Ireland, Israel, Italy, Japan, Korea Rep, Mexico, Netherlands, New Zealand, Norway, Poland, Russia, Saudi Arabia, Serbia, Singapore, Slovenia, Spain, Sweden, Switzerland, UK, Uruguay, USA. [2021/XD3983/v/**D**]

♦ International Society for Facial Expression (ISFE) 15112

Contact Dept of Psychology, Univ of Geneva, Blvd du Pont d'Arve 40, 1205 Geneva, Switzerland. T. +41223799216. Fax +41223799019.
Contact Dept of Psychology, Univ of Geneva, Blvd du Pont d'Arve 40, 1205 Geneva, Switzerland. T. +41223799216. Fax +41223799019.
Contact Inst of Psychology, Univ of Innsbruck, Innrain 52, 6020 Innsbruck, Austria. T. +4351250756011. Fax +4351250756199. E-mail: eva.baenninger-huber@uibk.ac.at.

History Proposed, 2001, Innsbruck, at 9th European Conference on Facial Expression – Measurement and Meaning. Original title: *International Society for Facial Expression – Measurement and Meaning.* **Aims** Improve scientific exchange between researchers working with facial expression. **Structure** Informal. **Languages** English. **Staff** Voluntary. **Finance** No budget. **Events** *European Conference on Facial Expression / European Conference on Facial Expression – Measurement and Meaning* Geneva (Switzerland) 2015, *European Conference on Facial Expression / European Conference on Facial Expression – Measurement and Meaning* Lisbon (Portugal) 2012, *European Conference on Facial Expression – Measurement and Meaning* Essen (Germany) 2010, *European Conference on Facial Expression – Measurement and Meaning* Geneva (Switzerland) 2008, *European Conference on Facial Expression – Measurement and Meaning* Durham (UK) 2005. **Publications** Proceedings; articles; books. **NGO Relations** *International Society for Research on Emotion (ISRE, #15420).*
[2015.06.01/XJ7644/**F**]

♦ International Society for Facial Expression – Measurement and Meaning / see International Society for Facial Expression (#15112)
♦ International Society of Facilities Executives (inactive)
♦ International Society for Fair Elections and Democracy (internationally oriented national body)

♦ International Society for Fall Protection (ISFP) 15113

Contact 2500 Newmark Drive, Miamisburg OH 45342, USA. T. +19372596350. Fax +19372595100. E-mail: info@isfp.org.
URL: http://www.isfp.org/

History 1988. **Aims** Reduce fall-related injuries and fatalities by promoting research and facilitating communication among industry professionals. **Structure** Board of Directors of 8 members. **Finance** Sources: members' dues. **Events** *Symposium* Las Vegas, NV (USA) 2013, *Symposium* Düsseldorf (Germany) 2011, *Symposium* Baltimore, MD (USA) 2010, *Symposium* Las Vegas, NV (USA) 2008, *Symposium* Seattle, WA (USA) 2006. **Members** Individual; Corporate. Membership countries not specified. [2014/XJ7022/**C**]

♦ International Society of Family Law (ISFL) 15114

Association internationale de droit de la famille – Internationale Gesellschaft für Familienrecht

SG address not obtained.
Pres address not obtained.
URL: https://www.isflhome.org/home

History Apr 1973, Birmingham (UK). Principles adopted at 1st Annual General Meeting, 12 Apr 1975, Berlin West (Germany FR). **Aims** Encourage study and discussion of family law and family policy; promote laws and policies supportive of families and members in society; advance legal education in family law by all practical means, including exchange of teachers, students, judges and practising lawyers. **Structure** Executive Council. Officers: President; Immediate Past-President; 6 Vice-Presidents; Secretary-General; Treasurer; Editor. **Languages** English, French. **Finance** Sources: members' dues. **Activities** Events/meetings; knowledge management/information dissemination; networking/liaising; research/documentation. **Events** *Triennial World Conference* Antwerp (Belgium) 2023, *Triennial World Conference* Bridgetown (Barbados) 2021, *Triennial World Conference* Bridgetown (Barbados) 2020, *Triennial World Conference* Buenos Aires (Argentina) 2020, *Asia Regional Conference* Hod Hasharon (Israel) 2019. **Publications** *Family Law Newsletter* (2 a year); *International Survey of Family Law* (annual). *An Aging World*; *Families Across Frontiers*; *Family Finances*; *Family Violence*; *Marriage and Cohabitation in Contemporary Societies*; *The Changing Family*; *The Child and the Law*; *The Family, the State and Individual Economic Security*; *The Resolution of Family Conflict*. Proceedings of world conferences.

Members Ordinary members of legal or related profession; Institutional interested organizations at the discretion of, and on terms approved by, Council; Honorary offered to distinguished persons by decision of Executive Council. Members (630) in 66 countries and territories:
Angola, Argentina, Australia, Austria, Belarus, Belgium, Botswana, Brazil, Bulgaria, Cameroon, Canada, China, Colombia, Costa Rica, Croatia, Cuba, Czechia, Denmark, Dominican Rep, Finland, France, Germany, Greece, Hong Kong, Hungary, Iceland, India, Indonesia, Iran Islamic Rep, Ireland, Israel, Italy, Jamaica, Japan, Korea Rep, Lebanon, Lesotho, Luxembourg, Malaysia, Malta, Namibia, Netherlands, New Zealand, Nigeria, Norway, Papua New Guinea, Philippines, Portugal, Russia, Serbia, Sierra Leone, Singapore, Slovenia, South Africa, Spain, Sweden, Switzerland, Tanzania UR, Thailand, Trinidad-Tobago, UK, Ukraine, USA, Zambia, Zimbabwe.

IGO Relations *UNESCO (#20322)*; *The Hague Conference on Private International Law (HCCH, #10850).*
[2020.03.03/XC5996/**C**]

♦ International Society of Farm Animal Endocrinology (inactive)

♦ International Society for Fat Research (ISF) 15115

Société internationale des matières grasses – Sociedad Internacional por Investigación de las Grasas – Internationale Gesellschaft für Fettwissenschaft

Secretariat c/o AOCS, PO Box 17190, Urbana IL 61803-7190, USA. T. +12173592344. Fax +12176934860.
Street address 2710 S Boulder Dr, Urbana IL 61802-6996, USA.
URL: https://www.aocs.org/isf/

History 24 Oct 1954, Hannover (Germany). Founded during session of Deutsche Gesellschaft für Fettwissenschaften and at the instigation of Prof Dr H P Kaufman. Initially an international forum with a minimum of organization and administration; became a formal federation, 11 May 1992, Toronto (Canada). **Aims** Provide for international exchange of information and technology pertaining to fats, *oils* and related materials. **Structure** Executive Board; Extended Board. **Languages** English. **Activities** Awards/prizes/competitions; events/meetings. **Events** *World Congress on Oleo Science* 2022, *World Congress* Kuala Lumpur (Malaysia) 2016, *World Congress* Rosario (Argentina) 2015, *World Congress* Antalya (Turkey) 2013, *World Congress on Olea Science* Sasebo (Japan) 2012.

Members Regional and national organizations (23). National organizations in 21 countries and territories:
Argentina, Australia, Canada, Czechia, Egypt, France, Germany, Hungary, India, Italy, Japan, Korea Rep, Malaysia, Netherlands, Pakistan, Poland, Russia, Spain, Taiwan, UK, USA.

Regional organizations (3):
American Oil Chemists' Society (AOCS) (Latin American Section); *European Federation for the Science and Technology of Lipids (Euro Fed Lipid, #07210)*; *Nordic Forum for Lipid Research and Technology (Nordic Lipidforum, #17299).* [2021/XF2485/y/**C**]

♦ International Society and Federation of Cardiology / see World Heart Federation (#21562)

♦ International Society of Feline Medicine (ISFM) 15116

Chief Executive c/o iCatCare, Place Farm, Chillmark Road, Tisbury, SP3 6LW, UK. T. +441747871872. E-mail: info@icatcare.org.
Events Manager address not obtained.
URL: https://icatcare.org/veterinary/isfm/

History 1996. Founded by *'Feline Advisory Bureau (FAB)'* (UK), the current *International Cat Care (iCatCare)*, as *European Society of Feline Medicine (ESFM)*. Current name adopted Apr 2010. **Aims** Provide a worldwide resource for *veterinarians* on feline medicine and *surgery*. **Languages** English. **Staff** 22.00 FTE, paid. **Finance** Members' dues. **Activities** Knowledge management/information dissemination; certification/accreditation; standards/guidelines; training/education; events/meetings. **Events** *Feline Congress* Hong Kong (Hong Kong) 2023, *Feline Congress* Hong Kong (Hong Kong) 2022, *Feline Congress* London (UK) 2022, *Feline Congress* Rhodes (Greece) 2022, *World Feline Congress* Tisbury (UK) 2021. **Publications** *ISFM Members' e-Package* (12 a year) – newsletter; *Journal of Feline Medicine and Surgery* (12 a year) – in 3 formats. Practice protocols; manuals; conference proceedings. **Members** Practice; Individual. Members in 49 countries. Membership countries not specified. **NGO Relations** Affiliated member of: *World Small Animal Veterinary Association (WSAVA, #21795).* [2022/XD6653/**E**]

♦ International Society for Fertility Preservation (ISFP) 15117

Sec Reproductive Services, Royal Women's Hosp, Grattan Str, Parkville VIC 3053, Australia. E-mail: info@isfp-fertility.org.
Pres Cleveland Clinic, 9500 Euclid Ave – A81, Cleveland OH 44195, USA. E-mail: falcont@ccf.org.
URL: http://www.isfp-fertility.org/

History 2008. Registration: USA, Kansas. **Aims** Facilitate networking between scientists and clinicians worldwide; advocate patient rights and educate the public as well as medical professionals; share current knowledge and new discoveries; promote multidisciplinary collaborative research; develop consensus and guidelines on fertility preservation; serve and unite communities. **Structure** Board of Directors. **Languages** English. **Staff** 1.00 FTE, voluntary. **Finance** Sources: donations; members' dues. **Activities** Events/meetings. **Events** *World Congress* Brussels (Belgium) 2022, *World Congress* New York, NY (USA) 2019, *World Congress* Vienna (Austria) 2017, *World Congress* Shanghai (China) 2015, *World Congress* Valencia (Spain) 2013. **Publications** *Recommendations for Fertility Preservation in Patients with Lymphoma, Leukemia, and Breast Cancer* (2012). **Members** in 68 countries (not specified). [2022/XJ7026/**C**]

♦ International Society of the Fetus as a Patient / see International Society – The Fetus as a Patient (#15118)

♦ International Society – The Fetus as a Patient 15118

Pres c/o Lenox Hill Hospital, Dept of OB/GYN, 100 East 77th Street, New York NY 10075, USA.

History 1984. Founded on the initiative of Asim Kurjak (1942-). Former names and other names: *International Society of the Fetus as a Patient (ISFAP)* – alias. **Aims** Promote development of fetal *medicine*. **Structure** Board. **Languages** English. **Staff** 2.00 FTE, paid. **Finance** Source: annual meeting. **Activities** Events/meetings; training/education. **Events** *Congress* 2021, *Congress* Moscow (Russia) 2019, *Congress* Slovenia 2018, *Congress* Brazil 2017, *Annual Congress* Tirana (Albania) 2016. **Publications** *Fetal Diagnosis and Therapy* – journal, jointly with International Foetal Medicine and Surgery Society.

Members Individuals in 36 countries:
Albania, Argentina, Australia, Belgium, Bosnia-Herzegovina, Canada, China, Croatia, Czechia, Egypt, Finland, France, Germany, Greece, Hungary, India, Indonesia, Israel, Italy, Japan, Korea Rep, Netherlands, Norway, Philippines, Portugal, Qatar, Russia, Serbia, Spain, Sweden, Switzerland, Thailand, Türkiye, UK, Uruguay, USA.

NGO Relations Cooperates with (3): *International Cooperation Agency for Maternal and Infant Health (Matres Mundi International)*; *International Fetal Medicine and Surgery Society (#13592)*; *World Association of Perinatal Medicine (WAPM, #21170).* Instrumental in setting up (1): *International Academy of Perinatal Medicine (IAPM, #11568).* [2021/XF2716/v/**F**]

♦ International Society for Fibrinolysis and Proteolysis (ISFP) 15119

Exec Dir Thrombosis and Atherosclerosis Research Inst, Rm C5-105 DBRI, 237 Barton St E, Hamilton ON L8L 2X2, Canada. T. +19055212100 ext 40781. E-mail: fibrinolysis.org@gmail.com.
URL: http://www.fibrinolysis.org/

History Founded by *International Committee on Fibrinolysis (ICP, inactive)*. Previously registered in accordance with Belgian law. Former names and other names: *International Society for Fibrinolysis and Thrombolysis (ISFT)* – former (26 Jul 2001). Registration: Canada. **Aims** Promote scientific research relating to fundamental and medical aspects of fibrinolysis, proteolysis and *thrombolysis*; encourage exchange of information in the field. **Structure** General Meeting (annual); Council; Advisory Board. **Languages** English. **Staff** 1.50 FTE, paid. **Activities** Events/meetings. **Events** *Congress* Caen (France) 2022, *International Workshop on Molecular and Cellular Biology of Plasminogen Activation* Caen (France) 2022, *Congress* Edinburgh (UK) 2018, *Congress* Shizuoka (Japan) 2016, *International Workshop on Molecular and Cellular Biology of Plasminogen Activation* Shizuoka (Japan) 2016.

Members Active; Sponsoring. Individuals (260) in 41 countries and territories:
Argentina, Australia, Austria, Belgium, Brazil, Bulgaria, Canada, China, Denmark, Egypt, Estonia, Finland, France, Germany, Greece, Hong Kong, Hungary, Iceland, India, Ireland, Israel, Italy, Japan, Korea Rep, Mexico, Netherlands, Norway, Poland, Portugal, Russia, Saudi Arabia, Slovakia, Slovenia, South Africa, Spain, Sweden, Switzerland, Taiwan, UK, USA, Venezuela.
[2021.07.02/XC0080/v/**C**]

♦ International Society for Fibrinolysis and Thrombolysis / see International Society for Fibrinolysis and Proteolysis (#15119)
♦ International Society of Fire Service Instructors (internationally oriented national body)

♦ International Society for First World War Studies 15120

Pres School of History, Univ of Leeds, Woodhouse Lane, Leeds, LS2 9JT, UK. E-mail: president@firstworldwarstudies.org.
URL: http://www.firstworldwarstudies.org/

History 2001. **Aims** Promote the study of the First World War; foster international collaboration; encourage the comparative history of the war; facilitate exchanges across disciplines and generations of scholars. **Structure** Board of Directors. **Languages** English, French. **Activities** Events/meetings; publishing activities. **Events** *Technology* 2021, *Legacies* Leeds (UK) 2019, *Recording, Narrating and Archiving the First World War* Melbourne, VIC (Australia) 2018, *War Time* Oxford (UK) 2016, *Landscapes of the Great War* Trento (Italy) / Padua (Italy) 2015. **Publications** *First World War Studies* – journal. Books. **Members** Individuals (214) in 23 countries. Membership countries not specified. [2022.10.19/XJ5272/**D**]

♦ International Society for Fish Endocrinology (ISFE) 15121

Pres IFREMER, Univ de Brest – CNRS – IRD – LEMAR, 29280 Plouzané, France. E-mail: contact@isfendo.com.
URL: http://isfendo.com/

History 2015. Launched after having organized symposia since 1988. **Aims** Stimulate research on all aspects of the endocrine systems in fishes, including living hagfish, lampreys, cartilaginous and bony fish. **Structure** International Council; Executive Office. **Activities** Awards/prizes/competitions; events/meetings. **Events** *Conference of European Comparative Endocrinologists (CECE) & International Symposium of Fish Endocrinology* Faro (Portugal) 2022, *International Symposium* Faro (Portugal) 2021, *International Symposium* Guangzhou (China) 2020, *Quadrennial International Symposium* Gothenburg (Sweden) 2016, *Symposium* Buenos Aires (Argentina) 2012. **NGO Relations** Cooperates with (1): *European Society for Comparative Endocrinology (ESCE, #08558).* [2021/XM4451/**C**]

♦ International Society of Fish and Shellfish Immunology (ISFSI) 15122

Treas Malmoyveien 34b, 0198 Oslo, Norway.
URL: http://www.isfsim.org/

History 1990. Founded within *Nordic Council of Ministers (NCM, #17260)*. Former names and other names: *Projektstyregruppen for Fiskeimmunologi* – former (1990 to 1993); *Nordic Society of Fish Immunology* – former (1993 to 2007); *Nordisk Forening for Fiskeimmunologi (NOFFI)* – former (1993 to 2007); *European Organisation of Fish Immunology (EOFFI)* – former (2007 to 2010). **Aims** Enhance cooperation between international scientists in the fields of fish and shellfish immunology and vaccinology. **Structure** General Assembly; Board. **Languages** English. **Finance** Sources: members' dues. **Activities** Events/meetings; publishing activities. **Events** *Conference* Bodø (Norway) 2022, *Conference* Las Palmas de Gran Canaria (Spain) 2019, *Conference* Maine (USA) 2016, *ISFSI symposium and general assembly* Vigo (Spain) 2013, *EOFFI symposium and general assembly* Viterbo (Italy) 2010. [2019/XD9402/**D**]

♦ International Society for Fluoride Research (ISFR) 15123

Co-Sec Biochemistry Dept, Pomeranian Medical Univ, al Powstancow Wlkp 72, 70-111 Szczecin, Poland.
Co-Sec Preventive Medicine Dept, Kitasato Univ School of Medicine, Kitasato 1-15-1, Sagamihara KANAGAWA, 228-8555 Japan.
URL: http://www.fluorideresearch.org/

History 1962, Detroit MI (USA), at a meeting of American Society for Fluoride Research. Originally a US organization. **Structure** Officers: President, Vice President, Second Vice President, Secretary and Treasurer. Editorial Board of 37 Members. **Finance** Members' dues: US$ 50 per person, per year. **Activities** Conducts research on biological, chemical, ecological, industrial, toxicological and clinical aspects of inorganic and organic fluoride compounds. **Events** *Conference* Harbin (China) 2022, *Conference* Guiyang (China) 2018, *Conference* Hyderabad (India) 2016, *Biennial Conference* Chiang Mai (Thailand) 2014, *Biennial Conference* Jaipur (India) 2010. **Publications** *Fluoride* (4 a year) – journal. Conference proceedings, research reports and reviews, abstracts and comments. **Members** Researchers and individuals. Membership countries not specified. [2015/XG5409/**C**]

♦ **International Society for Folk Narrative Research (ISFNR)** **15124**
Société internationale de recherche sur le folklore oral
Sec Center of German Studies, Jawaharlal Nehru Univ, Delhi 110067, DELHI 110067, India. T. +919971989781. E-mail: nisfnr@gmail.com.
Pres address not obtained.
URL: http://www.isfnr.org/
History Founded 1959, Copenhagen (Denmark). Statutes adopted by 7th General Assembly, Aug 1979, Edinburgh (UK); amended by the 10th General Assembly, Jan 1995, Mysore (India). A scientific body. **Aims** Develop scholarly work in the field of folk narrative research; stimulate contacts and exchange of views among members. **Structure** General Assembly (at least every 4 years); Executive Committee; Membership Committee; Ad hoc Special Committees. **Languages** English, French, German, Russian, Spanish. **Staff** 3.00 FTE, voluntary. **Finance** Sources: members' dues. **Activities** Events/meetings; research/documentation. **Events** *Congress and General Assembly* Zagreb (Croatia) 2021, *Congress and General Assembly* Zagreb (Croatia) 2020, *Congress and General Assembly* Miami, FL (USA) 2016, *Interim Conference* Ankara (Turkey) 2015, *Congress and general assembly / Congress* Vilnius (Lithuania) 2013. **Publications** *ISFNR Newsletter* (annual). Congress reports.
Members Individuals (750) in 76 countries and territories:
Argentina, Armenia, Australia, Austria, Bangladesh, Belgium, Brazil, Bulgaria, Cameroon, Canada, Chile, China, Congo DR, Croatia, Cyprus, Czechia, Denmark, Egypt, Estonia, Faeroe Is, Finland, France, Georgia, Germany, Ghana, Greece, Greenland, Guyana, Hungary, Iceland, India, Iran Islamic Rep, Ireland, Israel, Italy, Japan, Kazakhstan, Kenya, Korea Rep, Latvia, Lithuania, Malawi, Malta, Mauritius, Netherlands, New Zealand, Nigeria, North Macedonia, Northern Ireland, Norway, Poland, Portugal, Romania, Russia, Scotland, Serbia, Sicily, Slovakia, Slovenia, South Africa, Spain, Sri Lanka, Sudan, Sweden, Switzerland, Taiwan, Tajikistan, Tanzania UR, Thailand, Tunisia, Türkiye, UK, Ukraine, USA, Venezuela, Vietnam. [2022/XC4556/v/**C**]

♦ International Society of Follicular Unit Extraction Surgeons (no recent information)

♦ **International Society of Food, Agriculture and Environment (ISFAE)** **15125**
Gen Manager WFL Publisher, PL 48, FI-00981 Helsinki, Finland. T. +3580505051135. E-mail: isfae09@gmail.com – contact@wflpublisher.com.
URL: http://world-food.net/isfae-ry/
History Originated, 2000. Formally founded in 2003. **Aims** Disseminate news and information on food, agriculture and environment; promote science and development in the field; assist scientists, professionals, experts and students to publish recent findings in our scientific journal. **Structure** Executive Committee; Executive Secretariat, headed by Secretary-General; Sections (3); Sub-Sections (28). **Languages** English, Finnish, French. **Staff** 6.00 FTE, voluntary. **Finance** Members' dues. **Activities** Knowledge management/ information dissemination; events/meetings. **Events** *International conference on cassava plant breeding, biotechnology and ecology* Brasilia (Brazil) 2006, *Conference on innovations in postharvest* Dublin (Ireland) 2006, *International symposium on sustainable agriculture for subtropical region* Changsha (China) 2005, *International conference on soilless culture* Singapore (Singapore) 2005, *International conference on sustainable agriculture for food, energy and industry* St Catharines, ON (Canada) 2005. **Publications** *Agri Food: Research and News*; *ISFAE* – journal. **Members** Full (about 1,600). Membership countries not specified.
[2019.10.23/XM0117/**D**]

♦ **International Society of Food Applications of Nanoscale Science (ISFANS)** **15126**
Chair LSU and LSU AgCenter, 141 E B Doran Bldg, Louisiana State Univ, Baton Rouge LA 70803, USA. T. +12255781055.
URL: http://www.biodelivery.lsu.edu/ISFANS Website/index.html
History Aug 2010. A Special Interest Group of *International Union of Food Science and Technology (IUFoST, #15773)*. **Aims** Strengthen research, communication, dissemination of information and networking for technology transfers and international collaborations among interested parties from academia, industry, government, consumers, and other stakeholders around the world in food nanoscale science and *nanotechnology*. **Structure** Executive Committee. **Activities** Events/meetings; research/documentation. **Events** *Symposium* Jeju (Korea Rep) 2017. [2015/XM6593/**E**]

♦ **International Society of Food Engineering (ISFE)** **15127**
Contact BsysE/WSU, Pullman WA 99164-6120, USA. T. +15093356188. Fax +15093352722. E-mail: secretariat@iufost.org.
URL: http://www.iufost.org/isfe/main.html
History 2004. A Food Engineering Disciplinary Group within *International Union of Food Science and Technology (IUFoST, #15773)*. **Aims** Provide a forum to facilitate communication and cooperation among professionals working on food engineering and related topics in academia, industry and government worldwide. **Structure** General Assembly. Executive Committee, comprising Chairman, Chairman-Elect and Secretary. **Publications** *ISFE Newsletter* (2 a year). [2017/XM0078/**E**]

♦ **International Society for Forensic Genetics (ISFG)** **15128**
Internationale Gesellschaft für Forensische Genetik
Sec Inst of Legal Medicine, Univ of Cologne, Melatengürtel 60/62, 50823 Cologne, Germany.
URL: http://www.isfg.org/
History 24 Jun 1968, Mainz (Germany). Founded at founding assembly. Former names and other names: *Society of Forensic Haemogenetics* – former (24 Jun 1968 to 1989); *International Society for Forensic Haemogenetics (ISFH)* – former (1989 to 1999); *Internationalen Gesellschaft für Forensische Hämogenetik* – former (1989 to 1999). Registration: Start date: 31 Jul 1968, Germany FR. **Aims** Promote scientific knowledge in the field of genetic markers as applied to forensic science. **Structure** General Assembly (every 2 years at scientific conference); Executive Committee; language-based Working Parties; Canine DNA Working Group. **Languages** English, German. **Staff** No permanent staff. **Finance** Sources: members' dues. **Activities** Events/ meetings; knowledge management/information dissemination; publishing activities. **Events** *ISFG Congress* Santiago de Compostela (Spain) 2024, *Congress* Washington, DC (USA) 2022, *Congress* Washington, DC (USA) 2021, *Congress* Prague (Czechia) 2019, *Congress* Seoul (Korea Rep) 2017. **Publications** *Forensic Science International: Genetics* – official journal. Congress proceedings.
Members Honorary; Full. Individuals in 81 countries and territories:
Argentina, Australia, Austria, Barbados, Belgium, Bermuda, Bolivia, Bosnia-Herzegovina, Botswana, Brazil, Canada, Chile, China, Colombia, Costa Rica, Croatia, Cyprus, Czechia, Denmark, Dominican Rep, Ecuador, Egypt, El Salvador, Estonia, Finland, France, Germany, Ghana, Greece, Guatemala, Hong Kong, Hungary, India, Iraq, Ireland, Israel, Italy, Japan, Korea Rep, Kuwait, Lebanon, Lithuania, Luxembourg, Malaysia, Malta, Mauritania, Mexico, Montenegro, Netherlands, New Zealand, North Macedonia, Norway, Pakistan, Panama, Paraguay, Peru, Philippines, Poland, Portugal, Puerto Rico, Qatar, Romania, Russia, Saudi Arabia, Senegal, Serbia, Sierra Leone, Singapore, Slovakia, Slovenia, South Africa, Spain, Sweden, Switzerland, UK, United Arab Emirates, Uruguay, USA, Venezuela, Zimbabwe.
NGO Relations Instrumental in setting up: *European DNA Profiling Group (EDNAP, #06934)*.
[2022/XD1363/v/**C**]

♦ International Society for Forensic Haemogenetics / see International Society for Forensic Genetics (#15128)
♦ International Society of Forensic Odonto-Stomatology / see International Organization for Forensic Odonto-Stomatology (#14448)

♦ **International Society of Forensic Radiology and Imaging (ISFRI)** . . . **15129**
Sec USF Health, Dept of Radiology, 2 Tampa General Circle, STC 7033, Tampa FL 33606, USA. T. +18132598782. E-mail: isfri@congresscompany.com.
URL: http://www.isfri.org/
Aims Strengthen and develop the field of forensic radiology and imaging worldwide. **Structure** Board. **Events** *Congress* Tokyo (Japan) 2022, *Congress* Krakow (Poland) 2021, *Congress* Albuquerque, NM (USA) 2020, *Congress* Berlin (Germany) 2019, *Congress* Melbourne, VIC (Australia) 2018. **Publications** *Journal of Forensic Radiology and Imaging*. **NGO Relations** Cooperates with: *International Association of Forensic Radiographers (IAFR)*. [2018/XJ8646/**D**]

♦ **International Society for Fracture Repair (ISFR)** **15130**
Exec Dir Rizzoli Orthopaedic Inst, Via GC Pupilli 1, 40136 Bologna BO, Italy. T. +39516366581. Fax +39516366581. E-mail: isfr.fractures@gmail.com.
Contact c/o Inst of Orthopaedics, Stanmore, London, HA7 4LP, UK. T. +447971686434. Fax +447971136741.
URL: http://www.fractures.com/
History 1987, Helsinki (Finland) and Stockholm (Sweden) (simultaneously). A temporary working group was set up in 1982. **Aims** Advance science of fracture repair and its application for the improvement of patient care. **Structure** Board of Directors, comprising President, First Vice-President/President Elect, Second Vice-President, Past President, Secretary General, Membership Secretary, Treasurer, Publication and Publicity Secretary, Meeting Chairman, Programme and Award Secretary, Senior Member at Large and 3 Members at Large. Executive Committee. **Activities** Advocacy/lobbying/activism; events/meetings. **Events** *Biennial General Meeting* Kyoto (Japan) 2018, *Biennial General Meeting* New York, NY (USA) 2014, *Biennial General Meeting / Biennial Meeting* Kyoto (Japan) 2012, *Biennial general meeting / Biennial Meeting* London (UK) 2010, *Workshop on osteoporotic fractures in the spine* London (UK) 2009. **Publications** *Journal of Orthopaedic Trauma*. [2018/XD7958/**D**]

♦ International Society of Franchising (internationally oriented national body)

♦ **International Society for Free Radical Research (ISFRR)** **15131**
SG King's British Heart Foundation Cntr of Excellence, School of Cardiovascular Medicine and Sciences, King's College London, 150 Stamford St, London, SE1 9NH, UK. T. +442078484306. Fax +442078484500.
Pres Univ de Valencia, Av de Blasco Ibañez 13, 46010 Valencia, Spain. T. +34983864650.
URL: http://www.sfrr.org/
History 9 Jul 1982. Most recent constitution: 1992. Former names and other names: *Society for Free Radical Research International (SFRR)* – alias. **Aims** Promote interest in research into understanding redox signalling in living cells, reactions and properties of reactive oxygen species, including their physical, chemical, biological and medical roles; advance education in redox biology, reactive oxidants and exogenous and cellular antioxidant defence pathways. **Structure** General Meeting (every 2 years); International Committee; Regional groups (5): *Society for Free Radical Research Africa (SFRR-Africa, #19559)*; *Society for Free Radical Research Asia (SFRR ASIA, #19560)*; *Society for Free Radical Research – Europe (SFRRE, #19561)*; *Society for Redox Biology and Medicine (SfRBM, #19628)* (for North and South America); *Society for Redox Research Australasia (#19629)*. **Languages** English. **Staff** 4.00 FTE, voluntary. **Finance** Sources: donations; members' dues; sponsorship. **Activities** Events/meetings; financial and/or material support; training/education. **Events** *Biennial Conference* Punta del Este (Uruguay) 2023, *Biennial Conference* 2021, *Africa Meeting* Cape Town (South Africa) 2021, *Biennial Conference* Taipei (Taiwan) 2020, *Biennial Conference* Lisbon (Portugal) 2018. **Publications** *Free Radical Biology and Medicine* (12 a year) – journal; *Free Radical Research* (12 a year) – journal; *Redox Biology*; *Redox Report*. **Members** Societies representing over 2,800 individual researchers. Membership countries not specified. **NGO Relations** Member of (1): *International Union of Biochemistry and Molecular Biology (IUBMB, #15759)*. [2021.06.16/XD5477/**C**]

♦ **International Society of Friendship and Good Will (ISFGW)** **15132**
Société internationale d'amitié et de bonne volonté – Sociedad Internacional de Amistad y Buena Voluntad – Internacia Societo de Amikeco kaj Bonvolo
Pres 3119 Lassiter St, Durham NC 277707-3888, USA.
URL: http://www.friendshipandgoodwill.org/
History Founded 8 Mar 1978. **Aims** Encourage and foster the advancement of international *understanding*, better human relations, *peace*, friendship and good will. **Structure** President; President Emeritus; 2 Vice-Presidents; Secretary General; Treasurer. **Languages** English, Esperanto. **Staff** Voluntary. **Finance** Members'dues. Budget (annual): US$ 25,000. **Activities** Sponsors and promotes: *'Universal Letter Writing Week'* each year 1-7 January; *'Celebration of Love Week'* during second full week in February; *'International Friendship Week'* last week in February; *'Universal Women's Week'* 8-14 March; *'Universal Amateur Radio Month'* 1-30 April; *'Universal Family Week'* second week in May; *'International Volunteers Week'* 1-7 June; *'Freedom Week'* 4-10 July; *'Self Improvement Month'* 1-30 September; *'Universal Children's Week'* 1-7 October; *'Peace Friendship and Good Will Week'* 24-31 October; *'World Communication Week'* 1-7 November; *'Human Rights Week'* 10-16 December, distributing copies of the Universal Declaration of Human Rights; *'Interlanguage Week'* 15-21 December; *'Human Rights Month'* 1-31 December; *'International Hall of Fame'* honouring persons who have made significant contributions to humanity through their service in government, business, industry, education, and the arts and sciences. Offers home-study courses in Esperanto. Holds annual meetings usually the last week in Jul or the first week in Aug in conjunction with UEA World Congress. Operates a book service for members. **Events** *Annual Meeting* Orlando, FL (USA) 2003, *Annual meeting* Prague (Czech Rep) 1996, *Annual meeting* Finland 1995, *Annual meeting* Seoul (Korea Rep) 1994, *Annual meeting* Valencia (Spain) 1993. **Publications** *ISFGW Bulletin* (4 a year) in English; *ISFGW Esperanto-Bulteno* (4 a year) in Esperanto.
Members Individuals: men and women worldwide who subscribe to the objectives of the Society. Members in 188 countries and territories:
Afghanistan, Albania, Algeria, Andorra, Angola, Antigua-Barbuda, Argentina, Armenia, Australia, Austria, Azerbaijan, Bahamas, Bahrain, Bangladesh, Barbados, Belarus, Belgium, Belize, Benin, Bhutan, Bolivia, Bosnia-Herzegovina, Botswana, Brazil, Brunei Darussalam, Bulgaria, Burkina Faso, Burundi, Cambodia, Cameroon, Canada, Canaries, Cape Verde, Central African Rep, Chad, Chile, China, Colombia, Comoros, Congo Brazzaville, Congo DR, Costa Rica, Côte d'Ivoire, Croatia, Cuba, Cyprus, Czechia, Denmark, Djibouti, Dominica, Dominican Rep, Ecuador, Egypt, El Salvador, Equatorial Guinea, Estonia, Eswatini, Ethiopia, Fiji, Finland, France, Gabon, Gambia, Georgia, Germany, Ghana, Greece, Grenada, Guatemala, Guinea, Guinea-Bissau, Guyana, Haiti, Holy See, Honduras, Hong Kong, Hungary, Iceland, India, Indonesia, Iran Islamic Rep, Iraq, Ireland, Israel, Italy, Jamaica, Japan, Jordan, Kazakhstan, Kenya, Korea DPR, Korea Rep, Kuwait, Kyrgyzstan, Laos, Latvia, Lebanon, Lesotho, Liberia, Libya, Liechtenstein, Lithuania, Luxembourg, Madagascar, Malawi, Malaysia, Maldives, Mali, Malta, Marshall Is, Mauritania, Mauritius, Mexico, Micronesia FS, Moldova, Monaco, Mongolia, Morocco, Mozambique, Myanmar, Namibia, Nepal, Netherlands, New Zealand, Nicaragua, Niger, Nigeria, North Macedonia, Northern Ireland, Norway, Oman, Pakistan, Panama, Papua New Guinea, Paraguay, Peru, Philippines, Poland, Portugal, Qatar, Romania, Russia, Rwanda, Samoa, San Marino, Sao Tomé-Principe, Saudi Arabia, Senegal, Serbia, Seychelles, Sierra Leone, Singapore, Slovakia, Slovenia, Solomon Is, Somalia, South Africa, Spain, Sri Lanka, St Kitts-Nevis, St Lucia, St Vincent-Grenadines, Sudan, Suriname, Sweden, Switzerland, Syrian AR, Taiwan, Tajikistan, Tanzania UR, Thailand, Togo, Trinidad-Tobago, Tunisia, Türkiye, Turkmenistan, Uganda, UK, Ukraine, United Arab Emirates, Uruguay, USA, Vanuatu, Venezuela, Vietnam, Yemen, Zambia, Zimbabwe.
IGO Relations *United Nations (UN, #20515)*. **NGO Relations** *Universal Esperanto Association (UEA, #20676)*.
[2015/XD3935/v/**F**]

♦ International Society of the Friends of Notocacti (internationally oriented national body)

♦ **International Society for Frontotemporal Dementias (ISFTD)** **15133**
Contact 1124 Frederick Drive S, Indianapolis IN 46260, USA. T. +13173394700. E-mail: isftd.org@gmail.com.
URL: http://www.isftd.org/
History Founded 2011, following a series of conferences organized since 1986. **Structure** Executive Committee. **Finance** Members' dues. **Activities** Events/meetings. **Events** *Congress* Lille (France) 2022, *Congress* 2021, *Congress* Minneapolis, MN (USA) 2020. [2019/XM8005/c/**E**]

♦ International Society of Functional Linguistics (#19492)
♦ International Society for Functional Metagenomics / see Functional Metagenomics International (#10017)
♦ International Society of Functional Thin Film Materials and Devices (unconfirmed)

♦ **International Society for Fungal Conservation (ISFC)** **15134**
Société Internationale pour la Conservation Fongique – Sociedad Internacional para la Conservación de los Hongos – Sociedade Internacional para a Conservação dos Fungos
Pres c/o CABI, Bakeham Lane, Egham, TW20 9TY, UK. T. +441491829031. E-mail: ffunecol@gmail.com.
URL: http://www.fungal-conservation.org/

History Aug 2010. **Aims** Promote conservation of fungi globally. **Structure** General Assembly. Council, comprising Governing Committee, 4 elected Councillors, Chair of each fungal special group within *International Union for Conservation of Nature and Natural Resources (IUCN, #15766)* – Species Survival Commission (SSC), representative of *International Mycological Association (IMA, #14203)* and 17 Regional Delegates. Governing Committee, comprising Offices, 2 non-office-holding Council members. Officers: President; Vice-President; Secretary; Treasurer; Membership Secretary; Editor; Communications Officer. **Events** *Meeting on Fungal Conservation in a Changing Europe* Ohrid (Macedonia) 2017, *Congress* Mugla (Turkey) 2013, *Congress* Whitby (UK) 2009, *Congress* Córdoba (Spain) 2007. [2020/XJ5782/**B**]

♦ International Society on the Fusion of Science and Technologies (unconfirmed)

♦ International Society of Gastroenterological Carcinogenesis (ISGC) 15135

Chairman Dept of Surgery, Tokushima Univ, 3-18-15 Kuramoto, Tokushima, 770-8503 Japan. T. +81886337139. Fax +81886319698.
URL: http://www.j-sgc.org/isgc/

History 1996, Hiroshima (Japan), during the 1st International Conference on Gastroenterological Carcinogenesis. **Aims** Encourage and develop research and communication in the areas of gastroenterological biology and oncology in both basic and clinical aspects. **Structure** General Assembly (annual); Board of Directors. **Languages** English, Japanese. **Staff** 2.00 FTE, paid. **Finance** Members' dues. **Activities** Events/meetings. **Events** *Conference* Kumamoto (Japan) 2017, *Conference* Fukuoka (Japan) 2014, *Conference* Philadelphia, PA (USA) 2013, *Conference* Houston, TX (USA) 2010, *Conference* Oxford (UK) 2008. **Publications** *ISGC Newsletter*.
Members Full in 12 countries and territories:
Australia, Canada, China, Finland, France, Germany, Italy, Korea Rep, Taiwan, Türkiye, UK, USA. [2018.09.05/XD7404/**D**]

♦ International Society for Gastrointestinal Hereditary Tumours (InSiGHT) 15136

UK Secretariat The Polyposis Registry, St Mark's Hospital, Watford Road, Harrow, HA1 3UJ, UK.
Netherlands Secretariat Netherlands Foundation for the Detection of Hereditary Tumours, Poortgebouw Zuid, Rijnsburgerweg 10, 2333 AA Leiden, Netherlands.
URL: https://www.insight-group.org/

History 2005. Established by merger of *International Collaborative Group for Hereditary Non-Polyposis Colorectal Cancer (ICG-HNPOC, inactive)* and Leeds Castle Polyposis Group. Registration: Companies House, No/ID: 7358100, England and Wales, England and Wales; Charities Commission, No/ID: 1139700, England and Wales. **Aims** Improve the quality of care of patients and families with any hereditary condition resulting in gastrointestinal tumours. **Structure** Council, comprising Chairman, Chairman Elect, Immediate Past Chairman, Secretary, Treasurer and 6 members. **Languages** English. **Staff** 2.00 FTE, voluntary. **Finance** Sources: members' dues. **Activities** Events/meetings; healthcare; knowledge management/information dissemination; research and development; training/education. **Events** *Biennial Conference* Jersey City, NJ (USA) 2022, *Biennial Conference* Auckland (New Zealand) 2019, *Biennial Conference* Florence (Italy) 2017, *Biennial Conference / Biennial Scientific Meeting* Sao Paulo (Brazil) 2015, *Biennial Conference / Biennial Scientific Meeting* Cairns, QLD (Australia) 2013.
Members Individuals in 29 countries:
Argentina, Australia, Austria, Brazil, Canada, Chile, China, Cyprus, Czechia, Denmark, Finland, France, Germany, India, Ireland, Israel, Italy, Japan, Korea Rep, Lithuania, Malaysia, Netherlands, New Zealand, Norway, Spain, Sweden, Switzerland, UK, USA. [2022/XM0073/**D**]

♦ International Society of Gender Medicine (IGM) 15137

Pres MedUni Vienna, Dept of Medicine III, Währinger Gürtel 18-20, 1090 Vienna, Austria. T. +4314040043000. Fax +4314040043060. E-mail: info@isogem.eu.
URL: http://www.isogem.eu/

History 1999. New name adopted Jul 2006, Berlin (Germany), following 1st World Congress on Gender Specific Medicine. Former names and other names: *International Society for Gender Specific Medicine (ISGSM)* – former (1999 to 2006). **Aims** Establish and develop gender medicine in an international context by promoting interdisciplinary research on sex/gender differences in basic sciences, clinical medicine and public health. **Structure** General Assembly (every 2 years); Board, comprising President, Secretary, Treasurer and ex-officio members. **Languages** English. **Staff** Voluntary. **Finance** Low budget. **Activities** Events/meetings; knowledge management/information dissemination; publishing activities; standards/guidelines; training/education. **Events** *Congress* Padua (Italy) 2022, *Congress* Florence (Italy) 2021, *Congress* Vienna (Austria) 2019, *Joint Meeting* Washington, DC (USA) 2019, *Congress* Miyagi (Japan) 2017. **Publications** Textbook on gender medicine; congress proceedings.
Members National; Individual. National associations in 8 countries:
Austria, Germany, Israel, Italy, Japan, Netherlands, Sweden, USA. [2019/XM2528/**D**]

♦ International Society for Gender Specific Medicine / see International Society of Gender Medicine (#15137)
♦ International Society of General Practice (inactive)

♦ International Society on General Relativity and Gravitation (ISGRG) 15138

Commission internationale sur la relativité générale et la gravitation
Sec/Treas Dept of Physics, Oakland Univ, Rochester MI 48309, USA. T. +12483703411.
Pres Dept of Physics and Astronomy, The Johns Hopkins Univ, Baltimore MD 21218, USA. T. +14105162535.
URL: http://www.isgrg.org/

History 1957. Former names and other names: *International Committee on General Relativity and Gravitation* – former (1957 to 1971); *GRG Committee* – former (1957 to 1971); *International Commission on General Relativity and Gravitation* – alias (1971); *GRG Society* – alias (1971). **Aims** Promote study of GRG and exchange information in the interest of members and the profession. **Structure** General Assembly (every 3 years, at International Conference); Commission; Executive Council; Nominating Committee. **Languages** English. **Staff** Voluntary. **Finance** Sources: members' dues. Annual budget: 5,000 USD. **Activities** Events/meetings; knowledge management/information dissemination. **Events** *International Conference on General Relativity and Gravitation* Beijing (China) 2022, *Edoardo Amaldi Conference on Gravitational Waves* Valencia (Spain) 2019, *International Conference on General Relativity and Gravitation* Valencia (Spain) 2019, *Edoardo Amaldi Conference on Gravitational Waves* Pasadena, CA (USA) 2017, *International Conference on General Relativity and Gravitation* New York, NY (USA) 2016. **Publications** *General Relativity and Gravitation* (12 a year) – journal.
Members Full in 49 countries and territories:
Argentina, Australia, Austria, Belgium, Brazil, Canada, China, Colombia, Czechia, Denmark, Egypt, Estonia, France, Georgia, Germany, Greece, Hungary, Iceland, India, Iran Islamic Rep, Ireland, Israel, Italy, Japan, Kazakhstan, Korea Rep, Kuwait, Malaysia, Malta, Mexico, Moldova, Netherlands, New Zealand, Norway, Oman, Pakistan, Poland, Portugal, Qatar, Romania, Russia, South Africa, Spain, Sweden, Switzerland, Taiwan, Türkiye, UK, USA.
NGO Relations Affiliated with (1): *International Union of Pure and Applied Physics (IUPAP, #15810)* (as Affiliated Commission of). [2023.02.26/XD4359/**C**]

♦ International Society for General Semantics (inactive)
♦ International Society for General Systems Research / see International Society for the Systems Sciences (#15500)

♦ International Society for Genetic Eye Diseases and Retinoblastoma (ISGEDR) 15139

President Jules-Gonin Eye Hospital, 15 Avenue de France, 1002 Lausanne VD, Switzerland.
Exec Vice-Pres i32, 9500 Euclid Ave, Cleveland OH 44195, USA.
URL: http://www.isgedr.com/

History 1975, Oxford (UK). **Aims** Bring together individuals interested in the field of genetic diseases of the eye and in Retinoblastoma; provide a forum for researchers in the field of genetic diseases of the eye and to share information; promote international collaboration in the study of genetic diseases of the eye and in Retinoblastoma; disseminate scientific knowledge. **Structure** Executive Committee. Membership open. **Languages** English. **Staff** 1.00 FTE, paid. **Finance** Sources: members' dues. **Activities** Events/meetings. **Events** *Meeting* Lausanne (Switzerland) 2021, *Meeting* Giesen (Germany) 2019, *Meeting* Leeds (UK) 2017, *Meeting* Halifax, NS (Canada) 2015, *Meeting* Ghent (Belgium) 2013. **Publications** *Ophthalmic Genetics* – official journal.
Members Active; Associate. Individuals in 13 countries and territories:
Australia, Brazil, Canada, France, Germany, Lebanon, Netherlands, Puerto Rico, Saudi Arabia, Spain, Switzerland, UK, USA.
IGO Relations None. **NGO Relations** Member of (4): *International Council of Ophthalmology (ICO, #13057)*; *International Pediatric Ophthalmology and Strabismus Council (IPOSC, #14544)*; World Congress of Ophthalmology; *World Society of Paediatric Ophthalmology and Strabismus (WSPOS, #21807)*. Cooperates with (1): *Société internationale d'ophtalmologie pédiatrique (no recent information)*. [2022.04.13/XD7555/**D**]

♦ International Society for Genomic and Evolutionary Microbiology (unconfirmed)

♦ International Society of Geographical and Epidemiological Ophthalmology (ISGEO) 15140

Société internationale d'ophtalmologie géographique et épidémiologique – Sociedad Internacional de Oftalmologia Geografica y Epidemiológica
Sec c/o ICEH LSHTM, Keppel Street, London, WC1 E7HT, UK. T. +442079588333. Fax +442079588325. E-mail: isgeomembers@gmail.com.
URL: https://iceh.lshtm.ac.uk/isgeo/

History Jun 1970, Canada. Jun 1970, Fort Smith (Canada), as *International Society of Geographic Ophthalmology (ISGO) – Société internationale d'ophtalmologie géographique – Sociedad Internacional de Oftalmologia Geografica*. Registered in accordance with Canadian law and the law of North West Territories (Canada), under patronage of *International Council of Ophthalmology (ICO, #13057)* and of *International Federation of Ophthalmological Societies (IFOS, inactive)*. **Aims** Promote the science of geographic and epidemiologic ophthalmology, including the epidemiological, clinical, educational, environmental and cultural aspects of eye disease, prevention of blindness, preservation of sight and visual rehabilitation; provide a forum for presentation and discussion of research in ophthalmology and support for ophthalmic research in developing countries. **Structure** Executive Council, comprising the Executive Committee – President, Past President, Vice-President, Treasurer and Secretary – and 10 Councillors. **Languages** English, French, German, Spanish. **Staff** Voluntary. **Finance** Members' dues (annual): US$ 100. Meeting fees. **Activities** Sends lecturers, ophthalmic technicians, ophthalmologists and other experts to developing countries to estimate needs of programmes for prevention and cure of ocular diseases, focusing in particular on the epidemiology and public health aspects of eye disease and the evaluation of different interventions; provides funds for students from developing countries; collects and compiles bibliographical information. Organizes International Congress (every 2 years). Local members of the Executive Council organize zonal and regional meetings. **Events** *International Congress* Singapore (Singapore) 2020, *International Congress* Hyderabad (India) 2018, *International Congress* Durban (South Africa) 2016, *International Congress* London (UK) 2014, *International Congress* Hyderabad (India) 2012. **Publications** *Ophthalmic Epidemiology* – journal.
Members Honorary Life; Full; Associate. Health professionals in 55 countries and territories:
Albania, Argentina, Australia, Belgium, Bolivia, Brazil, Bulgaria, Canada, Chile, China, Colombia, Denmark, Egypt, Ethiopia, Finland, France, Gambia, Germany, Ghana, Greece, India, Indonesia, Ireland, Israel, Italy, Japan, Kenya, Korea Rep, Liberia, Malawi, Mali, Mexico, Mongolia, Morocco, Nepal, Netherlands, Nigeria, Norway, Pakistan, Russia, Saudi Arabia, Singapore, South Africa, Sweden, Switzerland, Taiwan, Tanzania UR, Thailand, Tunisia, Türkiye, Uganda, UK, USA, Zambia, Zimbabwe.
NGO Relations Representative member of: *International Agency for the Prevention of Blindness (IAPB, #11597)*. [2020/XC4598/v/**C**]

♦ International Society of Geographical Pathology (inactive)
♦ International Society of Geographic Ophthalmology / see International Society of Geographical and Epidemiological Ophthalmology (#15140)

♦ International Society for Geometry and Graphics (ISGG) 15141

Contact Unit Geometry and Surveying, Univ Innsbruck, Technikerstr 13, 6020 Innsbruck, Austria.
Pres Politecnico Milano, Dipto di Architettura e Studi Urbani, Via Bonardi 3, 20133 Milan MI, Italy.
URL: http://www.isgg.net/

Aims Foster international collaboration; stimulate scientific research and teaching methodology in the fields of geometry and graphics. **Structure** Board Committee. **Languages** English. **Finance** Sources: members' dues. **Activities** Events/meetings; publishing activities. **Events** *Conference* Sao Paulo (Brazil) 2022, *Conference* Sao Paulo (Brazil) 2021, *Conference* Sao Paulo (Brazil) 2020, *Conference* Milan (Italy) 2018, *Conference* Beijing (China) 2016. **Publications** *Journal for Geometry and Graphics*.
Members Institutional members in 19 countries:
Australia, Austria, Brazil, Canada, China, Croatia, Czechia, Egypt, Germany, Hungary, Italy, Japan, Poland, Romania, Russia, Slovakia, Switzerland, Ukraine, USA.
Included in the above, 1 organization listed in this Yearbook:
Institute of Electrical and Electronics Engineers (IEEE, #11259). [2022.10.12/XJ6520/y/**C**]

♦ International Society of Geriatric Oncology (#19493)

♦ International Society for Gerontechnology 15142

SG Matrix 1-05, Eindhoven Univ of Technology, PO Box 513, 5600 MB Eindhoven, Netherlands.
URL: http://www.gerontechnology.org/

History 3 Sep 1997. A Standing Committee of *International Association of Gerontology and Geriatrics (IAGG, #11920)*. **Aims** Encourage and promote research and development of technological innovations in products and services that address older peoples' ambitions and functional needs on the basis of scientific knowledge about ageing processes, including cultural and socioeconomic aspects. **Structure** General Assembly (every é years); Executive Board; Committees; Working Groups; Regional Chapters. **Languages** English. **Staff** 8.00 FTE, voluntary. **Finance** Members' dues. Conferences. **Activities** Events/meetings; training/education. **Events** *World Conference of Gerontechnology* 2024, *World Conference of Gerontechnology* Daegu (Korea Rep) 2022, *World Conference of Gerontechnology* 2020, *World Conference of Gerontechnology* Trondheim (Norway) 2020, *Evolving designs for our future selves* St Petersburg, FL (USA) 2018. **Publications** *Gerontechnology* (4 a year) – journal.
Members Full in 22 countries and territories:
Argentina, Australia, Austria, Brazil, Canada, Finland, France, Germany, Hong Kong, Ireland, Israel, Italy, Japan, Malaysia, Netherlands, Norway, Slovakia, Sweden, Switzerland, Taiwan, UK, USA. [2022/XD7096/**D**]

♦ International Society for Gesture Studies (ISGS) 15143

Pres Dept Psychological and Brain Sciences, Colgate Univ, 13 Oak Dr, Hamilton NY 13346, USA.
URL: http://www.gesturestudies.com/

History 6 Jun 2002, Austin TX (USA), during the conference 'Gesture – the living medium'. Official founding follows organizing activities initiated in 1998. Previously referred to as *International Association for Gesture Research*. **Aims** Promote gesture studies worldwide; facilitate dialogue among researchers, professionals and the interested public, across disciplinary and institutional boundaries; integrate the study of gesture with investigations into a diverse range of forms of cognitive, communicative and cultural life of human groups. **Structure** Executive Board. **Events** *Congress* Chicago, IL (USA) 2021, *Congress* Cape Town (South Africa) 2018, *Congress* Paris (France) 2016, *The communicative body in development* Lund (Sweden) 2012, *Gesture – evolution, brain and linguistic structures* Frankfurt-Oder (Germany) 2010. **Publications** *Gesture* – journal.
NGO Relations *International Association for Semiotic Studies (IASS-AIS, #12160)*. [2020.03.11/XD7913/**D**]

♦ International Society for Glaucoma Surgery (ISGS) 15144

Pres Service d'Ophtalmologie, Hôpitaux Univ de Genève, Rue Alcide Jentzer 22, 1211 Geneva, Switzerland.
URL: https://isgs.info/

Aims Promote the art and science of glaucoma surgery. **Structure** Executive Board. Committees (3): Senior Advisory; Associate Advisory; Right for Vision. **Activities** Events/meetings; knowledge management/information dissemination; research/documentation; training/education. **Events** *International Congress on Glaucoma Surgery* Geneva (Switzerland) 2022, *International Congress on Glaucoma Surgery* London (UK) 2020, *Congress* Montréal, QC (Canada) 2018, *Congress* Muscat (Oman) 2016, *Congress* Singapore (Singapore) 2014. **Members** Membership countries not specified. **NGO Relations** Member of: *World Glaucoma Association (WGA, #21540)*. [2019/XD9410/**C**]

♦ International Society of Global Health (ISOGH) 15145

Pres Caledonian Exchange, 19A Canning Street, Edinburgh, EH3 8HE, UK. E-mail: secretariat@isogh.org.
URL: https://isogh.org/

History 2019, Edinburgh (UK). Registration: No/ID: SC630328, Scotland. **Aims** Promote global health as a field of scientific research and health care practice nationally and internationally. **Structure** Board of Governors; Secretariat. **Activities** Knowledge management/information dissemination; research/documentation; training/education. **Events** *Conference on Global Health* Dubrovnik (Croatia) 2022. **Publications** *Journal of Global Health*; *Journal of Global Health Reports*.
Members Individuals in 79 countries and territories:
Albania, Argentina, Australia, Austria, Belgium, Botswana, Brazil, Bulgaria, Burkina Faso, Cambodia, Cameroon, Canada, China, Colombia, Congo DR, Côte d'Ivoire, Croatia, Cyprus, Czechia, Egypt, Ethiopia, Finland, Gambia, Germany, Ghana, Greece, Guinea, Haiti, Hong Kong, Hungary, Iceland, India, Indonesia, Iran Islamic Rep, Iraq, Ireland, Italy, Jamaica, Japan, Jordan, Kenya, Korea Rep, Latvia, Lesotho, Malaysia, Malta, Mexico, Mongolia, Morocco, Mozambique, Namibia, Nepal, Netherlands, New Zealand, Nigeria, Norway, Paraguay, Peru, Philippines, Poland, Portugal, Qatar, Russia, Rwanda, Saudi Arabia, Serbia, Slovenia, South Africa, Spain, Sudan, Sweden, Switzerland, Taiwan, Tanzania UR, Uganda, UK, Uruguay, USA, Vietnam.
[AA2952/v/C]

♦ International Society of Global Optimization (iSoGO) 15146

Pres Univ of Florida, PO Box 116595, Gainesville FL 32611-6595, USA.
URL: http://www.globaloptimization.org/

History Jun 2009, Changsha (China). Proposed at 1st World Congress on Global Optimization. **Aims** Promote common understanding of all disciplines in related fields of global optimization; advance the theory and methodology for academicians and practitioners. **Structure** Advisory Board. **Activities** Awards/prizes/competitions; events/meetings. **Events** *HUGO – Workshop on Global Optimization* Szeged (Hungary) 2022, *World Congress on Global Optimization* Athens (Greece) 2021, *World Congress on Global Optimization* Metz (France) 2019, *LeGO – International Workshop on Global Optimization* Leiden (Netherlands) 2018, *World Congress on Global Optimization* College Station, TX (USA) 2017. [2021/AA2471/C]

♦ International Society for Gravitational Physiology (ISGP) 15147

Chair Dir Nutritional Sci, Profil Inst, Hellerbergstrasse 9, 41460 Neuss, Germany. T. +4915751469753.
URL: http://www.isgp1979.org/

Events *Annual Meeting* College Station, TX (USA) 2021, *Annual Meeting* College Station, TX (USA) 2020, *Annual Meeting* Nagoya (Japan) 2019, *Annual Meeting* Toulouse (France) 2016, *Annual Meeting* Ljubljana (Slovenia) 2015. **Publications** *Journal of Gravitational Physiology.* [2016/XD8877/D]

♦ International Society of Grid Generation (ISGG) 15148

Contact address not obtained. E-mail: bsoni@tntech.edu.
URL: http://www.isgg.org/

Aims Promote, foster, organize and coordinate various activities in *computer*-assisted *mathematical* grid generation. **Events** *Conference* Las Palmas de Gran Canaria (Spain) 2012, *Conference* Montréal, QC (Canada) 2011, *Conference* Moscow (Russia) 2010, *Conference* Montréal, QC (Canada) 2009, *International conference on numerical grid generation* Montréal, QC (Canada) 2009.
Members Corporate; Individual; Institutional; Student. Members in 17 countries:
Brazil, Canada, France, Germany, India, Iran Islamic Rep, Italy, Japan, Korea Rep, Netherlands, Norway, Russia, Singapore, Spain, Switzerland, UK, USA. [2012/XM0170/D]

♦ International Society of Groundwater for Sustainable Development (ISGSD) 15149

Sociedad Internacional de Agua Subterranea para el Desarrollo Sostenible

Main Office Teknikringen 10B, SE-100 44 Stockholm, Sweden. T. +4687907399.
Vice-Pres Institute for Life Sciences and the Environment, Toowoomba Campus, Univ of Southern Queensland, Toowoomba QLD 4350, Australia.
URL: http://www.isgsd.org/

Aims Improve understanding of groundwater resources; facilitate their sustainable management for a social and economic human development. **Structure** Executive Board, comprising President, Vice-President, Executive Secretary, Joint Secretary, Treasurer and 10 members. **Finance** Sources: members' dues. **Activities** Events/meetings. **Events** *International Congress on Arsenic in the Environment* Wageningen (Netherlands) 2021, *International Congress on Arsenic in the Environment* Wageningen (Netherlands) 2020, *International Congress on Arsenic in the Environment* Beijing (China) 2018, *International Congress on Arsenic in the Environment* Stockholm (Sweden) 2016, *International Congress on Arsenic in the Environment* Buenos Aires (Argentina) 2014. **NGO Relations** Supported by: *Fondation de la maison des sciences de l'homme (MSH).*
[2020/XM2936/C]

♦ International Society for Group Theory in Cognitive Science (no recent information)
♦ International Society of Gynaecological Pathologists / see International Society of Gynecological Pathologists (#15151)

♦ International Society of Gynecological Endocrinology (ISGE) 15150

Associazione Internazionale di Ginecologia Endocrinologica

Pres Univ degli Studi di Pisa, Div Ginecologia e Ostetricia, Via Rome 35, 56100 Pisa PI, Italy. E-mail: isge@tiscali.it.
Exec Sec address not obtained.
URL: https://www.isgesociety.com/

History 1986, Geneva (Switzerland). Registration: Switzerland. **Aims** Promote science and research into all aspects of gynaecological endocrinology and of communication between scientists interested in these subjects. **Structure** Board; Executive Committee. **Languages** English, Italian. **Activities** Events/meetings; training/education. **Events** *World Congress* Florence (Italy) 2022, *World Congress* Florence (Italy) 2020, *World Congress* Florence (Italy) 2020, *World Congress* Florence (Italy) 2018, *World Congress* Florence (Italy) 2016. **Publications** *Gynecological Endocrinology* (12 a year); *Gynecological and Reproductive Endocrinology and Metabolism (GREM)* – open-Access Journal. *ISGE Series.*
Members Full in 34 countries:
Albania, Argentina, Brazil, Bulgaria, Chile, Denmark, Dominican Rep, Egypt, Estonia, Finland, France, Germany, Greece, Hungary, Iran Islamic Rep, Israel, Italy, Japan, Libya, Lithuania, Malta, Netherlands, New Zealand, Nigeria, Poland, Romania, Russia, Spain, Sweden, Switzerland, Taiwan, UK, USA, Venezuela. [2023/XD3447/D]

♦ International Society of Gynecological Pathologists (ISGyP) 15151

Société internationale des pathologistes en gynécologie

Sec Univ of California San Francisco, 1701 Divisadero St, San Francisco CA 94115, USA.
Pres Vancouver General Hosp, 899 W 12th Ave, Vancouver BC V5Z 1M9, Canada.
URL: http://www.isgyp.org/

History Founded 1976, Washington DC (USA). Also referred to as *International Society of Gynaecological Pathologists.* **Aims** Foster education, research and international communication in gynaecological pathology. **Structure** Board of Directors. **Languages** English. **Staff** Voluntary. **Finance** Sources: members' dues. **Activities** Events/meetings; publishing activities. **Events** *Symposium* San Diego, CA (USA) 2007, *Symposium* Atlanta, GA (USA) 2006, *Symposium* Montréal, QC (Canada) 2006, *Symposium* Vancouver, BC (Canada) 2004, *Symposium* Washington, DC (USA) 2003. **Publications** *International Journal of Gynaecological Pathology* (6 a year); *ISGyP Newsletter.* **Members** Individuals. Membership countries not specified. **IGO Relations** *WHO (#20950).* **NGO Relations** *European Society of Pathology (ESP, #08689)*; *Fédération Internationale de Gynécologie et d'Obstétrique (FIGO, #09638)*; *International Academy of Pathology (IAP, #11567)*; *International Collaboration on Cancer Reporting (ICCR, #12637)*; *International Gynecologic Cancer Society (IGCS, #13767)*; *United States and Canadian Academy of Pathology (USCAP)*; national associations.
[2017.10.13/XD1318/v/C]

♦ International Society for Gynecologic Endoscopy (ISGE) 15152

Secretariat Viale Vasco De Gama 271, 00121 Rome RM, Italy. E-mail: secretariat@isge.org.
URL: http://www.isge.org/

History 1989, Orlando, FL (USA). **Aims** Establish an international forum to exchange information and new ideas between gynaecologic endoscopists of all nations; provide leadership and unprejudiced academic excellence in the field; promote development of new instrumentation, techniques and therapy; promote safety and competence in endoscopy through proper education of all involved persons. **Structure** Board of 24. Executive Committee. Committees (4): Conference; Scientific; Training; Website. **Languages** English. **Staff** 1.00 FTE, paid. **Finance** Sources: sponsorship. **Activities** Events/meetings. **Events** *Annual Congress* Split (Croatia) 2021, *Gynecological Endocrinology World Congress* Florence (Italy) 2020, *Gynecological Endocrinology World Congress* Florence (Italy) 2020, *Annual Congress* Split (Croatia) 2020, *Joint Conference* Cape Town (South Africa) 2019. **Publications** *ISGE Newsletter.*
Members Full in 25 countries:
Argentina, Australia, Belgium, Cameroon, Canada, Chile, China, France, Germany, Hong Kong, India, Italy, Malaysia, Mexico, Netherlands, New Zealand, Portugal, Singapore, South Africa, Spain, Taiwan, Thailand, Türkiye, UK, USA.
NGO Relations Affiliated with: *Australasian Gynaecological Endoscopy and Surgery (AGES).* Cooperates with: *Middle East Society for Gynecological Endoscopy (MESGE, #16789).* [2005.10.21/XD2747/B]

♦ International Society of Haemofiltration / see International Society of Blood Purification (#14978)
♦ International Society of Haemorheology / see International Society of Biorheology (#14972)
♦ International Society of Haemotherapy and Graft Engineering / see International Society for Cell & Gene Therapy (#15000)
♦ International Society of Hair Restoration Surgery (internationally oriented national body)
♦ International Society of Hand and Composite Tissue Allotransplantation / see International Society of Vascularized Composite Allotransplantation (#15536)

♦ International Society for Haptics (ISFH) 15153

Address not obtained.

History 18 Feb 2003. **Aims** Promote and exchange knowledge in the field of haptics, encompassing all aspects of the sense of *touch*, including: research in perception and action; the development of interfaces and applications to allow human-machine interaction and communication through touch. **Languages** English. **Staff** 1.00 FTE, paid. **Finance** Contributions from members. **Activities** Organizes seminars and on-line lectures.
Members in 18 countries:
Austria, Brazil, Canada, China, Finland, France, Germany, India, Ireland, Israel, Italy, Korea Rep, Mexico, Netherlands, Norway, Sweden, UK, USA. [2010/XM0324/F]

♦ International Society for HDX-MS (IS-HDXMS) 15154

Admin Dir Univ of Copenhagen, Copenhagen, Denmark.
URL: http://hdxms.net/

History 2018. Founded to provide support and a legal structure for the *International Conference for HDX-MS (IC-HDXMS).* "HDX-MS" is an acronym of *Hydrogen Deuterium Exchange Mass Spectrometry.* Registration: Denmark. **Aims** Support the International Conference for HDX-MS (IC-HDXMS). **Structure** General Assembly; Board. **Events** *International Conference on Hydrogen Deuterium Exchange Mass Spetrometry* London (UK) 2022, *International Conference on Hydrogen Deuterium Exchange Mass Spetrometry* Banff, AB (Canada) 2019, *International Conference on Hydrogen Deuterium Exchange Mass Spetrometry* Gothenburg (Sweden) 2017.
[2022/AA3223/c/E]

♦ International Society of Healthcare Ethics and Compliance Professionals (ethics) 15155

SG 9 place Vendôme, 75002 Paris, France. E-mail: contact@ethicspros.com.
URL: http://www.ethicspros.com/

History Registered in accordance with French law, Jan 2012. **Aims** Develop and enhance the highest professional standards for compliance and ethics professionals in the healthcare sector. **Structure** General Assembly (annual); Board of Directors; Strategic Committee. **Languages** English, French. **Events** *General Assembly* Paris (France) 2021, *International Pharmaceutical and Medical Devices Compliance Congress* Athens (Greece) 2019, *Asia Pacific Pharmaceutical and Medical Device Compliance Congress* Singapore (Singapore) 2018, *International Pharmaceutical and Medical Devices Compliance Congress* Vienna (Austria) 2018, *International Pharmaceutical Compliance Congress and Best Practices Forum* Lisbon (Portugal) 2017.
[2018/XJ6982/t/D]

♦ International Society for Health and Human Rights (ISHHR) 15156

Sociedad Internacional para la Salud y Derechos Humanos

Secretariat PO Box 203, Fairfield NSW 2165, Australia. T. +61297941900. Fax +61297941910. E-mail: coordinator@ishhr.com.
URL: http://ishhr.com/

History 1993. **Aims** Gather knowledge about the effects of human rights violations on health; exchange experiences and information about treatment methods, psychosocial and psychological care; contribute to development of psychosocial interventions for individuals and communities. **Structure** General Meeting (annual); Council; Executive Committee. **Languages** English, Spanish. **Staff** 0.50 FTE, paid. **Finance** Members' dues. **Activities** Events/meetings; networking/liaising; knowledge management/information dissemination; research and development; capacity building. **Events** *Conference* Medellin (Colombia) 2021, *Conference* Medellin (Colombia) 2020, *Mental health, mass people displacement and ethnic minorities* Novi Sad (Serbia) 2017, *Conference* Tbilisi (Georgia) 2011, *Conference* Lima (Peru) 2008. **Publications** Conference Report. **Members** Individuals (about 1,000); organizations. Membership countries not specified. **IGO Relations** Provincial Secretariats for Health and for Social Policy, Demography and Gender Equality, Novi Sad (Serbia).
[2017/XF4704/D]

♦ International Society of Health Psychology Research (no recent information)

♦ International Society for Heart and Lung Transplantation (ISHLT) . . 15157

Main Office 14673 Midway Rd, Ste 200, Addison TX 75001, USA. T. +19724909495. Fax +19724909499. E-mail: ishlt@ishlt.org.
URL: http://www.ishlt.org/

History 1981. Former names and other names: *International Society for Heart Transplantation* – former (1981). **Aims** Advance the science and treatment of end-stage heart and lung diseases; provide ongoing, current information on worldwide thoracic organ transplant experience; bring together persons interested in heart and lung transplantation, end-stage heart and lung disease and related sciences; encourage and stimulate basic and clinical research in these disciplines; promote new therapeutic strategies. **Structure** Annual Meeting; Board of Directors; Programme Committee; Scientific Councils. **Languages** English. **Staff** 9.00 FTE, paid. **Finance** Annual budget: 1,200,000 USD. **Activities** Events/meetings; knowledge management/information dissemination; networking/liaising. **Events** *Annual Meeting* Toronto, ON (Canada) 2026, *Annual Meeting* Boston, MA (USA) 2025, *Annual Meeting* Prague (Czechia) 2024, *Annual Meeting* Denver, CO (USA) 2023, *Annual Meeting* Boston, MA (USA) 2022. **Publications** *Journal of Heart and Lung Transplantation* (12 a year). Registry of international heart and lung transplant statistics.
Members Individuals cardiologists and cardiac surgeons (2,000) in 44 countries:
Argentina, Australia, Austria, Belgium, Brazil, Canada, Chile, China, Colombia, Cuba, Denmark, Dominican Rep, Finland, Germany, Greece, Hong Kong, India, Ireland, Israel, Italy, Japan, Korea DPR, Korea Rep, Malaysia, Mexico, Netherlands, New Zealand, Norway, Philippines, Portugal, Puerto Rico, Romania, Saudi Arabia, Singapore, Slovenia, South Africa, Spain, Sweden, Switzerland, Taiwan, Thailand, Türkiye, UK, USA. [2021/XD4556/v/C]

♦ International Society for Heart Research (ISHR) 15158

Société internationale de recherches cardiaques

Exec Sec PO Box 52643, Durham NC 27717-2643, USA. T. +19194934418.
International Pres address not obtained.
Pres address not obtained. E-mail: glopasch@ualberta.com.
URL: http://www.ishrworld.org/

History Founded 1967, as *International Study Group for Research in Cardiac Metabolism (ISGRCM).* Current title adopted 1976, but for some years from 1989 known also in English as *International Society for Cardiovascular Research.* **Aims** Promote multidisciplinary approaches to the solutions to the problems of heart diseases. **Structure** World Congress (every 3 years); Council of 18. Regional Sections (8): American,

Australasian, Chinese, CIS, European, Indian, Japanese, Latin American. **Languages** English. **Activities** Each regional section meets annually, but all members from all sections are entitled to attend each meeting. World Meeting every 3 years. Working Group on Peripheral Circulation. **Events** *World Congress* Nara (Japan) 2025, *European Congress* Porto (Portugal) 2023, *World Congress* Berlin (Germany) 2022, *Annual Meeting* Nagoya (Japan) 2021, *European Congress* Turin (Italy) 2021. **Publications** *Journal of Molecular and Cellular Cardiology* (12 a year); *Heart News and Views* (3 a year). **Members** Medical and research doctors. Individuals (about 400); Regional Sections (with total membership about 3,000). Membership countries not specified. **NGO Relations** *European Society of Cardiology (ESC, #08536); The NCD Alliance (NCDA, #16963); World Heart Federation (WHF, #21562).* [2018/XD2622/v/C]

♦ International Society for Heart Transplantation / see International Society for Heart and Lung Transplantation (#15157)

♦ International Society of Hematology (ISH) 15159

Société internationale d'hématologie (SIH)

SG Yeditepe Univ, Fac of Medicine,, 26 Ağustos Yerleşimi, İnönü Mah. Kayişdaği Cad., 34755 Istanbul/ Istanbul, Türkiye. T. +81529510559.
URL: http://www.ishworld.org/

History 1946, Dallas, TX (USA). Founded at Conference held simultaneously also in Mexico City (Mexico). Amalgamated, Aug 1966, with *European Society of Hematology (inactive)*, set up 1947, Turin (Italy). **Aims** Provide a forum for discussion of haematological problems at international level and encourage scientific investigation of such problems; promote the advance of haematology and its recognition as a branch of *biological sciences*; standardize haematological methods and nomenclature at international level; foster better understanding of basic scientific principles of haematology among scientific investigators, practitioners and general physicians. **Structure** Council. Officers: Chairman of the Council (Chief Executive Officer); President (International Congress Organizer); Vice-Presidents (3 for each Division); Secretary-General (one for each Division). Board of Counsellors and Counsellors at large (meets at time of International Congress). Regional Divisions (3): Asian and Pacific; European and African; Inter-American. Special Committees (5): Science and Education; Nomenclature, Terminology, Quantities and Units; Scientific; Nomination; Standing. **Languages** English. **Finance** Members' dues (anual): US$ 40. **Activities** Aims of the Society are carried out and implemented by the Regional Divisions. Principal areas of concern: anaemias; polycythaemias; myeloproliferative disorders; haematological malignancies; haemostasis and thrombosis; prophylaxis of haematological disorders; apheresis and transfusion medicine; stem cell transplantation; molecular haematology; therapeutic aspects. Organizes international congresses and divisional meetings (every 2 years). **Events** *Biennial Congress* Barcelona (Spain) 2022, *Biennial Congress* Vancouver, BC (Canada) 2018, *Biennial Congress* Glasgow (UK) 2016, *Biennial Congress* Beijing (China) 2014, *Biennial Congress* Cancún (Mexico) 2012. **Publications** *ISH Newsletter* (2 a year); *International Journal of Hematology.*
Members National societies; individuals (ordinary, honorary, emeritus). Members in 80 countries and territories:
Algeria, Argentina, Australia, Austria, Azerbaijan, Belgium, Bolivia, Bosnia-Herzegovina, Brazil, Bulgaria, Cameroon, Canada, Chile, Colombia, Congo DR, Costa Rica, Côte d'Ivoire, Croatia, Cuba, Cyprus, Czechia, Denmark, Egypt, Ethiopia, Finland, France, Germany, Ghana, Greece, Hong Kong, Hungary, India, Ireland, Israel, Italy, Japan, Kenya, Korea DPR, Korea Rep, Kuwait, Latvia, Lebanon, Liberia, Lithuania, Mexico, Morocco, Mozambique, Netherlands, New Zealand, Nigeria, North Macedonia, Norway, Oman, Pakistan, Panama, Peru, Philippines, Poland, Portugal, Puerto Rico, Romania, Russia, Saudi Arabia, Serbia-Montenegro, Singapore, Slovakia, South Africa, Spain, Sudan, Sweden, Switzerland, Taiwan, Thailand, Türkiye, UK, Ukraine, Uruguay, USA, Venezuela, Zimbabwe.
International organizations (2):
International Council for Standardization in Haematology (ICSH, #13078); WHO (#20950).
Consultative Status Consultative status granted from: *ECOSOC (#05331)* (Ros C). **IGO Relations** Accredited by (1): *United Nations Office at Vienna (UNOV, #20604).* Cooperates with (1): *WHO Regional Office for Europe (#20945).* **NGO Relations** Member of (1): *Council for International Organizations of Medical Sciences (CIOMS, #04905).* [2022/XB2546/v/B]

♦ International Society for Hemodialysis (ISHD) 15160

Pres UCL Centre for Nephrology, Royal Free Hosp, Gower Street, London, WC1E 6BT, UK. T. +442074726457.
Sec 9 rue des Carmelites, 34090 Montpellier, France.
URL: http://www.ishd.net/

History 26 Feb 2000, San Francisco CA (USA), during annual Dialysis Conference. Registered in the State of Illinois (USA). **Aims** Improve care for patients with *kidney* failure; upgrade teaching of dialysis; promote dialysis research; facilitate dissemination of dialysis knowledge. **Structure** Board of Directors. **Languages** English. **Staff** 1.00 FTE, paid. **Finance** Members' dues. **Events** *Congress* Shanghai (China) 2019, *Congress* Abu Dhabi (United Arab Emirates) 2018, *Congress* Cartagena de Indias (Colombia) 2018, *Congress* Bangkok (Thailand) 2017, *ISN-EMAN Update in Nephrology Congress* Dubai (United Arab Emirates) 2017. **Publications** *Hemodialysis International* (4 a year).
Members Individuals in 33 countries and territories:
Argentina, Australia, Belgium, Brazil, Canada, Croatia, Finland, France, Germany, Hong Kong, Hungary, India, Indonesia, Italy, Japan, Korea Rep, Malaysia, Mexico, Morocco, Philippines, Poland, Portugal, Romania, Russia, Saudi Arabia, Singapore, Spain, Suriname, Sweden, Switzerland, UK, Uruguay, USA. [2016.06.01/XM0633/D]

♦ International Society for Hepatic Encephalopathy and Nitrogen Metabolism (ISHEN) 15161

Pres UCL Medical School, Royal Free Hosp, Rowland Hill Street, London, NW3 2PF, UK.
Treas Clinica Medica 5, Via Giustiniani 2, 35128 Padua PD, Italy.
Registered Office c/o Hepatos Foundation, Via Martiri Giuliani e Dalmati 2/A, 35129 Padua PD, Italy.
URL: http://www.ishen.org/

History 2005, Düsseldorf (Germany) at 12th Symposium on Ammonia Metabolism, the first one organized May 1972, Budapest (Hungary). Officially registered, 6 Apr 2006, Italy. **Aims** Promote scientific and clinical research on nitrogen metabolism and brain disorders associated with liver disease; support research in neuroscience, hepatology, metabolism, nutrition and other scientific and/or clinical discipline contributing to the understanding of nitrogen metabolism and the pathophysiology, diagnosis or management of liver-related brain disorders; foster circulation of scientific ideas and encourage collaborative, interdisciplinary research and the exchange of information, material and personnel; provide a forum for the dissemination of specialist opinions and consensus information; promote medical knowledge and good clinical practice. **Structure** Executive Committee, comprising President, Secretary, Treasurer and 8 members. **Languages** English. **Activities** Organizes: international meetings; symposia; congresses; workshops. **Events** *Biennial Symposium* UK 2014, *Biennial Symposium* Grenå (Denmark) 2012, *Biennial Symposium* Val-David, QC (Canada) 2010, *Symposium* Val-David, QC (Canada) 2010, *Triennial Symposium* Abano Terme (Italy) 2008. **Publications** Guidelines; articles. **NGO Relations** Member of: *Council for International Organizations of Medical Sciences (CIOMS, #04905).* [2012.06.01/XJ0170/E]

♦ International Society for Hepatic Sinusoidal Research (ISHSR) 15162

Sec-Treas address not obtained.
URL: https://ishsr.net/

History Dec 2008. **Aims** Promote education, basic and translational research on the cells of the hepatic sinusoid including liver parenchymal cells. **Structure** Council; Standing Committee. **Finance** Sources: members' dues. **Activities** Events/meetings. **Events** *Liver Sinusoid Meeting* Shanghai (China) 2021, *Liver Sinusoid Meeting* Sydney, NSW (Australia) 2019, *International symposium on cells of the hepatic sinusoid* Tromsø (Norway) 2008, *International symposium on cells of the hepatic sinusoid* Kyoto (Japan) 1994, *International symposium on cells of the hepatic sinusoid* Antwerp (Belgium) 1992. **Members** Full (over 150) in 20 countries. Membership countries not specified. [2020/AA0814/C]

♦ International Society of Heterocyclic Chemistry (ISHC) 15163

Sec Dep of Chemistry, Univ of Western Ontario, London ON N6A 5B7, Canada. T. +5196612111 ext86354.
Treas Univ of Louisville, Dept Chem, 2320 South Brook St, Louisville KY 40208, USA. T. +15028527323 – +15022953469. Fax +15028528149.
Pres Dept of Chemistry, Shanghai Inst of Organic Chemistry, 345 Lingling Rd, 200032 Shanghai, China.
URL: http://www.ishc-web.org/

History 1968, Albuquerque NM (USA). **Aims** Provide a medium for dissemination of research in heterocyclic chemistry and for communication, cooperation and understanding among all persons concerned with the field; honour those making outstanding contributions; stimulate general interest in the field; encourage study of heterocyclic chemistry in institutions of higher learning at all levels and improve quality of teaching; encourage application of heterocyclic chemistry to the service of mankind through international cooperation among industry, governments, and other concerned institutions. **Structure** Executive Committee consisting of President, President-Elect, Past-President, Secretary-General, Treasurer, Vice-President; Publicity Chairperson; Fundraising Chairperson; Advisory Committee consisting of President-Elect and 6 members. **Languages** English. **Staff** None. **Finance** Sources: members' dues. Other sources: Funds. **Activities** Serves as primary sponsoring agency for *International Congress of Heterocyclic Chemistry.* **Events** *Biennial Congress* Kyoto (Japan) 2019, *Biennial Congress* Santa Barbara, CA (USA) 2015, *Biennial Congress / International Congress* Shanghai (China) 2013, *Biennial congress / International Congress* Glasgow (UK) 2011, *Biennial congress / International Congress* St John's, NL (Canada) 2009. **Publications** *Progress in Heterocyclic Chemistry.*
Members Individuals in 49 countries:
Argentina, Australia, Austria, Belgium, Brazil, Canada, Chile, Croatia, Czechia, Denmark, Egypt, Finland, France, Germany, Greece, Hong Kong, Hungary, India, Ireland, Israel, Italy, Japan, Jordan, Korea Rep, Latvia, Lithuania, Luxembourg, Mexico, Netherlands, New Zealand, Norway, Poland, Portugal, Romania, Russia, Serbia, Slovakia, Slovenia, South Africa, Spain, Sweden, Switzerland, Taiwan, Thailand, Türkiye, UK, Ukraine, USA, Venezuela. [2012/XD1372/v/C]

♦ International Society of Hildegard von Bingen Studies (ISHBS) 15164

Web Admin 787 Iowa Avenue West, St Paul MN 55117, USA.
Editor 155 Brookwood Drive, Tryon NC 28782, USA.
URL: http://www.hildegard-society.org/p/home.html

History 1983, Muncie IN (USA), by Professor Bruce Hozeski of Ball State University. **Aims** Promote study, criticism, research and exchange of ideas related to all aspects of the *scholasticism* of Hildegard von Bingen, 12th century *abbess.* **Staff** Voluntary. **Finance** Members' dues. **Activities** Events/meetings; networking/liaising. **Events** *Meeting / Annual Meeting* Philadelphia, PA (USA) 2008, *Annual meeting* Kalamazoo, MI (USA) 2004, *Meeting* Muncie, IN (USA) 2004, *Annual meeting* Kalamazoo, MI (USA) 2003, *Annual meeting* Kalamazoo, MI (USA) 2001. **Publications** *QUALELIBET* (2 a year) – newsletter.
Members Scholars and enthusiasts in 25 countries:
Australia, Austria, Belgium, Brazil, Canada, China, Croatia, Czechia, Denmark, Finland, France, Germany, Hungary, Ireland, Italy, Japan, Netherlands, New Zealand, Norway, Serbia, Spain, Sweden, Switzerland, UK, USA.
IGO Relations None. **NGO Relations** None. [2017.06.01/XN4152/E]

♦ International Society for Hip Arthroscopy (ISHA) 15165

Main Office c/o Warrender House, Haywood Road, Moffat, DG10 9BU, UK. E-mail: ishabureau@gmail.com – member@isha.net.
URL: http://www.isha.net/

History May 2008, Paris (France). **Aims** Be the premier international society for education and research in arthroscopic hip surgery. **Structure** Executive Committee. **Languages** English. **Finance** Sources: members' dues. **Activities** Events/meetings; training/education. **Events** *Annual Scientific Meeting* Cape Town (South Africa) 2023, *Annual Scientific Meeting* Glasgow (UK) 2022, *Annual Scientific Meeting* Las Vegas, NV (USA) 2021, *Annual Scientific Meeting* Ottawa, ON (Canada) 2020, *Annual Scientific Meeting* Madrid (Spain) 2019. **Members** Ordinary; Honorary; Associate; Affiliate; Emeritus. Membership countries not specified. [2020/XJ7871/C]

♦ International Society for Historical Linguistics (ISHL) 15166

Société internationale de linguistique historique

Contact University of Texas at San Antonio, 1 UTSA Circle, San Antonio TX 78249, USA.
URL: http://ichl23.utsa.edu/

History 30 Mar 1979, Stanford, CA (USA). Founded at 4th International Conference on Historical Linguistics. **Aims** Promote study of historical linguistics through holding conferences. **Structure** Executive Committee, consisting of President, Secretary, future conference Director, former conference Director and 3 other members. Nominating Committee, consisting of Chair and 3 other members. **Languages** English. **Finance** Sources: meeting proceeds; sponsorship. **Activities** Events/meetings. **Events** *Biennial Conference* Canberra, ACT (Australia) 2019, *Biennial Conference* San Antonio, TX (USA) 2017, *Biennial Conference* Naples (Italy) 2015, *Biennial conference / International Conference* Oslo (Norway) 2013, *Biennial conference / International Conference* Osaka (Japan) 2011. **Publications** Conference proceedings.
Members Regular and Student. Individuals in 32 countries:
Australia, Bangladesh, Belgium, Bulgaria, Canada, Denmark, Estonia, Finland, France, Germany, Ghana, Greece, Hungary, Iceland, Ireland, Israel, Italy, Japan, Korea Rep, Mexico, Netherlands, New Zealand, Norway, Russia, Serbia, Slovenia, South Africa, Spain, Sweden, Switzerland, UK, USA. [2016/XF5839/v/C]

♦ International Society for Historical and Systematic Research On Schoolbooks / see Internationale Gesellschaft für Schulbuch- und Bildungsmedienforschung (#13242)
♦ International Society for Historical and Systematic Research on Textbooks and Educational media / see Internationale Gesellschaft für Schulbuch- und Bildungsmedienforschung (#13242)
♦ International Society for the History of Arabic and Islamic Science and Philosophy (#19490)
♦ International Society of the History of Behavioral and Social Sciences / see CHEIRON – The International Society for the History of Behavioral and Social Sciences (#03857)

♦ International Society for History Didactics (ISHD) 15167

Société internationale pour la didactique de l'histoire – Internationale Gesellschaft für Geschichtsdidaktik

Pres Uni Augsburg, Philologisch-Historische Fak, Lehrstuhl Didaktik der Geschichte, Universitätsstr 10, 86159 Augsburg, Germany. T. +49821598 ext 5556.
Sec University of East Anglia, School of Education and Lifelong Learning, Zuckerman Bldg, Norwich, NR4 7TL, UK.
URL: http://ishd.co/

History Mar 1980, Germany FR. Mar 1980, Tutzing (Germany FR). **Aims** Promote through international professional cooperation the research of history teaching and learning, historical consciousness and historical culture as an integral part of history education in all forms and on all levels, not only through schools and other educational institutions but also through historical culture and extramural activities including education through mass media. **Structure** General Assembly (every 1-2 years); Board. **Languages** English, French, German. **Staff** 1.00 FTE, voluntary. **Finance** Members' dues (annual): euro 30. Annual budget: 3,500 EUR. **Activities** Events/meetings. **Events** *Annual Conference* Providence, RI (USA) 2024, *Annual Conference* Tallinn (Estonia) 2023, *Annual Conference* Poznań (Poland) 2022, *Annual Conference* Lucerne (Switzerland) 2021, *Annual Conference* Poznań (Poland) 2021. **Publications** *International Society for History Didactics Yearbook* (periodical) in English – abstracts in German/French. *Worldwide Teaching of History – Present and Future* (2006) in English, French, German; *Historical Consciousness and History Teaching in a Globalizing Society* (2001); *International Bibliography for History Didactics* (1994).
Members Full (212) of which 5 corporate. Members in 38 countries:
Australia, Austria, Belgium, Botswana, Brazil, Canada, Chile, China, Congo DR, Cyprus, Czechia, Denmark, Estonia, Finland, France, Germany, Greece, Hungary, Italy, Japan, Korea Rep, Latvia, Mexico, Morocco, Nigeria, Norway, Portugal, Romania, Singapore, Slovakia, South Africa, Spain, Sweden, Switzerland, UK, USA, Venezuela, Zimbabwe.
NGO Relations Affiliated to: *International Committee of Historical Sciences (ICHS, #12777).* Associate member of: *European Association of History Educators (EUROCLIO, #06069).* [2020/XD0501/C]

♦ International Society for the History of East Asian Science Technology and Medicine (ISHEASTM) 15168

Société internationale pour l'histoire de la science, de la technologie et de la médecine en asie orientale

Sec Inst for the History of Natural Sciences, Chinese Ac of Sciences, 55 Zhong Guan Cun East Road, 100190 Beijing, China.
Pres Dept of History of Science and Technology, Jinzhai Road 96, Hefei, 230026 Anhui, China.
URL: http://www.isheastm.org/

History 4 Aug 1990, Cambridge (UK). Founded at 6th International Conference on the History of Science in China. Also serves as East Asia Commission of *International Union of History and Philosophy of Science and Technology (IUHPST, #15779)* – Division of History of Science and Technology. **Aims** Promote research into the history of pre-modern and modern science, technology and medicine in East Asia; facilitate meetings of scholars in the field. **Structure** General Assembly; Council; Executive Committee. **Languages** English. **Finance** Sources: contributions; members' dues; sale of products. **Activities** Awards/prizes/competitions; events/meetings; publishing activities. **Events** *Triennial Conference on the History of Science in East Asia* Jeonju (Korea Rep) 2019, *Triennial Conference on the History of Science in East Asia* Paris (France) 2015, *Triennial Conference* Hefei (China) 2011, *Triennial conference on the history of science in East Asia / Triennial Conference* Baltimore, MD (USA) 2008, *Triennial conference on the history of science in East Asia / Triennial Conference* Munich (Germany) 2005. **Publications** *East Asian Science, Technology and Medicine* (2 a year) – journal.
Members Individuals and organizations in 26 countries and territories:
Australia, Belgium, Canada, China, Czechia, Denmark, France, Germany, Hong Kong, India, Israel, Italy, Japan, Korea Rep, Mexico, Netherlands, Philippines, Portugal, Russia, Singapore, Spain, Switzerland, Taiwan, UK, USA, Vietnam.
[2022.02.27/XD7574/**D**]

♦ International Society for the History of Ideas (inactive)

♦ International Society for the History of Islamic Medicine (ISHIM) .. 15169

Pres Weber State Univ, Ogden UT 84408, USA.
SG address not obtained.
URL: http://www.ishim.net/

History 1 Dec 2000, Doha (Qatar). **Aims** Bring to light the contributions of Arab and Muslim physicians to the history of medicine. **Structure** General Assembly (every 2 years); Executive Committee. **Languages** Arabic, English. **Finance** Members' dues. Donations. **Activities** Research/documentation; awareness raising; knowledge management/information dissemination; publishing activities; events/meetings; awards/prizes/competitions; networking/liaising. **Events** *International Congress* Van (Türkiye) 2019, *International Congress* Van (Türkiye) 2014, *International Congress* Istanbul (Türkiye) 2010, *International Congress* Tripoli (Libyan AJ) 2008, *International Congress* Doha (Qatar) 2007. **Publications** *Journal of the INTERNATIONAL SOCIETY FOR THE HISTORY OF ISLAMIC MEDICINE (JISHIM).* **Members** from over 15 countries. Membership countries not specified. **IGO Relations** No direct relationships. **NGO Relations** Cooperative relationships.
[2020.03.11/XD9350/**D**]

♦ International Society for the History of the Map (ISHMap) 15170

Sec address not obtained. E-mail: ishmap.secretary@gmail.com.
URL: http://ishmap.wordpress.com/

History 2011. **Aims** Promote the study of map history. **Structure** Annual General Meeting; Council. **Finance** Sources: members' dues. **Activities** Awards/prizes/competitions; events/meetings; training/education. **Events** *Symposium* Berlin (Germany) 2023, *Symposium* Montevideo (Uruguay) 2022, *Symposium* Sao Paulo (Brazil) 2020, *Survey, state, map* Portland, ME (USA) 2018. **Members** in North and South America, Europe and Asia. Membership countries not specified.
[2019.03.13/XM7065/**C**]

♦ International Society for the History of Medicine (ISHM) 15171

Société Internationale d'Histoire de la Médecine (SIHM) – Societas Internationalis Historiae Medicinae (SIHM)

Gen Sec Grigore T Popa Univ of Medicine and Pharmacy, 16, University Street, 700115 Iasi, Romania. T. +40740142210. E-mail: ishmsecretariat@gmail.com.
Pres Dpt Historia y Filosofia, Fac de Medicina – UNAM, Brasil 33, col Centro, 06020 Mexico City CDMX, Mexico.
URL: http://www.biusante.parisdescartes.fr/ishm/

History 1 Jul 1921, Paris (France). Founded following 1st International Congress on the History of Medicine, 12 Aug 1920, Antwerp (Belgium). Former names and other names: *Sociedad Internacional de Historia de la Medicina* – former. **Aims** Assist, support and disseminate historical study of all questions relating to medical and allied sciences and, in general, to all fields of the art of *healing*. **Structure** International Congress (every 2 years); Administrative Council; Executive Committee (Bureau); Councillors; National Delegates. **Languages** English, French. **Staff** 40.00 FTE, voluntary. **Finance** Sources: members' dues. **Activities** Events/meetings. Active in all member countries. **Events** *Biennial Congress* Iasi (Romania) 2022, *Biennial Congress* Riga (Latvia) 2021, *Biennial Congress* Riga (Latvia) 2020, *International Meeting* Oaxaca (Mexico) 2019, *Biennial Congress* Lisbon (Portugal) 2018. **Publications** *Analecta Histórico Médica* (2 a year) in English, French, Spanish; *Vesalius – Acta Internationalia Historiae Medicinae* (2 a year) in English, French; *ISHM Electronic Newsletter.* Congress and meeting abstracts and proceedings.
Members National delegates, ordinary members, some forming National Groups, in 48 countries and territories:
Algeria, Argentina, Australia, Austria, Belgium, Bolivia, Brazil, Canada, China, Costa Rica, Cyprus, Denmark, Dominican Rep, Egypt, Estonia, Finland, France, Georgia, Germany, Greece, Iran Islamic Rep, Ireland, Israel, Italy, Japan, Latvia, Malaysia, Mexico, Morocco, Netherlands, New Zealand, Panama, Paraguay, Poland, Portugal, Puerto Rico, Qatar, Romania, Russia, Spain, Sweden, Switzerland, Türkiye, UK, Ukraine, Uruguay, USA, Venezuela.
NGO Relations Member of (1): *Association of Learned and Professional Society Publishers (ALPSP, #02786).*
[2022.06.30/XB2547/**C**]

♦ International Society for the History of the Neurosciences (ISHN) .. 15172

Sec College of Medical Sciences, Nova Southeastern University, Fort Lauderdale FL 33328, USA.
Pres Mayo Clinic, 200 1st St SW, Rochester MN 55905, USA. E-mail: wijde@mayo.edu.
URL: http://www.ishn.org/

History 14 May 1995, Montréal QC (Canada). **Aims** Improve communication between individuals and groups interested in the history of neuroscience; promote research, education in, and stimulate interest for the history of neuroscience. **Structure** Board of Directors. **Languages** English. **Finance** Members' dues. **Events** *Annual Meeting* Rennes (France) 2023, *Annual Meeting* Rome (Italy) 2022, *Annual Meeting* 2021, *Annual Meeting* Rennes (France) 2020, *Annual Meeting* Vilnius (Lithuania) 2019. **Publications** *Journal of the History of the Neurosciences – Basic and Clinical Perspectives.*
Members Individuals in 23 countries:
Australia, Belgium, Brazil, Canada, China, Denmark, France, Germany, Greece, Ireland, Israel, Italy, Luxembourg, Malaysia, Mexico, Netherlands, Russia, Spain, Sweden, Switzerland, Taiwan, UK, USA.
NGO Relations Contacts with the Research Group for the History of the Neurosciences of: *World Federation of Neurology (WFN, #21461).*
[2019.10.21/XD5977/v/**D**]

♦ International Society for History of Pharmacy (ISHP) 15173

Société internationale d'histoire de la pharmacie – Internationale Gesellschaft für Geschichte der Pharmacie

SG Univ of Belgrade, Fac of Pharmacy, 450 Vojvode Stepe, Belgrade, PAK 11221, Serbia. T. +381113951383. Fax +381113972840.
Pres Pharmaziezentrum, Althanstrasse 14, 1090 Vienna, Austria.
URL: http://www.histpharm.org/

History 1926, Innsbruck (Austria). New constitution adopted 1999. **Aims** Handle all matters of a pharmaceutical historical nature without commercial interests. **Structure** Congress (every 2 years); Executive Committee. **Activities** Research/documentation; training/education; knowledge management/information dissemination. **Events** *Biennial Congress* Washington, DC (USA) 2019, *Biennial Congress* Warsaw (Poland) 2017, *Biennial Congress* Istanbul (Turkey) 2015, *Biennial Congress* Paris (France) 2013, *Biennial Congress* Berlin (Germany) 2011. **Publications** *ISHP Newsletter.*
Members Organizations in 21 countries and territories:
Australia, Austria, Belgium, Canada, Colombia, Denmark, France, Germany, Hungary, Italy, Japan, Netherlands, Norway, Poland, Romania, Serbia, Spain, Sweden, Switzerland, UK, USA.
Individuals in 1 country:
Argentina.
Included in the above, 1 organization listed in this Yearbook:
Cercle Benelux d'histoire de la pharmacie (#03827).
NGO Relations Sponsors joint congress with: *International Academy of the History of Pharmacy (no recent information).*
[2014.09.23/XD5485/**D**]

♦ International Society for the History of Philosophy of Science (HOPOS) 15174

Exec Sec SUNY Albany Philosophy, 1400 Washington Ave, Albany NY 12222, USA. T. +15184424262.
URL: http://hopos.org/

History 1992. Founded following a meeting of the Philosophy of Science Association (PSA), Oct 1990, Minneapolis MN (USA). Adopted a more formal organizational structure, Oct 1994. Former names and other names: *The History of Philosophy of Science Working Group* – former. **Aims** Promote serious, scholarly research on the history of the philosophy of science, including topics in the history of related disciplines and in all historical periods, studied through diverse methodologies; encourage exchange among scholars. **Structure** Steering Committee. **Languages** English. **Staff** None. **Finance** Sources: members' dues. **Activities** Events/meetings. **Events** *Biennial Congress* Singapore (Singapore) 2020, *Biennial Congress* Groningen (Netherlands) 2018, *Biennial Congress* Minneapolis, MN (USA) 2016, *Biennial Congress* Ghent (Belgium) 2014, *Biennial Congress* Halifax, NS (Canada) 2012. **Publications** *HOPOS Journal* (2 a year). **Members** Individuals (several hundred). Membership countries not specified. **NGO Relations** Member of: *International Federation of Philosophical Societies (FISP, #13507).*
[2020.06.25/XM2697/**D**]

♦ International Society for the History of Physical Education and Sport (ISHPES) 15175

Société internationale d'histoire de l'éducation physique et du sport – Internationale Gesellschaft für die Geschichte der Leibeserziehung und des Sports

Pres Ludwigsburg Univ of Education, Postfach 220, 71602 Ludwigsburg, Germany. E-mail: info@ishpes.org – president@ishpes.org.
URL: http://ishpes.org/

History 25 May 1989. Founded on merger of *International Association for the History of Physical Education and Sport (HISPA, inactive)* (founded 1973) and *International Committee for History of Sport and Physical Education (ICOSH, inactive)* (founded 1967), following a decision at ICOSH and HISPA General Assemblies, 23 May 1989, Olympia (Greece). Statutes most recently revised 2017. **Aims** Promote research and teaching in the area of physical education and sport; facilitate and improve communication and cooperation between sport history associations at regional and national levels, and between scholars. **Structure** General Assembly; Council; Executive Committee; President. **Languages** English. **Staff** Voluntary. **Finance** Sources: members' dues. **Activities** Awards/prizes/competitions; events/meetings; knowledge management/information dissemination; training/education. **Events** *Congress* Lausanne (Switzerland) 2023, *Congress* Oslo (Norway) 2022, *Congress* Cape Town (South Africa) 2021, *Sport History and Interdisciplinary Relations* Sapporo (Japan) 2020, *Milestones in the histories of sport and physical culture* Madrid (Spain) 2019.
Members Organizations and individuals in 34 countries and territories:
Australia, Austria, Belgium, Brazil, Canada, China, Croatia, Denmark, Egypt, Estonia, Finland, France, Germany, Hungary, India, Iran Islamic Rep, Israel, Italy, Japan, Netherlands, Nigeria, Norway, Poland, Portugal, Qatar, Romania, South Africa, Spain, Sweden, Switzerland, Taiwan, Türkiye, UK, USA.
NGO Relations Affiliated with (1): *International Council of Sport Science and Physical Education (ICSSPE, #13077).*
[2022.02.02/XD2106/**C**]

♦ International Society for the History of Radiology (ISHRAD) 15176

Contact c/o German Röntgen Museum, Schwelmer Str 41, 42897 Kingston, Germany. T. +492191163384. Fax +492191163145. E-mail: info@ishrad.org.
URL: http://www.ishrad.org/

History 5 Mar 2011, at *European Society of Radiology (ESR, #08720).* Registered in accordance with German law. **Aims** Advance scientific research and information exchange in the field of the history of radiology and radiological technology and practice. **Structure** Board, comprising Chairman, Vice-Chairman, Honorary Secretary, Honorary Treasurer and 4 Coopted members. **Languages** English. **Finance** Members' dues. **Events** *Symposium* Brussels (Belgium) 2019, *Symposium* Eindhoven (Netherlands) 2018, *Symposium* Erlangen (Germany) 2017, *Annual Meeting* Würzburg (Germany) 2015, *Symposium* Würzburg (Germany) 2015. **Publications** *ISHRAD Newsletter.*
[2015/XJ7201/**E**]

♦ International Society for the History of Rhetoric (ISHR) 15177

SG Dept of English, Univ of Denver, 2199 S University Blvd, Denver CO 80208, USA. E-mail: lbenselmeyers@hotmail.com.
Pres Louisiana State Univ, 114 West David Boyd, Baton Rouge LA 70803, USA.
URL: http://www.ishr-web.org/

History 30 Jun 1977, Zurich (Switzerland), when constitution was adopted. Constitution amended 2 Sep 1985, Oxford (UK); 24 Jul 1993, Turin (Italy); 3 Oct 1994, Edinburgh (UK). **Aims** Promote study of the theory and practice of rhetoric in all periods and languages and the relationship of rhetoric to poetics, literary theory and criticism, philosophy, politics, religion, law and other aspects of cultural context. **Structure** Board of Directors. Congress meets in host country of current President. **Languages** English, French, German, Italian, Spanish. **Events** *Biennial Conference* Nijmegen (Netherlands) 2022, *Biennial Conference* New Orleans, LA (USA) 2019, *Biennial Conference* London (UK) 2017, *Biennial Conference* Tübingen (Germany) 2015, *Biennial Conference* Chicago, IL (USA) 2013. **Publications** *Rhetorica: A Journal of the History of Rhetoric* (4 a year); *Rhetoric Newsletter* (irregular). *International Studies in the History of Rhetoric* – monograph series.
Members Individuals (about 400) in 39 countries and territories:
Argentina, Australia, Austria, Belgium, Brazil, Bulgaria, Canada, China, Czechia, Denmark, Finland, France, Germany, Greece, Hong Kong, Hungary, Iceland, India, Ireland, Italy, Japan, Korea Rep, Malta, Mexico, Netherlands, New Zealand, Poland, Portugal, Romania, Russia, Serbia, South Africa, Spain, Sweden, Switzerland, Taiwan, UK, USA, Venezuela.
[2019/XD0494/v/**C**]

♦ International Society for the History and Theory of Intellectual Property (ISHTIP) 15178

Dir address not obtained.
Dir address not obtained.
URL: https://www.ishtip.org/

History 20 Mar 2008, London (UK). Current constitution adopted 2014. **Aims** Promote and support scholarly investigation of the national histories of patent, copyright, and "related" rights. **Structure** Executive Committee; Governing Board; Advisory Board. **Activities** Events/meetings; knowledge management/information dissemination; training/education. **Events** *ISHTIP Workshop* Sydney, NSW (Australia) 2019.
[2020/AA0813/**C**]

♦ International Society for HIV/AIDS Education and Prevention (inactive)
♦ International Society for Holistic Medicine (unconfirmed)
♦ International Society of Holter Monitoring / see International Society for Holter and Noninvasive Electrocardiology (#15179)

♦ International Society for Holter and Noninvasive Electrocardiology (ISHNE) 15179

Contact address not obtained. E-mail: contact@ishne.org.
URL: http://www.ishne.org/

History 1984. Former names and other names: *International Society of Holter Monitoring (ISHM)* – former; *International Society for Noninvasive Electrocardiology* – alias. **Aims** Promote and advance the science of noninvasive electrocardiology; encourage continuing education in the field. **Structure** Officers: President; Past-President; President-Elect; Vice-President; Secretary; Treasurer. **Languages** English. **Staff** 10.00 FTE, paid. **Finance** Members' dues. **Activities** Organizes: biennial congress; educational sessions; virtual symposia. **Events** *International Congress of Electrocardiology (ICE)* Zakopane (Poland) 2021, *Congress* Lyon (France) 2015, *Congress* Timisoara (Romania) 2013, *Congress* Moscow (Russia) 2011, *Winter young investigator meeting* Zakopane (Poland) 2011. **Publications** *Annals of Noninvasive Electrocardiology* (4 a year). **Members** in over 30 countries. Membership countries not specified. **NGO Relations** Associate member of: *World Heart Federation (WHF, #21562).* Member of: *The NCD Alliance (NCDA, #16963).*
[2021/XD7823/**D**]

♦ International Society for Homotoxicology and Antihomotoxicological Therapy / see Internationale Gesellschaft für Homöopathie und Homotoxikologie

♦ International Society for Horticultural Science (ISHS) 15180

Exec Dir Corbeekhoeve, Pastoriestraat 2, 3360 Korbeek-Lo, Belgium.
Mailing Address PO Box 500, 3001 Leuven, Belgium. T. +3216229427. Fax +3216229450.
General: https://www.ishs.org/

History 27 Apr 1959, Paris (France). Founded, replacing, according to resolutions adopted by Congresses in 1955, Scheveningen (Netherlands), and 1958, Nice (France), the *International Committee for Horticultural Congresses (inactive)*, set up 19 Sep 1927, The Hague (Netherlands). Origins date back to 1864. Former names and other names: *Société internationale de la science horticole* – alias; *Sociedad Internacional de la Ciencia Horticola* – alias; *Internationale Gesellschaft für Gartenbauwissenschaften* – alias. Registration: Banque-Carrefour des Entreprises, No/ID: 0472.448.990, Start date: 10 Aug 2000, Belgium. **Aims** Promote and encourage research and education in all branches of horticultural science; facilitate cooperation and knowledge transfer on a global scale. **Structure** Board; Council; Executive Committee; Working Groups. **Languages** English, French. **Staff** 5.00 FTE, paid. **Finance** Sources: members' dues. **Activities** Events/meetings; knowledge management/information dissemination; networking/liaising; research/documentation. **Events** *International Horticultural Congress* Kyoto (Japan) 2026, *International Symposium on the Processing Tomato* Budapest (Hungary) 2024, *International Symposium on Plant Cryopreservation* Oslo (Norway) 2023, *Asian Horticultural Congress* Tokyo (Japan) 2023, *Quadrennial Congress* Angers (France) 2022. **Publications** *Chronica Horticulturae* (4 a year) – magazine; *Acta Horticulturae* – journal; *Fruits: The International Journal of Tropical and Subtropical Horticulture*; *The European Journal of Horticultural Science (eJHS)*. *Scripta Horticulturae*.

Members Affiliated Organizations; Individuals. Organizations in 53 countries and territories:
Australia, Austria, Belgium, Bosnia-Herzegovina, Brazil, Bulgaria, Canada, Chile, Cyprus, Czechia, Denmark, Egypt, France, Germany, Greece, Hungary, India, Indonesia, Iran Islamic Rep, Ireland, Israel, Italy, Japan, Jordan, Kenya, Korea Rep, Latvia, Lithuania, Luxembourg, Mexico, Morocco, Netherlands, New Zealand, Nigeria, North Macedonia, Norway, Papua New Guinea, Peru, Poland, Portugal, Romania, Saudi Arabia, Serbia, South Africa, Spain, Sweden, Switzerland, Taiwan, Tanzania UR, Thailand, Türkiye, UK, USA.
Included in the above, 8 organizations listed in this Yearbook:
AVRDC – The World Vegetable Center (#03051); *CABI (#03393)*; *Centre de coopération internationale en recherche agronomique pour le développement (CIRAD, #03733)* (FLHOR); *International Peatland Society (IPS, #14538)*; *Mediterranean Agronomic Institute of Chania (MAICh, #16642)*; *Mediterranean International Association of the Processing Tomato (#16659)*; *Warwick HRI*.
Individuals (7,000) in 146 countries and territories:
Afghanistan, Albania, Algeria, Argentina, Armenia, Australia, Austria, Bahamas, Bahrain, Bangladesh, Barbados, Belarus, Belgium, Belize, Benin, Bhutan, Bolivia, Bosnia-Herzegovina, Botswana, Brazil, Bulgaria, Burkina Faso, Cambodia, Cameroon, Canada, Chad, Chile, China, Colombia, Congo Brazzaville, Costa Rica, Côte d'Ivoire, Croatia, Cuba, Curaçao, Cyprus, Czechia, Denmark, Dominican Rep, Ecuador, Egypt, Estonia, Eswatini, Ethiopia, Fiji, Finland, France, Gambia, Georgia, Germany, Ghana, Greece, Guadeloupe, Guatemala, Guernsey, Guyana, Haiti, Honduras, Hong Kong, Hungary, Iceland, India, Indonesia, Iran Islamic Rep, Ireland, Israel, Italy, Jamaica, Japan, Jordan, Kenya, Korea Rep, Kuwait, Kyrgyzstan, Latvia, Lebanon, Liberia, Libya, Lithuania, Luxembourg, Madagascar, Malawi, Malaysia, Mali, Malta, Mauritius, Mexico, Micronesia FS, Moldova, Morocco, Myanmar, Namibia, Nepal, Netherlands, New Caledonia, New Zealand, Nicaragua, Niger, Nigeria, North Macedonia, Norway, Oman, Pakistan, Palestine, Panama, Papua New Guinea, Peru, Philippines, Poland, Portugal, Puerto Rico, Réunion, Romania, Russia, Rwanda, Saudi Arabia, Senegal, Serbia, Singapore, Slovakia, Slovenia, South Africa, Spain, Sri Lanka, St Lucia, St Vincent-Grenadines, Sudan, Sweden, Switzerland, Syrian AR, Taiwan, Tanzania UR, Thailand, Trinidad-Tobago, Tunisia, Türkiye, Uganda, UK, Ukraine, United Arab Emirates, Uruguay, USA, Venezuela, Vietnam, Zambia, Zimbabwe.

Consultative Status Consultative status granted from: *ECOSOC (#05331)* (Ros C); *FAO (#09260)* (Liaison Status). **NGO Relations** Member of (3): *Global Horticulture Initiative (GlobalHort, #10412)* (Founding); *International Association of Botanical and Mycological Societies (IABMS, #11730)*; *International Union of Biological Sciences (IUBS, #15760)* (Scientific). Partner of (1): *InterAmerican Society of Tropical Horticulture (ISTH, #11451)*. [2021.03.04/XB2488/y/**B**]

♦ International Society for Human and Animal Mycology (ISHAM) . . . 15181

Société internationale de mycologie humaine et animale (SIMHA) – Sociedad Internacional de Micologia Humana y Animal – Internationale Gesellschaft für Humane und Animale Mykologie – Societas Internationalis Mycologiae Humanae et Animalis

Secretariat PO Box 440, 5201 AK 's Hertogenbosch, Netherlands. E-mail: secretary@isham.org.
URL: http://www.isham.org/

History Jul 1954, Paris (France). Founded by a group of scientists from 10 different nations during 8th International Congress of Botany. Present Statutes and By-Laws adopted at General Assembly, 13 Jun 1997, Parma (Italy). Registration: Switzerland. **Aims** Encourage the practice and study of all aspects of *medical* and *veterinary* mycology; facilitate international exchange of ideas in the field. **Structure** General Assembly (at least every 3 years); Council. Membership open, subject to approval of Committee. **Languages** English, French. **Staff** Voluntary. **Finance** Sources: members' dues. **Events** *Congress* Delhi (India) 2022, *Congress* Delhi (India) 2021, *Congress* Amsterdam (Netherlands) 2018, *Congress* Melbourne, VIC (Australia) 2015, *From laboratory to clinic* Berlin (Germany) 2012. **Publications** *Medical Mycology* (6 a year); *Mycoses Newsletter* (2 a year).

Members Affiliated national organizations in 24 countries and territories:
Argentina, Belgium, Brazil, Bulgaria, Canada, China, Denmark, Finland, France, India, Indonesia, Israel, Italy, Japan, Korea Rep, Mexico, Netherlands, Philippines, Poland, Slovakia, Spain, Sweden, UK.
Affiliated international organizations (6):
Asian Pacific Society for Medical Mycology (APSMM, #01638); *Australasian Federation for Medical and Veterinary Mycology (AFMVM)*; *Deutschsprachige Mykologische Gesellschaft (DMykG, #05051)*; *European Confederation of Medical Mycology (ECMM, #06712)*; *Latin American Association for Mycology (#16248)*; *Medical Mycological Society of the Americas (MMSA, #16625)*.
Individuals (over 1,000) in 74 countries and territories:
Argentina, Australia, Austria, Azerbaijan, Bangladesh, Belgium, Bolivia, Brazil, Brunei Darussalam, Bulgaria, Canada, Chile, China, Colombia, Costa Rica, Croatia, Cuba, Czechia, Denmark, Dominican Rep, Ecuador, Egypt, Finland, France, Gabon, Germany, Greece, Guatemala, Hong Kong, Hungary, India, Indonesia, Iran Islamic Rep, Iraq, Ireland, Israel, Italy, Japan, Korea Rep, Kuwait, Malaysia, Mali, Mexico, Morocco, Netherlands, New Zealand, Nigeria, Pakistan, Panama, Peru, Philippines, Poland, Portugal, Puerto Rico, Russia, Saudi Arabia, Senegal, Singapore, Slovenia, South Africa, Spain, Sri Lanka, Sudan, Sweden, Switzerland, Taiwan, Thailand, Tunisia, Türkiye, UK, Uruguay, USA, Venezuela, Zimbabwe.

Consultative Status Consultative status granted from: *ECOSOC (#05331)* (Ros C). **IGO Relations** *Pan American Health Organization (PAHO, #18108)*. **NGO Relations** Partner of (1): *Global Action For Fungal Infections (GAFFI, #10166)*. Associated society of *International Union of Microbiological Societies (IUMS, #15794)*. Through IUMS, relations with: *International Council for Science (ICSU, inactive)*. [2019.03.06/XB2489/y/**B**]

♦ International Society for Human Ethology (ISHE) 15182

Sec Dept of Psychology, St Mary's Univ, Halifax NS B3H 3C3, Canada.
URL: http://www.ishe.org/

History 1972. Merged with *European Sociobiological Society (ESS, inactive)*, Sep 2000. **Aims** Promote ethological perspectives in the scientific study of humans worldwide; encourage empirical research in all fields of human behavior using the full range of methods developed in biology and the human behavioral sciences and operating within the conceptual framework provided by evolutionary theory; promote the exchange of knowledge and opinions concerning human ethology with all the other empirical sciences of human behavior; administer its funds to support this purpose. **Structure** Meeting (every 2 years); Board of Trustees; Officers (elected). Committees. **Languages** English. **Staff** 3.00 FTE, voluntary. **Finance** Members' dues: US$ 20; US$ 50 for 3 years; US$ 75 for 5 years. **Events** *Biennial Conference* Würzburg (Germany) 2022, *Biennial Conference* Liverpool (UK) 2020, *Biennial Conference* Santiago (Chile) 2018, *Biennial Conference* Stirling (UK) 2016, *Biennial Conference* Belém (Brazil) 2014. **Publications** *Human Ethology Bulletin* (4 a year). *Membership Directory*.

Members Individuals in 30 countries:
Argentina, Australia, Austria, Belgium, Brazil, Canada, China, Colombia, Denmark, France, Germany, Hungary, India, Israel, Italy, Japan, Mexico, Netherlands, Norway, Portugal, Russia, South Africa, Spain, Sri Lanka, Sweden, Switzerland, UK, Ukraine, Uruguay, USA. [2012/XD1386/v/**C**]

♦ International Society for Human Rights (ISHR) 15183

Société internationale pour les droits de l'homme (SIDH) – Sociedad Internacional para los Derechos Humanos (SIDH) – Internationale Gesellschaft für Menschenrechte (IGFM)

Pres Borsigallee 9, 60388 Frankfurt-Main, Germany. T. +49694201080. Fax +496942010833. E-mail: info@ishr.org.
SG address not obtained. T. +41794591802. E-mail: info@igfm.ch.
URL: http://www.ishr.org/

History Founded Apr 1972, Frankfurt-Main (Germany FR), as *Society for Human Rights – Gesellschaft für Menschenrechte*. Present title adopted 1981. **Aims** Achieve universal respect for and observance of human rights; provide support and relief to victims of discrimination, but not to those using or advocating force or totalitarianism; support the Universal Declaration of Human Rights and other international human rights instruments. **Structure** International Council. Regional Committees (3): ISHR Eurasia (GUS states); ISHR Pan-American; ISHR West Africa. **Languages** English, French, German, Russian, Spanish. **Staff** 25.00 FTE, paid. Voluntary. **Finance** Sources: grants. Each national section has its own budget. Annual budget: 1,500,000 EUR. **Activities** Events/meetings; guidance/assistance/consulting; knowledge management/information dissemination; publishing activities. **Events** *International congress* Batumi (Georgia) 2000, *Annual international session on human rights education* Moscow (Russia) 2000, *Meeting on the murder of the Caucasian peoples* Tbilisi (Georgia) 1998, *Annual meeting* Prague (Czech Rep) 1995, *International seminar on racism yesterday and today* Prague (Czech Rep) 1995. **Publications** *Charter* (4 a year) in English; *Droit de regard* (4 a year) in French; *Für die Menschenrechte* (4 a year) in German; *Menschenrechte* (4 a year) in German; *Yearbook on Religious Freedom* in German.

Members National Sections; National Groups; Regional Committees; Regional Working Groups; Individuals. National Sections in 41 countries and territories:
Australia, Austria, Azerbaijan, Belarus, Benin, Bosnia-Herzegovina, Cameroon, Canada, Cape Verde, Colombia, Congo DR, Croatia, Cuba, France, Gambia, Georgia, Germany, Guatemala, Kenya, Kosovo, Latvia, Lithuania, Mali, Mauritius, Moldova, Nepal, Nicaragua, Nigeria, North Macedonia, Romania, Russia, Senegal, Serbia, Slovakia, Sweden, Switzerland, Togo, UK, Ukraine, USA, Uzbekistan.

Consultative Status Consultative status granted from: *African Commission on Human and Peoples' Rights (ACHPR, #00255)* (Observer); *ECOSOC (#05331)* (Ros A). **IGO Relations** Observer status with: *OAS (#17629)*. Associated with Department of Global Communications of the United Nations. **NGO Relations** Member of: *EarthAction (EA, #05159)*. [2014.07.18/XF0109/**C**]

♦ International Society for Human Values (inactive)

♦ International Society for Humor Studies (ISHS) 15184

Exec Sec Holy Names Univ, Oakland CA 94619, USA. T. +15104361532. E-mail: ishs@hnu.edu.
URL: http://www.humorstudies.org/

History 1 Apr 1980, Tempe AZ (USA), as *Western Humor and Irony Membership*. Name changed: 1985, to *World Humor and Irony Membership (WHIM)*; 1988, to *World Humor and Irony Movement*. Current title adopted, 1989. **Aims** Promote humor research across multiple academic disciplines and professional areas, including psychology, sociology, anthropology, linguistics, literary studies, performing and fine arts, business, education and health care. **Structure** Executive Board; Committees. **Finance** Members' dues. **Events** *Annual International Conference* Tallinn (Estonia) 2018, *Annual International Conference* Montréal, QC (Canada) 2017, *Annual International Conference* Dublin (Ireland) 2016, *Annual International Conference* Oakland, CA (USA) 2015, *Annual International Conference* Utrecht (Netherlands) 2014. **Publications** *Humor: International Journal of Humor Research*; *Humorous Times* – newsletter.

Members Individuals (mostly in USA) in 28 countries and territories:
Argentina, Australia, Brazil, Canada, Chile, China, Egypt, France, Germany, India, Ireland, Israel, Italy, Japan, Luxembourg, Nepal, Netherlands, New Zealand, Norway, Poland, Russia, South Africa, Spain, Sweden, Switzerland, Taiwan, UK, USA. [2019.02.12/XF4223/v/**F**]

♦ International Society for Hunter Gatherer Research (ISHGR) 15185

Sec Dept of Social and Cultural Anthropology, Univ of Vienna, Universitätsstr 7, 1010 Vienna, Austria.

History Oct 2014. Registration: Companies House, No/ID: 08923018, Start date: 5 Mar 2014, End date: 23 May 2017, England. **Aims** Promote research and better knowledge about hunter gatherer societies in the past and present; promote respect for the rights of hunter gatherer societies. **Structure** General Meeting; Board. **Activities** Events/meetings. Organizes the Conference on Hunting and Gathering Societies (CHAGS) **Events** *Conference on Hunting and Gathering Societies (CHAGS)* Dublin (Ireland) 2022, *Conference on Hunting and Gathering Societies (CHAGS)* Penang (Malaysia) 2018, *Conference on Hunting and Gathering Societies* Vienna (Austria) 2015. **Publications** *Hunter Gatherer Research* (4 a year) – journal; *ISHGR Newsletter*. [2022/XM4757/**C**]

♦ International Society for Hyaluronan Sciences (ISHAS) 15186

Pres University of Manchester, Michael Smith Bldg, Oxford Road, Manchester, M13 9PT, UK.
URL: https://ishas.org/

History 2004. Founded following discussions initiated in 2003. Registration: 501(c)(3), USA. **Aims** Advance knowledge on the structure, function and therapeutic application of hyaluronan and its role in the structure and function of the extracellular matrix and cells. **Structure** Board. **Activities** Awards/prizes/competitions; events/meetings. **Events** *International Conference on Hyaluronan* Portland, OR (USA) 2023, *International Conference on Hyaluronan* Cardiff (UK) 2019, *International Conference on Hyaluronan* Cleveland, OH (USA) 2017, *International Conference on Hyaluronan* Florence (Italy) 2015, *International Conference on Hyaluronan* Oklahoma City, OK (USA) 2013. [2023/AA3118/**C**]

♦ International Society for Hybrid Microelectronics (inactive)

♦ International Society for Hydrocephalus and Cerebrospinal Fluid Disorders (ISHCSF) 15187

Main Office c/o ARTION, 74 Ethnikis Antistaseos, Sigma Bl 1 1st fl, 551 33 Kalamaria, Greece. E-mail: contact@ishcsf.com.
URL: http://ishcsf.com/

History Sep 2008. Former names and other names: *Hydrocephalus Society* – alias. **Aims** Advance the art and science of the field of clinical care and research in hydrocephalus and CSF disorders, so as to promote the best possible care for patients with hydrocephalus and CSF disorder. **Structure** Board. **Activities** Events/meetings; healthcare; training/education. **Events** *Hydrocephalus Meeting* Toulouse (France) 2025, *Hydrocephalus Meeting* Nagoya (Japan) 2024, *Hydrocephalus Meeting* Hamburg (Germany) 2023, *Hydrocephalus Meeting* Gothenburg (Sweden) 2022, *Hydrocephalus Meeting* 2021. **Publications** Global Webinar Series. [2022.02.15/XJ1797/**D**]

♦ International Society for Hydrothermal Techniques (#19497)

♦ International Society of Hymenopterists (ISH) 15188

Sec address not obtained.
Pres address not obtained.
URL: http://www.hymenopterists.org/

History 2 Dec 1982, Toronto, ON (Canada). **Aims** Encourage scientific research and promote the diffusion of scientific knowledge concerning Hymenoptera. **Structure** Executive Committee. **Languages** English. **Staff** 6.00 FTE, voluntary. **Finance** Sources: members' dues. **Activities** Awards/prizes/competitions; events/meetings. **Events** *Congress* Iasi (Romania) 2022, *Congress* Matsuyama City (Japan) 2018, *Quadrennial Conference* Cusco (Peru) 2014, *Meeting* Daegu (Korea Rep) 2012, *Quadrennial conference / Quadrennial Conference and Meeting* Köszeg (Hungary) 2010. **Publications** *Journal of Hymenoptera Research* (2 a year); *ISH Newsletter*.

Members Individuals in 52 countries:
Algeria, Argentina, Australia, Bangladesh, Belgium, Brazil, Bulgaria, Canada, China, Colombia, Costa Rica, Cuba, Czechia, Denmark, Egypt, France, Germany, Ghana, Hungary, India, Indonesia, Iran Islamic Rep, Israel, Italy, Japan, Kazakhstan, Kenya, Korea Rep, Lithuania, Malaysia, Mexico, Netherlands, New Zealand, Nicaragua, Norway, Panama, Paraguay, Portugal, Romania, Russia, South Africa, Spain, Sweden, Switzerland, Thailand, Trinidad-Tobago, Türkiye, Uganda, UK, Ukraine, USA, Venezuela. [2021/XD7562/v/**D**]

♦ International Society for Hymnological Studies (#13213)

♦ **International Society of Hypertension (ISH)** **15189**
Société internationale d'hypertension
Secretariat c/o C J Association Management, Peershaws, Berewyk Hall Court/ Bures Road, White Colne, Colchester, CO6 2QB, UK. T. +4401787226995. E-mail: secretariat@ish-world.com.
URL: http://www.ish-world.com/
History 1966, Cleveland, OH (USA). Registration: Charity Commission, No/ID: 1122135, England and Wales. **Aims** Promote and encourage advancement of scientific knowledge in all aspects of research in hypertension and connected *cardiovascular* diseases. **Structure** Biennial Meeting; Scientific Council; Officers. **Languages** English. **Staff** 1.00 FTE, paid. Association management company employed to manage other Secretariat duties including membership, communications and governance. **Finance** Sources: members' dues. **Activities** Awareness raising; events/meetings; projects/programmes. **Events** *Biennial Scientific Meetingp* Kyoto (Japan) 2022, *Biennial Scientific Meeting* 2021, *Biennial Scientific Meeting* Glasgow (UK) 2020, *Biennial Scientific Meeting* Beijing (China) 2018, *Pulse of Asia Meeting* Seoul (Korea Rep) 2016. **Publications** *Journal of Hypertension* (12 a year). **Members** Individuals in over 80 countries and territories. Membership countries not specified. **NGO Relations** Set up: *World Hypertension League (WHL, #21574).* Links with national and regional societies of hypertension and councils of hypertension, including: *Asian-Pacific Society of Hypertension (#01634); European Society of Hypertension (ESH, #08627); Inter-American Society of Hypertension (IASH, #11449); Latin American Society of Hypertension (LASH, #16372); Pan African Society of Cardiology (PASCAR, #18066).* [2022.02.04/XC2329/**C**]

♦ International Society on Hypertension in Blacks (internationally oriented national body)

♦ **International Society of Hypnosis (ISH)** **15190**
Société internationale d'hypnose
Address not obtained.
URL: http://ishhypnosis.org/
History 1973, Uppsala (Sweden). **Aims** Promote hypnosis in the broader context of psychological and *neurological* science and as a therapeutic modality for use by health professionals; improve clinical practice and research; promote professional study and experimentation; encourage cooperative relationships among relevant scientific disciplines; increase formal and informal communication among members. **Structure** Board of Directors; Central Office in Berwyn PA (USA). **Languages** English. **Staff** 1.00 FTE, paid. **Finance** Sources: members' dues. Annual budget: 30,000 USD. **Events** *World Congress of Medical and Clinical Hypnosis* Krakow (Poland) 2024, *World Congress of Medical and Clinical Hypnosis* Krakow (Poland) 2022, *World Congress of Medical and Clinical Hypnosis* Krakow (Poland) 2021, *Triennial Congress* Montréal, QC (Canada) 2018, *Triennial Congress* Paris (France) 2015. **Publications** *International Journal of Clinical and Experimental Hypnosis* – official journal; *ISH Newsletter.* Membership directory (every 3 years).
Members Individual physicians, dentists, psychologists and other health professionals using hypnosis in the context of their work, in 42 countries:
Argentina, Australia, Austria, Belgium, Brazil, Bulgaria, Canada, Chile, Czechia, Denmark, Finland, France, Germany, Hong Kong, Hungary, Iceland, India, Iran Islamic Rep, Ireland, Israel, Italy, Japan, Jordan, Korea Rep, Libya, Malaysia, Mexico, Netherlands, New Zealand, Nigeria, Poland, Romania, Russia, Serbia, Singapore, Slovakia, South Africa, Sweden, Switzerland, Türkiye, UK, USA.
Confédération Francophone d'Hypnose et Thérapies brèves (CFHTB).
National Constituent Societies in 28 countries and territories:
Australia, Austria, Belgium, Brazil, Canada, Denmark, Finland, France, Germany, Hungary, Iceland, India, Iran Islamic Rep, Italy, Japan, Mexico, Netherlands, New Zealand, Norway, Poland, Portugal, Russia, South Africa, Sweden, Switzerland, Türkiye, UK, USA.
NGO Relations Affiliated to: *World Federation for Mental Health (WFMH, #21455).* [2021/XC0145/**C**]

♦ International Society on Hypospadias and Intersex Disorders (inactive)
♦ International Society of Ichthyology and Hydrobiology (inactive)

♦ **International Society for IGF Research (IGF Society)** **15191**
Contact address not obtained. E-mail: igfsociety@gmail.com.
URL: http://www.igf-society.org/
History Former names and other names: *International Society for Insulin-like Growth Factor Research* – former; *International IGF Research Society* – alias. **Finance** Members' dues. **Events** *Joint Congress* Foz do Iguaçu (Brazil) 2020, *Joint Congress* Seattle, WA (USA) 2018, *Joint Congress* Tel Aviv (Israel) 2016, *Joint Congress / Meeting* Singapore (Singapore) 2014, *Joint Symposium* Munich (Germany) 2012. **Publications** *Growth Hormone and IGF Research.* **NGO Relations** Joint publication with: *Growth Hormone Research Society (GRS, #10798).* Member of: *European Society of Endocrinology (ESE, #08594).* [2019/XD7846/**D**]

♦ International Society for IHC and Molecular Morphology / see International Society for Immunohistochemistry and Molecular Morphology (#15192)
♦ International Society of Immuno-Allergology of the Nasal Sinuses (inactive)

♦ **International Society for Immunohistochemistry and Molecular Morphology (ISIMM)** **15192**
Contact address not obtained. E-mail: info@isimm.org.
URL: http://isimm.org/
History Mar 2016, Seattle, WA (USA). Former names and other names: *International Society for IHC and Molecular Morphology* – alias. **Aims** Promote knowledge, innovation and excellence in slide-based techniques such as immunohistochemistry and in situ hybridization. **Structure** Board. **Languages** English. **Activities** Events/meetings; knowledge management/information dissemination. [2022.06.08/XM6250/**D**]

♦ **International Society for Immunology of Reproduction (ISIR)** **15193**
Société internationale pour l'immunologie de la reproduction
Pres Dept Obstetrics and Gynecology, Univ of Toyama, 3190 Gofuku, Toyama City TOYAMA, 930-8555 Japan.
SG Robinson Research Inst and School of Medicine, Univ of Adelaide, Adelaide SA 5005, Australia.
URL: http://www.isir.org.in/
History Founded 1975, by *International Coordination Committee for Immunology of Reproduction (ICCIR, #12958).* **Aims** Advance the study of the immunological and genetic aspects of the reproductive process; facilitate contact between persons interested in this and allied fields; disseminate widely all (new) information. **Structure** Officers (5); Councillors (8). **Languages** English. **Staff** voluntary. **Finance** Sources: members' dues. **Activities** Events/meetings. **Events** *Triennial Congress* Nara (Japan) 2019, *Triennial Congress* Erfurt (Germany) 2016, *Triennial Congress / International Congress on Reproductive Immunology* Boston, MA (USA) 2013, *Triennial congress / International Congress on Reproductive Immunology* Palm Cove, QLD (Australia) 2010, *International symposium for immunology or reproduction* Suita (Japan) 2010. **Publications** *American Journal of Reproductive Immunology* (periodical); *Journal of Reproductive Immunology* (periodical).
Members Scientists and physicians in 26 countries:
Argentina, Australia, Belgium, Brazil, Bulgaria, Canada, China, Croatia, Czechia, France, Germany, Greece, Hungary, India, Indonesia, Ireland, Italy, Japan, Netherlands, Philippines, Poland, Russia, Sweden, UK, Ukraine, USA.
[2018.09.10/XD8600/v/**C**]

♦ **International Society for Immunonutrition (ISIN)** **15194**
Contact Phase 20, c/o AAYG Ltd Unit 412, Bon Mache Ctr, 241-251 Ferndale Road, London, SW9 8BJ, UK. E-mail: info@phase20events.co.uk.
URL: http://www.immunonutrition-isin.org/
History May 2014, by *International Forum of Immunonutrition for Education and Research (i-FINER),* set up 2007. **Aims** Promote education and research in the transdisciplinary area comprising the interaction between *nutrition* and *immunology*, through advancement of its understanding and publication and communication of its results. **Structure** Board. **Activities** Events/meetings; networking/liaising; research/documentation; training/education. **Events** *International Symposium* Barcelona (Spain) 2021, *International Symposium* Barcelona (Spain) 2020, *International Symposium* London (UK) 2018, *International Symposium* Madrid (Spain) 2017. [2017/XM6140/**C**]

♦ International Society on Immunopharmacology (inactive)
♦ International Society on Immuno-Rehabilitation / see World Immunopathology Organization (#21576)

♦ **International Society of Impact Engineering (ImpactEng)** **15195**
Address not obtained.
URL: http://www.impacteng.org/
History Proposed during 4th International Conference on Impact Loading of Lightweight Structures (ICILLS), Jan 2014, Cape Town (South Africa). **Aims** Congregate engineers, scientists and policy makers to develop the field of impact engineering. **Structure** Biennial General Meeting; Board. **Languages** English. **Activities** Awards/prizes/competitions; events/meetings. **Events** *International Conference on Impact Loading of Structures and Materials* Trondheim (Norway) 2022, *International Conference on Impact Loading of Structures and Materials* Trondheim (Norway) 2020, *Biennial International Conference on Impact Loading of Structures and Materials* Xian (China) 2018, *Biennial International Conference on Impact Loading of Structures and Materials* Trondheim (Norway) 2016. **Members** Individuals. Membership countries not specified. [2020/AA0448/**E**]

♦ International Society for Impotence Research / see International Society for Sexual Medicine (#15441)
♦ International Society for the Improvement and Teaching of Dialectical Behavior Therapy (internationally oriented national body)
♦ International Society for Improving Training Quality (no recent information)
♦ International Society for Individual Liberty / see Liberty International (#16457)
♦ International Society for Individual Psychology / see International Association of Individual Psychology (#11960)

♦ **International Society of Indoor Air Quality and Climate (ISIAQ)** **15196**
Sec c/o Infinity Conference, 1035 Sterling Rd, Ste 202, Herndon VA 20170, USA. T. +17039259455. Fax +17039259453. E-mail: info@isiaq.org.
URL: http://www.isiaq.org/
History Apr 1992. Founded when constitution came into force on approval by founding members, following 5th International Conference on Indoor Air Quality and Climate, 1990, Toronto (Canada). **Aims** Support the creation of healthy, comfortable and productivity-encouraging indoor environments by: advancing the science and technology of indoor air quality and climate as it relates to indoor environment design, construction, operation and maintenance, measurement and health science; facilitating international and interdisciplinary communication and information exchange through publication and fostering of publications, organization, sponsoring and support of initiatives and development, adaptation and maintenance of codes, standards and guidelines; cooperating with governments and other agencies and societies with an interest in the indoor environment. **Structure** Board of Directors; Administrative Secretariat in the State of California (USA). Task Forces (10). Since 2005, includes former *International Academy of Indoor Air Sciences (IAIAS, inactive),* which became *Academy of Fellows.* **Languages** English. **Finance** Sources: members' dues; sale of publications. Other sources: conference promotion; grants from government agencies, companies and societies for the Journal, Task Forces and other activities. **Activities** Events/meetings; research/documentation. **Events** *Healthy Buildings Conference* Aachen (Germany) 2023, *Healthy Buildings Asia* Tianjin (China) 2023, *Indoor Air : International Conference on Indoor Air Quality and Climate* Kuopio (Finland) 2022, *Healthy Building Conference* Oslo (Norway) 2021, *Indoor Air : International Conference on Indoor Air Quality and Climate* Seoul (Korea Rep) 2020. **Publications** *Indoor Air: International Journal of Indoor Air Quality and Climate* (6 a year); *ISIAQ E-Newsletter* (6 a year). *Indoor Air Quality: A Comprehensive Reference Book* (1995). Conference proceedings – paper, CD-ROM and flash drive; Task Force Reports.
Members Individual; corporate; affiliate; sponsor. Individuals in 34 countries and territories:
Andorra, Australia, Austria, Belgium, Brazil, Canada, China, Czechia, Denmark, Finland, France, Germany, Greece, Hong Kong, Hungary, India, Israel, Italy, Japan, Korea Rep, Luxembourg, Netherlands, New Zealand, Norway, Portugal, Singapore, Slovakia, Slovenia, Spain, Sweden, Switzerland, Taiwan, UK, USA.
National chapters in 4 countries:
Finland, Netherlands, Norway, Sweden.
NGO Relations Memorandum of understanding with: *International Council for Research and Innovation in Building and Construction (CIB, #13069).* [2022/XC0027/**C**]

♦ **International Society for Industrial Ecology (ISIE)** **15197**
Exec Dir 195 Prospect St, New Haven CT 06511-2189, USA. T. +12034326953. Fax +12034325556. E-mail: info@is4ie.org.
URL: http://is4ie.org/
History Feb 2001. **Aims** Promote the use of industrial ecology in research, education, policy, community development and industrial practices. **Structure** Council. **Languages** English. **Staff** 0.50 FTE, paid. 0.5 FTE, paid. **Finance** Sources: members' dues. **Events** *Biennial Conference* Leiden (Netherlands) 2021, *Americas Regional Conference* New Haven, CT (USA) 2020, *Biennial Conference* Beijing (China) 2019, *Conference* Berlin (Germany) 2019, *Asia-Pacific Conference* Qingdao (China) 2018. **Publications** *Journal of Industrial Ecology* (6 a year); *ISIE News* (4 a year).
Members Individuals in 42 countries and territories:
Australia, Austria, Bangladesh, Belgium, Brazil, Canada, China, Colombia, Croatia, Denmark, Finland, France, Germany, Greece, Grenada, Hong Kong, Hungary, India, Italy, Japan, Korea Rep, Malaysia, Mauritius, Mexico, Netherlands, New Zealand, Nigeria, Norway, Peru, Philippines, Portugal, Singapore, South Africa, Spain, Sri Lanka, Sweden, Switzerland, Taiwan, Thailand, Türkiye, UK, USA. [2022/XD3878/t/**D**]

♦ **International Society for Industrial Process Tomography (ISIPT)** ... **15198**
Pres address not obtained. E-mail: admin@isipt.org.
URL: http://www.isipt.org/
History 2007, Bergen (Norway). Founded during 5th WCIPT. **Activities** Events/meetings. **Events** *World Congress on Industrial Process Tomography* Mexico City (Mexico) 2025, *World Congress on Industrial Process Tomography* Tianjin (China) 2023, *World Congress on Industrial Process Tomography* 2021, *World Congress on Industrial Process Tomography* Bath (UK) 2018, *World Congress on Industrial Process Tomography* Foz do Iguaçu (Brazil) 2016. **Publications** *Industrial Process Tomography – Systems and Applications* (2015) by M Wang; *Process Imaging for Automatic Control* (2005) by D M Scott and H McCann; *Frontiers in Industrial Process Tomography* (1995) by D M Scott and R A Williams; *Imaging of Industrial Flows: Applications of Electrical Process Tomography* (1995) by A Plaskowski and M S Beck et al; *Process Tomography – Principles, Techniques and Applications* (1995) by R A Williams and M S Beck; *Tomographic Techniques for Process Design and Operation* (1993) by M S Beck and E Campogrande et al. Congress reports; articles. **Members** Membership countries not specified. [2021.06.11/XJ8071/t/**D**]

♦ International Society of Infant Psychiatrics (inactive)
♦ International Society on Infant Studies / see International Congress of Infant Studies

♦ **International Society for Infectious Diseases (ISID)** **15199**
Secretariat 9 Babcock St, 3rd Floor, Brookline MA 02446, USA. T. +16172770551. Fax +16172789113. E-mail: media@isid.org – info@isid.org.
Secretariat: http://www.isid.org/
History 1986. Founded by merger of *International Society for the Study of Infectious and Parasitic Diseases (inactive)* and *International Congress of Infectious Diseases (inactive).* **Aims** Maintain and encourage worldwide perspective on infectious diseases; generate discussion and share information on the ways that new and older technologies and knowledge can be applied to populations throughout the world; monitor discovery of new agents of disease, specific geographic characteristics of certain infections and potential for control and for spread. **Structure** Council organized according to WHO regions. Executive Committee. Committees. **Languages** English. **Staff** 11.00 FTE, paid. **Finance** No membership fee. **Activities** Awards/prizes/competitions; events/meetings; financial and/or material support; research/documentation. **Events** *International Congress on Infectious Diseases* Kuala Lumpur (Malaysia) 2022, *International Meeting on Emerging Diseases and Surveillance* Boston, MA (USA) 2021, *International Congress on Infectious Diseases* Kuala Lumpur (Malaysia) 2020, *Congress* Buenos Aires (Argentina) 2018, *International Meeting on Emerging Diseases and Surveillance* Vienna (Austria) 2018. **Publications** *IJID Regions* in English; *International Journal of Infectious Diseases* in English; *ISID News* in English. **Information Services** *ProMED-mail* in English – Electronic reporting system for outbreaks of emerging infectious diseases and toxins. **NGO Relations** Partner of (1): *Global Action For Fungal Infections (GAFFI, #10166).* [2022.03.04/XD3106/v/**D**]

♦ International Society for Infectious Diseases in Obstetrics and Gynaecology (ISIDOG) 15200

Contact Gasthuismolenstraat 31, 3300 Tienen, Belgium.
URL: http://www.isidog.com/

History 28 Oct 2015, Riga (Latvia). Founded at 1st ISIDOG European Congress. Principles created, 2013, London (UK), at 9th European meeting of *European Society for Infectious Diseases in Obstetrics and Gynaecology (ESIDOG, no recent information)*. Registration: Banque Carrefour des Entreprises, No/ID: 0645.503.920, Start date: 28 Oct 2015, Belgium. **Structure** Executive Board; Scientific Board. **Finance** Sources: members' dues. **Activities** Awards/prizes/competitions; events/meetings; research/documentation; training/education. **Events** *Congress* Budapest (Hungary) 2021, *Congress* Porto (Portugal) 2019, *Congress* Vienna (Austria) 2017, *Congress* Riga (Latvia) 2015. **NGO Relations** Cooperates with (1): *European Board and College of Obstetrics and Gynaecology (EBCOG, #06357).* [2021/AA1347/**D**]

♦ International Society of Inflammation and Allergy of the Nose (ISIAN) 15201

Sec Hospital of the University of Pennsylvania, Otorhinolaryngology – Head and Neck Surgery Dept, 5 Silverstein, 313, Philadelphia PA 19104, USA. T. +12156622777.
URL: http://www.isian.org/

History 1976, Tokyo (Japan). Founded by Ryo Takahashi, superseding *International Society of Immuno-Allergology of the Nasal Sinuses (inactive)*, set up 1946, Tokyo. Former names and other names: *International Society of Otorhinolaryngologic Allergy and Immunology* – former alias; *International Symposium on Infection and Allergy of the Nose (ISIAN)* – former (1976 to 2014). **Aims** Contribue to the international promotion of *rhinology*; provide a forum for scientific interchange, discussion and presentation, with primary focus on allergic, inflammatory and *infectious* problems in the nose, and with aspects of the science and clinical practice of rhinology also considered. **Structure** Board of Directors, comprising representatives from each region. President (rotates on annual basis); Secretary General (appointed for 5-year term). **Languages** English. **Staff** 2.00 FTE, voluntary. Full-time staff added prior to meetings. **Finance** Registration fee; meeting variable, depending on venue. **Activities** Organizes annual meeting, with biennially organized with *European Rhinologic Society (ERS, #08388)*. **Events** *Congress* Tokyo (Japan) 2024, *Congress* Sofia (Bulgaria) 2023, *Rhinology World Congress* St Petersburg (Russia) 2022, *International Symposium* Thessaloniki (Greece) 2021, *International Symposium* Thessaloniki (Greece) 2020. **Publications** Symposium proceedings. **Members** Participating members in over 50 countries and territories. Membership countries not specified. **NGO Relations** Close links with: *European Rhinologic Society (ERS, #08388)*; *International Rhinologic Society (IRS, #14753)*; American Rhinologic Society (ARS). [2021/XD2070/cv/**F**]

♦ International Society for Influenza and other Respiratory Virus Diseases (isirv) 15202

Registered Address 54a Castle Road, Isleworth, London, TW7 6QS, UK. E-mail: membership@isirv.org.
URL: http://www.isirv.org/

History 2005. Registration: Companies House, No/ID: 6021083, England and Wales; Charity Commission, No/ID: 1118829, England and Wales. **Aims** Promote prevention, detection, treatment and control of influenza and other respiratory virus diseases. **Structure** Board, including Chair, Deputy Chair, Secretary and Treasurer. Finance Group. Special Interest Group: Antiviral, previously *Neuraminidase Inhibitor Susceptibility Network (NISN)*. **Staff** 1.50 FTE, paid. **Finance** Members' dues (pounds85 a year). Other sources: surplus from scientific meetings; journal royalties. **Activities** Organizes 'Option for the Control of Influenza' conference (every 3-4 years). **Events** *Options for the Control of Influenza Conference* Singapore (Singapore) 2019, *Options for the Control of Influenza Conference* Singapore (Singapore) 2019, *Workshop on Health Technology Assessment for Vaccine* Singapore (Singapore) 2019, *Conference* Stockholm (Sweden) 2019, *Symposium on Neglected Influenza Viruses* Brighton (UK) 2018. **Publications** *isirv Newsletter* (4 a year); *Influenza and other Respiratory Viruses* – journal. Reports; proceedings. **Members** Individual scientists, clinicians, public health experts and others with direct interest and involvement in relevant areas. Membership countries not specified. **NGO Relations** Memorandum of Understanding with: *Asia-Pacific Alliance for the Control of Influenza (APACI, #01822).* [2022/XJ6395/**C**]

♦ International Society of Information Fusion (ISIF) 15203

Vice-Pres Communications address not obtained.
Sec Compunetix, 2420 Mosside Blvd, Monroeville PA 15146, USA.
URL: http://www.isif.org/

History 1998. Statutes drafted 1 Mar 2000; approved 15 Apr 2000. **Aims** Advance science, engineering and application of information fusion *technology*; serve both professional and public interests by fostering the open interchange of information and by promoting the highest professional and ethical standards; support advancement of the standing of members of the professions ISIF serves. **Structure** Members' Meeting. Board of Directors (meets annually) elects Executive Board, comprising 9 Directors and ex-officio Directors from Executive Committee. Executive Committee, consisting of President, Secretary and Treasurer, and other members appointed by President with approval of the Board. Standing Committees (5): Conference; Membership; Publications; Communications; Working Groups. **Languages** English. **Staff** 17.00 FTE, voluntary. **Finance** Members' dues. Conference surplus revenue. **Activities** Develops Data Information Fusion research community; organizes annual International Conference on Information Fusion; sponsors workshops and conferences. **Events** *Conference* Linköping (Sweden) 2022, *Conference* Sun City (South Africa) 2021, *Conference* 2020, *Conference* Ottawa, ON (Canada) 2019, *Conference* Cambridge (UK) 2018. **Publications** *Journal of Advances in Information Fusion* (2 a year) – online. Conference proceedings.
Members Categories Member; Student Member. Members in 38 countries:
Argentina, Australia, Austria, Belgium, Brazil, Bulgaria, Canada, China, Denmark, Estonia, Finland, France, Germany, Greece, Iran Islamic Rep, Israel, Italy, Japan, Lebanon, Luxembourg, Mexico, Morocco, Netherlands, Norway, Poland, Portugal, Romania, Russia, Singapore, South Africa, Spain, Sweden, Switzerland, Tunisia, Türkiye, UK, Ukraine, USA. [2013.06.28/XD7764/**D**]

♦ International Society for Information Studies / see International Society for the Study of Information (#15477)

♦ International Society of Infrared, Millimeter and Terahertz Waves (IRMMW-THz) 15204

Gen Sec 5166 Oakwood Ave, La Canada Flintridge CA 91101, USA.
URL: http://www.irmmw-thz.org/

History 7 May 2009. Founded to incorporate and formalize the *International Conference on Infrared, Millimeter and Terahertz Waves*, begun in 1974. Registration: Start date: 5 Nov 2009, USA, California; IRS 501(c)3, Start date: 10 Jun 2016, USA. **Aims** Promote worldwide collection, dissemination and exchange of scientific and technical knowledge in the areas and disciplines involving infrared, millimeter and terahertz waves. **Structure** International Board of Directors. **Languages** English. **Staff** 32.00 FTE, voluntary. **Finance** Sources: meeting proceeds; revenue from activities/projects. Annual budget: 50,000 USD (2022). **Events** *International Conference on Infrared, Millimeter and Terahertz Waves* Perth, WA (Australia) 2024, *International Conference on Infrared, Millimeter and Terahertz Waves* Montréal, QC (Canada) 2023, *Annual International Conference on Infrared, Millimeter and Terahertz Waves* Delft (Netherlands) 2022, *Annual International Conference on Infrared, Millimeter, and Terahertz Waves* Chengdu (China) 2021, *Annual International Conference on Infrared, Millimeter, and Terahertz Waves* Buffalo, NY (USA) 2020. **Publications** *Digest International Conference on Infrared, Millimeter and Terahertz Waves*; *IEEE Transactions on Terahertz Science and Technology*; *Journal of Infrared, Millimeter and Terahertz Waves.*
Members Individuals (32) in 17 countries:
Australia, Canada, China, Denmark, France, Germany, Hong Kong, Italy, Japan, Korea Rep, Mexico, Netherlands, Russia, Sweden, Switzerland, UK, USA.
Emeritus IOC members (Advisory) (13) in 7 countries:
Australia, France, Germany, Japan, Switzerland, UK, USA.
NGO Relations Cooperates with: *Institute of Electrical and Electronics Engineers (IEEE, #11259).* [2022.05.04/XJ1423/**E**]

♦ International Society for Inhaled Medical Gases and Therapies (inactive)

♦ International Society for Insulin-like Growth Factor Research / see International Society for IGF Research (#15191)

♦ International Society for Integrated Disaster Risk Management (IDRiM Society) 15205

Managing Dir DRS – DPRI, Kyoto Univ, Uji Campus, Gokasho – Uji, Kyoto, 611-0011 Japan. T. +81774384043. Fax +81774384044. E-mail: society@idrim.org.
URL: http://idrim.org/

History 15 Oct 2009, Kyoto (Japan). Founded at 9th IIASA-DPRI Forum on Integrated Disaster Risk Management (IDRiM Forum). **Aims** Promote knowledge sharing, interdisciplinary research and development on integrated disaster risk management contributing to the implementation of success models for efficient and equitable disaster risk management options. **Structure** Board of Directors. Committees. **Events** *International Conference* Roorkee (India) 2023, *International Conference* 2022, *IDRiM Conference* Kyoto (Japan) 2021, *IDRiM Conference* Kyoto (Japan) 2020, *Conference* Sydney, NSW (Australia) 2018. **Publications** *IDRiM Journal*; *IDRiM Society Newsletter.* [2020/XJ5401/**C**]

♦ International Society for Intellectual History (ISIH) 15206

Main Office Faculty of History, University of Oxford, Old Boy's High School, George Street, Oxford, OX1 2RL, UK. E-mail: isih@history.ox.ac.uk.
URL: http://isih.history.ox.ac.uk/

History Founded 1994. **Aims** Promote the study and teaching of intellectual history in all its forms; foster communication and interaction among the global community of scholars in the field. **Structure** Executive Committee, comprising President, General Secretary, Communications Director, Announcements Editor, Editors of Intellectual History Review, Editor of Intellectual News (1996-2010), Membership Secretariats and representatives at large. Standing Committee of 11 members. **Languages** English, French, German. **Staff** 0.50 FTE, paid; 3.00 FTE, voluntary. **Finance** Members' dues. Support from private foundation. **Activities** Organizes international conferences; offers Charles Schmitt Prize. **Events** *Change and Exchange* San Domenico di Fiesole (Italy) 2020, *Revolutions and evolutions in international history* Brisbane, QLD (Australia) 2019, *Conference* St Andrews (UK) 2018, *Conference* Sofia (Bulgaria) 2017, *Conference* Rethymnon (Greece) 2016. **Publications** *Intellectual History Review* (4 a year). *International Dictionary of Intellectual Historians.* **Members** Individuals – scholars working in the histories of philosophy and theology; science, medicine and technology; legal and political thought; literature; visual arts; music; as well as in social and cultural history more generally. Membership countries not specified. [2013.06.01/XD7394/**D**]

♦ International Society of Intellectuals (inactive)

♦ International Society for Intelligence Research (unconfirmed)

♦ International Society of Intelligent Unmanned Systems (ISIUS) 15207

Vice-Pres Operations Dept of Aerospace-IT Fusion Engineering, Konkuk Univ, Engineering Bldg C – 383-1, 1 Hwayang-dong, Gwangjin-gu, Seoul 143-701, Korea Rep. T. +8224503817. Fax +8224446670.
URL: http://www.isiusys.org/

History 3 Nov 2010, Bali (Indonesia). 3-5 Nov 2010, Bali (Indonesia), during 6th International Conference on Intelligent Unmanned Systems. **Aims** Promote advancement of technologies relevant to unmanned *vehicles* in underwater, ground, aerial and space domains for humanitarian uses. **Structure** Committee. **Languages** English. **Staff** 4.00 FTE, paid. **Finance** Sponsorship from various international and governmental research institutes. **Activities** Events/meetings. **Events** *International Conference on Intelligent Unmanned Systems* Tokushima (Japan) 2022, *International Conference on Intelligent Unmanned Systems* Ho Chi Minh City (Vietnam) 2021, *International Conference on Intelligent Unmanned Systems* Jeju (Korea Rep) 2019, *International Conference on Intelligent Unmanned Systems* Jeju (Korea Rep) 2018, *International Conference on Intelligent Unmanned Systems* New Taipei City (Taiwan) 2017. **Publications** *International Journal of Intelligent Unmanned Systems.* **Members** Scientists, engineers, academia and practitioners from over 60 countries. Membership countries not specified. [2014.06.01/XJ4657/**E**]

♦ International Society for the Interaction of Mechanics and Mathematics (ISIMM) 15208

Société internationale pour l'action réciproque entre la mécanique et les mathématiques

Sec c/o Dept of Engineering, Univ Roma TRE, via Vito Volterra 62, 00146 Rome RM, Italy.
URL: http://isimm.unipg.it/

History 1977, Porabka-Kozubnik (Poland), during an international symposium on trends in applications of pure mathematics in mechanics. **Aims** Foster dynamic interaction between the disciplines of mathematics and mechanics in the international scientific community. **Structure** Executive Committee. **Languages** English. **Staff** None. **Finance** Voluntary contributions. **Activities** Events/meetings. **Events** *STAMM : Biennial Symposium on Trends in Applications of Mathematics to Mechanics* Oxford (UK) 2018, *STAMM : Biennial Symposium on Trends in Applications of Mathematics to Mechanics* Rome (Italy) 2016, *STAMM : Biennial Symposium on Trends in Applications of Mathematics to Mechanics* Poitiers (France) 2014, *STAMM : Biennial Symposium on Trends in Applications of Mathematics to Mechanics* Haifa (Israel) 2012, *STAMM : Biennial Symposium on Trends in Applications of Mathematics to Mechanics* Berlin (Germany) 2010. **Publications** *Interaction of Mechanics and Mathematics Series.* Symposium proceedings.
Members Ordinary; Honorary. Individuals in 39 countries:
Armenia, Austria, Belgium, Bosnia-Herzegovina, Brazil, Bulgaria, Canada, Chile, China, Czechia, Denmark, Estonia, France, Georgia, Germany, Greece, Hungary, India, Iran Islamic Rep, Ireland, Israel, Italy, Japan, Latvia, Mexico, Montenegro, Netherlands, Norway, Poland, Portugal, Russia, Serbia, Slovakia, South Africa, Sweden, Türkiye, UK, Ukraine, USA.
NGO Relations Associated with: *International Mathematical Union (IMU, #14121)*; *International Union of Theoretical and Applied Mechanics (IUTAM, #15823).* [2020.03.07/XD9214/v/**D**]

♦ International Society for Intercommunication of New Ideas (ISINI) 15209

Pres DCEA Univ de Sonora – Ed 10J, Planta Baja Rosales y Blvd Luis Encinas, Hermosillo, CP 83000 Sonora, Mexico. T. +526622592167. Fax +526622592166. E-mail: frankysolid@gmail.com – fvargas@guaymas.uson.mx.
URL: https://www.isini.info/

History 1988, as *International Society for Intercommunications of New Ideas.* **Aims** Prepare, spiritually and materially, the objective foundation of a better world, crystallized in the ideals of a free, just and stable society and economy with a truly democratic form of government of limited delegated powers; open and promote a free and unfettered communication of new ideas in a spirit of special brotherhood in the world of ideas, where differing points of view are not considered divisive but a challenge for further exploration and a sign of spiritual vitality; foster and support discovery of new ideas in theory – analysis; arrange for their testing (logical or empirical) in the realm of various possible social, economic and political systems, including history of analysis and social-ethical issues; initiate and maintain continuous contact consultation among economists, sociologists and political scientists and between social and natural scientists including men of arts and letters; study systematically, using practical reason, the application of new ideas to problems of the real world according to various existing social regimes, levels of development and historical circumstances; call on political leaders to allow controlled experiments in small areas to test empirical validity of scientific principles or relationships directly related to the wellbeing of a nation and which are questioned or open for debate. **Structure** Executive Committee, comprising: President; 1st, 2nd and 3rd Vice-Presidents; Executive Secretary-Treasurer. Consultative Council, consisting of 12 members. Members, referred to as 'Innovators', grouped in national Chapters, each with a Coordinator elected every 2 years by regular members. **Languages** English. **Finance** Members' dues: US$ 20. **Activities** Develops economic, monetary, financial and social stabilization plans in those countries where ISINI is represented. **Events** *International Conference* Wroclaw (Poland) 2020, *International Conference* Groningen (Netherlands) 2016, *International Conference* Hermosillo (Mexico) 2011, *International Conference* Bucharest (Romania) 2009, *International Conference* Bacau (Romania) 2007. **Publications** *The International Journal of New Ideas* (2 a year).
Members National Chapters, grouping individuals ('Innovators'). Membership categories or sections (7) I – History, statistics; II – Theory, new concepts, principles, interpretations, explanations (positive science); III – Ethics, what ought to be, general stable equilibrium (normative science); IV – Policy, how to achieve a certain given goal without creating other problems; V – Doctrines, history of thought; VI – Arts, letters, humanities; VII – General supporters. Members in 31 countries and territories:

Argentina, Australia, Belarus, Belgium, Brazil, Canada, Chile, Colombia, France, Germany, Greece, Hungary, India, Israel, Italy, Japan, Kazakhstan, Korea Rep, Mexico, Moldova, Netherlands, New Zealand, Poland, Romania, Russia, Switzerland, Taiwan, UK, Ukraine, USA, Venezuela. [2020/XF1745/**F**]

- ♦ International Society for Intercommunications of New Ideas / see International Society for Intercommunication of New Ideas (#15209)
- ♦ International Society for Inter-cultural Studies and Research / see International Society for Intercultural Studies and Research
- ♦ International Society for Intercultural Studies and Research (internationally oriented national body)
- ♦ International Society for Interdisciplinary Medical Check-up (inactive)

♦ International Society for the Interdisciplinary Study of Symmetry (SIS-Symmetry) 15210

Pres Budapest, Tisza u. 7, Budapest 1029, Hungary.
Chairperson 43 Charlick Circuit, Adelaide SA 5000, Australia.
Treasurer 1 las Maratou Street, Zografou, 157 73 Athens, Greece.
URL: http://symmetry-us.com/

History 1989, Budapest (Hungary). Charter Articles adopted 16 Aug 1989; modified 20 Aug 1995, 12 July 2001 and 29 May 2022. Former names and other names: *ISIS-S* – former; *International Symmetry Society (SIS)* – alias. Registration: Fővárosi Bíróság (Court of the Capital City), Budapest, Hungary, No/ID: Pk. 60.315/1989, Start date: 1989, Hungary, Budapest. **Aims** Bring together artists, philosophers, scientists, engineers, educators, students, and practitioners in seeking a broad, interdisciplinary perspective on symmetry and using the intellectual experience of the study of symmetry to promote coordinated inquiries of diverse structures with the ultimate goal to develop a unified view of reality. **Structure** General Assembly, hosted by Congress (every 3 years); Executive Board; Oversight Committee; International Advisory Board. **Languages** English. **Activities** Events/meetings. Active in: Argentina, Australia, Austria, Belgium, Brazil, Canada, China, Finland, Germany, Greece, Hungary, India, Israel, Italy, Japan, Poland, Portugal, Russia, Switzerland, UK, Ukraine, USA. **Events** *Congress* Porto (Portugal) 2022, *Congress* Kanazawa (Japan) 2019, *Logics of Image* Kolymbari (Greece) 2018, *Congress* Adelaide, SA (Australia) 2016, *Logics of Image* Santorini Is (Greece) 2016. **Publications** *Symmetry: Art and Science* (4 a year).
Members Honorary. Individuals in 7 countries:
Austria, Germany, Hungary, Israel, Japan, Switzerland, USA.
NGO Relations Links with national organizations. [2023.01.16/XJ9262/**C**]

- ♦ International Society for Interferon and Cytokine Research / see International Cytokine and Interferon Society (#13127)
- ♦ International Society for Interferon Research / see International Cytokine and Interferon Society (#13127)
- ♦ International Society of Interior Designers / see International Interior Design Association (#13946)

♦ International Society for Intermedial Studies (ISIS) 15211

Address not obtained.
URL: http://isis.digitaltextualities.ca/

History 1996, as *Nordic Society for Interarts Studies – Nordisk Selskap for Interartstudier (NorSIS)*. Subsequently changed title to *Nordic Society for Intermedial Studies*. Current statutes adopted 12 Dec 2011. **Aims** Promote intermedial research and *postgraduate* education. **Structure** General Assembly; Executive Board; Advisory Board. **Activities** Events/meetings. **Events** *Conference* Nancy (France) 2021, *Keeping silent, listening, speaking up* Nancy (France) 2020, *General Assembly* Hangzhou (China) 2018, *Intermedial practice and theory in comparison* Hangzhou (China) 2018, *General Assembly* Montréal, QC (Canada) 2017.
Members Individuals in 20 countries and territories:
Austria, Belgium, Brazil, Canada, Czechia, Denmark, Finland, France, Germany, India, Italy, Netherlands, Norway, Poland, Spain, Sweden, Switzerland, Taiwan, UK, USA. [2019/XD7883/v/**D**]

♦ International Society of Internal Medicine (ISIM) 15212

Société internationale de médecine interne – Sociedad Internacional de Medicina Interna – Internationale Gesellschaft für Innere Medizin

SG University of Bern, Faculty of Medicine, Murtenstrasse 11, 3008 Bern, Switzerland.
Pres PO Box 2896, Alberton, 1450, South Africa. T. +27119078827.
URL: http://www.isim-online.org/

History 29 Sep 1948, Basel (Switzerland). New Statutes adopted 12 Apr 1973, Chicago IL (USA); 29 Sep 2004, Grenada. **Aims** Act as a federation of national societies of internal medicine; promote scientific knowledge and unity in internal medicine; develop educational facilities; encourage friendship between *physicians* in all countries. **Structure** General Assembly (during Congress); International Committee; Executive Committee. **Languages** English. **Staff** 2.00 FTE, voluntary. **Finance** Sources: members' dues. **Activities** Events/meetings. **Events** *Biennial Congress* Prague (Czechia) 2024, *Biennial Congress* Punta Cana (Dominican Rep) 2023, *Biennial Congress* Cancún (Mexico) 2021, *Biennial Congress* Cancún (Mexico) 2020, *Biennial Congress* Cape Town (South Africa) 2018. **Publications** Congress reports in English, French, German.
Members Categories Society; Individual; Life; Honorary. National societies in 61 countries and territories:
Argentina, Australia, Austria, Bangladesh, Belarus, Belgium, Bolivia, Brazil, Bulgaria, Chile, China, Colombia, Croatia, Cuba, Czechia, Dominican Rep, Ecuador, Estonia, Finland, France, Georgia, Germany, Ghana, Great Britain, Hungary, India, Indonesia, Iran Islamic Rep, Israel, Italy, Japan, Korea Rep, Latvia, Lithuania, Mexico, Netherlands, Nicaragua, Nigeria, Norway, Panama, Paraguay, Peru, Philippines, Poland, Portugal, Romania, Russia, Serbia, Singapore, Slovakia, Slovenia, South Africa, Spain, Sweden, Switzerland, Taiwan, Türkiye, Ukraine, Uruguay, USA, Venezuela.
Individuals in 55 countries:
Argentina, Australia, Austria, Belgium, Brazil, Canada, Chile, Colombia, Costa Rica, Cuba, Denmark, Dominican Rep, Ecuador, Egypt, El Salvador, Finland, France, Germany, Greece, Guatemala, Hungary, India, Indonesia, Iran Islamic Rep, Iraq, Israel, Italy, Japan, Kenya, Lebanon, Mexico, Netherlands, Nicaragua, Norway, Panama, Paraguay, Peru, Philippines, Poland, Portugal, Puerto Rico, Romania, Saudi Arabia, Serbia, South Africa, Spain, Sweden, Switzerland, Tanzania UR, Türkiye, UK, Uruguay, USA, Venezuela, Zimbabwe.
NGO Relations Member of (1): *Council for International Organizations of Medical Sciences (CIOMS, #04905).* [2023/XB2551/**B**]

- ♦ International Society of Internet Professionals (inactive)

♦ International Society for Interpersonal Acceptance and Rejection (ISIPAR) 15213

Exec Dir U-1058 Human Development and Family Studies, Univ of Connecticut, Storrs CT 06269-1058, USA. T. +18604860073. Fax +18604863452.
URL: http://isipar.uconn.edu/

History Founded 4 Jun 2006, when initial constitution was ratified by participants at first International Congress on Interpersonal Acceptance and Rejection, Istanbul (Turkey). Current revision ratified, 23 Jul 2007 and 5 Jul 2008. Registered in the State of Connecticut (USA). **Aims** Support and encourage research and practice related to issues of interpersonal acceptance and rejection, including but not limited to parental, peer, intimate adult relationships and all other attachment relationships throughout the lifespan. **Structure** Executive Council; Regional Representatives. **Languages** English. **Staff** 0.50 FTE, paid; 1.00 FTE, voluntary. **Finance** Members' dues. **Activities** Events/meetings. **Events** *Biennial International Congress* Geneva, NY (USA) 2022, *Biennial International Congress* Porto (Portugal) 2020, *Biennial International Congress* Athens (Greece) 2018, *Biennial International Congress* Madrid (Spain) 2016, *Biennial International Congress* Chisinau (Moldova) 2014. **Publications** *Interpersonal Acceptance* (3 a year) – newsletter. Books; selected readings from congresses.
Members Full in 34 countries:
Australia, Austria, Bangladesh, Botswana, Bulgaria, Canada, Colombia, Croatia, Egypt, Estonia, Greece, India, Iran Islamic Rep, Iraq, Israel, Italy, Jordan, Korea Rep, Kuwait, Malaysia, Netherlands, New Zealand, Nigeria, Norway, Pakistan, Portugal, Puerto Rico, Romania, Spain, Sweden, Türkiye, UK, USA, Zimbabwe. [2019/XJ0116/**D**]

♦ International Society of Intraoperative Neurophysiology (ISIN) 15214

Main Office c/o GCB, Griffeweg 5, 9724 GE Groningen, Netherlands. T. +31503168877. E-mail: info@gcb.nl.
URL: http://www.neurophysiology.org/

History Founded 2005, Rome (Italy). Registered in accordance with Italian law. **Aims** Advance excellence in intra and perioperative neurophysiology. **Structure** General Business Meeting (annual). Executive Board of 6 members. **Finance** Members' dues. **Events** *Congress* Vienna (Austria) 2019, *Congress* Seoul (Korea Rep) 2017, *Congress* Rio de Janeiro (Brazil) 2015, *Congress* Cape Town (South Africa) 2013, *Congress* Barcelona (Spain) 2011. [2020.03.04/XM3132/**D**]

♦ International Society of Intraoperative Radiation Therapy (ISIORT) 15215

Sec Policlinico Universitario A Gemelli, Largo Francesco Vito 1, 00168 Rome RM, Italy. T. +39630154376. Fax +39630155908.
URL: http://www.isiort.org/

History 1998. Also referred to as *International Society of IORT*. **Aims** Foster scientific and clinical development of Intraoperative Radiation Therapy; promote research, education and treatment of *cancer* patients by intraoperative radiation therapy 8ISIORT9 by orthovoltage, electron beam or HDR brachytherapy; encourage liaison among specialists and scientists concerned with the treatment of cancer patients. **Structure** General Meeting (every 2 years). Board of Directors (meets every 2 years), comprising President, Past-President, President-Elect, Founding President; Secretary; Treasurer and 3 members-at-large. Committees (9): Arrangements; Clinical Liaison; Clinical Research; Commercial Liaison; Constitution and Bylaws; Education and Publication; Membership and Credentials; Nominating; Web. IORT Protocol Study Group. Membership managed by International Meeting Managers Inc. **Languages** English. **Finance** Members' dues (initiation and biennial). **Events** *General Meeting* Scottsdale, AZ (USA) 2010, *International conference / General Meeting* Madrid (Spain) 2008, *International conference / General Meeting* Montpellier (France) 2007, *International conference / General Meeting* Miami, FL (USA) 2005, *International conference / General Meeting* Aachen (Germany) 2002.
Members Active; Senior; Inactive; Corporate; Associate over 1,000 members in 15 countries:
Argentina, Austria, Brazil, China, France, Germany, Italy, Japan, Korea Rep, Netherlands, Spain, Sweden, Switzerland, UK, USA. [2012/XD8863/**D**]

♦ International Society for Inventory Research (ISIR) 15216

Contact Kiraly u 12, Budapest 1061, Hungary. T. +3612678740. Fax +3612678740. E-mail: isir@isir.hu.
URL: http://isir.hu/

History 26 Aug 1982, Budapest (Hungary), at 2nd Symposium on Inventories, following recommendations of 1st Symposium, 1-5 Sep 1980, Budapest. **Aims** Provide those engaged in inventory research with an opportunity to exchange views and experience on an international and interdisciplinary basis; provide a framework for dissemination of results of research in members' countries; take the initiative in developing research and higher education. **Structure** General Assembly; Executive Committee; Sections (3). **Languages** English. **Staff** 2.50 FTE, paid. **Finance** Members' dues. Contributions; other sources. **Activities** Events/meetings; training/education; research/documentation; awards/prizes/competitions. **Events** *Biennial Symposium* Budapest (Hungary) 2014, *Biennial Symposium* Budapest (Hungary) 2010, *Biennial Symposium* Budapest (Hungary) 2008, *Biennial Symposium* Budapest (Hungary) 2006, *Biennial Symposium* Budapest (Hungary) 2004. **Publications** *ISIR Newsletter*. *International Bibliography of Inventory Literature* – in 3 vols. Proceedings of symposia and summer schools.
Members Organizations and individuals in 41 countries and territories:
Australia, Austria, Belgium, Brazil, Bulgaria, Canada, China, Croatia, Czechia, Denmark, Estonia, Finland, France, Germany, Greece, Hungary, India, Israel, Italy, Japan, Korea Rep, Latvia, Lebanon, Netherlands, New Zealand, Nigeria, Norway, Poland, Portugal, Russia, Serbia, Slovakia, Slovenia, Spain, Sweden, Switzerland, Taiwan, Thailand, Türkiye, UK, USA.
NGO Relations Affiliated member of: *European Logistics Association (ELA, #07710).* Maintains links with other international and national organizations in the field (not specified). [2020/XD4235/**D**]

♦ International Society for Invertebrate Morphology (ISIM) 15217

Sec Evolutionary Biology – Morpholoy, Univ Wien, Althanstr 14, 1090 Vienna, Austria.
Pres Dept Organismic and Evolutionary Board, Harvard Univ, 504 MCZ Labs, 26 Oxford St, Museum of Comparative Zoology, Cambridge MA 02138, USA.
URL: http://zoologi.snm.ku.dk/english/Forskning/Invertebrates/isim/

History Aug 2008, Copenhagen (Denmark), during 1st International Congress. **Aims** Promote international collaboration and provide educational opportunities and training on invertebrate morphology; organize and promote the international congresses of invertebrate morphology, international meetings and other forms of scientific exchange. **Structure** Officers: President; President-Elect; Secretary; Treasurer. **Events** *International Congress on Invertebrate Morphology* Vienna (Austria) 2022, *International Congress on Invertebrate Morphology* Vienna (Austria) 2020, *International Congress on Invertebrate Morphology* Moscow (Russia) 2017, *International Congress on Invertebrate Morphology* Berlin (Germany) 2014, *International congress on invertebrate morphology / Congress* Cambridge, MA (USA) 2011. [2013/XJ1993/**D**]

- ♦ International Society for Invertebrate Neurobiology (inactive)
- ♦ International Society of Invertebrate Reproduction / see International Society of Invertebrate Reproduction and Development (#15218)

♦ International Society of Invertebrate Reproduction and Development (ISIRD) 15218

Sec Max F Perutz Labs, Univ of Vienna, Dr Bohr-Gasse 9/4, 1030 Vienna, Austria. T. +431427754616.
Pres Wayne State Univ, 42 Warren Ave, Detroit MI 48202, USA.
URL: http://www.isird.org/

History 11 Sep 1975, Calicut (India), during International Symposium on Reproductive Physiology of Invertebrates. Original title: *International Society of Invertebrate Reproduction (ISIR).* **Aims** Promote coordinated scientific research on reproductive biology of invertebrates on a global basis with a view to understanding the mechanisms involved in their sexuality, reproduction and development. **Structure** Committee. **Languages** English. **Finance** Sources: members' dues. **Events** *Triennial Congress* Qingdao (China) 2021, *Triennial Congress* Qingdao (China) 2020, *Triennial Congress* Naples (Italy) / Florence (Italy) 2017, *Triennial Congress* Hyderabad (India) 2016, *Triennial Congress* Detroit, MI (USA) 2013. **Publications** *Invertebrate Reproduction and Development* (6 a year). Proceedings of symposia.
Members Individuals (252, participating actively in events) in 40 countries and territories:
Argentina, Australia, Belgium, Brazil, Canada, Chile, China, Denmark, Egypt, France, Germany, Greece, Hong Kong, India, Ireland, Israel, Italy, Japan, Korea Rep, Netherlands, New Zealand, Philippines, Russia, Scotland, South Africa, Spain, Sweden, Switzerland, Taiwan, Thailand, Türkiye, UK, USA, Vietnam.
NGO Relations Scientific member of: *International Union of Biological Sciences (IUBS, #15760).* [2015.03.26/XD5170/v/**C**]

- ♦ International Society for the Investigation of Stress (inactive)
- ♦ International Society of IORT / see International Society of Intraoperative Radiation Therapy (#15215)
- ♦ International Society for Iranian Studies / see Association for Iranian Studies

♦ International Society for Islamic Legal Studies (ISILS) 15219

Sec/Treas address not obtained.
URL: http://www.isils.net/

History 2003, Murcia (Spain). Conceived following conferences organized since 1994. Registration: Start date: 2004, USA, State of Massachusetts. **Aims** Encourage scholarship on, and foster communication about, Islamic law and related subjects. **Structure** Executive Board. **Finance** Sources: members' dues. **Activities** Events/meetings. **Events** *Conference* Helsinki (Finland) / Tampere (Finland) 2018. [2020.11.16/XM7929/c/**E**]

♦ International Society for Islamic Philosophy (ISIP) 15220

Regional Coordinator address not obtained.

History Jul 2008, Seoul (Korea Rep), during 22nd World Congress of Philosophy. **Aims** Solidify a global network of individuals and institutions from diverse geographical and cultural contexts collaborating in critical reflection on philosophic issues within their specific cultures and across societies in civilizational exchange; refresh the creative spirit of the Islamic intellectual and ethical heritage; integrate timeless philosophic concerns and values into our contemporary scene. **Structure** General Assembly (during quinquennial Congress of FISP). Executive Committee, including President, Secretary General and Treasurer. Advisory Board. **Finance** Sources: members' dues. **Events** *International Conference* Teheran (Iran Islamic Rep) 2009.

Publications *Philosophica Islamic* – journal. **Members** Full; Honorary; Student; Institutional. Membership countries not specified. **NGO Relations** Recognized organization of: *International Federation of Philosophical Societies (FISP, #13507).* [2012/XJ5082/C]

♦ International Society for Islamic Secularization / see Institute for the Secularization of Islamic Society

♦ International Society for Japanese Kampo Medicine (ISJKM) 15221

Treas 36 Bankhurst Road, London, SE6 4XN, UK. E-mail: mail@isjkm.com.
Pres address not obtained.
URL: http://www.isjkm.com/

History 2009, Tokyo (Japan). **Aims** Promote communication and collaboration among English speaking researchers and practitioners who are dedicated to and identify with Japanese Kampo Medicine. **Structure** General Meetings; Executive Board. **Languages** English. **Finance** Sources: members' dues. **Activities** Events/meetings. **Events** *International Symposium for Japanese Kampo Medicine* Oxford (UK) 2023, *International Symposium* Oxford (UK) 2022, *International Symposium* Hannover (Germany) 2019, *International Symposium* Berlin (Germany) 2017, *International Symposium* Vienna (Austria) 2015. **Members** Full in 8 countries. Membership countries not specified. [2022/XM4873/D]

♦ International Society for Japanese Philately (ISJP) 15222

Pres 5011 Gundry Ave, Long Beach CA 90807, USA. E-mail: president@isjp.org.
Vice Pres PO Box 1283, Haddonfield NJ 08033, USA. E-mail: publisher@isjp.org.
URL: http://www.isjp.org/

History 1 Mar 1945, Canada. **Aims** Promote interest in philately and *postal* history of Japan and former Japanese colonies (Korea, Sakhalin /Karafuto/, Taiwan), territories (Kwantung, South Manchurian Railway Zone, and mandated Caroline, Mariana, and Marshall Islands) and occupied area (China and Southeast Asia), including Manchukuo, Ryukyu Islands, Japanese seapost offices and other civilian and military post offices abroad and foreign offices in Japan. **Structure** Board of Governors; Chapters. **Languages** English. **Staff** Voluntary. **Finance** Sources: investments; members' dues. **Activities** Guidance/assistance/consulting; knowledge management/information dissemination; networking/liaising. **Publications** *Japanese Philately* (4-5 a year) in English. *ISJP Monographs* – series. Annual and cumulative indexes; CD-ROM monographs; Flash Drive containing all publications.

Members Individuals in 28 countries and territories:
Andorra, Argentina, Australia, Belgium, Canada, China, Denmark, Finland, France, Germany, India, Israel, Italy, Japan, Korea Rep, Netherlands, New Zealand, Norway, Poland, Singapore, Spain, Sweden, Switzerland, Taiwan, Thailand, UK, USA, Virgin Is USA. [2022.10.18/XF0958/v/E]

♦ International Society for Justice Research (ISJR) 15223

Pres Duke Univ – Fuqua School of Business, 100 Fuqua Drive, Durham NC 27708, USA. T. +19196603737. E-mail: isjr@isjr.org – schloesser.thomas@fh-swf.de.
URL: http://www.isjr.org/

History Jul 1997, Potsdam (Germany). Registration: Germany. **Aims** Promote interdisciplinary justice research; communicate research findings; advance application of justice theory and research findings in various fields of practice. **Structure** Board, comprising President, Past-President or President-Elect, Treasurer, Secretary, Newsletter Editor and organizer of the following meeting. **Languages** English. **Staff** 6.00 FTE, voluntary. **Finance** Members' dues (annual): US$ 75 for people who hold permanent positions; US$ 40 for others; Associate, US$ 10. Budget (annual): US$ 9,000. **Activities** Events/meetings; awards/prizes/competitions. **Events** *International Social Justice Conference* Munich (Germany) 2023, *International Social Justice Conference* Lisbon (Portugal) 2021, *International Social Justice Conference* Atlanta, GA (USA) 2018, *International Social Justice Conference* Canterbury (UK) 2016, *International Social Justice Conference* New York, NY (USA) 2014. **Publications** *ISJR Newsletter*, *Social Justice Research* – journal.

Members Full scholars whose work is related to justice; Associate students interested in justice research. Individuals in 26 countries:
Australia, Austria, Belgium, Brazil, Canada, Croatia, Czechia, Finland, France, Germany, India, Israel, Italy, Latvia, Lithuania, Netherlands, New Zealand, Norway, Pakistan, Philippines, Portugal, Spain, Sweden, Switzerland, UK, USA. [2020/XD8279/v/D]

♦ International Society of the Knee (inactive)

♦ International Society for Knowledge Organization (ISKO) 15224

Société internationale pour l'organisation des connaissances – Internationale Gesellschaft für Wissenorganisation

Sec/Treas School of Information, Kent State Univ, PO Box 5190, Kent OH 44242-0001, USA. E-mail: secr@isko.org.
Pres Dept of Economics, Tory Bldg 8-19, Univ of Alberta, Edmonton AB T6G 2H4, Canada. E-mail: president@isko.org.
URL: http://www.isko.org/

History Set up 22 Jul 1989, Frankfurt-Main (Germany FR). **Aims** Promote research, development and application of methods for the organization of knowledge in general or of particular fields, by integrating conceptual approaches of classification research and *artificial intelligence*. **Structure** General Assembly (every 2 years); Executive Board; Scientific Advisory Council; Regional Chapters (15); National Coordinators (10); National and International Working Groups (4). **Languages** English. **Staff** None. **Finance** Sources: members' dues. **Activities** Events/meetings; knowledge management/information dissemination; training/education. **Events** *Biennial Conference* Aalborg (Denmark) 2022, *Biennial Conference* Aalborg (Denmark) 2020, *Biennial Conference* Porto (Portugal) 2018, *International Colloquium* Paris (France) 2017, *Biennial Conference* Rio de Janeiro (Brazil) 2016. **Publications** *Knowledge Organization. Knowledge Organization in Subject Areas KOSA* (1995); *Advances in Knowledge Organization (AKO).*

Members Representatives, mainly in the information science field, in research and application of logic, system theory, organization science, psychology, science theory, informatics, semiotics, linguistics and philosophy, particularly epistemology. Regular (individuals and bodies); Sponsoring (individual and bodies); Honorary (individuals). Members (about 500) in 50 countries and territories:
Algeria, Australia, Austria, Belgium, Benin, Brazil, Cameroon, Canada, China, Croatia, Denmark, Estonia, Finland, France, Germany, Ghana, Hungary, India, Iran Islamic Rep, Ireland, Israel, Italy, Japan, Korea Rep, Latvia, Mexico, Morocco, Netherlands, New Zealand, Nigeria, Norway, Papua New Guinea, Poland, Portugal, Romania, Russia, Saudi Arabia, Singapore, Slovakia, Slovenia, South Africa, Spain, Sweden, Switzerland, Taiwan, Togo, Tunisia, UK, USA, Venezuela.

IGO Relations Cooperates with: *European Commission (EC, #06633); UNESCO (#20322).* **NGO Relations** Cooperates with: *International Organization for Standardization (ISO, #14473).* [2020.03.03/XD2048/C]

♦ International Society for Knowledge and Systems Sciences (internationally oriented national body)
♦ International Society for Krishna Consciousness (religious order)

♦ International Society for Laboratory Hematology (ISLH) 15225

Project Leader 2111 Chestnut Ave, Ste 145, Glenview IL 60025, USA. T. +18479833519. Fax +13128965614. E-mail: admin@islh.org – info@islh.org.
URL: http://www.islh.org/

History 1992. **Aims** Serve as a forum for exchange of new ideas and information on laboratory haematology; advance research in laboratory haematology; promote laboratory haematology as a profession. **Structure** Board. **Languages** English. **Activities** Events/meetings; publishing activities. **Events** *International Symposium on Technical Innovations in Laboratory Hematology* New Orleans, LA (USA) 2023, *International Symposium on Technical Innovations in Laboratory Hematology* Bologna (Italy) 2022, *International Symposium on Technical Innovations in Laboratory Hematology* 2021, *International Symposium on Technical Innovations in Laboratory Hematology* 2020, *Annual Symposium* Vancouver, BC (Canada) 2019. **Publications** *International Journal of Laboratory Hematology* (6 a year). **Members** Individuals. Membership countries not specified. **NGO Relations** Member of (1): *World Association of Societies of Pathology and Laboratory Medicine (WASPaLM, #21191).* [2021.09.14/XN9916/C]

♦ International Society for Labour Law and Social Security / see International Society for Labour and Social Security Law (#15226)

♦ International Society for Labour and Social Security Law (ISLSSL) . 15226

Société internationale de Droit du Travail et de la Sécurité Sociale (SIDTSS) – Sociedad Internacional de Derecho del Trabajo y de la Seguridad Social (SIDTSS)

SG c/o ITC of the ILO, Viale Maestri del Lavoro 10, 10127 Turin TO, Italy.
Pres Wharton School, Univ of Pennsylvania, 672 Jon M Huntsman Hall, 3730 Walnut Street, Philadelphia PA 19104, USA. T. +12158986820.
URL: http://islssl.org/

History 13 Jun 1958, Brussels (Belgium). Established as a result of the merger of *International Social Law Society (SIDS, inactive)*, which had held congresses in 1954, Sao Paulo (Brazil) and 1958, Brussels, with *'International Congress of Labour Law'*, held 1951, Trieste (Italy) and 1957, Geneva (Switzerland). Former names and other names: *International Society for Labour Law and Social Security* – former; *Internationale Gesellschaft für das Recht der Arbeit und der Sozialen Sicherheit* – former. **Aims** Study labour and social security law at national and international level; promote exchange of ideas and information; encourage collaboration among academics, lawyers and other experts within the fields of labour and social security law. **Structure** General Assembly (every 3 years); Executive Committee. **Languages** English, French, Spanish. **Staff** Voluntary. **Finance** Sources: gifts, legacies; grants; members' dues. **Activities** Events/meetings. **Events** *European Regional Congress* Ghent (Belgium) 2023, *World Congress* Lima (Peru) 2021, *European Regional Congress* Lisbon (Portugal) 2021, *American Regional Congress* Córdoba (Argentina) 2019, *World Congress* Turin (Italy) 2018. **Publications** *ISLSSL Bulletin*. Congress proceedings. **Members** National associations in 60 countries. Membership countries not specified. [2020.09.02/XD2491/B]

♦ International Society for Language Studies (ISLS) 15227

CEO 1968 S Coast Hwy 142, Laguna Beach CA 92651, USA. E-mail: john@isls.co – webby@isls.co.
Pres Dept of Spanish and Portuguese Studies, University of Florida, PO Box 117405/170 Dauer Hall, Gainesville FL 32611, USA. T. +13523922463.
URL: http://www.isls.co/

History 2002. Registered in Delaware (USA). **Aims** Encourage and improve scholarship on language studies. **Structure** Board, including President, Vice-President and Secretary-Treasurer. **Events** *Intersections of peace and language studies* Hong Kong (Hong Kong) 2019, *Conference* Waterloo, ON (Canada) 2018, *Intersections of peace and language studies* Honolulu, HI (USA) 2017, *A critical examination of language and society* Normal, IL (USA) 2016, *Critical language studies – focusing on community* Albuquerque, NM (USA) 2015. **Publications** *Critical Inquiry in Language Studies* (4 a year).

Members Individuals in 32 countries and territories:
Australia, Bangladesh, Brazil, Canada, China, Denmark, Finland, Greece, Hong Kong, India, Indonesia, Iran Islamic Rep, Jamaica, Japan, Kenya, Korea Rep, Malaysia, New Zealand, Nigeria, Philippines, Poland, Portugal, Singapore, South Africa, Spain, Sweden, Taiwan, Thailand, Türkiye, UK, United Arab Emirates, USA. [2016/XD9384/D]

♦ International Society of Laparoscopic Colorectal Surgery (ISLCRS) . 15228

Headquarters 5019 W 147th St, Leawood KS 66224, USA. T. +19134027102. Fax +19132739940. E-mail: events@lp-etc.com.
URL: http://www.islcrs.org/

Aims Provide a forum to support collaboration between surgeons and scientists interested in the advancement of laparoscopic colorectal surgical techniques; help in the education of surgeons wishing to learn these techniques. **Structure** Executive Council, including President, Past-President, President-Elect, Vice-President and Secretary/Treasurer. **Events** *Annual Congress* Singapore (Singapore) 2015, *Annual Congress / Congress* Baltimore, MD (USA) 2013, *Annual Congress / Congress* Hong Kong (Hong Kong) 2012, *Annual congress / Congress* Colchester (UK) 2011, *Annual congress / Congress* Fort Lauderdale, FL (USA) 2007. [2013/XM2680/D]

♦ International Society for the Laser in Ophthalmology (inactive)
♦ International Society for Lasers in Dentistry / see World Federation for Laser Dentistry (#21451)
♦ International Society for Laser Surgery / see International Society for Laser Surgery and Medicine (#15229)

♦ International Society for Laser Surgery and Medicine (ISLSM) 15229

Contact No 9-5 Chandrabagh Ave, Mylapore, Chennai, Tamil Nadu 600 004, Chennai TAMIL NADU 600 004, India. T. +914428473777 – +914428473577 – +914428473804.
SG Billroth Hosp, 54 2nd Pain Road, RA Puram, Chennai, Tamil Nadu 600028, Chennai TAMIL NADU 600028, India.
URL: http://islsminfo.com/

History 1975, Tel Aviv (Israel). Founded as *International Society for Laser Surgery*. **Aims** Promote application of lasers in surgery and medicine; train and educate medical personnel; cooperate with physicists and industry in performing research to produce adequate instrumentation for preventing misuse of lasers. **Structure** Board. **Languages** English. **Staff** None. **Finance** Sources: donations; members' dues. **Events** *LASER FLORENCE : International Congress on Laser Medicine and Surgery* Florence (Italy) 2019, *LASER FLORENCE : International Congress on Laser Medicine and Surgery* Florence (Italy) 2017, *LASER FLORENCE : International Congress on Laser Medicine and Surgery* Florence (Italy) 2015, *Biennial Congress* Indore (India) 2015, *Biennial Congress* Paris (France) 2013. **Publications** *Medical Laser Application.*

Members Full in 78 countries and territories:
Argentina, Australia, Austria, Bahrain, Belgium, Bolivia, Bosnia-Herzegovina, Brazil, Brunei Darussalam, Canada, Chile, China, Colombia, Croatia, Cuba, Czechia, Denmark, Ecuador, Egypt, Estonia, Finland, France, Germany, Greece, Hong Kong, Hungary, Iceland, India, Indonesia, Iran Islamic Rep, Iraq, Ireland, Israel, Italy, Japan, Kenya, Korea Rep, Kuwait, Lithuania, Luxembourg, Malaysia, Mexico, Netherlands, New Zealand, Nicaragua, Nigeria, Norway, Oman, Pakistan, Paraguay, Peru, Philippines, Poland, Portugal, Qatar, Romania, Russia, Saudi Arabia, Serbia, Singapore, Slovakia, Slovenia, South Africa, Spain, Sudan, Sweden, Switzerland, Syrian AR, Taiwan, Thailand, Türkiye, UK, Ukraine, United Arab Emirates, Uruguay, USA, Venezuela, Vietnam. [2019/XD8344/C]

♦ International Society of Lawyers for Public Service (no recent information)

♦ International Society of the Learning Sciences (ISLS) 15230

Exec Officer 1071 Educational Sci, 1025 W Johnson St, Madison WI 53706-1706, USA. E-mail: info@isls.org.
URL: http://www.isls.org/

History Sep 2002. **Aims** Promote the communication of scientific research in the interdisciplinary field of the learning sciences. **Structure** Board of Directors, including President, Past-President, President-Elect, Executive Officer and Financial Officer. **Finance** Sources: members' dues. **Activities** Events/meetings. **Events** *Annual Meeting* Hiroshima (Japan) 2022, *Annual Meeting* Bochum (Germany) 2021, *Biennial Conference of the Learning Sciences* Nashville, TN (USA) 2020, *International Conference on Computer-Supported Collaborative Learning* Lyon (France) 2019, *Biennial Conference of the Learning Sciences* London (UK) 2018. **Publications** *International Journal of Computer Support for Collaborative Learning (IJCSCL); ISLS Newsletter, Journal of the Learning Sciences (JLS).* [2014/XM0072/C]

♦ International Society of Leather Trades Chemists (inactive)

♦ International Society of Limb Salvage (ISOLS) 15231

Office Manager c/o Vienna Medical Acad, Alser Str 4, 1090 Vienna, Austria. T. +4314051383 – +43121. Fax +4314078274. E-mail: office@isols.com.
URL: http://www.isols.info/

History 1989, Saint-Malo (France). Former names and other names: *Internationale Gesellschaft für Extremitätenerhaltung* – legal name. Registration: Austria. **Aims** Promote researcch, education and clinical practice related to musculoskeletal tumors; improve patient care related to limb salvage interventions. **Structure** Board. **Events** *ISOLS General Meeting* Los Angeles, CA (USA) 2022, *ISOLS General Meeting* Los Angeles, CA (USA) 2021, *Symposium* Athens (Greece) 2019, *Symposium* Kanazawa (Japan) 2017, *Symposium* Orlando, FL (USA) 2015. [2021/XD9488/D]

♦ International Society of Limnology 15232

Societas Internationalis Limnologiae (SIL)

Managing Dir c/o UQAM, PO Box 8888, Succ Centre-Ville, Montréal QC H3C 3P8, Canada.
Pres IGB Leibniz-Inst of Freshwater Ecology and Inland Fisheries, Müggelseedamm 301/310, 12587 Berlin, Germany.
URL: http://limnology.org/

History 3 Aug 1922, Kiel (Germany). Former names and other names: *International Limnological Society* – former; *Société internationale de limnologie* – former; *International Association of Theoretical and Applied Limnology (IAL)* – former; *Association internationale de limnologie théorique et appliquée (AIL)* – former; *Asociación Internacional de Limnologia Teórica y Aplicada (AIL)* – former; *Internationale Vereinigung für Theoretische und Angewandte Limnologie (IVL)* – former; *Societas Internationalis Limnologiae Theoreticae et Applicatae (SIL)* – former. **Aims** Foster and support international scientific networks of freshwater research; develop and maintain partnerships for sustainable management of freshwater ecosystems and water resources; contribute to addressing global environmental and societal issues through a strategic alignment with the UN SDGs; empower researchers of tomorrow and facilitate knowledge-transfer to promote limnology to a wider audience. **Structure** General Assembly (every 2 years at Congress); Executive Board; International Committee; National Representatives; Special Committees; Working Groups (15). **Languages** English. **Staff** 1.00 FTE, paid; 15.00 FTE, voluntary. **Finance** Sources: members' dues; sale of publications. **Activities** Events/meetings; projects/programmes; publishing activities; training/education. **Events** *Congress* Berlin (Germany) 2022, *Congress* Gwangju (Korea Rep) 2021, *Congress* Gwangju (Korea Rep) 2020, *Congress* Nanjing (China) 2018, *Congress* Turin (Italy) 2016. **Publications** *Inland Waters*; *SILnews*.
Members Individuals: regular; student; early career; emeritus; life. Members in 72 countries and territories:
Afghanistan, Algeria, Angola, Argentina, Australia, Austria, Belgium, Botswana, Brazil, Bulgaria, Cambodia, Cameroon, Canada, Chile, China, Colombia, Congo DR, Costa Rica, Cuba, Czechia, Denmark, Ecuador, Egypt, Estonia, Finland, France, Germany, Greece, Hong Kong, Hungary, Iceland, India, Indonesia, Ireland, Israel, Italy, Japan, Kenya, Korea Rep, Luxembourg, Malaysia, Malta, Mexico, Mongolia, Netherlands, New Zealand, Nigeria, Norway, Peru, Philippines, Poland, Portugal, Puerto Rico, Romania, Russia, Rwanda, Serbia, Slovakia, South Africa, Spain, Sri Lanka, Sweden, Switzerland, Taiwan, Tanzania UR, Türkiye, Uganda, UK, Ukraine, Uruguay, USA, Zimbabwe.
NGO Relations Member of (2): *Environment Liaison Centre International (ELCI, no recent information)*; *International Union for Conservation of Nature and Natural Resources (IUCN, #15766)*. Affiliated with (1): *International Union of Biological Sciences (IUBS, #15760)* (forming its Section of Limnology).
[2021.04.06/XB1362/**B**]

♦ International Society for the Linguistics of English (ISLE) 15233

Sec address not obtained.
Pres address not obtained.
URL: http://www.isle-linguistics.org/
History 8 Oct 2008, Freiburg (Germany). Founded 2008 during 1st Conference in Freiburg (Germany). **Aims** Promote the study of English *language*, that is, the study of the structure and history of standard and non-standard varieties of English, in terms of both form and function, at an international level. **Structure** Executive Committee, comprising President, President-elect, Past President, Secretary, 3 Vice-Presidents (Research, Teaching, Profession), Treasurer and Webmaster. Committees (3): Executive; Nominating; Prize. **Activities** Awards/prizes/competitions; capacity building; events/meetings; networking/liaising; research and development; training/education. **Events** *Conference* Joensuu (Finland) 2021, *Conference* Joensuu (Finland) 2020, *Conference* London (UK) 2018, *Conference* Poznań (Poland) 2016, *Conference* Zurich (Switzerland) 2014. [2022.05.11/XJ0639/**D**]

♦ International Society of Lipo-Suction Surgery (no recent information)

♦ International Society of Liquid Biopsy (ISLB) 15234

Sociedad Internacional de Biopsia Liquida
Sec Dr Oloriz 16 Street, 18012 Granada, Spain. E-mail: admin@isliquidbiopsy.org.
URL: https://www.isliquidbiopsy.org/
History 2017, Granada (Spain). Registration: Spanish Registry of Association, No/ID: 612859, Spain. **Aims** Be the link of all stakeholders in the liquid biopsy theme. **Structure** Committee; Board of Directors. **Finance** Sources: members' dues. **Activities** Events/meetings; training/education. **Events** *Annual Congress* Barcelona (Spain) 2020. [2021/AA1749/**C**]

♦ International Society of Liver Surgeons (ISLS) 15235

Office InSession Intl Convention Services Inc, 4Fl 10, Yeoksam-ro 7-gil, Gangnam-Gu, Seoul 06244, Korea Rep. T. +82234527245. Fax +8225218683. E-mail: isls-liversurgeon@insession.co.kr.
URL: http://www.isls-liversurgeon.org
History Founded 2016. Current by-laws approved at Inaugural Council Meeting, 12 Apr 2018. **Aims** Contribute to academic development and education by establishing the advanced standards in surgery for liver and pancreas diseases. **Structure** Council. **Activities** Events/meetings. **Events** *International Advanced Liver and Pancreas Surgery Symposium* Busan (Korea Rep) 2021, *International Advanced Liver and Pancreas Surgery Symposium* Busan (Korea Rep) 2020, *International Advanced Liver and Pancreas Surgery Symposium* Istanbul (Turkey) 2019, *International Advanced Liver and Pancreas Surgery Symposium* Seoul (Korea Rep) 2018, *International Advanced Liver and Pancreas Surgery Symposium* Ankara (Turkey) 2017. [2020/XM8301/**C**]

♦ International Society of Livestock Husbandry 15236

Société international pour la garde des animaux de ferme – Internationale Gesellschaft für Nutztierhaltung (IGN)
Contact Lehrstuhl für Tierschutz/Verhaltenskunde / Tierhygiene und Tierschutz, Veterinärstr 13, 80539 Munich, Germany. T. +4988218078300. Fax +4988218078333.
URL: http://www.ign-nutztierhaltung.ch/
History 1978. **Aims** Increase research in livestock husbandry; promote proper housing of *farm animals*. **Structure** Managing Committee. **Languages** English, French, German. **Staff** 0.50 FTE, paid; 6.00 FTE, voluntary. **Finance** Members' dues. Support from organizations. **Activities** Events/meetings; awards/prizes/competitions; research and development; guidance/assistance/consulting. **Events** *Symposium* Munich (Germany) 2020, *Conference* Freiburg-Breisgau (Germany) 2019, *Conference* Celle (Germany) 2014, *Conference* Freiburg (Germany) 2014, *Conference* Vienna (Austria) 2014. **Publications** *Nutztierhaltung im Fokus* (annual); *Nutztierhaltung Spezial* (annual). Advisory opinions; books.
Members in 7 countries:
Austria, Canada, Denmark, Netherlands, Slovenia, Sweden, Switzerland.
NGO Relations Links with various national organizations, mainly in Austria, Germany and Switzerland.
[2020.03.03/XD9237/**D**]

♦ International Society of Logotherapy and Existential Analysis (#13241)

♦ International Society for Low Vision Research and Rehabilitation (ISLRR) 15237

Chairperson c/o Dana Bakir, School of Optometry, 3744 Jean Brillant, Montréal QC H3T 1H3, Canada. T. +15143436111 ext 31537. Fax +15143432382. E-mail: inquiries@islrr.org.
URL: http://www.islrr.org/
Aims Stimulate scientific research in the field of low vision and in the field of rehabilitation of people with low vision; promote exchange of information in these fields. **Structure** Executive Committee of 10 members; Board of Directors of 5 members. **Languages** English. **Activities** Training/education; events/meetings; publishing activity; networking/liaising. **Events** *International Conference on Low Vision Vision2022* Dublin (Ireland) 2022, *International Conference on Low Vision Vision2020+1* Dublin (Ireland) 2020, *International Conference on Low Vision Vision2020* Dublin (Ireland) 2020, *International Conference on Low Vision* The Hague (Netherlands) 2017, *International Conference on Low Vision* Melbourne, VIC (Australia) 2014. **Publications** *ISLRR Low Vision Newsletter*.
Members Individuals and societies in 41 countries and territories:
Argentina, Australia, Austria, Bangladesh, Belgium, Brazil, Canada, China, Colombia, Czechia, Denmark, Finland, France, Germany, Greece, Hong Kong, India, Ireland, Israel, Italy, Japan, Malaysia, Netherlands, New Zealand, Nigeria, Norway, Peru, Puerto Rico, Russia, Saudi Arabia, South Africa, Spain, Sweden, Switzerland, Thailand, Türkiye, UK, Uruguay, USA, Vietnam, Zimbabwe. [2020/XD7523/**D**]

♦ International Society of Lymphology (ISL) 15238

Société internationale de lymphologie – Internationale Gesellschaft für Lymphologie
SG Dept of Surgery, Univ of Arizona, College of Medicine, PO Box 245200, 1501 N Campbell Ave, Room 4402J, Tucson AZ 85724-5200, USA. T. +15206266118. Fax +15206260822. E-mail: lymph@u.arizona.edu.
Office Manager address not obtained.
URL: http://www.u.arizona.edu/~witte/ISL.htm
History 19 Jul 1966, Zurich (Switzerland). Founded during 1st International Symposium on Lymphology. Registration: Swiss Civil Code, Switzerland. **Aims** Further and assist in activities to advance and disseminate knowledge in the field; stimulate and strengthen experimental and clinical investigation; stimulate research; establish relations between basic researchers and clinicians working in the field; further personal contact and exchange among lymphologists. **Structure** General Assembly (held simultaneously with international Congress); Executive Board; Nominating Committee; International Working Groups (3). **Languages** English, French, German. **Staff** 1.00 FTE, paid. **Finance** Sources: members' dues. **Activities** Events/meetings; knowledge management/information dissemination; networking/liaising; training/education. **Events** *World Congress of Lymphology* Genoa (Italy) 2023, *Biennial Congress* Athens (Greece) 2021, *Biennial Congress* Buenos Aires (Argentina) 2019, *Biennial Congress* Barcelona (Spain) 2017, *Biennial Congress* San Francisco, CA (USA) 2015. **Publications** *LYMPHOLOGY Journal* (4 a year).
Members Individuals in 37 countries and territories:
Argentina, Australia, Austria, Bangladesh, Belgium, Brazil, Bulgaria, Canada, China, Czechia, Denmark, Egypt, Finland, France, Germany, Greece, Hungary, India, Indonesia, Israel, Italy, Japan, Korea Rep, Mexico, Netherlands, Norway, Poland, Portugal, Puerto Rico, Romania, Russia, Saudi Arabia, Spain, Sweden, Switzerland, UK, USA. [2021.08.31/XC2552/v/**C**]

♦ International Society of Lyophilization- Freeze Drying (ISL-FD) 15239

Contact 917 Lexington Way, Waunakee WI 53597, USA. T. +16085776790.
History 2001. Registration: USA. **Activities** Events/meetings. **Events** *Biennial Conference* Ghent (Belgium) 2019, *Biennial Conference* Havana (Cuba) 2017, *Biennial Conference* Barcelona (Spain) 2015.
[2020/AA0272/**C**]

♦ International Society for MacIntyrean Enquiry (internationally oriented national body)

♦ International Society of Magnetic Resonance (ISMAR) 15240

Société mondiale de résonance magnétique
SG Dept of Chemistry, New York Univ, 100 Washington Square East, New York NY 10003, USA.
URL: http://www.weizmann.ac.il/ISMAR/welcome-ismar/
History 1971. Constitution amended: June 1992; May 1998; Dec 2001; Jan 2008; Apr 2014; Sep 2015. Registration: Start date: 8 Dec 1982, USA, Illinois. **Aims** Advance and disseminate knowledge of the principles, recent developments and applications of magnetic resonance in physics, chemistry, biology, medicine and other disciplines; foster scientific interaction among magnetic resonance spectroscopists throughout the world. **Structure** General Meeting; Council; Executive Committee; Standing Committees (4). **Languages** English. **Staff** Temporary. **Finance** Members' dues. **Activities** Events/meetings. **Events** *Conference* Brisbane, QLD (Australia) 2023, *Biennial Conference* Tokyo (Japan) 2021, *Biennial Conference* Berlin (Germany) 2019, *Biennial Conference* Québec, QC (Canada) 2017, *Biennial Conference* Shanghai (China) 2015. **Publications** *ISMAR News*. **Members** Membership countries not specified. **NGO Relations** Associated organization of: *International Union of Pure and Applied Chemistry (IUPAC, #15809)*. [2021/XD6046/**D**]

♦ International Society for Magnetic Resonance in Medicine (ISMRM) 15241

Exec Dir One Concord Center, 2300 Clayton Rd, Ste 620, Concord CA 94520, USA. T. +15108411899. Fax +15108412340. E-mail: info@ismrm.org.
URL: http://www.ismrm.org/
History 1 Jan 1994. Founded on merger of 'Society of Magnetic Resonance in Medicine' (established 1981) and 'Society for Magnetic Resonance Imaging' (established 1982). **Aims** Promote communication, research, development and applications in the field of magnetic resonance in medicine and biology and other related topics; develop and provide channels and facilities for continuing education in this field. **Structure** Hosts: study groups (23) on focused topics; international chapters (9). **Languages** English. **Staff** 17.00 FTE, paid. **Finance** Sources: members' dues. Annual budget: 8,000,000 USD. **Activities** Events/meetings; training/education. **Events** *Annual Meeting* Honolulu, HI (USA) 2025, *Annual Meeting* Singapore (Singapore) 2024, *Annual Meeting* Toronto, ON (Canada) 2023, *Annual Meeting* London (UK) 2022, *Annual Meeting* Vancouver, BC (Canada) 2021. **Publications** *Journal of Magnetic Resonance Imaging (FMRI)* (12 a year); *Magnetic Resonance in Medicine (MRM)* (12 a year). **Members** Associate; Full; Student; Emeritus. Individuals involved in magnetic resonance in medicine, biology or other related topics, research, education, manufacture or practice in over 60 countries. Membership countries not specified. **NGO Relations** Cooperates with (1): *European Society of Magnetic Resonance in Medicine and Biology (ESMRMB, #08644)*. [2023.02.14/XD5577/v/**C**]

♦ international Society for Maintenance and Rehabilitation of Transport infrastructures (iSMARTi) 15242

Exec Sec address not obtained. E-mail: ismarti2016@gmail.com.
URL: http://ismarti.org/
History Founded 6 Jul 2003, Guimarães (Portugal). Statutes and By-laws adopted Jun 2006. **Aims** Promote international cooperation among engineers, scientists and other professionals for the worldwide dissemination, advancement and implementation of knowledge in the field of maintenance and rehabilitation of transport infrastructures. **Structure** Board of Governors; Executive Council; Secretariat. Regions (10): Africa; Asia – Far East; Asia – Southeast and South Asian; Australia, New Zealand and Pacific Islands; Central Asian Republics and Russia; China; Europe; Middle East; North America; South America, Central America and the Caribbean. Standing Committees (14). **Languages** English. **Finance** Sources: members' dues; sale of publications. **Activities** Awards/prizes/competitions; events/meetings; knowledge management/information dissemination; networking/liaising. **Events** *International Conference on Transportation Infrastructure* Lima (Peru) 2022, *International Conference on Maintenance and Rehabilitation of Constructed Infrastructure Facilities* Bogota (Colombia) 2021, *International Conference on Maintenance and Rehabilitation of Pavements* Zurich (Switzerland) 2020, *International Conference on Smart Cities* Seoul (Korea Rep) 2019, *International Conference on Transportation Infrastructure* Pretoria (South Africa) 2018. **Publications** *MDPI Infrastructures* – journal. **Members** Founder; Patron; Regular; Honorary; Associate; Student; Supporting. Membership countries not specified. [2019/XM7374/**B**]

♦ International Society of Management Engineers (ISME International) 15243

Chair Universiti Teknologi Petronas – UTP, Dept of Computer and Information Sciences, 32610 Seri Iskandar, Perak, Malaysia. T. +6053687517. E-mail: imip2010@gmail.com.
URL: http://www.ismeip.org/
History Apr 2003. **Aims** Support the innovation and research on management engineering. **Structure** Committee; Board; Executive Board. Executive Chair. **Events** *Symposium* Kitakyushu (Japan) 2017, *Symposium* Kitakyushu (Japan) 2015, *Symposium* Hangzhou (China) 2013, *International Conference on Genetic and Evolutionary Computing* Kitakyushu (Japan) 2012, *International Symposium on Management Engineering* Kitakyushu (Japan) 2012. [2018/XJ1477/**C**]

♦ International Society of Managing and Technical Editors (ISMTE) . . 15244

Exec Dir 3739 National Dr, Ste 202, Raleigh NC 27612, USA. E-mail: info@ismte.org.
URL: http://www.ismte.org/
History Aug 2007. **Aims** Connect the community of professionals committed to peer review and publication of academic and scholarly *journals*. **Structure** Board of Directors. **Languages** English. **Finance** Sources: members' dues; sponsorship. **Activities** Awards/prizes/competitions; events/meetings; financial and/or material support; publishing activities. **Events** *ISMTE Global Event* 2022, *Annual European Conference* Raleigh, NC (USA) 2020, *Asia Pacific Conference* Raleigh, NC (USA) 2020, *North America Annual Meeting* Raleigh, NC (USA) 2020, *Annual European Conference* Oxford (UK) 2019. **Publications** *Editorial Office News*.
Members Individuals (1,000) in 38 countries and territories:
Australia, Bangladesh, Bosnia, Canada, China, Denmark, Egypt, England, Ethiopia, France, Germany, Hong Kong, India, Iraq, Ireland, Israel, Italy, Japan, Korea Rep, Malaysia, Myanmar, Nepal, Netherlands, New Zealand, Nigeria, Northern Ireland, Norway, Pakistan, Portugal, Romania, Scotland, Singapore, Sri Lanka, Switzerland, Taiwan, Uganda, UK, USA.
NGO Relations Cooperates with: *European Association of Science Editors (EASE, #06201)*; national organizations. [2022/XJ9858/**C**]

♦ International Society for Mangrove Ecosystems (ISME) 15245

Société internationale pour l'étude des écosystèmes de la mangrove

Exec Dir c/o Fac of Agriculture, Univ of the Ryukyus, Nishihara, Okinawa, 903 0129 Japan. T. +81988956601. Fax +81988956602. E-mail: isme@mangrove.or.jp.
URL: http://www.mangrove.or.jp/isme/english/index.htm

History 1990. **Aims** Promote research, surveys and contacts with other scientists and organizations with the purpose of promoting *conservation*, rational management and sustainable utilization of mangroves; serve as an international data-bank on mangrove ecosystems. **Structure** Council, consisting of 18 members. Executive, comprising 6 members. Officers: President, 3 Vice-Presidents, Treasurer, Executive Secretary. Secretariat. **Languages** English. **Staff** 4.00 FTE, paid; 1.00 FTE, voluntary. **Finance** Sources: donations; members' dues; subsidies. Other sources: support by the government of Okinawa Prefecture. **Activities** Organizes and co-sponsors conferences, seminars, working group meetings, lectures and courses. Supports and implements research projects and programmes. **Events** *General Assembly* Ho Chi Minh City (Vietnam) 2002, *Workshop on Asia-Pacific cooperation on research and conservation of mangroves* Okinawa (Japan) 2000, *General Assembly* Bali (Indonesia) 1999, *General Assembly* Hat Yai (Thailand) 1996, *Symposium on significance of mangrove ecosystems for coastal people* Hat Yai (Thailand) 1996. **Publications** *Mangroves* (1-2 a year) – newsletter. *ISME Mangrove Ecosystems Occasional Papers*; *ISME Mangrove Ecosystems Proceedings*; *ISME Mangrove Ecosystems Technical Reports*. *Know Your Mangroves* – ISME slide kit programme for children. ISME slide kit programme for children. ISME/ITTO Project: non-technical publication; technical manual; atlas.

Members Organizations and individuals. Members (800) in 77 countries and territories:
Antigua-Barbuda, Australia, Bangladesh, Belgium, Belize, Benin, Brazil, Cameroon, Canada, Chile, China, Colombia, Costa Rica, Côte d'Ivoire, Cuba, Denmark, Dominica, Dominican Rep, Ecuador, Fiji, France, Germany, Ghana, Grenada, Guinea, Guinea-Bissau, Honduras, Hong Kong, India, Indonesia, Italy, Jamaica, Japan, Kenya, Macau, Madagascar, Malaysia, Mauritius, Mexico, Micronesia FS, Mozambique, Myanmar, Nepal, Netherlands, New Zealand, Nigeria, Oman, Pakistan, Panama, Papua New Guinea, Peru, Philippines, Portugal, Puerto Rico, Qatar, Samoa, Saudi Arabia, Senegal, Sierra Leone, Singapore, Solomon Is, Spain, Sri Lanka, St Lucia, Sudan, Sweden, Taiwan, Tanzania UR, Thailand, Trinidad-Tobago, UK, United Arab Emirates, USA, Venezuela, Vietnam, Virgin Is UK, Virgin Is USA.

Consultative Status Consultative status granted from: *ECOSOC (#05331)* (Ros A). **IGO Relations** Cooperates with: *UN Environment Programme World Conservation Monitoring Centre (UNEP-WCMC, #20295)*; *UNESCO Office, Jakarta – Regional Bureau for Sciences in Asia and the Pacific (#20313)*. Associated with Department of Global Communications of the United Nations. **NGO Relations** Member of: *Action for Mangrove Reforestation (ACTMANG, no recent information)*. Cooperates with: *International Union for Conservation of Nature and Natural Resources (IUCN, #15766)*. [2014/XD2693/**C**]

♦ International Society for Mannosidosis and Related Diseases / see International Advocate for Glycoprotein Storage Diseases (#11592)

♦ International Society for Markets and Development (ISMD) 15246

Pres c/o Hanken School, PO Box 479, FI-00101 Helsinki, Finland.
Pres c/o Dept of Marketing, Birmingham Business School, University House, Birmingham, B15 2TT, UK. T. +441214145658.
URL: https://ismd.info/

History Registered in the State of Indiana (USA), 1992, following 2nd Conference, Delhi (India). **Aims** Advance research and exchange of ideas relating to how markets and other institutions connect to socio-economic development. **Structure** Board of 10. Executive, comprising President, President-Elect, Past-President and Executive Director/Treasurer. **Events** *Biennial Conference* Accra (Ghana) 2023, *Biennial Conference* Tiruchirappalli (India) 2021, *Biennial Conference* Tiruchirappalli (India) 2020, *Biennial Conference* Chisinau (Moldova) 2018, *Biennial Conference* Lima (Peru) 2016. **Publications** *Markets and Development Network* (2 a year) – newsletter. [2017/XJ6480/**E**]

♦ International Society for Mark Studies (SIGNUM) 15247

Contact Paço de Rianxinho 30-BA, 15920 Rianxo, La Coruña, Spain. E-mail: markstudiesinfo@gmail.com.
URL: http://markstudies.org/

History Founded 2010. **Aims** Advance the study of human mark use; support scholars and other specialists involved with mark studies as a distinct field of inquiry. **Structure** Executive Secretariat. **Languages** English. **Staff** 10.00 FTE, voluntary. **Finance** No financing. **Events** *Conference* Berlin (Germany) 2017, *Conference* Mainz (Germany) 2015, *Conference* Leiden (Netherlands) 2014, *Conference* Leiden (Netherlands) 2013, *Conference* Stockholm (Sweden) 2012. **Publications** *Re:marks* – journal. Academic publications.

Members Individuals (66) in 22 countries:
Australia, Belgium, Canada, Czechia, France, Germany, Hungary, Italy, Japan, Kazakhstan, Netherlands, Norway, Poland, Portugal, Russia, South Africa, Spain, Sweden, Türkiye, UK, USA, Uzbekistan. [2015.09.02/XJ7408/v/**C**]

♦ International Society of Mathematical Biology (inactive)

♦ International Society for Matrix Biology (ISMB) 15248

Past Pres ICBMS, UMR 5246, Univ Lyon 1, Lederer Bldg, 43 bd du 11 novembre 1918, 69622 Villeurbanne CEDEX, France. E-mail: ismb@ismb.org.
Registered Office c/o Institut pour la Biologie, 7 passage du Vercors, 69367 Lyon CEDEX 7, France.
URL: http://ismb.org/

History 29 Oct 1992. Registration: Start date: 29 Oct 1992, France. **Aims** Promote matrix biology on a global scale. **Structure** General Assembly (at least once every 2 years); Council; Executive Committee. **Languages** English. **Staff** No permanent staff. **Finance** Members' dues. **Activities** Events/meetings; financial and/or material support; publishing activities; awards/prizes/competitions. **Events** *International Conference on Proteoglycans* Kanazawa (Japan) 2019, *International Conference on Proteoglycans* Seoul (Korea Rep) 2015, *Meeting* Oulu (Finland) 2006. **Publications** *ISMB Newsletter*.

Members in 30 countries and territories:
Australia, Austria, Belgium, Brazil, Bulgaria, Canada, China, Denmark, Finland, France, Germany, Greece, Hong Kong, Hungary, India, Ireland, Israel, Italy, Japan, Netherlands, New Zealand, Norway, Portugal, Russia, Singapore, Spain, Sweden, Switzerland, UK, USA.

NGO Relations National societies for matrix biology. [2021/XM1792/**D**]

♦ International Society for Maxillofacial Rehabilitation (ISMR) 15249

Contact 4425 Cass St, Suite A, San Diego CA 92109, USA. T. +18582721018. Fax +1858272687. E-mail: ismr@res-inc.com.
URL: http://www.ismr-org.com/

History Oct 1996. Completely restructured 2008. Current constitution revised 2010. Former names and other names: *International Congress of Maxillofacial Prosthetics* – former (Oct 1996 to 7 Jan 2002). **Aims** Advance interdisciplinary maxillofacial rehabilitation throughout the world. **Structure** Board of Councilors; Executive Officers. **Staff** 7.00 FTE, paid. **Finance** Sources: members' dues. **Activities** Events/meetings. **Events** *Conference* India 2021, *Meeting* San Francisco, CA (USA) 2017, *Conference* Belgrade (Serbia) 2016, *Conference / Regional Conference* Groningen (Netherlands) 2015, *Conference / Congress* Xian (China) 2014. **Publications** *ISMR E-Bulletin*. **Members** Constituent; Life; Organizational; Honorary. [2018/XJ8888/**C**]

♦ International Society on MCDM / see International Society on Multiple Criteria Decision Making (#15283)

♦ International Society for the Measurement of Physical Behaviour (ISMPB) 15250

Sec address not obtained.
URL: https://ismpb.org/

History Registration: Netherlands. **Aims** Promote and facilitate the study and applications of objective measurement and quantification of free-living physical behavior(s) and its related constructs (e.g. energy expenditure, context) using wearable devices. **Structure** General Membership Meeting; Board of Directors. **Activities** Events/meetings. **Events** *Biennial International Conference on Ambulatory Monitoring of Physical Activity and Movement* Keystone, CO (USA) 2021, *Biennial International Conference on Ambulatory Monitoring of Physical Activity and Movement* Maastricht (Netherlands) 2019, *Biennial International Conference on Ambulatory Monitoring of Physical Activity and Movement* Bethesda, MD (USA) 2017, *Biennial International Conference on Ambulatory Monitoring of Physical Activity and Movement* Limerick (Ireland) 2015, *Biennial International Conference on Ambulatory Monitoring of Physical Activity and Movement* Amherst, MA (USA) 2013. **Publications** *ISMPB Newsletter*; *Journal for the Measurement of Physical Behaviour*. [2021/AA0382/**C**]

♦ International Society for Mechanical Circulatory Support (ISMCS) . 15251

Contact c/o Center for Medical Physics, Waehringer Guertel 18-20, 1090 Vienna, Austria. E-mail: info@ismcs.org.
URL: http://www.ismcs.org/

History 1992. Founded following the *International Workshop on Rotary Blood Pumps* events organized in 1988 and 1991 by Georg M Wieselthaler. Former names and other names: *International Society for Rotary Blood Pumps (ISRBP)* – former (1992 to 2015). **Aims** Provide a forum for discussion of research, development, clinical use and social acceptance of rotary blood pumps. **Structure** Board; Board of Trustees. **Languages** English. **Events** *Annual Meeting* Utsunomiya (Japan) 2024, *Annual Meeting* Dallas, TX (USA) 2023, *Annual Meeting* Hannover (Germany) 2021, *Annual Meeting* Bologna (Italy) 2019, *Congress* Tokyo (Japan) 2018. **Publications** *Artificial Organs* (12 a year) – journal.

Members Individuals in 13 countries:
Australia, Austria, Belgium, Canada, Germany, Italy, Japan, Netherlands, Singapore, Switzerland, Türkiye, UK, USA.

NGO Relations Joint journal with: *International Federation for Artificial Organs (IFAO, #13357)*. [2022/XD8097/**C**]

♦ International Society of Mechanobiology (unconfirmed)
♦ International Society of Mechanocardiography / see International Society of Non-invasive Cardiology (#15308)

♦ International Society for Media, Religion, and Culture (ISMRC) 15252

Address not obtained.
URL: https://www.ismrc.org/

History Proposed 2008, Toronto ON (Canada), with meetings dating back to 1994. **Structure** Board of Directors; Executive Committee. **Activities** Events/meetings. **Events** *International Conference on Media, Religion and Culture* Bochum (Germany) 2023, *Rethinking Religion, Media & Secularities* 2021, *International Conference on Media, Religion and Culture* Sigtuna (Sweden) 2021, *International Conference on Media, Religion and Culture* Sigtuna (Sweden) 2020, *International Conference on Media, Religion and Culture* Boulder, CO (USA) 2018. **Publications** *Journal of Religion, Media and Digital Culture (RMDC)* (3 a year). [2021/XM5739/**E**]

♦ International Society for Medical and Applied Malacology (no recent information)

♦ International Society of Medical Doctors for Biophysical Information Therapy (BIT) 15253

Société internationale des médecins pour la thérapie de l'information biophysique – Sociedad Internacional de Médicos para la Terapia de Informaciones-Biofisicas – Internationale Ärztegesellschaft für biophysikalische Informationstherapie

Pres Wilhelmstr 10, 79098 Freiburg, Germany. E-mail: bit-aerzte@t-online.de.
URL: http://www.bit-org.de/

History 1980. Former names and other names: *Bioresonanz-Ärztegesellschaft* – former; *MORA-Ärztegesellschaft* – former. **Aims** Promote research and practice of magnetic field therapy. **Members** Individuals (650). Membership countries not specified. **NGO Relations** Member of: *European Council of Doctors for Plurality in Medicine (ECPM, #06816)*. [2021/XD7211/v/**D**]

♦ International Society of Medical Hydrology / see International Society of Medical Hydrology and Climatology (#15254)

♦ International Society of Medical Hydrology and Climatology (ISMH) 15254

Société internationale d'hydrologie et de climatologie médicale – Internationale Gesellschaft für Medizinische Balneologie und Klimatologie

Pres Rua Marta Mesquita da Câmara 110 A-3, 4 Esquerdo, 4150-485 Porto, Portugal. T. +351919360635. E-mail: ismh@doki.net.
SG 12 rue Albert 1er, 73100 Aix-les-Bains, France. T. +44479350247.
URL: http://www.ismh-direct.net/

History 9 Dec 1921, London (UK). Statutes modified: 1954, 1966, 1993. Former names and other names: *International Society of Medical Hydrology* – former; *Société internationale d'hydrologie médicale* – former; *Internationale Gesellschaft für Wissenschaftliche Bäderkunde* – former. **Aims** Promote scientific, clinical and experimental studies of medical *balneology* and climatology and of related fields within health resort medicine. **Structure** General Assembly (every 4 years); Executive Committee; International Council. **Languages** English. **Finance** Sources: members' dues. Voluntary contributions from national associations. **Activities** Awards/prizes/competitions; events/meetings; knowledge management/information dissemination; training/education. **Events** *World Congress* Salsomaggiore Terme (Italy) 2022, *Congress* Dax (France) 2021, *Congress* Dax (France) 2020, *Congress* Wieliczka (Poland) 2019, *Congress* Amarante (Portugal) 2018. **Publications** *Archives of Medical Hydrology* (4 a year); *Archives of Health Resort Medicine* (2 a year). *Lischi Editori* (1966); *Health Resort Medicine*; *History of the ISMH* by M Messini; *Medizinische Bäder*, *Physikalische Medizin Balneologie Klimatologie*; *Radon in der Kurortmedizin*; *Sulphure in Health Resort Medicine*.

Members National associations; Individuals. Members in 46 countries:
Algeria, Argentina, Australia, Austria, Belgium, Brazil, Bulgaria, Canada, Chile, China, Croatia, Cuba, Cyprus, Czechia, Ecuador, Egypt, Estonia, Finland, France, Germany, Greece, Hungary, Israel, Italy, Japan, Latvia, Lithuania, Luxembourg, Netherlands, New Zealand, Nigeria, Poland, Portugal, Romania, Russia, Saudi Arabia, Serbia, Slovakia, Slovenia, Spain, Switzerland, Tunisia, Türkiye, United Arab Emirates, Uruguay, USA.

NGO Relations Instrumental in setting up: *Organisation mondiale du thermalisme (OMTh, #17820)*, in collaboration with *Latin American Federation of Thermalism and Climatism (FLT, no recent information)*; *Société internationale de technique hydrothermale (SITH, #19497)*. *Asia Pacific Association of Medical Hydrology and Climatology (no recent information)*, FLT and AEMThB are represented on Council. [2022/XD2554/**C**]

♦ International Society for Medical Innovation and Technology (ISMIT) 15255

Contact Falkenweg 19, 65527 Niedernhausen, Germany. Fax +4961288606801. E-mail: office@smit.de.
URL: http://www.ismit.org/

History 1989, London (UK). Former names and other names: *Society for Minimally Invasive Therapy* – former (1989 to 2000); *Society for Medical Innovation and Technology (SMIT)* – former (2000). **Aims** Promote multidisciplinary advancement of minimally invasive therapy intended to reduce patient trauma after traditional surgical or radiological interventions. **Structure** Steering Committee. **Languages** English. **Finance** Members' dues. Donations. **Activities** Knowledge management/information dissemination; events/meetings. **Events** *Annual Conference* Munich (Germany) 2026, *Annual Conference* Washington, DC (USA) 2025, *Annual Conference* Caceres (Spain) 2024, *Annual Conference* Taichung (Taiwan) 2023, *Annual Conference* Oslo (Norway) 2022. **Publications** *Minimally Invasive Therapy and Allied Technologies (MITAT)* (6 a year) – journal.

Members Full in 23 countries:
Australia, Austria, Canada, China, Czechia, Denmark, France, Germany, Hungary, Ireland, Israel, Italy, Japan, Korea Rep, Netherlands, Norway, Portugal, Romania, Spain, Switzerland, Türkiye, UK, USA.

NGO Relations Affiliated with: Society of Laparoendoscopic Surgeons (SLS). Member of: *European Alliance for Medical and Biological Engineering and Science (EAMBES, #05873)*. [2021/XD8143/**D**]

♦ International Society for Medical Laser Applications (ISLA) 15256

Chair c/o Weber Medical, Lönsstr 10, 37697 Lauenförde, Germany. T. +495373367780. Fax +4953733677829. E-mail: info@isla-laser.org.
URL: http://www.isla-laser.org/

History Registered in accordance with German law: VR 2852. **Structure** Board. **Finance** Members' dues. **Activities** Events/meetings; research/documentation. **Events** *International Conference* Frankfurt-Main (Germany) 2020, *Congress* Bangkok (Thailand) 2017, *Seminar on Innovation Laser Therapy and Regenerative Medicine* Vienna (Austria) 2017, *Annual Congress* Beverungen (Germany) 2014. **Publications** Handbooks. **Members** Individuals. Membership countries not specified. **NGO Relations** Partners with: *International Council of Medical Acupuncture and Related Techniques (ICMART, #13046)*; *World Association for Laser Applications (WALA, #21152).* [2020/XJ5397/**D**]

♦ International Society for Medical and Psychological Hypnosis (ISMPH) 15257

Société internationale d'hypnose médicale et psychologique – Centro Internazionale di Ipnosi Medica e Psicologica (CIIMP)

Dir Corso XXII Marzo 57, 20129 Milan MI, Italy. T. +39270126489 – +3927388427. Fax +3927491051.

URL: http://www.uim.mi.it/

History 5 Apr 1985, Milan (Italy). **Aims** Carry out and promote counselling, practical applications and research in the field of medical and psychological hypnosis. **Structure** Founders and Presidents (3); General Deputy; Director; Secretary-General; International Scientific Board of 8 members. **Languages** English, Italian. **Staff** 22 voluntary in Italy and around the world. **Finance** Members' dues. Grants. Budget (annual): about euro 1,000. **Activities** Carries out research; provides counselling; performs practical applications in the field of hypnosis, hypnotherapy, creative hypnosis, hypnosis in pedagogy and psychosomatic medicine; provides autogenous training; organizes courses on medical and psychological hypnosis for physicians and psychologists. **Events** *Conference* Milan (Italy) 1996, *Meeting on hypnotherapy and psychology of handwriting* Milan (Italy) 1988.
Members National representatives in 25 countries:
Argentina, Australia, Bolivia, Brazil, Bulgaria, China, Czechia, Ecuador, El Salvador, France, Germany, India, Israel, Italy, Japan, Mexico, Nigeria, Poland, Russia, Serbia, Spain, Sweden, UK, USA, Venezuela. [2009.06.01/XF1390/**F**]

♦ International Society for Medical Publication Professionals (internationally oriented national body)

♦ International Society for Medical Shockwave Therapy (ISMST) 15258

Main Office Ebelsberger Schlossweg 5, 4030 Linz, Austria. T. +43732302373. Fax +43732303375. E-mail: shockwave@ismst.com.

URL: http://www.ismst.com/

History 12 Sep 1997, Vienna (Austria). Former names and other names: *European Society for Musculoskeletal Shockwave Therapy (ESMT)* – former (12 Sep 1997 to 1999); *International Society for Musculoskeletal Shockwave Therapy (ISMST)* – former (1999 to 2007). Registration: Austria. **Aims** Promote development of *musculoskeletal* shock wave therapy worldwide. **Structure** General Meeting (annual). Managing Board, comprising President, 2 Vice Presidents, General Secretary and Treasurer, Membership Secretary, Scientific Treasurer, Honorary President. **Languages** English. **Staff** 0.50 FTE, paid. **Finance** Sources: meeting proceeds; members' dues; sponsorship. **Activities** Events/meetings. **Events** *Congress* Daegu (Korea Rep) 2023, *Congress* Prague (Czechia) 2022, *Congress* Vienna (Austria) 2021, *Congress* Vienna (Austria) 2020, *Congress* Beijing (China) 2019. **Publications** *ISMST Newsletter.*
Members Individuals in 51 countries and territories:
Argentina, Australia, Austria, Belarus, Belgium, Brazil, Bulgaria, Canada, Chile, Colombia, Costa Rica, Croatia, Cyprus, Czechia, Denmark, Ecuador, Egypt, France, Germany, Greece, India, Iran Islamic Rep, Ireland, Israel, Italy, Japan, Jordan, Korea Rep, Kuwait, Luxembourg, Malaysia, Mexico, Nepal, Netherlands, New Zealand, Norway, Poland, Russia, Saudi Arabia, Singapore, Slovakia, Spain, Sweden, Switzerland, Taiwan, Thailand, Tunisia, Türkiye, UK, USA, Venezuela. [2023/XD7864/**D**]

♦ International Society of Medical Writers (inactive)
♦ International Society for Medieval Theology (#13243)

♦ International Society of Mediterranean Ecology (ISOMED) 15259

Seat Centro de Ecologia Aplicada Prof Baeta Neves, Tapada da Ajuda, 1349-017 Lisbon, Portugal. E-mail: medecosxiii@gmail.com.

History Founded 1984, Perth (Australia), as *Society of Mediterranean Ecologists*, at 4th *International Congress of Mediterranean-climate Ecosystems (MEDECOS).* Present name and structure adopted 2004. **Aims** Promote communication among ecologists working in the five Mediterranean-climate regions of the world through the continuation of the international conferences as well as through special symposia and exchanges of personnel. **Structure** General Assembly; Executive Committee; Secretariat. **Finance** Members' dues. **Activities** Meeting activities. **Events** *MEDECOS : International Mediterranean Ecosystems Conference* Langebaan (South Africa) 2021, *MEDECOS : International Mediterranean Ecosystems Conference* Langebaan (South Africa) 2020, *MEDECOS : International Mediterranean Ecosystems Conference* Seville (Spain) 2017, *MEDECOS : International Mediterranean Ecosystems Conference* Olmué (Chile) 2014, *MEDECOS : international Mediterranean ecosystems conference* Los Angeles, CA (USA) 2011. **Publications** *ISOMED Newsletter* (occasional).
Members Full from 21 countries:
Algeria, Argentina, Australia, Chile, Egypt, France, Germany, Greece, Israel, Italy, Jordan, Mexico, Morocco, New Zealand, Portugal, South Africa, Spain, Tunisia, Türkiye, UK, USA. [2014/XE0946/**D**]

♦ International Society for Men's Health (ISMH) 15260

Internationale Gesellschaft für Männergesundheit

Secretariat 100 Walnut Ave, Ste 103, Clark NJ 07066, USA. T. +19735201832. E-mail: office@ismh.org.

URL: http://www.ismh.org/

History 1999. Former names and other names: *International Society for Men's Health and Gender (ISMH)* – alias; *Internationale Gesellschaft für Männergesundheit und Geschlechtsspezifische Medizin* – alias. **Aims** Focus on issues concerning men and gender from the medical, sociological political, biological and public-health perspective; create a foundation for men's health and gender-specific medical research; enhance the awareness of this topic among a wide range of the medical society. **Structure** International Scientific Board of over 50 members. **Languages** English. **Activities** Organizes symposia and world congresses; coorganizes "International Men's Health Week". **Events** *World Congress* Kuching (Malaysia) 2023, *World Congress* Kuching (Malaysia) 2022, *World Congress* Kuching (Malaysia) 2021, *World Congress* Kuching (Malaysia) 2020, *World Congress* Florence (Italy) 2017. **Publications** *Journal of Men's Health and Gender (JMHG)*; *Men's Health Newsletter.* **Information Services** *ISMH elearning* – online.
Members Full in 50 countries and territories:
Australia, Austria, Belgium, Brazil, Bulgaria, Canada, Chile, China, Colombia, Costa Rica, Croatia, Dominican Rep, Ecuador, El Salvador, Finland, France, Germany, Guatemala, Honduras, Hong Kong, Hungary, Indonesia, Ireland, Italy, Korea Rep, Lebanon, Malaysia, Mexico, Netherlands, Nicaragua, Norway, Panama, Philippines, Poland, Russia, Singapore, Slovenia, South Africa, Spain, Sweden, Switzerland, Taiwan, Thailand, Türkiye, UK, Ukraine, United Arab Emirates, Uruguay, USA, Venezuela, Vietnam. [2020/XD8969/**D**]

♦ International Society for Men's Health and Gender / see International Society for Men's Health (#15260)
♦ International Society for Mental Imagery Techniques / see Société internationale des techniques d'imagerie mentale onirique (#19498)

♦ International Society for Mental Training and Excellence (ISMTE) 15261

Pres Hagalundsvägen 4, SE-702 30 Örebro, Sweden. T. +4619332233 – +4619(46706091973. E-mail: info@siu.nu.

URL: http://www.wcecongress.com/

History 1989 at World Congress on Sport Psychology, Singapore. **Aims** Promote excellence in sport, performance, education, work, health and life in general; create, collect, produce and provide practical material and educational opportunities; serve as a vehicle for on-going improvement in the quality of knowledge, education and consulting in mental training and excellence. **Structure** World Congress (every 4 years); Board. **Languages** English. **Staff** 0.50 FTE, paid. **Finance** Congress proceedings; sale of the Journal. **Activities** Events/meetings; publishing activities. **Events** *Quadrennial Congress* Gävle (Sweden) 2019, *Quadrennial Congress* Chandigarh (India) 2015, *Quadrennial Congress* Pristina (Kosovo) 2011, *Quadrennial Congress* Beijing (China) 2008, *Quadrennial Congress* St Petersburg (Russia) 2003. **Publications** *Journal of Excellence* (6 a year). [2018.06.01/XD8784/**D**]

♦ International Society for Mesotherapy 15262

Société internationale de mésothérapie – Sociedad Internacional de Mesoterapia

Pres 50 rue du Progrès, 69100 Villeurbanne, France.

History 1983, by Dr Michel Pistor. **Languages** French. **Finance** Members' dues. **Events** *Congress* Moscow (Russia) 2010, *Congress* Mexico City (Mexico) 2008, *Congress* Madeira (Portugal) 2006, *Congress* Algiers (Algeria) 2003, *Congress* Paris (France) 2000.
Members Societies in 23 countries:
Algeria, Argentina, Belgium, Brazil, Colombia, France, Germany, Greece, Israel, Italy, Japan, Kazakhstan, Lebanon, Mexico, Morocco, Portugal, Russia, Spain, Switzerland, Tunisia, Türkiye, UK, Venezuela.
Individuals in 38 countries and territories:
Andorra, Austria, Bulgaria, Canada, Chad, Chile, Congo Brazzaville, Costa Rica, Côte d'Ivoire, Czechia, Haiti, Hungary, Ireland, Jordan, Kazakhstan, Lithuania, Luxembourg, Madagascar, Mauritania, Mauritius, Monaco, Morocco, Netherlands, Niger, Oman, Palestine, Paraguay, Peru, Poland, Romania, Senegal, Serbia, Syrian AR, Ukraine, United Arab Emirates, Uruguay, USA, Uzbekistan. [2016.06.01/XD2032/**D**]

♦ International Society on Metabolic Eye Diseases (ISMED) 15263

Société internationale des maladies métaboliques de l'oeil

Address not obtained.

History 1971. **Aims** Apply the fields of metabolism, nutrition, genetics and paediatrics and other disciplines of medicine, including neurochemistry and enzymology, to *ophthalmology.* **Languages** English. **Staff** Voluntary. **Events** *Symposium* Russia 2012, *Symposium* Canada 2010, *Symposium* USA 2010, *Symposium* Iceland 2009, *Symposium* Guangzhou (China) 2008. **Publications** *Metabolic, Paediatric and Systemic Ophthalmology* (periodical); *Nutritional and Metabolic Ophthalmology.*
Members Ophthalmologists, paediatricians and other specialists (600) in 23 countries and territories:
Australia, Austria, Belgium, Brazil, Canada, China, Colombia, Denmark, Egypt, France, Germany, Greece, Hong Kong, Israel, Italy, Japan, Netherlands, Norway, Spain, Sweden, Switzerland, UK, USA. [2017/XD5957/v/**D**]

♦ International Society for Metal Music Studies (ISMMS) 15264

Sec address not obtained. E-mail: ismmswebmaster@gmail.com.

Events Manager address not obtained.

URL: https://metalstudies.org/

History 2011, Prague (Czechia). **Aims** Encourage and facilitate trans / interdisciplinary and international academic research regarding processes and phenomena related to heavy metal music and culture; support the recognition of such research as a significant contribution to academic communities. **Structure** Executive Board. **Activities** Events/meetings. **Events** *Biennial Research Conference* Mexico City (Mexico) 2022, *Biennial Research Conference* Mexico City (Mexico) 2021, *International Conference on Modern Heavy Metal* Helsinki (Finland) 2015. **Publications** *Metal Music Studies.* **Members** Individuals (116) in about 25 countries. Membership countries not specified. [2021.09.07/AA1857/**C**]

♦ International Society for Metaphysics (ISM) 15265

Société internationale de métaphysique

Pres Dept of Philosophy, East China Normal Univ, 500 Dongchuan Road, 200241 Shanghai, China. T. +86215435125. Fax +86215435125.

Sec Dept of Philosophy, East China Normal Univ, 500 Dongchuan Road, 200241 Shanghai, China. T. +86215435125. Fax +86215435125.

URL: http://www.i-s-m-philosophy.org/

History 1973, Varna (Bulgaria). **Aims** Promote critical reflection and metaphysical discourse on the reality of personal, social, cultural, national, international and global life through philosophical meetings, conferences and exchanges at diverse regional levels as well as on international and intercultural levels. **Structure** Council; President; Secretary. **Languages** Chinese, English. **Staff** Voluntary. **Finance** Sources: contributions. **Activities** Events/meetings; knowledge management/information dissemination; networking/liaising; research/documentation. **Events** *Past, present and future* Shanghai (China) 2014, *Round Table* Athens (Greece) 2013, *Metaphysics – East and West* Shanghai (China) 2013, *Meeting* Wuhan (China) 2012, *Meeting* Vienna (Austria) 2011. **Publications** *Cultural Heritage and Contemporary Change*; *Philosophical Challenges and Opportunities of Globalization* – in 2 vols. *On Human Action and Practical Wisdom* (2016); *The Mutual Cultivation of Self and Things* (2016); *Person and God*; *Person and Nature*; *Person and Society.*
Members Individuals in 77 countries and territories:
Algeria, Argentina, Australia, Austria, Bangladesh, Belgium, Bolivia, Brazil, Bulgaria, Burundi, Cameroon, Canada, Chad, Chile, China, Colombia, Congo Brazzaville, Congo DR, Costa Rica, Côte d'Ivoire, Croatia, Czechia, Denmark, Dominican Rep, Ecuador, Egypt, El Salvador, Ethiopia, France, Georgia, Germany, Ghana, Greece, Holy See, Hong Kong, Hungary, India, Iran Islamic Rep, Ireland, Israel, Italy, Japan, Kenya, Lesotho, Mexico, Morocco, Netherlands, New Zealand, Nicaragua, Nigeria, Norway, Pakistan, Paraguay, Peru, Philippines, Poland, Puerto Rico, Russia, Rwanda, Senegal, Serbia, Slovakia, Slovenia, South Africa, Spain, Sri Lanka, Sweden, Switzerland, Taiwan, Tanzania UR, Thailand, Uganda, Ukraine, USA, Venezuela, Zambia, Zimbabwe.
NGO Relations Member of: *International Federation of Philosophical Societies (FISP, #13507).* [2017.11.04/XD5288/v/**C**]

♦ International Society for Microbial Ecology (ISME) 15266

Exec Dir PO BOX 50, 6700 AB Wageningen, Netherlands. T. +31317473467. E-mail: office@isme-microbes.org.

URL: http://www.isme-microbes.org/

History 1998. Replaces *International Committee on Microbial Ecology (ICOME, inactive).* Formerly incorporated in the State of Michigan. Registration: Handelsregister, No/ID: 09191073, Netherlands, Arnhem. **Aims** Promote exchange of scientific information on microbial ecology and related disciplines. **Structure** International Board of Directors of 12 members. World Ambassadors; Executive Director; Event Manager; Membership Manager; Editorial Board. **Languages** Dutch, English. **Staff** None. **Finance** Sources: members' dues. **Activities** Events/meetings; guidance/assistance/consulting; research and development; training/education. **Events** *International Symposium on Microbial Ecology (ISME)* Auckland (New Zealand) 2026, *International Symposium on Microbial Ecology (ISME)* Cape Town (South Africa) 2024, *International Symposium on Microbial Ecology (ISME)* Lausanne (Switzerland) 2022, *International Symposium on Microbial Ecology (ISME)* Cape Town (South Africa) 2020, *PAM : International Conference on Polar and Alpine Microbiology* Hamilton (New Zealand) 2019. **Publications** *The ISME Journal* (12 a year); *ISME Communications* (Open Access). **Members** Individuals (about 1,000). Membership countries not specified. **NGO Relations** Member of (2): *Associations and Conference Forum (AC Forum, #02909)*; *International Union of Microbiological Societies (IUMS, #15794).* [2022.05.10/XD7922/**D**]

♦ International Society for Microbial Electrochemistry and Technology (ISMET) 15267

Pres Dept Environmental Technology, Wageningen Univ and Research, 6708 PB Wageningen, Netherlands.

URL: http://www.is-met.org/

History Sep 2011. **Aims** Link researchers from various areas of science and engineering towards studying the complex interactions of microorganisms and electrodes, while finding novel ways to use them for sustainability applications. **Structure** Board; Committees (6). **Activities** Awards/prizes/competitions; events/meetings. **Events** *International Meeting* Chania (Greece) 2022, *European Meeting* Girona (Spain) 2021, *Asia Pacific Meeting* Harbin (China) 2021, *European Meeting* Girona (Spain) 2020, *North America Meeting* Los Angeles, CA (USA) 2020. **Publications** *ISMET Newsletter.* [2021/XJ9462/**C**]

♦ International Society for Microbiology / see International Union of Microbiological Societies (#15794)

♦ International Society of Microbiota (ISM) 15268

Chairman Kanaya Bldg 4F, 4-11-3, Hatchobori Chuo-ku, Tokyo, 104-0032 Japan. E-mail: microbiota@microbiota-site.com.

URL: http://www.microbiota-site.com/

History 2013. **Aims** Bring a new level of understanding of microbiata science out of the classical existing point of view. **Structure** Steering Committee; Scientific Committee. **Finance** Sources: members' dues. **Events** *World Congress on Targeting Microbiota* Paris (France) 2021, *World Congress on Targeting Microbiota* Paris (France) 2020, *World Congress on Targeting Microbiota* Krakow (Poland) 2019, *World Congress on Targeting Microbiota* Porto (Portugal) 2018, *World Congress on Targeting Microbiota* Berlin (Germany) 2017. **Publications** *ISM Newsletter.* [2021/XJ9006/**C**]

♦ International Society for Mild Approaches in Assisted Reproduction (ISMAAR) 15269

Pres St George's University Hospital, Blackshaw Road, Tooting, London, SW17 0QT, UK. Fax +442089445800.
URL: http://www.ismaar.org/

History Registration: Charity, No/ID: 1123677, England and Wales. **Activities** Events/meetings. **Events** *Symposium* Copenhagen (Denmark) 2020, *World Congress* London (UK) 2018, *Symposium* London (UK) 2015, *World Congress* Monterrey (Mexico) 2015, *World Congress* Sydney, NSW (Australia) 2014. [2021/XM3580/**D**]

♦ International Society for Military Ethics (internationally oriented national body)

♦ International Society for Military Law and the Law of War 15270

Société internationale de droit militaire et de droit de la guerre – Sociedad Internacional de Derecho Militar y Derecho de la Guerra

SG Av de la Renaissance 30, 1000 Brussels, Belgium. T. +3224413797. E-mail: brussels@ismllw.org.
URL: http://www.ismllw.org/

History 22 Mar 1988, Brussels (Belgium). Established deriving inspiration from ideals and principles of an international society of the same name set up 1956, Strasbourg (France), and registered according to French law. Registration: Banque-Carrefour des Entreprises, No/ID: 0433.914.850, Start date: 20 Apr 1988, Belgium. **Aims** Study military law and the law of armed *conflict*; carry out research into the harmonization of internal systems of law both reciprocally, having regard to international conventions and the rules of international law relating to these fields, and also to the promotion of a body of military law and of the law of armed conflict established with respect to *human rights*. **Structure** General Assembly; Board of Directors; Specialized Committees (4). **Languages** English, French. **Staff** 2.00 FTE, paid. **Finance** Sources: government support; grants; meeting proceeds; members' dues; sale of publications. **Activities** Awards/prizes/competitions; events/meetings. **Events** *Seminar for Legal Advisors of the Armed Forces* West Point, NY (USA) 2023, *Silent Leges Inter Arma Conference* Bruges (Belgium) 2022, *Triennial International Congress* Florence (Italy) 2022, *Silent Leges Inter Arma Conference* Bruges (Belgium) 2021, *International Conference* Aix-en-Provence (France) 2020. **Publications** *Military Law and the Law of War Review – Revue de droit militaire et de droit de la guerre* (annual) in Dutch, English, French, German, Italian, Spanish. Information Services: Documentation centre/library. **Members** University professors, civilian and military magistrates, high-ranking public servants, lawyers, general and field officers, either in national groups or individually, admitted on the basis of their competence on matters within the scope of the Society. Individuals (about 700) in 50 countries. Membership countries not specified. **Consultative Status** Consultative status granted from: *ECOSOC (#05331)* (Ros A). [2020/XC2562/v/**B**]

♦ International Society of Military Sciences (ISMS) 15271

Sec address not obtained.
Pres address not obtained.
URL: http://www.isofms.org/

History 22 Oct 2008, Copenhagen (Denmark). **Aims** Build a network for the creation, development, exchange and diffusion of research and knowledge about war, conflict management and peace support efforts. **Structure** Council. **Events** *Annual Conference* Kingston, ON (Canada) 2021, *Annual Conference* Helsinki (Finland) 2020, *Annual Conference* Helsinki (Finland) 2020, *Annual Conference* Vienna (Austria) 2019, *Annual Conference* Warsaw (Poland) 2018.
Members National member institutions in 9 countries:
Austria, Belgium, Canada, Denmark, Finland, Netherlands, Norway, Poland, Sweden.
Regional member (1):
Baltic Defence College (BALTDEFCOL, #03110). [2021/XM4678/**D**]

♦ International Society for Mine Surveying (ISM) 15272

Société internationale de topographie minière – Sociedad Internacional de Topografia Minera – Internationale Gesellschaft für Markscheidewesen – Mezdunarodnoe Obscestvo po Marksejderskomu Delu

Pres Natl Research Irkutsk State Tech Univ, Dept Mine Surveying and Geodesy, 83 Lermontov Street, IRKUTSK, Russia, 664074. T. +73952405102. E-mail: president@ism-minesurveying.org.
URL: http://www.ism-minesurveying.org/

History 1969, Prague (Czech Rep), during 1st Symposium on Mine Surveying. Operates as a permanent international body affiliated to *World Mining Congress (WMC, #21654)*, set up 1958, Warsaw (Poland). Maintains an independent Secretariat. Statutes revised 2001-2002. **Aims** Encourage developments and international collaboration in the various fields of mine surveying and related disciplines. **Structure** Members' Assembly (on the occasion of International Congress, at least every 3 years); Praesidium; Executive Praesidium; Scientific Commissions (6); Secretariat. **Languages** English, German, Russian. **Staff** 1.00 FTE, voluntary. **Finance** Members' dues. No central budget. **Activities** Networking/liaising; events/meetings. **Events** *Triennial Congress* Xuzhou (China) 2023, *Triennial Congress* Irkutsk (Russia) 2019, *Triennial Congress* Brisbane, QLD (Australia) 2016, *International Symposium on Mobile Mapping Technology* Sydney, NSW (Australia) 2015, *Praesidium Meeting* Sydney, NSW (Australia) 2014. **Publications** Congress proceedings.
Members Regular associations, corporate bodies and individuals; Sponsoring scientific and technical institutions, societies, associations, companies and other corporations. Honorary individuals. Members in 44 countries:
Albania, Australia, Austria, Belarus, Bolivia, Bulgaria, Canada, Chile, China, Colombia, Czechia, Finland, France, Germany, Ghana, Hungary, India, Indonesia, Iran Islamic Rep, Ireland, Kazakhstan, Liberia, Malaysia, Mongolia, Montenegro, Nigeria, Norway, Poland, Romania, Russia, Serbia, Slovakia, Slovenia, South Africa, Spain, Sweden, Switzerland, UK, Ukraine, USA, Uzbekistan, Vietnam, Zambia, Zimbabwe.
IGO Relations Cooperates with: *International Hydrographic Organization (IHO, #13825).* **NGO Relations** Cooperates with: China Coal Society (CCS); *International Copper Association (ICA, #12962); International Federation of Surveyors (FIG, #13561).* [2016.11.07/XE5115/**E**]

♦ International Society for Minimal Intervention in Spinal Surgery (ISMISS) 15273

Europe Office Klinik für Neurochirurgie, Universitätsklinikum des Saarlandes, Gebäude 90.5, Kirrbergerstraße 100, 66421 Homburg-Saar, Germany. T. +4968411624400. Fax +4968411624480.
URL: http://www.ismiss.com/

History 1988, Brussels (Belgium). Founded during the meeting of *International Group for Study of Intervertebral Spine Approaches (#13757)*. An affiliate of *International Society of Orthopaedic Surgery and Traumatology (#15335)*. **Aims** Develop and promote minimally invasive techniques in spine surgery. **Structure** Presidential Board; Administrative Board; National Representatives. **Languages** English, French, German. **Finance** Sources: members' dues. **Activities** Events/meetings. **Events** *World ISMISS Conference* Homburg (Germany) 2021, *International Symposium Minimal Invasive and Instrumented Surgery of the Spine* Kharkiv (Ukraine) 2019, *ISMISS World Meeting* Homburg (Germany) 2018, *International Symposium Minimal Invasive and Instrumented Surgery of the Spine* Kharkiv (Ukraine) 2018, *Meeting* Paris (France) 2017.
Members Full in 29 countries:
Argentina, Australia, Bahrain, Belgium, Brazil, Canada, China, Colombia, Cyprus, France, Germany, Hungary, India, Israel, Italy, Japan, Korea Rep, Netherlands, Peru, Portugal, Slovenia, Spain, Sweden, Switzerland, Tunisia, Türkiye, UK, Ukraine, USA. [2022.05.16/XD2551/**E**]

♦ International Society for Minimally Invasive Cardiac Surgery / see International Society for Minimally Invasive Cardiothoracic Surgery (#15274)

♦ International Society for Minimally Invasive Cardiothoracic Surgery (ISMICS) 15274

Exec Dir 500 Cummings Center, Ste 4550, Beverly MA 01915, USA. T. +19789278330. Fax +19785248790. E-mail: ismics@prri.com.
URL: http://www.ismics.org/

History 31 May 1997, Paris (France). Founded by participants at the '*World Congress of Minimally Invasive Cardiac Surgery*'. Former names and other names: *International Society for Minimally Invasive Cardiac Surgery* – former. **Aims** Organize and centralize the various surgical centers concerned with patient outcomes, techniques, and progressive development of less invasive forms of *heart* surgery. **Structure** Board of Directors. **Languages** English. **Staff** None. **Events** *Meeting* Warsaw (Poland) 2022, *Meeting* Beverly, MA (USA) 2021, *Winter Workshop* Cairns, QLD (Australia) 2021, *Winter Workshop* Delhi (India) 2021, *Meeting* Warsaw (Poland) 2021. **Publications** *Innovations: Technology and Techniques in Cardiothoracic and Vascular Surgery* (6 a year). [2021/XD7424/**D**]

♦ International Society of Minimally Invasive Neurosurgery (ISMINS) 15275

Operating Secretariat OIC Srl, Viale Matteotti 7, 50121 Florence FI, Italy. T. +395550351. Fax +39555001912. E-mail: info@theismins.com.
Registered Office Viale Papiniano 42, 20123 Milan MI, Italy.
URL: http://www.theismins.com/

History 10 Feb 2011, Milan (Italy). Registration: Italy. **Aims** Propagate minimally invasive neurosurgery throughout the world. **Structure** Assembly. Officers: President; Vice-President; 3 Co-Vice-Presidents; Secretary; Treasurer; Assistant Secretary. **Activities** Events/meetings. **Events** *Congress of the International Society of Minimally Invasive Neurosurgery* Surabaya (Indonesia) 2021, *Congress of the International Society of Minimally Invasive Neurosurgery* Moscow (Russia) 2018, *Congress* Cairo (Egypt) 2016, *Congress* Xian (China) 2014, *Congress* Florence (Italy) 2012. [2022/XJ7653/**C**]

♦ International Society of Mini- and Micro-Computers (inactive)

♦ International Society for Mobile Youth Work (ISMO) 15276

Internationale Gesellschaft für Mobile Jugendarbeit

Chair ISMO, c/o Diakonisches Werk der evangelischen Kirche Württemberg, Heilbronnerstrasse 180, 70194 Stuttgart, Germany. T. +4971111656231.
ISMO Office Stafflenbergstrasse 76, 70184 Stuttgart, Germany. E-mail: board@ismo-online.org.
URL: http://www.ismo-online.org/

History 1992. **Aims** Discuss, analyse and develop the approach of Mobile Youth Work (MYW) on a global level so as to improve effectively the living situation of children and youth at *risk*. **Structure** Board, comprising Chair and 2 Vice-Chairs. **Languages** English, German. **Finance** Members' dues. Donations and grants. Budget (annual): euro 50,000. **Activities** Carries out projects, consisting of training seminars. Organizes symposia. **Events** *Symposium* Limuru (Kenya) 2003, *Symposium* St Petersburg (Russia) 1998, *Symposium* Solothurn (Switzerland) 1995, *Symposium* Santiago (Chile) 1994, *Symposium* Stuttgart (Germany) 1991. [2015/XD7583/**D**]

♦ International Society for Molecular Electronics and Biocomputing (inactive)
♦ International Society for Molecular Nutrition and Therapy (no recent information)

♦ International Society for Molecular Plant-Microbe Interactions (IS-MPMI) 15277

Executive Vice-Pres 3352 Sherman Ct, Ste 202, St Paul MN 55121, USA. T. +16514547250. Fax +16514540766. E-mail: ismpmi@scisoc.org.
URL: https://www.ismpmi.org/

History 7 Sep 1990. Registration: USA, Minnesota. **Aims** Advance interdisciplinary science pertaining to molecular interactions of plants with microbes and parasitic angiosperms, nematodes and insect pests (molecular plant-microbe interactions), affecting plant growth and productivity on a worldwide basis. **Structure** Board of Directors (meets at least once a year), comprising President/CEO, President-Elect, Immediate Past-President, Secretary, Treasurer, Immediate Past-President and members. Committees: Finance; Nominations; Conference. **Finance** Members' dues. **Events** *Congress* Glasgow (UK) 2019, *Congress* Portland, OR (USA) 2016, *Biennial Congress / Congress* Rhodes Is (Greece) 2014, *Biennial Congress / Congress* Kyoto (Japan) 2012, *Biennial congress / Congress* Québec, QC (Canada) 2009. **Publications** *Molecular Plant-Microbe Interactions* (12 a year) – journal; *IS-MPMI Reporter* (3 a year) – newsletter. **Members** Full; Post doctorate; Student; Corporate. Membership countries not specified. [2020/XN5604/**D**]

♦ International Society for Molecular Recognition (ISMR) 15278

Pres Dept of Biochemistry, Tel Aviv University, Tel Aviv, Israel. E-mail: gidifl@post.tau.ac.il.
URL: http://www.ismr.org/

History 1985, USA. Constitution and bylaws adopted 2 Sep 1985; amended 31 Mar 1986 and 7 Feb 1990. **Aims** Promote knowledge and cooperation in the area of molecular recognition. **Structure** International Council; President; Vice-President; Meeting Organizer. **Languages** English. **Staff** 4.00 FTE, voluntary. About 8 part-time, voluntary. **Finance** Members' dues. Other sources: contributions; meeting registration. Budget (annual): US$ 100,000. **Events** *Affinity Conference* Stockholm (Sweden) 2021, *Affinity Conference* Stockholm (Sweden) 2019, *Affinity Conference* Paris (France) 2017, *Affinity Conference* Puerto Vallarta (Mexico) 2015, *Affinity Conference* Vienna (Austria) 2013. **Publications** *Journal of Molecular Recognition.* [2013/XJ4361/**D**]

♦ International Society of Monarchists (inactive)
♦ International Society of Money Box Collectors (inactive)

♦ International Society for Monitoring Molecules in Neuroscience (MMiN) 15279

Main Office 2661 Queenswood Dr, Victoria BC V8N 1X6, Canada. E-mail: admin@monitoringmolecules.org – mmin@podiumconferences.com.
URL: http://www.monitoringmolecules.org/

History 1982, Nottingham (UK). Originally a UK national meeting. Other national meetings: Oxford 1984; Cambridge (UK) 1987. Former names and other names: *International Conference on In Vivo Methods* – former; *International Conference on Monitoring Molecules in Neuroscience* – former. **Aims** Provide a platform to facilitate the development and refinement of methods for time-resolved detection of chemicals in the living brain. **Structure** Organizing Committee; Scientific Advisory Board. **Events** *International MMiN Conference* Chapel Hill, NC (USA) 2024, *International MMiN Conference* Lyon (France) 2022, *International MMiN Conference* Lyon (France) 2021, *International MMiN Conference* Lyon (France) 2020, *International MMiN Conference* Oxford (UK) 2018. [2022/XM0608/c/**E**]

♦ International Society of Motor Control (ISMC) 15280

Sec address not obtained.
URL: http://www.i-s-m-c.org/

History 25 Mar 2002. Registered in the state of Delaware (USA). **Activities** Biennial meeting 'Progress in Motor Control'. **Events** *Progress in Motor Control Conference* Auckland (New Zealand) 2021, *Progress in Motor Control Conference* Miami, FL (USA) 2019, *Progress in Motor Control Conference* Miami, FL (USA) 2017, *Progress in Motor Control Conference* Budapest (Hungary) 2015, *Meeting* Montréal, QC (Canada) 2013. **Members** Membership countries not specified. [2020/XJ8088/**D**]

♦ International Society for Mountain Medicine (ISMM) 15281

Pres 111 Roy E, Montréal QC H2W 1M1, Canada. T. +14387938633.
URL: http://www.ismm.org/

History Dec 1985, Geneva (Switzerland). **Aims** Bring together physicians, members of paramedical professions and organizations or societies interested in mountain medicine; encourage research, studies, discussion and publications concerning all medical aspects of mountains, mountain peoples and mountaineers. **Structure** General Assembly (every 2 years); Executive Committee. **Languages** English. **Staff** 1.00 FTE, paid. **Finance** Members' dues. **Activities** Organizes and co-sponsors congresses of international character; awards the ISMM Prize. **Events** *World Congress of Mountain Medicine* Interlaken (Switzerland) 2021, *World Congress of Mountain Medicine* Interlaken (Switzerland) 2020, *World Congress of Mountain Medicine* Kathmandu (Nepal) 2018, *World Congress of Mountain Medicine* Telluride, CO (USA) 2016, *World Congress of High Altitude Medicine and Physiology* Bolzano (Italy) 2014. **Publications** *High Altitude Medicine and Biology* (4 a year) – journal.
Members Individuals (300) in 41 countries and territories:

Argentina, Australia, Austria, Belgium, Bolivia, Brazil, Canada, Chile, China, Colombia, Czechia, Denmark, Ecuador, France, Germany, Greece, India, Ireland, Italy, Japan, Kyrgyzstan, Nepal, Netherlands, New Zealand, Norway, Pakistan, Peru, Poland, Russia, Singapore, Slovakia, Slovenia, Spain, Sweden, Switzerland, Taiwan, Türkiye, UK, Ukraine, USA, Venezuela.
NGO Relations Cooperates with: *International Commission for Alpine Rescue (ICAR, #12662)*; *Union internationale des associations d'alpinisme (UIAA, #20420)*; *Wilderness Medical Society (WMS).* [2018/XD1415/v/**D**]

♦ International Society of Multiphysics 15282

Sec address not obtained.
URL: https://www.multiphysics.org/

Aims Address the latest advances in theoretical developments, numerical modelling and industrial applications so as to promote the concept of simultaneous engineering. **Activities** Awards/prizes/competitions; events/meetings. **Events** *International Conference of Multiphysics* Oslo (Norway) 2021, *International Conference of Multiphysics* 2020, *International Conference of Multiphysics* Dubai (United Arab Emirates) 2019, *International Conference of Multiphysics* Krakow (Poland) 2018, *International Conference of Multiphysics* Beijing (China) 2017. [2021/AA1830/**C**]

♦ International Society on Multiple Criteria Decision Making 15283

Pres Office IE 218, Industrial Eng, METU, Ankara/Ankara, Türkiye. E-mail: secretary@mcdmsociety.org.
URL: http://www.mcdmsociety.org/

History New bylaws adopted 11 Jun 1998, Charlottesville VA (USA), during Business Meeting; revised 6 Aug 2015, Hamburg (Germany). Also referred to as *International Society on MCDM.* **Aims** Develop, test, evaluate and apply methodologies for solving multiple criteria decision making problems; foster interaction and research in the scientific field of multiple criteria decision making; cooperate with other organizations in the study of management from a quantitative perspective. **Structure** Business Meeting (every 2 years, in conjunction with International Conference); Executive Committee. **Activities** Awards/prizes/competitions; events/meetings; training/education. **Events** *International Conference on Multiple Criteria Decision Making* Portsmouth (UK) 2022, *Conference* Portsmouth (UK) 2021, *Conference* Istanbul (Turkey) 2019, *Conference* Ottawa, ON (Canada) 2017, *Bridging disciplines* Hamburg (Germany) 2015. **Publications** Newsletter (2 a year); Special issues. **Members** Individuals (2,402) in 96 countries. Membership countries not specified. [2021/XN7229/v/**C**]

♦ International Society for Musculoskeletal Imaging in Rheumatology (ISEMIR) 15284

Contact address not obtained. T. +18605867576.

Aims Bring together rheumatologists, radiologists and other specialists dedicated to the furtherance of the art and science of imaging as applied to musculoskeletal diseases. **Structure** Board of Directors. Committees (3): Education; Research; Regulator Affairs. **Activities** Events/meetings. **Events** *CME Conference* Santa Monica, CA (USA) 2015, *CME Conference* Santa Monica, CA (USA) 2014. **Members** Founding; Regular; Associate; Organizational; Retired. Membership countries not specified. [2014/XJ8585/**C**]

♦ International Society of Musculoskeletal and Neuronal Interactions (ISMNI) 15285

Pres Charité – Univ of Medicine Berlin, Campus Benjamin Franklin, Hindenburgdamm 30, 12203 Berlin, Germany. T. +493084453046.
URL: http://www.ismni.org/

History 1999. Registration: Greece. **Aims** Enhance knowledge of interactions between tissues and organs coordinating in the function of the musculoskeletal and neuronal interactions. **Structure** General Assembly (twice a year); Advisory Board (Council); Board. **Languages** English. **Finance** Members' dues. **Activities** Events/meetings. **Events** *International Workshop* Montréal, QC (Canada) 2017, *Workshop* Ipswich (UK) 2012, *Workshop* Bergisch-Gladbach (Germany) 2010, *Workshop* Cologne (Germany) 2008, *Workshop* Porto Heli (Greece) 2006. **Publications** *Journal of Musculoskeletal and Neuronal Interactions (JMNI)* (4 a year). *The Utah Paradigm of Skeletal Physiology* by H M Frost – in 2 vols.
Members Regular in 22 countries and territories:
Argentina, Australia, Belgium, Canada, Cyprus, Czechia, Finland, Germany, Greece, Hong Kong, Italy, Japan, Lebanon, Netherlands, New Zealand, Portugal, Sweden, Switzerland, UK, Ukraine, Uruguay, USA. [2017/XD8727/**D**]

♦ International Society for Musculoskeletal Shockwave Therapy / see International Society for Medical Shockwave Therapy (#15258)
♦ International Society for Musculoskeletal Ultrasound (inactive)

♦ International Society for Mushroom Science (ISMS) 15286

Société internationale scientifique des champignons comestibles

Sec 1507 Valley Rd, Coatesville PA 19350, USA. T. +16103845031. Fax +16103840390. E-mail: isms@lambertspawn.com.
Pres address not obtained.
URL: http://www.isms.biz/

History Founded 1968 when statutes were adopted, an informal committee having existed since 2nd *International Conference on Mushroom Science*, 1953, Belgium. 1st Conference had been held in 1950, Peterborough (UK). Statutes revised: 1980; 1984; 1991; 1996; 2004; 2007; 2013. Former names and other names: *International Commission on Mushroom Science (ICMS)* – former. **Aims** Further development of the mushroom industry globally through application and communication of science. **Structure** Council, comprising an appointed representative of each corporate member and 5 members elected by individual members. Officers: President; Vice-President; Secretary; Treasurer; Past-President. A Commission of: *International Union of Biological Sciences (IUBS, #15760).* **Languages** English. **Staff** Voluntary. **Finance** Sources: members' dues. **Activities** Events/meetings; knowledge management/information dissemination; research and development; research/documentation. **Events** *International e-Congress on the Science and Cultivation of Edible and Medicinal Fungi* 2021, *International Congress on the Science and Cultivation of Edible Fungi* Amsterdam (Netherlands) 2016, *International Congress on the Science and Cultivation of Edible Fungi* Beijing (China) 2012, *International congress on the science and cultivation of edible fungi* Cape Town (South Africa) 2008, *International congress on the science and cultivation of edible fungi* Miami, FL (USA) 2004. **Publications** *ISMS Update* (4 a year) – newsletter. *Mushroom Science* – in 16 vols. Symposium proceedings.
Members Individuals, organizations or businesses interested in mushrooms; corporate, national organizations of mushroom growers; Honorary Life Members. Members in 40 countries and territories:
Australia, Austria, Barbados, Belgium, Canada, Colombia, Czechia, Egypt, Finland, France, Germany, Greece, Hong Kong, Hungary, India, Ireland, Israel, Italy, Japan, Kenya, Korea Rep, Malta, Mexico, Netherlands, New Zealand, Norway, Philippines, Poland, Romania, Singapore, South Africa, Spain, Sweden, Switzerland, Taiwan, Tanzania UR, Thailand, UK, Ukraine, USA.
NGO Relations Member of (2): *International Association of Botanical and Mycological Societies (IABMS, #11730)*; *International Mycological Association (IMA, #14203).* [2022.02.02/XC1564/**C**]

♦ International Society of Music (inactive)

♦ International Society for Music Education (ISME) 15287

Société internationale pour l'éducation musicale – Sociedad Internacional de Educación Musical – Internationale Gesellschaft für Musik-Erziehung

Admin Office Ste 148, 45 Glenferrie Road, Malvern VIC 3144, Australia. E-mail: admin@isme.org.
URL: http://www.isme.org/

History 1953, Brussels (Belgium). Founded at International Conference on Music Education convened by *UNESCO (#20322)* and attended by music educators from 40 countries. **Aims** Build and maintain a worldwide community of music educators characterized by mutual respect and support; foster global intercultural understanding and cooperation among the world's music educators; promote music education for people of all ages in all relevant situations. **Structure** Conference (every 2 years); Board of Directors; Executive Committee; Commissions (7). **Languages** English. **Staff** 3.00 FTE, paid. **Finance** Sources: meeting proceeds; members' dues; sale of publications; sponsorship. **Activities** Events/meetings; research/documentation; training/education. **Events** *World Conference* Helsinki (Finland) 2024, *European Regional Conference* Lyon (France) 2023, *A Visible Voice 2022*, *Music Education Today – Renewing Views and Contexts of Change* Cancún (Mexico) 2021, *Biennial Asia-Pacific Symposium on Music Education Research* Tokyo (Japan) 2021. **Publications** *International Journal of Music Education* (4 a year); *ISME Newsletter* (2-3 a year). *Games Children Sing Malaysia*; *ISME Fanfares*; *ISME History Book*; *Music Education and Music Ethnomusicology: A (Usually) Harmonious Relationship*; *Songs of Latin America*; *Traditional Songs of Singing Cultures: A World Sampler.* Conference proceedings; monographs; special editions. **Members** Affiliated National Organizations representatives of music education organizations, institutes and individual music educators. Group Members (i) Organizations of international, regional or national music educators or others who wish to keep informed; (ii) Institutions devoted wholly or partly to music education; (iii) Companies. Members in over 90 countries and territories. Membership countries not specified. **NGO Relations** Member of: *European Music Council (EMC, #07837)*; *International Music Council (IMC, #14199)*; *World Alliance for Arts Education (WAAE, #21078).* [2021/XB2492/**B**]

♦ International Society for Music Information Retrieval (ISMIR) 15288

Sec address not obtained.
URL: http://www.ismir.net/

History 2000. Registration: Start date: 4 Jul 2008, Canada. **Aims** Foster the exchange of ideas; stimulate research, development and improvement in teaching in all branches of music information retrieval; encourage publication and distribution of theoretical, empirical and applied studies; cooperate with representatives of other organizations and disciplines. **Structure** Business Meeting (annual). Board of Directors, comprising President, Treasurer, Secretary, President-Elect and 3 members. **Events** *Conference* 2023, *Conference* Bangalore (India) 2022, *Conference* 2021, *Conference* Montréal, QC (Canada) 2020, *Conference* Delft (Netherlands) 2019. **Publications** Conference proceedings. [2021/XJ3480/**C**]

♦ International Society for Music in Medicine (ISMM) 15289

Internationale Gesellschaft für Musik in der Medizin

Main Office Hochstr 65, 58511 Lüdenscheid, Germany. E-mail: ismmoffice@t-online.de.
URL: https://musicmedicine1.jimdo.com/

History 1982, Lüdenscheid (Germany). Founded at 1st International Symposium on 'Anxiety, Pain and Music'. **Aims** Understand the mechanisms of music in medical treatment and coaching; improve patient care through research, education and communication. **Structure** Scientific Committee, including President and 4 Vice-Presidents. Executive Director. Central Office in Lüdenscheid (Germany). Regional Chapters (2): USA; Europe. **Languages** English. **Staff** 2.00 FTE, paid. **Finance** Members' dues: US$ 80. **Events** *Symposium* Hamburg (Germany) 2003, *Symposium* Hamburg (Germany) 2002, *Symposium* Lüdenscheid (Germany) 2000, *Symposium* Melbourne, VIC (Australia) 1998, *Symposium* Austin, TX (USA) 1996. **Publications** *IJAM – International Journal of Arts Medicine.* Books.
Members Full; Individuals (health care professionals and scientists) in 21 countries:
Argentina, Australia, Austria, Canada, China, Finland, France, Germany, Greece, India, Italy, Japan, Netherlands, Norway, Poland, South Africa, Spain, Sweden, Switzerland, UK, USA.
NGO Relations Cooperates with (1): *International Association for Music and Medicine (IAMM, #12043).* [2020/XD5779/**D**]

♦ International Society for Mycotoxicology (ISM) 15290

Contact c/o CNR – ISPA, Via G Amendola 122/0, 70126 Bari BA, Italy. T. +39805929357. Fax +39805929374. E-mail: ism-secretary@mycotox-society.org.
Gen Sec Univ of Natural Resources and Life Sciences Vienna, Dept for Agrobiotechnology – IFA-Tulln, Konrad-Lorenz-Str 20, 3430 Tulln, Austria. T. +43227266280401.
URL: http://www.mycotox-society.org/

History 7 Nov 2005, Bari (Italy). **Aims** Increase scientific knowledge concerning biology, chemistry and any sciences/disciplines related to mycotoxins and toxigenic fungi. **Structure** Council; Executive Committee; Continental Representatives; Branches. **Languages** English. **Staff** 1.00 FTE, voluntary. **Finance** Sources: meeting proceeds; members' dues; sponsorship. Budget (annual): euro 35,000 – euro 80,000. **Activities** Events/meetings; networking/liaising; research/documentation; training/education. **Events** *International Mycotoxin Conference* Beijing (China) 2014, *International Conference Europe* Martina Franca (Italy) 2013, *International Conference North America* Ottawa, ON (Canada) 2012, *International Conference* Cape Town (South Africa) 2011, *ISM International Conference* Mendoza (Argentina) 2011. **Publications** *Food Additives and Contaminants (FAC)*; *Mycotoxicology Newsletter (MTNL).* **Members** Ordinary; Student; Honorary; Retired; Sustaining. Membership countries not specified. **NGO Relations** Instrumental in setting up (1): *African Society of Mycotoxicology (ASM).* [2021/XJ5403/**C**]

♦ International Society for Myriapodology (#03759)

♦ International Society for Nanomanufacturing (ISNM) 15291

CEO Inst of Material Research and Innovation, Univ of Bolton, Deane Road, Bolton, BL3 5AB, UK.
URL: http://www.isnm.org/

History 2008. **Aims** Advance nanomanufacturing *technology* to better serve the community. **Structure** Executive Board. **Languages** English. **Staff** 3.00 FTE, voluntary. **Events** *International Conference on Nanomanufacturing* Bolton (UK) 2022, *International Conference on Nanomanufacturing* Xian (China) 2021, *International Conference on Nanomanufacturing* Xian (China) 2020, *International Conference on Nanomanufacturing* London (UK) 2018, *International Conference on Nanomanufacturing* Macau (Macau) 2016. **Publications** *International Journal of Nanomanufacturing.*
Members Fellow; Member; Student; Corporate. Members in 13 countries:
Australia, Canada, China, France, Germany, Israel, Italy, Japan, Netherlands, Singapore, Switzerland, UK, USA. [2014.07.07/XJ7117/**C**]

♦ International Society of Naturalists (internationally oriented national body)
♦ International Society for Neglected Tropical Diseases (unconfirmed)

♦ International Society for Neonatal Screening (ISNS) 15292

Office Manager Reigerskamp 273, 3607 HP Maarssen, Netherlands. T. +31642078327.
URL: http://www.isns-neoscreening.org/

History 1991, Leura, NSW (Australia). Registration: No/ID: 34122624, Start date: 1999, Netherlands; EU Transparency Register, No/ID: 809390039113-90, Start date: 31 Jul 2020. **Aims** Promote appropriate screening of *foetal*, neonatal and infant illnesses and disorders worldwide. **Structure** Council. **Languages** English. **Staff** None. **Finance** Sources: members' dues. Annual budget: 10,000 EUR. **Activities** Awards/prizes/competitions; events/meetings; knowledge management/information dissemination. **Events** *European Regional Meeting* Luxembourg (Luxembourg) 2021, *European Regional Meeting* Luxembourg (Luxembourg) 2020, *European Regional Meeting* The Hague (Netherlands) 2016, *Meeting* The Hague (Netherlands) 2016, *Asia Pacific Regional Meeting* Penang (Malaysia) 2015. **Publications** *International Journal for Neonatal Screening (IJNS)*; *ISNS Newsletter.*
Members Individuals in 85 countries and territories:
Albania, Algeria, Argentina, Armenia, Australia, Austria, Bahrain, Bangladesh, Belgium, Bosnia-Herzegovina, Brazil, Bulgaria, Cambodia, Canada, Chile, China, Colombia, Costa Rica, Croatia, Cyprus, Czechia, Denmark, Egypt, Estonia, Finland, France, Germany, Greece, Guatemala, Hong Kong, Hungary, Iceland, India, Indonesia, Iran Islamic Rep, Iraq, Ireland, Israel, Italy, Japan, Jordan, Kazakhstan, Korea Rep, Kuwait, Latvia, Lebanon, Libya, Lithuania, Luxembourg, Malaysia, Malta, Mexico, Moldova, Mongolia, Morocco, Netherlands, New Zealand, Nigeria, North Macedonia, Norway, Oman, Pakistan, Panama, Peru, Philippines, Poland, Portugal, Qatar, Romania, Russia, Saudi Arabia, Serbia, Singapore, Slovakia, Slovenia, Spain, Sri Lanka, Sweden, Switzerland, Taiwan, Thailand, UK, United Arab Emirates, Uruguay, USA.
NGO Relations Member of (1): *Health First Europe (HFE, #10881).* [2021/XF3487/v/**C**]

♦ International Society for Neoplatonic Studies (ISNS) 15293

Gen Sec Dept of Philosophy, Univ of San Diego, 5998 Alcala Park, San Diego CA 92110-2492, USA. T. +16192604600ext4705. Fax +16192604227.
URL: http://www.isns.us/

History Founded 1973, Richmond KY (USA). **Aims** Promote the study of Neoplatonism. **Structure** Board of Directors, comprising Presidents of national and regional sections and 8 additional members. International Officers: President; Vice-President; General Secretary. National and regional sections (8), each having a President, Vice-President and Secretary-Treasurer: US; Canada; UK; Ireland; Ibero-American; France; Poland; Spain. **Languages** English, French. **Staff** 6.00 FTE, voluntary. **Finance** Fees from sub-sections. **Activities** Organizes annual Conference; maintains international study centre. Cooperates in *'Center for Neoplatonic Studies'* Nashville TN (USA). Joint meetings with US national philosophical societies. **Events** *Annual Conference* Athens (Greece) 2022, *Annual Conference* San Diego, CA (USA) 2021, *Annual Conference* Ottawa, ON (Canada) 2019, *Annual Conference* Los Angeles, CA (USA) 2018, *Annual Conference* Olomouc (Czechia) 2017. **Publications** *ISNS Newsletter* (2 a year); *Journal of Neoplatonic Studies. Studies in Neoplatonism: Ancient and Modern.* Series of books.

Members Scholars in 25 countries:
Argentina, Australia, Austria, Belgium, Brazil, France, Germany, Greece, India, Israel, Italy, Japan, Korea Rep, Mexico, Netherlands, New Zealand, Norway, Papua New Guinea, Portugal, Russia, Spain, Sweden, Switzerland, UK, USA.
[2013/XD5474/**C**]

♦ International Society of Nephrology (ISN) 15294

Société internationale de néphrologie – Sociedad Internacional de Nefrologia

Exec Dir Global Operations Center, Av des Arts 1-2, 1210 Brussels, Belgium. T. +3228080420. Fax +3228084454. E-mail: info@theisn.org.
Americas Operations Center 340 North Ave, 3rd Floor, Cranford NJ 07016, USA. T. +15672489703. Fax +19082727101.
URL: http://www.theisn.org/

History 3 Sep 1960, Geneva (Switzerland). Founded at 1st International Congress on Nephrology. Registration: Start date: 1962, France. **Aims** Advance diagnosis, treatment and prevention of *kidney disease*. **Structure** Congress (every 2 years); Executive Committee; Council; Nominating Committee; Regional Boards; Headquarters in Brussels (Belgium) and Cranford NJ (USA). **Languages** English. **Staff** Paid. **Finance** Sources: meeting proceeds; members' dues; sponsorship. Other sources: journal royalties. **Activities** Awards/prizes/competitions; events/meetings; financial and/or material support; guidance/assistance/consulting; research/documentation; training/education. **Events** *World Congress of Nephrology* Bangkok (Thailand) 2023, *World Congress of Nephrology* Kuala Lumpur (Malaysia) 2022, *World Congress of Nephrology* Montréal, QC (Canada) 2021, *World Congress of Nephrology* Abu Dhabi (United Arab Emirates) 2020, *Frontiers Meeting* Gothenburg (Sweden) 2019. **Publications** *Kidney International* (12 a year); *ISN Insight*; *ISN News*; *Kidney Internatonal Reports*.

Members Affiliated national societies in 83 countries and territories:
Albania, Australia, Bangladesh, Belgium, Bolivia, Bosnia-Herzegovina, Brazil, Bulgaria, Cameroon, Canada, Chile, China, Colombia, Costa Rica, Croatia, Cuba, Denmark, Ecuador, Egypt, El Salvador, Estonia, France, Georgia, Germany, Ghana, Greece, Guatemala, Hong Kong, Hungary, India, Indonesia, Iran Islamic Rep, Iraq, Ireland, Israel, Italy, Japan, Jordan, Kazakhstan, Kenya, Korea Rep, Kuwait, Latvia, Lebanon, Malaysia, Mexico, Moldova, Mongolia, Morocco, Myanmar, Netherlands, New Zealand, Nigeria, North Macedonia, Norway, Pakistan, Panama, Paraguay, Peru, Philippines, Poland, Portugal, Romania, Russia, Saudi Arabia, Senegal, Serbia, Slovenia, South Africa, Spain, Sweden, Switzerland, Syrian AR, Taiwan, Tanzania UR, Thailand, Tunisia, Türkiye, UK, United Arab Emirates, Uruguay, USA, Yemen.

Individuals in 150 countries and territories:
Afghanistan, Albania, Algeria, Argentina, Armenia, Australia, Austria, Azerbaijan, Bahamas, Bahrain, Bangladesh, Barbados, Belarus, Belgium, Benin, Bolivia, Bosnia-Herzegovina, Botswana, Brazil, Brunei Darussalam, Bulgaria, Burkina Faso, Burundi, Cambodia, Cameroon, Canada, Chad, Chile, China, Colombia, Congo DR, Costa Rica, Côte d'Ivoire, Croatia, Cuba, Curaçao, Cyprus, Czechia, Denmark, Dominican Rep, Ecuador, Egypt, El Salvador, Estonia, Eswatini, Ethiopia, Fiji, Finland, France, Gambia, Georgia, Germany, Ghana, Greece, Guadeloupe, Guatemala, Guinea, Haiti, Honduras, Hong Kong, Hungary, Iceland, India, Indonesia, Iran Islamic Rep, Iraq, Ireland, Israel, Italy, Jamaica, Japan, Jordan, Kazakhstan, Kenya, Korea Rep, Kuwait, Laos, Latvia, Lebanon, Libya, Lithuania, Luxembourg, Malawi, Malaysia, Mali, Malta, Mauritania, Mexico, Moldova, Monaco, Mongolia, Morocco, Mozambique, Myanmar, Namibia, Nepal, Netherlands, New Zealand, Nicaragua, Niger, Nigeria, North Macedonia, Norway, Oman, Pakistan, Palestine, Panama, Paraguay, Peru, Philippines, Poland, Portugal, Qatar, Romania, Russia, Rwanda, San Marino, Saudi Arabia, Senegal, Serbia, Sierra Leone, Singapore, Slovakia, Slovenia, South Africa, Spain, Sri Lanka, Sudan, Suriname, Sweden, Switzerland, Syrian AR, Taiwan, Tajikistan, Tanzania UR, Thailand, Togo, Trinidad-Tobago, Tunisia, Türkiye, UK, Ukraine, United Arab Emirates, Uruguay, USA, Uzbekistan, Venezuela, Vietnam, Zambia, Zimbabwe.

Includes 6 regional organizations listed in this Yearbook:
African Association of Nephrology (AFRAN, #00209); *Arab Society of Nephrology and Renal Transplantation (ASNRT, #01047)*; *Asian-Pacific Society of Nephrology (APSN, #01640)*; *European Renal Association – European Dialysis and Transplant Association (ERA-EDTA, #08353)*; *Panamerican Society for Dialysis and Transplantation (PSDT, inactive)*; *Sociedad Latinoamericana de Nefrologia e Hipertensión (SLANH, #19415)*.

Consultative Status Consultative status granted from: *WHO (#20950)* (Official). **NGO Relations** Member of: *Associations and Conference Forum (AC Forum, #02909)*. [2022/XB2559/y/**B**]

♦ International Society for Neronian Studies (#19484)
♦ International Society on Neurobiology and Psychopharmacology (internationally oriented national body)

♦ International Society for Neurochemistry (ISN) 15295

Société internationale de neurochimie

Executive Manager c/o Kenes Group, Piet Heinkade 55, 1019 GM Amsterdam, Netherlands. E-mail: secretariat@neurochemistry.org.
URL: http://www.neurochemistry.org/

History 1966. Founded an organizing committee having been formed in 1962. First meeting held Jul 1967, Strasbourg (France). **Aims** Advance education in neurochemistry throughout the world. **Structure** Council. Elected officers (3); appointed officers (2). Committees (7): Membership; Standing Rules and Ad Hoc; Programme; Publication; Aid in Neurochemistry; Small Conferences and Education; Travel Grant. **Languages** English. **Staff** 3.50 FTE, paid. Voluntary. **Finance** Annual budget: 400,000 USD. **Activities** Events/meetings; financial and/or material support; training/education. **Events** *Biennial Meeting* Porto (Portugal) 2023, *Joint Meeting* Porto (Portugal) 2023, *ISN-APSN Meeting* Honolulu, HI (USA) 2022, *Biennial Meeting* Kyoto (Japan) 2021, *Biennial Meeting* Montréal, QC (Canada) 2019. **Publications** *Journal of Neurochemistry* (12 a year); *ISN News* (2 a year).

Members Neurochemists (over 1,700) in 56 countries and territories:
Argentina, Armenia, Australia, Austria, Belgium, Brazil, Bulgaria, Canada, Chile, China, Czechia, Denmark, Egypt, Estonia, Finland, France, Germany, Greece, Hong Kong, Hungary, India, Iran Islamic Rep, Ireland, Israel, Italy, Japan, Korea Rep, Latvia, Libya, Malaysia, Mexico, Netherlands, New Zealand, Nigeria, Norway, Pakistan, Peru, Poland, Portugal, Puerto Rico, Romania, Russia, Serbia, Singapore, Slovakia, Slovenia, Spain, Sweden, Switzerland, Taiwan, Türkiye, UK, Ukraine, Uruguay, USA, Venezuela.

NGO Relations Associated member of: *International Union of Biochemistry and Molecular Biology (IUBMB, #15759)*. *European Society for Neurochemistry (ESN, #08662)* is member. Instrumental in setting up: *Asian Pacific Society for Neurochemistry (APSN, #01641)*; [2021/XD2493/v/**C**]

♦ International Society for Neuroemergencies (inactive)
♦ International Society of Neuroendocrinology (inactive)

♦ International Society for Neuroethology (ISN) 15296

Manager 810 E 10th St, Lawrence KS 66044, USA. T. +17858659215. Fax +17858436153. E-mail: isn@allenpress.com.
Sec Dept of Biology, University of Washington, Box 351800, Seattle WA 98195-1800, USA.
URL: http://www.neuroethology.org/

Aims Advance understanding of the *neural* bases of *behaviour* in all animals, vertebrate and invertebrate. **Structure** Council. Executive Committee, comprising President, President-Elect, Past-President, Secretary and Treasurer. Committees (9): Congress; Local Organizing; Heiligenberg Student Travel Award; Long-Range Planning; Membership; Nominating; Young Investigator Awards Review; Web Oversight and Education; Education. **Finance** Sources: members' dues. **Events** *Biennial Congress* Berlin (Germany) 2024, *Biennial Congress* Lisbon (Portugal) 2022, *Biennial Congress* Estoril (Portugal) 2020, *Biennial Congress* Brisbane, QLD (Australia) 2018, *Biennial Congress* Montevideo (Uruguay) 2016. **Publications** *ISN Newsletter* – online.

Members Regular; Life; Special; Student; Emeritus. Members in 35 countries and territories:
Argentina, Australia, Austria, Brazil, Canada, Chile, China, Cuba, Denmark, France, Germany, Greece, Hungary, India, Ireland, Israel, Italy, Japan, Lithuania, Mexico, Netherlands, New Zealand, Norway, Poland, Puerto Rico, Russia, Spain, Sweden, Switzerland, Taiwan, Türkiye, UK, Uruguay, USA, Venezuela. [2020/XC0058/v/**C**]

♦ International Society for Neurofeedback and Research (internationally oriented national body)
♦ International Society of Neurogastronomy (internationally oriented national body)

♦ International Society for Neuroimaging in Psychiatry (ISNIP) 15297

Secretariat Psychiatric Neurophysiology Dept, Univ Hospital of Psych – Waldau, 3000 Bern 60, Switzerland. T. +41319309716. Fax +41319309961.
URL: http://www.isnip.org/

History 1988, Munich (Germany), during a meeting of *Collegium Internationale Neuropsychopharmacologicum (CINP, #04115)*. **Events** *Joint Annual Meeting* Halifax, NS (Canada) 2022, *BACI : International Conference on Basic and Clinical Multimodal Imaging* Naples (Italy) 2021, *Joint Annual Meeting* Toronto, ON (Canada) 2020, *BACI : International Conference on Basic and Clinical Multimodal Imaging* Chengdu (China) 2019, *BACI : International Conference on Basic and Clinical Multimodal Imaging* Bern (Switzerland) 2017. **Members** Individuals. Membership countries not specified. **NGO Relations** Joint meetings with: *International Society for Brain Electromagnetic Topography (ISBET, #14984)*; *Electroencephalography and Clinical Neuroscience Society (ECNS, #05422)*. [2015/XJ8110/**D**]

♦ International Society of Neuroimmunology (ISNI) 15298

Sec-Treas c/o Hellenic Pasteur Inst, Dept of Immunology, 127 Vassilissis Sophias Ave, 115 21 Athens, Greece.
Secretariat c/o EEM Srl, Via Italia 1, 00040 Rocca di Papa RM, Italy. E-mail: secretariat@isniweb.org.
URL: http://www.isniweb.org/

History 1988. Training/education through: *European School for Neurolmmunology (ESNI)*, set up 1999; *Americas School of Neuroimmunology (ASNI)*; *Asia-Pacific School of Neuroimmunology (APSNI)*. **Aims** Carry out studies and research on immune system nervous system interactions. **Structure** International Advisory Board; Executives. **Languages** English. **Finance** Sources: donations; meeting proceeds; members' dues; sponsorship. **Activities** Events/meetings; training/education. **Events** *International Congress of Neuroimmunology* Québec, QC (Canada) 2023, *Congress* Nice (France) 2021, *Congress* Nice (France) 2020, *Congress* Brisbane, QLD (Australia) 2018, *Congress* Jerusalem (Israel) 2016.

Members Individuals in 34 countries and territories:
Australia, Austria, Bahrain, Belgium, Bosnia-Herzegovina, Brazil, Canada, Cuba, Denmark, Finland, France, Germany, Greece, Ireland, Israel, Italy, Japan, Kazakhstan, Lebanon, Luxembourg, Montenegro, Netherlands, Norway, Poland, Portugal, Russia, Serbia, Spain, Sweden, Switzerland, Taiwan, Türkiye, UK, Ukraine, USA.

NGO Relations Memorandum of Understanding with (1): *European Academy of Neurology (EAN, #05803)*. Member of (1): *Federation of Clinical Immunology Societies (FOCIS, #09472)*. [2021.06.25/XD3451/v/**C**]

♦ International Society for NeuroImmunoModulation (ISNIM) 15299

SG AG Immunphysiologie, Univ of Marburg, Deutschhausstrasse 2, 35037 Marburg, Germany. T. +4964212862175. E-mail: isnim@aol.com.
URL: http://www.isnim.org/

History Founded Jun 1987, Zagreb (Yugoslavia), at the European Congress of Immunology, having previously existed as *International Working Group on Neuroimmunomodulation (IWGN)*. **Aims** Understand the communication and regulatory mechanisms integrating the *nervous system* and the *immune* system; investigate neural and endocrine mechanisms of immune regulation as well as the effects of peripheral and central immune responses of brain function. **Structure** Regular Meeting (at least every 3 years). Executive Committee, comprising 5 officers and 13 members. **Languages** English. **Staff** 0.50 FTE, paid. **Finance** Sources: contributions; meeting proceeds; members' dues. **Activities** Events/meetings. **Events** *Triennial World Congress* Rome (Italy) 2017, *Triennial World Congress* Liège (Belgium) 2014, *Triennial World Congress* Dresden (Germany) 2011, *Triennial world congress* Rio de Janeiro (Brazil) 2008, *Iberoamerican congress on neuroimmunomodulation* Madrid (Spain) 2007. **Publications** *NeuroImmunoModulation* – official journal. **Information Services** *INFONIM System*.

Members Regular; Student; Retired; Corporate. Individuals in 20 countries and territories:
Argentina, Brazil, Canada, Croatia, Czechia, France, Germany, Greece, Hungary, Israel, Italy, Japan, Lebanon, Netherlands, Russia, Spain, Switzerland, Taiwan, UK, USA.

Organizations in 2 countries:
France, Russia. [2020/XD0828/**C**]

♦ International Society for Neuronal Regulation / see International Society for Neurofeedback and Research

♦ International Society of Neuropathology (ISN) 15300

Société internationale de neuropathologie – Internationale Gesellschaft für Neuropathologie

SG Neuropath Dept, Level 1 West Wing, John Radcliffe Hosp, Oxford, OX3 9DU, UK.
URL: http://www.intsocneuropathol.com/

History 1972, superseding *International Committee of Neuropathology*, set up in 1950. **Aims** Foster formation of national and regional societies of neuropathology and promote cooperation between them; advance knowledge of *pathology* of the *nervous system* at research, educational and service levels. **Structure** General Council; Executive Committee. **Languages** English. **Staff** No permanent staff. **Finance** Annual budget: 4,500 USD. **Activities** Awards/prizes/competitions; events/meetings. **Events** *Congress* Berlin (Germany) 2023, *Congress* Berlin (Germany) 2022, *A gateway to modern neuroscience* Tokyo (Japan) 2018, *Congress* Rio de Janeiro (Brazil) 2014, *Congress* Salzburg (Austria) 2010. **Publications** *Brain Pathology*.

Members National associations in 34 countries:
Argentina, Australia, Austria, Belgium, Brazil, Bulgaria, Canada, China, Croatia, Czechia, Denmark, Finland, France, Germany, Greece, Hungary, Iceland, India, Ireland, Italy, Japan, Latvia, Mexico, Netherlands, New Zealand, Norway, Poland, Portugal, Romania, Russia, Spain, Sweden, Switzerland, USA.

Individuals in 36 countries. Membership countries not specified. [2019.06.27/XD5257/**C**]

♦ International Society of Neuro-Semantics (ISNS) 15301

Contact PO Box 8, Clifton CO 81520, USA. T. +19705237877. E-mail: meta@acsol.net.
URL: https://www.neurosemantics.com/

History 1 Sep 1994, USA. Established in order to raise the quality and professionalism of Neuro-Linguistics. Registration: USA, State of Colorado. **Aims** Study, research, and present the Neuro-Semantic models that enables self-actualization, the synergy of meaning and performance, in order to facilitate individuals and groups to develop to their best. **Structure** Includes the Meta-Coach Foundation which governs Meta-Coaches. **Finance** Sources: members' dues.

Members Institutes in 11 countries and territories:
Australia, Brazil, Egypt, Hong Kong, Indonesia, Italy, Malaysia, Mexico, Philippines, South Africa, USA.

NGO Relations Member of (1): *NLP Global Body*. [2022.01.26/XG9714/**C**]

♦ International Society for Neurosurgical Technology and Instrument Invention (inactive)

♦ International Society for NeuroVascular Disease (ISNVD) 15302

Contact 30200 Telegraph Rd, Ste 140, Bingham Farms MI 48025, USA. T. +12487126798.
URL: http://www.isnvd.org/

Aims Further the development of research for neurovascular related diseases. **Structure** Executive Committee; Committees (11). **Events** *Annual Meeting* New York, NY (USA) 2022, *Annual Meeting* New York, NY (USA) 2020, *Annual Meeting* Ferrara (Italy) 2019, *Annual Meeting* Zhengzhou (China) 2018, *Annual Meeting* Taormina (Italy) 2017. **Publications** *Neurovascular Perspectives* – newsletter. [2017.11.28/XJ6265/**C**]

♦ International Society for NeuroVirology (ISNV) 15303

Office Dept Neuroscience, Temple Univ School of Medicine, Room 740 MERB, 3500 N Broad St, Philadelphia PA 19140 19140, USA. T. +12157079788. Fax +12157079838. E-mail: mail@isnv.org.
URL: http://www.isnv.org/

History 1998, Philadelphia PA (USA). **Aims** Advance collaboration among scientists in all aspects of neurovirology and related disciplines so as to further knowledge in the area; promote the clinical application of this knowledge to prevent and treat neurodegenerative and neoplastic disease in the nervous system. **Structure** Board of Directors. Officers: President; Vice-President; Treasurer; Secretary. Sub-Committees (7). **Events** *Symposium* 2021, *Symposium* Atlanta, GA (USA) 2019, *Symposium* Chicago, IL (USA) 2018, *Symposium* Toronto, ON (Canada) 2016, *Symposium* Washington, DC (USA) 2013. **Publications** *Journal of NeuroVirology* (6 a year). [2015/XM8281/**C**]

♦ International Society for Neutron Capture Therapy (ISNCT) 15304

SG address not obtained.
Pres address not obtained.
URL: http://www.isnct.net/

History 1983, Cambridge, MA (USA). **Aims** Promote research and therapy on neutron capture therapy. **Structure** Executive Board and President (executive); Board of Councillors (legislative). **Languages** English. **Staff** 0.50 FTE, paid. **Finance** Primarily registration fees at Biennial Congress. No annual budget. **Activities** Organizes: International Congress; Young BNCT Researchers Meeting. **Events** *International Congress on Neutron Capture Therapy – ICNCT* Granada (Spain) 2021, *Young Member's Boron Neutron Capture Therapy (YBNCT) Meeting* Helsinki (Finland) 2019, *International Congress on Neutron Capture Therapy – ICNCT* Taipei (Taiwan) 2018, *International Congress on Neutron Capture Therapy – ICNCT* Missouri (USA) 2016, *International Congress on Neutron Capture Therapy – ICNCT* Helsinki (Finland) 2014. **Publications** Special issue in "Applied Radiation and Isotopes" (every 2 years). Selected papers from Biennial Congress. **Members** Membership countries not specified. **NGO Relations** Links with national organizations. [2021/XD9486/**D**]

♦ International Society for Neutron Radiology (ISNR) 15305

Sec Technische Uni München, Radiochemie München RCM, Walther-Meissner-Str 3, Room 209, Ernst-Reuter-Platz 1, 85748 Garching, Germany. T. +498928914328. Fax +498928914347.
Pres address not obtained.
URL: http://www.isnr.de/

History Constitution operational, Jun 1996. **Aims** Support and promote any activities for development, improvement and application of neutron imaging techniques; assist collaborations among members and users of their facilities; transfer knowledge on neutron imaging techniques to students, users and other interested groups; initiate cooperation to other related organizations and units. **Structure** Board, comprising President, Vice-President and Secretary and up to 12 members. **Finance** No members' dues. **Activities** Organizes *World Conference on Neutron Radiography (WCNR)*. **Events** *International Topical Meeting on Neutron Radiography* Buenos Aires (Argentina) 2020, *World Conference on Neutron Radiography* Sydney, NSW (Australia) 2018, *International Topical Meeting on Neutron Radiography* Beijing (China) 2016, *World Conference on Neutron Radiography / World Conference* Grindelwald (Switzerland) 2014, *International Topical Meeting on Neutron Radiography* Kingston, ON (Canada) 2012. **Publications** *NR Newsletter*.
Members Individuals (149) – researchers and users of methods in neutron imaging – in 34 countries:
Algeria, Argentina, Australia, Austria, Bangladesh, Belgium, Brazil, Canada, China, Egypt, France, Germany, Greece, Hungary, India, Israel, Italy, Japan, Korea Rep, Malaysia, Morocco, Netherlands, New Zealand, Pakistan, Poland, Romania, Russia, South Africa, Spain, Sweden, Switzerland, Thailand, UK, USA. [2016/XM3855/v/**C**]

♦ International Society for New Institutional Economics / see Society for Institutional and Organizational Economics (#19576)

♦ International Society for Nomenclature of Paediatric and Congenital Heart Disease (ISNPCHD) 15306

Société internationale de nomenclature des maladies pédiatriques et congénitales du coeur (SINMPCC)

Sec address not obtained. E-mail: fredebailliard@googlemail.com.
URL: http://ipccc.net/

History Set up Oct 2000, Frankfurt-Main (Germany), as *International Nomenclature Committee for Paediatric and Congenital Heart Disease*. Current title adopted Jan 2005. **Aims** Unify paediatric cardiac disease under a single terminology. **Structure** Board of Directors; Executive Committee. International Working Groups (3): Mapping and Coding of Nomenclatures for Paediatric and Congenital Heart Disease (Nomenclature Working Group – NWG); Defining the Nomenclatures for Paediatric and Congenital Heart Disease (Definitions Working Group – DWG); Archiving and Cataloguing the Images and Videos of the Nomenclatures for Paediatric and Congenital Heart Disease (Archiving Working Group – AWG). **Events** *Meeting* 2021, *Meeting* Warsaw (Poland) 2020, *Meeting* Montréal, QC (Canada) 2019, *Meeting* Montréal, QC (Canada) 2019, *Meeting* Manaus (Brazil) 2018. **Publications** *Cardiology in the Young* – official journal. **Members** Individuals. Membership countries not specified. [2018/XM6602/v/**C**]

♦ International Society of Non-Antibiotics (ISN) 15307

Sec Sungade 54, 6320 Egernsund, Denmark. T. +4574632888. E-mail: malthe@dadlnet.dk.
Contact Szeged, Medicine Fac, Dóm tér 10, Szeged 6720, Hungary.
URL: http://www.non-antibiotics.com/

History 1990, as *International Society for Antimicrobial Activity of Non-Antibiotics (ISAAN)*. Current name adopted 2001. **Aims** Encourage the discovery of antimicrobial activity of agents primarily employed for treatment of *non-infectious pathology*. **Events** *International conference on reversal of resistance* Copenhagen (Denmark) 2009. **Members** Membership countries not specified. **NGO Relations** Member of: *Federation of European Societies for Chemotherapy and for Infections (FESCI, #09546)*; *International Society of Antimicrobial Chemotherapy (ISAC, #14925)*. [2016/XD2183/**D**]

♦ International Society of Non-invasive Cardiology (ISCN) 15308

Société internationale de cardiologie non-invasive

Sec Cardiology Dept, UZ Gasthuisberg O-N1 704, Herestraat 49, 3000 Leuven, Belgium. T. +3216330022. Fax +3216345844.

History 1980, Leuven (Belgium), as *International Society of Mechanocardiography (ISM) – Société internationale de mécanocardiographie (SIM)*. **Aims** Study the heart and circulation by non-invasive means, including phonocardiography, mechanocardiography, echo-doppler cardiography, NMR, impedance cardiography, nuclear cardiography, ECG, heart rate variability. **Structure** Branches (4): Asian; Europe-African; North-American; South-American. **Languages** English. **Staff** 0.50 FTE, paid. **Finance** Sources: registration; industrial exhibits. Meeting budget (annual): US$ 100,000. **Activities** International postgraduate exchange programme in Europe (Western and Central Europe) and USA. **Events** *Annual European Conference* Barcelona (Spain) 2009, *Annual European Conference* Munich (Germany) 2008, *Annual European Conference* Vienna (Austria) 2007, *Nordic meeting* Vaasa (Finland) 2006, *Annual European conference* Leuven (Belgium) 2004. **Publications** Proceedings published in 'Acta Cardiologica'.
Members Cardiologists, internists, biologists, pharmacologists, medical physicists, biological engineers. Members in 52 countries and territories:
Albania, Algeria, Argentina, Australia, Austria, Belgium, Bulgaria, Canada, China, Congo DR, Croatia, Cuba, Cyprus, Czechia, Egypt, Finland, France, Germany, Greece, Hong Kong, Hungary, Iceland, India, Indonesia, Israel, Italy, Japan, Korea Rep, Luxembourg, Mexico, Montenegro, Morocco, Netherlands, North Macedonia, Norway, Paraguay, Philippines, Poland, Portugal, Romania, Russia, Serbia, Slovakia, Slovenia, South Africa, Spain, Sweden, Switzerland, Taiwan, Türkiye, UK, USA. [2013/XD8470/v/**C**]

♦ International Society for Noninvasive Electrocardiology / see International Society for Holter and Noninvasive Electrocardiology (#15179)

♦ International Society for NonParametric Statistics (ISNPS) 15309

Treas Dept of Statistics, Pennsylvania State Univ, 414 Thomas, University Park PA 16802, USA. E-mail: mga@stat.psu.edu.
URL: http://www.isnpstat.org/

History 2010. **Aims** Foster research and practice of nonparametric statistics; promote dissemination of new developments in the field. **Structure** Council; Board of Directors. **Activities** Awards/prizes/competitions; events/meetings. **Events** *Conference* Paphos (Cyprus) 2022, *Conference* Paphos (Cyprus) 2021, *Conference* Paphos (Cyprus) 2020, *Conference* Salerno (Italy) 2018, *Conference* Avignon (France) 2016. [2020.03.11/XJ6805/**C**]

♦ International Society for Non Verbal Psychotherapy (inactive)
♦ International Society for Normal and Abnormal Ethnopsychology (inactive)

♦ International Society for Nubian Studies (ISNS) 15310

Hon Sec c/o British Museum, Dept of Ancient Egypt and Sudan, Great Russell Str, London, WC1B 3DG, UK. E-mail: isns@britishmuseum.org.
URL: http://nubianstudiessociety.wordpress.com/

History Jun 1972, Warsaw (Poland). **Aims** Provide a focus for those interested in the archaeology and history of Nubia and Sudan; promote awareness of the rich cultural heritage of this region. **Structure** General Meeting (every 4 years). **Languages** English, French. **Staff** Voluntary. **Finance** No budget. **Activities** Active in: Egypt, Sudan. **Events** *International Conference for Nubian Studies* Warsaw (Poland) 2022, *International Conference for Nubian Studies* Paris (France) 2018, *International Conference for Nubian Studies* Neuchâtel (Switzerland) 2014, *International Conference on Nubian Studies* London (UK) 2010, *International Conference on Nubian Studies* Warsaw (Poland) 2006. **Publications** Proceedings. **IGO Relations** *UNESCO (#20322)*. **NGO Relations** None. [2015.06.01/XG7945/v/**C**]

♦ International Society for Nucleosides, Nucleotides and Nucleic Acids (IS3NA) 15311

Sec Dept of Chemistry & Biochemistry, UMBC, 1000 Hilltop Circle, Baltimore MD 21250, USA. T. +33467143855. Fax +33467549610.
URL: http://www.is3na.org/

History 2000. Founded following a proposal during XIII Round Table on Nucleosides, Nucleotides and their Biological Applications, Montpellier (France) 1998. Has taken over activities of *International Society of Nucleic Acids Chemistry (ISNAC, inactive)*. **Aims** Promote and advance scientific knowledge in the area of nucleosides, nucleotides, oligonucleotides and nucleic acids. **Structure** Board of Directors, comprising President, Vice-President, Immediate Past-President, Chairman of next Round Table Secretary and Treasurer. Committees (7): Awards; Finance; Membership; Nomination; Programme; Publication and Publicity; Site-Selection. **Events** *International Round Table* Stockholm (Sweden) 2022, *Symposium* Baltimore, MD (USA) 2021, *International Round Table* Stockholm (Sweden) 2021, *International Round Table* Stockholm (Sweden) 2020, *International Round Table* San Diego, CA (USA) 2018. **Publications** *Nuclear Aids Research*; *Nucleosides, Nucleotides and Nucleic Acids*. [2021/XD8828/**D**]

♦ International Society for Nurses in Cancer Care (ISNCC) 15312

Main Office Suite 700, 1201 West Pender St, Vancouver BC V6E 2V2, Canada. E-mail: info@isncc.org.
URL: http://www.isncc.org/

History 1984. **Aims** Maximize the influence of nursing to reduce the global burden of cancer. **Structure** Board of Directors; Executive Committee. Committees. Secretariat. **Languages** English. **Finance** Sources: meeting proceeds; members' dues. **Activities** Events/meetings; knowledge management/information dissemination; networking/liaising; politics/policy/regulatory; research and development. **Events** *International Conference on Cancer Nursing (ICCN)* 2022, *International Conference on Cancer Nursing* London (UK) 2021, *International Conference on Cancer Nursing* London (UK) 2020, *International Conference on Cancer Nursing* Auckland (New Zealand) 2018, *International Conference on Cancer Nursing* Anaheim, CA (USA) 2017. **Publications** *Cancer Nursing* (6 a year) – official journal; *International Cancer Nursing News*. Positions papers.
Members Full – national cancer nursing societies; Associate – organizations, institutions or agencies involved/interested in issues of cancer; Sustaining – supporting corporations, organizations or individuals; Honorary. Full in 45 countries and territories:
Algeria, Australia, Botswana, Brazil, Bulgaria, Canada, Chile, China, Colombia, Costa Rica, Cyprus, Czechia, Denmark, France, Georgia, Germany, Greece, Guyana, Iceland, India, Indonesia, Japan, Kenya, Korea Rep, Mongolia, Netherlands, New Zealand, Nigeria, Pakistan, Panama, Peru, Philippines, Poland, Portugal, Romania, Russia, Serbia, Singapore, Sweden, Taiwan, Thailand, Türkiye, UK, USA, Zimbabwe.
Associations in 34 countries and territories:
Antigua-Barbuda, Argentina, Australia, Brazil, Canada, China, Czechia, Egypt, Ethiopia, Germany, Ghana, India, Indonesia, Japan, Jordan, Kenya, Mongolia, Nepal, Nicaragua, Nigeria, Pakistan, Philippines, Saudi Arabia, Singapore, South Africa, Sudan, Suriname, Taiwan, Thailand, Türkiye, UK, USA, Venezuela, Zambia.
Consultative Status Consultative status granted from: *ECOSOC (#05331)* (Ros C). **IGO Relations** Accredited by: *United Nations Office at Vienna (UNOV, #20604)*. Associated with Department of Global Communications of the United Nations. **NGO Relations** Memorandum of Understanding with (3): *Asian Oncology Nursing Society (AONS, #01590)*; *European Oncology Nursing Society (EONS, #08086)*; *Multinational Association of Supportive Care in Cancer (MASCC, #16895)*. Member of (2): *The NCD Alliance (NCDA, #16963)*; *Union for International Cancer Control (UICC, #20415)*. Cooperates with (1): *Breast Health Global Initiative (BHGI, #03318)*. Affiliated with (2): *International Council of Nurses (ICN, #13054)*; *International Psycho-Oncology Society (IPOS, #14665)*. [2022/XD1684/**C**]

♦ International Society of Nurses in Genetics (internationally oriented national body)

♦ International Society for Nutraceuticals and Functional Foods (ISNFF) 15313

Sec address not obtained. E-mail: isnffsecretary@gmail.com.
URL: https://www.isnff.org/

History 2007. Set up as a Disciplinary Interest Group of *International Union of Food Science and Technology (IUFoST, #15773)*. **Aims** Provide a forum to foster communication among professionals; provide technology transfer and facilitate communication among inventors, investors and other interested parties; foster cooperative endeavours. **Structure** Executive Board. **Activities** Events/meetings; awards/prizes/competitions. **Events** *Conference* Honolulu, HI (USA) 2023, *Conference* Istanbul (Türkiye) 2022, *Annual Conference* Kobe (Japan) 2019, *Annual Conference* Vancouver, BC (Canada) 2018, *Annual Conference* Gunsan (Korea Rep) 2017. **Publications** *ISNFF Newsletter*; *Journal of Food Bioactives (JFB)*. [2022/XM4790/**E**]

♦ International Society of Nutrigenetics / Nutrigenomics (ISNN) 15314

Sec 800 Eastowne Dr, Ste 100, 135 Dauer Drive, Campus Box 7461, Chapel Hill NC 27514 27514, USA. T. +19194083320. Fax +19194080674. E-mail: info@nutritionandgenetics.org.
URL: http://www.isnn.info/

History 2005. **Aims** Increase understanding through research and education of professionals and the general public of the role of *genetic* variation and *dietary* response and the role of *nutrients* in gene expression. **Structure** Board of Directors. **Activities** Events/meetings; research/documentation; training/education. **Events** *Congress* Timisoara (Romania) 2020, *Congress* Cambridge (UK) 2019, *Congress* Winnipeg, MB (Canada) 2018, *Congress* Tel Aviv (Israel) 2016, *Congress* Chapel Hill, NC (USA) 2015.
Members Individuals in 27 countries:
Australia, Belgium, Bulgaria, Canada, China, Costa Rica, Finland, France, Germany, Greece, India, Indonesia, Israel, Italy, Korea Rep, Lebanon, Mexico, Netherlands, New Zealand, Norway, South Africa, Spain, Sweden, Switzerland, UK, USA, Venezuela. [2020/XM2396/v/**C**]

♦ International Society of Nutrition and Metabolism in Renal Disease / see International Society of Renal Nutrition and Metabolism (#15418)
♦ International Society of Obstetrical Psycho-Prophylaxis (inactive)
♦ International Society of Obstetric Medicine (no recent information)
♦ International Society of Occupational Ergonomics and Safety Research (internationally oriented national body)
♦ International Society of Ocean and Polar Engineers / see International Society of Offshore and Polar Engineers (#15318)
♦ International Society for Ocular Fluorophotometry (no recent information)
♦ International Society of Ocular Oncology / see International Society of Ocular Trauma (#15317)

♦ International Society of Ocular Oncology (ISOO) 15315

Exec Sec Ocular Oncology Service, Wills Eye Hospital, 840 Walnut St, Philadelphia PA 19107, USA. Fax +12159281140. E-mail: contact@isoo.org.
URL: http://www.isoo.org/

History Jan 2004, Hyderabad (India), during 11th Congress of Ocular Oncology. **Aims** Advance *ophthalmic* oncology. **Structure** Council, comprising President, Vice President, Chairman, Secretary, Treasurer and 5 further members. **Finance** Membership fees. **Activities** *International Congress of Ocular Oncology (ICOO)*. **Events** *Biennial Congress* Leiden (Netherlands) 2021, *Biennial Congress* Los Angeles, CA (USA) 2019, *Biennial Congress* Sydney, NSW (Australia) 2017, *Biennial Congress* Paris (France) 2015, *Biennial Congress* Cambridge (UK) 2009. **Publications** *ISOO Newsletter* (12 a year). [2017/XM2105/**D**]

♦ International Society of Ocular Toxicology (ISOT) 15316

Sec-Treas Loma Linda Univ Faculty Medicine, Dept of Ophthalmology, 11370 Anderson St, Suite 1800, Loma Linda CA 92354, USA.
URL: http://www.isot.org/

History 1986, Bonn (Germany FR). **Aims** Encourage research, training, publication and dissemination of knowledge in all aspects of ocular toxicology. **Structure** Board of Directors, comprising President, President-Elect, Immediate Past President, Secretary-Treasurer and 6 members. **Languages** English. **Staff** 4.50 FTE, voluntary. **Finance** Members' dues: Family – US$ 115; Regular – US$ 100; Associate – US$ 60; Student – US$ 50; Retired – US$ 50. **Activities** Main programmes: In Vitro; Clinical Applications; Advances in Ocular Physiology; Advances in Ocular Toxicology; Ocular Metabolism; Cataract Genesis; Retinal Function. **Events** *Biennial Congress* Kanazawa (Japan) 2014, *Biennial Congress* Portland, OR (USA) 2011, *Biennial Congress* Portland, OR (USA) / Stevenson, WA (USA) 2011, *Biennial Congress* Philadelphia, PA (USA) 2008, *Congress / Biennial Congress* Königswinter (Germany) 2006.
Members Individuals in 15 countries:
Argentina, Canada, Cuba, Denmark, France, Germany, Italy, Japan, Korea Rep, Russia, Spain, Sweden, Switzerland, UK, USA.
Also members in Africa (countries not specified). [2014/XD6647/v/**D**]

♦ **International Society of Ocular Trauma (ISOT)** **15317**

Pres 1201 11th Ave South, Ste 300, Birmingham AL 35205, USA. Fax +12059331341.

History Previously also referred to as *International Society of Ocular Oncology.* **Aims** Further the cause of ocular traumatology through prevention, epidemiology and treatment. **Structure** Board of Directors. **Languages** English. **Finance** Members' dues. **Activities** Maintains *World Eye Injury Registry.* Evens/meetings. **Events** *Congress* Portoroz (Slovenia) 2018, *Congress* Singapore (Singapore) 2016, *Congress* Dubrovnik (Croatia) 2014, *Congress* Jaipur (India) 2012, *Congress* Buenos Aires (Argentina) 2010. [2022/XJ3362/**D**]

♦ International Society of Oculoplastic, Plastic and Reconstructive Surgery (internationally oriented national body)

♦ **International Society of Offshore and Polar Engineers (ISOPE)** **15318**

Exec Dir PO Box 189, Cupertino CA 95015-0189, USA. T. +16502541871. Fax +16502542038. E-mail: info@isope.org.

Street address 495 North Whisman Road, Suite 300, Mountain View CA 94043-5711, USA.

URL: http://www.isope.org/

History Sep 1989. Absorbed *Offshore Mechanics and Polar Engineering Council (OMPEC, inactive),* Jun 1995. Former names and other names: *International Society of Ocean and Polar Engineers (ISOPE)* – alias. Registration: Section 501(c)(3), Start date: Oct 1999, USA, State of California; Start date: 1989, USA, State of Colorado. **Aims** Advance at an international level technological progress in the interdisciplinary fields of offshore, ocean and polar (Arctic and Antarctic) engineering and related technologies; provide opportunities for maintenance and expansion of interest in these fields for benefit of the engineering profession. **Structure** Board of Directors; Technical Committees (11), including *International Hydrodynamics Committee (IHC, see: #15318)*; Technical Program Committee; Ad-hoc Committees; Working Groups. **Languages** English. **Staff** 4.00 FTE, paid. **Finance** Sources: meeting proceeds; members' dues; sale of publications; sponsorship. **Activities** Awards/prizes/competitions; events/meetings; financial and/or material support; knowledge management/information dissemination. **Events** *Annual Conference* Ottawa, ON (Canada) 2023, *Annual Conference* Shanghai (China) 2022, *Annual Conference* Rhodes (Greece) 2021, *PACOMS : Biennial Pacific/Asia Offshore Mechanics Symposium* Dalian (China) 2020, *Annual Conference* Shanghai (China) 2020. **Publications** *International Journal of Offshore and Polar Engineering (IJOPE)* (4 a year); *Journal of Ocean and Wind Energy* (4 a year); *Ocean and Polar Update* – newsletter. Conference and symposium proceedings; special scientific and technical reports.

Members Membership covers 82 countries and territories:

Algeria, Argentina, Australia, Austria, Bangladesh, Belgium, Brazil, Bulgaria, Canada, China, Colombia, Croatia, Cuba, Cyprus, Czechia, Denmark, Ecuador, Egypt, Estonia, Finland, France, Germany, Greece, Hong Kong, Hungary, India, Indonesia, Iran Islamic Rep, Iraq, Ireland, Israel, Italy, Jamaica, Japan, Kazakhstan, Korea DPR, Korea Rep, Kuwait, Latvia, Libya, Luxembourg, Malaysia, Mexico, Morocco, Mozambique, Myanmar, Namibia, Nepal, Netherlands, New Zealand, Nigeria, Norway, Pakistan, Panama, Papua New Guinea, Peru, Philippines, Poland, Portugal, Puerto Rico, Qatar, Romania, Russia, Saudi Arabia, Serbia, Singapore, Slovakia, Slovenia, South Africa, Spain, Sri Lanka, Sweden, Switzerland, Taiwan, Thailand, Türkiye, UK, Ukraine, United Arab Emirates, USA, Venezuela, Vietnam.

NGO Relations Links with a large number of national bodies interested in the field. [2022/XD3491/**C**]

♦ **International Society of Oil Palm Agronomists (ISOPA)** **15319**

Contact c/o MPOB, 6 Persiaran Institusi, Bandar Baru Bangi, 43000 Kajang, Selangor, Malaysia.

History 29 Jan 1994, Kuala Lumpur (Malaysia). **Aims** Advance knowledge of oil palm agronomy through international cooperation. **Structure** Officers: President; Immediate Past President; Vice President; Honorary Secretary; Honorary Treasurer; Editor. **Languages** English. **Staff** 2.00 FTE, voluntary. **Finance** Members' dues. Income from meetings, sales, private sponsors. **Activities** Organizes conference, seminars and study visits. **Events** *Oil palm developments in agronomy in the new millennium* Krabi (Thailand) 2000, *Conference* Kuala Lumpur (Malaysia) 1999, *Conference* Bali (Indonesia) 1998, *International conference on developments in oil palm plantation industry for the 21st century* Nusa Dua (Indonesia) 1998. **Publications** *ISOPA Newsletter.* Conference proceedings.

Members in 12 countries:

Benin, Colombia, Costa Rica, Côte d'Ivoire, France, India, Indonesia, Malaysia, Nigeria, Papua New Guinea, Singapore, Thailand. [2015/XD6591/**D**]

♦ **International Society for Oil Palm Breeders (ISOPB)** **15320**

Pres c/o MPOB, No 6 Persiaran Inst, Bandar Baru Bangi, 43000 Kajang, Selangor, Malaysia. E-mail: zulkifly@mpob.gov.my.

URL: http://isopb.mpob.gov.my/

History 1983. Registration: No/ID: 3437/83, Malaysia, Selangor. **Aims** Advance knowledge of oil palm breeding through international cooperation. **Structure** General Meeting (every 4 years); Officers: President, Vice-President, Secretary, Treasurer, Committee Members (4), Editor; Regional Representatives. **Languages** English. **Staff** 1.00 FTE, voluntary. **Finance** Sources: meeting proceeds; members' dues. **Activities** Events/meetings; training/education. **Events** *International Seminar on Digitalisation Of Data For Oil Palm Breeding* Kajang (Malaysia) 2021, *International Seminar on Status of Oil Palm Tissue Culture Technology* Medan (Indonesia) 2018, *International Seminar on Gearing Oil Palm Breeding and Agronomy for Climate Change* Kuala Lumpur (Malaysia) 2015, *Colloquium on Harnessing the Oil Palm Genome for Breeding* Bali (Indonesia) 2014, *International Seminar on Oil Palm Breeding* Kuala Lumpur (Malaysia) 2013. **Publications** Proceedings.

Members Full (200) in 18 countries:

Cameroon, Colombia, Costa Rica, Ecuador, France, Germany, Ghana, India, Indonesia, Iran Islamic Rep, Malaysia, Mexico, Nigeria, Papua New Guinea, Philippines, Thailand, UK, USA. [2021/XD1857/**D**]

♦ **International Society for Olfaction and Chemical Sensing (ISOCS)** .. **15321**

Pres School of Engineering, Univ of Warwick, Coventry, CV4 7AL, UK.

Contact House of Associations, Boîte F2, 2 rue des Corroyeurs, 21068 Dijon CEDEX, France.

URL: http://www.olfactionsociety.org/

History May 2008, by GOSPEL – EU Network of Excellence in artificial olfaction. UK Registered Charity: 1151074. Registered under French law May 2017, no: W212009300. **Aims** Advance education of the public in general (and particularly among scientists) in the fields of olfaction and chemical sensing; promote research for the public benefit in all aspects of that subject and publish useful results. **Structure** Executive Board; Thematic Chairs; Steering Committee. **Finance** Members' dues. **Activities** Events/meetings; training/education. **Events** *International Symposium on Olfaction and Electronic Nose* 2025, *International Symposium on Olfaction and Electronic Nose* 2021, *International Symposium on Olfaction and Electronic Nose* Fukuoka (Japan) 2019, *International Symposium on Olfaction and Electronic Nose* Montréal, QC (Canada) 2017, *International Symposium on Olfaction and Electronic Nose* Dijon (France) 2015. [2019.06.27/XJ8963/**D**]

♦ **International Society of Olympic Historians (ISOH)** **15322**

SG Vogelrijd 16, 8428 HJ Fochteloo, Netherlands. T. +31516588520. Fax +31516588260. E-mail: isohsocial@outlook.com.

URL: http://www.isoh.org/

History 5 Dec 1991, London (UK). **Aims** Promote and study the history of the Olympic movement and the Olympic *Games.* **Structure** Executive Committee (meets annually). **Languages** English. **Staff** None. **Finance** Members' dues. Subvention by: *International Olympic Committee (IOC, #14408).* **Activities** Events/meetings. **Events** *Quadrennial meeting* London (UK) 2012, *Extraordinary Meeting* Vancouver, BC (Canada) 2010, *Quadrennial Meeting* Beijing (China) 2008, *Quadrennial meeting* Athens (Greece) 2004, *Quadrennial meeting* Sydney, NSW (Australia) 2000. **Publications** *The Journal of Olympic History* (3 a year).

Members Organizations in 22 countries and territories:

Australia, Canada, Estonia, Finland, Germany, Greece, Hong Kong, Iran Islamic Rep, Israel, Italy, Mexico, Netherlands, New Zealand, Poland, Portugal, Russia, Slovakia, Spain, Sweden, Switzerland, UK, USA.

Individuals in 52 countries and territories:

Argentina, Australia, Austria, Belgium, Botswana, Brazil, Bulgaria, Canada, China, Colombia, Cuba, Cyprus, Czechia, Denmark, Finland, France, Germany, Greece, Hungary, India, Iran Islamic Rep, Ireland, Israel, Italy, Japan, Latvia, Luxembourg, Malaysia, Mexico, Mongolia, Netherlands, New Zealand, Norway, Peru, Poland, Portugal, Puerto Rico, Qatar, Romania, Russia, Serbia, Singapore, Slovakia, Slovenia, South Africa, Spain, St Kitts-Nevis, Sweden, Switzerland, UK, Ukraine, USA. [2020/XD5215/**E**]

♦ International Society for Oncodevelopmental Biology and Medicine / see International Society for Oncology and BioMarkers (#15323)

♦ **International Society for Oncology and BioMarkers (ISOBM)** **15323**

Contact 14 City Quay, Dundee, DD1 3JA, UK.

URL: http://www.isobm.org/

History Founded 1972, Sapporo (Japan), as *International Research Group for Carcinoembryonic Proteins (IRGCP) – Groupe international de recherche sur les protéines carcinoembryoniques.* 1986, name changed to *International Society for Oncodevelopmental Biology and Medicine (ISOBM).* **Aims** Bridge the gap between basic science and clinical application; provide a unique forum for discussion and development of novel approaches to clinical problems in cancer; support good communication between scientific interests, clinicians and commercial groups. **Structure** Executive Board. **Languages** English. **Finance** Sources: members' dues. **Activities** Awards/prizes/competitions; events/meetings; research and development. **Events** *Annual Congress* Bled (Slovenia) 2022, *Annual Congress* Bled (Slovenia) 2021, *Annual Congress* Bled (Slovenia) 2020, *Annual Congress* Hamburg (Germany) 2018, *Annual Congress* Rio de Janeiro (Brazil) 2017. **Publications** *Tumor Biology* (6 a year) – scientific journal.

Members Ordinary; Senior; Honorary; Corporate. Individuals in 28 countries:

Argentina, Austria, Belgium, Brazil, Canada, China, Czechia, Denmark, Finland, France, Germany, Greece, Hungary, India, Israel, Italy, Japan, Korea Rep, Netherlands, Norway, Poland, Portugal, Russia, Slovakia, Spain, Sweden, Switzerland, UK, USA. [2019/XD6042/**C**]

♦ **International Society of Oncology Pharmacy Practitioners (ISOPP)** . **15324**

Main Office c/o Sea to Sky Inc, Ste 206, 201 Bewicke Ave, Vancouver BC V7M 3M7, Canada. E-mail: info@isopp.org.

URL: http://www.isopp.org/

History Aug 1988, Rotorua (New Zealand). Founded during 1st international meeting. Registration: Start date: 1996, Germany. **Aims** Promote and enhance oncology pharmacy practice worldwide through networking, education, research and advocacy in order to improve cancer patient care. **Structure** Board (Secretariat), comprising President, President-Elect, Treasurer, Secretary, 4 general members and 5 committee chairs (education; publications, including newsletter; research; standards; finance and membership). **Languages** English. **Staff** Part-time, voluntary. **Finance** Sources: meeting proceeds; members' dues. **Activities** Organizes: scientific meetings; workshops. **Events** *International Symposium on Oncology Pharmacy Practice* Seville (Spain) 2023, *International Symposium on Oncology Pharmacy Practice* 2022, *International Symposium on Oncology Pharmacy Practice* London (UK) 2019, *International Symposium on Oncology Pharmacy Practice* Santiago (Chile) 2016, *International Symposium on Oncology Pharmacy Practice* Montréal, QC (Canada) 2014. **Publications** *ISOPP Newsletter* (4 a year); *Journal of Oncology Pharmacy Practice (JOPP).* **Members** Full in about 40 countries. Membership countries not specified. [2023.02.17/XJ0706/**C**]

♦ **International Society of Oncoplastic Endocrine Surgeons (ISOPES)** . **15325**

Secretariat address not obtained. T. +8227657996. Fax +8230334417996. E-mail: isopes.hq@gmail.com.

URL: http://www.isopes.org/

History 20 Jun 2013. **Aims** Advance the science and art of oncoplastic endocrine surgery; maintain high standards in the practice and art of oncoplastic endocrine surgery; provide a forum for scientific presentations and discussions; encourage basic and clinical research in the field of oncoplastic endocrine surgery. **Structure** General Assembly; Board of Directors. Committees. **Events** *Congress* Seoul (Korea Rep) 2021, *Congress* Lucknow (India) 2019, *Congress* Hangzhou (China) 2017, *Congress* Hong Kong (Hong Kong) 2015, *Congress* Busan (Korea Rep) 2014. [2021/AA1858/**D**]

♦ International Society of Ondol (unconfirmed)

♦ International Society for Oneiric Mental Imagery Techniques (#19498)

♦ International Society of Ophthalmic Pathology (internationally oriented national body)

♦ International Society for Ophthalmic Ultrasound / see Societas Internationalis de Diagnostica Ultrasonica in Ophthalmologia (#19443)

♦ International Society on Optics Within Life Sciences / see OWLS Society (#17921)

♦ **International Society for Oral Laser Applications (SOLA International)** **15326**

Main Office c/o Univ Clinic of Dentistry, Sensengasse 2a, 1090 Vienna, Austria. T. +431400705401. E-mail: office@sola-laser.com.

Registered Office Griesgasse 2, 2340 Mödling, Austria.

URL: http://www.sola-laser.com/

History 24 Oct 1999, Austria. Former names and other names: *European Society for Oral Laser Applications (ESOLA)* – former. Registration: Austria. **Aims** Initiate, support and coordinate research and increase and spread knowledge in the use of lasers in dentistry and in oral/maxillofacial surgery, as well as propagate relevant equipment and techniques throughout the world. **Structure** Executive Board. **Languages** English, German. **Activities** Certification/accreditation; training/education. **Events** *Congress* Teheran (Iran Islamic Rep) 2017, *Congress / World Congress* Beijing (China) 2014, *Congress* Taipei (Taiwan) 2013, *Congress* Delhi (India) 2012, *Congress / World Congress* Vienna (Austria) 2009. **Members** Individual, Associate, Sustaining, Corporate, Honorary. Membership countries not specified. [2022.02.15/XD7807/**D**]

♦ International Society for Oral Literature in Africa / see International Society for the Oral Literatures of Africa (#15327)

♦ **International Society for the Oral Literatures of Africa (ISOLA)** **15327**

Société Internationale pour les Littératures Orales d'Afrique

Pres Univ of Fort Hare, Alice, 5701, South Africa. E-mail: rosopondo@gmail.com.

Sec address not obtained.

URL: http://www.africaisola.org/

History 23 Oct 1998, Cape Town (South Africa). Founded following earlier conferences held in 1991 and 1995. Former names and other names: *International Society for Oral Literature in Africa (ISOLA)* – former (1998 to 2006). **Aims** Celebrate, study and promote the oral arts of Africa. **Structure** General meeting; Council. **Languages** English, French. **Staff** 2.00 FTE, paid. **Finance** Sources: members' dues. **Events** *Conference* 2027, *Conference* 2025, *Conference* Paris (France) 2023, *Conference* Nairobi (Kenya) 2021, *Transitions, transformations, and translocations in African oral traditions and (re)imagined boundaries* Nairobi (Kenya) 2020. **Publications** Conference papers. **NGO Relations** Member of (1): *International Federation for Modern Languages and Literatures (#13480).* [2022.06.06/XD7770/**D**]

♦ International Society of Oral Oncology / see International Society for Oral Oncology (#15328)

♦ **International Society for Oral Oncology (ISOO)** **15328**

Sec Dept of Dentistry, Vennelyst Boulevard 9, Building 1613, 8000 Aarhus C, Denmark.

URL: http://www.mascc.org/isoo/

History 1984, as *'Society for Clinical and Experimental Oral Oncology'.* Title changed: 1985, to *'Society for Oral Oncology'*; and 1992, to *International Society of Oral Oncology.* Current title adopted 2006. Alliance with *Multinational Association of Supportive Care in Cancer (MASCC, #16895)*: formally implemented 1998; renewed 2008. **Aims** Promote scientific exchange among health care professionals in oncology, *cytotoxic* therapy and its impact on the oral environment. **Structure** Board of Directors, comprising President, Immediate Past-President, President-Elect, Treasurer, Secretary, Vice-President of Communications, 2 Members at Large and 2 Liaison members. **Events** *MASCC/JASCC/ISOO Annual Meeting* Nara (Japan) 2023, *International Symposium on Supportive Care in Cancer* Toronto, ON (Canada) 2022, *International Symposium on Supportive Care in Cancer* Seville (Spain) 2021, *International Symposium on Supportive Care in Cancer* Seville (Spain) 2020, *International Symposium on Supportive Care in Cancer* San Francisco, CA (USA) 2019. **Publications** *ISOO Newsletter.* **NGO Relations** Joint meetings with: *Multinational Association of Supportive Care in Cancer (MASCC, #16895).* [2017/XD5479/**C**]

♦ International Society for Orbital Disorders (no recent information)

♦ **International Society of Organbuilders (ISO)** **15329**

Société internationale de facteurs d'orgues

Main Office Langesthal 130, 4700 Eupen, Belgium. E-mail: info@iso-organ.org.

URL: https://www.international-organbuilders.com/

History 1957, Amsterdam (Netherlands). Registration: Belgium. **Structure** Board, comprising President, 2 Vice-Presidents, Treasurer and 5 members. Secretariat, headed by Secretary. **Languages** English, French, German. **Activities** Organizes: Congress (every 2 years); workshops; exchange of trainees. **Events** *World Congress of Organ Builders* Strasbourg (France) 2022, *Congress* Austria 2018, *Biennial Congress* London (UK) 2016, *Biennial Congress* Bucharest (Romania) 2014, *Biennial Congress* Switzerland 2012. **Publications** *ISO Journal* (3 a year) in English, French, German. Newsletter.
Members Manufacturers of organs and suppliers of organ parts (over 280) in 31 countries and territories:
Australia, Austria, Belgium, Canada, Croatia, Denmark, Estonia, Faeroe Is, Finland, France, Germany, Iceland, Ireland, Italy, Japan, Latvia, Lithuania, Luxembourg, Malta, Mexico, Netherlands, New Zealand, Norway, Poland, Portugal, Slovenia, Spain, Sweden, Switzerland, UK, USA. [2021/XD1698/**D**]

♦ International Society for Organ Donation and Procurement (ISODP) . 15330
Address not obtained.
URL: http://www.tts.org/isodp/
History 1990. Founded following earlier symposia. Formally incorporated, 2003. 2004, became section of *The Transplantation Society (TTS, #20224)*. Former names and other names: *International Society for Organ Sharing (ISOS)* – former (1990). **Aims** Foster, promote and develop all aspects of organ and tissue donation and procurement. **Structure** Council. **Activities** Events/meetings. **Events** *Congress* Dubai (United Arab Emirates) 2019, *Congress* Geneva (Switzerland) 2017, *Congress* Seoul (Korea Rep) 2015, *Congress* Sydney, NSW (Australia) 2013, *Congress* Buenos Aires (Argentina) 2011. [2017/XK2397/**E**]

♦ International Society of Organic Farming Research (ISOFAR) 15331
Internationale Gesellschaft der Forschung im ökologischen Landbau
Secretariat Thuenen-Institute of Organic Farming, Trenthorst 32, 23847 Westerau, Germany. T. +4945398880200. E-mail: isofar@isofar.online.
URL: http://www.isofar.org/
History Current statutes adopted Sep 2011, Korea Rep. Registration: No/ID: 30/299/82907, Germany. **Aims** Promote and support research in all areas of organic agriculture. **Structure** General Assembly (every 3 years); Board of Directors; Executive Board. **Languages** English, German. **Finance** Sources: members' dues. **Activities** Events/meetings; publishing activities. **Events** *Scientific conference on organic farming research* Adelaide, SA (Australia) 2005. **NGO Relations** Member of: *TP Organics – European Technology Platform (TP Organics, #20180)*. Partner of: *IFOAM Organics Europe (#11104)*. [2020/XM3019/**D**]

♦ International Society for the Organization of World Psychiatric Congresses (inactive)
♦ International Society for Organ Sharing / see International Society for Organ Donation and Procurement (#15330)

♦ International Society of Oriental Medicine (ISOM) 15332
Headquarters 26-27 Gayang-dong, Gangseo-gu, Seoul 157-801, Korea Rep. T. +82226575000. Fax +82226575005.
URL: http://www.isom.or.kr/
History 1976. Former names and other names: *International Oriental Medicine Society* – alias. **Aims** Develop oriental medicine through intensive research works; promote health and welfare of human beings through allegiance to objective of traditional medicine as advocated by WHO. **Structure** Board of Directors; Board of Executive Directors; Secretariat. Officers: President, 2 Vice-Presidents, Honorary President, Secretary-General, Vice-Secretary-General and Directors. **Languages** English. **Staff** 3.00 FTE, paid. **Finance** Members' dues. **Activities** Promotes research, mutual exchange and cooperation required for the development of oriental medicine. Gathers and disseminates information in the field. Provides specific medical service of oriental medicine. Undertakes a cooperative project related to oriental medicine on the initiative of WHO. **Events** *International Congress of Oriental Medicine (ICOM)* Korea Rep 2022, *Traditional Medicine evolving into Integrative Medicine* Seoul (Korea Rep) 2021, *Congress* Seoul (Korea Rep) 2020, *Congress* Ginowan (Japan) 2016, *The future of medicine, traditional medicine* Seoul (Korea Rep) 2012.
Members Full in 43 countries and territories:
Australia, Austria, Bangladesh, Bulgaria, Canada, China, Czechia, Ethiopia, Fiji, France, Germany, Greece, Hong Kong, Hungary, India, Iran Islamic Rep, Israel, Italy, Japan, Korea Rep, Mongolia, Myanmar, Netherlands, Nigeria, Pakistan, Philippines, Poland, Romania, Russia, Serbia, Singapore, Slovakia, Spain, Sri Lanka, Sweden, Switzerland, Taiwan, Tanzania UR, Thailand, Tunisia, UK, USA, Vietnam. [2022/XD7340/**D**]

♦ International Society for Oriental Research (no recent information)

♦ International Society for Orthodox Church Music (ISOCM) 15333
Chairman School of Theology, Univ of Eastern Finland, Joensuu Campus, PO Box 111, FI-80101 Joensuu, Finland.
Sec address not obtained.
URL: http://www.isocm.com/
History Founded 18 Jun 2005, Joensuu (Finland), during 1st International Conference on Orthodox Church Music. **Aims** Foster development and knowledge of church music traditions based on Byzantine and other Eastern Christian heritage; provide an open platform for different traditions, researchers, composers and chanters of Eastern rite church to communicate, exchange information and cooperate; promote communication between East and West. **Structure** Meeting (annual); Board. **Languages** English, Russian. **Staff** Voluntary. **Finance** Members' dues. **Activities** Meeting activities. **Events** *Church Music and Topography: City, Village, and Monastery* Joensuu (Finland) 2021, *The Sounds of the Holy: From Manuscript to Performance* Joensuu (Finland) 2019, *Conference* Joensuu (Finland) 2017, *Conference* Joensuu (Finland) 2015, *Conference* Joensuu (Finland) 2013. **Publications** *Journal of the International Society for Orthodox Church Music (JISOCM)*. Conference proceedings; anthologies.
Members Members (64) in 19 countries:
Austria, Bosnia-Herzegovina, Bulgaria, Canada, Cyprus, Finland, France, Greece, Mexico, Netherlands, Poland, Portugal, Romania, Russia, Serbia, Sweden, UK, Ukraine, USA. [2014.01.30/XM2709/**D**]

♦ International Society for Orthomolecular Medicine (ISOM) 15334
Contact 16 Florence Ave, Toronto ON M2N 1E9, Canada. T. +14167332117.
URL: https://isom.ca/
History 29 Apr 1994, Vancouver, BC (Canada). Former names and other names: *Associazione Internationale di Medicina Ortomolecolare (AIMO)* – former. Registration: Charity, No/ID: 845552355 RR 0001, Canada. **Aims** Further the advancement of orthomolecular medicine, using most appropriate nutrients – vitamins, minerals and other essential compounds – in most appropriate therapeutic amounts according to an individual's particular biochemical requirements in order to establish optimum health; raise awareness of this cost-effective means of health care and educate health professionals in the benefit and practice of it's use; unite groups operating in the field. **Languages** English. **Finance** Sources: members' dues. **Activities** Events/meetings. **Events** *Orthomolecular Medicine Today Conference* Toronto, ON (Canada) 2021, *Orthomolecular Medicine Today Conference* Vancouver, BC (Canada) 2019, *Annual Conference* Tokyo (Japan) 2018, *Annual Conference* Vancouver, BC (Canada) 2012, *Annual Conference* Vancouver, BC (Canada) 2011. **Publications** *Journal of Orthomolecular Medicine* (4 a year); *ISOM Newsletter* (2 a year). **Information Services** *ISOM International Referral Database*.
Members Organizations in 18 countries:
Algeria, Australia, Belgium, Brazil, Canada, Denmark, France, Germany, India, Italy, Japan, Korea Rep, Mexico, Netherlands, Spain, Switzerland, UK, USA. [2021/XD6271/**D**]

♦ International Society of Orthopaedic Surgery / see International Society of Orthopaedic Surgery and Traumatology (#15335)

♦ International Society of Orthopaedic Surgery and Traumatology ... 15335
Société internationale de chirurgie orthopédique et de traumatologie (SICOT)
SG Rue de la Loi 26 – bte 13, 1040 Brussels, Belgium. T. +3226486823. E-mail: hq@sicot.org.
Events Dept address not obtained. E-mail: congress@sicot.org.
URL: http://www.sicot.org/
History 10 Oct 1929, Paris (France). Statutes modified: 1996; 2002; 2009. Former names and other names: *International Society of Orthopaedic Surgery* – former (1929 to 1936); *Société internationale de chirurgie orthopédique* – former (1929 to 1936). Registration: Banque-Carrefour des Entreprises, No/ID: 0408.289.826, Start date: 13 Dec 1949, Belgium. **Aims** Advance the science and art of orthopaedics and traumatology at international level. **Structure** General Assembly (annual); International Council; Board of Directors; Executive Committee; Academies (2); Councils (2); Board of Subspecialties; Committees (20); Sub-specialty Committees (15). **Languages** English, French. **Staff** 3.00 FTE, paid. **Finance** Sources: meeting proceeds; members' dues. **Activities** Awards/prizes/competitions; events/meetings; research and development; training/education. **Events** *Orthopaedic World Congress* Cairo (Egypt) 2023, *Orthopaedic World Congress* Kuala Lumpur (Malaysia) 2022, *Orthopaedic World Congress* Budapest (Hungary) 2021, *Orthopaedic World Congress* Budapest (Hungary) 2020, *Orthopaedic World Congress* Muscat (Oman) 2019. **Publications** *International Orthopaedics* (12 a year) – journal; *SICOT e-Newsletter*, *SICOT e-Science Bulletin*; *SICOT-J* – journal SICOT Newsletter. Books.
Members Individuals (over 3,000): qualified orthopaedic surgeons and traumatologists actively engaged in the field, in 106 countries and territories:
Algeria, Argentina, Armenia, Australia, Austria, Azerbaijan, Bahrain, Belarus, Belgium, Bosnia-Herzegovina, Brazil, Bulgaria, Cameroon, Canada, Chile, China, Colombia, Congo DR, Côte d'Ivoire, Croatia, Cuba, Curaçao, Cyprus, Czechia, Denmark, Dominican Rep, Egypt, El Salvador, Estonia, Finland, France, Georgia, Germany, Greece, Guatemala, Haiti, Honduras, Hong Kong, Hungary, Iceland, India, Indonesia, Iran Islamic Rep, Iraq, Ireland, Israel, Italy, Japan, Jordan, Kenya, Korea Rep, Kuwait, Latvia, Lebanon, Libya, Luxembourg, Malaysia, Mauritania, Mexico, Mongolia, Montenegro, Morocco, Netherlands, New Zealand, Nicaragua, Nigeria, North Macedonia, Norway, Oman, Pakistan, Panama, Peru, Philippines, Poland, Portugal, Puerto Rico, Qatar, Romania, Russia, Saudi Arabia, Senegal, Serbia, Singapore, Slovakia, Slovenia, South Africa, Spain, Sri Lanka, Sweden, Switzerland, Syrian AR, Taiwan, Tanzania UR, Thailand, Togo, Trinidad-Tobago, Tunisia, Türkiye, UK, Ukraine, United Arab Emirates, USA, Venezuela, Vietnam, Yemen, Zambia.
Affiliated Societies (9) including 8 listed in this Yearbook:
Association for the Rational Treatment of Fractures (ARTOF, #02885); *International Federation of Paediatric Orthopaedic Societies (IFPOS, #13497)*; *International Musculoskeletal Laser Society (IMLAS, no recent information)*; *International Society for Minimal Intervention in Spinal Surgery (ISMISS, #15273)*; Orthopaedic Association of SAARC Countries (OASAC); *Société Internationale de Recherche Orthopédique et Traumatologique (SIROT, #19495)*; *World Federation of Hemophilia (WFH, #21437)*; *World Orthopaedic Concern (WOC, #21699)*; *World Society for Reconstructive Microsurgery (WSRM, #21811)*.
Consultative Status Consultative status granted from: *WHO (#20950)* (Official Relations). **IGO Relations** Cooperates with (1): *WHO (#20950)*. **NGO Relations** Member of (1): *Global Alliance for Musculoskeletal Health (G-MUSC, #10213)*. Cooperates with (1): *Bureau international des Médecins sans frontières (MSF International, #03366)*. Affiliated with (1): *Orthopedic Association of SAARC Countries (OASAC)*. Links with national organizations. [2022.10.11/XB2561/v/**B**]

♦ International Society for Orthopedagogics (inactive)

♦ International Society of Osteoarthritis Imaging (ISOAI) 15336
Contact 601 Albany Street, Ground Floor, Boston MA 02118, USA. T. +16176804473. E-mail: info@isoai.org.
URL: https://www.isoai.org/
History Registration: 501(c)(3) non-profit, USA. **Aims** Coordinate, promote and foster the advancement of scientific research and clinical practice in osteoarthritis imaging. **Structure** Board. **Activities** Events/meetings. **Events** *International Workshop for Osteoarthritis Imaging* Tokyo (Japan) 2022, *International Workshop for Osteoarthritis Imaging* Rotterdam (Netherlands) 2021, *International Workshop for Osteoarthritis Imaging* Rotterdam (Netherlands) 2020. **Publications** *International Journal on Osteoarthritis Imaging*. [2021/AA1711/**C**]

♦ International Society for Otological Surgery / see Politzer Society (#18424)
♦ International Society of Otoneurology (unconfirmed)
♦ International Society of Otorhinolaryngologic Allergy and Immunology / see International Society of Inflammation and Allergy of the Nose (#15201)

♦ International Society on Oxygen Transport to Tissue (ISOTT) 15337
Sec Inst of Physiology, Martin-Luther-Univ Halle, Magdeburger Str 6, 06112 Halle (Saale), Germany. T. +49345554048. Fax +493455574019.
URL: http://www.isott.org/
History 1973, Charleston SC (USA). **Aims** Facilitate exchange of scientific information among those interested in any aspect of oxygen transport in the body. **Structure** Executive Committee. **Languages** English. **Staff** None. **Finance** Sources: members' dues. **Events** *Annual Meeting* Ascona (Switzerland) 2021, *Annual Meeting* Ascona (Switzerland) 2020, *Annual Meeting* Albuquerque, NM (USA) 2019, *Annual Meeting* Seoul (Korea Rep) 2018, *Annual Meeting* Halle (Saale) (Germany) 2017. **Publications** Meeting proceedings.
Members Individuals in 31 countries:
Argentina, Australia, Austria, Belgium, Canada, Chile, China, Denmark, Finland, France, Germany, Greece, Hungary, Israel, Italy, Japan, Korea Rep, Mexico, Montenegro, Netherlands, New Zealand, Norway, Poland, Russia, Serbia, Spain, Sweden, Switzerland, Türkiye, UK, USA. [2020.03.03/XD1054/v/**C**]

♦ International Society of Paddy and Water Environment Engineering (PAWEES) 15338
SG Kinki Univ, Dept of Environmental Management – School of Agriculture, 3327-204 Nakamachi, Nara, 631-8505 Japan. T. +81742439264. Fax +81742431593.
URL: http://pawees.net/
History 1 Jan 2003. **Aims** Advance science and technology of paddy and water environmental disciplines so as to improve and rationalize *sustainable paddy farming* systems while protecting nature and environment, giving special attention to harmonization of nature, society and humans. **Structure** Executive Board, including President, 3 Vice-Presidents and Secretary General. Presidium, comprising President, Vice-Presidents, Immediate Past President and Secretary General. **Activities** Organizes conferences, symposia and/or workshops; encourages research and studies; offers awards and honours to contributors to the field. **Events** *International Conference* Seoul (Korea Rep) 2019, *International Conference* Nara (Japan) 2018, *Conference* Daejeon (Korea Rep) 2016, *Conference* Cheongju (Korea Rep) 2013, *Conference* Taipei (Taiwan) 2011. **Publications** *Paddy and Water Environment Journal (PWE)*.
Members Full; Corporate. National Society Members in 3 countries and territories:
Japan, Korea Rep, Taiwan.
NGO Relations *International Network for Water and Ecosystem in Paddy Fields (INWEPF, #14340)*. [2011/XJ2729/**D**]

♦ International Society of Paediatric Oncology 15339
Société internationale d'oncologie pédiatrique (SIOP) – Sociedad Internacional de Oncologia Pediatrica
Secretariat Industriestrasse 25, 6312 Steinhausen ZG, Switzerland. T. +41796879163. E-mail: info@siop-online.org.
SG Univ of Tennessee Health Science Center, 920 Madison Ave, Memphis TN 38163, USA. T. +19016085086.
URL: http://www.siop-online.org/
History 6 Nov 1969, Madrid (Spain), at first annual meeting, deriving from a *Paediatric Oncology Club – Club d'oncologie pédiatrique* formed 3 Jul 1967, Paris (France), and subsequently meeting 1968, Paris. Registered according to the Swiss Civil Code. **Aims** Increase knowledge about all aspects of childhood *cancer*. **Structure** General Meeting (annual, at Conference); Board; Scientific Committee; Continental branches (6): *SIOP Europe (SIOPE, #19288)*, South America, North America, Asia, Australia, Africa; Secretariat and Organizing Secretariat. **Languages** English. **Staff** 1.00 FTE, paid. **Finance** Sources: members' dues. **Activities** Events/meetings; research and development. **Events** *Annual Conference* Amsterdam (Netherlands) 2025, *Annual Conference* Honolulu, HI (USA) 2024, *Annual Conference* Ottawa, ON (Canada) 2023, *Annual Conference* Barcelona (Spain) 2022, *Asia Congress* Guangzhou (China) 2022. **Publications** *Pediatric Blood and Cancer* (12 a year) – official journal; *SIOP Newsletter* (2 a year).
Members Founding; Ordinary; Associate. Individuals (about 1,000) in 74 countries and territories:

Algeria, Argentina, Armenia, Australia, Austria, Bangladesh, Belarus, Belgium, Brazil, Bulgaria, Canada, Chile, China, Colombia, Costa Rica, Côte d'Ivoire, Croatia, Cuba, Cyprus, Czechia, Denmark, Ecuador, Egypt, Finland, France, Germany, Greece, Hong Kong, Hungary, Iceland, India, Iran Islamic Rep, Ireland, Israel, Italy, Japan, Jordan, Kenya, Korea DPR, Korea Rep, Kyrgyzstan, Malaysia, Mexico, Morocco, Netherlands, New Zealand, Norway, Pakistan, Paraguay, Peru, Philippines, Poland, Portugal, Romania, Russia, Saudi Arabia, Serbia, Singapore, Slovakia, Slovenia, South Africa, Spain, Sudan, Sweden, Switzerland, Taiwan, Trinidad-Tobago, Türkiye, UK, Ukraine, United Arab Emirates, Uruguay, USA, Venezuela.

Consultative Status Consultative status granted from: *WHO (#20950)* (Official Relations). **NGO Relations** Affiliate Society of: *International Pediatric Association (IPA, #14541).* [2019.02.12/XC3974/v/**C**]

♦ International Society of Paediatric Oncology European Neuroblastoma Research Network (SIOPEN-R-NET) 15340

Project Coordinator Children's Cancer Research Inst, Zimmermannplatz 10, 1090 Vienna, Austria. E-mail: rnm@siopen-r-net.org.
URL: https://www.siopen.net/

History 2009, with the support of *European Commission (EC, #06633)* – FP5. **Aims** Perform and facilitate clinical, translational and basic research in children and adolescents with neuroblastoma to improve the outcome of these patients through risk adapted strategies. **Structure** General Meeting (annual). **Languages** English. **Activities** Research/documentation. **Events** *Annual General Meeting* Barcelona (Spain) 2021, *Annual General Meeting* Barcelona (Spain) 2020, *Annual General Meeting* Berlin (Germany) 2017, *Annual General Meeting* Vienna (Austria) 2014, *Annual Meeting* Vienna (Austria) 2014.
Members Full in 30 countries and territories:
Australia, Austria, Belgium, Croatia, Czechia, Denmark, Finland, France, Germany, Greece, Hong Kong, Hungary, Iceland, Ireland, Israel, Italy, Japan, New Zealand, Norway, Poland, Portugal, Serbia, Singapore, Slovakia, Slovenia, Spain, Sweden, Switzerland, Türkiye, UK. [2021/XJ7363/**F**]

♦ International Society of Paediatric Surgical Oncology (IPSO) 15341

Sec c/o Surgery Centre for Children Pte Ltd, Mount Elisabeth Med. Centre Ste 10-08, 3 Mount Elisabeth, Singapore 228510, Singapore. E-mail: secretary@ipso-online.org.
URL: http://www.ipsosurgeons.org/

Events *Annual Congress* Singapore (Singapore) 2021, *Annual Congress* Lyon (France) 2019, *Annual Congress* Kyoto (Japan) 2018, *Annual Meeting* Washington, DC (USA) 2017, *Annual Congress* Dublin (Ireland) 2016. **Publications** *IPSO Newsletter* (2 a year). **NGO Relations** *International Society of Paediatric Oncology (#15339).* [2021/XD8940/**D**]

♦ International Society of Parametric Analysts / see International Cost Estimating and Analysis Association
♦ International Society of Parenteral Nutrition (inactive)

♦ International Society on Participatory Mapping (ISPM) 15342

Contact address not obtained. E-mail: contact@pmappingsociety.org.
URL: http://landscapevalues.org/ispm/

History 1 Jul 2017, Boston, MA (USA). Founded by Rudo Kemper, Dr Efraim D Roxas and Dr Charla M Burnett following first international conference on Participatory Mapping held at California Polytechnic University (USA). **Aims** Encourage and support the development, experimentation, evaluation, and application of participatory mapping methods globally so as to foster interaction and research in this scientific field; coordinate with other organizations in the study of participatory processes, mapping, and quantitative analyses. **Structure** Executive Committee. **Activities** Events/meetings; guidance/assistance/consulting; knowledge management/information dissemination; networking/liaising; publishing activities; research and development; training/education. **Events** *Conference* Espoo (Finland) 2019. [2023.02.15/AA0414/**C**]

♦ International Society for the Pastoral Care of Persons with Defective Hearing / see International Federation for the Pastoral Care to Hearing Impaired Persons (#13500)
♦ International Society for the Pastoral Care of Persons Hard of Hearing / see International Federation for the Pastoral Care to Hearing Impaired Persons (#13500)

♦ International Society for Pathophysiology (ISP) 15343

Société internationale de pathophysiologie

SG c/o Centre of Experimental Medicine, SAS, Dúbravská cesta 9, 841 04 Bratislava, Slovakia.
Pres address not obtained.
URL: https://ispweb.cc/

History 28 May 1991, Moscow (Russia). Founded at Constituent Congress. **Aims** Promote pathophysiology as a modern integrative *biomedical* science concerned with the basic mechanisms responsible for initiation, development, elimination and treatment of pathological processes; unite specialists of experimental physiology, clinical medicine and modern biology working on problems of human and animal pathophysiology; support research in pathophysiology; promote international collaboration and exchange of scientific information and experience obtained from pathophysiological studies and related fields of medical research throughout the medical and scientific community; support teaching of pathophysiology; develop ways to promote ISP goals, objectives, and accomplishments in the public media; by these activities contribute, in cooperation with other scientific societies, to better health in humans and animals. **Structure** General Assembly. Council, comprising 36 members. Executive Committee, consisting of President, Honorary President, Past President, 2 Vice-Presidents, Secretary General, Treasurer and Editor. **Languages** English. **Staff** 0.50 FTE, paid. **Finance** Sources: donations; members' dues. **Events** *International Congress of Pathophysiology* Moscow (Russia) 2022, *International Congress of Pathophysiology* Bratislava (Slovakia) 2018, *International Congress of Pathophysiology* Rabat (Morocco) 2014, *International Congress of Pathophysiology* Montréal, QC (Canada) 2010, *International symposium for pathophysiology teaching* Shanghai (China) 2009. **Publications** *Pathophysiology* (4 a year) – journal.
Members Individual (591); Collective (6, with total membership of 2,000 individuals). Members, totalling 2,591, in 54 countries:
Argentina, Armenia, Australia, Austria, Azerbaijan, Belarus, Brazil, Bulgaria, Canada, Chile, China, Croatia, Czechia, Denmark, Ethiopia, Finland, France, Georgia, Germany, Greece, Hungary, India, Indonesia, Iran Islamic Rep, Israel, Italy, Japan, Kazakhstan, Kyrgyzstan, Latvia, Moldova, Netherlands, New Zealand, Nigeria, Norway, Pakistan, Poland, Portugal, Romania, Russia, Serbia-Montenegro, Slovakia, Slovenia, South Africa, Sweden, Türkiye, Turkmenistan, UK, Ukraine, United Arab Emirates, Uruguay, USA, Uzbekistan, Vietnam.
NGO Relations Regional member of: *International Union of Physiological Sciences (IUPS, #15800). African Association of Physiological Sciences (AAPS, #00212)* is a member. [2020/XD2497/**B**]

♦ International Society for Pediatric and Adolescent Diabetes (ISPAD) 15344

Pres KIT Group GmbH, Assn and Conference Management Group, Kurfürstendamm 71, 10709 Berlin, Germany. T. +493024603210. Fax +493024603200. E-mail: secretariat@ispad.org.
SG Medical Director of Pediatric Diabetes, UH Rainbow Babies and Children's Hospital, 11100 Euclid Ave, Cleveland OH 44106, USA.
URL: http://www.ispad.org/

History 12 Jun 1974, Paris (France). Constitution and Regulations adopted: June 1976, Han-sur-Lesse (Belgium). Revised: May 1978, Netanya (Israel); Sep 1980, Palafrugell (Spain); 1988, Manly (Australia); Sep 1993, Athens (Greece), when present name adopted. New constitution approved: Sep 1995, Linköping (Sweden). Full revision of Constitution: Sep 2001, Siena (Italy). New constitution, 2008. Former names and other names: *International Study Group of Diabetes in Children and Adolescents (ISGD)* – former; *Groupe international d'étude du diabète de l'enfant et de l'adolescent* – former. Registration: Charity Commission, No/ID: 1126927, England and Wales. **Aims** Promote care of children and adolescents with all forms of diabetes; be an advocate for children and adolescents with diabetes; encourage and support basic, clinical, epidemiological, health, economic and all other relevant research concerning paediatric and adolescent diabetes. **Structure** Steering Committee; Advisory Council. **Languages** English. **Staff** Voluntary. **Finance** Members' dues, based on country of residence (World Bank classification). **Activities** Advocacy/lobbying/activism; events/meetings; research and development; training/education. **Events** *Annual Conference* Rotterdam (Netherlands) 2023, *Annual Conference* Abu Dhabi (United Arab Emirates) 2022, *Annual Conference* Lisbon (Portugal) 2021, *Annual Conference* Berlin (Germany) 2020, *Annual Meeting* Boston, MA (USA) 2019. **Publications** *Pediatric Diabetes* – official journal. *ISPAD Clinical Practice Consensus Guidelines* (2014).
Members Medical or paramedical personnel active in the field of paediatric, adolescent and young adult diabetology in 95 countries and territories:
Afghanistan, Albania, Algeria, Argentina, Armenia, Australia, Austria, Azerbaijan, Bangladesh, Barbados, Belarus, Belgium, Bolivia, Bosnia-Herzegovina, Brazil, Bulgaria, Canada, Chile, China, Colombia, Costa Rica, Croatia, Cuba, Cyprus, Czechia, Denmark, Dominican Rep, Ecuador, Egypt, Estonia, Fiji, Finland, France, Georgia, Germany, Ghana, Greece, Guinea, Hong Kong, Hungary, Iceland, India, Indonesia, Iraq, Ireland, Israel, Italy, Japan, Jordan, Kenya, Korea Rep, Kuwait, Latvia, Lebanon, Lithuania, Luxembourg, Malaysia, Mexico, Montenegro, Morocco, Netherlands, New Zealand, Nigeria, North Macedonia, Norway, Papua New Guinea, Peru, Philippines, Poland, Portugal, Puerto Rico, Romania, Russia, Saudi Arabia, Serbia, Singapore, Slovakia, Slovenia, South Africa, Spain, Sweden, Switzerland, Taiwan, Thailand, Tonga, Türkiye, Uganda, UK, United Arab Emirates, Uruguay, USA, Uzbekistan, Venezuela, Vietnam, Zimbabwe.
NGO Relations Member of (1): *European Foundation for the Study of Diabetes (EFSD, #07351).* [2023.02.20/XD6153/v/**C**]

♦ International Society of Pediatric Dermatology (ISPD) 15345

Sociedad Internacional de Dermatologia Pediatrica

Pres C/ Princesa 47, 28008 Madrid, Spain. T. +34912042600. E-mail: info@ispedderm.com.
URL: https://www.ispedderm.com/

History 18 Oct 1973, Mexico City (Mexico), when statutes were adopted. **Aims** Promote and improve pediatric dermatology for the general health of infants and adolescents, through: clinical practice; investigation; teaching; collaboration among members; consultation. Provide pediatric dermatologists with an opportunity to share their professional and personal experience and exchange and discuss clinical and scientific ideas. **Structure** General Assembly (every 3 years at Congress). Board. Executive Committee, consisting of 8 members. Officers: President, Secretary and Treasurer. Regional Delegates (6) for: Africa; Asia; Australasia; Europe; Central and North America; South America. **Languages** English. **Finance** Sources: members' dues. Annual budget: 6,000 USD. **Activities** Organizes conferences, courses and meetings, including triennial International Congress of Pediatric Dermatology. **Events** *World Congress* Edinburgh (UK) 2021, *World Congress* Chicago, IL (USA) 2017, *World Congress* Madrid (Spain) 2013, *World Congress* Bangkok (Thailand) 2009, *World Congress* Rome (Italy) 2004. **Publications** *Pediatric Dermatology Journal* (6 a year).
Members Full; Associate; Honorary. Individuals (330) in 41 countries:
Argentina, Australia, Austria, Belgium, Brazil, Canada, Colombia, Denmark, Egypt, El Salvador, France, Germany, Guatemala, Honduras, Hungary, India, Indonesia, Iran Islamic Rep, Ireland, Israel, Italy, Japan, Malaysia, Mexico, Netherlands, Nigeria, Peru, Philippines, Poland, Portugal, Puerto Rico, Serbia, South Africa, Spain, Sudan, Switzerland, Türkiye, UK, Uruguay, USA, Venezuela.
NGO Relations Member of: *International League of Dermatological Societies (ILDS, #14018).* [2020/XC0018/v/**C**]

♦ International Society of Pediatric Genetics (inactive)
♦ International Society for Pediatric Mechanical Cardiopulmonary Support (unconfirmed)

♦ International Society for Pediatric Neurosurgery (ISPN) 15346

Main Office c/o Kenes, Rue François-Versonnex 7, 1207 Geneva, Switzerland. E-mail: ispnoffice@kenes.com.
URL: http://www.ispneurosurgery.org/

History 1972, Chicago, IL (USA). **Aims** Serve as forum for communication among pediatric neurosurgeons and between them and basic scientists and specialists in related fields; serve as a medium for development of scientific knowledge, medical care, rehabilitation and prevention of disease in the area of pediatric neurosurgery; encourage high standards of training at an international level. **Structure** Annual Meeting. Executive Board, comprising President, President Elect, Secretary Treasurer and Annual Meeting Representative. Committees (13): Audit; Bylaws; Education; Ethics and Morals; Liaison; Membership; Nominations; Communications; Scientific Program; Ways and Means; Historian; Child's Nervous System; Web Site Subcommittee. **Languages** English. **Staff** None. **Finance** Sources: members' dues. **Activities** Events/meetings; training/education. **Events** *Annual Scientific Meeting* Lyon (France) 2025, *Annual Scientific Meeting* Toronto, ON (Canada) 2024, *Annual Scientific Meeting* Viña del Mar (Chile) 2023, *Annual Scientific Meeting* Singapore (Singapore) 2022, *Virtual Meeting* 2021. **Publications** *Child's Nervous System.*
Members Active; Candidate; Associate; Senior. Individuals in 42 countries and territories:
Algeria, Argentina, Australia, Austria, Brazil, Canada, Chile, China, Czechia, Denmark, Egypt, Finland, France, Germany, Hong Kong, India, Iran Islamic Rep, Ireland, Israel, Italy, Japan, Korea Rep, Kuwait, Mexico, Morocco, Netherlands, New Zealand, Nigeria, Norway, Panama, Poland, Romania, Russia, Saudi Arabia, Spain, Sweden, Switzerland, Taiwan, Türkiye, UK, USA, Venezuela. [2022/XD4604/v/**C**]

♦ International Society of Pediatric Ophthalmology (no recent information)
♦ International Society of Pediatric Surgeons / see World Federation of Associations of Pediatric Surgeons (#21411)

♦ International Society of Pediatric Wound Care (ISPeW) 15347

Organizing Secretariat CCI Centro Congressi Int'l, Via S Francesco da Paola 37, 10123 Turin TO, Italy.
URL: http://www.ispew.org/

History Oct 2011, Rome (Italy). **Aims** Set global standards for the assessment and treatment of pediatric wounds of varying etiologies; provide a forum for international, interprofessional collaboration among healthcare professionals, researchers, educators and industry leaders; promote and support clinical research focused on the prevention, assessment and treatment of pediatric wounds; provide evidence based pediatric wound care education. **Structure** Board. **Activities** Events/meetings; research/documentation; standards/guidelines; training/education. **Events** *Meeting* Houston, TX (USA) 2019, *Meeting* Rome (Italy) 2018, *Meeting* London (UK) 2017. [2019.07.12/XM6505/**C**]

♦ International Society for Pelviperineology (ISPP) 15348

CEO 24 Fisher Avenue, North, Wahroonga NSW 2076, Australia. E-mail: info@pelviperineology.com.
URL: http://www.pelviperineology.com/

History 1996, Australia. Former names and other names: *Association of Ambulatory Vaginal and Incontinence Surgeons (AAVIS)* – former (1996 to 2010). Registration: Australia, NSW. **Aims** Represent clinicians interested in the management of conditions relating to the pelvic floor and associated viscera. **Structure** Executive. **Languages** English. **Staff** 2.00 FTE, paid. **Finance** Sources: members' dues; sponsorship. **Activities** Events/meetings; training/education. **Events** *International Annual Congress on Pelvic Floor Disorders* 2021, *Annual Congress* Treviso (Italy) 2019, *Annual Conference* Bucharest (Romania) 2018, *Annual Conference* Hasselt (Belgium) 2017, *Annual Conference* Tel Aviv (Israel) 2016. **Publications** *Pelviperineology* – journal. [2021/XJ6277/**C**]

♦ International Society of Performance Analysis of Sport (unconfirmed)

♦ International Society of Performance Analysis of Sports Asia (ISPASA) 15349

SG Dept of Sport Studies, Fac of Educational Studies, Universiti Putra Malaysia, 43400 Serdang, Selangor, Malaysia. T. +60389468155. E-mail: admin@ispasa.org.
URL: http://www.ispasa.org/

History Founded as chapter of *International Society of Performance Analysis of Sport (ISPAS).* **Aims** Provide an infrastructure of professionalisation, information and training opportunities for all Performance Analysts, in the Asian and Australasian region. **Activities** Events/meetings; knowledge management/information dissemination. **Events** *Asia-Pacific Conference on Performance Analysis in Sport* Nagoya (Japan) 2019. [2019/AA0129/**E**]

♦ International Society for Performance Improvement (internationally oriented national body)
♦ International Society for the Performing Arts / see International Society for the Performing Arts Foundation (#15350)
♦ International Society of Performing Arts Administrators / see International Society for the Performing Arts Foundation (#15350)

♦ International Society for the Performing Arts Foundation (ISPA) . . . 15350

CEO 630 9th Ave, Ste 213, New York NY 10036-4752, USA. T. +12122068490. Fax +12122068603.
URL: http://www.ispa.org/

History 7 Mar 1949. Former names and other names: *International Association of Concert Managers* – former (7 Mar 1949 to 1970); *International Association of Concert and Festival Managers* – former (1970 to 1973); *International Society of Performing Arts Administrators (ISPAA)* – former (1973); *International Society for the Performing Arts* – former (1996); *Société internationale des administrateurs des arts et du spectacle* – former (1996). Registration: Start date: 7 Mar 1949, USA, New York. **Aims** Strengthen performing arts globally through advancement of leadership, exchange of ideas and fostering a diverse and engaged membership. **Structure** Congress (twice a year); Board; action-based Sub-Committees. **Languages** English. **Staff** 4.50 FTE, paid. **Finance** Annual budget: US$ 1,500,000. **Activities** Events/meetings; January Congress always held in New York NY (USA) and the International Congress rotates locations. **Events** *Congress* New York, NY (USA) 2024, *Congress* Perth, WA (Australia) 2024, *Congress* Manchester (UK) 2023, *Congress* New York, NY (USA) 2023, *Congress* Hong Kong (Hong Kong) 2022. **Publications** Membership directory (annual); newsletters. **Members** (526) in 60 countries. Membership countries not specified. **NGO Relations** Member of: *Association of Asia Pacific Performing Arts Centres (AAPPAC, #02387)*; *International Artist Managers' Association (IAMA, #11673)*.
[2020/XC0034/t/F]

♦ International Society of Perinatal Obstetricians (unconfirmed)

♦ International Society for the Perioperative Care of the Obese Patient (ISPCOP) 15351

Contact address not obtained. E-mail: ispcopmembership@gmail.com.
URL: http://www.ispcop.org/

History Registered in the State of Florida (USA). **Aims** Promote excellence in clinical management, research and education in the perioperative care of the obese patient; associate and affiliate into one organization, all physicians who are engaged in the practice of medicine dealing with the obese surgical patient, and non-physicians who are involved in the perioperative care of these individuals. **Structure** Board of Directors. **Languages** English. **Staff** 3.00 FTE, paid. **Finance** Sources: members' dues. **Activities** Events/meetings; knowledge management/information dissemination; standards/guidelines. **Publications** Articles; reports. **Members** Active; Resident/Fellow; Honorary; Affiliate; Emeritus; Inactive; Benefactor; Retired; Life. Members in about 25 countries. Membership countries not specified. **NGO Relations** *European Society for Perioperative Care of the Obese Patient (ESPCOP, #08694)*; *International Anesthesia Research Society (IARS)*; national organizations. [2019.02.24/XJ6894/C]

♦ International Society of Peripheral Neurophysiological Imaging (unconfirmed)

♦ International Society for Peritoneal Dialysis (ISPD) 15352

Society Coordinator Av des Arts 1-2, 1210 Brussels, Belgium. E-mail: admin@ispd.org.
URL: http://www.ispd.org/

History 1984. Former names and other names: *International Peritoneal Dialysis Organization* – former. **Aims** Increase global uptake, promote quality practice, and achieve optimal outcomes of peritoneal dialysis through enhanced advocacy, research, and education, in order to improve the health and well-being of people living with end-stage kidney disease or suffering from acute kidney injury. **Structure** Council; Executive Committee; Committees; Regional Chapters. **Languages** English. **Staff** 0.75 FTE, paid; 5.00 FTE, voluntary. Dozens of voluntary committee members all over the globe. **Finance** Sources: meeting proceeds; members' dues; sponsorship. **Activities** Events/meetings; financial and/or material support; publishing activities; research and development; training/education. **Events** *Biennial Congress* Dubai (United Arab Emirates) 2024, *Asia Pacific Chapter Meeting* New Delhi (India) 2023, *Biennial Congress* Singapore (Singapore) 2022, *Biennial Congress* 2021, *Latin American Chapter Meeting* Cartagena de Indias (Colombia) 2020. **Publications** *Peritoneal Dialysis International* (6 a year). **Members** Individuals; Institutions; Collective Membership; Corporate Members. Membership countries not specified. **NGO Relations** . [2022.06.20/XD9916/v/C]

♦ International Society of Personalized Medicine (internationally oriented national body)

♦ International Society for Pest Information (ISPI) 15353

Pres c/o JKI Inst for Plant Protection of Fruit Crops and Viticulture, Schwabenheimerstrasse 101, 69221 Dossenheim, Germany. E-mail: ispi@pestinfo.org.
URL: http://www.pestinfo.org/

History 31 Jan 2001, Darmstadt (Germany). Registered in accordance with German law. **Aims** Promote science and research in the area of pest management. **Structure** Executive Committee; Finance Committee; Technical Working Groups. **Staff** 5.00 FTE, paid. **Events** *Meeting* Dossenheim (Germany) 2020, *Meeting* Dossenheim (Germany) 2016, *Meeting* Frankfurt-Main (Germany) 2015, *Meeting* Göttingen (Germany) 2013, *Meeting* Dossenheim (Germany) 2012.
Members Individuals (22) in 9 countries:
Benin, Cameroon, China, Egypt, Germany, Ghana, India, Italy, USA. [2016.08.19/XD8827/D]

♦ International Society of Pharmaceutical Engineering / see ISPE (#16065)

♦ International Society for Pharmacoeconomics and Outcomes Research (ISPOR) 15354

Exec Dir 505 Lawrence Sq Blvd S, Lawrenceville NJ 08648, USA. T. +16095864981. E-mail: info@ispor.org.
URL: http://www.ispor.org/

History 1995. Former names and other names: *Association for Pharmacoeconomics and Outcomes Research (APOR)* – former (1995). **Aims** Promote the science of pharmacoeconomics (*health economics*) and outcomes research (the scientific discipline that evaluates the effect of health care interventions on patient well-being including clinical, economic and patient-centred outcomes) and facilitate the translation of this research into useful information for health care decision makers. **Structure** Board of Directors; Initiatives and Governance Groups; Special Interest Groups; Student Groups. Advisory Groups. Geographic Groups (3): Asia-Pacific, including *ISPOR Asia Consortium (#16066)*; Americas, including *ISPOR Latin America Consortium (#16067)*; Europe/Middle East/Africa, including Central and Eastern European Network, African Network and Arabic Network. **Languages** Arabic, Chinese, English, French, Polish, Portuguese, Russian, Spanish, Ukrainian. **Staff** 30.00 FTE, paid. **Activities** Events/meetings; research/documentation; training/education. **Events** *ISPOR Conference* Boston, MA (USA) 2023, *ISPOR Europe Conference* Copenhagen (Denmark) 2023, *ISPOR Europe Conference* Vienna (Austria) 2022, *ISPOR Conference* Washington, DC (USA) 2022, *Annual European Congress* 2020. **Publications** *ISPOR eBulletin* (12 a year); *ISPOR Connections* (6 a year) – journal; *ISPOR Student News*; *News Across Asia*; *News Across Central and Eastern Europe*; *News Across Latin America*; *Value in Health* – journal; *Value in Health Regional Issues*. *ISPOR Book of Terms (Lexicon)*; *ISPOR Taxonomy of Patient Registries: Classification, Characteristics and Terms*; *Reliability and Validity of Data Sources for Outcomes Research and Disease and Health Management Programs*; *Therapeutic and Diagnostic Device Outcomes Research*.
Members Full in 62 countries and territories:
Andorra, Argentina, Australia, Austria, Belgium, Bolivia, Brazil, Canada, China, Croatia, Czechia, Denmark, Egypt, Estonia, Finland, France, Germany, Greece, Hong Kong, Hungary, Iceland, India, Indonesia, Iran Islamic Rep, Ireland, Israel, Italy, Japan, Jordan, Korea DPR, Korea Rep, Latvia, Lebanon, Lithuania, Luxembourg, Malaysia, Malta, Mexico, Montenegro, Netherlands, New Zealand, Nigeria, Norway, Oman, Poland, Portugal, Puerto Rico, Russia, Saudi Arabia, Serbia, Singapore, Slovakia, Slovenia, South Africa, Spain, Sweden, Switzerland, Taiwan, Türkiye, UK, Ukraine, USA.
NGO Relations Member of: *European Patients' Academy on Therapeutic Innovation (EUPATI, #08170)*.
[2021/XN2375/C]

♦ International Society for Pharmacoepidemiology (ISPE) 15355

Exec Sec 4800 Hampden Ln, Ste 200, Bethesda MD 20814-2934, USA. T. +13017186500. Fax +13016560989. E-mail: info@pharmacoepi.org.
URL: http://www.pharmacoepi.org/

History 1989, New Jersey (USA). **Aims** Advance public health by providing a forum for the open exchange of scientific information and for the development of policy, education and advocacy for the field of pharmacoepidemiology. **Structure** Executive Committee; Board of Directors. Committees; Councils; Special Interest Groups; Student Chapters. Includes: *European Drug Utilization Research Group (EURODURG, #06948)*. **Languages** English. **Finance** Sources: meeting proceeds; members' dues. **Activities** Awards/prizes/competitions; events/meetings; research/documentation. **Events** *Annual Conference* Seattle, WA (USA) 2027, *Annual Conference* Berlin (Germany) 2024, *Annual Conference* Halifax, NS (Canada) 2023, *Mid-Year Meeting* Reykjavik (Iceland) 2023, *Asian Conference on Pharmacoepidemiology* Tainan (Taiwan) 2022. **Publications** *Pharmacoepidemiology and Drug Safety* – journal. **Members** Full (2,200) in 75 countries. Membership countries not specified. **NGO Relations** Member of (2): *Council for International Organizations of Medical Sciences (CIOMS, #04905)*; *International Network for Epidemiology in Policy (INEP, #14264)*.
[2021.03.18/XD7035/C]

♦ International Society of Pharmacometrics (internationally oriented national body)

♦ International Society of Pharmacovigilance (ISoP) 15356

Pres 140 Emmanuel Road, London, SW12 0HS, UK. T. +442032560027. Fax +442032560027. E-mail: administration@isoponline.org.
URL: http://www.isoponline.org/

History Former names and other names: *European Society of Pharmacovigilance (ESOP)* – former. **Aims** Foster pharmacovigilance both scientifically and educationally; enhance all aspects of the safe and proper use of medicines in all countries; serve as a forum for those interested in clinical and scientific aspects of drug safety. **Structure** Executive Committee; Advisory Board. **Languages** English. **Staff** 1.00 FTE, paid. **Finance** Sources: meeting proceeds; members' dues. Annual budget: 70,000 EUR. **Activities** Events/meetings; financial and/or material support; research/documentation; training/education. **Events** *Annual Meeting* Muscat (Oman) 2021, *Annual Meeting* Muscat (Oman) 2020, *Annual Meeting* Bogota (Colombia) 2019, *Annual Meeting* Geneva (Switzerland) 2018, *Annual Meeting* Liverpool (UK) 2017. **Publications** *ISoP Star* (2 a year); *Drug Safety* – official journal.
Members Academia, regulatory agencies, industry, practising health professionals and patients (830) in 101 countries and territories:
Algeria, Argentina, Australia, Austria, Bahrain, Bangladesh, Belgium, Benin, Bhutan, Bolivia, Botswana, Brazil, Bulgaria, Burkina Faso, Cambodia, Cameroon, Canada, Chile, Colombia, Congo Brazzaville, Costa Rica, Croatia, Czechia, Denmark, Ecuador, Egypt, Eritrea, Eswatini, Ethiopia, France, Georgia, Germany, Ghana, Greece, Guatemala, Guinea, Guinea-Bissau, Honduras, Hong Kong, Hungary, India, Indonesia, Iran Islamic Rep, Iraq, Ireland, Israel, Italy, Japan, Jordan, Kazakhstan, Kenya, Kuwait, Latvia, Lebanon, Liberia, Malawi, Malaysia, Mexico, Moldova, Morocco, Myanmar, Nepal, Netherlands, New Zealand, Nigeria, North Macedonia, Norway, Oman, Pakistan, Palestine, Panama, Peru, Philippines, Portugal, Romania, Russia, Saudi Arabia, Senegal, Serbia, Sierra Leone, Singapore, South Africa, Spain, Sri Lanka, Sudan, Sweden, Switzerland, Taiwan, Thailand, Togo, Trinidad-Tobago, Tunisia, Türkiye, Uganda, UK, Ukraine, United Arab Emirates, Uruguay, USA, Venezuela, Zimbabwe.
NGO Relations Member of (2): *Council for International Organizations of Medical Sciences (CIOMS, #04905)*; *European Association for Clinical Pharmacology and Therapeutics (EACPT, #05977)*.
[2021.02.17/XD8737/D]

♦ International Society of Phenomenology, Aesthetics and the Fine Arts (ISPAFA) 15357

Pres 1 Ivy Pointe Way, Hanover NH 03755, USA. T. +18022953487. Fax +18022955963.
URL: http://www.phenomenology.org/

History 1995, and affiliated to *World Phenomenology Institute (WPI, #21725)*. **Aims** Orchestrate the arts, especially those in which creative synergies enhance life aesthetics. **Finance** Members' dues. **Activities** Topics of interest include, but are not limited to, literature and music (i e opera, the art song), from text to performance, poetry and dance, the visual arts, stage design, architecture and human nature. Major activities include congresses worldwide on the ontopoeisis of life. Annual meetings in April, always in Cambridge MA (USA) since 1998. **Events** *Annual Meeting / Annual Congress* Cambridge, MA (USA) 2013, *Annual meeting / Annual Congress* Cambridge, MA (USA) 2008, *Annual meeting / Annual Congress* Cambridge, MA (USA) 2007, *Annual meeting* Cambridge, MA (USA) 2006, *Annual meeting* Cambridge, MA (USA) 2005. **Publications** *Phenomenological Inquiry* (annual); *Analecta Husserliana*.
Members Full in 37 countries:
Austria, Belgium, Brazil, Canada, Chile, China, Denmark, Egypt, Estonia, Finland, France, Germany, Greece, Holy See, Hungary, India, Israel, Italy, Japan, Kenya, Korea Rep, Latvia, Lithuania, Luxembourg, Mexico, Netherlands, Norway, Poland, Puerto Rico, Romania, Russia, Slovakia, Spain, Sweden, Switzerland, Tunisia, Zimbabwe. [2013/XK0678/E]

♦ International Society for Phenomenology and Literature (see: #21725)
♦ International Society for Phenomenology and the Sciences of Life (see: #21725)

♦ International Society for Philosophical Enquiry (ISPE) 15358

Pres 4196 Merchant Plaza, Suite 212, Woodbridge VA 22192, USA. E-mail: slevin@thousanders.com – president@thousanders.com.
URL: http://www.thethousand.com/

History 1974, Australia. Former names and other names: *The Thousand* – alias. Registration: USA. **Aims** Encourage individual *intellectual* growth and *creative* development of people of high *intelligence* in an environment of advanced studies, research and accomplishment. **Structure** Board of Trustees; Elected Officers; Key Appointed Volunteer Officers. **Languages** English. **Finance** Sources: members' dues. **Publications** *Telicom* (10 a year).
Members Individuals with IQ within the top one-tenth of 0.1 percentile of the general population in 62 countries and territories:
Argentina, Aruba, Australia, Austria, Bahamas, Barbados, Belgium, Belize, Bermuda, Bosnia-Herzegovina, Brazil, Canada, China, Colombia, Costa Rica, Croatia, Cyprus, Denmark, Dutch Caribbean, Egypt, England, Estonia, Finland, France, Germany, Greece, Hong Kong, Hungary, Iceland, India, Ireland, Israel, Italy, Japan, Jordan, Malta, Mexico, Montenegro, Morocco, Netherlands, New Zealand, Norway, Philippines, Poland, Portugal, Puerto Rico, Serbia, Singapore, Slovakia, South Africa, Spain, Sri Lanka, St Maarten, Sweden, Switzerland, Taiwan, Turkey, UK, Ukraine, United Arab Emirates, USA, Virgin Is USA.
[2022.11.08/XF1922/v/F]

♦ International Society for the Philosophy of Chemistry (ISPC) 15359

Contact Max Planck Institute for Mathematics in the Sciences, Inselstrasse 22, 04103 Leipzig, Germany.
URL: https://sites.google.com/site/socphilchem/home/

History Constitution adopted 7 Jul 1997. **Aims** Promote philosophy of chemistry. **Structure** Executive Committee. **Languages** English. **Staff** 9.00 FTE, voluntary. **Finance** Members' dues. **Activities** Events/meetings. **Events** *Conference* Buenos Aires (Argentina) 2023, *Conference* Lille (France) 2022, *Summer Symposium* Buenos Aires (Argentina) 2021, *Symposium* Buenos Aires (Argentina) 2021, *Summer Symposium* Buenos Aires (Argentina) 2020. **Publications** *Foundations of Chemistry*.
Members Individuals in 26 countries:
Argentina, Australia, Belgium, Brazil, Canada, China, Croatia, Denmark, Estonia, France, Germany, India, Indonesia, Iran Islamic Rep, Italy, Japan, Norway, Philippines, Poland, Russia, Saudi Arabia, Sweden, Switzerland, Taiwan, UK, USA.
[2022/XD7729/v/D]

♦ International Society for the Philosophy of Music Education (ISPME) 15360

Sec c/o NTU-NIE, Visual & Performing Arts, 50 Nanyang Avenue, Singapore 639798, Singapore. E-mail: ispme360@gmail.com.
URL: http://ispme.net/

History 1990, Bloomington, IN (USA). **Aims** Gather, consider, and disseminate ideas on the philosophy and practice of music as an integral part of music education; increase communications on philosophy among the various disciplines of the music profession that bear on education. **Structure** Executive Committee, comprising 2 Co-Chairs, Program Chair, Associate Program Chair, Recording Secretary and Treasurer. **Events** *Symposium* Oslo (Norway) 2023, *Symposium* Oslo (Norway) 2021, *Symposium* London, ON (Canada) 2019, *Symposium* Volos (Greece) 2017, *Symposium* Frankfurt-Main (Germany) 2015. **Publications** *Philosophy of Music Education Review* (2 a year). [2021/XJ4120/C]

♦ International Society of Phonetic Sciences (ISPhS) 15361

Société internationale des sciences phonétiques – Internationale Gesellschaft für Phonetische Wissenschaften

SG Speech Research Lab, Hungarian Acad of Sci, Benczúr u 33, Budapest 1068, Hungary. T. +3613214830ext172. Fax +3613229297.
Pres USF Communication Sci, 4202 E Fowler Ave, PCD 1017, Tampa FL 33647, USA. T. +18139743182. Fax +18139740822. E-mail: rbahr@usf.edu.
URL: http://www.isphs.org/

History Founded 6 Jan 1938, Amsterdam (Netherlands). Reorganized after 1945, and in its present form, 2 Mar 1961. **Aims** Establish and maintain a centre of information for phoneticians; develop contacts with kindred scientific organizations; promote training and research; effect practical application of phonetics in the teaching of foreign *languages*. **Structure** Assembly (every 4 years); Board of Directors; Council of Representatives; Executive Committee. **Languages** English. **Staff** Voluntary. **Finance** Sources: members' dues. Annual budget: 3,000 USD. **Activities** Awards/prizes/competitions; events/meetings. **Events** *International Congress of Phonetic Sciences* Saarbrücken (Germany) 2007, *Meeting* Prague (Czech Rep) 2004, *International Congress of Phonetic Sciences* Barcelona (Spain) 2003, *International Congress of Phonetic Sciences* San Francisco, CA (USA) 1999, *Meeting / Congress* Bellingham, WA (USA) 1998. **Publications** *Election to Fellow* (annual); *The Phonetician* (annual); *Kay Elemetrics Prize for Research in Phonetics* (every 2 years) – odd years; *Svend Smith Prize for Applied Phonetics Research* (every 2 years) – even years; *Society Honors* (every 4 years).
Members Full (150 individuals); Corporate or Affiliate (6); Corresponding (300 individuals) in 45 countries and territories:
Algeria, Argentina, Australia, Austria, Belgium, Brazil, Cameroon, Canada, Chile, Croatia, Czechia, Denmark, Estonia, Finland, France, Germany, Hungary, India, Ireland, Israel, Italy, Japan, Jordan, Latvia, Malta, Mauritius, Mexico, Morocco, Netherlands, Nigeria, Norway, Philippines, Poland, Romania, Russia, Saudi Arabia, Spain, Sweden, Switzerland, Taiwan, Türkiye, UK, Ukraine, USA, Venezuela. [2018.09.14/XC0106/**B**]

♦ International Society for Phosphoinositide Metabolism and Signalling (no recent information)
♦ International Society for Photogrammetry / see International Society for Photogrammetry and Remote Sensing (#15362)

♦ International Society for Photogrammetry and Remote Sensing (ISPRS) 15362

Société internationale de photogrammétrie et télédétection (SIPT) – Internationale Gesellschaft für Photogrammetrie und Fernerkundung (IGPF)

Pres Leibniz Univ Hannover, Inst Photogrammetry, Nienburger Str 1, 30167 Hannover, Germany. T. +495117622482. Fax +495117622483.
URL: http://www.isprs.org/

History 1910. Statutes adopted 1968; amended 2004, 2019. Former names and other names: *International Society for Photogrammetry (ISP)* – former (1910 to 1980); *Société internationale de photogrammétrie (SIP)* – former (1910 to 1980); *Internationale Gesellschaft für Photogrammetrie* – former (1910 to 1980). **Aims** Enhance international cooperation among organizations worldwide with interests in photogrammetry, remote sensing and spatial information sciences. **Structure** General Assembly (every 4 years, at Congress); Council (meets at least annually). Technical Commissions (5): Sensor Systems; Photogrammetry; Remote Sensing; Spatial Information Science; Education and Outreach. Financial Commission. Ad Hoc Committees. *ISPRS Foundation.* **Languages** English, French, German. **Staff** 0.50 FTE, paid. **Finance** Sources: members' dues. **Activities** Advocacy/lobbying/activism; events/meetings; research and development; training/education. **Events** *Quadrennial Congress* Toronto, ON (Canada) 2026, *Quadrennial Congress* Nice (France) 2022, *Quadrennial Congress* Hannover (Germany) 2021, *International Conference on Smart Data and Smart Cities* Stuttgart (Germany) 2021, *Meeting of the 2020 presentations of the 24th ISPRS Congress* Hannover (Germany) 2020. **Publications** *ISPRS Journal of Photogrammetry and Remote Sensing* (6 a year); *ISPRS Highlights* (3 a year) – electronic bulletin; *International Archives of Photogrammetry, Remote Sensing and Spatial Information Sciences. ISPRS Book Series.*
Members Ordinary: scientific and/or technical organizations (92) representing geographic areas; Associate: organizations (16) representing a community of photogrammetrists, remote sensing experts and/or spatial information experts not represented by the ordinary member of the country concerned; Regional: multinational associations (15) of photogrammetry and/or remote sensing organizations promoting regional cooperation; Sustaining: individuals, organizations, institutions or agencies (totalling 60 members) manufacturing or distributing instruments, equipment or supplies or operating or providing services in the field and/or undertaking research, and who contribute to the financial support of the Society; Honorary: individuals elected in recognition of distinguished services to ISPRS and its aims. Ordinary members in 92 countries and territories:
Ordinary members in 92 countries and territories:
Algeria, Argentina, Australia, Austria, Azerbaijan, Bangladesh, Belgium, Botswana, Brazil, Brunei Darussalam, Bulgaria, Burkina Faso, Cameroon, Canada, Chile, China, Colombia, Côte d'Ivoire, Croatia, Cuba, Cyprus, Czechia, Denmark, Egypt, El Salvador, Ethiopia, Finland, France, Germany, Ghana, Greece, Hong Kong, Hungary, India, Indonesia, Iran Islamic Rep, Iraq, Ireland, Israel, Italy, Japan, Jordan, Kenya, Korea Rep, Kuwait, Latvia, Libya, Lithuania, Malawi, Malaysia, Mexico, Mongolia, Morocco, Myanmar, Namibia, Nepal, Netherlands, New Zealand, Nigeria, Norway, Oman, Pakistan, Peru, Philippines, Poland, Portugal, Qatar, Romania, Russia, Saudi Arabia, Senegal, Slovakia, Slovenia, South Africa, Spain, Sri Lanka, Sweden, Switzerland, Syrian AR, Taiwan, Tanzania UR, Thailand, Türkiye, UK, Ukraine, United Arab Emirates, Uruguay, USA, Uzbekistan, Venezuela, Vietnam, Zimbabwe.
Associate members (15) in 14 countries and territories:
Azerbaijan, Chile, Colombia, Côte d'Ivoire, Iran Islamic Rep, Italy, Korea Rep, Morocco, Myanmar, Pakistan, Peru, Russia, Taiwan, Thailand.
Regional members (14), listed in this Yearbook:
African Association of Remote Sensing of the Environment (AARSE, #00216); African Regional Centre for Space Science and Technology Education – English (ARCSSTE-E, #00431); African Regional Institute for Geospatial Information Science and Technology (AFRIGIST, #00433); Asian Association on Remote Sensing (AARS, #01336); Association of Geographic Information Laboratories for Europe (AGILE, #02622); Centre for Space Science and Technology Education in Asia and the Pacific /Affiliated to the United Nations/ (CSSTEAP, see: #04277); EIS-AFRICA (#05402); European Association of Remote Sensing Laboratories (EARSeL, #06191); European Spatial Data Research (EuroSDR, #08806); Pacific GIS and Remote Sensing Council (PGRSC); Pan American Institute of Geography and History (PAIGH, #18113); Regional Centre for Mapping of Resources for Development (RCMRD, #18757); Regional Remote Sensing Centre for North African States (#18807); Sociedad Especialistas Latinoamericana en Percepción Remota (SELPER, #19358).
Sustaining members in 27 countries and territories:
Australia, Austria, Brazil, Bulgaria, Canada, China, Denmark, Germany, Hong Kong, India, Iran Islamic Rep, Israel, Italy, Japan, Kenya, Netherlands, Palestine, Portugal, Russia, Saudi Arabia, Serbia, Sweden, Switzerland, Türkiye, UK, United Arab Emirates, USA.
Honorary members in 8 countries:
Australia, China, Germany, Japan, Switzerland, Türkiye, UK, USA.
Consultative Status Consultative status granted from: *ECOSOC (#05331)* (Ros C). **IGO Relations** Observer status with (1): *Committee on the Peaceful Uses of Outer Space (COPUOS, #04277).* Member of (1): *International Committee on Global Navigation Satellite Systems (ICG, #12775).* Partner of (1): *United Nations Committee of Experts on Global Geospatial Information Management (UN-GGIM, #20540).* Cooperates with (1): *United Nations Office for Outer Space Affairs (UNOOSA, #20601).* Consultative relations with: *UNESCO (#20322).* Associated with Department of Global Communications of the United Nations. **NGO Relations** Member of (1): *International Science Council (ISC, #14796).* Cooperates with (6): *Geo-Information for Disaster Management (Gi4DM); International Association for Pattern Recognition (IAPR, #12069); International Geographical Union (IGU, #13713)* (Spatial Data Handling); *International Society of Biomechanics (ISB, #14966); International Union of Forest Research Organizations (IUFRO, #15774); SPIE (#19919).* Represented in: *Committee on Space Research (COSPAR, #04287).* In liaison with technical committees of: *International Organization for Standardization (ISO, #14473).* Liaises with: *EIS-AFRICA (#05402); International Council on Monuments and Sites (ICOMOS, #13049).* Formal agreement with: *Committee on Earth Observation Satellites (CEOS, #04249).* Represented on the management body of: *CIPA Heritage Documentation (CIPA, #03929).* [2023/XB2496/y/**B**]

♦ International Society of Photosynthesis Research (ISPR) 15363

Secretary Dept of Biochemistry, Univ of Otago, PO Box 56, 710 Cumberland Street, Dunedin 9054, New Zealand. T. +6434797865. E-mail: secretary@photosynthesis-research.org.
Pres School of Life Sciences, Arizona State Univ, PO Box 874501, 427 E Tyler Mall, Tempe AZ 85287-4501, USA. T. +14809656250. E-mail: president@photosynthesis-research.org.
URL: https://www.photosynthesis-research.org/

History 1968, Germany FR. Former names and other names: *International Photosynthesis Committee* – former (1968 to 1995); *Comité international de photosynthèse* – former (1968 to 1995). **Aims** Promote communication and cooperation in research devoted to photosynthesis and related disciplines. **Structure** Officers (3); elected Area Representatives (12). **Languages** English. **Staff** None. **Finance** Sources: donations; grants; members' dues. Other sources: registration fees. **Activities** Events/meetings. **Events** *International Congress on Photosynthesis Research* Dunedin (New Zealand) 2022, *Quadrennial Congress* New Zealand 2020, *Triennial Congress* Maastricht (Netherlands) 2016, *Triennial Congress* St Louis, MO (USA) 2013, *Triennial congress* Beijing (China) 2010. **Publications** *Photosynthesis Research Journal.* Congress proceedings.
Members Individuals in 49 countries and territories:
Argentina, Australia, Austria, Azerbaijan, Belgium, Botswana, Brazil, Bulgaria, Canada, Chile, China, Croatia, Czechia, Denmark, Egypt, Estonia, Finland, France, Germany, Greece, Hungary, India, Ireland, Israel, Italy, Japan, Korea Rep, Mexico, Netherlands, New Zealand, Norway, Panama, Philippines, Poland, Portugal, Romania, Russia, Saudi Arabia, Singapore, Slovakia, South Africa, Spain, Sweden, Switzerland, Taiwan, UK, Ukraine, United Arab Emirates, USA. [2021.09.07/XD6170/v/**C**]

♦ International Society of Phthirapterists (ISoP) 15364

Pres School Biological Sciences, Univ of Utah, 257 S 1400 E, Salt Lake City UT 84112, USA.
Sec Texas A&M Univ, Dept Ecology and Conservation Biology, 534 Kimbrough Blvd., College Station TX 77843, USA.
URL: http://phthiraptera.info/

Aims Advance the study of Phthiraptera (lice) and *louse*-borne *diseases* in all its aspects of theory, principles, methodology and practice. **Structure** Council, comprising officers (President, Program Chairperson, Secretary, Treasurer, Editor) and 2 General Councillors. **Finance** Sources: members' dues. **Events** *International Congress on Phthiraptera* Guangzhou (China) 2022, *International Congress on Phthiraptera* Brno (Czechia) 2018, *International Congress on Phthiraptera* Park City, UT (USA) 2014, *International congress on phthiraptera* Ürgüp (Turkey) 2010, *International Congress on Phthiraptera* Buenos Aires (Argentina) 2006. **Members** Individual clinicians, veterinary scientists, evolutionary biologists and taxonomists working on various aspects of parasitic louse biology (about 100). Membership countries not specified. [2021.09.09/XJ0513/**C**]

♦ International Society for Physical Activity and Health (ISPAH) 15365

Sec address not obtained. E-mail: info@ispah.org.
Pres Dept of Sports Science and Clinical Biomechanics, SDU, Campusvej 55, 5230 Odense, Denmark.
URL: http://www.ispah.org/

History By-laws adopted, 18 Feb 2008. Incorporated in the State of Illinois (USA), 2008. **Aims** Advance health through the scientific study and promotion of physical activity. **Structure** Board of Governors; Executive Committee. Councils (4): Global Advocacy for Physical Activity (GAPA) / Advocacy Council; Physical Activity Interventions (PAI); Physical Activity and Obesity (PAO); Environment and Physical Activity (CEPA). **Events** *Congress* Abu Dhabi (United Arab Emirates) 2022, *Holistic approach to health and wellness through physical activity* Vancouver, BC (Canada) 2021, *Holistic approach to health and wellness through physical activity* Vancouver, BC (Canada) 2020, *Congress* London (UK) 2018, *Congress* Bangkok (Thailand) 2016. **Publications** *GlobalPANet Newsletter* (bi-weekly); *Journal of Physical Activity and Health.* [2020/XJ0678/**B**]

♦ International Society of Physical Medicine (inactive)

♦ International Society of Physical and Rehabilitation Medicine (ISPRM) 15366

Exec Dir c/o AIM Group, Via G Ripamonti 129, 20141 Milan MI, Italy. E-mail: isprmoffice@aimgroup.eu.
URL: http://www.isprm.org/

History 13 Nov 1999. Founded by merger of *International Federation of Physical Medicine and Rehabilitation (IFPMR, inactive)* and *International Rehabilitation Medicine Association (IRMA, inactive).* **Aims** Continuously improve PRM practice and facilitate PRM input in international health organizations to contribute to optimal functioning and quality of life of people experiencing disability. **Structure** President's Cabinet; Executive Committee; Assembly of Delegates; Committees, Task Forces and Special Interest Groups. **Languages** English. **Staff** 3.00 FTE, paid. **Finance** Sources: meeting proceeds; members' dues; sponsorship. **Activities** Events/meetings; networking/liaising; politics/policy/regulatory; training/education. **Events** *World Congress* Cartagena de Indias (Colombia) 2023, *World Congress* Lisbon (Portugal) 2022, *World Congress* Milan (Italy) 2021, *World Congress* Orlando, FL (USA) 2020, *World Congress* Kobe (Japan) 2019. **Publications** *News and Views* (6 a year) – newsletter; *Journal of International Society of Physical and Rehabilitation Medicine (JISPRM); Journal of Rehabilitation Medicine.* **Members** Individuals (35,000); national societies (62). Membership countries not specified. **Consultative Status** Consultative status granted from: *WHO (#20950)* (Official Relations). **IGO Relations** Accredited by (1): *United Nations Office at Vienna (UNOV, #20604).* **NGO Relations** Member of (1): *International Industry Society in Advanced Rehabilitation Technology (IISART, #13840).* Instrumental in setting up (1): *Global Rehabilitation Alliance (#10565).* [2023/XB0007/**B**]

♦ International Society of Physiological Anthropology / see International Association of Physiological Anthropology (#12086)

♦ International Society of Pituitary Surgeons (ISPS) 15367

Contact Neurosurgery Emory Med School, 1365B Clifton Rd, MS B6169C, Atlanta GA 30322, USA. E-mail: noyesik@emory.edu.
URL: http://www.ispsurgeons.org/

History 1983. **Events** *Meeting* San Diego, CA (USA) 2018, *Meeting* Liverpool (UK) 2015, *Meeting* Mumbai (India) 2013, *Meeting* Montréal, QC (Canada) 2012, *Meeting* Sonoma, CA (USA) 2010. [2018/XM3627/**D**]

♦ International Society of Planetarium Educators / see International Planetarium Society (#14588)

♦ International Society for Plant Anaerobiosis (ISPA) 15368

Exec Sec address not obtained. E-mail: serres@ucr.edu.
URL: http://www.is-pa.org/

History 1985, following a series of symposia on plant anaerobiosis since 1975. **Aims** Increase understanding of responses of plants to impeded aeration. **Structure** General Meeting. Executive Committee, comprising President, Honorary President or Past President, Executive Secretary, Membership Secretary, Treasurer, Website Manager and International Conference Director. International Advisory Panel. **Finance** Members' dues. **Events** *Triennial Conference* Helsingør (Denmark) 2016, *Triennial Conference* Los Baños (Philippines) 2013, *Triennial Conference* Volterra (Italy) 2010, *Conference* Matsushima (Japan) 2007, *Triennial Conference* Sendai (Japan) 2007. [2014/XM1956/**D**]

♦ International Society for the Planting and Protection of Trees / see International Tree Foundation
♦ International Society of Plant Molecular Biology (inactive)

♦ International Society for Plant Molecular Farming (ISPMF) 15369

Sec address not obtained. E-mail: daoustma@medicago.com.
Pres address not obtained.
URL: http://www.ispmf.org/

History Current constitution adopted Feb 2014. **Aims** Promote and support excellence in research, scholarship and practice in plant molecular farming. **Structure** General Meeting; Management Committee. **Finance** Sources: members' dues. **Events** *Conference* 2021, *Conference* Helsinki (Finland) 2018.
Members Full (nearly 200) in 21 countries:
Australia, Austria, Belgium, Canada, China, Czechia, Denmark, Finland, Germany, Iceland, Iran Islamic Rep, Italy, Korea Rep, Malaysia, Norway, Portugal, South Africa, Spain, Sweden, UK, USA. [2019/XM7931/**C**]

♦ International Society of Plant Morphologists (ISPM) 15370

Société internationale des morphologistes de la vie végétale

Sec-Treas Dept of Botany, Univ of Delhi, Delhi 110007, DELHI 110007, India. E-mail: phytomorphology@gmail.com – phytomorphology@ispm.co.in.
URL: http://www.ispm.co.in/

History 4 Jan 1951, Bangalore (India). Founded at Pan-Indian Ocean Sciences Congress. Registration: Societies Registration Act XXI of 1860, India. **Aims** Promote international cooperation in the study and diffusion of useful knowledge in the fields of descriptive and experimental plant morphology, anatomy and *embryology, histochemistry* and *ultrastructure.* **Structure** Executive Council. **Languages** English. **Staff** 1.00 FTE, paid. **Finance** Sources: members' dues. **Activities** Publishing activities; research and development; research/documentation. **Publications** *Phytomorphology* (4 a year). *Plant Tissue and Organ Culture; Recent Advances in the Embryology of Angiosperms.*
Members Ordinary; Life. Organizations and individuals in 24 countries:
Australia, Bangladesh, Canada, China, Egypt, France, Germany, Greece, India, Israel, Italy, Japan, Korea Rep, Netherlands, New Zealand, Nigeria, Norway, Poland, Russia, Singapore, Spain, Switzerland, UK, USA. [2022.06.15/XC2564/**C**]

♦ International Society for Plant Pathology (ISPP) 15371

Société internationale de phytopathologie – Sociedad Internacional de Fitopatologia

Business Manager Largo Paolo Braccini 2, 10095 Grugliasco TO, Italy.
Sec Univ of Pretoria, Office 2-29 Agricultural Bldg, Lunnon Rd, Pretoria, 0028, South Africa. T. +27124206471. E-mail: ispp.secretary@isppweb.org.
URL: http://www.isppweb.org/

History 26 Jul 1968, UK. New statutes adopted 1981. **Aims** Promote development of plant pathology by initiating and maintaining international cooperation. **Structure** General Assembly; Council. Executive Committee; Secretariat; Committees. **Languages** English. **Staff** 5.00 FTE, paid. **Finance** Sources: gifts, legacies; grants; members' dues; sale of publications. **Activities** Awards/prizes/competitions; events/meetings; research/documentation. **Events** *International Congress of Plant Pathology (ICPP)* Gold Coast, QLD (Australia) 2028, *International Congress of Plant Pathology (ICPP)* Lyon (France) 2023, *International Plant Virus Epidemiology Symposium* Madrid (Spain) 2022, *International Plant Virus Epidemiology Symposium* Seoul (Korea Rep) 2019, *International Congress of Plant Pathology* Boston, MA (USA) 2018. **Publications** *ISPP Newsletter* (12 a year); *Food Security* – journal.

Members Affiliated national societies in 50 countries and territories:
Argentina, Australia, Bangladesh, Belgium, Brazil, Canada, Chile, China, Colombia, Denmark, Egypt, Ethiopia, Finland, France, Germany, Greece, Hungary, India, Indonesia, Iran Islamic Rep, Ireland, Israel, Italy, Japan, Kenya, Korea Rep, Kyrgyzstan, Malaysia, Mexico, Morocco, Netherlands, Nigeria, Norway, Pakistan, Peru, Philippines, Poland, Portugal, Russia, Serbia, South Africa, Spain, Sudan, Sweden, Switzerland, Taiwan, Thailand, UK, USA, Venezuela.
Regional societies (8), listed in this Yearbook:
Arab Society for Plant Protection (ASPP, #01049); Asian Association of Societies for Plant Pathology (AASPP, #01339); Asociación Latinoamericana de Fitopatologia (ALF, #02223); Association of Applied Biologists (AAB); Australasian Plant Pathology Society (APPS); International Committee on Taxonomy of Viruses (ICTV, see: #15794); Mediterranean Phytopathological Union (MPU, #16672); Southern African Society for Plant Pathology (SASPP, #19863).
Affiliated international societies (7), listed in this Yearbook:
European Society of Nematologists (ESN, #08661); International Mycological Association (IMA, #14203); International Organization for Mycoplasmology (IOM, #14456); International Society for Horticultural Science (ISHS, #15180); International Society of Sugar Cane Technologists (ISSCT, #15495); International Union of Forest Research Organizations (IUFRO, #15774); Society of Nematologists (SON, #19604).
Consultative Status Consultative status granted from: *ECOSOC (#05331)* (Ros C); *FAO (#09260)* (Liaison Status). **IGO Relations** *European and Mediterranean Plant Protection Organization (EPPO, #07773).* **NGO Relations** Member of: *International Association of Botanical and Mycological Societies (IABMS, #11730); International Union of Biological Sciences (IUBS, #15760); International Union of Microbiological Societies (IUMS, #15794).* [2023/XC5789/y/**B**]

♦ International Society for Plasma Medicine (ISPM) 15372

Sec Leibniz Inst for Plasma Science and Technology, Felix-Hausdorff-Straße 2, 17489 Greifswald, Germany. T. +4938345543915. Fax +493834554301.
URL: http://plasmamedizin.com/

History 2009. Founded to formalize the activities of the *International Conference of Plasma Medicine (ICPM).* **Structure** General Assembly; Board of Directors; Executive Committee. **Activities** Advocacy/lobbying/activism; events/meetings; training/education. **Events** *ICPM: International Conference on Plasma Medicine* Utrecht (Netherlands) 2022, *ICPM: International Conference on Plasma Medicine* Seoul (Korea Rep) 2021, *International Conference on Plasma Medicine* Philadelphia, PA (USA) 2018, *International Conference on Plasma Medicine* Bratislava (Slovakia) 2016, *International Conference on Plasma Medicine* Nara (Japan) 2014. **Publications** *Plasma Medicine.* [2022/AA2749/**C**]

♦ International Society of Plastic Engineers (no recent information)
♦ International Society of Plastic Regenerative Surgery (internationally oriented national body)

♦ International Society for Plastination (ISP) 15373

Pres Univ of Toledo, College of Medicine and Life Sciences, Dept of Neurosciences, Mail Stop 1007, Health Science Campus, 3000 Arlington Ave, Toledo OH 43614-2598, USA. T. +14193834283. Fax +14193833008.
Treas address not obtained. T. +15207907737ext360.
URL: http://isp.plastination.org/

History Founded 1986, San Antonio TX (USA), by Dr Harmon Bickley, during the 3rd International Conference on Plastination. **Aims** Provide for and maintain an international association for individuals and institutions who perform plastination techniques, or are interested in plastination preservation methods; serve as a forum for the exchange of information about plastination; define plastination as a specialty area of professional activity, encourage other institutions to adopt plastination *preservation* methods, and invite individuals to learn and practice plastination as a career in the sciences. **Structure** Council; Executive Committee; Permanent Committees. **Languages** English. **Finance** Members' dues. **Activities** Events/meetings. **Events** *International Conference on Plastination* Temuco (Chile) 2022, *International Conference on Plastination* Dalian (China) 2018, *International Conference on Plastination* Toledo, OH (USA) 2016, *Interim Meeting on Plastination* Vitória (Brazil) 2015, *International Conference on Plastination* St Petersburg (Russia) 2014. **Publications** *Journal of Plastination* (1-2 a year).

Members Regular; Associate; Distinguished; Emeritus. Individuals in 56 countries and territories:
Albania, Australia, Austria, Bahrain, Belize, Bolivia, Brazil, Canada, Chile, China, Colombia, Denmark, Egypt, Estonia, France, Georgia, Germany, Greece, Grenada, Hong Kong, Hungary, Iceland, India, Indonesia, Iran Islamic Rep, Ireland, Italy, Japan, Jordan, Latvia, Lebanon, Maldives, Mexico, Moldova, Netherlands, New Zealand, North Macedonia, Norway, Oman, Peru, Poland, Puerto Rico, Romania, Serbia, Slovakia, Slovenia, South Africa, Spain, Sweden, Switzerland, Taiwan, Thailand, Uganda, UK, Ukraine, USA. [2016.06.01/XD4592/**D**]

♦ International Society of Political Psychology (ISPP) 15374

Société internationale de psychologie politique

Exec Dir PO Box 1213, Columbus NC 28722, USA. T. +18288945422. E-mail: info@ispp.org.
URL: http://www.ispp.org/

History Jan 1978, Camarillo, CA (USA). Registration: Non-profit 501(c)(3), No/ID: 95-3325946., Start date: 1979, USA, CA. **Aims** Represent all fields of inquiry concerned with exploring the relationships between political and psychological processes. **Structure** Governing Council. **Languages** English. **Staff** 2.00 FTE, paid. **Finance** Sources: meeting proceeds; members' dues; sale of publications. **Activities** Awards/prizes/competitions; events/meetings. **Events** *Annual Conference* Montréal, QC (Canada) 2023, *Annual Conference* Athens (Greece) 2022, *Annual Conference* Montréal, QC (Canada) 2021, *Annual Conference* Columbus, NC (USA) 2020, *Annual Conference* Lisbon (Portugal) 2019. **Publications** *Political Psychology* (6 a year) – journal; *Advances in Political Psychology* (annual); *ISPP News* (9-10 a year) – newsletter. **Members** Individuals (about 1,100) in over 70 countries. Membership countries not specified. [2022.02.09/XD6724/v/**F**]

♦ International Society for Polycyclic Aromatic Compounds (ISPAC) . 15375

Sec Dept of Fisheries and Oceans, Bedford Inst of Oceanography, Dartmouth NS B2Y 4A2, Canada. E-mail: chris.marvin@ec.gc.ca.
URL: http://www.ispac.org/

History 1991, on merger of activities of *International Committee on Polycyclic Aromatic Compounds (ICPAC),* founded 1985 and *International Symposium on Polynuclear Aromatic Hydrocarbons,* organized since 1976. **Aims** Encourage research on, review, compile and disseminate information on and provide leadership in the field of polycyclic aromatic compounds by: providing fora for presentation and discussion of new methodologies and development of technology for research in the field; encouraging excellence in research; encouraging and facilitating exchange of information and providing information; identifying a comprehensive set of properties for identification and characterization of polycyclic aromatic compounds, ascertaining which data are currently available and compiling that data into usable format. **Structure** Board of Directors (11 members). Officers: President; President-Elect; Secretary; Treasurer. **Languages** English. **Staff** None. **Finance** Members' dues. Other sources: donations; proceeds from symposium. **Events** *Biennial Symposium* Corvallis, OR (USA) 2013, *Biennial Symposium* Münster (Germany) 2011, *Biennial Symposium* Charleston, SC (USA) 2009, *Biennial Symposium* Trondheim (Norway) 2007, *Biennial Symposium* Toronto, ON (Canada) 2005. **Publications** *Polycyclic Aromatic Compounds* – journal.

Members Individuals in 17 countries:
Canada, Czechia, Denmark, Estonia, Finland, France, Germany, Ireland, Italy, Japan, Netherlands, Norway, Poland, Sweden, Switzerland, UK, USA. [2012.06.01/XD3786/v/**D**]

♦ International Society for Porous Media (InterPore) 15376

Managing Dir Groenekanseweg 128, 3731 AK De Bilt, Netherlands. T. +31302537464. Fax +31302534900.
Exec Officer address not obtained.
URL: http://www.interpore.org/

History 2008. **Aims** Advance and disseminate knowledge for the understanding, description, and modelling of natural and industrial porous media systems. **Structure** Council. Executive Committee, comprising President, President-Elect, Immediate Past-President, Managing Director and Treasurer. Committees (4): Publicity; Honors and Awards; Elections; Meetings. **Languages** English. **Staff** 1.50 FTE, paid. **Finance** Sources: members' dues. **Activities** Organizes: Annual meeting; workshops; short courses. **Events** *International Conference on Porous Media* Edinburgh (UK) 2023, *International Conference on Porous Media* Abu Dhabi (United Arab Emirates) 2022, *International Conference on Porous Media* Edinburgh (UK) 2021, *International Conference on Porous Media* Qingdao (China) 2020, *International Conference on Porous Media* Valencia (Spain) 2019. **Publications** *InterPore Newsletter* (24 a year). [2019/XJ7183/**C**]

♦ International Society of Portuguese Philately (ISPP) 15377

Sec/Treas 1491 Bonnie View Rd, Hollister CA 95023-5117, USA. E-mail: cjh1491@sbcglobal.net.
Pres PO Box 43146, Philadelphia PA 19129, USA.
URL: http://www.portugalstamps.com/

History 1961. **Aims** Promote and encourage the study and collection of philatelic material of Portugal and her past and present *overseas territories.* **Structure** A unit of American Philatelic Society. Officers: President; Secretary; Treasurer. Directors. **Finance** Members' dues. **Publications** *Portu-Info* (4 a year).

Members Individuals (mainly in North America) in 32 countries and territories:
Angola, Argentina, Australia, Austria, Belgium, Brazil, Canada, Cape Verde, Central African Rep, Denmark, Finland, France, Germany, Hong Kong, Indonesia, Israel, Italy, Luxembourg, Macau, Mexico, Mozambique, Netherlands, New Zealand, Norway, Portugal, Puerto Rico, Sao Tomé-Principe, South Africa, Spain, Sweden, UK, USA. [2016/XE3950/v/**E**]

♦ International Society of Postmasters (inactive)

♦ International Society for Postural and Gait Research (ISPGR) 15378

Société internationale de recherche sur la posture et la marche

Contact 2661 Queenswood Drive, Victoria BC V8N 1X6, Canada. T. +12504727644. Fax +12504727664. E-mail: ispgr@ispgr.org.
URL: http://www.ispgr.org/

History Founded 1969, Amsterdam (Netherlands), as *International Society of Posturography.* Current name adopted 1983. **Aims** Present and discuss the latest research and clinical findings relating to control of posture and gait and related disorders; facilitate interaction between members; promote the broad discipline of posture and gait research. **Structure** General Assembly (every 2 years, at Business Meeting); Executive Board. **Languages** English. **Staff** 1.00 FTE, paid. **Finance** Members' dues. Other sources: registration fees; sponsorships; exhibitor registrations. **Activities** Events/meetings. **Events** *World Congress* Montréal, QC (Canada) 2022, *World Congress* Edinburgh (UK) 2019, *World Congress* Fort Lauderdale, FL (USA) 2017, *World Congress* Seville (Spain) 2015, *World Congress* Vancouver, BC (Canada) 2014.

Members Individuals in 27 countries and territories:
Argentina, Australia, Austria, Belgium, Brazil, Bulgaria, Canada, China, Czechia, Denmark, France, Germany, Hong Kong, Ireland, Israel, Italy, Japan, Netherlands, New Zealand, Norway, Poland, Portugal, Spain, Sweden, Switzerland, UK, USA. [2017/XF5971/**F**]

♦ International Society of Posturography / see International Society for Postural and Gait Research (#15378)

♦ International Society of Precision Agriculture (ISPA) 15379

Sec 109 East Main St, Monticello IL 61856-1968, USA. T. +12177627955. E-mail: info@ispag.org.
URL: http://www.ispag.org/

History 2010, Denver, CO (USA). Registration: USA, Illinois. **Aims** Advance the science of precision agriculture globally. **Structure** Officers: President; President-Elect; Secretary; Treasurer. Country Representatives. **Languages** English. **Staff** 1.00 FTE, paid. **Activities** Events/meetings; knowledge management/information dissemination. **Events** *European Conference on Precision Agriculture (ECPA)* Bologna (Italy) 2023, *Congreso Latinoamericano de Agricultura de Precisión (CLAP)* Córdoba (Argentina) 2022, *International Conference on Precision Agriculture* Minneapolis, MN (USA) 2022, *African Conference on Precision Agriculture* Nairobi (Kenya) 2022, *Asian-Australian Conference on Precision Agriculture (ACPA)* 2021. **Publications** *ISPA e-newsletter* (4 a year); *Precision Agriculture* – journal. **Members** Individuals (400) in 51 countries. Membership countries not specified. **NGO Relations** Cooperates with (1): *African Plant Nutrition Institute (APNI, #00418).* [2021/XJ5846/**C**]

♦ International Society of Precision Cancer Medicine (ISPCM) 15380

Main Office Rm 11629 SNUH, 101 Daehak-ro, Jongno-gu, Seoul 03080, Korea Rep. T. +82220723143. Fax +8227411901. E-mail: ispcm2017@naver.com.
URL: http://www.ispcm.org/

History Launched following 1st International Conference for Precision Cancer Medicine (ICPCM), held Jun 2017, Tokyo (Japan). **Aims** Contribute to the eradication of cancer through innovative research and active exchange of knowledge. **Structure** Council; Executive Committee; Board. **Languages** English. **Finance** Sources: members' dues. **Activities** Events/meetings; research and development. **Events** *Annual Meeting* Seoul (Korea Rep) 2021, *Annual Meeting* Seoul (Korea Rep) 2020, *Annual Meeting* Tokyo (Japan) 2020, *Annual Meeting* Seoul (Korea Rep) 2019, *Annual Meeting* Busan (Korea Rep) 2018. [2020.02.18/XM8308/**C**]

♦ International Society for Prenatal Diagnosis (ISPD) 15381

Exec Dir 154 Hansen Rd, Ste 201, Charlottesville VA 22911, USA. T. +14349794773. Fax +14349771856. E-mail: info@ispdhome.org.
URL: http://www.ispdhome.org/

History 1996. Derived from meetings of the International Congresses on Early Prenatal Diagnosis (which became the current series of ISPD congresses). Original meetings convened in the UK with the purpose of serving as an exchange for the evolving procedure of chorionic villus sampling. This initial goal expanded in response to need of the international scientific community for focused communication in the discipline. **Aims** Bring together medical and scientific professionals with interests and expertise in clinical and research aspects of prenatal diagnosis and *fetal* care. **Structure** Board. **Languages** English. **Staff** Provided by US company. **Finance** Sources: contributions; fees for services; grants; meeting proceeds; members' dues. **Activities** Events/meetings; training/education. **Events** *International Conference on Prenatal Diagnosis and Therapy* Edinburgh (UK) 2023, *International Conference on Prenatal Diagnosis and Therapy* Montréal, QC (Canada) 2022, *International Conference on Prenatal Diagnosis and Therapy* 2021, *International Conference on Prenatal Diagnosis and Therapy* Montréal, QC (Canada) 2020, *Congress* Singapore (Singapore) 2019. **Publications** *Prenatal Diagnosis.*

Members Full in 44 countries and territories:
Albania, Argentina, Australia, Belgium, Brazil, Canada, Chile, China, Czechia, Denmark, Egypt, France, Germany, Greece, Hong Kong, Hungary, India, Iran Islamic Rep, Ireland, Israel, Italy, Jamaica, Japan, Korea Rep, Latvia, Mexico, Netherlands, New Zealand, Panama, Peru, Poland, Portugal, Qatar, Romania, Russia, Singapore, Slovakia, Spain, Sweden, Taiwan, UK, Ukraine, Uruguay, USA. [2021.06.15/XD7194/**D**]

♦ International Society for Prenatal and Perinatal Psychology and Medicine / see International Society for Pre- and Perinatal Psychology and Medicine (#15382)

♦ International Society for Pre- and Perinatal Psychology and Medicine (ISPPM) 15382

Internationale Gesellschaft für Prä- und Perinatale Psychologie und Medizin

Main Office Limburger Str 33, 65604 Elz, Germany. E-mail: info@isppm.ngo.
URL: https://isppm.ngo/

History 20 Jul 1971, Vienna (Austria). Statutes adopted 20 Jul 1973, Paris (France); modified 31 Mar 1978, Salzburg. Juridical status refounded in 2010. Former names and other names: *International Study Group for Prenatal Psychology* – former; *Internationale Studiengemeinschaft für Pränatale Psychologie (ISPP)* – former; *International Society for Prenatal and Perinatal Psychology and Medicine* – former; *Internationale Gesellschaft für Pränatale und Perinatale Psychologie und Medizin* – former. Registration: Start date: 31 Oct 2010,

Germany. **Aims** Support the fundamental idea that the psychological and physical development of the human being must be understood as an indivisible whole from conception until death. **Structure** Board; Extended Board. **Languages** English, German. **Staff** Voluntary. **Finance** Members' dues. **Events** *Prenatal Sciences Global Conference* 2022, *Congress* Stolpen (Germany) 2016, *Congress* Berlin (Germany) 2015, *Congress / Annual Conference* Maastricht (Netherlands) 2014, *Congress / Annual Conference* Stolpen (Germany) 2013. **Publications** *International Journal for Prenatal and Perinatal Psychology and Medicine* (4 a year). Yearbook, in German.
Members Gynaecologists, obstetricians, neonatologists, paediatricians, endocrinologists, midwives, birth educators, sociologists, therapists and counselors (240) in 18 countries:
Austria, Brazil, China, France, Germany, Greece, Hungary, India, Israel, Italy, Netherlands, Norway, Poland, Russia, Sweden, Switzerland, Thailand, USA. [2014.06.23/XD7893/v/**D**]

♦ International Society for Presence Research (ISPR) 15383

Pres Dept of BTMM, Temple Univ, Annenberg Hall 011-00, Philadelphia PA 19122, USA. T. +12152047182. Fax +12152045402.
URL: http://ispr.info/
History Jan 2002. **Aims** Support academic research related to the concept of (tele) presence, defined as an illusion of non-mediation in which users of any technology overlook or misconstrue its role in their experience. **Structure** Board of Directors. **Events** *Conference* Orlando, FL (USA) 2020, *Annual Workshop* Prague (Czechia) 2018, *Conference* Vienna (Austria) 2016, *Annual Workshop* Vienna (Austria) 2014, *Annual Workshop* Philadelphia, PA (USA) 2012. [2016/XJ3088/**D**]

♦ International Society for Preservation of the Tropical Rainforest (ISPTR) 15384

Sociedad Internacional para la Conservación del Bosque Tropical
CEO/Exec Dir/Founder 72902 Raymond Way, Twentynine Palms CA 92277, USA. T. +13103039050. E-mail: pard_expeditions@yahoo.com.
URL: http://isptr.org/
History Founded 1986. Commenced simultaneously with *Preservation of the Amazonian River Dolphin (ISPTR/PARD)*, also referred to as *PARD*. Registered in accordance with Peruvian law, 1990. Registered in accordance with US law. **Aims** Promote, through education, sustainable positive alternatives to native people in the tropical rainforests of South America; purchase, preserve and protect land in pristine tropical rainforest to conserve for future generations; patrol rivers with the Environmental Forest Police to stop illegal commercial fishing, logging and animal poaching; distribute free medicines. **Languages** English, Quechua (macrolanguage), Spanish. **Staff** 16.00 FTE, voluntary. **Finance** Private donations; grants. Annual budget: US$ 50,000. **Activities** Research/documentation; training/education; awareness raising; advocacy/lobbying/activism. **Events** *International dolphin conference* Iquitos (Peru) 2005. **Publications** *Amazon Frontline* (2-3 a year). Videos; information packets.
Members Honorary Directors; Directors; Supporting. Individuals in 13 countries:
Belgium, Brazil, China, Denmark, Germany, Italy, Mexico, Peru, Spain, Sweden, Switzerland, UK, USA.
NGO Relations Member of: *EarthAction (EA, #05159)*. [2019.06.25/XF5430/v/**F**]

♦ International Society for Prevention of Child Abuse and Neglect (ISPCAN) 15385

CEO 8547 E Arapahoe Rd, Unit J-384, Greenwood Village CO 80112, USA. E-mail: execdirector@ispcan.org – memberships@ispcan.org.
URL: http://www.ispcan.org/
History 7 Jul 1977, Geneva (Switzerland). Founded by Dr C Henry Kempe. Former names and other names: *Société internationale pour la prévention des mauvais traitements et négligences envers les enfants* – former. Registration: Section 501(c)(3), USA, Colorado. **Aims** Empower professionals to lead in the global effort to prevent child abuse and neglect with access to the latest information, best practices and a multidisciplinary worldwide network. **Structure** Board of Directors **Languages** Arabic, Chinese, Dutch, English, French, Russian, Spanish. **Staff** 4.00 FTE, paid. **Finance** Sources: contributions; fundraising; grants; in-kind support; meeting proceeds; members' dues; private foundations; revenue from activities/projects; sale of publications. **Activities** Events/meetings; training/education. **Events** *Europe Congress* Edinburgh (UK) 2023, *Americas Congress* Québec, QC (Canada) 2022, *Europe Congress* Tallinn (Estonia) 2022, *Biennial Congress* Adelaide, SA (Australia) 2021, *World Summit* USA 2021. **Publications** *Child Abuse and Neglect: The International Journal* (12 a year); *Child Protection and Practice* (12 a year) – launched 2023; *World Perspectives* (every 5 years); *ISPCAN News* – newsletter.
Members Individuals, group memberships and Country Partners in over 90 countries. Member countries not specified.
Over 90 countries are represented in our membership via individual memberships, group memberships or Country Partners.
Consultative Status Consultative status granted from: *WHO (#20950)* (Official Relations); *UNICEF (#20332)*.
IGO Relations Partner of (3): Centers for Disease Control and Prevention; *UNICEF (#20332)*; *WHO (#20950)*. Consultative status with national organizations. **NGO Relations** Partner of (11): *Alliance for Child Protection in Humanitarian Action (The Alliance, #00667)*; *Arigatou International*; *Child Helpline International (CHI, #03870)*; *End Child Prostitution, Child Pornography and Trafficking of Children for Sexual Purposes (ECPAT, #05456)*; *Global Partnership to End Violence Against Children (End Violence Against Children, #10533)*; *International Centre for Missing and Exploited Children (ICMEC, #12505)*; *International Pediatric Association (IPA, #14541)*; *International Society for Social Pediatrics and Child Health (ISSOP, #15448)*; *Together for Girls*; *WePROTECT Global Alliance (#20860)*; *World Vision International (WVI, #21904)*. Also links with various national organizations. [2023.01.27/XD9205/v/**B**]

♦ International Society for the Prevention of Iatrogenic Complications (inactive)

♦ International Society for the Prevention and Mitigation of Natural Hazards (ISPMNH) 15386

Contact Inst of Geodynamics, Nat Observatory of Athens, PO Box 20048, 118 10 Athens, Greece. T. +302103490165 – +302103490195. Fax +302103490165 – +302103490180.
Contact Natural Hazards Society, PO Box 49511, 80 Glen Shields Avenue, Concord ON L4K 4P6, Canada.
History 9 Aug 1988, Enseñada (Mexico). Also known as *International Natural Hazards Society (INHS)*. **Aims** Promote research in all aspects of natural hazards; assist in distribution of national preparedness and emergency-response plans worldwide; assist in drawing up and implementing education programmes on hazard prevention and mitigation. **Finance** Members' dues: General US$ 30; Student US$ 10; Corporate US$ 150 (minimum). **Activities** Organizes international symposia about every 2 years. **Events** *International symposium on natural and technological hazards / International Symposium* Hyderabad (India) 2004, *International symposium on natural and technological hazards / International Symposium* Antalya (Turkey) 2002, *International symposium on natural and technological hazards / International Symposium* Tokushima (Japan) 2000, *International symposium on natural and technological hazards / International Symposium* Qingdao (China) 1993, *International symposium on natural and technological hazards / International Symposium* Perugia (Italy) 1991. **Publications** *Natural Hazards: An International Journal of Hazards Research and Prevention* (regular).
Members Individuals; societies; institutes; laboratories; groups; organizations. International scientists and policy makers actively engaged in natural hazards studies or in the prevention and mitigation of natural disasters. Membership countries not specified. [2013/XD1830/**D**]

♦ International Society for the Prevention of Tobacco Induced Diseases (PTID Society) 15387

Pres Center for Global Tobacco Control, Harvard School of Public Health, 401 Park Drive, 4th West Landmark Center, Boston MA 02215, USA.
URL: http://www.isptid.org/
History Oct 2000, Essen (Germany), by Prof Dr Ed Nelson. Registered in accordance with German law. **Aims** Foster scientific medical studies and any effort to prevent tobacco-abuse, tobacco-addiction and tobacco-induced and/or worsened diseases in humans; foster scientific medical studies and any effort to prevent induced and/or worsened diseases through involuntary passive smoking; facilitate communication and dissemination of knowledge among scientists involved in such studies; promote and foster public health education. **Structure** General Meeting (annual). Executive Committee of up to 15 members, including President, Secretary, Treasurer and 5 further members. **Languages** English. **Finance** Sources: contributions; donations; meeting proceeds; members' dues; sale of publications. **Activities** Committees (3): Membership; Nomination; Publication. Sections (7): Behavioural Psychology; Clinical Sciences; Epidemiology; Laboratory Sciences; Law Practice; School Health Education; Social Sciences. **Events** *Annual Meeting* Brussels (Belgium) 2016, *Annual Meeting* Athens (Greece) 2013, *Annual Meeting* Daegu (Korea Rep) 2012, *Annual meeting* Vienna (Austria) 2011, *Annual meeting* Boston, MA (USA) 2010. **Publications** *PTID Newsletter*, *Tobacco Induced Diseases* – international journal.
Members Individuals in 17 countries and territories:
Australia, Canada, Denmark, Finland, France, Germany, Hong Kong, India, Iran Islamic Rep, Italy, Japan, Jordan, New Zealand, Norway, Philippines, Poland, USA. [2013/XD8309/v/**C**]

♦ International Society for Preventive Oncology (no recent information)

♦ International Society on Priorities in Health Care 15388

Address not obtained.
URL: http://www.org.uib.no/healthcarepriorities/
History 1996. **Aims** Provide forum for policy makers, researchers, practitioners and others involved in priority setting to exchange ideas and practical experiences on priority setting methods and approaches; promote application and dissemination of good practices in priority setting; promote informed understanding among politicians, policy makers, health professionals, managers, patients, the media and the general public of priority setting; encourage research and disseminate research findings and other information or knowledge on priority setting. **Structure** Annual Meeting. Management Committee (meets at least every 2 years) of 14 members including officers (Chairman, Deputy Chairman, Secretary and Treasurer). Executive Committee; Standing Committees. **Languages** English. **Finance** Members' dues. **Events** *Biennial Conference* Melbourne, VIC (Australia) 2014, *Biennial Conference* Cape Town (South Africa) 2010, *Biennial Conference* Gateshead (UK) 2008, *Biennial Conference* Newcastle upon Tyne (UK) 2008, *Biennial Conference* Toronto, ON (Canada) 2006.
Members Individual; Student; Non-Profit Institutional; Corporate. Individuals in 15 countries:
Argentina, Belgium, Canada, Finland, Israel, Kenya, Netherlands, New Zealand, Norway, Portugal, Sweden, Switzerland, Uganda, UK, USA.
Corporate members in 8 countries:
Canada, Germany, Israel, Netherlands, New Zealand, Norway, Sweden, UK. [2014/XD7759/**D**]

♦ International Society for Product Innovation Management / see International Society for Professional Innovation Management (#15389)
♦ International Society for Productivity Enhancement / see International Society of Transdisciplinary Engineering (#15514)
♦ International Society for Productivity and Quality Research (no recent information)
♦ International Society of Professional Auditorium Administrators / see International Association of Venue Managers
♦ International Society of Professional Heilpaedagogic Organizations (#13240)

♦ International Society for Professional Innovation Management (ISPIM) 15389

Exec Dir PO Box 18, Worsley, Manchester, M28 1XP, UK. T. +441617039411. Fax +441617039412. E-mail: conn@ispim.org – admin@ispim.org.
URL: https://www.ispim-innovation.com/
History 15 Jun 1983, Trondheim (Norway), as *International Society for Product Innovation Management*, taking over from *Need Assessment and Information Behaviour (NAIB Programme)*, active from the early 1970s on the initiative of Prof Knut Holt. Current title adopted 1991 to reflect the wider area of interest. **Aims** Create a worldwide network of excellence in the field of innovation management; enhance collaboration between members; be at the forefront of research on innovation. **Structure** Board, comprising 6 Directors (Events; Research; Publications; Association Development; Membership and Finance; Scientific Affairs). On of the directors is nominated as the Executive Director. **Languages** English. **Staff** 6.00 FTE, paid. **Finance** Members' dues. **Activities** Manages network of innovation professionals; organizes conferences; participates in research projects; publishing activity. **Events** *Connects Meeting* Osaka (Japan) 2023, *Innovation Conference* Copenhagen (Denmark) 2022, *Connects Meeting* Osaka (Japan) 2022, *Innovation Conference* 2021, *Innovation Conference* 2020. **Publications** *International Journal of Innovation Management* (4 a year); *ISPIM Newsletter* (4 a year); *Memobiblio* (4 a year); *Conference Book of Outlines* (2 a year); *Conference Special Issues* (2 a year). Conference proceedings (2 a year).
Members Personal; Institutional; National academics, business leaders, consultants and other professionals (359 as of 1 May 2009) in 45 countries and territories:
Australia, Austria, Belgium, Brazil, Canada, China, Croatia, Czechia, Denmark, Estonia, Finland, France, Germany, Greece, India, Ireland, Israel, Italy, Japan, Korea Rep, Lithuania, Luxembourg, Malaysia, Mexico, Netherlands, New Zealand, Norway, Poland, Portugal, Russia, Saudi Arabia, Serbia, Singapore, Slovakia, Slovenia, Spain, Sweden, Switzerland, Taiwan, Thailand, Türkiye, UK, United Arab Emirates, USA, Venezuela.
NGO Relations Member of: *International Network for Small and Medium Sized Enterprises (INSME, #14325)*. Affiliated with: *Northern Dimension Institute (NDI, #17585)*. Close links with: *European Association for Creativity and Innovation (EACI, #05997)*; *European Association for the Transfer of Technologies, Innovation and Industrial Information (TII, #06259)*; *International Association for Management of Technology (IAMOT, #12010)*. [2020/XD3449/t/**D**]

♦ International Society for the Promotion and Investigation of Wind Music / see Internationale Gesellschaft zur Erforschung und Förderung der Blasmusik (#13237)
♦ International Society for the Promotion and Research of Wind Music (#13237)
♦ International Society for Prophylactic Medicine and Social Hygiene (inactive)

♦ International Society for Prosthetics and Orthotics (ISPO) 15390

Sociedad Internacional de Protésica y Ortesica
Main Office Rue du Luxembourg 22-24, 1000 Brussels, Belgium. T. +3222131356. Fax +3222131313. E-mail: ispo@ispoint.org.
URL: http://www.ispoint.org/
History 15 Nov 1970, Copenhagen (Denmark). Former names and other names: *Société internationale de prothèse et orthèse* – alias; *Sociedad Internacional de Prótesis y Ortosis* – alias. **Aims** Serve as coordinating, correlating and advisory body on prosthetics, orthotics, *rehabilitation* engineering and other technical matters related to the neuro-muscular and skeletal system; improve the quality of life for persons who may benefit from prosthetic, orthotic, mobility and assistive devices. **Structure** World Congress (every 2 years); International Committee; Executive Board; Standing Committees; Ad Hoc Committees; International Task Officers; Head Office in Brussels (Belgium). **Languages** English. **Staff** 3.00 FTE, paid. Voluntary. **Finance** Sources: gifts, legacies; grants; meeting proceeds; members' dues; sale of publications. Other sources: contracts. **Activities** Events/meetings; networking/liaising; research and development; standards/guidelines; training/education. **Events** *World Congress* Guadalajara (Mexico) 2023, *Global Educators Meeting* 2022, *Global Educators Meeting* Adelaide, SA (Australia) 2022, *RehabWeek* Rotterdam (Netherlands) 2022, *World Congress* 2021. **Publications** *Prosthetics and Orthotics International* (6 a year). Reports on consensus conferences, special topic workshops and seminars. **Members** Full; Fellows; Emeritus Fellows or Members; Sponsored; Sponsoring; Institutional; Affiliated Societies; Student. Members in 103 countries. Membership countries not specified. **Consultative Status** Consultative status granted from: *ECOSOC (#05331)* (Special); *WHO (#20950)* (Official Relations). **NGO Relations** In liaison with technical committee of: *International Organization for Standardization (ISO, #14473)*. Founding member of: *Global Rehabilitation Alliance (#10565)*. Links indcated by: *D-Foot International (#05061)*; *Global Alliance of Assistive Technology Organizations (GAATO, #10185)*; *International Society of Wheelchair Professionals (ISWP)*; *World Federation of Occupational Therapists (WFOT, #21468)*. [2019/XB4010/**B**]

♦ International Society for the Protection of Animals (inactive)
♦ International Society for the Protection and Breeding of Aurochs (inactive)
♦ International Society for the Protection of the Sponge Fishermen (inactive)

♦ **International Society of Protein Termini (ISPT)** 15391

Contact address not obtained. E-mail: protein.termini@gmail.com.
URL: https://ispt.world/

History Founded 2018, following an N-term conference, held 2017, Halle (Germany). **Aims** Gather researchers in the fields of the N-end rule pathway as well as all aspects of protein termini. **Structure** Council. **Finance** Sources: members' dues. **Activities** Events/meetings; knowledge management/information dissemination. **Events** *Annual Meeting* Seoul (Korea Rep) 2019. **Members** Individuals. Membership countries not specified. [2020/XM8909/**C**]

♦ **International Society of Protistologists (ISOP)** 15392

Exec Sec Dept of Zoology, Fac of Science, Charles Univ, Vinicna 7, 128 00 Prague, Czechia.
Pres Dept of Science and Technology, Bryant Univ, 1150 Douglas Pike, Smithfield RI 02917, USA.
URL: https://protistologists.org/

History 1947, Chicago, IL (USA). Former names and other names: *Society of Protozoologists* – former (1947). **Aims** Foster development and advancement of the science of protistology. **Structure** Executive Committee; Standing Committees; ad hoc Committees. **Languages** English. **Activities** Awards/prizes/competitions; events/meetings. **Events** *International Congress of Protistology* Seoul (Korea Rep) 2025, *ECOP-ISOP joint meeting* Vienna (Austria) 2023, *International Congress of Protistology* Seoul (Korea Rep) 2022, *International Congress of Protistology* Seoul (Korea Rep) 2021, *Meeting* Rome (Italy) 2019. **Publications** *Journal of Eukaryotic Microbiology*. **NGO Relations** Cooperates with (1): *International Society for Evolutionary Protistology (ISEP, #15104)*. [2022.10.11/XM1407/**C**]

♦ International Society for Proton Dynamics in Cancer / see International Society of Cancer Metabolism (#14991)
♦ International Society of Protozoologists (internationally oriented national body)
♦ International Society for Psychiatric Consultation Liaison Nurses (internationally oriented national body)
♦ International Society for Psychiatric Disorders of Childbearing / see International Marcé Society for Perinatal Mental Health (#14089)

♦ **International Society of Psychiatric Genetics (ISPG)** 15393

Main Office 5034-A Thoroughbred Ln, Brentwood TN 37027, USA. T. +16156493086. Fax +18884173311. E-mail: info@ispg.net.
URL: http://www.ispg.net/

History 1993. Founded following the first two editions of the World Congress of Psychiatric Genetics (WCPG). **Aims** Promote and facilitate research in the genetics of psychiatric disorders, substance use disorders and allied traits; promote education, both of the scientific community and of the lay public; encourage communication and collaboration between researchers; encourage the development of research methods and, where possible, encourage comparability and replicability of results; strive for the highest ethical standards in research and the application of findings from genetic research in clinical psychiatric practice. **Structure** Board of 18 members. Officers: President; Vice-President; Secretary; Treasurer. **Activities** Grants the Lifetime Achievement Award annually. **Events** *World Congress of Psychiatric Genetics (WCPG)* Montréal, QC (Canada) 2023, *World Congress of Psychiatric Genetics (WCPG)* Florence (Italy) 2022, *World Congress of Psychiatric Genetics (WCPG)* Montréal, QC (Canada) 2021, *World Congress of Psychiatric Genetics (WCPG)* Brentwood, TN (USA) 2020, *World Congress of Psychiatric Genetics (WCPG)* Los Angeles, CA (USA) 2019. [2022/XD7445/**D**]

♦ International Society of Psychiatric-Mental Health Nurses (internationally oriented national body)
♦ International Society for Psychic Research (inactive)

♦ **International Society of Psychoanalysis and Philosophy (ISPP)** 15394

Société Internationale de Psychanalyse et Philosophie (SIPP)

Contact Depto de Filosfia, Univ de Sao Paulo, Av Prof Luciano Gualberto 315, sala 1007, Sao Paulo SP, 05508-900, Brazil. T. +551130913709. E-mail: sipp.ispp.website@gmail.com.
URL: https://www.sipp-ispp.com/

History Mar 2008. **Aims** Facilitate international university exchange at doctoral and post-doctoral levels; provide firm support for the work being done by colleagues in this emerging interdisciplinary research area. **Structure** Executive Committee of 4. **Events** *Annual Colloquium* Nicosia (Cyprus) 2020, *Annual Colloquium* Stockholm (Sweden) 2019, *Annual Colloquium* Paris (France) 2018, *Annual Colloquium* Munich (Germany) 2014, *Annual Meeting* Nijmegen (Netherlands) / Ghent (Belgium) 2013.
Members Individuals in 15 countries:
Belgium, Brazil, Chile, Finland, France, Germany, Israel, Japan, Netherlands, Slovenia, South Africa, Sweden, Switzerland, UK, USA. [2020/XJ5090/**C**]

♦ **International Society for the Psychoanalytic Study of Organizations (ISPSO)** 15395

Exec Dir 265 Exhibition Street, Melbourne VIC 3000, Australia. E-mail: admin@ispso.org.
URL: http://www.ispso.org/

History Founded 1985. Registered in the State of Kansas (USA). **Aims** Promote research, teaching and consultation in the area of psychoanalytic study of organizations. **Structure** Board of Directors. **Staff** 3.00 FTE, paid. **Finance** Members' dues. Surpluses on events. **Activities** Events/meetings. **Events** *Annual Meeting* Berlin (Germany) 2021, *Annual Meeting* Berlin (Germany) 2020, *Annual Meeting* New York, NY (USA) 2019, *Annual Meeting* Dublin (Ireland) 2018, *Annual Meeting* Copenhagen (Denmark) 2017.
Members Individuals in 28 countries and territories:
Argentina, Australia, Belgium, Brazil, Bulgaria, Canada, Chile, Denmark, France, Germany, Hungary, Ireland, Israel, Japan, Malaysia, Mexico, Netherlands, Norway, Peru, Poland, Puerto Rico, Russia, South Africa, Spain, Sweden, Switzerland, UK, USA. [2017/XM3673/v/**D**]

♦ **International Society for Psychological and Social Approaches to Psychosis (ISPS)** 15396

Organiser Paktolou 7-9, Ano Glyfada, 165 61 Athens, Greece. T. +302109618012. E-mail: isps@isps.org.
URL: http://www.isps.org/

History 1956. Founded to organize the International Symposium for Psychotherapy of Schizophrenia. In 1997, infrastructure underwent development to become an international association. Adopted the *'ISPS Charter of Good Practice in Psychological Therapies for People Experiencing Psychosis'*. Former names and other names: *International Society for the Psychological Treatments of the Schizophrenias and Other Psychoses* – former. Registration: USA; Norway. **Aims** Promote psychotherapy and psychological treatments for persons with psychosis. **Structure** Executive Committee. **Languages** English. **Finance** Sources: meeting proceeds; members' dues. **Activities** Events/meetings. **Events** *International Congress* Perugia (Italy) 2022, *International Congress* Perugia (Italy) 2021, *International Trauma, Dissociation and Psychosis Conference* Kristiansand (Norway) 2019, *International Congress* Rotterdam (Netherlands) 2019, *International Congress* Liverpool (UK) 2017. **Publications** *ISPS Newsletter* (4 a year); *Psychosis* (4 a year) – journal. *ISPS Book Series*.
Members Institutions/Organizations; Individual. Institutions in 4 countries:
Norway, Poland, Portugal, Spain.
Local groups in 21 countries:
Australia, Croatia, Denmark, Finland, Germany, Greece, India, Israel, Italy, Korea Rep, Netherlands, New Zealand, Norway, Poland, Russia, Slovenia, Spain, Sweden, Switzerland, UK, USA.
NGO Relations Member of: *World Psychiatric Association (WPA, #21741)*. [2021/XD9391/**C**]

♦ International Society for the Psychological Treatments of the Schizophrenias and Other Psychoses / see International Society for Psychological and Social Approaches to Psychosis (#15396)

♦ **International Society for Psychology as the Discipline of Interiority (ISPDI)** 15397

Pres 10417 Saskatchewan Dr, Edmonton AB T6E 4R8, Canada. E-mail: tispdi@gmail.com.
URL: http://www.ispdi.org/

Structure Executive Committee. **Finance** Members' dues. **Activities** Meeting activities. **Events** *The psychological difference* Berlin (Germany) 2014, *Conference* Berlin (Germany) 2012. **Publications** *ISPDI Newsletter*. [2014/XJ8291/**D**]

♦ **International Society of Psychology of Handwriting (ISPH)** 15398

Société internationale de psychologie de l'écriture (SIPE) – Sociedad Internacional de Psicologia de la Escritura (SIPE) – Internationale Gesellschaft der Schriftpsychologie (IGSP) – Società Internazionale di Psicologia della Scrittura (SIPS)

Contact address not obtained. T. +39270126489 – +3927388427. Fax +3927491051.

History 10 Dec 1961, Milan (Italy), at 1st Congress, as *International Society for the Psychology of Writing (ISPW)*. Also known in English as *International Handwriting Psychology Society (IHPS)*. **Aims** Develop scientific research on the psychological interpretation of handwriting style; spread knowledge of such research in scientific circles and utilize it for psychological and social *wellbeing* and improvement of human *morale*. **Structure** President, Secretary and 4 Directors, elected for 3-year term. **Languages** English, Italian. **Staff** 23.00 FTE, voluntary. **Finance** Members' dues. Grants. Budget (annual): about euro 1,000. **Activities** Organizes: handwriting psychology courses for teachers; lecture-debates; conventions; national and international congresses. **Events** *Meeting on hypnotherapy and psychology of handwriting* Milan (Italy) 1988, *International congress* Milan (Italy) 1986. **Publications** Books – by Marco and Rolando Marchesan and other authors – in Italian/some translated into Spanish.
Members Individuals in 13 countries:
Brazil, Canada, Colombia, Czechia, El Salvador, Germany, Italy, Nigeria, Slovenia, Spain, Sweden, Switzerland, USA.
NGO Relations Affiliated to: *World Federation for Mental Health (WFMH, #21455)*. [2009.06.01/XC2517/v/**F**]

♦ International Society for the Psychology of Writing / see International Society of Psychology of Handwriting (#15398)
♦ International Society for Psychomotor Therapy (no recent information)

♦ **International Society of Psychoneuroendocrinology (ISPNE)** 15399

Société internationale de psychoneuroendocrinologie

Exec Dir FAU Erlangen-Nürnberg, Schlossplatz 4, 91054 Erlangen, Germany. E-mail: ispne@ispne.net.
Events & Marketing Manager address not obtained.
URL: http://www.ispne.net/

History 1969, Milan (Italy). Former names and other names: *International Psychoneuroendocrine Society* – alias. **Aims** Coordinate the experiences of research in neurobiochemistry, neurology, neuroanatomy, neurophysiology, neuroendocrinology, neuropharmacology, behavioural genetics, psychology and psychiatry to further understanding normal and abnormal functional states of the brain in relation to endocrine function. **Structure** Executive Committee. **Languages** English. **Staff** 3.00 FTE, paid. **Finance** Members' dues. **Activities** Networking/liaising; research/documentation; events/meetings. **Events** *Annual Conference* Chicago, IL (USA) 2022, *Psychoneuroendocrinology across the lifespan* Chicago, IL (USA) 2021, *Psychoneuroendocrinology across the lifespan* Erlangen (Germany) 2020, *Congress* Milan (Italy) 2019, *Diversity, health, and resilience – taking science beyond discoveries* Irvine, CA (USA) 2018. **Publications** *Psychoneuroendocrinology* (8 a year) – journal.
Members Full in 37 countries:
Argentina, Austria, Belgium, Brazil, Canada, China, Croatia, Czechia, Denmark, Dominican Rep, Finland, France, Germany, Greece, Hungary, India, Iran Islamic Rep, Ireland, Israel, Italy, Japan, Luxembourg, Mexico, Netherlands, Norway, Pakistan, Portugal, Romania, Russia, Serbia, Spain, Sweden, Switzerland, Türkiye, UK, USA, Venezuela.
NGO Relations Member of: *International Brain Research Organization (IBRO, #12392)*. [2022/XD2385/**D**]

♦ International Society of Psychopathology of the Expression / see International Society for Psychopathology of Expression and Art-Therapy (#15400)

♦ **International Society for Psychopathology of Expression and Art-Therapy** 15400

Société internationale de psychopathologie de l'expression et d'art-thérapie (SIPE) – Sociedad Internacional de Psicopatologia de la Expresión – Internationale Gesellschaft für Psychopathologische Ausdrucksformen

Contact 10 rue du Fer à Cheval, 64000 Pau, France. T. +33559326610.
URL: https://sipe-at.org/

History 20 Oct 1959, Verona (Italy). Founded following 1st 'Symposium sull'Arte Psicopatologica'. Statutes adopted 9 Oct 1960, Catania (Italy), and modified 23 May 1964, Barcelona (Spain); modified Oct 1997, Biarritz (France). Former names and other names: *International Society of Psychopathology of the Expression* – alias; *International Society of Art and Psychopathology* – alias. Registration: France. **Aims** Group specialists interested in the problem of expression and artistic activities in relation to psychiatric, sociological and psychological research, including the application of methods employed in fields other than those of neurology and *mental illness*. **Structure** General Assembly (every 3 years). Board (Management Committee). Executive Committee, comprising: President; 2 Honorary Presidents; 14 Vice-Presidents; Secretary-General; Assistant Secretary-General in charge of international relations; Treasurer. **Languages** English, French, German. **Staff** Voluntary. **Finance** Sources: members' dues. **Activities** Organizes: congresses/exhibitions; panels; symposia; colloquia. **Events** *Triennial Congress* Belgrade (Serbia) 2015, *Triennial Congress* Toulouse (France) 2012, *Colloquium* Budapest (Hungary) 2010, *Triennial Congress* Lisbon (Portugal) 2009, *Triennial congress* Belfast (UK) 2006. **Publications** *Confinia Psychopathologica* – online journal.
Members Doctors (at least two thirds of total) PLUS specialists from other disciplines aestheticians, critics, artists and writers, psychologists, ethnologists, historians, linguists, criminologists. Individuals (about 700), national societies and cultural associations in 42 countries:
Algeria, Argentina, Australia, Austria, Belgium, Brazil, Canada, Chile, Colombia, Croatia, Denmark, Finland, France, Germany, Greece, Hungary, India, Ireland, Israel, Italy, Japan, Korea Rep, Lebanon, Morocco, Netherlands, New Zealand, Papua New Guinea, Peru, Poland, Portugal, Romania, Senegal, Serbia, Spain, Sweden, Switzerland, Tunisia, Türkiye, UK, Uruguay, USA, Venezuela.
NGO Relations Member of: *Council for International Organizations of Medical Sciences (CIOMS, #04905)*; *World Federation for Mental Health (WFMH, #21455)*; *World Psychiatric Association (WPA, #21741)*. [2022/XC2526/**C**]

♦ **International Society for Psychophysics (ISP)** 15401

Treas Tech Univ of Darnstadt, Karolinenplatz 5, 64289 Darmstadt, Germany. T. +496151165315.
Pres Psychology Fac, Smith College, Northampton MA 01063, USA. T. +14135853902. E-mail: mteghtso@smith.edu.
URL: http://www.ispsychophysics.org/

History 22 Oct 1985, Cassis (France). Registered in accordance with French law. **Aims** Further theoretical and applied research and teaching; encourage international communication and cooperation within the field of psychophysics. **Structure** Executive Committee of 5 members, comprising President, Vice-President, Secretary, Treasurer and Chairman of the Organizing Committee responsible for the next year's meeting. **Languages** English. **Staff** Voluntary. **Finance** Members' dues: Full – US$ 100; Student – US$ 30. **Activities** Participates in international congresses of psychology; organizes symposia; organizes 'Fechner Day'. **Events** *Annual Meeting* Darmstadt (Germany) 2020, *Annual Meeting* Antalya (Turkey) 2019, *Annual Meeting* Lüneburg (Germany) 2018, *Annual Meeting* Fukuoka (Japan) 2017, *Annual Meeting* Ottawa, ON (Canada) 2012. **Publications** Meeting proceedings (annual).
Members Individuals in 30 countries and territories:
Argentina, Australia, Belgium, Brazil, Bulgaria, Canada, China, Denmark, Finland, France, Germany, India, Ireland, Israel, Italy, Japan, Lithuania, Montenegro, Netherlands, New Zealand, Poland, Portugal, Puerto Rico, Russia, Serbia, Spain, Sweden, Switzerland, UK, USA. [2014/XD1417/v/**C**]

♦ **International Society of Psychosomatic Obstetrics and Gynaecology (ISPOG)** 15402

Société internationale d'obstétrique et de gynécologie psychosomatiques

SG Hilvarenbeekseweg 60, PO Box 90151, 5000 LC Tilburg, Netherlands.
URL: http://www.ispog.org/

History 27 Oct 1972, Geneva (Switzerland). Founded following informal meetings at congresses 1962-1971. Registration: Switzerland. **Aims** Promote the study and education of psychosomatic problems in obstetrics and gynaecology; organize, prepare and join international meetings and congresses on psychosomatic obstetrics and gynaecology and related subjects; advance knowledge and status of members. **Structure** General Assembly (every 3 years); Executive Committee. **Languages** English, French. **Staff** Voluntary. **Finance** Members' dues. Donations. **Events** *Congress* Seoul (Korea Rep) 2025, *Congress* Vienna (Austria) 2022, *Triennial Congress* The Hague (Netherlands) 2019, *Triennial Congress* Malaga (Spain) 2016, *Triennial Congress* Berlin (Germany) 2013. **Publications** *Journal of Psychosomatic Obstetrics and Gynaecology* (4 a year).

Members Organizations national or regional professional associations; Individuals. Members in 22 countries:
Argentina, Australia, Austria, Belgium, Canada, France, Germany, Greece, Hungary, India, Israel, Italy, Japan, Korea Rep, Netherlands, Portugal, South Africa, Spain, Sweden, Switzerland, UK, USA.
NGO Relations Member of: *Global Alliance for Maternal Mental Health (GAMMH, #10208).*
[2022/XD6552/**D**]

♦ International Society of Pteridinology (ISP) 15403

Internationalen Gesellschaft für Pteridinologie

Sec Inst für Innere Medizin, Medizinische Univ Innsbruck, Christoph-Probst-Platz 1, Innrain 52 A, 6020 Innsbruck, Austria.
Contact Div of Biological Chemistry, Biocenter, Innsbruck Medical Univ, Innrain 80, 6020 Innsbruck, Austria.
URL: http://www.pteridines.org/

History Registered in accordance with Austrian law. **Aims** Represent the interests of pteridinology and of people who work in this area. **Structure** General Meeting; Management Committee. **Languages** English. **Finance** Members' dues. **Events** *International Winter Workshop on Clinical, Chemical and Biochemical Aspects of Pteridines and Related Topics* Innsbruck (Austria) 2019, *International Winter Workshop on Clinical, Chemical and Biochemical Aspects of Pteridines and Related Topics* Innsbruck (Austria) 2018, *International Winter Workshop on Clinical, Chemical and Biochemical Aspects of Pteridines and Related Topics* Innsbruck (Austria) 2016, *International Winter Workshop on Clinical, Chemical and Biochemical Aspects of Pteridines and Related Topics* Innsbruck (Austria) 2015, *International Winter Workshop on Clinical, Chemical and Biochemical Aspects of Pteridines and Related Topics / International Winterworkshop* Innsbruck (Austria) 2014. **Publications** *Pteridines* – journal. **Members** Full (40). Membership countries not specified.
[2020.03.03/XJ9623/**D**]

♦ International Society of Public Law (ICON-S) 15404

Co-Chair IMT School for Advanced Studies Lucca, Piazza S Ponziano 6, 55100 Lucca LU, Italy.
Co-Chair Univ of New South Wales, The Law Bldg, Sydney NSW 2052, Australia.
URL: http://icon-society.org/

History Launched Jun 2014, Florence (Italy). **Structure** Council; Executive Committee. **Staff** 2.00 FTE, paid. **Finance** Sources: members' dues. **Activities** Events/meetings. **Events** *Conference* Auckland (New Zealand) 2023, *Conference* Wroclaw (Poland) 2022, *Mundo Conference* Lucca (Italy) 2021, *Conference* Wroclaw (Poland) 2021, *Seminar on (Un)Gendering Public Law in Asia* Singapore (Singapore) 2020. **Publications** *International Journal of Constitutional Law (ICON).* [2021/XM5059/**C**]

♦ International Society for Quality Assurance in Health Care / see International Society for Quality in Health Care (#15405)

♦ International Society for Quality in Health Care (ISQua) 15405

CEO Suite G01, 48 Mount Street Upper, Dublin, 2, CO. DUBLIN, D02 YY23, Ireland. E-mail: info@isqua.org.
URL: http://www.isqua.org/

History 1985, Stockholm (Sweden). New Constitution adopted in 1995. Permanent Secretariat in Australia from 1995 to 2008; moved to Ireland in 2008. Former names and other names: *International Society for Quality Assurance in Health Care* – former (1985). Registration: Start date: 1995, Australia, Victoria; No/ID: 20072445, Start date: 2008, Ireland. **Aims** Inspire and empower people to advocate for, and facilitate improvements in, the quality and safety of healthcare worldwide. **Structure** Executive Board; Secretariat, headed by Chief Executive Officer. **Languages** English. **Staff** 13.00 FTE, paid. **Finance** Sources: grants; members' dues. Annual budget: 1,000,000 EUR. **Activities** Events/meetings; publishing activities; training/education. **Events** *Conference* Sao Paulo (Brazil) 2025, *Conference* Istanbul (Türkiye) 2024, *International Conference* Seoul (Korea Rep) 2023, *Conference* Brisbane, QLD (Australia) 2022, *Conference* Florence (Italy) 2021. **Publications** *International Journal for Quality in Health Care* (6 a year); *ISQua Bulletin* (6 a year).
Members Institutional in 58 countries and territories:
Argentina, Australia, Austria, Belgium, Brazil, Canada, Chile, China, Côte d'Ivoire, Croatia, Denmark, Estonia, Eswatini, Finland, France, Germany, Greece, Hong Kong, India, Indonesia, Ireland, Israel, Italy, Jamaica, Jordan, Kazakhstan, Korea Rep, Kuwait, Lebanon, Lithuania, Malaysia, Mexico, Mongolia, Netherlands, New Zealand, Nigeria, Norway, Pakistan, Peru, Portugal, Qatar, Romania, Saudi Arabia, Senegal, Serbia, Singapore, South Africa, Spain, Switzerland, Taiwan, Tanzania UR, Thailand, Trinidad-Tobago, Tunisia, Türkiye, UK, United Arab Emirates, USA.
Asian Society for Quality in Health Care (ASQua, #01737); GS1 (#10809); International Hospital Federation (IHF, #13812); Joint Commission International (JCI, #16123); Planetree International (#18385).
Consultative Status Consultative status granted from: *WHO (#20950)* (Official Relations). **IGO Relations** *International Bank for Reconstruction and Development (IBRD, #12317)* (World Bank). **NGO Relations** Member of (1): *World Patients Alliance (WPA).* Instrumental in setting up (1): *International Society for Quality in Health Care External Evaluation Association (ISQua EEA, #15406).* Recognizes: *Council for Health Service Accreditation in Southern Africa (Cohsasa).* [2022/XD1128/**D**]

♦ International Society for Quality in Health Care External Evaluation Association (ISQua EEA) 15406

Contact Multifiduciaire Genève, Carrefour de Rive 1, Case Postale 3369, 1211 Geneva 3, Switzerland. E-mail: support@ieea.ch.
URL: https://ieea.ch/

History 2018. Founded by *International Society for Quality in Health Care (ISQua, #15405).* Commenced operations 2019. Registration: Switzerland. **Aims** Deliver evaluation services. **Structure** Board of Directors; External Evaluation Award Committee; Accreditation Council. **Activities** Awards/prizes/competitions; certification/accreditation; monitoring/evaluation. [2022/AA2864/**E**]

♦ International Society for Quality of Life Research (ISOQOL) 15407

Exec Dir 555 East Wells St, Ste 1100, Milwaukee WI 53202, USA. T. +14149189797. Fax +14142763349. E-mail: info@isoqol.org.
URL: http://www.isoqol.org/

History Founded 1994. **Aims** Promote scientific study of quality of life relevant to *health* and *healthcare.* **Structure** Annual Conference. **Languages** English. **Events** *Annual Conference* Dublin (Ireland) 2018, *Annual Conference* Philadelphia, PA (USA) 2017, *Annual Conference* Copenhagen (Denmark) 2016, *Annual Conference* Vancouver, BC (Canada) 2015, *Annual Conference* Berlin (Germany) 2014. **Publications** *Journal of Patient-Reported Outcomes (JPRO).* [2019.12.11/XF4898/**F**]

♦ International Society for Quality-of-Life Studies (ISQOLS) 15408

Exec Dir PO Box 118, Gilbert AZ 85299, USA. E-mail: office@isqols.org.
URL: http://isqols.org/

History 1995. Bylaws revised and effective, Jan 1998. Registration: USA, Virginia. **Aims** Promote and encourage research, discussion, contributions to the research literature and teaching in quality-of-life (QOL) studies; provide a liaison among academic, public sector and private sector researchers, scholars and teachers in the managerial, behavioural, social, medical as well as the applied natural sciences. **Structure** Board of Directors (meets annually); Executive Committee; Nominating Committee. **Languages** English. **Staff** 1.00 FTE, paid. **Finance** Sources: donations; fees for services; members' dues; sale of publications. **Activities** Awards/prizes/competitions; events/meetings; networking/liaising. **Events** *Annual Conference* Borneo (Malaysia) 2024, *Annual Conference* Rotterdam (Netherlands) 2023, *Annual Conference* Burlington, VT (USA) 2022, *Annual Conference* Gilbert, AZ (USA) 2021, *Annual Conference* Rotterdam (Netherlands) 2020. **Publications** *Social Indicators Network News (SINET)* (4 a year) – newsletter; *Applied Research in Quality of Life (ARQOL)* – journal; *Journal of Happiness Studies; Journal of Macromarketing; Social Indicators Research (SIR); Social-Psychological Intervention.*
Members Regular; Student; Emeritus; Charter; Institutional. Individuals in 35 countries and territories:
Argentina, Australia, Austria, Belgium, Bosnia-Herzegovina, Brazil, Canada, Colombia, Croatia, Denmark, Finland, France, Germany, Greece, Hong Kong, India, Ireland, Israel, Italy, Japan, Korea Rep, Lebanon, Mexico, Netherlands, New Zealand, Norway, Philippines, Singapore, South Africa, Spain, Sweden, Switzerland, Thailand, UK, USA.
University and Non-University Affiliations. Membership countries not specified. [2022/XD6558/**D**]

♦ International Society of Quantum Biology and Pharmacology (ISQBP) 15409

Past Pres Ctr for Structural Biochemistry, Dept of Biosciences and Nutrition, Karolinska Inst, SE-141 57 Huddinge, Sweden. T. +4686089228. Fax +4686089290.
URL: https://www.isqbp.org

History 1970. **Aims** Provide a forum for chemists, pharmacologists and biologists to discuss and extend the impact of computational methodologies in the fields of biology, chemistry, medicinal chemistry, chemical biology, drug discovery, pharmacology, bioinformatics, genomics and proteomics. **Structure** Executive Council, comprising President, Vice-President, Secretary, Past-President, Treasurer and 4 Councillors. Advisory Board. **Events** *Biennial Presidents Meeting* Strasbourg (France) 2021, *Biennial Presidents Meeting* Strasbourg (France) 2020, *Biennial Presidents Meeting* Barcelona (Spain) 2018, *Biennial Presidents Meeting* Bergen (Norway) 2016, *Biennial Presidents Meeting* Stockholm (Sweden) 2012. [2021/XJ6624/**C**]

♦ International Society for Racial Health (inactive)
♦ International Society for Radiation Oncology (inactive)
♦ International Society of Radiographers and Radiological Technicians / see International Society of Radiographers and Radiological Technologists (#15410)

♦ International Society of Radiographers and Radiological Technologists (ISRRT) 15410

CEO address not obtained. E-mail: admin@isrrt.org.
URL: http://www.isrrt.org/

History Jul 1959, Munich (Germany). Founded at 9th International Congress of Radiology. Constitution and Regulations produced and approved 1965, Rome (Italy). Former names and other names: *International Secretariat of Radiographers and Radiological Technicians* – former (Jul 1057 to Aug 1962); *International Society of Radiographers and Radiological Technicians* – former (Aug 1962 to 1992). **Aims** Advance the science and practice of medical imaging and radiation therapy and allied subjects by promoting improved standards of education and of research in the technical aspects of medical imaging, radiation therapy and radiation protection; make the results of research and experience in medical imaging, radiation therapy and radiation protection available to practitioners throughout the world. **Structure** Council (meets every 2 years, at World Congress); Board of Management; Committees. Manages: *World Radiography Education Trust Fund (WRETF, see: #15410).* **Languages** English. **Staff** 1.50 FTE, paid. **Finance** Sources: members' dues. **Activities** Advocacy/lobbying/activism; knowledge management/information dissemination; research/documentation; training/education. **Events** *World Congress* Aalborg (Denmark) 2024, *World Congress* Bangkok (Thailand) 2022, *Biennial World Congress* Dublin (Ireland) 2021, *Asian Australasian Regional Conference* Tokyo (Japan) 2021, *Biennial World Congress* Dublin (Ireland) 2020. **Publications** *ISRRT Newsletter* (2 a year). Teaching guides; meeting proceedings.
Members National societies in 82 countries and territories:
Australia, Bangladesh, Barbados, Belgium, Benin, Botswana, Brazil, Burkina Faso, Cameroon, Canada, Congo DR, Côte d'Ivoire, Croatia, Cyprus, Czechia, Denmark, El Salvador, Estonia, Ethiopia, Fiji, Finland, France, Gabon, Gambia, Germany, Ghana, Greece, Guyana, Hong Kong, Hungary, Iceland, India, Indonesia, Ireland, Italy, Jamaica, Japan, Kenya, Korea Rep, Latvia, Lebanon, Macau, Malaysia, Malta, Mexico, Morocco, Namibia, Nepal, Netherlands, New Zealand, Nigeria, North Macedonia, Norway, Pakistan, Panama, Peru, Philippines, Poland, Portugal, Senegal, Serbia, Seychelles, Singapore, Slovenia, South Africa, Spain, Sri Lanka, Sweden, Taiwan, Tanzania UR, Thailand, Togo, Trinidad-Tobago, Tunisia, Türkiye, Uganda, UK, Ukraine, USA, Vietnam, Zambia, Zimbabwe.
Consultative Status Consultative status granted from: *ECOSOC (#05331)* (Ros C); *WHO (#20950)* (Official). **IGO Relations** Accredited by (1): *United Nations Office at Vienna (UNOV, #20604).* Affiliated with (1): *International Atomic Energy Agency (IAEA, #12294).* Associated with Department of Global Communications of the United Nations. [2021/XB2565/**B**]

♦ International Society of Radiolabelled Blood Elements (ISORBE) . . . 15411

Sec AKH – Vienna General Hospital, Währinger Gürtel 18-20, 1090 Vienna, Austria.
Pres Nuclear Medicine Dept, University of Pretoria/Steve Biko Academic Hospital, Private Bag X169, Pretoria, 0001, South Africa. E-mail: mike.sathekge@up.ac.za.
Registered Address c/o Atherosclerosis Research Group, Nadlergasse 1, 1090 Vienna, Austria.
URL: http://www.isorbe.com/

History Founded 1989, Vienna (Austria), at 5th International Symposium on Radiolabelled Blood Elements, the 1st Symposium having been held in Nov 1979, New York NY (USA). Registered in accordance with Austrian law, 20 Aug 1990, Vienna. **Aims** Serve as a forum for discussion and collaboration among scientists involved in the study of inflammation, infection and *atherosclerosis*; maintain scientific contacts and exchange research experience in the field worldwide; promote research, resolve controversial issues and support young researchers in this area. **Structure** Members' Assembly (every 2 years), comprising Ordinary and Honorary members. Board of Directors of 22 members. Executive board, comprising President, Past President, Secretary, Treasurer, Editor-in-Chief of Newsletter and 3 members. **Languages** English. **Staff** 2.00 FTE, paid. **Finance** Members' dues (annual): US$ 50. Other sources: grants; donations. **Activities** Organizes: International Symposium on Radio-Labeled Blood Elements (every 2 years); meetings; practical courses; discusses technical aspects leading to international publications; promotes development of new radiopharmaceuticals; standardizes and improves techniques and makes them available to the scientific community interested in basic and applied research in the field. **Events** *International Symposium / International Congress* Izmir (Turkey) 2015, *International Workshop on Cell Therapies and Cell Labelling* Helsinki (Finland) 2014, *International Symposium* Pretoria (South Africa) 2013, *International Congress* Nijmegen (Netherlands) 2011, *International Congress* Antalya (Turkey) 2009. **Publications** *ISORBE Newsletter* (2 a year). Books; scientific papers; technical brochures.
Members Ordinary; Corporate; Honorary individuals and organizations in 43 countries and territories:
Argentina, Australia, Austria, Belgium, Brazil, Bulgaria, Canada, Chile, China, Croatia, Czechia, Denmark, Dominican Rep, Egypt, France, Germany, Greece, Hong Kong, Hungary, India, Iran Islamic Rep, Israel, Italy, Japan, Kuwait, Mexico, Netherlands, Pakistan, Peru, Portugal, Russia, Saudi Arabia, Singapore, South Africa, Spain, Switzerland, Syrian AR, Taiwan, Türkiye, UK, United Arab Emirates, USA, Venezuela. [2015/XD5899/**C**]

♦ International Society of Radiology (ISR) 15412

Société internationale de radiologie – Sociedad Internacional de Radiologia – Internationale Gesellschaft für Radiologie

Manager ACR, 1891 Preston White Drive, Reston VA 20191, USA. T. +17036488360. Fax +17036488361. E-mail: info@isradiology.org.
Europe – Office c/o European Society of Radiology, Neutorgasse 9, 1010 Vienna, Austria. T. +4315334064. Fax +4315357041. E-mail: internationalaffairs@myesr.org.
URL: http://www.isradiology.org/

History Jul 1953, Copenhagen (Denmark), at 7th *International Congress of Radiology (ICR)*, in succession to *Standing Committee for International Congresses of Medical Electrology and Radiology (inactive)*, set up 18 Sep 1912. **Aims** Contribute to coordination of progress in *medical* radiology; act as the continuing body between International Congresses of Radiology. **Structure** International Congress on Radiology (every 2 years); Executive Committee. and 10 members. National Board of Management, responsible for the next Congress. Standing Committees (3): *International Commission on Radiological Education (ICRE, #12723);* Program Planning Committee (PPC); *International Commission on Radiological Quality and Safety (ICRQS),* set up when *International Radiology Quality Network (IRQN, inactive)* merged into ISR, 2013. **Languages** English. **Staff** 1.00 FTE, paid. **Finance** Sources: members' dues. **Activities** Training/education. **Events** *Biennial Congress* Muscat (Oman) 2020, *Biennial Congress* Buenos Aires (Argentina) 2016, *Meeting* Chicago, IL (USA) 2015, *Biennial Congress* Dubai (United Arab Emirates) 2014, *Biennial congress / Biennial International Congress on Radiology – ICR* Sao Paulo (Brazil) 2012. **Publications** Commission publications.
Members Societies in 70 countries and territories:
Algeria, Argentina, Australia, Bangladesh, Belgium, Benin, Brazil, Burkina Faso, Burundi, Cameroon, Canada, Central African Rep, Chad, Chile, China, Colombia, Congo Brazzaville, Congo DR, Côte d'Ivoire, Czechia, Denmark, Ecuador, Estonia, Ethiopia, Finland, France, Gabon, Georgia, Germany, Greece, Guinea, Hong Kong, Hungary, Iceland, India, Ireland, Italy, Japan, Kenya, Korea Rep, Kuwait, Latvia, Lebanon, Malaysia, Mali, Mauritania, Mexico, Mongolia, Morocco, Netherlands, New Zealand, Niger, Portugal, Rwanda, Senegal, Serbia, Singapore, South Africa, Spain, St Vincent-Grenadines, Sweden, Switzerland, Syrian AR, Taiwan, Thailand, Togo, Tunisia, Türkiye, UK, USA.
Included in the above, 6 organizations listed in this Yearbook:

Caribbean Society of Radiologists (CSR, #03556); Inter-American College of Radiology (IACR, #11409); International Commission on Radiation Units and Measurements (ICRU, #12722); International Commission on Radiological Protection (ICRP, #12724); International Society of Radiographers and Radiological Technologists (ISRRT, #15410); World Federation for Ultrasound in Medicine and Biology (WFUMB, #21497).
Consultative Status Consultative status granted from: *WHO (#20950)* (Official Relations). **IGO Relations** Affiliated with: *International Atomic Energy Agency (IAEA, #12294).* [2019/XB2566/y/**B**]

♦ International Society for Radiopharmaceutical Chemistry and Biology / see Society of Radiopharmaceutical Sciences (#19627)
♦ International Society for Rapid Respond Systems (internationally oriented national body)

♦ International Society of Rare Sugars (ISRS) 15413

Secretariat c/o I Inst of Rare Sugar Research, 2393 Ikenobe, Miki, Takamatsu KAGAWA, 761-0795 Japan. T. +81878913099. Fax +81878913021.
URL: http://isrs.kagawa-u.ac.jp/
History 2001. **Aims** Perform worldwide activities for scientific society on rare sugars by international scientists with a variety of research fields. **Structure** International Committee, comprising President, Vice President and 12 members. Head Office. **Events** *Rare Sugar Congress* Takamatsu (Japan) 2019, *Congress* Kagawa (Japan) 2014, *Congress* Takamatsu (Japan) 2014, *Congress* Kagawa (Japan) 2011, *Congress* Takamatsu (Japan) 2011. [2019/XJ5483/**E**]

♦ International Society for Reconstructive Microsurgery (inactive)

♦ International Society of Reconstructive Neurosurgery (ISRN) 15414

Contact address not obtained. T. +8223615624. Fax +8223939979. E-mail: jchang@yuhs.ac.
History 19 Jun 2004, Hong Kong. **Aims** Facilitate the communications among neurosurgeons, basic scientists who are interested in neurorehabilitation and neuromodulation therapy. **Structure** Executive Committee; President; Secretary-General. **Languages** English. **Staff** 6.00 FTE, paid. **Finance** No budget. **Activities** New technology and translational research of neurotrauma and neurodegenerative disorders. **Events** *Congress* Rome (Italy) 2009, *New technology and translational research of neurotrauma and neurodegenerative disorders* Taipei (Taiwan) 2007, *Congress* Seoul (Korea Rep) 2005. [2010.06.01/XM1622/**D**]

♦ International Society for Reef Studies / see International Coral Reef Society (#12966)
♦ International Society for Reef Studies Corporation / see International Coral Reef Society (#12966)

♦ International Society for the Reform of Criminal Law (ISRCL) 15415

Treas Ste 231, Allard Hall, 1822 East Mall, Vancouver BC V6T 1Z1, Canada. T. +16048229443. Fax +16048229317. E-mail: secretariat@isrcl.com.
Pres address not obtained.
URL: http://isrcl2019.com/
History Founded 1987. **Aims** Work actively on the administration of criminal *justice*, both in the jurisdictions of members and internationally. **Structure** Council; Board of Directors; Management Committee. **Languages** English, French. **Events** *Annual Conference* Vancouver, BC (Canada) 2020, *Annual Conference* Brisbane, QLD (Australia) 2019, *Annual Conference* Montréal, QC (Canada) 2018, *Annual Conference* San Francisco, CA (USA) 2017, *Annual Conference* Halifax, NS (Canada) 2016. **Publications** *Criminal Law Forum* – journal.
Members Individuals in 28 countries and territories:
Australia, Bahamas, Barbados, Belgium, Botswana, Cameroon, Canada, China, Finland, Germany, Hong Kong, India, Israel, Japan, Malta, Netherlands, New Zealand, Nigeria, Papua New Guinea, Seychelles, South Africa, Sweden, Switzerland, Tanzania UR, Trinidad-Tobago, Uganda, UK, USA.
NGO Relations Founding member of: *International Centre for Criminal Law Reform and Criminal Justice Policy (ICCLR).* [2018/XN8322/v/**C**]

♦ International Society of Refractive Keratoplasty / see International Society of Refractive Surgery of the American Academy of Ophthalmology (#15416)
♦ International Society of Refractive Surgery / see International Society of Refractive Surgery of the American Academy of Ophthalmology (#15416)
♦ International Society of Refractive Surgery of the American Academy of Ophthalmology / see International Society of Refractive Surgery of the American Academy of Ophthalmology (#15416)

♦ International Society of Refractive Surgery of the American Academy of Ophthalmology (ISRS) 15416

Events Coordinator PO Box 7424, San Francisco CA 94109-7424, USA. T. +14154470398. E-mail: isrscommunity@aao.org.
Street address 655 Beach Street, San Francisco CA 94109-1336, USA.
URL: https://www.isrs.org/
History Nov 1979, San Francisco CA (USA), by Prof José Barraquer. Original title: *International Society of Refractive Keratoplasty (ISRK) – Société internationale de kératoplastie réfractive (SIKR).* Name changed to *International Society of Refractive Surgery (ISRS) – Société internationale de chirurgie réfractive.* Since 2003, when joined with Refractive Surgery Interest Group of American Academy of Ophthalmology, full title is: *International Society of Refractive Surgery of the American Academy of Ophthalmology (ISRS/AAO).* **Aims** Advance the art and science of refractive surgery worldwide. **Structure** Executive Committee of 14 members. **Languages** English. **Staff** 12.00 FTE, paid. **Finance** Sources: members' dues; sponsorship. Other sources: course fees. **Activities** Events/meetings; projects/programmes. **Events** *Annual Meeting* Chicago, IL (USA) 2016, *Annual Meeting* Las Vegas, NV (USA) 2015, *Annual Meeting* Chicago, IL (USA) 2014, *Annual Meeting* New Orleans, LA (USA) 2013, *Annual Meeting* Chicago, IL (USA) 2012. **Publications** *Journal of Refractive Surgery* (12 a year); *Refractive Surgery Outlook Newsletter* (12 a year). **Members** Over 2,200 members in over 80 countries. Membership countries not specified. [2019/XD0316/y/**C**]

♦ International Society of Regulatory Toxicology and Pharmacology (internationally oriented national body)
♦ International Society for Rehabilitation of the Disabled / see RI Global (#18948)

♦ International Society for Religion, Literature and Culture (ISRLC) . . 15417

Sec Religion, School of Arts and Humanities, University of Stirling, Stirling, FK9 4LA, UK. T. +441786466240.
URL: http://www.isrlc.org/
History Founded 1991, Durham (UK), as *European Society for Religion Literature and Culture (ESRLC)*, during 10th Annual Conference on Religion and Literature. Previously referred to as *European Society for Religion Literature and Arts (ESRLA).* Present name adopted Sep 2000. **Aims** Promote the study of literature, religion and arts, as they intersect with each other in both theoretical and cultural contexts. **Structure** International Committee. **Languages** Danish, Dutch, English, French, German, Italian, Swedish. **Staff** Voluntary. **Finance** Funds generated through biennial conference. **Activities** Events/meetings. **Events** *Biennial Conference* Chester (UK) 2022, *Biennial Conference* Chester (UK) 2021, *Biennial Conference* Chester (UK) 2020, *Biennial Conference* Uppsala (Sweden) 2018, *Biennial Conference* Glasgow (UK) 2016. **Publications** *ISRLC Online Newsletter.* **Members** Individuals (over 650) worldwide. Membership countries not specified. [2015.01.15/XM0114/**D**]

♦ International Society of Renal Nutrition and Metabolism (ISRNM) . . 15418

Secretariat address not obtained. E-mail: secretariat@isrnm.org.
URL: https://www.isrnm.org/
History 1976. Previously referred to as *International Society of Nutrition and Metabolism in Renal Disease.* **Aims** Advance the knowledge of and foster communication about nutrition and metabolism in renal disease and renal failure. **Structure** Council, consisting of President, President-Elect, Past President, Secretary, Treasurer, 6 at-Large members, Ex-Officio member and Associate Council member. **Languages** English. **Staff** None. **Finance** Members' dues: Full – US$ 120; Associate – US$ 100. **Activities** Organizes symposia and national meetings. Produces scientific statements. **Events** *Congress* Guangzhou (China) 2022, *Biennial Congress* Guangzhou (China) 2021, *Biennial Congress* Guangzhou (China) 2020, *Biennial Congress* Genoa (Italy) 2018, *Biennial Congress* Okinawa (Japan) 2016. **Publications** *International Renal Dietitians Newsletter, ISRNM E-Newsletter, Journal of Renal Nutrition.* Meeting reports; scientific statements.
Members Full in 43 countries and territories:
Australia, Austria, Belgium, Brazil, Canada, Chile, China, Colombia, Czechia, Denmark, Estonia, Finland, France, Germany, Greece, Hong Kong, Iceland, Ireland, Italy, Japan, Korea Rep, Latvia, Mexico, Netherlands, New Zealand, North Macedonia, Norway, Poland, Portugal, Russia, Saudi Arabia, Singapore, Slovakia, South Africa, Spain, Sweden, Switzerland, Taiwan, Trinidad-Tobago, Tunisia, Türkiye, UK, USA. [2021/XD3782/**D**]

♦ International Society for the Renewal of Sacred Catholic Music (inactive)

♦ International Society for Research on Aggression (ISRA) 15419

Exec Sec Georgia State Univ, Dept of Psychology, 140 Decatur St SE, Atlanta GA 30303, USA. T. +14044136287.
URL: http://www.israsociety.com/
History 1972, St Louis MO (USA). **Aims** Disseminate information regarding the causes and consequences of, and solutions to, aggressive behaviour in all its forms. **Structure** World Meeting; Council. **Languages** English. **Staff** None. **Finance** Sources: members' dues. **Activities** Awards/prizes/competitions; events/meetings; projects/programmes. **Events** *World Meeting* Ottawa, ON (Canada) 2022, *World Meeting* Ottawa, ON (Canada) 2020, *World Meeting* Paris (France) 2018, *World Meeting* Sydney, NSW (Australia) 2016, *World Meeting* Atlanta, GA (USA) 2014. **Publications** *Aggressive Behavior* (6 a year) – journal; *ISRA Bulletin* (2 a year). **Members** Fellow; Associate; Life Fellow; Student. Members mostly in USA. Membership countries not specified. **IGO Relations** Accredited by: *United Nations Office at Vienna (UNOV, #20604).* Associated with Department of Global Communications of the United Nations. [2019.12.18/XC4344/v/**C**]

♦ International Society for Research in Child and Adolescent Psychopathology (internationally oriented national body)
♦ International Society for Research on Civilization Diseases and Environment (inactive)
♦ International Society for Research on Civilization Diseases and Vital Substances (inactive)
♦ International Society for Research into DCD (unconfirmed)

♦ International Society for Research on Emotion (ISRE) 15420

Main Office 1545 Newton St NW, Washington DC 20010, USA.
URL: http://www.isre.org/
History Mar 1984, USA. Current bylaws adopted 29 Jul 2011. Registration: USA, Washington DC. **Aims** Provide a forum for the exchange of information; foster critical discussion of new ideas and findings on emotion; encourage collaboration on, or joint exploration of, new research areas; organize workshops and training institutes on new techniques and paradigms. **Structure** Board of Directors. **Finance** Sources: members' dues. **Activities** Events/meetings; training/education. **Events** *Conference* Los Angeles, CA (USA) 2022, *Meeting* Amsterdam (Netherlands) 2019, *Meeting* Geneva (Switzerland) 2015, *Meeting* Berkeley, CA (USA) 2013. **Publications** *Emotion Review* (4 a year) – journal; *Emotion Researcher* – newsletter. **Members** Full; Associate. Membership countries not specified. **NGO Relations** *International Society for Facial Expression (ISFE, #15112).* [2021/XJ9460/**C**]

♦ International Society for Research in EPH-Gestosis / see Organization Gestosis (#17869)
♦ International Society for Research on the Frontiers of Medicine (inactive)

♦ International Society for Research in Human Milk and Lactation (ISRHML) 15421

Executive Office 18 Avenue Louis Casai, 1209 Geneva, Switzerland. E-mail: info@isrhml.com.
URL: https://isrhml.org/
History 1988. **Aims** Promote excellence in research and the dissemination of research findings in the field of human milk and lactation. **Structure** Council; Executive. **Languages** English. **Staff** 2.00 FTE, paid. **Finance** Members' dues. Donations. **Activities** Events/meetings; awards/prizes/competitions; financial and/or material support. **Events** *Conference* Panama (Panama) 2022, *Congress* 2021, *Conference* Stockholm (Sweden) 2020, *Protecting, promoting and supporting breastfeeding from biology to policy* Hayama (Japan) 2018, *Conference* Stellenbosch (South Africa) 2016. **Publications** Monographs; conference proceedings.
Members Full; Associate; Trainee. Individuals in 27 countries:
Argentina, Australia, Austria, Belgium, Brazil, Czechia, Denmark, Finland, France, Germany, Greece, Iraq, Italy, Japan, Korea Rep, Mexico, Netherlands, New Zealand, Norway, Russia, Singapore, Slovenia, Spain, Sweden, Switzerland, UK, USA. [2022/XD7667/v/**D**]

♦ International Society for Research on Identity (ISRI) 15422

Sec address not obtained.
Pres address not obtained.
URL: http://identityisri.org/
History 2000. Former names and other names: *Society for Research on Identity Formation (SRIF)* – former (2000 to 2015). **Aims** Provide a nonpartisan forum within which identity researchers from a variety of areas can communicate their findings and stay apprised of the findings of others, especially among those who use different technical vocabularies. **Structure** Board of Directors; Advisory Board; Program Committee. **Languages** English. **Finance** Members' dues. **Activities** Events/meetings. **Events** *Conference* 2021, *Conference* Naples (Italy) 2019, *Conference* Groningen (Netherlands) 2017. **Publications** *Identity: An International Journal for Theory and Research on Identity.* [2022/XM6416/**D**]

♦ International Society for Research on Internet Interventions (ISRII) 15423

Contact 500 Westover Dr No 8131, Sanford NC 27330, USA. E-mail: info@isrii.org.
URL: http://www.isrii.org/
History 18 Sep 2004, Stockholm (Sweden). **Aims** Promote exchange of ideas and experience among researchers involved in *health* treatment and intervention research using the Internet. **Structure** Board of Directors. **Finance** Sources: members' dues. **Activities** Events/meetings. **Events** *Meeting* Auckland (New Zealand) 2019, *Making e/mHealth impactful in people's lives* Berlin (Germany) 2017, *Technologies for a digital world, improving health across the lifespan* Seattle, WA (USA) 2016, *Meeting* Valencia (Spain) 2014, *Meeting* Chicago, IL (USA) 2013. **Publications** *Internet Interventions* – journal. **NGO Relations** *European Society for Research on Internet Interventions (esrii, #08727).* [2017/XM0074/**C**]

♦ International Society for Research on Moor (inactive)
♦ International Society for Research on the Reticuloendothelial System (inactive)
♦ International Society for Research in Stereoencephalotomy / see World Society for Stereotactic and Functional Neurosurgery (#21812)

♦ International Society for the Research and Study of Diaconia and Christian Social Practice (ReDi) 15424

Sec address not obtained.
URL: https://www.diaconiaresearch.org/
Structure General Assembly; Executive Board. **Finance** Sources: members' dues. **Activities** Awards/prizes/competitions; events/meetings; networking/liaising; research/documentation. **Events** *International ReDi Conference* Oslo (Norway) 2023, *International ReDi Conference* Oslo (Norway) 2020, *International ReDi Conference* Berlin (Germany) 2018, *International ReDi Conference* Helsinki (Finland) 2016, *International ReDi Conference* Stockholm (Sweden) 2014. **Publications** *Diaconia – Journal for the Study of Christian Social Practice.*
Members Institutional; Individual; Regional. Institutional (13) in 5 countries:
Czechia, Finland, Germany, Norway, Sweden.
European Federation for Diaconia (Eurodiaconia, #07099); World Council of Churches (WCC, #21320).
Individuals (about 50). Membership countries not specified.
Regional and Thematic Networks (3).
International Academy for Diaconia and Social Action, Central & Eastern Europe (interdiac, #11545). [2021/AA1821/jy/**C**]

♦ International Society for Research on Textbooks and Educational media (#13242)

♦ International Society for Respiratory Protection (ISRP) 15425
Contact Private Bag 1001, Mona Vale NSW 2103, Australia. E-mail: secretary@isrp.com.
URL: http://www.isrp.com/
History 1983. **Aims** Enhance health and safety of persons that use or need to use respiratory protective devices; promote research into respiratory hazards, respiratory protective devices and evaluation techniques. **Structure** Regional Sections (4): Americas; European; Australasia; Asia. **Staff** Voluntary. **Finance** Sources: meeting proceeds; members' dues. Annual budget: 40,000 USD. **Activities** Knowledge management/ information dissemination; projects/programmes; standards/guidelines; training/education. **Events** *Biennial Conference* Oxford (UK) 2021, *Biennial Conference* Oxford (UK) 2020, *Biennial Conference* Denver, CO (USA) 2018, *Biennial Conference* Yokohama (Japan) 2016, *Biennial Conference* Prague (Czech Rep) 2014. **Publications** *ISRP Journal* (2 a year). Membership Directory. **Members** Technical and professional people involved in all aspects of non-medical occupational respiratory protection. Membership countries not specified. [2021/XD2621/**D**]

♦ International Society for Restorative Neurology (ISRN) 15426
Exec Dir 2020 Peachtree Rd NW, Atlanta GA 30309, USA. E-mail: ams@bcm.edu.
URL: http://restorativeneurology.org/
Aims Foster an environment for advancing knowledge in the field of restorative neurology through understanding of mechanisms of neurologic impairments, challenging unproven practices, and developing new interventions and assessment methods to facilitate the translation of discoveries into the clinical arena. **Structure** Board of Directors. **Events** *Asian Prosthetic and Orthotic Scientific Meeting* Taipei (Taiwan) 2014, *Meeting* Taipei (Taiwan) 2014, *Meeting* Melbourne, VIC (Australia) 2012. **Publications** *ISRN Newsletter*. **NGO Relations** *Asia Oceanian Society of Physical and Rehabilitation Medicine (AOSPRM, #01804)*. [2015/XJ9573/**C**]

♦ International Society for Rheumatic Therapeutics (no recent information)

♦ International Society for River Science (ISRS) 15427
Contact Kansas Biological Survey, W-113 Takeru Higuchi Hall Univ of Kansas, 2101 Constant Avenue, Lawrence KS 66047, USA. T. +17858641532. Fax +17858641537 – +17858641534.
URL: http://riversociety.org/
History Founded in 2009, following the meeting series *International Symposium on Regulated Rivers* and *International Symposium on Regulated Streams (ISORS)*. which began in 1985. **Aims** Promote river research, conservation and management. **Activities** Awards/prizes/competitions; events/meetings. **Events** *Biennial Congress* Vienna (Austria) 2019, *Biennial Congress* Hamilton (New Zealand) 2017, *Biennial Congress* La Crosse, WI (USA) 2015, *Biennial congress / Congress* Beijing (China) 2013, *Biennial congress / Congress* Berlin (Germany) 2011. **Publications** *River Research and Applications (RRA)* – official journal. **NGO Relations** *International Association for Hydro-Environment Engineering and Research (IAHR, #11950)*. [2018/XM0346/**C**]

♦ International Society for Rock Mechanics / see International Society for Rock Mechanics and Rock Engineering (#15428)

♦ International Society for Rock Mechanics and Rock Engineering (ISRM) 15428
SG c/o LNEC, Av Brasil 101, 1700-066 Lisbon, Portugal. T. +351218443419. Fax +351218443021. E-mail: secretariat@isrm.net.
Main: http://www.isrm.net/
History 1962, Salzburg (Austria). Founded as a result of enlarging the *'Salzburger Kreis'* and the efforts of Prof L Müller. Statutes approved 1991, Aachen (Germany); 2021. Former names and other names: *International Society for Rock Mechanics (ISRM)* – former (1962 to 2021). **Aims** Encourage teaching, research and advancement of knowledge in rock mechanics and international collaboration and exchange of ideas and information among rock mechanics practitioners; promote high standards of professional practice among rock engineers so as to ensure that civil, *mining* and *petroleum engineering* works are safer, more economic and less disruptive to the environment. **Structure** Council; Board; Commissions (17); Secretariat in Lisbon (Portugal). **Languages** English. **Staff** Voluntary. **Finance** Sources: members' dues. **Activities** Awards/prizes/ competitions; events/meetings; research and development; training/education. **Events** *ISRM International Congress on Rock Mechanics* Salzburg (Austria) 2023, *EUROCK : European Regional Symposium* Helsinki (Finland) 2022, *EUROCK : European Regional Symposium* Rome (Italy) 2021, *International Conference on Coupled Processes in Fractured Geological Media: Observation, Modeling, and Application* Seoul (Korea Rep) 2020, *EUROCK : European Regional Symposium* Trondheim (Norway) 2020. **Publications** *ISRM Newsletter* (3 a year); *ISRM News Journal* (annual). Congress proceedings; educational documents – published by commissions; slide sheets; videos; educational software. **Information Services** *ISRM Digital Library*.
Members National groups, individual (6,621), corporate (140) and corresponding members (162, 'C' indicate corresponding members only) in 68 countries:
Algeria (C), Argentina, Australia, Austria, Bahrain (C), Belgium, Bolivia, Bosnia-Herzegovina, Botswana (C), Brazil, Bulgaria (C), Canada, Chile, China, Colombia, Costa Rica, Croatia, Czechia, Denmark, Ecuador (C), Egypt (C), Ethiopia (C), Finland, France, Germany, Ghana (C), Greece, Guatemala (C), India, Indonesia, Iran Islamic Rep, Iraq (C), Ireland (C), Israel, Italy, Japan, Korea Rep, Malaysia (C), Malta (C), Mexico (C), Nepal, Netherlands, New Zealand, Nigeria (C), North Macedonia (C), Norway, Pakistan (C), Paraguay, Peru, Poland, Portugal, Romania (C), Russia, Serbia, Singapore, Slovakia, Slovenia, South Africa, Spain, Sri Lanka (C), Sweden, Switzerland, Türkiye, UK, United Arab Emirates (C), USA, Venezuela, Zambia (C).
Included in the above, 1 regional organization listed in this Yearbook:
Southeast Asian Geotechnical Society (SEAGS, #19769).
NGO Relations Member of (1): *Federation of International Geo-Engineering Societies (FedIGS, #09673)*. Affiliated member of: *International Union of Geological Sciences (IUGS, #15777)*. Observers at Council meetings: *International Association of Engineering Geology and the Environment (IAEG, #11872)*; *International Commission on Large Dams (ICOLD, #12696)*; *International Society for Soil Mechanics and Geotechnical Engineering (ISSMGE, #15452)*; *International Tunnelling and Underground Space Association (ITA, #15744)*; *Society of Petroleum Engineers (SPE, #19616)*; *World Mining Congress (WMC, #21654)*. Related organizations: *International Association for Computer Methods and Advances in Geomechanics (IACMAG, #11802)*; *International Association for Earthquake Engineering (IAEE, #11855)*; *International Association of Hydrogeologists (IAH, #11953)*; *International Association of Seismology and Physics of the Earth's Interior (IASPEI, #12157)*; *Réunion internationale des laboratoires d'essais et de recherches sur les matériaux et les constructions (RILEM, #18930)*. [2022/XC2505/**C**]

♦ International Society of Root Research (ISRR) 15429
Exec Sec c/o FZ-J, IBG-2, Wilhelm-Johnen-Str, 52428 Jülich, Germany. E-mail: isrr@fz-juelich.de.
Pres address not obtained.
URL: http://www.rootresearch.org/
History 1982. **Aims** Increase communication, cooperation and research into root, *rhizosphere* and related topics. **Structure** Executive Committee. **Languages** English. **Staff** None. **Finance** Voluntary laws. **Activities** Events/meetings. **Events** *International Symposium* China 2027, *International Symposium* Leipzig (Germany) 2024, *Symposium* Columbia, MO (USA) 2021, *Exposing the hidden half* Maale HaHamisha (Israel) 2018, *Roots down under – Belowground solutions to global challenges* Canberra, ACT (Australia) 2015. **Publications** *ISRR Newsletter*. Symposium proceedings.
Members Organizations in 11 countries:
Australia, China, France, Germany, Japan, Kazakhstan, Netherlands, Russia, Sweden, UK, USA.
Individuals in 72 countries:
Argentina, Armenia, Australia, Austria, Belgium, Bolivia, Brazil, Bulgaria, Burundi, Canada, Central African Rep, Chile, China, Czechia, Denmark, Ecuador, Egypt, Estonia, Ethiopia, Finland, France, Georgia, Germany, Greece, Haiti, Hungary, Iceland, India, Indonesia, Iraq, Ireland, Israel, Italy, Jamaica, Kenya, Kuwait, Latvia, Lesotho, Liberia, Lithuania, Luxembourg, Malaysia, Mexico, Nepal, Netherlands, New Zealand, Nigeria, Norway, Pakistan, Peru, Poland, Portugal, Romania, Russia, Rwanda, Serbia, Singapore, Slovakia, South Africa, Spain, Sri Lanka, Sweden, Switzerland, Tajikistan, Thailand, Tunisia, Uganda, UK, Ukraine, Uzbekistan, Venezuela, Zambia. [2023.03.01/XD1021/**D**]

♦ International Society of the Rorschach and Projective Methods (IRS) 15430
Société internationale du Rorschach et des méthodes projectives (SIR) – Sociedad Internacional de Rorschach y Métodos Proyectivos – Internationale Rorschach-Gesellschaft (IGROF)
Pres 4-12-16-617 Bunkyo-ku Hongo, Tokyo, 1130033 Japan.
Gen Sec address not obtained.
URL: http://www.rorschach.com/
History 1952, Bern (Switzerland). Original French title: *Société internationale du test de Rorschach et autres méthodes projectives*. Subsequently changed title to *International Rorschach Society (IRS) – Société Rorschach internationale (SIR)*. Registered in accordance with Swiss law. **Aims** Develop international contacts between *psychologists* specializing in the Rorschach method; promote theoretical and practical knowledge of Rorschach and projective techniques; safeguard and develop the archives of Rorschach and projective tests. **Structure** Assembly of Delegates; Executive Board. Membership open; meetings closed. **Languages** English, French, Japanese, Spanish. **Staff** None. **Finance** Members' dues. Other sources: donations; grants; profits from scientific activities. **Activities** Knowledge management/information dissemination; training/ education; projects/programmes. **Events** *Triennial Congress* Geneva (Switzerland) 2022, *Triennial Congress* Geneva (Switzerland) 2021, *Triennial Congress* Paris (France) 2017, *Triennial Congress* Istanbul (Turkey) 2014, *Summer Seminar* San Remo (Italy) 2012. **Publications** *IRS Bulletin* (annual); *IRS Newsletter* (annual); *Rorschachiana*. Online access to archives.
Members National societies or groups in 21 countries:
Argentina, Austria, Brazil, Canada, Cuba, Czechia, Finland, France, Israel, Italy, Japan, Mexico, Netherlands, Peru, Spain, Sweden, Switzerland, Türkiye, UK, USA, Venezuela.
Individuals (over 100) in 12 countries:
Austria, Denmark, Dominican Rep, Germany, Greece, India, Ireland, Norway, Philippines, Poland, Tunisia, UK.
IGO Relations Instrumental in setting up: *ALFA Programme (inactive)*. [2017.07.19/XE2422/**E**]

♦ International Society for Rotary Blood Pumps / see International Society for Mechanical Circulatory Support (#15251)

♦ International Society for Salt Lake Research (ISSLR) 15431
Pres Chinese Ac of Geological Sciences, 100037 Beijing, China. E-mail: shengmp2010@126.com.
Sec/Treas PO Box 176, Darlington WA 6070, Australia.
URL: http://www.isslr.org/
History 1988, Banyoles (Spain), as *International Consortium for Salt Lake Research*. Present name adopted 1994. Incorporated in the State of California (USA). **Aims** Establish effective liaison between persons interested in any aspect of inland saline waters, encourage these interests and educate the public in scientific use, management and conservation of salt lakes. **Structure** Board of Directors. **Languages** English. **Staff** 50.00 FTE, voluntary. **Finance** Members' dues. **Activities** Active in: Argentina, Austria, Bolivia, Canada, China, Germany, Israel, Laos, Russia, Spain, USA. **Events** *Triennial Conference* Grand Epoch City (China) 2014, *Triennial Conference* Langfang (China) 2014, *Triennial Conference* Córdoba (Argentina) 2011, *Triennial Conference* Salt Lake City, UT (USA) 2008, *Triennial Conference* Perth, WA (Australia) 2005. **Publications** Conference proceedings. **Members** Membership countries not specified. [2015.06.26/XD9178/**D**]

♦ International Society for Sandplay Therapy (ISST) 15432
Internationale Gesellschaft für Sandspiel Therapie – Associazione Internationale della Sandplay Therapy
Admin Sec address not obtained. E-mail: isst.office@gmail.com.
URL: http://www.isst-society.com/
History Founded 13 Aug 1985, Zollikon (Switzerland). Registered in accordance with Swiss Civil Code. **Structure** Board. **Activities** Events/meetings; knowledge management/information dissemination; networking/ liaising; research/documentation. **Events** *Congress* Berlin (Germany) 2019, *Congress* Amsterdam (Netherlands) 2018.
Members Societies in 14 countries and territories:
Brazil, Canada, Germany, Hong Kong, Ireland, Israel, Italy, Japan, Latvia, Netherlands, Switzerland, Taiwan, UK, USA.
Individual members in 13 countries:
Australia, Belgium, China, Denmark, France, Korea Rep, New Zealand, Poland, Romania, Russia, Singapore, South Africa, Uruguay. [2019/XM8022/**C**]

♦ International Society for Sandwich Construction and Bonding (inactive)

♦ International Society of Schema Therapy (ISST) 15433
Permanent Address Glossop-Ring 35, 61118 Bad Vilbel, Germany. E-mail: office@isstonline.com – schemasociety@gmail.com.
URL: https://schematherapysociety.org/
History Statutes adopted at founding assembly 11 Oct 2008, Coimbra (Portugal). Statutes revised, 8 Jul 2010, Berlin (Germany); May 2012, New York NY (USA); May 2015, New York NY (USA). Registered in accordance with German law. **Aims** Support *health care* of the population of member countries. **Structure** Membership Assembly (at Conference); Board. **Languages** English, German. **Staff** 0.50 FTE, paid; 7.00 FTE, voluntary. **Finance** Sources: members' dues. **Activities** Events/meetings; knowledge management/information dissemination; monitoring/evaluation; research and development. **Events** *INSPIRE Conference* Copenhagen (Denmark) 2022, *ISST Virtual Summmit* Bad Vilbel (Germany) 2021, *INSPIRE Conference* Copenhagen (Denmark) 2021, *INSPIRE Conference* Copenhagen (Denmark) 2020, *Summit* Frankfurt-Main (Germany) 2020. **Publications** *Schema Therapy Bulletin*. Books. **Members** Full (574); Associate (44); Supporting (31); Honorary (2). Membership EU (494); non-EU (157); majority (173) in Germany. [2021/XJ5008/**C**]

♦ International Society for the Scholarship of Teaching and Learning (ISSOTL) 15434
Sec Academic Excellence and Assessment, Communications Studies, Creighton University, 2500 California Plaza, Omaha NE 68178, USA. T. +14023802535. E-mail: maddam@creighton.edu.
URL: http://www.issotl.com/
History Mar 2003, Bloomington IN (USA). **Aims** Foster and disseminate inquiry on the factors that improve and articulate post-secondary learning and teaching; encourage application of the results. **Events** *Annual Conference* Atlanta, GA (USA) 2019, *Annual Conference* Bergen (Norway) 2018, *Annual Conference* Calgary, AB (Canada) 2017, *Annual Conference* Los Angeles, CA (USA) 2016, *Annual Conference / Conference* Melbourne, VIC (Australia) 2015. [2015/XM0076/**D**]

♦ International Society for the Science of Engineering Design (inactive)

♦ International Society for Science and Religion (ISSR) 15435
Exec Dir 2B Gregory Ave, Coventry, CV3 9ED, UK. T. +447471773152. E-mail: admin@issr.org.uk – execassist@issr.org.uk.
Main Website: http://www.issr.org.uk/
History 23 Aug 2002, Granada (Spain). Registration: No/ID: 1100273, UK. **Aims** Promote education through support of inter-disciplinary learning and research in the fields of science and religion conducted where possible in an international and multi-faith context. **Structure** Executive Committee. **Languages** English. **Staff** 2.00 FTE, paid. **Activities** Events/meetings; knowledge management/information dissemination; research/documentation. **Events** *Religion, Evolution, and Social Bonding* Oxford (UK) 2019, *Being Human in a Technological Age* Pretoria (South Africa) 2018, *Joint Conference on Religion, Society and the Science of Life* Oxford (UK) 2017, *North American Regional Conference* Atlanta, GA (USA) 2015, *ISSR Vienna Conference* Vienna (Austria) 2015. **Publications** *A 21st Century Debate on Sciencce and Religion* (2017); *Why the Science and Religion Dialogue Matters* (2006).
Members Fellowship by invitation only. Associates may register at any time. Members in 26 countries and territories:
Australia, Canada, China, Denmark, Estonia, France, Germany, India, Israel, Italy, Japan, Korea Rep, Netherlands, New Zealand, Norway, Pakistan, Poland, Romania, South Africa, Sweden, Taiwan, Türkiye, UK, United Arab Emirates, USA. [2023.02.14/XD8936/**D**]

♦ International Society of Scientist-Artists / see Leonardo/International Society for the Arts, Sciences and Technology (#16444)

♦ International Society for Scientometrics and Informetrics (ISSI) ... 15436
Internationale Gesellschaft für Szientometrie und Informetrie
Sec-Treas Ctr for R & D Monitoring, KU Leuven, Naamsestraat 61 – PO box 3551, 3000 Leuven, Belgium. T. +3216325713. Fax +3216325799.

URL: http://www.issi-society.org/
History 5 Oct 1994, Utrecht (Netherlands). **Aims** Advance the theory, method and explanation of: (1) quantitative studies of scientific, technological and other scholarly and substantive information; the science of science and technology, social sciences, arts and humanities; generation, diffusion and use of information; information systems, including libraries, archives and databases; (2) mathematical, statistical and computational modelling and analysis of information processes. **Structure** Board. **Languages** English. **Staff** 8.00 FTE, voluntary. **Events** *International Conference* Bloomington, IN (USA) 2023, *International Conference* Leuven (Belgium) 2021, *International Conference* Rome (Italy) 2019, *International Conference* Wuhan (China) 2017, *International Conference* Istanbul (Turkey) 2015. **Publications** *ISSI Newsletter*. Proceedings.
Members Individuals in 35 countries:
Australia, Bangladesh, Belgium, Brazil, Canada, China, Cuba, Czechia, Denmark, Finland, France, Germany, Hungary, India, Indonesia, Iran Islamic Rep, Israel, Italy, Japan, Latvia, Mexico, Netherlands, New Zealand, Nigeria, Philippines, Poland, Romania, Russia, Singapore, South Africa, Spain, Türkiye, UK, Uruguay, USA.
NGO Relations Instrumental in setting up: *Centre for Inquiry – Europe.* [2020/XD4793/v/**D**]

♦ International Society on Scoliosis Orthopaedic and Rehabilitation Treatment (SOSORT) 15437

Coordinator c/o ISICO, Via Roberto Bellarmino 13/1, 20141 Milan MI, Italy. T. +39284161700.
Sec address not obtained.
URL: https://www.sosort.org/
History Founded Jan 2004, Barcelona (Spain), as *International Society on Spinal Orthopaedic and Rehabilitation Treatment.* **Aims** Foster best conservative management of *scoliosis* and other spinal deformities; encourage multidisciplinary team work. **Structure** Board; President. **Languages** English. **Staff** Voluntary. **Finance** Sources: members' dues. **Activities** Events/meetings; networking/liaising; standards/guidelines; training/education. **Events** *International Conference on Conservative Management of Spinal Deformities* San Sebastian (Spain) 2022, *International Conference on Conservative Management of Spinal Deformities* San Sebastian (Spain) 2021, *International Conference on Conservative Management of Spinal Deformities* Milan (Italy) 2020, *International Conference on Conservative Management of Spinal Deformities* San Francisco, CA (USA) 2019, *International Conference on Conservative Management of Spinal Deformities* Dubrovnik (Croatia) 2018. **Publications** *Scoliosis and Spinal Disorders Journal.* Guidelines; consensus papers.
Members Individuals in 42 countries and territories:
Algeria, Australia, Austria, Belgium, Brazil, Bulgaria, Canada, Chile, China, Croatia, Czechia, Denmark, France, Germany, Greece, Hong Kong, Hungary, India, Indonesia, Ireland, Israel, Italy, Japan, Korea Rep, Latvia, Netherlands, North Macedonia, Norway, Poland, Portugal, Romania, Russia, Singapore, Slovakia, South Africa, Spain, Switzerland, Taiwan, Türkiye, UK, Ukraine, USA. [2020.03.03/XJ0423/**C**]

♦ International Society of Securities Administrators / see International Securities Services Association (#14824)

♦ International Society for Seed Science (ISSS) 15438

Sec Royal Botanic Gardens, Wellcome Trust Millennium Bldg, Wakehurst Place, Ardingly, Haywards Heath, RH17 6TN, UK. T. +441444894142. Fax +441444894110.
URL: http://www.seedscisoc.org/
History 1999. Founded during 6th International Workshop on Seeds. **Aims** Foster and promote research, education and communication in the scientific understanding of seeds. **Structure** Executive Committee; Regional Representatives (10). **Languages** English. **Staff** Voluntary. **Activities** Events/meetings. **Events** *Seed innovation systems for the 21st century* Brighton (UK) 2021, *Seed innovation systems for the 21st century* Brighton (UK) 2020, *International Symposium on Plant Dormancy* Kyoto (Japan) 2018, *Conference* Monterey, CA (USA) 2017, *Conference* Changsha (China) 2014. **Publications** *ISSS Newsletter*, *Seed Science Research* – official journal. Annual Report; books. **Members** Individuals. Membership countries not specified. [2021.02.24/XM4078/**C**]

♦ International Society of Seed Technologists (no recent information)
♦ International Society of Service Innovation Professionals (internationally oriented national body)
♦ International Society for Sexual and Impotence Research / see International Society for Sexual Medicine (#15441)

♦ International Society for Sexuality and Cancer (ISSC) 15439

Contact COMM Santé, 76 rue Marcel Sembat, 33323 Bègles CEDEX, France. T. +33557970088. Fax +33557971915. E-mail: secretariat@issc.nu.
URL: http://www.issc.nu/
History Founded Oct 2002. **Aims** Serve as a forum for research, treatment, care and prevention aspects of sexual problems in cancer; encourage highest standards of practice, education and research in the field of sexuality and cancer. **Structure** General Meeting; Board of Directors; Committees (6): Nominations; Scientific Programme; Meetings; On-line Services; Education; Membership. **Languages** English. **Staff** None. **Finance** Members' dues. **Activities** Organizes international congress. **Events** *Symposium on Cancer and Sexuality* Lyon (France) 2012, *Symposium on cancer and sexuality / Congress* Rotterdam (Netherlands) 2010, *Symposium on cancer and sexuality / Congress* Rotterdam (Netherlands) 2006.
Members Categories Active; Student; Senior; Affiliated; Business. Cancer clinicians, experts in sexual medicine, social workers, nurses and psychologists. Members in 8 countries:
Australia, France, Israel, Italy, Netherlands, Poland, UK, USA. [2013.11.27/XD9357/v/**D**]

♦ International Society for Sexually Transmitted Diseases Research (ISSTDR) 15440

SG UAB Med School, 1720 2nd Ave S, FOT 1203, Birmingham AL 35294-3412, USA. E-mail: bvanderp@uab.edu.
URL: http://www.isstdr.org/
History 1977. **Aims** Promote research in all aspects of sexually transmitted infections, including: microbiology, virology, pathogenesis, behavioural and social sciences; clinical sciences; epidemiology; prevention. **Structure** Board (elected on rotating basis for 6-year terms), comprising President, President-Elect, Past President and 12 members. President chairs upcoming international meeting. *ISSTDR Conference Support Foundation.* **Languages** English. **Staff** None. **Finance** Sources: meeting registrations; donations; grants. **Activities** Organizes biennial meeting in odd numbered years and in venues that alternate between Europe and North America. **Events** *Congress (STI and HIV 2019 World Congress)* Vancouver, BC (Canada) 2019, *Congress* Rio de Janeiro (Brazil) 2017, *STI and HIV World Congress* Rio de Janeiro (Brazil) 2017, *Biennial Congress* Brisbane, QLD (Australia) 2015, *STI and HIV World Congress* Brisbane, QLD (Australia) 2015. **Publications** Abstracts of meeting papers. [2015/XD1479/**D**]

♦ International Society for Sexual Medicine (ISSM) 15441

Exec Dir Zaanweg 119a, 1521 DS Wormerveer, Netherlands. T. +31756476372. Fax +31756476371. E-mail: secretariat@issm.info.
SG Lawson Research Inst, 268 Grosvenor St, London ON N6A 4V2, Canada.
URL: http://www.issm.info/
History 1982. Former names and other names: *International Society for Impotence Research (ISIR)* – former; *International Society for Sexual and Impotence Research (ISSIR)* – former. **Aims** Be the most respected and trusted source of information, education and professional development on human sexual health. **Structure** Executive Committee. Continental or regional professional societies (7): *Asia Pacific Society for Sexual Medicine (APSSM, #02045)*; *European Society for Sexual Medicine (ESSM, #08733)*; *International Society for the Study of Women's Sexual Health (ISSWSH)*; *Middle East Society for Sexual Medicine (MESSM, #16791)*; Sexual Medicine Society of North America (SMSMA); *Sociedad Latinoamericana de Medicina Sexual (SLAMS, #19413)*; *South Asian Society for Sexual Medicine (SASSM, #19743)*. **Languages** English. **Staff** 1.50 FTE, paid. **Finance** Sources: members' dues. **Activities** Events/meetings; knowledge management/information dissemination; publishing activities; training/education. **Events** *Biennial World Congress* Yokohama (Japan) 2021, *Biennial World Congress* Yokohama (Japan) 2020, *Biennial World Congress* Lisbon (Portugal) 2018, *Biennial World Congress* Beijing (China) 2016, *International Consultation on Sexual Medicine* Madrid (Spain) 2015. **Publications** *Journal for Sexual Medicine* (12 a year); *Sexual Medicine Review* (4 a year); *Sexual Medicine* – open access journal; *Video Journal on Prosthetic Urology.*
Members Full in 87 countries and territories:
Algeria, Argentina, Armenia, Australia, Austria, Bahrain, Bangladesh, Belarus, Belgium, Brazil, Bulgaria, Canada, Chile, China, Colombia, Cyprus, Czechia, Denmark, Dominican Rep, Ecuador, Egypt, Eswatini, Ethiopia, Finland, France, Georgia, Germany, Greece, Hong Kong, Hungary, India, Indonesia, Iran Islamic Rep, Ireland, Israel, Italy, Japan, Kazakhstan, Korea Rep, Kuwait, Lebanon, Libya, Lithuania, Malaysia, Mali, Mexico, Mongolia, Netherlands, New Zealand, Nigeria, Norway, Pakistan, Paraguay, Peru, Philippines, Poland, Portugal, Puerto Rico, Qatar, Romania, Russia, Saudi Arabia, Senegal, Serbia, Singapore, Slovakia, Slovenia, South Africa, Spain, Sri Lanka, Sudan, Sweden, Switzerland, Syrian AR, Taiwan, Thailand, Tunisia, Türkiye, UK, Ukraine, United Arab Emirates, Uruguay, USA, Uzbekistan, Venezuela, Vietnam, Zambia. [2022.02.02/XD5699/**C**]

♦ International Society for Shamanistic Research (inactive)

♦ International Society for Simulation Surgery (ISSiS) 15442

Address not obtained.
URL: http://www.issis.org/
History Dec 1992, Tokyo (Japan), during inaugural meeting. 1993, merged into *International Society for Computer Aided Surgery (ISCAS, #15028)*, eventually becoming dormant. Revived 2004. **Events** *Biennial congress / Meeting* Seoul (Korea Rep) 2012, *Biennial Congress* Honolulu, HI (USA) 2010, *Meeting* Waikiki, HI (USA) 2010, *Biennial congress / Meeting* Taipei (Taiwan) 2008, *Biennial congress / Meeting* Chiang Mai (Thailand) 2006. **Members** Membership countries not specified. [2012/XJ8078/**D**]

♦ International Society for Skiing Safety (ISSS) 15443

Société internationale pour la sécurité en ski – Internationaler Arbeitskreis Sicherheit beim Skilauf (IAS)
Sec-Treas PO Box 284, Martinborough 5781, New Zealand. T. +6421968919.
URL: http://www.isssweb.com/
History 1975, Sweden. 1975, Riksgrenzen (Sweden). Has been referred to as *International Organization for Safety in Skiing.* **Aims** Act as a forum to discuss all aspects of skiing safety; find internationally accepted means of preventing ski injuries. **Structure** General Assembly; Board. **Languages** English. **Staff** 5.00 FTE, voluntary. **Finance** Annual budget: US$ 10,000. **Events** *Biennial Congress* Serre Chevalier (France) 2022, *Biennial Congress* USA 2019, *Biennial Congress* Innsbruck (Austria) 2017, *Biennial Congress* San Vito di Cadore (Italy) 2015, *Biennial Congress* Bariloche (Argentina) 2013. **Publications** Information letters; symposium papers.
Members Individual and industrial in 20 countries:
Argentina, Australia, Croatia, Czechia, Denmark, Finland, France, Germany, Greece, Italy, Japan, Korea Rep, Netherlands, New Zealand, Norway, Spain, Sweden, Switzerland, UK, USA. [2018.08.02/XD8800/**D**]

♦ International Society for Skin Imaging (inactive)

♦ International Society of Skin Pharmacology and Physiology (ISP) 15444

Secretariat c/o S Karger AG, Allschwilerstrasse 10, PO Box, 4009 Basel BS, Switzerland.
History 2003, Basel (Switzerland), on the initiative of Joachim W Fluhr and other physicians. **Events** *Meeting* La Grande Motte (France) 2008, *Meeting* Washington, DC (USA) 2007, *Meeting* Hamburg (Germany) 2005, *Meeting* Orlando, FL (USA) 2004. **Publications** *Journal of Skin Pharmacology and Skin Physiology* (periodical). [2011/XM8213/**D**]

♦ International Society for Ski Traumatology and Medicine of Winter Sport 15445

Société internationale de traumatologie de ski et de médecine des sports d'hiver (SITEMSH) – Internationale Gesellschaft für Skitraumatologie und Wintersport-Medizin – Società Internazionale di Traumatologia dello Sciismo e della Medicina degli Sport Invernali
Sec-Treas address not obtained. E-mail: sitemsh.andorra@gmail.com.
URL: http://www.sitemsh.org/
History 1954, France. Founded 1954, Chambéry-Courchevel (France). Registered in accordance with Swiss Civil Code. **Aims** Promote international exchange of medical experiences in treating and preventing winter sports injuries and mountaineering accidents. **Structure** Congress; Executive Board. **Languages** English. **Staff** Voluntary. **Finance** Members' dues. Other sources: voluntary contributions; grants. **Events** *Congress* Serre Chevalier (France) 2022, *Congress* Escaldes-Engordany (Andorra) 2020, *Congress* Inawashiro (Japan) 2016, *Congress* Teheran (Iran Islamic Rep) 2015, *Congress* Flachau (Austria) 2014. **Publications** Congress reports.
Members Doctors; societies. Members in 15 countries:
Andorra, Argentina, Austria, Chile, Czechia, France, Germany, Greece, Hungary, Italy, Kazakhstan, Spain, Switzerland, UK, USA. [2019.12.15/XD2506/**D**]

♦ International Society for Small and Medium Enterprises (ISSME) 15446

Contact RZ-71A/10, Tughlakabad Extension, Delhi 110019, DELHI 110019, India. T. +911129993844. Fax +911129993845.
Facebook: https://www.facebook.com/issme.org/
History Founded 29 Jul 2010. An ISO 9001:2008 Certified International Non-Governmental Organization. Registered in accordance with Indian law: S/69544. **Aims** Foster, promote and coordinate international cooperation and put in place a framework for sustained growth of SMEs at national, regional and international levels. **Structure** Council (General Assembly); Governing Board; Secretariat, located at Delhi (India). **Languages** English, Hindi. **Staff** 19.00 FTE, paid. **Finance** Sources: members' dues. Other sources: sponsorship for events, programmes, studies and research projects; subscriptions and publication sales; advertising and brand building; consultancy and business development services; skill development and training programmes; business matchmaking and exposure tours. **Activities** Advocacy/lobbying/activism; capacity building; events/meetings; guidance/assistance/consulting; knowledge management/information dissemination; training/education. **Events** *Annual World Conference* Ho Chi Minh City (Vietnam) 2016, *World Conference* Durban (South Africa) 2015, *World Conference on Best Practices in Promoting SMEs / Annual World Conference* Delhi (India) 2013. **Publications** *SME Voice* (12 a year) – magazine; *International Journal for Small and Medium Enterprises* (4 a year); *International Journal on Innovation and Technology Transfer* (4 a year); *International Journal on Rural Industralisation* (4 a year); *International Journal on Women Entrepreneurship* (4 a year); *World Directory of SME Experts* (annual); *World SME Directory* (annual); *Global SME Watch* (24 a year) – bulletin.
Members Full (342) in 35 countries:
Australia, Austria, Bangladesh, Bhutan, Botswana, Brazil, Cambodia, Canada, China, Colombia, Eswatini, Fiji, Germany, Ghana, India, Ireland, Kenya, Laos, Nepal, New Zealand, Nigeria, Peru, Portugal, South Africa, Spain, Sri Lanka, Tanzania UR, Thailand, UK, Ukraine, United Arab Emirates, USA, Vietnam, Zambia, Zimbabwe.
Consultative Status Consultative status granted from: *ECOSOC (#05331)* (Special). **IGO Relations** Cooperates with: UNDESA; *United Nations Economic and Social Commission for Asia and the Pacific (ESCAP, #20557)*. **NGO Relations** Cooperates with: *United Nations Global Compact (#20567).* [2020/XJ6529/**C**]

♦ International Society of Social Defence / see International Society of Social Defence and Humane Criminal Policy (#15447)

♦ International Society of Social Defence and Humane Criminal Policy (ISSD) 15447

Société internationale de défense sociale pour une politique criminelle humaniste (SIDS) – Sociedad Internacional de Defensa Social para una Politica Criminal Humanista – Società Internazionale de Defense Sociale pour une Politique Criminelle Humaniste
SG c/o CNPDS, Via Palestro 12, 20121 Milan MI, Italy. T. +39286460714. E-mail: cnpds.ispac@cnpds.it.
Pres Calle Altagracia 50, CIUDAD, 13071 Real, Ourense, Spain.
URL: https://defensesociale.org/
History 1946, Genoa (Italy). Name subsequently changed together with the adoption of the present statutes 1949, Liège (Belgium), when the Institute became the scientific and teaching instrument of the Society. Statutes revised: 1956; 1966; 1984. Former names and other names: *International Institute for the Studies of Social Defence* – former (1946 to 1949); *Institut international pour les études de défense sociale* – former (1946 to 1949); *International Society of Social Defence* – former (1949); *Société internationale de défense sociale* – former (1949); *Sociedad Internacional de Defensa Social* – former (1949). **Aims** Combat crime by promoting action to be taken both before and after the occurrence of offences, so as to both

protect society against criminals and prevent citizens from being tempted into criminal action. **Structure** General Assembly; Board; Bureau. **Languages** English, French, Spanish. **Staff** 1.00 FTE, voluntary. **Finance** Sources: members' dues. **Activities** Events/meetings. **Events** *Quinquennial International Congress* Mexico City (Mexico) 2012, *International Congress on Social Defence* Toledo (Spain) 2007, *European Seminar* Bogota (Colombia) 2005, *European seminar* Bogota (Colombia) 2005, *Quinquennial international congress on social defence / International Congress on Social Defence* Lisbon (Portugal) 2002. **Publications** *Cahiers de défense sociale* (annual) in English, French. Transactions of congresses, seminars and colloquia.

Members Legal, medical experts, criminologists and sociologists in 37 countries:
Argentina, Armenia, Australia, Austria, Belarus, Belgium, Brazil, Canada, Colombia, Costa Rica, Denmark, Egypt, Finland, France, Georgia, Germany, Greece, Hungary, India, Italy, Japan, Moldova, Netherlands, Nigeria, Norway, Poland, Portugal, Russia, Slovenia, Spain, Sudan, Sweden, Switzerland, UK, Ukraine, USA, Venezuela.

NGO Relations Member of: *Alliance of NGOs on Crime Prevention and Criminal Justice (#00709)*. Partner of: *Global Forum on Law, Justice and Development (GFLJD, #10373)*. [2019.09.25/XB2507/v/**B**]

♦ International Society for Socialist Studies (inactive)

♦ International Society for Social Pediatrics and Child Health (ISSOP) 15448

Treas address not obtained. E-mail: webmaster@essop.org.
URL: http://www.essop.org/

History 1977. Promotes *United Nations Convention on the Rights of the Child (CRC, 1989)*. Former names and other names: *European Society for Social Paediatrics (ESSOP)* – former (1977). **Aims** Stimulate the highest possible quality of research in social paediatrics; promote the teaching of social paediatrics at the undergraduate and postgraduate level in medical and related curricula; work for a better understanding among policy-makers for the consequences of social policy on children's well-being; promote a European strategy for 'health for all children' in cooperation with other international organizations. **Structure** General Assembly; Council; Executive Committee. **Languages** English. **Staff** 0.50 FTE, voluntary. **Finance** Sources: members' dues. **Activities** Events/meetings. **Events** *Annual Congress* Beirut (Lebanon) 2019, *Annual Congress* Bonn (Germany) 2018, *Annual Congress* Budapest (Hungary) 2017, *Annual Congress* Santiago (Chile) 2016, *Annual Congress* Geneva (Switzerland) 2015. **Publications** *ISSOP e-Bulletin* (6-8 a year).

Members Individuals in 29 countries:
Australia, Belgium, Bulgaria, Canada, Croatia, Czechia, Denmark, Finland, France, Germany, Greece, Hungary, Israel, Italy, Lithuania, Netherlands, New Zealand, Norway, Poland, Portugal, Romania, Russia, Slovakia, Spain, Sweden, Switzerland, Türkiye, UK, USA.

NGO Relations Member of (2): *End Corporal Punishment (#05457)*; *International Pediatric Association (IPA, #14541)*. [2019/XD4660/v/**C**]

♦ International Society of Social Science (inactive)

♦ International Society for the Social Sciences of Sport (ISSSS) 15449

Contact Monika Piatkowska, Jozef Pilsudski Univ of Physical Education, Marymoncka 34, 00-968 Warsaw, Poland. E-mail: pcssr@awf.edu.pl.
URL: http://www.issss.net/

History 13 Feb 2009, Poland, on the initiative of Jerzy Kosiewicz, Registered in accordance with Polish law. **Aims** Develop and popularize philosophical, sociological, psychological, pedagogical and historical knowledge concerning cultural, anthropological, axiological, moral, aesthetic, educational and organizational assumptions of broadly and variously understood sport, considered both from the historical and the present day perspective. **Structure** General Assembly; Executive Board. **Finance** Members' dues. Support from: Polish Society for the Social Sciences of Sport; universities. **Activities** Knowledge management/information dissemination; publishing activities; events/meetings. **Events** *Conference* Budapest (Hungary) 2015, *Sport and leisure management – tendencies and challenges* Kaunas (Lithuania) 2014, *Conference* Porto (Portugal) 2013, *Conference* Kranjska Gora (Slovenia) 2012, *Conference* Olomouc (Czech Rep) 2011. **Publications** *Physical Culture and Sport: Studies and Research* (4 a year) – journal. Monographs; book collections.

Members Full in 33 countries and territories:
Albania, Austria, Canada, China, Czechia, Denmark, Egypt, Estonia, Finland, France, Germany, Greece, Hungary, Iran Islamic Rep, Iraq, Italy, Japan, Latvia, Lithuania, Nigeria, Norway, Poland, Portugal, Qatar, Russia, Slovakia, Spain, Sweden, Taiwan, Türkiye, UK, Ukraine, USA. [2019/XJ6312/**D**]

♦ International Society for the Sociology of Knowledge (inactive)

♦ International Society for the Sociology of Music Education (iSSME) 15450

Address not obtained.
URL: https://www.internationalsocietyforthesociologyofmusiceducation.com/

History Jan 2021. Took over organization of *International Symposium on the Sociology of Music Education*. **Aims** Curate and disseminate dialogue and discussion in the field of sociology of music education. **Structure** Steering Committee. **Activities** Events/meetings. **Events** *International Symposium on the Sociology of Music Education* Xalapa (Mexico) 2023, *International Symposium on the Sociology of Music Education* Norway 2021. [2022/AA2570/c/**E**]

♦ International Society for the Sociology of Religions (ISSR) 15451

Société internationale de sociologie des religions (SISR)

Gen Sec Queen's Univ Belfast, University Road, Belfast, BT7 1NN, UK. T. +442890973581. E-mail: general_secretary@sisr-issr.org – administration@sisr-issr.org – contact@sisr-issr.org.
Treas Ctr Maurice Halbwachs, UMR 8097, École Normale Supérieure, 48 boulevard Jourdan, 75014 Paris, France.
URL: https://www.sisr-issr.org/

History 3 Apr 1948, Leuven (Belgium). New statutes adopted: 1971; 1985; 1989; 2001; 2003; 2014. Former names and other names: *International Conference for the Sociology of Religions (ICSR)* – former (3 Apr 1948 to 1989); *Conférence internationale de sociologie des religions (CISR)* – former (3 Apr 1948 to 1989). **Aims** Advance sociology and related sciences in the analysis and interpretation of religious and related phenomena. **Structure** General Assembly (every 2 years); Council; Executive Committee; General Secretariat. **Languages** English, French. **Staff** 0.50 FTE, paid. **Finance** Sources: fees for services; gifts, legacies; members' dues. Annual budget: 50,000 EUR. **Events** *Biennial Conference* Taipei (Taiwan) 2023, *Biennial Conference* 2021, *Biennial Conference* Barcelona (Spain) 2019, *Biennial Conference* Lausanne (Switzerland) 2017, *Biennial International Conference* Louvain-la-Neuve (Belgium) 2015. **Publications** *Network/Réseau* (3 a year) in English, French. Mailing list. **Information Services** *Who's Who*.

Members Individuals (about 400) in 50 countries and territories:
Argentina, Australia, Austria, Belgium, Brazil, Bulgaria, Canada, Chile, Czechia, Denmark, El Salvador, Eswatini, Finland, France, Germany, Greece, Hong Kong, Hungary, Iceland, India, Iran Islamic Rep, Ireland, Israel, Italy, Japan, Lebanon, Lithuania, Mexico, Morocco, Netherlands, Norway, Poland, Portugal, Romania, Russia, Senegal, Serbia, Slovakia, Slovenia, South Africa, Spain, Sweden, Switzerland, Tunisia, Türkiye, UK, Ukraine, Uruguay, USA, Venezuela. [2023/XF1684/v/**C**]

♦ International Society for Soilless Culture (inactive)

♦ International Society for Soil Mechanics and Foundation Engineering / see International Society for Soil Mechanics and Geotechnical Engineering (#15452)

♦ International Society for Soil Mechanics and Geotechnical Engineering (ISSMGE) 15452

Société internationale de mécanique des sols et de la géotechnique (SIMSG)

SG c/o City Univ London, Northampton Square, London, EC1V 0HB, UK. T. +442070408154. Fax +442070408832. E-mail: secretariat@issmge.org.
URL: http://www.issmge.org/

History 1936, Cambridge, MA (USA). Reconstituted at 2nd International Conference, 1948, Rotterdam (Netherlands). Statutes modified 1953, Zurich (Switzerland), on formal organization of the Society. Statutes subsequently modified: 1957, London (UK); 1961, Paris (France); 1965, Montréal QC (Canada). New Statutes adopted 1969, Mexico City (Mexico), revised: 1971, Sydney (Australia); 1973, Moscow (USSR); 1975, Istanbul (Turkey); 1977, Tokyo (Japan); 1979, Oaxaca (Mexico). New statutes adopted 1989. Statutes revised 1999, Amsterdam (Netherlands); 2005, Osaka (Japan); 2009, Alexandria (Egypt); 2011, Toronto ON (Canada); 2013, Paris (France); 2015, Edinburgh (UK); 2017, Seoul (Korea Rep). Former names and other names: *International Society for Soil Mechanics and Foundation Engineering (ISSMFE)* – former (1936 to 1997); *Société internationale de mécanique des sols et de travaux de fondations* – former (1936 to 1997); *Internationale Gesellschaft für Landbautechnik* – former (1936 to 1997). **Aims** Promote international cooperation among engineers and scientists for the advancement of knowledge in the field of geotechnics and its engineering applications. **Structure** Council (meeting every 2 years); Board; Regions (6); International Committees (31). Autonomous Technical Committees set up to investigate special problems. Meetings closed. **Languages** English, French. **Staff** 1.50 FTE, paid. **Finance** Sources: members' dues. **Activities** Events/meetings; knowledge management/information dissemination. **Events** *European Conference on Numerical Methods in Geotechnical Engineering* London (UK) 2023, *International Conference on Physical Modelling in Geotechnics (ICPMG 2022)* Daejeon (Korea Rep) 2022, *International Conference on Stress Wave Theory and Design and Testing Methods for Deep Foundations* Rotterdam (Netherlands) 2022, *International Conference on Soil Mechanics and Geotechnical Engineering* Sydney, NSW (Australia) 2022, *Asiafuge : International Conference on Physical Modelling in Geotechnics* Singapore (Singapore) 2021. **Publications** *ISSMGE Bulletin* – online. *Multilingual Lexicon of Soil Mechanics Terms*. Proceedings of international, regional and specialist conferences.

Members National societies in 88 countries and territories (Czechia and Slovakia form a single society):
Albania, Algeria, Argentina, Australia, Austria, Bangladesh, Belarus, Belgium, Bolivia, Bosnia-Herzegovina, Brazil, Bulgaria, Canada, Chile, China, Colombia, Costa Rica, Croatia, Cuba, Cyprus, Czechia, Denmark, Egypt, Estonia, Finland, France, Georgia, Germany, Ghana, Greece, Guatemala, Hong Kong, Hungary, Iceland, India, Indonesia, Iran Islamic Rep, Iraq, Ireland, Israel, Italy, Japan, Kazakhstan, Korea Rep, Kyrgyzstan, Latvia, Lebanon, Lithuania, Malaysia, Mexico, Mongolia, Morocco, Mozambique, Nepal, Netherlands, New Zealand, Nigeria, North Macedonia, Norway, Pakistan, Paraguay, Peru, Poland, Portugal, Romania, Russia, Serbia, Singapore, Slovakia, Slovenia, South Africa, Spain, Sri Lanka, Sudan, Sweden, Switzerland, Syrian AR, Taiwan, Tajikistan, Thailand, Tunisia, Türkiye, UK, Ukraine, USA, Uzbekistan, Venezuela, Vietnam.

Regional societies (2):
Comité transnational des géotechniciens d'Afrique (CTGA, #04199); *Southeast Asian Geotechnical Society (SEAGS, #19769)*.

NGO Relations Member of (1): *Federation of International Geo-Engineering Societies (FedIGS, #09673)*. Affiliated member of: *International Union of Geological Sciences (IUGS, #15777)*. In liaison with technical committees of: *International Organization for Standardization (ISO, #14473)*. Founder member of: Federation of International Geo-Engineering Societies (FedIGS). [2023.02.14/XB2509/**B**]

♦ International Society of Soil Sciences / see International Union of Soil Sciences (#15817)

♦ International Society for Solid State Ionics (ISSI) 15453

Sec SNU Materials Sci, Rm 33-116, College of Engineering, Seoul 151-742, Korea Rep.
URL: http://issi.snu.ac.kr/

History 8 Sep 1987, Garmisch-Partenkirchen (Germany). 8 Sep 1987, Garmisch Partenkirchen (Germany FR), during 6th International Conference on Solid State Ionics. **Aims** Promote science and technology related to all aspects of ionic transport in solids; provide an international and interdisciplinary forum for scientists in this field. **Structure** Council (meets at least every 2 years); Executive Committee. **Languages** English. **Finance** Members' dues. **Activities** Events/meetings. **Events** *Biennial Conference* Pyeongchang (Korea Rep) 2019, *Biennial Conference* Padua (Italy) 2017, *International Conference on Solid State Ionics* Keystone, CO (USA) 2015, *Biennial Conference / International Conference on Solid State Ionics* Kyoto (Japan) 2013, *Biennial conference / International Conference on Solid State Ionics* Warsaw (Poland) 2011. **Publications** *ISSI Letters* (4 a year).

Members Professionals in solid-state-ionics. Individuals in 47 countries and territories:
Argentina, Australia, Austria, Belarus, Belgium, Brazil, Canada, China, Denmark, Finland, France, Germany, Greece, Hong Kong, Hungary, Iceland, India, Indonesia, Ireland, Israel, Italy, Japan, Korea Rep, Lithuania, Luxembourg, Malaysia, Mexico, Netherlands, New Zealand, Norway, Poland, Portugal, Romania, Russia, Singapore, Slovakia, South Africa, Spain, Sweden, Switzerland, Taiwan, Türkiye, UK, USA, Venezuela, Vietnam. [2019.04.25/XD3490/v/**D**]

♦ International Society of Sophrology (inactive)

♦ International Society for Southeast Asian Agricultural Sciences (ISSAAS) 15454

Philippines Office Rm 41 1a, Vega Centre, 4031 Los Baños LAG, Philippines. T. +43495365816. E-mail: issaasphil@gmail.com – secretariat_phil@issaas.org.
Japan Office Dept of Intl Agricultural Development, Fac of Intl Food Studies, Tokyo Univ of Agriculture, 1-1-1 Sakuragaoka, Setagaya, Tokyo, 156-8502 Japan. E-mail: issaas.secretariat@gmail.com.
URL: http://issaasphil.org/home/

Aims Encourage the holistic approach to problems and promote progress and development of science and technology related to agricultural sciences through research and publication. **Structure** General Meeting. Executive Board. **Activities** Events/meetings; awards/prizes/competitions. **Events** *International Congress* Manila (Philippines) 2023, *International Congress* Bogor (Indonesia) 2022, *International Congress* Thailand 2021, *International Congress* Seri Kembangan (Malaysia) 2019, *International Congress* Kuching (Malaysia) 2018. **Publications** *Journal of ISSAAS* (2 a year).

Members Full; Honorary; Student; Supporting; Life. Members in 6 countries:
Indonesia, Japan, Malaysia, Philippines, Thailand, Vietnam. [2023/XM4693/**D**]

♦ International Society on Spinal Orthopaedic and Rehabilitation Treatment / see International Society on Scoliosis Orthopaedic and Rehabilitation Treatment (#15437)

♦ International Society of Sport Psychology (ISSP) 15455

Pres c/o Laurentian Univ, F534 Fraser Auditorium, 935 Ramsey Lake Road, Sudbury ON P3E 2C6, Canada. T. +17056751151 ext 1045. E-mail: socialmedia@issponline.org.
SG address not obtained.
URL: http://www.issponline.org/

History 1965, Rome (Italy). Founded at 1st World Congress of Sports Psychology. **Aims** Initiate and upgrade standards related to sports psychology research, information services, programs, guidelines and ultimately to all sports and physical activity; provide a medium for exchange of ideas to promote mutually beneficial understanding; stimulate scientific activities and programmes. **Structure** General Assembly (every 4 years); Executive Committee; Managing Council. **Languages** English. **Finance** Sources: members' dues. Annual budget: 4,000 USD. **Activities** Events/meetings; guidance/assistance/consulting. **Events** *World Congress in Sport Psychology* 2025, *World Congress* Taipei (Taiwan) 2021, *World Congress* Seville (Spain) 2017, *World Congress* Beijing (China) 2013, *World Congress* Marrakech (Morocco) 2009. **Publications** *International Journal of Sport and Exercise Psychology* (4 a year). Monographs; congress proceedings; position papers; ethical guidelines.

Members Group national or international associations representing the interests of sport psychology and/or related disciplines. Associations in 16 countries:
Australia, Belarus, Belgium, Brazil, China, France, Germany, Greece, Japan, Morocco, Nigeria, Norway, Poland, South Africa, Spain, Taiwan.

Individual persons with professional interest in sport psychology; Fellow individuals who have made a contribution to the development or prestige of sport psychology. Individuals in 73 countries and territories:
Albania, Argentina, Armenia, Australia, Austria, Azerbaijan, Bangladesh, Belarus, Belgium, Belize, Bolivia, Brazil, Bulgaria, Cambodia, Canada, China, Costa Rica, Croatia, Czechia, Denmark, Dominican Rep, Egypt, Estonia, Finland, France, Germany, Greece, Guatemala, Hong Kong, Hungary, India, Indonesia, Iraq, Ireland, Israel, Italy, Jamaica, Japan, Kazakhstan, Kenya, Korea Rep, Kyrgyzstan, Latvia, Lithuania, Malaysia, Mexico, Morocco, Netherlands, New Zealand, Nigeria, Norway, Paraguay, Peru, Philippines, Poland, Portugal, Puerto Rico, Qatar, Russia, Samoa, Serbia, Singapore, South Africa, Spain, Sweden, Switzerland, Taiwan, Thailand, Trinidad-Tobago, Türkiye, UK, USA, Venezuela.

NGO Relations Member of: *International Council of Sport Science and Physical Education (ICSSPE, #13077)*. Contacts with: *International Olympic Committee (IOC, #14408)*. Instrumental in developing: American Association of Applied Sport Psychology; *Asian-South Pacific Association of Sport Psychology (ASPASP, #01755)*; *European Federation of Sport Psychology (#07218)*; *North American Society for Sport Psychology and Physical Activity (NASPSPA)*; *South American Sport Psychology Society (SOSUPE, no recent information)*. [2021/XC4347/**C**]

♦ International Society of SR Spectroscopy (ISMS) 15456

Sec ISIS Facility, Rutherford Appleton Lab, Chilton, OX11 0QX, UK. T. +441235446117. Fax +441235445103.
URL: https://www.musr.org/

Aims Promote worldwide advancement of muon spin rotation, relaxation and resonance æSR. **Structure** General Assembly. Executive Committee, comprising President, 3 Vice-Presidents, Secretary, Treasurer and Webmaster. Chapters (3). **Finance** Members' dues. **Events** *International Conference on Muon Spin Rotation, Relaxation and Resonance* Parma (Italy) 2022, *International Conference on Muon Spin Rotation, Relaxation and Resonance* Parma (Italy) 2020, *International Conference on Muon Spin Rotation, Relaxation and Resonance* Sapporo (Japan) 2017, *International Conference on Muon Spin Rotation, Relaxation and Resonance* Grindelwald (Switzerland) 2014, *International conference on muon spin rotation, relaxation and resonance / Conference* Cancún (Mexico) 2011. [2020/XM0085/**D**]

♦ International Society of Statistical Science (inactive)

♦ International Society for Stem Cell Research (ISSCR) 15457

CEO 5215 Old Orchard Rd, Ste 270, Skokie IL 60077, USA. T. +12245925700. E-mail: isscr@isscr.org.
URL: http://www.isscr.org/

History 2002. **Aims** Promote and foster exchange and dissemination of information relating to stem cells; encourage education and research in stem cells. **Structure** Board of Directors of 15 members. Officers: President; President-Elect; Vice-President; Clerk; Treasurer; Past President. **Activities** Awards/prizes/competitions; events/meetings; standards/guidelines; training/education. **Events** *Annual Meeting* Boston, MA (USA) 2023, *Spatial Transcriptomics – From Methods to Insights* 2022, *Boston International Symposium* Boston, MA (USA) 2022, *Annual Meeting* San Francisco, CA (USA) 2022, *Cellular Barcoding* Skokie, IL (USA) 2022. **Publications** *The Pulse* – electronic newsletter. Reports; guidelines; handbooks; policy briefs. **Members** Full (over 4,100) in over 60 countries. Membership countries not specified. **NGO Relations** Member of (1): *Alliance for Regenerative Medicine (ARM).* [2022.02.02/XQ0309/**C**]

♦ International Society for Stereology / see International Society for Stereology and Image Analysis (#15458)

♦ International Society for Stereology and Image Analysis (ISSIA) . . . 15458

Sec c/o Mines ParisTech, Centre de Morphologie Mathématique, 60 Bd St. Michel, 75272 Paris CEDEX 06, France. E-mail: info@issia.net.
Pres Dept of Biology, Biotechnology, Univ of Ljubljana, Večna pot 111, Office V.2.15, 1000 Ljubljana, Slovenia.
Registered Address Jetelová 3255/9a, Záběhlice, 106 00 Prague 10, Czechia.
URL: https://www.issia.net/

History 12 May 1963, Neustadt (Germany). In 1979 took over the functions of *International Society for Automatic Image Analysts (inactive)*. By-Laws updated 1 Jan 1983. Former names and other names: *International Society for Stereology (ISS)* – former (12 May 1963). **Aims** Promote research on theory, practice and results of stereology, as an inter-disciplinary science to characterize three-dimensional structures from their sections, using image analysis to help clarify micro-*morphometrical* problems, particularly problems of quantitative *microscopy* and mathematical *morphology*. **Structure** Board; Committees (10). **Languages** English, French, German. **Finance** Sources: members' dues. **Activities** Events/meetings; knowledge management/information dissemination; research/documentation; training/education. **Events** *Quadrennial International Congress* Aarhus (Denmark) 2019, *Quadrennial European Congress* Kaiserslautern (Germany) 2017, *Quadrennial International Congress* Liège (Belgium) 2015, *Quadrennial European Congress* Kaiserslautern (Germany) 2013, *Quadrennial international congress* Beijing (China) 2011. **Publications** *Image Analysis and Stereology* (3 a year).
Members Regular; Honorary; Student; Due-Free. Individuals in 39 countries and territories:
Argentina, Australia, Austria, Belgium, Brazil, Canada, China, Croatia, Czechia, Denmark, Estonia, Finland, France, Germany, Hong Kong, Hungary, India, Ireland, Italy, Japan, Kuwait, Netherlands, New Zealand, Norway, Poland, Portugal, Russia, Saudi Arabia, Serbia, Slovenia, South Africa, Spain, Sweden, Switzerland, Tunisia, Türkiye, UK, Ukraine, USA.
Organizations in 3 countries:
China, India, South Africa. [2022/XC2510/**C**]

♦ International Society for Strategic Studies / Africa / (no recent information)

♦ International Society for Strategic Studies in Radiology (IS3R) 15459

Main Office Am Gestade 1, 1010 Vienna, Austria. E-mail: office@is3r.org.
URL: http://www.is3r.org/

History 1999. Founded following the Oxford International Symposium on the Cost and Benefits of Radiology events. Former names and other names: *ISSSR* – alias. Registration: No/ID: ZVR: 27937871, Austria. **Aims** Define and investigate strategic, scientific and economic issues of global importance to the field of radiology. **Structure** General Assembly; Executive Board. **Languages** English. **Staff** 1.00 FTE, paid; 1.00 FTE, voluntary. **Finance** Members' dues. **Events** *Biennial Symposium* Berlin (Germany) 2023, *Biennial Symposium* Budapest (Hungary) 2019, *Biennial Symposium* Washington, DC (USA) 2017, *Biennial Symposium* Amsterdam (Netherlands) 2015, *Biennial Symposium* Beijing (China) 2013. **Publications** *Historical Perspectives*. Proceedings.
Members in 19 countries:
Australia, Austria, Belgium, Canada, China, Czechia, France, Germany, Greece, India, Italy, Japan, Netherlands, Russia, Singapore, Sweden, Switzerland, UK, USA. [2022/XJ0478/**D**]

♦ International Society for Structural Health Monitoring of Intelligent Infrastructure (ISHMII) 15460

Contact Univ of Manitoba, Agricultural and Civil Engineering Bldg, A250 – 96 Dafoe Road, Winnipeg MB R3T 2N2, Canada. T. +12044748506. Fax +12044747519. E-mail: central@ishmii.org.
URL: http://www.ishmii.org/

Aims Advance understanding and application of structural health monitoring in the civil *engineering* infrastructure, in the service of the engineering profession and society. **Structure** Council. Executive Committee, comprising President, 6 Vice-Presidents, Treasurer, Secretary, Conference Chair and Newsletter Editor. Advisory Committee. Working Groups (5). **Finance** Members' dues. **Activities** Working Groups: Code Implementation Strategies; International SHM Guidelines; Marketing and Communications; SHM Applications; Technology Transfer, Education and Training. **Events** *International Conference on Structural Health Monitoring of Intelligent Infrastructure* Montréal, QC (Canada) 2022, *International Conference on Structural Health Monitoring of Intelligent Infrastructure* Porto (Portugal) 2021, *International Conference on Structural Health Monitoring of Intelligent Infrastructure* St Louis, MO (USA) 2019, *International Conference on Structural Health Monitoring of Intelligent Infrastructure* Brisbane, QLD (Australia) 2017, *International Conference on Structural Health Monitoring of Intelligent Infrastructure* Turin (Italy) 2015. **Publications** *The Monitor* (annual).
Members Institutions and companies (16) in 8 countries:
Austria, Canada, Germany, Hong Kong, Japan, Sweden, Switzerland, USA. [2014/XM2045/**D**]

♦ International Society for Structural and Multidisciplinary Optimization (ISSMO) 15461

SG c/o Dept Civil Engineering, Johns Hopkins Univ, Baltimore MD, USA. T. +14105168680.
Pres c/o State Key Lab for Structural Analysis of Industrial Equipment, Dalian Univ of Technology, Dalian, 116024 Liaoning, China. T. +8641184706599.
URL: http://www.issmo.net/

History 1991, Berchtesgaden (Germany), as the *International Society for Structural Optimization*. Present name adopted, 1993. **Aims** Stimulate and promote research into all aspects of optimal design of structures as well as multidisciplinary design optimization where the involved disciplines deal with analysis of solids, fluids or other field problems; encourage practical applications of optimization methods and corresponding software development in all branches of technology; foster interchange of ideas among various fields contributing to structural and multidisciplinary optimization; provide a framework for organization of meetings, fora and other means for dissemination of knowledge on structural and multidisciplinary optimization; promote teaching of structural and multidisciplinary optimization. **Structure** General Meeting (every 2 years); Executive Committee. **Languages** English. **Staff** Voluntary. **Finance** Portion of registration fees for World Congresses. **Activities** Events/meetings. **Events** *Biennial World Congress* Sydney, NSW (Australia) 2015, *China-Japan-Korea Joint Symposium on Optimization of Structural and Mecanical Systems* Gyeongju (Korea Rep) 2014, *EngOpt : International Conference on Engineering Optimization* Lisbon (Portugal) 2014, *Biennial World Congress* Orlando, FL (USA) 2013, *Biennial world congress* Shizuoka (Japan) 2011. **Publications** *Structural and Multidisciplinary Optimization (SMO)* – journal.
Members Full; Associate (800 in total) in 54 countries:
Australia, Austria, Bahrain, Belarus, Belgium, Bosnia-Herzegovina, Brazil, Bulgaria, Canada, Chile, China, Colombia, Czechia, Denmark, Estonia, Finland, France, Germany, Ghana, Greece, Hungary, India, Indonesia, Iran Islamic Rep, Ireland, Israel, Italy, Japan, Korea Rep, Latvia, Libya, Moldova, Netherlands, New Zealand, Norway, Poland, Portugal, Puerto Rico, Qatar, Romania, Russia, Saudi Arabia, Singapore, Slovakia, Slovenia, South Africa, Spain, Sri Lanka, Sweden, Türkiye, UK, Ukraine, USA, Venezuela.
NGO Relations Affiliated with: *International Union of Theoretical and Applied Mechanics (IUTAM, #15823)*; national organizations. [2018.09.05/XD5726/**D**]

♦ International Society for Structural Optimization / see International Society for Structural and Multidisciplinary Optimization (#15461)

♦ International Society of Students of Translation and Interpretation (no recent information)

♦ International Society for the Study of the Aging Male (ISSAM) 15462

Admin Office c/o Kenes International Organisers of Congresses, Rue François-Versonnex 7, PO Box 6053, 1211 Geneva 6, Switzerland. T. +41229080485. Fax +41227322607. E-mail: issammem@kenes.com.
URL: http://www.issam.ch/

History Founded 1997, UK. **Aims** Encourage physicians and other healthcare professionals to understand male illness in the context of the ageing process. **Structure** Executive Council comprising 2 officers and 6 members. **Languages** English. **Staff** 1.50 FTE, paid; 2.00 FTE, voluntary. **Finance** Meetings funded by members' dues and donations. **Activities** Research/documentation; networking/liaising; events/meetings; financial and/or material support; awareness raising; guidance/assistance/consulting; politics/policy/regulatory. **Events** *World Congress on the Aging Male* St Petersburg (Russia) 2022, *World Congress on the Aging Male* Prague (Czech Rep) 2015, *World Congress on the Aging Male* Almaty (Kazakhstan) 2014, *World Congress on the Aging Male* Moscow (Russia) 2013, *European congress on the aging male* Budapest (Hungary) 2009. **Publications** *The Aging Male* (4 a year) – journal.
Members Individual; group. Members in 16 countries:
Argentina, Australia, Brazil, Bulgaria, Canada, Finland, France, Germany, Italy, Japan, Mexico, Nigeria, Qatar, Sweden, Switzerland, USA. [2019.02.13/XD6927/**D**]

♦ International Society for the Study of l'Altra Medicina (inactive)

♦ International Society for the Study of Argumentation (ISSA) 15463

Contact Dept of Speech Communication-Argumentation Theory-Rhetoric, University of Amsterdam, Spuistraat 134, 1012 VB Amsterdam, Netherlands. T. +31205254716. Fax +31205254644. E-mail: issa-fgw@uva.nl.
URL: http://cf.hum.uva.nl/issa/

History 1986, Amsterdam (Netherlands). **Aims** Promote and improve the extent and quality of research in the field of argumentation theory and its application; facilitate cooperation in the field of argumentation. **Structure** Board of 3 members. **Activities** Awards/prizes/competitions; events/meetings. **Events** *ISSA Conference on Argumentation* Amsterdam (Netherlands) 2018, *Quadrennial Conference* Amsterdam (Netherlands) 2014, *Quadrennial Conference* Amsterdam (Netherlands) 2006, *Quadrennial Conference* Amsterdam (Netherlands) 2002, *Quadrennial conference* Amsterdam (Netherlands) 1998. **Publications** Proceedings. [2018/XD8226/**D**]

♦ International Society for the Study of Behavioral Addictions (ISSBA) 15464

Contact address not obtained. E-mail: issba@ppk.elte.hu.
URL: http://www.issba.elte.hu/

Aims Study behavioral addictions; help developing the interface of behavioral addiction science on the international stage. **Structure** Board. **Activities** Events/meetings; research/documentation; training/education. **Events** *International Conference on Behavioral Addictions* Nottingham (UK) 2021, *International Conference on Behavioral Addictions* Nottingham (UK) 2020, *International Conference on Behavioral Addictions* Yokohama (Japan) 2019, *International Conference on Behavioral Addictions* Cologne (Germany) 2018, *International Conference on Behavioral Addictions* Haifa (Israel) 2017. **Publications** *Journal of Behavioral Addictions (JBA).* [2019/XM7487/**C**]

♦ International Society for the Study of Behavioural Development (ISSBD) 15465

Société internationale pour l'étude du développement du comportement

SG c/o Inst of Psychology, Univ of Jena, Am Steiger 3/1, 07743 Jena, Germany. T. +493641945221. Fax +493641945202.
Pres Institute for Social Research, LSA University of Michigan, 2217 Easy Hall, 530 Church St, Ann Arbor MI 48109-1043, USA. T. +17347649192.
URL: http://www.issbd.org/

History 3 May 1969. Statutes amended Jul 1972; Sep 1977, Pavia (Italy); 1992. Registration: Start date: 14 Jul 1972, Netherlands, Amsterdam. **Aims** Promote discovery, dissemination and application of scientific knowledge about behavioural development throughout life – infancy, childhood, adolescence, adulthood and old age; promote application of findings to improving lives of people at all stages in life; promote interaction and collaboration within the international community of behavioural scientists. Objectives: integration of research into the behaviour of different age groups; integration of methods of and approaches to study of development; integration of different national research projects in similar areas; exchange of information concerning planned and current research. **Structure** General Assembly (at least every 2 years). Executive Committee, comprising Steering Committee (President, Past President, President-Elect, Secretary General and Treasurer/Membership Secretary) and 8 members. Editor. Conference Committee, comprising Chairman (chosen by Executive Committee), Secretary General and members. **Languages** English. **Staff** 2.00 FTE, paid. **Finance** Members' dues: Regular, US$ 95 (annual)/US$ 160 (2 years); Student, Spouse and Emeritus, US$ 47 (annual)/US$ 80 (2 years). **Activities** Organizes: biennial international conferences; research training seminars; occasional symposia; colloquia; workshops. Performs outreach to scholars from developing countries. Together with IUPsyS, instrumental in setting up the previous *International Network of Human Development and Child Research Centres (inactive)*. **Events** *Biennial Meeting* Rhodes (Greece) 2022, *Biennial Meeting* Rhodes (Greece) 2020, *Biennial Congress* Gold Coast, QLD (Australia) 2018, *Biennial Congress* Vilnius (Lithuania) 2016, *Biennial Congress* Shanghai (China) 2014. **Publications** *International Journal of Behavioural Development* (6 a year); *ISSBD Bulletin* (2 a year). *World Directory of Human Development Research Centres.* Books.
Members Individual scientists having completed postgraduate training and actively involved in behavioural research in such areas as psychology, education, sociology, anthropology, social work and medicine (over 1,200) in 56 countries and territories:
Australia, Belarus, Belgium, Brazil, Cameroon, Canada, Chile, China, Costa Rica, Côte d'Ivoire, Croatia, Cyprus, Czechia, Estonia, Finland, France, Germany, Ghana, Greece, Hong Kong, Hungary, Iceland, India, Indonesia, Ireland, Israel, Italy, Japan, Kenya, Korea Rep, Latvia, Lithuania, Luxembourg, Malaysia, Mexico, Netherlands, New Zealand, Norway, Peru, Philippines, Poland, Portugal, Russia, Singapore, South Africa, Spain, Sweden, Switzerland, Taiwan, Türkiye, Uganda, UK, United Arab Emirates, USA, Zambia, Zimbabwe.
NGO Relations Member of: *International Union of Psychological Science (IUPsyS, #15807).* [2022/XC4858/v/**C**]

♦ International Society for the Study of Bladder Pain Syndrome (ESSIC) 15466

Pres Via San Marco 33, 29122 Piacenza PC, Italy. T. +39523338391. Fax +395231860018. E-mail: info@essic.org.
URL: http://www.essic.org/

History 5 Jun 2004, Copenhagen (Denmark). Former names and other names: *European Society for the Study of Interstitial Cystitis – Painful Bladder Syndrome* – former (5 Jun 2004); *European Society for the Study of Interstitial Cystitis – Bladder Pain Syndrome (ESSIC)* – former; *International Society for the Study of Interstitial Cystitis – Bladder Pain Syndrome (ESSIC)* – former; *International Society for the Study of BPS* – alias. **Aims** Promote and support study and research of Interstitial Cystitis/Bladder Pain Syndrome (IC/BPS); provide a forum for professional scientific communication among individuals and groups involved in studies and research concerned with IC/BPS. **Structure** Annual Meeting. **Events** *Annual Meeting* Amsterdam

(Netherlands) 2019, *Annual Meeting* Florence (Italy) 2018, *Annual Meeting* Budapest (Hungary) 2017, *Annual Meeting* Delhi (India) 2016, *Annual Meeting* Rome (Italy) 2015. **NGO Relations** *International Painful Bladder Foundation (IPBF, #14499).* [2019.11.11/XJ3912/**D**]

♦ International Society for the Study of BPS / see International Society for the Study of Bladder Pain Syndrome (#15466)

♦ International Society for the Study of Celiac Disease (ISSCD) 15467

Address not obtained.
URL: http://www.isscd-global.org/

History Founded 21 Jun 2011, Oslo (Norway). Registered in accordance with Dutch law: 57523703ISSCD. **Aims** Promote scientific knowledge regarding the field of celiac disease and gluten-mediated human disease. **Structure** General Assembly; Governing Board. **Activities** Events/meetings; research/documentation. **Events** *International Celiac Disease Symposium* Sorrento (Italy) 2022, *International Celiac Disease Symposium* Sorrento (Italy) 2021, *International Celiac Disease Symposium* Paris (France) 2019, *International Celiac Disease Symposium* Delhi (India) 2017, *International Celiac Disease Symposium* Prague (Czech Rep) 2015. **NGO Relations** *Association of European Coeliac Societies (AOECS, #02504).* [2019/XM8524/**C**]

♦ International Society for the Study of Chinese Overseas (ISSCO) ... 15468

Secretariat c/o Kaisa Heritage Center, 32 Anda cor Cabildo Sts, Intramuros, 1002 Manila, Philippines. E-mail: isscosecretariat@gmail.com.
URL: http://issco.info/

History 1992, Berkeley CA (USA). **Aims** Advance research and scholarly exchange in the study of Chinese overseas. **Events** *Conference* Melbourne, VIC (Australia) 2018, *Conference* Nagasaki (Japan) 2017, *Conference* Kuala Lumpur (Malaysia) 2013, *Conference* Singapore (Singapore) 2010, *Conference* Beijing (China) 2007. **Publications** *ISSCO Bulletin.* **Members** Membership countries not specified. [2014/XD9158/**D**]

♦ International Society for the Study of Comparative Oncology (inactive)
♦ International Society of Study, Correspondence and Exchange (inactive)
♦ International Society for the Study of Custom Prostheses / see International Society for Technology in Arthroplasty (#15502)
♦ International Society for the Study of Diseases of the Colon and Rectum (inactive)
♦ International Society for the Study of Dissociation / see International Society for the Study of Trauma and Dissociation (#15488)

♦ International Society for the Study of Drug Policy (ISSDP) 15469

Sociedad Internacional para el Estudio de la Política de Drogas

Sec University of York, Seebohm Rowntree Building, Heslington, YO10 5DD, UK. E-mail: enquiries@issdp.org.
URL: http://www.issdp.org/

History Registration: Charity Commission, No/ID: 1132454, England and Wales. **Aims** Develop relations among analysts and thus strengthen the field; be a forum for high quality drug policy analysis; develop the scientific base for policy decisions; improve the interface between researchers and policy makers. **Structure** Coordinating Committee, comprising President, Vice-President, Secretary and 5 members. **Events** *Annual Conference* Marrakech (Morocco) 2022, *Annual Conference* Aguascalientes (Mexico) 2021, *Annual Conference* Aguascalientes (Mexico) 2020, *Annual Conference* Paris (France) 2019, *Annual Conference* Vancouver, BC (Canada) 2018. **Publications** *International Journal of Drug Policy.* [2020/XJ0682/**C**]

♦ International Society for the Study of European Ideas (ISSEI) 15470

Société internationale pour l'étude des idées européennes

Contact c/o The European Legacy – Toward New Paradigms, 99 Ahad Ha'am Street, 6425307 Tel Aviv, Israel. Fax +972737946132. E-mail: eleg@013net.net.

History 1984, Bellagio (Italy), at 1st Conference of the Editorial Board of the History of European Ideas, set up 1979. **Aims** Study European intellectual and cultural history and the emerging paradigms of thought in the making of the New Europe. **Languages** English. **Finance** Members' dues. **Activities** Events/meetings. **Events** *Biennial Conference* Lódz (Poland) 2016, *Biennial Conference* Porto (Portugal) 2014, *Biennial Conference* Nicosia (Cyprus) 2012, *Biennial Conference* Ankara (Turkey) 2010, *Biennial conference* Helsinki (Finland) 2008. **Publications** *ISSEI* (7 a year); *The European Legacy: Toward New Paradigms* (7 a year).
Members Subscribers individuals in 28 countries and territories:
Australia, Austria, Belgium, Brazil, Bulgaria, Canada, Cyprus, Denmark, Finland, France, Germany, Hungary, Ireland, Israel, Italy, Japan, Kyrgyzstan, Netherlands, New Zealand, Norway, Poland, Singapore, South Africa, Sweden, Switzerland, Türkiye, UK, USA. [2017.01.11/XF1220/v/**F**]

♦ International Society for the Study and Exchange of evidence from Clinical research And Medical experience (ISSECAM) 15471

Main Office Leopoldplein 39 B1, 2500 Lier, Belgium. T. +3234918270. Fax +3234918271. E-mail: info@issecam.org.
URL: http://www.issecam.org/

Aims Provide integrated editorial-technological solutions for professional development that accelerate the adoption of evidence into daily practice and remedy variations from best practice. **Structure** Group of specialists. **Languages** English. **Activities** Training/education; events/meetings. **Events** *Global Congress on Bladder Cancer (BLADDR)* Ghent (Belgium) 2021, *Global Congress on Prostate Cancer (PROSCA)* Ghent (Belgium) 2021, *Global Congress on Bladder Cancer* Krakow (Poland) 2020, *Global Congress on Bladder Cancer* Paris (France) 2019, *Global Congress on Prostate Cancer* Paris (France) 2019. [2021/XM7688/**D**]

♦ International Society for the Study of Fatty Acids and Lipids (ISSFAL) 15472

Administrator 4301 50th Street NW, Suite 300 PMB 1032, Washington DC 20016, USA. T. +12025216743. Fax +12028333636. E-mail: admin@issfal.org.
Membership Coordinator address not obtained.
URL: http://www.issfal.org/

History Mar 1991. Founded following proposals during the Second International Conference on the Health Effects of Omega-3 Polyunsaturated Fatty Acids in Seafoods, Washington DC (USA), Mar 1990. **Aims** Increase awareness through research and education of the role of dietary fatty acids and lipids in health and disease. **Structure** Board of Directors of 15 members; Executive Committee, comprising President, Vice-President, President-Elect, Past-President, Honorary Treasurer and Honorary Secretary. **Languages** English. **Staff** 0.50 FTE, paid. **Events** *Congress* Nantes (France) 2023, *Congress* Washington, DC (USA) 2021, *Congress* Qingdao (China) 2020, *Congress* Las Vegas, NV (USA) 2018, *Congress* Stellenbosch (South Africa) 2016. **Publications** *Prostaglandins, Leukotrienes and Essential Fatty Acids* – official journal.
Members Individuals in 35 countries:
Argentina, Australia, Austria, Belgium, Brazil, Canada, Chile, China, Cuba, Cyprus, Denmark, Finland, France, Germany, Iceland, India, Indonesia, Ireland, Israel, Italy, Japan, Netherlands, New Zealand, Nigeria, Norway, Philippines, Romania, Russia, South Africa, Spain, Sudan, Sweden, UK, USA, Venezuela. [2023.02.27/XD3714/v/**D**]

♦ International Society for the Study of Gregorian Chants (#02991)
♦ The International Society for the Study of Harmful Algae / see International Society for the Study of Harmful Algae (#15473)

♦ International Society for the Study of Harmful Algae (ISSHA) 15473

Société internationale pour l'étude des algues nuisibles

Sec c/o EEMIS – Linnæus University, School of Natural Sciences, SE-391 82 Kalmar, Sweden.
URL: https://issha.org/

History 1997. Former names and other names: *The International Society for the Study of Harmful Algae (ISSHA)* – legal name. Registration: Denmark. **Aims** Promote study, research and training in harmful algae and collect, evaluate and disseminate information. **Structure** General Assembly (every 3 years). Council of up to 20 members. Executive Committee, comprising President, 3 Vice-Presidents, Treasurer and Secretary. **Finance** Sources: members' dues. **Activities** Organizes and co-sponsors conferences, seminars, symposia and working group meetings; organizes lectures and courses; supports and implements research projects and programmes. **Events** *International Conference on Harmful Algae (ICHA)* Punta Arenas (Chile) 2025, *International Conference on Harmful Algae (ICHA)* Hiroshima (Japan) 2023, *International Conference on Harmful Algae* Hiroshima (Japan) 2022, *International Conference on Harmful Algae* La Paz (Mexico) 2021, *International Conference on Harmful Algae* La Paz (Mexico) 2020.

Members Individuals (66) in 29 countries and territories:
Argentina, Australia, Belgium, Brazil, Canada, Chile, Cuba, Denmark, France, Germany, Hong Kong, Italy, Kenya, Korea Rep, Latvia, Lebanon, Mexico, Morocco, New Zealand, Norway, Philippines, Qatar, Romania, Spain, Sweden, Taiwan, Thailand, UK, USA.
IGO Relations *Intergovernmental Oceanographic Commission (IOC, #11496); IOC Intergovernmental Panel on Harmful Blooms (IPHAB, #16002).* **NGO Relations** Part of: *International Union of Biological Sciences (IUBS, #15760)* through: *International Association of Biological Oceanography (IABO, #11726).* [2023/XC0115/**C**]

♦ International Society for the Study of the Human-Companion Animal Bond / see International Association of Human-Animal Interaction Organizations (#11944)

♦ International Society for the Study of Human Ideas on Ultimate Reality and Meaning (URAM) 15474

Associate Editor Dept Health Management and Policy, Univ of Michigan, M5049 SPH II, 1415 Washington Hts, Ann Arbor MI 48109-2029, USA.
Editor Ac Dean Jesuit First Studies Program, Loyola Univ, 6324 North Kenmore Ave, Chicago IL 60660, USA.
Main Website: https://utpjournals.press/uram

History 1978. **Aims** Promote *interdisciplinary* studies and *research* related to ideas on ultimate reality and human efforts to find meaning in our world. **Structure** Governing Council. **Languages** English. **Finance** Sources: grants; members' dues. **Activities** Events/meetings; research/documentation. **Events** *Biennial Meeting* Toronto, ON (Canada) 2017, *Biennial Meeting* Toronto, ON (Canada) 2015, *Biennial Meeting* Toronto, ON (Canada) 2013, *Biennial Meeting* Toronto, ON (Canada) 2011, *Biennial Meeting* 2009. **Publications** *Ultimate Reality and Meaning: Interdisciplinary Studies in the Philosophy of Understanding* (4 a year). Monographs.
Members Individuals in 16 countries:
Australia, Canada, Germany, Holy See, Hungary, India, Italy, Kenya, Mexico, Pakistan, Poland, Romania, Slovakia, South Africa, UK, USA.
IGO Relations Member of (1): *Sistema Económico Latinoamericano (SELA, #19294).* [2020.12.24/XF0571/v/**F**]

♦ International Society for the Study of Hypertension in Pregnancy (ISSHP) 15475

Société internationale pour l'étude de l'hypertension de la grossesse – Sociedade Internacional para o Estudo da Hipertensão na Gravidez

Treas c/o INFANT Centre, Cork Univ Maternity Hosp, Wilton, Cork, CO. CORK, T12 YE02, Ireland. E-mail: info@isshp.org – isshpsociety@gmail.com.
URL: http://www.isshp.org/

History 1976. Registration: Charity Commission, No/ID: 1015890, England and Wales. **Aims** Conduct research in the field of hypertension in pregnancy and disseminate the results; advance education in the field; encourage research activity by encouraging junior research fellows, especially from Third World countries, to attend Society meetings. **Structure** General Meeting (every 2 years, in conjunction with Congress); International Council, consisting of one representative from each country with at least 6 active members; Executive Committee (2-year term). **Languages** English. **Staff** 0.50 FTE, paid. **Finance** Sources: members' dues. **Activities** Awards/prizes/competitions; events/meetings. **Events** *World Congress* Bangalore (India) 2023, *World Congress* Nara (Japan) 2021, *World Congress* Nara (Japan) 2020, *European Congress* Lund (Sweden) 2019, *World Congress* Amsterdam (Netherlands) 2018. **Publications** *Hypertension in Pregnancy* (3 a year) – journal.
Members Individuals in 37 countries:
Argentina, Australia, Austria, Belgium, Brazil, Canada, Chile, Egypt, Finland, France, Germany, Hungary, Iceland, India, Indonesia, Ireland, Israel, Italy, Japan, Kyrgyzstan, Netherlands, New Zealand, Norway, Pakistan, Peru, Portugal, Russia, Saudi Arabia, South Africa, Spain, Sweden, Switzerland, Türkiye, UK, United Arab Emirates, USA, Venezuela.
IGO Relations Cooperates with: *WHO (#20950).* **NGO Relations** Member of (2): *PMNCH (#18410); World Hypertension League (WHL, #21574).* Cooperates with (2): *Fédération Internationale de Gynécologie et d'Obstétrique (FIGO, #09638); Organization Gestosis (OG, #17869).* [2023/XD7881/v/**C**]

♦ International Society for the Study of Individual Differences (ISSID) 15476

Pres Dept of Psychology, City University of London, Northampton Square, London, EC1 0HB, UK.
Sec-Treas Chief Scientist – Center for Innovative Assessments Professional Examination Service, 475 Riverside Drive, Suite 600, New York NY 10115, USA.
URL: http://www.issid.org/

History Jul 1983, London (UK). **Aims** Foster research on individual differences in temperament, intelligence, attitudes and abilities; investigate the major dimensions of individual differences in the context of experimental, physiological, pharmacological, clinical, medical, genetic, statistical and social *psychology* and seek the determinants, causes and concomitants of individual differences, using concepts derived from these disciplines. **Structure** Members' Assembly. Executive Office, comprising Past President, President, President-elect and Secretary-Treasurer. Board of Directors, comprising Executive Office as ex-officio members and 8 additional members. Committees. **Languages** English. **Activities** Organizes scientific meetings; publishes scientific papers. **Events** *Biennial Meeting* London, ON (Canada) 2015, *Biennial Meeting* Barcelona (Spain) 2013, *Biennial Meeting / Biennial Conference* Evanston, IL (USA) 2009, *Biennial meeting / Biennial Conference* Giesen (Germany) 2007, *Biennial Meeting* Sydney, NSW (Australia) 2005. **Publications** *ISSID Newsletter* (every 2 years); *Personality and Individual Differences (PAID)* – official journal. Annual Report.
Members Individuals in 30 countries and territories:
Australia, Austria, Belgium, Brazil, Canada, Canaries, Czechia, Denmark, Estonia, France, Germany, Greece, Iceland, Ireland, Israel, Italy, Japan, Korea Rep, Kuwait, Netherlands, Norway, Poland, Puerto Rico, Russia, Slovenia, Spain, Sweden, Switzerland, UK, USA. [2016/XF0518/v/**F**]

♦ International Society for the Study of Infectious and Parasitic Diseases (inactive)

♦ International Society for the Study of Information (IS4SI) 15477

SG Gartengasse 18/12, 1050 Vienna, Austria.
URL: http://www.is4si.org/

History 2010, Beijing (China). Proposed Aug 2010 at 4th International Conference on the Foundations of Information Science. Former names and other names: *International Society for Information Studies (ISIS)* – former. Registration: Start date: 24 Jun 2011, Austria. **Aims** Promote global cooperation in the sciences of information, information technology and the information society as a field in its own right through development of common concepts whose translation into practice contributes to global problem solving in the information age. **Structure** General Assembly; Board; Secretariat. **Finance** Sources: members' dues. **Activities** Events/meetings. **Events** *Summit* Beijing (China) 2023, *Summit* Sendai (Japan) 2021, *Summit* Berkeley, CA (USA) 2019, *Summit* Gothenburg (Sweden) 2017, *Summit* Vienna (Austria) 2015. **Members** Individual; Institutional. Membership countries not specified. [2022.10.11/XM7824/**C**]

♦ International Society for the Study of Interstitial Cystitis – Bladder Pain Syndrome / see International Society for the Study of Bladder Pain Syndrome (#15466)

♦ International Society for the Study of Itch (IFSI) 15478

Sec Dept Clinical Social Medicine, Occupational and Environmental Dermatology, Thibautstr 3, 69115 Heidelberg, Germany.
URL: http://www.itchforum.net/

History 25 Sep 2005, Heidelberg (Germany). Registered in accordance with the laws of the State of North Carolina, USA. **Aims** Improve understanding and treatment of pruritus for the benefit of suffering *patients* worldwide. **Structure** Board of Directors, comprising President, Secretary, Treasurer and 9 members. **Languages** English. **Activities** Organizes International Workshop for the Study of Itch (every 2 years); offers Herman Handwerker Prize. **Events** *World Congress* Sydney, NSW (Australia) 2019, *World Congress* Wroclaw (Poland) 2017, *World Congress* Nara (Japan) 2015, *International workshop* Brest (France) 2011, *International workshop* Tokyo (Japan) 2009. **Publications** *Acta Dermato-Venereologica* – official journal. Newsletter.
Members Clinical practitioners, researchers and scientists in 22 countries:
Argentina, Brazil, Bulgaria, China, Croatia, Denmark, France, Germany, India, Italy, Japan, Korea Rep, Mexico, Netherlands, Poland, Russia, Sweden, Switzerland, Türkiye, Uganda, UK, USA. [2014/XJ1891/**C**]

♦ International Society for the Study of the Lumbar Spinal (ISSLS) . . . 15479

Société internationale d'étude de la colonne vertébrale lombaire

Administrator Mungårdsgatan 37, SE-426 53 Västra Frölunda, Sweden. T. +46760354125.
URL: http://www.issls.org/

History 1974. Former names and other names: *International Society for the Study of Lumbar Spine Pain* – alias. **Aims** Bring together individuals active or interested in the field of lumbar spine; serve as a forum for information exchange of an investigative and clinical nature, relating to low back pain and disability. **Languages** English. **Staff** 1.00 FTE, paid. **Activities** Events/meetings; training/education. **Events** *Annual Meeting* Milan (Italy) 2024, *Annual Meeting* Melbourne, VIC (Australia) 2023, *Annual Meeting* Boston, MA (USA) 2022, *Annual Meeting* 2021, *Annual Meeting* Melbourne, VIC (Australia) 2020. **Publications** *The Lumbar Spine* – in 2 volumes.
Members Individuals in 29 countries and territories:
Australia, Austria, Belgium, Brazil, Canada, China, Denmark, Egypt, Finland, France, Germany, Greece, Hong Kong, India, Israel, Italy, Japan, Korea Rep, Netherlands, New Zealand, Norway, Poland, Singapore, South Africa, Spain, Sweden, Switzerland, UK, USA. [2021.08.17/XD8783/v/**C**]

- ♦ International Society for the Study of Lumbar Spine Pain / see International Society for the Study of the Lumbar Spinal (#15479)
- ♦ International Society for the Study of Medieval Philosophy (#19483)

♦ International Society for the Study of Medieval Theatre 15480

Société internationale pour l'étude du théâtre médiéval (SITM)

Pres Justus-Liebig-Univ Giessen, Otto-Behagel-Strasse 10b, 35394 Giesen, Germany. T. +496419928170.
Sec/Treas Univ de les Iles Balears, Dept de Filologia Catalana i Lungüistica General, Cra de Valldemossa km 7-5, Palma, Spain.
URL: http://www.sitm.info/

History 1974. **Aims** Foster research in medieval European theatre and drama, including para-dramatic forms of performative art such as processions, rites, dances, show executions, etc. **Structure** General Assembly; Board; National/Regional Representatives. **Languages** English, French. **Finance** Members' dues. **Activities** Events/meetings. **Events** *Triennial Colloquium* Genoa (Italy) 2019, *Triennial Colloquium* Durham (UK) 2016, *Triennial Colloquium* Poznań (Poland) 2013, *Triennial Colloquium* Giesen (Germany) 2010, *Triennial Colloquium* Lille (France) 2007. **Publications** *European Medieval Drama (EMD).*
Members Individuals in 19 countries:
Austria, Belgium, Canada, Czechia, France, Germany, Hungary, Israel, Italy, Japan, Mexico, Netherlands, Poland, Portugal, South Africa, Spain, Switzerland, UK, USA. [2018.10.05/XD8133/v/**D**]

- ♦ International Society for the Study of Multiple Personality and Dissociation / see International Society for the Study of Trauma and Dissociation (#15488)
- ♦ International Society for the Study of Narrative (internationally oriented national body)
- ♦ International Society for the Study of the Origin of Life / see International Society for the Study of the Origin of Life – International Astrobiology Society (#15481)

♦ International Society for the Study of the Origin of Life – International Astrobiology Society (ISSOL) 15481

Société internationale pour l'étude de l'origine de la vie

Pres address not obtained.
Sec c/o Fac de Ciencias UNAM, Apdo 70-407, 04510 Mexico City CDMX, Mexico. E-mail: issol.society@gmail.com.
URL: http://www.issol.org/

History 29 Feb 1972, Washington, DC (USA). Founded on the initiative of Alexander Oparin, Sidney Fox, Cyril Ponnamperuma et al, following the initial three *International Conference of the Origin of Life (ICOL)* events. Former names and other names: *International Society for the Study of the Origin of Life (ISSOL)* – former (1972 to 2005). Registration: USA. **Aims** Promote research (experimental and theoretical) into the question of the origin of life; encourage international activity on this subject and facilitate exchange of data. **Structure** Meeting of Members (every 3 years) elects Executive Council (17). Membership Committee, consisting of President and 8 members of the Executive Council appointed by President. **Languages** English, French, Russian. **Staff** Voluntary. **Finance** Members' dues. **Activities** Exchanges and publishes scientific data on the origin of life; organizes regional meeting. **Events** *Virtual Meeting* 2021, *International Conference on the Origin of Life* Galapagos (Ecuador) 2020, *International Conference on the Origin of Life* La Jolla, CA (USA) 2017, *Congress* Nara (Japan) 2014, *Joint Conference / Congress* Montpellier (France) 2011. **Publications** *Origins of Life and Evolution of Biospheres* (6 a year) – journal.
Members Individuals in 20 countries:
Belgium, Brazil, Bulgaria, Canada, China, Czechoslovakia, France, Germany, India, Israel, Italy, Japan, Mexico, Netherlands, Poland, Spain, Sweden, Switzerland, UK, USA.
Members also in the former USSR; countries not specified. [2021/XD4099/v/**D**]

- ♦ International Society for the Study of the Origins and Evolution of Language (no recent information)

♦ International Society for the Study of Personality Disorders (ISSPD) 15482

Contact U Mich Rm 201, Attn: Ashley Stauffer, 914 Hill St, Ann Arbor MI 48109-1234, USA. E-mail: admin@isspd.com.
URL: http://www.isspd.com/

History 1988, Copenhagen (Denmark), during 1st International Congress on the Study of Personality Disorders. **Aims** Stimulate and improve collaboration in research and education, and in the exchange of clinical experience in the field of personality disorders. **Structure** Board, including President, 4 Vice-Presidents and Treasurer/Secretary. Regions (4): Asian/Australian; European; Latin American; North American. **Activities** Events/meetings; training/education. **Events** *Personality Disorder Congress / World Congress* Oslo (Norway) 2021, *International Congress* Vancouver, BC (Canada) 2019, *International Congress* Heidelberg (Germany) 2017, *International Congress* Montréal, QC (Canada) 2015, *International Congress* Copenhagen (Denmark) 2013. **Publications** *Journal of Personality Disorders* (6 a year). **NGO Relations** Close cooperation with: *European Society for the Study of Personality Disorders (ESSPD, #08746).* [2020/XM3162/**B**]

♦ International Society for the Study of Pleura and Peritoneum (ISSPP) 15483

Sec c/o Natl Ctr for Pleura and Peritoneum, Univ Hops Tübingen, Hoope-Seyler-Str 3, 72076 Tübingen, Germany. E-mail: secretary@isspp.org.

History Founded Sep 2018, Paris (France). Registered in accordance with German law: VR 724220. **Aims** Continuously improve therapy for *diseases* of the pleura, peritoneum and other serosa diseases through promotion of research, innovation, further training and education, patient care and interprofessional dialogue. **Structure** General Assembly; Executive Committee. **Languages** English, German. **Finance** Sources: donations; grants; meeting proceeds; members' dues. **Activities** Events/meetings; research/documentation; training/education. **Events** *Congress* Singapore (Singapore) 2019. **Publications** *Pleura and Peritoneum* – journal. **Members** Individual; Corporate. Membership countries not specified. [2020.03.13/XM8444/**C**]

- ♦ International Society for the Study and Prevention of Infant Death / see International Society for the Study and Prevention of Perinatal and Infant Death (#15484)

♦ International Society for the Study and Prevention of Perinatal and Infant Death (ISPID) 15484

Sec address not obtained.
Contact 1314 Bedford Ave, Suite 210, Baltimore MD 21208, USA.
URL: http://www.ispid.org/

History 2004, by merger of *European Society for the Study and Prevention of Infant Death (ESPID, inactive)* and Global Strategy Task Force of *SIDS International (inactive).* SIDS International completely merged into ISPID 2007. Original title: *International Society for the Study and Prevention of Infant Death.* Registered in accordance with German law. **Aims** Advance research and increase knowledge in areas of perinatal and infant health and mortality; serve as a centralized resource for sharing of information worldwide and connecting organisations and individuals. **Structure** General Meeting (annual). Executive Board, consisting of 5 individual members, 6 members representing organizations and 2 ex-officio members, and including Chairperson, Deputy Chair, Secretary and Treasurer. Working Groups. **Languages** English. **Finance** Members' dues. **Activities** Presents: 'ISPID Junior Investigator Award'; 'ISPID Senior Investigator Award'; 'ISPID Travel Award'. Working Groups (4): Epidemiology; Pathology; Physiology; Stillbirth. **Events** *Biennial International Conference on Stillbirth, SIDS and Baby Survival* Brisbane, QLD (Australia) 2021, *Biennial International Conference on Stillbirth, SIDS and Baby Survival* Brisbane, QLD (Australia) 2020, *Biennial International Conference on Stillbirth, SIDS and Baby Survival* Glasgow (UK) 2018, *Biennial International Conference on Stillbirth, SIDS and Baby Survival* Montevideo (Uruguay) 2016, *Biennial International Conference on Stillbirth, SIDS and Baby Survival* Amsterdam (Netherlands) 2014.
Members National organizations (21) in 20 countries:
Argentina, Australia, Austria, Belgium, Canada, Denmark, Finland, France, Germany, Ireland, Israel, Italy, Japan, Netherlands, New Zealand, Norway, Slovakia, Sweden, UK, USA.
IGO Relations *WHO (#20950).* **NGO Relations** *International Stillbirth Alliance (ISA, #15608).*
[2021/XM0810/**D**]

- ♦ International Society for the Study of Questions of Assistance (inactive)
- ♦ International Society for Study of Religion and Culture (inactive)

♦ International Society for the Study of Religion, Nature and Culture (ISSRNC) 15485

Exec Dir Dept of Religion, Univ of Florida, PO Box 117410, 107 Anderson Hall, Gainesville FL 32611-7410, USA. T. +13523921625ext235.
Pres address not obtained. E-mail: president@issrnc.org.
URL: http://www.religionandnature.com/society/index.htm

History Apr 2005. **Aims** Promote critical, interdisciplinary inquiry into relationships among human beings and their diverse cultures, environments, and religious beliefs and practices. **Structure** Board of Directors. Standing Committee. **Events** *Conference* Phoenix, AZ (USA) 2023, *Conference* Phoenix, AZ (USA) 2021, *Conference* Cork (Ireland) 2019, *Conference* New York, NY (USA) 2017, *Conference* Gainesville, FL (USA) 2016. **Publications** *ISSRNC Newsletter.* **Members** Institutional; Student; Founding; Sustaining; Society Patron; Honorary. Membership countries not specified. **NGO Relations** Member of: *International Association for the History of Religions (IAHR, #11936).* [2017.12.13/XJ1507/**C**]

- ♦ International Society for the Study of Religious Psychology (inactive)
- ♦ International Society for the Study of Romance Languages (inactive)
- ♦ International Society for the Study of Solute-Solvent Interactions (inactive)
- ♦ International Society for the Study of Subtle Energies and Energy Medicine (internationally oriented national body)

♦ International Society for the Study of Tension in Performance (ISSTIP) 15486

Head Office 6 Jonathans, Dene Road, Northwood, HA6 2AD, UK. T. +442071937037. E-mail: isstip@gmail.com.
URL: http://www.isstip.org/

History 1981. UK Registered Charity: 328203. **Aims** Increase and disseminate scientific information in the area of physical and psychological tension in performance; foster international communication in the area; provide an international forum of researchers, educators and practitioners to present their work. **Structure** Board of Trustees; Executive Committee; Advisory Council. **Languages** English. **Staff** Voluntary. **Finance** Members' dues. Donations. **Activities** Organizes international symposia, seminars, workshops, courses and conferences. Participates in advisory services for the performing artists. **Events** *Conference* London (UK) 2002. **Publications** *Tension in Performance* (2 a year) – journal. **Members** Membership countries not specified. [2014/XD3435/**D**]

♦ International Society for the Study of Time (ISST) 15487

Exec Sec 442 Brookhurst Ave, Narberth PA 19072, USA. E-mail: isst@studyoftime.org.
URL: http://www.studyoftime.org/

History Founded Jan 1966, New York NY (USA), by Dr J T Fraser. Constitution adopted 1 Sep 1974. Registered as an educational organization in USA. **Aims** Encourage the interdisciplinary study of time in all its aspects. **Structure** Conference (normally every 3 years); Council. Committees (5): Nominating; Membership; Admissions; Prize; Conference. **Languages** English. **Staff** Voluntary. **Finance** Sources: grants; members' dues. **Activities** Disseminates information, especially by the organization of international conferences and publication of selected papers. Plans setting up publications database and electronic information exchange. **Events** *Triennial Conference* Yamaguchi (Japan) 2023, *Triennial Conference* Yamaguchi (Japan) 2022, *Triennial Conference* Los Angeles, CA (USA) 2019, *Triennial Conference* Edinburgh (UK) 2016, *Triennial Conference* Chania (Greece) 2013. **Publications** *KronoScope* (2 a year) – journal. *The Study of Time* – 13 vols of conference papers (peer reviewed). **Information Services** *Kronomedia – Study of Time Wiki*; *TimeLine – Bibliography of Time Studies.*
Members Individual scientists, humanists and professionals (300) in 34 countries:
Argentina, Australia, Austria, Belgium, Brazil, Bulgaria, Canada, China, Denmark, Finland, France, Germany, Hungary, India, Iran Islamic Rep, Ireland, Israel, Italy, Japan, Kenya, Mexico, Netherlands, New Zealand, Norway, Poland, Portugal, Romania, Russia, South Africa, Spain, Sweden, Switzerland, UK, USA. [2020/XC4348/v/**C**]

♦ International Society for the Study of Trauma and Dissociation (ISSTD) 15488

Secretariat 4201 Wilson Blvd, 3rd Floor, Arlington VA 22103, USA. T. +18449947783. Fax +18889660310. E-mail: info@isst-d.org.
URL: http://www.isst-d.org/

History 1982. Former names and other names: *International Society for the Study of Multiple Personality and Dissociation (ISSMPD)* – former (1982 to 1994); *International Society for the Study of Dissociation (ISSD)* – former (1994 to 2006). **Aims** Advance clinical, scientific and societal understanding about the prevalence and consequences of chronic trauma and dissociation. **Structure** Board of Directors makes all major decisions and sets the direction for the organization. Committees work to carry out the mission and to suggest new directions for the future. **Languages** English. **Activities** Research/documentation; knowledge management/ information dissemination. **Events** *Annual Conference* Seattle, WA (USA) 2022, *Annual Conference* Arlington, VA (USA) 2021, *Annual Conference* San Francisco, CA (USA) 2020, *Annual Conference* Chicago, IL (USA) 2018, *Annual Conference* Washington, DC (USA) 2017. **Publications** *ISSD News* (6 a year); *Journal of Trauma and Dissociation* – official journal. *ISSD Membership Directory.* Bibliographies and reference lists. Conference proceedings.
Members Categories of membership Member; Affiliate member; Student member; Retiree member. Individuals (mainly in USA) in 18 countries:
Australia, Belgium, Canada, Denmark, Germany, India, Japan, Korea Rep, Mexico, Netherlands, New Zealand, Norway, South Africa, Spain, Sweden, Switzerland, Türkiye, UK.
Consultative Status Consultative status granted from: *ECOSOC (#05331)* (Special). [2021/XD5787/v/**D**]

♦ International Society for the Study of Trophoblastic Disease (ISSTD) 15489

Société internationale pour l'étude des maladies du trophoblaste

Contact c/o Radboud UMC, Geert Grooteplein-Zuid 26-28, Bur 791, 6525 GA Nijmegen, Netherlands.
URL: http://www.isstd.org/

History 1982, Nairobi (Kenya). **Aims** Disseminate information on trophoblastic disease. **Structure** Includes *Nurses International Society for the Study of Trophoblastic Diseases (NISSTD).* **Languages** English. **Staff** 5.00 FTE, voluntary. **Events** *World Congress* Toronto, ON (Canada) 2019, *World Congress* Amsterdam (Netherlands) 2017, *World Congress* Bali (Indonesia) 2015, *World Congress* Chicago, IL (USA) 2013, *World congress* Budapest (Hungary) 2011. **Publications** *ISSTD Newsletter.* **Members** Membership countries not specified. **NGO Relations** Recognized by: *Fédération Internationale de Gynécologie et d'Obstétrique (FIGO, #09638).*
[2020/XD1312/**D**]

♦ **International Society for the Study of Vascular Anomalies (ISSVA)** . **15490**
Sec Arkansas Children's Hospital, 1 Children's Way, Slot 836, Little Rock AR 72202, USA. T. +15013642656. Fax +15013644790.
Pres address not obtained.
URL: http://www.issva.org/
History Founded 1992, following a decision taken during the 1990 International Workshop on Vascular Anomalies held in Amsterdam (Netherlands). The creation of ISSVA formalized the Workshop series initiated in 1976 by John Mulliken and Anthony Young. Registered in accordance with Belgian law. **Aims** Promote research into all aspects of vascular anomalies. **Structure** General Assembly; Executive Board; Scientific Committee. **Languages** English. **Activities** Biennial workshop. **Events** *Workshop* Vancouver, BC (Canada) 2022, *Workshop* Little Rock, AR (USA) 2020, *Workshop* Amsterdam (Netherlands) 2018, *Workshop* Buenos Aires (Argentina) 2016, *Workshop* Melbourne, VIC (Australia) 2014. [2015.11.09/XM8210/**D**]

♦ International Society for the Study of Vernacular Settlements (unconfirmed)
♦ International Society for the Study of Vulvar Disease / see International Society for the Study of Vulvovaginal Disease (#15491)

♦ **International Society for the Study of Vulvovaginal Disease (ISSVD)** **15491**
Exec Dir PO Box 586, Waxhaw NC 28173, USA. T. +17047093511. E-mail: issvd@issvd.org.
URL: http://www.issvd.org/
History 1970. Founded at 6th World Congress of *Fédération Internationale de Gynécologie et d'Obstétrique (FIGO, #09638)*. Inaugural session, 5 May 1971, San Francisco CA (USA). Former names and other names: *International Society for the Study of Vulvar Disease* – former; *Société internationale pour l'étude des maladies vulvaires* – former. **Aims** Promote international communication among *gynaecologists*, pathologists, dermatologists and related disciplines; establish international agreement on terminology and definitions of vulvovaginal diseases; promote clinical investigation, basic research and dissemination of knowledge in this field. **Structure** Executive Committee. **Languages** English. **Staff** 1.50 FTE, paid. **Finance** Sources: members' dues. **Activities** Events/meetings; training/education. **Events** *World Congress* Dublin (Ireland) 2022, *World Congress* Turin (Italy) 2019, *World Congress* Chicago, IL (USA) 2018, *World Congress* New York, NY (USA) 2015, *World Congress* 2013. **Publications** *Journal of Lower Genital Tract Disease*.
Members Founding Fellow; Active Fellow; Active; Honorary; Life Fellow. Individuals (350) active in disciplines related to vulvovaginal diseases in 38 countries:
Argentina, Australia, Austria, Belgium, Brazil, Canada, Chile, China, Costa Rica, Czechia, Denmark, Ecuador, Finland, France, Germany, India, Ireland, Israel, Italy, Jamaica, Japan, Mexico, Netherlands, New Zealand, Norway, Peru, Philippines, Poland, Portugal, Singapore, South Africa, Spain, Sweden, Switzerland, Uganda, UK, Uruguay, USA.
NGO Relations Recognized by: *Fédération Internationale de Gynécologie et d'Obstétrique (FIGO, #09638)*. [2022.06.16/XD1317/v/**C**]

♦ International Society for the Study of Women's Sexual Health (internationally oriented national body)

♦ **International Society for the Study of Work and Organizational Values (ISSWOV)** **15492**
Sec-Treas School of Business, Louisiana State Univ Shreveport, One University Place, Shreveport LA 71115, USA.
Pres Indian Inst of Management, Diamond Harbour Road, Joka, Kolkata, West Bengal 700104, Kolkata WEST BENGAL 700104, India.
URL: http://www.isswov.net/
History 1988, Budapest (Hungary). Founded by participants at 1st International Conference on Work Values, at the instigation of Prof Dov Elizur and Prof Istvan Magyari-Beck. **Aims** Advance the study of work and organizational values and related aspects of the organization; encourage exchange of ideas and interaction among scholars engaged in these topics; collect, generate, preserve, decipher and disseminate data and information relating to work and organizational values; encourage and initiate publications concerning research on these themes. **Structure** Executive Committee; Program Committee; Organizing Committee; Regional Representatives. **Languages** English. **Staff** None. **Finance** Sources: meeting proceeds; members' dues. **Activities** Knowledge management/information dissemination; publishing activities; research/documentation. **Events** *Conference* 2024, *Biennial Conference* Brasov (Romania) 2022, *Virtual Conference* 2021, *Biennial Conference* Brasov (Romania) 2020, *Biennial Conference* Trieste (Italy) 2018. **Publications** *ISSWOV Newsletter* (2 a year). Conference proceedings.
Members Full in 56 countries and territories:
Argentina, Australia, Austria, Barbados, Belgium, Brazil, Bulgaria, Cameroon, Canada, Cayman Is, Chile, China, Czechia, Denmark, Ecuador, Estonia, Fiji, Finland, France, Germany, Greece, Hong Kong, Hungary, India, Ireland, Israel, Italy, Japan, Latvia, Lithuania, Malaysia, Mexico, Netherlands, New Zealand, Nigeria, Norway, Pakistan, Poland, Portugal, Romania, Russia, Serbia, Singapore, Slovakia, Slovenia, South Africa, Spain, Sri Lanka, Sweden, Switzerland, Taiwan, Türkiye, UK, Ukraine, USA, Venezuela. [2022.06.22/XC0055/**C**]

♦ **International Society for the Study of Xenobiotics (ISSX)** **15493**
Admin Officer 2025 M St NW, Ste 800, Washington DC 20036, USA. T. +12023671160. Fax +12023672160.
URL: http://www.issx.org/
History 1981, New Jersey (USA). 1981, New Jersey NJ (USA), under the aegis of the Gordon Research Conference on Drug Metabolism. Registered in the State of New Jersey (USA). **Aims** Promote study of xenobiotics and their interactions with living systems; facilitate and encourage cooperation between scientists working in the field; promote dissemination of results, public awareness and education and training; promote public awareness of chemical metabolism and its social and environmental implications. **Structure** Council (meets annually), comprising President, Immediate Past President, Secretary, Treasurer, Officers Elect of the society and 12 members. Standing Committees (7): Executive; Finance; Membership Affairs; Scientific Affairs; Publication; Exhibits; Society Awards. Since Mar 2007, incorporates *European Society of Biochemical Pharmacology (ESBP, inactive)*. **Languages** English. **Finance** Members' dues. Other sources: sponsorship from corporate benefactors for meetings and other functions; individual donors. **Activities** Disseminates, discusses and publishes results of research and related matters of interest in metabolism; provides financial support for scientific meetings related to the science of drug metabolism. Organizes: International Meeting (every 3 years); regular regional meetings and workshops in Europe, Asia/Pacific and North America. Offers awards: R T Williams Distinguished Scientific Achievement; Regional Scientific Achievement; New Investigator; Frederick J Di Carlo Distinguished Service. **Events** *European Meeting* Geneva (Switzerland) 2020, *Asia Pacific Meeting* Hangzhou (China) 2018, *North American Meeting* Montréal, QC (Canada) 2018, *European Meeting* Cologne (Germany) 2017, *North American Meeting* Providence, RI (USA) 2017. **Publications** *ISSX Newsletter* (4 a year). Conference proceedings; membership directory. **Members** Regular; Student; Emeritus; Honorary Life; Sustaining; Corporate. Individuals (over 2,800) in about 50 countries in North America, Europe and Asia Pacific. Membership countries not specified. **NGO Relations** *European Federation for Pharmaceutical Sciences (EUFEPS, #07192)*. [2014/XD6664/**D**]

♦ International Society of Substance Use Prevention and Treatment Professionals (unconfirmed)

♦ **International Society for Subsurface Microbiology (ISSM)** **15494**
Sec Natl Research Program, US Geological Survey, Boulder CO 80225-0046, USA. T. +13035413034.
Pres Univ Duisburg-Essen, Fak Chemie, S05 V03 F26, Campus Essen – Biofilm Ctr, Universitätsstr 5, 45141 Essen, Germany.
URL: http://www.subsurfacemicrobiology.com/
History Set up following 1999 ISSM Symposium. Ratified at 2002 Symposium. **Aims** Serve as a resource for the field of subsurface microbiology; provide guidance and support for the International Subsurface Microbiology Symposia. **Structure** International Committee; International Advisory Board. **Languages** English. **Staff** All voluntary. **Finance** Corporate sponsorship; conference registrations; "in-kind" services. Budget per conference: less than US$ 250,000. **Activities** Events/meetings. **Events** *Triennial International Symposium for Subsurface Microbiology* Ermelo (Netherlands) 2021, *Triennial International Symposium for Subsurface Microbiology* Ermelo (Netherlands) 2020, *Triennial International Symposium for Subsurface Microbiology* Rotorua (New Zealand) 2017, *Triennial International Symposium for Subsurface Microbiology* Pacific Grove, CA (USA) 2014, *Triennial International Symposium for Subsurface Microbiology* Garmisch-Partenkirchen (Germany) 2011. **Publications** No regular publication. **Members** Individuals (330). Membership countries not specified. [2015.06.01/XJ9572/c/**E**]

♦ International Society of Subterranean Biology / see International Society of Biospeleology (#14975)

♦ **International Society of Sugar Cane Technologists (ISSCT)** **15495**
Société internationale des techniciens de la canne à sucre – Sociedad Internacional de Tecnólogos Azucareros
Gen Sec Jean Espitalier Noël Bldg, MSIRI Complex, Moka Road, Réduit 80835, Mauritius. T. +2304639791. Fax +2304639789. E-mail: issct@intnet.mu.
URL: http://www.issct.org/
History 1924, Honolulu, HI (USA). **Aims** Promote research, advancement and exchange of knowledge on cultivation of cane, manufacture of sugar and valorization of co-products. **Structure** Congress (every 3 years); Council; Executive Committee; Technical Programme Committee; Commissions (5); Sections (10); Councillors appointed by Affiliated members. **Languages** English, French, Spanish. **Staff** 3.00 FTE, paid. **Finance** Sources: members' dues. **Activities** Events/meetings. **Events** *Congress* Hyderabad (India) 2023, *Congress* San Miguel de Tucuman (Argentina) 2019, *Germplasm and Breeding Workshop* Onna (Japan) 2018, *Molecular Biology Workshop* Onna (Japan) 2018, *Congress* Chiang Mai (Thailand) 2016. **Publications** Congress proceedings; congress newsletters; technical newsletters; electronic circulars, bulletin. **Members** Affiliated; Associate; Individual; Institutional; Corporate; Honorary Life. Members in 64 countries. Membership countries not specified. **NGO Relations** Member of: *International Society for Plant Pathology (ISPP, #15371)*, through Standing Committee for Sugar Cane Disease. [2021.10.26/XB2570/**B**]

♦ **International Society of Surgery (ISS)** **15496**
Société internationale de chirurgie (SIC)
Secretariat Seefeldstr 88, 8008 Zurich ZH, Switzerland. T. +41445337650. Fax +41445337659. E-mail: surgery@iss-sic.com.
URL: http://www.iss-sic.com/
History 1902, Brussels (Belgium). Headquarters moved to Switzerland, 1979. Current constitution adopted 13 Sep 1989, Toronto (Canada), at General Assembly of 33rd World Congress of Surgery – International Surgical Week; amended: 1991; 1993; 1995, 2005. Registration: Banque-Carrefour des Entreprises, No/ID: 0408.369.406, Start date: 19 Dec 1938, Belgium; Switzerland. **Aims** Advance the science and art of surgery by research, education and nurturing of surgical practice worldwide. **Structure** General Assembly (every 2 years, at Congress); Council; Programme Committee; National Chapters; Associated Societies. **Languages** English. **Staff** 4.00 FTE, paid. **Finance** Sources: donations; meeting proceeds; members' dues; sale of publications. **Activities** Awards/prizes/competitions; events/meetings; training/education. **Events** *Biennial Congress* Vienna (Austria) 2022, *International Surgical Week ISW* 2021, *Biennial Congress* Kuala Lumpur (Malaysia) 2021, *Biennial Congress* Krakow (Poland) 2019, *Biennial Congress* Basel (Switzerland) 2017. **Publications** *World Journal of Surgery* (12 a year); *ISS Newsletter* (2 a year). Congress information.
Members Active; Senior; Honorary. Membership limited to qualified surgeons, currently over 3,000 in 101 countries and territories:
Albania, Algeria, Argentina, Armenia, Australia, Austria, Azerbaijan, Bahrain, Bangladesh, Belgium, Bosnia-Herzegovina, Botswana, Brazil, Bulgaria, Cameroon, Canada, Chile, Colombia, Croatia, Cuba, Cyprus, Czechia, Denmark, Ecuador, Egypt, Estonia, Finland, Georgia, Germany, Ghana, Greece, Guatemala, Hong Kong, Hungary, Iceland, India, Indonesia, Iran Islamic Rep, Iraq, Ireland, Israel, Italy, Japan, Jordan, Kazakhstan, Kenya, Korea Rep, Kuwait, Latvia, Lebanon, Lithuania, Luxembourg, Malaysia, Maldives, Malta, Mexico, Moldova, Mozambique, Myanmar, Namibia, Netherlands, New Zealand, Nigeria, North Macedonia, Norway, Oman, Panama, Peru, Philippines, Poland, Portugal, Qatar, Romania, Russia, Saudi Arabia, Serbia, Singapore, Slovakia, Slovenia, South Africa, Spain, Sri Lanka, Sudan, Sweden, Switzerland, Taiwan, Tajikistan, Thailand, Timor-Leste, Trinidad-Tobago, Tunisia, Türkiye, UK, Ukraine, United Arab Emirates, Uruguay, USA, Uzbekistan, Venezuela, Vietnam, Yemen.
National chapters in 51 countries and territories:
Argentina, Australia, Austria, Belgium, Canada, Chile, China, Cuba, Denmark, Ecuador, Egypt, Estonia, Finland, France, Germany, Greece, Guatemala, Hong Kong, India, Iran Islamic Rep, Iraq, Ireland, Israel, Japan, Jordan, Korea Rep, Latvia, Malaysia, Mexico, Moldova, Netherlands, New Zealand, Nigeria, Poland, Portugal, Romania, Saudi Arabia, Singapore, South Africa, Spain, Sri Lanka, Sweden, Switzerland, Taiwan, Thailand, Türkiye, UK, Ukraine, USA, Uzbekistan, Vietnam.
Collective Member Societies (6), listed in this Yearbook:
Alliance for Surgery and Anesthesia Presence (ASAP, #00723); *Breast Surgery International (BSI, #03320)*; *International Association for Surgical Metabolism and Nutrition (IASMEN, #12217)*; *International Association for Trauma Surgery and Intensive Care (IATSIC, #12239)*; *International Association of Endocrine Surgeons (IAES, #11868)*; *International Society for Digestive Surgery (ISDS, #15060)*.
IGO Relations *WHO (#20950)*. **NGO Relations** Member of (1): *International Federation of Surgical Colleges (IFSC, #13560)*. [2022/XB2571/y/**B**]

♦ International Society of Sustainability Professionals (internationally oriented national body)
♦ International Society for Sustainable Development and Agriculture (inactive)

♦ **International Society of Sympathetic Surgery (ISSS)** **15497**
Sec Fac of Medicine, Technion – Israel Inst of Technology, 3200003 Haifa, Israel. E-mail: isss.secretary@isss.net.
Pres address not obtained. E-mail: isss.president@isss.net.
URL: http://www.isss.net/
History 2001, Tampere (Finland), following a series of symposia on sympathetic surgery held between 1993-2001. **Aims** Promote interchange of knowledge and experience; advance the science and technique of sympathetic surgery. **Structure** Board. **Languages** English. **Staff** None. **Finance** None. **Events** *Biennial Symposium* Santiago (Chile) 2015, *Biennial Symposium* Melbourne, VIC (Australia) 2013, *Biennial Symposium* Odense (Denmark) 2011, *Biennial Symposium* New York, NY (USA) 2009, *Biennial Symposium* Porto de Galinhas (Brazil) 2007. **NGO Relations** Associate member of: *European Federation of Autonomic Societies (EFAS, #07059)*. [2019.02.23/XM0329/**D**]

♦ International Society for Systematic and Comparative Musicology (inactive)

♦ **International Society of Systemic Auto-Inflammatory Diseases (ISSAID)** **15498**
Pres UOC Clinica Pediatrica e Reumatologia, IRCCS Ist Giannina Gaslini, Via Gerolamo Gaslini 5, 16147 Genoa GE, Italy.
Sec LHSC Victoria Hosp, Dept of Paediatrics, Western's Bone and Joint Inst, University Hosp B6-200, London ON N6G 2V4, Canada.
URL: http://www.issaid.org/
History 2000. **Aims** Promote knowledge of Systemic Auto-Inflammatory Diseases. **Structure** Steering Committee. **Languages** English. **Staff** None. **Finance** Undisclosed. **Activities** Awards/prizes/competitions; events/meetings; networking/liaising; politics/policy/regulatory; research/documentation; standards/guidelines; training/education. **Events** *Congress* Toronto, ON (Canada) 2023, *Congress* Genoa (Italy) 2019, *Familial Mediterranean fever and systemic auto-inflammatory diseases* Dresden (Germany) 2015, *Congress* Lausanne (Switzerland) 2013, *Congress* Amsterdam (Netherlands) 2010. **Members** Individuals in 54 countries. Membership countries not specified. [2019.12.19/XJ6323/**D**]

♦ **International Society for Systems Biology (ISSB)** **15499**
Contact address not obtained. E-mail: admin@issb.org.
URL: http://www.issb.org/
Aims Advance worldwide systems biology research by providing a forum for scientific discussions and various academic services. **Structure** Executive Board, headed by Chair. **Activities** Meeting activities. **Events** *International Conference on Systems Biology* Okinawa (Japan) 2019, *International Conference on Systems Biology* Lyon (France) 2018, *International Conference on Systems Biology* Blacksburg, VA (USA) 2017, *International Conference on Systems Biology* Barcelona (Spain) 2016, *International Conference on Systems Biology* Shanghai (China) 2015. [2018/XJ7186/**E**]

♦ International Society for System Science in Health Care (no recent information)

♦ **International Society for the Systems Sciences (ISSS)** **15500**
Vice-Pres for Administration 47 Southfield Road, Pocklington, YO42 2XE, UK. T. +441759302718. Fax +441759302718. E-mail: enquiryisss@gmail.com.
URL: http://www.isss.org/

History 1954, as *Society for the Advancement of General Systems Theory*; subsequently became *Society for General Systems Research (SGSR)*; name changed, 1988, to *International Society for General Systems Research (ISGSR)*. Present name adopted 1991. **Aims** Encourage development of theoretical systems applicable to more than one traditional department of knowledge; develop theoretical systems of concepts, relationships and models; investigate the isomorphy of concepts, laws and models in various fields; enhance comparisons and help in useful transfers from one field to another; minimize duplication of theoretical effort in different fields; promote the unity of science through improving and breaking the barriers of communication among specialists in various scientific fields. **Structure** Annual Meeting; Board of Directors; Executive Committee. Special Integration Groups; Regional Chapters. **Languages** English. **Staff** Voluntary. **Finance** Members' annual dues. **Activities** Events/meetings; awards/prizes/competitions. **Events** *Annual Meeting* 2021, *Annual Meeting* Cape Town (South Africa) 2020, *Annual Meeting* Corvallis, OR (USA) 2019, *Annual Meeting* Corvallis, OR (USA) 2018, *Annual Meeting* Vienna (Austria) 2017. **Publications** *General Systems Bulletin*; *General Systems Yearbook*; *Systems Research and Behavioral Science* – journal. Annual Conference Proceedings.
Members Institutional; Individual. Members in 28 countries:
Argentina, Australia, Austria, Botswana, Brazil, Bulgaria, Canada, Chile, China, Denmark, Estonia, Finland, France, Germany, Greece, Hungary, India, Ireland, Italy, Japan, Korea Rep, Mexico, Netherlands, South Africa, Sweden, Switzerland, UK, USA.
International member (1):
International Federation for Systems Research (IFSR, #13564).
IGO Relations *UNESCO (#20322).* **NGO Relations** Affiliated with: *American Association for the Advancement of Science (AAAS)*; *World Organisation of Systems and Cybernetics (WOSC, #21686).* [2018/XC4167/F]

♦ International Society of Takuboku Studies (unconfirmed)

♦ International Society for Teacher Education (ISfTE) 15501

SG Fac of Education, Brock Univ, 1812 Sir Isaac Brock Way, St Catharines ON L2S 3A1, Canada.
URL: http://isfte.org/

History 1981. Constitution amended 1997, Canada; 2004, Minneapolis MN (USA). **Aims** Provide an international forum for discussion and exchange of views on teacher education. **Structure** Annual Seminar of ISfTE (also meeting); Executive Board (meets annually); Regional Representatives (9). **Languages** English. **Staff** Voluntary. **Finance** Sources: members' dues. **Events** *Annual Seminar* Florianópolis (Brazil) 2022, *Annual Seminar* Paro (Bhutan) 2020, *Annual Seminar* Niagara Falls, ON (Canada) 2019, *Annual Seminar* Niigata (Japan) 2018, *Annual Seminar* Aarhus (Denmark) 2017. **Publications** *ISfTE Newsletter*, *JISTE* – journal. Directory; seminar proceedings.
Members Regular; Honorary individuals in 64 countries and territories:
Argentina, Australia, Austria, Bahrain, Belarus, Bhutan, Botswana, Brazil, Brunei Darussalam, Cameroon, Canada, Chile, China, Czechia, Denmark, England, Estonia, Fiji, Finland, Germany, Ghana, Greenland, Hong Kong, India, Indonesia, Israel, Japan, Kenya, Kiribati, Kosovo, Kuwait, Lesotho, Malaysia, Namibia, Nauru, Netherlands, New Zealand, Nigeria, Norway, Oman, Pakistan, Papua New Guinea, Philippines, Portugal, Qatar, Russia, Saudi Arabia, Scotland, Singapore, Slovakia, Slovenia, South Africa, Spain, Sweden, Taiwan, Tanzania UR, Thailand, Türkiye, Ukraine, United Arab Emirates, USA, Vietnam, Zambia, Zimbabwe.
IGO Relations *UNESCO (#20322).* [2019.02.22/XC0087/v/C]

♦ International Society for Technology in Arthroplasty (ISTA) 15502

Office 1246 P St, Sacramento CA 95814, USA. E-mail: ista@istaonline.org.
SG Suntenwiesenweg 5, 8803 Rüschlikon ZH, Switzerland. T. +41793538231.
URL: http://www.istaonline.org/

History 1988, Switzerland. Former names and other names: *International Society for the Study of Custom Prostheses (ISSCP)* – former. **Aims** Promote public awareness of, and education and research in, arthroplasty. **Structure** Board. **Finance** Sources: members' dues. **Events** *Congress* Maui Is (USA) 2022, *Congress* Maui Is (USA) 2020, *Congress* Toronto, ON (Canada) 2019, *Congress* London (UK) 2018, *Annual Congress* Seoul (Korea Rep) 2017. **Members** Individuals. Membership countries not specified. [2021/XD7982/v/D]

♦ International Society for Technology Assessment (inactive)
♦ International Society of Technology Assessment in Health Care (inactive)
♦ International Society for Technology in Education (internationally oriented national body)
♦ International Society for Technology, Law and Insurance (no recent information)

♦ International Society of Teledermatology (ISTD) 15503

Treas Auenbruggerplatz 8, A-8036, Graz, Austria. T. +433163852423. E-mail: info@teledermatology-society.org.
URL: http://www.teledermatology-society.org/

History 2003. Replaces *European Confederation of Telemedical Organizations in Dermatology (ECTODerm, inactive).* Registration: ZVR, No/ID: 029041502, Start date: 7 Feb 2003, Austria, Graz. **Aims** Promote teledermatology. **Structure** General Assembly (every 2 years); Executive Board. Continental representatives; International Advisory Board. **Events** *World Congress* Singapore (Singapore) 2023, *World Congress* 2021, *World Congress* 2020, *World Congress* Houston, TX (USA) 2018, *World Congress* London (UK) 2016.
Members Individuals in 46 countries:
Australia, Austria, Brazil, Bulgaria, Canada, China, Colombia, Costa Rica, Croatia, Cyprus, Czechia, Egypt, Ethiopia, Georgia, Ghana, Greece, Hungary, India, Iran Islamic Rep, Israel, Italy, Japan, Korea Rep, Lithuania, Malaysia, Mauritius, Mexico, Morocco, Netherlands, New Zealand, Pakistan, Peru, Philippines, Poland, Romania, Serbia, Slovenia, Spain, Switzerland, Syrian AR, Türkiye, UK, Ukraine, United Arab Emirates, USA, Venezuela. [2023/XM1539/D]

♦ International Society for Telemedicine / see International Society for Telemedicine and e-Health (#15504)

♦ International Society for Telemedicine and e-Health (ISfTeH) 15504

Pres Gellertstrasse 19, 4052 Basel BS, Switzerland. T. +41613778844. Fax +41613778820. E-mail: president@isfteh.org.
Registered Office St Urbangasse 2, 8001 Zurich ZH, Switzerland.
URL: http://www.isfteh.org/

History Jun 1997, Kobe (Japan). Re-started under current title, 14 Sep 2003, Tromsø (Norway). Former names and other names: *International Society for Telemedicine (ISfT)* – former (1997 to 2003). Registration: Switzerland. **Aims** Facilitate the international dissemination of knowledge and experience on Telemedicine and e-Health; provide access to recognized experts in the field worldwide. **Structure** General Assembly (annually). Board of 9. Executive, comprising President, Vice-President, Secretary and Treasurer. Working Groups (6): Education; Best Practice and Nomenclature; Bylaws; Students; Tele-nursing; Communication and Newsletters. **Languages** English. **Staff** None. **Finance** Sources: members' dues. **Activities** Organizes annual Med-e-Tel, International Educational and Networking Forum for eHealth, Telemedicine and Health ICT (always in Luxembourg). **Events** *International Conference on the Medical Aspects of Telemedicine* Japan 2021, *International Conference on the Medical Aspects of Telemedicine* Gunma (Japan) 2020, *International Conference on the Medical Aspects of Telemedicine* Lisbon (Portugal) 2019, *International Conference on the Medical Aspects of Telemedicine* Helsinki (Finland) 2018, *International Conference on the Medical Aspects of Telemedicine* Casablanca (Morocco) 2017. **Publications** *ISfTeH Newsletter.*
Members National Associations; Associate; Institutional; Corporate; Individual; Student; Nurse. National in 44 countries:
Albania, Argentina, Armenia, Australia, Austria, Bangladesh, Bosnia-Herzegovina, Brazil, Chile, Congo DR, Croatia, Czechia, Denmark, Finland, France, Georgia, Germany, Ghana, Hungary, India, Indonesia, Italy, Japan, Kenya, Kosovo, Malaysia, Moldova, Morocco, Nepal, Netherlands, New Zealand, Nigeria, Pakistan, Philippines, Poland, Russia, Slovenia, South Africa, Switzerland, Tunisia, Uganda, UK, Ukraine, Venezuela.
Included in the above, 1 organization listed in this Yearbook:
Australasian TeleHealth Society (ATHS).
Associate in 3 countries:
Brazil, France, Russia.
Institutional (20) in 17 countries and territories:
Belgium, Bolivia, Brazil, Bulgaria, Colombia, Denmark, Estonia, Greenland, Lithuania, Mali, Mexico, Norway, Pakistan, Russia, Spain, USA, Uzbekistan.
Included in the above, 2 organizations listed in this Yearbook:
Institute of Tropical Medicine Antwerp (IMT); *International Virtual e-Hospital Foundation (IVeH).*
Consultative Status Consultative status granted from: *WHO (#20950)* (Official Relations). **NGO Relations** *Australasian TeleHealth Society (ATHS).* [2021/XF4743/y/C]

♦ International Society for Terminal Care (inactive)

♦ International Society for Terrain-Vehicle Systems (ISTVS) 15505

Association internationale de matériel de terrassement

Gen Sec c/o CNR-IMAMOTER, Via Canal Bianco 28, 44124 Ferrara FE, Italy. T. +39532735636.
Deputy Gen Sec c/o CRREL, 72 Lyme Rd, Hanover NH 03755, USA. T. +16036466321.
URL: http://www.istvs.org/

History 4 Oct 1962, Durham, NC (USA). Incorporated under the laws of the State of North Carolina (USA). **Aims** Advance knowledge in terrain-vehicle systems for improvements in engineering practice and innovation. **Structure** Members elect President, Vice-Presidents and National/Regional Secretaries every 3 years. **Languages** English. **Staff** Voluntary. **Finance** Sources: members' dues; sale of publications. **Activities** Events/meetings; knowledge management/information dissemination; research and development; standards/guidelines. **Events** *Triennial Conference* 2024, *European-African Regional Conference* 2023, *Asia-Pacific Regional Conference* Harbin (China) 2023, *Americas Regional Conference* Montréal, QC (Canada) 2021, *Triennial Conference* Montréal, QC (Canada) 2021. **Publications** *ISTVS Newswire* (12 a year); *Journal of Terramechanics* (6 a year). Conference proceedings.
Members Professionally Active Individuals in 25 countries:
Austria, Canada, China, Czechia, Denmark, Egypt, Estonia, Finland, France, Germany, Hungary, India, Israel, Italy, Japan, Korea Rep, Poland, Russia, South Africa, Spain, Sweden, Switzerland, UK, Ukraine, USA.
National/Regional Secretariats in 24 countries and territories:
Austria, Belgium, Brazil, Canada, China, Denmark, Egypt, Finland, France, Hong Kong, Hungary, India, Israel, Italy, Japan, Kenya, Korea Rep, Mexico, Nigeria, Philippines, Singapore, Thailand, UK, USA. [2020/XC2511/C]

♦ International Society for Testate Amoeba Research (unconfirmed)

♦ International Society for Theoretical Chemical Physics (ISTCP) 15506

Pres Dept of Chemistry, Univ of Uppsala, Box 538, SE-751 21 Uppsala, Sweden.
URL: http://www.istcp.org/

History Nov 1990. **Aims** Provide a forum for researchers working in different disciplines of theoretical chemical physics; promote dissemination of information; support and promote cross-field communication, thus cross-fertilizing all fields leading to new results and general development of chemical physics. **Structure** International Board of Directors; Honorary Board; National Representatives. **Languages** English. **Staff** Voluntary. **Activities** Events/meetings; knowledge management/information dissemination. **Events** *World Congress* Shandong (China) 2024, *World Congress* Tromsø (Norway) 2019, *World Congress* Grand Forks, ND (USA) 2016, *World Congress* Budapest (Hungary) 2013, *World congress* Tokyo (Japan) 2011. **Publications** *Advances in Quantum Chemistry* (First edition 2020) by Prof Kenneth Ruud and Erkki Brändas – vol. 81. Conference proceedings.
Members Individuals and societies in 33 countries and territories:
Argentina, Australia, Belgium, Brazil, Bulgaria, Canada, China, Croatia, Czechia, Denmark, France, Germany, Greece, Hungary, India, Ireland, Italy, Japan, Mexico, Netherlands, New Zealand, Norway, Poland, Portugal, Russia, Slovakia, Slovenia, Spain, Sweden, Taiwan, UK, Ukraine, USA.
NGO Relations Cooperates with (3): *European Physical Society (EPS, #08207)*; International Academy of Quantum Molecular Science; *World Association of Theoretical and Computational Chemists (WATOC, #21198).* [2022.10.19/XD3078/v/D]

♦ International Society for Theoretical Psychology (ISTP) 15507

Sec address not obtained.
Pres address not obtained.
URL: https://istp.wildapricot.org/

History 1985, Plymouth (UK). **Aims** Support the study of theoretical psychology by stimulating theoretical arguments and innovations, fostering integration across areas and research traditions, and promoting interdisciplinary and transdisciplinary approaches to psychological questions. **Structure** Executive Committee. **Languages** English. **Staff** 12.00 FTE, voluntary. **Finance** Sources: members' dues. Annual budget: 16,000 EUR. **Events** *Meeting* Sacramento, CA (USA) 2022, *Biennial Conference* Copenhagen (Denmark) 2019, *Biennial Conference* Tokyo (Japan) 2017, *Biennial Conference* Coventry (UK) 2015, *Biennial Conference* Santiago (Chile) 2013. **Publications** *Theory and Psychology* (6 a year). *Contemporary Theorizing in Psychology: Global Perspectives* (2005); *Theoretical Psychology: Critical Contributions* (2003); *Theoretical Issues in Psychology* (2001); *Challengens to Theoretical Psychology* (1999); *Problems of Theoretical Psychology* (1996); *Trends and Issues in Theoretical Psychology* (1995); *Current Issues in Theoretical Psychology* (1987); *Recent Trends in Theoretical Psychology* – Vol I 1988, Vol II 1990, Vol III 1993.
Members in 28 countries:
Australia, Brazil, Canada, Chile, Croatia, Denmark, Egypt, Germany, Greece, India, Ireland, Japan, Korea Rep, Lithuania, Netherlands, New Zealand, Norway, Portugal, Russia, South Africa, Spain, Sweden, Switzerland, Taiwan, Türkiye, UK, USA, Venezuela. [2021/XD6424/C]

♦ International Society for the Theory and Application of Multi-Objective Decision Analysis (inactive)

♦ International Society for Therapeutic Jurisprudence (ISTJ) 15508

Contact address not obtained. E-mail: intsoctj@gmail.com.
URL: http://www.intltj.com/

History Founding meeting Jul 2017, Prague (Czech Rep). A US 501(c)(3) non-profit. **Aims** Advance therapeutic jurisprudence. **Structure** Board of Trustees; Global Advisory Council. **Finance** Sources: members' dues. **Activities** Advocacy/lobbying/activism; events/meetings; knowledge management/information dissemination; training/education. **Publications** *International Journal of Therapeutic Jurisprudence.* [2018/XM7074/C]

♦ International Society for Therapeutic Ultrasound (ISTU) 15509

SG PO Box 17592, Seattle WA 98127, USA. T. +12063105148. E-mail: admin@istu.org.
Pres address not obtained.
URL: http://www.istu.org/

History 2001. **Aims** Organize meetings on all aspects of therapeutic ultrasound, bringing together experts in this field. **Structure** Board. **Languages** English. **Events** *Symposium* Gyeongju (Korea Rep) 2021, *Symposium* Gyeongju (Korea Rep) 2020, *Symposium* Barcelona (Spain) 2019, *Symposium* Nashville, TN (USA) 2018, *Symposium* Nanjing (China) 2017.
Members Full in 16 countries:
Australia, Austria, China, Cyprus, France, Germany, Israel, Italy, Japan, Korea Rep, Netherlands, Russia, Singapore, Spain, UK, USA. [2021/XD8962/D]

♦ International Society for Third-Sector Research (ISTR) 15510

Exec Dir 1340 Smith Avenue, Suite 200, Baltimore MD 21209, USA. T. +14435705606. Fax +14107354201. E-mail: secretariat@istr.org.
Director of Programs address not obtained.
URL: http://www.istr.org/

History Mar 1992, Baltimore, MD (USA). Took over activities of *Steering Committee for an International Association on Third Sector Research (inactive).* Inaugural conference: 4-7 Jul 1994, Pécs (Hungary). Former names and other names: *International Research Society for Voluntary Associations, Nonprofit Organizations and Philanthropy* – former (Mar 1992). **Aims** Promote development of high quality research and education internationally on Third Sector related issues, theories and policies; enhance dissemination and application of knowledge about the subject worldwide. **Structure** Board of Directors; Executive Committee. Regional networks: *International Society for Third-Sector Research Africa Regional Network (ISTRAN, see: #15510)*; *ISTR Arab-Speaking Network (no recent information)*; *ISTR Asia/Pacific Third Sector Network (see: #15510)*; *ISTR European Third-Sector Network (see: #15510)*; *ISTR Latin America and the Caribbean Network (see: #15510).* **Languages** English. **Staff** 2.00 FTE, paid. **Finance** Sources: international organizations; meeting proceeds; members' dues. Supported by: *Charles Stewart Mott Foundation*; *Ford Foundation (#09858)*; *W K Kellogg Foundation (WKKF).* **Activities** Awards/prizes/competitions; events/meetings. **Events** *International Conference* Antwerp (Belgium) 2024, *Latin America and the Caribbean Regional Conference* Sao Paulo (Brazil) 2023, *Asia-Pacific Regional Conference* Kota Kinabalu (Malaysia) 2022, *International Conference* Montréal, QC (Canada) 2022, *International Conference* Baltimore, MD (USA) 2021. **Publications** *Inside ISTR* (5 a year) – newsletter; *Voluntas – International Journal of Voluntary and Nonprofit Organizations. Conference Working Paper Series*; *ISTR Report.* Membership Directory.

Members Individual (Member; Sponsor; Supporting); Student; Institutional (non-voting); Supporting (non-voting). Members in 83 countries and territories:
Argentina, Australia, Austria, Bangladesh, Belgium, Belize, Benin, Brazil, Burkina Faso, Cambodia, Cameroon, Canada, Chile, China, Congo Brazzaville, Costa Rica, Croatia, Czechia, Denmark, Dominican Rep, Egypt, El Salvador, Estonia, Ethiopia, Finland, France, Germany, Ghana, Greece, Guatemala, Honduras, Hong Kong, Hungary, India, Indonesia, Ireland, Israel, Italy, Japan, Kenya, Korea Rep, Kuwait, Mali, Mexico, Morocco, Nepal, Netherlands, New Zealand, Nicaragua, Niger, Nigeria, Norway, Pakistan, Peru, Philippines, Poland, Portugal, Puerto Rico, Romania, Russia, Serbia, Singapore, Slovakia, Slovenia, South Africa, Spain, Sri Lanka, Sweden, Switzerland, Taiwan, Tajikistan, Thailand, Türkiye, Uganda, UK, Ukraine, United Arab Emirates, Uruguay, USA, Uzbekistan, Venezuela, Vietnam, Zambia.
Institutional in 19 countries:
Austria, Belgium, Canada, Czechia, Denmark, Germany, Ghana, Italy, Liechtenstein, Mexico, Netherlands, Pakistan, South Africa, Spain, Sweden, Switzerland, Türkiye, UK, USA.
NGO Relations Member of (2): *CIVICUS: World Alliance for Citizen Participation (#03962)*; *Worldwide Initiatives for Grantmaker Support (WINGS, #21926).* [2023/XD3124/**B**]

♦ International Society for Third-Sector Research Africa Regional Network (see: #15510)

♦ International Society on Thrombosis and Haemostasis (ISTH) 15511

Société internationale de thrombose et d'hémostase

Exec Dir 610 Jones Ferry Rd, Ste 205, Carrboro NC 27510, USA. T. +19199293807. Fax +19199293935. E-mail: headquarters@isth.org.
Events Dir address not obtained.
URL: https://www.isth.org/

History 19 Oct 1969, Bath (UK). Founded following unanimous vote of the *'International Committee on Thrombosis and Haemostasis (ICTH)'* during its 15th Annual Meeting. ICTH was established in 1954 when a small group of investigators with seed money from the *'National Heart, Lung and Blood Institute'*. **Aims** Advance understanding, prevention, diagnosis and treatment of thrombotic and bleeding disorders; encourage transformative scientific discoveries and clinical practices, development of young professionals, and education of physicians, scientists and allied health professionals. **Structure** Meeting (annual); Council; Scientific and Standardization Committee (SSC); Scientific Subcommittees; Working Parties (about 20). **Languages** English. **Staff** 25.00 FTE, paid. **Finance** Sources: gifts, legacies; members' dues. **Activities** Events/meetings; research/documentation; standards/guidelines; training/education. **Events** *Annual Congress* Montréal, QC (Canada) 2023, *Annual Meeting* Montréal, QC (Canada) 2023, *Annual Congress* London (UK) 2022, *Annual Meeting* London (UK) 2022, *Annual Meeting* Philadelphia, PA (USA) 2021. **Publications** *Journal of Thrombosis and Haemostasis* (12 a year) – official journal; *Research and Practice in Thrombosis and Haemostasis* – open access journal.
Members Individuals (over 5,000) in 108 countries and territories:
Algeria, Argentina, Armenia, Australia, Austria, Azerbaijan, Bahrain, Bangladesh, Belgium, Bosnia-Herzegovina, Brazil, Brunei Darussalam, Bulgaria, Cameroon, Canada, Chile, China, Colombia, Congo DR, Costa Rica, Croatia, Cyprus, Czechia, Denmark, Dominican Rep, Ecuador, Egypt, Estonia, Finland, France, Georgia, Germany, Ghana, Greece, Guatemala, Hong Kong, Hungary, Iceland, India, Indonesia, Iran Islamic Rep, Iraq, Ireland, Israel, Italy, Japan, Jordan, Kenya, Korea Rep, Kosovo, Kuwait, Kyrgyzstan, Latvia, Lebanon, Lithuania, Madagascar, Malaysia, Mali, Malta, Mexico, Moldova, Mongolia, Morocco, Myanmar, Nepal, Netherlands, New Zealand, Nicaragua, Nigeria, North Macedonia, Norway, Oman, Pakistan, Panama, Paraguay, Peru, Philippines, Poland, Portugal, Puerto Rico, Qatar, Romania, Russia, Saudi Arabia, Senegal, Serbia, Sierra Leone, Singapore, Slovakia, Slovenia, South Africa, Spain, St Vincent-Grenadines, Sudan, Sweden, Switzerland, Taiwan, Thailand, Tunisia, Türkiye, Uganda, UK, Ukraine, United Arab Emirates, Uruguay, USA, Venezuela, Vietnam.
Consultative Status Consultative status granted from: *WHO (#20950)* (Official Relations). **NGO Relations** Member of (2): *European Thrombosis and Haemostasis Alliance (ETHA, #08911)*; *World Patients Alliance (WPA).* Supports (1): *International Symposium on Women's Health Issues in Thrombosis and Haemostasis (WHITH).* Over 600 partners and related societies participate in ISTH's World Thrombosis Day. [2023/XC4456/v/**C**]

♦ International Society for Thymology and Immunotherapy (inactive)

♦ International Society on Toxinology (IST) 15512

Société Internationale de Toxinologie

Sec/Treas Natural Toxins Center, Texas A&M Univ, 975 W Ave B, AL Kleberg Hall, MSc224, Kingsville TX 78363, USA. T. +13615933796. E-mail: istsecretarytreasurer@gmail.com.
Pres Toxinology Dept, Women's & Children's Hosp, 72 King William Road, North Adelaide SA 5006, Australia. T. +61881617000.
URL: http://www.toxinology.org/

History 1962. **Aims** Advance knowledge on the properties and clinical aspects of poisons, toxins and antitoxins derived from animals, plants and microorganisms, and antivenoms and other treatments for toxin-induced illness; bring together scholars and clinicians interested in these substances; support training and credentialing of medical doctors in this specialty. **Structure** Council; Regional sections (4): Pan-American, European, Asia-Pacific, African & Middle East. **Languages** English, French, German, Spanish. **Staff** 3.00 FTE, voluntary. **Finance** Sources: members' dues. **Activities** Events/meetings. **Events** *World Congress* Abu Dhabi (United Arab Emirates) 2022, *World Congress* St Petersburg (Russia) 2022, *Asia-Pacific Section Meeting* Cairns, QLD (Australia) 2021, *Asia-Pacific Section Meeting* Cairns, QLD (Australia) 2020, *World Congress* Buenos Aires (Argentina) 2019. **Publications** *IST Newsletter* (about 2 a year); *Toxicon* (16 a year).
Members Full: individuals who have conducted and published meritorious investigations in the field; Associate, individuals not eligible for full membership but interested in the field. Members in 69 countries and territories:
Argentina, Armenia, Australia, Belgium, Benin, Brazil, Bulgaria, Canada, China, Colombia, Costa Rica, Croatia, Cuba, Czechia, Denmark, Egypt, Estonia, Finland, France, Germany, Greece, Guatemala, Hong Kong, Hungary, India, Iran Islamic Rep, Ireland, Israel, Italy, Japan, Kenya, Korea Rep, Macau, Madagascar, Malaysia, Mexico, Mongolia, Netherlands, New Caledonia, New Zealand, Nigeria, Norway, Pakistan, Panama, Papua New Guinea, Peru, Philippines, Poland, Polynesia Fr, Portugal, Russia, Saudi Arabia, Singapore, Slovenia, South Africa, Spain, Sri Lanka, Sudan, Sweden, Switzerland, Taiwan, Thailand, Türkiye, UK, Uruguay, USA, Venezuela, Vietnam, Zimbabwe. [2021.02.24/XC4641/v/**C**]

♦ International Society of Trace Element Biogeochemistry (no recent information)

♦ International Society for Trace Element Research in Humans (ISTERH) 15513

Pres Dept of Molecular Pharmacology, Albert Einstein College of Medicine, 1300 Morris Park Ave, Bronx NY 10463, USA. T. +17184302317.
Sec USARIEM, Kansas St, Building 42, Natick MA 01760, USA.
URL: http://www.isterh.org/

History Founded 1984. Previously also referred to as *International Society for Trace Elements in Humans.* **Aims** Encourage and promote increased scientific and clinical research on the causes, alleviation of suffering and the cure of trace element disorders; accumulate information about trace elements, and promote its dissemination to scientists and physicians and other parties concerned; educate the general public and medical profession about the existence, diagnosis and treatment of trace element disorders. **Structure** Executive Board. **Languages** English. **Staff** Voluntary. **Finance** Members' dues. Registration fees for meetings. **Events** *Triennial Conference* Tokyo (Japan) 2013, *Triennial Meeting* Antalya (Turkey) 2011, *Triennial conference / Triennial Meeting* Hersonissos (Greece) 2007, *Triennial conference / Triennial Meeting* Bangkok (Thailand) 2004, *Triennial Conference* Québec, QC (Canada) 2002.
Members Individuals in 39 countries:
Australia, Austria, Belgium, Brazil, Canada, Chile, China, Croatia, Denmark, Egypt, Finland, France, Germany, Iceland, India, Indonesia, Italy, Japan, Kenya, Korea Rep, Kuwait, Libya, Mexico, Mozambique, New Zealand, Norway, Poland, Portugal, Romania, Russia, Saudi Arabia, Slovenia, Spain, Sri Lanka, Sweden, Thailand, Türkiye, UK, USA. [2014.06.19/XD1670/v/**D**]

♦ International Society for Trace Elements in Humans / see International Society for Trace Element Research in Humans (#15513)

♦ International Society of Transdisciplinary Engineering (ISTE) 15514

Gen Sec TUD Fac Luchtvaart, Gebouw 62, Kluyverweg 1, 2629 HS Delft, Netherlands.
URL: https://intsoctransde.org/

History 1984, USA. Former names and other names: *International Society for Productivity Enhancement (ISPE)* – former (1984 to 2004); *ISPE Inc* – former (2004 to 2017). Registration: Chamber of Commerce, No/ID: 71835237, Start date: 2017, Netherlands, Delft; Start date: 2004, End date: 2017, USA, New York. **Aims** Support and improve international exchange of ideas and scientific knowledge in the field of technological development and application. **Structure** Executive Board. Set up: *International Institute of Concurrent Engineering (IICE).* **Languages** English. **Activities** Events/meetings; knowledge management/information dissemination; networking/liaising; research/documentation. **Events** *International Conference on Transdisciplinary Engineering (TE)* Bath (UK) 2021, *International Conference on Transdisciplinary Engineering (TE)* Warsaw (Poland) 2020, *International Conference on Transdisciplinary Engineering* Tokyo (Japan) 2019, *International Conference on Transdisciplinary Engineering* Modena (Italy) 2018, *International Conference on Transdisciplinary Engineering* Singapore (Singapore) 2017. **Publications** Research papers. [2021/XG6403/**C**]

♦ International Society of Transference-Focused Psychotherapy (ISTFP) 15515

Exec Officer Dept of Psychoanalysis and Psychotherapy, Medical Univ of Vienna, Währinger Gürtel 18-20, 1090 Vienna, Austria. T. +431404002519 – +431404003061. Fax +4314066803. E-mail: victor.blueml@meduniwien.ac.at.
URL: http://istfp.org/

History Sep 2011, New York NY (USA). Registered in accordance with Austrian law, 27 Oct 2011. **Aims** Promote development, research, application and dissemination of Transference Focused Psychotherapy (TFP). **Structure** Executive Board, comprising President, Vice-President/Executive Officer, Treasurer, 2 Coordinators (research and scientific issues; training and certification issues) and 3 members-at-large. **Events** *Biennial Conference* Innsbruck (Austria) 2022, *Biennial Conference* Innsbruck (Austria) 2020, *Biennial Conference* Barcelona (Spain) 2018, *Biennial Conference* New York, NY (USA) 2016, *Biennial Conference* Parma (Italy) 2014.
Members National and regional TFP societies and groups in 14 countries:
Austria, Brazil, Canada, Chile, Denmark, Germany, Italy, Mexico, Netherlands, Spain, Sweden, Switzerland, UK, USA. [2013/XJ6891/**C**]

♦ International Society for Transgenic Technologies (ISTT) 15516

Main Office Roswell Park Inst, Elm and Carlton St, Buffalo NY 14263, USA. T. +17168455843. Fax +17168455908. E-mail: istt@transtechsociety.org.
URL: http://www.transtechsociety.org/

History 18 Jan 2006. Founded following activities initiated with the Transgenic Technology Meeting series. Registration: No/ID: 586922, Start date: 12 Apr 2006, End date: 3 Mar 2015, Spain; Start date: 2 Sep 2014, USA, New York. **Aims** Foster and encourage knowledge generation, discussion, training and education, and the diffusion of the technologies and specific research used for the genetic modification of animals, in particular those aimed at generating and/or analysing transgenic and mutant animals as particularly useful experimental models in the biology, biomedicine and biotechnology disciplines. **Structure** General Assembly; Council. **Languages** English. **Events** *Transgenic Technology Meeting* Houston, TX (USA) 2023, *Transgenic Technology Meeting* Helsinki (Finland) 2022, *Transgenic Technology Meeting* Kobe (Japan) 2019, *Transgenic Technology Meeting* Salt Lake City, UT (USA) 2017, *Transgenic Technology Meeting* Prague (Czech Rep) 2016. **NGO Relations** Member of: *AAALAC International.* [2023/XJ4625/**C**]

♦ International Society for Translational Medicine (ISTM) 15517

Exec VP address not obtained.
URL: http://www.istmed.org/

Aims Provide a forum for interdisciplinary exchange of current knowledge and concepts on translational medicine; accelerate the development and clinical application of new therapeutic strategies and diagnostic tools; promote interaction and cooperation among physicians, scientists, researchers, policy makers, investors, business developers in academics, industries, funding agencies and governments; provide professional recognition for engagement in translational medicine; promote outstanding and innovative studies in the field. **Structure** Board of Directors, comprising President, Past President, Senior Vice-President, Executive Vice President, Treasurer, Secretary General (Director of Administration) and 4 Directors (Education; Research; Development; Communication). Advisory Board. **Publications** *ISTM Newsletter.* **NGO Relations** Member of (1): *European Society of Pharmacogenomics and Personalised Therapy (ESPT, #08696).* [2016/XJ6434/**C**]

♦ International Society of Transport Aircraft Trading (internationally oriented national body)

♦ International Society for Traumatic Stress Studies (ISTSS) 15518

Exec Dir 111 West Jackson Blvd, Ste 1412, Chicago IL 60604, USA. T. +18476862234. Fax +18476862251. E-mail: info@istss.org.
URL: https://istss.org/

History 1990. Founded as an international organization, having existed since Mar 1985 as *'Society for Traumatic Stress Studies'.* **Aims** As an international, interdisciplinary, professional organization, promote advancement and exchange of knowledge about traumatic stress. **Structure** Meeting (twice a year); Board of Directors; Executive Committee; Committees. **Languages** English. **Staff** 8.00 FTE, paid. **Finance** Sources: members' dues. **Activities** Events/meetings; research/documentation; training/education. **Events** *Annual Meeting* Atlanta, GA (USA) 2022, *Trauma in Context – Moving Beyond the Individual* Chicago, IL (USA) 2021, *Annual Meeting* Chicago, IL (USA) 2020, *Annual Meeting* Boston, MA (USA) 2019, *Annual Meeting* Dallas, TX (USA) 2016. **Publications** *Journal of Traumatic Stress* (6 a year); *Traumatic StressPoints* (6 a year) – electronic newsletter. *ISTSS Membership Directory* – online.
Members Mental health, medical, education, social service, religious, research and legal professionals (over 2,000). Regular Members in 43 countries and territories:
Afghanistan, Argentina, Armenia, Australia, Austria, Belgium, Brazil, Cambodia, Canada, Chile, Croatia, Czechia, Denmark, Finland, France, Germany, Ghana, Iceland, India, Ireland, Israel, Italy, Japan, Jordan, Kenya, Korea Rep, Mexico, Netherlands, New Zealand, Norway, Pakistan, Panama, Portugal, Russia, Singapore, South Africa, Spain, Sweden, Switzerland, Taiwan, Türkiye, UK, USA.
Consultative Status Consultative status granted from: *UNICEF (#20332).* **IGO Relations** *United Nations Commission on Crime Prevention and Criminal Justice (CCPCJ, #20530).* Associated with Department of Global Communications of the United Nations. [2021/XD3493/**C**]

♦ International Society of Travel Medicine (ISTM) 15519

Société internationale de la médecine des voyages

Secretariat 1200 Ashwood Parkway, Ste 310, Dunwoody GA 30338, USA. T. +14043738282. Fax +14043738283. E-mail: istm@istm.org.
URL: http://www.istm.org/

History 12 May 1991, Atlanta, GA (USA). The first biennial Conference of the ISTM, CISTM1 took place in Zurich, Switzerland, April 5-8, 1988. Please join us 21-25 May, 2023 in Basel, Switzerland for CISTM18, where our theme will be: Dawn of a New Era in Travel Medicine. Registration: 501(c)(3), USA. **Aims** Promote healthy, safe and responsible travel of all people crossing international borders; contribute to the advancement of travel and migration medicine globally. **Structure** Executive Board, consisting of: President; President-Elect; Past-President; Secretary-Treasurer; 4 Counsellors; Executive Director. Secretariat, managed by the Executive Director. **Languages** English. **Staff** 8.00 FTE, paid. **Activities** Events/meetings; knowledge management/information dissemination; research and development; standards/guidelines; training/education. **Events** *Conference* Basel (Switzerland) 2023, *Conference* Kuala Lumpur (Malaysia) 2021, *Conference* Washington, DC (USA) 2019, *Conference* Barcelona (Spain) 2017, *Conference* Québec, QC (Canada) 2015. **Publications** *Journal of Travel Medicine* (6 a year) – Editor-in-Chief: Annelies Wilder-Smith, United Kingdom Deputy Editor: Eli Schwartz, Israel; *Travel Medicine News TMN* (3 a year) – newsletter. **Members** Individual: doctoral; non-doctoral, in 90 countries and territories. Membership countries not specified. [2022.05.03/XF3799/v/**F**]

♦ International Society for Trenchless Technology (ISTT) 15520

Exec Dir 600 Woodland Terrace, Alexandria VA 22302, USA.
URL: http://www.istt.com/

History Sep 1986, London (UK). Founded following conference and exhibition, Apr 1985, London. Registration: Charity Commission, No/ID: 295274, Start date: 1986, England and Wales. **Aims** Advance the science and practice of installing, renovating and replacing underground utility services with minimum excavation (trenchless technology) for public benefit; promote education, training, study and research in the field; serve those involved with provision of gas, water, sewerage, telecommunication and electrical services, plant manufacturers and contractors, highway engineers concerned with integrity of road works and those engaged in research and development of underground systems. **Structure** Board of Directors, representing 21 national organizations and including Chairman, Vice-Chairman, Chairman Emeritus. Executive Sub-Committee of 7 members. Executive Secretary; Technical Secretary; Membership Secretary; Trenchless Research Editor-in-Chief. **Languages** English. **Staff** 3.00 FTE, paid. **Finance** Annual budget: 150,000 GBP. **Activities** Organizes No-Dig series of international conferences and exhibitions (at least one annually) plus national or more localized events including seminars, demonstrations, technical visits and social activities arranged by national societies; offers annual *'No-Dig Awards'*. **Events** *NO-DIG conference* Panama (Panama) 2023, *NO-DIG conference* Helsinki (Finland) 2022, *NO-DIG conference* Kuala Lumpur (Malaysia) 2021, *NO-DIG conference* Florence (Italy) 2019, *NO-DIG conference* Cape Town (South Africa) 2018. **Publications** *Trenchless Technology International* (6 a year) – magazine; *Tunnelling and Underground Space Technology* (2-3 a year) – research journal. Information Services: Technical literature. **Information Services** *Trenchless Technology Database* – CD-ROM.

Members Affiliated societies, of which their corporate members are automatically granted ISTT membership, in 27 countries and territories:
Australia, Austria, Brazil, Canada, China, Czechia, Denmark, Finland, France, Germany, Hong Kong, Hungary, Italy, Japan, Netherlands, New Zealand, Norway, Poland, Portugal, Russia, South Africa, Spain, Sweden, Taiwan, UK, Ukraine, USA.
Included in the above, 4 regional organizations listed in this Yearbook:
Australasian Society for Trenchless Technology (ASTT); *North American Society for Trenchless Technology (NASTT)*; *Scandinavian Society for Trenchless Technology (SSTT, #19121)*; *Southern African Society for Trenchless Technology (SASTT, #19864)*.
Corporate members in 5 countries:
Lithuania, Romania, Russia, Saudi Arabia, United Arab Emirates.
Individuals in 58 countries and territories:
Argentina, Australia, Austria, Belgium, Brazil, Bulgaria, Canada, China, Colombia, Cyprus, Czechia, Denmark, Dominican Rep, Egypt, Eswatini, Finland, France, Germany, Greece, Grenada, Hong Kong, Hungary, India, Ireland, Israel, Italy, Japan, Korea DPR, Korea Rep, Kuwait, Lithuania, Luxembourg, Malaysia, Mexico, Netherlands, New Zealand, Norway, Philippines, Poland, Portugal, Qatar, Romania, Russia, Saudi Arabia, Singapore, Slovakia, Slovenia, South Africa, Spain, Sweden, Switzerland, Taiwan, Thailand, Türkiye, UK, Ukraine, United Arab Emirates, USA. [2021/XD4568/y/**C**]

♦ International Society for Tropical Crop Research and Development (no recent information)
♦ International Society of Tropical Dermatology / see International Society of Dermatology (#15048)

♦ International Society for Tropical Ecology (ISTE) 15521

Société internationale d'écologie tropicale

Sec Dept of Botany, Banaras Hindu Univ, Varanasi, Uttar Pradesh 221 005, Varanasi UTTAR PRADESH 221 005, India. E-mail: secretary.iste@gmail.com.
Pres Baruch Inst Coastal Ecology Forest Science, Clemson Univ, Highway 17 North, PO Box 596, Georgetown SC 29442-0596, USA. E-mail: skipvb@clemson.edu.
URL: http://www.tropecol.com/

History 1956, Varanasi (India), during a UNESCO/CCTA symposium on vegetation in relation to the soil, following decision taken 1956, Bombay (India), during 47th session of Indian Science Congress. Registered in India. **Aims** Promote the study of ecology and *conservation* of *natural resources* in the tropics and sub-tropics. **Structure** General Meeting (every 4 years); Executive Committee. **Languages** English, French, Portuguese, Spanish. **Staff** 15.00 FTE, paid. Voluntary. **Finance** Sources: members' dues; sale of publications. **Activities** Events/meetings; knowledge management/information dissemination; training/education. **Events** *Tropical Ecology Congress* Dehra Dun (India) 2014, *Tropical ecology congress* Dehra Dun (India) 2007, *Conference / International Conservation Conference* Nepal 2002, *International conference on conservation of tropical species, communities and ecosystems* Thiruvananthapuram (India) 1998, *International conference on land-water interaction* Delhi (India) 1991. **Publications** *Tropical Ecology* (4 a year). *ISTE Directory and Handbook*. Symposia proceedings.

Members Individual; Institutional. Members in 59 countries:
Argentina, Australia, Bangladesh, Belgium, Bhutan, Brazil, Canada, China, Colombia, Costa Rica, Cuba, Denmark, Egypt, Ethiopia, Finland, France, Germany, Ghana, Honduras, India, Indonesia, Ireland, Israel, Italy, Japan, Kenya, Korea Rep, Lesotho, Madagascar, Malaysia, Mexico, Nepal, Netherlands, New Zealand, Nigeria, Oman, Pakistan, Papua New Guinea, Peru, Philippines, Poland, Portugal, Puerto Rico, Russia, Saudi Arabia, Sierra Leone, Singapore, South Africa, Spain, Sri Lanka, Sweden, Switzerland, Tanzania UR, Thailand, Trinidad-Tobago, Turkmenistan, UK, USA, Venezuela.
[2018.09.04/XB2524/**B**]

♦ International Society of Tropical Foresters (ISTF) 15522

Société internationale des forestiers tropicaux – Sociedad Internacional de Forestales Tropicales

Contact address not obtained. E-mail: tropicalforesters@gmail.com.
URL: https://tropicalforesters.org/

History 1950, Washington, DC (USA). Inactive 1972-1980. Dormant between 2012 and 2017, when it was revived. Former names and other names: *Société internationale des ingénieurs forestiers tropicaux* – alias; *Sociedad Internacional de Ingenieros Forestales Tropicales* – alias. Registration: Puerto Rico Department of State, No/ID: 448965, Start date: 12 Aug 2020, Puerto Rico; USA, District of Columbia. **Aims** Facilitate and promote sharing of best practices for the effective management, protection, and equitable and ecologically sustainable use of tropical forests and natural resources in the tropical and subtropical regions across the globe. **Structure** Board of Directors. **Languages** English. some Spanish. **Staff** 3.00 FTE, voluntary. **Finance** Sources: donations; grants. **Activities** Events/meetings; knowledge management/information dissemination; research/documentation. **Events** *Conference on people in parks* New Haven, CT (USA) 2004, *Annual meeting* Washington, DC (USA) 2002, *Annual meeting* Washington, DC (USA) 2000, *Annual meeting* Washington, DC (USA) 1999, *Joint meeting* Washington, DC (USA) 1999. **Publications** *ISTF Newsletter* (4 a year) in English; *ISTF Update* (irregular). **Members** Members in 109 countries. Membership countries not specified. **NGO Relations** Partner of (3): *Global EverGreening Alliance (#10350)*; Initiative 20x20 for Latin America; *RECOFTC – The Center for People and Forests (RECOFTC, #18628)*. [2022.12.11/XB5367/y/**B**]

♦ International Society for Tropical Medicine (inactive)

♦ International Society of Tropical Pediatrics (ISTP) 15523

Exec Dir National Inst of Health, UP Manila, 623 Pedro Gil Street, Ermita 1000, 2346 Manila, Philippines.
URL: http://www.istpediatrics.org/

History 1986, Manila (Philippines). **Aims** Promote paediatrics in tropical and subtropical countries; encourage interested paediatricians to familiarize themselves with childhood conditions in these countries. **Structure** General Assembly (every 3 years); Standing Committee; Executive Committee. **Languages** English. **Staff** None. **Finance** Sources: members' dues. **Activities** Events/meetings. **Events** *Triennial Congress* Cairo (Egypt) 2021, *Triennial Congress* Cairo (Egypt) 2020, *Triennial Congress* Yogyakarta (Indonesia) 2017, *Triennial Congress* Nairobi (Kenya) 2014, *Triennial Congress* Bangkok (Thailand) 2011.

Members Full in 31 countries:
Australia, Bahrain, Bangladesh, Belgium, Brazil, Canada, Ecuador, Egypt, Finland, France, Germany, India, Indonesia, Israel, Kenya, Malaysia, Myanmar, Netherlands, Nigeria, Papua New Guinea, Philippines, Saudi Arabia, Singapore, South Africa, Spain, Sri Lanka, Sudan, Tanzania UR, Thailand, UK, USA.
NGO Relations Affiliate Society of: *International Pediatric Association (IPA, #14541)*. [2020/XD0530/**C**]

♦ International Society for Tropical Root Crops (ISTRC) 15524

Sec Intl Inst of Tropical Agriculture, PMB 5320, Oyo Road, Ibadan, Oyo, Nigeria. T. +2347031982887.
Pres Food Science and Technology, Fed Univ of Agriculture, Alabata Road, PMB 2240, Abeokuta, Ogun, Nigeria. T. +2348033469883.
URL: http://www.istrc.org/

History Apr 1967, at *University of the West Indies (UWI, #20705)*, St Augustine (Trinidad-Tobago). **Aims** Foster, stimulate, and support activities leading to general improvement of tropical root crop production and utilization, such as cassava, yams, sweet potatoes, potatoes, aroids and other tuberous crops of tropical origin. **Structure** General Meeting; Council. **Languages** English. **Staff** All voluntary. **Finance** Sources: members' dues. **Activities** Awards/prizes/competitions; events/meetings; financial and/or material support; knowledge management/information dissemination; networking/liaising; research and development. Active: worldwide. **Events** *Exploring climate smart, nutritious and healthy root and tuber crops for African business solutions* Lusaka (Zambia) 2021, *Exploring climate smart, nutritious and healthy root and tuber crops for African business solutions* Lusaka (Zambia) 2020, *Symposium* Cali (Colombia) 2018, *World Congress on Root and Tuber Crops* Nanning (China) 2016, *Symposium* Nanning (China) 2015. **Publications** Proceedings.

Members Full in 61 countries and territories:
Argentina, Australia, Barbados, Belgium, Benin, Brazil, Burundi, Cameroon, Canada, Chile, Colombia, Congo Brazzaville, Congo DR, Costa Rica, Côte d'Ivoire, Ecuador, Egypt, Fiji, France, Gabon, Germany, Ghana, India, Indonesia, Italy, Japan, Kenya, Liberia, Madagascar, Malawi, Malaysia, Mexico, Morocco, Mozambique, Netherlands, Nigeria, Papua New Guinea, Peru, Philippines, Rwanda, Senegal, Sierra Leone, Singapore, Sri Lanka, St Lucia, Sudan, Sweden, Syrian AR, Taiwan, Tanzania UR, Thailand, Togo, Trinidad-Tobago, Uganda, UK, USA, Vanuatu, Venezuela, Vietnam, Zambia, Zimbabwe.
IGO Relations *Inter-American Institute for Cooperation on Agriculture (IICA, #11434)*. **NGO Relations** Scientific member of: *International Union of Biological Sciences (IUBS, #15760)*. [2019.12.16/XD2111/**C**]

♦ International Society for Tryptophan Research (ISTRY) 15525

Address not obtained.
URL: https://www.istry.org/

History 1971. Former names and other names: *International Study Group for Tryptophan Research (ISTRY)* – former. **Aims** Advance knowledge on the biochemistry, nutrition, pathology, physiology, food science, regulation of tryptophan metabolism, and chemistry of tryptophan; bring together those scholars interested in these objectives through a common society. **Structure** Executive Committee. **Activities** Events/meetings. **Events** *Conference* Jena (Germany) 2021, *Meeting* Jena (Germany) 2020, *Meeting* Hikone (Japan) 2018, *Meeting* Grand Rapids, MI (USA) 2015, *Meeting* Sydney, NSW (Australia) 2012. [2022/AA1860/**C**]

♦ International Society for Twin Studies (ISTS) 15526

Société internationale d'études gémellaires – Internationale Gesellschaft für Zwillingsforschung

Treas QIMR Berghofer Medical Research Inst, Royal Brisbane Hosp, Brisbane QLD 4029, Australia. E-mail: ists@qimrberghofer.edu.au.
Pres address not obtained.
URL: https://twinstudies.org/

History 2 Nov 1974, Rome (Italy). Founded at 1st International Congress on Twin Studies. **Aims** Promote research and social action in all fields related to twin studies, for the mutual benefit of *twins* and their *families*, and of scientific research. **Structure** General Assembly (every 3 years); Board of Directors. **Languages** English. **Staff** None. **Finance** Sources: donations; grants; members' dues. **Activities** Awards/prizes/competitions; events/meetings. **Events** *Congress* Budapest (Hungary) 2023, *Congress* Budapest (Hungary) 2021, *Congress* Hong Kong (Hong Kong) 2019, *Congress* Madrid (Spain) 2017, *Congress* Budapest (Hungary) 2014. **Publications** *Twin Research and Human Genetics* (6 a year) – journal; *ISTS Newsletter*.

Members Individual; Collective. Members in 26 countries:
Australia, Belgium, Canada, Denmark, Finland, France, Germany, Hong Kong, Ireland, Israel, Italy, Japan, Korea Rep, Netherlands, New Zealand, Norway, Poland, Portugal, South Africa, Spain, Sri Lanka, Sweden, Switzerland, Türkiye, UK, USA.
NGO Relations Partner of (1): *International Council of Multiple Birth Organisations (ICOMBO, #13050)*. Cooperates with (1): *World Congress on Twin Pregnancy*. [2023.02.16/XC0102/**C**]

♦ International Society of Typographic Designers (internationally oriented national body)
♦ International Society on Ultrasonic Diagnostics in Ophthalmology (#19443)
♦ International Society of Ultrasonic Surgery (inactive)

♦ International Society of Ultrasound in Obstetrics and Gynaecology (ISUOG) 15527

Société internationale pour les ultrasons en obstétrique et gynécologie

CEO 122 Freston Road, London, W10 6TR, UK. T. +442074719955. Fax +442074719959. E-mail: info@isuog.org.
Dir Operations address not obtained.
URL: http://www.isuog.org/

History 1990. Registration: Charity Commission, No/ID: 1030406, England and Wales; Companies House, No/ID: 02722770, England and Wales. **Aims** Improve women's health though provision, advancement and dissemination of the highest quality education, standards and research information around ultrasound in obstetrics and gynaecology. **Structure** Board. **Languages** English. **Staff** 30-35. **Finance** Sources: meeting proceeds; members' dues; sale of publications. **Activities** Events/meetings; networking/liaising; publishing activities; research/documentation; standards/guidelines; training/education. **Events** *World Congress* 2023, *World Congress* London (UK) 2022, *International Symposium* London (UK) 2021, *World Congress* London (UK) 2021, *World Congress* London (UK) 2020. **Publications** *ISUOG Newsletter* (12 a year); *Ultrasound in Obstetrics and Gynecology* (12 a year) – journal. **Members** Individuals (over 13,000) in 127 countries. Membership countries not specified. **NGO Relations** Member of (1): *Associations and Conference Forum (AC Forum, #02909)*. Partner of (1): *World Association of Trainees in Obstetrics & Gynecology (WATOG, #21199)*. Cooperates with (3): *Bureau international des Médecins sans frontières (MSF International, #03366)*; *Partners in Health (PIH)*; *PMNCH (#18410)*. [2022.05.24/XD2489/v/**D**]

♦ International Society on Underground Freight Transportation (ISUFT) 15528

Contact Postbus 5030, 2600 GA Delft, Netherlands. T. +31152783005. Fax +31152784422.
Street Address Jaffalaan 9, 2628 BX Delft, Netherlands.
URL: http://isuft.org/

History Set up 2008, following 5 editions of the *International Symposium on Underground Freight Transportation*. Full title: *International Society on Underground Freight Transportation by Capsule Pipelines and Other Tube/Tunnel Systems (ISUFT)*. EU Transparency Register: 43232835676-74. **Aims** Present progress in research in developing underground freight and capsule *pipeline* transportation concepts. **Structure** Steering Committee. **Activities** Events/meetings; research/documentation. **Events** *International Symposium* Arlington, TX (USA) 2016, *International Symposium* Shanghai (China) 2010, *International Symposium* Arlington, TX (USA) 2008, *International Symposium* Shanghai (China) 2005, *International Symposium* Bochum (Germany) 2002. [2017/XM5646/**E**]

♦ International Society on Underground Freight Transportation by Capsule Pipelines and Other Tube/Tunnel Systems / see International Society on Underground Freight Transportation (#15528)
♦ International Society for the Understanding, Prevention and Treatment of Mental Illness Relating to Child Bearing / see International Marcé Society for Perinatal Mental Health (#14089)

♦ International Society for Universal Dialogue (ISUD) 15529

Chairman 1 University Drive, Gandhi Hall, Aliso Viejo CA 92656, USA. T. +19492906818.
Editor-in-Chief Inst Filozofii i Socjologii PAN, ul Nowy Swiat 72, 00-330 Warsaw, Poland. E-mail: dialogueanduniversalism@ifispan.waw.pl.
URL: http://www.worldialogue.org/

History Nov 1989, Warsaw (Poland). Founded by Professor Janusz Kuczynski of the University of Warsaw. Current constitution amended and adopted Jul 2016, Warsaw (Poland). Former names and other names: *International Society for Universalism (ISU)* – former. Registration: USA, Maine. **Aims** Promote an intellectual environment for discussion/papers/congresses regarding values of Human Dignity, Respect, Human Rights, Social Justice, Environmental Justice, Equality of Opportunities regardless of gender, race, religion. **Structure** Board of Directors; Executive Committee. **Languages** English. Languages of congress locations. **Staff** All officers are voluntary. **Finance** Sources: meeting proceeds; members' dues; sale of publications; subscriptions. Annual budget: 8,000 USD (2022). **Activities** Awards/prizes/competitions; events/meetings; publishing activities. **Events** *World Congress* Lima (Peru) 2018, *World Congress* Warsaw (Poland) 2016, *World Congress* Craiova (Romania) 2014, *World Congress* Olympia (Greece) 2012, *World congress* Beijing (China) 2010. **Publications** *Dialogue and Universalism* (3 a year). **Members** Diverse international membership. Membership countries not specified. **NGO Relations** Member of (1): *International Federation of Philosophical Societies (FISP, #13507)*. [2022.02.03/XN4573/**C**]

♦ International Society for Universalism / see International Society for Universal Dialogue (#15529)

♦ International Society of University Colon and Rectal Surgeons (ISUCRS) 15530

Société internationale des professeurs en maladies du côlon et du rectum – Societas Internationalis Universitaria Chirurgorum Colonis et Recti

Exec Dir 100 Kathleen Court, Penn Hills PA 15090, USA. E-mail: isucrs@valor.com.tr – admin@isucrs.org.
URL: http://www.isucrs.org/

History 24 Nov 1962, Mexico City (Mexico). Most recent statutes adopted 1990. **Aims** Contribute to the progress of colon and anorectal surgery; organize international meetings and congresses for exchange of scientific knowledge. **Structure** Congress (normally every 2 years); International Advisory Committee; Executive Council; Continental Vice-Presidents; Committees (6). **Languages** English. **Staff** Voluntary. **Finance** Sources: members' dues. Annual budget: 50,000 USD. **Activities** Events/meetings; knowledge management/information dissemination. **Events** *Biennial Congress* Seoul (Korea Rep) 2024, *Biennial Congress* Istanbul (Türkiye) 2022, *Biennial Congress* Yokohama (Japan) 2020, *Biennial Congress* London (UK) 2018, *Biennial Congress* Mumbai (India) 2016. **Publications** *World Journal of Colorectal Surgery* (4 a year) – print and online.
Members National Committees or individuals in 46 countries and territories:
Argentina, Austria, Belgium, Brazil, Canada, Chile, China, Colombia, Costa Rica, Czechia, Denmark, Egypt, France, Germany, Greece, Hong Kong, Hungary, Iceland, India, Iran Islamic Rep, Iraq, Israel, Italy, Japan, Korea DPR, Korea Rep, Mexico, Netherlands, Pakistan, Peru, Philippines, Portugal, Puerto Rico, Romania, Russia, Saudi Arabia, Singapore, Spain, Sweden, Switzerland, Thailand, Türkiye, UK, Uruguay, USA, Venezuela. [2023.02.15/XC2519/C]

♦ International Society for University Educators, Researchers and Creators of Dance (inactive)
♦ International Society of Urological Endoscopy (inactive)

♦ International Society of Urological Pathology (ISUP) 15531

Sec c/o Aquesta, PO Box 1878, Toowong QLD 4066, Australia. E-mail: info@isupweb.org.
URL: https://isupweb.org/

History 1990, USA. **Aims** Promote the development and progress of urogenital pathology as a medical discipline. **Languages** English. **Staff** 6.00 FTE, voluntary. **Finance** Members' dues. **Events** *Annual scientific meeting* Vancouver, BC (Canada) 2012, *Annual scientific meeting* San Antonio, TX (USA) 2011, *Annual scientific meeting* Washington, DC (USA) 2010, *Annual scientific meeting* Boston, MA (USA) 2009, *Annual scientific meeting* New Orleans, LA (USA) 2006. **Publications** *International Journal of Urologic Pathology.* **NGO Relations** *International Collaboration on Cancer Reporting (ICCR, #12637).* [2017/XD7451/D]

♦ International Society of Uterus Transplantation (ISUTx) 15532

Contact Sahlgrenska Univ Hosp, Blå stråket 6, SE-413 45 Gothenburg, Sweden. T. +46313429285.
URL: http://www.isutx.org/

History Founded Jan 2016, Gothenburg (Sweden). Bylaws approved 19 Sep 2017. **Aims** Stimulate scientific innovation and advances in *medical* care in the field of uterus transplantation. **Structure** Executive Committee; Board. **Finance** Sources: members' dues. **Activities** Events/meetings; knowledge management/information dissemination. **Events** *State-of-the-Art Meeting* Paris (France) 2022, *Congress* Tübingen (Germany) 2021, *Seminar* Prague (Czechia) 2020, *Congress* Cleveland, OH (USA) 2019, *State-of-the-Art Meeting* Ghent (Belgium) 2018. **Members** Founding (individuals); Active; Corporate. Membership countries not specified. [2020.02.12/XM7893/C]

♦ International Society for Utilitarian Studies (internationally oriented national body)
♦ International Society for Vaccination and Immunotherapy (inactive)

♦ International Society for Vaccines (ISV) 15533

Congress Secretariat 364 Plantation Street, Worcester MA 01605, USA. E-mail: info@isvcongress.org – info@isv-online.org.
Director of Operations address not obtained.
Main Website: http://www.isv-online.org/

History 1994, USA. Founded following discussions held in 1992. Registration: No/ID: EIN 26-2521865, USA. **Aims** Engage, support, and sustain the professional goals of a diverse membership in all areas relevant to vaccines. **Structure** General Meeting (annual, during Congress); Board; Officers; Congress Secretariat. **Finance** Sources: meeting proceeds; members' dues; sponsorship. **Activities** Events/meetings; projects/programmes. Active in all member countries. **Events** *ISV Annual Congress* Québec, QC (Canada) 2022, *ISV Virtual Congress Series Meeting* USA 2021, *ISV Virtual Congress Series Meeting* 2020, *ISV Annual Congress* Ghent (Belgium) 2019, *ISV Annual Congress* Atlanta, GA (USA) 2018. **Publications** *Vaccine* – journal. **Members** Vaccine researchers; professors; students; postdoctoral fellows; journalists. Membership countries not specified. [2022.06.28/XN9717/C]

♦ International Society for Value Inquiry (internationally oriented national body)

♦ International Society for Vascular, Behavioural and Cognitive Disorders (Vas-Cog) 15534

SG c/o Inst for Ageing and Health, NIHR Biomedical Research Bldg 1st Fl, Newcastle Univ Campus Ageing and Vitality, Newcastle upon Tyne, NE4 5PL, UK. T. +441912481352. E-mail: vascogsoc@gmail.com – d.c.k.little@ncl.ac.uk.
Chair address not obtained.
URL: http://www.vas-cog.org/

History 31 Aug 2003, Gothenburg (Sweden), during inaugural meeting. **Aims** Advance and promote knowledge and treatment of behavioural, psychiatric and cognitive disorders associated with cardiovascular and cerebrovascular diseases. **Events** *Congress* Amsterdam (Netherlands) 2016, *Biennial Congress / Congress* Tokyo (Japan) 2015, *Biennial Congress* Toronto, ON (Canada) 2013, *Biennial Congress* Lille (France) 2011, *Biennial congress / Congress* Singapore (Singapore) 2009. [2013/XJ4385/D]

♦ International Society of Vascular Health (ISVH) 15535

Contact address not obtained. T. +33174710362. Fax +33172349222.
URL: http://www.isvh.net/

History Dec 2005. **Aims** Stimulate clinical research in vascular medicine; catalyze cooperation between the medical profession, health educators and industrial partners to demonstrate a commitment to vascular health and well-being; unite the clinical and patient-oriented aspects of societies, including cardiology, angiology, hypertension, lipidology, atherosclerosis, endocrinology, diabetes, nephrology, ultrasound, vascular devices and nutrition. **Structure** Executive Board; Scientific Board. Officers: President; Treasurer; Secretary-General; Vice-President; Deputy Treasurer; Deputy Secretary. **Languages** English. **Finance** Members' dues. **Activities** Organizes congresses and workshops. **Events** *Congress* Paris (France) 2007, *Asian-Pacific congress* Beijing (China) 2006, *International workshop on controversies in vascular health management* Paris (France) 2006. **Publications** *Vascular Health and Risk Management.* [2016/XM2559/D]

♦ International Society of Vascularized Composite Allotransplantation (ISVCA) 15536

Pres c/o TTS, Intl HQ, 505 Boulevard René-Lévesque Ouest, Ste 1401, Montréal QC H2Z 1Y7, Canada. T. +15148741717. Fax +15148741716. E-mail: suzanne.landis@tts.org – info@tts.org.
URL: http://www.tts.org/

History Set up as *International Society of Hand and Composite Tissue Allotransplantation (IHCTAS).* Section of *The Transplantation Society (TTS, #20224).* **Aims** Promote and encourage research and training relevant to the transplantation of vascularized peripheral tissues as a functional unit, also known as composite tissue allotransplantation (CTA) or vascularized composite allografts (VCA); provide a scientific forum for exchange and discussion of clinical and experimental results and experiences relevant to transplantation of CTA of VCA; promote and encourage contacts between clinical and experimental researchers from different institutions and all pertinent disciplines, irrespective of their country of origin; promote and facilitate support in the planning and execution of collaborative studies, and pursue collaboration with other associations, societies, and/or organizations serving similar purposes. **Structure** Council. **Languages** English. **Staff** 1.00 FTE, paid. **Activities** Events/meetings; networking/liaising. **Events** *Biennial Congress* Delhi (India) 2019, *Biennial Congress* Salzburg (Austria) 2017, *International Chauvet Workshop on the Psychosocial Care of VCA Patients* Paris (France) 2016, *Biennial Congress* Philadelphia, PA (USA) 2015, *Biennial Congress* Wroclaw (Poland) 2013. **Publications** *ISVCA Quarterly Newsletter.* **Members** Membership worldwide. Membership countries not specified. [2018/XJ0743/E]

♦ International Society for Vascular Specialists (inactive)
♦ International Society of Vascular Surgeons / see Association of International Vascular Surgeons (#02765)

♦ International Society for Vascular Surgery (ISVS) 15537

Exec Dir 10062 SE Osprey Pointe Dr, Hobe Sound FL 33455, USA. T. +16319793780.

History 2003. **Aims** Promote Vascular Surgery as a distinct medical specialty worldwide through dissemination of administrative, scientific and clinical knowledge and the creation of strategic alliances; educate other healthcare professionals, government agencies and the general public concerning the unique services and valuable benefits provided by Vascular Surgery practitioners who are well trained and committed to the specialty in all its nuances; identify and provide recognition to individuals who meet certain guidelines, which qualify them as, committed and accomplished vascular surgeons; provide scholarships, travel, poster and abstract awards to fellows in training, in an effort to improve the delivery of care in their respective country. **Structure** Executive Council of 10 members; Regional Councillors (14). Committees (5): International Government Relations; Case Presentations; Membership; Vascular Supplements; Endovascular Program Evaluation and Endorsement. **Languages** English. **Staff** 1.00 FTE, paid. **Finance** Sources: grants; members' dues. **Activities** Events/meetings. **Events** *Congress* Sibiu (Romania) 2017, *Congress* Athens (Greece) 2015, *Congress* Guangzhou (China) 2014, *Congress* Miami, FL (USA) 2013, *Congress* Miami, FL (USA) 2012. **Publications** *VASCULAR* (6 a year). [2017/XM8209/C]

♦ International Society of Vertebrate Morphology (ISVM) 15538

Sec address not obtained.
URL: https://www.isvm-icvm.org/

History Aug 1994, Chicago, IL (USA). Founded during 4th International Congress, such congresses having been held since 1983. **Aims** Promote international collaboration and cooperation in vertebrate morphology and other biological sciences. **Structure** Executive Committee, consisting of President, President-Elect, Secretary, Treasurer and 14 members. Congress Convenors, appointed by the President, also serve on Executive Committee. Nomination Committee of 3 members. **Languages** English. **Staff** Voluntary. **Finance** Sources: members' dues. Other sources: members' contributions; international congresses financed by attendance fees and grants. **Activities** Sponsors and promotes *International Congress of Vertebrate Morphology* (every 3-4 years). **Events** *International Congress of Vertebrate Morphology* Cairns, QLD (Australia) 2023, *International Congress of Vertebrate Morphology* Prague (Czechia) 2019, *International Congress of Vertebrate Morphology* Barcelona (Spain) 2013, *International Congress of Vertebrate Morphology* Punta del Este (Uruguay) 2010, *International Congress of Vertebrate Morphology* Paris (France) 2007.
Members Individuals in 44 countries and territories:
Argentina, Australia, Austria, Azerbaijan, Belgium, Brazil, Canada, China, Czechia, Denmark, Egypt, Estonia, Finland, France, Germany, Hong Kong, Hungary, India, Israel, Italy, Japan, Kenya, Korea Rep, Latvia, Malaysia, Mexico, Netherlands, Norway, Poland, Portugal, Puerto Rico, Romania, Russia, Singapore, South Africa, Spain, Sweden, Switzerland, Uganda, UK, Ukraine, Uruguay, USA, Uzbekistan.
NGO Relations Scientific member of: *International Union of Biological Sciences (IUBS, #15760).* [2022/XD5045/v/C]

♦ International Society of Veterinary Dermatopathology (ISVD) 15539

Sec Tierdermatologie Deisenhofen, Schäftlarner Weg 1a, 82041 Oberhaching, Germany. E-mail: s-bettena@t-online.de.
Treas DVM, 14810 15th Ave NE, Shoreline WA 98155, USA.
URL: http://www.isvd.org/

Aims Encourage emerging technologies for the diagnosis of skin diseases in animals; further understanding of veterinary dermatopathology by promoting training of pathology and dermatology residents in dermatopathology; provide the opportunity for graduate veterinarians to learn advanced techniques and new concepts in veterinary dermatopathology. **Structure** Executive Board. **NGO Relations** Affiliate member of: *World Association for Veterinary Dermatology (WAVD, #21203).* [2015/XJ9412/C]

♦ International Society for Veterinary Epidemiology and Economics (ISVEE) 15540

Société internationale pour l'épidémiologie et l'économie vétérinaires

Sec c/o UADY, Calle 37 No 491, 62A y 62B, Colonia Centro, Mérida CHIS, Mexico. E-mail: dabimer@uady.mx.
URL: http://isvee.net/

History Former names and other names: *World Veterinary Epidemiology Society (WVES)* – former; *Organisation internationale d'épidémiologie animale* – former; *International Society for Epidemiology and Economics* – alias. **Structure** International Management Committee, consisting of Chairman, Secretary and 7 members. **Languages** English. **Staff** 3.00 FTE, voluntary. **Finance** Members' dues. **Events** *International Symposium of Veterinary Epidemiology and Economics (ISVEE16)* Halifax, NS (Canada) 2022, *Symposium* Chiang Mai (Thailand) 2018, *Symposium* Mérida (Mexico) 2015, *Symposium* Maastricht (Netherlands) 2012, *Symposium* Durban (South Africa) 2009.
Members Individuals (540) in 61 countries:
Argentina, Australia, Austria, Belgium, Botswana, Brazil, Burkina Faso, Cambodia, Canada, Chad, Chile, Colombia, Costa Rica, Côte d'Ivoire, Czechia, Denmark, Ethiopia, Finland, France, Gambia, Germany, Ghana, Greece, India, Indonesia, Iran Islamic Rep, Ireland, Israel, Italy, Japan, Kenya, Madagascar, Mali, Mauritania, Morocco, Netherlands, New Zealand, Niger, Nigeria, Norway, Pakistan, Paraguay, Philippines, Poland, Portugal, Romania, Russia, Senegal, Slovenia, Spain, Sweden, Switzerland, Thailand, Togo, Tunisia, Uganda, UK, Ukraine, USA, Zambia, Zimbabwe.
NGO Relations Associate member of: *World Veterinary Association (WVA, #21901).* [2021/XE1248/v/D]

♦ International Society of Veterinary Ophthalmology (ISVO) 15541

Sec-Treas c/o AMC, 510 East 62nd St, New York NY 10065, USA.
URL: http://www.isvo.info/

History 1980, Barcelona (Spain). **Aims** Acts as a society of veterinarians interested in ophthalmology. **Structure** Board of 5. **Languages** English. **Staff** None. **Finance** Members' dues. **Activities** Organizes scientific meetings (every 2 years). **Events** *Meeting* Auckland (New Zealand) 2013, *Scientific Meeting* Sao Paulo (Brazil) 2009, *Meeting / Scientific Meeting* Genoa (Italy) 2007, *Scientific Meeting* Mexico City (Mexico) 2005, *Scientific meeting* Cambridge (UK) 2003. **Publications** *The Globe* (2 a year) – newsletter. **NGO Relations** Affiliated member of: *World Small Animal Veterinary Association (WSAVA, #21795).* [2014/XD6292/D]

♦ International Society of Veterinary Perinatology (no recent information)

♦ International Society of Violin and Bow-Makers (ISVBM) 15542

Entente Internationale des Maîtres Luthiers et Archetiers d'Art (EILA) – Internationale Vereinigung der Geigenbau- und Bogenmacher-Meister – Unione Internazionale dei Maestri Liutai e Archettai d'Arte

Gen Sec 8 Elm St, Huntington NY 11743, USA. E-mail: secretairegeneral@eila.org.
URL: http://eila.org/

History Founded 18 Aug 1950, Geneva (Switzerland). Also referred to as *Entente Internationale des Luthiers et Archetiers.* **Aims** Promote and develop the art of violin and bow making; assure proper working conditions; facilitate exchange of knowledge and techniques; provide information to *musicians,* whether amateurs of professionals. **Structure** Executive Board. **Languages** English, French, German, Italian. **Finance** Members' dues. Other sources: gifts, subsidies, funds raised for an exceptional project. **Activities** Events/meetings. **Events** *Biennial Convention* Stockholm (Sweden) 2015, *Biennial Convention* Scottsdale, AZ (USA) 2009, *Biennial Convention* Aix-en-Provence (France) 2007, *Biennial Convention* Barcelona (Spain) 2005, *Biennial Convention* Baveno (Italy) 2003.
Members Master violin and bow makers in 25 countries:
Australia, Austria, Belgium, Canada, China, Czechia, Denmark, Finland, France, Germany, Iceland, Ireland, Israel, Italy, Japan, Netherlands, Norway, Portugal, Singapore, Spain, Sweden, Switzerland, Taiwan, UK, USA.
NGO Relations Member of: *European Alliance for Culture and the Arts (#05866).* [2020.03.03/XD0832/D]

♦ International Society for Virtual Rehabilitation (ISVR) 15543

Pres 29 Lambiance Court, Highland Park NJ 08904, USA.
CEO address not obtained.
URL: http://isvr.org/

History Jan 2009. Statutes amended Feb 2012; Dec 2019. **Aims** Facilitate interaction between communities interested in employing new technologies for physical, psychological, cognitive, and social rehabilitation applications. **Structure** Executive Committee; Board; Committees. **Finance** Sources: meeting proceeds; members' dues. **Activities** Events/meetings; standards/guidelines. **Events** *RehabWeek* Rotterdam (Netherlands) 2022, *International Conference on Virtual Rehabilitation* 2021, *International Conference on Virtual Rehabilitation* Tel Aviv (Israel) 2019, *International Conference on Virtual Rehabilitation* Montréal, QC (Canada) 2017, *International Conference on Virtual Rehabilitation* Valencia (Spain) 2015. **Members** Individuals and organizations (98) interested in the field of virtual rehabilitation and/or tele-rehabilitation. Categories: Regular; Student; Corporate; Clinical. Membership countries not specified. **NGO Relations** Member of (1): *International Consortium for Rehabilitation Technology (ICRT, #12921)*. Affiliated with (2): *European Federation for NeuroRehabilitation Societies (EFNR, #07178)*; *International Industry Society in Advanced Rehabilitation Technology (IISART, #13840)*. Also affiliated with: International Conference on Sport Sciences Research and Technology Support (iCSPORTS); International Consortium on Rehabilitation Technologies (ICRT); USC SensoriMotor Assessment and Rehabilitation Training in Virtual Reality Center (USC SMART-VR Center); VR4REHAB. Sponsors: *International Conference on Disability, Virtual Reality and Associated Technologies (ICDVRAT)*. [2021.09.01/XM4425/**C**]

♦ International Society on Virtual Systems and Multimedia (VSMM Society) 15544

Exec Officer Dept ASRO KU Leuven, Kasteelpark Arenberg 1, 3001 Leuven, Belgium. T. +3216321699. Fax +3216321983.
URL: https://vsmm.org/

History 1995, Gifu (Japan), on the initiative of Takeo Ojika. **Events** *Conference* Toronto, ON (Canada) 2019, *International Conference on Virtual Systems & Multimedia (VSMM2018)* San Francisco, CA (USA) 2018, *International Conference on Virtual Systems and Multimedia (VSMM2017)* Dublin (Ireland) 2017, *International Conference on Virtual Systems and Multimedia* Kuala Lumpur (Malaysia) 2016, *International Conference on Virtual Systems and Multimedia* Granada (Spain) 2015. **Members** Membership countries not specified. [2013/XD8116/**D**]

♦ International Society of Vitamins and Related BioFactors (no recent information)

♦ International Society for In Vitro Fertilization (ISIVF) 15545

Société Internationale pour la Fécondation In Vitro (SIFIV)

Secretariat 6980 Cote St Luc Road, Ste 502, Montréal QC H4V 3A4, Canada. T. +15142412537. E-mail: barcap@sympatico.ca.
URL: http://www.isivf.com/

History Registered in accordance with Canadian law. **Aims** Promote research and clinical development in the field of in vitro fertilization of human oocytes (IVF) and various forms of Assisted Reproductive Technology (ART) for the prevention and treatment of infertility and other indicated conditions; promulgate ethical practice and standards of practice for such treatments; foster collaboration between the various centres in the world that offer IVF and ART. **Structure** Board of Directors; Executive Committee. Scientific Committee. **Finance** Members' dues. **Activities** Events/meetings. **Events** *Congress* Barcelona (Spain) 2019, *Congress* Istanbul (Turkey) 2017, *World Congress* Copenhagen (Denmark) 2015, *World Congress* Tunis (Tunisia) 2013, *World congress* Tokyo (Japan) 2011. **Publications** *ISIVF News*. [2017.03.09/XM3569/**E**]

♦ International Society for In Vitro Methods (unconfirmed)
♦ International Society for Water Solutions (internationally oriented national body)

♦ International Society for Wearable Technology in Healthcare (WATCH Society) 15546

Address not obtained.
URL: http://www.watch-society.com/

History Initiated 2014. Legally founded 28 Apr 2015. **Aims** Bring together health experts, care professionals, developers, soft-and hardware manufacturers of portable technology to form a melting pot of innovation and collaboration, so as to research and validate development of portable technology for healthcare professionals and patients, and where possible improve and support this object by spreading knowledge and insights gained worldwide. **Structure** Board. **Activities** Events/meetings. **Events** *Conference* Toronto, ON (Canada) 2018. [2018/XM8029/**C**]

♦ International Society for Web Engineering (ISWE) 15547

Treas Mannheimer Str 8, 76344 Eggenstein Leopoldshafen, Germany. Fax +497247953901. E-mail: ec@iswe-ev.de.
URL: http://www.iswe-ev.de/

History Jul 2005, Sydney (Australia), during 5th International Conference on Web Engineering. Formally founded, 16 Dec 2005, Karlsruhe (Germany). Registered in accordance with German law 9 Nov 2006. **Aims** Promote science and research in the entire field of web engineering. **Structure** Steering Committee. **Activities** *International Conference on Web Engineering (ICWE)*. **Events** *International Conference on Web Engineering* Helsinki (Finland) 2020, *International Conference on Web Engineering* Daejeon (Korea Rep) 2019, *International Conference on Web Engineering* Caceres (Spain) 2018, *International Conference on Web Engineering* Rome (Italy) 2017, *International Conference on Web Engineering* Rotterdam (Netherlands) 2015.
Members Individuals in 16 countries:
Argentina, Australia, Austria, Brazil, Croatia, Denmark, France, Germany, Hungary, Italy, Japan, Netherlands, Slovakia, Spain, Switzerland, USA. [2020/XJ5404/**E**]

♦ International Society for Weigh-In-Motion (ISWIM) 15548

Gen Sec FHWA, 1200 New Jersey Ave SE, Washington DC 20590, USA.
Information Officer address not obtained.
Contact Via Ai Crott 5, 6702 Bellinzona TI, Switzerland.
URL: https://www.is-wim.net

History 2007. Registration: Swiss Civil Code, Switzerland. **Aims** Support advances in Weigh-In-Motion technologies and more widespread application of WIM systems and data. **Structure** General Assembly; Board; Executive Board; Technical Committees; Scientific Committee; Vendors & Consultants College. **Activities** Awareness raising; events/meetings; publishing activities; research/documentation; standards/guidelines; training/education. **Events** *Conference* Prague (Czechia) 2019, *Conference* Foz do Iguaçu (Brazil) 2016, *Conference* Dallas, TX (USA) 2012, *Conference* Paris (France) 2008, *Conference* Taipei (Taiwan) 2005. **Members** Individuals, institutions, vendors and consultants. Membership countries not specified. **NGO Relations** Accredited by (1): *World Road Association (PIARC, #21754)*. [2021.06.16/XJ8102/**D**]

♦ International Society for Welding Technology (#10144)
♦ International Society for the Welfare of Cripples / see RI Global (#18948)
♦ International Society for Welfare of Cripples / see International Cerebral Palsy Society (#12531)
♦ International Society of Wheelchair Professionals (internationally oriented national body)

♦ International Society of Wildlife Endocrinology (ISWE) 15549

Sec Cornell University, College of Veterinary Medicine, S1-088 Schurman Hall, Ithaca NY 14853, USA. T. +16072533796. Fax +16072534213. E-mail: njp27@cornell.edu.
Chair South East Zoo Alliance for Reproduction and Conservation, c/o White Oak, 581705 White Oak Rd, Yulee FL 32097, USA. T. +19042253285. E-mail: information@sezarc.com.
URL: http://www.iswe-endo.org/

History 2010. **Aims** Advance the field of wildlife endocrinology by promoting stronger inter-disciplinary collaboration among wildlife and conservation biologists to optimize animal health, reproduction, and welfare in support of global conservation efforts. **Structure** Board, comprising Chair, 2 Vice-Chairs, Treasurer, Secretary, Communications Chair, Conference Planning Chair and 2 members. **Events** *Conference* Nainital (India) 2023, *Conference* Ithaca, NY (USA) 2021, *Conference* South Africa 2019, *Conference* Lake Buena Vista, FL (USA) 2017, *Annual Conference* Berlin (Germany) 2015. [2015/XJ6620/**C**]

♦ International Society for Wildlife and Environment Non Profit Society (inactive)

♦ International Society of Women Airline Pilots (ISA+21) 15550

Chairwoman 6920 S Cimarron Road, Las Vegas NV 89113, USA. E-mail: chairwoman@iswap.org – secretary@iswap.org.
URL: http://www.iswap.org/

History Founded 1978, Las Vegas NV (USA), as *International Social Affiliation of Women Airline Pilots*. Current title adopted, 1984. **Aims** As an organization of career women airline pilots: celebrate friendships and achievements; support informational exchange and networking; provide aviation scholarship opportunities for airline pilot career-seeking women; educational outreach. **Structure** Board; Committees. **Languages** English. **Staff** 9.00 FTE, voluntary. **Finance** Members' dues: between US$ 40 and US$ 55. Accepts donations from institutions and the general public. **Activities** Through ISA Aviatrix Scholarship Trust, awards: International Career Scholarship; Fiorenza de Bernardi Merit Award; Holly Mullins Memorial Scholarship. Members participate in Educational Outreach. **Events** *Annual Convention* Sydney, NSW (Australia) 2019, *Annual Convention* Berlin (Germany) 2015, *Annual Convention / Annual Meeting* San Antonio, TX (USA) 2014, *Annual Convention / Annual Meeting* Budapest (Hungary) 2013, *Annual Convention / Annual Meeting* Seattle, WA (USA) 2012. **Publications** *ISA News* (3 a year). Information Services: Information bank provides network of assistance with members' questions.
Members Individuals (430) in 20 countries and territories:
Austria, Belarus, Belgium, Canada, Denmark, France, Germany, India, Ireland, Israel, Italy, Jamaica, Netherlands, New Zealand, Russia, Spain, Switzerland, Taiwan, Ukraine, USA.
NGO Relations *International Federation of Air Line Pilots' Associations (IFALPA, #13349)*. [2020/XD0163/v/**D**]

♦ International Society for Working Time and Health Research / see Working Time Society (#21062)
♦ International Society for Yad Vashem (internationally oriented national body)

♦ International Society for Zinc Biology (ISZB) 15551

Contact address not obtained. E-mail: iszb.org@gmail.com.
URL: http://iszb.org/

History 2007. **Aims** Bring together scientists from a diversity of fields with a common interest in the structural, biochemical, genetic and physiological aspects of zinc biology. **Structure** Board; Committees (4). **Languages** English. **Events** *Meeting* Kyoto (Japan) 2019, *Meeting* Larnaca (Cyprus) 2017, *Meeting* Asilomar, CA (USA) 2014, *Meeting* Melbourne, VIC (Australia) 2012, *Meeting* Jerusalem (Israel) 2009.
Members Individuals in 15 countries:
Australia, China, Denmark, France, Germany, Hungary, Israel, Italy, Japan, Korea Rep, Sweden, Türkiye, UK, Ukraine, USA.
NGO Relations *International Biometals Society (IBS, #12353)*. [2019.12.23/XJ6531/**C**]

♦ International Society of Zoological Sciences (ISZS) 15552

SG Inst of Zoology, Chinese Ac of Sciences, 1 Beichen West Rd, 100101 Beijing, China. T. +861064807295. Fax +861064807295. E-mail: iszs@ioz.ac.cn.
Exec Dir address not obtained.
URL: http://www.globalzoology.org.cn/index.html

History 1889, Paris (France). Ceased to exist after the 1972 meeting. Reinstated Athens (Greece) 2000, as *Permanent Committee of International Zoological Congresses – Comité permanent des congrès internationaux de zoologie (CPCIZ)*. Re-established under current title, 2004, Beijing (China). **Aims** Promote zoological science by improving communication between zoologists and zoological organizations; increase availability of resources needed to conduct zoological research; promote coordination, collaboration and cooperation between different fields of zoology. **Structure** Committee of 11 members. Secretariat. **Languages** English. **Staff** 4.00 FTE, paid. **Finance** Donations; income from congresses, other organizations and journal publication. **Activities** Organizes: training courses; symposia. **Events** *International Congress of Zoology* Cape Town (South Africa) 2021, *International Congress of Zoology* Cape Town (South Africa) 2020, *International Symposium of Integrative Zoology (ISIZ)* Auckland (New Zealand) 2019, *International Symposium of Integrative Zoology (ISIZ)* Beijing (China) 2018, *International Symposium of Integrative Zoology (ISIZ)* Xining (China) 2017. **Publications** *Integrative Zoology* (4 a year) – journal. **Members** Institutional (112), representing over 30,000 zoologists; Individual (1,086). Members in over 80 countries. Membership countries not specified. **NGO Relations** Member of: *International Union of Biological Sciences (IUBS, #15760)*. Affiliate Member of: *International Society of Biometeorology (ISB, #14969)*. [2021/XE1722/**E**]

♦ International Socioeconomics Laboratory (unconfirmed)

♦ International Sociological Association (ISA) 15553

Association internationale de sociologie (AIS) – Internationale Vereinigung für Soziologie – Asociación Internacional de Sociologia – Mezdunarodnaja Sociologiceskaja Associacija

Exec Sec Fac de CC Politicas y Sociologia, Universidad Complutense, 28223 Madrid, Spain. T. +34913527650. Fax +34913524945. E-mail: isa@isa-sociology.org.
URL: http://www.isa-sociology.org/

History 11 Sep 1949, Oslo (Norway). Founded at Constituent Congress, on the initiative of *UNESCO (#20322)*, when Statutes were adopted. Statutes modified and individual membership introduced Sep 1970, Varna (Bulgaria); last modifications: 1986, Delhi (India); Aug 1993, Gävle (Sweden); Jul 1994, Bielefeld (Germany); Jul 2002, Brisbane (Australia); Jul 2010, Gothenburg (Sweden); Jul 2014, Yokohama (Japan). **Aims** Represent sociologists regardless of school of thought, scientific approach or ideological opinion; advance sociological knowledge. **Structure** Assembly (every 4 years at World Congress); Council of National Associations; Research Council; Executive Committee; Research Committees; Working Groups; Thematic Groups; Secretariat. **Languages** English, French, Spanish. **Staff** 1.50 FTE, paid. **Finance** Sources: members' dues; sale of publications. **Activities** Events/meetings; knowledge management/information dissemination; research/documentation. **Events** *Forum of Sociology* Kyoto (Japan) 2024, *World Congress of Sociology* Melbourne, VIC (Australia) 2023, *Research Committee on Urban and Regional Development Conference* Antwerp (Belgium) 2021, *Forum of Sociology* Porto Alegre (Brazil) 2021, *Research Committee on Social Stratification Spring Meeting* Turku (Finland) 2021. **Publications** *Current Sociology* (6 a year); *International Sociology* (6 a year); *eSymposium* – online; *Global Dialogue* – online; *ISA Directory of Members*; *Isagram* – electronic newsletter. *Sage Studies in International Sociology* – book series.
Members Individual (about 6,360) and Collective: Regular and Affiliated (about 160). Members in 127 countries and territories:
Albania, Algeria, Angola, Argentina, Armenia, Australia, Austria, Azerbaijan, Bahrain, Bangladesh, Barbados, Belarus, Belgium, Benin, Bolivia, Bosnia-Herzegovina, Brazil, Brunei Darussalam, Bulgaria, Burkina Faso, Cambodia, Cameroon, Canada, Cape Verde, Chile, China, Colombia, Congo Brazzaville, Congo DR, Costa Rica, Croatia, Cuba, Cyprus, Czechia, Denmark, Ecuador, Egypt, El Salvador, Eritrea, Estonia, Ethiopia, Faeroe Is, Fiji, Finland, France, Georgia, Germany, Ghana, Greece, Guam, Guatemala, Honduras, Hong Kong, Hungary, India, Indonesia, Iran Islamic Rep, Ireland, Israel, Italy, Jamaica, Japan, Jordan, Kazakhstan, Kenya, Korea Rep, Kuwait, Kyrgyzstan, Latvia, Lebanon, Libya, Lithuania, Malaysia, Mali, Malta, Mauritius, Mexico, Mongolia, Morocco, Mozambique, Namibia, Nepal, Netherlands, New Zealand, Nicaragua, Nigeria, North Macedonia, Norway, Pakistan, Palestine, Paraguay, Peru, Philippines, Poland, Portugal, Puerto Rico, Réunion, Romania, Russia, Saudi Arabia, Senegal, Serbia, Singapore, Slovakia, Slovenia, South Africa, Spain, Sri Lanka, Sweden, Switzerland, Taiwan, Tanzania UR, Thailand, Trinidad-Tobago, Tunisia, Türkiye, Turkmenistan, UK, Ukraine, United Arab Emirates, USA, Uzbekistan, Venezuela, Vietnam, Virgin Is UK, Zambia, Zimbabwe.
Consultative Status Consultative status granted from: *ECOSOC (#05331)* (Special). **IGO Relations** Associated with Department of Global Communications of the United Nations. **NGO Relations** Member of (1): *International Science Council (ISC, #14796)*. Instrumental in setting up (3): *Asociación Iberoamericana de Investigación en Sociología de las Organizaziones y Comunicación (AISOC, #02145)*; *Association de recherche coopérative internationale (ARCI, no recent information)*; *Oñati International Institute for the Sociology of Law (IISL, #17725)*. [2021.11.05/XB2575/**B**]

♦ International Sociological and Legal Research Centre / see International Public Foundation (#14667)

♦ International Sociology of Sport Association (ISSA) 15554

Pres Montpetit Hall MNT-375, 125 University Private, Ottawa ON K1N 1A2, Canada. E-mail: president@issa1965.org.
Gen Sec address not obtained. E-mail: general.secretary@issa1965.org – conferences@issa1965.org.
URL: http://issa1965.org/

History 1965. Founded as a Committee of *International Council of Sport Science and Physical Education (ICSSPE, #13077)*. Previously referred to as *International Committee of Sociology of Sport (ICSS)*. **Aims** Foster research in the social scientific study of sport; encourage international communication among scholars; promote collaborative cross-national research projects; develop scholarly exchange. **Structure** Executive Board. **Languages** English. **Staff** Voluntary. **Finance** Members' dues. **Activities** Events/meetings; networking/liaising. **Events** *World Congress of Sociology of Sport* Ottawa, ON (Canada) 2023, *World Congress of Sociology of Sport* Tübingen (Germany) 2022, *World Congress of Sociology of Sport* Viña del Mar (Chile) 2021, *World Congress of Sociology of Sport* Viña del Mar (Chile) 2020, *World Congress of Sociology of Sport* Dunedin (New Zealand) 2019. **Publications** *IRSS e-Bulletin* (4 a year); *International Review for the Sociology of Sport* (8 a year).

Members Regular; Special; Institutional. Members in 51 countries and territories:
Argentina, Australia, Austria, Bahamas, Belgium, Brazil, Canada, Chile, China, Croatia, Cuba, Cyprus, Czechia, Denmark, Estonia, Finland, France, Germany, Greece, Hungary, Iceland, Iran Islamic Rep, Ireland, Israel, Italy, Jamaica, Japan, Korea Rep, Malaysia, Malta, Mexico, Morocco, Netherlands, New Zealand, Norway, Poland, Portugal, Russia, Singapore, Slovenia, South Africa, Spain, Sweden, Switzerland, Taiwan, Türkiye, UK, Uruguay, USA, Venezuela, Zimbabwe.

IGO Relations *UNESCO (#20322)*. [2022/XE2050/**E**]

♦ International Softball Federation (inactive)
♦ International Soft Drinks Council / see International Council of Beverages Associations (#12999)
♦ International Softswitch Consortium / see IP Multimedia Subsystems Forum
♦ International Soft Tennis Association / see International Soft Tennis Federation (#15555)

♦ International Soft Tennis Federation (ISTF) 15555

Main Office MIJU B/D 4F 361-1, 3Ga Dongin-Dong, Jung-Gu, Daegu, Korea Rep. T. +82534267117. E-mail: softtennisistf@gmail.com – parksh7117@hanmail.net.

History Former names and other names: *International Soft Tennis Association* – alias. **Events** *General Assembly* Anseong (Korea Rep) 2007, *General Assembly* Seoul (Korea Rep) 1999, *General Assembly* Seoul (Korea Rep) 1989.

Members Organizations in 32 countries and territories:
Bangladesh, Brazil, Brunei Darussalam, Canada, China, Congo DR, Costa Rica, Dominican Rep, Hong Kong, India, Indonesia, Japan, Kazakhstan, Korea DPR, Korea Rep, Kyrgyzstan, Malaysia, Maldives, Mongolia, Nepal, Pakistan, Philippines, Puerto Rico, Singapore, Sri Lanka, Taiwan, Thailand, UK, USA, Uzbekistan, Venezuela, Vietnam.

Individuals in 7 countries:
Australia, Germany, Hungary, Italy, Mexico, Russia, Spain.

NGO Relations Member of (2): *Alliance of Independent recognised Members of Sport (AIMS, #00690)*; *Olympic Movement (#17719)*. Recognized by: *International Olympic Committee (IOC, #14408)*. [2016/XD8260/**D**]

♦ International Software Benchmarking Standards Group (ISBSG) . . . 15556

Exec Dir Level 1, 147 Cecil St, Melbourne VIC 3205, Australia. T. +614124399976. E-mail: ceo@isbsg.org.
URL: http://www.isbsg.org/

History Jul 1994, as a cooperation between a group of national associations. Formally founded, 1997. **Aims** Improve the management of *information technology* resources by both *business* and *government*, through provision and exploitation of public repositories of software engineering knowledge that are standardized, verified, recent and representative of current technology. **Structure** Board of Directors; Executive Officer. Administration Office based in Australia. **Staff** 3.00 FTE, paid. **Finance** Members' dues. Other sources: industry sponsors; sale of product. **Activities** Standards/guidelines; knowledge management/information dissemination. **Events** *Annual IT Confidence Conference* Mexico City (Mexico) 2018, *Annual IT Confidence Conference* Beijing (China) 2017, *Annual IT Confidence Conference* Los Angeles, CA (USA) 2016, *Annual IT Confidence Conference* Florence (Italy) 2015, *Annual IT Confidence Conference* Tokyo (Japan) 2014. **Publications** *Benchmark Release 10* (2008); *Software Metrics Compendium* (2005). Special analyses reports. **Information Services** *Data Collection Package*.

Members IT and metrics associations in 12 countries:
Australia, China, Finland, Germany, India, Italy, Japan, Mexico, Netherlands, Spain, Switzerland, USA.
[2017.10.24/XE3410/**E**]

♦ International Software Consulting Network (ISCN) 15557

Head Office Freiraum Business Ctr, Liebenauer Hauptstr 2-6, 8041 Graz, Austria. T. +43316815910. Fax +43316815912.
Ireland ISCN Intl Software Consulting Network LTD, Florence House, 1 Florence Villas, Bray, CO. WICKLOW, Ireland. T. +35312050020. Fax +35312050021.
URL: http://www.iscn.com/

History 1 Sep 1994, Ireland. Registered in accordance with Irish law. **Aims** Set up a resource pool of *experts* involved in well known process improvement projects and initiatives. **Structure** Team of 12. **Activities** Events/meetings; training/education; guidance/assistance/consulting. **Events** *EuroAsiaSPI : European and Asian System, Software and Service Process Improvement and Innovation Conference* Graz (Austria) 2016, *EuroAsiaSPI : European and Asian System, Software and Service Process Improvement and Innovation Conference* Ankara (Turkey) 2015, *EuroSPI : annual European systems and software process improvement and innovation conference* Kirchberg (Luxembourg) 2014, *EuroSPI : Annual European Systems and Software Process Improvement and Innovation Conference* Dundalk (Ireland) 2013, *EuroSPI Conference* Vienna (Austria) 2012. **Publications** Annual Report. Seminar proceedings.

Members Organizations and individuals in 24 countries:
Austria, Belgium, Canada, Chile, Denmark, Finland, France, Germany, Greece, Hungary, India, Ireland, Italy, Latvia, Mexico, Netherlands, Norway, Poland, Romania, Slovenia, Spain, Sweden, UK, USA.

NGO Relations Member of: *European Certification and Qualification Association (ECQA, #06511)*.
[2018/XF3084/**F**]

♦ International Software Engineering Research Network (ISERN) 15558

Contact Fraunhofer IESE, Fraunhofer-Platz 1, 67663 Kaiserslautern, Germany. T. +4963168002260.
URL: http://isern.iese.de/

Events *Annual Meeting* Porto de Galinhas (Brazil) 2019, *Annual Meeting* Oulu (Finland) 2018, *Annual Meeting* Toronto, ON (Canada) 2017, *Annual Meeting* Ciudad Real (Spain) 2016, *Annual Meeting* Beijing (China) 2015.

Members Centres, institutes and universities (37) in 13 countries:
Australia, Austria, Brazil, Canada, Finland, Germany, Italy, Japan, Norway, Spain, Sweden, UK, USA. [2020/XF4670/**F**]

♦ International Software Product Line Conference (meeting series)

♦ International Software Testing Qualifications Board (ISTQB) 15559

Secretariat Blvd du Souverain 280, 1160 Brussels, Belgium. T. +3227431540. E-mail: info@istqb.org.
Registered Office Ave du Roi 206, 1190 Brussels, Belgium.
URL: http://www.istqb.org/

History Nov 2002, Edinburgh (UK). Registered in accordance with Belgian law. **Aims** Support a single, universally accepted, international qualification scheme aimed at software and system testing professionals. **Structure** General Assembly; Executive Committee; Working Groups; Secretariat. **Activities** Certification/accreditation. **Events** *General Assembly* Yerevan (Armenia) 2019, *General Assembly* Toronto, ON (Canada) 2018, *General Assembly* Seoul (Korea Rep) 2016, *Meeting* Copenhagen (Denmark) 2015, *Test Conference* Hurtigruten (Norway) 2012.

Members National Testing Boards in 34 countries:
Australia, Austria, Bangladesh, Belgium, Brazil, Canada, China, Czechia, Denmark, Finland, France, Germany, India, Israel, Italy, Japan, Korea Rep, Latvia, Malaysia, Netherlands, New Zealand, Nigeria, Norway, Poland, Portugal, Russia, Slovakia, Spain, Sweden, Switzerland, Türkiye, UK, Ukraine, USA.

Regional Testing Boards (2):
Hispanic America Software Testing Qualifications Board (HASTQB, #10923); *South East European Testing Board (SEETB, #19820)*. [2020/XM3092/y/**E**]

♦ International Soil Carbon Network (unconfirmed)

♦ International Soil Conservation Organization (ISCO) 15560

Organisation internationale de conservation des sols

Chair Dept Natural Resources/Environmental Management, College of Tropical Agriculture/Human Resources, Univ of Hawai'i at Manoa, 1910 East-West Rd, Honolulu HI 96822, USA. T. +18089566343 – +18082772598. Fax +18089566539. E-mail: elswaify@hawaii.edu.
URL: http://www.isco.org/

History 1983, Honolulu HI (USA), to organize biennial *International Soil and Water Conservation Conference*. **Aims** Advocate *sustainable*, productive and efficient use and management of soil, *water* and other *natural resources* through improved science-based understanding of resource management issues, enhanced communication and strategic publications. **Structure** Board of Directors. **Languages** English. **Staff** Voluntary. **Finance** Conference registration fees; host institution budgeting; sponsor and donor contributions. Budget varies. **Events** *Conference* Delhi (India) 2019, *CONSOWA : World Conference on Soil and Water Conservation under Global Change* Lleida (Spain) 2017, *Conference* Lleida (Spain) 2017, *Conference / International Soil Conservation Conference* El Paso, TX (USA) 2015, *Conference / International Soil Conservation Conference* Medellin (Colombia) 2013. **Publications** Conference proceedings; issue papers.

Members No formal membership. Professional colleagues in 75 countries and territories:
Algeria, Argentina, Australia, Austria, Belgium, Brazil, Burkina Faso, Cameroon, Canada, Chile, China, Colombia, Costa Rica, Côte d'Ivoire, Czechia, Denmark, Egypt, Eswatini, Ethiopia, Fiji, France, Germany, Ghana, Guatemala, Hungary, Iceland, India, Indonesia, Iran Islamic Rep, Iraq, Israel, Italy, Japan, Jordan, Kenya, Lebanon, Lesotho, Malaysia, Mexico, Morocco, Nepal, Netherlands, New Zealand, Nigeria, Peru, Philippines, Puerto Rico, Russia, Rwanda, Saudi Arabia, Senegal, Serbia, Singapore, Somalia, South Africa, Sri Lanka, Sudan, Sweden, Switzerland, Syrian AR, Taiwan, Tanzania UR, Thailand, Togo, Tonga, Tunisia, Türkiye, UK, Ukraine, USA, Venezuela, Vietnam, Zambia, Zimbabwe.

IGO Relations Links with several international institutes within *CGIAR System Organization (CGIAR, #03843)*.
[2017.03.09/XD1174/**F**]

♦ International Soil Moisture Network (unconfirmed)
♦ International Soil Museum / see ISRIC – World Soil Information (#16068)

♦ International Soil and Plant Analysis Council 15561

Contact 347 North Shores Circle, Windsor CO 80550, USA. T. +19706865702.
URL: http://www.spcouncil.com/

Events *Symposium* Kailua-Kona, HI (USA) 2015, *Symposium* Queenstown (New Zealand) 2013, *Symposium* Chania (Greece) 2011, *Symposium* Santa Rosa, CA (USA) 2009, *Symposium* Budapest (Hungary) 2007.
[2009/XM0554/**E**]

♦ International Soil Reference and Information Centre / see ISRIC – World Soil Information (#16068)

♦ International Soil Tillage Research Organization (ISTRO) 15562

Organisation internationale de recherche de travail du sol

SG Aarhus Univ, Blichers Allé 20, 8830 Tjele, Denmark.
URL: http://www.istro.org/

History 27 Sep 1973, Wageningen (Netherlands). Founded during 6th International Conference on Soil Tillage; new Constitution adopted 25 Jun 1982; revised 12 Jul 1991. Registration: No/ID: KVK 40024956, Netherlands. **Aims** Promote contacts among scientists undertaking research in soil tillage and field traffic and their relationships with soil environment, *land use* and crop production; stimulate scientific research in soil tillage and related fields; further application of results of such research in *agricultural* and environmental practice. **Structure** General Assembly of members (every 3 years at International Conference); Board. **Languages** English. **Staff** Voluntary. **Finance** Sources: donations; grants; members' dues. Other sources: profit from properties and transactions. Annual budget: 13,000 EUR. **Activities** Events/meetings; networking/liaising. **Events** *Triennial Conference* USA 2024, *Triennial Conference* Dublin (Ireland) 2022, *Triennial Conference* Dublin (Ireland) 2021, *Triennial Conference* Paris (France) 2018, *Triennial Conference* Nanjing (China) 2015. **Publications** *ISTRO-Info* (4 a year); *Soil and Tillage Research* (periodical). Conference proceedings; bibliographies.

Members Individual (540), Corporate, Honorary, Retired members in 78 countries and territories:
Argentina, Australia, Austria, Belgium, Bolivia, Bosnia-Herzegovina, Botswana, Brazil, Bulgaria, Burkina Faso, Cameroon, Canada, China, Colombia, Costa Rica, Côte d'Ivoire, Croatia, Czechia, Denmark, Egypt, Estonia, Finland, France, Germany, Ghana, Greece, Hungary (*), India, Indonesia, Iran Islamic Rep, Ireland, Israel, Italy, Japan, Kazakhstan, Kenya, Lithuania, Mexico, Moldova, Morocco, Netherlands, New Zealand, Niger, Nigeria, Norway, Pakistan, Paraguay, Peru, Philippines, Poland, Portugal, Puerto Rico, Romania, Russia, Saudi Arabia, Serbia, Slovakia, Slovenia, South Africa, Spain, Sudan, Sweden, Switzerland, Syrian AR, Taiwan, Tanzania UR, Thailand, Trinidad-Tobago, Türkiye, UK, Ukraine, United Arab Emirates, Uruguay, USA, Venezuela, Yemen, Zambia, Zimbabwe.

As of Jul 1992, formal agreements with Academies of Science of Russia, Ukraine and Kazakhstan to collaborate on joint conferences and scientific exchanges. " indicates formal branch (recognized by government authorities in country concerned).

IGO Relations Partner of (1): *Global Soil Partnership (GSP, #10608)*. [2022.10.14/XC6905/**B**]

♦ International Solar Alliance (ISA) 15563

Alliance solaire internationale (ASI)

Communication Lead Surya Bhawan, Natl Inst of Solar Energy Campus, Gwal Pahari, Faridabad-Gurugram Road, Gurugram, Gurugram, Haryana 122003, Gurugram HARYANA 122003, India. T. +911242853084. E-mail: info@isolaralliance.org.
Dir General address not obtained. T. +911242853090.
URL: http://www.isolaralliance.org/

History Launched 30 Nov 2015, Paris (France), by Indian Prime Minister and French President, at COP21 UN Climate Change Conference. Founding ceremony, Mar 2018. **Aims** Boost *solar energy* in *developing countries*. **Structure** Assembly; International Steering Committee; Secretariat. **Events** *Forum* Abu Dhabi (United Arab Emirates) 2019, *Assembly* Noida (India) 2019, *Global RE-Invest India-ISA Partnership Renewable Energy Investors Meeting* Noida (India) 2019, *Assembly* Noida (India) 2018, *Global RE-Invest India-ISA Partnership Renewable Energy Investors Meeting* Noida (India) 2018. **Publications** *ISA Journal*. **Members** Countries (about 120). Membership countries not specified. **IGO Relations** Partners: *European Bank for Reconstruction and Development (EBRD, #06315)*; *European Investment Bank (EIB, #07599)*; *International Energy Agency (IEA, #13270)*; *International Renewable Energy Agency (IRENA, #14715)*; *Regions of Climate Action (R20, #18820)*; *UNDP (#20292)*; *The World Bank Group (#21218)*. **NGO Relations** Partners: *Climate Parliament (#04019)*. [2019/XM4318/**C***]

♦ International Solar Commission (inactive)
♦ International Solar Energy Agency / see International Renewable Energy Agency (#14715)

♦ International Solar Energy Society (ISES) 15564

Société d'énergie solaire

Contact Villa Tannheim, Wiesentalstr 50, 79115 Freiburg, Germany. T. +49761459060. E-mail: public.relations@ises.org – hq@ises.org.
URL: http://www.ises.org/

History 24 Dec 1954, Phoenix, AZ (USA). Former names and other names: *Association for Applied Solar Energy* – former (1954 to 29 Jan 1963); *Solar Energy Society* – former (29 Jan 1963 to 9 May 1971). Registration: USA, State of Arizona. **Aims** Transition to 100% renewable energy for all. **Structure** Board of Directors; Committees; Regional Offices (5). **Languages** English. **Staff** 4.00 FTE, paid. **Finance** Sources: meeting proceeds; members' dues; sale of publications. **Activities** Events/meetings; knowledge management/information dissemination; projects/programmes; training/education. **Events** *Biennial World Congress* Santiago (Chile) 2019, *International Photovoltaic Power Generation Conference* Shanghai (China) 2018, *Biennial World Congress* Abu Dhabi (United Arab Emirates) 2017, *International Conference on Solar Air-Conditioning* Abu Dhabi (United Arab Emirates) 2017, *EuroSun Congress* Palma (Spain) 2016. **Publications** *ISES Newsletter* (12 a year) in English – Monthly Newsletter on society activites, section news, member & partner news; *Solar Energy* (12 a year) in English; *Solar Energy Advances* (irregular) in English – Fully Open Access Journal (founded in 2021). Position papers; white papers; reference books; infographic series. **Information Services** *Conference Proceedings Database*; *ISES Online Bookshop*.

Members National sections, representing 10,000 contacts, in 52 countries and territories:
Argentina, Australia, Austria, Belgium, Brazil, Bulgaria, Canada, Central African Rep, China, Costa Rica, Croatia, Cyprus, Czechia, Denmark, Egypt, Finland, France, Georgia, Germany, Ghana, Greece, Hungary, India, Israel, Italy, Japan, Korea Rep, Lebanon, Lithuania, Mexico, Nepal, Netherlands, Norway, Pakistan, Peru, Philippines, Poland, Portugal, Romania, Russia, Slovakia, Slovenia, South Africa, Spain, Sweden, Switzerland, Taiwan, Türkiye, UK, Ukraine, USA, Zimbabwe.

Also 3 regional sections:
Arab; *Solar Energy Society of Central Africa (SESCA)*; *Sustainable Energy Society of Southern Africa (SESSA)*.
Individuals in 113 countries and territories:
Antigua-Barbuda, Argentina, Australia, Austria, Bahrain, Bangladesh, Barbados, Belgium, Bolivia, Botswana, Brunei Darussalam, Bulgaria, Chile, China, Colombia, Cook Is, Croatia, Cuba, Cyprus, Czechia, Denmark, Dominican Rep, Ecuador, Egypt, El Salvador, Eswatini, Fiji, Finland, France, Gabon, Germany, Ghana, Greece, Guam, Guatemala, Guyana, Honduras, Hong Kong, Hungary, India, Indonesia, Ireland, Israel, Italy, Jamaica, Japan, Jordan, Kazakhstan, Kenya, Kiribati, Korea Rep, Kuwait, Lesotho, Libya, Lithuania, Luxembourg, Malawi, Malaysia, Malta, Mexico, Morocco, Mozambique, Namibia, Netherlands, New Zealand, Nigeria, Norway, Oman, Pakistan, Palau, Papua New Guinea, Paraguay, Peru, Philippines, Poland, Portugal, Puerto Rico, Qatar, Romania, Russia, Samoa, Saudi Arabia, Senegal, Serbia, Singapore, Slovakia, Slovenia, Solomon Is, South Africa, Spain, Sri Lanka, Sudan, Sweden, Switzerland, Tahiti Is, Taiwan, Tanzania UR, Thailand, Tonga, Trinidad-Tobago, Tunisia, Türkiye, Tuvalu, Uganda, UK, Ukraine, USA, Vanuatu, Venezuela, Yemen, Zambia, Zimbabwe.

Consultative Status Consultative status granted from: *ECOSOC (#05331)* (Ros A); *UNESCO (#20322)* (Consultative Status). **IGO Relations** Accredited by (3): *Green Climate Fund (GCF, #10714)*; *United Nations Framework Convention on Climate Change – Secretariat (UNFCCC, #20564)*; *United Nations Office at Vienna (UNOV, #20604)*. Contacts with: *European Commission (EC, #06633)*; *FAO (#09260)*; *Global Environment Facility (GEF, #10346)*; *International Bank for Reconstruction and Development (IBRD, #12317)*; *International Energy Agency (IEA, #13270)*; *UNDP (#20292)*; *United Nations Commission on Sustainable Development (CSD, inactive)*. **NGO Relations** Member of: *Global 100% RE (#10160)*; *Global Solar Council (GSC, #10609)*; *International Network for Sustainable Energy (INFORSE, #14331)*. In liaison with technical committees of: *International Organization for Standardization (ISO, #14473)*. Contacts with: *ASEAN Solar Energy Network (ASEN, no recent information)*; *Solar Heat Europe (SHE, #19674)*; *EUROSOLAR – European Association for Renewable Energy (#09183)*; *Fondation énergies pour le monde*; *Greenpeace International (#10727)*; *International Sustainable Energy Organization (ISEO, inactive)*; *Planetary Association for Clean Energy (PACE, #18381)*; *SolarPower Europe (#19676)*. Together with *World Wind Energy Association (WWEA, #21937)*, *World Bioenergy Association (WBA, #21231)*, *International Hydropower Association (IHA, #13828)* and *International Geothermal Association (IGA, #13717)*, founded: *International Renewable Energy Alliance (Ren Alliance, #14716)*. Set up: *Australian New Zealand Solar Energy Society (ANZSES, inactive)*, now Australian Solar Energy Society (AuSES). [2023.02.15/XC3244/**B**]

- International Solar Fuels Conference (meeting series)
- International Solar Yoga Teachers' Association (internationally oriented national body)

♦ International Sol-Gel Society (ISGS) 15565

Postal Address UCLA Materials Science, 6531 Boelter Hall, Los Angeles CA 90095, USA.
Contact address not obtained. T. +33965003735.
Treas IBM Almaden Research Center, Advanced Organic Materials, 650 Harry Road, K-17/E-1, San Jose CA 95120, USA.
URL: http://www.isgs.org/

History Aug 2003, Sydney (Australia), during the 12th International Sol-Gel Conference. **Aims** Coordinate promotion of sol-gel science and *technology* in the scientific and industrial community; foster communication among researchers; encourage education, training and research in the field. **Structure** Board of Directors, comprising President, Vice-President, Secretary, Chairman, Chief Financial Officer and 4 further members. **Finance** Members' dues. **Events** *Biennial Conference* Lyon (France) 2022, *Biennial Conference* Lyon (France) 2021, *Biennial Conference* St Petersburg (Russia) 2019, *Biennial Conference* Kyoto (Japan) 2015, *Biennial Conference* Madrid (Spain) 2013. [2012/XJ3864/**E**]

- International Solidarity Centre, Saguenay Lac-Saint-Jean (internationally oriented national body)
- International Solidarity for Development and Investment (internationally oriented national body)
- International Solidarity Foundation (internationally oriented national body)
- International Solidarity Foundation of the Company of Mary (#10034)
- International Solidarity and Human Rights Institute (internationally oriented national body)
- International Solidarity Movement (internationally oriented national body)
- International Solidarity Work / see International Solidarity Foundation

♦ International Solid State Dosimetry Organisation (ISSDO) 15566

Chairperson Centre for Medical Radiation Physics, Univ of Wollongong, Wollongong NSW 2522, Australia. T. +61242214574. E-mail: anatoly@uow.edu.au.
Sec CIEMAT, Environmental Dept, Av Complutense 40, 28040 Madrid, Spain. T. +34913466732. Fax +34913466604. E-mail: jm.gomezros@ciemat.es.
URL: http://www.issdo.org/

History Founded 1992. Constitution adopted 1995. **Aims** Promote and assist in organization and ensure continuity of the International Conferences of Solid State Dosimetry, as well as the School on Solid State Dosimetry. **Structure** Executive Officers; Secretary; Scientific Advisory Committee; Election Committee. **Languages** English. **Staff** Voluntary. **Finance** Proceeds from conferences and summer schools. **Activities** Events/meetings; training/education. **Events** *Triennial Conference* Hiroshima (Japan) 2019, *Triennial Conference* Munich (Germany) 2016, *Triennial conference / International Conference* Recife (Brazil) 2013, *International Conference* Sydney, NSW (Australia) 2010, *International Conference* Delft (Netherlands) 2007. **Publications** Proceedings published in an international peer reviewed scientific journal.
Members Individuals in 24 countries:
Argentina, Australia, Austria, Belgium, Brazil, China, Croatia, Czechia, Denmark, France, Germany, India, Israel, Italy, Japan, Korea Rep, Mexico, Netherlands, Poland, Russia, Spain, UK, Ukraine, USA.
IGO Relations None. **NGO Relations** None. [2018.09.05/XJ2968/cv/**F**]

♦ International Solid Waste Association (ISWA) 15567

Association internationale pour les résidus solides – Internationaler Verband für Abfallbeseitigung
Managing Dir Stationsplein 45, A4-004, 3013 AK Rotterdam, Netherlands. T. +31108083990. E-mail: iswa@iswa.org.
URL: http://www.iswa.org/

History 1931, London (UK). Merged, 1970, with *International Research Group on Refuse Disposal (inactive)*. Current Statutes adopted by General Assembly, 14 Oct 1995, Vienna (Austria). Former names and other names: *International Association of Public Cleansing (INTAPUC)* – former (1931 to 1970); *Association internationale du nettoiement public* – former (1931 to 1970); *International Solid Wastes and Public Cleansing Association* – former (1970); *Association internationale pour les résidus solides et du nettoiement des villes* – former (1970); *Internationaler Verband für Abfallbeseitigung und Städtereinigung* – former (1970). **Aims** Promote and develop sustainable and professional waste management worldwide and the transition to a circular economy. **Structure** General Assembly (annual, at Congress); Board; Working Groups; Scientific and Technical Committee; Task Forces; General Secretariat. **Languages** English. **Staff** 12.00 FTE, paid. **Finance** Sources: meeting proceeds; members' dues; sale of publications. **Activities** Awards/prizes/competitions; events/meetings; knowledge management/information dissemination; training/education. **Events** *ISWA World Congress* Argentina 2025, *ISWA World Congress* South Africa 2024, *ISWA World Congress* Singapore (Singapore) 2022, *ISWA World Congress* Athens (Greece) 2021, *Beacon Conference* Singapore (Singapore) 2020. **Publications** *Waste Management and Research* (6 a year) – journal; *ISWA Newsletter*, *Waste Management World* – magazine. Guidelines; technical policy papers; position papers.
Members National; Platinum; Gold; Silver. National in 46 countries:
Argentina, Austria, Belgium, Bosnia-Herzegovina, Brazil, Canada, Chile, China, Denmark, Finland, France, Greece, Hungary, Iceland, India, Indonesia, Israel, Italy, Japan, Jordan, Latvia, Lebanon, Liberia, Malaysia, Mexico, Mongolia, Netherlands, New Zealand, Nigeria, North Macedonia, Norway, Oman, Portugal, Romania, Serbia, Singapore, Slovenia, South Africa, Spain, Sweden, Türkiye, Uganda, UK, United Arab Emirates, Uruguay, USA.
Platinum in 6 countries:
Austria, Belgium, France, Germany, Italy, Oman.
Gold in 21 countries:
Argentina, Austria, Azerbaijan, Belgium, Chile, Denmark, France, Germany, Hungary, Italy, Japan, Netherlands, North Macedonia, Portugal, Romania, Spain, Sweden, Switzerland, Türkiye, UK, USA.
Silver in 37 countries and territories:
Austria, Belgium, Brazil, Canada, China, Colombia, Denmark, Finland, France, Germany, Ghana, Greece, Iceland, India, Italy, Japan, Jordan, Kazakhstan, Luxembourg, Malta, Netherlands, Nigeria, Norway, Pakistan, Peru, Portugal, Romania, Russia, Serbia, South Africa, Sweden, Switzerland, Taiwan, Türkiye, UK, Ukraine, USA.
Included in the above, 3 organizations listed in this Yearbook:
Confederation of European Waste-to-Energy Plants (CEWEP, #04535); *Energy and Resources Institute (TERI)*; *European Investment Bank (EIB, #07599)*.
Consultative Status Consultative status granted from: *ECOSOC (#05331)* (Ros A); *WHO (#20950)* (Official Relations); *UNEP (#20299)*. **IGO Relations** Accredited by (1): *Green Climate Fund (GCF, #10714)*. **NGO Relations** Member of (5): *Climate and Clean Air Coalition (CCAC, #04010)*; *Climate Technology Centre and Network (CTCN, #04023)*; *Global Methane Initiative (GMI, #10471)* (ProjectNetwork); *LEDS Global Partnership (LEDS GP, #16435)*; *Pacific Basin Consortium for Environment and Health (PBC, #17937)*. [2022/XC2577/**B**]

- International Solid Wastes and Public Cleansing Association / see International Solid Waste Association (#15567)
- International Soling Association (see: #21760)
- International Solvent Extraction Committee / see International Committee for Solvent Extraction (#12804)

♦ International Solvothermal and Hydrothermal Association (ISHA) . . 15568

Pres Penn State – Materials Research Inst, Agronomoy Dept – College of Agricultural Sciences, 205 Materials Research Lab Bldg, University Park PA 16802, USA. T. +18148651542. Fax +18148652326.
Conference Contact address not obtained.

History on merger of *International Symposium on Hydrothermal Reactions (ISHR)* with *International Conference on Solvothermal Reactions (ICSTR)*, 2007. **Events** *Conference* Sendai (Japan) 2018, *Conference* Tainan (Taiwan) 2016, *Conference* Bordeaux (France) 2014, *Conference* Austin, TX (USA) 2013, *Conference* Beijing (China) 2010. [2013/XJ1832/c/**E**]

♦ International Sonnenberg Association (ISA) 15569

Internationaler Arbeitskreis Sonnenberg
Contact c/o Internationales Haus Sonnenberg, Clausthaler Str 11, 37444 St Andreasberg, Germany. T. +4955829440. Fax +495582944100. E-mail: info@sonnenberg-international.de.
URL: http://www.sonnenberg-international.de/

History Founded Jan 1949, when 1st Sonnenberg Conference was held between German and Danish teachers in the Harz Rural Centre "Sonnenberg". **Aims** Promote *international cooperation* and *understanding* between people of all walks of life and different political and religious convictions, irrespective of their national and ethnic origins. **Structure** Annual General Meeting; Committee; Officers; Secretariat Office; Conference centre: *International House Sonnenberg*. **Languages** English, German. **Staff** Voluntary. **Finance** Affiliated countries pay annually at least 20% of their collected membership fee to ISA. Public subsidies. **Activities** Training/education; events/meetings. **Events** *Conference on Brazil, nation in the spotlight* St Andreasberg (Germany) 2006, *Conference on cooperation in the development field* St Andreasberg (Germany) 2006, *Conference on imprisoned in Europe, but yearning in spirit for the land of the Yanks* St Andreasberg (Germany) 2006, *Conference on participation and town planning in Germany and developing countries* St Andreasberg (Germany) 2006, *Conference on politics from below* St Andreasberg (Germany) 2006. **Publications** *Sonnenberg Tagungen und Seminare* (annual) in English, French, German.
Members Groups and individuals in 25 countries:
Austria, Belgium, Bulgaria, Croatia, Czechia, Denmark, Finland, France, Germany, Greece, Hungary, Israel, Italy, Latvia, Luxembourg, Malta, Netherlands, Norway, Poland, Romania, Russia, Sweden, Switzerland, UK, USA.
Also individuals in countries that no longer have national associations. Membership countries not specified. [2019.10.15/XF5040/**F**]

♦ International SOS Foundation (ISOS Foundation) 15570

Main Office John M Keynesplein 3, Say Buildings – Bldg 5, 1066 EP Amsterdam, Netherlands.
URL: http://www.internationalsosfoundation.org/

History 25 Oct 2011. Officially launched Mar 2012. Established with a grant from the health and safety services company known as *International SOS*. Former names and other names: *International SOS Foundation – Ambassadors for Duty of Care* – full title; *Stichting International SOS* – legal name. Registration: Netherlands. **Aims** Improve the safety, security, health and welfare of people working *abroad* or on remote assignments through the study, understanding and mitigation of potential *risks*. **Structure** Board. Independent Chapter: *Asia Remote Health Committee (ARHC)*. **Staff** None paid. **Activities** Research/documentation; knowledge management/information dissemination; training/education; advocacy/lobbying/activism. **Events** *Annual Conference* Singapore (Singapore) 2019, *Duty of Care Summit* Berlin (Germany) 2017, *Forum on Duty of Care in Asia / Forum* Singapore (Singapore) 2012. **NGO Relations** Member of: *Global Road Safety Partnership (GRSP, #10581)*. Sustaining member of: *International Commission on Occupational Health (ICOH, #12709)*. [2021/XJ7115/f/**F**]

- International SOS Foundation – Ambassadors for Duty of Care / see International SOS Foundation (#15570)

♦ International Source Suppliers and Producers Association (ISSPA) . 15571

Sec International Isotopes Inc, 4137 Commerce Circle, Idaho Falls ID 83401, USA. T. +12085245300. Fax +12085241411.
URL: http://www.isspa.com/

History Founded 2005. **Aims** Ensure that the beneficial use of *radioactive* sources continues to be regarded by the public, the media, legislators, and regulators as a safe, secure, viable technology for medical, industrial, and research applications. **Events** *General Assembly* Berlin (Germany) 2013.
Members Full in 8 countries:
Argentina, Canada, Germany, Hungary, Russia, Sweden, UK, USA.
IGO Relations Affiliated with: *International Atomic Energy Agency (IAEA, #12294)*. [2015/XJ0788/**C**]

- International South American Union for the Regulation of Private International Law (inactive)
- International Spa Association (internationally oriented national body)
- International Space Conference of Pacific-Basin Societies (meeting series)

♦ International Space Environment Service (ISES) 15572

Dir c/o NOAA Space Weather Prediction Center, 325 Broadway, Boulder CO 80305, USA.
Deputy Dir c/o INPE, Av dos Astronautas 1758, Jd Granja, São José dos Campos SP, 12227-010, Brazil. T. +551232086000.
General: http://www.ises-spaceweather.org/

History 1962, with the title *International URSIgram and World Days Service (IUWDS) – Service international des ursigrammes et jours mondiaux*, combining the former *International World Days Service*, initiated in 1959, and the former *URSI Central Committee of URSIgrams*, initiated in 1928. Current title adopted Jan 1997. Previously a permanent service of *Federation of Astronomical and Geophysical Data Analysis Services (FAGS, inactive)*, under the auspices of *Union radio-scientifique internationale (URSI, #20475)*, in association with *International Astronomical Union (IAU, #12287)* and *International Union of Geodesy and Geophysics (IUGG, #15776)*. **Aims** Improve, coordinate and deliver operational space *weather* services. **Structure** Directing Board. **Activities** Research/documentation; knowledge management/information dissemination. **Events** *Annual European space weather week* Namur (Belgium) 2011, *European space weather week* Brussels (Belgium) 2008, *Solar terrestrial predictions workshop* Boulder, CO (USA) 2000, *Solar terrestrial predictions workshop* Tokyo (Japan) 1996, *Solar terrestrial prediction workshop* Ottawa, ON (Canada) 1992. **Publications** *Spacewarn Bulletin* (12 a year) – for COSPAR, summarizing the status of satellites in each orbit and in interplanetary space; *International Geophysical Calendar* (annual). *ISES Code Book*. Collections of workshop papers.
Members Regional Warning Centres in 15 countries:
Australia, Austria, Belgium, Brazil, Canada, China, Czechia, India, Japan, Korea Rep, Poland, Russia, South Africa, Sweden, USA.
Included in the above, 1 centre listed in this Yearbook:
Solar Influences Data Analysis Centre (SIDC, #19675).
IGO Relations Collaborative Expert Centre at: *European Space Agency (ESA, #08798)*. Collaborates with: *WMO Space Programme (see: #21649)*. **NGO Relations** Network member of: *ISC World Data System (ISC-WDS, #16024)*. [2015/XF4061/**F**]

♦ International Space Exploration Coordination Group (ISECG) 15573

Address not obtained.
URL: http://www.globalspaceexploration.org/

History May 2007, by 14 space agencies. **Aims** Acts as a voluntary, non-binding international coordination mechanism through which individual space agencies may exchange information regarding interests, objectives, and plans in space exploration so as to strengthen both individual exploration programmes as well as collective effort. **Events** *Meeting* Noordwijk (Netherlands) 2009, *Meeting* Yokohama (Japan) 2009, *Meeting* Montréal, QC (Canada) 2008, *Meeting* Berlin (Germany) 2007.

Members Space agencies in 14 countries:
Australia, Canada, China, France, Germany, India, Italy, Japan, Korea Rep, Russia, UK, Ukraine, United Arab Emirates, USA.
Regional organization:
European Space Agency (ESA, #08798). [2017/XJ7448/**F***]

♦ International Space Safety Foundation (internationally oriented national body)
♦ International Space Science Institute (internationally oriented national body)

♦ International Space Station (ISS) 15574

Station spatiale internationale

Public Information Office c/o NASA Headquarters, Ste 5K39, Washington DC 20546-0001, USA. T. +12023581100.
URL: http://www.nasa.gov/mission_pages/station/main/index.html

History as a partnership of USA, Russia, Japan, Canada and *European Space Agency (ESA, #08798).* [2010/XF6514/**F***]

♦ International Space Syntax Symposium (meeting series)
♦ International Space Theatre Consortium / see Giant Screen Cinema Association (#10148)

♦ International Space University (ISU) 15575

Université international de l'espace (UIE)

Contact Parc d'Innovation, 1 rue Jean-Dominique Cassini, 67400 Illkirch-Graffenstanden, France. T. +33388655430. Fax +33388655447.
URL: http://www.isunet.edu/

History 1987, Boston, MA (USA). Permanent central campus near Strasbourg (France) links a network of affiliated campuses. **Aims** Establish an international institution of higher *learning*, dedicated to the exploration and development of *outer space* for peaceful purposes through international, multidisciplinary and intercultural education and research programmes for the benefit of all humanity. **Structure** Governing members: Academic Council; College of Teachers; Board of Trustees of 28 members; Board of Advisers of 22 members; Chancellor, with President and 3 Vice-Presidents; faculty for academic programmes. Executive Officers: President; Vice-President for North American Operations; Dean. Campus system comprises: Central Campus; affiliates and other institutions which host summer sessions and short courses and which receive Master of Space Studies, Master of Space Management and Executive MBA students on professional placement. Former students' association: *ISU European Alumni Association (EAA, no recent information).* **Languages** English. **Staff** 19.00 FTE, paid. **Finance** Sponsors: governmental space agencies and departments; private sector; educational institutes; foundations, associations and organizations; individuals. Includes the following organizations listed in this Yearbook: *American Film Institute (AFI)*; EAA; *European Organisation for the Exploitation of Meteorological Satellites (EUMETSAT, #08096)*; *European Space Agency (ESA, #08798)*; *Fondation pour la recherche stratégique (FRS)*; *Planetary Society (PS)*; *SETI League*; *UNESCO (#20322).* Budget (annual): euro 4.5 million. **Activities** Projects/programmes; research/documentation; training/education. **Events** *Annual Symposium* Strasbourg (France) 2013, *Annual Symposium* Strasbourg (France) 2012, *Annual Symposium* Strasbourg (France) 2011, *Annual Symposium* Strasbourg (France) 2010, *Annual Symposium* Strasbourg (France) 2009. **Publications** *Keys to Space* (1999); *The Farthest Shore.*

Members Governing Members Institutional; Industrial; Corporate; Individual. Membership countries not specified. Affiliates universities, university departments and research or educational institutions (currently 23) in 13 countries:
Australia, Belgium, Canada, China, France, Italy, Netherlands, Russia, Spain, Sweden, Türkiye, UK, USA.
Liaisons (24) in 19 countries:
Austria, Belgium, Canada, Chile, China, Finland, Germany, India, Italy, Japan, Kenya, Morocco, Netherlands, Norway, Russia, Sweden, Switzerland, UK, USA.
Points of contact (4) in 4 countries:
Argentina, Israel, Slovenia, USA.

IGO Relations Observer status with: *Committee on the Peaceful Uses of Outer Space (COPUOS, #04277).* Cooperative agreements with: national space agencies of France, Canada, USA and Japan; ESA. **NGO Relations** Member of: *Asia-Pacific Regional Space Agency Forum (APRSAF, #02010).* Students at the University set up: *Earth Council.* [2021/XF3229/**F**]

♦ International Spa and Fitness Association / see International Spa Association

♦ International Special Dietary Food Industries (ISDI) 15576

Fédération internationale des industries des aliments diététiques

SG Av de Tervuren 188A – bte 4, 1150 Brussels, Belgium. T. +3227611680. E-mail: secretariat@isdi.org.
Registered address 3200 Windy Hill Road, Marietta GA 30339, USA.
URL: http://www.isdi.org/

History 1965, as the *International Secretariat for the Dietetic Industry.* In 1984 took the name *International Society of Dietetic including all Infant and Young Children Food Industry – Fédération internationale des industries des produits diététiques incluant tous les aliments de l'enfance*, when it added to its members International Association of Infant Food Manufacturers, and a number of national associations in Europe, America and the Pacific Region. Registered under US law. **Aims** Develop a common policy on minimum composition, utilization, labelling and marketing of foods for special dietary uses. **Structure** General Assembly; Council of Presidents. **Languages** English. **Staff** 3.00 FTE, paid. **Finance** Members' dues. **Activities** Knowledge management/information dissemination; standards/guidelines; guidance/assistance/consulting; politics/policy/regulatory.

Members Full: associations in 23 countries:
Australia, Austria, Belgium, Brazil, China, France, Germany, Indonesia, Ireland, Italy, Malaysia, Mexico, Morocco, Netherlands, New Zealand, Philippines, Portugal, South Africa, Spain, Sweden, Switzerland, UK, USA.

Consultative Status Consultative status granted from: *ECOSOC (#05331)* (Ros C). **IGO Relations** Participates as observer in the activities of: *Codex Alimentarius Commission (CAC, #04081).* [2018.10.01/XD6420/t/**D**]

♦ International Special Events Society / see International Live Events Association
♦ International Specialized Terminology Organization (no recent information)
♦ International Special Tooling Association / see International Special Tooling and Machining Association (#15577)

♦ International Special Tooling and Machining Association (ISTMA) 15577

Sec Avenida Dom Dinis, 17, 2430-263 Marinha Grande, Portugal. T. +351244575150. E-mail: secretariat@istma.org.
Pres Romagnani Stampi, Via Trieste 2 Pioltello, 20096 Milan MI, Italy. T. +3929267237. Fax +39292161141.
URL: http://www.istma.org/

History 28 Sep 1973, Frankfurt-Main (Germany FR), as *International Special Tooling Association (ISTA).* **Aims** Help national *industry* associations and their member companies achieve business success in the global economy; enhance the reputation of the industry and its employees; maintain contacts and provide a channel of communication between members; defend the interests of members with regard to international organizations, authorities and other associations; promote efficiency and profitability of firms within their member associations; review training and educational standards for skilled workers employed by the industry, particularly in times of rapid technological changes; establish standard recommendations for the standard tooling components on a worldwide basis. **Structure** Board of Directors, comprising President, President of European Branch, President of American Branch and 2 additional members. Supervisory Board of 3 members. **Languages** English. **Staff** 1.00 FTE, paid. **Activities** Provides means for exchange of experience on economic and technical questions; establishes mutual contacts through the organization of meetings, reunions and company visits; organizes conferences, fora, workshops and study sessions. **Events** *Triennial Conference* Shanghai (China) 2022, *European Meeting* Marinha Grande (Portugal) 2020, *Triennial Conference* Shanghai (China) 2020, *European Meeting* Brussels (Belgium) 2019, *European Meeting* Celje (Slovenia) 2017. **Publications** *ISTMA Statistical Year Book* (2009, 2010, 2011); *Regional Business Conditions Report.* Market analyses and studies. **Information Services** *ISTMA Terminology* – web service.

Members National associations representing the interests of manufacturers of the following products dyes for pressing, stamping, punching and forming; injection and compression moulds; dye casting dyes; patterns and pattern equipment; jigs and fixtures; standard tooling components; precision machining; related products produced by tool-makers. Members in 19 countries:
Canada, Czechia, Estonia, Finland, France, Germany, Hungary, Italy, Latvia, Poland, Portugal, Slovenia, South Africa, Spain, Sweden, Switzerland, Türkiye, UK, USA.

IGO Relations Recognized by: *European Commission (EC, #06633)*; national governments. [2012/XD4321/**D**]

♦ International Species Information System / see Species360 (#19915)
♦ International Species Inventory System / see Species360 (#19915)

♦ International Speech Communication Association (ISCA) 15578

Association Européenne pour la Communication Parlée

Secretariat 4 rue des Fauvettes, Lous Tourils, 66390 Baixas, France. Fax +33468385827. E-mail: secretariat@isca-speech.org.
URL: http://www.isca-speech.org/

History Statutes deposited 1988 and last modified 2010. Former names and other names: *European Speech Communication Association (ESCA)* – former (1988 to 1999). Registration: Start date: 23 Feb 1988, France. **Aims** Promote speech communication science and technology, both in the industrial and academic areas. **Structure** General Assembly (annual); Board; Advisory Council; Secretariat. Special Interest Groups. **Languages** English, French. **Staff** 1.00 FTE, paid; 14.00 FTE, voluntary. **Finance** Self-financing membership income. **Activities** Since 2000, conferences organized under common label 'INTERSPEECH Events'. Supports several workshops. **Events** *INTERSPEECH Conference* Incheon (Korea Rep) 2022, *INTERSPEECH Conference* Brno (Czechia) 2021, *INTERSPEECH Conference* Shanghai (China) 2020, *International Conference on Speech Prosody* Tokyo (Japan) 2020, *Odyssey – Speaker and Language Recognition Workshop* Tokyo (Japan) 2020. **Publications** *ISCApad* (12 a year) – internal bulletin; *Speech Communication Journal.*

Members Individuals in 49 countries and territories:
Argentina, Australia, Austria, Belarus, Belgium, Brazil, Bulgaria, Canada, China, Croatia, Czechia, Denmark, Egypt, Estonia, Finland, France, Germany, Greece, Hong Kong, Hungary, India, Iran Islamic Rep, Ireland, Israel, Italy, Japan, Korea Rep, Lithuania, Luxembourg, Malta, Netherlands, Norway, Poland, Portugal, Romania, Russia, Singapore, Slovakia, Slovenia, South Africa, Spain, Sweden, Switzerland, Taiwan, Türkiye, UK, Ukraine, USA, Venezuela.

NGO Relations Supports: *Expert Advisory Group on Language Engineering Standards (EAGLES, inactive).* [2020/XD4269/**D**]

♦ International Spenser Society (ISS) 15579

Sec address not obtained.
URL: https://www.english.cam.ac.uk/spenseronline/iss/

History 1980. **Aims** Promote the reading and study of the works of Edmund Spenser. **Structure** Executive Committee. **Activities** Awards/prizes/competitions; events/meetings; research/documentation. **Publications** *The Spenser Review* (3 a year) – online. [2020/AA0284/**E**]

♦ International Spill Accreditation Association (internationally oriented national body)

♦ International Spill Control Organization (ISCO) 15580

Sec 169 Free Trade Wharf, 340 The Highway, London, E1W 3EU, UK. T. +447834556989. E-mail: info@spillcontrol.org.
URL: https://spillcontrol.org/

History Oct 1984. Registration: Companies House, No/ID: 01853936, Start date: 9 Oct 1984, England and Wales. **Aims** Raise worldwide preparedness and cooperation in response to oil and chemical spills; promote technical development and professional competency; provide a focus for making knowledge and experience of spill control professionals available to IMO, UNEP and other organizations. **Structure** Annual General Meeting; Executive Committee; Non-Executive Council. **Languages** English. **Finance** Sources: subscriptions. Other source: loan capital. **Activities** Advocacy/lobbying/activism; events/meetings; guidance/assistance/consulting; knowledge management/information dissemination; networking/liaising; standards/guidelines. **Events** *Annual General Meeting* London (UK) 2021, *Annual General Meeting* London (UK) 2020, *SPILLCON : Asia Pacific oil spill conference* Perth, WA (Australia) 2016, *Annual General Meeting* Amsterdam (Netherlands) 2015, *International Forum on Sinking Oils* Detroit, MI (USA) 2014. **Publications** *ISCO Newsletter* (weekly).

Members Individual; Corporate; Associate. Members in 46 countries and territories:
Australia, Azerbaijan, Belgium, Belize, Brazil, Canada, China, Colombia, Denmark, Egypt, Estonia, Faeroe Is, Finland, France, Ghana, Greece, Indonesia, Iran Islamic Rep, Ireland, Israel, Italy, Kazakhstan, Kenya, Kuwait, Luxembourg, Malaysia, Malta, Mexico, Netherlands, Nigeria, Norway, Poland, Portugal, Saudi Arabia, Singapore, South Africa, Sweden, Taiwan, Tunisia, Türkiye, UK, Ukraine, United Arab Emirates, Uruguay, USA, Virgin Is UK.
Sea Alarm Foundation (#19164).

Consultative Status Consultative status granted from: *International Maritime Organization (IMO, #14102).* **IGO Relations** Observer status with (1): *International Oil Pollution Compensation Funds (IOPC Funds, #14402).* [2022/XD6663/y/**D**]

♦ International Spinal Cord Society (ISCoS) 15581

Exec Administrator c/o NSIC, Stoke Mandeville Hosp, Aylesbury, HP21 8AL, UK. T. +441296315866. E-mail: admin@iscos.org.uk.
Pres address not obtained.
URL: http://www.iscos.org.uk/

History Jul 1961, Aylesbury (UK). Founded on the occasion of the Scientific Meeting on Paraplegia held in conjunction with *International Stoke Mandeville Wheelchair Sports Federation (ISMWSF, inactive).* Former names and other names: *International Medical Society of Paraplegia (IMSoP)* – former (Jul 1961 to Sep 2001). Registration: Private Limited Company by guarantee, No/ID: 03452747, Start date: 20 Oct 1997, England. **Aims** Study problems concerning traumatic and non-traumatic afflictions of the spinal cord, particularly advancement in medical and surgical treatment and social integration of the paralysed. **Structure** Officers (4). **Languages** English. **Staff** 1.00 FTE, paid. **Finance** Sources: subscriptions. **Activities** Events/meetings. **Events** *Annual Scientific Meeting* Edinburgh (UK) 2023, *Annual Scientific Meeting* Vancouver, BC (Canada) 2022, *Annual Scientific Meeting* Aylesbury (UK) 2021, *Annual Scientific Meeting* Aylesbury (UK) 2020, *Annual Scientific Meeting* Nice (France) 2019. **Publications** *Spinal Cord* (12 a year); *Spinal Cord Series and Cases* – continuous online journal.

Members Individuals in 86 countries and territories:
Argentina, Armenia, Australia, Austria, Bangladesh, Belgium, Botswana, Brazil, Cambodia, Canada, Chile, China, Costa Rica, Croatia, Cuba, Cyprus, Czechia, Denmark, Egypt, Estonia, Finland, France, Gabon, Germany, Greece, Honduras, Hong Kong, Hungary, Iceland, India, Indonesia, Iran Islamic Rep, Iraq, Ireland, Israel, Italy, Japan, Jordan, Kenya, Korea DPR, Korea Rep, Laos, Latvia, Lithuania, Malaysia, Mexico, Mongolia, Montenegro, Morocco, Myanmar, Nepal, Netherlands, New Zealand, Nigeria, Norway, Pakistan, Palestine, Philippines, Poland, Portugal, Puerto Rico, Romania, Russia, Saudi Arabia, Senegal, Serbia, Singapore, Slovakia, Slovenia, South Africa, Spain, Sri Lanka, Sweden, Switzerland, Taiwan, Tanzania UR, Thailand, Türkiye, Uganda, UK, United Arab Emirates, USA, Venezuela, Vietnam, Yemen, Zimbabwe.
Affiliated societies (19), include the following 6 organizations listed in this Yearbook:
Asian Spinal Cord Network (ASCoN, #01757); *Association francophone internationale des groupes d'animation de la paraplégie (AFIGAP, #02614)*; *Deutschsprachige Medizinische Gesellschaft für Paraplegie (DMGP)*; *Nordic Spinal Cord Society (NoSCoS, #17436)*; *Sociedad Latinoamericana de Paraplejia (SLAP, #19420)*; *Southern African Spinal Cord Association (SASCA).*

Consultative Status Consultative status granted from: *ECOSOC (#05331)* (Ros C); *WHO (#20950)* (Official). **IGO Relations** Accredited by (1): *United Nations Office at Vienna (UNOV, #20604).* **NGO Relations** Member of (1): *Global Rehabilitation Alliance (#10565)* (as Founding member). Affiliated with a large number of international and national paraplegia organizations. [2022.12.06/XD2254/y/**C**]

♦ International Spinal Pain Society (ISPS) 15582

SG 0705 – 240 Gangnam-daerom, Gangnam-gu, Seoul 06267, Korea Rep. T. +82553602753. Fax +82553602149. E-mail: pain@pusan.ac.kr.
URL: http://www.spinemeeting.org/

History Resulting from 1st International Congress on Spain Pain, 2016. **Aims** Develop and encourage the highest quality of total spinal care and research. **Structure** Committee. **Activities** Events/meetings. **Events** *Congress* Gwangju (Korea Rep) 2016. **Publications** *ISPS Newsletter.* [2017/XM5764/E]

♦ International Spinal Research Trust (internationally oriented national body)

♦ International Spin Chemistry Committee 15583

Chair Dept of Chemistry – Univ of Oxford, Physical and Theoretical Chemistry Lab, South Parks Road, Oxford, OX1 3QA, UK. T. +441865275415. Fax +441865275410.
URL: http://spinportal.chem.ox.ac.uk/

History Founded 1991. **Activities** Events/meetings. **Events** *International Symposium on Spin and Magnetic Field Effects in Chemistry and Related Phenomena* St Petersburg (Russia) 2019, *International Symposium on Spin and Magnetic Field Effects in Chemistry and Related Phenomena* Bad Hofgastein (Austria) 2013. [2020/XM8734/c/E]

♦ International Spine Research Foundation (INSPIRE) 15584

Contact 101 South Roosevelt Avenue, Chandler AZ 85226, USA. T. +14807858448. Fax +14807853916. E-mail: info@helpinspire.org – info@neuromechanical.com.
URL: http://helpinspire.org/

History Founded by Dr Chris Colloca. Registration: USA, Arizona. **Aims** Raise funds to support scientific research for the purpose of advancing the understanding of spinal related disorders and improving patient care. **Finance** Members' dues. **Activities** Research and development; events/meetings; financial and/or material support. **Events** *Symposium* Cape Town (South Africa) 2015, *International Conference on Spinal Manipulation* Sydney, NSW (Australia) 2014. [2017/XJ9171/f/F]

♦ International Spin Physics Symposium (meeting series)

♦ International Spiritist Council (ISC) 15585

Conselho Espirita Internacional (CEI)

SG Av L2 Norte-Q. 603, Conjunto F (SGAN), Brasilia DF, 70830-030, Brazil. E-mail: cei.secretariado@gmail.com.
URL: http://cei-spiritistcouncil.com/

History 28 Nov 1992, Madrid (Spain). **Activities** Advocacy/lobbying/activism; events/meetings; knowledge management/information dissemination; training/education. **Events** *World Spiritist Congress* Nice (France) 2022, *World Spiritist Congress* Mexico City (Mexico) 2019, *World Spiritist Congress* Porto (Portugal) 2016, *World Spiritist Congress* Havana (Cuba) 2013, *World Spiritist Congress* Valencia (Spain) 2010. **Publications** *ISC Newsletter* (4 a year); *The Spiritist Magazine* (4 a year).

Members Organizations in 25 countries:
Argentina, Belgium, Bolivia, Brazil, Canada, Colombia, Cuba, El Salvador, France, Germany, Guatemala, Ireland, Italy, Mexico, Netherlands, Paraguay, Peru, Portugal, Spain, Sweden, Switzerland, UK, Uruguay, USA, Venezuela.
Member countries in 10 countries:
Angola, Australia, Austria, Chile, Honduras, Luxembourg, Mozambique, New Zealand, Norway, Panama. [2022/XJ8695/C]

♦ International Spiritualist Federation (ISF) 15586

Fédération spirite internationale (FSI) – Federación Espiritista Internacional

Membership Sec 128 Malvern Road, Billingham, Stockton-on-Tees, TS23 2JP, UK.
Pres 78 Greys Road, Eastbourne, BN20 8AZ, UK.
URL: http://www.theisf.com/

History 1923, Liège (Belgium). Reorganized Jul 1947, Bournemouth (UK). **Aims** Cooperate in study and spread of understanding of psychic phenomena from scientific and philosophical points of view, recognizing the existence of a creative life force, the existence of a spiritual link between all forms of life and the survival of physical death by the individual human spirit; spread awareness of spiritualist philosophy and phenomena while recognizing differences of interpretation in different countries due to cultural factors. **Structure** Committee. **Languages** English. **Staff** 11.00 FTE, voluntary. **Finance** Members' dues. Donations. **Activities** Events/meetings; training/education. **Events** *Biennial Congress* Eastbourne (UK) 2014, *Biennial Congress* Scotland (UK) 2010, *Biennial Congress* St Andrews (UK) 2010, *Biennial Congress* Eastbourne (UK) 2008, *Biennial Congress* Eastbourne (UK) 2006. **Publications** *Yours Fraternally* (4 a year). Leaflets.

Members Affiliated organizations and individuals in 27 countries:
Australia, Austria, Belgium, Canada, Cyprus, Denmark, Egypt, Finland, France, Germany, Greece, Iceland, India, Israel, Japan, Korea Rep, Netherlands, New Zealand, Norway, Philippines, Portugal, South Africa, Spain, Sweden, Switzerland, USA, Zambia. [2015.01.19/XD2236/D]

♦ International Spiroll Producers Association / see International Prestressed Hollowcore Association (#14638)
♦ International Splash Class Association (see: #21760)
♦ International Sponge Symposium (meeting series)
♦ International Sponsorship of War Orphans (inactive)
♦ International Sport for All Federation (#09661)

♦ International Sport and Culture Association (ISCA) 15587

SG Vesterbrogade 6D, 1620 Copenhagen, Denmark. E-mail: info@isca-web.org.
URL: https://www.isca.org/

History 10 Feb 1995, Copenhagen (Denmark). Statutes revised, 1999, Montréal QC (Canada); May 2002, Prague (Czech Rep); Oct 2019, Budapest (Hungary). **Aims** Promote international understanding through sports and cultural activities; emphasize the view of sport as a bearer of local, regional or national cultural identity; encourage participation in sporting and cultural activities among members. **Structure** General Assembly (annual, at World Congress); Executive Committee. **Languages** English. **Staff** 4.50 FTE, paid. **Finance** Sources: members' dues. Other sources: national and international donors, including governments, foundations and organizations. **Activities** Events/meetings; training/education. **Events** *General Assembly* Brussels (Belgium) 2021, *MOVE Congress* Brussels (Belgium) 2021, *General Assembly* Budapest (Hungary) 2019, *MOVE Congress* Budapest (Hungary) 2019, *MOVE Congress* Birmingham (UK) 2017. **Publications** *CultureSports* – magazine; *ISCA Newsletter.*

Members Organizations (128) in 61 countries and territories:
Albania, Argentina, Belgium, Bhutan, Bosnia-Herzegovina, Botswana, Brazil, Bulgaria, Burundi, Canada, Chile, Colombia, Costa Rica, Côte d'Ivoire, Czechia, Denmark, Estonia, Eswatini, Faeroe Is, Finland, France, Germany, Ghana, Iceland, Indonesia, Ireland, Italy, Japan, Kenya, Korea Rep, Kuwait, Latvia, Lithuania, Malaysia, Mauritius, Montenegro, Mozambique, Myanmar, Netherlands, Nigeria, Pakistan, Paraguay, Philippines, Poland, Portugal, Romania, Russia, Senegal, Serbia, Sierra Leone, Slovakia, Spain, Sri Lanka, Taiwan, Thailand, Uganda, UK, USA, Venezuela, Vietnam, Zimbabwe.
Included in the above, 3 organizations listed in this Yearbook:
International Federation of Celtic Wrestling (IFCW, #13383); Organizzazione Europea Vigili del Fuoco Volontari di Protezione Civile (OEVFVPC); World Pahuyuth Federation (WPF, #21706).

IGO Relations Represented on Board of: *Enlarged Partial Agreement on Sport (EPAS, #05487).* **NGO Relations** Member of (1): *Lifelong Learning Platform – European Civil Society for Education (LLLP, #16466).* Supports (1): *European Alliance for the Statute of the European Association (EASEA, #05886).* [2022/XC0110/y/C]

♦ International Sport for Development and Peace Association (unconfirmed)

♦ International Sporting Cinema and Television Federation (FICTS) 15588

Fédération internationale du cinéma et de la télévision sportifs (FICTS)

Pres Via de Amicis 17, 20123 Milan MI, Italy. T. +39289409076. Fax +3928375973. E-mail: info@ficts.com.
Gen Sec address not obtained.
URL: http://www.sportmoviestv.com/

History Constitution adopted 31 May 1982, Turin (Italy). **Aims** Encourage young people to use their creativity to become creators and consumers of sports contents, including Olympic images, through modern technologies and social media. **Structure** General Assembly (every 4 years, during Festival); Board of Trustees. **Languages** English, French. **Staff** 10.00 FTE, paid. **Finance** Sources: members' dues. **Activities** Events/meetings; knowledge management/information dissemination; networking/liaising. **Publications** *FICTS Newsletter.* Press releases. **Members** Individual; Collective (Committees, Federations, Networks, etc). Full in 216 countries and territories. Membership countries not specified. **NGO Relations** Recognized by: *International Olympic Committee (IOC, #14408).* [2022/XD5357/D]

♦ International Sporting Federation of Catholic Schools 15589

Fédération internationale sportive de l'enseignement catholique (FISEC)

Secretariat 277 rue Saint-Jacques, 75005 Paris, France. E-mail: fisec.secretarybureau@gmail.com.
Pres address not obtained.
URL: http://www.fisec.org/

History Founded 1946, Paris (France). Operational from 1948, Monaco, at first games for young men. Registered under French law. Also referred to in English as *International Federation of Sport in Catholic Education.* **Aims** Promote and integrate physical and sports education into general education; contribute to the development of sport in schools; look into problems of sport in conjunction with other international organizations; promote friendship and understanding among young people in line with the educative project of Catholic education, and bring about meetings and exchanges among them. **Structure** General Assembly (annual); Executive Bureau; International Technical Commission (CTI); *International Commission for Educational and Pastoral Reflection (CIRPP, see: #15589).* A branch of: *Catholic International Education Office (#03604),* agreement on close cooperation having been signed 4 Dec 1971. **Languages** English, French, Spanish. **Staff** Voluntary. **Finance** Members' dues. Other sources: individual expenses of participants in events; donations. Annual budget: euro 50,000. **Activities** Events/meetings; sporting activities. **Events** *General Assembly* Paris (France) 2015, *General Assembly* Torremolinos (Spain) 2012, *General Assembly* Naples (Italy) 2009, *General Assembly* Delft (Netherlands) 2008, *General Assembly* Paris (France) 2007. **Publications** *FISEC News* (4 a year); *FICEP-FISEC Congress News* – special magazine (up to Apr 1998).

Members Full in 12 countries:
Austria, Belgium, Brazil, France, Germany, Hungary, Italy, Malta, Netherlands, Portugal, Spain, UK.

NGO Relations Recognized by: *International Olympic Committee (IOC, #14408).* [2018.01.24/XD4172/D]

♦ International Sporting Union of the PTT (inactive)
♦ International Sport Jujitsu Association (internationally oriented national body)

♦ International Sport Karate Association (ISKA) 15590

World Headquarters 333 SW 140th Terrace, Jonesville FL 32669, USA. T. +13523310260. Fax +13523312119.
Pres address not obtained. E-mail: schafriska@aol.com.
URL: http://www.iska.com/

History 16 Jul 1986. In Europe also referred to as *International Sport Kickboxing Association.* **Aims** Serve as a regulatory body for combat sports and competitive martial arts. **Activities** Championships. [2014/XD4451/D]

♦ International Sport Kickboxing Association / see International Sport Karate Association (#15590)

♦ International Sport Lawyers Association (ISLA) 15591

Internationale Vereinigung der Sportanwälte

Admin Coordinator Kirchenweg 8, 8034 Zurich ZH, Switzerland. T. +491626139468. E-mail: info@islasportlawyer.com.
Pres Mit Recht im Sport, Hoeferweg 14, 61184 Karben, Germany. E-mail: info@sportrechtsanwaeltin.de.
URL: https://www.islasportlawyer.com/

History Registration: Swiss Civil Code, Switzerland. **Aims** Connect sport lawyers around the world; help stakeholders in the sport, such as athletes and sports clubs worldwide, to define and defend their interests. **Structure** Board. **Languages** English, French, German, Spanish. **Staff** None. **Finance** Sources: members' dues; sponsorship. Annual budget: 100,000 EUR. **Events** *International Sports Law Conference* Hamburg (Germany) 2015, *Sports Rights Convention / Congress* Berlin (Germany) 2007, *Congress* Innsbruck (Austria) 2007, *Congress* Berlin (Germany) 2006, *Congress* Zurich (Switzerland) 2005.

Members Individuals in 27 countries:
Algeria, Austria, Belarus, China, Costa Rica, Czechia, Ecuador, Germany, Greece, India, Iran Islamic Rep, Italy, Japan, Malta, Monaco, Morocco, Netherlands, Nigeria, Panama, Portugal, Russia, Switzerland, Turkey, Uganda, UK, United Arab Emirates, USA.

NGO Relations Member of (2): *International Council of Sport Science and Physical Education (ICSSPE, #13077); The Association for International Sport for All (TAFISA, #02763).* [2022.10.27/XJ4274/D]

♦ International Sport for Life Society (internationally oriented national body)
♦ International Sport Management Alliance (inactive)

♦ International Sport Network Organization (ISNO) 15592

Gen Sec address not obtained. T. +41766168894. E-mail: info@internationalsportnetworkorganization.org.
URL: http://www.internationalsportnetworkorganization.org/

History 2018, Switzerland. **Aims** Assist members around the world; organize sport games and activities; support anti-doping programs; serve as European federation. **Structure** Board. **Languages** English, Italian. **Activities** Awards/prizes/competitions; certification/accreditation; events/meetings; guidance/assistance/consulting; knowledge management/information dissemination; networking/liaising; projects/programmes; sporting activities; training/education. Active Worldwide.

Members International; Continental; National; Club. National in 19 countries and territories:
Afghanistan, Brazil, China, Colombia, Gambia, Hong Kong, India, Iran Islamic Rep, Italy, Macau, Malaysia, Pakistan, Poland, Portugal, Russia, Sierra Leone, Spain, Switzerland, Taiwan.
International federations include 34 listed in this Yearbook:
- *Bukido World Federation (BWF, #03356);*
- *Federation International Football Skating (FIFS, #09671);*
- *International Association of Combative Sports (IACS, #11789);*
- *International Council of Sqay (ICS);*
- *International Diabolo Association (IDA, #13166);*
- *International Kempo Federation (IKF, #13981);*
- *International Pacific Sports Federation (IPSF);*
- *International Parkour Federation (IPF, #14516);*
- *International Pole Dance Fitness Association (IPDFA, #14609);*
- *International Taekwon-do Forum (ITF);*
- *Pole Sports & Arts World Federation (POSA, #18414);*
- *World Aerial Sports & Arts Federation (WAS&AF, #21071);*
- *World Association of Majorette-sport and Twirling (WAMT);*
- *World Boxing League (WBL);*
- *World Dodgeball Association (WDA, #21365);*
- *World Ethnosport Society (#21392);*
- *World Freerunning Parkour Federation (WFPF);*
- *World Futsal Association (#21532);*
- *World Hatha Yog Federation (#21554);*
- *World Heavy Events Association (WHEA);*
- *World Inclusive Dance Association (WIDA);*
- *World Kabaddi Federation (WKF, #21606);*
- *World Kettlebell Sport Federation (WKSF);*
- *World Kickboxing League (WKL);*
- *World Ninja Federation (WNF);*
- *World O-Sport Federation (WOF, #21700);*
- *World Rope Skipping Federation (WRSF);*
- *World Silambam Association (WSA);*
- *World Slingshot Sports Federation (WSSF, #21794);*
- *World Sport Council (WCS);*
- *World Strongmen Federation (WSF, #21832);*
- *World Wellness Weekend (WWW);*

– *World Yoga Association.*
Continental members include 11 organizations listed in this Yearbook:
Asia and Pacific Jump Rope Federation (APJRF, #01938); Asia Diabolo Association (ADA); Asia Freerunning Parkour Union (AFPU); Asian Bukido Federation (ABF); Asian O-Sport Federation (AOSF); Asian Weightlifting Federation (AWF, #01781); European Boxing League (EBL); Judo Union of Asia (JUA, #16162); Pan American Electronic Sports Confederation (PAMESCO, #18096); Silambam Asia (#19276); Sqay Organization of Asia (SOA, #19932).
NGO Relations Memorandum of Understanding with (1): Associazioni Sportive Sociali Italiane. Partner of (5): *General Association of Asia Pacific Sports Federations (GAAPSF, #10106); International Fitness and Bodybuilding Federation (IFBB, #13610);* International Humanitarian Games Association; *International Sport Organization (ISO);* World Sports University. [2021.09.03/AA1068/y/**C**]

- ♦ International Sport Organization (unconfirmed)
- ♦ International Sports Association of the Blind / see International Blind Sports Federation (#12363)
- ♦ International Sports Chanbara Association (unconfirmed)
- ♦ International Sports Council (internationally oriented national body)

♦ International Sports Engineering Association (ISEA) 15593

Contact Centre for Sports Engineering, Broomgrove Teaching Block, Sheffield Hallam Univ, Sheffield, S10 2LX, UK. T. +441142252258. Fax +441142254356. E-mail: isea@shu.ac.uk.
URL: http://www.sportsengineering.org/
History 1996, Sheffield (UK). Registration: Companies House, No/ID: 281119, England and Wales. **Aims** Serve the global community of sports engineers by promoting technical aspects of sports engineering and by providing a collaborative environment for collection and dissemination of knowledge in the field of sports engineering and technology. **Structure** Executive Committee. **Languages** English. **Events** *Conference* West Lafayette, IN (USA) 2022, *Conference* Tokyo (Japan) 2020, *Conference* Brisbane, QLD (Australia) 2018, *Conference* Delft (Netherlands) 2016, *Conference* Sheffield (UK) 2014. **Publications** *Sports Engineering* – journal. Information Services: Database of researchers' expertise in sports engineering; database of over 7,000 sports-related references and papers.
Members Individuals in 19 countries and territories:
Australia, Austria, Belgium, Canada, France, Germany, Ireland, Italy, Japan, Korea Rep, New Zealand, Slovenia, South Africa, Spain, Sweden, Switzerland, Taiwan, UK, USA. [2020/XD7168/v/**D**]

- ♦ International Sports Federation for the Intellectually Disabled / see Virtus: World Intellectual Impairment Sport (#20793)
- ♦ International Sports Federation for Persons with an Intellectual Disability / see Virtus: World Intellectual Impairment Sport (#20793)
- ♦ International Sports Federation for Persons with Mental Handicap / see Virtus: World Intellectual Impairment Sport (#20793)
- ♦ International Sports Goods Organization / see World Federation of the Sporting Goods Industry (#21487)
- ♦ International Sports Organization for the Disabled (inactive)
- ♦ International Sports Press Association (#02729)

♦ International Sports Sciences Association (ISSA) 15594

Head Office 11201 N. Tatum Blvd, Suite 300, PMB 28058, Phoenix AZ 85028-6039, USA. T. +18554780340. Fax +18057458119. E-mail: media@issaonline.com – support@issaonline.com.
URL: https://www.issaonline.com/
History 1988. . **Structure** Officers: President; Executive Director. Administrators: Director of Finance; Vice President of Operations; Director of Continuing Education; Director of Program Development; Business Director; Director of Marketing; Director of Student Services; Art Director. Program Directors (10): Youth Sports; Fitness Therapy; Nutritional Sciences; Sport Sciences; Aquatic Sciences; Senior Fitness; Adapted Fitness; Police Fitness; Bodybuilding Sciences; Fitness Sciences. Regional offices (6): Australia; Hong Kong; Iceland; Italy; Egypt; Neth Antilles. **Activities** Offers Certification and Continuing Education Programs: Certified Fitness Trainer; Specialist in Performance Nutrition; Fitness Therapy; Specialist in Senior Fitness; Specialist in Weight Management; Specialist in Martial Arts Conditioning; Youth Fitness Trainer; Water Fitness Trainer; Specialist in Fitness for the Physically Limited; Aerobic Fitness Trainer; Golf Fitness Trainer. [2022/XD7167/e/**D**]

- ♦ International Sports Sciences-Human Movement-Fitness Training and Nutrition Association (internationally oriented national body)
- ♦ International Sport Strategy Foundation (internationally oriented national body)

♦ International Sports Travel Agencies Association (ISTAA) 15595

SG c/o Libra Law SA, Maison du Sport Intl, Avenue de Rhodania 54, 1007 Lausanne VD, Switzerland. E-mail: info@istaa.org.
URL: http://www.istaa.org/
History Jun 2009, as a partnership of Sports Travel agencies. **Aims** Develop and secure sports travel, promoting a positive image of sports events; support and promote members' business and cooperation; share best practices; promote sports events and its destinations; support and promote group synergies; build relations with the relevant organizations and bodies in the sports, hospitality and travel fields. **Structure** Annual General Meeting; Board of Directors. **Languages** English. **Staff** 1.00 FTE, paid; 9.00 FTE, voluntary. **Finance** Sources: members' dues. **Activities** Awards/prizes/competitions; events/meetings. **Events** *Annual General Meeting* Tokyo (Japan) 2019, *Annual General Meeting* Herzliyya (Israel) 2018, *Annual General Meeting* St Petersburg (Russia) 2017, *Annual General Meeting* Berlin (Germany) 2016. **Members** Active; Associate; Partners. Members in over 50 countries. Membership countries not specified. [2017.12.06/XM5623/**C**]

♦ International Sprout Growers Association (ISGA) 15596

Pres 685 Bald Hill Rd, Box No 8, Warwick RI 02886, USA. T. +15086574742. E-mail: office@isga-sprouts.org – isgasprouts2022@gmail.com.
URL: http://www.isga-sprouts.org/
History 1989. **Aims** Promote the sprout industry; encourage exchange of information among sprout growers and *suppliers*. **Structure** Officers: President; 2 Vice-Presidents; Treasurer; Secretary. Directors (13). **Languages** English. **Staff** 1.00 FTE, paid. **Finance** Contributions. **Activities** Meeting activities. **Events** *Convention* Sydney, NSW (Australia) 2019, *Annual Convention* Rotterdam (Netherlands) 2015, *Annual Convention* Orlando, FL (USA) 2014, *Annual Convention* Cancún (Mexico) 2008, *Annual Convention* San Francisco, CA (USA) 2005. **Publications** *ISGA Newsletter* (2 a year). *Sanitation Guidelines for the Growing and Packing for Sale of Fresh Sprouted Beans and Seeds.*
Members Individuals in 17 countries:
Argentina, Australia, Canada, Chile, Denmark, Greece, Ireland, Italy, Japan, Korea Rep, Mexico, Netherlands, New Zealand, Singapore, Thailand, UK, USA. [2022/XE3438/v/**E**]

- ♦ International Squash Players Association / see Professional Squash Association (#18517)
- ♦ International Squash Rackets Federation / see World Squash Federation (#21826)
- ♦ International Stability Operations Association (internationally oriented national body)

♦ International Staff Association of UNESCO (ISAU) 15597

Association internationale du personnel de l'UNESCO (AIPU)
Secretariat 1 rue Miollis, Bât Bonvin 1-28, 75015 Paris CEDEX 15, France. T. +33145684961 – +33145684962. Fax +33145685783. E-mail: aipu@unesco.org.
URL: https://www.aipu-isau-unesco.org/
History 1981. Founded to represent staff members of *UNESCO (#20322).* **Aims** Defend interests of UNESCO *personnel*, allowing their cultural diversity to mutually enrich and enhance creativity. **Structure** Collegiate. Executive Committee. Bureaux (3): Cultural Affairs; Social Welfare; Legal Affairs. **Languages** English, French. **Staff** 2.50 FTE, paid. **Finance** Sources: members' dues; subsidies. Supported by: *UNESCO (#20322).* **Activities** Regular meetings concerning personnel questions; cultural events. **Events** *General Assembly* Paris (France) 2001, *Colloque sur la francophonie* Paris (France) 1989, *Conférence sur l'eudiatologie, la sophrologie et l'énergétique* Paris (France) 1988, *Conférence sur l'eudiatologie, la sophrologie énergétique* Paris (France) 1988, *Conférence sur les artistes pour l'Afrique australe* Paris (France) 1988. **Members** Membership varies from year to year. **NGO Relations** Member of (1): *United Nations International Civil Servants Federation (UNISERV, #20579).* [2021/XE0250/v/**E**]

- ♦ International Stained-Glass Centre (internationally oriented national body)
- ♦ International Stainless Steel Forum / see world stainless association (#21828)
- ♦ International Stamp Collectors Association (inactive)
- ♦ International Standard Book Number / see International ISBN Agency (#13955)
- ♦ International Standard for Maritime Pilot Organizations / see International Users Group of ISPO-certified organizations (#15837)
- ♦ International Ständiger Verband für Schiffahrtkongresse / see PIANC (#18371)
- ♦ International Standing Bureau for Mutual Assistance Studies and Statistics and International Federation of Free Mutual Assistance (inactive)
- ♦ International Standing Committee for History of Education / see International Standing Conference for History of Education (#15599)

♦ International Standing Committee of the International Congress on Animal Reproduction 15598

Comité permanent international du Congrès international de la reproduction animale
SG Fac of Veterinary Science, Univ of Sydney, Sydney NSW 2006, Australia. T. +61293513363. Fax +61293513957. E-mail: info@animalreproduction.org.
URL: http://animalreproduction.org/
History 3 Jun 1948, Milan (Italy). Founded to organize the *International Congress on Animal Reproduction.* Constitution and By-Laws adopted, 1992; modified, 2002. Former names and other names: *International Standing Committee of the International Congress on Animal Reproduction and Artificial Insemination* – former; *Comité permanent international du Congrès international de la reproduction animale et de l'insémination artificielle* – former. **Aims** Organize, in cooperation with international organizations in allied fields, congresses dealing with physiological and pathological problems of animal reproduction, methodological and practical problems of biotechnology of animals, legislative and organizational problems of artificial insemination and of animal reproduction. **Structure** International Standing Committee; Executive Committee. **Languages** English. **Staff** None. **Finance** Congress fees. **Events** *International Congress on Animal Reproduction (ICAR)* Bologna (Italy) 2022, *International Congress on Animal Reproduction (ICAR)* Bologna (Italy) 2021, *International Congress on Animal Reproduction (ICAR)* Bologna (Italy) 2020, *International Congress on Animal Reproduction (ICAR)* Tours (France) 2016, *Quadrennial Congress* Vancouver, BC (Canada) 2012. **Publications** Conference proceedings (every 4 years).
Members Individuals in 46 countries:
Argentina, Australia, Austria, Belgium, Brazil, Canada, Chile, China, Czechia, Denmark, Egypt, Estonia, Finland, France, Germany, Greece, Hungary, Iceland, India, Indonesia, Iran Islamic Rep, Ireland, Israel, Italy, Japan, Korea Rep, Malaysia, Mexico, Netherlands, New Zealand, Nigeria, Norway, Poland, Portugal, Romania, Russia, Slovenia, South Africa, Spain, Sri Lanka, Sweden, Switzerland, UK, United Arab Emirates, Uruguay, USA. [2022/XF2589/cv/**F**]

- ♦ International Standing Committee of the International Congress on Animal Reproduction and Artificial Insemination / see International Standing Committee of the International Congress on Animal Reproduction (#15598)
- ♦ International Standing Committee for Mycenaean Studies / see Comité international permanent des études mycéniennes (#04181)

♦ International Standing Conference for History of Education (ISCHE) 15599

Sec ISCHE Office, Feurigstrasse 22, 10827 Berlin, Germany. E-mail: ische-office@ische.org.
URL: http://www.ische.org/
History 1978. First conference Sep 1979, Leuven (Belgium). Previously also referred to as *International Standing Committee for History of Education.* Current constitution approved 27 Jul 2007, Hamburg (Germany). Admitted, 1990, Madrid (Spain), as an internal committee of ICHS; Aug 2000, transformed into a full-fledged affiliated organization of ICHS. **Aims** Foster research in the field of history of education; facilitate international contact, intellectual exchange and cooperation between all those work in the field; develop an appreciation of the history of education and its contribution to an understanding of education; encourage the teaching of the subject; arrange and promote sessions. **Structure** General Meeting; Executive Committee. **Languages** English, French, German, Portuguese, Spanish. **Finance** Members' dues. **Activities** Events/meetings; training/education. **Events** *Annual Conference* Milan (Italy) 2022, *Annual Conference* Örebro (Sweden) 2021, *Annual Conference* Örebro (Sweden) 2020, *Annual Conference* Porto (Portugal) 2019, *Annual Conference* Berlin (Germany) 2018. **Publications** *Paedagogica Historica – International Journal of the History of Education* (1-2 a year); *ISCHE-News.* **Members** Individuals; associations and institutions. Members in 40 countries. Membership countries not specified. [2019.04.25/XE1198/**E**]

♦ International Standing Conference on Philanthropy (INTERPHIL) . . . 15600

Conférence internationale permanente pour la philanthropie
Pres INTERPHIL Headquarters, CIC Case 20, 1211 Geneva 20, Switzerland. T. +41227336717. Fax +41227347082.
Correspondent for CIS c/o INTERLEGAL, Krupskaya 17/19 – No 126, Moscow MOSKVA, Russia, 117331. T. +7951384380. Fax +7951384408.
History 1969, following an international conference in Evian (France) at the initiative of international, American and European non-profit organizations. Restructured at General Assembly, 6 Jun 1984, London (UK). Also referred to in French as *Conférence internationale pour l'étude et l'encouragement de la philanthropie.* Registered in accordance with Swiss Civil Code. **Aims** Promote development of *civil society*, and specifically the idea and practice of modern philanthropy. **Structure** General Assembly; Board of Directors; Secretariat, headed by Executive Director. **Languages** English, French, German. **Staff** 2.00 FTE, voluntary. **Finance** Members' dues. Other sources: donations; grants; sale of literature. Annual budget: about pounds30,000. **Activities** Knowledge management/information dissemination; advocacy/lobbying/activism; networking/liaising; projects/programmes; events/meetings. **Events** *Conference* Montréal, QC (Canada) 2010, *International Meeting* Montréal, QC (Canada) 2010, *Conference / International Meeting* Utrecht (Netherlands) 2007, *Conference / International Meeting* Kiev (Ukraine) 2004, *Conference / International Meeting* Geneva (Switzerland) 2002. **Publications** *Studies in Philanthropy; Tax Treatment of Donors to Charity in 35 Countries.* Reports in English, French.
Members Corporate; Individual. Members in 26 countries:
Australia, Brazil, Bulgaria, Canada, Costa Rica, Estonia, France, Germany, India, Ireland, Israel, Italy, Kenya, Mexico, Netherlands, Norway, Romania, Russia, Singapore, Slovenia, Spain, Switzerland, Türkiye, UK, Ukraine, USA.
NGO Relations Member of: *Fédération des Institutions Internationales établies à Genève (FIIG, #09599).* Cooperation agreement with: *International Public Foundation (INTERLEGAL, #14667).*
[2017.09.16/XD2980/**F**]

- ♦ International Standing Seminar on Religious Education and Value Potential / see International Seminar on Religious Education and Values (#14832)
- ♦ International Star Class Yacht Racing Association (see: #21760)
- ♦ International State Crime Research Consortium (internationally oriented national body)
- ♦ International States Parliament for Safety and Peace – New Society of the Nations / see International Parliament for Safety and Peace
- ♦ International Static Studies College (internationally oriented national body)

♦ International Stationary Press Association (ISPA) 15601

Gen Sec Technopôle Agroparc, Bâtiment Icare, 160 rue Lawrence Durrell, BP 51269, 84911 Avignon CEDEX 9, France. T. +33490893300. Fax +33490882849.
URL: http://www.ispa.club/
History 1978. **Aims** Promote collaboration between industry publishers; encourage editorial exchange of information; increase advertising opportunities. **Languages** English. **Finance** Members' dues. **Activities** Offers 'ISPA Award'. **Events** *Meeting* Frankfurt-Main (Germany) 2012, *Meeting* Frankfurt-Main (Germany) 2011, *Meeting* Frankfurt-Main (Germany) 2010, *Meeting* Frankfurt-Main (Germany) 2009, *Meeting* Frankfurt-Main (Germany) 2008.
Members Magazines in 20 countries:
Argentina, Belgium, Brazil, Czechia, Denmark, France, Germany, Hungary, India, Italy, Japan, Korea Rep, Mexico, Netherlands, Poland, Slovakia, Spain, Switzerland, Türkiye, UK. [2020/XD8689/**D**]

- ♦ International Statistical Ecology Conference (meeting series)

♦ **International Statistical Education Centre (ISEC)** **15602**

Member Sec 202 Barrackpore Trunk Road, Kolkata, West Bengal 700108, Kolkata WEST BENGAL 700108, India. T. +913325752016 – +913325752027 – +913325752028. Fax +913325781834.
URL: https://www.isical.ac.in/~isecweb/

History 1950, Kolkata (India). Previously operated jointly by *International Statistical Institute (ISI, #15603)* – as part of its *'International Statistical Education Programme (ISEP)'* – and Indian Statistical Institute. Currently operated by Indian Statistical Institute under the auspices of Indian Government. **Aims** Provide courses in theoretical and applied statistics at various levels to selected participants from the countries of the Middle East, South and South-East Asia, Pacific area and the Commonwealth countries of Africa and other developing countries. **Structure** Board of Directors. **Languages** English. **Staff** 6.00 FTE, paid. Drawn from faculty of Indian Statistical Institute and officers of NSSO/NSSTA, Government of India. **Finance** Financed by Government of India through Indian Statistical Institute. **Activities** Training/education. **Publications** *Prospectus* (annual). Annual Report.

Members Applicants for Courses from 65 countries and territories:
Afghanistan, Australia, Bangladesh, Bhutan, Brunei Darussalam, Cambodia, China, Côte d'Ivoire, Cuba, Egypt, El Salvador, Eswatini, Ethiopia, Fiji, Gambia, Georgia, Ghana, Grenada, Hong Kong, India, Indonesia, Iran Islamic Rep, Iraq, Israel, Japan, Kazakhstan, Kenya, Korea Rep, Laos, Liberia, Malawi, Malaysia, Maldives, Mauritius, Mongolia, Myanmar, Namibia, Nepal, New Zealand, Niger, Nigeria, Oman, Pakistan, Papua New Guinea, Philippines, Samoa, Senegal, Seychelles, Sierra Leone, Singapore, Somalia, South Africa, Sri Lanka, St Kitts-Nevis, St Lucia, Sudan, Syrian AR, Tanzania UR, Thailand, Tonga, Uganda, United Arab Emirates, Uzbekistan, Vietnam, Zambia. [2022/XE0847/v/**E**]

♦ **International Statistical Institute (ISI)** **15603**

Institut international de statistique (IIS) – Instituto Internacional de Estadistica – Internationales Statistisches Institut – Istituto Internazionale di Statistica – Internationaal Statistisch Instituut – Internationella Statistiska Institutet – Mezdunarodnyj Statisticeskij Institut

Dir PO Box 24070, 2490 AB The Hague, Netherlands. T. +31703375737. Fax +31703860025.
Street Address c/o Centraal Bureau voor de Statistiek, CBS, Henri Faasdreef 312, 2492 JP The Hague, Netherlands.
URL: http://www.isi-web.org/

History 24 Jun 1885, Brussels (Belgium). Founded at inaugural conference, to provide an organizational foundation to *International Statistical Congress – Congrès internationaux de statistique* which had been held: 1853, Brussels; 1855, Paris (France); 1857, Vienna (Austria); 1860, London (UK); 1863, Berlin (Germany); 1867, Florence (Italy); 1869, The Hague (Netherlands); 1872, St Petersburg (Russia); 1876, Budapest (Hungary). The Institute assumed the character of an international organization seeking international uniformity in statistical procedures and practices; it formulated recommendations to national governments in this connection at biennial sessions. It administered first the *International Commission for the Revision of Nomenclature of Causes of Death (inactive)*, 1900-1911, and subsequently, from recommendations 19 Oct 1929, Paris, and subsequent adoption of *International Agreement Relating to Statistics of Causes of Death (1934)* 19 Jun 1934, London, until the outbreak of World War II, the *International Commission for the Decennial Revision of the International Lists of Diseases and Causes of Death (inactive)*. Reconstituted as an international professional society in 1948. Statutes revised Aug 1972, 2003 and 2011. Current Statutes effective 29 Nov 2011. Registration: Handelsregister, No/ID: KVK 40408414, Netherlands. **Aims** Develop and improve statistical methods and their application throughout the world; encourage international association of statisticians, exchange among them of professional knowledge, and growth among them of a collective interest in advancement of such knowledge; aid in establishment of such relations among statistical societies and other official and unofficial organizations having statistical interests as will further the international integration of statistics; establish and maintain professorships, lecturerships and fellowships for advanced studies in statistics; study statistical theories, appraise statistical methods and practices, encourage statistical research and further the use of statistical methods in diverse subject-matter fields wherever useful; promote the use in all countries of the most appropriate statistical methods; further international comparability of statistical data; foster public appreciation of sound statistical practice and the usefulness of statistical methods.

Structure General Assembly (every 2 years); Council (representatives of specified statistical interest groups may be entitled to membership in the Council without voting rights); Executive Committee. Permanent Office; Affiliated Organizations. Meetings on invitation.
Specialized Associations (7):
- *Bernoulli Society for Mathematical Statistics and Probability (BSMSP, #03212)*, formed in 1961, as *'International Association for Statistics in Physical Sciences (IASPS)'*;
- *International Association of Survey Statisticians (IASS, #12218)*, created in 1973;
- *International Association for Statistical Computing (IASC, #12183)*, founded Dec 1977, Delhi (India);
- *International Association for Official Statistics (IAOS, #12052)*, set up Aug 1985, Amsterdam (Netherlands) – this section replaces *International Association for Regional and Urban Statistics (IARUS, inactive)*, set up 22 Oct 1958, Geneva (Switzerland), as *'International Association of Municipal Statisticians'*, which merged with IAOS in 1989;
- *International Association for Statistics Education (IASE, #12184)*, founded in 1991;
- *International Society on Business and Industrial Statistics (ISBIS, #14989)*, founded in 2005;
- *International Environmetrics Society (TIES, #13284)*, founded in 1989.

Since 1949, administers *'International Statistical Education Programme (ISEP)'* with support from UNESCO and other sources.

Languages Arabic, Chinese, English, French, German, Italian, Russian, Spanish. **Staff** 8.00 FTE, paid. **Finance** Sources: government support; grants; members' dues; sale of publications. **Activities** Awards/prizes/competitions; events/meetings; knowledge management/information dissemination. **Events** *World Statistics Congress* The Hague (Netherlands) 2025, *IAOS-ISI Conference* Livingstone (Zambia) 2023, *World Statistics Congress* Ottawa, ON (Canada) 2023, *World Statistics Congress* 2021, *World Statistics Congress* Kuala Lumpur (Malaysia) 2019. **Publications** *Bernouilli* (4 a year) – journal; *International Statistical Review* (3 a year) – 1933-present; *Bulletin of the International Statistical Institute* (usually every 2 years) – (1886-present) proceedings of ISI World Statistics Congresses, CD, DVD and/or paper; *Dictionary of Statistical Terms*. *Identifying the Poor* (1999); *Assessment Challenge in Statistics Education* (1997); *Economic Statistics – Accuracy, Timeliness and Relevance* (1997); *Teaching Statistics in Schools throughout the World* (1982). *Statistical Theory and Method Abstracts* – DVD and online. Multilingual glossary of statistical terms; code of ethics in statistics; survey of national and international training efforts; proceedings; occasional papers; studies.

Members Honorary (11). Elected (2,000). Ex officio – individuals holding leading positions in official national statistical agencies and international organizations designated by the Council (over 1,000) and representatives of organizations affiliated with the Institute (about 50 intergovernmental organizations, international and national statistical societies). Corporate (43) – national or international statistical agencies, certain cultural, educational and scientific institutions, commercial, industrial and business enterprises which share or support the aims of the Institute. Members in 101 countries and territories:
Albania, Algeria, Argentina, Armenia, Australia, Austria, Bangladesh, Barbados, Belgium, Benin, Botswana, Brazil, Bulgaria, Cameroon, Canada, Central African Rep, Chile, China, Colombia, Congo DR, Croatia, Cyprus, Czechia, Denmark, Egypt, Estonia, Ethiopia, Finland, France, Georgia, Germany, Ghana, Greece, Hong Kong, Hungary, Iceland, India, Indonesia, Iran Islamic Rep, Iraq, Ireland, Israel, Italy, Jamaica, Japan, Jordan, Kenya, Korea Rep, Laos, Latvia, Lebanon, Madagascar, Malawi, Malaysia, Mexico, Morocco, Myanmar, Netherlands, New Zealand, Nigeria, North Macedonia, Norway, Oman, Pakistan, Panama, Peru, Philippines, Poland, Portugal, Puerto Rico, Romania, Russia, Saudi Arabia, Senegal, Serbia, Sierra Leone, Singapore, Slovakia, Slovenia, South Africa, Spain, Sri Lanka, Sudan, Suriname, Sweden, Switzerland, Tanzania UR, Thailand, Trinidad-Tobago, Tunisia, Türkiye, Uganda, UK, Ukraine, Uruguay, USA, Uzbekistan, Venezuela, Vietnam, Zambia, Zimbabwe.

Affiliated national organizations (43) in 34 countries:
Argentina, Australia, Austria, Bangladesh, Belgium, Brazil, Canada, China, Colombia, Denmark, Estonia, Finland, France (3), Germany (3), Greece, Hungary, India (4), Israel, Italy (2), Japan, Korea Rep, Netherlands, New Zealand, Norway, Philippines, Poland, Portugal, Singapore, Slovenia, Spain, Sweden, Switzerland (2), UK, USA.

Affiliated international and regional organizations (8):
American Society for Quality (ASQ); European Organization for Quality (EOQ, #08112); Institute of Mathematical Statistics (IMS, #11282); Inter-American Statistical Institute (IASI, #11452); International Association for Research in Income and Wealth (IARIW, #12134); International Biometric Society (#12354); International Society for Clinical Biostatistics (ISCB, #15014); International Union for the Scientific Study of Population (IUSSP, #15814).

Consultative Status Consultative status granted from: *ECOSOC (#05331)* (Special); *UNESCO (#20322)* (Consultative Status); *UNIDO (#20336)*. **IGO Relations** Accredited by (1): *United Nations Office at Vienna (UNOV, #20604)*. Cooperates with (1): *United Nations Population Fund (UNFPA, #20612)*. Associated with Department of Global Communications of the United Nations. **NGO Relations** Cooperates with (1): *International Organization for Standardization (ISO, #14473)*. Instrumental in setting up (2): *International Statistical Institute Research Centre (ISIRC, inactive); World Fertility Survey (WFS, inactive).* [2023/XA2590/jy/**A**]

♦ International Statistical Programs Center / see International Programs Center
♦ International Statistics Programs Center / see International Programs Center
♦ International Steel Guitar Convention (meeting series)
♦ International Steering Committee for Carbohydrate Symposia / see Joint IUBMB-IUPAC International Carbohydrate Organization (#16138)

♦ **International Steering Committee on Integral Methods in Science and Engineering (IMSE)** **15604**

Chairman Dept of Mathematical and Computer Sciences, Univ of Tulsa, 800 South Tucker Drive, Tulsa OK 74104, USA. T. +19186313068. Fax +19186313077.

History 1990. Consortium founded following first two conferences. Former names and other names: *International Consortium on Integral Methods in Science and Engineering (IMSE)* – alias. **Structure** Informal structure. Steering Committee, comprising Chairman, Co-Chairman and 11 members. **Events** *International Conference on Integral Methods in Science and Engineering (IMSE)* 2022, *International Conference on Integral Methods in Science and Engineering (IMSE)* St Petersburg (Russia) 2021, *International Conference on Integral Methods in Science and Engineering (IMSE)* Brighton (UK) 2018, *International Conference on Integral Methods in Science and Engineering (IMSE)* Padua (Italy) 2016, *International Conference on Integral Methods in Science and Engineering (IMSE)* Karlsruhe (Germany) 2014. [2022/XJ6508/c/**E**]

♦ International Steering Committee for People with HIV/AIDS / see Global Network of People Living with HIV/AIDS (#10494)
♦ International ST-EP Organization / see UNWTO Sustainable Tourism for Eliminating Poverty Foundation (#20725)

♦ **International Step by Step Association (ISSA)** **15605**

Exec Dir Kinderrechtenhuis, Hooglandse Kerkgracht 17R, 2312 HS Leiden, Netherlands. T. +31715161222. E-mail: info@issa.nl.
URL: http://www.issa.nl/

History 1999, Netherlands. Founded by independent organizations implementing the Step by Step Programme, initially funded by *Open Society Foundations (OSF, #17763)*. Registration: EU Transparency Register, No/ID: 053125133094-59, Start date: 5 Nov 2018. **Aims** Empower each *child* to reach her or his unique potential; embrace values of social justice and equity. **Structure** Council; Board; Committees (2); Secretariat based in Leiden (Netherlands). **Languages** English. **Staff** 12.00 FTE, paid. **Finance** Sources: fees for services; grants; members' dues; sale of products. Annual budget: 1,800,000 EUR. **Activities** Advocacy/lobbying/activism; awareness raising; capacity building; events/meetings; knowledge management/information dissemination; networking/liaising. developing professional resources. **Events** *Conference* Leiden (Netherlands) 2019, *Conference* Ghent (Belgium) 2017, *Conference* Vilnius (Lithuania) 2016, *Conference* Budapest (Hungary) 2014, *Conference* Opatija (Croatia) 2012. **Publications** *ISSA Principles of Quality Pedagogy; Quality Framework for Birth to Three Services.* Annual Report; guidebooks; tools; studies; reports.

Members Organizations in 41 countries:
Albania, Armenia, Austria, Azerbaijan, Belarus, Belgium, Bosnia-Herzegovina, Bulgaria, Croatia, Czechia, Estonia, France, Georgia, Greece, Hungary, India, Ireland, Italy, Kazakhstan, Kosovo, Kyrgyzstan, Latvia, Lithuania, Malawi, Moldova, Mongolia, Montenegro, Netherlands, North Macedonia, Pakistan, Poland, Romania, Russia, Serbia, Slovakia, Slovenia, Tajikistan, Türkiye, UK, Ukraine, USA.

International organizations (2):
International Child Development Initiatives (ICDI); Mother Child Education Foundation (ACEV).

IGO Relations Cooperates with: *UNICEF (#20332)*. Participant in Fundamental Rights Platform of: *European Union Agency for Fundamental Rights (FRA, #08969)*. **NGO Relations** Member of: *Early Childhood Development Action Network (ECDAN, #05155)*. Cooperates with organizations concerned with child education and development including: *Bernard van Leer Foundation (BvLF); Diversity, Early Childhood Education and Training (DECET, #05106); Early Childhood Peace Consortium (ECPC, #05156); International Child Development Initiatives (ICDI); Mother Child Education Foundation (ACEV)*; National Association for the Education of Young Children (NAEYC); *Open Society Foundations (OSF, #17763).* [2022/XD8859/**D**]

♦ **International Stereoscopic Union (ISU)** **15606**

Union Stéréoscopique Internationale

Treas PO Box 102634, 70022 Stuttgart, Germany. T. +497115208768-3. Fax +497115208768-9. E-mail: isu@stereoscopy.com.
URL: https://isu3d.org/

History 1975, Netherlands. **Aims** Promote 3D *photographic* imaging in its various forms worldwide; provide opportunities for developing improved *stereographic* practice and skills; provide a framework for disseminating stereographic educational and information materials. **Structure** Congress (every 2 years); Union Council; Board of Directors. **Languages** English. **Staff** Voluntary. **Finance** Sources: donations; members' dues; sale of products. **Events** *Biennial Congress* Tsukuba (Japan) 2023, *Biennial Congress* Cesky Krumlov (Czechia) 2022, *Biennial Congress* Lübeck (Germany) 2019, *Biennial Congress* Irvine, CA (USA) 2017, *Biennial Congress* Busan (Korea Rep) 2015. **Publications** *Stereoscopy* (4 a year).

Members Organizations (35) in 18 countries:
Australia, Austria, Canada, Czechia, Denmark, France, Germany, Italy, Japan, Korea Rep, Netherlands, New Zealand, Poland, Slovenia, Sweden, Switzerland, UK, USA.

Individuals in 47 countries and territories:
Australia, Austria, Bahrain, Belarus, Belgium, Brazil, Canada, Chile, China, Croatia, Czechia, Denmark, Finland, France, Germany, Greece, Hong Kong, Hungary, Iceland, India, Indonesia, Iran Islamic Rep, Ireland, Israel, Italy, Japan, Korea Rep, Malaysia, Mexico, Netherlands, New Zealand, Norway, Pakistan, Philippines, Poland, Portugal, Russia, Slovenia, South Africa, Spain, Sweden, Switzerland, Thailand, Türkiye, UK, Ukraine, USA. [2021.06.16/XD2925/**C**]

♦ **International Stereotactic Radiosurgery Society (ISRS)** **15607**

Contact c/o MCO Congrès Villa Gaby 285, Corniche Kennedy, 13007 Marseille, France. E-mail: secretariat@isrsy.org.
URL: http://www.isrsy.org/

History 1991, Pittsburgh, PA (USA). **Aims** Advance the field of Stereotactic Radiosurgery (SRS) and Stereotactic Body Radiation Therapy (SBRT) through multidisciplinary education and knowledge-sharing, collaborative research, and the definition and dissemination of best practices and clinical outcomes. **Structure** Biennial Meeting; Board of Directors; Committees (7). **Languages** English. **Finance** Sources: international organizations; members' dues. **Activities** Events/meetings; knowledge management/information dissemination; networking/liaising; research and development; standards/guidelines; training/education. **Events** *Biennial Congress* Milan (Italy) 2022, *Biennial Congress* Brisbane, QLD (Australia) 2021, *Biennial Congress* Rio de Janeiro (Brazil) 2019, *Biennial Congress* Montreux (Switzerland) 2017, *Biennial Congress* Yokohama (Japan) 2015. **Publications** *ISRS Newsletter* (4 a year); *Journal of Radiosurgery and SBRT* (2 a year). Annual Report

Members Active – neurosurgeons, radiation oncologists, medical physicists, radiation biologists, dosimetrists, nurses and radiologists; Associate – professionals whose work involves research applicable to the practice of stereotactic radiosurgery (SRS) and stereotactic body radiation therapy (SBRT). Members in 46 countries and territories:
Australia, Austria, Belgium, Brazil, Bulgaria, Canada, Chile, China, Denmark, Egypt, England, Finland, France, Germany, Greece, Hungary, India, Indonesia, Iran Islamic Rep, Israel, Italy, Japan, Korea Rep, Mexico, Netherlands, New Zealand, Norway, Peru, Poland, Portugal, Romania, Russia, Scotland, Singapore, South Africa, Spain, Sweden, Switzerland, Taiwan, Thailand, Turkey, Türkiye, UK, Ukraine, USA, Venezuela. [2022.10.22/XD3247/v/**C**]

♦ International Stevia Council (unconfirmed)

♦ **International Stillbirth Alliance (ISA)** **15608**

Contact 61 Kings Drive, Stoke Gifford, Bristol, GS34 8RD, UK. E-mail: info@stillbirthalliance.org.
URL: http://www.stillbirthalliance.org/

History 2002. Registration: 501(c)(3), USA. **Aims** Raise awareness, educate on recommended precautionary practices and facilitate research on the prevention of stillbirth. **Structure** Board; Scientific Advisory Committee. Committees (2): Communications; Scientific Advisory. Working Groups. **Finance** Sources: donations. **Activities** Events/meetings; research/documentation. **Events** *Annual Conference* Salt Lake City, UT (USA) 2022, *Biennial International Conference on Stillbirth, SIDS and Baby Survival* Brisbane, QLD (Australia) 2021, *Biennial International Conference on Stillbirth, SIDS and Baby Survival* Brisbane, QLD (Australia) 2020, *Annual Conference* Madrid (Spain) 2019, *Biennial International Conference on Stillbirth, SIDS and Baby Survival* Glasgow (UK) 2018. **Publications** *ISA Newsletter*.
Members Organizations in 24 countries:
Argentina, Australia, Canada, Chile, China, Denmark, Georgia, Guatemala, Ireland, Italy, Japan, Kenya, Mexico, Netherlands, New Zealand, Norway, Paraguay, Russia, South Africa, Spain, Sweden, UK, USA, Vietnam.
Included in the above, 1 organization listed in this Yearbook:
Global Alliance to Prevent Prematurity and Stillbirth (GAPPS).
NGO Relations Member of (1): *PMNCH (#18410)*. Partner of (1): *Healthy Newborn Network (HNN, #10894)*. *Neonatal Nursing Association of Southern Africa (NNASA)* is member. [2022.10.21/XM0809/**F**]

♦ International Stomatological Association (inactive)

♦ International Strabismological Association (ISA) 15609

Association internationale de strabisme

Main Office 1160 W Michigan St, Ste 220, Indianapolis IN 46202, USA. Fax +13173288864. E-mail: info@isahome.org.
URL: http://www.isahome.org/

History 1966. By-laws revised Apr 1990. **Aims** Disseminate knowledge on all *sensory* and motor aspects of strabismus and other *disorders* of *ocular motility*; foster clinical and experimental research; encourage and support countries wishing to set up organizations for the study and treatment of strabismus and associated sensory disorders; create, as far as possible, a common terminology and a *standardization* of *diagnostic* and *therapeutic* procedures. **Structure** General Business Meeting (every 4 years). Administrative Council (meets every 4 years), consisting of 20 members. Executive Committee, composed of President, 1st and 2nd Vice-President, Secretary-Treasurer, Transactions Editor, Newsletter Editor and any other officers the Council wishes to appoint. Nominating Committee; Program Committee; Bielschowsky Lecture and Linksz Award Committee; Committee on Terminology. **Events** *Meeting* Cancún (Mexico) 2022, *Quadrennial Congress* Paris (France) 2021, *Quadrennial Congress* Washington, DC (USA) 2018, *Quadrennial Congress* Kyoto (Japan) 2014, *Quadrennial Congress* Istanbul (Turkey) 2010.
Members Charter; Active; Associate; Honorary; Emeritus. Ophthalmologists and orthoptics (about 500) specializing in strabismus in 44 countries and territories:
Argentina, Australia, Austria, Belgium, Brazil, Canada, Chile, China, Colombia, Denmark, Ecuador, Egypt, Finland, France, Germany, Greece, India, Iran Islamic Rep, Israel, Italy, Japan, Korea Rep, Lebanon, Malaysia, Mexico, Netherlands, Norway, Peru, Poland, Portugal, Puerto Rico, Russia, Serbia, Singapore, South Africa, Spain, Sweden, Switzerland, Taiwan, Türkiye, UK, Uruguay, USA, Venezuela.
NGO Relations Member of: *International Pediatric Ophthalmology and Strabismus Council (IPOSC, #14544)*. Relates closely with: *International Council of Ophthalmology (ICO, #13057)*, officially representing the specialty at the International Congress of Ophthalmology. [2020/XD6877/v/**C**]

♦ International La Strada Association / see La Strada International (#20002)
♦ International Strategic Management Association (#02717)
♦ International Strategic Management Conference (meeting series)
♦ International Strategic Research Organisation (internationally oriented national body)
♦ International Strategic Technology Alliance (internationally oriented national body)
♦ International Straw, Fodder and Peat Trade Confederation (no recent information)
♦ International Street Painting Society (unconfirmed)

♦ International Stress and Behavior Society (ISBS) 15610

Conference Secretariat 309 Palmer Court, Slidell LA 70458, USA. T. +12408999571. E-mail: info@stressandbehavior.com – isbs.congress@gmail.com.
URL: http://www.stressandbehavior.com/

History 2007, resulting from Annual International Stress and Behavior Conferences. **Aims** Work with a wide range of topics in the field of translational neuroscience, neurobehavioral sciences, biopsychology and biopsychiatry, with a particular focus of stress, stress-related neurobehavioral phenotypes, their neural, molecular and genetic mechanisms, as well as stress-evoked neuropsychiatric disorders. **Structure** President; Vice-President. **Languages** English. **Staff** 1.00 FTE, paid. **Finance** Members' dues. **Activities** Meeting activities; Education. **Events** *International Neuroscience and Biological Psychiatry Regional Asia Conference* Saitama (Japan) 2022, *Annual International Neuroscience and Biopsychiatry Conference* St Petersburg (Russia) 2020, *Annual International Neuroscience and Biopsychiatry Conference* St Petersburg (Russia) 2020, *Annual International Neuroscience and Biopsychiatry Conference* St Petersburg (Russia) 2019, *Annual International Neuroscience and Biopsychiatry Conference* St Petersburg (Russia) 2018. **NGO Relations** Partner of national organizations. Member of: *World Federation of Societies of Biological Psychiatry (WFSBP, #21483)*. [2013.09.19/XM3192/**D**]

♦ International Stress Management Association (ISMA) 15611

Chair 85 Gordon Avenue, Stanmore, HA7 3QR, UK. T. +442089541593.
URL: http://www.isma.org.uk/

History Founded 1973, Chicago IL (USA), as *'American Association for the Advancement of Tension Control'*. Name changed, 1981, to *International Stress and Tension Control Society (ISTCS)*. Present title adopted, Sep 1989. **Aims** Promote sound knowledge and best practice in prevention and reduction of human stress. **Structure** Board of Trustees; Chair. **Languages** English. **Staff** 1.00 FTE, paid. Several voluntary. **Finance** Members' dues. Donations. **Activities** Research/documentation; knowledge management/information dissemination; networking/liaising; events/meetings. **Events** *International conference* Montréal, QC (Canada) 2007, *Joint conference on peak performance* Philadelphia, PA (USA) 2005, *International forum on quality of work life* Porto Alegre (Brazil) 2005, *International conference* Warwick (UK) 2001, *International conference* Houston, TX (USA) 1999. **Publications** *ISMAUK Stress and Wellbeing News Daily*; *The International Journal of Stress Prevention and Wellbeing*.
Members Professionals concerned with stress research and management; national branches. Members in 9 countries:
Austria, Belgium, Brazil, France, India, Netherlands, Nigeria, Sweden, UK.
NGO Relations Member of: *National Council for Voluntary Organizations (NCVO)*. [2018.06.01/XD1968/v/**F**]

♦ International Stress and Tension Control Society / see International Stress Management Association (#15611)

♦ International Stroke Genetics Consortium (ISGC) 15612

Contact address not obtained.
URL: http://www.strokegenetics.org/

History Founded Apr 2007. **Aims** Further understanding of the genetic basis of stroke. **Structure** Steering Committee; Scientific Committee. Working Groups. **Activities** Events/meetings. **Events** *Workshop* Cambridge (UK) 2019, *Workshop* Baltimore, MD (USA) 2018, *Workshop* Kyoto (Japan) 2018, *Workshop* Houston, TX (USA) 2017, *Workshop* Utrecht (Netherlands) 2017. **Members** Individuals (over 200). Membership countries not specified. [2019/XM4974/c/**C**]

♦ International Stroke Society (inactive)
♦ International Structural Genomics Organization (inactive)
♦ International Student Association of Indonesia / see Indonesian Students Association for International Studies
♦ International Student Association of Japan (internationally oriented national body)
♦ International Student Christian Services / see Friends International Ministries
♦ International Student Exchange Program (internationally oriented national body)
♦ International Student Exchange Programs (internationally oriented national body)
♦ International Student Federation 'Corda Fratres' (inactive)
♦ International Student Identity Card Association / see ISIC Association (#16029)
♦ International Student Information Service (inactive)
♦ International Student Insurance Services Association / see International Association for Student Insurance Services (#12190)
♦ International Student Office / see International Branch of the YMCA, New York
♦ International Student One Health Alliance (unconfirmed)
♦ International Student Pugwash / see International Student/Young Pugwash (#15614)
♦ International Students (internationally oriented national body)
♦ International Students' Association of Village Concept Projects (inactive)
♦ International Students' Bureau (inactive)
♦ International Student Service / see World University Service (#21892)

♦ International Students of History Association (ISHA) 15613

Sec FSI Geschichte, Humboldt Univ zu Berlin, Friedrichstrasse 191-193a, 10099 Berlin, Germany. E-mail: info@isha.international.
URL: https://ishainternational.wordpress.com/

History 9 May 1990, Budapest (Hungary). Secretariat subsequently moved to: Leuven (Belgium); Zurich (Switzerland); Berlin (Germany). **Aims** Enable international cooperation and exchange between students of history and other related disciplines. **Structure** General Assembly; International Board; Council; Committees; Local Sections. **Languages** English. **Staff** Voluntary. **Finance** Member's dues. Other sources: sponsoring; donations; grants. **Activities** Events/meetings; networking/liaising. **Events** *Spring Seminar* Belgrade (Serbia) 2019, *Summer Seminar* Berlin (Germany) 2019, *Annual Conference* Budapest (Hungary) 2019, *Memory spaces* Marburg (Germany) 2019, *Autumn Seminar* Skopje (Macedonia) 2018. **Publications** *Carnival* – journal.
Members Sections: university associations of history students and students with similar subjects and interests in 27 countries:
Argentina, Austria, Belgium, Bosnia-Herzegovina, Brazil, Bulgaria, Chile, Colombia, Croatia, Cyprus, Czechia, Finland, Germany, Greece, Hungary, Italy, Lithuania, Netherlands, North Macedonia, Poland, Romania, Russia, Serbia, Slovenia, Switzerland, Türkiye, UK.
NGO Relations Associate member of: *European Students' Union (ESU, #08848)*. *Network of Concerned Historians (NCH, #17001)* is affiliate member. Partner to: *European Association for Urban History (EAUH, #06262)*; *European Geography Association for Students and Young Geographers (EGEA, #07388)*; *International Committee of Historical Sciences (ICHS, #12777)*; national organizations. [2020/XD4784/**D**]

♦ International Students House (internationally oriented national body)
♦ International Students Trust / see International Students House
♦ International Student Theatre Union (inactive)
♦ International Student Travel Confederation (inactive)
♦ International Student Visitor Services / see InterExchange

♦ International Student/Young Pugwash (ISYP) 15614

Board c/o London Pugwash Office, 63-A Great Russell Street, London, WC1B 3BJ, UK. E-mail: office@isyp.org.
URL: http://www.isyp.org/

History 1979, USA. Founded following student attendance at *Pugwash Conferences on Science and World Affairs (#18574)*, 1978, Varna (Bulgaria). Restructured under current name 1997, Lillehammer (Norway). Former names and other names: *International Student Pugwash (ISP)* – former (1979 to 1997). **Aims** Provide the next generation of scientists, policy-makers and managers of technology with a forum to address and resolve complex *global problems*; stimulate *self-education*, empowering people by giving them the tools to educate themselves. **Structure** Executive Board. **Activities** Events/meetings. **Events** *Conference* Istanbul (Turkey) 2013, *Conference* Berlin (Germany) 2011, *Conference* The Hague (Netherlands) 2009, *Conference* The Hague (Netherlands) 2009, *Conference* Bari (Italy) 2007. **Publications** *ISYP Journal on Science and World Affairs* (2 a year). **Members** National Groups; Individuals. Membership countries not specified. [2022/XG9699/**E**]

♦ International Studies Association (ISA) 15615

Association des études internationales – Associacija Mezdunarodnyh Issledovanij

Dir Operations 362 Fairfield Way, Unit 4013, Storrs CT 06269-4013, USA. T. +18604865850. E-mail: isa@isanet.org.
Exec Dir address not obtained.
URL: http://www.isanet.org/

History 1959. **Aims** Advance development of research and communications on international *politics*, *international relations* and international studies among the global community of international studies scholars. **Structure** Meeting of Members (annual); Governing Council; Regional Divisions; Interdisciplinary Sections; Committees. **Languages** English. **Staff** 15.00 FTE, paid. **Finance** Members' dues. Other sources: host institution subvention; publication and convention proceeds. **Activities** Events/meetings. **Events** *Annual Convention* Baltimore, MD (USA) 2030, *Annual Convention* Las Vegas, NV (USA) 2029, *Annual Convention* New Orleans, LA (USA) 2028, *Annual Convention* Atlanta, GA (USA) 2027, *Annual Convention* Columbus, OH (USA) 2026. **Publications** *Foreign Policy Analysis*; *International Interactions*; *International Political Sociology*; *International Studies Perspectives*; *International Studies Quarterly*; *International Studies Review*; *Journal of Global Security Studies*. **Members** Individual (7,500); Institutional (12). Individuals represented in 112 countries. Membership countries not specified. **Consultative Status** Consultative status granted from: *ECOSOC (#05331)* (Ros B). **IGO Relations** Associated with Department of Global Communications of the United Nations.
NGO Relations Member of: *International Science Council (ISC, #14796)*. Participates in: *FIM-Forum for Democratic Global Governance (FIM, #09761)*. Cooperating organizations include the following listed in this Yearbook:
– *African Politics Conference Group (APCG)*;
– *American Society of International Law (ASIL)*;
– *Association des internationalistes (#02752)*;
– *Atlantic Council*;
– *Austrian Institute for International Affairs (oiip)*;
– *British International Studies Association (BISA)*;
– *Central and East European International Studies Association (CEEISA, #03700)*;
– *European Consortium for Political Research (ECPR, #06762)*;
– *European International Studies Association (EISA, #07589)*;
– *European Union Studies Association (EUSA)*;
– *Foreign Policy Association (FPA)*;
– *Institute for Cultural Diplomacy (ICD, #11252)*;
– *Institute for Development and International Relations (IRMO)*;
– *Instituto Brasileiro de Relações Internacionais (IBRI)*;
– *International Association for Political Science Students (IAPSS, #12095)*;
– *International Political Science Association (IPSA, #14615)*;
– *International Relations and Security Network (ISN, inactive)*;
– *International Social Science Council (ISSC, inactive)*;
– *International Society for the Comparative Study of Civilizations (ISCSC)*;
– *Jadavpur Association of International Relations (JAIR)*;
– *Japan Association of International Relations, Tokyo (JAIR)*;
– *Korean Association of International Studies (KAIS)*;
– *Mexican International Studies Association (AMEI)*;
– *Middle East Studies Association (MESA)*;
– *Nordic International Studies Association (NISA, #17325)*;
– *Organization for Social Science Research in Eastern and Southern Africa (OSSREA, #17888)*;
– *Peace Science Society – International (PSSI)*;
– *Policy Studies Organization (PSO)*;
– *Russian International Studies Association (RISA)*;
– *Toda Institute for Global Peace and Policy Research*;
– *University Association for Contemporary European Studies (UACES, #20697)*;
– *World International Studies Committee (WISC, #21595)*. [2019.12.11/XF0234/**F**]

♦ International Studies Association, Prague (internationally oriented national body)
♦ International Studies Association, University of Wyoming (internationally oriented national body)
♦ International Studies Conference (inactive)

- ♦ International Studies and Cooperation Centre, Montréal / see Canadian Centre for International Studies and Cooperation
- ♦ International Studies Coordinating Committee / see World International Studies Committee (#21595)
- ♦ International Studies Schools Association (internationally oriented national body)

♦ International Study of Arctic Change (ISAC) 15616

Exec Dir Arctic Inst North America, Univ of Calgary 2500 University Drive NW, Calgary AB T2N 1N4, Canada. T. +14032207294.
URL: http://www.arcticchange.org/

History as a long-term, multidisciplinary programme to study the effects of environmental changes. Initiated 2003 by *International Arctic Science Committee (IASC, #11668)* and *Arctic Ocean Sciences Board (AOSB, inactive)*. Serves as an IASC network. **Aims** Observe and understand the characteristics of the entire Arctic System, including the social domain and its responses to change so as to develop the best adaptation and mitigation strategies to counteract negative effects due to *greenhouse warming* and other anthropogenic activities, as well as to changes caused by natural variability affecting the region. **Structure** Science Steering Group. ISAC International Program Office, Stockholm (Sweden), headed by Executive Director. **Events** *Biennial Arctic Observing Summit* Tromsø (Norway) 2022, *Biennial Arctic Observing Summit* Akureyri (Iceland) 2020, *Biennial Arctic Observing Summit* Davos (Switzerland) 2018, *Annual Arctic Science Summit* Fairbanks, AK (USA) 2016, *Biennial Arctic Observing Summit* Fairbanks, AK (USA) 2016. [2016/XJ1203/**E**]

♦ International Study Association on Teachers and Teaching (ISATT) . 15617

Admin Dir address not obtained.
URL: http://www.isatt.org/

History Oct 1983, Tilburg (Netherlands). Founded during a Symposium for Research on Teacher Thinking. Former names and other names: *International Study Association on Teacher Thinking* – former (1983). **Aims** Promote, present, discuss and disseminate research on teachers and teaching; contribute to theory formation in this field. **Structure** Members' meeting (at least every 2 years); Executive Committee. **Languages** English. **Staff** 0.50 FTE, paid. **Finance** Members' dues. Other sources: royalties; conference proceeds. **Activities** Events/meetings; awards/prizes/competitions; financial and/or material support. **Events** *Conference* Bari (Italy) 2023, *Biennial Conference* Sibiu (Romania) 2019, *Biennial Conference* Salamanca (Spain) 2017, *Biennial Conference* Auckland (New Zealand) 2015, *Biennial Conference* Ghent (Belgium) 2013. **Publications** *ISATT Newsletter* (2 a year); *Teachers and Teaching: Theory and Practice – International Journal* (8 a year). *ISATT Publication Series*. Books.
Members Individuals in 50 countries and territories:
Algeria, Australia, Austria, Belgium, Brazil, Canada, Chile, China, Croatia, Cyprus, Czechia, Denmark, Finland, France, Germany, Greece, Hong Kong, Iceland, India, Iran Islamic Rep, Ireland, Israel, Italy, Jamaica, Japan, Macau, Malaysia, Malta, Netherlands, New Zealand, Nigeria, Norway, Pakistan, Philippines, Portugal, Romania, Russia, Singapore, Slovenia, South Africa, Spain, Sweden, Taiwan, Thailand, Trinidad-Tobago, Türkiye, UK, United Arab Emirates, USA, Zimbabwe. [2021/XD1286/v/**D**]

- ♦ International Study Association on Teacher Thinking / see International Study Association on Teachers and Teaching (#15617)
- ♦ International Study Committee of Catholic Nursing Associations / see International Catholic Committee of Nurses and Medico-social Assistants (#12451)
- ♦ International Study Group for Biothermokinetics / see International Study Group for Systems Biology (#15619)
- ♦ International Study Group on Cerebral Circulation (inactive)
- ♦ International Study Group on Copper / see International Copper Study Group (#12963)
- ♦ International Study Group for the Detection and Prevention of Cancer (inactive)
- ♦ International Study Group of Diabetes in Children and Adolescents / see International Society for Pediatric and Adolescent Diabetes (#15344)

♦ International Study Group on Ethnomathematics (ISGEm) 15618

Grupo de Estudio Internacional de Etnomatematica – Gruppo di Studio Internazionale di Etnomatematica

Sec Elementary Education Dept, UMC 2805, Utah State Univ, Logan UT 84341, USA.
URL: http://isgem.rpi.edu/

History 1985. **Structure** Executive Board, comprising President, 3 Vice Presidents, Past President, Secretary, Treasurer and 2 further members. **Events** *Conference* Maputo (Mozambique) 2014, *Conference* Auckland (New Zealand) 2006, *Conference* Ouro Preto (Brazil) 2002, *Conference* Towson, MD (USA) 2000, *Conference* Granada (Spain) 1998. **Publications** *ISGEm Newsletter* (2 a year). [2015/XE3906/**E**]

- ♦ International Study Group for Mathematics Learning (inactive)
- ♦ International Study Group on Music Archaeology (internationally oriented national body)
- ♦ International Study Group on Neuroendoscopy / see International Federation on Neuroendoscopy (#13489)
- ♦ International Study Group for Prenatal Psychology / see International Society for Pre- and Perinatal Psychology and Medicine (#15382)
- ♦ International Study Group for the Relations between the History and Pedagogy of Mathematics (see: #14121)
- ♦ International Study Group for Research in Cardiac Metabolism / see International Society for Heart Research (#15158)
- ♦ International Study Group for Steroid Hormones (no recent information)
- ♦ International Study Group on Systematic Examinations in Preventive Medicine and in Medicine (inactive)

♦ International Study Group for Systems Biology (ISGSB) 15619

Chair Biological and Medical Sciences, Oxford Brookes Univ, Gypsy Lane, Headington, OX3 0BP, UK.
URL: http://sysbio.brookes.ac.uk/

History 1980's. Previously known as *International Study Group for Biothermokinetics (BTK)*. Present name adopted, 2006. A loose collective of individual researchers. **Aims** Advance biological sciences through exploring the interplay between theory and experiment. **Structure** International Scientific Advisory Committee. **Languages** English. **Staff** None. **Finance** No budget. **Activities** Organizes biennial workshop. **Events** *Biennial Workshop* Innsbruck (Austria) 2022, *Conference* Innsbruck (Austria) 2020, *Biennial Workshop* Stellenbosch (South Africa) 2020, *Biennial Workshop* Tromsø (Norway) 2018, *Biennial Workshop* Groningen (Netherlands) 2012. **Publications** Workshop proceedings. **Members** Not a membership organization. [2012.06.01/XM3967/**F**]

- ♦ International Study Group for Tryptophan Research / see International Society for Tryptophan Research (#15525)
- ♦ International Study Institution of the Middle Classes (inactive)

♦ International Study of Religion in Eastern and Central Europe Association (ISORECEA) 15620

Gen Sec Amruseva 11, HR-10000 Zagreb, Croatia.
Pres address not obtained.
URL: http://www.isorecea.net/

History Set up Dec 1995, following series of conferences organized since 1991. **Aims** Develop and exchange scientific information concerning religions and Churches in Eastern and Central Europe. **Structure** General Assembly; Executive Board; Audit Commission. **Languages** English. **Staff** None. **Finance** Members' dues. **Activities** Events/meetings. **Events** *Conference* Warsaw (Poland) 2022, *Conference* Olomouc (Czechia) 2021, *Conference* Olomouc (Czechia) 2020, *Conference* Szeged (Hungary) 2018, *Religion and non-religion in contemporary societies* Zadar (Croatia) 2016. **Publications** *Religions and Society in Central and Eastern Europe* – journal.
Members Individuals in 22 countries:
Belgium, Bosnia-Herzegovina, Canada, Croatia, Czechia, Denmark, Estonia, Germany, Hungary, Italy, Latvia, Lithuania, Netherlands, Poland, Portugal, Russia, Slovakia, Slovenia, Spain, Switzerland, UK, USA.
NGO Relations Affiliate member of: *International Association for the History of Religions (IAHR, #11936)*. [2020.03.10/XM6373/**D**]

- ♦ International Study Society for the Exploration of Arctic Regions by Airship (inactive)
- ♦ International Study Weeks for Child Victims of the War (inactive)
- ♦ International Sturgeon Research Institute (internationally oriented national body)

♦ International Stuttering Association (ISA) 15621

Contact 1018 South Payne St, New Ulm MN 56073, USA. E-mail: admin@isastutter.org.
URL: http://www.isastutter.org/

History 25 Jul 1995, Linköping (Sweden). Constitution updated 2001. **Aims** Improve conditions of people whose lives are affected by stuttering in all countries. **Structure** Members Meeting (every 3 years, at World Congress; Board of Directors. Working Groups. **Finance** Sources: members' dues. **Activities** Awareness raising; events/meetings; guidance/assistance/consulting. **Events** *World Congress* Liverpool (UK) 2022, *Joint World Congress on Stuttering and Cluttering* Montréal, QC (Canada) 2022, *Joint World Congress on Stuttering and Cluttering* Montréal, QC (Canada) 2021, *World Congress* Hveragerøi (Iceland) 2019, *Joint World Congress on Stuttering and Cluttering* Hiroshima (Japan) 2018. **Publications** *One Voice* (2 a year) – newsletter.
Members National associations in 45 countries:
Argentina, Australia, Austria, Belgium, Benin, Brazil, Bulgaria, Burkina Faso, Cameroon, Canada, Croatia, Denmark, Dominican Rep, Estonia, Finland, France, Germany, Hungary, Iceland, Iran Islamic Rep, Ireland, Israel, Japan, Kosovo, Kyrgyzstan, Lithuania, Luxembourg, Mali, Mauritania, Nepal, Netherlands, New Zealand, Nigeria, Norway, Pakistan, Poland, South Africa, Spain, Sweden, Switzerland, Togo, Uganda, UK, USA, Zambia.
Included in the above, 1 organization listed in this Yearbook:
European League of Stuttering Associations (ELSA, #07673).
NGO Relations Cooperates with (2): *International Cluttering Association (ICA, #12603)*; *International Fluency Association (IFA, #13617)*. [2022/XD6933/**C**]

♦ International Substance Abuse and Addiction Coalition (ISAAC) ... 15622

Gen Sec 65 Anderson Avenue, Earley, Reading, RG6 1HD, UK. T. +447818047650.
URL: http://www.isaac-international.org/

History Founded 1997, USA, at an international meeting with representatives from 20 countries, as a coalition of diverse Christian organizations and ministries. Includes a UK Registered Charity and Australian NGO, with other local NGOs in the process of being set up to support international membership. **Aims** Build capacity among *Christians* who are working with addicted people worldwide, so as to maximize their effectiveness, through networking, training and professional development; connect, encourage and equip members in their individual work with those affected by addiction. **Structure** International Steering Group; Secretariat. **Languages** English, Russian, Spanish. **Staff** 1.50 FTE, paid; 5.00 FTE, voluntary. **Finance** Voluntary gifts from grant-making trusts, foundations, individuals. **Activities** Capacity building; networking/liaising; training/education. **Events** *Conference* Phnom Penh (Cambodia) 2013, *Conference* Prague (Czech Rep) 2012, *Conference* Kuala Lumpur (Malaysia) 2010, *Conference* Lima (Peru) 2009, *Conference* Netherlands 2007.
Members Individual; Organizational. Members and contacts in 114 countries, including the following 84 countries (some countries omitted for security reasons):
Albania, Argentina, Australia, Austria, Bangladesh, Belgium, Bolivia, Bosnia, Brazil, Bulgaria, Cambodia, Canada, Chad, Chile, China, Colombia, Costa Rica, Croatia, Czechia, Denmark, Egypt, Estonia, Ethiopia, Fiji, Finland, France, Germany, Ghana, Greece, Iceland, India, Indonesia, Ireland, Italy, Kazakhstan, Kenya, Korea Rep, Kosovo, Kyrgyzstan, Latvia, Lebanon, Liberia, Lithuania, Malawi, Malaysia, Mexico, Moldova, Mongolia, Montenegro, Mozambique, Myanmar, Nepal, Netherlands, New Zealand, Nigeria, Norway, Pakistan, Papua New Guinea, Peru, Philippines, Poland, Portugal, Romania, Russia, Rwanda, Serbia, Sierra Leone, Singapore, South Africa, Spain, Sri Lanka, Sweden, Switzerland, Tajikistan, Tanzania UR, Thailand, Togo, Uganda, UK, Ukraine, USA, Uzbekistan, Zambia, Zimbabwe.
NGO Relations Cooperates with: *ACET International*; *African Youths Initiative on Crime Prevention (AYICRIP)*; *Church Mission Society (CMS)*; *Global Teen Challenge*; International Society of Substance User Professionals (ISSUP); *Mildmay International*; *Radstock Ministries*; *Tearfund, UK*; *World Federation Against Drugs (WFAD, #21408)*; *World Federation of Therapeutic Communities (WFTC, #21491)*; *Youth with a Mission (YWAM, #22020)*. [2019.12.16/XF5561/**F**]

- ♦ International Subterranean Heritage Association (no recent information)
- ♦ International Suffrage Alliance / see International Alliance of Women (#11639)
- ♦ International Sufi Movement (religious order)
- ♦ International Sugar Agreement, 1953 (1953 treaty)
- ♦ International Sugar Agreement, 1958 (1958 treaty)
- ♦ International Sugar Agreement, 1968 (1968 treaty)
- ♦ International Sugar Agreement, 1973 (1973 treaty)
- ♦ International Sugar Agreement, 1977 (1977 treaty)
- ♦ International Sugar Agreement, 1984 (1984 treaty)
- ♦ International Sugar Agreement, 1987 (1987 treaty)
- ♦ International Sugar Agreement, 1992 (1992 treaty)
- ♦ International Sugar Committee (inactive)
- ♦ International Sugar Confectionery Manufacturers Association (inactive)
- ♦ International Sugar Council (inactive)

♦ International Sugar Organization (ISO) 15623

Organisation internationale du sucre (OIS) – Organización Internacional del Azúcar – Mezdunarodnaja Organizacija po Saharu

Exec Dir 1 Canada Square, Canary Wharf, London, E14 5AA, UK. T. +442075131144. Fax +442075131146. E-mail: exdir@isosugar.org.
Assistant address not obtained.
URL: http://www.isosugar.org/

History Established to administer *International Sugar Agreement, 1968 (1968)*, as a successor to *International Sugar Council (inactive)*, which was set up in May 1937, London (UK), and terminated its activity by operating *International Sugar Agreement, 1958 (1958)*. Various ISAs followed. Present Agreement entered into force on 20 Jan 1993. Initial life span scheduled for 5 years with no limit on the number of 2-year extensions which may be made. Agreements registered: *International Sugar Agreement, 1953 (1953)* in *'UNTS 1/3677'*; 1958 in *'UNTS 1/5534'*; 1968 in *'UNTS 1/9369'*; *International Sugar Agreement, 1973 (1973)* in *'UNTS 1/12951'*; *International Sugar Agreement, 1977 (1977)* in *'UNTS 1/16200'*; *International Sugar Agreement, 1984 (1984)*; *International Sugar Agreement, 1987 (ISA, 1987)*; *International Sugar Agreement, 1992 (1992)*. **Aims** Ensure enhanced international cooperation in connection with world sugar matters and related issues; provide a forum for intergovernmental consultations on sugar and on ways to improve the world sugar economy; facilitate trade by collecting and providing information on the world sugar market and other *sweeteners*; encourage increased demand for sugar, particularly for non-traditional uses. **Structure** International Sugar Council (meets twice a year); Administrative Committee; Market Evaluation, Consumption and Statistics Committee (MECAS). **Languages** English, French, Russian, Spanish. **Staff** 10.00 FTE, paid. **Finance** Sources: government support. Annual budget: 1,000,000 GBP. **Activities** Events/meetings; knowledge management/information dissemination; management of treaties and agreements. Manages the following treaties/agreements: *International Sugar Agreement, 1953 (1953)*; *International Sugar Agreement, 1973 (1973)*; *International Sugar Agreement, 1977 (1977)*; *International Sugar Agreement, 1984 (1984)*; *International Sugar Agreement, 1987 (ISA, 1987)*; *International Sugar Agreement, 1992 (1992)*. **Events** *Joint Conference* Moscow (Russia) 2021, *Annual Seminar* London (UK) 2020, *Joint Conference* Moscow (Russia) 2020, *Annual Seminar* London (UK) 2019, *Annual Seminar* London (UK) 2018. **Publications** *Market Report and Press Summary* (12 a year); *Statistical Bulletin* (12 a year); *Quarterly Market Outlook* (4 a year); *Sugar YearBook* (annual). Studies; proceedings of seminars and workshops.
Members 87 member countries, representing 87% of world sugar production, 68% of world sugar consumption, 90% of world exports and 40% of world imports. Governments of 59 countries and the European Community, with its 28 member countries, 87 countries in all:
Argentina, Australia, Austria, Barbados, Belarus, Belgium, Belize, Brazil, Bulgaria, Cameroon, Chad, Colombia, Congo Brazzaville, Costa Rica, Côte d'Ivoire, Croatia, Cuba, Cyprus, Czechia, Denmark, Dominican Rep, Ecuador, Egypt, El Salvador, Estonia, Eswatini, Ethiopia, Fiji, Finland, France, Germany, Ghana, Greece, Guatemala, Guyana, Honduras, Hungary, India, Indonesia, Iran Islamic Rep, Ireland, Italy, Jamaica, Kenya, Korea Rep, Latvia, Lithuania, Luxembourg, Madagascar, Malawi, Malta, Mauritius, Mexico, Moldova, Morocco, Mozambique, Netherlands, Nicaragua, Nigeria, Pakistan, Panama, Paraguay, Philippines, Poland, Portugal, Romania, Russia, Serbia, Slovakia, Slovenia, South Africa, Spain, Sri Lanka, Sudan, Sweden, Switzerland, Tanzania UR, Thailand, Tunisia, Türkiye, Uganda, UK, Ukraine, United Arab Emirates, Vietnam, Zambia, Zimbabwe.

Regional integration EU entity (1):
European Union (EU, #08967).
IGO Relations Cooperates with (2): *FAO (#09260)*; *UNCTAD (#20285).* [2022.10.11/XB2606/**B***]

♦ International Sugar Union (inactive)

♦ International Sumo Federation (IFS) 15624

SG 1-15-20 Hyakuninchó, Shinjuku-ku, Tokyo, 169-0073 Japan. T. +81333603911. Fax +81333604020. E-mail: office2@ifs-sumo.org.
URL: http://www.ifs-sumo.org/

History 10 Dec 1992. **Aims** Promote and advance the sport of sumo *wrestling*. **Structure** General Assembly (annual); Board of Directors; Continental federations (5): *African Sumo Union (#00477)*; *Asian Sumo Federation (#01762)*; *European Sumo Federation (ESF, #08855)*; Oceanian; Pan American. Committees (8). **Languages** English, Japanese. **Finance** Sources: members' dues. **Activities** Sporting activities.
Members National federations in 92 countries and territories:
Algeria, Argentina, Armenia, Australia, Austria, Belarus, Bosnia-Herzegovina, Brazil, Bulgaria, Cameroon, Canada, Chile, China, Colombia, Congo Brazzaville, Côte d'Ivoire, Croatia, Cuba, Czechia, Denmark, Dominican Rep, Egypt, Estonia, Fiji, Finland, France, Georgia, Germany, Haiti, Hong Kong, Hungary, Iceland, India, Indonesia, Iran Islamic Rep, Israel, Italy, Jamaica, Japan, Kazakhstan, Kenya, Kiribati, Korea Rep, Kyrgyzstan, Lithuania, Madagascar, Malaysia, Mali, Mauritius, Mexico, Moldova, Mongolia, Montenegro, Nepal, Netherlands, New Zealand, Nigeria, North Macedonia, Norway, Pakistan, Paraguay, Philippines, Poland, Portugal, Puerto Rico, Romania, Russia, Samoa, Senegal, Serbia, Slovakia, Slovenia, South Africa, Sri Lanka, Sweden, Switzerland, Syrian AR, Taiwan, Tajikistan, Thailand, Togo, Tonga, Türkiye, Turkmenistan, Uganda, UK, Ukraine, Uruguay, USA, Uzbekistan, Vietnam, Zimbabwe.
NGO Relations Member of (3): *Association of the IOC Recognized International Sports Federations (ARISF, #02767)*; *International World Games Association (IWGA, #15914)*; *Olympic Movement (#17719)*. Recognized by: *International Olympic Committee (IOC, #14408).* [2022/XC0091/**C**]

♦ International Sunday Observance Federation (inactive)
♦ International Sunfish Class Association (see: #21760)

♦ International Sunflower Association (ISA) 15625

Association internationale du tournesol (AIT)
Main Office 11 rue de Monceau, CS 60003, 75378 Paris CEDEX 8, France. E-mail: contact@isasunflower.org.
URL: http://isasunflower.org

History 1993, Paris (France). Current constitution adopted 5 Jun 2000, Paris. Registration: France. **Aims** Develop research and development of sunflower; improve international cooperation on the *agronomic*, technical and nutritional levels; promote sunflower research and development by: improving international cooperation in the study of agronomic, technical and nutritional problems; exchange of views; dissemination of results. **Structure** General Assembly (every 2 years); Board of Directors; Executive Committee; Secretariat; Commissions; Committees; Working Groups. **Languages** English. **Finance** Members' dues. Other sources: sponsors; donations; legacies; grants. **Activities** Events/meetings. **Events** *International Sunflower Conference* Novi Sad (Serbia) 2022, *Conference* Novi Sad (Serbia) 2021, *Conference* Novi Sad (Serbia) 2020, *Symposium on Broomrape* Bucharest (Romania) 2018, *Symposium on Sunflower and Climate Change* Toulouse (France) 2018. **Publications** *ISA Newsletter*. Conference and symposium proceedings.
Members Active Members; Individuals (about 180) in 27 countries:
Argentina, Australia, Austria, Belgium, Bulgaria, Canada, China, Czechia, Finland, France, Germany, Hungary, India, Italy, Moldova, Morocco, Nigeria, Romania, Russia, Serbia, South Africa, Spain, Türkiye, Uganda, UK, Ukraine, USA. [2022/XD8569/v/**D**]

♦ International Super-Cricket Committee (ISCC) 15626

Headquarters Office 512, Parsvnath Planet Plaza, TCG – 8/8 and 9/9 Vibhuti Khand, Gomti Nagar, Lucknow, Uttar Pradesh 226010, Lucknow UTTAR PRADESH 226010, India. E-mail: info@iscc-super-cricket.org – info@non-olympic.org.
URL: http://www.iscc-super-cricket.org/

History 14 Oct 2004, India, by *International Non-Olympic Committee (INOC, #14374)*. **Aims** Promote the sport of super-cricket worldwide. **NGO Relations** Member of: *World Council for Regular and Distance Education (WCRDE, #21338).* [2008/XM0693/**E**]

♦ International Superphosphate Manufacturers' Association / see International Fertilizer Association (#13589)
♦ International Supervision, Control and Arbitration Commission (#04228)

♦ International Superyacht Society (ISS) 15627

Administrator 757 SE 17th St, Ste 744, Fort Lauderdale FL 33316, USA. T. +19545256625. Fax +19545255325. E-mail: info@superyachtsociety.org.
URL: http://superyachtsociety.org/

History 1989. **Aims** Ensure sustainability and excellence in the global yachting industry. **Structure** Board. **Activities** Awards/prizes/competitions; events/meetings; training/education. **Events** *Asia Pacific Superyacht Conference* Singapore (Singapore) 2019, *Asia Pacific Superyacht Conference* Singapore (Singapore) 2018. **Publications** *ISS Newsletter*. **NGO Relations** *Professional Yachting Association (PYA, #18519).* [2015.08.10/XJ9873/**C**]

♦ International Supporting Association for War Victims (internationally oriented national body)

♦ International Support Vessel Owners' Association (ISOA) 15628

Sec Walsingham House, 35 Seething Lane, London, EC3N 4AH, UK. E-mail: isoa@isoaoffshore.org.
URL: https://www.isoaoffshore.org/

History 1985. **Aims** Act as focus point for international operators of supply vessels in the offshore industry. **Structure** Executive Committee; General Membership. **Languages** English. **Staff** 1.00 FTE, paid. **Finance** Sources: members' dues.
Members Full in 13 countries:
Australia, Brazil, Canada, Denmark, France, India, Italy, Netherlands, Norway, Singapore, UK, United Arab Emirates, USA.
NGO Relations Secretariat serviced by: *International Chamber of Shipping (ICS, #12535)* (Marisec); [2022.10.18/XD1336/**D**]

♦ International Surety Association (ISA) 15629

Exec Dir/Sec 6299 Airport Road, Suite 709, Mississauga ON L4V 1N3, Canada. T. +19056771353. E-mail: sness@suretycanada.com – surety@suretycanada.com.
URL: http://www.suretyinternational.org/

History 1 Feb 2000, London (UK). Founded by *International Credit Insurance & Surety Association (ICISA, #13103)*, the Surety and Fidelity Association of America (SFAA) and national surety associations of Australia, Canada and Mexico. *Panamerican Surety Association (PASA, #18134)* joined in 2018. Registration: Swiss Civil Code, Switzerland. **Aims** Promote acceptance and development of surety products worldwide. **Languages** English. **Activities** Events/meetings. **Events** *Meeting* Washington, DC (USA) 2019, *Meeting* Stockholm (Sweden) 2018, *Meeting* Lisbon (Portugal) 2017, *Meeting* Tel Aviv (Israel) 2016, *Meeting* Toronto, ON (Canada) 2015.
Members National associations in 4 countries:
Australia, Canada, Mexico, USA.
International organizations:
International Credit Insurance & Surety Association (ICISA, #13103); *Panamerican Surety Association (PASA, #18134).* [2022.05.10/XD7931/**D**]

♦ International Surfing Association (ISA) 15630

Main Office 5726 La Jolla Blvd, La Jolla CA 92037, USA. T. +18585518580. Fax +18585518563. E-mail: info@isasurf.org.
URL: http://www.isasurf.org/

History Nov 1976, Hawaii (USA). Successor to *International Surfing Federation (ISF)*, set up 1964, Sydney (Australia), at 1st World Surfing Championships. **Aims** Promote the interests of surfing in all its forms; bring together surfing and bodyboarding nations to compete at international level and to agree rules and regulations on matters concerning international surfing; represent surfing within international *sport* organizations; organize championships and competitions. **Structure** Executive Committee. **Languages** English, French, Portuguese, Spanish. **Staff** 3.00 FTE, paid. **Finance** Sources: members' dues; sponsorship. Other sources: grants from IOC; sanction fees. **Activities** Sporting activities. **Events** *General Meeting* Puntarenas (Costa Rica) 2009, *Biennial general Meeting / General Meeting* Costa da Caparica (Portugal) 2008, *General Meeting* Costa da Caparica (Portugal) 2007, *Annual General Meeting* 2006, *General Meeting* Huntington Beach, CA (USA) 2006. **Publications** *World Surfing News* (12 a year); *ISA Guide* (annual).
Members National governing bodies for surfing and bodyboarding (only one member per country/territory) in 54 countries and territories:
Argentina, Aruba, Australia, Austria, Bahamas, Barbados, Brazil, Bulgaria, Canada, Cape Verde, Chile, Colombia, Costa Rica, Dominican Rep, Ecuador, El Salvador, Fiji, France, Germany, Guam, Guatemala, Hawaii, India, Indonesia, Ireland, Israel, Italy, Jamaica, Japan, Korea Rep, Maldives, Mexico, Morocco, Namibia, Netherlands, New Zealand, Panama, Papua New Guinea, Peru, Philippines, Portugal, Puerto Rico, Senegal, Somalia, South Africa, Spain, Sweden, Switzerland, Tahiti Is, Trinidad-Tobago, UK, Uruguay, USA, Venezuela.
NGO Relations Member of (4): *Association of Summer Olympic International Federations (ASOIF, #02943)* (Associate); *Association of the IOC Recognized International Sports Federations (ARISF, #02767)*; *International World Games Association (IWGA, #15914)*; *Olympic Movement (#17719)*. Cooperates with (1): *International Testing Agency (ITA, #15678)*. Recognized by: *International Olympic Committee (IOC, #14408).* [2020/XD9165/**C**]

♦ International Surfing League (ISL) 15631

Address not obtained.

History 1940, Palm Beach FL (USA), as *International Professional Surfing Federation (IPSF)*. Registered in accordance with laws of the United States. Current financially reconstituted. To be incorporated in the State of Delaware (USA). **Aims** Provide annual salaries to new professional surfers. **Structure** Executive, comprising Commissioner of Surfing, Chaplain of Surfing, Chairman, CEO, President, General Council and Athlete Council. Board of Governors, including Chairman, Vice Chairman and Secretary-Treasurer. Amalgamated *International Surfing Federation (ISF, inactive)*. **Languages** English, French, Spanish. **Staff** 78.00 FTE, paid. **Finance** Members' dues. Other sources: sponsors; sanction fees; publication sales; contributions; grants; licensing of logos. **Activities** Functions as the international representative of 27 surfing events; competes in the 3 stellar Watersurfing events (Standup Surfing; Sailsurfing; Boatsurfing) and the stellar Snowsurfing events (Snowsurfing; Snowpipeing; Snowcrossing). Organizes Major and Minor League Games. **Events** *Annual meeting* Tokyo (Japan) 2008, *Annual meeting* Christchurch (New Zealand) 2007, *Annual meeting* Vancouver, BC (Canada) 2006, *Annual meeting* Mazatlan, SIN (Mexico) 2005, *Annual meeting* Perth, WA (Australia) 2004. **Publications** *Surfsports International* – newsletter. *ISL Icons*; *ISL International Surfing*; *ISL Surfing USA*; *Riding High*; *World Surfing*. Catalog; calendar; cards; books.
Members National ISL Committees grouping registered athletes (118,689,113 individuals) in 172 countries and territories:
Afghanistan, Albania, Algeria, Andorra, Angola, Antigua-Barbuda, Argentina, Armenia, Australia, Austria, Azerbaijan, Bahamas, Bahrain, Bangladesh, Barbados, Belarus, Belgium, Belize, Benin, Bermuda, Bhutan, Bolivia, Bosnia-Herzegovina, Botswana, Brazil, Brunei Darussalam, Bulgaria, Burkina Faso, Burundi, Cambodia, Cameroon, Canada, Cape Verde, Cayman Is, Central African Rep, Chile, China, Colombia, Comoros, Costa Rica, Côte d'Ivoire, Croatia, Cuba, Cyprus, Czechia, Denmark, Djibouti, Dominica, Dominican Rep, Ecuador, Egypt, El Salvador, Estonia, Fiji, Finland, France, Gabon, Georgia, Germany, Ghana, Greece, Greenland, Grenada, Guam, Guatemala, Guinea, Guinea-Bissau, Guyana, Haiti, Honduras, Hong Kong, Hungary, Iceland, India, Indonesia, Ireland, Israel, Italy, Jamaica, Japan, Jordan, Kazakhstan, Kenya, Kiribati, Korea Rep, Kuwait, Kyrgyzstan, Latvia, Lebanon, Lesotho, Liberia, Liechtenstein, Lithuania, Luxembourg, Madagascar, Malawi, Malaysia, Maldives, Mali, Malta, Mauritania, Mauritius, Mexico, Micronesia FS, Moldova, Monaco, Mongolia, Morocco, Mozambique, Myanmar, Namibia, Nepal, Netherlands, New Zealand, Nicaragua, Niger, Nigeria, Norway, Oman, Pakistan, Palestine, Panama, Papua New Guinea, Paraguay, Peru, Philippines, Poland, Portugal, Puerto Rico, Qatar, Romania, Russia, Samoa, San Marino, Sao Tomé-Principe, Saudi Arabia, Senegal, Serbia, Seychelles, Singapore, Slovakia, Slovenia, Solomon Is, South Africa, Spain, Sri Lanka, St Kitts-Nevis, St Lucia, Sweden, Switzerland, Tahiti Is, Taiwan, Tajikistan, Thailand, Tonga, Trinidad-Tobago, Tunisia, Türkiye, Turkmenistan, Tuvalu, Uganda, UK, Ukraine, Uruguay, USA, Uzbekistan, Vanuatu, Venezuela, Vietnam, Virgin Is USA, Zambia, Zimbabwe.
NGO Relations Instrumental in setting up a number of national, regional and world leagues, now merged into the ISL. [2011.06.01/XC7900/y/**F**]

♦ International Surgical Club / see International Association of Surgeons, Gastroenterologists and Oncologists (#12216)

♦ International Surgical Group (ISG) 15632

Secretariat address not obtained. E-mail: info@internationalsurgicalgroup.org.
URL: http://www.internationalsurgicalgroup.org/

History Inaugural meeting held Jul 1958, Edinburgh (UK). **Activities** Events/meetings. **Events** *Annual Meeting* Los Angeles, CA (USA) 2019, *Annual Meeting* Reykjavik (Iceland) 2018, *Annual Meeting* Johannesburg (South Africa) 2017, *Annual Meeting* Edinburgh (UK) 2016, *Annual Meeting* Helsinki (Finland) 1997.
Members on invitation only. Senior; Active; Honorary. Individuals in 26 countries:
Argentina, Australia, Belgium, Brazil, Canada, China, Denmark, Finland, France, Germany, Greece, Iceland, Ireland, Italy, Japan, Netherlands, New Zealand, Norway, Poland, South Africa, Spain, Sweden, Switzerland, Türkiye, UK, USA. [2018/XN8138/cv/**C**]

♦ International Survey Centre (internationally oriented national body)

♦ International Suspected Perioperative Allergic Reaction Group (ISPAR) 15633

Administration Room 8-30 Clinical Sciences Bldg, St James's Univ Hosp, Leeds, LS9 7JF, UK. T. +441132065274. E-mail: admin@perioperativeallergy.com.
URL: https://perioperativeallergy.com/

History Proposed 2019. **Aims** Improve treatment of perioperative allergy; improve investigation of perioperative allergy; generate evidence; better serve the patients who experience perioperative allergy; reduce the incidence of perioperative allergy. **Structure** Development Team. **Events** *Annual Meeting* Leeds (UK) 2022, *Annual Meeting* 2021. **NGO Relations** Partner of (1): *European Academy of Allergy and Clinical Immunology (EAACI, #05779)*. Specialty society of: *European Society of Anaesthesiology and Intensive Care (ESAIC, #08518)*. Also links with national organizations. [2021/AA1332/v/**C**]

♦ International Sustainability and Carbon Certification (internationally oriented national body)

♦ International Sustainability Standards Board (ISSB) 15634

Contact Opernplatz 14, 60313 Frankfurt-Main, Germany. E-mail: info@ifrs.org.
URL: https://www.ifrs.org/groups/international-sustainability-standards-board/

History 2021. Founded by *International Financial Reporting Standards Foundation (IFRS Foundation, #13603)*. **Aims** Deliver a comprehensive global baseline of sustainability-related disclosure standards that provide investors and other capital market participants with information about companies' sustainability-related risks and opportunities to help them make informed decisions. **Structure** Board. **Events** *Meeting* Frankfurt-Main (Germany) 2022. [2022/AA2882/**E**]

♦ International Sustainable Campus Network (ISCN) 15635

Co-Exec Dir c/o EPFL Sustainability, Bâtiment BS 101, Station 4, 1015 Lausanne VD, Switzerland. E-mail: iscn2020@epfl.ch.
URL: http://www.international-sustainable-campus-network.org/

History Jan 2007. **Aims** Provide a global forum to support leading colleges, universities, and corporate campuses in the exchange of information, ideas, and best practices for achieving sustainable campus operations and integrating sustainability in research and teaching. **Structure** Steering Committee. **Activities** Awards/prizes/competitions; events/meetings. **Events** *Conference* Lausanne (Switzerland) 2022, *Conference* Lausanne (Switzerland) 2021, *Conference* Lausanne (Switzerland) 2020, *Conference* Sao Paulo (Brazil) 2019, *Conference* Stockholm (Sweden) 2018.
Members Higher education institutes in 22 countries and territories:
Australia, Canada, China, Colombia, Cyprus, Denmark, France, Hong Kong, India, Italy, Japan, Luxembourg, Malaysia, Mexico, Netherlands, Peru, South Africa, Sweden, Switzerland, UK, USA, Vietnam.
NGO Relations *Nordic Sustainable Campus Network (NSCN, #17440).* [2020/XJ7902/**C**]

♦ International Sustainable Community Assistance (internationally oriented national body)
♦ International Sustainable Development Foundation (internationally oriented national body)
♦ International Sustainable Development Research Conference / see International Sustainable Development Research Society (#15636)

♦ International Sustainable Development Research Society (ISDRS) . 15636

Pres c/o Hull Univ, Cottingham Road, Hull, HU6 7RX, UK. E-mail: assistant@isdrs.org.
Vice Pres c/o Södertörn Univ, Alfred Nobels Allé 7, Flemingsberg, SE-141 89 Huddinge, Sweden. T. +46722372282. E-mail: vicepresident@isdrs.org.
URL: http://www.isdrs.org/

History 2005, Helsinki (Finland), on the initiative of Richard Welford and Jouni Korhonen, building on the work of the series *International Sustainable Development Research Conference*. Formally launched 2006. **Aims** Link researchers in academia and implementation practice from all continents to achieve a fair and clean sustainable society. **Structure** Board; Executive Committee. **Languages** English. **Finance** Members' dues. **Activities** Research/documentation; knowledge management/information dissemination; training/education; networking/liaising; events/meetings. **Events** *Annual Conference* Stockholm (Sweden) 2022, *Annual Conference* Sundsvall (Sweden) 2021, *Annual Conference* Budapest (Hungary) 2020, *Annual Conference* Nanjing (China) 2019, *Annual Conference* Messina (Italy) 2018. **Publications** *ISDRS Newsletter* (4 a year). **Members** Individuals (about 2,500). Membership countries not specified. [2019.04.24/XJ8083/**D**]

♦ International Sustainable Energy Organization (inactive)

♦ International Suzuki Association (ISA) 15637

CEO PO Box 21065, New York NY 10023-7910, USA. T. +12122625005. E-mail: info@internationalsuzuki.org.
URL: http://www.internationalsuzuki.org/

History 1983, Dallas TX (USA). *'Suzuki Method'* based on the "Mother Tongue Method" principle that all children possess ability which can be developed and enhanced through a nurturing environment, furthermore, all children learn to speak their own language with relative ease and if the same natural learning process is applied in teaching other skills, these can be acquired as successfully. **Aims** Encourage, promote, enlarge and coordinate the *'Suzuki Method'* throughout the world; serve as a coordination centre; protect the "Suzuki" name and rights. **Structure** Board of Directors; Instrument Committees. **Languages** English. **Staff** 0.50 FTE, paid. Voluntary. **Finance** Members' dues. General contributions. Annual budget: about US$ 70,000. **Activities** Events/meetings. **Events** *Biennial Suzuki Method World Convention / World Convention* Matsumoto (Japan) 2013, *Suzuki method world convention* Melbourne, VIC (Australia) 2009, *Biennial Suzuki method world convention* Turin (Italy) 2006, *Asia conference* Taiwan 2004, *World Convention* USA 2001. **Publications** *International Suzuki Journal* – online.
Members Regional organizations (5), each with national association members representing 8,000 – 10,000 teacher members:
Asia Region SUZUKI Association (ARSA, #02086); *European Suzuki Association (ESA, #08867)*; *Pan Pacific Suzuki Association (PPSA)*; *Suzuki Association of the Americas (SAA)*; Talent Education Research Institute (TERI). [2018.09.05/XE2298/y/**E**]

♦ International Swap Dealers Association / see International Swaps and Derivatives Association (#15638)

♦ International Swaps and Derivatives Association (ISDA) 15638

CEO 360 Madison Ave, 16th Fl, New York NY 10017, USA. T. +12129016000. Fax +12129016001. E-mail: isda@isda.org.
European Office One Bishops Square, London, E1 6AD, UK. E-mail: isdaeurope@isda.org.
URL: http://www.isda.org/

History 1985, when chartered in the USA. Originally referred to as *International Swap Dealers Association*. EU Transparency Register: 46643241096-93. **Aims** Promote sound *risk* management practices and processes; engage constructively with policymakers and legislators around the world to advance understanding and treatment of derivatives as a risk management tool. **Structure** Board of Directors; Main office in New York NY (USA), headed by Executive Director/Chief Executive Officer. Offices in London (UK), Hong Kong, Singapore and Tokyo (Japan). Committees (13). **Languages** English, French, German, Japanese, Spanish. **Staff** 27.00 FTE, paid. **Finance** Sources: meeting proceeds; members' dues; sale of publications. **Activities** Events/meetings; knowledge management/information dissemination; research/documentation. **Events** *Annual General Meeting* Chicago, IL (USA) 2023, *Annual General Meeting* Madrid (Spain) 2022, *Annual General Meeting* 2021, *Annual General Meeting* Hong Kong (Hong Kong) 2019, *Symposium* Tokyo (Japan) 2019. **Publications** *ISDA Master Agreement. ISDA Guides*; *ISDA Statements. ISDA Definitions* (1991) – supplement 2000; *1998 FX and Currency Option Definitions* – with annexes. Standard form contracts; master agreements; amendments to master agreements; bond option documentation; municipal transactions documentation. **Members** Primary; Associate; Subscriber. Over 900 member institutions in 71 countries and territories. Membership countries not specified. [2020/XD3562/y/**C**]

♦ International SWAT4LS Workshop (meeting series)

♦ International Sweeteners Association (ISA) 15639

Association Internationale pour les Edulcorants (AIE) – Internationaler Süsstoff-Verband (ISV)
SG Av de Tervueren 13 A, Bte 7, 1040 Brussels, Belgium. T. +3227365354. Fax +3227323427. E-mail: admin@isasecretariat.org.
URL: http://www.sweeteners.org/

History 1972. Statutes modified June 2012; Jun 2014. Registration: No/ID: 0424.301.259, Start date: 26 Jul 1983, Belgium; EU Transparency Register, No/ID: 11667896576-60, Start date: 5 Sep 2011. **Aims** Promote introduction, growth and development of safe, calorie-free or low-calorie sweeteners. **Structure** General Assembly (annual); Board of Directors; Executive Committee; Committees (2); Ad hoc Working Groups. **Languages** English. **Staff** None. **Finance** Sources: members' dues. **Events** *Conference* London (UK) 2018, *Conference* Brussels (Belgium) 2014, *Meeting on Aspartame* Brussels (Belgium) 2011, *World conference on low-calories sweeteners* Barcelona (Spain) 1999, *Annual conference* Lisbon (Portugal) 1992.
Members Companies and associations (19) in 10 countries and territories:
Belgium, China, France, Germany, Italy, Netherlands, Switzerland, Taiwan, UK, USA.
IGO Relations Participates as observer in the activities of: *Codex Alimentarius Commission (CAC, #04081)*.
NGO Relations Member of (1): *EU Specialty Food Ingredients (#09200)*. Cooperates with (1): *International Chewing Gum Association (ICGA, #12545)*. [2021.06.25/XD1793/**D**]

♦ International Swimming Federation / see World Aquatics (#21100)
♦ International Swimming Statisticians Association (inactive)

♦ International Symbiosis Society (ISS) 15640

Communications Officer address not obtained.
Pres address not obtained.
URL: http://www.iss-symbiosis.org/

History 15 Apr 1997, Woods Hole, MA (USA). Founded at 2nd International Symbiosis Congress. **Aims** Promote and advance the science of *symbiology*. **Events** *International Congress* Lyon (France) 2022, *Triennial Congress* Corvallis, OR (USA) 2018, *Triennial Congress* Lisbon (Portugal) 2015, *Triennial Congress* Krakow (Poland) 2012, *Triennial congress* Madison, WI (USA) 2009. **Publications** *Symbiosis International Journal*; *Symbiosis News*.
Members Members in 20 countries:
Belgium, Canada, Czechia, Egypt, Finland, France, Germany, India, Israel, Italy, Japan, New Zealand, Panama, Portugal, Russia, Spain, Sweden, Switzerland, Thailand, USA. [2022/XF6528/**F**]

♦ International Symmetry Association (ISA) 15641

Mailing Address c/o Symmetrion, 29 Eötvös St, Budapest 1067, Hungary. E-mail: sym@freemail.hu.
CEO University of Mining and Geology St. Ivan Rilski, 1700 Sofia, Bulgaria.
URL: http://symmetry.hu/

History 17 Aug 2003, Budapest (Hungary). **Aims** Bring together artists, scientists, engineers, designers, educators and students devoted to, or interested in, research and understanding of the concept and application of symmetry, asymmetry and dissymmetry; provide regular information to the general public about developments and events in symmetrology; ensure regular fora for all interested in the field. **Structure** Assembly; Executive Board; Advisory Board; Board of Electors; Discussion Groups (7); Headquarters in Budapest (Hungary). **Languages** English. **Staff** Voluntary. **Finance** No budget. **Activities** Events/meetings; training/education. Organizes the Symmetry Festival. **Events** *Symmetry Festival* Pécs (Hungary) 2023, *Symmetry Festival* Sofia (Bulgaria) 2021, *Symmetry Festival* Vienna (Austria) 2016, *Symmetry Festival* Delft (Netherlands) 2013, *Symmetry Festival* 2009. **Publications** Symposium proceedings; volumes of essays; text books and teaching aids; exhibition catalogues. Information Services: Ensures publishing in printed and electronic forms, including maintenance of website and interactive internet facilities.
Members Honorary; Ordinary – scientists, artists, educators and other specialists engaged in research or application of any field of symmetrology; Student; Corporate – institutions and associations. Members in 55 countries and territories:
Algeria, Armenia, Australia, Austria, Azerbaijan, Belarus, Belgium, Brazil, Bulgaria, Canada, China, Croatia, Czechia, Denmark, Estonia, Eswatini, Finland, France, Germany, Greece, Hungary, India, Indonesia, Iran Islamic Rep, Ireland, Israel, Italy, Japan, Kazakhstan, Korea Rep, Luxembourg, Mexico, Morocco, Mozambique, Netherlands, Norway, Oman, Philippines, Poland, Portugal, Romania, Russia, Serbia, Slovakia, Slovenia, South Africa, Spain, Sweden, Switzerland, Taiwan, Türkiye, UK, Ukraine, United Arab Emirates, USA.
NGO Relations Instrumental in setting up: *SYMMETRION (inactive)*. [2023/XC0014/**C**]

♦ International Symmetry Society / see International Society for the Interdisciplinary Study of Symmetry (#15210)
♦ International Symposium on Advanced Display Materials and Devices (meeting series)
♦ International Symposium on Advanced Material Research (meeting series)
♦ International Symposium on Advanced Organic Photonics (meeting series)
♦ International Symposium on Advances in Chromatography (meeting series)
♦ International Symposium on Advances in Technology Education (meeting series)
♦ International Symposium on the Aerodynamics, Ventilation and Fire in Tunnels (meeting series)
♦ International Symposium of Agrochimica (meeting series)
♦ International Symposium on Algorithms and Computation (meeting series)
♦ International Symposium on Analytical and Applied Pyrolysis (meeting series)
♦ International Symposium on Applied Bioinorganic Chemistry (meeting series)
♦ International Symposium on Archaeometry (meeting series)
♦ International Symposium on Arctic Geology (meeting series)
♦ International Symposium on Atomic Level Characterizations for New Materials and Devices (meeting series)
♦ International Symposium on Audit Research (meeting series)
♦ International Symposium on Avian Endocrinology (meeting series)
♦ International Symposium on Avian Viral Respiratory Diseases (meeting series)
♦ International Symposium on Bilingualism (meeting series)
♦ International Symposium on Biomechanics and Medicine in Swimming (meeting series)
♦ International Symposium on Biomechanics in Vascular Biology and Cardiovascular Disease (meeting series)
♦ International Symposium on Bioorganometallic Chemistry (meeting series)
♦ International Symposium on Boron, Borides and Related Materials (meeting series)
♦ International Symposium on Cable Dynamics (meeting series)
♦ International Symposium on Canine and Feline Reproduction (meeting series)
♦ International Symposium on Capture Gamma-Ray Spectroscopy and Related Topics (meeting series)
♦ International Symposium on Catalysis and Fine Chemicals (meeting series)
♦ International Symposium on Cerebral Impedance (meeting series)
♦ International Symposium Chemical Reaction Engineering (meeting series)
♦ International Symposium on Childhood, Adolescent and Young Adult Non-Hodgkin Lymphoma (meeting series)
♦ International Symposium of Child Neurology (meeting series)
♦ International Symposium on Chinese Language and Discourse (meeting series)
♦ International Symposium on Chirality (meeting series)
♦ International Symposium on Chlamydial Infections (meeting series)
♦ International Symposium on Chromatography (meeting series)
♦ International Symposium on Clinical Enzymology (meeting series)
♦ International Symposium on Clinical Nutrition (meeting series)
♦ International Symposium on Combinatorial Optimization (meeting series)
♦ International Symposium on Combustion Processes (meeting series)
♦ International Symposium on Compound Semiconductors (meeting series)
♦ International Symposium on Computer and Information Sciences (meeting series)
♦ International Symposium on Computer Music Multidisciplinary Research (meeting series)
♦ International Symposium on Concrete and Structures for Next Generation (meeting series)
♦ International Symposium on Controversies in Psychiatry (meeting series)
♦ International Symposium on Critical Bleeding (meeting series)
♦ International Symposium on Crop Protection (meeting series)
♦ International Symposium on Cutting Edge of Computer Simulation of Solidification, Casting and Refining (meeting series)
♦ International Symposium on Defects and Material Mechanisms (meeting series)
♦ International Symposium on Developmental Disabilities (meeting series)
♦ International Symposium on Diabetes, Hypertension, Metabolic Syndrome and Pregnancy (meeting series)
♦ International Symposium on Diffraction Structural Biology (meeting series)
♦ International Symposium on Digestive Physiology of Pigs (meeting series)
♦ International Symposium on Dredging Technology (meeting series)
♦ International Symposium on Dry Process (meeting series)
♦ International Symposium on Dynamics and Aerodynamics of Cables (meeting series)
♦ International Symposium on Ecological Networks (meeting series)
♦ International Symposium on Econometric Theory and Applications (meeting series)
♦ International Symposium on Education and Psychology (meeting series)
♦ International Symposium on Education and Social Sciences (meeting series)
♦ International Symposium on the Effects of Radiation on Structural Materials (meeting series)
♦ International Symposium on Electrocatalysis (meeting series)
♦ International Symposium on Electrokinetic Remediation (meeting series)
♦ International Symposium on Electroseparation and Liquid Phase-Separation Techniques (meeting series)
♦ International Symposium on Emerging Technologies for Education (meeting series)
♦ International Symposium on Endoscopic Ultrasonography (meeting series)
♦ International Symposium on Environmental Geochemistry (meeting series)
♦ International Symposium on Environmental Issues and Waste Management in Energy and Minerals Production (meeting series)
♦ International Symposium on Environmentally Conscious Design and Inverse Manufacturing (meeting series)
♦ International Symposium on Environmental Sociology in East Asia (meeting series)
♦ International Symposium on Epidemiology and Control of Salmonella and Other Foodborne Pathogens of Pork (meeting series)
♦ International Symposium on Equine Reproduction (meeting series)
♦ International Symposium on Essential Oils (meeting series)
♦ International Symposium on Feedstock Recycling of Polymeric Materials (meeting series)
♦ International Symposium on Field- and Flow-Based Separations (meeting series)
♦ International Symposium on Finite Element Methods in Flow Problems (meeting series)

- ♦ International Symposium on Fish Nutrition and Feeding (meeting series)
- ♦ International Symposium for Fish Parasitology (meeting series)
- ♦ International Symposium on Flavins & Flavoproteins (meeting series)
- ♦ International Symposium on Flow Visualization (meeting series)
- ♦ International Symposium on Fluorine Chemistry (meeting series)
- ♦ International Symposium on Foundations and Practice of Security (meeting series)
- ♦ International Symposium on Frontiers of Combining Systems (meeting series)
- ♦ International Symposium on Functional Equations (meeting series)
- ♦ International Symposium on Functionally Graded Materials (meeting series)
- ♦ International Symposium on Functional Materials (meeting series)
- ♦ International Symposium of Functional Neuroceptor Mapping of the Living Brain (meeting series)
- ♦ International Symposium on Fundamentals of Computation Theory (meeting series)
- ♦ International Symposium on Future Active Safety Technology toward zero-traffic-accident (meeting series)
- ♦ International Symposium on Geometric Function Theory and Applications (meeting series)
- ♦ International Symposium on GNSS (meeting series)
- ♦ International Symposium on Hearing (meeting series)
- ♦ International Symposium on Heating, Ventilation and Air Conditioning (meeting series)
- ♦ International Symposium on Hepatitis C Virus and Related Viruses (meeting series)
- ♦ International Symposium on Highly-Efficient Accelerators and Reconfigurable Technologies (meeting series)
- ♦ International Symposium on High Performance Liquid Phase Separations and Related Techniques (meeting series)
- ♦ International Symposium on HIV and Hepatitis (meeting series)
- ♦ International Symposium on Homogeneous Catalysis (meeting series)

♦ International Symposium on Human Factors in Telecommunications (HFT) 15642

Colloque international sur les facteurs humains dans les télécommunications

Chairman c/o Vonniman Consulting, Dalen 13, SE-132 45 Saltsjö-Boo, Sweden. T. +46733661234.
URL: http://www.hft.org/

History 1961, Cambridge (UK). **Aims** Provide an international forum to human factors experts and other professionals to exchange information, views and experiences in research and the application of excellent human factors, usability, accessibility and user experience principles in telecommunication, including information and communication technology equipment and services. **Structure** Permanent Steering Committee, comprising Chairman and 9 members. Symposia organized by National Organizing Committee for each symposium. **Languages** English. **Staff** None. **Finance** Conference fees; sponsorship. **Activities** Participating experts come from telecommunication administrations, service providers and manufacturers, and from related research and development organizations. **Events** *Biennial Symposium* Berlin (Germany) 2013, *Symposium / Biennial Symposium* Kuala Lumpur (Malaysia) 2008, *Biennial Symposium* France 2006, *Symposium* Sophia Antipolis (France) 2006, *Symposium / Biennial Symposium* Berlin (Germany) 2003. **Publications** Symposium proceedings.
Members Permanent Steering Committee members in 8 countries:
Austria, France, Germany, Netherlands, Spain, Sweden, UK, USA. [2013/XF5579/cv/**F**]

- ♦ International Symposium Hydrogen & Energy (meeting series)
- ♦ International Symposium on Hysteresis Modeling and Micromagnetics (meeting series)
- ♦ International Symposium on Image and Signal Processing and Analysis (meeting series)
- ♦ International Symposium on Imaging, Sensing, and Optical Memory (meeting series)
- ♦ International Symposium on Impact Engineering (meeting series)
- ♦ International Symposium on Impedance Methods for Brain Circulation Investigation (meeting series)
- ♦ International Symposium on Infection and Allergy of the Nose / see International Society of Inflammation and Allergy of the Nose (#15201)
- ♦ International Symposium on Innovations and Applications of Monitoring Perfusion, Oxygenation and Ventilation (meeting series)
- ♦ International Symposium on Inorganic and Environmental Materials (meeting series)
- ♦ International Symposium on Inorganic Ring Systems (meeting series)
- ♦ International Symposium on Integrative Bioinformatics (meeting series)
- ♦ International Symposium on Intensive Care and Emergency Medicine (internationally oriented national body)
- ♦ International Symposium Intra Articular Treatment (meeting series)
- ♦ International Symposium on Intracranial Pressure and Brain Monitoring (meeting series)
- ♦ International Symposium on Intrauterine Surveillance (meeting series)
- ♦ International Symposium on Ion-Atom Collisions (meeting series)
- ♦ International Symposium on Kallikreins and Kallikrein-Related Peptidases (meeting series)
- ♦ International Symposium on Laser-Aided Plasma Diagnostics (meeting series)
- ♦ International Symposium on Laser Precision Microfabrication (meeting series)
- ♦ International Symposium on Late Complications After Childhood Cancer (meeting series)
- ♦ International Symposium on Long-Term Clinical Trials (meeting series)
- ♦ International Symposium Loss Prevention and Safety Promotion in the Process Industries (meeting series)
- ♦ International Symposium on Machinery and Mechatronics for Agricultural and Biosystems Engineering (meeting series)
- ♦ International Symposium on Macrocyclic and Supramolecular Chemistry (meeting series)
- ♦ International Symposium on Magnesium (meeting series)
- ♦ International Symposium on Mechanical Design, Manufacture and Automation (meeting series)
- ♦ International Symposium for Mechanisms of Vasodilatation (meeting series)
- ♦ International Symposium on Media Innovations (meeting series)
- ♦ International Symposium on Metastable, Amorphous and Nanostructured Materials (meeting series)
- ♦ International Symposium on Microbial Sulfur Metabolism (meeting series)
- ♦ International Symposium on Microcalorimetric Applications in Biology / see International Society for Biological Calorimetry (#14963)
- ♦ International Symposium on Microwave/Terahertz Science and Applications (meeting series)
- ♦ International Symposium on Military Aspects of Blast and Shock (meeting series)
- ♦ International Symposium on Molecular Beams (meeting series)
- ♦ International Symposium on Molecular Spectroscopy (meeting series)
- ♦ International Symposium of Morphology (meeting series)
- ♦ International Symposium on Motivational and Cognitive Control (meeting series)
- ♦ International Symposium on Moyamoya Angiopathy (meeting series)
- ♦ International Symposium on Multiparticle Dynamics (meeting series)
- ♦ International Symposium on Nanomaterials and Membrane Science for Water, Energy and Environment (meeting series)
- ♦ International Symposium on Nasopharyngeal Carcinoma (meeting series)
- ♦ International Symposium on Naturally Occurring Radioactive Material (meeting series)
- ♦ International Symposium on Naval Medicine (unconfirmed)
- ♦ International Symposium on NDT in Aerospace (meeting series)
- ♦ International Symposium: Neurological Surgery of the Ear and Skull Base (meeting series)
- ♦ International Symposium on Neuroprotection and Neurorepair (meeting series)
- ♦ International Symposium on Neutron Induced Reactions (meeting series)
- ♦ International Symposium for Next Generation Infrastructure (meeting series)
- ♦ International Symposium on Nitrides (meeting series)
- ♦ International Symposium on Nitrogen Fixation with Non-Legumes (meeting series)
- ♦ International Symposium on Noise in Physical Systems (meeting series)
- ♦ International Symposium on Nonlinear Theory and its Applications (meeting series)
- ♦ International Symposium on Novel and Nano Materials (meeting series)
- ♦ International Symposium on Objective Measures in Auditory Implants (meeting series)
- ♦ International Symposium on Olefin Metathesis and Related Chemistry (meeting series)
- ♦ International Symposium on Open Collaboration (meeting series)
- ♦ International Symposium on Orthogonal Polynomials, Special Functions and Applications (meeting series)
- ♦ International Symposium PaCor – Parallel Corpora: Creations and Applications International Symposium (meeting series)
- ♦ International Symposium on Pediatric Neuro-Oncology (meeting series)
- ♦ International Symposium on Pediatric Surgical Research (meeting series)
- ♦ International Symposium on Performance Science (meeting series)
- ♦ International Symposium on Pharmaceutical and Biomedical Analysis (meeting series)
- ♦ International Symposium for Photosynthetic Prokaryotes (meeting series)
- ♦ International Symposium on Plant Lipids (meeting series)
- ♦ International Symposium on Plant Senescence (meeting series)
- ♦ International Symposium on Plant-Soil Interactions at Low PH (meeting series)

♦ International Symposium on Polymer Analysis and Characterization (ISPAC) 15643

Co-Chair Univ of Twente, MTP LA 1735, PO Box 217, 7500AE Enschede, Netherlands.
Co-Chair Tulane Physics Dept, 5068 Percival Stern Hall, New Orleans LA 70118, USA.
URL: http://ispac-conferences.org/

History 1987, Wilmington, DE (USA). Wilmington DE (USA) 1987. **Aims** Provide an international forum for the presentation of recent advances in the field of polymer analysis and characterization methodologies. **Structure** Governing Board of 14 members. **Languages** English. **Staff** Meeting arrangements by volunteer members of the Governing Board, assisted by meeting coordinators engaged part-time, paid, as needed. **Finance** Income from meetings, short courses and donations. **Activities** Organizes annual 3-day meetings with accompanying 1-day courses. **Events** *Annual Symposium* Como (Italy) 2021, *Annual Symposium* Como (Italy) 2020, *Annual Symposium* Sendai (Japan) 2019, *Annual Symposium* Bethesda, MD (USA) 2018, *Annual Symposium* Linz (Austria) 2017. **Publications** Lecture and Poster presentations at meetings; selected publications of these in the International Journal for Polymer Analysis and Characterization.
Members Individuals in 9 countries:
Canada, Czechia, France, Greece, Italy, Japan, Netherlands, South Africa, UK, USA. [2015/XF5921/c/**F**]

- ♦ International Symposium on Polymer Electrolytes (meeting series)
- ♦ International Symposium on Practical Design of Ships and other Floating Designs (meeting series)
- ♦ International Symposium on Preparative Chromatography and Allied techniques (meeting series)
- ♦ International Symposium on Principles and Practice of Declarative Programming (meeting series)
- ♦ International Symposium on Problems of Listeria and Listeriosis (meeting series)
- ♦ International Symposium for Production Research (meeting series)

♦ International Symposium on the Properties of Water (ISOPOW) 15644

Pres School of Food and Nutritional Science, Univ College Cork, Cork, CO. CORK, Ireland.
Contact Agrosup-Univ de Bourgogne, 26 bd Petitjean, BP 87999, 21079 Dijon CEDEX, France.
URL: http://www.isopow.org/

History First Symposium organized 1974, Glasgow (UK). Currently a Standing Committee of *International Union of Food Science and Technology (IUFoST, #15773)*. Current statutes adopted 2013. **Aims** Promote the ISOPOW Symposia series. **Structure** Central Committee; Executive Group. **Activities** Events/meetings. **Publications** Books. **Members** Individuals. Membership countries not specified. [2019.02.12/XM4791/c/**E**]

- ♦ International Symposium on Quantitative Mass Spectrometry in Life Sciences (meeting series)
- ♦ International Symposium Quantum Theory and Symmetries (meeting series)
- ♦ International Symposium on Radiation Resistance (meeting series)
- ♦ International Symposium on Radioimmunology, Lyon (meeting series)
- ♦ International Symposium on Relations between Homogeneous and Heterogeneous Catalysis (meeting series)
- ♦ International Symposium on Remote Sensing (meeting series)
- ♦ International Symposium on Reservoir Wettability and its Effects on Oil Recovery (meeting series)
- ♦ International Symposium on Rice Functional Genomics (meeting series)
- ♦ International Symposium on Root Development (meeting series)
- ♦ International Symposium on Ruminant Physiology (meeting series)
- ♦ International Symposium on the Science and Processing of Cast Iron (meeting series)
- ♦ International Symposium on Scientific Basis for Preparation of Heterogeneous Catalyser (meeting series)
- ♦ International Symposium on Scientific Computing, Computer Arithmetic and Validated Numerical Computations (meeting series)
- ♦ International Symposium on Security and Privacy in Social Networks and Big Data (meeting series)
- ♦ International Symposium on Sediment Management (meeting series)
- ♦ International Symposium on Selenium in Biology and Medicine (meeting series)
- ♦ International Symposium on Sentinel Node Biopsy in Head and Neck Cancer (meeting series)
- ♦ International Symposium on the Separation of Proteins, Peptides and Polynucleotides (meeting series)
- ♦ International Symposium on Sexuality and Disability (meeting series)
- ♦ International Symposium on Small Business / see International Small Business Congress (#14875)
- ♦ International Symposium on Small Business (meeting series)
- ♦ International Symposium on Society and Resource Management (meeting series)
- ♦ International Symposium on the Sociology of Music Education (meeting series)
- ♦ International Symposium on Soil Biology (meeting series)
- ♦ International Symposium on Space Technology and Science (meeting series)
- ♦ International Symposium on Spatial and Temporal Databases (meeting series)
- ♦ International Symposium on Spermatology (meeting series)
- ♦ International Symposium on Staphylococci and Staphylococcal Infections (meeting series)
- ♦ International Symposium on Superconductivity (meeting series)
- ♦ International Symposium on Symbolic and Algebraic Computation (meeting series)
- ♦ International Symposium on Tardigrada (meeting series)
- ♦ International Symposium on Temperature and Thermal Measurements in Industry and Science (meeting series)
- ♦ International Symposium for Textile Care Labelling / see Groupement International de l'Etiquetage pour l'Entretien des Textiles (#10761)
- ♦ International Symposium on Tilapia in Aquaculture (meeting series)
- ♦ International Symposium on Tonal Aspects of Languages (meeting series)
- ♦ International Symposium on Transport Network Reliability (meeting series)
- ♦ International Symposium on Trichoptera (meeting series)
- ♦ International Symposium on Tunnel Safety and Security (meeting series)
- ♦ International Symposium on Turbulence and Shear Flow Phenomena (meeting series)
- ♦ International Symposium on Ubiquitous Networking (meeting series)
- ♦ International Symposium on Ultrafine Grained Structures (meeting series)
- ♦ International Symposium on Ultrasonic Doppler Methods for Fluid Mechanics and Fluid Engineering (meeting series)
- ♦ International Symposium of Ultrasound for Regional Anesthesia (meeting series)
- ♦ International Symposium Use of Public Transit Automated Data for Planning and Operations (meeting series)
- ♦ International Symposium on Viral Hepatitis and Liver Disease (meeting series)
- ♦ International Symposium on Viruses of Lower Vertebrates (meeting series)
- ♦ International Symposium on VLSI Technology and Circuits (meeting series)
- ♦ International Symposium on Welding and Melting by Electron and Laser Beams (meeting series)
- ♦ International Symposium on Wetland Pollutant Dynamics and Control (meeting series)

♦ International Symposium on Wild Boar & Other Suids (meeting series)
♦ International Symposium on Wind Energy Systems (meeting series)
♦ International Symposium on Wireless Personal Multimedia Communications (meeting series)
♦ International Symposium on Women's Health Issues in Thrombosis and Haemostasis (meeting series)
♦ International Symposium on Wood, Fiber and Pulping Chemistry (meeting series)
♦ International Symposium on X- and Gamma-ray Sources and Applications (meeting series)
♦ International Symposium on Zootechny (meeting series)

♦ International Systemic Constellations Association (ISCA) 15645

Contact address not obtained. E-mail: info@isca-network.org – admin@isca-network.org.
URL: http://isca-network.org/

History Founding Assembly May 2007, Cologne (Germany). **Aims** Actively encourage development of a dynamic and reflective consciousness within the constellation community. **Structure** Board of Directors. **Finance** Members' dues. **Events** *Arab Impact Cratering and Astrogeology Conference* Algiers (Algeria) / Laghouat (Algeria) 2016, *Congress* Copenhagen (Denmark) 2013. [2016/XM4482/**D**]

♦ International Systemic Functional Linguistics Association (ISFLA) . 15646

Chair address not obtained. E-mail: isfla-chair@isfla.org.
URL: http://www.isfla.org/

History Jul 1993, Australia. Jul 1993, Victoria (Australia), when formally created, having previously existed for 21 years as *International Systemic Functional Linguistics Network*. **Aims** Promote scholarship and research in systematic functional linguistic theory and related fields; develop descriptions of the various world languages using a systematic functional linguistic framework. **Structure** Officers: Chair; Deputy Chair; Membership Secretary; Recording/Correspondence Secretary; Regional Treasurers. **Activities** Organizes annual International Systemic Congress; supports projects leading to courses, programmes, summer schools and other teaching activities; supports local and national events; maintains archives. **Events** *Annual Congress* Santiago (Chile) 2019, *Annual Congress* Boston, MA (USA) 2018, *Annual Congress* Wollongong, NSW (Australia) 2017, *Annual Congress* Aachen (Germany) 2015, *Annual Congress* Mendoza (Argentina) 2014.
Members in 36 countries and territories:
Argentina, Australia, Austria, Belgium, Brazil, Canada, Chile, China, Colombia, Denmark, Finland, France, Germany, Hong Kong, India, Indonesia, Iran Islamic Rep, Israel, Italy, Mexico, Netherlands, New Zealand, Nigeria, Norway, Pakistan, Portugal, Singapore, Slovenia, South Africa, Spain, Sweden, Switzerland, Thailand, UK, USA, Venezuela. [2014/XF2567/**C**]

♦ International Systemic Functional Linguistics Network / see International Systemic Functional Linguistics Association (#15646)
♦ International Systemics Organization (inactive)
♦ International System Safety Society (internationally oriented national body)

♦ International Systems Security Engineering Association (ISSEA) . . . 15647

Contact address not obtained. T. +16132564715. Fax +16133566262.

History 1999. **Aims** Advance systems security engineering as a defined and measurable discipline through the further development of its theory and practice. **Structure** Board of Directors; Working Groups. **Finance** Sources: members' dues. **Activities** Certification/accreditation; events/meetings; networking/liaising; training/education. **Events** *Annual Conference* Ottawa, ON (Canada) 2006. [2021/XM1952/**D**]

♦ International Szondi Association (ISA) 15648

Société Internationale Szondi – Internationale Szondi-Gesellschaft (ISG)

Sec Schakelveldstraat 5, 3211 Binkom, Belgium.
Pres Univ de Lisboa, Fac de Psicologia, Alameda da Universidade, 1649-013 Lisbon, Portugal.
URL: http://www.szondiassociation.org/index.php

History 1959. **Aims** Promote the work of *psychoanalyst* Leopold Szondi (1893-1986). **Structure** Secretariat. **Languages** English, French, German. **Staff** 0.50 FTE, paid. **Finance** Members' dues. **Events** *Congress* Pécs (Hungary) 2022, *Congress* Bucharest (Romania) 2020, *Congress* Budapest (Hungary) 2017, *Szondi with Schotte – to play, build, interpret, create* Brussels (Belgium) 2014, *Congress* Nice (France) 2011. **Publications** *Szondiana* (annual) – digital magazine.
Members in 16 countries:
Austria, Belgium, Brazil, France, Germany, Hungary, Japan, Poland, Portugal, Romania, Russia, Slovakia, Spain, Sweden, Switzerland, Ukraine. [2022/XE3931/**E**]

♦ International Table Soccer Federation (ITSF) 15649

Fédération internationale de football de table

Secretariat 3 rue de Clermont, 44000 Nantes, France. T. +33240479084. Fax +33240204459. E-mail: info@tablesoccer.org.
URL: http://www.table-soccer.org/

History 16 Aug 2002, Oberwart (Austria). Registration: Start date: 26 Aug 2002, France. **Aims** Promote development of table soccer worldwide; increase friendship between table soccer players. **Structure** General Assembly; Executive Committee. Commissions (13): Administrative; Anti-Doping; Communication; Data processing; Disciplinary; Federation Assessment; ITSF Development Fund; Media; Medical Ranking; Rules; Sports; Women. **Languages** English, French. **Staff** 3.50 FTE, paid. **Finance** Registration fees from members. Income from activities. **Activities** Organizes: Table Soccer World Cup; Table Soccer World Championships; World Championship Series. **Events** *Congress* Nantes (France) 2011.
Members National federations in 57 countries and territories:
Algeria, Argentina, Australia, Austria, Bahrain, Belgium, Bolivia, Brazil, Bulgaria, Cameroon, Canada, China, Costa Rica, Côte d'Ivoire, Czechia, Denmark, Estonia, France, Georgia, Germany, Hong Kong, Hungary, India, Iran Islamic Rep, Ireland, Israel, Italy, Japan, Korea Rep, Lithuania, Luxembourg, Malaysia, Malta, Mexico, Mongolia, Morocco, Netherlands, Nigeria, Norway, Pakistan, Peru, Poland, Portugal, Romania, Russia, Senegal, Slovakia, Slovenia, South Africa, Spain, Switzerland, Taiwan, Thailand, UK, Ukraine, United Arab Emirates, USA.
NGO Relations Member of (1): *Alliance of Independent recognised Members of Sport (AIMS, #00690)* (Observer). [2021/XM0371/**D**]

♦ International Table Tennis Federation (ITTF) 15650

Fédération internationale de tennis de table (FITT) – Federación Internacional de Tenis de Mesa

CEO MSI, Avenue de Rhodanie 54B 2, 1007 Lausanne VD, Switzerland. T. +41213407090. Fax +41213407099. E-mail: ittf@ittf.com.
SG address not obtained.
URL: http://www.ittf.com/

History Dec 1926, London (UK). **Aims** Uphold ITTF rules and develop a spirit of friendship and mutual assistance among associations and players; regulate relations among associations and between associations and other organizations; improve technical standard and participation in the sport worldwide; foster friendly sporting competition and eliminate unfair and unsporting practices such as drug use; establish and maintain the laws of table tennis and regulations for international *competitions*; encourage publication of the rules in different languages and check the accuracy of such publications; promote and supervise World, Olympic and Paralympic title competitions; employ funds as may be expedient in the interests of international table tennis. **Structure** General Meeting (at World Championship, annual since 2001), at which each association is entitled to 1 vote. Board of Directors. Olympics Commission. Committees (11): Equipment; Media; Ranking; Rules; Sports Science; Technical; Nomination; Veterans; Para Table Tennis; Umpires and Referees. Commission (2): Athletes; Junior. Calendar Panel; Merit Awards and Hall of Fame. **Languages** English, French, Spanish. **Staff** 26.00 FTE, paid. **Finance** Sources: members' dues. Other source: equipment approval; marketing and sponsorship; World Championships; World Cup; Olympic income; miscellaneous. **Activities** Organizes: World Championships (annual); World Team Cup; Men's World Cup; Women's World Cup; Pro-Tour Events; World Youth Championships. **Events** *Annual General Meeting* Houston, TX (USA) 2021, *Annual General Meeting* Seoul (Korea Rep) 2020, *Annual General Meeting* Budapest (Hungary) 2019, *Sports Science Congress* Budapest (Hungary) 2019, *Meeting* Busan (Korea Rep) 2019. **Publications** *ITTF News* (6 a year) – electronic; *Table Tennis Fascination* (every 2 years). *Handbook for Match Officials*; *Handbook for Tournament Referees*; *ITTF Directory*; *ITTF Handbook*; *ITTF Rules Booklet*; *Table Tennis Legends*; *Table Tennis – The Early Years*.
Members National associations in 215 countries and territories:
Afghanistan, Albania, Algeria, Andorra, Angola, Anguilla, Antigua-Barbuda, Argentina, Armenia, Aruba, Australia, Austria, Azerbaijan, Bahrain, Bangladesh, Barbados, Belarus, Belgium, Belize, Benin, Bermuda, Bhutan, Bolivia, Bosnia-Herzegovina, Botswana, Brazil, Brunei Darussalam, Bulgaria, Burkina Faso, Burundi, Cambodia, Cameroon, Canada, Cayman Is, Central African Rep, Chile, China, Colombia, Comoros, Congo Brazzaville, Congo DR, Cook Is, Costa Rica, Côte d'Ivoire, Croatia, Cuba, Curaçao, Cyprus, Czechia, Denmark, Djibouti, Dominica, Dominican Rep, Ecuador, Egypt, El Salvador, England, Equatorial Guinea, Estonia, Eswatini, Ethiopia, Faeroe Is, Fiji, Finland, France, Gabon, Gambia, Georgia, Germany, Ghana, Gibraltar, Greece, Greenland, Grenada, Guam, Guatemala, Guernsey, Guinea, Guyana, Haiti, Honduras, Hong Kong, Hungary, Iceland, India, Indonesia, Iran Islamic Rep, Iraq, Ireland, Isle of Man, Israel, Italy, Jamaica, Japan, Jersey, Jordan, Kazakhstan, Kenya, Kiribati, Korea DPR, Korea Rep, Kosovo, Kuwait, Kyrgyzstan, Laos, Latvia, Lebanon, Lesotho, Liberia, Libya, Liechtenstein, Lithuania, Luxembourg, Macau, Madagascar, Malawi, Malaysia, Maldives, Malta, Marshall Is, Mauritania, Mauritius, Mexico, Micronesia FS, Moldova, Monaco, Mongolia, Montenegro, Morocco, Mozambique, Myanmar, Namibia, Nauru, Nepal, Netherlands, New Caledonia, New Zealand, Nicaragua, Niger, Nigeria, Niue, Norfolk Is, North Macedonia, Northern Mariana Is, Norway, Oman, Pakistan, Palau, Palestine, Panama, Papua New Guinea, Paraguay, Peru, Philippines, Poland, Portugal, Puerto Rico, Qatar, Romania, Russia, Rwanda, Samoa, Samoa USA, San Marino, Saudi Arabia, Scotland, Senegal, Serbia, Seychelles, Sierra Leone, Singapore, Slovakia, Slovenia, Solomon Is, Somalia, South Africa, Spain, Sri Lanka, St Kitts-Nevis, St Lucia, St Vincent-Grenadines, Sudan, Suriname, Sweden, Switzerland, Syrian AR, Tahiti Is, Taiwan, Tajikistan, Tanzania UR, Thailand, Timor-Leste, Togo, Tokelau, Tonga, Trinidad-Tobago, Tunisia, Türkiye, Turkmenistan, Tuvalu, Uganda, Ukraine, United Arab Emirates, Uruguay, USA, Uzbekistan, Vanuatu, Venezuela, Vietnam, Virgin Is UK, Wales, Wallis-Futuna, Yemen, Zambia, Zimbabwe.
Continental federations (6):
African Table Tennis Federation (#00478); *Asian Table Tennis Union (ATTU, #01765)*; *European Table Tennis Union (ETTU, #08873)*; North america Table Tennis Federation; *Oceania Table Tennis Federation (OTTF, #17678)*; *Unión Latinoamericana de Tenis de Mesa (ULTM, #20453)*.
NGO Relations Memorandum of Understanding with (1): *International Esports Federation (IESF, #13303)*. Member of (7): *Association of Paralympic Sports Organisations (APSO, #02850)*; *Association of Summer Olympic International Federations (ASOIF, #02943)*; *International Committee for Fair Play (#12769)*; *International Council for Coaching Excellence (ICCE, #13008)*; *International Masters Games Association (IMGA, #14117)*; *International Paralympic Committee (IPC, #14512)*; *Olympic Movement (#17719)*. Cooperates with (1): *International Testing Agency (ITA, #15678)*. Instrumental in setting up (1): *International Table Tennis Federation Foundation (ITTF Foundation, #15651)*. Recognized by: *International Olympic Committee (IOC, #14408)*. Recognized organizations: *Caribbean Table Tennis Federation (CTTF, no recent information)*; *Central American Table Tennis Confederation (CTIC, #03673)*; *Commonwealth Table Tennis Federation (COMTAB, #04364)*; *Federación Iberoamericana de Tenis de Mesa (FIBE, #09322)*; *Federation of International Table-Tennis Manufacturers (FIT, #09679)*; *Francophonie pongiste internationale (#09983)*; *International Veterans Table Tennis Society (IVTTS, #15845)*; *Mediterranean Table Tennis Union (MTTU, #16684)*; *North European Table Tennis Union (NETU, #17599)*; *Confederación Sudamericana de Tenis de Mesa (CONSUTEME, #04493)*; *South Asia Table Tennis Federation (no recent information)*; *South East Asia Table Tennis Association (SEATTA, #19798)*; *Swaythling Club International (SCI, #20072)*. [2021/XB2611/y/**B**]

♦ International Table Tennis Federation Foundation (ITTF Foundation) 15651

Contact Richard-Wagner-Str 10, 04109 Leipzig, Germany. T. +49341999927944.
URL: http://www.ittffoundation.org/

History Founded by *International Table Tennis Federation (ITTF, #15650)*, as a financially and organizationally independent foundation. Registered in accordance with German law, Mar 2019. **Aims** Use table tennis as a tool for development and peace by connecting people all over the world; implement or support projects on the field and empower them to serve as models; make table tennis popular, universal and inclusive. **Structure** Board of Trustees; Governing Board; Management Team. **NGO Relations** Member of: *The Association for International Sport for All (TAFISA, #02763)*. [2019/XM8629/f/**F**]

♦ International Tactical Officers Training Association (internationally oriented national body)
♦ International Taekwondo Federation / see International Taekwon-Do Federation (#15652)

♦ International Taekwon-Do Federation (ITF) 15652

Sec Draugasse 3, 1210 Vienna, Austria. T. +4312928467. Fax +431292846789. E-mail: secretary@itfhq.org.
URL: https://www.itf-tkd.org/

History 22 Mar 1966, Seoul (Korea Rep). Founded by General Choi Hong Hi. Headquarters moved in 1972 to Toronto ON (Canada) and in 1985 to Vienna (Austria). Registered in accordance with Spanish law. Former names and other names: *International Taekwondo Federation* – alias. **Aims** Represent, promote and work for development of the practice of Taekwon-Do. **Structure** Board of Directors. Regional organizations include: *All Europe Taekwon-Do Federation (AETF, #00649)*; *Asia Taekwondo Federation (ATF, #02100)*; *North American Taekwondo Federation (no recent information)*. **Languages** English, Korean, Spanish. **Staff** Voluntary. **Activities** Regional and world championships; meeting activities; education and training. **Events** *Congress* Québec, QC (Canada) 2007, *Congress* Warsaw (Poland) 2003, *Congress* Buenos Aires (Argentina) 1999, *Congress* St Petersburg (Russia) 1997.
Members Associations (founding members) in 127 countries and territories:
Afghanistan, Albania, Algeria, Angola, Argentina, Armenia, Australia, Austria, Bahamas, Bangladesh, Belarus, Belgium, Belize, Bolivia, Bosnia-Herzegovina, Brazil, Bulgaria, Burkina Faso, Cambodia, Canada, Canaries, Chad, Chile, China, Colombia, Cook Is, Costa Rica, Croatia, Cuba, Cyprus, Czechia, Denmark, Dominica, Dominican Rep, Egypt (*), El Salvador, England, Estonia, Ethiopia, Faeroe Is, Fiji, Finland, France, Georgia, Germany (*), Greece, Grenada, Guatemala, Haiti, Honduras, Hong Kong, Hungary, India, Indonesia, Ireland, Israel, Italy (*), Jamaica, Japan, Kazakhstan, Kenya, Korea DPR, Korea Rep (*), Kuwait, Kyrgyzstan, Laos, Latvia, Lebanon, Liberia, Libya, Lithuania, Luxembourg, Madagascar, Malaysia (*), Mexico, Moldova, Mongolia, Mozambique, Nepal, Netherlands, New Zealand, Nicaragua, Nigeria, Norway, Pakistan, Palestine, Panama, Papua New Guinea, Paraguay, Peru, Philippines, Poland, Portugal, Puerto Rico, Romania, Russia, Saudi Arabia, Scotland, Serbia, Singapore (*), Slovakia, Slovenia, Solomon Is, South Africa, Spain, Suriname, Sweden, Switzerland, Syrian AR, Taiwan, Tajikistan, Tanzania UR, Thailand, Trinidad-Tobago, Türkiye (*), Turkmenistan, UK, Ukraine, United Arab Emirates, Uruguay, USA (*), Uzbekistan, Venezuela, Vietnam (*), Wales, Zambia, Zimbabwe.
NGO Relations Member of: *The Association for International Sport for All (TAFISA, #02763)*; *International Martial Art Games Committee (IMGC, #14107)*. [2019/XF3408/**F**]

♦ International Taekwon-do Forum (unconfirmed)

♦ International Tai Chi Chuan Association (ITCCA) 15653

Association internationale Tai Chi Chuan

Austria Contact YEE KUNG Zentrum, Mariahilfer Str 115, 1060 Vienna, Austria. T. +4315962681. E-mail: austria@yeekung.at – europe@originalyangstyle.org.
URL: https://www.itcca.com/

History Former names and other names: *International Tai Chuan Association* – former. Registration: Belgium. **Structure** No permanent secretariat.
Members National organizations in 6 countries:
Austria, Belgium, France, Germany, Italy, Switzerland. [2022/XF1756/**F**]

♦ International Tai Chi Federation (unconfirmed)
♦ International Tai Chuan Association / see International Tai Chi Chuan Association (#15653)
♦ International Tailor Employees Federation (inactive)
♦ International Tank Container Organisation / see International Tank Container Organization (#15654)

♦ International Tank Container Organization (ITCO) 15654

Sec Suite 3 Charter House, 26 Claremont Road, Surbiton, KT6 4QZJL, UK. T. +442083900000. E-mail: secretary@itco.org.
URL: https://international-tank-container.org/

History 1998, *International Tank Container Organization (ITCO)*, by merger of *European Portable Tank Association (EPTA, inactive)* and *International Tank Container Leasing Association (ITCLA, inactive)*. Merged with *Asian Tank Container Organisation (@TCO)*, 1 Jan 2018. **Aims** Promote and represent tank containers as safe, cost-efficient and flexible means of *transport*. **Structure** Board of Directors; Secretariat. Council. Membership divisions (4): Operators; Leasing companies; Manufacturers; Tank service providers. **Languages** English. **Staff** 1.50 FTE, paid; 8.00 FTE, voluntary. **Finance** Members' dues. **Activities** Events/meetings. **Events** *Members Meeting* Amsterdam (Netherlands) 2019, *General Meeting* Dubai (United Arab Emirates) 2016, *Meeting* Barcelona (Spain) 2002, *General Meeting* Berlin (Germany) 2001, *General Meeting* Paris (France) 2001. **Publications** *Acceptable Container Condition*; *Longer-term Trends and Developments of the Tank Container Industry*.
Members Manufacturers, lessors, operators, Depots, tank container trucking companies, inspection and registration organizations, service providers. Companies (over 170) in 16 countries:

Belgium, China, Finland, France, Germany, Ireland, Italy, Japan, Netherlands, Singapore, South Africa, Spain, Switzerland, Taiwan, UK, USA.
IGO Relations Involved in the work of: *United Nations Committee of Experts on the Transport of Dangerous Goods and on the Globally Harmonized System of Classification and Labelling of Chemicals (Committee of Experts on TDG and GHS, #20543).* [2019.02.13/XD8056/**D**]

- ♦ International Tanker Nominal Freight Scale Association Limited in London / see Worldscale Association (#21765)
- ♦ International Tanker Owners Pollution Federation / see ITOPF Ltd (#16073)
- ♦ International Tape Association / see Content Delivery and Storage Association (#04779)
- ♦ International Tape/Disc Association / see Content Delivery and Storage Association (#04779)

♦ International Tar Association (ITA) 15655

Association internationale du goudron (AIG) – Internationale Teervereinigung (ITV)
Mailing address 7208 West Sand Lake Rd, Ste 305, Orlando FL 32814, USA.
Administrator address not obtained. T. +19082407697. E-mail: administrator@itaorg.com.
Pres address not obtained. T. +19087977178. E-mail: president@itaorg.com.
URL: http://www.itaorg.com/

History 1952, Paris (France), as *International Road Tar Conference – Conférence internationale du goudron pour routes – Internationale Strassenteer Konferenz.* Previously also referred to as *International Tar Conference (ITC) – Conférence internationale du goudron (CIG) – Internationale Teerkonferenz (ITK).* Current name adopted 1992. **Aims** Investigate scientific and technical questions regarding *crude tar* and tar products; collect and exchange scientific and practical experience; unify practices and testing procedures. **Structure** Executive Committee; Steering Committee; Secretariat. Technical Committee. **Languages** English. **Staff** 1.50 FTE, paid. **Finance** Members' dues. **Activities** Events/meetings; grants/awards/prizes. **Events** *Annual Conference* Rome (Italy) 2021, *Conference* Orlando, FL (USA) 2020, *Annual Conference* Shanghai (China) 2019, *Annual Conference* San Francisco, CA (USA) 2018, *Annual Conference* Prague (Czechia) 2017. **Publications** Conference proceedings.
Members Organizations; Individuals. Members in 17 countries:
Australia, Belgium, Canada, Czechia, Denmark, France, Germany, Italy, Japan, Korea Rep, Netherlands, Poland, South Africa, Spain, UK, USA, Zimbabwe. [2020/XD2419/**D**]

- ♦ International Tar Conference / see International Tar Association (#15655)
- ♦ International Task Force on Canine Atopic Dermatitis / see International Committee on Allergic Diseases of Animals (#12744)

♦ International Task Force for the Rural Poor (INTAF) 15656

International Co-convenor 12 Eastleigh Avenue, South Harrow, HA2 0UF, UK. T. +442088644740.
Head Office Amarpurkashi, PO Bilari-202411, Moradabad, Uttar Pradesh, Moradabad UTTAR PRADESH, India. T. +919411809030. E-mail: apkgram@gmail.com.
URL: http://www.vri-online.org.uk/intaf/

History Founded 1989, following international seminar Dec 1988, India. An international programme of *'Volunteers for Rural India'* (UK). **Aims** Identify and publicize policies, programmes and projects of integrated *education* and *development* which contribute most to the all round development of the rural poor. **Structure** Triennial General Meeting; Coordinating Committee. **Languages** English, Hindi. **Staff** 3.00 FTE, voluntary. **Finance** Members' dues. Contributions. Separate budget for each chapter; very small international budget. **Activities** Events/meetings. Active in: India, UK. **Events** *World conference and general assembly / Conference* London (UK) 2011, *World conference and general assembly / Conference* Amarpurkashi (India) 2008, *World conference and general assembly / Conference* Harrow (UK) 2005, *Conference* India 2002, *World conference and general assembly* Konch (India) 2002. **Publications** *International Journal of Rural Studies (IJRS)* (2 a year) – jointly with VRI.
Members National and regional chapters in 11 countries:
Bangladesh, Belgium, Canada, China, Guyana, India, Slovakia, Sweden, Switzerland, Trinidad-Tobago, UK.
Individuals in 5 countries:
Australia, Canada, China, India, UK.
NGO Relations Member of: *EarthAction (EA, #05159).* [2015.11.03/XF5346/**F**]

♦ International Task Force on Teachers for Education 2030 15657

Secretariat UNESCO HQ Office, 7 place de Fontenoy, 75352 Paris, France. T. +33145682427. Fax +33145685626. E-mail: teacherstaskforce@unesco.org.
URL: https://teachertaskforce.org/

History Dec 2008, Oslo (Norway). Established by High Level Group meeting on Education for All. Former names and other names: *International Task Force on "Teachers for Education for All"* – former; *International Task Force on Teachers for EFA* – former. **Aims** Mobilize governments and other stakeholders for the advancement of teachers and quality teaching, acting as a catalyst of global, regional and national efforts through advocacy, knowledge creation and sharing, and country support and engagement. **Structure** Steering Committee, composed of all donors, one developing country representative from each of the regions of Arab countries, Asia/Pacific, Latin America/Caribbean and Sub-Saharan Africa, 2 members from global intergovernmental organizations, one member from a regional intergovernmental organization and 2 representatives of international NGOs. Secretariat. Teachers for EFA E-Network. **Languages** Arabic, English, French, Spanish. **Activities** Advocacy/lobbying/activism; capacity building; guidance/assistance/consulting; knowledge management/information dissemination; politics/policy/regulatory. **Publications** Articles; papers; presentations. **Members** Governments and organizations in about 160 countries. Membership countries not specified. **IGO Relations** Secretariat hosted by: *UNESCO (#20322).* [2021.09.05/XJ2270/y/**E***]

- ♦ International Task Force on "Teachers for Education for All" / see International Task Force on Teachers for Education 2030 (#15657)
- ♦ International Task Force on Teachers for EFA / see International Task Force on Teachers for Education 2030 (#15657)
- ♦ International Taskforce on Women and ICTs / see International Taskforce on Women and Information and Communication Technologies (#15658)

♦ International Taskforce on Women and Information and Communication Technologies (ITF) 15658

Contact c/o European Centre for Women and Technology, PO Box 822, 3007 Drammen, Norway. E-mail: info@ecwt.eu.
Chair Ayacucho 551, Buenos Aires, Argentina. T. +541152389337. Fax +541143751373.
URL: http://www.itfwomenict.org/

History 2005, Baltimore MD (USA). Also referred to as *International Taskforce on Women and ICTs.* **Events** *Conference* Kuala Lumpur (Malaysia) 2007, *Conference* Paris (France) 2006. **NGO Relations** *European Centre for Women and Technology (ECWT, #06504)* established on initiative of ITF-Europe. Instrumental in setting up: *Asia-Pacific Centre for Women and Technology (APCWT, #01869).* [2013/XM8203/**F**]

♦ International Tax and Investment Center 15659

Pres 1634 I St NW, Suite 500, Washington DC 20006, USA. T. +12025309799. Fax +12025307987. E-mail: info@iticnet.org.
Communications address not obtained.
URL: http://www.iticnet.org/

History Founded 1993. **Aims** Act as a clearinghouse for tax and investment policy information; serve as a training institute for key policy makers in the former Soviet Union and other transition economies. **Structure** Board of Directors, including President, Vice-President, Secretary and Treasurer. Offices (7): Baku (Azerbaijan); Almaty (Kazakhstan); Astana (Kazakhstan); Kiev (Ukraine); London (UK); Moscow (Russia); Washington DC (USA). **Events** *Global Excise Summit* Brussels (Belgium) 2012, *Asia Excice taxation conference* Singapore (Singapore) 2005. **Publications** *ITIC Bulletin* (12 a year). Annual report. **IGO Relations** Cooperates with: *Department for International Development (DFID, inactive); International Bank for Reconstruction and Development (IBRD, #12317)* (World Bank); *International Monetary Fund (IMF, #14180); European Commission (EC, #06633)* (EUTACIS Programme); *United States Agency for International Development (USAID).* [2018/XM1694/**E**]

♦ International Tax Planning Association (ITPA) 15660

Registrar PO Box 70653, London, SW1P 9XL, UK. T. +442078217399. Fax +442078346613. E-mail: registry@itpa.org.
URL: http://www.itpa.org/

History 1975. Registered in Cayman Is. **Aims** Disseminate and exchange information about international tax planning and related matters from the viewpoint of the taxpayer. **Structure** Committee. Membership limited to experts in the international tax field. **Languages** English. **Staff** 2.00 FTE, paid. **Finance** Sources: meeting proceeds; members' dues. Other sources: enrollment fees. **Activities** Events/meetings. **Events** *Conference* Estepona (Spain) 2019, *Conference* London (UK) 2018, *Meeting* Vienna (Austria) 2018, *Conference* Monte Carlo (Monaco) 2017, *Conference* Amsterdam (Netherlands) 2015. **Publications** *ITPA Journal* (3 a year); *ITPA News* (3 a year). *Green Book* – directory of services. Information Services: Online library. **Members** Full; Student and Subscribers. Bankers, trust officers, finance directors, accountants, lawyers and others concerned with tax aspects of cross-frontier transactions (over 1,000) in over 70 countries and territories. Membership countries not specified. [2018/XD1306/v/**C**]

- ♦ International TB-meeting – Inhaled Therapies for Tuberculosis and Other Infectious Diseases Conference (meeting series)
- ♦ Internationalt Bynetvaerk for Det gode Liv / see Cittaslow (#03958)

♦ International Tchoukball Federation (FITB) 15661

Fédération internationale de Tchoukball (FITB)
Sec P.O Box 33, Luzhu District, Kaohsiung 82106, Taiwan. T. +886905118464. E-mail: secretary@fitb.org – contactus@fitb.org.
Pres address not obtained.
URL: https://fitb.org/

History 1971. **Aims** Govern, manage and develop tchoukball so that it becomes a prominent team sport with high global awareness. **Structure** General Assembly (every 2 years); Executive Committee. **Languages** English, French. **Activities** Sporting activities.
Members National Federations in 51 countries and territories:
Argentina, Austria, Bangladesh, Benin, Brazil, Burkina Faso, Cameroon, Canada, China, Colombia, Congo DR, Costa Rica, Côte d'Ivoire, Czechia, France, Germany, Ghana, Guinea, Haiti, Hong Kong, Hungary, India, Indonesia, Italy, Japan, Kenya, Korea Rep, Macau, Malaysia, Mauritius, Mexico, Morocco, Nepal, Pakistan, Philippines, Poland, Rwanda, Senegal, Singapore, Spain, Sri Lanka, Switzerland, Tanzania UR, Thailand, Togo, Uganda, UK, United Arab Emirates, Uruguay, USA, Vietnam.
NGO Relations Member of (1): *The Association for International Sport for All (TAFISA, #02763).* [2023/XD4663/**C**]

♦ International Teacher Association (ITA) 15662

Editor Teglgården 8, 4220 Korsør, Denmark. T. +4558377891.
URL: http://www.international-teacher.dk/

Structure Executive Committee. **Activities** Training/education. **Publications** *International Teacher-post.* **NGO Relations** Member of: *International Peace Bureau (IPB, #14535).* [2018/XM6352/**C**]

- ♦ International Teachers Trade Union Cooperation Committee (inactive)

♦ International Teaching of Psychology Network (InterTOP) 15663

Contact Dept of Psychology, Aquinas College, 1607 Robinson Rd SE, Grand Rapids MI 49506, USA. T. +16166322155. E-mail: vk001@aquinas.edu.
URL: http://interteachpsy.org/

History following a series of conferences, starting in 2002. **Aims** Foster international professional development, broaden the worldwide knowledge base, provide new ideas and international experience and provide opportunities to discover resources available worldwide for teaching and training in psychology. **Languages** English. **Finance** Grants; institution supports. **Activities** Organizes meetings and conferences. **Events** *International Conference on Psychology Education / International Conference on Psychology Education – ICOPE* Cape Town (South Africa) 2012, *International conference on psychology education / International Conference on Psychology Education – ICOPE* Sydney, NSW (Australia) 2010, *International conference on the teaching of psychology / International Conference on Psychology Education – ICOPE* St Petersburg (Russia) 2008, *International conference on psychology education / International Conference on Psychology Education – ICOPE* Foz do Iguaçu (Brazil) 2005, *International conference on psychology education / International Conference on Psychology Education – ICOPE* St Petersburg (Russia) 2002. **Publications** *Teaching Psychology around the World* by S McCarthy et al – 3 vols published to date. Articles. [2013.07.19/XJ1995/**E**]

♦ International Tea Committee (ITC) 15664

Comité international du thé
Chief Exec 1st Floor, Millbank Tower, 21-24 Millbank Tower, London, SW1P 4QP, UK. T. +442036270898. E-mail: inteacom@globalnet.co.uk.
URL: http://www.inttea.com/

History 1933, London (UK). Founded to administer the *International Tea Agreement* signed by representatives of the tea industries in Ceylon, India, and Netherlands East Indies. Agreement renewed from time to time; last Agreement, entered into force 8 May 1950, between Ceylon (now Sri Lanka), India, Indonesia and Pakistan, was valid for 5 years, ending 31 Mar 1955; it was not formally renewed. Since 1959, Nyasaland (now Malawi), China and other countries have been represented on the Committee. New Constitution, adopted Jun 1979, extended membership to include consuming countries. Registration: Companies House, Start date: Jan 1987, England and Wales. **Aims** Act as information centre to collect and publish worldwide statistics on tea in respect of area, production, exports, imports, auction prices, stocks. **Structure** Chief Executive; Secretary; Statistician. **Languages** English. **Staff** 3.00 FTE, paid. **Finance** Partly financed (about 30%) by member countries. **Activities** Serves as a statistical and information centre, providing data covering the following trade-related subjects: acreage; production; exports by country of destination; imports by country of origin; FOB values of exports; CIF values of imports and weekly auction prices for all auction centres. **Publications** *Annual Bulletin of Statistics; Monthly Statistical Summary; Web Summary. World Tea Statistics 1910-1990* (1996).
Members Full producer/exporter members in 8 countries:
Bangladesh, China, India, Indonesia, Kenya, Malawi, Sri Lanka, Tanzania UR.
Full consumers in 3 countries:
Canada, Ireland, USA.
Associate (24) in 18 countries:
China, France, India, Italy, Japan, Kenya, Mozambique, Nepal, Netherlands, Pakistan, Russia, Rwanda, Sri Lanka, Tanzania UR, Uganda, UK, Vietnam, Zimbabwe.
Corporate members (42) in 19 countries:
Cameroon, Chile, China, France, Germany, India, Kenya, Morocco, Myanmar, Netherlands, Pakistan, South Africa, Sri Lanka, Switzerland, Tanzania UR, UK, United Arab Emirates, USA, Zimbabwe.
Consultative Status Consultative status granted from: *ECOSOC (#05331)* (Ros C); *FAO (#09260)* (Liaison Status). [2022/XC2614/**C**]

♦ International Teak Information Network (TEAKNET) 15665

Coordinator Kerala Forest Research Inst, Peechi, Thrissur, Kerala 680653, Thrissur KERALA 680653, India. T. +914872690396. Fax +914872690111. E-mail: coordinator@teaknet.org – secretariat@teaknet.org.
URL: http://www.teaknet.org/

History 1995, Rangoon (Myanmar). Founded during 2nd regional seminar on teak. Headquarters moved from Myanmar to India, 2008. Former names and other names: *Asia-Pacific Network on Research and Development of Teak (TEAK-NET)* – former (1995). **Aims** Address interests of all categories of stakeholders related to teak, whether they are growers, traders, researchers or other groups with a profound interest or concerned with teak. **Structure** International Steering Committee; Secretariat, based at Kerala (India). **Languages** English. **Staff** 1.00 FTE, paid; 9.00 FTE, voluntary. **Finance** Members' dues. Support from: *FAO Regional Office for Asia and the Pacific (RAP, #09266).* **Activities** Networking/liaising; events/meetings; knowledge management/information dissemination; training/education. **Events** *World Teak Conference* Accra (Ghana) 2022, *World Teak Conference* Accra (Ghana) 2021, *World Teak Conference* Guayaquil (Ecuador) 2015, *World Teak Conference* Bangkok (Thailand) 2013, *World Teak Conference* Costa Rica 2011. **Publications** *Teaknet Bulletin* (4 a year).
Members Institutional; Individual. Members in 47 countries:

Australia, Austria, Benin, Bolivia, Brazil, Canada, China, Colombia, Costa Rica, Czechia, Denmark, Ecuador, Fiji, Finland, France, Germany, Ghana, Guatemala, Honduras, India, Indonesia, Ireland, Italy, Japan, Malaysia, Mexico, Netherlands, New Zealand, Nicaragua, Nigeria, Norway, Panama, Peru, Singapore, Spain, Sri Lanka, Sudan, Switzerland, Tanzania UR, Thailand, Togo, Uganda, UK, United Arab Emirates, USA, Venezuela, Vietnam.
Included in the above, 2 organizations listed in this Yearbook:
Center for International Forestry Research (CIFOR, #03646); International Tropical Timber Organization (ITTO, #15737). [2019.07.01/XF6406/y/**F**]

♦ International Team for Implantology (ITI) 15666

CEO Peter Merian Weg 10, 4052 Basel BS, Switzerland. T. +41612708383. Fax +41612708384. E-mail: headquarters@iti.org.
URL: http://www.iti.org/

History 1980. Former names and other names: *International Team for Oral Implantology (ITI)* – former. **Aims** Provide a growing global network for life-long learning in implant *dentistry* through quality education and innovative research to the benefit of the patient. **Structure** General Assembly; Board of Directors; Committees. **Activities** Training/education; financial and/or material support. events/meetings. **Events** *Annual Congress* Lisbon (Portugal) 2023, *World Symposium* Basel (Switzerland) 2021, *World Symposium* Singapore (Singapore) 2020, *Annual General Meeting* Berlin (Germany) 2019, *Congress* Oslo (Norway) 2019. **Publications** *Forum Implantologicum* – journal. *ITI Treatment Guide* – series. **Information Services** *ITI Online Academy*. **Members** Fellows and Members (over 16,000) in 101 countries. Membership countries not specified. [2020/XF6807/**F**]

- ♦ International Team for Oral Implantology / see International Team for Implantology (#15666)
- ♦ International Teams (internationally oriented national body)
- ♦ International Team for Studying Sintering / see International Institute for the Science of Sintering (#13922)
- ♦ International Tea Promotion Association (inactive)
- ♦ International Technical Centre of Bottling / see International Technical Centre for Bottling and Packaging (#15667)

♦ International Technical Centre for Bottling and Packaging 15667

Centre technique international de l'embouteillage et du conditionnement (CETIE) – Internationales Zentrum für Abfüll- und Verpackungstechnik

Acting Gen Sec 114 rue la Boétie, 75008 Paris, France. T. +33142652645. E-mail: contact@cetie.org.
URL: http://www.cetie.org/

History 3 Jun 1960, Évian-les-Bains (France). Founded at 1st International Congress on Bottling. Former names and other names: *International Technical Centre of Bottling* – former; *Centre technique international de l'embouteillage* – former. **Aims** Promote cooperation among international organizations for bottling to exchange technical and economic data and to solve jointly the essential problems of bottling; study problems arising in the international field of packaging liquid foods and others; investigate materials best suited to present needs and prepare their standardization; promote technical and economic progress of bottling. **Structure** Board of Directors; Working Groups. **Languages** English, French, German. **Staff** 3.00 FTE, paid. **Finance** Sources: members' dues. Annual budget: 270,000 EUR. **Activities** Research/documentation. **Events** *Glass Plenary Meeting* UK 2021, *Glass Plenary Meeting* Paris (France) 2020, *Glass Plenary Meeting* Amsterdam (Netherlands) 2019, *Biennial Congress* Brussels (Belgium) 2007, *Biennial Congress* Munich (Germany) 2005. **Publications** Technical documents; codes of practice; recommendations. **Members** Companies, professional organizations and stakeholders in boottling (about 84). Membership countries not specified. **NGO Relations** In liaison with technical committees of: *International Organization for Standardization (ISO, #14473).* [2021.02.17/XD2616/**D**]

- ♦ International Technical Committee of Legal Experts on Air Questions (inactive)
- ♦ International Technical Committee on Masonry, Reinforced Concrete and Foundation Work in Modern Building (inactive)
- ♦ International Technical Committee for the Prevention and Extinction of Fire / see CTIF International Association of Fire and Rescue Services (#04979)
- ♦ International Technical Conference on Circuits/Systems, Computers and Communications (meeting series)
- ♦ International Technical Conference on the Enhanced Safety of Vehicles (meeting series)
- ♦ International Technical Cooperation / see ITECO – Centre de formation pour le développement
- ♦ International Technical Institute of Flight Engineers (inactive)
- ♦ International Technical Meeting on Air Pollution Modelling and its Application (meeting series)
- ♦ International Technical Meeting of the Nuclear Industries (meeting series)
- ♦ International Technical Training Office (inactive)

♦ International Technical Tropical Timber Association (ITTTA) 15668

Association technique internationale des bois tropicaux (ATIBT) – Asociación Técnica Internacional de las Maderas Tropicales – Internationaler Technischer Verband Tropenholz

General Manager Jardin Tropical, 45 bis av de la Belle Gabrielle, 94736 Nogent-sur-Marne CEDEX, France. E-mail: info@atibt.org.
URL: http://www.atibt.org/

History 11 Dec 1951, Paris (France). Sometimes referred to in German as *Internationaler Technischer Verband des Tropischen Holzes*. Bylaws most recently changed 2011. Registered in accordance with French law. **Aims** Ensure liaison among members and protection of their professional interests, nationally and internationally; promote research on problems concerning tropical timbers and development of their utilization, including transport, export, import, brokerage, transformation; promote, research and implement *sustainable* tropical forest management. **Structure** General Meeting (annual); Board of Directors; Presidency rotates among member countries (2-year term); Advisory Committee; Commissions (4); Scientific and Technical Committee; Arbitration Chamber; General Secretariat. **Languages** English, French. **Staff** 5.00 FTE, paid. **Finance** Sources: members' dues. **Activities** Networking/liaising; research and development; standards/guidelines. **Events** *Together towards global green supply chains* Shanghai (China) 2019, *Racewood meeting* Pointe Noire (Congo Brazzaville) 2011, *General Assembly* Rome (Italy) 2001, *International Tropical Timber Markets, Sustainable Forest Management* Rome (Italy) 2001, *Les bois tropicaux, marchés mondiaux et technologies d'avenir* Istanbul (Turkey) 2000. **Publications** *ATIBT Newsletter* (2 a year) in English, French; *ATIBT Directory* (annual) in English, French. *Tropical Timber Atlas – Vol 1: Africa* in English, French, German; *Tropical Timber Atlas – Vol 2: Asia* in English, French, German; *Tropical Timber Atlas – Vol 3: Latin America* in French, Spanish. Standards; guides; manuals; technical documents.
Members 'Collective' professional associations; 'Active' persons or companies exercising activities in the field. Members (220) in 34 countries and territories:
Algeria, Andorra, Angola, Belgium, Brazil, Cameroon, Central African Rep, Congo Brazzaville, Congo DR, Côte d'Ivoire, Denmark, Equatorial Guinea, Finland, France, Gabon, Germany, Ghana, Greece, Guinea, Guyana, Indonesia, Italy, Kenya, Morocco, Mozambique, Netherlands, Portugal, Singapore, Spain, Switzerland, Taiwan, Türkiye, USA, Vietnam.
Included in the above, 2 organizations listed in this Yearbook:
African Academy of Sciences (AAS, #00193); African Timber Organization (ATO, no recent information).
Consultative Status Consultative status granted from: *FAO (#09260)* (Liaison Status); *ECOSOC (#05331)* (Ros C). **IGO Relations** *Convention on International Trade in Endangered Species of Wild Fauna and Flora (CITES, 1973); European Commission (EC, #06633); International Bank for Reconstruction and Development (IBRD, #12317); International Tropical Timber Organization (ITTO, #15737).* Close cooperation with: *Centre de coopération internationale en recherche agronomique pour le développement (CIRAD, #03733).* **NGO Relations** Cooperates with (3): *European Sustainable Tropical Timber Coalition (STTC); International Wood Products Association (IWPA); Tropical Forest Foundation (TFF).* In liaison with technical committees of: *International Organization for Standardization (ISO, #14473).* Member of: *International Union of Forest Research Organizations (IUFRO, #15774).* Associate member of: *European Timber Trade Federation (ETTF, #08915)* Stakeholder of: *PEFC Council (#18288).* [2020/XC2621/y/**C**]

- ♦ International Technology Education Association / see International Technology and Engineering Educators Association
- ♦ International Technology and Engineering Educators Association (internationally oriented national body)

♦ International Technology Law Association (ITechLaw) 15669

Contact 401 Edgewater Place, Ste 600, Wakefield MA 01880, USA. T. +17818768877. Fax +17812241239. E-mail: office@itechlaw.org.
URL: http://www.itechlaw.org/

History 1971, as *Computer Law Association (CLA) – Association du droit de l'informatique*. **Aims** Inform and educate lawyers about the legal issues arising from the evolution, production, marketing, acquisition and use of computer and communications technology. **Structure** Executive Committee, including President, Vice-President, Immediate Past-President, Treasurer and Secretary. Advisory Board. **Finance** Members' dues. **Events** *World Technology Law Conference* San Francisco, CA (USA) 2022, *European Conference* Zurich (Switzerland) 2022, *European Conference* Lisbon (Portugal) 2021, *European Conference* Lisbon (Portugal) 2020, *World Technology Law Conference* Seattle, WA (USA) 2018. **Publications** *ITechLaw Bulletin*. **Members** Individuals (approx 2,000) in 40 countries. Membership countries not specified. **Consultative Status** Consultative status granted from: *World Federation of the Deaf (WFD, #21425)* (Observer Status). [2020/XD9355/**D**]

- ♦ International Technology Rental Association (internationally oriented national body)
- ♦ International Telecommunication Convention, 1973 (1973 treaty)
- ♦ International Telecommunication Convention, 1982 (1982 treaty)
- ♦ International Telecommunication Convention, 1989 (1989 treaty)
- ♦ International Telecommunications Convention, 1982 (1982 treaty)
- ♦ International Telecommunications Energy Conference (meeting series)
- ♦ International Telecommunications Regulation (1988 treaty)
- ♦ International Telecommunications Satellite Consortium / see International Telecommunications Satellite Organization (#15670)

♦ International Telecommunications Satellite Organization (ITSO) ... 15670

Organisation Internationale des Télécommunications par Satellites – Organización Internacional de Telecomunicaciones por Satélite

Dir Gen 4400 Jenifer St NW, Ste 332, Washington DC 20015, USA. T. +12022435096. Fax +12022435018. E-mail: itsomail@itso.int.
URL: http://www.itso.int/

History 20 Aug 1964, Washington DC (USA), as *International Telecommunications Satellite Consortium (INTELSAT)*, by adoption of interim arrangements for a global commercial communications satellite system. First satellite *'Early Bird'* launched in 1965. The Consortium was superseded by an organization with the listed title on entry into force, 12 Feb 1973, of definitive agreements: 'the Agreement' (concluded among governments), and 'the Operating Agreement' (concluded among governments or their designated public or private communications entities). Statutes registered in *'UNTS 1/19677'*. Intergovernmental organization restructured whereby certain assets, including satellites and orbital filings were transferred to Intelsat Ltd, a commercial company, 18 Jul 2001. **Aims** Act as the supervisory authority of Intelsat Ltd; ensure the performance of Core Principles for provision of international public telecommunications services by satellite, with high reliability and quality; promote international public telecommunications services by satellite to meet the needs of the information and communication society. **Structure** Assembly of Parties (once every 2 years) comprising all 140 Member States; Executive Organ, headed by Director General, who is responsible to Assembly of Parties. **Languages** English, French, Spanish. **Staff** 5.00 FTE, paid. **Finance** Annual financial requirements met from returns of Funding Agreement Contract, set up by INTELSET prior to privatization. **Events** *Meeting* Washington, DC (USA) 2020, *Signatories meeting* Singapore (Singapore) 1996, *Biennial meeting* Porlamar (Venezuela) 1994, *Digital seminar* Seoul (Korea Rep) 1993, *Symposium on global satellite communications* Nanjing (China) 1991. **Publications** Annual Report; brochure.
Members Governments (149):
Afghanistan, Algeria, Angola, Argentina, Armenia, Australia, Austria, Azerbaijan, Bahamas, Bahrain, Bangladesh, Barbados, Belgium, Benin, Bhutan, Bolivia, Bosnia-Herzegovina, Botswana, Brazil, Brunei Darussalam, Burkina Faso, Cameroon, Canada, Cape Verde, Central African Rep, Chad, Chile, China, Colombia, Comoros, Congo Brazzaville, Congo DR, Costa Rica, Côte d'Ivoire, Croatia, Cuba, Cyprus, Czechia, Denmark, Dominican Rep, Ecuador, Egypt, El Salvador, Equatorial Guinea, Estonia, Eswatini, Ethiopia, Fiji, Finland, France, Gabon, Gambia, Georgia, Germany, Ghana, Greece, Guatemala, Guinea, Guinea-Bissau, Haiti, Holy See, Honduras, Hungary, Iceland, India, Indonesia, Iran Islamic Rep, Iraq, Ireland, Israel, Italy, Jamaica, Japan, Jordan, Kazakhstan, Kenya, Korea DPR, Korea Rep, Kuwait, Kyrgyzstan, Lebanon, Libya, Liechtenstein, Luxembourg, Madagascar, Malawi, Malaysia, Mali, Malta, Mauritania, Mauritius, Mexico, Micronesia FS, Monaco, Mongolia, Montenegro, Morocco, Mozambique, Namibia, Nepal, Netherlands, New Zealand, Nicaragua, Niger, Nigeria, Norway, Oman, Pakistan, Panama, Papua New Guinea, Paraguay, Peru, Philippines, Poland, Portugal, Qatar, Romania, Russia, Rwanda, Saudi Arabia, Senegal, Serbia, Singapore, Somalia, South Africa, Spain, Sri Lanka, Sudan, Sweden, Switzerland, Syrian AR, Tajikistan, Tanzania UR, Thailand, Togo, Trinidad-Tobago, Tunisia, Türkiye, Uganda, UK, United Arab Emirates, Uruguay, USA, Uzbekistan, Venezuela, Vietnam, Yemen, Zambia, Zimbabwe.
IGO Relations Reports annually to: *United Nations (UN, #20515).* Formal agreements with: *African Telecommunications Union (ATU, #00482); Arab Satellite Communications Organization (ARABSAT, #01037); Association of Telecommunication Enterprises of the Andean Community (#02951); Comisión Técnica Regional de Telecomunicaciones (COMTELCA, #04144); European Telecommunications Satellite Organization (EUTELSAT IGO, #08896); International Mobile Satellite Organization (IMSO, #14174); Intersputnik International Organization of Space Communications (#15976).* Close working relations with: *International Telecommunication Union (ITU, #15673)*, especially its Radiocommunication and Development Sectors. Partnership agreement with: *Commonwealth Telecommunications Organisation (CTO, #04365).* Cooperation agreement with: *International Maritime Organization (IMO, #14102).* Invited to sessions of Intergovernmental Council of: *International Programme for the Development of Communication (IPDC, #14651).* **NGO Relations** Member of: *Pacific Islands Telecommunications Association (PITA, #17979).* In liaison with technical committees of: *International Organization for Standardization (ISO, #14473).* Formal agreement with: *Asociación Interamericana de Empresas de Telecomunicaciones (ASIET, #02160); European Telecommunications Standards Institute (ETSI, #08897).* [2020.02.10/XB2627/**B***]

♦ International Telecommunications Society (ITS) 15671

Sec 416 Wilverside Way SE, Calgary AB T2J 1Z7, Canada. T. +14038138949. Fax +14032719776. E-mail: secretariat@itsworld.org.
URL: http://www.itsworld.org/

History USA. **Aims** Encourage distribution of information, discussions and research concerning telecommunications issues, *legislative* and *policy* decisions. **Structure** Board of Directors, comprising Chairman, Vice Chairman, Treasurer and Secretary. Conference Committee. **Activities** Research/documentation; events/meetings. **Events** *European Regional Conference* Gothenburg (Sweden) 2022, *Biennial Conference* Stockholm (Sweden) 2021, *African Regional Conference* Cape Town (South Africa) 2020, *Asia Pacific Regional Conference* Bangkok (Thailand) 2019, *European Regional Conference* Espoo (Finland) 2019. **Publications** *Info* – official journal.
Members Individuals (400) professionals (academics and practitioners in operating companies, consultancies, government agencies) with an interest in the field of telecommunications planning, policy formulation and economic decision analyses. Membership countries not specified. Corporate members in 19 countries:
Corporate members in 19 countries:
Argentina, Australia, Austria, Belgium, Brazil, Canada, China, France, Germany, Greece, Hungary, Italy, Japan, Korea Rep, New Zealand, Spain, Sweden, Switzerland, UK. [2015/XF1415/**F**]

♦ International Telecommunications Users Group (INTUG) 15672

Chairperson Schrieksebaan 3, 3140 Keerbergen, Belgium. T. +3237781783. E-mail: post@intug.org.
URL: http://www.intug.org/

History Founded 7 Nov 1974, The Hague (Netherlands). Registered in accordance with Belgian law. **Aims** Promote the interests of users of international telecommunications; create new means of direct and continuous consultation and positive cooperation with international telecommunications authorities and other relevant bodies regarding both current needs and future planning; encourage removal of barriers to establishing an effective and efficient global digital economy. **Structure** General Meeting (annual); Council; Board. **Languages** English. **Staff** 1.00 FTE, paid; 3.00 FTE, voluntary. **Finance** Members' dues. Annual budget: euro 20,000. **Activities** Advocacy/lobbying/activism; networking/liaising. **Events** *Annual General*

Meeting Brussels (Belgium) 2015, *Annual General Meeting* Brussels (Belgium) 2014, *Annual General Meeting* Copenhagen (Denmark) 2014, *Annual General Meeting* Amsterdam (Netherlands) 2013, *Annual General Meeting* Mexico City (Mexico) 2013.
Members Full: national and international users' associations. Associate: companies with an interest as users in international communications. Correspondents and contacts: individuals and companies providing information to INTUG and presenting INTUG locally in 20 countries and territories:
Argentina, Australia, Belgium, Colombia, Denmark, France, Germany, Hong Kong, India, Indonesia, Mexico, Netherlands, New Zealand, Norway, South Africa, Spain, Sweden, Switzerland, UK, USA.
IGO Relations Cooperates with: *International Telecommunication Union (ITU, #15673)*. Member of: *Bureau de développement des télécommunications (BDT, #03358)*. [2016.10.28/XD6790/y/**F**]

♦ International Telecommunication Union (ITU) 15673
Union internationale des télécommunications (UIT) – Unión Internacional de Telecomunicaciones (UIT)

Headquarters Place des Nations, 1211 Geneva 20, Switzerland. T. +41227306039 – +41227305111. Fax +41227305939 – +41227337256. E-mail: itumail@itu.int.
URL: http://www.itu.int/

History 17 May 1985, Paris (France). Established on signature by 20 States of the *Convention télégraphique de Paris – International Telegraph Convention of Paris*, as *Union radiotélégraphique universelle – International Telegraph Union.* Convention entered into force 1 Jan 1866. Central secretariat created by *International Telegraph Conference*, 1868, Vienna (Austria-Hungary) and set up 1869, Bern (Switzerland), as *Bureau international des administration télégraphiques – International Bureau of Telegraphs*, which changed title to *Bureau de l'Union télégraphique*, 1908. *International Wireless Telegraph Convention (Radiotelegraph convention, 1906)* signed by 27 maritime nations, 3 Nov 1906, following the conclusion of *Final Protocol of the Preliminary Conference Respecting Wireless Telegraphy (1903)*, 13 Aug 1903, Berlin, at Preliminary Wireless Telegraphy Conference. *Bureau of International Telegraph Union* entrusted with administering the Convention with Radiotelegraph Section of the Bureau operational as of 1 May 1907. At International Telegraph Conference 1925, Paris (France), officially incorporated the Comité consultatif international des communications téléphoniques à grande distance – International Consultative Committee for Long Distance Telephone Communications, which later became known as Comité consultatif international téléphonique – International Telephone Consultative Committee (CCIF). During same conference, Comité consultatif international des communications télégraphiques – International Consultative Committee on Telegraph Communications was also created, which was later known as Comité consultatif international télégraphique (CCIT) – International Telegraph Consultative Committee. Comité consultatif international technique des communications radioélectriques – International Technical Consultative Committee for Radioelectric Communication, created 1927, Washington DC (USA), subsequently known as Comité consultatif international des radiocommunications – International Consultative Committee for Radiocommunications (CCIR). International Telegraph Conference and International Radiotelegraph Conference merged their respective conventions – *International Telegraph Convention – Convention télégraphique internationale* and *International Radiotelegraph Convention (1912)*, 1932. New convention signed 9 Dec 1932 and entered into force 1 Jan 1934, when current title was also adopted. Headquarters moved to Geneva (Switzerland) 1948. CCIF and CCIT merged to form *International Telegraph and Telephone Consultative Committee (CCITT, inactive)*, 1956. New Constitution and Convention for ITU adopted 1992 and in force since 1 Jul 1994. Based at *United Nations Office at Geneva (UNOG, #20597)*. Since 15 Nov 1947, a specialized agency of *United Nations (UN, #20515)* in the framework of *United Nations System (#20635)*, linked to *ECOSOC (#05331)*.
Legal status:
Convention of the International Telecommunication Union, 1992, signed 1992, Geneva (Switzerland); entered into force 1 Jul 1994, superseding *International Telecommunication Convention, 1982 (1982)*, signed 6 Nov 1982, Nairobi (Kenya); entered into force 1 Jan 1984, superseding *International Telecommunication Convention, 1973 (1973)*. *Radio Regulations (1979)* and *Additional Radio Regulations* signed 1979, Geneva, since partially revised by World Administrative Radio Conferences. *International Telecommunications Regulation (1988)*, signed 9 Dec 1988, Melbourne (Australia), entered into force 1 Jul 1990, replacing *Telegraph Regulations, Telephone Regulations (1973)*. New ITU Constitution and Convention, *International Telecommunication Convention, 1989 (1989)*, adopted May 1989, Nice (France). Statutes registered in: *'LNTS 1365'*; *'LNTS 1905'*; *'LNTS 3479'*.
Aims Coordinate the shared global use of the radio spectrum; promote international cooperation in assigning satellite orbits; improve communication infrastructure in the developing world; establish worldwide standards that foster seamless interconnection of a vast range of communications systems and technologies, and therefore contributing to connect the world; leverage the power of ICTs towards achievement of the SDGs.
Structure General Secretariat; Technical Bureaus (3): *ITU Radiocommunication Bureau (BR, no recent information)*; *Telecommunication Standardization Bureau (TSB, see: #15673)*; *Bureau de développement des télécommunications (BDT, #03358)*. Regional Offices (6): Africa; Americas; Arab States; Asia-Pacific; Commonwealth of Independent States (CIS); Europe. Area Offices. **Languages** Arabic, Chinese, English, French, Russian, Spanish. **Staff** About 700 from more than 100 countries. **Finance** Sources: contributions of member/participating states. At plenipotentiary conferences, each Member State declares its financial commitment through a free-choice system of contributory units intended to provide budgetary predictability and stability. Other sources, covering around 24 per cent of total funding: publications sales; satellite network filing fees; registration of Universal International Freephone Numbers (UIFN). **Activities** Events/meetings; politics/policy/regulatory; projects/programmes; research/documentation; standards/guidelines. **Events** *World Radiocommunication Conference* United Arab Emirates 2023, *Session* Geneva (Switzerland) 2022, *World Summit on the Information Society (WSIS) Forum* Geneva (Switzerland) 2022, *ITU/WHO Workshop on Artificial Intelligence for Health* Helsinki (Finland) 2022, *Meeting of the Focus Group on Artificial Intelligence for Health (ITU-T FG-AI4H)* Helsinki (Finland) 2022. **Publications** *ITU Journal: ICT Discoveries*; *ITU News Magazine.* Handbooks; proceedings; reports; software. Publications in Arabic, Chinese, English, french, Russian, Spanish. Databases.
Members Governments of 193 countries:
Afghanistan, Albania, Algeria, Andorra, Angola, Antigua-Barbuda, Argentina, Armenia, Australia, Austria, Azerbaijan, Bahamas, Bahrain, Bangladesh, Barbados, Belarus, Belgium, Belize, Benin, Bhutan, Bolivia, Bosnia-Herzegovina, Botswana, Brazil, Brunei Darussalam, Bulgaria, Burkina Faso, Burundi, Cambodia, Cameroon, Canada, Cape Verde, Central African Rep, Chad, Chile, China, Colombia, Comoros, Congo Brazzaville, Congo DR, Costa Rica, Côte d'Ivoire, Croatia, Cuba, Cyprus, Czechia, Denmark, Djibouti, Dominica, Dominican Rep, Ecuador, Egypt, El Salvador, Equatorial Guinea, Eritrea, Estonia, Eswatini, Ethiopia, Fiji, Finland, France, Gabon, Gambia, Georgia, Germany, Ghana, Greece, Grenada, Guatemala, Guinea, Guinea-Bissau, Guyana, Haiti, Holy See, Honduras, Hungary, Iceland, India, Indonesia, Iran Islamic Rep, Iraq, Ireland, Israel, Italy, Jamaica, Japan, Jordan, Kazakhstan, Kenya, Kiribati, Korea DPR, Korea Rep, Kuwait, Kyrgyzstan, Laos, Latvia, Lebanon, Lesotho, Liberia, Libya, Liechtenstein, Lithuania, Luxembourg, Madagascar, Malawi, Malaysia, Maldives, Mali, Malta, Marshall Is, Mauritania, Mauritius, Mexico, Micronesia FS, Moldova, Monaco, Mongolia, Montenegro, Morocco, Mozambique, Myanmar, Namibia, Nauru, Nepal, Netherlands, New Zealand, Nicaragua, Niger, Nigeria, North Macedonia, Norway, Oman, Pakistan, Panama, Papua New Guinea, Paraguay, Peru, Philippines, Poland, Portugal, Qatar, Romania, Russia, Rwanda, Samoa, San Marino, Sao Tomé-Principe, Saudi Arabia, Senegal, Serbia, Seychelles, Sierra Leone, Singapore, Slovakia, Slovenia, Solomon Is, Somalia, South Africa, South Sudan, Spain, Sri Lanka, St Kitts-Nevis, St Lucia, St Vincent-Grenadines, Sudan, Suriname, Sweden, Switzerland, Syrian AR, Tajikistan, Tanzania UR, Thailand, Timor-Leste, Togo, Tonga, Trinidad-Tobago, Tunisia, Türkiye, Turkmenistan, Tuvalu, Uganda, UK, Ukraine, United Arab Emirates, Uruguay, USA, Uzbekistan, Vanuatu, Venezuela, Vietnam, Yemen, Zambia, Zimbabwe.
Sector members: over 900 companies and 150 academic institutions and civil society organizations in 114 countries and territories. Membership countries not specified.
IGO Relations Observer status with: *United Nations Sustainable Development Group (UNSDG, #20634)*; *World Trade Organization (WTO, #21864)*. Member of: *United Nations Group on the Information Society (UNGIS, #20570)*. Agreement with: *Council of Europe (CE, #04881)*. Instrumental in setting up: *Broadband Commission for Sustainable Development (#03333)*; *Conférence européenne des administrations des postes et des télécommunications (CEPT, #04602)*; *Multi-Country Posts and Telecommunications Training Centre, Blantyre (MCTC, no recent information)*; *Multinational Higher School of Telecommunications of Dakar (#16898)*; *Regional African Satellite Communications Organization (RASCOM, #18748)*; *World Telecommunication Forum (TELECOM)*; *World Telecommunication Policy Forum (WTPF)*. **NGO Relations** ITU does not have NGO relations as defined by ECOSOC; consequently the term 'nongovernmental organization' is not used by the Union. Member of: World Standards Cooperation (WSC). Instrumental in setting up: *African Advanced Level Telecommunications Institute (AFRALTI, #00197)*; *International Amateur Radio Club (IARC)*.
[2022/XB2622/**B***]

♦ International Teleconferencing Association / see Interactive Multimedia and Collaborative Communications Alliance
♦ International Telegraph and Telephone Consultative Committee (inactive)
♦ International Telegraph Union / see International Telecommunication Union (#15673)
♦ International Telematic University UNINETTUNO (internationally oriented national body)
♦ International Telethons Organization (#17842)

♦ International Teletraffic Congress (ITC) 15674
Congrès international de télétrafic (CIT) – Congreso Internacional de Teletrafico

Communications Chair Univ of Würzburg, Fac of Mathematics and Informatics, Am Hubland, 97074 Würzburg, Germany. T. +499313186631. Fax +499313186632. E-mail: contact@i-teletraffic.org.
URL: http://www.i-teletraffic.org/

History 1955, Copenhagen (Denmark). Founded on the initiative of Arne Jensen (1920-2008), when 1st Congress was held. Subsidiary title: *Application of the Theory of Probability to Telecommunication Research, Engineering and Administration.* Full title of Congress: *International Congress on the Application of the Theory of Probability in Telephone Engineering and Administration.* Now subtitled as "The first international conference in networking science and practice". **Aims** Bring researchers and practitioners together toward operational understanding of all types of current and future networks; provide a forum for leading researchers from academia and industry to present and discuss key technological and methodological advances in the design, performance evaluation and control of communication networks like the Internet, protocols and applications, and in traffic measurement and management. **Structure** *International Advisory Council of the International Teletraffic Congress (see: #15674)*; Congress Secretariat for each congress. **Languages** English. **Staff** 1.00 FTE, voluntary. **Finance** No financing. Some surplus from past events feed next events. **Activities** Events/meetings. **Events** *International Teletraffic Congress* Shenzhen (China) 2022, *International Teletraffic Congress* Budapest (Hungary) 2019, *International Teletraffic Congress* Vienna (Austria) 2018, *International Teletraffic Congress* Genoa (Italy) 2017, *International Teletraffic Congress* Würzburg (Germany) 2016. **Publications** Congress proceedings. [2022/XD1268/c/**F**]

♦ International Television Committee (inactive)
♦ International Television Symposium (meeting series)

♦ International Telework Academy (ITA) 15675
Chair address not obtained.
URL: http://www.ita.fidt.org/

History 1995, as *International Telework Foundation (ITF).* Current name adopted 2003. Registered in accordance with Dutch law. **Aims** As an international *virtual* group of researchers, promote high-quality academic *research* in the field of telework and sharing the outcome with academics, businesses and government organizations. **Events** *Workshop and conference* Pori (Finland) 2009, *Workshop and conference / Conference* Krakow (Poland) 2008, *Workshop and conference / Conference* Lillehammer (Norway) 2007, *Workshop and conference / Conference* Preston (UK) / Liverpool (UK) 2005, *Workshop and conference / Conference* Heraklion (Greece) 2004. **Members** Membership countries not specified. [2013/XF6291/**F**]

♦ International Telework Foundation / see International Telework Academy (#15675)
♦ International Temperance Association / see International Health and Temperance Association
♦ International Temperance Bureau / see International Council on Alcohol and Addictions (#12989)
♦ International Temperance Educational and Cultural Association (inactive)
♦ International Temperance and Health League (no recent information)
♦ International Temperance Union / see International Council on Alcohol and Addictions (#12989)
♦ International Tempest Class Association (see: #21760)
♦ International Tenebrionoidea Symposium (meeting series)
♦ International Tennikoit Confederation (no recent information)

♦ International Tennis Federation (ITF) 15676
Fédération internationale de tennis (FIT) – Federación Internacional de Tenis (FIT)

Address not obtained.
URL: http://www.itftennis.com/

History 1 Mar 1913, Paris (France). Founded at a meeting of the *'Union des sociétés françaises de sport athlétique'*, evolving from an international committee set up by Duane Williams (USA), Charles Barde (Switzerland) and Henri Wallet (France). From Jan 1998, includes the former *International Wheelchair Tennis Federation (inactive)*; since 2007, includes Beach Tennis. Former names and other names: *International Lawn Tennis Federation* – former. **Aims** Foster growth and development of the *sport* of tennis on a worldwide basis; perform the functions of world governing body; make, amend, uphold and enforce the rules of tennis; promote universally the development of the game at all levels regardless of age, gender or disability. **Structure** General Assembly (annual); Board of Directors. Commissions (3); Committees (12). Membership open; meetings closed. **Languages** English, French, Spanish. **Staff** 83.00 FTE, paid. Also part-time staff. **Finance** Members' dues: US$ 729 per country plus US$ 43535 per share. **Activities** Sporting activities; standards/guidelines. **Events** *Annual General Meeting* Lisbon (Portugal) 2019, *Annual General Meeting* Dubai (United Arab Emirates) 2014, *Annual General Assembly* Paris (France) 2013, *Annual General Assembly* Copenhagen (Denmark) 2012, *Annual General Assembly* Bangkok (Thailand) 2011. **Publications** *ITFWorld* (3 a year) – magazine; *The ITF Year* (annual); *This Week* (52 a year) – bulletin; *Davis Cup by BNP Paribas: The Year in Tennis.* Annual Report; online media guides for the Davis Cup and Fed Cup.
Members National Associations in 210 countries and territories:
Afghanistan, Albania, Algeria, Andorra, Angola, Anguilla, Antigua-Barbuda, Argentina, Armenia, Aruba, Australia, Austria, Azerbaijan, Bahamas, Bahrain, Bangladesh, Barbados, Belarus, Belgium, Belize, Benin, Bermuda, Bhutan, Bolivia, Bosnia-Herzegovina, Botswana, Brazil, Brunei Darussalam, Bulgaria, Burkina Faso, Burundi, Cambodia, Cameroon, Canada, Cape Verde, Cayman Is, Central African Rep, Chad, Chile, China, Colombia, Comoros, Congo Brazzaville, Congo DR, Cook Is, Costa Rica, Côte d'Ivoire, Croatia, Cuba, Curaçao, Cyprus, Czechia, Denmark, Djibouti, Dominica, Dominican Rep, Ecuador, Egypt, El Salvador, Equatorial Guinea, Eritrea, Estonia, Eswatini, Ethiopia, Fiji, Finland, France, Gabon, Gambia, Georgia, Germany, Ghana, Greece, Grenada, Guam, Guatemala, Guinea, Guinea-Bissau, Guyana, Haiti, Honduras, Hong Kong, Hungary, Iceland, India, Indonesia, Iran Islamic Rep, Iraq, Ireland, Israel, Italy, Jamaica, Japan, Jordan, Kazakhstan, Kenya, Kiribati, Korea DPR, Korea Rep, Kosovo, Kuwait, Kyrgyzstan, Laos, Latvia, Lebanon, Lesotho, Liberia, Libya, Liechtenstein, Lithuania, Luxembourg, Macau, Madagascar, Malawi, Malaysia, Maldives, Mali, Malta, Marshall Is, Mauritania, Mauritius, Mexico, Micronesia FS, Moldova, Monaco, Mongolia, Montenegro, Morocco, Mozambique, Myanmar, Namibia, Nauru, Nepal, Netherlands, New Zealand, Nicaragua, Niger, Nigeria, Norfolk Is, North Macedonia, Northern Mariana Is, Norway, Oman, Pakistan, Palau, Palestine, Panama, Papua New Guinea, Paraguay, Peru, Philippines, Poland, Portugal, Puerto Rico, Qatar, Romania, Russia, Rwanda, Samoa, Samoa USA, San Marino, Saudi Arabia, Senegal, Serbia, Seychelles, Sierra Leone, Singapore, Slovakia, Slovenia, Solomon Is, Somalia, South Africa, Spain, Sri Lanka, St Kitts-Nevis, St Lucia, St Vincent-Grenadines, Sudan, Suriname, Sweden, Switzerland, Syrian AR, Tahiti Is, Taiwan, Tajikistan, Tanzania UR, Thailand, Togo, Tonga, Trinidad-Tobago, Tunisia, Türkiye, Turkmenistan, Turks-Caicos, Tuvalu, Uganda, UK, Ukraine, United Arab Emirates, Uruguay, USA, Uzbekistan, Vanuatu, Venezuela, Vietnam, Virgin Is UK, Virgin Is USA, Yemen, Zambia, Zimbabwe.
Affiliated Regional Associations (6), listed in this Yearbook:
Asian Tennis Federation (ATF, #01767); *Confederación de Tenis de Centroamérica y el Caribe (COTECC, #04496)*; *Confederation of African Tennis (#04507)*; *European Tennis Federation (#08898)* (Tennis Europe); *Oceania Tennis Federation (OTF, #17679)*; *South American Tennis Confederation (#19709)*.
NGO Relations Member of (8): *Association of Paralympic Sports Organisations (APSO, #02850)*; *Association of Summer Olympic International Federations (ASOIF, #02943)*; *International Committee for Fair Play (#12769)*; *International Council for Coaching Excellence (ICCE, #13008)*; *International Council of Sport Science and Physical Education (ICSSPE, #13077)*; *International Paralympic Committee (IPC, #14512)*; *Olympic Movement (#17719)*; *Sports Rights Owners Coalition (SROC, #19929)*. Recognized by: *International Olympic Committee (IOC, #14408)*. In liaison with technical committees of: *Comité européen de normalisation (CEN, #04162)*; *International Organization for Standardization (ISO, #14473)*. Stakeholder in: *World Anti-Doping Agency (WADA, #21096)*. Signatory to 'World Anti-Doping Code'. [2020/XB2190/y/**B**]

♦ International Tennis Hall of Fame (internationally oriented national body)
♦ International Tennis-Volleyball Federation (no recent information)

♦ International Test Commission (ITC) 15677
Contact c/o CEB, The Pavilion, 1 Atwell Place, Thames Ditton, KT7 0NE, UK. T. +442083358514. E-mail: secretary@intestcom.org.
URL: http://www.intestcom.org/

History Constitution approved Aug 1978, Munich (Germany FR). Amended: Jul 1982, Edinburgh (UK); Sep 1984, Acapulco (Mexico); Jul 1986, Jerusalem (Israel); Jul 1990, Kyoto (Japan); Jul 1994, Madrid (Spain); 1998, San Francisco CA (USA); 2000, Stockholm (Sweden); 2008, Berlin (Germany). Previously also known in French as *Commission internationale des Tests.* **Aims** Promote effective testing and assessment *policies* and proper development, evaluation and use of educational and psychological instruments; facilitate the exchange of information among members; further their cooperation on problems and issues relating to the construction, distribution and use of *psychological* tests and other methods that assess important personal qualities. **Structure** General Meeting (every 2 years); Council. **Languages** English. **Staff** 1.00 FTE, voluntary. **Finance** Members' dues. **Activities** Events/meetings; research/documentation; projects/programmes; standards/ guidelines. **Events** *Conference* Montréal, QC (Canada) 2018, *Conference* Vancouver, BC (Canada) 2016, *Global and local challenges for best practices in assessment* San Sebastian (Spain) 2014, *Conference* Amsterdam (Netherlands) 2012, *Conference* Hong Kong (Hong Kong) 2010. **Publications** *International Journal of Testing* (4 a year); *Testing International* (2 a year).
Members Full (national psychological associations and societies), Affiliate (any interested organization) and Individual members. Full in 20 countries:
Australia, Austria, Belgium, Denmark, Finland, France, Germany, India, Ireland, Japan, Lithuania, Netherlands, Russia, Singapore, Slovenia, South Africa, Spain, Sweden, UK, USA.
Affiliate (50) in 20 countries and territories:
Argentina, Australia, Belgium, Brazil, Canada, China, Croatia, Denmark, France, Germany, Hong Kong, Hungary, Israel, Mexico, Netherlands, New Zealand, Puerto Rico, Spain, Taiwan, UK.
NGO Relations Member of: *International Association of Applied Psychology (IAAP, #11705).* Cooperates with: *International Union of Psychological Science (IUPsyS, #15807).* [2015.09.04/XE3356/E]

♦ International Testing Agency (ITA) 15678
Agence de contrôles internationale (ACI)
Dir-Gen Avenue de Rhodanie 40B, 1007 Lausanne VD, Switzerland. T. +41216121212. E-mail: info@ ita.sport.
URL: https://ita.sport/
History 2018. Founded by *International Olympic Committee (IOC, #14408),* with the support of *World Anti-Doping Agency (WADA, #21096).* Current statutes adopted Dec 2019. Registration: Switzerland. **Aims** Manage anti-doping programs, independent from sporting or political powers, for International Federations (IFs), Major Event Organisers (MEOs) and all other anti-doping organisations requesting support. **Structure** Board; Executive Office; Director General. **Activities** Guidance/assistance/consulting; training/education.
NGO Relations Member of (1): *Olympic Movement (#17719).*
Cooperates with (58):
- *Badminton World Federation (BWF, #03060);*
- *Central European Anti-Doping Organization (CEADO, #03703);*
- *Confédération internationale de la pêche sportive (CIPS, #04562);*
- *European Olympic Committees (EOC, #08083);*
- *Fédération aéronautique internationale (FAI, #09397);*
- *Fédération internationale de basketball (FIBA, #09614);*
- *Fédération internationale de SAMBO (FIAS, #09655);*
- *Fédération Internationale de Savate (FISav, #09656);*
- *Fédération Internationale de Ski (FIS, #09659);*
- *Fédération Internationale de Teqball (FITEQ, #09663);*
- *Fédération Équestre Internationale (FEI, #09484);*
- *Global Association of Mixed Martial Arts (GAMMA, #10243);*
- *International Aikido Federation (IAF, #11605);*
- *International Bobsleigh and Skeleton Federation (IBSF, #12375);*
- *International Boxing Association (IBA, #12385);*
- *International Dragon Boat Federation (IDBF, #13197);*
- *International Federation of Muaythai Associations (IFMA, #13482);*
- *International Federation of Sport Climbing (IFSC, #13553);*
- *International Fistball Association (IFA, #13609);*
- *International Functional Fitness Federation (iF3, #13691);*
- *International Golf Federation (IGF, #13727);*
- *International Handball Federation (IHF, #13771);*
- *International Hockey Federation (#13802);*
- *International Judo Federation (IJF, #13975);*
- *International Life Saving Federation (ILS, #14040);*
- *International Luge Federation (FIL, #14066);*
- *International Orienteering Federation (IOF, #14485);*
- *International Racquetball Federation (IRF, #14683);*
- *International Skating Union (ISU, #14865);*
- *International Ski Mountaineering Federation (ISMF, #14871);*
- *International Surfing Association (ISA, #15630);*
- *International Table Tennis Federation (ITTF, #15650);*
- *International University Sports Federation (FISU, #15830);*
- *International Waterski and Wakeboard Federation (IWWF, #15872);*
- *International Weightlifting Federation (IWF, #15876);*
- *International Wheelchair Basketball Federation (IWBF, #15882);*
- *International World Games Association (IWGA, #15914);*
- *International Wushu Federation (IWUF, #15918);*
- *Ju-Jitsu International Federation (JJIF, #16164);*
- *Tug of War International Federation (TWIF, #20259);*
- *Union Cycliste Internationale (UCI, #20375);*
- *Union internationale Motonautique (UIM, #20431);*
- *United World Wrestling (UWW, #20665);*
- *World Aquatics (#21100);*
- *World Archery (#21105);*
- *World Association of Kickboxing Organizations (WAKO, #21151);*
- *World Baseball Softball Confederation (WBSC, #21222);*
- *World Bridge Federation (WBF, #21246);*
- *World Curling Federation (WCF, #21348);*
- *World DanceSport Federation (WDSF, #21354);*
- *World Karate Federation (WKF, #21608);*
- *World Lacrosse (#21616);*
- *World Rowing (#21756);*
- *World Skate (#21786);*
- *World Squash Federation (WSF, #21826);*
- *World Taekwondo (#21844);*
- *World Triathlon (#21872);*
- *World Underwater Federation (#21873).*

Recognized by: *International Olympic Committee (IOC, #14408).* Also cooperates with national anti-doping organizations and institutional partners worldwide. [2022/AA3048/t/F]

♦ International Textbook Institute / see Georg Eckert Institute for International Textbook Research
♦ International Textile and Apparel Association (internationally oriented national body)
♦ International Textile Care and Rental Association / see International Committee of Textile Care (#12809)
♦ International Textile, Garment and Leather Workers' Federation (inactive)

♦ International Textile Manufacturers Federation (ITMF) 15679
Fédération internationale des industries textiles – Internationale Vereinigung der Textilindustrie
Dir Gen Wiedingstrasse 9, 8055 Zurich ZH, Switzerland. T. +41442836380. Fax +41442836389. E-mail: secretariat@itmf.org.
URL: https://www.itmf.org/
History 1904, Zurich (Switzerland). Founded at meeting convened by the British cotton spinning industry. Reorganized and new Statutes adopted, May 1954. Headquarters transferred from Manchester (UK), to Zurich in 1963. Former names and other names: *International Federation of Master Cotton Spinners' and Manufacturers' Associations* – former (1904 to 1954); *International Cotton Federation* – former (1904 to 1954); *International Federation of Cotton and Allied Textile Industries (IFCATI)* – former (May 1954 to 1978); *Fédération internationale des industries textiles cotonnière et connexes* – former (May 1954 to 1978). **Aims** Monitor, protect and promote the common interests of members; provide a neutral meeting ground for textile *trade* associations in industrialized and developing countries for discussion of matters of common interest and for exchange of information and experience; act as an international spokesman in matters relating to raw materials and as a liaison agent between the textile industry and governmental and intergovernmental organizations. **Structure** Committee of Management (meets annually); Board; Secretariat; Sub-Committees of the Committee of Management (5). **Languages** English, French, German. **Staff** 3.00 FTE, paid. **Finance** Sources: members' dues. **Activities** Events/meetings; guidance/assistance/consulting; knowledge management/information dissemination; networking/liaising; research/documentation. **Events** *Annual Conference* Shaoxing (China) 2023, *Annual Conference* Davos (Switzerland) 2022, *Annual Conference* Davos (Switzerland) 2021, *Annual Conference* Seoul (Korea Rep) 2020, *Annual Conference* Porto (Portugal) 2019. **Publications** *ITMF Newsletter* (12 a year); *ITMF Directory* (every 2 years). Reports; statistics; surveys.
Members Full: associations or other duly constituted trade organizations of manufacturers of textiles 17 countries:
Argentina, Austria, Belgium, Brazil, China, Egypt, Germany, India, Indonesia, Italy, Japan, Korea Rep, Portugal, Spain, Switzerland, Türkiye, Uzbekistan.
Regional association:
African Cotton and Textile Industries Federation (ACTIF, #00271).
Associate in 9 countries and territories:
China, Egypt, Germany, India, Italy, Switzerland, Taiwan, UK, USA.
Corporate in 17 countries and territories:
Austria, Bangladesh, Canada, China, France, Germany, Hong Kong, India, Indonesia, Italy, Pakistan, Singapore, South Africa, Spain, Switzerland, USA, Vietnam.
Consultative Status Consultative status granted from: *ECOSOC (#05331)* (Ros A); *FAO (#09260)* (Liaison Status); *UNCTAD (#20285)* (General Category). **NGO Relations** Cooperates with (1): *International Organization for Standardization (ISO, #14473).* Associate Expert Group of *Business and Industry Advisory Committee to the OECD (BIAC, #03385).* [2023/XC1898/ty/C]

♦ International Textiles and Clothing Bureau (ITCB) 15680
Bureau international des textiles et de l'habillement (BITH) – Oficina Internacional de los Textiles y las Prendas de Vestir (OITP)
Contact address not obtained. T. +41229291616. Fax +41229291617.
History 1984, by a group of developing countries in response to problems arising from administration of the *Arrangement Regarding International Trade in Textiles (Multifibre agreement, 1973)* (1974-1994) governing international trade in textiles under the auspices of *General Agreement on Tariffs and Trade (GATT, inactive).* Also referred to in French as *Bureau international des textiles et de l'habillement.* **Aims** Achieve the elimination of *discriminatory* restrictions directed against members' exports of textiles and clothing in world markets, and the full application of rules and principles enunciated in the General Agreement on Tariffs and Trade of the WTO to world trade in textiles and clothing products. **Structure** Council of Representatives – governing body. Private sector consultative committee to advise on matters of interest to businesses. **Languages** English. **Finance** Members' contributions. **Activities** Monitors the evolution of trade and of developments in trade policy from the point of view of its impact on trade interests of members; assists them in their effective participation in relevant international fora, such as the WTO, and in their bilateral trade relations with major importing countries. In this context, focuses on issues related to WTO's non-agricultural market access negotiations, preferential agreements and rules of origin, among others. Organizes: session of the Council of Representatives (at least annually), often held in a member country; meetings of the Private Sector Consultative Committee; regular meetings in Geneva (Switzerland). **Events** *Textile trade policy and perspectives of textile trade* Brussels (Belgium) 1996. **Publications** *Threads* (6 a year) – newsletter. *International Trade Policy in Textiles – Fifty Years of Protectionism* by Sanjoy Bagchi; *Prospects for Exporting Textiles and Clothing to the United States Over the Next Decade* by Laura M Baughman; *The Drafting History of the Agreement on Textiles and Clothing* by Marcello Raffaelli and Tripti Jenkins; *The US Wool Industries: A Brief History of Protection and Assessment of Current Trends* by L Baugham.
Members Governments of developing countries who are exporters of textiles and clothing in 19 countries and territories:
Argentina, Brazil, China, Egypt, El Salvador, Guatemala, Honduras, Hong Kong, India, Indonesia, Korea DPR, Korea Rep, Macau, Maldives, Pakistan, Paraguay, Thailand, Uruguay, Vietnam.
Observers in 5 countries:
China, Cuba, India, Mauritius, Singapore.
Included in the above Observers, 3 organizations listed in this Yearbook:
International Trade Centre (ITC, #15703); UNCTAD (#20285); World Trade Organization (WTO, #21864).
IGO Relations Observer Status in: *International Trade Centre (ITC, #15703); UNCTAD (#20285); World Trade Organization (WTO, #21864).* Observer Status in the Textile Committee of: *ILO (#11123).* **NGO Relations** Links with national importers associations. [2009.09.08/XE6018/y/E*]

♦ International Textile Services Alliance (ITSA) 15681
Contact c/o ETSA, Rue Montoyer 24 – Bte 7, 1000 Brussels, Belgium. T. +3222820990.
History 2012, Frankfurt-Main (Germany). Launched at the initiative of *European Textile Services Association (ETSA, #08904)* and Textile Rental Services Association of America (TRSA), together with 2 federations in Germany and Belgium. **Aims** Create a cooperative international business-to-business ('B2B') textile services community. **Structure** Steering Committee. **Languages** English. **Staff** None paid. **Finance** No budget. **Events** *Annual Meeting* Frankfurt-Main (Germany) 2016, *Annual Meeting* Atlanta, GA (USA) 2015, *Annual Meeting* Milan (Italy) 2014, *Annual Meeting* New Orleans, LA (USA) 2013.
Members Full in 13 countries:
Australia, Belgium, Brazil, Denmark, Finland, France, Germany, Italy, Norway, Sweden, Switzerland, UK, USA.
Regional organization (1):
European Textile Services Association (ETSA, #08904).
IGO Relations None. [2019.12.12/XJ9311/y/C]

♦ Internationalt Forum (internationally oriented national body)

♦ International Thatching Society (ITS) 15682
Sec address not obtained. E-mail: info@thatchers.eu.
URL: http://thatchers.eu/
Aims Upgrade thatch to become a modern and competitive roof, acknowledging the historic skills and techniques for future reference. **Structure** Board. **Events** *Meeting* Netherlands 2023, *General Meeting* Kyoto (Japan) / Kobe (Japan) / Nantan (Japan) 2019, *Meeting* UK 2017, *Meeting* Sweden 2015.
Members Full in 8 countries:
Denmark, France, Germany, Japan, Netherlands, South Africa, Sweden, UK. [2023.02.15/AA0096/C]

♦ International Theatre Exchange (internationally oriented national body)

♦ International Theatre Institute (ITI) 15683
Institut International du Théâtre (IIT)
Dir Gen UNESCO, 1 rue Miollis, 75732 Paris CEDEX 15, France. T. +33145684880. E-mail: info@iti-worldwide.org.
Pres address not obtained. E-mail: afkham99@gmail.com.
URL: http://www.iti-worldwide.org/
History Founded 28 Jun 1948, Prague (Czech Rep), under the auspices of UNESCO and the international performing arts community, having existed unofficially since 1946. Charter/constitution last amended in 2014. **Aims** Promote international exchange of knowledge and practice in the domain of performing arts; stimulate creation and increase cooperation among performing arts people; increase public awareness of the need to take artistic creation into consideration in matters concerning development; deepen mutual understanding and contribute to consolidation of peace and friendship among peoples; defend the ideals and aims of *UNESCO*; combat all form of racism or social and political discrimination. **Structure** Congress of Members with General Assembly. Executive Council; Executive Board; Permanent Liaison Office at UNESCO House in Paris (France); headquarters in Shanghai (China). Regional bodies coordinate their respective regions. Committees and Project Groups each have their own programme of activities (16): Committees and Project Groups (16): International Dance; Music Theatre NOW Network; International Playwrights' Forum; Forum for Theatre Training and Education; Publications; Theatre in Conflict Zones Network; Network Theatre for Social Change; Network Identity, Migration, Heritage; Dramatic Theatre; Young Practitioners; New Project Group; International

Monodrama Forum; International Festival Forum. Forum; Action Committee for Artists Rights; International Stage Art Network; International Stage Directors Network. Organizes ITI/UNESCO Network for Higher Education in the Performing Arts. Maintains secretariat of *European Secretariat of Cultural NGOs in Germany*, as part of *Culture Action Europe (CAE, #04981)*. Founding and Leading Member of ITI/UNESCO Network for Higher Education in the Performing Arts. **Languages** English, French. **Staff** 8.00 FTE, paid. **Finance** Sources: donations; members' dues. Contributions from national centres; UNESCO contracts. **Activities** Awards/prizes/competitions; events/meetings; knowledge management/information dissemination; training/ education. **Events** *Acts! Performing arts transforming the world* Segovia (Spain) 2017, *Biennial Congress* Manaus (Brazil) 2016, *Biennial Congress* Yerevan (Armenia) 2014, *Biennial Congress* Xiamen (China) 2011, *Theatre of Nations Festival* Nanjing (China) 2008. **Publications** *ITI Info* (12 a year); *News from the ITI Secretariat* (12 a year); *World of Theatre* (every 2 years). *World Encyclopaedia of Contemporary Theatre* – 6 vols.
Members Centres and Cooperating members in 89 countries and territories:
Algeria, Argentina, Armenia, Austria, Azerbaijan, Bangladesh, Belarus, Belgium, Benin, Bosnia-Herzegovina, Brazil, Burkina Faso, Cameroon, Canada, Chad, China, Colombia, Congo Brazzaville, Congo DR, Costa Rica, Côte d'Ivoire, Croatia, Cuba, Cyprus, Czechia, Denmark, Dominican Rep, Egypt, Estonia, Faeroe Is, Finland, Georgia, Germany, Greece, Hungary, Iceland, India, Iran Islamic Rep, Iraq, Ireland, Israel, Italy, Japan, Jordan, Korea Rep, Kosovo, Kuwait, Latvia, Luxembourg, Mali, Mexico, Monaco, Mongolia, Morocco, Nepal, Netherlands, Niger, Nigeria, North Macedonia, Oman, Palestine, Papua New Guinea, Peru, Philippines, Puerto Rico, Qatar, Romania, Russia, Saudi Arabia, Senegal, Sierra Leone, Slovakia, Slovenia, South Sudan, Spain, Sri Lanka, Sudan, Sweden, Switzerland, Taiwan, Togo, Tunisia, Türkiye, Uganda, United Arab Emirates, USA, Venezuela, Vietnam, Zimbabwe.
Consultative Status Consultative status granted from: *ECOSOC (#05331)* (Ros C); *UNESCO (#20322)* (Associate Status). **IGO Relations** Cooperates with: *World Intellectual Property Organization (WIPO, #21593)*. Observer status with: *Intergovernmental Committee of the International Convention of Rome for the Protection of Performers, Producers of Phonograms and Broadcasting Organizations (#11474)*.
[2020.02.06/XB2630/j/**B**]

♦ International Theatre University (inactive)

♦ International Theological Commission 15684

Commission théologique internationale – Commissione Teologica Internazionale – Commissio Theologica Internationalis
Contact Palazzo del S Ufficio, 00120 Vatican City, Vatican. T. +39669895971.
URL: http://www.cti.va/
History Founded 11 Apr 1969, to aid the *Congregation for the Doctrine of the Faith (#04669)*, following recommendations of the Second Vatican Council and proposals, 1967, of *Synod of Bishops (#20083)*. Comes within the framework of the *Administrative Hierarchy of the Roman Catholic Church (#00117)*. **Aims** Offer services to the Holy See and to the Congregation for the Doctrine of the Faith in examining doctrinal questions of major importance. **Structure** General Assembly (annual, always in Rome). **Staff** 3.00 FTE, paid. **Activities** Events/meetings; guidance/assistance/consulting. **Events** *Annual General Assembly* Vatican City (Vatican) 2005, *Annual General Assembly* Vatican City (Vatican) 1998, *Annual general assembly* Rome (Italy) 1993, *Annual General Assembly* Rome (Italy) 1992, *Annual General Assembly* Rome (Italy) 1989.
Members Individuals in 25 countries:
Australia, Belgium, Brazil, Chile, Egypt, France, Germany, Hungary, India, Ireland, Italy, Japan, Lebanon, Mexico, Netherlands, Nigeria, Philippines, Poland, Portugal, Slovenia, Spain, Sweden, Switzerland, UK, USA. [2014.11.11/XF9065/v/**F**]

♦ International Theological Institute (internationally oriented national body)
♦ International Theological Institute – Catholic School of Theology / see International Theological Institute
♦ International Theological Institute for Studies on Marriage and the Family / see International Theological Institute
♦ International Theological Seminary (internationally oriented national body)
♦ International Theoretical Biophysics Symposium (meeting series)

♦ International Thermoelectric Academy (ITA) 15685

Sec Bldg 806, 11 Bozhenka Str, Kiev, 03150, Ukraine. T. +380372244422. Fax +380372241917.
Pres 1 Nauky Str, Chernivtsi, 58029, Ukraine.
History 14 Sep 1994, Ukraine. **Aims** Unite leading specialists to promote progress in the field, concentrating on scientific potential to solve thermoelectric problems of international significance. **Structure** General Meeting (every 2 years). President, Vice-Presidents. Honorary academicians. Corresponding members. **Languages** English, Russian, Ukrainian. **Staff** 3.00 FTE, paid. **Finance** Members' dues. Sponsors. **Activities** Organizes: biennial International Forum on Thermoelectricity; workshops; other festivities. **Events** *Biennial International Forum on Thermoelectricity* Paris (France) 2015, *Biennial International Forum on Thermoelectricity* Tallinn (Estonia) 2013, *Biennial International Forum on Thermoelectricity* Moscow (Russia) 2011, *Biennial International Forum on Thermoelectricity* Kiev (Ukraine) 2009, *Biennial International Forum on Thermoelectricity* Chernivtsi, Vinnytsia (Ukraine) 2007. **Publications** *Thermoelectricity* (6 a year). *Who's Who in Thermoelectricity*.
Members Individuals in 21 countries:
Australia, Azerbaijan, China, Czechia, France, India, Israel, Italy, Japan, Kazakhstan, Lithuania, Mexico, Moldova, Mozambique, Poland, Russia, Spain, Türkiye, Turkmenistan, Ukraine, USA.
NGO Relations Cooperation with: *International Thermoelectric Society (ITS, #15686)*. [2017/XM0190/v/**E**]

♦ International Thermoelectric Society (ITS) 15686

Address not obtained.
URL: http://www.its.org/
History 12 Jul 1989. Statutes adopted on founding. Statutes revised Mar 1990; Jun 1995. Registration: USA, California. **Aims** Advance thermoelectricity industry, science and engineering; promote collection and exchange of information and education. **Structure** Board of Directors. Executive Officers: President, Vice-President (President-Elect), Secretary, Treasurer and 9 Directors. Regional organization: *European Thermoelectric Society (ETS, #08909)*. **Languages** English. **Staff** 1.00 FTE, voluntary. **Finance** Members' dues. **Events** *International Conference on Thermoelectrics* Sendai (Japan) 2025, *Virtual Conference on Thermoelectrics (VCT2022)* 2022, *International Conference on Thermoelectrics* Sendai (Japan) 2022, *Conference* Krakow (Poland) 2021, *Conference* Seattle, WA (USA) 2020. **Publications** *ITSnews*.
Members Honorary; Full; Student. Individuals in 33 countries and territories:
Australia, Austria, Belgium, Brazil, Bulgaria, Canada, Czechia, Denmark, France, Georgia, Germany, Hong Kong, India, Ireland, Israel, Italy, Japan, Korea Rep, Lithuania, Luxembourg, Mexico, Moldova, Poland, Russia, Saudi Arabia, South Africa, Spain, Sweden, Switzerland, Taiwan, UK, Ukraine, USA. [2022/XD5181/v/**D**]

♦ International Thermonuclear Experimental Reactor / see ITER International Fusion Energy Organization (#16072)
♦ International Thermophiles Conference (meeting series)
♦ International Thespian Society (internationally oriented national body)

♦ International Think Tank for Landlocked Developing Countries (ITTLLDC) 15687

Exec Dir UN House, UN Street 14, Sukhbaatar district, Ulaanbaatar 14201, Mongolia. T. +97611351971. Fax +97611322127. E-mail: thinktank@land-locked.org.
URL: http://land-locked.org/
History Jul 2009, Ulaanbaatar (Mongolia). Established through the Multilateral Agreement for the Establishment of an International Think Tank for Landlocked Developing Countries. Proposed 2003, Almaty (Kazakhstan). Officially launched by *United Nations (UN, #20515)* Secretary-General, Ban Ki-moon and Mongolian Minister of Foreign Affairs, S Batbold. Former names and other names: *International Think Tank for LLDCs (ITT)* – alias. **Aims** Use top-quality research and advocacy to improve the ability of landlocked developing countries to build capacity with a view to benefiting from the international trade including WTO negotiations, with the ultimate aim of raising human development and reducing poverty. **Structure** Board of Governors; Secretariat. **Activities** Events/meetings; research/documentation.
Members Member States which have ratified the Agreement (14):
Afghanistan, Armenia, Azerbaijan, Bhutan, Burkina Faso, Ethiopia, Kazakhstan, Kyrgyzstan, Laos, Mongolia, Nepal, Niger, Paraguay, Tajikistan.
IGO Relations Observer status with (1): *United Nations (UN, #20515)* (General Assembly).
[2020/AA1015/**F***]

♦ International Think Tank for LLDCs / see International Think Tank for Landlocked Developing Countries (#15687)
♦ International Thorium Energy Organisation (unconfirmed)

♦ International Thorstein Veblen Association (ITVA) 15688

Pres Dept of Political Science, Vassar College, 124 Raymond Ave, Poughkeepsie NY 12604, USA.
URL: http://ITVA.Vassar.edu/
History 1992. **Aims** Facilitate and revive a critical and historical attitude in the *social sciences*; examine and evaluate Veblen's ideas and methods from the point of view of their applicability and utility for comprehending and analysing the contemporary world; make explicit the attitudes, perspectives and assumptions underlying Veblen's social, economic, political and religious frameworks; illuminate the relationship between Veblen's ideas and his linguistic, rhetorical and poetic style; foster and facilitate communication among Veblen scholars. **Structure** Board of 6 members, including President and Meeting Coordinator. **Languages** English. **Staff** None. **Finance** Members' dues: US$ 50. **Events** *Meeting* Columbia, MO (USA) 2011, *Meeting* Northfield, MN (USA) 2009, *Meeting* New York, NY (USA) 2007, *Meeting* Northfield, MN (USA) 2007, *Meeting* Northfield, MN (USA) 2004.
Members Individuals in 18 countries:
Australia, Austria, Belgium, Canada, Colombia, Denmark, Finland, Germany, Ireland, Italy, Japan, Mexico, Netherlands, Norway, Sweden, Switzerland, UK, USA. [2009.06.01/XE1996/v/**E**]

♦ International Thymic Malignancy Interest Group (ITMIG) 15689

Contact 6 Cold Spring Ct, Mount Kisco NY 10549, USA. E-mail: itmig@thymic.org.
URL: http://www.itmig.org/
History May 2010, New York, NY (USA). Founded at first conference; founding followed discussions which took place during the *International Conference on Thymic Malignancies* and other events organized by the (USA) *Foundation for Thymic Cancer Research (FTCR)*. **Aims** Promote the advancement of clinical and basic science pertaining to thymic and other mediastinal malignancies and related conditions. **Structure** Steering Committee, comprising Chair, Vice-Chair, Secretary, Treasurer and 4 members. Standing Committees (4): Research and Infrastructure; Education/Communication; Finance and Development; Nominating. **Events** *Meeting* Warsaw (Poland) 2022, *Meeting* Mount Kisco, NY (USA) 2021, *Meeting* Warsaw (Poland) 2020, *ITMIG Meeting* Niagara-on-the-Lake, ON (Canada) 2019, *Annual Meeting* Seoul (Korea Rep) 2018. **Members** Individuals (about 300). Membership countries not specified. **NGO Relations** Cooperates with: *International Association for the Study of Lung Cancer (IASLC, #12204)*; *Union for International Cancer Control (UICC, #20415)*. [2021/XJ5406/**C**]

♦ International Thyroid Congress (meeting series)
♦ International Tibet Independence Movement (internationally oriented national body)

♦ International Tibet Network 15690

Main Office 1310 Fillmore St, Ste 401, San Francisco CA 94115, USA. T. +919882255516. E-mail: mail@tibetnetwork.org.
URL: http://www.tibetnetwork.org/
History 2000, Berlin (Germany). Founded during the Third International Tibet Support Group Conference. Former names and other names: *International Tibet Support Network* – former (2000). Registration: USA. **Aims** Maximize effectiveness of the worldwide Tibet movement. **Structure** Steering Committee. **Activities** Training/education; capacity building; events/meetings. **NGO Relations** Member of: *World Heritage Watch (WHW)*. Cooperates with: *Global Call for Climate Action (GCCA, inactive)*. [2022/XJ5549/**F**]

♦ International Tibet Support Network / see International Tibet Network (#15690)
♦ International Tiger Coalition (unconfirmed)
♦ International Timber Committee (inactive)
♦ International Timber Floating Association / see International Timber Raftsmen Association (#15691)

♦ International Timber Raftsmen Association 15691

Association internationale des flotteurs et radeliers – Asociación Internacional de Navateros, Almadieros y Gancheros – Internationale Flösservereinigung – Associació Internacional de Raiers – Associazione Internazionale degli Zattieri – Internasjonale Tommerflotteroranisasjonen – Kansainvälinen Tukkilaisyhdiastys – Asociatia Internationala a Plutasilor – Internacionala Koku Pludinataju Asociacija – Mednarodna Zveza Splavarjev – Mezinarodni Asociace Plavcu A Voraru – Miedzynarodowe Stowarzyszenie Flisaków
Pres C/ Dr Casanovas 14, 25500 La Pobla de Segur, Lleida, Spain. T. +34973679592078. E-mail: forrallat@hotmail.com.
Gen Sec C/ Pallars 4, 25500 La Pobla de Segur, Lleida, Spain. T. +34973659585127. E-mail: raftsmeninternational@gmail.com.
URL: http://www.raftsmen.org/
History 11 Nov 1989, Barcelona (Spain). Former names and other names: *International Timber Floating Association* – alias. **Aims** Study and publicize information on old methods of transporting timber down rivers and over lakes so as to preserve this part of culture as part of ancestral ethnological roots. **Structure** General Assembly. **Languages** Catalan, English, French, German, Italian, Spanish. **Staff** 13.00 FTE, voluntary. **Finance** Members' dues. **Activities** Events/meetings; research/documentation. **Events** *International Timber Raftmen Meeting* Lieksa (Finland) 2020, *General Assembly* Sachsenburg (Austria) 2019, *International Timber Raftmen Meeting* Longarone (Italy) 2018, *General Assembly* Maribor (Slovenia) 2017, *International Timber Raftmen Meeting* Maribor (Slovenia) 2017. **Publications** Book and documentary about the history and tradition of timber-rafting in Europe.
Members Organizations (41) in 12 countries:
Austria, Bosnia-Herzegovina, Czechia, Finland, France, Germany, Italy, Latvia, Poland, Romania, Slovenia, Spain.
[2019/XD8706/**D**]

♦ International Time Bureau (inactive)
♦ International Timekeepers Federation (#09717)
♦ International Timekeeping Federation / see Federazione Internazionale Cronometristi (#09717)
♦ International Tin Agreement, 1954 (1954 treaty)
♦ International Tin Agreement, 1975 (1975 treaty)
♦ International Tin Agreement, 1981 (1981 treaty)

♦ International Tin Association 15692

CEO Unit 3, Curo Park, Frogmore, St Albans, AL2 2DD, UK. T. +441727875544. Fax +441727871341. E-mail: info@internationaltin.org.
Manager China Office Rm 1501, Office Tower 1, Henderson Centre, 18 Jianguomennei Street, Longcheng District, 100005 Beijing, China. T. +861068080915. Fax +861068080975.
URL: http://www.internationaltin.org/
History 1932, London (UK). Took over activities of *International Tin Research Council (ITRC, inactive)*. Former names and other names: *International Tin Research and Development Council* – former (1932 to 1942); *Tin Research Institute* – former (1942 to 1976); *International Tin Research Institute* – former (1976 to 1995); *ITRI* – former (1995 to 2018); *Institut international de recherches sur l'étain* – former. Registration: Company limited by guarantee, No/ID: 02994115, England; EU Transparency Register, No/ID: 781584236220-60, Start date: 15 Oct 2019. **Aims** Support and encourage use of *tin* in existing and new applications. **Structure** Management Board. **Languages** English. **Staff** 25.00 FTE, paid. **Finance** Sources: members' dues; revenue from activities/projects. **Activities** Events/meetings; guidance/assistance/consulting; networking/liaising; research and development. **Events** *International Tin Conference* Toronto, ON (Canada) 2022, *International Tinplate Conference* 2021, *International Tinplate Conference* London (UK) 2020, *International Tin Conference* Toronto, ON (Canada) 2020, *International Tin Conference* Budapest (Hungary) 2018. **Publications** *Tin in the News* (weekly); *Tin Annual Review*. Conference proceedings; specialized reports. **Information Services** *ITRI Database*.
Members Delegates representing the industry in 9 countries:
Australia, Belgium, Bolivia, China, Indonesia, Malaysia, Peru, Poland, Thailand.
NGO Relations Member of (1): *ResponsibleSteel (#18921)* (associate). Subscriber to: *ISEAL (#16026)*.
[2022.05.04/XD2633/**F**]

♦ International Tin Council (inactive)

- ♦ International Tinnitus and Hyperacusis Society (inactive)
- ♦ International Tin Research and Development Council / see International Tin Association (#15692)
- ♦ International Tin Research Institute / see International Tin Association (#15692)
- ♦ International Tin Study Group (no recent information)
- ♦ International Tire Association (no recent information)
- ♦ International Tissue Repair Society (inactive)

♦ International Tobacco Evidence Network (ITEN) 15693

Co-Dir Univ of Illinois at Chicago, Inst for Health Research and Policy, 1747 West Roosevelt Rd, Room 558 – M/C 275, Chicago IL 60608, USA. T. +13129961470. E-mail: fjc@uic.edu – iten@uic.edu.

Co-Dir address not obtained.

URL: http://www.tobaccoevidence.net/

History following a partnership between *International Bank for Reconstruction and Development (IBRD, #12317)* and *WHO (#20950)*. **Aims** Maintain a formal network of economists, epidemiologists, social scientists and other tobacco control experts able to provide rapid, policy-relevant research on country-level, regional or international tobacco control issues. **Structure** Steering Committee, comprising Chair and 8 members. **Events** *ECToH : European conference on tobacco or health* Warsaw (Poland) 2002. **Members** Membership countries not specified. [2009/XJ0244/**F**]

♦ International Tobacco Growers' Association (ITGA) 15694

Secretariat Apartado 5, 6001-081 Castelo Branco, Portugal. T. +351272325901. Fax +351272325906. E-mail: itga@tobaccoleaf.org.

URL: http://www.tobaccoleaf.org/

History 26 Nov 1984, Brazil, as *International Flue-Cured Tobacco Growers' Association (IFTGA)*. Present name adopted Nov 1988. **Aims** Represent the interests of growers worldwide; improve information exchange on crops, prices, political environment, etc. **Structure** Board of Directors, currently composed of 3 representatives from Founder Members. **Languages** English, Portuguese, Spanish. **Staff** 3.00 FTE, paid. **Finance** Members' dues. **Activities** Organizes annual and regional meetings. **Events** *Annual General Meeting* Arusha (Tanzania UR) 2011, *Annual General Meeting* Kentucky (USA) 2010, *Annual General Meeting* USA 2010, *Annual General Meeting* Hyderabad (India) 2009, *Annual General Meeting* Puerto Iguazú (Argentina) 2008. **Publications** *Tobacco Briefing*; *Tobacco Courier*; *Tobacco Farming Sustainable Alternatives ?*; *Tobacco Forum*; *Tobacco in the Developing World*; *Tobacco Trade or Aid ?*.

Members Full in 28 members:
Argentina, Brazil, Burundi, China, Colombia, Croatia, Cyprus, Dominican Rep, India, Indonesia, Italy, Kenya, Malawi, Malaysia, Mexico, Nigeria, Pakistan, Philippines, Poland, Portugal, South Africa, Tanzania UR, Thailand, Uganda, USA, Venezuela, Zambia, Zimbabwe.

NGO Relations Member of: *Eliminate Child Labour in Tobacco Foundation (ECLT Foundation, #05430)*. [2018/XD1807/**D**]

♦ International Tobacco Growers Union 15695

Union internationale des producteurs de tabac (UNITAB)

SG 19 rue Ballu, 75009 Paris, France. T. +33144534800. Fax +33142811686. E-mail: unitab@wanadoo.fr.

History 19 Jul 1952, Fribourg (Switzerland). Previously also referred to in French as *Union internationale des planteurs et producteurs de tabac*. Association under 1901 French law. EU Transparency Register: 14541128505-57. **Aims** Focus attention on the interests of European tobacco-growing; ensure improvements in the income and working conditions of tobacco growers, while keeping pace with environmental constraints and changing consumer tastes. **Languages** French. **Staff** 0.20 FTE, paid. **Finance** Members' dues. Grants. Annual budget: euro 120,000. **Activities** Events/meetings. **Events** *Congress* Brussels (Belgium) 2018, *Congress* Budapest (Hungary) 2012, *Congress* Mainz (Germany) 2006, *Congress* Strasbourg (France) 2002.

Members Associations in 11 countries:
Belgium, Bulgaria, France, Germany, Greece, Hungary, Italy, Poland, Portugal, Spain, Switzerland.

IGO Relations EU institutions. **NGO Relations** *European Leaf Tobacco Interbranch (ELTI)*. [2019.04.24/XD7039/**D**]

- ♦ International Tonnage Stabilization Association (inactive)
- ♦ International Topical Conference on High-Power Electron and Ion-Beam Research and Technology (meeting series)
- ♦ International Topical Steroid Awareness Network (internationally oriented national body)
- ♦ International Topper International Class Association (see: #21760)
- ♦ International Tornado Association (see: #21760)
- ♦ International Total Abstainers Association of Railway Workers (inactive)
- ♦ International Touring Alliance (#00694)
- ♦ International Tourism Partnership / see Sustainable Hospitality Alliance (#20061).

♦ International Tourism Studies Association (ITSA) 15696

London Office University of Greenwich, Old Royal Naval College, Park Row, London, SE10 9LS, UK. E-mail: itsa@gre.ac.uk.

China Office Fundan University, 220 Handan Rd, 200433 Shanghai, China.

Pres Marriott Hall, Room 257, Purdue University, 900 W. State Street, West Lafayette IN 47907-2115, USA.

URL: http://intltourismstudies.com/

History 15 Aug 2006, Hangzhou (China). Registration: Start date: Mar 2008, Hong Kong. **Aims** Bridge the gap between West and East in tourism and hospitality research; provide a forum for exchange of research ideas and good research practices in tourism studies among scholars around the world, with a particular focus on developing countries; diffuse research findings for the benefits of the tourism industry. **Structure** Executive Committee, including Chairman, Vice Chairman, President, Secretary-General, Vice-President, Treasurer and Symposium and Meeting Director. **Finance** Sources: members' dues. **Activities** Events/meetings. Organizes "Tourism and the New Asia International Conference (TNAIC)". **Events** *Biennial Conference* Las Palmas de Gran Canaria (Spain) 2022, *Biennial Conference* Jakarta (Indonesia) 2020, *Biennial Conference* Tshwane (South Africa) 2018, *Biennial Conference* London (UK) 2016, *Biennial Conference / TNAIC Conference* Perth, WA (Australia) 2014. **Publications** *Association Newsletter* (4 a year). **Members** Invited; General; Student. Membership countries not specified. [2022/XJ0721/**C**]

♦ International Tourism Trade Fairs Association (ITTFA) 15697

Address not obtained.

History 15 Jan 1992. No activity reported since 2000. Former names and other names: *European Tourism Trade Fairs Association (ETTFA)* – former. **Aims** Increase awareness of public opinion and tourism authorities of the major role *exhibitions* play as economic and social strength; improve and enhance high standards in services to all participants. **Structure** Chairman, President, Vice-President, Treasurer and Secretary. **Languages** English. **Staff** 1.50 FTE, paid. **Finance** Members' dues. **Activities** Designing an international media database. Exhibitions. **Events** *International ITF Slovakiatour travel seminar and workshop* Bratislava (Slovakia) 2008, *Holiday World : Central Europe tourism seminar and workshop* Prague (Czech Rep) 2008, *Holiday World : Central Europe tourism industry seminar and workshop* Prague (Czech Rep) 2007, *PHILOXENIA : international tourism conference and seminar* Thessaloniki (Greece) 2007, *PHILOXENIA : international tourism conference and seminar* Thessaloniki (Greece) 2006. **Publications** Manuals; information kits; leaflets.

Members Full in 15 countries:
Belgium, Czechia, Finland, Greece, Hungary, Italy, Norway, Portugal, Russia, Slovakia, Spain, Sweden, Switzerland, Türkiye, UK.

Associate members in 3 countries:
Croatia, Italy, Russia.

IGO Relations Affiliate member of: *World Tourism Organization (UNWTO, #21861)*. [2011/XD4204/**t/D**]

- ♦ International Tourist Health Association (no recent information)

♦ International Towing Tank Conference (ITTC) 15698

Conférence internationale des bassins d'essais de carènes

Secretariat c/o FORCE Tech, Hjortekaersvej 99, 2800 Lyngby, Denmark. T. +4572157700. Fax +4572157701. E-mail: aad@force.dk.

URL: http://ittc.info/

History 27 Jun 1932, Hamburg (Germany), during the *International Hydro-mechanical Congress* as *International Conference of Ship Tank Superintendents*. Current name adopted 1954, Scandinavia. Reorganized 1960, London (UK). **Aims** Stimulate progress on solving technical problems of importance to towing tank superintendents regularly responsible for giving advice and information based on experiments with ship models; recommend standard procedure for ship model experimentation; stimulate research in fields requiring improved knowledge of ship hydrodynamics in experimental modelling; formulate collective policy on matters of common interest; provide effective organization for information exchange. **Structure** Controlling Body (meets every 3 years); Executive Committee; Technical Committees. **Languages** English. **Finance** Members' dues. Budget (annual): US$ 100,000. **Events** *Conference* Nantes (France) 2021, *Conference* Nantes (France) 2020, *Conference* Wuxi (China) 2017, *Conference* Copenhagen (Denmark) 2014, *Conference* Rio de Janeiro (Brazil) 2011. **Publications** *ITTC Dictionary of Hydromechanics*; *ITTC Recommended Procedures and Guidelines*. Conference proceedings.

Members Towing tanks and ship-model laboratories. Members in 30 countries:
Argentina, Australia, Austria, Belgium, Brazil, Bulgaria, Canada, China, Croatia, Denmark, Finland, France, Germany, Greece, India, Indonesia, Iran Islamic Rep, Italy, Japan, Korea Rep, Malaysia, Netherlands, Norway, Poland, Russia, Spain, Sweden, Türkiye, UK, USA.

Consultative Status Consultative status granted from: *International Maritime Organization (IMO, #14102)*. [2021/XD3917/**F**]

- ♦ International Town and Port Association / see Association internationale villes et ports – réseau mondial des villes portuaires (#02751)
- ♦ International Towns Association (inactive)

♦ International Toy Library Association (ITLA) 15699

Association internationale des Ludothèques – Asociación Internacional de Ludotecas

Pres address not obtained. E-mail: info.itla@gmail.com – mediacomunication.itla@gmail.com – media.comunication@itla-toylibraries.org.

URL: http://www.itla-toylibraries.org/

History 1990, Turin (Italy). Proposed 28 May 1987, Toronto ON (Canada), at 4th International Conference of Toy Libraries. Set up 1990, Torino (Italy). Registration: Belgium. **Aims** Promote the concept of toy libraries as a means of bringing *play* and play material to people; serve as a link between national toy library organizations, providing an opportunity for international exchange of ideas and material; maintain a liaison with othre organizations and associations pertaining to development and social issues, health, education and play; promote development, production and creation of toys and *games* that foster educational, physical, psychological, social and cultural growth, and disseminate information about such toys. **Structure** General Assembly (at international congress); Board of Directors. **Languages** English. **Staff** No FTE, paid. **Finance** Members' dues. **Activities** Events/meetings. **Events** *International Toy Library Conference* Melbourne, VIC (Australia) 2023, *International Toy Library Conference* Johannesburg (South Africa) 2019, *International Toy Library Conference* Leiden (Netherlands) 2017, *Conference* Seoul (Korea Rep) 2014, *Conference* Sao Paulo (Brazil) 2011. **Publications** *ITLA Newsletter* (4 a year). **Members** Full in 45 countries. Membership countries not specified. [2022/XD3292/**D**]

♦ International Toy Research Association (ITRA) 15700

Association internationale pour la recherche sur le jouet

Sec Univ of Texas Austin, Dept of Anthropology, 3705 Laurel Ledge Lane, Austin TX 78731, USA.

URL: http://www.itratoyresearch.org/

History 10 Sep 1993, Utrecht (Netherlands). Registration: Start date: 1998, France, Angoulème. **Aims** Stimulate further research on the role of toys in everyday life, particularly toys for children in their home environment as well as in preschool and compulsory school to meet their demands of good, secure and fun toys for joy and learning. **Structure** Board comprising President, Secretary-Treasurer, 7 delegates. **Languages** English. **Staff** None. **Finance** Members' dues: US$ 50. **Activities** Initiate cross-national studies. **Events** *World Conference* Rochester, NY (USA) 2023, *Conference* Paris (France) 2018, *Conference* Braga (Portugal) 2014, *Conference* Bursa (Turkey) 2011, *World Congress* Nafplion (Greece) 2008. **Publications** *ITRA Newsletter* (2-4 a year).

Members Researchers in 22 countries:
Australia, Austria, Belgium, Brazil, Canada, Denmark, France, Germany, Greece, India, Israel, Italy, Japan, Korea Rep, Netherlands, Nigeria, Portugal, Spain, Sweden, Türkiye, UK, USA. [2022.09.23/XD6161/**v/D**]

♦ International Trachoma Initiative (ITI) 15701

Dir 330 West Ponce de Leon Ave, Decatur GA 30030, USA. T. +14043710466. Fax +14043171087. E-mail: info@taskforce.org.

URL: http://www.trachoma.org/

History 1998. Founded by *Edna McConnel Clark Foundation (EMCF)* and Pfizer. Since 2009, a part of *Task Force for Global Health (TFGH, #20098)*, formerly 'Task Force for Child Survival and Development'. **Aims** Eliminate blindness caused by trachoma. **Structure** Board of Directors. **Finance** Funders include: *Bill and Melinda Gates Foundation (BMGF)*; *Lions Clubs International (LCI, #16485)*; *The Rockefeller Foundation (#18966)*; national foundations; individuals. **Publications** Annual Report. **IGO Relations** Partners: *Institute for Tropical Ophthalmology in Africa (IOTA, inactive)*; *UNICEF (#20332)*; *United States Agency for International Development (USAID)*. **NGO Relations** Member of (2): *International Coalition for Trachoma Control (ICTC, #12624)*; *Neglected Tropical Diseased NGO Network (NNN, #16969)*. Supports the work of: *WHO Alliance for the Global Elimination of Trachoma (GET 2020, #20935)*. Partners: *Americares Foundation*; *The Carter Center*; *Earth Institute at Columbia University*; *International Agency for the Prevention of Blindness (IAPB, #11597)*; *Light for the World (#16474)*; *Lions Clubs International (LCI, #16485)*; national organizations; *Operation Eyesight Universal*; *ORBIS International (#17786)*; *Sightsavers International (#19270)*; *United States Fund for UNICEF (UNICEF USA)*; *WaterAid (#20822)*; *World Vision International (WVI, #21904)*. [2020/XM1205/**E**]

- ♦ International Tracing Service / see Arolsen Archives – International Center on Nazi Persecution (#01112)

♦ International Track and Field Coaches Association (ITFCA) 15702

Association internationale des entraîneurs d'athlétisme – Internationaler Leichtatletic Lehrer Verband

Contact address not obtained. T. +12693491008.

History 9 Jan 1959, Olympia (Greece), an organizing committee having been appointed 20 Jun 1956, Berkeley CA (USA). **Aims** Establish contact between track and field coaches in different countries; exchange coaching techniques and experience; collect and distribute to coaches throughout the world information as to research in sciences related to track and field; cooperate with *athletic* federations by providing advice and service. **Structure** Congress (at least every 2 years); Council. **Languages** English, French, German, Irish Gaelic. **Staff** President, Secretary, Treasurer: voluntary. **Finance** Members' dues. Donations. **Events** *Congress* Athens (Greece) 2004, *Congress* Edmonton, AB (Canada) 2001, *Congress* Sydney, NSW (Australia) 2000, *Congress* Atlanta, GA (USA) 1996, *Congress* Paris (France) 1994. **Publications** Membership directory; congress reports; bulletins.

Members Active (1,620 individuals) in 84 countries and territories:
Albania, Algeria, Argentina, Aruba, Australia, Austria, Bahamas, Bahrain, Belgium, Bermuda, Bosnia-Herzegovina, Botswana, Brazil, Canada, China, Cook Is, Croatia, Cuba, Cyprus, Czechia, Denmark, Djibouti, Egypt, El Salvador, Eritrea, Eswatini, Ethiopia, Fiji, Finland, France, Germany, Great Britain, Greece, Grenada, Guatemala, Hong Kong, India, Ireland, Israel, Italy, Jamaica, Japan, Kenya, Kiribati, Korea Rep, Lebanon, Liberia, Libya, Malawi, Maldives, Mexico, Nepal, Netherlands, New Zealand, Nigeria, Northern Ireland, Northern Mariana Is, Norway, Pakistan, Philippines, Poland, Portugal, Puerto Rico, Russia, Samoa, Saudi Arabia, Scotland, Slovakia, Slovenia, South Africa, Spain, Sweden, Switzerland, Taiwan, Trinidad-Tobago, Tunisia, Uganda, UK, United Arab Emirates, Uruguay, USA, Virgin Is UK, Zambia, Zimbabwe. [2010.07.29/XF2638/**v/F**]

♦ International Trade Centre (ITC) 15703

Centre du commerce international – Centro de Comercio Internacional

Exec Dir Palais des Nations, 1211 Geneva 10, Switzerland. T. +41227300111. Fax +41227334439. E-mail: itcreg@intracen.org.

Head Office Rue de Montbrillant 54-56, 1202 Geneva, Switzerland.

URL: http://www.intracen.org/

History Mar 1964, Geneva (Switzerland). Established by *General Agreement on Tariffs and Trade (GATT, inactive)*. Sponsored jointly by GATT and *UNCTAD (#20285)*, Jan 1968, following decisions taken by the General Assembly of *United Nations (UN, #20515)* and the GATT Council to combine the resources and activities of both bodies in the field of export promotion. Formally recognized, Dec 1974, as a joint subsidiary organ of GATT and the United Nations, the latter acting through UNCTAD. Since 1973, recognized by *ECOSOC (#05331)* as the focal point in *United Nations System (#20635)* for technical cooperation in trade promotion. Became an executing agency of *UNDP (#20292)* in 1984. Since 1 Jan 1995 jointly operated by *World Trade Organization (WTO, #21864)* and the United Nations, the latter continuing to act through UNCTAD. Former names and other names: *International Trade Centre UNCTAD/GATT* – former; *Centre du commerce international CNUCED/GATT* – former; *Centro de Comercio Internacional UNCTAD/GATT* – former; *International Trade Centre UNCTAD/WTO* – former (1 Jan 1995); *Centre du commerce international CNUCED/OMC* – former (1 Jan 1995); *Centro de Comercio Internacional UNCTAD/OMC* – former (1 Jan 1995); *CCI* – former. Registration: EU Transparency Register, No/ID: 158043841743-12, Start date: 16 Mar 2021. **Aims** Foster sustainable economic development and contribute to achieving the United Nations Global Goals for sustainable development in developing countries and transition economies through trade and international business development. **Structure** Office of the Executive Director; Senior Management Committee. Divisions (4): Country Programmes; Market Development; Enterprises and Institutions; Programme Support. Joint Advisory Group (meets annually); Consultative Committee of the ITC Trust Fund. **Languages** English, French, Spanish. **Staff** 314.00 FTE, paid. **Finance** Regular programme equally financed by UN and WTO. Donor governments and civil society organizations finance specific projects, based on demand from countries. Annual budget: 92,900,000 USD (2018). **Activities** Guidance/assistance/consulting; advocacy/lobbying/activism; financial and/or material support. **Events** *Conference on Trade Promotion Organizations* Accra (Ghana) 2021, *SheTrades Global Meeting* Dubai (United Arab Emirates) 2021, *Annual Session* Geneva (Switzerland) 2021, *Trade for Sustainable Development Forum* Geneva (Switzerland) 2021, *Annual Session* Geneva (Switzerland) 2020. **Publications** *International Trade Forum* (4 a year) – magazine; *SME Competitiveness Outlook* (annual). Reports.

Members No membership of its own. All member states of UN and WTO. Governments of 194 countries and territories:

Afghanistan, Albania, Algeria, Andorra, Angola, Antigua-Barbuda, Argentina, Armenia, Australia, Austria, Azerbaijan, Bahamas, Bahrain, Bangladesh, Barbados, Belarus, Belgium, Belize, Benin, Bhutan, Bolivia, Bosnia-Herzegovina, Botswana, Brazil, Brunei Darussalam, Bulgaria, Burkina Faso, Burundi, Cambodia, Cameroon, Canada, Cape Verde, Central African Rep, Chad, Chile, China, Colombia, Comoros, Congo Brazzaville, Congo DR, Costa Rica, Côte d'Ivoire, Croatia, Cuba, Cyprus, Czechia, Denmark, Djibouti, Dominica, Dominican Rep, Ecuador, Egypt, El Salvador, Equatorial Guinea, Eritrea, Estonia, Eswatini, Ethiopia, Fiji, Finland, France, Gabon, Gambia, Georgia, Germany, Ghana, Greece, Grenada, Guatemala, Guinea, Guinea-Bissau, Guyana, Haiti, Holy See, Honduras, Hungary, Iceland, India, Indonesia, Iran Islamic Rep, Iraq, Ireland, Israel, Italy, Jamaica, Japan, Jordan, Kazakhstan, Kenya, Kiribati, Korea DPR, Korea Rep, Kuwait, Kyrgyzstan, Laos, Latvia, Lebanon, Lesotho, Liberia, Libya, Liechtenstein, Lithuania, Luxembourg, Madagascar, Malawi, Malaysia, Maldives, Mali, Malta, Marshall Is, Mauritania, Mauritius, Mexico, Micronesia FS, Moldova, Monaco, Mongolia, Montenegro, Morocco, Mozambique, Myanmar, Namibia, Nauru, Nepal, Netherlands, New Zealand, Nicaragua, Niger, Nigeria, North Macedonia, Norway, Oman, Pakistan, Palau, Panama, Papua New Guinea, Paraguay, Peru, Philippines, Poland, Portugal, Qatar, Romania, Russia, Rwanda, Samoa, San Marino, Sao Tomé-Principe, Saudi Arabia, Senegal, Serbia, Seychelles, Sierra Leone, Singapore, Slovakia, Slovenia, Solomon Is, Somalia, South Africa, South Sudan, Spain, Sri Lanka, St Kitts-Nevis, St Lucia, St Vincent-Grenadines, Sudan, Suriname, Sweden, Switzerland, Syrian AR, Tajikistan, Tanzania UR, Thailand, Timor-Leste, Togo, Tonga, Trinidad-Tobago, Tunisia, Türkiye, Turkmenistan, Tuvalu, Uganda, UK, Ukraine, United Arab Emirates, Uruguay, USA, Uzbekistan, Vanuatu, Venezuela, Vietnam, Yemen, Zambia, Zimbabwe.

IGO Relations World Trade Organization (Observer Status). Recognized by: *European Commission (EC, #06633)*. Cooperates with:

- *African Development Bank (ADB, #00283)*;
- *Arab Organization for Agricultural Development (AOAD, #01018)*;
- *Banque centrale des Etats de l'Afrique de l'Ouest (BCEAO, #03167)*;
- *Banque de développement des Etats de l'Afrique centrale (BDEAC, #03168)*;
- *Banque de développement des Etats des Grands Lacs (BDEGL, inactive)*;
- *Banque ouest africaine de développement (BOAD, #03170)*;
- *Caribbean Development Bank (CDB, #03492)*;
- *Commonwealth Fund for Technical Cooperation (CFTC, #04331)*;
- *Commonwealth Secretariat (#04362)*;
- *Council of Arab Economic Unity (CAEU, #04859)*;
- *East African Development Bank (EADB, #05183)*;
- *FAO (#09260)*;
- *ILO (#11123)*;
- *Commission de l'Océan Indien (COI, #04236)*;
- *Inter-American Development Bank (IDB, #11427)*;
- *International Atomic Energy Agency (IAEA, #12294)*;
- *International Bank for Reconstruction and Development (IBRD, #12317)*;
- *International Computing Centre (ICC, #12839)*;
- *International Jute Organization (IJO, inactive)*;
- *International Olive Council (IOC, #14405)*;
- *International Pepper Community (IPC, #14557)*;
- *International Spice Group (inactive)*;
- *International Tropical Timber Organization (ITTO, #15737)*;
- *Islamic Development Bank (IsDB, #16044)*;
- *Preferential Trade Area for Eastern and Southern African States (PTA, inactive)*, currently *Common Market for Eastern and Southern Africa (COMESA, #04296)*;
- *UNIDO (#20336)*;
- *United Nations Economic Commission for Africa (ECA, #20554)*;
- *United Nations Economic Commission for Europe (UNECE, #20555)*;
- *United Nations Economic Commission for Latin America and the Caribbean (ECLAC, #20556)*;
- *United Nations Economic and Social Commission for Asia and the Pacific (ESCAP, #20557)*;
- *United Nations Economic and Social Commission for Western Asia (ESCWA, #20558)*;
- *United Nations Volunteers (UNV, #20650)*;
- *WHO (#20950)*.

NGO Relations Links with a large number of international organizations concerned with specific trade functions or product groups, not specified but including: *International Chamber of Commerce (ICC, #12534)*.

[2021/XE2639/t/**E***]

♦ International Trade Centre UNCTAD/GATT / see International Trade Centre (#15703)
♦ International Trade Centre UNCTAD/WTO / see International Trade Centre (#15703)
♦ International Trade Development Association (inactive)

♦ International Trade and Finance Association (IT and FA) 15704

Exec Vice-Pres 200 Evans St, Winnsboro SC 29180, USA.

URL: https://www.itfassociation.org

History 1988. **Aims** Promote study of international trade and finance; encourage internationalization of economics and business curricula. **Structure** Board of Directors. **Languages** English. **Staff** None. **Finance** Sources: members' dues. **Activities** Events/meetings. **Events** *Conference* Winnsboro, SC (USA) 2021, *Conference* Livorno (Italy) 2019, *Conference* Livorno (Italy) 2019, *Conference* Beijing (China) 2018, *Conference* Poznań (Poland) 2017. **Publications** *The Global Economy Journal*. [2017.10.12/XQ0310/t/**C**]

♦ International Trade and Forfaiting Association (ITFA) 15705

Chairman c/o Format-A AG, Pfingstweidstrasse 102b, 8005 Zurich ZH, Switzerland.

URL: http://itfa.org/

History Aug 1999, as *International Forfaiting Association (IFA)*. Current title adopted 11 Sep 2014. EU Transparency Register: 659141434941-88. **Aims** Bring together banks and financial institutions engaged in originating and distributing trade related risk and finding creative ways to mitigate threats. **Structure** Board. **Languages** English. **Staff** 1.00 FTE, paid. **Finance** Members' dues. **Events** *Annual Conference* Singapore (Singapore) 2020, *Annual Global Commodities Finance Conference* Geneva (Switzerland) 2017, *Annual Conference* Dubai (United Arab Emirates) 2015, *Annual Conference* Barcelona (Spain) 2014, *Annual Conference* Floriana (Malta) 2013.

Members Full; Associate. Companies and organizations in 35 countries and territories:

Albania, Australia, Austria, Belarus, Burundi, China, Czechia, Egypt, France, Germany, Greece, Hong Kong, Hungary, India, Indonesia, Ireland, Italy, Korea Rep, Kuwait, Lebanon, Luxembourg, Malta, Netherlands, North Macedonia, Norway, Oman, Poland, Saudi Arabia, South Africa, Spain, Switzerland, UK, Ukraine, United Arab Emirates, USA. [2020/XM0412/t/**D**]

♦ International Trade and Investment Organisation (no recent information)

♦ International Trademark Association (INTA) 15706

Communications Dir 675 Third Ave, 3rd Floor, New York NY 10017, USA. T. +12126421700. Fax +12127687796.

INTA Europe Rue Belliard 40, 1040 Brussels, Belgium. E-mail: europe@inta.org.

URL: http://www.inta.org/

History 21 Nov 1878, New York, NY (USA). Founded by 17 merchants and manufacturers. Current title adopted when membership covered 110 countries. Former names and other names: *United States Trademark Association (USTA)* – former (21 Nov 1878 to May 1993); *Association des marques des Etats-Unis* – former (21 Nov 1878 to May 1993). Registration: USA; EU Transparency Register, No/ID: 10141574843-32. **Aims** Support trademarks and complementary intellectual property (IP) to foster consumer trust, economic growth and innovation; commit to building a better society through brands. **Structure** Board of Directors; Officers/Committees. **Languages** English. **Staff** 64.00 FTE, paid. **Finance** Sources: meeting proceeds; members' dues. **Activities** Advocacy/lobbying/activism; events/meetings; knowledge management/information dissemination; networking/liaising; training/education. **Events** *Annual meeting* San Diego, CA (USA) 2025, *Annual Meeting* Washington, DC (USA) 2022, *Annual Meeting* Houston, TX (USA) 2021, *Annual Meeting* San Diego, CA (USA) 2021, *Annual meeting and Leadership Meeting* New York, NY (USA) 2020. **Publications** *The Trademark Reporter* (5 a year); *INTA Bulletin* (23 a year). **Members** Organizations (over 6,400) from 185 countries representing about 34,000 trademark professionals and brand owners from major corporations, SMEs, law firms and non-profits. Other members include agency officials, professors and students. Categories: Corporate; Associate; Government; Academic. Membership countries not specified. **Consultative Status** Consultative status granted from: *ECOSOC (#05331)* (Special); *World Intellectual Property Organization (WIPO, #21593)* (Permanent Observer Status); *UNCTAD (#20285)* (General Category). **IGO Relations** Official cooperation and consultative status with: *European Union Intellectual Property Office (EUIPO, #08996)*. Regular consultation with: *ASEAN (#01141)*. Memoranda of Understanding with: *African Intellectual Property Organization (#00344)*. **NGO Relations** Input/influence on aspects of development or regulation of: *Internet (#15948)*. Partnership with: *The European Law Students' Association (ELSA, #07660)*.

[2022.10.11/XB0011/t/**B**]

♦ International Trade Organization / see World Trade Organization (#21864)
♦ International Trade Parliamentary Conference (inactive)
♦ International Trade Secretariats / see Global Union Federations (#10638)
♦ International Trade Secretariats Liaison Office (inactive)

♦ International Trade Union Alliance of Public Utilities, Local Industry and Services Workers 15707

Pres 42 Leninsky Prospekt, Moscow MOSKVA, Russia, 119119. T. +74959388024. Fax +74959306537.

URL: http://en.vkp.ru/

Members Trade unions in the CIS region (membership countries not specified). **NGO Relations** Affiliated with: *General Confederation of Trade Unions (GCTU, #10108)*. [2014/XM2461/t/**D**]

♦ International Trade Union Association CCCWU / see Consultative Council of Cultural Workers' Unions (#04766)
♦ International Trade Union Committee for Youth and Educational Questions (inactive)

♦ International Trade Union Confederation (ITUC) 15708

Confédération syndicale internationale (CSI) – Confederación Sindical Internacional – Internationaler Gewerkschaftsbund (IGB)

Pres Bd du Roi Albert II 5, Bte 1, 1210 Brussels, Belgium. T. +3222240211. Fax +3222015815. E-mail: info@ituc-csi.org.

Deputy Gen Sec address not obtained.

URL: http://www.ituc-csi.org/

History 1 Nov 2006, Vienna (Austria). Founded by merger of *International Confederation of Free Trade Unions (ICFTU, inactive)*, *World Confederation of Labour (WCL, inactive)* and other independent trade unions, during inaugural congress. Registration: EU Transparency Register, No/ID: 51806831589-68, Start date: 27 Apr 2009. **Aims** Promote and defend workers' *rights* and interests through international cooperation among trade unions, global campaigning and advocacy within the major global institutions. **Structure** Congress (at least every 4 years). Constitutional Committees: General Council; Executive Bureau; Women Committee; Youth Committee. General Council (meets at least once a year), consisting of up to 78 titular members: 70 according regional distribution; 6 nominated by Women's Committee; 2 nominated by Youth Committee. Executive Bureau (meets at least twice a year), comprising President, General Secretary and up to 25 titular members of the General Council, including Chair and Vice-Chair of Women's Committee and Chair of Youth Committee. Human and Trade Union Rights Committee. Regional organizations and structure (4): *International Trade Union Confederation – African Regional Organization (#15709)*, Lomé (Togo); *ITUC – Asia Pacific (ITUC-AP, #16076)*, Singapore (Singapore); *Confederación Sindical de Trabajadores y Trabajadoras de las Américas (CSA, #04480)*, Sao Paulo (Brazil); *Pan-European Regional Council (PERC, #18180)*. Sub-Offices (6): Geneva (Switzerland); New Independent States – Moscow (Russia); Washington DC (USA); South-East European – Sarajevo (Bosnia-Herzegovina); Kowloon (Hong Kong); Amman (Jordan). Also includes: *ITUC Asia-Pacific Labour Network (APLN)*; Trade Union Development Cooperation Network (TUDCN). Head Office at *International Trade Union House, Brussels (ITUH)*. **Languages** English, French, German, Spanish. **Staff** 70.00 FTE, paid. **Finance** Sources: members' dues. **Activities** Advocacy/lobbying/activism; events/meetings; guidance/assistance/consulting. **Events** *World Congress* Melbourne, VIC (Australia) 2022, *World Peace Conference* New York, NY (USA) 2020, *World Youth Summit* Berlin (Germany) 2019, *Symposium on the Unchecked Power of Amazon in Today's Economy and Society* Brussels (Belgium) 2019, *Women and Youth Conference* Tokyo (Japan) 2019. **Publications** Available on website.

Members Affiliated organizations (340), totalling 182 million workers, in 164 countries and territories:

Afghanistan, Albania, Algeria, Angola, Antigua-Barbuda, Argentina, Armenia, Aruba, Australia, Austria, Azerbaijan, Bahrain, Bangladesh, Barbados, Belarus, Belgium, Belize, Benin, Bermuda, Bonaire Is, Bosnia-Herzegovina, Botswana, Brazil, Bulgaria, Burkina Faso, Burundi, Cambodia, Cameroon, Canada, Cape Verde, Central African Rep, Chad, Chile, Colombia, Comoros, Congo Brazzaville, Congo DR, Cook Is, Costa Rica, Côte d'Ivoire, Croatia, Curaçao, Cyprus, Czechia, Denmark, Djibouti, Dominica, Dominican Rep, Ecuador, Egypt, El Salvador, Eritrea, Estonia, Eswatini, Ethiopia, Fiji, Finland, France, Gabon, Gambia, Georgia, Germany, Ghana, Greece, Grenada, Guatemala, Guinea, Guinea-Bissau, Haiti, Holy See, Honduras, Hong Kong, Hungary, Iceland, India, Indonesia, Ireland, Israel, Italy, Japan, Jordan, Kazakhstan, Kenya, Kiribati, Korea Rep, Kosovo, Kuwait, Latvia, Lesotho, Liberia, Liechtenstein, Lithuania, Luxembourg, Madagascar, Malawi, Malaysia, Mali, Malta, Mauritania, Mauritius, Mexico, Moldova, Mongolia, Montenegro, Morocco, Mozambique, Myanmar, Namibia, Nepal, Netherlands, New Caledonia, New Zealand, Nicaragua, Niger, Nigeria, North Macedonia, Norway, Oman, Pakistan, Palestine, Panama, Paraguay, Peru, Philippines, Poland, Polynesia Fr, Portugal, Romania, Russia, Rwanda, Samoa, San Marino, Sao Tomé-Principe, Senegal, Serbia, Sierra Leone, Singapore, Slovakia, Somalia, South Africa, Spain, Sri Lanka, St Lucia, Sudan, Suriname, Sweden, Switzerland, Taiwan, Tanzania UR, Thailand, Togo, Tonga, Trinidad-Tobago, Tunisia, Türkiye, Uganda, UK, Ukraine, USA, Vanuatu, Venezuela, Yemen, Zambia, Zimbabwe.

Consultative Status Consultative status granted from: *ECOSOC (#05331)* (General); *UNESCO (#20322)* (Consultative Status); *ILO (#11123)* (General); *UNCTAD (#20285)* (General Category); *World Intellectual Property Organization (WIPO, #21593)* (Permanent Observer Status); *FAO (#09260)*; *UNIDO (#20336)*; *UNEP (#20299)*. **IGO Relations** Associated with Department of Global Communications of the United Nations. Observer to: *International Organization for Migration (IOM, #14454)*. Accredited to the Conference of the Parties of: *Secretariat of the United Nations Convention to Combat Desertification (Secretariat of the UNCCD, #19208)*. Accredited by: *Commonwealth Secretariat (#04362)*; *Green Climate Fund (GCF, #10714)*; *United Nations Framework Convention on Climate Change – Secretariat (UNFCCC, #20564)*; *United Nations Office at Vienna (UNOV, #20604)*. Francophonie syndicale (FS) accredited by: *Organisation internationale de la Francophonie (OIF, #17809)*. **NGO Relations** Member of (12): *Committee of NGOs on Human Rights, Geneva (#04275)*; *Federation of European and International Associations Established in Belgium (FAIB, #09508)*; *Fédération des Institutions Internationales établies à Genève (FIIG, #09599)*; *Global Labour University (GLU,*

#10448); *GoodElectronics (#10679)*; *Informal Working Group on Gender and Trade (IWGGT, no recent information)*; *UNCAC Coalition (#20283)*; *Vienna NGO Committee on the Family (#20774)*; *Women's Working Group on Financing for Development (WWG on FfD, #21036)*; *World Benchmarking Alliance (WBA, #21228)*; *World Organisation Against Torture (OMCT, #21685)*; *World Social Forum (WSF, #21797)*. Partner of (2): *Global Call for Climate Action (GCCA, inactive)*; *Green Economy Coalition (GEC, #10717)*. Supports (1): *Global Call for Action Against Poverty (GCAP, #10263)*. Instrumental in setting up (1): *Global Unions Committee on Workers' Capital (CWC, #10639)*. Board member of: *Conference of Non-Governmental Organizations in Consultative Relationship with the United Nations (CONGO, #04635)*. Member of *Global Union Federations (GUF, #10638)*, together with 10 other GUFs: *Building and Wood Workers' International (BWI, #03355)*; *Education International (EI, #05371)*; *IndustriALL Global Union (IndustriALL, #11177)*; *International Arts and Entertainment Alliance (IAEA, #11676)*; *International Federation of Journalists (IFJ, #13462)*; *International Transport Workers' Federation (ITF, #15726)*; *Public Services International (PSI, #18572)*; *Trade Union Advisory Committee to the OECD (TUAC, #20186)*; *UNI Global Union (#20338)*. Allied partner of: *Financial Transparency Coalition (FTC, #09772)*. [2023/XM2085/ty/**A**]

♦ International Trade Union Confederation – African Regional Organization 15709

SG CSI-Afrique, Route internationale d'Atakpamé, Centre FOPADESC Agoè-Zongo, Lomé, Togo. T. +22822250710. Fax +22822256113. E-mail: info@ituc-africa.org.
URL: http://www.ituc-africa.org/

History as a regional organization of *International Confederation of Free Trade Unions (ICFTU, inactive)*, as *ICFTU African Regional Organization (AFRO) – Organisation régionale africaine de la CISL (ORAf) – Organización Regional Africana de la CIOSL (ORAf) – Afrikanische Regionalorganisation des IBFG*. Following merger of IFCTU and *World Confederation of Labour (WCL, inactive)*, Nov 2006, into *International Trade Union Confederation (ITUC, #15708)*, adopted current title. **Aims** Work for full, productive and decent *employment* and elimination of *discrimination* based on race, sex, nationality or creed; seek universal recognition and application of trade union rights; strengthen international trade union *solidarity*, giving *relief* to oppression, repression victims and other sufferers due to natural and industrial disasters. **Staff** 16.00 FTE, paid. **Activities** Advocacy/lobbying/activism; politics/policy/regulatory; knowledge management/information dissemination. **Events** *Ordinary congress* Abuja (Nigeria) 2011, *Congress* Tunis (Tunisia) 2005, *Sustainable social justice in the global economy – an Africa trade union challenge in the century* Nairobi (Kenya) 2001, *Regional educational workshop* Nairobi (Kenya) 1999, *Congress* Dakar (Senegal) 1997. **Members** Trade union organizations (86) in 44 African countries representing 13 millions members. Membership countries not specified. **Consultative Status** Consultative status granted from: *African Commission on Human and Peoples' Rights (ACHPR, #00255)* (Observer); *ILO (#11123)* (Regional). [2017/XE3238/t/**E**]

♦ International Trade Union Confederation – Asian and Pacific Regional Organization / see ITUC – Asia Pacific (#16076)
♦ International Trade Union Confederation – Asia Pacific / see ITUC – Asia Pacific (#16076)

♦ International Trade Union "Elektroprofsoyuz" (Electrounion) 15710

Pres 42 Leninsky Prospekt, Moscow MOSKVA, Russia, 119119. T. +7959307416. Fax +7959387812.
History 17 Dec 1991, Moscow (Russia). **Members** Trade unions in the CIS region (membership countries not specified). **IGO Relations** *Commonwealth of Independent States (CIS, #04341)*. **NGO Relations** Affiliated with: *General Confederation of Trade Unions (GCTU, #10108)*. [2008.10.06/XM2478/t/**D**]

♦ International Trade Union House, Brussels (internationally oriented national body)

♦ International Traditional Federation of Karate (ITFK) 15711

Admin Office Av Com Franco 2885, Curitiba PR, 81520-230, Brazil. E-mail: secretary@itkf.global.
URL: https://itkf.global/

History 1974. Became part of *World Karate Federation (WKF, #21608)*, 1994. Former names and other names: *International Traditional Karate Federation* – former (1974); *International Amateur Karate Federation (IAKF)* – alias. **Aims** Provide international rules, regulations and competition standards for *amateur* karate. **Structure** Meeting (annual). **Activities** Organizes international and regional championships. **Events** *Meeting* Australia 1988. **Publications** *ITFK Official Circular* (2 a month).
Members National karate federations in 62 countries:
Albania, Antigua-Barbuda, Argentina, Armenia, Australia, Austria, Belarus, Belgium, Brazil, Canada, Chile, Colombia, Croatia, Cyprus, Czechia, Dominican Rep, France, Georgia, Germany, Greece, Hungary, India, Indonesia, Iran Islamic Rep, Ireland, Israel, Italy, Japan, Kyrgyzstan, Latvia, Lithuania, Malaysia, Malta, Mexico, Moldova, Netherlands, North Macedonia, Norway, Panama, Paraguay, Peru, Philippines, Poland, Portugal, Puerto Rico, Romania, Russia, Rwanda, Serbia, Slovakia, Slovenia, South Africa, Spain, Sri Lanka, Switzerland, Turkmenistan, UK, Ukraine, Uruguay, USA, Uzbekistan, Venezuela. [2022/XD0162/**B**]

♦ International Traditional Karate Federation / see International Traditional Federation of Karate (#15711)

♦ International Traditional Taekwon-Do Federation (ITTAF) 15712

Federación Internacional de Taekwon-do Tradicional

Headquarters PO Box 33, San Jaime Str No 11 – 3, Alcoy, 03801 Alicante, Castellón, Spain. T. +34965546980. Fax +34965546980. E-mail: ittafpresident@hotmail.com.
URL: http://www.ittaf.com/

History Current statutes adopted 2011. Registered in accordance with Spanish law. **Structure** Assembly; Executive Board. **Languages** English, Spanish. **NGO Relations** Member of: *The Association for International Sport for All (TAFISA, #02763)*; *International Council of Sport Science and Physical Education (ICSSPE, #13077)*. [2018.09.07/XM5484/**D**]

♦ International Traffic Medicine Association (ITMA) 15713

Association internationale de médecine du trafic – Asociación Internacional de Medicina del Trafico – International Gesellschaft für Verkehrsmedizin – Associazione Internazionale di Medicina del Traffico

Sec address not obtained.
Pres address not obtained.
URL: http://www.trafficmedicine.org/

History 1960, San Remo (Italy). Founded at 1st meeting of Italian national association. Constitution confirmed, 1963, Rome (Italy), at first IAATM Congress. Bylaws adopted 3 Nov 2000; amended: 24 Sep 2002; 27 Jan 2003; 25 Mar 2019. Former names and other names: *International Association for Accident and Traffic Medicine (IAATM)* – former (10 Dec 1960 to 3 Nov 2000); *Association internationale de médecine des accidents et du trafic* – former (10 Dec 1960 to 3 Nov 2000); *Asociación Internacional de Medicina de Accidentes y del Trafico* – former (10 Dec 1960 to 3 Nov 2000); *Internationale Gesellschaft für Unfall- und Verkehrsmedizin* – former (10 Dec 1960 to 3 Nov 2000); *Associazione Internazionale di Medicina degli Infortuni e del Traffico* – former (10 Dec 1960 to 3 Nov 2000). **Aims** Promote and develop the study of traffic medicine; promote and maintain contact with governments, supra-national and national organizations concerned with medicine-related traffic problems; sponsor efforts to unify and harmonize all legal aspects of medicine-related traffic problems; ensure diffusion of the results of studies carried out; support and develop mechanisms for prevention of traffic *crashes* and enhancement of safe mobility; educate concerning medical aspects of traffic *safety*. **Structure** Congress (every 1-2 years). Board of Directors, comprising President, President-Elect, Treasurer, Secretary, Immediate Past-President and 8 Regional Vice-Presidents (Africa; Australasia; Eastern Europe; Western Europe; Near and Middle East; Far East Asia; North America; South America). **Languages** English. **Staff** No permanent staff. **Finance** Sources: members' dues; subscriptions. Budget (annual): US$ 10,000 – 15,000. **Activities** Organizes world congress. **Events** *Congress* China 2022, *Congress* Shanghai (China) 2021, *Congress* Shanghai (China) 2020, *Congress* Curitiba (Brazil) 2018, *Congress* Beijing (China) 2016. **Publications** *Traffic Injury Prevention* (4-6 a year) – journal.
Members in 25 countries and territories:
Argentina, Australia, Belgium, Brazil, Canada, China, Egypt, Finland, France, Germany, Hong Kong, Hungary, Ireland, Israel, Japan, Korea Rep, Netherlands, New Zealand, Norway, Saudi Arabia, South Africa, Sweden, UK, United Arab Emirates, USA. [2020/XC1173/**C**]

♦ International Traffic Police and Road Transport Organization (no recent information)

♦ International Trail Running Association (ITRA) 15714

Contact address not obtained. T. +41215190208. E-mail: contact@itra.run.
URL: http://www.i-tra.org/

History Jul 2013, following a conference Sep 2012, Courmayeur (Italy). **Aims** Give a voice to parties involved in trail running so as to promote its strong values, diversity, safety of races and the health of runners; further development of trail running and ensure a constructive dialogue between national and international bodies with an interest in the sport. **Structure** General Meeting (annual); Steering Committee; Executive Committee. **Activities** Sporting activities. **Events** *General Assembly* Paris (France) 2015.
Members Full in 29 countries:
Argentina, Australia, Austria, Belgium, Brazil, Bulgaria, Canada, China, Croatia, Denmark, France, Germany, Hungary, Israel, Italy, Japan, Korea Rep, Latvia, Mexico, Nepal, Norway, Peru, Poland, Portugal, South Africa, Spain, Switzerland, Türkiye, UK. [2016/XM4702/**C**]

♦ International Training Center of Indigenous Peoples (ITCIP) 15715

Coordinator C P Holbøllsvej 11, PO Box 901, 3900 Nuuk Greenland, Denmark. T. +299539191.
History Dec 1997. Founded by Ingmar Egede and 17 international experts in human rights and indigenous people's issues. **Aims** Create a learning environment in which representatives for indigenous peoples' organizations and nations can expand upon their research skills and knowledge of international issues, including human rights issues in order for them to comfortably play central roles in the international decision-making process. **Structure** International Advisory Board. International faculty. **Activities** Training/education. Organizes annual training workshops to indigenous peoples worldwide focusing on Indigenous Peoples in the International System. [2021/XJ0539/**F**]

♦ International Training Center for Intangible Cultural Heritage in the Asia-Pacific Region under the auspices of UNESCO (CRIHAP) 15716

Dir Jia 1, Huixin Beili, Chaoyang District, 100029 Beijing, China. T. +861064966526. Fax +861064969281. E-mail: administration@crihap.cn.
URL: http://en.crihap.cn/

History Established 22 Feb 2012, Beijing (China), under Agreement between Government of China and *UNESCO (#20322)*. A UNESCO Category II Centre. Registered in accordance with Chinese law. **Aims** Promote the UNESCO Convention for the Safeguarding of the Intangible Cultural Heritage and contribute to its implementation in the Asia-Pacific Region; increase the participation of communities, groups and individuals in Safeguarding intangible cultural heritage in the region; enhance the capacity of Asia-Pacific Member States of UNESCO in safeguarding ICH, particularly by strengthening the capacities of concerned personnel; foster regional and international cooperation for safeguarding ICH. **Structure** Governing Board; Advisory Committee; Secretariat. **Activities** Events/meetings; training/education. **NGO Relations** *Regional Centre for the Safeguarding of Intangible Cultural Heritage in Africa*; *Regional Centre for the Safeguarding of the Intangible Cultural Heritage in South-Eastern Europe under the auspices of UNESCO (#18759)*. [2017/XM6090/**E**]

♦ International Training Centre for Appropriate Technology and Development / see Artefact – Centre for Energy, Appropriate Technology and International Development Cooperation
♦ International Training Centre on Human Rights and Peace Teaching, Geneva (see: #21184)

♦ International Training Centre of the ILO (ITC) 15717

Centre international de formation de l'OIT (CIF)

Acting Gen Dir Viale Maestri del Lavoro 10, 10127 Turin TO, Italy.
URL: http://www.itcilo.org/

History 1964. Founded by *ILO (#11123)* in collaboration with the Italian Government, as a training arm of the ILO. The Centre has matured from the technical and vocational institute of its early days into a focal point for advanced in-service training and post-experience specialization. Former names and other names: *International Centre for Advanced Technical and Vocational Training (CATVT)* – former (1964 to 5 Mar 1991); *Centre international de perfectionnement professionnel et technique* – former (1964 to 5 Mar 1991); *Centro Internacional de Perfeccionamiento Profesional y Técnico* – former (1964 to 5 Mar 1991); *ILO Turin Centre* – alias; *Centre de l'OIT à Turin* – alias; *Centro de la OIT en Turin* – alias; *Centro OIL a Turin* – alias; *Turin Centre* – alias; *Centre de Turin* – alias. **Aims** Through training and learning, develop human resources and institutional capacity in pursuit of ILO's primary goal of decent work men and women, focusing 4 strategic objectives: fundamental principles and rights at work, employment, social protection and social dialogue; contribute to strengthening the capacity of countries, organizations and individuals to manage development processes and interventions; design and deliver training programmes using the latest training technologies. **Structure** Governed by a tripartite Board, chaired by Director-General of ILO, composed of representatives of governments, employers and workers, including 24 members appointed by ILO Governing Body from among its own membership and representatives of the: *United Nations (UN, #20515)*; *UNDP (#20292)*; *UNESCO (#20322)*; *UNIDO (#20336)*; Italian Government; City of Turin; Piedmont Region; 'Unione Industriale di Turin'. **Languages** Arabic, Chinese, English, French, Italian, Portuguese, Russian, Spanish. **Staff** About 200, grouped in *Staff Union of the International Training Centre of the ILO (ITCILO Staff Union)*. *Administrative Tribunal of the International Labour Organization (ILO Tribunal, #00118)* is competent to settle disputes. **Finance** Core subsidies from ILO and the Italian Government. Training programmes eligible for funding by bilateral (central or regional) donors, multilateral agencies, development banks and commissions, foundations, recipient governments and other institutions. **Activities** Training/education; events/meetings. **Events** *Forum on Decent Work and Poverty Reduction* Doha (Qatar) 2011. **Publications** *Course Catalogue* (annual); *Director's Implementation Report* (annual); *GenderInfo* – online newsletter. Printed and non-printed training and learning materials; brochure. Information Services: Computerized documentation and information centre. **Members** Not a membership organization. **NGO Relations** Partnerships with national and international employer and worker organizations, and with national or regional training institutions. Ad-hoc partnership with NGOs for implementation of projects and training activities. [2022/XF2186/**E***]

♦ International Training Centre on Vital Statistics and Health Statistics for South-East Asia (inactive)
♦ International Training and Education Center on HIV (internationally oriented national body)

♦ International Training and Simulation Alliance (ITSA) 15718

Contact 2101 Wilson Boulevard, Ste 700, Arlington VA 22201-3061, USA. T. +17032479471. E-mail: cdwyer@ndia.org.
URL: http://www.itsassociation.org/

Aims Promote a better understanding worldwide of the importance of training and simulation technology for the use in every profession and endeavour known to mankind. **Events** *Asian defence training and simulation seminar* Kuala Lumpur (Malaysia) 2010.
Members Associations in 3 countries:
Australia, Korea Rep, USA.
International organization:
European Training and Simulation Association (ETSA, #08935). [2009.03.03/XM1905/y/**F**]

♦ International Trampoline Federation (inactive)

♦ International Transactional Analysis Association (ITAA) 15719

Association internationale d'analyse transactionnelle

Contact address not obtained. E-mail: info@itaaworld.org.
URL: http://www.itaaworld.org/

History 1958, San Francisco, CA (USA). Founded at the *Social Psychiatry Seminar*, by Dr Eric Berne (1910–1970). Registered as a non-profit educational corporation in the State of California (USA), 6 May 1960. Articles amended and present name adopted 20 Oct 1964. **Aims** Encourage the advancement of transactional analysis as a theory of personality, useful in *psychotherapy*, personal and social growth, education, business and other fields of human interaction. **Structure** Organizes Annual Conference and Spring Meeting, elects Board of Trustees for 3-year term and Officers for 2-year term. Training Standards Committee and Board of Certification. Standing and ad-hoc committees. **Languages** English. **Staff** 3.00 FTE, paid. **Finance** Sources: meeting proceeds; members' dues; sale of products; subscriptions. Other sources: rental income. **Activities** Grants the Eric Bern Memorial Scientific Award (annually). Library; information service. Annual Conferences; annual Spring Meeting. **Events** *Courage, Physis, and Resilience: Resources for a New Emerging World*. 2022,

Conference Daegu (Korea Rep) 2021, *Expanding the TA map – sharing learning across our fields* Birmingham (UK) 2020, *World Conference for Transactional Analysis* Birmingham (UK) 2020, *Joint Conference* Raleigh, NC (USA) 2019. **Publications** *Transactional Analysis Journal* (4 a year); *Script Newsletter* (9 a year). Mailing List – including psychologists, social workers, marriage and family counselors, organizational consultants, educators, sorted by geographic area or member level.
Members Regular Professional Individuals and Organizations (5,000) in 58 countries and territories:
Argentina, Aruba, Australia, Austria, Bangladesh, Belgium, Bolivia, Brazil, Canada, Chile, China, Colombia, Costa Rica, Croatia, Denmark, Dominican Rep, Ecuador, Finland, France, Germany, Greece, Honduras, Hong Kong, Hungary, India, Indonesia, Iran Islamic Rep, Ireland, Israel, Italy, Japan, Korea DPR, Malaysia, Mexico, Monaco, Mozambique, Netherlands, New Zealand, Norway, Pakistan, Paraguay, Peru, Philippines, Poland, Russia, Serbia-Montenegro, Singapore, South Africa, Spain, Sweden, Switzerland, Taiwan, Thailand, Türkiye, UK, Uruguay, USA, Venezuela.
Also in Caribbean.
NGO Relations Joint events with: *European Association for Transactional Analysis (EATA, #06257)*; *Latin American Transactional Analysis Association (ALAT, no recent information)*; *Western Pacific Association for Transactional Analysis (WPATA).* [2020/XC4383/**C**]

♦ International Transfer Live Lessons Network (unconfirmed)

♦ International Trans Fund (ITF) 15720

Fondo Internacional Trans (FIT)

Contact address not obtained. E-mail: info@transfund.org.
URL: https://www.transfund.org/

Aims Mobilize sustainable resources for strong, trans-led movements and collective action; address and eliminate funding gaps impacting trans groups across the globe. **Structure** Steering Committee; Grant Making Panel. **Languages** English, Spanish. **Activities** Financial and/or material support. **NGO Relations** Member of: *Global Philanthropy Project (GPP, #10546).* [2020.03.18/XM8811/f/**F**]

♦ International Transmembrane Transporter Society (ITTS) 15721

Sec Medical Univ of Vienna, Ctr for Physiology and Pharmacology, Inst of Pharmacology, Währingerstr 13a, 1090 Vienna, Austria. E-mail: ittsociety@ittsociety.org.
URL: http://www.ittsociety.org/

History Evolved from a meeting held Apr 2013, Cancún (Mexico). Formal founding 2014. Statutes adopted 20 Aug 2014; amended 8 Sep 2017; 15 May 2018; and 8 Nov 2020. **Aims** Promote transporter biologists and transporter-related research. **Structure** Council; Executive Committee. **Languages** English. **Staff** Voluntary. **Activities** Events/meetings. **Events** *Meeting* Copenhagen (Denmark) 2022, *Meeting* Copenhagen (Denmark) 2021, *Meeting* Copenhagen (Denmark) 2020, *Conference* Vienna (Austria) 2018. **Publications** *ITTS Newsletter* (2 a year).
Members Full in 17 countries:
Australia, Austria, Belgium, Canada, Chile, Denmark, France, Germany, Hungary, Israel, Italy, Japan, Netherlands, Spain, Switzerland, UK, USA. [2020.01.17/XM7998/**C**]

♦ International Transpersonal Association (ITA) 15722

Internationale Transpersoonlijke Associatie

Contact address not obtained. E-mail: itacontactpoint@gmail.com.
URL: http://www.transpersonalassociation.com/

History 31 Oct 1979, San Francisco CA (USA). Registered in accordance with California State Law, USA. Dissolved 2004. Relaunched 2008. Incorporated 27 May 2008. **Aims** Promote a transpersonal vision in research, scholarship, education, and therapeutic and practical spheres in which a spiritual orientation is beneficial. **Structure** Board. **Languages** English. **Staff** Voluntary. **Finance** Sources: organizing conferences; scientific activities. **Activities** Events/meetings; knowledge management/information dissemination. **Events** *International Transpersonal Conference* Prague (Czechia) 2017, *International conference* Palm Springs, CA (USA) 2004, *International conference* Manaus (Brazil) 1996, *International conference* Killarney (Ireland) 1994, *International conference* Prague (Czechoslovakia) 1992. **Publications** *International Journal of Transpersonal Studies.* **Members** Individuals, mainly in North America but in a number of countries (not specified). **NGO Relations** Cooperates with: *Association for Holotropic Breathwork International (AHBI, inactive)*; *City of Peace Foundation (no recent information)*; *European Transpersonal Association (EUROTAS- Global Transpersonal Network, #08937)*; *Green Earth Foundation*; *International Transpersonal Centre (ITC, no recent information)*; *South American Transpersonal Association (no recent information).* [2017/XD8236/**B**]

♦ International Transplant Coordinators Society (inactive)
♦ International Transplant Nurses Society (internationally oriented national body)

♦ International Transportation Economics Association (ITEA) 15723

Sec Ist di Scienze Economiche, Univ degli Studi di Urbino "Carlo Bo", Via Saffi 22, 61029 Urbino FM, Italy. T. +39722305563. Fax +39722305550.
URL: http://www.iteaweb.org/

History 10 Jul 2010, Valencia (Spain), when bylaws were adopted. Registered in accordance with Finnish law. **Aims** Promote the development and application of transport economics. **Structure** General Meeting (annual). Executive Committee, including President, Vice-President, Secretary and Treasurer. **Finance** Members' dues. **Activities** Meeting activities; awards; education. **Events** *Annual Conference* Paris (France) 2019, *Kuhmo Nectar Conference* Barcelona (Spain) 2017, *Kuhmo Nectar Conference* Santiago (Chile) 2016, *Kuhmo Nectar Conference* Oslo (Norway) 2015, *Kuhmo Nectar Conference* Toulouse (France) 2014. **Publications** *Economics of Transportation: Journal of ITEA*; *ITEA Newsletter.* [2014/XJ5407/**D**]

♦ International Transportation Safety Association (ITSA) 15724

Sec PO Box 95404, 2509 CK The Hague, Netherlands. T. +31703337000. Fax +31703337077. E-mail: itsa@ntsb.gov.
URL: http://www.itsasafety.org/

History 22 Oct 1993, Apeldoorn (Netherlands), on signature of an agreement by chairmen of national independent transport accident investigation boards of Netherlands, Sweden, USA and Canada. **Aims** Improve transport safety; promote independent investigation into causes and safety deficiencies of transportation accidents and incidents; exchange information on safety deficiencies, studies, recommendations, accident data, and investigation techniques and methodologies. **Structure** No formal structure. Member chairmen meet annually. Officers: President; Secretary. **Finance** No members' dues; no budget. Part-time secretariat financed by Dutch presidency. **Activities** Investigations and studies. **Events** *Chairman Meeting* Queenstown (New Zealand) 2014, *Chairman Meeting* Delhi (India) 2013, *World congress* 2003, *Transportation recorder symposium / Symposium* Washington, DC (USA) 1999, *World congress* Delft (Netherlands) 1998.
Members Independent national boards in 15 countries and territories:
Australia, Canada, Finland, France, India, Japan, Korea Rep, Netherlands, New Zealand, Norway, Russia, Sweden, Taiwan, UK, USA. [2021/XF4749/**F**]

♦ International Transport Forum (ITF) 15725

Forum international des transport – Weltverkehrsforum

SG 2 rue André Pascal, 75775 Paris CEDEX 16, France. T. +33145249710. Fax +33145249742 – +33145241322. E-mail: contact@itf-oecd.org.
URL: https://www.itf-oecd.org/

History 17 Oct 1953, Brussels (Belgium). Founded as an intergovernmental organization within the *OECD (#17693)* family, and on signature of a Protocol, following proposals adopted at European Inland Transport Conference, 18 Mar-17 June 1953, Paris (France). ECMT was supplanted by the International Transport Forum in 2006, following transformation into a global organization. Former names and other names: *European Conference of Ministers of Transport (ECMT)* – former; *Conférence européenne des ministres des transports (CEMT)* – former; *Europäische Konferenz der Verkehrsminister* – former. **Aims** As a global platform and meeting place for transport, logistics and mobility: foster a deeper understanding of the role of transport in economic growth, environmental sustainability and social inclusion and to raise the public profile of transport policy. **Structure** Summit of Ministers of Transport (annually), in Leipzig (Germany); Presidency, annually rotating among member countries; Transport Management Board, chaired by Presidency country; Task Force; Transport Research Centre; Corporate Partnership Board; Secretariat. **Languages** English, French. **Staff** Supplied by OECD. **Finance** Specific International Transport Forum budget managed by OECD. **Activities** Events/meetings; knowledge management/information dissemination. **Events** *Annual Summit* Leipzig (Germany) 2023, *Annual Summit* Leipzig (Germany) 2022, *IRTAD Conference* Lyon (France) 2022, *Annual Summit* Paris (France) 2021, *Annual Summit* Leipzig (Germany) 2020. **Publications** *Transport Outlook* (2 a year); *Summit Highlights* (annual); *ITF Newsletter*, *Policy Brief* – newsletter; *Statistics Brief* – newsletter. *Case-Specific Policy Analysis Report* – series; *Corporate Partnership Board Report* – series; *Discussion Paper* – series; *Research Report* – series; *Roundtable Report* – series. Documentation Centre.
Members Full: Governments of 64 countries:
Albania, Argentina, Armenia, Australia, Austria, Azerbaijan, Belarus, Belgium, Bosnia-Herzegovina, Bulgaria, Cambodia, Canada, Chile, China, Colombia, Croatia, Czechia, Denmark, Estonia, Finland, France, Georgia, Germany, Greece, Hungary, Iceland, India, Ireland, Israel, Italy, Japan, Kazakhstan, Korea Rep, Latvia, Liechtenstein, Lithuania, Luxembourg, Malta, Mexico, Moldova, Mongolia, Montenegro, Morocco, Netherlands, New Zealand, North Macedonia, Norway, Poland, Portugal, Romania, Russia, Serbia, Slovakia, Slovenia, Spain, Sweden, Switzerland, Tunisia, Türkiye, UK, Ukraine, United Arab Emirates, USA, Uzbekistan.
IGO Relations Cooperates with: *Asia-Pacific Economic Cooperation (APEC, #01887)*; *Central Commission for the Navigation of the Rhine (CCNR, #03687)*; *Commission du Danube (CD, #04210)*; *Committee on Inland Transport (#04262)*; *Council of Europe (CE, #04881)*; *European Commission (EC, #06633)*; *EUROCONTROL (#05667)*; *Organisation intergouvernementale pour les transports internationaux ferroviaires (OTIF, #17807)*; *International Bank for Reconstruction and Development (IBRD, #12317)* (World Bank); *International Civil Aviation Organization (ICAO, #12581)*; *International Maritime Organization (IMO, #14102)*; *Union for the Mediterranean (UfM, #20457)*; *United Nations Economic Commission for Europe (UNECE, #20555)*; *United Nations Framework Convention on Climate Change – Secretariat (UNFCCC, #20564)*; *World Customs Organization (WCO, #21350).* [2023.02.15/XD0695/**F***]

♦ International Transport Workers' Federation (ITF) 15726

Fédération internationale des ouvriers du transport – Federación Internacional de los Trabajadores del Transporte – Internationale Transportarbeiter-Föderation – Internationella Transportarbetarefederationen

SG ITF House, 49-60 Borough Road, London, SE1 1DR, UK. T. +442074032733. Fax +442073577871. E-mail: mail@itf.org.uk.
URL: http://www.itfglobal.org/

History 30 Jun 1896. Before foundation, meetings held previously in: 1893, Paris (France); 1894, Zurich (Switzerland); 1895, Milan (Italy); 1896, London (UK). Current Constitution adopted Nov 1998. Former names and other names: *International Federation of Ship, Dock and River Workers* – former (1896 to 1898); *International Association of Dock, Wharf and Riverside Workers* – alias; *Fédération internationale des dockers et marins* – alias. **Aims** Help and support affiliated unions and transport workers worldwide; fight for social justice, against unemployment and poverty, for decent wages and *working conditions* and for a safe and healthy working environment; foster the advancement of democratic trade unionism; promote and defend fundamental human and trade union rights; promote development of efficient public transport offering a quality service to users and safe working conditions to transport employees; provide research and information services to affiliates and general assistance to transport workers in difficulty. **Structure** Congress (every 4 years); Executive Board; Management Committee; Secretariat, headed by Secretary General. Regional Offices (7): Africa; African Francophone; Asia Pacific; Asian Sub-Region; Europe; Europe Sub-Region; Inter-American. Congresses open; other meetings and conferences closed. 'ITF Seafarers Trust' funds projects which benefit the seafarers and their families. **Languages** Arabic, English, French, German, Japanese, Russian, Spanish. **Staff** 120.00 FTE, paid. **Finance** Affiliation fees. **Activities** Advocacy/lobbying/activism; guidance/assistance/consulting; knowledge management/information dissemination; training/education. Industrial sections (7): railway workers; road transport workers; seafarers; dock workers; fishing workers; civil aviation workers; tourism services workers. **Events** *Civil Aviation Section Conference* Montréal, QC (Canada) 2022, *Management Committee Membership Working Group Meeting* Montréal, QC (Canada) 2019, *Quadrennial Congress* Singapore (Singapore) 2018, *Asia Pacific Regional Conference* Tokyo (Japan) 2016, *Quadrennial Congress* Sofia (Bulgaria) 2014. **Publications** *Transport International* (4 a year) in English, French, German, Japanese, Russian, Spanish, Swedish; *Message to Seafarers* (2 a year) – multilingual directory of maritime union contacts for seafarers; *Seafarers' Bulletin* (annual) in Chinese, English, French, German, Japanese, Polish, Russian, Spanish, Swedish – also in Pilipino; *African Bulletin* (occasional) in English, French; *Asia/Pacific News* (occasional) in English; *Civil Aviation Bulletin* (occasional) in English, French, German, Spanish, Swedish; *ITF Women* (occasional) in English, French, German, Spanish, Swedish; *Port Worker* (occasional) in Danish, English, French, German, Swedish. Pamphlets; documents; studies; posters; videos. Information Services: comprises about 6,000 books and pamphlets plus press cuttings, collective agreements, etc, dealing with working conditions, in particular those of transport workers.
Members About 670 transport workers unions representing over 19 million workers from about 147 countries and territories. Membership countries not specified. Included in the above, 7 organizations listed in this Yearbook:
Included in the above, 7 organizations listed in this Yearbook:
International Association of Machinists and Aerospace Workers (IAM); *International Brotherhood of Teamsters (IBT)*; *International Longshore and Warehouse Union (ILWU)*; *International Longshoremen's Association (ILA)*; *International Organization of Masters, Mates and Pilots (MMP)*; *Seafarers' International Union of North America (SIUNA)*; *Transportation Communications International Union (TCIU).*
Consultative Status Consultative status granted from: *ECOSOC (#05331)* (General); *International Civil Aviation Organization (ICAO, #12581)* (Observer). **IGO Relations** Accredited by (1): *International Whaling Commission (IWC, #15879).* Consultative status with: *International Maritime Organization (IMO, #14102).* **NGO Relations** Member of (5): *European Diving Technology Committee (EDTC, #06932)*; *Global Labour University (GLU, #10448)*; *Global Union Federations (GUF, #10638)*; *International Seafarers' Welfare and Assistance Network (ISWAN, #14815)*; *Maritime Piracy Humanitarian Response Programme (MPHRP, #16583).* Trade secretariat in cooperation with: *International Trade Union Confederation (ITUC, #15708)* (replacing *International Confederation of Free Trade Unions (ICFTU, inactive)*). Consultative member of: *Comité maritime international (CMI, #04192).* Partner of: *Partnership on Sustainable, Low Carbon Transport Foundation (SLoCaT Foundation, #18244).* Supports: *Seafarers International Research Centre (SIRC).* [2021/XB2644/y/**B**]

♦ International Trappist Association (ITA) 15727

Association internationale trappist – Asociación Internacional Trapense – Internationaler Verein Trappist – Associazione Internazionale Trappista – Internationale Vereniging Trappist (IVT)

Contact Vosheuvelstraat 39, 3950 Bocholt, Belgium.
URL: http://www.trappist.com/

History Founded Jan 1998. A union of monasteries of *Cistercian Order of the Strict Observance (Trappists)* who market their products. Registered in accordance with Belgian law: BE 0462 582 112. **Aims** Help monasteries protect the Trappist name and their common economic interests; watch over references to the religious order and ensures that information is correct; develop a system of solidarity and collaboration with other associations on an international level. **Languages** Dutch, English, French. **Staff** 1.00 FTE, paid. **Activities** Networking/liaising; advocacy/lobbying/activism; monitoring/evaluation. **Publications** *Newsletter ITA.*
Members Full Abbeys (20) in 8 countries:
Austria, Belgium, France, Germany, Italy, Netherlands, Spain, USA. [2016.08.05/XD7038/**D**]

♦ International Trauma-Healing Institute (internationally oriented national body)
♦ International Travel Association / see Association of Special Fares Agents (#02928)

♦ International Travel Insurance Alliance e.V. (ITIA) 15728

SG c/o ERGO Reiseversicherung AG, Thomas-Dehler-Str. 2, 81737 Munich, Germany. T. +498941661673. Fax +498941662673. E-mail: management@itia.biz.
Main Website: http://itia.biz

History 15 Oct 2018, Germany. Former names and other names: *Intereurop* – former (27 May 1933); *Internationaler Verein von Europäische Reiseversicherer (IVE)* – former (1951); *International Association of European Travel Insurers (IAE)* – former; *European Travel Insurance Group (ETIG Group)* – former (1 Oct 2002 to 2018). Registration: Amtsgericht München – Registergericht, No/ID: VR 208115, Start date: 16 Apr 2019, Germany, Bavaria. **Aims** Enable its members to compete with multinational competitors with international activities, and to meet the demands of the members' customers and business partners with regard to cross-border and international business; support the business development of every individual member and of the members as a group by pooling the collective experience of the members and by joint measures such as marketing, quality control and cooperation under a joint brand name and a joint brand logotype. **Structure**

General Assembly (annual); Board of Directors; Secretary-General. **Languages** English. **Finance** Sources: members' dues. **Activities** Events/meetings. e-Commerce Summits for members.
Members Insurance companies in 15 countries:
Bulgaria, Czechia, Denmark, Germany, Italy, Netherlands, Norway, Poland, Portugal, Spain, Sweden, Switzerland, Türkiye, UK, Ukraine. [2022.10.18/XD7923/D]

♦ International Travel Retail Confederation / see European Travel Retail Confederation (#08945)

♦ International Treatment Preparedness Coalition (ITPC) 15729

Coalition internationale de la préparation au traitement – Coalition Coalición Internacional de Preparación paa el Tratamie

Secretarait APN, 51/2 Soi Ruam Rudee, Ploenchit Rd, 3rd floor, Ruam Rudee Bldg III, Lumpini, Pathumwan, Bangkok, 10330, Thailand. T. +66225574778. Fax +6622557479. E-mail: editpc@ gmail.com.
URL: http://www.itpcglobal.org/

History Mar 2003, Cape Town (South Africa), during International Treatment Preparedness Summit. **Aims** Advocate universal and free access to treatment for *AIDS* for all *HIV+* people; increase input from HIV+ people in decisions that affect their lives. **Structure** International Steering Group of 30 members; Regional Advisory Committees. No Secretariat. **Staff** Voluntary. **Finance** Project funding. **Activities** Financial and/or material support. **Publications** *Missing the Target: A Report on HIV/AIDS Treatment Access from the Frontlines* (2005).
Members National and international organizations representing over 600 individuals. National organizations (12) in 8 countries:
Australia, Belarus, Costa Rica, India, Nepal, St Lucia, UK, USA.
International organizations (10):
AIDS Foundation East-West (AFEW); Asia-Pacific Council of AIDS Service Organizations (APCASO, #01875); Asia-Pacific Network of People Living with HIV/AIDS (APN+, #01973); European AIDS Treatment Group (EATG, #05850); Frontline AIDS (#10007); Global Network of People Living with HIV/AIDS (GNP+, #10494); Human Rights Watch (HRW, #10990); ICM Latin American Secretariat; *International Community of Women Living with HIV/AIDS (ICW, #12826); Latin American Network of People Living with HIV/AIDS (RED LA+, #16355).*
NGO Relations Participates in: *HIV Young Leaders Fund (HYLF, no recent information).* Cooperates with: *ICASO (#11040).* [2009/XM0877/y/F]

♦ International Treaty for the Limitation and Reduction of Naval Armament (1930 treaty)
♦ International Treaty on Plant Genetic Resources for Food and Agriculture (2001 treaty)
♦ International Tree Foundation (internationally oriented national body)
♦ International Tree Nut Council / see International Nut and Dried Fruit Council Foundation (#14387)
♦ International Tremor Foundation / see International Essential Tremor Foundation
♦ International Triathlon Union / see World Triathlon (#21872)

♦ International Tribology Council (ITC) 15730

Contact Jost Inst for Tribotechnology, School of Engineering, Univ of Central Lancashire, Fylde Road, Preston, PR1 2HE, UK. T. +441772893322.
URL: http://www.itctribology.net/

History Founded 24 Sep 1973, London (UK). **Aims** Maintain contact among tribology and kindred societies and groups worldwide; help them keep each other informed of activities, in particular of forward programmes; facilitate exchange of views, comments and opinions on tribological matters among member societies and groups; on request, advise and assist in founding tribology societies in countries where they do not exist; assist international cooperation in matters connected with tribology science, technology and education. **Structure** Executive Committee; President; Vice President. **Languages** English. **Activities** Events/meetings; guidance/assistance/consulting. **Events** *World Tribology Congress* Rio de Janeiro (Brazil) 2026, *World Tribology Congress* Lyon (France) 2022, *World Tribology Congress* Lyon (France) 2021, *World Tribology Congress* Beijing (China) 2017, *World Tribology Congress* Turin (Italy) 2013.
Members Full: national tribology societies, groups and divisions in 39 countries and territories:
Armenia, Austria, Belarus, Belgium, Brazil, Bulgaria, China, Czechia, Egypt, Finland, France, Georgia, Germany, Hungary, India, Israel, Italy, Japan, Korea Rep, Lithuania, Malaysia, Netherlands, Nigeria, Norway, Poland, Romania, Russia, Serbia, Slovakia, Slovenia, South Africa, Spain, Sweden, Switzerland, Taiwan, UK, Ukraine, USA, Vietnam.
Also corresponding individual members. Membership countries not specified.
NGO Relations *Asian Tribology Council (ATC, #01770).* [2019.07.23/XF0852/C]

♦ International Tribunal for the Law of the Sea (ITLOS) 15731

Tribunal international du droit de la mer – Tribunal Internacional del Derecho del Mar – Internationaler Seegerichtshof

Pres Am Internationalen Seegerichtshof 1, 22609 Hamburg, Germany. T. +494035607281. Fax +494035607287. E-mail: itlos@itlos.org – presidentoffice@itlos.org – registraroffice@itlos.org.
Registrar address not obtained.
URL: http://www.itlos.org/

History Set up by *United Nations Convention on the Law of the Sea (UNCLOS, 1982)*, which came into force 16 Nov 1994, as an independent judicial body. The *Preparatory Commission for the International Seabed Authority and for the International Tribunal for the Law of the Sea (LOS PrepCom, inactive)* made the necessary recommendations regarding the practical arrangements for the establishment of the Tribunal. The first 21 judges inaugurated 18 Oct 1996. Seat of the Tribunal is in the Free and Hanseatic City of Hamburg (Germany). **Aims** Adjudicate over disputes concerning the interpretation or application of the Convention, and over all matters specifically provided for in any other agreement which confers jurisdiction on the Tribunal. **Structure** 21 Judges are elected by States Parties to the Convention serving a 9-year-term, with one third of the Judges being elected every 3 years. A President and Vice-President of the Tribunal are elected by secret ballot by a majority of the Judges. Pursuant to the provisions of its Statute, the Tribunal has formed the following Chambers: the Chamber of Summary Procedure (5 Judges), the Chamber for Fisheries Disputes (9 Judges), the Chamber for Marine Environment Disputes (9 Judges) and the Chamber for Maritime Delimitation Disputes (9 Judges). Composed of 11 Judges, the Seabed Disputes Chamber is established in accordance with Part XI, section 5, of the Convention and article 14 of the Statute. The Registry is the legal and administrative secretariat, and is headed by the Registrar with the assistance of the Deputy Registrar. **Languages** English, French. **Staff** 38.00 FTE, paid. **Finance** Provided by the States Parties to UNCLOS. Annual budget: 23,443,900 EUR (2023). **Activities** Conflict resolution; events/meetings; guidance/assistance/consulting; management of treaties and agreements; training/education. Manages the following treaties/agreements: *Agreement on the Privileges and Immunities of the International Tribunal for the Law of the Sea (1997).* **Publications** *Reports of Judgments, Advisory Opinions and Orders – Recueil des arrêts, avis consultatifs et ordonnances* (annual); *Pleadings, Minutes of Public Sittings and Documents – Mémoires, procès-verbaux des audiences publiques et documents* – by case; *Yearbook – Annuaire. Basic Texts/Textes de Base 2015.*
Members 167 States Parties have ratified, acceded or succeeded to the Convention, as of Oct 2021:
Albania, Algeria, Angola, Antigua-Barbuda, Argentina, Armenia, Australia, Austria, Azerbaijan, Bahamas, Bahrain, Bangladesh, Barbados, Belarus, Belgium, Belize, Benin, Bolivia, Bosnia-Herzegovina, Botswana, Brazil, Brunei Darussalam, Bulgaria, Burkina Faso, Cameroon, Canada, Cape Verde, Chad, Chile, China, Comoros, Congo Brazzaville, Congo DR, Cook Is, Costa Rica, Côte d'Ivoire, Croatia, Cuba, Cyprus, Czechia, Denmark, Djibouti, Dominica, Dominican Rep, Ecuador, Egypt, Equatorial Guinea, Estonia, Eswatini, Fiji, Finland, France, Gabon, Gambia, Georgia, Germany, Ghana, Greece, Grenada, Guatemala, Guinea, Guinea-Bissau, Guyana, Haiti, Honduras, Hungary, Iceland, India, Indonesia, Iraq, Ireland, Italy, Jamaica, Japan, Jordan, Kenya, Kiribati, Korea Rep, Kuwait, Laos, Latvia, Lebanon, Lesotho, Liberia, Lithuania, Luxembourg, Madagascar, Malawi, Malaysia, Maldives, Mali, Malta, Marshall Is, Mauritania, Mauritius, Mexico, Micronesia FS, Moldova, Monaco, Mongolia, Montenegro, Morocco, Mozambique, Myanmar, Namibia, Nauru, Nepal, Netherlands, New Zealand, Nicaragua, Niger, Nigeria, Niue, North Macedonia, Norway, Oman, Pakistan, Palau, Palestine, Panama, Papua New Guinea, Paraguay, Philippines, Poland, Portugal, Qatar, Romania, Russia, Samoa, Sao Tomé-Principe, Saudi Arabia, Senegal, Serbia, Seychelles, Sierra Leone, Singapore, Slovakia, Slovenia, Solomon Is, Somalia, South Africa, Spain, Sri Lanka, St Kitts-Nevis, St Lucia, St Vincent-Grenadines, Sudan, Suriname, Sweden, Switzerland, Tanzania UR, Thailand, Timor-Leste, Togo, Tonga, Trinidad-Tobago, Tunisia, Tuvalu, Uganda, UK, Ukraine, Uruguay, Vanuatu, Vietnam, Yemen, Zambia, Zimbabwe.
Included in the above, one international organization listed in this Yearbook:
European Union (EU, #08967).
IGO Relations Observer status with (1): *United Nations (UN, #20515).* Member of (1): *United Nations Joint Staff Pension Fund (UNJSPF, #20581).* **NGO Relations** Member of (1): *Federation of International Civil Servants' Associations (FICSA, #09603).* [2022.12.16/XF2625/F*]

♦ International Trichoscopy Society 15732

Contact 132 – 4th Floor Calle de Emerson, 11560 Mexico City CDMX, Mexico. E-mail: info@ internationaltrichoscopysociety.org.
URL: https://www.internationaltrichoscopysociety.org/

History 4 May 2017, Mexico City (Mexico). **Aims** Teach trichoscopy as a diagnostic procedure for hair and scalp disorders and in general dermatology; promote the development of trichoscopy. **Structure** Scientific Board. **Activities** Events/meetings. **Events** *World Congress of Trichoscopy – Hair & Nail and Anti-Aging* Sorrento (Italy) 2021. **NGO Relations** Member of (1): *International League of Dermatological Societies (ILDS, #14018).* [2021/AA2130/v/C]

♦ International Triffin Foundation / see Robert Triffin International
♦ International Tripartite Rubber Organization, Thailand (inactive)

♦ International Triticale Association (ITA) 15733

Main Office U-Gent – Bioscience Eng, Valentin Vaerwyckweg 1, 9000 Ghent, Belgium. E-mail: ita.ugent@gmail.com.
URL: http://triticale.org/

History Feb 1986, Sydney, NSW (Australia). Founded uring 1st International Triticale Symposium. Formal ratification in 1987, Schwerin (German DR), at meeting of *EUCARPIA (#05571).* **Aims** International promotion of triticale production and utilization. **Structure** Executive. Sub-committees (3): Symposium; Editorial; Research. **Languages** English. **Staff** Voluntary. **Finance** Sources: members' dues. **Activities** Events/meetings. **Events** *Symposium* Radzików (Poland) 2022, *Symposium* Lethbridge, AB (Canada) 2019, *International Conference on Triticale and Wheat Biology, Breeding and Production* Erzurum (Turkey) 2018, *Symposium* Szeged (Hungary) 2016, *Symposium* Ghent (Belgium) 2013. **Publications** *Triticale Topics* (2 a year). Conference proceedings.
Members Full in 41 countries:
Algeria, Argentina, Australia, Austria, Bangladesh, Belgium, Brazil, Bulgaria, Canada, Chile, China, Czechia, Finland, France, Germany, Greece, Hungary, India, Italy, Japan, Madagascar, Mexico, Morocco, Netherlands, New Zealand, Norway, Pakistan, Poland, Portugal, Romania, Russia, South Africa, Spain, Sweden, Syrian AR, Thailand, Tunisia, UK, Ukraine, USA, Venezuela.
NGO Relations EUCARPIA; *International Maize and Wheat Improvement Center (#14077).* [2022/XD2185/C]

♦ International Triticeae Mapping Initiative (ITMI) 15734

Address not obtained.
URL: http://wheat.pw.usda.gov/ITMI/

History 1989, originally as a 5-year collaborative project. **Aims** Provide support in coordination of research efforts in molecular *genetics, genomics* and genetic analysis generally in the Triticeae; ensure data and information on the Triticeae is readily available to all researchers; help avoid duplication of research efforts; provide a framework for accessing international collaboration; help keep Triticeae research at the cutting edge of genetic research. **Events** *Workshop* Mexico City (Mexico) 2011, *Workshop* San Diego, CA (USA) 2010, *Workshop* Clermont-Ferrand (France) 2009, *Workshop* San Diego, CA (USA) 2008, *Workshop* Tiberias (Israel) 2007. **NGO Relations** *International Maize and Wheat Improvement Center (#14077).* [2013/XF3960/F]

♦ International Trombone Association (ITA) 15735

Exec Dir PO Box 3214, Henrico VA 23228, USA. T. +18882366241. Fax +18882366242. E-mail: info@trombone.net.
URL: http://www.trombone.net/

History Founded 1971. **Aims** Promote, celebrate and nurture trombone pedagogy, performance, research and literature. **Structure** Annual Meeting (at International Trombone Festival). **Languages** English. **Staff** 4.00 FTE, paid; 10.00 FTE, voluntary. **Finance** Members' dues (annual). **Activities** Events/meetings. **Events** *Annual Meeting* Valencia (Spain) 2015, *Annual Meeting* Rochester, NY (USA) 2014, *Annual Meeting* Columbus, GA (USA) 2013, *Annual meeting* Paris (France) 2012, *Annual meeting* Nashville, TN (USA) 2011. **Publications** *ITA Journal* (4 a year). *ITA Press Sheet Music Compositions.* **Members** Individuals (3,700) in 73 countries. Membership countries not specified. [2014.10.06/XD3978/v/D]

♦ International Trombone Union (internationally oriented national body)
♦ International Tropenbos Programme / see Tropenbos International

♦ International Tropical Fruits Network (TFNet) 15736

CEO Box 334, UPM Post Office, 43400 Serdang, Selangor, Malaysia. T. +60389416589 – +60389416590. Fax +60389416591. E-mail: info@itfnet.org.
URL: http://www.itfnet.org/

History Established 5 Jul 2001, officially established under the auspices of *FAO (#09260)*, with the support of *Intergovernmental Sub-Group on Tropical Fruits.* Office started operation 1 Aug 2000. **Aims** Promote sustainable global development of the tropical fruit industry in relation to production, consumption and trade. **Structure** General Assembly (every 3 years); Board of Trustees (meets at least annually) of 19 members, including a representative of FAO, 2 experts, country members and associate members. Secretariat in Malaysia. **Languages** English. **Staff** 7.00 FTE, paid. **Finance** Members' dues. Other sources: studies; consultancies; projects. **Activities** Strengthen data collection and analysis, documentation and dissemination of information on tropical fruits; improves awareness and understanding of tropical fruit markets; monitors impacts of regional and international agreements on production and trade policies; promotes research and development technologies of eco-regional importance; conducts seminars and workshops; strengthens linkages between tropical fruit producers and consumers; encourages financing and investment in the sector. **Events** *International symposium on papaya* Malaysia 2005, *Special assembly* Kuala Lumpur (Malaysia) 2001, *General Assembly* Kuala Lumpur (Malaysia) 2000. **Publications** *TFNet e-Newsletter.* Seminar proceedings; reports.
Members Governments of 13 countries:
Australia, Bangladesh, China, Fiji, India, Indonesia, Malaysia, Nigeria, Philippines, Sri Lanka, Sudan, Syrian AR, Vietnam.
Organizations and individuals (64) in 22 countries and territories:
China, Costa Rica, Côte d'Ivoire, Ecuador, Ghana, Hawaii, India, Indonesia, Iran Islamic Rep, Kenya, Malaysia, New Zealand, South Africa, Sri Lanka, Sudan, Switzerland, Taiwan, Thailand, Trinidad-Tobago, Uganda, Vietnam, Yemen.
Individuals (8) in 5 countries:
Costa Rica, Ecuador, Kenya, Malaysia, Vietnam. [2017/XF6479/F*]

♦ International Tropical Timber Agreement, 1983 (1983 treaty)
♦ International Tropical Timber Agreement, 1994 (1994 treaty)
♦ International Tropical Timber Agreement, 2006 (2006 treaty)

♦ International Tropical Timber Organization (ITTO) 15737

Organisation internationale des bois tropicaux (OIBT) – Organización Internacional de las Maderas Tropicales (OIMT)

Contact Intl Organizations Ctr, 5F Pacifico-Yokohama, 1-1-1 Minato-Mirai, Nishi-ku, Yokohama KANAGAWA, 220-0012 Japan. T. +81452231110. Fax +81452231111. E-mail: itto@itto.int.
URL: http://www.itto.int/

History Established Apr 1985, on coming into force of *International Tropical Timber Agreement, 1983 (ITTA, 1983)*, negotiated under the auspices of the Integrated Programme for Commodities of *UNCTAD (#20285).* Operational activities commenced Jan 1987, on opening of headquarters in Yokohama (Japan). New treaty, *International Tropical Timber Agreement, 1994 (1994)*, also negotiated under the auspices of UNCTAD, came into force on 1 Jan 1997. Successor agreement, *International Tropical Timber Agreement, 2006 (2006)* entered into force Dec 2011. **Aims** Develop internationally agreed policy documents to promote sustainable *forest* management and forest *conservation*; assist tropical member countries to adapt such policies to local circumstances and implement them in the field through projects. **Structure** International Tropical Timber Council (ITTC) meets annually on rotational basis between Headquarters (Japan) and a Producer member country, rotating among 3 tropical regions of Africa, Asia/Pacific and Latin America/Caribbean. Council; Committees (4): Economics, Statistics and Markets; Forest Industry; Reforestation and Forest Management; Finance ad Administration. Secretariat in Yokohama (Japan). **Languages** English, French, Spanish. **Staff** 26.00 FTE, paid. **Finance** *'Administrative Account'*, financing Secretariat, comprises member country contributions (50% from producing members and 50% from consuming members), calculated in proportion to the number of votes held, this being derived from trade values and volumes and areas of closed tropical moist forest. *'Special Account'*, financing project activities, comprises contributions from regional and international financial institutions and voluntary contributions from donor countries and governmental

and nongovernmental organizations. *'Thematic Programme Sub-Account'* under the Special Account for development, management, implementation and evaluation of Thematic Programmes. *'Bali Partnership Fund'*, assisting producing members in achieving the Year 2000 Objective, functions in a similar way to the Special Account. Combined project budget 1997-2014: over US$ 400 million. **Activities** Management of treaties and agreements; politics/policy/regulatory. Manages the following treaties/agreements: *Convention on Biological Diversity (Biodiversity convention, 1992)*. **Events** *Session* Yokohama (Japan) 2022, *Session* Yokohama (Japan) 2021, *Session* Yokohama (Japan) 2020, *Session* Lomé (Togo) 2019, *Session* Yokohama (Japan) 2018. **Publications** *ITTO Market News Services*. *ITTO Information Papers* – scientific information relevant to projects and activities; *ITTO Mission Reports* – results and reports of missions undertaken by consultants or fact-finding teams for the purpose of establishing baseline data; *ITTO Policy Development Series* – guidelines on various issues; *ITTO Technical Series* – reports of ITTO-funded technical research, studies and activities. *ITTO Tropical Forest Update*. Guidelines, criteria and indicators on sustainable tropical forest management, encompassing natural forests, planted forests, conservation of biological diversity, fire management and development of forest industries. Other publications.
Members Producers – 34 countries:
Benin, Brazil, Cambodia, Cameroon, Colombia, Congo Brazzaville, Congo DR, Costa Rica, Côte d'Ivoire, Czechia, Ecuador, Fiji, Gabon, Ghana, Guatemala, Guyana, Honduras, India, Indonesia, Liberia, Malaysia, Mali, Mexico, Mozambique, Myanmar, Panama, Papua New Guinea, Peru, Philippines, Suriname, Thailand, Togo, Trinidad-Tobago, Vietnam.
Consumers – 37 countries and the European Union:
Albania, Australia, Austria, Belgium, Bulgaria, China, Croatia, Cyprus, Czechia, Denmark, Estonia, Finland, France, Germany, Greece, Hungary, Ireland, Italy, Japan, Korea Rep, Latvia, Lithuania, Luxembourg, Malta, Netherlands, New Zealand, Norway, Poland, Portugal, Romania, Slovakia, Slovenia, Spain, Sweden, Switzerland, UK, USA.
IGO Relations Accredited by: *Secretariat of the United Nations Convention to Combat Desertification (Secretariat of the UNCCD, #19208)*. Cooperates with: *Common Fund for Commodities (CFC, #04293)*; *Japan International Cooperation Agency (JICA)*; *UNCTAD (#20285)*; *UNESCO Office, Jakarta – Regional Bureau for Sciences in Asia and the Pacific (#20313)*; *UNIDO (#20336)*; *United Nations Forum on Forests (UNFF, #20562)*. Member of: *Collaborative Partnership on Forests (CPF, #04100)*. **NGO Relations** Cooperates with all NGOs actively involved in promoting conservation, management and sustainable development of tropical forests (not specified). Member of: *International Teak Information Network (TEAKNET, #15665)*. Cooperates with: *Center for International Forestry Research (CIFOR, #03646)*; *International Union of Forest Research Organizations (IUFRO, #15774)*; *World Wide Fund for Nature (WWF, #21922)*. [2020/XB0100/**B***]

♦ International Trotting Association (ITA) 15738

Exec Sec USTA, 6130 S Sunbury Rd, Westerville OH 43081-9309, USA.
URL: http://www.ustrotting.com/
History 1938, Columbus OH (USA). **Aims** Promote the *sport* of *harness racing* and the *Standardbred* breed. **Structure** Board of Directors. **Languages** English. **Staff** 45.00 FTE, paid. **Finance** Members' dues. **Activities** Events/meetings; sporting activities. **Events** *Biennial Conference* Stockholm (Sweden) 2019, *Biennial Conference* Charlottetown, PE (Canada) 2017, *Biennial Conference* Sydney, NSW (Australia) 2015, *Biennial Conference* Paris (France) 2013, *Biennial conference / World Conference* Columbus, OH (USA) 2011. **Publications** *Hoof Beats* (12 a year) – magazine.
Members National organizations (18) in 18 countries:
Australia, Austria, Belgium, Canada, Denmark, Finland, France, Germany, Ireland, Italy, Netherlands, New Zealand, Norway, Russia, Sweden, Switzerland, UK, USA.
Associate member (1):
European Trotting Union (#08952). [2016.12.14/XD8481/y/**D**]

♦ International Trotting and Pacing Association (internationally oriented national body)
♦ International Trust Fund for Demining and Mine Victims Assistance / see ITF Enhancing Human Security
♦ International Trust for Traditional Medicine (internationally oriented national body)

♦ International Trypanotolerance Centre (ITC) 15739

Contact PMB 14, Banjul, Gambia. T. +2204462928. Fax +2204462924.
URL: http://www.itc.gm/
History 1982. **Aims** Contribute to the efforts in increasing *livestock* productivity and utilization in the West *African* region through the optimal and sustainable exploitation of the genetic resistance of indigenous breeds of livestock for the welfare of the human populations. **Structure** Council Executive; Programme Committees; Director General. **Finance** Donations and contributions. Main donor: Belgian government. Restricted (project) donations: *European Commission (EC, #06633)*; German government; *Directorate-General for Development Cooperation (DGDC)*; *European Development Fund (EDF, #06914)*; *International Development Research Centre (IDRC, #13162)*; Gambian government; Berlin (Germany) university; *African Development Bank (ADB, #00283)*; *Vlaamse Vereniging voor Ontwikkelingssamenwerking en Technische Bijstand (VVOB)*; *Centre for Tropical Veterinary Medicine, Edinburgh (CTVM)*; national organizations. **Activities** *'Research and Development Programme (RDP)'* – aims to enhance the food security and general welfare of the human populations through improved and sustainable livestock production and use. Medium Term Plan (2001-2004) contains 11 Institutional Projects under 3 Programmes: *'Low-Input Systems Improvement Programme (LISIP)'*; *'Market-Oriented Systems Improvement Programme (MOSIP)'*; *'Systems Overlaps and Linkages Improvement Programme (SOLIP)'*. Additional restricted funded projects. Training and networking; information exchange. **Publications** Annual report; conference proceedings.
Members Full in 5 countries:
Guinea, Guinea-Bissau, Liberia, Senegal, Sierra Leone.
IGO Relations Member of: *Mano River Union (MRU, #16566)*. [2008/XE4076/**E**]

♦ International Tsunami Information Center (ITIC) 15740

Centre international d'information sur le tsunami
Dir 1845 Wasp Boulevard, Building 176, Honolulu HI 96818, USA. T. +18087256050. Fax +18087256055. E-mail: itic.tsunami@noaa.gov.
URL: http://www.tsunamiwave.info/
History Established, 12 Nov 1965, Paris (France), alongside 'International Coordination Group for the Tsunami Warning System in the Pacific (ITSU)' – currently *Intergovernmental Coordination Group for the Pacific Tsunami Warning and Mitigation System (ICG/PTWS, #11481)*, by *Intergovernmental Oceanographic Commission (IOC, #11496)*, on recommendation by its Working Group Meeting on the International Aspects of the Tsunami Warning System in the Pacific, 27-30 Apr 1965, Honolulu HI (USA). **Aims** Mitigate the effects of tsunamis throughout the *Pacific*. **Structure** Programme administered by a Director with advice on its operation provided by IOC. **Languages** English, Spanish. **Staff** 6.00 FTE, paid. **Finance** Staff and office operations provided by USA and Chile; project and activity task provided by external support. **Activities** Guidance/assistance/consulting; training/education; awareness raising; knowledge management/information dissemination. **Events** *Biennial General Meeting* Ecuador 2007, *Biennial General Meeting* Melbourne, VIC (Australia) 2006, *Biennial session / Biennial General Meeting* Chile 2005, *Biennial session / Biennial General Meeting* Wellington (New Zealand) 2003, *Bienial session / Biennial General Meeting* Cartagena de Indias (Colombia) 2001. **Publications** Booklets; posters.
Members Member states of Intergovernmental Oceanographic Commission, mainly those states actively engaged in tsunami warning services in the Pacific. Members of International Coordination Group for the Tsunami Warning System in the Pacific (30):
Australia, Canada, Chile, China, Colombia, Cook Is, Costa Rica, Ecuador, El Salvador, Fiji, France, Guatemala, Indonesia, Japan, Korea DPR, Korea Rep, Malaysia, Mexico, New Zealand, Nicaragua, Papua New Guinea, Peru, Philippines, Russia, Samoa, Singapore, Thailand, Tonga, USA, Vietnam.
IGO Relations Cooperates with *Intergovernmental Coordination Group for the Pacific Tsunami Warning and Mitigation System (ICG/PTWS, #11481)* Service Providers: USA NOAA *Pacific Tsunami Warning Center (PTWC)*; Japan JMA *Northwest Pacific Tsunami Advisory Center (NWPTAC)*; China NMEFC *South China Sea Tsunami Center (SCSTAC)*; Nicaragua INETER *Central America Tsunami Advisory Center (CATAC)*. [2019/XC2646/**E***]

♦ International Tsunami Society / see Tsunami Society International (#20255)

♦ International Tube Association (ITA) 15741

Association internationale du tube – Asociación Internacional de Tubos – Internationaler Rohrverband – Associazione Internazionale dei Tubi Metallici
Gen Manager Heinz-Ingenstau-Strasse 9, 40474 Düsseldorf, Germany. T. +492119475650. Fax +492119473938. E-mail: info@itatube.org.
Exec Sec address not obtained.
URL: http://www.itatube.org/
History 1979, Birmingham (UK). Also known as *International Association for the Ferrous and Non-Ferrous Tube and Pipe Industries*. **Aims** Secure the interests of all persons involved in the manufacture, production and processing of non-ferrous and ferrous tubes and *pipes*. **Structure** International Executive Management Board; Management Boards (4); Committees (5). **Languages** Chinese, English, French, German, Italian, Russian, Spanish, Turkish. **Staff** 2.00 FTE, paid; 28.00 FTE, voluntary. **Finance** Sources: meeting proceeds; members' dues. **Activities** Awards/prizes/competitions; events/meetings; guidance/assistance/consulting; knowledge management/information dissemination; networking/liaising. **Events** *International Symposium on Innovative Tube/Pipe Manufacturing and Forming* Osaka (Japan) 2015, *Meeting* Düsseldorf (Germany) 2011, *International Symposium on Innovative Tube* Osaka (Japan) 2011, *Meeting* Pittsburgh, PA (USA) 2010, *Meeting* Istanbul (Turkey) 2009. **Publications** *Tube and Pipe Technology* (4 a year) – journal. Information Services: Database.
Members Individuals (about 1,000) and groups in 71 countries and territories:
Argentina, Armenia, Australia, Austria, Bahrain, Belarus, Belgium, Bolivia, Bosnia-Herzegovina, Brazil, Bulgaria, Canada, Chile, China, Colombia, Croatia, Cyprus, Czechia, Denmark, Egypt, Estonia, Finland, France, Germany, Greece, Hungary, India, Indonesia, Iran Islamic Rep, Ireland, Italy, Japan, Kenya, Korea Rep, Kuwait, Latvia, Lebanon, Lithuania, Malaysia, Mexico, Moldova, Morocco, Netherlands, New Zealand, North Macedonia, Norway, Oman, Pakistan, Poland, Portugal, Romania, Russia, Saudi Arabia, Serbia, Singapore, Slovakia, Slovenia, South Africa, Spain, Sweden, Switzerland, Taiwan, Tanzania UR, Thailand, Türkiye, Uganda, UK, Ukraine, United Arab Emirates, Uruguay, USA. [2017.10.12/XD2519/**C**]

♦ International Tube Cartel (inactive)
♦ Internationalt Uddannelsescenter i Svendborg (internationally oriented national body)
♦ International Tug Conference (meeting series)

♦ International Tundra Experiment (ITEX) 15742

Co-Chair address not obtained.
Co-Chair address not obtained.
URL: https://www.gvsu.edu/itex/
History 1990, Michigan (USA). Comes under *Programme on Man and the Biosphere (MAB, #18526)*. Dormant 2003; active in 2005. Former names and other names: *MAB-ITEX* – alias. **Aims** Examine the response of circumpolar cold adapted plant species and tundra ecosystems to environmental change, specifically to an increase in summer temperature as the best way to predict species response to climate change. **Structure** Steering Committee. **Languages** English. **Staff** 10.00 FTE, voluntary. **Finance** Sources: grants. **Activities** Events/meetings; knowledge management/information dissemination; monitoring/evaluation; research/documentation. **Events** *Workshop* Parma (Italy) 2019, *Workshop* Stirling (UK) 2018, *Workshop* Uppsala (Sweden) 2015, *Workshop* Bergün (Switzerland) 2013, *Workshop* El Paso, TX (USA) 2012. **Publications** *ITEX Update* (1-2 a year). *Global Change Biology* (1997).
Members Arctic and alpine sites (27) in 11 countries:
Austria, Canada, Finland, Greenland, Iceland, Japan, Norway, Russia, Sweden, Switzerland, USA.
Organizations and/or individuals (only individual membership) in 25 countries and territories:
Argentina (*), Australia (*), Austria, Belgium (*), Canada, China (*), Czechia (*), Denmark, Estonia (*), Finland, France (*), Germany (*), Iceland, Italy (*), Japan, Netherlands (*), Norway, Poland (*), Puerto Rico (*), Romania (*), Russia, Sweden, Switzerland, UK, USA.
NGO Relations Partner of (1): *Circumpolar Biodiversity Monitoring Program (CBMP, #03941)*. [2022.02.09/XF3652/**F**]

♦ International Tungsten Industry Association (ITIA) 15743

Association internationale de l'industrie du tungstène
SG 1st Floor, 454-458 Chiswick High Road, London, W4 5TT, UK. T. +442089962221. Fax +442089948728. E-mail: info@itia.info.
URL: http://www.itia.info/
History Founded Feb 1988, Brussels (Belgium), replacing *Primary Tungsten Association (PTA, inactive)*, which had been set up 1975, La Paz (Bolivia). Registered in accordance with Belgian law. **Aims** Promote the use of tungsten and tungsten products; provide a regular meeting forum; collate from different sources, comprehensive statistics covering tungsten production, processing, consumption and end-uses; prepare market reports; coordinate the industry's activities. **Languages** English. **Staff** All full-time, paid. **Finance** Annual budget: US$ 2,000,000. **Activities** Compiles statistics; organizes symposia. **Events** *Annual General Meeting* Stockholm (Sweden) 2016, *Annual General Meeting* Hanoi (Vietnam) 2015, *Annual General Meeting* Sydney, NSW (Australia) 2013, *Annual General Meeting* Beijing (China) 2012, *Annual General Meeting* Nice (France) 2011. **Publications** *International Tungsten Industry Association Newsletter* (2 a year). Brochure; members' directory.
Members Mining companies, processors/consumers, trading companies and assayers. Full (50) in 18 countries:
Australia, Austria, Belgium, Canada, China, France, Germany, Italy, Japan, Korea Rep, Luxembourg, New Zealand, Russia, Singapore, Sweden, UK, USA, Vietnam.
Consultative Status Consultative status granted from: *UNCTAD (#20285)* (Special Category). [2018.07.23/XC5577/t/**D**]

♦ International Tunnelling Association / see International Tunnelling and Underground Space Association (#15744)

♦ International Tunnelling and Underground Space Association (ITA) . 15744

Association internationale des tunnels et de l'espace souterrain (AITES)
Secretariat c/o MIE 2, Chemin de Balexert 9, 1219 Châtelaine, Switzerland. T. +41225477441. E-mail: secretariat@ita-aites.org.
URL: http://www.ita-aites.org/
History 25 Apr 1974, Oslo (Norway). Founded following a conference at government level, 1970, Washington DC (USA). Former names and other names: *International Tunnelling Association (ITA)* – former; *Association Internationale des Travaux en Souterrain (AITES)* – former. **Aims** Encourage use of the subsurface for the benefit of public, environment and sustainable development; promote advances in planning, design, construction, maintenance and safety of tunnels and underground space. **Structure** General Assembly (annual); Executive Council; Committees (5); Working Groups; Secretariat. **Languages** English, French. **Staff** 4.00 FTE, paid. **Finance** Sources: members' dues. **Activities** Awards/prizes/competitions; events/meetings; knowledge management/information dissemination; monitoring/evaluation; research and development. **Events** *World Tunnel Congress* Athens (Greece) 2023, *World Tunnel Congress* Copenhagen (Denmark) 2022, *World Tunnel Congress* Copenhagen (Denmark) 2021, *World Tunnel Congress* Kuala Lumpur (Malaysia) 2020, *ETS Tunnelling and underground Construction Conference* Luxor (Egypt) 2019. **Publications** *Tunnelling and Underground Space Technology* (4 a year); *ita'at'news*; *Scoop* – online publication, free; *Tribune*. *Muir Wood Lecture*. Assembly reports; Working Groups and Committees reports.
Members Full: Adhering national organizations in 78 countries:
Albania, Algeria, Argentina, Australia, Austria, Azerbaijan, Belarus, Belgium, Bhutan, Bolivia, Bosnia-Herzegovina, Brazil, Bulgaria, Cambodia, Canada, Chile, China, Colombia, Costa Rica, Croatia, Czechia, Denmark, Ecuador, Egypt, Finland, France, Germany, Greece, Guatemala, Hungary, Iceland, India, Indonesia, Iran Islamic Rep, Israel, Italy, Japan, Kazakhstan, Kenya, Korea Rep, Laos, Lebanon, Lesotho, Malaysia, Mexico, Montenegro, Morocco, Myanmar, Nepal, Netherlands, New Zealand, Nigeria, North Macedonia, Norway, Panama, Peru, Poland, Portugal, Qatar, Romania, Russia, Saudi Arabia, Serbia, Singapore, Slovakia, Slovenia, South Africa, Spain, Sweden, Switzerland, Thailand, Türkiye, UK, Ukraine, United Arab Emirates, USA, Venezuela, Vietnam.
Affiliate: Individuals (126) in 35 countries and territories:
Australia, Austria, Belgium, Brazil, Canada, China, Czechia, Denmark, Egypt, France, Germany, Greece, Hong Kong, India, Iran Islamic Rep, Ireland, Israel, Italy, Japan, Lebanon, Malaysia, Netherlands, Norway, Peru, Portugal, Romania, Saudi Arabia, South Africa, Spain, Sweden, Switzerland, Türkiye, UK, United Arab Emirates, USA.
Consultative Status Consultative status granted from: *ECOSOC (#05331)* (Special). **IGO Relations** Associated with Department of Global Communications of the United Nations. [2022.06.15/XC4435/**C**]

♦ International Turfgrass Society (ITS) 15745

Société internationale des gazons
Pres c/o STERF, PO Box 11016, SE-110 16 Stockholm, Sweden.
Sec c/o Dept of Plant Biology, Rutgers Univ, 59 Dudley Road, New Brunswick NJ 08901-8520, USA.

URL: http://turfsociety.com/
History 1969, Harrogate (UK). Founded at first meeting. **Aims** Encourage research and education in turf *grass* science; further the dissemination of technical information; strive toward uniform terminology and standard research evaluation techniques; maintain liaison with other scientific or educational bodies with interests in turfgrass science. **Structure** Members elect Directors; Directors elect Officers. **Languages** English. **Staff** Voluntary. **Finance** Sources: members' dues. Other sources: Savings. **Events** *International Turfgrass Research Conference (ITRC)* Saitama (Japan) 2025, *International Turfgrass Research Conference* Copenhagen (Denmark) 2022, *International Turfgrass Reseach Conference* Copenhagen (Denmark) 2021, *Quadrennial Conference* New Brunswick, NJ (USA) 2017, *Quadrennial Conference* Beijing (China) 2013. **Publications** *Conference Journal*; *ITS Newsletter*.
Members Individuals in 18 countries:
Australia, Canada, Chile, China, Denmark, France, Germany, Greece, Italy, Japan, Netherlands, New Zealand, Norway, Spain, Sweden, Switzerland, UK, USA.
NGO Relations *Scandinavian Turfgrass and Environment Research Foundation (STERF, #19126).*
[2021/XD4741/v/C]

♦ International TVA Network (ITVA) 15746

Contact Ctr for Visual Cognition, Dept of Psychology, Univ of Copenhagen, Øster Farimagsgade 2A, 1353 Copenhagen K, Denmark. T. +4535324860.
URL: http://itva.wordpress.com/
History Founded Jun 2010, Copenhagen (Denmark). **Aims** Coordinate research projects; share theoretical and empirical resources; organize joint meetings and other events. **Activities** Events/meetings; training/education. **Events** *Meeting* Copenhagen (Denmark) 2016.
Members Individuals in 10 countries:
Belgium, Denmark, France, Germany, Iceland, Ireland, Norway, Switzerland, UK, USA. [2016/XM5523/F]

♦ International Twins Congress (meeting series)
♦ International Typographers' Secretariat (inactive)
♦ International Tyre, Rubber and Recycling Federation (inactive)
♦ International UFO Congress (meeting series)

♦ International Ultraviolet Association (IUVA) 15747

Mailing Address 6935 Wisconsin Ave, Ste 207, Bethesda MD 20815, USA. E-mail: info@iuva.org.
URL: http://www.iuva.org/
History Apr 1999. **Aims** Promote collection, collaboration and research in ultraviolet technologies. **Structure** Board; Committees. **Events** *World Congress* 2021, *World Congress on Ultraviolet Technologies* Sydney, NSW (Australia) 2019, *World Congress on Ultraviolet Technologies* Dubrovnik (Croatia) 2017, *Symposium* Singapore (Singapore) 2017, *Symposium on UV Innovations* Tokyo (Japan) 2016. **Publications** *IUVA e-News* – online E-J journal. **Members** Membership countries not specified. [2013/XD9191/C]

♦ International Umbrella Organization for Road Transport of Goods under Controlled Temperatures / see Transfrigoroute International (#20213)

♦ International Underwriting Association (IUA) 15748

CEO London Underwriting Centre, 1 Minster Court, Mincing Lane, London, EC3R 7AA, UK. T. +442076174444. E-mail: info@iua.co.uk.
URL: https://www.iua.co.uk/
History 31 Dec 1998. Formed through the merger of the London International Insurance and Reinsurance Market Association (LIRMA), founded in 1991 to support non-marine insurance business and reinsurance, and the Institute of London Underwriters (ILU), established in 1884 as a formal representative underwriting association by senior members of marine insurance companies. This union brought together the representative bodies for the marine and non-marine sectors of the London company insurance market. **Aims** Promote and enhance the business environment for international insurance and reinsurance companies operating in or through London (UK). **Structure** Board; Management; Technical Committees. **Activities** Services. **Events** *Asian motor insurance and claims management conference* Singapore (Singapore) 2009, *Biennial Seminar* London (UK) 2003, *Biennial seminar* Gleneagles (UK) 2001. **Members** Ordinary; Associate; Affiliate; Affiliated Associations. Membership countries not specified. [2020.05.13/XE2959/E]

♦ International Unicycling Federation (IUF) 15749

Main Office 4100 Redwood Rd, Ste 257, Oakland CA 94619, USA. E-mail: contact@unicycling.org.
Pres address not obtained.
URL: http://iufinc.org/
History Jan 1985. **Aims** Foster awareness of and participation in unicycling as a *sport*; develop national associations; promote voluntary international standards for *competition* towards achieving Olympic status. **Structure** Board of Directors, comprising the Officers (President, Vice President, Secretary/Treasurer, Publications Manager and Advertising Manager) and 3 members. Committees (5): Convention; Rules; Public Relations; Nominating; Fund Raising. **Languages** English. **Staff** Voluntary. **Finance** Members' dues. **Events** *Biennial Convention and Competition* Bressanone (Italy) 2012, *Biennial Convention* Bressanone (Italy) 2012, *Biennial convention / Biennial Convention and Competition* Wellington (New Zealand) 2010, *Biennial Convention* Wellington (New Zealand) 2009, *Biennial convention / Biennial Convention and Competition* Denmark 2008. **Publications** *International Unicycling Federation Competition Rulebook* (every 2 years).
Members Members in 39 countries and territories:
Argentina, Australia, Austria, Belgium, Brazil, Canada, China, Czechia, Denmark, Finland, France, Germany, Hong Kong, Hungary, Ireland, Israel, Italy, Japan, Korea Rep, Luxembourg, Malaysia, Mexico, Netherlands, New Zealand, Norway, Poland, Portugal, Puerto Rico, Russia, Singapore, Slovakia, Slovenia, South Africa, Spain, Sweden, Switzerland, Taiwan, UK, USA.
[2015/XD0069/F]

♦ International Union of Abstaining Teachers (inactive)
♦ International Union of Academies (#20345)
♦ International Union of Advertisers Associations / see World Federation of Advertisers (#21407)

♦ International Union of Aerospace Insurers (IUAI) 15750

Union internationale des assureurs aéronautiques (UIAA) – Unión Internacional de Compañias de Seguros de Aviación – Mezdunarodnyj Sojuz Aviacionnogo Strahovanija
SG 32 Threadneedle Street, London, EC2R 8AY, UK. T. +442030538680.
URL: http://www.iuai.org/
History 4 Jun 1934, London (UK). Founded by 8 insurance organizations. Former names and other names: *International Union of Aviation Insurers (IUAI)* – former (4 Jun 1934). Registration: Companies House, No/ID: 9926124, England and Wales. **Aims** Represent and serve the global aerospace insurance and reinsurance industry. **Structure** General Meeting (annual); Study Groups (5). Meetings closed. **Languages** English. **Staff** 2.00 FTE, paid. **Finance** Sources: members' dues. **Events** *Annual General Meeting* Bordeaux (France) 2019, *Annual General Meeting* Tokyo (Japan) 2018, *Annual General Meeting* Taormina (Italy) 2017, *Annual General Meeting* Charleston, SC (USA) 2016, *Annual General Meeting* Bangalore (India) 2015. **Publications** *IUAI Aerospace Bulletin* (6 a year). *Aviation Liability Handbook*; *IUAI Statistical Handbook*. Yearbook.
Members Insurance pools, groups or associations whose participants are actively engaged in aerospace insurance either direct or by way of reinsurance. Members in 30 countries:
Australia, Bangladesh, Belgium, Bermuda, Bulgaria, China, Egypt, France, Germany, Hungary, India, Ireland, Israel, Italy, Japan, Korea Rep, Libya, Morocco, Poland, Portugal, Romania, Russia, Singapore, Spain, Sweden, Switzerland, UK, Ukraine, United Arab Emirates, USA.
Consultative Status Consultative status granted from: *ECOSOC (#05331)* (Ros C); *International Civil Aviation Organization (ICAO, #12581)* (Observer Status). **IGO Relations** Accredited by: *United Nations Office at Vienna (UNOV, #20604)*. Observer to: *European Civil Aviation Conference (ECAC, #06564)*. [2019.04.24/XC2693/C]

♦ International Union Against Alcoholism / see International Council on Alcohol and Addictions (#12989)
♦ International Union Against Cancer / see Union for International Cancer Control (#20415)
♦ International Union Against the Duel and for the Protection of Honour (inactive)
♦ International Union Against Racism (inactive)

♦ International Union against Sexually Transmitted Infections (IUSTI) 15751

SG Dept of Sexual Health, Level B, Royal South Hants Hosp, St Mary's Road, Southampton, SO14 0YG, UK. E-mail: secretary@iusti.org.
Treas Univ Hosps Birmingham NHS Foundation Trust, Whitall St Clinic, Whitall Street, Birmingham, B4 6DH, UK. T. +441212375721.
URL: https://www.iusti.org/
History Founded Jan 1923, Paris (France), as *International Union for Combating Venereal Diseases – Union internationale contre le péril vénérien*. Subsequently referred to in French as *Union internationales contre le péril vénérien et les tréponématoses*; name again changed to *International Union Against the Venereal Diseases and the Treponematoses (IUVDT) – Union internationale contre les maladies vénériennes et les tréponématoses (UIMVT)*. Most recent statutes and present name adopted 1997. **Aims** Unite all forces devoted to combating sexually-transmitted diseases (STDs), including *HIV-AIDS* and endemic treponematoses; promote worldwide activities aimed at research, prevention and control of these diseases; encourage members to contribute to *public health* programmes for control of STDs. **Structure** General Assembly (at least every 2 years); Executive Committee. Regional Offices (5): Africa; Asia-Pacific; Europe; Latin America – through *Asociación Latinoamericana y Caribeña para el control de las Infecciones de Transmisión (ALAC-ITS, #02191)*; North America. **Languages** English, French, Spanish. **Staff** Voluntary. **Finance** Sources: members' dues. **Activities** Awareness raising; events/meetings; guidance/assistance/consulting; training/education. **Events** *IUSTI World Congress* Victoria Falls (Zimbabwe) 2022, *Asia Pacific Congress* Shanghai (China) 2019, *European Regional Congress* Tallinn (Estonia) 2019, *World Congress (STI and HIV 2019 World Congress)* Vancouver, BC (Canada) 2019, *Asia Pacific Congress* Auckland (New Zealand) 2018. **Publications** *International Journal of STD and AIDS* – official journal; *Venereology* – official journal for Asia-Pacific. Assembly proceedings.
Members Individuals; national and international voluntary groups, associations, societies and organizations; national health administrations. Members in 64 countries:
Argentina, Australia, Austria, Bangladesh, Belgium, Bhutan, Brazil, Bulgaria, Canada, Chile, China, Costa Rica, Croatia, Czechia, Denmark, Estonia, Fiji, Finland, France, Germany, Greece, Guyana, Hungary, India, Indonesia, Iran Islamic Rep, Ireland, Italy, Jamaica, Japan, Korea Rep, Malaysia, Malta, Mexico, Monaco, Morocco, Myanmar, Nepal, Netherlands, New Zealand, Pakistan, Panama, Papua New Guinea, Peru, Philippines, Poland, Portugal, Senegal, Singapore, South Africa, Spain, Sri Lanka, Switzerland, Thailand, Tunisia, Türkiye, UK, Ukraine, Uruguay, USA, Venezuela, Vietnam, Zambia, Zimbabwe.
Consultative Status Consultative status granted from: *ECOSOC (#05331)* (Ros C); *WHO (#20950)* (Official Relations). **NGO Relations** Member of: *Commonwealth HIV and AIDS Action Group (Para55, no recent information)*; *Council for International Organizations of Medical Sciences (CIOMS, #04905)*; *International League of Dermatological Societies (ILDS, #14018)*; *Regional Network Supporting the HIV, Viral Hepatitis and Sexual Health Workforce in the Asia Pacific (Regional Network, #18802).* [2019.04.24/XC2650/C]

♦ International Union Against Traffic in Children (inactive)
♦ International Union Against Tuberculosis / see International Union Against Tuberculosis and Lung Disease (#15752)

♦ International Union Against Tuberculosis and Lung Disease (The Union) 15752

Union internationale contre la tuberculose et les maladies respiratoires – Unión Internacional contra la Tuberculosis y Enfermedades Respiratorias
Exec Dir 2 Rue Jean Lantier, 75001 Paris, France. E-mail: union@theunion.org.
URL: http://www.theunion.org/
History 20 Oct 1920, Paris (France). Founded to continue the activities of *Bureau central pour la prévention de la tuberculose (inactive)*, set up 1902, Berlin (Germany), following resolution of an international congress held in 1901, London (UK) (and several previous meetings from 1867 onwards). Statutes modified: Jul 1922, Brussels (Belgium); Aug 1924, Lausanne (Switzerland); Oct 1926, Washington DC (USA); Sep 1950, Copenhagen (Denmark); Oct 1954, Madrid (Spain); Jan 1957, Delhi (India); 1959; Jun 1961, Paris; Oct 1967, Amsterdam (Netherlands); Jul 1971, Moscow (USSR); Sep 1973, Tokyo (Japan); Sep 1975, Mexico; Jul 1980, Prague (Czechoslovakia); Nov 1986, Singapore (Singapore); Jun 1994, Mainz (Germany); Nov 1998, Bangkok (Thailand). Former names and other names: *International Union Against Tuberculosis (IUAT)* – former alias; *Union internationale contre la tuberculose (UICT)* – former alias; *International Association Against Tuberculosis* – former alias; *Association internationale contre la tuberculose* – former alias; *IUATLD* – former alias; *UICTMR* – former alias; *UICTER* – former alias. Registration: Start date: 23 Aug 1989, France. **Aims** Promote national autonomy within the framework of the priorities of each country by developing, implementing and assessing anti-tuberculosis and *respiratory* health programmes; gather and disseminate knowledge on all aspects of tuberculosis and lung disease, as well as on the resulting community health problems; alert doctors, decision makers, leaders of opinion and the general public to the dangers presented by tuberculosis and lung disease, as well as the community health problems associated with them; coordinate, assist and promote the work of its constituent members throughout the world; establish and maintain close links with WHO, other UN organizations and government and non-government institutions in the sectors of health and development. **Structure** General Assembly (every 4 years); Board of Directors; Executive Management Team; Senior Management Team; Coordinating Committee of Scientific Activities. Regions (7): Africa; Asia Pacific; South-East Asia; Latin America; Middle East; Europe; North America. Technical Departments (4): Tuberculosis and HIV; Tobacco Control; Research; Lung Health. **Languages** English, French, Spanish. **Staff** 20.00 FTE, paid. **Finance** Quotas from constituent members; dues from individual members. Other sources: voluntary contributions to mutual assistance programme; grants from official bodies. **Activities** Awards/prizes/competitions; events/meetings; knowledge management/information dissemination; research/documentation; training/education. **Events** *WCTOH : World Conference on Tobacco or Health* Dublin (Ireland) 2022, *Asia Pacific Region Conference* Hong Kong 2022, *WCTOH : World Conference on Tobacco or Health* Dublin (Ireland) 2021, *Summit on Tobacco Control* Paris (France) 2021, *World Conference on Lung Health* Paris (France) 2021. **Publications** *International Journal of Tuberculosis and Lung Disease* (12 a year) in Chinese, English, French, Russian, Spanish – with supplements; *IUATLD Newsletter* (2 a year) in English, French, Spanish. *Research Methods for Promotion of Lung Health – A guide to protocol development for low-income countries* (2001); *Management of Tuberculosis – A Guide for Low Income Countries* (5th ed 2000) in English, French, Spanish; *Epidemiological Basis of Tuberculosis Control* (1999) in English, French, Spanish; *Management of Asthma in Adults: A Guide for Low Income Countries* (1996) in English, French; *Clinical Tuberculosis* (2nd ed) in English, French.
Members Constituent; Organizational; Honorary; Individual; Benefactor. Constituent in 131 countries and territories:
Afghanistan, Albania, Algeria, Andorra, Angola, Australia, Austria, Bangladesh, Belgium, Benin, Bolivia, Botswana, Brazil, Bulgaria, Burkina Faso, Burundi, Cameroon, Canada, Central African Rep, Chad, Chile, China, Colombia, Congo Brazzaville, Congo DR, Costa Rica, Côte d'Ivoire, Croatia, Cuba, Czechia, Denmark, Djibouti, Dominican Rep, Ecuador, Egypt, El Salvador, Eritrea, Estonia, Ethiopia, Finland, Gambia, Germany, Ghana, Greece, Guatemala, Guinea, Haiti, Honduras, Hong Kong, Hungary, Iceland, India, Indonesia, Iran Islamic Rep, Iraq, Ireland, Israel, Italy, Japan, Jordan, Kenya, Korea DPR, Korea Rep, Kuwait, Laos, Latvia, Lebanon, Lesotho, Liberia, Libya, Lithuania, Luxembourg, Madagascar, Malawi, Malaysia, Mali, Mauritania, Mexico, Mongolia, Morocco, Mozambique, Myanmar, Namibia, Nepal, Netherlands, New Caledonia, New Zealand, Nicaragua, Niger, Nigeria, Norway, Oman, Pakistan, Panama, Papua New Guinea, Paraguay, Peru, Philippines, Poland, Portugal, Romania, Rwanda, Saudi Arabia, Senegal, Singapore, Slovakia, Somalia, South Africa, Spain, Sri Lanka, Sudan, Sweden, Switzerland, Syrian AR, Taiwan, Tanzania UR, Thailand, Togo, Trinidad-Tobago, Tunisia, Türkiye, Uganda, UK, United Arab Emirates, Uruguay, USA, Venezuela, Vietnam, Yemen, Zambia, Zimbabwe.
Included in the above, 2 organizations listed in this Yearbook:
SAARC Tuberculosis and HIV/AIDS Centre (STAC, see: #19721); *Vital Strategies*.
Individuals in 118 countries and territories:
Algeria, Angola, Argentina, Australia, Austria, Bangladesh, Belgium, Benin, Bolivia, Botswana, Brazil, Burkina Faso, Cambodia, Cameroon, Canada, Cape Verde, Central African Rep, Chad, Chile, China, Colombia, Côte d'Ivoire, Croatia, Cuba, Czechia, Denmark, Ecuador, Egypt, El Salvador, Eritrea, Estonia, Ethiopia, Fiji, Finland, France, Gambia, Georgia, Germany, Ghana, Greece, Guatemala, Guinea, Honduras, Hong Kong, Hungary, Iceland, India, Indonesia, Iran Islamic Rep, Ireland, Israel, Italy, Japan, Jordan, Kazakhstan, Kenya, Korea Rep, Kuwait, Laos, Latvia, Lebanon, Lithuania, Madagascar, Malawi, Malaysia, Maldives, Mali, Mauritius, Mexico, Mongolia, Morocco, Mozambique, Namibia, Nepal, Netherlands, New Caledonia, New Zealand, Nicaragua, Norway, Pakistan, Panama, Papua New Guinea, Paraguay, Peru, Philippines, Poland, Portugal, Romania, Russia, Saudi Arabia, Senegal, Serbia, Singapore, Slovakia, Somalia, South Africa, Spain, Sri Lanka, Sudan, Sweden, Switzerland, Syrian AR, Taiwan, Tanzania UR, Thailand, Tonga, Trinidad-Tobago, Tunisia, Türkiye, Uganda, UK, Ukraine, Uruguay, USA, Vietnam, Yemen, Zambia, Zimbabwe.
Consultative Status Consultative status granted from: *ECOSOC (#05331)* (Ros C); *ILO (#11123)* (Special List); *WHO (#20950)* (Official Relations); *UNICEF (#20332)*.
NGO Relations Member of:

– *CHS Alliance (#03911); CORE Group; Framework Convention Alliance (FCA, #09981); Global Alliance Against Chronic Respiratory Diseases (GARD, #10182); Global Coalition Against Child Pneumonia (#10290); The NCD Alliance (NCDA, #16963); NGO Committee on UNICEF (#17120); PMNCH (#18410); Union des organisations internationales non-gouvernementales établies en France (UOIF, inactive); Associations and Conference Forum (AC Forum, #02909).*

Cooperates with: *Council for International Organizations of Medical Sciences (CIOMS, #04905); Every Woman Every Child (EWEC, #09215); Global Smokefree Partnership (GSP, #10602); Stop TB Partnership (#19999). International Leprosy Association (ILA, #14029).* Supports: *Pan-African Thoracic Society (PATS, #18070).* Together with: *Union for International Cancer Control (UICC, #20415),* set up: *International Non Governmental Coalition Against Tobacco (INGCAT, no recent information).* Provides permanent secretariat of: *World Conference on Tobacco or Health (WCTOH).* [2022/XB2651/y/**B**]

♦ International Union Against the Venereal Diseases and the Treponematoses / see International Union against Sexually Transmitted Infections (#15751)
♦ International Union Against Vivisection (inactive)
♦ International Union of Agricultural Sciences (inactive)
♦ International Union of Agroforestry (unconfirmed)
♦ International Union of Air Pollution Prevention Associations / see International Union of Air Pollution Prevention and Environmental Protection Associations (#15753)

♦ International Union of Air Pollution Prevention and Environmental Protection Associations (IUAPPA) 15753

Union internationale des associations pour la prévention de la pollution de l'air et la protection de l'environnement (UIAPPA)

Dir Gen Oakwood House, 11 Wingle Tye Rd, Burgess Hill, RH15 9HR, UK. T. +447710153525.
URL: http://www.iuappa.org/

History Jun 1964, Washington, DC (USA). Founded at a meeting of representatives of 6 national air pollution associations, the constitution then drafted being subsequently ratified by member associations, 8 Jan 1965. Previous statute: agreed at a meeting of International Council, 19 May 1977, Tokyo (Japan); adopted, together with bye-laws, 23 Sep 1978. Statute and bye-laws amended: 24 Oct 1980; 28 Aug 1986; 14 Sep 1989; 3 Sep 1992. Current statute agreed by International Board, 15 Aug 2000. Permanent Secretariat established 1 Jan 1978, Brighton (UK). Former names and other names: *International Union of Air Pollution Prevention Associations* – former; *Union internationale des associations de prévention de la pollution atmosphérique* – former. **Aims** Promote progress in prevention and control of air pollution, protection of the environment and adoption of *sustainable development.* **Structure** International Board (meets annually); Permanent Secretariat. **Languages** English. **Finance** Sources: members' dues. Annual budget: 30,000 GBP. **Activities** Awards/prizes/competitions; events/meetings; knowledge management/information dissemination; monitoring/evaluation; networking/liaising; standards/guidelines. **Events** *Regional Conference* Suwon (Korea Rep) 2020, *World Clean Air Congress* Istanbul (Turkey) 2019, *World Clean Air Congress* Busan (Korea Rep) 2016, *Regional Conference* Amsterdam (Netherlands) 2014, *World Clean Air Congress* Cape Town (South Africa) 2013. **Publications** *IUAPPA Newsletter. Three Year Review* (2010). World conference and congress proceedings. **Members** Full; Associate; Observer. Members in 50 countries and territories. Membership countries not specified. **IGO Relations** Accredited by (1): *Convention on Long-range Transboundary Air Pollution (#04787).* **NGO Relations** Member of (1): *Climate and Clean Air Coalition (CCAC, #04010).* Mutual associate membership with: *European Federation of Clean Air and Environmental Protection Associations (EFCA, #07079).* [2019.04.23/XC2683/y/**C**]

♦ International Union of Allied, Novelty and Production Workers (internationally oriented national body)
♦ International Union of Alpinist Associations / see Union internationale des associations d'alpinisme (#20420)
♦ International Union of Amateur Astronomers (no recent information)
♦ International Union of Amateur Billiards Federations (inactive)
♦ International Union of Amateur Cinema / see Union internationale du cinéma (#20423)
♦ International Union of Amateur Film Makers / see Union internationale du cinéma (#20423)
♦ International Union of American Republics / see OAS (#17629)

♦ International Union of Angiology (IUA) 15754

Union internationale d'angiologie

Sec Via Germanico 211, 00192 Rome RM, Italy. E-mail: secretary@angiology.org.
SG address not obtained.
URL: http://www.angiology.org/

History Sep 1958, San Remo (Italy). Founded as successor to International Provisional Committee set up in 1951. Constitution modified 25 June 2006, Lisbon (Portugal); July 2012, Prague (Czech Rep). Former names and other names: *International Union of Angiology – Society for Vascular Medicine, Vascular Surgery and Endovascular Interventions* – full title; *Union internationale d'angiologie – société pour la Médecine et la Chirurgie Vasculaire ainsi que les Interventions Endovasculaires* – full title. Registration: Start date: 9 Oct 1982, France. **Aims** Stimulate at an international level scientific knowledge in the whole field of angiology, diseases of *blood vessels* and their social incidence. **Structure** General Assembly (annual, including every 2 years at Congress); Administrative Committee; Executive Board; Advisers to the Board (12); Councils (2); Chapters (9); Committees (8); National Delegates; Representative from other societies; Administrative Secretariat. **Languages** English, French. **Staff** 0.50 FTE, paid. **Finance** Sources: members' dues. **Activities** Events/meetings. **Events** *World Congress* Porto Alegre (Brazil) 2022, *Biennial World Congress* Prague (Czechia) 2020, *Biennial World Congress* Beijing (China) 2018, *Congress* Aswan (Egypt) 2017, *Congress* Graz (Austria) 2017. **Publications** *International Angiology* – journal. Textbooks.

Members Individual physicians in 60 countries:
Algeria, Argentina, Australia, Austria, Azerbaijan, Belgium, Bosnia-Herzegovina, Brazil, Bulgaria, Canada, Chile, China, Colombia, Côte d'Ivoire, Cuba, Cyprus, Czechia, Denmark, Ecuador, Finland, France, Georgia, Germany, Greece, Hungary, Iceland, India, Ireland, Israel, Italy, Japan, Korea Rep, Kyrgyzstan, Lebanon, Lithuania, Luxembourg, Mexico, Netherlands, New Zealand, Norway, Philippines, Poland, Portugal, Romania, Russia, Saudi Arabia, Serbia, Slovakia, Slovenia, South Africa, Spain, Sweden, Switzerland, Türkiye, UK, Ukraine, United Arab Emirates, Uruguay, USA, Uzbekistan.

NGO Relations Affiliated with (1): *Pan Arab Angiology College (PAAC, #18139).* Instrumental in setting up (1): *European Venous Forum (EVF, #09050).* [2023.02.17/XC2686/v/**C**]

♦ International Union of Angiology – Society for Vascular Medicine, Vascular Surgery and Endovascular Interventions / see International Union of Angiology (#15754)

♦ International Union of Anthropological and Ethnological Sciences (IUAES) 15755

Union Internationale des Sciences Anthropologiques et Ethnologiques (UISAE) – Unión Internacional de Ciencias Antropológicas y Etnológicas (UNICAE)

Permanent Address c/o Ctr for Intl Academic Exchange, National Museum of Ethnology, 10-1 Senri Expo Park, Suita, Osaka, 565-8511 Japan. T. +81668788235.
SG Anthropology – FSW – KU Leuven, Parkstraat 45 – bus 3615, 3000 Leuven, Belgium. T. +3216320159. E-mail: s-g@iuaes.org.
URL: https://www.waunet.org/iuaes/

History 23 Aug 1948, Brussels (Belgium). Founded at the 3rd *International Congress of Anthropological and Ethnological Sciences (ICAES, inactive),* when it was brought into one organization, de facto, with the latter. ICAES was itself set up in 1934 and acted as the follower of various Congresses of Anthropological Sciences, starting in 1865 as *Congrès international d'anthropologie et d'archéologie préhistoriques (CIAPP, inactive).* The two organizations were united, de jure, in 1968. Together with the *World Council of Anthropological Associations (WCAA, #21317),* became one of 2 distinctly separate but constituent chambers within *World Anthropological Union (WAU, #21093),* 2018. Former names and other names: *Internationale Union der Anthropologischen und Ethnologischen Wissenschaften* – former. **Aims** Enhance exchange and communication among anthropologists and ethnologists of all regions of the world, in a collective effort to expand human knowledge; contribute to a better understanding of human society, and to a sustainable future based on harmony between nature and culture. **Structure** General Assembly (every 4 years); Council of Commissions; Executive Committee; Commissions (32). **Languages** English. **Finance** Sources: grants; members' dues. **Activities** Events/meetings; research/documentation. **Events** *IUAES-WAU World Anthropology Congress* Delhi (India) 2023, *Congress* St Petersburg (Russia) 2022, *Congress* 2021, *Inter-Congress* Sibenik (Croatia) 2021, *Inter-Congress* Sibenik (Croatia) 2020. **Publications** *IUAES Newsletter* (2 a year). **Members** National; Institutional institutes, academies, university departments; Individual infranational organizations (museums, research laboratories, etc). Members in 57 countries and territories:
Argentina, Australia, Austria, Bangladesh, Belgium, Brazil, Cameroon, Canada, Chile, China, Colombia, Croatia, Cuba, Cyprus, Czechia, Denmark, Egypt, Finland, France, Germany, Greece, Hong Kong, Hungary, India, Israel, Italy, Japan, Kenya, Korea Rep, Lebanon, Libya, Malaysia, Mexico, Netherlands, New Zealand, Nigeria, Peru, Philippines, Poland, Portugal, Puerto Rico, Romania, Russia, Saudi Arabia, Slovenia, South Africa, Spain, Sweden, Switzerland, Taiwan, Tanzania UR, Türkiye, UK, Uruguay, USA, Venezuela, Zimbabwe.

IGO Relations Accredited by (1): *United Nations Office at Vienna (UNOV, #20604).* **NGO Relations** Member of (5): *International Committee for Social Science Information and Documentation (ICSSD, no recent information); International Council for Philosophy and Human Sciences (CIPSH, #13061); International Council of Museums (ICOM, #13051); NGO Committee on Financing for Development, New York (#17108)* (as Full member of); *World Council of Anthropological Associations (WCAA, #21317).* Affiliated with (1): *Coordinadora Latinoamericana de Cine et de Comunicación de los Pueblos Indígenas (CLACPI, #04806)* (Commission on Visual Anthropology). [2022.10.11/XB2687/**B**]

♦ International Union of Antimilitarist Ministers and Clergymen (inactive)
♦ International Union for Applied Ornithology (inactive)
♦ International Union of Architects (#20419)
♦ International Union for Arrangements concerning Laws and Customs during Wars on Land (inactive)
♦ International Union of Artists (inactive)
♦ International Union of Arts (inactive)
♦ International Union of Associations of Doctor-Motorists (no recent information)
♦ International Union of the Associations of Heating, Ventilating and Air Conditioning Contractors (inactive)
♦ International Union of Associations of Industrial Inventors and Artists (inactive)

♦ International Union of Associations of Mountain Guides 15756

Union internationale des associations de guides de montagne (UIAGM) – Internationale Vereinigung der Bergführerverbände (IVBV) – Unione Internazionale delle Associazione di Guide di Montagna

Main Office Heuberg 25, 4051 Basel BS, Switzerland. T. +41612611311. E-mail: office@uiagm.info.
URL: http://www.ifmga.info/

History 17 Oct 1965. Statutes adopted 22 Oct 1966, Sion (Switzerland); amended: 24 Jun 1987, Kippel-Lötschental (Switzerland); 8 Nov 1969, St Johann-Tirol (Austria); 30 Jun 1979, Bettmeralp (Switzerland). **Aims** Create close links between national organizations of mountain guides in order to: harmonize professional rules; facilitate practice of the profession; constitute a body for arbitration, conciliation and consultation; centralize information and encourage research. **Structure** General Assembly (annual); Bureau; Technical Committee. **Languages** English, French, German. **Staff** 7.00 FTE, voluntary. **Finance** Members' dues. **Activities** Events/meetings; training/education; knowledge management/information dissemination. **Events** *General Meeting* Bariloche (Argentina) 2019, *General Meeting* Schruns (Austria) 2018, *General Meeting* Obergurgl (Austria) 2014, *General Meeting* Tønsberg (Norway) 2014, *General Meeting* Huaraz (Peru) 2013. **Publications** *UIAGM Info Brochure.*

Members Professional guide associations in 21 countries:
Argentina, Austria, Bolivia, Canada, Czechia, France, Germany, Italy, Japan, Nepal, New Zealand, Norway, Peru, Poland, Slovakia, Slovenia, Spain, Sweden, Switzerland, UK, USA. [2020/XD2427/**D**]

♦ International Union of Aviation Insurers / see International Union of Aerospace Insurers (#15750)
♦ International Union of Bailiffs and Law Officers / see International Union of Judicial Officers (#15785)
♦ International Union of Bakers and Bakers-Confectioners / see International Union of Bakers and Confectioners (#15757)

♦ International Union of Bakers and Confectioners (UIBC) 15757

Unión Internacional de Panaderos y Pasteleros – Internationaler Verband der Bäcker und Konditoren

SG Calle Raimundo Fernandez Villaverde 61, E-28003, Madrid, Spain. E-mail: admin@worldbakersconfectioners.org.
Pres address not obtained.
URL: http://www.worldbakersconfectioners.org/

History Founded 1924, Brussels (Belgium), as *Union internationale de la boulangerie et de la boulangerie-pâtisserie (UIB) – International Union of Bakers and Bakers-Confectioners – Internationaler Verband der Bäcker und Bäcker-Konditoren.* Former titles: English – *International Union of Master Bakers and Bakers-Confectioners, Union of International Bakers;* French – *Union internationale des maîtres-boulangers.* Merged with *International Union of Confectioners, Pastrycooks and Ice Cream Makers (UIPCG, inactive)* and adopted current title, 2014. **Aims** Represent the cultural, economic and social interests of members; treat problems regarding formation, engineering, quality, sale, tax and all other problems related to the trade; consult and represent members and protect their interests. **Structure** Annual Congress; Presidium; Secretariat. **Languages** English, French, German, Spanish. **Activities** Awards/prizes/competitions; events/meetings. **Events** *Congress* Amsterdam (Netherlands) 2015, *Congress* Munich (Germany) 2015, *Congress* Poznań (Poland) 2014, *Congress* Taipei (Taiwan) 2014, *Congress* Granada (Spain) 2013.

Members National organizations in 35 countries and territories:
Algeria, Argentina, Australia, Brazil, Chile, China, Denmark, Finland, France, Germany, Greece, Hungary, Iceland, Iran Islamic Rep, Ireland, Israel, Italy, Japan, Mexico, Morocco, Netherlands, Norway, Peru, Poland, Portugal, Romania, Russia, Slovakia, South Africa, Spain, Sweden, Switzerland, Taiwan, Türkiye, Uruguay. [2018.09.07/XD8626/**D**]

♦ International Union of Bakers, Confectioners and Similar Trades (inactive)

♦ International Union of Basic and Clinical Pharmacology (IUPHAR) 15758

SG Univ of Kansas Medical Center, 3901 Rainbow Blvd, Mail Stop 4016, Kansas City KS 66160, USA. T. +19135887533. Fax +19135887373. E-mail: admin@iuphar.org.
URL: http://www.iuphar.org/

History 1959, Buenos Aires (Argentina), as Section of Pharmacology (SEPHAR) of *International Union of Physiological Sciences (IUPS, #15800).* Independent union established 1963 Prague (Czechoslovakia), as *International Union of Pharmacology (IUPHAR) – Union internationale de pharmacologie.* Statutes adopted 1966, Sao Paulo (Brazil). Present name adopted, 2006. **Aims** Promote international coordination of research, discussion, symposia, and publication in the field of pharmacology, including clinical pharmacology, drug metabolism and *toxicology;* organize permanent cooperation between representative societies throughout the world; contribute to the advancement of pharmacology in all its international aspects; cooperate with WHO in all matters concerning *drugs* and drug research; establish contacts with related international unions and sponsor joint scientific activities. **Structure** General Assembly (at Congress). Executive Committee, consisting of President, Past President, 1st Vice-President, 2nd Vice-President, Secretary General, Treasurer, Representative of the Division of Clinical Pharmacology and 5 Councillors. Auditors (2). Committees (4): International Advisory Board; Membership; Nominating; Receptor Nomenclature and Drug Classification. **Languages** English. **Staff** Voluntary. **Finance** Sources: members' dues. Other sources: royalties on congress proceedings; grants from ICSU. **Activities** Events/meetings; projects/programmes. **Events** *Quadrennial Congress on Pharmacology* Glasgow (UK) 2022, *ISCTICO : International Symposium on Cell/Tissue Injury and Cytoprotection/ Organoprotection* Budapest (Hungary) 2021, *Quadrennial Congress on Pharmacology* Kyoto (Japan) 2018, *World Conference on the Pharmacology of Natural and Traditional Medicine* Singapore (Singapore) 2015, *Quadrennial Congress on Pharmacology* Cape Town (South Africa) 2014. **Publications** *Pharmacology International* (2 a year) – to member societies; *Directory of IUPHAR* (annual). Congress proceedings; Compendium.

Members Full National societies in 52 countries and territories:
Argentina, Armenia, Australia, Austria, Belgium, Brazil, Bulgaria, Canada, Chile, China, Colombia, Croatia, Cuba, Czechia, Denmark, Egypt, Estonia, Finland, France, Germany, Greece, Hong Kong, Hungary, India, Indonesia, Iran Islamic Rep, Israel, Italy, Japan, Korea Rep, Latvia, Netherlands, Norway, Pakistan, Philippines, Poland, Portugal, Russia, Serbia, Singapore, Slovakia, Slovenia, South Africa, Spain, Sweden, Switzerland, Taiwan, Thailand, Türkiye, UK, USA, Venezuela.
Included in the above, 2 international organizations:
Australasian Society of Clinical and Experimental Pharmacology and Toxicology (ASCEPT); European Society for Developmental Perinatal and Paediatric Pharmacology (ESDPPP, #08581).
Associate (11), including 6 organizations listed in this Yearbook:

Asia Pacific Federation of Pharmacologists (APFP, #01903); European Association for Clinical Pharmacology and Therapeutics (EACPT, #05977); European College of Neuropsychopharmacology (ECNP, #06612); Federation of European Pharmacological Societies (EPHAR, #09527); Latin American Association of Pharmacology (LAP, #16249); Pacific Rim Association for Clinical Pharmacogenetics (PRACP, no recent information).
Consultative Status Consultative status granted from: *WHO (#20950)* (Official Relations). **NGO Relations** Member of: *Council for International Organizations of Medical Sciences (CIOMS, #04905); International Council for Medicinal and Aromatic Plants (ICMAP, #13047); International Science Council (ISC, #14796).* Represented in: *Committee on Data for Science and Technology (CODATA, #04247).* Joint meeting with: *European Association for Clinical Pharmacology and Therapeutics (EACPT, #05977).* [2019/XC3918/y/**C**]

♦ International Union of Biochemistry / see International Union of Biochemistry and Molecular Biology (#15759)

♦ International Union of Biochemistry and Molecular Biology (IUBMB) 15759

Union internationale de biochimie et de biologie moléculaire

Sec Univ of Manitoba, Dept of Biochemistry and Medical Genetics, Room 333A – Basic Medical Science Bldg, 745 Bannatyne Ave, Winnipeg MB R3E 0J9, Canada. T. +12042723174. Fax +12047893900.

Registered Office c/o MJ Meijer Notarissen, Keizersgracht 695-699, 1017 DW Amsterdam, Netherlands.
URL: http://www.iubmb.org/

History 5 Jan 1955, London (UK). Founded following decision, 1 Mar 1953, of *International Committee for Biochemistry (inactive)*, which had been constituted by the 1st International Congress of Biochemistry, 1949, Cambridge (UK). Present Statutes and By-Laws adopted at General Assembly, 2018, Seoul (Korea Rep). Former names and other names: *International Union of Biochemistry (IUB)* – former (5 Jan 1955 to 1991); *Union internationale de biochimie* – former (5 Jan 1955 to 1991). Registration: RSIN, No/ID: 806945138, Netherlands. **Aims** Advance the international molecular life sciences community. **Structure** General Assembly (every 3 years, normally in association with International Congress); Executive Committee; Nominating Committee; Editorial Boards. Interest Groups (11), each with its own Committee, include: *Joint IUBMB-IUPAC International Carbohydrate Organization (ICO, #16138).* Other Committees (8) include: *IUBMB-IUPAC Joint Commission on Biochemical Nomenclature (JCBN, #16078).* **Languages** English. **Staff** Voluntary. **Finance** Sources: donations; members' dues; sale of publications. Other sources: grants from ICSU and *UNESCO (#20322)*; contributions by foundations. **Activities** Events/meetings; financial and/or material support; guidance/assistance/consulting; networking/liaising; training/education. **Events** *World Congress / International Congress of Biochemistry & Molecular Biology* Melbourne, VIC (Australia) 2024, *The Biochemistry Global Summit* Lisbon (Portugal) 2022, *Meeting on Tissue Homeostasis in Health and Diseases* Lisbon (Portugal) 2019, *Meeting on Inhibitors of Protein Kinases, Kinase Inhibitors in Target Biology and Disease* Warsaw (Poland) 2019, *Triennial Congress* Seoul (Korea Rep) 2018. **Publications** *IUBMB Life* (12 a year) – journal; *Trends in Biochemical Sciences (TiBS)* (12 a year); *Biochemistry and Molecular Biology Education* (6 a year); *Biotechnology and Applied Biochemistry* (6 a year); *BioFactors* (4 a year); *IUBMB Newsletter* (2 a year). *Standards for the PhD Degree in the Molecular Biosciences* (2011); *Biochemical Nomenclature and Related Documents – a Compendium* (1992); *Enzyme Nomenclature* (1992). Congress and Focused Meeting reports; circulars.

Members Adhering Bodies; Associate Adhering Bodies; Special Membership (bodies with professional interests in biochemistry and in the aims of IUBMB). National Committees of the form 'Committee for International Relations in Biochemistry' in 49 countries and territories:
Argentina, Australia, Belgium, Brazil, Bulgaria, Canada, Chile, China, Croatia, Czechia, Denmark, Egypt, Finland, France, Germany, Greece, Hungary, India, Iran Islamic Rep, Ireland, Israel, Italy, Japan, Korea Rep, Malaysia, Mexico, Morocco, New Zealand, Nigeria, Norway, Pakistan, Peru, Philippines, Poland, Portugal, Russia, Serbia, Slovakia, Slovenia, South Africa, Spain, Sweden, Switzerland, Taiwan, Türkiye, UK, Ukraine, Uruguay, USA.
Associate members in 30 countries and territories:
Armenia, Bangladesh, Belarus, Benin, Bolivia, Cameroon, Cuba, Cyprus, Estonia, Georgia, Hong Kong, Iceland, Indonesia, Kazakhstan, Kenya, Latvia, Lithuania, Moldova, Myanmar, Nepal, Panama, Romania, Singapore, Sri Lanka, Thailand, Togo, Tunisia, Vietnam, Zambia, Zimbabwe.
International associated organizations (8), listed in this Yearbook:
Federation of African Societies of Biochemistry and Molecular Biology (FASBMB, #09410); Federation of Asian and Oceanian Biochemists and Molecular Biologists (FAOBMB, #09438); Federation of European Biochemical Societies (FEBS, #09494); International Federation of Clinical Chemistry and Laboratory Medicine (IFCC, #13392); International Society for Free Radical Research (ISFRR, #15131); International Society for Neurochemistry (ISN, #15295); International Society of Vitamins and Related BioFactors (ISVRB, no recent information); Pan American Association for Biochemistry and Molecular Biology (PABMB, #18080).

NGO Relations Cooperates with: *Federation of African Societies of Biochemistry and Molecular Biology (FASBMB, #09410); Federation of Asian and Oceanian Biochemists and Molecular Biologists (FAOBMB, #09438); Federation of European Biochemical Societies (FEBS, #09494); International Union for Pure and Applied Biophysics (IUPAB, #15808); International Union of Pure and Applied Chemistry (IUPAC, #15809); Pan American Association for Biochemistry and Molecular Biology (PABMB, #18080).* Member of: *Committee on Space Research (COSPAR, #04287); Scientific Committee on Problems of the Environment (SCOPE, #19150).* [2021/XC2697/y/**B**]

♦ International Union of Biological Sciences (IUBS) 15760

Union internationale des sciences biologiques (UISB) – Unión Internacional de Ciencias Biológicas – Internationaler Verein der Biologischen Wissenschaften

Exec Dir Univ Paris Sud XI, Bât 442, 91405 Orsay CEDEX, France. T. +33169155027. Fax +33169155747.

SG A. N. Severtsov Institute of Ecology and Evolution, Russian Academy of Sciences, Leninsky Prospect 33, Moscow MOSKVA, Russia, 119071.
URL: http://www.iubs.org/

History 1922, Brussels (Belgium). Founded following recommendations, 1919, of the then *'International Research Council (IRC)'*, and since 1931, *International Council for Science (ICSU, inactive).* In 1947, took over activities of *International Institute of Embryology (IIE, inactive)*, set up 4 Jun 1911, Utrecht (Netherlands). Statutes and By-Laws modified 1955 and 1970, and amended by: 19th General Assembly, 1976, India; 21st General Assembly, 1982, Ottawa (Canada); 22nd General Assembly, 1985, Budapest (Hungary); 28th General Assembly, 2004, Cairo (Egypt). **Aims** Promote study of biological sciences; initiate, facilitate and coordinate research and other scientific activities that require international cooperation; ensure discussion and dissemination of results of cooperative research; promote organization of international conferences and assist publication of their reports. **Structure** General Assembly (every 3 years); Executive Committee. Secretary General holds annual consultations with adhering organizations. Officers meet when necessary. Secretariat, headed by Executive Director. **Languages** English, French. **Staff** 2.00 FTE, paid. **Finance** Sources: contributions; members' dues. Contributions from other organizations supporting IUBS scientific programmes. Supported by: *UNESCO (#20322).*

Activities Research and development; research/documentation. /Sections and Commissions/:
- Aerobiology;
- Algology;
- Animal Genetics;
- Animal Physiology and Bio-chemistry;
- Arachnology;
- Bee Research;
- Bee Relationships;
- Biological Control;
- Bioindicators;
- Biometeorology;
- Biometry;
- Botanical Gardens;
- Botany;
- Botany, General;
- Bryzoology;
- Cell Biology;
- Coleopterology;
- Culture Collections;
- Developmental Biology;
- Dipterology;
- Ecology;
- Education;
- Endocrinology;
- Entomology;
- Environmental Mutagens;
- Eriksson Prize Fund;
- Ethological Conferences;
- Evolutionary Biology;
- Fungi Taxonomy;
- *General Committee on Botanical Nomenclature (no recent information);*
- Genetics;
- Herpetology;
- Histochemistry and Cytochemistry;
- Horticultural Science;
- Human Biology;
- Immunology;
- *International Commission for the Nomenclature of Cultivated Plants (ICNCP, see: #15760);*
- *International Commission for Small Scale Vegetation Mapping (no recent information);*
- *International Congress of Systematic and Evolutionary Biology (ICSEB);*
- *International Federation of Mammalogists (IFM, see: #15760);*
- *International Mycological Association (IMA, #14203);*
- *International Plant Growth Substances Association (IPGSA, #14591);*
- *International Plant Protection Congresses (IPPC);*
- *International Society of Mediterranean Ecology (ISOMED, #15259);*
- Invertebrate Pathology;
- Invertebrate Reproduction;
- Invertebrate Survey;
- Lichenology;
- Limnology;
- Malacology;
- Mammalogy;
- Mediterranean Ecology;
- Mediterranean Phyto-Taxonomy;
- Microbial Ecology; Mushroom Science;
- Microbiology, Nematology;
- Nomenclature of Cultivated Plants;
- Nomenclature of Plants;
- Oceanography, Biological;
- Ornithology;
- Palaeobotany;
- Palaeozoology;
- Palynology;
- Parasitology;
- Photobiology;
- Plant Growth Substances;
- Plant Information;
- Plant Pathology;
- Plant Physiology;
- Plant Protection;
- Plant Sexual Reproductive Research;
- Plant Taxonomy;
- Plant Taxonomy Databases;
- Polychaetology;
- Primatology;
- Protozoology, Radiobiology;
- Reticuloendotheliel Societies;
- Seed Technology;
- Skin Biology;
- Vegetation Mapping;
- Vertebrate Morphology;
- Science Editing;
- Senescence Research;
- Social Insects;
- Soil Zoology;
- Succulent Plants;
- Systematic and Evolutionary Biology;
- Tropical Root Crops;
- Vegetation Science;
- Zoological Nomenclature.

Events *Conference on Sustainability Science (ICSS)* Tokyo (Japan) 2022, *Triennial General Assembly* Oslo (Norway) 2019, *Triennial General Assembly* Berlin (Germany) 2015, *International Congress of Systematic and Evolutionary Biology* Seoul (Korea Rep) 2015, *Triennial General Assembly* Suzhou (China) 2012. **Publications** *Biology International (The News Magazine of the International Union of Biological Sciences)* (2 a year) – including special issues. *IUBS Monograph Series*; *Methodology Manual Series.* Proceedings of IUBS General Assemblies.

Members Ordinary Members: Academies of Science, National Research Councils, national science associations, similar organizations. National Adhering Organizations in 47 countries and territories:
Argentina, Australia, Austria, Belgium, Brazil, Bulgaria, Chile, China, Cuba, Czechia, Denmark, Ecuador, Egypt, Finland, France, Germany, Hungary, India, Ireland, Israel, Italy, Japan, Korea Rep, Lebanon, Mexico, Monaco, Mongolia, Netherlands, New Zealand, Norway, Philippines, Poland, Portugal, Romania, Russia, Saudi Arabia, Slovakia, South Africa, Spain, Sweden, Switzerland, Taiwan, Tunisia, UK, Uruguay, USA, Venezuela.
Scientific Members: international scientific associations, societies, commissions or sections in various biological and related disciplines. Commissions or organizations representing commissions (74):
- *All Union Theriological Society* (Section of Mammalogy of);
- *Asociación Europea de Coleopterologia (AEC, #02125);*
- *Biodiversity Information Standards (TDWG, #03243);*
- *Council for International Congresses of Dipterology (CICD, #04899);*
- *Council for International Congresses of Entomology (ICE Council, #04900);*
- *European Association of Science Editors (EASE, #06201);*
- *European Society for Comparative Endocrinology (ESCE, #08558);*
- *European Society for Comparative Skin Biology (ESCSB, inactive);*
- *European Society of Nematologists (ESN, #08661);*
- *General Committee on Botanical Nomenclature (no recent information);*
- *International Association for Aerobiology (IAA, #11691);*
- *International Association for Ecology (INTECOL, #11856);*
- *International Association for Lichenology (IAL, #12000);*
- *International Association for Plant Taxonomy (IAPT, #12092);*
- *International Association for Radiation Research (IARR, #12119);*
- *International Association for the Plant Protection Sciences (IAPPS, #12091);*
- *International Association for Vegetation Science (IAVS, #12253);*
- *International Association of Biological Oceanography (IABO, #11726);*
- *International Association of Botanical and Mycological Societies (IABMS, #11730);*
- *International Association of Botanic Gardens (IABG, #11731);*
- *International Association of Comparative Physiology and Biochemistry (IACPB, #11798);*
- *International Association of Environmental Mutagenesis and Genomics Societies (IAEMGS, #11877);*
- *International Association of Human Biologists (IAHB, #11945);*
- *International Association of Sexual Plant Reproduction Research (IASPRR, #12161);*
- *International Bee Research Association (IBRA, #12330);*
- *International Biometric Society (#12354);*
- *International Bryozoology Association (IBA, #12403);*
- *International Commission for Plant-Pollinator Relationships (ICPPR, #12716);*
- *International Commission for Small Scale Vegetation Mapping (no recent information);*
- *International Commission for the Nomenclature of Cultivated Plants (ICNCP, see: #15760);*
- *International Commission on Bioindicators (#12667);*
- *International Commission on Protozoology (ICOP, no recent information);*
- *International Commission on the Taxonomy of Fungi (ICTF, #12734);*
- *International Commission on Zoological Nomenclature (ICZN, #12737);*
- *International Council for Medicinal and Aromatic Plants (ICMAP, #13047);*

- *International Ethological Committee (no recent information)*;
- *International Federation for Cell Biology (IFCB, #13382)*;
- *International Federation of Palynological Societies (IFPS, #13498)*;
- *International Federation of Societies for Histochemistry and Cytochemistry (IFSHC, #13548)*;
- *International Genetics Federation (IGF, #13711)*;
- *International Organisation for Biological Control (IOBC, #14424)*;
- *International Organization for Plant Information (IOPI, no recent information)*;
- *International Organization for Succulent Plant Study (IOS, #14477)*;
- *International Organization for Systematic and Evolutionary Biology (IOSEB, #14479)*;
- *International Organization of Palaeobotany (IOP, #14459)*;
- *International Ornithological Congress (IOC, #14486)*;
- *International Ornithologists' Union (IOU, #14487)*;
- *International Palaeontological Association (IPA, #14501)*;
- *International Phycological Society (IPS, #14576)*;
- *International Polychaetology Association (#14617)*;
- *International Seed Testing Association (ISTA, #14829)*;
- *International Society for Animal Genetics (ISAG, #14921)*;
- *International Society for Horticultural Science (ISHS, #15180)*;
- *International Society for Mushroom Science (ISMS, #15286)*;
- *International Society for Plant Pathology (ISPP, #15371)*;
- *International Society for Tropical Root Crops (ISTRC, #15524)*;
- *International Society of Arachnology (ISA, #14935)*;
- *International Society of Biometeorology (ISB, #14969)*;
- *International Society of Developmental Biologists (ISDB, #15052)*;
- *International Society of Invertebrate Reproduction and Development (ISIRD, #15218)*;
- *International Society of Limnology (#15232)*;
- *International Society of Vertebrate Morphology (ISVM, #15538)*;
- *International Society of Zoological Sciences (ISZS, #15552)*;
- *International Union for the Study of Social Insects (IUSSI, #15819)*;
- *International Union of Photobiology (IUPB, #15798)*;
- *International Union of Reticuloendothelial Societies (IURES, no recent information)*;
- *International Union of Soil Sciences (IUSS, #15817)* (Soil Zoology Sub-Commission of);
- *IUBS Commission for Biological Education (IUBS-CBE, #16079)*;
- *Organization for the Phyto-Taxonomic Investigation of the Mediterranean Area (OPTIMA, #17884)*;
- *Unitas Malacologica (#20495)*;
- *World Congress of Herpetology (WCH, #21307)*;
- *World Federation for Culture Collections (WFCC, #21424)*;
- *World Federation of Parasitologists (WFP, #21471)*.

Consultative Status Consultative status granted from: *ECOSOC (#05331)* (Ros C); *FAO (#09260)* (Liaison Status). **IGO Relations** Accredited by (1): *United Nations Office at Vienna (UNOV, #20604)*. Associated with Department of Global Communications of the United Nations. **NGO Relations** Member of (1): *International Science Council (ISC, #14796)*. Cooperates with (4): *International Botanical Congress (IBC)*; *International Commission on Trichinellosis (#12735)*; *International Committee on Systematics of Prokaryotes (ICSP, #12807)*; *Permanent Service, Type Culture Collection of Drosophila (no recent information)*. Instrumental in setting up (1): *IUPS Commission on Comparative Physiology (see: #15800)*. Represented in inter-union commissions and scientific committees: *Committee on Data for Science and Technology (CODATA, #04247)*; *Committee on Space Research (COSPAR, #04287)*; *Scientific Committee on Antarctic Research (SCAR, #19147)*; *Scientific Committee on Oceanic Research (SCOR, #19149)*; *Scientific Committee on Problems of the Environment (SCOPE, #19150)*. Participates in international bodies concerned with biological problems: *International Union of Basic and Clinical Pharmacology (IUPHAR, #15758)*; *International Union of Biochemistry and Molecular Biology (IUBMB, #15759)*; *International Union of Nutritional Sciences (IUNS, #15796)*; *International Union of Physiological Sciences (IUPS, #15800)*; *International Union for Pure and Applied Biophysics (IUPAB, #15808)*. [2021/XB2698/y/**B**]

♦ International Union of Blacksmithing and Forging / see European Metal Union (#07785)
♦ International Union of Bricklayers and Allied Craftsmen / see International Union of Bricklayers and Allied Craftworkers
♦ International Union of Bricklayers and Allied Craftworkers (internationally oriented national body)

♦ International Union of Building Centres 15761

Union internationale des centres du bâtiment (UICB) – Internationale Union der Bauzentren

Pres NSC Nat'l Bldg Ctr, Bauerova 10, 603 00 Brno, Czechia. T. +420541152861.
URL: http://www.uicb.org/

History 1958, Brussels (Belgium), as *Standing International Conference of Building Centres – Conférence permanente internationale des centres du bâtiment (CICB)*. Constitution and present name adopted 6 Jun 1963, Essen (Germany FR); present articles adopted Oct 1986, Budapest (Hungary). Registered in accordance with French law. **Aims** Strengthen social, cultural and professional ties among national and regional building *information* centres; encourage exchange of documentation and information on all developments relevant to building. **Structure** General Assembly (every 3 years); Executive Committee; General Secretary; Treasurer. **Languages** English. **Staff** 0.50 FTE, paid. **Finance** Sources: members' dues. Annual budget: 20,000 EUR. **Activities** Organizes: exchange of technical documents, information, building processes and materials; architectural exhibitions, annual ad hoc seminars, study tours; working groups. **Events** *Annual Meeting* Manchester (UK) 2010, *Annual meeting* Istanbul (Turkey) 2008, *Triennial general assembly* Istanbul (Turkey) 2008, *Annual meeting* Stuttgart (Germany) 2007, *Annual meeting* Prague (Czech Rep) 2006. **Publications** *UICB Bulletin* (2 a year). *Directory of Quality Approval Systems* (1990).

Members Organizations (18) in 12 countries:
Belgium, Czechia, Denmark, Estonia, Finland, France, Germany, Netherlands, Norway, Russia, Sweden, Türkiye.

IGO Relations Cooperates with: *United Nations Economic Commission for Europe (UNECE, #20555)*. Accredited by: *United Nations Office at Vienna (UNOV, #20604)*. Associated with Department of Global Communications of the United Nations. [2012/XD2700/**C**]

♦ International Union of Building Societies and Savings Associations / see International Union for Housing Finance (#15780)
♦ International Union of Building Societies and Savings and Loan Associations / see International Union for Housing Finance (#15780)
♦ International Union of Catholic Employers' Associations / see International Christian Union of Business Executives (#12566)
♦ International Union of the Catholic Press / see International Christian Organisation of the Media (#12563)
♦ International Union of Catholic Women's Leagues / see World Union of Catholic Women's Organisations (#21876)
♦ International Union of Chemistry / see International Union of Pure and Applied Chemistry (#15809)
♦ International Union of Children's NGOs / see International Union of Children's Organizations (#15762)

♦ International Union of Children's Organizations (UPO-FCO) 15762

Contact Novaya Plostchad dom 8, stroyeniye 1, Moscow MOSKVA, Russia, 109012. T. +7959281733. Fax +7959281733.
Pres address not obtained. T. +7952068550. Fax +7959219840.

History 1990. Founded as *International Federation of Children's Organizations*. Previously also known as *International Union of Children's NGOs*. Also known as *Union of Pioneer Organizations – Federation of Children's Organizations*. Registration: Russia. **Aims** Strive to create optimal conditions for children to acquire knowledge of their world; promote and protect international cooperation of children and their associations; promote children's development by means of associative, life and non-formal education. **Structure** General Assembly (every 4 years). Council, comprising President, Vice President and member representatives. **Languages** English, French, German, Russian. **Staff** 10.00 FTE, paid. **Finance** Members' dues. Other sources: public funds; sponsorship; revenues from activities; sales of publications. **Activities** Organizes: international assemblies; international fora of leaders of children's NGOs; conferences; meetings; symposia; programmes covering children's needs and interests in games, mass media, culture and tradition, creativity and sports, including camps, festivals and international exchanges. **Events** *International forum of leaders of children's NGOs* Russia 2006, *International multicultural children's meeting* Moscow (Russia) 2005, *International forum of leaders of children's NGOs / International Forum* Budapest (Hungary) 2004, *Conference on children's self-management within a children's association* Ufa (Russia) 2004, *General assembly / International Assembly* Moscow (Russia) 2003. **Publications** Monographs; reports; dictionaries; educational tools.

Members Organizations in 12 countries:
Armenia, Azerbaijan, Belarus, Georgia, Kazakhstan, Kyrgyzstan, Moldova, Russia, Tajikistan, Turkmenistan, Ukraine, Uzbekistan. [2005.07.08/XD6983/**D**]

♦ International Union for Child Welfare (inactive)
♦ International Union of Christian-Democratic and Conservative Students / see European Democrat Students (#06901)

♦ International Union of Cinemas 15763

Union internationale des cinémas (UNIC) – Unión Internacional de Cines – Internationale Filmtheaterunion – Unione Internazionale dei Cinema

CEO Avenue des Arts 10-11, 1210 Brussels, Belgium. T. +3228809939.
URL: http://www.unic-cinemas.org/

History 1964, Cannes (France), when formally set up under present title by presidents of 6 national associations, these presidents having met informally since 11 Sep 1952, Venice (Italy), as *International Union of Cinematograph Exhibitors – Union internationale de l'exploitation cinématographique (UIEC) – Unión Internacional de Explotación Cinematografica – Internationaler Verein der Kino-Betreiber*. EU Transparency Register: 74301917747-65. **Aims** Defend the interests of member associations, groups or unions of *cinematograph* exhibitors in relation to other professional organizations and public authorities; promote exchange of information; coordinate and facilitate relations between exhibitors in different countries; promote and protect the cinema, maintain its high public profile and promote the importance of the cinema exhibition industry. **Structure** General Assembly (annual) with rotating chairmanship, usually at Cannes Film Festival. Executive Committee. Permanent Secretariat General. Meetings closed. **Languages** English, French. **Staff** Part-time, paid. **Finance** Members' dues. **Activities** Undertakes studies based on information received from national associations. Current concerns: common observance of release patterns of films throughout the audiovisual media, maintaining the cinema as the correct place for first showing; reduction of VAT on cinema tickets; decreased rental charges; harmonization of film release throughout Europe; freedom of choice in programming. Annual General Meeting (always in Cannes). Documentation centre, including large archives on: Europe; Sinti and Romanies; Near East; Africa; Asia; the Pacific; the Americas; Asylum; general information on minorities and indigenous peoples. On-line service. **Events** *CINEEUROPE Convention* Barcelona (Spain) 2021, *CINEEUROPE Convention* Barcelona (Spain) 2015, *CINEEUROPE Convention* Barcelona (Spain) 2013, *ECS : European cinema summit congress* Brussels (Belgium) 2009, *Annual General Meeting* Cannes (France) 2008. **Publications** *Bulletin UNIC* (6 a year) in English, French.

Members National organizations (15) representing the owners of the majority of cinemas in each country, in 15 countries:
Austria, Belgium, Denmark, Finland, France, Germany, Hungary, Israel, Italy, Luxembourg, Netherlands, Norway, Spain, Switzerland, UK.

Consultative Status Consultative status granted from: *World Intellectual Property Organization (WIPO, #21593)* (Permanent Observer Status). **IGO Relations** Recognized by: *European Commission (EC, #06633)*. Observer to: *Intergovernmental Committee of the International Convention of Rome for the Protection of Performers, Producers of Phonograms and Broadcasting Organizations (#11474)*; *Union for the International Registration of Audiovisual Works (#20444)*. **NGO Relations** Participated in the foundation of: *Caribbean Digital Library Consortium (no recent information)*; *MEDIA Salles (#16620)*. Member of: *Federation of the Staff Associations of the United Nations and its Specialized Agencies and their Affiliated Bodies in Denmark (FUNSA Denmark)*. Affiliated to: *International Centre of Films for Children and Young People (#12493)*. Part of: *Europa Cinemas (#05744)*. [2017/XD2703/**D**]

♦ International Union of Cinematograph Exhibitors / see International Union of Cinemas (#15763)

♦ International Union for Circumpolar Health (IUCH) 15764

Sec c/o ICHR, PO Box 11050, Yellowknife NT X1A 3X7, Canada.
Pres c/o SSI, 5 Artillerivej, 2300 Copenhagen S, Denmark.
URL: http://iuch.net/

History 1981, Copenhagen (Denmark). Founded at the meeting of 5th International Congress of Circumpolar Health. The first Constitution drafted and adopted in May 1986, amended Jun 2000. Registration: 501(c)3, USA, Alaska. **Aims** Promote international cooperation in circumpolar health; encourage and support research and exchange of scientific information in the circumpolar health sciences; promote education and public awareness of circumpolar health; provide a means of communication with other scientific organizations; promote and encourage the participation of indigenous peoples in circumpolar health affairs. **Structure** Council of 13 members. Officers: President; Vice-President; Secretary; Treasurer. **Languages** English. **Staff** Voluntary. **Finance** Public donations; government grants. Budget (annual): about US$ 30,000. **Activities** Collects and disseminates information on circumpolar health and Arctic medicine. Organizes (every 3 years) an *International Congress on Circumpolar Health (ICCH)*. Working groups on specific health problems of the circumpolar regions, including matters relating to: birth defects and genetics; cancer; environmental health; indigenous people; infectious diseases; injury prevention; occupational safety and health; HIV/STDs; women's health. **Events** *International Congress on Circumpolar Health (ICCH)* Canada 2023, *International Congress on Circumpolar Health (ICCH)* St Petersburg (Russia) 2022, *International Congress on Circumpolar Health (ICCH)* St Petersburg (Russia) 2021, *International Congress on Circumpolar Health (ICCH)* Copenhagen (Denmark) 2018, *International Congress on Circumpolar Health (ICCH)* Oulu (Finland) 2015. **Publications** *International Journal of Circumpolar Health*. Congress proceedings.

Members Adhering bodies (5) in 5 countries:
Canada, Denmark, Finland, Russia, USA.
Affiliated members (5) in 5 countries:
Canada, Finland, Iceland, Sweden, UK.
Included in the above, 3 organizations listed in this Yearbook:
Circumpolar Health Research Network (CirchNet, #03942); *Nordic Society for Circumpolar Health (NSCH, #17412)*; *Scientific Committee on Antarctic Research (SCAR, #19147)*. [2022/XD2143/y/**D**]

♦ International Union of Civil Register Officials (inactive)
♦ International Union of Colleges Working for World Understanding (inactive)
♦ International Union for Combating Venereal Diseases / see International Union against Sexually Transmitted Infections (#15751)

♦ International Union for Combined Road – Rail Transport (UIRR) . . . 15765

Union internationale des sociétés de transport combiné rail – route (UIRR) – Internationale Vereinigung der Gesellschaften für den Kombinierten Verkehr Schiene-Strasse (UIRR)

Pres/Dir Gen Rue Montoyer 31, Bte 11, 1000 Brussels, Belgium. T. +3225487890. E-mail: headoffice.brussels@uirr.com.
Main Website: http://www.uirr.com/

History 1970. Converted from a "de facto" association into a cooperative company in 1991. Former names and other names: *Internationale Vereinigung der Huckepackgesellschaften* – former; *Unione Internazionale delle Società per il Trasporto Combinato Strada – Rotaia* – former; *International Union of Combined Road-Rail Transport Companies* – former. Registration: Banque-Carrefour des Entreprises, No/ID: 0443.774.307, Start date: 15 Apr 1991, Belgium, Brussels. **Aims** Promote combined transport, exchange of information, management of common assets and relations with international organizations. **Structure** Central liaison office in Brussels (Belgium). **Languages** English, French, German. **Staff** 5.00 FTE, paid. **Finance** Sources: members' dues. Other sources: participation in EU research projects. **Activities** Events/meetings; projects/programmes; research/documentation. **Events** *European Intermodal Summit (EIS)* 2022, *European Intermodal Summit (EIS)* 2021, *European Intermodal Summit (EIS)* 2020, *Annual General Assembly* Paris (France) 2013, *Annual General Assembly* Brussels (Belgium) 2012. **Publications** *UIRR Newsletter* (4 a year). Annual Report; position papers.

Members Operators of combined transport and terminals in 19 countries:
Austria, Belgium, Bulgaria, Croatia, Czechia, Estonia, France, Germany, Greece, Hungary, Italy, Luxembourg, Netherlands, Poland, Romania, Slovenia, Spain, Switzerland, UK.

IGO Relations Participates in the work of: *United Nations Economic Commission for Europe (UNECE, #20555)*. **NGO Relations** Member of (3): *European Logistics Platform (ELP, #07711)*; *European Technology Platform ALICE (ALICE, #08888)*; *Rail Forum Europe (RFE, #18607)*. [2022.10.21/XF5055/**F**]

♦ International Union of Combined Road-Rail Transport Companies / see International Union for Combined Road – Rail Transport (#15765)

♦ International Union of Commercial Agents and Brokers / see Internationally United Commercial Agents and Brokers (#14072)

♦ International Union of Confectioners, Pastrycooks and Ice Cream Makers (inactive)

♦ International Union for Conservation of Nature and Natural Resources (IUCN) 15766

Union mondiale pour la conservation de la nature et de ses ressources – Unión Internacional para la Conservación de la Naturaleza y de los Recursos Naturales (UICN)

Dir Gen Rue Mauverney 28, 1196 Gland VD, Switzerland. T. +41229990000. Fax +41229990002. E-mail: membership@iucn.org.

Pres address not obtained. E-mail: president@iucn.org.

URL: http://www.iucn.org/

History 5 Oct 1948, Fontainebleau (France). Founded at an international conference convened by UNESCO and the French Government. Establishment followed the setting up, Oct 1928, Brussels (Belgium), of *Office international de documentation et de corrélation pour la protection de la nature*, as the delayed result of the decision of an intergovernmental conference, 1913, Bern (Switzerland); subsequently becoming *International Office for the Protection of Nature (inactive)*, 1934, on registration under Belgian law; reactivated in 1945 and documentation transferred to the IUPN on its setting up in 1948. Present Statutory name adopted Edinburgh (UK). Statutes adopted 5 Oct 1948; revised 4 Oct 1978; amended 2 and 5 Dec 1990; revised 22 Oct 1996 and 13 Oct 2008; last amended 13 Oct 2015. Established pursuant to Swiss Civil Code. Former names and other names: *International Union for the Protection of Nature (IUPN)* – former (5 Oct 1948); *Union internationale pour la protection de la nature (UIPN)* – former (5 Oct 1948); *World Conservation Union* – former alias (Dec 1990 to Mar 2008); *Union mondiale pour la nature* – former (Dec 1990 to Mar 2008); *Unión Mundial para la Naturaleza* – former (Dec 1990 to Mar 2008). **Aims** Influence, encourage and assist societies throughout the world to conserve the integrity and diversity of nature and ensure that any use of natural resources is equitable and *ecologically sustainable*; develop and support cutting edge conservation science, particularly in species, ecosystems and *biodiversity* and the impact these have on human *livelihoods*. **Structure** World Conservation Congress (every 4 years). Council, comprising President, 4 Vice Presidents (elected among members), Treasurer, Commission Chairs, 3 Regional Councillors from each Statutory Region and a Councillor from Switzerland (where IUCN has its seat). Bureau. Secretariat, headed by Director-General. Offices in over 45 countries. Scientists and experts (over 10,000) structured in 6 Commissions: Commission on Education and Communication (CEC); Commission on Environmental, Economic and Social Policy (CEESP); *World Commission on Environmental Law (WCEL)*; Commission on Ecosystem Management (CEM); Species Survival Commission (SSC); *World Commission on Protected Areas (WCPA)*. Also includes: IUCN Sustainable Use and Livelihoods Specialist Group (SULi). Statutory Regions (8): Africa; Meso and South America; North America and the Caribbean; South and East Asia; West Asia; Oceania; East Europe; North and Central Asia; West Europe. Members can organizes themselves into National and Regional Committees. Instrumental in setting up: *International Wader Study Group (IWSG, see: #15766)*. **Languages** English, French, Spanish. **Staff** 950.00 FTE, paid. Staff in 51 countries worldwide. **Finance** Sources: members' dues. Other sources: funding from framework partners for core activities (Swiss Fr 19.6 million); funding for targeted project activities (Swiss Fr 77.2 million). Budget (2014): Swiss Fr 115.8 million. **Activities** Events/meetings; guidance/assistance/consulting; knowledge management/information dissemination; monitoring/evaluation; politics/policy/regulatory; projects/programmes; training/education. Programme is implemented through combined force of the Secretariat – via global thematic programmes and regional programmes – working together with the 3 IUCN Commissions, with members who provide knowledge for Programme implementation. On a global basis, monitors status of threatened species and ecosystems, protected areas and areas in need of protection, major actual or impending ecological changes and their causes and consequences and major issues regarding the management of natural resources. Management of treaties and agreements: *Convention on Biological Diversity (Biodiversity convention, 1992)*; *Convention on Wetlands of International Importance Especially as Waterfowl Habitat (Convention on Wetlands, 1971)*; *United Nations Framework Convention on Climate Change (UNFCCC, 1992)*. **Events** *International Marine Protected Area Congress* Vancouver, BC (Canada) 2023, *IUCN Leaders Forum* Jeju (Korea Rep) 2022, *Africa Protected Areas Congress* Kigali (Rwanda) 2022, *People-Nature Culture Forum* Suwon (Korea Rep) 2022, *Measuring the Effectiveness of Environmental Law through Legal Indicators* Sceaux (France) 2021. **Publications** *Red List of Threatened Species* – describing all threatened species of mammals, amphibians and reptiles, fish, plants and invertebrates; *United Nations List of National Parks and Protected Areas*. *Best Practice Guidelines*. Commission newsletters; Environmental Policy and Law Papers; books on environmental management, marine issues, protected area management, sustainable development, wetlands and water, forests, and biodiversity; newsletters.

Members total over 1,300 members. Affiliate (41) in 15 countries:
Brazil, Canada, China, Czechia, France, Germany, Indonesia, Italy, Kenya, Monaco, Netherlands, South Africa, Spain, UK, USA.

Government agencies (127) in 55 countries:
Argentina, Australia, Austria, Belgium, Benin, Bulgaria, Canada, China, Congo DR, Côte d'Ivoire, Croatia, Czechia, Dominican Rep, Ecuador, Ethiopia, Gabon, Germany, Guatemala, Guinea-Bissau, Hungary, India, Indonesia, Iraq, Ireland, Israel, Italy, Jamaica, Japan, Jordan, Korea DPR, Korea Rep, Kuwait, Malta, Mauritania, Monaco, Montenegro, Mozambique, Namibia, New Zealand, North Macedonia, Norway, Pakistan, Panama, Portugal, Romania, Serbia, Slovenia, South Africa, Spain, Sri Lanka, Sweden, UK, United Arab Emirates, Uruguay, USA.

International non-governmental organizations (107) in 31 countries:
Argentina, Barbados, Belgium, Costa Rica, Czechia, Denmark, Egypt, Fiji, France, Gabon, Germany, Hungary, Italy, Kenya, Liechtenstein, Mexico, Namibia, Nepal, Netherlands, Pakistan, Peru, Philippines, Senegal, Sweden, Switzerland, Thailand, Trinidad-Tobago, Uganda, UK, Ukraine, USA.

National non-governemntal organizations (962) in 127 countries:
Albania, Algeria, Argentina, Armenia, Australia, Austria, Azerbaijan, Bahamas, Bahrain, Bangladesh, Belize, Benin, Bhutan, Bolivia, Bosnia-Herzegovina, Botswana, Brazil, Bulgaria, Burkina Faso, Burundi, Cambodia, Cameroon, Canada, Chile, China, Colombia, Comoros, Congo Brazzaville, Congo DR, Cook Is, Costa Rica, Croatia, Cyprus, Czechia, Denmark, Dominican Rep, Ecuador, Egypt, El Salvador, Eswatini, Fiji, Finland, France, Georgia, Germany, Ghana, Greece, Guatemala, Guinea-Bissau, Haiti, Honduras, Hungary, Iceland, India, Iran Islamic Rep, Ireland, Israel, Italy, Jamaica, Jordan, Kazakhstan, Kenya, Korea Rep, Kuwait, Kyrgyzstan, Laos, Lebanon, Lithuania, Luxembourg, Madagascar, Malawi, Maldives, Mali, Mauritania, Mauritius, Mexico, Montenegro, Morocco, Myanmar, Namibia, Nepal, Netherlands, New Zealand, Nicaragua, Nigeria, Niue, Oman, Pakistan, Palau, Palestine, Panama, Papua New Guinea, Paraguay, Peru, Philippines, Poland, Portugal, Qatar, Romania, Russia, Rwanda, Senegal, Seychelles, Sierra Leone, Singapore, South Africa, Spain, Sri Lanka, St Lucia, Sweden, Syrian AR, Tajikistan, Tanzania UR, Thailand, Togo, Tunisia, Türkiye, Uganda, UK, United Arab Emirates, Uruguay, USA, Venezuela, Vietnam, Yemen, Zambia, Zimbabwe.

State Organizations (89) in 89 countries:
Albania, Angola, Australia, Azerbaijan, Bangladesh, Belgium, Bhutan, Botswana, Burkina Faso, Burundi, Cameroon, Canada, Central African Rep, China, Congo Brazzaville, Costa Rica, Côte d'Ivoire, Cyprus, Czechia, Denmark, Ecuador, Egypt, El Salvador, Estonia, Eswatini, Fiji, Finland, France, Gabon, Georgia, Germany, Guinea, Guinea-Bissau, Iceland, India, Iraq, Italy, Japan, Jordan, Kenya, Korea Rep, Kuwait, Laos, Lesotho, Liechtenstein, Luxembourg, Madagascar, Malaysia, Mali, Mauritius, Mexico, Monaco, Mongolia, Morocco, Myanmar, Nauru, Nepal, Netherlands, New Zealand, Niger, Nigeria, Norway, Oman, Pakistan, Palau, Panama, Peru, Russia, Rwanda, Samoa, Saudi Arabia, Senegal, Seychelles, Solomon Is, South Africa, Spain, Sri Lanka, Sweden, Switzerland, Thailand, Tonga, Tunisia, Türkiye, Uganda, UK, USA, Vanuatu, Vietnam, Zambia.

Indigenous People organizations (17) in 10 countries:
Australia, Bangladesh, Canada, Ecuador, Guatemala, Honduras, Panama, Peru, South Africa, USA.

Member organizations listed in this Yearbook (179):
- *African Conservation Trust (ACT)*;
- *African Wildlife Foundation (AWF, #00498)*;
- *Africa Resources Trust*;
- *Agencia Española de Cooperación Internacional para el Desarrollo (AECID)*;
- *Antarctic and Southern Ocean Coalition (ASOC, #00849)*;
- *Arab Group for the Protection of Nature (APN, #00970)*;
- *Arab NGO Network for Environment and Development (RAED, #01017)*;
- *A Rocha International (#18965)*;
- *Asia-Pacific Centre for Environmental Law, Singapore (APCEL)*;
- *Association for Tropical Biology and Conservation (ATBC, #02963)*;
- *Associazione di Cooperazione Rurale in Africa e America Latina (ACRA)*;
- *ASUDEC*;
- *Bat Conservation International (BCI)*;
- *Bears in Mind*;
- *BirdLife International (#03266)*;
- *Blue Ventures*;
- *Born Free Foundation*;
- *Both ENDS (#03307)*;
- *Caribbean Natural Resources Institute (CANARI, #03525)*;
- *Caribbean Research and Management of Biodiversity (CARMABI)*;
- *Caucasus Environmental NGO Network (CENN, #03613)*;
- *Center for International Environmental Law (CIEL)*;
- *Center for International Forestry Research (CIFOR, #03646)*;
- *Center for Meso American Studies on Appropriate Technology (#03650)*;
- *Central Africa Protected Areas Network (#03656)*;
- *Centre Africain de Recherches Forestières Appliquées et de Développement (CARFAD)*;
- *Centre de coopération internationale en recherche agronomique pour le développement (CIRAD, #03733)*;
- *Centre for Environment and Development for the Arab Region and Europe (CEDARE, #03738)*;
- *Centro Cientifico Tropical, Costa Rica (CCT)*;
- *Centro Desarrollo y Pesca Sustenable (CeDePesca, #03796)*;
- *Charles Darwin Foundation for the Galapagos Islands (CDF, #03852)*;
- *Cheetah Conservation Fund (CCF)*;
- *Christensen Fund (TCF)*;
- *CIPRA International (#03930)*;
- *Coalition Clean Baltic (CCB, #04053)*;
- *Coastal Oceans Research and Development – Indian Ocean (CORDIO East Africa, #04073)*;
- *Confederation of European Forest Owners (CEPF, #04525)*;
- *Conservation Force (#04729)*;
- *Conservation International (CI)*;
- *Conservation Through Public Health (CTPH)*;
- *Coordinadora de las Organizaciones Indígenas de la Cuenca Amazónica (COICA, #04811)*;
- *Cousteau Society*;
- *Deutsche Gesellschaft für Internationale Zusammenarbeit (GIZ)*;
- *Durrell Wildlife Conservation Trust*;
- *Earth Day Network (EDN, #05164)*;
- *Earthwatch Europe*;
- *EcoAgriculture Partners (#05290)*;
- *Eco Forum Global (EFG)*;
- *EcoHealth Alliance*;
- *Ecologic Institut (#05303)*;
- *Endangered Wildlife Trust (EWT)*;
- *Environment Africa (EA)*;
- *Environmental Defense Fund (EDF)*;
- *Environmental Foundation for Africa (EFA)*;
- *Environment Liaison Centre International (ELCI, no recent information)*;
- *Environnement et développement du Tiers-monde (enda, #05510)*;
- *EuroNatur – Europeän Nature Heritage Fund (#05738)*;
- *EUROPARC Federation (#05768)*;
- *European Association of Zoo and Wildlife Veterinarians (EAZWV, #06284)*;
- *European Association of Zoos and Aquaria (EAZA, #06283)*;
- *European Bureau for Conservation and Development (EBCD, #06412)*;
- *European Foundation Il Nibbio (FEIN)*;
- *European Herpetological Society (#07481)*;
- *European Institute for Environmental Education, Interpretation and Training (PANGEA Institute)*;
- *European Outdoor Conservation Association (EOCA, #08121)*;
- *Fauna & Flora International (FFI, #09277)*;
- *Federation of Associations for Hunting and Conservation of the EU (#09459)*;
- *Fondation Internationale pour la Gestion de la Faune (Fondation IGF)*;
- *Forest Peoples Programme (FPP, #09865)*;
- *Forest Stewardship Council (FSC, #09869)*;
- *Forest Trends (#09870)*;
- *Fundación Futuro Latinoamericano (FFLA, #10022)*;
- *Fundación Monte Mediterraneo (FMM)*;
- *Game Rangers Association of Africa (GRAA)*;
- *George Wright Society*;
- *Global Change Impact Studies Centre (GCISC)*;
- *Global Institute of Sustainability*;
- *Global Land Cover Facility (GLCF)*;
- *Global Nature Fund (GNF, #10479)*;
- *Green Earth Organization (GEO, inactive)*;
- *Indigenous Peoples of Africa Coordinating Committee (IPACC, #11163)*;
- *Instituto para el Desarrollo Sustentable en Mesoamérica, Mexico (IDESMAC)*;
- *International Association for Falconry and Conservation of Birds of Prey (IAF, #11888)*;
- *International Association for Impact Assessment (IAIA, #11956)*;
- *International Association for the Conservation of the Geological Heritage (ProGEO, #11810)*;
- *International Centre for Integrated Mountain Development (ICIMOD, #12500)*;
- *International Centre of Comparative Environmental Law (#12483)*;
- *International Cooperative University (ICU, #12952)*;
- *International Council for Game and Wildlife Conservation (#13024)*;
- *International Council of Environmental Law (ICEL, #13018)*;
- *International Crane Foundation (ICF, #13102)*;
- *International Dialogue for Environmental Action (IDEA)*;
- *International Fund for Animal Welfare (IFAW, #13693)*;
- *International Fur Federation (IFF, #13696)*;
- *International Institute for Environment and Development (IIED, #13877)*;
- *International Institute for Sustainable Development (IISD, #13930)*;
- *International Network of Engaged Buddhists (INEB, #14259)*;
- *International Primate Protection League (IPPL, #14641)*;
- *International Primatological Society (IPS, #14642)*;
- *International Society of Naturalists (INSONA)*;
- *International Wildlife Crimestoppers (IWC)*;
- *Inuit Circumpolar Council (ICC, #15995)*;
- *Island Conservation (CI)*;
- *Leadership for Conservation in Africa (LCA, #16415)*;
- *Lighthawk (LH)*;
- *Local Governments for Sustainability (ICLEI, #16507)*;
- *Mare Terra – Fundació Medeterrània (Mare Terra)*;
- *marinecultures.org*;
- *MarViva Foundation (#16591)*;
- *Mediterranean Institute for Nature and Anthropos (MedINA)*;
- *NatureServe*;
- *Non-Timber Forest Products Exchange Programme for South and Southeast Asia (NTFP-EN, #17151)*;
- *Nordic Hunters' Alliance (NHA, #17313)*;
- *Oceanidas*;
- *Oiseaux migrateurs du paléarctique occidental (OMPO, #17712)*;
- *Organization for the Phyto-Taxonomic Investigation of the Mediterranean Area (OPTIMA, #17884)*;
- *Peace Parks Foundation (#18281)*;
- *PEFC Council (#18288)*;
- *Peoples Trust for Endangered Species (PTES)*;
- *Pew Charitable Trusts*;
- *Plantlife International*;
- *Project AWARE Foundation*;
- *Pro-Natura International (#16951)*;
- *Rainforest Alliance*;
- *Rainforest Concern*;
- *Rainforest Trust*;
- *Rare*;
- *RECOFTC – The Center for People and Forests (RECOFTC, #18628)*;
- *Red Panda Network (RPN, #18726)*;
- *Re:wild*;
- *Rewilding Europe (#18933)*;
- *Safari Club International (SCI)* (Foundation);
- *Safeguard for Agricultural Varieties in Europe (SAVE Foundation, #19027)*;
- *SaharaConservation (SC, #19032)*;
- *Save our Seas Foundation (SOSF)*;
- *SHARKPROJECT International (#19259)*;
- *Smithsonian Institution*;

- *Sociedad Mesoamericana para la Biología y la Conservación (SMBC, #19429)*;
- *Society for Conservation Biology (SCB, #19534)*;
- *Society for Ecological Restoration International (SERI)*;
- *Southern African Faith Communities' Environment Institute (SAFCEI)*;
- *Southern African Foundation for the Conservation of Coastal Birds (SANCCOB)*;
- *Southern African Natural Products Trade Association (PhytoTrade Africa, #19852)*;
- *Southern African Wildlife College (SAWC)*;
- *Species360 (#19915)*;
- *Synchronicity Earth*;
- *The International Ecotourism Society (TIES, #13225)*;
- *The Nature Conservancy (TNC)*;
- *Tree Aid*;
- *Tropenbos International (TBI)*;
- *Tropical Agriculture Research and Higher Education Center (#20246)*;
- *Tropical Resources Institute (TRI)*;
- *Turtle Conservancy (TC)*;
- *Turtle Survival Alliance (TSA, #20264)*;
- *United States Agency for International Development (USAID)*;
- *University of the South Pacific (USP, #20703)*;
- *Van Tienhoven Foundation for International Nature Protection*;
- *Verdens Skove*;
- *West Asia-North Africa Institute (WANA Institute)*;
- *Western Indian Ocean Marine Science Association (WIOMSA, #20916)*;
- *Western Pacific Regional Fishery Management Council*;
- *Wetlands International (#20928)*;
- *Wilderness Foundation Africa*;
- *WILD Foundation (WILD, #20956)*;
- *Wildfowl and Wetlands Trust (WWT)*;
- *Wildlife Alliance (#20957)*;
- *Wildlife Conservation Society (WCS)*;
- *Wildlife Protection Solutions (WPS)*;
- *Wildscreen*;
- *World Agroforestry Centre (ICRAF, #21072)*;
- *World Association of Zoos and Aquariums (WAZA, #21208)*;
- *World Business Council for Sustainable Development (WBCSD, #21254)*;
- *World Environment Center (WEC, #21386)*;
- *World Land Trust (WLT)*;
- *World Parrot Trust (WPT, #21713)*;
- *World Resources Institute (WRI, #21753)*;
- *World Underwater Federation (#21873)*;
- *World Wide Fund for Nature (WWF, #21922)*;
- *Yves Rocher Foundation*.

Consultative Status Consultative status granted from: *FAO (#09260)* (Special Status); *International Maritime Organization (IMO, #14102)*; *OAS (#17629)*; *UN Environment Programme World Conservation Monitoring Centre (UNEP-WCMC, #20295)*; *UNCTAD (#20285)* (Special Category); *UNESCO (#20322)* (Associate Status); *World Intellectual Property Organization (WIPO, #21593)* (Permanent Observer Status); *World Meteorological Organization (WMO, #21649)*. **IGO Relations** Accredited by (3): *Green Climate Fund (GCF, #10714)*; *United Nations Framework Convention on Climate Change – Secretariat (UNFCCC, #20564)*; *United Nations Office at Vienna (UNOV, #20604)*. Memorandum of Understanding with (1): *United Nations Population Fund (UNFPA, #20612)*. Member of (3): *Collaborative Partnership on Forests (CPF, #04100)*; *Congo Basin Forest Partnership (CBFP, #04662)*; *High Seas Task Force (HSTF, inactive)*. Cooperates with (2): *United Nations Institute for Training and Research (UNITAR, #20576)*; *UN-Water (#20723)*. Observer status with: *United Nations (UN, #20515)*, including the right to attend and speak at all meetings of *ECOSOC (#05331)* and at all other UN meetings; *Committee of International Development Institutions on the Environment (CIDIE, no recent information)*; *International Council for the Exploration of the Sea (ICES, #13021)*; *International Oil Pollution Compensation Funds (IOPC Funds, #14402)*; *Secretariat for Eastern African Coastal Area Management (SEACAM, no recent information)*. Partnerships – Formal working relations with a wide range of intergovernmental and international organizations, especially: FAO; UNEP; UNESCO. Accredited to the Conference of the Parties of: *Secretariat of the United Nations Convention to Combat Desertification (Secretariat of the UNCCD, #19208)*. Associated with Department of Global Communications of the United Nations. **NGO Relations** Member of (8): BFSD; *Dinaric Arc Initiative (DAI, no recent information)*; *EarthAction (EA, #05159)*; *GEF CSO Network (GCN, #10087)*; *High Seas Alliance (HSA, #10918)*; *Mountain Forum (MF, #16861)*; *Water and Climate Coalition (WCC, no recent information)*; *World Water Council (WWC, #21908)*. Instrumental in setting up (11): *Biodiversity and Economics for Conservation (BIOECON, #03240)*; *Biodiversity Conservation Information System (BCIS, inactive)*; *Botanic Gardens Conservation International (BGCI, #03306)*; *EcoAgriculture Partners (#05290)*; *Global Coral Reef Monitoring Network (GCRMN, #10306)*; *International Ombudsman Centre for the Environment and Development (OmCED, no recent information)*; IUCN/SSC Sir Peter Scott Action Plan Fund; *Network of Marine Protected Area Managers in the Mediterranean (MEDPAN, #17048)*; *Red Latinoamericana de Derecho Ambiental (no recent information)*; *South and Southeast Asia Network for Environmental Education (SASEANEE, no recent information)*; *UNEP-IOC-WMO-IUCN Long-Term Global Monitoring System of Coastal and Near-Shore Phenomena Related to Climate Change (inactive)*. Together with: *Environment and Development Resource Centre (EDRC)*, Netherlands Committee set up: *Institute for Environmental Security (IES)*. [2023/XA2654/y/**A**]

- ♦ International Union for Cooperation in Solar Research (inactive)
- ♦ International Union of Cooperative and Associated Tourism (inactive)
- ♦ International Union of Cooperative Wholesale Societies (inactive)

♦ International Union of Credit and Investment Insurers (Bern Union) 15767

Union d'assureurs des crédits et des investissements internationaux (Union de Berne) – Unión de Seguros y de Créditos Internacionales (Unión de Berna) – Internationale Union der Kreditversicherer (Berner Union)

Secretariat 1st Floor, 27-29 Cursitor Street, London, EC4A 1LT, UK. T. +442078411110. Fax +442074300375. E-mail: bu-sec@berneunion.org.
URL: http://www.berneunion.org/

History 1934, Bern (Switzerland), as *Union d'assureurs pour le contrôle des crédits internationaux*. Statutes amended and name changed, 1957, to *Union d'assureurs des crédits internationaux*. Statutes revised to admit only organizations engaged in insuring or guaranteeing export credit transactions and/or foreign investments as new members, and present name adopted Jun 1974. Secretariat moved from Paris (France) to London (UK), Jul 1975. Registered in accordance with Swiss Civil Code. **Aims** Enhance trade and investment flows globally through export credit, trade finance and investment facilities. **Structure** General Meeting (Plenary); Committee Meetings (INV/MLT/PC/ST); Management Committee; Secretariat. **Languages** English. **Staff** 8.00 FTE, paid. **Finance** Sources: members' dues. **Activities** Events/meetings; knowledge management/information dissemination; networking/liaising. **Events** *Spring Meeting* Brussels (Belgium) 2023, *Spring Meeting* Istanbul (Turkey) 2022, *Annual General Meeting* Kigali (Rwanda) 2022, *Annual General Meeting* Budapest (Hungary) 2021, *Spring Meeting* London (UK) 2021. **Publications** *Yearbook*.

Members Government backed export credit agencies, private export credit insurers and multilateral agencies from 73 countries. Membership countries not specified. Multilateral members include 4 organizations listed in this Yearbook:

Multilateral members include 4 organizations listed in this Yearbook:

African Trade Insurance Agency (ATI, #00485); *Arab Investment and Export Credit Guarantee Corporation (DHAMAN, #00997)*; *Islamic Corporation for the Insurance of Investment and Export Credit (ICIEC, #16041)*; *Multilateral Investment Guarantee Agency (MIGA, #16888)*.

IGO Relations Regular cooperation with: *Bank for International Settlements (BIS, #03165)*; *European Bank for Reconstruction and Development (EBRD, #06315)*; *International Bank for Reconstruction and Development (IBRD, #12317)* (World Bank); *International Monetary Fund (IMF, #14180)*; *OECD (#17693)*; *UNCTAD (#20285)*; *World Trade Organization (WTO, #21864)*; other regional development banks. [2018.06.01/XC2707/**C**]

♦ International Union of Crystallography (IUCr) 15768

Union internationale de cristallographie – Unión Internacional de Cristalografica – Internationale Union für Kristallographie

Secretariat 2 Abbey Square, Chester, CH1 2HU, UK. E-mail: execsec@iucr.org.
URL: http://www.iucr.org/

History 7 Apr 1947, London (UK). Founded following the formation at an International Conference on Crystallography, Jul 1946, London, of a *Provisional International Crystallographic Committee – Comité provisoire international de cristallographie*. Statutes and By-Laws adopted by 4th General Assembly, 1957, and amended by the following General Assemblies: 1960 (5th); 1963 (6th); 1966 (7th); 1969 (8th); 1972 (9th); 1975 (10th); 1978 (11th); 1996 (17th); 1999 (18th); 2010 (postal agreement); 2011 (22nd). Registration: Swiss Civil Code, Switzerland. **Aims** Promote international cooperation in crystallography and structural science; contribute to all aspects of crystallography and structural science; promote publication of research; facilitate standardization of methods, units, nomenclatures and symbols; form a focus for relations of crystallography to other sciences. **Structure** General Assembly (every 3 years); Executive Committee; Finance Committee; Advisory Committees; Commissions. **Languages** English. **Staff** 25.00 FTE, paid. **Finance** Sources: investments; members' dues; sale of publications. **Activities** Awards/prizes/competitions; events/meetings; networking/liaising; research and development; training/education. **Events** *Congress and General Assembly* Melbourne, VIC (Australia) 2023, *Triennial International Conference on Aperiodic Crystals* Sapporo (Japan) 2022, *Congress and General Assembly* Prague (Czechia) 2021, *Triennial International Conference on Aperiodic Crystals* Sapporo (Japan) 2021, *Triennial General Assembly and Congress* Prague (Czechia) 2020. **Publications** *IUCr Newsletter* (4 a year). Scientific journals; international tables; books; book series; teaching pamphlets.

Members Adhering: national committees; regional associate; scientific associate. Adhering in 55 countries:
Albania, Algeria, Argentina, Australia, Austria, Bangladesh, Belgium, Brazil, Bulgaria, Cameroon, Canada, Chile, China, Costa Rica, Croatia, Czechia, Denmark, Egypt, Finland, France, Germany, Greece, Guatemala, Hungary, India, Ireland (currently suspended), Israel, Italy, Japan, Korea Rep, Kosovo, Mexico, Morocco (currently suspended), Netherlands, New Zealand, Norway, Pakistan, Poland, Portugal, Russia, Serbia, Singapore, Slovakia, Slovenia, South Africa, Spain, Sweden, Switzerland, Tunisia, Türkiye, UK, United Arab Emirates, Uruguay, USA, Venezuela.

Regional Associates (4):
American Crystallographic Association (ACA); *Asian Crystallographic Association (AsCA, #01416)*; *European Crystallographic Association (ECA, #06867)*; *Latin American Crystallographic Association (LACA)*.

Scientific Associates (3):
International Centre for Diffraction Data (ICDD); *International Organization for Crystal Growth (IOCG, #14443)*; *Worldwide Protein Data Bank Foundation (wwPDB, #21932)*.

IGO Relations *UNESCO (#20322)*. **NGO Relations** Member of (4): *Association of Learned and Professional Society Publishers (ALPSP, #02786)*; Coalition of Society Publishers; *International Science Council (ISC, #14796)*; *International Union of Pure and Applied Chemistry (IUPAC, #15809)* (Inter-Divisional Committee on Terminology, Nomenclature and Symbols). Represented in: *Committee on Data for Science and Technology (CODATA, #04247)*; *Committee on Space Research (COSPAR, #04287)*. [2022.02.08/XC2708/y/**C**]

- ♦ International Union for Cultural Cooperation (inactive)
- ♦ International Union of Cycle and Motor-Cycle Trade and Repair (inactive)
- ♦ International Union of Department Stores (inactive)
- ♦ International Union for the Development of Grape Farms and the Consumption of Grapes (inactive)
- ♦ International Union of Directors of Zoological Gardens / see World Association of Zoos and Aquariums (#21208)
- ♦ International Union for the Distribution of Combined Railway Tickets (inactive)
- ♦ International Union of Dolls, Toys, Playthings, Novelties and Allied Products of the US and Canada / see International Union of Allied, Novelty and Production Workers
- ♦ International Union of Doll and Toy Workers of the United States and Canada / see International Union of Allied, Novelty and Production Workers
- ♦ International Union of Drivers of Long-Distance Lorries and Similar Vehicles / see International Union of Professional Drivers (#15802)

♦ International Union of Economists (IUE) 15769

Pres 22a Tverskaya Street, Moscow MOSKVA, Russia, 125009. T. +74956090766. Fax +74956940283. E-mail: iue@iuecon.org – inform@iuecon.org.
URL: http://www.iuecon.org/

History 1991, Sandanski (Bulgaria). **Aims** Promote economic reform; develop projects, programs and integrations processes in order to accelerate economic growth and stabilize economies; render practical assistance in development of small and medium business; ensure exchange of information and expand collaboration with national and international organizations, unions and associations in the fields of socio-economic, scientific and technical ideas. **Structure** General Meeting (annual). Administrative Board, consisting of President, First Vice-President and 15 Vice-Presidents. Executive Committee, comprising General Director and 2 Directors. **Languages** English, Russian. **Staff** 50.00 FTE, paid. **Finance** Members' dues and entrance fees. Other sources: voluntary contributions and donations. **Activities** Organizes and participates in economic fora and congresses. Organizes General Meeting. Runs programmes and projects. **Events** *General Meeting* St Petersburg (Russia) 2023, *Conference* Moscow (Russia) 2021, *Meeting* St Petersburg (Russia) 2018, *Meeting* Vienna (Austria) 2017, *Meeting* Moscow (Russia) 2016. **Publications** *Econom* (4 a year) – magazine; *Documents* – collection of legislative documents (since 1992); *Economic News from Russia and CIS* – newspaper (since 1992); *The Customs Bulletin* – newspaper (since 1992); *Transactions of the International Union of Economists and the Free Economic Society of Russia* – scientific publication (since 1994). Newspapers; journals bulletins; brochures; booklets; proceedings.

Members Organizations; individuals. Members (over 400). Branches and representation in 21 countries and territories:
Armenia, Australia, Azerbaijan, Belarus, Bulgaria, France, Georgia, Hong Kong, Hungary, Kazakhstan, Kyrgyzstan, Luxembourg, Malaysia, Moldova, Russia, Tajikistan, Turkmenistan, UK, Ukraine, USA, Uzbekistan.

Consultative Status Consultative status granted from: *ECOSOC (#05331)* (General). **IGO Relations** Cooperates with *United Nations (UN, #20515)* on regular basis. Associated with Department of Global Communications of the United Nations. **NGO Relations** Member of: *Union internationale des associations et organismes scientifiques et techniques (UATI, #20421)*. Instrumental in setting up: *"Eurasian Economic Club of Scientists" Association (EECSA, no recent information)*; *European Banking Industry Committee (EBIC, #06314)*. [2023/XD2961/**D**]

- ♦ International Union for the Education of Country People by Scientific Films and Slides (inactive)
- ♦ International Union of Electrical, Radio and Machine Workers / see International Union of Electronic, Electrical, Salaried, Machine and Furniture Workers

♦ International Union for Electricity Applications 15770

Union internationale pour les applications de l'électricité (UIE)

Gen Sec Dept Electrical Engineering, Div ELECTA, Kasteelpark Arenberg 10, 3001 Leuven, Belgium.
Pres Inst für Elektroprozesstechnik, Leibniz Univ Hannover, Wilhelm-Busch-Str 4, 30167 Hannover, Germany. T. +495117623248. Fax +495117623275.
URL: http://www.uie.org/

History Founded May 1953, Paris (France), at 3rd International Congress for Electroheat, as *Bureau international d'électrothermie (BIE)*. Statutes amended: 28 May 1970; 20 Jun 1984; 2 Jun 1994; 7 Sep 2005; 4 Dec 2012. Name changed, 1957, to *International Union for Electroheat – Union internationale d'électrothermie – Internationale Elektrowärme Union*. Present name adopted 1994. Registered in accordance with French law. **Aims** Promote and develop applications of electricity in line with principles of energy efficiency, protection of the environment, economic viability and social acceptance. **Structure** General Assembly (annual); Management Committee; Working Groups. **Languages** English. **Staff** Freelance. **Finance** Members' dues. **Activities** Research/documentation; training/education; networking/liaising. **Events** *Quadrennial Congress* Pilsen (Czechia) 2021, *Quadrennial Congress* Pilsen (Czechia) 2020, *Quadrennial Congress* Hannover (Germany) 2017, *Quadrennial Congress* St Petersburg (Russia) 2012, *Quadrennial Congress* Krakow (Poland) 2008. **Publications** Reports of meetings; congress proceedings; progress reports of Study Committees (occasional); technical documentation on applications of electricity and on power quality.

Members Organizations and individuals in 9 countries:
Belgium, Czechia, France, Germany, Italy, Poland, Russia, South Africa, USA.

NGO Relations Member of: *Fédération internationale pour la sécurité des usagers de l'électricité (FISUEL, #09658)*. Cooperates with: *Association for Microwave Power in Europe for Research and Education (AMPERE Europe, #02806)*; *International Organization for Standardization (ISO, #14473)*; *Union of the Electricity Industry – Eurelectric (#20379)*. [2019.12.12/XD2658/**D**]

- ♦ International Union of Electricity Stations (inactive)
- ♦ International Union for Electrodeposition and Surface Finishing (no recent information)
- ♦ International Union for Electroheat / see International Union for Electricity Applications (#15770)
- ♦ International Union of Electronic, Electrical, Salaried, Machine and Furniture Workers (internationally oriented national body)
- ♦ International Union of Elevator Constructors (internationally oriented national body)
- ♦ International Union of Esperantist Philologists (inactive)
- ♦ International Union of Esperanto Vegetarians / see World Esperantist Vegetarian Association (#21389)

♦ International Union of Esthetics Medicine 15771

Union internationale de médecine esthétique (UIME) – Unión Internacional de Medicina Estética

SG Société Française de Médecine Esthétique, 154 rue Armand Silvestre, 92400 Courbevoie, France. E-mail: info@sfme.info.

Pres 12/3 Fotievoi Street, Pol No 3 – Off 512, Moscow MOSKVA, Russia, 119333.

URL: http://www.sfme.info/union-internationale-de-medecine-esthetique/

History 1974, France. **Aims** Promote medical continuous education in aesthetic medicine worldwide. **Languages** English, French. **Staff** 1.50 FTE, voluntary. **Finance** Sources: sponsorship. **Events** *Biennial Congress* Warsaw (Poland) 2019, *European Congress of Aesthetic Medicine* Brussels (Belgium) 2018, *Biennial Congress* Istanbul (Turkey) 2017, *Biennial Congress* Miami, FL (USA) 2015, *Biennial Congress* Cape Town (South Africa) 2013. **Publications** *Journal International de Médecine Esthétique et de Chirurgie Dermatologiaue* (4 a year).

Members Full in 31 countries:

Algeria, Argentina, Belgium, Bolivia, Brazil, Canada, Chile, China, Colombia, Croatia, Ecuador, France, Georgia, India, Italy, Kazakhstan, Mexico, Morocco, Peru, Poland, Portugal, Romania, Russia, South Africa, Spain, Switzerland, Türkiye, Ukraine, Uruguay, USA, Venezuela. [2021.02.17/XD1327/**D**]

- ♦ International Union of Ethical Societies (inactive)
- ♦ International Union of European Guides and Scouts / see Union Internationale des Guides et Scouts d'Europe – Fédération du Scoutisme Européen (#20426)
- ♦ International Union of Family Organizations / see World Family Organization (#21399)
- ♦ International Union of Flower Wholesale Trade / see UNION FLEURS (#20408)

♦ International Union of Food, Agricultural, Hotel, Restaurant, Catering, Tobacco and Allied Workers Associations (IUF) 15772

Union internationale des travailleurs de l'alimentation, de l'agriculture, de l'hôtellerie-restauration, du tabac et des branches connexes (UITA) – Unión Internacional de Trabajadores de la Alimentación, Agricolas, Hoteles, Restaurantes, Tabaco y Afines (UITA) – Internationale Union der Lebensmittel-, Landwirtschafts-, Hotel-, Restaurant-, Café- und Genussmittelarbeiter-Gewerkschaften (IUL) – Internationella Unionen för Livsmedels-, Njutningsmedels- och Lantarbetareförbund Samt Förbund Inom Hotell- och Restaurangbranschen (IUL)

SG Rampe du Pont-Rouge 8, Petit-Lancy, 1213 Geneva, Switzerland. T. +41227932233. Fax +41227932238. E-mail: iuf@iuf.org.

URL: http://www.iuf.org/

History 1920, Zurich (Switzerland). Founded by merger of International Secretariats of bakery, brewery and meat workers. Further mergers: in 1958, with *International Federation of Tobacco Workers (inactive)*, set up in 1886, Brussels (Belgium); in 1961, with *International Union of Hotel, Restaurant and Bar Workers (inactive)*, formed in May 1908; on 1 Jan 1994, with *International Federation of Plantation, Agricultural and Allied Workers (IFPAAW, inactive)*, formed Dec 1959, Brussels, itself replacing *Plantation Workers' International Federation (inactive)*, formed in 1957, and having subsequently merged with *European Landworkers' Federation (ELF, inactive)*, set up Aug 1920, as *International Landworkers' Federation (ILFA) – Fédération internationale des travailleurs agricoles – Europäische Landarbeiter Föderation*. Current title adopted on merger with IFPAAW. Statutes adopted 29 Jan – 1 Feb 1973, Geneva (Switzerland); amended: 1977, 1981, 1985, 1989, 1993, 2002, 2007. Former names and other names: *International Union of Food and Drink Workers (IUFD)* – former; *Union internationale des fédérations des ouvriers et ouvrières de l'alimentation (UIA)* – former; *Internationale Union der Organisationen der Arbeiter und Arbeiterinnen der Lebens und Genussmittelindustrien* – former; *International Union of Food and Drink Workers' Associations* – former; *Union internationale des syndicats des industries alimentaires* – former; *Unión Internacional de Asociaciones de Trabajadores de Alimentos y Bebidas* – former; *Internationale Union der Gewerkschaften der Lebens- und Genussmittelbranchen* – former; *International Union of Food and Allied Workers Associations* – former; *Union internationale des travailleurs de l'alimentation et des branches connexes (UITA)* – former; *Unión Internacional de Trabajadores de la Alimentación y Afines (UITA)* – former; *Internationale Union der Lebens- und Genussmittelarbeiter-Gewerkschaften (IUL)* – former; *Internationale Union af Levneds- og Nydelsesmiddelarbejder-Forbund (IUL)* – former; *International Union of Foodworkers* – former. **Aims** Defend the general and specific interests of workers of all countries employed in food and allied industries by: aiding affiliated unions in organization, education and efforts to improve living and *working conditions* of members; establishing unions in areas where none exists; assisting coordination of policies engaging in common projects. Promote national legislation and international agreements in the interests of members or of the working population as a whole; promote organization of the world's food resources for the common good of all; seek participation of labour and consumer interests at all stages of national and international policy making. **Structure** Congress (every 5 years); Executive Committee (meets annually). Regions: Africa; Caribbean; Asia; Continental Western Europe; Eastern Europe and Central Asia; Eastern Mediterranean; Latin America; Nordic Countries; North America; Pacific; United Kingdom and Ireland. Regional organization: *European Federation of Food, Agriculture and Tourism Trade Unions (EFFAT, #07125)*. Administrative Committee; Secretariat. Membership open; meetings closed. **Languages** English, French, German, Spanish, Swedish. **Staff** 17.00 FTE, paid. **Finance** Sources: subscriptions. **Activities** Advocacy/lobbying/activism; conflict resolution; events/meetings; guidance/assistance/consulting; knowledge management/information dissemination; training/education. **Events** *Quinquennial Congress* Geneva (Switzerland) 2017, *Meeting* Geneva (Switzerland) 2012, *Quinquennial Congress* Geneva (Switzerland) 2012, *Meeting* Geneva (Switzerland) 2011, *Meeting* Geneva (Switzerland) 2010.

Members Unions (422), totalling over 2.6 million members in 133 countries and territories:

Algeria, Antigua, Argentina, Armenia, Australia, Austria, Azerbaijan, Bahamas, Bangladesh, Barbados, Belarus, Belgium, Belize, Benin, Bermuda, Bolivia, Bosnia-Herzegovina, Brazil, Bulgaria, Burkina Faso, Cambodia, Cameroon, Canada, Chile, Colombia, Costa Rica, Côte d'Ivoire, Croatia, Cyprus, Czechia, Denmark, Dominica, Dominican Rep, Ecuador, Egypt, El Salvador, Eswatini, Ethiopia, Faeroe Is, Fiji, Finland, France, Georgia, Germany, Ghana, Greece, Grenada, Guatemala, Guinea, Guyana, Haiti, Honduras, Hong Kong, Hungary, Iceland, India, Indonesia, Iran Islamic Rep, Ireland, Israel, Italy, Jamaica, Japan, Jordan, Kazakhstan, Kenya, Korea Rep, Kosovo, Kyrgyzstan, Latvia, Lebanon, Liberia, Lithuania, Luxembourg, Malawi, Malaysia, Maldives, Mali, Malta, Mauritania, Mauritius, Mexico, Moldova, Montenegro, Mozambique, Myanmar, Nepal, Netherlands, New Zealand, Nicaragua, Niger, Nigeria, North Macedonia, Norway, Pakistan, Palestine, Panama, Papua New Guinea, Paraguay, Peru, Philippines, Poland, Portugal, Romania, Russia, Rwanda, Senegal, Serbia, Sierra Leone, Slovakia, Slovenia, Somalia, South Africa, Spain, Sri Lanka, St Lucia, Sweden, Switzerland, Tanzania UR, Thailand, Timor-Leste, Togo, Trinidad-Tobago, Tunisia, Türkiye, Uganda, UK, Ukraine, Uruguay, USA, Venezuela, Zambia, Zimbabwe.

Consultative Status Consultative status granted from: *ECOSOC (#05331)* (Ros C); *FAO (#09260)*. **IGO Relations** Cooperates with (1): *World Tourism Organization (UNWTO, #21861)*. **NGO Relations** Member of (9): *European Banana Action Network (EUROBAN, #06310)*; *European Responsible Investment Network (ERIN)*; *European Trade Union Liaison Committee on Tourism (ETLC, #08929)*; *Fédération des Institutions Internationales établies à Genève (FIIG, #09599)*; *Global Union Federations (GUF, #10638)*; *ILGA World (International Lesbian, Gay, Bisexual, Trans and Intersex Association, #11120)* (Associate); *International Land Coalition (ILC, #13999)*; *International NGO/CSO Planning Committee for Food Sovereignty (IPC, #14365)*; *Women in Informal Employment: Globalizing and Organizing (WIEGO, #21003)*. Cooperates with (4): *Amnesty International (AI, #00801)*; *Ethical Trading Initiative (ETI)*; *Pesticide Action Network (PAN, #18336)*; *World Organisation Against Torture (OMCT, #21685)*. [2022/XB2719/**B**]

- ♦ International Union of Food and Allied Workers Associations / see International Union of Food, Agricultural, Hotel, Restaurant, Catering, Tobacco and Allied Workers Associations (#15772)
- ♦ International Union of Food and Drink Workers / see International Union of Food, Agricultural, Hotel, Restaurant, Catering, Tobacco and Allied Workers Associations (#15772)
- ♦ International Union of Food and Drink Workers' Associations / see International Union of Food, Agricultural, Hotel, Restaurant, Catering, Tobacco and Allied Workers Associations (#15772)

♦ International Union of Food Science and Technology (IUFoST) 15773

Union internationale de science et de technologie alimentaires

General Secretariat c/o University of Guelph, Dept of Food Science, Room 106, 50 Stone Road E, Guelph ON N1G 2M7, Canada. T. +16128018315. E-mail: secretariat@iufost.org.

Pres address not obtained.

URL: http://www.iufost.org/

History 14 Aug 1970, Washington, DC (USA). Established as a successor to *International Committee of Food Science and Technology (inactive)*, set up 1962. **Aims** Promote international cooperation and exchange of scientific/technical *information* among working scientists and specialists of member countries; support international progress in theoretical and applied areas of food science; advance technology in the processing, manufacturing, preservation and distribution of *food products*; stimulate education and training in food science and technology. **Structure** General Assembly (every 2 years); Governing Council; Board; Scientific Council; *International Academy of Food Science and Technology (IAFoST)* and its own Executive Council. Special Interest Groups (5): *International Society of Food Engineering (ISFE, #15127)*; *International Society for Nutraceuticals and Functional Foods (ISNFF, #15313)*; *International Symposium on the Properties of Water (ISOPOW, #15644)*; *International Food Research Collaboration (IFRC)*; *International Society of Food Applications of Nanoscale Science (ISFANS, #15126)*. Working Groups. **Languages** English. **Staff** 1.50 FTE, paid. **Finance** Sources: members' dues. **Activities** Events/meetings; training/education. **Events** *Biennial Congress* Singapore (Singapore) 2022, *Biennial Congress* Auckland (New Zealand) 2020, *Biennial Congress* Mumbai (India) 2018, *Symposium* Jeju (Korea Rep) 2017, *Biennial Congress* Dublin (Ireland) 2016. **Publications** *International Review of Food Science and Technology* – journal; *IUFoST Newsline* – newsletter; *Lebensmittel-Wissenschaft und Technologie* – official journal; *Trends in Food Science and Technology* – official journal. *IUFoST Handbook*. Information statements; scientific information bulletins; technical reports; proceedings.

Members National food science organizations representing over 200,000 food scientists and technologists, in 69 countries and territories:

Albania, Argentina, Australia, Austria, Belgium, Benin, Botswana, Brazil, Bulgaria, Canada, Chile, China, Colombia, Costa Rica, Croatia, Czechia, Denmark, Egypt, Finland, France, Germany, Ghana, Greece, Hungary, India, Indonesia, Ireland, Italy, Japan, Kazakhstan, Kenya, Korea Rep, Kuwait, Lebanon, Lesotho, Lithuania, Malawi, Malaysia, Mexico, Mozambique, Netherlands, New Zealand, Nigeria, North Macedonia, Norway, Pakistan, Philippines, Poland, Portugal, Qatar, Russia, Saudi Arabia, Singapore, Slovenia, South Africa, Spain, Sweden, Switzerland, Taiwan, Thailand, Türkiye, Uganda, UK, Ukraine, Uruguay, USA, Vietnam, Zambia, Zimbabwe.

Regional organizations (4), listed in this Yearbook:

Asociación Latinoamericano y del Caribe de Ciencia y Tecnologia de los Alimentos (ALACCTA, #02276); *European Federation of Food Science and Technology (EFFoST, #07126)*; *Federation of Institutes of Food Science and Technology of ASEAN (FIFSTA, #09598)*; *West African Association of Food Science and Technology (WAAFoST, #20869)*.

Consultative Status Consultative status granted from: *ECOSOC (#05331)* (Ros C); *FAO (#09260)* (Special Status); *UNIDO (#20336)*. **NGO Relations** Member of: *International Science Council (ISC, #14796)*. Instrumental in setting up: *Network of International Food Science Communicators (no recent information)*. [2021/XB1610/y/**B**]

- ♦ International Union of Foodworkers / see International Union of Food, Agricultural, Hotel, Restaurant, Catering, Tobacco and Allied Workers Associations (#15772)
- ♦ International Union of Foreign Language Associations (inactive)
- ♦ International Union of Forest Experiment Stations / see International Union of Forest Research Organizations (#15774)

♦ International Union of Forest Research Organizations (IUFRO) 15774

Union Internationale des Instituts de Recherches Forestières – Unión Internacional de Organizaciones de Investigación Forestal – Internationaler Verband Forstlicher Forschungsanstalten

Exec Dir Marxergasse 2, 1030 Vienna, Austria. T. +43187701510. Fax +431877015150. E-mail: office@iufro.org.

URL: https://www.iufro.org/

History 17 Aug 1892, Eberswalde (Germany). Founded after initiative at International Congress, 1890, Vienna (Austria), and according to the Statutes agreed upon on 18 Sep 1891, Badenweiler (Germany). Decision to reconstitute the Union adopted 1926, Rome (Italy); reconstitution brought into being and new name adopted at 7th Congress, 1929, Stockholm (Sweden). New Statutes and Internal Regulations adopted at 13th Congress, 1961, Vienna. Statutes renewed and approved at 15th Congress, 1971, Gainesville FL (USA), 1971; revised at 19th Congress, 1990, Montréal QC (Canada). Current Statutes approved and present name adopted at 21st Congress, 2000, Kuala Lumpur (Malaysia); revised in 2003, 2005, 2007, 2010, 2014 and 2017. Former names and other names: *International Union of Forest Experiment Stations* – former (17 Aug 1982); *Union internationale des instituts d'essais forestiers* – former (17 Aug 1982). **Aims** Advance research excellence and knowledge sharing, and foster development of science-based solutions to forest-related challenges for the benefit of forests and people worldwide. **Structure** Congress in plenary session acts as the General Assembly and meets every 5 years; International Council; Board; Scientific Divisions; Task Forces; Special Programmes; Projects and IUFRO-led Initiatives. **Languages** English, French, German, Spanish. **Staff** 11.00 FTE, paid. **Finance** Sources: members' dues. **Activities** Awards/prizes/competitions; events/meetings; knowledge management/information dissemination; networking/liaising; projects/programmes; research/documentation. **Events** *World Congress* Stockholm (Sweden) 2024, *International Conference on Acid Deposition* Niigata (Japan) 2023, *World Teak Conference* Accra (Ghana) 2022, *European Forum on Urban Forestry* Belgrade (Serbia) 2022, *Small-Scale Forestry International Conference* Ginowan (Japan) 2022. **Publications** *IUFRO-News* (10 a year) – electronic; *IUFRO Annual Report* in English. *IUFRO Research Series* – 11 vols; *IUFRO World Series* – 38 vols; *Occasional Papers* – 31 vols. Congress proceedings; other publications edited in the name of or in connection with IUFRO by Member Institutions and/or Research Groups.

Members Member Organizations: forest research organizations or organizations involved in research into subjects related to forests and forest-related science. Individual Members: (1) Full: individuals belonging to a Member Organization who are engaged, or have been engaged, in research in forests or related subjects and wish to participate in Union activities; (2) Associate: individuals who are engaged, or have been engaged, in research in forests or related subjects; (3) Honorary. Members totalling 15,000 scientists in 650 member organizations, in 121 countries and territories:

Albania, Algeria, Argentina, Australia, Austria, Bangladesh, Belarus, Belgium, Benin, Bolivia, Bosnia-Herzegovina, Brazil, Bulgaria, Burkina Faso, Cambodia, Cameroon, Canada, Chad, Chile, China, Colombia, Congo Brazzaville, Congo DR, Costa Rica, Côte d'Ivoire, Croatia, Cuba, Cyprus, Czechia, Denmark, Ecuador, Egypt, Estonia, Eswatini, Ethiopia, Fiji, Finland, France, Georgia, Germany, Ghana, Greece, Guatemala, Haiti, Honduras, Hungary, Iceland, India, Indonesia, Iran Islamic Rep, Iraq, Ireland, Israel, Italy, Japan, Kenya, Korea DPR, Korea Rep, Kosovo, Kyrgyzstan, Laos, Latvia, Liberia, Lithuania, Luxembourg, Madagascar, Malaysia, Mali, Mexico, Moldova, Mongolia, Morocco, Myanmar, Namibia, Nepal, Netherlands, New Zealand, Nicaragua, Niger, Nigeria, North Macedonia, Norway, Pakistan, Panama, Papua New Guinea, Paraguay, Peru, Philippines, Poland, Portugal, Romania, Russia, Rwanda, Senegal, Serbia, Slovakia, Slovenia, Solomon Is, South Africa, Spain, Sri Lanka, Sudan, Sweden, Switzerland, Taiwan, Tanzania UR, Thailand, Togo, Trinidad-Tobago, Tunisia, Türkiye, Uganda, UK, Ukraine, Uruguay, USA, Vanuatu, Venezuela, Vietnam, Zambia, Zimbabwe.

Included in the above, 12 organizations listed in this Yearbook:

Bioversity International (#03262); *CABI (#03393)*; *Center for International Forestry Research (CIFOR, #03646)*; *Centre de coopération internationale en recherche agronomique pour le développement (CIRAD, #03733)*; *European Forest Institute (EFI, #07297)*; *International Network for Bamboo and Rattan (INBAR, #14234)*; *International Technical Tropical Timber Association (ITTTA, #15668)*; *Tropical Agriculture Research and Higher Education Center (#20246)*; *UN Environment Programme World Conservation Monitoring Centre (UNEP-WCMC, #20295)*; *United States Agency for International Development (USAID)*; *World Agroforestry Centre (ICRAF, #21072)*; *World Forestry Center, Portland (WFC)*.

Consultative Status Consultative status granted from: *ECOSOC (#05331)* (Ros C); *FAO (#09260)* (Special Status); *UNEP (#20299)*. **IGO Relations** Accredited by (3): *Ministerial Conference on the Protection of Forests in Europe (FOREST EUROPE, #16817)*; *UNEP (#20299)*; *United Nations Office at Vienna (UNOV, #20604)*. Member of (1): *Collaborative Partnership on Forests (CPF, #04100)*. Partner of (1): *United Nations Forum on Forests (UNFF, #20562)*. Accredited to the Conference of the Parties of: *Convention on International Trade in Endangered Species of Wild Fauna and Flora (CITES, 1973)*; *Secretariat of the Convention on Biological Diversity (SCBD, #19197)*; *Secretariat of the United Nations Convention to Combat Desertification (Secretariat of the UNCCD, #19208)*; *United Nations Framework Convention on Climate Change – Secretariat (UNFCCC, #20564)*. **NGO Relations** Memorandum of Understanding with: *Northeast Asian Forest Forum (NEAFF)*.

Member of: *International Foundation for Science (IFS, #13677)*; *International Science Council (ISC, #14796)*; *International Society for Plant Pathology (ISPP, #15371)*. Forest History Group is member of: *International Consortium of Environmental History Organizations (ICEHO, #12912)*. Partner of: *Forestry Research Network for Sub-Saharan Africa (FORNESSA, #09866)*. Cooperates with: *International Society for Photogrammetry and Remote Sensing (ISPRS, #15362)*. Contacts with: *SYLVA-WORLD for Development and the Protection of Forests and the Environment*. Special relationship with: *International Union for Conservation of Nature and Natural Resources (IUCN, #15766)*. [2022.02.02/XB2721/y/B]

♦ International Union of Game Biologists (IUGB) 15775

Union internationale des biologistes du gibier (UIBG)

Contact Av de la Gare 81, L-9233 Diekirch, Luxembourg. T. +3524022011.

URL: http://www.iugb2013.be/

History Founded 1954, Düsseldorf (Germany FR), during 'International Exposition for Fish and Game'. **Aims** Promote improvement of knowledge about game biology and any other skill related to wildlife, such as wise use of animal populations and conservation of their habitats. **Structure** Board; Presidency rotates every 2 years. **Languages** English. **Finance** No budget. **Events** *Biennial Congress* Budapest (Hungary) 2021, *Biennial Congress* Kaunas (Lithuania) 2019, *Biennial Congress* Montpellier (France) 2017, *Perdix Symposium* Montpellier (France) 2017, *Biennial Congress* Puebla (Mexico) 2015. **Publications** Congress abstracts.

Members Regular. Individuals in 18 countries:

Austria, Belgium, Czechia, Finland, France, Germany, Greece, Luxembourg, Netherlands, Poland, Portugal, Russia, Slovakia, Slovenia, Spain, Sweden, Switzerland, USA. [2019/XD3769/v/F]

♦ International Union of Geodesy and Geophysics (IUGG) 15776

Union géodésique et géophysique internationale (UGGI)

Exec Sec Helmholtz Centre Potsdam, GFZ German Research Ctr for Geosciences, Telegrafenberg A17, 14473 Potsdam, Germany. T. +493312881759. E-mail: secretariat@iugg.org.

URL: http://www.iugg.org/

History 28 Jul 1919, Brussels (Belgium). Founded as constituent union of *International Research Council (IRC) – Conseil international des recherches (CIR)*, latterly referred to as *International Council for Science (ICSU, inactive)* that merged, 2018, with *International Social Science Council (ISSC, inactive)* to become *International Science Council (ISC, #14796)*. Statutes adopted 1946, Cambridge (UK); modified: 1957, 1960, 1967, 1971, 1979, 1983, 1991, 1995, 1999, 2003, Sapporo (Japan); 2007, Perugia (Italy); 2011, Melbourne (Australia); 2015, Prague (Czech Rep); 2018. Former names and other names: *Internationaler Verein für Geodäsie und Geophysik* – former. **Aims** Advance, promote and communicate knowledge of the Earth system, its space environment, and the dynamical processes causing change. **Structure** General Assembly (every 4 years); Council; Executive Committee; Bureau; Finance Committee. Semi-autonomous Associations (8): *International Association of Cryospheric Sciences (IACS, #11829)*; *International Association of Geodesy (IAG, #11914)*; *International Association of Geomagnetism and Aeronomy (IAGA, #11916)*; *International Association of Hydrological Sciences (IAHS, #11954)*; *International Association of Meteorology and Atmospheric Sciences (IAMAS, #12031)*; *International Association for the Physical Sciences of the Oceans (IAPSO, #12082)*; *International Association of Seismology and Physics of the Earth's Interior (IASPEI, #12157)*; *International Association of Volcanology and Chemistry of the Earth's Interior (IAVCEI, #12259)*. **Languages** English, French. **Finance** Sources: members' dues. **Activities** Events/meetings. **Events** *General Assembly* Berlin (Germany) 2023, *Conference on Mathematical Geophysics* Seoul (Korea Rep) 2022, *International Tsunami Symposium* Sendai (Japan) 2021, *General Assembly* Montréal, QC (Canada) 2019, *Conference on Mathematical Geophysics* Nizhniy Novgorod (Russia) 2018. **Publications** *E-Journals* (12 a year). Annual Report; Yearbook; proceedings of General Assemblies; special publications.

Members Adhering bodies and national committees in 73 countries and territories:

Albania, Algeria, Argentina, Armenia, Australia, Austria, Azerbaijan, Belgium, Bolivia, Bosnia-Herzegovina, Brazil, Bulgaria, Canada, Chile, China, Colombia, Congo DR, Costa Rica, Croatia, Czechia, Denmark, Egypt, Estonia, Finland, France, Georgia, Germany, Ghana, Greece, Hungary, Iceland, India, Indonesia, Iran Islamic Rep, Ireland, Israel, Italy, Japan, Jordan, Korea Rep, Latvia, Luxembourg, Mauritius, Mexico, Morocco, Mozambique, Netherlands, New Zealand, Nicaragua, Nigeria, North Macedonia, Norway, Pakistan, Peru, Poland, Portugal, Romania, Russia, Saudi Arabia, Serbia, Slovakia, Slovenia, South Africa, Spain, Sweden, Switzerland, Taipei, Thailand, Türkiye, UK, Uruguay, USA, Vietnam.

Affiliate members (6):

American Geosciences Institute (AGI); *Commission for the Geological Map of the World (CGMW, #04216)*; *International Association for Geoethics (IAGETH, #11915)*; *International Association for Mathematical Geosciences (IAMG, #12017)*; *International Consortium on Landslides (ICL, #12917)*; *Promoting Earth Science for Society (YES Network, #18541)*.

Consultative Status Consultative status granted from: *ECOSOC (#05331)* (Ros C). **IGO Relations** Recognized by: Consultative Committee for Time and Frequency of *Bureau international des poids et mesures (BIPM, #03367)*; *Group on Earth Observations (GEO, #10735)*; ICSU-ISSC-UNISDR Scientific Committee on Integrated Research on Disaster Risk (IRDR); *Intergovernmental Oceanographic Commission (IOC, #11496)*; *Intergovernmental Panel on Climate Change (IPCC, #11499)*; *International Civil Aviation Organization (ICAO, #12581)*; *International Hydrological Programme (IHP, #13826)*; *Pan American Institute of Geography and History (PAIGH, #18113)*; *United Nations Committee of Experts on Global Geospatial Information Management (UN-GGIM, #20540)*; *World Meteorological Organization (WMO, #21649)*. **NGO Relations** Member of (1): *COmON Foundation*. Partner of (7): *Committee on Data for Science and Technology (CODATA, #04247)*; *Committee on Space Research (COSPAR, #04287)*; *ISC World Data System (ISC-WDS, #16024)*; *Scientific Committee on Antarctic Research (SCAR, #19147)*; *Scientific Committee on Oceanic Research (SCOR, #19149)*; *Scientific Committee on Solar-Terrestrial Physics (SCOSTEP, #19151)*; *World Climate Research Programme (WCRP, #21279)*. Instrumental in setting up (2): *IASPEI/IAVCEI Commission on Volcano Seismology (#11008)*; *International Commission on Atmospheric Electricity (ICAE, #12665)*. [2023/XA2722/y/A]

♦ International Union of Geological Sciences (IUGS) 15777

Union internationale des sciences géologiques (UISG) – Unión Internacional de Ciencias Geológicas (UICG) – Internationale Union für Geologische Wissenschaften

Dir 26 Baiwanzhuang Road, Xicheng District, 100037 Beijing, China. T. +861058584808 – +861068310893. Fax +861068310893. E-mail: secretariat@iugs.org.

SG Dept of Geological Sciences, California State Univ, Long Beach CA 90840, USA.

Pres The Lyell Centre, Heriot-Watt University, Edinburgh, EH14 4AP, UK.

URL: http://www.iugs.org/

History 10 Mar 1961, Paris (France). Derives from *International Geological Congress (IGC)*, set up in 1875, Buffalo NY (USA). Original statutes accepted by Constitutive Assembly, 9 Mar 1961; ratified 28 Sep 1961, when became a member of *International Council for Science (ICSU, inactive)*; amended by Council at subsequent International Geological Congresses in 1964, 1968, 1972 and 1976. Current Bye-Laws adopted by Council at 34th Congress, 9 Aug 2012, Brisbane (Australia). **Aims** Promote development of *earth sciences* through support of broad-based scientific studies relevant to the entire earth-system; apply results of these and other studies to preserving Earth's natural *environment*, using all *natural resources* wisely and improving the prosperity of nations and the quality of human life; strengthen public awareness of geology and advance geological education in the widest sense; foster dialogue and communication among the various specialists in earth sciences around the world.

Structure Council (normally meets every 4 years in ordinary session at International Geological Congress); Executive Committee; Bureau; Permanent Secretariat. Committees (2): Nominating; International Geological Congress. Committees (4): *International Geological Congress (IGC)*; Nominating; Publications; Strategic Implementation. Ad Hoc Review Committees. Task Groups (2).

Scientific Commissions (7):

Commission on Geoheritage; *Commission on Global Geochemical Baselines*; *Geoscience Education, Training and Technology Transfer (COGE)*; *International Commission on the History of Geological Sciences (INHIGEO, #12685)*; *IUGS Commission on Management and Application of Geoscience Information (CGI, #16081)*; *International Commission on Stratigraphy (ICS, #12730)*;

IUGS Commission on Tectonics and Structural Geology (TECTASK).

Joint Programmes (4): *International Geoscience Programme (IGCP, #13715)*; *International Lithosphere Program (ILP, #14059)*; Isotope Geology and Geochronology (TGIG); *Commission for the Geological Map of the World (CGMW, #04216)*.

Task Groups (2).

Languages English. **Staff** No permanent staff. **Finance** Sources: grants; members' dues. **Activities** Events/meetings; training/education. **Events** *International Geological Congress* St Petersburg (Russia) 2028, *International Geological Congress* Busan (Korea Rep) 2024, *Symposium on Offshore Wind Development in Active Margins* Tokyo (Japan) 2023, *Symposium of Offshore Wind Power Generation at Active Margins* Tokyo (Japan) 2022, *International Geological Congress* Delhi (India) 2021. **Publications** *IUGS Electronic Bulletin* (12 a year); *Episodes* (4 a year) – newsletter and journal. Annual Report.

Members Adhering Organizations countries (or defined geographical areas), appointed academies, geological surveys or similar national agencies (121). Active Adhering members in 66 countries and territories:

Australia, Azerbaijan, Bangladesh, Belgium, Bosnia-Herzegovina, Botswana, Brazil, Canada, China, Costa Rica, Croatia, Cuba, Cyprus, Czechia, Denmark, Egypt, Estonia, Finland, France, Germany, Greece, Hungary, Iceland, India, Iraq, Ireland, Israel, Italy, Japan, Jordan, Korea Rep, Kosovo, Lebanon, Lithuania, Luxembourg, Malaysia, Mexico, Mongolia, Morocco, Mozambique, Namibia, Netherlands, New Zealand, Norway, Poland, Portugal, Romania, Russia, Saudi Arabia, Serbia, Slovakia, Slovenia, South Africa, Spain, Sweden, Switzerland, Taiwan, Tajikistan, Thailand, Tunisia, Türkiye, UK, USA, Uzbekistan, Vietnam, Yemen.

Pending Active Adhering members in 10 countries:

Albania, Argentina, Austria, Chile, Colombia, Gambia, Ghana, Kenya, Korea DPR, Peru.

Affiliated Organizations (56):

- *African Association of Women in Geosciences (AAWG, #00219)*;
- *American Association of Petroleum Geologists (AAPG)*;
- *American Geophysical Union (AGU)*;
- American Geosciences Institute;
- *Arab Geologists' Association (AGA, #00967)*;
- *Association internationale pour l'étude des argiles (AIPEA, #02688)*;
- *Association of Applied Geochemists (AAG, #02372)*;
- *Association of European Geological Societies (AEGS, #02513)*;
- *Association of Geoscientists for International Development (AGID, #02623)*;
- *Balkan Geophysical Society (BGS, #03074)*;
- Canadian Federation of Earth Sciences;
- *Carpathian Balkan Geological Association (CBGA, #03586)*;
- *Centre international pour la formation et les échanges en géosciences (CIFEG, #03754)*;
- *Circum-Pacific Council (CPC, #03939)*;
- *Commission for the Geological Map of the World (CGMW, #04216)*;
- *Coordinating Committee for Geoscience Programmes in East and Southeast Asia (CCOP, #04816)*;
- DOSECC;
- *Earth Science Matters Foundation (ESM, #05169)*;
- *EuroGeoSurveys (#05686)*;
- *European Association of Science Editors (EASE, #06201)*;
- *European Federation of Geologists (EFG, #07133)*;
- *European Geoparks Network (EGN, #07389)*;
- *European Mineralogical Union (EMU, #07807)*;
- *Geochemical Society*;
- Geological Association of Canada;
- *Geological Society of Africa (GSAf, #10135)*;
- *Geological Society of America (GSA)*;
- Geological Society of France;
- Geological Society of India;
- Geologische Vereinigung;
- *International Association for Geoethics (IAGETH, #11915)*;
- *International Association for Mathematical Geosciences (IAMG, #12017)*;
- *International Association for Promoting Geoethics (IAPG, #12107)*;
- *International Association for the Conservation of the Geological Heritage (ProGEO, #11810)*;
- *International Association of Engineering Geology and the Environment (IAEG, #11872)*;
- *International Association of GeoChemistry (IAGC, #11913)*;
- *International Association of Geomorphologists (IAG, #11917)*;
- *International Association of Hydrogeologists (IAH, #11953)*;
- *International Association of Sedimentologists (IAS, #12155)*;
- *International Association on the Genesis of Ore Deposits (IAGOD, #11910)*;
- *International Consortium on Landslides (ICL, #12917)*;
- *International Federation of Palynological Societies (IFPS, #13498)*;
- *International Geoscience Education Organization (IGEO, #13714)*;
- *International Medical Geology Association (IMGA, #14133)*;
- *International Mineralogical Association (IMA, #14165)*;
- *International Palaeontological Association (IPA, #14501)*;
- *International Permafrost Association (IPA, #14558)*;
- *International Society for Rock Mechanics and Rock Engineering (ISRM, #15428)*;
- *International Society for Soil Mechanics and Geotechnical Engineering (ISSMGE, #15452)*;
- Italian Federation of Earth Sciences;
- *Meteoritical Society (#16738)*;
- National Groundwater Association;
- *Promoting Earth Science for Society (YES Network, #18541)*;
- *Society for Geology Applied to Mineral Deposits (#19565)*;
- *Society for Sedimentary Geology (SEPM)*;
- *Society of Economic Geologists (SEG, #19546)*.

NGO Relations Instrumental in setting up (1): *International Union for Quaternary Research (INQUA, #15811)*. Member of: *International Science Council (ISC, #14796)* and its committees: *Committee on Data for Science and Technology (CODATA, #04247)*; *Committee on Space Research (COSPAR, #04287)*; *Scientific Committee on Antarctic Research (SCAR, #19147)*; *Scientific Committee on Problems of the Environment (SCOPE, #19150)*; *ISC World Data System (ISC-WDS, #16024)*. [2023/XA2723/y/A]

♦ International Union of Glaziers / see European Glaziers Association (#07394)
♦ International Union of Gospel Missions / see Association of Gospel Rescue Missions
♦ International Union of Guides and Scouts of Europe – Federation of European Scouting (#20426)
♦ International Union of Hairdressers' Employees (inactive)
♦ International Union of Hat Workers (inactive)
♦ International Union for Health Education / see International Union for Health Promotion and Education (#15778)

♦ International Union for Health Promotion and Education (IUHPE) 15778

Union internationale de promotion de la santé et d'éducation pour la santé (UIPES) – Unión Internacional de Promoción de la Salud y de Educación para la Salud

Headquarters c/o Santé publique France, 12 rue du Val d'Osne, 94415 Saint-Maurice, France. T. +33786487477. E-mail: iuhpe@iuhpe.org.

Int'l Secretariat c/o École de Santé Publique, Université de Montréal, 7101 ave du Parc, porte 3187, Montréal QC H3N 1X9, Canada. T. +15143437945.

URL: http://www.iuhpe.org/

History May 1951, Paris (France). Founded as *Interim Commission*. Definitive statutes adopted May 1953, Paris; revised: Jul 1962, Philadelphia PA (USA); Sep 1969, Buenos Aires (Argentina); 1973, Paris; 1982, Hobart (Australia); 1985, Dublin (Ireland); 1988 Houston TX (USA); 1998, Puerto Rico; 2007, Vancouver BC (Canada). Former names and other names: *Union internationale pour l'éducation sanitaire de la population* – former; *International Union for Health Education (IUHE)* – former (1974 to 1993); *Union internationale d'éducation pour la santé (UIES)* – former (1974 to 1993); *Unión Internacional de Educación para la Salud* – former (1974 to 1993). **Aims** Promote global health and contribute to achievement of equity in health between and within countries; advocate activities to promote the health of populations worldwide; develop the knowledge base for health promotion and health education; improve and advance the quality and effectiveness of health promotion and health education practice and knowledge; contribute to development of countries' capacity to undertake health promotion and health education activity. **Structure** General Assembly (every 3 years, at World Conference). Board of Trustees, comprising Executive Committee (President and 12 Vice-Presidents), globally elected members and ex-officio members (accredited representatives of organizations with national trustee membership and Regional Directors). Membership and meetings open. **Languages** English, French, Spanish. **Staff** 5.00 FTE, paid. **Finance** Sources: grants; members' dues; sale of publications. **Activities** Strategies: strengthening IUHPE capacity; advocacy; knowledge development; professional and technical development; networking; partnership building. Organizes: triennial World Conference; regional conferences; seminars. **Events** *World Conference on Health Promotion and General Assembly* Montréal, QC (Canada) 2022, *World Conference on Health Promotion and General Assembly* Rotorua (New Zealand) 2019, *Latin American*

Conference on Health Promotion and Education Sao Paulo (Brazil) 2018, *European Conference* Trondheim (Norway) 2018, *Triennial World Conference and General Assembly* Curitiba (Brazil) 2016. **Publications** *Promotion and Education* (4 a year) – journal with supplement issues; *Critical Public Health* – associated journal; *Health Education Research* – associated journal; *Health Promotion International (HIP)* – associated journal; *Internal Journal of Mental Health Promotion* – associated journal; *International Journal of Public Health* – associated journal. **Members** 'Trustee' organizations of national scope responsible for organizing and/or supporting health promotion in their country. 'Institutional' organizations (international, national, sub-national or local) whose main purposes include undertaking, teaching, research or promotion of some aspect of health promotion/education. 'Individual' individuals who support IUHPE mission, goals and objectives. 'Honorary' organizations or individuals. Members in over 150 countries (countries not specified). **Consultative Status** Consultative status granted from: *UNESCO (#20322)* (Consultative Status); *UNICEF (#20332)*. **IGO Relations** Official Relationship with: *WHO (#20950)*; *WHO Regional Office for Europe (#20945)*. Accredited by: *United Nations Office at Vienna (UNOV, #20604)*. Associated with Department of Global Communications of the United Nations. **NGO Relations** Member of: *Conference of Non-Governmental Organizations in Consultative Relationship with the United Nations (CONGO, #04635)*; *Framework Convention Alliance (FCA, #09981)*; *International Non Governmental Coalition Against Tobacco (INGCAT, no recent information)*. Associate member of: *European Public Health Association (EUPHA, #08298)*. [2021/XB2659/**B**]

- ♦ International Union of Heat Distributors / see Euroheat and Power (#05694)
- ♦ International Union of Historic House Associations / see European Historic Houses Association (#07491)
- ♦ International Union for History and Methodological Sciences (inactive)
- ♦ International Union of the History and Philosophy of Science / see International Union of History and Philosophy of Science and Technology (#15779)

♦ International Union of History and Philosophy of Science and Technology (IUHPST) 15779

SG IUHPST/DHST, Observatoire de Paris, 61 avenue de l'Observatoire, 75014 Paris, France.
General: http://www.iuhpst.org/

History 1956. Founded by the federation of *International Union of the History of Sciences (inactive)*, set up in 1947, and *Union internationale de logique, méthodologie et philosophie des sciences (UIPS, inactive)*, formed 12 Jun 1949. The federating bodies became Divisions of the Union. Former names and other names: *International Union of the History and Philosophy of Science (IUHPS)* – former (1956 to 2015); *Union internationale d'histoire et de philosophie des sciences* – former (1956 to 2015); *Unión Internacional de Historia y Filosofía de las Ciencias* – former (1956 to 2015); *Internationaler Verband für Geschichte und Philosophie der Wissenschaften* – former (1956 to 2015). **Aims** Coordinate and promote research on the history and philosophy of science, contributing to the unity of science in general and establishing links between different branches of knowledge. **Structure** General Assembly; Council; Executive Committee. Historical Commissions (13) include: *International Society for the History of East Asian Science Technology and Medicine (ISHEASTM, #15168)*; *International Commission on History of Meteorology (ICHM, #12687)*. Inter-Union Commissions (5): *International Astronomical Union (IAU, #12287)*; *International Geographical Union (IGU, #13713)*; *International Commission on the History of Geological Sciences (INHIGEO, #12685)*, with *International Union of Geological Sciences (IUGS, #15777)*; *International Commission on the History of Mathematics (ICHM, #12686)*, with *International Mathematical Union (IMU, #14121)*; *International Union of Soil Sciences (IUSS, #15817)*. Independent Scientific Sections: *International Committee for the History of Technology (ICOHTEC, #12778)*; *International Association for Science and Cultural Diversity (IASCUD, #12150)*. Commissions (3). **Languages** English. **Staff** None. **Finance** Sources: members' dues. **Activities** Events/meetings. **Events** *International Congress* Buenos Aires (Argentina) 2023, *International Congress of History of Science and Technology* Prague (Czechia) 2021, *International Congress* Prague (Czechia) 2019, *International Congress of History of Science and Technology* Rio de Janeiro (Brazil) 2017, *International congress* Helsinki (Finland) 2015.

Members DHST membership consists of National committees in 47 countries and territories:
Argentina, Australia, Belgium, Brazil, Bulgaria, Canada, Chile, China, Colombia, Croatia, Cuba, Czechia, Denmark, Egypt, Finland, France, Germany, Greece, Hungary, India, Iran Islamic Rep, Ireland, Israel, Italy, Japan, Korea Rep, Kyrgyzstan, Mexico, Netherlands, New Zealand, Norway, Poland, Portugal, Romania, Russia, Serbia, Slovakia, South Africa, Spain, Sweden, Switzerland, Syrian AR, Taiwan, Tunisia, Türkiye, UK, USA.
Also membership in Baltic Republics. DLMPST Ordinary members in 35 countries and territories:
DLMPST Ordinary members in 35 countries and territories:
Argentina, Australia, Austria, Belgium, Brazil, Canada, China, Croatia, Czechia, Denmark, Estonia, Finland, France, Germany, Hungary, India, Iran Islamic Rep, Ireland, Israel, Italy, Japan, Korea Rep, Netherlands, New Zealand, Norway, Poland, Romania, Serbia, South Africa, Spain, Sweden, Switzerland, Taiwan, UK, USA.
International members (12) include 4 organizations listed in this Yearbook:
Association for Symbolic Logic (ASL, #02945); *Association of Logic, Language and Information (FoLLI, #02789)*; *European Philosophy of Science Association (EPSA, #08202)*; *Institut Wiener Kreis*.
NGO Relations Member of (1): *International Science Council (ISC, #14796)*. Joint commissions with: *International Astronomical Union (IAU, #12287)*; *International Geographical Union (IGU, #13713)*; *International Union of Soil Sciences (IUSS, #15817)*; *International Union of Geological Sciences (IUGS, #15777)*. DLMPST is member of: *International Federation of Philosophical Societies (FISP, #13507)*. [2022.10.11/XC2786/y/**C**]

- ♦ International Union of the History of Sciences (inactive)
- ♦ International Union of Hotel Concierges "The Golden Keys" (#20424)
- ♦ International Union of Hotel, Restaurant and Bar Workers (inactive)

♦ International Union for Housing Finance (IUHF) 15780

Main Office Rue Montoyer 25, 1000 Brussels, Belgium. T. +3222310371. Fax +3222308245. E-mail: info@housingfinance.org.
URL: https://www.housingfinance.org/

History 11 Aug 1914, London (UK). Founded following development, 1893, of a USA conference *'World Congress of Building and Loan Associations'*; commencement of truly international activities at International Congress, 1931, Philadelphia PA (USA). Statutes adopted 15 Sep 1938, when transformed from an 'ad hoc' organization arranging conferences to a permanent body; reconstituted 3 May 1956; statutes amended 1971; new statutes adopted 1986; 4 Oct 1988; 1995, London; current statutes adopted 21 Sep 2006. Offices have alternated between USA, UK and Belgium. Former names and other names: *International Union of Building Societies and Savings and Loan Associations* – former; *International Union of Building Societies and Savings Associations (IUBSSA)* – former; *International Organization for Housing Finance Institutions* – former; *International Union of Housing Finance Institutions (IUHFI)* – former; *Union internationale des sociétés d'épargne et de prêts immobiliers* – former; *Internationaler Verband für Haus Finanzierungen* – former; *Unión Internacional de Asociaciones de Ahorros y Préstamo para la Vivienda* – former; *União Internacional das Entidades de Crédito Imobiliario e Poupança* – former. **Aims** Facilitate global contact between member organizations and their officers and directors, and be a source of international leadership in housing finance; promote exchange of knowledge about housing finance issues and serve as a recognized primary source of information on international housing finance; influence opinion leaders to adopt policies and initiatives to promote housing; facilitate business opportunities between member institutions; promote and facilitate development of housing finance systems in developing countries; encourage cooperation between public and private sectors in housing finance sectors. **Structure** World Congress (every 2 years, open registration); Executive Committee; Council of Members; Nominating Committee. **Languages** English. **Staff** None. **Finance** Sources: meeting proceeds; members' dues; sale of publications. Annual budget: 100,000 EUR. **Activities** Events/meetings; guidance/assistance/consulting; knowledge management/information dissemination; networking/liaising; research/documentation; training/education. **Events** *World Congress* Cape Town (South Africa) 2019, *World Congress* Washington, DC (USA) 2017, *World Congress* Rio de Janeiro (Brazil) 2015, *World Congress* Vienna (Austria) 2013, *International housing summit* Rotterdam (Netherlands) 2011. **Publications** *Housing Finance International* (4 a year) – journal. *International Housing Finance Sourcebook* (2000); *Secondary Mortgage Markets: International Perspectives* by Michael Lea; *Securitization: The Financial Instrument of the New Millennium* by Vinod Kothari.
Members National banking associations, mortgage lending institutions, consultants, economists, academics, government agencies, international institutes. Members (109) in 46 countries and territories:
Algeria, Austria, Azerbaijan, Belgium, Botswana, Brazil, Canada, Chile, Croatia, Cyprus, Czechia, Denmark, Dominican Rep, Estonia, Finland, France, Germany, Hungary, India, Indonesia, Jamaica, Japan, Kenya, Korea Rep, Lithuania, Malaysia, Malta, Mongolia, Palestine, Peru, Philippines, Poland, Romania, Russia, Slovakia, South Africa, Sri Lanka, St Lucia, Sweden, Syrian AR, Tanzania UR, Thailand, Uganda, UK, USA, Zimbabwe.
Regional affiliates, 5 organizations listed in this Yearbook:
African Union for Housing Finance (AUHF, #00491); *Caribbean Association of Housing Finance Institutions (CASHFI, #03447)*; *European Federation of Building Societies (EFBS, #07064)*; *Inter-American Housing Union (#11433)*; *International Bank for Reconstruction and Development (IBRD, #12317)* (World Bank). [2021.10.26/XC2701/y/**B**]

- ♦ International Union of Housing Finance Institutions / see International Union for Housing Finance (#15780)
- ♦ International Union of Hunting / see Fédération Internationale de Tir aux Armes Sportives de Chasse (#09665)

♦ International Union of Immunological Societies (IUIS) 15781

Union internationale des sociétés d'immunologie

Pres c/o KIT Group GmbH, Kufürstendamm 71, 10709 Berlin, Germany. T. +4930246030. E-mail: info@iuis.org.
SG address not obtained.
URL: https://iuis.org/

History 5 May 1969, Bruges (Belgium). Founded following recommendations of a meeting, 1968, Interlaken (Switzerland). Official constitution adopted 1971, Washington DC (USA). Constitution revised: 1986, Toronto ON (Canada); 1995, San Francisco CA (USA); 2014, Nairobi (Kenya); 2019, Beijing (China). **Aims** Organize international cooperation in immunology; promote communication between the various branches of immunology and allied subjects; encourage cooperation between societies representing the interests of immunology within each scientifically independent territory. **Structure** Council and Executive Committee (3-year rotation); Standing Committees (10). **Languages** English. **Finance** Sources: meeting proceeds; members' dues. Other sources: journal subscriptions. **Activities** Events/meetings; projects/programmes; training/education. International Day of Immunology (April 29). **Events** *International Congress of Immunology – ICU* Cape Town (South Africa) 2023, *International Congress of Immunology – ICU* Cape Town (South Africa) 2022, *International Congress of Immunology – ICU* Beijing (China) 2019, *International Congress of Immunology – ICU* Melbourne, VIC (Australia) 2016, *International Veterinary Immunology Symposium* Milan (Italy) 2013. **Publications** *Frontiers in Immunology* – official journal. Congress proceedings.
Members Regular: societies, representing over 35,000 immunologists in 83 countries and territories:
Algeria, Argentina, Armenia, Australia, Austria, Belgium, Bolivia, Bosnia-Herzegovina, Brazil, Bulgaria, Cameroon, Canada, Chile, China, Colombia, Congo DR, Côte d'Ivoire, Croatia, Cuba, Czechia, Denmark, Egypt, Estonia, Finland, France, Gambia, Georgia, Germany, Greece, Hong Kong, Hungary, Iceland, India, Iran Islamic Rep, Ireland, Israel, Italy, Japan, Kazakhstan, Kenya, Korea Rep, Kosovo, Latvia, Lithuania, Luxembourg, Malawi, Mali, Mexico, Montenegro, Morocco, Netherlands, New Zealand, Nigeria, Norway, Pakistan, Papua New Guinea, Paraguay, Peru, Philippines, Poland, Portugal, Romania, Russia, Senegal, Serbia, Singapore, Slovakia, Slovenia, South Africa, Spain, Sweden, Switzerland, Taiwan, Tanzania UR, Thailand, Tunisia, Türkiye, UK, Ukraine, Uruguay, USA, Venezuela, Zimbabwe.
Included in the above, 2 organizations listed in this Yearbook:
Australasian Society for Immunology (ASI); *Scandinavian Society for Immunology (SSI, #19110)*.
Regional federations (4), listed in this Yearbook:
European Federation of Immunological Societies (EFIS, #07142); *Federation of African Immunological Societies (FAIS, #09403)*; *Federation of Immunological Societies of Asia-Oceania (FIMSA, #09594)*; *Latin American and Caribbean Association of Immunology (ALACI, #16265)*.
International Affiliate members (8), listed in this Yearbook:
Federation of Clinical Immunology Societies (FOCIS, #09472); *International Council for Laboratory Animal Science (ICLAS, #13039)*; *International Council for Science (ICSU, inactive)*; *International Society for Immunology of Reproduction (ISIR, #15193)*; *International Society of Developmental and Comparative Immunology (ISDCI, #15053)*; *Society for Mucosal Immunology (SMI, #19601)*; *WHO (#20950)*; *World Allergy Organization – IAACI (WAO, #21077)*.
Consultative Status Consultative status granted from: *WHO (#20950)* (Official). **NGO Relations** Member of: *International Council for Laboratory Animal Science (ICLAS, #13039)*; *International Science Council (ISC, #14796)*. Through Standardization Committee, liaises with: *Collegium Internationale Allergologicum (CIA, #04114)*; *International Council for Standardization in Haematology (ICSH, #13078)*; *International Federation of Clinical Chemistry and Laboratory Medicine (IFCC, #13392)*; *International League of Associations for Rheumatology (ILAR, #14016)*; *International Society of Hematology (ISH, #15159)*; *International Society for Human and Animal Mycology (ISHAM, #15181)*; *World Association of Societies of Pathology and Laboratory Medicine (WASPaLM, #21191)*. [2023.02.15/XC4222/y/**C**]

- ♦ International Union of Independent Laboratories (#20429)
- ♦ International Union of Individuals of Mixed Parentage (inactive)
- ♦ International Union for Inland Navigation (inactive)

♦ International Union of Institutes of Archaeology, History and Art History in Rome 15782

Union internationale des instituts d'archéologie, d'histoire et d'histoire de l'art de Rome – Unione Internazionale degli Istituti di Archeologia, Storia e Storia dell'Arte in Roma

SG Via di Sant'Eufemia 13, 00187 Rome RM, Italy.
URL: http://www.unioneinternazionale.it/

History 9 Jan 1946, Rome (Italy). Founded on signature of a document by the Directors of Ecole Française de Rome, American Academy in Rome, Istituto Svedese di Studi Classici a Roma and the President of Istituto Nazionale di Archeologia e Storia dell'Arte. Statutes adopted 6 Feb 1906; modified: 1960 and 1980. New statutes approved June 1990; amended July 1996. Registration: Italy. **Structure** Presidency. **Activities** Events/meetings; training/education. **Publications** *Annuario dell'Unione Internazionale degli Istituti di Archeologia, Storia e Storia dell'Arte in Roma*. *Catalogo delle Edizioni di Testi Classici esistenti nelle Biblioteche degli Istituti Stranieri di Roma* (1969); *Catalogo delle Pubblicazioni Periodiche esistenti in Varie Biblioteche di Roma e Firenze* (1955); *Catalogo dei Periodici esistenti in Biblioteche di Roma* (1935).
Members Institutes (25) representing 17 countries:
Austria, Belgium, Canada, Denmark, Finland, France, Germany, Holy See, Italy, Netherlands, Norway, Poland, Spain, Sweden, Switzerland, UK, USA.
International institutes (2):
Associazione Internazionale di Archeologia Classica (AIAC, #02988); *Pontifical Institute of Christian Archaeology (#18449)*.
NGO Relations Affiliate member of: *International Committee of Historical Sciences (ICHS, #12777)*. *Association internationale pour l'étude de la mosaïque antique (AIEMA, #02689)*; *Fédération internationale des associations d'études classiques (FIEC, #09607)*. [2020/XD9758/**D**]

♦ International Union for Intercultural and Interfaith Dialogue and Peace Education (ADIC) 15783

Contact address not obtained. E-mail: info@adicinterfaith.org.
URL: http://www.adicinterfaith.org/

History Founded in Paris (France) 1989, as *Association for Muslim-Christian Dialogue – Association pour le dialogue international islamo-chrétien (ADIC)*, on the initiative of Adel Amer (died 1995) and Fr Lelong. Later known as *International Union of Jewish-Islamic-Christian Dialogue and Peace Education (ADIC)*. Present name adopted, 2010. **Aims** Build relationships among the three monotheistic religions. **Structure** Board of Directors; Management Team. [2017/XD2165/**E**]

♦ International Union for an International Classification of the Figurative Elements of Marks (Vienna Union) 15784

Contact c/o WIPO, 34 chemin des Colombettes, Case Postale 18, 1211 Geneva 20, Switzerland. T. +41227309111. Fax +41227335428.
URL: http://www.wipo.int/treaties/en/classification/vienna/

History 9 Aug 1985, on entry into force of *Vienna Agreement Establishing an International Classification of the Figurative Elements of Marks (Vienna Agreement, 1973)*, concluded 12 Jun 1973, Vienna (Austria). A union within *World Intellectual Property Organization (WIPO, #21593)*. **Activities** Agreement establishes a classification system for marks which consist of or contain figurative elements; the competent national office of each contracting State must indicate in official documents and publications relating to registration and renewals of marks the applicable symbols of the International Classification. Committee of Experts, set up under the Agreement, periodically revises the Classification.
Members Open to States party to the Vienna Agreement. States party to the Agreement, as of Feb 2016 (32):
Armenia, Austria, Bosnia-Herzegovina, Bulgaria, Croatia, Cuba, France, Guinea, Jamaica, Jordan, Korea Rep, Kyrgyzstan, Luxembourg, Malaysia, Mexico, Moldova, Montenegro, Netherlands, North Macedonia, Poland, Romania, Serbia, Slovenia, St Lucia, Sweden, Trinidad-Tobago, Tunisia, Türkiye, Turkmenistan, UK, Ukraine, Uruguay. [2016.02.16/XF2259/**F***]

♦ International Union of Jewish-Islamic-Christian Dialogue and Peace Education / see International Union for Intercultural and Interfaith Dialogue and Peace Education (#15783)
♦ International Union of Journeymen and Allied Trades (internationally oriented national body)
♦ International Union of Journeymen Horseshoers / see International Union of Journeymen and Allied Trades
♦ International Union of Journeymen, Horseshoers and Allied Trades / see International Union of Journeymen and Allied Trades
♦ International Union of Journeymen Horseshoers of the United States and Canada / see International Union of Journeymen and Allied Trades

♦ International Union of Judicial Officers 15785

Union internationale des huissiers de justice et officiers judiciaires (UIHJ) – Internationale Union der Gerichtsvollzieher und Gerichtlichen Beamten – Internationale Unie van Gerechtsdeurwaarders en Gerechtelijke Officieren

SG 6 place du Colonel Fabien, 75019 Paris, France. T. +33142408948. Fax +33142409615. E-mail: uihj@uihj.com.
URL: http://www.uihj.com/

History 21 Apr 1952, Paris (France). Registered by French Ministerial Decree, 19 Jan 1954. Former names and other names: *International Association of Sheriff Officers and Judicial Officers* – alias; *International Union of Bailiffs and Law Officers* – alias. **Aims** Represent members to international organizations and ensure collaboration with national professional bodies; work to improve national procedural lax and international treaties; promote ideas, projects and initiatives which help to move forward and elevate the independent status of officers of Court. **Structure** International Congress (every 3 years); Permanent Council; Bureau. **Languages** English, French. **Staff** 1.50 FTE, paid. **Finance** Sources: members' dues. **Activities** Events/meetings; networking/liaising; training/education. **Events** *Congress* Rio de Janeiro (Brazil) 2024, *Triennial Congress* Dubai (United Arab Emirates) 2021, *Triennial Congress* Bangkok (Thailand) 2018, *Triennial Congress* Madrid (Spain) 2015, *Triennial congress* Marseille (France) 2009. **Publications** *Global Code of Digital Enforcement – Code mondial de l'exécution digitale* (Bruylant 2021); *Global Code of Enforcement*; *Juris-Union*; *Reports on the efficiency of enforcement in the World*. Congress proceedings; guides and guidelines.
Members Official bodies representing the profession of judicial officer and enforcement agent (93) in 90 countries and territories:
Albania, Algeria, Antigua-Barbuda, Argentina, Armenia, Austria, Barbados, Belgium, Belize, Benin, Brazil, Bulgaria, Burkina Faso, Cameroon, Chad, Chile, Congo Brazzaville, Côte d'Ivoire, Cuba, Cyprus, Czechia, Denmark, Dominica, Dubai, Egypt, England, Estonia, Eswatini, Finland, France, Gabon, Georgia, Germany, Greece, Grenada, Guinea, Guyana, Haiti, Hungary, Italy, Jamaica, Kazakhstan, Kenya, Latvia, Lesotho, Lithuania, Luxembourg, Madagascar, Malawi, Mali, Mauritania, Mauritius, Moldova, Mongolia, Montenegro, Morocco, Namibia, Netherlands, Niger, North Macedonia, Norway, Poland, Portugal, Québec, Romania, Russia, Scotland, Senegal, Serbia, Slovakia, Slovenia, South Africa, Spain, St Kitts-Nevis, St Lucia, St Vincent-Grenadines, Suriname, Sweden, Switzerland, Thailand, Togo, Trinidad-Tobago, Tunisia, Uganda, Ukraine, USA, Uzbekistan, Wales, Zambia, Zimbabwe.
Consultative Status Consultative status granted from: *Council of Europe (CE, #04881)* (Participatory Status); *ECOSOC (#05331)* (Special). **IGO Relations** Observer status with (1): *Commission européenne pour l'efficacité de la justice (CEPEJ, #04213)*. Technical partner of: *Organisation pour l'Harmonisation en Afrique du Droit des Affaires (OHADA, #17806)*. Associated with Department of Global Communications of the United Nations. **NGO Relations** Member of (1): *World Union of Professions (WUP, #21882)*. Partner of (1): *Global Forum on Law, Justice and Development (GFLJD, #10373)*. [2022.10.23/XD2694/v/**D**]

♦ International Union of Kettlebell Lifting (IUKL) 15786

SG address not obtained.
Exec Dir address not obtained. E-mail: evvwork@gmail.com.
Pres address not obtained.
URL: http://www.giri-iukl.com/

History 1992. Former names and other names: *European Union of Weightball Lifting (EUWL)* – former. **Structure** Executive Committee. **Events** *International Forum* Seoul (Korea Rep) 2017.
Members National federations and representatives in 60 countries and territories:
Argentina, Australia, Belarus, Belgium, Brazil, Bulgaria, Cameroon, Canada, Chile, China, Costa Rica, Croatia, Czechia, Denmark, England, Estonia, Finland, France, Germany, Greece, Hungary, India, Indonesia, Ireland, Italy, Japan, Jordan, Kazakhstan, Korea Rep, Kyrgyzstan, Latvia, Lithuania, Malaysia, Mauritius, Mexico, Mongolia, Nepal, Netherlands, New Zealand, Nigeria, Norway, Philippines, Poland, Puerto Rico, Russia, Scotland, Serbia, Singapore, Slovakia, Slovenia, South Africa, Spain, Sweden, Switzerland, Taiwan, Ukraine, USA, Uzbekistan, Venezuela, Wales.
NGO Relations Member of (2): *Alliance of Independent recognised Members of Sport (AIMS, #00690)* (Observer); *The Association for International Sport for All (TAFISA, #02763)*. [2020/XJ6355/**D**]

♦ International Union of Laboratories and Experts in Construction Materials, Systems and Structures (#18930)
♦ International Union of Landed Property Owners / see International Union of Property Owners (#15804)

♦ International Union for Land Value Taxation and Free Trade (The IU) 15787

Union internationale pour la taxation de la valeur de la terre – – Unión Internacional pro Impuesto sobre el Valor de la Tierra y el Librecambio – Internationale Union für Grundstückwertbesteuerung und Freihandel

Administrator/Dir c/o Earth Rights Institute – West Coast Office, 1127 18th Street, Suite 4, Santa Monica CA 90403, USA. E-mail: annie@earthrightsinstitute.org.
Contact 41 Coleraine Road, London, N8 0QJ, UK.
URL: http://www.theIU.org/

History Jul 1926, Copenhagen (Denmark), at 3rd International Conference on Land Value Taxation and Free Trade. Constitution confirmed Aug 1955, St Andrews (UK); amended: Aug 1979, San Francisco CA (USA). 1997, adopted subtitle *The International Georgist Union*. Previously referred to as *Union internationale pour la taxation des biens fonciers et le libre-échange – Unión Internacional para la Imposición de los Bienes Raices y el Comercio Libre – Internationale Union für Grundstückbesteuerung und Freihandel*. **Aims** Stimulate in all countries a public opinion favourable to permanent peace and prosperity for all people, through the progressive removal of the basic *economic* causes of poverty and war, as these causes are demonstrated in the writings of Henry George (1839-1897); specifically towards the realization of these objects, favour the raising of public revenues by public collection of the rental value of land apart from improvements and the abolition of taxes, tariffs, or imposts of every sort that interfere with the free production and exchange of wealth. **Structure** Executive Committee, composed of President, Deputy President, Vice Presidents, Treasurer, General Secretary, Assistant General Secretary and not more than 20 other members, elected at International Conference. **Languages** English. **Staff** 0.50 FTE, paid. Others voluntary. **Finance** Sources: contributions; donations; members' dues. **Activities** Meetings; correspondence with members; bureau of information; international conferences. **Events** *Conference / International Conference* London (UK) 2013, *Conference* Buenos Aires (Argentina) 2012, *Conference / International Conference* London (UK) 2010, *Conference / International Conference* London (UK) 2006, *Conference / International Conference* Madrid (Spain) 2004. **Publications** *The Georgist Journal* (2 a year); *IU Newsletter*. Books; pamphlets.
Members Individual; Full Corporate; Associate Corporate. Members in 32 countries:
Argentina, Australia, Belgium, Canada, Cayman Is, Colombia, Denmark, Dominican Rep, Ethiopia, France, Germany, Greece, Hungary, Ireland, Israel, Japan, Kenya, Korea Rep, Mali, Malta, Netherlands, New Zealand, Nicaragua, Nigeria, Philippines, Russia, Senegal, South Africa, Spain, Thailand, UK, USA.
Consultative Status Consultative status granted from: *ECOSOC (#05331)* (Special). **IGO Relations** Associated with Department of Global Communications of the United Nations. [2017/XB2661/t/**C**]

♦ International Union of Latin Notaries / see International Union of Notaries (#15795)
♦ International Union of Lawyers / see Union Internationale des Avocats (#20422)
♦ International Union of Leather Chemists Societies / see International Union of Leather Technologists and Chemists Societies (#15788)

♦ International Union of Leather Technologists and Chemists Societies (IULTCS) 15788

Union internationale des sociétés de techniciens et chimistes des industries du cuir – Unión Internacional de Sociedades de Quimicos y Técnicos del Cuero – Internationale Union der Ledertechniker und -Chemiker Verbände

Sec c/o TFL AG, Rothausstrasse 61 (Bau 914B), 4132 Muttenz BL, Switzerland.
Pres address not obtained.
URL: http://www.iultcs.org/

History 1948. Founded on dissolution of *International Society of Leather Trades Chemists (inactive)*, set up 28 Sep 1897, London (UK). Statutes adopted 3 Sep 1965. Former names and other names: *International Union of Leather Chemists Societies (IULCS)* – former (1948 to 1978); *Union internationale des sociétés de chimistes du cuir* – former (1948 to 1978). **Aims** Encourage international collaboration in the field of leather technology and chemistry. **Structure** General Conference (every 2 years); Executive Committee; Council of Delegates; Special Commissions. Membership open; meetings closed. **Languages** English. **Staff** Voluntary. **Finance** Subscriptions based on representation. **Activities** Events/meetings; research and development; standards/guidelines; training/education. **Events** *Biennial Congress* Chengdu (China) 2023, *Biennial Congress* Addis Ababa (Ethiopia) 2021, *Biennial Congress* Dresden (Germany) 2019, *Biennial Congress* Chennai (India) 2017, *Biennial Congress* Novo Hamburgo (Brazil) 2015. **Publications** *IULTCS Leather Test Methods*.
Members National societies; other societies. Members in 25 countries:
Argentina, Australia, Bangladesh, Brazil, China, Colombia, Ethiopia, France, Germany, India, Indonesia, Italy, Japan, Mexico, New Zealand, Portugal, Romania, South Africa, Spain, Switzerland, Tunisia, Türkiye, UK, Uruguay, USA.
Consultative Status Consultative status granted from: *ECOSOC (#05331)* (Ros C); *FAO (#09260)* (Special Status); *UNIDO (#20336)*. **IGO Relations** *UNESCO (#20322)*. **NGO Relations** In liaison with technical committees of: *International Organization for Standardization (ISO, #14473)*. Cooperates with: *International Council of Tanners (ICT, #13084)* and *International Council of Hides, Skins and Leather Traders Associations (ICHSLTA, #13029)* on *Global Leather Coordinating Committee (GLCC)*. [2022/XC2734/t/**C**]

♦ International Union of Liberal Christian Women / see International Association of Liberal Religious Women (#11999)
♦ International Union for the Liberty of Education (inactive)
♦ International Union of Lipoplastic Surgery Societies (#20438)
♦ International Union of Local Authorities (inactive)
♦ International Union for the Logic, Methodology and Philosophy of Sciences (inactive)
♦ International Union of Lorry Drivers / see International Union of Professional Drivers (#15802)

♦ International Union of Marine Insurance (IUMI) 15789

Union internationale d'assurances transports – Unión Internacional de Seguros de Transportes – Internationaler Dachverband der Transportversicherer – Unione Internazionale Assicurazioni Trasporti

SG Grosse Elbstr 36, 22767 Hamburg, Germany. T. +494020007470. Fax +4940200074715. E-mail: info@iumi.com.
URL: https://iumi.com/

History 8 Jan 1874, Berlin (Germany). Reorganized 1946. New statutes adopted 1950. Statutes revised: 1960; 1974; 1985; 1996; 2014. Office moved to Hamburg (Germany), Feb 2013. Registration: EU Transparency Register, No/ID: 456150222492-25. **Aims** Secure representation, safeguarding and development of marine insurance interests. **Structure** Council; Executive Committee; Secretariat; Nomination Committee. Meetings closed. **Languages** English. **Staff** 2.50 FTE, paid. **Finance** Annual contribution fixed according to Premium volume of previous year. **Activities** Advocacy/lobbying/activism; events/meetings; guidance/assistance/consulting. **Events** *Annual Congress* Hong Kong 2029, *Annual Congress* Belgium 2028, *Annual Congress* Japan 2027, *Annual Congress* Rotterdam (Netherlands) 2026, *Annual Congress* Singapore (Singapore) 2025. **Publications** *IUMI Eye Newsletter* (4 a year). Technical reports, papers and pamphlets on cargo loss prevention.
Members National or market marine associations, boards of marine underwriters, marine underwriters' committees or similar organizations in 43 countries and territories:
Albania, Australia, Austria, Belgium, Bermuda, Canada, China, Croatia, Cyprus, Denmark, Egypt, Finland, France, Germany, Greece, Hong Kong, India, Israel, Italy, Japan, Kazakhstan, Korea Rep, Malaysia, Morocco, Myanmar, Netherlands, New Zealand, Nigeria, Norway, Philippines, Poland, Singapore, Slovenia, South Africa, Spain, Sweden, Switzerland, Taiwan, Thailand, Türkiye, UK, United Arab Emirates, USA.
Consultative Status Consultative status granted from: *ECOSOC (#05331)* (Ros A); *UNCTAD (#20285)* (General Category); *International Maritime Organization (IMO, #14102)*. **NGO Relations** Member of (3): *Conference of Non-Governmental Organizations in Consultative Relationship with the United Nations (CONGO, #04635)*; *International Maritime Statistics Forum (IMSF, #14105)*; *International Salvage Union (ISU, #14779)*. Cooperates with (1): *International Organization for Standardization (ISO, #14473)*. Consultative member of: *Comité maritime international (CMI, #04192)*. [2022.10.21/XC2737/**C**]

♦ International Union of Master Bakers and Bakers-Confectioners / see International Union of Bakers and Confectioners (#15757)

♦ International Union of Materials Research Societies (IUMRS) 15790

Global Headquarters Block N4.1 Level 1, 50 Nanyang Avenue, Singapore 639798, Singapore. E-mail: admin@iumrs.org.
Admin Office 907 Old Hills Rd, McKeesport PA 15135, USA. T. +14127513888. E-mail: mdriverphd@gmail.com.
URL: https://iumrs.org/

History 1991. **Aims** Facilitate international cooperation among materials research organizations; contribute to the advancement of materials research in all its aspects. **Structure** Officers: President; 2 Past-Presidents; 2 Vice-Presidents; Secretary; Treasurer; General Secretary. The *Global Materials Network (GMN)*, for young researchers, was founded during the IUMRS-ICYRAM event in 2012. **Activities** Events/meetings. **Events** *International Conference of Young Researchers on Advanced Materials (ICYRAM)* Fukuoka (Japan) 2022, *ICEM : International Conference on Electronic Materials* Foz do Iguaçu (Brazil) 2021, *International Conference in Asia (IUMRS-ICA)* Jeju (Korea Rep) 2021, *ICEM : International Conference on Electronic Materials* Foz do Iguaçu (Brazil) 2020, *International Conference of Young Researchers on Advanced Materials (ICYRAM)* Warsaw (Poland) 2020.
Members National organizations in 10 countries and territories:
Australia, China, India, Japan, Korea Rep, Mexico, Russia, Singapore, Taiwan, USA.
Regional organization (2):
African Materials Research Society (African MRS, #00369); *European Materials Research Society (E-MRS, #07753)*.
NGO Relations Member of: *International Science Council (ISC, #14796)*. [2022/XD9058/**D**]

♦ International Union of Mathematics (inactive)

♦ International Union of Medical Advisers Associations 15791

Union internationale des associations de délégués médicaux (UIADM) – Unión Internacional de Asociaciones de Visitadores Médicos – Internationale Vereinigung der Pharmaberater-Verbände

Pres 22 Marni St, 104 33 Athens, Greece. T. +302105244822. Fax +302105240883. E-mail: president@uiadm.net – info@uiadm.net.
URL: http://www.uiadm.org/

History by *Union européenne des associations de délégués médicaux (UEADM, inactive)*. **Aims** Promote exact and objective *pharmaceutical* information based on powerful deontological rules that will contribute to promotion of public health and equivalent access to new pharmaceutical therapies. **Structure** Board; Controllers of Accounts (2). **Languages** English, French, Irish Gaelic, Italian. **Staff** 2.00 FTE, paid; 15.00 FTE, voluntary. **Finance** Members' dues. Donations to support events, conferences, etc. **Events** *International Congress* Athens (Greece) 2012.
Members Members in 14 countries:
Argentina, Austria, Belgium, Cyprus, France, Germany, Greece, Italy, Malta, Morocco, Romania, Spain, Switzerland, Tunisia.
Also member Federation of States of Latin America. [2016.12.27/XD9497/**D**]

♦ International Union of Medical and Applied Bio-Electrography (IUMAB) 15792

Unión Internacional de Bioelectrografia Médica y Aplicada

Pres Ligovski 56E, St Petersburg SANKT-PETERBURG, Russia, 191040. T. +79219368394. E-mail: seminar@iumab.org.
Contact Kerese 20, 21008 Narva, Estonia.
URL: http://www.iumab.org/

History 1978. **Aims** Develop scientific approaches to the investigation into the complex biological field of the human being; investigate the altered states of consciousness in different types of activities (mental training, meditation, healing, top-level athletes, theatre, etc); promote the scientific status of bio-electrography through scientific research and unification of Western and Eastern scientific approaches; bring together people involved in various aspects of bio-electrographic investigation so as to exchange experience and results; develop bio-electrographic research within a strict scientific framework, especially concerning health aspects. **Structure** Officers: President; Executive Vice-President; 2 Vice-Presidents; Secretary General. **Languages** English, Russian, Spanish. **Staff** 3.00 FTE, paid; 11.50 FTE, voluntary. **Finance** Private financing. **Activities** Events/meetings. **Events** *Conference* St Petersburg (Russia) 2015, *Conference* St Petersburg (Russia) 2014, *Conference* St Petersburg (Russia) 2013, *Conference* St Petersburg (Russia) 2012, *Conference* St Petersburg (Russia) 2011. **Publications** Books.
Members Individuals; Institutes. Members in 30 countries:
Argentina, Australia, Austria, Belarus, Brazil, Canada, Chile, China, Colombia, Czechia, Denmark, Finland, France, Germany, India, Japan, Korea Rep, Malaysia, Mexico, Mongolia, Netherlands, Poland, Slovenia, Spain, Switzerland, Türkiye, UK, Ukraine, USA, Uzbekistan. [2020.03.03/XD7138/**D**]

♦ International Union of the Medical Press (no recent information)
♦ International Union of Medical Sciences (inactive)
♦ International Union for Mental Health (no recent information)

♦ International Union of Microbeam Analysis Societies (IUMAS) 15793

Sec NIST MS 8371, 100 Bureau Dr, Gaithersburg MD 20899-8371, USA.
Pres 625-3 Yodang-ri, Yanggam-myun, Hwaseong GYEONGGI 445-935, Korea Rep.
URL: http://iumas.org/

History 1994, Bethlehem PA (USA). **Aims** Promote worldwide cooperation in all aspects of microbeam analysis. **Structure** Council. Officers: President and Secretary/Treasurer. **Languages** English. **Staff** None. **Finance** Members' dues: US$ 200. **Events** *Meeting* Banff, AB (Canada) 2023, *Meeting* Konstanz (Germany) 2017, *Meeting* Hartford, CT (USA) 2014, *Meeting* Seoul (Korea Rep) 2011, *Meeting* Perth, WA (Australia) 2008.
Members Full in 7 countries:
Australia, Brazil, Canada, China, Japan, Korea Rep, USA.
International member (1), included in this Yearbook:
European Microbeam Analysis Society (EMAS, #07791). [2014/XD7356/y/**D**]

♦ International Union of Microbiological Societies (IUMS) 15794

Union internationale des sociétés de microbiologie (UISM) – Unión Internacional de las Sociedades de Microbiologia – Internationale Vereinigung der Mikrobiologischen Gesellschaften

SG Westerdijk Fungal Biodiversity Inst, PO Box 85167, 3508 AD Utrecht, Netherlands. T. +31302122600. Fax +31302512097.
Pres Dept Molecular Microbiology and Biotechnology, George S Wise Fac of Life Sciences, Tel Aviv Univ, 69978 Tel Aviv, Israel.
URL: http://www.iums.org/

History 1927. 1st International Congress of Microbiology held in 1930, Paris (France). In 1953 assumed the activities of *International Federation of Culture Collection of Microbic Types (IFCC, inactive)*, set up 1947, by taking over the functions of *Centre of Collections of Microbial Species (inactive)*, which was formed in 1945, Switzerland. Statutes revised by General Assembly: Aug 1982, Sep 1986; Aug 2005; Sep 2011. Former names and other names: *International Society for Microbiology* – former (1927); *Société internationale de microbiologie* – former (1927); *International Association of Microbiological Societies (IAMS)* – former; *Association internationale des sociétés de microbiologie (AISM)* – former. Registration: Banque-Carrefour des Entreprises, Belgium. **Aims** Promote the study of microbiological sciences internationally; initiate, facilitate and coordinate research and other scientific activities which involve international cooperation; promote the publication of international study and research; promote the organization of international conferences, symposia, and meetings and assist in the publication of their reports; represent microbiological sciences in ICSU and maintain contact with other international organizations.
Structure General Assembly (triennial, at Congress), consists of representatives of National Member Societies, Divisions and COMCOFs (Committees, Commissions and Federations) together with members of the Executive Board. Executive Board (meets annually); Steering Committee.
'Subsidiary Bodies':
- *IUMS Division of Bacteriology and Applied Microbiology (BAM, see: #15794)*, including:
  - *International Committee on Food Microbiology and Hygiene (ICFMH, #12770)*;
  - *International Committee on Systematics of Prokaryotes (ICSP, #12807)* (with 25 sub-committees);
  - *Medical Microbiology Interdisciplinary Commission (MEMIC, no recent information)*;
  - *International Commission on Microbiological Specifications for Foods (ICMSF, #12703)* (with 4 regional sub-commissions).
- *IUMS Division of Mycology (see: #15794)*, including:
  - *International Commission on Antigens and Molecular Diagnostics (ICAMD, see: #15794)*;
  - *International Commission on the Taxonomy of Fungi (ICTF, #12734)*;
  - *International Commission on Yeasts (ICY, see: #15794)*;
  - *International Commission on Penicillium and Aspergillus (ICPA, see: #15794)*;
  - *International Commission on Food Mycology (ICFM, see: #15794)*;
- *IUMS Division of Virology (see: #15794)*, including:
  - *International Committee on Taxonomy of Viruses (ICTV, see: #15794)* with 7 sub-committees (Coordination; Bacterial Virus; Fungal Virus (with 5 study groups); Invertebrate Virus (with 4 study groups); Plant Virus (with 10 study groups); Vertebrate Virus (with a number of study groups); Virus Data).

'International Federations':
- *International Federation for Enteric Phage Typing (IFEPT, #13413)*;
- *World Federation for Culture Collections (WFCC, #21424)* (with 7 Committees).

Languages English, French, German. **Finance** Sources: contributions; grants; members' dues; revenue from activities/projects. Grants from ICSU. Supported by: *UNESCO (#20322)*. **Activities** Awards/prizes/competitions; events/meetings. **Events** *IUMS Congress* Rotterdam (Netherlands) 2022, *International Congress on Yeasts* Vienna (Austria) 2021, *International Congress of Bacteriology and Applied Microbiology* Daejeon (Korea Rep) 2020, *International Congress of Mycology and Eukariotic Microbiology* Daejeon (Korea Rep) 2020, *International Congress of Virology* Daejeon (Korea Rep) 2020. **Publications** *International Journal of Food Microbiology (ICFMH)*; *International Journal of Systematic Evolutionary Microbiology*; *Microbiological Sciences. Microbial Ecology of Foods (ICMSF)* – in 2 vols; *Microorganisms in Food (ICMSF)* – in 2 vols. Conference proceedings; reports.
Members Full; Associate; Supporting. National microbiological Societies (114), totalling about 100,000 members, in 71 countries and territories (indicates associate member):
Algeria, Argentina, Armenia, Australia, Austria, Bangladesh, Belarus (*), Belgium, Brazil, Bulgaria, Cameroon, Canada, Chile, China, Croatia, Cuba, Czechia, Denmark, Egypt, Estonia, Finland, France, Germany, Ghana (*), Greece, Guinea (*), Hong Kong, Hungary, Iceland, India, Indonesia, Iran Islamic Rep, Iraq, Israel, Italy, Japan, Korea Rep, Kuwait, Latvia, Lithuania (*), Mexico, Morocco, Netherlands, New Zealand, Nigeria, North Macedonia, Norway, Pakistan (*), Peru, Philippines, Poland, Portugal, Romania, Russia, Saudi Arabia, Singapore, Slovakia, Slovenia, South Africa, Spain, Sweden, Switzerland, Thailand, Türkiye, UK, Uruguay, USA, Uzbekistan, Venezuela, Zambia, Zimbabwe (*).
International associate members (10):
African Regional Network for Microbiology (ARNM, no recent information); *European Society for Clinical Virology (ESCV, #08552)*; *European Society for Veterinary Virology (ESVV, #08786)*; *Federation of European Microbiological Societies (FEMS, #09516)*; *Foundation for African Development through International Biotechnology (FADIB, #09939)*; *International Organization for Biotechnology and Bioengineering (IOBB, no recent information)*; *International Society for Human and Animal Mycology (ISHAM, #15181)*; *International Society for Microbial Ecology (ISME, #15266)*; *International Society for Plant Pathology (ISPP, #15371)*; *UNESCO World Network of Microbiological Resources Centres MIRCEN (no recent information)*.
Consultative Status Consultative status granted from: *ECOSOC (#05331)* (Ros C); *FAO (#09260)* (Liaison Status); *WHO (#20950)* (Official Relations). **IGO Relations** Observer status with (1): *Codex Alimentarius Commission (CAC, #04081)*. **NGO Relations** Member of (3): *Council for International Organizations of Medical Sciences (CIOMS, #04905)* (as Associate member); *International Science Council (ISC, #14796)*; *Scientific Committee on Problems of the Environment (SCOPE, #19150)*. Instrumental in setting up (4): *Global Society for Industrial Microbiology (GIM, #10606)*; *International Alliance for Biological Standardization (IABS, #11622)*; *International Committee on Bionomenclature (ICB, #12748)*; *Medical Microbiology Interdisciplinary Commission (MEMIC, no recent information)*. Represented in: *Committee on Data for Science and Technology (CODATA, #04247)*. In liaison with technical committees of: *International Organization for Standardization (ISO, #14473)*. [2022.02.02/XB1314/y/**B**]

♦ International Union for Moral and Social Action (inactive)
♦ International Union of Motor Manufacturers (inactive)
♦ International Union of Muslim Scholars (internationally oriented national body)
♦ International Union of Muslim Scouts (no recent information)
♦ International Union of National Federations and Associations of Shooting / see International Shooting Sport Federation (#14852)

♦ International Union of Notaries 15795

Union internationale du Notariat (UINL) – Unión Internacional del Notariado – Unione Internazionale del Notariato

Dir Via Flaminia 160, Pal A-I, 00196 Rome RM, Italy. T. +3963208384. Fax +3963212269. E-mail: uinl@uinl.org.
Pres 2020-2022 address not obtained.
URL: http://www.uinl.org/

History 2 Oct 1948, Buenos Aires (Argentina). Previous statutes approved 25 May 1989, Amsterdam (Netherlands); modified: 30 Apr 1992, Cartagena de Indias (Columbia); 12 Feb 1994, Vienna (Austria); 30 Sep 2001, Athens (Greece); 20 Oct 2002, Valencia (Spain). Current statutes approved 8 Nov 2005, Rome (Italy). Former names and other names: *International Union of Latin Notaries* – former; *Union internationale du notariat latin (UINL)* – former; *Unión Internacional del Notariado Latino* – former; *Unione Internazionale del Notariato Latino* – former. **Aims** Promote study and standardization of notarial legislation; secure progress, stability and advancement of the Latin notarial system; contribute experience and advice to those practising law in the sphere of individual rights, whether commercial, family, inheritance or property matters; establish offices for international notarial exchange. **Structure** General Meeting of Member Chambers of Notaries; Permanent General Council; Executive Steering Committee; Supervisory Financial Council; International Congress of Notaries (every 3 years); President (elected every 3 years); Administrative Secretariat; Working Groups. Continental Commissions (4): *Commission for African Affairs (CAAf, see: #15795)*; *Commission for American Affairs (CAA, see: #15795)*; Commission for Asian Affairs (CAAs); *Commission for European Affairs (CAE, see: #15795)*. Intercontinental Commissions: *Commission for International Notarial Cooperation (CCNI, see: #15795)*; Advisory (CC); Themes and Congresses (CTC); Notarial Social Security (CSSN); Notarial Deontology (CDN); Human Rights (CDH). **Languages** English, French, Spanish. **Staff** 3.00 FTE, paid. Expert consultants as needed. **Finance** Sources: members' dues. **Activities** Advocacy/lobbying/activism; events/meetings; guidance/assistance/consulting; knowledge management/information dissemination; research/documentation. **Events** *Congress* Jakarta (Indonesia) 2019, *Joint Meeting* Madrid (Spain) 2018, *Congress* Paris (France) 2016, *Congress* Lima (Peru) 2013, *Plenary Session* Tirana (Albania) 2011. **Publications** *Notarius International* (4 a year) – review, in 5 languages; *Revista Internacional del Notariado (RIN)* (annual) in English, French, Spanish; *IT Bulletin* – electronic. Studies, particularly on comparative law. Publications produced, exchanged and disseminated in collaboration with IRENE and CNUE.
Members National organizations and groups of notaries in 91 countries and territories:
Albania, Algeria, Andorra, Argentina, Armenia, Austria, Belarus, Belgium, Benin, Bolivia, Bosnia-Herzegovina, Brazil, Bulgaria, Burkina Faso, Cameroon, Canada, Central African Rep, Chad, Chile, China, Colombia, Congo Brazzaville, Costa Rica, Côte d'Ivoire, Croatia, Cuba, Czechia, Dominican Rep, Ecuador, El Salvador, Estonia, France, Gabon, Georgia, Germany, Greece, Guatemala, Guinea, Haiti, Holy See, Honduras, Hungary, Indonesia, Italy, Japan, Kazakhstan, Korea Rep, Kosovo, Latvia, Lebanon, Lithuania, Luxembourg, Madagascar, Mali, Malta, Mauritania, Mauritius, Mexico, Moldova, Monaco, Mongolia, Montenegro, Morocco, Netherlands, Nicaragua, Niger, North Macedonia, Panama, Paraguay, Peru, Poland, Portugal, Puerto Rico, Romania, Russia, San Marino, Senegal, Serbia, Slovakia, Slovenia, Spain, Switzerland, Togo, Tunisia, Türkiye, UK, Ukraine, Uruguay, Uzbekistan, Venezuela, Vietnam.
Consultative Status Consultative status granted from: *ECOSOC (#05331)* (Special); *UNESCO (#20322)* (Consultative Status); *FAO (#09260)* (Liaison Status); *OAS (#17629)*. **IGO Relations** Cooperates with (7): *Court of Justice of the European Union (CJEU, #04938)*; *European Parliament (EP, #08146)*; *International Court of Justice (ICJ, #13098)*; *International Institute for the Unification of Private Law (UNIDROIT, #13934)*; *Secretaria Permanente del Tratado General de Integración Económica Centroamericana (SIECA, #19195)*; *The Hague Conference on Private International Law (HCCH, #10850)*; *United Nations Economic Commission for Latin America and the Caribbean (ECLAC, #20556)*. **NGO Relations** Member of (2): *Global Land Tool Network (GLTN, #10452)*; *Union Internationale des Avocats (UIA, #20422)*. Cooperates with (5): *Conference of Non-Governmental Organizations in Consultative Relationship with the United Nations (CONGO, #04635)*; *Hispano-Luso-American Institute of International Law (#10924)*; *International Association of Judges (IAJ, #11978)*; *International Bar Association (IBA, #12320)*; *International Law Association (ILA, #14003)*. Instrumental in setting up (1): *Office notarial permanent d'échange international (ONPI, see: #15795)*. [2022.02.14/XC2732/**C**]

♦ International Union of Nutritional Sciences (IUNS) 15796

Union internationale des sciences de la nutrition (UISN) – Unión Internacional de Ciencias de la Nutrición – Internationale Union der Ernährungswissenschaften

Pres Catedratico de Nutrición, Depto de Fisiologia y Nutrición, Univ de Navarra, Edificio de Investigación, C/Irunlarrea 1, 31008 Pamplona, Navarre, Spain.
URL: http://www.iuns.org/

History 10 Jun 1948, London (UK). Founded at a meeting of an International Committee set up following recommendations, 4-20 Jul 1946, London, at 1st International Congress of Nutrition. Elected as member of *International Council for Science (ICSU, inactive)* in 1968. New Statutes and Rules of Procedure revised and adopted by General Assembly, 29 Aug 1978, Rio de Janeiro (Brazil) and further revised 16 Aug 1981, San Diego CA (USA). Current Statutes and Rules of Procedure revised and adopted by General Assembly, 29 Aug 2001. **Aims** Promote advancement in nutrition science, research and development through international cooperation at the global level; encourage communication and collaboration among nutrition scientists; disseminate information in nutritional sciences through modern communications technology. **Structure** General Assembly (every 4 years, at International Congress); Council. Task Forces and Committees: Nutrition and Cancer; Sustainable Diets; Dietary Fat Quality; Benefit-Risk and Cost Effectiveness of Micronutrient Interventions; Precision Nutrition; Capacity Development in Nutrition; International Malnutrition; Traditional and Indigenous Food Systems and Nutrition; Towards a Multi-Dimensional Index to Child Growth; Archive. **Languages** English. **Staff** Provided by secretariat agency, Kenes office in Netherlands. **Finance** Subscriptions from Adhering Bodies. Annual fee from US$ 100 to US$ 6,000 depending on category. Grants from ICSU; subventions from *UNESCO (#20322)* through ICSU. **Activities** Events/meetings. **Events** *International Congress of Nutrition (ICN)* Paris (France) 2025, *International Congress of Nutrition (ICN)* Tokyo (Japan) 2022, *International Congress of Nutrition* Tokyo (Japan) 2021, *Quadrennial Congress* Buenos Aires (Argentina) 2017, *Quadrennial Congress / International Congress* Granada (Spain) 2013. **Publications** *IUNS Newsletter*. Annual Report; Task Force reports – some also online; miscellaneous publications.
Members Adhering Bodies: principal academies, National Research Councils and other appropriate scientific groups in 84 countries and territories:
Argentina, Australia, Austria, Bangladesh, Belgium, Benin, Brazil, Bulgaria, Burkina Faso, Cameroon, Canada, Chile, China, Congo DR, Costa Rica, Côte d'Ivoire, Cuba, Czechia, Denmark, Egypt, Finland, France, Gambia, Germany, Ghana, Guinea, Haiti, Hungary, Iceland, India, Indonesia, Iran Islamic Rep, Ireland, Israel, Italy, Japan, Kazakhstan, Kenya, Korea Rep, Kuwait, Lebanon, Libya, Madagascar, Malaysia, Mexico, Mongolia, Morocco, Netherlands, New Zealand, Nigeria, Norway, Pakistan, Palestine, Paraguay, Peru, Philippines, Poland, Portugal, Romania, Russia, Rwanda, Saudi Arabia, Senegal, Serbia, Sierra Leone, Singapore, Slovakia, South Africa, Spain, Sri Lanka, Sudan, Sweden, Switzerland, Taiwan, Tanzania UR, Thailand, Tunisia, Uganda, UK, United Arab Emirates, USA, Venezuela, Vietnam, Zimbabwe.
Affiliated Bodies include 16 organizations listed in this Yearbook:

Accademia Europea di Scienza della Nutrizione (#00045); African Nutrition Society (ANS, #00400); Asia Pacific Clinical Nutrition Society (APCNS, #01871); Federation of African Nutrition Societies (FANUS, #09409); Federation of Asian Nutrition Societies (FANS, #09437); Federation of European Nutrition Societies (FENS, #09524); Groupe de recherche en pédiatrie (no recent information); International Confederation of Dietetic Associations (ICDA, #12856); International Symposium on Clinical Nutrition (ISCN); International Zinc Nutrition Consultative Group (iZiNCG, #15943); Iodine Global Network (IGN, #16004); Micronutrient Forum (#16748); Middle East and North Africa Nutrition Association (MENANA, #16782); Sociedad Latinoamericana de Nutrición (SLAN, #19417); World Obesity (#21678); World Public Health Nutrition Association (WPHNA, #21742).
Consultative Status Consultative status granted from: *ECOSOC (#05331)* (Ros C); *FAO (#09260)* (Special Status); *UNICEF (#20332)*; *WHO (#20950)* (Official Relations). **IGO Relations** *Arab Centre for the Studies of Arid Zones and Dry Lands (ACSAD, #00918); Codex Alimentarius Commission (CAC, #04081); FAO (#09260); International Atomic Energy Agency (IAEA, #12294); International Fund for Agricultural Development (IFAD, #13692); UNESCO (#20322); UNICEF (#20332); United Nations Office at Vienna (UNOV, #20604); United Nations University (UNU, #20642); UN System Network on Rural Development and Food Security (no recent information)* – SCN; *WHO (#20950); WHO Regional Office for Europe (#20945).* Associated with Department of Global Communications of the United Nations. **NGO Relations** *African Graduate Nutrition Students Network (#00330); Committee on Data for Science and Technology (CODATA, #04247); Global Alliance for the Prevention of Obesity and Related Chronic Disease (#10219); International Council for Laboratory Animal Science (ICLAS, #13039); International Malnutrition Task Force (IMTF, #14079); International Science Council (ISC, #14796); International Union of Biological Sciences (IUBS, #15760); International Union of Food Science and Technology (IUFoST, #15773); International Union of Nutritional Sciences (IUNS, #15796); International Union of Pure and Applied Chemistry (IUPAC, #15809); Scaling Up Nutrition Movement (SUN Movement, #19064); Survey in Europe on Nutrition and the Elderly (SENECA, #20046).* [2022/XB2743/y/**B**]

- ♦ International Union of Oenologists (#20432)
- ♦ International Union of Old Catholics (inactive)
- ♦ International Union of Operating Engineers (internationally oriented national body)
- ♦ International Union for Oriental and Asian Studies (inactive)
- ♦ International Union of Painters and Allied Trades (internationally oriented national body)
- ♦ International Union of Peace Societies (inactive)
- ♦ International Union of Penal Law (inactive)
- ♦ International Union of Pharmacology / see International Union of Basic and Clinical Pharmacology (#15758)

♦ International Union of Phlebology 15797

Union Internationale de Phlébologie (UIP)

Contact Level 5, 7 Help St, Chatswood NSW 2067, Australia. E-mail: uip@uipmail.org.
URL: http://www.uip-phlebology.org/

History 1959, Aix-en-Provence (France). **Aims** Represent phlebology societies aiming to improve the standards of education, research and healthcare in the management of venous and lymphatic disorders and to provide a platform for scientific exchange and dialogue amongst its members and the wider community; strengthen collaboration and foster harmony between its member societies to achieve a higher standard of healthcare, education, training and scientific research in phlebology; promote organizational transparency, member accountability and objectivity; encourage formation of phlebology societies especially in countries where the field needs further development. **Structure** Congress (every 2 years); General Council; Executive Committee. **Languages** English, French, Spanish. **Staff** 2.00 FTE, paid; 1.00 FTE, voluntary. **Finance** Sources: members' dues; sponsorship. **Activities** Awards/prizes/competitions; awareness raising; events/meetings; knowledge management/information dissemination; networking/liaising; research/documentation; standards/guidelines; training/education. **Events** *World Congress* Buenos Aires (Argentina) 2025, *World Congress* Miami, FL (USA) 2023, *World Congress* Istanbul (Türkiye) 2022, *Congress* Krakow (Poland) 2019, *World Congress* Melbourne, VIC (Australia) 2018. **Publications** *Phlebology* – official journal. Consensus documents.
Members National societies or sections (78) in 63 countries:
Argentina, Armenia, Australia, Austria, Belarus, Belgium, Bolivia, Brazil, Bulgaria, Canada, Chile, China, Colombia, Costa Rica, Cuba, Czechia, Denmark, Dominican Rep, Ecuador, Egypt, El Salvador, Estonia, France, Georgia, Germany, Greece, Guatemala, Hungary, India, Indonesia, Iran Islamic Rep, Italy, Japan, Kazakhstan, Korea Rep, Latvia, Lithuania, Luxembourg, Mexico, Netherlands, New Zealand, Norway, Panama, Paraguay, Peru, Poland, Portugal, Romania, Russia, Serbia, Singapore, Slovakia, Slovenia, Spain, Sweden, Switzerland, Thailand, Türkiye, UK, Ukraine, Uruguay, USA, Venezuela.
NGO Relations Instrumental in setting up (1): *European Venous Forum (EVF, #09050).*
[2022.12.23/XC2750/**B**]

♦ International Union of Photobiology (IUPB) 15798

SG CNRS UMR3347, Inst Curie – Centre de Recherche, Centre Universitaire, 91405 Orsay CEDEX, France.
Pres Food Futures Inst, Murdoch Univ, Perth WA, Australia.
URL: http://www.iuphotobiology.org/

History 11 Sep 1928, Lausanne (Switzerland). Former names and other names: *International Light Committee* – former (1928 to 1951); *Comité international de la lumière (CIL)* – former (1928 to 1951); *International Committee of Photobiology* – former (1951 to 1976); *Comité international de photobiologie (CIP)* – former (1951 to 1976); *Internationale Komitee für Photobiologie* – former (1951 to 1976); *Association internationale de photobiologie (AIP)* – former (1976 to 2000); *International Photobiology Association* – former. **Aims** Stimulate scientific research in photobiology physics, chemistry and climatology of non-ionizing radiation (ultraviolet, visible and infrared) in relation to their biological effects, and the effects of the application of non-ionizing radiation in biology and medicine. **Structure** General Assembly. **Languages** English. **Staff** Voluntary. **Finance** Sources: donations; grants; members' dues. **Activities** Awards/prizes/competitions; events/meetings. **Events** *Quniquennial International Photobiology Congress* Barcelona (Spain) 2019, *Quinquennial International Photobiology Congress* Córdoba (Argentina) 2014, *Quinquennial international photobiology congress* Düsseldorf (Germany) 2009, *Quadrennial international photobiology congress* Jeju (Korea Rep) 2004, *South-East Asian workshop on photobiology in the tropics* Yogyakarta (Indonesia) 2000. **Publications** Congress reports.
Members National groups in 14 countries:
Australia, France, Germany, Hungary, India, Italy, Japan, Korea Rep, Netherlands, Norway, Poland, Russia, UK, USA.
NGO Relations Commission of: *International Union of Biological Sciences (IUBS, #15760).*
[2022.03.04/XC1615/**D**]

- ♦ International Union of Photography (inactive)

♦ International Union for Physical and Engineering Sciences in Medicine (IUPESM) 15799

Union internationale des sciences physiques et technologiques en médecine

SG School of Engineering, Univ of Warwick, Coventry, CV4 7AL, UK. T. +442476573383.
Pres Medical Physics and Research Dept, Hong Kong Sanatorium and Hospital, Happy Valley, Hong Kong, Central and Western, Hong Kong. T. +85228357002.
URL: http://www.iupesm.org/

History 1979, Jerusalem (Israel). Founded by *International Federation for Medical and Biological Engineering* and *International Organization for Medical Physics*, following extensive planning by a working group; acts as representative for IFMBE and IOMP with *International Council for Science (ICSU, inactive)*, since it was accepted, Sep 1982, as a scientific associate. Officers approved, 1985, Helsinki (Finland), at 1st General Assembly. **Aims** Contribute to advancement of medical science and *technology*; organize international cooperation and promote communication among those engaged in *health care* science and technology; represent interests and views of engineering and physical scientists as one health *care* community. **Structure** General Assembly (every 3 years); Administrative Council; Health Technology and Training Task Group (HTTTG). **Languages** English. **Staff** 1.50 FTE, paid. **Finance** Members' dues. **Activities** Training/education; guidance/assistance/consulting; capacity building. **Events** *World Congress on Medical Physics & Biomedical Engineering* 2028, *World Congress on Medical Physics and Biomedical Engineering (WCMPBE)* Adelaide, SA (Australia) 2025, *IUPESM World Congress on Medical Physics and Biomedical Engineering (IUPESM WC2022)* Singapore (Singapore) 2022, *World Congress on Medical Physics and Biomedical Engineering* Singapore (Singapore) 2021, *World Congress on Medical Physics and Biomedical Engineering* Prague (Czechia) 2018. **Publications** *Health and Technology* (4 a year) – journal. Conference proceedings (every 3 years).
Members National Adhering Bodies; national academies of science, research councils or similar bodies; scientific or engineering societies or groups of societies; other specific national bodies. Members in 88 countries and territories:
Argentina, Australia, Austria, Bangladesh, Belgium, Brazil, Bulgaria, Cameroon, Canada, Chile, China, Colombia, Croatia, Cuba, Cyprus, Czechia, Denmark, Ecuador, Egypt, Estonia, Finland, France, Georgia, Germany, Ghana, Greece, Hong Kong, Hungary, Iceland, India, Indonesia, Iran Islamic Rep, Iraq, Ireland, Israel, Italy, Japan, Jordan, Korea Rep, Kuwait, Latvia, Lebanon, Lithuania, Macau, Malaysia, Mexico, Moldova, Mongolia, Morocco, Myanmar, Nepal, Netherlands, New Zealand, Nigeria, North Macedonia, Norway, Pakistan, Panama, Peru, Philippines, Poland, Portugal, Qatar, Romania, Russia, Saudi Arabia, Serbia, Singapore, Slovakia, Slovenia, South Africa, Spain, Sri Lanka, Sudan, Sweden, Switzerland, Taiwan, Tanzania UR, Thailand, Trinidad-Tobago, Türkiye, Uganda, UK, Ukraine, United Arab Emirates, USA, Venezuela, Vietnam.
Founding constituent international organizations (2):
International Federation for Medical and Biological Engineering (IFMBE, #13477); International Organization for Medical Physics (IOMP, #14453).
NGO Relations Member of: *International Science Council (ISC, #14796).* [2020/XC1749/y/**E**]

♦ International Union of Physiological Sciences (IUPS) 15800

Union internationale des sciences physiologiques – Unión Internacional de Ciencias Fisiológicas

Manager Dept of Physiology and Biophysics, Case Western Reserve Univ, 10900 Euclid Ave, Cleveland OH 44106-4970, USA. T. +12163685520. Fax +12163685586.
URL: http://www.iups.org/

History Sep 1953, Montréal QC (Canada), at 19th International Physiological Congress. Functions previously administered by *Permanent Committee of International Physiological Congresses (inactive)*, set up in 1891. **Aims** Encourage advancement of physiological sciences; facilitate dissemination of knowledge in the field; promote the International Congress and similar meetings as may be useful to advance physiological sciences, and other measures that contribute to its development in developing countries. **Structure** General Assembly (every 4 years, at Congress); Council; Executive Committee. Committees and Commissions: *IUPS Commission on Locomotion (see: #15800); IUPS Commission on Circulation – Respiration (see: #15800); IUPS Commission on Endocrine, Reproduction and Development (see: #15800); IUPS Commission on Neurobiology (see: #15800); IUPS Commission on Secretion and Absorption (see: #15800); IUPS Commission on Molecular and Cellular Physiology (see: #15800); IUPS Commission on Comparative Physiology (see: #15800); IUPS Commission on Genomics and Biodiversity (see: #15800)*; Education Committee; Physiome and Systems Biology Committee. **Languages** English. **Staff** 1.00 FTE, paid. **Finance** Sources: members' dues. **Activities** Events/meetings; training/education. **Events** *Quadrennial Congress* Beijing (China) 2022, *Quadrennial Congress* Beijing (China) 2021, *Quadrennial Congress* Rio de Janeiro (Brazil) 2017, *Quadrennial Congress* Birmingham (UK) 2013, *Teaching workshop* Kobe (Japan) 2009. **Publications** *Physiology*. Proceedings of Congresses.
Members National or regional physiological societies in 50 countries and territories:
Argentina, Australia, Austria, Belarus, Belgium, Brazil, Bulgaria, Canada, Chile, China, Czechia, Denmark, Egypt, Finland, France, Georgia, Germany, Greece, Hungary, India, Indonesia, Iran Islamic Rep, Israel, Italy, Japan, Kazakhstan, Korea Rep, Mexico, New Zealand, Nigeria, Norway, Pakistan, Philippines, Poland, Romania, Russia, Serbia, Slovakia, Slovenia, South Africa, Spain, Sweden, Switzerland, Taiwan, Thailand, Türkiye, UK, Ukraine, USA, Venezuela.
Associate members in 13 countries:
Armenia, Cameroon, Cuba, Estonia, Georgia, Ghana, Indonesia, Kenya, Latvia, Lithuania, Myanmar, Portugal, Uruguay.
Affiliated international members (2), listed in this Yearbook:
International Society for Pathophysiology (ISP, #15343); International Society of Nephrology (ISN, #15294).
Regional members (5), listed in this Yearbook:
African Association of Physiological Sciences (AAPS, #00212); Federation of Asian and Oceanian Physiological Societies (FAOPS, #09440); Federation of European Physiological Societies (FEPS, #09530); Latin American Association of Physiological Sciences (#16250); Scandinavian Physiological Society (SPS, #19097).
NGO Relations Associate member of: *Council for International Organizations of Medical Sciences (CIOMS, #04905).* Member of: *International Brain Research Organization (IBRO, #12392); International Council for Laboratory Animal Science (ICLAS, #13039); International Science Council (ISC, #14796).* Represented in: *Committee on Space Research (COSPAR, #04287); Scientific Committee on Antarctic Research (SCAR, #19147). Scientific Committee on Problems of the Environment (SCOPE, #19150).* Special links with: *International Union of Biological Sciences (IUBS, #15760).* [2019/XB2752/y/**B**]

- ♦ International Union of the Pluralist-Secular Scout-Guide Associations (no recent information)
- ♦ International Union of Police Associations (internationally oriented national body)
- ♦ International Union of Police Federations (inactive)
- ♦ International Union of Practitioners in Advertising (inactive)
- ♦ International Union of Prayer of Banneux Notre-Dame (religious order)

♦ International Union of Prehistoric and Protohistoric Sciences 15801

Union internationale des sciences préhistoriques et protohistoriques (UISPP) – Unión Internacional de Ciencias Prehistóricas y Protohistóricas – Internationaler Verein der Prähistorischen und Protohistorischen Wissenschaften – União Internacional das Ciências Pré-Históricas e Proto-Históricas

SG Dipartimento di Studi Umanistici, Università di Ferrara, Corso Ercole I d'Este 32, 44121 Ferrara FE, Italy. T. +39532293736. E-mail: rzrmrt@unife.it.
URL: http://www.uispp.org/

History 27 May 1931, Bern (Switzerland). Founded as a successor to *Congrès international d'anthropologie et d'archéologie préhistoriques (CIAPP, inactive)* which had existed since Sep 1985 – when referred to as *'Congrès paléoethnologique international (CPI)'* – but which ceased functioning with the onset of World War I. Current name adopted Lund (Sweden). Present Constitution adopted by the Permanent Council, 25-30 Aug 1958, Hamburg (Germany FR), and amended by Permanent Council meetings: 11 Sep 1964, Saragossa (Spain); 30 Sep 1974, Ferrara (Italy); 21 May 1979, Zeist (Netherlands); 4 Sep 1989, Dublin (Ireland); 6 Sep 2011 at General Assembly, Florianópolis (Brazil). Former names and other names: *International Congress of Prehistoric and Protohistoric Sciences* – former (27 May 1931 to 8 Jul 1956); *Congrès international de sciences préhistoriques et protohistoriques (CISPP)* – former (27 May 1931 to 8 Jul 1956). **Aims** Unite all sciences related to prehistoric and protohistoric studies. **Structure** General Assembly (every 3 years, at Congress); Board; Executive Committee; Scientific Commissions (30). Membership open; meetings closed. **Languages** English, French. **Staff** Voluntary. **Finance** Sources: meeting proceeds; members' dues. Scientific commissions carry out activities with autonomous budgets. **Activities** Events/meetings; projects/programmes; publishing activities; research/documentation. **Events** *Evolution of the Human Societies of Prehistory to Protohistory* Meknès (Morocco) 2021, *Conference* Ferrara (Italy) 2020, *Adaptation and sustainability of prehistoric and protohistoric societies confronted to climate change* Paris (France) 2018, *Meeting* Melbourne, VIC (Australia) 2017, *Congress* Burgos (Spain) 2014. **Publications** *UISPP Journal*. *Corpus de l'ambre ancien*; *Encyclopédie berbère*; *Fiches Travail de l'Os Préhistorique*; *Inventaria Archaeologica*; *Prähistorische Bronzefunde*; *Sidérurgie ancienne*. Congress proceedings; proceedings of commission symposia. **Members** Individual; Affiliated. Members from over 100 countries. Membership countries not specified. **IGO Relations** *Council of Europe (CE, #04881)* (Cultural Heritage Division); *UNESCO (#20322)*. **NGO Relations** Member of: *International Council for Philosophy and Human Sciences (CIPSH, #13061).* [2021/XB2755/y/**B**]

- ♦ International Union of Press Associations (inactive)
- ♦ International Union for Preventing the Spreading of Phylloxera (inactive)
- ♦ International Union of Private Hospitals (no recent information)
- ♦ International Union of Private Law (inactive)
- ♦ International Union of Private Railway Wagon Owners' Associations / see International Union of Wagon Keepers (#15827)
- ♦ International Union of Private Sanatoria (inactive)
- ♦ International Union of Private Wagons / see International Union of Wagon Keepers (#15827)

♦ International Union of Professional Drivers 15802

Union internationale des chauffeurs routiers (UICR) – Unión Internacional de Conductores por Carreteras – Internationale Union der Berufskraftfahrer

Contact Liebhartsgasse 53, 1160 Vienna, Austria. T. +436642023470. E-mail: info@uicr.org.
URL: http://www.uicr.org/

History Founded 12 Dec 1951, Madrid (Spain). Structure modified to present form, 7 Apr 1968, Paris (France). Previously referred to in English as *International Union of Drivers of Long-Distance Lorries and Similar Vehicles* and as *International Union of Lorry Drivers*. Registered in Munich (Germany). **Aims** Unite national associations of professional drivers so as to allow them representation in deliberations affecting further growth of the private car and commercial traffic in harmony with society and ecology through reduction in accidents and increased environmental awareness; represent rights of professional drivers with national and international institutions; improve traffic education so as to improve road safety in general and the image of professional drivers in particular; cooperate in matters related to road haulage, especially with regard to harmonization within EU states. **Structure** General Assembly (every 2 years, in a different country by rotation); Board; Presidency; Technical and Legal Committees. Disputes are settled by a Court of Arbitration. **Languages** English, French, German. **Staff** Voluntary. **Finance** Members' dues. **Activities** Awards/prizes/competitions; training/education; advocacy/lobbying/activism. **Events** *General Assembly* Zagreb (Croatia) 2019, *General Assembly* Zolder (Belgium) 2017, *General Assembly* Split (Croatia) 2011, *General Assembly* Eernewoude (Netherlands) 2009, *General Assembly* Martigny (Switzerland) 2007. **Publications** *UICR Newsletter*. Assembly reports and communiques – published in national journals.

Members Trade unions and driver-safety organizations (19), totalling over 1.2 million members, mainly in Western Europe but in total in 33 countries:

Austria, Belgium, Canada, Croatia, Czechia, Denmark, Estonia, Finland, France, Germany, Greece, Hungary, Iceland, Ireland, Israel, Italy, Liechtenstein, Luxembourg, Netherlands, Norway, Poland, Portugal, Romania, Slovakia, Slovenia, South Africa, Spain, Sweden, Switzerland, Türkiye, UK, Uruguay, Zimbabwe. [2016.11.10/XD2713/t/**D**]

♦ International Union of Professional Engineers 15803

Union Internationale des Ingénieurs Professionnels (UIDIP)

Pres Friedrich-Ebert Strasse 22, 42781 Haan, Germany. T. +4921298932. Fax +492129341747. E-mail: eit_uidip@web.de.

Vice-Pres Schöller Werke Deutschland, Im Kirschseiffen, 53940 Hellenthal, Germany. T. +49248281166.

Registered Seat 127 rue Amelot, 75011 Paris, France.

History 3 Jul 1953. Registered according to French law, 1 Dec 1954. Current statutes adopted 1990. New objectives adopted 22 Dec 2008. **Aims** Promote relations between engineers and international exchanges; further training in the field. **Structure** General Assembly (annual); Council/Bureau; European Register of Professional Engineers (set up 1987). **Languages** German. **Finance** Members' dues. **Events** *General Assembly* Hannover (Germany) 1999, *General Assembly* Paris (France) 1998, *General Assembly* Neustadt (Germany) 1997, *General Assembly* Luxembourg (Luxembourg) 1996, *General Assembly* Brussels (Belgium) 1995. **Members** Societies of professional engineers. Membership countries not specified. **NGO Relations** *Conservatoire européen de l'ingénierie et des sciences appliquées (no recent information)* (set up 1990, as a division of UIDIP although now independent); *Union des organisations internationales non-gouvernementales établies en France (UOIF, inactive)*. [2016.09.01/XD0677/t/**D**]

♦ International Union of Professors and Lecturers in Technical and Scientific Universities and in Post-Graduate Institutes for Technical and Scientific Studies (inactive)

♦ International Union for the Promotion of Work (inactive)

♦ International Union of Property Owners 15804

Union internationale de la propriété immobilière (UIPI) – Unión Internacional de la Propiedad Urbana – Internationaler Verein des Haus und Grundbesitzer – Unione Internazionale de la Proprietà Immobiliaria

SG Bd de l'Empereur 24, 1000 Brussels, Belgium. T. +3225022318. E-mail: office@uipi.com – mail@uipi.com.

Pres address not obtained.

URL: http://www.uipi.com/

History 1923, Paris (France). *Congrès international de la propriété immobilière* organized before foundation: 1900, Paris (France), and 5-8 May 1912, Berlin (Germany). Officially established 1923, following First World War. Activities interrupted during Second World War; reconstructed 1948. Statutes modified: 1978, Torremolinos (Spain); 26 Sep 1990, Brussels (Belgium). Current statutes adopted May 2006, London (UK). Former names and other names: *International Union of Landed Property Owners* – former; *Union internationale de la propriété foncière bâtie (UIPFB)* – former (1923). Registration: Banque Carrefour des Entreprises, No/ID: 0882.810.955, Start date: 1 Aug 2006, Belgium; EU Transparency Register, No/ID: 57946843667-42, Start date: 25 May 2010. **Aims** Protect and promote the interests, needs and concerns of home owners and landlords at national, European and international levels. **Structure** General Assembly; Executive Committee; Headquarters in Brussels (Belgium). Officers: President; Elected General Secretary; Secretariat. **Languages** English, French. **Staff** 4.00 FTE, paid. **Finance** Sources: members' dues; revenue from activities/projects. **Activities** Guidance/assistance/consulting; knowledge management/information dissemination. **Events** *Boosting Energy Communities in the EU* Brussels (Belgium) 2022, *UIPI Renovation Tour – Basque Owners on Board* Bilbao (Spain) 2021, *Board meeting* Brussels (Belgium) 2021, *UIPI Renovation Tour – Hungarian Owners on Board* Budapest (Hungary) 2021, *UIPI Renovation Tour – Wallonie Owners on Board* Liège (Belgium) 2021. **Publications** *UIPI Book* (every 2 years) – on occasion of international Congress, presents the work of UIPI.

Members National associations in 28 countries:

Albania, Austria, Belgium, Bulgaria, Croatia, Cyprus, Czechia, Denmark, Estonia, Finland, France, Germany, Greece, Hungary, Ireland, Italy, Monaco, Netherlands, Norway, Poland, Portugal, Serbia, Slovakia, Slovenia, Spain, Sweden, Switzerland, UK.

IGO Relations Cooperates with (3): *European Commission (EC, #06633)* (Sustainable Energy Europe Campaign); *European Economic and Social Committee (EESC, #06963)*; *European Parliament (EP, #08146)* (URBAN and Water Intergroups). **NGO Relations** Member of (3): *Construction 2050 Alliance (#04760)*; *European Housing Forum (EHF, #07504)*; *International Property Measurement Standards Coalition (IPMSC, #14656)*. [2021.09.01/XC2731/**C**]

♦ International Union for the Protection of Industrial Property (Paris Union) 15805

Union internationale pour la protection de la propriété industrielle (Union de Paris) – Unión Internacional para la Protección de la Propiedad Industrial (Unión de Paris)

Dir Gen WIPO, Chemin des Colombettes 34, 1211 Geneva 20, Switzerland. T. +41223389111. Fax +41227335428.

URL: http://www.wipo.int/treaties/en/ip/paris/index.html

History 20 Mar 1883, Paris (France). Established by *Paris Convention for the Protection of Industrial Property, 1883 (1883)*, revised: Brussels (Belgium) 4 Dec 1900; Washington DC (USA) 2 Jun 1911; The Hague (Netherlands) 6 Nov 1925; 2 Jun London (UK) 1934; Lisbon (Portugal) 31 Oct 1958; Stockholm (Sweden) 14 Jul 1967. Amended 1979. Both the Paris Union and its Convention come within the framework of *World Intellectual Property Organization (WIPO, #21593)*. The Convention provides for all or any of the member States to conclude separate, special agreements on particular aspects of industrial property. These are:

- (1) *Madrid Agreement for the Repression of False or Deceptive Indications of Source on Goods, 1891 (Madrid Agreement, 1891)*, concluded 14 Apr 1891, Madrid (Spain); revised Washington DC 1911, The Hague 1925, London 1934, Lisbon 1958, and complemented by the additional act of Stockholm 1967;
- (2) *Madrid Agreement Concerning the International Registration of Marks, 1891 (1891)*, concluded 14 Apr 1891, revised 1900 Brussels, 1911 Washington DC and 1925 The Hague – *Revision of Agreement of Madrid of 14 Apr 1891 Concerning International Registration of Commercial and Industrial Trade Marks (1911)*, 1934 London, 1957 Nice, 1967 Stockholm and amended 1979;
- (3) *Protocol to the Madrid Agreement Concerning the International Registration of Marks (1989)*, adopted 27 Jun 1989, amended 2006 and 2007;
- (4) *The Hague Agreement Concerning the International Deposit of Industrial Designs (1925)*, concluded 6 Nov 1925; revised 1934, London; 1960, The Hague 1960; and completed by *Additional Act to the 1925 Agreement Concerning the International Deposit of Industrial Designs (1961)*, signed 1961, Monaco, by *Complementary Act to the 1925 Hague Agreement Concerning the International Deposit of Industrial Design (1967)*, signed 1967, Stockholm, amended 1979 and the Geneva Act adopted by the Diplomatic Conference, 2 Jul 1999;
- (5) *Nice Agreement Concerning the International Classification of Goods and Services for the Purposes of the Registration of Marks (1957)*, concluded 15 Jun 1957; revised 1967 Stockholm, 1977 Geneva, and amended 1979;
- (6) *Lisbon Agreement for the Protection of Appellations of Origin and Their International Registration (Lisbon Agreement, 1958)*, signed 31 Oct 1958; revised 1967, Stockholm, and amended 1979;
- (7) *Locarno Agreement Establishing an International Classification for Industrial Design (1968)*, concluded 8 Oct 1968, and amended 1979;
- (8) *Patent Cooperation Treaty (PCT, 1970)*, signed 19 Jun 1970, amended 1979, modified 1984 and 2001;
- (9) *Strasbourg Agreement Concerning the International Patent Classification (IPC Agreement, 1971)*, signed 24 Mar 1971, and amended 1979;
- (10) *Vienna Agreement Establishing an International Classification of the Figurative Elements of Marks (Vienna Agreement, 1973)*, concluded 12 Jun 1973, amended 9 Aug 1985;
- (11) *Vienna Agreement for the Protection of Type Faces and Their International Deposit (Vienna Agreement, 1973)*, concluded 12 Jun 1973, not yet in force;
- (12) *Budapest Treaty on the International Recognition of the Deposit of Microorganisms for the Purposes of Patent Procedure (Budapest Treaty of 1977, 1977)*, in force 19 Aug 1980, amended 1980;
- (13) *Geneva Treaty on the International Recording of Scientific Discoveries (Geneva Treaty, 1978)*, not yet in force;
- (14) *Nairobi Treaty on the Protection of the Olympic Symbol (Nairobi Treaty, 1981)*, in force 25 Sep 1982.
- (15) *Trademark Law Treaty (TLT, 1994)*, adopted 27 Oct 1994;
- (16) *Patent Law Treaty (PLT, 2000)*, adopted 1 Jun 2000;
- (17) *Singapore Treaty on the Law of Trademarks (Singapore Treaty, 2006)*, in force 16 Mar 2009.

Each of these treaties has its own union, these being described separately. Specialized agency of: *United Nations (UN, #20515)*.

Aims Ensure and develop the international protection of industrial property including patents, marks, industrial designs, utility models, *trade names*, geographical indications, and the repression of unfair competition. **Structure** Assembly; Executive Committee; Committees of Experts. **Languages** English, French. **Finance** Supported by: *World Intellectual Property Organization (WIPO, #21593)*. **Activities** Events/meetings; knowledge management/information dissemination. Convention applies to industrial property in the widest sense, including not only inventions, trademarks, service marks and industrial designs, but also utility models (a kind of small patent provided for by the laws of a few countries), trade names (designations under which an industrial or commercial activity is carried on), geographical indications (indications of source and appellations of origin) and the repression of unfair competition. The Paris Convention, which is the basic international treaty in the field of industrial property, establishes a system of international cooperation for the protection of industrial property. The principal elements of that system are: the establishment of the Paris Union; the principal of national treatment; a right of priority in respect of applications filed in another member State for an industrial property title (patent, utility model, trademark or industrial design); common rules concerning the protection of industrial property; the maintenance by each member State of a special industrial property service and a central office for communication to the public of information on titles of industrial property; the possibility for member States of the Paris Union to make special agreements in respect of the subject matters covered by the Paris Convention, provided that those special agreements are not incompatible with the Paris Convention. **Events** *Meeting* Madrid (Spain) 2003, *Assembly* Geneva (Switzerland) 1994, *Assembly* Geneva (Switzerland) 1993, *Assembly session* Geneva (Switzerland) 1991. **Publications** *Patent Cooperation Treaty (PCT) Gazette* (bi-weekly) in English, French; *International Designs Bulletin* (12 a year) in English, French; *Les marques internationales* (12 a year); *Industrial Property* (4 a year) in Spanish; *Les appellations d'origine. Manual of Industrial Property Convention*; *Trade Names and Acts of Unfair Competition*. Conference documents; collection of industrial property laws.

Members States party to the convention as of 14 Jan 2020 (177):

Afghanistan, Albania, Algeria, Andorra, Angola, Antigua-Barbuda, Argentina, Armenia, Australia, Austria, Azerbaijan, Bahamas, Bahrain, Bangladesh, Barbados, Belarus, Belgium, Belize, Benin, Bhutan, Bolivia, Bosnia-Herzegovina, Botswana, Brazil, Brunei Darussalam, Bulgaria, Burkina Faso, Burundi, Cambodia, Cameroon, Canada, Central African Rep, Chad, Chile, China, Colombia, Comoros, Congo Brazzaville, Congo DR, Costa Rica, Côte d'Ivoire, Croatia, Cuba, Cyprus, Czechia, Denmark, Djibouti, Dominica, Dominican Rep, Ecuador, Egypt, El Salvador, Equatorial Guinea, Estonia, Eswatini, Finland, France, Gabon, Gambia, Georgia, Germany, Ghana, Greece, Grenada, Guatemala, Guinea, Guinea-Bissau, Guyana, Haiti, Holy See, Honduras, Hungary, Iceland, India, Indonesia, Iran Islamic Rep, Iraq, Ireland, Israel, Italy, Jamaica, Japan, Jordan, Kazakhstan, Kenya, Korea DPR, Korea Rep, Kuwait, Kyrgyzstan, Laos, Latvia, Lebanon, Lesotho, Liberia, Libya, Liechtenstein, Lithuania, Luxembourg, Madagascar, Malawi, Malaysia, Mali, Malta, Mauritania, Mauritius, Mexico, Moldova, Monaco, Mongolia, Montenegro, Morocco, Mozambique, Namibia, Nepal, Netherlands, New Zealand, Nicaragua, Niger, Nigeria, North Macedonia, Norway, Oman, Pakistan, Panama, Papua New Guinea, Paraguay, Peru, Philippines, Poland, Portugal, Qatar, Romania, Russia, Rwanda, Samoa, San Marino, Sao Tomé-Principe, Saudi Arabia, Senegal, Serbia, Seychelles, Sierra Leone, Singapore, Slovakia, Slovenia, South Africa, Spain, Sri Lanka, St Kitts-Nevis, St Lucia, St Vincent-Grenadines, Sudan, Suriname, Sweden, Switzerland, Syrian AR, Tajikistan, Tanzania UR, Thailand, Togo, Tonga, Trinidad-Tobago, Tunisia, Türkiye, Turkmenistan, Uganda, UK, Ukraine, United Arab Emirates, Uruguay, USA, Uzbekistan, Venezuela, Vietnam, Yemen, Zambia, Zimbabwe.

IGO Relations Working Agreements with: *Council of Europe (CE, #04881)*; *ECOSOC (#05331)*; *International Olive Council (IOC, #14405)*; *International Organisation of Vine and Wine (OIV, #14435)*; *OAS (#17629)*; *WHO (#20950)*. [2021.05.03/XF2669/t/**F***]

♦ International Union for the Protection of Literary and Artistic Works (Bern Union) 15806

Union internationale pour la protection des oeuvres littéraires et artistiques (Union de Berne) – Unión Internacional para la Protección de las Obras Literarias y Artisticas (Unión de Berna)

Dir Gen WIPO, Chemin des Colombettes 34, 1211 Geneva 20, Switzerland. T. +41223389111. Fax +41227335428.

URL: http://www.wipo.int/treaties/en/ip/berne/index.html

History 9 Sep 1886, Bern (Switzerland). Established by *Bern Convention for the Protection of Literary and Artistic Works, 1886 (1886)*, completed 1896, Paris (France), and revised: 1908, Berlin (Germany); 1914, Bern; 1928, Rome (Italy); 1948, Brussels (Belgium); 1967, Stockholm (Sweden); 1971, Paris. Amended 1979. Neighbouring Rights: *Intergovernmental Committee of the International Convention of Rome for the Protection of Performers, Producers of Phonograms and Broadcasting Organizations (#11474)*, 26 Oct 1961, Rome; *International Convention for the Protection of Performers, Producers of Phonograms and Broadcasting Organizations (Rome Convention, 1961)*, 26 Oct 1961, Rome; *Convention for the Protection of Producers of Phonograms Against Unauthorized Duplication of Their Phonograms (Geneva Convention, 1971)*, 29 Oct 1971, Geneva (Switzerland); *Convention Relating to the Distribution of Programme-carrying Signals Transmitted by Satellite (Brussels Convention, 1974)*, 21 May 1974, Brussels. The Bern Union is currently a Union within *World Intellectual Property Organization (WIPO, #21593)*. **Aims** Give creators the right to control and receive payment for their creative works on an international level. **Structure** Assembly; Executive Committee; Committees of Experts. **Languages** English, French. **Finance** Supported by: *World Intellectual Property Organization (WIPO, #21593)*. **Activities** Events/meetings; knowledge management/information dissemination; research/documentation. **Publications** *Collective Management of Copyright and Related Rights*; *Copyright Collective Management in Music*; *From Artist to Audience*; *From Script to Screen*; *Glossary of Copyright and Related Rights Terms*; *Guide to the Bern Convention for the Protection of Literary and Artistic Works (Paris Act, 1971)*; *Guide to the Copyright and Related Rights Treaties Administered by WIPO*; *Guide to the Rome Convention and to the Phonograms Convention*; *How to Make a Living from Music*; *Managing Intellectual Property in the Advertising Industry*; *Managing Intellectual Property in the Book Publishing Industry*; *Mastering the Game: Business and Legal Issues for Video Game Developers*.

Members Convention is open to all states; as of 3 March 2021, 178 states were party to the Convention:

Afghanistan, Albania, Algeria, Andorra, Antigua-Barbuda, Argentina, Armenia, Australia, Austria, Azerbaijan, Bahamas, Bahrain, Bangladesh, Barbados, Belarus, Belgium, Belize, Benin, Bhutan, Bolivia, Bosnia-Herzegovina, Botswana, Brazil, Brunei Darussalam, Bulgaria, Burkina Faso, Burundi, Cameroon, Canada, Cape Verde, Central African Rep, Chad, Chile, China, Colombia, Comoros, Congo Brazzaville, Congo DR, Costa Rica, Côte d'Ivoire, Croatia, Cuba, Cyprus, Czechia, Denmark, Djibouti, Dominica, Dominican Rep, Ecuador, Egypt, El Salvador, Equatorial Guinea, Estonia, Eswatini, Fiji, Finland, France, Gabon, Gambia, Georgia, Germany, Ghana, Greece, Grenada, Guatemala, Guinea, Guinea-Bissau, Guyana, Haiti, Holy See, Honduras, Hungary, Iceland, India, Indonesia, Ireland, Israel, Italy, Jamaica, Japan, Jordan, Kazakhstan, Kenya, Kiribati, Korea DPR, Korea Rep, Kuwait, Kyrgyzstan, Laos, Latvia, Lebanon, Lesotho, Liberia, Libya, Liechtenstein, Lithuania, Luxembourg, Madagascar, Malawi, Malaysia, Mali, Malta, Mauritania, Mauritius, Mexico, Micronesia FS, Moldova, Monaco, Mongolia, Montenegro, Morocco, Mozambique, Namibia, Nauru, Nepal, Netherlands, New Zealand, Nicaragua, Niger, Nigeria, Niue, North Macedonia, Norway, Oman, Pakistan, Panama, Paraguay, Peru, Philippines, Poland, Portugal, Qatar, Romania, Russia, Rwanda, Samoa, San Marino, Sao Tomé-Principe, Saudi Arabia, Senegal, Serbia, Singapore, Slovakia, Slovenia, Solomon Is, South Africa, Spain, Sri Lanka, St Kitts-Nevis, St Lucia, St Vincent-Grenadines, Sudan, Suriname, Sweden, Switzerland, Syrian AR, Tajikistan, Tanzania UR, Thailand, Togo, Tonga, Trinidad-Tobago, Tunisia, Türkiye, Turkmenistan, Tuvalu, UK, Ukraine, United Arab Emirates, Uruguay, USA, Uzbekistan, Vanuatu, Venezuela, Vietnam, Yemen, Zambia, Zimbabwe.

States party to the Convention but not members of the Assembly (3):

Lebanon, Madagascar, New Zealand.

Affiliate Members, including one organization listed in this Yearbook:

Islamic Corporation for the Insurance of Investment and Export Credit (ICIEC, #16041).

IGO Relations Working Agreements with: *ILO (#11123)*; *UNESCO (#20322)*; *Council of Europe (CE, #04881)*; *OAS (#17629)*. [2021.03.31/XF2670/**F***]

♦ International Union for the Protection of Nature / see International Union for Conservation of Nature and Natural Resources (#15766)
♦ International Union for the Protection of New Varieties of Plants (#20436)
♦ International Union for the Protection of Trade in War-Time (inactive)
♦ International Union for the Protection of Very Early Childhood (inactive)

♦ International Union of Psychological Science (IUPsyS) 15807

SG Entabeni Hospital, 148 Mazisi Kunene Road, 148 Mazisi Kunene Road, Durban, 4001, South Africa. T. +27312618288. E-mail: secretariat@iupsys.org – karl.swain@iupsys.org.
URL: http://www.iupsys.net/

History 15 Jul 1951, Stockholm (Sweden). Founded at 13th International Congress of Psychology, developing from International Organizing Committees of the earliest Congresses, the first *International Congress of Psychology* having been held in 1889, Paris (France). Statutes most recently modified in 2012. Former names and other names: *Comité permanent des Congrès internationaux de psychologie* – former; *Union internationale de psychologie scientifique* – former. **Aims** Develop, represent and advance psychology as a basic and applied science nationally, regionally and internationally. **Structure** General Assembly (every 2 years, at international congress); Executive Committee; Standing Committees (3). Assembly meetings open; Officer and Executive Committee meetings closed. **Languages** English. **Staff** Voluntary. **Finance** Sources: grants; members' dues; sale of publications. **Activities** Events/meetings; networking/liaising; projects/programmes. **Events** *International Congress of Psychology (ICP)* Melbourne, VIC (Australia) 2028, *International Congress of Psychology* Rio de Janeiro (Brazil) 2025, *International Congress of Psychology* Prague (Czechia) 2021, *International Congress of Psychology* Prague (Czechia) 2020, *International Congress of Psychology* Yokohama (Japan) 2016. **Publications** *International Journal of Psychology* in English – with abstracts in English/French/Spanish. Congress abstracts and proceedings; monographs; research reports; book series.
Members National organizations; regional organizations; affiliated international organizations. Membership countries not specified. **Consultative Status** Consultative status granted from: *ECOSOC (#05331)* (Special); *WHO (#20950)* (Official Relations). **IGO Relations** Associated with Department of Global Communications of the United Nations. **NGO Relations** Accredited by (7): *European Federation of Psychologists Associations (EFPA, #07199)*; *Fondation Mattei Dogan (FMD, #09826)*; *International Brain Research Organization (IBRO, #12392)*; *International School Psychology Association (ISPA, #14788)*; *International Test Commission (ITC, #15677)*; *NGO Committee on Mental Health, New York NY (#17111)*; *NGO Committee on the Family, New York NY (#17107)*. Member of (3): *International Science Council (ISC, #14796)*; *Scientific Committee on Problems of the Environment (SCOPE, #19150)*; *Standing Committee of Presidents of International NGOs Concerned with Mental Health Issues (no recent information)*. Represented in *Committee on Data for Science and Technology (CODATA, #04247)*. Represented on: *International Committee for Social Science Information and Documentation (ICSSD, no recent information).* [2022.02.09/XA2764/y/**A**]

♦ International Union for the Publication of Customs Tariffs / see International Customs Tariffs Bureau (#13124)
♦ International Union for Public Welfare (inactive)

♦ International Union for Pure and Applied Biophysics (IUPAB) 15808

Union internationale de biophysique pure et appliquée – Unión Internacional de Biofisica Pura y Aplicada – Internationale Vereinigung für Reine und Angewandte Biophysik

SG Room 517, School of Chemistry (F11), Univ of Sydney, Sydney NSW 2006, Australia.
URL: https://iupab.org/

History 2 Aug 1961, Stockholm (Sweden). Founded during International Congress of Biophysics convened on the initiative of *International Union of Pure and Applied Physics (IUPAP, #15810)*; a preliminary meeting, Jul 1960, Amsterdam (Netherlands), having set up a Steering Committee and a Constitution Committee. Former names and other names: *Organisation Internacional de Biofisica Pura y Aplicada* – former; *Internationale Vereinigung für Reine und Angewandte Biophysik* – former. Registration: France. **Aims** Organize international cooperation in biophysics; promote communication among the various branches of the subject and, within each country, cooperation among societies representing the interests of biophysics. **Structure** General Assembly (every 3 years); Council; Task Forces. **Languages** English. **Staff** 1.00 FTE, paid. **Finance** Sources: members' dues. Annual budget: 70,000 USD. **Activities** Events/meetings; research and development. **Events** *Congress* Berlin (Germany) 2027, *Congress* Kyoto (Japan) 2024, *Triennial Congress* Sao Paulo (Brazil) 2021, *Triennial Congress* Foz do Iguaçu (Brazil) 2020, *Triennial Congress* Edinburgh (UK) 2017. **Publications** *IUPAB News* (periodical); *Biophysical Review.*
Members Categories 1, 2, 3 in 39 countries and territories:
Argentina, Australia, Austria, Belgium, Brazil, Canada, China, Croatia, Czechia, Denmark, Egypt, Finland, France, Germany, Hungary, India, Israel, Italy, Japan, Netherlands, New Zealand, Norway, Poland, Portugal, Romania, Russia, Serbia, Singapore, Slovakia, Slovenia, South Africa, Spain, Sweden, Switzerland, Taiwan, Türkiye, UK, Uruguay, USA.
Included in the above, 3 organizations listed in this Yearbook:
Asian Biophysics Association (ABA, #01358); *International Society of Biorheology (ISB, #14972)*; *Latin American Federation of Biophysical Societies (LAFeBS, #16317).*
Observers in 11 countries and territories:
Armenia, Azerbaijan, Belarus, Bulgaria, Chile, Colombia, Greece, Hong Kong, Ukraine, Venezuela, Vietnam.
IGO Relations Official relations with: *WHO (#20950)*. **NGO Relations** Represented in: *Committee on Data for Science and Technology (CODATA, #04247)*. Coordinating Committees with: *Federation of European Biochemical Societies (FEBS, #09494)*; *International Union of Biochemistry and Molecular Biology (IUBMB, #15759)*; *International Union of Pure and Applied Chemistry (IUPAC, #15809)*; *Pan American Association for Biochemistry and Molecular Biology (PABMB, #18080)*. Member of: *International Science Council (ISC, #14796)*; *Scientific Committee on Problems of the Environment (SCOPE, #19150)*. Instrumental in setting up: *IUPS Commission on Comparative Physiology (see: #15800).* [2023/XC2766/y/**C**]

♦ International Union of Pure and Applied Chemistry (IUPAC) 15809

Union internationale de chimie pure et appliquée (UICPA) – Unión Internacional de Quimica Pura y Aplicada – Internationale Union für Reine und Angewandte Chemie

Exec Dir PO Box 13757, Research Triangle Park NC 27709-3757, USA. T. +19194858700. E-mail: secretariat@iupac.org.
Street Address 794 T W Alexander Drive, Building 4501, Suite 190, Research Triangle Park NC 27709, USA.
URL: http://www.iupac.org/

History 1919, Paris (France). Founded to carry on the work of *International Association of Chemistry Societies (inactive)*, set up 26 Apr 1911, London (UK). Title abbreviated to *International Union of Chemistry – Union internationale de chimie* in 1930, but the full title was resumed 1951. Statutes and Bylaws adopted by the Council 9 Sep 1975, Madrid (Spain); additions and amendments approved: 9-10 Sep 1979, Davos (Switzerland); 1-2 Sep 1981, Leuven (Belgium); 25-26 Aug 1983, Lyngby (Denmark); 6-7 Sep 1985, Lyon (France); 16-17 Aug 1989, Lund (Sweden); 14-15 Aug 1991, Hamburg (Germany); 11-12 Aug 1993, Lisbon (Portugal); 10-11 Aug 1995, Guildford (UK); 20-30 Aug 1997, Geneva (Switzerland); 13-14 Aug 1999, Berlin (Germany); 7-8 Jul 2001, Brisbane (Australia); 5-6 Aug 2009, Glasgow (UK). **Aims** Contribute to the worldwide understanding and application of chemical sciences and to the betterment of the human condition; address international issues in the chemical sciences utilizing expert volunteers from member countries; provide leadership, facilitation and encouragement of chemistry; promote norms, values, standards and ethics of science and free exchange of scientific information. **Structure** General Assembly (every 2 years, in odd years – in conjunction with Congress since 1997); Council (meets at General Assembly); Executive Committee; Bureau. Other Standing Committees (9): *Chemical Research Applied to World Needs (CHEMRAWN Committee, #03861)*; Chemistry and Industry (COCI); Chemistry Education (CCE); Publications and Cheminformatics Data Standards (CPCDS); Interdivisional Committee on Terminology, Nomenclature and Symbols (ICTNS); Evaluation; Finance; Project; Pure and Applied Chemistry Editorial Advisory Board (PAC-EAB). Sub-committees. Divisions (8): Physical and Biophysical Chemistry; Inorganic Chemistry; Organic and Biomolecular Chemistry; Polymer; Analytical Chemistry; Chemistry and the Environment; Chemistry and Human Health; Chemical Nomenclature and Structure Representation. *IUBMB-IUPAC Joint Commission on Biochemical Nomenclature (JCBN, #16078).* **Languages** English. **Staff** 5.00 FTE, paid. **Finance** Members' dues: National – according to chemical turnover; individual (affiliate) – as a portion of fees paid nationally. Grants from *UNESCO (#20322)*. **Activities** Events/meetings; knowledge management/information dissemination; networking/liaising; research/documentation. Active in over 60 countries. **Events** *MACRO : World Polymer Congress* Kuching (Malaysia) 2026, *International Biotechnology Symposium* Maastricht (Netherlands) 2024, *International Symposium on Plasma Chemistry* Kyoto (Japan) 2023, *International Conference on Chemical Thermodynamics* Osaka (Japan) 2023, *International Symposium on Organometallic Chemistry Directed Toward Organic Synthesis (OMCOS)* Vancouver, BC (Canada) 2023. **Publications** *Pure and Applied Chemistry* (12 a year) – IUPAC journal; *Chemistry International* (6 a year) – IUPAC news magazine; *Chemical Education International* – online newsletter; *Macromelecular Symposia* – journal. *IUPAC Solubility Data Series.* Books; major technical reports and recommendations; provisional recommendations; definitive volumes of chemical data and nomenclature; handbooks; conference reports.
Members National Adhering Organizations in 56 countries and territories (" including chemical society located in Taipei):
Argentina, Australia, Austria, Bangladesh, Belgium, Brazil, Bulgaria, Canada, Chile, China (*), Croatia, Cuba, Czechia, Denmark, Egypt, Finland, France, Germany, Greece, Hungary, India, Ireland, Israel, Italy, Jamaica, Japan, Jordan, Kazakhstan, Korea Rep, Kuwait, Malaysia, Nepal, Netherlands, New Zealand, Nigeria, Norway, Pakistan, Poland, Portugal, Puerto Rico, Russia, Senegal, Serbia, Slovakia, Slovenia, South Africa, Spain, Sri Lanka, Sweden, Switzerland, Thailand, Türkiye, UK, Ukraine, Uruguay, USA.
Associate National Adhering Organizations in 1 country:
Ghana.
Affiliated individuals (about 5,000) in 65 countries and territories:
Argentina, Australia, Austria, Bangladesh, Belgium, Brazil, Bulgaria, Cameroon, Canada, Chile, China, Cuba, Cyprus, Denmark, Ecuador, Egypt, Ethiopia, Finland, France, Germany, Ghana, Hong Kong, Hungary, India, Indonesia, Iran Islamic Rep, Ireland, Israel, Italy, Jamaica, Japan, Kenya, Malaysia, Mauritius, Mexico, Nepal, Netherlands, New Zealand, Nigeria, Oman, Pakistan, Panama, Philippines, Poland, Portugal, Romania, Russia, Saudi Arabia, Serbia, Sierra Leone, Singapore, Slovenia, South Africa, Spain, Sri Lanka, Sudan, Sweden, Switzerland, Taiwan, Trinidad-Tobago, Türkiye, UK, Uruguay, USA, Venezuela.
Associated Organizations (31):
- African Network of Analytical Chemists;
- *AOAC INTERNATIONAL (#00863)*;
- Chemical Heritage Foundation;
- *EURACHEM (#05595)*;
- *European Chemical Society (EuCheMS, #06524)*;
- *European Chemistry Thematic Network (ECTN, #06526)*;
- *European Federation of Chemical Engineering (EFCE, #07074)*;
- *European Federation of Corrosion (EFC, #07090)*;
- *European Photochemistry Association (EPA, #08204)*;
- *Federation of African Societies of Chemistry (FASC, #09411)*;
- *Federation of Asian Chemical Societies (FACS, #09431)*;
- *Federation of Asian Polymer Societies (FAPS, #09447)*;
- *International Association of Catalysis Societies (IACS, #11757)*;
- *International Association of Colloid and Interface Scientists (IACIS, #11788)*;
- *International Association of GeoChemistry (IAGC, #11913)*;
- *International Association on Chemical Thermodynamics (IACT, #11764)*;
- *International Board on the Applications of the Mössbauer Effect (IBAME, #12365)*;
- International Chemistry Olympiad (IChO);
- *International Committee for Imaging Science (ICIS, #12779)*;
- *International Confederation for Thermal Analysis and Calorimetry (ICTAC, #12871)*;
- *International Conference on Organometallic Chemistry (ICOMC)*;
- *International Conference on Solution Chemistry (ICSC)*;
- *International Federation of Clinical Chemistry and Laboratory Medicine (IFCC, #13392)*;
- *International Mechanochemical Association (IMA, #14126)*;
- *International Organization for Chemical Sciences in Development (IOCD, #14440)*;
- *International Organization for Crystal Growth (IOCG, #14443)*;
- *International Society of Electrochemistry (ISE, #15079)*;
- *International Society of Magnetic Resonance (ISMAR, #15240)*;
- *International Zeolite Association (IZA, #15941)*;
- *Joint IUBMB-IUPAC International Carbohydrate Organization (ICO, #16138)*;
- *Latin American Federation of Chemical Societies (#16320).*

Company Associates in 12 countries:
Belgium, Canada, China, Denmark, Germany, Hungary, Japan, Russia, Sweden, Switzerland, UK, USA.
Regional organization (1), listed in this Yearbook:
Joint Research Centre (JRC, #16147).
Consultative Status Consultative status granted from: *ECOSOC (#05331)* (Ros C); *FAO (#09260)* (Special Status). **IGO Relations** Observer status with: *Codex Alimentarius Commission (CAC, #04081)*. **NGO Relations** Member of: *Collaborative International Pesticides Analytical Council (CIPAC, #04099)*; *International Science Council (ISC, #14796)*. Represented in: *Committee on Data for Science and Technology (CODATA, #04247)*; *Committee on Space Research (COSPAR, #04287)*; *Scientific Committee on Antarctic Research (SCAR, #19147)*; *Scientific Committee on Oceanic Research (SCOR, #19149)*. Cooperates with: *International Union of Basic and Clinical Pharmacology (IUPHAR, #15758)*; *International Union of Biochemistry and Molecular Biology (IUBMB, #15759)*; *International Union of Crystallography (IUCr, #15768)*; *International Union of Food Science and Technology (IUFoST, #15773)*; *International Union of Nutritional Sciences (IUNS, #15796)*; *International Union for Pure and Applied Biophysics (IUPAB, #15808)*; *International Union of Pure and Applied Physics (IUPAP, #15810)*; *International Union of Toxicology (IUTOX, #15824)*. Instrumental in setting up: *Chemical Research Applied to World Needs (CHEMRAWN Conference).* [2020/XC2767/y/**B**]

♦ International Union of Pure and Applied Physics (IUPAP) 15810

Union internationale de physique pure et appliquée (UIPPA) – Unión Internacional de Fisica Pura y Aplicada

Secretariat Fondazione Internazionale Trieste, c/o ICTP, Strada Costiera 11, 34151 Trieste TS, Italy. T. +390406759109. E-mail: secretariat@iupap.org.
URL: http://www.iupap.org/

History 1922, Brussels (Belgium). Founded following a decision of the then *'International Research Council (IRC) – Conseil international des recherches (CIR)'*, subsequently, since 1931, *International Council for Science (ICSU, inactive)*. Statutes adopted 1931; amended: 1948, 1954, 1981, 1987, 1990, 1996, 1999, 2002, 2005, 2021. Registration: Swiss Civil Code, Switzerland. **Aims** Stimulate and promote international cooperation in physics; sponsor suitable international meetings, and assist organizing committees; foster the preparation and the publication of abstracts of papers and tables of physical constants; promote international agreements on the use of symbols, units, nomenclature and standards; foster free circulation of scientists; encourage research and education. **Structure** General Assembly (annual; in-person every 3 years); Executive Council. Internal Commissions (19). Affiliate Commissions (6) include: *International Commission for Optics (ICO, #12710)*; *International Society on General Relativity and Gravitation (ISGRG, #15138)*; *International Commission for Acoustics (ICA, #12658)*. Working Groups (15) include: *International Committee for Future Accelerators (ICFA, #12774)*; *International Committee on Ultrahigh Intensity Lasers (ICUIL, #12810)*; *Gravitational Wave International Committee (GWIC, #10697)*. **Languages** English, French. **Staff** None. **Finance** Sources: members' dues. Contributions from liaison committees in proportion to physics activity. Possible annual grant from *UNESCO (#20322)*, depending on programmes being offered. **Activities** Awards/prizes/competitions; events/meetings; research and development; research/documentation. **Events** *International Symposium on Lepton Photon Interactions at High Energies* Melbourne, VIC (Australia) 2023, *STATPHYS : International Conference on Statistical Physics* Tokyo (Japan) 2023, *INPC : Triennial International Nuclear Physics Conference* Cape Town (South Africa) 2022, *Triennial General Assembly* Geneva (Switzerland) 2022, *STATPHYS : International Conference on Statistical Physics* Yokohama (Japan) 2022. **Publications** *Cosray News* (periodical); *IUPAP News Bulletin* (about 2 a year); *Newsletter on Physics Education* (periodical). *Physics 50 Years Later* (1973) by Sanborn C Brown; *Physics 2000*; *Sunamco Document: Guide to Correct Usage of Symbols, Units and Nomenclature* – in several languages. General reports (every 3 years); reports of meetings.
Members Full and Liaison in 60 countries and territories:
Algeria, Argentina, Australia, Austria, Belgium, Brazil, Cameroon, Canada, Chile, China, Colombia, Costa Rica, Croatia, Cuba, Cyprus, Czechia, Denmark, Egypt, Estonia, Ethiopia, Finland, France, Germany, Ghana, Greece, Hungary, India, Iran Islamic Rep, Ireland, Israel, Italy, Japan, Kenya, Korea Rep, Latvia, Lithuania, Mexico, Mongolia, Netherlands, New Zealand, Norway, Peru, Philippines, Poland, Portugal, Romania, Russia, Saudi Arabia, Senegal, Singapore, Slovakia, Slovenia, South Africa, Spain, Sweden, Switzerland, Taiwan, Tunisia, UK, USA.
NGO Relations Member of (1): *International Science Council (ISC, #14796)*. Cooperates with (5): *International Electrotechnical Commission (IEC, #13255)*; *International Organization for Crystal Growth (IOCG, #14443)*; *International Union of Pure and Applied Chemistry (IUPAC, #15809)*; *Scientific Committee on Problems of the*

Environment (SCOPE, #19150); *Scientific Committee on Solar-Terrestrial Physics (SCOSTEP, #19151)*. Supports (1): *Inter-American Council on Physics Education (#11424)*. Instrumental in setting up (1): *International Union for Pure and Applied Biophysics (IUPAB, #15808)*. Represented in: *Committee on Data for Science and Technology (CODATA, #04247)*; *Committee on Space Research (COSPAR, #04287)*; *International Union of Theoretical and Applied Mechanics (IUTAM, #15823)*. In liaison with technical committees of: *International Organization for Standardization (ISO, #14473)*. [2022.06.15/XC2768/**C**]

♦ International Union for Quaternary Research (INQUA) 15811

Union internationale pour l'étude du Quaternaire – Unión Internacional para el Estudio del Cuaternario – Internationale Quartärvereinigung – Mezdunarodnyj Sojuz po Izuceniju Cetverticnogo Perioda

Contact MTA-MTM-ELTE Research Group for Paleontology, Eötvös University, Pázmány Péter Stny 1/C, Budapest 1117, Hungary. E-mail: info@inqua.org.
URL: http://www.inqua.org/

History 1928, Copenhagen (Denmark). Founded by the then *International Geological Congress (IGC)*, currently *International Union of Geological Sciences (IUGS, #15777)*. Former names and other names: *International Association for the Study of the European Quaternary* – former (1928 to 1932); *Association internationale pour l'étude du quaternaire européen* – former (1928 to 1932); *International Association on Quaternary Research* – former (1932 to 1964); *Association internationale pour l'étude du quaternaire* – former (1932 to 1964). **Aims** Promote collaboration among scientists around the world by coordinating and facilitating research on all aspects of the Quaternary Era and placing particular emphasis on supporting and encouraging early career and developing country researchers. **Structure** General Assembly of Congress (every 4 years) ratifies decisions of International Council of Member Countries. Executive Committee, elected by International Council for one inter-congress period. Commissions (5): Coastal and Marine Processes; Humans and the Biosphere; Palaeoclimates; Stratigraphy and Chronology; Terrestrial Processes, Deposits and History. Venue for each Congress decided by International Council at preceding Congress. **Languages** English. **Staff** Voluntary. **Finance** Sources: members' dues. **Activities** Events/meetings. **Events** *Quadrennial Congress* Rome (Italy) 2023, *Quadrennial Congress* Dublin (Ireland) 2019, *Conference on the Impacts of Sea Level Rise* Utrecht (Netherlands) 2018, *International Workshop on Paleoseismology, Active Technoics and Archeoseismology* Blenheim (New Zealand) 2017, *PeriBaltic Working Group Symposium* Utrecht (Netherlands) 2015. **Publications** *Quaternary Perspective* (2 a year); *Quaternary International* (8 a year) – journal. Congress proceedings; guides to excursions.

Members Group membership in 48 countries and territories:
Argentina, Australia, Austria, Belarus, Belgium, Brazil, Canada, China, Colombia, Croatia, Czechia, Denmark, Egypt, Estonia, Finland, France, Georgia, Germany, Greece, Hungary, India, Indonesia, Ireland, Israel, Italy, Japan, Korea Rep, Latvia, Lithuania, Mexico, Moldova, Mozambique, Netherlands, New Zealand, Norway, Poland, Portugal, Romania, Russia, Serbia, South Africa, Spain, Sweden, Switzerland, Taiwan, UK, Ukraine, USA.
Also in Eastern and Western Africa. Membership countries not specified.
Groups applying for election in 4 countries:
Iran Islamic Rep, Slovenia, Tunisia, Venezuela.

NGO Relations Accredited by (4): *International Association of Engineering Geology and the Environment (IAEG, #11872)*; *International Geographical Union (IGU, #13713)*; *International Union of Geodesy and Geophysics (IUGG, #15776)*; *Past Global Changes (PAGES, #18257)*. Member of (3): *International Science Council (ISC, #14796)*; *Scientific Committee on Antarctic Research (SCAR, #19147)*; *Scientific Committee on Problems of the Environment (SCOPE, #19150)*. Cooperates with (1): *International Union of Soil Sciences (IUSS, #15817)* (through Commission C-6). [2021.03.25/XC2663/**C**]

♦ International Union of Radical, Liberal and Democratic Youth (inactive)
♦ International Union of Radioecologists / see International Union of Radioecology (#15812)

♦ International Union of Radioecology (IUR) 15812

Union internationale de radioécologie (UIR)

Sec IRSN-DS/Dir Centre d'Etudes de Cadarache, Bât 229 BP 3, 13115 Saint-Paul-lez-Durance, France. T. +33442199735. Fax +33442199154. E-mail: per.strand@nrpa.no – contact@iur-uir.org.
Gen Sec address not obtained.
URL: http://www.iur-uir.org/

History Mar 1978, Oupeye (Belgium), as *International Union of Radioecologists (IUR) – Union internationale des radioécologistes (UIR)*. Most recent statutes adopted 2007. Registered in accordance with Belgian law. **Aims** Reduce exposure of humans and other living beings to ionizing *radiation*. **Structure** General Assembly (annual); Administrative Council; Board; Permanent Secretary. **Languages** English, French. **Staff** 1.00 FTE, paid; 12.00 FTE, voluntary. **Finance** Sources: members' dues. Annual budget: 120,000 EUR. **Activities** Events/meetings; guidance/assistance/consulting; knowledge management/information dissemination; training/education. **Events** *International Conference on Radioecology and Environmental Radioactivity* Oslo (Norway) 2022, *IERR : International Conference on Impacts of Environmental Radioactivity and Advances in Radioecology* Fukushima (Japan) 2021, *International Conference on Radioecology and Environmental Radioactivity* Oslo (Norway) 2021, *International Conference on Radioecology and Environmental Radioactivity* Oslo (Norway) 2021, *International Conference on Radioecology and Environmental Radioactivity* Amsterdam (Netherlands) 2020. **Publications** *IUR Newsletter* (4 a year); *UIR Information Bulletin*. Reports of working groups and taskforces. **Information Services** *Database on Transfer Factors of Sr-90, Cs-137 and Transuranics*.

Members Active (having at least 5 years experience in the field); Adhering; Honorary. Individuals (over 800) in 101 countries and territories:
Algeria, Argentina, Australia, Austria, Azerbaijan, Bangladesh, Belarus, Belgium, Bosnia-Herzegovina, Brazil, Bulgaria, Cambodia, Cameroon, Canada, Chile, China, Colombia, Croatia, Cuba, Cyprus, Czechia, Denmark, Dominica, Egypt, Estonia, Ethiopia, Finland, France, Gabon, Georgia, Germany, Ghana, Greece, Hong Kong, Hungary, Iceland, India, Indonesia, Iran Islamic Rep, Ireland, Israel, Italy, Jamaica, Japan, Jordan, Kazakhstan, Kenya, Korea DPR, Korea Rep, Kuwait, Kyrgyzstan, Latvia, Lebanon, Libya, Liechtenstein, Lithuania, Luxembourg, Madagascar, Mali, Malta, Marshall Is, Mauritania, Mexico, Monaco, Morocco, Netherlands, New Zealand, Niger, North Macedonia, Norway, Pakistan, Palestine, Philippines, Poland, Portugal, Romania, Russia, Rwanda, Saudi Arabia, Senegal, Serbia, Singapore, Slovakia, Slovenia, South Africa, Spain, Sri Lanka, Sweden, Switzerland, Syrian AR, Taiwan, Tajikistan, Thailand, Tunisia, Türkiye, UK, Ukraine, United Arab Emirates, USA, Venezuela, Vietnam.

IGO Relations Cooperating member of: *Arctic Monitoring and Assessment Programme (AMAP, #01100)*. Affiliated with: *International Atomic Energy Agency (IAEA, #12294)*. **NGO Relations** Joint meeting with: *European Society for New Methods in Agricultural Research (ESNA, #08666)*. [2017.11.22/XD7418/v/**C**]

♦ International Union of Radiologists (unconfirmed)
♦ International Union of Radio Science (#20475)
♦ International Union of Railway Medical Services (#20437)
♦ International Union of Railway Press (#20434)

♦ International Union of Railways 15813

Union internationale des chemins de fer (UIC) – Internationaler Eisenbahnverband

Dir-Gen 16 rue Jean Rey, 75015 Paris, France. T. +33144492020. Fax +33144492029. E-mail: info@uic.org.
URL: http://www.uic.org/

History 20 Oct 1922, Paris (France). Established following intergovernmental conferences, 23 Nov 1921, Portorose (Yugoslavia), and 3 May 1922, Genoa (Italy). On 16 Oct 1979, Paris, took over activities of *International Wagon Union (RIV, inactive)*, set up 25 Apr 1921, Stresa (Italy). Current Statutes approved by General Assembly, 2009. Registration: France. **Aims** Promote rail transport globally with the objective of responding effectively to current and future challenges relating to mobility and sustainable development; develop and facilitate all forms of international cooperation among members and promote sharing of best practice; promote interoperability and develop and publish solutions to railway system related issues (IRSs); support members in their efforts to develop new business and areas of activity; propose new ways to improve the technical and environmental performance of rail transport, increase competitiveness and reduce costs. **Structure** General Assembly (2 a year); Executive Board of 21 CEOs, with geographical representation of 6 regions. UIC Regional Assemblies (Europe, Asia, Africa, Middle East, North America, Latin America). Headquarters in Paris (France). Special groups include: *Union internationale des services médicaux des chemins de fer (UIMC, #20437)*. **Languages** English, French, German. **Staff** 135.00 FTE, paid. **Finance** Expenses shared by members in proportion to votes in General Assembly. **Activities** Events/meetings; guidance/assistance/consulting; knowledge management/information dissemination; networking/liaising; research and development; standards/guidelines. **Events** *Global Security Congress* Jaipur (India) 2023, *HIGHSPEED : World Congress on High Speed Rail* Marrakech (Morocco) 2023, *Asset Management Conference* Paris (France) 2023, *Future Railway Mobile Communication System Conference* Paris (France) 2023, *World Congress on Rail Training* Paris (France) 2022. **Publications** *UIC e-News* (weekly); *International Railway Statistics* (annual). *UIC Code* – over 700 technical leaflets regularly updated. *RailLexic: International Railway Terminology* (2011) – CD-ROM in 22 languages. Technical and research reports; policy papers; manuals; pamphlets; documentary studies. **Consultative Status** Consultative status granted from: *ECOSOC (#05331)* (Special); *UNCTAD (#20285)* (Special Category).

IGO Relations United Nations and UN institutions:
- *ILO (#11123)*;
- *International Bank for Reconstruction and Development (IBRD, #12317)* (World Bank);
- *United Nations Committee of Experts on the Transport of Dangerous Goods and on the Globally Harmonized System of Classification and Labelling of Chemicals (Committee of Experts on TDG and GHS, #20543)*;
- *United Nations Economic Commission for Africa (ECA, #20554)*;
- *United Nations Economic Commission for Europe (UNECE, #20555)* (Working Party on Facilitation of International Trade Procedures);
- *United Nations Economic Commission for Latin America and the Caribbean (ECLAC, #20556)*;
- *United Nations Economic and Social Commission for Asia and the Pacific (ESCAP, #20557)*;
- *United Nations Economic and Social Commission for Western Asia (ESCWA, #20558)*.

Other intergovernmental organizations:
- *Asian Development Bank (ADB, #01422)*;
- *Conference of General Directors of OSJD Railways (see: #17803)*;
- *Council of Europe (CE, #04881)*;
- *Council of the European Union (#04895)*;
- *European Bank for Reconstruction and Development (EBRD, #06315)*;
- *European Commission (EC, #06633)*;
- *European Investment Bank (EIB, #07599)*;
- *European Union Agency for Railways (#08973)*;
- *European Youth Foundation (EYF, #09141)*;
- *Organisation intergouvernementale pour les transports internationaux ferroviaires (OTIF, #17807)*;
- *International Institute for the Unification of Private Law (UNIDROIT, #13934)*;
- *International Telecommunication Union (ITU, #15673)*;
- *International Transport Forum (ITF, #15725)*;
- *OECD (#17693)*;
- *Organisation for Cooperation between Railways (OSJD, #17803)*;
- *Phare Programme (inactive)*;
- *Railway Transport Committee of the Maghreb (#18609)*;
- *Southern African Transport and Communications Commission (SATCC, no recent information)*;
- *Statistical Office of the European Union (Eurostat, #19974)*;
- *Trans-European Railway Project (TER, #20210)*;
- *Union of African Railways (UAR, #20347)*;
- *World Customs Organization (WCO, #21350)*;
- *World Tourism Organization (UNWTO, #21861)*.

Accredited by: *United Nations Framework Convention on Climate Change – Secretariat (UNFCCC, #20564)*. Invited to attend the meetings of: *International Civil Aviation Organization (ICAO, #12581)*.
NGO Relations Member of (1): *Rail Forum Europe (RFE, #18607)* (Associate). Cooperates with (4): *Association of the European Rail Supply Industry (UNIFE, #02536)*; *Collaboration des services de police ferroviaire et de sécurité (COLPOFER, #04096)*; *European Rail Infrastructure Managers (EIM, #08324)*; *International Association of Public Transport (#12118)*. Instrumental in setting up (3): *European Rail Research Advisory Council (ERRAC, #08325)*; *HIT Rail (#10933)*; *International Railway Strategic Management Institute (IRSMI)*. Railway organizations linked to UIC by the 1951 Agreement: *Comité international des transports ferroviaires (CIT, #04188)*; *Forum Train Europe (FTE, #09930)*. In liaison with technical committees of: *International Organization for Standardization (ISO, #14473)*. Cooperation agreement with: *European Committee for Electrotechnical Standardization (CENELEC, #06647)*.
Other railway and professional organizations:
- *Bureau international des containers et du transport intermodal (BIC, #03364)*;
- *European Travel Commission (ETC, #08943)*;
- *Fédération internationale des associations de transitaires et assimilés (FIATA, #09610)*;
- *International Air Transport Association (IATA, #11614)*;
- *International Association of Tariff-Specialists – Organization of Tariff and Transport Experts (#12219)*;
- *International Chamber of Commerce (ICC, #12534)*;
- *International Road Transport Union (IRU, #14761)*;
- *International Union for Combined Road – Rail Transport (UIRR, #15765)*;
- *International Union of Wagon Keepers (#15827)*;
- *United Federation of Travel Agents' Associations (UFTAA, #20509)*. [2023.02.15/XB2772/**B**]

♦ International Union of Registered Nurses (inactive)
♦ International Union of Religious Socialists / see International League of Religious Socialists (#14022)
♦ International Union for Research of Communication (inactive)
♦ International Union of Resistance and Deportee Movements (no recent information)
♦ International Union of Revolutionary Writers (inactive)
♦ International Union for the Roerich Pact (inactive)
♦ International Union of Romani / see International Romani Union (#14765)
♦ International Union of Roofing and Plumbing Contractors (inactive)
♦ International Union for the Scientific Investigation of Population Problems / see International Union for the Scientific Study of Population (#15814)
♦ International Union for the Scientific Press (inactive)
♦ International Union of Scientific Radiotelegraphy / see Union radio-scientifique internationale (#20475)

♦ International Union for the Scientific Study of Population (IUSSP) . . 15814

Union internationale pour l'étude scientifique de la population (UIESP) – Unión Internacional para el Estudio Científico de la Población (UIECP)

Exec Dir Campus Condorcet, 9 cours des Humanités, CS 50004, 93322 Aubervilliers cedex, France. T. +33156062173. Fax +33156062204. E-mail: contact@iussp.org.
Pres Dépt de Démographie, Univ de Montréal, CP 6128, Succ Centre-ville, Montréal QC H3C 3J7, Canada. T. +15143436111 ext 1972. Fax +15143432309.
URL: http://www.iussp.org/

History Jul 1928, Paris (France). Restructured Sep 1947, Washington DC (USA). Constitution adopted 8 Sep 1969, London (UK); amended: 30 Aug 1973, Liège (Belgium); Jun 1985, Florence (Italy); Sep 1989, Delhi (India); Aug 1993, Montréal (Canada); Oct 1997, Beijing (China); Jul 2005, Tours (France); Nov 2017, Cape Town (South Africa). Former names and other names: *International Union for the Scientific Investigation of Population Problems* – former (Jul 1928 to Sep 1947); *Union internationale pour l'étude scientifique des problèmes de la population* – former (Jul 1928 to Sep 1947). **Aims** Promote the scientific study of population, encourage exchange between researchers and stimulate interest in population issues. **Structure** General Assembly (every 4 years at General Conference); Council (serving 4-year terms); Committees (2); Scientific Panels (15); Secretariat, located in Paris (France). **Languages** English, French. **Staff** 4.00 FTE, paid. **Finance** Sources: contributions; government support; international organizations; members' dues; sale of publications. Supported by: *United Nations Population Fund (UNFPA, #20612)*. **Activities** Events/meetings; training/education. **Events** *International Population Conference* Hyderabad (India) 2021, *International Symposium on Lifespan Extension with Varying Cause-of-Death Trajectories in European Societies* Ebsdorfergrund (Germany) 2019, *Research workshop on Digital Demography in the Era of Big Data* Seville (Spain) 2019, *Workshop on Uncertainty and Complexity of Migration* London (UK) 2018, *Seminar on Incidence and Safety of Abortion* Watamu (Kenya) 2018. **Publications** *N-IUSSP* (weekly); *IUSSP Bulletin* (4 a year). *International Studies in Population (ISIP)* – Springer series. Working papers; conference papers; policy and research papers; guidelines; seminar reports; special issues; statements. **Members** Full (1,939); Student Associate (814). Members representing 133 nationalities in 125 countries. Membership countries not specified. **Consultative Status** Consultative status granted from: *ECOSOC (#05331)* (Special); *ILO (#11123)* (Special List); *United Nations Population Fund (UNFPA, #20612)*. **IGO Relations** Cooperates with (8): *Institut de formation et de recherche démographiques (IFORD, #11304)*; *International Bank for Reconstruction and Development (IBRD,*

#12317) (World Bank); *United Nations Economic and Social Commission for Asia and the Pacific (ESCAP, #20557)*; *United Nations Economic and Social Commission for Western Asia (ESCWA, #20558)*; *United Nations Economic Commission for Africa (ECA, #20554)*; *United Nations Economic Commission for Europe (UNECE, #20555)*; *United Nations Economic Commission for Latin America and the Caribbean (ECLAC, #20556)*; *WHO (#20950)*. Associated with Department of Global Communications of the United Nations. **NGO Relations** Member of (1): *International Science Council (ISC, #14796)*. Cooperates with (3): *European Association for Population Studies (EAPS, #06158)*; national population organizations; *Union for African Population Studies (UAPS, #20346)*. Instrumental in setting up (1): *Population Environment Research Network (PERN, #18459)*. [2021.08.30/XC2676/v/**B**]

♦ International Union of Scientific and Technical Associations and Organizations (#20421)
♦ International Union of Secondary School Students (no recent information)
♦ International Union of Shoe Industry Technicians (#20439)
♦ International Union for Slavonic Archeology (inactive)
♦ International Union of Social Democratic Teachers / see International Social Democratic Union for Education (#14881)
♦ International Union of Socialist Teetotallers (inactive)

♦ International Union of Socialist Youth (IUSY) 15815

Union internationale des jeunesses socialistes – Unión Internacional de Juventudes Socialistas

SG Amtshausgasse 4, 1050 Vienna, Austria. T. +431525231267. Fax +4315252312679. E-mail: iusy@iusy.org.
URL: http://www.iusy.org/

History 24 Aug 1907, Stuttgart (Germany). Suspended during World War I, the *International of the Socialist Youth (inactive)* was set up May 1923, Hamburg (Germany). Activities were again suspended during World War II. Re-established under its current name, 30 Sep 1946, Paris (France). Structural changes: Oct 1954, Copenhagen (Denmark); Oct 1957, Rome (Italy); Oct 1960, Vienna (Austria); Aug 1963, Oslo (Norway); Jun 1966, Vienna; Dec 1969, Rome; Jun 1973, Malta; Sep 1991, Sec (Czechoslovakia); Nov 1993, Montevideo (Uruguay). Current Statutes adopted by 21st Congress, 1995, Modena (Italy); 22nd Congress, Nov 1997, Lillehammer (Norway). Part of the general *International Youth Movement (inactive)*. Registered in accordance with Austrian law. **Aims** Propagate the principles of free and democratic socialism amongst the younger generation; further practical cooperation among democratic socialist youth and student organizations of all countries so as to strengthen international solidarity among young socialists worldwide in the fight against fascism, racism, discrimination and for the liberation of man and particularly women from all exploitation and for the right of all peoples to free and independent development, for protection of environment and for human rights. **Structure** World Congress (every 2 years); Council (meets every 2 years between Congresses); Praesidium; Working Groups (2); Regional Committees (5); Control Commission; Arbitrating Body; Membership limited to socialist youth and student organizations covering age groups 14-35. Meetings closed. **Languages** English, French, Spanish. **Staff** 3.00 FTE, paid. **Finance** Sources: members' dues. Other sources: proceeds from activities; donations, inheritance and other allocations; subventions from national, European and international institutions. **Activities** Events/meetings; networking/liaising; politics/policy/regulatory; training/education. **Events** *Biennial Congress* Panama (Panama) 2021, *Biennial Congress* Panama (Panama) 2020, *Leadership Meeting* Gaborone (Botswana) 2019, *Asia Pacific Leadership Meeting* Medan (Indonesia) 2019, *Global Seminar* Stockholm (Sweden) 2019. **Publications** *IUSY Newsletter* (4 a year) in English, Spanish; *IUSY Magazine* (annual) in English, Spanish. Congress reports; posters; stickers; leaflets.

Members Full member organizations in 90 countries and territories:
Albania, Angola, Argentina, Armenia, Austria, Belarus, Belgium, Benin, Bhutan, Bosnia-Herzegovina, Brazil, Bulgaria, Burkina Faso, Canada, Cape Verde, Chad, Chile, Colombia, Costa Rica, Croatia, Cyprus, Czechia, Denmark, Dominican Rep, Equatorial Guinea, Estonia, Eswatini, Faeroe Is, Finland, France, Georgia, Germany, Ghana, Great Britain, Greece, Greenland, Honduras, Hungary, Iceland, Indonesia, Iran Islamic Rep, Iraq, Israel, Italy, Jamaica, Japan, Latvia, Lebanon, Lithuania, Luxembourg, Malaysia, Mali, Malta, Mexico, Moldova, Mongolia, Montenegro, Morocco, Myanmar, Nepal, Netherlands, New Zealand, Niger, North Macedonia, Norway, Palestine, Panama, Paraguay, Philippines, Poland, Portugal, Romania, Sahara West, Senegal, Serbia, Slovakia, Slovenia, South Africa, Spain, Sweden, Switzerland, Tanzania UR, Togo, Tunisia, Türkiye, Uganda, Ukraine, Uruguay, USA, Venezuela.

Observer members in 21 countries and territories:
Botswana, Central African Rep, Congo Brazzaville, Cyprus, Gabon, Gambia, India, Iran Islamic Rep, Kenya, Myanmar, Namibia, Nicaragua, Northern Ireland, Serbia, Taiwan, Tibet, Timor-Leste, Türkiye, Ukraine, Venezuela, Zimbabwe.

Consultative Status Consultative status granted from: *ECOSOC (#05331)* (Special); *FAO (#09260)* (Liaison Status); *ILO (#11123)* (Special List); *UNICEF (#20332)*; *Council of Europe (CE, #04881)* (Participatory Status). **IGO Relations** Contacts with: European Union Institutions. Accredited by: *United Nations Office at Vienna (UNOV, #20604)*. Associated with Department of Global Communications of the United Nations. **NGO Relations** Member of: *Espacio Iberoamericano de Juventud (EIJ, no recent information)*; *European Youth Forum (#09140)*; *Foro Latinoamericano de Juventud (FLAJ, #09881)*; *International Campaign to Abolish Nuclear Weapons (ICAN, #12426)*; *NGO Committee on Disarmament, Peace and Security, New York NY (#17106)*; *NGO Committee on UNICEF (#17120)*; *Socialist International (SI, #19340)*; *UNITED for Intercultural Action – European Network Against Nationalism, Racism, Fascism and in Support of Migrants and Refugees (UNITED, #20511)*. Supports: *Global Call for Action Against Poverty (GCAP, #10263)*. Instrumental in setting up: *Global Progressive Youth Forum (GPYF, #10558)*. [2018.10.18/XB2778/**B**]

♦ International Union for Social Studies (inactive)

♦ International Union of Societies for Biomaterials Science and Engineering (IUSBSE) 15816

Sec CSIRO Manufacturing, Bayview Ave, Clayton VIC 3168, Australia. T. +61395452599.
Pres Natl Engineering Research Ctr for Biomaterials, Sichuan Univ, 17 Renmin S Rd 3rd Section, Chengdu, Wuhou District, 610000 Sichuan, China.
URL: http://www.worldbiomaterials.org/

History Evolved from an International Liaison Committee (ILC) of biomaterials societies. **Aims** Promote biomaterials science and engineering for application in surgical implants, prosthetics, artificial organs, tissue engineering and regenerative medicine. **Structure** Committee (meets annually). **Languages** English. **Staff** Voluntary. **Finance** No budget. **Events** *World Biomaterials Congress* Daegu (Korea Rep) 2024, *World Biomaterials Congress* 2020, *World Biomaterials Congress* Montréal, QC (Canada) 2016, *Meeting* Chengdu (China) 2012, *World Biomaterials Congress* Chengdu (China) 2012. **Publications** *World Congress Transactions* (every 4 years).

Members Biomaterials Societies (10), including the following 3 organizations listed in this Yearbook:
Australasian Society for for Biomaterials and Tissue Engineering (ASBTE); *European Society for Biomaterials (ESB, #08530)*; *Latin American Society on Biomaterials, Artificial Organs and Tissue Engineering (#16370)*. [2017.10.11/XM3856/y/**C**]

♦ International Union of Societies of Foresters (no recent information)
♦ International Union of Societies of Teachers of Dancing (inactive)

♦ International Union of Soil Sciences (IUSS) 15817

Union internationale de la science du sol (UISS) – Internationale Bodenkundliche Union (IBU)

Sec Umweltbundesamt (Environment Agency Austria), Spittelauer Laende 5, 1090 Vienna, Austria. E-mail: iuss@umweltbundesamt.at.
URL: http://www.iuss.org/

History 19 May 1924, Rome (Italy). Founded at 4th International Conference of Pedology. Reconstituted during 4th International Congress of Soil Science, 1950, Amsterdam (Netherlands). Present name adopted at World Congress, Montpellier (France), Aug 1998. Former names and other names: *International Society of Soil Sciences (ISSS)* – former (1950 to 1998); *Association internationale de la science du sol (AISS)* – former (1950 to 1998); *Sociedad Internacional de la Ciencia del Suelo (SICS)* – former (1950 to 1998); *Internationale Bodenkundliche Gesellschaft (IBG)* – former (1950 to 1998). Registration: United States Patent and Trademark Office, No/ID: 6,400,386, Start date: 21 Jun 2021, End date: 21 Jun 2031, USA. **Aims** Foster all branches of soil science and its applications; promote contacts among scientists and other persons engaged in study and application of soil science; stimulate scientific research and further application of such research for the benefit of mankind. **Structure** Officers: President; Vice-President Congress; President-Elect; Past-President; Secretary; Treasurer. Executive Committee, consisting of the four Presidents, Treasurer, Chairpersons of four Divisions and four Standing Committees; Divisions comprise Commissions (22) and Working Groups (16). **Languages** English. **Staff** 1.00 FTE, paid; 0.50 FTE, voluntary. **Finance** Sources: members' dues. **Activities** Awards/prizes/competitions; awareness raising; events/meetings; knowledge management/information dissemination; monitoring/evaluation; publishing activities; research and development; standards/guidelines. **Events** *Congress* Florence (Italy) 2024, *World Congress of Soil Science* Glasgow (UK) 2022, *International Conference on Soil Micromorphology (ICoSM)* Krakow (Poland) 2022, *WMESS : World Multidisciplinary Earth Sciences Symposium* Prague (Czechia) 2022, *International Conference on Soil Micromorphology (ICoSM)* Krakow (Poland) 2020. **Publications** *IUSS Alert* (12 a year) in English; *IUSS Bulletin* (2 a year) in English. *International Decade of Soils 2015-2024* (2015-2024) in English.

Members National Societies or National Academies of Science (or their equivalent) in 61 countries and territories:
Argentina, Australia, Austria, Bangladesh, Belgium, Bolivia, Bosnia-Herzegovina, Brazil, Bulgaria, Burkina Faso, Canada, Chile, China, Colombia, Costa Rica, Croatia, Cuba, Czechia, Denmark, Dominican Rep, Ecuador, El Salvador, Estonia, Finland, France, Georgia, Germany, Ghana, Guatemala, Honduras, Hungary, India, Indonesia, Italy, Japan, Korea Rep, Lithuania, Malaysia, Mexico, Netherlands, New Zealand, Nigeria, Norway, Pakistan, Panama, Paraguay, Peru, Poland, Portugal, Serbia, Slovakia, South Africa, Spain, Switzerland, Taiwan, Türkiye, UK, Ukraine, USA, Uzbekistan, Venezuela.

Consultative Status Consultative status granted from: *ECOSOC (#05331)* (Ros C); *FAO (#09260)* (Special Status); *World Meteorological Organization (WMO, #21649)*. **IGO Relations** Partner of: *Global Soil Partnership (GSP, #10608)*. Cooperates in related fields of interest with: *UNEP (#20299)*. Accredited to the Conference of the Parties of: *Secretariat of the United Nations Convention to Combat Desertification (Secretariat of the UNCCD, #19208)*. **NGO Relations** Scientific union member of: *Committee on Data for Science and Technology (CODATA, #04247)*; *International Union of Biological Sciences (IUBS, #15760)*. Member of: *International Science Council (ISC, #14796)*. In liaison with technical committees of: *International Organization for Standardization (ISO, #14473)*. Instrumental in setting up: *International Biochar Initiative (IBI, #12342)*. [2022.10.12/XB2568/**B**]

♦ International Union of Speleology 15818

Union internationale de spéléologie (UIS) – Internationale Union für Speläologie

SG Mednarodna speleološka zveza – UIS, Titov trg 2, 6230 Postojna, Slovenia. E-mail: secretary@uis-speleo.org.
Pres address not obtained.
URL: http://www.uis-speleo.org/

History 16 Sep 1964, Ljubljana (Slovenia). Founded during 4th *International Speleological Congress (CIS) – Congrès international de spéléologie*, the Congresses having been initiated 12 Sep 1953, Paris (France), after a preliminary meeting 1949, Valence-sur-Rhône (France). Statutes modified: 1969, Stuttgart (Germany FR); 1977, Sheffield (UK); 1981, Bowling Green KY (USA); 1997, Chaux-de-Fonds (Switzerland). **Aims** Develop relations between speleologists in all countries and coordinate their activities at the international level. **Structure** General Assembly (every 4 years); Permanent Bureau; Commissions on Karst and Cave Protection, Research, Documentation, Exploration, Education and Teaching etc. **Languages** English, French, German, Italian, Russian, Spanish. **Staff** None. **Finance** Sources: meeting proceeds; members' dues; sale of publications. **Activities** Events/meetings. **Events** *Quadrennial Congress and General Assembly* Lyon (France) 2022, *International Vulcanospeleology Symposium* Catania (Italy) 2021, *Quadrennial Congress and General Assembly* Lyon (France) 2021, *International Vulcanospeleology Symposium* Catania (Italy) 2020, *Quadrennial Congress and General Assembly* Sydney, NSW (Australia) 2017. **Publications** *UIS-Bulletin* (2 a year); *International Journal of Speleology*. *International Speleological Bibliography*. Congress and symposia proceedings; commission reports.

Members National Groups in 67 countries:
Albania, Argentina, Armenia, Australia, Austria, Belgium, Bolivia, Bosnia-Herzegovina, Brazil, Bulgaria, Canada, China, Colombia, Costa Rica, Croatia, Cuba, Czechia, Denmark, Dominican Rep, France, Germany, Greece, Honduras, Hungary, Iceland, India, Indonesia, Iran Islamic Rep, Ireland, Israel, Italy, Jamaica, Japan, Korea Rep, Lebanon, Lithuania, Luxembourg, Malaysia, Mexico, Mongolia, Namibia, Netherlands, New Zealand, North Macedonia, Norway, Pakistan, Peru, Philippines, Poland, Portugal, Puerto Rico, Romania, Russia, Serbia, Slovakia, Slovenia, South Africa, Spain, Switzerland, Tunisia, Türkiye, UK, Ukraine, USA, Uzbekistan, Venezuela, Vietnam.

IGO Relations *UNESCO (#20322)*. **NGO Relations** Affiliated member of: *International Geographical Union (IGU, #13713)*. Member of: *International Science Council (ISC, #14796)*. Instrumental in setting up: *Fédération Spéléologique Européenne (FSE, #09705)*; *Speleological Federation of Latin America and the Caribbean (#19917)*; *Balkan Speleological Union (BSU, #03087)*. Additional regional society: *Asian Federation of Speleology (AFS, #01474)*. [2022.10.12/XC2580/**C**]

♦ International Union of Steam and Operating Engineers / see International Union of Operating Engineers
♦ International Union of Students in Architecture (inactive)

♦ International Union for the Study of Social Insects (IUSSI) 15819

Union internationale pour l'étude des insectes sociaux (UIEIS) – Unión Internacional para el Estudio de los Insectos Sociales – Internationale Union zum Studium der Sozialen Insekten

SG School of Life and Environmental Sciences, Univ of Sydney, Room 239c, Macleay A12, Sydney NSW 2006, Australia.
URL: http://www.iussi.org/

History Founded 13 Jun 1952, Paris (France), following initial steps taken at Entomological Congress. **Aims** Link all scientists studying social insects and facilitate mutual exchange of scientific information. **Structure** General Assembly (every 4 years); Executive Committee. **Languages** English. **Staff** 4.00 FTE, voluntary. **Finance** Sources: grants; members' dues; sale of publications. **Events** *Quadrennial Congress* San Diego, CA (USA) 2022, *Quadrennial Congress* Guajará (Brazil) 2018, *European Meeting* Helsinki (Finland) 2016, *Quadrennial Congress* Cairns, QLD (Australia) 2014, *Quadrennial Congress* Copenhagen (Denmark) 2010. **Publications** *Insectes sociaux – Social Insects – International Journal for the Study of Social Arthropods* (4 a year). Congress and symposium proceedings.

Members National/Regional sections in 18 countries:
Australia, Austria, Belgium, Brazil, Canada, Denmark, Finland, France, Germany, India, Japan, Netherlands, New Zealand, Norway, South Africa, Sweden, UK, USA.

Also in South America and Caribbean regions (not specified).

Individuals in 43 countries and territories:
Argentina, Australia, Austria, Brazil, Canada, China, Colombia, Costa Rica, Côte d'Ivoire, Czechia, Denmark, Egypt, Finland, France, Germany, Hong Kong, Hungary, India, Ireland, Israel, Italy, Japan, Kenya, Malaysia, Mexico, Netherlands, Nigeria, Norway, Panama, Peru, Poland, Portugal, Russia, Senegal, South Africa, Spain, Sri Lanka, Sweden, Switzerland, Taiwan, UK, USA, Venezuela.

NGO Relations Member of: *International Union of Biological Sciences (IUBS, #15760)*. [2019.12.11/XD4256/**C**]

♦ International Union of Superiors General 15820

Union internationale des supérieures générales (UISG) – Unione Internazionale Superiore Generali

Address not obtained.
URL: http://www.uisg.org/

History 8 Dec 1965, Rome (Italy). **Aims** Represent Congregations of *Women Religious* throughout the world. **Structure** Plenary Assembly (every 3 years); Executive Committee; Regional Representatives. **Languages** Dutch, English, French, German, Italian, Portuguese, Spanish. **Staff** 10.00 FTE, paid. **Finance** Members' dues. Other sources: grants; donations. **Activities** Guidance/assistance/consulting; knowledge management/information dissemination; events/meetings; religious activities; projects/programmes; training/education. **Events** *General Assembly* Rome (Italy) 2016, *General Assembly* Rome (Italy) 2007, *General Assembly* Warsaw (Poland) 2005, *General Assembly* Rome (Italy) 2001, *General Assembly* Rome (Italy) 2001. **Publications** *UISG Bulletin* (3 a year) in Dutch, English, French, German, Italian, Portuguese, Spanish. Newsletters; information communiqués. **Members** Superiors General of apostolic religious institutes of women and societies of apostolic life (1,960) in over 100 countries and territories. Membership countries not specified. **NGO Relations** Represented with: *Agrimissio (no recent information)*; *Association of Advisers on Education in International Religious Congregations (EDUC International, no recent information)*; *Ecumenical Group of Women (KAIRE, #05348)*; *Service of Documentation and Studies on Global Mission (#19241)*; *World Union of Catholic Women's Organisations (WUCWO, #21876)*; Pontifical Commissions and Councils. *Missionary Sisters of Our Lady of Africa (White Sisters)* is a member. Joint commission, *Commission for Justice, Peace and Integrity of Creation*

– *USG/UISG (#04230)*, and joint consultation, *Permanent International Ecumenical Consultation of Religious (PIECR, #18326)*, with: *Union of Superiors General (#20484)*. Member of: *Religious in Europe Networking Against Trafficking and Exploitation (RENATE, #18833)*. Preparatory meetings with: *Congregation for Catholic Education – for Seminaries and Educational Institutions (CEC, #04665)*; *Congregation for the Evangelization of Peoples (CEP, #04670)*; *'Congregation for Institutes of Consecrated Life and Societies of Apostolic Life (CIVCSVA)'*; representatives of national conferences. Instrumental in setting up: *Talitha Kum – International Network against Trafficking in Persons (Talitha Kum, #20090)*. [2017.10.10/XF5934/v/**F**]

♦ International Union for Surface Finishing (IUSF) 15821

SG c/o MFAI, 202-203 Atlanta Estate, Vitbhatti, Goregaon, Mumbai, Maharashtra 400063, Mumbai MAHARASHTRA 400063, India. E-mail: relianceatotech@yahoo.com.
URL: https://www.iusf.world/

History by *International Union for Electrodeposition and Surface Finishing (no recent information)*. Former names and other names: *INTERFINISH* – former. **Structure** Council, comprising President, 2 Vice Presidents, Treasurer, Deputy Treasurer, Secretary General and Assistant Secretary General. **Events** *Interfinish World Congress* India 2028, *Interfinish World Congress* Hong Kong (Hong Kong) 2024, *Interfinish World Congress* Mumbai (India) 2021, *Quadrennial World Congress* Nagoya (Japan) 2020, *Quadrennial world congress* Beijing (China) 2016.

Members Full in 24 countries and territories:
Argentina, Australia, Austria, Belgium, Brazil, China, Denmark, Finland, France, Germany, Hong Kong, India, Israel, Italy, Japan, Korea Rep, Netherlands, Norway, Singapore, Spain, Sweden, Switzerland, UK, USA.
Included in the above, 1 organization listed in this Yearbook:
European Academy of Surface Technology (EAST, #05816). [2020/XD8838/**D**]

- ♦ International Union for Surveys and Mapping (inactive)
- ♦ International Union of Teachers of Jaques-Dalcroze / see International Federation of Eurhythmics Teachers (#13418)
- ♦ International Union of Technical Associations and Organizations / see Union internationale des associations et organismes scientifiques et techniques (#20421)
- ♦ International Union of Technical Cinematograph Associations (inactive)
- ♦ International Union for Technical and Cultural Education of Adults (inactive)

♦ International Union of Tenants (IUT) 15822

Union internationale des locataires – Internationale Mieterallianz

SG PO Box 7514, SE-103 92 Stockholm, Sweden. T. +4684591120. E-mail: info@iut.nu.
EU Liaison Office Av de Rogations 28, 1200 Brussels, Belgium. T. +3225130784.
URL: http://www.iut.nu/

History 21 May 1926, Zurich (Switzerland). Founded at 1st Congress. Secretariat set up in Vienna (Austria). Existence disrupted by political changes leading to World War II. Restarted, Jun 1955, Vienna; statutes adopted 17 Jun 1958, Stuttgart (Germany FR) and amended 1985, Sorrento (Italy) and 1988, London (UK). New statutes adopted 24 Aug 1994, Munich (Germany); updated 27 Oct 2013, Krakow (Poland)/Munich (Germany). Former names and other names: *Union of International Tenant Associations* – former; *International League of Tenants* – former. Registration: EU Transparency Register, No/ID: 94035285059-91. **Aims** Safeguard the interests of tenants and promote them in national governments, European Union and similar institutions worldwide; work to realize the right of everyone to affordable good housing and residential environment; realize residential/tenants democracy; encourage establishment of national tenants associations. **Structure** Conference (every 3 years); Board; Committees (4). **Languages** English. **Finance** Sources: members' dues. **Activities** Events/meetings; knowledge management/information dissemination; training/education. **Events** *World Conference* Lisbon (Portugal) 2023, *World Conference* Vienna (Austria) 2019, *Congress* Glasgow (UK) 2016, *Congress* Krakow (Poland) 2013, *Congress* Prague (Czech Rep) 2010. **Publications** *Brussels EU News*; *The Global Tenant*.

Members National tenants' associations in 45 countries:
Australia, Austria, Belgium, Benin, Canada, Congo DR, Côte d'Ivoire, Croatia, Czechia, Denmark, Estonia, Finland, France, Germany, Greece, Greenland, Hungary, India, Israel, Italy, Japan, Kenya, Latvia, Liberia, Nepal, Netherlands, New Zealand, Nigeria, North Macedonia, Norway, Poland, Portugal, Romania, Russia, Slovakia, Slovenia, South Africa, Spain, Sweden, Switzerland, Tanzania UR, Togo, Uganda, UK, USA.

Consultative Status Consultative status granted from: *ECOSOC (#05331)* (Ros A); *Council of Europe (CE, #04881)* (Participatory Status). **IGO Relations** Member of (1): *European Economic and Social Committee (EESC, #06963)* (Liaison Group). **NGO Relations** Member of (5): *Asia-Pacific Network for Housing Research (APNHR, #01967)*; *European Housing Forum (EHF, #07504)*; *Habitat International Coalition (HIC, #10845)*; *International Property Measurement Standards Coalition (IPMSC, #14656)*; *Social Platform (#19344)*. [2023/XD2783/**C**]

- ♦ International Union of Testing and Research Laboratories for Materials and Structures / see Réunion internationale des laboratoires d'essais et de recherches sur les matériaux et les constructions (#18930)

♦ International Union of Theoretical and Applied Mechanics (IUTAM) . 15823

Union internationale de mécanique théorique et appliquée – Unión Internacional de Mecanica Teórica y Aplicada – Internationale Union für Theoretische und Angewandte Mechanik

SG Inst of Fundamental Technological Research, Polish Ac of Sciences, Pawinskiego 5B, 02-106 Warsaw, Poland.
URL: http://www.iutam.net/

History Founded Sep 1946, Paris (France). Statutes adopted 1948; modified: 1950, 1960, 1964, 1984, 1990, 1992, 1994, 2004, 2008. **Aims** Link individuals and national or international organizations concerned with theoretical and experimental scientific work in mechanics or related sciences. **Structure** General Assembly (every 2 years). Bureau (meets annually), consisting of President, retiring President who serves as Vice-President, Secretary-General, Treasurer and 4 members. Congress Committee (meets at least once at every Congress). Meetings closed. **Languages** English, French, German. **Finance** Sources: grants; international organizations; members' dues. Supported by: *UNESCO (#20322)* (grant). **Activities** Events/meetings; training/education. **Events** *Quadrennial International Congress* Milan (Italy) 2021, *Symposium on Computational Methods for Large Scale and Complex Wave Problems* Tokyo (Japan) 2021, *Quadrennial International Congress* Milan (Italy) 2020, *Symposium on Laminar-Turbulent Transition* London (UK) 2019, *Symposium on Fluid Structure Interaction* Montréal, QC (Canada) 2019. **Publications** *IUTAM Newsletter*. Annual Report; proceedings of congresses and symposia.

Members National organizations and societies (also elected members-at-large) and individuals in 49 countries and territories:
Australia, Austria, Belgium, Brazil, Bulgaria, Canada, Chile, China, Croatia, Cyprus, Czechia, Denmark, Egypt, Estonia, Finland, France, Georgia, Germany, Greece, Hong Kong, Hungary, India, Ireland, Israel, Italy, Japan, Korea Rep, Latvia, Netherlands, New Zealand, Norway, Poland, Portugal, Romania, Russia, Saudi Arabia, Serbia, Slovakia, Slovenia, South Africa, Spain, Sweden, Switzerland, Taiwan, Türkiye, UK, Ukraine, USA, Vietnam.
Affiliated organizations (21):
- *Asian Fluid Mechanics Committee (AFMC, #01484)*;
- Beijing International Center for Theoretical and Applied Mechanics (BICTAM);
- *Centre International des Sciences Mécaniques (CISM, #03766)*;
- *EUROMECH – European Mechanics Society (#05713)*;
- *International Association for Boundary Element Methods (IABEM, #11732)*;
- *International Association for Computational Mechanics (IACM, #11800)*;
- *International Association for Hydromagnetic Phenomena and Applications (HYDROMAG, #11955)*;
- *International Association for Multibody System Dynamics (IMSD, #12037)*;
- *International Association for Structural Control and Monitoring (IASCM, #12186)*;
- *International Association for Vehicle System Dynamics (IAVSD, #12255)*;
- *International Centre for Heat and Mass Transfer (ICHMT, #12496)*;
- *International Commission for Acoustics (ICA, #12658)*;
- *International Committee on Rheology (ICR, #12802)*;
- *International Congresses on Thermal Stresses (ICTS, #12893)*;
- *International Congress on Fracture (ICF, #12894)*;
- *International Congress on Mechanical Behaviour of Materials (ICM, #12897)*;
- *International Institute of Acoustics and Vibration (IIAV, #13858)*;
- *International Society for Structural and Multidisciplinary Optimization (ISSMO, #15461)*;
- *International Society for the Interaction of Mechanics and Mathematics (ISIMM, #15208)*;
- *Latin American and Caribbean Conference on Theoretical and Applied Mechanics (LACCOTAM, #16269)*;
- *World Council for Biomechanics (WCB, #21319)*.

NGO Relations Member of: *International Science Council (ISC, #14796)*. Represented in: *Committee on Space Research (COSPAR, #04287)*; *International Union of Pure and Applied Physics (IUPAP, #15810)*; *Scientific Committee on Problems of the Environment (SCOPE, #19150)*. [2020/XC2788/y/**C**]

- ♦ International Union of Therapeutics (inactive)
- ♦ International Union for Thermal Medicine and Climatothalassotherapy (inactive)
- ♦ International Union of Tourism Managers (no recent information)

♦ International Union of Toxicology (IUTOX) 15824

Headquarters 11190 Sunrise Valley Dr, Ste 300, Reston VA 20191, USA. T. +17034383103. E-mail: iutoxhq@iutox.org.
URL: http://www.iutox.org/

History Jul 1980. **Aims** Foster international scientific cooperation among toxicologists; promote global acquisition, dissemination and utilization of toxicological knowledge; ensure continued training and development of toxicologists worldwide. **Structure** Executive Committee, comprising President, President-Elect, Vice-President, Secretary General, Treasurer, Past President and 5 members. Standing Commissions (6). **Languages** English. **Staff** 5.50 FTE, voluntary. **Finance** Sources: members' dues. **Activities** Major programmes are covered by Standing Commissions (6): Marketing and Promotion; Science; Communication; Finance; Membership and Society Development; Education and Development. Organizes: International Congress of Toxicology; Congress on Toxicology in Developing Countries. Promotes education in developing countries and in Central and Eastern European countries; promotes increase in exchange of scientific information and individuals between Western and Eastern European countries and between developing countries and Western Europe, Japan and USA; holds Risk Assessment Summer School. **Events** *Congress of Toxicology in Developing Countries* Santiago (Chile) 2024, *International Congress of Toxicology* Maastricht (Netherlands) 2022, *Congress of Toxicology in Developing Countries* Kuala Lumpur (Malaysia) 2021, *Triennial Congress* Honolulu, HI (USA) 2019, *Triennial Congress of Toxicology in Developing Countries* Belgrade (Serbia) 2018. **Publications** *IUTOX Newsletter* (annual). Congress proceedings.

Members Societies of toxicology (47) representing over 19,000 toxicologists in 32 countries and territories:
Australia, Brazil, Bulgaria, Canada, China, Croatia, Denmark, Egypt, Estonia, Finland, France, Germany, Greece, Hungary, India, Iran Islamic Rep, Ireland, Israel, Italy, Japan, Korea Rep, Latvia, Mexico, Netherlands, Norway, Poland, Russia, Slovenia, Spain, Sweden, Taiwan, Thailand, Türkiye, UK, USA.
Included in the above, 6 organizations listed in this Yearbook:
Asian Society of Toxicology (ASIATOX, #01744); *Asociación Latinoamericana de Toxicologia (ALATOX, #02274)*; *Australasian Society of Clinical and Experimental Pharmacology and Toxicology (ASCEPT)*; *European Association of Poisons Centres and Clinical Toxicologists (EAPCCT, #06155)*; *EUROTOX (#09191)*; *International Neurotoxicology Association (INA, #14359)*.

Consultative Status Consultative status granted from: *WHO (#20950)* (Official Relations). **NGO Relations** Member of: *International Science Council (ISC, #14796)*. Represented on the Committee of: EUROTOX. Collaborates with: *International Federation of Societies of Toxicologic Pathologists (IFSTP, no recent information)*. [2018/XC0385/y/**C**]

- ♦ International Union of Tramways, Local Railways and Public Motor Transport / see International Association of Public Transport (#12118)
- ♦ International Union of Transgenics / see International Union of Transgenics and Synthetic Biology (#15825)

♦ International Union of Transgenics and Synthetic Biology (IUT) 15825

SG Benjoe Inst of System Bio-Engineering, North 354 – Bldg 15, Science Tech Park, Changzhou, New District, 213022 Guangdong, China.
URL: http://www.sysbioeng.net

History 1996. Since 1999, a division of *World Associates for Biosystem Science and Engineering (WABSE)*. Former names and other names: *International Union of Transgenics (IUT)* – former (1996). **Aims** Improve research of transgenics and synthetic biology, which explores artificial biosystems with the methods of biotechnology and bio-computation; promote investigation of biosystem patterning from bio-molecules, cellular phenotypes to organic systems and development of bionic intelligence, transgenic organisms, etc for advancement of bio-medicine and bio-industrials. **Structure** Council; Chairperson; Secretary-General. **Languages** Chinese, English. **Staff** 5.00 FTE, paid. **Finance** Sources: revenue from activities/projects. Proceeds from exhibitions, training courses, bio-informatic services and conferences. **Activities** Events/meetings; knowledge management/information dissemination; training/education. **Events** *ICBSE Conference* China 2014, *ICTA Conference* Guangzhou (China) 2005, *Conference* UK 2004, *ICTA Conference* Shanghai (China) 2002, *Conference* USA 2002. **Publications** *Structurity Bulletin – Biosystem Analytics*, *Genbrain Biosystem Network*. Gallery on Bio-machine. Conference proceedings; training books.

Members Individuals in 18 countries:
Australia, Austria, Belgium, Canada, China, Denmark, France, Germany, Greece, India, Israel, Italy, Japan, Netherlands, Russia, Slovakia, UK, USA. [2020.06.18/XD7761/v/**D**]

- ♦ International Union, United Automobile, Aerospace and Agricultural Implement Workers of America (internationally oriented national body)
- ♦ International Union, United Automobile, Aircraft and Agricultural Implement Workers of America / see International Union, United Automobile, Aerospace and Agricultural Implement Workers of America
- ♦ International Union, United Welders / see International Union of Operating Engineers

♦ International Union for Vacuum Science, Technique and Applications (IUVSTA) 15826

Union internationale pour la science, la technique et les applications du vide (UISTAV) – Internationale Union für Vakuum-Forschung, -Technik und -Anwendung (IUVFTA)

SG Technische Uni Wien, Inst für Festkörperphysik – 138, Wiedner Hauptstr 8-10, 1040 Vienna, Austria. T. +4315880113774. Fax +43180113899.
URL: http://www.iuvsta.org/

History Founded 13 Jun 1958, Namur (Belgium), as *International Organization for Vacuum Science and Technology (IOVST) – Organisation internationale pour la science et la technique du vide (OISTV) – Internationale Organisation für Vakuum- Physik und -Technik (IOVPT)*, at 1st International Congress on Vacuum Techniques. Present name adopted Dec 1962. Statutes adopted: 7 Aug 1959 and 2 May 1963. Statutes modified: 11 May 1972; 5 Dec 1974; 14 Jun 1978. Statutes revised and adopted 13 Mar 2011. Registered in accordance with Belgian law. **Aims** Promote, encourage and develop vacuum sciences, techniques and applications in all countries. **Structure** General Assembly (every 3 years); General Meeting (annual); Executive Council; Scientific and Technical Directorate; Scientific Divisions (9); Standing Committees (8). **Languages** English, French. **Staff** None. **Finance** Sources: donations; investments; members' dues. **Activities** Events/meetings; research and development. **Events** *IVC : Triennial International Vacuum Congress* Sapporo (Japan) 2022, *ECOSS : European conference on surface science* Luxembourg (Luxembourg) 2021, *ECOSS : European conference on surface science* Luxembourg (Luxembourg) 2020, *IVC : Triennial International Vacuum Congress* Malmö (Sweden) 2019, *Vacuum and Surfaces Sciences Conference of Asia and Australia* Sydney, NSW (Australia) 2018. **Publications** *IUVSTA News Bulletin* (2 a year).

Members National Committees in 34 countries:
Argentina, Australia, Austria, Belgium, Brazil, Bulgaria, China, Croatia, Czechia, Finland, France, Germany, Hungary, India, Iran Islamic Rep, Israel, Italy, Japan, Korea Rep, Mexico, Netherlands, Pakistan, Philippines, Poland, Portugal, Romania, Slovakia, Slovenia, Spain, Sweden, Switzerland, UK, Ukraine, USA.

Consultative Status Consultative status granted from: *UNESCO (#20322)* (Consultative Status). **IGO Relations** Cooperates with: *UNESCO (#20322)*. **NGO Relations** Member of: *International Science Council (ISC, #14796)*. Cooperates with: *International Organization for Standardization (ISO, #14473)*. [2018.09.06/XC2677/**C**]

♦ International Union of Wagon Keepers 15827

Union internationale des wagons-privés – Internationale Privatgüterwagen-Union

SG Rue Montoyer 23, 1000 Brussels, Belgium. T. +3226728847. Fax +3226728114. E-mail: info@uiprail.org.

URL: http://www.uiprail.org/
History 18 Apr 1950, Switzerland. Former names and other names: *International Union of Private Railway Wagon Owners' Associations* – former (1950); *Union internationale d'associations de propriétaires de wagons de particuliers* – former (1950); *Unión Internacional de Asociaciones de Propietarios de Vagones Particulares* – former (1950); *Internationale Union von Verbänden der Privatgüterwagen-Besitzer* – former (1950); *International Union of Private Wagons (UIP)* – former. Registration: Banque-Carrefour des Entreprises, No/ID: 0464.623.367, Start date: 24 Aug 1998, Belgium. **Aims** Ensure the future of freight wagons by working towards a coordinated *transport* policy, which no longer discriminates against *rail*. **Structure** General Assembly (annual); Executive Board. Topical Committees; National Associations Committee. **Languages** English. **Finance** Sources: members' dues. **Activities** Research/documentation; standards/guidelines. **Events** *General Assembly* Berlin (Germany) 2019, *General Assembly* Vienna (Austria) 2018, *General Assembly* Amsterdam (Netherlands) 2017, *General Assembly* Rome (Italy) 2016, *Congress* Brussels (Belgium) 2013. **Publications** *UIP Newsletter*. Annual Report.
Members National associations in 14 countries:
Austria, Belgium, Czechia, France, Germany, Hungary, Italy, Netherlands, Romania, Slovakia, Spain, Sweden, Switzerland, UK.
NGO Relations In liaison with technical committees of: *Comité européen de normalisation (CEN, #04162)*. Associate member of: *Rail Forum Europe (RFE, #18607)*. [2022/XD2758/**D**]

♦ International Union of War Orphans (inactive)
♦ International Union of Wine, Spirits, Brandy and Liqueur Industrialists and Wholesalers / see FIVS (#09789)

♦ International Union of Women Architects (IUWA) 15828

Union internationale des femmes architectes (UIFA)

Pres 14 rue Dumont d'Urville, 75116 Paris, France. T. +33147208882. Fax +33147233864. E-mail: info@uifa.fr.

History 8 Sep 1963, on the initiative of the French Union of Women Architects. **Aims** In the spirit of the United Nations Charter and the Universal Declaration of Human Rights: establish friendly relations and exchanges among women architects and *town planners* in all countries; consolidate their efforts to ensure that careers in these fields are opened to women; collect information concerning their status and professional life; provide opportunities for women architects to express and diffuse their ideas. **Structure** Congress elects Executive Committee. **Languages** English, French. **Staff** Voluntary. **Finance** Sources: gifts, legacies; members' dues. **Activities** Distributes technical information to members; organizes study tours, international exhibitions, exchanges among different countries. **Events** *Congress* Washington, DC (USA) 2015, *Congress* Washington, DC (USA) 2015, *Congress* Ulaanbaatar (Mongolia) 2013, *Congress* Seoul (Korea Rep) 2010, *Congress* Bucharest (Romania) 2007.
Members Associations and individuals (over 1,000) in 74 countries and territories:
Algeria, Argentina, Armenia, Australia, Austria, Belgium, Bolivia, Brazil, Bulgaria, Burkina Faso, Cameroon, Canada, Central African Rep, Chile, China, Côte d'Ivoire, Croatia, Cyprus, Czechia, Denmark, Egypt, Estonia, Finland, France, Georgia, Germany, Greece, Hong Kong, Hungary, India, Iran Islamic Rep, Ireland, Israel, Italy, Jamaica, Japan, Jordan, Kazakhstan, Korea DPR, Latvia, Lebanon, Lithuania, Luxembourg, Malaysia, Mauritius, Mexico, Monaco, Mongolia, Montenegro, Netherlands, New Zealand, Niger, Nigeria, Norway, Palestine, Peru, Philippines, Poland, Portugal, Romania, Russia, Senegal, Serbia, Slovakia, South Africa, Spain, Sweden, Switzerland, Syrian AR, Trinidad-Tobago, Tunisia, Türkiye, UK, USA.
NGO Relations Member of: *Union des organisations internationales non-gouvernementales établies en France (UOIF, inactive)*. Cooperates with: *International Archive of Women in Architecture (IAWA)*. [2014/XC2793/**B**]

♦ International Union of Young Christian Democrats (inactive)

♦ International Union of Young Farmers (IUYF) 15829

Internationale Vereinigung von Jungen Landwirten (IVJL) – Starptautiska Jauno Fermeru Apvieniba (SJFA) – Tarptautine Jaunuju Ukininku Sajunga (TJUS)

Sec Kunkiu g 12, Darguziai, LT-92384 Klaipeda, Lithuania. T. +37064575953. Fax +37046301174. E-mail: info@iuyf.org.
URL: http://www.iuyf.org/

History Founded 2000, by call of UN General Assembly resolution 54/120, 1999, Articles 3, 14 and 15, to implement articles 17, 47 of the World Programme of Action for Youth to the Year 2000 and Beyond, adopted by the UN General Assembly resolution 50/81, 1995. Registered in accordance with Austrian law. Secretariat registered in Lithuania. **Aims** Represent interests of young farmers and *rural* youth; provide a platform for communication and cooperation among members. **Structure** Assembly; Board. **Languages** English, Russian. **Staff** 4.00 FTE, paid. **Finance** Members' dues. **Activities** Networking/liaising; research/documentation. **Events** *Assembly* Vienna (Austria) 2014, *Congress* Klaipeda (Lithuania) 2013, *Congress* Klaipeda (Lithuania) 2011. **Publications** *Development of Agriculture in the Context of Food Security* (2011).
Members Associations and individuals in 17 countries:
Armenia, Austria, Belarus, Czechia, Estonia, Germany, Ireland, Italy, Kazakhstan, Latvia, Lithuania, Moldova, Poland, Russia, UK, Ukraine, USA.
IGO Relations Cooperates with: *FAO Regional Office for Europe and Central Asia (FAO/REU, #09267)*. **NGO Relations** Cooperates with: *International Institute of Political Sciences (IIPS)*. [2017.09.20/XM3915/**E**]

♦ International Unity for Equality (unconfirmed)
♦ International and Universal Federation of Cremation Societies (inactive)
♦ International University (inactive)
♦ International University of Africa (internationally oriented national body)
♦ International University Association of Wine (unconfirmed)
♦ International University of Business Agriculture and Technology (internationally oriented national body)
♦ International University Conference (inactive)
♦ International University Consortium for Executive Education (internationally oriented national body)
♦ International University Contact for Management Education (inactive)
♦ International University of Entreprenology (internationally oriented national body)
♦ International University Equestrian Federation (#02694)
♦ International University Federation for the Principles of the League of Nations (inactive)
♦ International University of Japan (internationally oriented national body)
♦ International University of Kyrgyzstan (internationally oriented national body)
♦ International University of Monaco (internationally oriented national body)
♦ International University Network for Cooperation with Palestinian Higher Education Institutions / see Programme for Palestinian-European-American Cooperation in Education (#18527)
♦ International University of Peoples Institutions for Peace (internationally oriented national body)
♦ International University for Social Studies 'Guido Carli' (internationally oriented national body)

♦ International University Sports Federation (FISU) 15830

Fédération Internationale du Sport Universitaire (FISU) – Federación Internacional del Deporte Universitario (FISU)

SG/CEO FISU Headquarters, Quartier UNIL-Centre, Bât Synathlon, 1015 Lausanne VD, Switzerland. T. +41216926400. E-mail: fisu@fisu.net.
Main Website: https://www.fisu.net/

History 1949, Merano (Italy). Statutes modified: 1967, Tokyo (Japan); 1975, Rome (Italy); 1977, Sofia (Bulgaria); 1979, Mexico City (Mexico); 1981, Bucharest (Romania); 1983, Edmonton (Canada); 1987, Zagreb; 1989, Duisburg (Germany FR); 1995, Fukuoka (Japan); 2001, Beijing (China); 2003, Daegu (Korea Rep); 2005, Izmir (Turkey). Registration: Swiss Civil Code, Start date: 2011, Switzerland; Banque-Carrefour des Entreprises, End date: 2011, Belgium. **Aims** Provide opportunity for all students to participate in physical activity while acting for the health and wellbeing of students and thereby helping them to become active members of global society. **Structure** General Assembly (every 2 years); Executive Committee; Committees (15); ad hoc Commissions (3). **Languages** English. **Staff** 42.00 FTE, paid. **Finance** Sources: meeting proceeds; members' dues. Other sources: television rights. **Activities** Events/meetings; sporting activities; training/education. **Events** *Winter Universiade Sports Science Conference* Lucerne (Switzerland) 2021, *Winter Universiade Sports Science Conference* Krasnoyarsk (Russia) 2019, *Summer Universiade Conference* Naples (Italy) 2019, *Winter Universiade Sports Science Conference* Almaty (Kazakhstan) 2017, *Summer Universiade Conference* Taipei (Taiwan) 2017. **Publications** *FISU Yearbook* (annual). *FISU 70th Anniversary Book: FISU's achievements over the past 70 years* (2019).
Members National University Sports Organizations in 164 countries and territories:
Afghanistan, Albania, Algeria, Angola, Argentina, Armenia, Australia, Austria, Azerbaijan, Bahamas, Bangladesh, Barbados, Belarus, Belgium, Benin, Bhutan, Bosnia-Herzegovina, Botswana, Brazil, Bulgaria, Burkina Faso, Burundi, Cambodia, Cameroon, Canada, Cape Verde, Central African Rep, Chile, China, Colombia, Comoros, Congo Brazzaville, Congo DR, Costa Rica, Côte d'Ivoire, Croatia, Cuba, Cyprus, Czechia, Denmark, Dominican Rep, Ecuador, Egypt, El Salvador, Estonia, Eswatini, Ethiopia, Fiji, Finland, France, Gabon, Gambia, Georgia, Germany, Ghana, Greece, Guatemala, Guinea, Haiti, Honduras, Hong Kong, Hungary, India, Indonesia, Iran Islamic Rep, Iraq, Ireland, Israel, Italy, Jamaica, Japan, Jordan, Kazakhstan, Kenya, Korea DPR, Korea Rep, Kosovo, Kuwait, Kyrgyzstan, Latvia, Lebanon, Libya, Liechtenstein, Lithuania, Luxembourg, Macau, Madagascar, Malawi, Malaysia, Mali, Malta, Marshall Is, Mexico, Micronesia FS, Moldova, Mongolia, Montenegro, Morocco, Mozambique, Namibia, Nepal, Netherlands, New Zealand, Nicaragua, Niger, Nigeria, North Macedonia, Northern Mariana Is, Norway, Oman, Pakistan, Palestine, Panama, Papua New Guinea, Paraguay, Peru, Philippines, Poland, Portugal, Puerto Rico, Romania, Russia, Samoa, San Marino, Sao Tomé-Principe, Saudi Arabia, Senegal, Serbia, Sierra Leone, Singapore, Slovakia, Slovenia, Somalia, South Africa, Spain, Sri Lanka, Suriname, Sweden, Switzerland, Syrian AR, Taipei, Taiwan, Tajikistan, Tanzania UR, Thailand, Timor-Leste, Trinidad-Tobago, Tunisia, Türkiye, Turkmenistan, Uganda, UK, Ukraine, United Arab Emirates, Uruguay, USA, Uzbekistan, Venezuela, Vietnam, Virgin Is UK, Virgin Is USA, Yemen, Zambia, Zimbabwe.
Associate Members: continental associations (5):
Asian University Sports Federation (AUSF, #01775); *European University Sports Association (EUSA, #09036)*; *Federation of African University Sports (FASU, #09412)*; *FISU Oceania (#09785)*; *Organización Deportiva Universitaria Panamericana (FISU América, #17835)*.
IGO Relations Member of: *Enlarged Partial Agreement on Sport (EPAS, #05487)*. **NGO Relations** Member of (4): *Association of the IOC Recognized International Sports Federations (ARISF, #02767)*; *International Committee for Fair Play (#12769)*; *International Council of Sport Science and Physical Education (ICSSPE, #13077)*; *Olympic Movement (#17719)*. Cooperates with (1): *International Testing Agency (ITA, #15678)*. Recognized by: *International Olympic Committee (IOC, #14408)*. Instrumental in setting up: *International Foundation for the Development of University Sport (IFDUS, inactive)*. Memorandum of Understanding with: *International Esports Federation (IESF, #13303)*. *World Penthathlon (UIPM, #21720)* is member. [2022.02.03/XB2799/**B**]

♦ International University Statistical Bureau (inactive)
♦ International University on Sustainable Development (internationally oriented national body)

♦ International University Theatre Association (IUTA) 15831

Association internationale du théâtre à l'université (AITU) – Asociación Internacional de Teatro Universitario

Main Office 2305 Rue Joliette, Montréal QC H1W 3G7, Canada. T. +15147816364. E-mail: contact@aitu-iuta.org.
SG Théâtre Univ Royal de Liège, Univ de Liège, Que Roosevelt 1b, 4000 Liège, Belgium. T. +3243665295. Fax +3243665672.
URL: http://iuta-aitu.org/

History 15 Oct 1994, Liège (Belgium). **Aims** Develop and promote recognized post-secondary activity in theatre training, creation, research and theoretical and practical research, throughout the world, at the level of university or higher studies. **Structure** Executive Committee. **Languages** English, French, Spanish. **Staff** Voluntary. **Finance** Members' dues. **Events** *World Congress* Manila (Philippines) 2020, *World Congress* Moscow (Russia) 2018, *World Congress* Manizales (Colombia) 2016, *World Congress* Liège (Belgium) 2014, *World Congress* Minsk (Belarus) 2012. **Publications** *Theater Without Frontiers* (2002) in English, French, Spanish; *Studying Theatre* (2001) in English, French, Spanish; *Theatre in the University: a Genre of its Own* (1996) in English, French, Spanish. **Members** Full in over 50 countries. Membership countries not specified.
NGO Relations Associated with: *International Theatre Institute (ITI, #15683)*. [2018.06.01/XD4662/**D**]

♦ International Uranium Group (see: #11910)

♦ International Urban Development Association (INTA) 15832

Association internationale du développement urbain – Asociación Internacional para el Desarrollo Urbano – Internationaler Stadtentwicklungsverband – Associazione Internazionale per lo Sviluppo Urbano

SG 18 rue Daval, 75011 Paris, France. T. +33158303452. E-mail: intainfo@inta-net.org.
URL: http://www.inta-aivn.org/

History Nov 1975, Paris (France). Founded as *International New Towns Association (INTA) – Association internationale des villes nouvelles (AIVN)*. Present name adopted 1992. From 1984-1992, also referred to as *International Association for the Development and Management of Existing and New Towns – Association internationale pour le développement et la gestion des villes anciennes et nouvelles*. Also known as *International Network for Urban Development*. . Registration: Start date: 15 Dec 2000, France. **Aims** Gather public and private policy-makers and urban practitioners to share knowledge, experience and performing tools for integrated urban development. **Structure** General Assembly (annual); Board; Board of Governors; Executive Committee. **Languages** English, French. **Staff** 4.00 FTE, paid. **Finance** Sources: meeting proceeds; members' dues; subsidies. **Activities** Events/meetings; guidance/assistance/consulting; training/education. **Events** *Congress* Paris (France) 2022, *Congress* Paris (France) 2020, *Partnerships for sustainable cities and communities* Malmö (Sweden) 2018, *Congress* Rostock (Germany) 2018, *Congress* Lisbon (Portugal) 2016. **Publications** *INTA Newsletter* (24 a year). Directory; reports; brochures; conference proceedings. Information Services: Publications referral service.
Members National; corporate; individual. Policymakers of national, regional and local government; business leaders in real estate development, construction, engineering, service provision, product development; preeminent thinkers and research institutes; influential architecture and urbanism firms. Members in 48 countries and territories:
Australia, Austria, Belgium, Benin, Canada, China, Colombia, Denmark, Ecuador, Egypt, Estonia, France, Gabon, Germany, Hong Kong, India, Indonesia, Iran Islamic Rep, Israel, Italy, Japan, Laos, Latvia, Malaysia, Mauritania, Mauritius, Mexico, Morocco, Netherlands, New Zealand, Norway, Palestine, Peru, Poland, Portugal, Russia, Senegal, Slovenia, South Africa, Spain, Sweden, Switzerland, Taiwan, Thailand, UK, USA, Venezuela, Vietnam.
IGO Relations Consultative status with: *ECOSOC (#05331)*. Cooperates with: *United Nations Economic Commission for Europe (UNECE, #20555)*. Associated with Department of Global Communications of the United Nations. **NGO Relations** Member of: *Global Alliance for Buildings and Construction (GlobalABC, #10187)*. [2019/XC7282/**C**]

♦ International Urban Food Network (internationally oriented national body)

♦ International Urban Planning and Environment Association (IUPEA) 15833

Chair Univ of Washington, Dept of Urban Design and Planning, 410 Gould Hall, Box 355740, Seattle WA 98195-5740, USA. T. +12065437355. Fax +12066859597.
URL: http://www.iupea.net/

History Founded 1952. **Aims** Foster dialogue on issues of urban environmental planning; help develop practical solutions; encourage research concerning ways in which urban planning can aid understanding and solving of urban environmental conflicts. **Structure** Board of Directors; Advisory Committee. **Languages** English. **Staff** 3.50 FTE, paid. **Finance** Symposium registration fees; sponsorships. **Activities** Networking/liaising; events/meetings. **Events** *Symposium* Lisbon (Portugal) 2016, *Symposium* Buenos Aires (Argentina) 2014, *Symposium* La Plata (Argentina) 2014, *Symposium* Sydney, NSW (Australia) 2012, *Symposium* Guangzhou (China) 2010. **Publications** *Urban Planning and Environment* – 21 vols published to date. **NGO Relations** Links with universities and national governmental agencies. [2015.08.26/XJ0069/**E**]

♦ International Urban Symposium (IUS) 15834

Contact School of Anthropology and Conservation, Univ of Kent, Canterbury, CT2 7NR, UK.
Registered Office Via Riviera di Chiaia 276, 80121 Naples NA, Italy.
URL: https://www.internationalurbansymposium.com/

History 2015, Italy. Established on the initiative of Italo Pardo and Giuliana B. Prato, both at the University of Kent, UK. Initial founders included 13 international scholars and 2 non-academic professionals from the legal and media fields. Registration: Agenzia delle Entrate UT NA 1, No/ID: 1T-16945, Start date: 25 Sep 2015, Italy. **Aims** Promote, support, coordinate and conduct scientific research and initiatives in urban areas, charting new directions on topical issues such as social and economic justice, old and new forms of inequality, individual and public health, the relationship between citizenship and governance, and between processes of legitimacy and democratic institutions; promote the significance of ethnographic research to intellectual debates and new theoretical directions and to society more broadly, stimulating critical scholarship and exchange of ideas among different disciplines and engaging in exchange of ideas and collaboration with non-academics who operate in society. **Structure** General Assembly; Executive Board; Officers. **Languages** English. **Staff** 3.00 FTE, voluntary. **Finance** Sources: donations; members' dues. **Activities** Events/meetings; knowledge management/information dissemination; networking/liaising; projects/programmes; publishing activities; research and development; training/education. **Events** *Urban Ethnography and Theory* Montecatini Terme (Italy) 2022, *Legitimacy and the Right to Health* Montecatini Terme (Italy) 2021, *Urbanimaginary. Mégalopoles, métropoles, villes à la campagne, ville décroissante : quels imaginaires pour la ville de demain ?* Saint-Étienne (France) 2021, *Legitimacy and Health* Montecatini Terme (Italy) 2020, *Urban Inequalities: Ethnographic Insights* Corinth (Greece) 2019. **Publications** *Urbanities-Journal of Urban Ethnography* (2 a year) in English – open-access; peer-reviewed; *IUS Newsletter*, *Urbanities-IUS Supplements* – Revised and expanded versions of papers discussed in the IUS meetings are brought together in edited collections and published as Supplements to Urbanities-Journal of Urban Ethnography (https://www.anthrojournal-urbanities.com/the-ius-supplements/). *Greek Crisis and Inequalities* (2022) in English – Special Issue of Urbanities-Journal of Urban Ethnography, Vol. 12, Suppl. 5; *Healthcare and Public Health: Questions of Legitimacy* (2022) in English – Special Issue of Urbanities-Journal of Urban Ethnography, Vol. 12, Suppl. 6; *City Life and Beyond in Times of Pandemic* (2020) in English – Special Issue of Urbanities-Journal of Urban Ethnography, Vol.10, Suppl.4; *Ethnographies of Urbanity in Flux: Theoretical Reflections* (2020) in English – Special issue of Urbanities, Vol. 10, Suppl 3; *On Legitimacy: Multidisciplinary Reflections* (2019) in English – Special Issue of Urbanities, Vol. 9, Suppl 2; *Ethnographers Debate Legitimacy* (2018) in English – Special issue of Urbanities, Vol. 8, Suppl 1. *Urban Inequalities: Ethnographically Informed Reflections* (2021) by Italo Pardo and Giuliana B Prato in English – Edited volume. Series "Palgrave Studies in Urban Anthropology"; *Legitimacy: Ethnographic and Theoretical Insights* (2018) by I Pardo and G B Prato in English – edited volume, published in the Series "Palgrave Studies in Urban Anthropology". #

Members Individuals in 23 countries:
Albania, Argentina, Austria, Canada, Colombia, Czechia, France, Greece, Hungary, India, Ireland, Israel, Italy, Japan, Lithuania, New Zealand, Poland, Portugal, Spain, Switzerland, Türkiye, UK, USA. [2022.06.21/XM4991/**C**]

♦ International Urogynecological Association (IUGA) 15835

Sec 14305 Southcross Drive, Ste 100, Burnsville MN 55306, USA. T. +19526839037. E-mail: office@iuga.org – meeting@iuga.org.
Europe Contact Zaanweg 119A, 1521 DS Wormerveer, Netherlands. T. +31756476365. Fax +31756476371.
URL: http://www.iuga.org/

History 1975, USA. By-Laws revised 19 Sep 1996; 1 Aug 2008. Registration: Nonprofit 501(c)(3), No/ID: EIN: 36-4045817, Start date: 1996, USA. **Aims** Advance urogynecological knowledge and patient care through education and the promotion of basic and clinical research on disorders of the female pelvic floor. **Structure** Board; Committees (8). **Languages** English. **Staff** Staffed by Association Management Company. **Finance** Sources: grants; meeting proceeds; members' dues; sale of publications. **Activities** Events/meetings; financial and/or material support; training/education. **Events** *Annual Meeting* The Hague (Netherlands) 2023, *Annual Meeting* Austin, TX (USA) 2022, *Annual Meeting* Burnsville, MN (USA) 2021, *Annual Meeting* Burnsville, MN (USA) 2020, *Annual Meeting* Nashville, TN (USA) 2019. **Publications** *International Urogynecology Journal* (12 a year).

Members Regular; Lifetime; Honorary; Affiliate Societies. Individuals in 84 countries and territories:
Afghanistan, Albania, Argentina, Australia, Austria, Azerbaijan, Bahrain, Belgium, Bolivia, Brazil, Cambodia, Canada, Cayman Is, Chile, China, Colombia, Costa Rica, Croatia, Czechia, Denmark, Ecuador, Egypt, Estonia, Finland, France, Germany, Ghana, Greece, Guatemala, Honduras, Hong Kong, Iceland, India, Indonesia, Iran Islamic Rep, Ireland, Israel, Italy, Japan, Jordan, Kenya, Korea Rep, Kuwait, Lebanon, Lithuania, Malaysia, Mexico, Nepal, Netherlands, New Zealand, Nicaragua, Nigeria, North Macedonia, Norway, Oman, Pakistan, Panama, Peru, Philippines, Poland, Portugal, Puerto Rico, Romania, Russia, Saudi Arabia, Serbia, Singapore, Slovakia, Slovenia, South Africa, Spain, Sweden, Switzerland, Taiwan, Thailand, Türkiye, UK, Ukraine, United Arab Emirates, Uruguay, USA, Venezuela, Vietnam, Zimbabwe.
Affiliated societies include 3 organizations listed in this Yearbook:
Australasian Gynaecological Endoscopy and Surgery (AGES); *Mediterranean Incontinence and Pelvic Floor Society (MIPS, #16656)*; *UroGynaecological Society of Australasia (UGSA)*. [2021/XD5137/y/**C**]

♦ International Urolithiasis Society (IUS) 15836

Chair Dept of Urology, Klinikum Coburg GmbH, Academic Hosp Julius-Maximilians-Univ Würzburg, Ketschendorfer Strasse 33, 96450 Coburg, Germany. T. +499561226301. Fax +499561226391.
URL: http://iusint.com/

History 1968, Leeds (UK). **Structure** Board. **Languages** English. **Activities** Events/meetings. **Events** *Symposium* Chiba (Japan) 2016, *Symposium* Ouro Preto (Brazil) 2012, *Symposium* Nice (France) 2008, *Symposium* Hong Kong (Hong Kong) 2004, *Symposium* Cape Town (South Africa) 2000. **Publications** *Urolithaisis* – official journal. [2017.10.04/XM3978/**E**]

♦ International URSIgram and World Days Service / see International Space Environment Service (#15572)

♦ International Users Group of ISPO-certified organizations (IUG) . . . 15837

Contact PO Box 830, 3000 AV Rotterdam, Netherlands. T. +31889002500. Fax +31889002588. E-mail: iug@ispo-standard.com – info@ispo-standard.com.
Street Address Markweg 200, EUROPOORT, 3198 NB Rotterdam, Netherlands.
URL: http://www.ispo-standard.com/

History *International Standard for Maritime Pilot Organizations (ISPO)* developed by Dutch Maritime Pilot's Association and Lloyds Register, in close cooperation with *European Maritime Pilots' Association (EMPA, #07743)*. Standard first employed 2005. **Aims** Maintain and further develop the standard; communicate between ISPO-certified organizations adn inform them and other interested parties; support potential members and other interested parties in relation to the implementation of the standard; recognize and authorize classification societies as independent bodies for ISPO-certification; administer certificates. **Structure** Board. **Activities** Certification/accreditation; events/meetings. **Events** *International Standard for Maritime Pilot Organizations (ISPO) Annual Conference* Rotterdam (Netherlands) 2017, *International Standard for Maritime Pilot Organizations (ISPO) Annual Conference* Safat (Kuwait) 2015, *International Standard for Maritime Pilot Organizations (ISPO) Annual Conference* Liverpool (UK) 2014, *International Standard for Maritime Pilot Organizations (ISPO) Annual Conference* Port-of-Spain (Trinidad-Tobago) 2013.

Members Full in 11 countries:
Australia, Belgium, Bulgaria, Ireland, Kuwait, Netherlands, Spain, Trinidad-Tobago, Türkiye, UK, United Arab Emirates. [2016/XM4898/**E**]

♦ International Uveitis Study Group (IUSG) 15838

Main Office Rue de l'Industrie 24, 1040 Brussels, Belgium. E-mail: office@iusg.net.
URL: http://www.iusg.net/

History 1979. Registration: 501(c)3, USA; Start date: 1986, France. **Aims** Advance the knowledge of uveitis within the framework of *ophthalmology*. **Structure** An *International Uveitis Study Group Foundation (IUSG Foundation)* was set up, 1995, in accordance with Belgian law. **Languages** English. **Staff** Voluntary. **Finance** Members' dues. Meeting support from pharmaceutical companies. **Activities** Events/meetings; knowledge management/information dissemination; training/education. **Events** *International Symposium on Uveitis (ISU)* Utrecht (Netherlands) 2022, *Quadrennial Symposium* Singapore (Singapore) 2020, *Quadrennial Symposium* Dublin (Ireland) 2016, *Quadrennial Symposium* Chalkidiki (Greece) 2012, *Quadrennial Symposium* Germany 2008. **Publications** *Ocular Immunology and Inflammation* – journal. Case reports; articles.

Members Individuals. Active (120) in 35 countries and territories:
Argentina, Australia, Austria, Belgium, Brazil, Bulgaria, Canada, China, Colombia, Finland, France, Germany, Greece, India, Iran Islamic Rep, Ireland, Israel, Italy, Japan, Korea Rep, Netherlands, Qatar, Saudi Arabia, Serbia, Singapore, Spain, Sweden, Switzerland, Taiwan, Thailand, Tunisia, Türkiye, UK, USA, Venezuela. [2022/XF1494/v/**F**]

♦ International Vaccine Access Center (internationally oriented national body)

♦ International Vaccine Institute (IVI) 15839

Institut international de vaccins (IIV) – Instituto Internacional de Vacunas

Dir Gen IVI Headquarters, SNU Research Park, 1 Gwanak-ro, Gwanak-gu, Seoul 08826, Korea Rep. T. +8228722801. Fax +8228722803. E-mail: iviinfo@ivi.int.
IVI European Regional Office 7A Posthuset, 6th floor, Vasagatan 28, SE-111 20 Stockholm, Sweden. E-mail: ivieurope@ivi.int.
URL: http://www.ivi.int/

History 29 May 1997. Established at the initiative of *UNDP (#20292)*. Formally set up after 3 signatories, including *WHO (#20950)*, ratified the Establishment Agreement. **Aims** Discover, develop and deliver safe, effective and affordable vaccines for global public health. **Structure** Board of Trustees; Scientific Advisory Group; Institutional Support Council; Director General's Office; Divisions (4); Headquarters in the Republic of Korea. **Languages** English. **Staff** 190.00 FTE, paid. **Finance** Funded by member states, international organizations, other agencies, manufacturers and private institutions, including: governments of Korea, Sweden, India, and Finland; *Bill and Melinda Gates Foundation (BMGF)*; *Korea International Cooperation Agency (KOICA)*. **Activities** Events/meetings; financial and/or material support; research and development; research/documentation; training/education. technology transfers. **Events** *Seminar on COVID-19 and Public Governance* Seoul (Korea Rep) 2021, *Seminar on Curbing the Invisible Pandemic* Seoul (Korea Rep) 2021, *Forum for Enhancement of Cooperation* Seoul (Korea Rep) 2020, *Bord of Trustees Meeting* Seoul (Korea Rep) 2019, *Forum for Enhancement of Cooperation* Seoul (Korea Rep) 2019. **Publications** *The IVI Newsletter* (4 a year). Annual Report; Strategic Plan.

Members State Parties to IVI Establishment Agreement (24):
Bangladesh, Brazil, China, Ecuador, Finland, India, Korea Rep, Liberia, Mongolia, Netherlands, Oman, Pakistan, Panama, Peru, Philippines, Rwanda, Spain, Sri Lanka, Sweden, Thailand, United Arab Emirates, Uzbekistan, Vietnam.
WHO (#20950).
Signatory Statues (17):
Bhutan, Egypt, Indonesia, Israel, Jamaica, Kazakhstan, Kyrgyzstan, Lebanon, Myanmar, Nepal, Panama, Papua New Guinea, Romania, Senegal, Tajikistan, Thailand, Türkiye.

IGO Relations Collaborates with: *ICDDR,B (#11051)*. Adheres to: *Global Partnership for Effective Development Co-operation (GPEDC, #10532)*. Settlement of disputes: *International Court of Justice (ICJ, #13098)*. **NGO Relations** Member of (5): *Coalition against Typhoid (CaT, #04049)*; *Developing Countries Vaccine Manufacturers Network (DCVMN, #05052)*; *Global Coalition Against Child Pneumonia (#10290)*; *Global Dengue and Aedes-transmitted Diseases Consortium (GDAC, #10316)*; *Global Health Technologies Coalition (GHTC)*. Instrumental in setting up (1): *Dengue Vaccine Initiative (DVI, #05038)*. [2022.10.11/XE2717/j/**E***]

♦ International Vacuum Insulation Symposium (meeting series)
♦ International Vacuum Nanoelectronics Conference (meeting series)
♦ International Valuation Standards Committee / see International Valuation Standards Council (#15840)

♦ International Valuation Standards Council (IVSC) 15840

Head Office 20 St Dunstan's Hill, London, EC3R 8HL, UK. T. +442037953140. Fax +442037953140. E-mail: contact@ivsc.org.
URL: http://www.ivsc.org/

History Oct 1981. Primary operations in the UK. Former names and other names: *International Assets Valuation Standards Committee* – former (Oct 1981 to Mar 1995); *International Valuation Standards Committee* – former (Mar 1995 to 2008). Registration: USA. **Aims** Develop a single set of globally recognized valuation standards, acceptable to the world's capital markets organizations, regulators and market participants; protect the public interest by promoting strong ethical values, encouraging quality practice and supporting the development of all sectors of the valuation profession around the world. **Structure** Annual General Meeting; Board of Trustees; Standards Review Board; Business Valuation Board (technical); Financial Instruments Board (technical); Tangible Assets Board (technical); Membership and Standards Recognition Board; Europe Board; Advisory Forum Working Group. **Languages** English. **Staff** 6.00 FTE, paid. **Finance** Sources: members' dues; sponsorship. **Activities** Standards/guidelines. **Events** *Annual General Meeting* Fort Lauderdale, FL (USA) 2022, *IVAS-IVSC Business Valuation Conference* Singapore (Singapore) 2021, *IVSC-WAVO Global Valuation Conference* Seoul (Korea Rep) 2020, *Annual General Meeting* Singapore (Singapore) 2019, *Business Valuation Conference* Singapore (Singapore) 2019. **Publications** *IVSC E-News*. *International Valuation Standards (IVS)*.

Members Valuation Professional Organisation (VPO); Associate Valuation Professional Organisation (AVPO); Institutional; Corporate; Academic. VPOs and AVPOs represent national organisations of qualified valuers in 56 countries and territories:
Australia, Azerbaijan, Bangladesh, Belarus, Bosnia-Herzegovina, Botswana, Brazil, Canada, China, Colombia, Costa Rica, Croatia, Egypt, Finland, Georgia, Germany, Hong Kong, India, Indonesia, Ireland, Israel, Italy, Japan, Kazakhstan, Kenya, Korea Rep, Kosovo, Latvia, Malaysia, Mexico, Mongolia, Montenegro, Nepal, Netherlands, New Zealand, Nigeria, North Macedonia, Norway, Peru, Philippines, Romania, Russia, Rwanda, Serbia, Singapore, Slovenia, South Africa, Spain, Sri Lanka, Sweden, Thailand, Türkiye, Turkmenistan, UK, Ukraine, USA.
Institutional in 38 countries:
Australia, Austria, Bahrain, Bangladesh, Belarus, Brazil, Bulgaria, Canada, France, Georgia, Germany, India, Italy, Japan, Korea Rep, Kuwait, Lithuania, Malaysia, Mexico, Mongolia, Namibia, Nigeria, North Macedonia, Pakistan, Philippines, Russia, Saudi Arabia, Singapore, South Africa, Spain, Sri Lanka, Uganda, UK, Ukraine, United Arab Emirates, USA, Uzbekistan, Vietnam.
Corporate in 10 countries and territories:
Brazil, China, France, Hong Kong, Japan, Kuwait, Qatar, Türkiye, UK, USA.
Academic in 14 countries:
Austria, Canada, Czechia, India, Ireland, Italy, Malawi, Oman, Russia, Singapore, Switzerland, Türkiye, UK, USA.

Consultative Status Consultative status granted from: *ECOSOC (#05331)* (Ros A). **NGO Relations** Member of (1): *International Ethics Standards Coalition (IES Coalition, #13307)*. [2021.06.23/XD5197/**C**]

♦ International Vascular Biology Meeting (meeting series)
♦ International Vasculitis and ANCA Workshop (meeting series)

♦ International VAT Association (IVA) 15841

Association internationale des représentants fiscaux

Sec address not obtained.
URL: http://www.vatassociation.org/

History Founded 1993. Registered in accordance with Belgian law, 2003. EU Transparency Register: 41440872023-73. **Aims** Provide a forum for value added tax (VAT) reclaim agents and intermediaries; facilitate the exchange of ideas and information on VAT matters; further the study and knowledge of VAT law and practice; establish links between VAT reclaim agents or intermediaries and governmental authorities. **Structure** General Meeting (annual). Council, comprising Chairman, Deputy Chairman, Secretary and Treasurer. Technical Committee. **Finance** Members' dues. **Events** *Autumn Conference* Athens (Greece) 2019, *Spring Conference* Munich (Germany) 2019, *Spring Conference* Nice (France) 2018, *Autumn Conference* Stockholm (Sweden) 2018, *Autumn Conference* Brussels (Belgium) 2017. [2016/XD8634/**D**]

♦ International Vaurien Class Association (see: #21760)

♦ International Vegetarian Union (IVU) 15842

Union internationale végétarienne – Unión Internacional Vegetariana – Internationale Vegetarier Union – Unione Vegetariana Internazionale – Internacia Vegetara Unuigxo

Chair address not obtained. E-mail: chair@ivu.org.
URL: http://www.ivu.org/

History 18 Aug 1908, Dresden (Germany), as *Union végétarienne internationale*, successor body of *Vegetarian Federal Union*, set up 1889. New Constitution adopted Aug 1955, Paris (France); amended Aug 1960, Hannover (Germany FR); revised Sep 1971 The Hague (Netherlands). New Constitution adopted 1982, Ulm (Germany FR); fully revised 1990, Tel Aviv (Israel); amended 1994, The Hague. **Aims** Coordinate the work of regional and national vegetarian societies and encourage formation of new ones; collect and disseminate news of vegetarian interest; ensure that vegetarianism is represented at international bodies. **Structure** Congress (every 2 years); International Council, comprising Officers and Councillors. **Languages** English, Spanish. **Staff** Voluntary. **Finance** Sources: gifts, legacies; members' dues. Business partnerships. **Activities** Organizes World and Regional Congresses. Carries out studies and research into all aspects of vegetarianism and encourages the holding of conferences on vegetarian nutrition. Acts as a contact organization for any enquiry about vegetarianism from any part of the world. Instrumental in setting up: *Asia Pacific Vegetarian Union (APVU, #02074)*; *European Vegetarian Union (EVU, #09048)*. **Events** *World Vegfest Congress* Beijing (China) 2021, *World Vegfest Congress* Beijing (China) 2020, *World Vegfest Congress* Berlin (Germany) 2019, *World Vegfest Congress* Nairobi (Kenya) 2018, *World Vegfest Congress* Taipei (Taiwan) 2017. **Publications** *IVU News* (2 a year).

Members National Societies and individuals. Members in 45 countries and territories:
Armenia, Australia, Austria, Barbados, Belgium, Bosnia-Herzegovina, Botswana, Brazil, Bulgaria, Canada, Congo DR, Croatia, Denmark, Finland, France, Germany, Ghana, Hong Kong, India, Indonesia, Ireland, Israel, Italy, Japan, Kenya, Korea Rep, Luxembourg, Malta, Mexico, Mongolia, New Zealand, Nigeria, Norway, Puerto Rico, Russia, Singapore, Spain, Sri Lanka, Sweden, Switzerland, Tanzania UR, Thailand, Uganda, UK, USA. [2021/XB2800/**B**]

♦ International Ventilator Users Network (internationally oriented national body)

♦ International Venture Philanthropy Center (IVPC) 15843

Street Address Sguirrels Chase, Crossfield Place, Weybridge, KT13, UK. E-mail: pcarttar@ivpc.global.
URL: https://ivpc.global/

History 2015. **Aims** Engage more human, intellectual and financial capital to support social-purpose investment globally; increase the effectiveness of that capital in generating meaningful social impact. **Structure** Board. **Languages** English. **Staff** 4.00 FTE, paid. **Finance** Annual budget: 1,000,000 USD. **Activities** Capacity building; knowledge management/information dissemination; networking/liaising. **Members** Not a membership organization. **NGO Relations** Member of (1): *Worldwide Initiatives for Grantmaker Support (WINGS, #21926)*. Partner of (3): *African Venture Philanthropy Alliance (AVPA)*; *Asian Venture Philanthropy Network (AVPN, #01778)*; *European Venture Philanthropy Association (EVPA, #09053)*.
[2022.02.02/XM8814/**C**]

♦ International Vereinigung zur Förderung innovativer Ansätze der Auseinandersetzung mit global Herausforderungen (#11687)
♦ International Vereinigung der Lebenswerten Städte / see Cittaslow (#03958)
♦ International Vereinigung der Unternehmungen für Elektrische Ausrüstung / see EuropeOn (#09166)
♦ International Vessel Operators Dangerous Goods Association (internationally oriented national body)
♦ International Vessel Operators Hazardous Materials Association / see International Vessel Operators Dangerous Goods Association

♦ International Veteran Cycle Association (IVCA) 15844

Sec Berthold-Haupt-Str 89, 01259 Dresden, Germany. E-mail: veterancykel@gmail.com.
Pres address not obtained.
URL: http://www.ivca-online.org/

History 1986, Lincoln (UK). Founded by vintage cyclist clubs. **Aims** Serve as a forum and coordinating body for matters relating to *historical bicycles* and other cycles; encourage research and classification of their history. **Structure** General Meeting (annual during rally); Executive Committee. **Languages** English, French, German. **Staff** Voluntary. **Finance** Sources: members' dues. **Activities** Events/meetings; knowledge management/information dissemination. **Events** *Annual General Meeting* Germany 2028, *Annual General Meeting* France 2026, *Annual General Meeting* Australia 2025, *Annual General Meeting* Ostrava (Czechia) 2024, *Annual General Meeting* Cremona (Italy) 2023. **Publications** *IVCA Newsletter* (2 a year).
Members Full in 28 countries:
Australia, Austria, Belgium, Canada, Czechia, Denmark, Estonia, Finland, France, Germany, Hungary, Indonesia, Ireland, Italy, Japan, Latvia, Liechtenstein, Netherlands, New Zealand, Norway, Poland, Russia, Slovakia, South Africa, Spain, Sweden, Switzerland, UK, USA.
[2021.06.09/XJ3100/**D**]

♦ International Veterans Society / see International Veterans Table Tennis Society (#15845)

♦ International Veterans Table Tennis Society (IVTTS) 15845

SG address not obtained.
Pres 11 Hurdlow Avenue, Birmingham, B18 5QQ, UK.
URL: http://www.tt-veterans-international.com/

History Founded 21 Apr 2001, Potsdam (Germany). Also referred to as *International Veterans Society (IVS)* and *Veterans International*. **Aims** Promote Veterans Table Tennis Sport all over the world; uphold and further the interests of the organization and of members; support the efforts of national and international table tennis organizations to further Veterans Table Tennis Sport all over the world; establish rules and regulations for the teams that take part in the International Table Tennis Team Championships for Veterans Societies/Groups. **Structure** General Meeting (every 2 years); Executive Board; Working Groups. **Languages** English. **Activities** Advocacy/lobbying/activism; events/meetings. **Events** *General Meeting* Bremen (Germany) 2013.
Members National organizations or group representing the interests of table tennis veterans matters, 8 countries:
Australia, Bulgaria, Denmark, Georgia, Germany, Netherlands, Türkiye, UK.
[2015.01.05/XD9433/**C**]

♦ International Veterinary Academy on Disaster Medicine (inactive)
♦ International Veterinary Academy of Pain Management (internationally oriented national body)

♦ International Veterinary Acupuncture Society (IVAS) 15846

Contact 1730 South College Ave Ste 301, Fort Collins CO 80525, USA. T. +19702660666. Fax +19702660777. E-mail: office@ivas.org.
URL: http://www.ivas.org/

History 1972, Athens GA (USA). Incorporated 1974. **Aims** Promote and encourage scientific investigation and research into the technique of veterinary acupuncture; maintain high standards of treatment and diagnosis using acupuncture as an integral part of the total veterinary health care system. **Languages** English. **Staff** 3.00 FTE, paid. **Activities** International conferences (every year); courses in basic veterinary acupuncture (at regular intervals). **Events** *Annual Congress* Aalborg (Denmark) 2010, *Annual Congress* Aalborg (Denmark) 2010, *Annual Congress* San Antonio, TX (USA) 2009, *Annual Congress* Keystone, CO (USA) 2008, *Annual congress* Niedernhausen (Germany) 2007. **Publications** *Veterinary Acupuncture Newsletter* (4 a year); *International Journal of Veterinary Acupuncture* (2 a year).
Members Full in 23 countries:
Australia, Austria, Belgium, Brazil, Canada, Denmark, Finland, France, Germany, Ireland, Italy, Japan, Mexico, Netherlands, New Zealand, Norway, South Africa, Sweden, Switzerland, Taiwan, UK, United Arab Emirates, USA.
[2014/XD7624/**D**]

♦ International Veterinary Association for Animal Production (inactive)
♦ International Veterinary Auxiliary (inactive)

♦ International Veterinary Biosafety Workgroup (IVBW) 15847

Contact address not obtained. E-mail: uwemd@gmx.net.
URL: http://ivbw.camp9.org/

Aims Promote best practice in microbiological biocontainment and safety in veterinary laboratories that have national responsibility for the health of large animals, and which operate at biosafety level 3 and 4. **Structure** Executive Group; Core Group; President. **Languages** English. **Staff** All voluntary. **Finance** Sources: members' dues. **Events** *Workshop* Pirbright (UK) 2014, *Workshop* Pretoria (South Africa) 2012, *Workshop* Copenhagen (Denmark) 2011, *Workshop* Ames, IA (USA) 2009, *Workshop* Buenos Aires (Argentina) 2008.
Members Full in 24 countries:
Argentina, Australia, Canada, Cuba, Denmark, France, Germany, Guatemala, India, Ireland, Italy, Kenya, Malaysia, Netherlands, New Zealand, Oman, Singapore, South Africa, Spain, Sweden, Switzerland, Uganda, UK, USA.
NGO Relations Member of: *International Federation of Biosafety Associations (IFBA, #13373)*.
[2015.03.02/XJ8868/**C**]

♦ International Veterinary Chiropractic Association (IVCA) 15848

Main Office Neunäckervörde 14, 31139 Hildesheim, Germany. E-mail: contact@ivca.de.
URL: http://www.ivca.de/

Aims Promote excellence in the field of veterinary chiropractic. **Structure** Annual General Meeting held along with the conference. **Events** *Annual Conference* Minneapolis, MN (USA) 2021, *Annual Conference* Minneapolis, MN (USA) 2020, *Annual Conference* Hamburg (Germany) 2019, *Annual Conference* Oslo (Norway) 2016, *Annual Conference* Berlin (Germany) 2015.
[2021/XM3729/**D**]

♦ International Veterinary Ear, Nose and Throat Association (IVENTA) 15849

Contact address not obtained. E-mail: gert.terhaar@anicura.nl.
URL: http://www.wsava.org/iventa.htm

Events *Meeting* Rhodes Is (Greece) 2004, *Meeting* Bangkok (Thailand) 2003, *Meeting* Granada (Spain) 2002, *Annual meeting* Vancouver, BC (Canada) 2001. **NGO Relations** Affiliated member of: *World Small Animal Veterinary Association (WSAVA, #21795)*.
[2013/XD6289/**D**]

♦ International Veterinary Nurses and Technicians Association (internationally oriented national body)

♦ International Veterinary Radiology Association (IVRA) 15850

Association internationale de radiologie vétérinaire

Treas 11321 NW 122 Terrace, Alachua FL 32610, USA.
Sec 305 Selby St North, Osborne Park WA 6017, Australia. T. +61892040400. Fax +61892045677.
URL: https://www.ivraimaging.org/

History Founded 1968, Dublin (Ireland). **Aims** Encourage and promote all forms of scientific endeavours and research involving veterinary radiology; disburse knowledge of veterinary radiology throughout the world; represent the radiology discipline in other veterinary organizations; encourage training in veterinary radiology. **Structure** Membership Meeting (every 3 years). Board of Directors of 6-20 members (serving 3-year terms), including 5 officers. Committees (4): Directors Nominating; Finance; Scientific Meeting; Travel Fellowship. **Languages** English. **Staff** 4.00 FTE, voluntary. **Finance** Sources: members' dues. Annual budget: 20,000 USD. **Events** *Scientific Meeting* Dublin (Ireland) 2021, *Scientific Meeting* Fort Worth, TX (USA) 2018, *Scientific Meeting* Fremantle, WA (Australia) 2015, *Scientific Meeting* Bursa (Turkey) 2012, *Scientific Meeting* Armação de Búzios (Brazil) 2009. **Publications** *Veterinary Radiology and Ultrasound* – official journal.
Members Full in 36 countries:
Australia, Austria, Belgium, Brazil, Canada, Chile, China, Denmark, Egypt, Finland, France, Germany, Greece, India, Ireland, Israel, Italy, Japan, Korea Rep, Netherlands, New Zealand, Norway, Poland, Portugal, Romania, Russia, Saudi Arabia, Serbia, Slovenia, South Africa, Spain, Sweden, Switzerland, Türkiye, UK, USA.
Regional organizations (3), listed in this Yearbook:
Australasian Association of Veterinary Diagnostic Imaging (AAVDI); *European Association of Veterinary Diagnostic Imaging (EAVDI, #06269)*; *European College of Veterinary Diagnostic Imaging (ECVDI, #06623)*.
[2019/XD1378/y/**C**]

♦ International Veterinary Students' Association (IVSA) 15851

Office Rue Victor Oudart 7, 1030 Brussels, Belgium. E-mail: secretarygeneral@ivsa.org – mod@ivsa.org.
URL: http://www.ivsa.org/

History Jul 1953, Giessen (Germany). Former names and other names: *International Veterinary Students Union* – former (1953 to 1968). Registration: Federale Overheidsdienst Justitite, No/ID: 0678547860, Belgium, brussels. **Aims** Benefit animals and humans by harnessing the potential and dedication of veterinary students to promote international application of veterinary skills, education and knowledge. **Structure** General Assembly (twice a year); Executive Committee; Secretariat, Regional Representatives (6): Asia, Americas, Pacific, MENA, SSA, Europe; Committees (6); ad hoc Taskforces. **Languages** English. **Staff** Voluntary. **Finance** Annual budget: 35,000 EUR. **Activities** Awards/prizes/competitions; events/meetings; financial and/or material support; networking/liaising. **Events** *IVSA Symposium* Guadalajara (Mexico) 2022, *Annual Congress* Sao Paulo (Brazil) 2022, *Annual Congress* 2021, *Annual Congress* 2020, *Annual Congress* Thessaloniki (Greece) / Volos (Greece) 2020. **Publications** *IVSA Bulletin* (12 a year); *IVSA Journal* (4 a year) – online.
Members Organizations in 51 countries and territories:t
Algeria, Austria, Bangladesh, Belgium, Brazil, Cameroon, China, Colombia, Croatia, Czechia, Denmark, Egypt, Estonia, Finland, France, Germany, Ghana, Greece, Hungary, Indonesia, Iraq, Ireland, Italy, Japan, Korea Rep, Kosovo, Malaysia, Morocco, Namibia, Nepal, Netherlands, Nigeria, North Macedonia, Norway, Philippines, Poland, Portugal, Romania, Russia, Slovakia, South Africa, Spain, Sweden, Switzerland, Taiwan, Tanzania UR, Thailand, Tunisia, Türkiye, UK, USA.
Consultative Status Consultative status granted from: *ECOSOC (#05331)* (Special). **IGO Relations** Formal contacts with: *FAO (#09260)*; *OIE – World Organisation for Animal Health (#17703)*. **NGO Relations** Member of (4): *European Association of Veterinarians in Education, Research and Industry (EVERI, #06267)*; *Informal Forum of International Student Organizations (IFISO, #11193)*; *World Health Students' Alliance (WHSA, #21559)*; *World Small Animal Veterinary Association (WSAVA, #21795)*. Partner of (3): *European Association of Establishments for Veterinary Education (EAEVE, #06031)*; *Federation of Veterinarians of Europe (#09713)*; *International Student One Health Alliance (ISOHA)*. Cooperates with (1): *World Veterinary Association (WVA, #21901)*.
[2022.10.18/XD2802/**C**]

♦ International Veterinary Students Union / see International Veterinary Students' Association (#15851)

♦ International Video Federation (IVF) 15852

Fédération internationale de la vidéo

Dir Gen Rue Ducale 83, 1000 Brussels, Belgium. T. +3225034063. Fax +3225033719. E-mail: info@ivf-video.org.
URL: http://www.ivf-video.org/

History Oct 1988, Paris (France). Registered according to Belgian law. EU Transparency Register: 7013477846-25. **Aims** Represent at the international level, national associations of entities exploiting copyright works and/or by other content delivery models such as dissemination or distribution of copyright works on networks, including on the Internet, in particular as regards: collection and dissemination of statistics and other information; coordination of legislative and lobbying activities in the field of fiscal treatment of the video media; abolition of trade barriers, censorship/classification systems and anti-piracy/ copyright. **Structure** General Assembly. Board of Directors (5-9 members). Officers: Chairman and Treasurer. Director General. **Languages** English. **Staff** 2.00 FTE, paid. **Finance** Subventions. **Publications** *European Video Yearbook* (annual).
Members National associations in 11 countries:
Belgium, Denmark, Finland, France, Germany, Italy, Netherlands, Spain, Sweden, UK, USA.
Consultative Status Consultative status granted from: *World Intellectual Property Organization (WIPO, #21593)* (Permanent Observer Status). **NGO Relations** In liaison with technical committees of: *International Organization for Standardization (ISO, #14473)*. Member of: *Creative Media Business Alliance (CMBA, #04947)*. Associate member of: *European Internet Forum (EIF, #07591)*.
[2016/XD3004/**D**]

♦ International Videotex Industry Association (inactive)

♦ International Vienna Council (IVC) 15853

Conseil international de Vienne

Secretariat 13 Blaasstrasse, 1190 Vienna, Austria.
URL: http://www.ivc-europe.eu/

History Mar 1979, Vienna (Austria), as *International Council for New Initiatives in East-West Cooperation – Conseil international pour de nouvelles initiatives de coopération Est-Ouest*, following the East-West Conferences Vienna I and II. Vienna III and IV were held in 1986 and 1992 respectively. **Aims** Bring together the *industrial countries* of the *West* and the states of *Central/Eastern Europe* and *South-East Europe* at *economic* and *financial* level; work together in solving problems, bring together leading personalities in the economic sphere and establish a reliable information network for all National Committees of the Council. **Structure** Praesidium, serves as an executive board, comprised of the Chairman, Honorary Chairman, 6 to 8 Vice-Chairmen and the Secretary General. Executive Committee (meets twice a year), composed of the Praesidium and the Chairmen of the National Committees. **Finance** Members' dues. **Activities** Brings together businessmen, finance experts and top economists whenever possible. Organizes meetings (such as seminars, symposia, round tables) and study trips in all regions of the reforming countries. **Events** *The Danube region* Vienna (Austria) 1999, *Conference / Meeting* Vienna (Austria) 1998, *Conference / Meeting* Trieste (Italy) 1996, *Meeting* Moscow (Russia) 1995, *Conference / Meeting* Vienna (Austria) 1994. **Publications** *Danube Region Recommendations* (1998).
Members National Committees in 16 countries:
Armenia, Austria, Bulgaria, Croatia, Czechia, France, Germany, Hungary, Italy, Moldova, Poland, Romania, Russia, Slovakia, Slovenia, Spain.
Individuals in 1 country:
Belgium.
IGO Relations *Organization for Security and Cooperation in Europe (OSCE, #17887)*; *UNIDO (#20336)*. **NGO Relations** Co-founder of: *Association for Euro-Atlantic Cooperation (AEAC, no recent information)*.
[2012/XF5546/**F**]

♦ International Vine and Wine Office / see International Organisation of Vine and Wine (#14435)

♦ International Vintage Poster Dealers Association (IVPDA) 15854

Contact PO Box 501, Old Chelsea Station, New York NY 10113-0501, USA.
URL: http://www.ivpda.com/

History 1996. **Aims** Inform and educate the public, collectors and other buyers; help promote the appreciation of vintage posters worldwide. **Structure** Board of Directors (USA); European Board. President; US Vice-President; European Vice-President; Secretary. **Languages** Dutch, English, French, German. **Staff** Part-time, voluntary. **Finance** Members' dues.
Members in 15 countries and territories:
Australia, Belgium, Canada, France, Germany, Hawaii, Israel, Italy, Netherlands, Poland, Spain, Sweden, Switzerland, UK, USA. [2019/XM1169/**D**]

♦ International Viola Society (IVS) 15855

Pres 7995 Sartre, Brossard QC J4X 1S3, Canada.
Sec address not obtained.
URL: http://www.internationalviolasociety.org/

History 1968. Former names and other names: *Société internationale de l'alto* – former; *Internationale Viola-Gesellschaft* – former. **Aims** Serve as umbrella organization to govern and support existing and future national and regional organized groups or "National Sections" of viola players; promote and support activities serving the common good for all friends of the viola; promote increasing standards of excellence in viola performance; encourage and support research in the history of the viola, its performers, teachers, makers and *composers*; promote publication of relevant music and books. Encourage: building of new, high quality instruments and bows; development of new viola repertoire and publication of new music; organization of viola events and activities in regions not represented by a member section; national and international organization of viola sections in professional *orchestras*; exchange of information and professional contact among friends of the viola. **Languages** English. **Staff** 7.00 FTE, voluntary. **Finance** Sources: members' dues. **Activities** Advocacy/lobbying/activism; events/meetings; financial and/or material support; knowledge management/information dissemination. **Events** *International Viola Congress* Salaya (Thailand) 2023, *International Viola Congress* Columbus, GA (USA) 2022, *International Viola Congress* Castelo Branco (Portugal) 2020, *International Viola Congress* Poznań (Poland) 2019, *International Viola Congress* Rotterdam (Netherlands) 2018. **Publications** *IVS e-News*.
Members Member societies representing viola players, teachers and amateurs and musicologists in 22 countries and territories:
Australia, Brazil, Canada, China, Finland, France, Germany, Iceland, Italy, Netherlands, New Zealand, Nigeria, Norway, Poland, Portugal, South Africa, Sweden, Switzerland, Thailand, Türkiye, UK, USA. [2023.03.01/XF1520/**F**]

♦ International Virtual Aviation Organisation (IVAO) 15856

Main Office IVAO VZW, Werfstraat 89, 1570 Galmaarden, Belgium. E-mail: vzw@ivao.aero.
URL: http://ivao.aero/

History 1998. Registered in accordance with Belgian law, 2010. **Aims** Provide an online platform for *flight* simulation enthusiasts to enjoy their hobby in a simulated real-world environment, in company of other people, flying or providing Air Traffic Control services. **Structure** Board of Governors; Executive Council; HQ Departments; HQ Divisions. **Languages** English. **Staff** 500.00 FTE, voluntary. **Finance** Sources: donations; members' dues; sponsorship. **Activities** Awards/prizes/competitions; events/meetings; guidance/assistance/consulting; networking/liaising; research/documentation; training/education. **Publications** *Virtual Sky* – magazine. Information Services: Documentation Library; Route Database.
Members Registered users (over 200,000) in 78 countries and territories:
Algeria, Angola, Argentina, Aruba, Australia, Austria, Bahamas, Bahrain, Belgium, Botswana, Brazil, Canada, Chile, Colombia, Croatia, Czechia, Denmark, Dominican Rep, Egypt, Finland, France, Germany, Greece, Hong Kong, Hungary, India, Indonesia, Iran Islamic Rep, Iraq, Ireland, Italy, Jordan, Kazakhstan, Korea Rep, Kuwait, Lebanon, Luxembourg, Macau, Malaysia, Mexico, Morocco, Mozambique, Namibia, Netherlands, New Caledonia, New Zealand, Norway, Oman, Peru, Philippines, Poland, Polynesia Fr, Portugal, Qatar, Romania, Russia, Saudi Arabia, Senegal, Slovakia, Slovenia, South Africa, Spain, Sudan, Sweden, Switzerland, Syrian AR, Taiwan, Thailand, Tunisia, Türkiye, UK, Ukraine, United Arab Emirates, Uruguay, USA, Vietnam, Zimbabwe.
IGO Relations None. **NGO Relations** None. [2021/XM4262/v/**C**]

♦ International Virtual e-Hospital Foundation (internationally oriented national body)

♦ International Virtual Laboratory for Enterprise Interoperability (INTEROP-VLab) 15857

General Manager Univ Bordeaux – IMS A31, 351 cours de la Libération, 33405 Talence CEDEX, France. T. +33540003752. E-mail: info@interop-vlab.eu.
Admin HQ Bureau Nouvell Région Aquitaine Europe, Rue Montoyer 21, 1000 Brussels, Belgium.
URL: http://interop-vlab.eu/

History Mar 2007. Created mar 2007. Also known under the acronym *I-VLab*. Registered in accordance with Belgian law. **Aims** Maintain and develop the defragmentation of the ERA (European Research Area) in cooperation with other regions of the world. **Structure** General Assembly; Board of Directors. **Activities** Research/documentation; training/education. **Events** *International Conference on Interoperability of Enterprise Software and Applications* Tarbes (France) 2020, *International Conference on Interoperability of Enterprise Software and Applications* Berlin (Germany) 2018. **Publications** *I-VLab Newsletter*.
Members Poles representing 12 countries:
Belgium, China, Finland, France, Germany, Italy, Luxembourg, Norway, Portugal, Spain, Sweden, UK. [2021/XM8368/**F**]

♦ International Virtual Observatory Alliance (IVOA) 15858

Sec address not obtained.
Chair address not obtained.
URL: http://www.ivoa.net/

History Jun 2002. **Aims** Facilitate international coordination and collaboration for development and deployment of the tools, systems and organizational structures necessary to enable international utilization of astronomical archives as an integrated and interoperating virtual observatory. **Structure** Executive Committee; Technical Coordination Group; Committee for Science Priorities; Working Groups (6); Interest Groups (8). **Languages** English. **Staff** No formal staff. **Finance** No budget. Activities funded by participating organizations. **Activities** Events/meetings; projects/programmes. **Events** *Interoperability Meeting* 2022, *Interoperability Meeting* 2021, *Interoperability Meeting* 2021, *Interoperability Meeting* 2020, *Interoperability Meeting* 2020. **Publications** *IVOA Newsletter*.
Members National virtual observatories in 20 countries:
Argentina, Armenia, Australia, Brazil, Canada, Chile, China, France, Germany, Hungary, India, Italy, Japan, Netherlands, Russia, South Africa, Spain, UK, Ukraine, USA.
NGO Relations Member of (1): *ISC World Data System (ISC-WDS, #16024)*. [2022.06.15/XM1803/**F**]

♦ International Virtual Ophthalmic Research Center (unconfirmed)

♦ International Visegrad Fund 15859

Contact Hviezdoslavovo namestie 9, 811 02 Bratislava, Slovakia. T. +421259203811. E-mail: visegradfund@visegradfund.org.
URL: http://www.visegradfund.org/

History 9 Jun 2000. Established by *Visegrad Group (#20794)*. **Aims** Promote regional *cooperation* through grant, scholarship and fellowship funding of civil society and citizens of the Visegrad Group countries and other countries in Central and Eastern Europe, particularly the Western Balkans and Eastern Partnership countries. **Structure** Conference of Ministers of Foreign Affairs; Council of Ambassadors; Executive Director; Deputy Executive Director; Secretariat. **Languages** English. **Staff** 15.00 FTE, paid. **Finance** Sources: contributions; members' dues. Annual budget: 10,000,000 EUR (2022). **Activities** Capacity building; financial and/or material support; training/education.
Members in 4 countries:
Czechia, Hungary, Poland, Slovakia. [2022.10.11/XF6941/f/**F***]

♦ International Visual Communication Association (inactive)
♦ International Visual Literacy Association (internationally oriented national body)
♦ International Visual Sociology Association (internationally oriented national body)
♦ International Vitamin Conference (meeting series)
♦ International Vladimir Nabokov Society (internationally oriented national body)

♦ International VLBI Service for Geodesy and Astrometry (IVS) 15860

Dir Coordinating Ctr, NASA Goddard Space Flight Ctr (GSFC), Space Geodesy Lab, Code 698-2, Greenbelt MD 20771, USA. E-mail: ivscc@lists.nasa.gov.
URL: http://ivscc.gsfc.nasa.gov/

History 1999, within the framework of *International Association of Geodesy (IAG, #11914)*. **Aims** Provide a service to support *geodetic*, *geophysical* and astrometric research and operational activities; promote research and development for VLBI; interact with user of VLBI products. **Structure** Directing Board. Coordinating Center of Coordinators (3): Networks; Technology; Analysis. Operation Centers; Data Centers; Analysis Centers; Network Stations; Correlators. **Activities** Data provision; Research. Acts as coordinating centre for *International Earth Rotation and Reference Systems Service (IERS, #13216)*. **Events** *General Meeting* Tsukuba (Japan) 2024, *East-Asian VLBI Workshop* Mito (Japan) 2019, *General Meeting* Longyearbyen (Norway) 2018, *General Meeting* Johannesburg (South Africa) 2016, *General Meeting* Shanghai (China) 2014. **Publications** *IVS Newsletter* (3 a year).
Members Organizations in 20 countries:
Australia, Austria, Brazil, Canada, Chile, China, France, Germany, Italy, Japan, Korea Rep, New Zealand, Norway, Russia, South Africa, Spain, Sweden, Türkiye, Ukraine, USA.
NGO Relations Network member of: *ISC World Data System (ISC-WDS, #16024)*. [2020/XK2121/**E**]

♦ International VLBI Technology Workshop (meeting series)

♦ International Vocational Education and Training Association (IVETA) 15861

Exec Dir 5439 Red Bank Rd, Galena OH 43021, USA. T. +16142034361. E-mail: iveta@visi.com.
URL: https://iveta.global/

History Dec 1984. Founded as an affiliate of Association for Career and Technical Education. **Aims** Foster and promote professional links among international vocational educators and trainers; serve as a forum for sharing vocational education and training problems and solutions worldwide; assist in further development of vocational education and training as an international enterprise; facilitate worldwide dissemination of information in the field. **Structure** Executive Secretariat. Regions: Africa; East Asia and Pacific; Eastern Europe and Central Asia; Europe; Latin America and Caribbean; Middle East and North Africa; North America; South Asia. **Languages** English. **Staff** 0.50 FTE, paid; 20.00 FTE, voluntary. **Finance** Sources: members' dues. **Activities** Advocacy/lobbying/activism; events/meetings; knowledge management/information dissemination. **Events** *International Conference* Cape Town (South Africa) 2018, *International Conference* Queenstown (New Zealand) 2017, *International Conference* Suva (Fiji) 2016, *International Conference* Kuching (Malaysia) 2015, *International Conference* Helsinki (Finland) / St Petersburg (Russia) 2014. **Publications** *IVETA Hotline* (4 a year) – online; *International Journal of Vocational Education and Training* (2 a year); *Membership Directory* (regular) – online.
Members Individual professionals representing international agencies, government organizations, training, business and industrial organizations, private volunteer organizations, universities and technical institutes; administrators, students, teachers and researchers in the field. Individuals in 62 countries and territories:
Afghanistan, Armenia, Australia, Austria, Barbados, Botswana, Brazil, Canada, China, Eswatini, Ethiopia, Fiji, Finland, France, Georgia, Germany, Greece, India, Indonesia, Italy, Jamaica, Jordan, Kazakhstan, Kiribati, Korea Rep, Liberia, Malawi, Malaysia, Maldives, Mauritius, Mongolia, Netherlands, New Zealand, Nigeria, Norway, Pakistan, Palau, Palestine, Philippines, Poland, Russia, Saudi Arabia, Scotland, Somalia, South Africa, Sri Lanka, Sweden, Switzerland, Taiwan, Tajikistan, Tanzania UR, Thailand, Trinidad-Tobago, Türkiye, Uganda, UK, Ukraine, United Arab Emirates, USA, Yemen, Zambia, Zimbabwe.
NGO Relations Member of (1): *Skillman Network (#19306)* (Alliance). [2022/XD5123/v/**D**]

♦ International Vocational Training Centre, Arnhem (internationally oriented national body)
♦ International Vocational Training Organization / see WorldSkills International (#21791)
♦ International Voice of Justice (internationally oriented national body)
♦ International Volcanic Health Hazard Network (see: #12259)
♦ International Volleyball Federation (#09670)
♦ International Voluntary Action and Voluntary Research Organization (inactive)
♦ International Voluntary Organisation for Women, Education and Development (internationally oriented national body)
♦ International Voluntary Service / see Service Civil International (#19238)
♦ International Voluntary Service / see Service Volontaire International (#19245)
♦ International Voluntary Service for Peace / see Peace Corps
♦ International Voluntary Service, UK (internationally oriented national body)
♦ International Volunteer Academy (unconfirmed)
♦ International Volunteer Expeditions (internationally oriented national body)
♦ International Volunteering Service (#19245)
♦ International Volunteerism Organization for Women, Education, Development (#20806)
♦ International Volunteers for African Development (internationally oriented national body)
♦ International Volunteers for Development (internationally oriented national body)
♦ International Wader Study Group (see: #15766)
♦ International Wages Due Lesbians (internationally oriented national body)
♦ International Wagon Union (inactive)
♦ International WAGR Syndrome Association (internationally oriented national body)
♦ International Waldenstrom's Macroglobulinemia Foundation (internationally oriented national body)
♦ International Waldorf Kindergarten Association / see International Association for Steiner/Waldorf Early Childhood Education (#12185)
♦ International Wallcovering Manufacturers Association / see IGI – The Global Wallcoverings Association (#11107)

♦ International Walras Association 15862

Association internationale Walras (AIW)

Co-Pres Univ de Lausanne, 1015 Lausanne VD, Switzerland.
Sec/Treas address not obtained.
URL: http://www.unil.ch/walras/

History 3 Oct 1997, by Prof Donald Walker. **Aims** Promote research on the works of Léon Walras (1834-1910), furthering its diffusion and encouraging communication among scholars active in this field. **Structure** Committee, comprising 2 Co-Presidents, Vice-President, Secretary-Treasurer and 2 members. **Events** *Biennial Conference* Lyon (France) 2015, *Conference* Paris (France) 2015, *Biennial Conference / Conference* Toulouse (France) 2012, *Biennial conference / Conference* Lyon (France) 2010, *Biennial conference / Conference* Kyoto (Japan) 2008. **Publications** Conference proceedings.
Members Individuals in 8 countries:
Australia, Belgium, France, Italy, Japan, Switzerland, UK, USA. [2016.08.27/XJ2361/v/**E**]

♦ International Walter Benjamin Society (IWBS) 15863

Webmaster Inst für Germanistik, Ludwig Wucherer 2, 06108 Halle (Saale), Germany.
Registered Address Schützenstr 18, 10117 Berlin, Germany.
URL: http://walterbenjamin.info/

History 14 Sep 2009, Antwerp (Belgium). Founded on merger of *Internationale Walter Benjamin Gesellschaft (IWBG, inactive)* and *International Walter Benjamin Association (inactive)*. Registration: Berlin District court, No/ID: VR 31761, Start date: 28 Aug 2012, Germany. **Aims** Bring together scholars and readers interested in the works of the philosopher Walter Benjamin (1892-1940). **Structure** Executive Board. **Finance** Sources: members' dues. **Activities** Awards/prizes/competitions; events/meetings; knowledge management/information dissemination. **Events** *Conference* Berlin (Germany) 2021, *International Walter Benjamin Conference* Bern (Switzerland) 2019, *International Walter Benjamin Conference* Oxford (UK) 2017, *International Walter Benjamin Conference* Tel Aviv (Israel) 2015, *International Walter Benjamin Congress* Frankfurt-Main (Germany) 2013. [2021/AA2017/v/**E**]

♦ International War Tribunal (inactive)

♦ International Waste Working Group (IWWG) 15864

Managing Dir c/o Hamburg Univ of Technology, Harburger Schlossstrasse 36, 20179 Hamburg, Germany. T. +4940428782053. Fax +4940428782375. E-mail: info@iwwg.eu.
URL: http://www.iwwg.eu/

History 2002. **Aims** Serve as a forum for the scientific and professional community; answer a need for the international promotion and dissemination of developments in the waste management industry; provide an intellectual forum to encourage and support integrated and sustainable waste management; promote practical scientific development in the field. **Structure** Board of up to 12 members. Scientific Advisory Panel. Task Groups. General Secretariat. **Languages** English. **Staff** Voluntary. **Finance** Members' dues. **Activities** Organizes conferences, seminars, workshops and courses. **Events** *Asian Regional Symposium* Seoul (Korea Rep) 2017, *International waste management and landfill symposium* Santa Margherita di Pula (Italy) 2011, *Asian Pacific landfill symposium* Seoul (Korea Rep) 2010, *BOKU waste conference* Vienna (Austria) 2009, *International waste management and landfill symposium* Santa Margherita di Pula (Italy) 2005. **Publications** *Waste Management* – official journal. Monographs. **Members** Full in 41 countries. Membership countries not specified. [2014.06.01/XM0555/**E**]

♦ International Water Association (IWA) 15865

Headquarters Export Building, First Floor, 1 Clove Crescent, London, E14 2BA, UK. T. +442076545500. Fax +442076545555. E-mail: water@iwahq.org.
Global Office Technology Innovation Center, No 1 Xiankun Road, Nanjing, Jianye, 210019 Jiangsu, China.
URL: http://www.iwa-network.org/

History 7 Sep 1990, Buenos Aires (Argentina). Founded by merger of *International Association on Water Quality (IAWQ, inactive)* and *International Water Services Association (IWSA, inactive)*. Registration: Charity Commission, No/ID: 107690, England and Wales. **Aims** Bring together people from across the water profession to deliver equitable and sustainable water solutions for our world. **Structure** Governing Assembly; Board of Directors; Executive Management; Strategic Council. *Young Water Professionals (IWA YWPs)*; Clusters; Task Groups. Regional groups (6): *American Water Works Association (AWWA, #00791)*; Danube and the Black Sea Region; *European Federation of National Associations of Water and Waste Water Services (#07170)*; *Inter-American Association of Sanitary and Environmental Engineering (#11400)*; *IWA Asia Pacific Region Grouping (IWA-ASPIRE, #16083)*. **Languages** English. **Staff** 39.00 FTE, paid. **Finance** Sources: meeting proceeds; members' dues; sale of publications. **Activities** Advocacy/lobbying/activism; awards/prizes/competitions; events/meetings. **Events** *Leading Edge Conference on Water and Wastewater Technologies* Daegu (Korea Rep) 2023, *World Water Congress* Copenhagen (Denmark) 2022, *International Symposium on Waste Management Problems in Agro-Industries* Gdansk (Poland) 2022, *International Conference on Sewer Processes and Networks* Graz (Austria) 2022, *International Conference on Wetland Systems for Water Pollution Control* Lyon (France) 2022. **Publications** *Water21* (6 a year) – magazine; *IWA Newsletter*.
Members Governing; Corporate; Individual. Governing membership in 88 countries and territories:
Algeria, Argentina, Australia, Austria, Bangladesh, Belgium, Benin, Botswana, Brazil, Bulgaria, Cameroon, Canada, Chile, China, Congo Brazzaville, Côte d'Ivoire, Croatia, Cyprus, Czechia, Denmark, Egypt, Eswatini, Finland, France, Gabon, Germany, Ghana, Gibraltar, Greece, Hong Kong, Hungary, India, Indonesia, Iran Islamic Rep, Ireland, Israel, Italy, Japan, Jordan, Kenya, Korea Rep, Kuwait, Lebanon, Lesotho, Lithuania, Luxembourg, Macau, Malawi, Malaysia, Mauritius, Mexico, Morocco, Mozambique, Namibia, Nepal, Netherlands, New Zealand, North Macedonia, Norway, Philippines, Portugal, Romania, Russia, Senegal, Serbia, Seychelles, Singapore, Slovakia, Slovenia, South Africa, Spain, Sri Lanka, Sweden, Switzerland, Taiwan, Thailand, Togo, Trinidad-Tobago, Tunisia, Türkiye, Uganda, UK, Ukraine, Uruguay, USA, Uzbekistan, Venezuela, Vietnam.
Consultative Status Consultative status granted from: *ECOSOC (#05331)* (Ros B); *FAO (#09260)* (Special Status); *WHO (#20950)* (Official Relations). **IGO Relations** Accredited by: *United Nations Office at Vienna (UNOV, #20604)*. Associated with Department of Global Communications of the United Nations. Member of: *Regional Centre on Urban Water Management, Teheran (RCUWM, #18761)*. Partner of: *UN-Water (#20723)*. **NGO Relations** Cooperative agreement or joint activities with: *European Water Association (EWA, #09080)*; *International Association for Hydro-Environment Engineering and Research (IAHR, #11950)*; *International Union of Pure and Applied Chemistry (IUPAC, #15809)*. Member of: *Water Europe (WE, #20828)*; *Global Water Operators' Partnerships Alliance (GWOPA, #10652)*; *International Science Council (ISC, #14796)*; *Water and Climate Coalition (WCC, no recent information)*; *World Water Council (WWC, #21908)*. In liaison with technical committees of: *International Organization for Standardization (ISO, #14473)*. Partner of: *International Rainwater Harvesting Alliance (IRHA, #14695)*; *Rainwater Partnership (no recent information)*; *Sanitation and Water for All (SWA, #19051)*; *Sustainable Sanitation Alliance (SuSanA, #20066)*. Special relationship with: *International Union for Conservation of Nature and Natural Resources (IUCN, #15766)*. [2021/XC0103/**C**]

♦ International Water Association Asia Pacific Group / see IWA Asia Pacific Region Grouping (#16083)
♦ International WaterCentre (internationally oriented national body)
♦ International Waterfowl and Wetlands Research Bureau (inactive)

♦ International Water History Association (IWHA) 15866

Treas Australian National Univ School of History, RSSS Bldg Room 6-17, 146 Ellery Cres, Canberra ACT 2601, Australia.
URL: https://internationalwaterhistory.org/

History 2001, Bergen (Norway). **Aims** Promote understanding of the history of the control and use of freshwater resources throughout the world. **Languages** English. **Events** *Biennial Conference* Stellenbosch (South Africa) 2022, *Biennial Conference* Delft (Netherlands) 2020, *Biennial Conference / Conference* Delft (Netherlands) 2015, *Biennial conference / Conference* Montpellier (France) 2013, *Biennial Conference* South Africa 2011. **NGO Relations** Member of: *International Consortium of Environmental History Organizations (ICEHO, #12912)*; *International Water-Related Associations' Liaison Committee (IWALC, #15869)*. [2022/XD4371/**D**]

♦ International Water Industry Conference (meeting series)
♦ International Waterlogging and Salinity Research Institute (internationally oriented national body)

♦ International Water Management Institute (IWMI) 15867

Dir-Gen PO Box 2075, Colombo, Sri Lanka. T. +94112880000. Fax +94112786854. E-mail: iwmi@cgiar.org – iwmi-comms@cgiar.org.
Street address 127 Sunil Mawatha, Pelawatte, Battaramulla, Sri Lanka.
URL: http://www.iwmi.cgiar.org/

History Dec 1984, Sri Lanka. Founded by agreement between the Government of Sri Lanka and *Ford Foundation (#09858)*. An international agricultural research centre under the auspices of *CGIAR System Organization (CGIAR, #03843)*. Absorbed activities of *International Board for Soil Research and Management (IBSRAM, inactive)*, Apr 2001. Former names and other names: *International Irrigation Management Institute (IIMI)* – former; *Institut international de management de l'irrigation* – former. **Aims** Provide evidence-based solutions to sustainably managed water and land resources for food security, people's livelihoods and environment. **Structure** International Board of Governors; Regional Offices; IWMI Representatives; Headquarters in Colombo (Sri Lanka). **Languages** Afrikaans, Chinese, Dutch, English, French, German, Hindi, Nepali, Russian, Sinhala, Spanish, Swahili, Tamil, Thai, Urdu. **Staff** 241.00 FTE, paid. Staff includes scientific team of 71 staff of whom 63 recruited internationally and regionally. **Finance** Sources: donations; government support; international organizations. Principal donor governments: Australia, Germany, India, Netherlands, Sweden, Switzerland, UK, USA. Supported by: *Asian Development Bank (ADB, #01422)*; *Australian Centre for International Agricultural Research (ACIAR)*; *Bill and Melinda Gates Foundation (BMGF)*; *European Commission (EC, #06633)*; Helmsley Charitable Trust; *International Bank for Reconstruction and Development (IBRD, #12317)* (World Bank). Annual budget: 36,290,000 USD (2022). **Activities** Advocacy/lobbying/activism; awards/prizes/competitions; events/meetings; research and development; research/documentation. **Events** *International Conference on Water Security through Rainwater Harvesting* Colombo (Sri Lanka) 2018, *Regional Workshop on Building Drought Resilience in Agriculture* Bangkok (Thailand) 2017, *International forum on water resources and sustainable development* Wuhan (China) 2009, *International conference on regional cooperation in transboundary river basins* Dushanbe (Tajikistan) 2005, *East African integrated river basin management conference* Morogoro (Tanzania UR) 2005. **Publications** Annual Report; research reports; working papers; books; case studies series; country papers; bibliographies; maps; conference and workshop proceedings; policy briefings; issue briefs; corporate communications material (brochures, flyers, posters). **IGO Relations** Accredited by (1): *United Nations Framework Convention on Climate Change – Secretariat (UNFCCC, #20564)*. Member of (1): *International Information System for the Agricultural Sciences and Technology (AGRIS, #13848)*. Partner of (3): *Group on Earth Observations (GEO, #10735)*; *UN-Water (#20723)*; *West African Science Service Center on Climate Change and Adapted Land Use (WASCAL, #20897)*. Functions as Regional Support Office of: *United Nations Platform for Space-based Information for Disaster Management and Emergency Response (UN-SPIDER, #20610)*. Cooperates with the other CGIAR supported centres: *Africa Rice Center (AfricaRice, #00518)*; *Bioversity International (#03262)*; *International Center for Agricultural Research in the Dry Areas (ICARDA, #12466)*; *International Crops Research Institute for the Semi-Arid Tropics (ICRISAT, #13116)*; *International Livestock Research Institute (ILRI, #14062)*; *International Rice Research Institute (IRRI, #14754)*. **NGO Relations** Member of (11): *Alliance for Water Stewardship (AWS, #00727)*; *Climate Technology Centre and Network (CTCN, #04023)*; *Extractive Industries Transparency Initiative (EITI, #09229)*; *Inland Valley Consortium (IVC, no recent information)*; *International Foundation for Science (IFS, #13677)*; *International Network of Resource Centers on Urban Agriculture and Food Security (RUAF Foundation, #14319)*; *International Union for Conservation of Nature and Natural Resources (IUCN, #15766)*; *Network of Asian River Basin Organizations (NARBO, #16993)*; *Sustainable Sanitation Alliance (SuSanA, #20066)*; *WaterNet (#20832)*; *World Water Council (WWC, #21908)*. Partner of (1): *Wetlands International (#20928)*. Cooperates with (1): *Bellanet Alliance of Social Entrepreneurs (BASE, #03196)*. Participates in: *Agricultural Libraries Network (AGLINET, #00571)*; *Movement of Spiritual Inner Awareness (MSIA)*. Cooperates with other CGIAR supported centres: *Center for International Forestry Research (CIFOR, #03646)*; *International Centre for Tropical Agriculture (#12527)*; *International Food Policy Research Institute (IFPRI, #13622)*; *International Institute of Tropical Agriculture (IITA, #13933)*; *International Maize and Wheat Improvement Center (#14077)*; *International Potato Center (#14627)*; *World Agroforestry Centre (ICRAF, #21072)*; *WorldFish (#21507)*. [2022.11.15/XE0387/j/**E**]

♦ International Water Mist Association (IWMA) 15868

Gen Manager Poststrasse 33 (im HBC), 20354 Hamburg, Germany. T. +494035085215. Fax +49403508580. E-mail: info@iwma.net.
URL: http://www.iwma.net/

History 4 Apr 1998. Registration: Germany. **Aims** Promote research, development and application of innovative *firefighting* methods, in particular in the area of the water mist technology. **Structure** Assembly of Members; Board; Scientific Council; Marketing Group; Technical Committee. **Languages** English. **Staff** 1.00 FTE, paid; 10.00 FTE, voluntary. **Finance** Sources: members' dues. **Activities** Awards/prizes/competitions; events/meetings; standards/guidelines; training/education. **Events** *Annual Conference* Berlin (Germany) 2019, *Annual Conference* London (UK) 2018, *Annual Conference* Rome (Italy) 2017, *Annual Conference* Vienna (Austria) 2016, *Annual Conference* Amsterdam (Netherlands) 2015. **Publications** *IWMA Newsletter* (4 a year). Conference proceedings; position papers; standards and guidelines; reports; scientific articles.
Members Individuals, corporations (mostly manufacturers), institutions and fire departments (60) from 20 countries:
Australia, Austria, Bahrain, China, Denmark, Egypt, Finland, France, Germany, India, Italy, Netherlands, Norway, South Africa, Spain, Sweden, Switzerland, UK, United Arab Emirates, USA.
Consultative Status Consultative status granted from: *International Maritime Organization (IMO, #14102)*. **IGO Relations** Observer status with: European Commission – Expert Group on Marine Equipment. **NGO Relations** In liaison with technical committees of: *Comité européen de normalisation (CEN, #04162)*. [2021.06.09/XD3824/**D**]

♦ International Water Power Consortium (unconfirmed)
♦ International Waterproofing Association / see European Waterproofing Association (#09084)
♦ International Water-Related Associations Liaison Committee / see International Water-Related Associations' Liaison Committee (#15869)

♦ International Water-Related Associations' Liaison Committee (IWALC) 15869

Comité de liaison des associations internationales relevant de l'eau

Sec c/o ICID, 48 Nyaya Marg, Chanakyapuri, Delhi 110 021, DELHI 110 021, India. T. +911126116837 – +911126115679. Fax +911126115962. E-mail: icid@icid.org.
URL: http://www.icid.org/

History 23 Nov 1994, Cairo (Egypt). Also referred to as *International Water-Related Associations Liaison Committee*. **Aims** Initiate integrative approaches for combined involvement of various specializations; review activities in the field of global water issues; share experiences on organizational and financial matters. **Structure** Committee of 14 international water-related associations, represented by their Secretaries General or Presidents and of 2 international organizations as Observers: *International Hydrological Programme (IHP, #13826)*; *World Meteorological Organization (WMO, #21649)*. Coordinating secretariat supported by *International Commission on Irrigation and Drainage (ICID, #12694)*, Delhi (India). **Languages** English. **Staff** Voluntary. **Finance** Free secretariat and organizational support provided by ICID. **Activities** Events/meetings. **Events** *Meeting* Montréal, QC (Canada) 1997. **Publications** Booklet.
Members International organizations (13):
International Association for Hydro-Environment Engineering and Research (IAHR, #11950); *International Association of Hydrogeologists (IAH, #11953)*; *International Association of Hydrological Sciences (IAHS, #11954)*; *International Commission on Irrigation and Drainage (ICID, #12694)*; *International Commission on Large Dams (ICOLD, #12696)*; *International Hydrological Programme (IHP, #13826)*; *International Hydropower Association (IHA, #13828)*; *International Water Association (IWA, #15865)*; *International Water History Association (IWHA, #15866)*; *International Water Resources Association (IWRA, #15871)*; *PIANC (#18371)*; *World Association for Sedimentation and Erosion Research (WASER, #21186)*; *World Meteorological Organization (WMO, #21649)*. [2015.09.03/XE2445/y/**E**]

♦ International Water and Resource Economics Consortium (IWREC) . 15870

Contact Water Science / Geology 2228A, UC Riverside, 900 University Ave, Riverside CA 92521, USA. T. +19518272875. Fax +19518272711.
URL: http://wspc.ucr.edu/iwrec/home.html

Structure Advisory Board. **Events** *Meeting / Conference* Washington, DC (USA) 2014, *Annual meeting / Conference* Stockholm (Sweden) 2012, *Annual meeting* Banff, AB (Canada) 2011, *Conference* Banff, AB (Canada) 2011, *Conference* Berkeley, CA (USA) 2009. **Members** Individuals. Membership countries not specified. **NGO Relations** *Stockholm International Water Institute (SIWI)*. [2014/XN8088/v/**E**]

♦ International Water Resources Association (IWRA) 15871

Association internationale des ressources en eau (AIRE) – Asociación Internacional de Recursos Hidricos (AIREH)

Exec Dir 51 rue Salvador Allende, 92027 Nanterre CEDEX, France. T. +33140201628. E-mail: office@iwra.org.
URL: https://www.iwra.org/

History 1971. Former names and other names: *International Association of Water Resources (IAWR)* – alias. **Aims** Improve and expand understanding of water issues through education, research and information exchange among countries and across disciplines. **Structure** General Assembly (every 3 years); Board of Directors; Council; Executive Committee; Geographical Committees; Standing Committees. **Languages** English. **Staff** 9.00 FTE, paid. **Finance** Sources: grants; meeting proceeds; members' dues; sponsorship. Other sources: journal subscriptions. **Activities** Awards/prizes/competitions; events/meetings; projects/programmes; publishing activities. **Events** *World Water Congress* 2025, *World Water Congress* Beijing (China) 2023, *World Water Congress* Daegu (Korea Rep) 2021, *Triennial World Congress* Daegu (Korea Rep) 2020, *Triennial World Congress* Cancún (Mexico) 2017. **Publications** *IWRA Update* (4 a year) – newsletter; *Water International (WIN): Official Journal of the IWRA* (8 a year). Book series; policy briefs.
Members Individual (over 1,100): Regular; Special (Student, Retiree, Fellow); Organizational (Institution, Corporation). Full in 84 countries and territories:
Angola, Argentina, Australia, Austria, Azerbaijan, Bahrain, Bangladesh, Belgium, Botswana, Brazil, Cambodia, Canada, Cape Verde, Chile, Côte d'Ivoire, Croatia, Denmark, Egypt, Eswatini, Finland, France, Germany, Ghana, Greece, Hong Kong, Hungary, India, Indonesia, Iran Islamic Rep, Ireland, Israel, Italy, Japan, Jordan, Kenya, Korea Rep, Kuwait, Lesotho, Luxembourg, Malaysia, Mexico, Morocco, Namibia, Nepal, Netherlands, New Zealand, Nigeria, Norway, Oman, Pakistan, Palestine, Panama, Peru, Philippines, Poland, Portugal, Romania, Russia, Saudi Arabia, Singapore, Slovenia, South Africa, Spain, Sri Lanka, Sudan, Suriname, Sweden, Switzerland, Taiwan, Tanzania UR, Thailand, Tonga, Tunisia, Türkiye, Uganda, UK, United Arab Emirates, Uruguay, USA, Uzbekistan, Venezuela, Vietnam, Zambia, Zimbabwe.
IGO Relations Partner of: *Global Alliances for Water and Climate (GAfWaC, #10230)*; *UN-Water (#20723)*. **NGO Relations** Member of: *World Water Council (WWC, #21908)*. In liaison with technical committees of: *International Organization for Standardization (ISO, #14473)*. [2022/XB4125/**B**]

♦ International Water Services Association (inactive)
♦ International Water Ski Federation / see International Waterski and Wakeboard Federation (#15872)
♦ International Water Ski Union / see International Waterski and Wakeboard Federation (#15872)

♦ International Waterski and Wakeboard Federation (IWWF) 15872

SG The Forum, Hanworth Lane, Chertsey, KT16 8JX, UK. E-mail: info@iwwfed.com – executive@iwwfed.com.
URL: https://iwwf.sport/

History 29 Jul 1946. Statutes adopted 3-4 Nov 1947, Brussels (Belgium), at first Congress. Restructured, 12 Aug 1955, Beirut (Lebanon), on merger with *World Water Ski Federation (WWSF, inactive)*. Former names and other names: *International Water Ski Union* – former (1946); *Union internationale de ski nautique (UISN)* – former (1946); *World Water Ski Union (WWSU)* – former (1955); *Union mondiale de ski nautique (UMSN)* – former (1955); *International Water Ski Federation (IWSF)* – former (1989). **Aims** Promote and support development of water skiing and wakeboard worldwide. **Structure** World Congress (every 2 years); World Executive Board; Bureau; Athletes Commission; World Councils (8); World Commissions (2); Regional Confederations (5). **Languages** English. **Staff** 1.00 FTE, paid; 6.00 FTE, voluntary. **Finance** Regional sections' dues and other membership fees. Other sources: sanction fees for World Titled Events; television rights and other funding from water skiing events organized by or under the auspices of IWWF; IOC, ARISF, government or other public or private subsidies, sponsorship, donations and legacies; investment income; various contributions depending on circumstances and needs. **Activities** Sporting activities. **Events** *Biennial Congress* Putrajaya (Malaysia) 2019, *Biennial Congress* Paris (France) 2017, *Biennial Congress* Chapala (Mexico) 2015, *Team Managers Meeting* Busan (Korea Rep) 2013, *World Wakeboard Judges Meeting* Busan (Korea Rep) 2013.

Members National federations in 80 countries and territories:
Argentina, Australia, Austria, Belarus, Belgium, Brazil, Cameroon, Canada, Chile, China, Colombia, Costa Rica, Croatia, Cyprus, Czechia, Denmark, Dominican Rep, Ecuador, Egypt, England, Finland, France, Georgia, Germany, Ghana, Great Britain, Greece, Guatemala, Hong Kong, Hungary, India, Indonesia, Iran Islamic Rep, Ireland, Israel, Italy, Japan, Korea DPR, Korea Rep, Kuwait, Latvia, Lebanon, Lithuania, Luxembourg, Malaysia, Mauritius, Mexico, Monaco, Morocco, Namibia, Netherlands, New Zealand, Nigeria, Norway, Panama, Paraguay, Peru, Philippines, Poland, Portugal, Puerto Rico, Qatar, Romania, Russia, Serbia, Singapore, Slovakia, Slovenia, South Africa, Spain, Sweden, Switzerland, Taiwan, Thailand, Türkiye, UK, Ukraine, United Arab Emirates, USA, Zimbabwe.

NGO Relations Member of (3): *Association of the IOC Recognized International Sports Federations (ARISF, #02767)*; *International World Games Association (IWGA, #15914)*; *Olympic Movement (#17719)*. Cooperates with (1): *International Testing Agency (ITA, #15678)*. Recognized by: *International Olympic Committee (IOC, #14408)*. Oceania region is member of: *Organisation of Sports Federations of Oceania (OSFO, #17828)*.
[2023.02.15/XC0151/**B**]

♦ International Waters Learning Exchange and Resource Network (IW-LEARN) 15873

Project Manager c/o Intergovernmental Oceanographic Commission, 7 Place de Fontenoy, 75007 Paris, France. E-mail: info@iwlearn.org.
Program Manager GRID-Arendal, Teaterplassen 3, 4836 Arendal, Norway. E-mail: iwlearn@grida.no.
URL: http://www.iwlearn.net/

History Founded as a project of *Global Environment Facility (GEF, #10346)*. **Aims** Build an Internet-based community to protect, restore and sustain the world's aquifers, great lakes and river basins, coastal zones, seas and oceans. **Events** *Water Information Summit* Delft (Netherlands) 2003. **Members** Membership countries not specified. **IGO Relations** Partners: *International Bank for Reconstruction and Development (IBRD, #12317)*; *UNDP (#20292)*; *UNEP (#20299)*. **NGO Relations** Member of: *Network for Capacity Building in Integrated Water Resources Management (CAP-Net, #17000)*.
[2020/XF6968/**F**]

♦ International Weather and Climate Forum (meeting series)

♦ International Webmasters Association (IWA) 15874

Association internationale des webmasters – Asociación Internacional de Webmasters

Exec Dir 556 S Fair Oaks Ave, Ste 101-200, Pasadena CA 91105, USA. T. +16264493709ext706. Fax +18666071773. E-mail: support@iwanet.org.
URL: http://www.iwanet.org/

History Merged with *HTML Writers Guild (HWG, inactive)*, 2001. Also referred to as *IWA-HWG*. **Structure** Regional branches (6). **Events** *Meeting* Santa Barbara, CA (USA) 2001.

Members Head office () and regional branches in 7 countries:
Brazil, France, Germany, Iceland, Serbia, Spain, USA (*).
[2017/XD6624/**D**]

♦ International Weed Science Society (IWSS) 15875

Société internationale de malherbologie sur le désherbage

Sec UFPEI-FAEM, Pelotas RS, 96010-610, Brazil. E-mail: vice-president@iwss.info.
Pres Haryana Agricultural Univ, Main Rd, Azad Nagar, Hisar, Haryana 125004, Hisar HARYANA 125004, India. T. +14795753955.
URL: http://www.iwss.info/

History 5 Feb 1975. Founded by 50 individuals from Europe, North American, South America and the Asian-Pacific area, at 15th annual meeting of Weed Science Society of America. **Aims** Encourage, promote and assist development of global weed science and weed control technology. **Structure** Executive Committee. Regional societies (6): *Asian Pacific Weed Science Society (APWSS, #01646)*; *European Weed Research Society (EWRS, #09089)*; *Latin American Weed Society (#16394)*; Weed Science Society of Eastern Africa (WSSEA); *Weed Science Society of America (WSSA)*; *West African Weed Science Society (WAWSS, #20899)*. **Languages** English. **Staff** None. **Finance** Sources: members' dues. **Activities** Events/meetings; guidance/assistance/consulting; networking/liaising; training/education. **Events** *International Weed Science Congress* Jerusalem (Israel) 2024, *International Weed Science Congress* Bangkok (Thailand) 2022, *International Weed Science Congress* Bangkok (Thailand) 2021, *International Weed Science Congress* Bangkok (Thailand) 2020, *Quadrennial Congress* Prague (Czech Rep) 2016. **Publications** *IWSS Newsletter* (2 a year). *Bibliography of Weed Science* (1981). Membership directory.

Members Categories Individual (554); Affiliate (9); Sustaining (17). Members in 82 countries and territories:
Argentina, Australia, Bahamas, Bangladesh, Belgium, Benin, Bolivia, Brazil, Bulgaria, Burkina Faso, Canada, Chile, China, Colombia, Costa Rica, Côte d'Ivoire, Cuba, Cyprus, Czechia, Denmark, Ecuador, Egypt, Ethiopia, Fiji, Finland, France, Germany, Ghana, Greece, Honduras, Hungary, India, Indonesia, Iraq, Ireland, Israel, Italy, Japan, Jordan, Kenya, Korea Rep, Lebanon, Lithuania, Luxembourg, Malaysia, Mexico, Mozambique, Nepal, Netherlands, New Zealand, Nigeria, Pakistan, Palau, Palestine, Panama, Paraguay, Peru, Philippines, Poland, Portugal, Puerto Rico, Russia, Serbia, Singapore, Slovenia, South Africa, Spain, Sri Lanka, Sudan, Suriname, Sweden, Switzerland, Syrian AR, Taiwan, Tanzania UR, Thailand, Türkiye, UK, Uruguay, USA, Venezuela, Vietnam.
[2022.10.11/XB9533/**B**]

♦ International Weightlifting Federation (IWF) 15876

Fédération internationale d'haltérophilie – Federación Internacional de Halterofilia

Pres House of Hungarian Sports, Istvanmezei út 1-3, Budapest 1146, Hungary. T. +3613530530. Fax +3613530199. E-mail: iwf@iwfnet.net.
URL: http://www.iwf.net/

History 1905, Paris (France), as *Fédération internationale haltérophile (FIH)*. Name changed, 1950, Paris, to *International Weightlifting and Physical Culture Federation – Fédération internationale haltérophile et culturiste (FIHC)*, and, 1968, Mexico City (Mexico), to *Fédération haltérophile internationale (FHI)*. Present title adopted 1972, Munich (Germany FR). **Aims** Organize, control and develop weightlifting on an international scale; assist national federations; set up rules; regulate and control world and international *championships* and competitions; resolve disputes between affiliated organizations; train and examine referees; supervise the activities of continental federations; register world records. **Structure** Congress (annual). Executive Board, consisting of President, General Secretary/Treasurer, 1st Vice-President, 5 Vice-Presidents, 8 Executive Members, 6 Continental Presidents and Assistant Secretary. Committees (5): Technical; Scientific and Research; Medical; Auditors; Athletes. **Activities** Organizes the Junior and Senior World Weightlifting Championships. **Events** *Annual congress* Pattaya (Thailand) 2019, *Quadrennial Electoral Congress* Bangkok (Thailand) 2017, *Quadrennial electoral congress* Madrid (Spain) 2009, *Annual congress* Budapest (Hungary) 2005, *Annual Congress* Doha (Qatar) 2005. **Publications** *World Weightlifting* (4 a year).

Members Member federations (174) in 174 countries and territories:
Afghanistan, Albania, Algeria, Antigua-Barbuda, Argentina, Armenia, Aruba, Australia, Austria, Azerbaijan, Bahamas, Bahrain, Bangladesh, Barbados, Belarus, Belgium, Belize, Bhutan, Bolivia, Bosnia-Herzegovina, Brazil, Brunei Darussalam, Bulgaria, Cambodia, Cameroon, Canada, Cayman Is, Chile, China, Colombia, Comoros, Congo Brazzaville, Congo DR, Cook Is, Costa Rica, Croatia, Cuba, Cyprus, Czechia, Denmark, Dominican Rep, Ecuador, Egypt, El Salvador, Estonia, Eswatini, Ethiopia, Fiji, Finland, France, Georgia, Germany, Ghana, Greece, Guam, Guatemala, Guyana, Haiti, Honduras, Hong Kong, Hungary, Iceland, India, Indonesia, Iran Islamic Rep, Iraq, Ireland, Israel, Italy, Japan, Jordan, Kazakhstan, Kenya, Kiribati, Korea DPR, Korea Rep, Kuwait, Kyrgyzstan, Latvia, Lebanon, Lesotho, Libya, Lithuania, Luxembourg, Macau, Madagascar, Malaysia, Mali, Malta, Marshall Is, Mauritius, Mexico, Micronesia FS, Moldova, Monaco, Mongolia, Morocco, Myanmar, Nauru, Nepal, Netherlands, New Zealand, Nicaragua, Nigeria, Niue, Norfolk Is, Northern Mariana Is, Norway, Oman, Pakistan, Palau, Palestine, Panama, Papua New Guinea, Paraguay, Peru, Philippines, Poland, Polynesia Fr, Portugal, Puerto Rico, Qatar, Romania, Russia, Samoa, Samoa USA, San Marino, Saudi Arabia, Scotland, Senegal, Serbia-Montenegro, Seychelles, Sierra Leone, Singapore, Slovakia, Slovenia, Solomon Is, Somalia, South Africa, Spain, Sri Lanka, St Vincent-Grenadines, Sudan, Suriname, Sweden, Switzerland, Syrian AR, Taiwan, Tajikistan, Tanzania UR, Thailand, Timor-Leste, Tonga, Trinidad-Tobago, Tunisia, Türkiye, Turkmenistan, Tuvalu, Uganda, UK, Ukraine, United Arab Emirates, USA, Uzbekistan, Vanuatu, Venezuela, Vietnam, Virgin Is USA, Wales, Yemen, Zambia, Zimbabwe.

Continental members (5):
Asian Weightlifting Federation (AWF, #01781); *European Weightlifting Federation (EWF, #09090)*; *Oceania Weightlifting Federation (OWF, #17682)*; *Pan American Weightlifting Confederation (PAWC, #18137)*; *Weightlifting Federation of Africa (WFA, #20854)*.

NGO Relations Member of (3): *Asociación de Confederaciones Deportivas Sudamericanas (ACODESU, no recent information)*; *Association of Summer Olympic International Federations (ASOIF, #02943)*; *Olympic Movement (#17719)*. Cooperates with (1): *International Testing Agency (ITA, #15678)*. Recognized by: *International Olympic Committee (IOC, #14408)*. Partner of: *General Association of Asia Pacific Sports Federations (GAAPSF, #10106)*.
[2019/XB2809/y/**B**]

♦ International Weightlifting and Physical Culture Federation / see International Weightlifting Federation (#15876)
♦ International Wellbeing at Work Conference (meeting series)

♦ International Well Control Forum (IWCF) 15877

Main Office Inchbraoch House, South Quay, Montrose, DD10 9UA, UK. T. +441674678120. Fax +441674678125. E-mail: iwcfinformation@iwcf.org.
URL: http://www.iwcf.org/

History 1 Dec 1992. Former names and other names: *European Well Control Forum (EWCF)* – former (1 Dec 1992 to 1994); *Stichting The International Well Control Forum* – legal name. Registration: Start date: 1992, Netherlands; Charity Commission, No/ID: SC045842, Scotland. **Aims** Develop standards for assessing of well control skills and knowledge. **Structure** International Board, comprising 2 elected representatives from each of 7 national and 7 regional branches, elects Chairman from among its members. **Languages** Chinese, Croatian, Dutch, English, French, German, Hungarian, Indonesian, Italian, Norwegian, Polish, Portuguese, Russian, Spanish, Thai, Turkish. **Staff** 6 full-time and 15 part-time staff manage the accreditation and certification programmes worldwide from Montrose, Scotland, with assistance from 7 national branches and over 50 contracted third party agencies. **Finance** Members' dues (annual): pounds200; joining fee – pounds100. **Activities** Annual General Meeting. **Publications** *IWCF Newsletter*.

Members Membership open to companies involved in provision or utilization of "Well Control" training or operations. Companies and organizations in 66 countries:
Algeria, Angola, Argentina, Australia, Austria, Azerbaijan, Bahrain, Bangladesh, Brazil, Brunei Darussalam, Bulgaria, Canada, China, Colombia, Congo Brazzaville, Croatia, Cuba, Cyprus, Denmark, Ecuador, Egypt, France, Gabon, Germany, Hungary, India, Indonesia, Iran Islamic Rep, Ireland, Italy, Jordan, Kazakhstan, Kuwait, Libya, Malaysia, Mexico, Morocco, Myanmar, Netherlands, New Zealand, Nigeria, Norway, Oman, Pakistan, Papua New Guinea, Peru, Philippines, Poland, Qatar, Romania, Russia, Saudi Arabia, Singapore, South Africa, Spain, Syrian AR, Thailand, Trinidad-Tobago, Tunisia, Türkiye, UK, Ukraine, United Arab Emirates, USA, Venezuela, Vietnam.

NGO Relations Together with: *International Association of Drilling Contractors (IADC)*, instrumental in setting up: International Alliance for Well Control.
[2021/XF4608/y/**F**]

♦ International Wernicke-Kleist-Leonhard Society (WKL) 15878

Internationale Wernicke-Kleist-Leonhard Gesellschaft

Contact Klinik und Poliklinik für Psychiatrie, Psychosomatik und Psychotherapie, Universitätklinikum Würzburg, Margarete-Höppel-Platz 1, 97080 Würzburg, Germany. T. +4993120176370. Fax +4993120177020. E-mail: info@wkl-society.com.
URL: http://www.wkl-society.de/

History 1989. **Aims** Support and encourage the development of *psychopathology* and *nosology* of psychic diseases according to the classification system of Leonhard and Kleist based on modern *neurobiology* in order to improve *diagnosis* and therapy in *psychiatry* and support research in this field. **Structure** General Assembly (every 3 years). Executive Committee, consisting of President, 2 Vice-Presidents, Secretary/Treasurer, Associate Secretary-Treasurer and 4 Honorary Fellows. Scientific Council of 5 members. **Finance** Members' dues. Other sources: donations; sales of publications. **Events** *Psychiatric congress* Würzburg (Germany) 2002, *Psychiatric congress* Würzburg (Germany) 2000, *Psychiatric congress / Congress* Göttingen (Germany) 1998, *Congress* Budapest (Hungary) 1996, *Congress* Berlin (Germany) 1994. **Publications** Books; conference proceedings.

Members Individuals and organizations () in 25 countries:
Algeria, Argentina (*), Australia, Austria, Belgium, Brazil, Bulgaria, Canada, China, France, Germany, Hungary, India, Indonesia, Israel, Italy, Japan, Korea Rep, Morocco, Netherlands, Poland, Romania, Russia, UK, USA.
[2017/XE3909/**E**]

♦ International West African Conference (inactive)
♦ International Whales Network (see: #20147)

♦ International Whaling Commission (IWC) 15879

Commission baleinière internationale (CBI) – Comisión Ballenera Internacional

Exec Sec The Red House, 135 Station Road, Impington, CB24 9NP, UK. T. +441223233971. Fax +441223232876. E-mail: secretariat@iwc.int.
URL: http://www.iwc.int/

History 2 Dec 1946, Washington, DC (USA). Established under the *International Convention for the Regulation of Whaling (1946)*, which came into force 10 Nov 1948, and which contains the regulations governing the actual operations of whaling by the nationals of Contracting Governments. These may be amended by the Commission. **Aims** Provide for proper conservation of whales and the management of whaling. **Structure** Commission (meets every 2 years). Committees/Sub-Committees/Working Groups (6). Any Government may adhere to the Convention by notification in writing to the Depository Government (USA). Meetings attended by observers from more than 100 accredited non-governmental organisations as well as media. **Languages** English, French, Spanish. **Staff** 19.00 FTE, paid. **Finance** Sources: contributions; members' dues. **Activities** Capacity building; knowledge management/information dissemination; monitoring/evaluation; research/documentation. **Events** *Meeting* Cambridge (UK) 2022, *Biennial Meeting* Portoroz (Slovenia) 2022, *Virtual Special Meeting* Impington (UK) 2021, *Biennial Meeting* Portoroz (Slovenia) 2021, *Biennial Meeting* Portoroz (Slovenia) 2020. **Publications** *Journal of Cetacean Research and Management* (up to 3 a year with annual Supplement); *Special Issues* (occasional). IWC biennial meeting report (annual until 2014); report of the intersessional period.

Members As of Sept 20, governments of 88 countries:
Antigua-Barbuda, Argentina, Australia, Austria, Belgium, Belize, Benin, Brazil, Bulgaria, Cambodia, Cameroon, Chile, China, Colombia, Congo Brazzaville, Costa Rica, Côte d'Ivoire, Croatia, Cyprus, Czechia, Denmark, Dominica, Dominican Rep, Ecuador, Egypt, Eritrea, Estonia, Finland, France, Gabon, Gambia, Germany, Ghana, Grenada, Guinea, Guinea-Bissau, Hungary, Iceland, India, Ireland, Israel, Italy, Kenya, Kiribati, Korea Rep, Laos, Lithuania, Luxembourg, Mali, Marshall Is, Mauritania, Mexico, Monaco, Mongolia, Morocco, Nauru, Netherlands, New Zealand, Nicaragua, Norway, Oman, Palau, Panama, Peru, Poland, Portugal, Romania, Russia, San Marino, Sao Tomé-Principe, Senegal, Slovakia, Slovenia, Solomon Is, South Africa, Spain, St Kitts-Nevis, St Lucia, St Vincent-Grenadines, Suriname, Sweden, Switzerland, Tanzania UR, Togo, Tuvalu, UK, Uruguay, USA.

IGO Relations Relationship agreement with: *FAO (#09260)*. Agreement of cooperation with: *International Maritime Organization (IMO, #14102)*. Observer to: *International Council for the Exploration of the Sea (ICES, #13021)*.

NGO Relations Accredited NGOs include the following international and internationally-orientated national bodies:
– *Advisory Committee on Protection of the Sea (ACOPS, #00139)*;
– *American Friends Service Committee (AFSC)*;
– *Antarctic and Southern Ocean Coalition (ASOC, #00849)*;

– *AAALAC International*;
– *Born Free Foundation*;
– *Campaign Whale*;
– *Caribbean Conservation Association (CCA, #03481)*;
– *Cetacean Society International (CSI)*;
– *Cousteau Society*;
– *Earth Island Institute (EII)*;
– *Earthtrust*;
– *EarthVoice*;
– *Eastern Caribbean Coalition for Environmental Awareness (ECCEA, #05233)*;
– *Environmental Investigation Agency (EIA)*;
– *Eurogroup for Animals (#05690)*;
– *Friends of the Earth International (FoEI, #10002)*;
– *Global Animals Protection Trust (no recent information)*;
– *Greenpeace International (#10727)*;
– *High North Alliance (inactive)*;
– *Humane Society International (HSI, #10966)*;
– *Indigenous World Association (#11166)*;
– *International Association for Religious Freedom (IARF, #12130)*;
– *International Dolphin Watch (IDW, #13189)*;
– *International Environmental Advisers (no recent information)*;
– *International Fund for Animal Welfare (IFAW, #13693)*;
– *International Institute for Environment and Development (IIED, #13877)*;
– *International Primate Protection League (IPPL, #14641)*;
– *International Transport Workers' Federation (ITF, #15726)*;
– *International Wildlife Coalition (IWC, inactive)*;
– *Inuit Circumpolar Council (ICC, #15995)*;
– *Living Earth Foundation*;
– *Minority Rights Group International (MRG, #16820)*;
– *The Nature Conservancy (TNC)*;
– *Nordic Council for Animal Welfare (inactive)*;
– *Oceana*;
– *Sino Cetacean International Institute (no recent information)*;
– *Survival International (#20047)*;
– *Whale and Dolphin Conservation (WDC)*;
– *Whales Alive*;
– *Women's International League for Peace and Freedom (WILPF, #21024)*;
– *World Animal Protection (#21092)*;
– *World Conservation Trust (IWMC, #21312)*;
– *World Council of Whalers (WCW, #21341)*;
– *World Wide Fund for Nature (WWF, #21922)*. [2022.10.11/XC2811/**C***]

♦ International Wheat Agreement, 1971 (treaty)
♦ International Wheat Agreement, 1986 (1986 treaty)
♦ International Wheat Convention (1986 treaty)
♦ International Wheat Council / see International Grains Council (#13731)
♦ International Wheat Genetics Symposium (meeting series)

♦ International Wheat Genome Sequencing Consortium (IWGSC) 15880

Exec Dir 4620 Village Terrace Ct, Eau Claire WI 54701, USA. T. +13016189543. Fax +18662066124. E-mail: contact@iwgsc.org.
Communications Dir address not obtained.
URL: http://www.wheatgenome.org/

History 2005. Registration: Section 501(c)(3), Start date: 2014, USA. **Aims** Develop tools and resources that serve as a foundation for accelerated development of improved varieties and empowers all aspects of basic and applied wheat science. **Structure** Board of Directors; Coordinating Committee. **Languages** English. **Staff** 2.50 FTE, paid. **Finance** Sources: contributions; sponsorship. Annual budget: 125,000 USD. **Activities** Events/meetings; knowledge management/information dissemination; projects/programmes; research and development; research/documentation.
Members Individuals (3,300) in 71 countries and territories:
Algeria, Argentina, Australia, Austria, Azerbaijan, Bangladesh, Belarus, Belgium, Brazil, Bulgaria, Canada, Chile, China, Czechia, Denmark, Ecuador, Egypt, Estonia, Ethiopia, Finland, France, Germany, Greece, Hungary, Iceland, India, Indonesia, Iran Islamic Rep, Iraq, Ireland, Israel, Italy, Japan, Jordan, Kazakhstan, Kenya, Korea Rep, Lebanon, Malaysia, Mexico, Mongolia, Morocco, Nepal, Netherlands, New Zealand, Nigeria, Norway, Pakistan, Peru, Poland, Portugal, Romania, Russia, Saudi Arabia, Serbia, Singapore, South Africa, Spain, Sri Lanka, Sudan, Sweden, Switzerland, Syrian AR, Taiwan, Thailand, Tunisia, Türkiye, UK, Ukraine, Uruguay, USA. [2022.06.17/XM4497/v/**C**]

♦ International Wheat Gluten Association (internationally oriented national body)

♦ International Wheelchair and Amputee Sports Federation (IWAS) .. 15881

CEO c/o Aylesbury College, Oxford Road, Aylesbury, HP21 8PD, UK. T. +441296780212. E-mail: info@iwasf.com.
URL: http://www.iwasf.com/

History 2004. Founded by merger of *International Sports Organization for the Disabled (ISOD, inactive)* and *International Stoke Mandeville Wheelchair Sports Federation (ISMWSF, inactive)*. Registration: Charity Commission, No/ID: 1011552, England and Wales. **Aims** Promote welfare and social change across the globe through the medium of sport; create barrier-free opportunities for all, in countries where IWAS has a presence. **Structure** General Assembly of Nations (every 2 years); Executive Board. Includes: *Wheelchair Sports Worldwide (see: #15881)*. **Languages** English. **Activities** Awards/prizes/competitions; events/meetings; sporting activities. **Publications** *IWAS E-news* (12 a year).
Members National organizations in 66 countries and territories:
Argentina, Australia, Austria, Azerbaijan, Bahrain, Belarus, Belgium, Brazil, Bulgaria, Canada, Chile, China, Colombia, Costa Rica, Croatia, Cyprus, Czechia, Denmark, Estonia, Finland, France, Georgia, Germany, Great Britain, Greece, Hong Kong, Hungary, India, Indonesia, Iran Islamic Rep, Iraq, Ireland, Italy, Japan, Kazakhstan, Korea Rep, Kuwait, Latvia, Lebanon, Lithuania, Luxembourg, Macau, Malaysia, Morocco, Netherlands, Nigeria, Norway, Poland, Portugal, Qatar, Romania, Russia, Saudi Arabia, Singapore, Slovakia, Slovenia, South Africa, Spain, Sweden, Switzerland, Taiwan, Thailand, Türkiye, Ukraine, United Arab Emirates, USA.
Consultative Status Consultative status granted from: *ECOSOC (#05331)* (Special). **IGO Relations** Accredited by (1): *United Nations Office at Vienna (UNOV, #20604)*. **NGO Relations** Member of (2): *Association of Paralympic Sports Organisations (APSO, #02850)*; *International Paralympic Committee (IPC, #14512)*. [2020.10.13/XB0016/**B**]

♦ International Wheelchair Basketball Federation (IWBF) 15882

Fédération internationale de basketball en fauteuil roulant (FIBR)
SG c/o FIBA, Route Suisse 5, 1295 Mies VD, Switzerland. T. +41225450000. Fax +41225450039. E-mail: info@iwbf.org.
URL: http://iwbf.org/

History Founded 1993, UK. **Aims** Promote and develop the sport of wheelchair basketball worldwide. **Structure** World Congress. Executive Committee. Zones (4): IWBF Africa; IWBF Americas; IWBF Asia Oceania; IWBF Europe. **Languages** English. **Staff** 1.00 FTE, voluntary. **Finance** Annual budget: 250,000 USD. **Events** *World Congress* Dubai (United Arab Emirates) 2022, *World Congress* Hamburg (Germany) 2018, *World Congress* Incheon (Korea Rep) 2014, *World congress* Birmingham (UK) 2010, *World congress* Amsterdam (Netherlands) 2006.
Members Full in 84 countries and territories:
Algeria, Argentina, Australia, Austria, Bahrain, Belgium, Bosnia-Herzegovina, Brazil, Cameroon, Canada, Chile, China, Colombia, Costa Rica, Croatia, Cuba, Czechia, Denmark, Ecuador, Egypt, El Salvador, Eritrea, Finland, France, Gabon, Germany, Ghana, Greece, Guatemala, Guinea, Hong Kong, India, Iran Islamic Rep, Iraq, Ireland, Israel, Italy, Jamaica, Japan, Jordan, Kenya, Korea Rep, Kuwait, Latvia, Lebanon, Lithuania, Malaysia, Mauritius, Mexico, Morocco, Netherlands, New Zealand, Nigeria, Oman, Palestine, Panama, Peru, Philippines, Poland, Portugal, Puerto Rico, Qatar, Russia, Saudi Arabia, Serbia, Singapore, Slovakia, Slovenia, South Africa, Spain, Sudan, Sweden, Switzerland, Syrian AR, Taiwan, Thailand, Türkiye, UK, Ukraine, United Arab Emirates, Uruguay, USA, Venezuela, Zimbabwe.
NGO Relations Member of (2): *Association of Paralympic Sports Organisations (APSO, #02850)*; *International Paralympic Committee (IPC, #14512)*. Cooperates with (1): *International Testing Agency (ITA, #15678)*. Officially recognized by: *Fédération internationale de basketball (FIBA, #09614)*. [2021/XC0127/**C**]

♦ International Wheelchair Rugby Federation (IWRF) 15883

Head Office 4 Park Square, Newton Chambers Road, Sheffield, S35 2PH, UK. T. +447792329470. E-mail: info@iwrf.com.
URL: http://www.iwrf.com/

History within the framework of *International Stoke Mandeville Wheelchair Sports Federation (ISMWSF, inactive)*. Became a fully independent body, 2010. **Aims** Inspire and support people throughout the world to participate in wheelchair rugby. **Structure** Board of 8 Directors. Regional zones (3): Americas; Europe; Asia-Oceania. **Languages** English. **Staff** 0.50 FTE, paid. **Finance** Sources: grants; international organizations; members' dues; sponsorship. Other sources: sanction and capitation fees. Supported by: *International Paralympic Committee (IPC, #14512)*. **Activities** Sanctions international competitions in wheelchair rugby, including Paralympic Games, World and Zone Championships, and invitational tournaments. Establishes rules and regulations for the sport, including rules of play, athlete classification rules, and competition regulations. Conducts development activities to increase national and international participation. Trains and certifies wheelchair rugby officials.
Members Organizations in 25 countries:
Argentina, Australia, Austria, Belgium, Brazil, Canada, China, Colombia, Czechia, Denmark, Finland, France, Germany, Great Britain, Ireland, Japan, Korea Rep, Netherlands, New Zealand, Norway, Poland, South Africa, Sweden, Switzerland, USA.
NGO Relations Member of (2): *Association of Paralympic Sports Organisations (APSO, #02850)*; *International Paralympic Committee (IPC, #14512)*. In partnership with: *World Rugby (#21757)*. [2021/XD8575/**C**]

♦ International Wheelchair Tennis Federation (inactive)
♦ International Wheelset Congress (meeting series)
♦ International Whistleblowing Research Network (unconfirmed)
♦ International Wholesale and Foreign Trade Centre (inactive)
♦ International Wiesenthal Center / see Simon Wiesenthal Center
♦ International Wilderness Leadership Foundation / see WILD Foundation (#20956)
♦ International Wildlife Crimestoppers (internationally oriented national body)
♦ International Wildlife Film Makers Symposium (meeting series)
♦ International Wildlife Management Consortium / see World Conservation Trust (#21312)

♦ International Wildlife Ranching and Conservation Alliance (IWRCA) 15884

Address not obtained.
URL: http://iwrca.org/

History Formally set up at founding meeting, Nov 2018, Iceland. Previously functioned as *International Wildlife Ranching Symposium (IWRS)*. **Structure** Coordinating Committee. **Activities** Events/meetings. **Events** *Conference* Hveragerdi (Iceland) 2019, *Conference* Hveragerdi (Iceland) 2018. [2019.02.20/XM6840/**E**]

♦ International Wildlife Ranching Symposium / see International Wildlife Ranching and Conservation Alliance (#15884)

♦ International Wildlife Rehabilitation Council, The (IWRC) 15885

Exec Dir PO Box 3197, Eugene OR 97403, USA. T. +18668711869. Fax +14088766153. E-mail: office@theiwrc.org.
URL: http://theiwrc.org/

History 1972, USA. Former names and other names: *Wildlife Rehabilitation Council (WRC)* – former (1972 to 1986). **Aims** Provide evidence-based education and resources on wildlife rehabilitation to move the field of wildlife rehabilitation forward; promote wildlife conservation and welfare; mitigate human-wildlife conflicts worldwide, through better understanding of wild animal ecology, behavior, and welfare. **Structure** Board of Directors; Executive Director. **Languages** English, Spanish. **Staff** 3.75 FTE, paid. **Finance** Sources: donations; fees for services; grants; members' dues. Annual budget: 300,000 USD. **Activities** Certification/accreditation; knowledge management/information dissemination; networking/liaising; politics/policy/regulatory; publishing activities; standards/guidelines; training/education. Active in all member countries. **Events** *Annual Symposium* Cincinnati, OH (USA) 2014, *Annual Conference* Victoria, BC (Canada) 2013, *Annual Symposium* Appleton, WI (USA) 2012, *Annual Symposium* Fort Lauderdale, FL (USA) 2011, *Annual Symposium* Albuquerque, NM (USA) 2010. **Publications** *IWRC Newsletter*; *Journal of Wildlife Rehabilitation*. *Wildlife Rehabilitation: A Comprehensive Approach* (2nd ed 2021) by Dr Katie McInnis and Julissa Favela et al in English; *Standards for Wildlife Rehabilitation* (1st ed 2021) by Dr Erica Miller and Jenny Schlieps in English – copublished with NWRA; *Body Masses of North American Birds* (2018) by Dr John Dunning in English; *Wildlife Rehabilitation: A Comprehensive Approach* (1st ed 2016) by Rebekah Weiss and Kim Poisson in English; *Minimum Standards in Wildlife Rehabilitation* (4th ed 2012) by Erica Miller in English – Out of print – replaced with Standards of Wildlife Rehabilitation Copublished with NWRA; *Initial Wildlife Care* (3rd ed 2011) by Dr Renee Schott and Dr Jan White in English; *Wildlife Feeding and Nutrition* (2nd ed 2004) by Dr Janine Perlman and Astrid MacLead in English.
Members Organizations and individuals in 23 countries and territories:
Australia, Belgium, Belize, Canada, Cyprus, France, Germany, Hong Kong, India, Ireland, Japan, Latvia, Lebanon, Netherlands, New Zealand, Singapore, South Africa, St Kitts-Nevis, Sweden, Switzerland, Trinidad-Tobago, UK, USA, Venezuela.
NGO Relations Also links with national and local NGOs. [2021.09.01/XF5491/**F**]

♦ International Willi Hennig Society 15886

Treas Inv Zoology AMNH, Central Park W at 79th St, New York NY 10024, USA. T. +12127695638. Fax +12127695277.
Sec Molekylärsystematiska lab, Naturhistoriska riksmuseet, Box 50007, SE-104 05 Stockholm, Sweden.
URL: http://www.cladistics.org/

History Incorporated in the District of Columbia, USA Office registered in the state of New York, USA. **Aims** Promote the work of Willi Hennig, notably in the field of *cladistics* – a method of hypothesizing relationships among *organisms*, notably in *phylogenetic analysis*. **Structure** General Meeting. Council, consisting of President, Vice-President, Treasurer, Secretary, Membership Secretary, Editor, Past Presidents and 9 Councillors, elected from among the Fellows. Nominating Committee, comprising Chairman and 2 Fellows. **Finance** Members' dues: individuals US$ 55/pounds28; students US$ 35/pounds22. **Events** *Annual Meeting* Mexico City (Mexico) 2024, *Annual Meeting* Ithaca, NY (USA) 2023, *Annual Meeting* Helsinki (Finland) 2022, *Annual Meeting* Helsinki (Finland) 2021, *Annual Meeting* Helsinki (Finland) 2020. **Publications** *Cladistics* – journal.
Members Elected fellows. Members in 42 countries:
Argentina, Australia, Austria, Belgium, Brazil, Canada, Chile, China, Colombia, Czechia, Denmark, Dominican Rep, Ecuador, Egypt, Finland, France, Germany, Iceland, Italy, Japan, Korea DPR, Korea Rep, Malaysia, Mexico, Netherlands, New Zealand, Norway, Paraguay, Poland, Portugal, Puerto Rico, Russia, Slovenia, South Africa, Spain, Sweden, Switzerland, Taiwan, Türkiye, UK, USA, Venezuela. [2017/XD5837/**E**]

♦ International Window Film Association (internationally oriented national body)

♦ International Windship Association (IWSA) 15887

Sec 71-75 Shelton St, Covent Garden, London, WC2H 9JQ, UK. E-mail: secretary@wind-ship.org.
URL: https://www.wind-ship.org/

History 1 Jul 2014. Registration: EU Transparency Register, No/ID: 753008748493-71, Start date: 29 Dec 2022. **Aims** Facilitate and promote *wind propulsion* for commercial *shipping* worldwide; bring together all parties in the development of a wind-ship sector to shape industry and government attitudes and policies. **Structure** Executive Committee. **Finance** Members' dues. **Events** *Wind Propulsion Conference* 2023.
Members Companies; Organizations; Individuals. Full; Associate; Supporter. Members in 9 countries:
Finland, France, Germany, Italy, Japan, Netherlands, Norway, UK, USA.
IGO Relations *University of the South Pacific (USP, #20703)*. [2023/XJ8984/**D**]

♦ International Windsurfing Association (IWA) 15888

Gen Sec Kemp House, 152 – 160 City Road, London, EC1V 2NX, UK. E-mail: iwaoffice@internationalwindsurfing.com.
URL: http://www.internationalwindsurfing.com/

History Jan 2001. **Structure** General Meeting (annual); Executive Committee, including President and Honorary Secretary; Sub-Committees (4). **Languages** English. **Finance** Sources: members' dues. **Activities** Awards/prizes/competitions; networking/liaising; sporting activities; training/education. **Events** *Annual General Meeting* Martigues (France) 2010.

Members National organizations and companies in 73 countries and territories:
Algeria, Argentina, Australia, Austria, Barbados, Belarus, Belgium, Bonaire Is, Brazil, Bulgaria, Canada, Chile, China, Colombia, Croatia, Cuba, Cyprus, Czechia, Denmark, Dominican Rep, Ecuador, Estonia, Finland, France, Germany, Greece, Hong Kong, Hungary, India, Indonesia, Ireland, Israel, Italy, Jamaica, Japan, Korea Rep, Latvia, Lebanon, Lithuania, Macau, Malaysia, Malta, Mexico, Namibia, Netherlands, New Zealand, North Macedonia, Norway, Pakistan, Peru, Poland, Portugal, Russia, Seychelles, Singapore, Slovakia, Slovenia, South Africa, Spain, Sri Lanka, Sweden, Switzerland, Taiwan, Thailand, Trinidad-Tobago, Tunisia, UK, Ukraine, Uruguay, USA, Venezuela, Virgin Is UK, Virgin Is USA.
Included in the above, 4 organizations listed in this Yearbook:
International Formula Windsurfing Class (see: #21760); International Funboard Class Association (IFCA, see: #21760); International Raceboard Class Association (see: #21760); Professional Windsurfers Association (PWA). [2022.02.08/XB0014/y/**B**]

♦ International Wine Clubs Association (IWCA) **15889**
CEO Intl Wine and Spirit Centre, 39/45 Bermondsey Street, London, SE1 3XF, UK. T. +442070893877. Fax +442070893870.
URL: http://www.internationalwineclubsassociation.com/
History 1991. Registered in accordance with Spanish law. **Aims** Promote the distance selling wine industry; encourage enjoyment and appreciation of quality wine. **Structure** Committee, comprising Chairman, Treasurer, Secretary and at least 5 members. **Languages** English. **Staff** 0.50 FTE, paid. **Finance** Subscriptions. Budget (annual): euro 75,000. **Activities** Organizes congresses and workshops. **Events** *Workshop* Paris (France) 2016, *Workshop* Palermo (Italy) 2014, *Congress* Gaiole in Chianti (Italy) 2012, *Congress* Edinburgh (UK) 2010, *Biennial congress / Congress* Buenos Aires (Argentina) 2008. **Publications** *Crystal Ball*; *IWCA Newsletter*.
Members Full; Associate. Clubs and merchants (39) in 17 countries:
Argentina, Australia, Austria, Brazil, Canada, France, Germany, Italy, Netherlands, Poland, Portugal, South Africa, Spain, Switzerland, UK, Uruguay, USA. [2016/XD9192/**D**]

♦ International Wine and Food Society (IWFS) **15890**
Société internationale du vin et de l'alimentation
Administrator Naval and Military Club, 4 St James' Square, London, SW1Y 4JU, UK. T. +442078275732. Fax +442078275733. E-mail: sec@iwfs.org.
URL: http://www.iwfs.org/
History 1933, by André L Simon (1877-1970). **Aims** Increase knowledge and appreciation of good wine and food. **Structure** Local branches; geographical areas (3). **Languages** English. **Staff** 1.00 FTE, paid; 200.00 FTE, voluntary. **Finance** Sources: members' dues. **Activities** Awards/prizes/competitions; events/meetings; knowledge management/information dissemination; training/education. **Events** *Area Festival* Vancouver, BC (Canada) 2014, *Area Festival* Sydney, NSW (Australia) 2010, *Area Festival* Cape Town (South Africa) 2009, *Area Festival* Australia 2006, *Area Festival* Italy 2003. **Publications** *North American Newsletter* (4 a year); *European Newsletter* (3 a year); *Asian Pacific Newsletter* (2 a year).
Members Branches (137), with over 6,000 individual members, in 33 countries and territories:
Australia, Canada, Cayman Is, China, Dominican Rep, Estonia, Finland, France, Hong Kong, Hungary, India, Indonesia, Ireland, Japan, Korea Rep, Malaysia, Mexico, New Zealand, Norway, Philippines, Puerto Rico, Russia, Singapore, South Africa, Sweden, Switzerland, Taiwan, Thailand, UK, USA, Vietnam, Zambia, Zimbabwe. [2016.04.11/XD3815/**C**]

♦ International Wine Law Association (IWLA) **15891**
Association internationale des juristes du droit de la vigne et du vin (AIDV)
Acting SG 18 rue d'Aguesseau, 75008 Paris, France. T. +33144948095. Fax +33142669063. E-mail: contact@aidv.org.
URL: http://www.aidv.org/
History 1985. Registered in accordance with French law, 13 Nov 1985. **Aims** Review and analyse *legal* issues affecting international wine community and commerce; provide a forum for wine lawyers, regulators, academics and business people to discuss issues of common concern; support national and international organizations involved in the vine and wine sector on the means of harmonizing international wine regulations; serve as a clearing house for legal documentation concerning the worldwide wine industry. **Structure** General Assembly (annual). Board of Directors (meets annually) of maximum 30 members elected for 3 years by the General Assembly. Bureau, chosen from Board of Directors, comprising President, one or more Vice-Presidents, Secretary General (and if necessary, Deputy Secretary General) and Treasurer (and Deputy Treasurer, if necessary). Regional Sections (5), whose Presidents are members of right of the Board of Directors: Australasia; Europe; USA; Italy; Scandinavia. Headquarters located in Paris (France). **Languages** English, French. **Finance** Members' dues (annual): Institutional euro 600; Individual euro 125. Other sources: subsidies; gifts; legacies. **Events** *European Conference* Avignon (France) 2019, *Wine law for a new generation* Lausanne (Switzerland) 2019, *European Conference* Mainz (Germany) 2018, *Conference* Napa, CA (USA) 2018, *Conference* Bordeaux (France) 2017. **Publications** *AIDV Bulletin* (4 a year) in English, French.
Members Individual; Institutional; Honorary. Members (over 350) in 27 countries and territories:
Argentina, Australia, Belgium, Brazil, Canada, Chile, Colombia, France, Germany, Hong Kong, Hungary, Italy, Japan, Luxembourg, Netherlands, New Zealand, Norway, Peru, Portugal, South Africa, Spain, Sweden, Switzerland, Türkiye, UK, Uruguay, USA.
Consultative Status Consultative status granted from: *World Intellectual Property Organization (WIPO, #21593)* (Permanent Observer Status). **IGO Relations** Observer to: *International Organisation of Vine and Wine (OIV, #14435).* [2016/XD7639/**D**]

♦ International Wine Office / see International Organisation of Vine and Wine (#14435)
♦ International Wine Technical Summit (unconfirmed)

♦ International Wire and Cable Symposium (IWCS) **15892**
CEO 6920-B Braddock Rd, PMB 650, Annandale VA 22003, USA. T. +17039144927.
Operations Manager address not obtained.
URL: http://www.iwcs.org/
History Incorporated 7 Jan 1987, with symposia staring 1952. Reorganized 2000. **Structure** Board of Directors; Symposium Committee. **Events** *Symposium* Providence, RI (USA) 2014, *Symposium* Wallingford, CT (USA) 2013, *Symposium* Providence, RI (USA) 2012, *Symposium* Charlotte, NC (USA) 2011, *Symposium* Providence, RI (USA) 2010. [2019/XJ8650/c/**E**]

♦ International Wireless Telegraph Convention (1906 treaty)

♦ International Wire and Machinery Association (IWMA) **15893**
Association internationale du fil métallique et des machines – Internationaler Draht und Maschinenverband – Associazione Internazionale del Filo Metallico e Macchinario
Exec Manager Wellington House, Starley Way, Birmingham Intl Park, Solihull, B37 7HB, UK. T. +441217817367. Fax +441217817404. E-mail: info@iwma.org.
Main: http://www.iwma.org/
History 1970. **Aims** Promote new technology, education and growth within the wire, cable and wire product industries. **Structure** General Meeting (annual); Executive Board. **Languages** English, Mandarin Chinese, Russian, Spanish, Turkish. **Staff** 3.00 FTE, paid; 20.00 FTE, voluntary. **Finance** Sources: meeting proceeds; members' dues. **Activities** Events/meetings; networking/liaising. **Events** *Meeting* Düsseldorf (Germany) 2010, *Annual General Meeting* Knutsford (UK) 2010, *Technical seminar* Bangkok (Thailand) 2009, *Educational seminar* Singapore (Singapore) 2003, *International technical conference* Stresa (Italy) 2003. **Publications** *WCN – Wire and Cable News*. **Members** International wire and cable industry manufacturers and suppliers. Membership countries not specified. [2016.06.01/XD5180/**C**]

♦ International Wolf Center (internationally oriented national body)
♦ International Wolf Federation – Environment Action (inactive)
♦ International Woman Suffrage Alliance / see International Alliance of Women (#11639)
♦ International Women Communication Centre (internationally oriented national body)

♦ International Women Count Network (IWCN) **15894**
Contact c/o Crossroads Women's Centre, PO Box 287, London, NW6 5QU, UK. T. +442074822496. Fax +442072094761.
Street address 25 Wolsey Mews, London, NW5 2DX, UK.
URL: http://www.allwomencount.net/
History 1985. **Aims** Advance measuring and valuing of unwaged caring work in national accounts and in all policies affecting women. **Structure** International network. **Languages** English, French, German, Italian, Spanish. **Staff** Voluntary. **Finance** Donations. **Activities** Events/meetings; networking/liaising. **Publications** *The Milk of Human Kindness – Defending breastfeeding from the global market and the AIDS industry* (2002). Pamphlets; advertising materials.
Members Full in 28 countries:
Barbados, Belgium, Brazil, Canada, China, France, Germany, Greece, Guyana, Haiti, India, Ireland, Italy, Japan, Mexico, Netherlands, Norway, Pakistan, Peru, Philippines, Spain, Sweden, Switzerland, Tanzania UR, Trinidad-Tobago, UK, USA, Venezuela.
NGO Relations Coordinated by: *Global Women's Strike (GWS, #10660).* [2019.07.02/XF5732/**F**]

♦ International Women and Family Foundation (internationally oriented national body)

♦ International Women and Mining Network **15895**
Red Internacional "Mujeres y Mineria" (RIMM)
International Secretariat Dhaatri Resource Ctr for Women and Children, 307 Manasarovar Heights, Phase-1 – Tirumalgherry, Secunderabad, Hyderabad, Telangana 500009, Hyderabad TELANGANA 500009, India. T. +914040121365. Fax +914040121365. E-mail: dhaatri@gmail.com.
URL: http://www.rimmrights.org/
History 1997. **Aims** Make visible the serious problems of women in mining across countries, governments, NGOs, human rights groups, trade unions, mining struggle groups and communities and all others concerned with the exploitation of women in mining. **Publications** *RIMM Newsletter*. **NGO Relations** Member of: *International Network for Economic, Social and Cultural Rights (ESCR-Net, #14255).* [2011/XJ4704/**F**]

♦ International Women's Alliance (unconfirmed)
♦ International Women's Coffee Alliance (internationally oriented national body)
♦ International Women's Committee for a Durable Peace / see Women's International League for Peace and Freedom (#21024)

♦ International Women's Convocation (IWC) **15896**
Contact 7811 S 113th St, Seattle WA 98178, USA. E-mail: admin@icuuw.com.
Exec Dir 5202 Crawford St, Unit 19, Houston TX 77004, USA. T. +17135245608.
URL: https://www.intlwomensconvo.org/
History 2009. Former names and other names: *International Convocation of Unitarian Universalist Women (ICUUW)* – legal name. Registration: 501(c)(3) charitable organization, USA, Texas. **Aims** Enable women to achieve their human rights, including access to economic opportunities, health care and security, education, and political expression. **Structure** General Assembly; Board of Directors; *Global Sisters' Council*. **Activities** Events/meetings. **Consultative Status** Consultative status granted from: *ECOSOC (#05331)* (Special). [2020/XJ7688/**C**]

♦ International Women's Cricket Council (inactive)
♦ International Women's Democracy Center (internationally oriented national body)

♦ International Women's Democracy Network (IWDN) **15897**
Contact c/o WLP, 4343 Montgomery Avenue, Ste 201, Bethesda MD 20814, USA. E-mail: wlp@learningpartnership.org.
URL: http://www.learningpartnership.org/iwdn/
History Set up 2004, Durban (South Africa), by *Women's Learning Partnership for Rights, Development and Peace (WLP, #21031)* at 3rd Assembly *World Movement for Democracy (#21661).* **Aims** Provide a virtual resource center and a forum for exchange of information and knowledge and therefore support women's roles and agency in the development of democratic practices and institutions at the community, national, and international levels in order to ensure women's full participation. **Publications** Articles; facts; interviews; reports; resources; training manuals. [2012.10.26/XJ1963/**E**]

♦ International Women's Democrat Union (IWDU) **15898**
Contact c/o Jarl Hjalmarson Foundation, Stora Nygatan 30, Box 2080, SE-103 12 Stockholm, Sweden. T. +4686788108.
History 1990, Canada, within the framework of *International Democrat Union (IDU, #13147).* **Aims** Provide a link for women in centre right and like minded parties world-wide; encourage the participation of women in politics and the political process; promote freedom and free enterprise particularly as they relate to and concern women and women's affairs; promote and support the principles of the IDU in all women's forums; extend the political influence of women in member parties. **Structure** Includes Chairman (who is ex officio Officer of IDU). **Events** *Meeting* Philadelphia, PA (USA) 2000. [2012/XE2077/**E**]

♦ International Women's Development Agency (internationally oriented national body)
♦ International Women's Federation of Commerce and Industry (internationally oriented national body)

♦ International Women's Forum (IWF) **15899**
Main Office 1155 15th St NW, Suite 1000, Washington DC 20005, USA. T. +12023871010. Fax +12023871009. E-mail: iwf@iwforum.org.
URL: http://www.iwforum.org/
History 1982, USA. Founded as an organization of preeminent women by Elinor "Elly" Guggenheimer, Muriel Siebert, Eleanor Holmes and Muriel Fox. 2021, merged with support organization the *Leadership Foundation*, founded in 1990. **Aims** Provide a platform for women leaders to meet in a non-competitive environment where friendships and alliances can grow. **Structure** Board of Directors, comprising President, Vice-President, Treasurer and 18 Directors. Includes *'Leadership Foundation'*. **Staff** 7.00 FTE, paid. **Activities** Training/eucation; events/meetings; networking/liaising. **Events** *World Leadership Conference* Seattle, WA (USA) 2025, *World Leadership Conference* New York, NY (USA) 2024, *World Leadership Conference* Detroit, MI (USA) 2023, *World Leadership Conference* Las Vegas, NV (USA) 2022, *Cornerstone Conference* Santiago (Chile) 2022.
Members Affiliate forums representing women (7,000) in 33 countries and territories:
Argentina, Australia, Austria, Bahamas, Bermuda, Canada, Chile, Ecuador, Egypt, Germany, Hong Kong, India, Ireland, Israel, Italy, Jamaica, Jordan, Lebanon, Mexico, Morocco, Philippines, Poland, Russia, Singapore, South Africa, Spain, Sweden, Trinidad-Tobago, Türkiye, UK, United Arab Emirates, USA, Venezuela.
Consultative Status Consultative status granted from: *ECOSOC (#05331)* (Special). [2021/XF7064/**F**]

♦ International Women's Grail Movement / see The Grail – International Movement of Christian Women (#10689)
♦ International Women's Health Coalition (internationally oriented national body)

♦ International Women's Initiative (IWI) **15900**
Founder/Exec Dir 712 H Street NE, Ste 1828, Washington DC 20002, USA. T. +13162850125. E-mail: hello@theiwi.org.
URL: https://www.theiwi.org/
History Incorporated 2012. Registered in accordance with UK law: 08178514. **Aims** Address issues central to women's communities, including but not limited to reproductive and medical rights, freedom from violence, education and other fundamental human rights. **Activities** Training/education; networking/liaising; knowledge management/information dissemination. **Publications** *IWI Newsletter* (12 a year); *The Lead*. [2022/XJ5802/**F**]

♦ International Women's Insolvency and Restructuring Confederation (internationally oriented national body)

♦ International Women's Media Foundation (IWMF) **15901**
Main Office 1625 K St NW, Ste 1275, Washington DC 20006, USA. T. +12024961992. Fax +12024961977. E-mail: info@iwmf.org.
URL: http://www.iwmf.org/
History 1990, USA. **Aims** Strengthen the role of women in the news media around the world, based on the belief that no press is truly free unless women share an equal voice. **Structure** Board of Directors, comprising 2 Co-Chairs, Executive Director and 15 members. **Staff** 13.00 FTE, paid. **Finance** Donations from organizations, corporations and individuals, including: *Ford Foundation (#09858)*; Howard G Buffett Foundation. **Activities** Projects/programmes; training/education; awards/prizes/competitions. **Publications** *Global Report on the Status of Women in the News Media*. **IGO Relations** *UNESCO (#20322)* Global Alliance on Media and Gender. **NGO Relations** Member of (1): *Ethical Journalism Network (EJN, #05554).* [2021/XF6910/f/**F**]

♦ International Women's Network Against Militarism (unconfirmed)
♦ International Women's Partnership for Peace and Justice (internationally oriented national body)
♦ International Women's Peace Group (internationally oriented national body)
♦ International Women's Peace Service (internationally oriented national body)

♦ International Women's Rights Action Watch Asia Pacific (IWRAW Asia Pacific) 15902

Exec Dir 10-2 Jalan Bangsar Utama 9, Bangsar Utama, 59000 Kuala Lumpur, Malaysia. T. +60322822255. E-mail: iwraw-ap@iwraw-ap.org.
URL: http://www.iwraw-ap.org/

History 1993. Founded to monitor implementation of *Convention on the Elimination of all Forms of Discrimination Against Women (CEDAW, 1979)*. **Aims** Work towards the realisation of women's human rights. **Structure** Advisory Committee; Board of Directors; Resource and Management Team. **Staff** 17.00 FTE, paid. **Finance** Sources: donations. Supported by: Channel Foundation; *Open Society Foundations (OSF, #17763)*; *Oxfam Novib*; *Swiss Agency for Development and Cooperation (SDC)*. **Activities** Advocacy/lobbying/activism; events/meetings; training/education. **Publications** *Occasional Paper Series*. Guides; manual. **Members** Not a membership organization. **Consultative Status** Consultative status granted from: *ECOSOC (#05331)* (Special). **NGO Relations** Member of (3): *Coalition for Sexual and Bodily Rights in Muslim Societies (CSBR, #04068)*; *End Corporal Punishment (#05457)*; *International Network for Economic, Social and Cultural Rights (ESCR-Net, #14255)*. Supports (2): *Equipo Latinoamericano de Justicia y Género (ELA)*; *KARAT Coalition (#16179)*. Instrumental in setting up (1): *Southeast Asia Women's Caucus on ASEAN (WC, #19800)*.
[2022.11.09/XF6805/**F**]

♦ International Women's Rights Project (internationally oriented national body)
♦ International Women's Writing Guild (internationally oriented national body)

♦ International Woodball Federation (IWbF) 15903

Contact No 37 – Ln 99, Sec 3, Kangning Rd, Taipei 11485, Taiwan. T. +886226318761. Fax +886226318763. E-mail: iwbf@iwbf-woodball.org.
URL: http://iwbf-woodball.org/

Aims Popularize the modern sport, Woodball, internationally; improve mutual communication among international member organizations. **Structure** General Assembly; Executive Committee. Committees Technical; Legal; Equipment; Financial. **Languages** Chinese, English. **Events** *General Assembly* Taichung (Taiwan) 2022, *General Assembly* Kaohsiung (Taiwan) 2021, *General Assembly* Kaohsiung (Taiwan) 2020, *General Assembly* Taipei (Taiwan) 2019, *General Assembly* Jeju (Korea Rep) 2016. **Publications** *IWbF News Letter* (4 a year).
[2022.05.11/XM5680/**D**]

♦ International Wood Culture Society (unconfirmed)
♦ International Wood Products Association (internationally oriented national body)
♦ International Wood Research Society (inactive)
♦ International Wool Secretariat (inactive)
♦ International Wool Study Group (inactive)

♦ International Wool Textile Organisation (IWTO) 15904

Fédération lainière internationale (FLI) – Internationale Wollvereinigung

SG Rue de l'Industrie 4, 1000 Brussels, Belgium. T. +3225054010. E-mail: iwto@iwto.org.
Events and Office Manager address not obtained.
URL: http://www.iwto.org/

History 1929, Paris (France). Founded following Arbitration Agreement, 1924, between Bradford (UK) and Roubaix-Tourcoing (France) Chambers of Commerce, subsequently signed by wool-textile organizations meeting in Belgium, Germany, Italy and other countries. Registration: Banque-Carrefour des Entreprises, No/ID: 0541.803.891, Start date: 12 Nov 2013, Belgium. **Aims** Connect all parts of the wool supply chain in order to strengthen wool's credentials as the world's leading *sustainable* fibre. **Structure** General Assembly; Heads of Delegation Council; Executive Committee; Committees (7); Groups (7). **Languages** English. **Staff** 4.00 FTE, paid. **Finance** Sources: subscriptions. **Activities** Events/meetings. **Events** *Congress* Kyoto (Japan) 2023, *Congress* Puyuan-Tongxiang (China) 2022, *Annual Conference* Brussels (Belgium) 2021, *Annual Conference* Brussels (Belgium) 2020, *Annual Conference* Venice (Italy) 2019. **Publications** *Blue Book* (annual); *IWTO Market Information* (annual); *The Ticker* (irregular) – newsletter.
Members National Committees representing all stages of trade and processing in the wool textile industry in 10 countries:
Australia, China, Germany, Italy, New Zealand, South Africa, Türkiye, UK, Uruguay, USA.
Associate in 17 countries and territories:
Australia, Bulgaria, Canada, Falklands/Malvinas, France, Germany, India, Italy, Japan, Lesotho, Luxembourg, Mongolia, Norway, Switzerland, Thailand, UK, Uruguay.
Consultative Status Consultative status granted from: *ECOSOC (#05331)* (Ros C); *FAO (#09260)* (Liaison Status). **IGO Relations** Cooperates with (1): *OIE – World Organisation for Animal Health (#17703)*. **NGO Relations** Member of (1): *Federation of European and International Associations Established in Belgium (FAIB, #09508)*. Partner of (1): *Livestock Environmental Assessment and Performance Partnership (LEAP, #16500)*. Cooperates with (3): *Comité européen de normalisation (CEN, #04162)*; *International Organization for Standardization (ISO, #14473)*; *Office international de l'élevage (OIE, no recent information)*.
[2022.07.01/XC2817/**C**]

♦ International Workcamps (internationally oriented national body)
♦ International Workers' Aid / see SOLIDAR (#19680)
♦ International Workers Aid, 1925 (inactive)

♦ International Workers and Amateurs in Sports Confederation 15905

Confédération Sportive Internationale Travailliste et Amateur (CSIT)

Admin Sec Steinergasse 12, 1230 Vienna, Austria. T. +4367684746425. E-mail: office@csit.tv – administration@csit.tv.
URL: https://www.csit.sport/

History 10 May 1913, Ghent (Belgium). After being affected by World War I and II and other political events in Europe, reconstituted 1946, Brussels (Belgium). Reconstituted, 1993, Eilat (Israel). Former names and other names: *International Workers Sport Association* – former (10 May 1913); *Labour Sports International* – former (1946); *Comité sportif international du travail* – former (1946); *International Workers Sports Confederation* – former (1993); *Confédération sportive internationale du travail (CSIT)* – former (1993); *International Labour Sports Confederation* – former alias. Registration: Start date: 2009, Austria. **Aims** As an open, international sports organization, aim for establishment of structures and setting up of activities, especially in the field of amateur sports and sports for all, sports within working places and sports for leisure. **Structure** Congress (annual); Executive Committee; Secretariat in Vienna (Austria), headed by General Secretary. **Languages** English, French. **Finance** Sources: members' dues; sponsorship. Other sources: registration fees; sports events; subventions. **Activities** Events/meetings; sporting activities. Organizes the *CSIT World Sport Games* on a approximately biennial schedule. **Events** *Congress* Rome (Italy) 2022, *Annual Congress* Zagreb (Croatia) 2020, *Annual Congress* Rome (Italy) 2019, *Annual Congress* Tortosa (Spain) 2018, *Annual Congress* Eilat (Israel) 2017. **Publications** *CSIT News* (2 a year) in English, French – magazine.
Members Total membership covers about 230 individuals. Full: national federations (55) in 37 countries:
Algeria, Angola, Austria, Belgium, Bulgaria, China, Croatia, Cyprus, Denmark, Estonia, Finland, France, Germany, Greece, Haiti, India, Iran Islamic Rep, Iraq, Ireland, Israel, Italy, Korea Rep, Kosovo, Latvia, Lithuania, Mali, Mexico, Netherlands, Peru, Portugal, Russia, Slovenia, Spain, Switzerland, Tunisia, Türkiye, Ukraine.
Regional federation:
Confederación Panamericana del Deporte de los Trabajadores (COPADET, #04473).
IGO Relations *UNESCO (#20322)*. **NGO Relations** Member of (2): *International Council of Sport Science and Physical Education (ICSSPE, #13077)*; *Olympic Movement (#17719)*. Cooperates with (6): *European Fair Play Movement (EFPM, #07025)*; *European Non-Governmental Sports Organization (ENGSO, #08054)*; *International Sport and Culture Association (ISCA, #15587)*; *International Working Group on Women and Sport (IWG, #15912)*; *The Association for International Sport for All (TAFISA, #02763)*; *World Anti-Doping Agency (WADA, #21096)*. Recognized by: *International Olympic Committee (IOC, #14408)*. Associated with: *Socialist International (SI, #19340)*.
[2023.02.22/XD2818/y/**C**]

♦ International Workers' Association (IWA) 15906

Asociación Internacional de los Trabajadores (AIT) – Internacia Laboristo Asocio (ILA)

Secretariat Boks 1977 Vika, 0121 Oslo, Norway. T. +4723140177. Fax +4723305465.
URL: http://www.iwa-ait.org/

History Founded 8 Sep 1866, Geneva (Switzerland). **Aims** Organize and press for revolutionary struggle in all countries with the aim of destroying once and for all the present political and economic régimes and to establish Libertarian Communism; give economic unionist organizations a national and industrial base and, where that already exists, strengthen those organizations which are determined to fight for the destruction of capitalism and the State; prevent infiltration of any political parties into the economic unionist organizations and resolutely fight every attempt by political parties to control unions; where circumstances demand it, establish through a course of action that is not in contradiction with the above, provisional alliances with other proletarian, union and revolutionary organizations, with the objective of planning and carrying out common international actions in the interest of the working class; unmask and fight the arbitrary violence of all governments against revolutionaries dedicated to the cause of the Social Revolution; examine all problems of concern to the world proletariat in order to strengthen and develop movements, in one country or several, which help to defend the rights and new conquests of the working class or to organize the revolution for emancipation itself; undertake actions of mutual aid in the event of important economic struggles or critical struggles against the overt or covert enemies of the working class; give moral and material help to the working class movements in each country in which the leadership of the struggle is in the hands of the national economic organization of the proletariat. **Languages** English. **Activities** Events/meetings.
Members Sections; Groups; Friends. Members in 20 countries:
Argentina, Australia, Brazil, Bulgaria, Chile, Colombia, Czechia, France, Germany, Italy, Nigeria, Norway, Portugal, Russia, Serbia, Slovakia, Spain, Switzerland, UK, Venezuela.
[2015/XD7543/**C**]

♦ International Workers' Compensation Foundation (internationally oriented national body)
♦ International of Workers in Education (inactive)
♦ International Workers Sport Association / see International Workers and Amateurs in Sports Confederation (#15905)
♦ International Workers Sports Confederation / see International Workers and Amateurs in Sports Confederation (#15905)
♦ International Workers' Swimming Commission (inactive)
♦ International Work Group on Death, Dying and Bereavement (unconfirmed)

♦ International Work Group for Indigenous Affairs (IWGIA) 15907

Groupement international de travail pour les peuples autochtones – Grupo Internacional del Trabajo sobre Asuntos Indigenos

Exec Dir Prinsessegade 29-B, 3rd Floor, 1422 Copenhagen, Denmark. T. +4553732830. E-mail: iwgia@iwgia.org.
URL: http://www.iwgia.org/

History Aug 1968, Stuttgart (Germany). Founded at 38th International Congress of Americanists. Statutes amended 10 Mar 1978; 20 Feb 1981; 1 June 1985; Dec 1989; 28 May 1994; 27 May 2000; 2017; Jan 2022. Former names and other names: *Indigenous Affairs* – alias; *Groupement international de travail pour les affaires indigènes* – former. Registration: CVR, No/ID: 81294410, Denmark. **Aims** Promote, protect and defend Indigenous Peoples' rights. **Structure** General Meeting (annual); Board; Executive; Secretariat, headed by Executive Director. **Languages** Danish, English, Spanish. **Staff** 18.00 FTE, paid. **Finance** Sources: donations; grants; members' dues. Supported by: *Christensen Fund (TCF)*; *Comic Relief*; *DANIDA*; *Deutsche Gesellschaft für Internationale Zusammenarbeit (GIZ)*; *European Commission (EC, #06633)*; *FAO (#09260)*; *Ford Foundation (#09858)*; *ILO (#11123)*; *International Fund for Agricultural Development (IFAD, #13692)*; *Nordic Council of Ministers (NCM, #17260)*; *Wallace Global Fund*. **Activities** Advocacy/lobbying/activism; awareness raising; capacity building; events/meetings; financial and/or material support; knowledge management/information dissemination; politics/policy/regulatory; projects/programmes; publishing activities; research and development; research/documentation; training/education. **Events** *The indigenous peoples in Africa* Greve (Denmark) 1993, *Seminar* Amsterdam (Netherlands) 1988, *Arctic seminar* Copenhagen (Denmark) 1988. **Publications** *The Indigenous World* (annual). Annual Report; IWGIA Reports; briefings; books. **Consultative Status** Consultative status granted from: *African Commission on Human and Peoples' Rights (ACHPR, #00255)* (Observer); *ECOSOC (#05331)* (Special); *ILO (#11123)* (Special List); *UNESCO (#20322)* (Consultative Status). **IGO Relations** Accredited by (1): *Green Climate Fund (GCF, #10714)*. **NGO Relations** Member of (1): *European Network on Indigenous Peoples (ENIP, #07932)*. Also links with national organizations.
[2022.11.04/XF4515/**F**]

♦ International Working Conference on Requirements Engineering: Foundation for Software Quality (meeting series)
♦ International Working Conference on Stored-Product Protection (meeting series)
♦ International Working Dog Breeding Association (unconfirmed)
♦ International Working Group for Biopsychosocial Cancer Research (no recent information)
♦ International Working Group for the Construction of Sports and Leisure Facilities / see Internationale Vereinigung Sport- und Freizeiteinrichtungen (#13319)

♦ International Working Group on Data Protection in Telecommunications (IWGDPT) 15908

Contact Berliner Beauftragte für Datenschutz und Informationsfreiheit, Friedrichstrasse 219, 10969 Berlin, Germany. T. +4930138890. Fax +49302155050. E-mail: iwgdpt@datenschutz-berlin.de – mailbox@datenschutz-berlin.de.
URL: http://www.berlin-privacy-group.org/

History 1983, in the framework of *Global Privacy Assembly (GPA, #10555)*. **Aims** Improve data protection and privacy in telecommunications services and on the Internet. **Languages** English. **Activities** Events/meetings. **Events** *Meeting* Oslo (Norway) 2016, *Meeting* Seoul (Korea Rep) 2015.
[2020.01.08/XE4621/**E**]

♦ International Working Group on the Diabetic Foot / see D-Foot International (#05061)
♦ International Working Group on the Diabetic Foot – Implementation / see D-Foot International (#05061)

♦ International Working Group on Education (IWGE) 15909

Groupe international de travail sur l'éducation (GITE)

Dir c/o IIEP, 7-9 rue Eugène-Delacroix, 75116 Paris, France. E-mail: info@iiep.unesco.org.
Info Services address not obtained. T. +33145037773. Fax +33140728366.
URL: http://www.iiep.unesco.org/en/our-expertise/iwge/

History 1972, Bellagio (Italy), as *Bellagio Group – Groupe de Bellagio*. Current name adopted 1982, Mont Sainte Marie (Canada). An informal group of intergovernmental (multilateral and bilateral) and non-governmental agencies and foundations for discussing topics of common interest. **Aims** Offer multilateral and bilateral *development agencies* a forum for exchanging ideas and strengthening their cooperation in projects of mutual interest. **Structure** Planning Committee, comprising: *Aga Khan Foundation (AKF, #00545)*; *Deutsche Gesellschaft für Internationale Zusammenarbeit (GIZ)*; *International Bank for Reconstruction and Development (IBRD, #12317)* (World Bank); *Swedish International Development Cooperation Agency (Sida)*; *UNESCO (#20322)*; *UNICEF (#20332)*; *United States Agency for International Development (USAID)*. Secretariat: *International Institute for Educational Planning (IIEP, #13874)*. **Languages** English, French. **Staff** 1.00 FTE, paid. **Finance** Each agency covers its own cost of participation in the Working Group. Planning Committee members share the cost of Secretariat activities. **Activities** Knowledge management/information dissemination. **Events** *Inclusion – rethinking education for all* Berlin (Germany) 2014, *Meeting* Stockholm (Sweden) 2010, *Meeting* Long Island, NY (USA) 2008, *Meeting* Rome (Italy) 2006, *Meeting* Washington, DC (USA) 2004. **Publications** Reports; case studies.
Members Participating agencies (45) in 20 countries:
Australia, Austria, Belgium, Canada, Denmark, Finland, France, Germany, Iceland, Ireland, Italy, Japan, Netherlands, Norway, Portugal, Sweden, Switzerland, Thailand, UK, USA.
Included in the above, 17 organizations listed in this Yearbook:

African Development Bank (ADB, #00283); Aga Khan Foundation (AKF, #00545); Asian Development Bank (ADB, #01422); Association for the Development of Education in Africa (ADEA, #02471); Bernard van Leer Foundation (BvLF); Carnegie Corporation of New York; Commonwealth Secretariat (#04362); European Commission (EC, #06633); FAO (#09260); ILO (#11123); International Bank for Reconstruction and Development (IBRD, #12317) (World Bank); *International Institute for Educational Planning (IIEP, #13874); OECD (#17693); The Rockefeller Foundation (#18966); UNDP (#20292); UNESCO (#20322); UNICEF (#20332); WHO (#20950).* [2016.10.19/XE0333/y/**E**]

♦ International Working Group on Educational Data Mining / see International Educational Data Mining Society (#13229)

♦ International Working Group on Endoscopic Ear Surgery (IWGEES) . 15910

Gen Sec address not obtained.
Pres address not obtained.
URL: https://iwgees.org/

Aims Foster excellence in technique, instrument development and research in the field of endoscopic ear surgery. **Structure** Founding Board; Executive Board. **Activities** Events/meetings; training/education. **Events** *World Congress on Endoscopic Ear Surgery* Kyoto (Japan) 2022, *World Congress on Endoscopic Ear Surgery* Boston, MA (USA) 2019, *World Congress on Endoscopic Ear Surgery* Bologna (Italy) 2017, *World Congress on Endoscopic Ear Surgery* Dubai (United Arab Emirates) 2015. [2022.02.04/AA1537/**C**]

♦ International Working Group on Medical Geology / see International Medical Geology Association (#14133)
♦ International Working Group on Neuroimmunomodulation / see International Society for NeuroImmunoModulation (#15299)
♦ International Working Group on Plant Viruses with Fungal Vectors (inactive)

♦ International Working Group on Satellite-Based Emergency Mapping (IWG-SEM) 15911

Address not obtained.
URL: https://un-spider.org/institutions-guides/international-working-group-satellite-emergency-mapping-iwg%E2%80%90sem

History Apr 2012, as a voluntary group of organizations. **Aims** Support *disaster* response by improving international cooperation in satellite based emergency mapping. **Structure** Rotating Chair. **Languages** English. **Events** *Autumn Meeting* Beijing (China) 2018, *Autumn Meeting* Rome (Italy) 2017, *Autumn Meeting* Salzburg (Austria) 2016, *Spring Meeting* Vienna (Austria) 2016, *Autumn Meeting* Vienna (Austria) 2015. **Members** Participants in 9 countries:
Argentina, France, Germany, Italy, Japan, Kenya, Nigeria, UK, USA.
Included in the above, 14 organizations listed in this Yearbook:
African Regional Institute for Geospatial Information Science and Technology (AFRIGIST, #00433); EC – Humanitarian Aid and Civil Protection; *European Commission (EC, #06633)* (Enterprise and Industry); *European Space Agency (ESA, #08798); Group on Earth Observations (GEO, #10735); Human Rights Watch (HRW, #10990); Information Technology for Humanitarian Assistance, Cooperation and Action (ITHACA); International Bank for Reconstruction and Development (IBRD, #12317)* (World Bank); *International Centre for Integrated Mountain Development (ICIMOD, #12500); Joint Research Centre (JRC, #16147)* (EC); *Pacific Disaster Center (PDC); United Nations Institute for Training and Research (UNITAR, #20576)* (UNOSAT); *United Nations Platform for Space-based Information for Disaster Management and Emergency Response (UN-SPIDER, #20610); World Food Programme (WFP, #21510).* [2015.06.01/XJ9505/y/**F**]

♦ International Working Group for the Study of Viruses and Virus Diseases of the Grapevine / see International Council for the Study of Virus and Virus-like Diseases of the Grapevine (#13080)
♦ International Working Group on Taxonomic Databases / see Biodiversity Information Standards (#03243)
♦ International Working Group on Taxonomic Databases for Plant Sciences / see Biodiversity Information Standards (#03243)

♦ International Working Group on Women and Sport (IWG) 15912

Groupe de travail international sur les femmes et le sport (GTI) – Grupo de Trabajo Internacionales sobre la Mujer y el Deporte

Contact c/o UK Sport, 6th Floor, 10 South Colonnade, London, E14 4PU, UK. E-mail: info@uksport.gov.uk.
URL: http://www.iwg-gti.org/

History 1994, Brighton (UK). Founded at first World Conference on Women and Sport. **Aims** Foster a sustainable sporting culture that enables and values the full involvement of women in every aspect of sport. **Structure** Chair; 2 Co-Chairs; Regional Representatives (Africa; Americas; Asia; Europe; Oceania); 2 International NGO Representatives (IAPESGW; WSI); Coopted members. **Languages** English, French, Japanese. **Staff** 5.00 FTE, paid. **Activities** Events/meetings. **Events** *World Conference on Women & Sport* Birmingham (UK) 2026, *World Conference on Women & Sport* Auckland (New Zealand) 2022, *Quadrennial World Conference* Gaborone (Botswana) 2018, *Meeting* Stockholm (Sweden) 2016, *Quadrennial World Conference* Helsinki (Finland) 2014. **Publications** *The Catalyst* (4 a year) – newsletter. Annual Report. **Members** Olympic committees; sports councils; associations; commissions; sports federations and organizations; governmental bodies; women and sport bodies. Members in 116 countries. Membership countries not specified. **NGO Relations** Representatives from: *International Association of Physical Education and Sport for Girls and Women (IAPESGW, #12081); WomenSport International (WSI, #21033).* [2022/XE4404/**E**]

♦ International Working Men's Association, 1864 (inactive)
♦ International Working Men's Association, 1923 (inactive)
♦ International Working Party for the Documentation and Conservation of Buildings, Sites and Neighbourhoods of the Modern Movement / see Documentation and Conservation of the Modern Movement (#05110)
♦ International Working Union of Socialist Parties (inactive)
♦ International of the Working Youth (inactive)
♦ International Work Platform Association (inactive)
♦ International Workshop on Adaptive Multimedia Retrieval (meeting series)
♦ International Workshop on Advanced Image Technology (meeting series)
♦ International Workshop on Advanced Learning Sciences (meeting series)
♦ International Workshop on Alloantigeneic Systems in the Rat (meeting series)
♦ International Workshop on the Arithmetic of Finite Fields (meeting series)

♦ International Workshop for Astronomy (IWA) 15913

Pres c/o IAYC, Elterleinplatz 1/9A, 1170 Vienna, Austria.
URL: http://www.iayc.org/

History *International Astronomical Youth Camp (IAYC)* set up 1969. Former participants are asked to join IWA as leaders. Registered as a non-profit, in accordance with German law: VR 1743. **Aims** Promote knowledge of astronomy and astronomy related sciences in a unique international atmosphere. **Languages** English. **Staff** Voluntary. **Activities** Events/meetings. **Publications** Articles; report book. [2016.06.01/XJ6754/**E**]

♦ International Workshop on Atmospheric Icing of Structures (meeting series)
♦ International Workshop on Baryon and Lepton Number Violation (meeting series)
♦ International Workshop on Bayesian Inference and Maximum Entropy Methods in Science and Engineering (meeting series)
♦ International Workshop on the Biology of Fish Gametes (meeting series)
♦ International Workshop on Boolean Functions and their Applications (meeting series)
♦ International Workshop on Brominated Flame Retardants (meeting series)
♦ International Workshop on Bubble and Drop Interfaces (meeting series)
♦ International Workshop on Business Data Collection Methodology (meeting series)
♦ International Workshop on Complex Systems and Networks (meeting series)
♦ International Workshop on Computer Science and Engineering (meeting series)
♦ International Workshop on Crystal Growth of Organic Materials (meeting series)
♦ International Workshop on Crystalline Silicon for Solar Cells (meeting series)
♦ International Workshop on Electrostatic Storage Devices (meeting series)
♦ International Workshop On Entrepreneurship, Electronic And Mobile Business (meeting series)
♦ International Workshop in Financial Markets and Nonlinear Dynamics (meeting series)
♦ International Workshop on Greenhouse Gas Measurements from Space (meeting series)
♦ International Workshop on High Aspect Ratio Micro and Nano System Technology (meeting series)
♦ International Workshop on Humanized Mice (meeting series)
♦ International Workshop on Instrumentation for Planetary Missions (meeting series)
♦ International Workshop on Laser Interaction and Related Plasma Phenomena (meeting series)
♦ International Workshop on Matrices and Statistics (meeting series)
♦ International Workshop on Measurement and Computation of Turbulent Nonpremixed Flames (meeting series)
♦ International Workshop on Methane Hydrate Research and Development (meeting series)
♦ International Workshop on Microplasmas (meeting series)
♦ International Workshop on Mining and Learning with Graphs (meeting series)
♦ International Workshop on Model Reduction in Reacting Flows (meeting series)
♦ International Workshop on Multiple Partonic Interactions at the LHC (meeting series)
♦ International Workshop on Neutrinos from Accelerators (meeting series)
♦ International Workshop on Nitride Semiconductors (meeting series)
♦ International Workshop on Non-Crystalline Solids (meeting series)
♦ International Workshop on Non-Hodgkin Lymphoma (meeting series)
♦ International Workshop on OpenMP (meeting series)
♦ International Workshop of Operative Digestive Endoscopy (meeting series)
♦ International Workshop on Operator Theory and its Applications (meeting series)
♦ International Workshop on Oxide Electronics (meeting series)
♦ International Workshop on Pattern Recognition in Neuroimaging (meeting series)
♦ International Workshop on Piezoelectric Materials and Applications in Actuators (meeting series)
♦ International Workshop on Qualitative Reasoning (meeting series)
♦ International Workshop on Quantitative Musculoskeletal Imaging (meeting series)
♦ International Workshop on (Quantitative) Structure-Activity Relationships in Environmental and Health Sciences (meeting series)
♦ International Workshop on Quantum Reactive Scattering (meeting series)
♦ International Workshop on Radiation Imaging Detectors (meeting series)
♦ International Workshop on Railway Noise (meeting series)
♦ International Workshop on Rare-Earth Permanent Magnets and their Applications (meeting series)
♦ International Workshop on Renal Failure in Children (meeting series)
♦ International Workshop on Retroviral Pathogenesis (meeting series)
♦ International Workshop on Satisfiability Modulo Theories (meeting series)
♦ International Workshop on Security (meeting series)
♦ International Workshop on the Sharing Economy (meeting series)
♦ International Workshop on Streptococcus suis (meeting series)
♦ International Workshop on Theory and Practice of Provenance (meeting series)
♦ International Workshop on Thermal Investigations of ICs and Systems (meeting series)
♦ International Workshop on Treebanks and Linguistic Theory (meeting series)
♦ International Workshop on the Trefftz Method (meeting series)
♦ International Workshop on UV Materials and Devices (meeting series)
♦ International Workshop on Variability Modelling of Software-Intensive Systems (meeting series)
♦ International Workshop on Weak Interactions and Neutrinos (meeting series)
♦ International World Calendar Association / see The World Calendar Association – International (#21255)

♦ International World Games Association (IWGA) 15914

Gen Manager Av de la Gare 12, 1003 Lausanne VD, Switzerland. T. +41216010321. E-mail: office@iwga.sport.
CEO An den Wieen 87, 47239 Duisburg, Germany. T. +491755811492. E-mail: ceo@iwga.sport.
URL: http://www.theworldgames.org/

History 21 May 1980, Seoul (Korea Rep). Founded at Assembly of GAISF. New constitution adopted by General Meeting, 27 May 2021, replacing previous Constitution adopted remotely 06 Nov 2020. Former names and other names: *World Games Council (WGC)* – former (1980 to 1984). Registration: Register of Commerce of the canton de Vaud, No/ID: CHE-100.602.518, Start date: 3 Oct 1986, Switzerland, Vaud. **Aims** Develop the popularity of sports governed by Member Federations; unite and develop communities in and through sport; provide global exposure and a unique experience for athletes and cities; engage with and inspire communities by promotion of Sport values. **Structure** Annual General Meeting; Executive Committee; CoCom Meeting. **Languages** English. **Staff** 3.00 FTE, paid. **Finance** Sources: contributions; members' dues; revenue from activities/projects. Other sources: commercial activities in, or in direct connection with, the organization of The World Games. **Activities** Awards/prizes/competitions; events/meetings; sporting activities. **Events** *Media Workshop* Lausanne (Switzerland) 2023, *Annual General Meeting* Lausanne (Switzerland) 2021, *Annual General Meeting* Lausanne (Switzerland) 2020, *Media Workshop* Lausanne (Switzerland) 2020, *Media Workshop* Madrid (Spain) 2019. **Publications** *The Anti-Doping Rules of the IWGA* (2017); *Bidding for TWG 2025; Sportcal Study; The Rules of The World Games; The World Games 2029 Candidature Brochure and Trifold; The World Games Brochure.*
Members International Sports Federations (39):
– *Fédération aéronautique internationale (FAI, #09397);*
– *Fédération internationale de gymnastique (FIG, #09636);*
– *Fédération internationale de SAMBO (FIAS, #09655);*
– *International Aikido Federation (IAF, #11605);*
– *International Bowling Federation (IBF, #12384);*
– *International Canoe Federation (ICF, #12437);*
– *International Casting Sport Federation (ICSF, #12447);*
– *International Federation of Muaythai Associations (IFMA, #13482);*
– *International Federation of Sport Climbing (IFSC, #13553);*
– *International Fistball Association (IFA, #13609);*
– *International Fitness and Bodybuilding Federation (IFBB, #13610);*
– *International Floorball Federation (IFF, #13615);*
– *International Handball Federation (IHF, #13771);*
– *International Hockey Federation (#13802);*
– *International Korfball Federation (IKF, #13992);*
– *International Life Saving Federation (ILS, #14040);*
– *International Orienteering Federation (IOF, #14485);*
– *International Powerlifting Federation (IPF, #14630);*
– *International Racquetball Federation (IRF, #14683);*
– *International Sumo Federation (IFS, #15624);*
– *International Surfing Association (ISA, #15630);*
– *International Waterski and Wakeboard Federation (IWWF, #15872);*
– *International Wushu Federation (IWUF, #15918);*
– *Ju-Jitsu International Federation (JJIF, #16164);*
– *Tug of War International Federation (TWIF, #20259);*
– *World Archery (#21105);*
– *World Association of Kickboxing Organizations (WAKO, #21151);*
– *World Baseball Softball Confederation (WBSC, #21222);*
– *World Confederation of Billiards Sports (WCBS, #21291);*
– *World DanceSport Federation (WDSF, #21354);*
– *World Flying Disc Federation (WFDF, #21509);*
– *World Karate Federation (WKF, #21608);*
– *World Lacrosse (#21616);*
– *World Netball (WN, #21668);*
– *World Pétanque and Bowls Federation (WPBF, #21721);*
– *World Rugby (#21757);*
– *World Skate (#21786);*

- *World Squash Federation (WSF, #21826);*
- *World Underwater Federation (#21873).*

NGO Relations Accredited by (1): *International Olympic Committee (IOC, #14408).* Member of (1): *Olympic Movement (#17719).* Cooperates with (1): *International Testing Agency (ITA, #15678).* [2022.12.01/XE4001/y/**E**]

♦ International World Travellers Club (IWTC) 15915

Club international des grands voyageurs (CIGV) – Club Internacional de los Grandes Viajeros – Internationaler Club der Weltreisenden

SG Avenue Bourguiba 26, 2013 Ben Arous, Tunisia. T. +21671383266 – +21671382390. Fax +21671382257. E-mail: cigv-hq@planet.tn.
Pres address not obtained.
URL: http://www.cigv-online.com/

History 4 Aug 1982, Puerto Rico. Founded at 1st world travellers' meeting. The creation of IWTC was a common decision of the Club's Headquarters in Tunisia and members throughout the world. **Aims** Unite people who have visited at least 50 countries; foster between world travellers of the 5 continents the bonds of friendship, a common enthusiasm and mutual aid, in order to contribute to a worldwide dialogue of *peace* and *friendship*. **Languages** Dutch, English, French, German, Italian, Spanish. **Staff** 5.50 FTE, paid; 1.00 FTE, voluntary. **Finance** Members' dues. **Activities** Awards/prizes/competitions. **Events** *World Congress* Hammamet (Tunisia) 2016, *World Congress* Mahdia (Tunisia) 2013, *World Congress* Mauritius 2011, *World congress* Hammamet (Tunisia) 2009, *World congress* Barcelona (Spain) 2006. **Publications** *CIGV-News* (12 a year); *Astrolabe* (4 a year); *World Directory* (2 a year); *Astrolabe-Plus* (annual). **Members** National Clubs in 194 countries. Membership countries not specified. [2022/XF1892/**F**]

♦ International World Wide Web Conference Committee (internationally oriented national body)

♦ International Wound Infection Institute (IWII) 15916

Secretariat Schofield Healthcare Media, 1 03 Enterprise House, 1-2 Hatfields, London, SE1 9PG, UK.
URL: http://www.woundinfection-institute.com/

Aims Provide a global perspective on the latest developments in wound infection. **Structure** General Meeting (annual); Executive Committee; Secretariat. **Activities** Events/meetings; knowledge management/information dissemination; networking/liaising. **Events** *Annual General Meeting* Las Vegas, NV (USA) 2019, *Annual General Meeting* Adelaide, SA (Australia) 2018, *Annual General Meeting* Toronto, ON (Canada) 2017, *Annual General Meeting* Melbourne, VIC (Australia) 2016, *Annual General Meeting* Gold Coast, QLD (Australia) 2014. **NGO Relations** Partner of: *European Wound Management Association (EWMA, #09121).* [2019/XM4361/**C**]

♦ International Writers Guild (inactive)
♦ International Writers' Reunion (meeting series)
♦ International Writing Centers Association (internationally oriented national body)

♦ International Wrought Copper Council (IWCC) 15917

Pres 1 Burwood Place, London, W2 2UT, UK. T. +442037552940. Fax +442037552944. E-mail: iwcc@coppercouncil.org.
URL: http://www.coppercouncil.org/

History 7 Oct 1953, Amsterdam (Netherlands). **Aims** Promote the interests of copper and copper alloy fabricating industries in member countries; encourage friendly relations within the industry and exchange of information; cooperate with other associations of similar interests and with international governmental bodies. **Structure** General Assembly (annual); Executive Board; Committees (3). Meetings closed. **Languages** English. **Staff** 4.00 FTE, paid. **Finance** Sources: members' dues. **Activities** Events/meetings; knowledge management/information dissemination. **Events** *Joint Meeting* Montréal, QC (Canada) 2020, *Joint Meeting* Santiago (Chile) 2019, *Technical Seminar* Chicago, IL (USA) 2018, *Joint Meeting* Seville (Spain) 2018, *General Assembly* Kuala Lumpur (Malaysia) 2017. **Publications** *World Trade in Copper and Copper Alloy Semi-Manufactures* (annual).

Members Wrought copper producing companies in 23 countries and territories:
Australia, Austria, Belgium, Bulgaria, China, Finland, France, Germany, Greece, India, Italy, Japan, Korea Rep, Malaysia, Netherlands, South Africa, Spain, Sweden, Switzerland, Taiwan, Türkiye, UK, USA.

Consultative Status Consultative status granted from: *UNCTAD (#20285)* (Special Category). [2020/XD2823/**C**]

♦ International Wushu Federation (IWUF) 15918

Dir Av de Rhodanie 58, 1007 Lausanne VD, Switzerland. T. +41213122583. E-mail: iwuf@iwuf.org.
Beijing Office 9 Huaweili, Chaoyang District, 100021 Beijing, China. T. +861087774492.
URL: http://www.iwuf.org/

History 3 Oct 1990, Beijing (China). Former names and other names: *IWF* – former. **Aims** Promote and develop wushu throughout the world; encourage friendship and understanding between people worldwide through the spirit of sport. **Structure** Congress (every 2 years); Executive Board; Secretariat; Committees (7); Working Groups (3). **Languages** Chinese, English. **Staff** 15.00 FTE, paid. **Finance** Sources: members' dues; sponsorship. **Activities** Events/meetings; sporting activities; training/education. **Publications** *IWUF Yearbook* (annual); *WUSHU Magazine* (annual).

Members National federations in 146 countries and territories:
Afghanistan, Algeria, Andorra, Argentina, Armenia, Australia, Austria, Azerbaijan, Bangladesh, Barbados, Belarus, Belgium, Benin, Bermuda, Bolivia, Bosnia-Herzegovina, Botswana, Brazil, Brunei Darussalam, Bulgaria, Cambodia, Cameroon, Canada, Chile, China, Colombia, Comoros, Congo Brazzaville, Congo DR, Costa Rica, Côte d'Ivoire, Croatia, Cuba, Cyprus, Czechia, Dominica, Ecuador, Egypt, Estonia, Ethiopia, Fiji, Finland, France, Gabon, Georgia, Germany, Greece, Guinea, Guyana, Hong Kong, Hungary, Iceland, India, Indonesia, Iran Islamic Rep, Iraq, Ireland, Israel, Italy, Jamaica, Japan, Jordan, Kazakhstan, Kenya, Korea DPR, Korea Rep, Kuwait, Kyrgyzstan, Laos, Latvia, Lebanon, Liberia, Libya, Lithuania, Luxembourg, Macau, Madagascar, Malawi, Malaysia, Maldives, Mali, Malta, Mauritania, Mauritius, Mexico, Moldova, Monaco, Mongolia, Montenegro, Morocco, Mozambique, Myanmar, Nepal, Netherlands, New Caledonia, New Zealand, Nigeria, Norway, Pakistan, Palestine, Paraguay, Peru, Philippines, Poland, Portugal, Puerto Rico, Romania, Russia, Rwanda, San Marino, Senegal, Serbia, Seychelles, Sierra Leone, Singapore, Slovakia, Slovenia, Somalia, South Africa, Spain, Sri Lanka, St Lucia, Sudan, Sweden, Switzerland, Syrian AR, Taiwan, Tajikistan, Tanzania UR, Thailand, Togo, Trinidad-Tobago, Tunisia, Türkiye, Turkmenistan, Uganda, UK, Ukraine, Uruguay, USA, Uzbekistan, Venezuela, Vietnam, Yemen, Zambia, Zimbabwe.

Continental federations (5):
African Wushu Federation; *European Wushu Kungfu Federation (EWUF, #09126)*; Oceania Wushu Federation; Panamerican Wushu Federation; *Wushu Federation of Asia (WFA, #21964).*

NGO Relations Member of (2): *Association of the IOC Recognized International Sports Federations (ARISF, #02767); Olympic Movement (#17719).* Partner of (1): *General Association of Asia Pacific Sports Federations (GAAPSF, #10106).* Cooperates with (1): *International Testing Agency (ITA, #15678).* Recognized by: *International Olympic Committee (IOC, #14408).* [2022/XD4119/**C**]

♦ International XAFS Society / see International X-ray Absorption Society (#15920)

♦ International Xenotransplantation Association (IXA) 15919

Sections Manager c/o TTS, 505 Boulevard René-Lévesque Ouest, Ste 1401, Montréal QC H2Z 1Y7, Canada. T. +15148741717. Fax +15148741716.
URL: https://www.tts.org/ixa/home

History Jul 1998, Montréal (Canada). Section of *The Transplantation Society (TTS, #20224).* **Aims** Promote the science of xenotransplantation as a safe, ethical, and effective therapeutic modality by: promoting ethical and pre-clinical research, productive discourse, and collaboration; educating health care providers and lay persons through participation in interactive public debate; guiding the development of public policy that is responsive to new develoments in the field and acknowledges varying social, ethical and legal frameworks. **Structure** Council. **Activities** Events/meetings. **Events** *Joint Congress* 2021, *Joint Meeting* 2021, *Joint Congress* San Diego, CA (USA) 2021, *Biennial Congress* Munich (Germany) 2019, *Biennial Congress* Baltimore, MD (USA) 2017. **Publications** *Xenotransplantation* (4 a year).

Members Individuals in 28 countries and territories:
Argentina, Australia, Austria, Belgium, Brazil, Canada, Cyprus, Denmark, Egypt, Finland, France, Germany, Hong Kong, Israel, Italy, Japan, Korea DPR, Korea Rep, Netherlands, Norway, Pakistan, Portugal, Spain, Sweden, Switzerland, Taiwan, UK, USA. [2019.12.05/XD7756/**E**]

♦ International X-ray Absorption Society (IXAS) 15920

Chairperson c/o Inst for Catalysis, Kita 21 Nishi 10, Kita-ku, Sapporo HOKKAIDO, 001-0021 Japan.
URL: https://xrayabsorption.org/

History 26 Aug 1992, Japan. Charter and bylaws approved by the membership, 29 Aug 1994. Former names and other names: *International XAFS Society (IXS)* – former (Aug 1992 to Jul 2007). **Aims** Promote and develop *X-Ray* Absorption Fine Structure (XAFS) and related disciplines; act as a representative for the community to other professional organizations; provide for education in the field; disseminate relevant information. **Structure** Executive Committee. **Languages** English. **Staff** 4.50 FTE, voluntary. **Finance** Sources: conference registration fees; web portal business. **Activities** Training/education; knowledge management/information dissemination. **Events** *International Conference on X-Ray Absorption and Fine Structure (XAFS)* Sydney, NSW (Australia) 2022, *International Conference on X-Ray Absorption Fine Structure* Sydney, NSW (Australia) 2021, *International Conference on X-Ray Absorption Fine Structure* Krakow (Poland) 2018, *International Conference on X-ray Absorption Fine Structure* Karlsruhe (Germany) 2015, *International Conference on X-ray Absorption Fine Structure* Beijing (China) 2012. **Publications** *IXAS Magazine* (4 a year).

Members Individuals (1,263), including students, in 35 countries and territories:
Argentina, Australia, Austria, Belgium, Brazil, Canada, China, Czechia, Denmark, Finland, France, Germany, Greece, India, Iran Islamic Rep, Israel, Italy, Japan, Korea Rep, Latvia, Mexico, Morocco, Netherlands, Norway, Poland, Romania, Russia, Senegal, Slovenia, Spain, Sweden, Switzerland, Taiwan, UK, USA. [2022/XE2834/v/**E**]

♦ International X-Ray Analysis Society (inactive)
♦ International X-ray Observatory (inactive)
♦ International X-Ray and Radium Protection Committee / see International Commission on Radiological Protection (#12724)
♦ International X-Ray Unit Committee / see International Commission on Radiation Units and Measurements (#12722)
♦ International Yacht Racing Union / see World Sailing (#21760)
♦ International YAG Laser Society (unconfirmed)
♦ International Yakult Symposium (meeting series)
♦ International YCS / see International Young Catholic Students (#15926)
♦ International YCS Center of Documentation and Information / see International Young Catholic Students (#15926)
♦ International Year of Shelter for the Homeless Trust / see Reall
♦ International Yeast 2.0 Synthetic Genomics Conference (meeting series)

♦ International Yeats Society 15921

Contact address not obtained. E-mail: contact@iwbys.org.
URL: http://www.internationalyeatssociety.org/

History 2014. **Aims** Allow a wide range of academic researches to share and present their work and make that work widely and easily available; facilitate communication amongst scholars, teachers and postgraduate students; foster productive teams of researchers, especially across national borders; advance awareness of Yeats studies in wider academic and public communities; promote the study of Yeats as well as Irish literature and culture, in a global context. **Structure** Executive Board. **Languages** English. **Staff** All voluntary. **Finance** Members' dues. **Activities** Events/meetings; training/education. **Events** *Conference* Paris (France) 2019, *Symposium* Kyoto (Japan) 2018, *Conference* New York, NY (USA) 2017, *Symposium on Yeats and Asia* Barcelona (Spain) 2016, *Conference* Limerick (Ireland) 2015. **Publications** *International Yeats Studies* – journal.

Members Individuals in 18 countries and territories:
Australia, Belgium, Canada, France, Hong Kong, Hungary, India, Ireland, Italy, Japan, Korea Rep, Norway, Poland, Russia, Spain, Taiwan, UK, USA. [2019/XM5536/**E**]

♦ International Yehudi Menuhin Foundation (IYMF) 15922

Exec Vice-Pres Bd du Souverain 36, 1170 Brussels, Belgium. T. +3226733504. E-mail: info@menuhin-foundation.com.
URL: http://www.menuhin-foundation.com/

History 18 Oct 1991, Brussels (Belgium), as *International Menuhin Association (IMA).* Present name adopted May 1994. Registered in accordance with Belgian law. EU Transparency Register: 34694767407-27. **Aims** Improve the environment of the *child* by music, arts and all disciplines necessary to its entire fulfilment; promote *musical expression* and encounters of different *cultures*; encourage expression and protection of cultural identities, especially those that are endangered; coordinate and implement cultural projects initiated by Lord Menuhin and spread them throughout Europe. **Structure** General Assembly; International Board. **Languages** English, French. **Staff** 1.50 FTE, paid. **Finance** Main source: public administrations, such as: *Council of Europe (CE, #04881); European Commission (EC, #06633); UNESCO (#20322)*; the Region of Brussels (Belgium); the French Community of Belgium. Other sources: activities of the Foundation; sponsors; private donors; foundations, including *Alfried Krupp von Bohlen und Halbach Foundation.* **Activities** Events/meetings; projects/programmes. **Events** *International seminar* Altea (Spain) 2000, *Annual international seminar* Brussels (Belgium) 1998, *Symposium of the assembly of European cultures* Brussels (Belgium) 1997, *Annual international seminar* Perpignan (France) 1997. **Publications** *MUS-E Newsletter.* DVDs; CDs.

Members Categories (1) Active; (2) Associate; (3) Honorary; (4) Adhering; (5) Artists associated with the Foundation. Members in 13 countries and territories:
Belgium, Brazil, Estonia, Finland, France, Germany, Hungary, Israel, Italy, Portugal, Scotland, Spain, Switzerland.

IGO Relations Joint projects with: *Parliamentary Assembly of the Council of Europe (PACE, #18211).* [2020/XE3193/f/**F**]

♦ International YMCA – International Branch of the YMCA, New York (internationally oriented national body)
♦ International Yngling Class Association (see: #21760)
♦ International Yoga Centre, Tokyo (internationally oriented national body)

♦ International Yoga Federation (IYF) 15923

Federación Internacional de Yoga

Pres address not obtained. E-mail: fiy@yoganet.org.
URL: http://www.internationalyogafederation.net/

History 1988. Former names and other names: *International Yoga Teachers and Instructors Federation* – former. **Aims** Promote yoga and yoga *therapy* worldwide. **Structure** General Assembly; Executive Board; Supervise Commission; Secretariat. **Events** *International Conference* Santiago (Chile) 2014, *International Conference* Paris (France) 2013, *International Conference* Belgrade (Serbia) 2012, *International Conference* Montevideo (Uruguay) 2011, *International yogatherapy and ayurveda conference* Punta del Este (Uruguay) 2011.

Members National organizations (134) in 53 countries and territories:
Argentina, Australia, Bangladesh, Bolivia, Brazil, Bulgaria, Canada, Chile, China, Costa Rica, Cuba, Czechia, France, Germany, Gibraltar, Iceland, India, Iran Islamic Rep, Ireland, Israel, Italy, Japan, Kenya, Mauritius, Mexico, Moldova, Nepal, Netherlands, New Zealand, North Macedonia, Norway, Pakistan, Panama, Paraguay, Peru, Philippines, Portugal, Romania, Russia, Senegal, Slovakia, Slovenia, South Africa, Spain, Sweden, Switzerland, Thailand, Türkiye, UK, Ukraine, Uruguay, USA, Venezuela.

Included in the above, 3 organizations listed in this Yearbook:
Integral Yoga Academy of Australasia (IYAA); International Yoga Centre, Tokyo; Open International University for Alternative Medicines (no recent information).

Continental organizations (8):
Africa Yoga Federation (AYF); Asian Union of Yoga (AUOY, no recent information); European Yoga Alliance (EYA, #09129); European Yoga Council (EYC, #09130); European Yoga Union (#09131); Ibero-American Yoga Association (no recent information); União Latino Americana de Yoga (ULY, #20329); Yoga Alliance of South America (no recent information).

International organizations (24):
- *International Academy of Ayurveda (IAA);*
- *International Association of Yoga Science Centres (IAYSC, no recent information);*
- *International Black Yoga Teachers Association (IABYT);*
- *International Centre for Yoga Education and Research (ICYER);*
- *International Centre for Yogic Arts and Sciences (ICYAS, no recent information);*
- *International College of Ayurveda (Joytinat, no recent information);*
- *International Integral Yoga Fellowship Movement (no recent information);*

- *International School of Ayurveda;*
- *International Society of Yoga Education (ISYE, no recent information);*
- *International Solar Yoga Teachers' Association (ISYTA);*
- *International Yoga Academy, Coimbatore (no recent information);*
- *International Yoga Foundation (no recent information);*
- *International Yoga Institute (no recent information);*
- International Yoga Institute of Canada;
- International Yoga Institute of Poland;
- *International Yoga Society (IYS);*
- *International Yoga Sport Federation (IYSF, #15924);*
- *International Yoga Studies (IYS, no recent information);*
- *International Yoga Therapy Association (IYA, no recent information);*
- *World Clinical Yoga Society, India (no recent information);*
- *World Vaisnava Association (WVA, #21897);*
- *World Yoga Council (no recent information);*
- *World Yoga Foundation;*
- *World Yoga Society.* [2020/XB0015/y/**B**]

♦ International Yoga Society (internationally oriented national body)

♦ International Yoga Sport Federation (IYSF) 15924

Sec address not obtained. E-mail: secretary@yogasports.org.
URL: http://yogasports.org/

History Founded 1989, Montevideo (Uruguay). **Events** *World Yoga Sport Cup* Madrid (Spain) 2004, *World Yoga Sport Cup* Santa Maria da Feira (Portugal) 2003, *World Yoga Sport Cup* Rio de Janeiro (Brazil) 2002, *World Yoga Sport Cup* Buenos Aires (Argentina) 2001, *World Yoga Sport Cup* Delhi (India) 2000. **Publications** *Yoga Sport Journal.*
Members National organizations in 4 countries:
Argentina, Brazil, Italy, Uruguay.
IGO Relations *UNESCO (#20322).* **NGO Relations** Member of (1): *International Yoga Federation (IYF, #15923).* Partner of (1): *European Esports Observatory (EEO).* [2014/XD5986/**D**]

♦ International Yoga Teachers Association (IYTA) 15925

Acting Pres GPO Box 57, Sydney NSW 2001, Australia. E-mail: membership@iyta.com.au.
URL: http://www.iyta.com.au/

History 1967, Sydney, NSW (Australia). **Aims** Promote the physical, mental, emotional and spiritual benefits of yoga. **Structure** Committee. **Languages** English. **Staff** 12.00 FTE, paid. **Finance** Sources: fees for services; members' dues. **Activities** Events/meetings; training/education. **Events** *Conference* Sydney, NSW (Australia) 2017, *World Yoga Convention* Sydney, NSW (Australia) 2016, *World Yoga Convention* Cairns, QLD (Australia) 2013, *World yoga convention* Sydney, NSW (Australia) 2010, *General Meeting* Barcelona (Spain) 2006. **Publications** *IYTA E-Newsletter* (12 a year); *International Light* (3 a year).
Members Individuals in 23 countries and territories:
Australia, Austria, Belgium, Brazil, Canada, Fiji, France, Germany, Greece, Hong Kong, India, Indonesia, Israel, Malaysia, New Zealand, Oman, Puerto Rico, Singapore, South Africa, Spain, Sri Lanka, Switzerland, UK.
NGO Relations National yoga associations. [2023/XD6223/v/**D**]

♦ International Yoga Teachers and Instructors Federation / see International Yoga Federation (#15923)
♦ International Yoga Therapy Association (no recent information)
♦ International Yoshinkan Aikido Federation / see Aikido Yoshinkai Foundation (#00595)

♦ International Young Catholic Students (IYCS) 15926

Jeunesse étudiante catholique internationale (JECI) – Juventud Estudiantil Católica Internacional (JECI) – Internationale Katholische Studierende Jugend (IKSJ)

SG 7 Impasse Reille, 75014 Paris, France. T. +33145481472. E-mail: mail@iycs-jeci.org.
URL: http://www.iycs-jeci.org/

History 1929. At the first YCS International Meeting, Fribourg (Switzerland), 1-8 Sep 1946, 8 national movements came together and decided to set up the *Centre international de documentation et d'information (CIDI) – International YCS Center of Documentation and Information* in Paris (today the International Secretariat) for the service of all YCS groups throughout the world. An International Commission (currently "International Team") was mandated to work for all existing YCS mouvements in the world. Present name adopted Aug 1954, Brussels (Belgium). Current statutes approved, Aug 2007, Kampala (Uganda). Registration: French Ministry of Interior, No/ID: 59/972, Start date: 14 Oct 1959, France, Paris. **Aims** Evangelize the student milieu and promote the lay apostolate among students, at both secondary and tertiary levels; bring together students seeking community, formation and action, in the framework of the Catholic Church; promote global solidarity, freedom, justice and peace, and work with all concerned women and men for joint reflection and action leading to a more just and social order; give students resources, pedagogies, and methodologies to help them integrate their Christian faith into their lives at all levels and in their efforts to build a more just society; be a voice for its student members by representing them in regional and international forums. **Structure** World Council (meeting every 4 years); International Committee (meeting every year); Advisory Body; International Secretariat; Regional Coordinations; National Movements. **Languages** English, French, Spanish. **Staff** 11.00 FTE, paid. **Finance** Sources: contributions; members' dues. **Activities** Advocacy/lobbying/activism; networking/liaising; projects/programmes; training/education. Active in all member countries. **Events** *World Council Meeting* Abuja (Nigeria) 2019, *World Council Meeting* Tagaytay (Philippines) 2015, *Quadrennial World Council Meeting* Delhi (India) 2011, *Quadrennial world council meeting* Kampala (Uganda) 2007, *Meeting* Barcelona (Spain) 2003. **Publications** *International Newsletter* (4 a year) in English, French, Spanish; *SPES: Boletín de Información para los Movimientos de América Latina* (4 a year); *YCS African Newsletter* (4 a year) in English, French; *Confrontation Europe* in English, French; *Info-Rapid* – published by European Secretariat; *YCS Asian Newsletter.* Series of publications, in English and French, published by the Pan African Documentation Centre – in Spanish, published by the 'Centro de Documentación del SLA'.
Members Member movements in 65 countries and territories:
Australia, Austria, Bangladesh, Belgium, Benin, Bolivia, Burkina Faso, Burundi, Cameroon, Canada, Catalunya, Central African Rep, Chad, Chile, China, Congo Brazzaville, Congo DR, Côte d'Ivoire, Dominican Rep, Ecuador, Egypt, France, Gabon, Gambia, Germany, Ghana, Greece, Guinea, India, Indonesia, Italy, Jordan, Kenya, Korea Rep, Lebanon, Lesotho, Luxembourg, Madagascar, Malawi, Malaysia, Mali, Nepal, Nigeria, Palestine, Peru, Philippines, Portugal, Rwanda, Senegal, Sierra Leone, Singapore, South Africa, South Sudan, Spain, Sri Lanka, Sudan, Syrian AR, Taiwan, Tanzania UR, Thailand, Togo, Uganda, Vietnam, Zambia, Zimbabwe.
Collaborator Movements in 8 countries:
Cuba, Haiti, Ireland, Liberia, Namibia, Niger, Pakistan, Slovakia.
Contact Movements in 13 countries:
Croatia, Cuba, Czechia, Eritrea, Ethiopia, Fiji, Hungary, Laos, Lithuania, Myanmar, Slovenia, United Arab Emirates, USA.
There are 2 Contact Movements in USA [Chicago YCS and US Vietnamese YCS].
Consultative Status Consultative status granted from: *UNESCO (#20322)* (Consultative Status); *Council of Europe (CE, #04881)* (Participatory Status). **IGO Relations** Accredited by (1): *United Nations Office at Vienna (UNOV, #20604).* **NGO Relations** Member of (1): *Forum of Catholic Inspired NGOs (#09905).* [2023.02.15/XB2825/**B**]

♦ International Young Christian Workers (IYCW) 15927

Jeunesse ouvrière chrétienne internationale (JOCI) – Juventud Obrera Cristiana Internacional (JOCI)

International Pres Av Georges Rodenbach 4, 1030 Brussels, Belgium. T. +3222421811. Fax +3222424800. E-mail: joci@jociycw.net.
Treas address not obtained.
URL: http://joci.org/

History 1945, Brussels (Belgium). *JOC Europe (#16118)* set up 1925, Belgium, and continuing its links with IYCW. Statutes ratified Sep 1957, Rome (Italy); modified: 1975, Linz (Austria); 2000, Brussels (Belgium). Former names and other names: *JOC internationale* – alias. Registration: Banque-Carrefour des Entreprises, No/ID: 0408.299.130, Start date: 9 May 1968, Belgium. **Aims** Allow young workers to discover the meaning of their lives and live in accordance with personal and collective dignity; train them to assume responsibilities and find solutions to their own situations; educate and motivate them to take actions for better working and living conditions; promote inter-religious dialogue and create an intercultural society where solidarity and justice prevail. **Structure** Council (every 4 years); Executive Committee. Meetings closed. **Languages** English, French, Spanish. **Staff** 4.00 FTE, paid. **Finance** Sources: contributions; donations; grants; members' dues. **Activities** Events/meetings; networking/liaising; training/education. **Events** *Quadrennial Meeting* Aachen (Germany) 2016, *Quadrennial Meeting* Accra (Ghana) 2012, *Quadrennial Meeting* Thanjavur (India) 2008, *Quadrennial meeting* Venezuela 2004, *Quadrennial meeting* Dworp (Belgium) 2000. **Publications** *Making Life Happen Bulletin* (4 a year) in English; *Africa Info* (annual) in English, French; *Continental Bulletin of America* (annual) in French, Spanish; *IYCW Bulletin. Eurotelegramme* in French, Spanish.
Members National organizations in 42 countries and territories:
Australia, Austria, Belgium, Bolivia, Brazil, Canada, Chile, China, Colombia, Congo Brazzaville, Congo DR, Costa Rica, Côte d'Ivoire, Dominican Rep, Ecuador, Egypt, Gabon, Germany, Ghana, Guatemala, Haiti, Hong Kong, India, Indonesia, Ireland, Japan, Malaysia, Namibia, Nicaragua, Pakistan, Paraguay, Peru, Philippines, Singapore, South Africa, Spain, Sri Lanka, Thailand, USA, Venezuela, Zambia, Zimbabwe.
Consultative Status Consultative status granted from: *UNESCO (#20322)* (Consultative Status); *FAO (#09260)* (Liaison Status); *ILO (#11123)* (Special List). **IGO Relations** Accredited by (1): *United Nations Office at Vienna (UNOV, #20604).* Associated with Department of Global Communications of the United Nations. **NGO Relations** Founding member of: *Social Alert International (inactive).* Member of: *UNITED for Intercultural Action – European Network Against Nationalism, Racism, Fascism and in Support of Migrants and Refugees (UNITED, #20511).* Instrumental in setting up: *International Cardijn Association (ICA).* [2020/XC2826/**B**]

♦ International Young Democrat Union (IYDU) 15928

SG Mies-van-der-Rohe-Str 1, 80807 Munich, Germany.
URL: http://www.iydu.org/

History Mar 1991, Washington DC (USA). A previous Union with the same title had been set up Jul 1981, Washington DC, and subsequently ceased to exist. Constitution last amended Dec 2010, with changes ratified Feb 2011. **Aims** Promote and defend the ideals and cultural heritage of pluralist democracies; promote free markets and individual freedoms; contribute to and participate in the workings of IDU; extend and strengthen cooperation among member organizations. **Structure** Council; Executive Committee. **Languages** English. **Staff** 1.00 FTE, paid. **Finance** Sources: members' dues. **Activities** Events/meetings. **Events** *Meeting* Munich (Germany) 2021, *Mini Meeting* Munich (Germany) 2020, *Meeting* Brussels (Belgium) 2019, *Meeting* Helsinki (Finland) 2018, *Meeting* Sydney, NSW (Australia) 2012.
Members Full and associate member organizations in 61 countries and territories:
Albania, Anguilla, Argentina, Armenia, Australia, Austria, Azerbaijan, Bolivia, Brazil, Canada, Chile, Colombia, Croatia, Cyprus, Czechia, Denmark, Dominican Rep, El Salvador, Estonia, Faeroe Is, Finland, France, Georgia, Germany, Ghana, Greece, Grenada, Honduras, Hungary, Iceland, India, Israel, Italy, Korea Rep, Latvia, Lebanon, Liechtenstein, Lithuania, Mongolia, Montserrat, Nepal, New Zealand, Norway, Poland, Portugal, Romania, Serbia, Slovakia, Slovenia, Spain, St Kitts-Nevis, St Lucia, St Vincent-Grenadines, Sweden, Taiwan, Tanzania UR, Uganda, UK, Ukraine, USA, Venezuela.
Regional member organizations (7):
Asia Pacific Democrat Youth (APDY, no recent information); Caribbean Young Democrat Union (CYDU); Democrat Youth Community of Europe (DEMYC, #05037); European Democrat Students (EDS, #06901); European Young Conservatives (EYC, no recent information); Nordens Konservativa Studentunion (NKSU, #17161); Nordic Young Conservative Union (NYCU, #17473).
Associate members in 4 countries:
Georgia, Guyana, Uruguay, Zambia.
NGO Relations Part of: *International Democrat Union (IDU, #13147).* [2019/XD6612/y/**C**]

♦ International Young Nature Friends (IYNF) 15929

Internationale des jeunes amis de la nature (IJAN) – Naturfreundejugend Internationale (NFJI)

Secretariat Senovazné namvesti 24, 110 00 Prague 1, Czechia. T. +420234621573. Fax +420234621574. E-mail: iynf@iynf.org.
SG address not obtained.
Pres address not obtained.
Pres address not obtained.
URL: https://www.iynf.org/

History Official legal status, 2005. Existed prior to 1975 as the Youth Branch of Naturefriends International (listed in this Yearbook as *Internationale amis de la nature (IAN, #14780)*). Former names and other names: *Natuurvrienden Jongeren Internationale* – former. **Aims** Represent members at European level and facilitate cooperation between them; focus on value-driven meetings and capacity building, nature-friendly activities for its members, partners, supporters and interested individuals. **Structure** General Assembly (every 2 years); Council (annual); Secretariat based in Prague (Czech Rep). **Languages** Czech, English, German. **Staff** 3.00 FTE, paid; 2.00 FTE, voluntary. **Finance** Sources: fees for services; grants; sale of products; sale of publications; sponsorship. Supported by: *Council of Europe (CE, #04881); European Commission (EC, #06633); European Youth Foundation (EYF, #09141); Internationale amis de la nature (IAN, #14780).* **Activities** Advocacy/lobbying/activism; capacity building; events/meetings; networking/liaising; training/education. **Events** *Social-Ecological Transformation: A Naturefriendly way to Sustainable Tourism* Zell am See (Austria) 2021, *Networking Conference* Volterra (Italy) 2014, *Networking Conference* Rajecké Teplice (Slovakia) 2013, *Networking Conference* Mariahalom (Hungary) 2012, *Networking Conference* Eben am Achensee (Austria) 2010. **Publications** *Courier* (bi-weekly) – newsletter. *Green Toolbox – Manual for Sustainable Youth Work and Organizational Management.*
Members National organizations (18) and partner organizations (14), representing 120,000 individual members in more than 1,000 local groups, in 15 countries:
Austria, Belgium, Czechia, Denmark, Finland, France, Germany, Hungary, Italy, Netherlands, North Macedonia, Poland, Sweden, Switzerland, UK.
NGO Relations Member of (3): *European Youth Forum (#09140); Generation Climate Europe (GCE, #10114); UNITED for Intercultural Action – European Network Against Nationalism, Racism, Fascism and in Support of Migrants and Refugees (UNITED, #20511).* [2021.06.21/XD5719/**C**]

♦ International Young Professionals Foundation (IYPF) 15930

Contact Rosen Dimov, Unit 1/50 Northlink Place, Virginia QLD 4014, Australia. E-mail: rosendimov@iypf.org – secretariat@iypf.org.
URL: http://www.iypf.org/

History 4 Oct 2001, Brisbane (Australia). **Aims** Inform, inspire and equip young professionals as *sustainability* practitioners and social change agents. **Structure** General Meeting (annual); Advisory Council; Board of Directors; International Secretariat. **Languages** English. **Staff** 7.00 FTE, paid. **Finance** Members' dues. Other sources: grants; corporate and private investments; crowd sourcing. **Activities** Events/meetings. **Events** *International young professionals summit* Manchester (UK) 2008, *International young professionals summit* Brisbane, QLD (Australia) 2004, *International young professionals summit* Brisbane, QLD (Australia) 2001, *International Young Professionals Summit* Gold Coast, QLD (Australia) 2001. **Publications** *The Chronicle* (daily); *IYPF News* (12 a year). **Members** Full (400); Members (11,500). Members in 130 countries. Membership countries not specified. **Consultative Status** Consultative status granted from: *ECOSOC (#05331)* (Special). **NGO Relations** Partners include: *Global Youth Action Network (GYAN); International Youth Parliament (IYP, no recent information).* Member of: *United Nations Global Compact (#20567); World Alliance for Efficient Solutions.* [2019.03.02/XF6698/ft/**F**]

♦ International Youth Aid Council (internationally oriented national body)

♦ International Youth Alliance for Family Planning (IYAFP) 15931

Exec Dir PO Box 96503 – 97923, Washington DC 20090, USA. E-mail: contact@iyafp.org.
URL: http://iyafp.org/

History 2013. Registration: Section 501(c)(3), No/ID: 47-5049026, USA, Washington DC. **Aims** Support youth to learn about and advocate for family planning, sexual and reproductive health and rights. **Structure** Executive Committee; Executive Team; Country Coordinators. **Languages** English. **Staff** 4.00 FTE, paid. Several voluntary. **Finance** Sources: donations. Supported by: *Bill and Melinda Gates Foundation (BMGF); Institute for Population and Reproductive Health.* **Activities** Advocacy/lobbying/activism; events/meetings; knowledge management/information dissemination.
Members Coordinators in 79 countries:
Afghanistan, Albania, Argentina, Bangladesh, Belgium, Benin, Bhutan, Bolivia, Botswana, Brazil, Burkina Faso, Burundi, Cambodia, Cameroon, Canada, Central African Rep, Chad, Congo Brazzaville, Congo DR, Costa Rica, Côte d'Ivoire, Denmark, Egypt, Ethiopia, Fiji, Gambia, Germany, Ghana, Guatemala, Guinea, Haiti, India, Indonesia, Iraq, Jamaica, Kenya, Lebanon, Lesotho, Liberia, Libya, Madagascar, Malawi, Malaysia, Mali, Mauritania, Mexico, Mongolia, Morocco, Myanmar, Namibia, Nepal, Nicaragua, Niger, Nigeria, Pakistan, Palestine, Peru, Philippines, Rwanda, Senegal, Sierra Leone, Singapore, Somalia, South Africa, St Vincent-Grenadines, Sudan, Switzerland, Syrian AR, Tajikistan, Tanzania UR, Togo, Trinidad-Tobago, Tunisia, Türkiye, Uganda, USA, Vietnam, Zambia, Zimbabwe.

NGO Relations Member of: *Global Climate and Health Alliance (GCHA, #10288)*; *PMNCH (#18410)*. [2020.08.26/XM7018/v/**C**]

- ♦ International Youth Centre (internationally oriented national body)
- ♦ International Youth Centre for Development, Brussels (internationally oriented national body)
- ♦ International Youth Centre San Lorenzo (internationally oriented national body)
- ♦ International Youth Civic Association (internationally oriented national body)
- ♦ International Youth Climate Movement / see Youth Climate (#22010)
- ♦ International Youth Committee (internationally oriented national body)
- ♦ International Youth Confederation (inactive)
- ♦ International Youth Council (internationally oriented national body)
- ♦ International Youth Cultural Exchange Federation (internationally oriented national body)

♦ International Youth Federation 15932

Fédération Internationale des Jeunes – Federación Internacional de la Juventud

Contact Intl House, 24 Holborn Viaduct, London, EC1A 2BN, UK. T. +447031897782. E-mail: info@iydg.org.

URL: http://www.iyfweb.org/

History 2014, London (UK). Current statutes approved Apr 2016. Registration: Swiss Civil Code, Switzerland. **Aims** Oversee international youth participation, empowering youth and encouraging their engagement among the national youth associations. **Structure** General Assembly; Executive Board; President; Secretariat; Commissions (6). **Languages** Arabic, English, Spanish. **Activities** Advocacy/lobbying/activism.

Members In 51 countries and territories:

Afghanistan, Albania, Algeria, Azerbaijan, Bahrain, Bangladesh, Brazil, Cameroon, Canada, Congo Brazzaville, Ecuador, Ethiopia, Gambia, Guatemala, Haiti, Indonesia, Iraq, Jordan, Kenya, Kurdish area (Iraq), Kuwait, Lebanon, Lesotho, Libya, Luxembourg, Madagascar, Malawi, Malaysia, Mexico, Morocco, Namibia, Nepal, Oman, Pakistan, Palestine, Peru, Rwanda, Saudi Arabia, Senegal, Sierra Leone, Slovakia, South Africa, South Sudan, Sudan, Suriname, Tanzania UR, Tunisia, Uganda, UK, USA, Yemen.

NGO Relations Accredited organizations include: *African Network for Prevention and Protection Against Child Abuse and Neglect (ANPPCAN, #00393)*; *African Youth Growth Foundation (AYGF)*; *African Youths Initiative on Crime Prevention (AYICRIP)*; *Alliance of Young Nurse Leaders and Advocates International (AYNLA)*; *Euro-Mediterranean Human Rights Monitor (Euro-Med Monitor, #05721)*; *International Centre for Youth Development on Information Communication Technology (ICYDICT)*; *International Islamic Youth League – African Youth Development Centre (IIYL-AYDC)*; *International Youth Committee (IYC)*; *Network of African Youths for Development (NAYD, #16989)*; *World Assembly of Youth (WAY, #21113)*; *Youth Initiative for Sustainable Human Development in Africa (YiSHDA)*; *Youth for Transparency International (YTI)*. [2023.02.17/XM7325/**C**]

- ♦ International Youth Federation for Environmental Studies and Conservation (inactive)
- ♦ International Youth Fellowship (internationally oriented national body)
- ♦ International Youth Foundation (internationally oriented national body)
- ♦ International Youth Foundation of Great Britain (internationally oriented national body)

♦ International Youth Health Organization (YHO) 15933

SG Gregorciceva ulica 7, 1000 Ljubljana, Slovenia. T. +38612009563. E-mail: secretary.general@apyn.org.

URL: http://www.apyn.org/

History Founded 2011, as a direct outcome of the work developed by *European Youth Forum (#09140)* together with *European Alcohol Policy Alliance (Eurocare, #05856)*, 2005-2006. Original title: *Alcohol Policy Youth Network (APYN)*. Current title adopted 2018. **Aims** Empower young people to work on youth health. **Structure** Annual Meeting. Secretariat, including 5 departments: Training; Alcohol Policy; Institutional Follow-up; Press and Communications; Finances. **Activities** Training/education; networking/liaising. **Events** *European Alcohol Policy Youth Conference* Bled (Slovenia) 2016.

Members Full; Associate; Observing. Full in 6 countries:

Estonia, Lithuania, Montenegro, Romania, Slovenia, Türkiye.

Included in the above, 4 organizations listed in this Yearbook:

European Medical Students' Association (EMSA, #07764); *International Federation of Medical Students' Associations (IFMSA, #13478)*; *World Peace Initiative (WPI, #21718)*; *Youth for Exchange and Understanding (YEU, #22016)*.

Associate in 6 countries:

Croatia, Georgia, Malta, Moldova, North Macedonia, Türkiye.

Included in the above, 1 organization listed in this Yearbook:

European Pharmaceutical Students' Association (EPSA, #08197).

Observing in 5 countries:

Croatia, Italy, Lithuania, Slovenia, UK.

IGO Relations Support from: DG SANCO of *European Commission (EC, #06633)*. Cooperates with: *UNICEF (#20332)*; *WHO (#20950)*. **NGO Relations** Member of: *European Alcohol Policy Alliance (Eurocare, #05856)*. [2019/XJ0600/**E**]

- ♦ International Youth Hostel Federation / see Hostelling International (#10950)
- ♦ International Youth Hostels' Association / see Hostelling International (#10950)

♦ International Youth Human Rights Movement (YHRM) 15934

Contact PO 152, CENTRE, VORONEZH, Russia, 394000. T. +74732545529. Fax +74732545529. E-mail: int@yhrm.org.

URL: http://www.yhrm.org/

History 2001. **Structure** Coordinating Council. Administrative Centre. **Events** *Conference on combating racism* Voronezh (Russia) 2010. **Members** Membership countries not specified. **Consultative Status** Consultative status granted from: *Council of Europe (CE, #04881)* (Participatory Status). [2020/XJ0981/**F**]

♦ International Youth Leadership Network (IYLN) 15935

Exec Dir Youth Leadership Europe, Civic Concepts Intl, Ripska 547/24, 130 00 Prague 3, Czechia.

Facebook: https://www.facebook.com/groups/InternationalYouthLeadershipNetwork/

History 2001. **Aims** Push participants who show potential to better themselves in various fields, particularly in politics and business. **Activities** Events/meetings. **Events** *International Youth Leadership Conference* Dubai (United Arab Emirates) 2018, *International Youth Leadership Conference* Prague (Czechia) 2018, *International Youth Leadership Conference* Dubai (United Arab Emirates) 2015, *Dubai Conference* Dubai (United Arab Emirates) 2014, *International Conference* Prague (Czech Rep) 2013. [2020/XJ6705/**F**]

♦ International Youth Library (IYL) 15936

Bibliothèque internationale de la jeunesse – Biblioteca Internacional de la Juventud (BIJ) – Internationale Jugendbibliothek (IJB)

Dir Schloss Blutenburg, 81247 Munich, Germany. T. +49898912110. Fax +498989121138. E-mail: direktion@ijb.de – juliajerosch@ijb.de – info@ijb.de.

URL: http://www.ijb.de/

History Dec 1948, Munich (Germany). Since 1953 an associated project of *UNESCO (#20322)*. Became a foundation in 1996. **Aims** Promote global children's and youth *literature* of high aesthetic and literary calibre and of significance for cultural literacy; systematically collect literature for *children* and youth of all countries and languages and *reference* literature so as to make it available to children's *book* specialists and the general public; promote international understanding by means of youth literature. **Structure** Administered by the *International Youth Library Foundation (IYL Foundation)*. **Languages** Chinese, Dutch, English, German, Greek, Irish Gaelic, Japanese. Roman languages. **Staff** 32.00 FTE, paid. **Finance** Sources: government support. German Federal Ministry for Families, Seniors, Women and Youth; Bavarian State Ministry for Education and Culture, Science and Art; Cultural Department of the Munich City Council; German Federal Foreign Office. **Activities** Advocacy/lobbying/activism; awards/prizes/competitions; events/meetings; knowledge management/information dissemination. **Events** *Tolerance and international understanding* Munich (Germany) 1999, *Workshop* Munich (Germany) 1993, *Children's literature in lesser used languages and language minorities* Munich (Germany) 1992, *Origami* Munich (Germany) 1991, *Symposium on Portuguese children's and youth literature* Munich (Germany FR) 1989. **Publications** *Das Bücherschloss* (annual) in German; *The White Ravens* (annual). Bibliographies and thematic catalogues; exhibition catalogues. **Information Services** *Bavarian Library Network* – Library holdings catalogued online. **Members** Not a membership organization. **NGO Relations** Member of: *International Federation of Library Associations and Institutions (IFLA, #13470)*; *UNESCO Network of Associated Libraries (UNAL, #20311)*. [2020.05.06/XE0353/**E**]

♦ International Youth Neuroscience Association (IYNA) 15937

Contact 2764 Pleasant Rd Ste A800, Fort Mill SC 29708, USA. E-mail: support@youthneuro.org – info@youthneuro.org.

URL: https://youthneuro.org/

History 20 Mar 2016, USA. Founded as Youth Neuroscience Clubs of America (YNCA). Registration: 509(a)(2) Public Charity – 501(c)(3), Start date: 19 Apr 2017, USA. **Aims** Advance the international collaboration of young neuroscientists from all backgrounds by educating them about the brain and inspiring them to fight neurological diseases. **Structure** Board of Directors; Executive Team; Advisory Board. **Publications** *IYNA Journal*. **NGO Relations** Partner of: *International Brain Bee (IBB, #12390)*; *International Neuroethics Society (INS, #14350)*. [2020/AA0238/**C**]

♦ International Youth Nuclear Congress Network (IYNC Network) 15938

Pres c/o EdF Lab Paris Saclay, 7 boulevard Gaspard Monge, 91120 Palaiseau, France.

Exec Sec address not obtained.

URL: https://www.iync.org/

History 2000, Bratislava (Slovakia). Proposed 1997. **Aims** Transfer knowledge from the current generation of leading scientists and engineers to the next generation. **Structure** Board of Directors. **Activities** Events/meetings. **Events** *International Youth Nuclear Congress* Kōriyama (Japan) 2022, *International Youth Nuclear Congress* Sochi (Russia) 2022, *International Youth Nuclear Congress* Sydney, NSW (Australia) 2020, *International Youth Nuclear Congress* Bariloche (Argentina) 2018, *International Youth Nuclear Congress* Hangzhou (China) 2016. **Publications** *IYNC Bulletin*. [2021/AA1725/c/**F**]

- ♦ International Youth Reformation Organization (unconfirmed)
- ♦ International Youth Union for the Conservation of Nature (no recent information)
- ♦ International Youth Work Coordination Agency (internationally oriented national body)

♦ International Zebrafish Society (IZFS) 15939

Main Office 555 East Wells St, Ste 1100, Milwaukee WI 53202, USA. E-mail: info@izfs.org.

URL: https://www.izfs.org/

History 2015. Founded as the successor to *Society for Zebrafish Research (SZR)*, which had provided the framework for the *International Conferences on Zebrafish Development and Genetics* and other conferences. Registration: 501(c)3, USA. **Aims** Promote zebrafish research in efforts to better human health. **Structure** Board of Directors. Committees. **Finance** Sources: members' dues. **Activities** Advocacy/lobbying/activism; awards/prizes/competitions; events/meetings; knowledge management/information dissemination; training/education. **Events** *International Zebrafish Conference* Japan 2024, *International Zebrafish Conference* Montréal, QC (Canada) 2022, *International Zebrafish Conference* Milwaukee, WI (USA) 2021, *International Zebrafish Conference* 2020, *International Zebrafish Conference* Suzhou (China) 2019. **Members** Individuals (Regular; Postdoctoral; Student; Associate; Corporate). Membership countries not specified. [2023/AA3189/v/**C**]

♦ International Zen Association 15940

Association Zen internationale (AZI)

Main Office c/o Temple de La Gendronnière, 41120 Valaire, France. E-mail: lagendronniere@zen-azi.org.

URL: http://www.zen-azi.org/

History Founded 1970, Paris (France), as *European Zen Association – Association Zen d'Europe*, by Deshimaru Roshi. Present name adopted 1978. Registered in accordance with French law. **Aims** Spread and promote the teaching and practice of Zen as it was transmitted by its founders; promote exchange among cultures and civilizations of East and West and contribute to development of a new humanism so as to bring peace and wisdom in the contemporary world. **Structure** Honour Committee, comprising 24 Members. Bureau, comprising about 12 Members of the Honour Committee and including President, 2 Vice-Presidents, Secretary General, Deputy Secretary General and Deputy Treasurer. **Languages** English, French, German, Italian, Spanish. **Activities** Organizes: international training periods (9-day); conferences; cultural events; film showings. **Events** *Future of the Sangha* Valaire (France) 1999, *Wisdom* Valaire (France) 1999, *Rules in a zen temple* Valaire (France) 1998. **Publications** *I Shin den Shin* (2 a year); *Zen* (2 a year). Complete oral teachings of Deshimaru Roshi.

Members Dojos and groups in 12 countries:

Austria, Belgium, France, Germany, Ireland, Italy, Portugal, Spain, Sweden, Switzerland, UK, Venezuela.

Correspondants in 24 countries:

Argentina, Austria, Belgium, Colombia, France, Germany, Hungary, Ireland, Italy, Laos, Luxembourg, Morocco, New Zealand, Norway, Portugal, Romania, Spain, Sweden, Switzerland, Tunisia, UK, United Arab Emirates, USA, Venezuela.

NGO Relations Founding member of: *European Buddhist Union (EBU, #06407)*. [2022/XD4572/**D**]

♦ International Zeolite Association (IZA) 15941

President CNRS ENSICAEN Normandy Univ-Caen, 6 bd Marechal Juin, 14050 Caen, France.

Sec National Inst of Chemistry, Hajdrihova 19, 1000 Ljubljana, Slovenia.

URL: http://www.iza-online.org/

History 1967. Statutes adopted 10 July 1992, Montréal QC (Canada), replacing the interim constitution and bylaws, 6 Sep 1973, Zurich (Switzerland), of *International Molecular Sieve Conference*. Most recently adjusted 23 June 2016, Rio de Janeiro (Brazil). Registration: USA, State of Delaware. **Aims** Promote and encourage all aspects of science and technology of *zeolites*, *molecular sieves* and other *microporous* and *mesoporous* materials with related properties or structure. **Structure** General Assembly (triennial, at Conference); Council; Executive Committee; Educational Commissions (5). **Languages** English. **Staff** None. **Finance** Sources: meeting proceeds; sponsorship. **Activities** Events/meetings; training/education. **Events** *International Zeolite Conference* Philadelphia, PA (USA) 2028, *International Zeolite Conference* Dalian (China) 2025, *International Zeolite Conference* Valencia (Spain) 2022, *Triennial Conference* Perth, WA (Australia) 2019, *Triennial Conference* Rio de Janeiro (Brazil) 2016. **Publications** Textbooks; conference proceedings.

Members Full: individuals in 75 countries and territories:

Albania, Algeria, Argentina, Armenia, Australia, Austria, Azerbaijan, Belgium, Bosnia-Herzegovina, Brazil, Bulgaria, Burkina Faso, Canada, China, Croatia, Cuba, Czechia, Denmark, Egypt, Estonia, Finland, France, Georgia, Germany, Ghana, Greece, Hungary, India, Indonesia, Iran Islamic Rep, Ireland, Israel, Italy, Jamaica, Japan, Kazakhstan, Kenya, Korea DPR, Korea Rep, Lebanon, Lithuania, Malaysia, Mexico, Mongolia, Morocco, Netherlands, New Zealand, North Macedonia, Norway, Pakistan, Philippines, Poland, Portugal, Romania, Russia, Saudi Arabia, Serbia, Singapore, Slovakia, Slovenia, South Africa, Spain, Sweden, Switzerland, Taiwan, Thailand, Tunisia, Türkiye, UK, Ukraine, United Arab Emirates, USA, Venezuela, Vietnam, Yemen.

NGO Relations Associated organization of: *International Union of Pure and Applied Chemistry (IUPAC, #15809)*. [2022.10.12/XD1168/v/**C**]

♦ International Zinc Association (IZA) 15942

Exec Dir Av de Tervueren 168 – Bte 4, 1150 Brussels, Belgium. T. +3227760070. Fax +3227760089. E-mail: rchart@zinc.org – contact@zinc.org.

Main Office 2530 Meridian Parkway, Suite 115, Durham NC 27713, USA.

URL: http://www.zinc.org/

History 11 Oct 1990. Registration: Banque-Carrefour des Entreprises, No/ID: 0644.591.229, Start date: 1 Jan 2016, Belgium; EU Transparency Register, No/ID: 017018214013-57, Start date: 18 Jul 2014. **Aims** Represent the global zinc industry; promote the necessity of zinc in present and potential product applications, human health and crop nutrition and through highlighting its contribution to sustainable development. **Structure** General Assembly (annual); Board of Directors; Executive Committee; Regional Offices in China and India. **Languages** English. **Staff** 20.00 FTE, paid. **Finance** Sources: members' dues; revenue from activities/projects. Annual budget: 6,000,000 USD. **Activities** Events/meetings; projects/programmes; training/education. **Events** *International Zinc Conference Europe* Istanbul (Turkey) 2022, *Zinc Die Casting Seminar* 2021, *International Galvanizing Symposium* Changzhou (China) 2021, *International Zinc Recycling Conference* Charlotte, NC (USA) 2021, *Zinc Metal Round Table* Charlotte, NC (USA) 2021. **Publications** *Zinc in Soils and Crop Nutrition*. *Zinc Protects*. Technical, scientific and promotional publications. **Members** Full (35): mining, refining and recycling companies. Affiliate (150): First-users. Associate (60): national, environmental and other industry associations. Membership countries not specified. **IGO Relations** Permanent observer to: *International Lead and Zinc Study Group (ILZSG, #14012).* **NGO Relations** Member of (3): *Federation of European and International Associations Established in Belgium (FAIB, #09508); METALS FOR BUILDINGS (#16737); ResponsibleSteel (#18921).* Supports (1): *International Zinc Nutrition Consultative Group (iZiNCG, #15943).* [2021.09.01/XD1259/y/**C**]

♦ International Zinc Nutrition Consultative Group (iZiNCG) 15943

Dir c/o UCSF Benioff Children's Hosp, Children's Hosp Oakland Research Inst, 5700 Martin Luther King Jr Way, Oakland CA 94609, USA. T. +15104507939. E-mail: secretariat@izincg.org.
URL: http://www.izincg.org/

History Jun 2000. **Aims** Promote and assist efforts to reduce zinc deficiency worldwide. **Structure** Steering Committee. **Languages** English. **Finance** Supported by: *Bill and Melinda Gates Foundation (BMGF).* **Activities** Research/documentation; knowledge management/information dissemination; networking/liaising; guidance/assistance/consulting. **Events** *Conference* Stockholm (Sweden) 2000. **Publications** Technical documents and briefs. **IGO Relations** *UNICEF (#20332); WHO (#20950).* **NGO Relations** Affiliated Member of: *International Union of Nutritional Sciences (IUNS, #15796).* [2021/XM3543/**F**]

♦ International Zionist Organization / see World Zionist Organization (#21961)

♦ International Zoo Educators Association (IZE) 15944

Contact Saint Louis Zoo (Education), One Government Drive, St Louis MO 63110, USA. E-mail: ize.centraloffice@izea.net – izeaoffice@gmail.com.
Main Website: http://www.izea.net/

History 1972, Frankfurt-Main (Germany). Former names and other names: *International Association of Zoo Educators* – former. **Aims** Expand the educational impact of zoos and aquariums worldwide by improving education programmes in the facilities of members, providing access to the latest thinking, techniques and information in conservation education and supporting excellence in animal care and welfare. **Structure** Board; President; President Elect; Immediate Past President; Secretary/Treasurer; Journal Editor; Website Editor; Social Media Editor; Membership Coordinator; Regional Representatives (7); Upcoming Conference Host; Administrator. **Languages** English. **Staff** 0.50 FTE, paid. **Finance** Sources: members' dues. **Activities** Events/meetings; knowledge management/information dissemination; training/education. **Events** *Biennial Congress* Wellington (New Zealand) 2023, *Biennial Congress* San Diego, CA (USA) 2020, *Biennial Congress* Al Ain (United Arab Emirates) 2018, *Biennial Congress* Buenos Aires (Argentina) 2016, *Biennial Congress* Hong Kong (Hong Kong) 2014. **Publications** *Journal of the International Zoo Educators Association* (annual). **Members** Institutional; Individual; Associate. Members (about 400) from 55 countries. Membership countries not specified. **NGO Relations** Member of (1): *World Association of Zoos and Aquariums (WAZA, #21208).* [2022.04.18/XD1308/**C**]

♦ International Zoom 8 Class Association 15945

Pres Björksalavägen 50, SE-139 56 Värmdö, Sweden. T. +46707606073.
URL: http://www.zoom8.org

NGO Relations Recognized Class Association of: *World Sailing (#21760).* [2019/XM2795/**E**]

♦ International Zurkhaneh Sports Federation (IZSF) 15946

Pres No 8 Sepidar Alley, Africa Blvd, Teheran, 1518943865, Iran Islamic Rep. T. +9888203115. Fax +9888203314.
URL: http://www.izsf.net/

History Founded 11 Oct 2004, Teheran (Iran Islamic Rep), with the support of Iran Physical Education Organization, National Olympic nd Paralympic Committee, TAFISA, presidency of Prof Urgen Palm, and representatives of 84 countries. Registered in accordance with Swiss Civil Code (020 6 001 197-4) and in accordance with Iranian law (22959). **Aims** Develop Zurkhaneh Sport all around the world; develop the sport's values and skills, peace and friendship, and achieve a sense of accomplishment throughout Zurkhaneh Sport; establish strong partnerships with indigenous communities and leaders in promoting Zurkhaneh Sport. **Structure** General Assembly; Executive Committee; Bureau; Technical Committee. **Languages** English, Persian. **Staff** 4.00 FTE, paid. **Finance** Sources: sponsorship. Other sources: Parliament of Iran Islamic Rep, Ministry of Sports and Youth. **Activities** Events/meetings; training/education. **Events** *General Assembly* Dushanbe (Tajikistan) 2015, *General Assembly* Teheran (Iran Islamic Rep) 2012, *General Assembly* Dhaka (Bangladesh) 2011, *General Assembly* Busan (Korea Rep) 2008, *General Assembly* Teheran (Iran Islamic Rep) 2006.
Members in 84 countries and territories:
Afghanistan, Argentina, Australia, Austria, Azerbaijan, Bangladesh, Belarus, Belgium, Belize, Benin, Bolivia, Brazil, Burkina Faso, Cameroon, Canada, Chile, Colombia, Congo DR, Costa Rica, Côte d'Ivoire, Cuba, Denmark, Dominican Rep, Ecuador, El Salvador, Estonia, Finland, France, Georgia, Germany, Guatemala, Honduras, Hungary, India, Indonesia, Iran Islamic Rep, Iraq, Japan, Kazakhstan, Kenya, Korea Rep, Kyrgyzstan, Latvia, Liberia, Lithuania, Malawi, Malaysia, Mali, Mauritania, Mexico, Moldova, Mongolia, Mozambique, Nepal, Nicaragua, Niger, Nigeria, Pakistan, Paraguay, Peru, Philippines, Poland, Puerto Rico, Russia, Serbia, Singapore, Slovakia, South Africa, Sri Lanka, Switzerland, Taiwan, Tajikistan, Tanzania UR, Thailand, Togo, Türkiye, Uganda, Ukraine, Uruguay, USA, Uzbekistan, Venezuela, Zambia, Zimbabwe.
NGO Relations Instrumental in setting up: *Asian Zurkhaneh Sports Confederation.* Member of: *The Association for International Sport for All (TAFISA, #02763); International Council of Traditional Sports and Games (ICTSG, #13088).* [2020/XM0893/**C**]

♦ Internation Council for Sustainable Energy (ICSE) 15947

Contact 505 9th St NW, Ste 800, Washington DC 20004, USA. T. +12027850507. Fax +12027850514. E-mail: info@i-cse.org.
URL: http://www.i-cse.org/

History Dec 2007. **Aims** Influence international negotiations on sustainable energy and climate change issues.
Members Founding members (4) in 3 countries:
Australia, UK, USA.
Included in the above, 1 organization listed in this Yearbook:
European Business Council for a Sustainable Energy Future (e5, #06417). [2015/XJ8946/**C**]

♦ Internationella Bandyförbundet / see Federation of International Bandy (#09601)
♦ Internationella Byggnads- och Träindustriarbetar-Unionen (inactive)
♦ Internationella Föreningen för Betonghåltagare (#11806)
♦ Internationella Grafiska Federationen (inactive)
♦ Internationella Guideklubben (inactive)
♦ Internationella Kemi-, Energi- och Fabriksarbetarefederationen (inactive)
♦ Internationella Kommittén för Insamlingskontroll (inactive)
♦ Internationella Kommunistiska Strömningen (#12818)
♦ Internationella Kristna Förbundet för Förebyggande av Alkoholism och Narkomani (no recent information)
♦ Internationella Kvinnoförbundet för Fred och Frihet / see Women's International League for Peace and Freedom (#21024)
♦ Internationella Metallarbetarfederationen (inactive)
♦ Internationella Nätverket för Progressiv Politik / see Policy Network (#18417)
♦ Internationella Statistiska Institutet (#15603)
♦ Internationella Transportarbetarefederationen (#15726)
♦ Internationella Unionen för Livsmedels-, Njutningsmedels- och Lantarbetareförbund Samt Förbund Inom Hotell- och Restaurangbranschen (#15772)
♦ Internationell Förening Mot Tortyren (no recent information)
♦ Internationell Registrering för Världsmedborgare / see Registre des Citoyens du Monde (#18822)
♦ Internationellt Center för Lärande för Hållbar Utveckling (internationally oriented national body)
♦ Internationellt Centrum för Lokal Demokrati (internationally oriented national body)
♦ Internationellt Nätverk för Städer där man lever det goda livet / see Cittaslow (#03958)
♦ InterNations Exchange (unconfirmed)
♦ Inter-Nations Liaison Commission Mars and Mercury / see Mars and Mercury Europe – Industrial and Commercial Circles of Officers and Reserve Officers Inter-Nations Coordination Commission (#16589)
♦ Internazionale dei Forum del Campo Lacaniano / see Internationale des Forums – Ecole de Psychanalyse des Forum du Champ Lacanien (#13234)
♦ Internazionale dei Forums – Scuola di Psicoanalisi dei Forums del Campo Lacaniano (#13234)

♦ Internet 15948

Address not obtained.

History as a development/expansion/combination of the computer network *ARPAnet*, set up in 1975 within Advanced Research Project Agency (ARPA) of the USA Department of Defense, and *NSFnet*, a computer network of US National Science Foundation (NSF). ARPAnet was conceived and designed in 1963, by Larry Roberts. The combination of ARPAnet and NSFnet used a common set of communication protocols (based on data packet switching) which allowed other computer networks to become interconnected in a system which was a fundamentally decentralized network. Now international in scope, the name "Internet" refers specifically to this network of networks and is derived from the term "internetworking" which was used to describe the protocols which ARPA and others developed and standardized for allowing computers to exchange information.
Some consider 1 Jan 1983 to be the most logical date of origin for the Internet. On this day, ARPANET switched from using the NCP protocol to the TCP/IP protocol. Six months later it split into two subnets – ARPANET and MILNET which were connected by internet gateways.
Aims Allow any user with basic *computer* equipment and a *phone* line to connect, communicate and host *information* internationally at low cost. **Structure** The "internet" is defined as the network of all computers which have a dedicated connection to the internet structure or "backbone". Related to it are constituent networks and appointed committees, working groups, consortiums and special interest groups (SIGs).
Members Not a membership organization. **IGO Relations** Organizations with input or influence on aspects of development or regulation of the network include: *ASEAN (#01141); Asia-Pacific Economic Cooperation (APEC, #01887); European Commission (EC, #06633); International Telecommunication Union (ITU, #15673); World Intellectual Property Organization (WIPO, #21593).*
NGO Relations Organizations with input or influence on aspects of development or regulation of the network include:
- *Asia-Pacific Networking Group (APNG, #01968);*
- *Asian-Pacific Network Information Centre (APNIC);*
- *Center for Democracy and Technology (CDT);*
- *CommerceNet Consortium;*
- *Electronic Frontier Foundation (EFF);*
- *FidoNet (no recent information);*
- *Forum of Incident Response and Security Teams (FIRST, #09918);*
- *International Organization for Standardization (ISO, #14473);*
- *International Trademark Association (INTA, #15706);*
- *International World Wide Web Conference Committee (IW3C2);*
- *Internet Assigned Numbers Authority (IANA);*
- *Internet Engineering and Planning Group (IEPG, no recent information);*
- *Internet Mail Consortium (IMC, inactive);*
- *Internet Society (ISOC, #15952);*
- *Internet Systems Consortium (ISC);*
- *Network Computer Consortium (no recent information);*
- *North American Network Operators' Group (NANOG);*
- *Organization of Internet Users (no recent information);*
- *Public-Root;*
- *RIPE Network Coordination Centre (RIPE NCC, #18951);*
- *Trans-European Research and Education Networking Association (TERENA, inactive);*
- *World Wide Web Consortium (W3C, #21935).* [2008/XF4583/**F**]

♦ Internet Assigned Numbers Authority (internationally oriented national body)
♦ Internet Centre Anti-Racism Europe (internationally oriented national body)

♦ Internet Corporation for Assigned Names and Numbers (ICANN) . . . 15949

European Office Rond Point Schuman 6, 1040 Brussels, Belgium. T. +3228947400. Fax +3222801221.
Head Office 12025 Waterfront Drive, Suite 300, Los Angeles CA 90094-2536, USA. T. +13103015800. Fax +13108238649.
URL: http://www.icann.org/

History Founded 26 Oct 1998, New York NY (USA), when Board was elected, following proposal of Dr Postel on behalf of a broad coalition of internet stakeholders. Set up in response to a request by USA that a non-profit organization should take on responsibility of *Internet Assigned Numbers Authority (IANA)* for the Internet Domain Name System (DNS) coordination. **Aims** Preserve the operational stability of the Internet; promote competition; achieve broad representation of global Internet communities; develop policy appropriate to its mission through bottom-up, consensus-based processes. **Structure** Board of Directors; Advisory Committee; Address Supporting Organization; Generic Names Supporting Organization; Country Code Names Supporting Organization; At-Large Advisory Committee; Security and Stability Advisory Committee; Root Server System Advisor Committee; Technical Liaison Group. Regional At-Large Organizations (RALOs): Africa – *AFRALO*; Asia, Australasian and Pacific Islands – *APRALO*; Europe – *EURALO*; Latin American and the Caribbean Islands – *LACRALO*; North America – *NARALO*. **Activities** Knowledge management/information dissemination; standards/guidelines. **Events** *Meeting* 2023, *Meeting* 2023, *Meeting* 2022, *Meeting* 2022, *Meeting* 2022. **Publications** *ICANN Newsletter.* **IGO Relations** Observer to: *United Nations Group of Experts on Geographical Names (UNGEGN, #20569).* 31 IGOs act as Observers in ICANN's Governmental Advisory Committee (GAC). **NGO Relations** Member of: *International Governance Forum Support Association (IGFSA, #13730); Internet Society (ISOC, #15952).* [2021/XF5550/**F**]

♦ Internet Governance Forum (IGF) 15950

Secretariat Villa Bocage, Palais des Nations, 1211 Geneva 10, Switzerland. T. +41229173678. E-mail: igf@un.org.
URL: http://www.intgovforum.org/

History Established in Paragraph 72 of the Tunis Agenda of the World Summit on the Information Society (WSIS), 2005, of the *United Nations (UN, #20515)* Inaugural meeting 30 Oct-2 Nov 2006, Athens (Greece). **Aims** Bring people together from various stakeholder groups as equals, in discussions on public policy issues relating to the Internet. **Structure** Secretariat. **Finance** Funded through donations from various stakeholder groups; host countries bear majority of costs holding annual meeting; Secretariat funded through extra-budgetary contributions paid into a multi-donor Trusts Fund administered by UNDESA. Also supported by: *International Governance Forum Support Association (IGFSA, #13730).* **Activities** Events/meetings; politics/policy/regulatory. **Events** *Annual Meeting* Katowice (Poland) 2021, *Annual Meeting* Geneva (Switzerland) 2020, *Internet Governance Forum* Katowice (Poland) 2020, *Annual Meeting* Berlin (Germany) 2019, *Annual Meeting* Paris (France) 2018. **Publications** Conference papers. [2021/XM2081/**F***]

♦ Internet Governance Project (internationally oriented national body)
♦ Internet Hotline Providers in Europe Association / see International Association of Internet Hotlines (#11970)
♦ INTERNET International Human Rights Documentation Network / see Human Rights Internet (#10986)
♦ INTERNET – International Project Management Association / see International Project Management Association (#14655)
♦ INTERNET Red Internacional de Documentación sobre los Derechos Humanos / see Human Rights Internet (#10986)

♦ Internet Research Task Force (IRTF) 15951

Chairman c/o NetApp, Sonnenallee 1, 85551 Kirchheim unter Teck, Germany. T. +4915112055791. E-mail: irtf-chair@irtf.org.
Main: http://www.irtf.org/

Aims Promote research of importance to the evolution of the future *Internet.* **Structure** Chairman appointed by Internet Architecture Board; Steering Group. **Languages** English. **Finance** Internet Engineering Task Force (IETF). **Activities** Meeting activities. **Publications** *Requests for Comments (RFCs)* – on IRTF FRC Stream. [2014.06.01/XE4753/**E**]

♦ INTERNET Réseau international de documentation sur les droits humains / see Human Rights Internet (#10986)

♦ Internet Sans Frontières (unconfirmed)

♦ Internet Society (ISOC) 15952

Pres and CEO 11710 Plaza America Drive, Ste 400, Reston VA 20190, USA. T. +17034392120. E-mail: isoc@isoc.org.
Geneva Rue Vallin 2, 1201 Geneva, Switzerland. T. +41228071444. Fax +41228071445.
General: http://www.internetsociety.org/

History Jan 1992. Society announced at an international networking conference, Jun 1991, Copenhagen (Denmark). Registration: Start date: 1992, USA, Washington. **Aims** Provide leadership in Internet related standards, education and policy; ensure the open development, evolution and use of the Internet for the benefit of all worldwide. **Structure** Board of Trustees; Secretariat, headed by President/CEO; Offices (2); Regional Bureaus (5). **Languages** English. **Staff** Paid. **Finance** Members' dues. Other sources: donations; contributions from supporting organizations; *Public Interest Registry (PIR, #18567).* **Activities** Knowledge management/information dissemination; training/education; standards/guidelines; politics/policy/regulatory. **Events** *IETF Meeting* London (UK) 2022, *IETF Meeting* San Francisco, CA (USA) 2021, *Africa Domain Name System (DNS) Forum* Gaborone (Botswana) 2019, *IETF Meeting* Montréal, QC (Canada) 2019, *IETF Meeting* Singapore (Singapore) 2019. **Publications** *IETF Journal* (3 a year). Members' newsletter.
Members Individuals (over 82,000) and organizations (over 85). Chapters (over 120) in 113 countries and territories:
Afghanistan, Argentina, Armenia, Australia, Bahrain, Bangladesh, Barbados, Belgium, Benin, Bolivia, Botswana, Brazil, Bulgaria, Burkina Faso, Burundi, Cameroon, Canada, Chad, Chile, Colombia, Congo Brazzaville, Congo DR, Costa Rica, Côte d'Ivoire, Dominica, Dominican Rep, Ecuador, Egypt, El Salvador, Estonia, Finland, France, Gambia, Georgia, Germany, Ghana, Guatemala, Guinea, Guyana, Haiti, Honduras, Hong Kong, Hungary, India, Indonesia, Ireland, Israel, Italy, Japan, Kazakhstan, Kenya, Korea Rep, Kyrgyzstan, Lebanon, Lesotho, Liberia, Luxembourg, Madagascar, Malaysia, Mali, Malta, Mauritania, Mexico, Montenegro, Morocco, Namibia, Nepal, Netherlands, Nicaragua, Niger, Nigeria, Norway, Pakistan, Palestine, Panama, Paraguay, Peru, Philippines, Poland, Portugal, Puerto Rico, Qatar, Romania, Russia, Rwanda, Senegal, Serbia, Sierra Leone, Singapore, Slovenia, Somalia, South Africa, Spain, Sri Lanka, St Vincent-Grenadines, Sudan, Sweden, Switzerland, Taiwan, Tanzania UR, Thailand, Togo, Trinidad-Tobago, Tunisia, Türkiye, Uganda, UK, United Arab Emirates, Uruguay, USA, Venezuela, Yemen, Zimbabwe.
Regional chapter:
Pacific Islands Chapter (PICISOC, #17963).
Organizations include ç organizations listed in this Yearbook:
AFRINIC (#00533); Asian-Pacific Network Information Centre (APNIC); Association for Computing Machinery (ACM, #02447); DotAsia Organisation (DotAsia, #05124); Eastern Caribbean Telecommunications Authority (ECTEL, #05237); European Telecommunications Network Operators' Association (ETNO, #08895); Internet Corporation for Assigned Names and Numbers (ICANN, #15949); Latin American and Caribbean Internet Address Registry (LACNIC, #16281); NORDUnet (#17553).
Consultative Status Consultative status granted from: *ECOSOC (#05331)* (Special); *UNESCO (#20322)* (Consultative Status). **IGO Relations** Permanent Observer status at: *World Intellectual Property Organization (WIPO, #21593).* Consultative status with: *International Telecommunication Union (ITU, #15673); OECD (#17693).* Affiliates: *African Telecommunications Union (ATU, #00482); Caribbean Telecommunications Union (CTU, #03560);* **NGO Relations** In liaison with technical committees of: *International Organization for Standardization (ISO, #14473).* Member of: *European Policy Centre (EPC, #08240); International Governance Forum Support Association (IGFSA, #13730); Network of Internet and Society Research Centers (NoC, #17045).* Associate member of: *European Internet Forum (EIF, #07591).* Set up: *Global Internet Liberty Campaign (GILC, inactive); Public Interest Registry (PIR, #18567).* Affiliates: *Access Now (#00052); CANTO (#03416); Center for Democracy and Technology (CDT); Global Cyber Alliance (GCA); Messaging, Malware and Mobile Anti-Abuse Working Group (M3AAWG).* Links with organizations worldwide in the areas of Internet and ICT development, education and project funding, including: *Council of European National Top-Level Domain Registries (CENTR, #04892); Transforming Education Through Information Technologies (EDUCAUSE).* [2021/XF5267/**F**]

♦ Internet Software Consortium / see Internet Systems Consortium
♦ Internet Systems Consortium (internationally oriented national body)
♦ Internet Watch Foundation (internationally oriented national body)
♦ Internews (internationally oriented national body)

♦ Internews Europe 15953

Contact 43-51 New North Road, London, N1 6LU, UK. T. +442075663300.
URL: http://www.internews.org/

History Sep 1995. Registration: Start date: 1995, France; Charity Commission, No/ID: 1148404, England and Wales; EU Transparency Register, No/ID: 003453329147-26, Start date: 30 Nov 2017. **Aims** Achieve the vision of open, independent, local media helping to stabilize *civil society* in every nation, through capacity-building partnerships with indigenous media outlets and NGOs in countries worldwide. **Structure** General Assembly. Board, comprising President, General Secretary, Treasurer and 4 members. **Languages** English, French. **Staff** 26.50 FTE, paid. **Finance** Support from: *Council of Europe (CE, #04881); Department for International Development (DFID, inactive); European Commission (EC, #06633); International Bank for Reconstruction and Development (IBRD, #12317)* (World Bank); *Irish Aid; Organization for Security and Cooperation in Europe (OSCE, #17887); Swedish International Development Cooperation Agency (Sida); UNDP (#20292); UNHCR (#20327); UNESCO (#20322);* Ministries of Foreign Affairs of Belgium, Denmark, Netherlands, France, Norway and Germany; Open Society Institute; Taiwan Democracy Fund; Virgin Unit; several European television channels. **Activities** Advocacy/lobbying/activism; financial and/or material support; knowledge management/information dissemination; events/meetings. **Events** *Media and diversity seminar* Prague (Czech Rep) 2009. **Publications** *Media4Diversity: Taking the Pulse of Diversity in the Media* (2009); *The Promise of Ubiquity, Mobile as Media Platform in the Global South* (2008); *Media Matters, Perspectives on Advancing Governance and Development form the Global Forum for Media Development* (2006). **IGO Relations** *Council of Europe (CE, #04881); European Commission (EC, #06633); Organization for Security and Cooperation in Europe (OSCE, #17887); UNESCO (#20322).* **NGO Relations** Member of (4): *Climate Knowledge Brokers (CKB, #04016); Communicating with Disaster Affected Communities Network (CDAC Network, #04379); Ethical Journalism Network (EJN, #05554); Global Forum for Media Development (GFMD, #10375).* Supports (1): *International News Safety Institute (INSI, #14364).* [2019.10.14/XG9000/**F**]

♦ InterNIC (internationally oriented national body)
♦ **InterNICHE** International Network for Humane Education (#14285)

♦ Inter Nordic Guide Club (IGC) 15954

Internordiska Guideklubben

Treas Upplandsgatan 49, 6tr, SE-113 28 Stockholm, Sweden. E-mail: info@nordicguides.org.
Pres address not obtained.
URL: http://nordicguides.org/

Events *Annual Meeting* Turku (Finland) 2011, *Meeting* Iceland 2010, *Annual Congress* Odense (Denmark) 2009, *Annual Congress* Stavanger (Norway) 2008, *Annual congress / Meeting* Vaasa (Finland) 2002. **Publications** *IGC-Nytt* – newsletter.
Members National organizations in 5 countries:
Denmark, Finland, Iceland, Norway, Sweden. [2021/XD5963/**F**]

♦ Internordiska Guideklubben (#15954)
♦ INTERNOTO – International Society of the Friends of Notocacti (internationally oriented national body)
♦ Interns for Peace (internationally oriented national body)
♦ Interoceanmetal / see Interoceanmetal Joint Organization (#15955)

♦ Interoceanmetal Joint Organization (IOM) 15955

Dir-Gen ul Cyryla i Metodego 9, 71-541 Szczecin, Poland. T. +48914539398. Fax +48914539399. E-mail: iom@iom.gov.pl.
URL: http://www.iom.gov.pl/

History 27 Apr 1987, based on an intergovernmental agreement originally signed by Bulgaria, Vietnam, German Democratic Republic, Cuba, Poland, USSR and Czechoslovakia. Operations started, Dec 1987. Also referred to as *Interoceanmetal.* **Aims** Carry out prospecting and exploration of polymetallic nodules in the North East Pacific ocean; prepare for future commercial development of nodule resources; develop mining technology to cause minimal disturbance to the marine environment; broaden the spectrum of potential uses for the nodules; ensure that deep-sea mining using clean technology becomes an attractive alternative to environmentally destructive land mining. **Structure** Council (meets twice a year); Board of Directors; Auditory Commission; Ad Hoc Technical Advisors Group; Technical and Scientific Experts Group; Finance and Administration Division. **Languages** English, Russian. **Staff** 6 experts (as official representatives of the sponsoring States) at headquarters; 15-25 experts in Ad Hoc Group; 6 in Administration Division. **Finance** Members' dues. **Activities** Activities take place mainly in the claim area, covering 75,000 square km in the eastern part of the Clarion-Clipperton Fracture Zone in the Pacific Ocean and are determined by such international regulations as *United Nations Convention on the Law of the Sea (UNCLOS, 1982),* and Regulations on Prospecting and Exploration for Polymetallic Nodules in the Area approved by the International Seabed Authority on 13 Jul 2000 (ISBA/6/A/18). According to provisions of the 15-year contract for exploration, signed 29 Mar 2001 with the International Seabed Authority, current exploration of IOM aims to obtain geological data and information of nodule deposits and reserves within the claim area, as well as to collect data on physical, chemical, geological and biological components of marine environment required to establish environmental baseline in the exploration area against which to assess and prevent harmful effects of its activities. Takes part in the international *'Benthic Impact Experiment (BIE)'* to study the impact of a simulated mining operation. Programme of activities also included research on development of a conceptual design for a future mining system and work on the optimization of existing technological schemes for extraction valuable components from polymetallic nodules, and development of the basic technological schemes for polymetallic nodules processing in the future. Arranges international conferences, workshops and symposia. **Events** *Symposium* Szczecin (Poland) 2008, *Ocean mining symposium* Tsukuba (Japan) 2003, *Ocean mining symposium* Szczecin (Poland) 2001. **Publications** Annual reports for ISBA and IOM's Council; books; papers; proceedings.
Members Governments of 6 countries:
Bulgaria, Cuba, Czechia, Poland, Russia, Slovakia. [2011.09.05/XD1796/e/**F***]

♦ **INTEROP-VLab** International Virtual Laboratory for Enterprise Interoperability (#15857)

♦ Inter-Organization Programme for the Sound Management of Chemicals (IOMC) 15956

Contact c/o WHO, 20 avenue Appia, 1211 Geneva 27, Switzerland. T. +41227911286. E-mail: ipcsmail@who.int.
URL: http://www.iomc.info/

History Established 1995, as an international coordinating group following recommendations of the 1992 *United Nations Conference on Environment and Development (UNCED),* in particular those in Chapter 19 of the conference report (Agenda 21) about toxic chemicals. The *FAO (#09260), ILO (#11123), OECD (#17693), UNEP (#20299), UNIDO (#20336)* and *WHO (#20950)* were the first to join IOMC, followed by *United Nations Institute for Training and Research (UNITAR, #20576)* in 1997, *International Bank for Reconstruction and Development (IBRD, #12317)* (World Bank) in 2010, and *UNDP (#20292)* in 2012. **Aims** Strengthen international cooperation in the field of chemicals; increase the effectiveness of the individual organizations' international chemicals programmes; promote coordination of policies and activities, pursued jointly or separately, to achieve the sound management of chemicals in relation to human health and the environment. **Structure** Inter-Organization Coordinating Committee (IOCC – meets twice year), consisting of representatives of the Participating Organizations and with annually rotating Chairmanship. Observers may attend IOCC meetings. WHO is the current administering agency and provides secretariat services to the IOCC. **Languages** English. **Staff** Secretariat staff provided by Participating Organizations. **Finance** Contributions from Participating Organizations. **Activities** Scientific and technical work is carried out through existing structures of Participating Organizations, either individually or jointly. Support for achievement of the objectives in the SAICM Overall Orientation and Guidance and the United Nations Sustainable Development Goals. Key activity areas include: risk reduction; knowledge and information; governance; capacity-building and technical cooperation; illegal traffic. **Events** *International conference on chemicals management* Dubai (United Arab Emirates) 2006. **Publications** *Developing a Capacity Assessment for the Sound Management of Chemicals and National SAICM Implementation; National Implementation of SAICM: a Guide to Resource, Guidance and Training Materials of IOMC Participating Organzations.* Online inventory and calendar; strategy documents; reports; various documents; flyers. **Information Services** *IOMC Analysis of Work Done to Implement the SAICM Global Plan of Action; IOMC Matrix of Activities in Countries; IOMC Toolbox on Sound Chemicals Management.* [2016.06.21/XE2966/**E***]

♦ Inter-Pacific Bar Association (IPBA) 15957

Secretariat Roppongi Hills North Tower 7F, 6-2-31 Roppongi, Minato-ku, Tokyo, 106-0032 Japan. T. +81357866796. Fax +81357866778. E-mail: ipba@ipba.org.
URL: https://ipba.org

History Apr 1991, Tokyo (Japan). Founded at 1st conference. Registration: No/ID: 201526931R, Singapore. **Aims** Provide members with the opportunity to: contribute to development of the legal profession, its status and organization in the "Region", comprising Asia and the jurisdiction within, or bordering the Pacific; contribute to development of law and legal structures within the Region; meet and exchange ideas with other lawyers who live in or are interested in the Region; share information on legal developments affecting the Region; promote the rule of law. **Structure** Council; Committees; Secretariat. **Languages** English. **Staff** 2.00 FTE, paid. **Activities** Events/meetings; networking/liaising; projects/programmes; publishing activities; standards/guidelines. **Events** *Conference and Annual Meeting* Dubai (United Arab Emirates) 2023, *Annual Conference* Tokyo (Japan) 2022, *Annual Conference* Shanghai (China) 2021, *Annual Conference* Shanghai (China) 2020, *Mid-Year Council Meeting and Regional Conference* Milan (Italy) 2019. **Publications** *IPBA Journal* (4 a year); *Eye on IPBA* (irregular). **Members** Individuals (over 1,300) in over 60 countries. Membership countries not specified. **NGO Relations** Formal contacts with: *International Association of Young Lawyers (#12282); International Bar Association (IBA, #12320).* Observer to: *Presidents of Law Associations in Asia (POLA, #18486).* [2021.09.01/XD3679/v/**D**]

♦ **INTERPA** International Association of Police Academies (#12093)
♦ Inter Pares (internationally oriented national body)
♦ Interparlamentarische Union (#15961)
♦ Interparliamentary Assembly of CIS / see Interparliamentary Assembly of Member Nations of the Commonwealth of Independent States (#15958)

♦ Interparliamentary Assembly of Member Nations of the Commonwealth of Independent States (IPA CIS) 15958

Mezparlamentskaja Assambleja Gosudarstv Ucastnikov Sodruzestva Nezavissimyh Gosudarstv (MPA SNG)

SG Shpalernaya Str 47, Tavrichesky Palace, St Petersburg SANKT-PETERBURG, Russia, 191015. T. +78123266982. Fax +78122722248. E-mail: kanz@iacis.ru.
URL: http://www.iacis.ru/

History 27 Mar 1992, under the *'Alma-Ata Agreement',* signed by heads of parliaments of Armenia, Belarus, Kazakhstan, Tajikistan, Uzbekistan, Kyrgyzstan and Russia. In 1993-1995 the parliaments of Azerbaijan, Georgia and Moldova became members of the Assembly. In 1999 Ukraine joined the *'Alma-Ata Agreement'.* Since 16 Jan 1996 recognized as an interstate organization within the system of the organs of the *Commonwealth of Independent States (CIS, #04341).* Previously also referred to as *Parliamentary Assembly of the Commonwealth of Independent States – Assemblée parlementaire de la Communauté des Etats indépendants.* Also referred also to as *Interparliamentary Assembly of CIS – Assemblée interparlementaire de la CEI – Mezparlamentskaja Assambleja SNG.* **Aims** Draft model laws and recommendations for member nations; harmonize national laws to promote comprehensive integration; monitor elections. **Structure** IPA CIS comprises parliamentary delegations of member nations; parliamentary delegations consist of representatives of member nations, elected or appointed by each member nation parliament from among its members in accordance with internal regulations and procedures. Council, consisting of the Heads of Parliamentary Delegations. Permanent Commissions (10): Economy and Finance; Social Policy and Human Rights; Political Issues and International Cooperation; Legal Issues; Defence and Security Issues; Culture, Information, Tourism and Sport; Practices of State-Building and Local Government; Agrarian Policy, Natural Resources and Ecology; Science and Education; Budget Oversight Commission. Joint Commission for Harmonization of National Laws Related to Security, Countering Emerging Threats and Challenges. Secretariat is a permanent body of the IPA CIS Council. **Languages** Russian. **Staff** Variable. **Finance** Contributions from member states. **Activities**

Politics/policy/regulatory; events/meetings; standards/guidelines; networking/liaising. Set up: *International Institute of Monitoring Democracy Development, Parliamentarianism and Suffrage Protection for the Citizens of the IPA CIS Member Nations (IIMDP, #13902).* Relevant treaty: *Convention on Standards of Democratic Elections, Electoral Rights and Freedoms in Member Nations of the Commonwealth of Independent States (2002).* **Events** *Plenary Session* St Petersburg (Russia) 2005, *Plenary Session* St Petersburg (Russia) 2004, *SPIEF : Annual St Petersburg International Economic Forum* St Petersburg (Russia) 2004, *Plenary Session* St Petersburg (Russia) 2003, *International forum on combating terrorism* St Petersburg (Russia) 2002. **Publications** *Dialog: politika, pravo, ekonomika* (periodical) in Russian – journal; *Informatsionny bulleten* (periodical) in Russian; *Vestnik Mezparlamentskoj Assamblei* (periodical) in Russian – newsletter.

Members Parliaments of 9 CIS member nations:

Armenia, Azerbaijan, Belarus, Kazakhstan, Kyrgyzstan, Moldova, Russia, Tajikistan, Ukraine.

IGO Relations Agreements and treaties with:

- *Parlamento Centroamericano (PARLACEN, #18201);*
- *Congress of Local and Regional Authorities of the Council of Europe (#04677);*
- *European Bank for Reconstruction and Development (EBRD, #06315);*
- *European Commission for Democracy through Law (Venice Commission, #06636);*
- *International Organization for Migration (IOM, #14454);*
- *Pan-African Parliament (PAP, #18058);*
- *Parlamento Latinoamericano (PARLATINO, #18203);*
- *Parliamentary Assembly of the Council of Europe (PACE, #18211);*
- *Parliamentary Assembly of the Mediterranean (PAM, #18212);*
- *Parliamentary Assembly of the Organization of the Black Sea Economic Cooperation (PABSEC, #18213);*
- *Parliamentary Assembly of the Organization for Security and Cooperation in Europe (OSCE PA, #18214);*
- *Parliamentary Union of the OIC Member States (PUIC, #18220);*
- UNDESA;
- *UNESCO (#20322);*
- *UNIDO (#20336);*
- *United Nations Economic Commission for Europe (UNECE, #20555);*
- *United Nations Population Fund (UNFPA, #20612);*
- *WHO Regional Office for Europe (#20945);*
- *World Intellectual Property Organization (WIPO, #21593).*

Regular relations with:

- *Asia-Pacific Economic Cooperation (APEC, #01887);*
- *Baltic Sea Parliamentary Conference (BSPC, #03146);*
- *Collective Security Treaty Organization (CSTO, #04103);*
- *Commonwealth of Independent States Anti-Terrorism Center (CIS ATC, #04342);*
- *Comprehensive Nuclear-Test-Ban Treaty Organization (CTBTO, #04420);*
- *European Commission (EC, #06633);*
- *European Parliament (EP, #08146);*
- *ILO (#11123);*
- *International Bank for Reconstruction and Development (IBRD, #12317)* (World Bank);
- *International Telecommunication Union (ITU, #15673);*
- *Nordic Council (NC, #17256);*
- *Office of the United Nations High Commissioner for Human Rights (OHCHR, #17697);*
- *OSCE – Office for Democratic Institutions and Human Rights (OSCE/ODIHR, #17902);*
- *Parliamentary Assembly of Turkic Speaking Countries (TURKPA, #18215);*
- *Shanghai Cooperation Organization (SCO, #19256);*
- *Standing Committee of Parliamentarians of the Arctic Region (SCPAR, #19958);*
- *UNHCR (#20327);*
- *United Nations Commission on International Trade Law (UNCITRAL, #20531);*
- *United Nations Human Settlements Programme (UN-Habitat, #20572);*
- *United Nations Office on Drugs and Crime (UNODC, #20596).*

NGO Relations Agreements with: *Arab Inter-Parliamentary Union (Arab IPU, #00995); Association of European Election Officials (ACEEEO, #02508); International Committee of the Red Cross (ICRC, #12799); International Federation of Red Cross and Red Crescent Societies (#13526).* Regular relations with: *ASEAN Inter-Parliamentary Assembly (AIPA, #01205); Asian Parliamentary Assembly (APA, #01653); Baltic Development Forum (#03111); Commonwealth Parliamentary Association (CPA, #04355); General Confederation of Trade Unions (GCTU, #10108); GLOBE International (#10668); Inter-Parliamentary Assembly on Orthodoxy (IAO, #15959); International Congress of Industrialists and Entrepreneurs (ICIE, #12895).* [2020/XF2508/**F***]

♦ Inter-Parliamentary Assembly on Orthodoxy (IAO) 15959

SG 22-24 Vasilissis Amalias Ave, 105 57 Athens, Greece. E-mail: info@eiao.org.
URL: http://www.eiao.org/

History following a proposal Jul 1993, Ormylia (Greece). Original title: *European Inter-Parliamentary Assembly on Orthodoxy (EIAO).* New name adopted 2001. **Aims** Encourage contact between parliamentary, political, ecclesiastical, academic and spiritual figures or institutions for both development of Orthodox cultural heritage and for its contribution to contemporary global dialogue on human rights and peaceful coexistence of peoples. **Structure** General Assembly (annual); International Secretariat; Committees (8). **Languages** English, Irish Gaelic, Russian. **Finance** Members' dues. **Events** *Annual General Assembly* Athens (Greece) 2018, *Annual General Assembly* Rome (Italy) 2017, *Annual General Assembly* Thessaloniki (Greece) 2016, *Annual General Assembly* Vienna (Austria) 2015, *Annual General Assembly* Moscow (Russia) 2014. **Publications** *IAO Annual Bulletin.*

Members Parliamentarians of Orthodox faith of 21 countries:

Albania, Armenia, Belarus, Bulgaria, Cyprus, Czechia, Estonia, Finland, Georgia, Greece, Kazakhstan, Latvia, Lithuania, Moldova, Montenegro, Poland, Romania, Russia, Serbia, Slovakia, Ukraine.

Also groups of Members of Parliaments from Africa, Australasia, Middle East and orth America. Membership countries not specified.

IGO Relations Observer Status with: *Parliamentary Assembly of the Organization of the Black Sea Economic Cooperation (PABSEC, #18213).* **NGO Relations** Observer Status with: *Inter-Parliamentary Union (IPU, #15961); World Council of Churches (WCC, #21320).* [2021/XF5833/**F**]

♦ Inter-parliamentary Coalition for Combating Antisemitism (ICCA) .. 15960

Chair c/o House of Commons, London, SW1A 0AA, UK. T. +442072198345. E-mail: mail@antisemitism.org.uk.
URL: http://www.antisemitism.org.uk

History 2008. Previously also referred to as *International Coalition to Combat Anti-Semitism.* **Aims** Share knowledge, experience, best practice, and recommendations, encouraging dissemination in an attempt to deal more effectively with contemporary antisemitism. **Structure** Steering Committee. [2017.10.18/XM4637/**C**]

♦ Inter-Parliamentary Conference / see Inter-Parliamentary Union (#15961)
♦ Inter-Parliamentary Consultative Council of Benelux / see Benelux Inter-Parliamentary Consultative Council (#03201)
♦ Inter-Parliamentary Forum of the Americas / see ParlAmericas (#18206)

♦ Inter-Parliamentary Union (IPU) 15961

Union interparlementaire (UIP) – Unión Interparlamentaria – Interparlamentarische Union

SG Chemin du Pommier 5, CP 330, Grand-Saconnex, 1218 Geneva, Switzerland. T. +41229194150. Fax +41229194160. E-mail: postbox@ipu.org.
Office of Permanent Observer of IPU to the UN 336 East 45th St, Tenth Floor, New York NY 10017, USA. T. +12125575880. Fax +12125573954. E-mail: ny-office@ipu.org.
URL: https://www.ipu.org/

History Proposal adopted Jun 1888. Founded 30 Jun 1889, Paris (France), on the initiative of French and British parliamentarians, with the aim of promoting international arbitration. Original title: *Inter-Parliamentary Conference – Conférence interparlementaire.* Headquarters: up to 1911, Bern (Switzerland); 1911 to 1914, Brussels (Belgium); 1914 to 1920, Oslo (Norway); since 1921, Geneva (Switzerland). Statutes adopted 1922, at Vienna conference and modified at subsequent conferences. Current statutes adopted 1976, revised Oct 1983, and amended Apr 2003, Oct 2013 and Mar 2016. Statutes and Rules made gender neutral at conference, 1996, Beijing (China). **Aims** Promote democratic governance, institutions and values, working with parliaments and parliamentarians to articulate and respond to the needs and aspirations of the people. **Structure** Assembly; Governing Council; Executive Committee; Secretariat. Standing Committees reporting to Assembly (4): Peace and International Security; Sustainable Development; Democracy and Human Rights; United Nations Affairs. Groups under Governing Council (8): Committee on the Human Rights of Parliamentarians; Committee on Middle East Questions; Group of Facilitators for Cyprus; Committee to Promote Respect for International Humanitarian Law; Advisory Group on Health; High-Level Advisory Group on Countering Terrorism and Violent Extremism; Forum of Women Parliamentarians; Forum of Young Parliamentarians. Bodies under Executive Committee (2): Gender Partnership Group; Sub-Committee on Finance. **Languages** Arabic, English, French, Spanish. **Staff** Aims for gender equality. Salary scale based on the UN system. Adheres to *United Nations Joint Staff Pension Fund (UNJSPF, #20581).* The *Administrative Tribunal of the International Labour Organization (ILO Tribunal, #00118)* is competent to settle disputes. **Finance** Members' contributions. Other sources: internal staff assessment; program support cost charges; interest; fund income; meeting room rentals; voluntary funding for technical cooperation projects and activities. **Activities** Events/meetings; guidance/assistance/consulting; politics/policy/regulatory. **Events** *Global Parliamentary Summit on Counter-Terrorism* Vienna (Austria) 2021, *Global Summit of Women Speakers of Parliament* Vienna (Austria) 2021, *World Conference of Speakers of Parliament* Vienna (Austria) 2021, *Global Summit of Women Speakers of Parliament* Geneva (Switzerland) 2020, *World Conference of Speakers of Parliament Virtual Segment* Geneva (Switzerland) 2020. **Publications** *Women in Parliament.* IPU Annual Report; results of IPU Assembly and related meetings; summary records of Inter-Parliamentary Assemblies; handbooks for parliamentarians on different thematic areas; miscellaneous publications on gender, democracy, health, youth and human rights. **Information Services** *New PARLINE* – online database on national parliaments – information on structures, working methods, gender parity, women's caucuses, youth and MPs'human rights; *Women in Politics* – online statistics concerning women's representation in national parliaments, global and regional averages.

Members As of 1 Jan 2020 (179):

Afghanistan, Albania, Algeria, Andorra, Angola, Argentina, Armenia, Australia, Austria, Azerbaijan, Bahrain, Bangladesh, Belarus, Belgium, Benin, Bhutan, Bolivia, Bosnia-Herzegovina, Botswana, Brazil, Bulgaria, Burkina Faso, Burundi, Cambodia, Cameroon, Canada, Cape Verde, Central African Rep, Chad, Chile, China, Colombia, Comoros, Congo Brazzaville, Congo DR, Costa Rica, Côte d'Ivoire, Croatia, Cuba, Cyprus, Czechia, Denmark, Djibouti, Dominican Rep, Ecuador, Egypt, El Salvador, Equatorial Guinea, Estonia, Eswatini, Ethiopia, Fiji, Finland, France, Gabon, Gambia, Georgia, Germany, Ghana, Greece, Guatemala, Guinea, Guinea-Bissau, Guyana, Haiti, Honduras, Hungary, Iceland, India, Indonesia, Iran Islamic Rep, Iraq, Ireland, Israel, Italy, Japan, Jordan, Kazakhstan, Kenya, Korea DPR, Korea Rep, Kuwait, Kyrgyzstan, Laos, Latvia, Lebanon, Lesotho, Libya, Liechtenstein, Lithuania, Luxembourg, Madagascar, Malawi, Malaysia, Maldives, Mali, Malta, Marshall Is, Mauritania, Mauritius, Mexico, Micronesia FS, Moldova, Monaco, Mongolia, Montenegro, Morocco, Mozambique, Myanmar, Namibia, Nepal, Netherlands, New Zealand, Nicaragua, Niger, Nigeria, North Macedonia, Norway, Oman, Pakistan, Palau, Palestine, Panama, Papua New Guinea, Paraguay, Peru, Philippines, Poland, Portugal, Qatar, Romania, Russia, Rwanda, Samoa, San Marino, Sao Tomé-Principe, Saudi Arabia, Senegal, Serbia, Seychelles, Sierra Leone, Singapore, Slovakia, Slovenia, Somalia, South Africa, South Sudan, Spain, Sri Lanka, St Lucia, Sudan, Suriname, Sweden, Switzerland, Syrian AR, Tajikistan, Tanzania UR, Thailand, Timor-Leste, Togo, Tonga, Trinidad-Tobago, Tunisia, Türkiye, Turkmenistan, Tuvalu, Uganda, UK, Ukraine, United Arab Emirates, Uruguay, Uzbekistan, Vanuatu, Venezuela, Vietnam, Yemen, Zambia, Zimbabwe.

Associate members (13):

Andean Parliament (#00820); Arab Parliament (#01023); Communauté économique et monétaire d'Afrique centrale (CEMAC, #04374) (Parliament of); *East African Legislative Assembly (EALA, #05185); European Parliament (EP, #08146); Interparliamentary Assembly of Member Nations of the Commonwealth of Independent States (IPA CIS, #15958); Parlamento Centroamericano (PARLACEN, #18201); Parlamento Latinoamericano (PARLATINO, #18203); Parliamentary Assembly of the Council of Europe (PACE, #18211); Parliamentary Assembly of the Organization of the Black Sea Economic Cooperation (PABSEC, #18213); Parliament of the Economic Community of West African States (ECOWAS Parliament, #18221); Union économique et monétaire Ouest africaine (UEMOA, #20377)* (Inter-Parliamentary Committee of).

Consultative Status Consultative status granted from: *FAO (#09260)* (Special Status).

IGO Relations United Nations and related organizations:

- *FAO (#09260);*
- *ILO (#11123);*
- *International Bank for Reconstruction and Development (IBRD, #12317)* (World Bank);
- *International Fund for Agricultural Development (IFAD, #13692);*
- *International Monetary Fund (IMF, #14180);*
- *International Organization for Migration (IOM, #14454);*
- *International Organization of Supreme Audit Institutions (INTOSAI, #14478);*
- *Joint United Nations Programme on HIV/AIDS (UNAIDS, #16149);*
- *Organisation for the Prohibition of Chemical Weapons (OPCW, #17823);*
- *PMNCH (#18410);*
- *Preparatory Commission for the Comprehensive Nuclear-Test-Ban Treaty Organization (CTBTO, #18482);*
- *UN Women (#20724);*
- *UNCTAD (#20285);*
- *UNDP (#20292);*
- *UNESCO (#20322);*
- *UNHCR (#20327);*
- *UNICEF (#20332);*
- *United Nations (UN, #20515)* (1996), with the right to circulate IPU documents (2002);
- *United Nations Population Fund (UNFPA, #20612);*
- *WHO (#20950);*
- *World Trade Organization (WTO, #21864).*

Regional inter-governmental organizations:

- *African Union (AU, #00488);*
- *League of Arab States (LAS, #16420);*
- *OAS (#17629).*

Parliamentary assemblies or associations:

- *ACP-EU Joint Parliamentary Assembly (#00077);*
- *African Parliamentary Union (APU, #00412);*
- *Amazonian Parliament (#00767);*
- *Arab Inter-Parliamentary Union (Arab IPU, #00995);*
- *ASEAN Inter-Parliamentary Assembly (AIPA, #01205);*
- *Asian Parliamentary Assembly (APA, #01653);*
- *Assemblée parlementaire de la Francophonie (APF, #02312);*
- *Association of Senates, Shoora and Equivalent Councils in Africa and the Arab World (ASSECAA, #02913);*
- *Baltic Assembly (BA, #03094);*
- *Commonwealth Parliamentary Association (CPA, #04355);*
- Parliamentary Assembly of *Comunidade dos Países de Língua Portuguesa (CPLP, #04430);*
- *Consultative Council of the Arab Maghreb Union (#04765);*
- Parliamentary Assembly of *Economic Cooperation Organization (ECO, #05313);*
- *Global Organization of Parliamentarians Against Corruption (GOPAC, #10518);*
- Inter-Parliamentary Union of the Member States of *Intergovernmental Authority on Development (IGAD, #11472);*
- *Inter-Parliamentary Assembly on Orthodoxy (IAO, #15959);*
- Forum of Parliaments of *International Conference on the Great Lakes Region (ICGLR, #12880);*
- *Nordic Council (NC, #17256);*
- *Pan-African Parliament (PAP, #18058);*
- *ParlAmericas (#18206);*
- *Parliamentarians for Nuclear Non-Proliferation and Disarmament (PNND, #18210);*
- *Parliamentary Assembly of the Mediterranean (PAM, #18212);*
- *Parliamentary Assembly of the Organization for Security and Cooperation in Europe (OSCE PA, #18214);*
- *Parliamentary Assembly of Turkic Speaking Countries (TURKPA, #18215);*
- Parliamentary Assembly of the Union of Belarus and Russia;
- *Parliamentary Assembly – Union for the Mediterranean (PA – UfM, #18216);*
- *Confederación Parlamentaria de las Américas (COPA, #04479);*
- *Parliamentary Union of the OIC Member States (PUIC, #18220);*
- *SADC Parliamentary Forum (SADC PF, #19023);*
- *World Scout Parliamentary Union (WSPU, #21773).*

International non-governmental organizations:

- *Amnesty International (AI, #00801);*
- *Global Fund to Fight AIDS, Tuberculosis and Malaria (Global Fund, #10383);*
- *Human Rights Watch (HRW, #10990);*
- *Penal Reform International (PRI, #18290);*
- *World Federation of United Nations Associations (WFUNA, #21499).*

International political party federations:

- *Centrist Democrat International (CDI, #03792);*
- *Liberal International (LI, #16454);*
- *Socialist International (SI, #19340).*

Other partner organizations:
- *Geneva Centre for Security Sector Governance (DCAF, #10121)*;
- *International Committee of the Red Cross (ICRC, #12799)*;
- *International Federation of Red Cross and Red Crescent Societies (#13526)*;
- *International Institute for Democracy and Electoral Assistance (International IDEA, #13872)*.

Associated with Department of Global Communications of the United Nations.
NGO Relations Permanent Observer Status granted to:
- *African Parliamentary Union (APU, #00412)*;
- *Amnesty International (AI, #00801)*;
- *Arab Inter-Parliamentary Union (Arab IPU, #00995)*;
- *ASEAN Inter-Parliamentary Assembly (AIPA, #01205)*;
- *Asian Parliamentary Assembly (APA, #01653)*;
- *Assemblée parlementaire de la Francophonie (APF, #02312)*;
- *Association of Senates, Shoora and Equivalent Councils in Africa and the Arab World (ASSECAA, #02913)*;
- *Centrist Democrat International (CDI, #03792)*;
- *Commonwealth Parliamentary Association (CPA, #04355)*;
- *Global Organization of Parliamentarians Against Corruption (GOPAC, #10518)*;
- *Human Rights Watch (HRW, #10990)*;
- *Inter-Parliamentary Assembly on Orthodoxy (IAO, #15959)*;
- *International Committee of the Red Cross (ICRC, #12799)*;
- *International Federation of Red Cross and Red Crescent Societies (#13526)*;
- *International Organization of Supreme Audit Institutions (INTOSAI, #14478)*;
- *Parliamentarians for Nuclear Non-Proliferation and Disarmament (PNND, #18210)*;
- *PMNCH (#18410)*;
- *Penal Reform International (PRI, #18290)*;
- *SADC Parliamentary Forum (SADC PF, #19023)*;
- *Socialist International (SI, #19340)*;
- *World Federation of United Nations Associations (WFUNA, #21499)*. [2020.02.11/XB2832/y/**B**]

♦ Interpeace 15962

Pres Chemin Eugène-Rigot 2E, 1202 Geneva, Switzerland. T. +41224045900. E-mail: noble@interpeace.org – info@interpeace.org.
Europe Office Av des Arts 24, Boîte 8, 1000 Brussels, Belgium.
URL: http://www.interpeace.org/

History Jun 1994, as *War-torn Societies Project (WSP)*, by *United Nations Research Institute for Social Development (UNRISD, #20623)* and *Centre on Conflict, Development and Peacebuilding (CCDP)*. Name changed to *WSP Transition Programme (WSP-TP)* in 1999 and *WSP International* in 2000, when it became independent of the UN. Subsequently Changed title to *International Peacebuilding Alliance (Interpeace) – Alliance internationale pour la consolidation de la paix – Alianza Internacional para la Consolidación de la Paz*, 2006. Currently only known under shortened title. Officially recognized as an international entity by Federal Council of Switzerland, 15 Jan 2018. **Aims** Harness the strengths of societies to manage conflict in non-violent ways by establishing processes of change that connect local communities, civil society, governments and the international community. **Structure** Governing Council; Advisory Council; Headquarters in Geneva (Switzerland). Offices in: Abidjan (Côte d'Ivoire), Brussels (Belgium), Guatemala (Guatemala), Nairobi (Kenya), New York NY (USA). **Languages** English, French, Spanish. **Staff** 67.00 FTE, paid. **Finance** Voluntary contributions from governments, multilateral organizations, foundations and private individuals. Annual expenditure (2017): US$ 14,882,942. **Activities** Conflict resolution; events/meetings. Active in: Burundi, Colombia, Congo DR, Côte d'Ivoire, Cyprus, Guinea-Bissau, Kenya, Mali, Palestine, Rwanda, Somalia, Sweden, Timor-Leste. **Events** *Geneva Peace Talks* Stockholm (Sweden) 2015, *Geneva Peace Talks* Geneva (Switzerland) 2014. **Publications** *Constitution-making and Reform: Options for the Process* (2011) in Arabic, English, French, Russian, Vietnamese. Annual Report; case studies. **Members** Not a membership organization. **Consultative Status** Consultative status granted from: *ECOSOC (#05331)* (Special). **IGO Relations** Agreement with: *United Nations (UN, #20515)* Department of Political Affairs. Cooperates with: *United Nations Office for Project Services (UNOPS, #20602)*. Partnership with: UN Peacebuilding Support Office (PBSO). **NGO Relations** *European Peacebuilding Liaison Office (EPLO, #08176)*; *Geneva Peacebuilding Platform (GPP)*. Partners with international and national NGOs, including: *Civil Society Platform for Peacebuilding and Statebuilding (CSPPS, #03970)*; *Peace One Day*; *Swisspeace*. [2020/XG9802/y/**F**]

♦ **INTERPHIL** International Standing Conference on Philanthropy (#15600)
♦ INTERPHOTO – International Photographic Dealers' Association (inactive)
♦ INTERPLAST / see ReSurge International
♦ INTERPOL / see International Criminal Police Organization – INTERPOL (#13110)
♦ **InterPore** International Society for Porous Media (#15376)

♦ InterPortPolice 15963

Pres Port of Los Angeles Police Dept, 425 S Palos Verdes St, San Pedro CA 90731, USA. T. +18889748883. E-mail: info@interportpolice.org.
SG address not obtained.
URL: http://www.interportpolice.org/

History Mar 1970, Boston MA (USA), as *International Association of Port Police*. Reorganized, 1974, when expanded to include aviation and title changed to *International Association of Airport and Seaport Police (IAASP) – Association internationale de la police des ports et des aéroports – Asociación Internacional de Policia de Puertos y Aeropuertos*. Expanded to include transport and border jurisdictions, 2010, when current title was adopted. Registered in the State of Washington (USA) and in Province of British Columbia (Canada). **Aims** Influence standards of safety and security in ports; prevent and detect criminal activity affecting safety and welfare of the public and passengers, crew members, ground and dock workers involved in international commerce; study and recommend methods and uniform practices for establishing safeguards for movement of international passengers and cargo; encourage and develop exchange of information and material among *law enforcement* agencies concerned with criminal activity at international airports and seaports; share information and experience; encourage cooperation among all segments of the international trade community so as to develop improved *security* measures for passengers and cargo moving internationally. **Structure** General Meeting (annual, at Conference). Board of Directors (meets twice a year), consisting of President, Executive Vice President, Immediate Past President, 5 Regional Vice-Presidents (Africa, Americas, Asia Pacific, Europe and Mid East), Secretary, Treasurer and 2 Co-opted Directors. Secretariat in Coquitlam (Canada), headed by Executive Director. Committees (6): Executive; Finance; Development and Information; Maritime; Aviation; Conference Coordinating. **Languages** English. **Staff** 2.00 FTE, paid. **Finance** Sources: members' dues. **Activities** Training; programmes; meeting activities; information dissemination. **Events** *World Port Security Summit* London (UK) 2018, *World Port Security Summit* Hamburg (Germany) 2012, *World Port Security Summit* Los Angeles, CA (USA) 2010, *World Port Security Summit* Hong Kong (Hong Kong) 2009, *Annual Conference* Los Angeles, CA (USA) 2003. **Publications** *IAASP News* (4 a year) – newsletter; *IAASP Annual Year Book*. *Security Recommendations and Standards for Cargo Security at Airports and Seaports*. Security audit; position papers; emergency response investigation checklists; special reports; manuals.
Members Full; Associate; Retired; Life; Honorary; Sustaining. Police forces, customs authorities or individuals having law enforcement powers or security responsiblities at airports, seaports or railways in 36 countries and territories:
Australia, Austria, Bahamas, Bahrain, Belgium, Belize, Canada, Dubai, Egypt, Finland, France, Greece, Israel, Jamaica, Japan, Jordan, Kenya, Korea Rep, Lebanon, Liberia, Netherlands, Papua New Guinea, Philippines, Saudi Arabia, Singapore, South Africa, Sri Lanka, St Lucia, Taiwan, Tanzania UR, Thailand, Trinidad-Tobago, UK, United Arab Emirates, USA.
Consultative Status Consultative status granted from: *ECOSOC (#05331)* (Ros A); *International Maritime Organization (IMO, #14102)*. **IGO Relations** Accredited by: *United Nations Office at Vienna (UNOV, #20604)*. **NGO Relations** *European Association of Airport and Seaport Police (EAASP, #05934)*. [2016/XC6080/**C**]

♦ InterPrayer (internationally oriented national body)

♦ Inter Press Service (IPS) 15964

IPS – World News Agency – IPS – Agence de presse du monde – IPS – Agencia de Prensa del Mundo – IPS – Welt Nachrichtenagentur

Contact Via Sabotino 45, 00195 Rome RM, Italy. E-mail: info@ips.org.
URL: http://ips.org/

History 1964, as *IPS – Third World News Agency*, as an organ of *IPS – Inter Press Service International Association (#16013)*. Also previously referred as *Inter Press Service Third World (IPS)*. **Aims** Facilitate and improve the exchange of information within, and the quality of information about, developing countries through independent news and analyses with focus on civil society and development issues; report on the globalization process and its impacts. **Finance** Sources: sale of news and feature services. **Activities** Knowledge management/information dissemination; publishing activities. **Publications** *IPS News and Feature Service* (daily) – wire service. 20 special weekly, monthly and bimonthly bulletins on regional, interregional and international levels on issues related to women, population and development, investment and development, environment, energy, agriculture, Church and The Group of 77. **Members** Correspondents and stringers serving media outlets and organizations worldwide in over 150 countries. Membership countries not specified.
IGO Relations IPS international users and cooperating bodies.
(1) *'United Nations system'*:
- Department of Global Communications of the United Nations;
- *FAO (#09260)*;
- *International Fund for Agricultural Development (IFAD, #13692)*;
- *UNEP (#20299)*;
- *UNDP (#20292)*;
- *UNESCO (#20322)*;
- *UNICEF (#20332)*;
- *United Nations Economic Commission for Latin America and the Caribbean (ECLAC, #20556)*;
- *United Nations Population Fund (UNFPA, #20612)*.

(2) *'Intergovernmental organizations'*:
- *European Commission (EC, #06633)*;
- *Group of 77 (G-77, #10732)*;
- *OPEC Fund for International Development (OFID, #17745)*;
- *Pan-African News Agency (PANA, inactive)* – now replaced by private company 'PANAPRESS';
- *Sistema Económico Latinoamericano (SELA, #19294)*.

(3) *'Governmental organizations'*:
- *Canadian International Development Agency (CIDA, inactive)*;
- *DANIDA*;
- *Department for International Development Cooperation*;
- *Norwegian Agency for Development Cooperation (Norad)*;
- *Swedish International Development Cooperation Agency (Sida)*.

Member of: *Asia-Pacific Institute for Broadcasting Development (AIBD, #01934)*.
NGO Relations IPS international users and cooperating bodies: *Association for Progressive Communications (APC, #02873)*; *Ford Foundation (#09858)*; *Friedrich-Ebert-Stiftung (FES)*; *Global Information Network (GIN)*; *International Co-operative Alliance (ICA, #12944)*; *Latin American Association for Human Rights (#16243)*; *MacArthur Foundation*; *Oxfam Novib*; *Society for International Development (SID, #19581)*; *World Association for Christian Communication (WACC, #21126)*; *Worldview International Foundation (WIF, #21903)*. Instrumental in setting up: *Latin American Feature Service on Women and Population (no recent information)*. Member of: *International Campaign to Abolish Nuclear Weapons (ICAN, #12426)*. [2020/XF6706/**F**]

♦ Inter Press Service Third World / see Inter Press Service (#15964)
♦ **Interpret Europe** European Association for Heritage Interpretation (#06067)

♦ InterPride 15965

Main Office 4306 S MacGregor Way, Houston TX 77021, USA. E-mail: info@interpride.org.
URL: http://www.interpride.org/

History Oct 1982, Boston, MA (USA). Former names and other names: *National Association of Lesbian and Gay Pride Coordinators* – former; *International Association of Lesbian and Gay Pride Coordinators* – former; *International Association of Lesbian, Gay, Bisexual and Transgender Pride Coordinators* – former. **Aims** Represent producers of pride events for the LGBT community that celebrate lesbian, gay, bisexual, and transgender culture and pride. **Structure** Board of Directors; Committees; Working Groups; Global Advisory Council; Consultants; Caucuses. **Languages** English, French, Portuguese, Spanish. **Activities** Advocacy/lobbying/activism; awareness raising; events/meetings; financial and/or material support; networking/liaising; projects/programmes; publishing activities; research and development; training/education. **Events** *General Meeting and World Conference* Guadalajara (Mexico) 2022, *General Meeting and World Conference* 2021, *General Meeting and World Conference* 2020, *General Meeting and World Conference* Montréal, QC (Canada) 2013, *General Meeting and World Conference* Montréal, QC (Canada) 2003. **Publications** *Pride Radar*. **Members** Over 400 members from over 70 countries. Membership countries not specified. **NGO Relations** Cooperates with (1): *ILGA World (International Lesbian, Gay, Bisexual, Trans and Intersex Association, #11120)*. [2022.05.10/XD7652/**D**]

♦ Interprofessional.Global (#10305)
♦ Inter-professional Organization Serving Temperature-Controlled Transport and Logistics / see Transfrigoroute International (#20213)
♦ Interprofessionelle Organisation im Dienste des Transports und der Logistik Temperaturgeführter Güter / see Transfrigoroute International (#20213)
♦ **INTERRAD** International Association of Radiolarian Palaeontologists (#12120)

♦ INTERREG V 15966

Contact Interreg Europe, Les Arcuriales, Entrée D, 5e étage, 45 rue de Tournai, 59000 Lille, France. T. +33328144100. Fax +33328144109.
URL: http://interreg.eu/

History 1990, as an initiative of *European Community (inactive)*, implemented by *European Commission (EC, #06633)*. Original title 'INTERREG', replacing the previous *REGEN (inactive)* (completion of trans-European energy networks). This was followed from 15 Jun 1994, by 'INTERREG II'. INTERREG III, covered 2000-2006, under guidelines approved by the Commission, 28 Apr 2000, as set out in Article 20 of Council Regulation (EC) No 1260/1999; INTERREG IV covered 2007-2013. Method of implementing cooperation activities set out in Communication of the Commission to Member States, 7 May 2001 'Interregional cooperation' Strand C; guidelines amended, 23 Aug 2001; present consolidated guidelines replace those decided on 28 Apr 2000. Current programme *INTERREG V* covers 2014-2020. Previously also known as *European Territorial Cooperation (ETC)*. **Aims** Promote a harmonious economic, social and territorial development of the Union as a whole. **Finance** under *European Regional Development Fund (ERDF, #08342)*. Total budget: euro 10,100,000 million. **Activities** Over 100 cooperation programmes between regions and territorial, social and economic partners, subdivided into 3 chapters: Cross-border INTERREG VA; Transnational INTERREG VG; Interregional INTERREG VC, containing: *INTERREG Europe*; INTERACT III; URBACT; *European Observation Network on Territorial Development and Cohesion (ESPON, #08070)*. **Events** *AlpWeek* Brig (Switzerland) 2022, *EU Interregional Cooperation Forum* Brussels (Belgium) 2019, *Seminar on Decarbonising Cities with Geothermal District Heating : How to Finance It ?* Brussels (Belgium) 2019, *Conference* Vaasa (Finland) 2019, *STREFOWA Conference on Food Waste Prevention and Management* Austria 2018. **Publications** Newsletter.
Members Eligible countries (28):
Austria, Belgium, Bulgaria, Croatia, Cyprus, Czechia, Denmark, Estonia, Finland, France, Germany, Greece, Hungary, Ireland, Italy, Latvia, Lithuania, Luxembourg, Malta, Netherlands, Poland, Portugal, Romania, Slovakia, Slovenia, Spain, Sweden, UK.
IGO Relations Supports: *International Commission of the Schelde River (#12727)*. **NGO Relations** Instrumental in setting up: *European Chemical Regions Network (ECRN, #06522)*; *Bio Base Europe*; *Nordisk Transportpolitisk Nettverk (NTN, #17542)*. Supports: *Baltic Palette Cooperation Network (no recent information)*; *Eucor – The European Campus (#05578)*; *Cap Business Océan Indien (#03419)*. [2018/XK0469/**E***]

♦ Inter-Regional Cooperative Research Network on Buffalo (Buffalo Network) 15967

Coordinator c/o CREA/ZA, Via Salaria 31, Monterotondo, 00015 Rome RM, Italy. T. +39690614942.
URL: http://www.agrowebcee.net/buffalo-network-website/home/

History 1992, with the title *European Cooperative Research Network on Buffalo*, as part of *European System of Cooperative Research Networks in Agriculture (ESCORENA, #08871)* within *FAO (#09260)*, through its *European Commission on Agriculture (ECA)*. **Aims** Promote research and development in buffalo, in close relationship with activities of International Buffalo Federation. **Structure** Working Groups (4): Reproduction and Biotechnology; Farming Systems; Products; Genetic Resources. **Languages** English. **Staff** 12.00 FTE, paid. **Finance** Funding for publications and meetings from FAO. Some funding from: *International Buffalo*

Federation (IBF, #12408). **Activities** Knowledge management/information dissemination; research/documentation; training/education. **Events** *Symposium on animal recording to attain breeding objectives / Biennial Session / Symposium* Bled (Slovenia) 2000. **Publications** *Buffalo Newsletter.*
Members Institutions in 31 countries:
Argentina, Australia, Bolivia, Brazil, Bulgaria, Canada, China, Colombia, Costa Rica, Cuba, Ecuador, Egypt, Germany, Greece, Guatemala, Hungary, Indonesia, Iran Islamic Rep, Iraq, Italy, Mexico, Pakistan, Philippines, Romania, Sri Lanka, Thailand, Trinidad-Tobago, Türkiye, UK, USA, Venezuela. [2017.06.30/XK0917/**E**]

♦ Inter-Regional Cooperative Research Network on Cotton for the Mediterranean and Middle East Regions 15968

Contact address not obtained.
URL: http://www.agrowebcee.net/cotton/
History 1988, as part of *European System of Cooperative Research Networks in Agriculture (ESCORENA, #08871)* within *FAO (#09260)*, through its *European Commission on Agriculture (ECA).* **Aims** Develop cooperation between researchers on cotton in the *Mediterranean* basin and the *Middle East.* **Structure** Working Groups (10). **Languages** English. **Finance** Sources: funding received principally from national institutions; some support from FAO and ICAC. **Activities** Programmes within working groups, including workshops and consultations. Working Groups (10): Cotton Breeding; Variety Trials; Growth Regulators; Cotton Nutrition; Plant Growth Modelling; Water Management; Integrated Pest Management; Cotton Technology; Biotechnology; Economy. Organizes working group meetings and Plenary Meeting. **Events** *Plenary meeting* Luxor (Egypt) 2018, *Plenary meeting* Sharm el Sheikh (Egypt) 2015, *Plenary meeting* Antalya (Turkey) 2012, *Plenary Meeting* Alexandroupoli (Greece) 2008, *Plenary Meeting* Ouagadougou (Burkina Faso) 2008. **Publications** REU Technical Series. Information Services: Card index (updated annually) of researchers on cotton in the Mediterranean basin and the Middle East.
Members Full in 25 countries:
Algeria, Belgium, Bulgaria, Burkina Faso, China, Egypt, Ethiopia, France, Germany, Greece, India, Iran Islamic Rep, Iraq, Israel, Italy, Morocco, Pakistan, Poland, Spain, Sudan, Syrian AR, Türkiye, UK, USA, Uzbekistan. [2018/XF3484/**E**]

♦ Inter-Regional Cooperative Research Network on Olives 15969

Réseau coopératif européen de recherche sur l'olivier – Red Cooperativa Europea de Investigación del Olivo
Coordinator IFAPA Ctr "Alameda del Obispo", Av Menéndez Pidal s/n, 14004 Córdoba, Spain. T. +34957016020. Fax +34957016043.
URL: http://www.agrowebcee.net/olive-network/
History Sep 1974, Córdoba (Spain), under the name of *European Cooperative Research Network on Olives*, as part of *European System of Cooperative Research Networks in Agriculture (ESCORENA, #08871).* Comes within the framework of *FAO (#09260)*, through its *European Commission on Agriculture (ECA).* **Structure** Working Groups (4): Genetic Resources and Plant Material; Production Techniques and Productivity; Plant Protection; Oil Technology and Quality. **Finance** Partially supported by FAO but research programme fully paid by each Cooperating Centre. **Activities** Characterization of existing varieties; exchange of germplasm; dissemination of information; soil conservation and erosion control; improvement of fertilizer applications, irrigation practices and oil quality. **Events** *Plant protection workshop* Marrakech (Morocco) 1994, *Plant material, cultural techniques, plant protection, olive oil quality* Bornova (Turkey) 1991, *Meeting on plant protection* Izmir (Turkey) 1990, *International symposium on olive growing* Córdoba (Spain) 1989. **Publications** *Olea* – newsletter.
Members Research institutes in 17 olive-producing countries of the Mediterranean Basin:
Albania, Algeria, Cyprus, Egypt, France, Greece, Israel, Italy, Lebanon, Libya, Morocco, Portugal, Serbia, Spain, Syrian AR, Tunisia, Türkiye. [2011/XF1150/**E**]

♦ Interregionaler Parlamentarier-Rat (#04696)

♦ Inter-regional FAO-CIHEAM Network for Research and Development in Sheep and Goats 15970

Contact Inst de la Recherche et de l'Enseignement Supérieur Agricoles, 30 rue Alain Savary, Belvédère, 1002 Tunis, Tunisia. T. +21671752897.
Contact IAMZ-CIHEAM, Avda Montañana 1005, 50059 Saragossa, Spain. E-mail: iamz@iamz.ciheam.org.
URL: http://www.iamz.ciheam.org/research/networks/sheep_and_goats/
History 1979, as part of *European System of Cooperative Research Networks in Agriculture (ESCORENA, #08871)* within *FAO (#09260)*, through its *FAO Regional Office for Europe and Central Asia (FAO/REU, #09267); CIHEAM – International Centre for Advanced Mediterranean Agronomic Studies (CIHEAM, #03927).* Original title: *FAO/CIHEAM Network of Cooperative Research on Sheep and Goats – Réseau FAO-CIHEAM de recherches coopératives sur les ovins et les caprins.* Also referred to as *European Research Network on Sheep and Goat Production (NCRSG).* **Aims** Study and improve the sheep and goat production systems in the Mediterranean Region. **Structure** Sub-networks (3): Nutrition; Production Systems. Working groups of limited duration inside each sub-network. **Languages** English, French. **Finance** Supported by FAO (REU and RNE) and CIHEAM. **Activities** Events/meeting; knowledge management/information dissemination; research/documentation. **Events** *Joint Seminar* Vitoria-Gasteiz (Spain) 2017, *Joint Seminar* Montpellier (France) 2015, *Seminar* Tangiers (Morocco) 2013, *Meeting* Córdoba (Spain) 2005, *Meeting* Granada (Spain) 2003. **Publications** *Options méditerranéennes* – journal. *Sheep and Goat Contacts.* REU Technical Series. Activities report; proceedings; special issues of journals.
Members Individuals (277) and institutions (78) in 38 countries:
Albania, Algeria, Austria, Belgium, Bulgaria, Croatia, Cyprus, Czechia, Egypt, Ethiopia, Finland, France, Germany, Greece, Hungary, Ireland, Israel, Italy, Lebanon, Malta, Morocco, Netherlands, Norway, Oman, Poland, Portugal, Romania, Russia, Serbia, Slovakia, Slovenia, Spain, Sweden, Switzerland, Syrian AR, Tunisia, Türkiye, UK.
NGO Relations *European Federation of Animal Science (EAAP, #07046).* [2017.06.30/XK0733/**E**]

♦ Inter-Regional Meeting of Bishops of Southern Africa (IMBISA) ... 15971

Reunião Inter-Regional dos Bispos da Africa Austral
SG 88 Broadlands Road, PO Box EH99 Emerald Hill, Harare, HARARE, Zimbabwe. T. +263242336775. Fax +263242336909. E-mail: imbisa@imbisa.com.
URL: http://imbisa.africa
History 22 Apr 1975. Founded following Synod of 1974. Constitution approved 1978. Secretariat established in Manzini (Swaziland), 1980. Amended Statutes approved 3 Dec 1993. Permanent Secretariat now located in Harare (Zimbabwe). Former names and other names: *Réunion inter-régionale des évêques de l'Afrique australe* – former. **Aims** Promote the spirit of collegiality and the prophetic role of the Church and Companion. **Structure** Plenary; Standing Committee; General Secretariat. **Languages** English, Portuguese. **Staff** 8.00 FTE, paid. **Finance** Sources: members' dues. Support from: Archdiocese of Cologne; *Catholic Agency for Overseas Development (CAFOD); Catholic Relief Services (CRS, #03608);* United States Conference of Catholic Bishops (USCCB). **Activities** Advocacy/lobbying/activism; awareness raising; projects/programmes; research/documentation; training/education. **Events** *Triennial Plenary Meeting* Luanda (Angola) 2007, *Triennial Plenary Meeting* Harare (Zimbabwe) 2004, *Triennial plenary meeting / African Synod* Harare (Zimbabwe) 2001, *Triennial plenary meeting* Manzini (Swaziland) 1998, *Triennial plenary meeting* Windhoek (Namibia) 1995. **Publications** *The Role of Young People in Endorsing the Gospel and Strengthening the Core Values of the Church* (2019); *Inculturation* (1993); *Justice and Peace in Southern Africa* (1988). Occasional papers.
Members Episcopal Conferences (4 national and 2 international) representing members in 9 countries:
Angola, Botswana, Eswatini, Lesotho, Mozambique, Namibia, Sao Tomé-Principe, South Africa, Zimbabwe.
International Conferences of Bishops:
Episcopal Conference of Angola and São Tomé (CEAST); *Southern African Catholic Bishops' Conference (SACBC, #19838).* [2023.02.14/XD2437/y/**D**]

♦ Inter-regional Network on Cotton in Asia and North Africa (INCANA) 15972

Secretariat c/o CRI, Shahid Beheshti St, PO Box 49175-483, Gorgan GOLESTAN, 49166-85915, Iran Islamic Rep. T. +981712254950 – +981712236401. Fax +981712227781. E-mail: info@cottonnetwork.ir.
URL: http://www.areeo.ac.ir/HomePage.aspx?TabID=8923&Site=AREEO&Lang=en-US/.%3C/
History 2002, by support of *Global Forum on Agricultural Research (GFAR, #10370), Association of Agricultural Research Institutions in the Near East and North Africa (AARINENA, #02364), Asia-Pacific Association of Agricultural Research Institutions (APAARI, #01830), Central Asia and the Caucasus Association of Agricultural Research Institutions (CACAARI, #03678), International Center for Agricultural Research in the Dry Areas (ICARDA, #12466),* Agricultural Research, Education and Extension Organization (AREEO), Iran. **Aims** Increase cotton yield in member countries through research collaboration and exchange of scientific knowledge, success stories and new technologies.
Members in 12 countries:
Azerbaijan, Egypt, India, Iran Islamic Rep, Kazakhstan, Kyrgyzstan, Pakistan, Sudan, Syrian AR, Tajikistan, Turkmenistan, Uzbekistan. [2007/XJ1940/**F**]

♦ Interregional Parliamentary Council (#04696)
♦ Interregional Union of Life Help for Mentally Handicapped Persons (unconfirmed)
♦ Inter Religious Federation for World Peace / see Twelve Gates Foundation
♦ Interreligious Foundation for Community Organization (internationally oriented national body)
♦ Interreligious and International Federation for World Peace / see Universal Peace Federation (#20681)
♦ Inter-Religious League (inactive)
♦ Inter-réseau européen des initiatives éthiques et solidaires (#07593)
♦ Inter-réseaux / see Inter-réseaux Développement rural
♦ Inter-réseaux Développement rural (internationally oriented national body)

♦ InterRidge (IR) 15973

Contact Seoul Natl Univ, 1 Gwanak-ro, Gwanak-gu, Seoul 08826, Korea Rep. E-mail: interridge@gmail.com.
URL: http://www.interridge.org/
History 1992, originally for 10 years (InterRidge Initial Science Plan), divided into 3 phases: 1992-1994; 1995-1997; 1997-2003. Prolonged for 2004-2013 (IR Next Decade Plan), and subsequently for 2014-2023 (IR Third Decade Plan). **Aims** Promote interdisciplinary, international studies of *oceanic* spreading centres by creating a global research community, planning and coordinating new science programmes, exchanging scientific information and sharing new technologies and facilities. **Structure** Steering Committee; National Correspondents (21); Programme Coordinator; Working Groups (4). Coordinated through InterRidge Office. **Languages** English. **Staff** 1700.00 FTE, paid. **Finance** Members' dues. Annual budget: US$ 150,000. **Activities** Events/meetings; knowledge management/information dissemination; projects/programmes. **Events** *Meeting on Mid-Ocean Ridges and other Geological features of the Indian Ocean* Goa (India) 2018, *Workshop on Oceanic Transform Faults* Plouzané (France) 2018, *MoHole workshop* Kanazawa (Japan) 2010, *Workshop on tectonic and oceanic processes along the Indian ocean ridge system* Goa (India) 2005, *Workshop on interactions among physical, chemical, biological and geological processes in backarc spreading systems on back-arc basins and back-arc spreading systems* Jeju (Korea Rep) 2004. **Publications** *InterRidge News* (annual). Meeting and workshop reports; Steering Committee Report; fliers. **Information Services** *InterRidge Vents Database* – global database on Active Submarine Hydrothermal Vent Fields.
Members Principal in 4 countries:
China, France, Norway, USA.
Regular in 6 countries:
Canada, Germany, India, Japan, Korea Rep, UK.
Corresponding in 11 countries and territories:
Australia, Brazil, Chile, Italy, Mauritius, New Zealand, Philippines, Poland, Portugal, Russia, South Africa.
Included in the above Corresponding Members, one organization listed in this Yearbook:
Pacific Islands Applied Geoscience Commission (SOPAC, inactive). [2022/XF4714/vy/**F**]

♦ Inter-Secretariat Committee on Scientific Programmes Relating to Oceanography (inactive)
♦ Intersections International (internationally oriented national body)

♦ Interserve 15974

International Dir c/o Link Coordination Sdn Bhd, No 5, Lorong 11/6A, Section 11, 46200 Petaling Jaya, Selangor, Malaysia. T. +60379609180. Fax +60379606594. E-mail: oaatio@gmail.com.
URL: http://www.interserve.org/
History 1852, UK, as 'Indian Female Normal School and Instruction Society (Zenana Mission)'. Subsequently known as *Bible Medical and Missionary Fellowship (BMMF).* Since 1976, includes *Woman's Union Missionary Society of America for Heathen Lands,* founded 1854, USA. **Aims** Second *health, development* and other professional *assistance* to *Asian* and *Middle Eastern* people; promote integral development of individuals and communities. **Publications** *Go* (4 a year).
Members Individuals (doctors, pharmacists, nurses, teachers, engineers) in 19 countries and territories:
Australia, Brazil, Canada, England, Germany, Hong Kong, India, Ireland, Korea Rep, Malaysia, Netherlands, New Zealand, Pakistan, Scotland, Singapore, South Africa, Switzerland, USA, Wales.
NGO Relations Member of: *Vereniging voor Personele Samenwerking met Ontwikkelingslanden (PSO, inactive); ECHO – International Health Services; Global Connections; United Mission to Nepal (UMN).* [2019/XF4961/v/**F**]

♦ INTERSHOE – International Federation of the Independent Shoe Trade (inactive)

♦ Interski International (INTERSKI) 15975

SG Siedlung Mooserkreuz 16, 6580 St Anton am Arlberg, Austria. Fax +435446400025.
Pres address not obtained.
URL: http://www.interski.org/
History First congress held 1951. Former names and other names: *World Association of the Ski Teaching System* – alias; *Weltverbandes für das Skilehrwesen* – alias. Registration: Switzerland. **Aims** Function as an umbrella organization for ski and *snowsports instruction* organizations. **Structure** Main working bodies: *International Federation of Snowsport Instructors (IFSI, #13542); International Ski Instructors Association (ISIA, #14870); International Association of Education in Science and Snowsports (IAESS, #11864).* **Events** *Congress* Sirkka (Finland) 2023, *Congress* Levi (Finland) 2021, *Congress* Pamporovo (Bulgaria) 2019, *Congress* Ushuaia (Argentina) 2015, *Congress / World Congress* St Anton am Arlberg (Austria) 2011.
Members Organizations in 37 countries and territories:
Andorra, Argentina, Australia, Austria, Belgium, Bulgaria, Canada, Chile, Croatia, Czechia, Denmark, Finland, France, Germany, Greece, Hungary, Ireland, Israel, Italy, Japan, Korea Rep, Liechtenstein, Montenegro, Netherlands, New Zealand, Norway, Poland, Romania, Russia, San Marino, Slovenia, Spain, Sweden, Switzerland, Türkiye, UK, USA. [2023/XJ8166/**B**]

♦ **INTERSKI** Interski International (#15975)
♦ Inter-Society Color Council (internationally oriented national body)
♦ Inter-Society for the Electronic Arts / see ISEA International (#16025)
♦ INTERSOS (internationally oriented national body)

♦ Intersputnik International Organization of Space Communications . 15976

Organisation Internationale des Télécommunications Spatiales Intersputnik – Organización Internacional de Telecomunicaciones Cósmicas Interspoutnik
Dir Gen 2nd Smolensky pereulok 1/4, Moscow MOSKVA, Russia, 121099. T. +74956414420. Fax +74956414440. E-mail: dir@intersputnik.int.
Exec Dir address not obtained.
URL: http://www.intersputnik.int/
History Established by 9 governments, on signing *Agreement on Establishment of the Intersputnik International System and Organization of Space Communications,* 15 Nov 1971. Agreement registered with United Nations, 27 Mar 1973: No 12343. Also governed by the following international agreements: Protocol of 4 Nov 2002, on Amendments to the Agreement on the Establishment of the Intersputnik International System and Organization of Space Communications; Agreement of 20 Sep 1976 on the Legal Capacity, Privileges and Immunities of the Intersputnik International Organization of Space Communications; Agreement of 15 Sep 1977 between Intersputnik International Organization of Space Communications and Government of the Union of Soviet Socialist Republics on the Settlement of Issues Related to the Seat of Intersputnik in the USSR (under this Agreement, legal successor is Government of Russia). Intersputnik Operating Agreement entered into force, 4 Feb 2003. **Aims** Contribute to strengthening and development of economic, scientific, technical, cultural, and other relations by communications, radio and television broadcasting via satellites, as well as ensure cooperation and coordination of efforts in design, establishment, operation and development

of satellite communications systems. **Structure** Board (meets annually); Operations Committee; Directorate, headed by Director General. **Languages** English, French, Russian, Spanish. **Staff** 38.00 FTE, paid. **Activities** Research and development. **Events** *Annual Board Session* Baku (Azerbaijan) 2023, *Annual Board Session* 2022, *Operations Committee Session* Moscow (Russia) 2022, *Annual Board Session* 2021, *Operations Committee Session* 2021. **Publications** *Intersputnik Newsletter* (irregular) in English – newsletter on the current topics in Satellite communications and Broadcasting Industry.
Members Member States (26):
Afghanistan, Azerbaijan, Belarus, Bulgaria, Cuba, Czechia, Georgia, Germany, Hungary, India, Kazakhstan, Korea DPR, Kyrgyzstan, Laos, Mongolia, Nicaragua, Poland, Romania, Russia, Somalia, Syrian AR, Tajikistan, Turkmenistan, Ukraine, Vietnam, Yemen.
IGO Relations Observer status with (2): *Committee on the Peaceful Uses of Outer Space (COPUOS, #04277)*; *Regional Commonwealth in the Field of Communications (RCC, #18767)*. Member of (1): *International Telecommunication Union (ITU, #15673)* (Radiocommunication Sector (ITU-R) and Telecommunication Development Sector (ITU-D)). Cooperates with (3): *European Telecommunications Satellite Organization (EUTELSAT IGO, #08896)*; *International Mobile Satellite Organization (IMSO, #14174)*; *International Telecommunications Satellite Organization (ITSO, #15670)*. **NGO Relations** Member of (2): *Global Satellite Operators' Association (GSOA, #10586)*; *International Astronautical Federation (IAF, #12286)*. [2022.10.28/XC2682/**C***]

♦ Interstate Aviation Committee (IAC) 15977

Mezhgosudarstvennyj aviacionnyj komitet (MAK)

Main Office Bolshaya Ordynka str 22/2/1, Moscow MOSKVA, Russia, 119017. T. +74959531244. Fax +74959533508. E-mail: press@mak.ru.
URL: https://mak-iac.org/en/

History 30 Dec 1991, on signing of 'Agreement on civil aviation and use of airspace'. Also referred to in English as *Intergovernmental Aviation Committee (IAC)*.
Members Participants (11):
Armenia, Azerbaijan, Belarus, Kazakhstan, Kyrgyzstan, Moldova, Russia, Tajikistan, Turkmenistan, Ukraine, Uzbekistan. [2021/XD6325/**D***]

♦ Interstate Bank 15978

Banque inter-Etats – Mezhgosudarstvennyi Bank

Pres 15 Shukhov St, Moscow MOSKVA, Russia, 115162. T. +74959544354. Fax +74959549258. E-mail: info@isbnk.org.
URL: http://www.isbnk.org/en/

History 22 Jan 1993, Minsk (Belarus), by 10 Member States of *Commonwealth of Independent States (CIS, #04341)*, namely Armenia, Belarus, Kazakhstan, Kyrgyzstan, Moldova, Russia, Tajikistan, Turkmenistan, Uzbekistan and Ukraine. Memorandum and Articles of Association signed by heads of the 10 CIS Members States 22 Jan 1993. Bilateral agreements with the governments of Russia, Armenia and Kyrgyzstan concerning the terms of the Bank operating within those countries were signed and ratified. Has also signed agreements with the central (national) banks of Russia, Armenia, Belarus, Kyrgyzstan and Tajikistan concerning procedures for and rules of the Bank's carrying out banking operations in territories of these States. **Aims** Facilitate economic integration and development of the national economies of CIS countries by means of creation of the mechanism of settlements for effecting cross-border payments in national currencies and crediting foreign trade operations of CIS countries in national currencies. **Structure** An international banking institution. Head office in Moscow (Russia). Representative offices (3): Yerevan (Armenia); Minsk (Belarus); Bishkek (Kyrgyzstan). **Languages** Russian. **Staff** 70.00 FTE, paid. **Finance** 100% of capital belongs to member countries of CIS. **Activities** Offers settlement services, both in national currencies of CIS countries and in freely convertible currencies, to financial institutions, IGOs, NGOs and companies. Being a member of the national payment systems of 6 countries (Armenia, Belarus, Kazakhstan, Kyrgyzstan, Russia and Tajikistan), provides the opportunity of effecting payments in national currencies directly through these payment systems. Active in foreign exchange and money market operations in CIS and other countries. **Publications** Statistical reviews – electronic.
Members Governments of 9 of the 12 countries of the Commonwealth of Independent States:
Armenia, Belarus, Kazakhstan, Kyrgyzstan, Moldova, Russia, Tajikistan, Turkmenistan, Ukraine.
IGO Relations Contacts include: Executive Committee of *Commonwealth of Independent States (CIS, #04341)*. Member of: Financial and Banking Council of CIS and the Business Centre for CIS Economic Development. [2017.03.09/XF3219/**F***]

♦ Inter-State Commission on Drugs (no recent information)

♦ Inter-State Commission for Water Coordination of Central Asia (ICWC) 15979

Mezgosudarstvennaja Koordinacionnaja Vodohozjajstvennaja Comissija Centralnoj Azii (MKVK)

Contact SIC ICWC, Karasu-4, Building 11 – BWO Syrdarya building, 5th Floor, Tashkent, Uzbekistan, 100187. T. +998712650836. E-mail: vdukhovniy@gmail.com.
URL: http://www.icwc-aral.uz/

History 1992. Established by 'Agreement on cooperation in joint management, use and protection of interstate water sources', signed by 5 Ministers of Water Resources of Central Asian States. First included as a subdivision of *Interstate Council of the Central Asia States on the Aral Sea Basin Problems (inactive)* and subsequently of *International Fund for Saving the Aral Sea (IFAS, #13694)*, 23 Mar 1993. **Aims** Be responsible for cooperation among Aral Sea Basin countries in joint management of *transboundary* water *resources* – surface, ground and return water; direct water resources management and development and maintenance of sustainable natural and hydro *ecological* processes on transboundary water resources; help to avoid conflict related to water; help control water *usage*; consider environmental programmes related to the Aral Sea drying and water sources exhaustion and to the establishment of annual volumes of inflow to river deltas and the Aral Sea. **Structure** Executive bodies: Secretariat; 2 basin organizations – BWO "Amudarya" and BWO "Syrdarya"; *Scientific Information Centre of Interstate Coordination Water Commission of Central Asia (SIC ICWC, #19152)*; *'Coordination Metrological Centre (CMC ICWC)'*. **Languages** Russian. **Activities** Events/meetings. Active in all member countries. **Events** *Meeting* Almaty (Kazakhstan) 2008, *Meeting* Ashgabat (Turkmenistan) 2008, *Meeting* Ashgabat (Turkmenistan) 1998, *Meeting* Cholpon-Ata (Kyrgyzstan) 1998, *Meeting* Shymkent (Kazakhstan) 1998. **Publications** *ICWC Central Asia Bulletin* (4 a year). Newsletters; abstracts collection; collection of legal documents and scientific papers. **Information Services** *SIC ICWC* – develops cooperative relations on water-saving technology, produces publications, provides information services, coordinates international projects and arranges training courses.
Members Riparian States of the Aral Sea (5):
Kazakhstan, Kyrgyzstan, Tajikistan, Turkmenistan, Uzbekistan. [2021.10.26/XE2805/**E***]

♦ Inter-State Council for Anti-Monopoly Policies of the Commonwealth of Independent States (no recent information)
♦ Interstate Council of the Central Asia States on the Aral Sea Basin Problems (inactive)
♦ Interstate Council on Hydrometeorology of the Countries of the Commonwealth of Independent States (unconfirmed)
♦ Interstate Council on the Protection of Industrial Property (inactive)
♦ Inter-State Customs School of CACEU / see Ecole Inter-Etats des Douanes de la CEMAC (#05297)
♦ Inter-State Customs School of CAEMC (#05297)
♦ Inter-State Ecological Council (no recent information)
♦ Inter-State Economic Committee of the Economic Union of the Commonwealth of Independent States (no recent information)

♦ Interstate Federation of Atomic Energy Workers' Unions 15980

Pres 8-a Novoryazanskaya St, Moscow MOSKVA, Russia, 107078. T. +74999753432. Fax +74992618506. E-mail: ck@profatom.ru – epk@union.kiev.ua.

Members Trade unions in the CIS region (membership countries not specified). **NGO Relations** Member of: *General Confederation of Trade Unions (GCTU, #10108)*. [2014/XM2456/**D**]

♦ Inter-State Institution of Higher Learning and Research in the Areas of Water, Energy, Environment and Public Work / see Institut International d'Ingénierie de l'Eau et de l'Environnement (#11313)
♦ Inter-State Monetary Committee (inactive)
♦ Inter-State Organization for Advanced Technicians of Hydraulics and Rural Equipment (inactive)
♦ Inter-State Rail Committee of the CIS (inactive)

♦ Inter-State School of Hydraulic and Rural Engineering for Senior Technicians 15981

Ecole inter-Etats des techniciens supérieurs de l'hydraulique et de l'équipement rural (ESTHER)

Contact address not obtained. T. +226319203 – +226319204 – +226301314. Fax +226314093.

History 1972, Burkina Faso. 1972, Kamboinsé (Burkina Faso), as a joint venture of Member States of *African and Mauritian Common Organization (OCAM, inactive)* (dissolved 1985). Statutes adopted by the Governing Board, Jul 1985. Agreement signed 21 Dec 1977. **Aims** Educate senior technicians able to promote and realize necessary *infrastructure* development in the rural areas of member countries. **Structure** Governing Board, consisting of designated ministers of Member States, appoints Director. Improvement Council. **Finance** Funded by member states, UN agencies, certain IGOs, NGOs and governments. **Activities** Organizes continuing education training courses, inter-state sessions, in road construction, irrigation, agricultural water management, water supplies.
Members Governments of 14 countries:
Benin, Burkina Faso, Cameroon, Central African Rep, Chad, Congo Brazzaville, Côte d'Ivoire, Equatorial Guinea, Gabon, Mali, Mauritania, Niger, Senegal, Togo.
Partners (6):
Canada, China, France, Germany, Netherlands, Switzerland.
Intergovernmental partner (1):
European Union (EU, #08967).
IGO Relations Member of: *Intergovernmental Organizations Conference (IGO Conference, #11498)*. **NGO Relations** *International Training Network for Water and Waste Management (ITN, no recent information)*. [2009/XF5374/**F***]

♦ Inter-State School of Veterinary Sciences and Medicine 15982

Ecole inter-Etats des Sciences et Médecine Vétérinaires (EISMV)

Dir-Gen BP 5077, Dakar, Senegal. T. +221338651008. Fax +221338244283. E-mail: directiongenerale@eismv.org – contact@eismv.org.
URL: http://www.eismv.org/

History 29 Jan 1968, Fort-Lamy (Chad). Established as a joint venture of the then *African and Mauritian Common Organization (OCAM, inactive)*, dissolved in 1985. Commenced operations Oct 1968. **Aims** Train veterinary *doctors* and encourage research in veterinary science and medicine. **Structure** Board of Directors. **Languages** French. **Staff** 100.00 FTE, paid. 100 **Finance** Sources: contributions of member/participating states; fees for services; grants; members' dues. Annual budget: 1,723,000,000 XOF (2021). **Activities** Awards/prizes/competitions; events/meetings; projects/programmes; publishing activities; research and development; research/documentation. Active in all member countries. **Events** *Colloque sur le rôle du vétérinaire de demain dans les pays du Nord et du Sud dans les filières agroalimentaires* 1993. **Publications** *RASPA*.
Members Governments of 14 countries:
Benin, Burkina Faso, Burundi, Cameroon, Central African Rep, Chad, Congo Brazzaville, Côte d'Ivoire, Gabon, Mali, Mauritania, Niger, Senegal, Togo.
IGO Relations Member of (1): *African and Malagasy Council for Higher Education (#00364)*. **NGO Relations** Member of (4): African Association of Veterinary Education Establishments; *Agence universitaire de La Francophonie (AUF, #00548)*; *Association des établissements d'enseignement vétérinaire totalement ou partiellement de langue française (AEEVTPLF, no recent information)*; *Association of Institutions of Tropical Veterinary Medicine (AITVM, #02648)*. Provides secretariat for: *Union inter-africaine des organisations professionnelles d'éleveurs (UIOPE, no recent information)*. [2022.11.18/XF7389/**F***]

♦ Interstate Statistical Committee of the Commonwealth of Independent States (CIS-Stat) 15983

Chairman bldg 1, 39 Myasnitskaya Street, Moscow MOSKVA, Russia, 107450. T. +74956074086. Fax +74956074592. E-mail: cisstat@cisstat.org.
URL: http://www.cisstat.org/

History Established 30 Dec 1991, within the framework of *Commonwealth of Independent States (CIS, #04341)*. **Aims** Coordinate activities of statistical organizations of CIS countries; develop and implement a unified statistical methodology on the basis of mutual consultations; secure comparability and continuity of statistical elaborations; facilitate wide-scale information exchange in the framework of the CIS. **Structure** Departments (4): Administrative; Economic Statistics; Information and Publishing; Socio-Demographic Statistics. **Languages** Russian. **Staff** 65.00 FTE, paid. **Finance** Members' dues. **Activities** Guidance/assistance/consulting; standards/guidelines; research/documentation; knowledge management/information dissemination; events/meetings. **Publications** *Commonwealth of Independent States* in English, Russian – statistical yearbook. Abstracts; statistical results.
Members Governments of 11 States:
Armenia, Azerbaijan, Belarus, Kazakhstan, Kyrgyzstan, Moldova, Russia, Tajikistan, Turkmenistan, Ukraine, Uzbekistan. [2018.10.05/XE4241/**E***]

♦ **INTERSTENO** Fédération internationale pour le traitement de l'information et de la communication (#09667)
♦ **INTERSUN** International Research Programme on Health, Solar UV Radiation and Environmental Change (#14740)
♦ Inter-syndicale des pharmaciens d'Afrique (inactive)
♦ **INTERTANKO** International Association of Independent Tanker Owners (#11959)
♦ INTERTEAM – Fachleute im Entwicklungseinsatz (internationally oriented national body)

♦ Inter-Territorial Catholic Bishops' Conference (ITCABIC) 15984

SG Santanno House, 10 Howe St, Freetown, Sierra Leone. T. +23276381506. Fax +232228252.

History 18 Feb 1971, Freetown (Sierra Leone), as *Inter-Territorial Episcopal Conference (ITEC)*. **Aims** Promote cooperation in pastoral matters among Roman Catholic communities in English-speaking West Africa. **Structure** Commissions (8): Biblical and Catechetical; Ecumenism; Education; Justice and Peace; Liturgical; Mission and Laity; Social Communications; Vocations. St Paul's Major Seminary, temporarily transferred from Gbarnga (Liberia) to Makeni (Sierra Leone) and *Inter-Territorial Pastoral and Social Development Centre*, Kenema (Sierra Leone) are responsible to ITCABIC. **Languages** English. **Staff** 2.00 FTE, paid. **Finance** Tax levy on each Bishop. Budget (annual): US$ 12,000. **Activities** Commission meetings – at diocesan and national levels at regular intervals and then at inter-territorial level in a three-yearly cycle. Plenary Meetings (once a year) in one of the countries in rotation. **Events** *Plenary Meeting* Banjul (Gambia) 2004, *Plenary Meeting* Banjul (Gambia) 2003, *Plenary Meeting* Banjul (Gambia) 2002, *Plenary Meeting* Banjul (Gambia) 2001, *Joint plenary assembly* Ouagadougou (Burkina Faso) 2000. **Publications** *ITCABIC Newsletter* (12 a year); *ITCABIC Ordo* (annual); *ITCABIC Directory* (annual or every 2 years). Monographs; pamphlets.
Members Bishops (5) of 2 countries:
Gambia, Sierra Leone. [2015.01.23/XD8860/v/**D**]

♦ Inter-Territorial Episcopal Board of Eastern Africa / see Association of Member Episcopal Conferences in Eastern Africa (#02805)
♦ Inter-Territorial Episcopal Conference / see Inter-Territorial Catholic Bishops' Conference (#15984)
♦ Intertextilmash – International Production Amalgamation for Manufacturing Textile Technological Equipment (inactive)
♦ **InterTOP** International Teaching of Psychology Network (#15663)
♦ INTERTOTO – International Association of Toto and Lotto Organizations (inactive)
♦ Inter-Union Commission on Frequency Allocations for Radio Astronomy and Space Science / see Scientific Committee on Frequency Allocations for Radio Astronomy and Space Science (#19148)
♦ Inter-Union Commission on the Lithosphere / see International Lithosphere Program (#14059)
♦ Inter-Union Commission on Solar-Terrestrial Physics / see Scientific Committee on Solar-Terrestrial Physics (#19151)
♦ Inter-Union IUBS/IUMS International Commission on Bionomenclature / see International Committee on Bionomenclature (#12748)

♦ Interuniversitair Centrum voor Scandinavische Studies, Gent (internationally oriented national body)
♦ Interuniversitair Centrum voor Studie en Documentatie van Latijns-Amerika / see Centre for Latin American Research and Documentation

♦ Interuniversity Benelux Group of Transport Economists 15985

Groupement interuniversitaire Benelux des économistes des transports (GIBET) – Benelux Interuniversitaire Groepering van Vervoerseconomen (BIVEC)

Pres Krijgslaan 281, Box S-8, 9000 Ghent, Belgium. T. +3292644553. Fax +3292644985.
URL: http://www.bivec.eu/

History Founded 21 Jun 1978, Brussels (Belgium), under the auspices of *Benelux Union (#03207)*. Registered in accordance with Belgian law, 30 Aug 1978. **Aims** Encourage cooperation between Benelux education and research institutions concerning transport economy and policy. **Structure** General Assembly (annual); Administrative Board. **Languages** Dutch, English, French. **Staff** 0.50 FTE, paid. **Finance** Members' dues. **Activities** Knowledge management/information dissemination; events/meetings; awards/prizes/competitions. **Events** *Benelux port study days* Antwerp (Belgium) 1997, *Liberalisation of European inland navigation in the year 2000* Antwerp (Belgium) 1997, *Colloquium* Heerlen (Netherlands) 1993, *Colloquium* Brussels (Belgium) 1992, *Transports and environment* Brussels (Belgium) 1990.
Members Active (80); Associate Individual (49); Associate Collective (4); Corresponding (2). Members in 3 countries:
Belgium, Luxembourg, Netherlands.
Corresponding members in 2 countries:
France, Switzerland. [2021/XD7158/F]

♦ Inter-University Centre for Advanced Studies (IUC) 15986

Centre inter-universitaire des études avancées – Interuniverzitetski centar za napredne sutdije

Dir Gen Don Frana Bulica 4, PO Box 104, HR-20000 Dubrovnik, Croatia. T. +38520413626 – +38520413627. Fax +38520413628. E-mail: iuc@iuc.hr.
URL: http://www.iuc.hr/

History Founded 1972, Dubrovnik (Yugoslavia), as *Inter-University Centre of Post-Graduate Studies (IUC) – Centre inter-universitaire des études post-universitaires – Interuniverzitetski centar za postdiplomski studij*. Inaugurated in 1974. **Aims** Further graduate and postgraduate studies (courses, conferences and colloquia) and research among *scholars* and *students* from universities and institutes of higher learning throughout the world on themes of international importance. **Structure** Council; Executive Committee; Secretariat. **Languages** English, German. **Staff** 3.00 FTE, paid. **Finance** Members' dues. Courses and conferences funded by organizing universities. Support from: Croatian Ministry of Science, Education and Sports; University of Zagreb; many different foundations. **Activities** Research/documentation; training/education; networking/liaising; events/meetings. **Events** *Annual Conference of Human Dignity and Humiliation Studies* Dubrovnik (Croatia) 2016, *Conference on Graded Structures in Algebra and its Applications* Dubrovnik (Croatia) 2016, *Conference on Information Technology and Journalism* Dubrovnik (Croatia) 2016, *Conference on Three and Four Manifold Topology and Geometry* Dubrovnik (Croatia) 2016, *International Conference on the Interfaces among Mathematics, Chemistry and Computer Sciences* Dubrovnik (Croatia) 2016.
Members Universities and scientific institutions (170) in 45 countries:
Albania, Austria, Belgium, Bosnia-Herzegovina, Bulgaria, Canada, China, Croatia, Czechia, Denmark, Egypt, Estonia, Ethiopia, Finland, France, Germany, Greece, Hungary, Iran Islamic Rep, Ireland, Israel, Italy, Japan, Kenya, Korea Rep, Kosovo, Malaysia, Montenegro, Netherlands, North Macedonia, Norway, Poland, Portugal, Romania, Russia, Serbia, Slovenia, Spain, Sweden, Switzerland, Türkiye, UK, Ukraine, USA, Venezuela.
Included in the above 3 institutions listed in this Yearbook:
Central European University (CEU, #03717); *Florida International University (FIU)*; *Research Centre for Islamic History, Art and Culture (IRCICA, #18852)*.
Associate members (9) in 7 countries:
Austria, Croatia, Germany, Italy, Netherlands, Serbia, USA.
Included in the above Associate members, 2 organizations listed in this Yearbook:
Council for Research in Values and Philosophy (RVP, #04915); *World Academy of Art and Science (WAAS, #21065)*. [2016.10.20/XF4277/y/E]

♦ Interuniversity Centre for Latin American Research and Documentation / see Centre for Latin American Research and Documentation
♦ Inter-University Centre of Post-Graduate Studies / see Inter-University Centre for Advanced Studies (#15986)
♦ Interuniversity Centre for Scandinavian Studies, Ghent (internationally oriented national body)
♦ Inter-University Centre for Social Studies / see Centre for Southeast Asian Social Studies
♦ Inter-University Centre for Terrorism Studies (unconfirmed)
♦ Inter-University Committee of Coordination for the Development of Oriental Studies in Latin America (inactive)
♦ Inter-University Committee for East Africa (inactive)
♦ Interuniversity Conference for Agricultural and Related Sciences in Europe / see Association for European Life Science Universities (#02519)
♦ Interuniversity Consortium for Agricultural and Related Sciences in Europe / see Association for European Life Science Universities (#02519)
♦ Inter-University Consortium for Arab Studies and Middle Eastern Studies (internationally oriented national body)
♦ Inter-University Consortium on International Social Development / see International Consortium for Social Development (#12922)
♦ Inter-University Consortium for Political Research / see Inter-University Consortium for Political and Social Research
♦ Inter-University Consortium for Political and Social Research (internationally oriented national body)

♦ Inter-University Council for East Africa (IUCEA) 15987

Exec Sec Plot M833, Kigobe Road, Kyambogo, PO Box 7110, Kampala, Uganda. T. +256414256251 – +256414256252. Fax +256414342007. E-mail: exsec@iucea.org – info@iucea.org.
URL: http://www.iucea.org/

History 1980, Arusha (Tanzania UR). Established following a memorandum of understanding (MoU) between the vice-chancellors of the national universities of Dar es Salaam (Tanzania), Makerere (Uganda) and Nairobi (Kenya), to maintain cooperation between the three universities under the framework of former *Inter-University Committee for East Africa (inactive)* (IUC), set up 1 Jul 1970, Kampala (Uganda), under the auspices of the *East African Community – 1967 (EAC, inactive)*. 2002, became a legal body corporate of re-established *East African Community (EAC, #05181)*, and was effectively integrate into its operational framework in 2009, when the IUCEA Act was enacted by the East African Legislative Assembly (EALA). Instrumental in setting up: *Lake Victoria Research Initiative (VicRes, inactive)*. **Aims** Facilitate networking among universities in East Africa and with universities outside the region; provide a forum for discussion on a wide range of academic and other matters relating to higher education in East Africa; facilitate maintenance of internationally comparable education standards in East Africa so as to promote the region's competitiveness in higher education; advise EAC Partner States on higher education matters. **Structure** Governing Board; Executive Committee; Specialized Committees; Standing Committees. Secretariat, headed by Executive Secretary, and hosted in Kampala (Uganda). **Languages** English, French, Swahili. **Staff** 42.00 FTE, paid. **Finance** Sources: contributions of member/participating states. Contributions from East African governments, member universities/university colleges and corporate members. Annual budget: 1,203,870 USD. **Activities** Guidance/assistance/consulting; monitoring/evaluation; networking/liaising; projects/programmes; research and development; standards/guidelines. Active in all member countries. **Publications** *Inter-University Newsletter* (2 a year).
Members Public and private universities and degree awarding institutions (138); councils and commissions regulating higher education. Members in 7 Partner States of EAC:
Burundi, Congo DR, Kenya, Rwanda, South Sudan, Tanzania UR, Uganda. [2022.12.14/XE2774/y/E*]

♦ Inter-University European Institute on Social Welfare (IEISW) 15988

Institut européen interuniversitaire de l'action sociale (IEIAS)

Sec Rue du Débarcadère 179, 6001 Marcinelle, Belgium. T. +3271447266 – +3271447267. Fax +3271472744. E-mail: carinelorent@hotmail.com.
Gen Dir address not obtained.
URL: http://www.hainaut.be/social/dgas/template/template.asp?page=ieias

History 1970. Inter-University status acquired 1972. Registered in accordance with Belgian law. **Aims** Promote, execute and disseminate scientific research in the field of social welfare. **Structure** Administrative Council, comprising President, 3 Vice-Presidents, Administrator-Delegate, Secretary and 36 members. Executive Committee; Scientific Council. **Languages** English, French. **Finance** Funded by Province of Hainaut (Belgium). **Activities** Main activities (3): training/education; research/scientific cooperation; documentation/publications. Annual colloquium in social gerontology. In 1975 set up the first Belgian University for Senior Citizens. Instrumental in setting up the now defunct *Conseil international de coordination des associations d'études et d'action en matière de vieillissement (CICAV, inactive)*. **Events** *Colloque Européen du Réseau REFUTS* Paris (France) 2019, *Colloque Européen du Réseau REFUTS* Charleroi (Belgium) 2011, *International colloquium* Charleroi (Belgium) 2006, *International colloquium* Charleroi (Belgium) 2003, *International colloquium* Charleroi (Belgium) 2000. **Publications** Books; study session proceedings; reports.
Members Cooperating universities in 7 countries:
Belgium, France, Germany, Italy, Spain, Switzerland, UK.
Consultative Status Consultative status granted from: *ECOSOC (#05331)* (Ros A). **IGO Relations** Accredited by: *United Nations Office at Vienna (UNOV, #20604)*. **NGO Relations** Instrumental in setting up (1): *Réseau Européen de Formation Universitaire en Travail Social (REFUTS)*. [2013.06.24/XE4410/j/E]

♦ Interuniversity Research Centre on Southern Europe (internationally oriented national body)
♦ Inter-University Union of Federalists (inactive)
♦ Interuniverzitetski centar za napredne sutdije (#15986)
♦ Interuniverzitetski centar za postdiplomski studij / see Inter-University Centre for Advanced Studies (#15986)

♦ INTERVac – International Home Exchange Holiday Service 15989

Service international d'échanges de maisons pour les vacances

Contact 230 boulevard Voltaire, 75011 Paris, France. E-mail: info@intervac.fr.
URL: http://www.intervac.com/

History Founded 1953, as *International Holiday Service Home Exchange – Service international de vacances – Internationaler Feriendienst*. Absorbed, 1984, the *International Home Exchange Service (IHES)*. Registered in accordance with Swedish law. **Aims** Develop interglobal *personal relationships* through exchange of living *accommodation*. **Structure** Annual General Meeting; Board of Directors; national representatives. **Languages** Chinese, Czech, Danish, Dutch, English, Finnish, French, German, Icelandic, Irish Gaelic, Italian, Norwegian, Polish, Portuguese, Romanian, Russian, Slovakian, Spanish, Swedish. **Finance** Members' dues. **Activities** Active in over 50 countries. **Events** *Annual General Meeting* France 2015, *Annual General Meeting* Germany 2013, *Annual General Meeting* Bologna (Italy) 2012, *Annual General Meeting* Italy 2012, *Annual General Meeting* Belgium 2011. **Publications** Printed books from 1969-2007; on the Internet since 1999.
Members Organizers in 41 countries:
Algeria, Argentina, Australia, Austria, Belgium, Brazil, Canada, Cyprus, Czechia, Denmark, El Salvador, Finland, France, Germany, Greece, Guatemala, Hungary, Iceland, Ireland, Israel, Italy, Japan, Liechtenstein, Lithuania, Luxembourg, Mexico, Morocco, Netherlands, New Zealand, Norway, Poland, Portugal, Romania, Russia, Slovakia, South Africa, Spain, Sweden, Switzerland, UK, USA.
Members also in the former USSR; countries not specified. [2014.11.18/XF1337/e/F]

♦ Interventional Radiology Olbert Symposium (meeting series)
♦ Intervention and Coiled Tubing Association (internationally oriented national body)
♦ Interventionell Radiologisches Olbert Symposium (meeting series)
♦ INTERVENTION – International Convention Relating to Intervention on the High Seas in Cases of Oil Pollution Casualties (1969 treaty)
♦ INTERVENTION PROT 1973 – Protocol Relating to Intervention on the High Seas in Cases of Marine Pollution by Substances other Than Oil (1973 treaty)
♦ Intervodoochistka (inactive)
♦ **Intervoice** The International Hearing Voices Network (#13785)
♦ INTERVUZ – Mezhdunarodnaya Assotsiatsiya Rabotnikov Agrarnykh (no recent information)
♦ **INTERWOOLLABS** International Association of Wool Textile Laboratories (#12275)

♦ Intestinal Rehabilitation and Transplant Association (IRTA) 15990

Sections Manager c/o TTS, 505 Bd René-Lévesque Ouest, Ste 1401, Montréal QC H2Z 1Y7, Canada. T. +15148741717. Fax +15148741716. E-mail: sections@tts.org.
URL: http://www.tts.org/irta-home/home/welcome-to-ita/

History Jul 2005, Brussels (Belgium), as a section of *The Transplantation Society (TTS, #20224)*. Original title: *Intestinal Transplantation Association (ITA)*. Registered in accordance with Delaware (USA) law. **Aims** Save and enhance the lives of patients with intestinal failure using innovative nutritional, medical, surgical and transplant therapies through education, policy development and research. **Structure** Council. **Activities** Events/meetings. **Events** *International Congress* Auckland (New Zealand) 2021, *International Congress* Paris (France) 2019, *International Congress* New York, NY (USA) 2017, *Biennial International Small Bowel Transplant Symposium* Buenos Aires (Argentina) 2015, *Biennial international small bowel transplant symposium* Washington, DC (USA) 2011. **NGO Relations** Instrumental in setting up: *Intestinal Transplant Registry (ITR, #15991)*. [2019.12.05/XJ4168/E]

♦ Intestinal Transplantation Association / see Intestinal Rehabilitation and Transplant Association (#15990)

♦ Intestinal Transplant Registry (ITR) 15991

Address not obtained.
URL: http://www.intestinaltransplant.org/

History 1994. Managed by *Intestinal Rehabilitation and Transplant Association (IRTA, #15990)*. **Aims** Collect, verify, analyse and index all *documentation* material relating to intestinal transplants. **Activities** Prepares reports based on data collection for *International Small Bowel Transplant Symposium*.
Members Centres in 19 countries:
Argentina, Austria, Belgium, Brazil, Canada, China, France, Germany, Iran Islamic Rep, Italy, Japan, Mexico, Netherlands, Portugal, Spain, Sweden, Switzerland, UK, USA. [2015/XF7213/F]

♦ INTF – International Nonviolence Training Fund (internationally oriented national body)
♦ **INTGLIM** International NGO Task Group on Legal and Institutional Matters (#14369)
♦ INTH – International Network for Theory of History (unconfirmed)
♦ INTI – Energies Solidaires (internationally oriented national body)
♦ Intifada mondiale (unconfirmed)
♦ INTI – INTI – Energies Solidaires (internationally oriented national body)
♦ **INTiP** International Network Theatre in Prison (#14333)
♦ **INTISA** International Network of Translation and Interpreting Studies Associations (#14335)
♦ **INTLawyers** International-Lawyers.Org (#14008)
♦ IntNSA – International Nurses Society on Addictions (internationally oriented national body)
♦ **INTO** International National Trusts Organisation (#14214)
♦ **INTOSAI** International Organization of Supreme Audit Institutions (#14478)

♦ Intra-Africa Metrology System (AFRIMETS) 15992

Système Intra-Africain de Métrologie

Secretariat NMISA, Bldg Private Bag X34, Lynnwood Ridge, Pretoria, South Africa.
URL: http://www.afrimets.org/

History 2006, by *Southern African Development Community (SADC, #19843)* – Cooperation in Measurement Traceability (SADCMET). **Aims** Promote metrology and quality infrastructure/related activities in Africa so as to facilitate intra-African and international trade (especially to overcome technical, sanitary and phytosanitary barriers to trade) and ensure safety, health, consumer and environmental protection. **Structure** General Assembly; Executive Committee; Technical Committees; Secretariat. **Languages** English, French. **Staff** Voluntary. **Finance** Supported by: *African Union (AU, #00488)* Commission (AUC); *New Partnership for Africa's Development (NEPAD, #17091)*; collaboration partners; institutions in South Africa. **Activities** Events/meetings; training/education. **Events** *General Assembly* Cairo (Egypt) 2019, *General Assembly* Enugu (Nigeria) 2018, *General Assembly* Pretoria (South Africa) 2017.

Members Principal: country scientific metrology institutes and legal metrology bodies or institutes which are members of a sub-regional metrology organization; Ordinary: countries that do not belong to a sub-regional metrology organization; Associate: institutes outside Africa; Observer: interested parties involved in metrology.
Principal in 44 countries:
Algeria, Angola, Benin, Botswana, Burkina Faso, Burundi, Cameroon, Central African Rep, Chad, Congo Brazzaville, Congo DR, Côte d'Ivoire, Egypt, Equatorial Guinea, Eswatini, Ethiopia, Gabon, Ghana, Guinea-Bissau, Kenya, Lesotho, Libya, Madagascar, Malawi, Mali, Mauritania, Mauritius, Morocco, Mozambique, Namibia, Niger, Nigeria, Rwanda, Senegal, Seychelles, South Africa, South Sudan, Sudan, Tanzania UR, Togo, Tunisia, Uganda, Zambia, Zimbabwe.
Ordinary in 2 countries:
Gambia, Sierra Leone.
Associate in 5 countries:
France, Ghana, Madagascar, Nigeria, Tanzania UR.
Regional Associate member:
International Atomic Energy Agency (IAEA, #12294).
Observer organizations (8):
African Accreditation Cooperation (AFRAC, #00196); African Committee of Metrology (#00258); African Electrotechnical Standardization Commission (AFSEC, #00295); African Organisation for Standardisation (ARSO, #00404); Arab Federation for Metrology (AFM); Asia Pacific Metrology Programme (APMP, #01957); European Association of National Metrology Institutes (EURAMET, #06129); Inter-American Metrology System (#11440).
IGO Relations *African Union (AU, #00488)* Commission; *Bureau international des poids et mesures (BIPM, #03367); International Organization of Legal Metrology (#14451); New Partnership for Africa's Development (NEPAD, #17091).* **NGO Relations** *African Committee of Metrology (#00258);* Pan-African Quality Infrastructure (PAQI). [2019.02.12/XM5897/**F***]

- ♦ INTRAC – International NGO Training and Research Centre, Oxford (internationally oriented national body)
- ♦ **INTRAC** International Research Network on Transitions to Adulthood from Care (#14738)
- ♦ INTRADE – International Trade Development Association (inactive)

♦ Intra-European Organization of Tax Administrations (IOTA) 15993

Exec Sec Wesselényi u 16, Budapest 1077, Hungary. T. +3614783030. Fax +3613415177. E-mail: iota@iota.hu.
URL: http://www.iota-tax.org/

History Founded following a proposal during the Conference of Tax Administrations of Central and Eastern Europe and Baltic Countries, Oct 1996, and supported by *European Commission (EC, #06633), International Monetary Fund (IMF, #14180), OECD (#17693), Inter-American Centre for Tax Administrations (#11405)* and USA. Became operational 1 Mar 1997. Registered in accordance with Hungarian law. **Aims** Promote cooperation between tax administrations in the European region through sharing of experience and best practice; be a source of professional knowledge and expertise about practical tax administration issues. **Structure** General Assembly (annual); Executive Council; Secretariat. **Languages** English. **Staff** 11.00 FTE, paid. **Finance** Members' dues. **Activities** Networking/liaising; knowledge management/information dissemination; events/meetings. **Events** *General Assembly* Zurich (Switzerland) 2022, *General Assembly* Budapest (Hungary) 2021, *General Assembly* Budapest (Hungary) 2020, *General Assembly* Brussels (Belgium) 2019, *General Assembly* Bratislava (Slovakia) 2018. **Publications** *IOTA Newsletter, Tax Tribune Magazine.* Reports, guides.
Members Full: tax administrations in 44 countries and territories:
Albania, Armenia, Austria, Azerbaijan, Belarus, Belgium, Bosnia-Herzegovina, Bulgaria, Croatia, Cyprus, Czechia, Denmark, Estonia, Finland, France, Georgia, Germany, Greece, Hungary, Ireland, Italy, Kazakhstan, Latvia, Lithuania, Luxembourg, Malta, Moldova, Montenegro, Netherlands, North Macedonia, Norway, Poland, Portugal, Romania, Russia, Serbia, Slovakia, Slovenia, Spain, Srpska, Sweden, Switzerland, UK, Ukraine. [2021/XD9029/**D**]

- ♦ INTRAH / see IntraHealth International
- ♦ IntraHealth International (internationally oriented national body)
- ♦ Intraocular Implant Club / see International Intra-Ocular Implant Club (#13948)

♦ Intraoperative Imaging Society (iOIS) 15994

Sec Dep of Neurosurgery, Univ Marburg, Biegenstr 10, 35037 Marburg, Germany.
Pres Dept of Neurosurgery, Univ Hosp Zurich, Frauenklinkstr 10, 8091 Zurich ZH, Switzerland. T. +41442553587. Fax +41442555741.
Sec Dept of Neurosurgery, Sheba Medical Ctr, 52621 Tel Hashomer, Israel. T. +97235302550. Fax +97235354413.
URL: http://www.intraopimaging.org/

Aims Provide a forum for comparison of alternate imaging techniques in the operating room, and the determination of their clinical efficacy. **Structure** Officers: President; Vice-President; Treasurer; Secretary. **Events** *Biennial Meeting* Houston, TX (USA) 2019, *Biennial Meeting* Hannover (Germany) 2017, *Biennial Meeting* Gurgaon (India) 2015, *Biennial Meeting* St Louis, MO (USA) 2013, *Biennial Meeting* Zurich (Switzerland) 2011. [2014/XJ1058/**C**]

- ♦ The Intrepid Foundation (unconfirmed)
- ♦ **INTROM** Inter-Islamic Network on Tropical Medicine (#11512)
- ♦ INTSH / see Anti-Smoking International Alliance (#00861)
- ♦ **INTS** International Neurotrauma Society (#14361)
- ♦ **INTS** International Nuclear Track Society (#14384)
- ♦ **INTUG** International Telecommunications Users Group (#15672)
- ♦ Intuition Network (internationally oriented national body)
- ♦ **INU** International Network of Universities (#14337)
- ♦ Inuit Circumpolar Conference / see Inuit Circumpolar Council (#15995)

♦ Inuit Circumpolar Council (ICC) 15995

Conseil circumpolaire inuit – Council Circumpolar Inuit – Inuit Isittormiut Siunnersuisogatigiiffiat

Pres PO Box 204, 3900 Nuuk Greenland, Denmark. T. +299323632. Fax +299323001. E-mail: iccgreenland@inuit.org.
Head of Secretariat address not obtained.
URL: http://www.inuit.org/

History Jun 1977, Barrow AK (USA), during 1st Conference, when interim *'Inuit Circumpolar Committee'* appointed to develop Charter. Original title: *Inuit Circumpolar Conference (ICC) – Conférence circumpolaire inuit – Conferencia Circumpolar Inuit – Inuit Isittormiut Kattuffiat.* **Aims** Strengthen unity among Inuit of the circumpolar region; promote Inuit *rights* and interests on an international level; develop and encourage long-term policies that safeguard the Arctic *environment*; seek full and active partnership in the political, economic and social development of circumpolar regions. **Structure** General Assembly (every 4 years); Executive Council. **Languages** English, Inuktitut, Inupiaq, Kalaallisut, Russian, Yup'ik languages. **Staff** 7.00 FTE, paid. **Finance** Funds from members, public and private foundations. **Activities** Projects/programmes; politics/policy/regulatory. **Events** *Triennial General Assembly* Inuvik, NT (Canada) 2014, *Triennial General Assembly* Inuvik, NT (Canada) 2014, *Triennial General Assembly* Nuuk (Greenland) 2010, *Triennial General Assembly* Barrow, AK (USA) 2006, *Triennial General Assembly* Kuujjuaq, QC (Canada) 2002. **Publications** *ICC Arctic Policy Review.* Declarations.
Members Official delegates representing about 160,000 Inuit people from each of 4 countries and territories:
Alaska, Canada, Greenland, Russia.
Consultative Status Consultative status granted from: *ECOSOC (#05331)* (Special); *UNEP (#20299).* **IGO Relations** Permanent Participant in: *Arctic Council (#01097); Emergency, Prevention, Preparedness and Response (EPPR, #05437); Standing Committee of Parliamentarians of the Arctic Region (SCPAR, #19958).* Accredited by: *International Whaling Commission (IWC, #15879); United Nations Framework Convention on Climate Change – Secretariat (UNFCCC, #20564).* 4-year mandate on: *Global Action Plan for Environment and Development in the 21st Century (Agenda 21, inactive).* **NGO Relations** Founding member of: *NGO Forum on Environment (FOE, #17125).* Member of: *Conference of Non-Governmental Organizations in Consultative Relationship with the United Nations (CONGO, #04635); International Union for Circumpolar Health (IUCH, #15764); International Union for Conservation of Nature and Natural Resources (IUCN, #15766).* Permanent Participant of: *Circumpolar Biodiversity Monitoring Program (CBMP, #03941).* Partner of: *Many Strong Voices (MSV, #16568).* [2016/XD3603/**F**]

- ♦ Inuit Isittormiut Kattuffiat / see Inuit Circumpolar Council (#15995)
- ♦ Inuit Isittormiut Siunnersuisogatigiiffiat (#15995)
- ♦ Inuit Pisinnaatitaaffiinut Instituti (internationally oriented national body)
- ♦ INUNDV / see International Council for the Day of VESAK (#13012)
- ♦ **INURA** International Network for Urban Research and Action (#14338)
- ♦ Inuvialuit Game Council, Canada (internationally oriented national body)

♦ Invadosome Consortium (IvC) 15996

Co-Pres address not obtained.
Co-Pres address not obtained.
URL: http://invadosomes.org/

History 2007. **Structure** General Assembly; Board. Offices in: Germany; USA. **Activities** Events/meetings. **Events** *Meeting* Sète (France) 2022, *Meeting* Roehampton (UK) 2019.
Members Individuals in 18 countries:
Australia, Belgium, Brazil, Canada, Czechia, France, Germany, Israel, Italy, Japan, Korea Rep, Luxembourg, Netherlands, Poland, Spain, Switzerland, UK, USA. [2022.10.13/AA0304/v/**C**]

- ♦ Invasive Bacterial Infections Surveillance Network / see European Invasive Bacterial Diseases Surveillance Network (#07598)
- ♦ Inveneo (internationally oriented national body)
- ♦ Inverse Problems International Association (unconfirmed)
- ♦ Invest Africa (unconfirmed)
- ♦ Investeringsfonden for Østlandene (internationally oriented national body)
- ♦ Investeringsfonden for Udviklingslande (internationally oriented national body)
- ♦ **Invest Europe** Invest Europe – The Voice of Private Capital (#15997)

♦ Invest Europe – The Voice of Private Capital (Invest Europe) 15997

SG Bastion Tower, Place du Champ de Mars 5, 1050 Brussels, Belgium. T. +3227150020. Fax +3227250704. E-mail: info@investeurope.eu.
URL: http://www.investeurope.eu/

History Founded 1983, Brussels (Belgium), when statutes were adopted, following Seminar, Jun 1982, organized by the Commission of the European Communities (currently European Commission). Original title: *European Venture Capital Association – Association européenne de capital à risque.* Previously also referred to in French as *Association européenne du capital investissement.* Subsequently changed title to *European Private Equity and Venture Capital Association (EVCA) – Association européenne de capital investissement et capital risque.* Statutes approved 30 Jul 1984. Current title adopted 1 Oct 2015. Registered in accordance with Belgian law. European Transparency Register: 60975211600-74. **Aims** Shape the future direction of the industry while promoting it to stakeholders such as entrepreneurs, business owners and employee representatives; explain private equity to the public and help shape public policy so that members can conduct their business effectively; develop the industry's professional standards, demanding accountability, good governance and transparency from members; spread best practice. **Structure** General Assembly (annual); Board of Directors; Executive Committee. Operating Committees (4): Investor Relations; Professional Standards; Tax and Legal; National Associations. **Languages** English, French, German. **Staff** 25.00 FTE, paid. **Finance** Members' dues. Other sources: registration for conferences and training courses; sponsorship. **Activities** Training/education; events/meetings. **Events** *Venture Capital Forum* Paris (France) 2019, *CFO Forum* Lisbon (Portugal) 2018, *Venture Capital Forum* Paris (France) 2018, *CFO Forum* Berlin (Germany) 2017, *Meeting* Brussels (Belgium) 2017. **Publications** Annual Report; guides to regulation; activity data. **Members** Full covers the full range of private equity activity, from early-stage venture capital to the largest private equity firms, investors such as pension funds, insurance companies, fund-of-funds and family offices. Associate members from related professions. Member firms (over 650) and affiliate members (500). Membership countries not specified. **NGO Relations** Member of: *International Employee Stock Option Coalition (no recent information).* [2020.03.03/XD9599/**D**]

- ♦ Investigación y Aplicación de Financiamientos Alternativos al Desarrollo / see Fondation RAFAD – Recherches et applications de financements alternatifs au développement (#09827)
- ♦ Investigaciones Cooperativas del Caribe y Regiones Adyacentes (inactive)
- ♦ Investigations coopératives dans les Caraïbes et les régions adjacentes (inactive)
- ♦ Investimentos, Comércio e Turismo de Portugal / see aicep Portugal Global – Trade and Investment Agency
- ♦ Investment Analysts Society of Southern Africa (internationally oriented national body)
- ♦ Investment Casting Institute (internationally oriented national body)

♦ Investment Climate Facility for Africa (ICF) 15998

CEO 2nd Floor, 50 Mirambo Street, PO Box 9114, Dar es Salaam, Tanzania UR. T. +255222129211. Fax +255222129210. E-mail: info@icfafrica.org.
Communications Manager address not obtained.
URL: http://www.icfafrica.org/

History Publicly launched Jun 2006, Cape Town (South Africa), at *World Economic Forum (WEF, #21367)* Africa Summit. Agreement with Tanzanian government signed, Apr 2007, to establish headquarters in Dar es Salaam (Tanzania UR). **Aims** Improve the climate for investment in Africa by removing barriers to doing business. **Structure** Board; Management Team. **Languages** English. **Staff** 14.00 FTE, paid. **Finance** Funding from African governments, and development and corporate partners. **Activities** Financial and/or material support. Active in: Burkina Faso, Cape Verde, Côte d'Ivoire, Ethiopia, Kenya, Lesotho, Liberia, Mali, Mauritius, Mozambique, Nigeria, Rwanda, Sao Tomé-Principe, Senegal, Seychelles, Sierra Leone, South Africa, Tanzania UR, Togo, Tunisia, Zambia. **Publications** Annual Report. **IGO Relations** Cooperates with: *Common Market for Eastern and Southern Africa (COMESA, #04296); East African Community (EAC, #05181); Organisation pour l'Harmonisation en Afrique du Droit des Affaires (OHADA, #17806).* [2016.10.19/XJ8428/**F***]

- ♦ Investment Fund for Central and Eastern Europe (internationally oriented national body)
- ♦ Investment Fund for Developing Countries (internationally oriented national body)

♦ Investment Migration Council (IMC) 15999

Contact Rue Maunoir 16, 1211 Geneva, Switzerland. T. +41225331333. E-mail: info@investmentmigration.org.
URL: http://investmentmigration.org/

History Registration: Swiss Civil Code, Start date: Oct 2014, Switzerland. **Aims** Improve public understanding of the issues faced by clients and governments in the area of investor migration and citizenship-by-investment; promote education and high professional standards among members. **Structure** Governing Board; Advisory Committee. **Languages** English, French. **Staff** 4.50 FTE, paid. **Finance** Sources: members' dues. **Activities** Events/meetings; projects/programmes; research/documentation. **Events** *Investment Migration Forum* Brussels (Belgium) 2022, *Investment Migration Forum* 2021, *Investment Migration Forum* Geneva (Switzerland) 2017. **Publications** *IM Yearbook* (annual) in English – A global reference tool for the industry by the industry, providing comprehensive, in-depth information about the global Investment Migration industry.; *IMC Bulletin. Investment Migration Policy Briefs; Investment Migration Research Papers.* Working papers; reports.
Members Active (over 300) in 40 countries and territories:
Antigua-Barbuda, Australia, Austria, Belgium, Canada, China, Croatia, Cyprus, France, Germany, Grenada, Hong Kong, Hungary, India, Indonesia, Ireland, Italy, Japan, Latvia, Libya, Liechtenstein, Malaysia, Malta, Netherlands, Norway, Panama, Poland, Portugal, Romania, Russia, Serbia, Singapore, South Africa, Spain, St Kitts-Nevis, St Lucia, Switzerland, UK, Ukraine, USA. [2022.06.23/XM5546/**C**]

- ♦ Investment, Trade and Tourism of Portugal / see aicep Portugal Global – Trade and Investment Agency
- ♦ Investor Group on Climate Change (internationally oriented national body)
- ♦ Invitación a la Vida (#16000)
- ♦ Invitation to Life International (#16000)

♦ Invitation à la vie internationale 16000

Invitation to Life International – Invitación a la Vida

Secretariat 26 rue des Peupliers, 92100 Boulogne, France. T. +33146082364. E-mail: ivi.france@gmail.com.

URL: http://www.invitation-a-la-vie.org/
History Founded 1983, France, by Yvonne Trubert, as 'Invitation à la vie internationale'. **Aims** Promote the application of *Christian Love* to modern life. **Structure** General Assembly (annual); Executive Committee of up to 4 members. **Finance** Members' dues. **Events** *Great Gathering* Colombia 2008, *Great Gathering* Mexico 2005, *Great Gathering* Brazil 2002, *Great Gathering* France 1999.
Members Founding members (4) in 4 countries:
Belgium, France, Germany, Netherlands. [2014/XD4405/**F**]

♦ INVITROM – International Society for In Vitro Methods (unconfirmed)
♦ INVSR – Inter-Islamic Network on Veterinary Science Research, Khartoum (unconfirmed)
♦ **INWA** International Nordic Walking Federation (#14375)
♦ **INWAT Europe** International Network of Women Against Tobacco – Europe (#14344)
♦ **INWAT** International Network of Women Against Tobacco (#14343)
♦ **INWEPF** International Network for Water and Ecosystem in Paddy Fields (#14340)
♦ **INWES** International Network of Women Engineers and Scientists (#14345)
♦ **INWF** Prospera – International Network of Women's Funds (#18545)
♦ **INWRDAM** Inter-Islamic Network on Water Resources Development and Management (#11513)
♦ **INWR** International Network for Whaling Research (#14342)
♦ **INWTC** International Network of Water Training Centres (#14341)
♦ **INZA** International Natural Zeolite Association (#14218)
♦ **IO3C** International Ozone Commission (#14495)
♦ IOA / see ISITC
♦ IOAAP – International Organization for the Advancement of Africa Policy (unconfirmed)
♦ **IOAG** Interagency Operations Advisory Group (#11389)
♦ **IOA** International Olympic Academy (#14406)
♦ IOA – International Ombudsman Association (internationally oriented national body)
♦ **IOA** International Opticians Association (#14415)
♦ IOA – International Optoelectronics Association (inactive)
♦ **IOA** International Orthoptic Association (#14489)
♦ **IOA** International Ostomy Association (#14491)
♦ IOA – International Ostrich Association (no recent information)
♦ **IOA** International Ozone Association (#14494)
♦ IOAP / see Bureau international d'audiophonologie (#03362)
♦ **IOAPA** International Olympic Academy Participants' Association (#14407)
♦ **IOAPT** International Organisation of Aquatic Physical Therapists (#14423)
♦ IOAR – International Organization for Aid to Revolutionaries (inactive)

♦ IOAS 16001

Exec Dir Operations 122 1/2 North Broadway, Fargo ND 58102, USA. T. +17013533353. E-mail: info@ioas.org.
URL: http://www.ioas.org/
History 1997. Founded *IFOAM – Organics International (IFOAM, #11105).* Currently only known under its acronym. Former names and other names: *International Organic Accreditation Service (IOAS)* – former (1997). Registration: USA, North Dakota. **Aims** Stimulate the organic and other *eco-labels* market by providing a transparent and respected system of accreditation and assessment against nationally and internationally-agreed standards. **Structure** Board; Committees. **Languages** English. **Staff** 14.00 FTE, paid. **Finance** Sources: fees for services. **Activities** Certification/accreditation; monitoring/evaluation; standards/guidelines. . **Publications** *IOAS Newsletter.* Annual report. **NGO Relations** Member of (2): *Asia Pacific Accreditation Cooperation (APAC, #01816); International Accreditation Forum (IAF, #11584).* Cooperates with (1): *IFOAM – Organics International (IFOAM, #11105).* [2018.09.05/XG9426/**F**]

♦ **IOAT** International Organization Against Trachoma (#14436)
♦ IOB / see International Brewers' Guild
♦ IOBB – International Organization for Biotechnology and Bioengineering (no recent information)
♦ IOBC / see International Organisation for Biological Control (#14424)
♦ **IOBC** International Organisation for Biological Control (#14424)
♦ **IOBCr** International Organization for Biological Crystallization (#14438)
♦ IOB – Instituut voor Ontwikkelingsbeleid en -beheer, Universiteit Antwerpen (internationally oriented national body)
♦ **IOB** Internationale Organisation für naturnahe Badegewässer (#14457)
♦ IOCAFRICA – IOC Sub-Commission for Africa and the Adjacent Island States (see: #11496)
♦ **IOCA** International Olympic Collectors Association (#02677)
♦ **IOCARIBE** IOC Sub-Commission for the Caribbean and Adjacent Regions (#16003)
♦ **IOCCG** International Ocean Colour Coordinating Group (#14392)
♦ IOCC – International Office of Cocoa and Chocolate (inactive)
♦ IOCC – International Orthodox Christian Charities (internationally oriented national body)
♦ IOC Committee for GOOS / see Intergovernmental Committee for the Global Ocean Observing System (#11473)
♦ **IOCD** International Organization for Chemical Sciences in Development (#14440)
♦ IOCEA – IOC Regional Committee for the Central Eastern Atlantic (inactive)
♦ **IOCE** International Organisation for Cooperation in Evaluation (#14426)
♦ IOCE – International Organization on Computer Evidence (inactive)
♦ **IOCES** Indian Ocean Comparative Education Society (#11159)
♦ IOC-FAO Intergovernmental Panel on Harmful Algal Blooms / see IOC Intergovernmental Panel on Harmful Blooms (#16002)
♦ **IOCG** International Organization for Crystal Growth (#14443)
♦ IOC Group of Experts on the Global Sea-Level Observing System (see: #11496)
♦ IOCHC / see Medicus Mundi International – Network Health for All (#16636)
♦ IOCHS / see Organization for Industrial, Spiritual and Cultural Advancement International (#17872)
♦ **IOC** Indian Ocean Commission (#04236)
♦ IOCINDIO – IOC Regional Committee for the Central Indian Ocean (see: #11496)
♦ **IOC** Intergovernmental Oceanographic Commission (#11496)

♦ IOC Intergovernmental Panel on Harmful Blooms (IPHAB) 16002

Groupe intergouvernemental COI chargé d'étudier les efflorescences algales nuisibles
Technical Sec IOC Science and Communication Centre on Harmful Algae, Univ of Copenhagen, Universitetsparken 4, 2100 Copenhagen, Denmark. T. +4523260246. E-mail: h.enevoldsen@unesco.org.
Contact c/o IOC, UNESCO, 7 place de Fontenoy, Cedex 07 SP, 75352 Paris, France. T. +33145680318. E-mail: hab.ioc@unesco.org.
URL: http://www.ioc-unesco.org/hab/
History Founded by *Intergovernmental Oceanographic Commission (IOC, #11496)* and *FAO (#09260)*, following resolution XVI-4 of IOC Assembly, 7-21 Mar 1991, Paris. Former names and other names: *IOC-FAO Intergovernmental Panel on Harmful Algal Blooms* – former; *Groupe intergouvernemental COI-FAO chargé d'étudier les efflorescences algales nuisibles* – former. **Aims** Foster effective management of, and scientific research on, harmful algal blooms in order to understand their causes, predict their occurrence and mitigate their effects. **Structure** Officers: Chair; Vice-Chair; Technical Secretary. **Languages** English. **Staff** 1.50 FTE, paid. **Finance** Funded by IOC member states. **Activities** Guidance/assistance/consulting; knowledge management/information dissemination; monitoring/evaluation; projects/programmes; research and development. **Events** *Session* Paris (France) 2019, *Session* Paris (France) 2017, *Session* Paris (France) 2015, *Session* Paris (France) 2013, *Session* Paris (France) 2011.
Members Representatives of 30 IOC member states:
Brazil, Canada, Chile, Colombia, Croatia, Cuba, Denmark, Egypt, Finland, France, Germany, India, Iran Islamic Rep, Italy, Japan, Malaysia, Mexico, Morocco, Namibia, New Zealand, Nigeria, Norway, Philippines, Slovenia, Spain, Sweden, Tunisia, UK, Uruguay, USA.
IGO Relations Close liaison with: *IOC Sub-Commission for the Caribbean and Adjacent Regions (IOCARIBE, #16003); IOC Sub-Commission for the Western Pacific (WESTPAC, see: #11496); ICES-IOC Working Group on the Dynamics of Harmful Algae Blooms.* Represented in membership: *International Atomic Energy Agency (IAEA, #12294); WHO (#20950).* **NGO Relations** Represented in membership: *IOC Science and Communication Centre on Harmful Algae (see: #11496).* [2020.08.27/XE3195/**E***]

♦ IOC – International Oat Conference (meeting series)
♦ **IOC** International Olive Council (#14405)
♦ **IOC** International Olympic Committee (#14408)
♦ **IOC** International Ornithological Congress (#14486)
♦ IOC / see International Ornithologists' Union (#14487)
♦ IOCLP – International Organization for Consultation-Liaison Psychiatry (inactive)
♦ **IOCOM** International Organization for Collaborative Outcome Management (#14442)
♦ IOCOMSA / see International Organization for Collaborative Outcome Management (#14442)
♦ IOC Regional Committee for the Central Eastern Atlantic (inactive)
♦ IOC Regional Committee for the Central Indian Ocean (see: #11496)
♦ IOC Regional Committee for the Western Indian Ocean (inactive)
♦ IOC Science and Communication Centre on Harmful Algae (see: #11496)
♦ IOCS – Institute for Ocean Conservation Science (internationally oriented national body)
♦ IOC Sub-Commission for Africa and the Adjacent Island States (see: #11496)

♦ IOC Sub-Commission for the Caribbean and Adjacent Regions (IOCARIBE) 16003

Sous-commission de la COI pour la mer des Caraïbes et les régions adjacentes – Subcomisión de la COI para el Caribe y Regiones Adyacentes
Sec UNESCO IOC Regional Secretariat, Ed Chambacu – Cra 3B 26-78, Apartado Aéro 1108, Cartagena de Indias, Bolivar, Colombia. T. +5756640955. Fax +5756640288.
Chair c/o NOAA, Southeast Fisheries Science Center – Natl Marine Fisheries Svc SE Miami Lab, 75 Virginia Beach Drive, Miami FL 33149, USA. T. +13053614264. Fax +13053614219.
URL: http://iocaribe.ioc-unesco.org/
History Nov 1982, by *Intergovernmental Oceanographic Commission (IOC, #11496)*, as successor to *IOC Association for the Caribbean and Adjacent Regions – Association COI pour la mer des Caraïbes et les régions adjacentes – Asociación COI para el Caribe y Regiones Adyacentes*, set up Nov 1975, by Resolution IX-13 of the 9th session of the IOC, itself successor to *Cooperative Investigations of the Caribbean and Adjacent Areas (CICAR, inactive)*, created by IOC in 1968 for a 6-year period. **Aims** Promote, develop and coordinate IOC's global scientific and research programmes and ocean services in the Caribbean region and adjacent regions; consider IOC's priorities and follow 3 main interactive lines of action: *oceans* and *climate*; ocean *ecosystems* science; *marine* science for integrated *coastal* area management. **Structure** Board of Officers; National Focal Points; Regional Secretariat. **Languages** English, Spanish. **Staff** 4.00 FTE, paid. **Finance** Supported by the Colombian Government and by the following international organizations: *Canadian International Development Agency (CIDA, inactive); European Commission (EC, #06633); Global Environment Facility (GEF, #10346); International Bank for Reconstruction and Development (IBRD, #12317)*; IOC; *Norwegian Agency for Development Cooperation (Norad); Swedish International Development Cooperation Agency (Sida); United States Agency for International Development (USAID).* **Activities** Research and development; knowledge management/information dissemination; projects/programmes; monitoring/evaluation. **Events** *Session* Panama (Panama) 2013, *Session* Miami, FL (USA) 2011, *Session* Puerto La Cruz (Venezuela) 2008, *Session* Cartagena de Indias (Colombia) 2006, *Session* Recife (Brazil) 2004. **Publications** *IOCARIBE News* (3-4 a year) in English, Spanish.
Members Governments of 30 countries and territories:
Antigua, Aruba, Bahamas, Barbados, Belize, Brazil, Colombia, Costa Rica, Cuba, Dominica, Dominican Rep, France, Grenada, Guatemala, Guyana, Haiti, Honduras, Jamaica, Mexico, Netherlands, Nicaragua, Panama, St Kitts-Nevis, St Lucia, St Vincent-Grenadines, Suriname, Trinidad-Tobago, UK, USA, Venezuela.
IGO Relations Regional component of: *Global Ocean Observing System (GOOS, #10511).* Cooperates with UN bodies: *FAO (#09260); International Atomic Energy Agency (IAEA, #12294); International Maritime Organization (IMO, #14102); UNDP (#20292); UNEP (#20299); UNESCO (#20322); United Nations Economic Commission for Latin America and the Caribbean (ECLAC, #20556); World Meteorological Organization (WMO, #21649).* **NGO Relations** Cooperates with: *Comité maritime international (CMI, #04192); Gulf and Caribbean Fisheries Institute (GCFI, #10823).* [2016.06.01/XE5376/**E***]

♦ IOC Sub-Commission for the Western Pacific (see: #11496)
♦ IOCU / see Consumers International (#04773)
♦ **IOCV** International Organization of Citrus Virologists (#14441)
♦ IOCWIO – IOC Regional Committee for the Western Indian Ocean (inactive)
♦ IODA – International Optimist Dinghy Association (see: #21760)
♦ **IODA** International Organization Development Association (#14444)
♦ IODE (internationally oriented national body)
♦ **IODE** International Oceanographic Data and Information Exchange (#14396)

♦ Iodine Global Network (IGN) 16004

Exec Dir 6016 1st Ave NW, Seattle WA 98017, USA. E-mail: info@ign.org.
Registered Office PO Box 51030, 375 des Epinettes, Ottawa ON K1E 3E6, Canada.
URL: https://www.ign.org/
History 1984. Founded with the acronym *ICCIDD.* Subsequently changed title to *International Council for Control of Iodine Deficiency Disorders (ICCIDD Global Network)*, when *Network for Sustained Elimination of Iodine Deficiency (Iodine Network, inactive)* merged with ICCIDD, 2012. Registration: Start date: 1986, Canada. **Aims** Be the authoritative voice for iodine *nutrition*; support and catalyze global and national iodine programmes, working with key public, private, scientific and civic stakeholders, and focusing on universal salt iodization as the most cost-effective and sustainable solution for prevention of iodine deficiency disorders. **Structure** Management Council; Board; Executive. Regions (10): Americas; Western and Central Europe; Eastern Europe and Central Asia; West and Central Africa; Southern Africa; Eastern Africa; Middle East and North Africa; South Asia; China and East Asia; South East Asia and Pacific. **Languages** Arabic, Chinese, English, French, Russian, Spanish. **Finance** Grants for core support and operations from: *Australian Aid (inactive); Canadian International Development Agency (CIDA, inactive); UNICEF (#20332).* Contracts for specific national assignments and international reviews. **Activities** Advocacy/lobbying/activism; awards/prizes/competitions; events/meetings; guidance/assistance/consulting; knowledge management/information dissemination. **Events** *Regional Workshop on Strengthening Monitoring Systems in Countries of South-Eastern Europe and Central Asia* Tbilisi (Georgia) 2018, *Regional Meeting* Pisa (Italy) 2012, *Regional Meeting* Zurich (Switzerland) 2012, *Regional Meeting* Boston, MA (USA) 2011, *Regional Meeting* Washington, DC (USA) 2010. **Publications** *IDD Newsletter* (4 a year); *Regional IDD Newsletter* (4 a year). *Towards the Global Elimination of Brain Damage Due to Iodine Deficiency* (2004); *SOS for a Billion II: The Conquest of Iodine Deficiency Disorders* (1998). Scientific monographs; technical manuals; training aids. Information Services: Global database on IDD control programmes is operational.
Members Individual professionals in 101 countries:
Albania, Algeria, Argentina, Armenia, Australia, Austria, Bangladesh, Belarus, Belgium, Benin, Bhutan, Bolivia, Bosnia-Herzegovina, Brazil, Bulgaria, Cameroon, Canada, Chile, China, Colombia, Congo Brazzaville, Congo DR, Croatia, Cuba, Czechia, Denmark, Djibouti, Ecuador, Egypt, El Salvador, Ethiopia, Fiji, Finland, France, Germany, Ghana, Greece, Guatemala, Guinea, Hungary, India, Indonesia, Iran Islamic Rep, Iraq, Israel, Italy, Jamaica, Japan, Jordan, Kazakhstan, Kenya, Laos, Lebanon, Lithuania, Madagascar, Malawi, Malaysia, Maldives, Mali, Mauritius, Mexico, Morocco, Myanmar, Nepal, Netherlands, Niger, Nigeria, Oman, Pakistan, Panama, Papua New Guinea, Paraguay, Peru, Philippines, Poland, Russia, Saudi Arabia, Senegal, Serbia, Slovakia, South Africa, Spain, Sri Lanka, Sudan, Sweden, Switzerland, Syrian AR, Tanzania UR, Thailand, Togo, Türkiye, Uganda, UK, Ukraine, United Arab Emirates, USA, Uzbekistan, Venezuela, Vietnam, Yemen, Zimbabwe.
Consultative Status Consultative status granted from: *ECOSOC (#05331)* (Roster); *WHO (#20950)* (Official Relations). **IGO Relations** Partners: *UNICEF (#20332); WHO (#20950).* **NGO Relations** Affiliated body of: *International Union of Nutritional Sciences (IUNS, #15796).* Partners include: *Every Woman Every Child (EWEC, #09215); European Salt Producers Association (EUsalt, #08425); Global Alliance for Improved Nutrition (GAIN, #10202); Kiwanis International (#16195); Salt Institute*; national associations. Member of: *PMNCH (#18410).* Working relationship with: *Thyroid Federation International (TFI, #20158)* and the regional associations: *Asia and Oceania Thyroid Association (AOTA, #01810); European Thyroid Association (ETA, #08913); Latin American Thyroid Society (LATS, #16390).* [2023/XC0077/v/**B**]

♦ **IoD** Institute of Directors (#11254)
♦ **IÖD** Internationale der Öffentlichen Dienste (#18572)
♦ IODMM – International Office of Documentation on Military Medicine (inactive)
♦ **IODP** International Ocean Discovery Program (#14393)

♦ **IOD World Class Association** International One Design World Class Association (#14412)
♦ IOED – International Organization for Educational Development (internationally oriented national body)
♦ IOE – Instituto por Oficialigo de Esperanto (inactive)
♦ **IOE** International Organisation of Employers (#14428)
♦ IOEMT – International Organization of Emergency Medical Technicians (unconfirmed)
♦ IOES – International Ophthalmic Exchange Society (inactive)
♦ IOFA / see International Organization of Folk Art (#14447)

♦ IO – Facilitating Space for Feminist Conversations (Io) 16005

Secretariat 3 Marunong Street, Barangay Central, 1100 Quezon City, Philippines. T. +6329281956 – +6329287785. Fax +6329241065. E-mail: hello@feminists.io.
URL: https://www.feminists.io/

History Nov 1974, Rome (Italy). Founded as an information and documentation centre with offices in Rome and Geneva (Switzerland). In 1980, the 2 offices became independent of one another, the Rome office retaining the title Isis International, while the Geneva office became *Isis Women's International Cross Cultural Exchange (ISIS-WICCE, #16031)*, based in Kampala (Uganda) since 1994. A third office *Isis Internacional, Santiago de Chile (#16030)* was established in Santiago (Chile) in 1984, to facilitate networking activities of Isis International in the Latin American and Caribbean region. In early 1990, the 3 offices became independent of each other and are now known as the 3 sister organizations. Secretariat located in Manila (Philippines) since 1991. Former names and other names: *Women's International Information and Communication Service (ISIS)* – former; *Service féminin international d'information et de communication* – former; *Servicio Femenino Internacional de Información y de Comunicación* – former; *Isis International* – former. Registration: Philippines. **Aims** Promote South-South and South-North dialogues to enhance *diversity* and collaboration within the global women's mouvement; strengthen growing *social justice* mouvements in the South. **Structure** General Assembly; Board of Trustees; Management Committee; Office of the Executive Director Team. **Staff** 19.00 FTE, paid. **Finance** Funded by partner donors and development agencies, including the following organizations listed in this Yearbook: *DANIDA*; *ICCO – Interchurch Organization for Development Cooperation*; *Norwegian Agency for Development Cooperation (Norad)*; *Oxfam International (#17922)*; *Oxfam Novib*; *Swedish International Development Cooperation Agency (Sida)*; *UNDP (#20292)*; *Unitarian Universalist Service Committee (UUSC)*; Global Ministries of *The United Methodist Church (UMC, #20514)*. **Activities** Advocacy/lobbying/activism; knowledge management/information dissemination; networking/liaising; research/documentation. **Events** *Conference on domestic violence in the Americas* Washington, DC (USA) 1997, *Conference on women empowering communication* Bangkok (Thailand) 1994. **Publications** *We!* (12 a year) – electronic and printed newsletter; *Info-Cache* (6 a year) – newsletter; *Women in Action (WIA)* (3 a year) – magazine. *Isis Book of Descriptors* – thesaurus of words or terms in multi-disciplinary scope related to women's issues. Books; occasional papers; media packs. **Information Services** *Human Resources Database (HuRes)*; *Watch-It !* – film review and forum; *Web-enabled Isis Library Management Automation System (WILMA)*; *Web-Hosting Service*. **Members** Individual and Organizational Membership. Network of over 50,000 contacts internationally. Membership countries not specified. **IGO Relations** *UNESCO (#20322)*; *United Nations Commission on the Status of Women (CSW, #20536)*; *United Nations Economic and Social Commission for Asia and the Pacific (ESCAP, #20557)*; *United Nations International Research and Training Institute for the Advancement of Women (UN-INSTRAW, inactive)*; *International Telecommunication Union (ITU, #15673)*; *Partners in Population and Development (PPD, #18247)*. **NGO Relations** Member of (3): *Asian Women's Resource Exchange (AWORC, no recent information)*; *ILGA World (International Lesbian, Gay, Bisexual, Trans and Intersex Association, #11120)*; *Just Net Coalition (JNC, #16173)*. [2020/XF5310/**F**]

♦ **IofC** Initiatives of Change International – Caux (#11213)
♦ **IOFI** International Organization of the Flavor Industry (#14446)
♦ **IOF** Internationale Orientierungslauf Föderation (#14485)
♦ **IOF** International Orienteering Federation (#14485)
♦ **IOF** International Osteoporosis Foundation (#14490)
♦ IOFM / see Islamic Countries Forensic Medicine Organization (#16042)
♦ **IOFOS** International Organization for Forensic Odonto-Stomatology (#14448)
♦ **IOGP** International Association of Oil and Gas Producers (#12053)
♦ IOGT International / see Movendi International (#16871)
♦ IOGT / see Movendi International (#16871)
♦ **IOHA** International Occupational Hygiene Association (#14391)
♦ IOHA – International Oral Health Association (unconfirmed)
♦ **IOHA** International Oral History Association (#14417)
♦ **IOHE** Inter-American Organization for Higher Education (#11442)
♦ IOHE – International Organization for Human Ecology (inactive)
♦ IOIAEA – Indian Ocean Islands Association for Environmental Assessment (inactive)
♦ IOIA / see International Organic Inspectors Association (#14421)
♦ **IOIA** International Organic Inspectors Association (#14421)
♦ **IOIBD** International Organization for the Study of Inflammatory Bowel Disease (#14475)
♦ IOIC – International Organization for Intellectual Cooperation (inactive)
♦ IOI – Independent Organization International (unconfirmed)
♦ **IOI** International Ocean Institute (#14394)
♦ **IOI** International Ombudsman Institute (#14411)
♦ IOI / see International Ozone Association (#14494)
♦ **Io** IO – Facilitating Space for Feminist Conversations (#16005)
♦ IOI-PI – International Ocean Institute – Pacific Islands (see: #14394)
♦ IOIRD – International Organization of Indigenous Resource Development (no recent information)
♦ **IOIS** International Ocular Inflammation Society (#14397)
♦ **iOIS** Intraoperative Imaging Society (#15994)
♦ IOJ – International Organization of Journalists (inactive)
♦ **IOJT** International Organization for Judicial Training (#14450)
♦ **IOK** Internationaal Olympisch Komitee (#14408)
♦ IOK / see International Olympic Committee (#14408)
♦ IOK – International Order of Kabbalists (religious order)
♦ **IOLDCs** International Organisation for Least Developed Countries (#14430)

♦ IOMAC Association 16006

Secretariat c/o Pedro Puig Adam s/n Edificio 7, Depto de Construcción e Ingeniera de Fabricación, Univ Oviedo, 33204 Oviedo, Asturias, Spain. E-mail: iomac@uniovi.es.
URL: https://www.iomac.info/

History 2015, Spain. Set up to run *International Operational Modal Analysis Conference (IOMAC)*. **Aims** Study, analyze, and apply operational modal analysis to all types of structures and mechanical systems. **Structure** General Assembly; Permanent Committee; Scientific Committee. **Activities** Events/meetings. **Events** *International Operational Modal Analysis Conference* Vancouver, BC (Canada) 2022, *International Operational Modal Analysis Conference* Copenhagen (Denmark) 2019, *International Operational Modal Analysis Conference* Ingolstadt (Germany) 2017. [2022/AA2485/c/**E**]

♦ IOMAC – International Operational Modal Analysis Conference (meeting series)
♦ IOMA – International Options Markets Association (inactive)
♦ **IOMA** International Oxygen Manufacturers Association (#14493)
♦ **IOMC** Inter-Organization Programme for the Sound Management of Chemicals (#15956)
♦ IOM Geneva Headquarters Staff Association / see IOM Global Staff Association Committee (#16008)
♦ IOM Geneva Staff Association / see IOM Global Staff Association Committee (#16008)

♦ IOM Global Migration Data Analysis Centre (GMDAC) 16007

Dir Taubenstr 20-22, 10117 Berlin, Germany. T. +493027877820 – +493027877821. Fax +493027877899. E-mail: gmdac@iom.int.
URL: http://gmdac.iom.int/

History Sep 2015, Berlin (Germany). Established at the invitation of the Government of Germany to respond to calls for better international migration data and analysis in order to inform migration governance, improve programming and promote a better public understanding of migration. Functions within *International Organization for Migration (IOM, #14454)*. **Aims** Strengthen the role of data in global migration governance (e.g. Global Compact for Migration, Sustainable Development Goals); support IOM Member States' capacities to collect, analyse and use migration data; promote evidence-based policies by compiling, sharing and analysing IOM and other sources of data. **Structure** Advisory Board; Team. **Languages** English. **Staff** 43.00 FTE, paid. **Activities** Capacity building; knowledge management/information dissemination; research/documentation; training/education. **Publications** *GMDAC Newsletter*. Data bulletins; Data Briefing series. [2022.10.19/XM6234/**E**]

♦ IOM Global Staff Association Committee (GSAC) 16008

Secretariat c/o IOM, Annex 1-108, Route des Morillons 15, CP 71, 1211 Geneva 19, Switzerland. T. +41227179229. E-mail: gsacmbx@iom.int.
URL: http://www.iom.int/

History Founded as *ICM Geneva Headquarters Staff Association*, to represent all staff at Geneva and Bern headquarters of *International Organization for Migration (IOM, #14454)*, plus officials at IOM's field offices. As *IOM Staff Association Committee (SAC)* represented Headquarter employees in Geneva and international staff worldwide. Previously also referred to as *IOM Geneva Headquarters Staff Association*; *IOM Geneva Staff Association*. Global Staff Association officially established, 19 Jun 2017 to replace former SAC. **Aims** Promote and safeguard the rights and defend the interests of IOM staff members by promoting improvement of conditions of employment, career development, and work and welfare; ensure conditions of employment and work to permit efficient performance and discharge of duties; promote harmonious working relations; serve as a channel of communication with the Administration; contribute towards achievement of the general objectives set up in the IOM Constitution. **Structure** Committee; Chairperson; Secretariat. **Languages** English, French, Spanish. **Finance** Members' dues. **Activities** Training/education. **Publications** *GSAC News*.
Members General Services, National Programme Officers and Professional (11,700) Staff of the International Organization for Migration in 172 IOM Member States:
Afghanistan, Albania, Algeria, Angola, Antigua-Barbuda, Argentina, Armenia, Australia, Austria, Azerbaijan, Bahamas, Bangladesh, Belarus, Belgium, Belize, Benin, Bolivia, Bosnia-Herzegovina, Botswana, Brazil, Bulgaria, Burkina Faso, Burundi, Cambodia, Cameroon, Canada, Cape Verde, Central African Rep, Chad, Chile, China, Colombia, Comoros, Congo Brazzaville, Congo DR, Cook Is, Costa Rica, Côte d'Ivoire, Croatia, Cuba, Cyprus, Czechia, Denmark, Djibouti, Dominica, Dominican Rep, Ecuador, Egypt, El Salvador, Eritrea, Estonia, Eswatini, Ethiopia, Fiji, Finland, France, Gabon, Gambia, Georgia, Germany, Ghana, Greece, Grenada, Guatemala, Guinea, Guinea-Bissau, Guyana, Haiti, Holy See, Honduras, Hungary, Iceland, India, Iran Islamic Rep, Ireland, Israel, Italy, Jamaica, Japan, Jordan, Kazakhstan, Kenya, Kiribati, Korea Rep, Kyrgyzstan, Laos, Latvia, Lesotho, Liberia, Libya, Lithuania, Luxembourg, Madagascar, Malawi, Maldives, Mali, Malta, Marshall Is, Mauritania, Mauritius, Mexico, Micronesia FS, Moldova, Mongolia, Montenegro, Morocco, Mozambique, Myanmar, Namibia, Nauru, Nepal, Netherlands, New Zealand, Nicaragua, Niger, Nigeria, North Macedonia, Norway, Pakistan, Palau, Panama, Papua New Guinea, Paraguay, Peru, Philippines, Poland, Portugal, Romania, Rwanda, Samoa, Sao Tomé-Principe, Senegal, Serbia, Seychelles, Sierra Leone, Slovakia, Slovenia, Solomon Is, Somalia, South Africa, South Sudan, Spain, Sri Lanka, St Kitts-Nevis, St Lucia, St Vincent-Grenadines, Sudan, Suriname, Sweden, Switzerland, Tajikistan, Tanzania UR, Thailand, Timor-Leste, Togo, Tonga, Trinidad-Tobago, Tunisia, Türkiye, Turkmenistan, Tuvalu, Uganda, UK, Ukraine, Uruguay, USA, Vanuatu, Venezuela, Vietnam, Yemen, Zambia, Zimbabwe.
Officials and Geneva employees (General Service Staff) of the International Organization for Migration in 8 Observer States:
Bahrain, Bhutan, Indonesia, Kuwait, Qatar, Russia, San Marino, Saudi Arabia.
NGO Relations Member of: *Federation of International Civil Servants' Associations (FICSA, #09603)*. [2019.03.22/XE1653/v/**E**]

♦ IOMHQ / see Holy Qu'ran Memorization International Organization (#10938)
♦ IOMICA – International One Metre International Class Association (see: #14687)
♦ **IOM** International Organization for Migration (#14454)
♦ **IOM** International Organization for Mycoplasmology (#14456)
♦ **IOM** Interoceanmetal Joint Organization (#15955)
♦ IOMMMS – International Organization of Materials, Metals and Minerals Societies (no recent information)
♦ **IOMP** International Organization for Medical Physics (#14453)
♦ **IOMS** International Organization for Masoretic Studies (#14452)
♦ IOMS – Islamic Organization for Medical Sciences (inactive)
♦ IOMSN / see International Organization of Multiple Sclerosis Nurses
♦ IOMSN – International Organization of Multiple Sclerosis Nurses (internationally oriented national body)
♦ IOM Staff Association Committee / see IOM Global Staff Association Committee (#16008)
♦ IOMTR – International Organization for Motor Trades and Repairs (inactive)
♦ **IONA** International Ophthalmic Nurses Association (#14414)
♦ **IONA** International Organization New Acropolis (#14458)
♦ **IONA** Organización Internacional Nueva Acrópolis (#14458)
♦ **IONC** International Ocean Noise Coalition (#14395)
♦ **ION** International Orality Network (#14418)
♦ **IONS** Institute of Noetic Sciences (#11284)
♦ IOOB – International Order of Old Bastards (internationally oriented national body)
♦ IOOC / see International Olive Council (#14405)
♦ IOOF – Independent Order of Odd Fellows (religious order)
♦ IOOL / see World Council of Optometry (#21335)
♦ **IOPB** International Organization of Plant Biosystematists (#14463)
♦ **IOPC Funds** International Oil Pollution Compensation Funds (#14402)
♦ **IOPER** International Offshore Petroleum Environmental Regulators (#14401)
♦ IOPHR – International Organisation to Preserve Human Rights (unconfirmed)
♦ IOPI – International Organization for Plant Information (no recent information)
♦ **IOP** International Organization of Palaeobotany (#14459)
♦ **IOP** International Organization of Psychophysiology (#14466)
♦ **IOPS** International Organisation of Pension Supervisors (#14432)
♦ **IOPS** International Organization for a Participatory Society (#14460)
♦ **IOPTMH** International Organization of Physical Therapists in Mental Health (#14461)
♦ **IOPTP** International Organisation of Physical Therapists in Paediatrics (#14433)
♦ **IOPTPWH** International Organization of Physical Therapists in Pelvic and Women's Health (#14462)
♦ IOPTWH / see International Organization of Physical Therapists in Pelvic and Women's Health (#14462)
♦ **IOQS** International Organization for Qumrân Studies (#14467)
♦ **IORA** Indian Ocean Rim Association (#11161)
♦ IOR-ARC / see Indian Ocean Rim Association (#11161)
♦ IORD – International Organization for Rural Development (inactive)
♦ IOREF – International Youth Reformation Organization (unconfirmed)
♦ **IORG** Indian Ocean Research Group (#11160)
♦ IORG – International Order of the Rainbow for Girls (internationally oriented national body)
♦ IORI – International Odonata Research Institute (internationally oriented national body)
♦ IORS – International Orders Research Society (inactive)
♦ IOSC – International Oil Spill Conference (meeting series)
♦ **IOSCO** International Organization of Securities Commissions (#14470)
♦ **IOSCS** International Organization for Septuagint and Cognate Studies (#14471)
♦ IOSDE – International Organization for Self-Determination and Equality (unconfirmed)
♦ IOSD – International Organization for Sustainable Development (internationally oriented national body)
♦ **IOSEB** International Organization for Systematic and Evolutionary Biology (#14479)
♦ **IOSF** International Otter Survival Fund (#14492)
♦ IOSGT – International Organization for the Study of Group Tensions (inactive)
♦ IOSHD – International Organization for the Study of Human Development (inactive)
♦ IOSH – Institution of Occupational Safety and Health (internationally oriented national body)

♦ **IOSH** International Order of Saint Hubertus (#14419)
♦ IOS – Institut für Ost- und Südosteuropaforschung (internationally oriented national body)
♦ **IOS** International Oak Society (#14388)
♦ IOS – International Observatory on Statelessness (internationally oriented national body)
♦ **IOS** International Orem Society for Nursing Science and Scholarship (#14420)
♦ **IOS** International Organization for Succulent Plant Study (#14477)
♦ **IOSN** International Open Source Network (#14413)
♦ **IOSOT** International Organization for the Study of the Old Testament (#14476)
♦ IOSTA – International Organization for Spice Trade Associations (internationally oriented national body)
♦ **IOSTE** International Organization for Science and Technology Education (#14469)
♦ **IOSTE** Organisation internationale pour l'éducation scientifique et technique (#14469)
♦ **IOSTE** Organización Internacional para la Educación Científica y Tecnológica (#14469)
♦ IOST / see International Social Tourism Organisation (#14889)
♦ IOSTT / see Organisation Internationale des Scénographes, Techniciens et Architectes de Théâtre (#17811)
♦ IOTA/ES – International Occultation Timing Association / European Section (unconfirmed)

♦ IOTA Foundation 16009

IOTA Stiftung

Chairman c/o Nextland, Strassburger Str 55, 10405 Berlin, Germany.
URL: https://www.iota.org/

History Registration: EU Transparency Register, No/ID: 500027331119-04, Start date: 9 Apr 2018. **Aims** Develop next generation protocols for the connected world. **Structure** Board of Directors; Supervisory Board; Executive Team. **NGO Relations** Member of (3): *Climate Ledger Initiative (CLI, #04017)*; *Eclipse Foundation (#05286)*; *International Association of Trusted Blockchain Applications (INATBA)*. [2021/AA1976/I/F]

♦ IOTA – Institut d'ophtalmologie tropicale africaine (inactive)
♦ **IOTA** International Occultation Timing Association (#14390)
♦ IOTA – International Orthodox Theological Association (internationally oriented national body)
♦ **IOTA** International Orthopaedic Trauma Association (#14488)
♦ **IOTA** Intra-European Organization of Tax Administrations (#15993)
♦ IOTA Stiftung (#16009)
♦ **IOTC** Indian Ocean Tuna Commission (#11162)
♦ **IOTC** International Olympic Truce Centre (#14409)
♦ **IOTF** International Olympic Truce Foundation (#14410)
♦ **IOT** Internationale van Oorlogstegenstanders (#20818)
♦ IOTOD – Improving Outcomes in the Treatment of Opioid Dependence Conference (meeting series)
♦ IOTO – Organisation touristique de l'Océan indien (no recent information)
♦ IOTPD – International Organization for the Transition of Professional Dancer (no recent information)
♦ **IOTS** International Organization for Targumic Studies (#14480)
♦ IOTTC – International Ophthalmology Teacher Training Council (internationally oriented national body)
♦ **IOTU Education and Science** International Organisation of Trade Unions of Educational and Scientific Workers (#14434)
♦ IOUC / see International Oracle Users Community (#14416)
♦ **IOUC** International Oracle Users Community (#14416)
♦ IOUF / see Intercultural Open University Foundation (#11466)
♦ **IOU** Intercultural Open University Foundation (#11466)
♦ **IOU** International Ornithologists' Union (#14487)
♦ IOVA – International Organization for Victim Assistance (internationally oriented national body)
♦ **IOV** Internationale Organisation für Volkskunst (#14447)
♦ IOVPT / see International Union for Vacuum Science, Technique and Applications (#15826)
♦ IOVS / see International Observatory of Violence in the School Environment (#14389)
♦ **IOVS** International Observatory of Violence in the School Environment (#14389)
♦ IOVST / see International Union for Vacuum Science, Technique and Applications (#15826)
♦ **IOV World** International Organization of Folk Art (#14447)
♦ IOWater / see International Office for Water (#14399)
♦ IOW – Institut für Ostseeforschung Warnemünde (internationally oriented national body)
♦ **IOW** International Office for Water (#14399)
♦ **IOWME** International Organization of Women and Mathematics Education (#14483)
♦ IOYR – International Organization of Youth with Rheumatism (inactive)
♦ IØ – Investeringsfonden for Østlandene (internationally oriented national body)
♦ **IP5** Five IP Offices (#09787)
♦ IPA / see Tube and Pipe Association International
♦ **IPACC** Indigenous Peoples of Africa Coordinating Committee (#11163)
♦ **IPACCMS** International Pan-Arab Critical Care Medicine Society (#14503)
♦ IPAC – International Particle Accelerator Conference (meeting series)
♦ **IPAC** International Personal Armour Committee (#14559)
♦ IPAC – International Pharmaceutical Aerosol Consortium (unconfirmed)
♦ **IPA CIS** Interparliamentary Assembly of Member Nations of the Commonwealth of Independent States (#15958)
♦ IPAC-RS – International Pharmaceutical Aerosol Consortium on Regulation and Science (internationally oriented national body)
♦ IPACS – Conrad Grebel College Institute of Peace and Conflict Studies (internationally oriented national body)
♦ IPACS – Institute of Peace and Conflict Studies, Waterloo ON (internationally oriented national body)
♦ **IPACS** International Physics and Control Society (#14579)
♦ IPADE / see IPADE Business School
♦ IPADE Business School (internationally oriented national body)
♦ IPADE – Instituto de Promoción y Apoyo al Desarrollo (internationally oriented national body)
♦ IPAEI – Institute for Public Administration and European Integration (internationally oriented national body)
♦ **IPA Europe** International Probiotics Association Europe (#14646)
♦ **IPAF** International Powered Access Federation (#14629)
♦ **IPAF** International Public AMC Forum (#14666)
♦ **IPAG** Institut panafricain de géopolitique (#11351)
♦ IPAID – Institute for Poverty Alleviation and International Development (internationally oriented national body)
♦ IPAI / see International Aluminium Institute (#11643)
♦ **IPAI** International Platform Against Isolation (#14598)
♦ iPAIN – International Pain Foundation (internationally oriented national body)
♦ IPA – Innovations for Poverty Action (internationally oriented national body)
♦ **IPA** International Palaeontological Association (#14501)
♦ **IPA** International Paleolimnology Association (#14502)
♦ IPA / see International Peace Institute (#14536)
♦ **IPA** International Pediatric Association (#14541)
♦ **IPA** International Permafrost Association (#14558)
♦ **IPA** International Phalaenopsis Alliance (#14563)
♦ **IPA** International Phonetic Association (#14573)
♦ **IPA** International Photodynamic Association (#14574)
♦ IPA – International Photographers Association (inactive)
♦ IPA – International Piezosurgery Academy (internationally oriented national body)
♦ IPA / see International Platinum Group Metals Association (#14602)
♦ **IPA** International Platinum Group Metals Association (#14602)
♦ IPA / see International Play Association (#14604)
♦ **IPA** International Play Association (#14604)
♦ **IPA** International Police Association (#14612)
♦ **IPA** International Pompe Association (#14618)
♦ **IPA** International Presentation Association (#14635)
♦ **IPA** International Press Association (#02868)
♦ **IPA** International Probiotics Association (#14645)
♦ **IPA** International Professional Pool Players' Association (#14648)
♦ **IPA** International Protea Association (#14659)
♦ **IPA** International Psychoanalytical Association (#14662)
♦ **IPA** International Psychogeriatric Association (#14664)
♦ IPA – International Psychohistorical Association (internationally oriented national body)
♦ **IPA** International Publishers Association (#14675)
♦ IPAIT – International Parliamentarians' Association for Information Technology (inactive)
♦ **IPALA** International Pediatric Academic Leaders Association (#14540)
♦ IPAM – Initiatives Pour un Autre Monde (internationally oriented national body)
♦ IPAM – Instituto de Pesquisa Ambiental da Amazônia (internationally oriented national body)
♦ **IPA** Parents International (#18198)
♦ **IPAP** Immunization Partners in Asia Pacific (#11131)
♦ IPARA – International Publishers Advertising Representatives Association (inactive)

♦ IPAS 16010

Pres/CEO PO Box 9990, Chapel Hill NC 27515, USA. T. +19199677052. Fax +19199290258. E-mail: media@ipas.org – info@ipas.org.
URL: http://www.ipas.org/

History 1973, Chapel Hill, NC (USA). Former names and other names: *International Projects Assistance Services* – former. **Aims** Reduce *maternal* morbidity and mortality in developing countries due to *abortion* complications; provide training programs for medical personnel in the manual vacuum aspiration abortion technique, with a focus on contraceptive follow-up. **Structure** Board of Directors. **Languages** English, French, Spanish. **Staff** 19.00 FTE, paid. **Activities** Training/education; guidance/assistance/consulting; projects/programmes. **Events** *Global safe abortion conference* London (UK) 2007. **Publications** *Advances in Abortion Care* – technical bulletin; *Initiatives* – newsletter. *Issues in Abortion Care* – series.
Members Organizations in 23 countries:
Bangladesh, Bolivia, Brazil, Chile, Ecuador, Ethiopia, Ghana, Guatemala, Kenya, Malawi, Mexico, Nicaragua, Nigeria, Paraguay, Peru, Romania, South Africa, Tanzania UR, Uganda, USA, Vietnam, Zambia, Zimbabwe.
Consultative Status Consultative status granted from: *ECOSOC (#05331)* (Special). **IGO Relations** *International Bank for Reconstruction and Development (IBRD, #12317)*; *Swedish International Development Cooperation Agency (Sida)*; *WHO (#20950)*. **NGO Relations** Member of: *Extractive Industries Transparency Initiative (EITI, #09229)*; *International Consortium for Emergency Contraception (ICEC, #12911)*; *NonProfit Organizations Knowledge Initiative (NPOKI)*; *PMNCH (#18410)*; *Abortion and Postabortion Care Consortium (APAC, #00007)*; *Reproductive Health Supplies Coalition (RHSC, #18847)*. Partner of: *Every Woman Every Child (EWEC, #09215)*. Supports: *DKT International*. [2021/XF4221/F]

♦ IPATH – International Professional Association for Transport & Health (internationally oriented national body)
♦ IPA Trust / see International Psychoanalytical Association (#14662)
♦ IPAVS / see EngenderHealth
♦ **IPBA** International Place Branding Association (#14587)
♦ **IPBA** Inter-Pacific Bar Association (#15957)
♦ **IPBES** Intergovernmental Science-Policy Platform on Biodiversity and Ecosystem Services (#11500)
♦ **IPBF** International Painful Bladder Foundation (#14499)
♦ IPBF – International Pony Breeders Federation (inactive)
♦ IPBFWG – International Plant Based Foods Working Group (unconfirmed)
♦ **IPB** International Peace Bureau (#14535)
♦ **IPBIS** International Paediatric Brain Injury Society (#14497)
♦ **IPBN** Indigenous Peoples' Biodiversity Network (#11164)
♦ IPC (internationally oriented national body)
♦ **IPCAA** International Pharmaceutical Congress Advisory Association (#14564)
♦ IPC Agreement – Strasbourg Agreement Concerning the International Patent Classification (1971 treaty)
♦ IPCA – Indo-Pacific Conservation Alliance (internationally oriented national body)
♦ IPCA / see International Energy Credit Association (#13271)
♦ IPCA / see International Pediatric Academic Leaders Association (#14540)
♦ **IPCA** International Physically Disabled Chess Association (#14577)
♦ **IPCA** International Prison Chaplains' Association (#14643)
♦ IPCAN / see Infection Control Africa Network (#11184)
♦ IPCC / see IP Multimedia Subsystems Forum
♦ **IPCC** Intergovernmental Panel on Climate Change (#11499)
♦ IPCCS – International Primary Care Cardiovascular Society foundation (unconfirmed)
♦ IPC European Committee / see European Paralympic Committee (#08140)
♦ IPC Groene Ruimte – Innovatie en Praktijk Centrum Groene Ruimte, Arnhem (internationally oriented national body)
♦ **IPC-IG** UNDP International Policy Centre for Inclusive Growth (#20289)
♦ **IPCI** Islamic Presentation Centre International (#16047)
♦ **IPC** International NGO/CSO Planning Committee for Food Sovereignty (#14365)
♦ **IPC** International Paralympic Committee (#14512)
♦ IPC – International Peace Centre, Sarajevo (internationally oriented national body)
♦ IPC – International Peace Commission (internationally oriented national body)
♦ IPC – International People's College (internationally oriented national body)
♦ **IPC** International Pepper Community (#14557)
♦ **IPC** International Personnel Certification Association (#14560)
♦ IPC – International Photographic Council (internationally oriented national body)
♦ IPC – International Police Commission (internationally oriented national body)
♦ **IPC** International Poplar Commission (#14619)
♦ **IPC** International Post Corporation (#14624)
♦ **IPC** International Poultry Council (#14628)
♦ IPC – International Press Centre (internationally oriented national body)
♦ IPC – International Programs Center (internationally oriented national body)
♦ IPC – International Prostitutes Collective (internationally oriented national body)
♦ **IPC** International Psoriasis Council (#14661)
♦ **IPCP** International Platform for Citizen Participation (#14599)
♦ **IPCRG** International Primary Care Respiratory Group (#14640)
♦ IPCRI / see Israel-Palestine: Creative Regional Initiatives
♦ IPCRI – Israel-Palestine: Creative Regional Initiatives (internationally oriented national body)
♦ **IPCSA** International Port Community Systems Association (#14623)
♦ IPCS – Institute of Peace and Conflict Studies (internationally oriented national body)
♦ IPCS – Institute of Postcolonial Studies (internationally oriented national body)
♦ IPCS / see International Federation of Pigment Cell Societies (#13512)
♦ **IPCS** International Plasma Chemistry Society (#14596)
♦ **IPCS** International Playing-Card Society (#14605)
♦ **IPCS** International Programme on Chemical Safety (#14650)
♦ IPC / see UNDP International Policy Centre for Inclusive Growth (#20289)
♦ **IPC Union** Union for the International Patent Classification (#20443)
♦ IPDA – International Private Drivers Association (inactive)
♦ IPDA – International Publishing Distribution Association (unconfirmed)
♦ IPDC – International Panel Data Conference (meeting series)
♦ **IPDC** International Programme for the Development of Communication (#14651)

- ♦ **IPDFA** International Pole Dance Fitness Association (#14609)
- ♦ **IPDGC** International Parkinson Disease Genomics Consortium (#14514)
- ♦ IPDI – Institute for Peace, Development and Integration (internationally oriented national body)
- ♦ IPD – Initiative for Policy Dialogue (internationally oriented national body)
- ♦ **IPD** Institut panafricain pour le développement (#18053)
- ♦ **IPDLN** International Population Data Linkage Network (#14620)
- ♦ IPDS – International Perinatal Doppler Society (inactive)
- ♦ **IPEA** Institut pontifical d'études arabes et d'islamologie (#18448)
- ♦ IPEALT / see Institut Pluridisciplinaire pour les Études sur les Amériques à Toulouse
- ♦ IPEAT – Institut Pluridisciplinaire pour les Études sur les Amériques à Toulouse (internationally oriented national body)
- ♦ **IPEBLA** International Pension and Employee Benefits Lawyers Association (#14555)
- ♦ IPEC-Americas – International Pharmaceutical Excipients Council of the Americas (internationally oriented national body)
- ♦ IPEC / see Para Equestrian (#05521)
- ♦ **IPEC Europe** International Pharmaceutical Excipients Council Europe (#14565)

♦ IPEC Federation 16011

Main Office Rue Marie de Bourgogne, 52, 1000 Brussels, Belgium. T. +3222137440. E-mail: info@ipec-federation.org.
URL: http://www.ipec.org/

History First created 1991, USA. Created under current title, Jan 2010, Cannes (France). Former names and other names: *International Pharmaceutical Excipients Council (IPEC)* – former. **Aims** Promote development of appropriate, scientifically valid, worldwide harmonized *regulations* of the inactive ingredients (excipients) in pharmaceutical formulations. **Structure** Board. **Finance** Each regional association has its own budget and dues structure. **Events** *China International Pharmaceutical Industry Forum* Beijing (China) 2012, *Joint seminar* Brussels (Belgium) 2006, *Regulatory affairs conference* Alexandria, VA (USA) 2003, *Symposium on macromolecules used as pharmaceutical excipients* Stockholm (Sweden) 1997, *Current and novel applications of excipients in pharmaceutical dosage forms – the challenge of the global market* Nice (France) 1994. **Publications** Position papers.
Members Organizations (5):
International Pharmaceutical Excipients Council Europe (IPEC Europe, #14565); International Pharmaceutical Excipients Council of the Americas (IPEC-Americas); IPEC China; IPEC India; IPEC Japan.
NGO Relations Member of (1): *International Council on Harmonisation of Technical Requirements for Registration of Pharmaceuticals for Human Use (ICH, #13027)* (Observer). [2021.05.31/XF3146/**F**]

- ♦ **IPEC+** International Programme on the Elimination of Child Labour and Forced Labour (#14652)
- ♦ IPEC / see IPEC Federation (#16011)
- ♦ IPEDA – Independant Pan European Digital Association (unconfirmed)
- ♦ **IPEEC** International Partnership for Energy Efficiency Cooperation (#14520)
- ♦ **IPEF** Indo-Pacific Economic Framework for Prosperity (#11170)
- ♦ **IPEF** Instituto Panamericano de Educación Fisica (#11348)
- ♦ **IPEG** International Pediatric Endosurgery Group (#14542)
- ♦ **IPEG** International Pharmaco EEG Society (#14569)
- ♦ IPEMB / see Institute of Physics and Engineering in Medicine
- ♦ **IPEMED** Institut de Prospective économique du Monde Méditerranéen (#11352)
- ♦ IPEM – Institute of Physics and Engineering in Medicine (internationally oriented national body)
- ♦ **IPEN** Instituto Panamericano de Engenharia Naval (#11349)
- ♦ **IPEN** International Pollutants Elimination Network (#14616)
- ♦ **IPES-Food** International Panel of Experts on Sustainable Food Systems (#14505)
- ♦ **IPES** International Police Executive Symposium (#14613)
- ♦ I and P Europe Imaging and Printing Association (internationally oriented national body)
- ♦ I and P Europe – I and P Europe Imaging and Printing Association (internationally oriented national body)
- ♦ IPEV – International Private Equity and Venture Capital Valuation Association (inactive)
- ♦ **IPFA** International Payments Framework Association (#14534)
- ♦ **IPFA** International Plasma and Fractionation Association (#14597)
- ♦ **IPFA** International Project Finance Association (#14654)
- ♦ IPFC / see Asia-Pacific Fishery Commission (#01907)
- ♦ **IPFD** International Partnership for Dogs (#14519)
- ♦ **IPFDS** International Pelvic Floor Dysfunction Society (#14551)
- ♦ IPFEO – Institut des producteurs de ferro-alliages d'Europe occidentale (inactive)
- ♦ IPF / see Federation of International Polo (#09675)
- ♦ IPF – Instituto Paulo Freire (internationally oriented national body)
- ♦ IPF – Instituto Politica Familiar Federación Internacional (internationally oriented national body)
- ♦ **IPF** International Parkour Federation (#14516)
- ♦ **IPF** International Pen Friends (#14554)
- ♦ IPF – International Polar Foundation (internationally oriented national body)
- ♦ **IPF** International Powerlifting Federation (#14630)
- ♦ **IPFP** IberoPanamerican Federation of Periodontics (#09328)
- ♦ **IPG/CF** International Physiotherapy Group for Cystic Fibrosis (#14581)
- ♦ **IPGH** Instituto Panamericano de Geografia e Historia (#18113)
- ♦ **IPG** International Practice Group (#14632)
- ♦ IPGRI / see Bioversity International (#03262)
- ♦ **IPGSA** International Pierre Gy Sampling Association (#14583)
- ♦ **IPGSA** International Plant Growth Substances Association (#14591)
- ♦ **IPHAB** IOC Intergovernmental Panel on Harmful Blooms (#16002)
- ♦ **iPHA** International Passive House Association (#14527)
- ♦ **IPHA** International Prestressed Hollowcore Association (#14638)
- ♦ **IPHA** International Professional Hunters Association (#14647)
- ♦ **IPHC** ICOMOS International Polar Heritage Committee (#11071)
- ♦ IPHC – International Pacific Halibut Commission (internationally oriented national body)
- ♦ IPHC – International Pentecostal Holiness Church (internationally oriented national body)
- ♦ IPHC – International People's Health Council (internationally oriented national body)
- ♦ IPHC – International Prostate Health Council (inactive)
- ♦ IPHD – International Partnership for Human Development (internationally oriented national body)
- ♦ **IPHE** International Partnership for Hydrogen and Fuel Cells in the Economy (#14521)
- ♦ **IPH** International Association of Paper Historians (#12066)
- ♦ IPHR – International Partnership for Human Rights (internationally oriented national body)
- ♦ IPIA – International Packaged Ice Association (internationally oriented national body)
- ♦ IPIA – International Pig Iron Association (inactive)
- ♦ IPIA – International Private Infrastructure Association (internationally oriented national body)
- ♦ IPIA – Inverse Problems International Association (unconfirmed)
- ♦ IPIC – International Physical Internet Conference (meeting series)
- ♦ IPIC – Treaty on the Protection of Intellectual Property in Respect of Integrated Circuits (1989 treaty)
- ♦ **IPIECA** International Petroleum Industry Environmental Conservation Association (#14562)
- ♦ **IPIFF** International Platform of Insects for Food and Feed (#14600)
- ♦ IPI – International Packaging Institute (internationally oriented national body)
- ♦ **IPI** International Peace Institute (#14536)
- ♦ **IPI** International Pharmacopuncture Institute (#14570)
- ♦ **IPI** International Potash Institute (#14626)
- ♦ **IPI** International Press Institute (#14636)
- ♦ IPILIR – Institute of International Public Law and International Relations of Thessaloniki (internationally oriented national body)
- ♦ IPIMIGEO – Instituto Panamericano de Ingeneria de Minas y Geologia (inactive)
- ♦ **IPIN** Instituto Panamericano de Ingenieria Naval (#11349)
- ♦ IPIS – Institute for Political and International Studies, Teheran (internationally oriented national body)
- ♦ IPIS – International Peace Information Service (internationally oriented national body)
- ♦ **IPITA** International Pancreas and Islet Transplant Association (#14504)
- ♦ **IPI-TBE** International Patient Information Board on Tick-Borne Encephalitis (#14532)
- ♦ **IPJET** International Platform of Jurists for East Timor (#14601)
- ♦ **IPJJ** Interagency Panel on Juvenile Justice (#11390)
- ♦ IPJ – Joan B Kroc Institute for Peace and Justice (internationally oriented national body)
- ♦ **IPJM** Instituto Internacional de Periodismo 'José Martí' (#11340)
- ♦ IP Justice (internationally oriented national body)
- ♦ IPLA / see Asociación Petroquimica y Quimica Latinoamericana (#02294)
- ♦ IPLAC – Instituto Pedagógico Latinoamericano y del Caribe (unconfirmed)
- ♦ IPLE – Institut für Produktives Lernen in Europa (internationally oriented national body)
- ♦ IPLI Foundation (unconfirmed)
- ♦ **IPLOCA** International Pipe Line and Offshore Contractors Association (#14586)
- ♦ IPMA / see International Public Management Association for Human Resources
- ♦ IPMA-HR – International Public Management Association for Human Resources (internationally oriented national body)
- ♦ IPMA – International Primary Market Association (inactive)
- ♦ IPMA – International Professional Managers Association (internationally oriented national body)
- ♦ **IPMA** International Project Management Association (#14655)
- ♦ IPMB Congress – International Congress of Plant Molecular Biology (meeting series)
- ♦ IPMEN – International Pacific Marine Educators Network (unconfirmed)
- ♦ IPMI – International Precious Metals Institute (internationally oriented national body)
- ♦ **IPM** Inner Peace Movement (#11220)
- ♦ IPM – International Conference for Integrated Pest Management for Cultural Heritage (meeting series)
- ♦ IPM-International – Institute of Psychotraumatology and Mediation (unconfirmed)
- ♦ IPM-International – Institut de Psychotraumatologie et Médiation (unconfirmed)
- ♦ **IPM** International Partners in Mission (#14526)
- ♦ **IPMN** International Public Management Network (#14668)
- ♦ IP/MPLS Forum / see Broadband Forum (#03334)
- ♦ **IPMSC** International Property Measurement Standards Coalition (#14656)
- ♦ **IPMSDL** Indigenous Peoples Movement for Self-determination and Liberation (#11165)
- ♦ IPMS – International Polar Motion Service (inactive)
- ♦ IPMT – Institute for the Preservation of Medical Traditions (internationally oriented national body)
- ♦ IPMU – International Conference on Information Processing and Management of Uncertainty (meeting series)
- ♦ IP Multimedia Subsystems Forum (internationally oriented national body)
- ♦ **IPMWC** International NGO Platform on the Migrant Workers' Convention (#14367)
- ♦ **IPNA** International Pediatric Nephrology Association (#14543)
- ♦ **IPNC** International Plant Nutrition Council (#14592)
- ♦ IPNDV – International Partnership for Nuclear Disarmament Verification (unconfirmed)
- ♦ **IPNEd** International Parliamentary Network for Education (#14518)
- ♦ **IPNFA** International Proprioceptive Neuromuscular Facilitation Association (#14658)
- ♦ **IPN** International Partnership Network (#14523)
- ♦ IPN – International Policy Network (internationally oriented national body)
- ♦ **IPNLF Africa** IPNLF Africa NPC (#14610)
- ♦ IPNLF Africa NPC (#14610)
- ♦ **IPNLF** International Pole and Line Foundation (#14610)
- ♦ IPNLF Maldives (#14610)
- ♦ **IPNLF-M** IPNLF Maldives (#14610)
- ♦ **IPNLF NL** Stichting International Pole and Line (#14610)
- ♦ IPOA / see International Stability Operations Association
- ♦ **IPO** International Pasta Organisation (#14528)
- ♦ **IPO** International Progress Organization (#14653)
- ♦ IPO – Istituto per l'Oriente Carlo Alfonso Nallino (internationally oriented national body)
- ♦ **IPOKRaTES** International Postgraduate Organization for Knowledge Transfer Research and Teaching Excellent Students (#14625)
- ♦ **IPONS** International Philosophy of Nursing Society (#14572)
- ♦ IPOP / see Global Strategies
- ♦ **IPOPI** International Patient Organization for Primary Immunodeficiencies (#14533)
- ♦ **IPOSC** International Pediatric Ophthalmology and Strabismus Council (#14544)
- ♦ **IPOS** International Psycho-Oncology Society (#14665)
- ♦ **IPPA** Indo-Pacific Prehistory Association (#11171)
- ♦ **IPPA** International Paediatric Pathology Association (#14498)
- ♦ **IPPA** International Panel Physicians Association (#14507)
- ♦ **IPPA** International Pectin Producers' Association (#14539)
- ♦ IPPA / see International Private Physical Therapy Association (#14644)
- ♦ **IPPA** International Public Policy Association (#14669)
- ♦ IPPA – International Public Procurement Association (inactive)
- ♦ IPPA / see International Public Procurement Conference (#14670)
- ♦ IPPCE – Initiative pour un Pacte Climat européen (unconfirmed)
- ♦ IPPC – International Penal and Penitentiary Commission (inactive)
- ♦ IPPC – International Plant Protection Convention, 1951 (1951 treaty)
- ♦ **IPPC** International Public Procurement Conference (#14670)
- ♦ **IPPC Secretariat** International Plant Protection Secretariat (#14595)
- ♦ **IPPF** Independent Power Producers Forum (#11153)
- ♦ **IPPF** International Penal and Penitentiary Foundation (#14553)
- ♦ **IPPF** International Planned Parenthood Federation (#14589)
- ♦ **IPPFoRB** International Panel of Parliamentarians for Freedom of Religion or Belief (#14506)
- ♦ IPPIA / see Plasma Protein Therapeutics Association (#18392)
- ♦ IPPIC / see World Coatings Council (#21283)
- ♦ IPPI – International Public Policy Institute (internationally oriented national body)
- ♦ **IPPL** International Primate Protection League (#14641)
- ♦ **IPPN** International Pediatric Peritoneal Dialysis Network (#14545)
- ♦ **IPPN** International Plant Phenotyping Network (#14593)
- ♦ **IPPN** International Porphyria Patient Network (#14621)
- ♦ IPPNO / see International Philosophers for Peace and the Elimination of Nuclear and Other Threats to Global Existence (#14571)
- ♦ **IPPNO** International Philosophers for Peace and the Elimination of Nuclear and Other Threats to Global Existence (#14571)
- ♦ **IPPNW** International Physicians for the Prevention of Nuclear War (#14578)
- ♦ **IPPS** International Parasitic Plant Society (#14513)
- ♦ IPPS – International Pelvic Pain Society (internationally oriented national body)
- ♦ **IPPS** International Plant Propagators' Society (#14594)
- ♦ **IPPTA** International Private Physical Therapy Association (#14644)
- ♦ IPR / see Austrian Study Centre for Peace and Conflict Resolution

♦ IPRA-CINDER – International Property Registries Association (IPRA-CINDER) 16012

Gen Sec c/ Diego de León 21 – 5a, 28006 Madrid, Spain. T. +34912701790. Fax +34915626737. E-mail: secretaria@cinder.info.
URL: http://ipra-cinder.info/

History 2 Dec 1972, Buenos Aires (Argentina). Former names and other names: *Centro Internacional de Derecho Registral (CINDER)* – former (1972); *International Centre of Registration Law* – former (1972). **Aims** Promote and foster the study of registration *law*. **Structure** General Assembly. **Languages** English, Spanish. **Activities** Events/meetings. **Events** *Congress* Costa Rica 2024, *Congress* Porto (Portugal) 2022, *Congress* Cartagena de Indias (Colombia) 2018, *Congress* Dubai (United Arab Emirates) 2016, *Congress* Santiago (Chile) 2014. **Publications** *IPRA-CINDER Newsletter.*

Members in 45 countries:
Angola, Argentina, Armenia, Belarus, Bolivia, Brazil, Canada, Cape Verde, Chile, Colombia, Costa Rica, Ecuador, El Salvador, England, France, Greece, Guatemala, Guinea-Bissau, Honduras, Italy, Latvia, Libya, Mexico, Morocco, Mozambique, Netherlands, Panama, Paraguay, Peru, Portugal, Puerto Rico, Romania, Russia, Sao Tomé-Principe, Scotland, Slovakia, Spain, Switzerland, Tunisia, Uganda, Ukraine, United Arab Emirates, Uruguay, USA, Venezuela. [2020.11.20/XU2521/E]

- ♦ **IPRA-CINDER** IPRA-CINDER – International Property Registries Association (#16012)
- ♦ IPRADA – International Peanut Research and Development Association (no recent information)
- ♦ **IPRA** International Peace Research Association (#14537)
- ♦ **IPRA** International Pension Research Association (#14556)
- ♦ IPRA – International Philosophy of Religion Association (unconfirmed)
- ♦ **IPrA** International Pragmatics Association (#14634)
- ♦ IPRA – International Property Rights Association (unconfirmed)
- ♦ **IPRA** International Public Relations Association (#14671)
- ♦ IPRAIS – International Pediatric Respiratory, Allergy and Immunology Society (no recent information)
- ♦ I Prasini sto Evropaiko Kinovulio / see Group of the Greens – European Free Alliance (#10781)
- ♦ IPRAS – International Confederation for Plastic, Reconstructive and Aesthetic Surgery (inactive)
- ♦ IPRCC – International Poverty Reduction Center in China (unconfirmed)
- ♦ IPRE – Institutul pentru Politici si Reforme Europene (internationally oriented national body)
- ♦ iPRES – International Conference on Digital Preservation (meeting series)
- ♦ IPRI – Instituto Português de Relações Internacionais (internationally oriented national body)
- ♦ **IPRI** International Prevention Research Institute (#14639)
- ♦ IPRI – Italian Peace Research Institute (internationally oriented national body)
- ♦ IPR – Institut Pierre Richet (no recent information)
- ♦ **IPR** Interregionaler Parlamentarier-Rat (#04696)
- ♦ IPRIS – Instituto Português de Relações Internacionais e Segurança (internationally oriented national body)
- ♦ IPRI-UNL / see Instituto Português de Relações Internacionais
- ♦ IPRM – International Conference on Indium Phosphide and Related Materials (meeting series)
- ♦ **IPRN** International Public Relations Network (#14672)
- ♦ **IPRP** International Pharmaceutical Regulators Programme (#14567)
- ♦ **IPRRG** International Pest Risk Research Group (#14561)
- ♦ IPS – Agence de presse du monde (#15964)
- ♦ IPS – Agencia de Prensa del Mundo (#15964)
- ♦ **IPSA** International Pediatric Sleep Association (#14547)
- ♦ **IPSA** International Political Science Association (#14615)
- ♦ **IPSA** International Professional Security Association (#14649)
- ♦ **IPS** Arctic Council Indigenous Peoples' Secretariat (#01098)
- ♦ **IPSASB** International Public Sector Accounting Standards Board (#14673)
- ♦ IPSCC – International PhD Student Cancer Conference (meeting series)
- ♦ **IPSC** International Practical Shooting Confederation (#14631)
- ♦ IPSE – Institute for European Social Protection (internationally oriented national body)
- ♦ IPSE – Institut de la protection sociale européenne (internationally oriented national body)
- ♦ IPSERA – International Purchasing and Supply Education and Research Association (internationally oriented national body)
- ♦ IPSFC – International Pacific Salmon Fisheries Commission (inactive)
- ♦ IPSF – Indigenous Peoples Survival Foundation (internationally oriented national body)
- ♦ IPSF – International Pacific Sports Federation (unconfirmed)
- ♦ **IPSF** International Pharmaceutical Students' Federation (#14568)
- ♦ **IPSF** International Pole Sports Federation (#14611)
- ♦ IPSF / see International Surfing League (#15631)
- ♦ **IPSG** International Patellofemoral Study Group (#14529)
- ♦ IPSHU / see Hiroshima Peace Institute
- ♦ IPSI / see Global Training and Development Institute
- ♦ IPSIA – Istituto Pace Sviluppo Innovazione ACLI (internationally oriented national body)
- ♦ **IPSI** International Partnership for the Satoyama Initiative (#14525)
- ♦ IPSI – International Peace and Security Institute (internationally oriented national body)
- ♦ IPSI – International Political Science Institute (inactive)
- ♦ **IPS** Imaging and Perimetric Society (#11125)
- ♦ IPS – Institute for Palestine Studies (internationally oriented national body)
- ♦ **IPS** Institute for Planetary Synthesis (#11287)
- ♦ IPS – Institute for Policy Studies, Singapore (internationally oriented national body)
- ♦ IPS – Institute for Policy Studies, Washington DC (internationally oriented national body)
- ♦ IPS – International Palm Society (internationally oriented national body)
- ♦ IPS / see International Peatland Society (#14538)
- ♦ **IPS** International Peatland Society (#14538)
- ♦ **IPS** International Peeling Society (#14550)
- ♦ **IPS** International Phycological Society (#14576)
- ♦ **IPS** International Phytotechnology Society (#14582)
- ♦ **IPS** International Planetarium Society (#14588)
- ♦ **IPS** International Primatological Society (#14642)
- ♦ **IPS** International Proteolysis Society (#14660)
- ♦ **IPS** International Pyrotechnics Society (#14676)
- ♦ IPS / see Inter Press Service (#15964)
- ♦ **IPS** Inter Press Service (#15964)
- ♦ IPS – Inter Press Service Asociación Internacional (#16013)
- ♦ IPS – Inter Press Service association internationale (#16013)
- ♦ IPS – Inter Press Service coopératif international / see IPS – Inter Press Service International Association (#16013)
- ♦ IPS – Inter Press Service Cooperativa Internacional / see IPS – Inter Press Service International Association (#16013)

♦ IPS – Inter Press Service International Association 16013

IPS – Inter Press Service association internationale – IPS – Inter Press Service Asociación Internacional

Dir-Gen IPS Headquarters, c/o FAO, Viale delle Terme di Caracalla, 00153 Rome RM, Italy. T. +39657050053. Fax +39657050052. E-mail: headquarters@ips.org.
Main: http://www.ips.org/

History 14 Apr 1964, as *IPS – Inter Press Service International Cooperative – IPS – Inter Press Service coopératif international – IPS – Inter Press Service Cooperativa Internacional.* Current title adopted in 2001, when became an international association. **Aims** Contribute to development by promoting free communication and a professional flow of information to reinforce technical and economic cooperation among developing countries, within the context of globalization and its impacts. **Structure** Ordinary General Meeting (annual); Board of Trustees; Board of Directors; Executive Committee; Other Committees (2). **Finance** Members' dues. Other sources: own revenues and revenues from governmental and inter-governmental organizations, including the following listed in this Yearbook: *Canadian International Development Agency (CIDA, inactive); DANIDA; Department for International Development Cooperation; Friedrich-Ebert-Stiftung (FES); Norwegian Agency for Development Cooperation (Norad); Oxfam Novib; Swedish International Development Cooperation Agency (Sida); UNEP (#20299); UNDP (#20292); UNICEF (#20332); United Nations Population Fund (UNFPA, #20612).* **Activities** Knowledge management/information dissemination; training/education; networking/liaising. **Events** *International conference for the reform of international institutions* Geneva (Switzerland) 2006, *Workshop on media and NGOs plan strategy for human rights drive in Great Lakes region* Kampala (Uganda) 1997, *European parliamentarian conference* Bonn (Germany) 1993. **Publications** *IPS Daily News Service* – on the activities of the United Nations; *IPS Daily Wire Service* in English, Spanish – selections in 10 other languages; *IPS Monthly Journal on the Group of 77.* Specialized bulletins (regularly). **Members** Individuals journalists and professional communicators with a specific interest in development; non-governmental organizations (). Members in 150 countries. Membership countries not specified. **Consultative Status** Consultative status granted from: *ECOSOC (#05331)* (General). **IGO Relations** Cooperates closely with the United Nations, its specialized agencies and many intergovernmental organizations including: *International Fund for Agricultural Development (IFAD, #13692).* Associated with Department of Global Communications of the United Nations. **NGO Relations** Cooperates with: *Alliance of Communicators for Sustainable Development (COMplus, #00669); Society for International Development (SID, #19581); South Commission (inactive).* Member of: *Conference of Non-Governmental Organizations in Consultative Relationship with the United Nations (CONGO, #04635); International Association for Media and Communication Research (IAMCR, #12022); World Social Forum (WSF, #21797).* Instrumental in setting up: *Women's Feature Service (WFS, #21017).* Memorandum of Understanding with: Supports: *Global Call for Action Against Poverty (GCAP, #10263).*
[2017.10.11/XF2515/F]

- ♦ IPS – Inter Press Service International Cooperative / see IPS – Inter Press Service International Association (#16013)
- ♦ **IPSO** International and European Public Services Organisation (#13311)
- ♦ **IPSO** International Pediatric Stroke Organization (#14548)
- ♦ **IPSO** International Psychoanalytical Studies Organization (#14663)
- ♦ **IPSO** International Society of Paediatric Surgical Oncology (#15341)
- ♦ **IPSP** International Panel on Social Progress (#14508)
- ♦ **IPS** Polish-Scandinavian Research Institute (#18420)
- ♦ IPSRG – International Plastic Surgery Residents Group (internationally oriented national body)
- ♦ **IPSS** International Pediatric Simulation Society (#14546)
- ♦ IPSTC – International Peace Support Training Centre (unconfirmed)
- ♦ IPS – Third World News Agency / see Inter Press Service (#15964)
- ♦ IPSUL – Initiative for Peace Studies in the University of London (internationally oriented national body)
- ♦ IPS – Welt Nachrichtenagentur (#15964)
- ♦ **IPSWG** International Portable Sanitation Working Group (#14622)
- ♦ IPS – World News Agency (#15964)
- ♦ IPTA – International Parcel Tankers Association (internationally oriented national body)
- ♦ **IPTA** International Pediatric Transplant Association (#14549)
- ♦ **IPTA** International PhotoTherapy Association (#14575)
- ♦ IPTC – International Particle Toxicology Conference (meeting series)
- ♦ IPTC – International Petroleum Technology Conference (meeting series)
- ♦ **IPTC** International Press Telecommunications Council (#14637)
- ♦ **IPTF** Indo-Pacific Theosophical Federation (#11172)
- ♦ **IPT-HOPE** International Physiotherapists for HIV/AIDS, Oncology, Palliative Care Empowerment (#14580)
- ♦ IPTIC / see Global Pulse Confederation (#10562)
- ♦ IPTI – International Police Training Institute (unconfirmed)
- ♦ **IPTI** International Property Tax Institute (#14657)
- ♦ IPTO – International Pet Trade Organization (inactive)
- ♦ **IPTOP** International Association for Physical Therapists Working with Older People (#12083)
- ♦ **IPTRN** International Polar Tourism Research Network (#14608)
- ♦ **IPU** Inter-Parliamentary Union (#15961)
- ♦ IPU – Islamic Press Union (inactive)

♦ IPv6 Forum 16014

President c/o Univ Luxembourg, Maison du Nombre, 6 Av de la Fonte, L-4364 Esch-sur-Alzette, Luxembourg.
URL: http://www.ipv6forum.com/

History 1999. Founded on the initiative of Latif Ladid. Registration: Luxembourg. **Aims** Promote IPv6 applications, websites, web servers and ISPs. **Activities** Certification/accreditation; events/meetings; awards/prizes/competitions.

Members Chapters in 63 countries and territories:
Australia, Belgium, Brazil, Canada, Chad, China, Colombia, Cuba, Denmark, Egypt, Estonia, Finland, France, Germany, Ghana, Greece, Grenada, Hong Kong, Hungary, India, Indonesia, Iran Islamic Rep, Ireland, Israel, Italy, Japan, Jordan, Korea Rep, Luxembourg, Malaysia, Mexico, Morocco, Netherlands, New Zealand, Nigeria, Norway, Oman, Pakistan, Palestine, Peru, Philippines, Poland, Portugal, Romania, Russia, Saudi Arabia, Senegal, Serbia, Singapore, Slovenia, Spain, Sudan, Sweden, Switzerland, Taiwan, Thailand, Tunisia, Türkiye, UK, United Arab Emirates, USA, Vietnam, Yemen. [2020/XM7623/F]

- ♦ IPV – Associazione Internazionale IUS Primi Viri (internationally oriented national body)
- ♦ IPVEA / see SOLARUNITED (#19677)
- ♦ IPV – Internationale Posaunenvereinigung (internationally oriented national body)
- ♦ **IPVS** International Papillomavirus Society (#14511)
- ♦ **IPVS** International Pig Veterinary Society (#14584)
- ♦ IPV Society / see International Papillomavirus Society (#14511)
- ♦ IPWH / see Workability International (#21049)
- ♦ IPW – International Probabilistic Workshop (meeting series)
- ♦ **IPWSO** International Prader-Willi Syndrome Organisation (#14633)
- ♦ IPYG – International Peace Youth Group (unconfirmed)
- ♦ IQd – Initiative for Quiet diplomacy (internationally oriented national body)
- ♦ **IQ International** Information Quality International (#11197)
- ♦ IQ / see International Quorum of Motion Picture Producers (#14680)
- ♦ **IQ** International Quorum of Motion Picture Producers (#14680)
- ♦ **IQKDF** International Qwan Ki Do Federation (#14682)
- ♦ **IQLA** International Quantitative Linguistics Association (#14678)
- ♦ **IQNet** International Certification Network (#12532)
- ♦ **IQSA** International Qajar Studies Association (#14677)
- ♦ **IQSA** International Quantum Structures Association (#14679)
- ♦ **IQSA** International Qur'anic Studies Association (#14681)

♦ IQsensato 16015

Contact address not obtained. T. +41223414819. Fax +41225457534.
URL: http://www.iqsensato.org/

Aims Shape international policy-making on development by harnessing research and analysis talent in and from *developing countries.* **Structure** General Assembly. Board of Directors, comprising President, Executive and 3 Non-executives. Board of Advisors. **Publications** *In Focus* – series; *IQsensato Studies.* Annual Report. Working papers. **Consultative Status** Consultative status granted from: *UNCTAD (#20285)* (General Category); *World Intellectual Property Organization (WIPO, #21593)* (Observer Status). [2011/XM3769/F]

- ♦ IR / see PPL/IR Europe
- ♦ IRA / see Life for Relief and Development
- ♦ IRACM – Institute of Research Against Counterfeit Medicines (internationally oriented national body)
- ♦ **IRAHSSE** International Research Association for History and Social Sciences Education (#14718)
- ♦ IRA – Institut des régions arides, Tunisia (internationally oriented national body)
- ♦ IRA / see International Literacy Association (#14057)
- ♦ **IRA** International Retrovirology Association (#14747)
- ♦ **IRA** International Rubber Association (#14769)
- ♦ **IRAK** Islamic Research Academy (#16049)
- ♦ **IRAM** Institut de radio-astronomie millimétrique (#11353)

- ♦ IRAM – Institut de recherches et d'applications des méthodes de développement (internationally oriented national body)
- ♦ IRAM – International Reformed Agency for Migration (inactive)
- ♦ Iranian Association for International Studies (internationally oriented national body)
- ♦ Iranian Christians International (internationally oriented national body)
- ♦ Iran Organization / see Organization for Investment, Economic and Technical Assistance of Iran
- ♦ **iRAP** International Road Assessment Programme (#14757)
- ♦ Iraqi National Accord (internationally oriented national body)
- ♦ Iraq Survey Group (inactive)
- ♦ IRASEC – Institut de recherche sur l'Asie du Sud-Est contemporaine (internationally oriented national body)
- ♦ IRAS – Institute on Religion in an Age of Science (internationally oriented national body)
- ♦ IRATA International (internationally oriented national body)
- ♦ **IRATDE** International Research Association for Talent Development and Excellence (#14720)
- ♦ IRATE International – Industrial Rope Access Trade Association / see IRATA International
- ♦ IRA / see World Leisure Organization (#21624)
- ♦ IRAZ – Institut de recherche agronomique et zootechnique (no recent information)
- ♦ **IRBDSG** International REM Sleep Behavior Study Group (#14714)
- ♦ IRB / see World Rugby (#21757)
- ♦ IRC / see International Relations Center

♦ IRC 16016

Dir PO Box 82327, 2508 EH The Hague, Netherlands. T. +31703044000. Fax +31703044044. E-mail: info@ircwash.org.
URL: http://www.ircwash.org/

History 1968. Founded by an agreement between *WHO (#20950)* (for which it acts as a Collaborating Centre for Community Water Supply and Sanitation) and the Netherlands Government. Since 1981, operates as an independent, non-profit organization with the title *IRC – International Water and Sanitation Centre – Centre international de l'eau et de l'assainissement*. Currently known only by its acronym. Former names and other names: *International Reference Centre for Community Water Supply and Sanitation (IRC)* – former; *Centre international de référence pour l'approvisionnement en eau collective et l'assainissement (CIR)* – former; *Centre international de référence pour l'approvisionnement collectif en eau et l'assainissement* – former; *IRC – International Water and Sanitation Centre* – former; *Centre international de l'eau et de l'assainissement* – former. **Aims** Support partner districts to bring sustainable *water, sanitation* and *hygiene* (WASH) to everyone. **Structure** Supervisory Board; Executive Team. **Languages** English, French, Spanish. **Staff** 80.00 FTE, paid. **Finance** Core budget from the Netherlands Government. Additional funds from bilateral and multilateral agencies for specific programmes and projects, and charity funds. **Activities** Advocacy/lobbying/activism; guidance/assistance/consulting; knowledge management/information dissemination; networking/liaising; research and development. Active in: Burkina Faso, Ethiopia, Ghana, Honduras, India, Mali, Niger, Uganda. **Events** *All systems go!* The Hague (Netherlands) 2019, *Symposium on Monitoring Sustainable WASH Service Delivery* Addis Ababa (Ethiopia) 2013, *SACOSAN : South Asian Conference on Sanitation* Kathmandu (Nepal) 2013, *Conference* The Hague (Netherlands) 2010, *Symposium on sanitation practices* Delft (Netherlands) 2008. **Publications** *Amplify: building sustainable WASH systems* (12 a year) – newsletter. Annual Report; working papers; briefing and policy papers; technical paper series; occasional paper series; thematic overview papers. **Information Services** *WASH Systems Academy* – online learning platform. **Members** Not a membership organization. **IGO Relations** Collaborates with: *Centro Panamericano de Ingenieria Sanitaria y Ciencias del Ambiente (CEPIS, no recent information)*; *DANIDA*; *Department for International Development (DFID, inactive)*; *Department for International Development Cooperation*; *Deutsche Gesellschaft für Technische Zusammenarbeit (GTZ, inactive)*; *International Bank for Reconstruction and Development (IBRD, #12317)*; *Norwegian Agency for Development Cooperation (Norad)*; *Pan American Health Organization (PAHO, #18108)*; *Swedish International Development Cooperation Agency (Sida)*; *UNEP (#20299)*; *UNDP (#20292)*; *UNICEF (#20332)*; *Water and Sanitation Programme (WSP, #20837)*. **NGO Relations** Member of: *End Water Poverty (EWP, #05464)*; *Global Handwashing Partnership (GHP, #10396)*; *Millennium Water Alliance (MWA)*; *IHE Delft Institute for Water Education (#11110)*; *World Water Council (WWC, #21908)*. Founding member of: *Water Integrity Network (WIN, #20830)*. Partner of: *Sanitation and Water for All (SWA, #19051)*; *WASH Alliance International (WAI)*; *Wetlands International (#20928)*. Close contacts with: *Water, Engineering and Development Centre (WEDC)*. Collaborates with: *Bill and Melinda Gates Foundation (BMGF)*; *Kreditanstalt für Wiederaufbau (KfW)*; *SNV Netherlands Development Organisation (SNV)*; *Network for Water and Sanitation International (NETWAS International, #17064)*; *Sustainable Sanitation Alliance (SuSanA, #20066)*; *Water and Sanitation for Africa (WSA, #20836)*. Instrumental in setting up: *Globetree Foundation*. Supports: *Rural Water Supply Network (RWSN, #19006)*. *Society for Participatory Research in Asia (PRIA)*. Also links with a number of national organizations interested in the field. [2022.05.19/XE9614/**E**]

- ♦ IRCAD / see European Institute of Tele-Surgery
- ♦ IRCAI – International Research Center for Artificial Intelligence under the auspices of UNESCO (unconfirmed)
- ♦ IRCA – International Railway Congress Association (inactive)
- ♦ **IRCICA** Research Centre for Islamic History, Art and Culture (#18852)
- ♦ **IRCI** International Research Centre for Intangible Cultural Heritage in the Asia-Pacific Region under the Auspices of UNESCO (#14721)
- ♦ IRC – International Medical Rehabilitation Center (internationally oriented national body)
- ♦ **IRC** International Radiation Commission (#14684)
- ♦ IRC – International Rainwear Council (inactive)
- ♦ **IRC** International Rangeland Congress (#14696)
- ♦ IRC – International Relations Center (internationally oriented national body)
- ♦ **IRC** International Rescue Committee (#14717)
- ♦ IRC – International Rescue Corps (internationally oriented national body)
- ♦ IRC – International Rice Commission (inactive)
- ♦ IRC – International Water and Sanitation Centre / see IRC (#16016)
- ♦ **IRCK** Internationale Raad van Christelijke Kerken (#13005)
- ♦ **IRCK** Internationaler Rat Christlicher Kirchen (#13005)
- ♦ IRCMS – International Radio-Controlled Models Society (inactive)
- ♦ IRCOBI / see International Research Council on the Biomechanics of Injury (#14723)
- ♦ **IRCOBI** International Research Council on the Biomechanics of Injury (#14723)
- ♦ IRCOD – Institut régional de coopération et de développement (internationally oriented national body)
- ♦ **IRCOI** International Research Committee of Oral Implantology (#14722)
- ♦ **IRCO** International Rubber Conference Organisation (#14770)
- ♦ **IRCRA** International Rock Climbing Research Association (#14763)
- ♦ **IRCSA** International Rainwater Catchment Systems Association (#14694)
- ♦ **IRCS** International Raymond Carver Society (#14700)
- ♦ **IRCTA** Initiative Régionale pour la Lutte contre le Tabac en Afrique (#00524)
- ♦ **IRCT** International Rehabilitation Council for Torture Victims (#14712)
- ♦ IRD / see Blumont International
- ♦ IRDAC – International Research and Development Actions (internationally oriented national body)
- ♦ IrDA – Infrared Data Association (internationally oriented national body)
- ♦ IRDC – International Rubber Development Committee (inactive)
- ♦ IRD-Geneva – International Institute for Rights and Development-Geneva (unconfirmed)
- ♦ IRD – Institut de recherche pour le développement (internationally oriented national body)
- ♦ **IRDiRC** International Rare Diseases Research Consortium (#14699)
- ♦ IRECE – International Research in Early Childhood Education Conference (meeting series)
- ♦ **I-REC Standard** International REC Standard Foundation (#14705)
- ♦ **IRED** Innovations et réseaux pour le développement (#05057)
- ♦ IRED – International Conference on the Integration of Renewable and Distributed Energy Resources (meeting series)
- ♦ **IREFREA** European Institute of Studies on Prevention (#07573)
- ♦ Irefrea Network / see European Institute of Studies on Prevention (#07573)
- ♦ IREG / see IREG Observatory on Academic Ranking and Excellence (#16017)

♦ IREG Observatory on Academic Ranking and Excellence (IREG Observatory) 16017

Managing Dir Nowogrodzka 31, 00-511 Warsaw, Poland. T. +48226295326. Fax +48226291617. E-mail: secretariat@ireg-observatory.org.
Registered Office Rue Washington 40, 1050 Brussels, Belgium. T. +32493452931.
URL: http://www.ireg-observatory.org/

History 2009, Brussels (Belgium). Founded as an informal group called *International Ranking Expert Group (IREG)*, set up by *UNESCO – European Centre for Higher Education (UNESCO-CEPES, inactive)*, organized conferences since 2002. Registration: Banque-Carrefour des Entreprises, No/ID: 0821.026.311, Start date: 1 Dec 2009, Belgium. **Aims** Improve the quality of international and national ranking of higher education institutions, strengthening understanding of rankings and academic excellence with special consideration to standards and good practices. **Structure** General Assembly; Executive Committee; Managing Director; Secretariat. **Languages** English. **Staff** 2.00 FTE, paid. **Finance** Members' dues. **Activities** Events/meetings; awards/prizes/competitions; standards/guidelines. **Events** *Ranking Conference* Budapest (Hungary) 2021, *Conference* Beijing (China) 2020, *Conference* Bologna (Italy) 2019, *Ranking and Accreditation – two roads to the same goal?* Hasselt (Belgium) 2018, *Excellence as the university driving force* Doha (Qatar) 2017. **Publications** *IREG Guidelines for Stakeholders of Academic Rankings*; *IREG Inventory on International Rankings*; *IREG Inventory on National Rankings*; *IREG List of International Academic Awards*.
Members Universities and academic institutions in 22 countries and territories:
China, Denmark, France, Germany, Hungary, Indonesia, Italy, Kazakhstan, Poland, Portugal, Qatar, Romania, Russia, Saudi Arabia, Slovakia, Slovenia, Spain, Sweden, Taiwan, UK, Ukraine, USA.
NGO Relations Member of: *Federation of European and International Associations Established in Belgium (FAIB, #09508)*. [2021/XJ8859/**E**]

- ♦ **IREG Observatory** IREG Observatory on Academic Ranking and Excellence (#16017)
- ♦ IREI – International Real Estate Institute (internationally oriented national body)
- ♦ IRE – Institute of the Regions of Europe (internationally oriented national body)
- ♦ IRE – Institut der Regionen Europas (internationally oriented national body)
- ♦ Ireland Aid / see Irish Aid
- ♦ IREM / see Istituto di Studi sul Mediterraneo
- ♦ **IREMAM** Institut de recherches et d'études sur le monde arabe et musulman (#11354)

♦ IRENA Coalition for Action 16018

Contact address not obtained. E-mail: coalition@irena.org.
URL: https://coalition.irena.org/

History Jan 2014. Founded by *International Renewable Energy Agency (IRENA, #14715)* and 35 players in renewable energy. **Aims** Promote the wider and faster uptake of renewable energy technologies. **Structure** Working Groups. Secretariat provided by *International Renewable Energy Agency (IRENA, #14715)*.
Members Members (over 120) include private sector companies, industry associations, civil society, research institutes and intergovernmental organizations. Organizations include 38 listed in this Yearbook:

- *Alliance for Rural Electrification (ARE, #00719)*;
- *Climate Action Network (CAN, #03999)*;
- *ECOWAS Centre for Renewable Energy and Energy Efficiency (ECREEE, #05335)*;
- *EKOenergy (#05412)*;
- *Energy Watch Group (EWG)*;
- *Environnement et développement du Tiers-monde (enda, #05510)*;
- *European Renewable Energies Federation (EREF, #08355)*;
- *Global Solar Council (GSC, #10609)*;
- *Global Wind Energy Council (GWEC, #10656)*;
- *Global Women's Network for the Energy Transition (GWNET, #10659)*;
- *Greenpeace International (#10727)*;
- *Humanistisch Instituut voor Ontwikkelingssamenwerking (Hivos)*;
- *Institut de la Francophonie pour le développement durable (IFDD, #11305)*;
- *International Geothermal Association (IGA, #13717)*;
- *International Hydropower Association (IHA, #13828)*;
- *International Network for Sustainable Energy (INFORSE, #14331)*;
- *International Renewable Energy Agency (IRENA, #14715)*;
- *International Solar Energy Society (ISES, #15564)*;
- *International Windship Association (IWSA, #15887)*;
- *Local Governments for Sustainability (ICLEI, #16507)*;
- *Middle East Solar Industry Association (MESIA)*;
- *Nordic Folkecenter for Renewable Energy*;
- *Ocean Energy Europe (EU-OEA, #17649)*;
- *RE100*;
- *Regional Center for Renewable Energy and Energy Efficiency (RCREEE, #18754)*;
- *REN21 (#18836)*;
- *Renewable Energy and Energy Efficiency Partnership (REEEP, #18837)*;
- *Renewable Energy Solutions for Africa (RES4Africa)*;
- *Renewables Grid Initiative (RGI, #18839)*;
- *SolarPower Europe (#19676)*;
- *The Nature Conservancy (TNC)*;
- *United Nations Foundation (UNF, #20563)*;
- *World Bioenergy Association (WBA, #21231)*;
- *World Business Council for Sustainable Development (WBCSD, #21254)*;
- *World Future Council Foundation (WFC, #21533)*;
- *World Resources Institute (WRI, #21753)*;
- *World Wide Fund for Nature (WWF, #21922)*;
- *World Wind Energy Association (WWEA, #21937)*. [2022/AA2825/y/**E**]

- ♦ **IRENA** International Renewable Energy Agency (#14715)
- ♦ IREO – Intergovernmental Renewable Energy Organization (inactive)
- ♦ IREPAS (unconfirmed)
- ♦ IREPD / see Institute of International Integration and Industrial Economics
- ♦ IRESCO – Institut de recherche sur les sociétés contemporaines, Paris (internationally oriented national body)
- ♦ **IRESD** Centre régional pour l'enseignement supérieur et le développement de la SEAMEO (#19174)
- ♦ **IRES** International Real Estate Society (#14702)
- ♦ **IRES-RDEC** Institut Régional d'Enseignement Supérieur et de Recherche en Développement Culturel (#11355)
- ♦ **IRETA** Institute for Research, Extension and Training in Agriculture (#11291)

♦ IREX Europe 16019

Dir 11 rue Aimé Collomb, 69003 Lyon, France. T. +339850527829. Fax +33998527829. E-mail: info@irexeurope.eu.
URL: http://irex-europe.fr/

History 2004, Lyon (France). Set up as a sister organization of *International Research and Exchanges Board (IREX)*. Registered in accordance with French law. Registration: France. **Aims** Provide services, programs, infrastructure and technology to improve the quality of *education*, strengthen independent media, foster pluralistic civil society development and reduce conflict. **Structure** Board. **NGO Relations** Member of: *Eastern Partnership Civil Society Forum (EaP CSF, #05247)*. [2020/XM5655/**E**]

- ♦ IREX – International Research and Exchanges Board (internationally oriented national body)
- ♦ IRF / see International Road Federation (#14759)
- ♦ IRFB / see World Rugby (#21757)
- ♦ IRFCAM – International Research Forum on Children and Media (internationally oriented national body)
- ♦ **IRFD** International Research Foundation for Development (#14724)
- ♦ IRF / see Federation of International Retail Associations (#09676)
- ♦ **IRFF** International Relief Friendship Foundation (#14713)

♦ **IRF Global** International Road Federation (#14759)
♦ **IRF** International Racquetball Federation (#14683)
♦ **IRF** International Rafting Federation (#14691)
♦ **IRF** International Ranger Federation (#14697)
♦ **IRF** International Recovery Foundation (#14703)
♦ **IRF** International Regulators' Forum (#14710)
♦ IRF – International Rehabilitation Forum (internationally oriented national body)
♦ IRF – International Religious Fellowship (no recent information)
♦ IRF – International Religious Freedom Alliance (unconfirmed)
♦ IRF – International Renaissance Foundation (internationally oriented national body)
♦ **IRF** International Rhino Foundation (#14752)
♦ IRF – International River Foundation (internationally oriented national body)
♦ **IRF** International Road Federation (#14758)
♦ **IRF** International Rogaining Federation (#14764)
♦ IRFT – International Resources for Fairer Trade, India (internationally oriented national body)
♦ IRF / see World Rowing (#21756)
♦ IRFWP / see Twelve Gates Foundation
♦ **IRGC** International Research Group on Charophytes (#14727)
♦ **IRGC** International Risk Governance Council (#14756)
♦ IRGCP / see International Society for Oncology and BioMarkers (#15323)
♦ IRGCVD / see International Colour Vision Society (#12656)
♦ **IRGFPSA** International Research Group for Psycho-Societal Analysis (#14732)
♦ IRG – Institute for Research and Debate on Governance (internationally oriented national body)
♦ **IRG** Internacional de Resistentes a la Guerra (#20818)
♦ **IRG** Internationale Gesellschaft für Regenbogenfische (#14693)
♦ **IRG** Internationale des résistants/résistantes à la guerre (#20818)
♦ **IRG** International Research Group on Wood Protection (#14733)
♦ **IRGLUS** International Research Group on Law and Urban Space (#14729)
♦ **IRGO** International Research Group on Ostracoda (#14730)
♦ **IRHA** International Rainwater Harvesting Alliance (#14695)
♦ IRHA – International Rural Housing Association (inactive)
♦ IRHD – Internationaler Rat der Hauspflegedienste (inactive)
♦ IRH – Institute for Reproductive Health (internationally oriented national body)
♦ IRI / see International Research Institute for Climate and Society
♦ IRIC / see Asian Research Centre for Migration
♦ IRIC – Institut des relations internationales du Cameroun (internationally oriented national body)
♦ IRIC – Islamic Research and Information Center (internationally oriented national body)
♦ IRI Europe – Initiative and Referendum Institute Europe (internationally oriented national body)
♦ IRI – Instituto de Relações Internacionais (internationally oriented national body)
♦ IRI – International Republican Institute (internationally oriented national body)
♦ IRI – International Research Institute for Climate and Society (internationally oriented national body)
♦ IRI – Islamic Reporting Initiative (unconfirmed)
♦ IRI – Islamic Research Institute (internationally oriented national body)
♦ IRIJW / see Hadassah-Brandeis Institute
♦ IRIN News / see The New Humanitarian (#17087)
♦ **IR** InterRidge (#15973)
♦ IRIPAZ – Instituto de Relaciones Internacionales y de Investigación para la Paz (internationally oriented national body)
♦ Irish Aid (internationally oriented national body)
♦ Irish Association of Development Workers / see Comhlamh
♦ Irish Association of Non-Governmental Development Organisations (internationally oriented national body)
♦ Irish Association of Returned Development Workers for the Promotion of International Development Cooperation / see Comhlamh
♦ Irish Centre for Human Rights (internationally oriented national body)
♦ Irish College Leuven / see Leuven Institute for Ireland in Europe
♦ Irish Council for International Students (internationally oriented national body)
♦ Irish Council for Overseas Students / see Irish Council for International Students
♦ Irish in Europe Association (internationally oriented national body)
♦ Irish in Europe Association International / see Irish in Europe Association
♦ Irish Institute for European Affairs, Leuven / see Leuven Institute for Ireland in Europe
♦ Irish League of Credit Unions International Development Foundation (internationally oriented national body)
♦ Irish Missionary Union (internationally oriented national body)
♦ Irish Peace Institute (internationally oriented national body)
♦ Irish Peace Institute Research Centre / see Centre for Peace and Development Studies, Limerick
♦ Irish Refugee Council (internationally oriented national body)
♦ IRIS – Incorporated Research Institutions for Seismology (internationally oriented national body)
♦ **IRIS** Information Systems Research in Scandinavia (#11200)
♦ IRIS – Institute for Regional and International Studies, Sofia (internationally oriented national body)
♦ IRIS – Institut de relations internationales et stratégiques (internationally oriented national body)
♦ **Iris** International Research Institutes (#14734)
♦ IRIS – International Research Institute of Stavanger (internationally oriented national body)
♦ IRIS – International Rest Investigators Society (no recent information)
♦ IRIS – International Symposium on Inorganic Ring Systems (meeting series)
♦ **IRIS** Inter-réseau européen des initiatives éthiques et solidaires (#07593)
♦ IRIS / see Isfahan Regional Center for Technology Incubators and Science Park Development (#16028)
♦ **IRIS** Isfahan Regional Center for Technology Incubators and Science Park Development (#16028)
♦ **IRIST** International Research Group in Immunoscintigraphy and Immunotherapy (#14728)
♦ IRIS / see World Immunopathology Organization (#21576)
♦ IRIWI / see Wheat Initiative (#20931)
♦ **IRKA** Internationale Regierungskommission Alpenrhein (#13293)
♦ IRKA – International Rhino Keeper Association (internationally oriented national body)
♦ IRK / see International Canoe Federation (#12437)
♦ IRLA – International Religious Liberty Association (internationally oriented national body)
♦ IRLCO-CSA – International Red Locust Control Organization for Central and Southern Africa (no recent information)
♦ IRLCS – International Red Locust Control Service (inactive)
♦ **IRLF** International Right to Life Federation (#14755)
♦ IRL – International Radioecology Laboratory (internationally oriented national body)
♦ **IRL** International Rugby League (#14773)
♦ IRLSSG – International Restless Legs Syndrome Study Group (unconfirmed)
♦ IRMA / see Content Delivery and Storage Association (#04779)
♦ **IRMA** Initiative for Responsible Mining Assurance (#11212)
♦ IRMA – International Rail Makers Association (inactive)
♦ IRMA – International Rectal Microbicide Advocates (unconfirmed)
♦ IRMA – International Rehabilitation Medicine Association (inactive)
♦ Irmãos de Nossa Senhora de Lourdes (religious order)
♦ Irmã Sacramentinas de Bérgamo (religious order)
♦ Irmas de Caridade de Montreal (religious order)
♦ Irmãs Franciscanas Hospitaleiras de Imaculada Conceição (religious order)
♦ Irmãs Franciscanas dos Pobres (religious order)
♦ Irmãs Missionarias de Jesus Crucificado (religious order)
♦ Irmas Missionarias do Precioso Sangue (religious order)
♦ Irmãs Missionarias de San Carlos Borromeo (religious order)
♦ Irmãs de Nossa Senhora (religious order)
♦ Irmãs de la Sagrada Familia (religious order)
♦ Irmãs da Santa Cruz (religious order)
♦ Irmãs dos Santos Anjos (religious order)
♦ IRMA / see World Instant Noodles Association (#21586)
♦ Irmãzinhas da Assunção (religious order)
♦ Irmãzinhas dos Pobres (religious order)
♦ IRMC – Institut de recherche sur le Maghreb contemporain, Tunis (internationally oriented national body)
♦ **IRMCT** International Residual Mechanism for Criminal Tribunals (#14746)
♦ **IRMG** Internationale Robert-Musil-Gesellschaft (#14762)
♦ IRM – Institute of Risk Management (internationally oriented national body)
♦ **IRM** International Raelian Movement (#14690)
♦ **IRMMW-THz** International Society of Infrared, Millimeter and Terahertz Waves (#15204)
♦ IRMO – Institut za Rasvoj i Medunarodne Odnose (internationally oriented national body)
♦ IRN / see International Rivers
♦ IRNC – Institut de recherche sur la résolution non-violente des conflits (internationally oriented national body)
♦ IRN – International Redox Network (unconfirmed)
♦ **IRN** International Revival Network (#14749)
♦ **IRNOP** International Research Network on Organizing by Projects (#14736)
♦ IRN-TP / see International Research Network on Time Perspective (#14737)
♦ IROA – International Range Officers Association (internationally oriented national body)
♦ IROC – International Robot Olympiad Committee (unconfirmed)
♦ IRO-FIET – Organisation régionale interaméricaine de la Fédération internationale des employés, techniciens et cadres / see UNI Global Union – Americas Regional Office (#20340)
♦ **IROICA** European Network of International Relations Officers at Higher Education Institutions for Agricultural and Related Sciences (#07935)
♦ **IRO** Internationale Rettungshunde Organisation (#14817)
♦ IRO – International Refugee Organization (inactive)
♦ **IRO** International Search and Rescue Dog Organisation (#14817)
♦ Iron Lung Polios and Multiplegics / see Post-Polio Health International
♦ IROS – Interventional Radiology Olbert Symposium (meeting series)
♦ IROS – Interventionell Radiologisches Olbert Symposium (meeting series)
♦ IROWS – Institute for Research on World Systems (internationally oriented national body)
♦ **IRPA** International Radiation Protection Association (#14686)
♦ IRPA / see Retina International (#18926)
♦ IRPC – International Rural Poultry Centre (internationally oriented national body)
♦ IRPEPS – Inspectorans Rerum Publicarum Europaeorum Pharmacopopularum Societas (no recent information)
♦ IRPF – International Real Property Foundation (internationally oriented national body)
♦ **IRP** International Recovery Platform (#14704)
♦ IRPP – Institute for Research on Public Policy (internationally oriented national body)
♦ **IRPS** International Radiation Physics Society (#14685)
♦ IRRB – International Rubber Research Board (inactive)
♦ **IRRDB** International Rubber Research and Development Board (#14771)
♦ IRRI / see Egmont Institute
♦ Irrigation Association (internationally oriented national body)
♦ **IRRI** International Refugee Rights Initiative (#14708)
♦ **IRRI** International Rice Research Institute (#14754)
♦ IRRI México – Instituto Internacional de Recursos Renovables (internationally oriented national body)
♦ IRR – Institute of Race Relations (internationally oriented national body)
♦ IRR – Internationale Rheinregulierung (internationally oriented national body)
♦ IRRP / see International Development and Relief Foundation
♦ **IRRPA** International Road Racing Press Association (#14760)
♦ IRRS – International Ruminant Reproduction Symposium (meeting series)
♦ **IRRTO** International Reading Recovery Trainers Organization (#14701)
♦ IRSA / see US Committee for Refugees and Immigrants
♦ IRSA – Association of Quality Clubs / see International Health, Racquet and Sportsclub Association (#13783)
♦ IRSA / see International Health, Racquet and Sportsclub Association (#13783)
♦ **IRSA** International Radio Sailing Association (#14687)
♦ **IRSA** International Radiostereometry Society (#14688)
♦ IRSA / see International Rett Syndrome Foundation (#14748)
♦ **IRSA** International Rural Sociology Association (#14774)
♦ **IRSCL** International Research Society for Children's Literature (#14742)
♦ IRSEA – Institut de recherche sur le sud-est Asiatique (internationally oriented national body)
♦ **IRSE** Institut Robert Schuman pour l'Europe (#18959)
♦ **IRSE** Robert Schuman Institute for Europe (#18959)
♦ IRSFC / see CIRFS – European Man-made Fibres Association (#03944)
♦ IRSF – International Refugee Sport Federation (unconfirmed)
♦ **IRSF** International Rett Syndrome Foundation (#14748)
♦ IRSF – International Rope Skipping Federation (inactive)
♦ **IRSG** International Rubber Study Group (#14772)
♦ IRSI – Institutul Român de Studii Internationale – Nicolae Titulescu (internationally oriented national body)
♦ IRS – Institute of Regional Studies, Islamabad (internationally oriented national body)
♦ **IRS** International Ragweed Society (#14692)
♦ **IRS** International Rhinologic Society (#14753)
♦ IRS / see International Society of the Rorschach and Projective Methods (#15430)
♦ **IRS** International Society of the Rorschach and Projective Methods (#15430)
♦ **IRSL** International Roundtable for the Semiotics of Law (#14767)
♦ IRSMI – International Railway Strategic Management Institute (internationally oriented national body)
♦ **IRSO** International Research Ship Operators (#14741)
♦ **IRSPM** International Research Society for Public Management (#14743)
♦ **IRSSD** International Research Society of Spinal Deformities (#14744)
♦ **IRSS** International Rough Set Society (#14766)
♦ IRSTA – International Roller Skating Trainer Association (no recent information)
♦ IRTAC / see International Association for Counselling (#11821)
♦ IRTA – International Refrigerated Transportation Association (internationally oriented national body)
♦ IRTA – International Road Racing Teams Association (internationally oriented national body)
♦ **IRTA** Intestinal Rehabilitation and Transplant Association (#15990)
♦ **IRTCES** International Research and Training Centre on Erosion and Sedimentation (#14745)
♦ **IRTF** Internet Research Task Force (#15951)
♦ **IRTI** Islamic Research and Training Institute, Jeddah (#16050)
♦ IRT – International Refugee Trust (internationally oriented national body)
♦ IRTSL / see International Roundtable for the Semiotics of Law (#14767)
♦ IRTU – International Railway Temperance Union (inactive)
♦ **IRUG** Infrared and Raman Users' Group (#11205)
♦ **IRU** Internationale Raiffeisen Union e.V. (#13291)
♦ **IRU** International Raiffeisen Union (#13291)
♦ IRU – International Relief Union (inactive)
♦ **IRU** International Road Transport Union (#14761)

- ♦ **IRU** International Romani Union (#14765)
- ♦ **IRU** Unión Internacional Raiffeisen (#13291)
- ♦ **IRU** Union internationale Raiffeisen (#13291)
- ♦ IRV / see BirdLife International (#03266)

♦ Irving Fisher Committee on Central Bank Statistics (IFC) 16020

Secretariat c/o BIS, 4002 Basel BS, Switzerland. T. +41612808940. E-mail: ifc.secretariat@bis.org.
URL: http://www.bis.org/ifc/index.htm

History 1995, Beijing (China). Founded at the Session of *International Statistical Institute (ISI, #15603)*. Inaugural meeting during 51st ISI session, 1997, Istanbul (Turkey). A BIS-hosted committee and formally a Section of ISI. Secretariat provided by *Bank for International Settlements (BIS, #03165)*. **Aims** Promote exchange of views amongst central bank economists, statisticians and policy makers as well as others who want to participate in discussing statistical issues of interest to central banks, including those relating to economic, monetary and financial stability; strengthen the relationship between compilers of statistics and the community of users and analysts of statistical information, both in and outside central banks. **Structure** Governors's Meeting; Committee; Executive; Secretariat, hosted by BIS. **Languages** English. **Staff** 1.00 FTE, paid. **Finance** Supported by: *Bank for International Settlements (BIS, #03165)*. **Activities** Events/meetings; knowledge management/information dissemination. For more details on the events: https://www.bis.org/ifc/events.htm?m=3%7C46%7C93. **Events** *Biennial Conference* Basel (Switzerland) 2022, *Biennial Conference* Basel (Switzerland) 2020, *Biennial Conference* Basel (Switzerland) 2018, *Biennial Conference* Basel (Switzerland) 2016, *Biennial Conference* Basel (Switzerland) 2014. **Publications** Annual Report; bulletins; reports; working papers.

Members Full institutional (97); Associate institutional; Associate individual; Honorary. Full (Central banks and monetary authorities) in 97 countries and territories:
Albania, Algeria, Angola, Argentina, Armenia, Australia, Austria, Azerbaijan, Barbados, Belarus, Belgium, Bolivia, Bosnia-Herzegovina, Brazil, Bulgaria, Cambodia, Canada, Cayman Is, Chile, China, Colombia, Croatia, Cyprus, Czechia, Denmark, El Salvador, Estonia, Finland, France, Georgia, Germany, Greece, Hong Kong, Hungary, Iceland, India, Indonesia, Iran Islamic Rep, Ireland, Israel, Italy, Japan, Kazakhstan, Korea Rep, Kuwait, Latvia, Lebanon, Lithuania, Luxembourg, Macau, Malaysia, Malta, Mauritius, Mexico, Montenegro, Morocco, Mozambique, Namibia, Netherlands, New Zealand, Nigeria, North Macedonia, Norway, Pakistan, Peru, Philippines, Poland, Portugal, Romania, Russia, Sao Tomé-Principe, Saudi Arabia, Serbia, Singapore, Slovakia, Slovenia, South Africa, Spain, Sri Lanka, Suriname, Sweden, Switzerland, Thailand, Timor-Leste, Tunisia, Türkiye, UK, Ukraine, United Arab Emirates, Uruguay, USA, Venezuela, Vietnam.
see IFC members at: https://www.bis.org/ifc/members.htm?m=3%7C46%7C92.
Regional authority (1):
European Union (EU, #08967).
Other Full institutional members (3):
Center for Latin American Monetary Studies (#03648); Central American Monetary Council (#03672); South East Asian Central Banks Research and Training Centre (SEACEN Centre, #19760).
NGO Relations Affiliated with (1): *International Statistical Institute (ISI, #15603).* [2022.11.08/XM3584/y/**E***]

- ♦ IRWA – International Right of Way Association (internationally oriented national body)
- ♦ IRWC / see Registre des Citoyens du Monde (#18822)
- ♦ **IRWC** Registry of World Citizens (#18822)
- ♦ **IRWF** International Raoul Wallenberg Foundation (#14698)
- ♦ **IRWW** Islamic Relief Worldwide (#16048)
- ♦ IRZ – Deutsche Stiftung für Internationale Rechtliche Zusammenarbeit (internationally oriented national body)
- ♦ IRZ Foundation – German Foundation for International Legal Cooperation (internationally oriented national body)
- ♦ **IS3NA** International Society for Nucleosides, Nucleotides and Nucleic Acids (#15311)
- ♦ **IS3R** International Society for Strategic Studies in Radiology (#15459)
- ♦ IS4E – International Society for Endomicroscopy (unconfirmed)
- ♦ **IS4SI** International Society for the Study of Information (#15477)
- ♦ ISA / see International Society of Automation
- ♦ ISA / see Global Impact
- ♦ ISA / see International Sign Association
- ♦ ISA / see Indonesian Students Association for International Studies
- ♦ ISA / see International Seabed Authority (#14813)
- ♦ **ISA+21** International Society of Women Airline Pilots (#15550)

♦ ISAA Agrochemical Network 16021

Contact PO Box 7, Mullica Hill NJ 08062, USA. E-mail: info@isaanetwork.org.
URL: http://www.isaanetwork.org/

History Founded to provide a backbone for the ISAA symposia, organized since 1986. Relaunched 2019 under present title. Former names and other names: *International Society for Agrochemical Adjuvants (ISAA)* – former (2005). Registration: Netherlands. **Aims** Organize the International Symposium for Agrochemical Adjuvants (ISAA); promote the use of adjuvants in agriculture. **Structure** Board. **Staff** 2.00 FTE, paid. **Events** *ISAA Symposium* Bordeaux (France) 2022, *Triennial Symposium* Bordeaux (France) 2021, *Triennial Symposium* Bordeaux (France) 2020, *Triennial Symposium* Monterey, CA (USA) 2016, *Triennial Symposium* Foz do Iguaçu (Brazil) 2013. **Publications** Symposia proceedings. [2022/XM2315/**D**]

- ♦ **ISAAA** International Service for the Acquisition of Agri-biotech Applications (#14839)
- ♦ **ISAAC** International Society for Analysis, its Applications and Computation (#14916)
- ♦ **ISAAC** International Society for Archaeoastronomy and Astronomy in Culture (#14937)
- ♦ **ISAAC** International Society for Augmentative and Alternative Communication (#14949)
- ♦ **ISAAC** International Substance Abuse and Addiction Coalition (#15622)
- ♦ ISAAC – International Symposium on Algorithms and Computation (meeting series)
- ♦ ISAA – International Shrine Aviation Association (internationally oriented national body)
- ♦ ISAA – International Spill Accreditation Association (internationally oriented national body)
- ♦ ISAA / see ISAA Agrochemical Network (#16021)
- ♦ ISAAN / see International Society of Non-Antibiotics (#15307)
- ♦ ISAAS – Indian Society for Afro-Asian Studies (internationally oriented national body)
- ♦ **ISABB** International Society for Artificial Cells, Blood Substitutes and Biotechnology (#14942)
- ♦ ISABC – International Symposium on Applied Bioinorganic Chemistry (meeting series)
- ♦ **ISABE** International Society of Air Breathing Engines (#14913)
- ♦ ISABI / see International Society for Artificial Cells, Blood Substitutes and Biotechnology (#14942)
- ♦ **ISAB** International Society for Adaptive Behavior (#14893)
- ♦ ISAB – International Society for Anaerobic Bacteria (no recent information)
- ♦ ISABR / see International Society for Animal Genetics (#14921)
- ♦ **ISABS** International Society for Applied Biological Sciences (#14928)

♦ ISACA 16022

Headquarters 1700 E Golf Rd, Ste 400, Schaumburg IL 60173, USA. T. +18472531545. Fax +18472531443.
URL: http://www.isaca.org/

History 1969. Founded as '*EDP Auditors Association*' (USA). Former names and other names: *Information Systems Audit and Control Association (ISACA)* – former. **Aims** As a global organization for information governance, security, control and *audit* professionals, lead the *information technology* community and provide necessary elements for professionals in an evolving industry. **Structure** General Meeting (annual); Board of Directors; Board of Trustees. Includes the affiliated *'IT Governance Institute (ITGI)'*, established in 1998. **Staff** 135.00 FTE, paid. **Activities** Knowledge management/information dissemination; certification/accreditation; advocacy/lobbying/activism; training/education. **Events** *EuroCACS : European Computer Audit Control and Security Conference* Helsinki (Finland) 2021, *From Open Banking to Open Finance and Open Data Seminar* Singapore (Singapore) 2020, *Seminar on Enhancing your Career Excellence with Mental Health Resilience* Singapore (Singapore) 2020, *Seminar on Trends and Challenges in Automotive Security Engineering* Singapore (Singapore) 2020, *EuroCACS : European Computer Audit Control and Security Conference* Vienna (Austria) 2020. **Publications** *atISACA* (12 a year) – membership newsletter; *ISACA Journal* (6 a year); *COBIT Focus Newsletter* (4 a year). Books; handbooks; manuals; white papers; CISA, CISM, CGEIT and CRISC examination reference materials. **Members** Chapters (nearly 200, representing over 100,000 members) in over 180 countries. Membership countries not specified. **NGO Relations** Cooperates with: *Association of Certified Anti-Money Laundering Specialists (ACAMS); Institute of Internal Auditors (IIA, #11272).* [2020/XF1362/**F**]

- ♦ ISACB / see International Society of Animal Clinical Pathology (#14920)
- ♦ **ISACB** International Society for Applied Cardiovascular Biology (#14929)
- ♦ ISACCD / see International Society for Adult Congenital Heart Disease (#14898)
- ♦ ISACC – Instituto Sindical para América Central y el Caribe (internationally oriented national body)
- ♦ **ISACHD** International Society for Adult Congenital Heart Disease (#14898)
- ♦ ISAC – International and Security Affairs Centre (internationally oriented national body)
- ♦ ISAC / see International Society for Advancement of Cytometry (#14900)
- ♦ **ISAC** International Society for Advancement of Cytometry (#14900)
- ♦ **ISAC** International Society of Antimicrobial Chemotherapy (#14925)
- ♦ **ISAC** International Society of Arterial Chemoreception (#14939)
- ♦ **ISAC** International Study of Arctic Change (#15616)
- ♦ ISA CIP / see Collaboration on International ICT Policy-Making for East and Southern Africa
- ♦ **ISACM** International Society for the Advancement of Clinical Magnetoencephalography (#14899)
- ♦ ISACPA – Independent South Asian Commission on Poverty Alleviation (see: #19721)
- ♦ **ISACP** International Society of Animal Clinical Pathology (#14920)
- ♦ ISAD – International Society of Abortion Doctors (inactive)
- ♦ **ISAD** International Society for Affective Disorders (#14910)
- ♦ **ISAD** International Society of Atopic Dermatitis (#14947)
- ♦ **ISAE** Internacia Scienca Asocio Esperantlingva (#13301)
- ♦ **ISAE** International Society for Applied Ethology (#14930)
- ♦ ISAFA – International Science And Football Association (unconfirmed)
- ♦ ISAF – International Security Assistance Force (inactive)
- ♦ ISAFIS – Indonesian Students Association for International Studies (internationally oriented national body)
- ♦ ISAF RSD (Radio Sailing Division) / see International Radio Sailing Association (#14687)
- ♦ ISAF / see World Sailing (#21760)
- ♦ ISAF/World Sailing Speed Record Council / see World Sailing Speed Record Council (#21761)
- ♦ ISAF/WSSRC / see World Sailing Speed Record Council (#21761)
- ♦ **ISAGA** International Simulation and Gaming Association (#14861)
- ♦ **ISAG** International Society for Animal Genetics (#14921)
- ♦ **ISAH** International Society for Animal Hygiene (#14922)
- ♦ **ISAI** International Society of Applied Intelligence (#14931)
- ♦ ISA – Independent Scholars of Asia (internationally oriented national body)
- ♦ ISA – Institute for the Study of the Americas (internationally oriented national body)
- ♦ ISA – The Instrumentation, Systems and Automation Society / see International Society of Automation
- ♦ ISA / see International Association of Seismology and Physics of the Earth's Interior (#12157)
- ♦ ISA – International Federation of National Standardizing Associations (inactive)
- ♦ **ISA** International Sauna Association (#14782)
- ♦ **ISA** International Schools Association (#14789)
- ♦ **ISA** International Scientists Association (#14811)
- ♦ ISA – International Seabuckthorn Association (internationally oriented national body)
- ♦ **ISA** International Seaweed Association (#14819)
- ♦ **ISA** International Security Association (#14825)
- ♦ ISA – International Seminar on Apterygota (meeting series)
- ♦ **ISA** International Shakespeare Association (#14843)
- ♦ **ISA** International Shuffleboard Association (#14857)
- ♦ ISA – International Silk Association (inactive)
- ♦ ISA – International Pro Ski Instructors Association (internationally oriented national body)
- ♦ **ISA** International Society of Amyloidosis (#14915)
- ♦ **ISA** International Society of Andrology (#14918)
- ♦ **ISA** International Society of Arachnology (#14935)
- ♦ **ISA** International Society of Arboriculture (#14936)
- ♦ ISA – International Society of Ascension (no recent information)
- ♦ **ISA** International Society of Audiology (#14948)
- ♦ ISA – International Society of Automation (internationally oriented national body)
- ♦ **ISA** International Sociological Association (#15553)
- ♦ **ISA** International Solar Alliance (#15563)
- ♦ ISA – International Soling Association (see: #21760)
- ♦ **ISA** International Sonnenberg Association (#15569)
- ♦ **ISA** International Stillbirth Alliance (#15608)
- ♦ **ISA** International Strabismological Association (#15609)
- ♦ ISA – International Student Association of Japan (internationally oriented national body)
- ♦ **ISA** International Studies Association (#15615)
- ♦ **ISA** International Stuttering Association (#15621)
- ♦ ISA – International Sugar Agreement, 1987 (1987 treaty)
- ♦ **ISA** International Sunflower Association (#15625)
- ♦ **ISA** International Surety Association (#15629)
- ♦ **ISA** International Surfing Association (#15630)
- ♦ **ISA** International Suzuki Association (#15637)
- ♦ **ISA** International Sweeteners Association (#15639)
- ♦ **ISA** International Symmetry Association (#15641)
- ♦ ISA – International Symposium on Archaeometry (meeting series)
- ♦ **ISA** International Szondi Association (#15648)
- ♦ ISAIO / see International Federation for Artificial Organs (#13357)
- ♦ **ISAJE** International Society of Addiction Journal Editors (#14895)
- ♦ ISAKE – Internacia Societo de Arkitektoj kaj Konstruistoj Esperantistoj (inactive)
- ♦ **ISAK** International Society for the Advancement of Kinanthropometry (#14901)
- ♦ **ISAKOS** International Society of Arthroscopy, Knee Surgery and Orthopaedic Sports Medicine (#14941)
- ♦ ISAL – International Society of African Lawyers (inactive)
- ♦ **ISAL** International Society of Artificial Life (#14943)
- ♦ ISAMA – International Scientific Association for Micronutrients in Agriculture (inactive)
- ♦ **ISAM** International Society for Adaptive Medicine (#14894)
- ♦ **ISAM** International Society of Addiction Medicine (#14896)
- ♦ **ISAM** International Society for Aerosols in Medicine (#14907)
- ♦ **ISAM** International Society of Aesthetics and Mesotherapy (#14909)
- ♦ **ISAM** International Society of Agile Manufacturing (#14911)
- ♦ ISAMR – International Symposium on Advanced Material Research (meeting series)
- ♦ ISANA – International Education Association (internationally oriented national body)
- ♦ ISANH – International Society of Antioxidant in Nutrition and Health (internationally oriented national body)
- ♦ **ISAN-IA** ISAN International Agency (#16023)

♦ ISAN International Agency (ISAN-IA) 16023

Managing Dir Cours de Rive 2, 1204 Geneva, Switzerland. T. +41225451000. Fax +41225451040. E-mail: info@isan.org.
URL: http://www.isan.org/

History 2003. Founded by *Association for the International Collective Management of Audiovisual Works (AGICOA, #02658)*, *Confédération internationale des sociétés d'auteurs et compositeurs (CISAC, #04563)* and *International Federation of Film Producers' Associations (#13429)*, to introduce the International Standard Audiovisual Number (ISAN), a voluntary numbering system for the identification of audiovisual works and their related versions. **Aims** Manage the International Standard *Audiovisual* Number (ISO 15706) as the ISAN registration authority mandated by ISO. **Languages** English, French. **Activities** Knowledge management/ information dissemination; standards/guidelines.
Members Registration agencies in 14 countries:
Belgium, Canada, Denmark, France, Germany, Italy, Netherlands, Poland, Portugal, Serbia, Spain, Switzerland, Türkiye, USA.
[2022.05.04/XM1197/E]

- ♦ **ISAN** International Society for Autonomic Neuroscience (#14952)
- ♦ ISAO / see International Federation for Artificial Organs (#13357)
- ♦ ISAOP – International Symposium on Advanced Organic Photonics (meeting series)
- ♦ ISA / see Organization of the Islamic Shipowners' Association (#17876)
- ♦ ISAPA / see International Coalition for Aging and Physical Activity (#12606)
- ♦ ISAPAM / see African Physical Society (#00417)
- ♦ **ISAP** Institut de statistique pour l'Asie et le Pacifique (#19972)
- ♦ ISAP – International Society of Acrylic Painters (internationally oriented national body)
- ♦ ISAP / see International Society for Adolescent Psychiatry and Psychology (#14897)
- ♦ ISAP – International Society for Anaesthetic Pharmacology (internationally oriented national body)
- ♦ **ISAP** International Society for Anti-Infective Pharmacology (#14924)
- ♦ **ISAP** International Society for Applied Phycology (#14932)
- ♦ **ISAP** International Society for Arabic Papyrology (#14934)
- ♦ **ISAP** International Society for Archaeological Prospection (#14938)
- ♦ **ISAP** International Society for Asphalt Pavements (#14944)
- ♦ **ISAPL** International Society of Applied Psycholinguistics (#14933)
- ♦ **ISAPP** International Scientific Association for Probiotics and Prebiotics (#14801)
- ♦ **ISAPP** International Society for Adolescent Psychiatry and Psychology (#14897)
- ♦ **ISAPS** International Society of Aesthetic Plastic Surgery (#14908)
- ♦ ISAP – South American Petroleum Institute (inactive)
- ♦ **ISAR** Intergovernmental Working Group of Experts on International Standards of Accounting and Reporting (#11503)
- ♦ **ISAR** International Society for Aeolian Research (#14906)
- ♦ ISAR – International Society for Animal Rights (internationally oriented national body)
- ♦ **ISAR** International Society for Antiviral Research (#14926)
- ♦ **ISAR** International Society of Arthroplasty Registries (#14940)
- ♦ **ISAR** International Society for Astrological Research (#14945)
- ♦ **ISAR** International Society for Auricular Reconstruction (#14950)
- ♦ ISAR – International Symposium on Audit Research (meeting series)
- ♦ **ISARM** Internationally Shared Aquifer Resources Management (#14071)
- ♦ ISAROB – International Society of Artificial Life and Robotics (internationally oriented national body)
- ♦ **ISARP** International Society for the Advancement of Respiratory Psychophysiology (#14902)
- ♦ **ISARRA** International Society for Atmospheric Research Using Remotely Piloted Aircraft (#14946)
- ♦ ISARRS / see International Society for Academic Research on Shamanism (#14891)
- ♦ **ISARS** International Society for Academic Research on Shamanism (#14891)
- ♦ ISARS / see International Society of Acoustic Remote Sensing of the Atmosphere and Oceans (#14892)
- ♦ **ISARS** International Society of Acoustic Remote Sensing of the Atmosphere and Oceans (#14892)
- ♦ ISASA – Independent Schools Association of Southern Africa (unconfirmed)
- ♦ ISASE – International Society of Affective Science and Engineering (internationally oriented national body)
- ♦ **ISASF** International Society for the Advancement of Supercritical Fluids (#14904)
- ♦ **ISASI** International Society of Air Safety Investigators (#14914)
- ♦ ISAS – Institute of South Asian Studies (internationally oriented national body)
- ♦ ISAS – International School for Advanced Studies, Trieste (internationally oriented national body)
- ♦ ISAS – International Society of African Scientists (internationally oriented national body)
- ♦ **ISAS** International Society of Anglo-Saxonists (#14919)
- ♦ **ISASS** International Society for the Advancement of Spine Surgery (#14903)
- ♦ ISASS – Society for the Advancement of Spine Surgery / see International Society for the Advancement of Spine Surgery (#14903)
- ♦ **ISATAP** International Society of Autogenic Training and Psychotherapy (#14951)
- ♦ ISATE – International Symposium on Advances in Technology Education (meeting series)
- ♦ **ISAT** International Society of Analytical Trilogy (#14917)
- ♦ **ISATT** International Study Association on Teachers and Teaching (#15617)
- ♦ **ISAU** International Staff Association of UNESCO (#15597)
- ♦ ISAVCP – International Students' Association of Village Concept Projects (inactive)
- ♦ ISAW – International Society of Aviation Writers (inactive)
- ♦ Isawiyyah (religious order)
- ♦ **ISAWR** International Society for the Advancement of Writing Research (#14905)
- ♦ ISAWV – International Supporting Association for War Victims (internationally oriented national body)
- ♦ **ISAZ** International Society for Anthrozoology (#14923)
- ♦ ISB / see World Services for the Blind
- ♦ ISBAB – International Society of Biocatalysis and Agricultural Biotechnology (unconfirmed)
- ♦ **ISBA** International Seabed Authority (#14813)
- ♦ **ISBA** International Short Break Association (#14853)
- ♦ **ISBA** International Society for Bayesian Analysis (#14953)
- ♦ ISBB / see International Society on Brain and Behaviour
- ♦ ISBB / see International Society of Biometeorology (#14969)
- ♦ ISBB – International Society on Brain and Behaviour (internationally oriented national body)
- ♦ ISBB – International Symposium on Boron, Borides and Related Materials (meeting series)
- ♦ **ISBC** International Small Business Congress (#14875)
- ♦ **ISBC** International Society for Biological Calorimetry (#14963)
- ♦ **ISBC** International Society for Bioluminescence and Chemiluminescence (#14965)
- ♦ **ISBCR** International Society for Body Composition Research (#14981)
- ♦ **ISBD** International Society for Behçet's Disease (#14958)
- ♦ **ISBD** International Society for Bipolar Disorders (#14977)
- ♦ **ISBEE** International Society of Business, Economics and Ethics (#14988)
- ♦ ISBE / see International Society for Behavioral Ecology (#14954)
- ♦ **ISBE** International Society for Behavioral Ecology (#14954)
- ♦ **ISBE** International Society of Bionic Engineering (#14970)
- ♦ ISBE – International Society for Boundary Elements (no recent information)
- ♦ **ISBE** International Society of the Built Environment (#14985)
- ♦ **ISBEM** International Society for Bioelectromagnetism (#14960)
- ♦ ISBEM – Istituto Scientifico Biomedico Euro Mediterraneo (internationally oriented national body)
- ♦ **ISBER** International Society for Biological and Environmental Repositories (#14964)
- ♦ **ISBET** International Society for Brain Electromagnetic Topography (#14984)
- ♦ **ISBF** International Society for Biofabrication (#14962)
- ♦ ISBGFH – International Society for British Genealogy and Family History (internationally oriented national body)
- ♦ **ISBI** International Society for Burn Injuries (#14986)
- ♦ **ISB** International Society for Biocuration (#14959)
- ♦ **ISB** International Society of Bioethics (#14961)
- ♦ **ISB** International Society of Biomechanics (#14966)
- ♦ **ISB** International Society of Biometeorology (#14969)
- ♦ **ISB** International Society of Biorheology (#14972)
- ♦ ISB – International Symposium on Bilingualism (meeting series)
- ♦ **ISBIS** International Society on Business and Industrial Statistics (#14989)
- ♦ **ISBITM** International Society for Business Innovation and Technology Management (#14990)
- ♦ **ISBM** International Schools of Business Management (#14790)
- ♦ **ISBM** International Society of Behavioral Medicine (#14955)
- ♦ **ISBM** International Society of Bone Morphometry (#14983)
- ♦ ISBN / see International ISBN Agency (#13955)
- ♦ **ISBN** International Society for Behavioural Neuroscience (#14957)
- ♦ **ISBNPA** International Society of Behavioral Nutrition and Physical Activity (#14956)
- ♦ ISBO / see Islamic Broadcasting Union (#16033)
- ♦ ISBOMC – International Symposium on Bioorganometallic Chemistry (meeting series)
- ♦ ISBOR – International Society of Breath Odor Research (inactive)
- ♦ **ISBP** International Society for Bonding Psychotherapy (#14982)
- ♦ ISBP – International Society of Breast Pathology (internationally oriented national body)
- ♦ **ISBRA** International Society for Biomedical Research on Alcoholism (#14968)
- ♦ **ISBR** International Society for Biosafety Research (#14973)
- ♦ **ISBSG** International Software Benchmarking Standards Group (#15556)
- ♦ ISBS – International Society for Biochemical Systematics (inactive)
- ♦ ISBS – International Society for Bioengineering and the Skin (inactive)
- ♦ **ISBS** International Society of Biomechanics in Sports (#14967)
- ♦ ISBS – International Society for Biopharmaceutical Statistics (unconfirmed)
- ♦ **ISBS** International Society for Biophysics and Imaging of Skin (#14971)
- ♦ **ISBS** International Society for Biosemiotic Studies (#14974)
- ♦ **ISBS** International Stress and Behavior Society (#15610)
- ♦ ISBSTP – International Society of Bone and Soft Tissue Pathology (internationally oriented national body)
- ♦ ISBT – International Society of Beverage Technologists (internationally oriented national body)
- ♦ **ISBT** International Society of Blood Transfusion (#14979)
- ♦ ISC / see Internet Systems Consortium
- ♦ ISC / see IP Multimedia Subsystems Forum
- ♦ ISC20C – ICOMOS International Committee on Twentieth Century Heritage (see: #13049)
- ♦ **ISC2** International Information Systems Security Certification Consortium (#13849)
- ♦ ISCaC / see International Society of Cancer Prevention (#14992)
- ♦ **ISCAEE** International Society for Ceramic Art Education and Exchange (#15001)
- ♦ **ISCAE** International Society for Comparative Adult Education (#15022)
- ♦ **ISCAID** International Society for Companion Animal Infectious Diseases (#15021)
- ♦ **ISCA** International Sailing Coaches Association (#14776)
- ♦ ISCA – International Sailing Craft Association (inactive)
- ♦ ISCA – International School Counselor Association (internationally oriented national body)
- ♦ **ISCA** International Sea Cadet Association (#14814)
- ♦ ISCA – International Senior Citizens Association (inactive)
- ♦ **ISCA** International Show Caves Association (#14856)
- ♦ ISCA – International Shrine Clown Association (internationally oriented national body)
- ♦ ISCA – International Society of Caricature Artists (internationally oriented national body)
- ♦ ISCA / see International Society of Christian Artists (#15009)
- ♦ **ISCA** International Speech Communication Association (#15578)
- ♦ **ISCA** International Sport and Culture Association (#15587)
- ♦ ISCA – International Sports Chanbara Association (unconfirmed)
- ♦ ISCA – International Stamp Collectors Association (inactive)
- ♦ ISCA – International Sunfish Class Association (see: #21760)
- ♦ ISCA – International Sustainable Community Assistance (internationally oriented national body)
- ♦ **ISCA** International Systemic Constellations Association (#15645)
- ♦ **ISCAIP** International Society for Child and Adolescent Injury Prevention (#15005)
- ♦ **ISCaM** International Society of Cancer Metabolism (#14991)
- ♦ **ISCaP** International Society of Cancer Prevention (#14992)
- ♦ **ISCAR** International Scientific Committee on Research in the Alps (#14804)
- ♦ **ISCAR** International Society for Cultural and Activity Research (#15042)
- ♦ **ISCARSAH** ICOMOS International Scientific Committee on Analysis and Restoration of Structures of Architectural Heritage (#11072)
- ♦ **ISCAS** International Society for Computer Aided Surgery (#15028)
- ♦ **ISCBFM** International Society of Cerebral Blood Flow and Metabolism (#15003)
- ♦ ISCB – International Society of Cell Biology (inactive)
- ♦ **ISCB** International Society for Clinical Bioethics (#15013)
- ♦ **ISCB** International Society for Clinical Biostatistics (#15014)
- ♦ **ISCB** International Society for Computational Biology (#15026)
- ♦ ISCB – International Symposium on Critical Bleeding (meeting series)
- ♦ ISC for Body-Psychotherapy – International Scientific Committee for Body-Psychotherapy (unconfirmed)
- ♦ ISCC / see Canadian Centre for International Studies and Cooperation
- ♦ **ISCCBE** International Society for Computing in Civil and Building Engineering (#15030)
- ♦ **ISCC** International Super-Cricket Committee (#15626)
- ♦ ISCC – International Sustainability and Carbon Certification (internationally oriented national body)
- ♦ **ISCCL** ICOMOS – IFLA International Scientific Committee on Cultural Landscapes (#11059)
- ♦ **ISCCSG** ICOMOS International Scientific Committee for the Conservation of Stained Glass (#11074)
- ♦ **ISCD** International Society for Clinical Densitometry (#15015)
- ♦ ISCD – International Society for Community Development (inactive)
- ♦ ISCD – International Society of Computerized Dentistry (internationally oriented national body)
- ♦ **ISCD** International Society of Cosmetic Dermatology (#15036)
- ♦ ISCD – International Symposium on Cable Dynamics (meeting series)
- ♦ ISCD – International Symposium on Chirality (meeting series)
- ♦ ISCEBS – International Society of Certified Employee Benefit Specialists (internationally oriented national body)
- ♦ ISCED – International Society of Continuing Education in Dentistry (inactive)
- ♦ ISCEH – International Society for Clinical and Experimental Hypnosis (inactive)
- ♦ **ISCE** International Society of Chemical Ecology (#15004)
- ♦ ISCE – International Society for Child Ecology (inactive)
- ♦ ISCE / see International Society for Enzymology (#15098)
- ♦ ISCEP – International Society of Cardiovascular Disease Epidemiology and Prevention (unconfirmed)
- ♦ ISCERG / see International Society for Clinical Electrophysiology of Vision (#15016)
- ♦ **ISCES** ICOMOS International Scientific Committee on Energy and Sustainability (#11075)
- ♦ ISCES – International Society for Complex Environmental Studies (inactive)
- ♦ ISCEST Nigeria – International Society of Comparative Education, Science and Technology (internationally oriented national body)
- ♦ **ISCEV** International Society for Clinical Electrophysiology of Vision (#15016)
- ♦ ISCFB – International Society of Cranio-Facial Biology (inactive)
- ♦ ISC-Foundation (internationally oriented national body)
- ♦ ISCFR – International Symposium on Canine and Feline Reproduction (meeting series)
- ♦ **ISCFS** International Society of Craniofacial Surgery (#15037)
- ♦ ISCG – International Society of Cosmetogynecology (unconfirmed)
- ♦ ISCHE – International Society for Children's Health and the Environment (internationally oriented national body)
- ♦ **ISCHE** International Standing Conference for History of Education (#15599)

- ♦ ISCHF / see International Society of Cardiomyopathy, Myocarditis and Heart Failure (#14993)
- ♦ **ISCH** International Society for Clinical Haemorheology (#15017)
- ♦ **ISCH** International Society for Cultural History (#15043)
- ♦ **ISCHOM** International Society of Chocolate and Cocoa in Medicine (#15008)
- ♦ **ISCHP** International Society of Critical Health Psychology (#15039)
- ♦ ISCID – Institut supérieur de commerce international de Dunkerque (internationally oriented national body)
- ♦ ISCIH – ICOMOS International c Committee on Industrial Heritage (unconfirmed)
- ♦ **ISCI** International Society for Child Indicators (#15006)
- ♦ ISC – Imaging Supplies Coalition for International Intellectual Property Protection (internationally oriented national body)
- ♦ ISC – Institute for Sustainable Communities (internationally oriented national body)
- ♦ **ISC** Inter-American Scout Committee (#11445)
- ♦ **ISC** Inter-American Society of Cardiology (#11448)
- ♦ **ISC** International Conference on Electrical Machines Steering Committee (#12878)
- ♦ ISC – International Conference on Sublobar Resections for Lung Cancer (meeting series)
- ♦ **ISC** Internationale Scheldecommissie (#12727)
- ♦ **ISC** International Saxophone Committee (#14784)
- ♦ **ISC** International School Connection (#14786)
- ♦ **ISC** International Science Council (#14796)
- ♦ **ISC** International Scientific Committee for Tuna and Tuna-like Species in the North Pacific Ocean (#14807)
- ♦ **ISC** International Seismological Centre (#14830)
- ♦ **ISC** International Sericultural Commission (#14837)
- ♦ ISC – International Silambam Committee (internationally oriented national body)
- ♦ ISC – International Slavistic Committee (inactive)
- ♦ ISC / see International Society of Antimicrobial Chemotherapy (#14925)
- ♦ **ISC** International Society for Chronobiology (#15010)
- ♦ **ISC** International Society of Citriculture (#15011)
- ♦ **ISC** International Society of Criminology (#15038)
- ♦ **ISC** International Society of Cryosurgery (#15040)
- ♦ ISC – International Society of Cryptozoology (inactive)
- ♦ **ISC** International Spiritist Council (#15585)
- ♦ ISC – International Stevia Council (unconfirmed)
- ♦ ISC – International Symposium on Chromatography (meeting series)
- ♦ ISC – Internet Systems Consortium (internationally oriented national body)
- ♦ ISCIS – International Symposium on Computer and Information Sciences (meeting series)
- ♦ ISCLD – International Symposium on Chinese Language and Discourse (meeting series)
- ♦ **ISCL** International Society for Cutaneous Lymphomas (#15044)
- ♦ **ISCLR** International Society for Contact Lens Research (#15033)
- ♦ **ISCLS** International Society of Contact Lens Specialists (#15034)
- ♦ ISCMA – International Sugar Confectionery Manufacturers Association (inactive)
- ♦ ISC / see Mediterranean Society of Chemotherapy and Infection (#16675)
- ♦ ISCME – International Society for Computational Methods in Engineering (inactive)
- ♦ **ISCMF** International Society of Cardiomyopathy, Myocarditis and Heart Failure (#14993)
- ♦ **ISCM** International Society for Ceramics in Medicine (#15002)
- ♦ **ISCM** International Society for Contemporary Music (#15035)
- ♦ ISCM – International Society of Cybernetic Medicine (inactive)
- ♦ **ISCMNS** International Society for Condensed Matter Nuclear Science (#15031)
- ♦ **ISCMP** ICOMOS International Scientific Committee on Mural Paintings (#11078)
- ♦ **ISCMR** International Society for Complementary Medicine Research (#15025)
- ♦ ISCNG / see International Skin-Care Nursing Group (#14872)
- ♦ **ISCN** International Society of Non-invasive Cardiology (#15308)
- ♦ **ISCN** International Software Consulting Network (#15557)
- ♦ ISCN – International Soil Carbon Network (unconfirmed)
- ♦ **ISCN** International Sustainable Campus Network (#15635)
- ♦ ISCN – International Symposium on Clinical Nutrition (meeting series)
- ♦ **ISCO3** International Scientific Committee on Ozone Therapy (#14803)
- ♦ ISCoAH – ICOMOS International Committee on Aerospace Heritage (unconfirmed)
- ♦ ISCOD – Instituto Sindical de Cooperación al Desarrollo, Madrid (internationally oriented national body)
- ♦ ISCO – International Society of Cellular Oncology (no recent information)
- ♦ ISCO – International Society of Corvette Owners (no recent information)
- ♦ **ISCO** International Soil Conservation Organization (#15560)
- ♦ **ISCO** International Spill Control Organization (#15580)
- ♦ ISCO – International Symposium on Combinatorial Optimization (meeting series)
- ♦ ISCOME – International Society for Communication Science and Medicine (internationally oriented national body)
- ♦ ISCOMET / see International Scientific Conference Minorities for Europe of Tomorrow (#14808)
- ♦ **ISCOMET** International Scientific Conference Minorities for Europe of Tomorrow (#14808)
- ♦ ISCOPS – International Space Conference of Pacific-Basin Societies (meeting series)
- ♦ ISCORD-AQ / see International Association of Cold Regions Development Studies (#11786)
- ♦ ISCORN – International Scientific Committee of Radionuclides in Nephrourology (inactive)
- ♦ ISCOS / see Institute for Cooperation in Space
- ♦ ISCOS / see Istituto Sindicale per la Cooperazione allo Sviluppo
- ♦ ISCOS Cisl – Istituto Sindicale per la Cooperazione allo Sviluppo (internationally oriented national body)
- ♦ **ISCOS** Inter-Governmental Standing Committee on Shipping (#11501)
- ♦ **ISCoS** International Spinal Cord Society (#15581)
- ♦ **ISCOWA** International Society for Construction with Alternative Materials (#15032)
- ♦ **ISCPES** International Society for Comparative Physical Education and Sport (#15023)
- ♦ **ISCP** International Society of Cardiovascular Pharmacotherapy (#14996)
- ♦ **ISCP** International Society for Chinese Philosophy (#15007)
- ♦ **ISCP** International Society for Coaching Psychology (#15019)
- ♦ **ISCP** International Society for Comparative Psychology (#15024)
- ♦ ISCPP – International Society of Crime Prevention Practitioners (internationally oriented national body)
- ♦ ISCP / see World Association of Societies of Pathology and Laboratory Medicine (#21191)
- ♦ **ISCRA** International Society for Cartilage Repair of the Ankle (#14999)
- ♦ **ISCRAM** International Community on Information Systems for Crisis Response and Management (#12824)
- ♦ ISCRAT – International Society for Cultural Research and Activity Theory (inactive)
- ♦ ISCRC – International School Choice and Reform Conference (meeting series)
- ♦ ISCRC – International State Crime Research Consortium (internationally oriented national body)
- ♦ ISCRE – International Symposium Chemical Reaction Engineering (meeting series)
- ♦ ISCS / see Friends International Ministries
- ♦ ISCSBH / see ICOMOS International Scientific Committee on Shared Built Heritage (#11081)
- ♦ ISCSC – International Society for the Comparative Study of Civilizations (internationally oriented national body)
- ♦ **ISCS** ICOMOS International Scientific Committee for Stone (#11082)
- ♦ ISCS – International Symposium on Compound Semiconductors (meeting series)
- ♦ **ISCSP** International Scientific Committee on Shot Peening (#14805)
- ♦ **ISCSS** International Society for Computational Social Science (#15027)
- ♦ **ISCST** International Society of Coating Science and Technology (#15020)
- ♦ ISC – TIMSS and PIRLS International Study Center (internationally oriented national body)
- ♦ ISCT / see International Society for Cell & Gene Therapy (#15000)
- ♦ **ISCT** International Society for Cell & Gene Therapy (#15000)
- ♦ ISCT – International Society for the Classical Tradition (inactive)
- ♦ ISCTM – International Society for CNS Clinical Trials and Methodology (internationally oriented national body)
- ♦ **ISCTRC** International Scientific Council for Trypanosomiasis Research and Control (#14809)
- ♦ **ISCTR** International Society for Cardiovascular Translational Research (#14997)
- ♦ ISCTS / see World Society of Cardiovascular & Thoracic Surgeons (#21800)
- ♦ **ISCU** International School Chess Union (#14785)
- ♦ **ISCU** International Society of Cardiovascular Ultrasound (#14998)
- ♦ **ISCVDP** International Society for Cardiovascular Disease Prevention (#14994)
- ♦ **ISCVID** International Society of Cardiovascular Infectious Diseases (#14995)
- ♦ **ISCWater** ICOMOS International Scientific Committee on Water and Heritage (#11083)
- ♦ **ISC-WDS** ISC World Data System (#16024)

♦ ISC World Data System (ISC-WDS) 16024

Main Office c/o UT-Oak Ridge Innovation Inst, 1345 Circle Park, 421B Communications Bldg, Knoxville TN 37996, USA. E-mail: wds-ipo@utk.edu.
URL: https://www.worlddatasystem.org/

History 1957. Founded within the framework of *International Council for Science (ICSU, inactive)*, when World Data Centres (WDCs) were set up to provide archives for the observational data resulting from the 'International Geophysical Year' (IGY), with activities guided by IGY Coordinator in Brussels (Belgium). The System has since expanded and evolved to cover an ever wider variety of geophysical and environmental data, guided and coordinated since 1968 by *'ICSU Panel on World Data Centres'*. At ICSU General Assembly, Oct 2008, Maputo (Mozambique), it was decided to merge *World Data Center System (WDCs) – Système des centres mondiaux de données* with *Federation of Astronomical and Geophysical Data Analysis Services (FAGS, inactive)* into a new system under current title. Currently functions within *International Science Council (ISC, #14796)*. **Aims** Form a worldwide 'community of excellence' for multidisciplinary scientific data to ensure long-term stewardship and provision of quality-assessed data and data services to the international science community and other stakeholders. **Structure** Scientific Committee (WDS-SC), headed by Chair and comprised of 12 members; International Program Office (IPO), hosted by the University of Tennessee Oak Ridge Innovation Institute in Knoxville TN (USA), headed by an Executive Director; Working Groups. **Languages** English. **Staff** 4.00 FTE, paid. **Finance** Support from: *International Council for Science (ICSU, inactive)*. IPO supported by US Department of Energy through the University of Tennessee. Members financed by sponsoring institutions. **Activities** Events/meetings. **Events** *SCIDATACON : International Conference on Data Sharing and Integration for Global Sustainability* Salzburg (Austria) 2023, *SCIDATACON : International Conference on Data Sharing and Integration for Global Sustainability* Seoul (Korea Rep) 2022, *SCIDATACON : International Conference on Data Sharing and Integration for Global Sustainability* Seoul (Korea Rep) 2021, *SCIDATACON : International Conference on Data Sharing and Integration for Global Sustainability* Gaborone (Botswana) 2018, *Workshop on Earth Observation in Support of the Sustainable Development Goals* Tokyo (Japan) 2017. **Publications** Annual Report; Strategic Plan.

Members Regular (57); Network (10); Partner (4); Associate (19). Regular in 15 countries and territories:
Australia, Belgium, Canada, China, Denmark, France, Germany, India, Japan, Russia, South Africa, Sweden, Taiwan, UK, Ukraine, USA.
Included in the above, 6 organizations listed in this Yearbook:
Incorporated Research Institutions for Seismology (IRIS); *International Service for Geomagnetic Indices (ISGI, #14840)*; *ISRIC – World Soil Information (#16068)*; *Strasbourg Astronomical Data Centre (#20003)*; *WFCC-MIRCEN World Data Centre for Microorganisms (WDCM, #20929)*; *World Glacier Monitoring Service (WGMS, #21539)*.
Network members include 7 organizations listed in this Yearbook:
International DORIS Service (IDS, #13192); *International GNSS Service (IGS, #13724)*; *International Laser Ranging Service (ILRS, see: #11914)*; *International Oceanographic Data and Information Exchange (IODE, #14396)*; *International Space Environment Service (ISES, #15572)*; *International Virtual Observatory Alliance (IVOA, #15858)*; *International VLBI Service for Geodesy and Astrometry (IVS, #15860)*.
Partner members include 2 organizations listed in this Yearbook:
International Environmental Data Rescue Organization (IEDRO); *International Union of Geodesy and Geophysics (IUGG, #15776)*.
Associate members include 9 organizations listed in this Yearbook:
Committee on Data for Science and Technology (CODATA, #04247) (ISC); *International Association of Hydrological Sciences (IAHS, #11954)*; *International Association of Scientific, Technical and Medical Publishers (STM, #12154)*; *International Commission for Acoustics (ICA, #12658)*; *International Council for Scientific and Technical Information (ICSTI, #13070)*; *International Mathematical Union (IMU, #14121)* (Committee on Electronic Information and Communication); *International Union of Geological Sciences (IUGS, #15777)*; *International Union of History and Philosophy of Science and Technology (IUHPST, #15779)* (Division of History of Science and Technology); *Research Data Alliance (RDA, #18853)*.
IGO Relations Participates in: *Group on Earth Observations (GEO, #10735)*. **NGO Relations** Member of (1): *International Council for Scientific and Technical Information (ICSTI, #13070)*. [2023.02.15/XE1185/y/**F**]

- ♦ ISCYRA – International Star Class Yacht Racing Association (see: #21760)
- ♦ ISD / see International Society of Dermatopathology (#15049)
- ♦ ISDAC – International Symposium on Dynamics and Aerodynamics of Cables (meeting series)
- ♦ ISDA – International Sino-Dance Association (inactive)
- ♦ **ISDA** International Swaps and Derivatives Association (#15638)
- ♦ IsDB / see Islamic Development Bank (#16044)
- ♦ **ISDB** International Society of Developmental Biologists (#15052)
- ♦ **ISDB** International Society of Drug Bulletins (#15066)
- ♦ **IsDB** Islamic Development Bank (#16044)
- ♦ **ISDCI** International Society of Developmental and Comparative Immunology (#15053)
- ♦ ISDC / see International Council of Beverages Associations (#12999)
- ♦ ISDC – International Security and Development Center (internationally oriented national body)
- ♦ **ISDCL** International Society for Deuterocanonical and Cognate Literature (#15051)
- ♦ **ISD and DE** International Society of Dacryology and Dry Eye (#15045)
- ♦ **ISDDE** International Society for Design and Development in Education (#15050)
- ♦ **ISDE** International Society for Digital Earth (#15061)
- ♦ **ISDE** International Society for Diseases of the Esophagus (#15064)
- ♦ **ISDE** International Society of Doctors for the Environment (#15065)
- ♦ ISDF – International Sustainable Development Foundation (internationally oriented national body)
- ♦ **ISDG** International Society of Dynamic Games (#15067)
- ♦ **ISDH** International Society for Digital Health (#15062)
- ♦ **ISDI** International Special Dietary Food Industries (#15576)
- ♦ **ISD** Institute for Strategic Dialogue (#11296)
- ♦ ISD – Institute for the Study of Diplomacy (internationally oriented national body)
- ♦ ISD – International Sealing Distribution Association (internationally oriented national body)
- ♦ ISD / see International Society of Dermatology (#15048)
- ♦ **ISD** International Society of Dermatology (#15048)
- ♦ **ISD** International Society of Differentiation (#15059)
- ♦ **ISDIS** International Society for Digital Imaging of the Skin (#15063)
- ♦ ISDL – Jagadguru Shree Kripaluji Maharaj / see Jagadguru Kripalu Parishat (#16086)
- ♦ ISDM – International Shared Decision Making Conference (meeting series)
- ♦ ISDM – International Shared Decision Making Society (unconfirmed)
- ♦ ISDM – International Society of Disaster Medicine (inactive)
- ♦ ISDMM – International Symposium on Defects and Material Mechanisms (meeting series)
- ♦ **ISDN** International Society for Developmental Neuroscience (#15054)
- ♦ ISDNP – International Society for the Development of Natural Products (internationally oriented national body)

- ♦ ISDPA – International Sport for Development and Peace Association (unconfirmed)
- ♦ ISDP – Institute for Security and Development Policy (internationally oriented national body)
- ♦ **ISDP** International Society of Dermatopathology (#15049)
- ♦ ISDP – International Society for Developmental Psychobiology (internationally oriented national body)
- ♦ ISDP – RAND International Security and Defense Policy Center (internationally oriented national body)
- ♦ ISDQP – International Society for Diagnostic Quantitative Pathology (inactive)
- ♦ ISDRA – International Sled Dog Racing Association (internationally oriented national body)
- ♦ **ISDR** International Society of Dental Regulators (#15046)
- ♦ **ISDR** International Society for Diatom Research (#15058)
- ♦ **ISDRS** International Sustainable Development Research Society (#15636)
- ♦ ISDSB – International Symposium on Diffraction Structural Biology (meeting series)
- ♦ ISDS – Institute for Strategic and Development Studies, Quezon City (internationally oriented national body)
- ♦ ISDS – International Skeletal Dysplasia Society (unconfirmed)
- ♦ **ISDS** International Society for Dermatologic Surgery (#15047)
- ♦ **ISDS** International Society for Dialogical Science (#15057)
- ♦ **ISDS** International Society for Digestive Surgery (#15060)
- ♦ **ISDUE** International Social Democratic Union for Education (#14881)
- ♦ ISDU – International Society for Dynamics of the Upper Urinary Tract (inactive)
- ♦ ISDVD – International Society of Diabetes and Vascular Disease (inactive)
- ♦ **ISDVMA** International Sled Dog Veterinary Medical Association (#14874)
- ♦ ISE / see Institution of Structural Engineers (#11322)
- ♦ ISEA / see International Society of Exposure Science
- ♦ ISEA Foundation – Foundation of International Servant Leadership Exchange Association (internationally oriented national body)
- ♦ ISEA – Institute for the Study of English in Africa (internationally oriented national body)
- ♦ ISEA – Inter-American Society for Educational Administration (inactive)

♦ ISEA International 16025

Exec Dir Univ of Brighton, School of Media, Grand Parade, Brighton, BN2 0JY, UK. T. +441273643042. E-mail: info@isea-web.org.
URL: http://www.isea-web.org/

History 1990, Netherlands. Founded following 1st International Symposium on Electronic Art, 1988, Utrecht (Netherlands). Former names and other names: *Inter-Society for the Electronic Arts (ISEA)* – former (1990 to 2009); *Société des arts électroniques* – alias. Registration: No/ID: KVK 24440251, Netherlands. **Aims** Foster *interdisciplinary* and *cross-cultural* academic discourse and exchange among culturally diverse organizations and individuals working with art, science and technology. **Structure** International Foundation Board. **Languages** English. **Staff** 1.00 FTE, paid. **Finance** Private and public foundations. **Activities** Events/meetings. **Events** *International Symposium on Electronic Art* Paris (France) 2023, *International Symposium on Electronic Art* Barcelona (Spain) 2022, *International Symposium on Electronic Art* Barcelona (Spain) 2021, *International Symposium on Electronic Art* Montréal, QC (Canada) 2020, *International Symposium on Electronic Art* Montréal, QC (Canada) 2020. **Publications** Symposium proceedings; academic papers; art exhibition catalogues.
Members Institutions, organizations and individuals in 43 countries and territories:
Argentina, Australia, Austria, Belgium, Brazil, Bulgaria, Canada, China, Colombia, Denmark, Egypt, Finland, France, Germany, Hong Kong, Hungary, India, Indonesia, Ireland, Italy, Japan, Lithuania, Macau, Mexico, Netherlands, New Zealand, North Macedonia, Norway, Peru, Poland, Qatar, Russia, Serbia, Singapore, South Africa, Spain, Sri Lanka, Switzerland, Thailand, Türkiye, UK, United Arab Emirates, USA.
IGO Relations *European Union (EU, #08967).* [2022/XD5976/**D**]

- ♦ ISEA / see International Renewable Energy Agency (#14715)
- ♦ **ISEA** International Sports Engineering Association (#15593)
- ♦ ISEA / see ISEA International (#16025)

♦ ISEAL 16026

Contact 244-354 Cambridge Heath Rd, Green House, London, E2 9DA, UK. E-mail: info@isealalliance.org.
URL: http://www.iseal.org/

History 2002. Founded by 8 standards and certification organizations: *Forest Stewardship Council (FSC, #09869); IFOAM – Organics International (IFOAM, #11105); Fairtrade International (FLO, #09240); Marine Stewardship Council (MSC, #16580); IOAS (#16001); Marine Aquarium Council (MAC, inactive); Rainforest Alliance; Social Accountability International (SAI).* Former names and other names: *International Social and Environmental Accreditation and Labelling Alliance (ISEAL Alliance)* – former. Registration: Companies House, No/ID: 04625800, Start date: 30 Dec 2002, England and Wales; EU Transparency Register, No/ID: 234563541838-29, Start date: 17 Mar 2021. **Aims** Support ambitious sustainability systems and their partners to tackle the world's most pressing challenges; drive impact and make markets a force for good. **Structure** Board of Directors; Senior Management Team; Committees (3); Stakeholder Council. **Languages** English. **Finance** Sources: government support; grants; international organizations; members' dues; private foundations. URL: https://www.isealalliance.org/get-involved/resources/iseal-annual-reports **Activities** Awareness raising; events/meetings; standards/guidelines. **Events** *Innovation and Credibility across a Range of Sustainability System* 2022, *Global Sustainability Standards Symposium* The Hague (Netherlands) 2019, *Global Sustainability Standards Conference* Sao Paulo (Brazil) 2018, *Global Sustainability Standards Conference* Berlin (Germany) 2015, *Global Sustainability Standards Symposium* Sao Paulo (Brazil) 2015. **Publications** *ISEAL Codes of Good Practice; ISEAL Credibility Principles; ISEAL Sustainability Claims Good Practice Guide.* **Members** Sustainability systems and accreditation bodies (not specified). **IGO Relations** *Deutsche Gesellschaft für Internationale Zusammenarbeit (GIZ); FAO (#09260); International Trade Centre (ITC, #15703); UNEP (#20299).* **NGO Relations** Participant of: *United Nations Global Compact (#20567).* Member of: *World Benchmarking Alliance (WBA, #21228).* [2022.10.28/XD7817/y/**D**]

- ♦ ISEAL Alliance / see ISEAL (#16026)
- ♦ **ISEAM** International Society of Engineering Asset Management (#15088)
- ♦ **ISEAN** Islands of Southeast Asian Network on Male and Transgender Sexual Health (#16063)
- ♦ **ISEAPA** International Society for Efficiency and Productivity Analysis (#15075)
- ♦ **ISEAPT** International Society for Electrophysical Agents in Physical Therapy (#15080)
- ♦ ISEAS / see ISEAS – Yusof Ishak Institute
- ♦ ISEAS – ISEAS – Yusof Ishak Institute (internationally oriented national body)
- ♦ ISEAS – Yusof Ishak Institute (internationally oriented national body)
- ♦ ISEAT – Instituto Superior Ecuménico Andino de Teologia (internationally oriented national body)
- ♦ ISEBE – International Society of Energy and Built Environment (unconfirmed)
- ♦ **ISEBI** International Society for Electrical Bio-Impedance (#15077)
- ♦ ISEBI / see International Society of Environmental Indicators (#15095)
- ♦ ISEB – International Society for Educational Biography (internationally oriented national body)
- ♦ **ISEB** International Society for Environmental Biogeochemistry (#15090)
- ♦ **ISEB** International Society for Environmental Biotechnology (#15091)
- ♦ ISEB – International Society of Environmental Botanists (internationally oriented national body)
- ♦ **ISEBTT** International Society for Electroporation-Based Technologies and Treatments (#15082)
- ♦ **ISECG** International Space Exploration Coordination Group (#15573)
- ♦ ISEC – International Statistical Ecology Conference (meeting series)
- ♦ **ISEC** International Statistical Education Centre (#15602)
- ♦ ISEC – Inter-State Economic Committee of the Economic Union of the Commonwealth of Independent States (no recent information)
- ♦ ISEC / see Local Futures (#16506)
- ♦ **ISECS** International Society for Eighteenth-Century Studies (#15076)
- ♦ **ISEC** UNIDO International Solar Energy Centre for Technology Promotion and Transfer (#20334)
- ♦ ISEEES – Institute of Slavic, East European and Eurasian Studies, Berkeley CA (internationally oriented national body)
- ♦ ISEE – International Seminar Earthworks in Europe (meeting series)
- ♦ **ISEE** International Society for Ecological Economics (#15069)
- ♦ ISEE – International Society for Environmental Education (inactive)
- ♦ **ISEE** International Society for Environmental Epidemiology (#15092)
- ♦ **ISEE** International Society for Environmental Ethics (#15094)
- ♦ ISEE – International Society of Explosives Engineers (internationally oriented national body)
- ♦ ISEG – International Society for Environmental Geotechnology (no recent information)
- ♦ ISEG – International Symposium on Environmental Geochemistry (meeting series)
- ♦ ISEGT – International Conference on Sustainable Energy and Green Technology (meeting series)
- ♦ **ISEHC** International Society for Evidence-Based Health Care (#15103)
- ♦ **ISEH** International Society for Experimental Hematology (#15107)
- ♦ ISEH – Society for Hematology and Stem Cells / see International Society for Experimental Hematology (#15107)
- ♦ **ISEI** International Society on Early Intervention (#15068)
- ♦ **ISEI** International Society of Environmental Indicators (#15095)
- ♦ **ISEI** International Society of Exercise and Immunology (#15106)
- ♦ **ISE** Initiative for Science in Europe (#11214)
- ♦ **ISE** Institut syndical européen (#08928)
- ♦ ISE – International Society of Ecoacoustics (unconfirmed)
- ♦ **ISE** International Society of Electrocardiology (#15078)
- ♦ **ISE** International Society of Electrochemistry (#15079)
- ♦ ISE – International Society for Electrostimulation (inactive)
- ♦ **ISE** International Society of Endocrinology (#15086)
- ♦ **ISE** International Society of Endocytobiology (#15087)
- ♦ **ISE** International Society for Enzymology (#15098)
- ♦ **ISE** International Society of Ethnobiology (#15101)
- ♦ **ISE** International Society for Ethnopharmacology (#15102)
- ♦ **ISE** International Society for Extremophiles (#15110)
- ♦ ISEIS – International Society for Environmental Information Sciences (internationally oriented national body)
- ♦ ISE – Istituto di Studi Europei 'Alcide de Gasperi' (internationally oriented national body)

♦ ISEKI-Food Association 16027

SG ImpactHub Vienna, Lindengasse 56, 18-19, 1070 Vienna, Austria. E-mail: office@iseki-food.net.
URL: http://www.iseki-food.net/

History 2005. Followed the establishment of the Thematic Network FoodNet, 1998, and its enlargement worldwide. Network included *Integrating Safety and Environment Knowledge in Food towards European Sustainable Development (ISEKI-Food 4, inactive).* Former names and other names: *European Association for Integrating Food Science and Engineering Knowledge into the Food Chain (ISEKI)* – former (2005); *Europäische Gesellschaft für die Integration der Lebensmittelwissenschaft und-Technologie in die Lebensmittelversorgungskette* – former (2005). Registration: ZVR, No/ID: 541528038, Austria. **Aims** Maintain a network among stakeholders in the food chain (research, education, industry); promote integration of *science* and *engineering* knowledge into the food chain; tune curricula and certify food studies; develop teaching materials and teaching methods. **Structure** General Assembly (every 3 years); Board; Committees (2); ISEKI Teams; Special Interest Groups. **Languages** English. **Staff** 7.00 FTE, paid. **Finance** Sources: meeting proceeds; members' dues; revenue from activities/projects. **Activities** Certification/accreditation; events/meetings. **Events** *Conference* Paris (France) 2023, *Conference* Vienna (Austria) 2021, *Conference* Nicosia (Cyprus) 2020, *Shelf Life International Meeting* Naples (Italy) 2019, *Conference* Stuttgart (Germany) 2018. **Publications** *International Journal of Food Studies* – electronic. *ISEKI Food Series.* Newsletter.
Members in 59 countries:
Albania, Argentina, Australia, Austria, Belgium, Bosnia-Herzegovina, Brazil, Bulgaria, Canada, Chile, Costa Rica, Croatia, Cyprus, Czechia, Ecuador, Egypt, Estonia, Finland, France, Germany, Greece, Hungary, Iceland, India, Indonesia, Iran Islamic Rep, Ireland, Israel, Italy, Kazakhstan, Korea Rep, Latvia, Lithuania, Malta, Mexico, Moldova, New Zealand, Nigeria, North Macedonia, Norway, Pakistan, Peru, Poland, Portugal, Romania, Russia, Rwanda, Serbia, Singapore, Slovakia, Slovenia, South Africa, Spain, Switzerland, Thailand, Türkiye, UK, Ukraine, USA.
Consultative Status Consultative status granted from: *UNIDO (#20336).* **NGO Relations** Member of (3): *Association for European Life Science Universities (ICA, #02519)* (Standing Committee); *European Alliance of Subject-Specific and Professional Accreditation and Quality Assurance (EASPA, #05887); Whole Grain Initiative (WGI, #20939).* [2023.02.17/XM3604/**D**]

- ♦ ISEKI / see ISEKI-Food Association (#16027)
- ♦ **ISEK** International Society of Electrophysiology and Kinesiology (#15081)
- ♦ ISELP – International Society for Equine Locomotor Pathology (internationally oriented national body)
- ♦ **ISEM** International Society of Ecological Modelling (#15070)
- ♦ **ISEM** International Society for Experimental Microsurgery (#15108)
- ♦ **ISEMIR** International Society for Musculoskeletal Imaging in Rheumatology (#15284)
- ♦ **ISEMMM** International Society of Environmental Micropaleontology, Microbiology and Meiobenthology (#15096)
- ♦ **ISEMPH** International Society for Evolution, Medicine and Public Health (#15105)
- ♦ ISEN – International Society for ECT and Neurostimulation (internationally oriented national body)
- ♦ ISEO – International Sustainable Energy Organization (inactive)
- ♦ ISEO – International Symposium on Essential Oils (meeting series)
- ♦ **ISEP** International Society for Ecological Psychology (#15071)
- ♦ ISEP – International Society for Educational Planning (internationally oriented national body)
- ♦ ISEP – International Society of Educators in Physiotherapy (no recent information)
- ♦ **ISEP** International Society for Environmental Protection (#15097)
- ♦ **ISEP** International Society for Evolutionary Protistology (#15104)
- ♦ ISEP – International Student Exchange Program (internationally oriented national body)
- ♦ ISEP – International Symposium on Education and Psychology (meeting series)
- ♦ ISEPP – International Society of Existential Psychology and Psychotherapy (internationally oriented national body)
- ♦ **ISEqH** International Society for Equity in Health (#15100)
- ♦ ISER / see Sir Arthur Lewis Institute of Social and Economic Studies
- ♦ **ISER** International Society for Eye Research (#15111)
- ♦ **ISERN** International Software Engineering Research Network (#15558)
- ♦ **ISERT** International Society for Empirical Research in Theology (#15084)
- ♦ ISES / see International Live Events Association
- ♦ ISES / see International Society of Endovascular Specialists
- ♦ ISESEA – International Symposium on Environmental Sociology in East Asia (meeting series)
- ♦ ISES – Institute for Social and European Studies (internationally oriented national body)
- ♦ ISES / see International Baccalaureate (#12306)
- ♦ ISES / see International Ship Engineering Service Association (#14848)
- ♦ **ISES** International Ship Engineering Service Association (#14848)
- ♦ **ISES** International Society for Equitation Science (#15099)
- ♦ ISES – International Society of Exposure Science (internationally oriented national body)
- ♦ **ISES** International Solar Energy Society (#15564)
- ♦ **ISES** International Space Environment Service (#15572)
- ♦ **ISESP** International Society for Electrostatic Precipitation (#15083)
- ♦ **ISESSAH** International Society for Economics and Social Sciences of Animal Health (#15072)
- ♦ ISESS – International Symposium on Education and Social Sciences (meeting series)
- ♦ **ISET-International** Institute for Social and Environmental Transition–International (#11294)
- ♦ ISETU – International Secretariat for Arts, Mass Media and Entertainment Trade Unions (inactive)
- ♦ ISEU – International Sakharov Environmental University (internationally oriented national body)
- ♦ ISEU – International Social Environmental Union (internationally oriented national body)
- ♦ **ISEV** International Society for Extracellular Vesicles (#15109)

♦ ISEVS – International Society of Endovascular Specialists (internationally oriented national body)
♦ ISE / see World Endoscopy Organization (#21380)
♦ ISFADPM – International Society for the Abolition of Data Processing Machines (inactive)
♦ ISFAE – International Society of Farm Animal Endocrinology (inactive)
♦ **ISFAE** International Society of Food, Agriculture and Environment (#15125)

♦ Isfahan Regional Center for Technology Incubators and Science Park Development (IRIS) 16028

Dir Isfahan Science and Technology, Isfahan Univ of Technology Blvd, PO Box 84155/666, Isfahan, Iran Islamic Rep. T. +983133860619. Fax +983133862355.
URL: http://www.unesco-iris.com/

History Established May 2010. Full title: *Isfahan Regional Center for Technology Incubators and Science Park Development – Under the Auspices of UNESCO (IRIS)*. A *UNESCO (#20322)* Category II centre. **Aims** Address and resolve the problems currently limiting the success of Science Parks and Technology Incubators in developing countries. **Structure** Governing Board. **Activities** Capacity building; guidance/assistance/consulting; knowledge management/information dissemination; research/documentation; training/education. **Publications** *IRIS Newsletter*. **IGO Relations** *African Union (AU, #00488)*; *International Science, Technology and Innovation Centre for South-South Cooperation under the auspices of UNESCO (ISTIC, #14799)*; *OIC Ministerial Standing Committee on Scientific and Technological Cooperation (COMSTECH, #17702)*. Memorandum of Understanding with: *ECO Science Foundation (ECOSF, #05328)*. **NGO Relations** *Asian Science Park Association (ASPA, #01693)*; *International Association of Science Parks and Areas of Innovation (IASP, #12151)*; *World Technopolis Association (WTA, #21850)*. [2017/XM6152/**E***]

♦ Isfahan Regional Center for Technology Incubators and Science Park Development – Under the Auspices of UNESCO / see Isfahan Regional Center for Technology Incubators and Science Park Development (#16028)
♦ ISFA – International Scientific Film Association (inactive)
♦ **ISFA** International Society for Apheresis (#14927)
♦ **ISFANS** International Society of Food Applications of Nanoscale Science (#15126)
♦ ISFAP / see International Society – The Fetus as a Patient (#15118)
♦ ISFC – International Scholarship Fund Committee (inactive)
♦ **ISFC** International Short Film Conference (#14854)
♦ **ISFC** International Society for Fungal Conservation (#15134)
♦ ISFC – International Symposium on Fluorine Chemistry (meeting series)
♦ ISFC / see World Heart Federation (#21562)
♦ ISFD – Islamic Solidarity Fund for Development (see: #16044)
♦ ISF "DRC" – International Scientific Forum 'Danube – River of Cooperation' (internationally oriented national body)
♦ ISFED – International Society for Fair Elections and Democracy (internationally oriented national body)
♦ **ISFE** Interactive Software Federation of Europe (#11380)
♦ **ISFE** International Society for Facial Expression (#15112)
♦ ISFE – International Society of Facilities Executives (inactive)
♦ **ISFE** International Society for Fish Endocrinology (#15121)
♦ **ISFE** International Society of Food Engineering (#15127)
♦ **ISFG** International Society for Forensic Genetics (#15128)
♦ ISFGMS – International Symposium on Functionally Graded Materials (meeting series)
♦ **ISFGW** International Society of Friendship and Good Will (#15132)
♦ ISFH / see International Society for Forensic Genetics (#15128)
♦ **ISFH** International Society for Haptics (#15153)
♦ **ISF** Information Security Forum (#11198)
♦ ISF – Ingénieurs assistance internationale (internationally oriented national body)
♦ ISF – Ingénieurs sans frontières (internationally oriented national body)
♦ ISF – Institut Séculier Féminin du Coeur de Jésus (religious order)
♦ ISF / see Interamerican Scout Foundation (#11446)
♦ **ISF** Interamerican Scout Foundation (#11446)
♦ ISF – International Federation of the Seed Trade (inactive)
♦ **ISF international** Ingénieurs sans frontières international (#05481)
♦ **ISF** International School Sport Federation (#14792)
♦ **ISF** International Seed Federation (#14828)
♦ ISF – International Self-Care Foundation (internationally oriented national body)
♦ **ISF** International Sepsis Forum (#14836)
♦ ISF – International Shinto Foundation (internationally oriented national body)
♦ ISF – International Shipping Federation (inactive)
♦ **ISF** International Skyrunning Federation (#14873)
♦ ISF – International Snowboard Federation (inactive)
♦ **ISF** International Society for Fat Research (#15115)
♦ ISF – International Softball Federation (inactive)
♦ ISF – International Solar Fuels Conference (meeting series)
♦ ISF – International Solidarity Foundation (internationally oriented national body)
♦ **ISF** International Spiritualist Federation (#15586)
♦ ISF – International Sport Strategy Foundation (internationally oriented national body)
♦ ISF – Internet Sans Frontières (unconfirmed)
♦ **ISF** Islamic Solidarity Fund (#16051)
♦ **ISFLA** International Systemic Functional Linguistics Association (#15646)
♦ **ISFL** International Society of Family Law (#15114)
♦ **ISFM** International Society of Feline Medicine (#15116)
♦ ISFM – International Symposium on Functional Materials (meeting series)
♦ ISFNF – International Symposium on Fish Nutrition and Feeding (meeting series)
♦ **ISFNR** International Society for Folk Narrative Research (#15124)
♦ ISFOS / see International Organization for Forensic Odonto-Stomatology (#14448)
♦ **ISFP** International Society for Fall Protection (#15113)
♦ **ISFP** International Society for Fertility Preservation (#15117)
♦ **ISFP** International Society for Fibrinolysis and Proteolysis (#15119)
♦ ISFPX – International Symposium for Fish Parasitology (meeting series)
♦ **ISFRI** International Society of Forensic Radiology and Imaging (#15129)
♦ **ISFR** International Society for Fluoride Research (#15123)
♦ **ISFR** International Society for Fracture Repair (#15130)
♦ ISFR – International Symposium on Feedstock Recycling of Polymeric Materials (meeting series)
♦ **ISFRR** International Society for Free Radical Research (#15131)
♦ ISFSI – International Society of Fire Service Instructors (internationally oriented national body)
♦ **ISFSI** International Society of Fish and Shellfish Immunology (#15122)
♦ **ISFTD** International Society for Frontotemporal Dementias (#15133)
♦ **ISfTeH** International Society for Telemedicine and e-Health (#15504)
♦ **ISfTE** International Society for Teacher Education (#15501)
♦ ISFT / see International Society for Fibrinolysis and Proteolysis (#15119)
♦ ISFT – International Society on the Fusion of Science and Technologies (unconfirmed)
♦ ISfT / see International Society for Telemedicine and e-Health (#15504)
♦ ISFUES – International Society of Follicular Unit Extraction Surgeons (no recent information)
♦ ISFV – International Symposium on Flow Visualization (meeting series)
♦ ISG / see International Forum of Towns and Villages in Graz
♦ **ISGAC** International Safflower Germplasm Advisory Committee (#14775)
♦ **ISGA** International Sprout Growers Association (#15596)
♦ **ISGAN** International Smart Grid Action Network (#14877)
♦ ISGAP – Institute for the Study of Global Antisemitism and Policy (internationally oriented national body)
♦ **ISGC** International Society of Gastroenterological Carcinogenesis (#15135)
♦ **ISGC** International Stroke Genetics Consortium (#15612)
♦ ISGD / see International Society for Pediatric and Adolescent Diabetes (#15344)
♦ **ISGEDR** International Society for Genetic Eye Diseases and Retinoblastoma (#15139)
♦ **ISGE** International Society of Gynecological Endocrinology (#15150)
♦ **ISGE** International Society for Gynecologic Endoscopy (#15152)
♦ **ISGEm** International Study Group on Ethnomathematics (#15618)
♦ **ISGEO** International Society of Geographical and Epidemiological Ophthalmology (#15140)
♦ **ISGF** International Scout and Guide Fellowship (#14812)
♦ **ISGG** International Society for Geometry and Graphics (#15141)
♦ **ISGG** International Society of Grid Generation (#15148)
♦ ISGHPM – International Study Group for the Relations between the History and Pedagogy of Mathematics (see: #14121)
♦ **ISGI** International Service for Geomagnetic Indices (#14840)
♦ ISGI – Istituto di Studi Giuridici Internazionali (internationally oriented national body)
♦ ISG – Institute for the Study of Genocide, New York (internationally oriented national body)
♦ **ISG** Internationale Heinrich-Schütz-Gesellschaft (#13248)
♦ ISG – Internationales Städteforum Graz (internationally oriented national body)
♦ **ISG** Internationale Szondi-Gesellschaft (#15648)
♦ **ISG** International Shoulder Group (#14855)
♦ **ISG** International Surgical Group (#15632)
♦ ISG – Iraq Survey Group (inactive)
♦ ISGlobal – Barcelona Institute for Global Health (internationally oriented national body)
♦ ISGMA – International Study Group on Music Archaeology (internationally oriented national body)
♦ ISGML – International Study Group for Mathematics Learning (inactive)
♦ ISGNE / see International Federation on Neuroendoscopy (#13489)
♦ ISGNSS – International Symposium on GNSS (meeting series)
♦ ISGO / see International Society of Geographical and Epidemiological Ophthalmology (#15140)
♦ ISGO – International Structural Genomics Organization (inactive)
♦ **ISGP** International Society for Gravitational Physiology (#15147)
♦ ISGRCM / see International Society for Heart Research (#15158)
♦ **ISGRG** International Society on General Relativity and Gravitation (#15138)
♦ **ISGSB** International Study Group for Systems Biology (#15619)
♦ **ISGSD** International Society of Groundwater for Sustainable Development (#15149)
♦ ISGSH – International Study Group for Steroid Hormones (no recent information)
♦ **ISGS** International Salivary Gland Society (#14778)
♦ ISGS – International Society for General Semantics (inactive)
♦ **ISGS** International Society for Gesture Studies (#15143)
♦ **ISGS** International Society for Glaucoma Surgery (#15144)
♦ **ISGS** International Sol-Gel Society (#15565)
♦ ISGSM / see International Society of Gender Medicine (#15137)
♦ ISGSR / see International Society for the Systems Sciences (#15500)
♦ **ISGyP** International Society of Gynecological Pathologists (#15151)
♦ ISHAGE / see International Society for Cell & Gene Therapy (#15000)
♦ ISHA – International Social History Association (unconfirmed)
♦ **ISHA** International Society for Hip Arthroscopy (#15165)
♦ **ISHA** International Solvothermal and Hydrothermal Association (#15568)
♦ **ISHA** International Students of History Association (#15613)
♦ ISHA – International Subterranean Heritage Association (no recent information)
♦ **ISHAM** International Society for Human and Animal Mycology (#15181)
♦ **ISHAS** International Society for Hyaluronan Sciences (#15186)
♦ **ISHBS** International Society of Hildegard von Bingen Studies (#15164)
♦ ISHCI – International Symposium on Chlamydial Infections (meeting series)
♦ **ISHC** International Society of Heterocyclic Chemistry (#15163)
♦ ISHC – International Symposium on Homogeneous Catalysis (meeting series)
♦ **ISHCSF** International Society for Hydrocephalus and Cerebrospinal Fluid Disorders (#15187)
♦ **ISHD** International Society for Hemodialysis (#15160)
♦ **ISHD** International Society for History Didactics (#15167)
♦ **IS-HDXMS** International Society for HDX-MS (#15154)
♦ **ISHEASTM** International Society for the History of East Asian Science Technology and Medicine (#15168)
♦ ISHEID – International Symposium on HIV and Hepatitis (meeting series)
♦ **ISHE** International Society for Human Ethology (#15182)
♦ **ISHEN** International Society for Hepatic Encephalopathy and Nitrogen Metabolism (#15161)
♦ ISHEP – International Society for HIV/AIDS Education and Prevention (inactive)
♦ **ISHGR** International Society for Hunter Gatherer Research (#15185)
♦ ISHHC – International Symposium on Relations between Homogeneous and Heterogeneous Catalysis (meeting series)
♦ **ISHHR** International Society for Health and Human Rights (#15156)
♦ ISHIB – International Society on Hypertension in Blacks (internationally oriented national body)
♦ ISHID – International Society on Hypospadias and Intersex Disorders (inactive)
♦ ISHI – International Society for the History of Ideas (inactive)
♦ **ISHIM** International Society for the History of Islamic Medicine (#15169)
♦ **ISH** International Society of Hematology (#15159)
♦ **ISH** International Society of Hymenopterists (#15188)
♦ **ISH** International Society of Hypertension (#15189)
♦ **ISH** International Society of Hypnosis (#15190)
♦ ISH – International Students House (internationally oriented national body)
♦ ISH – International Symposium on Hearing (meeting series)
♦ **ISHL** International Society for Historical Linguistics (#15166)
♦ **ISHLT** International Society for Heart and Lung Transplantation (#15157)
♦ **ISHMap** International Society for the History of the Map (#15170)
♦ **ISHMII** International Society for Structural Health Monitoring of Intelligent Infrastructure (#15460)
♦ **ISHM** International Society for the History of Medicine (#15171)
♦ ISHM / see International Society for Holter and Noninvasive Electrocardiology (#15179)
♦ ISHM – International Society for Hybrid Microelectronics (inactive)
♦ **ISHNE** International Society for Holter and Noninvasive Electrocardiology (#15179)
♦ **ISHN** International School Health Network (#14787)
♦ **ISHN** International Society for the History of the Neurosciences (#15172)
♦ **ISHPES** International Society for the History of Physical Education and Sport (#15175)
♦ **ISHP** International Society for History of Pharmacy (#15173)
♦ ISHPR – International Society of Health Psychology Research (no recent information)
♦ **ISHRAD** International Society for the History of Radiology (#15176)
♦ ISHRI – International Solidarity and Human Rights Institute (internationally oriented national body)
♦ ISHR – Institute for the Study of Human Rights, Columbia University (internationally oriented national body)
♦ **ISHR** International Service for Human Rights (#14841)
♦ **ISHR** International Society for Heart Research (#15158)
♦ **ISHR** International Society for the History of Rhetoric (#15177)
♦ **ISHR** International Society for Human Rights (#15183)
♦ ISHRS – International Society of Hair Restoration Surgery (internationally oriented national body)
♦ **ISHS** International Society for Horticultural Science (#15180)
♦ **ISHS** International Society for Humor Studies (#15184)
♦ **ISHSR** International Society for Hepatic Sinusoidal Research (#15162)

- ♦ **ISHTIP** International Society for the History and Theory of Intellectual Property (#15178)
- ♦ ISHVAC – International Symposium on Heating, Ventilation and Air Conditioning (meeting series)
- ♦ ISHV – International Society for Human Values (inactive)
- ♦ ISIA / see International Snowmobile Manufacturers Association
- ♦ ISIA / see International Pro Ski Instructors Association
- ♦ ISIAC – International Symposium on Ion-Atom Collisions (meeting series)
- ♦ **ISIA** International Serum Industry Association (#14838)
- ♦ **ISIA** International Ski Instructors Association (#14870)
- ♦ ISIAN / see International Society of Inflammation and Allergy of the Nose (#15201)
- ♦ **ISIAN** International Society of Inflammation and Allergy of the Nose (#15201)
- ♦ **ISIAQ** International Society of Indoor Air Quality and Climate (#15196)
- ♦ ISIAT – International Symposium Intra Articular Treatment (meeting series)

♦ ISIC Association 16029

Chair ISIC Global Office BV, Keizersgracht 174-176, 1016 DW Amsterdam, Netherlands. T. +31205200847. Fax +31204212810. E-mail: admin@isic.org.
URL: http://www.isic.org/

History 1968. Founded within *International Student Travel Confederation (ISTC, inactive)*, by ISTC and *International Union of Students (IUS, inactive)*; became independent under ISTC umbrella on signature of a Convention by IUS and ISTC, 21 Apr 1989. Since 1993, features *UNESCO (#20322)* logo on the card. Former names and other names: *ISTC Student Identity Card Scheme* – former (1968); *International Student Identity Card Association* – alias. Registration: Netherlands. **Aims** Increase access to educational opportunities, facilitate student life, foster intercultural understanding and education exchange, and forge stronger relationships between students of all nationalities and the global academic community. **Structure** General Meeting (annual); Board; Global Office, based in Amsterdam (Netherlands). **Languages** English. **Staff** 1162.00 FTE, paid. **Finance** Financed through sale of ISIC cards. Annual budget: about euro 3,000,000. **Activities** Awards/prizes/competitions. **Events** *ISIC Event* Belgrade (Serbia) 2022, *ISIC Event* Dubai (United Arab Emirates) 2021, *ISIC Event* 2020, *ISIC Event* Thessaloniki (Greece) 2019, *ISIC Event* Taipei (Taiwan) 2018. **Publications** *ISIC Benefit Applications*. Annual Report.

Members Student travel organizations; national student unions; academic and educational organizations; companies. Issuers in 133 countries and territories:
Andorra, Angola, Argentina, Armenia, Australia, Austria, Azerbaijan, Bahrain, Bangladesh, Belarus, Belgium, Benin, Bolivia, Bosnia-Herzegovina, Botswana, Brazil, Brunei Darussalam, Bulgaria, Cameroon, Canada, Chile, China, Colombia, Costa Rica, Croatia, Cuba, Cyprus, Czechia, Denmark, Dominican Rep, Ecuador, Egypt, El Salvador, Estonia, Faeroe Is, Fiji, Finland, France, Gambia, Georgia, Germany, Ghana, Gibraltar, Greece, Greenland, Guatemala, Holy See, Hong Kong, Hungary, Iceland, India, Indonesia, Iran Islamic Rep, Iraq, Ireland, Israel, Italy, Jamaica, Japan, Jordan, Kazakhstan, Kenya, Korea Rep, Kosovo, Kuwait, Kyrgyzstan, Latvia, Lebanon, Libya, Liechtenstein, Lithuania, Luxembourg, Macau, Malaysia, Mali, Malta, Mauritius, Mexico, Moldova, Monaco, Mongolia, Montenegro, Nepal, Netherlands, New Zealand, Nicaragua, Nigeria, North Macedonia, Norway, Oman, Pakistan, Panama, Paraguay, Peru, Philippines, Poland, Portugal, Puerto Rico, Qatar, Romania, Russia, San Marino, Saudi Arabia, Senegal, Serbia, Singapore, Slovakia, Slovenia, South Africa, South Sudan, Spain, Sri Lanka, Suriname, Sweden, Switzerland, Syrian AR, Taiwan, Tajikistan, Tanzania UR, Thailand, Tunisia, Türkiye, Uganda, UK, Ukraine, United Arab Emirates, Uruguay, USA, Venezuela, Vietnam, Yemen, Zambia, Zimbabwe.

Consultative Status Consultative status granted from: *UNESCO (#20322)* (Consultative Status). **IGO Relations** *United Nations Alliance of Civilizations (UNAOC, #20520)*; *World Tourism Organization (UNWTO, #21861)*. **NGO Relations** Affiliate to: *International Association of Universities (IAU, #12246)*. [2021/XK0261/**E**]

- ♦ ISICEM – International Symposium on Intensive Care and Emergency Medicine (internationally oriented national body)
- ♦ **ISIC** Institute for Scientific Information on Coffee (#11293)
- ♦ **ISIC** Institute for the Study of Islam and Christianity (#11297)
- ♦ ISICR / see International Cytokine and Interferon Society (#13127)
- ♦ ISIDA – International Service Innovation Design Association (unconfirmed)
- ♦ ISID – Institute for the Study of International Development (internationally oriented national body)
- ♦ ISID / see International Interior Design Association (#13946)
- ♦ **ISID** International Societies for Investigative Dermatology (#14890)
- ♦ **ISID** International Society for Infectious Diseases (#15199)
- ♦ **ISIDOG** International Society for Infectious Diseases in Obstetrics and Gynaecology (#15200)
- ♦ **ISIE** International Society for Industrial Ecology (#15197)
- ♦ ISIE – International Symposium on Impact Engineering (meeting series)
- ♦ ISIEM – International Symposium on Inorganic and Environmental Materials (meeting series)
- ♦ **ISIF** Institut pour la solidarité internationale des femmes (#19298)
- ♦ **ISIF** International Society of Information Fusion (#15203)
- ♦ ISIG – Istituto di Sociologia Internazionale di Gorizia (internationally oriented national body)
- ♦ **i-SIGMA** International Secure Information Governance and Management Association (#14823)
- ♦ **ISIH** International Society for Intellectual History (#15206)
- ♦ ISIH – In Sickness and In Health International Conference (meeting series)
- ♦ **ISIIL** Internacia Scienca Instituto Ivo Lapenna (#11525)
- ♦ **ISI** Informing Science Institute (#11201)
- ♦ **ISI** Institute on Statelessness and Inclusion (#11295)
- ♦ **ISI** Institut Sexocorporel International (#11358)
- ♦ **ISI** International Sediment Initiative (#14827)
- ♦ ISI – International Semiotics Institute, Imatra (internationally oriented national body)
- ♦ **ISI** International Statistical Institute (#15603)
- ♦ ISI – International Students (internationally oriented national body)
- ♦ ISIL – Indian Society of International Law (internationally oriented national body)
- ♦ ISIL / see Liberty International (#16457)
- ♦ **ISILS** International Society for Islamic Legal Studies (#15219)
- ♦ **ISIM** International Society of Internal Medicine (#15212)
- ♦ **ISIM** International Society for Invertebrate Morphology (#15217)
- ♦ **ISIMM** International Society for Immunohistochemistry and Molecular Morphology (#15192)
- ♦ **ISIMM** International Society for the Interaction of Mechanics and Mathematics (#15208)
- ♦ **ISINI** International Society for Intercommunication of New Ideas (#15209)
- ♦ **ISIN** International Society for Immunonutrition (#15194)
- ♦ **ISIN** International Society of Intraoperative Neurophysiology (#15214)
- ♦ ISIN – International Society for Invertebrate Neurobiology (inactive)
- ♦ ISIO – International Security Industry Organization (internationally oriented national body)
- ♦ **ISIORT** International Society of Intraoperative Radiation Therapy (#15215)
- ♦ **ISIPAR** International Society for Interpersonal Acceptance and Rejection (#15213)
- ♦ ISIP – International Society on Immunopharmacology (inactive)
- ♦ ISIP – International Society of Internet Professionals (inactive)
- ♦ **ISIP** International Society for Islamic Philosophy (#15220)
- ♦ **ISIPT** International Society for Industrial Process Tomography (#15198)
- ♦ ISIR / see International Sakharov Environmental University
- ♦ ISIRC – International Social Innovation Research Conference (meeting series)
- ♦ **ISIRD** International Society of Invertebrate Reproduction and Development (#15218)
- ♦ ISIR / see International Cytokine and Interferon Society (#13127)
- ♦ **ISIR** International Society for Immunology of Reproduction (#15193)
- ♦ ISIR – International Society for Intelligence Research (unconfirmed)
- ♦ **ISIR** International Society for Inventory Research (#15216)
- ♦ ISIR / see International Society of Invertebrate Reproduction and Development (#15218)
- ♦ ISIR / see International Society for Sexual Medicine (#15441)
- ♦ **isirv** International Society for Influenza and other Respiratory Virus Diseases (#15202)
- ♦ ISIS / see International Congress of Infant Studies
- ♦ ISIS / see Association for Iranian Studies
- ♦ ISIS / see School of International Studies, Delhi
- ♦ **ISISA** International Small Islands Studies Association (#14876)
- ♦ ISISAR – International Society for Intercultural Studies and Research (internationally oriented national body)
- ♦ ISIS / see ASEAN Institutes for Strategic and International Studies (#01200)
- ♦ ISIS Association / see International Association for Student Insurance Services (#12190)
- ♦ ISISC / see Siracusa International Institute for Criminal Justice and Human Rights (#19289)
- ♦ The ISIS Foundation / see Adara Development (#00110)
- ♦ ISIS – Institute for Science and International Security (internationally oriented national body)
- ♦ ISIS – Institute for the Secularization of Islamic Society (internationally oriented national body)
- ♦ ISIS – Institute of Security and International Studies, Bangkok (internationally oriented national body)
- ♦ ISIS – Institute for Security and International Studies, Sofia (internationally oriented national body)
- ♦ ISIS – Institute of Strategic and International Studies, Malaysia (internationally oriented national body)

♦ Isis Internacional, Santiago de Chile 16030

Contact address not obtained. T. +5622695506.

History Jan 1984, when ISIS was transformed into 3 organizations, the sister organizations being *IO – Facilitating Space for Feminist Conversations (Io, #16005)* and *Isis Women's International Cross Cultural Exchange (ISIS-WICCE, #16031)*. **Aims** As an information and communication service for *women*, participate in the *development* process; serve as a reliable source of information and bibliographical service on the studies of women; provide a centre of permanent consultation for women and men interested in the subject. **Activities** Programmes: No Violence Against Women; Women and Health; Information and Communication Technologies. Information and Documentation Centre. **Publications** *Agenda Salud*; *Las Mujeres*; *Perspectivas*. Bulletins (also electronic). **Members** Membership countries not specified. [2011/XF7029/**F**]

- ♦ Isis International / see IO – Facilitating Space for Feminist Conversations (#16005)
- ♦ ISIS / see International Association for Student Insurance Services (#12190)
- ♦ ISIS – International Security Information Service (internationally oriented national body)
- ♦ **ISIS** International Society for Intermedial Studies (#15211)
- ♦ ISIS – International Society for the Investigation of Stress (inactive)
- ♦ ISIS / see International Society for the Study of Information (#15477)
- ♦ ISIS – International Student Information Service (inactive)
- ♦ ISIS / see IO – Facilitating Space for Feminist Conversations (#16005)
- ♦ ISIS / see Isis Women's International Cross Cultural Exchange (#16031)
- ♦ ISIS-NIT / see International Association of Users and Developers of Electronic Libraries and New Information Technologies (#12252)
- ♦ ISIS-S / see International Society for the Interdisciplinary Study of Symmetry (#15210)
- ♦ ISIS / see Species360 (#19915)
- ♦ **ISIS-WICCE** Isis Women's International Cross Cultural Exchange (#16031)

♦ Isis Women's International Cross Cultural Exchange (ISIS-WICCE) . 16031

Exec Dir Plot 23 Bukoto St, Kampala, Uganda. T. +256414543953. Fax +256414543954.
URL: https://www.isis-wicce.org/

History 1974, Geneva (Switzerland), when operated as a *Women's International Information and Communication Service (ISIS) – Service féminin international d'information et de communication – Servicio Femenino Internacional de Información y de Comunicación*. Reconstituted under present title, Jan 1984, when ISIS was transformed into 3 organizations, the sister organizations being *IO – Facilitating Space for Feminist Conversations (Io, #16005)* and *Isis Internacional, Santiago de Chile (#16030)*. ISIS-WICCE re-located, Sep 1993, to Kampala (Uganda) in order to tap the voices of African women and link their issues and concerns to the debates and campaigns taking place at the international level. A global action oriented women's organization that emulates "Isis", the ancient Egyptian goddess of Wisdom, Creativity and Knowledge. **Aims** Promote justice, equality and mutual relationship between women and men and empowerment of women through documenting violations of women's *rights* and facilitating exchange of skills and information to strengthen women's capacities, potential and visibility. **Structure** International Board of Directors; Secretariat. **Languages** English, French. **Staff** 8.00 FTE, paid. **Finance** through: *DANIDA*; Evangelische Zentraistelle für Entwicklungsilfe (EED); *Forum for Kvinner og Utviklingsspørsmål (FOKUS)*; Global Human Rights Fund; *Global Ministries of The United Methodist Church (GM-UMC)*; *Humanistisch Instituut voor Ontwikkelingssamenwerking (Hivos)*; Kerkinactie; *Norwegian Agency for Development Cooperation (Norad)*; *Norwegian Council for Africa (NCA)*; *World Medical Association (WMA, #21646)*. **Activities** *'Exchange'*: organizes annual thematic event offering the opportunity for women activists working on women's human rights issues to meet and share ideas, exchange skills, strategies and experience and plan on future networking. *'Information and Documentation'*: coordinates research projects documenting women's experiences in armed conflict. **Events** *Know-how conference* Kampala (Uganda) 2002, *International women and health tribunal and meeting / International Women's Health and Meeting* Manila (Philippines) 1990, *European women and health conference* Madrid (Spain) 1989, *Meeting* Bangalore (India) 1987. **Publications** *Women's World* (2 a year) in English, French; *Impact* (annual). Research reports; video tapes on women in armed conflict and peacebuilding. **Information Services** *Women's International Resource Centre*. **Members** Not a membership organization. **Consultative Status** Consultative status granted from: *ECOSOC (#05331)* (Special). [2014/XF0271/**F**]

- ♦ ISITC (internationally oriented national body)

♦ ISITC Europe 16032

Main Office 59-60 Russell Square, London, WC1B 4HP, UK. E-mail: admin@isitc-europe.com.
URL: http://www.isitc-europe.com/

History Jan 1992. ISITC stands for *Industry Standardisation for Institutional Trade Communication Committee*. Previously also referred to as *International Securities Association for Institutional Trade Communication – International Operations Association (ISITC-IOA)*. **Aims** Promote operational efficiency in the global financial industry through education, design, standardization and recommendation. **Structure** ISITC Europe Leadership Group (IELG); Board; Advisory Board. Working Groups. **Finance** Members' dues. **Activities** Events/meetings. **Events** *Europe Market Inovation Summit* London (UK) 2019, *European spring conference* Amsterdam (Netherlands) 2005, *Annual European conference* London (UK) 2005. **Members** Membership countries not specified. **NGO Relations** In liaison with technical committees of: *International Organization for Standardization (ISO, #14473)*. [2020/XD9094/**D**]

- ♦ ISITC-IOA / see ISITC
- ♦ ISITC-IOA / see ISITC Europe (#16032)
- ♦ ISITDBT – International Society for the Improvement and Teaching of Dialectical Behavior Therapy (internationally oriented national body)
- ♦ ISIT – Institut supérieur international du tourisme (internationally oriented national body)
- ♦ ISITQ – International Society for Improving Training Quality (no recent information)
- ♦ **ISIUS** International Society of Intelligent Unmanned Systems (#15207)
- ♦ **ISIVF** International Society for In Vitro Fertilization (#15545)
- ♦ ISJA – International Sport Jujitsu Association (internationally oriented national body)
- ♦ ISJC / see International Jumping Officials Club (#13976)
- ♦ **ISJKM** International Society for Japanese Kampo Medicine (#15221)
- ♦ **ISJP** International Society for Japanese Philately (#15222)
- ♦ **ISJR** International Society for Justice Research (#15223)
- ♦ **ISKA** Internationalen för Stats- och Kommunalsanställda (#18572)
- ♦ **ISKA** International Sport Karate Association (#15590)
- ♦ ISKCON – International Society for Krishna Consciousness (religious order)
- ♦ ISK – Internacia Scienca Kolegio (see: #00617)
- ♦ **ISK** Internationale Seidenbau Kommission (#14837)
- ♦ **ISK** Internationales Sachsenhausen-Komitee (#04187)
- ♦ ISK – International Society of the Knee (inactive)
- ♦ ISK – International Symposium on Kallikreins and Kallikrein-Related Peptidases (meeting series)
- ♦ **ISKO** International Society for Knowledge Organization (#15224)
- ♦ ISKSS – International Society for Knowledge and Systems Sciences (internationally oriented national body)
- ♦ ISLA – International Securities Lending Association (internationally oriented national body)

♦ **ISLA** International Service Logistics Association (#14842)
♦ ISLA – International Sign Language Association (inactive)
♦ **ISLA** International Society for Medical Laser Applications (#15256)
♦ **ISLA** International Sport Lawyers Association (#15591)
♦ ISLA – Istituto di Studi Latinoamericani, Milano (internationally oriented national body)
♦ Islamic Academy of Sciences / see Islamic World Academy of Sciences (#16057)
♦ Islamic Army for the Liberation of the Holy Places / see Al-Qa'ida (#00748)
♦ Islamic Asian Coordinating Council (inactive)

♦ Islamic Broadcasting Union (IBU) 16033

SG PO Box 6351, Jeddah 21442, Saudi Arabia. T. +96626722269 – +9662672111. Fax +96626722600.

History 1975, Jeddah, as *Islamic States Broadcasting Organization (ISBO) – Organisation de radiodiffusion des Etats islamiques*, in accordance with a resolution adopted by 6th *Council of Foreign Ministers (CFM, see: #17813)*, 12-15 Jul 1975, Jeddah (Saudi Arabia). A Specialized Organ of *Organisation of Islamic Cooperation (OIC, #17813)*. **Aims** Propagate the principles of the Islamic Da'wa; acquaint people with the cause of Islam and ensure its defence; strengthen the spirit of brotherhood among the *Muslim* people; explain the political, social and economic basis of Islamic solidarity; develop cooperation between Islamic technical organizations and institutions of Member States engaged in the field of *radio* and *television*; promote teaching of the *Arabic* language using audiovisual aids. **Structure** General Assembly (every 2 years), comprising representatives of broadcasting organizations in OIC Member States. Executive Council (annual), consisting of 15 members, including (ex officio): the host country, Saudi Arabia, which heads the Council; Palestine; OIC Secretariat General. Permanent Committees (2): Programmes; Administration and Finance. **Languages** Arabic, English, French. **Staff** 21.00 FTE, paid. **Finance** Contributions and donations from Member States. Other sources: voluntary grants; resources from services rendered. **Activities** Organizes competitions and symposia; produces recordings; maintains library. **Events** *Session* Cairo (Egypt) 1991, *General Assembly* Jeddah (Saudi Arabia) 1987.

Members Governmental radio and TV institutions in 53 states:
Afghanistan, Albania, Algeria, Azerbaijan, Bahrain, Bangladesh, Benin, Brunei Darussalam, Burkina Faso, Cameroon, Chad, Comoros, Djibouti, Egypt, Gabon, Gambia, Guinea, Guinea-Bissau, Indonesia, Iran Islamic Rep, Iraq, Jordan, Kazakhstan, Kuwait, Kyrgyzstan, Lebanon, Libya, Malaysia, Maldives, Mali, Mauritania, Morocco, Mozambique, Niger, Nigeria, Oman, Pakistan, Palestine, Qatar, Saudi Arabia, Senegal, Sierra Leone, Somalia, Sudan, Syrian AR, Tajikistan, Togo, Tunisia, Türkiye, Turkmenistan, Uganda, United Arab Emirates, Yemen.

IGO Relations Special agreement with: *UNESCO (#20322)*. Invited to sessions of Intergovernmental Council of: *International Programme for the Development of Communication (IPDC, #14651)*. Cooperates with: *Islamic World Educational, Scientific and Cultural Organization (ICESCO, #16058)*. [2015/XD8624/**C***]

♦ Islamic Call College 16034

Contact address not obtained. T. +218214800059. Fax +218214800059.
URL: http://www.islamic-call.net/

History Founded 2 Nov 1974, Tripoli (Libyan AJ), within the framework of *World Islamic Call Society (WICS, inactive)*. **Aims** Help the Muslim community by granting educational scholarships; sponsor cultural conferences and exchange experience among visiting professors. **Activities** Trains students to BA Level at College in Tripoli (Libyan AJ) and a branch college in Damascus (Syrian AR). Supervises teaching courses in Arabic for non-native speakers; provides health care, full board accommodation and pocket money to students; works to enhance quality assurance of the College's curriculum programme; organizes seminars and conferences. **Publications** *Bulletin of the Faculty of Islamic Call* (11 a year). *Series of Islamic Heritage*. Studies. [2013.09.26/XF0183/**F**]

♦ Islamic Capitals Organization / see Organization of Islamic Capitals and Cities (#17875)
♦ Islamic-Catholic Liaison Committee (see: #09682)
♦ Islamic Cement Association (inactive)

♦ Islamic Centre for Development of Trade (ICDT) 16035

Centre islamique pour le développement du commerce (CIDC)

Dir Gen Tour des Habous, Avenue des FAR, BP 13545, 20000 Casablanca, Morocco. T. +212522314974. Fax +212522310110. E-mail: icdt@icdt-oic.org.
URL: http://www.icdt-oic.org/

History Founded as a subsidiary organ of *Organisation of Islamic Cooperation (OIC, #17813)*, in accordance with resolution of 3rd *Islamic Summit of Kings and Heads of States and Governments (#16053)*, Jan 1981, Makkah/Taif. Commenced operations Jan 1983, Casablanca (Morocco). Former names and other names: *OIC Trade Centre* – alias; *Casablanca Centre* – alias; *Islamic Trade Centre* – alias. **Aims** Encourage regular trade exchanges among Member States; promote investments likely to develop trade flows; contribute to promotion of Member States' products and encourage access to foreign markets; promote trade information; assist Member States in fields of trade promotion and international negotiations; extend assistance to enterprises and economic operators. **Structure** General Assembly (annual), comprising representatives of *Islamic Commission for Economic, Cultural and Social Affairs (ICECSA, #16038)*. Board of Directors (meeting once a year), consisting of 8 elected members and the permanent representative of Morocco, the host country; OIC Secretary General and the Director General of the Centre are ex-officio members. **Languages** Arabic, English, French. **Staff** 25.00 FTE, paid. **Finance** Annual contributions from Member States. Other sources: remuneration for services rendered; donations and similar funds. **Activities** Capacity building; events/meetings; knowledge management/information dissemination; projects/programmes; training/education. **Events** *World Islamic economic forum* Petaling Jaya (Malaysia) 2005, *Les groupements économiques régionaux dans le monde* 1997, *Seminar* Agadir (Morocco) 1997, *Seminar* Tunis (Tunisia) 1996, *Réunion des organismes de promotion commerciale des pays islamiques* Pakistan 1990. **Publications** *Tijaris* (6 a year) in Arabic, English, French; *Rapport annuel sur les Etats Membres de l'Organisation de la Conférence Islamique* (annual) in Arabic, English, French.

Members Governments (57):
Afghanistan, Albania, Algeria, Azerbaijan, Bahrain, Bangladesh, Benin, Brunei Darussalam, Burkina Faso, Cameroon, Chad, Comoros, Côte d'Ivoire, Djibouti, Egypt, Gabon, Gambia, Guinea, Guinea-Bissau, Guyana, Indonesia, Iran Islamic Rep, Iraq, Jordan, Kazakhstan, Kuwait, Kyrgyzstan, Lebanon, Libya, Malaysia, Maldives, Mali, Mauritania, Morocco, Mozambique, Niger, Nigeria, Oman, Pakistan, Palestine, Qatar, Saudi Arabia, Senegal, Sierra Leone, Somalia, Sudan, Suriname, Syrian AR, Tajikistan, Togo, Tunisia, Türkiye, Turkmenistan, Uganda, United Arab Emirates, Uzbekistan, Yemen.

IGO Relations Relationship agreement signed with: *UNIDO (#20336)*. Member of: *Intergovernmental Organizations Conference (IGO Conference, #11498)*. **NGO Relations** *Islamic Chamber of Commerce, Industry and Agriculture (ICCIA, #16036)*; *Islamic Chamber Council for Textile (ICCT, inactive)*. Maintains close links with trade and marketing centres and with external trade organizations in Member States. [2020/XE0681/t/**E***]

♦ Islamic Centre for Genetic Engineering and Biotechnology / see Inter-Islamic Network on Genetic Engineering and Biotechnology (#11507)
♦ Islamic Centre for Technical and Vocational Training and Research / see Islamic University of Technology (#16055)
♦ Islamic Chamber / see Islamic Chamber of Commerce, Industry and Agriculture (#16036)
♦ Islamic Chamber of Commerce and Industry / see Islamic Chamber of Commerce, Industry and Agriculture (#16036)

♦ Islamic Chamber of Commerce, Industry and Agriculture (ICCIA) . . 16036

Chambre Islamique de Commerce, d'Industrie et d'Agriculture (CICIA)

International Relations ST 2/A – Block 9, KDA Scheme 5 Clifton, PO Box 3831, Karachi 75600, Pakistan. T. +922135874756 – +922135874910. Fax +922135870765 – +922135874212. E-mail: icciaoic@gmail.com – info@iccia.com.
SG address not obtained.
URL: http://iccia.com/

History 17 Oct 1977. Founded 17-21 Oct 1977, at 1st Conference, following recommendations, 12-15 May 1976, Istanbul (Turkey), of 7th *Council of Foreign Ministers (CFM, see: #17813)*. Foundation was preceded by the setting up, Dec 1949, Karachi (Pakistan), of *International Federation of Islamic Chambers of Commerce and Industry (inactive)*, which no longer exists. Statutes adopted 17 Dec 1978. Originally known as *Islamic Chamber of Commerce, Industry and Commodity Exchange (ICCICE) – Chambre islamique de commerce, d'industrie et d'échange de marchandises*. Subsequently changed title to *Islamic Chamber of Commerce and Industry (ICCI) – Chambre islamique de commerce et d'industrie (CICI)*, Nov 1992, Teheran (Iran Islamic Rep). Also referred to as *Islamic Chamber*. **Aims** Strengthen closer collaboration in the field of trade, commerce, information technology, banking, promotion of investment opportunities and joint ventures in the Member countries. **Structure** General Assembly (annual); Board of Directors; Executive Committee; Financial Committee; General Secretariat, headed by Secretary General. **Languages** Arabic, English, French. **Staff** 11.00 FTE, paid. **Finance** Members' dues. **Activities** Capacity building; projects/programmes; events/meetings. **Events** *Challenges Facing Microfinance Institutions* Karachi (Pakistan) 2022, *International Conference on Tackling the Covid-19 Pandemic* Jakarta (Indonesia) 2021, *Seminar on Introduction to Islamic Banking and Finance* 2015, *Annual General Assembly* Kampala (Uganda) 2015, *Forum for Businesswomen in Islamic Countries* Kampala (Uganda) 2015.

Members National Chambers or Councils and Federations of Chambers of Commerce and Industry and Agriculture in 57 Member States of OIC (one per country or territory):
Afghanistan, Albania, Algeria, Azerbaijan, Bahrain, Bangladesh, Benin, Brunei Darussalam, Burkina Faso, Cameroon, Chad, Comoros, Côte d'Ivoire, Djibouti, Egypt, Gabon, Gambia, Guinea, Guinea-Bissau, Guyana, Indonesia, Iran Islamic Rep, Iraq, Jordan, Kazakhstan, Kuwait, Kyrgyzstan, Lebanon, Libya, Malaysia, Maldives, Mali, Mauritania, Morocco, Mozambique, Niger, Nigeria, Oman, Pakistan, Palestine, Qatar, Saudi Arabia, Senegal, Sierra Leone, Somalia, Sudan, Suriname, Syrian AR, Tajikistan, Togo, Tunisia, Türkiye, Turkmenistan, Uganda, United Arab Emirates, Uzbekistan, Yemen.
Observers in 6 countries:
Bosnia-Herzegovina, New Zealand, Northern Cyprus, Philippines, Singapore, Thailand.
Affiliated members in 2 countries:
Brazil, Ghana.

Consultative Status Consultative status granted from: *ECOSOC (#05331)* (Ros A); *UNIDO (#20336)*. **IGO Relations** Cooperates with: *International Trade Centre (ITC, #15703)*; *Islamic Centre for Development of Trade (ICDT, #16035)*; *Islamic Development Bank (IsDB, #16044)*; *Islamic University of Technology (IUT, #16055)*; *Organisation of Islamic Cooperation (OIC, #17813)*; *Statistical, Economic and Social Research and Training Centre for Islamic Countries (SESRIC, #19971)*; *UNDP (#20292)*; *UNESCO (#20322)*; *United Nations Office for South-South Cooperation (UNOSSC, #20603)*. [2022/XF0345/t/**F**]

♦ Islamic Chamber of Commerce, Industry and Commodity Exchange / see Islamic Chamber of Commerce, Industry and Agriculture (#16036)
♦ Islamic Chamber Council for Textile (inactive)

♦ Islamic Chamber Research and Information Center (ICRIC) 16037

Contact Apr 14 – No 6, 15 Khordad Alley, Taleghani Ave, Teheran, Iran Islamic Rep. T. +982188810527 – +982188346803. Fax +982188308332. E-mail: info@icricinternational.org.
URL: http://www.icricinternationa.org/

History Set up 2003. **Aims** Strengthen closer collaboration among OIC countries in the field of trade, insurance, shipping, banking and promotion of joint ventures. **Structure** Board of Directors. **Activities** Research/documentation.

Members Full in 54 countries:
Afghanistan, Albania, Algeria, Azerbaijan, Bahrain, Benin, Brunei Darussalam, Burkina Faso, Cameroon, Chad, Comoros, Côte d'Ivoire, Djibouti, Egypt, Gabon, Gambia, Guinea, Guinea-Bissau, Guyana, Indonesia, Iran Islamic Rep, Iraq, Jordan, Kazakhstan, Kuwait, Kyrgyzstan, Lebanon, Libya, Malaysia, Maldives, Mali, Morocco, Mozambique, Niger, Nigeria, Oman, Pakistan, Palestine, Qatar, Saudi Arabia, Senegal, Sierra Leone, Somalia, Sudan, Suriname, Syrian AR, Tajikistan, Togo, Türkiye, Turkmenistan, Uganda, United Arab Emirates, Uzbekistan, Yemen.

Consultative Status Consultative status granted from: *ECOSOC (#05331)* (Special); *UNCTAD (#20285)* (General). **IGO Relations** *Organisation of Islamic Cooperation (OIC, #17813)*. [2017/XM5849/**E**]

♦ Islamic Commission for Economic, Cultural and Social Affairs (ICECSA) 16038

Bureau c/o OIC, PO Box 178, Jeddah 21411, Saudi Arabia. T. +96626515222. Fax +96626512288.
URL: http://www.oic-oci.org/

History Jan 1977, as a specialized committee of *Organisation of Islamic Cooperation (OIC, #17813)*, in accordance with resolution adopted, 1976, Istanbul (Turkey), by the 7th *Council of Foreign Ministers (CFM, see: #17813)*. Also known under the acronym *ICESC*. **Aims** Formulate, implement and follow-up progress of economic, cultural and social cooperation; review and follow-up decisions and resolutions adopted and examine and study economic, social and cultural issues for submission to CFM. **Structure** A special committee of OIC. **Languages** Arabic, English, French. **Activities** Formulates, implements and follows up progress of economic, cultural and social cooperation; reviews and follows up decisions and resolutions adopted and examines and studies economic, social and cultural issues for submission to the CFM; acts as the general assembly responsible for examining budget and all activity programmes in the economic, cultural and social fields of OIC Subsidiary Organs, namely: *Islamic Centre for Development of Trade (ICDT, #16035)*; *International Islamic Fiqh Academy (IIFA, #13960)*; *Islamic University of Technology (IUT, #16055)*; *Research Centre for Islamic History, Art and Culture (IRCICA, #18852)*; *Statistical, Economic and Social Research and Training Centre for Islamic Countries (SESRIC, #19971)*. **Events** *Meeting* Jeddah (Saudi Arabia) 2011, *Meeting* Jeddah (Saudi Arabia) 2010, *Meeting* Jeddah (Saudi Arabia) 2009, *Meeting* Jeddah (Saudi Arabia) 2008, *Meeting* Jeddah (Saudi Arabia) 2007. **Members** Representatives of all OIC Member States. [2011.08.22/XE2848/**E***]

♦ Islamic Commission for the International Crescent / see Islamic Committee for International Crescent (#16039)

♦ Islamic Committee for International Crescent (ICIC) 16039

Contact PO Box 17434, Benghazi, Libya. T. +218612238080. Fax +218612220037. E-mail: info@icic-oic.org.
URL: http://www.icic-oic.org/

History 1980, Benghazi (Libyan AJ). Established as a specialized institution of *Organisation of Islamic Cooperation (OIC, #17813)*; creation having been approved, Aug 1982, Niamey (Niger), at 13th *Council of Foreign Ministers (CFM, see: #17813)*. Headquarters in Benghazi (Libyan AJ). Former names and other names: *Islamic Commission for the International Crescent* – former. **Aims** Provide humanitarian assistance and alleviate suffering caused by natural disasters and humanitarian crises; offer assistance to international and local organizations serving humanity; establish close relations and cooperation with organizations working in the field. **Structure** Members' Committee; Executive Director; President. **Languages** Arabic, English, French. **Finance** Sources: contributions. Contributions from OIC Member States and from OIC; own resources. **Activities** Humanitarian/emergency aid. **Publications** *Al-wasiya Journal on IHL Islamic Sharia*. Activities report. [2022/XE0695/**E***]

♦ Islamic Community (#16097)
♦ Islamic Conference of Kings and Heads of States and Governments / see Islamic Summit of Kings and Heads of States and Governments (#16053)

♦ Islamic Conference Youth Forum for Dialogue and Cooperation (ICYF-DC) 16040

Contact Istanbul World Trade Center, A3 Block 7th Floor, Yesilkoy, 34149 Istanbul/Istanbul, Türkiye. T. +902124653939. Fax +902124653670. E-mail: office@icyf-dc.org.
URL: http://www.icyf-dc.org/

Aims Facilitate resolution of socio-economic, moral and cultural problems faced by young people in the OIC region; promote the exchange of ideas, experiences and mutual understanding between young people. **Structure** General Assembly (annual). Board of 9 members, including President and Secretary General. Secretariat; Advisory Committee. **Languages** Arabic, English. **Finance** Members' dues. **Publications** *ICYFDC Newsletter*.

Members National youth organizations in 32 countries:
Afghanistan, Albania, Algeria, Azerbaijan, Bangladesh, Bosnia-Herzegovina, Côte d'Ivoire, Guinea, Guyana, Iran Islamic Rep, Iraq, Jordan, Kazakhstan, Kuwait, Kyrgyzstan, Lebanon, Libya, Malaysia, Niger, Pakistan, Palestine, Saudi Arabia, Sierra Leone, Somalia, Sudan, Syrian AR, Tajikistan, Tunisia, Türkiye, Turkmenistan, Uzbekistan, Yemen.
International organizations (3):
Eurasian International Development Association (EIDA, no recent information); *Forum of European Muslim Youth and Student Organisations (FEMYSO, #09909)*; *Istanbul International Brotherhood and Solidarity Association (IBS)*.

IGO Relations Affiliated institution of: *Organisation of Islamic Cooperation (OIC, #17813)*. Cooperates with: *Islamic World Educational, Scientific and Cultural Organization (ICESCO, #16058)*. [2016/XM2762/y/**F**]

♦ Islamic Corporation for the Development of the Private Sector (see: #16044)

♦ Islamic Corporation for the Insurance of Investment and Export Credit (ICIEC) 16041

Société Islamique pour l'Assurance des Investissements et des Crédits à l'Exportation (SIACE)

Main Office PO Box 15722, Jeddah 21432, Saudi Arabia. T. +96626445666. Fax +96626379755 – +96626443447. E-mail: communication@isdb.org.
URL: https://iciec.isdb.org/

History 1 Aug 1994. Founded as an autonomous international multilateral export credit insurance agency affiliated to *Islamic Development Bank (IsDB, #16044)* Group. Commenced operations in 1995. **Aims** Encourage exports from member countries and facilitate the flow of foreign direct investments to member countries by providing and encouraging the use of Sharia compatible export credit and investment insurance as credit and political risk mitigation instruments. **Structure** Board of Governors (BOG); Board of Directors; CEO. Departments (6): Business Development; Trade Credit Insurance; Structured Finance and Investment Insurance; Legal and Claims; Accounting and Finance; Human Resources Management and Corporate Services. Promotion and Inernational Relations Unit; Risk Management Divisions. **Staff** 55.00 FTE, paid. **Finance** Authorized capital – US$ 232 million; subscribed capital – US$ 230 million; paid up – US$ 114 million; net reserves – US$ 41 million. Total number of shares issued: 148,990. **Activities** Financial and/or material support; events/meetings. **Events** *Annual meeting* Sanaa (Yemen) 2011, *Annual meeting* Baku (Azerbaijan) 2010. **Publications** Newsletter (4 a year). Annual report and financial statements; brochures.
Members Shareholders in 40 countries:
Albania, Algeria, Bahrain, Bangladesh, Benin, Brunei Darussalam, Burkina Faso, Cameroon, Chad, Côte d'Ivoire, Djibouti, Egypt, Gabon, Gambia, Guinea, Indonesia, Iran Islamic Rep, Jordan, Kazakhstan, Kuwait, Lebanon, Libya, Malaysia, Mali, Mauritania, Morocco, Niger, Nigeria, Oman, Pakistan, Qatar, Saudi Arabia, Senegal, Sudan, Syrian AR, Tunisia, Türkiye, Uganda, United Arab Emirates, Yemen.
One organization:
Islamic Development Bank (IsDB, #16044).
IGO Relations Member of: *International Union for the Protection of Literary and Artistic Works (Bern Union, #15806)* and its Prague Club. **NGO Relations** Member of: *Global Network of Export-Import Banks and Development Finance Institutions (G-NEXID, #10489); International Union of Credit and Investment Insurers (Bern Union, #15767).* Instrumental in setting up: *Aman Union (#00763).* Affiliated to: *Accounting and Auditing Organization for Islamic Financial Institutions (AAOIFI, #00062); Islamic Financial Services Board (IFSB, #16045).* [2021/XK1712/e/**E***]

♦ Islamic Council of Europe (no recent information)

♦ Islamic Countries Forensic Medicine Organization (ICFMO) 16042

Secretariat No 6-8, Farshi Moghaddam (16th) St, Upper than Jalal Al Ahmad Exp Way, Northern Kargar Ave, Teheran, Iran Islamic Rep. T. +982184130. Fax +982188330686.
URL: http://www.icfmo.org/

History 23 Jun 2004, Teheran (Iran Islamic Rep), during 1st Islamic Countries Forensic Medicine Congress, as *Islamic Organization of Forensic Medicine (IOFM).* Subsequently changed title to *Islamic Countries Organization of Forensic Medicine (ICOFM).* Constitution adopted during 2nd Congress, 2006, Amman (Jordan). Final constitution ratified, Jun 2007, Teheran (Iran Islamic Rep), when activities officially commenced. **Aims** Coordinate and exchange expertise and knowledge in scientific, ethical and legal issues in the Islamic countries; promote forensic medicine in member countries to the highest level of international standards and in consistency with the holy rules and teaching of Islam; facilitate and enhance scientific and technical exchange; provide standards, manuals and guidelines for forensic medicine related processes and creating unanimity among member countries in this regard; provide appropriate solutions for new challenges in forensic medicine; propose reforms in the structures of forensic medicine institutions in member countries in harmony with internal laws and regulations; provide research and educational opportunities. **Structure** General Assembly. Executive Committee. President. Permanent secretariat in Teheran (Iran Islamic Rep). **Languages** Arabic, English, Persian. **Finance** Members' dues. Other sources: grants by other Islamic organizations and governments; income generating activities. **Activities** Commissions (7): Abortion and Artificial Insemination; Blood Money and Mulct; Brain Death and Organ Transplantation; Growth Determination; Medical Ethics; Medical Updates; Transsexualism and Sex Change Operation. Meeting activities; research; education. **Events** *Congress* Istanbul (Turkey) 2016, *Congress / Islamic Countries Forensic Medicine Congress* Semarang (Indonesia) 2013, *Congress* Algiers (Algeria) 2010, *Congress* Khartoum (Sudan) 2008, *Islamic Countries Forensic Medicine Congress* Tripoli (Libyan AJ) 2008. **Publications** *ICFMO Journal.*
Members in 22 countries:
Afghanistan, Algeria, Azerbaijan, Egypt, Indonesia, Iran Islamic Rep, Iraq, Jordan, Kuwait, Kyrgyzstan, Lebanon, Libya, Malaysia, Palestine, Qatar, Saudi Arabia, Sudan, Syrian AR, Tajikistan, Tunisia, Uzbekistan, Yemen. [2013/XM2043/**D**]

♦ Islamic Countries Organization of Forensic Medicine / see Islamic Countries Forensic Medicine Organization (#16042)

♦ Islamic Countries Society of Statistical Sciences (ISOSS) 16043

Secretariat Plot No 44-A, Civic Centre, Liaqat Chowk, Sabzazar Scheme, Multan Road, Lahore, Pakistan. T. +924237495789 – +924235878583. E-mail: secretary@isoss.net.
URL: http://www.isoss.net/

History 1988. **Structure** Executive Board; Office Bearers. **Finance** Members' dues. **Events** *International Conference* Karachi (Pakistan) 2016, *International Conference / International Conference on Statistical Sciences* Peshawar (Pakistan) 2015, *Islamic Conference / Islamic Countries Conference on Statistical Sciences* Bogor (Indonesia) 2014, *International Conference / International Conference on Statistical Sciences* Karachi (Pakistan) 2014, *International Conference* Dera Ghazi Khan (Pakistan) 2013. **Publications** *Journal of Applied Probability and Statistics.* [2018/XJ9991/**D**]

♦ Islamic Development Bank (IsDB) 16044

Banque islamique de développement (BID)

Contact 8111 King Khalid Street, Al Nuzlah Al Yamania District, Unit No 1, Jeddah 22332-2444, Saudi Arabia. T. +966126361400. Fax +966126366871. E-mail: idbarchives@isdb.org.
URL: http://www.isdb.org/

History 12 Aug 1974, Jeddah (Saudi Arabia), on signature of Agreement during *Council of Foreign Ministers (CFM, see: #17813),* following recommendations of the 2nd Foreign Ministers Conference, Dec 1970, Karachi (Pakistan) and declaration of intent, Dec 1973, Jeddah (Saudi Arabia). A specialized organ of *Organisation of Islamic Cooperation (OIC, #17813).* Became fully operational within OIC framework, 20 Oct 1975. A multilateral aid institution of *Organization of the Petroleum Exporting Countries (OPEC, #17881).* Former names and other names: *IsDB* – former. **Aims** Promote comprehensive human development. **Structure** Board of Governors (meets once a year); Board of Executive Directors; President is Chief Executive of the Bank, acts as Chairman of the Board of Executive Directors and is elected by the Board of Governors; Regional Hubs; Headquarters in Jeddah (Saudi Arabia). Entities of the IDB Group: IDB; *Islamic Research and Training Institute, Jeddah (IRTI, #16050),* founded 1981; *Islamic Corporation for the Insurance of Investment and Export Credit (ICIEC, #16041),* established 1994; *Islamic Corporation for the Development of the Private Sector (ICD, see: #16044),* founded 1999; *International Islamic Trade Finance Corporation (ITFC),* founded 2005. Specialized Funds: *Islamic Solidarity Fund for Development (ISFD, see: #16044);* Awqaf Properties Investment Fund (APIF); *World WAQF Foundation (WWF, #21906);* Waqf Fund; Unit Investment Fund (UIF). **Languages** Arabic, English, French. **Staff** 1178.00 FTE, paid. **Finance** Subscribed capital 2018: Islamic Dinar 50,200 million. **Activities** Financial and/or material support; research and development. **Events** *Annual Meeting of Board of Governors* Jeddah (Saudi Arabia) 2020, *Annual Meeting of Board of Governors* Marrakech (Morocco) 2019, *The Role of Consulting Engineers as well as the Procurement Function in Realizing Sustainable Development Goals (SDGs)* Marrakesh-Safi (Morocco) 2019, *Why We Need Arbitration?* Marrakesh-Safi (Morocco) 2019, *Islamic Finance Tools, IsDB Procurement Procedures and Relations Between: IFIs, Public Institutes and Consultant* Tashkent (Uzbekistan) 2019. **Publications** Annual Report; project stories.
Members 57 member countries (all members of Organisation of Islamic Cooperation (OIC):
Afghanistan, Albania, Algeria, Azerbaijan, Bahrain, Bangladesh, Benin, Brunei Darussalam, Burkina Faso, Cameroon, Chad, Comoros, Côte d'Ivoire, Djibouti, Egypt, Gabon, Gambia, Guinea, Guinea-Bissau, Guyana, Indonesia, Iran Islamic Rep, Iraq, Jordan, Kazakhstan, Kuwait, Kyrgyzstan, Lebanon, Libya, Malaysia, Maldives, Mali, Mauritania, Morocco, Mozambique, Niger, Nigeria, Oman, Pakistan, Palestine, Qatar, Saudi Arabia, Senegal, Sierra Leone, Somalia, Sudan, Suriname, Syrian AR (currently on hold), Tajikistan, Togo, Tunisia, Türkiye, Turkmenistan, Uganda, United Arab Emirates, Uzbekistan, Yemen.
Consultative Status Consultative status granted from: *World Trade Organization (WTO, #21864)* (Observer Status). **IGO Relations** Observer status with (1): *United Nations (UN, #20515)* (General Assembly). Special agreements with: *WHO (#20950); UNESCO (#20322); UNIDO (#20336).* Memorandum of Understanding with: *World Customs Organization (WCO, #21350).* Permanent Observer to: *ECOSOC (#05331).* Founding member of: *International Islamic Financial Market (IIFM, #13959).* Cooperation agreement with: *International Fund for Agricultural Development (IFAD, #13692); Islamic World Educational, Scientific and Cultural Organization (ICESCO, #16058).* Participates in the activities of: *UNCTAD (#20285).* Member of: *Arab Potash Company (APC, #01029); Central Asia Regional Economic Cooperation (CAREC, #03684).* Partner of: *African Development Institute (ADI, #00286); African Training and Research Centre in Administration for Development (CAFRAD, #00486).* Supports: *CIS-7 Initiative (no recent information); Inter-Islamic Network on Space Sciences and Technology (ISNET, #11511); Regional Organization for the Conservation of the Environment of the Red Sea and Gulf of Aden (PERSGA, #18804); UNESCO Regional Bureau for Education in Africa (BREDA, inactive).* Zero-risk weighted multilateral development bank, designated by *European Commission (EC, #06633).* **NGO Relations** Member of: *Accounting and Auditing Organization for Islamic Financial Institutions (AAOIFI, #00062); Global Development Learning Network (GDLN, #10317); International Council on Archives (ICA, #12996).* Multilateral agency of: *Coordination Group of Arab National and Regional Development Institutions (#04826).* Partner of: *Global Forum on Law, Justice and Development (GFLJD, #10373).* Instrumental in setting up: *General Council for Islamic Banks and Financial Institutions (CIBAFI, #10111); Islamic International Rating Agency (IIRA, #16046).* Representatives from: *Association internationale des traducteurs de conférence (AITC, #02748).* Supports: *Forum for African Women Educationalists (FAWE, #09896).* [2019.05.08/XF4542/**F***]

♦ Islamic Economics Research Bureau (internationally oriented national body)
♦ Islamic Federation of Research Institutes (inactive)

♦ Islamic Financial Services Board (IFSB) 16045

Secretariat Level 5 – Sasana Kijang, Bank Negara Malaysia, 2 Jalan Dato'Onn, 50480 Kuala Lumpur, Malaysia. T. +60391951400. E-mail: ifsb_sec@ifsb.org.
URL: http://www.ifsb.org/

History 3 Nov 2002, Kuala Lumpur (Malaysia), following a series of meetings since Mar 2001. Commenced operations Mar 2003. **Aims** Promote development of a prudent and transparent Islamic financial services industry through introducing new, or adapting existing, international standards consistent with Shari'ah principles and recommend them for adoption. **Structure** General Assembly (annual), comprising Full, Associate and Observer Members. Council (meets twice a year), comprising 1 senior executive officer or other senior representative of each Full Member (limited to one Full Member per country). Secretariat in Kuala Lumpur (Malaysia), headed by Secretary-General. **Languages** English. **Staff** 25.00 FTE, paid. **Finance** Members' dues. **Activities** As an international standard setting organization mandated to promote and enhance the soundness and stability of the Islamic financial services industry, issues global prudential standards and guiding principles for the industry, broadly defined to include banking, capital markets and insurance sectors. Standards follow a lengthy due process as outlined in the Guidelines and Procedures for the Preparation of Standards/Guidelines, which involves, among others, the issuance of exposure drafts, holding of workshops and where necessary, public hearings. Conducts research and coordinates initiatives on industry-related issues; organizes roundtables, seminars and conferences for regulators and industry stakeholders; works closely with relevant international, regional and national organizations, research/educational institutions and market players. **Events** *Summit* Jeddah (Saudi Arabia) 2021, *Joint Seminar Development of Sukuk Markets in the Middle East and Africa* Abu Dhabi (United Arab Emirates) 2019, *Summit* Jakarta (Indonesia) 2019, *Summit* Abu Dhabi (United Arab Emirates) 2017, *Summit* Almaty (Kazakhstan) 2015. **Publications** *IFSB Bulletin.* Standards; Guides; Reports.
Members Full and Associate regulatory and supervisory authorities (central banks, insurance and securities commissions, international inter-governmental organizations). Observer may include financial institutions, market players, professional firms and industry associations involved in Islamic financial services industry.
Full in 22 countries:
Bahrain, Bangladesh, Brunei Darussalam, Djibouti, Egypt, Indonesia, Iran Islamic Rep, Jordan, Kuwait, Malaysia, Maldives, Mauritius, Morocco, Nigeria, Oman, Pakistan, Qatar, Saudi Arabia, Singapore, Sudan, Türkiye, United Arab Emirates.
Included in the above, 2 organizations listed in this Yearbook:
Islamic Corporation for the Insurance of Investment and Export Credit (ICIEC, #16041); Islamic Development Bank (IsDB, #16044).
Associate in 14 countries and territories:
China, Hong Kong, Indonesia, Lebanon, Libya, Luxembourg, Malaysia, Palestine, Philippines, Senegal, Sudan, Tunisia, United Arab Emirates, Zambia.
Included in the above, 5 organizations listed in this Yearbook:
Asian Development Bank (ADB, #01422); Bank for International Settlements (BIS, #03165); Banque centrale des Etats de l'Afrique de l'Ouest (BCEAO, #03167); International Bank for Reconstruction and Development (IBRD, #12317) (World Bank); *International Monetary Fund (IMF, #14180).*
Observer in 28 countries and territories:
Afghanistan, Bahrain, Bangladesh, Egypt, France, Germany, Hong Kong, Iran Islamic Rep, Japan, Jordan, Kenya, Korea Rep, Kuwait, Lebanon, Malaysia, Nigeria, Northern Cyprus, Oman, Pakistan, Saudi Arabia, South Africa, Sudan, Switzerland, Tajikistan, Thailand, Türkiye, UK, United Arab Emirates.
Included in the above, 2 organizations listed in this Yearbook:
Islamic Corporation for the Development of the Private Sector (ICD, see: #16044); Japan Bank for International Cooperation (JBIC). [2023/XD8733/y/**D**]

♦ Islamic Fiqh Academy / see International Islamic Fiqh Academy (#13960)
♦ Islamic Food Council of Europe / see Halal Food Council of Europe
♦ Islamic Foundation for Ecology and Environmental Sciences (internationally oriented national body)
♦ Islamic Foundation for Science, Technology and Development (inactive)
♦ Islamic Group / see Jemaah Islamiya (#16097)
♦ Islamic Human Rights Commission (internationally oriented national body)
♦ Islamic Institute of Oceanography / see Inter-Islamic Science and Technology Network on Oceanography (#11514)
♦ Islamic Institute of Space Science Research / see Inter-Islamic Network on Space Sciences and Technology (#11511)
♦ Islamic Institute of Technology / see Islamic University of Technology (#16055)
♦ Islamic Institute of Tropical Medicine / see Inter-Islamic Network on Tropical Medicine (#11512)
♦ Islamic Institute of Water Resources Management / see Inter-Islamic Network on Water Resources Development and Management (#11513)
♦ Islamic and Interfaith Middle Eastern Peace Studies Association (internationally oriented national body)

♦ Islamic International Rating Agency (IIRA) 16046

Board Secretary Office 81, Bldg 474 (Dream Tower 1), Road 1010, Sanabis 410, PO Box 20582, Manama 973, Bahrain. T. +97317211606. Fax +97317211605. E-mail: iira@iirating.com.
URL: http://www.iirating.com/

History Jul 2005. Founded by *Islamic Development Bank (IsDB, #16044).* **Aims** Provide capital markets and the *banking* sector in predominantly Islamic countries with a rating spectrum that encompasses the full array of capital instruments and specialty Islamic *financial* products; enhance the level of analytical expertise in those markets. **Structure** Board of Directors. [2021.09.01/XM3783/**F**]

♦ Islamic Inter-Parliamentary Union / see Parliamentary Union of the OIC Member States (#18220)
♦ Islamic Jihad / see Al-Jihad (#00637)
♦ Islamic Jihad for the Liberation of Palestine / see Hezbollah Internationale (#10912)
♦ Islamic Liberation Front (#10936)
♦ Islamic Medical Association of North America (internationally oriented national body)
♦ Islamic Medical Association of the US and Canada / see Islamic Medical Association of North America
♦ Islamic Medical Conference (meeting series)
♦ Islamic Missionaries Guild of the Caribbean and South America (inactive)
♦ Islamic Network of Water Resources Development and Management / see Inter-Islamic Network on Water Resources Development and Management (#11513)

♦ Islamic Organization of Forensic Medicine / see Islamic Countries Forensic Medicine Organization (#16042)
♦ Islamic Organization for Medical Sciences (inactive)
♦ Islamic Peace Studies Association / see Islamic and Interfaith Middle Eastern Peace Studies Association

♦ Islamic Presentation Centre International (IPCI) 16047

Chairperson 426-434 Coventry Road, Small Heath, Birmingham, B10 0UG, UK. T. +441217730137. Fax +441217668577. E-mail: info@ipci-iv.co.uk.
URL: http://www.ipci-iv.co.uk/

History Founded 1984, Birmingham (UK), as *Islamic Propagation Centre International*. UK Registered Charity. **Aims** Present information on Islam to those who seek it. **Finance** Members' dues. **Activities** Produces free literature; organizes talks and meetings on Islam. **Publications** *IPCI Annual Catalogue*. Booklets, pamphlets.
Members Individuals in 30 countries:
Algeria, Australia, Bangladesh, Canada, Denmark, Egypt, Ethiopia, Finland, France, Germany, Ghana, Iceland, India, Ireland, Italy, Malaysia, Mauritius, Nigeria, Norway, Pakistan, Philippines, Russia, Saudi Arabia, Sierra Leone, Spain, Sri Lanka, Sweden, Türkiye, UK, USA. [2013.10.22/XF1321/v/**E**]

♦ Islamic Press Union (inactive)
♦ Islamic Propagation Centre International / see Islamic Presentation Centre International (#16047)
♦ Islamic Relief / see Islamic Relief Worldwide (#16048)

♦ Islamic Relief Worldwide (IRWW) 16048

Head Office 19 Rea Street South, Digbeth, Birmingham, B5 6LB, UK. T. +441216055555.
URL: https://www.islamic-relief.org/

History 1984, UK. Former names and other names: *Islamic Relief* – alias. Registration: Charity Register, No/ID: 328158, England and Wales; Company, No/ID: 02365572, England and Wales; Charity, No/ID: SC042020, Scotland. **Aims** Create a caring world where communities are empowered, social obligations are fulfilled and people respond as one to the suffering of others. **Structure** Board of Trustees; Board of Directors. **Languages** Arabic, English, French, Italian, Spanish. **Finance** Sources: donations; grants; gifts. **Activities** Humanitarian/emergency aid. **Events** *Annnual seminar* UK 1999. **Publications** *Partnership* (4 a year) – newsletter. Annual Report.
Members Full in 22 countries and territories:
Afghanistan, Albania, Bangladesh, Belgium, Bosnia-Herzegovina, Egypt, France, Germany, Indonesia, Italy, Kosovo, Mali, Mauritius, Netherlands, Pakistan, Palestine, Russia, Sudan, Sweden, Switzerland, UK, USA.
Consultative Status Consultative status granted from: *ECOSOC (#05331)* (Special); *UNEP (#20299)*. **IGO Relations** Partner of: *UNHCR (#20327)*.
NGO Relations Member of:
– *CHS Alliance (#03911); Confédération européenne des ong d'urgence et de développement (CONCORD, #04547); Conference of Non-Governmental Organizations in Consultative Relationship with the United Nations (CONGO, #04635); Global WASH Cluster (GWC, #10651); International Campaign to Ban Landmines – Cluster Munition Coalition (ICBL-CMC, #12427); International Islamic Council for Dawah and Relief (no recent information); International Partnership on Religion and Sustainable Development (PaRD, #14524); Joint Learning Initiative on Faith and Local Communities (JLI, #16139); Keeping Children Safe; Start Network (#19969); UNCAC Coalition (#20283); Voluntary Organisations in Cooperation in Emergencies (VOICE, #20809).*
Shareholder in: *International Civil Society Centre (#12589).* [2020/XF4129/**F**]

♦ Islamic Reporting Initiative (unconfirmed)

♦ Islamic Research Academy (IRAK) 16049

Académie des recherches islamiques

Dir D-35, Block 5, Federal 'B' Area, Karachi 75950, Pakistan. T. +922136349840. Fax +922136361040. E-mail: irak.pk@gmail.com.
URL: http://www.irak.pk/

History Sep 1963, Karachi (Pakistan). Also referred to as *Islamic Research Academy Karachi*. **Aims** Promote serious academic research in aspects of Islam – religion, law, culture and history – so as to bring out the relevance of its teachings to problems that confront mankind in general and Muslims in particular; make treasures of classical Islamic scholarship available to all interested in the study of Islam; promote studies on Muslim countries, in particular on Pakistan; enable wide dissemination of outstanding works on Islamic subjects by contemporary Muslim scholars; prepare and publish books, textbooks and educational documents to enable intelligent laymen to better understand the religion, culture and history of Islam and problems of the contemporary Muslim world; give education a constructive, Islamic basis and content. **Structure** Managing Committee of not less than 12 members. Officers: Chairman, 2 Vice-Chairmen, Secretary-General and Treasurer. **Finance** Financed by sale proceeds of publications. Donations. **Activities** Translation of books from Arabic and English into Urdu and from Urdu into English. Writing of original books in both English and Urdu. Library. **Publications** *Maarif Feature* (24 a year) in Urdu. Books. **Members** Not a membership organization. [2012.08.08/XF3216/**F**]

♦ Islamic Research Academy at Al-Azhar Al-Sharif (internationally oriented national body)
♦ Islamic Research Academy Karachi / see Islamic Research Academy (#16049)
♦ Islamic Research Association (inactive)
♦ Islamic Research and Information Artistic and Cultural Institute / see Islamic Research and Information Center
♦ Islamic Research and Information Center (internationally oriented national body)
♦ Islamic Research Institute (internationally oriented national body)

♦ Islamic Research and Training Institute, Jeddah (IRTI) 16050

Institut islamique de recherches et de formation (IIRF)

Main Office 8111 King Khalid St Al Nuzlah Al Yamania Dist Unit No 1, Jeddah 22332-2444, Saudi Arabia. T. +96626361400. Fax +96626378927. E-mail: irti@isdb.org.
URL: http://www.irti.org/

History 1981, as the research and training unit of *Islamic Development Bank (IsDB, #16044)*. **Aims** Undertake research, deliver training and knowledge-based solutions in Islamic *economics* and *banking* issues. **Structure** Board of Governors; Board of Executive Directors; Management Committee; Operational Divisions; Units. **Languages** Arabic, English, French. **Activities** Events/meetings; knowledge management/information dissemination; capacity building; training/education. **Events** *International conference on Islamic economics and finance* Doha (Qatar) 2011, *Singapore international waqf conference* Singapore (Singapore) 2007. **Publications** *Islamic Economic Studies* (2 a year) in Arabic, English, French – journal. Global reports on Islamic finance; social finance reports; country finance reports; research papers; background and discussion papers; textbooks; training manuals; conference proceedings; research papers. **Information Services** *IRTI Information Centre of the Islamic Research and Training Institute (IRTIC)*. **NGO Relations** Member of; *International Partnership on Religion and Sustainable Development (PaRD, #14524).*
[2019.11.10/XK0669/j/**E**]

♦ Islamic Salvation Foundation / see Al-Qa'ida (#00748)
♦ Islamic Sharia Council / see International Shari'ah Council of the AAOIFI (#14844)
♦ Islamic Shipowners' Association / see Organization of the Islamic Shipowners' Association (#17876)

♦ Islamic Solidarity Fund (ISF) 16051

Fonds de solidarité islamique

Executive Bureau c/o OIC, PO Box 178, Jeddah 21411, Saudi Arabia. T. +96626800800. Fax +96626876568. E-mail: oic_isf@hotmail.com.
URL: http://www.isf-fsi.com/

History Feb 1974, Lahore (Pakistan), as a subsidiary organ of *Organisation of Islamic Cooperation (OIC, #17813)*, in accordance with Resolution No 6/2 (I S) issued by the Second *Islamic Summit of Kings and Heads of States and Governments (#16053)*. Commenced operations in 1975. **Aims** Take all possible steps to raise the intellectual and moral levels of Muslims; provide *assistance* to alleviate the adverse after effects of crises, calamities and natural catastrophes that may occur or hit the Islamic States and *Muslim* communities in non-member countries; extend assistance in support of the steadfastness of the Palestinian people and resistance to the judaization of Al-Quds Ashareef; grant assistance to Muslim minorities and communities so as to improve their religious, social and cultural standards; contribute to the establishment of mosques, hospitals, Islamic schools, universities, scientific research institutes, centres and societies; finance Islamic Da'wa programmes and Muslim youth welfare. **Structure** General Assembly, comprising members of *Islamic Commission for Economic, Cultural and Social Affairs (ICECSA, #16038)*. Permanent Council, composed of OIC Secretary General, ex officio, and 13 members from among representatives of OIC Member States elected by *Council of Foreign Ministers (CFM, see: #17813)* every 2 years. Executive Bureau at OIC General Secretariat. **Finance** Annual budget financed by: voluntary contributions of Member States; donations and grants made by public and private bodies and by individuals; revenues of the endowment (Waqf) of the Fund, whose capital of US$ 100 million is also covered by contributions of OIC Member States, public and private bodies and individuals. **Activities** Does not extend loans – assistance is either in the form of grants or given in kind, much of which goes to educational institutions and social welfare activities. **Events** *Session* Jeddah (Saudi Arabia) 1993.
Members Council members from 13 countries:
Burkina Faso, Egypt, Iran Islamic Rep, Jordan, Kuwait, Libya, Morocco, Pakistan, Palestine, Saudi Arabia, Tunisia, Türkiye, United Arab Emirates.
IGO Relations Contributes to: *Al-Quds Fund (no recent information); Islamic Solidarity Sports Federation (ISSF, #16052); Islamic University in Niger (#16054).* [2015/XF9010/f/**F***]

♦ Islamic Solidarity Fund for Development (see: #16044)

♦ Islamic Solidarity Sports Federation (ISSF) 16052

Fédération sportive pour la solidarité islamique

Contact Al Diwan St, Ar Rafiah, Riyadh 12921, Saudi Arabia. T. +966112810895. E-mail: info@issf.sa.
URL: https://issf.sa/en/

History 6 May 1985, on resolutions of 11th *Council of Foreign Ministers (CFM, see: #17813)*, May 1980, Islamabad (Pakistan) and 3rd *Islamic Summit of Kings and Heads of States and Governments (#16053)*, Jan 1981, Makkah/Taif. An affiliated institution of *Organisation of Islamic Cooperation (OIC, #17813)*. Previously also referred to as *Sports Federation of Islamic Solidarity Games*. **Aims** Serve the needs of OIC member countries in all aspects of sports activities. **Structure** General Assembly (every 2 years); Executive Board. **Languages** Arabic, English, French. **Staff** 1.00 FTE, paid. **Finance** Members' admission fees and dues. Percentage of revenues of sports competitions and games organized by the Federation among Member States; revenues from TV broadcasting, sponsorships and advertising; donations and grants from OIC governments; annual subsidies of OIC and *Islamic Solidarity Fund (ISF, #16051)*.
Members States (57):
Afghanistan, Albania, Algeria, Azerbaijan, Bahrain, Bangladesh, Benin, Brunei Darussalam, Burkina Faso, Cameroon, Chad, Comoros, Côte d'Ivoire, Djibouti, Egypt, Gabon, Gambia, Guinea, Guinea-Bissau, Guyana, Indonesia, Iran Islamic Rep, Iraq, Jordan, Kazakhstan, Kuwait, Kyrgyzstan, Lebanon, Libya, Malaysia, Maldives, Mali, Mauritania, Morocco, Mozambique, Niger, Nigeria, Oman, Pakistan, Palestine, Qatar, Saudi Arabia, Senegal, Sierra Leone, Somalia, Sudan, Suriname, Syrian AR, Tajikistan, Togo, Tunisia, Türkiye, Turkmenistan, Uganda, United Arab Emirates, Uzbekistan, Yemen.
Observers Governments of (5) countries:
Bosnia-Herzegovina, Central African Rep, Northern Cyprus, Russia, Thailand.
Observers Muslim communities (1) Moro National Liberation Front.
IGO Relations Cooperates with: *Union of OIC News AGencies (UNA, #20467); Islamic Broadcasting Union (IBU, #16033); Islamic Centre for Development of Trade (ICDT, #16035); Islamic Development Bank (IsDB, #16044); Islamic World Educational, Scientific and Cultural Organization (ICESCO, #16058); Islamic Solidarity Fund (ISF, #16051)*; Ministries of Youth and Sports in Islamic States. [2022/XE1322/**E***]

♦ Islamic States Broadcasting Organization / see Islamic Broadcasting Union (#16033)
♦ Islamic States Telecommunications Union (inactive)

♦ Islamic Summit of Kings and Heads of States and Governments . . . 16053

Bureau c/o OIC, 6 Km Makkah Al-Mukarramah Rd, PO Box 178, Jeddah, Saudi Arabia. T. +96626800800. Fax +96626876568.
Contact 130 East 40th St, 5th Florr, New York NY 10016, USA. T. +12128830140. Fax +12128830143. E-mail: oicny@un.int.

History 25 Sep 1969, Rabat (Morocco), at first Conference. Has also been referred to as: *Conference of Islamic Kings and Heads of State and Government*; *Conference of Kings and Heads of States and Governments of Islamic Countries*; *Islamic Conference of Kings and Heads of States and Governments*. The supreme authority of *Organisation of Islamic Cooperation (OIC, #17813)*. **Aims** Define the *strategy* for Islamic policies and actions. **Structure** Sessions (normally every 3 years) elect Chairman who holds the office until the next session. Special sessions may be convened between regular sessions if so required. Intersessional meetings of the Joint Bureaux of the Islamic Summit and *Council of Foreign Ministers (CFM, see: #17813)* are held on specific issues, such as: Palestine and Al-Quds; Bosnia-Herzegovina. Bureau. **Activities** Among other activities, working on the establishment of *Islamic Common Market (no recent information)*. **Events** *Special Session* Makkah (Saudi Arabia) 2005, *Special Session* Doha (Qatar) 2003, *Triennial Islamic Summit Conference* Putrajaya (Malaysia) 2003, *Triennial Islamic Summit Conference* Doha (Qatar) 2000, *Special Session* Islamabad (Pakistan) 1997. **NGO Relations** *Organization of the Islamic Shipowners' Association (OISA, #17876).* [2008/XF4974/c/**F***]

♦ Islamic Trade Centre / see Islamic Centre for Development of Trade (#16035)
♦ Islamic Universities League / see League of Islamic Universities (#16425)

♦ Islamic University in Niger 16054

Université islamique au Niger

Contact BP 11507, Niamey, Niger. T. +227784020 – +227723903 – +227784021. Fax +227733796.

History Dec 1984, Sanaa (Yemen), at 15th *Council of Foreign Ministers (CFM, see: #17813)*, following recommendations at 2nd *Islamic Summit of Kings and Heads of States and Governments (#16053)*, Feb 1974, Lahore (Pakistan). Commenced activities, 1986. Situated in Say (near Niamey). Comes within the framework of *Organisation of Islamic Cooperation (OIC, #17813)*. Also referred to as *Oum Al Qura University of Niger* and previously in French as *Université islamique de l'Afrique de l'Ouest*. **Aims** Respond to the needs of *Muslim* populations in *Africa* and of the Muslim world in general. **Structure** Board of Trustees (meets annually), comprising 15 members, including: 4 members appointed by the Government of Niger; Chairman of the Permanent Council of *Islamic Solidarity Fund (ISF, #16051)*; Secretary General of OIC; 4 men of letters and scientists of the Islamic world regardless of nationality; 3 members appointed from among Muslim candidates proposed by French-speaking African States; Rector of the University; one representative of the faculty. Executive Board (meets monthly), provisionally comprising: Rector and Secretary General of the University; 2 Vice Rectors; Deans of Faculties; 2 elected members of the teaching staff. **Staff** 22.00 FTE, paid. **Finance** Sources: grants from the Islamic Solidarity Fund; OIC member States' contributions; donations; legacies; income yields and their management; sales of publications; fees. Building costs (US$ 31,200,000) paid one third by the Government of Niger and two thirds by ISF. **Activities** Provides courses of study leading to recognized university diplomas and degrees, currently in 2 units: Arabic language; Shari'a. Islam is a guiding principle of learning and teaching in academic research and the students' development programme. **IGO Relations** Cooperates with: *Islamic World Educational, Scientific and Cultural Organization (ICESCO, #16058)*. **NGO Relations** Member of: *Federation of the Universities of the Islamic World (FUIW, #09710).*
[2008/XF5213/**F***]

♦ Islamic University of Rotterdam (internationally oriented national body)

♦ Islamic University of Technology (IUT) 16055

Université islamique de technologie

Registrar Board Bazar, IUT Administrative Building, Room 315 and Room 319, Gazipur 1704, Bangladesh. T. +88029291252. Fax +88029291260. E-mail: registrar@iut-dhaka.edu.
URL: http://www.iutoic-dhaka.edu/

History 1979. Set up by decision of 9th *Council of Foreign Ministers (CFM, see: #17813)*, Apr 1978, Dakar (Senegal), as a Subsidiary Organ of *Organisation of Islamic Cooperation (OIC, #17813)*. Commenced operations in 1981, with the title *Islamic Centre for Technical and Vocational Training and Research (ICTVTR) – Centre islamique pour la formation professionnelle et technique et de recherches*. Subsequently changed title to *Islamic Institute of Technology (IIT) – Institut islamique de technologie*, 1994. Current name adopted, 27 Jun 2001, ICFM Resolution 48/28E. Also referred to as *Dhaka Centre*. **Aims** Help develop *human resources* of OIC Member States and train the technical *manpower* of international standard needed for industrial, economic and social *development* of the Ummah; initiate, promote and guide technological and industrial research for technological development; promote technical cooperation and exchange technical know-how and disseminate basic information in the field of human resources development in general; act as a focal point for human resources development in technical and vocational *education* for OIC Member States under UN-OIC Cooperation. **Structure** Council of Foreign Ministers (CFM). General Assembly, comprising members of *Islamic Commission for Economic, Cultural and Social Affairs (ICECSA, #16038)*. Governing Board; Syndicate; Academic Council. Vice Chancellor, who is responsible to OIC Secretary General. **Languages** Arabic, English, French. **Staff** 210.00 FTE, paid. **Finance** Members' contributions. Other sources: voluntary contributions; grants; donations; proceeds from services. Budget (annual): US$ 3.26 million. **Activities** Training/education; research/documentation; events/meetings. **Events** *International conference on computer and information technology* Dhaka (Bangladesh) 2005, *Workshop on ubiquitous computing* Dhaka (Bangladesh) 2005, *International workshop on innovative approaches in teaching for teachers of technical and vocational education* Dhaka (Bangladesh) 2004, *International seminar* Dhaka (Bangladesh) 1999, *Seminar on curriculum development in technical and vocational education* Dhaka (Bangladesh) 1999. **Publications** *IUT Newsletter* (5 a year); *Journal of Engineering and Technology* (2 a year); *Calendar* (annual); *IUT News Bulletin* (annual). Academic Regulations; calendar; annoucements; brochures; research results; workshop papers.
Members All OIC members in 57 countries and territories:
Afghanistan, Albania, Algeria, Azerbaijan, Bahrain, Bangladesh, Benin, Brunei Darussalam, Burkina Faso, Cameroon, Chad, Comoros, Côte d'Ivoire, Djibouti, Egypt, Gabon, Gambia, Guinea, Guinea-Bissau, Guyana, Indonesia, Iran Islamic Rep, Iraq, Jordan, Kazakhstan, Kuwait, Kyrgyzstan, Lebanon, Libya, Malaysia, Maldives, Mali, Mauritania, Morocco, Mozambique, Niger, Nigeria, Oman, Pakistan, Palestine, Qatar, Saudi Arabia, Senegal, Sierra Leone, Somalia, Sudan, Suriname, Syrian AR, Tajikistan, Togo, Tunisia, Türkiye, Turkmenistan, Uganda, United Arab Emirates, Uzbekistan, Yemen.
IGO Relations Contacts with the following UN bodies: *FAO (#09260)*; *ILO (#11123)*; *International Fund for Agricultural Development (IFAD, #13692)*; *International Telecommunication Union (ITU, #15673)*; *UNEP (#20299)*; *UNDP (#20292)*; *UNESCO (#20322)*; *UNIDO (#20336)*; *United Nations Economic and Social Commission for Asia and the Pacific (ESCAP, #20557)*; *United Nations International Research and Training Institute for the Advancement of Women (UN-INSTRAW, inactive)*. [2023/XE3961/**E***]

♦ Islamic University in Uganda (IUIU) 16056

Rector Box 2555, Mbale, Uganda. T. +256393512100. Fax +256393280525. E-mail: rector@iuiu.ac.ug – us@iuiu.ac.ug.
URL: http://www.iuiu.ac.ug./

History Feb 1988, following decision of 2nd *Islamic Summit of Kings and Heads of States and Governments (#16053)*, Feb 1974, Lahore (Pakistan). Sponsored by the *Organisation of Islamic Cooperation (OIC, #17813)*. **Aims** Function as a highly academic and cultural institutions based on Islam and the love of country; promote and enhance civilization and scientific influence of Islam and the physical world to produce well cultured, morally upright graduates of sound character, equipped with useful skills and knowledge who are able to participate positively in the development process of their countries. **Structure** University Council (meets at least annually); Council Committees (4); Executive Board; Management Committee; Rectorship; other Campuses (3). **Languages** Arabic, English, Swahili. **Staff** Main Campus: 250 Academic; 84 Senior Administrative; 89 Supporting. Kampala (Uganda) Campus: 213 Academic; 42 Senior Administrative; 48 Supporting. Females Campus: 99 Academic; 21 Administrative, 29 Supporting. Arua (Uganda) Campus: 33 Academic; 5 Administrative; 6 Supporting. **Finance** Financed by OIC. Other sources: student fees; endowments. **Activities** Training/education; projects/programmes. **Events** *Annual Ramadan convention* Mbale (Uganda) 1998, *Annual Ramadan convention* Mbale (Uganda) 1997, *Annual Ramadan convention* Mbale (Uganda) 1996. **Publications** *IUIU Gazette* (12 a year); *Dawah Voice* (2 a year); *Islamic University Multidisciplinary Journal* (2 a year); *IUIU Faculty of Education Journal* (annual); *IUIU Faculty of Law Journal* (annual); *IUIU Faculty of Science Journal* (annual); *IUIU Bulletin* (4-12 a year). **Members** All OIC Member States (57) and observers. **NGO Relations** Member of (2): *Association of African Universities (AAU, #02361)*; *Association of Commonwealth Universities, The (ACU, #02440)*. [2019.02.28/XF5214/**F***]

♦ Islamic World Academy of Sciences (IAS) 16057

Dir Gen PO Box 830036 Zahran, Amman 11183, Jordan. T. +96265522104 – +96265523385. Fax +96265511803. E-mail: ias@iasworld.org.
URL: http://www.iasworld.org/

History 28 Oct 1986, Amman (Jordan). Founded following recommendations of Standing Committee for Scientific and Technological Cooperation of *Organisation of Islamic Cooperation (OIC, #17813)* and subsequent approval at the 4th Islamic Summit, 1984, Casablanca. Acts within the framework of COMSTECH. Former names and other names: *Islamic Academy of Sciences* – former (1986 to 2006). **Aims** Serve as a consultative organization of the Islamic and developing world, and institutions of member states of OIC on matters related to science and *technology*; encourage and promote research on major problems of importance facing Islamic countries and identify future technology of relevance for possible adoption and utilization. **Structure** General Assembly of Founding and Elected Fellows; Council; Director; Technical Affairs Director; Standing Committees (5). **Languages** Arabic, English. **Staff** 8.00 FTE, paid. **Finance** Sources: government support; grants; international organizations. Annual budget: 750,000 USD. **Activities** Awards/prizes/competitions; events/meetings; networking/liaising; publishing activities; research and development; standards/guidelines; training/education. **Events** *Biodiversity Conference* Amman (Jordan) 2021, *Landscape of Science, Technology and Innovation in the Islamic Countries* Amman (Jordan) 2020, *Landscape of Science, Technology and Innovation in the Islamic Countries* Amman (Jordan) 2020, *Science, Technology and Innovation for Global Peace and Prosperity* Konya (Turkey) 2017, *Annual Conference* Teheran (Iran Islamic Rep) 2015. **Publications** *Medical Journal of the Islamic World Academy of Sciences* (4 a year); *IAS Newsletter* (2 a year); *Islamic Thought and Scientific Creativity* (2 a year). Proceedings and reports of conferences and seminars.
Members Founding and elected fellows (106) in 44 countries and territories:
Albania, Algeria, Australia, Azerbaijan, Bangladesh, Bosnia-Herzegovina, Canada, Cyprus, Egypt, France, Germany, India, Indonesia, Iran Islamic Rep, Iraq, Italy, Jordan, Kazakhstan, Kuwait, Kyrgyzstan, Lebanon, Malaysia, Mali, Mauritania, Morocco, Oman, Pakistan, Palestine, Qatar, Russia, Saudi Arabia, Senegal, Singapore, South Africa, Sudan, Switzerland, Syrian AR, Tatarstan, Tunisia, Türkiye, Turkmenistan, UK, USA, Uzbekistan.
IGO Relations Cooperation agreement with: *Islamic World Educational, Scientific and Cultural Organization (ICESCO, #16058)*. Affiliated to: OIC. **NGO Relations** Member of: *InterAcademy Partnership (IAP, #11376)*; *Network of Academies of Sciences in Countries of Organization of Islamic Conference (NASIC, #16981)*. Associate member of: *Union académique internationale (UAI, #20345)*. [2020.05.01/XF2129/v/**F**]

♦ Islamic World Educational, Scientific and Cultural Organization (ICESCO) 16058

Organisation du Monde Islamique pour l'Education (ICESCO)

Contact Avenue des FAR-Hay Ryad, PO Box 2275, 10104 Rabat, Morocco. T. +212537566052. E-mail: scecgcs@icesco.org – contact@icesco.org.
URL: https://www.icesco.org/

History May 1982, Fez (Morocco). Established at Founding Conference, held in furtherance of the recommendation adopted by the 6th Session of the Islamic Commission for Economic, Cultural and Social Affairs, Nov 1980, Jeddah (Saudi Arabia). Organization creation plan developed over a period of four years (1978-1981): recommendation in Resolution No 9/9-C during the 9th *Council of Foreign Ministers (CFM, see: #17813)*, 24-28 apr 1978, Dakar (Senegal); recommendation confirmed during the 10th CFM, 8-12 May 1979, Fez; resolution and ratification of Statutes (Charter) by virtue of resolution No 2/11-C of the 11th CFM, 17-22 May 1980, Islamabad (Pakistan); final resolution at 3rd *Islamic Summit of Kings and Heads of States and Governments (#16053)*, 25-28 Jan 1981, Makkah Al-Mukarramah (Saudi Arabia). A specialized organ of *Organisation of Islamic Cooperation (OIC, #17813)*. **Aims** Strengthen, promote and consolidate cooperation among member states in the fields of education, science, culture and communication; develop and upgrade these fields within the framework of the civilizational reference of the Islamic world and in light of human Islamic values and ideals; consolidate understanding among peoples within and outside member states; contribute to the achievement of world peace and security, particularly through education, science, culture and communication; publicize the correct image of Islam and Islamic culture; promote dialogue among civilizations, cultures and religions; work towards spreading the values of justice and peace and the principles of freedom and human rights, in accordance with the Islamic civilizational perspective; encourage cultural interaction and support cultural diversity in member states, while preserving their cultural identity and protecting independence of thought; consolidate complementarity and coordination among the specialized institutions of the OIC in education, science, culture and communication, and among member states, and promote cooperation and partnership with similar governmental and nongovernmental institutions sharing the same interest, within and outside member states; increase interest in Islamic culture, highlight its specificities and publicize its landmarks in intellectual studies, scientific research and educational curricula; work to establish complementarity and correlation among educational systems of member states; support the efforts of educational, scientific and cultural institutions for Muslims in non-member states. **Structure** General Conference (regular session every 3 years); Executive Council; General Directorate. Directorates (5); Divisions (20); Planning, Information and Documentation Centre; ISESCO Center for Promotion of Scientific Research. **Languages** Arabic, English, French. **Staff** 160.00 FTE, paid. **Finance** Sources: contributions of member/participating states; international organizations. Other sources: subsidies and donations offered by member or non-member states; subsidies and donations provided by bodies or individuals. Supported by: *ECOSOC (#05331)*. **Activities** Awareness raising; capacity building; events/meetings; guidance/assistance/consulting; knowledge management/information dissemination; politics/policy/regulatory; research and development; research/documentation; training/education. **Events** *Executive Council Session* Abu Dhabi (United Arab Emirates) 2020, *World Forum on Intercultural Dialogue* Baku (Azerbaijan) 2019, *World Forum on Intercultural Dialogue* Baku (Azerbaijan) 2017, *International Workshop on Applications of ICTs in Education, Healthcare and Agriculture* Amman (Jordan) 2016, *World Forum on Intercultural Dialogue* Baku (Azerbaijan) 2015. **Publications** *Guide to ISESCO* (annual); *ISESCO Newsletter* (periodical) in Arabic, English, French; *Islam Today* (periodical) in Arabic, English, French – journal. *Commemorative Book*. Documentary films.
Members Full member states of the OIC become members of ISESCO upon officially signing the Charter, and having completed the membership legal and legislative formalities and informed, in writing, the General Directorate of ISESCO. Member states and territories (52):
Afghanistan, Algeria, Azerbaijan, Bahrain, Bangladesh, Benin, Brunei Darussalam, Burkina Faso, Cameroon, Chad, Comoros, Côte d'Ivoire, Djibouti, Egypt, Gabon, Gambia, Guinea, Guinea-Bissau, Guyana, Indonesia, Iran Islamic Rep, Iraq, Jordan, Kazakhstan, Kuwait, Kyrgyzstan, Lebanon, Libya, Malaysia, Maldives, Mali, Mauritania, Morocco, Niger, Nigeria, Oman, Pakistan, Palestine, Qatar, Saudi Arabia, Senegal, Sierra Leone, Somalia, Sudan, Suriname, Syrian AR, Tajikistan, Togo, Tunisia, Uganda, United Arab Emirates, Yemen.
IGO Relations Memorandum of Understanding with: *Arab Women Organization (AWO, #01078)*. Cooperates with:
- *African Development Bank (ADB, #00283)*;
- *African Training and Research Centre in Administration for Development (CAFRAD, #00486)*;
- *Arab Bank for Economic Development in Africa (#00904)*;
- *Arab Bureau of Education for the Gulf States (ABEGS, #00910)*;
- *Arab Centre for Medical Literature (ACML, no recent information)*;
- *Arab League Educational, Cultural and Scientific Organization (ALECSO, #01003)*;
- *Center for Mediterranean Integration (CMI, #03649)*;
- *Centre régional africain des sciences et technologies de l'espace en langue française /Affilié à l'Organisation des nations unies/ (CRASTE-LF, see: #04277)*;
- *Commission on Science and Technology for Sustainable Development in the South (COMSATS, #04239)*;
- *Council of Europe (CE, #04881)* – Directorate of Youth and Sport;
- *FAO (#09260)*;
- *Federation of Arab Scientific Research Councils (FASRC, no recent information)*;
- *Institut du monde arabe (IMA, #11324)*;
- *International Bank for Reconstruction and Development (IBRD, #12317)* (World Bank);
- *International Fund for Agricultural Development (IFAD, #13692)*;
- *International Islamic Fiqh Academy (IIFA, #13960)*;
- *International Organization for Migration (IOM, #14454)*;
- *International Science, Technology and Innovation Centre for South-South Cooperation under the auspices of UNESCO (ISTIC, #14799)*;
- *Islamic Broadcasting Union (IBU, #16033)*;
- *Islamic Development Bank (IsDB, #16044)*;
- *Islamic Solidarity Sports Federation (ISSF, #16052)*;
- *Islamic University in Niger (#16054)*;
- *King Abdullah Bin Abdulaziz International Centre for Interreligious and Intercultural Dialogue (KAICIID, #16193)*;
- *Naif Arab University for Security Sciences (NAUSS, #16929)*;
- *Office of the United Nations High Commissioner for Human Rights (OHCHR, #17697)*;
- *OIC Ministerial Standing Committee on Scientific and Technological Cooperation (COMSTECH, #17702)*;
- *Organisation internationale de la Francophonie (OIF, #17809)*;
- *Parliamentary Union of the OIC Member States (PUIC, #18220)*;
- *Regional Council for Adult Education and Literacy in Africa (CREAA, no recent information)*;
- *Regional Organization for the Conservation of the Environment of the Red Sea and Gulf of Aden (PERSGA, #18804)*;
- *Research Centre for Islamic History, Art and Culture (IRCICA, #18852)*;
- *Southeast Asian Ministers of Education Organization (SEAMEO, #19774)*;
- *UNEP (#20299)*;
- *UNDP (#20292)*;
- *UNESCO (#20322)*;
- *UNESCO Institute for Information Technologies in Education (IITE, #20304)*;
- *UNHCR (#20327)*;
- *UNICEF (#20332)*;
- *UNIDO (#20336)*;
- *United Nations (UN, #20515)*;
- *United Nations Alliance of Civilizations (UNAOC, #20520)*;
- *United Nations Office for Disaster Risk Reduction (UNDRR, #20595)* – Africa;
- *United Nations Population Fund (UNFPA, #20612)*;
- *WHO (#20950)*;
- *World Food Programme (WFP, #21510)*;
- *World Intellectual Property Organization (WIPO, #21593)*;
- *World Meteorological Organization (WMO, #21649)*.

NGO Relations Member of: *Asian Coordinating Group for Chemistry (ACGC, no recent information)*; *Consortium on Science, Technology and Innovation for the South (COSTIS, no recent information)*.
Cooperates with:
- *Afro-Arab Institute for Culture and Strategic Studies (AACI, #00534)*;
- *Arab Thought Forum (ATF, #01055)*;
- *Arab Thought Foundation (ATF, #01056)*;
- *Asia-Pacific International Molecular Biology Network (A-IMBN, #01935)*;
- *Association for the Development of Education in Africa (ADEA, #02471)*;
- *Bayt Mal Alqods Asharief Agency*;
- *Center of Arab Women for Training and Research, Tunis (CAWTAR, #03637)*;
- *Federation of Islamic Organisations in Europe (FIOE, #09682)*;
- *Foundation for Environmental Education (FEE, #09949)*;
- *Holy Qu'ran Memorization International Organization (#10938)*;
- *International Academy of Rapprochement between Islamic Madhahib*;
- *International Institute of Islamic Thought (IIIT, #13894)*;
- *International Islamic Centre for Population Studies and Research (IICPSR, #13956)*;
- *International Islamic Charitable Organization (IICO, #13957)*;
- *International Islamic Relief Organization (IIRO)*;
- *International Literacy Institute (ILI)*;
- *International Muslim Organization for Woman and Family (IMOWF)*;
- *International Union of Muslim Scouts (IUMS, no recent information)*;
- *International University of Africa (IUA)*;
- *Islamic Chamber of Commerce, Industry and Agriculture (ICCIA, #16036)*;
- *Islamic Civilization Institute, Moscow (no recent information)*;
- *Islamic Conference Youth Forum for Dialogue and Cooperation (ICYF-DC, #16040)*;
- *Islamic World Academy of Sciences (IAS, #16057)*;
- *League of Islamic Universities (#16425)*;
- *Muslim World League (MWL, #16917)*;
- national and local organizations;
- *Oxford Centre for Islamic Studies (OCIS)*;

- *Prince Abdul Mohsin Bin Jalawi Centre for Research and Islamic Studies, Sharjah*;
- *Regional Information Technology and Software Engineering Centre (RITSEC, #18789)*;
- World Conference of *Religions for Peace (RfP, #18831)*;
- *Royal Aal al-Bayt Institute for Islamic Thought*;
- Centre for Near and Middle Eastern Studies of *School of Oriental and African Studies (SOAS)*;
- *Texas International Education Consortium (TIEC)*;
- *World Assembly of Muslim Youth (WAMY, #21112)*;
- *World Association of Industrial and Technological Research Organizations (WAITRO, #21145)*;
- *World Family Organization (WFO, #21399)*;
- *World Islamic Call Society (WICS, inactive)*;
- *World Organization of the Scout Movement (WOSM, #21693)* – Arab Scout Region;
- *World Renewable Energy Network (WREN, #21750)*;
- *Zayed Bin Sultan Al Nahayan Charitable and Humanitarian Foundation.* [2021/XD8574/**C***]

♦ Islamische Universiteit Rotterdam (internationally oriented national body)
♦ Islamrat für Europa (no recent information)
♦ Islam Ülkeleri Osinografi Bilim ve Teknoloji Agi (#11514)
♦ Island Conservation (internationally oriented national body)

♦ Island Dynamics 16059

Dir Lyneborggade 21 St, 2300 Copenhagen S, Denmark.
URL: http://www.islanddynamics.org/

History Founded 2009, initially as an outgrowth of the Elphinstone Institute, University of Aberdeen (UK). Based in Copenhagen (Denmark). **Aims** Create and communicate island studies knowledge through international, interdisciplinary conferences and workshops. **Languages** Danish, English. **Staff** Voluntary. **Finance** Mainly self-financing; additional funding provided by project partners. **Activities** Research/documentation; events/meetings. **Events** *Islands, resources and society, sustainable development under globalization and urbanization* Hangzhou (China) 2018, *Folk belief and traditions of the supernatural and the supernatural in literature and film* Longyearbyen (Norway) 2017, *Culture in urban space* Copenhagen (Denmark) 2016, *Island cities and urban archipelagos* Hong Kong (Hong Kong) 2016, *Indigenous resources – decolonization and development* Nuuk (Greenland) 2015. **Publications** *Urban Island Studies* – peer reviewed, online open access journal. [2016.10.19/XJ5934/**F**]

♦ Islands of the Baltic Sea (B7) 16060

Chairperson Leigri v 5, 92401 Kärdla, Estonia.
URL: http://www.b7.org/

History Established 1989, at a joint meeting of 6 Baltic Islands, subsequently joined by Rügen (Germany). Previously also referred to as *Council of the Baltic Islands* and as *Baltic Sea 7 Islands*. **Aims** In general: promote international cooperation on environment, culture, economics and other issues of common interest; develop tourism; sustain economic conditions at large for the wellbeing of island communities in a regional and European context. 'Common Strategy Programme for the Twenty-First Century' aims to: create positive development on the islands through common effort and by taking advantage of the strong development potential in the Baltic Sea area; create a foundation for new job opportunities, sustainable development and mutual enrichment of the islands and the world that surrounds them; revitalize the islands; achieve a positive development spiral; strengthen personal relations and communications among the islands. **Structure** Conference of Political Leaders (annual). Steering Group and Secretariat rotating with Chairmanship. B7 Representation in Brussels (Belgium). Civil Servant Group. Working Groups (2): Environment (B7 WGE); People to People. **Languages** English. **Staff** 1.00 FTE, paid. **Finance** Members' dues. **Activities** Functions as a cooperation organization for the 7 large island regions in the Baltic Sea region. Common strategy for the future adopted May 2002. Areas of common effort (6): joint action to achieve increased influence on national and international level; exchange of knowledge and experience; tourism; environment; business; democracy. **Events** *Annual Conference* Estonia 2014, *Meeting* Bornholm (Denmark) 2013, *Annual Conference* Mariehamn (Finland) 2013, *Annual Conference* Åland (Finland) 2006, *Annual conference* Visby (Sweden) 2005. **Publications** *B7 Newsletter* (4 a year); *B7 SUSWAT – Planning and Managagement of Sustainable Water Supply in the Baltic Sea Islands* – newsletter of the Work Group for Environmnent. *Baltic Sea Islands – a Common Strategy for the Future*. Basic document on application for EU Action Programme.
Members Baltic islands (7) in 5 countries:
Denmark (Bornholm), Estonia (Hiiumaa – Saaremaa), Finland (Åland), Germany (Rügen), Sweden (Gotland – Öland).
IGO Relations Special participant status with: *Council of the Baltic Sea States (CBSS, #04870)*. Representative in Board of: *Baltic Sea States Subregional Cooperation (BSSSC, #03150)*. [2018/XD5515/**D***]

♦ Islands Commission 16061

Commission des îles – Comisión de las Islas – Insel-Kommission – Comissão das Ilhas – Commissione delle Isole – Epitropi ton Nision – Ö-kommissionen – Saarte komisjon – Kummissjoni ta'Gżejjer – Ø Kommission

Exec Sec 6 rue Saint-Martin, 35700 Rennes, France. T. +33299354050. Fax +33299350919. E-mail: anne.lezin@crpm.org – islands@crpm.org.
Twitter: https://twitter.com/cpmr_islands

History 1979, Santiago de Compostela (Spain). Founded within the framework of *Conference of Peripheral Maritime Regions of Europe (CPMR, #04638)*. **Aims** Urge European Institutions and Member States to pay special attention to the islands, acknowledge permanent handicaps resulting from their insularity, and implement policies best suited to their condition; foster interregional cooperation between islands, especially on issues in direct relation with their insularity. **Structure** Assembly; Political Bureau; President; Executive Secretary. **Languages** English, French, Irish Gaelic, Italian, Portuguese, Spanish, Swedish. **Finance** Members' dues. **Events** *Seminar on Island Transport* Palma (Spain) 2016, *General Assembly* Rhodes Is (Greece) 2016, *General Assembly* Rhodes Is (Greece) 2014, *General Assembly* UK 2009, *General Assembly* Spain 2008.
Members Regions in 11 countries:
Cyprus, Denmark, Estonia, France, Greece, Italy, Malta, Portugal, Spain, Sweden, UK.
NGO Relations *Conference of Chambers of Commerce and Industry of the Island Regions of the European Union.* [2016/XK0231/**E**]

♦ Islands of Peace / see Friends of the Islands of Peace
♦ Islands of Peace Association / see Friends of the Islands of Peace
♦ Islands of Peace – Friends of the Islands of Peace (internationally oriented national body)

♦ Islands and Small States Institute, Malta (ISSI) 16062

Dir University of Malta, Msida, MSD 2080, Malta. T. +35623402117 – +35623403308. Fax +35621344879. E-mail: islands@um.edu.mt.
URL: http://www.um.edu.mt/islands/

History 1989, Malta. Initially set up at the *Foundation for International Studies, University of Malta (FIS, inactive)*, Valletta. Restructured in 1993 as an Institute with the principal aim of enabling the organization to offer academic courses. Former names and other names: *Islands and Small States Programme* – former (1989 to 1993). **Aims** Promote *research* and training in economic, social, cultural, ecological and geographical aspects of islands and small states. **Structure** Board; Scientific Advisory Council. **Languages** English. **Staff** 2.50 FTE, paid. **Finance** Funded by the University of Malta; self-funded projects. **Activities** Events/meetings; guidance/assistance/consulting; networking/liaising; projects/programmes; research and development; training/education. See projects at: https://www.um.edu.mt/issi/ourprojects. **Events** *Island dynamics conference on taking Malta out of the box* Valletta (Malta) 2011, *Conference on sustainable tourism with special reference to islands and small states* Valletta (Malta) 2006, *Workshop on building the economic resilience of small states* Gozo Is (Malta) 2005, *Conference on competitiveness and the Lisbon agenda* Valletta (Malta) 2005, *Workshop on maximising the competitiveness potential of small states* Gozo Is (Malta) 2004. **Publications** *Small States and Territories (SST)* (2 a year) in English – SST is a scholarly, open-access journal dedicated exclusively to the study of the nature and workings of small sovereign states (however defined) and non-sovereign territories. *Assessing the vulnerability of small island developing states to sea-level rise* in English – This paper attempts to estimate the areas that would be inundated as a result of a given degree of sea-level rise (SLR) on thirty-nine Small Island Developing States (SIDS); *A vulnerability/resilience framework applied to climate change with special reference to small island states* in English – This presentation was delivered during the University College, London workshop on SIDS and Climate Change held on 24-25 May 2016; *Climate change and Small Island States with reference to Malta* in English – This presentation was a public Lecture at University College London on 25 May 2016 on the theme Climate Change and Small Island States with reference to Malta; *Has overtourism reached the Maltese Islands?* in English – Occasional Papers on Islands and Small States, 1; *The human development index with a focus on small states* in English – The human development index with a focus on small states: with a focus on Mauritius; *The vulnerability and resilience framework applied to the public health system* in English – This presentation was presented at the World Health Organisation (WHO) High-Level meeting of the European Small Countries in Monaco, 11-12 October 2016. Case studies; conference proceedings; periodic reports; occasional papers; scientific papers; articles. **Information Services** *ISSI 30th Anniversary Commemorative Publication* in English. **NGO Relations** Member of (1): *Global Islands Network (GIN, #10437)*. [2022/XE1727/j/**E**]

♦ Islands and Small States Programme / see Islands and Small States Institute, Malta (#16062)

♦ Islands of Southeast Asian Network on Male and Transgender Sexual Health (ISEAN) 16063

Secretariat Jl Tebet Barat Dalam X-E No 3, Jakarta Selatan, Jakarta 12810 DKI, Indonesia. T. +622140838094.
Facebook: https://www.facebook.com/isean.asia/

History 2009. **Aims** Advocate understanding of sexual orientation and gender identity (SOGI), socially and culturally within ISEAN countries; promote health and human rights within ASEAN; enable community empowerment among members. **Structure** Board; Governing Board; Advisory Board; Secretariat. **Languages** English. **Staff** 6.00 FTE, paid; 1.00 FTE, voluntary. **Finance** Supported by *Global Fund to Fight AIDS, Tuberculosis and Malaria (Global Fund, #10383)* via *Humanistisch Instituut voor Ontwikkelingssamenwerking (Hivos)*. **Activities** Advocacy/lobbying/activism. **Publications** *ISEAN Bulletin* (4 a year). Reports.
Members Full in 6 countries:
Brunei Darussalam, Indonesia, Malaysia, Philippines, Singapore, Timor-Leste.
NGO Relations Member of: *Asia Pacific Coalition on Male Sexual Health (APCOM, #01872)*. Cooperates with: *MPact Global Action for Gay Men's Health and Rights (MPact, #16875).* [2018/XJ9352/**F**]

♦ Islas de Paz / see Friends of the Islands of Peace
♦ Islas de Paz – Amigos de Islas de Paz (internationally oriented national body)
♦ **ISLB** International Society of Liquid Biopsy (#15234)
♦ ISLCCC – International Symposium on Late Complications After Childhood Cancer (meeting series)
♦ **ISLCRS** International Society of Laparoscopic Colorectal Surgery (#15228)
♦ ISLD / see World Federation for Laser Dentistry (#21451)
♦ ISLE – Institute of Sociology of Law for Europe (inactive)
♦ **ISLE** International Society for the Linguistics of English (#15233)
♦ **ISL-FD** International Society of Lyophilization- Freeze Drying (#15239)
♦ **ISLH** International Society for Laboratory Hematology (#15225)
♦ **ISL** International Society of Lymphology (#15238)
♦ ISL – International Socioeconomics Laboratory (unconfirmed)
♦ **ISL** International Surfing League (#15631)
♦ ISLP – International Senior Lawyers Project (internationally oriented national body)
♦ ISLPS – International Society of Lawyers for Public Service (no recent information)
♦ **ISLRR** International Society for Low Vision Research and Rehabilitation (#15237)
♦ **ISLS** International Society for Language Studies (#15227)
♦ **ISLS** International Society of the Learning Sciences (#15230)
♦ **ISLS** International Society of Liver Surgeons (#15235)
♦ **ISLSM** International Society for Laser Surgery and Medicine (#15229)
♦ **ISLSSL** International Society for Labour and Social Security Law (#15226)
♦ ISLT – International Snow Leopard Trust (internationally oriented national body)
♦ ISLWF – International Shoe and Leather Workers' Federation (inactive)
♦ **ISMAAP** International Self-Monitoring Association of Oral Anticoagulated Patients (#14831)
♦ **ISMAAR** International Society for Mild Approaches in Assisted Reproduction (#15269)
♦ ISMAB / see International Society for Biological Calorimetry (#14963)
♦ ISMAB – International Symposium on Machinery and Mechatronics for Agricultural and Biosystems Engineering (meeting series)
♦ ISMAF / see International Martial Arts Federation of the Deaf (#14109)
♦ ISMA / see InterManager (#11520)
♦ ISMA / see International Fertilizer Association (#13589)
♦ ISMA – International Ship Masters' Association (internationally oriented national body)
♦ ISMA – International Six Metre Class Association (see: #21760)
♦ **iSMA** International Social Marketing Association (#14882)
♦ **ISMA** International Social Media Association (#14883)
♦ **ISMA** International Stress Management Association (#15611)
♦ ISMANAM – International Symposium on Metastable, Amorphous and Nanostructured Materials (meeting series)
♦ **ISMAR** International Society of Magnetic Resonance (#15240)
♦ **iSMARTi** international Society for Maintenance and Rehabilitation of Transport infrastructures (#15242)
♦ **ISMB** International Society for Matrix Biology (#15248)
♦ ISMB – International Symposium on Molecular Beams (meeting series)
♦ ISMBM / see UNESCO-Hebrew University of Jerusalem International School for Molecular Biology and Microbiology and Science for Peace
♦ ISMC / see International Ski Mountaineering Federation (#14871)
♦ **ISMC** International Society of Motor Control (#15280)
♦ ISMC – International Strategic Management Conference (meeting series)
♦ **ISMCS** International Society for Mechanical Circulatory Support (#15251)
♦ **ISMD** International Society for Markets and Development (#15246)
♦ ISMD – International Symposium on Multiparticle Dynamics (meeting series)
♦ ISMDMA – International Symposium on Mechanical Design, Manufacture and Automation (meeting series)
♦ ISMEBC – International Society for Molecular Electronics and Biocomputing (inactive)
♦ **ISMED** International Society on Metabolic Eye Diseases (#15263)
♦ ISMed – Istituto di Studi sul Mediterraneo (internationally oriented national body)
♦ **ISME International** International Society of Management Engineers (#15243)
♦ ISME – International Society for MacIntyrean Enquiry (internationally oriented national body)
♦ **ISME** International Society for Mangrove Ecosystems (#15245)
♦ **ISME** International Society for Microbial Ecology (#15266)
♦ ISME – International Society for Military Ethics (internationally oriented national body)
♦ **ISME** International Society for Music Education (#15287)
♦ ISMEO – Associazione Internazionale di Studi sul Mediterraneo e l'Oriente (internationally oriented national body)
♦ **ISMET** International Society for Microbial Electrochemistry and Technology (#15267)
♦ **ISMF** International Ski Mountaineering Federation (#14871)
♦ ISMG – International Society for Inhaled Medical Gases and Therapies (inactive)
♦ **ISMH** International Society of Medical Hydrology and Climatology (#15254)
♦ ISMH / see International Society for Men's Health (#15260)
♦ **ISMH** International Society for Men's Health (#15260)
♦ **ISMICS** International Society for Minimally Invasive Cardiothoracic Surgery (#15274)
♦ ISMI – International Symposium on Media Innovations (meeting series)
♦ **ISMINS** International Society of Minimally Invasive Neurosurgery (#15275)
♦ ISM – Institut Séculier Masculin du Coeur de Jésus (religious order)
♦ ISM – International School of Management (internationally oriented national body)
♦ **ISM** International Society for Metaphysics (#15265)

- ♦ **ISM** International Society of Microbiota (#15268)
- ♦ **ISM** International Society for Mine Surveying (#15272)
- ♦ **ISM** International Society for Mycotoxicology (#15290)
- ♦ ISM / see International Society of Non-invasive Cardiology (#15308)
- ♦ ISM – International Solidarity Movement (internationally oriented national body)
- ♦ ISM – International Sufi Movement (religious order)
- ♦ **ISMIR** International Society for Music Information Retrieval (#15288)
- ♦ ISM / see ISRIC – World Soil Information (#16068)
- ♦ **ISMISS** International Society for Minimal Intervention in Spinal Surgery (#15273)
- ♦ ISM – Istituto Studi Mediterranei (internationally oriented national body)
- ♦ **ISMIT** International Society for Medical Innovation and Technology (#15255)
- ♦ ISMM – International Society of Mini- and Micro-Computers (inactive)
- ♦ **ISMM** International Society for Mountain Medicine (#15281)
- ♦ **ISMM** International Society for Music in Medicine (#15289)
- ♦ **ISMMS** International Society for Metal Music Studies (#15264)
- ♦ **ISMNI** International Society of Musculoskeletal and Neuronal Interactions (#15285)
- ♦ ISMN – International Soil Moisture Network (unconfirmed)
- ♦ ISMNT – International Society for Molecular Nutrition and Therapy (no recent information)
- ♦ **ISMO** International Society for Mobile Youth Work (#15276)
- ♦ ISMO – International Symposium of Morphology (meeting series)
- ♦ **ISMPB** International Society for the Measurement of Physical Behaviour (#15250)
- ♦ **ISMPH** International Society for Medical and Psychological Hypnosis (#15257)
- ♦ **IS-MPMI** International Society for Molecular Plant-Microbe Interactions (#15277)
- ♦ ISMPP – International Society for Medical Publication Professionals (internationally oriented national body)
- ♦ **ISMRC** International Society for Media, Religion, and Culture (#15252)
- ♦ ISMRD / see International Advocate for Glycoprotein Storage Diseases (#11592)
- ♦ **ISMRD** International Advocate for Glycoprotein Storage Diseases (#11592)
- ♦ **ISMR** International Society for Maxillofacial Rehabilitation (#15249)
- ♦ **ISMR** International Society for Molecular Recognition (#15278)
- ♦ **ISMRM** International Society for Magnetic Resonance in Medicine (#15241)
- ♦ ISMSC – International Symposium on Macrocyclic and Supramolecular Chemistry (meeting series)
- ♦ ISMSI – International Conference on Intelligent Systems, Metaheuristics & Swarm Intelligence (meeting series)
- ♦ **ISMS** International Society of Military Sciences (#15271)
- ♦ **ISMS** International Society for Mushroom Science (#15286)
- ♦ **ISMS** International Society of SR Spectroscopy (#15456)
- ♦ ISMS – International Symposium on Molecular Spectroscopy (meeting series)
- ♦ ISMSM – International Symposium on Microbial Sulfur Metabolism (meeting series)
- ♦ ISMST / see International Society for Medical Shockwave Therapy (#15258)
- ♦ **ISMST** International Society for Medical Shockwave Therapy (#15258)
- ♦ **ISMTE** International Society of Managing and Technical Editors (#15244)
- ♦ **ISMTE** International Society for Mental Training and Excellence (#15261)
- ♦ ISMU / see ISMU Foundation – Foundation for Initiatives and Studies on Multi-ethnicity
- ♦ ISMU Foundation – Foundation for Initiatives and Studies on Multi-ethnicity (internationally oriented national body)
- ♦ ISMUS – International Society for Musculoskeletal Ultrasound (inactive)
- ♦ **ISNCC** International Society for Nurses in Cancer Care (#15312)
- ♦ **ISNCT** International Society for Neutron Capture Therapy (#15304)
- ♦ **ISNET** Inter-Islamic Network on Space Sciences and Technology (#11511)
- ♦ **ISNFF** International Society for Nutraceuticals and Functional Foods (#15313)
- ♦ ISNGI – International Symposium for Next Generation Infrastructure (meeting series)
- ♦ **ISNG** International Skin-Care Nursing Group (#14872)
- ♦ ISNIE / see Society for Institutional and Organizational Economics (#19576)
- ♦ ISNI-IA – ISNI International Agency (unconfirmed)
- ♦ ISNI International Agency (unconfirmed)
- ♦ **ISNI** International Society of Neuroimmunology (#15298)
- ♦ **ISNIM** International Society for NeuroImmunoModulation (#15299)
- ♦ **ISN** International Shiatsu Network (#14847)
- ♦ **ISN** International Sjögren's Network (#14864)
- ♦ **ISN** International Society of Nephrology (#15294)
- ♦ **ISN** International Society for Neurochemistry (#15295)
- ♦ ISN – International Society of Neuroendocrinology (inactive)
- ♦ **ISN** International Society for Neuroethology (#15296)
- ♦ ISN – International Society of Neurogastronomy (internationally oriented national body)
- ♦ **ISN** International Society of Neuropathology (#15300)
- ♦ **ISN** International Society of Non-Antibiotics (#15307)
- ♦ **ISNIP** International Society for Neuroimaging in Psychiatry (#15297)
- ♦ **ISNM** International Society for Nanomanufacturing (#15291)
- ♦ ISNM – International Symposium on Naval Medicine (unconfirmed)
- ♦ **ISNN** International Society of Nutrigenetics / Nutrigenomics (#15314)
- ♦ ISNNM – International Symposium on Novel and Nano Materials (meeting series)
- ♦ **ISNO** International Sport Network Organization (#15592)
- ♦ **ISNPCHD** International Society for Nomenclature of Paediatric and Congenital Heart Disease (#15306)
- ♦ ISNP – International Society on Neurobiology and Psychopharmacology (internationally oriented national body)
- ♦ **ISNPS** International Society for NonParametric Statistics (#15309)
- ♦ ISNR – International Society for Neurofeedback and Research (internationally oriented national body)
- ♦ **ISNR** International Society for Neutron Radiology (#15305)
- ♦ **ISNS** International Sentinel Node Society (#14834)
- ♦ **ISNS** International Society for Neonatal Screening (#15292)
- ♦ **ISNS** International Society for Neoplatonic Studies (#15293)
- ♦ **ISNS** International Society of Neuro-Semantics (#15301)
- ♦ **ISNS** International Society for Nubian Studies (#15310)
- ♦ ISNTD – International Society for Neglected Tropical Diseases (unconfirmed)
- ♦ ISNTii – International Society for Neurosurgical Technology and Instrument Invention (inactive)
- ♦ ISNT – International Symposium on Nitrides (meeting series)
- ♦ **ISNVD** International Society for NeuroVascular Disease (#15302)
- ♦ ISNV – International School of Neurological Sciences (internationally oriented national body)
- ♦ **ISNV** International Society for NeuroVirology (#15303)
- ♦ ISNVP – International Society for Non Verbal Psychotherapy (inactive)
- ♦ ISOABE / see International Society of Air Breathing Engines (#14913)
- ♦ **ISOAI** International Society of Osteoarthritis Imaging (#15336)
- ♦ ISOA – International Stability Operations Association (internationally oriented national body)
- ♦ **ISOA** International Support Vessel Owners' Association (#15628)
- ♦ **ISOB** International Society on Biotelemetry (#14976)
- ♦ ISOBM / see International Society for Oncology and BioMarkers (#15323)
- ♦ **ISOBM** International Society for Oncology and BioMarkers (#15323)
- ♦ **ISOCARP** International Society of City and Regional Planners (#15012)
- ♦ **ISOC** Internet Society (#15952)

♦ ISO Class Association 16064

Chairman 40 Orpington Road, London, N21 3PG, UK. E-mail: chairman@isoracing.org.
Sec address not obtained. E-mail: secretary@isoracing.org.
URL: https://isoracing.org/

History Previously also referred to as *ISO International Class Association*. **Aims** Promote and coordinate international ISO dinghy racing *competitions* throughout the world under uniform Class Rules in cooperation with regional ISO Class Associations. **Languages** Dutch, English, German, Italian. **Staff** Voluntary. **Finance** Annual subscription. **Activities** Guidance/assistance/consulting; standards/guideline; sporting activities. **Members** ISO sailors (88) in 5 countries:
Belgium, Germany, Italy, Netherlands, UK. [2019.09.25/XK1763/**E**]

- ♦ **ISOCM** International Society for Orthodox Church Music (#15333)
- ♦ ISoCP – International Symposium on Combustion Processes (meeting series)
- ♦ **ISOCS** International Society for Olfaction and Chemical Sensing (#15321)
- ♦ ISODARCO – International School on Disarmament and Research on Conflicts (internationally oriented national body)
- ♦ ISOD – International Society for Orbital Disorders (no recent information)
- ♦ ISOD – International Sports Organization for the Disabled (inactive)
- ♦ **ISODP** International Society for Organ Donation and Procurement (#15330)
- ♦ **ISOE** Information System on Occupational Exposure (#11199)
- ♦ ISOES – International Society of Occupational Ergonomics and Safety Research (internationally oriented national body)
- ♦ **ISOFAR** International Society of Organic Farming Research (#15331)
- ♦ ISoF – International Society of Franchising (internationally oriented national body)
- ♦ ISOF – International Society for Ocular Fluorophotometry (no recent information)
- ♦ ISOGEM – International Society for Genomic and Evolutionary Microbiology (unconfirmed)
- ♦ **ISOGH** International Society of Global Health (#15145)
- ♦ **iSoGO** International Society of Global Optimization (#15146)
- ♦ ISOHA – International Student One Health Alliance (unconfirmed)
- ♦ **ISOH** International Society of Olympic Historians (#15322)
- ♦ ISO International Class Association / see ISO Class Association (#16064)
- ♦ **ISO** International Organization for Standardization (#14473)
- ♦ ISO – International Shopfitting Organisation (inactive)
- ♦ ISO – International Society of Ondol (unconfirmed)
- ♦ **ISO** International Society of Organbuilders (#15329)
- ♦ ISO – International Sport Organization (unconfirmed)
- ♦ **ISO** International Sugar Organization (#15623)
- ♦ ISOLA / see International Society for the Oral Literatures of Africa (#15327)
- ♦ **ISOLA** International Society for the Oral Literatures of Africa (#15327)
- ♦ Isole di Pace / see Friends of the Islands of Peace
- ♦ Isole di Pace – Amici delle Isole di Pace (internationally oriented national body)
- ♦ **ISOLS** International Society of Limb Salvage (#15231)
- ♦ **ISOMED** International Society of Mediterranean Ecology (#15259)
- ♦ ISOM / see International Research Ship Operators (#14741)
- ♦ ISOM – International Society of Obstetric Medicine (no recent information)
- ♦ **ISOM** International Society of Oriental Medicine (#15332)
- ♦ **ISOM** International Society for Orthomolecular Medicine (#15334)
- ♦ ISOM – International Symposium on Imaging, Sensing, and Optical Memory (meeting series)
- ♦ ISOM – International Symposium on Olefin Metathesis and Related Chemistry (meeting series)
- ♦ ISONEUREM – International Society for Neuroemergencies (inactive)
- ♦ ISONG – International Society of Nurses in Genetics (internationally oriented national body)
- ♦ **ISOO** International Society of Ocular Oncology (#15315)
- ♦ **ISOO** International Society for Oral Oncology (#15328)
- ♦ **ISOPA** European Diisocyanate and Polyol Producers Association (#06926)
- ♦ **ISOPA** International Society of Oil Palm Agronomists (#15319)
- ♦ **ISOPB** International Society for Oil Palm Breeders (#15320)
- ♦ ISOPE / see International Society of Offshore and Polar Engineers (#15318)
- ♦ **ISOPE** International Society of Offshore and Polar Engineers (#15318)
- ♦ **ISOPES** International Society of Oncoplastic Endocrine Surgeons (#15325)
- ♦ ISOP – International Society of Ophthalmic Pathology (internationally oriented national body)
- ♦ ISoP – International Society of Pharmacometrics (internationally oriented national body)
- ♦ **ISoP** International Society of Pharmacovigilance (#15356)
- ♦ **ISoP** International Society of Phthirapterists (#15364)
- ♦ **ISOP** International Society of Protistologists (#15392)
- ♦ ISOPOL – International Symposium on Problems of Listeria and Listeriosis (meeting series)
- ♦ **ISOPOW** International Symposium on the Properties of Water (#15644)
- ♦ **ISOPP** International Society of Oncology Pharmacy Practitioners (#15324)
- ♦ ISOPRS – International Society of Oculoplastic, Plastic and Reconstructive Surgery (internationally oriented national body)
- ♦ **ISOQOL** International Society for Quality of Life Research (#15407)
- ♦ **ISORBE** International Society of Radiolabelled Blood Elements (#15411)
- ♦ **ISORECEA** International Study of Religion in Eastern and Central Europe Association (#15620)
- ♦ ISOSC – International Society for Soilless Culture (inactive)
- ♦ **ISOS Foundation** International SOS Foundation (#15570)
- ♦ **ISOS** International Social Ontology Society (#14884)
- ♦ ISOS / see International Society for Organ Donation and Procurement (#15330)
- ♦ **ISOSS** Islamic Countries Society of Statistical Sciences (#16043)
- ♦ **ISOT** International Society of Ocular Toxicology (#15316)
- ♦ **ISOT** International Society of Ocular Trauma (#15317)
- ♦ **ISOTT** International Society on Oxygen Transport to Tissue (#15337)
- ♦ ISOU / see Societas Internationalis de Diagnostica Ultrasonica in Ophthalmologia (#19443)
- ♦ ISPA / see International Cost Estimating and Analysis Association
- ♦ ISPA / see International Spa Association
- ♦ ISPAA / see International Society for the Performing Arts Foundation (#15350)
- ♦ **ISPAC** International Scientific and Professional Advisory Council of the United Nations Crime Prevention and Criminal Justice Programme (#14810)
- ♦ **ISPAC** International Society for Polycyclic Aromatic Compounds (#15375)
- ♦ **ISPAC** International Symposium on Polymer Analysis and Characterization (#15643)
- ♦ **ISPAD** International Society for Pediatric and Adolescent Diabetes (#15344)
- ♦ **ISPAFA** International Society of Phenomenology, Aesthetics and the Fine Arts (#15357)
- ♦ **ISPAH** International Society for Physical Activity and Health (#15365)
- ♦ ISPA / see International Association of Physiological Anthropology (#12086)
- ♦ ISPA / see International Prestressed Hollowcore Association (#14638)
- ♦ **ISPA** International School Psychology Association (#14788)
- ♦ **ISPA** International Skat Players Association (#14866)
- ♦ **ISPA** International Society for the Performing Arts Foundation (#15350)
- ♦ **ISPA** International Society for Plant Anaerobiosis (#15368)
- ♦ **ISPA** International Society of Precision Agriculture (#15379)
- ♦ ISPA – International Society for the Protection of Animals (inactive)
- ♦ ISPA – International Spa Association (internationally oriented national body)
- ♦ **ISPA** International Stationary Press Association (#15601)
- ♦ ISPA – International Symposium on Image and Signal Processing and Analysis (meeting series)
- ♦ ISPA / see Professional Squash Association (#18517)
- ♦ **ISPAR** International Suspected Perioperative Allergic Reaction Group (#15633)
- ♦ **ISPASA** International Society of Performance Analysis of Sports Asia (#15349)

- ♦ ISPAS – International Society of Performance Analysis of Sport (unconfirmed)
- ♦ ISPC / see International Programs Center
- ♦ **ISPCAN** International Society for Prevention of Child Abuse and Neglect (#15385)
- ♦ ISPC / see International School Psychology Association (#14788)
- ♦ **ISPC** International Society for the Philosophy of Chemistry (#15359)
- ♦ ISPCJ – Institut Séculier des Prêtres du Coeur de Jésus (religious order)
- ♦ ISPCLN – International Society of Psychiatric Consultation Liaison Nurses (internationally oriented national body)
- ♦ **ISPCM** International Society of Precision Cancer Medicine (#15380)
- ♦ **ISPCOP** International Society for the Perioperative Care of the Obese Patient (#15351)
- ♦ ISPDC / see International Society of Cancer Metabolism (#14991)
- ♦ **ISPDI** International Society for Psychology as the Discipline of Interiority (#15397)
- ♦ ISPD – International School of Protocol and Diplomacy (unconfirmed)
- ♦ **ISPD** International Society of Pediatric Dermatology (#15345)
- ♦ **ISPD** International Society for Peritoneal Dialysis (#15352)
- ♦ **ISPD** International Society for Prenatal Diagnosis (#15381)
- ♦ ISPE Inc / see International Society of Transdisciplinary Engineering (#15514)

♦ ISPE 16065

Headquarters 6110 Executive Blvd, Ste 600, North Bethesda MD 20852, USA. E-mail: ask@ispe.org.
URL: http://www.ispe.org/

History 1980. Former names and other names: *International Society of Pharmaceutical Engineering* – full title. **Aims** Provide a neutral forum for pharmaceutical technical professionals and international agencies to discuss and solve CGMP challenges; provide pharmaceutical technical professionals opportunities to develop technical knowledge, exchange practice experience and collaborate with global regulatory agencies and industry leaders. **Structure** Board of Directors, comprising Chairman, Vice Chairman, Treasurer, Secretary and Directors. Executive Council. Regional Advisory Councils: Pacific Rim; Europe; Latin America; North America. Board Task Teams; Committees; International Affiliates; Chapters. Headquarters located in Tampa FL (USA); other offices (3): Brussels (Belgium); Shanghai (China); Singapore (Singapore). **Languages** Chinese, Czech, English, French, German, Italian, Japanese, Polish, Portuguese, Spanish, Thai, Turkish. **Staff** 78.00 FTE, paid. **Finance** Members' dues. **Activities** Leads global change and innovation in pharmaceutical technology and processes through: education and training via on-site and distance learning vehicles across a wide range of industry topics; knowledge on demand, CPIP – certification programme; full array of technical documents; local networking; peer-to-peer collaboration through Communities of Practice (COP); worldwide membership; interaction with regulators; global industry impact; sponsorship and exhibit opportunities. **Events** *Europe Conference* Amsterdam (Netherlands) 2023, *ISPE Biotechnology Conference* Dublin (Ireland) 2023, *Annual Meeting* Las Vegas, NV (USA) 2023, *Europe Conference* Madrid (Spain) 2022, *Conference* Singapore (Singapore) 2020. **Publications** *Pharmaceutical Engineering* (6 a year); *Membership Directory* (annual). *GAMP Publications*; *ISPE Good Practice Guides (GPGs)*. Clinical trial materials; GMP products.
Members Individuals (22,000) working in engineering, pharmaceutical, healthcare and quality control and assurance professions, in over 90 countries. Affiliates and Chapters represent 33 countries:
Argentina, Australia, Austria, Belgium, Brazil, Canada, China, Czechia, Denmark, Finland, France, Germany, Iceland, India, Indonesia, Ireland, Italy, Japan, Korea Rep, Netherlands, New Zealand, Norway, Philippines, Poland, Singapore, Slovakia, Spain, Sweden, Switzerland, Thailand, Türkiye, UK, USA. [2022/XD3485/v/**D**]

- ♦ ISPEC / see African University for Cooperative Development (#00494)
- ♦ **ISPE** International Society for Pharmacoepidemiology (#15355)
- ♦ **ISPE** International Society for Philosophical Enquiry (#15358)
- ♦ ISPE / see International Society of Transdisciplinary Engineering (#15514)
- ♦ ISPE – International Symposium on Polymer Electrolytes (meeting series)
- ♦ **ISPeW** International Society of Pediatric Wound Care (#15347)
- ♦ **ISPF** International Ski Patrol Federation (#09647)
- ♦ **ISPG** International Society of Psychiatric Genetics (#15393)
- ♦ **ISPGR** International Society for Postural and Gait Research (#15378)
- ♦ ISPHARMA – Inter-syndicale des pharmaciens d'Afrique (inactive)
- ♦ **ISPH** International Society of Psychology of Handwriting (#15398)
- ♦ **ISPhS** International Society of Phonetic Sciences (#15361)
- ♦ ISPIC – International Society for the Prevention of Iatrogenic Complications (inactive)
- ♦ **ISPID** International Society for the Study and Prevention of Perinatal and Infant Death (#15484)
- ♦ ISPI – International Society for Performance Improvement (internationally oriented national body)
- ♦ **ISPI** International Society for Pest Information (#15353)
- ♦ ISPI – Istituto per gli Studi di Politica Internazionale (internationally oriented national body)
- ♦ **ISPIM** International Society for Professional Innovation Management (#15389)
- ♦ ISP – Institute for Sustainable Power (internationally oriented national body)
- ♦ **ISP** Inter-American Society of Psychology (#11450)
- ♦ **ISP** Internacional de Servicios Públicos (#18572)
- ♦ **ISP** Internationale des Services Publics (#18572)
- ♦ **ISP** International Society for Pathophysiology (#15343)
- ♦ ISP / see International Society for Photogrammetry and Remote Sensing (#15362)
- ♦ **ISP** International Society for Plastination (#15373)
- ♦ ISP – International Society of Postmasters (inactive)
- ♦ **ISP** International Society for Psychophysics (#15401)
- ♦ **ISP** International Society of Pteridinology (#15403)
- ♦ **ISP** International Society of Skin Pharmacology and Physiology (#15444)
- ♦ ISP / see International Student/Young Pugwash (#15614)
- ♦ ISPL – International Society for Phenomenology and Literature (see: #21725)
- ♦ ISPL – International Symposium on Plant Lipids (meeting series)
- ♦ ISPMB – International Society of Plant Molecular Biology (inactive)
- ♦ ISPMCS – International Society for Pediatric Mechanical Cardiopulmonary Support (unconfirmed)
- ♦ **ISPME** International Society for the Philosophy of Music Education (#15360)
- ♦ **ISPMF** International Society for Plant Molecular Farming (#15369)
- ♦ ISPM – International School in Physics and Mathematics (internationally oriented national body)
- ♦ **ISPM** International Society on Participatory Mapping (#15342)
- ♦ ISPM – International Society of Personalized Medicine (internationally oriented national body)
- ♦ **ISPM** International Society of Plant Morphologists (#15370)
- ♦ **ISPM** International Society for Plasma Medicine (#15372)
- ♦ **ISPMNH** International Society for the Prevention and Mitigation of Natural Hazards (#15386)
- ♦ **ISPNE** International Society of Psychoneuroendocrinology (#15399)
- ♦ ISPNI – International Society of Peripheral Neurophysiological Imaging (unconfirmed)
- ♦ ISPN – International Society of Parenteral Nutrition (inactive)
- ♦ **ISPN** International Society for Pediatric Neurosurgery (#15346)
- ♦ ISPN – International Society of Psychiatric-Mental Health Nurses (internationally oriented national body)
- ♦ ISPNO – International Symposium on Pediatric Neuro-Oncology (meeting series)
- ♦ **ISPOG** International Society of Psychosomatic Obstetrics and Gynaecology (#15402)
- ♦ **ISPO** International Simultaneous Policy Organisation (#14862)
- ♦ ISPO – International Society of Perinatal Obstetricians (unconfirmed)
- ♦ ISPO – International Society for Preventive Oncology (no recent information)
- ♦ **ISPO** International Society for Prosthetics and Orthotics (#15390)
- ♦ ISPO / see International Users Group of ISPO-certified organizations (#15837)

♦ ISPOR Asia Consortium 16066

Chair Graduate School of Public Policy, Univ of Tokyo, 7-3-1 Hongo, Bunkyo-ku, Tokyo, 113-8656 Japan. T. +81358411349. E-mail: asiaconsortium@ispor.org.
URL: http://www.ispor.org/consortiums/asia.asp

History Aug 2004, when officially set up, following initiative Sep 2003, Kobe (Japan). A group within *International Society for Pharmacoeconomics and Outcomes Research (ISPOR, #15354)*. **Structure** Executive Committee. **Events** *Asia-Pacific Conference* Lawrenceville, NJ (USA) 2020, *Asia-Pacific Conference* Tokyo (Japan) 2018, *Asia-Pacific Conference* Singapore (Singapore) 2016, *Asia-Pacific Conference* Beijing (China) 2014, *Asia-Pacific Conference* Taipei (Taiwan) 2012.
Members Full in 17 countries and territories:
Australia, China, France, Hong Kong, India, Indonesia, Japan, Korea Rep, Malaysia, Mongolia, Pakistan, Philippines, Singapore, Switzerland, Taiwan, Thailand, USA. [2022/XJ0615/**E**]

- ♦ **ISPOR** International Society for Pharmacoeconomics and Outcomes Research (#15354)

♦ ISPOR Latin America Consortium 16067

Contact c/o IPSOR, 505 Lawrence Square Blvd South, Lawrenceville NJ 08648, USA. T. +16095864981. E-mail: info@ispor.org.
URL: http://www.ispor.org/consortiums/latin_america.asp

History as a group within *International Society for Pharmacoeconomics and Outcomes Research (ISPOR, #15354)*. **Structure** Executive Committee; Advisory Committee. **Languages** English, Spanish. **Events** *Latin America Conference* Bogota (Colombia) 2019, *Latin America Conference* Sao Paulo (Brazil) 2017, *Latin America Conference* Santiago (Chile) 2015, *Latin America Conference* Buenos Aires (Argentina) 2013, *Latin America conference* Mexico City (Mexico) 2011. **Publications** *News Across Latin America* – newsletter.
Members Regional chapters in 6 countries:
Argentina, Brazil, Chile, Colombia, Mexico, Venezuela. [2016/XJ0617/**E**]

- ♦ **ISPP** International Society for Pelviperineology (#15348)
- ♦ **ISPP** International Society for Plant Pathology (#15371)
- ♦ **ISPP** International Society of Political Psychology (#15374)
- ♦ **ISPP** International Society of Portuguese Philately (#15377)
- ♦ ISPP / see International Society for Pre- and Perinatal Psychology and Medicine (#15382)
- ♦ **ISPP** International Society of Psychoanalysis and Philosophy (#15394)
- ♦ **ISPPM** International Society for Pre- and Perinatal Psychology and Medicine (#15382)
- ♦ ISPPP – International Symposium on the Separation of Proteins, Peptides and Polynucleotides (meeting series)
- ♦ ISPQ / see Institute for Sustainable Power
- ♦ ISPQR – International Society for Productivity and Quality Research (no recent information)
- ♦ Ispra IES – Institute for Environment and Sustainability (inactive)
- ♦ ISPRES – International Society of Plastic Regenerative Surgery (internationally oriented national body)
- ♦ **ISPR** International Society of Photosynthesis Research (#15363)
- ♦ **ISPR** International Society for Presence Research (#15383)
- ♦ ISPR – International Symposium for Production Research (meeting series)
- ♦ **ISPRM** International Society of Physical and Rehabilitation Medicine (#15366)
- ♦ **ISPRS** International Society for Photogrammetry and Remote Sensing (#15362)
- ♦ **ISPS** International Society of Pituitary Surgeons (#15367)
- ♦ **ISPS** International Society for Psychological and Social Approaches to Psychosis (#15396)
- ♦ **ISPS** International Spinal Pain Society (#15582)
- ♦ ISPS – International Street Painting Society (unconfirmed)
- ♦ ISPS – International Symposium on Performance Science (meeting series)
- ♦ **ISPSO** International Society for the Psychoanalytic Study of Organizations (#15395)
- ♦ ISPSP / see International Parliament for Safety and Peace
- ♦ ISPSR – International Symposium on Pediatric Surgical Research (meeting series)
- ♦ **ISPT** International Society of Protein Termini (#15391)
- ♦ **ISPTR** International Society for Preservation of the Tropical Rainforest (#15384)
- ♦ ISPU – Institut supérieur de planification d'urgence – Centre d'étude Europa (now national)
- ♦ ISPW / see International Society of Psychology of Handwriting (#15398)
- ♦ **ISQBP** International Society of Quantum Biology and Pharmacology (#15409)
- ♦ **ISQOLS** International Society for Quality-of-Life Studies (#15408)
- ♦ **ISQua EEA** International Society for Quality in Health Care External Evaluation Association (#15406)
- ♦ **ISQua** International Society for Quality in Health Care (#15405)
- ♦ IsraAID – Israel Forum for International Humanitarian Aid (internationally oriented national body)
- ♦ Israel Association of Jewish Professionals from the Former Soviet Union (internationally oriented national body)
- ♦ Israel Forum for International Humanitarian Aid (internationally oriented national body)
- ♦ Israel Identity / see Christian Identity
- ♦ Israel-Lebanon Monitoring Group (no recent information)
- ♦ Israel/Palestine Centre for Research and Information / see Israel-Palestine: Creative Regional Initiatives
- ♦ Israel-Palestine: Creative Regional Initiatives (internationally oriented national body)
- ♦ **ISRA** International Ship Recycling Association (#14849)
- ♦ **ISRA** International Society for Research on Aggression (#15419)
- ♦ ISRBP / see International Society for Mechanical Circulatory Support (#15251)
- ♦ ISRCAP – International Society for Research in Child and Adolescent Psychopathology (internationally oriented national body)
- ♦ ISRCB / see Society of Radiopharmaceutical Sciences (#19627)
- ♦ **ISRCL** International Society for the Reform of Criminal Law (#15415)
- ♦ ISRD / see RI Global (#18948)
- ♦ **ISRE** International Society for Research on Emotion (#15420)
- ♦ **ISREV** International Seminar on Religious Education and Values (#14832)
- ♦ ISRFG – International Symposium on Rice Functional Genomics (meeting series)
- ♦ **ISRF** Independent Social Research Foundation (#11155)
- ♦ ISRF / see World Squash Federation (#21826)
- ♦ **ISRHML** International Society for Research in Human Milk and Lactation (#15421)
- ♦ ISRIC / see ISRIC – World Soil Information (#16068)

♦ ISRIC – World Soil Information 16068

Dir PO Box 353, 6700 AJ Wageningen, Netherlands. T. +31317483735.
URL: http://www.isric.org/

History 1 Jan 1966, Utrecht (Netherlands), as *International Soil Museum (ISM) – Musée international du sol – Museo Internacional de Suelos – Internationales Bodenkundliches Museum – Internationaal Bodemkundig Museum*, following recommendations of *International Union of Soil Sciences (IUSS, #15817)* (formerly ISSS) and *FAO (#09260)*, with support from the General Conference of UNESCO (1964). Museum transferred to Wageningen (Netherlands) in 1978 and officially opened 9 Mar 1979. Subsequently changed title to *International Soil Reference and Information Centre (ISRIC) – Centre international de référence et d'information pédologique – Centro Internacional de Referencia e Información en Suelos – Internationales Bodenreferenz und Informations-Zentrum – Internationaal Centrum voor Bodem-referentie en -informatie*, 1984, when new role was adopted. Current shorter title registered 2003. Became a foundation Dec 1994. Since 2002, a strategic association with Wageningen University and Research Centre. **Aims** Serve the international community with information about the world's soil resources to help address major global issues. **Structure** Managing Board, comprising representatives from Wageningen University and Research Centre (Wageningen UR). International Scientific Advisory Council (ISAC) reflects, discusses and advises on ISRIC's activities viewed from an international perspective. **Languages** Chinese, Dutch, English, French, German, Portuguese, Spanish. **Staff** 8 senior scientists; 7 scientists; 7 support staff for collection, database and website management/project administration; varying number of visiting scientists carry out targeted research for periods ranging from 1-12 months. **Finance** Foundation with a global mandate with core funds provided by the Netherlands Government; projects carried out with external funding by international and other donors. **Activities** Knowledge management/information dissemination; research/documentation; training/education. **Events** *Workshop on scaling of trace gas fluxes between terrestrial and aquatic ecosystems and the atmosphere* Bennekom (Netherlands) 1998, *Workshop on mapping of soil and terrain vulnerability* *in Central and Eastern Europe* Wageningen (Netherlands) 1997, *International conference on soils and the greenhouse effect* Wageningen (Netherlands) 1989. **Publications** *ISRIC Reports* – online. Report of Activities (annual). Scientific papers; books; chapters in books; workshop proceedings; consultancy/mission reports – online. **IGO Relations** Cooperation agreement with: *Joint Research Centre (JRC, #16147).* Memorandum of Understanding with: *FAO (#09260); UNEP (#20299)* (also associated institute). Accredited to the Conference of the Parties of: *Secretariat of the United Nations Convention to Combat Desertification (Secretariat of the UNCCD, #19208).* Partner of: *Global Soil Partnership (GSP, #10608).* Links also include: *International Fund for Agricultural Development (IFAD, #13692).* **NGO Relations** Regular member of: *ISC World Data System (ISC-WDS, #16024)* of *International Council for Science (ICSU, inactive).* Member of: *Global Open Data for Agriculture and Nutrition (GODAN, #10514).* Links with ICSU bodies, unions and scientific associations. Special links with *International Union of Soil Sciences (IUSS, #15817).* Partner of: *Earth Science Matters Foundation (ESM, #05169).* Links also include: *Africa Soil Science Society (ASSS, #00520); International Institute for Applied Systems Analysis (IIASA, #13861); International Institute for Environment and Development (IIED, #13877); Royal Tropical Institute (KIT); Stockholm Environment Institute (SEI, #19993);* Wageningen University and Research Centre (Wageningen UR); *West and Central African Association of Soil Science (WCAASS, no recent information); World Overview of Conservation Approaches and Technologies (WOCAT, see: #21192);* national land resources institutions. [2015/XF0893/**E**]

♦ ISRiG – Instytut Studiów Regionalnych i Globalnych (internationally oriented national body)
♦ **ISRII** International Society for Research on Internet Interventions (#15423)
♦ ISRI – Instituto Superior de Relaciones Internacionales 'Raúl Roa Garcia' (internationally oriented national body)
♦ **ISRI** International Society for Research on Identity (#15422)
♦ **ISR** International Society of Radiology (#15412)
♦ I.S. Rivers (meeting series)
♦ ISRKF – International Sendo-Ryu Karatedo Federation (internationally oriented national body)
♦ ISRK / see International Society of Refractive Surgery of the American Academy of Ophthalmology (#15416)
♦ **ISRLC** International Society for Religion, Literature and Culture (#15417)
♦ ISRM – International Society for Reconstructive Microsurgery (inactive)
♦ ISRM / see International Society for Rock Mechanics and Rock Engineering (#15428)
♦ **ISRM** International Society for Rock Mechanics and Rock Engineering (#15428)
♦ **ISRN** International Society of Reconstructive Neurosurgery (#15414)
♦ **ISRN** International Society for Restorative Neurology (#15426)
♦ **ISRNM** International Society of Renal Nutrition and Metabolism (#15418)
♦ ISRO – International Society for Radiation Oncology (inactive)
♦ ISRO-USAK – International Strategic Research Organisation (internationally oriented national body)
♦ **ISRP** International Society for Respiratory Protection (#15425)
♦ **ISRR** International Society of Root Research (#15429)
♦ iSRRS – International Society for Rapid Respond Systems (internationally oriented national body)
♦ **ISRRT** International Society of Radiographers and Radiological Technologists (#15410)
♦ ISRS/AAO / see International Society of Refractive Surgery of the American Academy of Ophthalmology (#15416)
♦ ISRS / see International Coral Reef Society (#12966)
♦ **ISRS** International Society of Rare Sugars (#15413)
♦ ISRS / see International Society of Refractive Surgery of the American Academy of Ophthalmology (#15416)
♦ **ISRS** International Society of Refractive Surgery of the American Academy of Ophthalmology (#15416)
♦ **ISRS** International Society for River Science (#15427)
♦ **ISRS** International Stereotactic Radiosurgery Society (#15607)
♦ ISRS – International Symposium on Remote Sensing (meeting series)
♦ ISRT – International Society for Rheumatic Therapeutics (no recent information)
♦ ISRT – International Spinal Research Trust (internationally oriented national body)
♦ ISRTP – International Society of Regulatory Toxicology and Pharmacology (internationally oriented national body)
♦ ISS / see International Branch of the YMCA, New York
♦ ISSA (internationally oriented national body)
♦ **ISSAAS** International Society for Southeast Asian Agricultural Sciences (#15454)
♦ ISSAC – International Symposium on Symbolic and Algebraic Computation (meeting series)
♦ **ISSAID** International Society of Systemic Auto-Inflammatory Diseases (#15498)
♦ **ISSA** International Sailing Schools Association (#14777)
♦ **ISSA** International Securities Services Association (#14824)
♦ ISSA – International Shinto Studies Association (internationally oriented national body)
♦ **ISSA** International Ship Suppliers and Services Association (#14850)
♦ **ISSA** International Social Security Association (#14885)
♦ **ISSA** International Society for the Study of Argumentation (#15463)
♦ **ISSA** International Sociology of Sport Association (#15554)
♦ **ISSA** International Sports Sciences Association (#15594)
♦ **ISSA** International Step by Step Association (#15605)
♦ ISSA – International Studies Schools Association (internationally oriented national body)
♦ ISSA – International Swimming Statisticians Association (inactive)
♦ **ISSAM** International Society for the Study of the Aging Male (#15462)
♦ ISSAV – International Seminar on Safety and Security of Autonomous Vessels (meeting series)
♦ **ISSBA** International Society for the Study of Behavioral Addictions (#15464)
♦ **ISSBD** International Society for the Study of Behavioural Development (#15465)
♦ ISSB / see International Society of Biospeleology (#14975)
♦ **ISSB** International Society for Systems Biology (#15499)
♦ **ISSB** International Sustainability Standards Board (#15634)
♦ ISSB – International Symposium on Small Business (meeting series)
♦ ISSBS – International School for Social and Business Studies (internationally oriented national body)
♦ ISSCB – International Society for Sandwich Construction and Bonding (inactive)
♦ ISSC Comparative Research Programme on Poverty 1100053199
♦ **ISSCD** International Society for the Study of Celiac Disease (#15467)
♦ ISSC – International Social Science Council (inactive)
♦ **ISSC** International Society for Sexuality and Cancer (#15439)
♦ ISSC – Inter-Society Color Council (internationally oriented national body)
♦ ISSCM – International Society for Systematic and Comparative Musicology (inactive)
♦ **ISSCO** International Society for the Study of Chinese Overseas (#15468)
♦ ISSCO – International Society for the Study of Comparative Oncology (inactive)
♦ ISSCP / see International Society for Technology in Arthroplasty (#15502)
♦ **ISSCR** International Society for Stem Cell Research (#15457)
♦ **ISSCT** International Society of Sugar Cane Technologists (#15495)
♦ ISSDA – International Society for Sustainable Development and Agriculture (inactive)
♦ **ISSD** International Society of Social Defence and Humane Criminal Policy (#15447)
♦ ISSD / see International Society for the Study of Trauma and Dissociation (#15488)
♦ **ISSDO** International Solid State Dosimetry Organisation (#15566)
♦ **ISSDP** International Society for the Study of Drug Policy (#15469)
♦ **ISSEA** Institut sous-régional de statistique et d'économie appliquée (#11356)
♦ **ISSEA** International Systems Security Engineering Association (#15647)
♦ **ISSECAM** International Society for the Study and Exchange of evidence from Clinical research And Medical experience (#15471)
♦ **ISSEI** International Society for the Study of European Ideas (#15470)
♦ ISSE – Information Security Solutions Europe (meeting series)
♦ **ISSE** International School-to-School Experience (#14791)
♦ **ISSFAL** International Society for the Study of Fatty Acids and Lipids (#15472)
♦ ISSF – International Seafood Sustainability Foundation (internationally oriented national body)
♦ **ISSF** International Shooting Sport Federation (#14852)
♦ ISSF – International Space Safety Foundation (internationally oriented national body)
♦ **ISSF** Islamic Solidarity Sports Federation (#16052)
♦ ISSF / see world stainless association (#21828)
♦ ISS GB / see Children and Families Across Borders
♦ ISSHA / see International Society for the Study of Harmful Algae (#15473)
♦ **ISSHA** International Society for the Study of Harmful Algae (#15473)
♦ ISSHCAB / see International Association of Human-Animal Interaction Organizations (#11944)
♦ **ISSHP** International Society for the Study of Hypertension in Pregnancy (#15475)
♦ **ISSIA** International Society for Stereology and Image Analysis (#15458)
♦ **ISSID** International Society for the Study of Individual Differences (#15476)
♦ **ISSI** International Society for Scientometrics and Informetrics (#15436)
♦ ISSI – International Society for Skin Imaging (inactive)
♦ **ISSI** International Society for Solid State Ionics (#15453)
♦ ISSI – International Space Science Institute (internationally oriented national body)
♦ **ISSI** Islands and Small States Institute, Malta (#16062)
♦ ISS – Institute for Security Studies (internationally oriented national body)
♦ ISS – Institute for Strategic Studies, Brno (internationally oriented national body)
♦ ISS – Institute for Strategic Studies, Ulaanbaatar (internationally oriented national body)
♦ ISS – International Institute of Social Studies, The Hague (internationally oriented national body)
♦ **ISS** International J A Schumpeter Society (#13974)
♦ **ISS** International Sansevieria Society (#14781)
♦ ISS / see International Sauna Association (#14782)
♦ ISS – International Schools Services (internationally oriented national body)
♦ ISS – International Seapower Symposium (meeting series)
♦ **ISS** International Skeletal Society (#14867)
♦ **ISS** International Social Service (#14886)
♦ ISS / see International Society for Stereology and Image Analysis (#15458)
♦ **ISS** International Society of Surgery (#15496)
♦ **ISS** International Space Station (#15574)
♦ **ISS** International Spenser Society (#15579)
♦ ISS – International Stroke Society (inactive)
♦ **ISS** International Superyacht Society (#15627)
♦ **ISS** International Symbiosis Society (#15640)
♦ ISS – International Symposium on Spermatology (meeting series)
♦ ISS – International Symposium on Superconductivity (meeting series)
♦ ISSIP – International Society of Service Innovation Professionals (internationally oriented national body)
♦ ISSIR / see International Society for Sexual Medicine (#15441)
♦ **ISSiS** International Society for Simulation Surgery (#15442)
♦ **ISSLR** International Society for Salt Lake Research (#15431)
♦ **ISSLS** International Society for the Study of the Lumbar Spinal (#15479)
♦ ISSM / see Istituto di Studi sul Mediterraneo
♦ **ISSME** International Society for Small and Medium Enterprises (#15446)
♦ **ISSME** International Society for the Sociology of Music Education (#15450)
♦ ISSMFE / see International Society for Soil Mechanics and Geotechnical Engineering (#15452)
♦ **ISSMGE** International Society for Soil Mechanics and Geotechnical Engineering (#15452)
♦ **ISSM** International Society for Sexual Medicine (#15441)
♦ **ISSM** International Society for Subsurface Microbiology (#15494)
♦ **ISSMO** International Society for Structural and Multidisciplinary Optimization (#15461)
♦ ISSMPD / see International Society for the Study of Trauma and Dissociation (#15488)
♦ **ISSNIC** ISSN International Centre (#16069)

♦ ISSN International Centre (ISSNIC) 16069

Centre international de l'ISSN (CIEPS)

Dir 45 rue de Turbigo, 75003 Paris, France. T. +33144882220. Fax +33140263243. E-mail: secretariat@issn.org.
URL: http://www.issn.org/

History 1975, Paris (France). Established as an intergovernmental organization within the framework of the *UNISIST – Intergovernmental Programme for Cooperation in the Field of Scientific and Technological Information (inactive)* of *UNESCO (#20322).* Former names and other names: *International Centre for the Registration of Serial Publications* – alias; *Centre international d'enregistrement des publications en série (CIEPS)* – alias. **Aims** Manage at international level the identification and description of serial publications and ongoing resources, print and online, in any subject. **Structure** General Assembly; Governing Board; National Centres. **Languages** Arabic, Chinese, English, French, Russian, Spanish. **Staff** 14.00 FTE, paid. **Finance** Sources: contributions of member/participating states; government support; sale of publications. Supported by: French Government; *UNESCO (#20322).* **Activities** Events/meetings; knowledge management/information dissemination. **Events** *Annual Directors Meeting* 2021, *Annual Directors Meeting* Paris (France) 2020, *Annual Directors Meeting* New Delhi (India) 2019, *Annual Directors Meeting* Washington, DC (USA) 2018, *Annual Directors Meeting* Rabat (Morocco) 2017. **Information Services** *ETAS; ISSN PORTAL; Keepers Registry; List of Title Word Abbreviations (LTWA)* – may also be used for the abbreviations of titles of non-serial publications, according to the rules of ISO4 standard; *ROAD.*

Members Governments of 93 countries:

Algeria, Argentina, Armenia, Australia, Austria, Bahrain, Belgium, Benin, Bolivia, Bosnia-Herzegovina, Brazil, Bulgaria, Burkina Faso, Canada, Chile, China, Colombia, Costa Rica, Croatia, Cyprus, Czechia, Denmark, Dominican Rep, Ecuador, Egypt, Estonia, Finland, France, Gambia, Georgia, Germany, Ghana, Greece, Hungary, Iceland, India, Indonesia, Iran Islamic Rep, Ireland, Italy, Jamaica, Japan, Korea Rep, Kyrgyzstan, Latvia, Lesotho, Lithuania, Luxembourg, Malaysia, Mali, Mauritius, Mexico, Moldova, Montenegro, Morocco, Namibia, Nepal, Netherlands, New Zealand, Niger, Nigeria, North Macedonia, Norway, Panama, Peru, Philippines, Poland, Portugal, Romania, Russia, Saudi Arabia, Senegal, Serbia, Seychelles, Singapore, Slovakia, Slovenia, Spain, Sri Lanka, Sudan, Sweden, Switzerland, Tanzania UR, Thailand, Tunisia, Türkiye, UK, Ukraine, Uruguay, USA, Uzbekistan, Venezuela, Vietnam.

Regional organization:
Publications Office of the European Union (Publications Office, #18562).

IGO Relations Recognizes jurisdiction of: *Administrative Tribunal of the International Labour Organization (ILO Tribunal, #00118).* **NGO Relations** Member of (4): *Association of Learned and Professional Society Publishers (ALPSP, #02786); International Council for Scientific and Technical Information (ICSTI, #13070); ISNI International Agency (ISNI-IA);* NISO. Partner of (2): DOAJ; *Sistema Regional de Información en Linea para Revistas Científicas de América Latina, el Caribe, España y Portugal (Latindex, #19297).* Consultative Status with: *International Federation of Library Associations and Institutions (IFLA, #13470).* Linked to technical committees of: *International Organization for Standardization (ISO, #14473).* [2022.10.13/XE4387/**E***]

♦ **ISSN** International Science Schools Network (#14797)
♦ ISSN – International Society for the Study of Narrative (internationally oriented national body)
♦ ISSOCO / see Fondazione Lelio e Lisli Basso – ISSOCO
♦ ISSODAC / see International School on Disarmament and Research on Conflicts
♦ ISSO – International Self-Service Organization (no recent information)
♦ ISSO – International Side-Saddle Organization (internationally oriented national body)
♦ ISSOL / see International Society for the Study of the Origin of Life – International Astrobiology Society (#15481)
♦ **ISSOL** International Society for the Study of the Origin of Life – International Astrobiology Society (#15481)
♦ **ISSOP** International Society for Social Pediatrics and Child Health (#15448)
♦ **ISSOTL** International Society for the Scholarship of Teaching and Learning (#15434)

- ♦ **ISSPA** International Source Suppliers and Producers Association (#15571)
- ♦ **ISSPD** International Society for the Study of Personality Disorders (#15482)
- ♦ ISSPh – Capri Institute for International Social Philosophy (internationally oriented national body)
- ♦ **ISSP** International Social Survey Programme (#14887)
- ♦ **ISSP** International Society of Sport Psychology (#15455)
- ♦ ISSP – International Society of Sustainability Professionals (internationally oriented national body)
- ♦ **ISSPP** International Society for the Study of Pleura and Peritoneum (#15483)
- ♦ ISSRI – Institute for Sustainable Rural Development Foundation (internationally oriented national body)
- ♦ **ISSR** International Society for Science and Religion (#15435)
- ♦ ISSR – International Society for Shamanistic Research (inactive)
- ♦ **ISSR** International Society for the Sociology of Religions (#15451)
- ♦ ISSRM – International Symposium on Society and Resource Management (meeting series)
- ♦ **ISSRNC** International Society for the Study of Religion, Nature and Culture (#15485)
- ♦ ISSSA – International Society for Strategic Studies / Africa / (no recent information)
- ♦ ISSSEEM – International Society for the Study of Subtle Energies and Energy Medicine (internationally oriented national body)
- ♦ ISSSHC – International Society for System Science in Health Care (no recent information)
- ♦ ISSSI – International Symposium on Staphylococci and Staphylococcal Infections (meeting series)
- ♦ **ISSS** International Association for Sports Surface Sciences (#12181)
- ♦ **ISSS** International Society for Seed Science (#15438)
- ♦ **ISSS** International Society for Skiing Safety (#15443)
- ♦ ISSS – International Society for Socialist Studies (inactive)
- ♦ IS-SS – International Society of Statistical Science (inactive)
- ♦ **ISSS** International Society of Sympathetic Surgery (#15497)
- ♦ **ISSS** International Society for the Systems Sciences (#15500)
- ♦ ISSS / see International Union of Soil Sciences (#15817)
- ♦ ISSSR / see International Society for Strategic Studies in Radiology (#15459)
- ♦ **ISSSS** International Society for the Social Sciences of Sport (#15449)
- ♦ **ISSTD** International Society for the Study of Trauma and Dissociation (#15488)
- ♦ **ISSTD** International Society for the Study of Trophoblastic Disease (#15489)
- ♦ **ISSTDR** International Society for Sexually Transmitted Diseases Research (#15440)
- ♦ **ISST** International Society for Sandplay Therapy (#15432)
- ♦ **ISST** International Society of Schema Therapy (#15433)
- ♦ ISST – International Society of Seed Technologists (no recent information)
- ♦ **ISST** International Society for the Study of Time (#15487)
- ♦ **ISSTIP** International Society for the Study of Tension in Performance (#15486)
- ♦ ISS UK / see Children and Families Across Borders
- ♦ ISSUP – International Society of Substance Use Prevention and Treatment Professionals (unconfirmed)
- ♦ **ISSVA** International Society for the Study of Vascular Anomalies (#15490)
- ♦ **ISSVD** International Society for the Study of Vulvovaginal Disease (#15491)
- ♦ ISSW – International Ship Stability Workshop (meeting series)
- ♦ **ISSW** International Snow Science Workshop (#14880)
- ♦ ISS / see World University Service (#21892)
- ♦ **ISSWOV** International Society for the Study of Work and Organizational Values (#15492)
- ♦ ISSWSH – International Society for the Study of Women's Sexual Health (internationally oriented national body)
- ♦ **ISSX** International Society for the Study of Xenobiotics (#15493)
- ♦ **ISTAA** International Sports Travel Agencies Association (#15595)
- ♦ ISTAART – International Society to Advance Alzheimer's Research and Treatment (internationally oriented national body)
- ♦ ISTAC – International Institute of Islamic Thought and Civilization (internationally oriented national body)
- ♦ **ISTAF** International Sepaktakraw Federation (#14835)

♦ IST-Africa 16070

Coordinator IST-Africa Institute/IIMC, 13 Docklands Innovation Park, 128 East Wall Road, Dublin, 3, CO. DUBLIN, Ireland. T. +35318170607. Fax +35318170606. E-mail: secretariat@ist-africa.org.
URL: http://www.ist-africa.org/

History 2005, with the support of *European Commission (EC, #06633)*. IST stands for *Information Society Technologies*. **Aims** Reduce the *digital* divide in Sub-Saharan *Africa*. **Events** *IST-Africa Conference* Dublin (Ireland) 2020, *IST-Africa Conference* Gaborone (Botswana) 2018, *IST-Africa Conference* Durban (South Africa) 2016, *IST-Africa Conference* Nairobi (Kenya) 2013, *IST-Africa Conference* Dar es Salaam (Tanzania UR) 2012.
[2018/XM2956/**E**]

- ♦ ISTAHC – International Society of Technology Assessment in Health Care (inactive)
- ♦ ISTA – Institut sous-régional multisectoriel de technologie appliquée, de planification et d'évaluation de projets (no recent information)
- ♦ ISTA – International Sail Training Association (inactive)
- ♦ **ISTA** International Schools Theatre Association (#14793)
- ♦ ISTA – International School of Temple Arts (unconfirmed)
- ♦ **ISTA** International School of Theatre Anthropology (#14794)
- ♦ ISTA – International School Traditional Aikido (internationally oriented national body)
- ♦ **ISTA** International Seed Testing Association (#14829)
- ♦ ISTA – International Sightseeing and Tours Association (inactive)
- ♦ **ISTA** International Society for Technology in Arthroplasty (#15502)
- ♦ ISTA – International Society for Technology Assessment (inactive)
- ♦ ISTA / see International Special Tooling and Machining Association (#15577)
- ♦ ISTA – International Strategic Technology Alliance (internationally oriented national body)
- ♦ Istanbul Commission / see Commission on the Protection of the Black Sea Against Pollution (#04237)
- ♦ Istanbul convention – Convention on Temporary Admission (1990 treaty)
- ♦ Istanbul International Brotherhood and Solidarity Association (internationally oriented national body)
- ♦ Istanbul Uluslararasi Kardeslik ve Yardimlasma Dernegi (internationally oriented national body)
- ♦ ISTAR – International Society for Testate Amoeba Research (unconfirmed)
- ♦ ISTAR Research Network – Individual Self-esteem and Transition to Adolescence with Respect Research Network (unconfirmed)
- ♦ ISTAT – International Society of Transport Aircraft Trading (internationally oriented national body)
- ♦ ISTC Commission on International Student Insurance Service / see International Association for Student Insurance Services (#12190)
- ♦ ISTC / see Giant Screen Cinema Association (#10148)
- ♦ **ISTC** International Science and Technology Center (#14798)
- ♦ **ISTC** International Social Theory Consortium (#14888)
- ♦ ISTC – International Student Travel Confederation (inactive)
- ♦ **ISTCP** International Society for Theoretical Chemical Physics (#15506)
- ♦ ISTCRAD – International Society for Tropical Crop Research and Development (no recent information)
- ♦ ISTCS / see International Stress Management Association (#15611)
- ♦ ISTC Student Identity Card Scheme / see ISIC Association (#16029)
- ♦ ISTD / see International Society of Dermatology (#15048)
- ♦ **ISTD** International Society of Teledermatology (#15503)
- ♦ ISTD – International Society of Typographic Designers (internationally oriented national body)
- ♦ ISTEB – International Society of Trace Element Biogeochemistry (no recent information)
- ♦ **ISTEC** Ibero-American Science and Technology Education Consortium (#11027)
- ♦ ISTED – Institut des sciences et des techniques de l'équipement et de l'environnement pour le développement (internationally oriented national body)
- ♦ ISTE – International Society for Technology in Education (internationally oriented national body)
- ♦ **ISTE** International Society of Transdisciplinary Engineering (#15514)
- ♦ **ISTE** International Society for Tropical Ecology (#15521)
- ♦ ISTEL92 / see ETIS – Global IT Association for Telecommunications (#05559)
- ♦ **ISTERH** International Society for Trace Element Research in Humans (#15513)
- ♦ **ISTF** International Society of Tropical Foresters (#15522)
- ♦ **ISTF** International Soft Tennis Federation (#15555)
- ♦ **ISTFP** International Society of Transference-Focused Psychotherapy (#15515)
- ♦ **ISTH** InterAmerican Society of Tropical Horticulture (#11451)
- ♦ **ISTH** International Society on Thrombosis and Haemostasis (#15511)
- ♦ **ISTIC** International Science, Technology and Innovation Centre for South-South Cooperation under the auspices of UNESCO (#14799)
- ♦ ISTIEE – Institute for the Study of Transport in European Integration (internationally oriented national body)
- ♦ **IST** International Society on Toxinology (#15512)
- ♦ Istitut Ewropew Tat-Teknologija / see European Institute of Innovation and Technology (#07562)
- ♦ Istituti di ricerca dell'agricoltura biologica (#18857)
- ♦ Istituto Affari Internazionali, Roma (internationally oriented national body)
- ♦ Istituto Africano di Diritto Internazionale Privato (#11234)
- ♦ Istituto Agricolo Coloniale Italiano / see Istituto Agronomico per l'Oltremare, Italy
- ♦ Istituto Agronomico Mediterraneo di Bari (#16641)
- ♦ Istituto Agronomico per l'Oltremare, Italy (internationally oriented national body)
- ♦ Istituto della Beata Vergine Maria (religious order)
- ♦ Istituto della Carità (religious order)
- ♦ Istituto Caritas Christi (religious order)
- ♦ Istituto Cavanis – Congregazione delle Scuole di Carità (religious order)
- ♦ Istituto per la Cooperazione Economica Internazionale (internationally oriented national body)
- ♦ Istituto per la Cooperazione Economica Internazionale e i Problemi dello Sviluppo (internationally oriented national body)
- ♦ Istituto per la Cooperazione Universitaria (#11331)
- ♦ Istituto per l'Europa Centro-Orientale e Balcanica (internationally oriented national body)
- ♦ Istituto Europea di Ricerca sull'Impresa Cooperative e Sociale (internationally oriented national body)
- ♦ Istituto Europeo di Design (internationally oriented national body)
- ♦ Istituto Europeo di Design e di Comunicazione / see Istituto Europeo di Design
- ♦ Istituto Europeo per l'Educazione e la Formazione Professionale per l'Ambiente / see European Institute for Environmental Education, Interpretation and Training
- ♦ Istituto Europeo per l'Educazione, l'Interpretazione e la Formazione Professionale per l'Ambiente (internationally oriented national body)
- ♦ Istituto Europeo per la Formazione Professionale (inactive)
- ♦ Istituto Europeo dell' Ombudsman (#08085)
- ♦ Istituto Europeo de Oncologia, Milano (internationally oriented national body)
- ♦ Istituto Europeo di Scienze Forensi e Biomediche (unconfirmed)
- ♦ Istituto Europeo di Tecnologia / see European Institute of Innovation and Technology (#07562)
- ♦ Istituto Internazionale per la Cinematografia Educativa (inactive)
- ♦ Istituto Internazionale per il Diritto dei Gruppi Etnici e il Regionalismo (#13300)
- ♦ Istituto Internazionale di Diritto per lo Sviluppo / see International Development Law Organization (#13161)
- ♦ Istituto Internazionale di Diritto Umanitario (#13885)
- ♦ Istituto Internazionale Jacques Maritain (#13967)
- ♦ Istituto Internazionale Maria Ausiliatrice delle Salesiane di Don Bosco (internationally oriented national body)
- ♦ Istituto Internazionale per le Scienza Archivistica / see International Institute for Archival Science of Trieste and Maribor (#13862)
- ♦ Istituto Internazionale per le Scienze Archivistiche di Trieste e Maribor (#13862)
- ♦ Istituto Internazionale di Statistica (#15603)
- ♦ Istituto Internazionale di Studi Asiatici Avanzati (internationally oriented national body)
- ♦ Istituto Internazionale di Studi Bancari (#12313)
- ♦ Istituto Internazionale di Studi del Ceto Medio (inactive)
- ♦ Istituto Internazionale di Studi sui Diritti dell' Uomo (internationally oriented national body)
- ♦ Istituto Internazionale di Studi Europei Antonio Rosmini (internationally oriented national body)
- ♦ Istituto Internazionale di Studi Genealogici e Storia di Famiglia (internationally oriented national body)
- ♦ Istituto Internazionale di Studi Liguri (#11311)
- ♦ Istituto Internazionale di Teologia Pastorale Sanitaria (#13906)
- ♦ Istituto Internazionale per l'Unificazione del Diritto Privato (#13934)
- ♦ Istituto Italiano per la Ricerca sulla Pace (internationally oriented national body)
- ♦ Istituto Italo-Latino Americano (#16071)
- ♦ Istituto Mahayana Internazionale (#14074)
- ♦ Istituto per il Mediterraneo (internationally oriented national body)
- ♦ Istituto Missioni Consolata (religious order)
- ♦ Istituto per le Missioni Estere di Yarumal (religious order)
- ♦ Istituto Mondiale di Ricerca e di Studi Avanscati di Fenomenologia / see World Phenomenology Institute (#21725)
- ♦ Istituto di Nostra Signora del Lavoro (religious order)
- ♦ Istituto di Nostra Signora della Misericordia (religious order)
- ♦ Istituto di Nostra Signora della Strada (religious order)
- ♦ Istituto Nostra Signora della Vita (religious order)
- ♦ Istituto per l'Oriente Carlo Alfonso Nallino (internationally oriented national body)
- ♦ Istituto Pace Sviluppo Innovazione ACLI (internationally oriented national body)
- ♦ Istituto dei Padri di Schönstatt (religious order)
- ♦ Istituto PANGEA / see European Institute for Environmental Education, Interpretation and Training
- ♦ Istituto PANGEA – Istituto Europeo per l'Educazione, l'Interpretazione e la Formazione Professionale per l'Ambiente (internationally oriented national body)
- ♦ Istituto Patristico Augustinianum (internationally oriented national body)
- ♦ Istituto delle Piccole Suore della Sacra Famiglia (religious order)
- ♦ Istituto del Prado (religious order)
- ♦ Istituto di Ricerche sull' Economia Mediterranea, Naples / see Istituto di Studi sul Mediterraneo
- ♦ Istituto Scientifico Biomedico Euro Mediterraneo (internationally oriented national body)
- ♦ Istituto Secolare Servita (religious order)
- ♦ Istituto Sindacale per la Cooperazione con i Paesi in Via di Sviluppo / see Istituto Sindicale per la Cooperazione allo Sviluppo
- ♦ Istituto Sindicale per la Cooperazione allo Sviluppo (internationally oriented national body)
- ♦ Istituto di Sociologia Internazionale di Gorizia (internationally oriented national body)
- ♦ Istituto Statistico delle Comunità Europee / see Statistical Office of the European Union (#19974)
- ♦ Istituto Statistico dell'Unione Europea (#19974)
- ♦ Istituto di Studi Europei 'Alcide de Gasperi' (internationally oriented national body)
- ♦ Istituto di Studi Federalisti Altiero Spinelli (internationally oriented national body)
- ♦ Istituto di Studi Giuridici sulla Comunità Internazionale del Consiglio Nazionale delle Ricerche, Roma / see Istituto di Studi Giuridici Internazionali
- ♦ Istituto di Studi Giuridici Internazionali (internationally oriented national body)
- ♦ Istituto di Studi Latinoamericani, Milano (internationally oriented national body)
- ♦ Istituto di Studi Latino-Americani e dei Paesi in Transizione / see Istituto di Studi Latinoamericani, Milano
- ♦ Istituto Studi Mediterranei (internationally oriented national body)
- ♦ Istituto per lo Studio della Società Contemporanea / see Fondazione Lelio e Lisli Basso – ISSOCO
- ♦ Istituto per lo Studio dei Trasporti nell'integrazione Economica Europea (internationally oriented national body)

♦ Istituto per gli Studi di Politica Internazionale (internationally oriented national body)
♦ Istituto di Studi Politici (internationally oriented national body)
♦ Istituto di Studi sulle Società del mediterraneo / see Istituto di Studi sul Mediterraneo
♦ Istituto di Studi sul Mediterraneo (internationally oriented national body)
♦ Istituto Superiore di Scienze Religiose – Magisterium Vitae / see Salesian Pontifical University (#19038)
♦ Istituto Svizzero per lo Sviluppo / see Swiss Academy for Development
♦ Istituto Tethys / see Tethys Research Institute
♦ Istituto Universitario Europeo (#09034)
♦ Istituto Universitario Orientale (internationally oriented national body)
♦ Istituto Universitario di Studi Europei (internationally oriented national body)
♦ Istituzione Teresiana (religious order)
♦ **ISTJ** International Society for Therapeutic Jurisprudence (#15508)
♦ ISTLI – International Society for Technology, Law and Insurance (no recent information)
♦ **ISTMA** International Special Tooling and Machining Association (#15577)
♦ **ISTM** International Society for Translational Medicine (#15517)
♦ **ISTM** International Society of Travel Medicine (#15519)
♦ ISTNA / see International Nonviolent Initiatives
♦ **ISTO** International Social Tourism Organisation (#14889)
♦ ISTO – International Specialized Terminology Organization (no recent information)
♦ **ISTP** International Society for Theoretical Psychology (#15507)
♦ **ISTP** International Society of Tropical Pediatrics (#15523)
♦ **ISTQB** International Software Testing Qualifications Board (#15559)
♦ ISTRA – International Interplanetary Space Travel Research Association (inactive)
♦ ISTRAN – International Society for Third-Sector Research Africa Regional Network (see: #15510)
♦ ISTR Asia/Pacific Third Sector Network (see: #15510)
♦ **ISTRC** International Society for Tropical Root Crops (#15524)
♦ ISTR European Third-Sector Network (see: #15510)
♦ **ISTR** International Society for Third-Sector Research (#15510)
♦ ISTR Latin America and the Caribbean Network (see: #15510)
♦ **ISTRO** International Soil Tillage Research Organization (#15562)
♦ **IStructE** Institution of Structural Engineers (#11322)
♦ ISTRY / see International Society for Tryptophan Research (#15525)
♦ **ISTRY** International Society for Tryptophan Research (#15525)
♦ ISTS – International Scientific Tendinopathy Symposium (meeting series)
♦ **ISTS** International Sea Turtle Society (#14818)
♦ **ISTS** International Society for Twin Studies (#15526)
♦ ISTS – International Symposium on Space Technology and Science (meeting series)
♦ **IS&T** Society for Imaging Science and Technology (#19572)
♦ **ISTSS** International Society for Traumatic Stress Studies (#15518)
♦ ISTSS – International Symposium on Tunnel Safety and Security (meeting series)
♦ ISTSU – International Science, Technology and Skill Union (internationally oriented national body)
♦ **ISTT** International Society for Transgenic Technologies (#15516)
♦ **ISTT** International Society for Trenchless Technology (#15520)
♦ **ISTU** International Society for Therapeutic Ultrasound (#15509)
♦ ISTU – International Student Theatre Union (inactive)
♦ ISTU – Islamic States Telecommunications Union (inactive)
♦ ISTUS – Internationale Studienkommission für Motorlosen Flug (inactive)
♦ **ISTVS** International Society for Terrain-Vehicle Systems (#15505)
♦ **ISUCRS** International Society of University Colon and Rectal Surgeons (#15530)
♦ **ISUD** International Society for Universal Dialogue (#15529)
♦ ISUD – International Symposium on Ultrasonic Doppler Methods for Fluid Mechanics and Fluid Engineering (meeting series)
♦ **ISUDO** International Society on Ultrasonic Diagnostics in Ophthalmology (#19443)
♦ ISUE – International Society of Urological Endoscopy (inactive)
♦ **ISUF** International Seminar on Urban Form (#14833)
♦ ISUFT / see International Society on Underground Freight Transportation (#15528)
♦ **ISUFT** International Society on Underground Freight Transportation (#15528)
♦ ISUGS – International Symposium on Ultrafine Grained Structures (meeting series)
♦ **ISU** Internationalen Stauden Union (#13277)
♦ **ISU** International Salvage Union (#14779)
♦ **ISU** International Skating Union (#14865)
♦ ISU / see International Society for Universal Dialogue (#15529)
♦ **ISU** International Space University (#15575)
♦ **ISU** International Stereoscopic Union (#15606)
♦ **ISUOG** International Society of Ultrasound in Obstetrics and Gynaecology (#15527)
♦ **ISUP** International Society of Urological Pathology (#15531)
♦ ISURA – International Symposium of Ultrasound for Regional Anesthesia (meeting series)
♦ ISUS – International Society of Ultrasonic Surgery (inactive)
♦ **ISUTx** International Society of Uterus Transplantation (#15532)
♦ **ISVA** International Sheep Veterinary Association (#14846)
♦ **ISVBM** International Society of Violin and Bow-Makers (#15542)
♦ **ISVCA** International Society of Vascularized Composite Allotransplantation (#15536)
♦ **ISVC** International Forum on Sustainable Value Chains (#13655)
♦ **ISVD** International Society of Veterinary Dermatopathology (#15539)
♦ **ISVEE** International Society for Veterinary Epidemiology and Economics (#15540)
♦ **ISVH** International Society of Vascular Health (#15535)
♦ ISVHLD – International Symposium on Viral Hepatitis and Liver Disease (meeting series)
♦ ISVI – International Society for Value Inquiry (internationally oriented national body)
♦ **ISV** Internationaler Süsstoff-Verband (#15639)
♦ **ISV** International Society for Vaccines (#15533)
♦ ISVIT – International Society for Vaccination and Immunotherapy (inactive)
♦ ISVLV – International Symposium on Viruses of Lower Vertebrates (meeting series)
♦ **ISVM** International Society of Vertebrate Morphology (#15538)
♦ **ISVO** International Society of Veterinary Ophthalmology (#15541)
♦ ISVP – International Society of Veterinary Perinatology (no recent information)
♦ ISVRB – International Society of Vitamins and Related BioFactors (no recent information)
♦ **ISVR** International Society for Virtual Rehabilitation (#15543)
♦ ISVS / see InterExchange
♦ ISVS – International Secretariat for Volunteer Service (inactive)
♦ ISVS – International Society for the Study of Vernacular Settlements (unconfirmed)
♦ ISVS – International Society for Vascular Specialists (inactive)
♦ **ISVS** International Society for Vascular Surgery (#15537)
♦ **ISWA** International Science Writers' Association (#14800)
♦ **ISWA** International Solid Waste Association (#15567)
♦ ISWAK – International Social Welfare Association of Korea (internationally oriented national body)
♦ **ISWAN** International Seafarers' Welfare and Assistance Network (#14815)
♦ ISWC International Agency (see: #04563)
♦ **ISWE** International Society for Web Engineering (#15547)
♦ **ISWE** International Society of Wildlife Endocrinology (#15549)
♦ ISWE – International Society for Wildlife and Environment Non Profit Society (inactive)
♦ ISWFPC – International Symposium on Wood, Fiber and Pulping Chemistry (meeting series)
♦ **ISWI** International Shock Wave Institute (#14851)
♦ **ISWIM** International Society for Weigh-In-Motion (#15548)
♦ **ISW** International Secretariat for Water (#14822)
♦ ISWP – International Society of Wheelchair Professionals (internationally oriented national body)
♦ ISWS – International Society for Water Solutions (internationally oriented national body)
♦ ISW-TBE – International Scientific Working Group on Tick-Borne Encephalitis (unconfirmed)
♦ ISWTHR / see Working Time Society (#21062)
♦ **ISYP** International Student/Young Pugwash (#15614)
♦ ISYTA – International Solar Yoga Teachers' Association (internationally oriented national body)
♦ **ISYVC** International Sivananda Yoga Vedanta Center (#14863)
♦ **ISZB** International Society for Zinc Biology (#15551)
♦ **ISZS** International Society of Zoological Sciences (#15552)
♦ ITA / see International Health and Temperance Association
♦ ITAA – International Textile and Apparel Association (internationally oriented national body)
♦ **ITAA** International Transactional Analysis Association (#15719)
♦ ITA / see Association of Special Fares Agents (#02928)
♦ **ITACAB** Instituto de Transferencia de Tecnologia Apropiada para Sectores Marginales del Convenio Andrés Bello (#11242)
♦ ITACA Europe / see European Association of Professionals Working in the Drug Field (#06169)
♦ **ITACA** European Association of Professionals Working in the Drug Field (#06169)
♦ ITAC – Institut du Travail d'Afrique Centrale (unconfirmed)
♦ Itäeuroopan Maiden Tutkimuksen Pohjoismainen Komitea (inactive)
♦ ITA – European Federation of International Trade Advisers (inactive)
♦ ITA – Information Technology Agreement (1996 treaty)
♦ ITA – Institute for Transnational Arbitration (internationally oriented national body)
♦ ITA – Institut du transport aérien (inactive)
♦ ITA, International Recording Media Association / see Content Delivery and Storage Association (#04779)
♦ **ITA** International Tar Association (#15655)
♦ **ITA** International Teacher Association (#15662)
♦ **ITA** International Telework Academy (#15675)
♦ **ITA** International Testing Agency (#15678)
♦ **ITA** International Thermoelectric Academy (#15685)
♦ ITA – International Tornado Association (see: #21760)
♦ **ITA** International Transpersonal Association (#15722)
♦ **ITA** International Trappist Association (#15727)
♦ **ITA** International Triticale Association (#15733)
♦ **ITA** International Trombone Association (#15735)
♦ **ITA** International Trotting Association (#15738)
♦ **ITA** International Tube Association (#15741)
♦ ITA / see International Tunnelling and Underground Space Association (#15744)
♦ **ITA** International Tunnelling and Underground Space Association (#15744)
♦ ITA / see Intestinal Rehabilitation and Transplant Association (#15990)
♦ Italian Association Amici di Raoul Follereau (internationally oriented national body)
♦ Italian Association for Women in Development ONLUS (internationally oriented national body)
♦ Italian Centre for Building Development in Emerging Nations (internationally oriented national body)
♦ Italian Centre of European Education (internationally oriented national body)
♦ Italian Centre of Solidarity (internationally oriented national body)
♦ Italian Consortium of Solidarity (internationally oriented national body)
♦ Italian Corporation for International Joint Ventures (internationally oriented national body)
♦ Italian Council for Refugees (internationally oriented national body)
♦ Italian Foundation for Voluntary Service (internationally oriented national body)
♦ Italian Institute for International Political Studies (internationally oriented national body)

♦ Italian-Latin American Institute (ILAI) 16071

Institut italo-latinoaméricain – Instituto Italo-Latinoamericano (IILA) – Istituto Italo-Latino Americano

SG Via Giovanni Paisiello 24, 00198 Rome RM, Italy. T. +396684921. Fax +3966872834. E-mail: info@iila.org.
Exec Dir address not obtained.
URL: http://www.iila.org/

History 1 Jun 1966, Rome (Italy), on signature of an international convention by representatives of 20 Latin American governments and Italy. **Aims** Increase economic, technical-scientific and cultural collaboration between Italy and Latin America; develop and coordinate research and documentation related to the problems, realizations and aims of member countries in cultural, economic, social and technical and scientific fields; publicize results of this research in member countries with a view to interchange and reciprocal assistance. **Finance** Contributions from Member State. Other sources: support from the government of Italy; co-financing agreements with the UE and other donors. **Activities** Networking/liaising; research/documentation; publishing activities. **Events** *SILAE congress / Congress* Havana (Cuba) 2009, *Ivano Morelli* Perugia (Italy) 2006, *Gonzalo Aguirre Beltran* Mexico City (Mexico) 2005, *FIEALC congress* Rome (Italy) 2005, *Italian-Latin American forum on development and the small and medium-sized enterprise* Verona (Italy) 2000. **Publications** Congress, conference, seminar and symposium reports and proceedings; catalogues, bibliographies; investement guides; fair calendar (annual); information booklets on Latin America.
Members Governments of 21 countries:
Argentina, Bolivia, Brazil, Chile, Colombia, Costa Rica, Cuba, Dominican Rep, Ecuador, El Salvador, Guatemala, Haiti, Honduras, Italy, Mexico, Nicaragua, Panama, Paraguay, Peru, Uruguay, Venezuela.
IGO Relations Observer status with (1): *United Nations (UN, #20515)* (General Assembly). Formal agreement with: *UNESCO (#20322)*. Relationship agreement with: *FAO (#09260)*. Participates in the activities of: *UNCTAD (#20285)*. Permanent Observer to: *ECOSOC (#05331)*. Observer to: *International Organization for Migration (IOM, #14454)*. [2020/XE2837/j/**E***]

♦ Italian Lay Centre for Missions (internationally oriented national body)
♦ Italian Peace Research Institute (internationally oriented national body)
♦ Italian Society for International Organization (internationally oriented national body)
♦ Italian Volunteers for Solidarity with Developing Countries (internationally oriented national body)
♦ Italo-Latin American Asian and African Ethnomedicine Society (#19439)
♦ Italo-Latin American Ethnomedicine Society / see Società Italo-Latino Americana di Etnomedicina (#19439)
♦ Itämeren alueen museoiden ja linnojen yhdistyksessä (#02815)
♦ ITBLAV – Internationale Textil-, Bekleidungs- und Lederarbeiter-Vereinigung (inactive)
♦ ITCA / see Interactive Multimedia and Collaborative Communications Alliance
♦ **ITCABIC** Inter-Territorial Catholic Bishops' Conference (#15984)
♦ ITCA – Instituto Tecnológico Centroamericano, Santa Tecla (internationally oriented national body)
♦ **ITCB** International Textiles and Clothing Bureau (#15680)
♦ **ITCCA** International Tai Chi Chuan Association (#15653)
♦ **ITCC** Innovative Therapies for Children with Cancer Consortium (#11222)
♦ ITC / see Committee on Inland Transport (#04262)
♦ ITC-CSCC – International Technical Conference on Circuits/Systems, Computers and Communications (meeting series)
♦ ITCF – International Tai Chi Federation (unconfirmed)
♦ ITCILO Staff Union – Staff Union of the International Training Centre of the ILO (internationally oriented national body)
♦ ITC / see International Tar Association (#15655)
♦ **ITC** International Tea Committee (#15664)
♦ **ITC** International Teletraffic Congress (#15674)
♦ **ITC** International Test Commission (#15677)
♦ ITC – International Tiger Coalition (unconfirmed)

- ♦ ITC – International Tin Council (inactive)
- ♦ **ITC** International Trade Centre (#15703)
- ♦ **ITC** International Training Centre of the ILO (#15717)
- ♦ **ITC** International Tribology Council (#15730)
- ♦ **ITC** International Trypanotolerance Centre (#15739)
- ♦ **ITCIP** International Training Center of Indigenous Peoples (#15715)
- ♦ ITCO / see International Tank Container Organization (#15654)
- ♦ **ITCO** International Tank Container Organization (#15654)
- ♦ ITCS – International Transplant Coordinators Society (inactive)
- ♦ ITDA / see Content Delivery and Storage Association (#04779)
- ♦ ITDG / see Practical Action (#18475)
- ♦ ITD – International Institute for Trade and Development (internationally oriented national body)
- ♦ ITDP – Institute for Transportation and Development Policy (internationally oriented national body)
- ♦ ITEA / see International Technology and Engineering Educators Association
- ♦ **ITEA** International Transportation Economics Association (#15723)
- ♦ ITEBE / see Bioenergy Institute
- ♦ ITEBEA / see Association of Member Episcopal Conferences in Eastern Africa (#02805)
- ♦ ITEBE – Bioenergy Institute (internationally oriented national body)
- ♦ ITECA – International Temperance Educational and Cultural Association (inactive)
- ♦ I-TECH – International Training and Education Center on HIV (internationally oriented national body)
- ♦ **ITechLaw** International Technology Law Association (#15669)
- ♦ ITEC / see Inter-Territorial Catholic Bishops' Conference (#15984)
- ♦ ITECO / see ITECO – Centre de formation pour le développement
- ♦ ITECO – Centre de formation pour le développement (internationally oriented national body)
- ♦ ITEEA – International Technology and Engineering Educators Association (internationally oriented national body)
- ♦ ITE Europäische Verkehrsinitiative (#11215)
- ♦ ITE European Transport Initiative (#11215)
- ♦ **ITE** Initiative Transport Europe (#11215)
- ♦ ITE Iniziativa Europea delle Trasporti (#11215)
- ♦ ITE – Internationale évangélique ouvrière (inactive)
- ♦ ITE – Internationale des travailleurs de l'enseignement (inactive)
- ♦ ITE – International Institute of Transportation Engineers (internationally oriented national body)
- ♦ ITE – International Theatre Exchange (internationally oriented national body)
- ♦ ITEM – Instituto del Tercer Mundo, Montevideo (internationally oriented national body)
- ♦ **ITEN** International Tobacco Evidence Network (#15693)
- ♦ **ITEPAL** Instituto Teológico Pastoral para América Latina (#11350)

♦ ITER International Fusion Energy Organization (ITER Organization) . 16072

Dir Gen CS 90 046, Route de Vinon-sur-Verdon, 13067 Saint-Paul-lez-Durance CEDEX, France. T. +33442176888 – +33442176612. E-mail: itercommunications@iter.org.
URL: http://www.iter.org/

History *Agreement on the Establishment of the ITER International Fusion Energy Organization for the Joint Implementation of the ITER Project (ITER Agreement)*, signed 21 Nov 2006, Paris (France) and which entered into force 24 Oct 2007, when organization was officially established. Idea launched Nov 1985, Geneva (Switzerland), as a proposal between USSR and USA. Agreement reached between *European Union (EU, #08967)* – *European Atomic Energy Community (Euratom, inactive)*, Japan, USSR and USA to jointly pursue conceptual design activities for an international fusion facility. Conceptual design started 1988 with final design approved 2001. China and Korea Rep joined 2003; India joined 2005. Procedure for the decision on the location of ITER Project in Cadarache (France) concluded Jun 2005. ITER is the acronym of *International Thermonuclear Experimental Reactor.* **Aims** Provide for and promote cooperation among Members on the ITER Project, which aims to demonstrate the scientific and technological feasibility of fusion energy for peaceful purposes, an essential feature of which would be achieving sustained fusion power generation. **Structure** ITER Council (meets at least twice a year), consisting of 4 representatives per ITER Member. Advisory Bodies (4): Science and Technology Advisory Committee (STAC); Management Advisory Committee (MAC); Financial Audit Board (FAB); Management Assessment. **Languages** English. **Staff** 1000.00 FTE, paid. **Finance** Sources: contributions of member/participating states. **Activities** Research and development. **Events** *International Tokamak Physics Activity Topical Group on Diagnostis Meeting* Chiba (Japan) 2022, *Business Forum* Marseille (France) 2022, *Remote Business Meeting* Saint-Paul-lez-Durance (France) 2021, *Business Forum* Antibes (France) / Juan-les-Pins (France) 2019, *International Conference on Tritium Science and Technology* Busan (Korea Rep) 2019. **Publications** *Newsline* (weekly); *ITER Mag* (2 a year).
Members Governments of 6 countries:
China, India, Japan, Korea Rep, Russia, USA.
Regional member:
European Union (EU, #08967) (via Fusion for Energy).
Consultative Status Consultative status granted from: *World Intellectual Property Organization (WIPO, #21593)* (Observer Status). **IGO Relations** Entitled to be represented at Sessions of General Conference of *International Atomic Energy Agency (IAEA, #12294).* [2021.02.25/XM1807/**D***]

- ♦ **ITER Organization** ITER International Fusion Energy Organization (#16072)
- ♦ ITESA / see Africa Development Solutions
- ♦ ITESO – Instituto Tecnológico y de Estudios Superiores de Occidente (internationally oriented national body)
- ♦ **ITEX** International Tundra Experiment (#15742)
- ♦ ITF / see International Essential Tremor Foundation
- ♦ ITF / see ITF Enhancing Human Security
- ♦ **IT and FA** International Trade and Finance Association (#15704)
- ♦ **ITFA** International Trade and Forfaiting Association (#15705)
- ♦ ITFCAD / see International Committee on Allergic Diseases of Animals (#12744)
- ♦ **ITFCA** International Track and Field Coaches Association (#15702)
- ♦ ITF Enhancing Human Security (internationally oriented national body)
- ♦ ITFF / see Collaborative Partnership on Forests (#04100)
- ♦ ITF / see International Holocaust Remembrance Alliance (#13803)
- ♦ **ITF** International Taekwon-Do Federation (#15652)
- ♦ ITF – International Taekwon-do Forum (unconfirmed)
- ♦ **ITF** International Taskforce on Women and Information and Communication Technologies (#15658)
- ♦ ITF / see International Telework Academy (#15675)
- ♦ **ITF** International Tennis Federation (#15676)
- ♦ **ITF** International Trans Fund (#15720)
- ♦ **ITF** International Transport Forum (#15725)
- ♦ **ITF** International Transport Workers' Federation (#15726)
- ♦ ITF – International Tree Foundation (internationally oriented national body)
- ♦ ITF – ITF Enhancing Human Security (internationally oriented national body)
- ♦ **ITFK** International Traditional Federation of Karate (#15711)
- ♦ ITFMLA / see Intergovernmental Action Group against Money Laundering in West Africa (#11471)
- ♦ **ITGA** International Tobacco Growers' Association (#15694)
- ♦ ITG – Internationale Tabakwissenschaftlichen Gesellschaft (inactive)
- ♦ ITGLWF – International Textile, Garment and Leather Workers' Federation (inactive)
- ♦ ITG – Prins Leopold Instituut voor Tropische Geneeskunde (internationally oriented national body)
- ♦ ITHACA – Information Technology for Humanitarian Assistance, Cooperation and Action (internationally oriented national body)
- ♦ ITHA – International Tourist Health Association (no recent information)
- ♦ ITHEO – International Thorium Energy Organisation (unconfirmed)
- ♦ **ITH** Internationale Tagung der Historikerinnen der Arbeiter- und Anderer Sozialer Bewegungen (#12881)
- ♦ ITHL – International Temperance and Health League (no recent information)
- ♦ ITHS – International Tinnitus and Hyperacusis Society (inactive)
- ♦ ITI / see International Theological Institute
- ♦ **ITIA** International Travel Insurance Alliance e.V. (#15728)
- ♦ **ITIA** International Tungsten Industry Association (#15743)
- ♦ **ITIC** International Tsunami Information Center (#15740)
- ♦ ITI Convention – Customs Convention on the International Transit of Goods (1971 treaty)
- ♦ ITI / see International Team for Implantology (#15666)
- ♦ **ITI** International Team for Implantology (#15666)
- ♦ ITI – International Technical Institute of Flight Engineers (inactive)
- ♦ **ITI** International Theatre Institute (#15683)
- ♦ ITI – International Theological Institute (internationally oriented national body)
- ♦ **ITI** International Trachoma Initiative (#15701)
- ♦ ITI – International Trauma-Healing Institute (internationally oriented national body)
- ♦ IT International / see Practical Action (#18475)
- ♦ ITIO – International Trade and Investment Organisation (no recent information)
- ♦ ITK / see International Tar Association (#15655)
- ♦ **ITLA** International Toy Library Association (#15699)
- ♦ **ITLOS** International Tribunal for the Law of the Sea (#15731)
- ♦ ITM / see Institute of Tropical Medicine Antwerp
- ♦ ITMA – International 12 Metre Class Association (see: #21760)
- ♦ **ITMA** International Traffic Medicine Association (#15713)
- ♦ ITMC – International Conference on Intelligent Textiles and Mass Customization (meeting series)
- ♦ **ITMF** International Textile Manufacturers Federation (#15679)
- ♦ **ITMIG** International Thymic Malignancy Interest Group (#15689)
- ♦ **ITMI** International Triticeae Mapping Initiative (#15734)
- ♦ ITM – Informatics for the Third World (inactive)
- ♦ ITNS – International Transplant Nurses Society (internationally oriented national body)
- ♦ ITO – Jewish Territorial Organization (inactive)

♦ ITOPF Ltd 16073

Managing Dir 1 Oliver's Yard, 55 City Road, London, EC1Y 1HQ, UK. T. +442075666999. Fax +442075666950. E-mail: central@itopf.org.
Assistant address not obtained.
URL: https://www.itopf.org/

History 24 Dec 1968, London (UK). Set up in accordance with *Tanker owners voluntary agreement concerning liability for oil pollution (TOVALOP, inactive)*, which was developed and signed by 7 leading oil companies, adopted 7 Jan 1969, London and entered in force, 6 Oct 1969. Agreement incorporating amendments passed by resolution of Members: 14 Jul 1972, to take effect from 20 Feb 1973; 11 Feb 1977 to take effect from 20 Feb 1977; 16 May 1978 to take effect 1 Jun 1978; 28 May 1980 to take immediate effect; 26 May 1981 to take effect Jun 1981; 30 Oct 1984 to take effect 1 Nov 1984; 21 May 1986 to take effect 1 Jun 1986; 9 Dec 1986 to take effect 20 Feb 1987; 25 Oct 1989 to take effect 20 Feb 1990; 30 Oct 1991 to take effect 20 Feb 1992; 13 Oct 1993 to take effect 20 Feb 1994; 15 Nov 1995 to take effect 20 Feb 1996. TOVALOP ceased definitively on 20 Feb 1997, when the voluntary agreement among shipowners was superseded by the wide adoption of the *International Convention on Civil Liability for Oil Pollution Damage (CLC, 1969).* Former names and other names: *International Tanker Owners Pollution Federation (ITOPF)* – former (2018); *Fédération internationale des armateurs pétroliers contre la pollution* – former (2018). Registration: Companies House, No/ID: 00944863, Start date: 24 Dec 1968, England and Wales. **Aims** Promote effective response to ship-source pollution incidents and thereby prevent or minimize damage to *coastal resources* and the *marine environment.* **Structure** Board of Directors (meets annually); Advisory Committee; Secretariat in London (UK). **Languages** English, French, Portuguese, Spanish. **Staff** 40.00 FTE, paid. **Finance** Sources: members' dues. Other sources: Associates' dues, according to tonnage; advisory assignments. **Activities** Events/meetings; guidance/assistance/consulting; knowledge management/information dissemination; training/education. Offers technical services to Members, Associates, their P and I insurers and other groups concerned with oil and cargo spills. **Events** *Offshore Arabia Biennial Conference* Dubai (United Arab Emirates) 2020, *Offshore Arabia Biennial Conference* Dubai (United Arab Emirates) 2018, *International seminar on spill preparedness, response and compensation* Singapore (Singapore) 2003. **Publications** *Ocean Orbit* (annual) – newsletter; *Oil Tanker Spill Statistics* – information pack. *Technical Information Papers. Response to Marine Oil Spills* (2012). Annual Review; briefing papers; leaflets; reports. **Information Services** *Oil Tanker Spill Database.* **Members** Full; Associate. Tanker owners in over 100 countries and territories. Membership countries not specified. **Consultative Status** Consultative status granted from: *International Maritime Organization (IMO, #14102); ECOSOC (#05331)* (Ros C). **IGO Relations** Observer status with (2): *International Maritime Organization (IMO, #14102); Regional Marine Pollution Emergency Information and Training Centre – Wider Caribbean (REMPEITC-Carib, #18794).* **NGO Relations** Member of (1): *Comité maritime international (CMI, #04192)* (as consultative member of). Partner of (1): *Mediterranean Oil Industry Group (MOIG, #16669)* (as technical partner of). [2022.12.06/XD5309/**B**]

- ♦ ITOPF / see ITOPF Ltd (#16073)
- ♦ **ITOP Forum** Inter-Island Tourism Policy Forum (#11515)
- ♦ ITOTA – International Tactical Officers Training Association (internationally oriented national body)
- ♦ ITO / see World Trade Organization (#21864)
- ♦ **ITPA** International Tax Planning Association (#15660)
- ♦ ITPA – International Tea Promotion Association (inactive)
- ♦ ITPA – International Trotting and Pacing Association (internationally oriented national body)
- ♦ **ITPC** International Treatment Preparedness Coalition (#15729)
- ♦ ITP – International Symposium on Electroseparation and Liquid Phase-Separation Techniques (meeting series)
- ♦ ITPRTO – International Traffic Police and Road Transport Organization (no recent information)
- ♦ ITP / see Sustainable Hospitality Alliance (#20061)
- ♦ ITRA – International Technology Rental Association (internationally oriented national body)
- ♦ **ITRA** International Toy Research Association (#15700)
- ♦ **ITRA** International Trail Running Association (#15714)
- ♦ ITRC / see European Travel Retail Confederation (#08945)
- ♦ ITRC MIR – Intergovernmental TV and Radio Corporation (no recent information)
- ♦ ITRI / see International Tin Association (#15692)
- ♦ ITRI – Inner Trip Reiyukai International (internationally oriented national body)
- ♦ **ITR** Intestinal Transplant Registry (#15991)
- ♦ ITRO – International Tripartite Rubber Organization, Thailand (inactive)
- ♦ ITRRF – International Tyre, Rubber and Recycling Federation (inactive)
- ♦ ITRW – Agreement Concerning International Direct Goods Traffic by Rail and Water (1959 treaty)
- ♦ ITSA / see Institute of Tropics and Subtropics, Prague
- ♦ **ITSA** International Textile Services Alliance (#15681)
- ♦ **ITSA** International Tourism Studies Association (#15696)
- ♦ **ITSA** International Training and Simulation Alliance (#15718)
- ♦ **ITSA** International Transportation Safety Association (#15724)
- ♦ ITSAN – International Topical Steroid Awareness Network (internationally oriented national body)
- ♦ **ITS AP** ITS Asia-Pacific (#16074)
- ♦ ITS / see Arolsen Archives – International Center on Nazi Persecution (#01112)

♦ ITS Asia-Pacific (ITS AP) 16074

SG address not obtained.
URL: http://itsasia-pacific.com/

History ITS stands for *Intelligent Transport Systems*. **Aims** Support economic growth and better quality of life by solving transport problems of a modal or multi-modal nature through the developing and deploying of ITS; establish a cooperation framework by building a foundation on which ITS Asia-Pacific members can share and find solutions for common problems. **Activities** Advocacy/lobbying/activism; events/meetings; networking/liaising. **Events** *World Congress on Intelligent Transport Systems and Services* Dubai (United Arab Emirates) 2024, *World Congress on Intelligent Transport Systems and Services* Suzhou (China) 2023, *Forum* Chengdu (China) 2022, *World Congress on Intelligent Transport Systems and Services* Los Angeles, CA (USA) 2022, *World Congress on Intelligent Transport Systems and Services* Hamburg (Germany) 2021.
Members Signatories to Memorandum of Understanding in 11 countries and territories:
Australia, China, Hong Kong, Indonesia, Japan, Korea Rep, Malaysia, New Zealand, Singapore, Taiwan, Thailand.
[2021/XM6817/**D**]

- ♦ ITSCC – International immunosuppression & Transplant Skin Cancer Collaborative (internationally oriented national body)
- ♦ IT Service Management Forum / see IT Service Management Forum International (#16075)

♦ IT Service Management Forum International (itSMF International) . 16075

Chairperson Ground Floor South, Burford House, Leppington, Bracknell, RG12 7WW, UK. T. +441189186500.
URL: http://www.itsmfi.org/

History 1991, UK. Founded when UK chapter started as foundation chapter. Former names and other names: *IT Service Management Forum* – former (1991); *Service Management Association Ltd* – legal name. Registration: Companies House, No/ID: 02661244, England and Wales. **Aims** Create and sustain the global itSMF member community; promote service management practices; raise awareness of service management and how service management professionals benefit global communities. **Structure** Executive Board. Largely autonomous chapters with separate legal entities. **Activities** Events/meetings. **Events** *Conference* Bracknell (UK) 2020, *Conference* Oslo (Norway) 2019, *Seminar on Knowledge Sharing on Automation with Tech-Data / Red Hat* Singapore (Singapore) 2019, *Seminar on the T-Shaped Talent and ITSM DevOps-Accelerating Digital Transformations* Singapore (Singapore) 2019, *Forum on Agile, Service Delivery Management and Devops* Singapore (Singapore) 2018.
Members Companies (over 6000). Chapters (57) in 57 countries and territories:
Argentina, Australia, Austria, Belgium, Bosnia-Herzegovina, Brazil, Canada, Chile, Costa Rica, Croatia, Cyprus, Czechia, Denmark, Estonia, Finland, France, Germany, Greece, Hong Kong, Hungary, India, Ireland, Israel, Italy, Japan, Kenya, Korea Rep, Latvia, Luxembourg, Malaysia, Mexico, Morocco, Netherlands, New Zealand, North Macedonia, Norway, Philippines, Poland, Portugal, Russia, Serbia, Singapore, Slovakia, Slovenia, South Africa, Spain, Sudan, Sweden, Switzerland, Taiwan, Thailand, Türkiye, UK, Ukraine, United Arab Emirates, USA, Venezuela. [2021/XJ9610/**F**]

- ♦ **ITSF** International Table Soccer Federation (#15649)
- ♦ ITSG – International Tin Study Group (no recent information)
- ♦ ITS / see Global Union Federations (#10638)
- ♦ ITS – Institute of Tropics and Subtropics, Prague (internationally oriented national body)
- ♦ ITS / see International Institute for the Science of Sintering (#13922)
- ♦ **ITS** International Telecommunications Society (#15671)
- ♦ **ITS** International Thatching Society (#15682)
- ♦ **ITS** International Thermoelectric Society (#15686)
- ♦ ITS – International Thespian Society (internationally oriented national body)
- ♦ **ITS** International Turfgrass Society (#15745)
- ♦ **itSMF International** IT Service Management Forum International (#16075)
- ♦ **ITS Nationals** Network of National ITS Associations (#17049)
- ♦ **ITSO** International Telecommunications Satellite Organization (#15670)
- ♦ It's a Penalty (internationally oriented national body)
- ♦ ITST – International Conference on Intelligent Transport Systems Telecommunications (meeting series)
- ♦ ITSU / see Intergovernmental Coordination Group for the Pacific Tsunami Warning and Mitigation System (#11481)
- ♦ ITSZ / see Institute of Tropics and Subtropics, Prague
- ♦ **ITTAF** International Traditional Taekwon-Do Federation (#15712)
- ♦ ITTA – International Tropical Timber Agreement, 1983 (1983 treaty)
- ♦ ITTCC – International Teachers Trade Union Cooperation Committee (inactive)
- ♦ **ITTC** International Towing Tank Conference (#15698)
- ♦ **ITTFA** International Tourism Trade Fairs Association (#15697)
- ♦ **ITTF Foundation** International Table Tennis Federation Foundation (#15651)
- ♦ **ITTF** International Table Tennis Federation (#15650)
- ♦ ITTF-Oceania / see Oceania Table Tennis Federation (#17678)
- ♦ Ittihad Al Massaref Al Arabiya (#20349)
- ♦ Ittijah – Union of Arab Community-Based Associations (internationally oriented national body)
- ♦ ITT / see International Think Tank for Landlocked Developing Countries (#15687)
- ♦ **ITTLLDC** International Think Tank for Landlocked Developing Countries (#15687)
- ♦ ITTM – International Trust for Traditional Medicine (internationally oriented national body)
- ♦ **ITTO** International Tropical Timber Organization (#15737)
- ♦ **ITTS** International Transmembrane Transporter Society (#15721)
- ♦ **ITTTA** International Technical Tropical Timber Association (#15668)
- ♦ **ITUC-AP** ITUC – Asia Pacific (#16076)

♦ ITUC – Asia Pacific (ITUC-AP) 16076

Secretariat 9th Floor, NTUC Centre, One Marina Boulevard, Singapore 018989, Singapore. T. +6563273590. Fax +6563273576. E-mail: gs@ituc-ap.org.
URL: http://www.ituc-ap.org/

History May 1951. Founded as regional organization of *International Confederation of Free Trade Unions (ICFTU, inactive)*. Rules and Standing Orders amended by 16th Regional Conference, 18-20 Dec 1996, Cebu City (Philippines). Current title adopted, following merger of IFCTU and *World Confederation of Labour (WCL, inactive)*, Nov 2006, into *International Trade Union Confederation (ITUC, #15708)*. ICFTU-APRO and the *Brotherhood of Asian Trade Unionists (BATU, inactive)* – WCL established ITUC-Asia Pacific on 4 Sep 2007. Former names and other names: *International Trade Union Confederation – Asia Pacific* – full title; *ICFTU Asian and Pacific Regional Organization (APRO)* – former (1984 to 2006); *International Trade Union Confederation – Asian and Pacific Regional Organization* – former; *Asian Regional Organization (ARO)* – former. **Aims** Defend and promote fundamental workers' rights for social justice, democracy and peace; promote cooperation between all *trade unions* so that the workers they represent will have greater bargaining power nationally and regionally. **Structure** Regional Conference (every 4 years); Regional Executive Bureau (meets as need arises). Regional General Council (meets at least once a year). Special Committees on finance, women and youth. Secretariat, headed by General Secretary. Divisions and Departments (6): Workers' Rights; Organizing; Women; Youth; Information; Finance. **Languages** English. **Staff** 12.00 FTE, paid. **Activities** Advocacy/lobbying/activism; events/meetings. **Events** *Annual Coordination Meeting with GUFs and TUSSOs* Singapore (Singapore) 2021, *Annual Coordination Meeting with GUFs and TUSSOs* Singapore (Singapore) 2020, *Future of Work Workshop* Singapore (Singapore) 2020, *Meeting* Singapore (Singapore) 2020, *Regional Executive Bureau Meeting* Singapore (Singapore) 2020.
Members National trade union centres (52) from Asia and the Pacific Region, affiliated to ITUC, in 29 countries and territories:
Australia, Bahrain, Bangladesh, Cook Is, Fiji, Hong Kong, India, Indonesia, Israel, Japan, Jordan, Kiribati, Korea Rep, Kuwait, Malaysia, Mongolia, Nepal, New Zealand, Pakistan, Philippines, Samoa, Singapore, Sri Lanka, Taiwan, Thailand, Tonga, Türkiye, Vanuatu, Yemen. [2021/XK0006/t/**E**]

- ♦ ITUC Asia-Pacific Labour Network
- ♦ **ITUC** International Trade Union Confederation (#15708)
- ♦ ITUH – International Trade Union House, Brussels (internationally oriented national body)
- ♦ **ITU** International Telecommunication Union (#15673)

♦ ITU Staff Union 16077

Headquarters c/o ITU Headquarters, Place des Nations, 1211 Geneva 20, Switzerland. T. +41227305795. E-mail: president@syndicat-uit.org – contact@syndicat-uit.org.
URL: http://www.syndicat-uit.org/

History Founded to represent staff members of *International Telecommunication Union (ITU, #15673)*. **Structure** Executive Committee. **Members** Staff members of the International Telecommunication Union. **NGO Relations** Member of (1): *Coordinating Committee for International Staff Unions and Associations of the United Nations System (CCISUA, #04818)*. [2022.10.19/XE1917/v/**E**]

- ♦ ITU / see World Triathlon (#21872)
- ♦ **ITVA** International Thorstein Veblen Association (#15688)
- ♦ **ITVA** International TVA Network (#15746)
- ♦ **ITV** Internationale Teervereinigung (#15655)
- ♦ ITVS – International Television Symposium (meeting series)
- ♦ ITVTP – Internationale Tierärztliche Vereinigung für Tierproduktion (inactive)
- ♦ ITWG-AnGR – Intergovernmental Technical Working Group on Animal Genetic Resources for Food and Agriculture (see: #09260)
- ♦ ITW – Imaging the World (internationally oriented national body)
- ♦ IUAA / see Union internationale des associations d'alpinisme (#20420)
- ♦ IUAA – Union internationale des astronomes amateurs (no recent information)
- ♦ IUAA / see World Federation of Advertisers (#21407)
- ♦ IUADM – International Union of Associations of Doctor-Motorists (no recent information)
- ♦ **IUAES** International Union of Anthropological and Ethnological Sciences (#15755)
- ♦ IUAF – International Union of Agroforestry (unconfirmed)
- ♦ IUAI / see International Union of Aerospace Insurers (#15750)
- ♦ **IUAI** International Union of Aerospace Insurers (#15750)
- ♦ **IUA** International Underwriting Association (#15748)
- ♦ **IUA** International Union of Angiology (#15754)
- ♦ IUA – International Union of Arts (inactive)
- ♦ IUA – International University of Africa (internationally oriented national body)
- ♦ **IUAPPA** International Union of Air Pollution Prevention and Environmental Protection Associations (#15753)
- ♦ IUAS – International Union of Agricultural Sciences (inactive)
- ♦ IUAT / see International Union Against Tuberculosis and Lung Disease (#15752)
- ♦ IUATLD / see International Union Against Tuberculosis and Lung Disease (#15752)
- ♦ IUAV / see UNESCO Institute for Lifelong Learning (#20305)
- ♦ IUBAT – International University of Business Agriculture and Technology (internationally oriented national body)
- ♦ IUB / see International Union of Biochemistry and Molecular Biology (#15759)
- ♦ **IUBMB** International Union of Biochemistry and Molecular Biology (#15759)

♦ IUBMB-IUPAC Joint Commission on Biochemical Nomenclature (JCBN) 16078

Sec SRI International, 333 Ravenswood Ave, Menlo Park CA 94025-3493, USA.
ExplorEnz – the Enzyme Database: http://www.enzyme-database.org/index.php

History 1977. Founded as a joint commission of *International Union of Biochemistry and Molecular Biology (IUBMB, #15759)* and *International Union of Pure and Applied Chemistry (IUPAC, #15809)*. **Aims** Seek to facilitate communication of biochemical information by encouraging scientists to use accurate, consistent, and generally understood *terminology*. **Languages** English. **Staff** None. **Finance** By IUBMB and IUPAC. **Publications** *Joint Commission on Biochemical Nomenclature (JCBN) Newsletters. Enzyme Nomenclature.* Recommendations. **Information Services** *ExplorEnz* – enzyme classification database.
Members Individuals in 7 countries:
Denmark, Germany, Ireland, Netherlands, Portugal, UK, USA. [2023.02.13/XE7233/v/**E**]

- ♦ **IUBS-CBE** IUBS Commission for Biological Education (#16079)
- ♦ IUBS Commission for Bioindicators / see International Commission on Bioindicators (#12667)

♦ IUBS Commission for Biological Education (IUBS-CBE) 16079

Commission UISB de l'enseignement en biologie

Exec Dir Bât 442, Univ Paris Sud 11, 91405 Orsay CEDEX, France. T. +33169155027. Fax +33169157947.
URL: http://iubscbe.org/

History 1977, within the framework of *International Union of Biological Sciences (IUBS, #15760)*. Also referred to as *International Commission for Biological Education (CBE) – Commission internationale de l'enseignement en biologie*. **Aims** Promote biology education worldwide; improve awareness of the social and individual relevance of biology. **Structure** Chair, Vice-Chair and Secretary General elected by Commission. **Finance** Financed by IUBS with additional support from *UNESCO (#20322)* and selected national sources for projects. **Activities** Special projects: Biology and community development; Biotechnology in education; Use of computers in biology education; Bioethics as an object of teaching; Biology as a science (the self-understanding of biology); Biology education and future human needs; Order and diversity in the living world – teaching about taxonomy and systematics in schools, teaching neurobiology and behaviour; Bioliteracy. **Events** *BIOED : world congress on biological education / International Congress* Canada 2006, *Round table on bioliteracy* Cairo (Egypt) 2004, *Symposium on biological education, ethics and society* Cairo (Egypt) 2004, *BIOED : world congress on biological education / International Congress* Rio de Janeiro (Brazil) 2004, *BIOED : world congress on biological education / International Congress* Paris (France) 2000. **Publications** *Community Based Biology – UNESCO IUBS Bioliteracy Series*. Monographs.
Members Individuals in 28 countries:
Argentina, Australia, Barbados, Belgium, Brazil, Canada, China, Egypt, Finland, France, Germany, Hungary, India, Italy, Japan, Jordan, Kenya, Malaysia, Mauritius, Morocco, Netherlands, Nigeria, Russia, Spain, Switzerland, Tunisia, UK, USA. [2012/XE0285/v/**E**]

- ♦ IUBS Commission on Taxonomic Databases / see Biodiversity Information Standards (#03243)
- ♦ **IUBS** International Union of Biological Sciences (#15760)
- ♦ IUBSSA / see International Union for Housing Finance (#15780)
- ♦ IUC / see International Education Centre of Svendborg
- ♦ IUCAB / see Internationally United Commercial Agents and Brokers (#14072)
- ♦ **IUCAB** Internationally United Commercial Agents and Brokers (#14072)
- ♦ **IUCAF** Scientific Committee on Frequency Allocations for Radio Astronomy and Space Science (#19148)
- ♦ IUCAT – International Union of Cooperative and Associated Tourism (inactive)
- ♦ **IUCEA** Inter-University Council for East Africa (#15987)
- ♦ IUCESD – Inter-American University Council for Economic and Social Development (no recent information)
- ♦ IUC-Europe – Internationalt Uddannelsescenter i Svendborg (internationally oriented national body)
- ♦ **IUCH** International Union for Circumpolar Health (#15764)
- ♦ IUC – Information Unit for Conventions /Environmental/ (inactive)
- ♦ IUC – International Union of Colleges Working for World Understanding (inactive)
- ♦ IUC – International University Contact for Management Education (inactive)
- ♦ IUC / see Inter-University Centre for Advanced Studies (#15986)
- ♦ **IUC** Inter-University Centre for Advanced Studies (#15986)
- ♦ IUCISD / see International Consortium for Social Development (#12922)
- ♦ IUCN Conservation Monitoring Unit / see UN Environment Programme World Conservation Monitoring Centre (#20295)
- ♦ **IUCN** International Union for Conservation of Nature and Natural Resources (#15766)

♦ IUCN WCPA Specialist Group on Cultural and Spiritual Values of Protected Areas (CSVPA) 16080

Co-Chair c/o EarthCollective – FSD, PO Box 570, 6700 AN Wageningen, Netherlands.
Co-Chair address not obtained.
URL: http://www.csvpa.org/

History 1998, as *Task Force on Non Material Values of Protected Areas*. Subsequently changed title to *Task Force on Cultural and Spiritual Values of Protected Areas*, 2003. Became a permanent Specialist Group 2009. Functions as a group of *International Union for Conservation of Nature and Natural Resources (IUCN, #15766)* and *World Commission on Protected Areas (WCPA / CMAP)*. **Aims** Identify, define, and provide guidelines for managing the cultural and spiritual dimensions of protected areas. **Structure** Steering Committee of 12. Co-Chairs (2). **NGO Relations** *Foundation for Gaia (#09957)*. [2011/XJ1587/**E**]

- ♦ **IUCr** International Union of Crystallography (#15768)
- ♦ IUCSTP / see Scientific Committee on Solar-Terrestrial Physics (#19151)
- ♦ IUCTS – Inter-University Centre for Terrorism Studies (unconfirmed)
- ♦ IUCW – International Union for Child Welfare (inactive)
- ♦ IUDZG / see World Association of Zoos and Aquariums (#21208)
- ♦ IUE / see International Union of Electronic, Electrical, Salaried, Machine and Furniture Workers
- ♦ IUEC – International Union of Elevator Constructors (internationally oriented national body)
- ♦ IUE-CWA – International Union of Electronic, Electrical, Salaried, Machine and Furniture Workers (internationally oriented national body)
- ♦ IUEE – Institut Universitari d'Estudis Europeus (internationally oriented national body)
- ♦ IUEF – Internacia Unuîgo de la Esperantistoj-Filologoj (inactive)
- ♦ IUEI / see Centre for International Information and Documentation, Barcelona
- ♦ **IUE** International Union of Economists (#15769)
- ♦ IUE – International University of Entreprenology (internationally oriented national body)
- ♦ **IUE** Istituto Universitario Europeo (#09034)
- ♦ IUEP – International Union of Esperantist Philologists (inactive)
- ♦ IUE / see UNESCO Institute for Lifelong Learning (#20305)
- ♦ IUEV / see World Esperantist Vegetarian Association (#21389)
- ♦ IUFD / see International Union of Food, Agricultural, Hotel, Restaurant, Catering, Tobacco and Allied Workers Associations (#15772)
- ♦ IUFE – International Unity for Equality (unconfirmed)
- ♦ **IUF** International Unicycling Federation (#15749)
- ♦ **IUF** International Union of Food, Agricultural, Hotel, Restaurant, Catering, Tobacco and Allied Workers Associations (#15772)
- ♦ IUFN – International Urban Food Network (internationally oriented national body)
- ♦ **IUFoST** International Union of Food Science and Technology (#15773)
- ♦ IUFO / see World Family Organization (#21399)
- ♦ **IUFRO** International Union of Forest Research Organizations (#15774)
- ♦ **IUGA** International Urogynecological Association (#15835)
- ♦ **IUGB** International Union of Game Biologists (#15775)
- ♦ IUGG / see International Radiation Commission (#14684)
- ♦ **IUGG** International Union of Geodesy and Geophysics (#15776)
- ♦ IUG – International Uranium Group (see: #11910)
- ♦ **IUG** International Users Group of ISPO-certified organizations (#15837)
- ♦ IUGM / see Association of Gospel Rescue Missions

♦ IUGS Commission on Management and Application of Geoscience Information (CGI) 16081

SG Development Research Ctr, China Geological Survey, 45 Fuwai Street, Xicheng District, 100037 Beijing, China. T. +861058584620. E-mail: cgisecretariat@bgr.de.
SG Regional Geoscience Div – Geolovical Survey of Namibia, 1 Avition Road, Windhoek, Namibia. T. +264612848101.
Chair c/o Bureau de Recherches Géologiques et Minière (BRGM), 3 ave Claude Guillemin, 46060 Orléans CEDEX 2, France. T. +33238643132. Fax +33238643840.
URL: http://www.cgi-iugs.org/

History Founded 1967, Ottawa ON (Canada), as a committee of *International Union of Geological Sciences (IUGS, #15777)*, with the title *IUGS Commission on Storage, Automatic Processing and Retrieval of Geological Data (COGEODATA)*. Restructured 5 Apr 1974, Paris (France); 23 Aug 1976, Sydney (Australia). Became a Commission of IUGS Jul 1980, Paris; restructured Jul 1989, Washington DC (USA). Combined with *IUGS Commission on Geological Documentation (COGEODOC, inactive)*. Reactivated Feb 2002, following several years of inactivity. Also formerly known by the initials *COGEOINFO*; new initials (CGI) adopted Oct 2002. **Aims** Foster interoperability and exchange of geoscience information, by active community leadership, collaboration, education and development, and promotion of geoscience information standards and best practice. **Structure** Council; Subcommissions; Regional Groups; Special Interest Groups; Working Groups (4). **Languages** English. **Staff** Voluntary. **Finance** Source: *International Union of Geological Sciences (IUGS, #15777)*. **Activities** Networking/liaising; knowledge management/information dissemination; standards/guidelines. **Events** *Annual Meeting* Liège (Belgium) 2006, *Meeting* Washington, DC (USA) 1989, *Meeting on computer applications in resource exploration* Helsinki (Finland) 1988, *Meeting on basin analysis* Budapest (Hungary) 1987, *Triennial Conference* Hannover (Germany FR) 1986. **Publications** Newsletters; posters; flyers.

Members Individuals (268) in 65 countries:
Albania, Algeria, Argentina, Australia, Belgium, Bolivia, Brazil, Bulgaria, Cambodia, Cameroon, Canada, Chile, China, Croatia, Cyprus, Czechia, Denmark, Dominican Rep, Egypt, Ethiopia, Finland, France, Germany, Ghana, Greece, India, Indonesia, Iran Islamic Rep, Iraq, Ireland, Italy, Japan, Korea Rep, Liberia, Lithuania, Mexico, Morocco, Mozambique, Namibia, Netherlands, New Zealand, Nigeria, Norway, Pakistan, Peru, Philippines, Poland, Portugal, Romania, Russia, Serbia, Slovenia, South Africa, Spain, Sweden, Switzerland, Thailand, Tunisia, Türkiye, UK, USA, Uzbekistan, Vietnam, Yemen, Zimbabwe.

IGO Relations Cooperates with: *Coordinating Committee for Geoscience Programmes in East and Southeast Asia (CCOP, #04816)*; *UNESCO (#20322)*. **NGO Relations** Cooperates with: *Committee on Data for Science and Technology (CODATA, #04247)*; *Geological Society of Africa (GSAf, #10135)*. Instrumental in setting up: *International Association for Mathematical Geosciences (IAMG, #12017)*; *Southeast Asian Network for a Geological Information System (SANGIS, #19778)*. [2017.10.11/XE5196/v/**E**]

- ♦ IUGS Commission on Storage, Automatic Processing and Retrieval of Geological Data / see IUGS Commission on Management and Application of Geoscience Information (#16081)
- ♦ **IUGS** International Union of Geological Sciences (#15777)
- ♦ IUHE / see International Union for Health Promotion and Education (#15778)
- ♦ IUHFI / see International Union for Housing Finance (#15780)
- ♦ **IUHF** International Union for Housing Finance (#15780)
- ♦ IUHHA / see European Historic Houses Association (#07491)
- ♦ **IUHPE** International Union for Health Promotion and Education (#15778)
- ♦ IUHPS / see International Union of History and Philosophy of Science and Technology (#15779)
- ♦ **IUHPST** International Union of History and Philosophy of Science and Technology (#15779)
- ♦ IUHR – Inter-African Union of Human Rights (inactive)
- ♦ IUIC – Institut Universitaire Intergouvernemental pour la Coopération (internationally oriented national body)
- ♦ IUIC – Intergovernmental University Institute of Co-operation (internationally oriented national body)
- ♦ IUIL – Institut universitaire international de Luxembourg (internationally oriented national body)
- ♦ IU – Interlingue-Union (inactive)
- ♦ **The IU** International Union for Land Value Taxation and Free Trade (#15787)
- ♦ **IUIS** International Union of Immunological Societies (#15781)
- ♦ **IUIU** Islamic University in Uganda (#16056)
- ♦ IUJAT – International Union of Journeymen and Allied Trades (internationally oriented national body)
- ♦ IUJCD – Internationale Union Junger Christlicher Demokraten (inactive)
- ♦ IUJHAT / see International Union of Journeymen and Allied Trades
- ♦ IUJ – International University of Japan (internationally oriented national body)
- ♦ IUK – International University of Kyrgyzstan (internationally oriented national body)
- ♦ **IUKL** International Union of Kettlebell Lifting (#15786)
- ♦ IULA – International Union of Local Authorities (inactive)
- ♦ IULA Working Group of Wholesale Markets / see World Union of Wholesale Markets (#21889)
- ♦ IULCS / see International Union of Leather Technologists and Chemists Societies (#15788)
- ♦ IULCW / see International Association of Liberal Religious Women (#11999)
- ♦ IULDUG / see ULD CARE (#20278)
- ♦ **IUL** Internationale Union der Lebensmittel-, Landwirtschafts-, Hotel-, Restaurant-, Café- und Genussmittelarbeiter-Gewerkschaften (#15772)
- ♦ IUL / see International Union of Food, Agricultural, Hotel, Restaurant, Catering, Tobacco and Allied Workers Associations (#15772)
- ♦ **IUL** Internationella Unionen för Livsmedels-, Njutningsmedels- och Lantarbetareförbund Samt Förbund Inom Hotell- och Restaurangbranschen (#15772)
- ♦ **IULTCS** International Union of Leather Technologists and Chemists Societies (#15788)
- ♦ **IUMAB** International Union of Medical and Applied Bio-Electrography (#15792)
- ♦ **IUMAS** International Union of Microbeam Analysis Societies (#15793)
- ♦ **IUMI** International Union of Marine Insurance (#15789)
- ♦ **IUMRS** International Union of Materials Research Societies (#15790)
- ♦ IUMS Division of Bacteriology and Applied Microbiology (see: #15794)
- ♦ IUMS Division of Mycology (see: #15794)
- ♦ IUMS Division of Virology (see: #15794)
- ♦ **IUMS** International Union of Microbiological Societies (#15794)
- ♦ IUMS – International Union for Moral and Social Action (inactive)
- ♦ IUMS – International Union of Muslim Scouts (no recent information)
- ♦ IUNRWA/UNESCO IE – UNRWA/UNESCO Institute of Education (no recent information)
- ♦ **IUNS** International Union of Nutritional Sciences (#15796)
- ♦ IUOAS – International Union for Oriental and Asian Studies (inactive)
- ♦ IUOE – International Union of Operating Engineers (internationally oriented national body)
- ♦ IUOIR – International Union of Radiologists (unconfirmed)
- ♦ **IUPAB** International Union for Pure and Applied Biophysics (#15808)
- ♦ **IUPAC** International Union of Pure and Applied Chemistry (#15809)
- ♦ IUPA – International Union of Police Associations (internationally oriented national body)
- ♦ IUPA – International Union of Practitioners in Advertising (inactive)
- ♦ IUPA – International Union of Press Associations (inactive)

♦ IUPAP Commission on Astrophysics 16082

Commission de l'UIPPA sur l'astrophysique

Secretariat c/o ICTP, Strada Costiera 11, 34151 Trieste TS, Italy. E-mail: secretariat@iupap.org.
URL: https://iupap.org/commissions/c19-astrophysics/

History 1984. Founded as a Commission C 19 of *International Union of Pure and Applied Physics (IUPAP, #15810)*. Currently serves as an internal commission. Former names and other names: *International Commission on Astrophysics* – alias; *Commission internationale sur l'astrophysique* – alias. **Aims** Promote activities of physicists working in gravitation, plasma physics, nuclear physics, high energy physics, atomic and molecular physics and condensed matter so as to synthesize their contributions into a better understanding of astrophysical phenomena and the nature of the cosmos. **Structure** Chairman, Vice-Chairman, Secretary and 11 members. **Finance** Supported by: *International Union of Pure and Applied Physics (IUPAP, #15810)*. **Activities** Awards/prizes/competitions; events/meetings. **Events** *International conference on particle physics, astrophysics and cosmology* Stanford, CA (USA) 1994, *MG7 – Triennial Marcel Grossmann Meeting on General Relativity* Stanford, CA (USA) 1994, *Conference* Kyoto (Japan) 1991, *Meeting on primordial nucleosynthesis and the evolution of early universe / Conference* Tokyo (Japan) 1990, *International conference on accretion of discs and jets in astrophysics* Wuhan (China) 1989.

Members Individuals in 14 countries:
Belgium, Canada, Chile, France, India, Italy, Japan, Korea Rep, Lithuania, Poland, South Africa, Spain, UK, USA.

Associate members (5) in 4 countries:
Greece, India, Romania, USA (2). [2022/XE0201/v/**E**]

- ♦ IUPAP Commission on Atomic and Molecular Physics and Spectroscopy / see International Commission on Atomic, Molecular and Optical Physics (#12666)
- ♦ IUPAP Commission on Biological Physics / see International Commission on Biological Physics (#12669)
- ♦ IUPAP Commission on Cosmic Rays / see International Commission on Astroparticle Physics (#12663)
- ♦ IUPAP Commission on Low Temperature Physics / see International Commission on Low Temperature Physics (#12698)
- ♦ IUPAP Commission on Magnetism / see International Commission on Magnetism (#12699)
- ♦ IUPAP Commission on Mathematical Physics / see International Commission on Mathematical Physics (#12701)
- ♦ IUPAP Commission on Nuclear Physics / see International Commission on Nuclear Physics (#12708)
- ♦ IUPAP Commission on Particles and Fields / see International Commission on Particles and Fields (#12712)
- ♦ IUPAP Commission on Physics for Development / see International Commission on Physics for Development (#12713)
- ♦ IUPAP Commission on Physics Education / see International Commission on Physics Education (#12714)
- ♦ IUPAP Commission on Plasma Physics / see International Commission on Plasma Physics (#12717)
- ♦ IUPAP Commission on Quantum Electronics / see International Commission on Laser Physics and Photonics (#12697)
- ♦ IUPAP Commission on the Structure and Dynamics of Condensed Matter / see International Commission on the Structure and Dynamics of Condensed Matter (#12731)
- ♦ IUPAP Commission on Symbols, Units, Nomenclature, Atomic Masses and Fundamental Constants / see International Commission on Symbols, Units, Nomenclature, Atomic Masses and Fundamental Constants (#12733)
- ♦ **IUPAP** International Union of Pure and Applied Physics (#15810)
- ♦ IUPAT – International Union of Painters and Allied Trades (internationally oriented national body)
- ♦ **IUPB** International Union of Photobiology (#15798)
- ♦ **IUPEA** International Urban Planning and Environment Association (#15833)
- ♦ **IUPESM** International Union for Physical and Engineering Sciences in Medicine (#15799)
- ♦ IUPHAR / see International Union of Basic and Clinical Pharmacology (#15758)
- ♦ **IUPHAR** International Union of Basic and Clinical Pharmacology (#15758)
- ♦ IUPIP – International University of Peoples Institutions for Peace (internationally oriented national body)
- ♦ IUPL – International Union of Penal Law (inactive)
- ♦ IUPN / see International Union for Conservation of Nature and Natural Resources (#15766)
- ♦ IUPS Commission on Circulation – Respiration (see: #15800)
- ♦ IUPS Commission on Comparative Physiology (see: #15800)
- ♦ IUPS Commission on Endocrine, Reproduction and Development (see: #15800)
- ♦ IUPS Commission on Genomics and Biodiversity (see: #15800)
- ♦ IUPS Commission on Locomotion (see: #15800)
- ♦ IUPS Commission on Molecular and Cellular Physiology (see: #15800)
- ♦ IUPS Commission on Neurobiology (see: #15800)
- ♦ IUPS Commission on Secretion and Absorption (see: #15800)
- ♦ **IUPS** International Union of Physiological Sciences (#15800)
- ♦ **IUPsyS** International Union of Psychological Science (#15807)
- ♦ IURC – International Union for Research of Communication (inactive)
- ♦ IUR / see International Union of Radioecology (#15812)

- ♦ **IUR** International Union of Radioecology (#15812)
- ♦ Iuris Canonici Medii Aevi Consociatio (#19593)
- ♦ IUR – Islamische Universiteit Rotterdam (internationally oriented national body)
- ♦ IURW – International Union of Revolutionary Writers (inactive)
- ♦ IUSA – International Union of Students in Architecture (inactive)
- ♦ **IUSBSE** International Union of Societies for Biomaterials Science and Engineering (#15816)
- ♦ IUSDE / see International Social Democratic Union for Education (#14881)
- ♦ IUSD – International University on Sustainable Development (internationally oriented national body)
- ♦ IUSDT / see International Social Democratic Union for Education (#14881)
- ♦ IUSE – Istituto Universitario di Studi Europei (internationally oriented national body)
- ♦ IUSESS – International Union of Secondary School Students (no recent information)
- ♦ IUSF – International Union of Societies of Foresters (no recent information)
- ♦ **IUSF** International Union for Surface Finishing (#15821)
- ♦ **IUSG** International Uveitis Study Group (#15838)
- ♦ **IUS** International Urban Symposium (#15834)
- ♦ **IUS** International Urolithiasis Society (#15836)
- ♦ **IUS LABORIS** International Employment Law, Pensions and Employee Benefits Alliance (#13265)
- ♦ IUSM – International Union for Surveys and Mapping (inactive)
- ♦ **IUSSI** International Union for the Study of Social Insects (#15819)
- ♦ **IUSS** International Union of Soil Sciences (#15817)
- ♦ **IUSSP** International Union for the Scientific Study of Population (#15814)
- ♦ **IUSTI** International Union against Sexually Transmitted Infections (#15751)
- ♦ **IUSY** International Union of Socialist Youth (#15815)
- ♦ **IUTA** International University Theatre Association (#15831)
- ♦ **IUTAM** International Union of Theoretical and Applied Mechanics (#15823)
- ♦ **IUT** International Union of Tenants (#15822)
- ♦ IUT / see International Union of Transgenics and Synthetic Biology (#15825)
- ♦ **IUT** International Union of Transgenics and Synthetic Biology (#15825)
- ♦ **IUT** Islamic University of Technology (#16055)
- ♦ **IUTOX** International Union of Toxicology (#15824)
- ♦ IUVAA – Internationale Unie van Verenigingen van Artsen-Automobilisten (no recent information)
- ♦ **IUVA** International Ultraviolet Association (#15747)
- ♦ IUVDT / see International Union against Sexually Transmitted Infections (#15751)
- ♦ **IUVFTA** Internationale Union für Vakuum-Forschung, -Technik und -Anwendung (#15826)
- ♦ **IUVSTA** International Union for Vacuum Science, Technique and Applications (#15826)
- ♦ **IUWA** International Union of Women Architects (#15828)
- ♦ IUWDS / see International Space Environment Service (#15572)
- ♦ IUYCD – International Union of Young Christian Democrats (inactive)
- ♦ **IUYF** International Union of Young Farmers (#15829)
- ♦ **IVAA** Internationale Vereinigung Anthroposophischer Ärztegesellschaften (#13314)
- ♦ IVAAP – International Veterinary Association for Animal Production (inactive)
- ♦ IVAB – Internationaler Verband für Austausch und Bildung von Kindern und Jugendlichen (no recent information)
- ♦ IVA / see Cargo Rail Europe (#03431)
- ♦ IVAC – International Vaccine Access Center (internationally oriented national body)
- ♦ IVADM – International Veterinary Academy on Disaster Medicine (inactive)
- ♦ IVA – Ieder Voor Allen (internationally oriented national body)
- ♦ **IVA** Internationaler Verband für Arbeiterbildung (#13580)
- ♦ **IVA** International VAT Association (#15841)
- ♦ IVA – International Veterinary Auxiliary (inactive)
- ♦ IVA – International Volunteer Academy (unconfirmed)
- ♦ IVAKV – Internationale Vereinigung Ärztlicher Kraftfahrer-Verbände (no recent information)
- ♦ **IVAO** International Virtual Aviation Organisation (#15856)
- ♦ IVAPM – International Veterinary Academy of Pain Management (internationally oriented national body)
- ♦ IVAR – International Voluntary Action and Voluntary Research Organization (inactive)
- ♦ **IVAS** International Veterinary Acupuncture Society (#15846)
- ♦ IVBF / see Fédération internationale de volleyball (#09670)
- ♦ **IVBH** Internationale Vereinigung für Brückenbau und Hochbau (#11737)
- ♦ **IVBS** Internationaler Verband der Betonbohr und Sägeunternehmungen (#11806)
- ♦ **IVBS** Internationale Vereinigung für binokulares Sehen (#13315)
- ♦ **IVBV** Internationale Vereinigung der Bergführerverbände (#15756)
- ♦ **IVBW** International Veterinary Biosafety Workgroup (#15847)
- ♦ **IVCA** International Veteran Cycle Association (#15844)
- ♦ **IVCA** International Veterinary Chiropractic Association (#15848)
- ♦ IVCA – International Visual Communication Association (inactive)
- ♦ **IVCC** Innovative Vector Control Consortium (#11223)
- ♦ **IVCG** Internationale Vereinigung Christlicher Geschäftsleute (#13316)
- ♦ **IVC** International Vienna Council (#15853)
- ♦ IVC – International Vitamin Conference (meeting series)
- ♦ **IvC** Invadosome Consortium (#15996)
- ♦ IVDK – Internationale Vereinigung der Kriegswaisen (inactive)
- ♦ IVECA – Center for International Virtual Schooling (unconfirmed)
- ♦ IVeH – International Virtual e-Hospital Foundation (internationally oriented national body)
- ♦ IVE – Internationale Vereinigung von Einkaufs- und Marketingverbänden (inactive)
- ♦ IVE / see International Federation of Hardware and Housewares Associations (#13437)
- ♦ IVE / see International Travel Insurance Alliance e.V. (#15728)
- ♦ IVEN – Internationaler Verband der Eisenbahner für Nüchternheit (inactive)
- ♦ **IVENTA** International Veterinary Ear, Nose and Throat Association (#15849)
- ♦ IVEP – Informationsverbund Entwicklungspolitik (internationally oriented national body)
- ♦ IVES – Internationaler Verband für Erziehung zu Suchmittelfreiem Leben (inactive)
- ♦ **IVETA** International Vocational Education and Training Association (#15861)
- ♦ IVEX – International Volunteer Expeditions (internationally oriented national body)
- ♦ IVfgR / see International Association for the Protection of Intellectual Property (#12112)
- ♦ **IVF** International Video Federation (#15852)
- ♦ IVF / see International Visegrad Fund (#15859)
- ♦ IVFL – Internationale Vereinigung Freier Lehrergewerkschaften (inactive)
- ♦ **IVFS** Internationale Vereinigung für Sportrecht (#12180)
- ♦ **IVfW** Internationale Vereinigung für Walsertum (#12262)
- ♦ **IVG** Internationale Vereinigung für Germanistik (#13317)
- ♦ IVGWP – Internationaler Verband der Gastronomie- und Weinbuau- Presse (inactive)
- ♦ IVHHN – International Volcanic Health Hazard Network (see: #12259)
- ♦ **IVHW** Internationaler Verband für Hauswirtschaft (#13447)
- ♦ IVIA – International Videotex Industry Association (inactive)
- ♦ **IVI** International Vaccine Institute (#15839)
- ♦ IV / see International Association for Christian Education (#11770)
- ♦ iV – International Conference Information Visualisation (meeting series)
- ♦ **IV** Internationaler Verband für Christliche Erziehung und Bildung (#11770)
- ♦ iViP / see ProSTEP iViP Association
- ♦ **IVIP** Internationale Vereinigung für Individualpsychologie (#11960)
- ♦ IVIS – International Vacuum Insulation Symposium (meeting series)
- ♦ IVJH – Internationale Vereinigung für Jugendhilfe (inactive)
- ♦ **IVJL** Internationale Vereinigung von Jungen Landwirten (#15829)
- ♦ IVKDF / see Von Karman Institute for Fluid Dynamics (#16182)
- ♦ IVK Europe – Industrieverband Kunststoffbahnen (unconfirmed)
- ♦ **IVK** Institut von Karman de dynamique des fluides (#16182)
- ♦ IVKMH – Internationale Vereinigung der Klein- und Mittelbetriebe des Handels (inactive)
- ♦ IVKMI – Internationale Vereinigung der Klein- und Mittelbetriebe der Industrie (inactive)
- ♦ I-VLab / see International Virtual Laboratory for Enterprise Interoperability (#15857)
- ♦ IVLA – International Visual Literacy Association (internationally oriented national body)
- ♦ IVLD – Internationale Vereinigung von Organisationen der Lebensmittel-Detaillanten (inactive)
- ♦ IVL / see International Society of Limnology (#15232)
- ♦ **IVMB** Internationale Vereinigung der Musikbibliotheken, Musikarchive und Musikdokumentationszentren (#12042)
- ♦ IVMS – Internationale Vereinigung für Mutterschutz und Sexualreform (inactive)
- ♦ IVNC – International Vacuum Nanoelectronics Conference (meeting series)
- ♦ **IVN** Internationaler Verband der Naturtextilwirtschaft (#14217)
- ♦ **IVN** Internationale Vereniging voor Neerlandistiek (#11854)
- ♦ IVNS – International Vladimir Nabokov Society (internationally oriented national body)
- ♦ IVNTA – International Veterinary Nurses and Technicians Association (internationally oriented national body)
- ♦ **IVOA** International Virtual Observatory Alliance (#15858)
- ♦ IVODGA – International Vessel Operators Dangerous Goods Association (internationally oriented national body)
- ♦ **IVO** Internationaler Verband der Orthopädie-Schuhtechniker (#12059)
- ♦ IVOJ – International Voice of Justice (internationally oriented national body)
- ♦ Ivo Lapenna International Scientific Institute (#11525)
- ♦ IVORC – International Virtual Ophthalmic Research Center (unconfirmed)
- ♦ Ivory For Elephants (internationally oriented national body)
- ♦ IVOWED – International Voluntary Organisation for Women, Education and Development (internationally oriented national body)
- ♦ IVOW – Internationale Vereniging van Oorlogswezen (inactive)
- ♦ IVPC – Internationaler Verband der Petroleum- und Chemiearbeiter (inactive)
- ♦ **IVPC** International Venture Philanthropy Center (#15843)
- ♦ **IVPDA** International Vintage Poster Dealers Association (#15854)
- ♦ **IVPE** Internationaler Verband Psychiatrischer Epidemiologie (#13521)
- ♦ IVPMO – Internationaler Verband Psychologisch-Medizinischer Organisationen (inactive)
- ♦ IVPO – Internationale Vereniging voor Plattelandsontwikkeling (inactive)
- ♦ **IVRA** International Veterinary Radiology Association (#15850)
- ♦ **IVR** Internationale Vereinigung für Rechts- und Sozialphilosophie (#13318)
- ♦ **IVR** Internationale Vereniging voor de Behartiging van de Gemeenschappelijke Belangen van de Binnenvaart en de Verzekering en voor het Houden van het Register van Binnenschepen in Europa (#12131)
- ♦ IVRS National Welfare Conference / see Catholic Relief Services (#03608)
- ♦ **IVSA** International Veterinary Students' Association (#15851)
- ♦ IVSA – International Visual Sociology Association (internationally oriented national body)
- ♦ **IVSBB** Internationale Vereinigung für Schul- und Berufsberatung (#11862)
- ♦ **IVSC** International Valuation Standards Council (#15840)
- ♦ **IVSI** Internationalen Verband der Schneesportinstruktoren (#13542)
- ♦ IVSI / see International Federation of Snowsport Instructors (#13542)
- ♦ **IVS** Internationale Verbindung für Schalentragwerke und Raumtragwerke (#12162)
- ♦ IVS / see International Veterans Table Tennis Society (#15845)
- ♦ **IVS** International Viola Society (#15855)
- ♦ **IVS** International VLBI Service for Geodesy and Astrometry (#15860)
- ♦ IVS – International Voluntary Service, UK (internationally oriented national body)
- ♦ IVSP / see Peace Corps
- ♦ **IVSP** Internationale Vereinigung für Selbstmordprophylaxe und Krisenintervention (#12213)
- ♦ **IVSR** Internationale Vereniging voor Sportrecht (#12180)
- ♦ **IVSS-Churchear** Internationaler Verband für Schwerhörigenseelsorge (#13500)
- ♦ IVS / see Service Civil International (#19238)
- ♦ IVSS / see International Association of Education in Science and Snowsports (#11864)
- ♦ **IVSS** Internationale Vereinigung für Soziale Sicherheit (#14885)
- ♦ iVTH – International Association for Technical Issues Related to Wood (internationally oriented national body)
- ♦ iVTH – Internationaler Verein für Technische Holzfragen (internationally oriented national body)
- ♦ **IVT** Internationaler Verband der Tarifeure – Organisation der Tarif- und Transportexperten (#12219)
- ♦ **IVT** Internationale Vereniging Trappist (#15727)
- ♦ IVTO / see WorldSkills International (#21791)
- ♦ **IVTTS** International Veterans Table Tennis Society (#15845)
- ♦ **IVU** Internationale Verleger-Union (#14675)
- ♦ **IVU** International Vegetarian Union (#15842)
- ♦ IVUN – International Ventilator Users Network (internationally oriented national body)
- ♦ IVV / see International Association for Vegetation Science (#12253)
- ♦ IVV – Internationaler Verband für Verkehrsschulung und Verkehrserziehung (inactive)
- ♦ **IVV** Internationaler Volkssportverband (#13515)
- ♦ **IVW** Internationaler Verband für Die Wärmebehandlung und Randschichttechnik (#13443)
- ♦ **IVWSR** Internationaler Verband für Wohnungswesen, Städtebau und Raumordnung (#13450)
- ♦ IW3C2 – International World Wide Web Conference Committee (internationally oriented national body)
- ♦ IWA Asia-Pacific Regional Group / see IWA Asia Pacific Region Grouping (#16083)

♦ IWA Asia Pacific Region Grouping (IWA-ASPIRE) 16083

Contact c/o IWA, Export Bldg 1st Fl, 2 Clove Crescent, London, E14 2BE, UK.
URL: https://iwa-network.org/

History within the framework of the since suspended *Asian and Pacific Council (ASPAC, inactive)*. Previously a regional water supply organization of *International Water Services Association (IWSA, inactive)* with title: *IWSA Asia Pacific Group (ASPAC)*. Since 1999 active in *International Water Association (IWA, #15865)*, under title: *International Water Association Asia Pacific Group (IWA-ASPAC)*. Current title adopted on merger with *Asian Waterqual Group of International Association on Water Quality (IAWQ, inactive)*. **Aims** Encourage communication and better understanding between those engaged in the public supply of water; secure concerted action in improving knowledge of public *water supply* – technical, legal and administrative. **Structure** Rotating Chairmanship. **Activities** Fosters communication among those engaged in public supply of water in the Asia-Pacific region. Encourages participation of the world water community in discussion of questions affecting the region. **Events** *IWA-ASPIRE Conference* Kaohsiung (Taiwan) 2023, *IWA-ASPIRE Conference* Kaohsiung (Taiwan) 2021, *Asia Pacific Regional Conference* Hong Kong (Hong Kong) 2019, *Asia Pacific Regional Conference* Kuala Lumpur (Malaysia) 2017, *Asia Pacific Regional Conference* Beijing (China) 2015.

Members Full in 13 countries and territories:
Australia, China, Hong Kong, Japan, Korea Rep, Macau, Malaysia, New Zealand, Philippines, Singapore, Taiwan, Thailand, Vietnam.
Also members in the Pacific. Membership countries not specified. [2019/XE0468/**E**]

- ♦ IWAAS – Institute of West Asian and African Studies, Beijing (internationally oriented national body)
- ♦ IWA-ASPAC / see IWA Asia Pacific Region Grouping (#16083)
- ♦ IWA-ASPIRE / see IWA Asia Pacific Region Grouping (#16083)
- ♦ **IWA-ASPIRE** IWA Asia Pacific Region Grouping (#16083)
- ♦ IWA-HWG / see International Webmasters Association (#15874)
- ♦ IWA – Institute of World Affairs (internationally oriented national body)
- ♦ **IWA** International Water Association (#15865)
- ♦ **IWA** International Webmasters Association (#15874)

- ♦ IWA – International Wheat Agreement, 1971 (treaty)
- ♦ IWA – International Wheat Agreement, 1986 (1986 treaty)
- ♦ **IWA** International Windsurfing Association (#15888)
- ♦ IWA – International Women's Alliance (unconfirmed)
- ♦ **IWA** International Workers' Association (#15906)
- ♦ **IWA** International Workshop for Astronomy (#15913)
- ♦ IWAIS – International Workshop on Atmospheric Icing of Structures (meeting series)
- ♦ IWAIT – International Workshop on Advanced Image Technology (meeting series)
- ♦ **IWALC** International Water-Related Associations' Liaison Committee (#15869)
- ♦ IWALS – International Workshop on Advanced Learning Sciences (meeting series)
- ♦ **IWAS** International Wheelchair and Amputee Sports Federation (#15881)
- ♦ IWA / see SOLIDAR (#19680)
- ♦ IWASRI – International Waterlogging and Salinity Research Institute (internationally oriented national body)
- ♦ **IWBF** International Wheelchair Basketball Federation (#15882)
- ♦ **IWbF** International Woodball Federation (#15903)
- ♦ IWB – Internationales Wissenschaftsforum Bonn (internationally oriented national body)
- ♦ **IWBS** International Walter Benjamin Society (#15863)
- ♦ IWBS – Sisters of the Incarnate Word and Blessed Sacrament (religious order)
- ♦ **IWCA** International Wine Clubs Association (#15889)
- ♦ IWCA – International Women's Coffee Alliance (internationally oriented national body)
- ♦ IWCA – International Writing Centers Association (internationally oriented national body)
- ♦ IWCA / see The World Calendar Association – International (#21255)
- ♦ IWCC – International Criminal Justice and Weapons Control Center (internationally oriented national body)
- ♦ IWCC – International Women Communication Centre (internationally oriented national body)
- ♦ IWCC – International Women's Cricket Council (inactive)
- ♦ **IWCC** International Wrought Copper Council (#15917)
- ♦ **IWCF** International Well Control Forum (#15877)
- ♦ IWCF – International Workers' Compensation Foundation (internationally oriented national body)
- ♦ IWC / see International Grains Council (#13731)
- ♦ IWC – International WaterCentre (internationally oriented national body)
- ♦ **IWC** International Whaling Commission (#15879)
- ♦ IWC – International Wildlife Crimestoppers (internationally oriented national body)
- ♦ **IWC** International Women's Convocation (#15896)
- ♦ **IWCN** International Women Count Network (#15894)
- ♦ **IWCS** International Wire and Cable Symposium (#15892)
- ♦ IWCS – International Wood Culture Society (unconfirmed)
- ♦ IWCSN – International Workshop on Complex Systems and Networks (meeting series)
- ♦ IWCSPP – International Working Conference on Stored-Product Protection (meeting series)
- ♦ IWDA – International Women's Development Agency (internationally oriented national body)
- ♦ IWDBA – International Working Dog Breeding Association (unconfirmed)
- ♦ IWDC – International Women's Democracy Center (internationally oriented national body)
- ♦ **IWDN** International Women's Democracy Network (#15897)
- ♦ **IWDU** International Women's Democrat Union (#15898)
- ♦ IWE – Institute for World Economics of the Hungarian Academy of Sciences (internationally oriented national body)
- ♦ IWEMB – International Workshop On Entrepreneurship, Electronic And Mobile Business (meeting series)
- ♦ IWEP – Institute of World Economics and Politics (internationally oriented national body)
- ♦ IWEP – Institute of World Economics and Politics, Hanoi (internationally oriented national body)
- ♦ IWF / see International Wushu Federation (#15918)
- ♦ IWFA – International Window Film Association (internationally oriented national body)
- ♦ IWFCI – International Women's Federation of Commerce and Industry (internationally oriented national body)
- ♦ IWFEA – International Wolf Federation – Environment Action (inactive)
- ♦ IWFF – International Women and Family Foundation (internationally oriented national body)
- ♦ IWF – International Weather and Climate Forum (meeting series)
- ♦ **IWF** International Weightlifting Federation (#15876)
- ♦ **IWF** International Women's Forum (#15899)
- ♦ IWF – Internet Watch Foundation (internationally oriented national body)
- ♦ **IWFS** International Wine and Food Society (#15890)
- ♦ IWGA – International Wheat Gluten Association (internationally oriented national body)
- ♦ **IWGA** International World Games Association (#15914)
- ♦ IWGBPSCR – International Working Group for Biopsychosocial Cancer Research (no recent information)
- ♦ IWGDF / see D-Foot International (#05061)
- ♦ **IWGDPT** International Working Group on Data Protection in Telecommunications (#15908)
- ♦ **IWGEES** International Working Group on Endoscopic Ear Surgery (#15910)
- ♦ **IWGE** International Working Group on Education (#15909)
- ♦ IWGGMS – International Workshop on Greenhouse Gas Measurements from Space (meeting series)
- ♦ **IWGIA** International Work Group for Indigenous Affairs (#15907)
- ♦ IWG – International Work Group on Death, Dying and Bereavement (unconfirmed)
- ♦ **IWG** International Working Group on Women and Sport (#15912)
- ♦ IWG – International Writers Guild (inactive)
- ♦ IWGN / see International Society for NeuroImmunoModulation (#15299)
- ♦ IWGPVFV – International Working Group on Plant Viruses with Fungal Vectors (inactive)
- ♦ **IWGSC** International Wheat Genome Sequencing Consortium (#15880)
- ♦ **IWG-SEM** International Working Group on Satellite-Based Emergency Mapping (#15911)
- ♦ IWGS – International Wheat Genetics Symposium (meeting series)
- ♦ **IWHA** International Water History Association (#15866)
- ♦ IWHC – International Women's Health Coalition (internationally oriented national body)
- ♦ IWHM – International Workshop on Humanized Mice (meeting series)
- ♦ IWIC – International Water Industry Conference (meeting series)
- ♦ **IWII** International Wound Infection Institute (#15916)
- ♦ **IWI** Inland Waterways International (#11217)
- ♦ **IWI** International Women's Initiative (#15900)
- ♦ IWIM – Institute for World Economics and International Management, Bremen (internationally oriented national body)
- ♦ **IW** InnovaWood (#11224)
- ♦ IW – Institut für Weltgesellschaft (internationally oriented national body)
- ♦ IWIRC – International Women's Insolvency and Restructuring Confederation (internationally oriented national body)
- ♦ IWIU / see United Food and Commercial Workers Union
- ♦ IWJ – Cummings Institute for World Justice (internationally oriented national body)
- ♦ **IWLA** International Wine Law Association (#15891)
- ♦ **IW-LEARN** International Waters Learning Exchange and Resource Network (#15873)
- ♦ IWLF / see WILD Foundation (#20956)
- ♦ **IWMA** International Water Mist Association (#15868)
- ♦ **IWMA** International Wire and Machinery Association (#15893)
- ♦ **IWMC** World Conservation Trust (#21312)
- ♦ IWMF – International Waldenstrom's Macroglobulinemia Foundation (internationally oriented national body)
- ♦ **IWMF** International Women's Media Foundation (#15901)
- ♦ **IWMI** International Water Management Institute (#15867)
- ♦ **IWM** Institut für die Wissenschaften vom Menschen (#11239)
- ♦ IWM – International Workshop on Microplasmas (meeting series)
- ♦ IWMRRF – International Workshop on Model Reduction in Reacting Flows (meeting series)
- ♦ IWMS – International Workshop on Matrices and Statistics (meeting series)
- ♦ IWNAM – International Women's Network Against Militarism (unconfirmed)
- ♦ IWNCS – International Workshop on Non-Crystalline Solids (meeting series)
- ♦ iwNHL – International Workshop on Non-Hodgkin Lymphoma (meeting series)
- ♦ IWN – Indigenous Women's Network (internationally oriented national body)
- ♦ IWN – International Whales Network (see: #20147)
- ♦ IWN – International Workshop on Nitride Semiconductors (meeting series)
- ♦ iWOE – International Workshop on Oxide Electronics (meeting series)
- ♦ IWO – Initiative Wohnungswirtschaft Osteuropa (internationally oriented national body)
- ♦ Iwokrama Centre international pour la preservation et le développement de la forêt tropicale (internationally oriented national body)
- ♦ Iwokrama Centro Internacional para a Conservação e Desenvolvimento de Florestas Humidas Tropicais (internationally oriented national body)
- ♦ Iwokrama Internationaal Centrum voor het Behoud en Duurzame Ontwikkeling van het Regenwoud (internationally oriented national body)
- ♦ Iwokrama International Centre for Rain Forest Conservation and Development (internationally oriented national body)
- ♦ IWOMP – International Workshop on OpenMP (meeting series)
- ♦ iWORiD – International Workshop on Radiation Imaging Detectors (meeting series)
- ♦ IWOTA – International Workshop on Operator Theory and its Applications (meeting series)
- ♦ IWPA – International Wood Products Association (internationally oriented national body)
- ♦ IWPA – International Work Platform Association (inactive)
- ♦ IWPC – International Water Power Consortium (unconfirmed)
- ♦ IWPG – International Women's Peace Group (internationally oriented national body)
- ♦ IWP – Institute of World Politics (internationally oriented national body)
- ♦ IWP – International Women's Partnership for Peace and Justice (internationally oriented national body)
- ♦ IWPMA – International Workshop on Piezoelectric Materials and Applications in Actuators (meeting series)
- ♦ **IWPR** Institute for War and Peace Reporting (#11302)
- ♦ IWPS – International Women's Peace Service (internationally oriented national body)
- ♦ **IWRA** International Water Resources Association (#15871)
- ♦ **IWRAW Asia Pacific** International Women's Rights Action Watch Asia Pacific (#15902)
- ♦ IWRB – International Waterfowl and Wetlands Research Bureau (inactive)
- ♦ **IWRCA** International Wildlife Ranching and Conservation Alliance (#15884)
- ♦ **IWRC** International Wildlife Rehabilitation Council, The (#15885)
- ♦ **IWREC** International Water and Resource Economics Consortium (#15870)
- ♦ **IWRF** International Wheelchair Rugby Federation (#15883)
- ♦ IWRN – International Whistleblowing Research Network (unconfirmed)
- ♦ IWRN – International Workshop on Railway Noise (meeting series)
- ♦ IWRP – International Women's Rights Project (internationally oriented national body)
- ♦ IWRS / see International Wildlife Ranching and Conservation Alliance (#15884)
- ♦ IWRS – International Wood Research Society (inactive)
- ♦ IWSA Asia Pacific Group / see IWA Asia Pacific Region Grouping (#16083)
- ♦ IWSA – International WAGR Syndrome Association (internationally oriented national body)
- ♦ IWSA – International Water Services Association (inactive)
- ♦ **IWSA** International Windship Association (#15887)
- ♦ IWSAW – Institute for Women's Studies in the Arab World (internationally oriented national body)
- ♦ IWSEC – International Workshop on Security (meeting series)
- ♦ IWSF / see International Waterski and Wakeboard Federation (#15872)
- ♦ IWSG – International Wader Study Group (see: #15766)
- ♦ IWSG – International Wool Study Group (inactive)
- ♦ IWS – International Wool Secretariat (inactive)
- ♦ **IWSS** International Weed Science Society (#15875)
- ♦ i-WSSM – UNESCO International Centre for Water Security and Sustainable Management (internationally oriented national body)
- ♦ **IWTC** International World Travellers Club (#15915)
- ♦ **IWTO** International Wool Textile Organisation (#15904)
- ♦ IWTS – International Wine Technical Summit (unconfirmed)
- ♦ **IWUF** International Wushu Federation (#15918)
- ♦ IWUMD – International Workshop on UV Materials and Devices (meeting series)
- ♦ IWVWW – Internationale Wissenschaftliche Vereinigung Weltwirtschaft und Weltpolitik (internationally oriented national body)
- ♦ **IWWF** International Waterski and Wakeboard Federation (#15872)
- ♦ **IWWG** International Waste Working Group (#15864)
- ♦ IWWG – International Women's Writing Guild (internationally oriented national body)
- ♦ IWW – Industrial Workers of the World (internationally oriented national body)
- ♦ **IXA** International Xenotransplantation Association (#15919)
- ♦ **IXAS** International X-ray Absorption Society (#15920)
- ♦ IXAS – International X-Ray Analysis Society (inactive)
- ♦ **IxDA** Interaction Design Association (#11379)
- ♦ ixo Foundation (unconfirmed)
- ♦ IXO – International X-ray Observatory (inactive)
- ♦ IXS / see International X-ray Absorption Society (#15920)
- ♦ IYAA – Integral Yoga Academy of Australasia (internationally oriented national body)
- ♦ Iyaco – International Youth Aid Council (internationally oriented national body)
- ♦ IYAF / see Aikido Yoshinkai Foundation (#00595)
- ♦ **IYAFP** International Youth Alliance for Family Planning (#15931)
- ♦ IYA – International Yngling Class Association (see: #21760)
- ♦ IYA – International Yoga Therapy Association (no recent information)
- ♦ IYCEF – International Youth Cultural Exchange Federation (internationally oriented national body)
- ♦ IYC – International Youth Centre (internationally oriented national body)
- ♦ IYC – International Youth Committee (internationally oriented national body)
- ♦ IYC – International Youth Council (internationally oriented national body)
- ♦ IYCM / see Youth Climate (#22010)
- ♦ **IYCS** International Young Catholic Students (#15926)
- ♦ **IYCW** International Young Christian Workers (#15927)
- ♦ **IYDU** International Young Democrat Union (#15928)
- ♦ **IYF** International Yoga Federation (#15923)
- ♦ IYF – International Youth Federation for Environmental Studies and Conservation (inactive)
- ♦ IYF – International Youth Fellowship (internationally oriented national body)
- ♦ IYF – International Youth Foundation (internationally oriented national body)
- ♦ IYHF / see Hostelling International (#10950)
- ♦ **IYL** International Youth Library (#15936)
- ♦ **IYLN** International Youth Leadership Network (#15935)
- ♦ **IYMF** International Yehudi Menuhin Foundation (#15922)
- ♦ **IYNA** International Youth Neuroscience Association (#15937)
- ♦ **IYNC Network** International Youth Nuclear Congress Network (#15938)
- ♦ **IYNF** International Young Nature Friends (#15929)
- ♦ **IYPF** International Young Professionals Foundation (#15930)
- ♦ IYRU / see World Sailing (#21760)

- ♦ **IYSF** International Yoga Sport Federation (#15924)
- ♦ IYSH Trust UK / see Reall
- ♦ IYS – International Yakult Symposium (meeting series)
- ♦ IYS – International Yoga Society (internationally oriented national body)
- ♦ **IYTA** International Yoga Teachers Association (#15925)
- ♦ IZA – Institute of Labor Economics (unconfirmed)
- ♦ **IZA** International Zeolite Association (#15941)
- ♦ **IZA** International Zinc Association (#15942)
- ♦ **IZAS** Internationales Zentrum für Ausbildungssysteme (#12487)
- ♦ IZD / see Service Civil International (#19238)
- ♦ **IZE** International Zoo Educators Association (#15944)
- ♦ **IZFS** International Zebrafish Society (#15939)
- ♦ IZG – Ingenieurs Zonder Grenzen (internationally oriented national body)
- ♦ **IZG Internationaal** Ingenieurs Zonder Grenzen Internationaal (#05481)
- ♦ IZIIS – Institute of Earthquake Engineering and Engineering Seismology (internationally oriented national body)
- ♦ **iZiNCG** International Zinc Nutrition Consultative Group (#15943)
- ♦ **IZSF** International Zurkhaneh Sports Federation (#15946)
- ♦ Izumi Foundation (internationally oriented national body)
- ♦ IZWA – Institute for Zero Waste in Africa (internationally oriented national body)
- ♦ **JA Africa** Junior Achievement Africa (#16167)
- ♦ JAA / see Joint Aviation Authorities Training Organisation (#16122)
- ♦ JAAPES / see Japan Association for Asian Studies
- ♦ JAAS – Japan Association for Asian Studies (internationally oriented national body)
- ♦ JAA T / see Joint Aviation Authorities Training Organisation (#16122)
- ♦ **JAA TO** Joint Aviation Authorities Training Organisation (#16122)
- ♦ Jabez International (internationally oriented national body)
- ♦ Jacob Blaustein Institute for the Advancement of Human Rights (internationally oriented national body)
- ♦ Jacob Blaustein Institute for Desert Research (internationally oriented national body)

♦ Jacobs Foundation (JF) 16084

Jacobs Stiftung

Managing Director Seefeldquai 17, Postfach, 8034 Zurich ZH, Switzerland. T. +41443886123. Fax +41443886137. E-mail: jf@jacobsfoundation.org.
URL: http://www.jacobsfoundation.org/

History Dec 1988, Zurich (Switzerland), by Klaus J Jacobs. Registered in accordance with the Swiss Civil Code. **Aims** Support projects that contribute to the *welfare*, *social* productivity and social inclusion of current and future generations of *young people* by understanding and promoting their personal development and employability, their respect for and integration with nature and culture and the challenges faced by social, economic or technological changes. **Structure** Board of Directors, comprising Chairman and 7 Directors. **Languages** English. **Staff** 10.00 FTE, paid. **Finance** Endowment. **Activities** Provides Grants in the area of Child and Youth Development for: innovative research; implementation of pilot interventions; roll-out to apply tested models systematically on a larger scale. Operates the *'Johann Jacobs Museum'* and the *'Marbach Castle Communications Centre'*; organizes conferences. **Events** *Psychosocial Support Forum (PSS Forum)* Windhoek (Namibia) 2019, *Southeast Asian International Regional Workshop* Songkhla (Thailand) 2017. **Publications** Annual Report. **NGO Relations** Member of (2): *Early Childhood Development Action Network (ECDAN, #05155)*; *Philanthropy Europe Association (Philea, #18358)*. Board member of: *International Cocoa Initiative (ICI, #12626)*. Sponsors: *Youth Employment Network (YEN, inactive)*. [2012/XF6187/f/F]

- ♦ Jacob Soetendorp Institute for Human Values (internationally oriented national body)
- ♦ Jacobs Stiftung (#16084)
- ♦ Jacques Delors Centre (internationally oriented national body)
- ♦ Jacques Delors Centre – Hertie School / see Jacques Delors Centre
- ♦ Jacques Delors European Information Centre (internationally oriented national body)
- ♦ Jacques Delors Information Centre / see Centro de Informação Europeia Jacques Delors
- ♦ Jacques Delors Institute (internationally oriented national body)
- ♦ Jadavpur Association of International Relations (internationally oriented national body)
- ♦ JADE / see Junior Enterprises Europe (#16169)

♦ JA Europe 16085

CEO Rue Victor Oudart 7, 1030 Brussels, Belgium. T. +3227359720. Fax +3227332189. E-mail: info@jaeurope.org.
URL: http://www.jaeurope.org/

History 2002. Set up by *Young Enterprise Europe – Jeunes entreprises Europe* and *JA Worldwide (#16091)*. Regional federation of JA Worldwide. Former names and other names: *Junior Achievement Young Enterprise Europe (JA-YE Europe)* – former; *Fédération des jeunes entreprises d'Europe* – former. Registration: Banque-Carrefour des Entreprises, No/ID: 0478.584.538, Start date: 24 Jul 2002, Belgium; EU Transparency Register, No/ID: 519955443616-55, Start date: 20 Jul 2021. **Aims** Work with education and business communities as well as governments to provide young people from primary school to university with experiences that build the skills and competences they will need to succeed in a global economy. **Structure** General Assembly; Board of Directors. **Events** *Launch Meeting of Virtual Guide for Entrepreneurial Learning* Brussels (Belgium) 2014, *Conference* Brussels (Belgium) 2008. **Publications** Annual Report.
Members Organizations in 38 countries and territories:
Albania, Armenia, Austria, Belgium, Bulgaria, Cyprus, Czechia, Denmark, Estonia, Finland, France, Germany, Greece, Hungary, Iceland, Ireland, Isle of Man, Israel, Italy, Latvia, Lithuania, Luxembourg, Malta, Moldova, Netherlands, North Macedonia, Norway, Poland, Portugal, Romania, Russia, Serbia, Slovakia, Spain, Sweden, Switzerland, Türkiye, UK.
NGO Relations Alumni group: *JA-YE Alumni Europe (#16092)*. [2021/XF3305/**E**]

- ♦ JAFSA / see Japan Network for International Education
- ♦ JAFSA: Japan Network for International Education / see Japan Network for International Education
- ♦ JAFSA – Japan Network for International Education (internationally oriented national body)

♦ Jagadguru Kripalu Parishat (JKP) 16086

Contact Mangarh, District Pratapgarh, Kunda, Uttar Pradesh 230204, Kunda UTTAR PRADESH 230204, India. T. +919759003000. E-mail: info@jkp.org.in.
URL: https://jkp.org.in/

History Founded 1975, India, as *International Society of Divine Love (ISDL) – Jagadguru Shree Kripaluji Maharaj*. **Aims** Reveal the eternal knowledge of the *Vedas*, Gita and Bhagwatam – the *Holy Scriptures*; impart the practical processes of divine uplifting based on the ancient path of raganuga *bhakti*.
Members Ashrams in 3 countries:
India, New Zealand, USA. [2016.02.04/XF4321/**F**]

- ♦ Jahanara Foundation (internationally oriented national body)
- ♦ JAICAF – Japan Association for International Collaboration of Agriculture and Forestry (internationally oriented national body)
- ♦ JAICI – Japan Association for International Chemical Information (internationally oriented national body)
- ♦ JAIF – Japan Atomic Industrial Forum (internationally oriented national body)
- ♦ JAIR – Jadavpur Association of International Relations (internationally oriented national body)
- ♦ JAIR – Japan Association of International Relations, Tokyo (internationally oriented national body)
- ♦ JALAS / see Latin American Society of Japan

♦ Jamaat ul-Fuqra 16087

Address not obtained.

History 1980, Brooklyn NY (USA). An offshoot of orthodox African-American Muslims. Also referred to as *Al-Fuqra*. **Aims** Use any means, *political* or *violent*, including *terrorism*, to purify *Islam*. **Structure** Leader based in Pakistan. Fuqra cells in several countries, particularly USA. **Activities** Members live communally in isolated, rural settings so as to practice their faith unaffected by modern (western) culture. Carries out attacks, mainly in Pakistan and USA, on those seen as enemies of Islam, including heretics and Hindus. **Members** Membership countries not available. [2009/XN7930/s/**F**]

- ♦ James Bond 007 International Fan Club / see James Bond International Fan Club (#16088)

♦ James Bond International Fan Club (JBIFC) 16088

Chairman PO Box 21, York, YO41 1WX, UK. E-mail: editor@007.info.
URL: http://www.007.info/

History Founded 1979, UK, as James Bond British Fan Club. Changed name, 1990, to: *James Bond 007 International Fan Club (JBIFC)*. **Activities** Events/meetings; knowledge management/information dissemination. **Publications** *Kiss Kiss Bang Bang* – magazine.
Members Individuals (3,500) in 38 countries and territories:
Argentina, Australia, Austria, Bahamas, Barbados, Belgium, Brazil, Canada, Cyprus, Dominican Rep, Fiji, Hong Kong, India, Iraq, Israel, Jamaica, Japan, Kenya, Malaysia, Malta, Mexico, Monaco, Netherlands, New Zealand, Norway, Pakistan, Poland, Portugal, Saudi Arabia, Singapore, South Africa, Spain, Sweden, Switzerland, Thailand, UK, United Arab Emirates, USA.
[2023/XF3501/v/**F**]

- ♦ James S Coleman African Studies Center, Los Angeles (internationally oriented national body)
- ♦ The James Hutton Institute (internationally oriented national body)
- ♦ JAMES – Japan Association for Middle East Studies (internationally oriented national body)
- ♦ James Martin Center for Nonproliferation Studies (internationally oriented national body)
- ♦ James M Cox Jr Center for International Mass Communication Training and Research (internationally oriented national body)
- ♦ Al Jami'a al Lubnaaniyya al Sakafiyya fil 'Aalam (#21622)
- ♦ Jami-ayyat al-'Awn al-Mubahsir (#05091)
- ♦ JAM International (internationally oriented national body)
- ♦ Jamuhuriya ya Afrika Yamashariki ya Wanafunzi na Wanakijana (internationally oriented national body)
- ♦ Jane Addams Peace Association (internationally oriented national body)

♦ Jane Goodall Institute (JGI) 16089

Jane Goodall Institute Global BWB Secretarial Ltd, 10 Queen Street Place, London, EC4R 1BE, UK. E-mail: mail@janegoodall.global.
Founding Dir 1595 Spring Hill Rd, Ste 550, Vienna VA 22182, USA. T. +17036829220. Fax +17036829312.
Europe Office Mundo-J, Rue de l'Industrie 10,, 1000 Brussels, Belgium. E-mail: info@janegoodall.be.
Global Website: https://www.thejanegoodallinstitute.com/

History 1977, as *Jane Goodall Institute for Wildlife Research, Education and Conservation*. **Aims** Support: *wildlife* research on *primates*, particularly *chimpanzees*, in both *zoo* (captive) and natural *environments*; *conservation* activities to ensure long-term preservation of their habitat, including reforestation; animal welfare activities to ensure their physical and psychological wellbeing; environmental and humanitarian education. Investigate and publicize the *endangered* status of chimpanzees in the wild. **Structure** Board of Directors; Executive Director. **Finance** Members' dues. **Activities** Projects/programmes; research/documentation; advocacy/lobbying/activism. **Events** *Conflicts and Mitigations Conference* Singapore (Singapore) 2019, *Human-wildlife Coexistence in Asia Conference* Singapore (Singapore) 2019. **Publications** *JGI World Report*. Fact sheets.
Members Regional offices in 25 countries and territories:
Australia, Austria, Belgium, Canada, China, Congo DR, France, Gabon, Germany, Hong Kong, Hungary, Italy, Japan, Kenya, Netherlands, Singapore, South Africa, Spain, Sweden, Switzerland, Taiwan, Tanzania UR, Uganda, UK, USA.
IGO Relations Member of: *Congo Basin Forest Partnership (CBFP, #04662)*. Associated with Department of Global Communications of the United Nations. **NGO Relations** Member of: *Africa Biodiversity Collaborative Group (ABCG)*; *Ape Alliance (#00871)*; *Asia for Animals Coalition (AfA, #01250)*; *Extractive Industries Transparency Initiative (EITI, #09229)*; *Ontario Council for International Cooperation (OCIC)*; *Pan African Sanctuary Alliance (PASA, #18064)*. Signatory to: *Global Whale Alliance (GWA, no recent information)*.
[2020/XE3402/j/**E**]

- ♦ Jane Goodall Institute for Wildlife Research, Education and Conservation / see Jane Goodall Institute (#16089)
- ♦ JANIC – Japanese NGO Center for International Cooperation (internationally oriented national body)
- ♦ Jan Masaryk Centre of International Studies (internationally oriented national body)
- ♦ Janz Team Ministries / see TeachBeyond
- ♦ JAPA – Jane Addams Peace Association (internationally oriented national body)
- ♦ Japan-Arab Association (internationally oriented national body)
- ♦ Japan Association for Asian Political and Economic Studies / see Japan Association for Asian Studies
- ♦ Japan Association for Asian Studies (internationally oriented national body)
- ♦ Japan Association for Foreign Student Affairs / see Japan Network for International Education
- ♦ Japan Association for International Chemical Information (internationally oriented national body)
- ♦ Japan Association for International Collaboration of Agriculture and Forestry (internationally oriented national body)
- ♦ Japan Association of International Relations, Tokyo (internationally oriented national body)
- ♦ Japan Association for Latin American Studies / see Latin American Society of Japan
- ♦ Japan Association for Middle East Studies (internationally oriented national body)
- ♦ Japan Atomic Industrial Forum (internationally oriented national body)
- ♦ Japan Bank for International Cooperation (internationally oriented national body)
- ♦ Japan Center for Conflict Prevention / see Reach Alternatives
- ♦ Japan Center for Preventive Diplomacy / see Reach Alternatives
- ♦ Japan Centre for International Exchange (internationally oriented national body)
- ♦ Japan Cooperation Centre for the Middle East (internationally oriented national body)
- ♦ Japan Council against A and H Bombs (internationally oriented national body)
- ♦ Japanese Association for International Law / see Japan Society of International Law
- ♦ Japanese Association for South Asian Studies (internationally oriented national body)
- ♦ Japanese Language Education Global Network / see Global Network of Japanese Language Education (#10492)
- ♦ Japanese NGO Center for International Cooperation (internationally oriented national body)
- ♦ Japanese Organization for International Cooperation in Family Planning (internationally oriented national body)
- ♦ Japanese Red Army (unconfirmed)

♦ Japanese Scandinavian Radiological Society (JSRS) 16090

Contact address not obtained. E-mail: jsrs@jsrs.tokyo – jsrs@pacs.dk.
URL: http://www.jsrs.dk/

History 1985. Founded by Prof Kumazaki and Prof Nordenström at a meeting in Hawaii (USA). **Aims** Facilitate scientific meetings and exchange of younger radiologists. **Structure** Japanese Board; Scandinavian Board. **Languages** English. **Activities** Events/meetings. **Events** *Symposium and 17th Nordic Japan Imaging Informatics Symposium* Stockholm (Sweden) 2023, *Symposium* Sapporo (Japan) 2021, *Symposium* Sapporo (Japan) 2020, *Symposium* Bergen (Norway) 2018.
Members Full in 6 countries:
Denmark, Finland, Iceland, Japan, Norway, Sweden. [2022/XM8066/c/**E**]

- ♦ Japan External Trade Organization (internationally oriented national body)
- ♦ Japan Forum on International Relations (internationally oriented national body)
- ♦ Japan Foundation (internationally oriented national body)
- ♦ Japan Foundation for Shipbuilding Advancement / see Ocean Policy Research Institute
- ♦ Japan Fund for Global Environment (internationally oriented national body)
- ♦ Japan ICU Foundation / see Japan International Christian University Foundation
- ♦ Japan Institute of International Affairs (internationally oriented national body)
- ♦ Japan International Christian University Foundation (internationally oriented national body)
- ♦ Japan International Cooperation Agency (internationally oriented national body)
- ♦ Japan International Cooperation Agency Ogata Sadako Research Institute for Peace and Development (internationally oriented national body)
- ♦ Japan International Cooperation Center (internationally oriented national body)
- ♦ Japan International Corporation of Welfare Services (internationally oriented national body)
- ♦ Japan International Forestry Promotion and Cooperation Center (internationally oriented national body)

- ♦ Japan International Labour Foundation (internationally oriented national body)
- ♦ Japan International Marine Science and Technology Federation (internationally oriented national body)
- ♦ Japan International Medical Technology Foundation (internationally oriented national body)
- ♦ Japan International Research Centre for Agricultural Sciences (internationally oriented national body)
- ♦ Japan International Technology Foundation / see Japan International Medical Technology Foundation
- ♦ Japan International Volunteer Centre (internationally oriented national body)
- ♦ Japan Network for International Education (internationally oriented national body)
- ♦ Japan Overseas Christian Medical Cooperative Service (internationally oriented national body)
- ♦ Japan Overseas Cooperation Volunteers (internationally oriented national body)
- ♦ Japan Overseas Cooperative Association (internationally oriented national body)
- ♦ Japan Shipbuilding Industry Foundation / see Nippon Foundation
- ♦ Japan Society for Afrasian Studies (internationally oriented national body)
- ♦ Japan Society for International Development (internationally oriented national body)
- ♦ Japan Society of International Law (internationally oriented national body)
- ♦ Japan Society for Southeast Asian History / see Japan Society for Southeast Asian Studies
- ♦ Japan Society for Southeast Asian Studies (internationally oriented national body)
- ♦ Japan Tropical Forest Action Network (internationally oriented national body)
- ♦ Jardins botaniques de France et des pays francophones (internationally oriented national body)
- ♦ Jardins du Monde (internationally oriented national body)
- ♦ JAR / see Joint Aviation Authorities Training Organisation (#16122)
- ♦ Jarl Hjalmarson Foundation (internationally oriented national body)
- ♦ Jarl Hjalmarson Stiftelsen (internationally oriented national body)
- ♦ Jarnvagsanställdas (inactive)
- ♦ Järnvägsmännens Internationella Nykterhetsförbund (inactive)
- ♦ JASAS – Japanese Association for South Asian Studies (internationally oriented national body)
- ♦ JASID – Japan Society for International Development (internationally oriented national body)
- ♦ JATAN – Japan Tropical Forest Action Network (internationally oriented national body)

♦ JA Worldwide 16091

Main Office 745 Atlantic Ave, 8th Fl Ste 800, Boston MA 02111, USA. T. +16173158563.
URL: https://www.jaworldwide.org/

History 1994, USA. 1994, as an affiliate of a US national body, set up 1919, Springfield MA (USA), whose international operations started in 1989 with the title *Junior Achievement International*. Current title adopted on merger with *'Junior Achievement Inc'*, 1 Jul 2004. **Aims** Inspire and prepare young people to succeed in a global economy. **Structure** Board of Directors, headed by Chair. Regional offices (6): *Junior Achievement Africa (JA Africa, #16167)*; Americas; Asia-Pacific; *JA Europe (#16085)*; Middle-East and North Africa; Junior Achievement USA. **Staff** 9.00 FTE, paid. **Finance** Supported by: international corporations; foundations; development organizations; individuals. **Activities** Training/education. **Publications** *International Dateline* (4 a year) – newsletter. Annual Report.

Members Offices in 118 countries and territories:
Albania, Algeria, Argentina, Armenia, Austria, Azerbaijan, Bahamas, Bahrain, Bangladesh, Belgium, Bolivia, Botswana, Brazil, Bulgaria, Burkina Faso, Canada, Cayman Is, Chile, China, Colombia, Costa Rica, Curaçao, Czechia, Denmark, Dominica, Dominican Rep, Ecuador, Egypt, Estonia, Eswatini, Finland, France, Gambia, Georgia, Germany, Ghana, Greece, Grenada, Guam, Guatemala, Honduras, Hong Kong, Hungary, Iceland, India, Indonesia, Ireland, Isle of Man, Israel, Italy, Jamaica, Japan, Jordan, Kazakhstan, Kenya, Korea Rep, Kuwait, Latvia, Lebanon, Lithuania, Luxembourg, Malaysia, Mali, Malta, Mauritius, Mexico, Morocco, Namibia, Nepal, Netherlands, New Zealand, Nicaragua, Nigeria, North Macedonia, Norway, Oman, Pakistan, Palestine, Panama, Paraguay, Peru, Philippines, Poland, Portugal, Puerto Rico, Qatar, Romania, Russia, Saudi Arabia, Senegal, Serbia, Singapore, Slovakia, South Africa, Spain, Sri Lanka, St Kitts-Nevis, St Lucia, Sweden, Switzerland, Tajikistan, Thailand, Togo, Trinidad-Tobago, Tunisia, Türkiye, Turkmenistan, Uganda, UK, United Arab Emirates, Uruguay, USA, Venezuela, Vietnam, Virgin Is USA, Yemen, Zambia, Zimbabwe.

NGO Relations Member of the Advisory Committee of: *Making Cents International*. [2020/XF4537/**F**]

- ♦ JAYCEES Internacional / see Junior Chamber International (#16168)
- ♦ JAYCEES International / see Junior Chamber International (#16168)

♦ JA-YE Alumni Europe 16092

Pres address not obtained. E-mail: info@alumnieurope.org.
SG address not obtained. E-mail: camilla@alumnieurope.org.
URL: http://alumni.ja-ye.org/

History 16 Sep 2004, Vilnius (Lithuania), when alumni of *JA Europe (#16085)* held their first conference. **Structure** Board. **Events** *Conference* Vienna (Austria) 2019, *Conference* Copenhagen (Denmark) 2015, *Conference / Annual Conference* Helsinki (Finland) 2014. **Publications** *Flying High* – newsletter. Annual Report.

Members Full in 15 countries:
Austria, Bulgaria, Czechia, Denmark, Estonia, Finland, Germany, Italy, Lithuania, Norway, Portugal, Serbia, Spain, Sweden, Switzerland. [2015/XJ9312/**E**]

- ♦ JA-YE Europe / see JA Europe (#16085)
- ♦ JBF – Jardins botaniques de France et des pays francophones (internationally oriented national body)
- ♦ JB GIS / see UN-GGO: Geospatial Societies (#20324)
- ♦ JBIC – Japan Bank for International Cooperation (internationally oriented national body)
- ♦ JBIFC / see James Bond International Fan Club (#16088)
- ♦ **JBIFC** James Bond International Fan Club (#16088)
- ♦ JBI – Jacob Blaustein Institute for the Advancement of Human Rights (internationally oriented national body)
- ♦ JCAHPO – Joint Commission on Allied Health Personnel in Ophthalmology (internationally oriented national body)
- ♦ JCall – European Jewish Call for Reason (unconfirmed)
- ♦ **JCAM** Jesuit Conference of Africa and Madagascar (#16098)
- ♦ **JCAP** Jesuit Conference of Asia Pacific (#16099)
- ♦ JCAR – Joint Commission on Applied Radioactivity (inactive)
- ♦ JCAS – Berkeley Stanford Joint Center for African Studies (internationally oriented national body)
- ♦ **JCBN** IUBMB-IUPAC Joint Commission on Biochemical Nomenclature (#16078)

♦ JCC Global 16093

Exec Dir 12 Hess St, 94185 Jerusalem, Israel. T. +97226251265ext67. Fax +97226247767. E-mail: info@jccglobal.org.
URL: http://jccglobal.org/

History Founded Jan 1947, as *World Federation of YMHA's and Jewish Community Centres – Fédération mondiale de la jeunesse hébraïque*, also referred to as *World Federation of Jewish Community Centres – Fédération mondiale des centres communautaires juifs*. Reconstituted, May 1977, as *World Confederation of Jewish Community Centres (WCJCC) – Confédération mondiale des centres communautaires juifs – Federación Mundial de los Centros Recreativos Judios – Weltvereinigung der Jüdischen Gesellschaftlichen Zentren*. **Aims** Provide services and programmes that build and strengthen *Jewish communal* life; provide Jewish educational experience to and for Jews of all ages and orientations. **Structure** Board of Directors (meeting twice a year); Executive Committee. **Languages** English, French, Hebrew, Russian, Spanish. **Staff** 2.00 FTE, paid. **Finance** Sources: members' dues. **Activities** Events/meetings; knowledge management/information dissemination; training/education. **Events** *Quadrennial World Conference* Jerusalem (Israel) 2015, *Quadrennial world conference* Tel Aviv (Israel) 2009, *European conference of Jewish community centers* Bucharest (Romania) 2008, *European conference of Jewish community centers* Vilnius (Lithuania) 2006, *Quadrennial world conference* Haifa (Israel) 2005. **Publications** *Lexicon of Terminology*; *World Directory of JCCs*. Newsletter; articles. Information Services: Acts as a centre for information and for referrals on: leadership contacts in various countries; sources for obtaining programme information and technical assistance.

Members National bodies grouping over 2 million members in 39 countries:
Bahamas, Belarus, Belgium, Brazil, Bulgaria, Canada, Chile, Colombia, Costa Rica, Croatia, Czechia, Estonia, Finland, France, Georgia, Germany, Guatemala, Hungary, India, Israel, Italy, Kazakhstan, Latvia, Lithuania, Mexico, Moldova, Montenegro, Netherlands, Poland, Romania, Russia, Serbia, Spain, Sweden, Switzerland, UK, Uruguay, USA, Venezuela.

Regional organizations (3), listed in this Yearbook:
Confederación Latinoamericana Macabea (CLAM, #04459); *European Association of Jewish Community Centres (EAJCC, #06097)*; *European Council of Jewish Communities (ECJC, #06825)*.

NGO Relations Sponsored by: *American Jewish Joint Distribution Committee (JDC, #00785)*; JCC Association of North America; *Maccabi World Union (MWU, #16537)*. [2015.09.07/XC3540/y/**C**]

- ♦ JCC – Joint Coordinating Committee between the Non-Aligned Movement and the Group of 77 (inactive)
- ♦ JCCME – Japan Cooperation Centre for the Middle East (internationally oriented national body)
- ♦ JCCP / see Reach Alternatives
- ♦ JCCTS – Jebsen Center for Counter-Terrorism Studies (internationally oriented national body)
- ♦ JCC – United States/Pacific Island Nations Joint Commercial Commission (internationally oriented national body)
- ♦ JCEA / see Jesuit Conference of Asia Pacific (#16099)
- ♦ JCEAO / see Jesuit Conference of Asia Pacific (#16099)
- ♦ JCEE / see Youth of European Nationalities (#22013)
- ♦ **JCEP** Jesuit Conference of European Provincials (#16100)
- ♦ JCGP – Joint Consultative Group on Policies (no recent information)
- ♦ JCHARS – Joint Commission on High Altitude Research Stations (inactive)
- ♦ **JCI** Camara Júnior Internacional (#16168)
- ♦ JCIE – Japan Centre for International Exchange (internationally oriented national body)
- ♦ **JCI** Jeune chambre internationale (#16168)
- ♦ **JCI** Joint Commission International (#16123)
- ♦ **JCI** Junior Chamber International (#16168)
- ♦ JCI – Justice Coopération Internationale (internationally oriented national body)
- ♦ **JCILF** José Carreras International Leukaemia Foundation (#16153)
- ♦ JCM – Jeunesse Canada Monde (internationally oriented national body)
- ♦ **JCOMM** Joint WMO-IOC Technical Commission for Oceanography and Marine Meteorology (#16151)
- ♦ JCP – Baltic Sea Joint Comprehensive Environmental Action Programme (inactive)
- ♦ JCPD / see Reach Alternatives
- ♦ JCPDS / see International Centre for Diffraction Data
- ♦ **JCPU** Multidisciplinary Joint Committee on Paediatric Urology (#16883)
- ♦ **JCSA** Jesuit Conference of South Asia (#16101)
- ♦ JCSCCF – Joint Commission of the Socialist Countries on Cooperation in the Field of Fisheries (inactive)
- ♦ JCSC / see Council of Commonwealth Societies (#04878)
- ♦ **JCSS** Joint Committee on Structural Safety (#16126)
- ♦ **JCTLM** Joint Committee for Traceability in Laboratory Medicine (#16127)
- ♦ JCUD / see Joint Committee of IAHR and IAW on Urban Drainage (#16124)
- ♦ **JCUD** Joint Committee of IAHR and IAW on Urban Drainage (#16124)
- ♦ JCUSD / see Joint Committee of IAHR and IAW on Urban Drainage (#16124)
- ♦ JCWI – Joint Council for the Welfare of Immigrants (internationally oriented national body)
- ♦ **JDC** American Jewish Joint Distribution Committee (#00785)
- ♦ JDCE – Jeunes démocrates-chrétiens européens (inactive)
- ♦ JDC-ICCD – JDC International Centre for Community Development (unconfirmed)
- ♦ JDC International Centre for Community Development (unconfirmed)
- ♦ JDF International / see Juvenile Diabetes Research Foundation International
- ♦ JDI – Jacques Delors Institute (internationally oriented national body)
- ♦ JDI – Just Detention International (internationally oriented national body)
- ♦ JDM – Jardins du Monde (internationally oriented national body)
- ♦ JDRF International – Juvenile Diabetes Research Foundation International (internationally oriented national body)
- ♦ Jean-Jaurès Foundation (internationally oriented national body)
- ♦ Jean Monnet Association (internationally oriented national body)
- ♦ Jean Monnet Foundation for Europe (#09825)

♦ Jean Piaget Society 16094

Treas address not obtained.
Contact address not obtained.
URL: https://piaget.org/

History 1970. Bylaws adopted Jan 1971; revised: 1981; Jun 1989; Oct 1989; Jan 1996; Jun 1999; Feb 2000; Jun 2001; Jan 2002; Jun 2009. Former names and other names: *Jean Piaget Society: Society for the Study of Knowledge and Development* – full title (1989). Registration: 501(c)(3), USA. **Aims** Provide an open forum for the presentation and discussion of scholarly work on issues related to human knowledge and its development. **Structure** Board of Directors. Standing Committees. **Finance** Sources: members' dues. **Activities** Awards/prizes/competitions; events/meetings; publishing activities. **Events** *Conference* Madrid (Spain) 2023, *Annual Meeting* Philadelphia, PA (USA) 2022, *Annual Meeting* Philadelphia, PA (USA) 2021, *Annual Meeting* Philadelphia, PA (USA) 2020, *Annual Meeting* Portland, OR (USA) 2019. **Publications** *Human Development* (4 a year) – journal. **Members** Regular; Student; Family. Membership countries not specified. [2023/XM8014/**E**]

- ♦ Jean Piaget Society: Society for the Study of Knowledge and Development / see Jean Piaget Society (#16094)
- ♦ **JEASA** Jesuit Educational Association of South Asia (#16102)
- ♦ J&E / see Association Justice and Environment, z.s. (#02774)
- ♦ **J&E** Association Justice and Environment, z.s. (#02774)
- ♦ Jebsen Center for Counter-Terrorism Studies (internationally oriented national body)
- ♦ JEC / see International Young Catholic Students (#15926)
- ♦ **JECFA** Joint FAO/WHO Expert Committee on Food Additives (#16129)
- ♦ **JECI** Jeunesse étudiante catholique internationale (#15926)
- ♦ **JECI** Juventud Estudiantil Católica Internacional (#15926)
- ♦ JEC Internacional / see International Young Catholic Students (#15926)
- ♦ JEC internationale / see International Young Catholic Students (#15926)
- ♦ **JEC** Journées européennes du Cortinaire (#16155)
- ♦ JECSE – Jesuit European Committee for Primary and Secondary Education (unconfirmed)
- ♦ **JEDA** Joint European Drones Associations (#16128)
- ♦ Jeddah convention – Convention for the Conservation of the Red Sea and Gulf of Aden Environment (1982 treaty)

♦ JEDEC 16095

Dir 3103 North 10th Street, Suite 240-S, Arlington VA 22201-2107, USA.
URL: https://www.jedec.org/

History 1944, USA. Former names and other names: *Joint Electron Tube Engineering Council (JETEC)* – former (1944 to 1958); *Joint Electron Device Engineering Council (JEDEC)* – full title (1958). **Aims** Develop open standards for the microelectronics industry. **Structure** Board of Directors. Committees. **Activities** Awards/prizes/competitions; events/meetings; standards/guidelines. **Events** *Meeting* Montréal, QC (Canada) 2019. **Members** Companies. Membership countries not specifiied. [2020/AA0406/**C**]

- ♦ JEDI – Joint European Disruptive Initiative (unconfirmed)
- ♦ JEE / see Spirit of Enterprise Group
- ♦ **JE Europe** Junior Enterprises Europe (#16169)
- ♦ Jeffreys Henry International / see JHI Association (#16116)
- ♦ **JEF** Jeunes européens fédéralistes (#21984)

♦ Jehovah's Witnesses 16096

Témoins de Jéhovah

Address not obtained.

URL: http://www.jw.org/

History 1870, USA. Incorporated 1884 as *Zion's Watch Tower Tract Society*. Name changed, 1896, to *Watch Tower Bible and Tract Society*. Organized under laws of Commonwealth of Pennsylvania (USA) and present name adopted, 1955, as *Watch Tower Bible and Tract Society of Pennsylvania*. Registration: USA, Pennsylvania. **Aims** Understand and apply the *Bible* in everyday life and teach the Bible to others; print and distribute Bibles and disseminate Bible truths in various languages; establish and maintain free private Bible schools and classes; teach, train, prepare and equip men and women as ministers, missionaries, evangelists, preachers, teachers and lecturers. **Structure** Organized without clergy or laity, each individual is dedicated to following only Christ Jesus. "Watch Tower Bible and Tract Society of Pennsylvania" is legal servant for "Governing Body of Jehovah's Witnesses", which directs all activities worldwide. Other legal corporations include: *International Bible Students Association (IBSA, #12338)*; *Watchtower Bible and Tract Society of New York*. Annual Conventions open. **Languages** English. **Staff** 20119.00 FTE, voluntary. **Finance** Sources: voluntary contributions and donations. **Activities** Jehovah's Witnesses follow the pattern of first century Christianity, recognizing and teaching the Bible as God's Word of truth, believing it and following its commandments, thus maintaining constant neutrality toward political issues and activities. They advocate in their public preaching that God's Kingdom in the hand of Jesus Christ is the agency through which mankind will enjoy peace and security with the purpose to have a perfect life in a paradise to be restored on earth. Emphasis is on Bible education by the printed page, by Christian meetings and by public ministry. Organizes: systematic house-to-house ministry; congregational and home Bible studies; preaching in- and out-of-doors; use of radio, printing press and other aids in Bible education. All Witnesses engage in such activities as volunteers, and are not paid for their work. Each congregation conducts at least 5 educational meetings a week; activities are coordinated through regional Branch Offices. Over 6 million people worldwide attend local sessions of the *Theocratic Ministry School* – evening teaching sessions on the Bible at Jehovah's Witness meeting places; literacy and reading improvement classes are also conducted in some localities. National branches hold their own annual conventions. Also coordinates a network to bring humanitarian help in war-torn areas of Africa and in places suffering national disaster. **Events** *Annual international meeting* Paris (France) 2010, *International convention* Seoul (Korea Rep) 2009, *International convention* Vienna (Austria) 2008, *International convention* Copenhagen (Denmark) 2003, *International convention* Sydney, NSW (Australia) 1998. **Publications** *Awake* (12 or 4 a year) – in 81 languages; *The Watchtower* (24 or 12 a year) – in 158 languages. *What Does the Bible Really Teach* (2005); *Pay Attention to Daniel's Prophecy* (1999); *The Secret of Family Happiness* (1996); *Knowledge That Leads to Everlasting Life* (1995); *Jehovah's Witnesses: Proclaimers of God's Kingdom* (1993); *The Greatest Man Who Ever Lived* (1991); *Mankind's Search for God* (1990); *Questions Young People Ask – Answers that Work* (1989); *Reasoning from the Scriptures* (1989); *Worldwide Security under the Prince of Peace*; *True Peace and Security – From What Source*; *The Truth That Leads to Eternal Life*; *Is This Life All There Is*; *Revelation – It's Grand Climax at Hand*; *New World Translation of the Holy Scriptures* – in 37 languages; *My Book of Bible Stories*; *Man's Salvation Out of World Distress at Hand*; *Life – How did it get here ? By Evolution or Creation*; *Let Your Kingdom Come*; *You Can Live Forever in Paradise on Earth*. Booklets; brochures; tracts.
Members Branch Offices (109, marked "), directing 6,613,829 active members in 98,269 congregations in a total of 234 countries and territories, of which 197 specified:
Alaska (*), Albania (*), Andorra, Angola (*), Anguilla, Antigua-Barbuda (*), Argentina (*), Armenia, Aruba, Australia (*), Austria (*), Azerbaijan, Azores, Bahamas (*), Bangladesh, Barbados (*), Belarus, Belgium (*), Belize, Benin (*), Bermuda, Bolivia (*), Bonaire Is, Bosnia-Herzegovina, Botswana, Brazil (*), Bulgaria, Burkina Faso, Burundi, Cambodia, Cameroon (*), Canada (*), Cape Verde, Cayman Is, Central African Rep (*), Chad, Chile (*), Colombia (*), Comoros, Congo Brazzaville, Congo DR (*), Cook Is, Costa Rica (*), Côte d'Ivoire (*), Croatia (*), Cuba, Curaçao (*), Cyprus (*), Czechia (*), Denmark (*), Dominica, Dominican Rep (*), Ecuador (*), El Salvador (*), Equatorial Guinea, Estonia (*), Eswatini, Ethiopia (*), Faeroe Is, Falklands/Malvinas, Fiji (*), Finland (*), France (*), Gabon, Gambia, Georgia, Germany (*), Ghana (*), Gibraltar, Greece (*), Greenland, Grenada, Guadeloupe (*), Guam (*), Guatemala (*), Guiana Fr (*), Guinea, Guinea-Bissau, Guyana (*), Haiti (*), Hawaii (*), Honduras (*), Hong Kong (*), Hungary (*), Iceland (*), India (*), Indonesia, Ireland (*), Israel, Italy (*), Jamaica (*), Japan (*), Kazakhstan, Kenya (*), Kiribati, Korea Rep (*), Kyrgyzstan, Latvia, Lebanon (*), Lesotho, Liberia (*), Liechtenstein, Lithuania, Luxembourg (*), Macau, Madagascar (*), Malawi (*), Malaysia (*), Mali, Malta, Marshall Is, Martinique (*), Mauritius (*), Mayotte, Mexico (*), Micronesia FS, Moldova, Mongolia, Montserrat, Mozambique (*), Myanmar (*), Namibia, Nauru, Nepal, Netherlands (*), New Caledonia (*), New Zealand (*), Nicaragua (*), Niger, Nigeria (*), Niue, Norfolk Is, North Macedonia, Northern Mariana Is (Saipan), Norway (*), Pakistan (*), Palau, Panama (*), Papua New Guinea (*), Paraguay (*), Peru (*), Philippines (*), Poland (*), Portugal (*), Puerto Rico (*), Réunion, Romania (*), Russia (*), Rwanda (*), Samoa (*), Samoa USA, San Marino, Sao Tomé-Principe, Senegal (*), Serbia, Seychelles, Sierra Leone (*), Slovakia (*), Slovenia (*), Solomon Is (*), South Africa (*), Spain (*), Sri Lanka (*), St Helena, St Kitts-Nevis, St Lucia, St Maarten, St Pierre-Miquelon, St Vincent-Grenadines, Suriname (*), Sweden (*), Switzerland (*), Tahiti Is (*), Taiwan (*), Tajikistan, Tanzania UR, Thailand (*), Timor-Leste, Togo (*), Tonga, Trinidad-Tobago (*), Türkiye (*), Turks-Caicos, Tuvalu, Uganda, UK (*), Ukraine, Uruguay (*), USA (*), Vanuatu, Venezuela (*), Virgin Is UK, Virgin Is USA, Wallis-Futuna, Zambia (*), Zimbabwe (*).
Represented in other countries and territories where activities are banned and records incomplete.

[2021/XF3423/**F**]

- ♦ **JEICP** Juristes et économistes internationaux contre la pauvreté (#14006)
- ♦ Jeju Forum – Jeju Forum for Peace and Prosperity (meeting series)
- ♦ Jeju Forum for Peace and Prosperity (meeting series)

♦ Jemaah Islamiya (JI) 16097

Islamic Community

Address not obtained.

History 1993, Malaysia. Around 1993, Johor (Malaysia). Also referred to as *Islamic Group*. An Islamic terrorist organization associated with the Bali bombings, 12 Oct 2002. **Aims** Create an *Islamic state* comprising Indonesia, Malaysia, Singapore (Singapore), southern Philippines and southern Thailand. **NGO Relations** *Al-Qa'ida (#00748)*.

[2009/XG9900/s/**F**]

- ♦ JEMS – Joint European Magnetics Symposia (meeting series)
- ♦ Jemstone Network Ltd / see Journalism in the Eastern Mediterranean – Strategy, Training, Organization (#16154)
- ♦ **JEMSTONE Network** Journalism in the Eastern Mediterranean – Strategy, Training, Organization (#16154)
- ♦ **JENA** Jesuit Justice and Ecology Network Africa (#16105)
- ♦ The Jenner Society / see Edward Jenner Vaccine Society (#05377)
- ♦ JEO / see Spirit of Enterprise Group
- ♦ JEPJ – Juifs Européens pour une Paix Juste (unconfirmed)
- ♦ Jersey Wildlife Preservation Trust / see Durrell Wildlife Conservation Trust
- ♦ Jerusalem Committee / see Al-Quds Committee (#00749)
- ♦ JESAM / see Jesuit Conference of Africa and Madagascar (#16098)
- ♦ **JESC** Jesuit European Social Centre (#16103)
- ♦ JESIUM – Joint European Stable Isotope Users group Meeting (meeting series)
- ♦ Jesuitas – Compañia de Jesús (religious order)

♦ Jesuit Conference of Africa and Madagascar (JCAM) 16098

Conférence des Jésuites d'Afrique et Madagascar – conferêcia dos Jesuitas de África e Madagascar

Pres PO Box 1540-00502, Nairobi, Kenya. T. +254203884528. E-mail: president@jesuits.africa.

Street Address Africama House, Dagoretti Road 260, Karen, Nairobi, Kenya.

URL: https://www.jesuits.africa/

History 1970, by *Society of Jesus (SJ)*. Previously also known as *Jesuit Superiors of Africa and Madagascar*. Also known as *Conference of Major Superiors of the Assistancy of Africa and Madagascar*. Until Jul 2018, known as *Jesuit Conference of Major Superiors of Africa and Madagascar (JESAM)*. **Aims** Advise Fr General of the Society of Jesus on matters relating to the Assistancy of Africa; help Major Superiors realize their responsibility for the Society and the Church in Africa and Madagascar; facilitate union, communication, common vision and effective leadership on formation and mission among Major Superiors. **Structure** Plenary meeting (twice a year); Secretariat. **Languages** English, French, Portuguese. **Finance** Members' dues. **Events** *Assembly* 2006, *Conference on peace and conflict transformation* Nairobi (Kenya) 2005. **Publications** *SJ Africa News* – electronic bulletin.
Members Full in 29 countries:
Angola, Benin, Burkina Faso, Burundi, Cameroon, Chad, Congo Brazzaville, Congo DR, Côte d'Ivoire, Czechia, Ethiopia, Gabon, Ghana, Kenya, Liberia, Madagascar, Malawi, Mozambique, Nigeria, Rwanda, Senegal, South Africa, South Sudan, Sudan, Tanzania UR, Togo, Uganda, Zambia, Zimbabwe.
NGO Relations Runs: *Jesuit Justice and Ecology Network Africa (JENA, #16105)*.

[2019/XF6824/c/**F**]

♦ Jesuit Conference of Asia Pacific (JCAP) 16099

Pres 3/F Sonolux Bldg, Ateneo de Manila Campus, Loyola Heights, 1108 Quezon City, Philippines. T. +63284265974. Fax +63284265974. E-mail: jcapsj@jcapsj.org.

URL: https://jcapsj.org/

History Founded within the framework of *Society of Jesus (SJ)*. Former names and other names: *Bureau of Asian Affairs (BAA)* – former; *East Asian Assistancy* – former; *Jesuit Conference of East Asia (JCEA)* – former; *East Asia and Oceania Assistancy* – former; *Jesuit Conference of East Asia and Oceania (JCEAO)* – former. **Aims** Coordinate and facilitate the mission of Jesuits in the region. **Structure** Major Superiors Assembly (twice a year); President. **Languages** English. **Staff** 8.00 FTE, paid. **Finance** Sources: contributions; donations; grants; members' dues. **Activities** Networking/liaising; projects/programmes. **Events** *Meeting of novice masters of the East Asian assistancy* Seoul (Korea Rep) 1992, *Meeting of rectors/superiors of Jesuit university communities* Hong Kong (Hong Kong) 1991, *Alumni conference* Sydney, NSW (Australia) 1991, *Meeting of the novice masters of East Asia* Hiroshima (Japan) 1990. **Publications** *Jesuits in Asia Pacific* (at least 20 a year) – bulletin. Annual Report.
Members Individuals (over 1,600) in 17 countries and territories:
Australia, Cambodia, China, Hong Kong, Indonesia, Japan, Korea Rep, Macau, Malaysia, Myanmar, New Zealand, Philippines, Singapore, Taiwan, Thailand, Timor-Leste, Vietnam.
NGO Relations Member of (1): *Laudato Si' Movement (#16403)*.

[2022.05.04/XF0725/v/**F**]

- ♦ Jesuit Conference of East Asia / see Jesuit Conference of Asia Pacific (#16099)
- ♦ Jesuit Conference of East Asia and Oceania / see Jesuit Conference of Asia Pacific (#16099)

♦ Jesuit Conference of European Provincials (JCEP) 16100

Jesuit conférence des provinciaux européens

Assistant Rue des Trévires 3, 1040 Brussels, Belgium. T. +3227387720. Fax +3227387729. E-mail: assistant@jesuits.eu.

URL: http://www.jesuits.eu/

History Set up within the framework of *Society of Jesus (SJ)*. Previously also referred to as *Committee of European Jesuit Provincials* and *Conference of European Provincials – SJ – Conférence des provinciaux européens – SJ*. **Aims** Improve collaboration between European Jesuit Provinces (European Union, East Europe, Middle East, Maghreb) in the *apostolic* field and in formation and training of Jesuits. **Structure** General Assembly; President. European Interprovincial Collaboration Groups: Charismatics – Liaison Committee of Jesuits connected with the Charismatic Renewal (CEL); Communities – Christian Life Communities (Euro CLC); Ecumenism – JesEcum; Education – *Jesuit European Committee for Primary and Secondary Education (JECSE)*; Faculties of Philosophy and Theology; Faith and Politics; Formation Delegates; Missions – *Xavier Network of European Jesuit Development NGOs*; Muslims – Les deux rives; Novices – Masters of Novices; Philosophy – Professors of Philosophy (JESPHIL); Prayer – Apostleship of Prayer; Refugees – *Jesuit Refugee Service Europe (JRS Europe, #16107)*; Reviews – Editors of Cultural Reviews; Scholastics – European Jesuits in Formation (EJIF); Sciencie – Jesuits in Science (EJS); Social – *European Jesuits in Social Sciences (EUROJESS, #07607)*; University Chaplains (JUPC-eu); Vocation Delegates; Webmasters – European Jesuit Webmasters (JesWeb). Common Works: *Jesuit European Social Centre (JESC, #16103)*; OCIPE; JRS Europe; *European Catholic Home*; European Schools Brussels; Chapel of the Resurrection. **Languages** English, French, Italian, Spanish. **Staff** 2.50 FTE, paid. **Finance** Jesuit Provinces. **Events** *General Assembly* Lviv (Ukraine) 2014, *General Assembly* Rome (Italy) 2013, *General Assembly* Rome (Italy) 2013, *General Assembly* Soutelo (Portugal) 2012, *General Assembly* Czestochowa (Poland) 2011. **Publications** *JCEP Newsletter* (12 a year).
Members Membership open to Provincials, Vice-Provincials and Regional Superiors of Europe. Full members in 32 countries:
Albania, Austria, Belgium, Bosnia-Herzegovina, Croatia, Czechia, Denmark, France, Germany, Greece, Hungary, Ireland, Italy, Latvia, Lithuania, Luxembourg, Malta, Netherlands, North Macedonia, Poland, Portugal, Romania, Russia, Serbia, Slovakia, Slovenia, Spain, Sweden, Switzerland, Türkiye, UK, Ukraine.
NGO Relations Cooperates with: *Jesuit European Volunteers (JEV, #16104)*; *Jesuit Refugee Service (JRS, #16106)* – Europe.

[2019.12.11/XE1551/**F**]

- ♦ Jesuit Conference of Major Superiors of Africa and Madagascar / see Jesuit Conference of Africa and Madagascar (#16098)
- ♦ Jesuit conférence des provinciaux européens (#16100)

♦ Jesuit Conference of South Asia (JCSA) 16101

Pres 225 Jor Bagh, Delhi 110 003, DELHI 110 003, India. T. +911124642862. E-mail: jcsa.prov@gmail.com.

URL: http://www.jcsaweb.org/

History 1976, within the framework of *Society of Jesus (SJ)*. **Aims** Facilitate unity, communication, common vision and effective leadership among the Jesuit Major Superiors in South Asia. **Structure** Board (meets twice a year). **Publications** *IGNIS: Review of Ignatian Spirituality*; *JIVAN: Jesuits News and Views*; *VIDYAJYOTI: Journal of Theological Reflection*. **Members** Jesuits (4036) in South Asia. Membership countries not specified. **NGO Relations** *Conferencia de Provinciales Jesuitas de América Latina y El Caribe (CPAL, #04658)*; *Jesuit Educational Association of South Asia (JEASA, #16102)*.

[2019.02.12/XF6823/v/**F**]

♦ Jesuit Educational Association of South Asia (JEASA) 16102

Secretary Jesuit Residence, 225 Jor Bagh, Delhi NEW 110 003, DELHI NEW 110 003, India. T. +919643907591. E-mail: jcsa.jea@gmail.com.

URL: http://www.jeasa.org/

History 1961, Delhi (India). Functions within *Jesuit Conference of South Asia (JCSA, #16101)*. **Aims** Bring all Jesuit schools of South Asia under one network; collectively bring out innovative, progressive, value-based education to students in South Asian countries. **Structure** Secretariat functions under *Jesuit Conference of South Asia (JCSA, #16101)*. **Languages** English. Also Asian languages. **Staff** 25.00 FTE, voluntary. **Finance** Supported by member schools. **Activities** Capacity building; certification/accreditation; events/meetings; humanitarian/emergency aid; monitoring/evaluation; research/documentation; standards/guidelines; training/education. **Publications** *JEASA Newsletter*. Educational books; research papers.
Members Jesuit schools in 7 countries:
Afghanistan, Bangladesh, Bhutan, India, Nepal, Pakistan, Sri Lanka.
NGO Relations *Federation of Asian Bishops' Conferences (FABC, #09430)*.

[2021/XM7588/**E**]

- ♦ Jesuiten Flüchtlingdienst (#16106)
- ♦ Jesuitenmission (internationally oriented national body)
- ♦ Jésuites – Compagnie de Jésus (religious order)
- ♦ Jésuites européens en sciences sociales (#07607)
- ♦ Jesuit European Committee for Primary and Secondary Education (unconfirmed)
- ♦ Jesuit European Office – OCIPE / see Jesuit European Social Centre (#16103)

♦ Jesuit European Social Centre (JESC) 16103

Main Office Rue du Cornet 51, 1040 Etterbeek, Belgium. T. +3227379720. E-mail: info@jesc.eu.

Registered Office 15 rue de la Toussaint, 67000 Strasbourg, France. T. +33388223185.

URL: http://www.jesc.eu/

History Founded 11 Dec 1956, Strasbourg (France), by the Bishop of Strasbourg, at the request of the laity, following foundation, 6 Nov 1949, of *Catholic Secretariat for European Problems – Secrétariat catholique pour les problèmes européens (SCPE)*. Original title *Catholic European Study and Information Centre – Office catholique d'information et d'initiative pour l'Europe (OCIPE) – Katholisches Sekretariat für Europäische Fragen – Europai Katolikus Informaciós Központ – Katolickie Biuro Informacji i Inicjatyw Europejskich*. Subsequent title: *Jesuit European Office – OCIPE*. Current title adopted Jan 2012. Registered in accordance with French law, Strasbourg. Offices in Strasbourg, Brussels (Belgium), Budapest (Hungary) and Warsaw (Poland). EU Transparency Register: 73391376305-20. **Aims** Promote reflection and engage in dialogue and advocacy on: political, social and economic problems dealt with by the European Union and the Council of Europe; ethical and spiritual problems arising from society's *responsibility* for its citizens, especially developing countries and the environment, with a special concern for relations between the EU and Africa; cultural and spiritual problems which concern human *values* such as peace, justice and human dignity. Serve as a centre for European initiatives which seeks to establish links between *Christian* organizations and European institutions, support European unification and act as a critical voice in its development. **Structure** Directed by *Society of Jesus (SJ)*. **Languages** English, French, German. **Finance** Financial support from: the Holy See; Society of Jesus; several European episcopal conferences; several private organizations. **Activities** Advocacy/lobbying/activism; monitoring/evaluation. **Events** *Réunion sur la marginalisation, l'intégration et la désintégration en Europe Centrale* Budapest (Hungary) 1995, *Conférence sur les relations Eglise-Etat et le dialogue interreligieux dans la Russie postcommuniste* Strasbourg (France) 1995, *Colloquium for national and European catholic organizations of the laity on a new concept of Europe after the changes in Central and Eastern Europe* Brussels (Belgium) 1990, *European meeting of Jesuits working with migrants, refugees and asylum seekers* Gap (France) 1990, *Session on Europe in the world of today* Lille (France) 1990. **Publications** *EUROPE-INFOS* (11 a year) in English, French, German, Polish. **Members** Not a membership organization. **IGO Relations** *Council of Europe (CE, #04881)*. **NGO Relations** Special relations with: *Commission of the Bishops' Conferences of the European Union (COMECE, #04205)*. Member of: *European Network for Central Africa (EurAc, #07874)*; *European Policy Centre (EPC, #08240)*; *Forum of Catholic Inspired NGOs (#09905)*; *Laudato Si' Movement (#16403)*; *Permanent Forum of European Civil Society (#18322)*. Supports: *European Sunday Alliance (#08856)*. [2020/XE0640/**E**]

♦ Jesuit European Volunteers (JEV) 16104

Address not obtained.
URL: http://www.jesuits-europe.org/jev/

History 1986, Germany FR, by *Jesuit Volunteers International (JVI)*. Comes within the framework of *Society of Jesus (SJ)*. **Aims** Offer young people the opportunity to work as full-time volunteers for justice and peace in activities consistent with their Christian faith, discovering or deepening their spiritual life, by working and living together with underprivileged people. **Structure** General Assembly (annual). Management Board, consisting of not less than 3 and not more than 8 members. **Staff** 1.00 FTE, paid. **Finance** Donations. Budget (annual): about euro 1,240. **Activities** Works with existing organizations concerned with human dignity, supporting their activities and offering the assistance of volunteers whose aptitudes and interests match the organizations' specific requirements. Volunteers (teachers, nurses, jurists, social workers, etc) assist marginalized people, the homeless, delinquents, prisoners, refugees, immigrants, children, old people, living with them and sharing their experience, convictions and hopes. Time is given for reflection and for private and communal prayer. Each community is accompanied by a Jesuit priest or a religious. Holds meetings for volunteers to get to know each other, share experiences, train and have recreation.
Members Volunteers in centres in 10 countries:
Austria, France, Germany, Hungary, Ireland, Philippines, Poland, Slovakia, UK, USA. [2014/XF0978/**F**]

- ♦ Jesuit International Ministries (internationally oriented national body)
- ♦ Jesuit International Volunteers / see Jesuit Volunteers International

♦ Jesuit Justice and Ecology Network Africa (JENA) 16105

Contact Africama House, 260 Dagoretti Road – Karen, Nairobi, 20100, Kenya. E-mail: jeodirector@jesuits.africa.
URL: https://www.jenaafrica.org

History Operates under the aegis of the Justice and Ecology Office of *Jesuit Conference of Africa and Madagascar (JCAM, #16098)*. **Aims** Enable people to unlock their potential, exercise their rights and manage their own lives. **Structure** Board of Governors; Advisory Board. **Consultative Status** Consultative status granted from: *UNEP (#20299)*. [2020/XM8520/**F**]

- ♦ Jesuit Missions (internationally oriented national body)

♦ Jesuit Refugee Service (JRS) 16106

Service jésuite des réfugiés (JRS) – Servicio Jesuita a Refugiados (JRS) – Jesuiten Flüchtlingdienst – Servizio dei Gesuiti per i Rifugiati – Serviço Jesuita aos Refugiados

International Office Borgo Santo Spirito 4, 00193 Rome RM, Italy. T. +39668977468. Fax +39668977461. E-mail: international.communications@jrs.net.
URL: http://www.jrs.net/

History Nov 1980, Rome (Italy), by the *Society of Jesus (SJ)*. Officially registered with the Holy See, 19 Mar 2000. Former names and other names: *Fondazione Pia Autonoma Servizio dei Gesuiti per i Rifugiati* – legal name. **Aims** Accompany, serve and advocate for the rights of refugees and other forcibly displaced persons. **Structure** Decentralized structure: International office in Rome (Italy), headed by International Director. Regional offices (10), mostly headed by Director: Eastern Africa; Asia Pacific; *Jesuit Refugee Service Europe (JRS Europe, #16107)*; Grands Lacs; South Asia; Southern Africa; Latin America and Caribbean; Middle East; West Africa; North America. Projects, each headed by Project Director. **Languages** English, French, Italian, Spanish. **Staff** 1800.00 FTE, paid. **Finance** Sources: private, public, church and Jesuit network donors. **Activities** Projects/programmes; advocacy/lobbying/activism. **Events** *International conference on child soldiers* Amman (Jordan) 2001. **Publications** *Servir* (3 a year); *JRS Dispatches* (22 a year). Annual Report; books.
Members National offices and/or representatives in 52 countries:
Afghanistan, Angola, Australia, Belgium, Bosnia-Herzegovina, Burkina Faso, Cambodia, Cameroon, Canada, Central African Rep, Chad, Colombia, Côte d'Ivoire, Ecuador, Ethiopia, France, Germany, India, Indonesia, Iraq, Ireland, Italy, Jordan, Kenya, Lebanon, Malawi, Malaysia, Malta, Nepal, North Macedonia, Panama, Papua New Guinea, Philippines, Portugal, Romania, Singapore, Slovenia, South Africa, South Sudan, Sri Lanka, Sudan, Sweden, Syrian AR, Thailand, Timor-Leste, Türkiye, Uganda, UK, Ukraine, USA, Venezuela, Zimbabwe.
Consultative Status Consultative status granted from: *ECOSOC (#05331)* (Special). **IGO Relations** Observer to: *International Organization for Migration (IOM, #14454)*. Partner of: *UNHCR (#20327)*. Participant in Fundamental Rights Platform of: *European Union Agency for Fundamental Rights (FRA, #08969)*.
NGO Relations Member of:
- *Consortium of Christian Relief and Development Association (CCRDA)*;
- *European Council on Refugees and Exiles (ECRE, #06839)*;
- *Forum of Catholic Inspired NGOs (#09905)*;
- *International Council of Voluntary Agencies (ICVA, #13092)*;
- *International NGO Platform on the Migrant Workers' Convention (IPMWC, #14367)*;
- *Joint Learning Initiative on Faith and Local Communities (JLI, #16139)*;
- *Latin American Working Group (LAWG)*;
- *NGO Forum on Cambodia (#17124)*;
- *Platform for International Cooperation on Undocumented Migrants (PICUM, #18401)*;
- *Refugee Council (#18739)*;
- *Religious in Europe Networking Against Trafficking and Exploitation (RENATE, #18833)*;
- *Southern Refugee Legal Aid Network (SRLAN, #19879)*;
- *UNITED for Intercultural Action – European Network Against Nationalism, Racism, Fascism and in Support of Migrants and Refugees (UNITED, #20511)*.

African service is member of: *Environment Liaison Centre International (ELCI, no recent information)*. Cambodian office is member of: *Cooperation Committee for Cambodia (CCC)*. Partner of: *WorldFish (#21507)*. [2020/XK0348/**E**]

♦ Jesuit Refugee Service Europe (JRS Europe) 16107

Communications Officer Chausée de Wavre 205, 1050 Brussels, Belgium. T. +3225540221. E-mail: europe.admin@jrs.net.
Regional Dir address not obtained.
URL: http://www.jrseurope.org/

History Mar 1992. A region of *Jesuit Refugee Service (JRS, #16106)* and a project of *Jesuit Conference of European Provincials (JCEP, #16100)*. Registration: Banque-Carrefour des Entreprises, No/ID: 452165993, Belgium. **Aims** Accompany, serve and advocate for the rights of refugees and others who are forcibly displaced. **Structure** General Assembly; Governing Council. **Languages** English. **Staff** 8.00 FTE, paid. **Finance** Private and institutional funding. **Activities** Advocacy/lobbying/activism. **Publications** *JRS Europe Newsletter* (12 a year). Annual Report; reports.
Members Full in 22 countries:
Austria, Belgium, Bosnia-Herzegovina, Croatia, France, Germany, Greece, Hungary, Ireland, Italy, Kosovo, Luxembourg, Malta, North Macedonia, Poland, Portugal, Romania, Serbia, Slovenia, Spain, Switzerland, UK.

IGO Relations Also links with EU institutions. **NGO Relations** Member of (3): *European NGO Platform Asylum and Migration (EPAM, #08051)*; *European Policy Centre (EPC, #08240)*; *International Campaign to Ban Landmines – Cluster Munition Coalition (ICBL-CMC, #12427)*. [2023.02.16/XJ9008/**E**]

- ♦ Jesuit Superiors of Africa and Madagascar / see Jesuit Conference of Africa and Madagascar (#16098)
- ♦ Jesuit Volunteers Corps / see Jesuit Volunteers International
- ♦ Jesuit Volunteers International (internationally oriented national body)

♦ Jesuit Worldwide Learning (JWS) 16108

Exec Pres Rue Jacques Dalphin 18, 1227 Carouge GE, Switzerland. E-mail: jwlinfo@jwl.org.
Germany Kaulbachstrasse 31/33, 80539 Munich, Germany.
URL: https://www.jwl.org/

History Former names and other names: *Jesuit Worldwide Learning – Higher Education at the Margins (JWS)* – full title. **Structure** Executive Committee. Founding Board; Global Advisory Board; Global Leadership Team. **Activities** Training/education. **NGO Relations** Member of (1): *Refugee and Migrant Education Network (RME Network, #18740)*. [2022/AA3001/**F**]

- ♦ Jesuit Worldwide Learning – Higher Education at the Margins / see Jesuit Worldwide Learning (#16108)
- ♦ Jesus Alive Ministries International (internationally oriented national body)
- ♦ Jesus to the Communist World / see The Voice of the Martyrs (#20804)
- ♦ JETACE – Joint European Trade Association for Combustion Equipment (inactive)
- ♦ JETEC / see JEDEC (#16095)
- ♦ JETRO – Japan External Trade Organization (internationally oriented national body)
- ♦ Jeugd met een Opdracht (#22020)
- ♦ Jeugdforum van de Europese Unie (inactive)
- ♦ Jeugdorkest van de Europese Gemeenschap / see European Union Youth Orchestra (#09024)
- ♦ Jeugdorkest van de Europese Union (#09024)
- ♦ Jeugd zonder Land / see Euro-Children
- ♦ Jeune chambre internationale (#16168)
- ♦ Jeune entrepreneur européen / see Spirit of Enterprise Group
- ♦ Jeune Europe, 1834 (inactive)
- ♦ Jeune francophonie (internationally oriented national body)
- ♦ Jeune francophonie: Association de soutien à la création d'un forum international des jeunes pour la Francophonie / see Jeune francophonie
- ♦ **JEUNE** Jeunes entrepreneurs de l'Union européenne (#16109)
- ♦ Jeune musique nordique (inactive)
- ♦ Jeune PPE / see Youth of the European People's Party (#22014)
- ♦ Jeunes ambassadeurs pour la paix et leaders des Nations / see Union internationale des jeunes écrivains et artistes pour la paix, l'amour et la justice
- ♦ Jeunes chirurgiens-dentistes du monde (#21981)
- ♦ Jeunes contre le racisme en Europe (#22003)
- ♦ Jeunes démocrates-chrétiens européens (inactive)
- ♦ Jeunes pour le développement et la coopération (inactive)
- ♦ Jeunes pour les droits de l'homme international (#22019)

♦ Jeunes entrepreneurs de l'Union européenne (JEUNE) 16109

Young Entrepreneurs of the European Union

Address not obtained.
URL: http://www.jeune-pme.eu/

History 1994. Registered in accordance with Belgian law. **Aims** Increase entrepreneurial culture throughout the European Union and in Third World countries; stimulate cross-border discussions and comparisons among members; inform members about developments in European policies and legislation; represent the interests, opinions and problems of members vis à vis the European institutions; promote European and national initiatives relating to the specific interests of members. **Structure** General Assembly (annual). Administrative Council, including President, Secretary-General and Treasurer. **Languages** English, French, Italian, Spanish. **Staff** 1.00 FTE, paid. **Finance** Members' dues. **Activities** Research and development. **Events** *Annual General Assembly* Brussels (Belgium) 2006. **Publications** Newsletter (4 a year).
Members Organizations (10) representing over 300,000 young craftsmen and SME entrepreneurs in 9 countries:
France, Germany, Greece, Hungary, Italy, Luxembourg, Poland, Romania, Spain.
NGO Relations Member of: *European Youth Forum (#09140)*. [2015/XE3231/**E**]

- ♦ Jeunes européens fédéralistes (#21984)
- ♦ Jeunes pour un monde uni (see: #09806)
- ♦ Jeunes professionnels de media européens (#21986)
- ♦ Jeunes Restaurateurs d'Europe / see JRE- Jeunes Restaurateurs (#16157)
- ♦ Les Jeunes Restaurateurs France / see JRE- Jeunes Restaurateurs (#16157)
- ♦ Jeunesse Canada Monde (internationally oriented national body)
- ♦ Jeunesse pour Christ (#22009)
- ♦ Jeunesse des communautés ethniques européennes / see Youth of European Nationalities (#22013)
- ♦ Jeunesse démocratique chrétienne d'Amérique (no recent information)
- ♦ Jeunesse pour l'échange et la compréhension (#22016)
- ♦ Jeunesse étudiante catholique internationale (#15926)
- ♦ Jeunesse européenne fédéraliste / see Young European Federalists (#21984)
- ♦ Jeunesse indépendante chrétienne internationale (no recent information)
- ♦ Jeunesse en mission (#22020)
- ♦ Jeunesse nordique libérale et radicale (no recent information)
- ♦ Jeunesse ouvrière chrétienne – Europe / see JOC Europe (#16118)
- ♦ Jeunesse ouvrière chrétienne européenne / see JOC Europe (#16118)
- ♦ Jeunesse ouvrière chrétienne internationale (#15927)
- ♦ Jeunesse ouvrière chrétienne internationale – Secrétariat européen / see JOC Europe (#16118)
- ♦ Jeunesse rurale européenne (#19007)
- ♦ Jeunesse sans frontière (internationally oriented national body)
- ♦ Jeunesses Mariales – Fédération Internationale des Enfants de Marie Immaculée (religious order)

♦ Jeunesses Musicales International (JMI) 16110

Exec Dir Sq Eugene Plasky 92-94, Box 13, 1030 Brussels, Belgium. Fax +3225144755. E-mail: mail@jmi.net.
URL: http://www.jmi.net/

History 17 Jul 1945, Brussels (Belgium). Former names and other names: *Fédération internationale des jeunesses musicales (FIJM)* – former; *International Federation of Musical Youth* – former; *Internationale Federatie van Jeugd en Muziek* – former. Registration: Banque-Carrefour des Entreprises, No/ID: 0820.748.177, Start date: 31 Aug 2009, Belgium. **Aims** Help young people to realise their potential through tailor made music programmess, productions and competitions; offer music opportunities that make a difference in the lives of young people and consequently their communities **Structure** General Assembly (annual); Board; Legal and Elections Commissions; Programme Committees. Includes: Euro-Arab Youth Music Centre; *Music Crossroads (#16912)*; *World Youth Choir (WYC, #21955)*. **Languages** English, French, Spanish. **Staff** 230.00 FTE, paid; 2300.00 FTE, voluntary. **Finance** Sources: fundraising; government support; grants; members' dues; revenue from activities/projects; subscriptions; subsidies. Supported by: BELSPO; *Council of Europe (CE, #04881)*; Creative Europe; *European Commission (EC, #06633)* (Erasmus+); *European Parliament (EP, #08146)*; *ILO (#11123)*; National Lottery Belgium; *Transparency International (TI, #20223)*. Annual budget: 1,300,000 EUR (2021). **Activities** Advocacy/lobbying/activism; awareness raising; capacity building; events/meetings; networking/liaising; projects/programmes; standards/guidelines; training/education. **Events** *Congress and General Assembly* Harare (Zimbabwe) 2023, *JMI Annual General Assembly* Banyoles (Spain) 2022, *JMI Annual General Assembly* Brussels (Belgium) 2021, *Congress and General Assembly* Cape Town (South Africa) 2020, *Congress and General Assembly* Suzhou (China) 2019. **Publications** *Ethno Newsletter* (4 a year); *JMI News* (4 a year); *Young Audiences Music Newsletter* (4 a year); *Fair Play Newsletter* (2 a year); *JMI Highlights* (annual).

Members Full; Associate. Members in 60 countries:
Albania, Algeria, Argentina, Australia, Austria, Azerbaijan, Belgium, Bosnia-Herzegovina, Brazil, Bulgaria, Cambodia, Cameroon, Canada, Chile, China, Croatia, Cyprus, Czechia, Denmark, Estonia, Finland, France, Germany, Ghana, Greece, Hungary, Iceland, India, Indonesia, Italy, Jordan, Lebanon, Luxembourg, Malawi, Montenegro, Mozambique, Netherlands, New Zealand, North Macedonia, Norway, Palestine, Poland, Portugal, Romania, Serbia, Slovakia, Slovenia, Solomon Is, Spain, Sweden, Switzerland, Tanzania UR, Tunisia, Türkiye, Uganda, UK, Uruguay, USA, Zimbabwe.
Consultative Status Consultative status granted from: *UNESCO (#20322)* (Consultative Status). **IGO Relations** Accredited by (1): *United Nations Office at Vienna (UNOV, #20604)*. **NGO Relations** Member of (2): *Culture Action Europe (CAE, #04981)*; *European Music Council (EMC, #07837)*. Instrumental in setting up (2): *Nordic Youth Orchestra (#17475)*; Young Euro Classic. Founder member of: *International Music Council (IMC, #14199)*. Observer member of: *European Youth Forum (#09140)*. Partnership agreements with: *European Choral Association – Europa Cantat (#06541)*; *International Federation for Choral Music (IFCM, #13388)*. [2022.06.15/XC2047/**C**]

- Jeunesse universelle (inactive)
- Jeunes Talents Cirque Europe / see CircusNext (#03943)
- Jeunes Turcs de Belfort / see COJEP International – Conseil pour la Justice, l'Egalité et la Paix (#04090)
- **JEV** Jesuit European Volunteers (#16104)
- **JEV** Jugend Europäischer Volksgruppen (#22013)

♦ Jewish Agency for Israel 16111

Agence juive pour Israël – Agencia Judia para Israel – Agência Judaica para Israel
CEO 48 King George Street, 9426218 Jerusalem, Israel. T. +97226202222. Fax +97226202303. E-mail: pniyottzibor@jafi.org.
URL: http://www.jewishagency.org/
History 1929. Founded when joined with non-Zionist Jewish groups as instrument through which world Jewry could assist in building up the Jewish national home. During the British Mandate in Palestine the Agency had semi-official status, acting as representative of Jewish people in all matters concerning rebuilding of the country. Towards the end of this period the Executive of the Agency became practically identical with the Executive of the World Zionist Organization. Since the emergence of the State of Israel in 1948, the Agency acts on behalf of Jews throughout the world who are concerned for the development of Israel, the immigration of Jews into the country and the unity of the Jewish people. Works in close cooperation with the Government of Israel. Former names and other names: *The Jewish Agency for Palestine* – former (1929 to 1948). **Aims** Promote Aliyah (immigration to Israel). **Structure** Assembly (at least once every two years); Board of Governors; Executive. **Languages** Amharic, English, French, German, Hebrew, Portuguese, Russian, Spanish. **Staff** 1240.00 FTE, paid. Thousands voluntary. **Finance** Sources: donations; fees for services; private foundations; revenue from activities/projects. Supported by: Jewish Federations of North America; *Keren Hayesod – United Israel Appeal (UIA, #16183)*. **Activities** Awareness raising; capacity building; financial and/or material support; networking/liaising; training/education. **Events** *Conference on communities in transition* Jerusalem (Israel) 2008, *Annual Assembly* Jerusalem (Israel) 2000, *Annual Assembly* Jerusalem (Israel) 1999, *Annual Assembly* Jerusalem (Israel) 1998, *Annual Assembly* Jerusalem (Israel) 1996. **NGO Relations** Member of (1): *World Jewish Restitution Organization (WJRO, #21601)*. [2020.06.23/XE2838/**E**]

- The Jewish Agency for Palestine / see Jewish Agency for Israel (#16111)
- Jewish Association for the Protection of Girls, Women and Children (inactive)
- The Jewish Foundation for the Righteous (internationally oriented national body)

♦ Jewish Law Association (JLA) 16112

Association du droit juif
Treas 108-26 65 Ave, Forest Hills NY 11375, USA.
URL: http://www.legaltheory.demon.co.uk/jlas/
History Founded 1978, Oxford (UK). **Aims** Promote study and research in Jewish law. **Structure** Members Meeting (every 2 years); Executive Committee. **Languages** English, Hebrew. **Finance** Members' dues (annual). **Activities** Events/meetings; knowledge management/information dissemination. **Events** *International Conference* Tel Aviv (Israel) 2016, *Biennial meeting / International Conference* Manchester (UK) 2008, *International Conference* Ramat Gan (Israel) 2006, *International Conference* Boston, MA (USA) 2004, *Biennial meeting / International Conference* Ramat Rahel (Israel) 2002. **Publications** *Jewish Law* (annual); *Newsletter of the Jewish Law Association*. *Jewish Law Association Studies*.
Members Individuals scholars; lawyers; rabbis and others interested in Jewish law, in 10 countries:
Belgium, France, Germany, Israel, Italy, Luxembourg, Spain, Switzerland, UK, USA. [2016/XE1072/v/**E**]

- Jewish Legal Heritage Society (internationally oriented national body)

♦ Jewish National Fund (JNF) 16113

Fonds national juif – Keren Kayemet Leisrael (KKL)
JNF-US 42 East 69th St, New York NY 10021, USA. E-mail: jewishnationalfund@jnf.org.
Israel Office 206 Jaffa St, 94383 Jerusalem, Israel. E-mail: pneyot-tzibur@kkl.org.il.
URL: https://www.kkl-jnf.org/
History 1901, Basel (Switzerland). Founded at 5th Zionist Congress, following suggestion of Prof Zvi Hermann Schapira, 1897, at 1st Congress. Original headquarters in Jerusalem; additionally incorporated in the USA, 26 Jan 1926. Registration: 501(c)3, No/ID: 13-1659627, USA. **Aims** Build for Israel's future; respond in times of crisis and need; improve the quality of life for all who live in the *Middle East*. Originally set up to purchase land in Palestine with the aim of: founding a Jewish state; establishing modern Jewish cities; setting up *collective* communities – *kibbutzim* – and workers' communities; act as an environmental agency; pioneer higher education and *Zionist* education, helping to connect Jewish communities to the homeland; reach out to every Jewish community worldwide. **Activities** Following setting up of State of Israel, May 1948, main focus on: settling new areas; absorbing immigrants and providing them with employment working the land; reclamation for agricultural purposes; afforestation and development projects; rehabilitating rivers and streams; developing tourism. Sets up and administers farms; organizes afforestation programmes; founds secondary schools; set up an experimental agricultural station as the the basis of most Israeli agriculture. *International Arid Lands Consortium (IALC)* set up 1991 by JNF-US, in partnership with other bodies. Land maintained by JNF cannot be sold, but only leased for periods of 49 years. As of 2012 has purchased and helped to develop land by planting over 240 million trees, building more than 200 dams and reservoirs, developing over 250,000 acres of land and creating over 1,000 parks. **Members** National funds in various countries. **IGO Relations** *UNESCO (#20322)*; *UNEP (#20299)*. [2023/XU5589/f/**F**]

- Jewish Organization of Prisoners of Fascist Concentration Camps, Ghettos 'RUF' (internationally oriented national body)
- Jewish Peace Fellowship (internationally oriented national body)
- Jewish Prisoner Services International (internationally oriented national body)
- Jewish Territorial Organization (inactive)
- Jewish Voice Ministries International (internationally oriented national body)
- Jewish Volunteer Corps of American Jewish World Service (internationally oriented national body)

♦ Jewish Women International (JWI) 16114

CEO 1129 20th St NW, Ste 801, Washington DC 20036, USA. T. +12028571300. Fax +12028571380.
URL: https://www.jwi.org
History 1897, USA. Originally operated within the framework of *B'nai B'rith International (BBI, #03290)*; now operates separately. Former names and other names: *Women's Supreme Council* – former (1897 to 1957); *B'nai B'rith Women (BBW)* – former (1957). **Aims** Strengthen the lives of women, children and families through education, advocacy and action. **Structure** Based in Washington DC (USA). **Activities** Programmes: domestic violence awareness; counteracting anti-semitism and prejudice; support for residential treatment centre in Israel. **Events** *International domestic violence conference* Baltimore, MD (USA) 2003. **Publications** *Jewish Women* – magazine.
Members Active in 5 countries:
Canada, Colombia, Israel, UK, USA.
IGO Relations Associated with Department of Global Communications of the United Nations. [2021/XE0076/**E**]

- Jewish Women's League of the United Synagogue of America / see Women's League for Conservative Judaism
- Jews for Jesus (internationally oriented national body)

♦ Jews for Judaism 16115

Baltimore Office 5806 Park Heights Ave, Baltimore MD 21215, USA. T. +14105005430. E-mail: baltimore@jewsforjudaism.org.
URL: http://east.jewsforjudaism.org/
History Founded 1983. **Aims** Counteract aggressive and deceptive proselytizing efforts of individuals and groups that target Jews for conversion to other faiths. **Structure** Offices in: Baltimore MD (USA); Los Angeles CA (USA); Toronto ON (Canada); Sydney (Australia). [2015.08.27/XF3840/**F**]

- **JFC Brunssum** Allied Joint Force Command Brunssum (#00734)
- **JFC** Jugend für Christus (#22009)
- **JFC Naples** Allied Joint Force Command Naples (#00735)
- **JFC** World Bank – Civil Society Joint Facilitation Committee (#21217)
- JFGE – Japan Fund for Global Environment (internationally oriented national body)
- JFIR – Japan Forum on International Relations (internationally oriented national body)
- **JF** Jacobs Foundation (#16084)
- JF – Jahanara Foundation (internationally oriented national body)
- JFJ – Jews for Jesus (internationally oriented national body)
- JFR – The Jewish Foundation for the Righteous (internationally oriented national body)
- **JGI** Jane Goodall Institute (#16089)
- **JHG** Julius-Hirschberg-Gesellschaft (#16166)

♦ JHI Association 16116

Contact PO Box 199, Hillside NJ 07205, USA. T. +19734661430. Fax +19734661431. E-mail: info@jhi.com.
URL: http://www.jhi.com/
History 1975, as a worldwide association of independent medium-sized accounting firms. Changed title to *Jeffreys Henry International*, 1977. Merged with *ACPA International (inactive)*, Jan 2005, when current title was adopted. **Aims** Provide a constant exchange of information and referrals on current *taxation*, *accounting* and *audit* practice, *business* incorporation and planning and industry matters; provide education and training and updates on best practices. **Structure** Executive Committee, consisting of Chairman and 7 members. Regions (3): Americas; Asia-Pacific; Europe/Middle East/Africa. **Languages** English. **Finance** Members' dues. **Activities** Facilitates introduction and referrals and transfers of knowledge among members, thereby enhancing their ability to offer the widest range of services. **Events** *International Conference* Singapore (Singapore) 2015, *Americas Region Meeting / Americas Conference* Philadelphia, PA (USA) 2013, *Europe, Middle East, Africa Region Meeting / European Region Meeting* Vienna (Austria) 2013, *Tax and Audit Conference* Lyon (France) 2012, *International Annual General Meeting* Melbourne, VIC (Australia) 2012. **Publications** Newsletter; regional bulletins. Annual Review.
Members Accountancy, business advisor and financial consultancy firms in 52 countries and territories:
Argentina, Australia, Austria, Belgium, Brazil, Bulgaria, Cameroon, Canada, Chile, China, Cyprus, Czechia, Dominican Rep, Ecuador, Egypt, El Salvador, France, Germany, Guatemala, Hong Kong, India, Indonesia, Ireland, Israel, Italy, Jamaica, Japan, Kenya, Korea Rep, Lebanon, Liechtenstein, Luxembourg, Malaysia, Mauritius, Mexico, Netherlands, New Zealand, Nigeria, Pakistan, Peru, Portugal, Puerto Rico, Russia, Singapore, Spain, Switzerland, Taiwan, Türkiye, UK, United Arab Emirates, Uruguay, USA. [2020/XF0964/**F**]

- JHPIEGO – Johns Hopkins Program for International Education in Gynecology and Obstetrics (internationally oriented national body)
- JIA – Junta Interamericana de Agricultura (see: #11434)
- JICA – Japan International Cooperation Agency (internationally oriented national body)
- JICA Ogata Research Institute / see Japan International Cooperation Agency Ogata Sadako Research Institute for Peace and Development
- JICA Research Institute / see Japan International Cooperation Agency Ogata Sadako Research Institute for Peace and Development
- JICA-RI / see Japan International Cooperation Agency Ogata Sadako Research Institute for Peace and Development
- JICE – Japan International Cooperation Center (internationally oriented national body)
- JICI – Jeunesse indépendante chrétienne internationale (no recent information)
- JICI – Juventud Independiente Cristiana Internacional (no recent information)
- JIC / see Joint Meetings Industry Council (#16140)
- JICUF Endowment / see Japan International Christian University Foundation
- JICUF – Japan International Christian University Foundation (internationally oriented national body)
- JICWELS – Japan International Corporation of Welfare Services (internationally oriented national body)
- **JID** Junta Interamericana de Defensa (#11425)
- **JIFE** Junta Internacional de Fiscalización de Estupefacientes (#14212)
- JIFPRO – Japan International Forestry Promotion and Cooperation Center (internationally oriented national body)
- Jihad Group / see Al-Jihad (#00637)
- JIIA – Japan Institute of International Affairs (internationally oriented national body)
- **JI** Jemaah Islamiya (#16097)
- JILAF – Japan International Labour Foundation (internationally oriented national body)
- Jimmy and Rosalynn Carter School for Peace and Conflict Resolution (internationally oriented national body)

♦ Jim Smith Society 16117

Public Relations Officer 390 Tina St, Hollister MO 65672, USA.
URL: http://www.jimsmithsociety.com/
History 1969. **Structure** Officers: President; Vice President; Secretary; Treasurer; Historian/Quartermaster; Public Relations Officer; Fun Fest Chairman. **Languages** English. **Staff** Voluntary. **Finance** Sources: meeting proceeds; members' dues; sale of publications. **Activities** Events/meetings. **Publications** *Jim Smith Society Newsletter* (4 a year).
Members Individuals (1,826) named Jim Smith, in 6 countries:
Australia, Canada, Ireland, New Zealand, UK, USA.
Also members in South America. Membership countries not specified. [2021.05.26/XE1927/**E**]

- JIMSTEF – Japan International Marine Science and Technology Federation (internationally oriented national body)
- JIMTEF – Japan International Medical Technology Foundation (internationally oriented national body)
- JIN Climate and Sustainability (internationally oriented national body)
- **JINR** Joint Institute for Nuclear Research (#16134)
- Jinrui Aizen Kai (#20678)
- JINT – Coördinatie-orgaan voor Internationale Jongerenwerking (internationally oriented national body)
- JIRCAS – Japan International Research Centre for Agricultural Sciences (internationally oriented national body)
- JITMM – Joint International Tropical Medicine Meeting (meeting series)
- Jiu-Jitsu International Federation / see Ju-Jitsu International Federation (#16164)
- **JIU** Joint Inspection Unit of the United Nations (#16133)
- JIV / see Jesuit Volunteers International
- JIVD / see JIVD-AER
- JIVD-AER (internationally oriented national body)
- **JIVE** Joint Institute for VLBI in Europe (#16135)
- **JJEU** Ju-Jitsu European Union (#16163)
- **JJIF** Ju-Jitsu International Federation (#16164)
- JJIF – Ju-Jitsu International Federation (inactive)
- **JKP** Jagadguru Kripalu Parishat (#16086)
- **JLA** Jewish Law Association (#16112)

- JLHS – Jewish Legal Heritage Society (internationally oriented national body)
- **JLI** Joint Learning Initiative on Faith and Local Communities (#16139)
- JLS – John Locke Society (unconfirmed)
- JMCIS – Jan Masaryk Centre of International Studies (internationally oriented national body)
- **JMIC** Joint Meetings Industry Council (#16140)
- **JMI** Jeunesses Musicales International (#16110)
- JMU – Jóvenes por un Mundo Unido (see: #09806)
- JMVI – Jewish Voice Ministries International (internationally oriented national body)
- **JNC** Just Net Coalition (#16173)
- **JNF** Jewish National Fund (#16113)
- Joan B Kroc Institute for International Peace Studies / see Kroc Institute for International Peace Studies
- Joan B Kroc Institute for Peace and Justice (internationally oriented national body)
- JOCA – Japan Overseas Cooperative Association (internationally oriented national body)

♦ JOC Europe 16118

Secretariat Anderlechtsesteenweg 4, 1000 Brussels, Belgium. T. +3225137912. Fax +3200000000. E-mail: joceurope@joceurope.org.

URL: http://www.joceurope.org/

History 1925, Belgium. Assisted in setting up, 1945, Brussels (Belgium), the *International Young Christian Workers (IYCW, #15927)*, known also as *'JOC internationale'*. Became international itself in 1957. Functions as the European branch of 'JOC internationale'. Former names and other names: *JOC internationale – Secrétariat européen de la Jeunesse ouvrière chrétienne (JOC européenne)* – former; *European Young Christian Workers (EYCW)* – former; *Jeunesse ouvrière chrétienne européenne (JOC)* – former; *Jeunesse ouvrière chrétienne internationale – Secrétariat européen* – former; *Young Christian Workers – Europe* – former; *Jeunesse ouvrière chrétienne – Europe (JOC Europe)* – former; *Juventud Obrera Cristiana – Europa* – former; *Christliche Arbeit Jugend – Europa* – former. **Aims** Find a global solution to current problems of young workers by promoting *educational* activities and facilitating exchange of experience. **Structure** Continental Meeting (annual); European Commission; Executive Bureau; Commissions; Working Groups. **Languages** Dutch, English, French, German, Spanish. **Staff** 2.00 FTE, paid. **Finance** Sources: national branches; european institutions; foundations. **Activities** Events/meetings; networking/liaising; training/education. **Events** *Seminar on improvement of living and working conditions of the working youth in the European Union and in Eastern Europe* Dworp (Belgium) 2003, *Commitment and motivation of youth in the year 2001* Strasbourg (France) 2001, *European charter of demands against exclusion* Luxembourg (Luxembourg) 1998, *Meeting on professional training in Europe* Strasbourg (France) 1996, *Seminar on unemployment* Strasbourg (France) 1996. **Publications** Dossiers.

Members National organizations (13) in 9 countries:
Austria, Belgium, Germany, Ireland, Italy, Luxembourg, Slovakia, Spain, Switzerland.
Associate bodies in 6 countries:
Czechia, Hungary, Netherlands, Poland, Romania, Ukraine. [2022.10.19/XD8365/**E**]

- JOC européenne / see JOC Europe (#16118)
- **JOCI** Jeunesse ouvrière chrétienne internationale (#15927)
- **JOCI** Juventud Obrera Cristiana Internacional (#15927)
- JOC internationale / see International Young Christian Workers (#15927)
- JOC internationale – Secrétariat européen de la Jeunesse ouvrière chrétienne / see JOC Europe (#16118)
- JOC / see JOC Europe (#16118)
- JOCS – Japan Overseas Christian Medical Cooperative Service (internationally oriented national body)
- JOCV – Japan Overseas Cooperation Volunteers (internationally oriented national body)
- **JODI** Joint Organisations Data Initiative (#16143)
- Joe Homan Trust / see International Children's Trust
- Johannes Wier Foundation for Health and Human Rights, Netherlands (internationally oriented national body)
- Johannes Wier Stichting voor Mensenrechten en Gezondheidszorg (internationally oriented national body)

♦ Johanniter International (JOIN) 16119

General Manager Rue Joseph II 166, 1000 Brussels, Belgium. T. +3222821045. E-mail: join.office@johanniter.org.

URL: http://www.johanniter.org/

History Brussels (Belgium). Proposed May 1999, by enterprises of *Order of St John* in Europe. Letter of intent agreed upon Jul 2000, Riga (Latvia). Resolution passed Oct 2000, Basel (Switzerland). Registration: Banque-Carrefour des Entreprises, Start date: Feb 2006, Belgium; EU Transparency Register, No/ID: 14505908784-58. **Aims** Serve humanity with *medical* services and *first aid*, *social care*, international *aid*, *disaster relief* and youth work. **Structure** Annual General Meeting; Board; Working Groups; Secretariat. **Languages** English, French, German. **Staff** 3.00 FTE, paid. **Finance** Sources: members' dues. **Activities** Advocacy/lobbying/activism; awareness raising; events/meetings; monitoring/evaluation; networking/liaising; projects/programmes; standards/guidelines. **Events** *Annual General Meeting* Brussels (Belgium) 2021, *Annual General Meeting* Brussels (Belgium) 2020, *Annual General Meeting* Zurich (Switzerland) 2019, *Annual General Meeting* Lignano Sabbiadoro (Italy) 2018. **Publications** *JOIN Newsletter*. Annual Review; first aid guidelines.

Members National charities in 16 countries and territories:
Austria, Cyprus, Denmark, England, Finland, France, Germany, Hungary, Israel, Italy, Latvia, Malta, Netherlands, Poland, Sweden, Switzerland.

IGO Relations Institutions of *European Union (EU, #08967)*. **NGO Relations** *Knights Hospitallers of the Sovereign Order of Saint John of Jerusalem, Knights of Malta – The Ecumenical Order*. [2021.09.01/XM6888/**E**]

♦ Johanniter-Unfall-Hilfe (JUH) 16120

Secretariat Lützowstr 94, 10785 Berlin, Germany. T. +4930269970. Fax +49306997444. E-mail: nicole.reinke@johanniter.de.

URL: http://www.johanniter.de/

History 1952. **Aims** Enable people to survive in dignity and reduce their vulnerability and that of their communities throughout humanitarian crises and immediately after a disaster. **Languages** English, French, German, Spanish. **Staff** 57.00 FTE, paid. **Finance** Annual budget (2017): euro 18,000,000. **Activities** Humanitarian/emergency aid. **Publications** Annual Report; project reports.

Members Organizations in 5 countries:
Austria, Finland, Hungary, Italy, Latvia.

IGO Relations *ECHO (inactive)*. **NGO Relations** Member of: *International Council of Voluntary Agencies (ICVA, #13092)*. [2018.09.10/XG2110/**E**]

- John Abraham Memorial Christian Relief Fund / see Christian Relief Fund
- John Bassett Moore Society of International Law (internationally oriented national body)
- John C Whitehead School of Diplomacy and International Relations (internationally oriented national body)
- John D and Catherine T MacArthur Foundation / see MacArthur Foundation
- John E Fogarty International Center (internationally oriented national body)
- John E Fogarty International Center for Advanced Study in the Health Sciences / see John E Fogarty International Center
- John E Mack Institute (internationally oriented national body)
- John F Kennedy Institute for North American Studies (internationally oriented national body)
- John F Kennedy Institut für Nordamerikastudien (internationally oriented national body)
- John F Kennedy School of Government (internationally oriented national body)
- John Knox International Reformed Centre (internationally oriented national body)
- John Locke Society (unconfirmed)
- John Merck Fund (internationally oriented national body)

♦ John Paul II Foundation for the Sahel 16121

Fondation Jean Paul II pour le Sahel

SG BP 4890, Ouagadougou, Burkina Faso. T. +22625365314. Fax +22625365393. E-mail: fond.jp2@fasonet.bf.

URL: https://www.fondationjp2sahel.org/en/presentation-2/

History 22 Feb 1984. **Aims** Improve social-economic conditions of local populations of the Sahel by promoting the protection of the environment and by fighting against *desertification*, *drought* and *poverty*; facilitate the training of competent persons who would put themselves at the disposal of their countries and brothers, without any discrimination, in a spirit of full and joint human promotion. **Structure** Board of Directors (meets once a year). Secretariat, headed by Secretary-General. Project Committee. **Languages** French. **Staff** 6.00 FTE, paid. **Activities** Projects/programmes; financial and/or material support; capacity building; training/education; awareness raising. **Publications** *Solidarité* (2 a year) – bulletin.

Members Active in 9 countries:
Burkina Faso, Cape Verde, Chad, Gambia, Guinea-Bissau, Mali, Mauritania, Niger, Senegal. [2019.07.03/XF2108/f/**F**]

- Johns Hopkins Foreign Policy Institute, Washington DC (internationally oriented national body)
- Johns Hopkins Program for International Education in Gynecology and Obstetrics (internationally oriented national body)
- Johns Hopkins University Center for Communications Programs (internationally oriented national body)
- John Sloan Dickey Center for International Understanding (internationally oriented national body)
- Johnson Foundation, The (internationally oriented national body)
- JOICFP – Japanese Organization for International Cooperation in Family Planning (internationally oriented national body)
- Joined Hands – Campaign Against Hunger / see Manos Unidas
- **JOIN** Johanniter International (#16119)
- Joint Administration of the Turkic Arts and Culture / see International Organization of Turkic Culture (#14482)
- Joint Africa Board (inactive)
- Joint Aid Management – JAM International (internationally oriented national body)
- Joint Airworthiness Authorities / see Joint Aviation Authorities Training Organisation (#16122)
- Joint Anti-Locust and Anti-Aviarian Organization (inactive)
- Joint Arab Defence Council (no recent information)
- Joint Arab Scientific Council for the Utilization of Atomic Energy / see Arab Atomic Energy Agency (#00901)
- Joint Aviation Authorities / see Joint Aviation Authorities Training Organisation (#16122)

♦ Joint Aviation Authorities Training Organisation (JAA TO) 16122

Mailing Address PO Box 3000, 2130 KA Hoofddorp, Netherlands. T. +31235679790. E-mail: reception@jaato.com.

URL: http://www.jaato.com/

History 1970. Founded to meet the needs of European industry for common certification codes for large aircraft and engines, especially those manufactured by international consortia. Activities commenced 1971; work extended, 1987, to operations, maintenance, licensing and certification/design standards for all classes of aircraft. Originally referred to as *European Joint Airworthiness Requirements Body (JAR)* or *Joint Airworthiness Authorities*. Subsequently known as *Joint Aviation Authorities (JAA)*. Since autumn 2003, rule making activities gradually transferred to *European Union Aviation Safety Agency (EASA, #08978)*, while the upcoming close-down of the former JAA-system was processed by means of a transition phase. Transferred into *Joint Aviation Authorities – Transition (JAA T)*, with Liaison Office (JAA LO) at EASA and Training Organization in Hoofddorp (Netherlands). All former responsibilities of JAA transferred to EASA, 19 Mar 2008; JAA LO disbanded, 30 Jun 2009. Training Organization continued under current title, registered in accordance with Dutch law, and as an associated body of *European Civil Aviation Conference (ECAC, #06564)*. Registration: Netherlands. **Aims** Offer quality training courses on European *aviation safety* rules and regulations to both authority and industry personnel; contribute to aviation safety as a whole by enhancing understanding aviation safety rules and regulations. **Structure** Advisory Board; Foundation Board. **Languages** English. **Staff** 15.00 FTE, paid. **Finance** Income from training courses. **Activities** Training/education. **Events** *Workshop on improving safety during approach and landing* Brussels (Belgium) 2003, *Annual Conference* Reykjavik (Iceland) 2003, *International workshop on runway safety* Brussels (Belgium) 2002, *Annual Conference* Phoenix, AZ (USA) 2002, *Annual Conference* Geneva (Switzerland) 2001. **IGO Relations** *European Union Aviation Safety Agency (EASA, #08978)*; *European Civil Aviation Conference (ECAC, #06564)*; *International Civil Aviation Organization (ICAO, #12581)*; national organizations. **NGO Relations** *International Aviation Training and Education Organisation (IATEO)*. [2021/XF1558/**F***]

- Joint Aviation Authorities – Transition / see Joint Aviation Authorities Training Organisation (#16122)
- Joint Board of Associations of Nordic Clergy (inactive)
- Joint Board of the Geospatial Information Societies / see UN-GGO: Geospatial Societies (#20324)
- Joint Board of Right-Wing Nordic Women (inactive)
- Joint Commercial Commission / see United States/Pacific Island Nations Joint Commercial Commission
- Joint Commission on Allied Health Personnel in Ophthalmology (internationally oriented national body)
- Joint Commission on Applied Radioactivity (inactive)
- Joint Commission for Dialogue between the Representatives of the Vatican and the the World Methodist Council / see International Joint Commission for Dialogue between the World Methodist Council and the Vatican (#13972)
- Joint Commission of the Empress Shôken Fund (internationally oriented national body)
- Joint Commission on High Altitude Research Stations (inactive)

♦ Joint Commission International (JCI) 16123

Pres – CEO JCI Headquarters, 1515 West 22nd St, Ste 1300W, Oak Brook IL 60523, USA. T. +16302684800 – +16302682900. E-mail: jciaccreditation@jointcommissioninternational.org.

URL: http://www.jointcommissioninternational.org/

History A division of *'Joint Commission Resources (JCR)'*. **Aims** Improve the safety and quality of *care* in the international community through the provision of education and consultation services and international *accreditation*. **Events** *Patient Experience Asia Summit* Singapore (Singapore) 2018, *Annual hospital management Asia conference* Singapore (Singapore) 2011, *Annual hospital management Asia conference* Seoul (Korea Rep) 2010, *Executive meeting* Singapore (Singapore) 2010, *Meeting on practicum on accreditation and quality improvement* Singapore (Singapore) 2010. [2020/XM1552/**F**]

- Joint Commission of the Socialist Countries on Cooperation in the Field of Fisheries (inactive)
- Joint Committee of Building and Woodworkers in the EEC / see European Federation of Building and Woodworkers (#07065)
- Joint Committee on Chemical Analysis by X-ray Diffraction Methods / see International Centre for Diffraction Data
- Joint Committee for the Classification of Agricultural Literature (inactive)
- Joint Committee of IAHR and IAWQ on Urban Drainage / see Joint Committee of IAHR and IAW on Urban Drainage (#16124)
- Joint Committee of IAHR and IAWQ on Urban Storm Drainage / see Joint Committee of IAHR and IAW on Urban Drainage (#16124)

♦ Joint Committee of IAHR and IAW on Urban Drainage (JCUD) 16124

Sec Natl Water Research Inst, 867 Lakeshore Road, Burlington ON L7R 4A6, Canada. T. +19053364899. Fax +19053364420.

Chairman IFAK Magdeburg, Wermer-Heisenberg Strasse 1, 39106 Magdeburg, Germany.

URL: http://www.jcud.org/

History Founded 1982, under the title *Joint Committee of IAHR and IAWQ on Urban Drainage (JCUD)*, as a joint committee of *International Association for Hydro-Environment Engineering and Research (IAHR, #11950)* and *International Association on Water Quality (IAWQ, inactive)*. Current title adopted following merger, 7 Sep 1999, of IAWQ and *International Water Services Association (IWSA, inactive)* to form *International Water Association (IWA, #15865)*. Previously also referred to as *Joint Committee of IAHR and IAWQ on Urban Storm Drainage (JCUSD)*. UK Registered Charity: 1076690. **Aims** Promote progressive and innovative approaches to urban drainage, emphasizing protection of urban *ecosystems*, cost-efficiency and sustainability. **Structure** 9-12 members selected from the memberships of IAHR and IWA. Working Groups. **Languages** English. **Staff** 1.00 FTE, paid. **Finance** Not financed on a regular basis; members secure their own funding for various activities. Contributions from IAHR and IWA available for specific projects. Some funding raised from co-sponsored events. **Events** *ICUD : Triennial International Conference on Urban Drainage* Melbourne, VIC (Australia) 2021, *ICUD : Triennial International Conference on Urban Drainage* Melbourne, VIC (Australia) 2020, *ICUD : Triennial International Conference on Urban Drainage* Prague (Czechia) 2017, *ICUD : Triennial International Conference on Urban Drainage* Kuching (Malaysia) 2014, *Annual Meeting* Lyon (France) 2013. **Publications** *Joint Committee on Urban Storm Drainage Newsletter* (annual); *IAHR/IWA Joint Specialist Group on Urban Drainage* – newsletter; *Waterlines* – journal. Conference and symposium proceedings.
Members Individuals – members of Executive Committee, in 10 countries:
Australia, Canada, China, Czechia, Denmark, Germany, Italy, Japan, Netherlands, USA. [2015.06.01/XE4054/v/E]

- ♦ Joint Committee of International Teachers' Federations (inactive)
- ♦ Joint Committee of Nordic Employers' Associations (inactive)
- ♦ Joint Committee on Nordic Marine Technology (inactive)

♦ Joint Committee of the Nordic Medical Research Councils 16125

Nordiska Samarbetsnämnden för Medicinsk Forskning (NOS-M) – Lääketieteellisen Tutkimuksen Pohjoismainen Yhteistyötoimikunta

Exec Sec c/o NordForsk, NOS-M secretariat, Stensberggata 25, 0170 Oslo, Norway. T. +4799380264.
URL: http://nos-m.org/

History Established 22 Apr 1968, as a cooperation body of *Nordic Council of Ministers (NCM, #17260)*. **Aims** Act as a joint forum for the Nordic medical research councils for the promotion of health research in Nordic countries. **Structure** Rotating Chairmanship between Nordic countries; NordForsk is Secretariat. **Languages** Danish, English, Faroese, Icelandic, Norwegian, Swedish. **Staff** 0.50 FTE, paid. **Finance** Members' dues (annual). Budget (annual): euro 72,500. **Activities** Coordinates and promotes medical research in the Nordic countries; monitors its progress; facilitates information exchange among the countries; promotes and initiates concrete, collaborative Nordic projects in medical research by regularly funding policy-oriented and strategic workshops. **Events** *Seminar on gene transfer and gene therapy* Stockholm (Sweden) 1997. **Publications** *Nordic White Paper on Medical Research.*
Members Nordic medical research councils (5):
Denmark, Finland, Iceland, Norway, Sweden.
Observers:
Baltic countries; *NordForsk (#17164)*; *Nordic Council of Ministers (NCM, #17260)*.
NGO Relations *NordForsk (#17164)*. [2018/XE5565/E*]

- ♦ Joint Committee of the Nordic Natural Science Research Councils (#17529)
- ♦ Joint Committee of Nordic Nurserymen (inactive)
- ♦ Joint Committee for Nordic Research Councils for the Humanities and the Social Sciences (#17530)
- ♦ Joint Committee of the Nordic Social Democratic Labour Movement (#19045)
- ♦ Joint Committee of Organizations for the Blind in the Nordic Countries (inactive)
- ♦ Joint Committee on Powder Diffraction Standards / see International Centre for Diffraction Data
- ♦ Joint Committee for the Promotion of Agricultural Cooperatives / see Committee for the Promotion and Advancement of Cooperatives (#04279)
- ♦ Joint Committee for Safety of Structures / see Joint Committee on Structural Safety (#16126)
- ♦ Joint Committee of Scandinavian Falcon Organizations / see Arbetarrörelsens Barnorganisationer i Norden (#01084)

♦ Joint Committee on Structural Safety (JCSS) 16126

Pres c/o Civil Eng, Thomas Manns vej 23, 9220 Aalborg O, Denmark. E-mail: mfn@civil.aau.dk.
URL: http://www.jcss.byg.dtu.dk/

History 1971, as *Joint Committee for Safety of Structures*, by *Liaison Committee of International Associations of Civil Engineering (#16453)*, which groups: *Euro-International Committee for Concrete (CEB, inactive)*; *European Convention for Constructional Steelwork (ECCS, #06779)*; *Fédération internationale de la précontrainte (FIP, inactive)*; *International Association for Bridge and Structural Engineering (IABSE, #11737)*; *International Council for Research and Innovation in Building and Construction (CIB, #13069)*; *Réunion internationale des laboratoires d'essais et de recherches sur les matériaux et les constructions (RILEM, #18930)*. **Aims** Improve general knowledge and understanding within the fields of safety, *risk*, *reliability* and *quality* assurance for all types of civil engineering and *building* structures, on the basis of sound scientific principles and with an open eye for the applications in practice; take care that inter-associational pre-normative research in the field of risk and reliability is performed in an effective and adequate way; strive for coordination between the inter-associational pre-normative research and normalization activities in ISO, Eurocode etc; provide appropriate support and technical coordination for the work of member associations. **Structure** Board (meets annually), comprising President (Chair), Former President, Reporter(s) and one Member-Specialist per Association. Working Parties (meet twice a year), consisting of about 10 active members selected by the Board and chaired by Reporters. **Languages** English. **Staff** Voluntary. **Finance** Donations. **Activities** Main activities are: development of JCSS Probabilistic Model Code (published on website); JCSS guideline on probabilistic based assessment of existing structures (published on website); guideline on engineering risk assessment. Updates guidance documents and prepares new documents as requested by the Plenum or by Member Associations through the Liaison Committee. **Events** *Meeting* Lyngby (Denmark) 2016, *Meeting* Copenhagen (Denmark) 2009, *Meeting* Delft (Netherlands) 2009, *Meeting* Paris (France) 2008, *Meeting* San Francisco, CA (USA) 2008.
Members Individuals in 25 countries:
Australia, Austria, Belgium, Brazil, Canada, China, Czechia, Denmark, France, Germany, Greece, Hungary, Israel, Italy, Japan, Netherlands, Norway, Portugal, Romania, South Africa, Spain, Sweden, Switzerland, UK, USA. [2015/XE1672/v/E]

- ♦ Joint Committee Swissaid – Swiss Catholic Lenten Fund – Bread for Brethren – Helvetas / see Alliance Sud, Swiss Alliance of Development Organisations Swissaid – Catholic Lenten Fund – Bread for All – Helvetas – Caritas – Interchurch Aid
- ♦ Joint Committee on Tall Buildings / see Council on Tall Buildings and Urban Habitat (#04921)
- ♦ Joint Committee for Theological Dialogue Between the Catholic Church and the Assyrian Church of the East (unconfirmed)

♦ Joint Committee for Traceability in Laboratory Medicine (JCTLM) .. 16127

Secretariat c/o BIPM, Pavillon de Breteuil, 92312 Sèvres CEDEX, France. T. +33145077070. Fax +33145342021. E-mail: jctlm@bipm.org.
URL: https://www.jctlm.org/

History 2002. Established through a declaration between *Bureau international des poids et mesures (BIPM, #03367)*, *International Federation of Clinical Chemistry and Laboratory Medicine (IFCC, #13392)* and *International Laboratory Accreditation Cooperation (ILAC, #13995)*, in response to implementation of European Community Directive 98-79/EC. **Aims** Promote global standardization of clinical laboratory test results; provide information on reference materials, reference measurement methods and services that are available from around the world. **Structure** Executive Committee; JCTLM Working Group for Traceability, Education and Promotion (WG-TEP; JCTLM Database Working Group (JCTLM DBWG). **Activities** Knowledge management/information dissemination; standards/guidelines. **Events** *Biennial Meeting and Workshop* Paris (France) 2021.
Members National, regional and stakeholder members in 20 countries:
Argentina, Australia, Belgium, Canada, China, Colombia, France, Germany, Greece, India, Italy, Japan, Kazakhstan, Korea Rep, Netherlands, Russia, Singapore, Türkiye, UK, USA.
Included in the above, 6 organizations listed in this Yearbook:
Bureau international des poids et mesures (BIPM, #03367); *European Organisation for External Quality Assurance Providers in Laboratory Medicine (EQALM, #08098)*; *International Council for Standardization in Haematology (ICSH, #13078)*; *International Federation of Clinical Chemistry and Laboratory Medicine (IFCC, #13392)*; *International Laboratory Accreditation Cooperation (ILAC, #13995)*; *Joint Research Centre (JRC, #16147)*. [2021.05.28/XM6157/y/E]

- ♦ Joint Commonwealth Societies' Council / see Council of Commonwealth Societies (#04878)
- ♦ Joint Consultative Committee of International Non-Governmental Organizations in the Field of Librarianism, Documentation and the Collection of Archives (inactive)
- ♦ Joint Consultative Group on Policies (no recent information)
- ♦ Joint Convention on the Safety of Spent Fuel Management and on the Safety of Radioactive Waste Management (1997 treaty)
- ♦ Joint Coordinating Committee between the Non-Aligned Movement and the Group of 77 (inactive)
- ♦ Joint Council of Nordic Countries' Civil Servants (no recent information)
- ♦ Joint Council of Nordic Federations of Industry (inactive)
- ♦ Joint Council of Nordic Lawyers' Associations (meeting series)
- ♦ Joint Council of Nordic Real Estate Credit Institutions (inactive)
- ♦ Joint Council for the Welfare of Immigrants (internationally oriented national body)
- ♦ Joint Declaration Concerning Fishing Problems in the South Pacific (1952 treaty)
- ♦ Joint Disarmament Committee of Christian International Organizations (inactive)
- ♦ Joint Electron Device Engineering Council / see JEDEC (#16095)
- ♦ Joint Electron Tube Engineering Council / see JEDEC (#16095)
- ♦ Joint European Disruptive Initiative (unconfirmed)

♦ Joint European Drones Associations (JEDA) 16128

Contact c/o FPDC, 15 rue Beaujon, 75008 Paris, France. E-mail: europe@federation-drone.org.
URL: https://fpdc.fr/jeda-joint-european-drone-associations

History 12 Nov 2021, Brussels (Belgium). **Aims** Represent the increased legislative and regulatory activity that affects everyone who flies a drone for personal and professional use; develop and maintain a common understanding of the seamless integration of UAS/RPAS into aviation and the European airspace system.
Members National Associations in 17 countries and territories:
Albania, Austria, Belgium, Bulgaria, Estonia, Finland, Flanders, France, Germany, Greece, Ireland, Italy, Latvia, Lithuania, Netherlands, Portugal, Switzerland.
Unmanned Aviation Association (UAV DACH). [2021/AA2954/y/D]

- ♦ Joint European Magnetics Symposia (meeting series)
- ♦ Joint European Stable Isotope Users group Meeting (meeting series)
- ♦ Joint European Trade Association for Combustion Equipment (inactive)
- ♦ Joint FAO/WHO Codex Alimentarius Commission / see Codex Alimentarius Commission (#04081)

♦ Joint FAO/WHO Expert Committee on Food Additives (JECFA) 16129

Comité mixte FAO/OMS d'experts des additifs alimentaires – Comité Mixto FAO/OMS de Expertos en Aditivos Alimentarios

FAO/JEFCA Secretariat c/o FAO, Viale delle Terme di Caracalla, 00153 Rome RM, Italy. T. +39657053283. Fax +39657055493. E-mail: jecfa@fao.org.
WHO/JECFA Secretariat c/o WHO, 1211 Geneva 27, Switzerland. T. +41227911439. Fax +41227914848. E-mail: jecfa@who.int.
URL: http://www.fao.org/food/food-safety-quality/scientific-advice/jecfa/en/

History 1956, within the framework of *FAO (#09260)* and *WHO (#20950)*, as an advisory body to *Codex Alimentarius Commission (CAC, #04081)* and to FAO/WHO member governments. **Aims** Serve as an independent scientific committee which performs risk assessments on food additives, contaminants and residues of veterinary drugs in food. **Structure** Session (annual or twice a year, always in Rome-Italy and Geneva-Switzerland); Committee. **Languages** English. **Staff** UN staff. **Finance** UN budget. **Activities** Monitoring/evaluation; knowledge management/information dissemination. **Events** *Session* Rome (Italy) 2010, *Session* Geneva (Switzerland) 2009, *Session* Geneva (Switzerland) 2008, *Session* Rome (Italy) 2008, *Session* Rome (Italy) 2005. **Publications** *FAO JECFA Monographs*; *WHO Food Additive Series*; *WHO Technical Report Series.*
Members Not a membership organization. [2019.12.11/XE6099/E*]

- ♦ Joint FAO/WHO Expert Committee on Nutrition (inactive)
- ♦ Joint FAO/WHO/OAU Regional Food and Nutrition Commission for Africa (inactive)
- ♦ Joint Force Command North / see Allied Joint Force Command Brunssum (#00734)
- ♦ Joint Force Command South / see Allied Joint Force Command Naples (#00735)

♦ Joint Forum 16130

Contact c/o Basel Committee – BIS, Centralbahnplatz 2, Postfach, 4002 Basel BS, Switzerland. T. +41612808080. Fax +41612809100. E-mail: baselcommittee@bis.org.
URL: http://www.bis.org/bcbs/jointforum.htm

History 1996, by *Basel Committee on Banking Supervision (BCBS, #03183)*, *International Association of Insurance Supervisors (IAIS, #11966)* and *International Organization of Securities Commissions (IOSCO, #14470)*, as *Joint Forum on Financial Conglomerates*. Current title adopted, 1999. **Aims** Deal with issues common to the *banking*, *securities* and *insurance* sectors, including the regulation of *financial* conglomerates. **Structure** Chairman. Forum meets 3 times a year. **Activities** Subgroups (3): Risk Assessment and Capital; Business Continuity; Customer Suitability.
Members Full in 13 countries:
Australia, Belgium, Canada, Denmark, France, Germany, Italy, Japan, Netherlands, Spain, Switzerland, UK, USA.
Observer member (1):
European Union (EU, #08967).
IGO Relations *European Insurance and Occupational Pensions Authority (EIOPA, #07578).* [2015/XE3865/E]

- ♦ Joint Forum on Financial Conglomerates / see Joint Forum (#16130)
- ♦ Joint Glycobiology Meeting (meeting series)
- ♦ Joint Group of Experts on the Scientific Aspects of Marine Environmental Protection / see Joint Group of Experts on the Scientific Aspects of Marine Environmental Protection (#16131)

♦ Joint Group of Experts on the Scientific Aspects of Marine Environmental Protection (GESAMP) 16131

Groupe mixte d'experts chargé d'étudier les aspects scientifiques de la protection de l'environnement marin – Grupo Mixto de Expertos sobre los Aspectos Científicos de la Protección del Medio Marino – Obedinennaja Gruppa Ekspertov po Naucnym Aspektam Zascity Morskoj Sredy

Admin Sec IMO, 4 Albert Embankment, London, SE1 7SR, UK. T. +442075873142. Fax +442075873210.
URL: http://www.gesamp.org/

History Established 1969, London (UK), as *Joint Group of Experts on the Scientific Aspects of Marine Pollution – Groupe mixte d'experts chargé d'étudier les aspects scientifiques de la pollution des mers – Grupo Mixto de Expertos sobre los Aspectos Científicos de la Contaminación de las Aguas del Mar – Obedinennaja Gruppa Ekspertov po Naucnym Aspektam Zagrjaznenija Morskoj Sredy*, at headquarters of IMO, with participation of 13 scientists and representatives from the following United Nations Agencies: IMO, FAO, UNESCO and WMO. Since 1970, WHO, IAEA, UN, UNEP and IOC joined subsequently as co-sponsors. Subsequently changed title to *IMO/FAO/UNESCO-IOC/WMO/WHO/IAEA/UN/UNEP Joint Group of Experts on the Scientific Aspects of Marine Environmental Protection (GESAMP) – Groupe mixte d'experts OMI/FAO/UNESCO-COI/OMM/OMS/AIEA/ONU/PNUE chargé d'étudier les aspects scientifiques de la protection de l'environnement marin – Grupo Mixto de Expertos OMI/FAO/UNESCO-COI/OMM/OMS/OIEA/Naciones Unidas/PNUMA sobre los Aspectos Científicos de la Protección del Medio Marino – IMO/FAO/JUNESKO-MOK/VMO/VOZ/MAGATE/OON/JUNEP Obedinennaja Gruppa Ekspertov po Naucnym Aspektam Zascity Morskoj Sredy*, 1993. UNIDO became co-sponsor 2006 and UNDP 2010; WHO withdrew prior to 2011. Also referred to as *Joint Group of Experts on the Scientific Aspects of Marine Environmental Protection – Groupe mixte d'experts chargé d'étudier les aspects scientifiques* *de la protection de l'environnement marin – Grupo Mixto de Expertos sobre los Aspectos Cientificos de la Protección del Medio Marino – Obedinennaja Gruppa Ekspertov po Naucnym Aspektam Zascity Morskoj Sredy.* **Aims** Provide authoritative, independent, interdisciplinary scientific advice to organizations and member governments to support the protection and sustainable use of the marine environment. **Structure** Executive Board, comprising Technical Secretaries of the nine UN agencies (IMO, FAO, UNESCO-IOC, WMO, IAEA, UN, UNDP, UNEP, UNIDO), along with the Administrative Secretary, nominated by IMO. Executive Committee, comprising representatives of each Sponsoring Organization (Technical Secretary) and the Chairperson and 2 Vice-Chairpersons. Working Groups (6); Task Team. **Languages** English. **Staff** Office supported in-kind by IMO. Staff resources allocated as needed, and includes Administrative Secretary, Technical Secretary and secretarial support. **Finance** Funded by United Nations organizations. Working Groups also co-funded by other stakeholders (eg: governments and industry). **Activities** Inter-sessional work carried out by GESAMP Working Groups in which members and additional scientists who are not members of GESAMP participate. **Events** *Annual Session* Malmö (Sweden) 2014, *Annual Session* Vienna (Austria) 2013, *Annual Session* New York, NY (USA) 2012, *Annual Session* Monte Carlo (Monaco) 2011, *Annual Session* Monte Carlo (Monaco) 2011. **Publications** Reports and studies, including reports of sessions and results of studies carried out by Working Groups. **Members** As of 2013, 13 experts who have been nominated by the Sponsoring Organizations (IMO, FAO, UNESCO-IOC, WMO, IAEA, UN, UNEP, UNIDO, UNDP) from the ranks of the GESAP Pool of Experts (internationally recognized marine scientists), who act in their individual capacities serving GESAMP as a whole. **IGO Relations** Sponsoring agencies: *FAO (#09260); Intergovernmental Oceanographic Commission (IOC, #11496); International Atomic Energy Agency (IAEA, #12294); International Maritime Organization (IMO, #14102); UNEP (#20299); UNDP (#20292); UNESCO (#20322); UNIDO (#20336); United Nations (UN, #20515)*; United Nations Division for Ocean Affairs and the Law of the Sea; *World Meteorological Organization (WMO, #21649).* [2013.06.12/XE4186/v/**E***]

♦ Joint Group of Experts on the Scientific Aspects of Marine Pollution / see Joint Group of Experts on the Scientific Aspects of Marine Environmental Protection (#16131)

♦ Joint ILO-UNESCO Committee of Experts on the Application of the Recommendation concerning the Status of Teachers / see Joint ILO/UNESCO Committee of Experts on the Application of the Recommendations Concerning Teaching Personnel (#16132)

♦ Joint ILO/UNESCO Committee of Experts on the Application of the Recommendations Concerning Teaching Personnel (CEART) 16132

Comité conjoint OIT/UNESCO d'experts sur l'application des recommandations concernant le personnel enseignant

Contact Sectoral Policies Dept, Intl Labour Office, 4 route des Morillons, 1211 Geneva 22, Switzerland.

Contact Section for Teacher Education – Div for Support and Coordination of Education 2030, UNESCO, 7 place de Fontenoy, 75352 Paris 07 SP, France.

History Founded 1967, following Recommendation of *ILO (#11123)* and *UNESCO (#20322)* concerning Status of Teachers (1966), as *Joint ILO-UNESCO Committee of Experts on the Application of the Recommendation concerning the Status of Teachers (CEART).* Field enlarged following adoption by UNESCO of a Recommendation concerning the Status of Higher Education Teaching Personnel, 1997. Present name adopted, 2000. **Aims** Examine reports on the application of recommendations submitted by governments, national organizations representing teachers and their employers, the ILO and UNESCO and by relevant intergovernmental or non-governmental organizations; communicate findings to the ILO and UNESCO, so that they may take appropriate action; examine allegations from teachers' organizations on non-observance of recommendations. **Structure** Joint Committee Session (every 3 years, alternatively at UNESCO Headquarters in Paris, France and at ILO in Geneva, Switzerland). **Languages** English, French. **Events** *Session* Geneva (Switzerland) 2018, *Session* Paris (France) 2015, *Session* Geneva (Switzerland) 2012, *Session* Paris (France) 2009, *Session* Geneva (Switzerland) 2006. **Publications** Session proceedings; reports. [2019.08.27/XE2937/**E**]

♦ Joint ILO/WHO Committee on Occupational Health / see Global Coalition for Occupation Safety and Health (#10294)

♦ Joint Industry Council / see Joint Meetings Industry Council (#16140)

♦ Joint Inspection Unit of the United Nations (JIU) 16133

Corps commun d'inspection des Nations Unies – Dependencia Común de Inspección de las Naciones Unidas

Exec Sec Palais des Nations, Room D 505, 1211 Geneva 10, Switzerland. T. +41229173044. Fax +41229170627. E-mail: jiu@unog.ch.

URL: http://www.unjiu.org/

History 1968. Established on an experimental basis, within the framework of *United Nations (UN, #20515)* under General Assembly resolution 2150 (XXI) of 4 Nov 1966 and extended under Assembly resolutions 2735 A (XXV) of 17 Dec 1970 and 2924 B (XXVII) of 24 Nov 1972. Statute, approved by UN General Assembly in 1976, came into effect from 1 Jan 1978. Functions as a subsidiary organ both of the UN General Assembly and also of specialized agencies within the UN system (and of IAEA) which accept JIU Statute; some of these (for constitutional reasons) cannot, however, recognize the Unit as a subsidiary organ of their legislative bodies. Based at *United Nations Office at Geneva (UNOG, #20597).* **Aims** Assist legislative organs of participating organizations in meeting their governance responsibilities in respect of their oversight function concerning management of human, financial and other resources by secretariats; help improve the efficiency and effectiveness of the respective secretariats in achieving the legislative mandates and the mission objectives established for the organizations; promote greater coordination between organizations of the United Nations system; identify best practices, propose benchmarks and facilitate information-sharing throughout the system. **Structure** Inspectors (11), including Chairman and Vice-Chairman, appointed by UN General Assembly for 5-year terms (renewable for 1 term) on the basis of their special experience and with due regard to the principles of equitable geographical distribution and reasonable rotation. Secretariat, headed by Executive Secretary. **Staff** 20.00 FTE, paid. **Finance** Budget included in the regular budget of the UN and expenditures are shared by participating organizations. Annual budget: 7,000,000 USD (2017). **Activities** Inspections; Investigations; Evaluations. **Publications** Annual Activity Report; reports; notes.

Members Participating organizations within the UN system (28):

- *FAO (#09260);*
- *ILO (#11123);*
- *International Atomic Energy Agency (IAEA, #12294);*
- *International Civil Aviation Organization (ICAO, #12581);*
- *International Maritime Organization (IMO, #14102);*
- *International Telecommunication Union (ITU, #15673);*
- *International Trade Centre (ITC, #15703);*
- *Joint United Nations Programme on HIV/AIDS (UNAIDS, #16149);*
- *UNCTAD (#20285);*
- *UNDP (#20292);*
- *UNEP (#20299);*
- *UNESCO (#20322);*
- *UNHCR (#20327);*
- *UNICEF (#20332);*
- *UNIDO (#20336);*
- *United Nations Human Settlements Programme (UN-Habitat, #20572);*
- *United Nations Office for Project Services (UNOPS, #20602);*
- *United Nations Office on Drugs and Crime (UNODC, #20596);*
- *United Nations Population Fund (UNFPA, #20612);*
- *United Nations Relief and Works Agency for Palestine Refugees in the Near East (UNRWA, #20622);*
- *United Nations (UN, #20515);*
- *Universal Postal Union (UPU, #20682);*
- *UN Women (#20724);*
- *WHO (#20950);*
- *World Food Programme (WFP, #21510);*
- *World Intellectual Property Organization (WIPO, #21593);*
- *World Meteorological Organization (WMO, #21649);*
- *World Tourism Organization (UNWTO, #21861).* [2020/XE9922/y/**E***]

♦ Joint Institute for Nuclear Research (JINR) 16134

Institut unifié des recherches nucléaires – Obedinennyj Institut Jadernyh Issledovanij (OIJAI)

Contact Joliot-Curie 6, Moscow Region, Dubna TULA, Russia, 141980. T. +74962165059. E-mail: post@jinr.ru.

URL: http://www.jinr.ru/

History Established 26 Mar 1956, Moscow (USSR), by Convention signed by representatives of 11 governments. Also referred to as *Dubna.* Previously referred to in other languages as: *Instituto Unificado de Investigaciones Nucleares – Vereinigtes Institut für Kernforschung – Az Egyesitett Atomkutató Intézet – Cemnijn Sinzilgeenij Negdsen Institut – Institutul Unificat de Cercetari Nucleare – Obedinen Institut za Jadreni Izsledvanija – Spojeny Ustav Jadernych Vyzjumú – Vién Liên Hiêp Nghiên Cú'u Nguyên Tú' – Zjednoczony Instytut Badan Jadrowych.* **Aims** Ensure joint theoretical and experimental research in *peaceful uses* of *nuclear physics* by scientists of Member States; secure exchange of experience and achievements; maintain contacts with national and international scientific institutions and other organizations for promoting the development of nuclear physics and finding new possibilities for peaceful use of *atomic energy.* **Structure** Committee of Plenipotentiaries of Member States (meets twice a year); Directorate; Finance Committee (meets twice a year); Scientific Council (meets twice a year); Programme Advisory Committees; Science and Technological Council; Bilateral Committees (JINR – an associated Member State representative); Laboratories (7); Experimental Physics Workshops. **Languages** English, Russian. **Staff** 5300.00 FTE, paid. **Finance** Member States' contributions. **Activities** Research/documentation; research and development; events/meetings; training/education. **Events** *Conference on New Trends in High Energy Physics* Kiev (Ukraine) 2021, *Conference on New Trends in High Energy Physics* Odessa (Ukraine) 2019, *Biennial Russian Particle Accelerator Conference* Protvino (Russia) 2018, *SQM : International Conference on Strangeness in Quark Matter* Dubna, Tula (Russia) 2015, *Joint Workshop* Jeju (Korea Rep) 2014. **Publications** *JINR News* (4 a year); *Particles and Nuclei – Letters* – journal; *Physics of Elementary Particles and the Atomic Nucleus* – journal. Annual Report. Conference proceedings. Technical reports; preprints.

Members Governments of 18 countries:

Armenia, Azerbaijan, Belarus, Bulgaria, Cuba, Czechia, Georgia, Kazakhstan, Korea DPR, Moldova, Mongolia, Poland, Romania, Russia, Slovakia, Ukraine, Uzbekistan, Vietnam.

Associate membership in 6 countries:

Egypt, Germany, Hungary, Italy, Serbia, South Africa.

NGO Relations Member of: *Astroparticle Physics European Consortium (APPEC, #02998).* Cooperates and maintains scientific contacts with more than 700 international and national scientific centers and universities around the world. [2018.07.13/XC2849/j/**F***]

♦ Joint Institute for VLBI in Europe (JIVE) 16135

Dir Oude Hoogeveensedijk 4, 7991 PD Dwingeloo, Netherlands. T. +31521596500. E-mail: secretary@jive.eu.

URL: http://www.jive.eu/

History 1993. Since Apr 2015, an *European Research Infrastructure Consortium (ERIC).* Registered in accordance with Dutch law. **Aims** Foster and support state-of-the-art research and development of the techniques of Very Long Baseline Interferometry (VLBI) in Europe for *astronomy.* **Structure** Council; Groups (2). **Languages** English. **Staff** 25.00 FTE, paid. **Finance** Contributions from organizations. Additional activities supported by grant from: *European Commission (EC, #06633).* Annual budget: euro 2,000,000. **Activities** Research and development. **Events** *Technology Workshop* Groningen (Netherlands) / Dwingeloo (Netherlands) 2014, *Symposium* Dwingeloo (Netherlands) 1998. **Publications** Annual Report.

Members Full in 10 countries:

China (partial), France, Germany, Italy, Latvia, Netherlands, South Africa, Spain, Sweden, UK.

NGO Relations Member of: *African-European Radio Astronomy Platform (AERAP); European VLBI Network (EVN, #09074).* [2018.10.04/XE3439/j/**E**]

♦ Joint International Commission for Theological Dialogue between the Catholic Church and the Oriental Orthodox Churches 16136

Address not obtained.

History by Pope John Paul II and the Orthodox Ecumenical Patriarch, as a unity-seeking joint theological dialogue. **Events** *Meeting* Etchmiadzin (Armenia) 2006, *Meeting* Rome (Italy) 2005, *Meeting* Cairo (Egypt) 2004. **NGO Relations** Sponsored by: *Pontifical Council for Promoting Christian Unity (PCPCU, #18446).* [2009/XM2148/**E**]

♦ Joint International Committee for the Protection of Telecommunication Lines and Ducts (inactive)

♦ Joint International Tropical Medicine Meeting (meeting series)

♦ Joint IOC/IHO Guiding Committee for the General Bathymetric Chart of the Oceans (GEBCO) 16137

Permanent Sec IHO, 4-b quai Antoine 1er, BP 445, 98011 Monte Carlo, Monaco. T. +37793108100. Fax +37793108140. E-mail: adso@iho.int.

URL: http://www.gebco.net/

History 1972. Founded as a joint committee of *International Hydrographic Organization (IHO, #13825)* and *Intergovernmental Oceanographic Commission (IOC, #11496). A Commission for the General Bathymetric Chart of the Oceans* was first set up in 1899, Berlin (Germany), by 7th International Geographic Congress, organized by *International Geographical Union (IGU, #13713)* and under the Chairmanship of Prince Albert I of Monaco. Production of the Chart was formally agreed when the Commission met, Apr 1903, Wiesbaden (Germany), initially organized and financed by Prince Albert. It transferred in 1929 to International Hydrographic Bureau (forerunner of IHO) in Monaco. Former names and other names: *Monaco Chart* – former. **Aims** Establish and maintain digital databases, comprising world coverage of bathymetric soundings and *geographical* names of *undersea* features; based on this, compile and publish digital gridded data sets and new editions of the General Bathymetric Chart of the Oceans. **Structure** Joint Guiding Committee; Technical Sub-Committees. **Languages** English, French. **Staff** Secretarial support and financial administration provided by secretariat of IHO. **Finance** Participants obtain funding from host organizations; annual grants from government of Monaco, IOC and IHO. **Activities** Events/meetings; knowledge management/information dissemination; projects/programmes; research/documentation. **Events** *Session* Paris (France) 2021, *Symposium* Paris (France) 2021, *Session* Portsmouth, NH (USA) 2019, *Session* Canberra, ACT (Australia) 2018, *Symposium* Canberra, ACT (Australia) 2018. **Publications** *Annual GEBCO grid -15 arc-second 2021 grid. GEBCO Gazetteer of Undersea Feature Names* in English, English, French, Russian; *GEBCO Global Cover of Bathymetric Charts*; *GEBCO World Ocean Bathymetry*; *Standardization of Undersea Feature Names* in Chinese, English, English, English, English, French, Japanese. *GEBCO Digital Atlas* (2003) – CD-ROM.

Members Individuals in 21 countries:

Australia, Belgium, Brazil, Canada, China, France, Germany, Ireland, Italy, Japan, Kenya, Korea Rep, Malaysia, Mexico, New Zealand, Norway, Poland, Russia, Sweden, UK, USA.

Also all Member States of IHO and IOC through these parent organizations.

NGO Relations Academic and related industry bodies, not specified. [2021.09.07/XE1593/**E**]

♦ Joint IOC/WMO/CPPS Working Group on the Investigation of El Niño / see Programa para el Estudio Regional del Fenómeno El Niño en el Pacifico Sudeste (#18523)

♦ Joint IOC-WMO-UNEP Committee for the Global Ocean Observing System / see Intergovernmental Committee for the Global Ocean Observing System (#11473)

♦ Joint IUBMB-IUPAC International Carbohydrate Organization (ICO) 16138

Sec School of Chemistry/Bio21 Molecular Science/Biotechnology Inst, Univ of Melbourne, Parkville VIC 3010, Australia. E-mail: sjwill@unimelb.edu.au.

URL: http://ico.chemistry.unimelb.edu.au/

History 1960, as a joint body of *International Union of Biochemistry and Molecular Biology (IUBMB, #15759)* and *International Union of Pure and Applied Chemistry (IUPAC, #15809).* Formerly known as *International Steering Committee for Carbohydrate Symposia.* **Aims** Encourage research, communication and education in *glycoscience.* **Structure** President; Secretary; National Representatives. **Languages** English. **Staff** 2.00 FTE, voluntary. **Activities** Awards/prizes/competitions. **Events** *Biennial Symposium* Japan 2036, *Biennial Symposium* Australia 2034, *Biennial Symposium* Ireland 2032, *Biennial Symposium* Taiwan 2030, *Biennial Symposium* Italy 2028.

Members Individuals in 33 countries:
Argentina, Australia, Austria, Brazil, Canada, China, Cuba, Czechia, Denmark, Finland, France, Germany, Hungary, India, Ireland, Israel, Italy, Japan, Korea Rep, Netherlands, New Zealand, Norway, Poland, Portugal, Russia, Slovakia, South Africa, Spain, Sweden, Switzerland, Taiwan, UK, USA.
NGO Relations Committee of IUB. Associated organization of IUPAC. Member of: *International Union of Pure and Applied Chemistry (IUPAC, #15809).* [2017.06.15/XE1181/v/E]

♦ Joint Learning Initiative on Faith and Local Communities (JLI) 16139

CEO 1220 L Street NW, Ste 100-514, Washington DC 200005, USA. T. +12024809597. E-mail: info@jliflc.com.
URL: https://jliflc.com/
History 2012. Registration: Charity, USA. **Aims** Collaborate on evidence for faith groups' role and contributions to local community health and wellbeing and ending poverty. **Structure** Board of Directors; Executive Committee; Advisory Group. **Staff** 4.00 FTE, paid. **Activities** Knowledge management/information dissemination; advocacy/lobbying/activism; events/meetings. **Publications** *JLI Newsletter*. Scoping reports; policy briefs; conference proceedings. **Information Services** *Learning Hubs*.
Members Organizations, including 71 listed in this Yearbook:
- *ACT Alliance (#00081);*
- *Adventist Development and Relief Agency International (ADRA, #00131);*
- *Alliance for Peacebuilding;*
- *American Jewish World Service (AJWS);*
- *Anglican Alliance (#00822);*
- *Arigatou International;*
- *Baha'i International Community (#03062);*
- *Caritas Internationalis (CI, #03580);*
- *Catholic Agency for Overseas Development (CAFOD);*
- *Catholic Medical Mission Board (CMMB);*
- *Catholic Organization for Relief and Development (Cordaid);*
- *Catholic Relief Services (CRS, #03608);*
- *Christian Aid;*
- *Christian AIDS Bureau for Southern Africa (CABSA);*
- *Christian Connections for International Health (CCIH);*
- *Concern Worldwide;*
- *Danmission;*
- *Department for International Development (DFID, inactive);*
- *Digni;*
- *Episcopal Relief and Development;*
- *European Council of Religious Leaders – Religions for Peace (ECRL, #06840);*
- *Food for the Hungry (fh, #09845);*
- *Global Fund to Fight AIDS, Tuberculosis and Malaria (Global Fund, #10383);*
- *Global Interfaith WASH Alliance (GIWA);*
- *IMA World Health (IMA);*
- *International Bank for Reconstruction and Development (IBRD, #12317)* (World Bank);
- *International Federation of Red Cross and Red Crescent Societies (#13526);*
- *International Interfaith Peace Corps (IIPC);*
- *International Justice Mission (IJM);*
- *International Partnership on Religion and Sustainable Development (PaRD, #14524);*
- *Irish Association of Non-Governmental Development Organisations (Dóchas);*
- *Islamic Relief Worldwide (IRWW, #16048);*
- *Jesuit Refugee Service (JRS, #16106);*
- *Joint United Nations Programme on HIV/AIDS (UNAIDS, #16149);*
- *King Abdullah Bin Abdulaziz International Centre for Interreligious and Intercultural Dialogue (KAICIID, #16193);*
- *Latin American Council of Churches (LACC, #16309);*
- *Lutheran World Relief (LWR);*
- *Mennonite Central Committee (MCC);*
- *Misean Cara;*
- *Mother Health International;*
- *Muslim Aid;*
- *Muslim Hands;*
- *Norwegian Church Aid;*
- *Organization of African Instituted Churches (OAIC, #17853);*
- *Oxford Centre for Mission Studies (OCMS);*
- *Religions for Peace (RfP, #18831);*
- *Salvation Army (#19041);*
- *Salvation Army World Service Office (SAWSO, see: #19041);*
- *Sexual Violence Research Initiative (SVRI, #19251);*
- *SIL International (#19278);*
- *Soka Gakkai International (SGI, #19672);*
- *Tear;*
- *Tearfund, UK;*
- *UNDP (#20292);*
- *UNESCO (#20322);*
- *UNHCR (#20327);*
- *UNICEF (#20332);*
- *United Methodist Committee on Relief (UMCOR);*
- *United Religions Initiative (URI, #20658);*
- *United States Agency for International Development (USAID);*
- *United States Institute of Peace (USIP);*
- *USPG (#20736);*
- *We Will Speak Out (WWSO);*
- *WHO (#20950);*
- *World Association for Christian Communication (WACC, #21126);*
- *World Council of Churches (WCC, #21320);*
- *World Evangelical Alliance (WEA, #21393);*
- *World Faiths Development Dialogue (WFDD);*
- *World Relief;*
- *World Renew;*
- *World Vision International (WVI, #21904).*

IGO Relations *UNICEF (#20332).* **NGO Relations** Member of: *International Partnership on Religion and Sustainable Development (PaRD, #14524).* [2023/XM7722/y/F]

♦ Joint Lutheran – Orthodox Commission / see Lutheran-Orthodox Joint Commission (#16530)
♦ Joint Meeting of International Trade Union Organizations and United Nations System (meeting series)
♦ Joint Meeting of Ministers of Economic Affairs and Public Works of Central America (meeting series)
♦ Joint Meetings of CPC and ACC (meeting series)

♦ Joint Meetings Industry Council (JMIC) 16140

Exec Dir c/o EMECA, Rue de l'Amazone 2, 1050 Brussels, Belgium. E-mail: jmic@themeetingsindustry.org.
URL: http://www.themeetingsindustry.org/
History Founded 1978, Geneva (Switzerland), when the first meeting was held, as *Joint Industry Council (JIC).* Present name adopted 4 Oct 1993, Brussels (Belgium). New charter and constittion adopted 2019. **Aims** Support industry networking; develop a collective voice to advance key issues and values. **Structure** An informal group composed of 1 or 2 permanent representatives of each international organization; not currently an organization but undergoing some degree of formalization. Rotating Chairmanship. Separate administrative entity. **Languages** English. **Staff** None. **Finance** Members' dues. Supported by: *Events Industry Council (EIC, #09212);* IMEX and Reed Travel Exhibitions. **Activities** Advocacy/lobbying/activism; awards/prizes/competitions; awareness raising; networking/liaising; events/meetings. **Events** *Global Industry Summit* Hannover (Germany) 2018, *Politicians Forum* Frankfurt-Main (Germany) 2016, *Politicians Forum* Frankfurt-Main (Germany) 2015, *Conference on the Value of Meetings / Conference* Paris (France) 2015, *AIBTM : Americas incentive business travel and meetings workshop* Orlando, FL (USA) 2014.
Members Representatives of 18 organizations:
ASAE; Asian Association of Convention and Visitor Bureaus (AACVB, #01319); Asociación de Centros de Convenciones del Caribe y Latinoamérica (ACCCLATAM, #02116); City Destinations Alliance (CityDNA, #03960); European Association of Event Centers (EVVC, #06032); European Major Exhibition Centres Association (EMECA, #07726); Federación de Entidades Organizadoras de Congresos y Afines de América Latina (COCAL, #09299); International Association of Convention Centres (AIPC, #11818); International Association of Exhibitions and Events (IAEE); International Association of Professional Congress Organisers (IAPCO, #12103); International Congress and Convention Association (ICCA, #12892); Meeting Professionals International (MPI, #16695); Professional Convention Management Association (PCMA); Singapore Association of Convention and Exhibition Organisers and Suppliers (SACEOS); *Society for Incentive Travel Excellence (SITE, #19574);* Society of Independent Show Organizers (SISO); *UFI – The Global Association of the Exhibition Industry (#20276); Union of International Associations (UIA, #20414).* [2022/XE4191/ty/E]

♦ Joint Ministerial Committee of the Boards of Governors of the Bank and the Fund on the Transfer of Real Resources to Developing Countries (Development Committee) 16141

Comité ministériel conjoint des conseils des gouverneurs de la Banque mondiale et du Fonds monétaire international sur le transfert de ressources réelles aux pays en voie de développement (Comité du développement) – Comité Ministerial Conjunto de las Juntas de Gobernadores del Banco y del Fondo para la Transferencia de Recursos Reales a los Paises en Desarrollo (Comité para el Desarrollo)
Exec Sec 1818 H St NW, Room MC12-231, Washington DC 20433, USA. T. +12024733970.
URL: http://www.devcommittee.org/
History Oct 1974, Washington DC (USA), as a joint committee of *International Bank for Reconstruction and Development (IBRD, #12317)* and *International Monetary Fund (IMF, #14180).* **Aims** Advise the Boards of Governors of the Bank and the Fund on critical development issues and on the financial resources required to promote economic development in developing countries. **Structure** Committee of 25 members; Chair; Executive Secretary. **Languages** English, French, Spanish. **Finance** The World Bank and the IMF make such financial appropriations, in equal proportions, as are necessary for carrying out the work of the Development Committee. **Activities** Events/meetings. **Events** *Half-Yearly Meeting* Washington, DC (USA) 2016, *Half-Yearly Meeting* Washington, DC (USA) 2016, *Half-Yearly Meeting* Lima (Peru) 2015, *Half-Yearly Meeting* Washington, DC (USA) 2015, *Half-Yearly Meeting* Washington, DC (USA) 2014. **Publications** *Development Issues*. Agendas; reports; statements.
Members 25 members represent 25 constituencies and full membership of the Bank and the Fund as of Apr 2019:
Austria, Bahrain, Brazil, Cameroon, Canada, China, Eswatini, France, Germany, Iceland, India, Italy, Japan, Korea Rep, Malaysia, Morocco, Netherlands, Russia, Saudi Arabia, South Africa, Spain, Switzerland, UK, Uruguay, USA.
IGO Relations Receives reports and recommendations from: *Intergovernmental Group of Twenty-Four on International Monetary Affairs (Group of Twenty-Four, #11495).* Invites the following 24 international and regional organizations as observers to meetings:
- *African Development Bank (ADB, #00283);*
- *Arab Bank for Economic Development in Africa (#00904);*
- *Arab Fund for Economic and Social Development (AFESD, #00965);*
- *Arab Monetary Fund (AMF, #01009);*
- *Asian Development Bank (ADB, #01422);*
- *Banque ouest africaine de développement (BOAD, #03170);*
- *Commonwealth Secretariat (#04362);*
- *Council of Europe Development Bank (CEB, #04897);*
- *European Bank for Reconstruction and Development (EBRD, #06315);*
- *European Commission (EC, #06633);*
- *FAO (#09260);*
- *Gulf Cooperation Council (GCC, #10826);*
- *ILO (#11123);*
- *Inter-American Development Bank (IDB, #11427);*
- *International Fund for Agricultural Development (IFAD, #13692);*
- *Islamic Development Bank (IsDB, #16044);*
- *Nordic Development Fund (NDF, #17271);*
- *Nordic Investment Bank (NIB, #17327);*
- *OECD (#17693);*
- *OECD Development Assistance Committee (DAC, see: #17693);*
- *OPEC Fund for International Development (OFID, #17745);*
- *UNCTAD (#20285);*
- *UNDP (#20292);*
- *United Nations (UN, #20515).*

Cooperative links with: *International Centre for Settlement of Investment Disputes (ICSID, #12515); International Development Association (IDA, #13155); International Finance Corporation (IFC, #13597); Multilateral Investment Guarantee Agency (MIGA, #16888).* Instrumental in setting up: *Global Environment Facility (GEF, #10346).* [2019.07.24/XE8201/E*]

♦ Joint Nordic Committee for Economic Cooperation (inactive)
♦ Joint Nordic Committee for Military UN Matters (inactive)
♦ Joint Nordic Development Research Conference (meeting series)
♦ Joint Nordic Matrix Biology Meeting (meeting series)
♦ Joint Nordic Organization for Lappish Culture and Reindeer Husbandry Affairs (no recent information)
♦ Joint Nordic Organization for Rural Youth / see Nordic Youth Organization (#17476)

♦ Joint Nordic Organization for Technical Testing 16142

Samnordiskt Organ inom Provningsområdet (NORDTEST) – Testausalan Yhteispohjoismainen Elin
Dir Slettetoften 9, 2630 Taastrup, Denmark. T. +4521214444. E-mail: nordtest@nordtest.info – info@nordtest.info.
URL: http://www.nordtest.info/
History 1973, by *Nordic Council of Ministers (NCM, #17260),* on the initiative of *Nordic Council (NC, #17256),* following decision of Nordic ministers of industry, 11 Dec 1972. Replaced *Nordiska Samarbetskommittén för Materialforskning och- Provning (NM, inactive).* Currently a part of *Nordic Innovation (#17320).* Statutes adopted 19 Feb 1979; 7 Mar 1997. Also referred to as *Gemensamt Nordiskt Organ inom Provnings- och Kontrollområdet,* as *Nordiskt Organ på Provnings- och Kontrollområdet – Koestus ja Tarkastustoiminnan Elin* and in English as *Nordic Cooperation Body for Technical Testing.* **Aims** Develop Nordic test methods and Nordic cooperation concerning conformity assessment. **Structure** Board; Market Groups; Expert Groups. Secretariat, headed by Executive Director. **Languages** Danish, English, Faroese, Icelandic, Norwegian, Swedish. **Staff** Secretariat: 4 FTE; total number of persons involved: about 300. **Finance** Activities of Board and Technical Groups financed by the institutions taking part. NMR finances projects, secretariat and activities. **Activities** Certification/accreditation. **Events** *Symposium* Copenhagen (Denmark) 1988. **Publications** *NORDTEST-Info* in English, Swedish; *NORDTEST Methods*; *NORDTEST Register of Test Methods.* Annual and technical reports.
Members Governments of 5 countries:
Denmark, Finland, Iceland, Norway, Sweden.
IGO Relations Cooperates with: *Nordic-Baltic Committee on Food Analysis (NMKL, #17215).* **NGO Relations** Member of: *International Laboratory Accreditation Cooperation (ILAC, #13995).* [2018/XD5365/D*]

♦ Joint Nordic Organ for Recreational Sports (inactive)
♦ Joint Oil Data Exercise / see Joint Organisations Data Initiative (#16143)

♦ Joint Organisations Data Initiative (JODI) 16143

Coordinator Energy Dialogue Div, Diplomatic Quarter, PO Box 94736, Riyadh 11614, Saudi Arabia. E-mail: jodinfo@ief.org.
URL: http://www.jodidata.org/
History Apr 2001, as *Joint Oil Data Exercise,* following the 7th International Energy Forum in Riyadh (Saudi Arabia), to raise the awareness of all oil market players of the need for more transparency in oil market data. Six international organizations were involved: *Asia-Pacific Economic Cooperation (APEC, #01887); Statistical Office of the European Union (Eurostat, #19974); International Energy Agency (IEA, #13270); Latin American Energy Organization (#16313); Organization of the Petroleum Exporting Countries (OPEC, #17881); United Nations Statistical Office (UNSTAT, inactive).* Within 6 months, 55 countries had participated in the exercise, and after one year there were over 70 participating countries representing 90 percent of global oil supply and demand. Following approval of the work commenced thus far at the 8th International Energy Forum, 2002 Osaka (Japan), the exercise became a permanent reporting mechanism and adopted the current title.

Aims Improve the availability and reliability of oil data. **Events** *Heads of JODI Partner Organisations Meeting* China 2020, *Inter-Secretariat Meeting* Riyadh (Saudi Arabia) 2020, *Energy Data Transparency Workshop for Sustainable Future* Cape Town (South Africa) 2019, *Data User Seminar* Tokyo (Japan) 2019, *Inter-Secretariat Meeting* Vienna (Austria) 2019. [2019/XM3813/**E**]

♦ Joint Organization of Nordic Women's Rights Associations (inactive)

♦ Joint Organization for Solar Observations (JOSO) 16144

Pres Inst for Geophysics/Astrophysics/Meteorology, Institute of Physics, University of Graz, Universitaetsplatz 5/11, 8010 Graz, Austria. T. +433163805255 – +433163805270. Fax +433163809825.
Sec address not obtained.

History 1968, through 1969, by solar physicists from Germany FR, France, Italy, Netherlands, Norway, Sweden and Switzerland. *'Statement of Intentions'* adopted 1970. Current aims and intentions adopted 9 Oct 1993, Graz (Austria). **Aims** Facilitate collaboration in solar physics, with special regard to integration of East European observatories; promote cooperation between different branches of observational solar physics – optical, radio and space research; assess existing instrumentation and observing and evaluation techniques and initiate new ones, especially as regards LEST. **Structure** No legal status and minimum of rules. Board, including President, 2 Vice-Presidents and Secretary. Working groups (3): Solar observing techniques; Coordination of software development and data handling; Coordination of SOHO and ground-based observations. **Finance** No membership fees; no budget; expenses covered ad hoc by voluntary contributions of adhering institutes. **Activities** Annual conference; workshops; joint observing programmes; information on available technical facilities – telescopes, instrumentation, computer hardware and software. **Events** *European meeting on solar physics* Prague (Czech Rep) 2002, *Annual Conference* Vico Equense (Italy) 2001, *European meeting on solar physics* Florence (Italy) 1999, *Advances in solar physics euroconference / Annual Conference* Potsdam (Germany) 1998, *Advances in solar physics Euroconference / Annual Conference* Ioannina (Greece) 1997. **Publications** Annual Reports.

Members Solar physicists (29) in 27 countries:
Australia, Austria, Belgium, Bulgaria, China, Croatia, Czechia, France, Germany, Greece, Hungary, Ireland, Israel, Italy, Netherlands, Norway, Poland, Romania, Russia, Slovakia, Spain, Sweden, Switzerland, Türkiye, UK, Ukraine, USA.

NGO Relations *Community of European Solar Radio Astronomers (CESRA, #04397).* [2008/XF3955/v/**F**]

♦ Joint Parliamentary Assembly of the Partnership Agreement between the African, Caribbean and Pacific Group of States and the European Community and its Member States / see ACP-EU Joint Parliamentary Assembly (#00077)

♦ Joint Policy Committee of the Societies of Epidemiology / see International Network for Epidemiology in Policy (#14264)

♦ Joint Programming Initiative on Agriculture, Food Security and Climate Change (FACCE-JPI) 16145

Program manager 147 rue de l'Université, 75007 Paris, France. T. +33142759000. Fax +33147059966. E-mail: ophelie.bonnet@inrae.fr.
URL: http://www.faccejpi.com/

History Set up as a Joint Programming initiative, introduced by *European Commission (EC, #06633).* **Aims** Build an integrated European Research Area addressing the interconnected challenges of sustainable agriculture, food security and impacts of climate change. **Structure** Governing Board; Scientific Advisory Body; Stakeholder Advisory Board; Secretariat. **Languages** English. **Activities** Research/documentation. **Events** *Meeting* Paris (France) 2020, *International Symposium on Non-CO2 Greenhouse Gases* Amsterdam (Netherlands) 2019.

Members Participating countries (24):
Austria, Belgium, Cyprus, Czechia, Denmark, Estonia, Finland, France, Germany, Hungary, Ireland, Israel, Italy, Latvia, Lithuania, Netherlands, New Zealand, Norway, Poland, Romania, Spain, Sweden, Switzerland, UK.
Participating entity:
European Commission (EC, #06633). [2020.08.27/XM6344/**E***]

♦ Joint Programming Initiative on Healthy and Productive Seas and Oceans (JPI Oceans) 16146

Exec Dir Rue du Trône 4, 1000 Brussels, Belgium. T. +3226261660. E-mail: info@jpi-oceans.eu – office@jpi-oceans.eu.
Office Manager address not obtained.
URL: http://www.jpi-oceans.eu/

History Current statutes approved Nov 2017. Registration: Banque-Carrefour des Entreprises, No/ID: 0691.970.779, Start date: 13 Mar 2018, Belgium. **Aims** Strive to increase the impact of national investments in marine and maritime research and innovation. **Structure** Management Board; Internal Advisory Committee; Secretariat. **Languages** English. **Finance** Sources: members' dues. **Publications** *JPI Oceans' Newsletter* (irregular) in English. Annual Report; activity reports.

Members Full in 19 countries:
Belgium, Croatia, Denmark, Estonia, France, Germany, Greece, Iceland, Ireland, Italy, Malta, Netherlands, Norway, Poland, Portugal, Romania, Spain, Sweden, UK.

NGO Relations Member of (1): *Federation of European and International Associations Established in Belgium (FAIB, #09508).* [2023/XM7506/**F**]

♦ Joint Protocol Relating to the Application of the Vienna Convention and the Paris Convention (1988 treaty)

♦ Joint Research Centre (JRC) 16147

Centre commun de recherche (CCR) – Centro Común de Investigación (CCI) – Gemeinsame Forschungsstelle (GFS) – Centro Comum de Investigação (CCI) – Centro Comune de Ricerca (CCR) – Gemeenschappelijk Centrum voor Onderzoek (GCO) – Gemensamma Forskningscentret – Det Faelles Forskningscenter – Koino Kentro Erevnon – Yhteinen Tutkimuskeskus – Airmhean Comhphairteach Taighde – Společné Vyzkumné Centrum – Spojené Vyskumné Centrum – Közös Kutatóközpont – Wspólnotowe Centrum Badawcze – Skupni Raziknovalni Center – Teądusuuringute Ühiskeskus – Kopigais Petniecibas centrs – Jungtinis Tyrimu Centras – Ic-Centru Kongunt Ghar-Ricerka – Centrul Comun de Cercetare

Dir Gen c/o European Commission, Rue du Champ de Mars 21, 1050 Brussels, Belgium. T. +3222991111. E-mail: jrc-esarda@ec.europa.eu.
URL: https://joint-research-centre.ec.europa.eu/

History 1957, Rome (Italy). Established under the *Treaty Establishing the European Atomic Energy Community (Treaty of Rome, 1957)* which set up *European Atomic Energy Community (Euratom, inactive).* Comprises a service of the *European Commission (EC, #06633)*, originally as part of Directorate-General XII, now a Directorate-General in its own right, under the Commissioner for Education, Culture, Youth and Sport. An institution of *European Union (EU, #08967).* **Aims** As the European Commission's *science* and knowledge service, support EU policies with independent evidence throughout the whole policy cycle. **Structure** Directorate General – Brussels (Belgium), assisted by Board of Governors Directorates (10): A. Strategy and Work Programme Coordination (Brussels, Belgium); B. Growth and Innovation (Seville, Spain); C. Energy, Transport and Climate (Petten, Netherlands); D. Sustainable Resources (Ispra, Italy); E. Space, Security and Migration (Ispra, Italy); F. Health, Consumers and Reference Materials (Geel, Belgium); G. Nuclear Safety and Security (Karlsruhe, Germany); H. Knowledge Management (Ispra, Italy); I. Competences (Ispra, Italy); R. Resources (Brussels, Belgium). **Languages** EU languages. **Staff** 3000.00 FTE, paid. **Finance** Funded by the EU's framework programme for research and innovation, Horizon 2020, for its non-nuclear work and by the EURATOM Research and Training Programme for its nuclear work. Annual budget: about euro 330,000,000. **Activities** Research and development; training/education; knowledge management/information dissemination. **Events** *ONE – Health Environment and Society Conference* Brussels (Belgium) 2022, *Real Utopias for a Social Europe – Working Time Reduction and the Four-Day Week* Brussels (Belgium) 2022, *World Conference on Photovoltaic Energy Conversion (WCPEC-8)* Milan (Italy) 2022, *Workshop on User and Policy Needs of the European Biodiversity Observation Network* Laxenburg (Austria) 2021, *European Photovoltaic Solar Energy Conference* Lisbon (Portugal) 2021. **Publications** Annual Report; institute annual reports; reference reports; information leaflets; topical reports; press releases; contributions to conferences; scientific and technical articles; technical notes; communications; reports on special activities; special publications. **Information Services** *Environmental Chemicals Data and Information Network (ECDIN)* – databank; *Radioactivity Environmental Monitoring (REM).*

Members European Union Member States (27):
Austria, Belgium, Bulgaria, Croatia, Cyprus, Czechia, Denmark, Estonia, Finland, France, Germany, Greece, Hungary, Ireland, Italy, Latvia, Lithuania, Luxembourg, Malta, Netherlands, Poland, Portugal, Romania, Slovakia, Slovenia, Spain, Sweden.

IGO Relations Collaborates with: *European Environment Agency (EEA, #06995); International Transport Forum (ITF, #15725).* Member of: *Abdus Salam International Centre for Theoretical Physics (ICTP, #00005); Congo Basin Forest Partnership (CBFP, #04662).* Cooperates with: *United Nations Institute for Training and Research (UNITAR, #20576).* Ispra Site of JRC serves as secretariat for: *European Safeguards Research and Development Association (ESARDA, #08417).* **NGO Relations** Member of (9): *Eurolib (#05703); European Biomass Industry Association (EUBIA, #06339); European Network of Environmental Research Organizations (ENERO, #07902); Global Alliance for Genomics and Health (GA4GH, #10199); Global Alliance of Disaster Research Institutes (GADRI, #10194); Integrated Assessment Modeling Consortium (IAMC, #11366); International Union of Pure and Applied Chemistry (IUPAC, #15809); Joint Committee for Traceability in Laboratory Medicine (JCTLM, #16127); Sustainable Nuclear Energy Technology Platform (SNETP, #20063).* Observer to: *European Umbrella Organization for Geographical Information (EUROGI, #08964).* Is chair of: *European Network of GMO Laboratories (ENGL, #07914).* In liaison with technical committees of: *International Organization for Standardization (ISO, #14473).* Instrumental in setting up: *ERAWATCH Network (EWN, inactive); European Association for Environmental Management Education (EAEME, inactive); International Committee for Radionuclide Metrology (ICRM, #12798).* Partner of: *European Partnership for Alternative Approaches to Animal Testing (EPAA, #08155).* Collaboration agreement with: *Network of Reference Laboratories for Monitoring of Emerging Environmental Pollutants (NORMAN Network, #17053).* [2018/XE5547/**E***]

♦ Joint Research Centre – Institute for Reference Materials and Measurements (inactive)
♦ Joint Research Centre on Transnational Crime (internationally oriented national body)
♦ Joint Scandinavian Committee for Home Economics Education (no recent information)

♦ Joint Secretariat of Agricultural Trade Associations 16148

Secrétariat des Associations du Commerce Agricole Réunies (SACAR)

Contact Rue de Trèves 49-51, Box 14, 1040 Brussels, Belgium. T. +3222310638. E-mail: office@sacar.be.
URL: http://sacar.be/

History 1980, Brussels (Belgium). Former names and other names: *European Secretariat of the United Agricultural Trade Associations* – former; *Secrétariat européen d'associations du commerce agricole réunies (SACAR)* – former. Registration: Banque-Carrefour des Entreprises, No/ID: 0420.055.530, Start date: 23 Jan 1980, Belgium; EU transparency Register, No/ID: 68973742523-49, Start date: 19 Oct 2009. **Aims** Monitor and analyse EU legislation and policies relevant to member associations; promote and defend the interests of member organizations; liaise with EU institutions; promote technical cooperation and the common management of the secretariats of member organizations. **Structure** General Assembly (annual); Board of Directors. **Languages** English. **Staff** 6.00 FTE, paid. **Finance** Members' dues. **Events** *Annual General Assembly* Brussels (Belgium) 2002, *Annual General Assembly* Brussels (Belgium) 2001, *Annual General Assembly* Brussels (Belgium) 2000, *Annual General Assembly* Brussels (Belgium) 1994, *Annual General Assembly* Brussels (Belgium) 1993. **Members** Agricultural trade associations (membership countries not specified). **Consultative Status** Consultative status granted from: *UNCTAD (#20285)* (Special Category). **NGO Relations** Member of: *Federation of European and International Associations Established in Belgium (FAIB, #09508).* [2021/XD9136/t/**D**]

♦ Joint Secretariat of UNIPEDE and EURELECTRIC / see Union of the Electricity Industry – Eurelectric (#20379)
♦ Joint Sub-Commission on Mediterranean Forestry Problems / see AFWC/EFC/NEFC Committee on Mediterranean Forestry Questions – Silva Mediterranea (#00542)
♦ Joint UNESCO/WMO Flood Initiative / see International Flood Initiative (#13613)

♦ Joint United Nations Programme on HIV/AIDS (UNAIDS) 16149

Programme commun des Nations unies sur le VIH/SIDA (ONUSIDA)

Exec Dir 20 avenue Appia, 1211 Geneva 27, Switzerland. T. +41227914722 – +41227913666. Fax +41227914179 – +41227914187. E-mail: communications@unaids.org.
URL: http://www.unaids.org/

History 26 Jul 1994. Established when endorsed by *ECOSOC (#05331)*, in resolution 1994/24, under the aegis of *United Nations (UN, #20515).* Operational from 1 Jan 1996, replacing and taking over activities of *WHO Global Programme on AIDS (GPA, inactive)* and uniting six organizations in a jointly co-sponsored programme: *International Bank for Reconstruction and Development (IBRD, #12317)* (World Bank); *UNDP (#20292); UNESCO (#20322); UNICEF (#20332); United Nations Population Fund (UNFPA, #20612); WHO (#20950).* These six co-sponsors were joined by: *United Nations Office on Drugs and Crime (UNODC, #20596)* in Mar 1999; *ILO (#11123)* in Oct 2001; *UNHCR (#20327)* in Jun 2004; *World Food Programme (WFP, #21510)* in 2003. Comes within the framework of *United Nations System (#20635).* New high-level organizational structure endorsed, July 2021; commenced mid-2022 in a phased manner. **Aims** As main advocate for the global response to HIV/AIDS, lead, strengthen and support efforts to prevent HIV transmission, provide *care* and support, reduce impact and alleviate individual and communal vulnerability to HIV/AIDS; expand and strengthen national response to HIV/AIDS in *developing countries*; increase strong political and financial commitment by all governments to an expanded response to HIV/AIDS; expand and strengthen UN system response to HIV/AIDS through enhanced collaboration, coordination and joint action on policies, strategies and programmes; develop and promote international best practices, based on sound policy, strategies and research, established as an integral element of the response to HIV/AIDS. **Structure** Programme Coordinating Board (PCB), meeting in annual session in Geneva (Switzerland) and thematic session in alternate years outside Geneva. PCB serves as governing body and comprises 22 governments representing all world regions, the co-sponsors and 5 NGOs, including associations of people living with HIV. Committee of Cosponsoring Organizations (CCO), meeting regularly, acts as standing committee of PCB and comprises representatives of the co-sponsors and the Secretariat. Secretariat in Geneva, operating at global level, comprises: Executive Office; External Relations Department; Policy, Advocacy, and Knowledge Branch; Programme Branch; Department of Management; Regional Support Teams (Asia Pacific; Eastern Europe and Central sia; Eastern and Southern Africa; Latin America and the Caribbean; Middle-East and Northern Africa; Western and Central Africa); Network of UNAIDS Country Offices. **Languages** English, French, Russian, Spanish. **Staff** As of Aug 2005: 244 at headquarters in Geneva (Switzerland); 195 in the field. Personnel negotiations through *UNAIDS Secretariat Staff Association (USSA, see: #16149).* **Finance** Voluntary contributions from governments, foundations, corporations, private groups (students, universities, sporting clubs, etc) and individuals. **Activities** Reinforces roles at country, intercountry and global levels, covering 3 functions: (1) source of globally-relevant policy on HIV/AIDS; developing, promoting and strengthening international best practice and research; (2) catalyzing, targeting and providing technical support to help build and strengthen capability for an expanded response to HIV/AIDS, particularly in developing countries; (3) advocating a well-resourced and strategically, ethically and technically sound, comprehensive, multisectoral response to HIV/AIDS. **Events** *International AIDS Conference* Montréal, QC (Canada) 2022, *Fast-Track Cities Conference* Seville (Spain) 2022, *Fast-Track Cities Conference* Lisbon (Portugal) 2021, *International AIDS Conference* 2020, *Consultative Meeting on Africa CDC Public Health Situation Room* Addis Ababa (Ethiopia) 2019. **Publications** *Aids Epidemic Update* (annual); *Report on the Global AIDS Epidemic* (every 2 years); *Best Practice Collection.* **IGO Relations** Collaborates with co-sponsors and with other UN and intergovernmental organizations (not specified). Member of: *United Nations Sustainable Development Group (UNSDG, #20634).* Letters of Agreement with: *FAO (#09260); International Organization for Migration (IOM, #14454).* Observer to: *International Fund for Agricultural Development (IFAD, #13692).* Cooperates with: *United Nations Institute for Training and Research (UNITAR, #20576).* Participates in UN regional commissions; observer as requested in the UN System Chief Executives Board for Coordination and related mechanisms; participates in numerous regional bodies, development banks and regional offices of UN System organizations. **NGO Relations** Ongoing relations with a range of civil society actors, including NGOs, faith-based organizations, trade unions, private sector, sports associations, etc, on global, regional and country levels. Instrumental in setting up: *Global Coalition on Women and AIDS (GCWA, #10297).* [2022/XE2288/**E***]

♦ **Joint Vienna Institute (JVI)** **16150**
Objedinennyj Venskij Institut
Contact Mariahilfer Straße 97, 1060 Vienna, Austria. T. +4317989495. E-mail: jvi@jvi.org.
URL: http://www.jvi.org/
History 1992. Originally established as a temporary institute, scheduled to close 1999, extended until 2004, but became permanent in 2002, with *International Monetary Fund (IMF, #14180)* and Austrian authorities as primary members. Contributing members include: *European Bank for Reconstruction and Development (EBRD, #06315)*; *European Investment Bank (EIB, #07599)*; Organisation for Economic Co-operation and Development (OECD); *International Bank for Reconstruction and Development (IBRD, #12317)*; *World Trade Organization (WTO, #21864)*; *European Commission (EC, #06633)* (Observer Status). **Aims** Provide policy-oriented training, primarily for public sector officials, in order to strengthen *economic policies* and institutions in Central, Eastern and Southeastern Europe, the Caucasus, Central Asia and other selected countries. **Structure** Executive Board; Director. **Languages** English, Russian. **Staff** 26.00 FTE, paid. **Finance** Sources: contributions of member/participating states; donations; government support. Supported by: *International Monetary Fund (IMF, #14180)*. **Activities** Training/education. **Publications** *JVI Newsletter*. Annual Program Brochure. [2020.05.12/XE1742/j/**E**]

♦ **Joint WMO-IOC Technical Commission for Oceanography and Marine Meteorology (JCOMM)** **16151**
Co-Pres Laboratorio SINCEM, Univ of Bologna, Via S Alberto 163, 48123 Ravenna RA, Italy. T. +39544937324.
Co-Pres South African Weather Service, Weather Office, PO Box 21, International Airport, Cape Town, 7525, South Africa. T. +27219340450.
URL: http://www.jcomm.info/
History 1999, by *World Meteorological Organization (WMO, #21649)* and *Intergovernmental Oceanographic Commission (IOC, #11496)*, by merger of *Integrated Global Ocean Services System (IGOSS, inactive)* and WMO Commission for Marine Meteorology. **Structure** Management Committee; Programme Area Coordination; Expert Groups. **Activities** Research/documentation; knowledge management/information dissemination. **Events** *Meeting of the Community of Practice on End-to-End Early Warning Systems for Flood Forecasting* Seoul (Korea Rep) 2019, *Capacity Building Workshop of the WMO/IOC Data Buoy Cooperation Panel for the North Pacific Ocean and its Marginal Seas* Busan (Korea Rep) 2015, *Session* Yeosu (Korea Rep) 2012, *Data buoy cooperation panel meeting* Geneva (Switzerland) 2011, *Data buoy cooperation panel meeting* Jeju (Korea Rep) 2007. **IGO Relations** Participates in: *Integrated Global Observing Strategy (IGOS, inactive)*. **NGO Relations** Participates in: *Partnership for Observation of the Global Oceans (POGO, #18239)*. [2014.11.03/XE3456/**E***]

♦ Joint Working Group for Justice and Peace / see Commission for Justice, Peace and Integrity of Creation – USG/UISG (#04230)

♦ **Joint Working Group between the Roman Catholic Church and the World Council of Churches (JWG)** **16152**
Address not obtained.
URL: http://www.oikoumene.org/
History 1965, Enugu (Nigeria), by *World Council of Churches (WCC, #21320)* and the Vatican authorities through *Pontifical Council for Promoting Christian Unity (PCPCU, #18446)*. Also referred to as *Vatican-WCC Joint Working Group*. Comes under the General Secretariat of WCC. **Aims** As the official consultative forum of WCC and the Roman Catholic Church (RCC), monitor adn strengthen cooperation between the parent bodies, especially between the various organs and programmes of the WCC and the RCC. **Structure** Plenary Meeting (annual); Executive. **Staff** 2.00 FTE, paid. **Finance** No budget of its own. Parent bodies share expenses. **Activities** Events/meetings; networking/liaising. **Events** *Plenary Session* Augsburg (Germany) 2018, *Plenary Session* Lisbon (Portugal) 2017, *Plenary session* Bossey (Switzerland) 2016, *Plenary session* Rabat (Malta) 2011, *Plenary session* Sednayah (Syrian AR) 2010. **Publications** Communiques. **Members** WCC membership and representations nominated by the Pontifical Council for Promoting Christian Unity. [2017/XE1464/**E**]

♦ Joint Workshop on New Technologies for Computer/Robot Assisted Surgery (meeting series)
♦ Join For Water (internationally oriented national body)
♦ Jonathan Napela Center for Hawaiian and Pacific Islands Studies (internationally oriented national body)
♦ Jonge Europese Federalisten (#21984)
♦ Jonge Europese Ondernemer / see Spirit of Enterprise Group
♦ Jongeren tegen Racisme in Europa (#22003)
♦ Jornadas Internacionales de Sindicatos Médicos (meeting series)

♦ **José Carreras International Leukaemia Foundation (JCILF)** **16153**
Fundación Internacional José Carreras para la Lucha contra la Leucemia (FIJC) – Fundació Internacional Josep Carreras per a la Lluita contra la Leucèmia (FIJC)
Gen Manager Muntaner 383, 2nd, 08021 Barcelona, Spain. T. +34934145566. Fax +34932010588. E-mail: fundacio@fcarreras.es – info@fcarreras.es.
URL: http://www.fcarreras.org/
History 14 Jul 1988, Barcelona (Spain). **Aims** Promote scientific research in the fight against leukaemia through yearly grants; provide infrastructure for hospitals and health care centres; promote *bone marrow* and cord *blood* donation; provide social services for leukaemia *patients* and their relatives. **Structure** Board of Trustees; National and International Scientific Committees; General Management. Bone Marrow Registry. **Finance** Sources: donations; endowments; hospital service fees; international registries. Budget (annual) euro 12 million. **Activities** Research and development; awares/prizes/competitions. **Events** *Annual International Meeting* Barcelona (Spain) 1996. **Publications** *FIJC Journal* (3 a year) in Catalan, Spanish. Annual Report. Newsletter.
Members Organizations in 4 countries:
Germany, Spain, Switzerland, USA.
IGO Relations *European Commission (EC, #06633)* – DG Sanco. [2020/XE3644/f/**E**]

♦ Josef Korbel School of International Studies (internationally oriented national body)
♦ José Marti International Institute of Journalism (#11340)
♦ Joseph H and Belle R Braun Center for Holocaust Studies / see ADL Braun Holocaust Institute
♦ Joseph H Lauder Institute of Management and International Studies (internationally oriented national body)
♦ Josephite Fathers (religious order)
♦ Josephite Fathers – St Joseph's Society of the Sacred Heart (religious order)
♦ Joséphites de Belgique (religious order)
♦ Joséphites de Murialdo (religious order)
♦ Joseph Lau Luen Hung Charitable Trust Asia Pacific Centre for Leadership and Change. / see Asia Pacific Centre for Leadership and Change
♦ Joseph Rowntree Charitable Trust (internationally oriented national body)
♦ **JOSO** Joint Organization for Solar Observations (#16144)

♦ **Journalism in the Eastern Mediterranean – Strategy, Training, Organization (JEMSTONE Network)** **16154**
Dir PO Box 850191, Amman 11185, Jordan. E-mail: info@jemstone.net.
URL: http://www.jemstone.net/
History 1993. Founded by *MEDIA Programme (MEDIA, inactive)*. Originally functioned within *UNESCO Mediterranean Programme (inactive)* as a network of *Mediterranean Media Network (no recent information)*. Former names and other names: *Journalism in the Euro-Med region: Strategy, Training, Organisation and Networks* – alias; *Stichting JourNetwork* – legal name; *Jemstone Network Ltd* – legal name. Registration: Companies House, England and Wales; Netherlands. **Aims** Support media supporting development. **Languages** Arabic, Dutch, English. **Finance** Project funding. **Activities** Organizes workshops; training courses; masterclasses; Round Table seminars. **Publications** *Jemstone Newsletter*. Style book for Arabic language press.
Members in 9 countries and territories:
Cyprus, Egypt, Jordan, Lebanon, North Macedonia, Palestine, Syrian AR, Türkiye, Yemen.
IGO Relations *UNESCO (#20322)*. [2022/XK1751/**E**]

♦ Journalism in the Euro-Med region: Strategy, Training, Organisation and Networks / see Journalism in the Eastern Mediterranean – Strategy, Training, Organization (#16154)
♦ Journalists Against Corruption (internationally oriented national body)
♦ Journalists' International Association for Studying Problems of Overseas Peoples (inactive)
♦ Journée internationale de l'enfance africaine / see International Day of the African Child and Youth (#13140)
♦ Journée internationale de l'enfance et la jeunesse africaine / see International Day of the African Child and Youth (#13140)

♦ **Journées européennes du Cortinaire (JEC)** **16155**
Chairman address not obtained.
URL: http://www.jec-cortinarius.org/
History 1983. **Aims** Establish contacts and scientific links between European mycologists interested in the study of the genus Cortinarius. **Structure** Committee. **Activities** Events/meetings. **Events** *Congress* Sarnonico (Italy) 2022, *Congress* Norway 2019, *Congress* Bálványos (Romania) 2018, *Congress* Potes (Spain) 2017, *Congress* Borgsjö (Sweden) 2016. **Publications** *Le Journal des J.E.C.*. [2022/AA0727/**D**]

♦ Journées Internationales de Ventilation à Domicile / see JIVD-AER
♦ Journées internationales du verre / see Association internationale pour l'histoire du verre (#02706)
♦ Jóvenes Demócrata Cristianos Europeos (inactive)
♦ Jóvenes por los Derechos Humanos Internacional (#22019)
♦ Jóvenes por un Mundo Unido (see: #09806)
♦ Jóvenes del Tercer Mundo (internationally oriented national body)
♦ Joven Europeo Emprendedor / see Spirit of Enterprise Group
♦ Joven Orquesta de la Comunidad Europea / see European Union Youth Orchestra (#09024)
♦ Joven Orquesta de la Unión Europea (#09024)
♦ Joventut Europea Federalista (#21984)
♦ Joyce Mertz-Gilmore Foundation / see Mertz Gilmore Foundation
♦ JOYST Youth Exchange International (internationally oriented national body)
♦ J Paul Getty Trust (internationally oriented national body)
♦ **JPC** Jeunesse pour Christ (#22009)
♦ **JPC** Juventud para Cristo (#22009)
♦ JPC-SE / see International Network for Epidemiology in Policy (#14264)
♦ JPF – Jewish Peace Fellowship (internationally oriented national body)
♦ J/P Haitian Relief Organization / see Community Organized Relief Effort
♦ JPIC / see Commission for Justice, Peace and Integrity of Creation – USG/UISG (#04230)

♦ **JPI Climate** **16156**
Exec Dir c/o Belgian Science Policy Office, Av Louise 231, 1050 Brussels, Belgium. T. +3222383702. E-mail: secretariat@jpi-climate.belspo.be.
URL: http://www.jpi-climate.eu/
History A *Joint Programme Initiative*. **Aims** Bring together existing and develop new scientific knowledge needed to assist practitioners to adequately transform society towards *climate* resilience: provide integrated climate knowledge and decision support services for societal innovation. **Structure** Governing Board; Transdisciplinary Advisory Board; Management Committee; Central Secretariat. Task Forces; Working Groups; Expert Panel of Working Groups. **Activities** Research/documentation; events/meetings. **Events** *Workshop on Climate Impact and Loss Data for Europe* Berlin (Germany) 2015, *Meeting* Madrid (Spain) 2015, *Symposium on Taking Stock and Inspiring the Future Started* Madrid (Spain) 2015, *Symposium on Greening the Research System* Potsdam (Germany) 2015, *Symposium on Designing Comprehensive Open Knowledge Policies to Face Climate Change* Vienna (Austria) 2015. **Publications** *JPI Climate Newsletter*.
Members Countries (13):
Austria, Belgium, Denmark, Finland, France, Germany, Ireland, Italy, Netherlands, Norway, Spain, Sweden, UK.
Observer countries (3):
Estonia, Slovenia, Türkiye.
Observer institutions (4):
European Climate Research Alliance (ECRA, #06576); *European Environment Agency (EEA, #06995)*; *European Space Agency (ESA, #08798)*; *NordForsk (#17164)*.
IGO Relations *European Commission (EC, #06633)* and its *European Research Area and Innovation Committee (ERAC)*. [2017.06.20/XM4306/**F***]

♦ **JPI Oceans** Joint Programming Initiative on Healthy and Productive Seas and Oceans (#16146)
♦ JPLP – Juristes pour la Paix (internationally oriented national body)
♦ JPR – Institute for Jewish Policy Research (internationally oriented national body)
♦ JPSI – Jewish Prisoner Services International (internationally oriented national body)
♦ JRA – Japanese Red Army (unconfirmed)
♦ JRC-IRMM, Geel – Joint Research Centre – Institute for Reference Materials and Measurements (inactive)
♦ **JRC** Joint Research Centre (#16147)
♦ **JRE** Jeunes contre le racisme en Europe (#22003)

♦ **JRE- Jeunes Restaurateurs (JRE)** **16157**
Contact Beemdstraat 26, 5652 AB Eindhoven, Netherlands. T. +31402260934. E-mail: info@jre.eu.
Sec address not obtained.
URL: http://www.jre.eu/
History 1990, France. Founded as an European organization, following an idea to found an organization for young restaurant owners by Nicole Seitz, Head External Relations at Grand Marnier (1953-1998). Former names and other names: *Les Jeunes Restaurateurs France (JRF')* – former (1974); *Jeunes Restaurateurs d'Europe (JRE)* – former (2016). **Aims** Bring together young restaurateurs and chefs who want to share their talent and passion for food with likeminded people. **Languages** Dutch, English, French, German, Italian, Spanish. **Staff** 3.00 FTE, paid; 15.00 FTE, voluntary. **Finance** Sources: meeting proceeds; members' dues. **Events** *Congress* Bruges (Belgium) 2019, *Congress* Lucerne (Switzerland) 2017, *Congress* Roermond (Netherlands) 2015, *Congress* Salzburg (Austria) 2013, *Congress* Madrid (Spain) 2011. **Publications** *Passion* – magazine. *National JRE Restaurant Guides*.
Members Restaurants (over 350) in 16 countries:
Austria, Belgium, Croatia, France, Germany, Ireland, Italy, Luxembourg, Netherlands, Poland, Romania, Serbia, Slovenia, Spain, Switzerland, UK. [2021.02.16/XD3143/v/**D**]

♦ JRE / see JRE- Jeunes Restaurateurs (#16157)
♦ **JRE** JRE- Jeunes Restaurateurs (#16157)
♦ JRF' / see JRE- Jeunes Restaurateurs (#16157)
♦ **JRS Europe** Jesuit Refugee Service Europe (#16107)
♦ **JRS** Jesuit Refugee Service (#16106)
♦ **JRS** Service jésuite des réfugiés (#16106)
♦ **JRS** Servicio Jesuita a Refugiados (#16106)
♦ JSAPMDD / see Jubilee South – Asian Peoples' Movement on Debt and Development (#16160)
♦ **JSAPMDD** Jubilee South – Asian Peoples' Movement on Debt and Development (#16160)
♦ JSAS – Japan Society for Afrasian Studies (internationally oriented national body)
♦ **JSCA** Justice Studies Centre of the Americas (#16171)
♦ JSCASC – James S Coleman African Studies Center, Los Angeles (internationally oriented national body)
♦ JSF – Jeunesse sans frontière (internationally oriented national body)
♦ JSIF / see Nippon Foundation
♦ JSIL – Japan Society of International Law (internationally oriented national body)
♦ **JSRS** Japanese Scandinavian Radiological Society (#16090)
♦ JSSAH / see Japan Society for Southeast Asian Studies
♦ JSSEAS – Japan Society for Southeast Asian Studies (internationally oriented national body)
♦ JSSS – Jungian Society of Scholarly Studies (internationally oriented national body)
♦ **JUA** Judo Union of Asia (#16162)

♦ Jubilee 2000 Coalition / see Jubilee Research (#16158)
♦ Jubilee Action / see Chance for Childhood (#03850)
♦ Jubilee Debt Campaign (internationally oriented national body)
♦ Jubilee Plus / see Jubilee Research (#16158)

♦ Jubilee Research 16158

Contact address not obtained. T. +442078206350. Fax +442078206350. E-mail: info@ jubileeplus.org.
URL: http://www.jubileeplus.org/

History Apr 1996, Keele (UK), by *Christian Aid, Catholic Agency for Overseas Development (CAFOD), Oxfam GB* and *Tearfund, UK*. Originally a short-life campaign with the title *Jubilee 2000 Coalition*. Subsequently changed title to *Jubilee Plus*. Current title adopted 2002. UK Registered Charity. **Aims** Provide up-to-date, accurate analyses, news and data on international *debt* and *finance*; generate and air new ideas and debates on debt and globalization; develop a new, more accountable and transparent process for sovereign lending, borrowing and debt negotiations; highlight and develop policies for financing *development* in a more self-reliant way, without recourse to dependency on foreign donors and creditors; open up international financial institutions and markets to democratic scrutiny and accountability by civil society. **Structure** Director; Head of Research; Research Team; Group Coordinator. Secretariat at: *New Economics Foundation (NEF, #17082)*. **Activities** Supports and provides information to debt campaigns worldwide and social movements. **Publications** Newsletter reports; international economic and financial news.
Members Coalitions in 67 countries and territories:
Angola, Argentina, Australia, Austria, Bangladesh, Belgium, Benin, Bolivia, Brazil, Burkina Faso, Cameroon, Canada, Colombia, Côte d'Ivoire, Cuba, Czechia, Denmark, Ecuador, Egypt, El Salvador, Eswatini, Finland, France, Germany, Ghana, Guatemala, Guyana, Haiti, Honduras, Hong Kong, India, Indonesia, Ireland, Italy, Jamaica, Japan, Kenya, Korea Rep, Madagascar, Malawi, Mali, Mauritius, Mexico, Mozambique, Netherlands, New Zealand, Nicaragua, Nigeria, Norway, Pakistan, Peru, Philippines, Poland, Portugal, Senegal, South Africa, Spain, Sri Lanka, Sweden, Tanzania UR, Togo, Uganda, UK, USA, Venezuela, Zambia, Zimbabwe.
Organizational members include 34 listed in this Yearbook:
– *ActionAid (#00087)*;
– *Action for Southern Africa (ACTSA)*;
– *BMS World Mission*;
– *Campaign Against Arms Trade (CAAT)*;
– *Catholic Agency for Overseas Development (CAFOD)*;
– *Christian Aid*;
– *Church Mission Society (CMS)*;
– *Commonwealth Trade Union Council (CTUC, inactive)*;
– *Crosslinks*;
– *Friends of the Earth International (FoEI, #10002)* (UK);
– *Global Justice Now*;
– *Institute for African Alternatives (IFAA, #11241)*;
– *International Institute for Environment and Development (IIED, #13877)*;
– *Medact*;
– *Methodist Church Britain – World Church Office*;
– *Mid-Africa Ministry – CMS (MAM, inactive)*;
– *Missionary Society of St Columban (SSCME)*;
– *New Economics Foundation (NEF, #17082)*;
– *Oxfam GB*;
– *People and Planet*;
– *Religious Society of Friends (Quakers, #18834)* (UK);
– *Salvation Army (#19041)*;
– *Save the Children UK (SC UK)*;
– *South American Mission Society (SAMS International, #19705)*;
– *Tearfund, UK*;
– *The Mothers' Union (#16860)*;
– *Tools for Self Reliance*;
– *Trocaire – Catholic Agency for World Development*;
– *UNICEF (#20332)*;
– *USPG (#20736)*;
– *Voluntary Service Overseas (VSO)*;
– *War on Want*;
– *World Vision International (WVI, #21904)* (UK);
– *World Young Women's Christian Association (World YWCA, #21947)*.
Consultative Status Consultative status granted from: *UNCTAD (#20285)* (Special Category). **NGO Relations** Member of: *Jubilee International Movement for Economic and Social Justice (JMI, no recent information)*. Supported by: *Brot für die Welt*; *International Trade Union Confederation (ITUC, #15708)*. Supports: *Global Call for Action Against Poverty (GCAP, #10263)*. [2016/XF4314/y/F]

♦ Jubilee South 16159

Subilee Sur
Intl Coordinator 34 Matiyaga, Central District Diliman, 1104 Quezon City, Philippines. T. +6329253036. Fax +6329253036.
URL: http://www.jubileesouth.org/

Aims Develop and strengthen a global South movement on *debt*. **Structure** Regions (3): Asia; Southern Africa; *Jubileo Sur / Americas*. *Jubilee South – Asian Peoples' Movement on Debt and Development (JSAPMDD, #16160)*. **Members** Debt campaigns, social movements, people's organizations, communities, NGOs and political formations representing 85 anti-debt groups in 40 countries (not specified) in Latin America and the Caribbean, Africa and Asia. **NGO Relations** South American area is member of: *Alianza Social Continental (ASC, #00635)*. South American and African areas are member of: *Climate Justice Now ! (CJN!, inactive)*. Working relationship with: *European Network on Debt and Development (EURODAD, #07891)*. Supports: *Global Call for Action Against Poverty (GCAP, #10263)*. [2015/XM3622/F]

♦ Jubilee South APMDD / see Jubilee South – Asian Peoples' Movement on Debt and Development (#16160)

♦ Jubilee South – Asian Peoples' Movement on Debt and Development (JSAPMDD) 16160

Coordinator 34 Matiyaga St, Barangay Central Distr, 1100 Quezon City, Philippines. Fax +6329253036.
URL: http://www.apmdd.org/

History Set up as *Jubilee South – Asia Pacific Movement on Debt and Development (JSAPMDD)*. Also referred to as *Jubilee South APMDD*.
Members Organizations, including the following listed in this Yearbook (4):
Asian Migrant Centre (AMC); *Focus on the Global South (Focus, #09807)*; *Migrant Forum in Asia (MFA, #16798)*; *South Asia Alliance for Poverty Eradication (SAAPE, #19712)*.
IGO Relations Accredited by: *Green Climate Fund (GCF, #10714)*. **NGO Relations** *Jubilee South (#16159)*. Member of: *Climate Justice Now ! (CJN!, inactive)*; *Financial Transparency Coalition (FTC, #09772)*; *NGO Forum on ADB (#17123)*. Partner of: *Panafrican Climate Justice Alliance (PACJA, #18046)*. [2020/XJ1936/y/F]

♦ Jubilee South – Asia Pacific Movement on Debt and Development / see Jubilee South – Asian Peoples' Movement on Debt and Development (#16160)
♦ Jubileo Sur / Americas (unconfirmed)

♦ Judaica Europeana 16161

Project Manager Uni Bib Johann Christian Senckenberg, Bockenheimer Landstr 134-138, 60325 Frankfurt-Main, Germany. T. +496979839665. Fax +496979839380. E-mail: judaica.europeana@ googlemail.com.
URL: http://www.judaica-europeana.eu/

History Launched as a project 2010, in the framework of the digitization programme eContentplus of *European Union (EU, #08967)*, as one of the building blocks for *Europeana Foundation (#05839)*. Second stage started 2012, when network of institutions set up, under leadership of *European Association for Jewish Culture (EAJC, no recent information)*, Frankfurt University Library (Germany) and National Library of Israel. **Aims** Identify relevant *digital* content which *documents Jewish* life in *Europe*; assist collection holders in the ingestion and uploading process to Europeana; raise awareness of the partners' digital collections. **Structure** Academic Advisory Group; Team. **Activities** Knowledge management/information dissemination; research/ documentation. **Publications** *Judaica Europeana Newsletter*.
Members Partners (about 30) in 14 countries:
Belgium, Czechia, Denmark, France, Germany, Greece, Hungary, Israel, Italy, Netherlands, Poland, Spain, UK, USA.
Included in the above, 1 organization listed in this Yearbook:
European Association for Jewish Culture (EAJC, no recent information). [2019/XM7032/F]

♦ JUDCA – Juventud Demócrata Cristiana de América (no recent information)
♦ Judicial Tribunal of the Organization of Arab Petroleum Exporting Countries (see: #17854)
♦ Jüdischer Weltkongress (#21599)

♦ Judo Union of Asia (JUA) 16162

Union asiatique de judo – Unión Asiatica de Judo
Pres Post Box 795, 13008 Safat, Kuwait.
Gen Sec C2/154, West Enclave, Pitam Pura, Delhi 110034, DELHI 110034, India.
URL: http://www.onlinejua.org/

History 1956, Tokyo (Japan). **Aims** Organize and protect the interests of judo movements throughout Asia; promote, spread and develop the spirit and technique of Kodokan Judo among member organizations and promote friendly and cordial relations among them; supervise judo activities in Asia, in particular organizing and conducting Asian Judo Championships and judo events held as part of the Asian Games; establish regulations relating to the organization and administration of judo activities in Asia. **Structure** Congress (every 2 years during Asian Judo Championships); Executive Committee (meets annually); Secretariat. Self-governing zones (5): West Asia; South Asia; Southeast Asia; East Asia; Central Asia. **Finance** Members' dues. Donations. **Activities** Sporting activities. **Events** *Biennial Congress* Tashkent (Uzbekistan) 2005, *Biennial Congress* Jeju (Korea Rep) 2003, *Meeting* Busan (Korea Rep) 2002, *Meeting* Osaka (Japan) 2001, *Biennial Congress* Ulaanbaatar (Mongolia) 2001. **Publications** *Judo News* (4 a year).
Members National and regional federations in 39 countries and territories:
Afghanistan, Bangladesh, Cambodia, China, Hong Kong, India, Indonesia, Iran Islamic Rep, Iraq, Japan, Jordan, Kazakhstan, Korea DPR, Korea Rep, Kuwait, Kyrgyzstan, Laos, Lebanon, Macau, Malaysia, Mongolia, Myanmar, Nepal, Pakistan, Palestine, Philippines, Qatar, Saudi Arabia, Singapore, Sri Lanka, Syrian AR, Taiwan, Tajikistan, Thailand, Turkmenistan, United Arab Emirates, Uzbekistan, Vietnam, Yemen.
NGO Relations Member of (1): *International Sport Network Organization (ISNO, #15592)*. Partner of (1): *General Association of Asia Pacific Sports Federations (GAAPSF, #10106)*. Continental Union of: *International Judo Federation (IJF, #13975)*. [2020/XD0930/D]

♦ Jugend für Christus (#22009)
♦ Jugend Dritte Welt (internationally oriented national body)
♦ Jugend Dritte Welt – Freunde und Förderer der Missionsprokur der Salesianer Don Boscos in Bonn / see Youth Third World
♦ Jugend Europäischer Volksgruppen (#22013)
♦ Jugendforum der Europäischen Union (inactive)
♦ Jugend für Menschenrechte International (#22019)
♦ Jugendorchester der Europäischen Gemeinschaft / see European Union Youth Orchestra (#09024)
♦ Jugendorchester der Europäischen Union (#09024)
♦ **JUH** Johanniter-Unfall-Hilfe (#16120)
♦ Juifs Européens pour une Paix Juste (unconfirmed)
♦ JU – Jeunesse universelle (inactive)

♦ Ju-Jitsu European Union (JJEU) 16163

Gen Sec Am Nepomuk-Platz 4, 76661 Philippsburg, Germany. E-mail: info@jjeu.eu.
URL: http://www.jjeu.eu/

History 1977, as *European Ju-Jitsu Federation (EJJF)*. Subsequently changed title to *European Ju-Jitsu Union (EJJU)*. Present name adopted 1987. Registered in accordance with Italian law. **Structure** General Assembly. Board, comprising President, Vice-President, General Secretary, Treasurer and members. Committees (4): Sports; Referee; Education; Development. **Events** *General Assembly* Almere (Netherlands) 2015, *General Assembly* Lund (Sweden) 2014.
Members Full in 33 countries:
Austria, Azerbaijan, Belgium, Bosnia-Herzegovina, Bulgaria, Croatia, Cyprus, Czechia, Denmark, Estonia, Finland, France, Germany, Greece, Hungary, Israel, Italy, Latvia, Montenegro, Netherlands, North Macedonia, Norway, Poland, Portugal, Romania, Russia, Serbia, Slovenia, Spain, Sweden, Switzerland, UK, Ukraine.
NGO Relations A continental union of: *Ju-Jitsu International Federation (JJIF, #16164)*. [2018/XJ1810/D]

♦ Ju-Jitsu International Federation (inactive)

♦ Ju-Jitsu International Federation (JJIF) 16164

Headquarters PO Box 110006, Abu Dhabi, United Arab Emirates. E-mail: mail@jjif.org – contact@ jjif.org – pr@jjif.org.
Pres PO Box 15, 194 00 Koropi, Greece. T. +302106624579. Fax +302106624579. E-mail: jjif.secretariat@ gmail.com.
URL: https://jjif.sport/

History 1987. Former names and other names: *International Ju-Jitsu Federation* – former; *Jiu-Jitsu International Federation* – alias. **Aims** Promote friendship and aide between jujitsu *martial arts* organizations worldwide. **Structure** General Assembly (annual); Board of Directors. Continental union: *Ju-Jitsu European Union (JJEU, #16163)*. **Languages** English. **Finance** Sources: members' dues. **Activities** Sporting activities. **Events** *World Championship and JJIF Congress* Toronto, ON (Canada) 2014, *World Championship and JJIF Congress* Hainau (Germany) 2012, *World Championship and JJIF Congress* Rio de Janeiro (Brazil) 2010. **Members** Membership countries not specified. **NGO Relations** Member of (3): *Alliance of Independent recognised Members of Sport (AIMS, #00690)*; *International World Games Association (IWGA, #15914)*; *Olympic Movement (#17719)*. Cooperates with (1): *International Testing Agency (ITA, #15678)*. Recognized by: *International Olympic Committee (IOC, #14408)*. [2021/XD9311/C]

♦ Jules Gonin Club 16165

Headquarters Hôpital Ophtalmique, Av de France 15, 1004 Lausanne VD, Switzerland. T. +41216268830. Fax +41216268831. E-mail: info@clubjulesgonin.com.
URL: http://www.clubjulesgonin.com/

History Previously also referred to as *Gonin Society* and *Club Jules Gonin Society*. **Aims** Investigate *eye surgery* and *retinal* problems. **Events** *Meeting* Zurich (Switzerland) 2014, *Meeting* Kyoto (Japan) 2010, *Meeting* St Moritz (Switzerland) 2008, *Meeting* Cape Town (South Africa) 2006, *Meeting* Athens (Greece) 2004. [2009.01.09/XJ9800/F]

♦ **JuLiA** Juventudes Liberales de las Américas (#16174)

♦ Julius-Hirschberg-Gesellschaft (JHG) 16166

Office Kirchgasse 6, 97291 Thüngersheim, Germany. T. +499364811543. Fax +499364811559.
URL: http://www.dog.org/jhg/

History 1986, Aachen (Germany FR). Registered in accordance with Austrian law: ZVR 975680498. **Structure** Bureau. **Finance** Members' dues. **Events** *Meeting* Düsseldorf (Germany) 2019, *Meeting* Linz (Austria) 2017, *Meeting* Bonn (Germany) 2014, *Meeting* Amsterdam (Netherlands) 2013, *Meeting* Cologne (Germany) 2010. **Publications** *Nuntia Documenta Annotationes* (2 a year).
Members Full in 3 countries:
Austria, Germany, Switzerland. [2014/XJ7952/E]

♦ Junge Europäische Föderalisten (#21984)
♦ Junge EVP / see Youth of the European People's Party (#22014)
♦ Jungend gegen Rassismus in Europa (#22003)
♦ Junges Europa, 1834 (inactive)
♦ Jungfraujoch Scientific Station, International Foundation / see International Foundation of the High Altitude Research Stations Jungfraujoch and Gornergrat (#13671)
♦ Jungian Society of Scholarly Studies (internationally oriented national body)
♦ Jungtinis Tyrimu Centras (#16147)

♦ Junior Achievement Inc / see JA Worldwide (#16091)

♦ **Junior Achievement Africa (JA Africa)** **16167**

CEO 52 Jungle Road, East Legon, Accra, Ghana. T. +233577680373. E-mail: info@ja-africa.org.
URL: http://ja-africa.org/

History Set up as a member of *JA Worldwide (#16091)*. **Aims** Provide *young* people with the tools and skills they need to be prepared for their professional futures either as entrepreneurs who create jobs for themselves and others or as employees who add value to their employers. **Structure** Board of Directors.
Members Full in 14 countries:
Botswana, Burkina Faso, Eswatini, Gabon, Ghana, Kenya, Mauritius, Nigeria, Senegal, South Africa, Tanzania UR, Uganda, Zambia, Zimbabwe.
NGO Relations Partner of: *UNLEASH*. [2017/XM5834/**E**]

♦ Junior Achievement International / see JA Worldwide (#16091)
♦ Junior Achievement Young Enterprise Europe / see JA Europe (#16085)
♦ Junior Chamber of Commerce International / see Junior Chamber International (#16168)
♦ Junior Chamber International / see Junior Chamber International (#16168)

♦ **Junior Chamber International (JCI)** **16168**

Jeune chambre internationale (JCI) – Camara Júnior Internacional (JCI)
World Headquarters 15645 Olive Blvd, Chesterfield MO 63017, USA. T. +16364493100. Fax +16364493107. E-mail: info@jci.cc.
URL: http://www.jci.cc/

History 11 Dec 1944, Mexico City (Mexico). Former names and other names: *Junior Chamber International* – former (11 Dec 1944); *Junior Chamber of Commerce International* – former; *JAYCEES International* – former (1972 to 1988); *JAYCEES Internacional* – former (1972 to 1988). **Aims** Contribute to the advancement of the global community by providing the opportunity for young people to develop the leadership skill, social responsibility, fellowship and *entrepreneurship* necessary to create positive change. **Structure** General Assembly (annual, at World Congress); Board of Directors; Executive Committee; Development Officers; Secretariat. **Languages** English, French, Japanese, Spanish. **Staff** 25.00 FTE, paid. **Finance** Sources: members' dues; sponsorship. **Activities** Advocacy/lobbying/activism; events/meetings; networking/liaising; training/education. **Events** *European Conference* Bruges (Belgium) 2022, *World Congress* Hong Kong (Hong Kong) 2022, *Asia Pacific Conference* Osaka (Japan) 2022, *World Congress* Johannesburg (South Africa) 2021, *Annual World Congress* Yokohama (Japan) 2020. **Publications** *JCI News* (12 a year) in English, French, Spanish. Kits on various subjects.
Members National organizations; Individuals. Full in 117 countries and territories:
Albania, Argentina, Australia, Austria, Bangladesh, Belgium, Benin, Bolivia, Botswana, Brazil, Bulgaria, Burkina Faso, Burundi, Cambodia, Cameroon, Canada, Chad, Chile, Colombia, Comoros, Congo Brazzaville, Congo DR, Côte d'Ivoire, Croatia, Curaçao, Cyprus, Czechia, Denmark, Djibouti, Dominican Rep, Ecuador, Egypt, Estonia, Finland, France, Gabon, Georgia, Germany, Ghana, Guinea, Haiti, Honduras, Hong Kong, Iceland, India, Indonesia, Ireland, Italy, Jamaica, Japan, Jordan, Kenya, Korea Rep, Kosovo, Latvia, Lebanon, Lesotho, Liberia, Lithuania, Luxembourg, Macau, Madagascar, Malawi, Malaysia, Maldives, Mali, Malta, Mauritius, Mexico, Moldova, Monaco, Mongolia, Morocco, Myanmar, Namibia, Nepal, Netherlands, New Zealand, Niger, Nigeria, Norway, Panama, Paraguay, Peru, Philippines, Poland, Puerto Rico, Romania, Russia, Rwanda, Senegal, Serbia, Singapore, Slovakia, Slovenia, South Africa, South Sudan, Spain, Sri Lanka, Suriname, Sweden, Switzerland, Syrian AR, Taiwan, Thailand, Timor-Leste, Togo, Tunisia, Türkiye, Uganda, UK, Ukraine, Uruguay, USA, Venezuela, Zambia, Zimbabwe.
Also members in West Indies. Membership countries not specified.
Consultative Status Consultative status granted from: *ECOSOC (#05331)* (General); *UNESCO (#20322)* (Associate Status); *ILO (#11123)* (Special List); *UNCTAD (#20285)* (General Category); *UNICEF (#20332)*; *OAS (#17629)*. **IGO Relations** Accredited by (1): *United Nations Office at Vienna (UNOV, #20604)*. Associated with Department of Global Communications of the United Nations. **NGO Relations** Memorandum of Understanding with (1): *World Chambers Federation (WCF, #21269)*. Member of (3): *Alliance of NGOs on Crime Prevention and Criminal Justice (#00709)*; *Conference of Non-Governmental Organizations in Consultative Relationship with the United Nations (CONGO, #04635)*; *NGO Committee on UNICEF (#17120)*. Partner of (1): *Every Woman Every Child (EWEC, #09215)*. Cooperates with (4): *AIESEC (#00593)*; *Inter-American Foundation (IAF, #11431)*; *International Chamber of Commerce (ICC, #12534)*; *World Chambers Network (WCN, #21270)*. Affiliated with (1): *United Nations Global Compact (#20567)*. [2020/XB2853/**B**]

♦ **Junior Enterprises Europe (JE Europe)** **16169**

Main Office Av du Frioul 51, 1140 Brussels, Belgium. E-mail: mail@juniorenterprises.eu.
URL: https://juniorenterprises.eu/

History 1992. Founded by 6 National Networks: CNJE (France); CEJE (Spain); BDSU (Germany); JADE Italia; JADE Switzerland; UniPartners (Netherlands). First Junior Enterprise set up 1967, France. Former names and other names: *European Confederation of Junior Enterprises (JADE)* – former. Registration: Belgium. **Aims** Develop and spread international activities of junior enterprises throughout Europe; strengthen recognition of the Junior Enterprise concept as both a complementary tool and a professional entity; widen horizons of single junior entrepreneurs. **Structure** General Assembly (quarterly); Council; Executive Board; One Big Team; Advisory Board. **Languages** English. **Staff** 30.00 FTE, voluntary. **Finance** Sources: grants; members' dues. Partnerships. **Activities** Advocacy/lobbying/activism; awareness raising; events/meetings; networking/liaising; standards/guidelines; training/education. **Events** *JEE Winter Conference* Brussels (Belgium) 2022, *JEE Spring Conference* Rezzato (Italy) 2022, *JEE Autumn Conference* Coimbra (Portugal) 2021, *Fall Conference* Lisbon (Portugal) 2020, *Summer Conference* Coimbra (Portugal) 2019. **Publications** *JE Newsletter* (4 a year) in English. Annual Report; articles; training handbooks; success stories; reports; media contributions.
Members Confederations in 10 countries:
Austria, Belgium, France, Germany, Italy, Netherlands, Portugal, Romania, Spain, Switzerland.
Consultative in 6 countries:
Croatia, Denmark, Ireland, Norway, Poland, UK.
Affiliate Sister Confederations in 2 countries:
Brazil, Tunisia.
NGO Relations Cooperates with: *Informal Forum of International Student Organizations (IFISO, #11193)*. Member of: *European Policy Centre (EPC, #08240)*. [2022.05.17/XD7241/**D**]

♦ Junta Interamericana de Agricultura (see: #11434)
♦ Junta Interamericana de Defensa (#11425)
♦ Junta Internacional de Fiscalización de Estupefacientes (#14212)
♦ Junta Internacional de Registro de Frecuencias (inactive)
♦ Jura Working Community / see Conférence TransJurassienne
♦ Juristes canadiens pour le respect des droits de la personne dans le monde (internationally oriented national body)
♦ Juristes et économistes internationaux contre la pauvreté (#14006)
♦ Juristes pour la Paix (internationally oriented national body)
♦ **JURIX** Foundation for Legal Knowledge Systems (#09966)

♦ **JUSCANZ Group** **16170**

Address not obtained.

History by governments of Japan, USA, Canada, Australia and New Zealand. **Aims** Oppose the adoption of international *environmental conventions* and resolutions.
Members Governments of 9 countries:
Australia, Canada, Iceland, Japan, Mexico, New Zealand, Norway, Switzerland, USA. [2008/XF7179/**F***]

♦ JUSSCANNZ Group (no recent information)
♦ Jus Semper Global Alliance (internationally oriented national body)
♦ Just Access (internationally oriented national body)
♦ Just Detention International (internationally oriented national body)
♦ Justdiggit (internationally oriented national body)
♦ Justice Africa (internationally oriented national body)
♦ Justice for Athletes / see Foundation for Global Sports Development
♦ Justice Coopération Internationale (internationally oriented national body)
♦ Justice and Environment / see Association Justice and Environment, z.s. (#02774)
♦ Justice Group – Human Rights and Justice Group International (internationally oriented national body)
♦ Justice in Motion (internationally oriented national body)
♦ Justice and Peace Commission of the USG/UISG / see Commission for Justice, Peace and Integrity of Creation – USG/UISG (#04230)
♦ Justice and Peace Nederland (internationally oriented national body)
♦ Justice and Peace Netherlands (internationally oriented national body)

♦ **Justice Studies Centre of the Americas (JSCA)** **16171**

Centro de Estudios de Justicia de las Américas (CEJA)
Exec Dir San Pio X 2460 oficina 1602, Providencia, 751 0041 Santiago, Santiago Metropolitan, Chile. T. +56222742911 – +56956112162. E-mail: info@cejamericas.org.
Events Manager address not obtained.
URL: http://www.cejamericas.org/

History Nov 1999. **Aims** Support the countries of the region in their justice reform processes. **Structure** General Assembly; Board of Directors; Office of the Executive Director. **Languages** English, Portuguese, Spanish. **Staff** 5.00 FTE, paid. **Finance** Sources: contributions of member/participating states; fees for services; international organizations. **Activities** Events/meetings; knowledge management/information dissemination; projects/programmes; research and development; training/education. **Events** *Pacific resolution of conflicts Americas meeting* Viña del Mar (Chile) 2004. **Publications** *Sistemas Judiciales* – journal. Information Services: Maintains virtual library.
Members Active members of the OAS; governments of 34 countries:
Antigua-Barbuda, Argentina, Bahamas, Barbados, Belize, Bolivia, Brazil, Canada, Chile, Colombia, Costa Rica, Dominica, Dominican Rep, Ecuador, El Salvador, Grenada, Guatemala, Guyana, Haiti, Honduras, Jamaica, Mexico, Nicaragua, Panama, Paraguay, Peru, St Kitts-Nevis, St Lucia, St Vincent-Grenadines, Suriname, Trinidad-Tobago, Uruguay, USA, Venezuela.
Associate Institutes (3) in 2 countries:
Argentina, Mexico. [2022.12.02/XE4659/**E***]

♦ **JUSTICIA – European Rights Network (JUSTICIA)** **16172**

Contact c/o Irish Council for Civil Liberties, Unit 11 First Fl, 34 Usher's Quay, Dublin, 8, CO. DUBLIN, Ireland. T. +35317994504. Fax +35317994512.
URL: https://www.iccl.ie/eu-justicia/

History 2012. **Aims** Make available information about EU criminal justice. **Activities** Training/education; events/meetings.
Members Organizations (19) in 18 countries:
Austria, Bulgaria, Croatia, Cyprus, Czechia, Estonia, Greece, Hungary, Ireland, Italy, Latvia, Lithuania, Poland, Romania, Slovenia, Spain, Sweden, UK.
Included in the above, 1 organization listed in this Yearbook:
Statewatch. [2020/XJ8850/y/**F**]

♦ **JUSTICIA** JUSTICIA – European Rights Network (#16172)
♦ JUST – International Movement for a Just World (internationally oriented national body)
♦ Justitia et Pax European Conference / see Conference of European Justice and Peace Commissions (#04596)

♦ **Just Net Coalition (JNC)** **16173**

Secretariat 393 17th Main Road 35th Cross, Jayanagar 4th, 'T' Block Bangalore, Bangalore, Karnataka 560041, Bangalore KARNATAKA 560041, India. T. +918026654134 – +918026536890. Fax +918041461055. E-mail: info@justnetcoalition.org – secretariat@justnetcoalition.org.
URL: http://justnetcoalition.org/

History Feb 2014, Delhi (India), when Delhi Declaration was adopted. **Aims** Promote democracy, human rights and social justice. **Structure** Steering Committee.
Members Full in 15 countries:
Bangladesh, Dominican Rep, Ecuador, France, Iceland, India, Ireland, Italy, Kenya, Lebanon, Nigeria, Philippines, Switzerland, Thailand, Uruguay.
Included in the above, 8 organizations listed in this Yearbook:
ActionAid (#00087); *Agencia Latinoamericana de Información (ALAI, #00551)*; *Arab NGO Network for Development (ANND, #01016)*; *Asia Pacific Forum on Women, Law and Development (APWLD, #01912)*; *Development Alternatives with Women for a New Era (DAWN, #05054)*; *Focus on the Global South (Focus, #09807)*; *Instituto del Tercer Mundo, Montevideo (ITEM)*; *Third World Network (TWN, #20151)*. [2018/XM4145/y/**C**]

♦ Just World International (internationally oriented national body)
♦ Just World Partners (internationally oriented national body)
♦ Just World Trust / see International Movement for a Just World
♦ Juvenile Diabetes Foundation International / see Juvenile Diabetes Research Foundation International
♦ Juvenile Diabetes Research Foundation International (internationally oriented national body)
♦ Juvenile Entente (inactive)
♦ **JUVENILIA** European Association of Young Opera Friends (#06282)
♦ Juventud para Cristo (#22009)
♦ Juventud Demócrata Cristiana de América (no recent information)
♦ Juventud para el Desarrollo y la Cooperación (inactive)
♦ Juventude Europeia Federalista (#21984)
♦ Juventude Federalista Europea Juventude (#21984)

♦ **Juventudes Liberales de las Américas (JuLiA)** **16174**

Liberal Youth of the Americas
Contact address not obtained. T. +573158500064 – +57315(5713210828.

History 2005, within *International Federation of Liberal Youth (IFLRY, #13469)*. **Aims** Promote cooperation among liberal youth on the American continent; promote, defend and strengthen political participation of youth liberals worldwide. [2010/XM0658/**E**]

♦ Juventudes de la ONU (internationally oriented national body)
♦ Juventud Estudiantil Católica Internacional (#15926)
♦ Juventud Independiente Cristiana Internacional (no recent information)
♦ Juventud Obrera Cristiana – Europa / see JOC Europe (#16118)
♦ Juventud Obrera Cristiana Internacional (#15927)
♦ Juventud con una Misión (#22020)
♦ JUWFI / see International Flood Initiative (#13613)
♦ JVC / see Jesuit Volunteers International
♦ JVC – Japan International Volunteer Centre (internationally oriented national body)
♦ JVC – Jewish Volunteer Corps of American Jewish World Service (internationally oriented national body)
♦ JVI – Jesuit Volunteers International (internationally oriented national body)
♦ **JVI** Joint Vienna Institute (#16150)
♦ **JWG** Joint Working Group between the Roman Catholic Church and the World Council of Churches (#16152)
♦ **JWI** Jewish Women International (#16114)
♦ JWI – Just World International (internationally oriented national body)
♦ JWPT / see Durrell Wildlife Conservation Trust
♦ JWS / see Jesuit Worldwide Learning (#16108)
♦ **JWS** Jesuit Worldwide Learning (#16108)
♦ JWS – Johannes Wier Stichting voor Mensenrechten en Gezondheidszorg (internationally oriented national body)
♦ K-For / see KFOR (#16187)

♦ **Ev-K2-CNR Committee** **16175**

Technical Secretariat Via San Bernardino 145, 24126 Bergamo BG, Italy. T. +39353230511. Fax +39353230551. E-mail: evk2cnr@evk2cnr.org.
URL: http://www.evk2cnr.org/

History Started as a research project, 1987. Launched in collaboration with the Italian National Research Council, 1989. Registration: Not-for-profit organization, Start date: 1989, Italy. **Aims** Contribute to the resolution of global problems concerning the *environment*, *health* and socio-economic *development* by creating, coordinating and promoting scientific research and cooperation initiatives with a particular focus on vulnerable environments and populations in developing countries; develop and strengthen infrastructure systems and technological instruments used for monitoring the climate and the environment within the Mediterranean area. **Structure** Assembly of Associates of 13 members. Executive Committee of 5 members. Scientific Council of 6 experts. **Languages** English, Italian. **Finance** Support from Italian government and private donors. **Events** *Global Workshop on Long-Term Observatories of Mountain Social-Ecological Systems* Reno, NV (USA) 2014. **Members** Membership countries not specified. **Consultative Status** Consultative status granted from: *ECOSOC (#05331)* (Ros A); *UNEP (#20299)*. **IGO Relations** Observer organization of: *United Nations Framework Convention on Climate Change (UNFCCC, 1992)*. **NGO Relations** Member of: *Climate and Clean Air Coalition (CCAC, #04010)*; *Mountain Partnership (MP, #16862)*. [2021/XJ0698/**E**]

- ♦ **K4DP** Knowledge for Development Partnership (#16199)
- ♦ **K4I** Knowledge4Innovation (#16198)
- ♦ KABE – Keep A Breast Foundation Europe (internationally oriented national body)
- ♦ Kabissa (internationally oriented national body)
- ♦ Kabitószer és Kabitószer-FüggOség Európai Megfigyelöközpontja (#07820)
- ♦ Kadervorming voor Afrikanen (internationally oriented national body)
- ♦ KAF – Kataliko Action for Africa (internationally oriented national body)
- ♦ KAF – Konrad Adenauer Foundation (internationally oriented national body)
- ♦ KAICIID Dialogue Centre / see King Abdullah Bin Abdulaziz International Centre for Interreligious and Intercultural Dialogue (#16193)
- ♦ **KAICIID** King Abdullah Bin Abdulaziz International Centre for Interreligious and Intercultural Dialogue (#16193)
- ♦ KAIDEC – Korean Association of International Development and Cooperation (internationally oriented national body)
- ♦ Kaiga Sangyo Jinzai Ikusei Kyoukai (internationally oriented national body)
- ♦ KAIPTC – Kofi Annan International Peacekeeping Training Centre (internationally oriented national body)
- ♦ **KAIRE** Ecumenical Group of Women (#05348)
- ♦ KAIROS – Canadian Ecumenical Justice Initiatives (internationally oriented national body)
- ♦ Kairos-Europe (internationally oriented national body)
- ♦ KAIROS Foundation (internationally oriented national body)

♦ Kairos Prison Ministry International 16176

Vice-Chair 100 DeBary Plantation Boulevard, DeBary FL 32713, USA. T. +14076294948. Fax +14076292668.
URL: http://www.kairosprisonministry.org/

History 1976, USA. **Aims** Expand *Christian* lay-led, ecumenical prison ministry in which men and women volunteers bring Christ's love and forgiveness to incarcerated individuals and to their loved ones. **Activities** Programmes (3): Men's and Women's Ministry, begun in 1976, addresses spiritual needs of prisoners. Teams of 30 to 40 volunteers go into prisons to pray, share the love and forgiveness of Jesus Christ, share meals and provide fellowship with those in prison on a one-to-one basis. *Kairos Outside*, begun in 1991, provides spiritual healing to families of those in prison, who often feel that they too are "doing time". *Kairos Torch*, begun in 1997, ministers to young offenders between the ages of 13 and 19.
Members Mainly in the USA but operating in a total of 9 countries:
Australia, Canada, Costa Rica, Honduras, Nicaragua, Peru, South Africa, UK, USA. [2013/XM7102/**F**]

- ♦ KAIS – Korean Association of International Studies (internationally oriented national body)
- ♦ KAIS – Korean Association of International Studies, Seoul (internationally oriented national body)
- ♦ K/A – Knights of the Altar International (religious order)
- ♦ Kalamata International Dance Centre (internationally oriented national body)
- ♦ Kalasantiner Kongregation (religious order)
- ♦ Kalatalouskysymysten Pohjoismainen Kontaktielin (inactive)
- ♦ Kaleidoscope Diversity Trust / see Kaleidoscope Trust
- ♦ Kaleidoscope Trust (internationally oriented national body)
- ♦ Kalmar Union (inactive)
- ♦ **KALME** Kommunikationsausschuss Lutherischer Minderheitskirchen in Europa (#16205)
- ♦ Kamer van Koophandel Belgie-Luxemburg-Arabische Landen (#00907)
- ♦ Kamer van Koophandel, Nijverheid en Landbouw België – Luxemburg – Afrika-Caraiben-Pacific (internationally oriented national body)
- ♦ KAMES – Korean Association of Middle East Studies (internationally oriented national body)
- ♦ Kampagne für ein Parlament bei der UNO (#03406)
- ♦ Kampagne für Saubere Kleidung (#03986)
- ♦ Kampala Convention – African Union Convention for the Protection and Assistance of Internally Displaced Persons in Africa (2009 treaty)
- ♦ Kampanjen Rena Kläder (#03986)

♦ Kangaroo Group – Free Movement and Security 16177

Dir The Kangaroo Group, Rue Wiertz 11, 1050 Brussels, Belgium. T. +3222806095. Fax +3222800784. E-mail: office@kangaroogroup.eu.
Office Manager address not obtained.
URL: http://www.kangaroogroup.eu/

History 1979, as the movement for free movement within *European Parliament (EP, #08146)*. Previously referred to as *Kangaroo Group – Movement for Free Movement*. Registered in accordance with Belgian law. **Aims** Enhance European unity step by step around the pursuit of common projects; further realization of the European Home Market with: a safe and prosperous Europe for its citizens; the removal of any remaining barriers to the four freedoms (free movement of goods, persons, services and capital); a regulatory environment in Europe which ensures and improves the competitiveness of European industry in world markets; a competitive social market economy founded on the principle of subsidiarity; the stability of the Euro; effective measures to make the external borders of the Union safe but at the same time open for trade and a common security and defence policy. **Structure** General Meeting (in Brussels-Belgium); Board; Committee of Vice-Presidents and Secretariat. **Activities** Acts as an informal forum in which politicians, officials and the social partners can come together to exchange information and views regarding topical issues and devise further initiatives for the development of the EU. Activities include: lunch/dinner debates; working groups; visits. **Events** *Annual conference* Brussels (Belgium) 2002, *Annual Conference* Brussels (Belgium) 2001, *Annual conference* Brussels (Belgium) 2000, *The Euro and the European innovative industry* Toulouse (France) 1997, *Annual conference* Prague (Czech Rep) 1995. **Publications** *Kangaroo Group Newsletter* (4 a year).
Members Individual members of the European Institutions – European Parliament, Council, European Commission – from all parties and corporate members in the 27 EU member countries:
Austria, Belgium, Bulgaria, Cyprus, Czechia, Denmark, Estonia, Finland, France, Germany, Greece, Hungary, Ireland, Italy, Latvia, Lithuania, Luxembourg, Malta, Netherlands, Poland, Portugal, Romania, Slovakia, Slovenia, Spain, Sweden, UK. [2017/XF1974/v/**F**]

- ♦ Kangaroo Group – Movement for Free Movement / see Kangaroo Group – Free Movement and Security (#16177)
- ♦ Kangourou sans Frontières / see Association Kangourou sans Frontières (#02775)
- ♦ Kangu (internationally oriented national body)
- ♦ Kansainvälinen Kirjailijakokous (meeting series)
- ♦ Kansainvälinen Saunaliitto (#14782)
- ♦ Kansainvälinen solidaarisuussäätiö / see International Solidarity Foundation
- ♦ Kansainvälinen soveltavan estetiikan instituutti (internationally oriented national body)
- ♦ Kansainvälinen Suoyhdistys (#14538)
- ♦ Kansainvälinen Tukkilaisyhdiastys (#15691)
- ♦ Kansainvälinen Turveyhdistys / see International Peatland Society (#14538)
- ♦ Kansainvälinen Yhteisvapaamuurarijärjestö (religious order)
- ♦ Kansainvälisen henkilövaihdon keskus / see Centre for International Mobility
- ♦ Kansainvälisen Liikkuvuuden ja Yhteistyön Keskus (internationally oriented national body)
- ♦ Kansalaisjärjestöjen Euroopan Yhdistys / see European Council for Non-Profit Organizations (#06834)
- ♦ Kansas African Studies Center (internationally oriented national body)
- ♦ Kansen voor Kinderen / see Education for Development
- ♦ Kan-Taiheiyo Shigaku Kyoiku Rengokai (inactive)

♦ Kant-Gesellschaft 16178

Sec c/o Philosophisches Seminar, Johannes Gutenberg-Univ Mainz, Kantstraße 2, 55122 Mainz, Germany. T. +4961313922793. Fax +4961313925593. E-mail: kant@uni-mainz.de – info@kant-gesellschaft.de.
URL: http://www.kant-gesellschaft.de/

History 1904, Halle (Saale) (Germany). **Aims** Support the spread of the study of Kant's philosophy. **Structure** General Assembly; Board. **Finance** Sources: members' dues. **Activities** Events/meetings; knowledge management/information dissemination; training/education. **Events** *International Kant Congress* Oslo (Norway) 2019, *International Kant Congress* Vienna (Austria) 2015, *International Kant congress* Pisa (Italy) 2010, *International Kant congress* Memphis, TN (USA) 1995, *International Kant congress* State College, PA (USA) 1985. **Publications** *Kant-Studien*. [2021.09.03/AA0700/v/**E**]

- ♦ Kaolin and Plastic Clay Europe / see European Kaolin and Plastic Clays Association (#07623)
- ♦ KAOW – Koninklijke Academie voor Overzeese Wetenschappen (internationally oriented national body)
- ♦ Karadeniz Sivil Toplum Kuruluslari Konfederasyonu (unconfirmed)
- ♦ KARAMA (internationally oriented national body)
- ♦ KARAMAH – Muslim Women Lawyers for Human Rights (internationally oriented national body)

♦ KARAT Coalition 16179

Stowarzyszenie Koalicja Karat
Exec Dir ul Walecznych 26/5, 03-916 Warsaw, Poland. T. +48226282003. Fax +48226282003. E-mail: contact@karat.org.pl.
URL: http://www.karat.org/

History Founded 1 Feb 1997, Warsaw (Poland). Registered in accordance with Polish law, 30 Oct 2001. **Aims** Enable *women's* organizations from Central and Eastern Europe and Central Asia to participate in policy debates on *socio-economic gender inequality* in the region, in particular women's access to decent work; improve women's ability to use national and international women's *rights* mechanisms; raise public awareness on women's human rights' backlash in the region; increase participation of women from the region in the "gender in development" discourse/process, emphasizing development needs of women from specific countries in the region and fostering links between the region, the Global South and the North. **Structure** General Assembly; International Board; Polish Board; Secretariat. **Languages** English. **Staff** 4.00 FTE, paid. **Finance** Subsidized by grants from public and private foundations, including: Foundation Open Society Institute; *Sigrid Rausing Trust*; EOG Funds; Dutch Embassy; Batory Foundation. **Activities** Advocacy/lobbying/activism; awareness raising; monitoring/evaluation; politics/policy/regulatory; capacity building; research/documentation; events/meetings; training/education. **Events** *General Assembly* Bucharest (Romania) 2010, *General Assembly* Warsaw (Poland) 2003, *General assembly and conference / General Assembly* St Petersburg (Russia) 2001, *Meeting* Ohrid (Macedonia) 2000. **Publications** *KARAT Newsletter* (12 a year). Reports; guides; brochures.
Members Organizations (61) and individuals (12) in 28 countries:
Albania, Armenia, Azerbaijan, Belarus, Bosnia-Herzegovina, Bulgaria, Croatia, Czechia, Estonia, Georgia, Germany, Hungary, Kazakhstan, Kyrgyzstan, Latvia, Lithuania, Moldova, Montenegro, North Macedonia, Poland, Romania, Russia, Serbia, Slovakia, Slovenia, Tajikistan, Ukraine, Uzbekistan. [2020/XE3745/**E**]

- ♦ Karibische Organisation der Obersten Rechnungskontrollbehörden (#03536)

♦ Karl Jaspers Foundation 16180

Fondation Karl Jaspers – Karl Jaspers Stiftung
Main Office Augustinergasse 5, Postfach 112, 4001 Basel BS, Switzerland. E-mail: info@jaspers-stiftung.ch.
URL: http://www.jaspers-stiftung.ch/

History 19 Dec 1973, Basel (Switzerland). **Aims** Promote research and study on *psychologist* and *philosopher* Karl Jaspers (1883-1969). **Languages** German. **Activities** Events/meetings. **Events** *International Conference* Basel (Switzerland) 2008, *International Conference* Naples (Italy) 2007, *International Conference* Moscow (Russia) 2005, *International Conference* Basel (Switzerland) 2002, *International Conference* Heidelberg (Germany) 1998. **Publications** Commentary and edition of works; letters and posthumous papers.
Members Organizations in 8 countries:
Austria, Germany, Italy, Japan, Korea Rep, Poland, UK, USA.
Individuals in 6 countries:
Austria, Germany, Italy, Poland, UK, USA. [2021/XF0552/f/**E**]

- ♦ Karl Jaspers Stiftung (#16180)
- ♦ Karl Kahane Foundation (internationally oriented national body)
- ♦ Karl Kübel Foundation / see Karl Kübel Foundation for Child and Family
- ♦ Karl Kübel Foundation for Child and Family (internationally oriented national body)
- ♦ Karl Kübel Stiftung / see Karl Kübel Foundation for Child and Family
- ♦ Karl Kübel Stiftung für Kind und Familie (internationally oriented national body)

♦ Karma Kagyu Buddhist Network (KKBN) 16181

Contact Buddhist Center Munich, Gabelsbergerstr 52/RGB, 80333 Munich, Germany. E-mail: info@diamondway-buddhism.org.
URL: http://www.diamondway-buddhism.org/

History Also referred to as *Diamond Way Buddhism Network (DWBN)*. **Events** *Meeting* Dharamsala (India) 2000.
Members Buddhist centres (350) in 39 countries:
Argentina, Australia, Austria, Belarus, Belgium, Bulgaria, Canada, Colombia, Cyprus, Czechia, Denmark, El Salvador, Finland, Germany, Greece, Guatemala, Hungary, Israel, Italy, Latvia, Lithuania, Mexico, Netherlands, New Zealand, Norway, Peru, Poland, Romania, Russia, Serbia, Slovakia, Spain, Sweden, Switzerland, UK, Ukraine, Uruguay, USA, Venezuela. [2010/XF6399/**F**]

♦ Von Karman Institute for Fluid Dynamics (VKI) 16182

Institut von Karman de dynamique des fluides (IVK)
Dir Chaussée de Waterloo 72, 1640 St-Genesius-Rode, Belgium. T. +3223599611 – +3223599404. Fax +3223599600. E-mail: secretariat@vki.ac.be.
URL: http://www.vki.ac.be/

History 4 Oct 1956, Paris (France), on the signature of a convention between Belgium and USA. Statutes adopted 20 Dec 1956; amended: 18 May 1960; 2 Dec 1971; 26 Mar 1992; 5 Apr 2006. Previously also known under the acronyms *VKIFD – IVKDF*. Registered in accordance with Belgian law. **Aims** Provide *post-graduate* educational programmes and encourage the practice of research in experimental, theoretical and numerical fluid dynamics; contribute to dissemination of knowledge in the field. **Structure** General Assembly. Board of Directors, consisting of Chairman, Vice-Chairman and Secretary. Director. Departments (3): Aeronautics/Aerospace; Environmental and Applied Fluid Dynamics; Turbomachinery and Propulsion. **Languages** English, French. **Finance** Subsidies from NATO countries; remunerations for services rendered. **Activities** Training/education; events/meetings. **Events** *European CubeSat Symposium* Palaiseau (France) 2021, *Myrte Final International Workshop* St-Genesius-Rode (Belgium) 2019, *Symposium of VKI PhD Reasearch* St-Genesius-Rode (Belgium) 2019, *European CubeSat Symposium* Toulouse (France) 2018, *European CubeSat Symposium* Ostend (Belgium) 2017. **Publications** *Von Karman Institute Lecture Series Monographs* (irregular); *Von Karman Institute Technical Memoranda*; *Von Karman Institute Technical Notes*.
Members NATO funding countries (19):
Belgium, Bulgaria, Czechia, Estonia, France, Germany, Hungary, Iceland, Italy, Latvia, Lithuania, Luxembourg, Norway, Portugal, Romania, Slovakia, Slovenia, Spain, Türkiye. [2016/XE3420/jv/**E**]

- ♦ Karmelietessen van het Goddelijk Hart van Jezus (religious order)
- ♦ Karpatho-Balkanische Geologische Assoziation (#03586)

- ♦ Karuna Center for Peacebuilding (internationally oriented national body)
- ♦ KASC – Kansas African Studies Center (internationally oriented national body)
- ♦ KASEUS – Korean Association of Slavic-Eurasian Studies (internationally oriented national body)
- ♦ Kashmir Foundation International (internationally oriented national body)
- ♦ KAS – Konrad-Adenauer Stiftung (internationally oriented national body)
- ♦ KASS / see Korean Association of Slavic-Eurasian Studies
- ♦ KASTOB – Karadeniz Sivil Toplum Kuruluslari Konfederasyonu (unconfirmed)
- ♦ Kataliko Action for Africa (internationally oriented national body)
- ♦ Kate Chopin International Society (internationally oriented national body)
- ♦ Katedra svetového zemedelstvi a lesnictvi / see Institute of Tropics and Subtropics, Prague
- ♦ KATE – Kontaktstelle für Umwelt-und Entwicklung (internationally oriented national body)
- ♦ Katholiek Beurzenfonds voor Afrikanen / see Formation de cadres africains
- ♦ Katholieke Arbeiders-Internationale (inactive)
- ♦ Katholieke Internationale Unie voor Maatschappelijk Werk (inactive)
- ♦ Katholikus Felnottképzés Europai Szövetsége (#05966)
- ♦ Katholische Arbeiter-Internationale (inactive)
- ♦ Katholische Bibelföderation (#03600)
- ♦ Katholische Frauenbewegung Österreichs (internationally oriented national body)
- ♦ Katholisches Sekretariat für Europäische Fragen / see Jesuit European Social Centre (#16103)
- ♦ Katholische Welt-Bibelföderation / see Catholic Biblical Federation (#03600)
- ♦ Katholische Weltunion der Presse / see International Christian Organisation of the Media (#12563)
- ♦ Katholische Zentralstelle für Entwicklungshilfe (internationally oriented national body)
- ♦ Katolickie Biuro Informacji i Inicjatyw Europejskich / see Jesuit European Social Centre (#16103)
- ♦ Kaunihera mo te Whakapakari Ao Whanui (internationally oriented national body)
- ♦ Käymäläseura Huussi ry (internationally oriented national body)
- ♦ Kazakhstan Institute for Strategic Studies (internationally oriented national body)
- ♦ Kazakhstan Strategic Studies Centre / see Kazakhstan Institute for Strategic Studies
- ♦ Kazoku Keikaku Kokusai Kyoryoku Zaidan / see Japanese Organization for International Cooperation in Family Planning
- ♦ KBA / see Formation de cadres africains
- ♦ KBA – Kadervorming voor Afrikanen (internationally oriented national body)
- ♦ **KBF** Katholische Bibelföderation (#03600)
- ♦ KBF – King Baudouin Foundation (internationally oriented national body)
- ♦ **KBGA** Karpatho-Balkanische Geologische Assoziation (#03586)
- ♦ KBO – Organization for the Management and Development of the Kagera River Basin (no recent information)
- ♦ KBS – Koning Boudewijnstichting (internationally oriented national body)
- ♦ **KBS Society** Kettil Bruun Society for Social and Epidemiological Research on Alcohol (#16185)
- ♦ KCA – Keep a Child Alive (internationally oriented national body)
- ♦ KCA – Kidney Cancer Association (internationally oriented national body)
- ♦ KCA – Knowledge Commercialisation Australasia (internationally oriented national body)
- ♦ KCA – Knowledge Commercialisation Australasia (internationally oriented national body)
- ♦ KCA – Kurash Confederation of Asia (inactive)
- ♦ **KCAO** Kurash Confederation of Asia-Oceania (#16211)
- ♦ KCE – Kultura Centro Esperantista (internationally oriented national body)
- ♦ K of C – Knights of Columbus (internationally oriented national body)
- ♦ KCOC – Korea NGO Council for Overseas Development Cooperation (internationally oriented national body)
- ♦ **KDIGO** Kidney Disease: Improving Global Outcomes (#16190)
- ♦ KDM / see Rééducateurs Solidaires
- ♦ **KDN** Kristdemokraterna i Norden (#17237)
- ♦ **KDT** European Partnership for Key Digital Technologies (#08158)
- ♦ KDUN / see Democracy Without Borders
- ♦ **KDUN** Kristendemokratisk Ungdom i Norden (#17236)
- ♦ KEC / see Conference of European Churches (#04593)
- ♦ KED / see Brot für die Welt
- ♦ **KEDO** Korean Peninsula Energy Development Organization (#16206)
- ♦ Keep A Breast Foundation Europe (internationally oriented national body)
- ♦ Keep a Child Alive (internationally oriented national body)
- ♦ Keeping Children Safe (internationally oriented national body)
- ♦ Kéeri Bozje Ljubavi (religious order)
- ♦ KEER – International Conference on Kansei Engineering and Emotion Research (meeting series)
- ♦ Kehitystutkimuksen Seura (internationally oriented national body)
- ♦ Kehitysyhteistyön Palvelukeskus Ry / see Kepa – the Finnish NGO platform for global development
- ♦ Kehitysyhteistyöosasto (internationally oriented national body)
- ♦ **KEI** Knowledge Ecology International (#16200)
- ♦ Keio University Global Research Institute (internationally oriented national body)
- ♦ KEK / see International Communist Esperantist Collective (#12819)
- ♦ **KEK** Konferenz Europäischer Kirchen (#04593)
- ♦ A Keleti-Alpok Térsége Tartomanyainak, Megyéinek, Régióinak es Köztarsasagainak Munkaközössége / see Alps-Adriatic-Alliance (#00747)
- ♦ Kelet-Közép-Európai Kulturalis Obszervatórium Alapitvany (internationally oriented national body)
- ♦ **KELI** Kristana Esperantista Ligo Internacia (#03901)
- ♦ Kendalc'h Keltiek (#03632)
- ♦ Kepa – the Finnish NGO platform for global development (internationally oriented national body)
- ♦ Kepa ry (internationally oriented national body)
- ♦ KEPA – Service Centre for Development Cooperation / see Kepa – the Finnish NGO platform for global development
- ♦ KeraLink International (internationally oriented national body)
- ♦ Keren Hayesod – The Foundation Fund / see Keren Hayesod – United Israel Appeal (#16183)

♦ Keren Hayesod – United Israel Appeal (UIA) 16183

Dir Gen PO Box 7583, 91074 Jerusalem, Israel. T. +97226701811. Fax +97226701925. E-mail: info@kh-uia.org.il.
URL: http://www.kh-uia.org.il/

History 1920, London (UK), by Chaim Weizmann and other Zionist leaders. Headquarters moved to Jerusalem (Israel) in 1926. Original title: *Keren Hayesod – The Foundation Fund.* National campaigns may be referred to as: *United Israel Appeal*; *United Jewish Appeal (UJA)*; *Joint Israel Appeal (JIA)*; *Israel United Appeal (IUA)*; *Solidarité avec Israel*; *Appel Unifié pour Israel.* United Israel Appeal USA became part of (US) United Jewish Communities. **Aims** Be the world's leading *fundraising* organization for the People of Israel. **Structure** Board of Trustees includes senior officials of world Jewish communities, some of whom are also members of governing bodies of *Jewish Agency for Israel (#16111)* and *World Zionist Organization (WZO, #21961).* Regional departments (4): English-speaking countries; Europe; Latin America; East countries. Professional Units. **Languages** Dutch, English, French, German, Hebrew, Italian, Portuguese, Russian, Spanish. **Staff** 85.00 FTE, paid. **Activities** Financial and/or material support. **Publications** *The Case of the Campaign* (annual); *Your Investment in Israel and the Jewish People* (annual). Annual calendar; Annual film. **Members** Affiliated campaigns (60) in 47 countries. Membership countries not specified. [2019.02.12/XE2894/f/**E**]

- ♦ Keren Kayemet Leisrael (#16113)
- ♦ Keren Mivtsa Mochin (#18535)
- ♦ Kerk van God Ministeriëel van Jezus Christus Internationaal (religious order)
- ♦ Kerk in Nood/Oostpriesterhulp (#00587)
- ♦ Keshet Ga'avah (#21306)

♦ KES International 16184

Main Office 2A St Martins Lane, York, YO1 6LN, UK. E-mail: enquiry@kesinternational.org.
URL: http://www.kesinternational.org/

History 2001. Registration: England and Wales. **Aims** As a *knowledge* transfer organization, provide high-quality conference events and publish opportunities for researchers. **Structure** Executive, comprising Executive Chair, Chair International Relations/Founder, Chair Academic Affairs, 2 Directors (Strategic Business Development, Administrative Affairs) and 4 Associate Chairs; Advisory Group. **Events** *International Conference on Knowledge Based and Intelligent Information and Engineering Systems* Athens (Greece) 2023, *International Conference on Knowledge-Based and Intelligent Information and Engineering Systems* Verona (Italy) 2022, *Annual Conference on Knowledge-Based and Information and Engineering Systems* Singapore (Singapore) 2015, *Annual Conference on Knowledge-Based and Information and Engineering Systems* Kitakyushu (Japan) 2013, *International Conference on Sustainability in Energy and Buildings* Stockholm (Sweden) 2012. **Publications** *KES Journal.* [2022.10.19/XJ1554/**F**]

- ♦ Keskipohjola-Toimikunta (#16796)
- ♦ Kesunyans Keltek (#03633)
- ♦ Keten van de Hoop – België (internationally oriented national body)

♦ Kettil Bruun Society for Social and Epidemiological Research on Alcohol (KBS Society) 16185

Treas c/o FHI, Dept of Substance Abuse, PO Box 4404, Nydalen, 0403 Oslo, Norway.
URL: http://www.kettilbruun.org/

History 1986. Originated in epidemiology section of *International Council on Alcohol and Addictions (ICAA, #12989).* **Aims** Promote social and epidemiological research on alcohol; foster a comparative understanding of alcohol use and alcohol problems in a spirit of international cooperation. **Structure** Officers: President, Vice-President, Secretary, Treasurer. Coordinating Committee. **Activities** Grants Ole-Jørgen Skog Award for Early Career Scientist. **Events** *Annual Alcohol Epidemiology Symposium* Johannesburg (South Africa) 2023, *Annual Alcohol Epidemiology Symposium* Warsaw (Poland) 2022, *Annual Alcohol Epidemiology Symposium* Helsinki (Finland) 2021, *Annual Alcohol Epidemiology Symposium* Utrecht (Netherlands) 2019, *Annual Alcohol Epidemiology Symposium* Chiang Mai (Thailand) 2018. **Publications** *KBS Journal.* [2021/XJ7012/**E**]

- ♦ Kevre Keltiek (#03633)

♦ Keystone Accountability 16186

UK Office 222 Kensal Road, Unit 121, London, W10 5BN, UK. T. +442037356367. E-mail: info@keystoneaccountability.org.
South Africa Office Andre Proctor, Brockford House, Office 4, Muizenberg, Cape Town, 7945, South Africa. T. +27217885685. Fax +27217885685.
URL: http://www.keystoneaccountability.org/

History 2004, as *ACCESS.* Comprised of independent not-for-profit organizations registered in South Africa, UK and USA. UK Registered Charity: 1118999. **Aims** Improve effectiveness of social change organizations. **Languages** English, French, German, Portuguese, Spanish. **Activities** Research and development; networking/liaising; monitoring/evaluation. **Publications** Technical note. **IGO Relations** Global partner of: *Global Partnership for Social Accountability (GPSA, #10541).* **NGO Relations** *Aga Khan Foundation (AKF, #00545)*; *The William and Flora Hewlett Foundation.* [2018.06.01/XM3942/**F**]

- ♦ Keystone Human Services International (internationally oriented national body)
- ♦ KFAED – Kuwait Fund for Arab Economic Development (internationally oriented national body)
- ♦ KFAW – Kitakyushu Forum on Asian Women (internationally oriented national body)
- ♦ KFBÖ – Katholische Frauenbewegung Österreichs (internationally oriented national body)
- ♦ KFF – Kvinnor för Fred (internationally oriented national body)

♦ KFOR 16187

Commander KFOR Headquarters, Pristina, Kosovo. T. +38922682070. Fax +38922682050. E-mail: pao@hq.kfor.nato.int – pio@hq.kfor.nato.int.
URL: http://www.aco.nato.int/kfor/

History 10 Jun 1999, in accordance with UN Security Resolution 1244, as multinational force under the command of *NATO (#16945)* and under the auspices of *United Nations (UN, #20515).* Also referred to as *K-For* and as *HQ Kosovo Force.* From Apr 2000, a core element of *Eurocorps (#05671).* From 1 Nov 2000 – Apr 2001, command of KFOR Communication Zone West was assumed by *EUROFOR (inactive).* Restructured, Oct 2010. **Aims** Contribute to a safe and secure environment in Kosovo; support the development of *security* institutions. **Structure** Multinational Battle Groups (MNBG): HQ MNBG East, Camp Bondsteel; HQ MNG West, Camp Villagio Italia. Also located at: Camp Film City. Commander KFOR (COMKFOR). **Staff** Troops, as of 5 Oct 2011: 6,240. **Activities** In anticipation of a settlement, an advance enabling force was stationed by NATO in North Macedonia, within the framework of *Allied Command Operations (ACO, #00731).*
Members Contributing nations (30):
Albania, Armenia, Austria, Bulgaria, Canada, Croatia, Czechia, Denmark, Estonia, Finland, France, Germany, Greece, Hungary, Ireland, Italy, Luxembourg, Morocco, Netherlands, Norway, Poland, Portugal, Romania, Slovenia, Sweden, Switzerland, Türkiye, UK, Ukraine, USA.
IGO Relations Close collaboration with: *UN Interim Administration Mission in Kosovo (UNMIK, #20343).* [2015.09.16/XF5744/**F***]

- ♦ KFPE – Kommission für Forschungspartnerschaft mit Entwicklungsländern (internationally oriented national body)
- ♦ KfW – Kreditanstalt für Wiederaufbau (internationally oriented national body)
- ♦ KGRE / see Congress of Local and Regional Authorities of the Council of Europe (#04677)
- ♦ KGRI – Keio University Global Research Institute (internationally oriented national body)
- ♦ Khalwatiya (religious order)
- ♦ **Khanya-aicdd** African Institute for Community-Driven Development (#00340)
- ♦ Khanya-managing rural change / see African Institute for Community-Driven Development (#00340)
- ♦ Khanya-mrc / see African Institute for Community-Driven Development (#00340)
- ♦ Khartoum International Institute for the Arabic Language (no recent information)
- ♦ **KHR** Internationale Kommission für die Hydrologie des Rheingebietes (#12693)
- ♦ KHSI – Keystone Human Services International (internationally oriented national body)

♦ KIBANDA – European Spiritan Centre for Cooperation and Development 16188

Centre spiritain européen pour la coopération au développement – Europees Spiritijns Centrum voor Ontwikkeling en Samenwerking

Exec Dir Brussels Office Centre, Av Frans Van Kalken 9/8, 1070 Brussels, Belgium. E-mail: kibandadirector@gmail.com.
URL: https://www.kibanda.be

History 21 Mar 2001, Brussels (Belgium). Founded by *Congregation of the Holy Spirit (Spiritans).* Former names and other names: *Centre spiritain européen pour la coopération au développement (CSECD)* – former. Registration: Banque-Carrefour des Entreprises, No/ID: 0474799855, Start date: 25 Mar 2001, Belgium, Brussels. **Aims** Promote development of *disadvantaged* people in *developing countries*; support work of Spiritan *missionaries*; defend *human rights* and peace in countries affected by conflict or natural disaster. **Structure** General Assembly (annual); Board of Directors. **Languages** English, French. **Staff** Voluntary. **Finance** Spiritan Congregation; public donations. **Activities** Active in 66 countries worldwide. **Publications** *KIBANDA Newsletter* (6 a year) in Dutch, English, French.
Members Individuals (17) in 5 countries:
Belgium, France, Germany, Ireland, Portugal.
NGO Relations Mainly NGOs in Europe and North America. [2022.10.21/XE4277/**E**]

- ♦ Kibi International University, Okayama (internationally oriented national body)
- ♦ KIC InnoEnergy SE / see EIT InnoEnergy (#05407)
- ♦ KIC – Kristdemokratiskt Internationellt Center (internationally oriented national body)

♦ **Kidlink Association** **16189**

Deputy Chairman Bondegärdet 19, Angered, SE-424 33 Gothenburg, Sweden. E-mail: info@kidlink.net.
URL: http://www.kidlink.org/

History 25 May 1990. Previously registered in accordance with Norwegian law. Former names and other names: *Kidlink Society* – former (25 May 1990 to 22 Mar 2009); *Réseau kidlink* – former (25 May 1990 to 22 Mar 2009); *Red Kidlink* – former (25 May 1990 to 22 Mar 2009); *Kidlink Netzwerk* – former (25 May 1990 to 22 Mar 2009); *Stiftelsen Kidlink* – former (25 May 1990 to 22 Mar 2009). Registration: Sweden. **Aims** Promote global dialogue among *young people* worldwide; empower *kids* and youth with free *educational* programmes to help them mature, get better control over their lives, encourage creativity, create social networks and collaborate with peers around the world, individually or through their classrooms. **Structure** Meeting (annual); Board of Directors. Technical and Support Management; Language Area Management; Kidlink Institute. **Languages** English. **Staff** Voluntary. **Finance** Sources: donations; grants; members' dues. **Activities** Awards/prizes/competitions; awareness raising; conflict resolution; events/meetings; knowledge management/information dissemination; training/education. **Events** *International teacher conference* Arendal (Norway) 2001. **Publications** *Kidlink Newsletter*.
Members Full in 12 countries and territories:
Brazil, Indonesia, Italy, Nepal, Norway, Russia, Spain, Sri Lanka, Sweden, Türkiye, Uruguay, USA. [2019/XF6526/**C**]

♦ Kidlink Netzwerk / see Kidlink Association (#16189)
♦ Kidlink Society / see Kidlink Association (#16189)
♦ Kidney Cancer Association (internationally oriented national body)

♦ **Kidney Disease: Improving Global Outcomes (KDIGO)** **16190**

Contact Avenue Louise 65, Ste 11, 1050 Brussels, Belgium. E-mail: kdigocommunications@kdigo.org.
URL: http://kdigo.org/

History 2003. Registered in accordance with Belgian law. **Aims** Improve the care and outcomes of kidney disease patients worldwide through development and implementation of global clinical practice guidelines. **Structure** Executive Committee. **Activities** Events/meetings; standards/guidelines. **Events** *Conference on Central, Peripheral and Arterial Disease in Chronic Kidney Disease* Dublin (Ireland) 2020, *Optimal Anemia Management in Chronic Kidney Disease Conference* Barcelona (Spain) 2019, *CKD-MBD Implementation Summit* Tokyo (Japan) 2018, *Conference on Gitelman Syndrome* Brussels (Belgium) 2016. [2017/XM5616/**C**]

♦ Kids Care International (unconfirmed)
♦ Kids in Deficient Situations (internationally oriented national body)
♦ KIDS – Kids in Deficient Situations (internationally oriented national body)
♦ Kids in Need of Defense Europe (internationally oriented national body)
♦ KidsRights (internationally oriented national body)
♦ Kiel Institute for World Economics / see Kiel Institute for the World Economy
♦ Kiel Institute for the World Economy (internationally oriented national body)
♦ Kielisopimus (1981 treaty)
♦ KIEP – Korea Institute for International Economic Policy (internationally oriented national body)
♦ Kiev International University / see Kyiv International University
♦ Kiev protocol – Protocol on Pollutant Release and Transfer Registers (2003 treaty)
♦ Kigali Amendment – Amendment to the Montreal Protocol on Substances that Deplete the Ozone Layer, 2016 (2016 treaty)
♦ KIIB / see Egmont Institute
♦ KIITEC – Kilimanjaro International Institute for Telecommunications, Electronics and Computers (internationally oriented national body)
♦ KI – Kleiwerks International (internationally oriented national body)
♦ Kilimanjaro International Institute for Telecommunications, Electronics and Computers (internationally oriented national body)
♦ Kiltegan Fathers – St Patrick's Society for the Foreign Missions (religious order)

♦ **Kimberley Process (KP)** **16191**

Address not obtained.
URL: http://www.kimberleyprocess.com/

History May 2000, Kimberley (South Africa). **Aims** Set up mechanisms to regulate the *export* and origin of rough *diamonds*. **Structure** Participants Meeting (annual). Working Bodies: Participation Committee; Selection Committee; Committee on Rules and Procedures; Working Group on Monitoring; Working Group on Statistics; Working Group of Diamond Experts; Working Group on alluvial-artisanal Production; Technical Assistance. **Activities** Adopted Kimberley Process Certification Scheme, Nov 2002.
Members Governments of 75 countries and territories:
Angola, Armenia, Australia, Austria, Bangladesh, Belarus, Belgium, Botswana, Brazil, Bulgaria, Canada, Central African Rep, China, Congo Brazzaville, Congo DR, Côte d'Ivoire, Croatia, Cyprus, Czechia, Denmark, Estonia, Finland, France, Germany, Ghana, Greece, Guinea, Guyana, Hungary, India, Indonesia, Ireland, Israel, Italy, Japan, Korea Rep, Laos, Latvia, Lebanon, Lesotho, Liberia, Lithuania, Luxembourg, Malaysia, Malta, Mauritius, Mexico, Namibia, Netherlands, New Zealand, Norway, Poland, Portugal, Romania, Russia, Sierra Leone, Singapore, Slovakia, Slovenia, South Africa, Spain, Sri Lanka, Sweden, Switzerland, Tanzania UR, Thailand, Togo, Türkiye, UK, Ukraine, United Arab Emirates, USA, Venezuela, Vietnam, Zimbabwe.
Regional organization (1):
European Union (EU, #08967). [2012/XF6931/**F***]

♦ **KIMO International** **16192**

Local Authorities International Environmental Organization

Exec Sec c/o Shetland Islands Council, 8 North Ness Business Park, Lerwick, ZE1 0LZ, UK. T. +441595744807. E-mail: info@kimo.shetland.org.
URL: http://www.kimointernational.org/

History Founded Aug 1990, Esbjerg (Denmark) as *Kommunenes Internationale Miljøorganisasjon (KIMO)*. **Aims** Prevent *pollution* of the seas and *coastal* waters of North Western Europe; protect coastal communities from impacts of *marine* pollution and *climate change*; represent member local authorities and associated members at international and national levels. **Structure** General Meeting of Members (annual); International Board of Directors; National Coordinators. **Languages** English. **Staff** 2.00 FTE, paid. **Finance** Members' dues. Secretariat partially sponsored by Shetland Islands Council. **Activities** Advocacy/lobbying/activism; projects/programmes; research/documentation. **Events** *Annual Conference and General Meeting* Thórshavn (Faeroe Is) 2022, *Annual Conference and General Meeting* Kirkwall (UK) 2015, *Annual Conference and General Meeting* Holstebro (Denmark) 2014, *Annual Conference and General Meeting* Thórshavn (Faeroe Is) 2013, *Annual Conference and General Meeting* Gothenburg (Sweden) 2012. **Publications** *KIMO Newsletter*. Studies; reports; guides; manuals; press releases.
Members Full (80) and Group (3), representing 180 communities and organizations in 9 countries and territories:
Belgium, Denmark, Faeroe Is, Germany, Lithuania, Netherlands, Norway, Sweden, UK.
IGO Relations Observer to: *Baltic Marine Environment Protection Commission – Helsinki Commission (HELCOM, #03126)*; *European Commission (EC, #06633)*; *North Sea Conference*; *OSPAR Commission for the Protection of the Marine Environment of the North-East Atlantic (OSPAR Commission, #17905)*. **NGO Relations** Partnership with: *Conference of Peripheral Maritime Regions of Europe (CPMR, #04638)*. Close links with: *Greenpeace International (#10727)*; *International Secretariat Committee of Nuclear Free Zone Local Authorities (#14820)* (UK section); *North Sea Commission (NSC, #17604)*; *Seas at Risk (SAR, #19189)*; *World Wide Fund for Nature (WWF, #21922)*; national organizations. [2020.03.03/XD4804/**D**]

♦ KIMO / see KIMO International (#16192)
♦ Kim Phuc Foundation International (internationally oriented national body)
♦ Kinderberg International (internationally oriented national body)
♦ Kinderen Derde Wereld (internationally oriented national body)
♦ Kindermissionswerk (internationally oriented national body)
♦ Kindermissionswerk / Die Sternsinger / see Holy Childhood
♦ Kindernothilfe (internationally oriented national body)
♦ KIND Europe – Kids in Need of Defense Europe (internationally oriented national body)
♦ Kinésithérapeutes du Monde / see Rééducateurs Solidaires
♦ King Abdulaziz Center for World Culture (internationally oriented national body)

♦ **King Abdullah Bin Abdulaziz International Centre for Interreligious and Intercultural Dialogue (KAICIID)** **16193**

Contact Schottenring 21, 1010 Vienna, Austria. T. +431313220. E-mail: press@kaiciid.org – office@kaiciid.org.
URL: http://www.kaiciid.org/

History 12 Nov 2012, Vienna (Austria). Foundation Declaration signed, 13 Oct 2011, Vienna (Austria), by Kingdom of Saudi Arabia, Republic of Austria and Kingdom of Spain. Inauguration ceremony, 27 Nov 2012, Vienna (Austria). Former names and other names: *KAICIID Dialogue Centre* – alias. **Aims** Equip religious communities with knowledge and skills about policy frameworks, human rights and sustainable development, while also training policymakers on religious literacy, interreligious dialogue and inclusion. **Structure** Council of Parties; Board of Directors; Advisory Forum. **Languages** Arabic, English, German, Spanish. **Staff** 71.00 FTE, paid. **Finance** Annual budget: 18,000,000 EUR (2020). **Activities** Networking/liaising; projects/programmes; training/education. **Events** *European Policy Dialogue Forum on Refugees and Migrants* Lisbon (Portugal) 2021, *Interreligious Dialogue for Peace Meeting* Vienna (Austria) 2019, *Meeting on the Power of Words* Vienna (Austria) 2019, *Interreligious Dialogue for Peace Meeting* Vienna (Austria) 2018, *Meeting on the Implementation of the Plan of Action for Religious Leaders and Actors to Prevent Incitement to Violence that Could Lead to Atrocity Crimes* Vienna (Austria) 2018. **Publications** Annual Report; action plan; toolkit; studies.
Members Member States (3):
Austria, Saudi Arabia, Spain.
Founding Observer:
Holy See.
IGO Relations Memorandum of Understanding with (4): *Islamic World Educational, Scientific and Cultural Organization (ICESCO, #16058)*; *Organisation of Islamic Cooperation (OIC, #17813)*; *UNDP (#20292)*; *UNESCO (#20322)*. **NGO Relations** Memorandum of Understanding with (3): *Religions for Peace (RfP, #18831)*; universities; *World Organization of the Scout Movement (WOSM, #21693)*. Member of (3): *International Partnership on Religion and Sustainable Development (PaRD, #14524)*; *Joint Learning Initiative on Faith and Local Communities (JLI, #16139)*; *Network for Religious and Traditional Peacemakers (#17054)*. Partner of (1): *G20 Interfaith Forum Association (IF20, #10055)*. [2022.02.09/XJ7974/**E***]

♦ King Baudouin Foundation (internationally oriented national body)
♦ Kingdom of Christ (internationally oriented national body)
♦ King Faisal Centre for Research and Islamic Studies (internationally oriented national body)
♦ The King's Daughters / see International Order of the King's Daughters and Sons
♦ Kingston International Group / see International Foundation of Security and Safety Sciences
♦ Kinotiko Grafio Fitikon Pikilion (#04404)
♦ Kinovulevtiki Omada tu Evropaiku Sisialistiku Kommatos / see Group of the Progressive Alliance of Socialists and Democrats in the European Parliament (#10786)
♦ Kinshasa Convention – Central African Convention for the Control of Small Arms and Light Weapons, Their Ammunition, Parts and Components That Can be Used for Their Manufacture, Repair and Assembly (2010 treaty)
♦ Kin-Viden Information Forskning (internationally oriented national body)
♦ Kinzoku to Kankyo Kokusai Hyogikai (inactive)
♦ **KIP International School** Knowledge, Innovations, Policies and Territorial Practices for the United Nations Millennium Platform (#16201)
♦ **KIPUS** Red Docente de América Latina y El Caribe (#20110)
♦ **KIPUS** Teacher Network of Latin America and the Caribbean (#20110)
♦ Kirche und Frieden (#03916)
♦ Kirche Gottes Ministerium Jesus Christi International (religious order)
♦ Kirche in Not/Ostpriesterhilfe (#00587)
♦ Kirchlicher Entwicklungsdienst / see Brot für die Welt
♦ Kirkens Nødhjelp (internationally oriented national body)
♦ Kirkon Ulkomaanapu Säätiö (internationally oriented national body)
♦ KISI – Kazakhstan Institute for Strategic Studies (internationally oriented national body)
♦ KITA – Kitayushu International Techno-cooperative Association (internationally oriented national body)
♦ KITA – Korea International Trade Association (internationally oriented national body)
♦ Kitakyushu Forum on Asian Women (internationally oriented national body)
♦ Kitakyushu International Training Association / see Kitayushu International Techno-cooperative Association
♦ Kitayushu International Techno-cooperative Association (internationally oriented national body)
♦ KIT – Koninklijk Instituut voor de Tropen (internationally oriented national body)
♦ KIT – Københavns International Teater (internationally oriented national body)
♦ KITLV – Koninklijk Instituut voor Taal-, Land- en Volkenkunde (internationally oriented national body)
♦ **Kituo Cha Katiba** Eastern Africa Centre for Constitutional Development (#05220)
♦ Kiva (internationally oriented national body)

♦ **Kiwanis Asia-Pacific (ASPAC)** **16194**

Chair address not obtained.
Contact address not obtained.
URL: https://www.kiwanisaspac.org/

History Set up within *Kiwanis International (#16195)*. Current bylaws approved Jul 2014. **Structure** Convention (annual); Executive Board. **Events** *ASPAC Convention* Adelaide, SA (Australia) 2024, *ASPAC Convention* Port Dickson (Malaysia) 2023, *ASPAC Convention* Manila (Philippines) 2022, *Asia Pacific Conference* Taipei (Taiwan) 2019, *Asia Pacific Conference* Petaling Jaya (Malaysia) 2018.
Members Districts and non-districted nations of 17 countries and territories:
Australia, Hong Kong, India, Indonesia, Japan, Korea Rep, Malaysia, Nepal, New Caledonia, New Zealand, Pakistan, Philippines, Polynesia Fr, Singapore, Sri Lanka, Taiwan, Vanuatu. [2021/XM5164/**E**]

♦ Kiwanis-Europe / see Kiwanis International – European Federation (#16196)
♦ Kiwanis European Federation / see Kiwanis International – European Federation (#16196)

♦ **Kiwanis International** **16195**

Exec Dir 3636 Woodview Trace, Indianapolis IN 46268-3196, USA. T. +13178758755. Fax +13178790204. E-mail: memberservices@kiwanis.org.
URL: http://www.kiwanis.org/

History Founded 21 Jan 1915, Detroit MI (USA), extending to Canada in 1916. Clubs established in other countries in 1961. **Aims** Give primacy to human and spiritual, rather than material values to life; encourage daily living of the Golden Rule in all human relationships; promote adoption and application of higher social, business and professional standards; develop, by precept and example, a more intelligent, aggressive and serviceable citizenship; through Kiwanis Clubs, provide a practical means to form enduring friendship, to render altruistic service and to build better communities; cooperate in creating and maintaining the sound public opinion and high idealism which make possible the increase of righteousness, justice, patriotism, and good will. **Structure** Convention. International Board. Districts (3): Americas; *Kiwanis International – European Federation (#16196)*; *Kiwanis Asia-Pacific (ASPAC, #16194)*. Clubs: Kiwanis; Aktion Club; *Circle K International*; Key Club; Builders Club; Kiwanis Kids. **Languages** Chinese, English, French, German, Italian, Japanese, Korean, Norwegian, Spanish. **Finance** Members' dues, fees and subscriptions. *Kiwanis International Foundation* functions as fundraising arm. **Activities** Projects/programmes; advocacy/lobbying/activism. **Events** *Annual Convention* Orlando, FL (USA) 2019, *Asia Pacific Conference* Taipei (Taiwan) 2019, *Annual Convention* Las Vegas, NV (USA) 2018, *Asia Pacific Conference* Petaling Jaya (Malaysia) 2018, *Annual Convention* Paris (France) 2017. **Publications** *Kiwanis Magazine* (10 a year); *The Kiwanis Leader* (8 a year); *Circle K Magazine*; *Keynoter*. Booklets; guides.
Members Individuals (over 292,000), in 8,280 clubs, in 83 countries and territories:

Albania, Antigua-Barbuda, Argentina, Australia, Austria, Bahamas, Bangladesh, Barbados, Belgium, Bermuda, Bulgaria, Canada, Cayman Is, Colombia, Costa Rica, Croatia, Czechia, Dominica, Ecuador, El Salvador, Estonia, Faeroe Is, Finland, France, Georgia, Germany, Guam, Guiana Fr, Guyana, Hong Kong, Hungary, Iceland, India, Indonesia, Italy, Jamaica, Japan, Kazakhstan, Kenya, Korea Rep, Latvia, Liechtenstein, Lithuania, Luxembourg, Malaysia, Martinique, Mexico, Moldova, Monaco, Netherlands, New Caledonia, New Zealand, Nigeria, North Macedonia, Norway, Panama, Philippines, Poland, Polynesia Fr, Portugal, Puerto Rico, Romania, Russia, San Marino, Serbia, Singapore, Slovakia, South Africa, Spain, Sri Lanka, St Lucia, Suriname, Sweden, Switzerland, Taiwan, Trinidad-Tobago, Tunisia, Türkiye, Turks-Caicos, UK, USA, Venezuela.
Consultative Status Consultative status granted from: *ECOSOC (#05331)* (Special); *UNICEF (#20332)*. **IGO Relations** Associated with Department of Global Communications of the United Nations. **NGO Relations** Partner of: *Iodine Global Network (IGN, #16004)*. [2021/XF0173/v/F]

♦ Kiwanis International – European Federation 16196

Dir Europe Leiekaai 25 B, 9000 Ghent, Belgium. T. +3292167776 – +3292167777. Fax +3292167770. E-mail: europeinfo@kiwanis.org.
URL: http://www.kiwanis.eu/

History Founded 1963, within *Kiwanis International (#16195)*. Previously referred to as *Kiwanis-Europe* or *Kiwanis European Federation*. Registered in accordance with Belgian law. **Aims** Serve *children* worldwide through creation and management of projects to improve the quality of the lives of children and their families. **Structure** Board, comprising 4 officers and 9 District Governors, supported by a Secretary and a Treasurer. **Languages** English. Working languages are all European languages. **Events** *Annual Congress* Vienna (Austria) 2022, *Annual Congress* Ghent (Belgium) 2021, *Annual Congress* Bruges (Belgium) 2020, *Annual Congress* Reykjavik (Iceland) 2019, *Annual Congress* Baveno (Italy) 2018.
Members Clubs (over 1,000) in 37 countries:
Albania, Austria, Belarus, Belgium, Bulgaria, Czechia, Estonia, Finland, France, Georgia, Germany, Greece, Hungary, Iceland, Italy, Latvia, Liechtenstein, Lithuania, Luxembourg, Malta, Monaco, Netherlands, North Macedonia, Norway, Poland, Portugal, Romania, Russia, San Marino, Serbia, Slovakia, Slovenia, Spain, Sweden, Switzerland, Türkiye, UK. [2018/XE1503/E]

- ♦ KIYO (internationally oriented national body)
- ♦ KIYO – Children's rights NGO / see KIYO
- ♦ KIYO – NGO voor Kinderrechten / see KIYO
- ♦ KIYO – ONG des droits de l'enfant / see KIYO
- ♦ KIYO – ONG para os direitos das crianças / see KIYO
- ♦ **KKBN** Karma Kagyu Buddhist Network (#16181)
- ♦ **KKL** Keren Kayemet Leisrael (#16113)
- ♦ Kleine Zusters van de Assumptie (religious order)
- ♦ Kleiwerks International (internationally oriented national body)
- ♦ Klima-Bündnis (#04005)
- ♦ Klima-Bündnis der europäischen Städte mit indigenen Völkern der Regenwälder / see Climate Alliance (#04005)
- ♦ **KLRCA** Kuala Lumpur Regional Centre for Arbitration (#16210)
- ♦ Klub Zastupnika Europske Pucke Stranke – Krscanski Demokrati (#10775)
- ♦ KMA – Service Tiers-monde (internationally oriented national body)
- ♦ KMK – Krestanska Mirova Konference (inactive)
- ♦ KMK – Perhaps Kids Meeting Kids can make a Difference (internationally oriented national body)
- ♦ KMMA – Koninklijk Museum voor Midden-Afrika (internationally oriented national body)
- ♦ **KMM-VIN** European Virtual Institute on Knowledge-Based Multifunctional Materials (#09063)
- ♦ KMNEG – Konfederacija Malyh Narodov i Etnicеskih Grupp (inactive)
- ♦ KMW – Know My World (internationally oriented national body)

♦ Kneipp Worldwide 16197

Pres Adolf-Scholz-Allee 6-8, 86825 Bad Wörishofen, Germany. T. +4982473002102. Fax +4982473002199. E-mail: ikk@kneippbund.de – kneippworldwide@kneippbund.de.
URL: http://kneippworldwide.kneippbund.de/

History 1962. Founded as *International Confederation of the Kneipp Movement (ICK) – Confédération internationale des associations Kneipp (CIAK) – Internationale Konföderation der Kneipp-Bewegung (IKK)*. Has also been referred to in German as *Internationalen Kneipp-Konföderation*. Since 2005 known under its shortened title. Registration: Bavaria District Court, No/ID: VR 1288, Start date: 16 Apr 1998, Germany, Memmingen. **Aims** Promote exchange of experience in Kneippian *natural therapies* and *health* sustaining projects, especially with children and young people, around the world. **Structure** Rotating Presidency; General Secretariat. **Languages** English, German. **Finance** Members' dues. **Events** *Congress* Vienna (Austria) 1997, *Congress* Vienna (Austria) 1992. **Publications** *Kneipp-Journal* (10 a year) in German.
Members National associations; professional associations; individuals. Members in 19 countries:
Australia, Austria, Belgium, Brazil, Bulgaria, Canada, Chile, Denmark, Germany, Hungary, India, Italy, Korea Rep, Liechtenstein, Lithuania, Netherlands, Slovenia, South Africa, Switzerland, Ukraine. [2022/XE3684/E]

- ♦ KNH – Kindernothilfe (internationally oriented national body)
- ♦ Knights of the Altar International (religious order)
- ♦ Knightsbridge International (internationally oriented national body)
- ♦ Knights of Columbus (internationally oriented national body)
- ♦ Knights Hospitallers of the Sovereign Order of Saint John of Jerusalem, Knights of Malta – The Ecumenical Order (religious order)
- ♦ Knights of the Immaculate (religious order)
- ♦ Knights of St John International (religious order)
- ♦ Knights Templar (inactive)

♦ Knowledge4Innovation (K4I) 16198

Contact Rui Guimard 7, 1040 Brussels, Belgium. T. +3222335451. E-mail: k4i@knowledge4innovation.eu.
Management Dir Square de Meeûs 35, 1000 Brussels, Belgium.
URL: http://www.knowledge4innovation.eu/

History Registration: No/ID: 0810.270.197, Start date: 9 Mar 2009, Belgium; EU Transparency Register, No/ID: 409204438202-29, Start date: 18 May 2020. **Structure** Governing Board; Management Board. *K4I Forum of the European Parliament*. **Activities** Events/meetings. **Events** *European Innovation Summit* Brussels (Belgium) 2020, *AI and Big Data Innovation Summit* Brussels (Belgium) 2019, *European Innovation Summit* Brussels (Belgium) 2018, *European Innovation Summit* Brussels (Belgium) 2017, *European Innovation Summit* Brussels (Belgium) 2016.
Members Association members in 10 countries:
Belgium, Bulgaria, Finland, Germany, Italy, Netherlands, Poland, Russia, Slovakia, USA.
Included in the above, 13 organizations listed in this Yearbook:
A.SPIRE (#02311); *Bio Base Europe*; *Conseil européen de l'industrie chimique (CEFIC, #04687)*; *CropLife Europe (#04965)*; *EGI Foundation (EGI.eu, #05395)*; *EUREC (#05619)*; *Eureka Association (Eureka, #05621)*; *European Cooperation in Science and Technology (COST, #06784)*; *European Gas Research Group (#07380)*; *Fédération Européenne d'Associations Nationales d'Ingénieurs (FEANI, #09558)*; *Institute of Electrical and Electronics Engineers (IEEE, #11259)*; *Joint Institute for Nuclear Research (JINR, #16134)*.
Individual members of the K4I Forum of European Parliament (EP) from 14 countries:
Austria, Croatia, Finland, Germany, Greece, Ireland, Italy, Netherlands, Poland, Portugal, Romania, Slovakia, Spain, UK.
IGO Relations *European Parliament (EP, #08146)*. [2020/XJ9517/y/F]

- ♦ Knowledge Commercialisation Australasia (internationally oriented national body)
- ♦ Knowledge Commercialisation Australasia (internationally oriented national body)

♦ Knowledge for Development Partnership (K4DP) 16199

Managing Dir Gersthofer Str 162, 1180 Vienna, Austria.
URL: https://k4dp.org/

History Set up 3 Apr 2017, Geneva (Switzerland) at Knowledge for Development: Global Partnership Conference. Registered in accordance with Austrian law. **Aims** Advance on a global level peaceful, wealthy, sustainable and inclusive knowledge societies; foster global knowledge partnerships for achieving the Sustainable Development Goals of the United Nations and successfully implementing the Agenda 2030; promote knowledge management in international organizations, governments, public bodies as well as in the private sector. **Structure** Board of Directors; Presidium. **Languages** English. **Staff** Voluntary. **Finance** Members' dues. Other sources: voluntary contributions; project funding. **Activities** Events/meetings. **Publications** *Knowledge for Development Partnership: Agenda Knowledge for Development – Strengthening Agenda 2030 and the Sustainable Development Goals* (3rd ed 2018). **Members** in 25 countries. Membership countries not specified. [2019.03.19/XM7090/E]

♦ Knowledge Ecology International (KEI) 16200

Dir 1621 Connectivut Ave NW, Ste 500, Washington DC 20009, USA. T. +12023322670. Fax +12023322673.
Geneva Office Route des Morillons 1, CP 2100, 1211 Geneva 2, Switzerland. T. +41227916727.
URL: http://keionline.org/

History Founded 2006, assimilating the staff and work programme of the 'Consumer Project on Technology (CPTech). **Aims** Search for better outcomes, including new solutions, to the management of knowledge resources with a focus on social justice, particularly for the most vulnerable populations, including low-income persons and marginalized groups. **Structure** Board of Directors, comprising Chair and 2 members. Board of Advisors of 3 members. **Staff** 6.00 FTE, paid. **Finance** Contributions. Grants from foundations, including the following listed in this Yearbook: *Ford Foundation (#09858)*; *MacArthur Foundation*; *The Rockefeller Foundation (#18966)*. **Activities** Research/documentation; knowledge management/information dissemination; advocacy/lobbying/activism; guidance/assistance/consulting; monitoring/evaluation. **Publications** *KES Journal*. **Consultative Status** Consultative status granted from: *World Intellectual Property Organization (WIPO, #21593)* (Observer Status); *WHO (#20950)* (Official Relations). **NGO Relations** Member of: *Copyright for Creativity (C4C, #04832)*; *European Alliance for Responsible R and D and Affordable Medicines (#05879)*. [2016/XM3770/F]

- ♦ Knowledge Gateway on Women's Economic Empowerment / see Empower Women (#05447)

♦ Knowledge, Innovations, Policies and Territorial Practices for the United Nations Millennium Platform (KIP International School) 16201

General Secretariat FAO – Bldg E – Rooms 121/122, Viale delle Termi di Caracalla 1, 00153 Rome RM, Italy. T. +39657050212. E-mail: info@kipschool.org.
URL: http://kipschool.org/

History 2011, following a period of presentations and consultations. **Structure** General Assembly; Scientific Committee; Presidency; General Secretariat; Joint Working Groups; Technical Committee. **Activities** Training/education. Includes: *Innovation for Development and South-South cooperation (IDEASS)*; *International Links and Services for Local Economic Development Agencies (ILS LEDA)*. **IGO Relations** Cooperates with: *FAO (#09260)*; *ILO (#11123)*; *Inter-American Development Bank (IDB, #11427)*; *International Fund for Agricultural Development (IFAD, #13692)*; *UNEP (#20299)*; *UN Women (#20724)*; *UNDP (#20292)* national offices; *UNESCO (#20322)*; *United Nations Human Settlements Programme (UN-Habitat, #20572)*; *United Nations Office for Project Services (UNOPS, #20602)*; *WHO (#20950)*. **NGO Relations** *Echanges culturels en Méditerranée (ECUME, #05281)*. [2018/XM6463/E]

- ♦ Know My World (internationally oriented national body)
- ♦ **KNS** Kommunalanställdas Nordiska Samarbete (#16204)
- ♦ KNVIR – Koninklijke Nederlandse Vereniging voor Internationaal Recht (internationally oriented national body)

♦ KNX Association 16202

CTO/CFO De Kleetlaan 5, Bus 11, 1831 Diegem, Belgium. T. +3227758590. Fax +3226755028. E-mail: info@knx.org.
URL: http://www.knx.org/

History May 1999, Belgium. Founded following convergence process, started in 1997, of *BatiBUS Club international (inactive)* and *European Home Systems Association (EHSA, inactive)* into *European Installation Bus Association (EIB Association, inactive)*. Former names and other names: *Konnex Association* – former; *EIBA (European Installation Bus Association)* – former. Registration: No/ID: BE0441460064, Belgium. **Aims** Support the market for *home and building electronic* systems; promote common, open *standards* for home and building *automation* ("smart home" / "smart building"). **Structure** General Assembly; Executive Board; Technical and Marketing Board; Working Groups. **Languages** English. **Staff** 21.00 FTE, paid. **Finance** Sources: members' dues; sale of products. **Activities** Research and development; standards/guidelines. **Publications** *KNX Standard*.
Members Companies (about 500) and partnership agreements (about 100,000). Member companies in 44 countries and territories. Membership countries not specified.
National groups in 45 countries. Membership countries not specified.
NGO Relations Cooperates with (1): *European Committee for Electrotechnical Standardization (CENELEC, #06647)*. In liaison with technical committees of: *Comité européen de normalisation (CEN, #04162)*; *International Electrotechnical Commission (IEC, #13255)*; *International Organization for Standardization (ISO, #14473)*. [2022.05.08/XE4461/E]

- ♦ Kobe Osaka International (no recent information)
- ♦ **KODEWES** Komittee voor de Opheffing van de Derde Wereld Schuld (#04148)
- ♦ Koepel van de Vlaamse Noord-Zuidbeweging – 11 11 11 (internationally oriented national body)
- ♦ Koerdisch Instituut van Brussel (internationally oriented national body)
- ♦ Koestus ja Tarkastustoiminnan Elin / see Joint Nordic Organization for Technical Testing (#16142)
- ♦ KOFF – Kompetenzzentrum Friedensförderung (internationally oriented national body)
- ♦ Kofi Annan Foundation (internationally oriented national body)
- ♦ Kofi Annan International Peacekeeping Training Centre (internationally oriented national body)
- ♦ KoFID – Korea Civil Society Forum on International Development Cooperation (internationally oriented national body)
- ♦ KOICA – Korea International Cooperation Agency (internationally oriented national body)
- ♦ KOICID – Korea International Cooperation for Infectious Diseases (internationally oriented national body)
- ♦ KOI – Kobe Osaka International (no recent information)
- ♦ Koino Kentro Erevnon (#16147)
- ♦ Kokke i de Europaeiske Faellesskaber / see Euro-Toques International (#09190)
- ♦ Kokusai Budoin (#14108)
- ♦ Kokusai Bunka Kaikan (internationally oriented national body)
- ♦ Kokusai Daigaku (internationally oriented national body)
- ♦ Kokusaiho Gakkai (internationally oriented national body)
- ♦ Kokusai Hoken Kyoryoku Shimin-No-Kai (internationally oriented national body)
- ♦ Kokusai Judo Renmei (#13975)
- ♦ Kokusai Kaihatsu Senta (internationally oriented national body)
- ♦ Kokusai Koryu Kikin (internationally oriented national body)
- ♦ Kokusai Koutsu Anzen Gakkai (#12235)
- ♦ Kokusai Kyodokumiai Hoken Rengo (#12948)
- ♦ Kokusai Nanmin Hoshikai / see Refugee Empowerment International
- ♦ Kokusai Nanmin Kyuen Hohshidan / see Refugee Empowerment International
- ♦ Kölczönär Garanciabistosítók Egvesülete / see European Association of Guarantee Institutions (#06061)
- ♦ Koli Calling – International Conference on Computing Education Research (meeting series)

♦ KOLPING INTERNATIONAL 16203

Gen Sec Kolpingplatz 5-11, 50667 Cologne, Germany. T. +492217788014. E-mail: info@kolping.net.
URL: http://www.kolping.net/

History 1849, Cologne (Germany). Founded by Adolph Kolping, as a Catholic based organization providing help to journeymen in their personal and professional problems. Expanded to include men and women of all ages and social levels. Former names and other names: *Oeuvre Kolping internationale* – former; *Opera Internazionale di Kolping* – former; *Internationaal Kolpingwerk* – former; *International Kolping Society* – former; *Obra Kolping Internacional* – former; *Internationales Kolpingwerk* – former. **Aims** Enable members to

present themselves as Christians to the world, in their occupations, their marriages and families, in society and state; serve the needs of members and of society as a whole; promote general welfare in a *Christian* spirit through active participation of individual members and their groups; cooperate in the continuous renewal and humanization of society. **Structure** International Convention (every 6 years); International Board of Directors (every 2 years); International Executive Board; National Convention (legislative body); National Board of Directors (directive body). Third World Section: KOLPING INTERNATIONAL Cooperation e.V. *(formerly: Sozial- und Entwicklungshilfe des Kolpingwerkes)*, set up 1969, Cologne (Germany FR). **Languages** English, French, German, Spanish. **Staff** 29.00 FTE, paid. **Finance** Sources: donations; government support; members' dues. **Activities** Events/meetings; monitoring/evaluation; networking/liaising; projects/programmes; religious activities; training/education. **Events** *Quinquennial Convention* Lima (Peru) 2017, *Quinquennial Convention / Quinquennial International Convention* Bensberg (Germany) 2012, *European Congress* Bratislava (Slovakia) 2009, *Quinquennial International Convention* Alsópahok (Hungary) 2007, *Quinquennial congress / Quinquennial International Convention* Tuxtla Gutiérrez (Mexico) 2002. **Publications** *International Newsletter* (12 a year); *Dialogue, The International Kolping Society's Journal for the Leadership* (annual).
Members Individuals (about 400,000); Kolping Families (about 9,100); National organizations (50). Members in 60 countries:
Albania, Argentina, Austria, Benin, Bolivia, Brazil, Burundi, Cameroon, Canada, Chile, Colombia, Congo DR, Costa Rica, Croatia, Czechia, Dominican Rep, Ecuador, El Salvador, Germany, Ghana, Honduras, Hungary, India, Indonesia, Italy, Kenya, Korea Rep, Kosovo, Lithuania, Luxembourg, Malawi, Mexico, Moldova, Myanmar, Netherlands, Nicaragua, Nigeria, Paraguay, Peru, Philippines, Poland, Portugal, Romania, Rwanda, Serbia, Slovakia, Slovenia, South Africa, Sri Lanka, Switzerland, Tanzania UR, Timor-Leste, Togo, Uganda, Ukraine, Uruguay, USA, Venezuela, Vietnam, Zambia.
Consultative Status Consultative status granted from: *ECOSOC (#05331)* (Special); *ILO (#11123)* (Special List); *Council of Europe (CE, #04881)* (Participatory Status). **IGO Relations** Accredited by (1): *United Nations Office at Vienna (UNOV, #20604)*. Associated with Department of Global Communications of the United Nations. **NGO Relations** Member of (4): *Conference of Non-Governmental Organizations in Consultative Relationship with the United Nations (CONGO, #04635)*; *Forum of Catholic Inspired NGOs (#09905)*; *International Partnership on Religion and Sustainable Development (PaRD, #14524)*; *Vienna NGO Committee on the Family (#20774)*. [2023.02.14/XE1180/**E**]

- Komision rajonal për vërtetimin e fakteve mbi krimet e luftës dhe shkeljet tjera të rënda të të drejtave të njeriut të kryera në ish-Jugosllavi që nga 1 janari 1991 deri më 31 dhjetor të vitit 2001 (unconfirmed)
- Komisja Europejska (#06633)
- Komissija Organizacii Obedinennyh Nacij po Pravu Mezdunarodnoj Torgovli (#20531)
- Komissija po Sohraneniju Morskih Zivyh Resursov Antarktiki (#04206)
- Komité for Bomulds- og Dermed Beslaegtede Textilindustrier i EF / see European Federation of Cotton and Allied Textiles Industries (#07093)
- Komitee für eine Arbeiterinternationale (#04290)
- Komitee Ärzte für die Dritte Welt / see German Doctors
- Komitee der Atlantischen Studien (no recent information)
- Komitee der Baumwoll und Verwandten Textilindustriën der EG / see European Federation of Cotton and Allied Textiles Industries (#07093)
- Komitee Cap Anamur / see Cap Anamur – Deutsche Not-Ärzte
- Komitee für eine Demokratische UNO / see Democracy Without Borders
- Komitee für ein Effektives Völkerstrafrecht (internationally oriented national body)
- Komitee der Europäischen Garten- und Landschaftsarchitekten (inactive)
- Komitee der Europäischen Hersteller von Einrichtungen zur Messung und Verteilung von Flüssigen Brennstoffen (#04167)
- Komitee der Europäischen Hersteller von Textilmaschinen (#06672)
- Komitee der Europäischen Nahrungsmittelmaschinen-und Verpackungsmaschinenhersteller (inactive)
- Komitee des Getreide- und Futtermittelhandels in der EG / see Committee of the Trade in Cereals, Oilseeds, Pulses, Olive Oil, Oils and Fats, Animal Feed and Agrosupply of the EU (#04289)
- Komitee der Hefeindustrie in der Europäische Union / see Confédération des Fabricants de Levure de l'Union Européenne (#04551)
- Komitee der internationalen Schülerspiele (#04264)
- Komitéen for Sygehusadministratorers Nordiske Samarbejde (inactive)
- Komiteen for Sykehusadministratorenes Nordiske Samarbeid (inactive)
- Komitee SOS / see Fair Trade Original
- Komitee der Verbände der Kunststoffverarbeitenden Industrie in Westeuropa (inactive)
- Komitee gegen den Vogelmord (internationally oriented national body)
- Komitet ds Przemyslu Bawelniarskiego i Pokrewnych Przemyslow Wlokienniczych / see European Federation of Cotton and Allied Textiles Industries (#07093)
- Komittee des Handels mit Getreide, Futtermitteln, Ölsaaten, Olivenöl, Ölen und Fetten und Landwirtschaftlichen Betriebsmitteln in der EU / see Committee of the Trade in Cereals, Oilseeds, Pulses, Olive Oil, Oils and Fats, Animal Feed and Agrosupply of the EU (#04289)
- Komittee voor de Opheffing van de Derde Wereld Schuld (#04148)
- Kommission der Bischofskonferenzen der Europäischen Gemeinschaft / see Commission of the Bishops' Conferences of the European Union (#04205)
- Kommission der Bischofskonferenzen der Europäischen Union (#04205)
- Kommissionen for de Europaeiske Faellesskaber / see European Commission (#06633)
- Kommission der Europäischen Gemeinschaften / see European Commission (#06633)
- Kommission für Forschungspartnerschaft mit Entwicklungsländern (internationally oriented national body)
- Kommission der Kirchen für Migranten in Europa (#03912)
- Kommission Reinhaltung der Luft im VDI und DIN – Normenausschuss (internationally oriented national body)
- Kommittee der Hefehersteller der Europäischen Union (#04551)
- Kommittén for Integrering av Skogsundervisningen i Norden (inactive)
- Kommittén för Nordiskt Ungdomssamarbete / see Nordic Children's and Youth Committee (#17235)

♦ Kommunalanställdas Nordiska Samarbete (KNS) 16204

Fédération nordique des employées municipaux – Nordische Föderation der Gewerkschaften der Kommunalbediensteten – Nordic Federation of Unions of Municipal Employees

SG Hagagatan 2, SE-113 48 Stockholm, Sweden.
URL: https://kns-kpy.org/

History 1907. Founded by Swedish and Danish unions of municipal employees. Activities ceased during Second World War, but resumed in 1945. From 1 Jan 1981, includes the previous *Nordiska Skorstensfejarunionen (inactive)*. Former names and other names: *Nordiske Kommunaltjenestemannessekretariatet* – alias. **Events** *Conference* Helsinki (Finland) 2014.
Members Full in 5 countries:
Denmark, Finland, Iceland, Norway, Sweden. [2021/XD1938/**D**]

- Kommunenes Internationale Miljøorganisasjon / see KIMO International (#16192)

♦ Kommunikationsausschuss Lutherischer Minderheitskirchen in Europa (KALME) 16205

Comité pour communications des Eglises luthériennes minoritaires d'Europe – Communication Committee for Lutheran Minority Churches in Europe

Contact Ruitenborghstraat 37, 7721 BB Dalfsen, Netherlands.

History 1977, Güstrow (Germany). 1977, Güstrov (German DR), to provide the framework for a communication project of *The Lutheran World Federation (LWF, #16532)*. **Aims** Promote the effective use of communication in church ministry. **Structure** General Assembly; Board of Directors. **Languages** English, German. **Finance** Members' dues. Other sources: Department for Mission and Development; Lutheran World Federation; additional funds from Lutheran churches. **Activities** Organizes seminars, workshops, exchanges and lectures on church press, audiovisuals and radio-work; exchanges strategies in communication. **Events** *Triennial General Assembly* Rome (Italy) 2010, *Triennial General Assembly* Amsterdam (Netherlands) / Utrecht (Netherlands) 2007, *Triennial General Assembly* Sibiu (Romania) 2004, *Triennial general assembly* Bielsko-Biala (Poland) 2001, *Triennial General Assembly* Poland 2001.
Members Churches (22) in European countries where Lutheranism is not the state or folk Church. Churches in 18 countries:
Austria, Croatia, Czechia, Estonia, France, Hungary, Ireland, Italy, Latvia, Lithuania, Netherlands, Poland, Romania, Russia, Serbia, Slovakia, Slovenia, UK. [2013/XE9550/**E**]

- Kommunikations- und Informationszentrum für Entwicklung, Frieden und Menschenrechte (internationally oriented national body)
- Kompetenzzentrum Friedensförderung (internationally oriented national body)
- KOMRA – Komision rajonal për vërtetimin e fakteve mbi krimet e luftës dhe shkeljet tjera të rënda të të drejtave të njeriut të kryera në ish-Jugosllavi që nga 1 janari 1991 deri më 31 dhjetor të vitit 2001 (unconfirmed)
- Komunista Esperantista Kolektivo / see International Communist Esperantist Collective (#12819)
- Konfederacija Malyh Narodov i Etniceskih Grupp (inactive)
- Konfederasyona Komalên Kurd li Ewrupa / see European Kurdish Democratic Societies Congress (#07632)
- Konferansen for Europas Maritime Utkantregioner (#04638)
- Konferencen for Perifere Maritime Regioner i Europa (#04638)
- Konferencija Evropejskih Cerkvej / see Conference of European Churches (#04593)
- Konferencija Evropejskih Statistikov (#04600)
- Konferencija Primorskih Okrainov v Evrope (#04638)
- Konferencja Peryferycznych Regionów Morskich (#04638)
- Konferensen för Europas Perifera Maritima Regioner (#04638)
- Konferenz der Europäischen Regionalen Gesetzgebenden Parlamente (#04582)
- Konferenz der Europäischen Verfassungsgerichte (#04594)
- Konferenz Europäischer Kirchen (#04593)
- Konferenz der Internationalen Katholischen Organisationen (inactive)
- Konferenz der Kirchen Am Rhein (#04646)
- Konferenz von Peripهären Küstenregionen der EG / see Conference of Peripheral Maritime Regions of Europe (#04638)
- Konferenz der Peripheren Küstenregionen Europas (#04638)
- Konferenz der Präsidenten der Europäischen Parlamentarischen Versammlungen (meeting series)
- Konferenz der Präsidenten der Regionalen Gesetzgebenden Versammlungen in der Europäischen Union / see Conférence des assemblées législatives régionales d'Europe (#04582)
- Konferenz für Regionalentwicklung in Nordwesteuropa (inactive)
- Konferenz für Sicherheit und Zusammenarbeit / see Organization for Security and Cooperation in Europe (#17887)
- Konferenz theologischer Berufsarbeiter der Inneren Mission / see Internationale Konferenz Theologischer Mitarbeiterinnen und Mitarbeiter in der Diakonie
- Konferenz Theologischer Mitarbeiter in der Diakonie / see Internationale Konferenz Theologischer Mitarbeiterinnen und Mitarbeiter in der Diakonie
- Konferenz der Übersetzungsdienste Europäischer Staaten (#04650)
- Konferenz und Vereinigung der Stahlgebiete (inactive)
- Konföderation der Europäischen Drogistenverbände (inactive)
- Konföderation der Europäischen Laryngektomierten / see European Confederation of Laryngectomees (#06709)
- Konföderation der Europäischen Pherologischen Organisationen (inactive)
- Konföderation der Internationalen Unternehmervereinigungen (#04558)
- Kongregace kn/ve/vzi Nejsv/vet/vej/vsi (religious order)
- Kongregace Sester Sv Syrila a Metodéje (religious order)
- Kongregacji Nauki Wiary (#04669)
- Kongregatie van de Broeders van de Onbevlekte Ontvangenis van de Heilige Maagd Maria (religious order)
- Kongregation für die Glaubenslehre (#04669)
- Kongregation der Diennerinnen des Heiligstens Herzens Jesu (religious order)
- Kongregation der Dillinger Franziskanerinnen (religious order)
- Kongregation für das Katholische Bildungswesen (#04665)
- Kongregation Schwestern von Jesus dem Göttlichen Meister (religious order)
- Kongregation der Schwestern vom Göttlichen Erlöser (religious order)
- Kongregation der Schwestern vom Heiligen Josef (religious order)
- Kongregation vom Heiligsten Sakrament (religious order)
- Kongreso de la Popoloj (internationally oriented national body)
- Kongress des Europäischen Volkes (inactive)
- Kongress der Gemeinden und Regionen des Europarates (#04677)
- Kongress der Gemeinden und Regionen Europas / see Congress of Local and Regional Authorities of the Council of Europe (#04677)
- König Baudouin Stiftung (internationally oriented national body)
- Königliches Museum für Zentral-Afrika (internationally oriented national body)
- Koning Boudewijnstichting (internationally oriented national body)
- Koninklijke Academie voor Overzeese Wetenschappen (internationally oriented national body)
- Koninklijke Nederlandse Vereniging voor Internationaal Recht (internationally oriented national body)
- Koninklijk Instituut voor Internationale Betrekkingen / see Egmont Institute
- Koninklijk Instituut voor Taal-, Land- en Volkenkunde (internationally oriented national body)
- Koninklijk Instituut voor de Tropen (internationally oriented national body)
- Koninklijk Museum voor Midden-Afrika (internationally oriented national body)
- Koninklijk Nederlands Instituut voor Onderzoek der Zee (internationally oriented national body)
- Koninklijk Nederlands Meteorologisch Instituut / see International Service for Geomagnetic Indices (#14840)
- KON-KURD / see European Kurdish Democratic Societies Congress (#07632)
- Konnex Association / see KNX Association (#16202)
- Konrad Adenauer Foundation (internationally oriented national body)
- Konrad-Adenauer Stiftung (internationally oriented national body)
- Kontaktkommitéen for Barnehager og Fritidshjem i Norden (inactive)
- Kontaktstelle für Umwelt-und Entwicklung (internationally oriented national body)
- Kontinentaler Reklame Verband (inactive)
- Kontinentaler Verband für Innere Mission und Diakonie / see European Federation for Diaconia (#07099)
- Kontinentalnaja Organizacija Latinoamerikanskih Studentov / see Organización Continental Latinoamericana y Caribeña de Estudiantes (#17834)
- Konvensjon om inndrivning av underholdsbidrag (1962 treaty)
- Konvensjon inneholdende internasjonal-privatrettslige bestemmelser om ekteskap, adopsjon og vergemål med sluttprotokoll (1931 treaty)
- Konvention angående indrivning av underhållsbidrag (1962 treaty)
- Konventionen om social bistand og sociale tjenester (1994 treaty)
- Konvention des Europarates gegen menschenhandel (2005 treaty)
- Konvention des Europarates über die vermeidung von staatenlosigkeit in zusammenhang mit staatennachfolge (2006 treaty)
- Konvention des Europarates über geldwäsche, terrorismusfinanzierung sowie ermittlung, beschlagnahme und einziehung von erträgen aus straftaten (2005 treaty)
- Konvention om inddrivelse af underholdsbidrag (1962 treaty)
- Konvention innehållande internationellt privaträttslig bestämmelser om äktenskap, adoption och förmynderskap (1931 treaty)
- Konvention zum schutze der menschenrechte und grundfreiheiten (1950 treaty)
- KOO – Koordinierungstelle der Österreichischen Bischofskonferenz für Internationale Entwicklung und Mission (internationally oriented national body)

- ♦ Kooperation Utan Gränser / see We Effect
- ♦ Koordination Südliches Afrika (internationally oriented national body)
- ♦ Koordinierendes Komitee der Fachverbände der Schaltgerätehersteller in der Europäischen Union / see European Coordinating Committee of Manufacturers of Electrical Switchgear and Controlgear (#06790)
- ♦ Koordinierungs-Ausschuss Jüdischer Organisationen (#04813)
- ♦ Koordinierungstelle der Österreichischen Bischofskonferenz für Internationale Entwicklung und Mission (internationally oriented national body)
- ♦ Koor van de Europese Gemeenschappen / see European Union Choir (#08980)
- ♦ Koor van de Europese Unie (#08980)
- ♦ Kopienas Augu Skirnu Birojs (#04404)
- ♦ Kopigais Petniecibas centrs (#16147)
- ♦ KOPRI – Korea Polar Research Institute (internationally oriented national body)
- ♦ Korabel – Trade Union International of Workers in Shipbuilding (no recent information)
- ♦ Körber Foundation (internationally oriented national body)
- ♦ Körber Stiftung (internationally oriented national body)
- ♦ Korea Civil Society Forum on International Development Cooperation (internationally oriented national body)
- ♦ Korea Institute for International Economic Policy (internationally oriented national body)
- ♦ Korea International Cooperation Agency (internationally oriented national body)
- ♦ Korea International Cooperation for Infectious Diseases (internationally oriented national body)
- ♦ Korea International Trade Association (internationally oriented national body)
- ♦ Korea International Volunteer Organization (internationally oriented national body)
- ♦ Korean Association of International Development and Cooperation (internationally oriented national body)
- ♦ Korean Association of International Relations / see Korean Association of International Studies
- ♦ Korean Association of International Studies (internationally oriented national body)
- ♦ Korean Association of International Studies, Seoul (internationally oriented national body)
- ♦ Korean Association of Middle East Studies (internationally oriented national body)
- ♦ Korean Association of Slavic-Eurasian Studies (internationally oriented national body)
- ♦ Korean Association for Slavic Studies / see Korean Association of Slavic-Eurasian Studies
- ♦ Korean Foundation for World Aid (internationally oriented national body)
- ♦ Korea NGO Council for Overseas Cooperation / see Korea NGO Council for Overseas Development Cooperation
- ♦ Korea NGO Council for Overseas Development Cooperation (internationally oriented national body)

♦ Korean Peninsula Energy Development Organization (KEDO) 16206

Address not obtained.
URL: http://www.kedo.org/

History 9 Mar 1995, by governments of Japan, Korea Rep and USA, following signature of the Agreement on the Establishment of KEDO, to implement key provisions of the Agreed Framework between USA and Korea DPR, which promised Korea DPR 2 light-water reactors (LWR) of the Korean Standard Nuclear Power Plant model in return for the country's freezing of its nuclear programme. LWR project terminated, 31 Mar 2006, following failure on the part of Korea DPR to perform the necessary steps. Organization continues to fulfill legal and financial obligations. **Structure** Executive Board.
Members Governments (12):
Argentina, Australia, Canada, China, Czechia, Indonesia, Japan, Korea Rep, New Zealand, Poland, USA, Uzbekistan.
Regional entity:
European Union (EU, #08967). [2018/XJ1027/**E***]

- ♦ Korean Studies Association of Australasia (internationally oriented national body)
- ♦ Korea Polar Research Institute (internationally oriented national body)
- ♦ Koresponda Servo Mondskala (#04849)
- ♦ Korkeakouluasteen Koulutuksen Pohjoismaisen Yhteistyön Johtoryhmä (inactive)
- ♦ KOSA – Koordination Südliches Afrika (internationally oriented national body)
- ♦ Kosmoglott, Société de langue internationale (inactive)
- ♦ Kosmoglott, Society of International Language (inactive)
- ♦ Kosmos, Alliance internationale de correspondance (inactive)
- ♦ Kosmos, International Alliance for Correspondence (inactive)
- ♦ Kotitalouden Pohjoismainen Yhteistyötoimikunta (no recent information)
- ♦ Közép-európai Egyetem (#03717)
- ♦ Közép-Európai Urológus Tarsasag (no recent information)
- ♦ Közösségi Növényfajta Hivatal (#04404)
- ♦ Közös Kutatóközpont (#16147)
- ♦ Københavns International Teater (internationally oriented national body)
- ♦ **KPC Europe** European Kaolin and Plastic Clays Association (#07623)
- ♦ **KP** Kimberley Process (#16191)
- ♦ **KPKR** Konferenz der Peripheren Küstenregionen Europas (#04638)

♦ KPro Study Group 16207

SG Associate Office DVC and VP, Univ of Western Sydney, Locked Bag 1797, Penrith NSW 2751, Australia.
URL: http://www.kpro.org/

History 1990. **Aims** Foster *clinical* and basic research on *keratoprosthesis*, synthetic *cornea* and artificial biocorneal *implants.* **Structure** Steering Committee. **Finance** Attendance fees. **Events** *International Keratoprothesen Meeting* Kyoto (Japan) 2016, *Symposium* San Diego, CA (USA) 2015, *International Keratoprothesen Meeting / Symposium* Salzburg (Austria) 2014, *Symposium* Miami, FL (USA) 2012. [2015/XJ9629/c/**C**]

- ♦ Kraft Institute / see CEPI ContainerBoard (#03824)
- ♦ Krankenschwestern des Heiligen Franziskus (religious order)
- ♦ KRdL – Kommission Reinhaltung der Luft im VDI und DIN – Normenausschuss (internationally oriented national body)
- ♦ Kreativiäts Akademie (unconfirmed)
- ♦ Kreditanstalt für Wiederaufbau (internationally oriented national body)
- ♦ KRENWE – Konferenz für Regionalentwicklung in Nordwesteuropa (inactive)
- ♦ Kresge Foundation (internationally oriented national body)
- ♦ Krestanska Mirova Konference (inactive)
- ♦ Krestintern – International Farmer and Peasant Council (inactive)
- ♦ Kreuzschwestern von Ingenbohl – Barmherzige Schwestern vom Heiligen Kreuz (religious order)
- ♦ Kreyssig Fund (inactive)

♦ KR Foundation 16208

Exec Dir Lædestræde 20, 1201 Copenhagen, Denmark. E-mail: info@krfnd.org.
URL: http://krfnd.org/

History 21 Dec 2014. **Aims** Help provide answers to, stimulate mind shifts about, and encourage action on the long-term challenges faced by current and future generations living on a planet with finite resources, fragile *ecosystems,* and *climate change.* **Structure** Board. **Languages** Danish, English. **Staff** 5.00 FTE, paid. **Activities** Advocacy/lobbying/activism; financial and/or material support. **NGO Relations** Supports (1): *Climate Action Network Europe (CAN Europe, #04001).* [2022.02.22/XM5489/f/**F**]

- ♦ **KrimG** Kriminologische Gesellschaft (#16209)
- ♦ KrimG – Wissenschaftliche Vereinigung Deutscher, Österreichischer und Schweizerischer Kriminologen / see Kriminologische Gesellschaft (#16209)
- ♦ Kriminologische Gesellschaft / see Kriminologische Gesellschaft (#16209)

♦ Kriminologische Gesellschaft (KrimG) 16209

Criminological Society of the German Speaking Countries (CrimS)

Contact Inst für Kriminologie, Univ Tübingen, Sand 7, 72076 Tübingen, Germany. T. +4970712972044. Fax +497071295104. E-mail: ifk@uni-tuebingen.de.
Pres Inst of Criminology, Luetzerode Street 9, 30161 Hannover, Germany. T. +49511348360.
URL: http://www.krimg.de/drupal/node/1/

History 1988. Founded as *Neue Kriminologische Gesellschaft*, merging both the former *Gessellschaft für die Gesamte Kriminologie* and the *Deutsche Kriminologische Gesselschaft.* Current title adopted, 21 Sep 2007. Full title: *Kriminologische Gesellschaft (KrimG) – Wissenschaftliche Vereinigung Deutscher, Österreichischer und Schweizerischer Kriminologen.* **Aims** Promote and enhance the empirical study of crime, criminality, offenders, victims and the system of state and societal reaction to crime and criminality; make available research results to practitioners, in particular to women and men in the fields of social work, policing and justice; disseminate policy relevant research findings among the public, in particular via mass media; enhance delinquency and crime prevention in all state, societal and community areas. **Structure** Board of Directors. **Languages** English, French, German, Spanish. **Staff** 3.00 FTE, paid. **Finance** Members' dues. Other sources: donations; sponsorship of conferences. **Activities** Events/meetings; awards/prizes/competitions; publishing activities. **Events** *Meeting* Hannover (Germany) 2022, *Meeting* Vienna (Austria) 2019, *Meeting* Münster (Germany) 2017, *Meeting* Cologne (Germany) 2015, *Meeting* Fribourg (Switzerland) 2013. **Publications** *KrimG-Nachrichtendienst* (usually 12 a year) – newsletter. *Neue Kriminologische Schriftenreihe* – book series. Conference Book Series. **Information Services** *KrimG-Aktuelles* – electronic news service. **Members** About 450, mainly from Germany, Austria and Switzerland, but also several members in West- and Middle-East Europe and other continents. Membership countries not specified. [2022/XJ2783/**D**]

- ♦ Kring voor de Geschiedenis van de Pharmacie in Benelux (#03827)
- ♦ Kristana Esperantista Ligo Internacia (#03901)
- ♦ Kristdemokraterna i Norden (#17237)
- ♦ Kristdemokrater i Norden (#17237)
- ♦ Kristdemokratiskt Internationellt Center (internationally oriented national body)
- ♦ Kristendemokratisk Ungdom i Norden (#17236)
- ♦ Kristlig-Demokratiske Partiers Nordiske Samarbeidsutvalg / see Nordic Christian Democrats (#17237)
- ♦ Kroc Institute for International Peace Studies (internationally oriented national body)
- ♦ KROM – Scandinavian Association for Penal Reform (inactive)
- ♦ KSAA – Korean Studies Association of Australasia (internationally oriented national body)
- ♦ KSEI – Kansainvälinen soveltavan estetiikan instituutti (internationally oriented national body)
- ♦ KSJ / see International Young Catholic Students (#15926)
- ♦ KSJ – Knights of St John International (religious order)
- ♦ **KSM** Koresponda Servo Mondskala (#04849)
- ♦ KSZE / see Organization for Security and Cooperation in Europe (#17887)

♦ Kuala Lumpur Regional Centre for Arbitration (KLRCA) 16210

Contact Jalan Sultan Hishamuddin, 50000 Kuala Lumpur, Malaysia. T. +60321420103 – +60321420702 – +60321420384. Fax +60321424513.
URL: http://klrca.org/

History 17 Aug 1978, Kuala Lumpur (Malaysia). Founded 17 Oct 1978, Kuala Lumpur (Malaysia), as an independent arbitral institution, set up under the auspices of *Asian-African Legal Consultative Organization (AALCO, #01303),* in cooperation and with the assistance of the Government of Malaysia. Also referred to as *Regional Centre for Arbitration Kuala Lumpur (RCAKL).* **Aims** Administer arbitration proceedings. **Languages** English, Malay. **Staff** 45.00 FTE, paid. **Finance** Financial assistance grants received from the Government of Malaysia; fees from cases. **Activities** Monitoring/evaluation; capacity building; knowledge management/ information dissemination; training/education; events/meetings. **Events** *International meeting* Kuala Lumpur (Malaysia) 2008, *Arbitrator development programme* Kuala Lumpur (Malaysia) 1992. **Publications** *Arbitration News* (4 a year).
Members Member countries and territories of AALCO (48):
Bahrain, Bangladesh, Botswana, Brunei Darussalam, Cameroon, China, Cyprus, Egypt, Gambia, Ghana, India, Indonesia, Iran Islamic Rep, Iraq, Japan, Jordan, Kenya, Korea DPR, Korea Rep, Kuwait, Lebanon, Libya, Malaysia, Mauritius, Mongolia, Myanmar, Nepal, Nigeria, Oman, Pakistan, Palestine, Philippines, Qatar, Saudi Arabia, Senegal, Sierra Leone, Singapore, Somalia, South Africa, Sri Lanka, Sudan, Syrian AR, Tanzania UR, Thailand, Türkiye, Uganda, United Arab Emirates, Yemen.
Permanent Observers with AALCO (2):
Australia, New Zealand.
NGO Relations Cooperates with: *Chartered Institute of Arbitrators (CIArb)*; several national arbitration councils. [2017.07.03/XE9995/**E**]

- ♦ **KÜDES** Konferenz der Übersetzungsdienste Europäischer Staaten (#04650)
- ♦ Kuijpers Resolution / see Mercator European Research Centre on Multilingualism and Language Learning (#16719)
- ♦ Kula II Fund for the Pacific Region (see: #04359)
- ♦ Kuljetuskysymysten Pohjoismainen Virkamieskomitea (inactive)
- ♦ Kulttuuriperintöjen Akatemia (unconfirmed)
- ♦ Kultura Centro Esperantista (internationally oriented national body)
- ♦ Kulturkontakt Nord (internationally oriented national body)
- ♦ KULU – Kvindernes U-Landsudvalg (internationally oriented national body)
- ♦ Kummisjoni ta'Gueįjer (#16061)
- ♦ Kungiyar Sada Zumunci Tsakanin Al'ummar Kasasha, Duniya / see Registre des Citoyens du Monde (#18822)
- ♦ Kunsill Ewropew (#06801)
- ♦ Kunsill ta' l-Unjoni Ewropea (#04895)
- ♦ Kunst Bildung – Neue Technologien in Europa (#02553)
- ♦ Kunst des Lebens Verein (internationally oriented national body)
- ♦ Kurash Confederation of Asia (inactive)

♦ Kurash Confederation of Asia-Oceania (KCAO) 16211

Contact 4 Shakhrisabz passage, Mirabad district, Tashkent, Uzbekistan, 10060. T. +998712336814. E-mail: info@kurash-kcao.org.
URL: http://kurash-kcao.org/

History Set up Nov 2016, on merger of *Kurash Confederation of Asia (KCA, inactive)* and *Oceania Kurash Confederation (inactive).* Continental federation of *International Kurash Association (IKA, #13993).* **Aims** Develop the sport of Kurash. **Structure** Officers. Standing Committees (12): Sports; Refereeing; Protocol; International Relations; Legal; Athletes; Education; Women in Sport; Ethics and Disciplinary; Medical; Finance; Press and PR.
Members Federations in 39 countries and territories:
Afghanistan, Bangladesh, Fiji, Hong Kong, India, Indonesia, Iran Islamic Rep, Iraq, Japan, Jordan, Kazakhstan, Korea Rep, Kuwait, Lebanon, Macau, Malaysia, Mongolia, Nepal, New Caledonia, New Zealand, Northern Mariana Is, Pakistan, Palestine, Papua New Guinea, Philippines, Polynesia Fr, Samoa, Samoa USA, Singapore, Sri Lanka, Syrian AR, Taiwan, Tajikistan, Thailand, Tonga, Turkmenistan, Uzbekistan, Vietnam, Yemen. [2018/XM6829/**D**]

- ♦ Kuratorium of the Danube Symposium for Psychiatry / see Danubian Psychiatric Association (#05008)
- ♦ Kuratorium für die Tagungen der Nobelpreisträger in Lindau (#04909)
- ♦ Kurdish Institute for the Defence of a Thousand Year Old Culture in Peril / see Kurdish Institute of Paris (#16212)

♦ Kurdish Institute of Paris 16212

Institut kurde de Paris

Secretariat 106 rue La Fayette, 75010 Paris, France. T. +33148246464. Fax +33148246466.
URL: http://www.institutkurde.org/

History Feb 1983, Paris (France). Known also as *Kurdish Institute for the Defence of a Thousand Year Old Culture in Peril – Institut kurde pour la défense d'une culture millénaire en péril*. Registered in accordance with French law. **Aims** Study and encourage research and study of Kurdish language, art, literature, history and the Kurdish *cultural heritage*; help safeguard, renew interest in and diffuse the Kurdish culture and promote a dialogue between it and other cultures; keep the Kurdish language and culture alive among Kurdish immigrants and help them adapt to their new environment; inform the public of the historical, cultural, social and political dimensions of the Kurdish question. **Structure** General Assembly (every 3 years); Administrative Council. **Activities** Departments: documentation (Documentation Centre), research (Research Centre), plastic arts, music, audio-visual, publishing, teaching. Services: library; teaching; socio-cultural activities. Organizes exhibitions, music concerts, artistic entertainments, film projections, lectures, seminars and conferences. Participates in international conferences on linguistic and cultural problems as well as in radio and television programs. Training activities. **Publications** *Bulletin de liaison et d'information* (12 a year) in English, French, German, Italian, Kurdish, Spanish, Turkish; *Hêvî* (2 a year); *Kurmancî* (2 a year); *Etudes Kurdes* (periodical).
Members Individuals in 36 countries:
Afghanistan, Algeria, Australia, Austria, Belgium, Bulgaria, Canada, Chile, Colombia, Denmark, Egypt, Finland, France, Germany, Greece, Indonesia, Iran Islamic Rep, Iraq, Israel, Italy, Japan, Jordan, Netherlands, Norway, Pakistan, Saudi Arabia, Serbia, Spain, Sweden, Switzerland, Syrian AR, Tunisia, Türkiye, UK, USA, Venezuela.
Members also in the former USSR. Membership countries not specified. [2011.10.20/XF1385/jv/**F**]

- ♦ KURVE Wustrow (internationally oriented national body)
- ♦ Kuwait Fund / see Kuwait Fund for Arab Economic Development
- ♦ Kuwait Fund for Arab Economic Development (internationally oriented national body)
- ♦ Kuwait Institute for Economic and Social Planning in the Middle East / see Arab Planning Institute (#01027)
- ♦ Kuwait Regional Convention for Cooperation on the Protection on the Marine Environment from Pollution (1978 treaty)
- ♦ Kuwait Society for the Advancement of Arab Children (internationally oriented national body)

♦ Kvarken Council 16213

Kvarkenrådet – Merenkurkun Neuvosto
Secretariat Finland Gerbyvägen 18, FI-65230 Vaasa, Finland. T. +358401545883. E-mail: info@kvarken.org.
URL: http://www.kvarken.org/

History 1972, as a public cross-border organization between Sweden and Finland in the Kvarken area. From 1979, comes within the framework *Nordic Council of Ministers (NCM, #17260)*, within the remit of Nordic Council of Ministers for Business, Energy and Regional Policy (MR-NER). Previously within *Nordic Committee of Senior Officials for Regional Policy (EK-R / NÄRP / NERP)*. Registered under Finnish law. **Aims** Enhance *cross-border cooperation* in the Kvarken region. **Structure** Board; Secretariat. **Languages** English, Finnish, Swedish. **Staff** 3.00 FTE, paid. **Finance** Regional funding from member organizations; part funding from Nordic Council of Ministers. **Activities** Projects/programmes; events/meetings; networking/liaising; advocacy/lobbying/activism.
Members Regional authorities in 2 countries:
Finland, Sweden. [2021/XK0833/**E***]

- ♦ Kvarkenrådet (#16213)
- ♦ Kvindernes U-Landsudvalg (internationally oriented national body)
- ♦ Kvinder i videnskab og teknologi (#06276)
- ♦ KVINFO – Kín-Viden Information Forskning (internationally oriented national body)
- ♦ Kvinna till Kvinna Foundation (internationally oriented national body)
- ♦ Kvinnenes Faglige Nordiske Komite (inactive)
- ♦ Kvinneuniversitetet Nord (internationally oriented national body)
- ♦ Kvinnor för Fred (internationally oriented national body)
- ♦ Kvinnor inom teknisk och naturvetenskaplig sektor (#06276)
- ♦ **KvKBLA** Kamer van Koophandel Belgie-Luxemburg-Arabische Landen (#00907)
- ♦ KVO International – Korea International Volunteer Organization (internationally oriented national body)
- ♦ Kwanmukan International Society (internationally oriented national body)
- ♦ KWBF / see Catholic Biblical Federation (#03600)
- ♦ Kyiv International University (internationally oriented national body)
- ♦ Kyoto convention – International Convention on the Simplification and Harmonization of Customs Procedures (1973 treaty)
- ♦ Kyoto Protocol to the United Nations Framework Convention on Climate Change (1997 treaty)
- ♦ Kyrkans Utlandshjälp (internationally oriented national body)
- ♦ L4L – Lawyers for Lawyers Foundation (internationally oriented national body)
- ♦ **L4WB** Learning for Well-being Foundation (#16431)
- ♦ **LA21** Local Agenda 21 (#16504)
- ♦ LAAD – Latin American Agribusiness Development Corporation (internationally oriented national body)
- ♦ LAAG / see Society for Latin American and Caribbean Anthropology
- ♦ **LAAHS** Latin American Aviation Historical Society (#16253)
- ♦ Lääketieteellisen Tutkimuksen Pohjoismainen Yhteistyötoimikunta (#16125)
- ♦ Lääketieteen Opetuksen Pohjoismainen Federaatio (no recent information)
- ♦ LAAPP – Latin American Association of Plant Physiology (no recent information)
- ♦ LAARP – Latin American Art Resource Project (internationally oriented national body)
- ♦ LABIC – Latin American Meeting on Biological Inorganic Chemistry (meeting series)
- ♦ **LABIP** Lactic Acid Bacteria Industrial Platform (#16216)
- ♦ LAB – Latin America Bureau, London (internationally oriented national body)
- ♦ **LABMT** Latin American Bone Marrow Transplantation Group (#16257)
- ♦ Laboratoire de coopération internationale dans le domaine de la physique des particules élémentaires (internationally oriented national body)
- ♦ Laboratoire d'Economie de la Production et de l'Intégration Internationale / see Institute of International Integration and Industrial Economics
- ♦ Laboratoire européen de biologie moléculaire (#07813)
- ♦ Laboratoire européen pour l'excellence industrielle et territoriale (internationally oriented national body)
- ♦ Laboratoire européen pour la physique des particules / see European Organization for Nuclear Research (#08108)
- ♦ Laboratoire européen de psychologie sociale (internationally oriented national body)
- ♦ Laboratoire européen de signatures micro-ondes (#07797)
- ♦ Laboratoire nordique du théâtre (internationally oriented national body)
- ♦ Laboratoires internationaux de physiologie du Mont-Rose (inactive)
- ♦ Laboratorio Andino de Maderas (no recent information)
- ♦ Laboratorio Europeo per l'Eccelenza Industriale e Territoriale (internationally oriented national body)
- ♦ Laboratório Ibérico Internacional de Nanotecnologia (internationally oriented national body)
- ♦ Laboratorio Latinoamericano de Evaluación de la Calidad de la Educación (#16346)

♦ Laboratorio Latinoamericano para la Protección contra los Virus Informaticos 16214

Latin American Laboratory for Protection Against Computer Viruses
Dir Gen Calle Zanja No 651, Centro Havana, 10300 Havana, Cuba. T. +5378735965. Fax +5378335965.

History 1993, Havana (Cuba), by *Intergovernmental Informatics Programme (IIP, inactive)*. **Aims** Study virus programmes and development of antivirus software. **Structure** General Manager. **Languages** Spanish. **Finance** by Segurmatica enterprise. **Activities** Organizes Iberoamerican Seminar of Information Technology Security (always in Havana, Cuba). **Events** *Iberian-American seminar of protection against computer viruses and security in information technologies* Havana (Cuba) 2009, *Iberian-American seminar of protection against computer viruses and security in information technologies* Havana (Cuba) 2007, *Iberian-American seminar of protection against computer viruses and security in information technologies* Havana (Cuba) 2004, *Iberian-American seminar of protection against computer viruses and security in information technologies* Havana (Cuba) 2002, *Iberian-American seminar of protection against computer viruses and security in information technologies* Havana (Cuba) 2000. [2008.06.01/XE4098/**E**]

- ♦ Laboratori Scientifici "A Mosso" sul Monte-Rosa (inactive)
- ♦ Laboratory of International Collaboration on Elementary Particle Physics / see International Center for Elementary Particle Physics, Tokyo
- ♦ Labor Council for Latin American Advancement (internationally oriented national body)
- ♦ Labour Action for Peace (internationally oriented national body)
- ♦ Labour behind the Label / see Clean Clothes Campaign (#03986)

♦ Labour Law Research Network (LLRN) 16215

Chair address not obtained. E-mail: labourlawresearch.net@gmail.com.
URL: http://labourlawresearch.net/

History 2011. Set up by research institutes/centers from all over the world dedicated to the study of labour law. **Aims** Advance research in labour law; facilitate the dissemination of research work and encourage open discussion of scholarship and ideas in this field. **Structure** Steering Committee; Advisory Committee. **Activities** Events/meetings; knowledge management/information dissemination.
Members Research centres (80) specialized in labour law in 31 countries and territories:
Australia, Austria, Belarus, Belgium, Brazil, Canada, Chile, China, Colombia, Denmark, Finland, France, Germany, Hungary, Israel, Italy, Japan, Korea Rep, Mexico, Netherlands, Norway, Poland, Russia, Slovakia, South Africa, Spain, Sweden, Taiwan, UK, USA, Zimbabwe.
European Working Group on Labour Law (EWLL, #09114); *Institut für Arbeitsrecht und Arbeitsbeziehungen in der Europäischen Union (IAAEU)*. [2023.02.14/AA2098/jy/**F**]

- ♦ Labour and Socialist International (inactive)
- ♦ Labour Sports International / see International Workers and Amateurs in Sports Confederation (#15905)
- ♦ Labour Treaty (1956 treaty)
- ♦ Labour Wireless International (inactive)
- ♦ **labphon** Association for Laboratory Phonology (#02777)
- ♦ LABQUALITY DAYS – International Congress on Quality in Laboratory Medicine (meeting series)
- ♦ The Lab – The Sustainability Laboratory (internationally oriented national body)
- ♦ **LABWA** Latin American Bottled Water Association (#16258)
- ♦ **LACAC** Latin American Civil Aviation Commission (#16297)
- ♦ **LACA** Latin American and Caribbean Alliance of YMCAs (#16264)
- ♦ LACA – Latin American Crystallographic Association (unconfirmed)
- ♦ **LACCASO** Latin American and Caribbean Council of AIDS Service Organizations (#16272)
- ♦ **LACCEI** Latin American and Caribbean Consortium of Engineering Institutions (#16270)
- ♦ LACC – Latin American and Caribbean Center, Miami FL (internationally oriented national body)
- ♦ **LACC** Latin American Council of Churches (#16309)
- ♦ **LACCOTAM** Latin American and Caribbean Conference on Theoretical and Applied Mechanics (#16269)
- ♦ **LACEA** Latin American and Caribbean Economics Association (#16274)
- ♦ **LACEC** Latin American Consortium on Emergency Contraception (#16306)
- ♦ LACE – Latin-American Symposium on Biotechnology, Biomedical, Biopharmaceutical, and Industrial Applications of Capillary Electrophoresis and Microchip Technology (meeting series)
- ♦ **LACFC** Latin American and Caribbean Forestry Commission (#16278)
- ♦ **LACG** Latin American Chronobiology Group (#16296)
- ♦ **LAChIN** Latin American Chemical Network (#18718)
- ♦ LACIF – Latin American Challenge Investment Fund (internationally oriented national body)
- ♦ LACIM – Les Amis d'un coin de l'Inde et du monde (internationally oriented national body)
- ♦ LACIS – Latin American Circle for International Studies (internationally oriented national body)
- ♦ **LACLO** Latin American Community of Learning Objects (#16301)
- ♦ **LACMA** Latin American and Caribbean International Movers Association (#16280)
- ♦ LACNET / see Plantain and Banana Research and Development Network for Latin America and the Caribbean (#18389)
- ♦ LAC-Net / see Red Iberoamericana de Bosques Modelo (#18659)
- ♦ **LACNIC** Latin American and Caribbean Internet Address Registry (#16281)
- ♦ LACNOG – Latin American and Caribbean Network Operators Group (unconfirmed)
- ♦ LACONA – Conference on Lasers in the Conservation of Artworks (meeting series)
- ♦ LACPA / see CropLife Latin America (#04967)
- ♦ **LACSC** Latin American and Caribbean Seismological Commission (#16285)
- ♦ LACSI – Latin American and Caribbean Studies Institute (internationally oriented national body)

♦ Lactic Acid Bacteria Industrial Platform (LABIP) 16216

Secretariat Kralingse Plaslaan 52 B, 3061 BA Rotterdam, Netherlands. T. +31104188997. E-mail: labip.secretary@kpnmail.nl.
URL: http://www.labip.com/

History 1994. Registration: European Economical Association, Netherlands. **Aims** Keep members informed and updated about progress in European research on Lactic Acid Bacteria (LAB); coordinate communication about topics of industrial relevance between science, industry and EU authorities; secure EU-funding for LAB and related research on a long-term basis in Europe; organize workshops concerning topics of industrial relevance. **Structure** General Assembly (annual); Steering Group. **Languages** English. **Staff** No FTE staff. **Finance** Sources: members' dues. **Activities** Awards/prizes/competitions; events/meetings.
Members Companies (22) in 10 countries:
Belgium, Bulgaria, Denmark, Finland, France, Germany, Ireland, Italy, Netherlands, Switzerland. [2023.02.14/XM5787/t/**F**]

- ♦ **LACTLD** Latin American and Caribbean Top Level Domains (#16287)
- ♦ **LACTRIMS** Comité Latinoamericano para el Tratamiento y la Investigación en Esclerosis Múltiple (#04190)
- ♦ LACUS – Linguistic Association of Canada and the United States (internationally oriented national body)
- ♦ **LACWHN** Latin American and Caribbean Women's Health Network (#16288)
- ♦ LADIA – Latin American Dental Industry and Trade Association (no recent information)

♦ Ladies Circle International (LCI) 16217

Contact address not obtained. E-mail: info@ladiescircleinternational.org.
URL: http://www.ladiescircleinternational.org/

History May 1959. Founded by Ladies' Circles from UK, Ireland, Sweden and Denmark. **Aims** Support community projects and raise funds for the needy. **Structure** General Meeting (annual); International Board. **Languages** English. **Activities** Networking/liaising; events/meetings; projects/programmes. **Events** *Annual International Conference* Lahti (Finland) 2022, *Annual International Conference* Rotterdam (Netherlands) 2019, *Annual International Conference* Haugesund (Norway) 2018, *Annual International Conference* Sønderborg (Denmark) 2017, *Annual International Conference* Cape Town (South Africa) 2016. **Publications** *LCI Newsletter* (2 a year).
Members Full in 41 countries:
Austria, Belgium, Botswana, Burundi, Cyprus, Denmark, Estonia, Finland, France, Germany, Great Britain, Hong Kong, Iceland, India, Ireland, Israel, Italy, Kenya, Latvia, Lithuania, Luxembourg, Madagascar, Malta, Mauritius, Morocco, Nepal, Netherlands, Norway, Portugal, Romania, Singapore, Slovenia, South Africa, Spain, Sri Lanka, Sweden, Switzerland, Tunisia, USA, Zambia, Zimbabwe. [2019.06.01/XE2335/**E**]

♦ Ladies European Tour (LET) 16218

Main Office c/o Buckinghamshire Golf Club, Denham Court Drive, Denham, UB9 5PG, UK. T. +441895831028. Fax +441895832301. E-mail: bethan.cutler@ladieseuropeantour.com – enquiries@ladieseuropeantour.com.
URL: http://www.ladieseuropeantour.com/

History 1978, as *Women Professional Golfers Association (WPGA)* by the Professional Golfers' Association of Great Britain and Ireland. Reconstituted as *Women's Professional Golf Association*, 1 Apr 1989. Present title adopted, 2000. **Aims** Provide a global platform for demonstrating a commitment to women's professional *sport*; provide opportunities for the most determined women and girls to succeed. **Structure** Board of Directors; Players Council. **Languages** English. **Activities** Sporting activities. **Members** Individuals (over 300) representing almost 40 different nationalities. Membership countries not specified. [2019.10.15/XN5420/F]

- ♦ Ladies' Hairdressers International (#13218)
- ♦ LADIMA – Laboratorio Andino de Maderas (no recent information)
- ♦ LADS – League of ASEAN Dermatological Societies (unconfirmed)
- ♦ LAEA – Language Association of Eastern Africa (no recent information)
- ♦ LAEBA – Latin America-Caribbean and Asia-Pacific Economics and Business Association (no recent information)
- ♦ LAECC – Groupe international 'Laïcat et communauté chrétienne' (inactive)
- ♦ **LAE** Library Assembly of Eurasia (#16458)
- ♦ LAF Austria – Lateinamerikaforschung Austria (internationally oriented national body)
- ♦ **LAFeBS** Latin American Federation of Biophysical Societies (#16317)
- ♦ **LAF** Literature Across Frontiers (#16492)
- ♦ LAFP / see Federación Iberolatinoamericana de Artistas Intérpretes y Ejecutantes (#09325)
- ♦ LAFTA – Latin American Free Trade Association (inactive)
- ♦ L-Agenzija Ewropea tas-Sigurtà ta' l-Avjazzjoni (#08978)
- ♦ Lagos-Mombasa Trans-African Highway Authority (inactive)
- ♦ **LAGPA/IIAS** Latin American Group for Public Administration (#16337)
- ♦ **LAHC** Latin American Heads Conference (#16338)
- ♦ Lahore Ahmadiyya Movement in Islam / see Lahore Ahmadiyya Society (#16219)

♦ Lahore Ahmadiyya Society 16219

Ahmadiyya Anjuman Lahore

SG Ahmadiyya Anjuman Lahore, 5 Usman Block, New Garden Town, PO Box Ferozepur Rd, Lahore PC 54600, Pakistan. T. +924235862956 – +924235863260. Fax +924235839202.
URL: http://www.aaiil.org/

History 1914, Lahore (Pakistan). Derives from *Sadar Anjuman Ahmadiyya*, founded in Qadain (India) by Hazrat Mirza Ghulam Ahmad, a Mujaddid (reformer) of the 14th century Hijra and Maseeh-i-Mauood (the Promised Messiah). He died in 1908 and was succeeded by Maulana Noor-ud-Din as the first religious head of the community. Upon the latter's death in 1914, the Jamaat split into 2 sections. The Secretary of the Jamaat, Maulana Muhammad Ali, together with 7 of the original 14 members of the Executive Committee formed by Hazrat Mirza Ghulam Ahmad, went to Lahore and founded *Ahmadiyya Society for the Propagation of Islam – Ahmadiyya Anjuman-i-Ishaat-i-Islam Lahore*, also referred to as *Lahore Group of Ahmadies*. Current title adopted in 1985, to meet legal and constitutional requirements of Pakistan. Also referred to as *Lahore Ahmadiyya Movement in Islam*. **Aims** Through *missionary* and literary work, present the original teaching of *Islam* based on the Holy *Quran* and the Holy Prophet's traditions: belief in the universality of prophet-hood among all nations, culminating in the *Prophet Muhammad* as the last prophet; no compulsion in religion; universal *brotherhood* of all humanity regardless of colour, creed or nationality; protection of the rights of women and children; the *family* as the basic unit of civilization; spiritual and moral as well as material uplift of mankind; fair distribution of wealth. **Structure** President; General Council (Majlis-i-Moatemideen); Executive Committee (Majlis-i-Muntanzimma); Secretary General. **Staff** 7.00 FTE, paid. **Finance** Sources: members' contributions; donations; income from assets. **Activities** Training; Conferences, convention and meetings; education. **Publications** *The Call* (12 a year); *Paigham-i-Sulh* (6 a year) in Urdu; *The Light* (6 a year); *Iqra* (2 a year) in Dutch. Books, translations and pamphlets by Hazrat Mirza Ghulam Ahmad, Maulana Noor-ud-Din, Maulana Muhammad Ali and other writers, mostly in Urdu, Arabic and Persian – some also translated into English and other languages.

Members Head office (") and affiliated societies in 20 countries:
Australia, Canada, Fiji, France, Germany, Guyana, India, Indonesia, Netherlands, New Zealand, Nigeria, Pakistan (*), Philippines, Poland, South Africa, Suriname, Thailand, Trinidad-Tobago, UK, USA. [2018/XE1929/E]

- ♦ Lahore Group of Ahmadies / see Lahore Ahmadiyya Society (#16219)
- ♦ **LAHRS** Latin American Heart Rhythm Society (#16339)
- ♦ LAHUPO – Latin American Human Proteome Organization (no recent information)
- ♦ LAI / see Latin American and Iberian Institute, Albuquerque
- ♦ **LAIA** Latin American Integration Association (#16343)
- ♦ LAI – Austrian Latin America Institute (internationally oriented national body)
- ♦ Laici Dehoniani (religious order)
- ♦ Laïcs Dehoniens (religious order)
- ♦ LAIGC – Latin American Investment Guarantee Corporation (no recent information)
- ♦ LAII – Latin American and Iberian Institute, Albuquerque (internationally oriented national body)
- ♦ LAI – Lateinamerika-Institut, Freie Universität Berlin (internationally oriented national body)
- ♦ LAI – Latvijas Arpolitikas Institūts (internationally oriented national body)
- ♦ **LAI** Life Ascending International (#20769)
- ♦ LAIS / see Nordic Institute of Latin American Studies
- ♦ **LAJC** Latin American Jewish Congress (#16344)
- ♦ Lajna Tahrir Al-Maghrib Al-Arabi (inactive)
- ♦ Läkarmissionen (internationally oriented national body)

♦ Lake Chad Basin Commission (LCBC) 16220

Commission du Bassin du Lac Tchad (CBLT)

Exec Sec PO Box 727, Ndjamena, Chad. T. +235524145. Fax +235524137. E-mail: cab@cblt.org – cblt.lcbc@gmail.com.
URL: http://www.cblt.org/

History 22 May 1964, Fort Lamy, currently Ndjamena (Chad), on signature of a Convention and Statute by Cameroon, Chad, Niger and Nigeria. Further Agreement signed Aug 1968, Lagos (Nigeria), covering the joint economic development of the area. In Dec 1977, Enugu (Nigeria), the 3rd Conference of Heads of State of the Commission signed the Protocol of the agreement to join regulations on the Fauna and Flora in the four member countries. Agreement applicable from Aug 1988, when ratified by all member States. Present status of LCBC reviewed during 30th Session and 5th Summit, 15-29 Apr 1985, Lagos. New staff status and financial regulations adopted Oct 1987, Ndjamena, at 34th Session. Restructured 1990 and again 2009-2010. **Aims** Regulate and rationalize the sustainable exploitation of Lake Chad and its resources; manage *water* and other natural resources of the Lake Chad Basin; conserve and protect the ecosystems of the Conventional Basin; preserve and promote integration, peace and trans-boundary security in the Conventional Basin; collect, evaluate and disseminate information on projects prepared by member States and recommend plans for common projects and joint research programmes in the Basin; keep close contact between the High Contracting Parties so as to ensure the most efficient use of the waters of the Basin; monitor the execution of studies and works in the basin and keep member States informed; draw up common rules regarding navigation and transport; draw up staff regulations and ensure their application. **Structure** Summit of Heads of State (annual); Council of Ministers (meets annually), consisting of 2 Commissioners per Member State; Executive Secretariat, headed by Executive Secretary; Technical Directorate; Administration and Finance Directorate. **Languages** English, French. **Staff** 121.00 FTE, paid. **Finance** Contributions from Member States: Cameroon 20%; Central African Rep 4%; Chad 11%; Libya AJ 18%; Nigeria 40%; Niger 7%. Technical and financial assistance from: *African Development Bank (ADB, #00283)*; *Deutsche Gesellschaft für Internationale Zusammenarbeit (GIZ)*; *European Commission (EC, #06633)*; *Facilité africaine de l'eau (FAE, #09233)*. **Events** *Workshop* Abuja (Nigeria) 2013, *Workshop* Ndjamena (Chad) 2013, *Workshop* Niamey (Niger) 2013, *Workshop* Yaoundé (Cameroon) 2013, *Summit Meeting* Libyan AJ 2011. **Publications** *LCBC Newsmagazine*. Decisions; action programmes; brochures.

Members Governments of 6 countries:
Cameroon, Central African Rep, Chad, Libya, Niger, Nigeria.
Observer members (4):
Congo Brazzaville, Congo DR, Egypt, Sudan.

IGO Relations Memorandum of Cooperation with: *Secretariat of the Convention of Wetlands (#19200)*. Member of: *Observatoire du Sahara et du Sahel (OSS, #17636)*. Partner of: *Commission des forêts d'Afrique centrale (COMIFAC, #04214)*; *Economic Community of Central African States (ECCAS, #05311)*; *Economic Community of West African States (ECOWAS, #05312)*; *International Commission of the Congo-Ubangui-Sangha Basin (#12674)*; *Niger Basin Authority (NBA, #17134)*. [2019.02.13/XD4496/E*]

- ♦ Lake Constance Foundation (#03297)

♦ Lake Constance International 16221

Internationale du Lac de Constance – Sozialistische Bodensee-Internationale (SBI)

Pres Washingtonstr 13, 9400 Rorschach SG, Switzerland. T. +41718417450.
Vice-Pres Grete-Gulbransson-Weg 16, 6700 Bludenz, Austria. T. +43555232736.
URL: http://www.bodensee-internationale.org/

History 1908, Switzerland. 1908, Constance (Switzerland). Current Statutes adopted 16 Jun 1984. **Aims** Unite *socialist* organizations in regions surrounding Lake Constance. **Structure** Assembly of Delegates (at least every 3 years). Management Board, consisting of President, 2 Vice-Presidents, Honorary President and members. Control Board. Executive Committee, consisting of President, 2 Vice-Presidents, Treasurer, Registrar and Head of the Control Board. The function of President rotates yearly. **Languages** German. **Finance** Financed by socialist parties SPÖ (Austria), SPS (Switzerland) and SPD (Germany). Budget: about euro 2,000. **Activities** Organizes an annual Frontier Rally. Meetings (several times a year). **Events** *Meeting / Major Meeting* Lindau (Germany FR) 1988, *Major Meeting* Bregenz (Austria) 1983.

Members Representatives of the socialist parties (Sozialistische Partei Österreichs (SPÖ) SPÖ Vorarlberg, Fraktion sozialistischer Gewerkschafter im Österreichischen Gewerkschaftsbund / Landesgruppe Vorarlberg (FSG Vorarlberg); Sozialdemokratische Partei Deutschland (SPD) Kreis Lindau, Kreis Ravensburg, Bodenseekreis (Friedrichshafen), Kreis Konstanz; Sozialdemokratische Partei Schweiz (SPS) SPS St Gallen, SPS Thurgau) in the countries bordering on Lake Constance (3):
Austria, Germany, Switzerland. [2010/XD5960/F]

- ♦ Lakes Tanganyika and Kivu Basin Commission (inactive)

♦ Lake Victoria Fisheries Organization (LVFO) 16222

Executive Secretary Bell Avenue, Plot 7B/E Busoga Square, P O Box 1625, Jinja, Uganda. T. +256434125000. E-mail: lvfo-sec@lvfo.org.
URL: http://www.lvfo.org/

History 30 Jun 1994, Kisumu (Kenya). Established upon signing of *Agreement on the Preparation of a Tripartite Environmental Management Programme for Lake Victoria (1994)* by Contracting Parties comprising the governments of Kenya, Tanzania UR and Uganda. Between 1991 and 1995 three seminars were held in the region, under the auspices of *'FAO Committee for Inland Fisheries of Africa (CIFA)'* Sub-Committee on Lake Victoria. Further consultation between riparian authorities led to drafting of the convention establishing the *'Lake Victoria Fisheries Commission'*. This draft was later approved by a Legal and Technical Consultation Meeting for the Establishment of Lake Victoria Fisheries Organization (LVFO), 12-25 Mar 1994, Dar es Salaam (Tanzania UR), followed by signing and adoption of the Convention at a conference of plenipotentiaries, 30 Jun 1994. Headquarters in Jinja (Uganda), with Secretariat operations started 1 Jul 1997. On signing of the treaty of *East African Community (EAC, #05181)*, 30 Nov 1999, officially became a specialized institution of EAC under Art 9 of EAC Treaty. Mandate re-affirmed in Art 8 of the Protocol for Sustainable Development of Lake Victoria Basin, 2003, which acts as the basis for establishing *Lake Victoria Basin Commission (LVBC)*. The Convention was extended in 1998 and Jan 2016 to accommodate for (a) extended scope and mandate of the organization to include all EAC Partner States; (b) extended focus beyond Lake Victoria into covering all water bodies in the EAC region; (c) increased prominence to aquaculture as a priority area of focus in addition to capture fisheries. LVFO is in the process of changing the name to *East African Fisheries Organization (EAFO)* as per the directives of the EAC Council of Ministers which has been necessitated by the expansion of scope and mandates of the organization. Registration: No/ID: 42611, Start date: 20 Aug 1997, USA, New York; No/ID: CD114, Start date: 11 Dec 1995, Uganda, Kampala. **Aims** Foster cooperation among the Contracting Parties; harmonize national measures for *sustainable utilization* of fisheries and aquaculture *resources* of the East African Water bodies; develop and adopt *conservation* and management measures. **Structure** Fisheries and Aquaculture Sectoral Council of Ministers (FASCoM) is the governing body of the organization, consisting of the Ministers responsible for Fisheries and Aquaculture of the Contracting Parties; Coordination Committee (CC) consists of Permanent Secretaries / Cabinet Secretary of the Ministries responsible for fisheries and aquaculture; Senior Officials (SOs)Committee consists of Directors of Fisheries and Aquaculture management and fisheries research institutions; Technical Committees; Sub-Technical Committees; Technical Working Groups; Beach Management Units (BMUs); Association of Industrial Fish Processors; Aquaculture Associations; Secretariat, headed by Executive Secretary. **Languages** English. **Staff** 27.00 FTE, paid. **Finance** Sources: contributions of member/participating states. Other sources: E€OFISH Programme; TRUEFISH programme; *EU-EAC True Fish Farming Story in Lake Victoria Basin*;German Federal Ministry for Economic Cooperation and Development (BMZ) through GIZ under the Responsible Fisheries Business Chains Project (RFBC) project; St. Andrews University, Scotland (UK). Annual budget: 3,077,934 USD (2020). **Activities** Events/meetings; knowledge management/information dissemination; monitoring/evaluation; research and development. **Events** *African Great Lakes Stakeholder Network Workshop* Entebbe (Uganda) 2019, *ScaleWAYS Project Start-up Workshop* Entebbe (Uganda) 2019, *African Great Lakes Conference* Entebbe (Uganda) 2017, *Meeting* Dar es Salaam (Tanzania UR) 2009, *Meeting* Nairobi (Kenya) 2007. **Publications** *Fisheries Management Plan-III for Lake Victoria* in English; *Strategic Plan* in English; *The Convention for the Establishment of Lake Victoria Fisheries Organization – English* in English.

Members Governments of 4 countries:
Burundi, Kenya, Tanzania UR, Uganda.

IGO Relations Partner of (1): *Intergovernmental Oceanographic Commission (IOC, #11496)*. Cooperates with (1): *Southern African Development Community (SADC, #19843)*. [2022.10.13/XE4240/E*]

- ♦ **LALICS** Latin American Network for Economics of Learning, Innovation and Competence Building Systems (#16352)
- ♦ **LA LIGA** La Liga Iberoamericana de Organizaciones de la Sociedad Civil (#16470)
- ♦ **LALMA** Latin American Lifestyle Medicine Association (#16347)
- ♦ LALN – Latin American and Caribbean Leadership Network for Nuclear Disarmament and Nonproliferation (unconfirmed)
- ♦ LAM – Les Afriques dans le monde (internationally oriented national body)
- ♦ Lama Gangchen International Global Peace Association / see Lama Gangchen International Global Peace Foundation
- ♦ Lama Gangchen International Global Peace Foundation (internationally oriented national body)
- ♦ Lama Gangchen Peace Foundation / see Lama Gangchen International Global Peace Foundation

♦ Lama Gangchen World Peace Foundation (LGWPF) 16223

CEO/UN Representative Via Zara 20, 28813 Albagnano di Bee, Italy. T. +39323569608. Fax +39323569608.
URL: http://www.lgpt.net/

History Founded 7 Jul 1992. **Aims** Develop a culture of peace and better living for world peace by cooperating in the humanitarian fields of health, education, the environment, spirituality, preservation of indigenous cultures and world heritage sites; engage in voluntary service in support of UN programmes devoted to helping developing countries towards self-sustainability. **Languages** Chinese, English, French, German, Italian, Portuguese, Spanish, Tibetan. **Activities** Humanitarian/emergency aid; financial and/or material support; events/meetings. **Events** *Annual International Interfaith Conference* Albagnano di Bee (Italy) 2014, *Annual Meeting* Kathmandu (Nepal) 2014, *Annual Conference* Madrid (Spain) 2014, *Annual Congress* Magelang (Indonesia) 2014, *Annual Congress* Madrid (Spain) 2012. **Publications** *Peace Times* (4 a year) – newspaper. *Links* – 10 vols published to date; *Seeds for Peace* – 8 vols published to date. Congress proceedings; foundation projects' update; Help in Action news reports; CD-ROMs; DVDs.

Members Affiliate organizations in 10 countries. Membership in 28 countries:
Argentina, Belgium, Brazil, Canada, Chile, China, Colombia, Ecuador, France, Germany, Greece, India, Indonesia, Italy, Malaysia, Mongolia, Nepal, Netherlands, Pakistan, Singapore, Spain, Sri Lanka, Switzerland, Thailand, Türkiye, UK, USA, Venezuela.

Consultative Status Consultative status granted from: *ECOSOC (#05331)* (Special). **IGO Relations** Associated with the Department of Global Communications of the United Nations. **NGO Relations** Member of: Italian Buddhist Union (UBI). [2019.06.28/XF4469/f/F]

♦ LAMA – Latin American Museological Association (inactive)
♦ Lamaze International (internationally oriented national body)
♦ Lambda Rowing International / see Gay and Lesbian Rowing Federation (#10079)

♦ Lambeth Conference of Bishops of the Anglican Communion 16224

Gen Sec Saint Andrew's House, 16 Tavistock Crescent, London, W11 1AP, UK. E-mail: aco@anglicancommunion.org – secretary.general@anglicancommunion.org.
Pres Archbishop of Canterbury, Lambeth Palace, London, SE1 7JU, UK. T. +442079288282. Fax +442072619836.
URL: http://www.anglicancommunion.org/

History 1867, London (UK). Founded as a conference for the diocesan bishops of the *Anglican Communion (#00827)*; convened at the personal invitation of the Archbishop of Canterbury. After the Lambeth Conference of 1958, a full-time officer, who became known as the Anglican Executive Officer, was appointed 'to collect and disseminate information, keep open lines of communication, and make contact when necessary with responsible authority'. The next Lambeth Conference in 1968 set up *Anglican Consultative Council (ACC, #00828)* which, with the consent of all the Provinces (or member Churches), came into being at the end of 1969 and whose members attend the Lambeth Conference. The appointment of Secretary General of the Council replaced that of Anglican Executive Officer. *Primates Meeting of the Anglican Communion (#18497)* was proposed at the 1978 Lambeth Conference and first met in 1979. **Structure** Conference takes place approximately every 10 years. **Events** *Decennial Conference* Canterbury (UK) 2022, *Decennial conference* Canterbury (UK) 2008, *Decennial conference* Canterbury (UK) 1998, *Decennial Conference* Canterbury (UK) 1988, *Decennial conference* London (UK) 1988.
Members Representatives of every Anglican diocese. From 1998, all Bishops of the United Churches are full members. Autonomous Churches of the Anglican Communion. National churches serving more than 165 countries and territories. Membership countries not specified.
Regional Provincial Churches (47), including the following 12 listed in this Yearbook:
Anglican Church in Aotearoa, New Zealand and Polynesia (#00823); Anglican Church of Southern Africa (ACSA, #00826); Anglican Church of the Province of the Indian Ocean (#00824); Church in the Province of the West Indies (CPWI, #03921); Church of the Province of Central Africa (#03917); Church of the Province of Melanesia (#03918); Church of the Province of South East Asia (#03919); Church of the Province of West Africa (CPWA, #03920); Domestic and Foreign Missionary Society of the Protestant Episcopal Church (DFMS); Episcopal Church in Jerusalem and the Middle East (#05513); Iglesia Anglicana de la Region Central de América (IARCA, #11108); The Anglican Church of South America (#00825).
All active bishops in the 42 national and regional independent-yet-interdependent Churches of the Anglican Communion.
NGO Relations Instrumental in setting up (1): *Five Talents International.* [2023.02.21/XF3759/y/**F**]

♦ **LAMCET** Latin American and Mediterranean Coalition for East Timor (#16348)
♦ LAMC – Latin American Center for Graduate Study of Music, Washington DC (internationally oriented national body)
♦ LAMM – Lutheran Association for Maritime Ministry (internationally oriented national body)
♦ **LAM Network** African Laser, Atomic and Molecular Sciences Network (#00356)
♦ LAMP – Liberal Association for the Movement of People (internationally oriented national body)
♦ **LAMRN** Lugina Africa Midwives Research Network (#16522)
♦ LAMSO – Asociación Latinoamericana de Mercadeo Social (unconfirmed)
♦ **Lanasjódur Vesturnordurlanda** Norraeni Tróunarsjódurinn fyrir hin Vestlaegu Nordurlönd (#20926)
♦ Lanaudière Regional Committee for International Development Education (internationally oriented national body)
♦ **LANBO** Latin American Network of Basin Organizations (#16351)
♦ Lancefield International Symposium on Streptococci and Streptoccocal Diseases (meeting series)

♦ The Lancefield Society 16225

Secretariat ASN Events Pty Ltd, PO Box 200, Barnarring VIC 3926, Australia. T. +61385604390. Fax +61386922035. E-mail: lancefield@asnevents.net.au.
URL: https://www.lancefieldsociety.org/

History 2019. Officially formed following vote by the International Scientific Committee of the 20th *Lancefield International Symposium on Streptococci and Streptoccocal Diseases (LISSSD)*, organized since 1960. Took over organization of LISSSD as of 21st Symposium. **Aims** Improve knowledge and understanding of streptococcal biology, pathogenesis, immunology and epidemiology; improve prevention and treatment of streptococcal diseases. **Structure** Committee. **Finance** Sources: members' dues. **Events** *Lancefield International Symposium for Streptococci and Streptococcal Diseases* Stockholm (Sweden) 2022, *Lancefield International Symposium for Streptococci and Streptococcal Diseases* Stockholm (Sweden) 2021, *Lancefield International Symposium for Streptococci and Streptococcal Diseases* Fiji 2017. [2022/AA2460/v/**E**]

♦ LANDac – LANDac – Netherlands Land Academy (internationally oriented national body)
♦ LANDac – Netherlands Land Academy (internationally oriented national body)

♦ Landcare International (LI) 16226

Contact World Agroforestry Centre, United Nations Ave, PO Box 30677-00100, Nairobi, Kenya. T. +254207224387. Fax +254207224001.
URL: http://landcareinternational.org/

Aims Enhance worldwide recognition and adoption of the Landcare approach as a viable model for *environment* and *natural resource conservation*, effective public-private partnerships and authentic stakeholder participation in community action and decision-making. **Events** *International landcare and sustainable rural landscape conference* Melbourne, VIC (Australia) 2006. **Publications** *LI Quarterly Newsletter.* **NGO Relations** Located at: *World Agroforestry Centre (ICRAF, #21072).* Member of: *International Partnership for the Satoyama Initiative (IPSI, #14525).* [2007/XM2847/**F**]

♦ Landesa – Landesa – Rural Development Institute (internationally oriented national body)
♦ Landesa – Rural Development Institute (internationally oriented national body)
♦ Land Governance for Equitable and Sustainable Development / see LANDac – Netherlands Land Academy

♦ Land Healers Foundation (LHF) 16227

Exec Dir address not obtained.
URL: http://landhealers.org/

History 2018. **Aims** Create a profession of land healers for *indigenous youth* in need of help in obtaining meaningful *employment.* **Structure** Women's Council. **NGO Relations** Member of: *World Alliance for Efficient Solutions.* [2018/XM7307/f/**F**]

♦ Ländlichkeit – Umwelt – Entwicklung (#19003)
♦ Landmine Survivors Network (internationally oriented national body)
♦ Land-Ocean Interactions in the Coastal Zone Project / see Future Earth Coasts (#10049)
♦ Land O'Lakes International Development (internationally oriented national body)

♦ Land Research Action Network (LRAN) 16228

Address not obtained.
URL: http://www.landaction.org/

History Founded and coordinated by *Fondation des maisons familiales rurales dans le monde, Focus on the Global South (Focus, #09807),* (Brazilian) Social Network for Justice and Human Rights and (South African) National Land Committee. **Aims** Promote and advance fundamental rights of individuals and communities to land, and to equitable access to the resources necessary for life with human dignity. **Publications** *LRAN Briefing Paper Series.* [2012/XJ6276/**F**]

♦ LandsAid – LandsAid – Verein für Internationale Humanitäre Hilfe (internationally oriented national body)
♦ LandsAid – Verein für Internationale Humanitäre Hilfe (internationally oriented national body)

♦ LANDSCAPE EUROPE 16229

Coordinator ILE SAS, Akademicka 2, 949 01 Nitra, Slovakia. T. +421220920351.
URL: http://www.landscape-europe.net/

History Full title: *International Network of Expertise on Landscapes (LANDSCAPE EUROPE).* Registered in accordance with Dutch law. **Aims** Develop and disseminate knowledge on European landscapes by actively involving and drawing upon the wide range of relevant disciplines so as to support landscape values as a central and cross-cutting environmental issue in policy, science, education and human living. **Structure** Assembly (annual). General Board, consisting of country representatives. Executive Board, comprising Chair, Secretary, Treasurer and 5 members. Coordinating Office. **Publications** *LANDSCAPE EUROPE Newsletter.*
Members Full; Associate. Members in 15 countries:
Austria, Belgium, Czechia, Denmark, Estonia, France, Germany, Hungary, Italy, Netherlands, Norway, Romania, Slovakia, Spain, UK. [2013.11.26/XJ4617/**F**]

♦ Landscape Institute (internationally oriented national body)
♦ **LANENT** Latin American Network for Education in Nuclear Technology (#16353)
♦ LANET – Lutheran AIDS Network (internationally oriented national body)

♦ Langham Partnership International 16230

Dir 19 Whitfield Place, London, W1T 5JX, UK.
URL: http://www.langhampartnership.org/

History 2001. Originates from (UK) Langham Trust, set up 1969, UK, and named after All Souls Church, Langham Place, London (UK). **Aims** Help partner *churches* in the majority world grow in maturity and be equipped for *mission,* through literature, scholarship and preaching training.
Members National organizations (6) in 7 countries and territories:
Australia, Canada, Hong Kong, Ireland, New Zealand, UK, USA.
NGO Relations UK section is member of: *Global Connections.* [2011.06.01/XM1984/**F**]

♦ Language Association of Eastern Africa (no recent information)
♦ Language and Intercultural Research Center / see David M Kennedy Center for International Studies
♦ Language Recordings International / see Global Recordings Network
♦ Languages in Contact and Conflict in Africa (inactive)

♦ Language Technology Industry Association (LT-Innovate) 16231

Exec Dir address not obtained.
URL: http://lt-innovate.org/

History Operated by LT-Innovate Ltd, which is registered in England and Wales: 8264944. **Aims** Encourage collaboration within the industry and with other stakeholders of the Language Technology value-chains; strengthen the Language Technology industry for increased competitiveness in the global markets; articulate the industry's collective interests vis-à-vis its clients, researcher partners, investors and policy makers; promote Language Technologies as driver of economic success, societal well-being and cultural integrity. **Structure** Board of Directors; Board of Advisors; Secretariat. **Finance** Members' dues. **NGO Relations** Member of: *Cracking the Language Barrier (#04942).* [2018/XM7348/t/**D**]

♦ Lanka Jathika Sarvodaya / see Sarvodaya Shramadana Movement
♦ Lanka Jathika Sarvodaya Shramadana Sangamaya (internationally oriented national body)
♦ Lanka Mahila Samiti (internationally oriented national body)
♦ **LANSA** Latin American Paper Money Society (#16359)
♦ Länsimaisen Buddhalaisen Veljeskunnan Ystävät / see Triratna Buddhist Community (#20243)
♦ Länsi-Pohjolan Neuvosto (#20925)
♦ Länsipohjolan Pohjoismainen Kehittämisrahasto (#20926)
♦ LAOHA – Latin American Oral Health Association (internationally oriented national body)
♦ LAPD – International Symposium on Laser-Aided Plasma Diagnostics (meeting series)
♦ **LAPEN** Latin American Physics Education Network (#16361)
♦ LAP – Labour Action for Peace (internationally oriented national body)
♦ **LAP** Latin American Association of Pharmacology (#16249)
♦ **LAP** LatinoAméricaPosible (#16402)
♦ **LAP** London Action Plan (#16509)
♦ Lappischer Rat (#19012)
♦ Lappischer Rat der Skandinavischen Länder / see Saami Council (#19012)
♦ LAPSS – Latin American Peace Science Society (unconfirmed)
♦ **LAQI** Latin American Quality Institute (#16364)
♦ **LA RED** Red de Estudios Sociales en Prevención de Desastres en América Latina (#17058)
♦ Larenstein International Agricultural College / see Van Hall Larenstein University of Applied Sciences
♦ Larenstein University of Professional Education / see Van Hall Larenstein University of Applied Sciences
♦ **LARES** Latin American Real Estate Society (#16366)

♦ Large Carnivore Initiative for Europe (LCIE) 16232

Chairman Dept of Biology and Biotechnology, University of Rome, Piazzale Aldo Moro 5, 00185 Rome RM, Italy.
URL: http://www.lcie.org/

History Founded Jun 1995, by *World Wide Fund for Nature (WWF, #21922).* **Aims** Maintain and restore, in coexistence with people, viable populations of large carnivores as an integral part of ecosystems and landscapes across Europe. **Members** Individuals and organizations in 29 countries. Membership countries not specified. **IGO Relations** Member of: *Standing Committee to the Bern Convention on the Conservation of European Wildlife and Natural Habitats (#19949).* [2016/XK2111/**E**]

♦ Large Cities Climate Leadership Group / see C40 (#03391)
♦ Large Format Cinema Association / see Giant Screen Cinema Association (#10148)
♦ LARGE-PD – Latin American Research consortium on the GEnetics of Parkinson's Disease (unconfirmed)
♦ Large Yacht Brokers Association (unconfirmed)
♦ LASAK – Latin American Studies Association of Korea (internationally oriented national body)
♦ **LASA** Latin American Shipowners Association (#16369)
♦ **LASA** Latin American Studies Association (#16388)
♦ Lasallian Developing World Projects / see Lasallian Projects
♦ Lasallian Projects (internationally oriented national body)
♦ LASBRA – Latin American Society for Biomedical Research on Alcoholism (unconfirmed)
♦ LASC – Latin America Solidarity Coalition (internationally oriented national body)
♦ LASCRS / see Asociación Latino Americana de Cirugia de Catarata, Segmento Anterior y Refractiva (#02194)
♦ **LASDB** Latin American Society for Developmental Biology (#16371)

♦ Laserlab-Europe AISBL 16233

Main Office Max Born Inst, Max-Born-Str 2A, 12489 Berlin, Germany. T. +493063921508. E-mail: office@laserlab-europe.eu.
Sec address not obtained.
Exec Dir ICFO, Carl Friedrich Gauss 3, 08860 Castelldefels, Barcelona, Spain. T. +34935534059.
Registered Address Rue du Trône 98, 1050 Brussels, Belgium.
URL: http://www.laserlab-europe.eu/

History Laser research infrastructures network started with FP5 LASERNET (2001-2004), followed by FP6 Laserlab-Europe (2004-2008), covering 9 European countries. Laserlab-Europe in FP7 (2009-2015) and in H2020 (2015-2019) expanded to 16 European countries. In Horizon Europe (from 2019) covering 22 countries. Former names and other names: *LASERLAB-EUROPE – The Integrated Initiative of European Laser Research Infrastructures* – full title. Registration: Banque-Carrefour des Entreprises, No/ID: 0701.800.839, Start date: 28 Aug 2018, Belgium; EU Transparency Register, No/ID: 889951444779-18, Start date: 26 Nov 2021. **Aims** Maintain a competitive, inter-disciplinary network of *European* national *laser laboratories*; strengthen the European role in laser *research*; offer transnational access to top-quality laser research facilities; increase the European basis in laser research and applications. **Structure** General Assembly; Management Board; Boards

(3). **Languages** English. **Finance** Supported by: *European Union (EU, #08967).* **Activities** Events/meetings; networking/liaising; research and development. **Events** *Laserlab-Europe Colloquim* 2022, *General Assembly* 2021, *General Assembly* Bucharest (Romania) 2019, *User Meeting* Coimbra (Portugal) 2019, *General Assembly* London (UK) 2019. **Publications** *Laserlab Europe Newsletter.*
Members Participating infrastructures (over 40) in 22 countries:
Austria, Bulgaria, Croatia, Czechia, Denmark, Finland, France, Germany, Greece, Hungary, Italy, Latvia, Lithuania, Netherlands, Poland, Portugal, Romania, Slovakia, Spain, Sweden, Switzerland, UK.
NGO Relations Member of (1): *Association of European-level Research Infrastructure Facilities (ERF-AISBL, #02518).* [2023.02.14/XJ8873/**E**]

- ♦ LASERLAB-EUROPE – The Integrated Initiative of European Laser Research Infrastructures / see Laserlab-Europe AISBL (#16233)
- ♦ LASFLA / see Asociación de Lingüística Sistémico Funcional de América Latina (#02279)
- ♦ LASGP / see Latinamerican Society for Pediatric Gastroenterology, Hepatology and Nutrition (#16382)
- ♦ **LASH** Latin American Society of Hypertension (#16372)
- ♦ LASHST – Latin American Society for the History of Sciences and Technology (no recent information)
- ♦ **LASID** Latin American Society for Immunodeficiencies (#16373)
- ♦ **LASIL** Latin American Society of International Law (#16374)
- ♦ LASJ – Latin American Society of Japan (internationally oriented national body)
- ♦ LAS – Latinoamérica Sustentable (unconfirmed)
- ♦ **LAS** League of Arab States (#16420)
- ♦ **LASL** Latin American Association for the Study of the Liver (#16252)
- ♦ Laspau Inc. (internationally oriented national body)
- ♦ LASPAU – Academic and Professional Programs for the Americas / see Laspau Inc.
- ♦ LASPGAN / see Latinamerican Society for Pediatric Gastroenterology, Hepatology and Nutrition (#16382)
- ♦ **LASPGHAN** Latinamerican Society for Pediatric Gastroenterology, Hepatology and Nutrition (#16382)
- ♦ LASPGNH / see Latinamerican Society for Pediatric Gastroenterology, Hepatology and Nutrition (#16382)
- ♦ LASPGN / see Latinamerican Society for Pediatric Gastroenterology, Hepatology and Nutrition (#16382)
- ♦ **LASRA** Latin American Society of Regional Anesthesia (#16384)
- ♦ LASSA – Lipid and Atherosclerosis Society of Southern Africa (internationally oriented national body)
- ♦ LASSAM – Latin American Society for the Study of the Aging Male (no recent information)
- ♦ Last Mile Health (internationally oriented national body)
- ♦ Lateinamerikaforschung Austria (internationally oriented national body)
- ♦ Lateinamerika-Institut, Freie Universität Berlin (internationally oriented national body)
- ♦ Lateinamerikanischer Verband des Strafrechts und der Kriminologie (unconfirmed)
- ♦ Lateinamerikanisches Institut für Psychosoziale Gesundheit und Menschenrechte (internationally oriented national body)
- ♦ Lateinamerika-Zentrum, Bonn (internationally oriented national body)
- ♦ LATICI – Latin American Technical Institute for Cooperative Integration (inactive)
- ♦ Latijnsamerikaanse Vereniging voor de Controle van Gezondheidsdiensten (#19392)
- ♦ Latin America Bureau, London (internationally oriented national body)
- ♦ Latin America-Caribbean and Asia-Pacific Economics and Business Association (no recent information)
- ♦ Latin America and Caribbean Model Forest Network / see Red Iberoamericana de Bosques Modelo (#18659)
- ♦ Latin America and the Caribbean Network / see Plantain and Banana Research and Development Network for Latin America and the Caribbean (#18389)
- ♦ Latin America and the Caribbean Network of TRANS People (#18699)
- ♦ Latin America Centre, Oxford (internationally oriented national body)
- ♦ Latin America Chiropractic Federation (#09367)
- ♦ Latin America-European Network on Technology Innovation Studies and Co-Development (internationally oriented national body)
- ♦ Latin America Food Law Association (internationally oriented national body)
- ♦ Latin America Institute, Moscow / see Institute of Latin America of the Russian Academy of Sciences
- ♦ Latin American Academy of Craniomandibular Disorders and Orofacial Pain / see Ibero-Latin American Academy of Craniomandibular Disorders
- ♦ Latin American Academy of Sciences (#00010)
- ♦ Latin American Adult Education Council / see Consejo de Educación de Adultos de América Latina (#04707)
- ♦ Latin American, African and Asian Low-Income Housing Service / see Servicio Latinoamericano, Africano y Asiatico de Vivienda Popular (#19246)
- ♦ Latin American, African and Asian Social Housing Service (#19246)
- ♦ Latin American Agreement on Port State Control of Vessels (1992 treaty)
- ♦ Latin American Agribusiness Development Corporation (internationally oriented national body)
- ♦ Latin American Agro-Ecological Movement / see Movimiento Agroecológico para Latinoamérica y El Caribe (#16872)
- ♦ Latin American Air Transport Association / see Latin American and Caribbean Air Transport Association (#16263)
- ♦ Latin American Alliance against Contraband (#00631)
- ♦ Latin American Alliance for the Family (#00633)
- ♦ Latin American Alliance for Global Health (inactive)
- ♦ Latin American Alliance for Rare Diseases (#00630)

♦ Latin American Anthropological Association 16234

Asociación Latinoamericana de Antropologia (ALA) – Associação Latino Americana de Antropologia

Pres Inst de Investigaciones Antropologicas, Circuito Exterior s/n, Cd Universitaria, Del Coyoacan, CP 04510 Mexico City CDMX, Mexico. T. +5556229573. Fax +5556190763. E-mail: bella@servidor.unam.mx – latinoamerica.ala@gmail.com.

History Apr 1990, Florianópolis (Brazil). Apr 1990, Florianopolis (Brazil). **Aims** Support, promote and advance the anthropological study and knowledge of Latin America and the Caribbean. **Structure** Board, including President and 5 Vice-Presidents. **Events** *Latin American anthropologies facing a world in transition* Mexico City (Mexico) 2015, *Congress* Santiago (Chile) 2012, *Congress* Rosario (Argentina) 2005. **NGO Relations** Member of: *Anthropology Southern Africa (#00851); World Council of Anthropological Associations (WCAA, #21317).* [2011/XM1078/**D**]

- ♦ Latin American Anthropology Group / see Society for Latin American and Caribbean Anthropology
- ♦ Latin American Anti-Communist Confederation (inactive)
- ♦ Latin American Area Center, Tucson / see Center for Latin American Studies, Tucson
- ♦ Latin American Art Resource Project (internationally oriented national body)
- ♦ Latin American Association of Advanced Studies in Agriculture (no recent information)

♦ Latin American Association of Advertising Agencies 16235

Asociación Latinoamericana de Agencias de Publicidad (ALAP) – Associação Latino-Americana de Agências de Publicidade

Contact Av Pernambuco 2623 – sala 601, CEP 90240-002, Floresta, Porto Alegre RS, 90240-002, Brazil. T. +555132225222. E-mail: alap@terra.com.br.
URL: http://www.alap.com.br/

History 9 Jul 1983, Gramado (Brazil). Registered in accordance with Brazilian law. **Aims** Provide agreements and partnerships among agencies and media within MERCOSUR and Latin America. **Structure** International President; President (Brazil); Secretary General; Chapter Representatives; Regional Vice-Presidents (15). **Activities** Promotes *'World Advertising Festival of Gamado'.* **Events** *International Festival of Advertising of Tourism and Ecology* Rio de Janeiro (Brazil) 2002. **Publications** *Publicidad* – bulletin.
Members Advertising agencies in 8 countries:
Argentina, Bolivia, Brazil, Chile, Ecuador, Peru, Uruguay, Venezuela. [2014/XD6902/**D**]

- ♦ Latin American Association for Aeronautical and Space Law (#02202)
- ♦ Latin American Association for Afro-Asian Studies / see Latin American Association for Asian and African Studies (#16236)
- ♦ Latin American Association of Agricultural Engineering / see Asociación Latinoamericana y del Caribe de Ingeniería Agrícola (#02190)
- ♦ Latin American Association of Agriculture and Cattle Insurance Companies / see Asociación Latinoamericana para el Desarrollo del Seguro Agropecuario (#02205)
- ♦ Latin American Association of Air Cargo Transporters (inactive)
- ♦ Latin American Association for Alternative Technologies (inactive)
- ♦ Latin American Association of Analysis and Behavioural Modification (#02179)
- ♦ Latin American Association for Analytic Philosophy (#02221)
- ♦ Latin American Association for Animal Production (#02257)
- ♦ Latin American Association for Apheresis and Cell Therapies (#02178)
- ♦ Latin American Association on Archives (#02183)

♦ Latin American Association for Asian and African Studies 16236

Association latino-américaine d'études afro-asiatiques – Asociación Latinoamericana de Estudios de Asia y Africa (ALADAA)

SG El Colegio de Mexico City, Camino al Ajusco 20, Pedregal de Santa Teresa 17040, 01000 Mexico City CDMX, Mexico. T. +5254493000ext4052. E-mail: aladaa@colmex.mx.
URL: http://aladaainternacional.com/

History 1976, Mexico. Also referred to as *Latin American Association for Afro-Asian Studies.* **Aims** Cooperate with centres of research and higher education in the training of specialists; promote academic exchange among members; contribute to general knowledge of Africa and Asia and their presence in Latin America. **Structure** General Assembly (every 3 years) elects Secretary-General, who appoint the Executive Committee. National Coordinators elected by ordinary members in each country. **Languages** Portuguese, Spanish. **Staff** Voluntary. **Finance** Members' dues. Funds from 'El Colegio de México'. **Activities** Organizes: colloquia; courses; series of conferences with *Center for Asian and African Studies, Mexico (CEAA)* and other academic institutions. **Events** *Congress* Quito (Ecuador) 2021, *Congress* Lima (Peru) 2018, *Congress* Santiago (Chile) 2016, *Congress* La Plata (Argentina) 2013, *The new South – theories and practices of Asia, Africa and Latin America in the 21st century* Bogota (Colombia) 2011. **Publications** Proceedings of national and international meetings.
Members Individual members in 15 countries:
Argentina, Brazil, Colombia, Costa Rica, Cuba, Dominican Rep, Ecuador, Guatemala, Mexico, Panama, Paraguay, Peru, Spain, USA, Venezuela.
NGO Relations Member of: *International Union for Oriental and Asian Studies (IUOAS, inactive).* [2018/XD0482/v/**D**]

- ♦ Latin American Association for Automated Highway Transport (inactive)
- ♦ Latin American Association of Aviation and Space Medicine / see Asociación Iberoamericana de Medicina Aerospacial (#02147)
- ♦ Latin American Association of Biological Anthropology (#02180)
- ♦ Latin American Association of Biomathematics – Association latinoaméricaine de biomathématique (inactive)
- ♦ Latin American Association of Bucco-Maxillo-Facial Surgery (#02195)
- ♦ Latin American Association of Cancer Registries (no recent information)
- ♦ Latin American Association of Capital Goods Manufacturers (no recent information)
- ♦ Latin American Association of Carcinology (#02188)
- ♦ Latin American Association of Cataract, Anterior Segment and Refractive Surgery (#02194)
- ♦ Latin American Association of Cataract and Anterior Segment Surgery / see Asociación Latino Americana de Cirugia de Catarata, Segmento Anterior y Refractiva (#02194)
- ♦ Latin American Association of Chemical Engineering Students (#02215)
- ♦ Latin American Association of Child Psychiatry / see Federación Latinoamericana de Psiquiatria de la Infancia, Adolescencia, Familia y Profesiones Afines (#09364)

♦ Latin American Association of Coloproctology (ALACP) 16237

Asociación Latinoamericana de Colo-Proctologia – Associação Latino-Americana de Colo-Proctologia

Secretariat Av Marechal Câmara 160/916, Ed Orly, Rio de Janeiro RJ, 20020-080, Brazil. T. +552122408927. Fax +552122205803. E-mail: alacp@alacp.org.
URL: http://www.alacp.org/

History 1957, Mar del Plata (Argentina), during first Congresso Internacional de Proctologia, as *Asociación Latinoamericana de Proctologia.* Present name adopted 1984. **Events** *Congress* El Salvador 2013, *General Assembly and Congress* San Salvador (El Salvador) 2013, *General assembly and congress* Mendoza (Argentina) 2011, *General assembly and congress / Congress* Havana (Cuba) 2007, *General assembly and congress / Congress* Asunción (Paraguay) 2005.
Members National organizations (10) in 10 countries:
Argentina, Bolivia, Brazil, Chile, Colombia, El Salvador, Mexico, Peru, Uruguay, Venezuela.
NGO Relations *International Council of Coloproctology (ICCP, #13009).* [2017/XD4061/**D**]

- ♦ Latin American Association of Communications Researchers (#02237)
- ♦ Latin American Association of Communicators of Demography (inactive)
- ♦ Latin American Association of Congress Organizers / see Federación de Entidades Organizadoras de Congresos y Afines de América Latina (#09299)
- ♦ Latin American Association of Constitutional Law (no recent information)
- ♦ Latin American Association of Control of Quality, Pathology and Recovery of Construction (#02199)
- ♦ Latin American Association of Cooperative Centres of Education (no recent information)
- ♦ Latin American Association for Cotton Research and Development (#02235)
- ♦ Latin American Association of Credit Bureaus / see Asociación Latinoamericana y del Caribe de Burós de Crédito (#02189)
- ♦ Latin American Association of Criminal Law and Criminology (unconfirmed)
- ♦ Latin American Association of Dental Schools (inactive)
- ♦ Latin American Association of Desalination and Water Reuse (#02204)

♦ Latin American Association of Design (ALADI) 16238

Asociación Latinoamericana de Diseño

Pres Av San Martin 5212, B1751AAW Lomas del Mirador, Buenos Aires, Argentina. T. +541146551633. Fax +541144543703. E-mail: prensad@disenioaladi.org – presidencia@disenioaladi.org.
URL: http://www.disenioaladi.org/

History 12 Nov 1980, Columbia, as *Latin American Association of Industrial Design (ALADI) – Association latinoaméricaine de dessin industriel – Asociación Latinoamericana de Diseño Industrial.* **Structure** Committee. **Events** *Congress* Santo Domingo (Dominican Rep) 2016, *Congress* Santiago (Chile) 2014, *Congress* Bento Gonçalves (Brazil) 2012, *Congress* Havana (Cuba) 2010, *Congress* Managua (Nicaragua) 2008.
Members National committees in 17 countries:
Argentina, Bolivia, Brazil, Chile, Colombia, Costa Rica, Cuba, Dominican Rep, Ecuador, El Salvador, Guatemala, Mexico, Nicaragua, Panama, Paraguay, Peru, Uruguay.
Delegates in 3 countries:
Colombia, Peru, Puerto Rico.
Representatives in 4 countries:
Germany, Italy, Japan, Spain.
NGO Relations Founding member of: *Asociación Latinoamericana de la Industria del Letrero (ALAIL, #02229).* [2022/XD2278/**D**]

- ♦ Latin American Association for the Development of Agricultural and Livestock Insurance / see Asociación Latinoamericana para el Desarrollo del Seguro Agropecuario (#02205)
- ♦ Latin American Association of Development of Crop and Livestock Insurance (#02205)
- ♦ Latin American Association of Development Financing Institutions (#02233)

- ♦ Latin American Association for the Development and Integration of Women (inactive)
- ♦ Latin American Association of Development Journalists (inactive)
- ♦ Latin American Association of Development Organizations (inactive)
- ♦ Latin American Association for Ecological Development (inactive)
- ♦ Latin-American Association of Economic Theory (#02271)
- ♦ Latin-American Association of Economy of the Energy (#02206)
- ♦ Latin American Association of Editors of Biological Periodicals (inactive)
- ♦ Latin American Association of Editors in the Earth Sciences (inactive)
- ♦ Latin American Association for Education and Research on Social Work (#02210)
- ♦ Latin American Association of Emergency Medicine and Disaster Cooperation (#02200)

♦ Latin American Association of Endoscopic Surgeons 16239

Asociación Latinoamericana de Cirujanos Endoscópistas (ALACE)

Exec Dir address not obtained. E-mail: alace@alaceweb.org.
URL: http://www.alaceweb.org/

History Nov 1993, Mexico City (Mexico). Also referred to as *Latin American Association of Endoscopic Surgery – Asociación Latinoamericana de Cirurgia Endoscópica.* **Languages** Spanish. **Staff** 12.00 FTE, voluntary. **Events** *Congress* Guatemala 2008, *Congress* Miami, FL (USA) 2006, *International symposium* Punta del Este (Uruguay) 2005, *Congress on endoscopy video surgery* Bahia Blanca (Argentina) 2004, *Congress* Cancún (Mexico) 2004.
Members Organizations and individuals. Members in 25 countries:
Argentina, Belgium, Bolivia, Brazil, Chile, Colombia, Costa Rica, Cuba, Dominica, Dominican Rep, Ecuador, El Salvador, France, Grenada, Guatemala, Honduras, Italy, Mexico, Nicaragua, Panama, Paraguay, Peru, Spain, Uruguay, Venezuela.
NGO Relations Member of: *International Federation of Societies of Endoscopic Surgeons (IFSES, #13546),* 1998. [2015/XD0679/**D**]

- ♦ Latin American Association of Endoscopic Surgery / see Latin American Association of Endoscopic Surgeons (#16239)

♦ Latin American Association of Environmental Mutagens, Carcinogens and Teratogens 16240

Association latinoaméricaine d'étude des mutagènes, carcinogènes et tératogènes présents dans l'environnement – Asociación Latinoamericana de Mutagenesis, Carcinogeneisi y Teratogenesis Ambiental (ALAMCTA) – Associação Latino-Americana de Mutagênese, Carcinogênese e Teratogênese Ambiental

Pres IIBCE, Avenida Italia 3318, 11600 Montevideo, Uruguay.

History 9 Jun 1980, Puebla (Mexico). **Aims** Represent scientists involved in research on *genetic* damage induced by environmental chemical and physical agents, on its mechanisms, its effects as well as its prevention. **Structure** Executive Council; Board of Directors. **Languages** English, Portuguese, Spanish. **Staff** Voluntary. **Finance** Funding of specific activities through international agencies. **Activities** Training/ education; events/meetings; knowledge management/information dissemination. **Events** *Congress* Asunción (Paraguay) 2019, *Congress* Montevideo (Uruguay) 2016, *Congress* Buenos Aires (Argentina) 2015, *ICEM : International Conference on Environmental Mutagens* Foz do Iguaçu (Brazil) 2013, *Congress* Viña del Mar (Chile) 2010. **Publications** *Boletin ALAMCTA.* Information Services: Establishing an information centre.
Members Individuals in 14 countries and territories:
Argentina, Brazil, Chile, Colombia, Costa Rica, Cuba, Ecuador, El Salvador, Mexico, Peru, Puerto Rico, Spain, Uruguay, Venezuela.
NGO Relations Member of: *International Association of Environmental Mutagenesis and Genomics Societies (IAEMGS, #11877).* [2019/XD6729/v/**D**]

♦ Latin American Association of Export Credit Insurance Companies . 16241

Asociación Latinoamericana de Organismos de Seguros de Crédito a la Exportación (ALASECE)

SG Calle 72 No 6 – 44 Piso 12, Bogota, Bogota DC, Colombia. T. +5713266969. Fax +5712110218.

History 1982, Rio de Janeiro (Brazil). **Aims** Promote development of export credit insurance in Latin America and the Caribbean; further technical cooperation among member companies. **Structure** General Assembly (annual) appoints President and Executive Secretary for 2-year term. **Languages** English, Portuguese, Spanish. **Staff** 2.00 FTE, voluntary. **Finance** Members' dues. Budget (annual): US$ 39,000. **Activities** Plans to establish an information system on bankruptcies in Latin America. Occasionally organizes international seminars. **Events** *General Assembly* Buenos Aires (Argentina) 2009, *General Assembly* Rio de Janeiro (Brazil) 2000, *General Assembly* Mexico 1999, *General Assembly* Rio de Janeiro (Brazil) 1997. **Publications** *ALASECE Bulletin* (2 a year). **Information Services** *Mutual Assistance Agreement on Commercial Information* – database.
Members Companies in 13 countries:
Argentina, Brazil, Chile, Colombia, Cuba, France, Germany, Luxembourg, Mexico, Peru, Spain, Trinidad-Tobago, Venezuela. [2017/XD2894/**D**]

- ♦ Latin American Association of Express Companies (#04654)
- ♦ Latin American Association of Food Processors (inactive)
- ♦ Latin American Association of Forensic Medicine and Medical Deontology (inactive)
- ♦ Latin American Association of Forensic Medicine and Medical Deontology and Ibero American Association of Forensic Science (no recent information)
- ♦ Latin American Association of Genetics (#02225)
- ♦ Latin American Association of Glass Producers (no recent information)

♦ Latin American Association for Groundwater Hydrology Development 16242

Asociación Latinoamericana de Hidrologia Subterranea para el Desarrollo (ALHSUD)

SG Goes 2419 of 804, 11800 Montevideo, Uruguay. Fax +59824030110. E-mail: secretaria.general@ alhsud.com.
URL: http://www.alhsud.com/

Aims Promote in Latin America and the Caribbean investigation, utilization, conservation and protection of groundwater hydrological resources and the training of human resources for its balanced an rational development. **Structure** General Assembly (meets every 4 years). Executive Board, consisting of President, 4 Vice-Presidents and Secretary General. Management Council (meets once a year), comprising President, 6 members from countries which have no Vice-President and Past-President. **Languages** Portuguese, Spanish. **Staff** Voluntary. **Activities** Research; exchange and dissemination of information; technical and scientific meetings. **Events** *Congress* Mérida (Mexico) 2016, *Congress* Cartagena de Indias (Colombia) 2012, *International Summit on Water* Chile 2012, *Subterranean waters and sustainable development of the Latin American population* Barquisimeto (Venezuela) 2010, *Congress* Quito (Ecuador) 2008.
Members Full; Institutional; Sponsoring; Affiliate; Honorary, in 18 countries:
Argentina, Bolivia, Brazil, Canada, Chile, Colombia, Costa Rica, Cuba, Dominican Rep, Ecuador, El Salvador, Mexico, Paraguay, Peru, Puerto Rico, Uruguay, USA, Venezuela.
NGO Relations *International Association of Hydrogeologists (IAH, #11953).* [2014/XD4206/**D**]

- ♦ Latin American Association for Health at the Workplace (#02264)
- ♦ Latin American Association of Home Educators (inactive)
- ♦ Latin American Association for Human Reproduction Research (#02238)

♦ Latin American Association for Human Rights 16243

Association latinoaméricaine pour les droits de l'homme – Asociación Latinoamericana para los Derechos Humanos (ALDHU)

Deputy SG Circunvalación Durango 14-29 of 3C, Montevideo, Uruguay. T. +5982682956. E-mail: aldhu.alc@gmail.com.
URL: https://aldhu.org/

History 13 Aug 1980. Founded initially in the context of re-democratization of South America and pacification of Central America. Working limits enlarged 1985 to include socio-economic, cultural and people's rights. **Aims** Defend, promote and protect human rights. **Structure** General Assembly. Ruling Council, comprising 55 members. Executive Committee of 9 members, including 2 from Southern Cone, 2 from the Andean area, one from Brazil, 2 from Central America and 2 from the Caribbean. Officers: President; Vice-President; Secretary-General. General Secretariat in Quito (Ecuador); Regional Section for the Southern Cone in Montevideo (Uruguay); Link Offices in La Paz (Bolivia) and Montevideo. **Languages** Spanish. **Staff** Total of 17 professionals and small permanent staff. **Finance** Annual budget: 500,000 USD.
Activities Events/meetings; projects/programmes. Coordinates with other organizations to avoid duplication of effort.
/Work Programmes/: *'Legal Protection of Human Rights'* Penal systems and human rights; civilian population and the human rights protection mechanisms; legislation and human rights protection. *'Population and Human Rights'* Refugees and displacement in Latin America; illegal immigration and marginality. *'Protection of the Amazon'* Installation of the Amazon Radio for Peace; social-cultural empowerment for indigenous communities; training for indigenous women leaders. *'Human Rights Education'* Educational events; drawing up methodologies; production of human rights educational materials. *'Training in Human Rights for the Armed Forces in Ecuador'* Educational program of consciousness building for officials, lower officials and troops of the armed forces; specialization in human rights. *'New Threats to Peace (drug trafficking and terrorism)'* Impact of drug trafficking and terrorism; creation of pro-peace and life culture; alternative community actions; legal intervention. *'Women's Rights'* Women and citizenship; women and development; women and violence; women and legislation. *'Children's Rights'* Legal protection of minors; children and development; education and publicizing children's rights. Investigates and systematizes information and makes proposals for effective protection of children.
Events *International conference on community mental health and human rights* Chile 1991, *Conferencia latinoamericana sobre realidad de los menores en situacion de riesgo* Guayaquil (Ecuador) 1991. **Publications** *ALDHU* (6 a year). Annual Report on Human Rights in Latin America and the Caribbean. Books; manuals; monographs.
Members Individual intellectual, political, social, religious and academic personalities; national and regional organizations. Members in 17 countries:
Argentina, Bolivia, Brazil, Chile, Colombia, Costa Rica, Cuba, Dominican Rep, El Salvador, Guatemala, Haiti, Jamaica, Nicaragua, Paraguay, Peru, Uruguay, Venezuela.
Consultative Status Consultative status granted from: *UNESCO (#20322)* (Consultative Status). **IGO Relations** Accredited by (1): *United Nations Office at Vienna (UNOV, #20604).* Participates in meetings of authorities within: *OAS (#17629),* especially: *Inter-American Commission on Human Rights (IACHR, #11411).* Associated with Department of Global Communications of the United Nations. **NGO Relations** Supports (1): *International Campaign Against Mass Surveillance (ICAMS, no recent information).* [2022.03.04/XD0360/**D**]

- ♦ Latin American Association of Immunology / see Latin American and Caribbean Association of Immunology (#16265)
- ♦ Latin American Association of Industrial Design / see Latin American Association of Design (#16238)
- ♦ Latin American Association of Institutional Research (inactive)
- ♦ Latin American Association of Insurance Supervisors (#02300)
- ♦ Latin American Association of Library and Information Science Schools (inactive)
- ♦ Latin American Association of Linguistics and Philology (#02278)

♦ Latin American Association of Manufacturers of Refractory Materials 16244

Association latinoaméricaine des matières réfractaires – Asociación Latinoamericana de Fabricantes de Materiales Refractarios (ALAFAR)

Exec Sec Praça Louis Ensch, 240 Cidade Industrial CEP, Contagem MG, 32210-902, Brazil. Fax +553133339490. E-mail: alafar@alafar.org.
URL: http://www.alafar.org/

History 1967, Montevideo (Uruguay). **Languages** Portuguese, Spanish. **Finance** Members' dues (annual): US$ 350. **Events** *Congress* Lima (Peru) 2024, *Congress* Foz do Iguaçu (Brazil) 2022, *Congress* Medellin (Colombia) 2018, *Congress* Bariloche (Argentina) 2016, *Congress* Santiago (Chile) 2014. **Publications** Congress proceedings.
Members Manufacturers (32) in 9 countries:
Argentina, Brazil, Chile, Colombia, Guatemala, Mexico, Peru, Uruguay, Venezuela.
NGO Relations Founding member of: *UNITECR International Executive Board (UNITECR IEB, #20496).* [2022/XD4795/**D**]

- ♦ Latin American Association of Market and Opinion Research (no recent information)
- ♦ Latin American Association of Meat Exporters (inactive)

♦ Latin American Association of Medical Faculties and Schools 16245

Association latinoaméricaine des facultés et écoles de médecine – Asociación Latinoamericana de Facultades y Escuelas de Medicina (ALAFEM)

Pres Univ Ciencias Médicas de La Habana, Calle 146 No 2504, entre 25 y 31, Siboney – Playa, 11300 Havana, Cuba.
URL: http://www.unam.mx/udual/Cooperacion/alafem.htm

History 9 Feb 1980, León (Nicaragua). 9 Feb 1980, Léon (Nicaragua), by decision of delegates at 13th Conference of Latin American Medical Faculties and Schools, under the auspices of *Association of Universities of Latin America and the Caribbean (#02970).* **Aims** Promote the development of *education*, research and social achievements in the field of *health care*; support member faculties and schools; cooperate with related regional and international bodies. **Structure** General Assembly (every 2 years). Executive Committee, consisting of President and six Counsellors. General Secretariat, headed by Secretary General. Technical Commissions. **Languages** Portuguese, Spanish. **Finance** Members' dues. Grants. **Activities** Studies and research. Exchange of professors, teachers, researchers, students and pupils. Awards 'Juan Cesar Garcia' International Prize. **Events** *Conference* Guatemala (Guatemala) 2007, *Conference* Guatemala (Guatemala) 2001, *Conference* La Paz (Bolivia) 1998, *Conference* Havana (Cuba) 1991. **Publications** *ALAFEM Informa* – information bulletin.
Members Medical faculties and schools in 18 countries:
Argentina, Bolivia, Brazil, Chile, Colombia, Costa Rica, Cuba, Dominican Rep, Ecuador, Guatemala, Honduras, Mexico, Nicaragua, Panama, Paraguay, Peru, Uruguay, Venezuela.
IGO Relations *UNICEF (#20332); WHO (#20950); Pan American Health Organization (PAHO, #18108).* [2016/XD7359/**D**]

♦ Latin American Association of Medical Physics 16246

Association latinoaméricaine de physique médicale – Asociación Latinoamericana de Fisica Médica (ALFIM) – Associação Latinoamericana de Fisica Médica

Pres IRD, Av Salvador Allende s/n, Barra da Tijuca, Rio de Janeiro RJ, 22783-127, Brazil.
URL: http://revistaalfim.org/

History 1984, Chicago IL (USA). **Languages** English, Spanish. **Events** *Congress* Costa Rica 2013, *Congress* Cusco (Peru) 2010, *Iberian Latin American and Caribbean congress of medical physics / Congress* Rio de Janeiro (Brazil) 2004, *Iberian Latin American and Caribbean congress of medical physics / Congress* Caracas (Venezuela) 2001, *Iberian Latin American and Caribbean congress of medical physics / Congress* Mexico City (Mexico) 1998.
Members National associations in 10 countries:
Argentina, Brazil, Chile, Colombia, Costa Rica, Cuba, Ecuador, Panama, Peru, Venezuela.
Representatives in 4 countries:
Bolivia, El Salvador, Nicaragua, Uruguay.
NGO Relations Member of: *International Organization for Medical Physics (IOMP, #14453).* [2015/XD1499/**D**]

- ♦ Latin American Association of Metros and Subways (#02242)

♦ Latin American Association of Microbiology 16247

Association latinoaméricaine de microbiologie – Asociación Latinoamericana de Microbiologia (ALAM)

Contact c/o AMM, Piñón 209, Nueva Santa Maria Azcapotzalco, 02800 Mexico City CDMX, Mexico.
URL: https://alam.science/

History Also referred to in English as *Association of Microbiologists for Latin America.* **Events** *Congress* Asunción (Paraguay) 2021, *Congress* Asunción (Paraguay) 2020, *Congress* Santiago (Chile) 2018, *Congress* Rosario (Argentina) 2016, *Congress* Cartagena de Indias (Colombia) 2014. **Publications** *Revista Latinoamericana de Microbiología* (4 a year). **Members** Membership countries not specified. [2017/XD1459/**D**]

♦ Latin American Association for Mycology 16248

Asociación Latinoamericana de Micologia (ALM)

Acting Gen Dir address not obtained. E-mail: almycol@gmail.com.
URL: https://indicasat.org.pa/asociacion-latinoamericana-de-micologia-alm/

History 1990, Havana (Cuba). Founded during 5th Latin American Congress of Botany. Statutes adopted during 1st Latin American Symposium of Mycology, 21-25 Jun 1993, Havana. Secretariat moved, Oct 1996, to Caracas (Venezuela); moved again to Brazil in Jun 2002; moved to Columbia, 2014; to Peru, 2017; to Chile, 2020; and to Panama 2023. **Aims** Promote mycological studies and research in the Latin American and Caribbean countries; further and develop the relations between members, favouring the scientific exchanges. **Structure** General Assembly; Rotating Council Board; Country or Area Representatives (11). **Languages** English, Portuguese, Spanish. **Staff** 2.50 FTE, voluntary. **Finance** Sources: members' dues. **Activities** Research/documentation. **Events** *Congress* Panama (Panama) 2023, *Congress* Santiago (Chile) 2020, *Congress* Lima (Peru) 2017, *Congress* Medellin (Colombia) 2014, *Congress* San Pedro (Costa Rica) 2011. **Publications** *ALM Boletin/ALM Newsletter* in English, Spanish.
Members Honorary; Active. Individuals in 26 countries and territories:
Argentina, Belgium, Bolivia, Brazil, Canada, Chile, Colombia, Costa Rica, Cuba, Ecuador, El Salvador, France, Germany, Guatemala, Guiana Fr, Jamaica, Mexico, Norway, Panama, Peru, Puerto Rico, Spain, Sweden, Uruguay, USA, Venezuela.
NGO Relations Affiliated with (1): *International Society for Human and Animal Mycology (ISHAM, #15181).* Regional Committee for Latin America of: *International Mycological Association (IMA, #14203).* [2022.03.21/XD2686/v/**D**]

- ♦ Latin American Association of National Academies of Medicine (#02175)
- ♦ Latin American Association of National Agrochemical Industries (#02230)
- ♦ Latin American Association of Navigational Law and Law of the Sea (no recent information)
- ♦ Latin American Association of Nursing Science Schools and Departments (#02211)
- ♦ Latin American Association of Organic Geochemistry (#02331)
- ♦ Latin American Association of Organizational Development (no recent information)
- ♦ Latin American Association of Paleobotany and Palynology (#02249)
- ♦ Latin American Association of Palliative Care (#02201)
- ♦ Latin American Association of Pharmaceutical Industries (#02232)

♦ Latin American Association of Pharmacology (LAP) 16249

Association latinoaméricaine de pharmacologie – Asociación Latinoamericana de Farmacologia (ALF)

Pres address not obtained.

History 1964. A regional society of *Red Latinoamericana de Ciencias Biológicas (RELAB, #18706).* **Aims** Promote teaching and research in the area of pharmacology. **Structure** General Assembly. Executive Committee. Committees (3): Selection; Scientific; Program. **Languages** English, Spanish. **Finance** Members' dues. **Activities** Organizes (every 3 years) the main Congresses in a different county of Latin America. Sponsors regional activities. **Events** *Congress / Triennial Congress* Havana (Cuba) 2013, *Congress / Triennial Congress* Coquimbo (Chile) 2008, *Congress* Caracas (Venezuela) 2003, *LAP congress* Cartagena de Indias (Colombia) 1997, *LAP congress / Triennial Congress* Santiago (Chile) 1994. **Publications** *Acta Physiologica et Pharmacologica*; *Archivos Venezolanos de Farmacologia y Terapéutica.*
Members Associations, grouping 1,070 individuals, in 20 countries:
Argentina, Bolivia, Brazil, Chile, Colombia, Costa Rica, Cuba, Dominican Rep, Ecuador, El Salvador, Guatemala, Honduras, Mexico, Nicaragua, Panama, Paraguay, Peru, Puerto Rico, Uruguay, Venezuela.
NGO Relations Regional member of: *International Union of Basic and Clinical Pharmacology (IUPHAR, #15758).* [2013/XD6984/v/**D**]

♦ Latin American Association of Physiological Sciences 16250

Association latinoaméricaine des sciences physiologiques – Asociación Latino-americana de Ciencias Fisiológicas (ALACF) – Associação Latino-Americana de Ciências Fisiológicas

Pres address not obtained. E-mail: alacfnew@gmail.com.
Facebook: https://www.facebook.com/ALACFdifusion/

History 1956. Regional society of *Red Latinoamericana de Ciencias Biológicas (RELAB, #18706).* Re-founded 2020. **Aims** Promote studies, experimental research and other initiatives aimed at advancing, diffusing and popularizing physiological science for the benefit of the community; encourage the teaching of the physiological sciences according to modern educational trends; promote training of teachers and research workers in this field. **Structure** General Meeting (annual); Officers: President, Elected President, Secretary, Treasurer. **Languages** English, Portuguese, Spanish. **Staff** 12.00 FTE, voluntary. **Finance** Sources: contributions; donations; gifts, legacies; grants. Annual budget: 4,000 USD (2022). **Activities** Events/meetings; networking/liaising. **Events** *Pan-American Physiological Sciences Congress* Puerto Varas (Chile) 2023, *Joint Congress* Puebla (Mexico) 2022, *Joint Meeting* Buenos Aires (Argentina) 2021, *Congress* Chile 2020, *Congress* Mexico 2012. **Publications** *Acta Physiologica et Pharmacologica et Therapeutica Latinoamericana* (4 a year); *Physiological Mini-reviews* (4 a year).
Members Individuals: Full, Honorary, Contributing; Societies. Members from affiliated societies in 11 countries:
Argentina, Brazil, Chile, Colombia, Cuba, Ecuador, Haiti, Honduras, Mexico, Uruguay, Venezuela.
NGO Relations Regional member of: *International Union of Physiological Sciences (IUPS, #15800).* [2022.10.25/XD2860/**D**]

- ♦ Latin American Association of Plant Physiology (no recent information)
- ♦ Latin American Association of Plant Sciences (inactive)
- ♦ Latin American Association of Plastic Industries (no recent information)
- ♦ Latin American Association of Poison Control Centers (inactive)
- ♦ Latin American Association for Political Consultants (#02198)
- ♦ Latin American Association of Political Science (#02193)
- ♦ Latin American Association of Popular Education and Communication (#02207)
- ♦ Latin American Association on Post-Harvest Grain Technology (inactive)
- ♦ Latin American association of Power Planners (inactive)
- ♦ Latin American Association of Project Evaluators (inactive)
- ♦ Latin American Association for the Promotion of Habitat, Architecture and Urbanism (inactive)
- ♦ Latin American Association for Psychological Sexology (inactive)
- ♦ Latin American Association of Public Administration (inactive)
- ♦ Latin American Association for Quality (inactive)
- ♦ Latin American Association of Radio Education / see Asociación Latinoamericana de Educación y Comunicación Popular (#02207)
- ♦ Latin American Association of Regional Development Corporations (inactive)
- ♦ Latin American Association of Responsible Self-care (#02184)
- ♦ Latin American Association of Risk and Insurance Administrators (#02275)
- ♦ Latin American Association of Schools and Faculties of Optometry (#02220)
- ♦ Latin American Association of Schools of Social Work (inactive)
- ♦ Latin American Association for Science and Technology Policy (inactive)
- ♦ Latin American Association of Security and Hygiene at Work (#02265)
- ♦ Latin American Association of Services Exporters (#02219)
- ♦ Latin American Association of Social Medicine (#02241)
- ♦ Latin American Association for Social Psychology (inactive)

♦ Latin American Association of Societies of Nuclear Biology and Medicine 16251

Association latinoaméricaine des sociétés de biologie et médecine nucléaires – Asociación Latinoamericana de Sociedades de Biologia y Medicina Nuclear (ALASBIMN)

Sec address not obtained. E-mail: secretariaalasbimn@gmail.com.
Pres address not obtained. E-mail: danfer.gh@gmail.com.
URL: http://www.alasbimn.net/

History 3 Oct 1961, Rio de Janeiro (Brazil). **Aims** Promote development of nuclear medicine in the region. **Structure** Executive Committee. **Languages** Portuguese, Spanish. **Staff** 1.00 FTE, paid. **Finance** Members' dues. Congress revenue. **Events** *Congress* Lima (Peru) 2019, *Congress* Santiago (Chile) 2017, *Congress* Punta del Este (Uruguay) 2015, *Congress* Cancún (Mexico) 2014, *Congress* Porto de Galinhas (Brazil) 2011. **Publications** *ALASBIMN Journal.*
Members National associations in 11 countries:
Argentina, Brazil, Chile, Colombia, Guatemala, Mexico, Paraguay, Peru, Portugal, Spain, Uruguay. [2019.02.12/XD2862/**D**]

- ♦ Latin American Association of Sociology (#02267)
- ♦ Latin American Association of Sociology of Work (#02268)
- ♦ Latin American Association of Solar Energy (inactive)
- ♦ Latin American Association of Space Geophysics (#02226)
- ♦ Latin American Association for Sport Management (#02227)
- ♦ Latin American Association of Sport, Physical Education and Dance (unconfirmed)

♦ Latin American Association for the Study of the Liver (LASL) 16252

Association latinoaméricaine pour l'étude du foie (ALEF) – Asociación Latinoamericana para el Estudio del Higado (ALEH) – Associação Latinoamericana para o Estudo do Figado (ALEF)

Main Office Av Pr Kennedy 5488, Oficina 303, Vitacura, Santiago, Santiago Metropolitan, Chile. E-mail: info@alehlatam.org.
URL: http://www.alehlatam.org/

History Apr 1968, Sao Paulo (Brazil). Former names and other names: *Latin American Society of Hepatology* – former (1968 to 1992); *Sociedad Latinoamericana de Hepatologia (SLH)* – former (1968 to 1992). **Aims** Establish communication among Latin American hepatologists; promote study of common problems; encourage development of hepatology and setting up of national organizations; stimulate and facilitate training, research in hepato-biliary diseases and progress in prevention, recognition and treatment of these diseases in the region. **Structure** Congress (every 2 years); Board. **Languages** Portuguese, Spanish. **Staff** Voluntary. **Finance** Members' dues. Other sources: contributions; grants; proceeds of meetings. **Activities** Events/meetings; projects/programmes. **Events** *Congress* Bogota (Colombia) 2023, *Congress* Buenos Aires (Argentina) 2022, *Biennial Congress* Santiago (Chile) 2021, *Biennial Congress* Rio de Janeiro (Brazil) 2020, *Biennial Congress* Punta Cana (Dominican Rep) 2018. **Publications** *Latinoamerican Association for the Study of the Liver Bulletin* (3 a year) in Portuguese, Spanish; *Annals of Hepatology Journal.*
Members National Associations of Hepatology and individuals in 16 countries:
Argentina, Bolivia, Brazil, Chile, Colombia, Costa Rica, Cuba, Dominican Rep, Ecuador, Guatemala, Mexico, Panama, Paraguay, Peru, Uruguay, Venezuela.
NGO Relations Constituent society of: *International Association for the Study of the Liver (IASL, #12203).* [2022/XD0375/**D**]

- ♦ Latin American Association of the Tanning Industry (inactive)
- ♦ Latin American Association of Technological Management / see Asociación Latino-Iberoamericana de Gestión Tecnológica y de la Innovación (#02277)
- ♦ Latin American Association of Toxicology (#02274)
- ♦ Latin American Association of Trading Companies (no recent information)
- ♦ Latin American Association of Universities of Public Relations Programmes (#02192)
- ♦ Latin American Association on Weeds / see Latin American Weed Society (#16394)
- ♦ Latin American Association of Wood Products Producers (no recent information)
- ♦ Latin American Association of Writing Studies in Higher Education and Professional Contexts (#02218)
- ♦ Latin American Association of Zoological Gardens and Aquariums / see Asociación Latinoamericana de Parques Zoológicos y Acuarios (#02252)
- ♦ Latin American Association of Zoos and Aquariums (#02252)
- ♦ Latin American Association of Zoos, Aquariums and Similar Sites / see Asociación Latinoamericana de Parques Zoológicos y Acuarios (#02252)

♦ Latin American Aviation Historical Society (LAAHS) 16253

Address not obtained.
URL: http://www.laahs.com/

Aims Promote research, preservation and dissemination of the history of the civilian and military aviation in Latin America. [2012/XD9436/**D**]

- ♦ Latin American Balanced Feed Federation (no recent information)
- ♦ Latin American Banana and Agroindustrial Workers' Union Coordination (#04810)
- ♦ Latin American Banana Workers' Union Coordination / see Coordinadora Latinoamericano de Sindicatos Bananeros en Agroindustriales (#04810)

♦ Latin American Banking Association 16254

Fédération bancaire latinoaméricaine – Federación Latinoamericana de Bancos (FELABAN)

General Secretariat Carrera 7 No 71-21, Torre A Ofic 401-2, Bogota, Bogota DC, Colombia. T. +5717451187. Fax +5716217659. E-mail: felabanonline@gmail.com – mangarita@felaban.com.
URL: http://www.felaban.net/

History 1965, Mar del Plata (Argentina). **Aims** Promote the integration of Latin American commercial banks; create a progressive and persistent rise in the standard of living of Latin American people by encouraging closer collaboration and common understanding among the sectors to which productive resources are entrusted. **Structure** Governing Board; Executive Council,; General Secretariat, headed by Secretary-General. Technical Committees (10): Comité Latinoamericano de Auditoria Interna y Evaluación de Riesgos (CLAIN); Comité Latinoamericano de Automatización Bancaria (CLAB); Comité Latinoamericano de Expertos en Seguridad Bancaria (CELAES); Comité Latinoamericano para la Prevención del Lavado de Activos y Financiamiento del Terrorismo (COPLAFT); Centro Latinoamericano de Comercio Exterior (CLACE); Comité Latinoamericano de Fideicomiso (COLAFI); Comité Latinoamericano de Economistas (CLEC); Comité Latinoamericano de Derecho Financiero (COLADE); Comité Latinoamericano de Riesgos (CLAR); Comité Latinoamericano de Educación e Inclusión Financiera (CLEIF). **Languages** Spanish. **Staff** 7.00 FTE, paid. **Finance** Annual budget: 751,000 USD. **Activities** Training/education; events/meetings; guidance/assistance/consulting. **Events** *General Assembly* Colombia 2020, *Annual Assembly* Hollywood, FL (USA) 2019, *Financial Technology and Innovation Conference* Hollywood, FL (USA) 2019, *Latin American Congress of Bank Security* Panama (Panama) 2019, *Congreso Latinoamericano de Fideicomiso* Santo Domingo (Dominican Rep) 2019. **Publications** *Boletin Noticias FELABAN* (6 a year); *Guia Bancaria Latinoamericana* (annual). *Biblioteca FELABAN* – series – 20 vols so far.
Members Banking associations in 19 countries:
Argentina, Bolivia, Brazil, Chile, Colombia, Costa Rica, Cuba, Dominican Rep, Ecuador, El Salvador, Guatemala, Honduras, Mexico, Nicaragua, Panama, Paraguay, Peru, Uruguay, Venezuela.
Adhering members (6):
Asociación de Administradoras de Fondos y Fideicomisos del Ecuador; *Asociación Latinoamericana y del Caribe de Burós de Crédito (ALACRED, #02189)*; *Association of Supervisors of Banks of the Americas (ASBA, #02944)*; *Banco Latinoamericano de Comercio Exterior (BLADEX, #03159)*; *Central American Bank for Economic Integration (CABEI, #03658)*; *Development Bank of Latin America (CAF, #05055).*
Corresponding members (9):
American Express; Asociación Española de Banca Privada; *Florida International Bankers' Association (FIBA)*; *Society for Worldwide Interbank Financial Telecommunication (SWIFT, #19661)*; Visa International.
Consultative Status Consultative status granted from: *OAS (#17629).* **NGO Relations** Partner of: *SME Finance Forum (#19323).* [2020/XD2864/y/**D**]

♦ Latin American Baptist Women's Union 16255

Union des femmes baptistes d'Amérique latine – Union Femenil Bautista de America Latina (UFBAL)

Sec Mario Urteaga D-1, URB Ramón Castilla, Cajamarca, Peru. E-mail: ufbalatina@outlook.es.
Pres Rua 5-Lote 10-Quadra 3, Parque Chaperó, Itajai SC, 23812-000 RJ, Brazil. Fax +552126882679.

URL: http://www.bwawd.org/ufbal
History 1950. Founded as one of 7 Continental Unions of the Women's Department of *Baptist World Alliance (BWA, #03176)*. **Activities** Organizes Continental Union Congresses. **Events** *Congress* Guayaquil (Ecuador) 2008, *Quinquennial Meeting* Chile 2003, *Congress for Mexico, Central America and Panama* Managua (Nicaragua) 2001, *Continental congress* Panama (Panama) 2001. **Members** National Conventions (25) in 19 countries.Membership countries not specified. [2016/XD8139/**E**]

- ♦ Latin American Beer Manufacturers Association (#03836)
- ♦ Latin American Biblical Seminary / see Universidad Biblica Latinoamericana
- ♦ Latin American Biblical University (internationally oriented national body)
- ♦ Latin American Biological Psychiatry Federation (no recent information)
- ♦ Latin American Biotechnology and Bioengineering Association (unconfirmed)

♦ Latin American Blind Union 16256

Union latinoaméricaine des aveugles – Unión Latinoamericana de Ciegos (ULAC)
Technical Sec Mercedes 1327 CP 11100, Montevideo, Uruguay. T. +59829019797ext22. Fax +5989019797ext21. E-mail: ulac@ulacdigital.org – oficinaulac@gmail.com.
SG address not obtained. E-mail: sgeneral@ulacdigital.org.
URL: http://www.ulacdigital.org/
History 15 Nov 1985, Mar del Plata (Argentina), at General Assembly, when constitution was adopted, on the initiative of *Pan-American Council for the Blind (CPPC, inactive)*, set up 1956, Lima (Peru), and *Latin American Organization for the Welfare of the Blind and Visually Handicapped (OLAP, inactive)*, formed 1977, Sao Paulo (Brazil), to unite the aspirations of these two organizations. **Aims** Work for the prevention of blindness; promote welfare of the blind and visually handicapped living in Latin America, securing for them equal opportunity and full participation in society; strengthen self-awareness of blind people, foster development of their personality and self-fulfilment; promote, sponsor and support creation of organizations of and for the blind; promote enactment of laws to abolish discrimination against the blind; promote scientific and technical research to improve and advance social, cultural and economic level of the blind; encourage exchange and technical cooperation among regional and international organizations. **Structure** Regional (Geographical) Union of the *World Blind Union (WBU, #21234)*. General Assembly (every 4 years at Latin American Congress of the Blind). Board of Directors. Executive Committee, consisting of Coordinators of Special Committees, Coordinator of Geographical Areas, President of Committee on Human Rights, International Member, and Officers of the Board (Chairman, First Vice-Chairman, Second Vice-Chairman – a blind or visually handicapped person by constitution – Past Chairman, Secretary and Treasurer) comprise the Executive Committee. Geographical areas (5): Mexico and Central America; the Caribbean; the Andean Region; Brazil; the South Cone. **Languages** Portuguese, Spanish. **Staff** 1.00 FTE, paid. **Finance** Members' dues, depending on membership category. **Activities** Standing Committee of Human Rights and Legislation. Technical-Professional Committees (10): Prevention of Blindness; Education; Basic Functional Rehabilitation and Low Vision; Professional Training and Employment; Access to Information and Culture; Physical Education, Recreation and Sports; Promotion of the Status of Blind Women; Promotion of the Status of Elderly Blind People; Promotion of the Status of Blind Young People; Deafblind Person's Activities. 'Basic Didactic Materials' program; needs surveys; project 'Textbooks for Blind Children'; assists national projects. **Events** *General Assembly* Mexico City (Mexico) 2012, *Quadrennial Congress* 2008, *Quadrennial General Assembly* 2008, *Quadrennial General Assembly* Quito (Ecuador) 2004, *Quadrennial congress / General Assembly* Quito (Ecuador) 2004. **Publications** *América Latina* (4 a year) in Spanish – in braille, ordinary print, on cassette.
Members National; international; associate; Honorary (life); sponsoring. Organizations in 19 countries:
Argentina, Bolivia, Brazil, Chile, Colombia, Costa Rica, Cuba, Dominican Rep, Ecuador, El Salvador, Guatemala, Honduras, Mexico, Nicaragua, Panama, Paraguay, Peru, Uruguay, Venezuela.
Non-Latin American member in 1 country:
Spain.
Consultative Status Consultative status granted from: *ECOSOC (#05331)* (Special). [2022/XD0477/**D**]

♦ Latin American Bone Marrow Transplantation Group (LABMT) 16257

Sec Rua Hadock Lobo 72, Room 407, Estacio, Rio de Janeiro RJ, 22260-132, Brazil. T. +552122738390. E-mail: info@labmt.net.
URL: http://www.labmt.net/
History Registration: Brazil. **Aims** Promote excellence in hematopoietic stem cell transplantation, stem cell donation, cellular therapy and accreditation in Latin America. **Structure** General Assembly; Board; Executive Committee. **NGO Relations** Member of (2): *Alliance for Harmonisation of Cellular Therapy Accreditation (AHCTA, #00686)*; *Worldwide Network for Blood and Marrow Transplantation (WBMT, #21929)*.
[2021/XJ9997/**D**]

- ♦ Latin American Botanical Association / see Asociación Latinoamericana de Botanica (#02187)

♦ Latin American Bottled Water Association (LABWA) 16258

Main Office Av Las Américas, Zona 13, 01013 Guatemala, Guatemala. T. +50223107342 – +50223107343. E-mail: info@labwa.org.
URL: http://www.labwa.org/
NGO Relations Member of (1): *International Council of Bottled Water Associations (ICBWA, #13001)*.
[2021/XM2245/**D**]

♦ Latin American Boxing Federation 16259

Federación Latinoamericana de Boxeo (FEDELATIN)
Pres address not obtained. E-mail: fedelatin@cwpanama.net.
URL: http://www.wbaboxing.com/category/regions-fedelatin/
History by *World Boxing Association (WBA, #21241)*. **Languages** Spanish. [2019.12.12/XD7726/**D**]

♦ Latin American Bryological Society 16260

Sociedad Latinoamericana de Briologia (SLB)
Contact Inst de Ciencias Naturales, Univ Nacional de Colombia, Cra 45, Bogota, Bogota DC, Colombia.
URL: http://briologia.blogspot.be/
History 15 Dec 1982. **Aims** Promote knowledge of regional *bryophyte* research and teaching; stimulate interaction among Latin American bryologists and all individuals interested in this topic. **Structure** Executive Committee. **Languages** Spanish. **Staff** 4.00 FTE, voluntary. **Finance** Sources: donations; contributions. **Activities** Events/meetings. **Events** *General Assembly and Symposium* La Serena (Chile) 2010, *General assembly and symposium* Santo Domingo (Dominican Rep) 2006, *General assembly and symposium* Bogota (Colombia) 2002, *General assembly and symposium / Symposium* Mexico City (Mexico) 1998, *General assembly and symposium / Symposium* Mar del Plata (Argentina) 1994. **Publications** *Briolatina* – electronic newsletter.
Members Governmental and national organizations in 27 countries:
Argentina, Bolivia, Brazil, Canada, Chile, Colombia, Costa Rica, Cuba, Dominican Rep, Ecuador, Egypt, Finland, France, Germany, Guatemala, India, Italy, Mexico, Netherlands, Panama, Peru, Puerto Rico, Spain, Sweden, UK, USA, Venezuela.
[2017.03.12/XD7471/**D**]

- ♦ Latin American Bureau of Society of Jesus (religious order)

♦ Latin American Business Council 16261

Consejo Empresario de América Latina (CEAL) – Conselho de Empresarios da América Latina
Main Office Of 305 – piso 3, Torre A, Torres de las Américas, Punta Pacifica, Panama, Panamá, Panama PANAMá, Panama. T. +5072706419. E-mail: ceal@ceal.co.
URL: http://www.ceal.co/
History 1990, Mexico City (Mexico). **Events** *Plenary Assembly* Madrid (Spain) 2014.
Members Full in 11 countries:
Argentina, Bolivia, Brazil, Chile, Colombia, Ecuador, Mexico, Paraguay, Peru, Uruguay, Venezuela.
NGO Relations Member of: *International Counterparts Network (#13095)*. [2018/XD7089/**D**]

- ♦ Latin American Business Credit Reporting Association (no recent information)

♦ Latin American Business Ethics Network 16262

Asociación Latinoamericana de Etica en los Negocios y Economia (ALENE)
Sec c/o ESAN, Alonso de Molina 1652, Monterrico, Surco, Lima, Peru. E-mail: kjauregui@esan.edu.pe.
History Founded Jul 1998. **Aims** Foster processes for improving ethics through teaching and consulting. **Structure** Central Committee. **Finance** Members' dues. Other sources: contributions from sponsors at annual congress. **Activities** Knowledge management/information dissemination. **Events** *Congress* Santiago (Chile) 2015, *Congress* Sao Paulo (Brazil) 2011, *Congress* Rio de Janeiro (Brazil) 2010, *Congress* Bogota (Colombia) 2009, *Congress* Lima (Peru) 2006. **Publications** Congress proceedings.
Members Individuals (40) in 7 countries:
Argentina, Brazil, Chile, Colombia, Ecuador, Mexico, USA.
NGO Relations Partner of: *Globethics.net Foundation (#10669)*. [2016/XF4759/**F**]

- ♦ Latin-American Campaign for the Right to Education (#03407)
- ♦ Latin American Candle Manufacturers Association (unconfirmed)
- ♦ Latin American Carbon Federation (#09347)
- ♦ Latin American Carbon Program (see: #05055)
- ♦ Latin American and Caribbean Agency for Communication (#00550)
- ♦ Latin American and Caribbean Agro-Ecological Movement (#16872)

♦ Latin American and Caribbean Air Transport Association 16263

Asociación Latinoamericana y del Caribe de Transporte Aéreo (ALTA)
Main Office 6355 NW 36th St, Ste 601, Miami FL 33166, USA. T. +17863880222.
URL: http://www.alta.aero/
History 8 Apr 1980, Bogota (Colombia), as *International Association for Latin American Air Transport – Asociación Internacional de Transporte Aéreo Latinoamericano (AITAL)*, by 11 members. Subsequently changed title to *Latin American Air Transport Association – Association du transport aérien latinoaméricain – Asociación Latinoamericana de Transporte*. **Aims** Facilitate the development of safer, more efficient and environmentally friendly air transport in the Latin American and Caribbean region. **Structure** General Assembly. Executive Committee. **Languages** English, Portuguese, Spanish. **Staff** 22.00 FTE, paid. **Finance** Members' dues (annual). **Activities** Main areas: Safety; Security; Maintenance; Training; Aeropolitical Affairs; Cargo; Distribution; Operations; Airports; Fuel. **Events** *Pan American Aviation Safety Summit* Panama (Panama) 2016, *Aviation Law Americas Conference* Cancún (Mexico) 2015, *Panamerican Safety Summit / Pan American Aviation Safety Summit* Medellin (Colombia) 2015, *Latin American and Caribbean Airline and Suppliers Annual Meeting / Latin American and Caribbean Airlines and Suppliers Annual Meeting (CCMA)* Punta Cana (Dominican Rep) 2015, *Annual Latin American Airline Leaders Forum / Latin American Airline Leaders Forum* San Juan (Puerto Rico) 2015. **Publications** *Latin America and Caribbean Capacity Analysis*. Yearbook; Directory.
Members Airlines. Full (36) in 20 countries and territories:
Antigua-Barbuda, Argentina, Bahamas, Brazil, Cayman Is, Chile, Colombia, Costa Rica, Cuba, Curaçao, Ecuador, El Salvador, Guatemala, Jamaica, Mexico, Panama, Paraguay, Peru, Suriname, Trinidad-Tobago.
Associate (8) in 5 countries:
Canada, Portugal, Spain, Türkiye, USA.
Affiliate (45) in 11 countries:
Belgium, Brazil, Canada, France, Germany, Italy, Japan, Russia, Spain, Switzerland, USA.
IGO Relations Co-sponsors Pan American Aviation Safety Summit with: *International Civil Aviation Organization (ICAO, #12581)* Regional Aviation Safety Group – Pan America. **NGO Relations** Member of: *Air Transport Action Group (ATAG, #00614)*. [2018/XD8730/**D**]

♦ Latin American and Caribbean Alliance of YMCAs (LACA) 16264

Alianza Latinoamericana y del Caribe de Asociaciones Cristianas de Jóvenes (ALCACJ)
Main Office Av Ejército Nacional 253, 1er Piso, Col Anahuac, Deleg Miguel Hidalgo, CP 11320 Mexico City CDMX, Mexico. T. +525555212091. E-mail: info@lacaymca.org.
URL: http://www.lacaymca.org/
History Founded 6 Jun 1914, Montevideo (Uruguay), as *South American Federation of YMCAs*. Regional organization of *World Alliance of Young Men's Christian Associations (YMCA, #21090)*. Name changed to *Latin American Confederation of YMCAs – Confédération latinoaméricaine des associations unions chrétiennes de jeunes gens – Confederação Latinoamericana das de Associações Cristãos de Moços*, 6 Jun 1917, when registered in accordance with Uruguayan law. Became *Latin American and Caribbean Confederation of YMCAs – Confederación Latinoamericana y del Caribe de Asociaciones Cristianas de Jóvenes (CLACJ) – Confederação Latinoamericana e do Caribe de Associações Cristãos de Moços*, 1990, when registered in accordance with Argentine law. Present name adopted 2003. **Aims** Strengthen the leadership, programmes and self-reliance of National Movements in Latin America and the Caribbean to advance *youth* and *community* development. **Structure** Assembly (every 4 years), Executive Committee of 10 volunteer members (meets annually). Executive Office in Mexico City (Mexico). Sub-regional Offices, each coordinated by an ad hoc executive: Central America; South Cone; Andes; Caribbean; Mesoamerica. Thematic Networks. **Languages** English, French, Portuguese, Spanish. **Staff** 3.00 FTE, paid. **Finance** Members' dues. Donations. **Activities** Guidance/assistance/consulting; financial and/or material support; projects/programmes; networking/liaising. Databanks: Scientific research concerning psoriasis; Available treatment and acceptance of these treatments by national health and insurance bodies in EU member countries. **Events** *Annual Conference* Oranjestad (Aruba) 2015, *General Assembly* Estes Park, CO (USA) 2014, *Annual Conference* Managua (Nicaragua) 2013, *Annual Conference* Viña del Mar (Chile) 2012, *Annual Conference* Lima (Peru) 2011. **Publications** *Carta Abierta* (4 a year). Study guides; manuals; technical publications; information bulletins; reports on international activities; brochures.
Members YMCAs in 28 countries and territories:
Aruba, Bahamas, Barbados, Belize, Bolivia, Brazil, Cayman Is, Chile, Colombia, Cuba, Dominican Rep, Ecuador, Guatemala, Guyana, Haiti, Honduras, Jamaica, Martinique, Mexico, Nicaragua, Panama, Paraguay, Peru, St Vincent-Grenadines, Suriname, Trinidad-Tobago, Uruguay, Venezuela.
IGO Relations Cooperates with: *FAO (#09260)*; *OAS (#17629)*; *UNDP (#20292)*; *UNEP (#20299)*; *UNESCO (#20322)*. **NGO Relations** Cooperates with: *Consejo Episcopal Latinoamericano (CELAM, #04709)*; *Earth Council Alliance (ECA, inactive)*; *ICCO – Interchurch Organization for Development Cooperation*; *Latin American Council of Churches (LACC, #16309)*; *Universidad Biblica Latinoamericana (UBL)*; different Christian churches and NGOs, foundations, official international and social organizations. Member of: *Espacio Iberoamericano de Juventud (EIJ, no recent information)*; *Foro Latinoamericano de Juventud (FLAJ, #09881)*.
[2015.09.03/XD0397/**D**]

- ♦ Latin American and Caribbean Association of Agricultural Economy (no recent information)
- ♦ Latin American and Caribbean Association of Air Freight and Transport Agents / see Latin American and Caribbean Federation of National Associations of Cargo (#16276)
- ♦ Latin American and Caribbean Association of Credit Bureaus (#02189)
- ♦ Latin American and Caribbean Association of Educators (unconfirmed)
- ♦ Latin American and Caribbean Association of Environmental and Resource Economists (inactive)

♦ Latin American and Caribbean Association of Immunology (ALACI) 16265

Asociación Latinoamericana y Caribeña de Inmunología (ALACI) – Associação Latino-Americana e do Caribe de Imunologia (ALACI)
Permanent Sec IIFP – Fac de Ciencias Exactas, Univ Nacional de La Plata, Calle 47 y 115 s/n, 1900 La Plata, Argentina. T. +542214250497 ext 45. E-mail: secretariat.alaci@gmail.com.
Secretary address not obtained.
URL: http://www.alaci.org
History Jun 1984, Buenos Aires (Argentina). Founded 1984 at Constitutive Assembly. Former names and other names: *Latin American Association of Immunology (ALAI)* – former; *Asociación Latinoamericana de Inmunología (ALAI)* – former; *Associação Latinoamericana de Imunologia (ALAI)* – former. **Aims** Promote contacts and cooperation between immunological societies in Latin America; facilitate exchange of scientific information and interrelationships among immunologists. **Structure** General Assembly (every 3 years at International Congress); Assembly of Representatives; Executive Committee. **Languages** English. **Staff** 4.00 FTE, voluntary. **Finance** Activities supported on an ad-hoc basis; no membership subscription. **Activities** Events/

meetings; training/education. **Events** *Latin American and Caribbean Congress of Immunology* Varadero (Cuba) 2022, *Latin American and Caribbean Congress of Immunology* Cancún (Mexico) 2018, *Latin American and Caribbean Congress of Immunology* Medellin (Colombia) 2015, *International Congress on Meningeal Disease Vaccines* Varadero (Cuba) 2013, *Latin American and Caribbean Congress of Immunology* Lima (Peru) 2012. **Members** Full: societies of immunology adhering to IUIS; Corresponding: individuals in countries not having a national society, or joining that of a neighboring country; Observer: societies in a non-defined situation. Full in 10 countries:
Argentina, Bolivia, Brazil, Chile, Colombia, Cuba, Honduras, Mexico, Peru, Uruguay.
Regional member: West Indian Immunology Society.
Corresponding members in 3 countries:
Ecuador, El Salvador, Guatemala.
Observer in 2 countries:
Paraguay, Venezuela.
NGO Relations Member of (1): *International Union of Immunological Societies (IUIS, #15781).*
[2023.02.14/XD0995/**D**]

♦ Latin American and Caribbean Association of Public Health Education (inactive)
♦ Latin American and Caribbean Association for Women's Studies (inactive)
♦ Latin American and Caribbean Association of Zoological Parks and Aquariums / see Asociación Latinoamericana de Parques Zoológicos y Acuarios (#02252)

♦ Latin American and Caribbean Bonsai Federation (FELAB) 16266

Fédération latinoaméricaine et caraïbéenne de bonsaï – Federación Latinoamericana y Caribeña de Bonsai

Contact address not obtained. T. +5624208604.
URL: http://www.revistadebonsai.com/

History Founded 21 Feb 1992, Cali (Colombia), as *Bonsai Latin American Federation – Federación Latino Americana de Bonsai.* **Aims** Advance the art of bonsai. **Structure** Board of Directors of 8 members, including President, 1st and 2nd Vice-Presidents, Secretary and Treasurer. Delegates (19) for each member country. **Languages** English, Spanish. **Staff** 8 voluntary (Board). **Finance** Members' dues. **Activities** Organizes congress (every 2 years); offers the "Pedro J Morales" Award. **Events** *Congress* Puerto Rico 2014, *Congress* Sao Paulo (Brazil) 2012, *Congress* Mexico 2010, *Biennial convention / Congress* Argentina 2009, *Biennial Convention* San Juan (Puerto Rico) 2007. **Publications** *FELAB Informa* in Spanish.
Members Organizations (19) in 19 countries and territories:
Argentina, Barbados, Brazil, Chile, Colombia, Costa Rica, Dominican Rep, Ecuador, Guadeloupe, Guiana Fr, Martinique, Mexico, Panama, Paraguay, Peru, Puerto Rico, St Croix Is, St Lucia, Venezuela.
NGO Relations Latin American region of: *World Bonsai Friendship Federation (WBFF, #21239).* Member of: *Bonsai Clubs International (BCI, #03301).* [2014/XD7998/**D**]

♦ Latin American and Caribbean Broadcasting Union (inactive)
♦ Latin American and Caribbean Center, Miami FL (internationally oriented national body)

♦ Latin American and Caribbean Centre on Health Sciences Information (BIREME) 16267

Centre Latinoaméricain et des Caraïbes d'Information dans les Sciences de la Santé – Centro Latinoamericano y del Caribe de Información en Ciencias de la Salud – Centro Latinoamericano e do Caribe de Informação em Ciências da Saúde

Contact BIREME/PAHO/WHO, Rua Vergueiro 1759 12th floor, Sao Paulo SP, 04101-000, Brazil. T. +551155769800. E-mail: birdir@paho.org.
URL: http://www.paho.org/bireme/

History 3 Mar 1967, Sao Paulo (Brazil), as *Regional Library of Medicine – Biblioteca Regional de Medicina,* a name under which it is still known. Renewed in 1978, 1982 and 1986, according to an agreement signed between *Pan American Health Organization (PAHO, #18108)* and the Brazilian government. Also previously known as *Latin American Health Sciences Information Centre – Centro Latinoamericano de Información en Ciencias de la Salud.* Present name adopted 1986. Most recent statutes approved by the 49th Directing Council of PAHO (CD49-R5), Oct 2009, when the new governance structure was also established. **Aims** Contribute to development of health in the countries of Latin America and the Caribbean through democratization of access, publication and use of scientific information, knowledge and evidence. **Structure** Member States; Advisory Committee; Scientific Committee; Secretariat. **Languages** English, Portuguese, Spanish. **Staff** 40.00 FTE, paid. **Finance** Sources: *Pan American Health Organization (PAHO, #18108); WHO (#20950);* Brazilian governmental institutions, including Ministries of Health and Secretary of Health of the State of Sao Paulo (SES-SP) and Secretary of Health of the Municipality of Sao Paulo. **Activities** Knowledge management/information dissemination; capacity building; research and development; networking/liaising; events/meetings. **Events** *ICML : world congress on health information and libraries* Salvador (Brazil) 2005, *Regional congress on health sciences information* Puebla (Mexico) 2003, *Meeting of specialists in digital scientific information* Sao Paulo (Brazil) 2002, *International conference on scientific electronic publishing in developing countries* Valparaiso (Chile) 2002, *Pan American congress on health sciences information* London (UK) 2000. **Publications** Tutorials, handouts and guides for management and operation portals and sites that follow the VHL model and methodology. Information Services: Health information sources produced by Latin American and Caribbean countries through the VHL. **Information Services** *DeCS – Health Science Descriptors* – translated version of NLM Medical Subject Headings to Portuguese and Spanish; *LILACS – Latin American and Caribbean Health Science Literature.* **Members** Categories (a) Members States – Member States, Participating States and Associated Members of PAHO; (b) Participating States – Members States of WHO; (c) Participating Organizations – public international organizations with specific qualification related to information and communication in the scientific and technical field. Membership countries not specified. **IGO Relations** A specialized centre of *Pan American Health Organization (PAHO, #18108)* and *WHO (#20950).*
[2019.07.17/XE6824/**E***]

♦ Latin American and Caribbean Committee for the Defense of Women's Rights 16268

Comité de América Latina y el Caribe para la Defensa de los Derechos de la Mujer (CLADEM)

Exec Sec Jirón Caracas 2426 Jesús María, 15076, Lima, Peru. T. +5114639237. Fax +5114635898. E-mail: infocom@cladem.org – coordi@cladem.org.
URL: http://www.cladem.org/

History 3 Jul 1987, San José (Costa Rica). Derives from 3rd World Forum Women, Law and Development, Jul 1985, Nairobi (Kenya). Former names and other names: *Latin American Committee for the Defense of Women's Rights* – former; *Comité Latinoamericano para la Defensa de los Derechos de la Mujer* – former. **Aims** Design strategies for regional action; exchange information and maintain the flow of communication among groups and persons working in the field; maintain archives on women and the *law*; propose issues for debate and reflection at regional level, whether through meetings or publications; channel *emergency* support through *solidarity* network. **Structure** Regional Assembly. Regional Coordinator supported by Decision-Making Committee of 5 members and Regional Office. **Languages** Spanish. **Staff** 5.00 FTE, paid. **Activities** Includes *Latin American Solidarity Network – Cadena Latinoamericano de Solidaridad* to respond to emergencies. **Events** *Penal normativity and women in Latin America* Sao Paulo (Brazil) 1992. **Publications** *Los Derechos de las Mujeres en Clave Feminista – Experiencias del Cladem* (2009); *Vigiladas y Castigadas*; *Women Watched and Punished.*
Members National organizations in 15 countries and territories:
Argentina, Bolivia, Brazil, Colombia, Dominican Rep, El Salvador, Guatemala, Honduras, Mexico, Nicaragua, Panama, Paraguay, Peru, Puerto Rico, Uruguay.
Consultative Status Consultative status granted from: *UNESCO (#20322)* (Consultative Status). **IGO Relations** Civil society network of: *OAS (#17629).* **NGO Relations** Member of: *International NGO Committee on Human Rights in Trade and Investment (INCHRITI, no recent information).* Supports: *Global Call for Action Against Poverty (GCAP, #10263).* [2012/XF2907/**F**]

♦ Latin American and Caribbean Confederation of Domestic Workers (unconfirmed)
♦ Latin American and Caribbean Confederation of YMCAs / see Latin American and Caribbean Alliance of YMCAs (#16264)

♦ Latin American and Caribbean Conference on Theoretical and Applied Mechanics (LACCOTAM) 16269

Sec Univ of The West Indies, Dept of Mathematics and Statistics, St Augustine Campus, St Augustine, Trinidad-Tobago. T. +18686622002. Fax +18686457132.

History Founded 1989, Trinidad-Tobago, as *Caribbean Congress of Fluid Dynamics (CACOFD).* Current name adopted, 2010. **Aims** Promote the study of mechanics as a branch of science and engineering in the region. **Structure** Executive Committee; Co-opted Executive Board. **Languages** English. **Events** *Conference / Triennial Conference* Caracas (Venezuela) 2012, *Triennial Conference* Port-of-Spain (Trinidad-Tobago) 2008, *Triennial international conference / Triennial Conference* Mexico City (Mexico) 1998, *Symposium on lubricated transport of viscous materials* Trinidad-Tobago 1997, *Triennial international conference / Triennial Conference* Caracas (Venezuela) 1995.
Members Participants from 7 countries:
Barbados, Brazil, Guatemala, Jamaica, Mexico, Trinidad-Tobago, Venezuela.
NGO Relations Affiliated member of and joint symposia with: *International Union of Theoretical and Applied Mechanics (IUTAM, #15823).* [2019.02.12/XF2915/c/**F**]

♦ Latin American and Caribbean Consortium against Unsafe Abortion (#04733)

♦ Latin American and Caribbean Consortium of Engineering Institutions (LACCEI) 16270

Exec Dir FAU Engineering, 777 Glades Rd, EE-525, Boca Raton FL 33431-0991, USA. T. +15612973899. Fax +15612971111. E-mail: admin@laccei.org – info@laccei.org.
URL: http://www.laccei.org/

History Feb 2002, Miami FL (USA). **Aims** Serve as the leading organization of Latin American and Caribbean engineering institutions that will bring innovations in engineering education and research; foster partnerships among academia, industry, government and private organizations. **Structure** Executive Board; Board of Trustees; Administrative Board. Secretariat. **Languages** English, French, Guarani, Portuguese, Spanish. **Staff** 2.00 FTE, paid. **Finance** Members' dues. Other sources: conference proceeds. Annual budget: about US$ 40,000. **Activities** Training/education. **Events** *Prospective and trends in technology and skills for sustainable social development* Buenos Aires (Argentina) 2021, *Engineering, integration, and alliances for a sustainable development, hemispheric cooperation for cometitiveness and prosperity on a knowledge-based economy* Boca Raton, FL (USA) 2020, *Conference* Montego Bay (Jamaica) 2019, *Conference* Lima (Peru) 2018, *Conference* Boca Raton, FL (USA) 2017. **Publications** *Journal of Engineering Education in the Americas.* Conference proceedings.
Members Universities and institutions (201) in 30 countries and territories:
Argentina, Belize, Brazil, Chile, Colombia, Costa Rica, Dominican Rep, Ecuador, El Salvador, France, Guatemala, Haiti, Honduras, Jamaica, Kazakhstan, Korea Rep, Mexico, Nicaragua, Panama, Peru, Portugal, Puerto Rico, Russia, Spain, Taiwan, Trinidad-Tobago, UK, Uruguay, USA, Venezuela.
IGO Relations Formal contacts with: *OAS (#17629).* **NGO Relations** Member of: *Engineering for the Americas (EftA, no recent information); International Federation of Engineering Education Societies (IFEES, #13412).* Associate member of: *European Network for Accreditation of Engineering Education (ENAEE, #07859).* Formal contacts with: *Global Engineering Deans Council (GEDC, #10344).* [2019/XM2584/y/**F**]

♦ Latin American and Caribbean Consortium to Support Cassava Research and Development 16271

Consorcio Latinoamericano y del Caribe de Apoyo a la Investigación y Desarrollo de la Yuca (CLAYUCA)

Contact Kilómetro 17 Recta Cali, Palmira 6713, Valle del Cauca, Colombia. T. +5724450157 – +5724450159. Fax +5724450073.

History Apr 1999.
Members in 9 countries:
Bolivia, Colombia, Cuba, Ecuador, Haiti, Mexico, Paraguay, Peru, Venezuela.
NGO Relations *International Centre for Tropical Agriculture (#12527).* [2014/XD9419/**D**]

♦ Latin American and Caribbean Council of AIDS Service Organizations (LACCASO) 16272

Consejo Latinoamericano y Caribeño de Organizaciones No Gubernamentales con Servicio en VIH/Sida – Conselho Latino-Americano e do Caribe de Organizações Nã Governamentais com Serviço em VIH/Aids

Contact c/o GESTOS, Rua dos Médicis 68, Boa Vista, Recife PE, 50070-290, Brazil. T. +558134217670. Fax +558132313880.
URL: http://www.laccaso.org/

History within *ICASO (#11040).* **Aims** Promote and defend human rights, through coordination, integration and capacity building of civil society organizations, so as to achieve an articulated and effective community and multi-sectoral response to the HIV/AIDS epidemic. **Staff** 2.00 FTE, paid. Plus contractual staff. **Activities** Coordinates sub-regional meetings; acts as focus for groups in Latin America and for international agencies/funders/donors looking for partnership with the community-based sector; is responsible developing, implementing and monitoring a variety of projects, including *Centro de Recursos e Información sobre Sexualidad y SIDA (CRISSOL).* **Events** *United Nations International Conference on Space-based Technologies for Disaster Management* Beijing (China) 2013, *Biennial Pan-American conference on AIDS* Salvador (Brazil) 1999, *Biennial Pan-American conference on AIDS* Lima (Peru) 1997, *Latin American congress on sexual transmitted diseases* Lima (Peru) 1997, *Biennial Pan-American conference on AIDS / Biennial Pan American Conference on AIDS* Santiago (Chile) 1995. **Publications** *LACCASO Newsletter* (4 a year) in Spanish. *Acción en SIDA.*
Members Full in 20 countries:
Argentina, Belize, Bolivia, Brazil, Colombia, Costa Rica, Cuba, Dominican Rep, Ecuador, El Salvador, Guatemala, Guyana, Haiti, Honduras, Mexico, Nicaragua, Panama, Peru, Uruguay, Venezuela.
NGO Relations Member of: *International AIDS Women's Caucus (IAWC, #11603).* Partner of: *Horizontal Technical Cooperation Group of Latin America and the Caribbean on HIV/AIDS (HTGC, #10945).*
[2014/XE2109/**E**]

♦ Latin American and Caribbean Council for Self-Management (inactive)

♦ Latin American and Caribbean Demographic Centre 16273

Centre latinoaméricain et de caraïbes de démographie – Centro Latinoamericano y Caribeño de Demografia (CELADE)

Contact c/o CEPAL, CELADE-Population Div, Casilla 179 D, Santiago, Santiago Metropolitan, Chile. T. +5622102002. Fax +5622080196.
URL: https://www.cepal.org/celade/proyecciones/basedatos_BD.htm/

History Aug 1957, Santiago (Chile), following technical assistance agreement between *United Nations (UN, #20515)* and the Government of Chile. From 1966 to 1974, functioned as a regional project financed by *UNDP (#20292)* and by governments which signed the corresponding Plan of Operations (Argentina, Chile, Colombia, Costa Rica and Venezuela). In May 1971, recognized as an autonomous organ under the aegis of the then Economic Commission for Latin America (ECLA), currently *United Nations Economic Commission for Latin America and the Caribbean (ECLAC, #20556).* Under ECLAC resolution 569 (XXVII), became the Population Division of ECLAC, whilst maintaining its original title. Previously also referred to as *Latin American Demographic Centre – Centro Latinoamericano de Demografía.* **Aims** Contribute to the socio-economic *development* of Latin America and the *Caribbean* in the field of *population* by assisting countries to increase their self-reliance and promote horizontal cooperation while providing services that can be furnished more effectively at the regional level; provide teaching, research, technical assistance and technical information services; analyse population growth and its interrelations with economic, social, environmental and political aspects of development; provide national institutions with the technical cooperation, training, services and technology required to utilize population information. **Structure** Headquarters in Santiago (Chile). **Languages** English, French, Portuguese, Spanish. **Staff** Centre: 8 international professionals; 7 local professionals; 5 administrative. **Finance** Sources: United Nations regular budget; *United Nations Population Fund (UNFPA, #20612).* Other donors: *Inter-American Development Bank (IDB, #11427); International Development Research Centre (IDRC, #13162); Pan American*

Health Organization (PAHO, #18108); *UNICEF (#20332)*; *Ibero-American General Secretariat (#11024)*; *Ibero-American Youth Organization (#11036)*; *Ford Foundation (#09858)*. **Activities** Executes ECLAC's population programs for Latin America and the Caribbean, involving promotion, organization and execution of: (a) training professionals in demographic analysis, interdisciplinary studies and specific techniques applied to the study of population; (b) research programme to broaden understanding of the demographic situation of the region, oriented towards formulation of government policies and plans; (c) technical assistance to develop national capacities in human resources, technology and institutional organization; (d) population documentation and technology for data processing, monitoring of population trends, keeping up-to-date a series of demographic indicators on inter-relations between population and development. These activities are organized into 3 interlinked sub-projects: integration of population variables in development planning; population information and technology for development; training in population and development. Sections (2): Population and Development; Demography and Population Information. Organizes workshops. **Events** *Workshop on Winredatam, Turgis application* Cayman Is 1996, *International seminar on socio-demographic information for public management* Montevideo (Uruguay) 1996, *Regional workshop on Winredatam* Santiago (Chile) 1996, *Workshop on the REDATAM system* San José (Costa Rica) 1987, *International symposium on aging* Santiago (Chile) 1987. **Publications** *Notas de Población* (2 a year); *Demographic Observatory* (2 a year); *Aging Bulletin* (annual); *REDATAM Bulletin* (annual). *Population and Development Series*. Books; monographs; conference papers. **Information Services** *Retrieval of Census Data for Small Areas by Microcomputer (REDATAM)*.

Members As for ECLAC, governments of 43 countries:
Antigua-Barbuda, Argentina, Bahamas, Barbados, Belize, Bolivia, Brazil, Canada, Chile, Colombia, Costa Rica, Cuba, Dominica, Dominican Rep, Ecuador, El Salvador, France, Germany, Grenada, Guatemala, Guyana, Haiti, Honduras, Italy, Jamaica, Japan, Mexico, Netherlands, Nicaragua, Panama, Paraguay, Peru, Portugal, Spain, St Kitts-Nevis, St Lucia, St Vincent-Grenadines, Suriname, Trinidad-Tobago, UK, Uruguay, USA, Venezuela.
Associate members (7):
Anguilla, Aruba, Montserrat, Puerto Rico, Virgin Is UK, Virgin Is USA.

NGO Relations International and regional organizations, especially: *International Planned Parenthood Federation (IPPF, #14589)*; *International Union for the Scientific Study of Population (IUSSP, #15814)*. Links also with: *Association of Economists of Latin America and the Caribbean (AELAC, #02480)*; *Centre Population et développement (Ceped)*. [2013/XD2867/E*]

♦ Latin American and Caribbean Economics Association (LACEA) . . . 16274

Asociación de Economia de Latinoamérica y el Caribe

Secretariat 1818 H Street, NW, MSN MC3-301, Washington DC 20433, USA. E-mail: lacea@lacea.org.
URL: http://www.lacea.org/

History Jul 1992. Former names and other names: *ADEALC* – former; *AEALC* – former. Registration: No/ID: 13-3999267, USA, New York State. **Aims** Encourage research and teaching related to the economies of Latin American and Caribbean countries; foster dialogue among researchers and practitioners whose work focuses on the economies of the region. **Structure** Executive Committee. **Languages** English, Portuguese, Spanish. **Staff** 2.00 FTE, paid; 15.00 FTE, voluntary. **Finance** Sources: contributions; donations; fundraising; grants; international organizations; members' dues; sale of publications. Annual budget: 300,000 USD. **Activities** Events/meetings; knowledge management/information dissemination; networking/liaising; projects/programmes; publishing activities. Active in all member countries. **Events** *Annual Meeting* Lima (Peru) 2022, *LAMES-LACEA Annual Meeting* Lima (Peru) 2022, *Annual Meeting* Bogota (Colombia) 2021, *Annual Meeting* Puebla (Mexico) 2019, *Annual Meeting* Guayaquil (Ecuador) 2018. **Publications** *Economia LACEA Journal* (2 a year) in English.

Members Full; Student; Institutional. Individuals in 26 countries:
Argentina, Brazil, Canada, Chile, Colombia, Costa Rica, Dominican Rep, Ecuador, El Salvador, France, Honduras, Italy, Jamaica, Japan, Korea Rep, Mexico, Netherlands, New Zealand, Peru, Puerto Rico, Spain, Sweden, Trinidad-Tobago, UK, USA, Venezuela.

NGO Relations Regional Network of: *Global Development Network (GDN, #10318)*. [2023.02.14/XD6396/D]

♦ Latin American and Caribbean Education Innovation Network (INNOVEMOS) 16275

Red de Innovaciones Educativas para América Latina y el Caribe – Rede de Innovações para a América Latina e o Caribe

Coordinator c/o UNESCO, Calle Enrique Delpiano 2058, Providencia, Santiago, Santiago Metropolitan, Chile. T. +5624724626. Fax +5626551046 – +5626551047.

History 2000, by *UNESCO Regional Bureau for Education in Latin America and the Caribbean (#20318)*, within *UNESCO (#20322)*. **Aims** Play a strategic role in educational *reform* in the region; contribute to improving *quality* and equity of education within different modalities and programmes and to changes in educational concepts and practices; guarantee quality, life-long learning for all, covering all levels of education for children, young people and adults but giving priority to broadened basic education. **Structure** Functions as a regional network of national networks, each country's network of schools, programmes, NGOs and ministries of education being coordinated by a university or research centre as "national coordinating institution". **Activities** Knowledge management/information dissemination.

Members Currently covers 13 countries:
Argentina, Bolivia, Chile, Colombia, Cuba, Dominican Rep, Ecuador, El Salvador, Mexico, Panama, Peru, Spain, Venezuela.
National coordinating institutions include 3 internationally-oriented national bodies listed in this Yearbook:
Centro de Estudios del Desarrollo, Caracas (CENDES); *Instituto Centroamericano de Administración y Supervisión de la Educación (ICASE, no recent information)*; *Universidad Iberoamericana, México (UIA)*. [2014/XK2336/y/E*]

- ♦ Latin American and Caribbean Federation of Bioethics Institutions (#09348)
- ♦ Latin American and Caribbean Federation of Exporters (inactive)
- ♦ Latin American and Caribbean Federation of Hotel, Gastronomy, Casino and Tourism Workers (inactive)
- ♦ Latin American and Caribbean Federation for Internet and Electronic Commerce (#09341)

♦ Latin American and Caribbean Federation of National Associations of Cargo 16276

Fédération latinoaméricaine et des Caraïbes des associations nationales de charge – Federación de Asociaciones Nacionales de Agentes de Carga de América Latina y del Caribe (ALACAT)

Secretariat Carrera 102A, no 25H-45 Of 106, Edif Centro Aéreo Int, Bogota, Bogota DC, Colombia. E-mail: secretario.ejecutivo@alacat.org – alacat@alacat.org.
Registered Address Zabala 1379, Of 405, 11000 Montevideo, Uruguay.
URL: http://www.alacat.org/

History 1982, Sao Paulo (Brazil), with the title *Latin American and Caribbean Association of Air Freight and Transport Agents – Asociación Latinoamericana y del Caribe de Agencias de Carga Aérea y Transporte*. Present name adopted 1986. **Aims** Promote and defend interests of *freight* forwarders in the region; organize national associations where there are none; obtain legal recognition for the *profession*; maintain educational institutes for members. **Structure** Executive Committee, comprising President, First Vice-President, Second Vice-President, Secretary, Treasurer, 4 Directors and one member. Permanent Secretariat. **Languages** Spanish. **Staff** 1.00 FTE, paid. 1 full-time paid. **Finance** Members' dues. Budget (annual): about US$ 7 million. **Activities** Educational studies include courses on dangerous goods. **Events** *Annual Congress* Punta Cana (Dominican Rep) 2020, *Annual Congress* Barcelona (Spain) 2019, *Annual Congress* Mexico City (Mexico) 2018, *Annual Congress* Panama (Panama) 2017, *Annual Congress* Barcelona (Spain) 2016. **Publications** *ALACAT News*.

Members National associations in 13 countries:
Argentina, Chile, Colombia, Costa Rica, Dominican Rep, Ecuador, Guatemala, Honduras, Mexico, Paraguay, Peru, Uruguay, Venezuela.
Affiliate members in 6 countries:
Canada, Italy, Portugal, Singapore, Spain, USA.
Included in the above, 2 organizations listed in this Yearbook:
Animal Transportation Association (ATA, #00844); *Federation of Asia Pacific Aircargo Associations (FAPAA, #09453)*.
Companies in 3 countries:
Argentina, Brazil, USA.

Consultative Status Consultative status granted from: *UNCTAD (#20285)* (Special Category). **IGO Relations** *Asociación Latinoamericana de Derecho Aeronautico y Espacial (ALADA, #02202)*; *Andean Community (#00817)*; *United Nations Economic Commission for Latin America and the Caribbean (ECLAC, #20556)*. **NGO Relations** *International Air Transport Association (IATA, #11614)*; *Fédération internationale des associations de transitaires et assimilés (FIATA, #09610)*. [2020/XD5151/D]

- ♦ Latin American and Caribbean Federation of Radiation Protection Societies (#09387)

♦ Latin American and Caribbean Feminist Network Against Domestic and Sexual Violence 16277

Red Feminista Latinoamericana y del Caribe contra la Violencia Doméstica y Sexual

Contact address not obtained. T. +5622695506.

History Aug 1992, Olinda (Brazil), at 1st meeting. Sometimes referred to in English simply as *Feminist Network Against Domestic and Sexual Violence* and in Spanish as *Red Feminista Latinoamericana y del Caribe por una vida sin violencia contra las mujeres*. **Aims** Raise awareness of *gender violence* and work for its eradication; strengthen the capability of action and proposal of member organizations. **Structure** Subregional sections (6): Andean; Brazil; Caribbean; Central America; Cono Sur; Mexico. **Finance** Source: international cooperation. **Activities** Information; publishing activity; periodical regional and subregional meetings; elaboration of legislative proposals and of international conventions and declarations in the field; participation in regional, continental and world forums. **Publications** *Boletin Red Feminista Latinoamericana y del Caribe contra la Violencia Doméstica y Sexual* (4 a year) in Spanish; *Hoja de Datos* in Spanish.

Members Covers 36 countries in the Latin American and the Caribbean Region:
Antigua-Barbuda, Argentina, Bahamas, Barbados, Belize, Bermuda, Bolivia, Brazil, Chile, Colombia, Costa Rica, Cuba, Dominica, Dominican Rep, Ecuador, El Salvador, Grenada, Guatemala, Guyana, Haiti, Honduras, Jamaica, Mexico, Neth Antilles, Nicaragua, Panama, Paraguay, Peru, Puerto Rico, St Kitts-Nevis, St Lucia, St Vincent-Grenadines, Suriname, Trinidad-Tobago, Uruguay, Venezuela. [2011/XF2898/F]

♦ Latin American and Caribbean Forestry Commission (LACFC) 16278

Commission des forêts pour l'Amérique latine et les Caraïbes – Comisión Forestal para America Latina y del Caribe (COFLAC)

Head Office FAO Regional Office Latin America and Caribbean, Av Dag Hammarskjöld 3241, Vitacura, Santiago, Santiago Metropolitan, Chile. T. +56229232100. Fax +56229232101.
URL: http://www.rlc.fao.org/es/agenda/27-reunion-de-la-coflac/

History Apr 1948, within the framework of *FAO (#09260)*, by Article VI-1 of the FAO Constitution, as *Latin American Forestry Commission*. Previously also referred to as *Commission des forêts pour l'Amérique latine – Comisión Forestal Latinoamericana (COFLA)* and *Comisión Forestal Latinoamericana y del Caribe*. Based at *FAO Regional Office for Latin America and the Caribbean (FAO/RLC, #09268)*. **Aims** Advise on formulation of forestry policy; review and coordinate its implementation at a regional level; exchange information and advise on suitable practices and action in regard to technical forestry problems. **Structure** Executive Committee, consisting of Chairman and 4 Vice-Chairmen of the Commission. **Languages** English, French, Spanish. **Finance** FAO regular programme fund; contribution of event hosting country. **Events** *Session* Asunción (Paraguay) 2012, *Session* Guatemala 2010, *Session* Quito (Ecuador) 2008, *Session* Santo Domingo (Dominican Rep) 2006, *Session* San José (Costa Rica) 2004.

Members Open to FAO member nations and associate members whose territories are situated wholly or partly in Latin America and the Caribbean or who are responsible for the international relations of any non-self-governing territory in that region, and who desire to be considered members. Current members governments of 31 countries:
Argentina, Barbados, Belize, Bolivia, Brazil, Chile, Colombia, Costa Rica, Cuba, Dominican Rep, Ecuador, El Salvador, France, Guatemala, Guyana, Haiti, Honduras, Jamaica, Mexico, Netherlands, Nicaragua, Panama, Paraguay, Peru, St Kitts-Nevis, Suriname, Trinidad-Tobago, UK, Uruguay, USA, Venezuela.
Observer government of 1 country:
Canada.

NGO Relations Links with many NGOs in the region. [2019.11.22/XE1755/E*]

- ♦ Latin American and Caribbean Institute of Auditing Sciences / see Organization of Latin American and Caribbean Supreme Audit Institutions (#17877)

♦ Latin American and Caribbean Institute for Economic and Social Planning 16279

Institut latinoaméricain et des Caraïbes de planification économique et sociale – Instituto Latinoamericano y del Caribe de Planificación Económica y Social (ILPES)

Dir Edificio ONU, Avda Dag Hammarskjöld 3477, Vitacura, 179-D Santiago, Santiago Metropolitan, Chile. T. +56222102507. E-mail: sigca@cepal.org.
URL: http://www.cepal.org/en/acerca-del-ilpes

History 11 Jun 1962. Established by virtue of Resolution adopted 6-7 Jun 1962, New York NY (USA), by meetings of the 'Committee of the Whole' of the then United Nations Economic Commission for Latin America (ECLA), currently *United Nations Economic Commission for Latin America and the Caribbean (ECLAC, #20556)*; endorsed by *ECOSOC (#05331)*, Apr 1962. ECLA Resolution 340 (AC66), Jan 1974, New York NY, includes ILPES as a permanent institution within ECLA (now ECLAC). Former names and other names: *Latin American Institute for Economic and Social Planning* – former (11 Jun 1962); *Instituto Latinoamericano de Planificación Económica y Social (ILPES)* – former (11 Jun 1962). **Aims** Cooperate in national modernization processes by strengthening basic planning and strategic public-management functions, by systematizing and disseminating experience in public administration and by providing human resource training for essential workers in national administrations. **Structure** *Consejo Regional de Planificación (CRP, #04725)* (meeting every 4 years), is the guiding body and comprises ministers or heads of national planning bodies of 39 governments of the Latin American and Caribbean region and of Spain. Presiding Officers of the Regional Council for Planning (MD/CRP), meeting more frequently, comprises 10 members elected by CRP plus a representative of the host country (Chile). *Conference of Ministers and Heads of Planning of Latin America and the Caribbean (see: #16279)*, established by member governments, exchanges experience and research results on planning and coordination of public policy. **Languages** English, French, Portuguese, Spanish. **Finance** Regular system of contributions by governments; United Nations regular budget; contributions from international institutions, mainly for specific projects; contributions from non-member governments (such as France and Italy). **Activities** Work is guided by CRP, MD/CRP and the Conference of Ministers and Heads of Planning, and through regular contact with national planning authorities. Work programme priorities: (a) building of strategic visions to strengthen the institutional structure of planning as a tool for government; (b) programming and evaluation of public-sector activities, including macro-fiscal rules, multi-year fiscal planning, management and banks of public investment projects and international cooperation, and follow-up and evaluation of public management; (c) processes of decentralization and planning and management of local and regional development, with emphasis on fiscal decentralization and territorial competitiveness. Also acts as central training body of ECLAC. *REDILPES (see: #16279)* seeks to provide a network for exchange of experience and permanent updating of knowledge in the strategic management of the state and basic functions of planning. **Events** *Conference of Ministers and Heads of Planning of Latin America and the Caribbean* Brasilia (Brazil) 2007, *Conference of Ministers and Heads of Planning of Latin America and the Caribbean* Madrid (Spain) 2002, *Conference of Ministers and Heads of Planning of Latin America and the Caribbean* Chile 1998, *Conference of ministers and heads of planning of Latin America and the Caribbean* Santiago (Chile) 1998, *Conference of ministers and heads of planning of Latin America and the Caribbean* Mexico City (Mexico) 1994. **Publications** *Boletin del Instituto – ILPES Bulletin* (2 a year) in English, Spanish. *Panorama de la gestión Pública* – series; *Serie Conferencias y Seminarios*; *Serie Gestión Pública*; *Serie Manuales*. Textbooks; reports; manuals; papers.

Members Governments of 40 countries and territories:
Antigua-Barbuda, Argentina, Aruba, Bahamas, Barbados, Belize, Bolivia, Brazil, Chile, Colombia, Costa Rica, Cuba, Dominica, Dominican Rep, Ecuador, El Salvador, Grenada, Guatemala, Guyana, Haiti, Honduras, Jamaica, Mexico, Montserrat, Neth Antilles, Nicaragua, Panama, Paraguay, Peru, Puerto Rico, Spain, St Kitts-Nevis, St Lucia, St Vincent-Grenadines, Suriname, Trinidad-Tobago, Uruguay, Venezuela, Virgin Is UK, Virgin Is USA.

IGO Relations Relationship agreement with: *UNIDO (#20336)*. [2018/XD2881/j/E*]

♦ Latin American and Caribbean International Movers Association (LACMA) 16280

Asociación Latinoamericana y del Caribe de Mudanzas Internacionales

Mailing Address PO Box 0819-07566, El Dorado, Panama, Panamá, Panama PANAMá, Panama. E-mail: lacma@lacmassoc.org.

URL: http://www.lacmassoc.org/

History 9 Feb 1969, Lima (Peru). **Aims** Unify *enterprises* involved in moving and *packing* in Latin America and the Caribbean; contribute to members' *commercial* development through cooperation, advice, collaboration, technical and economic assistance; propose, establish and maintain norms. **Structure** General Assembly (annual); Board of Directors of 6 members; Permanent Secretariat. **Languages** English, Spanish. **Staff** 5.00 FTE, paid. **Finance** Members' dues. Journal subscriptions. **Activities** Training/education; events/meetings; networking/liaising; humanitarian/emergency aid. **Events** *Annual General Assembly and Convention* Miami, FL (USA) 2022, *Annual General Assembly and Convention* Panama (Panama) 2019, *Annual General Assembly and Convention* Puerto Vallarta (Mexico) 2017, *Annual General Assembly and Convention* Bogota (Colombia) 2016, *Annual General Assembly and Convention* Punta del Este (Uruguay) 2015. **Publications** *LACMA Newsletter* (12 a year); *LACMA News* (4 a year) in English, Spanish; *Yearbook* (annual) – membership directory.

Members Active: Latin American and Caribbean companies, in 24 countries and territories:
Argentina, Bahamas, Bolivia, Brazil, Chile, Colombia, Costa Rica, Curaçao, Dominican Rep, Ecuador, El Salvador, Guatemala, Honduras, Jamaica, Mexico, Nicaragua, Panama, Paraguay, Peru, Puerto Rico, Trinidad-Tobago, Uruguay, Venezuela, Virgin Is USA.

Associate: Companies outside the region, in 37 countries and territories:
Australia, Austria, Bangladesh, Belgium, Canada, China, Denmark, Egypt, England, Finland, France, Germany, Ghana, Greece, Hong Kong, India, Italy, Japan, Jordan, Lebanon, Malaysia, Morocco, Netherlands, Nigeria, Norway, Poland, Portugal, Russia, Singapore, South Africa, Spain, Switzerland, Taiwan, Thailand, Tunisia, United Arab Emirates, USA. [2021/XD6585/**D**]

♦ Latin American and Caribbean Internet Address Registry (LACNIC) . 16281

Exec Dir Rambla República de México 6125, 11400 Montevideo, Uruguay. E-mail: comunicaciones@lacnic.net.

Social Media Editor address not obtained.

URL: http://www.lacnic.net/

History 2002, Montevideo (Uruguay). **Aims** Contribute to internet development in the region. **Structure** General Assembly (annual); Board of Directors; Commissions (2); Committees (5). **Languages** English, Portuguese, Spanish. **Staff** 55.00 FTE, paid. **Finance** Members' dues. **Activities** Events/meetings. **Events** *Meeting* Foz do Iguaçu (Brazil) 2017, *Meeting* Montevideo (Uruguay) 2017, *Meeting* Cancún (Mexico) 2014, *Meeting* Santiago (Chile) 2014, *Meeting* Willemstad (Curaçao) 2013. **Publications** *LACNIC News* (12 a year). Annual Report. **NGO Relations** Member of: *Internet Society (ISOC, #15952)*; *Number Resource Organization (NRO, #17625)*. Cooperates with: *Latin American and Caribbean Network Operators Group (LACNOG)*. [2017.06.01/XM2953/**D**]

- ♦ Latin American and Caribbean Law and Economics Association / see Latin American and Iberian Law and Economics Association (#16340)
- ♦ Latin American and Caribbean Leadership Network for Nuclear Disarmament and Nonproliferation (unconfirmed)
- ♦ Latin American and Caribbean Medical Confederation (#04463)
- ♦ Latin American and Caribbean Network Against Sexual Exploitation / see Coalition Against Trafficking in Women – Latin America (#04048)
- ♦ Latin American and Caribbean Network for the Conservation of Bats (#18703)
- ♦ Latin-American and Caribbean Network to Defend the Rights of Children and Adolescents (#18705)
- ♦ Latin American and Caribbean Network for Democracy (#18704)
- ♦ Latin American and Caribbean Network of Environmental Funds (#18656)
- ♦ Latin American and the Caribbean Network for Monitoring, Evaluation and Systematization (unconfirmed)
- ♦ Latin American and Caribbean Network Operators Group (unconfirmed)

♦ Latin American and Caribbean Network of Small Fairtrade Producers 16282

Coordinadora Latinoamericana y del Caribe de Pequeños Productores de Comercio Justo (CLAC)

Contact Av El Boquerón, Calle Ayagualo M-1A, Ciudad Merliot, Santa Tecla, La Libertad, El Salvador. T. +50322784635. E-mail: info@clac-comerciojusto.org.

URL: http://www.clac-comerciojusto.org/

History Aug 2004. **Aims** Represent organizations of small producers and workers who are democratically organized. **Structure** General Assembly; Board of Directors. **Publications** *CLAC Newsletter*.

Members Networks (over 800) in 25 countries and territories:
Argentina, Belarus, Bolivia, Brazil, Chile, Colombia, Costa Rica, Cuba, Dominican Rep, Ecuador, El Salvador, Grenadines, Guatemala, Guyana, Haiti, Honduras, Jamaica, Mexico, Nicaragua, Panama, Paraguay, Peru, St Lucia, St Vincent-Grenadines, Uruguay.

NGO Relations Regional member of: *Fairtrade International (FLO, #09240)*. Member of: *Intercontinental Network for the Promotion of the Social Solidarity Economy (INPSSE, #11463)*; *World Fair Trade Organization (WFTO, #21396)*. [2020/XM3278/t/**F**]

♦ Latin American and Caribbean Network for Social Ecology 16283

Red Americana y Caribeña de Ecologia Social (RedLACES)

Mailing Address c/o CLAES, Magallanes 1334, Casilla de Correo 13125, 11700 Montevideo, Uruguay. T. +59824030854. E-mail: claes@adinet.com.uy.

URL: http://www.ecologiasocial.com/

History 1989. Founded within the framework of *Latin American Center of Social Ecology (#16292)* which acts as coordinator. Former names and other names: *Latin American Network for Social Ecology (RedLAES)* – former. **Aims** Stress South-South communication in the region; strengthen Latin American NGOs as tools for the expression of local communities; recover an integrated perspective of human-human and human-environment relationships. **Structure** Annual Meeting; Latin American and Caribbean Council in which different regions are represented. **Languages** English, Portuguese, Spanish. **Staff** 14.00 FTE, paid. **Activities** Knowledge management/information dissemination; training/education. **Events** *Meeting* Montevideo (Uruguay) 1995, *Meeting* Montevideo (Uruguay) 1994, *Meeting* Rio de Janeiro (Brazil) 1992, *Meeting* Rosario (Argentina) 1991, *Meeting* Buenos Aires (Argentina) 1990. **Publications** *Teko-ha* (4 a year) – bulletin; *Studies on Social Ecology* (irregular) – monographs; *TEMAS CLAVE* (irregular). Books.

Members Full and subscribers (52) in 17 countries:
Argentina, Bolivia, Brazil, Chile, Colombia, Costa Rica, Dominican Rep, Ecuador, El Salvador, Honduras, Mexico, Nicaragua, Panama, Paraguay, Peru, Puerto Rico, Uruguay.

NGO Relations *Consejo de Educación de Adultos de América Latina (CEAAL, #04707)*. [2020/XF1538/**F**]

- ♦ Latin American and Caribbean Network of University Continuing Education / see Red Universitaria de Educación Continua de Latinoamérica y Europa (#18734)
- ♦ Latin American and the Caribbean Open Science Forum (meeting series)

♦ Latin American and Caribbean Research Network 16284

Coordinator IDB Research Dept, 1300 New York Ave NW, Washington DC 20577, USA. T. +12026231000. Fax +12026232481. E-mail: red@iadb.org.

URL: https://www.iadb.org/en/research-and-data/latin-american-and-caribbean-research-network

History 1991, as *Regional Research Network (RRN)*, by *Inter-American Development Bank (IDB, #11427)*. Later known as *Latin American Research Network*. Sixth phase funded in 2007. **Aims** Assist in study of the main economic and social problems in Latin America and the Caribbean through non-reimbursable technical cooperation *funding* to strengthen *policy* formulation and inform the institutional reform agenda in the region. **Activities** Financial and/or material support.

Members Open to institutions located in any IDB borrowing member country in Latin American / Caribbean. Institutions (over 300) in 28 participating countries:
Argentina, Bahamas, Barbados, Belize, Bolivia, Brazil, Canada, Chile, Colombia, Costa Rica, Dominican Rep, Ecuador, El Salvador, Guatemala, Guyana, Haiti, Honduras, Jamaica, Mexico, Nicaragua, Panama, Paraguay, Peru, Suriname, Trinidad-Tobago, Uruguay, USA, Venezuela.

Included in the above, 21 organizations listed in this Yearbook:
- *Academia de Centroamérica, San José*;
- *Caribbean Centre for Money and Finance (#03469)*;
- *Center for Andean Regional Studies 'Bartolomé de Las Casas' (#03636)*;
- *Center for the Study of State and Society, Buenos Aires (CEDES)*;
- *Centro de Estudios Internacionales, Bogota (CEI, no recent information)*;
- *Centro de Investigación Economica para el Caribe (CIECA)*;
- *Centro Internacional de Politica Económica para el Desarrollo Sostenible (CINPE)*;
- *Centro Latinoamericano de Estudios sobre Violencia y Salud 'Jorge Careli' (CLAVES)*;
- *Centro Latinoamericano para la Competitividad y el Desarrollo Sostenible (CLACDS)*;
- *Corporación de Investigaciones Económicas para Latinoamérica (CIEPLAN, no recent information)*;
- *Fundación Centroamericana para el Desarrollo Humano (FUMANITAS, no recent information)*;
- *Fundación Centroamericana para el Desarrollo Sostenible (FUCAD, no recent information)*;
- *Fundación de Investigaciones Económicas Latinoamericanas (FIEL)*;
- *Fundación Internacional para el Desafio Económico y Global (FIDEG, #10029)*;
- *Instituto Latinoamericano de Doctrinas y Estudios Sociales (ILADES, #11345)*;
- *Instituto Latinoamericano de Investigaciones Sociales (ILDIS, #11346)*;
- *Latin American Faculty of Social Sciences (#16316)*;
- *Secretaria Permanente del Tratado General de Integración Económica Centroamericana (SIECA, #19195)*;
- *United Nations Economic Commission for Latin America and the Caribbean (ECLAC, #20556)*;
- *Universidad CLAEH (#20688)*;
- *University of the West Indies (UWI, #20705)*.

IGO Relations *United Nations Commission on the Status of Women (CSW, #20536)*. [2022/XF2829/y/**F***]

♦ Latin American and Caribbean Seismological Commission (LACSC) 16285

Exec Sec Inst Astronomy Geophysics, Atmospheric Sciences, Univ of Sao Paulo, Sao Paulo SP, 05508-090, Brazil.

URL: http://www.iaspei.org/commissions/LACSC.html

History Proposed Sep 2012, Lima (Peru). Formally approved as a *International Association of Seismology and Physics of the Earth's Interior (IASPEI, #12157)* Commission, Jul 2013, Gothenburg (Sweden). **Aims** Promote the science of seismology in Latin America and Caribbean by encouraging research studies, extending and enhancing scientific cooperation and facilitating training of young scientists. **Structure** Assembly. Council, consisting of country representatives. Executive Committee, comprising President, Vice-President, Executive Secretary and 2 members. **Events** *Assembly* San José (Costa Rica) 2016, *Assembly* Bogota (Colombia) 2014.

Members Full in 11 countries:
Argentina, Bolivia, Brazil, Colombia, Costa Rica, Ecuador, Mexico, Paraguay, Peru, Trinidad-Tobago, Venezuela. [2013/XJ7421/**E**]

- ♦ Latin American and Caribbean Society for Environmental History (#19396)

♦ Latin-American and Caribbean Society of Medical Oncology 16286

Sociedad Latinoamericana y del Caribe de Oncologia Médica (SLACOM)

Contact Av Córdoba 2415 – 5th floor, C1120AAG Buenos Aires, Argentina. T. +541149610981. Fax +541149640504. E-mail: secretaria@slacom.org – consultas@slacom.org.

URL: http://www.slacom.org/

History 11 Aug 2003. Full title: *Sociedad Latinoamericana y del Caribe de Oncologia Médica – SLACOM Asociación Civil*. Registered in accordance with the law of Argentina. **Aims** Improve cancer care and prevention in Latin America and the Caribbean. **Structure** General Assembly; Board of Directors; Executive Committee. **Finance** Members' dues. Other sources: income from registration fees; pharmaceutical sponsorship; grants from NGOs. **Activities** Training/education; events/meetings. **Events** *Latin American Medical Education Workshop on Molecular Targeted Therapy of Cancer* Sao Paulo (Brazil) 2013, *Congress* Buenos Aires (Argentina) 2005. **Members** Full (over 900); Associate; Active Allied; Honorary; Emeritus. Membership countries not specified. **NGO Relations** Member of: *The NCD Alliance (NCDA, #16963)*; *Union for International Cancer Control (UICC, #20415)*. Participates in: *Breast Health Global Initiative (BHGI, #03318)*. [2016.06.27/XJ3564/**D**]

- ♦ Latin American and Caribbean Studies Institute (internationally oriented national body)
- ♦ Latin American and Caribbean Studies Network on Asia-Pacific (internationally oriented national body)

♦ Latin American and Caribbean Top Level Domains (LACTLD) 16287

Contact Rbla Rep de México 6125, CP 11400, Montevideo, Uruguay. E-mail: contacto@lactld.org.

URL: http://www.lactld.org/

History 20 Aug 1998, Buenos Aires (Argentina). **Aims** Represent the interests and promote development of ccTLDs in Latin America and the Caribbean. **Structure** General Assembly (annual). **Languages** English, Portuguese, Spanish. **Staff** 3.00 FTE, paid. **Events** *General Assembly* Punta Cana (Dominican Rep) 2019, *General Assembly* Panama (Panama) 2018. **Publications** *LACTLD Report* (irregular). **Members** Associates (26); Affiliates (6); Observers (11). Membership countries not specified. **NGO Relations** *International Governance Forum Support Association (IGFSA, #13730)*; *Internet Corporation for Assigned Names and Numbers (ICANN, #15949)*; *Latin American and Caribbean Internet Address Registry (LACNIC, #16281)*. [2018.06.01/XM0285/**F**]

- ♦ Latin American and Caribbean Water Supply and Sewerage Undertakings Association (no recent information)

♦ Latin American and Caribbean Women's Health Network (LACWHN) 16288

Réseau sanitaire pour les femmes d'Amérique latine et de Caraïbes – Red de Salud de las Mujeres Latinoamericanas y del Caribe (RSMLAC)

General Coordinator address not obtained. E-mail: scastaneda@reddesalud.org – secretaria@reddesalud.org.

URL: http://www.reddesalud.org/

History May 1984, Tenza (Colombia). Founded at 1st Regional Women and Health Meeting, at the request of 60 participating groups. **Aims** Promote health, the full exercise of women's civil and human rights and women's citizenship through the cultural, political and social transformation of our region and the world from a feminist perspective; develop and strengthen the Networks capacity to generate information and promote circulation of this knowledge; contribute to the improved epidemiological diagnosis of women's comprehensive health in Latin America and the Caribbean; develop and strengthen the Network as a political reference point within the women's health mouvement and the wider society in order to influence national and international public policies and to monitor these processes as part of civil society; develop and strengthen links among Latin American and Caribbean women's health organizations and publicize their experiences. **Structure** Assembly of Active Members; Board of Directors; Advisory Council; NationalLiaisons; General Coordination; Technical Team. **Languages** English, Spanish. **Staff** 8.00 FTE, paid; 23.00 FTE, voluntary. **Activities** Advocacy/lobbying/activism; events/meetings; monitoring/evaluation; projects/programmes; training/education. **Publications** *Women's Health Journal* (4 a year) in English; *Cuadernos Mujer Salud* (annual) in Spanish; *Revista Mujer Salud* (annual) in Spanish; *Women's Health Collection* (annual) in English. Brochures. Information Services: Databases on LACWHN's member groups and individuals, containing information on their research and activities.

Members Participating groups, institutions and individuals (about 2,500) in 56 countries:
Argentina, Australia, Bahamas, Bangladesh, Barbados, Belize, Bermuda, Bolivia, Brazil, Canada, Chile, China, Colombia, Costa Rica, Cuba, Dominica, Dominican Rep, Ecuador, Egypt, El Salvador, Fiji, France, Germany, Ghana, Greece, Grenada, Guatemala, Haiti, Honduras, India, Israel, Italy, Jamaica, Japan, Kenya, Malaysia, Mexico, Netherlands, New Zealand, Nicaragua, Nigeria, Pakistan, Panama, Paraguay, Peru, Philippines, Puerto Rico, Senegal, Spain, St Kitts-Nevis, Sweden, Switzerland, Trinidad-Tobago, Uruguay, USA, Venezuela.

IGO Relations Official links with: *Pan American Health Organization (PAHO, #18108)*. **NGO Relations** Member of (4): *Association for Women's Rights in Development (AWID, #02980)*; *Latin American and Caribbean Youth Network for Sexual and Reproductive Health and Rights (REDLAC, #16289)*; *Latin American Consortium on Emergency Contraception (LACEC, #16306)*; *Reproductive Health Supplies Coalition (RHSC, #18847)*. Partner of (1): *Global Coalition on Women and AIDS (GCWA, #10297)*. [2022.02.08/XF0881/**F**]

♦ Latin American and Caribbean Youth Network for Sexual and Reproductive Health and Rights (REDLAC) 16289

Red Latinoamericana y Caribeña de Jóvenes por los Derechos Sexuales y Reproductivos

Coordinator Parana 135 Piso 3-13, 1017 Buenos Aires, Argentina. T. +541143722763. Fax +541143722763. E-mail: redlac.dsdr@gmail.com.
URL: http://www.jovenesredlac.org/
History 1999. **Aims** Promote youth empowerment for the recognition and full exercise of the sexual and reproductive rights. **Structure** General Assembly (annual).
Members Organizations (16) in 14 countries:
Argentina, Bolivia, Brazil, Colombia, Costa Rica, Dominican Rep, Ecuador, El Salvador, Guatemala, Mexico, Nicaragua, Panama, Peru, Uruguay.
Included in the above, 1 organization listed in this Yearbook:
Latin American and Caribbean Women's Health Network (LACWHN, #16288).
NGO Relations Member of: *Espacio Iberoamericano de Juventud (EIJ, no recent information); Latin American Consortium on Emergency Contraception (LACEC, #16306).* [2010/XM0740/**F**]

♦ Latin American Center, Albuquerque / see Latin American and Iberian Institute, Albuquerque
♦ Latin American Center of Educational Technology for Health (inactive)
♦ Latin American Center for European Relations (internationally oriented national body)
♦ Latin American Center for Graduate Study of Music, Washington DC (internationally oriented national body)
♦ Latin American Center for Perinatology and Human Development / see Latin American Center for Perinatology/Unit of Woman and Reproductive Health (#16290)

♦ Latin American Center for Perinatology/Unit of Woman and Reproductive Health (CLAP/WR) 16290

Centro Latinoamericano de Perinatologia/Unidad de Salud de la Mujer y Reproductiva (CLAP/SMR)
Dir Avenue Brasil 2697 Ap 4, CP 11300 Montevideo, Uruguay. T. +59824872929. Fax +59824872929.
Street Address Hospital de Clinicas, Piso 16, Avenida Italia s/n, Montevideo, Uruguay.
URL: http://www.paho.org/clap/
History in 1970, by *Pan American Health Organization (PAHO, #18108)*, as *Latin American Center for Perinatology and Human Development – Centro Latinoamericano de Perinatologia y Desarrollo Humano (CLAP)*. Reorganized under current title on merger, in 2005. **Aims** Promote a gender, family and community perspective, using evidence based cost effective interventions, to strengthen the integral care addressed to women, *mothers* and neonatal health needs, throughout their life cycle; support countries to improve development and implementation of maternal-perinatal and *neonatal* health programs; promote the improvement of sexual and reproductive health and the sexual and reproductive rights of women and men; develop and promote strategies and interventions so as to diminish maternal-perinatal mortality; provide *epidemiological* surveillance, development and dissemination of best practices in health care, clinical and epidemiological research of health services and health professional training on health information managing and evidence based clinical practice. **Publications** *Salud Perinatal* (periodical). **Members** Western Hemisphere member countries of PAHO. Membership countries not specified. [2021/XE9292/**E***]

♦ Latin American Center for Research in the Social Sciences (inactive)

♦ Latin American Center for Service Learning 16291

Centro Latinoamericano de Aprendizaje y Servicio Solidario (CLAYSS)
Dir Yapeyu 283, C1202ACD Buenos Aires, Argentina. T. +541149815122. Fax +541149815122. E-mail: info@clayss.org.
Pres address not obtained.
URL: http://www.clayss.org.ar/
History Founded 26 Feb 2002, Buenos Aires (Argentina). **Aims** Contribute to the growth of a fraternal and participative culture in Latin America through development of educational social engagement projects. **Structure** Board of Directors. **Languages** English, Italian, Portuguese, Spanish. **Finance** Funded through support of private donors, both institutional and individual. Annual budget (2016): euro 661,600. **Activities** Financial and/or material support; training/education; guidance/assistance/consulting; research/documentation; networking/liaising; publishing activities; events/meetings. **IGO Relations** *OAS (#17629); Organization of Ibero-American States for Education, Science and Culture (#17871).* **NGO Relations** Member of: *Union de Responsabilidad Social Universitaria de Latinoamérica (URSULA, #20476).* [2017.11.07/XM3800/**F**]

♦ Latin American Center on Sexuality and Human Rights (#03814)

♦ Latin American Center of Social Ecology 16292

Centre latinoaméricain d'écologie sociale – Centro Latinoamericano de Ecologia Social (CLAES)
Exec Sec Magallanes 1334, 11200 Montevideo, Uruguay. T. +5982402. E-mail: claesd3e@gmail.com – claes@adinet.com.uy.
URL: http://www.ambiental.net/claes/
History Mar 1989, Montevideo (Uruguay). Founded as an outgrowth of *Latin American Group on Social Ecology*. **Aims** Promote activities in social *ecology*; study relationships of humans with their *environment*, integrating *biological* and *sociological* dimensions. **Structure** Latin American Council; Executive Board. **Languages** English, Portuguese, Spanish. **Staff** 6.00 FTE, paid. **Finance** Funds from national and international funding agencies. **Activities** Research and promotion programmes (currently 4): *'Participative Research'* developing participative procedures and practice with people in the outskirts of cities; *'Environment and Development'* with particular emphasis on environment and trade – *Southern Common Market (#19868)*; *'Dissemination and Training'* from the social ecology viewpoint (workshops, mail consultancies, data base); *Sustainable Development at the Local Level* with municipalities. Coordinates *Latin American and Caribbean Network for Social Ecology (#16283)* and *Uruguayan Forum on Sustainable Development*. **Events** *General Assembly* Borås (Sweden) 2006, *General Assembly* Bilbao (Spain) 2005, *Simposio de recursos geneticos para América latina y el caribe* Montevideo (Uruguay) 2005, *General Assembly* Lisbon (Portugal) 2004, *Social ecology, environment and development, environmental ethics, etc* Buenos Aires (Argentina) 1990. **Publications** *Cuadernos Latinoamericanos de Ecologia Social* (occasional) – journal; *Environment and Trade in Latin America* – bulletin; *Teko-ha* – newsletter. *Key Issues* – series. *Ecologia, Mercado y Desarollo* by Eduardo Gudynas; *La Praxis por la Vida* by Eduardo Gudynas and Graciela Evia; *Studies on Social Ecology* – monographs; *Vendiendo la Naturaleza, Impactos Ambiental del Comercio Internacional* by Eduardo Gudynas. Information Services: Information bank. **Information Services** *Bibliographic Database on Social Ecology (SIES).*
Members Represented in 16 countries:
Argentina, Bolivia, Brazil, Chile, Colombia, Costa Rica, Dominican Rep, Ecuador, El Salvador, Honduras, Mexico, Nicaragua, Paraguay, Peru, Puerto Rico, Uruguay.
IGO Relations *UNEP (#20299).* **NGO Relations** Member of: *Alliance for Zero Extinction (AZE, #00730); Climate Justice Now ! (CJN!, inactive); EarthAction (EA, #05159); International Confederation of Associations for Pluralism in Economics (ICAPE, #12849); Latin American Network on Environmental Conflicts (no recent information).* [1997.10.10/XD2123/**E**]

♦ Latin American Center for Studies in Informatics 16293

Centre latinoaméricain d'études en informatique – Centro Latinoamericano de Estudios en Informatica (CLEI)
Exec Sec Univ Nacional del Sur, Complejo Av Alem 1253 – 1 piso, 8000 Bahia Blanca, Argentina. T. +54914595100 – +54914595101.
URL: http://www.clei.cl/
History 2 Feb 1979, Valparaiso (Chile), conferences having been held since 1974. **Aims** Develop informatics in the Latin American region; promote exchanges among specialists leading to *technology transfer*. **Structure** Executive Committee, comprising President, Executive Secretary and Treasurer. Other officers: Past President; Honorary Member; Country Representatives. **Finance** Support from *UNESCO (#20322)* for Master Thesis competition. **Activities** Organizes annual Conference; until 1993 called *'PANEL-EXPODATA'*, from 1994 to 1997 called *'CLEI-PANEL'*, subsequently called *'CLEI'* from 1998 onwards. Runs Master Thesis competition. **Events** *Conference* Montevideo (Uruguay) 2014, *Conference* Naiguata (Venezuela) 2013, *Conference* Medellin (Colombia) 2012, *Conference* San José (Costa Rica) 2007, *Latin America networking conference* San José (Costa Rica) 2007. **Publications** *Boletin CLEI* (4 a year); *CLEI Electronic Journal* – online. Conference proceedings.
Members Academic institutions in relation with informatics; professional societies of informatics. Members (over 50) in 12 countries:
Argentina, Bolivia, Brazil, Chile, Colombia, Costa Rica, Ecuador, Mexico, Paraguay, Peru, Uruguay, Venezuela.
Extra-regional members in 2 countries:
Spain, USA. [2014/XE8929/**E**]

♦ Latin American Center for Theater Creation and Research (#03811)
♦ Latin American Central of Workers (inactive)

♦ Latin American Centre for Development Administration 16294

Centre latinoaméricain d'administration pour le développement – Centro Latinoamericano de Administración para el Desarrollo (CLAD)
SG Apartado Postal 4181, Caracas 1010 DF, Venezuela. T. +582122709211. Fax +582122709214. E-mail: clad@clad.org – cedai@clad.org.
Street address Av Principal de Los Chorros con Av 6, Casa CLAD, Urb Los Chorros, Municipio Sucre, Caracas 1071 DF, Venezuela.
URL: https://clad.org/
History 30 Jun 1972, Caracas (Venezuela). Established by Latin American and Caribbean governments, following recommendations of Resolution 2802 (XXVI) of the General Assembly of *United Nations (UN, #20515)* and and 15th Biennial Meeting of *United Nations Economic Commission for Latin America and the Caribbean (ECLAC, #20556).* **Aims** Integrate efforts towards updating and developing public administration systems; provide a forum for exchange of knowledge and experience; undertake and promote research and training; systematically disseminate information. **Structure** Directive Council; Programming and Evaluation Commission; Board of Directors; Scientific Council; General Secretariat located in Caracas (Venezuela). Maintains: Escuela Iberoamericana de Administración y Politicas Públicas (EIAPP); *Network of Institutions for the Fight Against Corruption and the Recovery of Public Ethics (RICOREP, see: #16294); Post-Graduate Network in Administration and Public Policy (REDAPP, see: #16294); Red de Escuelas e Institutos Gubernamentales en Asuntos Públicos (REIGAP, see: #16294).* **Languages** English, Portuguese, Spanish. **Staff** 16.00 FTE, paid. **Finance** Sources: members' dues. **Activities** Events/meetings; guidance/assistance/consulting; knowledge management/information dissemination; networking/liaising; publishing activities; research/documentation; training/education. Institutional activity currently focused on: social policy and management; decentralization; modernization of Presidency of the Republic-heads of government. **Events** *International Congress – Reforma del Estado y de la Administración Pública* Bolivia 2022, *International Congress* Bogota (Colombia) 2021, *International Congress – Reforma del Estado y de la Administración Pública* Lisbon (Portugal) 2020, *Annual International Congress* Buenos Aires (Argentina) 2019, *Annual World Government Summit* Dubai (United Arab Emirates) 2019. **Publications** *Revista del CLAD – Reforma y Democracia* (3 a year). *Documentos Clave* – series; *Documentos Debate* – series; *Documentos Reuniones Internacionales* – series; *Estudios de Casos* – series. Books. Information Services: *Red Latinoamericana de Documentación e Información en Administración Pública (REDIAP, see: #16294)* – assists exchange of documents and data among Spanish-speaking member countries which have previously received training and technical assistance. **Information Services** *Documentation and Analysis Information Centre – Centro de Documentación y Análisis de Información (CEDAI); Integrated and Analytical Information System on State Reform, Management and Public Policies – Sistema Integrado y Analítico de Información sobre Reforma del Estado, Gestión y Politicas Públicas (SIARE); REFORME* – discussion list for exchange among those interested in reforming the State, especially in modernizing public management in Latin America, the Caribbean, Spain and Portugal.
Members Governments of 24 countries:
Andorra, Angola, Argentina, Bolivia, Brazil, Chile, Colombia, Costa Rica, Cuba, Dominican Rep, Ecuador, El Salvador, Equatorial Guinea, Guatemala, Honduras, Mexico, Nicaragua, Panama, Paraguay, Peru, Portugal, Spain, Uruguay, Venezuela.
IGO Relations Agreements with: *Agencia Española de Cooperación Internacional para el Desarrollo (AECID); Deutsche Stiftung für Internationale Entwicklung (DSE, inactive); Development Bank of Latin America (CAF, #05055); ILO (#11123); Inter-American Development Bank (IDB, #11427); International Bank for Reconstruction and Development (IBRD, #12317)* (World Bank); *Latin American and Caribbean Institute for Economic and Social Planning (#16279); Pan American Health Organization (PAHO, #18108); UNDP (#20292); UNICEF (#20332).* Cooperates with: *Global Partnership for Social Accountability (GPSA, #10541); United Nations Public Administration Network (UNPAN, #20615).* **NGO Relations** Member of: *EarthAction (EA, #05159). Public Budget International Association (PBIA, #18564).* [2023.03.03/XE6058/**E***]

♦ Latin American Centre for Development and Participatory Communication (internationally oriented national body)
♦ Latin American Centre for Economic and Social Documentation (inactive)
♦ Latin American Centre of Human Economy / see Universidad CLAEH (#20688)
♦ Latin American Centre for Physics (#03815)
♦ Latin American Centre for the Study of Violence and Health 'Jorge Careli' (internationally oriented national body)
♦ Latin American Challenge Investment Fund (internationally oriented national body)
♦ Latin American Chemical Network (#18718)
♦ Latin American Child's Audiovisual Universe (internationally oriented national body)

♦ Latin American Chlor-Alkali and Derivatives Industry Association (CLOROSUR) 16295

Asociación Latinoamericana de la Industria del Cloro, Alcalis y Derivados – Associação Latinoamericana da Indústria de Cloro, Alkalis e Derivados
SG/Exec Dir Av Chedid Jafet 222, Bloco C-4o andar, Vila Olimpia, Sao Paulo SP, 04551-065, Brazil. T. +551121484780. Fax +551121484788.
URL: http://www.clorosur.org/
History 1 Mar 1997, New Orleans, LA (USA). Founded at annual meeting of *Chlorine Institute*. Former names and other names: *South American Association of the Chlor-Alkali and Derivatives Industry (CLOROSUR)* – former (Mar 1997 to Dec 2002); *Asociación Sudamericana del la Industria del Cloro-Soda y sus Derivados* – former (Mar 1997 to Dec 2002); *Associação Sul Americana da Indústria de Cloro-Soda e Derivados* – former (Mar 1997 to Dec 2002). Registration: Brazil. **Aims** Provide a forum for manufacturers and users of chlorine, alkalis and derivatives that represents their interests and enables them to communicate and exchange information related to the most important themes concerning the industry. **Staff** 1.00 FTE, paid. **Events** *Congress on safety transportation* Sao Paulo (Brazil) 2007.
Members Producer members in 6 countries:
Argentina, Brazil, Chile, Colombia, Cuba, Uruguay.
Non-Producer (Contributing) members in 8 countries:
Belgium, Brazil, Canada, Chile, India, Italy, Japan, USA.
NGO Relations Member of: *World Chlorine Council (WCC, #21274).* [2016/XD8269/t/**D**]

♦ Latin American Chronobiology Group (LACG) 16296

Contact EACH/USP, Rua Arlindo Bettio 1000, Sao Paulo SP, 03828-000, Brazil. T. +551130918123. E-mail: contato@temponavida.com.
URL: http://ischronobiology.org/information/Links.php
History 1991. **Aims** Integrate efforts in Latin America; share projects and lab facilities; organize student exchanges. **Structure** Informal organization of researchers. **Languages** English, Portuguese, Spanish. **Staff** Voluntary. **Finance** Receives support for symposia from Latin American agencies. Supported by: *Inter-Bank Research Organization (IBRO, inactive); NSF International.* **Activities** Events/meetings; research and development. **Events** *Biennial symposium* Buenos Aires (Argentina) 2021, *Symposium* Colonia del Sacramento (Uruguay) 2019, *Symposium* Valparaiso (Chile) 2017, *Symposium* Bragança Paulista (Brazil) 2015, *Symposium* Sao Paulo (Brazil) 2015. **Publications** *Cronobiologia: Principios e Aplicaçoes* (2003). **Information Services** *CronoLA* – virtual network used for communication.
Members Full in 12 countries:
Argentina, Brazil, Canada, Chile, Colombia, Cuba, Germany, Mexico, Netherlands, Spain, Uruguay, USA.
NGO Relations Member of (1): *World Federation of Societies of Chronobiology (WFSC, #21484).* [2022.05.05/XE4647/**E**]

♦ Latin American Cinematography Common Market (no recent information)
♦ Latin American Circle for International Studies (internationally oriented national body)

♦ Latin American Circle of Phenomenology (#03937)

♦ Latin American Civil Aviation Commission (LACAC) 16297

Comisión Latinoamericana de Aviación Civil (CLAC) – Comissão Latino-Americana de Aviação Civil

Sec Apartado Postal 27032, 15000, Lima, Peru. T. +5114226905 – +5114229367. Fax +5114228236. E-mail: clacsec@clac-lacac.org.
Street Address Av Victor Andrés Belaúnde 147, Edificio Real Cuatro, 3o Piso, Centro Empresarial Real, San Isidro, 15000, Lima, Peru.
URL: http://clacsec.lima.icao.int/

History Established 14 Dec 1973, Mexico City (Mexico), as regional body of civil aviation for Latin America. Statutes registered in *'UNTS 1/20170'*. **Aims** Provide civil aviation authorities of member states an appropriate framework within which to discuss and plan all the required measures for cooperation and coordination of all their civil aviation activities. **Structure** Assembly (every 2 years); Executive Committee; General Secretariat; GEPEJTA; AVSEC/FAL/RG/LACAC Group; Strategic Plan Management Group; ad hoc groups. **Languages** English, Portuguese, Spanish. **Staff** 5.00 FTE, paid. **Finance** Contribution of member states. **Activities** Events/meetings; knowledge management/information dissemination; training/education. **Events** *Biennial Assembly* Antigua (Guatemala) 2014, *Meeting* Bogota (Colombia) 2013, *Meeting* Panama (Panama) 2013, *Biennial Assembly* Brasilia (Brazil) 2012, *Meeting / Biennial Assembly* Brasilia (Brazil) 2012.
Members Governments of 22 countries:
Argentina, Aruba, Belize, Bolivia, Brazil, Chile, Colombia, Costa Rica, Cuba, Dominican Rep, Ecuador, El Salvador, Guatemala, Honduras, Jamaica, Mexico, Nicaragua, Panama, Paraguay, Peru, Uruguay, Venezuela. [2016.10.18/XD5456/**D***]

♦ Latin American Clinical Epidemiology Network 16298

Red Latinoamericana de Epidemiologia Clinica (LatinCLEN)

Pres Fac of Medicine, Pontificia Univ Javeriana – Hosp, Univ San Ignacio, Carrera 7 #45-62, Bogota, Bogota DC, Colombia. T. +5645325740. Fax +5645325741.
URL: http://www.inclentrust.org/

History Regional network of: *INCLEN Trust International (#11142)*. **Structure** Executive Committee of 4. President. **Events** *Congress* Barcelona (Spain) 2007, *Congress* Buenos Aires (Argentina) 2005, *Congress* Pucón (Chile) 2003, *Congress* Villarrica (Chile) 2002, *Congress* Cartagena de Indias (Colombia) 2001.
Members Institutes and universities (16) in 7 countries:
Argentina, Bolivia, Brazil, Chile, Colombia, Mexico, Peru. [2020/XF6156/**F**]

♦ Latin American Clinical Pathology and Laboratory Medicine (ALAPAC/ML) 16299

Asociación Latinoamericana de Patologia Clinica/Medicina de Laboratorio

Permanent Sec PO Box M-10295, La Paz, Bolivia. T. +59122796432. E-mail: alapac_ml@yahoo.com.
URL: http://alapacml.net/

History 23 Sep 1976, Lima (Peru). **Structure** Executive Committee, comprising President, Alternate President, Permanent Secretary, Secretary, Alternate Secretary and Treasurer. **Events** *Congress* Havana (Cuba) 2016, *Congress* Montevideo (Uruguay) 2014, *Congress* Punta del Este (Uruguay) 2014, *Congress* Cancún (Mexico) 2012, *Congress* Quito (Ecuador) 2010. **NGO Relations** *Asociación Iberoamericana de Telesalud y Telemedicina (AITT, #02155)*. [2017/XM3850/**D**]

♦ Latin American Club of Neuro Ophthalmology (#04036)
♦ Latin American Collaborative Study of Congenital Malformations (#05552)
♦ Latin American Committee for Civil Servants / see Coordinadora Latinoamericana de Trabajadores de los Servicios Públicos (#04809)
♦ Latin American Committee for the Coordination and Promotion of Appropriate Technology (inactive)
♦ Latin American Committee of Deans of Schools of Business Administration / see Latin American Council of Business Schools (#16308)
♦ Latin American Committee for the Defense of Women's Rights / see Latin American and Caribbean Committee for the Defense of Women's Rights (#16268)
♦ Latin American Committee for Energy Workers (inactive)
♦ Latin American Committee on Films on Indian Peoples / see Coordinadora Latinoamericana de Cine et de Comunicación de los Pueblos Indigenas (#04806)

♦ Latin American Committee on Macroeconomic and Financial Issues 16300

Comité Latinoamericano de Asuntos Financieros (CLAAF)

Chair c/o Center for Global Development, 2055 L St NW, Washington DC 20036, USA. T. +12024164000.
URL: http://www.claaf.org/

History Jul 2000, Rio de Janeiro (Brazil). Former names and other names: *Latin-American Shadow Financial Regulatory Committee* – former. **Aims** Identify and analyse trends and ongoing events that affect the appropriate functioning of financial markets in Latin America.
Members Individuals (12) in 8 countries:
Argentina, Brazil, Chile, Mexico, Panama, Peru, Uruguay, Venezuela.
Invited member (1) in 1 country:
Netherlands. [2021/XE4587/**E**]

♦ Latin American Committee on National Parks (inactive)
♦ Latin American Committee on Treatment and Research of Multiple Sclerosis (#04190)

♦ Latin American Community of Learning Objects (LACLO) 16301

Comunidad Latinoamericana de Objetos de Aprendizaje – Comunidade Latino Americana de Objetos de Aprendizagem

Coordinator Instituto de Informatica – UACh, Valdivia, Los Ríos, Chile. T. +5663221815.
Coordinator Ctr de Tecno de Infn – ESPOL, Campus Gustavo Galindo, Area de Tecnologias, 09-01-5863 Guayaquil, Ecuador.
URL: http://www.laclo.org/

History 27 Oct 2006. **Structure** Includes *Federación Latinoamericana de Repositorios de Objetos de Aprendizaje (FLOR)*. **Events** *Conference* Valdivia (Chile) 2013, *Conference* Guayaquil (Ecuador) 2012, *Conference* Montevideo (Uruguay) 2011, *Conference* Sao Paulo (Brazil) 2010, *Conference* Mérida (Mexico) 2009. [2012/XM4055/**D**]

♦ Latin American Confederation of Associations of University Professionals (#04453)
♦ Latin American Confederation of Centres of Ignatian Spirituality (#04455)
♦ Latin American Confederation of Clinical Biochemistry (#04454)
♦ Latin American Confederation of Communication Workers (no recent information)
♦ Latin American Confederation of Company Executives Associations (no recent information)
♦ Latin American Confederation of Congress Organizers / see Federación de Entidades Organizadoras de Congresos y Afines de América Latina (#09299)
♦ Latin American Confederation of Cooperative Workers (#04456)

♦ Latin American Confederation of Credit Unions 16302

Confédération latinoaméricaine des coopératives d'épargne et de crédit – Confederación Latinoamericana de Cooperativas de Ahorro y Crédito (COLAC)

Main Office Bd Punta Pacifica, Torres de las Américas, Torre B – piso 19 – oficina 1902, Panama, Panamá, Panama PANAMÁ, Panama. E-mail: info@colac.coop.
URL: http://www.colac.coop/

History 28 Aug 1970, Panama (Panama). Former names and other names: *Latin American Confederation of Savings and Loan Cooperatives* – alias. Registration: Panama. **Aims** Serve as the institution leader of the credit and savings sector in Latin America. **Structure** General Assembly (annual); Board of Directors; Executives (3); Maintains, since 1979, *Education Foundation of the Latin American Confederation of Credit Unions (FECOLAC, see: #16302)*. **Languages** English, Spanish. **Staff** 12.00 FTE, paid. **Finance** Supported by: *Inter-American Development Bank (IDB, #11427)*; *Overseas Private Investment Corporation (OPIC)*; *United States Agency for International Development (USAID)*. **Activities** Events/meetings; guidance/assistance/consulting; training/education. **Events** *Biennial Convention* Cancún (Mexico) 2014, *Biennial Convention* Cancún (Mexico) 2012, *Biennial Convention* Bavaro (Dominican Rep) 2010, *Biennial Convention* Punta Cana (Dominican Rep) 2010, *Biennial Convention* Panama (Panama) 2008. **Publications** Annual Report.
Members Organizations and credit unions in 16 countries:
Argentina, Brazil, Chile, Colombia, Costa Rica, Dominican Rep, Ecuador, Honduras, Mexico, Nicaragua, Panama, Paraguay, Peru, Uruguay, USA, Venezuela.
Associate members in 2 countries:
Canada, USA.
Consultative Status Consultative status granted from: *ECOSOC (#05331)* (General). **IGO Relations** Associated with Department of Global Communications of the United Nations. **NGO Relations** Member of (2): *Internationale Raiffeisen Union e.V. (IRU, #13291)*; *Oikocredit International (Oikocredit, #17704)*. Affiliated with (1): *International Co-operative Alliance (ICA, #12944)*. [2021/XE4466/**D**]

♦ Latin American Confederation of the Graphics Industry 16303

Confédération latinoaméricaine de l'industrie graphique – Confederación Latinoamericana de la Industria Grafica (CONLATINGRAF) – Confederação Latinoamericana da Industria Grafica

No permanent address. E-mail: comunicaciones@conlatingraf.net. address not obtained. E-mail: comunicaciones@conlatingraf.net.
URL: http://www.conlatingraf.net/

History Nov 1967, Mar del Plata (Argentina), as a sectorial member of *Latin American Industrialists Association (#16341)*. Current Statutes adopted 7-9 Oct 1985, Brasilia (Brazil). Registered in accordance with the law of Uruguay. **Aims** Group the official and representative bodies of the graphics industry in the various countries of Latin America. **Structure** General Assembly. Board of Directors, comprising President, 1st and 2nd Vice-Presidents and 2 Directors. Executive Director; Secretary-General; Administrative Secretary. **Languages** English, Portuguese, Spanish. **Finance** Members' dues. Budget (annual): about US$ 68,500. **Events** *Latin American Congress* Cancún (Mexico) 2010, *Latin American Congress* Buenos Aires (Argentina) 2008, *Congress* Cartagena de Indias (Colombia) 2006, *Latin American Congress* Colombia 2006, *Congress* Mexico City (Mexico) 2004.
Members Active in 15 countries:
Argentina, Brazil, Chile, Colombia, Costa Rica, Dominican Rep, Ecuador, El Salvador, Mexico, Nicaragua, Panama, Paraguay, Peru, Uruguay, Venezuela.
Associate in 2 countries:
Spain, USA. [2019/XD0504/t/**D**]

♦ Latin American Confederation of People in Social Marginality (#04461)

♦ Latin American Confederation of Public Sector Workers 16304

Confédération latinoaméricaine des travailleurs de l'Etat – Confederación Latinoamericana de Trabajadores Estatales (CLATE)

Main Office Av Parana 26, 6 piso E, C1017AAB Buenos Aires, Argentina. E-mail: presidencia@clate.org.
URL: https://clate.net/

History 1967. Former names and other names: *Latin American Official Workers Confederation* – alias. **Events** *Meeting* Toluca (Mexico) 2019, *Congress* Cartagena de Indias (Colombia) 2017, *Congress* Sao Paulo (Brazil) 1984, *Congress* Mar del Plata (Argentina) 1980.
Members Organizations in 18 countries and territories:
Argentina, Brazil, Chile, Colombia, Costa Rica, Cuba, Curaçao, Dominican Rep, Ecuador, El Salvador, Guatemala, Haiti, Mexico, Paraguay, Peru, Puerto Rico, Uruguay, Venezuela.
Consultative Status Consultative status granted from: *ECOSOC (#05331)* (Ros A). [2023/XD5230/**D**]

♦ Latin American Confederation of the Pulp and Paper Industry (no recent information)
♦ Latin American Confederation of Religious Orders (#04442)
♦ Latin American Confederation of Retired Workers, Pensioners and Senior Citizens (#04462)
♦ Latin American Confederation of Savings and Loan Cooperatives / see Latin American Confederation of Credit Unions (#16302)
♦ Latin American Confederation of Small and Medium Enterprises (no recent information)
♦ Latin American Confederation of Societies of Anesthesia / see Latin American Confederation of Societies of Anesthesiology (#16305)

♦ Latin American Confederation of Societies of Anesthesiology 16305

Confédération Latinoaméricaine des Sociétés d'Anesthésiologie – Confederación Latinoamericana de Sociedades de Anestesiología (CLASA)

SG address not obtained. E-mail: info@anestesiaclasa.org – secretariageneral@anestesiaclasa.org.
Pres address not obtained.
URL: https://www.anestesiaclasa.org/

History Oct 1962, Lima (Peru). Founded at 6th Latin American Congress of Anaesthesiology, in succession to *Organization of Latin American Congresses of Anaesthesiology (inactive)*, set up Nov 1949, Buenos Aires (Argentina). Regional section of *World Federation of Societies of Anaesthesiologists (WFSA, #21482)*. Former names and other names: *Latin American Confederation of Societies of Anesthesia* – alias; *Confédération latinoaméricaine des sociétés d'anesthésie* – alias; *Confederación Latinoamericana de Sociedades de Anestesia* – alias. Registration: Peru. **Aims** Improve the standard of anaesthesia in Latin America through close cooperation of member societies; disseminate scientific information; encourage research; establish basic standards for teaching and training; promote scholarships and fellowships. **Structure** General Assembly (every 2 years); Executive Committee. **Languages** Portuguese, Spanish. **Staff** 2.00 FTE, paid. **Finance** Sources: donations; grants; members' dues. **Activities** Healthcare; knowledge management/information dissemination; networking/liaising; publishing activities; standards/guidelines; training/education. **Events** *Latin American Congress of Anesthesiology* Rio de Janeiro (Brazil) 2023, *Biennial Latin American Congress* Buenos Aires (Argentina) 2019, *Biennial Latin American Congress* Punta del Este (Uruguay) 2017, *Biennial Latin American congress* Lima (Peru) 2015, *Congress* Asunción (Paraguay) 2013. **Publications** *Noticias de la CLASA* – newsletter.
Members National societies in 19 countries:
Argentina, Bolivia, Brazil, Chile, Colombia, Costa Rica, Cuba, Dominican Rep, Ecuador, El Salvador, Guatemala, Honduras, Mexico, Nicaragua, Panama, Paraguay, Peru, Uruguay, Venezuela. [2023.02.14/XD2870/**D**]

♦ Latin American Confederation of Tourism Organizations (#04466)
♦ Latin American Confederation of Tourism Press (no recent information)
♦ Latin American Confederation of YMCAs / see Latin American and Caribbean Alliance of YMCAs (#16264)
♦ Latin-American Conference on Bioimpedance (meeting series)
♦ Latin American Congress on Child Psychiatry and Allied Professions (meeting series)
♦ Latin American Congress to Defend the Rights of the Jewish Minority in the Soviet Union (meeting series)
♦ Latin American Conscientious Objection Network (inactive)

♦ Latin American Consortium on Emergency Contraception (LACEC) . 16306

Consorcio Latinoamericano de Anticoncepción de Emergencia (CLAE)

Contact Calle Hermano Deligne 101 C Gascue, Distrito Nacional, Santo Domingo, Dominican Rep. T. +8096826670. E-mail: claecoordinacion@gmail.com.
URL: http://clae-la.org/

History Oct 2000, New York NY (USA). **Events** *Conference* Quito (Ecuador) 2002.
Members National and international organizations in 20 countries:
Argentina, Bolivia, Brazil, Chile, Colombia, Costa Rica, Cuba, Dominican Rep, Ecuador, El Salvador, Guatemala, Honduras, Mexico, Nicaragua, Panama, Paraguay, Peru, Uruguay, USA, Venezuela.
Included in the above, 10 organizations listed in this Yearbook:
Center for Reproductive Rights; *International Planned Parenthood Federation (IPPF, #14589)*; *International Women's Health Coalition (IWHC)*; *Latin American and Caribbean Women's Health Network (LACWHN, #16288)*; *Latin American and Caribbean Youth Network for Sexual and Reproductive Health and Rights (REDLAC, #16289)*; *MSI Reproductive Choices*; *Pacific Institute for Women's Health (PIWH)*; *Pathfinder International (#18261)*; *Population Council (#18458)*; *Prosalud Inter Americana Foundation (PSIA, #18542)*.
NGO Relations Partner of: *International Consortium for Emergency Contraception (ICEC, #12911)*. Member of: *Reproductive Health Supplies Coalition (RHSC, #18847)*. [2015/XM0908/y/**F**]

♦ Latin American Consortium for Religious Liberty (#04732)
♦ Latin American Continental Students Organization / see Organización Continental Latinoamericana y Caribeña de Estudiantes (#17834)
♦ Latin American Cooperation of Advanced Networks (#04790)
♦ Latin American Cooperative Group on Haemostasis and Thrombosis (#10802)
♦ Latin American Coordination of Rural Organizations (#04808)

♦ Latin American Coordination Table for Fair Trade 16307

Mesa de Coordinación Latinoamericana de Comercio Justo (MCLACJ)

Coordinator c/o RPCJyCE, Jr Ezekiel Ossio Peñaranda 1799, Urbanizacicón Los Cipreses, 1, Lima, Peru. E-mail: alfonsocotera@yahoo.com.

History Oct 2004, Peru. **Events** *Meeting* Porto Alegre (Brazil) 2005. **NGO Relations** Member of: *Intercontinental Network for the Promotion of the Social Solidarity Economy (INPSSE, #11463).* [2014/XM1898/t/**F**]

♦ Latin American Coordinator of Public Service Workers (#04809)
♦ Latin American Corn Society (inactive)
♦ Latin American Council of Adult Education (#04707)
♦ Latin American Council for Biomedical Research (no recent information)

♦ Latin American Council of Business Schools 16308

Conseil latinoaméricain des écoles d'administration – Consejo Latinoamericano de Escuelas de Administración (CLADEA)

Exec Dir Av El Polo 670, of B-404, Santiago de Surco, 33, Lima, Peru. T. +5114363926. E-mail: direccionejecutiva@cladea.org – comunicaciones@cladea.org – info@cladea.org.
Exec Coordinator address not obtained. E-mail: molivos@cladea.org.
URL: http://www.cladea.org/

History 6 Mar 1967, Lima (Peru), under the name *Latin American Committee of Deans of Schools of Business Administration – Comité Latinoaméricano de Decanos de Escuelas de Administración*, having the same initials. **Aims** Improve management education at both graduate and undergraduate levels, and development and improvement of executive education; support management research relevant to the region's social and economic development; contribute to the long-term process of Latin American integration. **Structure** Assembly (annual); Executive Committee also acts as Advisory Board. **Languages** English, Portuguese, Spanish. **Staff** 6.00 FTE, paid. **Finance** Members' dues. Other sources: donations; grants. **Activities** Knowledge management/ information dissemination; research/documentation; events/meetings. **Events** *Annual Assembly* Medellin (Colombia) 2016, *Annual Assembly* Viña del Mar (Chile) 2015, *Annual Assembly* Barcelona (Spain) 2014, *Annual Assembly* Rio de Janeiro (Brazil) 2013, *Annual Assembly* Lima (Peru) 2012. **Publications** *ACADEMIA – Latin American Journal of Administration*; *CLADEA Newsletter*; *ISI Journal*. Academic resources; scientific papers; research documents.
Members Full; Associate; Observer; Institutional. Graduate schools and institutions related to management education and management research in 33 countries and territories:
Argentina, Australia, Austria, Belgium, Bolivia, Brazil, Canada, Chile, Colombia, Costa Rica, Cuba, Dominican Rep, Ecuador, France, Germany, Guatemala, Honduras, Italy, Mexico, Netherlands, New Zealand, Panama, Paraguay, Peru, Poland, Portugal, Puerto Rico, Scotland, Spain, Trinidad-Tobago, Uruguay, USA, Venezuela.
NGO Relations Cooperates with (1): *European Business Schools Librarians's Group (EBSLG, #06425).* Member of: *Conference of the Americas on International Education (CAIE, #04581)*; *Global University Network for Innovation (GUNI, #10641).* On Steering Committee of: *Principles for Responsible Management Education (PRME, #18500).* [2020.03.04/XD5826/y/**D**]

♦ Latin American Council of Catholic Women (inactive)

♦ Latin American Council of Churches (LACC) 16309

Conseil latinoaméricain des Eglises – Consejo Latinoamericano de Iglesias (CLAI) – Conselho Latinoamericano de Igrejas

SG Calle Inglaterra N32-113 y Mariana de Jesús, Quito, Ecuador. T. +59322504377. Fax +59322568373.
URL: http://www.reddeliturgia.org/

History 21 Sep 1982, Huampani (Peru). **Aims** Promote the unity of the people of God in Latin America, serving Jesus Christ and proclaiming His message to the Latin American continent. **Structure** General Assembly. Board of Directors (meets annually), consisting of President, First Vice-President, Second Vice-President, Secretary, Treasurer and 12 members. General Secretary, coordinating secretaries' work. Regional Secretariats (5) in: Andean region (Ecuador, Bolivia, Peru, Chile); Brazil; Caribbean and 'Gran Colombia' (Colombia, Cuba, Dominican Rep, Haiti, Puerto Rico, Venezuela); Central America, Panama and Mexico; River Plate (Argentina, Paraguay, Uruguay). Original Offices in: Argentina; Brazil; Chile; Costa Rica; Colombia. Secretariats and Pastoral Services: Women; Aboriginal Pastoral; Young People; Promotion and Communication. **Languages** English, Portuguese, Spanish. **Staff** 17.50 FTE, paid. **Finance** Members' dues. Contributions of church related agencies in Europe, USA and Canada. **Activities** Through regional and service secretariats, CLAI develops its work, which takes place mainly through workshops in local communities. Special programmes for: Faith and Economy; Children; Liturgy; Health; Solidarity; Action with Churches (ASI). Disseminates information. Circulates periodicals to interested parties in and outside Latin America. **Events** *General Assembly* Havana (Cuba) 2013, *General Assembly* Buenos Aires (Argentina) 2007, *General Assembly* Barranquilla (Colombia) 2001, *General Assembly* Barranquilla (Colombia) 2000, *General Assembly* Concepción (Chile) 1995. **Publications** *Nuevo Siglo* (12 a year) in Spanish; *Signos De Vida* (4 a year) in Spanish; *Latin American Ecumenical News – LAEN* (3 a year) in English; *Liturgical Resources Through Internet* in Portuguese, Spanish. Monographs. Various other publications.
Members Full; Associate; Fraternal. Churches and Christian bodies (over 150) in 21 countries:
Argentina, Bolivia, Brazil, Chile, Colombia, Costa Rica, Cuba, Dominican Rep, Ecuador, El Salvador, Guatemala, Haiti, Honduras, Mexico, Nicaragua, Panama, Paraguay, Peru, Puerto Rico, Uruguay, Venezuela.
Associate bodies in 9 countries:
Argentina, Brazil, Costa Rica, Ecuador, Mexico, Paraguay, Peru, Puerto Rico, Venezuela.
NGO Relations Member of: *ACT Alliance (#00081)*; *Environment Liaison Centre International (ELCI, no recent information)*; *Espacio Iberoamericano de Juventud (EIJ, no recent information)*; *Joint Learning Initiative on Faith and Local Communities (JLI, #16139)*; *Side by Side (#19265)*; *World Alliance of Young Men's Christian Associations (YMCA, #21090).* Instrumental in setting up: *Foro de Educación Teológica Ecuménica de América Latina y el Caribe (FETELAC).* [2018/XD8770/**D**]

♦ Latin American Council of Indigenous Film and Communication / see Coordinadora Latinoamericana de Cine et de Comunicación de los Pueblos Indigenas (#04806)
♦ Latin American Council for Journalism Education Accreditation (#04717)
♦ Latin American Council for Law and Development (inactive)
♦ Latin American Council of Neuro Ophthalmology / see Club Latinoamericano de Neuroftalmologia (#04036)
♦ Latin American Council on Oceanography (inactive)

♦ Latin American Council for Peace Research 16310

Conseil latinoaméricain de recherches sur la paix – Consejo Latinoamericano de Investigaciones para la Paz (CLAIP)

SG Sustainable Development, CRIM/UNAM, Av Universidad s/n Cto 2o Col Champilpa, Cuernavaca, 62210 Morelos, Mexico. E-mail: claip.secretariageneral@gmail.com.
Alternative Address Priv Rio Bravo num 1, Col Vista Hermosa 62290, Cuernavaca, Morelos, Mexico.
URL: https://claip.org/

History 17 Dec 1977, Oaxtepec (Mexico). Former names and other names: *Latin American Peace Research Council* – alias. **Aims** Coordinate research activities of Latin American scholars on violence, human rights, economic dependency, the New International Economic Order, peace education, conflict resolution, nonviolence, human, gender and environmental security and militarism. **Structure** General Assembly. Officers: 8 Honorary Presidents, 7 Vice-Presidents, Secretary General. Executive Committee, consisting of Secretary General and 16 members. Working and Research Commissions. **Languages** Spanish. **Staff** 2.00 FTE, paid. **Finance** Members' dues. Public support. **Events** *Congreso Latinoamericano de Investigación para la Paz* 2021, *Congress* Guatemala 2015, *Congress* Buenos Aires (Argentina) 2014, *Congress* Yautepec (Mexico) 2004, *Latin American conference on international relations and peace research* Buenos Aires (Argentina) 1997. **Publications** Books; brochures; videos; research papers.
Members Full in 27 countries:
Argentina, Austria, Belgium, Brazil, Canada, Chile, Colombia, Costa Rica, Cuba, Dominican Rep, Ecuador, El Salvador, Germany, Guatemala, Haiti, Italy, Mexico, Nicaragua, Norway, Paraguay, Peru, Sweden, Switzerland, UK, Uruguay, USA, Venezuela.
IGO Relations *UNESCO (#20322)*; *Contadora Group (inactive).* **NGO Relations** Regional organization of: *International Peace Research Association (IPRA, #14537).* Participant of: *United Nations Global Compact (#20567).* Member of: *International Peace Bureau (IPB, #14535).* [2021/XD8375/**D**]

♦ Latin American Council for Space Physics (inactive)
♦ Latin American Council of Strabismus (#04720)
♦ Latin American Council of Ultrasound in Ophthalmology (#04719)
♦ Latin American Crop Protection Association / see CropLife Latin America (#04967)
♦ Latin American Crystallographic Association (unconfirmed)
♦ Latin American Cultural Council (inactive)
♦ Latin American Customs Brokers and Forwarders Association / see Professional Customs Brokers Association of the Americas (#18512)
♦ Latin American Cystic Fibrosis Federation (no recent information)
♦ Latin American Cytology Society / see Sociedad Latinoamericana de Citopatologia (#19398)
♦ Latin American Cytopathology Society (#19398)
♦ Latin American Demographic Centre / see Latin American and Caribbean Demographic Centre (#16273)
♦ Latin American Dental Industry and Trade Association (no recent information)

♦ Latin American Diabetes Association 16311

Asociación Latinoamericana de Diabetes (ALAD)

Office Carrera 11 n-90 – 07 Of 306, Bogota, Bogota DC, Colombia. T. +5716103779. E-mail: contactoalad1619@gmail.com.
Sec address not obtained. E-mail: evgaladoax@gmail.com.
Pres address not obtained. E-mail: presidenciaalad1619@gmail.com.
URL: http://www.alad-americalatina.org/

History 1970. **Structure** Executive Board, consisting of President, Vice-President, Academic Secretary, Technical Secretary and 5 members. **Activities** Events/meetings. **Events** *Triennial Congress* Punta Cana (Dominican Rep) 2019, *Triennial Congress* Bogota (Colombia) 2016, *Triennial Congress* Cancún (Mexico) 2013, *Triennial Congress* Santiago (Chile) 2010, *Triennial Congress* Havana (Cuba) 2007. **Publications** *ALAD Review.*
Members Full in 18 countries:
Argentina, Bolivia, Brazil, Chile, Colombia, Costa Rica, Cuba, Dominican Rep, Ecuador, Honduras, Mexico, Panama, Paraguay, Peru, Puerto Rico, Uruguay, USA, Venezuela.
NGO Relations *Federação Latino Americana de Endocrinologia (FELAEN, #09286).* [2019/XD4966/**D**]

♦ Latin American Dredging Association (inactive)
♦ Latin American Dysphagia Society / see Sociedad Latinoamericana de Disfagia (#19400)
♦ Latin American Economic Research Foundation (internationally oriented national body)
♦ Latin American Economic System (#19294)

♦ Latin American Ecumenical Networking of Missiologists 16312

Rede Ecumênica Latino Americana de Missiologas (RELAMI)

Address not obtained.
URL: http://www.missiologia.org.br/

Events *United Nations/IAA Workshop on Small Satellites in the Service of Developing Countries* Toronto, ON (Canada) 2014. [2012/XM0464/**F**]

♦ Latin American Educational Film Institute / see Instituto Latinoamericano de la Comunicación Educativa (#11343)

♦ Latin American Energy Organization 16313

Organisation latinoaméricaine de l'énergie – Organización Latinoamericana de Energia (OLADE) – Organização Latinoamericana de Energia

Exec Sec Av Mariscal Antonio José de Sucre N58-63 y Fernandez Salvador, Sector San Carlos, PO Box 17-11-6413, Quito, Ecuador. T. +59322531674 – +59322598122 – +59322598280. Fax +59322531691 – +59322293526.
Head of Public Affairs address not obtained.
URL: http://www.olade.org/

History 2 Nov 1973, Lima (Peru), on signature of the Lima Agreement by 25 regional countries at 3rd Latin American Consultation of Ministers of Energy and Petroleum, following a series of meetings held since Aug 1972. Agreement became effective on 18 Dec 1974; Permanent Secretariat became operational in 1975. Scheme to restructure the Organization ratified by resolution of 26th Meeting of Ministers, Nov 1996, Guatemala (Guatemala). Statutes registered in *'LNTS 1/14670'.* **Aims** Function as: a centre for exchange of experience and information among high-level policymaking areas of the energy sector; a permanent advisory body for energy cooperation and integration among the countries of Latin America and the Caribbean; a forum for exchanging viewpoints so as to achieve regional and subregional stances regarding rational development of natural resources and the impact of their use on the region's environment. In the interest of implementation of policies and programmes compatible with demands stemming from globalization of the world's economy and energy systems and in harmony with world energy development objectives: (a) promote action among member countries to develop and defend the natural resources of their respective countries and of the region as a whole; (b) foster a policy for rational exploration, exploitation, transformation and marketing of member countries' energy resources; (c) enhance appropriate preservation of the region's energy resources by means of policies for rational use of energy; (d) promote direct negotiations among member states to ensure stable and efficient energy supplies; (e) contribute to coordination and complementarity of energy resources by furthering development of means of transport; (f) advance integration of a Latin American energy market; (g) ensure adoption of protective measures for effective energy efficiency, rational use of energy and protection of the environment; (h) foster technical cooperation and the exchange and dissemination of scientific, legal and technological information. **Structure** Meeting of Ministers (annual), comprises energy ministers or secretaries of state in charge of energy in member countries. Council of Experts meets 2 days before the Meeting of Ministers and makes recommendations primarily on technical and administrative matters. Strategy and Programming Committee, comprising experts of 7 countries, meets at least annually. Permanent Secretariat, headed by Executive Secretary. **Languages** English, French, Portuguese, Spanish. **Staff** 40.00 FTE, paid. **Finance** Member countries' annual quotas; extra-budgetary contributions from regional and extra-regional cooperation mechanisms, including resources obtained through memoranda of understanding between OLADE and state-owned energy companies and/or cooperation agreements with international organizations. **Activities** *'Reorientation of OLADE'* OLADE has been restructured in accordance with resolution of Nov 1996; further consolidation and enhancement of its political role through a new political and technical agenda is being considered by an Ad Hoc Working Group set up in Jun 1999, Rio de Janeiro (Brazil), at 30th Meeting of Ministers. Meanwhile the 3rd extraordinary Meeting of Ministers, Nov 1999, Quito (Ecuador), adopted new concepts for vision and strategy:
– Favouring bilateral and multilateral energy integration;
– Promoting adjustment of regulatory frameworks so as to dismantle barriers to integration;
– Promoting the most adequate and economical means for energy supply and integration;
– Preserving the environment and ensuring sustainable development of the continent.

he 31st Meeting of Ministers, 13-14 Oct 2000, Asunción (Paraguay), created 3 fora to consolidate ties with strategy players and sectors for regional energy development:
– *Forum of Supervisory Entities and Regulatory Agencies for Oil and Gas Activities*;
– *Forum of Supervisory Entities and Regulatory Agencies for Electrical Power Activities*;
– *Energy Sector Business Forum.*

The first 2 fora foster exchange of experience so as to optimize the work of relevant entities and agencies and support establishment of these agencies in countries requiring them; the 3rd forum acts as a vehicle for dialogue with the public sector and promotes energy sector integration, impetus and transformation by encouraging business associations, chambers of production and private-sector enterprises involved in energy sector development in Latin America and the Caribbean to analyse and discuss business opportunities and obstacles to investment and to exchange experience.

Unified Electrical Power Planning System (SUPER) – comprises 7 modules for planning expansion of electrical power generation and transmission interconnections, grouped in 4 areas: basic data; optimization; simulation; impacts. This service was developed with support from IDB and integrates such innovative aspects as hydrological risk, demand growth, fuel costs, project lead times and financial constraints. It is used by many Latin American power utilities; users meet annually for exchange of experience and to recommend improvements.
'Master's Degree in Energy and the Environment' – program implemented at OLADE Headquarters, Quito, jointly with University of Calgary (Canada) and with support from CIDA.
Events *Latin American Carbon Forum* Montevideo (Uruguay) 2018, *Latin American Climate Week* Montevideo (Uruguay) 2018, *Regional Energy Integration Forum* 2015, *Latin American and Caribbean Electricity Seminar* Lima (Peru) 2014, *Regional Energy Integration Forum* San Salvador (El Salvador) 2014. **Publications** *Energy Magazine* (4 a year); *Enery Report of Latin America and the Caribbean* (annual); *Final Report of the Meeting of Ministers* (annual); *Energy Indicators and Statistics* (every 2 years). *Preliminary Wind Map of Latin America and the Caribbean* in Spanish – 6 vols; *Shared Hydropower Developments* in Spanish – 6 vols. Manuals; guides; statistics; conference reports. Information Services: *Energy-Economic Information System for the Latin American and Caribbean Region (SIEE, see: #16313)* – provides the Permanent Secretariat and high-level decision-makers in member countries with an integrated software package for systematic, up-to-date, consistent and reliable information on the principal economic and energy variables of the Latin American and Caribbean countries, allowing comparison between countries and regions. The system permits analysis of relations between energy and macroeconomic trends, so as to support regional studies and analyses on which to base comprehensive energy planning, facilitate internal policy decisions and offer elements for greater regional integration.
Members Governments of 26 countries:
Argentina, Barbados, Bolivia, Brazil, Chile, Colombia, Costa Rica, Cuba, Dominican Rep, Ecuador, El Salvador, Grenada, Guatemala, Guyana, Haiti, Honduras, Jamaica, Mexico, Nicaragua, Panama, Paraguay, Peru, Suriname, Trinidad-Tobago, Uruguay, Venezuela.
IGO Relations Cooperates with: *International Energy Forum (IEF, #13272)*; *UNIDO (#20336)*; *United Nations Economic Commission for Latin America and the Caribbean (ECLAC, #20556)*. Participates in the activities of: *UNCTAD (#20285)*. Accredited by: *United Nations Framework Convention on Climate Change – Secretariat (UNFCCC, #20564)*. Observer to: *Sistema Económico Latinoamericano (SELA, #19294)*. **NGO Relations** In liaison with technical committees of: *International Organization for Standardization (ISO, #14473)*. Member of: *Climate Technology Centre and Network (CTCN, #04023)*; *International Network on Small Hydro Power (IN-SHP, #14324)*; *LEDS Global Partnership (LEDS GP, #16435)*. Instrumental in setting up: *Joint Organisations Data Initiative (JODI, #16143)*. [2014/XD5835/**D***]

♦ Latin American Engineering Association for Labour Security 16314

Asociación Latino-americana de Ingenieros de Seguransa del Trabajo (ALAIST) – Associação Latino-Americana de Engenharia de Segurança do Trabalho (ALAEST)

Contact Rua Estanislau Pampuche no 77, Campina do Siqueira, CEP 81 350-010, Curitiba PR, CEP 81 350-010, Brazil. T. +554130162303. Fax +554130162303. E-mail: alaest@alaest.org.
URL: http://www.alaest.org/

History Founded 25 Sep 1985, Curitiba (Brazil). **Events** *Conference* Curitiba (Brazil) 2000, *Conference* Rio de Janeiro (Brazil) 2000, *Conference* Rio de Janeiro (Brazil) 1993, *Conference* Ciudad del Este (Paraguay) 1989, *Conference* Buenos Aires (Argentina) 1987. **NGO Relations** Member of: *Consejo de las Asociaciones Profesionales de Ingenieros Civiles de Lengua Oficial Portuguesa y Castellana (CECPC-CICPC, #04702)*. [2017/XD8424/**D**]

- ♦ Latin American Environmental Protection Association (no recent information)
- ♦ Latin American Episcopal Conference / see Consejo Episcopal Latinoamericano (#04709)
- ♦ Latin American Episcopal Council (#04709)
- ♦ Latin American Ethnobotanical Group (no recent information)

♦ Latin America Network of Assisted Reproduction 16315

Red Latinoamericana de Reproducción Asistida (REDLARA) – Rede Latino-americana de Reprodução Assistida

Main Office Calle Manuel Aguilar 2, Fracc Anáhuac, Campo de Tiro, 36815 Irapuato GTO, Mexico. E-mail: info@redlara.com.
URL: http://www.redlara.com/

History 1995, Viña del Mar (Chile). Former names and other names: *RED* – former. **Aims** Offer training and education; disseminate information; maintain a quality control and accreditation programme; coordinate multi-centre research projects. **Structure** Board of Directors, comprising President, Vice-President, 5 Regional Directors and Executive Secretary. **Activities** Offers: Continuing Educational Programme, composed of annual conferences; Continuing Education Programme Online. **Events** *Regional Congress – Southern Cone* Asunción (Paraguay) 2022, *General Congress* Mérida (Mexico) 2019, *General Meeting* Barranquilla (Colombia) 2017, *General Meeting* Lima (Peru) 2015, *General Meeting* Cancún (Mexico) 2013.
Members Centres (141) in 14 countries:
Argentina, Bolivia, Brazil, Chile, Colombia, Costa Rica, Dominican Rep, Ecuador, Guatemala, Mexico, Panama, Peru, Uruguay, Venezuela.
NGO Relations Supports: *International Committee Monitoring Assisted Reproductive Technologies (ICMART, #12787)*. [2022/XJ4790/**D**]

- ♦ Latin American and European Network of University Continuing Education (#18734)
- ♦ Latin American Export Bank / see Banco Latinoamericano de Comercio Exterior (#03159)
- ♦ Latin American Faculty for Environmental Sciences / see Latin American Forum of Environmental Sciences (#16336)

♦ Latin American Faculty of Social Sciences 16316

Faculté latinoaméricaine de sciences sociales – Facultad Latinoamericana de Ciencias Sociales (FLACSO) – Faculdade Latinoamericana de Ciências Sociais

SG 300 Sur y 50 Oeste de MacDonald's Plaza del Sol, Curridabat, San José, San José, San José, 11801, Costa Rica. T. +50622530082. Fax +50622346696. E-mail: info@flacso.org – flacsosg@flacso.org.
URL: http://www.flacso.org/

History 1957, Santiago (Chile). Institutionalization strengthened as an autonomous regional organization of the Latin American and Caribbean States by an agreement concluded, 18 Jun 1971, Paris (France), under the auspices of UNESCO; came into force 19 Jun 1972; agreement modified 8 Jun 1979, San José (Costa Rica). Statutes registered in 'UNTS/1 14696'. Since 1973 has 15 academic units in Latin America and the Caribbean. **Aims** Assure training of specialists in social sciences in Latin America and the Caribbean through graduate *education* activities at doctoral, master and specialization levels; carry out research in the area of social sciences on subjects related to Latin American problems; disseminate knowledge of social sciences and the results of research; encourage exchange of social science teaching materials in the region and promote cooperation in the field; carry out academic activities related to social sciences that benefit development and integration in the region. **Structure** General Assembly (every 2 years); Higher Council (meets annually), comprising representatives of 7 State members and 6 Academic Councillors; Executive Committee. Academic Headquarters (7): Buenos Aires (Argentina); Brasilia (Brazil), San José (Costa Rica); Santiago (Chile); Quito (Ecuador); Guatemala (Guatemala); Mexico City (Mexico). Programmes (4): Habana (Cuba); San Salvador (El Salvador); Panama (Panama); Asunción (Paraguay); Santo Domingo (Dominican Rep); Montevideo (Uruguay). Projects (2): Tegucigalpa (Honduras); Salamanca (Spain). Regional body of: *International Federation of Social Science Organizations (IFSSO, #13543)*. **Languages** English, Portuguese, Spanish. **Staff** 1668.00 FTE, paid. **Finance** Members' dues. Grants and funding agencies. **Activities** Training/education; research/documentation. **Events** *Gender Summit North and Latin America* Mexico City (Mexico) 2016, *General Assembly* San José (Costa Rica) 2016, *Biennial General Assembly* Guatemala 2014, *General Assembly* Guatemala (Guatemala) 2014, *General Assembly* Guatemala (Guatemala) 2014. **Publications** In 2014, published 74 books, 151 chapters with external publishers, and 139 articles written by investigators in several journals. Journals (26) produced by Academic Units.
Members Governments of 18 countries:
Argentina, Bolivia, Brazil, Chile, Costa Rica, Cuba, Dominican Rep, Ecuador, El Salvador, Guatemala, Honduras, Mexico, Nicaragua, Panama, Paraguay, Peru, Suriname, Uruguay.

Observer (1):
Spain.
IGO Relations Agreements with: *ECOSOC (#05331)*; *European Commission (EC, #06633)*; *Ibero-American General Secretariat (#11024)*; *OAS (#17629)*; Spanish Agency for International Cooperation for Development (AECID); *UNDP (#20292)*; *UNESCO (#20322)*. Member of: *Latin American and Caribbean Research Network (#16284)*. Cooperates with: *Agencia Española de Cooperación Internacional para el Desarrollo (AECID)*; *International Development Research Centre (IDRC, #13162)*. **NGO Relations** Member of: *All Europe Taekwon-Do Federation (AETF, #00649)*; *Asociación Universitaria Iberoamericana de Postgrado (AUIP, #02307)*; *Global Network of Domestic Election Monitors (GNDEM, #10487)*; *Global University Network for Innovation (GUNI, #10641)*; *International Science Council (ISC, #14796)*; *Network for Social Studies on Disaster Prevention in Latin America (#17058)*; *Observatoire des relations Union Européenne – Amérique latine (OBREAL-EULARO, #17635)*; *Social Studies Network for Central America, Caribbean and Europe (no recent information)*. Cooperates with: *Confederación Universitaria Centroamericana (CSUCA, #04497)*; *Ford Foundation (#09858)*; *Friedrich-Ebert-Stiftung (FES)*. *Instituto Francés de Estudios Andinos (IFEA)*; *Red de Seguridad y Defensa de América Latina (RESDAL, #18730)*; *Real Instituto Elcano de Estudios Internacionales y Estratégicos*. [2021/XF6646/**F***]

- ♦ Latin American Federation of Adolescent Health Services (no recent information)
- ♦ Latin American Federation of Agricultural and Food Workers (inactive)
- ♦ Latin American Federation of Agricultural, Livestock and Affiliated Workers (no recent information)
- ♦ Latin American Federation of Animal Health (no recent information)
- ♦ Latin American Federation of Associations of Communication Schools / see Federación Latinoamericana de Facultades de Comunicación Social (#09353)
- ♦ Latin American Federation of Associations for Relatives of the Detained and Disappeared (#09344)
- ♦ Latin American Federation of Bank and Insurance Workers (#09373)

♦ Latin American Federation of Biophysical Societies (LAFeBS) 16317

Contact Inst Biofisica CC Filho, UFRJ Centro Ciencias Saude, Bloc G sala 52, Rio de Janeiro RJ, 21949900, Brazil. Fax +552125626572.
URL: http://www.lafebs.org/

History Founded 2007. Registered in accordance with Brazilian law. **Aims** Develop the basis for a more permanent interrelation between Latin American biophysical and related societies; promote regional development and human resources information in biophysics. **Structure** General Assembly; Council. **Languages** English, Portuguese, Spanish. **Finance** Members' dues. **Activities** Events/meetings; training/education; networking/liaising.
Members Full in 2 countries:
Argentina, Brazil.
NGO Relations Member of: *International Union for Pure and Applied Biophysics (IUPAB, #15808)*. [2015.06.24/XJ5656/**D**]

♦ Latin American Federation of Building, Wood and Building Materials Unions 16318

Fédération latino-américaine des syndicats des travailleurs de la construction et du bois – Federación Latinoamericana de la Edificación, Madera y Materiales de la Construcción (FLEMACON)

Pres Avenida Sete de Setembro no 71, Edificio Executivo, salas 613 e 614, Salvador BA, 40 060-001, Brazil. T. +557133213909. Fax +557132428496. E-mail: flemaconoficinabr@gmail.com.
URL: http://flemacon.org/

History Also referred to as *Latin American Wood and Building Workers Union*. **Events** *World religious leaders summit for peace* Sapporo (Japan) 2008, *Congress* Sao Paulo (Brazil) 2003, *Congress* Chile 2001. **NGO Relations** *Trades Union International of Workers in the Building, Wood, Building Materials and Allied Industries (UITBB, #20185)*. [2016/XD0408/**D**]

♦ Latin American Federation of Cancerology Societies 16319

Fédération des sociétés latinoaméricaines de cancérologie – Federación Latinoamericana de Sociedades de Cancerologia (FLASCA)

Secretariat Av Federico Lacroze 2252 2-A, C1426CPU Buenos Aires, Argentina. T. +541147787233 – +54113611. Fax +541147787233.
URL: http://www.flasca.com/

History 16 Sep 1965. **Aims** Coordinate the scientific aspects of the fight against cancer in Latin America, academic interchange, permanent relations with *medical* groups, *hospitals*, research centers, and others. **Languages** Spanish. **Finance** Meetings are held under governmental and non governmental support. **Activities** The main event: *Congreso Integrado Latinoamericano de Cancerologia (CILAC)*. Workshops, panels, symposia or regional meetings are usually organized in close cooperation with international bodies like: *International Agency for Research on Cancer (IARC, #11598)*; *Union for International Cancer Control (UICC, #20415)*; *Pan American Health Organization (PAHO, #18108)*. **Events** *Congress* Venezuela 2006, *Latin American conference on lung cancer* Guajará (Brazil) 2004, *Congress* Córdoba (Argentina) 2003, *CILAC congress* Havana (Cuba) 1999, *Congress* Havana (Cuba) 1998. **Publications** *Cancerologia*.
Members Scientific cancer societies; voluntary cancer societies in the fight against cancer in Latin American countries; individuals of recognized prestige as cancerologists. Members in 21 countries:
Argentina, Bolivia, Brazil, Chile, Colombia, Costa Rica, Cuba, Dominican Rep, Ecuador, El Salvador, Guatemala, Haiti, Honduras, Mexico, Nicaragua, Panama, Paraguay, Peru, Puerto Rico, Uruguay, Venezuela. [2018/XD7314/**D**]

- ♦ Latin American Federation of Catholic Doctors Associations (no recent information)
- ♦ Latin American Federation of Catholic Schools of Journalism (inactive)

♦ Latin American Federation of Chemical Societies 16320

Fédération latinoaméricaine des sociétés de chimie – Federación Latinoamericana de Asociaciones Quimicas (FLAQ)

Exec Sec Soc Quimica del Perú, Nicolas de Aranibar 696, Santa Beatriz, Lima, Peru. E-mail: flaq_se@yahoo.es – info@flaq2020.com – claq2020@gmail.com.
URL: http://www.flaq1959.org/

History 1959, Mexico City (Mexico). Founded during 7th Latin American Congress on Chemistry. Statutes adopted at 8th Congress, 1962, Buenos Aires (Argentina). **Aims** Promote establishment of chemical associations at local level; promote establishment of a code of ethics for practitioners of chemistry in Latin America; promote studie and exchange between higher education centers. **Structure** General Assembly; Board of Directors; Executive Secretariat; Counsellors; Committees. **Languages** English, Portuguese, Spanish. **Staff** None paid. **Finance** Sources: members' dues. **Activities** Events/meetings. **Events** *Latin American Congress on Chemistry* Cartagena de Indias (Colombia) 2021, *Latin American Congress on Chemistry* Cartagena de Indias (Colombia) 2020, *Biennial Congress* Havana (Cuba) 2018, *Biennial Congress* Concepción (Chile) 2016, *Biennial Congress* Lima (Peru) 2014. **Publications** Congress proceedings.
Members Associations in 16 countries and territories:
Argentina, Bolivia, Brazil, Chile, Colombia, Costa Rica, Cuba, Dominican Rep, Ecuador, El Salvador, Honduras, Mexico, Panama, Paraguay, Peru, Puerto Rico.
IGO Relations None. **NGO Relations** Associated organization of: *International Union of Pure and Applied Chemistry (IUPAC, #15809)*. Also links with national societies. [2021.03.02/XD7051/**D**]

- ♦ Latin-American Federation of Cinematographic and Audiovisual Producers / see Federación Iberoamericana de Productores Cinematograficos y Audiovisuales (#09318)
- ♦ Latin American Federation of Cities, Municipalities and Associations of Local Governments (#09350)
- ♦ Latin American Federation of Clothing Industries (inactive)
- ♦ Latin American Pro-Federation Committee of Public Entertainment Workers (inactive)
- ♦ Latin American Pro-Federation Committee of Trade Workers (inactive)
- ♦ Latin American Federation of Communication Schools (#09353)
- ♦ Latin American Federation of Consulting Engineers / see Federación Panamericana de Consultores (#09379)
- ♦ Latin American Federation for Education and Cultural Workers (#09375)

♦ Latin-American Federation of Exhibitors and Distributors of Independent Cinema 16321

Fédération latino-américaine des exploitants et distributeurs de cinéma indépendant – Federación Latino-Americana de Exhibidores y Distribuidores de Cine Independiente (FELCINE)
Pres 2da Av de Campo Alegre con Av Francisco de Miranda, Edificio Laino piso 5, oficina 51, Caracas AP 1060 DF, Venezuela. T. +582122669607. Fax +582122647346. [2012/XJ0595/**D**]

♦ Latin American Federation of Farmworkers (inactive)
♦ Latin American Federation of Fertility and Sterility Societies (inactive)

♦ Latin American Federation of Hospitals 16322

Fédération latinoaméricaine des hôpitaux – Federación Latinoamericana de Hospitales (FLH)
Pres Tucuman 1668, 1er Piso, 1050 Buenos Aires, Argentina. T. +541143732375. Fax +541143723229.
Dir address not obtained.
Twitter: https://twitter.com/flhnews1
History 1975, Mexico City (Mexico). Former names and other names: *Latin American Hospital Association* – former; *Latin American Hospital Federation* – former; *FELAH* – alias; *FELH* – alias. **Aims** Improve hospital and *medical care* in Latin America. **Structure** Board of Directors. **Languages** English, Spanish. **Staff** Paid. **Finance** Sources: members' dues. Staff paid by the host association of the Secretariat. Annual budget: 3,000 USD. **Activities** Projects/programmes. **Events** *Assembly* Santo Domingo (Dominican Rep) 1993, *Assembly* San José (Costa Rica) 1992, *Assembly* Washington, DC (USA) 1991, *Assembly* Buenos Aires (Argentina) 1990, *Congress* Mexico City (Mexico) 1989. **Publications** *Conesión Salud*; *Prensa Hospitalaria*.
Members Health associations in 15 countries:
Argentina, Brazil, Chile, Colombia, Costa Rica, Cuba, Dominican Rep, Guatemala, Mexico, Panama, Paraguay, Peru, Puerto Rico, Uruguay, Venezuela.
IGO Relations Official relations with: *Pan American Health Organization (PAHO, #18108)*. **NGO Relations** Member of (1): CENAS (Centro especializado para la Normatizacion y Acreditacion en Salud). [2021.06.09/XD7896/**D**]

♦ Latin American Federation of Industrial and Construction Workers (#09376)
♦ Latin American Federation of Industry Workers (inactive)
♦ Latin American Federation of Intensive Care Nurses (unconfirmed)
♦ Latin American Federation of International Transport Users' Councils (no recent information)

♦ Latin American Federation of Jesuit Schools 16323

Federación Latinoamericana de Colegios de la Compañia de Jesús (FLACSI)
Exec Sec Carrera 7 No 9-96, Bogota, Bogota DC, Colombia. T. +5714442530ext2267. E-mail: secretaria@flacsi.net.
Pres address not obtained. E-mail: presidencia@flacsi.net.
URL: http://www.flacsi.net/
History Founded May 2001, Rio de Janeiro (Brazil), as *Federation of Jesuit Schools in Latin America – Federación Latinoamericana de Colegios Jesuitas*, as a subsidiary of *Conferencia de Provinciales Jesuitas de América Latina y El Caribe (CPAL, #04658)*. Subsequently referred to as *Federation of Jesuit and Ignatians Schools in Latin America and the Caribbean – Federación Latinoamericana y del Caribe de Colegios Jesuitas e Ignacianos*. **Aims** Promote a sense of apostolic body in the educational mission of the Society of Jesus in Latin America. **Structure** General Assembly; Board of Directors. **Languages** Portuguese, Spanish. **Staff** 2.00 FTE, paid. **Finance** Members' dues. Budget (annual): US$ 100,000. **Events** *Assembly* Buenos Aires (Argentina) 2018, *Assembly* Rio de Janeiro (Brazil) 2017, *Assembly* Panama (Panama) 2016, *Assembly* Bogota (Colombia) 2015, *Assembly* Quito (Ecuador) 2014. **Publications** *FLACSI Newsletter*. School catalogue; editorials. Information Services: Virtual Center of Ignatian Pedagogy.
Members Schools (90) in 19 countries and territories:
Argentina, Bolivia, Brazil, Chile, Colombia, Dominican Rep, Ecuador, El Salvador, Guatemala, Honduras, Mexico, Nicaragua, Panama, Paraguay, Peru, Puerto Rico, Uruguay, USA, Venezuela. [2015.08.31/XD9462/**E**]

♦ Latin American Federation of Journalists and Writers in the Tourist Trade (inactive)
♦ Latin-American Federation of Leather Chemists and Technicians Federation (unconfirmed)
♦ Latin American Federation of Magicians Societies (#09371)

♦ Latin American Federation of Mastology 16324

Federación Latinoamericana de Mastología (FLAM)
Contact c/o Av Juan Tanca Marengo, Calle 13E NE, Omni Hosp Torre Vitalis 1 Piso 2 Cons 202, Guayaquil, Ecuador.
URL: http://www.flammastologia.org/
History 1972. Former names and other names: *Sociedad Latinoamericana de Mastología (SLAM)* – former (1972 to Jul 1983). **Structure** Board of Directors, comprising President, 5 Vice-Presidents, Secretary, Treasurer and 5 further members. **Events** *Congress* Santiago (Chile) 2019, *Congress* Santo Domingo (Dominican Rep) 2017, *Congress* Punta del Este (Uruguay) 2011, *Congress* Cusco (Peru) 2007, *Congress* Santiago (Chile) 2005. **Publications** *Revista Latinoamericana de Mastologia*. **NGO Relations** Scientific Center of: *Senologic International Society (SIS, #19230)*. [2021/XD8241/**D**]

♦ Latin-American Federation of Medical Students Scientific Societies (no recent information)
♦ Latin American Federation of Metalworkers and Miners (inactive)
♦ Latin American Federation of Music Publishers (inactive)
♦ Latin American Federation of Neurosurgery / see Latin American Federation of Neurosurgical Societies (#16325)

♦ Latin American Federation of Neurosurgical Societies 16325

Federación Latinoamericana de Neurocirugia (FLANC) – Federação Latinoamericana das Sociedades de Neurocirurgia
Pres SHIN QL 01 – Conj 06 C 05, Peninsula Norte, Brasilia DF, 71505 065, Brazil.
Exec Sec address not obtained.
URL: http://flanc.la/
History 1981, following series of congresses *Congress of Latin American Neurosurgery (CLAN)*. Previously also referred to as *Latin American Federation of Neurosurgery*. **Aims** Work on the integration of human and technological resources in neuroscience for the better treatment of patients. **Structure** Board of Directors, comprising President, Vice-President, Secretary-General, Executive Secretary, Treasurer, Editor and one Delegate per member association. Executive Committee. **Languages** Portuguese, Spanish. **Events** *International Conference on Recent Advances in Neurotraumatology (ICRAN)* Santa Cruz (Bolivia) 2023, *Congress* Rio de Janeiro (Brazil) 2012, *Congress* El Salvador 2010, *Congress* San Salvador (El Salvador) 2010, *Congress* Bogota (Colombia) 2008. **Publications** *Boletin FLANC*.
Members in 20 countries:
Argentina, Bolivia, Brazil, Chile, Colombia, Costa Rica, Cuba, Dominican Rep, Ecuador, El Salvador, Guatemala, Honduras, Mexico, Nicaragua, Panama, Paraguay, Peru, Puerto Rico, Uruguay, Venezuela.
NGO Relations *Southern Cone Society of Neurological Surgeons (#19869)* is member. [2017/XD7791/**D**]

♦ Latin American Federation of Nutritional Therapy, Clinical Nutrition and Metabolism 16326

Federación Latinoamericana de Terapia Nutricional, Nutrición Clinica y Metabolismo (FELANPE)
Secretariat address not obtained. E-mail: secretariafelanpe@gmail.com.
URL: http://www.felanpeweb.org/
History 1988, Curitiba (Brazil), as *Federación Latino-Americana de Nutrición Parenteral y Enteral (FELANPE)*. **Events** *Congreso Latinoamericano de Nutrición Clínica, Terapia Nutricional y Metabolismo* Guayaquil (Ecuador) 2021, *Congreso Latinoamericano de Nutrición Clínica, Terapia Nutricional y Metabolismo* 2020, *Congreso Latinoamericano de Nutrición Clínica, Terapia Nutricional y Metabolismo* Guadalajara (Mexico) 2018, *Congress* Florianópolis (Brazil) 2016, *Congress* Buenos Aires (Argentina) 2014. **Publications** *Boletin Felanpe*.
Members Organizations in 20 countries:
Argentina, Bolivia, Brazil, Chile, Colombia, Costa Rica, Cuba, Dominican Rep, Ecuador, El Salvador, Guatemala, Honduras, Mexico, Panama, Paraguay, Peru, Puerto Rico, Spain, Uruguay, Venezuela. [2020/XD9446/**D**]

♦ Latin American Federation of Obstetric and Gynecological Societies (#09372)

♦ Latin American Federation of Parasitologists 16327

Fédération latinoaméricaine des parasitologues – Federación Latinoamericana de Parasitólogos (FLAP)
Contact Univ of Guayaquil, Ayacucho 732 y Lorenzo de Garaicoa Mezanine, Guayaquil, Ecuador. T. +59342405098. Fax +59342562569. E-mail: dre_montalvo@yahoo.es.
History 6 Sep 1963, Rio de Janeiro (Brazil), during 7th World Congress on Tropical Medicine and Malaria. Also referred to as *Federación Latinoamericana de Parasitologia*. **Structure** Secretariat rotates. **Events** *Congress* Havana (Cuba) 2021, *Congress* Panama (Panama) 2019, *Biennial Congress* Guayaquil (Ecuador) 2013, *Biennial Congress* Bogota (Colombia) 2011, *Biennial Congress* Asunción (Paraguay) 2009. **Publications** *Parasitologia Ibero-Latinoamericana* (periodical).
Members Individuals in 16 countries:
Argentina, Bolivia, Brazil, Chile, Colombia, Costa Rica, Cuba, Ecuador, El Salvador, Guatemala, Honduras, Mexico, Paraguay, Peru, Uruguay, Venezuela.
NGO Relations Affiliated with: *World Federation of Parasitologists (WFP, #21471)*. [2019/XD2877/v/**D**]

♦ Latin American Federation of Performers / see Federación Iberolatinoamericana de Artistas Intérpretes y Ejecutantes (#09325)
♦ Latin American Federation of Perinatology (#09345)
♦ Latin American Federation of Petroleum Workers (inactive)

♦ Latin American Federation of the Pharmaceutical Industry 16328

Fédération latinoaméricaine de l'industrie pharmaceutique – Federación Latinoamericana de la Industria Farmacéutica (FIFARMA)
Exec Dir Porfirio Diaz No 102 Col Del Valle, Delegación Benito Juarez, CP 13100, 13100 Mexico City CDMX, Mexico. E-mail: secretariageneral@fifarma.org – info@fifarma.org.
URL: http://www.fifarma.org/
History 4 Aug 1962, Bogota (Colombia). Founded during 1st Inter American Conference of the Pharmaceutical Industry. Statutes amended 2014. **Aims** Be the regional voice of the innovative pharmaceutical industry, supporting development of a sustainable and patient centric healthcare system in Latin America. **Structure** Executive Committee; Steering Committee; Advisory Board; Working Groups. **Languages** English, Portuguese, Spanish. **Staff** 4.00 FTE, paid. **Finance** Annual budget: 70,000,000 USD. **Publications** *FIFARMA News Bulletin*. Conference proceedings.
Members Pharmaceutical association representatives (9) and pharmaceutical companies (11) in 8 countries:
Argentina, Brazil, Chile, Colombia, Ecuador, Mexico, Peru, Venezuela.
IGO Relations Accredited by (1): *United Nations Office at Vienna (UNOV, #20604)*. Official relations with: *Pan American Health Organization (PAHO, #18108)*. [2020/XD2878/t/**D**]

♦ Latin American Federation of Phonograms and Videograms Producers (inactive)
♦ Latin American Federation of Physics Societies (#09370)
♦ Latin American Federation of Press Workers / see Federación Latinoamericana de Trabajadores de la Cultura y de la Comunicación Social (#09374)
♦ Latin-American Federation of Psychology in Emergencies and Disasters (no recent information)

♦ Latin American Federation for Psychotherapy 16329

Federación Latinoamericana de psicoterapia (FLAPSI)
Pres c/o SUAMOC, Ejido 1415, Of 802, Montevideo, Uruguay. E-mail: flapsisec2@gmail.com – flpsicoterapia@gmail.com.
Contact Fundación AIGLE, Virrey Olaguer 2679, 1426 Buenos Aires, Argentina. T. +541147845363.
URL: http://www.flapsi.org/
History May 2000, Santiago (Chile). Founded following a meeting organized Buenos Aires (Argentina), 1999. A continental federation of *World Council for Psychotherapy (WCP, #21337)*. **Events** *Congreso Latinoamericano de Psicoterapia* Montevideo (Uruguay) 2021, *Congreso Latinoamericano de Psicoterapia* Monterrey (Mexico) 2018, *Congress* La Paz (Bolivia) 2017, *Congreso Latinoamericano de Psicoterapia* Sao Paulo (Brazil) 2015, *Congreso Latinoamericano de Psicoterapia* Quito (Ecuador) 2013.
Members in 10 countries:
Argentina, Bolivia, Brazil, Chile, Ecuador, Mexico, Panama, Peru, Uruguay, Venezuela. [2020/XM1290/**D**]

♦ Latin American Federation of Psychotherapy and Psychoanalysis Associations (#09362)

♦ Latin American Federation of Seed Associations 16330

Federación Latinoamericana de Asociaciones de Semillas (FELAS) – Federação Latino-Americana de Associações de Sementes
Sec address not obtained. E-mail: asosemillas@cotas.com.bo – felas@felas.org.
History 21 Nov 1986. Former names and other names: *Latin American Federation of Seed Producers Association* – former. **Aims** Strengthen functioning of national seed producers associations; promote international trade; serve as a forum for exchange of knowledge, training and integration. **Structure** General Assembly; Council. **Languages** Spanish. **Staff** 1.00 FTE, paid. **Finance** Sources: members' dues. **Events** *Biennial Pan American Seed Seminar* Santa Cruz (Bolivia) 2012, *Biennial Pan American Seed Seminar* Asunción (Paraguay) 2010, *Biennial Pan American seed seminar* Cartagena de Indias (Colombia) 2008, *Biennial Pan American seed seminar* Fortaleza (Brazil) 2006, *Biennial Pan American seed seminar* Asunción (Paraguay) 2004.
Members National associations (11) in 10 countries:
Bolivia, Brazil, Colombia, Dominican Rep, Ecuador, El Salvador, Guatemala, Mexico, Paraguay, Venezuela.
NGO Relations Member of (1): *Seed Association of the Americas (SAA, #19214)* (Affiliate). [2018/XD7011/**D**]

♦ Latin American Federation of Seed Producers Association / see Latin American Federation of Seed Associations (#16330)
♦ Latin-American Federation for Semiotic Studies (no recent information)

♦ Latin American Federation of Sexology and Sexual Education Societies 16331

Federación Latinoamericana de Sociedades de Sexologia y Educación Sexual (FLASSES)
Pres Praça Dom Feliciano 26, sala 402, Porto Alegre RS, Brazil.
SG address not obtained.
URL: http://www.flasses.net/
History 23 Mar 1980, Montevideo (Uruguay). Founded on the occasion of the 6th *Jornadas Latinoamericanas de Sociedades de Sexología y Educación Sexual*. A regional continental federation of *World Association for Sexual Health (WAS, #21187)*. **Structure** Board of Directors, comprising President, 2 Vice-Presidents, Secretary-General and Treasurer. Commissions (5): Consultative; Documentation and Publications Centre; Sexual Nomenclature; Accreditations; Ethics. **Languages** Portuguese, Spanish. **Activities** Organizes Latin American Congress of Sexology and Sexual Education (CLASES). **Events** *Congreso Latinoamericano de Sexología y Educación Sexual* Valencia (Spain) 2022, *Biennial Congress* Brasilia (Brazil) 2021, *Biennial Congress* Lima (Peru) 2020, *Biennial Congress* Buenos Aires (Argentina) 2018, *Biennial Congress* Madrid (Spain) 2016. **Publications** *Flasses Online* – electronic bulletin; *Revisto Latino Americana de Sexologia*. *Catalogos Latinoamericanos de Publicaciones* (12th ed).
Members Associations (about 80) in 14 countries:
Argentina, Bolivia, Brazil, Chile, Colombia, Costa Rica, Cuba, Dominican Rep, Ecuador, Mexico, Peru, Spain, Uruguay, Venezuela. [2022/XD7459/**D**]

♦ Latin American Federation of Social Tourism (inactive)

♦ Latin American Federation of Societies of Obesity 16332

Federación Latinoamericana de Sociedades de Obesidad (FLASO)
Pres Mariano Turrey N45-172 y Av Marco Jofre, Avda Gonzales Suarez y Rafael Leon, E14-107 PB Edif Qatar, Quito, Ecuador. E-mail: info@flaso.net.
URL: http://flaso.net/

History 9 Oct 1990, Santiago (Chile). **Aims** Develop medical meetings related to the latest advances in obesity; advise the public on the risks of obesity, on prevention and treatment. **Structure** General Committee of 12 members. Executive Committee, comprising President, Vice-President, Secretary and Treasurer. **Languages** Spanish. **Staff** 8.00 FTE, voluntary. **Finance** Members' dues. Other sources: Congress dues. **Events** *Congress* Mexico 2014, *Congress* Santiago (Chile) 2010, *Congress* Panama 2001, *Latin American summit on healthy weight* Rio de Janeiro (Brazil) 2000, *Congress* Buenos Aires (Argentina) 1999. **Publications** *Obesidad* (4 a year) – magazine. *Acta de Rio de Janeiro*; *Latin American consensuous.*
Members Organizations (12) in 12 countries:
Argentina, Bolivia, Brazil, Chile, Colombia, Cuba, Ecuador, Panama, Paraguay, Peru, Puerto Rico, Uruguay.
NGO Relations Affiliated with: *World Obesity (#21678).* [2022/XD7582/**D**]

♦ Latin-American Federation of Societies of Phoniatrics, Logopedics and Audiologists (inactive)

♦ Latin American Federation of Societies of Ultrasound in Medicine and Biology 16333

Federación Latinoamericana de Sociedades de Ultrasonido (FLAUS)
Pres address not obtained. T. +551132846680. E-mail: flaus@hybrida.com.br.
URL: http://www.flaus-us.org/
History 1983, Buenos Aires (Argentina), during the 1st Latin American Ultrasound Congress. **Aims** Encourage promotion of ultrasound through educational programmes and national congresses in affiliated countries. **Structure** Executive Committee. **Activities** Events/meetings. **Events** *Congress* San José (Costa Rica) 2015, *Congress* Sao Paulo (Brazil) 2013, *Congress* Asunción (Paraguay) 2011, *Biennial congress / Congress* Ecuador 2007, *Biennial congress / Congress* Cancún (Mexico) 2003.
Members National societies (15) in 15 countries:
Argentina, Bolivia, Brazil, Chile, Colombia, Costa Rica, Dominican Rep, Ecuador, Guatemala, Mexico, Nicaragua, Paraguay, Peru, Uruguay, Venezuela.
NGO Relations Affiliated with: *Inter-American College of Radiology (IACR, #11409)*; *World Federation for Ultrasound in Medicine and Biology (WFUMB, #21497).* [2014/XD3414/**D**]

♦ Latin American Federation of Textile Chemists (#09366)
♦ Latin American Federation of Therapeutic Communities (#09352)
♦ Latin American Federation of Thermalism and Climatism (no recent information)
♦ Latin American Federation of Transport Workers (no recent information)

♦ Latin American Federation of University Women 16334

Federación Latinoamericana de Mujeres Universitarias (FLAMU)
Pres Res El Vergel 2271, Dep 1001, Providencia, Santiago, Santiago Metropolitan, Chile. T. +5624153615. Fax +5624153615.
URL: http://www.ifuw.org/who-we-are/our-membership/regional-groups/
History Founded 20 Jul 1996, as a regional grouping of *Graduate Women International (GWI, #10688).* **Structure** General Assembly (annual). Executive Committee, comprising President, Vice President, General Secretary, Treasurer and 5 further members. **Languages** Portuguese, Spanish. **Staff** None. **Finance** Members' dues. **Events** *Women towards 21st century or women and citizenship* Santiago (Chile) 2000, *Meeting* Montevideo (Uruguay) 1999, *Meeting* Santiago (Chile) 1997, *Meeting* Uruguay 1996.
Members Individuals in 4 countries:
Bolivia, Brazil, Chile, Uruguay. [2016/XD6621/**D**]

♦ Latin American Federation of Workers of the Construction Industry, Wood and Building Materials (inactive)
♦ Latin American Federation of Workers of the Food, Hotel and Tobacco Industries (inactive)
♦ Latin American Federation of the Workers in Graphic and Paper Industries (inactive)
♦ Latin American Federation of Workers of the Textile, Clothing, Leather and Shoe Industries (inactive)
♦ Latin American Federation of Writers (inactive)
♦ Latin American Federation of Young Environmentalists (inactive)

♦ Latin American Fisheries Development Organization 16335

Organisation latinoaméricaine pour le développement de la pêche – Organización Latinoamericana de Desarrollo Pesquero (OLDEPESCA)
Assistant Exec Dir address not obtained. T. +51997153453. Fax +51947340146. E-mail: direc@oldepesca.com.
History 29 Oct 1982. Established by an agreement which entered into force 2 Nov 1984. Agreement amended 2 Nov 1984, Managua (Nicaragua). Arose from Action Committees of *Sistema Económico Latinoamericano (SELA, #19294)*, and replaced *Action Committee on Sea and Freshwater Products (CAPMAD)*, set up 1977, whose activities it took over, following decision of 3rd Annual Meeting of Ministers responsible for matters concerning fisheries. Officially commenced activities 1 Jan 1985. **Aims** Increase production and trade of marine and freshwater products; boost consumption of such products; promote the generation of sources of income and employment; promote rational exploitation of the potential of fisheries in the region; coordinate joint actions with Member States. **Structure** Conference of Ministers (annual), comprising Ministers or Secretaries of State responsible for matters related to the fishery sector, or their alternates. Governing Board (meets annually prior to Conference), consisting of an official representative and substitute appointed by each country. Executive Director appointed by Conference for 3-year term; Executive Management Board. Technical Committee for the Technological Development of Fish Products in Latin America and the Caribbean. **Languages** English, French, Portuguese, Spanish. **Staff** 7.00 FTE, paid. **Finance** Contributions from member states. **Activities** Regional cooperation concentrates mainly on: research on fishery resources; exploitation of fishery resources; industrialization and physical support infrastructure; aquaculture; technological development; marketing; training; international cooperation. Much of the work of coordination, negotiation and publication is the responsibility of the Technical Committee. Projects include: information mechanisms; regional training programme; starting up *East Pacific Tuna Organization (inactive)*; assessment of the main species in Lake Titicaca; regional aquacultural project; technological development of fishery projects in Latin America and the Caribbean; construction and repair of small- and medium-sized vessels; promotion of foreign trade in fishery products; promotion of fishery research in the Central American area; prospective study for fishery organization and development in Latin America and the Caribbean; regional cooperation on coastal fishing; development of fishery in Central America and Panama (with establishment of a Technical Secretariat in Panama); development of continental fishing. **Events** *Conference of Ministers* Campeche (Mexico) 2010, *Conference of ministers* Lima (Peru) 2004, *Conference of ministers* San Salvador (El Salvador) 2003, *Conference of ministers* Belize 1997, *Conference of ministers* Havana (Cuba) 1996. **Publications** *Aquarius* (4 a year); *Revista Latinoamericana de Acuicultura* (4 a year); *Vessel* (2 a year); *Documentos de Pesca* (irregular); *Revista sobre Embarcaciones Pesqueras de Pequeño y Mediano Porte* (irregular); *Revista Tecnologia de Alimentos Pesqueros* (irregular). Directories.
Members Members in 19 countries:
Argentina, Bolivia, Brazil, Chile, Colombia, Costa Rica, Cuba, Dominican Rep, Ecuador, El Salvador, Guatemala, Honduras, Mexico, Nicaragua, Panama, Paraguay, Peru, Uruguay, Venezuela.
IGO Relations Relationship agreement with: *FAO (#09260).* [2015/XD0335/**D***]

♦ Latin American Food Marketing Association (no recent information)
♦ Latin American Forestry Commission / see Latin American and Caribbean Forestry Commission (#16278)
♦ Latin American Forestry Institute (internationally oriented national body)

♦ Latin American Forum of Environmental Sciences 16336

Foro Latinoamericano de Ciencias Ambientales (FLACAM)
Main Office c/o CEPA, Calle 53 No 506, B1900BMF La Plata, Argentina. T. +54214256556. Fax +54214226800. E-mail: flacam@flacam-red.com.ar – cursosflacam@gmail.com.
URL: http://www.redflacam.com/
History 1989, as *Latin American Faculty for Environmental Sciences – Facultad Latinoamericana de Ciencias Ambientales (FLACAM).* Present name adopted, 1999. **Aims** Develop theory, principles and epistemology of environmental sciences and, particularly, their contribution to implement *sustainable development*; provide training in the field of the resolution of environmental and *development* conflicts. **Structure** Board of Directors. **Languages** English, Spanish. **Staff** 4.00 FTE, paid. **Finance** Funds from courses, programmes and congresses. **Activities** Training/education; projects/programmes; events/meetings. **Publications** *Sin Murallas* – magazine. *Voces de FLACAM* – book series. Books.
Members National and local offices (25) in 12 countries:
Argentina, Bolivia, Brazil, Chile, Colombia, Cuba, Honduras, Mexico, Paraguay, Peru, Spain, Venezuela. [2020/XF5379/**F**]

♦ Latin American Forum for Urban Security and Democracy (#09883)
♦ Latin American Foster Care Network (#18700)
♦ Latin American Foundation of Catholics for the Right to Decide (#03612)
♦ Latin American Foundation of Detained and Disappeared People / see Fundación Latinoamericana por los Derechos Humanos y el Desarrollo Social (#10036)
♦ Latin American Foundation for Distance Education (#10037)
♦ Latin American Foundation for Human Rights and Social Development (#10036)
♦ Latin American Free Trade Association (inactive)
♦ Latin American Glaucoma Society (#19357)
♦ Latin American Group of Cement and Concrete Institutions / see Federación Interamericana del Cemento (#09330)
♦ Latin American Group of Ocular Angiography, Laser and Vitreo-retinal Surgery / see Pan-American Retina and Vitreous Society (#18126)

♦ Latin American Group for Public Administration (LAGPA/IIAS) 16337

Grupo Latinoamericano por la Administración Pública (GLAP/IIAS) – Grupo Latino-americano pela Administração Pública (GLAP/IIAS)
Exec Sec Fundação Getuio Vargas, Praia de Botafogo no 190, 15o andar – Sala 1506, Botafogo, Rio de Janeiro RJ, CEP 22 250 900, Brazil.
URL: https://lagpa.iias-iisa.org/
History Aug 2010, Chiapas (Mexico). Founded as a Regional group of *International Institute of Administrative Sciences (IIAS, #13859).* Current bylaws adopted Oct 2015. **Aims** Strengthen liaisons among Latin American and the Caribbean specialists in Public Administration, both scholars and practitioners; promote innovative ideas, methods and techniques in order to develop the theory and management of public policies. **Structure** General Meeting (annual); Steering Committee; Secretariat. **Languages** Portuguese, Spanish. **Activities** Events/meetings. **Events** *Annual Conference* Barranquilla (Colombia) 2022, *Annual Conference* San Juan (Costa Rica) 2021, *Annual Conference* Bogota (Colombia) 2020, *Annual Conference* Quito (Ecuador) 2019, *Joint Conference* Lima (Peru) 2018. **Publications** *RAP-GLAP* (2 a year). [2022.11.02/XM8391/**E**]

♦ Latin American Group for the Study of Lupus (unconfirmed)

♦ Latin American Heads Conference (LAHC) 16338

Exec Officer Av Ricardo Elias Aparicio 240, 12, Lima, Peru.
URL: http://www.lahc.net/
History Apr 1996, Montevideo (Uruguay), The British Schools, as *Latin American Heads Conference of Schools Reflecting British Practice.* **Aims** As a network of heads and leaders of schools based on British educational principles and with an international focus, share good practice and provide mutual support through provision of professional development opportunities. **Structure** General Meeting (annual). Executive Committee, comprising Chair, Treasurer and 3 Officers (Education, Student, Communication). **Languages** English. **Staff** 2.50 FTE, paid. **Finance** Members' dues. Other sources: income from conference fees and training. **Activities** Organizes: Annual Members' Conference (early May, on rotational basis by country); Annual Student Conference (Sep/Oct) for students of member schools in the last 2 years of Secondary Education. Other activities: LAHC School Review – an evaluation of academic and other aspects, applied upon request; appraisal process for heads of school and section; training for senior and middle managers and teachers; exchanges for teachers and for pupils. **Events** *Student Conference* Lima (Peru) 2011, *Annual Conference* Bogota (Colombia) 2009, *Student Conference* Chile 2009, *Annual Conference* Santiago (Chile) 2008, *Annual members conference / Annual Conference* Quito (Ecuador) 2007. **Publications** Newsletter (3 a year), circulated to membership and accessible on website.
Members Heads of schools (42) in 11 countries:
Argentina, Brazil, Chile, Colombia, Ecuador, Mexico, Panama, Peru, Trinidad-Tobago, Uruguay, Venezuela. [2012.06.01/XF7084/**F**]

♦ Latin American Heads Conference of Schools Reflecting British Practice / see Latin American Heads Conference (#16338)
♦ Latin American Health Sciences Information Centre / see Latin American and Caribbean Centre on Health Sciences Information (#16267)

♦ Latin American Heart Rhythm Society (LAHRS) 16339

Sociedad Latinoamericana del Ritmo Cardiaco
Admin Office Av Garibaldi 2583, 11600 Montevideo, Uruguay.
URL: http://lahrs.org/
History Founded in 1979, as *Sociedad Latino Americana de Estimulación Cardiaca (SOLAEC).* 1996, name changed to *Sociedad Latinoamericana de Estimulación Cardiaca y Electrofisiología (SOLAECE) – Latin American Society of Cardiac Pacing and Electrophysiology.* 2017, present name adopted upon restructuring and legal registration. **Activities** Congress. **Events** *Scientific Sessions* Montevideo (Uruguay) 2021, *Scientific Sessions* Montevideo (Uruguay) 2020, *Scientific Sessions* Guadalajara (Mexico) 2019, *Scientific Sessions* Cartagena de Indias (Colombia) 2018, *International workshop on arrhythmias* Venice (Italy) 2007. [2018/XJ0860/**D**]

♦ Latin American Hemapheresis Group / see Asociación Latinoamericana de Aféresis y Terapias celulares (#02178)
♦ Latin American High Tech, Computer and Law Institute (#11341)
♦ Latin American Hospital Association / see Latin American Federation of Hospitals (#16322)
♦ Latin American Hospital Federation / see Latin American Federation of Hospitals (#16322)
♦ Latin American Human Proteome Organization (no recent information)
♦ Latin American Human Rights Education and Research Network (#18712)
♦ Latin American and Iberian Institute, Albuquerque (internationally oriented national body)

♦ Latin American and Iberian Law and Economics Association 16340

Asociación Latinoamericana e Ibérica de Derecho y Economia (ALACDE) – Associação Latino-Americana e Ibérica de Direito e Economia
Vice Pres Av República 105, 837-0089 Santiago, Santiago Metropolitan, Chile. E-mail: info@alacde.org.
URL: http://alacdeorg.com/
History 1994, as *Latin American Law and Economics Association – Asociación Latinoamericana de Derecho y Economia (ALADE).* Later known as *Latin American and Caribbean Law and Economics Association – Asociación Latinoamericana y del Caribe de Derecho y Economia (ALACDE) – Associação Latino Americana e do Caribe de Direito e Economia.* Present name adopted, 2016. **Structure** Board of Directors; Advisory Board. **Activities** Events/meetings; training/education; awards/prizes/competitions. **Events** *Congress* Santiago (Chile) 2016, *Congress* Lima (Peru) 2012, *Congress* Bogota (Colombia) 2011, *Congress* San Salvador (El Salvador) 2010, *Annual conference / Congress* Barcelona (Spain) 2009. **Publications** *L and E Journal.* **NGO Relations** *Corporación Latinoamericana para el Desarrollo (CLD, no recent information)* is a member. [2019/XD7316/**D**]

♦ Latin American Industrialists Association 16341

Association des industriels de l'Amérique latine – Asociación de Industriales Latinoamericanos (AILA) – Associação dos Industriais Latinoamericanos (AILA)
Main Office 300 Mts Sur de la Fuente de la Hispanidad, San Pedro, Nivel 12, San José, Montes de Oca, San Pedro, Costa Rica. T. +50622025600. E-mail: secretaria.tecnica@aila.lat.
URL: https://www.aila.lat/
History Founded Apr 1962, Buenos Aires (Argentina), at 1st Assembly of Industrialists of the countries of the then *Latin American Free Trade Association (LAFTA, inactive)*, currently, since 12 aug 1980, *Latin American Integration Association (LAIA, #16343).* **Aims** Defend the principles of free enterprise and private initiative; promote Latin American integration and international cooperation to assist industrial development and the formulation of a common economic policy; promote trade; coordinate development activities of members and promote cooperation between them. **Structure** Congress (annual); General Assembly (annual) elects

Executive Board; Council of Section Representatives; Officers (3). **Languages** Portuguese, Spanish. **Staff** 3.00 FTE, paid. **Activities** Projects/programmes. **Events** *Annual Congress* Guayaquil (Ecuador) 2008, *General assembly / Annual Congress* Chile 2007, *Annual general assembly and congress / Annual Congress* Mexico City (Mexico) 1992, *Annual Congress* San Juan (Puerto Rico) 1991, *Annual general assembly and congress / Annual Congress* Ecuador 1990. **Publications** *Boletín AILA*.

Members Active; Sectorial; Adherent. Active members in 17 countries:
Argentina, Bolivia, Brazil, Chile, Colombia, Costa Rica, Dominican Rep, Ecuador, El Salvador, Guatemala, Honduras, Mexico, Nicaragua, Panama, Peru, Uruguay, Venezuela.
International organization:
Federación de Cámaras y Asociaciones Industriales de Centroamérica y República Dominicana (FECAICA, #09294).

Consultative Status Consultative status granted from: *ECOSOC (#05331)* (Ros C); *ILO (#11123)* (Regional); *UNCTAD (#20285)* (General Category); *UNIDO (#20336)*; *OAS (#17629)*. **NGO Relations** Through Global Chamber Platform, links with: *Association des chambres de commerce et d'industrie européennes (EUROCHAMBRES, #02423).* [2021/XD7129/ty/**D**]

- ♦ Latin American Information Center on Migration / see Center for Information on Migration in Latin America (#03643)
- ♦ Latin American Information Technology Industry Association / see Federación de Asociaciones de América Latina, el Caribe, España y Portugal de Entidades de Tecnologias de Información y Comunicación (#09288)
- ♦ Latin American Institute for Advanced Technology, Computer Science and Law / see Instituto Latinoamericano de Alta Tecnologia, Informatica y Derecho (#11341)
- ♦ Latin American Institute of Agricultural Marketing (inactive)
- ♦ Latin American Institute, Albuquerque / see Latin American and Iberian Institute, Albuquerque
- ♦ Latin American Institute for Alternative Legal Services / see Latin American Institute for and Alternative Society and an Alternative Law
- ♦ Latin American Institute for and Alternative Society and an Alternative Law (internationally oriented national body)
- ♦ Latin American Institute of Auditing Sciences / see Organization of Latin American and Caribbean Supreme Audit Institutions (#17877)
- ♦ Latin American Institute, Berlin / see Lateinamerika-Institut, Freie Universität Berlin
- ♦ Latin American Institute of Communication Education / see Instituto Latinoamericano de la Comunicación Educativa (#11343)
- ♦ Latin American Institute of Comparative Law (inactive)
- ♦ Latin American Institute for Economic and Social Planning / see Latin American and Caribbean Institute for Economic and Social Planning (#16279)
- ♦ Latin American Institute of Educational Cinema / see Instituto Latinoamericano de la Comunicación Educativa (#11343)
- ♦ Latin American Institute of Educational Communication (#11343)
- ♦ Latin American Institute for Mental Health and Human Rights (internationally oriented national body)

♦ Latin American Institute for the Ombudsman 16342

Instituto Latino Americano del Ombudsman (ILO)

SG Corrientes 880 pis o7o, C1008AAG Buenos Aires, Argentina. E-mail: info@ilo-defensordelpueblo.org.
URL: http://www.ilo-defensordelpueblo.org/

History 15 Aug 1984, Caracas (Venezuela). Former names and other names: *Instituto Latinoamericano del Ombudsman – Defensor del Pueblo (ILO)* – full title. **Aims** Promote the figure of the Ombudsman in Latin America; contribute to the consolidation of democratic processes and respect for human rights; develop academic studies about the ombudsman institution. **Structure** Assembly (annual); Board of Directors. **Languages** Portuguese, Spanish. **Finance** No funding. **Events** *Annual Assembly* Brazil 2015. **Publications** *Éforos*. Books.

Members Full (85) in 19 countries and territories:
Argentina, Bolivia, Brazil, Chile, Colombia, Costa Rica, Curaçao, Ecuador, Honduras, Italy, Mexico, Paraguay, Romania, Spain, St Maarten, Trinidad-Tobago, Uruguay, USA, Venezuela. [2020/XN9977/j/**D**]

- ♦ Latin American Institute for Social Research (#11346)
- ♦ Latin American Institute of Social Studies 'Humberto Valdez' (inactive)
- ♦ Latin American Institute of Social Theory and Social Studies (#11345)
- ♦ Latin American Institute, Stockholm / see Nordic Institute of Latin American Studies

♦ Latin American Integration Association (LAIA) 16343

Association latinoaméricaine d'intégration (ALADI) – Asociación Latinoamericana de Integración (ALADI) – Associação Latino-Americana de Integração (ALADI)

SG Calle Cebollati 1461, Barrio Palermo, Casilla de Correo 20005, 12000 Montevideo, Uruguay. T. +59824101121 – +59824101125. Fax +59824190649. E-mail: sgaladi@aladi.org.
Undersecretary address not obtained.
Undersecretary address not obtained.
URL: http://www.aladi.org/

History 12 Aug 1980, Montevideo (Uruguay). Established when the new *Montevideo Treaty 1980 (1980)* was signed by the Ministers of Foreign Affairs of 11 Latin American countries. Replaced the former *Latin American Free Trade Association (LAFTA, inactive)*, which entered into force 2 Jun 1961, following ratification of the first *Montevideo Treaty (1960)*, signed 18 Feb 1960. LAIA entered into force 18 Mar 1981, after deposit of the first 3 ratification instruments by the signatory Governments. The new Montevideo Treaty, which has an indefinite duration, introduces fundamental changes to the orientation of the regional integration process. It is open to all Latin American nations and extends its scope of action to the rest of Latin America through multilateral links or partial agreements with other countries or integration movements in the continent. Similarly, the Treaty foresees horizontal cooperation with other integration schemes of the world. **Aims** Support creation of an area of *economic* preferences in the region, with the ultimate goal of a Latin American *common market*. **Structure** Council of Foreign Affairs Ministers; Evaluation and Convergence Conference; Committee of Representatives; General Secretariat (technical body). *'Montevideo Treaty 1980'* is the global legal framework that constitutes and rules the Association. **Languages** Portuguese, Spanish. **Staff** 65.00 FTE, paid. **Finance** Sources: contributions of member/participating states. **Activities** Monitoring/evaluation. **Events** *Annual Forum* 2021, *Forum* Montevideo (Uruguay) 2021, *ONLINE EDUCA : international conference on technology based education and training* Madrid (Spain) 2006, *Seminar on international negotiations on agriculture* Montevideo (Uruguay) 2000, *Meeting* Quito (Ecuador) 1994. **Publications** *Comercio exterior global : ALADI* (annual); *Tendencias del Comercio (TENCI)* (irregular). *Montevideo Treaty 1980* in English, Portuguese, Spanish. Periodicals; books; reports; technical studies; subscribed agreements between member countries; CD-ROMs.

Members Through the 'Montevideo Treaty 1980' any Latin American country can join LAIA; membership also open to all Latin American countries through agreements with other countries and integration areas of the continent, as well as to other developing countries or their respective integration areas outside Latin America. Members include the governments of 13 countries:
Argentina, Bolivia, Brazil, Chile, Colombia, Cuba, Ecuador, Mexico, Panama, Paraguay, Peru, Uruguay, Venezuela.

Consultative Status Consultative status granted from: *World Intellectual Property Organization (WIPO, #21593)* (Observer Status). [2021.11.09/XD2879/y/**D***]

- ♦ Latin American Investment Guarantee Corporation (no recent information)
- ♦ Latin American Iron and Steel Institute / see Asociación Latinoamericana del Acero (#02176)

♦ Latin American Jewish Congress (LAJC) 16344

Congrès juif latinoaméricain – Congreso Judio Latinoamericano (CJL) – Congresso Judaico Latino Americano

Contact Larrea 744, C1030AAP Buenos Aires, Argentina. T. +541149614534 – +541149625028. Fax +541149637056. E-mail: info@congresojudio.org.
URL: http://www.congresojudio.org/

Members Full in 21 countries:
Argentina, Bolivia, Brazil, Chile, Colombia, Costa Rica, Cuba, Dominican Rep, Ecuador, El Salvador, Guatemala, Guyana, Haiti, Honduras, Mexico, Nicaragua, Panama, Paraguay, Peru, Suriname, Venezuela.

NGO Relations Regional branch of: *World Jewish Congress (WJC, #21599).* [2013.08.16/XF0421/**E**]

♦ Latin American Journalism Centre 16345

Centro Latinoamericano de Periodismo (CELAP)

Contact address not obtained. E-mail: dilmar@celap.net.
URL: http://www.celap.net/

History May 1995. Took over the Journalism Program of *Florida International University (FIU)*. **Aims** Promote a free and responsible press through ongoing education and training of journalists. **Structure** General Assembly; Board of Directors. **Finance** Donations. **Activities** Specialized courses for journalists and media staff. **Events** *Congress* Panama (Panama) 2004, *Congress* Panama (Panama) 2001, *Interactive media conference* Santiago (Chile) 1996.

Members in 25 countries:
Argentina, Bahamas, Belize, Bolivia, Brazil, Chile, Colombia, Costa Rica, Cuba, Dominican Rep, Ecuador, El Salvador, Guatemala, Guyana, Haiti, Honduras, Jamaica, Mexico, Nicaragua, Panama, Paraguay, Puerto Rico, Suriname, Uruguay, Venezuela. [2016/XE4179/**E**]

♦ Latin American Laboratory for Assessment of Quality in Education . 16346

Laboratorio Latinoamericano de Evaluación de la Calidad de la Educación (LLECE)

Coordinator OREALC/UNESCO Santiago, Enrique Delpiano 2058, Plaza Pedro de Valdivia, Providencia, 7511019 Santiago, Santiago Metropolitan, Chile. T. +56234724600 – +56224724632.
URL: http://www.unesco.org/new/en/santiago/education/education-assessment-llece/

History 10 Nov 1994, Mexico City (Mexico). Coordinated by *UNESCO Regional Bureau for Education in Latin America and the Caribbean (#20318)*, Santiago (Chile), originally within the framework of *Major Project in the Field of Education in Latin America and the Caribbean (inactive)* before the latter's termination in Mar 2001. **Aims** As a new form of cooperation among countries of the region, improve quality and equity of education by adopting methodologies which provide greater clarity in discerning the processes and results of efforts undertaken by countries in this field; carry out assessment both in policy making and in tracking and carrying out educational policy. **Structure** Organized as the *'National Assessment Systems Network'* where each country is represented by its coordinator of the National Assessment or Evaluation and Measurement System. Technical Coordination Team, comprising Coordinator, Technical Assistant, Programme Assistant and Chief of the Section for Planning, Management, Monitoring and Evaluation. **Staff** 4.00 FTE, paid. **Finance** Grants from: *Inter-American Development Bank (IDB, #11427)*; *Ford Foundation (#09858)*; Statistics Canada. Contributions from: member countries; *UNESCO (#20322)*; *Convenio Andrés Bello de integración educativa, científica y cultural de América Latina y España (Convenio Andrés Bello, #04785)*. **Activities** Politics/policy/regulatory. **Events** *Meeting of National Coordinators* Havana (Cuba) 2004. **Publications** Reports; studies.

Members in 15 countries:
Argentina, Brazil, Chile, Colombia, Costa Rica, Dominican Rep, Ecuador, Guatemala, Honduras, Mexico, Nicaragua, Panama, Paraguay, Peru, Uruguay.

NGO Relations *Foro Hemisférico de Evaluación e Indicadores (no recent information)*; *Partnership for Educational Revitalization in the Americas (PREAL)*; national educational and development centres. [2017/XF4948/**F***]

- ♦ Latin American Laboratory for Protection Against Computer Viruses (#16214)
- ♦ Latin American Law and Economics Association / see Latin American and Iberian Law and Economics Association (#16340)
- ♦ Latin American Lay Movement (internationally oriented national body)
- ♦ Latin American League for the study of ADHD (unconfirmed)
- ♦ Latin American Leasing Federation (#09356)
- ♦ Latin American Leisure and Recreation Association (inactive)

♦ Latin American Lifestyle Medicine Association (LALMA) 16347

Asociación Latinoamericana de Medicina del Estilo de Vida

Contact Avenida Coronel Portillo 376, oficina 301, San Isidro, Lima, Peru. E-mail: info@lalma.co.
URL: http://www.lalma.co/

History Activities started 2014. Legally formalized 2018. **Aims** Promote the advancement and practice of Lifestyle Medicine, which is used as an intervention to prevent, treat and even reverse most chronic *diseases*, directly addressing the underlying causes. **Structure** Executive Council; Executive Board. **Languages** Spanish. **Staff** Voluntary. **Finance** Members' dues. Other sources: organization of academic and educational events. Annual budget: US$ 100,000. **Activities** Events/meetings; training/education; certification/accreditation. **Events** *Congress* Lima (Peru) 2020, *Congress* Cancún (Mexico) 2019, *Congress* Lima (Peru) 2018, *Congress* Lima (Peru) 2017.

Members Full in 11 countries:
Argentina, Bolivia, Brazil, Chile, Colombia, Costa Rica, Ecuador, Mexico, Panama, Paraguay, Peru.

NGO Relations *European Lifestyle Medicine Organization (ELMO, #07694)*; *Lifestyle Medical Global Alliance (LMGA, #16468).* [2020.01.17/XM7833/**D**]

- ♦ Latin American Light Network (#18673)
- ♦ Latin American Maccabi Confederation (#04459)
- ♦ Latin American Marketing Federation (no recent information)
- ♦ Latin American MCR Network / see Network for an Economical and Ecological Habitat (#17007)

♦ Latin American and Mediterranean Coalition for East Timor (LAMCET) 16348

Pres Via Emilio Morosini 36, 20135 Milan MI, Italy.
Sec Vicolo San Celso 14, 00186 Rome RM, Italy.

History Mar 1998, Santiago (Chile). Founded simultaneously in Sao Paulo (Brazil) and Lisbon (Portugal). **Aims** Provide *support* and facilitate advocacy for the people of Timor-Leste. **Structure** Executive Board; Standing Committee. **Languages** English, French, Italian, Portuguese, Spanish, Tetum. **Finance** Sources: donations; grants; members' dues. Annual budget: 30,000 USD. **Activities** Advocacy/lobbying/activism; events/meetings. **Events** *Workshop on Promoting Human Resource Development in East Timor* Rome (Italy) 2017, *Annual meeting* Dili (Timor-Leste) 2008, *Five years since independence, what next?* Lisbon (Portugal) 2008, *East Timor two years after freedom – what future?* 2002, *The UN administration in East Timor – an assessment* Barcelona (Spain) 2001. **Publications** *Viva Timor Leste* (4 a year).

Members Full in 61 countries and territories:
Angola, Argentina, Australia, Austria, Belgium, Brazil, Bulgaria, Canada, Cape Verde, Chile, China, Colombia, Costa Rica, Croatia, Cuba, Cyprus, Dominican Rep, Ecuador, Egypt, Ethiopia, France, Germany, Greece, Guatemala, Guinea-Bissau, Holy See, India, Indonesia, Ireland, Israel, Italy, Japan, Lithuania, Macau, Mauritania, Mexico, Monaco, Mozambique, Netherlands, New Zealand, North Macedonia, Norway, Paraguay, Peru, Philippines, Poland, Portugal, Russia, Sao Tomé-Principe, Slovenia, South Africa, Spain, Switzerland, Taiwan, Thailand, Timor-Leste, Türkiye, UK, Uruguay, USA, Venezuela.

NGO Relations Member of (2): Interfaith Encounter Association; *International Federation for East Timor (IFET, #13408).* [2021.05.18/XF6118/**F**]

- ♦ Latin American Meeting on Biological Inorganic Chemistry (meeting series)
- ♦ Latin American Millers' Association (no recent information)
- ♦ Latin American Motorcycling Union / see FIM Latin America (#09762)
- ♦ Latin American Mountain Forum / see Latin American Network on Andean Mountains (#16350)
- ♦ Latin American Multidisciplinary Association for Environmental Strategic Planning (inactive)
- ♦ Latin American Museological Association (inactive)
- ♦ Latin American Musical Education Forum (#09879)

♦ Latin American Nanotechnology and Society Network 16349

Red Latinoamericana de Nanotecnologia y Sociedad (ReLANS) – Rede Latinoamericana de Nanotecnologia e Sociedada

Address not obtained.
URL: http://www.relans.org/

History 2006, Zacatecas (Mexico). **Aims** Create a forum for discussion and information exchange that follows the process of nanotechnology development in Latin America. **Languages** Portuguese, Spanish. **Staff** All voluntary. **Finance** Project-based. No annual regular budget. **Activities** Events/meetings; training/education. **Events** *NANOSUR Community Workshop on Challenges of the Regional and International Cooperation in Nanoscience and Nanotechnology* Caracas (Venezuela) 2014, *Iberoamerican Seminar on Nanotechnologies* Zacatecas (Mexico) 2014, *Congress* Curitiba (Brazil) 2013. **Publications** Books.
Members Full in 13 countries:
Argentina, Bolivia, Brazil, Chile, Colombia, Costa Rica, Cuba, Mexico, Peru, Spain, Uruguay, USA, Venezuela.
NGO Relations *International Pollutants Elimination Network (IPEN, #14616).* [2015.02.12/XJ9258/F]

- Latin American Network Against Free Trade (internationally oriented national body)
- Latin American Network against Monoculture Tree Plantations (unconfirmed)

♦ Latin American Network on Andean Mountains (INfoAndina) 16350

Red Latinoamericana sobre Desarrollo Sostenible de Montañas
Contact c/o CONDESAN, Av La Molina 1895, Puerta No 3 del Centro Internacional de la Papa, Lima, Peru. T. +5116189400ext522. Fax +5116189415. E-mail: infoandina@condesan.org.
URL: http://www.infoandina.org/
History 1994. Serves as information programme of *Consortium for the Sustainable Development of the Andean Ecoregion (#04758).* Since 1996 a node of *Mountain Forum (MF, #16861).* Previously also referred to as *Latin American Mountain Forum – Foro de Montañas para América Latina.* **Aims** Promote knowledge generation, information exchange, and learning among different actors to create sustainable development of the mountain region. **Languages** English, Spanish. **Staff** 6.00 FTE, paid. **Finance** Support from: *Agencia Española de Cooperación Internacional para el Desarrollo (AECID); Swiss Agency for Development and Cooperation (SDC);* Other sources: information services provided to third parties. **Activities** *'InfoAndina'*, created in 1994, – knowledge management space aimed to promote information exchange in the Andean region. **Events** *Workshop on experiences in the management of biosphere reserves in mountainous regions of Latin America* 1998. [2014/XE3294/E]

♦ Latin American Network of Basin Organizations (LANBO) 16351

Réseau latino-américain des organismes de bassin (RELOB) – Red Latinoamericana de Organizaciones de Cuenca (RELOC)
Contact Agencia Nacl de Aguas de Brasil – ANA, Sector Polical – Area 5, Quadra 3, Bloco M, Sala 116, Brasilia DF, 70610-200 DF, Brazil. E-mail: relob@ana.gov.br.
History 9 Jul 1997, Brasilia (Brazil). 9-10 Jul 1997, Brasilia (Brazil), at Constituent Assembly. First General Assembly 4-6 Aug 1998, Santafé de Bogota (Colombia). Regional network of *International Network of Basin Organizations (INBO, #14235).* Registered in accordance with Mexican law. **Structure** General Assembly. **Activities** Knowledge management/information dissemination. **Events** *General Assembly* Fortaleza (Brazil) 2013, *General Assembly* Dakar (Senegal) 2010, *General Assembly* Foz do Iguaçu (Brazil) 2009, *General Assembly* Salvador (Brazil) 2008, *General Assembly* Québec, QC (Canada) 2002. [2015/XF1350/F]

- Latin American Network of Biological Sciences (#18706)
- Latin American Network for Community Marketing (#18707)
- Latin American Network on Debt, Development and Rights (#18711)
- Latin American Network for Documentation and Information on Public Management (see: #16294)

♦ Latin American Network for Economics of Learning, Innovation and Competence Building Systems (LALICS) 16352

Contact Calzada del Hueso 1100, Col Villa Quietud, Delegación Coyoacan, CP 04960 DF Mexico City CDMX, Mexico. E-mail: contacto@lalics.org – noticiaslalics@gmail.com.
URL: http://www.lalics.org/
History Originated 2004, Beijing (China), during 2nd *Global Network for Economics of Learning, Innovation and Competence Building Systems (GLOBELICS, #10488).* Set up 2011, Buenos Aires (Argentina), during GLOBELICS Conference. **Aims** Facilitate a forum for researchers, policy makers, students, entrepreneurs, and civil society organizations, in which they can share experiences and knowledge acquired through the implementation of public policies, theoretical frameworks and methodology, research results and new approaches to address the main challenges faced by the region; contribute to the global knowledge flow; add to the debate and advancement of knowledge in the area. **Structure** Scientific Board; Coordinator. **Languages** Spanish. **Staff** 1.00 FTE, paid; 3.00 FTE, voluntary. **Finance** No annual budget. **Activities** Research/documentation; capacity building; training/education; events/meetings. **Events** *ESOCITE-LALICS Congress* Montevideo (Uruguay) 2020, *Conference* Rio de Janeiro (Brazil) 2013. **IGO Relations** *Programa Iberoamericano de Ciencia y Tecnologia para el Desarrollo (CYTED, #18524).* **NGO Relations** Cooperates with (1): *Sociedad Latinoamericana de Estudios Sociales de la Ciencia y la Tecnologia (ESOCITE, #19407).* [2021/XJ9676/F]

♦ Latin American Network for Education in Nuclear Technology (LANENT) 16353

Red Latinoamericana para la Educación y la Capacitación en Tecnologia Nuclear
Contact c/o CNEA, Av Del Libertador 8250 (C1429BNP), Buenos Aires, Argentina. E-mail: medina.gironzini@gmail.com.
URL: http://www.lanentweb.org/
History Formally set up 8 Dec 2010, Lima (Peru), following a consultancy meeting held Apr 2009, San Carlos de Bariloche (Argentina), by *International Atomic Energy Agency (IAEA, #12294).* **Aims** Promote, develop and preserve nuclear knowledge to ensure the availability of qualified nuclear professionals in the future. **Structure** General Assembly; Coordinating Committee; Scientific Secretariat. **Activities** Training/education. **Events** *International Symposium on Radiological Protection in Medicine* Arequipa (Peru) 2017. **Publications** Bulletin. Abstracts.
Members Institutions in 17 countries:
Argentina, Bolivia, Brazil, Chile, Colombia, Costa Rica, Cuba, Ecuador, Guatemala, Mexico, Nicaragua, Panama, Paraguay, Peru, Spain, Uruguay, Venezuela.
International member:
Collaborator:
IGO Relations *Asian Network for Education in Nuclear Technology (ANENT, #01549).* **NGO Relations** *European Nuclear Education Network (ENEN, #08057).* [2019/XM6011/F]

- Latin American Network for Genocide and Mass Atrocity Prevention (#18716)
- Latin American Network of Independent Presenters of Contemporary Art / see Red de Promotores Culturales de Latinoamérica y el Caribe (#18727)
- Latin American Network Information Center, University of Texas (internationally oriented national body)
- Latin-American Network of Judges (#18714)
- Latin American Network of Masters in Children's Rights (#18715)

♦ Latin American Network of Non-Governmental Organizations of Persons with Disabilities and their Families 16354

Red Iberoamericana de Organizaciones No Gubernamentales de Personas con Discapacidad y sus Familias (RIADIS)
Contact Carrera 18A No 103 88, Bogota, Bogota DC, Colombia.
Contact Hernando de la Cruz 3254 y Mariana de Jesús Dpto 2, Quito, Ecuador. E-mail: info@riadis.org.
URL: http://www.riadis.org/
History Set up 17 Oct 2002, Caracas (Venezuela). Previously also referred to as *Ibero-American Network of Organizations and Persons with Disabilities.* **Aims** Promote and protect the rights of people with disabilities in Latin America and the Caribbean, promoting values of non-discrimination and inclusive development based on improving quality of life and social inclusion of persons with disabilities and their families. **Structure** General Assembly; Board of Directors; Committees (4); Fiscal Council. **Languages** Portuguese, Spanish. **Staff** 1.00 FTE, paid. **Finance** Members' dues. International funding. Annual budget (2014): US$ 396,972. **Activities** Knowledge management/information dissemination; events/meetings; training/education; advocacy/lobbying/activism. **Members** Organizations (49) in 19 countries. Membership countries not specified. **NGO Relations** Member of: *International Disability Alliance (IDA, #13176).* Alliances with: *Disabled Peoples' International (DPI, #05097); Humanity and Inclusion (HI, #10975); Inclusion International (#11145); Latin American Blind Union (#16256);* other NGOs, not specified. [2014.06.01/XF6958/F]

♦ Latin American Network of People Living with HIV/AIDS (RED LA+) 16355

Contact address not obtained. T. +5073965161. Fax +5073965160.
URL: http://www.gnpplus.net/
History Regional network of *Global Network of People Living with HIV/AIDS (GNP+, #10494).* Also referred to as *GNP Latin America.* **NGO Relations** Member of: *International Treatment Preparedness Coalition (ITPC, #15729).* Partner of: *Horizontal Technical Cooperation Group of Latin America and the Caribbean on HIV/AIDS (HTGC, #10945).* [2013/XF6339/F]

- Latin American Network for Rivers, River Communities and Water (#18709)
- Latin American Network of Silk (inactive)
- Latin American Network for Social Ecology / see Latin American and Caribbean Network for Social Ecology (#16283)
- Latin American Networks School (internationally oriented national body)
- Latin American Network of Women in Fisheries / see Network of Latin American Women of the Fishery Sector (#17046)
- Latin American Notaphilic Society / see Latin American Paper Money Society (#16359)
- Latin American Nutritional Information Council (internationally oriented national body)
- Latin American Observatory of Environmental Conflict, Chile (internationally oriented national body)
- Latin American Occupational Safety Association (no recent information)

♦ Latin American Occupational Therapists Confederation 16356

Confederación Latinoamericana de Terapeutas Ocupacionales (CLATO)
Contact Los Magnolios 0284, Maupú, Santiago, Santiago Metropolitan, Chile. E-mail: contacto@clatoterapiaocupacional.org – clatoterapiaocupacional@gmail.com.
Sec Cra 17 A, No 119 A-38, Bogota, Bogota DC, Colombia. E-mail: juliansto@gmail.com.
URL: https://www.clatoterapiaocupacional.org/
History Oct 1997, Venezuela. Founded during 3rd Latin American Congress on Occupational Therapists. **Structure** Officers: President; Vice-President; 2 Secretaries; Treasurer. **Events** *Congress* Argentina 2019, *Congress* Mexico 2017, *Congress* San José (Costa Rica) 2015, *Congress* Caracas (Venezuela) 2013, *Congress* Brazil 2011.
Members in 9 countries:
Argentina, Brazil, Chile, Colombia, Costa Rica, El Salvador, Mexico, Peru, Venezuela.
NGO Relations Member of: *World Federation of Occupational Therapists (WFOT, #21468).* [2020/XM0588/D]

♦ Latin American Odontological Federation 16357

Fédération odontologique de l'Amérique latine – Federación Odontológica Latinoamericana (FOLA)
Pres c/o FOE, Calle Luis Sodiro y Saa, Edif Cadena 5to 508, Quito, Ecuador. E-mail: gorkijm@yahoo.com.
URL: http://folalaro.com/
History 3 Oct 1917, Santiago (Chile). Statutes revised Oct 1972. Regional Organization of *FDI – World Dental Federation (#09281).* **Aims** Foster and strengthen links of friendship between odontologists and institutions in member countries; gather information concerning all socio-economic professional aspects and all advances in the field; coordinate joint activity among other such entities. **Structure** General Assembly (annual); Executive Committee of 8 members designated by headquarters country (rotates every 3 years). **Languages** Spanish. **Finance** Members' dues. **Events** *Congress* Havana (Cuba) 2005, *Latin American congress on health prevention and education* Havana (Cuba) 2005, *Congress* Quito (Ecuador) 2004, *Congress* Buenos Aires (Argentina) 2003, *Congress* Cartagena de Indias (Colombia) 2002. **Publications** *FOLA Information Bulletin* (periodical).
Members Odontological associations, representing at least 10% of the professionals, in 19 countries:
Bolivia, Brazil, Chile, Colombia, Costa Rica, Cuba, Dominican Rep, Ecuador, El Salvador, Guatemala, Haiti, Honduras, Mexico, Nicaragua, Panama, Paraguay, Peru, Uruguay, Venezuela.
NGO Relations Affiliated with: *World Federation of Orthodontists (#21469).* [2015/XE2885/D]

- Latin American Official Workers Confederation / see Latin American Confederation of Public Sector Workers (#16304)
- Latin American Operative Dentistry and Biomaterials Society (#02244)
- Latin American Oral Health Association (internationally oriented national body)
- Latin American Organization of Alcoholic Beverage Manufacturers (inactive)
- Latin American Organization of Intermunicipal Cooperation / see Ibero-American Union of Municipalists (#11034)
- Latin American Organization for Secretarial Development (no recent information)
- Latin American Organization for the Welfare of the Blind and Visually Handicapped (inactive)

♦ Latin American Packaging Federation 16358

Union latinoaméricaine d'emballage – Unión Latinoamericana del Embalaje (ULADE)
Main Office Inst Argentino del Envase, Av Jujuy 425, C1083AAE Buenos Aires, Argentina. T. +541149570350. Fax +541149561368.
History Dec 1971, Buenos Aires (Argentina). Founded under the auspices of: *FAO (#09260); UNIDO (#20336); United Nations Economic Commission for Latin America and the Caribbean (ECLAC, #20556).* **Aims** Study and perfect packaging techniques in Latin America; organize and maintain contacts with various packaging organizations, industrial producers, distributors and users' organizations; direct the activities of the industry in the form of joint projects and create a working community in Latin America that permits more harmonious development than at present; promote creation of national packaging organizations. **Structure** General Meeting (annual); Executive Council. **Languages** Spanish. **Staff** 5.00 FTE, paid. **Finance** Members' dues (annual), according to capacity. **Activities** Advocacy/lobbying/activism; knowledge management/information dissemination; events/meetings; training/education. **Events** *ENVASE* Buenos Aires (Argentina) 2007, *ENVASE* San José (Costa Rica) 2007, *ENVASE* Lima (Peru) 2006, *ENVASE* Buenos Aires (Argentina) 2005, *ENVASE* Lima (Peru) 2004. **Publications** *Informa ULADE* (4 a year).
Members Active national packaging organizations; Adhering organizations and institutes; Honorary. Members in 14 countries:
Argentina, Bolivia, Brazil, Chile, Colombia, Costa Rica, Cuba, Dominican Rep, Ecuador, Mexico, Paraguay, Peru, Uruguay, Venezuela.
NGO Relations Member of: *World Packaging Organisation (WPO, #21705).* In contact with packaging institutes and associations worldwide (unspecified). [2016/XD4225/D]

♦ Latin American Paper Money Society (LANSA) 16359

Sociedad Papel Moneda Latinoamericana
Pres 6602 Cambria Ter, Elkridge MD 21075, USA. T. +14107962559.
History 1973, London (UK), as *Latin American Notaphilic Society.* Present name adopted 1978. **Aims** Promote the study and *collection* of Latin American and *Iberian* paper money. **Languages** English, Spanish. **Finance** Members' dues. **Publications** *LANSA Bulletin.*
Members Individuals in 55 countries and territories:
Argentina, Australia, Austria, Bahamas, Belgium, Bolivia, Brazil, Canada, Chile, China, Colombia, Costa Rica, Croatia, Cuba, Czechia, Denmark, Dominican Rep, Ecuador, Estonia, Finland, France, Germany, Haiti, Honduras, Hong Kong, Hungary, India, Indonesia, Italy, Japan, Latvia, Lithuania, Mexico, Moldova, Netherlands, New Zealand, Nicaragua, Norway, Panama, Paraguay, Peru, Poland, Portugal, Puerto Rico, Qatar, Singapore, Slovenia, Spain, Switzerland, UK, Ukraine, Uruguay, USA, Venezuela. [2012/XF4564/v/F]

- Latin American Parliament (#18203)
- Latin American Peace and Justice Service (#19247)
- Latin American Peace Research Council / see Latin American Council for Peace Research (#16310)
- Latin American Peace Science Society (unconfirmed)

♦ Latin American Pediatric Association 16360

Association latinoaméricaine de pédiatrie – Asociación Latinoamericana de Pediatria (ALAPE)
Pres Hosp Centro Pediatrico Diagonal Luis Vasquez, 222 Colonia Médica, San Salvador, El Salvador. T. +50322253294. Fax +5037885086.
URL: http://www.alape.org/

History 1944, as *South American Confederation of Pediatric Societies – Confédération sud-américaine des sociétés de pédiatrie – Confederación Sudamericana de Sociedades de Pediatria*. Present name adopted 30 Jul 1963, Quito (Ecuador). **Aims** Foster research and diffusion of knowledge; stimulate local and regional meetings among members; promote medico-social works for benefit of children of Latin America. **Structure** Presidents of member associations. **Languages** Spanish. **Staff** 10.00 FTE, voluntary. **Finance** Members' dues. **Events** *Triennial Congress* Cartagena de Indias (Colombia) 2012, *Triennial Congress* Puerto Rico 2009, *Triennial Congress* Dominican Rep 2006, *Simposio internacional de cuidados intensivos neonatal y pediatrico* Havana (Cuba) 2005, *Triennial Congress* Montevideo (Uruguay) 2000. **Publications** *Criterio Pediatrico Latino Americano*.
Members Full: national pediatric societies in 24 countries:
Argentina, Belize, Bolivia, Brazil, Chile, Colombia, Costa Rica, Cuba, Dominican Rep, Ecuador, El Salvador, Guatemala, Haiti, Honduras, Italy, Mexico, Nicaragua, Panama, Paraguay, Peru, Portugal, Puerto Rico, Spain, Uruguay.
IGO Relations Official relations with: *Pan American Health Organization (PAHO, #18108)*. **NGO Relations** Affiliate Society of: *International Pediatric Association (IPA, #14541)*. [2019.10.24/XD6213/**D**]

♦ Latin American Pediatric Ophthalmology Society (#19430)
♦ Latin American Petrochemical Association (#02294)

♦ Latin American Physics Education Network (LAPEN) 16361

Exec Sec Univ Nac de San Luis, Ejercito de Los Andes 950, D5700HHW, San Luis, Argentina.
URL: http://www.lajpe.org/

History Nov 2005, Matanzas (Cuba). **Aims** Contribute to the improvement of physics education. **Structure** General Assembly. Coordinator Committee, comprising President, Vice-President, Executive Secretary and regional Coordinators. **Events** *World Conference on Physics Education* Hanoi (Vietnam) 2021, *World Conference on Physics Education* Hanoi (Vietnam) 2020, *World Conference on Physics Education* Sao Paulo (Brazil) 2016, *World Conference on Physics Education* Istanbul (Turkey) 2012. **Publications** *Latin-American Journal of Physics Education*. [2012/XJ5408/**F**]

♦ Latin American Physiotherapy and Kinesiology Confederation (#04458)
♦ Latin American Phytochemistry Society (inactive)
♦ Latin American Phytopathological Association (#02223)
♦ Latin American Plantation Workers' Federation (inactive)

♦ Latin American Plant Sciences Network 16362

Réseau latinoaméricain de botanique – Red Latinoamericana de Botanica (RLB)

Exec Dir Inst de Ecologia – Univ Nacional Autónoma de México, Cd Univ-Coyoacan DF, 04510 Coyoacan CHIS, Mexico. T. +522556229025. Fax +522556161976. E-mail: rlb@ecologia.unam.mx.
Pres address not obtained.
URL: http://www.uchile.cl/rlb/

History 1988. **Aims** Stimulate graduate studies and research in the plant sciences in the region, particularly as they bear on biodiversity, conservation, and sustainable use of natural resources. **Structure** Executive Committee, comprising President, Past President, 3 Directors and Executive Director (ex-officio). Scientific Committee; National Representatives; External Advisory Committee. **Languages** English, Spanish. **Finance** Private foundations and Latin American research and educational institutions, including the following organizations: Alice C Tyler Perpetual Trust; *Andrew W Mellon Foundation*; CONABIO; *MacArthur Foundation*; *The Rockefeller Foundation (#18966)*. **Activities** Organizes courses and scientific events; supports research projects; offers fellowships for graduate and short term studies. **Events** *Annual meeting* Bogota (Colombia) 1998, *Annual meeting* Santiago (Chile) 1997, *Conservacion y manejo de recursos naturales en Latinoamerica* Mexico City (Mexico) 1991. **Publications** *RLB Boletin Informativo* (4 a year).
Members Relies on regional graduate training centres in 6 countries:
Argentina, Brazil, Chile, Costa Rica, Mexico, Venezuela. [2013.10.29/XF1197/**F**]

♦ Latin American Potato Association (#02250)
♦ Latin American Poultry Association (#02185)

♦ Latin American Psychiatric Association 16363

Association latinoaméricaine de psychiatrie – Asociación Psiquiatria de América Latina (APAL)

Pres address not obtained. E-mail: secretariageneralapal@gmail.com.
URL: http://www.apalweb.org/

History 1962. Former names and other names: *Asociación Latinoamericana de Psiquiatria* – former. **Events** *APAL Congress* Lima (Peru) 2021, *APAL Congress* Brasilia (Brazil) 2018, *Congress* Cartagena de Indias (Colombia) 2014, *Congress* Buenos Aires (Argentina) 2012, *Congress* Puerto Vallarta (Mexico) 2010. **Members** Membership countries not specified. **NGO Relations** Affiliated association of *World Psychiatric Association (WPA, #21741)*. [2020/XD5204/**D**]

♦ Latin American Quality Institute (LAQI) 16364

CEO Via Ricardo J Alfaro, Century Tower – Of 401-03, Panama, Panamá, Panama PANAMá, Panama. T. +5072029505. Fax +5073605400. E-mail: info@laqi.org – info@laqualityinstitute.org.
URL: http://www.laqi.org/

History 28 Feb 2001, Panama (Panama). Registration: Registros Publicos de Panamá, No/ID: 29297533, Start date: 28 Feb 2001, Panama, Panama. **Aims** Promote good business practices, quality and sustainable development and ESG; establish and maintain a mindset of Total Quality and Total Responsibility in companies and institutions in Latin America. **Structure** CEO/Founder; Executive Directors; Evaluation Committee; Area Managers; Advisors. **Languages** English, Portuguese, Spanish. **Staff** 57.00 FTE, paid. **Finance** Sources: members' dues; revenue from activities/projects; sponsorship. Annual budget: 2,000,000 USD (2022). **Activities** Events/meetings. **Publications** *Quality Magazine* in English, Portuguese, Spanish. Reports.
Members Full in 18 countries:
Argentina, Bolivia, Brazil, Chile, Colombia, Costa Rica, Dominican Rep, Ecuador, El Salvador, Guatemala, Honduras, Mexico, Nicaragua, Paraguay, Peru, Puerto Rico, Uruguay, Venezuela.
IGO Relations Contacts with: *United Nations (UN, #20515)*. **NGO Relations** Member of (2): *Green Industry Platform (GIP, #10722)*; *Principles for Responsible Management Education (PRME, #18500)*. [2023.02.14/XJ2432/j/**D**]

♦ Latin American Railways Association 16365

Association latinoaméricaine des chemins de fer – Asociación Latinoamericana de Ferrocarriles (ALAF) – Associação Latinoamericana de Estradas de Ferro

SG Av Belgrano 863, 1o Piso, CP 1092 Buenos Aires, Argentina. T. +541143454006 – +541143427271. Fax +541143454996. E-mail: alaf@alaf.int.ar.
URL: https://alaf.int.ar/

History 27 Mar 1964, Chapadmalal (Argentina). Statutes adopted 28 Sep 1965, Rio de Janeiro (Brazil). Registration: Argentina. **Aims** Ensure regional integration in the field of rail *transportation*; foster safe, efficient and economic transport by rail; stimulate goods traffic; ensure standardization of material and equipment; obtain coordination and progress of the industry as a means of achieving social and economic integration of the Latin American peoples. **Structure** General Assembly (annual); Consultative Board (meets twice a year); Metropolitan Transport Group. Sectors (2): Technical; Administrative. Technical Secretariat in Buenos Aires (Argentina); north subregional office; regional groups. **Languages** Portuguese, Spanish. **Staff** 9.00 FTE, paid. **Finance** Sources: members' dues. **Activities** Events/meetings; training/education; financial and/or material support; guidance/assistance/consulting; knowledge management/information dissemination. **Events** *Challenges for Rail Integration in Latin America* Paris (France) 2021, *Annual General Assembly* Sao Paulo (Brazil) 2014, *Annual General Assembly* Caracas (Venezuela) 2005, *Annual General Assembly* Buenos Aires (Argentina) 1994, *Annual general assembly* San José (Costa Rica) 1993. **Publications** *ALAF-Tiempo Real* (12 a year); *Revista ALAF* (4 a year); *Anuario Estadistico Ferroviario Latinoamericano* (annual).
Members Full authorized national railways providing passenger and goods services; Associate; Supporting. Members in 20 countries:
Argentina, Bolivia, Brazil, Canada, Chile, Colombia, Costa Rica, Cuba, Ecuador, El Salvador, Guatemala, Honduras, Mexico, Nicaragua, Panama, Paraguay, Peru, Spain, Uruguay, Venezuela.
Consultative Status Consultative status granted from: *ECOSOC (#05331)* (Ros A). **IGO Relations** Cooperates with: *Meeting of Foreign Relations Ministers of the "Liberator's Corridor"*; *Meeting of Foreign Relations Ministers of the Plata Basin Countries*; *Meeting of Ministers Responsible for Transport in Central America (REMITRAN)*; *OAS (#17629)*; *Reunión de Ministros de Obras Públicas y de Transportes de los Países de l Cono Sur*; *Southern Common Market (#19868)*; *Secretaria Permanente del Tratado General de Integración Económica Centroamericana (SIECA, #19195)*; *United Nations Economic Commission for Latin America and the Caribbean (ECLAC, #20556)*. **NGO Relations** Member of (1): *International Union of Railways (#15813)*. [2022/XD2887/**D**]

♦ Latin American Real Estate Society (LARES) 16366

Sociedade Latino Americana de Estudos Imobiliarios

Sec PCC USP, Av Prof Almeida Prado, Ed Eng Civil, Sao Paulo SP, 05508-900, Brazil. E-mail: lares@lares.org.br.
URL: http://www.lares.org.br/

Events *Annual Conference* Sao Paulo (Brazil) 2010, *Annual Conference* Sao Paulo (Brazil) 2009, *Annual Conference* Sao Paulo (Brazil) 2008, *Annual Conference* Sao Paulo (Brazil) 2007, *Annual Conference* Rio de Janeiro (Brazil) 2006. **NGO Relations** Member of: *International Real Estate Society (IRES, #14702)*. [2010/XD8517/**D**]

♦ Latin American Regional Association of Pacific Ports (inactive)
♦ Latin American Research consortium on the GEnetics of Parkinson's Disease (unconfirmed)
♦ Latin American Research Network / see Latin American and Caribbean Research Network (#16284)

♦ Latin American Reserve Fund 16367

Fonds latinoaméricain de réserve – Fondo Latinoamericano de Reservas (FLAR)

Exec Pres Calle 84A 82, No 12-18 Piso 7, PO Box 241523, Bogota, Bogota DC, Colombia. T. +5716344360. Fax +5716344384. E-mail: flar@flar.net.
Gen Sec address not obtained.
URL: http://www.flar.net/

History Established Nov 1976, as *Andean Reserve Fund (ARF) – Fonds andin de réserve – Fondo Andino de Reservas (FAR)*, by representatives of the governments of Bolivia, Colombia, Ecuador, Peru and Venezuela, in accordance with Article 89 of *Andean Subregional Integration Agreement (Cartagena Agreement, 1969)*, providing for the creation of a Common Reserve Fund. Establishment followed meetings of Governors of the Central Banks of Cartagena Agreement member countries: 13-14 Feb 1976, Lima (Peru) (when a draft Treaty to establish the Fund was approved); 11 Nov 1976, Caracas (Venezuela) (when the Treaty was adopted). The Treaty was signed by plenipotentiary representatives, 12 Nov 1976, Caracas, and entered into force 8 Jun 1978. In 1987-1988 it was decided that ARF constituted a solid foundation on which to build a financial institution for balance of payments support at the Latin American level. The *'Agreement for the Establishment of the Latin American Reserve Fund'*, *LARF*, was signed 10 Jun 1988, Lima, and Articles of said Agreement (transforming ARF into LARF) took effect on 12 Mar 1991. As a consequence, the transformation allowed other Latin-American countries besides those of the Andean Community to become members of LARF. Costa Rica became the 6th member on 30 Mar 1999; Uruguay the 7th on 19 Jun 2007; Paraguay the 8th on 24 Nov 2013. LARF maintains close contacts with the *Andean Community (#00817)*, with its principal organs and with *Development Bank of Latin America (CAF, #05055)*. In this context, it is an organ of the *Sistema Andino de Integración (SAI, #19292)*. **Aims** Provide balance of payments assistance to member countries by extending credits or guaranteeing loans from third parties; contribute to harmonization of foreign exchange, monetary and financial policies of member countries by assisting them to fulfil their commitments within the framework of the Cartagena Agreement and the Montevideo Treaty of 1980; improve conditions for the investment of international reserves of member countries. **Structure** Assembly of Representatives (annual); Board of Directors (meets at least 3 times a year). Committees. **Languages** Spanish. **Staff** 52.00 FTE, paid. **Finance** Capital contributions; deposits; issued obligations. As of Jun 2019, subscribed capital: US$ 3,938,000,000, of which Colombia, Costa Rica, Peru and Venezuela subscribed US$ 656,000,000 each, and Bolivia, Ecuador, Paraguay and Uruguay US$ 328,000,000 each. For the financial year ended Jun 2019: Total assets: US$ 7,046,850,687; total liabilities: US$ 3,582,727,280; total net worth: US$ 3,464,123,408; net income for financial year ended Jun 2019: US$ 90,550,216. **Activities** Financial and/or material support; events/meetings. **Events** *Conference of Central Banks and Official Institutions* Cartagena de Indias (Colombia) 2018, *Economic Studies Conference* Cartagena de Indias (Colombia) 2018, *Financial Department Conference* Bogota (Colombia) 2017, *Seminar of Legal Counsel from Central Banks and Multilateral Institutions of Latin America* Bogota (Colombia) 2017, *Economic Studies Conference* Cartagena de Indias (Colombia) 2017. **Publications** *Agreement for the Establishment and By-Laws of the Fund* in English, Spanish; *Building a Latin American Reserve Fund – The 35 years of FLAR* in English, Spanish. Annual Report in Spanish/English; Economic Studies Conference's annual papers and proceedings in original language (either Spanish or English).
Members Governments of 8 countries:
Bolivia, Colombia, Costa Rica, Ecuador, Paraguay, Peru, Uruguay, Venezuela. [2019.12.11/XF5466/f/**F***]

♦ Latin American Resuscitation Council (inactive)
♦ Latin American Rhizobiology Association – Associação Latinoamericana de Rizobiologia (#02262)
♦ Latin American Rorschach Association (#02263)

♦ Latin American Rural Sociological Association 16368

Association latinoaméricaine de sociologie rurale – Asociación Latinoamericana de Sociologia Rural (ALASRU)

Main Office Constituyente 1502, 5º piso – Oficina 22, 11200 Montevideo, Uruguay. E-mail: alasru2022@gmail.com.
URL: http://www.alasru.org/

History 6 Nov 1969, Buenos Aires (Argentina). **Aims** Promote rural development in the region; foster the dissemination and advancement of rural sociology; support the creation of national centres to carry out research in the field. **Structure** General Assembly of 600 members. Steering Committee, consisting of President, 3 Vice-Presidents and Secretary-Treasurer. **Languages** Spanish. **Staff** 1.00 FTE, paid. **Finance** Annual contributions of members. Grants from IICA and *W K Kellogg Foundation (WKKF)*. Budget (annual): US$ 10,000. **Activities** Assists the creation of national and sociological associations. **Events** *Congreso Latinoamericano de Sociología Rural* Oaxaca (Mexico) 2022, *Congreso Latinoamericano de Sociología Rural* Montevideo (Uruguay) 2018, *Congress* Porto de Galinhas (Brazil) 2010, *Congress* Quito (Ecuador) 2006, *Sustainability and democratisation of rural society in Latin America* Porto Alegre (Brazil) 2002. **Publications** *Boletin ALASRU* (periodical).
Members National associations and individuals in 20 countries:
Argentina, Bolivia, Brazil, Chile, Colombia, Costa Rica, Dominica, Dominican Rep, Ecuador, El Salvador, Guatemala, Haiti, Honduras, Mexico, Nicaragua, Panama, Peru, Puerto Rico, Uruguay, Venezuela.
IGO Relations Cooperation agreement with: *Inter-American Institute for Cooperation on Agriculture (IICA, #11434)*. **NGO Relations** *European Society for Rural Sociology (ESRS, #08731)*; *International Rural Sociology Association (IRSA, #14774)*. Also links with a number of national peasants organizations. [2021/XD8734/**D**]

♦ Latin American Scholarship Program of American Universities / see Laspau Inc.
♦ Latin American School of Mathematics (meeting series)
♦ Latin American Scientific Society of Agroecology (#19354)
♦ Latin American Sepsis Institute (internationally oriented national body)
♦ Latin-American Shadow Financial Regulatory Committee / see Latin American Committee on Macroeconomic and Financial Issues (#16300)

♦ Latin American Shipowners Association (LASA) 16369

Association latinoaméricaine des armateurs – Asociación Latinoamericana de Armadores (ALAMAR) – Associação Latinoamericana de Armadores

Contact Blanco 869, Piso 3, Valparaiso, Valparaíso, Chile. T. +56322212057. Fax +5632212017. E-mail: info@armadores-chile.cl.

History 15 Jul 1963, Viña del Mar (Chile). Registered in accordance with Chilean and Uruguayan laws. In French also referred to as *Organisation d'associations nationales d'armateurs d'Amérique latine.* **Aims** Promote the development of merchant shipping in the countries of Latin American Integration Association (LAIA); cooperate in attaining the objectives of the Treaty of Montevideo (Uruguay) as regards zonal integration. **Structure** General Assembly; Governing Board; Executive Secretary; Administrative Under-Secretary; Auditing Committee. National Chapters. **Languages** Spanish. **Activities** Developed: *'Declaration of Shipping Policy'* (1965); *'General Agreement on Sea, River and Lake Transport'.* **Events** *General Assembly* Montevideo (Uruguay) 1992, *Joint seminar* Angra dos Reis (Brazil) 1991, *General Assembly* Buenos Aires (Argentina) 1991, *General Assembly* Guayaquil (Ecuador) 1990, *General Assembly* Montevideo (Uruguay) 1989. **Publications** *Boletin Informativo ALAMAR; Carta de la Secretariat. Anales de la Asamblea; Legislación Naviera; Manual de Documentación Naviera.*
Members National shipowners in 10 LAIA countries:
Argentina, Brazil, Chile, Colombia, Ecuador, Mexico, Paraguay, Peru, Uruguay, Venezuela.
Consultative Status Consultative status granted from: *ECOSOC (#05331)* (Ros C); *UNCTAD (#20285)* (Special Category). [2021/XD2890/**D**]

- ♦ Latin American Shoulder and Elbow Society (#19409)
- ♦ Latin American Sleep Society / see Federation of Latin American Sleep Societies (#09685)
- ♦ Latin American Social Sciences Council (#04718)
- ♦ Latin American Social Studies Association (internationally oriented national body)
- ♦ Latin American Society of Allergology / see Sociedad Latinoamericana de Alergia, Asma e Inmunologia (#19389)
- ♦ Latin American Society of Allergy, Asthma and Immunology (#19389)
- ♦ Latin American Society of Allergy and Immunology / see Sociedad Latinoamericana de Alergia, Asma e Inmunologia (#19389)
- ♦ Latin American Society of Aquatic Mammal Specialists (#19402)
- ♦ Latin American Society of Arthroscopy, Knee Surgery and Orthopaedic Sports Medicine (#19390)
- ♦ Latin American Society of Atherosclerosis (#19391)
- ♦ Latin American Society of Audit in Health Services (#19392)

♦ Latin American Society on Biomaterials, Artificial Organs and Tissue Engineering 16370

Sociedad Latino Americana de Biomateriales, Ingenieria de Tejidos y Organos Artificiales – Sociedade Latino Americana de Biomateriais, Engenharia de Tecidos e Orgãos Artificiais (SLABO)
Address not obtained.
URL: http://slabo.org.br/

History Dec 1998, Belo Horizonte (Brazil). **Events** *Biennial Congress* Natal (Brazil) 2012, *Biennial Congress* Gramado (Brazil) 2010, *Congress* Rio Grande do Sul (Brazil) 2010, *Biennial Congress* Caxambú (Brazil) 2008, *Congress* Ouro Preto (Brazil) 2008. **Members** Membership countries not specified. **NGO Relations** Member of: *International Union of Societies for Biomaterials Science and Engineering (IUSBSE, #15816).* [2015/XJ0961/**D**]

- ♦ Latin American Society for Biomedical Research on Alcoholism (unconfirmed)
- ♦ Latin American Society for Botany (#02187)
- ♦ Latin American Society on Breast Imaging (no recent information)
- ♦ Latin American Society for Buiatrics (#19394)
- ♦ Latin American Society of Cardiac Pacing and Electrophysiology / see Latin American Heart Rhythm Society (#16339)
- ♦ Latin American Society of Cataract and Refractive Surgeons / see Asociación Latino Americana de Cirugia de Catarata, Segmento Anterior y Refractiva (#02194)
- ♦ Latin American Society of Cytology / see Sociedad Latinoamericana de Citopatologia (#19398)

♦ Latin American Society for Developmental Biology (LASDB) 16371

Sociedad Latino Americana de Biologica del Desarrollo (SLBD)
Sec address not obtained. E-mail: lasdb.development@gmail.com.
URL: http://lasdb-development.org/

Aims Promote thestudy of development biology in Latin America. **Structure** Board. **Finance** Members' dues. **Activities** Events/meetings; training/education; awards/prizes/competitions. **Events** *Meeting* Buenos Aires (Argentina) 2019, *Meeting* Medellin (Colombia) 2017, *Meeting* Santos (Brazil) 2015, *Meeting* Cancún (Mexico) 2013, *Meeting* Buenos Aires (Argentina) 2008.
Members Full in 9 countries:
Argentina, Brazil, Chile, Colombia, Ecuador, Mexico, Peru, Uruguay, Venezuela.
NGO Relations Affiliated to: *International Society of Developmental Biologists (ISDB, #15052).* [2018/XD8857/**D**]

- ♦ Latin American Society of Electroencephalography (inactive)
- ♦ Latin-American Society of Environmental and Algal Biotechnology (#19393)
- ♦ Latin American Society of Forensic Genetics (#19408)
- ♦ Latin-American Society of Health Psychology (#02259)
- ♦ Latin American Society of Hepatology / see Latin American Association for the Study of the Liver (#16252)
- ♦ Latin American Society for the History of Sciences and Technology (no recent information)

♦ Latin American Society of Hypertension (LASH) 16372

Sociedad Latinoamericana de Hipertensión Arterial
Pres c/o FOSCAL, Urb el Bosque, Autopista a Floridablanca, Bucaramanga, Santander, Colombia.
URL: http://www.lash-hipertension.org/

History 1994, Caracas (Venezuela). **Structure** Executive Committee, comprising President, President-Elect, 2 Vice-Presidents and Secretary. **Events** *Congress* Porlamar (Venezuela) 2013, *Congress* Caracas (Venezuela) 2011, *Congress* Caracas (Venezuela) 2004, *Congress* Caracas (Venezuela) 2000, *Congress* Caracas (Venezuela) 1997. [2016/XJ3393/**D**]

♦ Latin American Society for Immunodeficiencies (LASID) 16373

Pres Centro de Inmunologia/Alergia y Pediatria, Hospital Ángeles Lomas, Col Valle de las Palmas, Hacienda de las Palmas, 52763 Huixquilucan MEX, Mexico. T. +525552474097 – +525552474098. E-mail: francisco.espinosa@iap.mx.
Registered Office Callao 3380, Las Condes, Santiago Metropolitan, Chile.
URL: http://www.lasid.org/

History Founded 2009, Santiago (Chile), when replaced *Grupo Latinoamericano de Inmunodeficiencias Primarias (LAGID, inactive).* **Aims** Increase awareness of Primary Immunodeficiency Diseases (PIDD) at all levels; develop diagnostic capabilities accessible to as many as possible patients; favour establishment of centres capable of offering effective management to PIDD patients. **Structure** Board; Committees. **Languages** English, Portuguese, Spanish. **Staff** 1.50 FTE, paid. **Finance** Members' dues (annual). Donations. **Events** *Meeting* Cancún (Mexico) 2019, *Meeting* Sao Paulo (Brazil) 2017, *Meeting* Buenos Aires (Argentina) 2015, *Meeting* Santiago (Chile) 2013, *Meeting* Mexico City (Mexico) 2011. **Publications** *Journal of Clinical Immunology.*
Members Full in 15 countries:
Argentina, Brazil, Chile, Colombia, Costa Rica, Cuba, El Salvador, Honduras, Mexico, Panama, Peru, Sweden, Uruguay, USA, Venezuela. [2019/XJ1708/**D**]

- ♦ Latin American Society of Inborn Errors of Metabolism and Neonatal Screening (#19401)
- ♦ Latin American Society of Internal Medicine (#19412)

♦ Latin American Society of International Law (LASIL) 16374

Société latino-américaine de droit international – Sociedad Latinoamericana de Derecho Internacional (SLADI) – Sociedade Latinoamericana de Direito Internacional
Exec Dir Fac de Direito da Univ de So Paulo, Largo So Francisco 95, Sao Paulo SP, 01005-010, Brazil. E-mail: info@lasil.org.
URL: http://www.lasil.org/

History Founded 2007, by a joint initiative of several Latin American jurists. **Aims** Constitute a space for discussion and contribution of international international *lawyers* to the reflection and development of international law in Latin America. **Structure** Executive Board; Advisory Board. **Languages** English, French, Portuguese, Spanish. **Staff** 7.00 FTE, paid. **Finance** Members' dues. Members' donations. **Activities** Events/meetings; networking/liaising. **Events** *Biennial Conference* Bogota (Colombia) 2014, *Biennial Conference* Rio de Janeiro (Brazil) 2012.
Members Full in 14 countries:
Argentina, Australia, Brazil, Chile, Colombia, France, Italy, Norway, Peru, Spain, UK, Uruguay, USA, Venezuela. [2022/XJ1204/**D**]

♦ Latin American Society for Interventional Cardiology 16375

Sociedad Latinoamericana de Cardiologia Intervencionista (SOLACI)
Communications Officer Adolfo Alsina 2653, Piso 2 H, C1090AAQ Buenos Aires, Argentina. T. +541149547173. E-mail: info@solaci.org.
URL: http://www.solaci.org/

History 1995. Founded following the activities of the *Grupo Latino Americano de Cardiólogos Intervencionistas (GLACI).* **Aims** Integrate, educate and promote research and standardize the practice of interventional cardiology in the Latinamerican region. **Languages** Portuguese, Spanish. **Events** *Congress* Buenos Aires (Argentina) 2021, *Congress* Sao Paulo (Brazil) 2019, *Congress* Mexico City (Mexico) 2018, *Congress* Buenos Aires (Argentina) 2017, *Congress* Rio de Janeiro (Brazil) 2016. [2021/XD5888/**D**]

- ♦ Latin American Society of Japan (internationally oriented national body)

♦ Latin American Society for Maternal Fetal Interaction and Placenta 16376

Sociedad Latinoamericana de Interacción Materno-Fetal y Placenta (SLIMP) – Sociedade Latino Americana de Interação Materno Fetal and Placenta (SLIMP)
Contact Lab of Biology of Reproduction, IFIBIO-CONICET, Univ of Buenos Aires, Viamonte 430, C1053 CABA, Buenos Aires, Argentina. T. +541152874786.
URL: http://www.slimp.org/

History 2000. Founded at the instigation of *Placenta Association of the Americas (PAA).* **Aims** Facilitate interaction between investigators of the region; promote education and spread awareness about issues affecting the Latin American community within the framework of the maternal fetal interaction and placenta; help collaboration on education and research to facilitate scientific exchange. **Languages** English. **Staff** 3.00 FTE, paid. **Activities** Events/meetings; training/education. **Events** *Latin-American Symposium on Maternal-Fetal Interaction and Placenta* Bogota (Colombia) 2022, *Latin-American Symposium on Maternal-Fetal Interaction and Placenta* Bogota (Colombia) 2021, *Latin-American Symposium on Maternal-Fetal Interaction and Placenta* Buenos Aires (Argentina) 2019, *Latin-American Symposium on Maternal-Fetal Interaction and Placenta* Puerto Varas (Chile) 2017, *Latin-American Symposium on Maternal-Fetal Interaction and Placenta* Mar del Plata (Argentina) 2015. **Publications** Meeting abstracts.
Members Representatives from 8 countries:
Argentina, Brazil, Chile, Colombia, Mexico, Peru, Uruguay, Venezuela. [2021.03.02/XM5799/**D**]

♦ Latin American Society for Mathematical Biology 16377

Sociedad Latinoamericana de Biologia Matematica (SOLABIMA)
Pres Unesp, Instituto de Biociências – Câmpus de Botucatu, Rua Prof. Dr. Antonio Celso Wagner Zanin 250, Botucatu SP, 18618-689, Brazil.
URL: https://www.dm2a.org/

History 2002, Guanajuato (Mexico). Founded by merger of *Asociación Latinoamericana de Biomatematica (SoLaBiMa, inactive)* and *Red Latino Americano de Ecologia Matematica (RedLEM, inactive).* **Aims** Develop and strengthen the interdisciplinary work of mathematical modelling in the biosciences; encourage the exchange of knowledge, education and cooperation in the field. **Structure** General Assembly. Board, comprising President, Vice-President, Secretary and Treasurer. **Languages** English, Portuguese, Spanish. **Staff** Voluntary. **Finance** Meetings financed by host countries, host institutions and foundations. **Activities** Events/meetings. **Events** *Congress* Brazil 2022, *Congress* 2021, *Congress* Campinas (Brazil) 2007, *Congress* Tandil (Argentina) 2005, *Congress* Armenia (Colombia) 2003.
Members in 9 countries:
Argentina, Brazil, Chile, Colombia, Ecuador, Mexico, Peru, USA, Venezuela.
NGO Relations *BIOMAT Consortium (#03250).* [2022/XM0897/**D**]

- ♦ Latin-American Society of Medical Research on Rare Diseases (no recent information)
- ♦ Latin American Society for Mycotoxicology (unconfirmed)
- ♦ Latin American Society of Nephrology and Hypertension (#19415)

♦ Latin American Society of Neuropsychology 16378

Société latino-américaine de neuropsychologie – Sociedad Latinoamericana de Neuropsicologia (SLAN) – Sociedade Latinoamericana de Neuropsicologia
Sec address not obtained.
Pres address not obtained.
URL: http://www.slan.org/

History 22 Jun 1989, Buenos Aires (Argentina). **Events** *Congreso Latinoamericano de Neuropsicología* Cuenca (Ecuador) 2024, *Congreso Latinoamericano de Neuropsicología* Montevideo (Uruguay) 2022, *Congreso Latinoamericano de Neuropsicología* Lima (Peru) 2019, *Congreso Latinoamericano de Neuropsicología* Natal (Brazil) 2017, *Congreso Latinoamericano de Neuropsicología* Medellin (Colombia) 2015. **Publications** *Revista SLAN.* [2023.02.23/XD8367/**D**]

- ♦ Latin American Society of Nutrition (#19417)
- ♦ Latin American Society for Orthopaedics and Traumatology (#19418)

♦ Latin American Society of Paediatric Nephrology 16379

Asociación Latinoamericana de Nefrologia Pediatrica (ALANEPE)
Pres Av. Presidente Kennedy 5488, Oficina 303, Vitacura, 763 0000 Santiago, Santiago Metropolitan, Chile. Fax +56232514970. E-mail: info@alanepe.org.
URL: http://www.alanepe.org/

History 27 Nov 1981, Buenos Aires (Argentina). **Aims** Bring together specialists in paediatric nephrology residing in Latin American countries. **Structure** Regional association of: *International Pediatric Nephrology Association (IPNA, #14543).* Zones (3). **Languages** English, Portuguese, Spanish. **Staff** 1.00 FTE, paid. **Activities** Events/meetings. **Events** *Triennial Congress* Mexico City (Mexico) 2021, *Triennial Congress* Mexico City (Mexico) 2020, *Triennial Congress* Santiago (Chile) 2017, *Triennial Congress* Cartagena de Indias (Colombia) 2014, *Triennial Congress* Sao Paulo (Brazil) 2011. **Publications** *Revista Archivos Latinoamericanos de Nefrologia Pediatrica.*
Members Individuals (500) practising paediatric nephrology in 20 countries and territories:
Argentina, Bolivia, Brazil, Chile, Colombia, Costa Rica, Cuba, Dominican Rep, Ecuador, Guatemala, Haiti, Honduras, Jamaica, Mexico, Panama, Paraguay, Peru, Puerto Rico, Uruguay, Venezuela. [2021/XD2139/**v**/**D**]

- ♦ Latin American Society of Paraplegia (#19420)

♦ Latin American Society of Pathology 16380

Société latinoaméricaine de pathologie – Sociedad Latinoamericana de Patologia (SLAP)
Admin Office Av Belgrano 1217, Piso 10 Of 104, ACJ1221C, Buenos Aires, Argentina. T. +541143826887. Fax +541143826887. E-mail: info@slap-patologia.org.
SG 10 Calle 2-45, Zona 14, Clinicas Bella Aurora, Guatemala, Guatemala.
URL: http://slap-patologia.org/

History 15 Dec 1955, Mexico City (Mexico). Registered in Argentina, Brazil, Mexico and Venezuela. **Aims** Promote advancement and exchange of scientific information among members; foster development of pathology in Latin America. **Structure** President, assisted by 2 Advisors, responsible for organizing the next Latin American Congress in his country; Vice-President, responsible for the Congress 4 years hence and assumes presidency 2 years later; Secretary-General; national chapters whose representatives coordinate with Secretary-General; Congress Organizing Committee. **Languages** English, Portuguese, Spanish. **Staff** 1.00 FTE, paid. **Finance** Members' dues. Proceeds from Congress. **Events** *Latin American Congress of Pathology* Santa Cruz (Bolivia) 2015, *Congress / Latin American Congress of Pathology* Oaxaca (Mexico) 2013,

Latin American Congress of Pathology Maceió (Brazil) 2011, *Latin American Congress of Pathology* Antigua (Guatemala) 2009, *Congress / Latin American Congress of Pathology* Havana (Cuba) 2005. **Publications** *Boletin SLAP* (4 a year) – supplement to journal; *Patologia* (4 a year) – official journal. Directory of Latin American pathologists. Information Services: Database of Spanish and Portuguese speaking pathologists.
Members Chapters in 24 countries:
Argentina, Bolivia, Brazil, Canada, Chile, Colombia, Costa Rica, Cuba, Dominican Rep, Ecuador, El Salvador, Guatemala, Honduras, Mexico, Nicaragua, Panama, Paraguay, Peru, Portugal, Puerto Rico, Spain, Uruguay, USA, Venezuela.
[2014/XD2893/**D**]

♦ Latin American Society of Pediatric Dermatology (inactive)

♦ Latin American Society for Pediatric Endocrinology 16381

Sociedad Latinoamericana de Endocrinología Pediatrica (SLEP) – Sociedade Latino-Americana de Endocrinologia Pediátrica

Secretariat c/o MCI Argentina, Av Córdoba 883, C1123AAO Buenos Aires, Argentina. E-mail: info@slep-endocrino.com.
Registered Office Alc Eduardo Castillo Velazco 1838, Ñuñoa, Santiago, Santiago Metropolitan, Chile.
URL: https://slep-endocrino.com/

History 1986, Buenos Aires (Argentina). **Aims** Improve pediatric endocrinology in Latin America. **Structure** Officers: President; President-Elect; General Secretary; Treasurer. Committees Admission; Scientific; Communication and Information; Education and Training; Ethics Advisory; International Relations; By-laws. **Languages** English, Portuguese, Spanish. **Staff** 7.00 FTE, paid. **Finance** Grants from non-governmental bodies, including proceeds from annual meeting. **Activities** Training/education; research/documentation; standards/guidelines; events/meetings; awards/prizes/competitions. **Events** *Congress* Bogota (Colombia) 2022, *Joint Meeting of Paediatric Endocrinology* Buenos Aires (Argentina) 2021, *Annual Meeting* Mérida (Mexico) 2020, *Annual Meeting* Florianópolis (Brazil) 2019, *Annual Meeting* Cusco (Peru) 2018.
Members Full in 11 countries:
Argentina, Bolivia, Brazil, Chile, Colombia, Costa Rica, Ecuador, Mexico, Peru, Uruguay, Venezuela.
NGO Relations Member of: *Global Pediatric Endocrinology and Diabetes (GPED, #10545).* [2022/XD3465/**D**]

♦ Latin-American Society of Pediatric Gastroenterology / see Latinamerican Society for Pediatric Gastroenterology, Hepatology and Nutrition (#16382)

♦ Latinamerican Society for Pediatric Gastroenterology, Hepatology and Nutrition (LASPGHAN) 16382

Sociedad Latinoamericana de Gastroenterologia, Hepatologia y Nutrición Pediatrica (SLAGHNP) – Sociedade Latino-Americana de Gastroenterologia, Hepatologia e Nutrição Pediatrica

Pres c/o Clinica Delgado, Av Angamos Oeste, cuadra 4, Esq con General Borgoño, Miraflores, Lima, Peru.
URL: http://laspghan.org/

History 10 Oct 1975, Sao Paulo (Brazil). 10 Oct 1975, San Pablo (Brazil), as *Latin-American Society of Pediatric Gastroenterology (LASGP).* Name changed, 1977, to *Latin American Society of Pediatric Gastroenterology and Nutrition (LASPGN) – Sociedad Latinoamericana de Gastroenterologia Pediatrica y Nutrición (SLAGPN) – Sociedade Latinoamericana de Gastroenterologia Pediatrica e Nutrição.* Previously referred to as *LASPGAN.* Later known as *Latin American Society for Pediatric Gastroenterology, Nutrition and Hepatology (LASPGNH) – Sociedad Latinoamericana de Gastroenterologia Pediatrica, Nutrición y Hepatologia (SLAGPNH) – Sociedade Latino-americana de Gastroenterologia Pediatrica, Nutrição e Hepatologia.* Present name adopted, 2003. **Aims** Promote research of the functions of *gastrointestinal tract, liver* and nutrition in normal and abnormal conditions in *children.* **Structure** Executive Council. **Languages** Portuguese, Spanish. **Finance** Members' dues. Annual budget: about US$ 25,000. **Activities** Training/education; research/documentation; events/meetings. **Events** *Congress* Quito (Ecuador) 2022, *Iberoamerican Congress* Quito (Ecuador) 2022, *Congress* Cancún (Mexico) 2019, *Iberoamerican Congress* Cancún (Mexico) 2019, *Iberoamerican Congress* Porto (Portugal) 2017. **Publications** *Acta Gastroenterologica Latinoamericana* – journal; *Arquivos de Gastroenterologia* – journal. **Information Services** *Electronic Journal of Pediatric Gastroenterology, Nutrition and Liver Diseases* – on Internet.
Members Individuals (about 300) in 21 countries:
Argentina, Bolivia, Brazil, Chile, Colombia, Costa Rica, Cuba, Dominican Rep, Ecuador, El Salvador, Guatemala, Honduras, Mexico, Nicaragua, Panama, Paraguay, Peru, Portugal, Spain, Uruguay, Venezuela.
NGO Relations Member of: *Federation of International Societies for Pediatric Gastroenterology, Hepatology and Nutrition (FISPGHAN, #09678).* [2019.04.24/XD6147/v/**D**]

♦ Latin American Society of Pediatric Gastroenterology and Nutrition / see Latinamerican Society for Pediatric Gastroenterology, Hepatology and Nutrition (#16382)
♦ Latin American Society for Pediatric Gastroenterology, Nutrition and Hepatology / see Latinamerican Society for Pediatric Gastroenterology, Hepatology and Nutrition (#16382)
♦ Latin American Society of Pediatric Infectious Diseases (#19410)

♦ Latin American Society for Pediatric Oncology 16383

Sociedad Latinoamericana de Oncologia Pediatrica (SLAOP)

Sec Tupungato 10070, Vitacura, 7650169 Santiago, Santiago Metropolitan, Chile. E-mail: slaop@slaop.org.
Pres address not obtained.
URL: http://slaop.org/

History 14 Nov 1974, Uruguay. **Aims** Represent medical multidisciplinary teams for the treatment of cancer in children in Latin America. **Languages** Portuguese, Spanish. **Staff** 6.00 FTE, paid. **Events** *Congress* Lima (Peru) 2016, *Congress* Puebla (Mexico) 2015, *Biennial Congress* Bogota (Colombia) 2013, *Annual Meeting* Sao Paulo (Brazil) 2009, *Biennial Congress* Sao Paulo (Brazil) 2009. [2015.01.20/XD3463/**D**]

♦ Latin American Society for Pediatric Pathology (#19421)
♦ Latin American Society for Pediatric Radiology (#19424)
♦ Latin American Society for Pediatric Research (#19411)
♦ Latin American Society of Phenomenology / see Circulo Latinoamericano de Fenomenologia (#03937)
♦ Latin American Society for Physical Therapy Teachers (inactive)
♦ Latin American Society of Plastic Surgery (inactive)

♦ Latin American Society of Regional Anesthesia (LASRA) 16384

Sociedad Latinoamericana de Anestesia Regional

Pres address not obtained.
Sec address not obtained.
URL: http://www.lasra.com.br/

History 1993, Brazil. **Events** *Annual Congress* 2019, *General Assembly* Sao Paulo (Brazil) 2019, *World Congress of Regional Anaesthesia and Pain Therapy* Cape Town (South Africa) 2014, *Annual Congress* Medellin (Colombia) 2014, *World Congress of Regional Anaesthesia and Pain Therapy* Sydney, NSW (Australia) 2013. [2019/XD7986/**D**]

♦ Latin American Society of Remote Sensing and Special Systems (#19358)
♦ Latin American Society for Rubber Technology (#19426)

♦ Latin American Society of Soil Science 16385

Sociedad Latinoamericana de la Ciencia del Suelo (SLCS) – Sociedade Latinoamericana de Ciencia do Solo

SG Miramar 54, Cumbria, CP 54740, Cuautitlan Izcalli MEX, Mexico. E-mail: lbrs@unam.mx.
Pres address not obtained.
URL: http://www.slcs.org.mx/

History 1955, Buenos Aires (Argentina). **Aims** Promote investigation and education in the field of soil science. **Structure** General Council; Executive Committee. **Languages** Spanish. **Staff** 2.50 FTE, voluntary. **Finance** Members' dues: US$ 200. **Events** *Todos los suelos en la mitad del mundo* Quito (Ecuador) 2016, *International Soil Congress* Havana (Cuba) 2015, *Congress* Cusco (Peru) 2014, *AgroEnviron International Symposium* Goiânia (Brazil) 2014, *Congress* Mar del Plata (Argentina) 2012. **Publications** *Boletin de la SLCS.*
Members National Societies of Soil Science in 19 countries:
Argentina, Bolivia, Brazil, Chile, Colombia, Costa Rica, Cuba, Dominica, Ecuador, El Salvador, Guatemala, Honduras, Mexico, Paraguay, Peru, Portugal, Spain, Uruguay, Venezuela.
IGO Relations Partner of: *Global Soil Partnership (GSP, #10608).* **NGO Relations** *International Union of Soil Sciences (IUSS, #15817).* [2016/XD0662/**D**]

♦ Latin American Society for Stereotactic and Functional Neurosurgery (LSSFN) 16386

Sociedad Latinoamericana de Neurocirugia Funcional y Esterotaxia (SLANFE)

Sec Fundacion FIRE, Barrio Ternera, Calle 1a El Edén, AA 604 y 5007, Cartagena de Indias, Bolivar, Colombia.

History Regional chapter of *World Society for Stereotactic and Functional Neurosurgery (WSSFN, #21812).* **Structure** Officers: President; Vice-President; Secretary; Past Secretary; Treasurer; Past Treasurer. **Events** *International Symposium* Cartagena de Indias (Colombia) 2011. [2011/XD7578/**D**]

♦ Latin American Society of Studies on Latin America and the Caribbean (#19406)
♦ Latin American Society for the Study of the Aging Male (no recent information)
♦ Latin American Society of Therapeutic Radiology and Oncology (#02272)

♦ Latin American Society of Toxicologic Pathology 16387

Asociación Latinoamericana de Patologia Toxicologica (ALAPT) – Associação Latinoamericana de Patologia Toxicológica

SG-Treas Univ Estadual Paulista Júlio de Mesquitau Filho, Fac de Medicina de Botucatu, Depto de Patologia, Distrito de Rubiã Jr, Sem No Laboratório TOXICAN, Botucatu SP, 18618 000, Brazil. T. +551438828255. Fax +551438152348.
URL: http://www.alaptox.net/

Events *Symposium on the role of toxicologic pathology in risk assessment* Rio de Janeiro (Brazil) 2008. [2013/XM3805/**D**]

♦ Latin American Society for Travel Medicine (#19414)
♦ Latin American Society of Tuberculosis and other mycobacteriosis (#19427)
♦ Latin American Sociological Association / see Asociación Latinoamericana de Sociologia (#02267)
♦ Latin American Steel Association (#02176)
♦ Latin American Student Zionist Federation – North (no recent information)
♦ Latin American Student Zionist Federation – South (inactive)

♦ Latin American Studies Association (LASA) 16388

Association d'études latinoaméricaines – Asociación de Estudios Latinoamericanos

Main Office 4338 Bigelow Boulevard, Pittsburgh PA 15213, USA. T. +14126487929. E-mail: lasa@lasaweb.org.
URL: https://www.lasaweb.org/en/

History 1966. Since 1986, hosted by University of Pittsburgh PA (USA). **Aims** Foster intellectual discussion, research, and teaching on Latin America, the Caribbean, and its people throughout the Americas; promote interests of its diverse membership; encourage civic engagement through network building and public debate. **Structure** Executive Council; LASA Sections (40). **Languages** English, French, Portuguese, Spanish. **Staff** 12.00 FTE, paid. **Finance** Sources: meeting proceeds; members' dues. Annual budget: 1,800,000 USD (2022). **Activities** Events/meetings; knowledge management/information dissemination; publishing activities; research/documentation. **Events** *International Congress* Vancouver, BC (Canada) 2023, *International Congress* San Francisco, CA (USA) 2022, *International Congress* Pittsburgh, PA (USA) 2021, *International Congress* Guadalajara (Mexico) 2020, *International Congress* Boston, MA (USA) 2019. **Publications** *LASA Forum* (4 a year); *Latin American Research Review* (4 a year). **Information Services** *LARC – Latin America Research Commons* – open access research portal on Latin America.
Members Membership categories: Regular; Student; Retired Academic; Independent or Non-Affiliated Scholar; Professional or Executive; Lifetime. Individuals (over 12,000) and institutions (35), in a total of 92 countries. Membership countries not specified.
Organizations include 1 listed in this Yearbook:
GIGA – German Institute of Global and Area Studies.
NGO Relations Member of (1): *Federación Internacional de Estudios sobre América Latina y el Caribe (FIEALC, #09338).* Instrumental in setting up (1): *Confederación Latinoamericana y del Caribe de Trabajadoras del Hogar (CONLACTRAHO).* [2023.02.17/XF4215/**F**]

♦ Latin American Studies Association of Korea (internationally oriented national body)
♦ Latin American Studies Center / see Center for Latin American and Caribbean Studies, Michigan
♦ Latin American Studies Center 'Justo Arosemena' (internationally oriented national body)
♦ Latin American Studies Centre, Tucson / see Center for Latin American Studies, Tucson
♦ Latin American Studies Collection / see Caribbean and Latin American Studies Library
♦ Latin American Supermarket Association (#02269)
♦ Latin-American Symposium on Biotechnology, Biomedical, Biopharmaceutical, and Industrial Applications of Capillary Electrophoresis and Microchip Technology (meeting series)
♦ Latin American System of Customs Training and Research (inactive)
♦ Latin American Systemic Functional Linguistics Association (#02279)
♦ Latin American Table Tennis Union (#20453)
♦ Latin American Tax Law Institute (#11344)
♦ Latin American Technical Institute for Cooperative Integration (inactive)
♦ Latin American Technological Information Network (see: #19294)
♦ Latin American Testing Board / see Hispanic America Software Testing Qualifications Board (#10923)
♦ Latin American Theological Information Network (#18713)
♦ Latin American Theoretical Informatics Conference / see Latin American Theoretical Informatics Symposium (#16389)

♦ Latin American Theoretical Informatics Symposium (LATIN) 16389

Chair Dept of Computer Science, Stony Brook Univ, 100 Nicolls Rd, Stony Brook NY 11794 -2424, USA.
URL: http://www.latintcs.org/

History Also referred to as *Latin American Theoretical Informatics Conference.* **Structure** Steering Committee, comprising last 3 Chairs of a LATIN conference, and 3 members-at-large. Program Committee. **Activities** Grants: Imre Simon Test-of-Time Paper Award. **Events** *Symposium* Montevideo (Uruguay) 2014, *Symposium* Arequipa (Peru) 2012, *Symposium* Oaxaca (Mexico) 2010, *Symposium* Rio de Janeiro (Brazil) 2008, *Symposium* Valdivia (Chile) 2006. [2020/XJ6780/c/**E**]

♦ Latin American Thoracic Association (#02273)

♦ Latin American Thyroid Society (LATS) 16390

Société latinoaméricaine de la thyroïde – Sociedad Latinoamericana de Tiroides (SLAT) – Sociedade Latinoamericana de Tireóide

Sec Dept de Bioquimica Clinica, Fac de Ciencias Quimicas, Univ Nacl de Cordoba, Haya de la Torre y Medina Allende, Ciudad Universitaria, Córdoba, Argentina.
URL: http://www.lats.org/

History 1974, Buenos Aires (Argentina). **Aims** Promote and publicize Latin American research on thyroid problems. **Structure** Commissions (3): Scientific; Financial; Prices. **Languages** English, Portuguese, Spanish. **Staff** Voluntary. **Finance** Members' dues. **Activities** Training/education; events/meetings. **Events** *Biennial Congress* Curitiba (Brazil) 2023, *Biennial Congress* 2021, *International Thyroid Congress* 2020, *Biennial Congress* Buenos Aires (Argentina) 2019, *Biennial Congress* Rio de Janeiro (Brazil) 2017. **Publications** *LATS Newsletter.* Congress proceedings.
Members Full, Honorary and Corresponding in 23 countries:
Argentina, Australia, Brazil, Canada, Chile, Colombia, Cuba, Ecuador, France, Germany, Guatemala, Italy, Japan, Mexico, Panama, Paraguay, Peru, Spain, Switzerland, UK, Uruguay, USA, Venezuela. [2020.03.03/XD1475/**D**]

♦ Latin American Tissue Banking Association (#02186)
♦ Latin American Tourism Operators Association (inactive)

- ♦ Latin American Transactional Analysis Association (no recent information)
- ♦ Latin American Transplantation Society (inactive)
- ♦ Latin American Union of Ecumenical Youth (no recent information)
- ♦ Latin American Unionized Workers Association (inactive)
- ♦ Latin American Union of Medical Advisors (no recent information)
- ♦ Latin American Union of Rescue Organisms (inactive)
- ♦ Latin American Union of Societies of Phthisiology (inactive)
- ♦ Latin American University of Science and Technology (internationally oriented national body)

♦ Latin-American Uro-oncology Association (UROLA) 16391

Asociación Latino-Americana del Uro-oncologia – Associação Latino-Americana de Uro-oncologia

Pres address not obtained.
URL: http://www.uro-onco.com.br/

History 18 Oct 2004. Since 2007, serves as Latin American representation within *World Uro Oncology Federation (WUOF, #21895).* **Aims** Promote integration of Latin American countries with regards to the work, the procedures and the experience exchanges in the area of Uro-oncology and its developments. **Structure** Executive Committee, including President, Vice-President, Secretary General and Treasurer. **Events** *Symposium* Campinas (Brazil) 2014, *Symposium* Córdoba (Argentina) 2012, *Symposium* Curitiba (Brazil) 2010, *Symposium* Monterrey (Mexico) 2008, *Symposium* Montevideo (Uruguay) 2006. [2014/XJ6722/**D**]

- ♦ Latin-American Vermiculture Network (unconfirmed)
- ♦ Latin American Veterinary Conference (meeting series)

♦ Latin American Veterinary Emergency and Critical Care Society (LAVECCS) 16392

Sociedad Latinoamericana de Medicina Veterinaria de Emergencia y Cuidados Intensivos

Contact 25 de Mayo 890, 20000 Maldonado, Uruguay. E-mail: info@laveccs.org.
URL: http://www.laveccs.org/

History 1 Apr 2007, Santiago (Chile). Registration: Uruguayan Ministry of Foreign Affairs. **Aims** Promote, spread and secure knowledge progression and elevated standards of practice in veterinary emergency and critical care medicine in Latin America. **Structure** General Assembly; Board Committee. **Languages** Portuguese, Spanish. **Activities** Certification/accreditation; training/education. **Events** *Congress* Mexico City (Mexico) 2018, *Congress* Punta del Este (Uruguay) 2017, *Congress* Monterrey (Mexico) 2016, *Congress* Sao Paulo (Brazil) 2015, *Congress* Medellin (Colombia) 2014. **Publications** *JLAVECCS.*

Members Associate in 16 Countries:
Argentina, Brazil, Chile, Colombia, Ecuador, El Salvador, Grenada, Mexico, Panama, Paraguay, Peru, Puerto Rico, Spain, Uruguay, USA, Venezuela.

NGO Relations Affiliate member of: *World Small Animal Veterinary Association (WSAVA, #21795).* Close relations with: Veterinary Emergency Critical Care Society (VECCS); national societies.
[2020.06.24/XJ1205/**D**]

- ♦ Latin American Vine and Grape Organization (inactive)

♦ Latin American Water Education and Training Network (LA-WETNET) 16393

Red Latinoamericana de Educación y Capacitación en Recursos Hidricos (LA-WETnet)

Coordinator Billinghurst 470, Planta A, Oficina 16, San Isidro B1642BDJ, Buenos Aires, Argentina. T. +541147233948. Fax +541147233948. E-mail: info@lawetnet.org.
Coordinator address not obtained.
URL: https://lawetnet.org/

History 17 Jul 2002, Lima (Peru). **Aims** Promote and strengthen educational activities and knowledge transfer on water issues in order to contribute to the development of capacities for the effective management of water resources and water related services in Latin America. **Events** *Regional workshop on training network development in Latin America* Bogota (Colombia) 2005. **IGO Relations** Participating organizations: *Centro Panamericano de Ingenieria Sanitaria y Ciencias del Ambiente (CEPIS, no recent information); Pan American Health Organization (PAHO, #18108); UNESCO (#20322); United Nations Economic Commission for Latin America and the Caribbean (ECLAC, #20556).* **NGO Relations** Participating organizations: *Global Water Partnership (GWP, #10653); Inter-American Association of Sanitary and Environmental Engineering (#11400).*
[2021/XM0559/**F**]

- ♦ Latin American Water Information System (#19295)
- ♦ Latin American Water Ski Federation (inactive)

♦ Latin American Weed Society 16394

Société latinoaméricaine de malherbologie – Asociación Latinoamericana de Malherbologia (ALAM)

Pres FAUBA, Av San Martin 4453, C1417DSE, Buenos Aires, Argentina.

History 1971. Former names and other names: *Latin American Association on Weeds* – alias; *Asociación Latinoamericana de Malezas* – alias. **Aims** Promote dissemination of research and interaction among researchers, organizations, industry and policymakers. **Languages** English, Portuguese, Spanish. **Activities** Events/meetings. **Events** *Congreso Latinoamericano de Malezas* San José (Costa Rica) 2019, *Congreso Latinoamericano de Malezas* Havana (Cuba) 2017, *Congress* Buenos Aires (Argentina) 2015, *Congress* Cancún (Mexico) 2013, *Congress* Viña del Mar (Chile) 2011. **Publications** *Series Técnicas de ALAM* in Portuguese, Spanish. **Members** Academic, governmental and industry research scientists, students and educators, extension educators and private land managers (about 500). Membership countries not specified.
[2017.07.14/XD6719/**D**]

- ♦ Latin American Wind Energy Association (#02209)
- ♦ Latin American Wireless Industry Association (no recent information)
- ♦ Latin American Women Association on Smoking Control (inactive)
- ♦ Latin American Women's Network for Economic Transformation / see Latin American Women's Network to Transform the Economy (#16395)

♦ Latin American Women's Network to Transform the Economy 16395

Red Latinoamericana Mujeres Transformando la Economia (REMTE)

Coordinator Av Ecuador 2519, La Paz, Bolivia. T. +5912417057 – +5912417953.
URL: http://www.movimientos.org/remte/

History 1997. Also referred to as *Latin American Women's Network for Economic Transformation.* **Members** Organizations (70) in 10 countries. Membership countries not specified. **NGO Relations** Member of: *Alianza Social Continental (ASC, #00635); World Social Forum (WSF, #21797).* [2014.11.07/XF6434/**F**]

- ♦ Latin American Wood and Building Workers Union / see Latin American Federation of Building, Wood and Building Materials Unions (#16318)
- ♦ Latin American Working Group (internationally oriented national body)
- ♦ Latin American Yoga Union (#20329)
- ♦ Latin American Youth Alliance / see World Youth Alliance Latin America (#21953)
- ♦ Latin American Youth Centre (internationally oriented national body)
- ♦ Latin American Youth Federation for Studies on the Human Environment (inactive)
- ♦ Latin American Youth Forum (#09881)
- ♦ Latin America Petrochemical Institute / see Asociación Petroquimica y Quimica Latinoamericana (#02294)
- ♦ Latin America Petroleum Association (#02231)
- ♦ Latin America Poultry Association (#02177)
- ♦ Latin America Social Marketing Association (unconfirmed)
- ♦ Latinamerica Society for Science and Technology (#19397)

♦ Latin America in Solidarity Action (ALAS Foundation) 16396

América Latina en Acción Solidaria (Fundación ALAS)

Exec Dir Vicente Bonilla Avenue, Bldg 120, City of Knowledge, Panama, Panamá, Panama PANAMá, Panama. E-mail: info@fundacionalas.org – mmoreno@fundacionalas.org.
URL: http://www.fundacionalas.org/

History by artists and philanthropists from Latin America and Spain. **Aims** Improve health and education of children in Latin America. **NGO Relations** Partner of: *1,000 Days.* [2019/XM3329/**E**]

- ♦ Latin America Solidarity Coalition (internationally oriented national body)
- ♦ Latinamerika-Institutet i Stockholm / see Nordic Institute of Latin American Studies
- ♦ **LATINAPSO** Red Latinoamericana de Psoriasis (#18717)
- ♦ **Latinautor** Organización Iberoamericana de Derechos de Autor (#17840)
- ♦ LatinCaribeBureau – Organization of Conventions Bureaus of Latin America and the Caribbean (no recent information)
- ♦ **LatinCLEN** Red Latinoamericana de Epidemiologia Clinica (#16298)
- ♦ Latin Coin Union (inactive)
- ♦ Latin Congress on Rheumatology (meeting series)
- ♦ Latin Culture Congress on Radiology (meeting series)
- ♦ **LATINDADD** Red Latinoamericana sobre Deuda, Desarrollo y Derechos (#18711)
- ♦ **Latindex** Sistema Regional de Información en Linea para Revistas Cientificas de América Latina, el Caribe, España y Portugal (#19297)
- ♦ Latin Europe-America Integration Committee (#04169)

♦ Latin Evangelical Alliance 16397

Alianza Evangélica Latina

Exec Dir Luis María Argaña e/ Cacique Sepe, Asunción, Paraguay. E-mail: info@aelatina.org – prensa@aelatina.org.
URL: https://www.aelatina.org/

History Nov 2001, as *Iberoamerican Forum for Evangelical Dialogue – Foro Iberoamericano de Dialogo Evangélico (FIDE).* Previously also referred to in English as *Forum for Ibero-American Dialogue of Evangelicals.* Transformed under current title, 2013. **Aims** Strengthen unity among the evangelical churches in Latin America; provide a forum for the national evangelical alliances; be the united voice for the Latin American evangelical church; maintain an active alliance with other regional alliances. **Finance** Voluntary donations.

Members National alliances in 19 countries:
Argentina, Belize, Bolivia, Brazil, Chile, Colombia, Costa Rica, Dominican Rep, Ecuador, El Salvador, Guatemala, Honduras, Mexico, Nicaragua, Panama, Paraguay, Peru, Uruguay, Venezuela.

NGO Relations Regional member of: *World Evangelical Alliance (WEA, #21393).* [2019/XJ4269/**F**]

- ♦ Latin Federation of Medical Electro-Radiological Societies (inactive)
- ♦ **LATINFOODS** Red Latinoamericana de Composición de Alimentos (#18708)

♦ Latin-Iberian-American Association of Operations Research Societies 16398

Société latino-ibéroaméricaine de recherche opérationnelle – Asociación Latino-Iberoamericana de Investigación Operativa (ALIO) – Asociación Latino-Ibero-Americana de Pesquisa Operacional

Sec address not obtained.
Pres address not obtained.

History Nov 1982. Founded as a regional group affiliated to *International Federation of Operational Research Societies (IFORS, #13493).* Former names and other names: *Latin-Ibero American Society of Operations Research* – alias; *Latin-Iberian-American Association of Operations Research and Systems Engineering Societies* – alias. **Aims** Promote the operations research discipline and its application in the decision-making process in the Latin-Iberian-American context by stimulating contact, exchange of results and experience among *professionals* and researchers in the field. **Structure** Officers: President; Vice President; Congress Vice-President; Secretary – all with 2-year terms. **Languages** English, Portuguese, Spanish. **Finance** Members' dues. Incomes from biennial conference. **Activities** Organizes: biennial conference; annual workshop targeted at young scholars interested in Operations Research; ALIO/EURO Conference on Applied Combinational Optimization; ELAVIO Summer School. **Events** *Biennial Conference* Madrid (Spain) 2021, *International Conference* Medellin (Colombia) 2021, *Biennial Conference* Madrid (Spain) 2020, *Biennial Conference* Lima (Peru) 2018, *Biennial Conference* Santiago (Chile) 2016. **Publications** *International Transactions in Operations Research; Investigación Operativa.*

Members Societies in 13 countries:
Argentina, Bolivia, Brazil, Chile, Colombia, Cuba, Ecuador, Mexico, Peru, Portugal, Spain, Uruguay, Venezuela.
[2020/XD0993/**E**]

- ♦ Latin-Iberian-American Association of Operations Research and Systems Engineering Societies / see Latin-Iberian-American Association of Operations Research Societies (#16398)
- ♦ Latin Ibero-American Association of Technological Management / see Asociación Latino-Iberoamericana de Gestión Tecnológica y de la Innovación (#02277)
- ♦ Latin Ibero-American Association of Technological Management and Innovation (#02277)
- ♦ Latin-Ibero-American Medical Law Association (no recent information)
- ♦ Latin-Ibero American Society for Computational Methods in Engineering (inactive)
- ♦ Latin-Ibero American Society of Operations Research / see Latin-Iberian-American Association of Operations Research Societies (#16398)
- ♦ Latin Languages Speaking Allergists and Immunologists (#10754)
- ♦ **LATIN** Latin American Theoretical Informatics Symposium (#16389)

♦ Latin Link 16399

Britain and Ireland Team Leader 87 London Street, Reading, RG1 4QA, UK. T. +441189577100. E-mail: info@latinlink.org.uk – international@latinlink.org.
Latin Link Europe PO Box 279, 8405 Winterthur ZH, Switzerland. T. +41522020884. E-mail: info@latinlink.ch.
URL: http://www.latinlink.org/

History 1991. Founded on merger of *Evangelical Union of South America (EUSA, inactive)* and Regions Beyond Missionary Union (RBMU Peru). Former names and other names: *Enlace Latino* – former. Registration: Registered Charity, No/ID: 1020826, England and Wales; Registered Charity, No/ID: SC052161, Scotland; Company limited by guarantee, No/ID: 2811525, England. **Aims** See *Christian* communities in every part of Latin America impact their neighbours, their societies and the wider world; in partnership with churches, send and receive individuals, families and teams to or from Latin American communities. **Structure** Based in UK; *Latin Link Europe* in Winterthur (Switzerland); *Latin Link International* in Lima (Peru). **Languages** Dutch, English, German, Portuguese, Spanish. **Staff** 15.00 FTE, paid. **Finance** Sources: donations. Annual budget: 2,000,000 GBP. **Activities** Events/meetings; projects/programmes; publishing activities; training/education.

Members Individuals in 16 countries:
Argentina, Bolivia, Brazil, Chile, Colombia, Costa Rica, Ecuador, Guatemala, Ireland, Mexico, Netherlands, Nicaragua, Peru, Spain, Switzerland, UK.

NGO Relations Member of (1): *Global Connections.* [2023.02.13/XG9761/**F**]

♦ Latin Mass Society 16400

Hon Sec 9 Mallow Street, London, EC1Y 8RQ, UK. T. +442074047284. E-mail: info@lms.org.uk.
URL: http://www.lms.org.uk/

History 24 Apr 1965. Inaugural meeting took place in Notre Dame Hall, Leicester Square, London (UK). Former names and other names: *The Latin Mass Society of England & Wales* – full title. Registration: Charity Commission, No/ID: 248388, UK, England and Wales. **Aims** Promote the traditional Latin liturgy of the Catholic Church, the teachings and practices integral to it, the musical tradition which serves it, and the Latin language in which it is celebrated. **Structure** Board of Trustees. **Languages** English, Latin. **Staff** 3.00 FTE, paid; 30.00 FTE, voluntary. **Finance** Sources: donations; gifts, legacies; members' dues. **Activities** Financial and/or material support; religious activities; training/education. **Publications** *Mass of Ages* (4 a year) – magazine; *Ordo – Liturgical* (annual). *Proper of Feasts Celebrated in the Dioceses of England & Wales* (2020); *Ordinary Prayers of the Traditional Latin Mass; Pilgrim's Handbook; Plain Man's Guide to the Traditional Roman Rite of Holy Mass; Simplicissimus* – Latin grammar textbook. Wall calendar; funeral guide; DVDs; greetings cards. **Members** Societies in 15 countries. Membership countries not specified. [2022.10.20/XE1895/**E**]

♦ The Latin Mass Society of England & Wales / see Latin Mass Society (#16400)
♦ Latin Medical Association (inactive)
♦ Latin Medical Union (inactive)

♦ Latin and Mediterranean Group of Sport Medicine 16401

Groupement latin et méditerranéen de médecine du sport (GLMMS) – Grupo Latino y Mediterraneo de Medicina del Deporte – Gruppo Latino e Mediterraneo di Medicina Sportiva – Grupul Latin Mediteranean de Medicina Sportiva – Grup Llati i Mediterrani de Medicina de l'Esport

SG 11 rue des Frères Ougalis, El Mouradia Golf, 16070 Algiers, Algeria. T. +21321547892.
Treas address not obtained.

History 1956, Paris (France), under the name *Groupement latin de médecine du sport*, as a group of *International Federation of Sports Medicine (#13554)*. Present name adopted Jan 1986. **Aims** Promote development of sport medicine; carry out research in sport medicine; group sport physicians. **Structure** General Assembly; Executive Board. Officers: President; Secretary General; 2 Deputy Secretaries General; Treasurer; Deputy Treasurer. Scientific Commission. **Languages** English, French, Latin. **Staff** Voluntary. **Finance** Sources: contributions; members' dues; sponsorship. **Activities** Organizes: congress (formerly every 2 years; since 1993 every 4 years); symposia. **Events** *Symposium* Digne les Bains (France) 2010, *Symposium* Genoa (Italy) 2010, *Quadrennial Congress* Pescara (Italy) 2009, *Symposium* Digne les Bains (France) 2007, *Quadrennial congress* Palma (Spain) 2005. **Publications** *Apunts* (6 a year); *Archivos de Medicina Deportiva* (6 a year); *Cinésiologie* (6 a year); *Medicina Osporto* (4 a year).

Members Full and Associate. National groups and individuals in 38 countries and territories:
Albania, Algeria, Angola, Belgium, Benin, Burkina Faso, Burundi, Cameroon, Côte d'Ivoire, Croatia, Cyprus, Czechia, Egypt, France, Gabon, Greece, Haiti, Italy, Japan, Luxembourg, Macau, Madagascar, Malta, Mauritania, Monaco, Morocco, Poland, Portugal, Romania, Russia, Senegal, Serbia, Spain, Switzerland, Togo, Tunisia, Türkiye, Vietnam.

NGO Relations Member of FIMS. [2014/XD8593/**C**]

♦ Latin Mediterranean Medical Union / see Surgery Society of the Latin Mediterranean (#20042)
♦ Latin Mediterranean Society of Pharmacy (#19508)
♦ Latin Monetary Union (inactive)
♦ **Latin NCAP** New Car Assessment Programme for Latin America and the Caribbean (#17077)
♦ Latinoamerican Institute for Quality Assurance (internationally oriented national body)
♦ Latino-American Underground Committee / see Asociación Latinoamericana de Metros y Subterraneos (#02242)

♦ LatinoAméricaPosible (LAP) 16402

Contact ç VIVA Services, Costado N de Nunciatura Apostólica, Blvd de Róhrmoser, San José, San José, San José, Costa Rica. T. +50622912244. E-mail: info@latinoamericaposible.net.
Contact address not obtained.
URL: http://www.latinoamericaposible.net/

History Also referred to as *Fundación LatinoAméricaPosible.* **Structure** Board of Directors. Praesidium. **Members** Membership countries not specified. [2017/XJ0685/f/**F**]

♦ Latinoamérica Sustentable (unconfirmed)
♦ **LATINPIN** Federación Latinoamericana de Asociaciones de Técnicos y Fabricantes de Pinturas y Tintas (#09346)
♦ LATIN / see Red Latinoamericana de Información Teologica (#18713)
♦ Latin Society of Otorhinolaryngology (inactive)
♦ Latin Society of Reproductive Medicine (#19387)
♦ Latin Union (inactive)
♦ LATOA – Latin American Tourism Operators Association (inactive)
♦ **LATS** Latin American Thyroid Society (#16390)
♦ **LATTU** Latin American Table Tennis Union (#20453)
♦ Latvian Centre for Human Rights and Ethnic Studies (internationally oriented national body)
♦ Latvian Federation of the Free World / see Pasaules Brivo Latviesu Apvieniba (#18250)
♦ Latvian Human Rights Committee (internationally oriented national body)
♦ Latvian Institute of International Affairs (internationally oriented national body)
♦ Latvijas Arpolitikas Instituts (internationally oriented national body)
♦ Latvijas Cilvèktiesibu Un Etnisko Studiju Centrs (internationally oriented national body)
♦ Latvijas Cilvektiesibu Komiteja (internationally oriented national body)

♦ Laudato Si' Movement 16403

Exec Dir 700 12th St NW, Suite 700, Washington DC 20005, USA. T. +18572728775. E-mail: katie@laudatosimovement.org.
URL: https://laudatosimovement.org/

History Founded Jan 2015. Registered in accordance with US law. Former names and other names: *Global Catholic Climate Movement (GCCM)* – former. **Aims** Serve the Catholic family worldwide to turn Pope Francis' Laudato Si' encyclical into action for climate justice. **Structure** Steering Committee; Board of Directors; Secretariat. **Staff** 12.00 FTE, paid.

Members Organizations (over 400) in 57 countries and territories:
Angola, Argentina, Australia, Austria, Bangladesh, Belgium, Belize, Bolivia, Brazil, Burundi, Canada, China, Colombia, Ecuador, El Salvador, Eswatini, Finland, France, Germany, Guatemala, Guyana, Honduras, Hong Kong, Hungary, India, Indonesia, Ireland, Italy, Japan, Kenya, Korea Rep, Malawi, Malaysia, Mexico, Nepal, New Zealand, Nicaragua, Nigeria, Norway, Pakistan, Panama, Paraguay, Peru, Philippines, Samoa, Sierra Leone, Singapore, Slovakia, South Africa, Spain, Sri Lanka, Taiwan, Togo, UK, Ukraine, USA, Zimbabwe.

Included in the above, 43 organizations listed in this Yearbook:
- *AGIOMONDO;*
- *Apostleship of Prayer;*
- *Association of Member Episcopal Conferences in Eastern Africa (AMECEA, #02805);*
- *Carmelite Sisters of Charity, Vedruna (CCV);*
- *Catholic Agency for Overseas Development (CAFOD);*
- *Catholics in Coalition for Justice and Peace (CCJP);*
- *Catholic Youth Network for Environmental Sustainability in Africa (CYNESA, #03611);*
- *Christian Life Community (CLC, #03905);*
- *CIDSE (CIDSE, #03926);*
- *Comité Catholique contre la Faim et pour le Développement-Terre Solidaire (CCFD-Terre Solidaire);*
- *Conference of European Justice and Peace Commissions (#04596);*
- *Development and Peace (CCODP);*
- *Dominican Sisters of the Congregation of the Most Holy Rosary (Adrian Dominican Sisters);*
- *Earth Link;*
- *European Alliance of Catholic Women's Organisations (ANDANTE, #05864);*
- FABC – Office of Human Development;
- *Federation of Asian Bishops' Conferences (FABC, #09430)* (Climate Change Desk);
- *Federazione Organismi Cristiani Servizio Internazionale Volontario (Volontari nel Mondo – FOCSIV);*
- *Forum international d'action catholique (FIAC, #09919);*
- *Franciscans International (FI, #09982);*
- *Fundação Gonçalo da Silveira (FGS);*
- *International Catholic Conference of Scouting (ICCS, #12453);*
- *Jesuit Conference of Asia Pacific (JCAP, #16099);*
- *Jesuit European Social Centre (JESC, #16103);*
- *Marianites of Holy Cross;*
- *Maryknoll Office for Global Concern (MOGC);*
- *Mercy International Association (MIA, #16723);*
- *Missionary Franciscan Sisters of the Immaculate Conception (MFIC);*
- *Missionary Society of St Columban (SSCME);*
- *Order of Friars Minor (OFM)* (English Speaking Conference);
- *Ordo Fratrum Minorum Capuccinorum (OFM Cap);*
- *Passionists International (PI, #18254);*
- *Pax Christi – International Catholic Peace Movement (#18266);*
- *RENEW International;*
- *Scottish Catholic International Aid Fund (SCIAF);*
- *Secular Franciscan Order (SFO);*
- *Sisters of Charity of Nazareth (SCN);*
- *Sisters of Our Lady of the Missions (RNDM);*
- *Sisters of the Congregation of Mary (Marist Sisters);*
- *Sisters of the Holy Cross;*
- *Society of African Missions (SMA);*
- *UNANIMA International (#20281).*

NGO Relations Member of: *Forum of Catholic Inspired NGOs (#09905).* [2019.06.18/XM6051/y/**E**]

♦ Laudes Foundation (internationally oriented national body)

♦ Laureate International Universities (LUI) 16404

CEO/Chairman 650 South Exeter St, Baltimore MD 21202-4382, USA. T. +14108436100.
URL: http://www.laureate.net/

Aims Make education more accessible and affordable so that more students can pursue their dreams. **Structure** Education Executive Committee; Operating Committee.

Members Institutions (43) in 19 countries:
Australia, Brazil, Chile, China, Costa Rica, Cyprus, Ecuador, France, Germany, Honduras, Malaysia, Mexico, Panama, Peru, Spain, Switzerland, Türkiye, UK, USA.

Included in the above, 3 organizations listed in this Yearbook:
Universidad de las Américas (UDLA); Universidad Latinoamericana de Ciencia y Tecnologia (ULACIT); Universidad Tecnológica Centroamericana (UNITEC). [2020/XJ2693/y/**F**]

♦ Laureus Sport for Good Foundation (unconfirmed)
♦ Laurier Centre for Global Relations, Governance and Policy (internationally oriented national body)

♦ Lausanne Committee for World Evangelization (LCWE) 16405

Exec Dir/CEO The Lausanne Movement, 1-4-10 Taiko, Nakamura-ku, Nagoya, Aichi, 470-0801 Japan. E-mail: info@lausanne.org.
URL: http://www.lausanne.org/

History 1974, Lausanne (Switzerland), at 1st Evangelization Congress, when Lausanne Covenant was written and agreed on. Committee created shortly after. Also popularly known as *Lausanne Movement.* **Aims** Connect influencers and ideas for global mission. **Finance** Donations. **Activities** Awareness raising; events/meetings. **Events** *East Asia Young Leaders Gathering* Jeju (Korea Rep) 2019, *International congress on world evangelization* Cape Town (South Africa) 2010, *Lausanne diaspora strategy consultation* Manila (Philippines) 2009, *Biennial international leadership meeting* Seoul (Korea Rep) 2009, *Lausanne diaspora educators consultation* Seoul (Korea Rep) 2009. **Publications** *Lausanne Global Analysis* (6 a year).

Members Individuals (about 80) in 47 countries and territories:
Angola, Argentina, Australia, Bangladesh, Brazil, Canada, Colombia, Congo DR, Côte d'Ivoire, Denmark, Egypt, England, France, Germany, Ghana, Guatemala, Hong Kong, India, Indonesia, Ireland, Israel, Italy, Jamaica, Japan, Kenya, Korea Rep, Malaysia, Mexico, Netherlands, New Zealand, Nigeria, Norway, Pakistan, Peru, Philippines, Scotland, Singapore, South Africa, Spain, Sri Lanka, Switzerland, Taiwan, Tanzania UR, Uganda, USA, Venezuela, Zimbabwe.

NGO Relations Instrumental in setting up: *Lausanne Consultation of Jewish Evangelism (LCJE, see: #16405).* [2014.06.01/XF1559/v/**F**]

♦ Lausanne Consultation of Jewish Evangelism (see: #16405)
♦ Lausanne Movement / see Lausanne Committee for World Evangelization (#16405)
♦ Lauterpacht Centre for International Law (internationally oriented national body)
♦ Lauterpacht Research Centre for International Law / see Lauterpacht Centre for International Law
♦ **LAVCA** Association for Private Capital Investment in Latin America (#02871)
♦ LAVC – Latin American Veterinary Conference (meeting series)
♦ **LAVE** Association volcanologique européenne (#09077)
♦ **LAVECCS** Latin American Veterinary Emergency and Critical Care Society (#16392)
♦ Law Asia Conference (meeting series)

♦ LAWASIA – Law Association for Asia and the Pacific 16406

Association juridique de l'Asie et du Pacifique

SG Suite 1101, Level 11, 170 Philip Street, Sydney NSW 2000, Australia. T. +61299260165. Fax +61292239652. E-mail: lawasia@lawasia.asn.au.
URL: http://www.lawasia.asn.au/

History 13 Aug 1966, Canberra, ACT (Australia). Former names and other names: *Law Association for Asia and the Western Pacific* – former. **Aims** Promote administration of justice, protection of human rights and maintenance of the rule of law; advance *legal* education; diffuse knowledge of laws of member countries; promote development of law and uniformity where appropriate; further international understanding and goodwill; foster relations and intercourse between lawyers; uphold and advance status of the legal profession in the region. **Structure** Council; Executive Committee; Secretariat; Standing Committees. **Languages** English. **Staff** 3.50 FTE, paid. **Finance** Sources: members' dues. **Activities** Knowledge management/information dissemination; networking/liaising; research and development; training/education. **Events** *LAWASIA Human Rights Conference* 2022, *LAWASIA Alternative Dispute Resolution Conference* Denarau (Fiji) 2022, *Annual Conference* Sydney, NSW (Australia) 2022, *World Congress on Family Law and Children's Rights* Singapore (Singapore) 2021, *Annual Conference* Sydney, NSW (Australia) 2021. **Publications** *LAWASIA Human Rights Section Update* (12 a year); *LAWASIA Monthly e-Newsletter* (12 a year).

Members National organizations and individuals in 43 countries, jurisdictions and territories:
Afghanistan, Australia, Azerbaijan, Bangladesh, Brazil, Brunei Darussalam, Cambodia, Canada, Chile, China, Fiji, Georgia, Germany, Guam, Hong Kong, India, Indonesia, Israel, Italy, Japan, Korea Rep, Kuwait, Macau, Malaysia, Maldives, Mongolia, Myanmar, Nepal, Netherlands, New Zealand, Pakistan, Papua New Guinea, Peru, Philippines, Russia, Samoa, Singapore, Sri Lanka, Switzerland, Thailand, UK, USA, Vietnam.

Consultative Status Consultative status granted from: *ECOSOC (#05331)* (Special); *World Intellectual Property Organization (WIPO, #21593)* (Permanent Observer Status). **IGO Relations** Accredited by (1): *United Nations Office at Vienna (UNOV, #20604).* **NGO Relations** Observer status with (1): *Presidents of Law Associations in Asia (POLA, #18486).* Instrumental in setting up (1): *Working Group for an ASEAN Human Rights Mechanism (Working Group).* [2022.02.09/XC2901/**C**]

♦ Law Association for Asia and the Western Pacific / see LAWASIA – Law Association for Asia and the Pacific (#16406)

♦ The Law and Development Institute (LDI) 16407

Contact address not obtained. E-mail: info@lawanddevelopment.net.
URL: https://www.lawanddevelopment.net/

History 2009. **Aims** Promote law and development studies and projects. **Activities** Events/meetings; networking/liaising; projects/programmes; research/documentation; training/education. **Events** *Law and Development Conference* Hamburg (Germany) 2021. **Publications** *Law and Development Review.*

Members Individuals in 8 countries:
Australia, Canada, Israel, Japan, Korea Rep, Singapore, UK, USA. [2020.09.20/AA0476/jv/**C**]

♦ Law and Development Research Network (LDRN) 16408

Contact address not obtained. E-mail: editor@lawdev.org.
URL: https://lawdev.org/

History Sep 2017, Antwerp (Belgium). **Aims** Enhance knowledge and understanding of the role of law, both domestic and international, in relation to development and governance, as perceived globally and locally. **Structure** Executive Committee. **Activities** Events/meetings; training/education. **Events** *Annual Conference* Port Elizabeth (South Africa) 2021, *Annual Conference* Berlin (Germany) 2019, *Annual Conference* Leiden (Netherlands) 2018, *Annual Conference* Leiden (Netherlands) 2017, *Annual Conference* Ostend (Belgium) 2016. **Publications** *LDRN Newsletter.* **Members** Individuals. Membership countries not specified. [2020/AA0751/v/**F**]

♦ **LAWEA** Latin American Wind Energy Association (#02209)

♦ Law Enforcement and HIV Network (LEAHN) 16409

Chair address not obtained.
URL: http://www.leahn.org/

Aims Build sustainable global and local partnerships to work more effectively with *vulnerable* groups, such as people who inject *drugs* (PWID), sex workers, prisoners, migrants and men who have sex with men (MSM). **Structure** International Police Advisory Group (IPAG); International Expert Advisory Group. Country Focal Points. **Activities** Knowledge management/information dissemination; advocacy/lobbying/activism.

Members Focal points in 15 countries:
Australia, Bangladesh, Brazil, Ethiopia, Ghana, Indonesia, Kenya, Kyrgyzstan, Moldova, Nepal, Tajikistan, Tanzania UR, Thailand, Ukraine, Vietnam.
NGO Relations Supports: *Women and Harm Reduction International Network (WHRIN, #21000).*
[2014/XJ8496/**F**]

- ♦ **LA-WETNET** Latin American Water Education and Training Network (#16393)
- ♦ **LA-WETnet** Red Latinoamericana de Desarrollo de Capacidades para la Gestión Integrada del Agua (#18710)
- ♦ **LA-WETnet** Red Latinoamericana de Educación y Capacitación en Recursos Hidricos (#16393)
- ♦ LAWG – Latin American Working Group (internationally oriented national body)
- ♦ Law Group / see Global Rights
- ♦ **LAW** Lawyers Associated Worldwide (#16410)
- ♦ **LAW** Legal Action Worldwide (#16438)
- ♦ LawPact (internationally oriented national body)
- ♦ Law of the Sea Institute (internationally oriented national body)
- ♦ LAWS – Lawyers Alliance for World Security (internationally oriented national body)
- ♦ Law and Society Association (internationally oriented national body)
- ♦ Lawyers for Africa / see LEX Africa (#16449)
- ♦ Lawyers Alliance for Nuclear Arms Control / see Lawyers Alliance for World Security
- ♦ Lawyers Alliance for World Security (internationally oriented national body)

♦ Lawyers Associated Worldwide (LAW) 16410

Exec Dir address not obtained. T. +17207959039. Fax +17207957040.
URL: http://www.lawyersworldwide.com/

History 1989, as an unincorporated association. Registered in accordance with Swiss Civil Code, 2001. **Structure** Executive Committee; Executive Director. **Events** *Europe, Africa and Middle East Regional Meeting* Aberdeen (UK) 2017, *Asia Pacific Regional Meeting* Adelaide, SA (Australia) 2017, *Americas Regional Meeting* Atlanta, GA (USA) 2017, *Annual General Meeting* Miami, FL (USA) 2017, *Annual General Meeting* London (UK) 2016. **Publications** *LAW Newsletter.*
Members Membership by invitation only. Firms (over 90) in 51 countries and territories:
Argentina, Australia, Austria, Barbados, Belgium, Brazil, Bulgaria, Canada, Chile, China, Colombia, Costa Rica, Cyprus, Denmark, Ecuador, England, Finland, France, Germany, Ghana, Greece, Guatemala, Hungary, Ireland, Israel, Italy, Japan, Korea Rep, Lebanon, Liechtenstein, Malaysia, Mexico, Netherlands, New Zealand, Nigeria, Norway, Panama, Peru, Philippines, Poland, Portugal, Russia, Scotland, South Africa, Spain, Sweden, Switzerland, Türkiye, Uruguay, USA, Venezuela.
[2018/XM4615/**C**]

- ♦ Lawyers Committee against Nuclear Proliferation / see Lawyers Committee on Nuclear Policy
- ♦ Lawyers Committee for Human Rights / see Human Rights First
- ♦ Lawyers Committee for International Human Rights / see Human Rights First
- ♦ Lawyers Committee on Nuclear Policy (internationally oriented national body)
- ♦ Lawyers for Human Rights International (internationally oriented national body)
- ♦ Lawyers for Lawyers Foundation (internationally oriented national body)
- ♦ Lawyers for Peace (internationally oriented national body)
- ♦ Lawyers' Rights Watch Canada (internationally oriented national body)
- ♦ LAYA / see World Youth Alliance Latin America (#21953)
- ♦ Lay Canossians (religious order)
- ♦ Lay Carmelite Order Calced (religious order)
- ♦ Lay Dehonians (religious order)
- ♦ Lay Volunteers International Association (internationally oriented national body)
- ♦ Lay Volunteers International Community / see Lay Volunteers International Association

♦ Lazarus Union 16411

Contact Spargelfeldstrasse 162, House 196, 1220 Vienna, Austria. E-mail: lazarus-union@chello.at.
URL: http://www.lazarus-union.org/

History 2007. Former names and other names: *Union Corps Saint Lazarus International (CSLI)* – full title. Registration: ZVR, No/ID: 023914681, Start date: 7 Sep 2010, Austria. **Aims** Support and provide service to the needy, sick, handicapped, or old persons so as to ease their everyday life. **Structure** General Assembly; Board of Management. **Activities** Awards/prizes/competitions; guidance/assistance/consulting. **Consultative Status** Consultative status granted from: *ECOSOC (#05331)* (General). [2020/AA1122/**F**]

- ♦ LAZ – Lateinamerika-Zentrum, Bonn (internationally oriented national body)
- ♦ LBI – Leo Baeck Institute (internationally oriented national body)
- ♦ LBI – Ludwig Boltzmann Institut für Grund- und Menschenrechte (internationally oriented national body)
- ♦ **LBMA** London Bullion Market Association (#16510)
- ♦ **LBS** LittleBigSouls (#16494)
- ♦ LBS Protocol – Protocol for the Protection of the Mediterranean Sea against Pollution from Land-Based Sources and Activities (1980 treaty)
- ♦ LBT – Lutheran Bible Translators (internationally oriented national body)
- ♦ LBV – Legiã do Boa Vontade (internationally oriented national body)
- ♦ **LCA** Leadership for Conservation in Africa (#16415)
- ♦ **LCBC** Lake Chad Basin Commission (#16220)
- ♦ LCCLG / see C40 (#03391)
- ♦ **LCC** Linear Collider Collaboration (#16481)
- ♦ LCC – Linked Content Coalition (unconfirmed)
- ♦ LC – Congregatio Legionariorum Christi (religious order)
- ♦ LCHR / see Human Rights First
- ♦ LCHRES – Latvian Centre for Human Rights and Ethnic Studies (internationally oriented national body)
- ♦ LCIA – London Court of International Arbitration (internationally oriented national body)
- ♦ **LCIE** Large Carnivore Initiative for Europe (#16232)
- ♦ **LCI** Ladies Circle International (#16217)
- ♦ **LCI** Life Cycle Initiative (#16464)
- ♦ **LCI** Lions Clubs International (#16485)
- ♦ LC Initiative / see Life Cycle Initiative (#16464)
- ♦ LCJE – Lausanne Consultation of Jewish Evangelism (see: #16405)
- ♦ LCLAA – Labor Council for Latin American Advancement (internationally oriented national body)
- ♦ LC – Legionaries of Christ (religious order)
- ♦ **LC** Lymphoma Coalition (#16535)
- ♦ LCM – Little Company of Mary (religious order)
- ♦ LCNP – Lawyers Committee on Nuclear Policy (internationally oriented national body)
- ♦ LCP – League of Coloured Peoples (inactive)
- ♦ **LCPPC** League of Canaanite, Phoenician and Punic Cities (#16421)
- ♦ LC Prot 1996 – 1996 Protocol to the Convention on the Prevention of Marine Pollution by Dumping of Wastes and other Matter (1996 treaty)
- ♦ **LCS-RNet** International Research Network for Low Carbon Societies (#14735)
- ♦ LCSTL / see European Speech and Language Therapy Association (#08812)
- ♦ LCT / see International Organization Against Trachoma (#14436)
- ♦ **LCTPi** Low Carbon Technology Partnerships Initiative (#16516)
- ♦ **LCWE** Lausanne Committee for World Evangelization (#16405)
- ♦ **LDAC** Commission on Livestock Development in Latin America and the Caribbean (#04233)
- ♦ **LDAC** Long Distance Advisory Council (#16511)
- ♦ LDA International / see International Lead Association (#14009)
- ♦ LDA / see International Lead Association (#14009)
- ♦ LDC – Convention on the Prevention of Marine Pollution by Dumping of Wastes and other Matter (1972 treaty)
- ♦ LDC Debt Traders Association / see EMTA (#05449)
- ♦ **LDC** Leaders of Design Council (#16414)

♦ LDC Watch 16412

Observatoire PMA

Secretariat Rural Reconstruction Nepal, PO Box 8130, Kathmandu, Nepal. T. +97714427823. Fax +97714004508-4443494. E-mail: info@ldcwatch.org.
European Coordination Office EUROSTEP, Rue Stevin 115, 1000 Brussels, Belgium. T. +3222311659. Fax +3222303780.
URL: http://www.ldcwatch.org/

History 2001. **Aims** Engage with governments and the international community to effect implementation of the Istanbul Programme of Action (IPoA) including other Internationally Agreed Development Goals (IADGs) such as the Sustainable Development Goals (SDGs). **Structure** Steering Committee; International Secretariat. **Activities** Advocacy/lobbying/activism; events/meetings; guidance/assistance/consulting; research/documentation. **Consultative Status** Consultative status granted from: *ECOSOC (#05331)* (Special); *UNCTAD (#20285)* (General Category). **IGO Relations** Accredited by: *Green Climate Fund (GCF, #10714)*; *United Nations Framework Convention on Climate Change – Secretariat (UNFCCC, #20564).* [2020/XJ0306/**F**]

- ♦ LDF – Leonardo DiCaprio Foundation (internationally oriented national body)
- ♦ LDGL – Ligue des droits de la personne humaine dans la région des Grands-Lacs (internationally oriented national body)
- ♦ **LDI** The Law and Development Institute (#16407)
- ♦ LDI – Life Decisions International (internationally oriented national body)
- ♦ LDR / see Alliance of Liberals and Democrats for Europe (#00702)
- ♦ **LDRN** Law and Development Research Network (#16408)
- ♦ LDR / see Renew Europe (#18840)
- ♦ LDS International Society (internationally oriented national body)
- ♦ LDWP / see Lasallian Projects
- ♦ Lead Development Association / see International Lead Association (#14009)
- ♦ Lead Development Association International / see International Lead Association (#14009)

♦ LEADER Inspired Network Community (LINC) 16413

Contact Meierhofgasse 9, 6361 Hopfgarten im Brixental, Austria. T. +43533520306. E-mail: office@foerderinfo.eu.
URL: http://www.info-linc.eu/

History Derives from the previous *Links between Actions for the Development of the Rural Economy (LEADER+, inactive).* LEADER stands for *Liaison Entre Actions de Développement de l'Économie Rurale.* Concept work for LINC started 2009. **Aims** Promote networking and exchange of experience among European LEADER Areas in an innovative way. **Structure** Informal structure. **Languages** English. **Staff** 21 FTE, temporary. **Activities** Events/meetings. **Events** *Meeting* Romania 2024, *Meeting* Italy 2023, *Meeting* Jesenik (Czechia) 2022, *Meeting* Jesenik (Czechia) 2021, *Meeting* Prague (Czechia) 2020.
Members Full in 10 countries:
Austria, Czechia, Estonia, Finland, Georgia, Germany, Hungary, Italy, Luxembourg, Romania.
NGO Relations *European Network for Rural Development (ENRD, #07995)*; national organizations.
[2019.03.20/XJ9634/c/**F**]

♦ Leaders of Design Council (LDC) 16414

Contact address not obtained. E-mail: hello@leadersofdesign.com.
URL: http://leadersofdesign.com/

Aims Improve the welfare of the design industry as a whole. **Activities** Events/meetings. **Events** *Annual Conference* Monaco (Monaco) 2021, *Annual Conference* Monaco (Monaco) 2020, *Annual Conference* Prague (Czechia) 2019, *Annual Conference* Kyoto (Japan) 2018, *Annual Conference* Dublin (Ireland) 2017. **Members** Full (over 200). Membership countries not specified. [2020.01.16/XJ8637/**C**]

♦ Leadership for Conservation in Africa (LCA) 16415

CEO address not obtained. T. +27124605323. E-mail: admin@lcafrica.org.
URL: http://lcafrica.org/

History Initiated Aug 2006, by South African National Parks, Gold Fields Limited and *International Union for Conservation of Nature and Natural Resources (IUCN, #15766).* **Aims** Influence, accelerate and bring about the protection of *rainforests* and selected *eco-systems* in Sub-Saharan Africa. **Structure** Board. **NGO Relations** Member of: *International Union for Conservation of Nature and Natural Resources (IUCN, #15766).*
[2018/XM6792/**F**]

- ♦ Leadership, Effectiveness, Accountability and Professionalism / see LEAP Africa

♦ Leadership for Environment and Development (LEAD International) 16416

Sec 14 Beech Walk, Epsom, KT17 1PU, UK. T. +442082249386.
URL: http://www.lead.org/

History 1991. Founded by *The Rockefeller Foundation (#18966).* Registration: Charity Commission, No/ID: 1086989, England and Wales. **Aims** Inspire leadership and change for a sustainable world by working with individuals and organizations to develop their leadership potential through innovative training and capacity programmes. **Structure** Board of Directors. **Languages** Chinese, English, French, Japanese, Portuguese, Russian, Spanish. **Finance** Support from various sources, including: *UNDP (#20292)*; *UNEP (#20299)*; *Department for International Development (DFID, inactive).* **Activities** Capacity building; events/meetings; training/education. **Publications** Reports; case studies; CD-ROM learning resources; books; regular publications from participants.
Members Based in UK. Regional offices in 13 countries:
Brazil, Canada, China, India, Indonesia, Japan, Malawi (for Southern Africa region), Mexico, Nigeria (for Anglophone West African region), Pakistan, Russia (for Commonwealth of Independent States), Senegal (for Francophone African region), USA.
Consultative Status Consultative status granted from: *ECOSOC (#05331)* (Special); *UNEP (#20299).* **IGO Relations** Observer Status with: *United Nations Framework Convention on Climate Change – Secretariat (UNFCCC, #20564).* **NGO Relations** Supports: *SEED (#19213).* [2021/XE3903/**E**]

- ♦ Leadership exCHANGE (internationally oriented national body)
- ♦ Leadership Initiative for Transformation and Empowerment (internationally oriented national body)
- ♦ The Leadership Program: Developmental Leaders, Elites and Coalitions / see Developmental Leadership Program (#05053)
- ♦ Leaders Network in Nordic Countries / see Ledernes Netvaerk i Norden (#16434)

♦ Leaders and Organizations of Community Organizations in Asia (LOCOA) 16417

Contact 25-A Mabuhay Street, Brgy Central, Quezon City, Philippines. T. +639258432 – +634264119. Fax +634264118. E-mail: info@locoa.org.
URL: https://www.locoa.org/

History Nov 1993, Baguio (Philippines). Established during meeting of Asian community organizations. Took over activities of *Asian Committee for People's Organization (ACPO, inactive)*, founded in 1971 and dissolved in early 1990's. **Aims** Introduce community organizations to countries where none as yet exist; train community organizations on long- and short-term basis (one to seven months); organize exposure trips for community organizations and their support groups; arrange workshops in which national groups can exchange tactics and experiences; circulate information; arrange for research and evaluation; work with other Asia-wide bodies to help make people's participation a reality; retain the ecumenical nature of the network and expand it to include Muslim, Hindu and Buddhist members. **Structure** Directors/Founders (11). **Activities** Events/meetings; projects/programmes; training/education. **Publications** Books; manuals; articles. **Members** Community organization groups in Asia. Membership countries not specified.
[2020/XD8662/**D**]

♦ Leading Centres of Europe 16418

Address not obtained.
URL: https://www.leadingcentres.com/

History Set up as an informal alliance. **Aims** Forge greater relationships with *conference clients* worldwide. **Activities** Networking/liaising; events/meetings.
Members Conference centres in 10 countries:
Austria, France, Germany, Italy, Netherlands, Portugal, Spain, Sweden, Switzerland, UK. [2019/XM8614/**F**]

- ♦ Leading Edge International Research Group (internationally oriented national body)
- ♦ Leading International Association of Lawyers, Accountants and Tax Specialists / see International Practice Group (#14632)

♦ Leading Women of Africa (LWA) 16419

Founder and Pres 6 Pringle Road, Tygerhof, Cape Town, 7441, South Africa. T. +27812184736. E-mail: info@leadingwomenofafrica.com.
URL: http://www.leadingwomenofafrica.com/

History May 2008. Registration: No/ID: 2010/006294/08, South Africa. **Aims** Advance leadership and economic development of women *entrepreneurs* in Africa, by putting African women at the heart of sustainable economic development in Africa. **Structure** Board of Directors; Executive Committee; Patron. **Languages** English, French. **Staff** 2.00 FTE, paid; 7.00 FTE, voluntary. **Finance** Sources: members' dues. Annual budget: 500,000 ZAR. **Activities** Advocacy/lobbying/activism; awards/prizes/competitions; events/meetings. **Events** *Roundtable* Cape Town (South Africa) / Johannesburg (South Africa) 2022. **Publications** *LWA – Our Journey So Far*; *LWA – Women Doing Business in SADC*.
Members Members in over 32 countries
Cameroon, Nigeria, South Africa, UK, Zambia, Zimbabwe. [2023.02.13/XM4400/**F**]

- ♦ **LEAD International** Leadership for Environment and Development (#16416)
- ♦ LEAD Network – Leading Executives Advancing Diversity / see Foundation LEAD Network (#09965)
- ♦ League of African Bloggers and Cyber-activists for Democracy (#16476)
- ♦ League of the Africa Zone for the Defense of the Rights of Children and Pupils (internationally oriented national body)
- ♦ League of the Arab Fatherland (inactive)

♦ League of Arab States (LAS) 16420

Ligue des Etats arabes (LEA)

SG 1 Midan Al-tahrir, Tahrir Square, Cairo, 11642, Egypt. T. +20225750511. Fax +20225752966.
Permanent Delegation to the United Nations Rue du Valais 9, 1202 Geneva, Switzerland. T. +4122323038 – +4122323030 – +4122323039. Fax +41227316947.
URL: http://www.leagueofarabstates.net/

History 22 Mar 1945, Cairo (Egypt), at the Arab General Congress, on signature by representatives of the then 7 independent Arab States of the *Pact of the League of Arab States*, also referred to as the *'Charter'*, which is the constituent instrument of the League. Establishment followed meetings 25 Sep 1944 – 7 Oct 1944, Alexandria, later known as the *Arab Unity Consultations*, at which the Arab League project, subsequently known as the *Alexandria Protocol*, had been signed. Two further documents may be regarded as complementing the Charter: *Treaty for Joint Defence and Economic Cooperation*, signed 13 Mar 1950; *Charter for National Economic Action*, issued 26 Nov 1980. The Charter also proposed to set up *Arab Court of Justice (ACJ)*. All LAS Member States have become parties to both instruments. LAS headquarters transferred temporarily from Cairo to Tunis (Tunisia) in Mar 1979 but returned to Cairo following a resolution dated 10 Sep 1990. LAS is also referred to as *Arab League – Ligue arabe*. **Aims** Foster and promote relations among member states in political, economic, social, financial, transport, cultural and health issues; coordinate the policies of member states so as to safeguard their national security and maintain their independence and sovereignty; promote the common interests of member states.
Structure *'Council of the League'* is the supreme policy-, planning- and decision-making body, and convenes at 3 levels: Heads of State; Foreign Ministers; Permanent Delegates to the League. The Council of the League supervises *Arab Peace and Security Council (see: #16420)* established 29 Mar 2006, with the aim of preventing inter-Arab conflicts and following up and studying developments affecting Arab national security. *Arab Economic and Social Council (AESC, #00937)*, set up in accordance with a resolution adopted by the Council of the League in 1977, comprises ministers concerned or their deputies. The AESC is responsible for the economic and social affairs of the League, for supervision of the specialized agencies and institutions and for following up their activities. *'General-Secretariat'*, supervised by the Secretary General, prepares the work of the Council and follows up progress in the implementation of its resolutions. *Arab Parliament (#01023)* was inaugurated 27 Dec 2005, Cairo (Egypt); it was expected to become fully operational by 2010. Specialized Ministerial Councils (14):
- Arab Interior Ministers' Council;
- *Council of Arab Ministers of Foreign Affairs*;
- *Arab Ministerial Council for Electricity*;
- *Council of Arab Ministers of Health (#04861)*;
- *Council of Arab Ministers for Housing and Reconstruction (CAMHR, #04862)*;
- *Council of Arab Ministers of Justice (no recent information)*;
- *Council of Arab Ministers Responsible for the Environment (CAMRE, #04863)*;
- *Council of Arab Ministers for Social and Economic Affairs (#04864)*;
- *Council of Arab Ministers of Tourism (#04865)*;
- *Council of Arab Ministers of Transport (no recent information)*;
- *Council of Arab Ministers for Youth and Sports (#04866)*;
- *Arab Telecommunication and Information Council of Ministers (#01054)*;
- *Council of Arab Ministers for Water Resources*;
- *Council of Arab Ministers Responsible for Media.*

General Secretariat Departments (50).
LAS missions (26): Delhi (India); Berlin (Germany); Brussels (Belgium); Beirut (Lebanon); New York NY (USA); Washington DC (USA); Geneva (Switzerland); Moscow (Russia); Paris (France); Vienna (Austria); London (UK); Madrid (Spain); Rome (Italy); Addis Ababa (Ethiopia); Beijing (China); Buenos Aires (Argentina); Brasilia (Brazil); Nairobi (Kenya); Moroni (Comoros); Mogadishu (Somalia); Juba (Sudan); Damascus (Syrian AR); Tunis (Tunisia); Baghdad (Iraq); Pretoria (South Africa); Turkey.
Affiliate organs (3):
- *Arab Fund for Technical Assistance to African Countries (AFTAAC, #00966)*;
- *Arab Academy of Music (AAM, #00890)*;
- *High Arab Institute for Translation (HAIT).*

Technical Committees: although expansion of the scope of cooperation among Member States had led to establishment of specialized ministerial councils and agencies to replace technical and specialized committees, some standing, technical committees continue to function regularly. These include committees on human rights, political affairs, information affairs and on legal affairs.
Auditing, administrative monitoring and judicial bodies:
- *Arab Human Rights Committee (no recent information)*;
- *Administrative Tribunal of the Arab League (no recent information)*, also referred to as *Administrative Court of the Arab League*, which has competence to examine and deliver verdicts on administrative cases filed by General Secretariat staff members;
- *Investment Tribunal*, which examines disputes between Member States that may arise in the process of implementing the Unified agreement on Arab capital investments in Member States;
- *Higher Auditing Board* comprising representatives of 7 Member States and undertaking financial and administrative examination duties.

'Arab-African Affairs'
The 1st Joint Meeting of Ministers of Foreign Affairs of LAS and OAU, Mar 1977, Cairo (Egypt), adopted a charter instituting the following organs: *Arabo-African Summit*; Ministerial Council; *Standing Commission for Afro-Arab Cooperation (no recent information)*, comprising 12 ministers of each organization and, in addition, the Secretaries-General, who with the 2 co-Presidents comprise the Coordination Committee; Specialized Groups (5), dealing with cooperation in finance, industry, agriculture, transport, communications and telecommunications, and education, culture and information. Organizations set up in parallel by LAS were the Arab Fund for Technical Assistance to African States and BADEA. The 2nd African Arab Summit, 2010, adopted strategy for the African Arab partnership plan of action 2011-2016 and Serte Declaration.
'Arab-European Affairs' Certain mechanisms for the pursuance of the Arab-European dialogue were set up, including the Higher Tripartite Committee, formed of 3 states from each side and the plenary committee. The former was created to address political matters and undertake overall supervision of the technical aspects of the dialogue process, while the latter was meant to take care of economic, developmental and social matters.
Languages Arabic. **Staff** 460.00 FTE, paid.
Activities Serves as a forum for member states to coordinate their policy positions in the political field; plays a role in reaching peaceful settlements of inter-Arab disputes; concludes agreements in the economic field to achieve Arab economic integration; in the social field, enhances women's statuts and promotes human rights, sponsors sponsors joint Arab strategies in the areas of child and youth care, social defence against crime, combating narcotics and drug abuse; plays a role in the harmonization of school curricula, the launching of literacy campaigns and fostering dialogue among civilizations. Executive programme, created 1 Jan 2005, to create Greater *Greater Arab Free-Trade Area (GAFTA, #10700).*
Arab specialized unions, approved and statutes ratified by LAS:
- *Arab Cooperative Union (UCA, inactive)*;
- *Arab Federation for Engineering Industries (AFEI, #00943)*;
- *Arab Federation of Fish Producers (AFFP, #00945)*;
- *Arab Federation for Food Industries (AFFI, #00946)*;
- *Arab Federation of Leather Industries (inactive)*;
- *Arab Federation for Paper, Printing and Packaging Industries (AFPPPI, #00950)*;
- *Arab Fertilizer Association (AFA, #00958)*;
- *Arab Iron and Steel Union (AISU, #00998)*;
- *Arab Sugar Federation (ASF, inactive)*;
- *Arab Union for Cement and Building Materials (AUCBM, #01065)*;
- *Arab Union of Land Transport (AULT, #01069)*;
- *Arab Union of Manufacturers of Pharmaceuticals and Medical Appliances (AUPAM, #01070)*;
- *Union of Maritime Ports of Arab Countries (no recent information).*

Fora:*Arab Chinese Forum (no recent information)*; *Arab India Cooperation Forum (#00980)*; Summit for the Arab and South American Countries.
Instrumental in setting up, organizing or maintaining:
- *Afro-Arab Investment Institution (no recent information)*;
- *Afro-Arab Preferential Trade Area (no recent information)*;
- *Arab African Institute for Culture and Strategic Studies* (proposed);
- *Arab Air Carriers Organization (AACO, #00896)*;
- *Arab Centre for Medical Research (ACMR, inactive)*;
- Arab Civil Aviation Commission;
- *Arab Committee of Seven (no recent information)*;
- *Arab Council for Medical Specializations (no recent information)*;
- *Arab Fisheries Company (AFC, #00959)*;
- *Arab Higher Committee for Pharmacological Affairs (no recent information)*;
- *Arab Human Rights Committee (no recent information)*;
- *Arab Information System Network (ARISNET, inactive)*;
- *Arab Institute for Forestry and Range (AIFR, no recent information)*;
- *Arab Oil Experts Committee (inactive)*;
- *Arab Permanent Committee for Meteorology (see: #16420)*;
- *Arab Permanent Military Commission (no recent information)*;
- *Arab Permanent Postal Commission (APPC, #01025)*;
- *Arab Potash Company (APC, #01029)*;
- *Arab Research Centre for Injuries (ARCI, inactive)*;
- *Arab Scientific Advisory Committee for Blood Transfer (no recent information)*;
- *Arab Technical Committee for Endemic Diseases (no recent information)*;
- *Arab Telecommunication Union (ATU, inactive)*;
- *Arab Tourism Organization (ATO, #01057)*;
- *Arab Trade Financing Programme (ATFP, #01060)*;
- *Arab Unified Military Command (no recent information)*;
- *Arab Women Organization (AWO, #01078)*;
- *Arab Women's Committee (no recent information)*;
- *Association of Arab Universities (AARU, #02374)*;
- *Bureau de promotion du tourisme culturel dans les pays arabes (no recent information)*;
- *Committee of Arab Experts on Cooperation (no recent information)*;
- *Committee of Arab Experts on Customs Tariffs (inactive)*;
- *Coordinating Committee between the League of Arab States, Organs Working within its Framework and Arab Specialized Organizations (inactive)*;
- *Egyptian Arab Land Bank*;
- *Federation of Arab News Agencies (FANA, #09423)*;
- *High Coordination Committee for Joint Arab Action (no recent information)*;
- *Institute of Arab Manuscripts (no recent information)*;
- *League of Arab and Islamic Peoples (inactive)*;
- *Pan Arab Project for Child Development (PAPCHILD, no recent information)*;
- *Regional Organization for the Conservation of the Environment of the Red Sea and Gulf of Aden (PERSGA, #18804).*

Agreements concluded under LAS auspices:
- Arab charter on human rights (in force since 16 Mar 2008);
- *Cultural Treaty (1945)*;
- *Treaty of Joint Defence and Economic Cooperation between the Arab League States (1950)*;
- *Agreement Relating to Writs and Letters of Request (1952)*;
- *Convention Affecting the Nationality of Arabs Resident in Countries to Which They Are Not Related by Origin (1952)*;
- *Extradition Agreement (1952)*;
- *Reciprocal Enforcement of Judgements Agreement (1952)*;
- *Convention for Facilitating Trade Exchange and the Regulation of Transit Trade between States of the Arab League (1953)*;
- *Convention of the Privileges and Immunities of the League of Arab States (1953)*;
- *Convention for the Settlement of Payments of Current Transaction and the Movements of Capital between States of the Arab League (1953)*;
- *Nationality Agreement (1954)*;
- *Arab Convention on the Suppression of Terrorism (1998)*;
- Treaty on Arab Judicial Cooperation (Riyadh);
- Treaty on Trade Adjudication (Amman).

Events *Arab Energy Conference* Qatar 2023, *Summit* Brussels (Belgium) 2022, *(COVID-19) pandemic on Arab food security* 2020, *Arab Ministerial Forum for Housing and Urban Development* Dubai (United Arab Emirates) 2019, *Summit* Sharm el Sheikh (Egypt) 2019. **Publications** *Arab Perspectives – Sh'oun Arabiyya* (12 a year); *Journal of Arab Affairs* (12 a year) in Arabic; *LAS Information Bulletin* in Arabic, English. Bulletins of treaties and agreements; studies; essays; regular publications for local circulation published by regional offices.
Members Governments of 22 countries:
Algeria (1962), Bahrain (1971), Comoros (1993), Djibouti (1977), Egypt (1945), Iraq (1945), Jordan (1945), Kuwait (1961), Lebanon (1945), Libya (1953), Mauritania (1973), Morocco (1958), Oman (1971), Palestine (1976), Qatar (1971), Saudi Arabia (1945), Somalia (1974), Sudan (1956), Syrian AR (1945), Tunisia (1958), United Arab Emirates (1971), Yemen (1945).
League of Arab States Specialized Agencies (30):
- *Arab Academy for Science, Technology and Maritime Transport (AASTMT, #00891)*;
- *Arab Academy of Banking and Financial Sciences (AABFS)*;
- *Arab Administrative Development Organization (ARADO, #00893)*;
- *Arab Agricultural Engineers Union (AAEU, #00895)*;
- *Arab Atomic Energy Agency (AAEA, #00901)*;
- *Arab Authority for Agricultural Investment and Development (AAAID, #00902)*;
- *Arab Bank for Economic Development in Africa (#00904)*;
- *Arab Centre for the Studies of Arid Zones and Dry Lands (ACSAD, #00918)*;
- *Arab Civil Aviation Organization (ACAO, #00920)*;
- *Arab Fund for Economic and Social Development (AFESD, #00965)*;
- *Arab Industrial Development, Standardization and Mining Organization (AIDSMO, #00981)*;
- *Arab Information and Communication Technologies Organization (AICTO, #00982)*;
- *Arab Interior Ministers' Council (AIMC, #00990)*;
- *Arab Investment and Export Credit Guarantee Corporation (DHAMAN, #00997)*;
- *Arab Investors Union (AIU, no recent information)*;
- *Arab Labour Organization (ALO, #01001)*;
- *Arab League Educational, Cultural and Scientific Organization (ALECSO, #01003)*;
- *Arab Monetary Fund (AMF, #01009)*;
- *Arab Organization for Agricultural Development (AOAD, #01018)*;
- *Arab Satellite Communications Organization (ARABSAT, #01037)*;
- *Arab States Broadcasting Union (ASBU, #01050)*;
- *Arab Towns Organization (ATO, #01059)*;
- Arab Women's Organization;
- *Cairo Demographic Centre (CDC, #03396)*;
- *Council of Arab Economic Unity (CAEU, #04859)*;
- *Federation of Arab Businessmen (#09418)*;
- General Union of Chambers for Trade, Industry and Agriculture;
- *Organization of Arab Petroleum Exporting Countries (OAPEC, #17854)*;
- *Union arabe des assurances (no recent information)*;
- *Union of Arab Banks (UAB, #20349).*

IGO Relations Special agreements with: *FAO (#09260)* (formal agreement came into force Nov 1959); *ILO (#11123)*; *International Atomic Energy Agency (IAEA, #12294)*; *International Civil Aviation Organization (ICAO, #12581)*; *Organisation internationale de la Francophonie (OIF, #17809)*; *UNESCO (#20322)*; *UNIDO (#20336)*; *WHO (#20950)*. Cooperation Agreement with: *International Fund for Agricultural Development (IFAD, #13692)*. Participates in the activities of: *UNCTAD (#20285)*. Permanent observer status with: *World Intellectual Property Organization (WIPO, #21593)*. Observer to: *Agricultural and Land and Water Use Commission for the Near East (ALAWUC, #00570)*; *Conference on Interaction and Confidence-Building Measures in Asia (CICA, #04609)*; *Intergovernmental Committee of the International Convention of Rome for the Protection of Performers, Producers of Phonograms and Broadcasting Organizations (#11474)*; *International Organization for Migration (IOM, #14454)*; *Non-Aligned Movement (NAM, #17146)*; General Assembly of *United Nations (UN, #20515)*. Participates as observer in the activities of: *Codex Alimentarius Commission (CAC, #04081)*. Mutual arrangements with: *OAS (#17629)*. Invited to meetings of: *Union for the Mediterranean (UfM, #20457)*. Special links with: *ECOSOC (#05331)*; *International Maritime Organization (IMO, #14102)*; *United Nations Economic and Social Commission for Western Asia (ESCWA, #20558)*. Cooperates with: *International Telecommunication Union (ITU, #15673)*. Member of: *Parliamentary Union of the OIC Member States (PUIC, #18220)*; *United Nations Committee on the Exercise of the Inalienable Rights of the Palestinian People (CEIRPP, #20539)*. Partner in: *Regional Remote Sensing Centre for North African States (#18807)*. Memorandum of Understanding with: *International Centre for Migration Policy Development (ICMPD, #12503)*. Accredited to the Conference of the Parties of: *Secretariat of the United Nations Convention to Combat Desertification (Secretariat of the UNCCD, #19208)*. Accredited by: *United Nations Framework Convention on Climate Change – Secretariat (UNFCCC, #20564)*. Invited to sessions of Intergovernmental Council of: *International Programme for the Development of Communication (IPDC, #14651)*. Supports setting up of: *World Solidarity Fund (#21818)*. Memorandum of Understanding with the governments of the following countries:
- Bolivian Republic of Venezuela (15/9/2006);
- Dominican Republic (10/10/2006);
- Georgia (12/4/2009);
- Independent Government of Andalusia (28/5/2002);
- People's Republic of China (4/1/1999);
- Republic of Argentina (6/5/2005);
- Republic of Armenia (19/1/2005);
- Republic of Azerbaijan (16/10/2005);
- Republic of Bolivia (5/3/2009);
- Republic of Bulgaria (27/9/2007);
- Republic of Chili (27/1/2005);
- Republic of Croatia (28/2/2007);
- Republic of Cuba (20/3/2005);
- Republic of Hungary (8/3/2009);
- Republic of India (6/3/2002);
- Republic of Italy (28/2/2008);
- Republic of Kazakhstan (13/3/2007);
- Republic of Malta (20/9/2006);
- Republic of Pakistan (21/9/2005);
- Republic of Peru (29/5/2007);
- Republic of Portugal (24/5/2007);
- Republic of Romania (31/10/2007);
- Republic of Turkey (22/9/2004);
- Republic of Uzbekistan (18/4/2007);
- Russian Federation (23/9/2003);
- San Polo (12/5/2005);
- Secretariat of the State of the Vatican City (23/4/2009);
- United States of Mexico (11/4/2006).

NGO Relations Observer to: *International Committee of the Red Cross (ICRC, #12799)*; *International Federation of Red Cross and Red Crescent Societies (#13526)*; *International Red Cross and Red Crescent Movement (#14707)*. In liaison with technical committees of: *International Organization for Standardization (ISO, #14473)*. Library is member of: *International Federation of Library Associations and Institutions (IFLA, #13470)*. Memorandum of Understanding and Declaration with: *Mediterranean Universities Union (UNIMED, #16687)*. Links with the following bodies:
- *African Parliamentary Union (APU, #00412)*;
- *Afro-Asian Philosophy Association (AAPA, inactive)*;
- *Arab-African Arbitrators Association (no recent information)*;
- *Arab Commission for International Law (no recent information)*;
- *Arab Council for Childhood and Development (ACCD, #00929)*;
- *Arab Federation of Chambers of Shipping (#00940)*;
- *Arab Federation for the Consumer (AFC, #00942)*;
- *Arab Institute for Human Rights (AIHR, #00983)*;
- *Arab Institute for Security Studies (#00986)*;
- *Arab Inter-Parliamentary Union (Arab IPU, #00995)*;
- *Arab NGO Network for Environment and Development (RAED, #01017)*;
- *Arab Organization for Human Rights (AOHR, #01020)*;
- *Arab Organization of Supreme Audit Institutions (ARABOSAI, #01021)*;
- *Arab Regional Branch of the International Council on Archives (ARBICA, see: #12996)*;
- *Arab Society of Nephrology and Renal Transplantation (ASNRT, #01047)*;
- *Arab Sports Confederation (ASC, inactive)*;
- *Arab Towns Organization (ATO, #01059)*;
- *Arab Union of Youth Hostels Associations (no recent information)*;
- *Chambre de commerce franco-arabe (CCFA)*;
- *Commission permanente de la coopération arabo-africaine (no recent information)*;
- *Council of Arab Business Women (CABW, no recent information)*;
- *Euro-Arab Management School (EAMS, no recent information)*;
- *Euro-Arab Secretariat (no recent information)*;
- *Euro-Mediterranean Tourism Organization (EMTO, no recent information)*;
- *Federation of Arab Journalists (FAJ, #09422)*;
- *General Arab Insurance Federation (GAIF, #10104)*;
- *General Union of Arab Publishers (no recent information)*;
- *Gulf Centre for Strategic Studies (GCSS, #10824)*;
- *Inter-Parliamentary Union (IPU, #15961)*;
- *International Centre for Environment Audit and Sustainable Development (iCED, #12489)*;
- *International Council on Monuments and Sites (ICOMOS, #13049)*;
- *International Electrotechnical Commission (IEC, #13255)*;
- *International Institute of Humanitarian Law (IIHL, #13885)*;
- *International Union of School and University Health and Medicine (IUSUHM, no recent information)*;
- *Japan-Arab Association*;
- *Mediterranean NGO Forum (no recent information)*;
- *Muslim World League (MWL, #16917)*;
- *Network of Arab Scientists and Technologists Abroad (ASTA, no recent information)*;
- *Pan Arab Society of Andrological Sciences (PASAS, #18155)*;
- *Parliamentary Assembly of the Mediterranean (PAM, #18212)*;
- *Parliamentary Association for Euro-Arab Cooperation (PAEAC, #18217)*;
- *Siracusa International Institute for Criminal Justice and Human Rights (SII, #19289)*;
- *Standing Conference of Eastern, Central and Southern African Librarians (SCECSAL, #19960)*;
- *Union of Arab Chambers (UAC, #20350)*;
- *Union of Arab Football Associations (UAFA, #20353)*;
- *Union of Arab Historians (UAH, no recent information)*;
- *Vienna NGO Committee on the Status of Women (#20775)*;
- *World Family Organization (WFO, #21399)*. [2020/XD2903/y/**D***]

♦ League of ASEAN Dermatological Societies (unconfirmed)
♦ League of Augsburg Treaty (1686 treaty)
♦ League of Buddhist Esperantists (#03348)

♦ League of Canaanite, Phoenician and Punic Cities (LCPPC) 16421

Ligue des Cités Cananéennes, Phéniciennes et Puniques

Contact c/o Fondation Tyr, 35 avenue Foch, 75116 Paris, France.
URL: http://www.lcppc.com/

Aims Be a link between these cities that are the heirs of a common *history* and a set of common values. **Events** *Forum* Cadiz (Spain) 2012.

Members Cities in 11 countries:
Cyprus, Egypt, Greece, Italy, Lebanon, Malta, Morocco, Spain, Syrian AR, Tunisia, Yemen. [2015/XJ8578/**E**]

♦ League of Coloured Peoples (inactive)
♦ League of Democracies (unconfirmed)

♦ League of Dermatologists in the GCC States 16422

Contact PO Box 280, 80000 Al Farwaniyah, Kuwait. T. +9654832067. Fax +9654814936. E-mail: gjdv@usa.net.
URL: http://www.gulfdermajournal.net/

History 1991. **Aims** Contribute to scientific advances in dermatology; cooperate in the field of dermatology with different societies in the Gulf States; exchange scientific materials, ideas, etc, with faculties and universities in the Gulf States; encourage and support dermatology residents; provide continual medical educational activities for the dermatologists in the Gulf States. **Structure** Board; Secretary-General; Deputy; Treasurer. **Languages** Arabic, English. **Finance** Sources: meeting proceeds; members' dues; sale of publications. **Activities** Events/meetings. **Events** *International GCC dermatology and venereology conference / Conference* Khobar (Saudi Arabia) 2007, *International GCC dermatology and venereology conference / Conference* Kuwait (Kuwait) 2005, *International GCC dermatology and venereology conference / Conference* Doha (Qatar) 2003, *International GCC dermatology and venereology conference / Conference* Dubai (United Arab Emirates) 2001. **Publications** *Gulf Journal of Dermatology and Venereology*. [2021/XD8904/**D**]

♦ League of European Research Libraries / see Association of European Research Libraries (#02540)

♦ League of European Research Universities (LERU) 16423

SG Minderbroerstraat 8 – bus 5101, 3000 Leuven, Belgium. T. +3216329971. E-mail: info@leru.org.
URL: http://www.leru.org/

History 2002. **Aims** Advocate the values of high quality teaching within an environment of internationally competitive research. **Structure** Rectors' Assembly; Board of Directors Committees (2): Membership; Research Policy. Working Groups (2): Doctoral Studies; Research Career Development. **Languages** English. **Staff** 3.50 FTE, paid. **Finance** Members' dues. **Activities** Training/education; events/meetings; research/documentation. **Events** *Rectors Assembly* Strasbourg (France) 2019, *Rectors Assembly* Dublin (Ireland) 2018, *European Research Project Managers Community Meeting* Helsinki (Finland) 2013, *BRIGHT Student Conference* Amsterdam (Netherlands) 2012, *Bright student conference* Stockholm (Sweden) 2007. **Publications** Annual Report. Position papers; reports.

Members Universities (23) in 9 countries:
Belgium, Denmark, Finland, France, Germany, Ireland, Italy, Netherlands, Spain, Sweden, Switzerland, UK.

Consultative Status Consultative status granted from: *ECOSOC (#05331)* (Special). [2018/XM3672/**F**]

♦ League of Free Nations Association / see Foreign Policy Association
♦ League of Free Nations Associations (inactive)
♦ League for Gay, Lesbian, Bisexual and Transsexual Esperantists / see Ligo de Samseksamaj Geesperantistoj (#16475)

♦ The League of Historical Cities (LHC) 16424

Ligue des villes historiques – Liga de las Ciudades Históricas

Acting Gen Sec International and Multicultural Affairs Office, Kyoto City Hall, Kyoto, 604-8571 Japan. T. +81752223072. Fax +81752223055. E-mail: lhcs@city.kyoto.lg.jp.
URL: https://www.lhc-s.org/

History 1987, Kyoto (Japan). Reorganized and present name adopted at 4th World Conference of Historical Cities, 1994, Kyoto. Covenant adopted by General Assembly, 10 Sep 1996, Xian (China). Former names and other names: *World Conference of Historical Cities Council* – former (1987 to 1994). **Aims** Promote enrichment of *culture*, emphasizing the fact that historical cities are assets created by the wisdom of mankind; contribute to world *peace*; deepen *mutual understanding* by transcending national boundaries; strengthen affiliations between member cities, foster exchange of experience and knowledge among them and contribute to their development. **Structure** General Assembly (at Conference); Board of Directors (meets annually); Secretariat. **Languages** English. **Staff** 5.00 FTE, paid. **Finance** Sources: members' dues. Annual budget: 50 USD (2021). **Activities** Awareness raising; capacity building; events/meetings; knowledge management/information dissemination; networking/liaising; politics/policy/regulatory; projects/programmes; publishing activities; research and development; research/documentation. **Events** *World Conference of Historical Cities* 2024, *World Conference of Historical Cities* Andong (Korea Rep) 2022, *World Conference of Historical Cities* Kazan (Russia) 2021, *World Conference of Historical Cities* Kazan (Russia) 2020, *World Conference of Historical Cities* Bursa (Turkey) 2018. **Publications** *World Historical Cities* (3 a year) in English – bulletin; *The League of Historical Cities Brochure* (annual) in English. Articles on members' original initiatives and practices are published in our bulletin.

Members Historical cities (125) in 65 countries and territories:
Algeria, Australia, Austria, Azerbaijan, Belarus, Belgium, Bosnia-Herzegovina, Bulgaria, Canada, China, Colombia, Croatia, Cyprus, Czechia, Ecuador, Egypt, France, Georgia, Germany, Greece, Hungary, India, Indonesia, Iran Islamic Rep, Iraq, Ireland, Israel, Italy, Japan, Korea DPR, Korea Rep, Latvia, Lithuania, Malta, Mexico, Mongolia, Morocco, Myanmar, Nepal, Netherlands, New Zealand, Pakistan, Palestine, Peru, Philippines, Poland, Portugal, Romania, Russia, Serbia, Slovakia, Slovenia, Spain, Sri Lanka, Sweden, Switzerland, Taiwan, Thailand, Tunisia, Türkiye, UK, Ukraine, USA, Uzbekistan, Vietnam. [2022.10.20/XF4242/**F**]

♦ League of Homosexual Esperantists (#16475)
♦ League of Institutes of Global and Area Studies / see Leiden Global

♦ League of Islamic Universities 16425

Ligue des universités islamiques

SG c/o Saleh Kamel Center, Al-Azhar University, Nasr City, Cairo, Egypt. T. +2024015565. Fax +2024015541.

History Founded 1953. Also referred to as *Islamic Universities League*.

Members Countries not specified. International members include 1 organization listed in this Yearbook: *Islamic World Educational, Scientific and Cultural Organization (ICESCO, #16058)*.

IGO Relations *International Islamic University Malaysia (IIUM, #13961)*. [2018/XE1861/**D**]

♦ League of Jewish Women (inactive)
♦ League of the Latin Race (inactive)
♦ League of Nations (inactive)
♦ League of Nations High Commission for Refugees (inactive)
♦ League of Norden Associations / see Föreningarna Nordens Förbund (#09859)
♦ League for Pastoral Peoples / see League for Pastoral Peoples and Endogenous Livestock Development
♦ League for Pastoral Peoples and Endogenous Livestock Development (internationally oriented national body)
♦ League of Red Cross and Red Crescent Societies / see International Federation of Red Cross and Red Crescent Societies (#13526)
♦ League of Red Cross Societies / see International Federation of Red Cross and Red Crescent Societies (#13526)
♦ League of the Societies of the Citizens of the European Community Living Abroad / see Europeans throughout the World (#08839)
♦ League for the United States of Europe – Young Europe (inactive)
♦ **LEAHN** Law Enforcement and HIV Network (#16409)
♦ **LEA** Ligue des Etats arabes (#16420)
♦ Lean HE Hub / see Lean in Higher Education (#16426)
♦ **Lean HE** Lean in Higher Education (#16426)

♦ Lean in Higher Education (Lean HE) 16426

Chairperson address not obtained.
Sec address not obtained.
URL: https://www.leanhe.org/

History Sep 2013, Coventry (UK). Former names and other names: *Lean HE Hub* – former (2016). **Aims** Ensure that continuous improvement philosophies and practitioners within Higher Education (HE) are themselves always improving. **Structure** Steering Group. Continental Divisions: Asia Pacific; Americas; Europe. **Activities** Events/meetings. **Events** *International Conference* Melbourne, VIC (Australia) 2022, *International Conference* Glasgow (UK) 2021, *Lean in Higher Education International Conference* Canberra, ACT (Australia) 2020, *Lean in Higher Education International Conference* Ann Arbor, MI (USA) 2019, *Lean in Higher Education International Conference* Tromsø (Norway) 2018. [2022/AA2795/F]

♦ LEAP Africa (internationally oriented national body)
♦ **LEAP** Livestock Environmental Assessment and Performance Partnership (#16500)
♦ LEAP – Low Energy Antiproton Physics Conference (meeting series)

♦ learn4dev 16427

Contact c/o BTC, Rue Haute 147, 1000 Brussels, Belgium.
URL: http://www.learn4dev.net/

History Derived from workshops, 2003, Glasgow (UK) and 2004, Copenhagen (Denmark). Former names and other names: *Train4Dev* – former. **Aims** As a joint competence development network, link bilateral and multilateral *donor* organizations committed to more effective and harmonized *development*.
Members Organizations (30):
Australia, Austria, Belgium, Canada, Denmark, Finland, France, Germany, Ireland, Luxembourg, Netherlands, New Zealand, Norway, Poland, Slovakia, Slovenia, Spain, Sweden, Switzerland.
- *Agence française de développement (AFD)*;
- *Agencia Española de Cooperación Internacional para el Desarrollo (AECID)*;
- *Austrian Development Agency (ADA)*;
- *Center of Excellence in Finance (CEF, #03640)*;
- *DANIDA*;
- *Deutsche Gesellschaft für Internationale Zusammenarbeit (GIZ)*;
- *Enabel*;
- *European Commission (EC, #06633)*;
- *FAO (#09260)*;
- *International Bank for Reconstruction and Development (IBRD, #12317)*;
- *International Organization for Migration (IOM, #14454)*;
- *International Training Centre of the ILO (ITC, #15717)*;
- *Irish Aid*;
- *Luxembourg Agency for Development Cooperation (LUXDEV)*;
- *Norwegian Agency for Development Cooperation (Norad)*;
- *Swedish International Development Cooperation Agency (Sida)*;
- *Swiss Agency for Development and Cooperation (SDC)*;
- *UNDP (#20292)*;
- *United Nations Human Settlements Programme (UN-Habitat, #20572)*;
- *United Nations System Staff College (UNSSC, #20637)*;
- *World Food Programme (WFP, #21510)*. [2019/XJ7243/y/F]

♦ Learner Research Network 16428

Contact c/o Common Ground Research Networks, Research Park, 2001 South First St, Ste 202, Champaign IL 61820, USA. T. +12173280405. Fax +12173280435.
URL: http://learningconference.com/

History 1989, Sydney (Australia), when 1st *International Conference of Learning* was organized. Original title: *International Literacy and Education Research Network (LERN)*. **Activities** Events/meetings. **Events** *International Conference on Learning* Krakow (Poland) 2021, *International Conference on Learning* Valencia (Spain) 2020, *International Conference on Learning* Belfast (UK) 2019, *International Conference on Learning* Athens (Greece) 2018, *International Conference on Learning* Manoa, HI (USA) 2017. **Publications** *The Learner Book Imprint*; *The Learner Collection*. [2017/XS0259/c/F]

♦ Learning2 (internationally oriented national body)
♦ Learning Environments Australasia (internationally oriented national body)

♦ Learning in Higher Education (LiHE) 16429

Exec Dir Institute for Learning in Higher Education, Ambassador's Building, Steelcase Active Learning Center, HC Andersens Blvd 48, 1553 Copenhagen V, Denmark. E-mail: info@lihe.info.
URL: http://www.lihe.info/

History 2007. Former names and other names: *International Academic Association for the Advancement of Learning-centred Higher Education – Learning in Higher Education (LiHE)* – full title. **Aims** Advance learning-centred higher education. **Events** *International Symposium for Collaborative Writing of the International Anthology / International Symposium* Adelaide, SA (Australia) 2014, *International Symposium for Collaborative Writing of the International Anthology* Aegina Is (Greece) 2014, *International Symposium* Greece 2014, *International Symposium* Greece 2013, *International Symposium* USA 2013. **Publications** *Learning in Higher Education* – book series. [2021/XJ7619/F]

♦ Learning Initiative on Citizen Participation and Local Governance (internationally oriented national body)
♦ Learning for Life (internationally oriented national body)
♦ Learning Network on Capacity Development (unconfirmed)

♦ The Learning Teacher Network (LTN) 16430

Co-Treas Box 5089, SE-650 05 Karlstad, Sweden. E-mail: info@learningteachernetwork.org.
URL: http://learningteachernetwork.org/

History 2003, as a network within Comenius 3 within *SOCRATES Programme (inactive)*, funded by *European Commission (EC, #06633)* (2003-2006). Subsequently developed into an independent non-profit association. Current statutes adopted 2 Oct 2006; amended 17 Jun 2009 and 23 Nov 2009. **Aims** Act as a European platform for professional debate in the vanguard of educational progress. **Structure** General Meeting (annual); Executive Committee. **Finance** Members' dues. **Activities** Events/meetings; training/education. **Events** *International Conference* Dubrovnik (Croatia) 2019, *International Conference* Zagreb (Croatia) 2015, *International Seminar on Education for Sustainable Develoment* Istanbul (Turkey) 2014, *International Conference* Lisbon (Portugal) 2013, *International Conference* Nice (France) 2012. **Publications** *The Learning Teacher Magazine* (4 a year); *The Learning Teacher Journal*.
Members Institutional in 20 countries and territories:
Belgium, Bulgaria, Czechia, Denmark, Faeroe Is, Finland, France, Germany, Hungary, Ireland, Italy, Nepal, Netherlands, Norway, Portugal, Romania, Slovenia, Sweden, UK, USA.
Included in the above, 1 organization listed in this Yearbook:
International Polar Foundation (IPF).
Individuals in 28 countries:
Austria, Belarus, Belgium, Croatia, Czechia, Denmark, Estonia, Finland, Germany, Greece, Hungary, Ireland, Italy, Latvia, Lithuania, Malta, Nepal, Netherlands, Nigeria, Poland, Portugal, Romania, Slovakia, Slovenia, Sweden, Türkiye, UK, USA. [2022/XJ5231/y/F]

♦ Learning for Well-being Foundation (L4WB) 16431

Managing Dir Van Leijenberghlaan 22, 2nd Floor, 1082 GM Amsterdam, Netherlands. T. +31642481361. E-mail: info@learningforwellbeing.org.
EU Policy Advisor Rue Amédée Lynen 8, 1210 Brussels, Belgium. T. +3223409629.
URL: http://learningforwellbeing.org/

History May 2004, Netherlands. Introduced at annual meeting of *European Foundation Centre (EFC, inactive)*, 2004. Former names and other names: *Universal Education Foundation (UEF)* – former. Registration: No/ID: 34206704, Netherlands; EU Transparency Register, No/ID: 265989548300-62, Start date: 6 Dec 2022. **Aims** Manifest a world where each of us can participate fully, in a holistic and systemic way, to discover and enrich our unique qualities and experience our common humanity, on the individual and collective level. **Structure** Board; Head Office in Amsterdam (Netherlands); Branch Office in Brussels (Belgium); Project Offices (3). **Languages** Dutch, English, French, Italian, Portuguese, Spanish. **Staff** Paid; voluntary. **Finance** Sources: donations; grants; international organizations. Supported by: EU Institutions. Annual budget: 900,000 EUR (2020). **Activities** Advocacy/lobbying/activism; capacity building; events/meetings; research and development; training/education. Active in: Belgium, Bolivia, Germany, Israel, Netherlands, Palestine, Portugal, USA. **Events** *2GETHERLAND Workshop* Amsterdam (Netherlands) 2020, *Unfolding Conference* Brussels (Belgium) 2013. **Publications** *The Learning for Well-being Magazine* in English – The Learning for Well-being Magazine was published online twice a year and the articles are free to download. *Personal archeology: discovering your inner diversity through childhood artefacts* in English, Portuguese – This article describes a self-exploration by the primary author through artefacts from his own childhood. **NGO Relations** Member of (4): *End Corporal Punishment (#05457)*; *Eurochild (#05657)*; *Lifelong Learning Platform – European Civil Society for Education (LLLP, #16466)*; *Philanthropy Europe Association (Philea, #18358)*. Operational partners: *European Institute of Education and Social Policy (EIESP, #07551)*; *Synergos (#20082)*. Global partners: *Bertelsmann Foundation*; *Evens Foundation (EF)*; *Freudenberg Foundation*; *Guerrand-Hermès Foundation for Peace (#10815)*; *International Partnership Network (IPN, #14523)*; *International Yehudi Menuhin Foundation (IYMF, #15922)*; *King Baudouin Foundation (KBF)*; *Robert Bosch Foundation*; national organizations. [2023/XM0215/f/F]

♦ **LEASEUROPE** European Federation of Equipment Leasing Company Associations (#07111)
♦ Leather Naturally (unconfirmed)
♦ Leather, Shoe, Fur and Leather-Products Workers Trade Unions International (inactive)

♦ Leather Working Group (LWG) 16432

Office Kings Park Road, Moulton Park, Northampton, NN3 6JD, UK. T. +441604679999. E-mail: info@leatherworkinggroup.com.
Registered Office The Pinnacle, 170 Midsummer Boulevard, Milton Keynes, MK9 1FE, UK.
URL: http://www.leatherworkinggroup.com/

History 2005. Registered in accordance with UK law. **Aims** Develop and maintain a protocol that assesses the *environmental* compliance and performance capabilities of leather manufacturers and promotes sustainable and appropriate environmental business practices within the leather industry. **Structure** Executive Committee. **Activities** Standards/guidelines; events/meetings. **Events** *Main Member Meeting* Hong Kong (Hong Kong) 2017, *Main Member Meeting* Milan (Italy) 2017. **Publications** *LWG Newsletter*. **Members** Brands; Suppliers; Audited tanners. Membership countries not specified. [2018.06.01/XM6001/D]

♦ Le'atid Europe – European Centre for Jewish Leadership (internationally oriented national body)
♦ **LE** Autonomous Traindrivers' Union in Europe (#03043)
♦ Leave it in the Ground Coalition (unconfirmed)
♦ Lebanese International Businessmen Associations' Network (internationally oriented national body)
♦ **LECE** Ligue européenne de coopération économique (#07669)

♦ La Leche League International (LLLI) 16433

Ligue internationale de la leche – Liga de la Leche Internacional – Internationale La Leche Liga
Exec Dir 110 Horizon Dr, Ste 210, Raleigh NC 27615, USA. T. +19194592617. E-mail: info@llli.org.
URL: http://www.llli.org/

History 17 Oct 1956, Franklin Park, IL (USA). Commenced activities 1960, Canada. Became officially international 1964. Registration: 501(c)3, USA, Illinois. **Aims** Help *mothers* worldwide to breastfeed through mother-to-mother support, encouragement, information and education; promote a better understanding of *breastfeeding* as an important element in the healthy development of *baby* and mother. **Structure** International Board of Directors; Health Advisory Council; Legal Advisory Council; Management Advisory Council. **Languages** English. **Staff** 7.00 FTE, paid. **Finance** Members' dues. Other sources: contributions; online store; publications; royalties; rental income. Budget (annual) US$ 1,323,839. **Activities** Knowledge management/information dissemination; guidance/assistance/consulting; events/meetings; training/education. **Events** *Conference* Chicago, IL (USA) 2021, *Journée Internationale de l'Allaitement* Paris (France) 2016, *Biennial conference* Chicago, IL (USA) 2007, *Seminar for physicians / Biennial International Conference / Annual Physicians' Seminar* Chicago, IL (USA) 2007, *Biennial Conference* Washington, DC (USA) 2005. **Publications** *Breastfeeding Today* (4-6 a year) – magazine; *Leaven* (4-6 a year) – magazine; *LLLI Catalogue* (1-2 a year). *Feed Yourself Feed Your Family*; *Sweet Sleep*; *The Womanly Art of Breastfeeding* (8th ed).
Members Leaders (6,800) are accredited to handle group discussion meetings; Groups 1,844 worldwide. Representatives in every state of the USA and in over 66 countries and territories. Members (60,000) in 50 countries and territories:
Argentina, Australia, Austria, Bahrain, Belgium, Bolivia, Brazil, Bulgaria, Canada, China, Colombia, Costa Rica, Croatia, Denmark, Ecuador, Finland, France, Germany, Greece, Guatemala, Honduras, Hong Kong, Hungary, India, Ireland, Israel, Italy, Japan, Lebanon, Luxembourg, Mexico, Netherlands, New Zealand, Paraguay, Peru, Poland, Portugal, Puerto Rico, Saudi Arabia, Serbia, Slovenia, South Africa, Spain, Sweden, Switzerland, Türkiye, UK, USA, Zambia, Zimbabwe.
Consultative Status Consultative status granted from: *ECOSOC (#05331)* (Ros A); *UNICEF (#20332)*. **NGO Relations** Member of: *Conference of Non-Governmental Organizations in Consultative Relationship with the United Nations (CONGO, #04635)*; *CORE Group*; *NGO Committee on UNICEF (#17120)*; *PMNCH (#18410)*. Founding member of: *World Alliance for Breastfeeding Action (WABA, #21079)*. [2021/XD5428/F]

♦ Lectorium Rosicrucianum – International School of the Golden Rosycross (religious order)
♦ Ledarnas Nordiska Nätverk (#16434)

♦ Ledernes Netvaerk i Norden (LNN) 16434

Nordic Network of Leaders – Ledarnas Nordiska Nätverk
Address not obtained.

History 2 Dec 1998, Oslo (Norway). Former names and other names: *Leaders Network in Nordic Countries (LNN)* – alias. **Activities** Events/meetings. **Events** *Conference* Helsinki (Finland) 2020, *Conference* Copenhagen (Denmark) 2018, *Conference* Reykjavik (Iceland) 2016.
Members Associations in 6 countries and territories:
Denmark, Faeroe Is, Finland, Iceland, Norway, Sweden. [2020/XM6297/F]

♦ LEDIA – International Conference on Light-Emitting Devices and Their Industrial Applications (meeting series)

♦ LEDS Global Partnership (LEDS GP) 16435

Global Secretariat address not obtained. E-mail: secretariat@ledsgp.org.
URL: http://ledsgp.org/

History Founded 2011. Full title: *Low Emission Development Strategies Global Partnership*. **Aims** Strengthen quality, coordinated support, and leadership of *climate*-resilient low emission development strategies by countries in all regions; foster effective implementation of LEDS; spur development of new LEDS by additional national and sub-national governments. **Structure** Steering Committee; Global Secretariat, consisting of *Climate and Development Knowledge Network (CDKN, #04012)*. Regional Platforms: *Africa LEDS Partnership (AfLP)*; *Asia LEDS Partnership (ALP)*; *LEDS Europe and Eurasia*; *LEDS Latin America and Caribbean Regional Platform (LEDS LAC)*. Working Groups (6): Agriculture, Forestry and Other Land Use; Benefits; Energy; Finance; Subnational Integration; Transport. **Events** *ACF : Africa Carbon Forum* Accra (Ghana) 2019, *ACF : Africa Carbon Forum* Nairobi (Kenya) 2018, *ACF : Africa Carbon Forum* Cotonou (Benin) 2017, *ACF : Africa Carbon Forum* Kigali (Rwanda) 2016.
Members Governmental; International. Governmental in 21 countries:
Australia, Chile, Colombia, Congo DR, Costa Rica, Denmark, Germany, Haiti, Honduras, Indonesia, Israel, Japan, Kenya, Mexico, Nepal, New Zealand, Norway, Peru, UK, USA, Vietnam.
Included in the above, 7 governmental organizations listed in this Yearbook:
Australian Aid (inactive); *Department for International Development (DFID, inactive)*; *Deutsche Gesellschaft für Internationale Zusammenarbeit (GIZ)*; *European Commission (EC, #06633)*; *Japan International Cooperation Agency (JICA)*; *Tropical Agriculture Research and Higher Education Center (#20246)*; *United States Agency for International Development (USAID)*.
Organizations include the following 55 listed in this Yearbook:
- *African Climate Policy Centre (ACPC, #00251)*;
- *African Development Bank (ADB, #00283)*;
- *Asian Development Bank (ADB, #01422)*;
- *Center for Clean Air Policy (CCAP)*;
- *CGIAR System Organization (CGIAR, #03843)*;
- *CLASP (#03979)*;
- *Clean Air Asia (#03983)*;
- *Climate and Development Knowledge Network (CDKN, #04012)*;
- *ClimateWorks Foundation (#04024)*;
- *Coalition for Rainforest Nations (CfRN, #04066)*;

- *Conservation International (CI);*
- *Development Bank of Latin America (CAF, #05055);*
- *E3G – Third Generation Environmentalism;*
- *ECOWAS Centre for Renewable Energy and Energy Efficiency (ECREEE, #05335);*
- *Energy and Resources Institute (TERI);*
- *Environmental Defense Fund (EDF);*
- *Environnement et développement du Tiers-monde (enda, #05510);*
- *European Climate Foundation (ECF, #06574);*
- *Global Environment Facility (GEF, #10346);*
- *Global Green Growth Forum (3GF);*
- *Global Green Growth Institute (GGGI, #10392);*
- *Global South Initiative (GSI);*
- *Green Growth Knowledge Platform (GGKP, #10719);*
- *Humane Society International (HSI, #10966);*
- *ILO (#11123);*
- *Institute for Sustainable Communities (ISC);*
- *Inter-American Development Bank (IDB, #11427);*
- *International Atomic Energy Agency (IAEA, #12294);*
- *International Bank for Reconstruction and Development (IBRD, #12317);*
- *International Energy Agency (IEA, #13270);*
- *International Institute for Sustainable Development (IISD, #13930);*
- *International Partnership on Mitigation and MRV (#14522);*
- *International Renewable Energy Agency (IRENA, #14715);*
- *International Research Network for Low Carbon Societies (LCS-RNet, #14735);*
- *International Solid Waste Association (ISWA, #15567);*
- *JIN Climate and Sustainability;*
- *Latin American Energy Organization (#16313);*
- *Local Governments for Sustainability (ICLEI, #16507);*
- *OAS (#17629);*
- *OECD (#17693);*
- *Pan African Vision for the Environment (PAVE);*
- *REN21 (#18836);*
- *Renewable Energy and Energy Efficiency Partnership (REEEP, #18837);*
- *SNV Netherlands Development Organisation (SNV);*
- *Stockholm Environment Institute (SEI, #19993);*
- *UNDP (#20292);*
- *UNEP (#20299);*
- *UNIDO (#20336);*
- *United Nations Economic and Social Commission for Asia and the Pacific (ESCAP, #20557);*
- *United Nations Economic Commission for Africa (ECA, #20554);*
- *United Nations Economic Commission for Latin America and the Caribbean (ECLAC, #20556);*
- *United Nations Human Settlements Programme (UN-Habitat, #20572);*
- *Winrock International;*
- *World Economic Forum (WEF, #21367);*
- *World Resources Institute (WRI, #21753).*

NGO Relations Member of: *Climate Technology Centre and Network (CTCN, #04023).* [2019/XM4413/y/F]

♦ **LEDS GP** LEDS Global Partnership (#16435)
♦ **LEF** – Living Economies Forum (internationally oriented national body)
♦ **LEF** Lobby européen des femmes (#09102)

♦ The Left in the European Parliament (The Left) 16436

Secretariat Rue Belliard 73, Trêves 1 -TRI 07V003 – B-1000, 1000 Brussels, Belgium. T. +32228422045. Fax +3222841382. E-mail: left.communications@europarl.europa.eu.
URL: https://left.eu/

History 1994. Set up to represent political grouping of the member parliamentarians in *European Parliament (EP, #08146)*. Former names and other names: *GUE/NGL* – former; *EUL/NGL* – former. **Aims** Bring together left-wing MEPs in the European Parliament. **Structure** Bureau (executive body). A confederal group where each component party retains its own identity and policies while pooling their efforts in pursuit of common political objectives. **Events** *Feminist Forum* Brussels (Belgium) 2022, *Cities for Future Communal Forum* Vienna (Austria) 2021, *Just Transition Conference* Brussels (Belgium) 2016, *Study days* Tampere (Finland) 1996.
Members Parliamentarians (39) of the European Parliament in 13 countries:
Belgium, Cyprus, Czechia, Denmark, Finland, France, Germany, Greece, Ireland, Netherlands, Portugal, Spain, Sweden.
NGO Relations Member of (2): *European Energy Forum (EEF, #06986)*; *European Network of Political Foundations (ENoP, #07972).* [2021.09.01/XF3739/F]

♦ **The Left** The Left in the European Parliament (#16436)

♦ Legacy International (LI) 16437

Contact 1020 Legacy Drive, Bedford VA 24523, USA. T. +15402975982. Fax +15402971860.
URL: http://www.legacyintl.org/

History 1979, USA. **Aims** Promote *peace* by strengthening *civil society* and fostering a culture of citizen participation worldwide. **Structure** Officers: Founder/President, Vice-Presidents, Comptroller. Advisory Board, consisting (currently) of 6 members. Main office in USA. **Languages** English. **Staff** 6.00 FTE, paid. Volunteers (fluctuating): 2-10. **Finance** Work funded by: tuition; individual donors; foundation grants; US government grants. **Activities** Up to 2010, trained and mentored over 7,000 community leaders, youths, professionals and public administrators. Programs: Global Youth Village; Indonesia Youth Leadership; Community Connections (Central Asia); Responsible Governance, Civic Education and Citizen Participation (Kazakhstan, Kyrgyzstan, Tajikistan); Arabic Language Institute (Morocco); Iraqi Youth Leadership Program; Religion and Society – a Dialogue (Indonesia). **Publications** *Building Bridges* – electronic newsletter; *Legacy Links* – electronic alumni newsletter. **Members** Not a membership organization. **IGO Relations** *UNEP (#20299)*. Associated with Department of Global Communications of the United Nations. [2010.08.02/XF1616/F]

♦ Lega Internazionale per l'Abolizione della Pena di Morte entro il 2000 / see Hands Off Cain – Citizens' and Parliamentarians' League for the Abolition of the Death Penalty Worldwide (#10857)
♦ Lega Internazionale dell'Insegnamento, dell'Educazione e della Cultura Popolare (#14023)
♦ Lega Internazionale Medici per l'Abolizione della vivisezione / see International Doctors – ILDAV (#13186)
♦ Lega Internazionale per la Tutela del Credito (#16463)

♦ Legal Action Worldwide (LAW) 16438

Exec Dir c/o Hodge, Jones and Allen, 180 North Gower Street, London, NW1 2NB, UK. T. +447921811591. E-mail: info@legalactionworldwide.org.
URL: http://legalactionworldwide.org/

History Jul 2013. **Aims** Provide innovative legal *assistance* to the least represented people, especially women and children, in fragile and conflict-affected states. **Structure** Advisory Council; UK, Dutch Board and Swiss Committee. **Activities** Advocacy/lobbying/activism; guidance/assistance/consulting; knowledge management/information dissemination. [2022/XM4340/F]

♦ Legal Commission for the Self-Development of the Indigenous Peoples of the Andes (#04139)

♦ Legal Network International (LNI) 16439

Contact Rue Jean-Gabriel Eynard 6, 1205 Geneva, Switzerland.
URL: http://www.lninternational.com/

History Merged with Organisation of Advocates Specialising in International Services (OASIS), May 2012. **Structure** Steering Committee. **Events** *Autumn Conference* Mexico City (Mexico) 2013, *Annual Conference* Helsinki (Finland) 2007, *Annual Conference* Oslo (Norway) 2003.
Members Law firms in 27 countries:
Argentina, Austria, Belgium, Brazil, Bulgaria, Canada, Chile, China, Colombia, Croatia, Cyprus, Denmark, Estonia, France, Germany, Hong Kong, Hungary, India, Indonesia, Ireland, Israel, Italy, Japan, Jersey, Lebanon, Liechtenstein, Luxembourg, Malaysia, Malta, Mexico, Netherlands, Norway, Panama, Peru, Poland, Portugal, Romania, Russia, Serbia, Singapore, Slovakia, Slovenia, South Africa, Spain, Sweden, Switzerland, Thailand, Türkiye, UK, USA, Virgin Is UK.
NGO Relations Member of (1): *Association of International Law Firm Networks (AILFN, #02753).* [2020/XF6929/F]

♦ Legal Protection International (LPI) 16440

SG Rue de l'Industrie 4, 1000 Brussels, Belgium. T. +3227323628. Fax +3227320622. E-mail: secretariat@legalprotectioninternational.com.
URL: https://legalprotectioninternational.com/

History Former names and other names: *Rencontres internationales des assureurs défense (RIAD)* – former; *Internationales Treffen der Rechtsschutzversicherer* – former; *RIAD-IALEX* – former (1993 to 2002); *Asociación Internacional del Seguro de Defensa Juridica* – former; *Internationale Vereniging van de Rechtsbijstandverzekering* – former; *Associazione Internazionale dell'Assicurazione di Difesa Legale* – former; *Internationale Vereinigung der Rechtsschutz-Versicherung* – former; *Association internationale de l'assurance de protection juridique* – former; *International Association of Legal Protection Insurance (RIAD)* – former. Registration: Banque-Carrefour des Entreprises, No/ID: 0879.083.284, Start date: 2 Feb 2006, Belgium; EU Transparency Register, No/ID: 5610333409-62, Start date: 19 Sep 2008. **Aims** Unite companies specializing in legal protection; promote, via global members, easy, affordable and high quality access to justice and the law. **Structure** General Council; Board; National Sections. **Languages** English, French, German. **Staff** 1.50 FTE, paid. **Finance** Sources: members' dues. **Events** *Congress* Vienna (Austria) 2021, *Congress* The Hague (Netherlands) 2020, *Collective redress/class action and its importance for our industry and partners* Berlin (Germany) 2019, *From claims settlement to solution management* Bratislava (Slovakia) 2018, *Congress* Dublin (Ireland) 2017. **Publications** *The Legal Protection Insurance Market in Europe* (annual).
Members Companies in 22 countries and territories:
Austria, Belgium, Canada, Czechia, Estonia, France, Germany, Gibraltar, Greece, Hungary, Ireland, Italy, Japan, Luxembourg, Netherlands, Norway, Poland, Slovakia, South Africa, Spain, Switzerland, UK. [2021/XF1691/F]

♦ LEGATO 16441

Contact Bauerstr 37, 80796 Munich, Germany. E-mail: info@legato-choirs.com.
URL: http://www.legato-choirs.com/

History 1 Nov 1997, Vienna (Austria). Statutes modified 25 Oct 1999, Stuttgart (Germany). Former names and other names: *Association of Gay and Lesbian Choruses in Europe (LEGATO)* – former; *Dachverband Schwuler und Lesbischer Chöre in Europa* – former; *Europäischer Dachverband Schwuler und Lesbischer Chöre* – alias; *LEGATO – European Association of LGBTQ+ Choirs* – full title. Registration: No/ID: VR 102885, Germany. **Aims** Serve as the umbrella organisation for lesbian and gay choirs and ensembles in Europe. **Structure** General Meeting (annual); Board. **Languages** English, German, Spanish. **Staff** Voluntary. **Finance** Sources: members' dues. **Activities** Events/meetings; networking/liaising; research/documentation. **Events** *Various Voices Festival* London (UK) 2009, *Various Voices Festival* Paris (France) 2005, *Various Voices Festival* Berlin (Germany) 2001, *Various Voices Festival* Munich (Germany) 1997, *Various Voices Festival* Groningen (Netherlands) 1995. **Publications** *LEGATO Newsletter.*
Members Choruses (143) with over 5,000 singers in 20 countries:
Belgium, Croatia, Czechia, Denmark, Estonia, Finland, France, Germany, Iceland, Ireland, Italy, Netherlands, Poland, Portugal, South Africa, Spain, Sweden, Switzerland, UK, Ukraine. [2022.05.10/XD7346/D]

♦ LEGATO – European Association of LGBTQ+ Choirs / see LEGATO (#16441)
♦ Legatum Foundation (internationally oriented national body)
♦ Léger Foundation – Fostering human dignity here and abroad / see Mission Inclusion
♦ Leger des Heils (#19041)
♦ Legiã do Boa Vontade (internationally oriented national body)
♦ Legio Mariae (religious order)
♦ Legionaries of Christ (religious order)
♦ Legion of Frontiersmen / see Corps of Imperial Frontiersmen of the Commonwealth (#04844)
♦ Legion of Good Will (internationally oriented national body)
♦ Légion de Marie (religious order)
♦ Legion of Mary (religious order)
♦ Légionnaires du Christ (religious order)
♦ LEGIPORT – International Association of Port Jurists (no recent information)
♦ LEGO Foundation (internationally oriented national body)
♦ **LEGS** Livestock Emergency Guidelines and Standards (#16499)
♦ **LEGUS** International Network of Law Firms (#14292)
♦ Leibniz Centre for Tropical Marine Ecology (internationally oriented national body)
♦ Leibniz-Institut für Agrarentwicklung in Mittel- und Osteuropa / see Leibniz-Institut für Agrarentwicklung in Transformationsökonomien
♦ Leibniz-Institut für Agrarentwicklung in Transformationsökonomien (internationally oriented national body)
♦ Leibniz Institute of Agricultural Development in Central and Eastern Europe / see Leibniz-Institut für Agrarentwicklung in Transformationsökonomien
♦ Leibniz Institute of Agricultural Development in Transition Economies (internationally oriented national body)
♦ Leibniz-Institut für Globale und Regionale Studien (internationally oriented national body)
♦ Leibniz-Institut Hessische Stiftung Friedens- und Konfliktforschung (internationally oriented national body)
♦ Leibniz-Zentrum für Marine Tropenökologie (internationally oriented national body)
♦ Leiden Global (internationally oriented national body)
♦ Leigos para o Desenvolvimento (internationally oriented national body)
♦ LEI – Literacy and Evangelism International (internationally oriented national body)

♦ LeishVet 16442

Contact Veterinary Fac – Univ Complutense de Madrid, Av Puerto de Hierro s/n, 28040 Madrid, Spain. E-mail: leishvet@ucm.es.
URL: https://www.leishvet.org/

History 2005, Palermo (Italy). Registration: National Register of Associations, Start date: 2008, Spain. **Aims** Offer a consensus statement on the clinical management of veterinarian leishmaniosis up-to-date with the current evidence-based knowledge on the disease; standardize criteria for the diagnosis of veterinarian leishmaniosis; develop initiative actions and research on leishmaniosis. **Structure** Executive Committee. **Activities** Events/meetings; research/documentation; standards/guidelines. **Events** *ALIVE – Animal Leishmaniosis International Veterinary Event Congress* Torremolinos (Spain) 2022.
Members Individuals in 6 countries:
France, Israel, Italy, Portugal, Spain, USA. [2021/AA2046/C]

♦ Leisure Marine Association-MENA (unconfirmed)
♦ **Leitourgia** Nordisk Liturgisk Netvaerk (#17522)
♦ **LEKKJ** Lutherische Europäische Kommission für Kirche und Judentum (#16528)
♦ LEM – Fondazione Livorno Euro Mediterranea (internationally oriented national body)
♦ LenCD – Learning Network on Capacity Development (unconfirmed)
♦ Leningrad International Management Institute / see International Management Institute, St Petersburg
♦ **LEN** Ligue européenne de natation (#16477)
♦ Lenten Campaign / see Broederlijk Delen
♦ LENTISCO – Latin America-European Network on Technology Innovation Studies and Co-Development (internationally oriented national body)
♦ Leo Baeck Institute (internationally oriented national body)

♦ Leonard Cheshire Disability 16443

Head Office 66 South Lambeth Road, London, SW8 1RL, UK. T. +442032420200. Fax +442032420250. E-mail: info@leonardcheshire.org.
URL: https://www.leonardcheshire.org/

History 1948, UK. First non-UK home opened 1955. Former names and other names: *Cheshire Foundation Homes for the Sick* – former (1955 to 1976); *Leonard Cheshire Foundation* – former (1976 to 1997); *Leonard Cheshire International* – former (1997 to 2007). Registration: Charity Commission, No/ID: 218186, England and Wales; Companies House, No/ID: 552847, England and Wales. **Aims** Work with local partner organizations to *support* people with disabilities in education, livelihoods, everyday living and campaigning. **Structure** International secretariat of a global alliance with independent partner organizations in 54 countries. Each

country has a National Council representing alliance members in that country. Regional Councils (7) represent National Councils on a regional level. Regional offices: Kenya; Sierra Leone; India; Thailand. **Languages** English. **Staff** 15.00 FTE, paid. **Finance** Annual revenue: pounds156,357,000; Expenditure: pounds155,189,000; Overseas expenditure: pounds3,540,000. **Activities** Advocacy/lobbying/activism; events/meetings; projects/programmes; research and development. **Events** *Biennial General Meeting* Kobe (Japan) 2012, *International Conference on East Asia and Pacific Regional Council of Cheshire Homes* Kobe (Japan) 2012, *International conference* London (UK) 1998, *International conference* London (UK) 1989. **Publications** *Poverty and Disability* (2010); *Disability and Inclusive Development* (2007).
Members Residential homes and outreach services in 54 countries and territories:
Argentina, Bangladesh, Barbados, Botswana, Canada, Channel Is, China, Colombia, Cyprus, Ecuador, Eswatini, Ethiopia, Ghana, Grenada, Guernsey, Guyana, Hong Kong, India, Indonesia, Ireland, Jamaica, Japan, Jersey, Kenya, Lesotho, Liberia, Malawi, Malaysia, Mauritius, Morocco, Namibia, Nicaragua, Nigeria, Pakistan, Papua New Guinea, Philippines, Portugal, Russia, Rwanda, Seychelles, Sierra Leone, Singapore, South Africa, Spain, Sri Lanka, Sudan, Tanzania UR, Thailand, Trinidad-Tobago, Uganda, UK, USA, Zambia, Zimbabwe.
Consultative Status Consultative status granted from: *ECOSOC (#05331)* (Special); *UNESCO (#20322)* (Consultative Status). **IGO Relations** Contacts with: *African Union (AU, #00488)*; *European Union (EU, #08967)*; *International Bank for Reconstruction and Development (IBRD, #12317)* (World Bank). Special consultative status with UNDESA. Co-organizes or has co-organized international conferences with: *United Nations Economic Commission for Africa (ECA, #20554)*; *United Nations Economic and Social Commission for Asia and the Pacific (ESCAP, #20557)*. **NGO Relations** Member of (2): *ILO Global Business and Disability Network (GBDN, #11122)*; *Keeping Children Safe*. Full member of: *British Overseas NGO's for Development (BOND)*; *Global Partnership for Disability and Development (GPDD, #10530)*; *International Disability and Development Consortium (IDDC, #13177)*. Associate member of: *European Disability Forum (EDF, #06929)*. Participates in: *Global Partnership on Children with Disabilities (GPcwd, #10529)*. [2022/XF0244/f/**F**]

♦ Leonard Cheshire Foundation / see Leonard Cheshire Disability (#16443)
♦ Leonard Cheshire International / see Leonard Cheshire Disability (#16443)
♦ Leonard Davis Institute for International Relations (internationally oriented national body)
♦ Leonardo DiCaprio Foundation (internationally oriented national body)

♦ Leonardo/International Society for the Arts, Sciences and Technology (Leonardo/ISAST) 16444

CEO 1201 Martin Luther King Jr Way, Suite 100, Oakland CA 94612, USA. E-mail: isast@leonardo.info.
'Leonardo' – Europe 8 rue Emile Dunois, 92100 Boulogne-Billancourt, France.
URL: http://www.leonardo.info/

History 1968, Paris (France). Moved to California (USA) in 1981. Former names and other names: *International Society of Scientist-Artists* – former. **Aims** Foster transformation at the nexus of art, science, and technology; empower an inclusive global network, a borderless community where all belong in pursuit of a more vibrant, just and regenerative world. **Structure** Board of Directors. **Languages** English. **Staff** 5.00 FTE, paid. **Finance** Sources: fundraising; members' dues; sale of publications. Annual budget: 200,000 USD. **Activities** Events/meetings; projects/programmes; publishing activities. **Events** *International Conference on the Histories of Media Art, Science and Technology* Melbourne, VIC (Australia) 2009, *International workshop on interstellar message design* Paris (France) 2003. **Publications** *Leonardo Electronic Almanac* (12 a year); *Leonardo* (5 a year); *Leonardo Music Journal* (annual); *Leonardo e-Newsletter*. *Leonardo Book Series*; *Leonardo Reviews*. Podcast.
Members Affiliate and Individual. Affiliate members in 11 countries:
Australia, Austria, Brazil, Canada, Colombia, Italy, Mexico, Poland, Russia, UK, USA.
Individual members in 48 countries and territories:
Argentina, Australia, Austria, Belgium, Brazil, Canada, Chile, China, Colombia, Croatia, Cyprus, Czechia, Denmark, Ecuador, Egypt, Finland, France, Germany, Greece, Hong Kong, Hungary, India, Indonesia, Iran Islamic Rep, Ireland, Israel, Italy, Japan, Korea Rep, Maldives, Mexico, Moldova, Netherlands, New Zealand, Norway, Peru, Poland, Portugal, Serbia, Singapore, Slovenia, Spain, Sweden, Switzerland, Taiwan, Türkiye, UK, Uruguay. [2022/XD6471/v/**D**]

♦ **Leonardo/ISAST** Leonardo/International Society for the Arts, Sciences and Technology (#16444)
♦ **LEO-NET** Leveraging Education into Organisations – Network (#16448)
♦ Leon H Sullivan Summit (meeting series)
♦ Léon Mba Foundation (internationally oriented national body)
♦ Leopold Zunz Centre for the Study of European Jewry (internationally oriented national body)
♦ Leopold-Zunz-Zentrum zur Erforschung des Europäischen Judentums (internationally oriented national body)

♦ Leo S Rowe Pan American Fund (Rowe Fund) 16445

Fondo Panamericano Leo S Rowe (Fondo Rowe)

Program Manager OAS Dept of Human Dev, 1889 F St NW, 7th Floor, Washington DC 20006, USA. T. +12023704910. E-mail: rowefund@oas.org.
URL: http://www.oas.org/en/rowefund/

History 1948, from a legacy bequeathed by Dr Leo S Rowe, ex-Director of the Pan American Union (precursor to *OAS (#17629)*). Statutes approved 19 Mar 1952, Washington DC (USA). Also known in French as *Fonds panaméricain Léo S Rowe (Fonds Rowe)* and Portuguese as *Fundo Panamericano Leo S Rowe (Fundo Rowe)*. **Aims** As a student loan program of the OAS, help citizens from Latin American and Caribbean countries finance their studies or research in accredited universities across the USA by awarding interest-free loans, made on the understanding that the recipients are to return to their respective countries within a year of completion of their studies to assist in their countries' development and further their welfare. **Structure** OAS Permanent Council is responsible for the administration of the Fund through a Committee consisting of 4 representatives of Member States and the OAS Secretary-General. **Languages** English, French, Portuguese, Spanish. **Finance** Income derived from the capital made up of a legacy bequeathed by Dr Leo S Rowe and the investment of that capital. **Events** *International symposium on Skythia textile* Kherson (Ukraine) 1998.
Members States (33):
Antigua-Barbuda, Argentina, Bahamas, Barbados, Belize, Bolivia, Brazil, Chile, Colombia, Costa Rica, Cuba, Dominica, Dominican Rep, Ecuador, El Salvador, Grenada, Guatemala, Guyana, Haiti, Honduras, Jamaica, Mexico, Nicaragua, Panama, Paraguay, Peru, St Kitts-Nevis, St Lucia, St Vincent-Grenadines, Suriname, Trinidad-Tobago, Uruguay, Venezuela. [2018.10.01/XF2970/f/**F***]

♦ LePAF – Leukemia Patient Advocates Foundation (unconfirmed)
♦ LEPH – International Conference on Law Enforcement and Public Health (meeting series)
♦ LEPII / see Institute of International Integration and Industrial Economics
♦ LEPRA / see LEPRA Health in Action
♦ LEPRA Health in Action (internationally oriented national body)
♦ Leprahilfe Emmaus Schweiz / see FAIRMED
♦ LEPRA – LEPRA Health in Action (internationally oriented national body)
♦ Leprosy Mission / see Leprosy Mission International (#16446)

♦ Leprosy Mission International (TLMI) 16446

Mission évangélique internationale contre la lèpre

International Dir 80 Windmill Road, Brentford, TW8 0QH, UK. T. +442083266767. Fax +442083266777. E-mail: friends@leprosymission.org.
URL: http://www.leprosymission.org/

History 1874, Ireland. Founded by Wellesley Bailey. Former names and other names: *Mission to Lepers in India and the East* – former (1893 to 1962); *Leprosy Mission (TLM)* – former (1962). Registration: Charity, No/ID: 1076356, Start date: 2 Jul 1999, England and Wales; Companies House, No/ID: 03591514, Start date: 2 Jul 1998, England and Wales. **Aims** Break the chains of leprosy, empowering people to attain healing, dignity and life. **Structure** International Board. **Staff** 1800.00 FTE, paid. **Finance** Donations from individuals, churches, organizations and government agencies. **Activities** Projects/programmes; guidance/assistance/consulting; training/education. **Events** *International Assembly* Toronto, ON (Canada) 2009, *International assembly* Switzerland 2007, *International assembly* Dublin (Ireland) 2005, *International assembly* Hoddesdon (UK) 2003, *International assembly* Bournemouth (UK) 2001. **Publications** *ASK Prayer Guide* (annual).
Members Individuals and missions in 30 countries and territories:
Australia, Bangladesh, Belgium, Chad, Congo DR, Denmark, England, Ethiopia, France, Germany, Hungary, India, Korea Rep, Mozambique, Myanmar, Nepal, Netherlands, New Zealand, Niger, Nigeria, Northern Ireland, Papua New Guinea, Scotland, South Africa, South Sudan, Sudan, Sweden, Switzerland, Timor-Leste, Wales.
Consultative Status Consultative status granted from: *ECOSOC (#05331)* (Special). **NGO Relations** Member of (12): *Association of Evangelicals in Africa (AEA, #02587)* (Associate); *British Overseas NGO's for Development (BOND)* (Full); *CHS Alliance (#03911)* (Full); *European Christian Organisations in Relief and Development (EU-CORD, #06545)*; *Global Connections*; *Global Partnership for Zero Leprosy (#10543)*; *International Disability and Development Consortium (IDDC, #13177)*; *International Federation of Anti-Leprosy Associations (ILEP, #13355)*; *Micah Global (#16741)*; *Neglected Tropical Diseased NGO Network (NNN, #16969)*; *Prisma*; *Restored*. Participates in: *Global Partnership on Children with Disabilities (GPcwd, #10529)*. [2023/XF6461/**F**]

♦ Leprosy Relief Canada (internationally oriented national body)
♦ Leprosy Relief Emmaus Switzerland / see FAIRMED
♦ Leprosy Relief Work Emmaus / see FAIRMED
♦ LEPS – Laboratoire européen de psychologie sociale (internationally oriented national body)
♦ Leraars zonder Grenzen (#05489)
♦ LERG – Leading Edge International Research Group (internationally oriented national body)
♦ LERN / see Learner Research Network (#16428)
♦ **LERU** League of European Research Universities (#16423)
♦ **LES-AC** Licensing Executives Society Arab Countries (#16459)
♦ LES Benelux – Licensing Executives Benelux (internationally oriented national body)
♦ **LES Europe** Licensing Executives Society Europe (#16460)
♦ **LESI** Licensing Executives Society International (#16461)
♦ **LES Scandinavia** Licensing Executives Society Scandinavia (#16462)
♦ Lessons for Life (internationally oriented national body)
♦ Lester B Pearson United World College of the Pacific (internationally oriented national body)
♦ **LET** Ladies European Tour (#16218)
♦ Let's Promote Europe (unconfirmed)
♦ **LETSystems** Local Employment Trading/Energy Transfer System (#16505)
♦ Letterstedtska Föreningen (#16447)
♦ Letterstedtska Föreningen för Industri, Vetenskap och Konst / see Letterstedt Society (#16447)

♦ Letterstedt Society 16447

Société Letterstedt – Letterstedtska Föreningen

Sec PO Box 1074, SE-101 39 Stockholm, Sweden. T. +4686547570. E-mail: info@letterstedtska.org.
URL: http://www.letterstedtska.org/

History 1875, Stockholm (Sweden), as *Letterstedt Society for Industry, Science and Art – Letterstedtska Föreningen för Industri, Vetenskap och Konst*. Commissions in each of the Nordic countries. **Aims** Promote *cultural* and other forms of cooperation between the *Nordic* countries. **Structure** Governing Body, consisting of Chairman, Permanent Secretary and 10 members. National Divisions (5): Denmark; Finland; Iceland; Norway; Sweden. **Finance** Budget (annual): Swedish Kr 6 million. **Publications** *Nordisk Tidskrift för Vetenskap, Konst och Industri* (4 a year) in Danish, Norwegian, Swedish – journal.
Members Individuals in 5 countries:
Denmark, Finland, Iceland, Norway, Sweden. [2018/XE1819/v/**E**]

♦ Letterstedt Society for Industry, Science and Art / see Letterstedt Society (#16447)
♦ Let There Be Light International (internationally oriented national body)
♦ Leuenberg Church Fellowship / see Community of Protestant Churches in Europe (#04405)
♦ Leuenberger Kirchengemeinschaft / see Community of Protestant Churches in Europe (#04405)
♦ Leukemia Patient Advocates Foundation / see CML Advocacy Network (#04040)
♦ Leukemia Patient Advocates Foundation (unconfirmed)
♦ Leuser International Foundation (internationally oriented national body)
♦ Leuven Centre for Global Governance Studies (internationally oriented national body)
♦ Leuven Centre for Transition Economics / see LICOS Center for Institutions and Economic Performance.
♦ Leuven Institute for Central and East European Studies / see LICOS Center for Institutions and Economic Performance.
♦ Leuven Institute for Ireland in Europe (internationally oriented national body)
♦ Leuvens Instituut voor Centraal- en Oost-Europese Studies / see LICOS Center for Institutions and Economic Performance.
♦ LEVA – Light Electric Vehicle Association (unconfirmed)

♦ Leveraging Education into Organisations – Network (LEO-NET) 16448

Exec Board De Rondom 70, Atlas Bldg fl 10, 5612 AP Eindhoven, Netherlands. E-mail: info@leo-net.org.
Secretariat Eindhoven Univ of Technology, MMP 1-43, PO Box 513, 5600MB Eindhoven, Netherlands. E-mail: info@leo-net.org.
URL: http://www.leo-net.org/

History 1999, and initiated at *European Association for International Education (EAIE, #06092)*, Maastricht (Netherlands). Registered in accordance with Dutch law: 56612842. **Aims** Build a community of experts involved in traineeship mobility and related fields to build bridges between education and work. **Structure** Board; Secretariat. **Staff** 0.10 FTE, paid. **Finance** Members' dues. **Activities** Events/meetings; training/education. **Members** Universities, colleges and intermediate organizations (about 100) in 17 EU countries. Membership countries not specified. **IGO Relations** *European Commission (EC, #06633)*. [2022/XJ0417/**F**]

♦ Leverhulme Centre for Research on Globalisation and Economic Policy / see Nottingham Centre for Research on Globalisation and Economic Policy
♦ Leverhulme Trust (internationally oriented national body)
♦ Levin Institute – Neil D Levin Graduate Institute of International Relations and Commerce (internationally oriented national body)
♦ Levi Strauss Foundation (internationally oriented national body)
♦ LEVS – World Light Electric Vehicle Summit (meeting series)

♦ LEX Africa 16449

Contact Private Bag 10015, Sandton, Johannesburg, 2146, South Africa. T. +27115358188. E-mail: lexenquiries@werksmans.com.
Street Address 95 Rivonia Rd, Sandton, Johannesburg, 2196, South Africa.
URL: http://www.lexafrica.com/

History 1993. Subtitles: *Lawyers for Africa – Advogados para África – Avocats/Conseils pour l'Afrique*. **Aims** Collaborate with member firms to drive business growth in Africa through best legal practice by attracting, developing and promoting world-class professional skills for the continuing success of the network and the broader African continent. **Structure** Annual General Meeting; Management Committee; Management Office. **Languages** English. Local languages. **Activities** Events/meetings.
Members Independent firms in 26 countries:
Angola, Botswana, Burkina Faso, Cameroon, Congo Brazzaville, Congo DR, Côte d'Ivoire, Eswatini, Ethiopia, Ghana, Guinea, Kenya, Lesotho, Malawi, Mauritius, Morocco, Mozambique, Namibia, Nigeria, Rwanda, Senegal, South Africa, Tanzania UR, Uganda, Zambia, Zimbabwe.
NGO Relations *African Business Law Firms Association (ABLFA)*; *African Labour Law Society (ALLS, #00354)*; *EuroCollectNet (ECN, #05664)*; *Interlex Group (#11518)*; *HLB International*; *International Association of Independent Law Firms (Interlaw, #11958)*; *ADVOC (#00141)*; *International Practice Group (IPG, #14632)*; *Multilaw (#16891)*; *Southern Africa Litigation Centre (SALC, #19832)*. [2020.02.10/XM6278/**F**]

♦ LEXIA Exchange International / see LEXIA International
♦ LEXIA International (internationally oriented national body)

♦ **Lex Mundi** **16450**

Main Office 2100 West Loop South, Ste 1000, Houston TX 77027, USA. T. +17133350122 – +17136269393. Fax +17136269933. E-mail: info@lexmundi.com.

URL: http://www.lexmundi.com/

History Sep 1989. **Aims** Provide member firms with a network of *law* firms that share similar values and a similar focus on quality through which they can access global legal resources that enable them to serve their clients better and improve continuously all aspects of their firms; through Pro Bono Foundation, provide pro bono legal assistance to social entrepreneurs around the world. **Structure** Board of Directors. Officers: President; Vice-President; 3 Directors (Marketing and Communications; Administration; Professional Development). **Languages** English. **Staff** 19.00 FTE, paid. **Finance** Members' dues. **Activities** Organizes: 4 annual regional conferences; Managing Partners Conference; Executive Directors Conference; Lex Mundi Institute. **Events** *Annual Europe-Middle East-Africa Regional Conference* Copenhagen (Denmark) 2020, *North America Regional Conference* Atlanta, GA (USA) 2019, *Annual Conference* London (UK) 2019, *Asia Pacific Regional Conference* Seoul (Korea Rep) 2019, *Asia Pacific Regional Conference* Bangkok (Thailand) 2018. **Publications** Guides; directory; reports; handbook.

Members Lawyers (21,000), Law firms (160) and offices (560) in 102 countries and territories:
Anguilla, Argentina, Australia, Austria, Bahamas, Bahrain, Bangladesh, Barbados, Belgium, Belize, Bermuda, Bolivia, Brazil, Bulgaria, Canada, Cayman Is, Chile, China, Colombia, Costa Rica, Côte d'Ivoire, Croatia, Curaçao, Cyprus, Czechia, Denmark, Dominican Rep, Ecuador, Egypt, El Salvador, Estonia, Finland, France, Germany, Ghana, Greece, Grenada, Guatemala, Guernsey, Honduras, Hong Kong, Hungary, Iceland, India, Indonesia, Ireland, Isle of Man, Israel, Italy, Jamaica, Japan, Jersey, Korea Rep, Kuwait, Latvia, Lebanon, Liechtenstein, Lithuania, Luxembourg, Malaysia, Malta, Mauritius, Mexico, Morocco, Namibia, Netherlands, New Zealand, Nicaragua, Nigeria, Northern Ireland, Norway, Pakistan, Panama, Paraguay, Peru, Philippines, Poland, Portugal, Romania, Russia, Scotland, Senegal, Serbia, Slovakia, Slovenia, South Africa, Spain, Sri Lanka, St Kitts-Nevis, Sweden, Switzerland, Taiwan, Thailand, Trinidad-Tobago, Türkiye, Turks-Caicos, Ukraine, United Arab Emirates, Uruguay, USA, Venezuela, Virgin Is UK.
[2020/XF6297/**F**]

♦ Ley modelo de la CNUDMI sobre conciliación comercial internacional (2002 treaty)
♦ LFA – Life For Africa (internationally oriented national body)
♦ LFCA / see Giant Screen Cinema Association (#10148)
♦ LFHRI – Lawyers for Human Rights International (internationally oriented national body)
♦ LFL – Learning for Life (internationally oriented national body)
♦ LGA – Liptako-Gourma Integrated Development Authority (no recent information)
♦ LGBT Humanists (internationally oriented national body)
♦ **LGDA Europe** LGD Alliance Europe (#16451)

♦ **LGD Alliance Europe (LGDA Europe)** **16451**

Address not obtained.

URL: http://www.lgda.eu

History 2010. **Aims** Create a community of *patients* throughout Europe; stimulate research in Complex Lymphatic Anomalies, like *Lymphangiomatosis* and *Gorham's Disease*. **Structure** Board; Executive Committee. **Languages** European languages. **Activities** Awareness raising; events/meetings. The entire European geographic area. **NGO Relations** Member of (1): *EURORDIS – Rare Diseases Europe (#09175)*.
[2021.06.17/XM7461/**D**]

♦ LGIB – Local Government International Bureau (internationally oriented national body)
♦ LGIGPA / see Lama Gangchen International Global Peace Foundation
♦ LGIGPF – Lama Gangchen International Global Peace Foundation (internationally oriented national body)
♦ LGM-AS – International Association on Layered and Graded Materials (inactive)
♦ LGW – Legion of Good Will (internationally oriented national body)
♦ **LGWPF** Lama Gangchen World Peace Foundation (#16223)
♦ **LHC** The League of Historical Cities (#16424)
♦ **LHF** Land Healers Foundation (#16227)
♦ LH – Lighthawk (internationally oriented national body)
♦ LHM International / see International Lutheran Hour Ministries
♦ LHRC – Latvian Human Rights Committee (internationally oriented national body)
♦ LIAC / see Van Hall Larenstein University of Applied Sciences
♦ **LIADA** Liga Iberoamericana de Astronomía (#11018)
♦ Liaison Entre Actions de Développement de l'Économie Rurale / see LEADER Inspired Network Community (#16413)
♦ Liaison Bureau of Ceramic Industries of the Common Market / see European Ceramic Industry Association (#06506)
♦ Liaison Bureau of the European / EEC / Union of Aromatic Products / see European Flavour Association (#07269)
♦ Liaison Bureau of Paint and Printing Ink Manufacturers' Associations of the Common Market Countries / see Conseil européen de l'industrie des peintures, des encres d'imprimerie et des couleurs d'art (#04688)
♦ Liaison Centre of the Meat Processing Industry in the EEC / see Liaison Centre for the Meat Processing Industry in the EU (#16452)

♦ **Liaison Centre for the Meat Processing Industry in the EU** **16452**

Centre de liaison des industries transformatrices de viandes de l'UE (CLITRAVI)

SG Bvd Baudouin 18, Bte 4, 1000 Brussels, Belgium. T. +3222035141. Fax +3222033244. E-mail: info@clitravi.eu.

Registered Office Bierstalpad 15, 1121 JK Landsmeer, Netherlands.

URL: http://www.clitravi.eu/

History 22 May 1958, Paris (France). Former names and other names: *Liaison Centre of the Meat Processing Industry in the EEC* – former (22 May 1958); *Centre de liaison des industries transformatrices de viandes de la CEE Verbindungsstelle der Fleischverwertungsindustrie der EWG-Länder* – former (22 May 1958); *Centro di Collegamento delle Industrie Trasformatrici delle Carni Macellate della CEE* – former (22 May 1958); *Verbindingscentrum van Vleesverwerkende Industrieën van de EEG* – former (22 May 1958); *Forbindelsescentret for det Europaeiske Økonomiske Faellesskabs Kog Forarbejdningsindustrier* – former (22 May 1958). Registration: Netherlands; EU Transparency Register, No/ID: 02978802379-31. **Aims** Represent and advance the interests of the meat processing industry in the EU. **Structure** General Assembly; Board; Management Council; Standing Committee; Secretariat; Permanent and ad hoc Working Groups. **Languages** English, French. **Staff** 3.00 FTE, paid. **Finance** Members' dues. **Activities** Politics/policy/regulatory; advocacy/lobbying/activism. **Events** *Annual General Assembly* Netherlands 2016, *Annual General Assembly* Milan (Italy) 2015, *Annual General Assembly* Bucharest (Romania) 2014, *Annual General Assembly* Valencia (Spain) 2013, *Annual General Assembly* Venice (Italy) 1995.

Members National associations in 22 countries:
Austria, Belgium, Bulgaria, Czechia, Denmark, Finland, France, Germany, Greece, Hungary, Ireland, Italy, Lithuania, Netherlands, Poland, Portugal, Romania, Slovakia, Slovenia, Spain, Sweden, UK.
Associate members in countries:
Norway, Türkiye.
Guest member in 1 country:
France.

IGO Relations Recognized by: *European Commission (EC, #06633)*. Observer to: *Codex Alimentarius Commission (CAC, #04081)*. **NGO Relations** Affiliated member of: *FoodDrinkEurope (#09841)*.
[2021/XE2913/t/**E**]

♦ Liaison Committee of Agricultural Engineers for the EEC Countries / see Confédération européenne des associations d'ingénieurs agronomes (#04538)
♦ Liaison Committee of the Associations of University Graduate Engineers of the European Union / see Council of Associations of Long Cycle Engineers of a University or Higher School of Engineering of the European Union (#04869)
♦ Liaison Committee for the Automotive Components and Equipment Industry / see European Association of Automotive Suppliers (#05948)
♦ Liaison Committee for the Automotive Equipment and Parts Industry / see European Association of Automotive Suppliers (#05948)
♦ Liaison Committee of Coachwork and Trailer Builders / see International Association of the Body and Trailer Building Industry (#11727)
♦ Liaison Committee Europe – Africa – Caribbean – Pacific for the promotion of ACP Horticultural Exports / see COLEACP (#04091)
♦ Liaison Committee of INGOs Enjoying Participatory Status with the Council of Europe / see Conference of INGOs of the Council of Europe (#04607)

♦ **Liaison Committee of International Associations of Civil Engineering** **16453**

Comité de liaison des associations internationales de génie civil

Secretariat c/o RILEM, 4 avenue Recteur Poincaré, 75016 Paris, France. T. +33145361020. Fax +33145366320.

URL: https://iabse.org/About/Liaison-Committee

History 1958. **Aims** Promote coordination of members' activities; harmonize members' activities and publications. **Structure** Liaison Committee (meets once a year), comprising Presidents and Secretaries of member associations or their representatives. Chair and Rotating Secretariat (every 2 years). **Languages** English. **Staff** 3.00 FTE, paid. **Finance** No expenses; no budget. **Activities** Sets up joint committees, when necessary. Organizes and co-sponsors international conferences on an irregular basis. **Events** *Conference* Malta 2001, *Conference* Innsbruck (Austria) 1999.

Members International associations (5):
European Convention for Constructional Steelwork (ECCS, #06779); Fédération internationale du béton (FIB, #09615); International Association for Bridge and Structural Engineering (IABSE, #11737); International Council for Research and Innovation in Building and Construction (CIB, #13069); Réunion internationale des laboratoires d'essais et de recherches sur les matériaux et les constructions (RILEM, #18930).

NGO Relations Instrumental in setting up: *Joint Committee on Structural Safety (JCSS, #16126)*.
[2017/XE1671/y/**E**]

♦ Liaison Committee for the International Congresses of Stenography (inactive)
♦ Liaison Committee of International Non-Governmental Organizations Enjoying Participatory Status with the Council of Europe / see Conference of INGOs of the Council of Europe (#04607)
♦ Liaison Committee for Major International Associations (inactive)
♦ Liaison Committee for the Manufacture of Automobile Equipment and Spare Parts / see European Association of Automotive Suppliers (#05948)
♦ Liaison Committee of Mediterranean Citrus Producing Countries (inactive)
♦ Liaison Committee of NGOs enjoying Consultative Status with the Council of Europe / see Conference of INGOs of the Council of Europe (#04607)
♦ Liaison Committee of NGOs enjoying Participatory Status with the Council of Europe / see Conference of INGOs of the Council of Europe (#04607)
♦ Liaison Committee for the Promotion of Tropical Fruits and Off-Season Vegetables Exported from ACP States / see COLEACP (#04091)
♦ Liaison Committee of Rural Women's and Homemakers' Organizations / see Associated Country Women of the World (#02338)
♦ Liaison Committee of Secretaries of Organizations for Christian-Jewish Cooperation / see International Council of Christians and Jews (#13006)
♦ Liaison Committee of Veterinarians of the EEC / see Federation of Veterinarians of Europe (#09713)
♦ Liaison Committee of Women's International Organizations (inactive)
♦ Liaison Group for the European Engineering Industries / see Orgalim – Europe's Technology Industries (#17794)
♦ Liaison Group of the European Mechanical, Electrical, Electronic and Metalworking Industries / see Orgalim – Europe's Technology Industries (#17794)
♦ Liaison Group of Modern History Lecturers of European Community Universities / see European Union Liaison Committee of Historians (#09000)
♦ Liaison internationale des industries de l'alimentation (inactive)
♦ Liaison Office of the European Ceramic Industries / see European Ceramic Industry Association (#06506)
♦ Liaison Office of the Rubber Industries of the European Common Market / see European Tyre and Rubber Manufacturers' Association (#08963)
♦ Liaison Office of the Rubber Industries of the European Communities / see European Tyre and Rubber Manufacturers' Association (#08963)
♦ Liaison Office of the Rubber Industries of the European Union / see European Tyre and Rubber Manufacturers' Association (#08963)
♦ LIAT 1974 Ltd (inactive)
♦ LIAT / see Alliance internationale de tourisme (#00694)
♦ LIBAN – Lebanese International Businessmen Associations' Network (internationally oriented national body)
♦ **LIBE** Ligo Internacia de Blindaj Esperantistoj (#14017)
♦ Liberación (internationally oriented national body)
♦ Liberal Association for the Movement of People (internationally oriented national body)
♦ Liberal, Democratic and Reformers' Group / see Alliance of Liberals and Democrats for Europe (#00702)
♦ Liberale Bewegung für ein Vereintes Europa (inactive)
♦ Liberale Internationale (#16454)
♦ Liberalen voor Ontwikkelingssamenwerking / see Horizon 2007
♦ Liberales para la Cooperación al Desarrollo / see Horizon 2007
♦ Liberal European Youth / see European Liberal Youth (#07690)
♦ Liberal Group / see Alliance of Liberals and Democrats for Europe (#00702)

♦ **Liberal International (LI)** **16454**

Internationale libérale – Internacional Liberal – Liberale Internationale

SG 1 Whitehall Place, London, SW1A 2HD, UK. T. +442078395905. E-mail: office@liberal-international.org.

URL: http://www.liberal-international.org/

History Apr 1947, Oxford (UK). Former names and other names: *World Liberal Union* – alias; *Union libérale mondiale* – alias; *Internacional Liberal y Progresista* – alias. **Aims** Win general acceptance worldwide of Liberal principles which are international in their nature; foster growth of a free society based on personal *liberty*, personal *responsibility* and social *justice*; provide the means of cooperation and exchange of information among member organizations and among men and women of all countries who accept these principles. **Structure** Congress (every 18 months); Executive Committee. **Languages** English, French, Spanish. **Staff** 4.00 FTE, paid. **Finance** Sources: contributions; revenue from activities/projects. **Activities** Awards/prizes/competitions; events/meetings. **Events** *Congress* 2021, *Extraordinary Congress* London (UK) 2020, *Congress* Sofia (Bulgaria) 2020, *Congress* Dakar (Senegal) 2018, *Congress* Escaldes-Engordany (Andorra) 2017. **Publications** *LI-News* (weekly); *Experiment in Internationalism*; *Liberalism in the World*; *Relations between USA, Canada and Western Europe*; *Spires of Liberty*. *Andorra Liberal Manifesto* (2017); *A Sense of Liberty – The History of the Liberal International* (1997); *Who's Who in International Liberalism* (1997); *A Sense of Liberty* (1994); *A Changing World* (1993); *Strengthening of the United Nations* (1992); *Liberal Manifesto 1981*. Pamphlets; reports; conference proceedings.

Members National political parties or groups and individuals. Full in 50 countries and territories:
Andorra, Belgium, Bulgaria, Burkina Faso, Burundi, Cambodia, Canada, Chile, Congo DR, Côte d'Ivoire, Croatia, Cuba, Denmark, Estonia, Finland, Georgia, Germany, Gibraltar, Guinea, Honduras, Iceland, Ireland, Israel, Kenya, Kosovo, Lebanon, Luxembourg, Madagascar, Mexico, Mongolia, Montenegro, Morocco, Netherlands, Nicaragua, North Macedonia, Norway, Paraguay, Philippines, Russia, Senegal, Slovenia, Somalia, South Africa, Spain, Sweden, Switzerland, Taiwan, Tanzania UR, Thailand, UK.
Included in the above, 4 organizations listed in this Yearbook:
Alliance of Liberals and Democrats for Europe Party (ALDE Party, #00703); International Federation of Liberal Youth (IFLRY, #13469); International Network of Liberal Women (INLW, #14294); Renew Europe (#18840).

Observer organizations in 15 countries:
Austria, Brazil, Burkina Faso, Comoros, Congo Brazzaville, Cyprus, Ghana, Italy, Madagascar, Malaysia, Mali, Mauritania, Moldova, Romania, Singapore.
Consultative Status Consultative status granted from: *Council of Europe (CE, #04881)* (Participatory Status); *ECOSOC (#05331)* (General). **IGO Relations** Associated with Department of Global Communications of the United Nations. **NGO Relations** Cooperates with (11): *Africa Liberal Network (ALN, #00187)*; *Alliance of Liberals and Democrats for Europe (ALDE, #00702)*; *Arabic Alliance for Freedom and Democracy (AAFD)*; *Council of Asian Liberals and Democrats (CALD, #04867)*; *European Liberal Youth (LYMEC, #07690)*; Fondazione Luigi Einaudi; *Friedrich Naumann Foundation for Freedom*; *Inter-Parliamentary Union (IPU, #15961)*; *National Democratic Institute for International Affairs (NDIIA)*; *Red Liberal de América Latina (RELIAL)*; *Swedish International Liberal Centre (SILC)*. [2021.05.20/XF2934/y/**F**]

- ♦ Liberalisok és Demokratak Szövetsége Európaért Képviselocsoport / see Renew Europe (#18840)
- ♦ A Liberalisok és Demokratak Szövetsége Európaért Part (#00703)
- ♦ Liberal Movement for a United Europe (inactive)
- ♦ Liberal and Radical Youth Movement of the European Union / see European Liberal Youth (#07690)
- ♦ Liberals for Development Cooperation / see Horizon 2007
- ♦ Liberalu ir Demokratu Aljanso uz Europa Frakcija / see Renew Europe (#18840)
- ♦ Liberalu ir Demokratu Aljanso uz Europa Partija (#00703)
- ♦ Liberal Youth of the Americas (#16174)
- ♦ Liberation (internationally oriented national body)
- ♦ Liberation Committee of the Arab West (inactive)
- ♦ Libera Università Internazionale degli Studi Sociali, Pro Deo / see Libera Università Internazionale degli Studi Sociali, Guido Carli
- ♦ Libera Università Internazionale degli Studi Sociali, Guido Carli (internationally oriented national body)
- ♦ Libéraux pour la coopération au développement / see Horizon 2007

♦ Liberian Shipowners Council (LSC) 16455

Main Office 99 Park Ave, Ste 1700, New York NY 10016, USA. T. +12129733896. Fax +12123173869. E-mail: info@liberianshipowners.com.
URL: http://www.liberianshipowners.com/

History 1974, New York NY (USA). **Aims** Promote the interests of the members; assist in the promotion of a *ship safety* inspection program. **Members** International shipowners and operators whose ships fly the Liberian flag; organizations connected with shipping (membership countries not specified). **NGO Relations** Member of: *International Chamber of Shipping (ICS, #12535)*. Associate Member of: *International Association of Independent Tanker Owners (INTERTANKO, #11959)*. [2009/XF0456/**F**]

- ♦ **LIBER** Ligue des Bibliothèques Européennes de Recherche (#02540)
- ♦ Libertarian Foundation for Human Assistance (internationally oriented national body)
- ♦ The Libertarian Research & Education Trust / see Statewatch
- ♦ Libertarisch Fonds voor Hulpacties / see Libertarian Foundation for Human Assistance
- ♦ Libertarisch Fonds voor Hulpakties (internationally oriented national body)

♦ Libertas International 16456

Contact Maestro Tarega 7, Onil, 03430 Alicante, Castellón, Spain. T. +34630587959. E-mail: infolibertasinternational@gmail.com.
URL: http://www.libertasinternational.com/

History 2009. **Aims** Foster mutual understanding between *young* people from different countries; develop education among children and young people; create activities that will empower youth and women. **Languages** English, French, Italian, Spanish. **Finance** Members' dues. Sponsored by Erasmus Plus. **Activities** Events/meetings; training/education; awareness raising. Active in: Morocco, Netherlands, Russia, Senegal, Spain. **Members** Individuals (about 250). Membership countries not specified. [2016.06.01/XJ7361/**F**]

- ♦ **Liberties** Civil Liberties Union for Europe (#03965)
- ♦ Liberty Asia (internationally oriented national body)

♦ Liberty International 16457

Contact 237 Kearny St n120, San Francisco CA 94108-4502, USA. T. +14158595174. E-mail: info@liberty-intl.org.
URL: https://liberty-intl.org/

History Founded 30 Aug 1989, as *International Society for Individual Liberty (ISIL)*, on merger of *Libertarian International (inactive)*, set up Jul 1980, Ann Arbor MI (USA), and *Society for Individual Liberty*, set up 1969, Philadelphia PA (USA). Registered in USA as a non-profit educational foundation 501(c)3: EIN 54-1512492. **Aims** Build a free and peaceful world, respect for individual rights and liberties and an open and competitive *economic* system based on voluntary exchange and *free trade*; provide networking opportunities and targeted project sponsorships to members. **Structure** Board of Directors. **Languages** English. **Staff** 2.00 FTE, paid; 25.00 FTE, voluntary. **Finance** Annual budget: US$ 200,000. **Activities** Events/meetings; financial and/or material support; knowledge management/information dissemination. **Events** *World Conference* Medellin (Colombia) 2021, *World Conference* Medellin (Colombia) 2020, *World Conference* Ulaanbaatar (Mongolia) 2019, *World Conference* Krakow (Poland) 2018, *World Conference* San Juan (Puerto Rico) 2017. **Publications** *LI News* (weekly) – electronic blog items. *Educational pamphlet* in English, Spanish – series. *The Adventures of Jonathan Gullible: A Free Market Odyssey* by Ken Schoolland. Periodic progress reports.
Members Individuals and organizations, mainly in North America but in a total of 63 countries and territories:
Argentina, Australia, Austria, Belarus, Belgium, Brazil, Canada, Chile, China, Colombia, Czechia, Denmark, Estonia, Eswatini, Ethiopia, Finland, France, Germany, Greece, Guatemala, Hong Kong, Hungary, Iceland, India, Ireland, Israel, Italy, Japan, Kenya, Kyrgyzstan, Latvia, Lithuania, Luxembourg, Mexico, Monaco, Mongolia, Nepal, Netherlands, New Zealand, Nigeria, North Macedonia, Norway, Pakistan, Panama, Peru, Poland, Romania, Russia, Serbia, Slovakia, Slovenia, Somalia, South Africa, Spain, Sweden, Switzerland, Thailand, Türkiye, UK, Ukraine, USA, Venezuela, Zimbabwe. [2019.08.11/XD1339/**F**]

- ♦ Libra Association (unconfirmed)
- ♦ Libraries Without Borders (#03229)
- ♦ Library for All (internationally oriented national body)

♦ Library Assembly of Eurasia (LAE) 16458

Assemblée des bibliothèques de l'Eurasie (ABE) – Bibliotheksassemblee Eurasiens – Bibliotechnoj Assamblei Evrazii (BAE)

Pres c/o RSL, 3-5 Vozdvizhenka Street, Moscow MOSKVA, Russia, 119019. T. +7952027371. Fax +7952906062.
URL: http://www.rsl.ru/en/s5/s41/s414258/lae

History 1992. New charter approved 2003. **Aims** Strengthen cooperation between libraries; contribute to building-up of a library policy in participating countries; facilitate collaboration in implementation of joint programmes, research and projects; support *professional* training. **Structure** General Assembly; Coordinating Bureau; Secretariat; Auditing Committee. **Languages** English, Russian. **Staff** 1.00 FTE, paid. **Finance** Member's dues. Other sources: sponsoring; sale of Bulletin. **Activities** Politics/policy/regulatory; networking/liaising; projects/programmes; events/meetings. Elaboration of a Unified Library Legislation for CIS countries; humanitarian book aid; international book exchange; cultural programmes. Organizes exhibitions and conferences. **Publications** *LAE Information Bulletin*. Conference proceedings; monographs.
Members National libraries (16) in 11 countries:
Armenia, Azerbaijan, Belarus, Kazakhstan, Kyrgyzstan, Moldova, Russia, Tajikistan, Turkmenistan, Ukraine, Uzbekistan.
IGO Relations *UNESCO (#20322)*. **NGO Relations** International association member of: *International Federation of Library Associations and Institutions (IFLA, #13470)*. Member of: *International Informatization Academy (#13850)*. Partner of: *World Business Council for Sustainable Development (WBCSD, #21254)*. [2016.07.12/XF3926/**F**]

- ♦ Library and Information Science Society for Asia and the Pacific / see International Library and Information Science Society (#14038)
- ♦ Library of Political and International Studies (internationally oriented national body)
- ♦ Libre organisation mondiale d'aide aux réfugiés (internationally oriented national body)
- ♦ LIBS – International Conference on Laser-Induced Breakdown Spectroscopy (meeting series)
- ♦ **LICAGE** Liver Intensive Care Group of Europe (#16497)
- ♦ LICA / see International League Against Racism and Antisemitism (#14014)
- ♦ LICCA – Languages in Contact and Conflict in Africa (inactive)
- ♦ LICCD / see Ligue internationale du droit de la concurrence (#16478)
- ♦ Licensing Executives Benelux (internationally oriented national body)

♦ Licensing Executives Society Arab Countries (LES-AC) 16459

Manager PO Box 921100, Amman 11192, Jordan. T. +96265100900. Fax +96265100901. E-mail: les@lesarab.org.
URL: http://www.lesarab.org/

History Founded as a regional society of *Licensing Executives Society International (LESI, #16461)*. Registered in accordance with Jordanian law. **Aims** Support LES societies in their efforts on behalf of individual members by providing organizational leadership and quality educational content to LES societies; play a role in interacting with global organizations and policy forums concerning the economic significance and importance of licensing and technology transfer and IPRs protection. **Structure** General Assembly; Board of Directors; Standing Committees. **Languages** Arabic, English. **Staff** 5.00 FTE, paid. **Finance** Members' dues. Other sources: donations; training and activities revenues. **Activities** Training/education; events/meetings; certification/accreditation; research/documentation. **Events** *Annual meeting* Abu Dhabi (United Arab Emirates) 2005, *Annual meeting* Amman (Jordan) 2004. **Publications** *Guidelines to Licensing and Technology Transfer Agreements* in Arabic, English; *How to Become an Arab Certified IP Licensing Practioner Guide*; *LESI Guide to Licensing Best Practices* in Arabic. Annual Report; seminar volumes.
Members Licensing and technology transfer professionals in 21 countries and territories:
Algeria, Bahrain, Egypt, Iran Islamic Rep, Iraq, Jordan, Kuwait, Lebanon, Libya, Morocco, Oman, Pakistan, Palestine, Qatar, Saudi Arabia, Sudan, Syrian AR, Tunisia, Türkiye, United Arab Emirates, Yemen. [2018/XJ3039/**E**]

♦ Licensing Executives Society Europe (LES Europe) 16460

Contact LES Benelux, c/o Assistance Office SWAN v o f, Lodewijk de Vromestraat 25, 3962 VG Wijk bij Duurstede, Netherlands. T. +31343575397. Fax +31343594566. E-mail: secretariat@les-benelux.org.
URL: http://www.les-europe.org/

History Regional society of *Licensing Executives Society International (LESI, #16461)*. **Aims** Encourage high standards, expertise and ethics among persons engaged in the business of licensing or transferring technology or other *intellectual property*; make governments, academics, business communities and professional bodies aware of the benefits of licensing and thus create an environment in which the business of licensing can flourish. **Structure** Meeting of LES Europe National Presidents, before each LES International Delegates Meeting. **Languages** English. **Activities** Assists members in improving their knowledge, skills and techniques, by: creating opportunities for networking between members both nationally and internationally; facilitating exchange of ideas related to all fields of licensing; sponsoring and providing educational activities and materials; publishing articles, reports, statistics and other materials; conducting special studies. Inform and advises the business and academic communities and professional and governing bodies of the significance and importance of licensing and the high professional standards and value of using LES members; works actively in the formation of laws, regulations and procedures that facilitate licensing. **Events** *Pan-European Conference* Istanbul (Turkey) 2016, *Pan-European Conference* Rome (Italy) 2014, *Pan-European Conference* Davos (Switzerland) 2013, *Pan-European Conference* Budapest (Hungary) 2010, *Pan-European Conference* Hungary 2010. **Publications** *Les News Exchange*; *Les Novelles*.
Members National organizations in 22 countries:
Austria, Belgium, Croatia, Czechia, Denmark, Finland, France, Germany, Hungary, Iceland, Ireland, Italy, Luxembourg, Netherlands, Norway, Poland, Portugal, Russia, Spain, Sweden, Switzerland, UK. [2008.08.18/XD9361/**D**]

♦ Licensing Executives Society International (LESI) 16461

Société internationale des cadres en transfert des technologies – Sociedad Internacional de Ejecutivos de Negocios de Tecnologia

Exec Dir 1800 M Street NW, Suite 500 South Tower, Washington DC 20036, USA. E-mail: nne@lesi.org.
URL: https://www.lesi.org/

History 1973, USA. Registration: Start date: 2000, USA. **Aims** As an umbrella organization, support Member Societies in their efforts on behalf of individual members in matters dealing with and related to *intellectual property*, including domestic and international licensing of intellectual property rights and transfer of technology. **Structure** Board of Directors; Board of Delegates; Management Committees (14); Industry, Professional and Regional Committees (15); ad hoc Committees; Working Groups. **Languages** English. **Staff** 1.00 FTE, paid. **Finance** Sources: meeting proceeds; members' dues. **Activities** Events/meetings; publishing activities; training/education. **Events** *Annual International Conference* Montréal, QC (Canada) 2023, *Annual International Conference* Venice (Italy) 2022, *Annual International Conference* 2021, *Asia Pacific Regional Conference* Singapore (Singapore) 2020, *Mediation and Arbitration Workshop* Singapore (Singapore) 2020. **Publications** *Global News* (4 a year) – electronic publication; *Les Nouvelles* (4 a year). Annual Report.
Members National and regional chapters or individuals (where no national chapter). Company or government officials, lawyers, patent and trademark agents, scientists, engineers and others engaged in some form of licensing activity. Local and regional societies (33) representing members in 62 countries and territories:
Algeria, Argentina, Australia, Austria, Bahrain, Belgium, Bolivia, Brazil, Canada, China, Colombia, Croatia, Czechia, Denmark, Ecuador, Egypt, Finland, France, Germany, Hungary, Iceland, India, Iraq, Ireland, Israel, Italy, Japan, Jordan, Korea Rep, Kuwait, Lebanon, Libya, Luxembourg, Malaysia, Mexico, Morocco, Netherlands, New Zealand, Norway, Oman, Palestine, Peru, Philippines, Poland, Portugal, Qatar, Russia, Saudi Arabia, Singapore, South Africa, Spain, Sudan, Sweden, Switzerland, Syrian AR, Taiwan, Tunisia, UK, United Arab Emirates, USA, Venezuela, Yemen.
Regional societies (4), listed in this Yearbook:
Licensing Executives Benelux (LES Benelux); *Licensing Executives Society Arab Countries (LES-AC, #16459)*; *Licensing Executives Society Europe (LES Europe, #16460)*; *Licensing Executives Society Scandinavia (LES Scandinavia, #16462)*.
Consultative Status Consultative status granted from: *ECOSOC (#05331)* (Ros C); *UNCTAD (#20285)* (Special Category); *UNIDO (#20336)*; *World Intellectual Property Organization (WIPO, #21593)* (Permanent Observer Status). **IGO Relations** Observer status with (1): *World Intellectual Property Organization (WIPO, #21593)*. Cooperates with (1): *European Patent Office (EPO, #08166)*. [2022.02.02/XD0147/y/**C**]

♦ Licensing Executives Society Scandinavia (LES Scandinavia) 16462

Pres Nuottaniementie 9, FI-02230 Espoo, Finland. T. +358415032187. E-mail: mdg@bechbruun.com – secretariat@les-scandinavia.org.
URL: http://www.les-scandinavia.org/

History 1970. Regional society of *Licensing Executives Society International (LESI, #16461)*. Registered in accordance with Norwegian law: 984 228 309. **Aims** Link individuals engaged in domestic and foreign transfer of technology, and intellectual property or industrial property. **Structure** General Assembly; Board. **Languages** English. **Staff** No permanent staff; part-time, paid staff engaged according to needs. **Finance** Members' dues. Minor income from conferences and seminars. Annual budget: about euro 60,000. **Events** *Annual Conference* Helsinki (Finland) 2021, *Annual Conference* Helsinki (Finland) 2020, *Annual Conference* Stockholm (Sweden) 2018, *Annual Conference* Copenhagen (Denmark) 2017, *Annual Conference* Helsinki (Finland) 2016. **Publications** *Les Nouvelles* (4 a year) – journal.
Members in 5 countries:
Denmark, Finland, Iceland, Norway, Sweden. [2020.03.03/XD9363/**D**]

- ♦ LICH – London International College of Homeopathy (internationally oriented national body)
- ♦ Licht für die Welt (#16474)

♦ LIC – League International for Creditors 16463

Ligue internationale pour la protection du crédit – Liga Internacional para la Protección del Crédito – Liga für Internationalen Creditschultz – Lega Internazionale per la Tutela del Credito

SG address not obtained. E-mail: licgensec@gmail.com.
URL: http://www.lic-international.com/

History 8 Mar 1962, as an association of independent commercial debt collection agencies, law offices and credit reporting agencies located all over the world. **Aims** Facilitate international debt collection among countries, exchange of credit information investments and legal advice for the benefit of members and their clients worldwide. **Structure** General Assembly (at least every 3 years). Meeting (annual). Executive Council, comprising Secretary General, President, Vice President, Treasurer and 5 members. **Languages** English. **Staff** 1.00 FTE, paid. **Finance** Members' dues. **Activities** Major project aims to reach some regulations governing collecting agencies at European level so as to protect the credit industry. Supplies traders with information and assistance before they deal with foreign parts (especially concerning status of limitation, reservation of titles and various laws with regard to the letter of exchange and cheques). **Events** *General Assembly* Lisbon (Portugal) 2014, *Biennial General Assembly / General Assembly* Cologne (Germany) 2012, *Biennial general assembly / General Assembly* Florence (Italy) 2010, *Biennial general assembly / General Assembly* Barcelona (Spain) 2008, *Biennial general assembly / General Assembly* Vienna (Austria) 2006. **Publications** Information Services: Data bank.

Members Full; Associate; Agent. Members in 136 countries and territories:
Algeria, Antigua-Barbuda, Argentina, Australia, Austria, Bahamas, Bahrain, Bangladesh, Barbados, Belgium, Belize, Benin, Bolivia, Botswana, Brazil, Brunei Darussalam, Bulgaria, Burkina Faso, Burundi, Cameroon, Canada, Cape Verde, Central African Rep, Chad, Chile, China, Congo DR, Costa Rica, Croatia, Cuba, Cyprus, Czechia, Denmark, Djibouti, Dominica, Dominican Rep, Ecuador, Egypt, El Salvador, Estonia, Eswatini, Ethiopia, Fiji, Finland, France, Gabon, Gambia, Germany, Ghana, Greece, Grenada, Guatemala, Guinea, Guyana, Haiti, Honduras, Hong Kong, Hungary, Iceland, Indonesia, Iran Islamic Rep, Iraq, Ireland, Israel, Italy, Jamaica, Jordan, Kenya, Korea Rep, Kuwait, Laos, Lebanon, Lesotho, Liberia, Libya, Madagascar, Malawi, Malaysia, Malta, Mauritania, Mauritius, Monaco, Morocco, Mozambique, Myanmar, Namibia, Nepal, Neth Antilles, New Zealand, Nicaragua, Niger, Nigeria, Norway, Oman, Pakistan, Panama, Papua New Guinea, Paraguay, Peru, Philippines, Poland, Portugal, Qatar, Romania, Russia, Rwanda, Saudi Arabia, Senegal, Sierra Leone, Singapore, Slovakia, Somalia, South Africa, Spain, Sri Lanka, St Lucia, Sudan, Suriname, Sweden, Switzerland, Syrian AR, Taiwan, Tanzania UR, Thailand, Trinidad-Tobago, Tunisia, Türkiye, Uganda, UK, United Arab Emirates, Uruguay, USA, Venezuela, Vietnam, Yemen, Zimbabwe. [2015/XF0080/v/**F**]

♦ LICOS / see LICOS Center for Institutions and Economic Performance.
♦ LICOS Center for Institutions and Economic Performance. (internationally oriented national body)
♦ **LICRA** Ligue internationale contre le racisme et l'antisémitisme (#14014)
♦ **LICR** Ludwig Institute for Cancer Research (#16520)
♦ Licross/Volags Steering Committee for Disasters / see Steering Committee for Humanitarian Response (#19978)
♦ **LIDC** Ligue internationale du droit de la concurrence (#16478)
♦ LIDC – London International Development Centre (internationally oriented national body)
♦ LIDIA – Liaison internationale des industries de l'alimentation (inactive)
♦ LIDI – Ligue internationale pour la défense des indigènes-races de couleur (inactive)
♦ Lie Detectors (internationally oriented national body)
♦ **LIEECP** Ligue internationale de l'enseignement, de l'éducation et de la culture populaire (#14023)
♦ Liefdezusters van de Heilige Carolus Borromeus (religious order)
♦ LIEIS – Luxembourg Institute for European and International Studies (internationally oriented national body)
♦ **LIEN** Ligue mondiale pour l'éducation nouvelle (#21370)
♦ LIEN – Transnational Network for Young European Women (see: #10689)
♦ LIEN / see World Education Fellowship (#21370)
♦ Les Lieux de Genève / see International Civil Defence Organization (#12582)
♦ Life For Africa (internationally oriented national body)
♦ Life Ascending International (#20769)

♦ Life Cycle Initiative (LCI) 16464

Contact 1 rue Miollis, Building VII, 75015 Paris, France. T. +33144377628. Fax +33144371474. E-mail: info@lifecycleinitiative.org.
URL: http://www.lifecycleinitiative.org/

History Founded 2002, by *UNEP (#20299)* and *Society of Environmental Toxicology and Chemistry (SETAC, #19551)*. Also referred to as *LC Initiative*. **Aims** Enable users around the world to put life cycle thinking into effective practice; promote life cycle thinking globally and facilitate knowledge exchange. **Structure** Board; Secretariat; Project Management Office. **Languages** Chinese, English, French, Japanese, Spanish. **Finance** Sponsors: Government sources of France, Japan, Germany, Brazil, Switzerland and USA. Corporate sources, including: Exxon Mobil Chemical; Thinkstep; Unilever; Product Ecology Consultants. Association and NGO sources, including: *Association of Plastics Manufacturers in Europe (Plastics Europe, #02862)*; *International Council on Mining and Metals (ICMM, #13048)*; *World Steel Association (worldsteel, #21829)*; Brazilian LCA Association; WRAP-UK; Fundación Chile; IBICT. **Activities** Projects/programmes; research/documentation; capacity building. **Events** *Seminar on the Assessment of the Contribution of Products to Avoided Greenhouse Gas Emissions* Tokyo (Japan) 2018. **Publications** *LCnet Newsletter*. Reports; articles; training material.
Members Networks Regional; National; Other. National networks in 27 countries:
Argentina, Australia, Brazil, Chile, China, Colombia, Costa Rica, Denmark, Estonia, Finland, France, Germany, Hungary, India, Italy, Japan, Korea Rep, Malaysia, Mexico, New Zealand, Peru, Poland, Spain, Sweden, Switzerland, Thailand, USA.
Regional networks include 5 organizations listed in this Yearbook:
African Life Cycle Assessment Network (ALCANET); *Association for Life Cycle Assessment in Latin America (ALCALA, no recent information)*; *Central and Southeast Europe LCA Network (CASE-LCA, #03720)*; *Nordic Life Cycle Association (NorLCA, #17337)*; *Red Iberoamericana de Ciclo de Vida (#18660)*.
Other networks include 3 organizations listed in this Yearbook:
Global Footprint Network (#10367); *International Society for Industrial Ecology (ISIE, #15197)*; *The Sustainability Consortium (TSC, #20049)*.
IGO Relations *UNEP (#20299)*. [2018/XJ7331/y/**E**]

♦ Life Decisions International (internationally oriented national body)
♦ Lifeline / see Samaritans
♦ Lifeline Energy (internationally oriented national body)

♦ LifeLine International (LLI) 16465

CEO Level 12, 70 Phillip Street, Sydney NSW 2000, Australia. E-mail: secretariat@lifeline-international.com.
Head of Policy address not obtained.
Main Website: https://lifeline-intl.com/

History 1966, Sydney, NSW (Australia). Registration: Australian Charities and Not For Profit Commission (ACNC), No/ID: ABN 12 639 930 206, Australia. **Aims** Provide crisis lines and related community support services for suicide prevention, mental health promotion and prevention. **Structure** Governing Board of non-Executive Directors; Chief Executive. **Languages** English. **Staff** 5.00 FTE, paid. **Finance** Sources: contributions; donations; members' dues. Annual budget: 800,000 AUD (2022). **Activities** Advocacy/lobbying/activism; capacity building; events/meetings; humanitarian/emergency aid; networking/liaising; standards/guidelines. Regional forums for LifeLine International are: Africa, Asia/Oceania, Northern America, and Europe/UK. **Events** *Asian Pacific Telephone Counselling Conference* Taichung (Taiwan) 2023, *General assembly / Triennial International Convention* Chicago, IL (USA) 2009, *Triennial convention / Triennial International Convention* Durban (South Africa) 2005, *Triennial convention / Triennial International Convention* Kaohsiung (Taiwan) 2002, *Triennial convention / Triennial International Convention* Cape Town (South Africa) 1999.
Members Members in 22 countries and territories:
Argentina, Australia, Botswana, Canada, China, Fiji, Ghana, Japan, Korea Rep, Malawi, Malaysia, Namibia, New Zealand, Northern Ireland, Papua New Guinea, Samoa, South Africa, Sri Lanka, Taiwan, Tonga, USA, Zambia. [2023.02.14/XF8603/**F**]

♦ Life Link / see Samaritans
♦ Life-Link Association / see Life-Link Friendship-Schools
♦ Life-Link Friendship-Schools (internationally oriented national body)

♦ Lifelong Learning Platform – European Civil Society for Education (LLLP) 16466

Director Rue de l'Industrie 10, 1000 Brussels, Belgium. T. +3228962515. Fax +3222346181. E-mail: director@lllplatform.eu – info@lllplatform.eu.
URL: https://lllplatform.eu/

History 2005. Former names and other names: *European Civil Society Platform on Lifelong Learning (EUCIS-LLL)* – former. Registration: Banque-Carrefour des Entreprises, No/ID: 0883.476.196, Start date: 13 Sep 2006, Belgium. **Aims** Build a citizen's voice on lifelong learning issues; propose concrete solutions based on expertise, competencies and experience of network experts and practitioners. **Structure** General Assembly (annual); Steering Committee; Secretariat, based in Brussels (Belgium). **Languages** English, French. **Staff** 10.00 FTE, paid. **Finance** Sources: members' dues. Annual budget: 500,000 EUR (2021). **Activities** Advocacy/lobbying/activism; events/meetings. **Events** *Lifelong Learning Week Meeting* Brussels (Belgium) 2022, *Lifelong Learning Week Meeting* Brussels (Belgium) 2020, *Annual Conference* Brussels (Belgium) 2019, *Lifelong Learning Week Meeting* Brussels (Belgium) 2019, *Lifelong Learning Week Meeting* Brussels (Belgium) 2018. **Publications** *LLLP Newsletter*. EU Guide; activity reports; conference and policy debate reports; presentation brochure. **Information Services** *LLLP Database* – Database of good practices in the field..
Members Full; Associate. Regional organizations (41) listed in this Yearbook:
– *ALL DIGITAL (#00646)*;
– *Association des états généraux des étudiants de l'Europe (AEGEE-Europe, #02495)*;
– *Association for Teacher Education in Europe (ATEE, #02949)*;
– *Democracy and Human Rights Education in Europe (DARE Network, #05031)*;
– *EDEN Digital Learning Europe (EDEN, #05356)*;
– *EMDR Europe Association (#05435)*;
– *Erasmus Student Network (ESN, #05529)*;
– *European Association for Catholic Adult Education (#05966)*;
– *European Association for the Education of Adults (EAEA, #06018)*;
– *European Association of History Educators (EUROCLIO, #06069)*;
– *European Association of Institutes for Vocational Training (#06085)*;
– *European Association of Institutions of Higher Education (EURASHE, #06086)*;
– *European Association of Regional and Local Authorities for Lifelong Learning (EARLALL, #06188)*;
– *European Council for Steiner Waldorf Education (ECSWE, #06844)*;
– *European Council of National Associations of Independent Schools (ECNAIS, #06833)*;
– *European Digital Learning Network (DLEARN, #06922)*;
– *European Educational Exchanges – Youth for Understanding (EEE-YFU, #06965)*;
– *European Federation for Intercultural Learning (EFIL, #07146)*;
– *European Forum for Freedom in Education (EFFE, #07311)*;
– *European Forum of Technical and Vocational Education and Training (EfVET, #07338)*;
– *European Parents' Association (EPA, #08142)*;
– *European School Heads Association (ESHA, #08431)*;
– *European Students' Union (ESU, #08848)*;
– *European University College Association (EucA, #09028)*;
– *European University Continuing Education Network (EUCEN, #09030)*;
– *European University Foundation – Campus Europae (EUF-CE, #09031)*;
– *European Vocational Training Association (EVTA, #09075)*;
– *Fédération européenne des écoles de cirque professionnelles (FEDEC, #09565)*;
– *Fondation des Régions Européennes pour la Recherche, l'Education et la Formation (FREREF, #09828)*;
– *ICC – the international language association (ICC, #11050)*;
– *International Federation of Training Centres for the Promotion of Progressive Education (#13572)*;
– *International Sport and Culture Association (ISCA, #15587)*;
– *Learning for Well-being Foundation (L4WB, #16431)*;
– *Mediterranean Universities Union (UNIMED, #16687)*;
– *Organising Bureau of European School Student Unions (OBESSU, #17829)*;
– *Réseau international des Cités des métiers (#18890)*;
– *SIRIUS – Policy Network on Migrant Education (SIRIUS, #19291)*;
– *SOLIDAR (#19680)*;
– *Volonteurope (#20807)*;
– *World Organization of the Scout Movement (WOSM, #21693)*;
– *Youth for Exchange and Understanding (YEU, #22016)*.

Consultative Status Consultative status granted from: *Council of Europe (CE, #04881)* (Participatory Status); *UNESCO (#20322)* (Consultative Status). **IGO Relations** Cooperates with (4): *European Commission (EC, #06633)*; *European Economic and Social Committee (EESC, #06963)*; *European Parliament (EP, #08146)*; *UNESCO Institute for Lifelong Learning (UIL, #20305)*. **NGO Relations** Member of (2): *Civil Society Europe*; *Conference of INGOs of the Council of Europe (#04607)*. Cooperates with (1): *ALL DIGITAL (#00646)*. Supports (1): *European Alliance for the Statute of the European Association (EASEA, #05886)*. [2022.11.04/XJ4239/y/**F**]

♦ **LIFE** Low Impact Fishers of Europe (#16517)
♦ LifeMosaic (unconfirmed)
♦ LifeNet International (internationally oriented national body)
♦ LIFE Network (unconfirmed)

♦ Life and Peace Institute (LPI) 16467

Exec Dir Kungsängsgatan 17, SE-753 22 Uppsala, Sweden. T. +4618660131. E-mail: info@life-peace.org.
URL: http://www.life-peace.org/

History Nov 1985, Uppsala (Sweden), by churches and ecumenical organizations. **Aims** Support and promote nonviolent approaches to conflict transformation through a combination of research and action that entails the strengthening of existing local capacities and enhancing preconditions for building peace. **Structure** International Board; Executive Committee; Strategic Leadership Team; Senior Management Team. **Languages** English, French. **Staff** 43.00 FTE, paid. **Finance** Funded by governments and organizations in Sweden, Belgium and USA, and by NGO financial partners. **Activities** Projects/programmes; events/meetings. **Events** *International interfaith peace conference* Stockholm (Sweden) 2004, *International peace research consultation* Uppsala (Sweden) 2003, *Justice and peace in Northeast Asia – the power of Japan and the reunification of Korea in the global context* Kyoto (Japan) 1994, *Joint meeting* Manila (Philippines) 1993, *Justice and peace – strategies and stumbling blocks* Uppsala (Sweden) 1993. **Publications** *Horn of Africa Bulletin* (6 a year). Research reports; conference reports and papers; working papers; occasional papers. **IGO Relations** Associated with Department of Global Communications of the United Nations. **NGO Relations** Member of: *European Peacebuilding Liaison Office (EPLO, #08176)*; *Global Partnership for the Prevention of Armed Conflict (GPPAC, #10538)*. [2018.08.13/XE3653/j/**E**]

♦ Life for Relief and Development (internationally oriented national body)
♦ Life Saving Association of the Nordic Countries (inactive)
♦ Life Sowing Ministries / see Child Legacy International

♦ Lifestyle Medical Global Alliance (LMGA) 16468

Dir address not obtained.
URL: https://lifestylemedicineglobal.org/

History Initiated 2015. **Aims** Unite national Lifestyle Medicine medical professional associations from around the world, so as to rein in the alarming rise in global obesity and lifestyle-related chronic *disease* trends; identify and eradicate the cause of disease. **Structure** Advisory Board. **Activities** Events/meetings; training/education. **NGO Relations** Sister organizations include: *Australasian Society of Lifestyle Medicine (ASLM)*; *Mediterranean Society of Lifestyle Medicine (MSLM)*; *South Pacific Society of Lifestyle Medicine (SPLSLM)*. [2020.03.13/XM7834/**C**]

♦ Lifewater International (internationally oriented national body)
♦ LifeWind International / see Medical Ambassadors International
♦ Lifewords / see SGM Lifewords
♦ Life and Work Movement (inactive)
♦ LIFHAS – Libertarian Foundation for Human Assistance (internationally oriented national body)
♦ LIF – Leuser International Foundation (internationally oriented national body)
♦ **LIF** Lipizzan International Federation (#16487)
♦ LIFPL / see Women's International League for Peace and Freedom (#21024)

♦ Lifting The Burden 16469

Sec 21-27 Lamb's Conduit Street, London, WC1N 3GS, UK. E-mail: admin@l-t-b.org.
URL: http://www.l-t-b.org/

History 24 Jun 2009. Registration: Charity, No/ID: 1130642, England and Wales. **Aims** Direct the Global Campaign against *headache*. **Structure** Board of Directors. **Consultative Status** Consultative status granted from: *WHO (#20950)* (Official). [2023.02.14/XM5092/**F**]

- ♦ Liga de Amistad Internacional / see International Friendship League (#13685)
- ♦ Liga Asiatica y del Pacifico de Medicina Fisica y Rehabilitación (inactive)
- ♦ Liga Catholica Internationalis Sobrietas (inactive)
- ♦ Liga de las Ciudades Históricas (#16424)
- ♦ Liga contra la Esclavitud / see Anti-Slavery International (#00860)
- ♦ Liga dos Escoteiros Esperantistas (#19309)
- ♦ Liga Europea de Cooperación Económica (#07669)
- ♦ Liga de Exploradores Esperantistas (#19309)
- ♦ Liga Filatélica Esperantista (#05545)
- ♦ Liga für Hirtenvölker und nachhaltige Viehwirtschaft (internationally oriented national body)
- ♦ Liga Homeopathica Internationalis / see Liga Medicorum Homoeopathica Internationalis (#16471)
- ♦ Liga Howard para la Reforma Penal (internationally oriented national body)
- ♦ Liga Iberoamericana de Astronomia (#11018)

♦ La Liga Iberoamericana de Organizaciones de la Sociedad Civil (LA LIGA) 16470

Ibero-American League of Civil Society Organizations – Liga Ibero-americana de Organizações da Sociedade Civil para a Superação da Probeza e da Exclusão Social

Contact Edificio Centre Esplai, Calle Riu Anoia 42-54, El Prat de Llobregat, 08820 Barcelona, Spain. T. +34934747474. E-mail: laliga@ligaiberoamericana.org.
URL: http://www.ligaiberoamericana.org/

History Founded Dec 1999, Santiago de Compostela (Spain). Registered in accordance with Spanish law. **Aims** Build equity, particularly focusing on citizens' rights and participation to overcome poverty and social exclusion. **Structure** Assembly; Board of Directors. **Events** *Forum* Barcelona (Spain) 2017, *Forum* Brasilia (Brazil) 2016.
Members Organizations (31) in 18 countries:
Argentina, Bolivia, Brazil, Chile, Colombia, Ecuador, El Salvador, Guatemala, Honduras, Mexico, Nicaragua, Panama, Paraguay, Peru, Portugal, Spain, Uruguay, Venezuela. [2018/XM6655/**D**]

- ♦ Liga Ibero-americana de Organizações da Sociedade Civil para a Superação da Probeza e da Exclusão Social (#16470)
- ♦ Liga Internacionais do Ensino e da Educação Permanente (#14023)
- ♦ Liga Internacional de Asociaciones pro Deficientes Mentales / see Inclusion International (#11145)
- ♦ Liga Internacional de Asociaciones en favor de las Personas con Deficiencia Mental / see Inclusion International (#11145)
- ♦ Liga Internacional de Asociaciones para la Reumatologia (#14016)
- ♦ Liga Internacional contra la Competencia Desleal / see Ligue internationale du droit de la concurrence (#16478)
- ♦ Liga Internacional contra el Reumatismo / see International League of Associations for Rheumatology (#14016)
- ♦ Liga Internacional de los Doctores Homeopatas (#16471)
- ♦ Liga Internacional de la Enseñanza, de la Educación y de la Cultura Popular (#14023)
- ♦ Liga Internacional de Lucha de los Pueblos (#14021)
- ♦ Liga Internacional de Mujeres pro la Paz y la Libertad / see Women's International League for Peace and Freedom (#21024)
- ♦ Liga Internacional para la Protección del Crédito (#16463)
- ♦ Liga Internacional de la Representación Comercial (inactive)
- ♦ Liga Internacional de Socialistas Religiosos (#14022)
- ♦ Liga Internacional de Sociedades Dermatológicas (#14018)
- ♦ Liga für Internationalen Creditschultz (#16463)
- ♦ Liga Latinoamericana par el Estudio del TDAH (unconfirmed)
- ♦ Liga Latinoamericana par o Estudo do TDAH (unconfirmed)
- ♦ Liga de la Leche Internacional (#16433)

♦ Liga Medicorum Homoeopathica Internationalis (LMHI) 16471

Ligue internationale des médecins homéopathes – Liga Internacional de los Doctores Homeopatas – Internationaler Verein der Homöopathischer Ärzte – International Homeopathic Medical League

Secretariat 1400 sk baysak 1 ishani n:9/3 Alsancak, 35220 Izmir/Izmir, Türkiye. T. +905300398386. E-mail: secretary@ligamedicorum.org.
Gen Sec Wallstr 45, 06366 Köthen, Germany.
URL: http://www.lmhi.org/

History 10 Sep 1925, Rotterdam (Netherlands). Founded following international congresses from 1876, and the setting up of a Council following the 8th Congress, London (UK), whose statutes had been adopted 22 Jul 1911. Constitution adopted 26 Jul 1934, Arnhem (Netherlands); revised and altered Jun 1953, Brussels (Belgium); modified 1966, Hannover (Germany FR); amended 1998, Amsterdam (Netherlands). Former names and other names: *Liga Homeopathica Internationalis* – former. Registration: Amtsgericht Stendal, No/ID: VR 3685, Germany; Swiss Civil Code, Switzerland. **Aims** Develop homeopathy worldwide; create a link between homeopaths with medical diplomas and also between societies and persons interested in homeopahty. bibliography and documentation. **Structure** International Council (meets annually); Executive Committee; General Secretaries; Executive Team; Working Groups. **Languages** English. **Staff** 1.00 FTE, paid; 12.00 FTE, voluntary. **Finance** Sources: members' dues. **Activities** Awareness raising; events/meetings; knowledge management/information dissemination; networking/liaising. **Events** *Annual Congress* Canada 2027, *Annual Congress* Dhaka (Bangladesh) 2026, *Annual Congress* Mexico 2026, *Annual Congress* Netherlands 2025, *Annual Congress* Spain 2024. **Publications** *The Homoeopathic Physician* (4 a year); *Liga Letter* (annual).
Members Institutional Full; Individual Full; Associate. Institutional in 63 countries and territories:
Afghanistan, Argentina, Armenia, Australia, Austria, Bangladesh, Belgium, Brazil, Bulgaria, Canada, China, Colombia, Croatia, Cuba, Czechia, Ecuador, Egypt, England, Estonia, France, Georgia, Germany, Ghana, Greece, Haiti, Hong Kong, Hungary, India, Iran Islamic Rep, Italy, Japan, Kazakhstan, Kyrgyzstan, Latvia, Lithuania, Malaysia, Mexico, Moldova, Nepal, Netherlands, Nigeria, Norway, Pakistan, Peru, Poland, Portugal, Romania, Russia, Serbia, Slovenia, South Africa, Spain, Sweden, Switzerland, Taiwan, Tajikistan, Thailand, Türkiye, Turkmenistan, UK, Ukraine, USA, Venezuela.
Included in the above, 1 organization listed in this Yearbook:
European Committee for Homeopathy (ECH, #06651). [2022.11.03/XC2106/**C**]

- ♦ Liga Mediterranea frente a las Enfermedades Tromboembólicas / see European and Mediterranean League Against Thrombotic Diseases (#07771)
- ♦ Liga Mundial pro Educación Nueva (#21370)
- ♦ LIGA – Österreichische Liga für Menschenrechte (internationally oriented national body)
- ♦ Liga Panamericana de Asociaciones de Reumatologia (#18118)
- ♦ Liga Panamericana de Associações de Reumatologia (#18118)
- ♦ Liga Panamericana contra el Reumatismo / see Pan American League of Associations for Rheumatology (#18118)
- ♦ Liga Panamericana contra o Reumatismo / see Pan American League of Associations for Rheumatology (#18118)
- ♦ Liga der Rotkreuz- und Rothalbmond-Gesellschaften / see International Federation of Red Cross and Red Crescent Societies (#13526)
- ♦ Liga de Sociedades de la Cruz Roja Liga der Rotkreuz-Gesellschaften / see International Federation of Red Cross and Red Crescent Societies (#13526)
- ♦ Liga de Sociedades de la Cruz Roja y de la Media Luna Roja / see International Federation of Red Cross and Red Crescent Societies (#13526)
- ♦ Liga Universal de Bienestar Público (inactive)
- ♦ LIGHT Africa (internationally oriented national body)
- ♦ Light Electric Vehicle Association (unconfirmed)
- ♦ Lighthawk (internationally oriented national body)

♦ LightingEurope 16472

Main Office Rue Belliard 205, 1040 Brussels, Belgium. T. +3227068608. E-mail: contact@lightingeurope.org.
URL: http://www.lightingeurope.org/

History 5 Dec 2012, Brussels (Belgium). During 2013, replaced *Committee of EU Luminaires Manufacturers Associations (CELMA, inactive)* and *European Lamp Companies Federation (ELC, inactive)*. Registration: No/ID: 0525.955.279, Start date: 12 Apr 2013, Belgium; EU Transparency Register, No/ID: 29789243712-03, Start date: 8 Jun 2010. **Aims** Promote efficient *lighting* practices for the benefit of the global environment, human comfort, and the health and safety of consumers. **Structure** General Assembly (annual); Board. **Languages** English. **Staff** 5.00 FTE, paid. **Finance** Sources: members' dues. **Events** *Why Indoor Environmental Quality (IEQ) Matters – Towards Healthier Buildings* Brussels (Belgium) 2022. **NGO Relations** Member of (6): *Alliance for Internet of Things Innovation (AIOTI, #00697); Coalition for Energy Savings (#04056); Energy Efficiency Industrial Forum (EEIF, #05470); Federation of European and International Associations Established in Belgium (FAIB, #09508); Global Lighting Association (#10459); Industry4Europe (#11181).* Liaison Organization of: *Comité européen de normalisation (CEN, #04162); European Committee for Electrotechnical Standardization (CENELEC, #06647).* Affiliate member of: *European Association of lighting WEEE compliance schemes (EucoLight, #06108).* [2020/XJ6860/**D**]

♦ Lighting Urban Community International (LUCI) 16473

Gen Manager 13 rue du Griffon, 69001 Lyon, France. T. +33427118537. Fax +33427118536. E-mail: luci@luciassociation.org.
URL: http://www.luciassociation.org/

History 2002. Founded on the initiative of the City of Lyon. **Aims** Promote high quality and carefully designed urban lighting to influence the process of urban development and regeneration in a decisive and positive way. **Structure** Includes: LUCI Regional Office for Asia (LROA). **Languages** English. **Staff** 5.00 FTE, paid. **Activities** Awards/prizes/competitions; awareness raising; capacity building; events/meetings; knowledge management/information dissemination; networking/liaising; projects/programmes; publishing activities. **Events** *Annual General Meeting* Busan (Korea Rep) 2022, *Asia Urban Lighting Workshop* Seoul (Korea Rep) 2021, *Annual General Meeting* Tartu (Estonia) 2021, *Annual General Meeting* Tartu (Estonia) 2020, *City under Microscope Meeting* Oulu (Finland) 2019. [2022.10.25/XM3735/**F**]

- ♦ Light on Life / see Nordic Safe Cities (#17403)

♦ Light for the World 16474

Licht für die Welt

Main Office Niederhofstr 26, 1120 Vienna, Austria. T. +4318101300. E-mail: info@licht-fuer-die-welt.at – info@light-for-the-world.org.
EU Office 10 Rue de l'Industrie, 1000 Brussels, Belgium. E-mail: eu@light-for-the-world.org.
URL: http://www.light-for-the-world.org/

History 1998. Founded by a group of Austrian individuals. Belgian group set up 1997; Czech group set 2007, which led to formal agreement of confederation, 2008. Dutch group joined Apr 2011. Registration: No/ID: 0858.373.586, Start date: 17 Mar 2003, Belgium; EU Transparency Register, No/ID: 74313108109-71, Start date: 20 Feb 2012. **Aims** Promote: prevention of *blindness*, restoration of eyesight and eye health; *rehabilitation* and inclusive *education* for persons with *disabilities*; inclusive development and *human rights* of persons with disabilities. **Finance** Budget (2011): nearly euro 20 million. **Events** *International meeting on the prevention of childhood blindness* London (UK) 1990. **Publications** *Activity Report* (annual); *Vision and Development* (1-2 a year). **IGO Relations** Contacts with: *European Community (inactive).* Participant in Fundamental Rights Platform of: *European Union Agency for Fundamental Rights (FRA, #08969).*
NGO Relations Member of:
- *Arbeitsgemeinschaft Evangelikaler Missionen (AEM);*
- *Fédération francophone et germanophone des associations de coopération au développement (ACODEV, #09587);*
- *Global Campaign for Education (GCE, #10264);*
- *Global Partnership for Disability and Development (GPDD, #10530);*
- *GLOBAL RESPONSIBILITY – Austrian Platform for Development and Humanitarian Aid;*
- *Human Rights and Democracy Network (HRDN, #10980);*
- *International Coalition for Trachoma Control (ICTC, #12624);*
- *International Council for Education of People with Visual Impairment (ICEVI, #13015);*
- *International Disability and Development Consortium (IDDC, #13177);*
- *Neglected Tropical Diseased NGO Network (NNN, #16969)*
- *Partnership Committee to the WHO Programme for the Prevention of Blindness (Partnership Committee, no recent information);*
- *Prisma;*
- *SDG Watch Europe (#19162).*

Participates in: *Global Partnership on Children with Disabilities (GPcwd, #10529).* Relations with: *Dana Center for Preventive Ophthalmology (DCPO, #04997).* Partner of: *International Trachoma Initiative (ITI, #15701).* Supports: *Eastern Africa College of Ophthalmologists (EACO, inactive).* [2020/XG1211/**F**]

- ♦ LIGI – Liu Institute for Global Issues (internationally oriented national body)
- ♦ LignoBiotech – Symposium of Biotechnology Applied to Lignocelluloses (meeting series)
- ♦ Ligo Internacia de Blindaj Esperantistoj (#14017)

♦ Ligo de Samseksamaj Geesperantistoj (LSG) 16475

League of Homosexual Esperantists

Pres address not obtained. E-mail: lsgesperanto@icloud.com.
Facebook: https://www.facebook.com/LSG.eo/

History 1977. Former names and other names: *League for Gay, Lesbian, Bisexual and Transsexual Esperantists* – former; *Association internationale des gays et lesbiennes espérantistes* – former. **Aims** Create international solidarity and cooperation among members, thereby supporting efforts to promote *Esperanto* and to fully integrate *gays* and *lesbians* in society; work towards the end of language discrimination by educating people in gay circles about the world's language problem and about how it can be solved with Esperanto; work towards the end of anti-gay discrimination by educating people in Esperanto circles about gay men and lesbians, their value in the world today, and the problems they face. **Structure** General Assembly (every 3 years); Board. **Languages** Esperanto. **Finance** Sources: members' dues. **Activities** Events/meetings. **Events** *Annual Meeting* Copenhagen (Denmark) 2010, *Annual Meeting* Bialystok (Poland) 2009, *Annual Meeting* Rotterdam (Netherlands) 2008, *Annual Meeting* Florence (Italy) 2006, *Annual Meeting* Vilnius (Lithuania) 2005. **Publications** *Forumo* (4 a year).
Members Individuals and associations/institutions in 40 countries:
Algeria, Argentina, Australia, Austria, Belarus, Belgium, Brazil, Canada, China, Cuba, Czechia, Denmark, Estonia, Finland, France, Germany, Hungary, Ireland, Israel, Italy, Japan, Latvia, Lithuania, Malta, Moldova, Netherlands, New Zealand, Nigeria, Poland, Russia, Serbia, Singapore, Slovakia, Spain, Sweden, Switzerland, Togo, UK, Ukraine, USA.
NGO Relations Member of (1): *Universal Esperanto Association (UEA, #20676).* [2022/XD8610/**D**]

- ♦ LIGO Scientific Collaboration (internationally oriented national body)
- ♦ Ligue Africaine des Associations en Rhumatologie (#00360)

♦ Ligue Africaine des Blogueurs et Cyber-activistes pour la Démocratie (AFRICTIVISTES) 16476

League of African Bloggers and Cyber-activists for Democracy (AFRICTIVISTES)

Contact rue 45 x 34 Medina, 24930 Dakar, Senegal. E-mail: info@africtivistes.org – cheikh.fall@africtivistes.org – aisha.dabo@africtivistes.org.
URL: https://www.africtivistes.org/

History Nov 2015. Registration: Senegal. **Aims** Seek to strengthen democracy, human rights and good governance in Africa through information and communication technologies. **Languages** English, French. **Staff** 200.00 FTE, voluntary. **Activities** Advocacy/lobbying/activism; capacity building; events/meetings; projects/programmes; publishing activities; training/education. Africa. **NGO Relations** Partner of (8): *ARTICLE 19 (#01121); Global Voices; International Research and Exchanges Board (IREX); Internet Sans Frontières (ISF); Internews; Open Society Foundations (OSF, #17763); Panos Network (#18183); Platform to Protect Whistleblowers in Africa (PPLAAF, #18402).* [2020.11.24/XM8844/**F**]

- ♦ Ligue africaine contre le rhumatisme / see African League of Associations for Rheumatology (#00360)

- Ligue d'amitié internationale / see International Friendship League (#13685)
- Ligue des anciens des armées du Commonwealth / see Royal Commonwealth Ex-Services League (#18989)
- Ligue des anciens des armées du Commonwealth britannique / see Royal Commonwealth Ex-Services League (#18989)
- Ligue arabe / see League of Arab States (#16420)
- Ligue de l'Asie Pacifique contre le rhumatisme (#01945)
- Ligue balkanique (inactive)
- Ligue des Bibliothèques Européennes de Recherche (#02540)
- Ligue bouddhiste espérantiste (#03348)
- Ligue celtique (#03633)
- Ligue des Cités Cananéennes, Phéniciennes et Puniques (#16421)
- Ligue communiste (inactive)
- Ligue contre le trachome / see International Organization Against Trachoma (#14436)
- Ligue danubienne contre la thrombose et les troubles hémorragiques (#05007)
- Ligue de Delos (inactive)
- Ligue des droits de la personne humaine dans la région des Grands-Lacs (internationally oriented national body)
- Ligue espérantiste baha'ie (#03061)
- Ligue espérantiste scoute (#19309)
- Ligue espérantiste universelle (inactive)
- Ligue des Etats arabes (#16420)
- Ligue pour les Etats-Unis d'Europe – Jeune Europe (inactive)
- Ligue européenne des associations d'aide aux handicapés mentaux / see Inclusion International (#11145)
- Ligue Européenne des Associations d'employeurs du spectacle / see Pearle – Live Performance Europe (#18284)
- Ligue européenne de bridge (#06402)
- Ligue européenne contre le rhumatisme / see European Alliance of Associations for Rheumatology (#05862)
- Ligue européenne de coopération économique (#07669)
- Ligue européenne d'hygiène mentale (inactive)
- Ligue européenne des imams et des aumôniers (inactive)

♦ Ligue européenne de natation (LEN) 16477

European Swimming Federation

Operations Manager 9 rue de la Morâche, 1260 Nyon VD, Switzerland. T. +41225529999. E-mail: lenoffice@len.eu.
URL: http://www.len.eu/

History 30 Aug 1927, Bologna (Italy). **Aims** Promote development of swimming, diving, water polo, synchronized swimming, open water swimming and masters swimming, diving and water polo in Europe; promote European *championships* and events. **Structure** Congress (annual); Bureau; Technical Sub-committees (7); Calendar Conference (annual). **Languages** English, French. **Staff** 6.00 FTE, paid. **Finance** Members' dues. Marketing and commercialization of events. Annual budget: about euro 4,000,000. **Activities** Sporting activities; training/education. **Events** *Congress* Budapest (Hungary) 2021, *Congress* St Petersburg (Russia) 2019, *Congress* Vienna (Austria) 2015, *Learn to Swim Seminar* Budapest (Hungary) 2011, *Congress* Limassol (Cyprus) 2010. **Publications** *LEN Magazine* (4 a year); *LEN Handbook* – rules and regulations; *LEN Yearbook*.
Members National swimming federations/associations in 52 countries and territories:
Albania, Andorra, Armenia, Austria, Azerbaijan, Belarus, Belgium, Bosnia-Herzegovina, Bulgaria, Croatia, Cyprus, Czechia, Denmark, Estonia, Faeroe Is, Finland, France, Georgia, Germany, Gibraltar, Greece, Hungary, Iceland, Ireland, Israel, Italy, Kosovo, Latvia, Liechtenstein, Lithuania, Luxembourg, Malta, Moldova, Monaco, Montenegro, Netherlands, North Macedonia, Norway, Poland, Portugal, Romania, Russia, San Marino, Serbia, Slovakia, Slovenia, Spain, Sweden, Switzerland, Türkiye, UK, Ukraine.
NGO Relations Founding member of: *Sport Integrity Global Alliance (SIGA, #19925)*. Member of: *World Aquatics (#21100)*; *Sports Rights Owners Coalition (SROC, #19929)*. Negotiates with: *European Broadcasting Union (EBU, #06404)*. [2017.11.29/XD2715/**D**]

- Ligue féminine d'Afrique orientale (internationally oriented national body)
- Ligue des femmes juives (inactive)
- Ligue hanséatique (inactive)
- Ligue Howard pour la réforme pénale (internationally oriented national body)
- Ligue ibéroaméricaine d'astronomie (#11018)
- Ligue internationale des adversaires de la prohibition (inactive)
- Ligue internationale des agriculteurs spécialistes espérantistes (inactive)
- Ligue internationale antivivisectionniste (inactive)
- Ligue internationale d'arbitrage (inactive)
- Ligue internationale des associations d'aide aux handicapés mentaux / see Inclusion International (#11145)
- Ligue internationale des associations pour les personnes handicapées mentales / see Inclusion International (#11145)
- Ligue internationale d'associations pour la rhumatologie (#14016)
- Ligue internationale des associations touristes / see Alliance internationale de tourisme (#00694)
- Ligue internationale des aveugles espérantistes (#14017)
- Ligue internationale des aviateurs (inactive)
- Ligue internationale de bridge / see European Bridge League (#06402)
- Ligue internationale catholique IKA (inactive)
- Ligue internationale catholique Sobrietas (inactive)
- Ligue internationale des chrétiens espérantistes (#03901)
- Ligue internationale contre l'abus des boissons spiritueuses (inactive)
- Ligue internationale contre l'antisémitisme / see International League Against Racism and Antisemitism (#14014)
- Ligue internationale contre la concurrence déloyale / see Ligue internationale du droit de la concurrence (#16478)
- Ligue internationale contre l'épilepsie (#14013)
- Ligue internationale contre les pogromes / see International League Against Racism and Antisemitism (#14014)
- Ligue internationale contre le racisme et l'antisémitisme (#14014)
- Ligue internationale contre le rhumatisme / see International League of Associations for Rheumatology (#14016)
- Ligue internationale contre la vaccination (inactive)
- Ligue internationale de coopérateurs espérantistes (inactive)
- Ligue internationale de culture (inactive)
- Ligue internationale pour la défense et le développement du protestantisme (inactive)
- Ligue internationale pour la défense des indigènes-races de couleur (inactive)
- Ligue internationale de défense juive (inactive)
- Ligue internationale pour la défense du soldat (inactive)

♦ Ligue internationale du droit de la concurrence (LIDC) 16478

International League of Competition Law – Internationale Liga für Wettbewerbsrecht

Secretariat Place Saint-François 1, 1002 Lausanne VD 7191, Switzerland. T. +41582003300. Fax +41582003311. E-mail: info@ligue.org.
Pres c/o Altius, Av du Port 86C B414, Tour & Taxis, Royal Depot, 1000 Brussels, Belgium.
Gen Sec c/o UGGC Avocats, 47 rue de Monceau, 75008 Paris, France.
URL: http://www.ligue.org/

History Founded 1930. Reconstructed 1946. Registered by French Ministerial Decree, 25 Jan 1955. Original title: *International League Against Unfair Competition – Ligue internationale contre la concurrence déloyale (LICCD) – Liga Internacional contra la Competencia Desleal – Internationale Liga gegen Unlauteren Wettbewerb*. Since 1965 also referred to as *Association internationale d'étude de la concurrence*. Present name adopted 1984. **Aims** Promote open and honest competition and combat *unfair*, illicit or improper practices at national and international levels; study competition problems; study and participate in international agreements; disseminate principles of fair competition; promote reforms at national and international levels. **Structure** General Assembly (annual); Council; Bureau. **Languages** English, French. **Staff** 1.00 FTE, paid; 5.00 FTE, voluntary. **Finance** Sources: members' dues. **Activities** Events/meetings. **Events** *Congress* Brussels (Belgium) 2020, *Congress* Paris (France) 2019, *Congress* Budapest (Hungary) 2018, *Congress* Rio de Janeiro (Brazil) 2017, *Congress* Geneva (Switzerland) 2016.
Members Regional groups in 18 countries and territories:
Austria, Belgium, Brazil, Czechia, Denmark, Finland, France, Germany, Hungary, Italy, Japan, Luxembourg, Norway, Sweden, Switzerland, UK, Ukraine, USA.
Correspondents in 16 countries and territories:
Algeria, Australia, Bulgaria, Cyprus, Estonia, Hong Kong, Kenya, Lithuania, Morocco, Netherlands, Poland, Portugal, Romania, Serbia, Spain, Taiwan.
Consultative Status Consultative status granted from: *World Intellectual Property Organization (WIPO, #21593)* (Permanent Observer Status). **IGO Relations** *European Commission (EC, #06633)*.
[2021/XC2197/**C**]

- Ligue Internationale d'Education Nouvelle / see World Education Fellowship (#21370)
- Ligue internationale pour l'éducation rationnelle de l'enfance (inactive)
- Ligue internationale des enseignants espérantistes / see ESPERANTO + EDUKADO (#05544)
- Ligue internationale de l'enseignement, de l'éducation et de la culture populaire (#14023)
- Ligue internationale espérantiste d'échecs (inactive)
- Ligue internationale de femmes pour la paix et la liberté / see Women's International League for Peace and Freedom (#21024)
- Ligue internationale de gymnastique moderne (inactive)
- Ligue internationale de la leche (#16433)
- Ligue internationale de la librairie ancienne (#14015)
- Ligue internationale de luttes des peuples (#14021)
- Ligue internationale des médecins homéopathes (#16471)
- Ligue internationale des mères et des éducatrices pour la paix (inactive)
- Ligue internationale des non-religieux et des athées (#14020)
- Ligue internationale d'optique / see World Council of Optometry (#21335)
- Ligue internationale des pacifistes catholiques (inactive)
- Ligue internationale de la paix et de la liberté (inactive)
- Ligue internationale et permanente de la paix (inactive)
- Ligue internationale des peuples (inactive)
- Ligue internationale des postiers espérantistes (inactive)
- Ligue internationale pour la protection du crédit (#16463)
- Ligue internationale pour la protection des primates (#14641)
- Ligue internationale des radio-amateurs espérantistes (#11524)
- Ligue internationale pour la réforme du calendrier (inactive)
- Ligue internationale de la représentation commerciale (inactive)
- Ligue internationale pour la sauvegarde de la main (inactive)

♦ Ligue internationale des scientifiques pour l'usage de la langue française (LISULF) 16479

Pres 1200 rue Latour, St Laurent QC H4L 4S4, Canada. T. +15147472308. E-mail: lisulf@lisulf.quebec – c3410@er.uqam.ca.
URL: http://www.er.uqam.ca/nobel/c3410/lisulf.htm

History 14 Oct 1988. **Structure** Includes offices in Paris (France) and Saint-Laurent (Canada). **Publications** *Sciences et Francophonie* (4 a year). [2016/XF4217/**F**]

- Ligue internationale des sociétés dermatologiques (#14018)
- Ligue internationale des sociétés de surveillance / see International Security Ligue (#14826)
- Ligue internationale pour la vie familiale (inactive)
- Ligue islamique mondiale (#16917)
- Ligue des Jeunes Africains pour la Paix et le Développement (unconfirmed)
- Ligue pour la lecture de la Bible – Conseil international (#19161)
- Ligue maritime espérantiste (inactive)
- Ligue de médecine physique et de réadaptation de l'Asie et le Pacifique (inactive)
- Ligue méditerranéenne de thrombose / see European and Mediterranean League Against Thrombotic Diseases (#07771)
- Ligue mondiale criminelle et de la police (inactive)
- Ligue mondiale pour l'éducation nouvelle (#21370)
- Ligue mondiale des étudiants espérantistes (inactive)
- Ligue mondiale de la liberté et de la démocratie (#21621)
- Ligue mondiale de la police (inactive)
- Ligue panafricaine contre le tribalisme, le sectarianisme et le racisme (inactive)
- Ligue panaméricaine des associations de rhumatologie (#18118)
- Ligue panaméricaine contre le rhumatisme / see Pan American League of Associations for Rheumatology (#18118)
- Ligue de la patrie arabe (inactive)
- Ligue des pays du Commonwealth (#04320)
- Ligue des peuples de couleurs (inactive)
- Ligue philatélique espérantiste (#05545)
- Ligue protestante universelle (inactive)
- Ligue de la race latine (inactive)
- Ligue des sociétés de la Croix-Rouge / see International Federation of Red Cross and Red Crescent Societies (#13526)
- Ligue des sociétés de la Croix-Rouge et du Croissant-Rouge / see International Federation of Red Cross and Red Crescent Societies (#13526)
- Ligue suisse des droits de l'homme (internationally oriented national body)
- Ligue tunisienne pour la défense des droits de l'homme (internationally oriented national body)
- Ligue universelle du bien public (inactive)
- Ligue universelle pour la réforme sexuelle (inactive)
- Ligue des universités islamiques (#16425)
- Ligue des villes historiques (#16424)
- Ligue de la zone afrique pour la défense des droits des enfants, étudiants et élèves (internationally oriented national body)
- Ligums par Konstituciju Eiropai (2004 treaty)
- LiHE / see Learning in Higher Education (#16429)
- **LiHE** Learning in Higher Education (#16429)
- LIIA – Latvian Institute of International Affairs (internationally oriented national body)
- LIJAPD – Ligue des Jeunes Africains pour la Paix et le Développement (unconfirmed)
- LIKE – Association des villes et régions de européennes pour la culture (#06554)
- **LIKE** European Cities and Regions for Culture (#06554)
- Likud Olami (#21625)
- **LILA** Ligue internationale de la librairie ancienne (#14015)
- **LI** Landcare International (#16226)
- LI – Landscape Institute (internationally oriented national body)
- LILAPETDAH – Liga Latinoamericana par el Estudio del TDAH (unconfirmed)

♦ **LI** Legacy International (#16437)
♦ Liliane Foundation (internationally oriented national body)
♦ **LI** Liberal International (#16454)
♦ LI – Ligue internationale de la représentation commerciale (inactive)
♦ Lima Convention – Convention for the Protection of the Marine Environment and Coastal Area of the Southeast Pacific (1981 treaty)
♦ LIMAV / see International Doctors – ILDAV (#13186)
♦ LIMEP – Ligue internationale des mères et des éducatrices pour la paix (inactive)
♦ LIMES Congress – International Congress of Roman Frontier Studies (meeting series)
♦ LIMI / see International Management Institute, St Petersburg

♦ Limmud FSU International Foundation 16480

Acting Dir 80 Central Park West, Central park 2D, New York NY 10023, USA.
URL: https://www.limmudfsu.org/

History 2006, Moscow (Russia). Registration: No/ID: EIN 26-1870256, USA. **Structure** International Steering Committee. **Activities** Events/meetings; training/education. **Events** *European Conference* Vienna (Austria) 2020, *European Conference* London (UK) 2017.
Members Communities in:
Australia, Belarus, Canada, Israel, Moldova, Ukraine, USA.
Also communities in West Europe. [2021/AA1454/**E**]

♦ LIMPAL / see Women's International League for Peace and Freedom (#21024)
♦ **LINC** LEADER Inspired Network Community (#16413)

♦ Linear Collider Collaboration (LCC) 16481

Office Fermilab, PO Box 500, Batavia IL 60510-5011, USA.
URL: http://www.linearcollider.org/

History 21 Feb 2013, as an organization bringing *International Linear Collider (ILC, #14052)* and Compact Linear Collider Study (CLIC) under one roof. **Aims** Coordinate and advance the global development work for the linear collider. **Structure** Board. **Events** *Asian Linear Collider Workshop* Fukuoka (Japan) 2018, *International Symposium on The Superconducting RF Technology for the International Linear Collider* Tokyo (Japan) 2018, *European Linear Collider Workshop* Santander (Spain) 2016, *Can the ILC Solve the Mystery of the Universe Symposium* Tokyo (Japan) 2013, *International Workshop on Future Linear Colliders* Tokyo (Japan) 2013. **Publications** *LC Newsline.* [2019/XJ6586/**E**]

♦ LINGO – Leave it in the Ground Coalition (unconfirmed)
♦ Linguapax Institute / see Linguapax International (#16482)

♦ Linguapax International 16482

Coordinator C/ de Maria Aurèlia Capmany 14-16, 08001 Barcelona, Spain. E-mail: info@linguapax.org – comunicacio@linguapax.org.
URL: http://www.linguapax.org/

History 1987, Kiev (Ukraine). Former names and other names: *Linguapax Programme* – former; *International Linguapax Committee* – former; *Linguapax Institute* – former (2001). Registration: Generalitat de Catalunya, No/ID: 24740, Spain, Catalunya. **Aims** Promote, coordinate and disseminate research in the field of *sociolinguistics*; provide advice and support to ideological, political and legislative processes encouraging protection of linguistic diversity and programmes at improving or revitalizing specific linguistic communities; promote development of *multilingual* education including local, national and international languages. **Structure** General Assembly; Board; Advisory Board. *Linguapax International Network*, subdivided into 7 regions: Africa; Asia; Eurasia; Europe; Latin America; North America; Pacific. **Languages** Catalan, English, French, Spanish. **Staff** 2.00 FTE, paid. **Activities** Awards/prizes/competitions; guidance/assistance/consulting; knowledge management/information dissemination; standards/guidelines; training/education. **Events** *International Conference* Barcelona (Spain) 2016, *International Meeting* Dakar (Senegal) 2011, *International Meeting* Addis Ababa (Ethiopia) 2008, *Congress* Barcelona (Spain) 2004, *World Congress on Language Policies / Congrés Mundial sobre Polítiques Lingüístiques* Barcelona (Spain) 2002. **Publications** *Linguapax Review* in Catalan, English – Annual Review; *Report on the World Languages. e-Linguapax* (2021) in Catalan, English – Bimensual electronic newsletter; *The Management of Linguistic Diversity and Peace Processes* (2010) in Catalan, English. **Members** Membership countries not specified. **Consultative Status** Consultative status granted from: *UNESCO (#20322)* (Consultative Status). [2022.10.20/XE4232/**E**]

♦ Linguapax Programme / see Linguapax International (#16482)
♦ Linguasphere Observatory (internationally oriented national body)
♦ Linguistevereniging van Suider-Afrika (internationally oriented national body)
♦ Linguistic Association of Canada and the United States (internationally oriented national body)
♦ Linguistic Society of Southern Africa (internationally oriented national body)
♦ Linguistics Society of Europe (#19448)
♦ Lingva Komitato / see Esperanto Academy (#05543)
♦ LINK / see Books Abroad
♦ Link Africa / see Link Community Development (#16483)

♦ Link Community Development (Link) 16483

Acting CEO Dolphin House, 4 Hunter Square, Edinburgh, EH1 1QW, UK. T. +441312253076. E-mail: link@lcd.org.uk.
URL: http://www.lcdinternational.org/

History 1989, as *Link Africa*. Partner organizations set up: South Africa (1995); Ghana (1999); Uganda (2000); Malawi (2006); Scotland (2006); Ireland (2006); Ethiopia (2007). **Structure** Group of 5 independent, legal organizations. Officers: CEO; Group Finance Director; International Programme Director; International Programme Officers. **NGO Relations** Member of: *Commonwealth Consortium for Education (CCfE, #04318)*. LCD Scotland is member of: *Scotland's International Development Alliance (the Alliance)*. [2016.08.24/XM3583/**F**]

♦ Linked Content Coalition (unconfirmed)
♦ Linked Hands – Campaign Against Hunger / see Manos Unidas
♦ **Link** Link Community Development (#16483)
♦ Links International (internationally oriented national body)

♦ Linux Foundation 16484

Main Office 548 Market St, PMB 57274, San Francisco CA 94104-5401, USA. E-mail: info@linuxfoundation.org.
Linux Foundation Europe Ave des arts 56, 1000 Brussels, Belgium.
URL: http://www.linuxfoundation.org/

History 2000. **Aims** Solve technology problems and accelerate open *technology* development and commercial adoption. **Structure** Board; Leadership. **Activities** Training/education; events/meetings; certification/accreditation. **Events** *Open Networking & Edge Summit Europe* Antwerp (Belgium) 2022, *Open Source Summit Japan* Tokyo (Japan) 2022, *Open Networking & Edge Summit North America* 2021, *Open Source Summit Japan* Tokyo (Japan) 2021, *Automotive Linux Summit* San Francisco, CA (USA) 2020. **NGO Relations** *Open Networking Foundation (ONF, #17759).* [2021/XM5248/f/**F**]

♦ Linux Plumbers Conference (meeting series)
♦ LIO International Conference on Flavour Physics (meeting series)

♦ Lions Clubs International (LCI) 16485

Main Office 300 W 22nd St, Oak Brook IL 60523-8842, USA. T. +16305715466. Fax +16305718890.
Representative at UNESCO 102 rue du Molinel, 59000 Lille, France. T. +33320027897.
URL: http://www.lionsclubs.org/

History 1917, Chicago, IL (USA). Founded by Melvin Jones. Initial membership consisted of 25 clubs located in the USA. In subsequent years, clubs were established in Canada (1920), Mexico (1925) and China (1926). Currently there are more than 46,000 clubs and 1.35 million members in over 200 countries and geographic areas. Statutes amended: 4 Jul 1988; 2 Jul 1988. Former names and other names: *Lions International* – former; *International Association of Lions Clubs* – full title; *Association internationale des Lions clubs* – full title; *Asociación Internacional de los Clubes de Leones* – full title; *Internationale Vereinigung der Lions-Club* – full title. Registration: USA. **Aims** Empower *volunteers* to serve their communities, meet *humanitarian* needs, encourage *peace* and promote international understanding. **Structure** *Lions Clubs International Foundation (LCIF)* is the registered charitable entity. International Convention; International Board; Executive Committee; Standing Committees (9). **Languages** Chinese, English, Finnish, French, German, Italian, Japanese, Korean, Portuguese, Spanish, Swedish. **Staff** 268.00 FTE, paid. **Finance** Members' dues: semi-annual per-capita dues of US$ 21.50; new members entrance fee US$ 25; certified family members, students and Leo club members – semi-annual per-capita of US$ 10.75. **Activities** Financial and/or material support; training/education; networking/liaising. **Events** *International Convention* Singapore (Singapore) 2028, *International Convention* Washington, DC (USA) 2027, *International Convention* Atlanta, GA (USA) 2026, *International Convention* Mexico City (Mexico) 2025, *International Convention* Melbourne, VIC (Australia) 2024. **Publications** *LION Magazine* (35 a year) in Chinese, Danish, Dutch, English, Finnish, French, French, German, Greek, Hindi, Italian, Japanese, Korean, Norwegian, Polish, Portuguese, Spanish, Swedish, Thai, Turkish. **Members** Clubs (over 46,000), totalling over 1.35 million members adhering to 'Lions Code of Ethics', in over 200 countries and geographic regions. Membership countries not specified. **Consultative Status** Consultative status granted from: *ECOSOC (#05331)* (General); *UNESCO (#20322)* (Consultative Status); *WHO (#20950)* (Official Relations); *UNICEF (#20332)*; *UNEP (#20299)*; *Council of Europe (CE, #04881)* (Participatory Status). **IGO Relations** Cooperates with: *UNHCR (#20327)*. Associated with Department of Global Communications of the United Nations. Sponsors: *Onchocerciasis Elimination Program for the Americas (OEPA, #17726)*. Accredited by: *United Nations Office at Geneva (UNOG, #20597)*; *United Nations Office at Vienna (UNOV, #20604)*. **NGO Relations** Member of (7): *Conference of Non-Governmental Organizations in Consultative Relationship with the United Nations (CONGO, #04635)*; *International Coalition for Trachoma Control (ICTC, #12624)*; *Neglected Tropical Diseased NGO Network (NNN, #16969)*; *New York NGO Committee on Drugs (NYNGOC, #17097)*; *NGO Committee on UNICEF (#17120)*; *Vienna NGO Committee on Drugs (VNGOC, #20773)*; *World Blind Union (WBU, #21234)*. Supports (1): *International Children's Trust (ICT)*. Instrumental in setting up (1): *Nordic Youth Orchestra (#17475)*. [2021/XF2936/**F**]

♦ Lions International / see Lions Clubs International (#16485)

♦ Lions Quest 16486

Manager Lions Clubs Intl Foundation, 300 W 22nd St, Oak Brook IL 60523-8842, USA. T. +16305715466. Fax +16305715735.
URL: http://www.lions-quest.org/

History 1975, as *Quest International*. Since 1984, a youth programme of *Lions Clubs International (LCI, #16485)*. **Aims** Empower and support adults worldwide in nurturing *responsibility* and *caring* in *young people* through a school-based life-skills program. **Structure** International Board of Directors (meets annually). President. **Finance** Mainly from Lions Clubs International Foundation. **Activities** *'Partnership'*: collaboration among professional, service and development organizations on local positive youth development initiatives. Programs (3): Skills for Growing; Skills for Adolescence; Skills for Action. *'Training Workshops'*: preparing participants for program implementation and staff development in-services. *'Products'*: support materials to reinforce program topics, enhance classroom management, support school climate and promote community involvement in positive youth development. *'Support Services'*: for trained teachers and others implementing programs.
Members Covers 50 countries and territories:
Argentina, Australia, Austria, Bangladesh, Belgium, Belize, Botswana, Brazil, Canada, Cayman Is, Colombia, Cyprus, Czechia, Denmark, Dominican Rep, Ecuador, Finland, Germany, Guyana, Hungary, Iceland, India, Italy, Japan, Kenya, Lebanon, Lithuania, Nepal, Netherlands, New Zealand, Nigeria, Norway, Pakistan, Paraguay, Peru, Poland, Romania, Russia, Singapore, South Africa, Sri Lanka, Suriname, Sweden, Tanzania UR, Thailand, Trinidad-Tobago, Uganda, Ukraine, Uruguay, USA. [2014/XF5510/**F**]

♦ Lions World Services for the Blind / see World Services for the Blind
♦ LIPA – Ligue panafricaine contre le tribalisme, le sectarianisme et le racisme (inactive)
♦ Lipid and Atherosclerosis Society of Southern Africa (internationally oriented national body)
♦ LIPIDFORUM / see Nordic Forum for Lipid Research and Technology (#17299)

♦ Lipizzan International Federation (LIF) 16487

SG I Rezeka 9, HR-42000 Varazdin, Croatia. T. +385997032128. E-mail: office@lipizzanonline.com.
Registered office B Henrycaan 13, 3650 Dilsen-Stokkem, Belgium.
URL: http://www.lipizzan-online.com/

History 20 Nov 1986, Brussels (Belgium). Registered in accordance with Belgian law. Also referred to as *International Federation for the Lipizzaner Horse*. **Aims** Perpetuate the ancient *breed* of Lipizzaner *horse* through international scientific research and cooperation. **Structure** General Assembly (annual); LIF Breeding Committee. **Languages** English, French, German. **Staff** 5.00 FTE, paid. **Activities** Knowledge management/information dissemination; standards/guidelines. **Events** *General Assembly* Vienna (Austria) 2016, *General Assembly* Szilvasvarad (Hungary) 2013, *General Assembly* Kelebija (Serbia) 2012, *General Assembly* Lipica (Slovenia) 2011, *General Assembly* Topol'cianky (Slovakia) 2010.
Members State studs and breeding organizations in 17 countries:
Austria, Belgium, Croatia, Denmark, France, Germany, Hungary, Italy, Netherlands, Norway, Romania, Serbia, Slovakia, Slovenia, Sweden, UK, USA.
IGO Relations Cooperation with Ministries of Agriculture of member countries. [2017.10.15/XD5772/**E**]

♦ **LIPP** Ligue internationale pour la protection des primates (#14641)
♦ Liptako-Gourma Integrated Development Authority (no recent information)
♦ Liqued Gas Europe The European LPG Association / see Liquid Gas Europe (#16488)

♦ Liquid Gas Europe 16488

Office Manager Rue de la Loi 38, 1000 Brussels, Belgium. T. +3228931120. Fax +3228931129. E-mail: info@liquidgaseurope.eu.
URL: https://liquidgaseurope.eu/

History 25 Nov 1968, Paris (France). Former names and other names: *European Liquefied Petroleum Gas Association* – former; *Association européenne des gaz de pétrole liquéfiés (AEGPL)* – former; *Europäischer Flüssiggasverband* – former; *Liqued Gas Europe The European LPG Association* – alias. Registration: Banque-Carrefour des Entreprises, No/ID: 0879.660.039, Start date: 28 Feb 2006; EU Transparency Register, No/ID: 63503202933-02, Start date: 4 Jan 2010. **Aims** Engage with EU decision-makers and the wider policy community in order to optimize the contribution that LPG, as a clean and immediately available energy source, can make to Europe's *energy* and *environmental* challenges. **Structure** General Assembly (twice a year); Steering Committee (Executive Committee) of up to 9 members; Ad hoc working groups. **Languages** English, French. **Staff** 6.00 FTE, paid. **Activities** Guidance/assistance/consulting; events/meetings. **Events** *European Liquid Gas Congress* Rome (Italy) 2023, *European LPG Congress* Barcelona (Spain) 2022, *Virtual Congress* Brussels (Belgium) 2021, *European LPG Congress* Barcelona (Spain) 2020, *Annual Congress* Amsterdam (Netherlands) 2019. **Publications** *AEGPL Communication* (4 a year). Congress papers; technical recommendations.
Members National associations in 17 countries:
Austria, Belgium, Czechia, Denmark, France, Germany, Hungary, Ireland, Italy, Netherlands, Norway, Poland, Portugal, Slovenia, Spain, Sweden, UK.
Affiliate in 11 countries:
Austria, Belgium, Denmark, France, Germany, Italy, Luxembourg, Norway, Portugal, Sweden, UK.
Consultative Status Consultative status granted from: *ECOSOC (#05331)* (Ros A). **IGO Relations** Recognized by: *European Commission (EC, #06633)*. **NGO Relations** Member of (3): *European Policy Centre (EPC, #08240)*; *Federation of European and International Associations Established in Belgium (FAIB, #09508)*; *Mobility for Prosperity in Europe (MPE, #16839)*. Cooperates with (2): *Comité européen de normalisation (CEN, #04162)*; *International Organization for Standardization (ISO, #14473)*. Associate partner of: *Intergroup on Rural, Mountainous and Remote Areas (RUMRA)*. [2023/XD0804/**D**]

♦ LIRC / see David M Kennedy Center for International Studies

♦ LIRMA / see International Underwriting Association (#15748)

♦ LIRNEasia 16489

Contact 12 Balcombe Place, Colombo, 08, Sri Lanka. T. +94112671160. Fax +94112675212. E-mail: helani@lirneasia.net – info@lirneasia.net.
URL: http://lirneasia.net/

History 2004. Registered in accordance with the law of Sri Lanka, Apr 2008. **Aims** Catalyze policy change through research to improve people's lives in the emerging Asia Pacific by facilitating their use of hard and soft *infrastructures* through use of knowledge, information and technology. **Structure** Board of Directors; International Advisory Board; CEO. **Languages** English. **Staff** 25.00 FTE, paid. **Finance** Funded by: *Department for International Development (DFID, inactive)*; *Ford Foundation (#09858)*; *International Bank for Reconstruction and Development (IBRD, #12317)* (World Bank); *International Development Research Centre (IDRC, #13162)*; *Open Society Foundations (OSF, #17763)*. **Activities** Research and development; training/education; capacity building; knowledge management/information dissemination. **Publications** Research papers; books. **NGO Relations** Member of: *Alliance for Affordable Internet (A4AI, #00651)*; *International Communication Association (ICA, #12814)*. Partners with: *International Telecommunications Society (ITS, #15671)*; *Regional Dialogue on the Information Society (#18777)*; *Research ICT Africa Network (RIA)*.
[2019.06.25/XJ4812/**D**]

♦ LIRS – Lutheran Immigration and Refugee Service (internationally oriented national body)

♦ LISA Consortium 16490

Contact Albert Einstein Inst Hannover, Callinstr 38, 30167 Hannover, Germany. T. +495117622229. Fax +495117622784.
URL: https://www.lisamission.org/

History Original title: *eLISA Consortium*. **Aims** Prepare, launch and operate the LISA *space mission* for the observation of low-frequency gravitational waves. **Structure** Executive Board; Consortium Board; Steering Committee; Working Groups. **Languages** English. **Finance** Funded by: *European Space Agency (ESA, #08798)* and its Member State agencies; NASA.
Members Full in 13 countries:
Denmark, France, Germany, Hungary, Italy, Netherlands, Portugal, Romania, Spain, Sweden, Switzerland, UK, USA.
IGO Relations *European Space Agency (ESA, #08798)*. [2017.10.26/XJ7416/**E**]

♦ Lisbon Agreement – Cooperation Agreement for the Protection of North-East Atlantic Coasts and Waters Against Pollution (1990 treaty)
♦ Lisbon Agreement – Lisbon Agreement for the Protection of Appellations of Origin and Their International Registration (1958 treaty)
♦ Lisbon Agreement for the Protection of Appellations of Origin and Their International Registration (1958 treaty)

♦ Lisbon Council for Economic Competitiveness and Social Renewal (Lisbon Council) 16491

Pres Intl Press Ctr, Residence Palace, Block C, Rue de la Loi 155, 1040 Brussels, Belgium. T. +3226479575. Fax +3226409828.
CEO address not obtained.
URL: http://www.lisboncouncil.net/

History 2003, Belgium. Registration: No/ID: 0860.905.088, Start date: 7 Oct 2003, Belgium; EU Transparency Register, No/ID: 6766950469-32, Start date: 5 Oct 2008. **Aims** Define and articulate mature, holistic and evidence-based strategies for managing current and future challenges; seek strategies based on inclusion, opportunity and sustainability that will make the benefits of modernization and technological advancement available to all citizens. **Structure** General Assembly; Board of Directors. ,. **Languages** English. **Events** *European Summit for Government Transformation* Brussels (Belgium) 2012. **Publications** *Lisbon Council Newsletter*. Annual Report. **NGO Relations** Member of (1): *Global Trade and Innovation Policy Alliance (GTIPA)*.
[2020/XJ4760/**E**]

♦ **Lisbon Council** Lisbon Council for Economic Competitiveness and Social Renewal (#16491)
♦ **Lisbon Union** Union for the Protection of Appellations of Origin and their International Registration (#20474)
♦ LISDINYS / see Jus Semper Global Alliance
♦ LISSAPAC / see International Library and Information Science Society (#14038)
♦ LISSSD – Lancefield International Symposium on Streptococci and Streptoccocal Diseases (meeting series)
♦ **LISULF** Ligue internationale des scientifiques pour l'usage de la langue française (#16479)
♦ LITCA – International Licensing, Innovation and Technology Consultants' Association (inactive)
♦ LITE-Africa – Leadership Initiative for Transformation and Empowerment (internationally oriented national body)
♦ Literacy Bridge / see Amplio
♦ Literacy and Evangelism International (internationally oriented national body)
♦ Literacy Research Centre / see International Literacy Institute
♦ Pro-Literacy Worldwide / see ProLiteracy Worldwide
♦ Literary Academy of Esperanto (no recent information)

♦ Literature Across Frontiers (LAF) 16492

Dir Mercator Inst for Media/Languages/Culture, Dept of Theatre/Film/Television Studies, Aberystwyth Univ, Aberystwyth, SY23 1NN, UK. T. +441612490235. Fax +441612490210.
URL: http://www.lit-across-frontiers.org/

History 2001. **Aims** Advance European cultural exchange in the field of literature and translation through multilateral cooperation. **Finance** Supported by Culture Programme of *European Commission (EC, #06633)*. **Activities** and projects creating opportunities for international literary collaborations. Researches, challenges and debates policy in the field of literature and translation. Offers translator training and skills development. Participates in international book fairs, literature festivals and fora. Organizes conferences, seminars and workshops. **Publications** *Transcript – European Internet Review of Books and Writing* – online magazine. **IGO Relations** Member of: *Anna Lindh Euro-Mediterranean Foundation for the Dialogue between Cultures (Anna Lindh Foundation, #00847)* Network. **NGO Relations** Member of: *Culture Action Europe (CAE, #04981)*; *European Civil Society Platform for Multilingualism (ECSPM, #06569)*. [2012.11.22/XJ6174/**E**]

♦ Lithuanians' World Centre for Advancement of Culture, Science and Education (Lithuanians' World Centre) 16493

Pasaulio Lietuviu Kulturos, Mokslo ir Šietimo Centras

Main office S Daukanto g 11 antras aukstas, Kaunas, Lithuania. T. +37037321320. Fax +37037320988. E-mail: info@lwc.lt.
URL: http://www.lwc.lt/

History 1989, USSR. 1989, Kaunas (USSR). **Aims** Preserve and develop Lithuanian national culture. **Structure** 2 Directors (one in Lithuania; one abroad). **Languages** English, Lithuanian. **Staff** 15.00 FTE, paid. **Finance** Members' dues. Other sources: donations; income from activities. **Activities** Events/meetings; publishing activities.
Members Individuals (Full and Supporting) in 6 countries:
Australia, Canada, Lithuania, Poland, UK, USA. [2011/XE0235/v/**E**]

♦ **Lithuanians' World Centre** Lithuanians' World Centre for Advancement of Culture, Science and Education (#16493)
♦ Little Apostles of Redemption (religious order)

♦ LittleBigSouls (LBS) 16494

CEO/Founder UK Office, 15 Abroath Gardens, Orton Northgate, Peterborough, PE2 6BS, UK. T. +448453721922. E-mail: info@littlebigsoulsghana.com.
URL: http://littlebigsoulsghana.com/

History A charitable non-profit organization. Also referred to as *LittleBigSouls International*. Incorporated in the UK, Nigeria, Ghana and South Africa. **Aims** Promote the health of *babies*; reduce *death* and *disability* for pre-term babies born in *Africa*. **Languages** English. **Staff** Paid and voluntary. **Activities** Advocacy/lobbying/activism; healthcare; financial and/or material support. **Members** Worldwide membership. Membership countries not specified. **NGO Relations** *European Foundation for the Care of Newborn Infants (EFCNI, #07344)*. Founding member of: *World Prematurity Network (#21736)*. [2021/XJ4549/**F**]

♦ LittleBigSouls International / see LittleBigSouls (#16494)
♦ Little Brothers of the Good Shepherd (religious order)
♦ Little Brothers of Jesus (religious order)
♦ Little Brothers of Mary (religious order)
♦ Little Company of Mary (religious order)
♦ Little Entente Treaty (1921 treaty)
♦ Little League Baseball (internationally oriented national body)
♦ Little League International Baseball and Softball / see Little League Baseball
♦ Little Missionary Sisters of Charity (religious order)
♦ Little Sisters of the Assumption (religious order)
♦ Little Sisters of the Holy Family (religious order)
♦ Little Sisters of the Holy Family, Verona (religious order)
♦ Little Sisters of Jesus (religious order)
♦ Little Sisters of the Poor (religious order)
♦ Little Sisters of the Poor and Aged (religious order)
♦ Little Sisters of the Sacred-Heart of Charles de Foucauld (religious order)
♦ Little Sisters of Saint Francis (religious order)
♦ Little Work of Divine Providence (religious order)
♦ LitWorld (internationally oriented national body)
♦ Liu Institute for Global Issues (internationally oriented national body)

♦ Live DMA European Network 16495

Coordinator 35 rue Crucy, 44000 Nantes, France. T. +33767005989.
URL: http://www.live-dma.eu/

History Set up Oct 2012. Registered in accordance with French law. **Aims** Listen to and promote the interests of live popular *music artists* in the broadest sense of the word; function as spokesperson for the European music venues and festivals for all artistic, *cultural*, social, political and economic issues. **Structure** Board. **Languages** English. **Staff** 2.00 FTE, paid. **Finance** Members' dues. Support from: Creative Europe; Erasmus+. Annual budget: about euro 185,000. **Activities** Advocacy/lobbying/activism; awareness raising; capacity building; events/meetings; guidance/assistance/consulting: networking/liaising; research/documentation. **Publications** Survey results.
Members Full: live music associations (17) in 13 countries:
Belgium, Denmark, France, Germany, Italy, Lithuania, Netherlands, Norway, Spain, Sweden, Switzerland, Türkiye, UK.
NGO Relations Member of: *European Alliance for Culture and the Arts (#05866)*; *European Music Council (EMC, #07837)*. [2017.10.11/XM4839/**F**]

♦ Live Music Now (LMN) 16496

Musique vivante d'aujourd'hui

Dir Intl Development 14 Lennox Street, Edinburgh, EH4 1QA, UK. T. +441313326356.
URL: http://www.livemusicnow.org.uk/

History 1977, London (UK), by Sir Yehudi Menuhin. UK Registered Charity. **Aims** Bring live music into everyday life of the community; provide performing experience, training and support to young and emerging professional *musicians*. **Languages** English. **Staff** 15.00 FTE, paid. **Finance** Public funding; private donations; charitable donations; earned income. **Activities** Events/meeting.
Members National directors and branches in 10 countries and territories:
Austria, Chile, Denmark, France, Germany, Ireland, Netherlands, Scotland, Switzerland, UK, USA. [2019.12.20/XF5060/**F**]

♦ Liver Intensive Care Group of Europe (LICAGE) 16497

Sec/Treas Dept of Anesthesia, Univ Medical Center Groningen, Hanzeplein 1, 9713 GZ Groningen, Netherlands.
Pres address not obtained.
Communications Officer address not obtained.
URL: https://licage.eu/

History 1987, UK. **Events** *Joint International Congress* Rotterdam (Netherlands) 2023, *Joint International Congress* Istanbul (Turkey) 2022, *Joint International Congress* Florence (Italy) 2021, *Joint International Congress* Istanbul (Turkey) 2020, *Meeting* Edinburgh (UK) 2019. **NGO Relations** Joint meetings with: *European Liver and Intestine Transplant Association (ELITA, #07705)*. [2022/XE2486/**E**]

♦ Liver Patients International (LPI) 16498

Registered Address Dreve du Pressoir 38, 1190 Brussels, Belgium. E-mail: info@liverpatients.international – liverpatientsinternational@gmail.com.
URL: https://liverpatientsinternational.org/

History 2019. Registration: Banque-Carrefour des Entreprises, No/ID: 0740.852.247, Start date: 3 Nov 2019, Belgium. **Aims** Improve care and treatment for people affected by, or at risk of, a liver condition. **Structure** General Assembly; Board of Directors. **Finance** Sources: members' dues.
Members Organizations in countries:
Argentina, Austria, Bulgaria, Germany, Greece, Italy, Netherlands, North Macedonia, Portugal, Romania, Switzerland, UK, USA.
Global Liver Institute (GLI).
NGO Relations Cooperates with (6): *ACHIEVE (#00068)*; *Correlation – European Harm Reduction Network (C-EHRN, #04848)*; *European Association for the Study of the Liver (EASL, #06233)*; *European Reference Networks (ERN, #08337)*; *Global Liver Institute (GLI)*; *Hepatitis B and C Public Policy Association (#10910)*.
[2021/AA2335/**D**]

♦ Liverpool School of Tropical Medicine (internationally oriented national body)

♦ Livestock Emergency Guidelines and Standards (LEGS) 16499

Coordinator c/o Vetwork UK, Vesey Farm, Little Clacton Road, Great Holland, CO13 0EX, UK. E-mail: coordinator@livestock-emergency.net.
URL: http://www.livestock-emergency.net/

History 2009. **Aims** Offer a set of international guidelines and standards for design, implementation and assessment of livestock interventions to assist people affected by humanitarian crises. **Structure** Steering Group of 6 members from *International Committee of the Red Cross (ICRC, #12799)*, *FAO (#09260)*, *African Union (AU, #00488)*, *Overseas Development Institute (ODI)*, Sphere India, Vetwork UK and *Feinstein International Center (FIC)*. Coordinator. **Languages** Arabic, English, French, Spanish. **Staff** 1.50 FTE, paid. **Finance** Donations, including from: *African Union (AU, #00488)*; *Department for International Development (DFID, inactive)*; *Donkey Sanctuary, The (#05120)*; *ECHO (inactive)*; *Feinstein International Center (FIC)*; *Intergovernmental Authority on Development (IGAD, #11472)* and *FAO (#09260)*; *International Committee of the Red Cross (ICRC, #12799)*; national organizations; *Oxfam GB*; *Trocaire – Catholic Agency for World Development*; *United States Agency for International Development (USAID)*; VSF Belgium. **Activities** Standards/guidelines; training/education. **Publications** Handbook; books; tools; policy briefs; briefing papers. **Members** No formal membership. **NGO Relations** Cooperates with: *The Sphere Project (#19918)*. Member of: Humanitarian Standards Partnership. [2018.06.08/XJ0741/**F**]

♦ Livestock Environmental Assessment and Performance Partnership (LEAP) 16500

Partenariat pour l'évaluation et la performance environnementales de l'élevage – Alianza sobre evaluación ambiental y desempeño ecológico de la ganadería

Secretariat c/o FAO Headquarters, Viale delle Terme di Caracalla, 00153 Rome RM, Italy. E-mail: livestock-partnership@fao.org.
URL: http://www.fao.org/partnerships/leap/en/

History Consultative process started Oct 2010. Launched 2012. **Aims** Improve the environmental performance of livestock supply chains, whilst ensuring its economic and social viability. **Structure** Steering Committee, composed of 3 stakeholder groups: Governments; Private Sector; Civil Society and Non-Governmental Organizations. Secretariat, hosted by Animal Production and Health Division of *FAO (#09260)*. Technical Advisory Groups (TAG). **Activities** Guidance/assistance/consulting; knowledge management/information dissemination; networking/liaising.
Members Governments (6):
France, Ireland, Italy, Netherlands, New Zealand, Switzerland.
Private sector – business associations include 8 organizations listed in this Yearbook:
African Union for Scientific Development (AUSD, inactive); Health for Animals (#10870); International Council of Tanners (ICT, #13084); International Dairy Federation (IDF, #13128); International Feed Industry Federation (IFIF, #13581); International Meat Secretariat (IMS, #14125); International Poultry Council (IPC, #14628); International Wool Textile Organisation (IWTO, #15904).
NGOs and CSOs include 5 organizations listed in this Yearbook:
International NGO/CSO Planning Committee for Food Sovereignty (IPC, #14365); International Union for Conservation of Nature and Natural Resources (IUCN, #15766); World Alliance of Mobile Indigenous Peoples (WAMIP); World Vision International (WVI, #21904); World Wide Fund for Nature (WWF, #21922).
Observer organizations (5):
European Commission (EC, #06633); International Organization for Standardization (ISO, #14473); MICCA; *OIE – World Organisation for Animal Health (#17703); UNEP (#20299).*
Organizations having signed the Partnership Agreement, include 3 organizations listed in this Yearbook:
League for Pastoral Peoples and Endogenous Livestock Development (LPP); OIE; *The Sustainability Consortium (TSC, #20049).* [2020/XM6171/y/**E**]

♦ Live Working Association (LWA) 16501

Pres c/o PTPiREE, ul Wolynska 22, 60-637 Poznań, Poland. E-mail: ptpiree@ptpiree.pl.
URL: http://www.icolim2014.org/

Aims Promote development of methods of live working in *power* networks and *switchyards.* **Structure** Steering Committee; Technical Committee. Officers: President; Vice-President; Chairman; Secretary. **Languages** English, French. **Activities** *International Conference on Live Maintenance (ICOLM).* **Events** *ICOLIM : Biennial Conference on Live Maintenance / Conference* Budapest (Hungary) 2014, *Conference* Zagreb (Croatia) 2011, *ICOLIM : biennial conference on live maintenance / Conference* Torun (Poland) 2008, *ICOLIM : biennial conference on live maintenance / Conference* Prague (Czech Rep) 2006, *ICOLIM : biennial conference on live maintenance / Conference* Bucharest (Romania) 2004.
Members in 8 countries:
Czechia, France, Germany, Hungary, Italy, Portugal, Romania, Spain. [2012/XM0156/**D**]

♦ Living Earth Foundation (internationally oriented national body)
♦ Living Economies Forum (internationally oriented national body)
♦ Living Goods (unconfirmed)

♦ Living Knowledge – The International Science Shop Network 16502

Contact Point Bonn Science Shop, Norbert Steinhaus, Reuterstr 157, 53113 Bonn, Germany. T. +492282016122. E-mail: livingknowledge@wilabonn.de.
URL: http://www.livingknowledge.org/

History 2000. As yet, still functions as a non-registered organization. **Aims** Provide scientific knowledge for citizens in an open, action-oriented and participatory way; bring civil society issues and interests to the scientific discussion; promote co-creation of knowledge among civil society organizations and researchers. **Structure** Open structure. **Languages** English. **Staff** 1.00 FTE, voluntary. **Activities** Events/meetings; knowledge management/information dissemination; projects/programmes. **Events** *Conference* Groningen (Netherlands) 2021, *Enriching science and community engagement* Budapest (Hungary) 2018, *Conference* Dublin (Ireland) 2016, *Conference* Copenhagen (Denmark) 2014, *Conference* Bonn (Germany) 2012. **Publications** *Living Knowledge.*
Members Contact points in 24 countries:
Australia, Austria, Belgium, Canada, China, Cyprus, Denmark, Estonia, France, Germany, Greece, Hungary, Israel, Italy, Latvia, Netherlands, Norway, Portugal, Romania, South Africa, Spain, Sweden, UK, USA.
NGO Relations Member of (1): *Asia-Pacific University – Community Engagement Network (APUCEN, #02072).* [2020.11.17/XJ9042/**F**]

♦ Living Water International (internationally oriented national body)
♦ Living Waters for the World (internationally oriented national body)
♦ Livonian Knights – Livonian Order (inactive)
♦ Livonian Order (inactive)
♦ Livorno Euro Mediterranea / see Fondazione Livorno Euro Mediterranea
♦ LIVOS / see Horizon 2007
♦ LIZADEEL – Ligue de la zone afrique pour la défense des droits des enfants, étudiants et élèves (internationally oriented national body)
♦ Ljubljana Charter on Reforming Health Care in Europe (1996 treaty)
♦ Llamado Mundial a la Acción Contra la Pobreza (#10263)
♦ Llangollen International Musical Eisteddfod (meeting series)
♦ **LLECE** Laboratorio Latinoamericano de Evaluación de la Calidad de la Educación (#16346)
♦ LLILAS – Teresa Lozano Long Institute of Latin American Studies, Austin (internationally oriented national body)
♦ **LLI** LifeLine International (#16465)
♦ LL – International Convention on Load Lines (1966 treaty)
♦ **LLLI** La Leche League International (#16433)
♦ **LLLP** Lifelong Learning Platform – European Civil Society for Education (#16466)
♦ LLMC – Convention on Limitation of Liability for Maritime Claims (1976 treaty)
♦ **LLRN** Labour Law Research Network (#16215)
♦ **LMA** Loan Market Association (#16503)
♦ LMA-MENA – Leisure Marine Association-MENA (unconfirmed)
♦ **LMGA** Lifestyle Medical Global Alliance (#16468)
♦ **LMHI** Liga Medicorum Homoeopathica Internationalis (#16471)
♦ **LMN** Live Music Now (#16496)
♦ LMU – Latin Monetary Union (inactive)
♦ LNDE – European Federation Lesch-Nyhan Disease (unconfirmed)
♦ **LNI** Legal Network International (#16439)
♦ LN – Leather Naturally (unconfirmed)
♦ LN – LifeNet International (internationally oriented national body)
♦ LNN / see Ledernes Netvaerk i Norden (#16434)
♦ **LNN** Ledernes Netvaerk i Norden (#16434)

♦ Loan Market Association (LMA) 16503

Chief Exec 10 Upper Bank Street, London, E14 5JJ, UK. T. +442070066007. Fax +442070063423. E-mail: lma@lma.eu.com.
URL: http://www.lma.eu.com/

History 1996. **Aims** Improve liquidity, efficiency and transparency in the primary and secondary syndicated loan markets in Europe, the Middle East and Africa (EMEA). **Structure** Board. **Publications** *LMANEWS.* [2020.06.22/XM8023/**D**]

♦ LOBBY / see European Women's Lobby (#09102)
♦ Lobby européen des femmes (#09102)

♦ Local Agenda 21 (LA21) 16504

Dir ICLEI World Secretariat, Kaiser Friedrich Strasse 7, 53113 Bonn, Germany. T. +4922897629900. Fax +4922897629901. E-mail: iclei@iclei.org.
URL: http://www.iclei.org/index.php?id=798

History within the framework of *Local Governments for Sustainability (ICLEI, #16507)*, to promote *Global Action Plan for Environment and Development in the 21st Century (Agenda 21, inactive)* at the local level. **Activities** Conducts international surveys on local authority response to Agenda 21; as of 2001, an estimated 6,000 communities have engaged in LA21 processes. Organizes: 'Incentive Grants Program (IGP)' through the 'Open Society Institute', New York NY (USA); *Local Authorities Self-Assessment of Local Agenda 21 (LASALA)*, coordinated through ICLEI European secretariat as a Europe-wide project identifying eco-efficient urban management as a contribution to *European Sustainable Cities and Towns Campaign (#08863)*, co-funded by DG Research of the European Commission; training courses in a joint project with *Union of the Baltic Cities (UBC, #20366)* and Åbo Akademi University, Turku (Finland); *LA21 Charters Project* (with IULA), establishing North-South partnerships for mutual assistance; capacity building for UNCHS Global Urban Indicators Project; *LA21 in Latin America Network (inactive); 'Asia Pacific Mayors' Action Plan for Sustainable Development and Local Agenda 21'.* ICLEI European Secretariat *'AQUA'* project supports integration of water protection into the LA 21 process. **Publications** *Asia-Pacific Local Agenda 21 Resource Guide; Best Practices of Innovative Models of Urban Governance; European LA21 Evaluation Report; LA21 Self-Assessment Manual; Local Agenda 21 Workshop Modules.* **IGO Relations** *European Commission (EC, #06633); United Nations Human Settlements Programme (UN-Habitat, #20572).* **NGO Relations** *Stakeholder Forum for a Sustainable Future (SF); World Organization of United Cities and Local Governments (UCLG, #21695).* [2012/XF6137/**E**]

♦ Local Authorities International Environmental Organization (#16192)

♦ Local Employment Trading/Energy Transfer System (LETSystems) . 16505

Address not obtained.
URL: http://www.gmlets.u-net.com/

History Nov 1987, Maleny (Australia). **Aims** Liberate wealth in local communities on the premise that this *wealth* lies in goods and services rather than money. **Structure** Not an organization but a community-based economic system, part of *Community Exchange System (CES, #04399).* **Finance** Members' dues. **Activities** Cashless trading between members for goods and services. Community credits and debits (LETS) are recorded for each individual on those transactions, and no interest is charged or paid on those transactions. Organizes annual national conference. **Publications** Online newsletter (4 a year).
Members Systems (several hundred) in 10 countries:
Australia, Brazil, Canada, Japan, Netherlands, New Zealand, South Africa, Sweden, UK, USA. [2013/XF2733/**F**]

♦ Local Futures 16506

USA Office PO Box 36, East Hardwick VT 05836, USA. T. +18024723505. E-mail: info@localfutures.org.
UK Office PO Box 239, Totnes, TQ9 9DP, UK.
URL: http://www.localfutures.org/

History 1975. Former names and other names: *International Society for Ecology and Culture (ISEC)* – former (2014). **Aims** Work to renew ecological, social and spiritual well-being by promoting a systemic shift towards localization. **Languages** English. **Staff** 0.50 FTE, paid. **Finance** Private donations. **Activities** Events/meetings; advocacy/lobbying/activism; guidance/assistance/consulting. **Events** *Economics of Happiness Conference* Jeonju (Korea Rep) 2022, *Economics of Happiness Conference* Jeonju (Korea Rep) 2021, *Economics of Happiness Conference* Jeonju (Korea Rep) 2020, *Economics of Happiness Conference* Jeonju (Korea Rep) 2019, *International Economics of Happiness Conference* Santa Fe, NM (USA) 2017. **Publications** *Ecologist* – magazine. Annual Report; books.
Members Full in 9 countries:
Australia, France, Germany, India, Japan, Korea Rep, Thailand, UK, USA.
NGO Relations Member of (1): *Wellbeing Economy Alliance (WEAll, #20856).* [2020/XD8084/**D**]

♦ Local Government International Bureau (internationally oriented national body)

♦ Local Governments for Sustainability (ICLEI) 16507

SG Kaiser-Friedrich-Str 7, 53113 Bonn, Germany. T. +4922897629900. Fax +4922897629901. E-mail: secretary.general@iclei.org – iclei.ws@iclei.org.
URL: http://www.iclei.org/

History 8 Sep 1990, New York, NY (USA). Founded when Charter was adopted at World Congress of Local Governments for a Sustainable Future, under the auspices of *UNEP (#20299).* Former names and other names: *International Council for Local Environmental Initiatives (ICLEI)* – former; *Conseil international pour les initiatives écologiques locales* – former; *Consejo Internacional para las Iniciativas Ambientales Locales* – former; *Internationale Rat für Kommunale Umweltinitiativen* – former. **Aims** Influence sustainability policy and drive local action for low emission, nature-based, equitable, resilient and circular development. **Structure** World Congress (every 3 years); Global Executive Committee; Council; World Secretariat in Bonn (Germany); Regional Secretariats; Country Offices; Subsidiary Offices. **Languages** Chinese, English, Filipino, French, German, Indonesian, Japanese, Korean, Mongolian, Portuguese, Spanish. **Staff** 30.00 FTE, paid. **Finance** Sources: grants; members' dues. **Activities** Capacity building; events/meetings; knowledge management/information dissemination. Initiatives include: *EcoMobility Alliance (#05308)*; EcoLogistics Community. **Events** *ICLEI World Congress (The Malmö Summit)* Malmö (Sweden) 2022, *Research Symposium* Malmö (Sweden) 2022, *Zero Carbon City International Forum* Tokyo (Japan) 2022, *ICLEI World Congress (The Malmö Summit) Launching Meeting* 2021, *Zero Carbon City International Forum* Tokyo (Japan) 2021. **Publications** *ICLEI iNews* (24 a year). *ICLEI Case Studies.* Annual Report; Global Report; briefing sheets; ICLEI Papers.
Members Local governments and local government associations; Associate partners; Institutional partners; Corporate partners. Members in 96 countries and territories:
Albania, Argentina, Armenia, Australia, Austria, Bangladesh, Belgium, Benin, Bhutan, Bolivia, Botswana, Brazil, Bulgaria, Burkina Faso, Burundi, Cameroon, Canada, Chile, China, Colombia, Costa Rica, Côte d'Ivoire, Croatia, Cyprus, Czechia, Denmark, Ecuador, Estonia, Eswatini, Ethiopia, Fiji, Finland, France, Germany, Ghana, Greece, Honduras, Hong Kong, Hungary, Iceland, India, Indonesia, Ireland, Italy, Japan, Jordan, Kenya, Korea Rep, Liberia, Luxembourg, Malawi, Malaysia, Maldives, Mali, Mauritania, Mauritius, Mexico, Mongolia, Morocco, Mozambique, Namibia, Nepal, Netherlands, New Zealand, Niger, Nigeria, Norway, Palestine, Peru, Philippines, Poland, Portugal, Romania, Rwanda, Saudi Arabia, Senegal, Serbia, Slovenia, Solomon Is, South Africa, Spain, Sri Lanka, Sweden, Switzerland, Taiwan, Tanzania UR, Thailand, Togo, Türkiye, Uganda, UK, Uruguay, USA, Vanuatu, Zambia, Zimbabwe.
Consultative Status Consultative status granted from: *ECOSOC (#05331)* (Special); *UNEP (#20299).* **IGO Relations** Accredited by (3): *ECOSOC (#05331); Green Climate Fund (GCF, #10714); United Nations Framework Convention on Climate Change – Secretariat (UNFCCC, #20564).* Memorandum of Understanding with (3): *UNEP (#20299); United Nations Human Settlements Programme (UN-Habitat, #20572); United Nations Office for Disaster Risk Reduction (UNDRR, #20595).* Member of (1): *NDC Partnership (#16964)* (Associate). Partner of (1): *Global Biodiversity Information Facility (GBIF, #10250).* Cooperates with (1): *UNDP (#20292).* **NGO Relations** Member of (8): *Climate Action Network (CAN, #03999); Climate and Clean Air Coalition (CCAC, #04010); European Network for Community-Led Initiatives on Climate Change and Sustainability (ECOLISE, #07882); GEF CSO Network (GCN, #10087); Global Alliance for Buildings and Construction (GlobalABC, #10187); Global Taskforce of Local and Regional Governments (Global Taskforce, #10622); International Union for Conservation of Nature and Natural Resources (IUCN, #15766); Sustainable Sanitation Alliance (SuSanA, #20066).* Participant in: *Global Partnership on Local and Subnational Action for Biodiversity (#10536).* Represented on the Board of: *International Green Purchasing Network (IGPN, #13736).* Joint projects with: *World Organization of United Cities and Local Governments (UCLG, #21695).* Cooperates with: *World Business Council for Sustainable Development (WBCSD, #21254); World Economic Forum (WEF, #21367).* Partner of: *C40 (#03391); Global Footprint Network (#10367);* IUCN; *World Mayors Council on Climate Change (WMCCC, #21643).* [2022/XF2316/y/**B**]

♦ Local Urban Development European Network (LUDEN) 16508

Dir Rue Vieux Marché aux Grains 48, 1000 Brussels, Belgium. T. +3225244545. Fax +3225244431.
URL: http://www.ludenet.org/

History 1989, as *Quartiers en crise*, an exchange programme for professionals in deprived urban areas. From 1991 to 1994, a network within the framework of *Regions and Cities of Europe (RECITE Programme, inactive).* Subsequently changed title to *Association for the Regeneration of Neighbourhoods in Crisis – Association internationale pour la revitalization des quartiers en crise*, 1994, when became a formal association registered in accordance with Belgian law. Later known as *Quartiers en Crise – European Regeneration Areas Network (QEC-ERAN).* Present name adopted, 2010. **Aims** Act as a network for mutual cooperation which focuses on major transitions that are taking place across the EU and touch cities, towns and the surrounding countryside.

Structure General Assembly (annual); Executive Bureau. **Languages** English, French, Italian. **Staff** 10.00 FTE, paid. **Finance** Members' dues. Support from *European Commission (EC, #06633)* through *European Regional Development Fund (ERDF, #08342)* and other EU funds. **Activities** Research and development; training/education; advocacy/lobbying/activism. **Events** *General Assembly* Modena (Italy) 2011, *General Assembly* Bobigny (France) 2010, *Conference / General Assembly* Brussels (Belgium) 2009, *Workshop* Brussels (Belgium) 2007, *General Assembly* Turin (Italy) 2005. **Publications** Reports. **Members** EU towns, cities, district councils, strategic NGOs, research institutes involved in national, regional and EU policies and programmes concerned with area-based regeneration. Membership countries not specified.
[2015/XF2775/**D**]

- ♦ **LoCARNet** Low Carbon Asia Research Network (#16515)
- ♦ Locarno Agreement Establishing an International Classification for Industrial Design (1968 treaty)
- ♦ **Locarno Union** Union for the International Classification for Industrial Designs (#20416)
- ♦ **LOCOA** Leaders and Organizations of Community Organizations in Asia (#16417)
- ♦ LOD – International Conference on Machine Learning, Optimization, and Data Science (meeting series)
- ♦ LO/FTF Council – Danish Trade Union Council for International Development Cooperation (internationally oriented national body)
- ♦ Loge unie des théosophes (#20512)
- ♦ La Loggia – Centro Internazionale di Scrittura Drammaturgica (internationally oriented national body)
- ♦ La Loggia – International Centre of Dramatic Writing (internationally oriented national body)
- ♦ Logistics Institute – Asia Pacific (internationally oriented national body)
- ♦ Logistics and Supply Chain Management Society (internationally oriented national body)
- ♦ LOG – Luftfahrt ohne Grenzen (internationally oriented national body)
- ♦ LOGMS – International Conference on Logistics and Maritime Systems (meeting series)
- ♦ LogoLink – Learning Initiative on Citizen Participation and Local Governance (internationally oriented national body)
- ♦ LOICZ / see Future Earth Coasts (#10049)
- ♦ Loi type de la CNUDCI sur l'arbitrage commercial international (1985 treaty)
- ♦ Loi type de la CNUDCI sur la conciliation commerciale internationale (2002 treaty)
- ♦ Loka Viyaptha Parisara Neethi Santhanaya (#05503)
- ♦ LOMAR – Libre organisation mondiale d'aide aux réfugiés (internationally oriented national body)
- ♦ Lomé convention – ACP-EEC Convention (1975 treaty)
- ♦ Lomé III – Third ACP-EEC Convention (1984 treaty)
- ♦ Lomé II – Second ACP-EEC Convention (1979 treaty)
- ♦ Lomé IV – Fourth ACP-EEC Convention (1989 treaty)

♦ London Action Plan (LAP) 16509

Address not obtained.
URL: http://londonactionplan.org/

History 11 Oct 2004, London (UK), by government and public agencies from 27 countries. Full title: *LONDON ACTION PLAN – International Cybersecurity Enforcement Network.* **Aims** Promote international spam enforcement cooperation and address spam related problems, such as *online* fraud and deception, phishing, and dissemination of viruses. **Activities** Guidance; training; partnerships. **Events** *Annual Conference* Tokyo (Japan) 2014.
Members Regulatory and Enforcement Authorities from 27 countries and territories:
Australia, Belgium, Brazil, Canada, Chile, China, Denmark, Finland, Hungary, Ireland, Japan, Korea Rep, Latvia, Lithuania, Malaysia, Mexico, Netherlands, New Zealand, Nigeria, Norway, Portugal, Spain, Sweden, Switzerland, Taiwan, UK, USA.
Industry participants in 12 countries:
Australia, Belgium, Canada, Chile, China, France, Germany, Malaysia, Netherlands, Spain, UK, USA.
Included in the above, 2 organizations listed in this Yearbook:
Federation of European Data & Marketing (FEDMA, #09499); Messaging, Malware and Mobile Anti-Abuse Working Group (M3AAWG).
Observers in 4 countries:
Belgium, France, Russia, UK.
Included in the above, 2 organizations listed in this Yearbook:
European Commission (EC, #06633) (DG Information Society and Media); *OECD (#17693)* (DSTI).
IGO Relations Cooperates with: *International Consumer Protection and Enforcement Network (ICPEN, #12930); Internet Governance Forum (IGF, #15950).* [2014/XJ7977/y/**E***]

- ♦ LONDON ACTION PLAN – International Cybersecurity Enforcement Network / see London Action Plan (#16509)
- ♦ London amendment – Amendment to the Montreal Protocol on Substances That Deplete the Ozone Layer, 1990 (1990 treaty)

♦ London Bullion Market Association (LBMA) 16510

Chief Exec 1-2 Royal Exchange Buildings, Royal Exchange, London, EC3V 3LF, UK. T. +442077963067. Fax +442072830030. E-mail: mail@lbma.org.uk.
URL: http://www.lbma.org.uk/

History 1987. Founded by Bank of England. **Aims** Ensure the highest levels of leadership, integrity and transparency for the global precious metals industry by advancing standards and developing market solutions. **Structure** Board. Committees (3): Finance; HR/Remuneration; Executive. **Events** *Global Precious Metals Conference* Lisbon (Portugal) 2022, *Global Precious Metals Conference* Lisbon (Portugal) 2021, *Annual Precious Metals Conference* Lisbon (Portugal) 2020, *Annual Precious Metals Conference* Barcelona (Spain) 2017, *Annual Precious Metals Conference* Singapore (Singapore) 2016. **Publications** *Alchemist* (4 a year) – journal. *Good Delivery Lists.* **Members** Companies (over 140). Membership countries not specified.
[2021/XJ9017/**F**]

- ♦ London Club / see Nuclear Suppliers Group (#17621)
- ♦ London Court of International Arbitration (internationally oriented national body)
- ♦ London Fisheries Convention (1964 treaty)
- ♦ London International College of Homeopathy (internationally oriented national body)
- ♦ London International Development Centre (internationally oriented national body)
- ♦ London International Insurance and Reinsurance Market Association / see International Underwriting Association (#15748)
- ♦ London School of Hygiene and Tropical Medicine (internationally oriented national body)

♦ Long Distance Advisory Council (LDAC) 16511

Conseil Consultatif de Pêche Lointaine – Consejo Consultivo de Flota de Larga Distancia en Aguas No Comunitarias

Exec Sec Calle del Doctor Fleming 7, 2o Dcha, 28036 Madrid, Spain. T. +34914323623. Fax +34914323624. E-mail: secretaria@ldac.eu.
Chair address not obtained.
URL: https://ldac.eu/

History Set up by virtue of *European Commission (EC, #06633)* Council Decision No 585/2004. Became operational May 2007. Recognized by the CFP Regulation (UE) No 1380/2013. Former names and other names: *Long Distance Regional Advisory Group* – former (2004); *Long Distance Advisory Group* – former; *Long Distance Advisory Council in non-EU waters* – legal name. **Aims** Promote participatory governance and stakeholders' involvement and engagement in the conservation of *marine biodiversity* and *sustainable* use of *fishing* resources outside EU waters, including EEZ third countries where EU has signed Sustainable Fisheries Partnership Agreements, and the high seas. **Structure** General Assembly; Executive Committee; Working Groups (5); Ad-hoc Focus Groups; Secretariat. **Languages** English, French, Spanish. **Staff** 3.00 FTE, paid. **Finance** Members' dues. Grant for operation from: *European Commission (EC, #06633).* Permanent funding subject to EU Financial Regulation. **Activities** Events/meetings; knowledge management/information dissemination; guidance/assistance/consulting; networking/liaising; politics/policy/regulatory; projects/programmes; research and development. **Events** *General Assembly* Lisbon (Portugal) 2016, *General Assembly* Dublin (Ireland) 2015, *General Assembly* Lisbon (Portugal) 2014. **Publications** Recommendations; position papers; advice; letters.

Members Organizations representing EU fisheries stakeholders (52) in 12 countries:
Denmark, Estonia, France, Germany, Ireland, Lithuania, Netherlands, Poland, Portugal, Spain, Sweden, UK.
Included in the above, 10 organizations listed in this Yearbook:
Brot für die Welt; Coalition for Fair Fisheries Agreements (CFFA, #04060); Confédération internationale de la pêche sportive (CIPS, #04562); European Bureau for Conservation and Development (EBCD, #06412); European Transport Workers' Federation (ETF, #08941); European Tropical Tuna Trade and Industry Committee (EUROTHON, #08951); European Union Fish Processors Association (#08989); Oceana; Seas at Risk (SAR, #19189); World Wide Fund for Nature (WWF, #21922).
IGO Relations Partner of: *European Union (EU, #08967)* – H2020 FarFish Project. [2019.12.11/XJ9735/y/**E**]

- ♦ Long Distance Advisory Council in non-EU waters / see Long Distance Advisory Council (#16511)
- ♦ Long Distance Advisory Group / see Long Distance Advisory Council (#16511)
- ♦ Long Distance Regional Advisory Group / see Long Distance Advisory Council (#16511)
- ♦ The Long Run (unconfirmed)
- ♦ A Long-Term Biodiversity, Ecosystem and Ecosystem Services Research and Awareness Network / see Alternet (#00756)

♦ Long-term Infrastructure Investors Association (LTIIA) 16512

Contact 4 place de l'Opéra, 75002 Paris, France. E-mail: info@ltiia.org.
URL: http://www.ltiia.org/

History 2014, Paris (France). Registered in accordance with French law. **Aims** Work with a wide range of stakeholders, including infrastructure investors, policy-makers and academia, on supporting long-term, responsible deployment of private capital to public infrastructure around the world. **Structure** General Meeting; Board of Directors; General Secretariat. **Languages** English. **Staff** 4.00 FTE, paid. **Finance** Sources: members' dues. **Activities** Advocacy/lobbying/activism; events/meetings; research/documentation; standards/guidelines; training/education. **Events** *Annual Meeting* Washington, DC (USA) 2015, *Annual Meeting* Paris (France) 2014. **Publications** *Environmental, Social and Governance Handbook for Long-Term Investors in Infrastructure* (2nd ed 2017). Articles. **Members** Institutional investors and fund managers (43), including 1 organization listed in this Yearbook: **NGO Relations** *Cities Climate Finance Leadership Alliance (CCFLA, #03952); European Association of Long-Term Investors (ELTI, #06112); Global Infrastructure Basel Foundation (GIB Foundation, #10418); Global Infrastructure Connectivity Alliance (GICA, #10419); Long-Term Investors Club (LTIC, #16513).* [2017.10.30/XJ9428/**C**]

♦ Long-Term Investors Club (LTIC) 16513

SG c/o European Investment Bank, Bvd Konrad Adenauer 98-100, L-2950 Luxembourg, Luxembourg. E-mail: ltic-secretary-general@eib.org.
URL: http://www.ltic.org/

History Set up 2009, by Caisse des Dépots (France), Cassa Depositi e Prestiti (Italy), *European Investment Bank (EIB, #07599)* and Kreditanstalt für Wiederaufbau (Germany). **Aims** Bring together major worldwide institutions to emphasize common identity as long-term investors, encourage cooperation and foster the right conditions for long-term investments in promoting growth. **Structure** Steering Committee. **Languages** English. **Staff** 0.50 FTE, paid; 1.00 FTE, voluntary. **Finance** Members' dues. Annual budget (2016): about euro 110,000. **Events** *Conference* Rabat (Morocco) 2013, *Conference* Luxembourg 2012, *Conference* Berlin (Germany) 2011, *Conference* Rome (Italy) 2009.
Members Institutions (18) in 14 countries:
Brazil, Canada, China, France, Germany, India, Italy, Japan, Luxembourg, Morocco, Poland, Russia, Spain, Türkiye.
Included in the above, 2 organizations listed in this Yearbook:
European Investment Bank (EIB, #07599); Japan Bank for International Cooperation (JBIC).
IGO Relations *OECD (#17693).* **NGO Relations** *Eurofi (#05679); Long-term Infrastructure Investors Association (LTIIA, #16512); European Association of Long-Term Investors (ELTI, #06112); World Economic Forum (WEF, #21367).* [2016.10.28/XJ9425/y/**F**]

- ♦ Long-term Trade Agreement (1967 treaty)
- ♦ Longview Foundation for Education in World Affairs and International Understanding (internationally oriented national body)

♦ The Loomba Trust – The Loomba Foundation 16514

Headquarters Loomba House, 622 Western Ave, London, W3 0TF, UK. T. +442081020351. E-mail: safdar@theloombafoundation.org.
USA Office c/o Gutenberg Communications, 555 Eighth Ave, Suite 1002, New York NY 10018, USA. T. +16467756314.
URL: http://www.theloombafoundation.org/

History 26 Jun 1997, UK. International sister organizations founded: India 1999; Scotland 2002; USA 2005; South Africa 2006. Former names and other names: *Shrimati Pushpa Wati Loomba Memorial Trust* – former. Registration: Charity Register, No/ID: 1064988, England and Wales. **Aims** Promote fundamental freedoms and human rights of *widows* and their children around the world; empower poor, impoverished widows so they can earn a living and lead a life of dignity; provide educational support to children of poor widows, suffering through poverty, illiteracy, GHIV/AIDS, conflict and social injustice. **Structure** President; Patron-in-Chief; Founder Chairman/Trustee. **Languages** English. **Staff** 10.00 FTE, paid. **Finance** Fundraising; funding from Loomba family. **Activities** Training/education; projects/programmes; awareness raising; events/meetings; financial and/or material support. **Publications** *20 Years of TLF* (2017); *The World Widows Report* (2015); *One Man Walking* (2014); *Hidden Calamity* (2011); *Invisible Forgotten Sufferers* (2010).
Members Individuals in 3 countries:
India, UK, USA.
NGO Relations In partnership with: *Oxfam GB*; Rotary India Literacy Mission (RILM); *Youth Business International (YBI).* [2018.02.26/XJ8229/f/**F**]

- ♦ LORCS / see International Federation of Red Cross and Red Crescent Societies (#13526)
- ♦ Loreto – Institute of the Blessed Virgin Mary, Irish Branch (religious order)
- ♦ LOSI – Law of the Sea Institute (internationally oriented national body)
- ♦ LO-TCO Biståndsnämnd (internationally oriented national body)
- ♦ LO-TCO Council of International Trade Union Cooperation / see LO-TCO Secretariat of International Trade Union Development Cooperation
- ♦ LO-TCO Secretariat of International Trade Union Development Cooperation (internationally oriented national body)
- ♦ Lotus World (internationally oriented national body)
- ♦ Louvain Coopération (internationally oriented national body)
- ♦ Louvain Development / see Louvain Coopération
- ♦ Louvain-développement / see Louvain Coopération
- ♦ Louvain Foundation for Cooperation to Development / see Louvain Coopération
- ♦ To Love Children Educational Foundation International (internationally oriented national body)
- ♦ Love Line / see Samaritans

♦ Low Carbon Asia Research Network (LoCARNet) 16515

Secretariat c/o IGES, 2108-11 Kamiyamaguchi, Hayama KANAGAWA, 240-0115 Japan. Fax +81468553809.
URL: http://lcs-rnet.org/

History Founded Apr 2012, at the "East Asia Low Carbon Growth Partnership Dialogue", following proposal for the Network at the ASEAN+3 Environmental Ministers' Meeting (EMM), Oct 2011, Cambodia, by the Japanese government and *Institute for Global Environmental Strategies (IGES, #11266).* Reports progress to the ASEAN+3 EMM every year. **Aims** Promote research for policies towards low-carbon growth by enabling dialogue between scientists and policy-makers while also encouraging collaboration amongst researchers in-country whose research capacity and scientific knowledge are firmly grounded in their home countries; increase research capacity in the region through knowledge sharing and information exchange in the context of not only north-south cooperation, but also south-south regional cooperation. **Structure** Annual Meeting. Secretariat provided by *Institute for Global Environmental Strategies (IGES, #11266).* **Languages** English. **Activities** Networking/liaising; capacity building; events/meetings. **Events** *Annual Meeting* Bangkok (Thailand) 2017, *International Conference of Low Carbon Asia and Beyond* Bangkok (Thailand) 2017, *Annual Meeting* Bogor (Indonesia) 2014, *Annual Meeting* Yokohama (Japan) 2013, *Annual Meeting* Bangkok (Thailand) 2012. **Publications** Synthesis reports of annual meetings and dialogues.

Members Experts from 4 ASEAN countries:
China, India, Japan, Korea Rep. [2019.06.28/XJ7845/**F**]

♦ Low Carbon Technology Partnerships Initiative (LCTPi) 16516

Contact c/o WBCSD, Maison de la Paix, Chemin Eugène-Rigot 2B, CP 2075, 1211 Geneva 1, Switzerland.
URL: http://lctpi.wbcsd.org/

History Set up at *United Nations Framework Convention on Climate Change (UNFCCC, 1992)* – COP21, 2015, Paris (France), under the auspices of *World Business Council for Sustainable Development (WBCSD, #21254).* Developed in coordination with *International Energy Agency (IEA, #13270)* and *Sustainable Development Solutions Network (SDSN, #20054).* **Aims** Accelerate development and scaling up deployment of low-carbon technology solutions to stay below the 2 degrees celcius ceiling. **Structure** Working Groups (6). **Languages** English. **Staff** 15.00 FTE, paid. **Finance** Budget of *World Business Council for Sustainable Development (WBCSD, #21254).* Annual budget for climate-related activities: Swiss Fr 5,000,000. **Activities** Advocacy/lobbying/activism; awareness raising. **Events** *Scaling our impact – connecting businesses and policymakers for low-carbon solutions* Brussels (Belgium) 2017. **Publications** Annual progress report. **Members** Companies (over 180). Membership countries not specified. **NGO Relations** Partners: *International Energy Agency (IEA, #13270); Local Governments for Sustainability (ICLEI, #16507); Sustainable Development Solutions Network (SDSN, #20054); World Business Council for Sustainable Development (WBCSD, #21254).* [2018.10.09/XM5815/**E**]

- ♦ Low Emission Development Strategies Global Partnership / see LEDS Global Partnership (#16435)
- ♦ Low Energy Antiproton Physics Conference (meeting series)
- ♦ Lowenstein Project / see Allard K Lowenstein International Human Rights Project
- ♦ Lower-Middle Income Countries Initiative / see Group of Eleven (#10753)

♦ Low Impact Fishers of Europe (LIFE) 16517

Communications Officer Rue Abbé Cuypers 3, 1040 Brussels, Belgium. T. +3227412433. Fax +3227412412. E-mail: communications@lifeplatform.eu.
URL: http://lifeplatform.eu/

History Registration: Start date: 2014, UK. **Aims** Unite small-scale fishers across Europe to achieve fair fisheries, healthy seas and vibrant communities. **Structure** Management Board; Secretariat, headed by Executive Director. **Languages** English, French, Spanish. **Staff** 7.00 FTE, paid. **Finance** Sources: grants; private foundations. Supported by: *European Commission (EC, #06633); MAVA Foundation.* Annual budget: 400,000 EUR (2016). **Activities** Advocacy/lobbying/activism; capacity building; projects/programmes.
Members Fishermen associations in 15 countries:
Croatia, Cyprus, Denmark, Finland, France, Germany, Ireland, Italy, Latvia, Netherlands, Poland, Romania, Spain, Sweden, UK.
NGO Relations Cooperates with (1): *European Network of Women's Organisations in Fisheries and Aquaculture (AKTEA, #08035).* Also links with national organizations. [2022.02.09/XM6472/**F**]

♦ Low Power Radio Association (LPRA) 16518

Membership Sec c/o Business Synergies Limited, Synergy House, 98 Hornchurch Road, Hornchurch, RM11 1JS, UK. T. +441268755394. E-mail: business.synergies@me.com.
URL: http://lpra.org/

History Registered in accordance with UK law. **Aims** Develop, promote and preserve the interests of all members and provide a better understanding of the Short Range Devices (SRD) industry within the European community. **Structure** Council; Secretariat. **Events** *Radio Solutions Conference* Groenlo (Netherlands) 2019, *Radio Solutions Conference* Groenlo (Netherlands) 2017, *Radio Solutions Conference* Sophia Antipolis (France) 2015.
Members Full in 12 countries:
Austria, Belgium, Canada, Denmark, France, Germany, Italy, Japan, Netherlands, Spain, UK, USA.
NGO Relations Member of (1): *European Telecommunications Standards Institute (ETSI, #08897).* [2020/XJ2138/**D**]

- ♦ Lowy Institute for International Policy (internationally oriented national body)
- ♦ Loyal Orange Association / see Orange Order (#17782)
- ♦ LPC – Linux Plumbers Conference (meeting series)
- ♦ LPE – Let's Promote Europe (unconfirmed)
- ♦ LPF – Lutheran Peace Fellowship (internationally oriented national body)
- ♦ **LPI** Legal Protection International (#16440)
- ♦ **LPI** Life and Peace Institute (#16467)
- ♦ **LPI** Liver Patients International (#16498)
- ♦ LPIS – Library of Political and International Studies (internationally oriented national body)
- ♦ LPM – International Symposium on Laser Precision Microfabrication (meeting series)
- ♦ LPP / see League for Pastoral Peoples and Endogenous Livestock Development
- ♦ LPP – League for Pastoral Peoples and Endogenous Livestock Development (internationally oriented national body)
- ♦ **LPRA** Low Power Radio Association (#16518)
- ♦ **LP&R** International Network on Leave Policies and Research (#14293)
- ♦ **LRAN** Land Research Action Network (#16228)
- ♦ **LRCICA** Regional Centre for International Commercial Arbitration, Lagos (#18756)
- ♦ **LRC** International Chemical Employers Labour Relations Committee (#12541)
- ♦ LRI / see Global Recordings Network
- ♦ LRI / see Gay and Lesbian Rowing Federation (#10079)
- ♦ LRTAP Convention / see Convention on Long-range Transboundary Air Pollution (#04787)
- ♦ LRWC – Lawyers' Rights Watch Canada (internationally oriented national body)
- ♦ LSACECC – Lutheran South-East Asia Christian Education Curriculum Committee (inactive)
- ♦ LSA – Law and Society Association (internationally oriented national body)
- ♦ LSA – Little Sisters of the Assumption (religious order)
- ♦ LSC – International Conference on Advances in Liquid Scintillation Spectrometry (meeting series)
- ♦ **LSC** Liberian Shipowners Council (#16455)
- ♦ LSC – LIGO Scientific Collaboration (internationally oriented national body)
- ♦ LSCMS – Logistics and Supply Chain Management Society (internationally oriented national body)
- ♦ LSCR / see International Federation of Red Cross and Red Crescent Societies (#13526)
- ♦ LSEC – European Network of Security Professionals, Research and Industry (internationally oriented national body)
- ♦ LSF – Levi Strauss Foundation (internationally oriented national body)
- ♦ **LSG** Ligo de Samseksamaj Geesperantistoj (#16475)
- ♦ LSHTM Centre for Global Non Communicable Diseases (internationally oriented national body)
- ♦ LSHTM – London School of Hygiene and Tropical Medicine (internationally oriented national body)
- ♦ LSI – Labour and Socialist International (inactive)
- ♦ LSI – Lynch Syndrome International (internationally oriented national body)
- ♦ **LSI** La Strada International (#20002)
- ♦ LSJF – Sud-ouest sans frontières (internationally oriented national body)
- ♦ LSK – European Light Steel Construction Association (no recent information)
- ♦ LSN – Landmine Survivors Network (internationally oriented national body)
- ♦ LSOSF – Little Sisters of Saint Francis (religious order)
- ♦ LSP – Little Sisters of the Poor (religious order)
- ♦ LSSA – Linguistic Society of Southern Africa (internationally oriented national body)
- ♦ **LSSFN** Latin American Society for Stereotactic and Functional Neurosurgery (#16386)
- ♦ LSST@Europe (meeting series)
- ♦ LSTM – Liverpool School of Tropical Medicine (internationally oriented national body)
- ♦ LTDH – Ligue tunisienne pour la défense des droits de l'homme (internationally oriented national body)
- ♦ **LTER-Europe** European Long-Term Ecosystem Research Network (#07712)
- ♦ **LTIC** Long-Term Investors Club (#16513)
- ♦ **LTIIA** Long-term Infrastructure Investors Association (#16512)
- ♦ **LT-Innovate** Language Technology Industry Association (#16231)
- ♦ **LT** Lucis Trust (#16519)
- ♦ **LTN** The Learning Teacher Network (#16430)
- ♦ Lubavitch Movement / see Chabad Lubavitch (#03844)
- ♦ LUBP – Ligue universelle du bien public (inactive)
- ♦ **LUCCEA** Lutheran Communion in Central and East Africa (#16525)
- ♦ **LuCE** Lung Cancer Europe (#16523)
- ♦ Luce et Vita (religious order)
- ♦ **LUCI** Lighting Urban Community International (#16473)

♦ Lucis Trust (LT) 16519

New York Office 866 UN Plz, Ste 482, New York NY 10017, USA. T. +12122920707. Fax +12122920808. E-mail: worldgoodwill.us@lucistrust.org.
Geneva Office Rue du Stand 40, 1204 Geneva, Switzerland. T. +41227341252. E-mail: geneva@lucistrust.org.
London Office Suite 54, 3 Whitehall Court, London, SW1A 2EF, UK. T. +442078394512 – +442078394513. Fax +442078395575. E-mail: worldgoodwill.uk@londonlucistrust.org.
URL: http://www.lucistrust.org/

History 1922, New York, NY (USA). Founded by Alice A Bailey, as a nonprofit and nonsectarian world service and spiritual organization, sponsoring no special creed or dogma. Registration: Charity Commission, No/ID: 216041, England and Wales; Section 501(c)(3), No/ID: 13-1674445, USA; Swiss Civil Code, No/ID: 080 018 750, Switzerland. **Aims** Help establish right *human relations,* world *cooperation* and *sharing,* and solve immediate problems of progress, through the constructive power of *goodwill;* hold the vision of the Divine Plan before humanity and the possibility of its restoration on earth; mobilize world goodwill by cooperating with and supporting the world service action of individuals, groups and organizations working for right human relations among men and between nations; aid in solving humanity's problems and in establishing right human relations by creating an informed and spiritually oriented public opinion based on goodwill. **Structure** International Board of Trustees, aided by additional elected Officers and members in different countries. **Languages** Dutch, English, French, German, Irish Gaelic, Italian, Russian, Spanish. **Staff** 25.00 FTE, paid. **Finance** Sources: donations; gifts, legacies. No set dues. **Activities** Financial and/or material support; knowledge management/information dissemination; publishing activities; training/education. Activities through: *Arcane School,* set up 1923; Lucis Publishing Companies; *Triangles,* set up 1937; *World Goodwill,* set up 1932: Lucis Productions. **Events** *Conference* Geneva (Switzerland) 1999, *Conference* New York, NY (USA) 1999, *Conference* Geneva (Switzerland) 1998, *Conference* London (UK) 1998, *Annual Conference* New York, NY (USA) 1998. **Publications** *The Beacon – Magazine of Esoteric Philosophy* (6 a year). Books and monographs published by the Lucis Publishing Company of New York NY and the Lucis Press Ltd of London.
Members Associated individuals and groups in 103 countries and territories:
Algeria, Argentina, Australia, Austria, Barbados, Belgium, Belize, Benin, Bermuda, Bolivia, Botswana, Brazil, Bulgaria, Cameroon, Canada, Chile, Colombia, Congo Brazzaville, Congo DR, Costa Rica, Côte d'Ivoire, Cyprus, Czechia, Denmark, Dominican Rep, Ecuador, Egypt, El Salvador, Finland, France, Gambia, Germany, Ghana, Gibraltar, Greece, Grenada, Guatemala, Haiti, Honduras, Hong Kong, Hungary, Iceland, India, Indonesia, Iran Islamic Rep, Iraq, Ireland, Israel, Italy, Jamaica, Japan, Jordan, Kenya, Korea Rep, Lebanon, Lesotho, Liberia, Luxembourg, Malaysia, Malta, Martinique, Mauritius, Mexico, Myanmar, Netherlands, New Zealand, Nicaragua, Nigeria, Norway, Pakistan, Panama, Paraguay, Peru, Philippines, Poland, Portugal, Puerto Rico, Romania, Russia, Saudi Arabia, Senegal, Sierra Leone, Slovakia, South Africa, Spain, Sri Lanka, Sudan, Sweden, Switzerland, Tanzania UR, Thailand, Togo, Trinidad-Tobago, Türkiye, Uganda, UK, Ukraine, Uruguay, USA, Venezuela, Vietnam, Zambia, Zimbabwe.
Consultative Status Consultative status granted from: *ECOSOC (#05331)* (Ros A). **IGO Relations** Accredited by (1): *United Nations Office at Vienna (UNOV, #20604).* **NGO Relations** Member of (3): *Conference of Non-Governmental Organizations in Consultative Relationship with the United Nations (CONGO, #04635); Fédération des Institutions Internationales établies à Genève (FIIG, #09599); NGO Alliance on Global Concerns and Values (NGO Alliance, #17102).* [2022.02.10/XF3547/**F**]

- ♦ **LUCSA** Lutheran Communion in Southern Africa (#16527)
- ♦ LUCWA / see Lutheran Communion in Central and Western Africa (#16526)
- ♦ **LUCWA** Lutheran Communion in Central and Western Africa (#16526)
- ♦ **LUDEN** Local Urban Development European Network (#16508)
- ♦ Ludmila Jivkova International Foundation / see St Cyril and St Methodius International Foundation
- ♦ Ludwig Boltzmann Institute of Fundamental and Human Rights (internationally oriented national body)
- ♦ Ludwig Boltzmann Institut für Grund- und Menschenrechte (internationally oriented national body)

♦ Ludwig Institute for Cancer Research (LICR) 16520

Pres/CEO 666 Third Ave, 28th Floor, New York NY 10017, USA. T. +12124501500. Fax +12124501565.
Registered Office Stadelhoferstrasse 22, Postfach 8024, 8001 Zurich ZH, Switzerland. T. +41442676262. Fax +41442676200.
URL: http://www.licr.org/

History 1971, Switzerland, by Daniel K Ludwig (1897-1992). Registered in accordance with Swiss Civil Code. **Aims** Improve understanding and control of cancer; translate research discoveries into applications for human benefit. **Structure** Board of Directors of 10 members, including Chairman. Administrative Offices (2); Research Branches (9); Translational/Clinical Center. **Languages** English. **Staff** 700.00 FTE, paid. **Finance** Endowment; licensing revenue; competitive research grant funding. **Activities** Carries out: laboratory research; translational and clinical cancer research, including the sponsorship of early-phase clinical trials. Offices for: Budget and Finance; Clinical Trials Management; Communications; Intellectual Property and Technology Licensing. **Events** *International conference on signal transduction* Dubrovnik (Croatia) / Cavtat (Croatia) 2000. **Publications** Annual Report.
Members Branches (10) in 7 countries:
Australia (2), Belgium, Brazil, Sweden (2), Switzerland, UK, USA (2).
NGO Relations Member of: *The NCD Alliance (NCDA, #16963); Union for International Cancer Control (UICC, #20415).* [2016/XE2949/j/**E**]

♦ Ludwig von Mises Institute Europe (LVMI Europe) 16521

Pres Rue d'Arlon 20, 1050 Brussels, Belgium. T. +32479722107. E-mail: annette.godart@vonmisesinstitute-europe.org – assistant@vonmisesinstitute-europe.org.
URL: http://www.vonmisesinstitute-europe.org/

History 12 Oct 2001, Brussels (Belgium). Named after Prof Ludwig von Mises (1881-1973). Registration: Banque-Carrefour des Entreprises, No/ID: 0863.327.417, Start date: 10 Feb 2004, Belgium. **Aims** Promote a free and open economy with particular focus on the ideas of the Austrian School of *economics* and *libertarian political* and *social* theory. **Structure** Board of Directors; Boards (3); High Patrons (5). **Languages** English. **Staff** 2.00 FTE, voluntary. **Finance** Members' dues. Other sources: sponsorship; corporate membership. **Activities** Events/meetings; training/education; awards/prizes/competitions. **Events** *Conference on Building a EU Defence* Brussels (Belgium) 2022, *Conference on the European Banking Union and the Future Financial Situation in Europe* Brussels (Belgium) 2019, *Conference on corporate governance* Brussels (Belgium) 2005, *Conference on Europe* Brussels (Belgium) 2004, *Conference on social responsible entrepreneurship* Brussels (Belgium) 2004. **Publications** *Better Regulation* (2009); *Hayek Revisited* (2001). Brochure.
Members Individuals in 13 countries:
Belgium, Estonia, France, Germany, Greece, Italy, Mexico, Netherlands, Poland, Spain, Switzerland, UK, USA.
[2023/XJ3319/j/**E**]

- ♦ L-Ufficcju Komunitarju tal-Varjetajcet ta' Pjanti (#04404)
- ♦ Luftfahrt ohne Grenzen (internationally oriented national body)
- ♦ Lugano Convention – Convention on Jurisdiction and the Enforcement of Judgements in Civil and Commercial Matters (1988 treaty)
- ♦ Lugano Convention – Convention on jurisdiction and the recognition and enforcement of judgments in civil and commercial matters (2007 treaty)

♦ Lugina Africa Midwives Research Network (LAMRN) 16522

Contact c/o School of Nursing, PO Box 19676-00202 KNH, Nairobi, Kenya. T. +254727466460. E-mail: info@lamrn.org.
URL: http://lamrn.org/

History 1992, Tanzania UR, as *African Midwives Research Network (AMRN)*, at a workshop sponsored by *Swedish Agency for Research Cooperation with Developing Countries (SAREC, inactive)*. 2013, present name adopted in honour of Dr Helen Lugina (died 2011). **Aims** Enhance research capabilities among midwives; provide opportunity for research collaboration and sharing research results; improve midwifery practice; foster coordination and collaboration in the region. **Activities** Research/documentation; training/education; events/meetings. **Events** *Triennial Conference* Lilongwe (Malawi) 2018, *Triennial Conference* Dar es Salaam (Tanzania UR) 2015. **NGO Relations** *Confederation of African Midwives Associations (CONAMA, #04506)*; *International Confederation of Midwives (ICM, #12863)*. [2017/XJ8950/F]

- ♦ **LUI** Laureate International Universities (#16404)
- ♦ LUISS / see Libera Università Internazionale degli Studi Sociali, Guido Carli
- ♦ LUISS – Libera Università Internazionale degli Studi Sociali, Guido Carli (internationally oriented national body)
- ♦ Lukiota ja ammatillisia oppilaitoksia koskeva pohjoismainen koulutusyhteistyö (2004 treaty)
- ♦ LULO / see DANAYA
- ♦ Lumbini World Peace Forum (internationally oriented national body)
- ♦ LUMDETR – International Conference on Luminescent Detectors and Transformers of Ionizing Radiation (meeting series)
- ♦ Lumen 2000 International (inactive)
- ♦ **LUMEN VITAE** International Centre for Studies in Religious Education (#12519)
- ♦ Lumière Project Association (inactive)
- ♦ Lumière et Vie (religious order)
- ♦ Luminate (internationally oriented national body)
- ♦ Lumos Foundation (internationally oriented national body)
- ♦ Lumos Foundation USA Inc / see Lumos Foundation
- ♦ Lundbeckfonden / see Grete Lundbeck European Brain Research Foundation
- ♦ Lundbeck Foundation / see Grete Lundbeck European Brain Research Foundation

♦ Lung Cancer Europe (LuCE) 16523

Contact c/o ETOP, Effingerstrasse 40, 3008 Bern, Switzerland. E-mail: luce@etop-eu.org.
URL: https://www.lungcancereurope.eu/

Aims Raise awareness about inequities regarding the access to lung cancer treatment and care in Europe. **Structure** Board; Scientific Advisory Board. **Activities** Advocacy/lobbying/activism; awareness raising; training/education. **Events** *European Cancer Forum* Brussels (Belgium) 2022.
Members National assocations. Full in 11 countries:
Denmark, Germany, Israel, Italy, Netherlands, Norway, Poland, Portugal, Spain, Sweden, UK.
Women against Lung Cancer in Europe (WALCE).
Associate in 12 countries:
Croatia, Finland, France, Germany, Greece, Italy, Latvia, Romania, Slovenia, Spain, Switzerland, Türkiye.
European School of Oncology (ESO, #08434); *European Thoracic Oncology Platform (ETOP, #08910)*.
NGO Relations Member of (3): *European Cancer Organisation (ECO, #06432)* (Patient Advisory Committee); *European Patients' Forum (EPF, #08172)*; *Workgroup of European Cancer Patient Advocacy Networks (WECAN, #21054)*. [2020/AA0350/y/D]

- ♦ Luonnontieteellisten Tutkimusneuvostojen Pohjoismainen Yhteistyölautakunta (#17529)
- ♦ **Lupus Academy** Stichting Lupus Academy Foundation (#19986)

♦ LUPUS EUROPE 16524

Main Office Rue d'Egmont 11, 1000 Brussels, Belgium. E-mail: secretariat@lupus-europe.org.
URL: http://www.lupus-europe.org/

History 1989, Leuven (Belgium). Headquarters moved to Brussels, 2021, following Brexit. Former names and other names: *European Lupus Erythematosus Federation (ELEF)* – former (1989 to 2008). Registration: Charity Commission, No/ID: 803768, England and Wales; No/ID: 0758.650.658, Belgium. **Aims** Encourage research, improve the knowledge and promote awareness of Systematic Lupus Erythematosus (SLE), an *auto-immune* disease; collect information on all aspects of the disease, both in the medical and sociological areas; encourage national support group creation. **Structure** Council; Board of Trustees; Secretariat. **Languages** English. **Staff** 6.00 FTE, voluntary. **Activities** Liaisons worldwide on Lupus issues. Supports establishing of new national groups. Develops projects to united national groups. **Events** *Convention* Leuven (Belgium) 2022, *Annual Convention* Romford (UK) 2020, *Annual Convention* Liverpool (UK) 2019, *Annual Convention* Brussels (Belgium) 2018, *Annual Convention* Venice (Italy) 2016. **Publications** *Newsflash* (4 a year); *Sharing and Caring* (annual) – newsletter.
Members Full in 19 countries:
Belgium, Cyprus, Denmark, Estonia, Finland, France, Germany, Greece, Hungary, Italy, Lithuania, Netherlands, Norway, Portugal, Slovakia, Spain, Sweden, Switzerland, UK.
Associate in 5 countries:
Iceland, Ireland, Israel, Romania, Slovenia.
NGO Relations Instrumental in setting up: *World Lupus Federation (WLF, #21630)*. Member of: *European Patients' Forum (EPF, #08172)*; *International Alliance of Patients' Organizations (IAPO, #11633)*. Associate member of: *EURORDIS – Rare Diseases Europe (#09175)*. [2022/XD5121/D]

- ♦ LUPUS – International Congress on Systemic Lupus Erythematosus (meeting series)
- ♦ Luso-American Development Foundation (internationally oriented national body)
- ♦ Luso-American Foundation / see Fundação Luso-Americana para o Desenvolvimento
- ♦ LUSOCOM – Federação de Associações Lusófonas de Ciências da Comunicação (unconfirmed)
- ♦ Luta pela Paz (internationally oriented national body)
- ♦ Lutheran AIDS Network (internationally oriented national body)
- ♦ Lutheran Association for Maritime Ministry (internationally oriented national body)
- ♦ Lutheran Bible Translators (internationally oriented national body)

♦ Lutheran Communion in Central and East Africa (LUCCEA) 16525

Secretariat PO Box 54128-00200, Nairobi, Kenya. T. +254724100195. E-mail: info@luccea.org.
Street Address Nile Road, off Jogoo Road, Nairobi, Kenya.
URL: www.luccea.org

History 1993, to coordinate member churches of *The Lutheran World Federation (LWF, #16532)* in the region.
Members Lutheran Churches (7) in 6 countries:
Congo Brazzaville, Eritrea, Ethiopia, Kenya, Madagascar, Tanzania UR. [2008/XE3679/E]

♦ Lutheran Communion in Central and Western Africa (LUCWA) 16526

Contact Evangelical Lutheran Church in Sierra Leone, Private Mail Bag 1155, Freetown, Sierra Leone. T. +23222222267. Fax +23222229188.
Contact c/o World Lutheran Federation, 50 route de Ferney, PO Box 2100, 1211 Geneva 2, Switzerland. T. +41227916111. Fax +41227916630. E-mail: info@lutheranworld.org.
URL: https://www.lutheranworld.org/content/africa/

History Founded 1993, as *Lutheran Communion in Western Africa (LUCWA)*.
Members Lutheran Churches (12) in 9 countries:
Cameroon, Central African Rep, Chad, Congo Brazzaville, Ghana, Liberia, Nigeria, Senegal, Sierra Leone.
NGO Relations Cooperates with: *The Lutheran World Federation (LWF, #16532)*. [2016/XE3681/E]

♦ Lutheran Communion in Southern Africa (LUCSA) 16527

Exec Dir PO Box 7170, Bonaero Park, 1622, South Africa. T. +27119797142. Fax +27113951615. E-mail: info@lucsa.org.
Street Address 24 Geldenhuys Rd, Bonaero Park, 1622, South Africa.
URL: http://www.lucsa.org/

History Founded 17 May 1991, Kempton Park (South Africa), taking over activities of *Federation of Evangelical Lutheran Churches in Southern Africa (FELCSA, inactive)*, set up 1966. Within *Evangelical Lutheran Church of Southern Africa (ELCSA)*. **Aims** Cooperate in theological training, adult education and *diaconal*, *mission* and *ecumenical* work; foster reconciliation; promote social and economic justice and human rights and responsibility for creation; promote stewardship and self reliance; encourage sharing of resources and skills within and among member churches. **Structure** General Conference (every 3 years); Council; Executive Committee. **Languages** English. **Staff** 10.00 FTE, paid; 1.00 FTE, voluntary. **Finance** Members' dues. Annual grant from: *The Lutheran World Federation (LWF, #16532)*; VELKD. **Activities** Projects/programmes; training/education; advocacy/lobbying/activism; events/meetings. **Events** *General Conference* Kempton Park (South Africa) 2004, *Seminar on NEPAD* Kempton Park (South Africa) 2004, *Seminar on NEPAD* Maputo (Mozambique) 2004, *General Conference* Botswana 2001, *General Conference* Windhoek (Namibia) 1998. **Publications** *LUCSA Update* (3 a year).
Members Independent Lutheran Churches (17) representing about 2 million individuals, in 10 countries:
Angola, Botswana, Eswatini, Lesotho, Malawi, Mozambique, Namibia, South Africa, Zambia, Zimbabwe.
NGO Relations Cooperates with: *The Lutheran World Federation (LWF, #16532)*. [2016.07.06/XE3218/E]

- ♦ Lutheran Communion in Western Africa / see Lutheran Communion in Central and Western Africa (#16526)

♦ Lutheran European Commission on the Church and the Jewish People 16528

Lutherische Europäische Kommission für Kirche und Judentum (LEKKJ)
Contact Amt der VELKD, Postfach 21 02 20, 30402 Hannover, Germany. E-mail: zentrale@velkd.de.
URL: http://www.lekkj.eu/

History 1976, under the auspices of *The Lutheran World Federation (LWF, #16532)*. Constitution adopted 30 Mar 1976, Christiansfeld (Denmark); amended 9 May 1993, Venice and 8 May 2004, Cluj-Napoca (Romania). **Aims** Encourage and promote consultation and cooperation among Lutheran churches and their agencies engaged in relations with Jews. **Structure** Board. **Languages** English, German. **Activities** Events/meetings; awards/prizes/competitions. **Events** *Annual Meeting* Venice (Italy) 2015, *Annual Meeting* Korneuburg (Austria) 2014, *Annual meeting* Oslo (Norway) 1995, *Annual meeting* Prague (Czech Rep) 1994, *Annual meeting* Venice (Italy) 1993. **Publications** *Luther's Heirs and the Jews* (2nd ed 1994) in German.
Members National bodies in 8 countries:
Austria, France, Germany, Hungary, Italy, Netherlands, Romania, Slovakia.
NGO Relations *International Jewish Committee on Interreligious Consultations (IJCIC, #13970)*. [2016.06.21/XE1430/E]

♦ Lutheran Foundation for Interconfessional Research 16529

Fondation luthérienne pour la recherche oecuménique – Lutherische Stiftung für Ökumenische Forschung
Secretariat 8 rue Gustave-Klotz, 67000 Strasbourg, France. T. +33388152575. Fax +33388152570. E-mail: strasecum@ecumenical-institute.org.
URL: http://www.ecumenical-institute.org/

History 1963, Strasbourg (France), to develop a programme approved by *The Lutheran World Federation (LWF, #16532)* in 1960. **Aims** Help Lutheran churches fulfil their *ecumenical* responsibility in the area of *theology*. **Structure** Board of Trustees. **Languages** English, French, German. **Staff** 6.00 FTE, paid. **Finance** Endowment fund; contributions from Lutheran churches; special donations. **Activities** Research/documentation; events/meetings; religious activities; networking/liaising; publishing activities. **Events** *Annual Seminar* Strasbourg (France) 2015, *Annual Seminar* Strasbourg (France) 2014, *Annual seminar* Strasbourg (France) 1986. **NGO Relations** Maintains, since 1 Feb 1965, *Institute for Ecumenical Research, Strasbourg (#11258)*. [2017.10.26/XF8285/f/F]

- ♦ Lutheran Hour International Ministries / see International Lutheran Hour Ministries
- ♦ Lutheran Immigration and Refugee Service (internationally oriented national body)
- ♦ Lutheran Office for World Community (internationally oriented national body)

♦ Lutheran-Orthodox Joint Commission 16530

Commission commune luthérienne-orthodoxe
Contact c/o LWF, PO Box 2100, Route de Ferney 150, 1211 Geneva 2, Switzerland. T. +41227916111. Fax +41227988616.

History Aug 1981, Helsinki (Finland), following preliminary contacts since 1978, between representatives of the *Ecumenical Patriarchate of Constantinople (#05349)* and of *The Lutheran World Federation (LWF, #16532)*. Also referred to as *Joint Lutheran – Orthodox Commission*. **Events** *Meeting* Bratislava (Slovakia) 2006, *Meeting* 1998, *Meeting* Limassol (Cyprus) 1995, *Meeting* Sønderborg (Denmark) 1993, *Authority in and of the Church* Moscow (USSR) 1991.
Members Representatives from 20 countries:
Bulgaria, Cyprus, Czechia, Denmark, Estonia, Ethiopia, Finland, France, Georgia, Germany, Greece, India, Italy, Poland, Romania, Russia, Serbia, Sweden, Türkiye, USA. [2010/XE1615/E]

- ♦ Lutheran Peace Fellowship (internationally oriented national body)

♦ Lutheran-Roman Catholic Commission on Unity 16531

Commission internationale catholique romaine-évangélique luthérienne
Co-Sec Lutheran World Federation, Route de Ferney 150, PO Box 2100, 1211 Geneva 2, Switzerland. T. +41227916357.
Co-Sec Pontificial Council for Promoting Christian Unity, c/o PCPCU, 00120 Vatican City, Vatican. T. +39669884385. Fax +39669885365.
URL: http://www.christianunity.va/content/unitacristiani/en/dialoghi/sezione-occidentale/luterani.html

History Mar 1973, as *Lutheran/Roman Catholic Joint Working Group*, following discussion by a previous commission between 1967 – 1971. In 1977, the Working Group became a Commission under the list title, also being referred to as: *Roman Catholic/Lutheran Joint Commission* and *Lutheran/Roman Catholic International Commission*. Second phase – 1973-1984; third phase – 1986-1993; fourth phase – 1995-2006; fifth phase 2009-present. Commission was appointed by *The Lutheran World Federation (LWF, #16532)* and Vatican *Pontifical Council for Promoting Christian Unity (PCPCU, #18446)*; not an autonomous body. **Events** *Annual meeting* Stuttgart (Germany) 1996, *Annual Meeting* Karis (Finland) 1995, *Annual meeting* Würzburg (Germany) 1993, *Annual meeting* Eisenach (Germany) 1992, *Annual meeting* Venice (Italy) 1991. **Publications** Reports.
Members Representative persons in 11 countries:
Brazil, Finland, France, Germany, Italy, Japan, Latvia, Norway, Tanzania UR, UK, USA. [2019/XE0269/E]

- ♦ Lutheran/Roman Catholic International Commission / see Lutheran-Roman Catholic Commission on Unity (#16531)
- ♦ Lutheran/Roman Catholic Joint Working Group / see Lutheran-Roman Catholic Commission on Unity (#16531)
- ♦ Lutheran South-East Asia Christian Education Curriculum Committee (inactive)
- ♦ Lutheran Women's Missionary League / see International Lutheran Women's Missionary League

♦ The Lutheran World Federation (LWF) 16532

Fédération luthérienne mondiale (FLM) – Lutherischer Weltbund (LWB) – Lutherska Världsförbundet – Federación Luterana Mundial
Assistant Route de Ferney 150, PO Box 2100, 1211 Geneva 2, Switzerland. T. +41227916111. Fax +41227916630. E-mail: info@lutheranworld.org.
URL: https://www.lutheranworld.org/

History 1947, Lund (Sweden). Founded in succession to *Lutheran World Convention*, set up 1923, Eisenach (Germany). Present constitution adopted 1990, Curitiba (Brazil), at 8th Assembly; amended 1997, Hong Kong and Jul 2010, Stuttgart (Germany). Registration: Swiss Civil Code, No/ID: 478, Start date: 27 Feb 1951, Switzerland. **Aims** As a communion of churches which confess the triune God, agree in the proclamation of the Word of God and are united in pulpit and altar fellowship: confess the one, holy, catholic and apostolic Church; resolve to serve Christian unity throughout the world; further the united witness to the Gospel of Jesus Christ and strengthen member churches in carrying out the missionary command and in their efforts towards *Christian unity* worldwide; further diaconic action worldwide among member churches, alleviating human need, promoting peace and human rights, social and economic justice, care for God's creation and sharing of resources; through cooperative study, further self-understanding and communion of member churches and help them to act jointly in common tasks; confess the Holy Scriptures of the Old and New Testaments to be the only source and norm of doctrine, life and service; in the three Ecumenical Creeds and in the Confessions of the Lutheran Church, and especially in the unaltered Augsburg Confession and the Small Catechism of Martin Luther, see a pure exposition of the Word of God. **Structure** Assembly (every 6 years); Council;

Meeting of Officers. Committees (7): Finance; Advocacy and Public Voice; Mission and Development; Theology and Ecumenical Relations; World Service; Standing Committee for Constitution and Membership; Standing Committee for Communications. Regional offices (2): India; USA. Departments (4): Mission and Development (DMD); Theology and Public Witness (DTPW); World Service (DWS); Planning and Operations (DPO). Offices (4): Communication Services (OCS); Finance (OF); Human Resources (OHR); General Secretary (GS). Lutheran Foundation for Interconfessional Research. **Languages** English, French, German, Spanish. **Staff** Geneva (Switzerland): about 65 of about 20 different nationalities. Also 40 international staff who work alongside 2,700 local staff in regional and country programmes. **Finance** Sources: members' dues. Appropriations from National Committees. LWF Foundation – Endowment Fund: for long-term financial support. Annual budget: 168,000,000 EUR (2019). **Activities** Events/meetings; humanitarian/emergency aid; religious activities; training/education. . **Events** *Assembly* Krakow (Poland) 2023, *Assembly* Windhoek (Namibia) 2017, *Assembly* Stuttgart (Germany) 2010, *Living in communion in the world today* Lund (Sweden) 2007, *European church leadership consultation* Greifswald (Germany) 2006. **Publications** *LWF Documentation* in English, German. Conference and Assembly proceedings; book series; studies; directories; promotional material, in electronic and traditional formats. Information Services: Audiovisual, editing and translation services.
Members Churches (148) in 99 countries and territories:
Angola, Argentina, Australia, Austria, Bangladesh, Bolivia, Botswana, Brazil, Cameroon, Canada, Central African Rep, Chile, Colombia, Congo Brazzaville, Congo DR, Costa Rica, Croatia, Cuba, Czechia, Denmark, El Salvador, Eritrea, Estonia, Ethiopia, Faeroe Is, Finland, France, Georgia, Germany, Ghana, Greenland, Guyana, Honduras, Hong Kong, Hungary, Iceland, India, Indonesia, Israel, Italy, Japan, Jordan, Kazakhstan, Kenya, Korea Rep, Kyrgyzstan, Latvia, Liberia, Liechtenstein, Lithuania, Madagascar, Malawi, Malaysia, Mexico, Mozambique, Myanmar, Namibia, Nepal, Netherlands, New Zealand, Nicaragua, Nigeria, Norway, Palestine, Papua New Guinea, Peru, Philippines, Poland, Romania, Russia, Rwanda, Senegal, Serbia, Sierra Leone, Singapore, Slovakia, Slovenia, South Africa, Sri Lanka, Suriname, Sweden, Switzerland, Taiwan, Tanzania UR, Thailand, UK, Ukraine, Uruguay, USA, Uzbekistan, Venezuela, Zambia, Zimbabwe.
Associate Members churches in 2 countries:
Australia, Japan.
National Committees in 24 countries:
Austria, Brazil, Czechia, Denmark, Finland, France, Germany, Hungary, Iceland, India, Indonesia, Italy, Kenya, Madagascar, Malawi, Namibia, Netherlands, Norway, Poland, Romania, Russia, Sweden, Tanzania UR, USA.
Recognized churches, councils and congregations in 11 countries:
Belgium, Bolivia, Colombia, Costa Rica, Ecuador, Germany, Guatemala, Ireland, Mexico, Peru, UK.
Consultative Status Consultative status granted from: *ECOSOC (#05331)* (Special); *UNCTAD (#20285)* (General Category); *UNEP (#20299)*. **IGO Relations** Observer status with (1): *International Organization for Migration (IOM, #14454)*. Cooperates with (5): *FAO (#09260)*; *UNHCR (#20327)*; *United Nations Office for the Coordination of Humanitarian Affairs (OCHA, #20593)*; *United Nations Relief and Works Agency for Palestine Refugees in the Near East (UNRWA, #20622)*; *World Food Programme (WFP, #21510)*. Associated with Department of Global Communications of the United Nations.
NGO Relations Bilateral dialogue at global level with: *Anglican Communion (#00827)*; Orthodox churches; Roman Catholic Church. Ecumenical conversations with: *General Conference of Seventh-Day Adventists (SDA, #10109)*. Close cooperation with: *Lutheran Foundation for Interconfessional Research (#16529)*. Partner to: *Development Innovations and Networks (#05057)*. Observer to: *ACT Alliance EU (#00082)*. Board member of: *The Sphere Project (#19918)*. International Associate of: *International Dalit Solidarity Network (IDSN, #13129)*. Supports: *Circle of Concerned African Women Theologians (CAWT, #03931)*; *Coordinadora Regional de Investigaciones Económicas y Sociales (CRIES, #04812)*.
Member of:
- *Child Rights International Network (CRIN, #03885)*;
- *CHS Alliance (#03911)*;
- *Committee of NGOs on Human Rights, Geneva (#04275)*;
- *Cooperation Committee for Cambodia (CCC)*;
- *Ecumenical Advocacy Alliance (EAA, inactive)*;
- *Fédération des Institutions Internationales établies à Genève (FIIG, #09599)*;
- *International Association for Mission Studies (IAMS, #12032)*;
- *International Campaign to Ban Landmines (ICBL, inactive)*;
- *International Council of Voluntary Agencies (ICVA, #13092)*;
- *International NGO Committee on Human Rights in Trade and Investment (INCHRITI, no recent information)*;
- *NGO Committee on the Status of Women, Geneva (#17117)*;
- *NGO Forum on Cambodia (#17124)*;
- *Oikocredit International (Oikocredit, #17704)*;
- *Steering Committee for Humanitarian Response (SCHR, #19978)*.

Partner of: *Global Camp Coordination and Camp Management Cluster (CCCM Cluster, #10268)*. Regular cooperation with:
- *Association francophone internationale de recherche scientifique en éducation (AFIRSE, #02615)*;
- *Associazione per la Promozione degli Scambi e della Solidarietà Internazionale (Lunaria, no recent information)*;
- *Brot für die Welt*;
- *Den Norske Israelmisjon (DNI)*;
- *Finn Church Aid (FCA)*;
- *Finnish Lutheran Overseas Mission*;
- *Folkekirkens Nødhjaelp (FKN)*;
- *Icelandic Church Aid*;
- *Lutheran Communion in Central and East Africa (LUCCEA, #16525)*;
- *Lutheran Communion in Central and Western Africa (LUCWA, #16526)*;
- *Lutheran Communion in Southern Africa (LUCSA, #16527)*;
- *Lutheran Immigration and Refugee Service (LIRS)*;
- *Lutheran World Relief (LWR)*;
- *Lutherans United in Communication (LUC, no recent information)*;
- *Martin Luther Federation*;
- *Norwegian Church Aid*;
- *United Evangelical Lutheran Church in Southern Africa (UELCSA)*.

Instrumental in setting up: *All Africa Anglican-Lutheran Commission (AAALC, #00638)*; *Anglican-Lutheran International Commission (ALIC, inactive)*; *Asian Program for the Enhancement of Lay Training (APELT, no recent information)*; *Institute for Ecumenical Research, Strasbourg (#11258)*; *Lutheran European Commission on the Church and the Jewish People (#16528)*; *Lutheran Office for World Community*; *Lutheran-Orthodox Joint Commission (#16530)*; *Lutheran-Roman Catholic Commission on Unity (#16531)*. [2022.02.02/XB2937/**B**]

- ♦ Lutheran World Relief (internationally oriented national body)
- ♦ Lutherische Europäische Kommission für Kirche und Judentum (#16528)
- ♦ Lutherischer Weltbund (#16532)
- ♦ Lutherische Stiftung für Ökumenische Forschung (#16529)
- ♦ Lutherska Världsförbundet (#16532)
- ♦ LuWQ – International Interdisciplinary Conference on Land Use and Water Quality (meeting series)
- ♦ LUX-DEVELOPMENT / see Luxembourg Agency for Development Cooperation
- ♦ LUXDEV – Luxembourg Agency for Development Cooperation (internationally oriented national body)
- ♦ Luxembourg Agency for Development Cooperation (internationally oriented national body)
- ♦ Luxembourg Institute for European and International Studies (internationally oriented national body)
- ♦ Luxembourg International University Institute (internationally oriented national body)
- ♦ Luxembourg Protocol to the Convention on International Interests in Mobile Equipment on Matters Specific to Railway Rolling Stock (2007 treaty)
- ♦ Luxembourg Protocol – Luxembourg Protocol to the Convention on International Interests in Mobile Equipment on Matters Specific to Railway Rolling Stock (2007 treaty)

♦ LUX EUROPA 16533

Managing Dir Deutsche Lichttechnische Gesellschaft eV, Burggrafenstr 6, 10787 Berlin, Germany. T. +493026369524. Fax +493026557873.
Contact German Lighting Engineering Soc, Working Group Communication, Kärtnerweg 13b, 22393 Hamburg, Germany.
URL: http://www.luxeuropa.eu/
History Current statutes approved Nov 1996. Registered in accordance with German law. **Aims** Promote *lighting* knowledge and practice in all fields through technical, scientific and cultural links and cooperation between member countries. **Structure** Council (meets every 2 years); Board of Directors; Advisory Committee; Secretariat. **Languages** English, French, German. **Activities** Events/meetings. **Events** *Quadrennial Conference* Ljubljana (Slovenia) 2017, *Quadrennial Conference* Krakow (Poland) 2013, *Quadrennial Conference* Istanbul (Turkey) 2009, *Quadrennial Conference* Berlin (Germany) 2005, *Quadrennial Conference* Reykjavik (Iceland) 2001.
Members National societies in 20 countries:
Austria, Belgium, Croatia, Czechia, France, Germany, Hungary, Iceland, Italy, Netherlands, Poland, Romania, Russia, Serbia, Slovakia, Slovenia, Spain, Switzerland, Türkiye, UK. [2016/XJ6682/**D**]

♦ Lux Pacifica – Association of Lighting Societies (Lux Pacifica) 16534

Chairperson c/o The Illuminating Engineering Inst of Japan, Suitaya Bldg 3F, 2-8-4 Kanda Tsukasa-cho, Chiyoda-ku, Tokyo, 101-0048 Japan. T. +81352940101. Fax +81352940102. E-mail: info@luxpacifica.org.
URL: http://www.luxpacifica.org/
Aims Provide an opportunity for lighting researchers and designers to present their ideas to an international audience. **Structure** Board of Directors. **Activities** Events/meetings. **Events** *Conference* St Petersburg (Russia) 2022, *Conference* St Petersburg (Russia) 2021, *Conference* St Petersburg (Russia) 2020, *Conference* Tokyo (Japan) 2018, *Conference* Bangkok (Thailand) 2013.
Members Societies in 15 countries and territories:
Australia, Canada, China, Colombia, India, Japan, Korea Rep, Mexico, New Zealand, Russia, South Africa, Taiwan, Thailand, USA, Vietnam.
Included in the above, 1 organization listed in this Yearbook:
Illuminating Engineering Society (IES). [2020/XM5246/**C**]

- ♦ **Lux Pacifica** Lux Pacifica – Association of Lighting Societies (#16534)
- ♦ **LVFO** Lake Victoria Fisheries Organization (#16222)
- ♦ LVIA – Lay Volunteers International Association (internationally oriented national body)
- ♦ **LVMI Europe** Ludwig von Mises Institute Europe (#16521)
- ♦ LVSA – Linguistevereniging van Suider-Afrika (internationally oriented national body)
- ♦ **LWA** Leading Women of Africa (#16419)
- ♦ **LWA** Live Working Association (#16501)
- ♦ **LWB** Libraries Without Borders (#03229)
- ♦ **LWB** Lutherischer Weltbund (#16532)
- ♦ **LWF** The Lutheran World Federation (#16532)
- ♦ **LWG** Leather Working Group (#16432)
- ♦ LWR – Lutheran World Relief (internationally oriented national body)
- ♦ LWSB / see World Services for the Blind
- ♦ LYBRA – Large Yacht Brokers Association (unconfirmed)
- ♦ **LYMEC** European Liberal Youth (#07690)

♦ Lymphoma Coalition (LC) 16535

CEO 8 Stavebank Road N, Unit 401, Mississauga ON L5G 2T4, Canada. E-mail: info@lymphomacoalition.org.
URL: http://www.lymphomacoalition.org/
History 2002. Founded as a network by lymphoma organizations in Canada, UK, Germany and USA. Registration: No/ID: 803211465, Start date: 2010, Canada; EU Transparency Register, No/ID: 809500545743-75, Start date: 8 Mar 2022. **Aims** Be the global source for lymphoma facts and statistics; improve awareness and understanding of lymphomas; build capacity for new and existing lymphoma groups. **Structure** Board of Directors; Medical Advisory Board. **Languages** English. **Activities** Awards/prizes/competitions; events/meetings. **Events** *Annual Lymphoma Coalition Global Summit* 2021, *Lymphoma Coalition Global Summit* Mississauga, ON (Canada) 2020, *Global Summit* San Diego, CA (USA) 2016.
Members Full (66) in 44 countries and territories:
Algeria, Argentina, Australia, Barbados, Belgium, Brazil, Bulgaria, Canada, Colombia, Croatia, Czechia, Denmark, France, Germany, Hong Kong, Hungary, India, Ireland, Israel, Italy, Japan, Latvia, Lithuania, Mexico, Netherlands, New Zealand, North Macedonia, Poland, Portugal, Russia, Serbia, Singapore, Slovakia, Slovenia, South Africa, Spain, Sweden, Switzerland, Türkiye, UK, Ukraine, Uruguay, USA, Venezuela.
Included in the above, 1 organization listed in this Yearbook:
International Waldenstrom's Macroglobulinemia Foundation (IWMF).
NGO Relations Member of (4): *European Cancer Organisation (ECO, #06432)* (Patient Advisory Committee); *Global Cancer Coalitions Network (GCCN, #10270)*; *The NCD Alliance (NCDA, #16963)*; *Union for International Cancer Control (UICC, #20415)*. Cooperates with (5): American Society of Clinical Oncology (ASCO); *European Hematology Association (EHA, #07473)*; *European Society for Medical Oncology (ESMO, #08648)*; InterLymph Research Consortium; Lymphoma Hub. [2021/XJ2063/y/**C**]

- ♦ Lynch Syndrome International (internationally oriented national body)
- ♦ LYPHYS' – International Laser Physics Workshop (meeting series)
- ♦ LZIF / see St Cyril and St Methodius International Foundation
- ♦ LZZ – Leopold-Zunz-Zentrum zur Erforschung des Europäischen Judentums (internationally oriented national body)
- ♦ **m2m** mothers2mothers (#16859)
- ♦ M2S – International Conference on Materials and Mechanisms of Superconductivity (meeting series)
- ♦ M3AAWG – Messaging, Malware and Mobile Anti-Abuse Working Group (internationally oriented national body)
- ♦ M3M – Médecine pour le Tiers-Monde (internationally oriented national body)
- ♦ M8 Alliance of Academic Health Centers, and Medical Universities / see M8 Alliance of Academic Health Centers, Universities and National Academies (#16536)

♦ M8 Alliance of Academic Health Centers, Universities and National Academies (M8 Alliance) 16536

Contact c/o Charité – Universitätsmedizin Berlin, Charitéplatz 1, 10117 Berlin, Germany. T. +4930450570003. Fax +4930450517944. E-mail: communications@worldhealthsummit.org.
URL: https://www.worldhealthsummit.org/m8-alliance.html
History 2009, Berlin (Germany). Founded at inaugural *World Health Summit*, as a collaborative network of academic institutions of education and research excellence. Former names and other names: *M8 Alliance of Academic Health Centers, and Medical Universities* – former. **Aims** Develop science-based solutions to health challenges all over the world. **Structure** Executive Committee. Academic platform of *World Health Summit Foundation (WHS Foundation, #21560)*. **Languages** English. **Activities** Events/meetings; publishing activities. **Events** *World Health Summit* Berlin (Germany) 2019, *World Health Summit* Berlin (Germany) 2018, *World Health Summit – Europe Regional Meeting* Coimbra (Portugal) 2018, *World Health Summit* Berlin (Germany) 2017, *World Health Summit – North America Regional Meeting* Montréal, QC (Canada) 2017. **Publications** *WHS Yearbook*. Statements.
Members Full (30) in 19 countries and territories:
Australia, Brazil, Canada, China, France, Germany, Iran Islamic Rep, Italy, Japan, Lebanon, Portugal, Russia, Singapore, Switzerland, Taiwan, Türkiye, Uganda, UK, USA.
Association of Academic Health Centers International (AAHC International); *Consortium of Universities for Global Health (CUGH)*; *InterAcademy Partnership (IAP, #11376)*; *London School of Hygiene and Tropical Medicine (LSHTM)*. [2021/XJ5340/y/**E**]

- ♦ **M8 Alliance** M8 Alliance of Academic Health Centers, Universities and National Academies (#16536)
- ♦ MAAAS – Mid-America Alliance for African Studies (internationally oriented national body)
- ♦ Maa- ja Metsätalouskysymysten Pohjoismainen Kontaktielin (inactive)
- ♦ **MAA** Marketing Agencies Association Worldwide (#16585)
- ♦ MAA – Medical Aid Abroad (internationally oriented national body)
- ♦ **mAAN** Modern Asian Architecture Network (#16841)
- ♦ MaaS Alliance – Mobility as a Service Alliance (unconfirmed)
- ♦ Maastricht Centre for European Governance (internationally oriented national body)
- ♦ Maastrichts Europees Instituut voor Transnationaal Rechtswetenschappelijk Onderzoek (internationally oriented national body)
- ♦ Maastricht Treaty – Treaty on European Union (1992 treaty)
- ♦ Maasverdrag (2002 treaty)

- ♦ Maataloustutkimuksen Pohjoismainen Kontaktielin / see Nordic Joint Committee for Agricultural and Food Research (#17332)
- ♦ Maat for Peace, Development, and Human Rights (internationally oriented national body)
- ♦ **Maaya** World Network for Linguistic Diversity (#21671)
- ♦ MAB-ITEX / see International Tundra Experiment (#15742)
- ♦ **MAB** Programme on Man and the Biosphere (#18526)
- ♦ MABS – International Symposium on Military Aspects of Blast and Shock (meeting series)
- ♦ MACALAN / see African Academy of Languages (#00192)
- ♦ MacArthur Foundation (internationally oriented national body)
- ♦ **MAC** Asociación de Museos del Caribe (#16909)
- ♦ **MAC** Association des Musées de la Caraïbe (#16909)

♦ Maccabi World Union (MWU) 16537

Unión Mundial Macabi (UMM)

Exec Dir Kfar Maccabiah,, 7 Peretz Bernstein st., 5224771 Ramat Gan, Israel. T. +97236715722. Fax +97236772426.

URL: http://maccabi.org/

History Founded 1921, as the parent body of Maccabi territorial organizations established wherever an organized Jewish community is to be found. **Aims** Promote the development and organization of the *Jewish* youth and adults through sports, cultural and educational activities, maintaining close connection with Jewish youth and adults in Israel. **Structure** Congress (every 4 years); Plenary Meeting (annual). World Executive, elected by the Congress; Israeli Executive (sub-committee of World Executive). Secretariat. **Languages** English, Hebrew, Spanish. **Staff** 18.00 FTE, paid. **Activities** Organizes: Maccabiah games (every 4 years); regional games and national games and sports carnivals; folk-dancing festivals, camps and competitions; summer camps; educational experience in Israel; leadership seminars; Menorah seminars; educational programmes. Organizes professional football and basketball teams plus amateur teams in virtually every branch of sport. Centre in Israel comprises hotel, country club, convention centre and museum. Network of emissaries from Israel to Maccabi clubs and institutions is funded by World Zionist Organization. **Events** *Quadrennial World Congress and Maccabiah Games* Israel 2005, *European Maccabi Games* Antwerp (Belgium) 2003, *Pan American Maccabi Games* Santiago (Chile) 2003, *Quadrennial World Congress and Maccabiah Games* Israel 2001, *Pan American Maccabi Games* Mexico 1999. **Publications** *Maccabi Newsletter*.

Members Organizations in 59 countries and territories:

Argentina, Australia, Austria, Azerbaijan, Belarus, Belgium, Bosnia-Herzegovina, Brazil, Bulgaria, Canada, Chile, Colombia, Costa Rica, Croatia, Cuba, Czechia, Denmark, Finland, France, Georgia, Germany, Greece, Guatemala, Hong Kong, Hungary, India, Israel, Italy, Kazakhstan, Latvia, Lithuania, Luxembourg, Mexico, Moldova, Netherlands, New Zealand, Norway, Panama, Paraguay, Peru, Poland, Portugal, Romania, Russia, Serbia, Singapore, Slovakia, South Africa, Spain, Sweden, Switzerland, Türkiye, UK, Ukraine, Uruguay, USA, Uzbekistan, Venezuela, Zimbabwe.

Regional confederations (6), of which 3 listed in this Yearbook:

Confederación Latinoamericana Macabea (CLAM, #04459); European Maccabi Confederation (EMC, #07720); North American Maccabi Confederation (no recent information).

NGO Relations Member of (1): *World Zionist Organization (WZO, #21961)*. Partner of (1): *International Esports Federation (IESF, #13304).* [2020/XD2938/y/**C**]

- ♦ MACCS – Mediterranean Association of Cardiology and Cardiac Surgery (no recent information)
- ♦ Macedonian Centre for International Cooperation (internationally oriented national body)
- ♦ Macedonian World Youth Congress
- ♦ MACHC – Meso-American-Caribbean Sea Hydrographic Commission (see: #13825)

♦ Machinery Information Management Open Systems Alliance (MIMOSA) 16538

Admin Office 2200 Jack Warner Pkwy, Ste 300, Tuscaloosa AL 35406, USA. T. +19496258616. E-mail: info@mimosa.org.

URL: http://www.mimosa.org/

Aims Develop and encourage adoption of open information standards for operations and maintenance and collaborative asset lifecycle management. **Activities** Organizes conferences and workshops. **Events** *Annual meeting* San Antonio, TX (USA) 2002, *European conference / Conference* Birmingham (UK) 1998.

Members Corporate; Individual; Corresponding. Members (34) in 9 countries:

Australia, Canada, Finland, Germany, Poland, Russia, Sweden, UK, USA. [2016/XF4775/**F**]

- ♦ MACJT – Movimiento Africano das Crianças e Jovens Trabalhadores (unconfirmed)
- ♦ MACLAS – Middle Atlantic Council of Latin American Studies (internationally oriented national body)
- ♦ **MAC** Market Advisory Council (#16584)
- ♦ **MAC** Mediterranean Arbitration Council (#16645)
- ♦ MAC – Meeting for African Collaboration (meeting series)
- ♦ **MAC** MEPs against Cancer (#16717)
- ♦ Macmillan Brown Centre for Pacific Studies (internationally oriented national body)
- ♦ MacMillan Center for International and Area Studies (internationally oriented national body)
- ♦ **MAC** Museums Association of the Caribbean (#16909)
- ♦ **MACQC** Massive Analysis and Quality Control Society (#16595)
- ♦ Macquarie University Centre for International and Environmental Law (internationally oriented national body)

♦ Macroeconomic and Financial Management Institute of Eastern and Southern Africa (MEFMI) 16539

Exec Dir 9 Earls Rd, Alexandra Park, PO Box A 1419, Avondale, Harare, HARARE, Zimbabwe. T. +2634745988 – +2634745989 – +2634745991. Fax +26347455547 – +26347455548. E-mail: capacity@mefmi.org.

URL: http://www.mefmi.org/

History Established 1994, as *Eastern and Southern African Initiative on Debt and Reserves Management (ESAIDARM)*, by senior economic officials and financial manager in Eastern and Southern Africa. Current title adopted Jan 1997, when mandate expanded. **Aims** Build sustainable capacity and foster best practices in central banks, ministries of finance and of planning in Eastern and Southern Africa; help identify emerging challenges, risks and opportunities. **Structure** Board of Governors; Executive Committee; Secretariat. **Languages** English, Portuguese. **Staff** 32.00 FTE, paid. **Finance** Member States contributions: about US$ 24,692,070. Project funding (2017-2021): about US$ 44,070,550. **Activities** Events/meetings; training/education; projects/programmes; standards/guidelines. **Events** *Annual seminar* Harare (Zimbabwe) 2000. **Publications** Studies; books; forum papers; manuals; guidelines; handbooks. **Information Services** *MEFMI E-learning Portal*; *Private Capital Monitoring System (PCMS)*.

Members Member States (14):

Angola, Botswana, Burundi, Eswatini, Lesotho, Malawi, Mozambique, Namibia, Rwanda, Tanzania UR, Uganda, Zambia, Zimbabwe.

IGO Relations Technical Cooperating Partners: *African Development Bank (ADB, #00283)*; Africa Regional Technical Assistance Centre (AFRITAC); *Bank for International Settlements (BIS, #03165)* and Affiliate Committees; Centre for Central Banking Studies (CCBS) of the Bank of England (BOE); *Commonwealth Secretariat (#04362)*; Federal Reserve Bank of New York; Federal Reserve Board; *Financial Stability Institute (FSI, #09771)*; *IMF Institute (see: #14180)*; *International Bank for Reconstruction and Development (IBRD, #12317)* (World Bank); *International Monetary Fund (IMF, #14180)*; *UNCTAD (#20285)*; *World Bank Institute (WBI, #21220)*. Networking Partner: *United Nations Institute for Training and Research (UNITAR, #20576)*. **NGO Relations** Networking Partners: *African Economic Research Consortium (AERC, #00292)*; *Center for International Development, Harvard University (CID)*; *Crown Agents for Overseas Governments and Administrations*. *Debt Relief International (DRI)*; *Direct Relief (DR)*. National Treasury of South Africa. [2018.09.07/XF3634/j/**E***]

- ♦ MACS – Mexican Association of Caribbean Studies (internationally oriented national body)
- ♦ MACS Worldwide – Mobile Air Conditioning Society Worldwide (internationally oriented national body)

♦ Madagascar Fauna and Flora Group (MFG) 16540

Exec Dir MFG c/o Naples Zoo, 1590 Goodlette Rd N, Naples FL 34102, USA. E-mail: info@savethelemur.org.

Contact BP 422 Morafino, Toamasina, Madagascar.

URL: http://www.madagascarfaunaflora.org/

History Founded 1987, following a meeting convened by *Wildlife Conservation Society (WCS)* and *International Union for Conservation of Nature and Natural Resources (IUCN, #15766)* – SSC Conservation Breeding Specialist Group (CBSG). Formalized 1988. Original title: *Madagascar Fauna Group – Groupe pour l'élevage et la conservation de la faune malgache*. **Aims** Provide technical support for Parc Ivoloina, a native fauna zoo in Tamatave, Madagascar; provide protection and support for the Betampona Natural Reserve; promote and fund field research on animals, plants and habitats; support captive breeding programmes for Malagasy species; undertake and promote rigorous conservation planning; education of zoo visitors. **Structure** Steering Committee (meets annually). **Staff** 50.00 FTE, paid.

Members Zoos, botanical gardens, aquariums, universities and related institutions (30) in 12 countries and territories:

Australia, Canada, Germany, Japan, New Zealand, South Africa, Spain, Switzerland, Taiwan, Thailand, UK, USA. [2022/XF4679/**F**]

- ♦ Madagascar Fauna Group / see Madagascar Fauna and Flora Group (#16540)
- ♦ Madaniya (religious order)
- ♦ **MADERA** Mission d'aide au développement des économies rurales afghanes (#16828)
- ♦ Mad'in Europe (unconfirmed)
- ♦ Madonna House Apostolate (religious order)
- ♦ Madras Institute of Development Studies (internationally oriented national body)
- ♦ MADRE (internationally oriented national body)
- ♦ Madres de San Columbano (religious order)
- ♦ MADRE – Women's Peace Network / see MADRE
- ♦ Madrid Agreement Concerning the International Registration of Marks, 1891 (1891 treaty)
- ♦ Madrid Agreement – Madrid Agreement for the Repression of False or Deceptive Indications of Source on Goods, 1891 (1891 treaty)
- ♦ Madrid Agreement for the Repression of False or Deceptive Indications of Source on Goods, 1891 (1891 treaty)
- ♦ Madrid Multilateral Convention – Multilateral Convention for the Avoidance of Double Taxation of Copyright Royalties and Additional Protocol (1979 treaty)
- ♦ Madrid Quartet / see Quartet Group (#18593)
- ♦ **Madrid Union** Union for the International Registration of Marks (#20445)
- ♦ MAEJT – Mouvement Africain des Enfants et Jeunes Travailleurs (unconfirmed)
- ♦ **MAELA** Movimiento Agroecológico para Latinoamérica y El Caribe (#16872)
- ♦ Maelkehandelens Europaeiske Union (inactive)
- ♦ MAEM – Mediterranean Academy of Emergency Medicine (unconfirmed)
- ♦ MAEN – Mezhdunarodnaya Assotsiatsia – Eposy Narodov Mira (no recent information)
- ♦ Maestral International (internationally oriented national body)
- ♦ Maestre Pie Filippini (religious order)
- ♦ MAF – Conference on Methods and Applications in Fluorescence (meeting series)

♦ Mafia 16541

Address not obtained.

History during 13th century in Sicily, as a hierarchically structured secret society of individuals using terrorist methods including blackmail, violence and murder, originally in protection of lands, orchards and marketing but subsequently penetrating the construction and entertainment industries and the illegal drug market. As a consequence of emigration, a network of such societies has been built up in a number of countries, notably the United States and South America, and is considered to be intimately linked to the various forms of internationally organized crime. Through investment may have extended its connections to legitimate business. Also known, especially in the USA, as *Cosa Nostra*. **NGO Relations** Possible links with: *Mara Salvatrucha (MS, #16570).* [2010/XF8640/s/**F**]

- ♦ MAF – International Conference on Mathematical and Statistical Methods for Actuarial Sciences and Finance (meeting series)
- ♦ **MAF** Mission Aviation Fellowship (#16829)
- ♦ **MAFS** Mediterranean Academy of Forensic Sciences (#16637)
- ♦ **MAFVA** Miniature Armoured Fighting Vehicle Association (#16810)
- ♦ Magasins du monde-Oxfam (internationally oriented national body)
- ♦ Magdalena Aulina Institute (religious order)
- ♦ Magee Womancare International (internationally oriented national body)

♦ Magellan Exchange 16542

Dir 920 Broadway St, Ste 312, One University Plaza, MS0130, Cape Girardeau MO 63701, USA. T. +15733357111. Fax +15733357110.

URL: http://www.magellanexchange.org/

Aims Provide opportunities for students and faculty to have an affordable educational and cultural immersion experience. **Finance** Members' dues.

Members Institutions in 13 countries:

Austria, Belgium, Costa Rica, Denmark, Finland, France, Germany, Korea Rep, Mexico, Netherlands, Serbia, Spain, USA.

Included in the above, 1 organization listed in this Yearbook:

Universidad Latinoamericana de Ciencia y Tecnologia (ULACIT). [2018/XJ6140/y/**F**]

♦ Magento Association 16543

Contact 330 North Wabash Suite 2000, Chicago IL 60611, USA. E-mail: info@magentoassociation.org.

URL: https://www.magentoassociation.org/

History 2018. Registered in the State of Illinois (USA). Registration: USA. **Aims** Advance and empower the global Magento community and commerce ecosystem through open collaboration, education, and thought leadership. **Structure** Board of Directors. **Finance** Sources: members' dues. **Activities** Events/meetings; training/education. [2020/AA0196/**C**]

- ♦ Maghreb Centre for Administrative Studies and Research (no recent information)
- ♦ Maghreb Electricity Committee (#04191)
- ♦ Maghreb Esparto Bureau (inactive)
- ♦ Maghreb Front (unconfirmed)

♦ Maghreb-Mashreq Alliance for Water 16544

Alliance Maghreb-Machrek pour l'eau (ALMAE)

Contact 53 Rond Point Mers Sultan, 21100 Casablanca, Morocco. T. +21222491573 – +21222484561. Fax +21222223397. E-mail: almae@wanadoopro.ma.

History 1993. Registration: Morocco. **Aims** Encourage communication and information exchange; promote the integrated and active participation of civil society in issues concerning *water resources*; act with respect for the diversity of member communities and countries; facilitate synergy for the success of civil society action; provide a forum in order to clearly define all issues concerning access and good governance of water resources. **Structure** General Assembly (annual); Coordinating Committee; Support Committee; Executive Committee; Secretariat in Casablanca (Morocco). **Languages** Arabic, English, French. **Staff** 3.00 FTE, paid. **Finance** Sources: members' dues. **Activities** Events/meetings; knowledge management/information dissemination; training/education. **Events** *Meeting* Cairo (Egypt) 1996, *Meeting* Casablanca (Morocco) 1996. **Publications** Directory of partners involved in water issues; proceedings of workshops and other events.

Members Covers 8 countries and territories:

Algeria, Egypt, Jordan, Lebanon, Mauritania, Morocco, Palestine, Tunisia.

NGO Relations Member of (2): *Mediterranean Information Office for Environment, Culture and Sustainable Development (MIO-ECSDE, #16657)*; *World Water Council (WWC, #21908).* [2015/XD3945/**D**]

- ♦ Maghreb Road Association (no recent information)

- Maghreb Social Forum (unconfirmed)
- Maghreb Studies Association (internationally oriented national body)
- Maghreb Union / see Arab Maghreb Union (#01004)
- Maghreb Union of Voluntary Associations (no recent information)

♦ Magic Circle, The 16545

Cercle magique

Secretariat 12 Stephenson Way, London, NW1 2HD, UK. T. +441923822589. E-mail: secretary@themagiccircle.co.uk.

Registered Office 12 Stephenson Way, London, NW1 2HD, UK. T. +442073872222. Fax +442073875114.

URL: http://www.TheMagicCircle.co.uk/

History Founded 1905, London (UK). **Aims** Promote and advance the art of magic. **Activities** Events/meetings; awards/prizes/competitions; knowledge management/information dissemination. **Events** *Nordic magical congress* Copenhagen (Denmark) 1999. **Publications** *The Magic Circular* (12 a year) – only for members. **Members** Full people who have knowledge of, and practical ability in, the art of magic; Apprentice people who are training to become full members, with sufficient knowledge and ability to pass an examination within 2 years. Individuals (1,500) in about 38 countries. Membership countries not specified.
[2016.06.21/XF2940/v/**F**]

- **MAGI** International Association of Medical Genetics (#12025)
- MAGIS – Movimento e Azione dei Gesuiti per lo Sviluppo (internationally oriented national body)

♦ Magistrats européens pour la démocratie et les libertés (MEDEL) . . 16546

European Magistrates for Democracy and Liberties

Contact Greifswalder Str 4, Briefkasten 42, 10405 Berlin, Germany.

URL: http://www.medelnet.eu/

History 15 Jun 1985, Strasbourg (France). Statutes adopted 29 Nov 1987, Paris (France). Former names and other names: *European Judges for Democracy and Liberties* – former. Registration: EU Transparency Register, No/ID: 981119221130-18; France. **Aims** Promote a European jurisdictional culture based on the legal values of democracy, essentially respect for human rights and fundamental freedoms; protect differences between human beings and the rights of minorities, especially of immigrants and the disadvantaged, with a view to social emancipation; support European integration in creating a European political union aimed at greater social justice; defend the independence of the judiciary from other authorities and specific interests; promote transparency of the judicial system, democratization of the magistrature and the right of judges to meet, to express themselves and to form unions; promote exchange of information and of a democratic legal culture between judges of different countries. **Structure** A federation of European judges and prosecutors' free associations and unions. Congress (annual). Board, elected by the Administrative Council for a renewable term of 2 years, comprising Chairman, Vice-President, Treasurer, Secretary-General and 4 members. **Languages** English, French. **Staff** Voluntary. **Finance** Members' dues. **Activities** Events/meetings; training/education. **Events** *Colloquium* Ankara (Turkey) 2009, *Colloquium* Hamburg (Germany) 2009, *Colloquium* Lampedusa (Italy) 2009, *Colloquium* Bucharest (Romania) 2008, *Colloquium* Palermo (Italy) 2008. **Publications** *Europeanrights* (12 a year) – magazine; *Medel Social* (12 a year) – magazine.
Members National associations of judges and public prosecutors (18) representing about 15,000 members, in 12 countries:
Belgium, Cyprus, Czechia, France, Germany, Greece, Italy, Poland, Portugal, Romania, Serbia, Spain.
Consultative Status Consultative status granted from: *Council of Europe (CE, #04881)* (Participatory Status). **IGO Relations** Observer status with: *Conseil consultatif de procureurs européens (CCPE, #04685); Consultative Council of European Judges (CCJE, #04767); Commission européenne pour l'efficacité de la justice (CEPEJ, #04213). European Committee on Crime Problems (CDPC, #06645).* [2021/XD5328/**D**]

- MAGMANet / see European Institute of Molecular Magnetism (#07566)
- Magmeet – International Conference on the Scientific and Clinical Applications of Magnetic Carriers (meeting series)
- MAG – Mines Advisory Group (internationally oriented national body)

♦ Magna Charta Observatory 16547

SG Via Zamboni 25, 40126 Bologna BO, Italy. T. +36512098709. Fax +36512098710. E-mail: magnacharta@unibo.it.

URL: http://www.magna-charta.org/

History Set up by *European University Association (EUA, #09027)* and University of Bologna (Italy). Full title: *Magna Charta Observatory of Fundamental University Values and Rights.* Magna Chart Universitatum signed, 1988, Bologna, by 388 Rectors of worldwide universities. **Aims** Gather information, express opinions and prepare documents relating to the respect for, and protection of, the fundamental *university values* and *rights* laid down in the Magna Charta Universitatum. **Structure** Council, comprising President, Vice-President, Honorary President and and 11 members. Secretariat, composed of Secretary-General and Administrator. **Events** *Annual Conference* Bologna (Italy) 2013, *Annual Conference* Bologna (Italy) 2012, *Annual Conference* Bologna (Italy) 2011, *Annual Conference* Bologna (Italy) 2010, *Annual Conference* Bologna (Italy) 2009.
Members Signatory universities (755) in 81 countries and territories:
Albania, Andorra, Argentina, Armenia, Australia, Austria, Azerbaijan, Bahrain, Belgium, Bosnia-Herzegovina, Brazil, Bulgaria, Cambodia, Canada, Chile, China, Colombia, Croatia, Cyprus, Czechia, Denmark, Dominican Rep, Ecuador, Egypt, El Salvador, Estonia, Finland, France, Georgia, Germany, Ghana, Greece, Guatemala, Hungary, Iceland, India, Indonesia, Iran Islamic Rep, Ireland, Israel, Italy, Japan, Kazakhstan, Kosovo, Kyrgyzstan, Latvia, Lebanon, Lithuania, Malta, Mexico, Moldova, Morocco, Netherlands, Nigeria, North Macedonia, Norway, Palestine, Paraguay, Peru, Philippines, Poland, Portugal, Puerto Rico, Romania, Russia, Serbia, Slovakia, Slovenia, South Africa, Spain, Sweden, Switzerland, Tunisia, Türkiye, Turkmenistan, UK, Ukraine, USA, Uzbekistan, Venezuela, Zimbabwe.
NGO Relations Affiliate of: *International Association of Universities (IAU, #12246).* [2017/XJ6309/**E**]

- Magna Charta Observatory of Fundamental University Values and Rights / see Magna Charta Observatory (#16547)
- Magnesium Association / see International Magnesium Association (#14073)

♦ Magnetic Imaging in Multiple Sclerosis (MAGNIMS) 16548

Contact Passeig Vall d'Hebron 119-129, 08035 Barcelona, Spain. T. +34934286034. Fax +34934286059.

Website Administrator address not obtained.

URL: http://www.magnims.eu/

Structure Steering Committee, comprising 2 Co-Chairs and 13 members. **Events** *Workshop and Plenary Meeting* Barcelona (Spain) 2016. [2013/XJ0462/**E**]

- Magnetics and Optics Research International Symposium (meeting series)
- Magnetic Union (inactive)
- Magnetospheres of the Outer Planets (meeting series)
- **MAGNIMS** Magnetic Imaging in Multiple Sclerosis (#16548)
- Magnus Hirschfeld Center for Human Rights (internationally oriented national body)
- Magyar Külügyi Intézet (internationally oriented national body)
- Magyar Nemzetközi Fejlesztési Segitségnyújtasi (internationally oriented national body)
- Magyar Okumenikus Segélyszervezet (internationally oriented national body)
- Magyar Tudomanyos Akademia Vilaggazdasagi Kutatointezet (internationally oriented national body)
- Magyar Zsidók Vilagszövetsége (#21439)
- Mahabodhi International Meditation Centre (internationally oriented national body)
- Maharishi International University / see Maharishi University of Management (#16549)

♦ Maharishi University of Management (MUM) 16549

Contact 1000 North Fourth St, Fairfield IA 52557, USA. T. +16414721110. Fax +16414721179. E-mail: admissions@mum.edu.

URL: http://www.mum.edu/

History 1971, by Maharishi Mahesh Yogi. Previously referred to as *Maharishi International University (MIU).* **Aims** Provide *consciousness*-based education to unfold the individual's *creative* potential; stimulate sustainability for life in *harmony* with natural law; fulfil the goals set by the founder. **Languages** English. **Finance** Grant support from US National Institutes of Health and other government agencies. **Activities** Training/education; events/meetings. **Publications** *The Review* (10 a year); *University Report* (annual). **Members** Not a membership organization. [2018.08.09/XF6397/**F**]

- Mahatma Gandhi Canadian Foundation for World Peace (internationally oriented national body)
- Mahatma Gandhi Human Rights Movement (internationally oriented national body)
- MAHCONF – International Conference on Modern Approach in Humanities (meeting series)
- MAI / see Medical Ambassadors International
- MAIB / see Mediterranean Agronomic Institute of Bari (#16641)
- **MAICh** Mediterranean Agronomic Institute of Chania (#16642)
- MAIC – Mine Action Information Center (internationally oriented national body)
- **MAIIF** Marine Accident Investigators' International Forum (#16577)
- MAI – Maison des Associations Internationales (internationally oriented national body)
- MAI – Media Associates International (internationally oriented national body)
- MAI – Missionary Athletes International (internationally oriented national body)
- MAI – Monash Asia Institute (internationally oriented national body)
- MAIN – Microfinance African Institutions Network (internationally oriented national body)
- Mains tendues – Organisme contre la faim et pour le développement des peuples / see Mani Tese
- La main tendue (internationally oriented national body)
- MAI – OECD multilateral agreement on investment (inactive)
- **MAIS** Mediterranean Association of International Schools (#16646)
- MAIS – Movimento per l'Autosviluppo, l'Interscambio et la Solidarietà (internationally oriented national body)
- Maison Afrique, La (internationally oriented national body)
- Maison de l'Amérique latine, Bruxelles (internationally oriented national body)
- Maison Asie Pacifique (internationally oriented national body)
- Maison des Associations Internationales (internationally oriented national body)

♦ Maison Chance Organization 16550

Association Maison Chance

Founder Take Wing Center – Trung Tam Chap Canh, 19A Duong so 1, KP. 9, P. Binh Hung Hoa A, Binh Tan District, Ho Chi Minh City HO CHI MINH 71912, Vietnam. T. +842862659566 – +842837670433. E-mail: vietnam@maison-chance.org.

URL: http://www.maison-chance.org/

History 1993, Vietnam. Founded on the initiative of Aline Rebeaud. Following setting up of similar houses in France and Switzerland (1996), Belgium (2006) and Canada and USA (2008), all joined together in one federation, 2009. Registration: Swiss Civil Code, Start date: 2012, Switzerland. **Aims** Help orphans and people with disabilities; provide a place for under-privileged children and the disabled can study and work; provide health care services; facilitate rehabilitation and reinsertion into social life. **Structure** Branches (6), each has its own Management Committee. **Languages** English, French, Vietnamese. **Staff** 117.00 FTE, paid; 10.00 FTE, voluntary. **Finance** Sources: fundraising. Annual budget: 1,000,000 USD. **Activities** Guidance/assistance/consulting; healthcare; training/education.
Members Houses in 6 countries:
Belgium, Canada, France, Switzerland, USA, Vietnam. [2021.05.24/XM2265/**F**]

- Maison des citoyens du monde (internationally oriented national body)
- Maison du Covenant (internationally oriented national body)
- Maison des Cultures du Monde (internationally oriented national body)
- Maison européenne de la protection sociale, Bruxelles (internationally oriented national body)
- Maison de l'Europe de Paris (internationally oriented national body)
- Maison de l'Europe de Paris – Centre de rencontres internationales / see Maison de l'Europe de Paris
- Maison de la grande région (internationally oriented national body)
- Maison internationale de l'environnement (internationally oriented national body)
- Maison méditerranéenne des sciences de l'homme (internationally oriented national body)
- Maison nordique des îles Faroe (internationally oriented national body)
- Maison nordique à Reykjavik / see Nordic House in Reykjavik
- Maison du Peuple d'Europe (internationally oriented national body)
- Maison de sagesse (internationally oriented national body)
- Maisons familiales rurales / see Union nationale des maisons familiales rurales d'éducation et d'orientation
- Maison syndicale internationale, Bruxelles (internationally oriented national body)
- Maison des Tiers Mondes, Montpellier / see Maison des Tiers monde et de la solidarité internationale
- Maison des Tiers monde et de la solidarité internationale (internationally oriented national body)
- Maison universelle des Séphardin (inactive)
- Maîtresses Pieuses Filippini (religious order)
- MAI of Zaragoza / see Mediterranean Agronomic Institute of Zaragoza (#16644)
- **MAIZ** Mediterranean Agronomic Institute of Zaragoza (#16644)
- **MAJIC** International Federation of Associations in the Field of Microwave and RF Power Engineering (#13362)
- Majles Addefaa al Arabi Almouchtarak (no recent information)
- El Majles el Ahla Liel Riadha Biifriqya (inactive)
- Majlis Da'wah Islamiah Serantau Asia Tenggara dan Pasifik (#18792)
- majmae alfiqh al'iislamii aldawli (#13960)

♦ Major Cities of Europe IT Users Group (MCE) 16551

Headquarters Postbox 210360, 27524 Bremerhaven, Germany. T. +494715902115. Fax +494715902022. E-mail: info@majorcities.eu.

URL: http://www.majorcities.eu/

History 1982, on initiative of the Greater London (UK) Council. **Aims** Promote voluntary exchange of ideas, visions and experience among members so as to improve performance of *local government* by using information and communication technology; represent collective interests of members in discussion with public authorities, suppliers of information technology and other relevant organizations at European level. **Structure** Group Annual Conference. Organizing Committee, including President, Vice-Presidents, Treasurer, Secretary and members. **Languages** English. **Staff** Voluntary. **Finance** Members' dues. Sponsorship. Budget (annual): about euro 15,000. **Activities** Organizes annual conference and workshops. **Events** *Annual Conference* Hamburg (Germany) 2015, *Annual Conference* Zurich (Switzerland) 2014, *Annual Conference* Ljubljana (Slovenia) 2013, *Annual Conference* Vienna (Austria) 2012, *Annual Conference* Prato, RN (Italy) 2011. **Publications** *MCE Newsletter.*
Members Representatives of 45 cities in 19 countries:
Austria, Bosnia-Herzegovina, Bulgaria, Croatia, Denmark, France, Germany, Greece, Ireland, Israel, Italy, Netherlands, Norway, Slovenia, Spain, Sweden, Switzerland, UK, USA. [2018/XF5925/**F**]

♦ Major Economies Forum on Energy and Climate (MEF) 16552

Contact US Dept of State, 1951 Constitution Ave, Washington DC 20240, USA. T. +12026474875. Fax +12026470191. E-mail: mef_secretariat@state.gov.

URL: http://www.majoreconomiesforum.org/

History 28 Mar 2009, as a partnership of 17 major economies. **Aims** Facilitate dialogue among major developed and developing economies; advance the exploration of concrete initiatives and joint ventures that increase the supply of clean energy while cutting greenhouse gas emissions. **Events** *Meeting of the Leaders Representatives* New York, NY (USA) 2016, *Meeting of the Leaders Representatives* New York, NY (USA) 2016, *Meeting of the Leaders Representatives* Luxembourg (Luxembourg) 2015, *Meeting of the Leaders Representatives* New York, NY (USA) 2015, *Meeting of the Leaders Representatives* Washington, DC (USA) 2015.
Members Economies of 16 countries:
Australia, Brazil, Canada, China, France, Germany, India, Indonesia, Italy, Japan, Korea Rep, Mexico, Russia, South Africa, UK, USA.
Regional entity:
European Union (EU, #08967). [2016/XJ1174/**F***]

♦ **Major Groups Partnership on Forests (MGPoF)** **16553**
Office Manager 1781 Paisley Avenue, Ottawa ON K2C 1A7, Canada. T. +16132364763.
Pres/CEO address not obtained.
History Originated in activities of Major Groups following UN forest policy debates with the inception of Intergovernmental Panel on Forests (IPF), 1995. Founded 2012. **Aims** Advance conservation and sustainable forest management in partnerships. **Structure** Board of Directors. **Consultative Status** Consultative status granted from: *ECOSOC (#05331)* (Special). **IGO Relations** Supports (1): *United Nations Forum on Forests (UNFF, #20562).* [2021/XM7244/**F**]

♦ Make-a-Wish Foundation / see Make-a-Wish Foundation International
♦ Make-a-Wish Foundation International (internationally oriented national body)
♦ Makedonischer Weltjugendkongress

♦ **Make Mothers Matter** **16554**
SG 5 rue de l'Université, 75007 Paris, France. T. +33142882728. E-mail: info@makemothersmatter.org.
URL: http://www.makemothersmatter.org/
History May 1947, Paris (France). Original title: *World Movement of Mothers (WMM) – Mouvement mondial des mères (MMM) – Movimiento Mundial de las Madres – Weltbewegung der Mütter.* Subsequently changed title to *Make Mothers Matter – International – Mouvement Mondial des Mères – International (MMM I).* New statutes adopted: 18 May 1962, Paris; 21 May 1992, Paris; 14 Jun 2001; 3 Jul 2009, Paris; 2 Dec 2010, Paris; 1 Jun 2012, Paris; 7 Apr 2014. Registration: RNA, No/ID: W751018133, Start date: 23 Aug 1949, France. **Aims** Advocate and support mothers as changemakers for a better world. **Structure** General Assembly (annual); Board of Governors; Executive Office. **Languages** English, French, Spanish. **Staff** Voluntary. **Finance** Sources: donations; fundraising; members' dues; sale of publications. **Activities** Events/meetings; knowledge management/information dissemination; networking/liaising. **Events** *Mothers and Health* Brussels (Belgium) 2016, *Annual Meeting* Beirut (Lebanon) 2003, *Annual meeting* Paris (France) 2002, *Annual Meeting* Brussels (Belgium) 2001, *Annual Meeting* Paris (France) 1999. **Publications** *La Lettre* – newsletter. *The Role of Women in Peace Building and Security.* Brochures; statements.
Members Honorary; Supporting; Affiliate; Associations. Member associations in 31 countries:
Austria, Bangladesh, Belgium, Cameroon, Central African Rep, Colombia, Congo DR, Côte d'Ivoire, France, Germany, Greece, Ireland, Italy, Lebanon, Luxembourg, Madagascar, Mali, Mauritius, Morocco, Nigeria, Romania, Rwanda, Slovakia, South Africa, Spain, Sweden, Switzerland, UK, Uruguay, USA, Zimbabwe.
Consultative Status Consultative status granted from: *ECOSOC (#05331)* (General); *UNESCO (#20322)* (Consultative Status); *FAO (#09260)* (Special Status); *UNICEF (#20332).* **IGO Relations** In relation with: *ILO (#11123).* Associated with Department of Global Communications of the United Nations. **NGO Relations** Member of: *Child Rights Connect (#03884); Conference of Non-Governmental Organizations in Consultative Relationship with the United Nations (CONGO, #04635); NGO Forum on Environment (FOE, #17125); NGO Committee on the Status of Women, Geneva (#17117); SDG Watch Europe (#19162); Vienna NGO Committee on the Family (#20774).* Associate member of: *Social Platform (#19344).* [2020/XC3560/**C**]

♦ Make Mothers Matter – International / see Make Mothers Matter (#16554)
♦ Making Cents International (internationally oriented national body)
♦ Making Change (internationally oriented national body)
♦ Making Drylands Food Secure / see Global Dryland Alliance (#10326)

♦ **Making Finance Work for Africa (MFW4A)** **16555**
Secretariat c/o ADB, Immeuble du CCIA, Avenue Jean-Paul II, 01 BP 1387, Abidjan 01, Côte d'Ivoire. E-mail: secretariat@mfw4a.org.
URL: https://www.mfw4a.org/
Aims Be *the* reference platform for advocacy, knowledge sharing and cooperation on financial sector development in Africa. **Structure** Supervisory Board. Secretariat, hosted at *African Development Bank (ADB, #00283).* Working Groups. **Activities** Events/meetings; knowledge management/information dissemination; networking/liaising.
Members Governing members (5):
African Development Bank Group (ADB Group, #00284); African Export-Import Bank (Afreximbank, #00305); Agence française de développement (AFD); Deutsche Gesellschaft für Internationale Zusammenarbeit (GIZ); European Investment Bank (EIB, #07599).
Partners (6):
African Crowdfunding Association (ACfA); African Union for Housing Finance (AUHF, #00491); Association of African Central Banks (AACB, #02352); Association of African Development Finance Institutions (AADFI, #02353); Caisse régionale de refinancement hypothécaire; *Centre for Affordable Housing Finance in Africa (CAHF, #03723).* [2023/XM5996/y/**E**]

♦ **MAK** Mezhgosudarstvennyj aviacionnyj komitet (#15977)

♦ **Maktab Tarighat Oveyssi Shahmaghsoudi (MTO Shahmaghsoudi)** . . **16556**
Ecole de Soufisme Islamique – School of Islamic Sufism
Public Relations Office PO Box 3620, Washington DC 20027, USA. T. +12023420022. Fax +17034306530. E-mail: info@mto.org.
URL: http://www.mto.org/
History 670, by Hazrat Oveys Gharani. Since then the 'Holy Cloak' of the Prophet has passed to Sufi teachers in unbroken succession. Also referred to as *Oveyssi School of Sufism.* **Aims** Educate and assist in understanding the reality of *religion* in the attainment of world peace and tranquility from the smallest unit, such as the family, to the world community. **Structure** Board of Directors, including Chairman, President, Vice Presidents, Secretary, Treasurer and Directors. Public Relations Representatives; Office Managers in each chapter. **Languages** Arabic, Chinese, Danish, English, French, German, Hebrew, Hindi, Hungarian, Italian, Norwegian, Pashto, Persian, Portuguese, Russian, Spanish, Swedish, Turkish, Urdu. **Staff** About 800, mostly voluntary. **Finance** Donations; fundraising. **Activities** Education. **Events** *Healing and AIDS* 1990, *Erfan* San Rafael, CA (USA) 1990, *Conference* India 1989, *Conference* Malta 1989, *Healing and AIDS* Sacramento, CA (USA) 1989. **Publications** Books.
Members International chapters (over 100, mainly in USA), grouping about 5400,000 individuals, in 14 countries:
Australia, Austria, Canada, Denmark, France, Germany, India, Italy, Netherlands, Spain, Sweden, Switzerland, UK, USA.
[2016/XF0115/**F**]

♦ Malacological Society of Australasia (internationally oriented national body)

♦ **Malala Fund** **16557**
CEO PO Box 73767, Washington DC 20056, USA. E-mail: info@malalafund.org.
URL: http://www.malala.org/
History 2013. Founded by Nobel Laureate Malala Yousafzai and her father Ziauddin. **Aims** Champion every *girl's* right to 12 years of free, safe, quality *education.* **Structure** Board of Directors. **Staff** 24.00 FTE, paid. **Activities** Advocacy/lobbying/activism; training/education; guidance/assistance/consulting. Active in: Pakistan, Afghanistan, India, Nigeria and countries housing Syrian refugees. **NGO Relations** Supports: *Women in Security, Conflict Management and Peace (WISCOMP).* [2022/XM6631/f/**F**]

♦ Malaria Consortium (internationally oriented national body)

♦ **Malaria Foundation International (MFI)** **16558**
Pres Emory Med School, Vaccine Research Ctr, 954 Gatewood Rd NE, Atlanta GA 30329, USA. T. +14047277214. Fax +14047277845.
URL: http://www.malaria.org/
History 1992. **Aims** Facilitate development and implementation of solutions to health, economic and social problems caused by malaria. **Structure** International Board; Board of Trustees; Scientific Advisory Board; Programme Directors. **NGO Relations** Partner of: *Global Health Advocates (#10400).* [2008/XF4769/f/**F**]

♦ Malaria No More (internationally oriented national body)
♦ MALAS – Midwest Association for Latin American Studies (internationally oriented national body)
♦ Male Contraceptive Initiative (internationally oriented national body)
♦ Mallorca Group / see European Hereditary Tumour Group (#07476)
♦ Mallorca – Missionari dei Sacri Cuori di Gesù e di Maria (religious order)

♦ **Malone Society** **16559**
Contact Dept of English, King's College London, Room 7 10, Virginia Woolf Building, Strand, London, WC2B 6LE, UK. T. +442078487837.
URL: http://malonesociety.com/
History 1906, Oxford/London. Registered Charity: 1027048. **Aims** *Publish* scholarly editions of inaccessible materials for the study of *Renaissance drama* in the UK. **Structure** General Meeting (annual); Council; Editorial Committee. **Finance** Members' dues. **Activities** Research/documentation; publishing activities. **Events** *Centenary conference / Conference* Oxford (UK) 2006, *Conference* Oxford (UK) 2002, *Annual General Meeting* Oxford (UK) 1992. **Publications** Texts of Renaissance plays and related manuscripts written before 1642 (over 180 volumes to date).
Members Libraries and individuals in 16 countries:
Australia, Canada, Denmark, Finland, France, Germany, Ireland, Italy, Netherlands, New Zealand, Norway, Spain, Sweden, Switzerland, UK, USA. [2017/XE3652/v/**E**]

♦ Malteser Foreign Aid Department (internationally oriented national body)
♦ Malteser Hilfsdienst (internationally oriented national body)
♦ Malteser International (internationally oriented national body)
♦ Maltheser Emergency Aid / see Malteser Foreign Aid Department

♦ **Mama Cash** **16560**
Contact PO Box 15686, 1001 ND Amsterdam, Netherlands. T. +31205158700. Fax +31205158799. E-mail: info@mamacash.org.
URL: http://www.mamacash.org/
History 1983. Former names and other names: *Mama Cash Fund for Women* – former; *Mama Cash fonds pour les femmes* – former; *Mama Cash Fundo para Mujeres* – former; *Mama Cash Fonds voor Vrouwen* – former. **Aims** Support women, girls, trans people and intersex people who fight for their rights. **Structure** Board of Directors. **Languages** Dutch, English, French, Russian, Spanish. **Staff** 45.00 FTE, paid. **Publications** *Mama Cash e-zine.* Annual Report. **Members** Not a membership organization. **NGO Relations** Member of (4): *Association for Women's Rights in Development (AWID, #02980); Global Philanthropy Project (GPP, #10546); Philanthropy Europe Association (Philea, #18358); Women's Funding Network.* Supports (1): *International Centre for Reproductive Health and Sexual Rights (INCRESE).* [2020.10.13/XN9931/f/**F**]

♦ Mama Cash fonds pour les femmes / see Mama Cash (#16560)
♦ Mama Cash Fonds voor Vrouwen / see Mama Cash (#16560)
♦ Mama Cash Fundo para Mujeres / see Mama Cash (#16560)
♦ Mama Cash Fund for Women / see Mama Cash (#16560)
♦ MAMA – Mobile Alliance for Maternal Action (internationally oriented national body)
♦ MAMBO – Mediterranean Association for Marine Biology and Oceanology (inactive)
♦ MAMCJ – Missionarias do Amor Misericordioso do Coração de Jesus (religious order)
♦ MAME – Myanmar Actions for Mission and Evangelism (internationally oriented national body)
♦ MAMH / see European Association of Intellectual Disability Medicine (#06089)
♦ **MAMH** European Association of Intellectual Disability Medicine (#06089)
♦ MAMI' / see AMC Institute
♦ Management, Arts and Culture International Association / see Association internationale de management de l'art et de la culture (#02716)
♦ The Management Centre / see The Management Centre of the Mediterranean

♦ **Management Centre Europe (MCE)** **16561**
Managing Dir Rue de l'Aqueduc 118, 1050 Brussels, Belgium. T. +3225432120. Fax +3225432400. E-mail: info@mce-ama.com.
URL: http://www.mce-ama.com/
History Founded 1961, Brussels (Belgium), as European headquarters of *American Management Association International (AMA, #00787).* **Aims** Provide human capital and management development programmes for international companies and public organizations worldwide. **Structure** Councils (2): Senior Human Resource; Marketing and Sales Executives. Includes: *Asia-Pacific Management Institute, Shanghai (no recent information); Middle East Management and Research Centre (no recent information);* Africa Management and Research Centre; South America and Canada Management and Research Centre. **Languages** English. **Staff** 800.00 FTE, paid. **Finance** Members' dues. **Activities** Training/education; guidance/assistance/consulting. **Events** *Meeting* Brussels (Belgium) 2016, *Rebranding Africa Forum* Brussels (Belgium) 2016, *Conference* Barcelona (Spain) 2005, *Annual international pharmaceutical conference* Brussels (Belgium) 2000, *International logistics conference* Brussels (Belgium) 2000. **Publications** *Management Review; MCE Knowledge* – email newsletter; *The Executive Issue.* Books. **Members** Managers and executives (over 100,000) in 65 countries, including in the Middle East, Central Asia and Europe. Membership countries not specified. **NGO Relations** Member of: *EFMD – The Management Development Network (#05387); International Consortium for Executive Development Research (ICEDR, #12913).* [2015.06.01/XF4224/**F**]

♦ The Management Centre of the Mediterranean (internationally oriented national body)
♦ Management for Development Foundation (internationally oriented national body)
♦ Management Sciences for Health (internationally oriented national body)

♦ **Management of Social Transformations (MOST)** **16562**
Gestion des transformations sociales
Contact c/o UNESCO, Research Policy and Foresight Section, 7 place de Fontenoy, 75007 Paris, France. T. +33145680359. Fax +33145685724. E-mail: r.siryani@unesco.org.
URL: http://www.unesco.org/new/en/social-and-human-sciences/themes/most-pro gramme/
History 1992, as a programme of *UNESCO (#20322).* Became operational in 1994. **Aims** Enhance the *social and human sciences* knowledge base to support an improved *policy research* interface to favour achievement of the 2030 Agenda for sustainable and inclusive development; thematic priority areas: social inclusion, environmental change, migration, peace and governance, digital transformations. **Structure** Intergovernmental Council (IGC) (meeting every 2 years); Scientific Advisory Committee (SAC); National Liaison Committees; International and regional partners (NGOs, research institutions, research networks, universities). MOST Secretariat. **Languages** English, French. **Staff** 6.00 FTE, paid. **Finance** Core institutional budget through regular budget of UNESCO. Substantive activities funded by contributions from UNESCO member states and from international and national funding agencies. **Activities** Research/documentation; capacity building; training/education; knowledge management/information dissemination. **Events** *Session* Paris (France) 2019, *Session* Kuala Lumpur (Malaysia) 2017, *Extraordinary Session* Paris (France) 2017, *Session* Paris (France) 2015, *Session* Paris (France) 2011. **Publications** *Inclusive Policy Lab Thinkpieces* (4 a year); *MOST Discussion Papers* (4 a year); *MOST Policy Papers* (2 a year). Books; training materials including MOOCs. **Information Services** *Inclusive Policy Lab* – global online service.
Members Member states of the Intergovernmental Council (2017-2019) in 29 countries:
Afghanistan, Argentina, Bahrain, Benin, Costa Rica, Cuba, Czechia, Dominican Rep, Ecuador, Egypt, Ethiopia, France, Ghana, Indonesia, Kenya, Madagascar, Malaysia, Pakistan, Philippines, Qatar, Russia, Saudi Arabia, Slovakia, Sri Lanka, Tanzania UR, Thailand, Togo, Türkiye, Zimbabwe.
IGO Relations Partners include:
- *African Development Bank (ADB, #00283);*
- *Centre for the Coordination of Research and Documentation in Social Science for Sub-Saharan Africa (no recent information);*
- *Instituto Latinoamericano de las Naciones Unidas para la Prevención del Delito y Tratamiento del Delincuente (ILANUD, #11347);*
- *International Bank for Reconstruction and Development (IBRD, #12317)* and its European Office;
- *Latin American Faculty of Social Sciences (#16316);*
- *OECD (#17693);*
- *Swiss Agency for Development and Cooperation (SDC);*
- *UNDP (#20292);*
- *UNESCO Environment and Development in Coastal Regions and Small Islands (UNESCO CSI Programme, see: #20322);*
- *UNICEF (#20332);*
- *United Nations Economic Commission for Latin America and the Caribbean (ECLAC, #20556);*
- Governing Council of

- *United Nations Human Settlements Programme (UN-Habitat, #20572)*;
- *United Nations Population Fund (UNFPA, #20612)*;
- *United Nations University (UNU, #20642)*.

NGO Relations Partners include:
- *Association of Asian Social Science Research Councils (AASSREC, #02382)*;
- *Association Internationale des Maires et responsables des capitales et métropoles partiellement ou entièrement Francophones (AIMF, #02715)*;
- *Centro de Estudios Municipales y de Cooperación Internacional (CEMCI)*;
- *Commission mondiale d'éthique des connaissances scientifiques et des technologies de l'UNESCO (COMEST, #04235)*;
- *Consejo Latinoamericano de Ciencias Sociales (CLACSO, #04718)*;
- *Council for the Development of Social Science Research in Africa (CODESRIA, #04879)*;
- *European and Mediterranean Network for the Social Sciences (EUMENESS, no recent information)*;
- *Groupement d'intérêt scientifique pour l'étude de la mondialisation et du développement (GEMDEV)*;
- *Habitat International Coalition (HIC, #10845)*;
- *Helen Keller International (HKI, #10902)*;
- *Ibero-American Union of Municipalists (#11034)*;
- *Instituto Tecnológico y de Estudios Superiores de Occidente (ITESO)*;
- *International Association for Social Science Information Service and Technology (IASSIST, #12169)*;
- *International Committee for Social Science Information and Documentation (ICSSD, no recent information)*;
- *International Council for Philosophy and Human Sciences (CIPSH, #13061)*;
- *International Society of City and Regional Planners (ISOCARP, #15012)*;
- *Netherlands Organization for International Cooperation in Higher Education (NUFFIC)*;
- *Social Science Research Council (SSRC)*;
- *Solidarités agricoles et alimentaires (SOLAGRAL)*;
- *Union internationale des associations et organismes scientifiques et techniques (UATI, #20421)*;
- *World Organization of United Cities and Local Governments (UCLG, #21695)*. [2018.06.13/XF5361/**F***]

♦ Managing the Environment Locally in Sub-Saharan Africa (no recent information)
♦ MANA – Musicians Against Nuclear Arms (internationally oriented national body)

♦ MANCEF 16563

Headquarters PO Box 3092, Wimberley TX 78676, USA. E-mail: row@mtu.edu.
URL: http://www.mancef.org/

History Founded 1996, following several conferences organized since 1994. Officially incorporated 26 Dec 2000, in the state of Florida (USA). Original title: *Micro and Nanotechnology Commercialization Education Foundation (MANCEF)*. Currently functions under acronym with subtitle: *Emergeing Tech Commercializaion*. **Aims** Connect a global community focused on commercializing micro and nanotechnologies through conferences and educational efforts. **Structure** Executive Board of Directors; Strategic Operations Board of Directors. **Activities** Events/meetings. **Events** *Annual Conference on the Commercialization of Micro-Nano Systems* Shenyang (China) 2021, *Annual Conference on the Commercialization of Micro-Nano Systems* Rockville, MD (USA) 2020, *Annual Conference on the Commercialization of Micro-Nano Systems* Montreux (Switzerland) 2018, *Annual Conference on the Commercialization of Micro-Nano Systems* Houston, TX (USA) 2016, *Annual Conference on the Commercialization of Micro-Nano Systems / COMS Conference* Enschede (Netherlands) 2013. **Members** Organizational; Charter; Individual; Student. Membership countries not specified. [2020/XJ6691/f/**F**]

♦ Manchester College Peace Studies Institute (internationally oriented national body)
♦ Mandat d'arrêt européen (2001 treaty)
♦ Mandat International (internationally oriented national body)

♦ Mande Studies Association (MANSA) 16564

Association du études Mande

Pres Dept of Religion, Florida State Univ, PO Box 3061520, Tallahassee FL 32306-1520, USA.
URL: http://mandestudies.org/

History 1 Nov 1986, Madison WI (USA). **Aims** Bring researchers, students and teachers together to share interests in the Mande-speaking people of *Africa* and the African diaspora, and in those who live and interact with Mande-speakers. **Structure** Executive Committee; Advisory Board; Ad-hoc Committees. **Languages** English, French, Mandingo. **Finance** Members' dues. Other sources: donations; contributions from countries and institutions hosting triennial conference. **Activities** Events/meetings; networking/liaising. **Events** *Conference* Bobo Dioulasso (Burkina Faso) 2014, *Conference* Bamako (Mali) 2011, *Conference* Lisbon (Portugal) 2008, *Conference* Conakry (Guinea) / Kankan (Guinea) 2005, *Conference* Leiden (Netherlands) 2002. **Publications** *Mande Studies* (annual).
Members Individuals in 21 countries:
Australia, Belgium, Benin, Burkina Faso, Canada, Congo Brazzaville, Côte d'Ivoire, France, Germany, Guinea, Ireland, Italy, Japan, Mali, Netherlands, Niger, Russia, Sweden, Switzerland, UK, USA.
NGO Relations Affiliate organization of: *African Studies Association (ASA)*. [2018.06.01/XE4427/**E**]

♦ MANEB / see International Academy of Ecology and Life Protection Sciences
♦ Man-Environment Research Association (internationally oriented national body)
♦ Manganese Centre / see International Manganese Institute (#14083)
♦ Mangrove Macrobenthos and Management Meeting (meeting series)
♦ Mangroves for the Future / see Mangroves for the Future (#16565)

♦ Mangroves for the Future (MFF) 16565

Coordinator c/o IUCN Asia Regional Office, 63 Soi 39 Sukhumvit Road, Wattana, Bangkok, 10110, Thailand. T. +6626624029ext144. E-mail: asia@iucn.org.
URL: http://www.mangrovesforthefuture.org/

History 2006. Full title: *Mangroves for the Future (MFF) – Investing in coastal ecosystems*. **Aims** Promote investment in *coastal ecosystem conservation* for sustainable development. **Structure** Co-Chaired by *International Union for Conservation of Nature and Natural Resources (IUCN, #15766)* and *UNDP (#20292)*. Regional Steering Committee; National Coordination Body. Secretariat. **Finance** Financed by: *DANIDA*; *Norwegian Agency for Development Cooperation (Norad)*; Royal Norwegian Embassy in Thailand; *Swedish International Development Cooperation Agency (Sida)*; core partners; private sector. **Activities** Financial and/or material support. **Events** *US-ASEAN Conference on Marine Environmental Issues* Bangkok (Thailand) 2017.
Members Participants. Co-Chairs (2):
International Union for Conservation of Nature and Natural Resources (IUCN, #15766); *UNDP (#20292)*.
National governments (11):
Bangladesh, Cambodia, India, Indonesia, Maldives, Myanmar, Pakistan, Seychelles, Sri Lanka, Thailand, Vietnam.
Institutional partners (8):
ASEAN Centre for Biodiversity (ACB, #01149); *DANIDA*; *FAO (#09260)*; *Norwegian Agency for Development Cooperation (Norad)*; Royal Norwegian Embassy – Thailand; *Swedish International Development Cooperation Agency (Sida)*; *UNEP (#20299)*; *Wetlands International (#20928)*. [2018/XM5423/y/**E**]

♦ Manila Accord (1963 treaty)
♦ Manila pact – Pacific Charter: Southeast Asia Collective Defence Treaty (1954 treaty)
♦ Mani Tese (internationally oriented national body)
♦ Mani Tese – Organismo contro la Fame e per lo Sviluppo dei Popoli / see Mani Tese
♦ Manitoba Council for International Cooperation (internationally oriented national body)
♦ Mankind 2000 (inactive)
♦ **MAN** MERLOT African Network (#16726)
♦ MAN – Mouvement pour une alternative non-violente (internationally oriented national body)
♦ Manna International (internationally oriented national body)
♦ Mannréttindaskrifstofa Islands (internationally oriented national body)

♦ Mano River Union (MRU) 16566

Union du fleuve Mano

Secretariat 32S Spur Loop, Wilberforce, Freetown, Sierra Leone.
Sub-office Guinea c/o Min of Cooperation, BP 1712, Conakry, Guinea.
Sub-office Liberia c/o Min of Planning, PM Bag 9050, Ministry of Planning and Economic Affairs, Monrovia, Liberia.
URL: http://www.manoriverunion.int/

History 3 Oct 1973, Malema, as a customs union between the Governments of Liberia and Sierra Leone, an arrangement in which all the other States in the Western African Sub-Region may participate. Protocols to the Declaration signed 1974, Bo (Liberia). **Aims** Expand trade; encourage productive capacity; progressively develop a common policy and cooperation as regards harmonization of tariffs and regulations related to customs, qualifications and postal services; promote joint development projects; secure a fair distribution of the benefits from economic cooperation. **Structure** Assembly of Heads of State. Joint Ministerial Council (meets at least once a year), consisting of Economics and Finance Ministers of member States. Technical Commissions, meet before Ministerial Council and present recommendations for approval. Divisions (3): Finance; Economic Affairs; Administration and Personnel. **Languages** English, French. **Staff** 65.00 FTE, paid. **Finance** Members' dues. **Activities** Common External Tariff instituted between Liberia and Sierra Leone, Apr 1977; extension to Guinea envisaged. Trade between Liberia and Sierra Leone liberalized 1 May 1981, for specific goods of local origin; Guinea was later incorporated into the trade liberalization scheme. Emphasizes cooperation through practical and feasible measures in areas of trade liberalization and facilitation, industry, agriculture, livestock and transport. **Events** *Annual meeting / Annual Council of Ministers* Sierra Leone 2000, *Annual meeting* Freetown (Sierra Leone) 1994, *Annual Council of Ministers* Sierra Leone 1994, *Meeting / Annual Council of Ministers* Guinea 1992, *Annual Council of Ministers* Sierra Leone 1991.
Members Governments of 3 countries:
Guinea, Liberia, Sierra Leone.
IGO Relations Relationship agreement with: *FAO (#09260)*. Under Lomé Conventions, links with: *European Commission (EC, #06633)*. Participates in the activities of: *UNCTAD (#20285)*. Instrumental in setting up: *Union Telecommunications and Postal Training Institute (UTTI, no recent information)*. [2014/XD0445/**D***]

♦ MANOSMED / see Mobile Mediterranean University of Mastology (#16836)
♦ **MANOSMED** Mobile Mediterranean University of Mastology (#16836)
♦ Manos Unidas (internationally oriented national body)
♦ Manos Unidas – Campaña contra el Hambre / see Manos Unidas
♦ **MANSA** Mande Studies Association (#16564)
♦ Manufacturers of Educational and Commercial Stationery European Association (inactive)
♦ Manufacturing Enterprise Solutions Association / see MESA International (#16728)
♦ Manufacturing Execution Systems Association / see MESA International (#16728)

♦ Manufuture 16567

Secretariat Daimler AG, Mercedesstr 137, 70327 Stuttgart, Germany. E-mail: info@manufuture.org.
URL: http://www.manufuture.org/

History Former names and other names: *European Technology Platform Manufuture* – alias; *Manufuture Technology Platform* – alias; *Manufuture-EU* – alias. **Aims** Propose, develop and implement a strategy based on research and innovation, capable of speeding up the rate of *industrial* transformation to *high-added-value* products, processes and services, securing high-skills employment and winning a major share of world *manufacturing* output in the future knowledge-driven economy. **Structure** High Level Group – HLG. Groups (4): Implementation Support; Industrial Advisory; National/Regional Manufuture Initiative. Working Groups. **Finance** Sources: none. **Activities** Events/meetings; knowledge management/information dissemination; monitoring/evaluation; research and development. **Events** *General Assembly Stakeholder Meeting* Cambridge (UK) 2015, *Biennial Conference / Conference* Luxembourg (Luxembourg) 2015, *Biennial Conference / Conference* Vilnius (Lithuania) 2013, *Biennial Conference / Conference* Wroclaw (Poland) 2011, *MANUFUTURE : European industrial technologies conference* Brussels (Belgium) 2010. **Publications** ManuFuture Vision 2030 – DIGITAL ISBN: 978–989–95853–7–9, PRINT ISBN: 978-989-95853-8-6. ManuFuture Strategic Research and Innovation Agenda 2030 (SRIA) – DIGITAL ISBN: 978-989-54695-0-5.
Members Full in 21 countries:
Austria, Belgium, Czechia, Denmark, Finland, France, Germany, Greece, Ireland, Italy, Luxembourg, Norway, Poland, Portugal, Romania, Slovakia, Slovenia, Spain, Sweden, Switzerland, UK.
NGO Relations Member of: *European Technology Platform ALICE (ALICE, #08888)*. [2020.05.13/XJ4817/**F**]

♦ Manufuture-EU / see Manufuture (#16567)
♦ Manufuture Technology Platform / see Manufuture (#16567)

♦ Many Strong Voices (MSV) 16568

Co-Dir c/o IRDR UCL, Gower Street, London, WC1E 6BT, UK.
Co-Dir c/o ICC Canada, 75 Albert Street – Suite 1001, Ottawa ON K1P 5E7, Canada.
URL: http://www.manystrongvoices.org/

History Programme launched, Dec 2005, Montréal QC (Canada) at Conference of Parties to *United Nations Framework Convention on Climate Change (UNFCCC, 1992)*. **Aims** Promote well-being, security and *sustainability* of *coastal* communities in the Arctic and Small *Island* Developing States (SIDS) by bringing these regions together to take action on *climate change* mitigation and adaptation, and to publicize their situation. **Structure** Steering Group. Coordinated by University College London (UCL) and *Global Resource Information Database (GRID, #10578)* – Arendal (Norway). **Finance** Financial and/or in-kind support from various organizations, including: *Caribbean Community Climate Change Centre (CCCCC, #03477)*; *Christensen Fund (TCF)*; *International Institute for Environment and Development (IIED, #13877)*; Norwegian Ministry of Foreign Affairs; *OAS (#17629)*; *UNEP (#20299)* and its Regional Office for North America (RONA); *United Nations Foundation (UNF, #20563)*. **IGO Relations** Partners include: *Arctic Athabaskan Council (AAC)*; *Caribbean Community Climate Change Centre (CCCCC, #03477)*; *Global Resource Information Database (GRID, #10578)*; *OAS (#17629)* Department for Sustainable Development; *Secretariat of the Pacific Regional Environment Programme (SPREP, #19205)*; *UNEP (#20299)* – Regional Office for North America; *United Nations Framework Convention on Climate Change (UNFCCC, 1992)*. **NGO Relations** Partners include: *Aleut International Association (AIA)*; *Centre for International Climate and Environmental Research, Oslo (CICERO)*; *Foundation for International Environmental Law and Development (FIELD, inactive)*; *Inuit Circumpolar Council (ICC, #15995)*; *Sea Level Rise Foundation (SLRF, no recent information)*; *Stockholm Environment Institute (SEI, #19993)*. [2019/XJ3012/**E**]

♦ **MAOC-N** Maritime Analysis and Operations Centre – Narcotics (#16581)
♦ MapAction (internationally oriented national body)
♦ **MAPG** Mezdunarodnaja Associacija 'Porodnennye Goroda' (#20271)
♦ Maphilindo (inactive)

♦ MAP International 16569

Office 4700 Glynco Parkway, Brunswick GA 31525-6910, USA. E-mail: map@map.org.
URL: http://www.map.org/

History 1954, as *Medical Assistance Programs*. Current name adopted 1975. **Aims** As a global *Christian health* organization, partner with people living in conditions of *poverty* to save lives and develop healthier families and communities. **Structure** Board; Management Team; Global Offices (9). **Languages** English, French, Spanish. **Finance** Sources: private contributions from individuals and churches; grants from foundations and government agencies; cost sharing by partner agencies. **Activities** Humanitarian/emergency aid; training/education. Active in over 115 countries. **Events** *Workshop on health, culture and the bible* Brunswick, GA (USA) 1998, *Workshop on transformation for better health* St Simons Is, GA (USA) 1997, *Workshop on transformation for better health* St Simons Is, GA (USA) 1997, *Triennial conference on Christian health ministries* St Simons Is, GA (USA) 1996, *Triennial conference on Christian health ministries* St Simons Is, GA (USA) 1993. **Publications** *MAP International Report*. Annual Report. **IGO Relations** *UNHCR (#20327)*. Associated with Department of Global Communications of the United Nations. **NGO Relations** Member of: *Accord Network*; *American Council for Voluntary International Action (InterAction)*; *Association of Evangelicals in Africa (AEA, #02587)*; *Ecumenical Advocacy Alliance (EAA, inactive)*; *Global Relief Alliance*; *Extractive Industries Transparency Initiative (EITI, #09229)*; *Integral (#11364)*. Through Kenya office, supports: *Media for Development International (MFDI)*. [2014.06.01/XF3818/**F**]

♦ Maple Leaf and Eagle Conference in North American Studies (meeting series)
♦ MAP – Medical Aid for Palestinians (internationally oriented national body)
♦ MAP / see Mediterranean Action Plan (#16638)
♦ **MAP** Mediterranean Action Plan (#16638)
♦ MAP Phase II / see Mediterranean Action Plan (#16638)
♦ MAPRIAL / see Mezdunarodnaja Associacija Prepodavatelej Russkogo Jazyka i Literatury (#16739)

♦ **MAPRYAL** Mezdunarodnaja Associacija Prepodavatelej Russkogo Jazyka i Literatury (#16739)
♦ MAPW – Medical Association for the Prevention of War, Australia (internationally oriented national body)
♦ MarAlliance (unconfirmed)
♦ Maranatha Community (internationally oriented national body)
♦ Marangopoulos Foundation for Human Rights (internationally oriented national body)

♦ Mara Salvatrucha (MS) 16570

Salvatrucha Gang

Address not obtained.

History in the 1980s, El Salvador, during the civil war. Also referred to as *MS-13* or *MS-18*. **Structure** Comprises various gangs, originally among Salvadoran emigrants living in Los Angeles CA (USA) but currently in other parts of North America, in Central America and in Europe. No known centralization or hierarchy among regions, although a coordination network is thought to be planned. **Activities** Member gangs carry out acts of violence including rape and murder. Members of groups may have training in firearms, explosives and booby traps. They use tattoos to express their allegiance and are expected to remain members for life – deserters are killed.

Members Estimated at about 60,000 individuals in 9 countries:
Belgium, Canada, El Salvador, Guatemala, Honduras, Italy, Mexico, Spain, USA.

NGO Relations Possible links with: *Mafia (#16541)*. [2009/XM7002/s/F]

♦ MARC / see Centre for Asian Studies

♦ MARCALLIANCE 16571

Manager Boulevard St Michel 11, 1040 Brussels, Belgium.
Registered Office Levels 20-21 – Bastion Tower, Place du Champ de Mars 5, 1050 Brussels, Belgium.
URL: http://www.marcalliance.com/

History Launched Jul 2013. Full title: *MARCALLIANCE for Global Law and Tax Practices*. Registered in accordance with Belgian law. **Aims** Provide clients with an access to a full range of legal and tax services, in all areas of business *law*. **Structure** General Meeting; Management Board. **Finance** Members' dues. **Activities** Guidance/assistance/consultancy.

Members Firms (22) in 20 countries:
Brazil, Denmark, Egypt, France, Germany, Ghana, Greece, Hungary, Italy, Korea Rep, Netherlands, Portugal, Russia, Slovakia, Spain, Thailand, Tunisia, Türkiye, UK, United Arab Emirates. [2018.01.18/XM6074/D]

♦ MARCALLIANCE for Global Law and Tax Practices / see MARCALLIANCE (#16571)
♦ Marcelline – Suore di Santa Marcellina (religious order)
♦ Marcel Mérieux Foundation / see Mérieux Foundation
♦ **Marcé Society** International Marcé Society for Perinatal Mental Health (#14089)
♦ Marcha Mundial de la Mujeres (#21632)
♦ Marchas Europeas Contra el Paro, la Precariedad y la Exclusión (#07735)
♦ Marché commun de l'Afrique de l'Est et de l'Afrique australe (#04296)
♦ Marché commun centroaméricain (#03666)
♦ Marché commun nordique (inactive)
♦ Marché commun du Sud (#19868)
♦ Marche mondiale des femmes (#21632)
♦ Marches européennes contre le chômage, la précarité et les exclusions (#07735)
♦ Marché de travail nordique commun (no recent information)
♦ MARCH / see Rehabilitation in Multiple Sclerosis (#18826)

♦ MARCOGAZ – Technical Association of the European Natural Gas Industry 16572

SG Rue Belliard 40, 1040 Brussels, Belgium. T. +3227863074. E-mail: marcogaz@marcogaz.org.
URL: http://www.marcogaz.org/

History 1968. Former names and other names: *Union of the Gas Industries of the Common Market Countries* – former; *Union des industries gazières des pays du Marché commun Union der Gas-Industrie des Gemeinsamen Marktes* – former. Registration: Banque-Carrefour des Entreprises, No/ID: 0877.785.464, Start date: 8 Dec 2005, Belgium; EU Transparency Register, No/ID: 57944346163-37, Start date: 7 Jul 2011. **Aims** Monitor and take influence when needed on European technical regulation, standardization and certification with respect to integrity and safety of pipeline systems, equipment, and rational use of energy. **Structure** General Assembly (annual); Executive Board; Standing Committees (3); Working Groups and Task Forces; Secretariat. **Languages** English. **Staff** 3.00 FTE, paid. **Finance** Sources: members' dues. **Activities** Certification/accreditation; events/meetings; knowledge management/information dissemination; monitoring/evaluation; networking/liaising; standards/guidelines. **Events** *European Gas Technology Conference (EGATEC)* Hamburg (Germany) 2022, *European Gas Technology Conference* Groningen (Netherlands) 2019, *European Gas Technology Conference* Vienna (Austria) 2015, *Annual Pipeline Integrity Management Forum* Berlin (Germany) 2014, *European Gas Technology Conference* Paris (France) 2013. **Publications** Annual Report; papers.

Members Organizations (28) in 20 countries:
Austria, Belgium, Czechia, Denmark, Finland, France, Germany, Greece, Ireland, Italy, Netherlands, Poland, Portugal, Romania, Slovakia, Spain, Sweden, Switzerland, UK, Ukraine.
Eurogas (#05682); *European Gas Research Group (#07380)*; *European Research Institute for Gas and Energy Innovation (ERIG, #08371)*.

IGO Relations Recognized by: *European Commission (EC, #06633)*. Participates in the work of: *United Nations Economic Commission for Europe (UNECE, #20555)*. **NGO Relations** Member of (3): *Eurogas (#05682)*; *European Association for the Streamlining of Energy Exchange-gas (EASEE-gas, #06224)*; *GasNaturally (#10074)*. In liaison with technical committees of: *Comité européen de normalisation (CEN, #04162)*. [2019.02.12/XE3083/ty/E]

♦ Mare Terra – Fundació Medeterrània (internationally oriented national body)
♦ Mare Terra – Mare Terra – Fundació Medeterrània (internationally oriented national body)
♦ MAREVIVO Associazione Ambientalista (internationally oriented national body)

♦ Marfan Europe Network (M.E.N.) 16573

Chair address not obtained. E-mail: chair@marfan.eu.
URL: http://www.marfan.eu/

History 1991. Founded by Diane L Rust at the meeting of 'European Heritable Connective Tissue Disorders', Ghent (Belgium). Former names and other names: *European Marfan Support Network (EMSN)* – former (1991 to 2014). **Aims** Support and encourage members by exchanging and sharing information and working for the benefit of people with Marfan syndrome or related disorders and their families. **Structure** Coordinating Committee. **Languages** English. **Staff** 7.00 FTE, voluntary. **Activities** Events/meetings; knowledge management/information dissemination; networking/liaising. **Events** *Meeting* Paris (France) 2022, *Meeting* Drammen (Norway) 2019, *Meeting* Ebeltoft (Denmark) 2010, *Meeting* Bergen (Norway) 2009, *Conference* Castelnaudary (France) 2006.

Members Organizations in 13 countries:
Austria, Belgium, Denmark, Finland, France, Germany, Luxembourg, Netherlands, Norway, Slovakia, Spain, Sweden, Switzerland.

NGO Relations Member of (1): *EURORDIS – Rare Diseases Europe (#09175)*. [2023.02.27/XF3551/F]

♦ Marfan World 16574

Pres c/o The Marfan Foundation, 22 Manhasset Ave, Port Washington NY 11050, USA. E-mail: cilla71@aol.com – research@marfan.org.
URL: http://www.marfanworld.org/

History 1992, San Francisco CA (USA), a symposium previously being organized in 1988, Baltimore MD (USA). Original title: *International Federation of Marfan Syndrome Organizations (IFMSO)*. Current title adopted 2014, at 9th Symposium. **Aims** Share current, accurate information about the Marfan syndrome and related disorders; facilitate communication among medical professionals; facilitate communication between organizations representing patients and families; support and foster global research; convene the International Symposia on Marfan Syndrome and Related Disorders. **Structure** President; Secretary; Treasurer. **Languages** English. **Staff** Voluntary. **Finance** Members' dues. **Activities** Events/meetings; research/documentation; knowledge management/information dissemination. **Events** *International Symposium* Amsterdam (Netherlands) 2018, *International Symposium* Paris (France) 2014, *International symposium* Warrenton, VA (USA) 2010, *International symposium* Ghent (Belgium) 2005, *International workshop for people with Marfan syndrome* Baltimore, MD (USA) 2002.

Members Organizations and individuals in 32 countries:
Argentina, Australia, Austria, Belgium, Brazil, Canada, China, Costa Rica, Cuba, Denmark, Finland, France, Germany, Greece, Guatemala, India, Ireland, Italy, Japan, Mexico, Netherlands, Norway, Peru, Poland, Portugal, Slovakia, South Africa, Spain, Sweden, Switzerland, UK, USA. [2017.10.27/XD5693/D]

♦ **MAR Fund** Mesoamerican Reef Fund (#09835)
♦ Marga Institute (internationally oriented national body)
♦ Margaret Sanger Center International (internationally oriented national body)
♦ Marian Alliance (see: #21334)
♦ Marian Fathers – Congregation of the Marian Clerics of the Immaculate Conception of the Most Blessed Virgin Mary (religious order)
♦ Mariani – Chierici Mariani sotto il titolo dell'Immacolata Concezione della Beata Vergine Maria (religious order)
♦ Marianische Aktion Kolbe (religious order)
♦ Marianische Preisterbewegung (#16575)
♦ Marianistas – Compañia de Maria (religious order)
♦ Marianiste – Figlie di Maria Immacolata (religious order)
♦ Marianistes – Filles de Marie-Immaculée (religious order)
♦ Marianistes – Société de Marie (religious order)
♦ Marianisti – Società di Maria (religious order)
♦ Marianist Lay Communities (see: #21334)
♦ Marianists – Society of Mary (religious order)
♦ Marianites of Holy Cross (religious order)

♦ Marian Movement of Priests (MMP) 16575

Mouvement sacerdotal marial – Movimiento Sacerdotal Mariano – Marianische Preisterbewegung – Movimento Sacerdotal Mariano (MSM)

International Office Via don Giovanni Bosco 3, 22100 Como CO, Italy. E-mail: info@msm-mmp.org.
URL: http://www.msm-mmp.org/

History 1973. **Activities** Religious activities. **Publications** *To the Priests, Our Lady's Beloved Sons*. [2022.02.09/XF4960/F]

♦ Mariannhiller Missionare (religious order)
♦ Marian Union of Beauraing (religious order)
♦ Marian Youth – International Federation of Children of Mary Immaculate (religious order)
♦ Marichem – International Conference on the Transportation, Handling and Storage of Bulk Chemicals (meeting series)

♦ Marie Curie Alumni Association (MCAA) 16576

Registered Office Avenue des Arts 24, 1000 Brussels, Belgium.
URL: http://www.mariecuriealumni.eu/

History Launched initially as a restricted-access website, 2012. Restructured when registered as an association in accordance with Belgian law, 7 Feb 2014. **Aims** Support, and contribute to, the advancement of knowledge for a global, diverse, and informed society. **Structure** General Assembly; Board; Executive Committee. Working Groups; Chapters. National/Regional Chapters. **Languages** English. **Staff** Voluntary. **Finance** Funding from *European Commission (EC, #06633)* – DG for Education and Culture. **Activities** Events/meetings. **Events** *Annual Conference and General Asssembly* Córdoba (Spain) 2023, *Conference and General Assembly* Vienna (Austria) 2019, *Conference and General Assembly* Leuven (Belgium) 2018, *Conference and General Assembly* Salamanca (Spain) 2017, *Conference and General Assembly* Venice (Italy) 2016. **Publications** *MCAA Newsletter* (4 a year) – online; *IRRADIUM* (1-2 a year) – online magazine. **Members** Individuals (about 10,000). Membership countries not specified. **NGO Relations** Member of: *Initiative for Science in Europe (ISE, #11214)*. [2023/XM6066/v/E]

♦ Marie Schlei Association – Assistance for Women in Africa, Asia and Latin America (internationally oriented national body)
♦ Marie-Schlei-Verein – Hilfe für Frauen in Afrika, Asien und Lateinamerika (internationally oriented national body)
♦ Marie-Schlei-Verein – Hilfe für Frauen in der Dritten Welt / see Marie-Schlei-Verein – Hilfe für Frauen in Afrika, Asien und Lateinamerika
♦ Marie Stopes International / see MSI Reproductive Choices
♦ **MARINALG International** World Association of Seaweed Processors (#21185)

♦ Marine Accident Investigators' International Forum (MAIIF) 16577

Gen Sec Opalham, The Street, Bramley, RG26 5BP, UK. T. +441256881697. E-mail: sec@maiif.org.
URL: http://www.maiif.org/

History 1992. Charter adopted, May 1994. Amended June 1996, Aug 1997, Aug 2000, Aug 2005, Nov 2010, Apr 2014, Nov 2015. **Aims** Provide a forum to promote and improve marine accident investigation and to foster cooperation and communication between marine accident investigators. **Structure** Officers: Chair; Deputy Chair; 2 Assistant Chairs; Treasurer; General Secretary. **Languages** English. **Activities** Events/meetings. **Events** *Annual Meeting* Lima (Peru) 2022, *Annual Meeting* Busan (Korea Rep) 2013, *Asia Forum* Busan (Korea Rep) 2013, *International Conference on the Safety Investigation into Marine Casualty* Busan (Korea Rep) 2013, *Annual Meeting* Hong Kong (Hong Kong) 2012.

Members Governments of 51 countries and territories:
Antigua-Barbuda, Argentina, Australia, Austria, Bahamas, Barbados, Belgium, Brazil, Canada, Cape Verde, Chile, China, Cyprus, Denmark, Ecuador, Estonia, Finland, France, Germany, Gibraltar, Hong Kong, Hungary, Iceland, Indonesia, Italy, Japan, Korea Rep, Latvia, Liberia, Luxembourg, Malta, Marshall Is, Mexico, Netherlands, New Zealand, Norway, Oman, Panama, Peru, Philippines, Portugal, Romania, Singapore, Slovenia, South Africa, St Kitts-Nevis, Sweden, Switzerland, Türkiye, UK, USA.

IGO Relations Agreement of cooperation with: *International Maritime Organization (IMO, #14102)*. [2023.02.15/XJ1608/F*]

♦ Marine Biodiversity Observation Network (unconfirmed)
♦ Marine Biological Association (internationally oriented national body)
♦ Marine Board – ESF / see European Marine Board (#07738)
♦ Marine Connection (internationally oriented national body)
♦ Marine Conservation Biology Institute / see Marine Conservation Institute
♦ Marine Conservation Initiative / see SeaWeb
♦ Marine Conservation Institute (internationally oriented national body)
♦ Marine Conservation Society (internationally oriented national body)
♦ marinecultures.org (internationally oriented national body)

♦ Marine Emergency Mutual Aid Centre (MEMAC) 16578

Dir PO Box 10112, Manama, Bahrain. T. +97317274554. Fax +97317274551. E-mail: memac@batelco.com.bh.
URL: http://www.memac-rsa.org/

History 4 Aug 1982, Manama (Bahrain). Founded following decision of the Ministerial Council of *Regional Organization for the Protection of the Marine Environment (ROPME, #18805)*, within the framework of *Kuwait Regional Convention for Cooperation on the Protection on the Marine Environment from Pollution (1978)* which established *Kuwait Action Plan (KAP, no recent information)*. Functions as a division of ROPME. **Aims** Strengthen capacities of contracting States to the Convention and facilitate cooperation among them to combat *pollution* by *oil* and other *harmful substances* in cases of marine emergencies. **Structure** Headed by Director. **Languages** Arabic, English. **Staff** 8.00 FTE, paid. **Finance** Sources: contributions of member/participating states. Annual budget: 1,000,000 KWD. **Activities** Events/meetings; guidance/assistance/consulting; knowledge management/information dissemination; networking/liaising; projects/programmes; standards/guidelines; training/education. **Events** *Regional conference* Manama (Bahrain) 2000, *Regional oil*

spill response and contingency planning in the Middle East conference Manama (Bahrain) 2000. **Publications** *Kuwait Regional Convention for Co-operation on the Protection of the Marine Environment from Pollution*; *Manual for investigating Mortality Incidents in the ROPME Sea Area*; *Manual of Oceanographic Observations and Pollutant Analyses methods (MOOPAM)*; *Marine Environment Protection Legislation Guide*; *Marine Pollution – Combat Directory* – directory of competent national authorities, key persons, contact points; *Oil Spill Incidents in ROPME Sea Area 1965-2002*; *Oil Spill Manual*; *Oil Spill Response Safety Guide*; *Regional Oil Spill Damage Assessment Guidelines*; *ROPME Region from Space*; *Use of Oil Spill Chemicals in the ROPME Sea Area*. Inventory of response capabilities – equipment, facilities and manpower – of member states and the region, including private sector, oil industry and regional organizations; guides; manuals; reports; protocols; workshop proceedings.
Members Contracting States (8):
Bahrain, Iran Islamic Rep, Iraq, Kuwait, Oman, Qatar, Saudi Arabia, United Arab Emirates. [2022.11.30/XE1245/**E***]

♦ Marine Environmental Data Information Referral System (no recent information)
♦ Marine Geological and Biological Habitat Mapping (unconfirmed)

♦ The Marine Ingredients Organisation (IFFO) 16579

Dir Gen Unit C, Printworks, 22 Amelia Street, London, SE17 3BZ, UK. T. +442030539195. E-mail: secretariat@iffo.com.
URL: http://www.iffo.com/

History 1959. Merged with Fishmeal Exporters Organization (FEO), 2001. Former names and other names: *International Association of Fish Meal Manufacturers (IAFMM)* – former; *Association internationale de fabricants de farine de poisson* – former; *Asociación Internacional de Fabricantes de Harina de Pescado* – former; *International Fish Meal and Oil Manufacturers Association (IFOMA)* – former; *International Fishmeal and Fish Oil Organisation (IFFO)* – former (2001 to 2012). **Aims** Organize and finance research and development and the exchange of technical and scientific information with a view to: efficient production of high quality fish meal and fish oil; development of new products from industrial *fish*; increased user benefits; represent the industry, particularly with United Nations and other international and regional bodies. **Structure** Conference (annual); Board of Directors; Management Team; Secretariat. **Languages** English, Spanish. **Staff** 12.00 FTE, paid. **Finance** Sources: members' dues. **Activities** Events/meetings; research/documentation; training/education. **Events** *Members Meeting* Miami, FL (USA) 2022, *Members Meeting* Madrid (Spain) 2019, *Annual Conference* Shanghai (China) 2019, *Annual Conference* Rome (Italy) 2018, *Annual Conference* Washington, DC (USA) 2017. **Publications** *Weekly Report* (weekly) in English, Spanish; *Update* (12 a year) in English, Spanish; *Digest of Selected Statistics* (annual); *Fish Oil Bulletins* (occasional); *Processing Bulletins* (occasional); *Technical Bulletins* (occasional) in Chinese, English, German, Spanish. Conference proceedings; technical reports.
Members Companies in 37 countries and territories:
Angola, Argentina, Australia, Canada, Chile, China, Cyprus, Denmark, Ecuador, Faeroe Is, France, Germany, Greece, Iceland, India, Italy, Japan, Korea Rep, Mauritania, Mauritius, Mexico, Morocco, Namibia, Netherlands, Norway, Panama, Peru, Russia, South Africa, Spain, Switzerland, Taiwan, Thailand, UK, United Arab Emirates, USA, Vietnam.
Consultative Status Consultative status granted from: *ECOSOC (#05331)* (Ros C); *FAO (#09260)* (Special Status). **IGO Relations** Accredited by (1): *United Nations Office at Vienna (UNOV, #20604)*. Observer status with (1): *Codex Alimentarius Commission (CAC, #04081)*. **NGO Relations** In liaison with technical committees of: *International Organization for Standardization (ISO, #14473)*. [2022.05.11/XD1282/**D**]

♦ Marine Librarians Association / see Maritime Information Association
♦ Marine Mammal Action Plan – Global Plan of Action for the Conservation, Management and Utilization of Marine Mammals (inactive)

♦ Marine Stewardship Council (MSC) 16580

CEO Marine House, 1 Snow Hill, London, ECIA 2DH, UK. T. +442072468900. Fax +442072468901. E-mail: info@msc.org.
URL: http://www.msc.org/

History Founded Feb 1997. Originally, a joint initiative funded by *World Wide Fund for Nature (WWF, #21922)* and Unilever. Now independent. UK Registered Charity: 1066806. **Aims** Contribute to the health of the world's oceans by recognizing and rewarding sustainable *fishing* practices, influencing the choices people make when buying *seafood* and working with partners to transform the seafood market to a sustainable basis. **Structure** Board of Trustees; Technical Advisory Board (TAB); Stakeholder Council (STAC); National and Regional Working Groups; Committees. Regional Offices; Local Offices. **Languages** Danish, Dutch, English, French, German, Icelandic, Italian, Japanese, Malay, Mandarin Chinese, Norwegian, Polish, Portuguese, Russian, Spanish, Swedish. **Staff** 260.00 FTE, paid. **Finance** Sources: donations; grants. Other sources: ecolabel licensing revenue. **Activities** Awareness raising; certification/accreditation; guidance/assistance/consulting; standards/guidelines. **Events** *Endangered Pollack Industry Sustainability Symposium* Busan (Korea Rep) 2021, *Sustainable Seafood Round Table* Singapore (Singapore) 2019, *Asia Pacific General Assembly* Busan (Korea Rep) 2018, *World Ocean Forum* Busan (Korea Rep) 2016. **Publications** *Global Impact Reports*. Annual Report; guides; certification requirements. **Members** Not a membership organization. **IGO Relations** Observer to: *Inter-American Tropical Tuna Commission (IATTC, #11454)*. **NGO Relations** Member of: *High Level Panel for a Sustainable Ocean Economy (Panel, #10917)* – Advisory Network; *ISEAL (#16026)*; *Market Advisory Council (MAC, #16584)*. Partner of: *1% for the Planet*. [2018.10.09/XD7013/**C**]

♦ Marine Technology Society (internationally oriented national body)
♦ Marine Zoological Station / see Royal Netherlands Institute for Sea Research
♦ Marin Interfaith Task Force on the Americas (internationally oriented national body)
♦ Marin Interfaith Task Force on Central America / see Marin Interfaith Task Force on the Americas
♦ Mario Einaudi Center for International Studies, Cornell University (internationally oriented national body)
♦ Marionettistes sans frontières (internationally oriented national body)
♦ Marist Brothers – Little Brothers of Mary (religious order)
♦ Maristenpatres – Gesellschaft Mariens (religious order)
♦ Mariste – Suore della Congregazione di Maria (religious order)
♦ Marist Fathers – Society of Mary (religious order)
♦ Marist International Solidarity Foundation Onlus (#09831)
♦ Marist Sisters – Sisters of the Congregation of Mary (religious order)
♦ Maritime Academy, Chittagong / see Bangladesh Maritime Academy

♦ Maritime Analysis and Operations Centre – Narcotics (MAOC-N) .. 16581

Centro de Analise e de Operações contra o Narcotrafico Maritimo

Exec Dir address not obtained. T. +351218686010. Fax +351218686112. E-mail: gab-inete.informacao@maoc.eu.
URL: http://www.maoc.eu/

History 30 Sep 2007, Lisbon (Portugal). Established by signature of International Agreement. **Aims** Collect and analyse information on *drug trafficking*; enhance intelligence exchange and cooperation; identify availability of naval and other assets to facilitate national drug interdiction operations. **Languages** Dutch, English, French, Italian, Portuguese, Spanish. **Finance** Financed by: *European Union (EU, #08967)*; partners' contributions. **Activities** Networking/liaising.
Members Governments of 7 countries:
France, Ireland, Italy, Netherlands, Portugal, Spain, UK. [2022.12.01/XM3328/**E***]

♦ Maritime Development Center (internationally oriented national body)
♦ Maritime Development Center of Europe / see Maritime Development Center
♦ Maritime Human Factors Conference (meeting series)
♦ Maritime Industry Foundation (unconfirmed)
♦ Maritime Information Association (internationally oriented national body)
♦ Maritime Labour Convention (2006 treaty)

♦ Maritime Organization of West and Central Africa (MOWCA) 16582

Organisation Maritime de l'Afrique de l'Ouest et du Centre (OMAOC) – Organização Maritima da Africa do Oeste e do Centro (OMAOC)

Contact BP V 257, Abidjan, Côte d'Ivoire. T. +22522406100. Fax +22522412154. E-mail: infos@omaoc.org.
URL: http://www.omaoc.org/

History 5 May 1975, Abidjan (Côte d'Ivoire). 5-7 May 1975, Abidjan (Côte d'Ivoire), as *Ministerial Conference of West and Central African States on Maritime Transport (MINCONMAR)* – *Conférence ministérielle des Etats de l'Afrique de l'Ouest et du Centre sur les transports maritimes (CMEAOC)*, at a meeting of Plenipotentiary Ministers and Representatives of 17 countries, by the adoption of a *Maritime Transport Charter for West and Central Africa* – *Charte des transports maritimes en Afrique de l'Ouest et du Centre*, commonly referred to as *Abidjan Charter – Charte d'Abidjan*. Restructured at an extra-ordinary session of Ministers of member States, 6th Aug 1999, Abidjan, when current title was adopted. **Aims** Provide an effective inter-governmental sub-regional platform for sectoral cooperation in the field of Maritime/Transit Transport in a maritime region where countries share common problems of demand and supply for *shipping* services and associated safety and environmental protection threats. **Structure** General Assembly of Ministers and Committee of Experts responsible for shipping matters (meet every 2 years); Bureau of Ministers; Permanent Secretariat, headed by Secretary-General, in Abidjan (Côte d'Ivoire). Specialized organs (3): *Association of African Shipowners*; *Port Management Association of West and Central Africa (PMAWCA, #18463)*; *Union of African Shippers' Councils (UASC, #20348)*. Regional Academies: *Regional Maritime University, Accra (RMU, #18796)*; *Regional Academy of Maritime Science and Technology (#18744)*. Specializes Committees (3): Maritime Safety and Marine and Inland Waterways Environmental Protection; Maritime Transport and Related Activities, Statistics and Economic Data; Facilitation of Transit Transport and Specific Concerns of Landlocked Member States. **Languages** English, French, Portuguese. **Staff** 22.00 FTE, paid. **Finance** Contributions from member states; Regional Maritime Fund. Target budget: US$ 5 million. **Activities** Projects/programmes; research/documentation; networking/liaising. Management of treaties and agreements: *Memorandum of Understanding on Port State Control in West and Central Africa (Abuja MOU, 1999)*. **Events** *Extraordinary Session / General Assembly* Kinshasa (Congo DR) 2011, *General Assembly* Dakar (Senegal) 2008, *Extraordinary Session* Dakar (Senegal) 2006, *General Assembly* Luanda (Angola) 2003, *General Assembly* Abuja (Nigeria) 2001. **Publications** *Afrique Maritime* – magazine. Biennial Report.
Members Governments of 25 countries:
Angola, Benin, Burkina Faso, Cameroon, Cape Verde, Central African Rep, Chad, Congo Brazzaville, Congo DR, Côte d'Ivoire, Equatorial Guinea, Gabon, Gambia, Ghana, Guinea, Guinea-Bissau, Liberia, Mali, Mauritania, Niger, Nigeria, Sao Tomé-Principe, Senegal, Sierra Leone, Togo.
IGO Relations Participates in the activities of: *UNCTAD (#20285)*. Cooperation agreement with: *African Union (AU, #00488)*; *International Hydrographic Organization (IHO, #13825)*; *International Maritime Organization (IMO, #14102)*. **NGO Relations** Cooperates with: *International Association of Marine Aids to Navigation and Lighthouse Authorities (IALA, #12013)*. [2015.10.14/XF1523/**F***]

♦ Maritime Piracy Humanitarian Response Programme (MPHRP) 16583

Exec Dir c/o ISWAN, 3rd Fl Suffolk House, George Street, Croydon, CR0 1PE, UK. T. +442073232737. E-mail: iswan@iswan.org.uk.
URL: http://www.mphrp.org/

History Founded 2012. Became a programme of *International Seafarers' Welfare and Assistance Network (ISWAN, #14815)*, 2015. UK registered charity. **Aims** Assist seafarers and their families with the humanitarian aspects of a traumatic incident caused by a piracy attack, armed robbery or being taken hostage; assist families of seafarers imprisoned abroad, missing at sea, or victims of suicide. **Structure** Board. **Languages** Arabic, Chinese, English, French, Hindi, Lithuanian, Russian, Spanish, Tagalog. **Staff** 5.00 FTE, paid. **Finance** Supported by: *International Transport Workers' Federation (ITF, #15726)* Seafarers' Trust; Seafarers UK; TK Foundation. **Publications** *MPHRP Newsletter*. *Good Practice Guides for Shipping Companies and Manning Agents for the Humanitarian Support of Seafarers and their Families Involved in Piracy Incidents*. Annual Report.
Members Partners (10):
BIMCO (#03236); *InterManager (#11520)*; *International Christian Maritime Association (ICMA, #12561)*; *International Federation of Shipmasters Associations (IFSMA, #13539)*; *International Group of P and I Clubs (#13751)*; *International Maritime Employers' Council (IMEC, #14098)*; *International Maritime Health Association (IMHA, #14099)*; *International Parcel Tankers Association (IPTA)*; *International Transport Workers' Federation (ITF, #15726)*; *Society of International Gas Tanker and Terminal Operators (SIGTTO, #19582)*.
Observers:
International Maritime Organization (IMO, #14102); NATO Shipping Centre. [2019.04.24/XJ5074/y/**F**]

♦ Maritime Preparedness and International Partnership in the High North Consortium (unconfirmed)

♦ Market Advisory Council (MAC) 16584

SG Rue de la Science 10, 1000 Brussels, Belgium. T. +3222303013. E-mail: secretary@marketac.eu.
URL: http://marketac.eu/

History Set up 2016. Registered in accordance with Belgian law: 0652 757 045. **Aims** Provide recommendations to the European Commission and Member States on matters relevant for the *EU* market of *fishery* and *aquaculture* products. **Structure** General Assembly; Executive Committee; Working Groups; Secretariat. **Languages** English, French, Spanish. **Staff** 1.00 FTE, paid. **Finance** Co-funded by *European Commission (EC, #06633)*. **Activities** Guidance/assistance/consulting; knowledge management/information dissemination.
Members European and national organizations in 11 countries:
Belgium, Denmark, France, Germany, Ireland, Italy, Netherlands, Poland, Spain, Sweden, UK.
Included in the above, 16 organizations listed in this Yearbook:
Association des organisations nationales d'entreprises de pêche de l'UE (EUROPECHE, #02841); *Coalition for Fair Fisheries Agreements (CFFA, #04060)*; *Comité des organisations nationales des importateurs et exportateurs de poisson de l'UE (CEP, #04194)*; *COPA – european farmers (COPA, #04829)*; *EuroCommerce (EC, #05665)*; *European Association of Fish Producers Organizations (EAPO, #06041)*; *European Fismeal and Fish Oil Producers (European Fishmeal, #07268)*; *European Tropical Tuna Trade and Industry Committee (EUROTHON, #08951)*; *European Union Fish Processors Association (#08989)*; *Federation of European Aquaculture Producers (FEAP, #09491)*; *General Confederation of Agricultural Cooperatives in the European Union (#10107)*; *Low Impact Fishers of Europe (LIFE, #16517)*; *Marine Stewardship Council (MSC, #16580)*; *Oceana*; *Seas at Risk (SAR, #19189)*; *World Wide Fund for Nature (WWF, #21922)*.
IGO Relations *European Committee of the Regions (CoR, #06665)*; *European Commission (EC, #06633)*; *European Economic and Social Committee (EESC, #06963)*; *European Parliament (EP, #08146)*. **NGO Relations** *Coalition for Fair Fisheries Agreements (CFFA, #04060)*; *Good Fish Foundation*; *Long Distance Advisory Council (LDAC, #16511)*; *Marine Stewardship Council (MSC, #16580)*; *Mediterranean Advisory Council (MEDAC, #16639)*; *Oceana*; *Seas at Risk (SAR, #19189)*; *World Wide Fund for Nature (WWF, #21922)*. [2020.03.03/XM7031/y/**D**]

♦ Marketing Agencies Association Worldwide (MAA) 16585

Pres address not obtained.
URL: https://www.maaworldwide.com/

History Former names and other names: *Council of Sales Promotion Agencies (CSPA)* – former; *Association of Promotion Marketing Agencies Worldwide (APMA Worldwide)* – former. **Aims** Understand and address the business and personal needs of Principals, CEOs, Presidents, Directors and Senior personnel of Marketing Communication companies. **Staff** 4.00 FTE, paid. **Finance** Single summit attendance fee. **Activities** Awards/prizes/competitions; events/meetings. **Events** *Summit* Montréal, QC (Canada) 2020, *Summit* Paris (France) 2019, *Summit* Washington, DC (USA) 2018, *Spring Conference* Amsterdam (Netherlands) 2013, *Fall Conference* New York, NY (USA) 2013.
Members Companies (87) in 16 countries and territories:
Argentina, Australia, Brazil, Canada, France, Germany, Ireland, Israel, Italy, Japan, Korea Rep, Puerto Rico, Sweden, Switzerland, UK, USA. [2021/XD4743/**D**]

♦ Marketing Communications Executives International (MCEI) 16586

Association internationale de cadres de marketing-communications

SG Rue Rousseau 30, 1201 Geneva 15, Switzerland. T. +41227982544. Fax +41227882075. E-mail: geneva@mcei.ch.
URL: http://www.mcei.org/

History 1954, New York NY (USA), as *Sales Promotion Executives Association International (SPEA)*. European Headquarters set up Feb 1960, Brussels (Belgium). Registered in the State of New York (USA) and in accordance with Belgian law. Present name adopted 1972. **Aims** Foster exchange of ideas, data and knowledge between marketing communications executives; raise ethical standards and practices as related to *sales* promotion; encourage development of improved scientific techniques in the evaluation and practice of marketing communications activities. **Structure** Annual Meeting; Board of Directors; Regional Directors. **Languages** English, French. **Staff** 4.00 FTE, paid. **Finance** Members' dues. **Activities** Events/meetings; awards/prizes/competitions. **Publications** *MCEI Newsletter* (12 a year); *The Communicator* (12 a year). Membership Roster; white papers; check lists.
Members Chapters (10) in 9 countries and territories:
Australia, Belgium, France, Italy, Japan, Peru, Switzerland, Taiwan, USA. [2015.01.14/XN5481/v/**D**]

♦ Mark Makers International (internationally oriented national body)
♦ MARPART Consortium – Maritime Preparedness and International Partnership in the High North Consortium (unconfirmed)
♦ MARPE / see MARPE Network (#16587)

♦ MARPE Network 16587

Leader address not obtained. E-mail: contact@marpenetwork.eu.
URL: http://marpenetwork.eu/
History 1988. Founded as a project of CERP Educational Research (now *European Public Relations Education and Research Association (EUPRERA, #08302)*). Former names and other names: *MARPE* – former. **Aims** Develop a European body of knowledge in public, organizational and civil society diplomacy. **Structure** A network of strategic and associated partners. **Languages** Dutch, English, French, Portuguese, Romanian, Spanish. Working language: English. **Staff** 8.00 FTE, voluntary. **Activities** Events/meetings; knowledge management/information dissemination; networking/liaising; projects/programmes; publishing activities; research and development; training/education. **Events** *MARPE Diplo Conference* Lisbon (Portugal) 2021, *MARPE Diplo Conference* Ghent (Belgium) 2019. **Publications** *MARPE Diplo Newsletter* (6 a year). *Diplomacy, Organisations and Citizens A European Communication Perspective* (2022) by Prof Dr Sonia Sebastião and Assoc Prof Susana de Carvalho Spínola in English.
Members Core Partners: universities (5) in 5 countries:
Belgium, France, Portugal, Romania, Spain. [2022.10.27/AA0274/**F**]

♦ MARPOL – International Convention for the Prevention of Pollution from Ships (1973 treaty)
♦ MARPOL PROT 1997 – Protocol of 1997 to Amend the International Convention for the Prevention of Pollution from Ships, 1973, as Modified by the Protocol of 1978 Relating Thereto (1997 treaty)

♦ MARQUES 16588

External Relations Officer Unit Q – Troon Way Business Centre, Humberstone Lane, Thurmaston, Leicester, LE4 9HA, UK. T. +441162747355. Fax +441162747365. E-mail: info@marques.org.
URL: http://www.marques.org/
History 1986, Vienna (Austria). Inaugural conference Sep 1986 after activities started in 1984 by a small group of in-house trade mark managers who felt that their companies' needs as trade mark owners should be represented more adequately in Europe. Steering Committee set up, formed of senior representatives from Rolls-Royce Motor Cars, Mars Incorporated, Rowntrees Distillers Company, Allied-Lyons, British Telecom and Beecham. This Steering Committee together with a group of other companies, including Lego (Denmark), Morgan Crucible (UK) and Volvo (Sweden), committed a significant measure of foundation funding to ensure the successful international launch and establishment of MARQUES. Former names and other names: *Association of European Trade Mark Proprietors* – former; *Association des propriétaires européens de marques de commerce (MARQUES)* – former; *MARQUES – European Association of Trade Mark Owners* – former; *Vereinigung Europäischer Markeninhaber* – former. Registration: Companies House, No/ID: 02210172, Start date: 11 Jan 1988, England and Wales; EU Transparency Register, No/ID: 97131823590-44. **Aims** Represent and be a trusted voice for brand owners; educate in the field of management and exploitation of IP rights; promote professional development of members; be a reliable partner in advancing these aims. **Structure** General Meeting (Annual Conference); Council; Executive Committee; Secretariat. **Languages** English. **Staff** 2.00 FTE, paid. **Finance** Sources: members' dues. No shareholders; issues no dividends; directors are expressly prohibited from being paid for their services. **Activities** Events/meetings; training/education. **Events** *Spring Team Meeting* 2021, *Annual Conference* The Hague (Netherlands) 2021, *Spring Team Meeting* Frankfurt-Main (Germany) 2020, *Annual Conference* Stockholm (Sweden) 2020, *Annual Conference* Dublin (Ireland) 2019. **Publications** *HouseMARQUES* (12 a year). Position papers; surveys; guides; other professional and educational material. **Members** Ordinary – Corporate or Expert; Honorary. Members in over 80 countries. Membership countries not specified. **Consultative Status** Consultative status granted from: *World Intellectual Property Organization (WIPO, #21593)* (Permanent Observer Status). **IGO Relations** Member of (1): Private Stakeholders Sector of the European Observatory on Infringements of Intellectual Property Rights. Cooperates with (1): *European Union Intellectual Property Office (EUIPO, #08996)*. **NGO Relations** Member of (1): *Global Anti-Counterfeiting Group (GACG, #10236)*. [2021/XD2451/y/**D**]

♦ MARQUES – European Association of Trade Mark Owners / see MARQUES (#16588)
♦ Marrakesh Treaty to Facilitate Access to Published Works for Persons Who Are Blind, Visually Impaired or Otherwise Print Disabled (2013 treaty)
♦ Marrakesh Treaty – Marrakesh Treaty to Facilitate Access to Published Works for Persons Who Are Blind, Visually Impaired or Otherwise Print Disabled (2013 treaty)
♦ Married Priests. Europe / see European Federation of Catholic Married Priests (#07069)
♦ **MARRI** Migration, Asylum, Refugees Regional Initiative (#16800)
♦ Marseille Center for Mediterranean Integration / see Center for Mediterranean Integration (#03649)
♦ Marshall Plan of the Mind Trust / see BBC Media Action
♦ Mars et Mercure Europe – Cercles industriels et commerciaux d'officiers et officiers de réserve Commission de coordination inter-nations (#16589)
♦ Mars et Mercure Europe – Commission de Coordination Inter-Nations / see Mars and Mercury Europe – Industrial and Commercial Circles of Officers and Reserve Officers Inter-Nations Coordination Commission (#16589)

♦ Mars and Mercury Europe – Industrial and Commercial Circles of Officers and Reserve Officers Inter-Nations Coordination Commission 16589

Mars et Mercure Europe – Cercles industriels et commerciaux d'officiers et officiers de réserve Commission de coordination inter-nations
Gen Sec Aardbruggenstraat 61, 3570 Alken, Belgium. T. +3211313599. E-mail: info@mars-mercurius.eu.
Registered Office Quartier Reine Elisabeth – Bloc Météo, Rue d'Evere 1, 1140 Evere, Belgium.
URL: https://mars-mercurius.eu/
History 1926, Belgium. Founded following WWI by former officers and reserve officers. Similar circles were set up following WWII in France (1958) and Germany (1959). Both signed a convention establishing *Inter-Nations Liaison Commission Mars & Mercury* in 1960. Became a Europe-wide organization, 1991, with member nations Belgium, Denmark, France, Germany, Luxembourg, Netherlands, Poland, Spain, Switzerland. Former names and other names: *Inter-Nations Liaison Commission Mars and Mercury* – former; *Commission de Liaison Inter-Nations Mars et Mercure (CLIMM)* – former; *Mars and Mercury Europe – Inter-Nations Coordination Commission* – alias; *Mars et Mercure Europe – Commission de Coordination Inter-Nations* – alias. **Aims** Develop close cooperation bounds among members of national Mars & Mercury Circles comprising officers, former officers or reserve officers active in commerce and industry; contribute to development of members' professional work at the international level, on a non-political and non-confessional basis. **Structure** Executive Committee; Board of Directors; National Circles. **Languages** English, French. **Staff** 5.00 FTE, voluntary. **Finance** Sources: members' dues. **Activities** Events/meetings. **Events** *General Assembly* Maastricht (Netherlands) 2022, *General Assembly* Alken (Belgium) 2020.
Members National Circles in 9 countries:
Belgium, Denmark, France, Germany, Luxembourg, Netherlands, Poland, Spain, Switzerland. [2022.05.16/XD1121/t/**E**]

♦ Mars and Mercury Europe – Inter-Nations Coordination Commission / see Mars and Mercury Europe – Industrial and Commercial Circles of Officers and Reserve Officers Inter-Nations Coordination Commission (#16589)
♦ **MARS Network** European Network of Marine Research Institutes and Stations (#07941)
♦ MARSS – International Conference on Manipulation, Automation and Robotics at Small Scales (meeting series)
♦ Martat / see Marttaliitto
♦ **Martens Centre** Wilfried Martens Centre for European Studies (#20962)
♦ Martha Organization (internationally oriented national body)
♦ Martial Arts Games Council of Asia (inactive)
♦ Martín-Baró Initiative for Wellbeing and Human Rights (internationally oriented national body)

♦ Martin Ennals Foundation 16590

Fondation Martin Ennals
Contact c/o OMCT, BP 21, 1211 Geneva 8, Switzerland. T. +41228094925. E-mail: info@martinennalsaward.org.
Street Address Rue du Vieux-Billard 8, 1205 Geneva, Switzerland.
URL: https://www.martinennalsaward.org/
Aims Award the Martin Ennals Award for Human Rights Defenders to honour individuals and organizations that have shown exceptional commitment to defending and promoting human rights, despite the risks involved. **Structure** Board; Secretariat. **Finance** Sources: donations. Donors also include: Swiss Federal Department of Foreign Affairs; City of Geneva; Canton of Geneva; Principality of Liechtenstein; Loterie Romande. Supported by: *Brot für die Welt*; *Irish Aid*; *Norwegian Human Rights Fund (NHRF)*. **Activities** Awards/prizes/competitions; projects/programmes. [2021/AA1298/f/**F**]

♦ Martin Institute for Peace Studies and Conflict Resolution (internationally oriented national body)
♦ Martin Luther Bund (internationally oriented national body)
♦ Martin Luther Federation (internationally oriented national body)
♦ Marttaliitto (internationally oriented national body)
♦ Martti Ahtisaari Centre / see Crisis Management Initiative
♦ Martyrernes Rost (#20804)
♦ Martyrs for Morocco / see Rejection of Sins and Exodus (#18829)

♦ MarViva Foundation 16591

Managing Dir address not obtained. T. +50622903657. Fax +5062231-4429. E-mail: info@marviva.net – info.colombia@marviva.net – info.panama@marviva.net.
URL: http://www.marviva.net/
History 2002. **Aims** Promote conservation and sustainable use of *marine* and *coastal* resources by protecting and supporting the Marine Spatial Planning process. **Structure** Board of Directors; National Offices (3). **Languages** English, Spanish. **Consultative Status** Consultative status granted from: *UNEP (#20299)*. **NGO Relations** Member of: *Global Seafood Ratings Alliance (GSRA)*; *High Level Panel for a Sustainable Ocean Economy (Panel, #10917)* – Advisory Network; *International Union for Conservation of Nature and Natural Resources (IUCN, #15766)*. Participates in: *Global Partnership for Oceans (GPO, #10537)*. [2019/XJ2244/f/**F**]

♦ Maryknoll Fathers – Catholic Foreign Missionary Society of America (religious order)
♦ Maryknoll Institute of African Studies (internationally oriented national body)
♦ Maryknoll Lay Missioners / see Maryknoll Mission Association of the Faithful
♦ Maryknoll Mission Association of the Faithful (internationally oriented national body)
♦ Maryknoll Office for Global Concern (internationally oriented national body)
♦ Maryknoll Office for Global Concerns: Peace, Social Justice and Integrity of Creation / see Maryknoll Office for Global Concern
♦ Maryknoll Sisters of Saint Dominic (religious order)
♦ di Maryknoll – Società per le Missioni Estere degli Stati Uniti d'America (religious order)
♦ Maryland United for Peace and Justice (internationally oriented national body)

♦ Marymount International Schools 16592

Registrar George Road, Kingston upon Thames, London, KT2 7PE, UK. T. +442089490571. E-mail: admissions@marymountlondon.com.
URL: http://www.marymountlondon.com/
History within the framework of *Religious of the Sacred Heart of Mary (RSHM)*. **Aims** Provide the International Baccalaureate programme; provide continuity in the *academic* careers of *students* whose educational programme has been disrupted by a family move abroad. **Languages** English, French, German, Japanese, Korean, Mandarin Chinese, Spanish. **Activities** Training/education.
Members Schools (5) in 4 countries:
France, Italy, UK, USA. [2022.10.19/XF2791/**F**]

♦ MASAD – Mediterranean Association for Science Advancement and Dissemination (no recent information)
♦ **MASCC** Multinational Association of Supportive Care in Cancer (#16895)
♦ **MASC** Multinational Arabidopsis Steering Committee (#16894)
♦ **MASEAN** Medical Association of South East Asian Nations (#16623)
♦ MASHAV – Centre for International Cooperation (internationally oriented national body)
♦ Masimanyane – Masimanyane Women's Rights International (unconfirmed)
♦ Masimanyane Women's Rights International (unconfirmed)
♦ MAS – Mission d'aménagement du fleuve Sénégal (inactive)

♦ Masonic Movement 16593

Mouvement de la Franc-maçonnerie
Address not obtained.
History prior to 1640, probably as a semi-secret brotherhood of masons travelling among the sites where cathedrals and other great buildings were being erected. Officially open to non-stonemasons from 1717 onwards. The term *'freemason'* is first recorded in 1376. **Structure** Lodges and chapters include: *Gran Oriente Latinoamericano (GOLA, no recent information)*; *Grande loge mixte universelle (no recent information)*; *Grand Masonic Lodge for Arab Countries (no recent information)*; *Grand Rite Malgache (GRM, see: #16593)*; *General Grand Chapter of Royal Arch Masons International*; *General Grand Chapter, Order of the Eastern Star*; *Grande loge nordique (no recent information)*. Instrumental in setting up: *DeMolay International*.
Members Lodges or otherwise active in 77 countries and territories:
Algeria, Argentina, Australia, Austria, Belgium, Bolivia, Brazil, Bulgaria, Cameroon, Canada, Chile, Colombia, Costa Rica, Croatia, Cuba, Czechia, Denmark, Egypt, El Salvador, England, Finland, France, Germany, Greece, Guatemala, Honduras, Hong Kong, Hungary, Iceland, India, Indonesia, Iran Islamic Rep, Ireland, Israel, Italy, Jamaica, Japan, Kenya, Lebanon, Liberia, Luxembourg, Madagascar, Malaysia, Mexico, Morocco, Netherlands, New Zealand, Nicaragua, Nigeria, Norway, Pakistan, Palestine, Panama, Paraguay, Peru, Philippines, Poland, Portugal, Puerto Rico, Romania, Russia, Scotland, Serbia, Slovakia, Slovenia, South Africa, Spain, Sweden, Switzerland, Syrian AR, Tanzania UR, Tunisia, Türkiye, Uganda, Uruguay, USA, Venezuela. [2008/XF2899/**F**]

♦ Mas Paz Menos SIDA Fundación (+ Paz – sida Fundación) 16594

More Peace Less AIDS Foundation (+ Peace – AIDS Foundation)
Argentina Office Santiago del Estero 454, 5th floor – room 22, C1036AAO Buenos Aires, Argentina. T. +541143817946. E-mail: info@maspazmenossida.org.
Panama Office City of Knowledge, Bldg 120 – Executive Offices, Panamá, Panamá, Panama PANAMá, Panama. T. +5073063710. E-mail: infopanama@maspazmenossida.org.
URL: https://maspazmenossida.org/
History Set up to develop the More Peace Less Aids campaign, which was set up 2007, by *International Community of Women Living with HIV/AIDS (ICW, #12826)*. **Aims** Build a peace culture so as to oppose violence that generates ignorance, prejudice, fanaticism and inequalities, all which are socio-economic-political factors that are potential roots of HIV/AIDS. **Structure** Administrative Board. **NGO Relations** Member of: *International Peace Bureau (IPB, #14535)*. [2019/XM6360/f/**F**]

♦ El Masraf el Arabi Lel Tanmia el Ectesadia fi Afriqya (#00904)
♦ **MASSEE** Mathematical Society of South Eastern Europe (#16602)

♦ Massive Analysis and Quality Control Society (MACQC) 16595

Exec Sec One Broadway 14th Fl, c/o Immuneering, Cambridge MA 02142, USA.
URL: http://www.maqcsociety.org/

History A US 501(c)(3) non-profit organization. **Aims** Communicate, promote, and advance reproducible science principles and quality control for analysis of the massive data generated from the existing and emerging technologies in solving biological, health, and medical problems. **Structure** Board of Directors. **Activities** Events/meetings. **Events** *Annual Meeting* Riva del Garda (Italy) 2019, *Annual Meeting* Shanghai (China) 2018, *Annual Meeting* Cary, NC (USA) 2017. [2018/XM7072/**C**]

- ♦ Massive Effort Campaign / see Global Health Advocates (#10400)
- ♦ Master Brewers Association of the Americas (internationally oriented national body)
- ♦ Mastercard Foundation (internationally oriented national body)
- ♦ Masters Games International / see International Masters Games Association (#14117)
- ♦ Mastology Association of Northern and Southern Mediterranean / see Mobile Mediterranean University of Mastology (#16836)
- ♦ Mastology North Mediterranean Association / see Mobile Mediterranean University of Mastology (#16836)
- ♦ **MASU** Mediterranean and African Society of Ultrasound (#16640)

♦ Matariki Network of Universities (MNU) 16596

Sec Durham Univ, Intl Office – Palatine Ctr, Stockton Road, Durham, DH1 3LE, UK.
URL: https://www.matarikinetwork.org/

History 2010, Dunedin (New Zealand). **Aims** Build upon the collective strengths of member institutions to develop international excellence in research and education and to promote social responsibility locally and globally. **Activities** Events/meetings; knowledge management/information dissemination; projects/programmes; research/documentation; training/education. **Publications** *News from the Matariki Network* – e-newsletter.
Members Universities in 7 countries:
Australia, Canada, Germany, New Zealand, Sweden, UK, USA. [2022.10.19/AA2757/**F**]

- ♦ MATCH / see Equality Fund
- ♦ MATCH International Centre / see Equality Fund
- ♦ The MATCH International Women's Fund / see Equality Fund

♦ MaterCare International (MCI) 16597

Founder – Exec Dir MCI Headquarters, 8 Riverview Avenue, St John's NL A1C 2S5, Canada. T. +17095796472. Fax +17095796501 – +17097533268. E-mail: info@matercare.org.
URL: http://www.matercare.org/

History 13 Oct 1995, Liverpool (UK), by a group of Catholic health professionals. **Aims** Improve the lives and health of *mothers* and their unborn children in accordance with the teaching contained in the Encyclical Evangelium Vitae (the Gospel of Life). **Languages** English. **Staff** 13.50 FTE, voluntary. **Finance** Grants and donations. Budget (annual): Canadian $ 230,000. **Activities** Events/meetings. **Publications** *MCI News and Comment Quarterly* (4 a year).
Members National affiliates in 6 countries:
Australia, Canada, Ghana, Ireland, UK, USA.
Consultative Status Consultative status granted from: *ECOSOC (#05331)* (Special). **IGO Relations** Associated with DPI of United Nations. **NGO Relations** Affiliated as obstetrical arm of *International Federation of Catholic Medical Associations (#13378)*. Member of: *Forum of Catholic Inspired NGOs (#09905)*. [2016/XD8431/**D**]

- ♦ Materials Australia / see Institute of Materials Engineering, Australasia

♦ Materials Development Association (MATSDA) 16598

Pres address not obtained.
Sec address not obtained.
URL: https://www.matsda.org/

History 1993. Founded by Brian Tomlinson. **Aims** Bring together researchers, publishers, writers and teachers to work towards the development of high quality materials for the learning of languages. **Structure** Committee. **Activities** Events/meetings. **Events** *Bilingual International School Conference* Rufina (Italy) 2023. **Publications** *Folio* (2 a year).
Members Full in 27 countries:
Argentina, Australia, Bulgaria, Canada, Germany, India, Indonesia, Italy, Japan, Korea Rep, Madagascar, Malaysia, Mozambique, Namibia, Netherlands, Norway, Oman, Poland, Portugal, Romania, South Africa, Spain, Sudan, Sweden, UK, United Arab Emirates, USA. [2023/AA3239/**C**]

♦ Materials Research Society (MRS) 16599

Exec Dir 506 Keystone Dr, Warrendale PA 15086-7537, USA. T. +17247793003. Fax +17247798313. E-mail: info@mrs.org.
URL: http://www.mrs.org/

History 1973, State College, PA (USA). **Aims** Promote communication for the advancement of interdisciplinary materials research to improve the quality of life. **Structure** Board of Directors, comprising President, Past President, Vice President, Secretary, Treasurer, Executive Director and Directors. **Events** *Spring Meeting* Seattle, WA (USA) 2025, *Spring Meeting* Seattle, WA (USA) 2024, *Spring Meeting* San Francisco, CA (USA) 2023, *Spring Meeting* Honolulu, HI (USA) 2022, *Fall Meeting* Boston, MA (USA) 2021. **Publications** *MRS Bulletin* (12 a year); *Journal of Materials Research (JMR)* (24 a year); *MRS Communications* – journal. *MRS Proceedings* – series. **Members** Full in over 80 countries. Membership countries not specified. **NGO Relations** Member of (1): *ABET*. [2021/XW0388/**D**]

- ♦ Materials World Network (internationally oriented national body)
- ♦ Maternal and Childhealth Advocacy International (internationally oriented national body)
- ♦ Maternity Foundation (internationally oriented national body)
- ♦ Maternity Worldwide (internationally oriented national body)

♦ Mathematical Council of the Americas (MCofA) 16600

Contact Math Dept – USC, 3620 S Vermont Ave, KAP 104, Los Angeles CA 90089-2532, USA. E-mail: susanfri@usc.edu.
URL: http://mcofamericas.org/

History First meeting held 2013, Guanajuto (Mexico), by national organizations in USA, Canada, Brazil and Mexico and by *Unión Matematica de América Latina y el Caribe (UMALCA, #20456)*. **Aims** Highlight the excellence of mathematical achievements in the Americas within the context of the international arena; foster scientific integration of all mathematical communities in the continent. **Structure** Council; Executive Committee. **Languages** English. **Staff** 3.00 FTE, voluntary. **Activities** Awards/prizes/competitions; events/meetings. **Events** *Mathematical Congress of the Americas* Buenos Aires (Argentina) 2021, *Mathematical Congress of the Americas* Montréal, QC (Canada) 2017, *Mathematical Congress of the Americas* Guanajuato (Mexico) 2013.
Members Societies and institutions. Members in 7 countries:
Argentina, Brazil, Canada, Chile, Colombia, Mexico, USA.
Associate members in 7 countries:
Bolivia, Costa Rica, Cuba, Ecuador, Paraguay, Peru, Venezuela.
NGO Relations Member of (1): *International Mathematical Union (IMU, #14121)* (Affiliate). [2021/XM6248/**D**]

- ♦ Mathematical Models in Ecology and Evolution (meeting series)

♦ Mathematical Optimization Society (MOS) 16601

Société pour l' optimisation mathématique

Office 3600 Market St, 6th Floor, Philadelphia PA 19104-9800, USA. T. +12153829800ext319. Fax +12153867999. E-mail: service@mathopt.org.
URL: http://www.mathopt.org/

History 1971, The Hague (Netherlands). Former names and other names: *Mathematical Programming Society (MPS)* – former (1971). **Aims** Advance knowledge of the theory, application and *computational* aspects of mathematical programming. **Structure** Council; Executive Committee; Committees. **Languages** English. **Staff** None. **Finance** Sources: members' dues. Royalties from Society Publications. **Activities** Awards/prizes/competitions; events/meetings. **Events** *International Symposium on Mathematical Programming (ISMP 2024)* Montréal, QC (Canada) 2024, *International Conference on Stochastic Programming* Davis, CA (USA) 2023, *International Conference on Continuous Optimization* Berlin (Germany) 2019, *International Conference on Stochastic Programming* Trondheim (Norway) 2019, *International Conference on Continuous Optimization* Tokyo (Japan) 2016. **Publications** *Mathematical Programming Computation*; *Optima Newsletter*. *Mathematical Programming – Series A*; *Mathematical Programming – Series B*.
Members Individuals (1,055) in 48 countries and territories:
Argentina, Australia, Austria, Belgium, Brazil, Bulgaria, Canada, Chile, China, Croatia, Czechia, Denmark, Ecuador, Finland, France, Germany, Greece, Hong Kong, Hungary, India, Israel, Italy, Japan, Korea Rep, Malaysia, Mexico, Netherlands, New Zealand, Norway, Oman, Peru, Poland, Portugal, Russia, Serbia, Singapore, Slovakia, Slovenia, South Africa, Spain, Sweden, Switzerland, Taiwan, Türkiye, UK, Uruguay, USA, Venezuela. [2021/XE3671/v/**C**]

- ♦ Mathematical Programming Society / see Mathematical Optimization Society (#16601)

♦ Mathematical Society of South Eastern Europe (MASSEE) 16602

Gen Sec MASSEE Secretariat, 34 Panepistimiou Street, 106 79 Athens, Greece. T. +302103616532. Fax +302103641025. E-mail: mgeorg@hms.gr – info@massee-org.eu.
Pres address not obtained.
General: http://www.massee-org.eu/

History 1 Mar 2003. Takes over activities of *Balkan Mathematical Union (UBM, inactive)*. Registered in accordance with Greek law. **Aims** Develop cooperation between and beyond communities involved; further collaboration for adding value to the common activities organized in the area to advance mathematics research and education. **Activities** Projects/programmes; events/meetings; awards/prizes/competitions. **Events** *International Conference on Mathematics* Nicosia (Cyprus) 2018, *Meeting* Protaras (Cyprus) 2016, *Triennial Congress* Athens (Greece) 2015, *Triennial Congress* Sarajevo (Bosnia-Herzegovina) 2012, *Triennial Congress* Ohrid (Macedonia) 2009. **Publications** *Mathematica Balkanica* – journal. Scientific journals.
Members National organizations in 9 countries:
Albania, Bosnia-Herzegovina, Bulgaria, Cyprus, Greece, Moldova, North Macedonia, Romania, Serbia. [2022/XD9245/**D**]

- ♦ Mathematical Union for Latin America and the Caribbean (#20456)

♦ Mathematical Views (MAVI-Group) 16603

Contact Piazza Sant'Eusebio 5, 13100 Vercelli VC, Italy. E-mail: board.of.mavi@gmail.com.
URL: https://www.mathematical-views.org/

History 1995. Initially a conference. During 2019 and 2021 conferences, idea of a board was suggested. Originated from a bi-national research group, with 'MAVI' deriving from the phrase: *Mathematical Views on Beliefs and Mathematical Education*. Former names and other names: *International Conference on Mathematical Views (MAVI)* – former. **Aims** Support research and collaboration in relation to the broad area of affect in mathematics education. **Structure** Board. **Languages** English. **Staff** 5.00 FTE, voluntary. **Finance** Sources: meeting proceeds. **Activities** Events/meetings; networking/liaising; publishing activities; research/documentation. **Events** *International Conference of Mathematical Views* Gijón (Spain) 2022, *International Conference on Mathematical Views* Bremen (Germany) 2021, *International Conference on Mathematical Views* 2020, *International Conference on Mathematical Views* Intra (Italy) 2019, *International Conference on Mathematical Views* Helsinki (Finland) 2018. **Publications** Conference proceedings.
Members Individuals (about 125) in 14 countries:
Australia, Austria, Canada, Cyprus, Denmark, Finland, Germany, Italy, New Zealand, Spain, Sweden, Switzerland, UK, USA. [2023.01.18/XS0337/cv/**E**]

- ♦ Mathematics Education Network for Central America and the Caribbean (#18646)

♦ Mathematics Education and Society (MES) 16604

Pres address not obtained. E-mail: bhe@msu.edu.
Contact address not obtained.
URL: http://mescommunity.info/

History 1998, Nottingham (UK). Founded at inaugural conference. **Aims** Bring together mathematics educators from around the world to provide a forum for discussion of the social, ethical and political dimensions of mathematics education for disseminating theoretical frameworks, discussing methodological issues, sharing and discussing research, planning for action and the development of a strong research network on mathematics education and society. **Structure** International Committee. **Languages** English. **Staff** None paid. **Finance** Sources: meeting proceeds. **Activities** Events/meetings. **Events** *International Mathematics Education and Society Conference* Klagenfurt am Wörthersee (Austria) 2021, *Conference* Hyderabad (India) 2019, *Conference* Volos (Greece) 2017, *Conference* Portland, OR (USA) 2015, *Conference* Cape Town (South Africa) 2013. **Publications** Conference proceedings.
Members Individuals in 18 countries:
Australia, Bhutan, Brazil, Canada, Colombia, Denmark, France, Germany, Greece, India, New Zealand, Norway, Portugal, South Africa, Spain, Sweden, UK, USA. [2020.05.06/XJ8842/c/**E**]

- ♦ MATHMET – European Centre for Mathematics and Statistics in Metrology (unconfirmed)
- ♦ Matres Mundi International – International Cooperation Agency for Maternal and Infant Health (internationally oriented national body)
- ♦ **MATSDA** Materials Development Association (#16598)
- ♦ MATS – Melanesian Association of Theological Schools (internationally oriented national body)
- ♦ Matsunaga Institute for Peace / see Spark M Matsunaga Institute for Peace and Conflict Resolution
- ♦ Matthew B Ridgway Center for International Security Studies (internationally oriented national body)
- ♦ **MAU** Miznarodna Asociaciia Ukrainistiv (#12243)
- ♦ Maurice Pate Institute for Human Survival (internationally oriented national body)
- ♦ Mauritius Convention on Transparency – United Nations Convention on Transparency in Treaty-based Investor-State Arbitration (2014 treaty)
- ♦ MAVA – Fondation pour la Nature (internationally oriented national body)
- ♦ MAVA Foundation (internationally oriented national body)
- ♦ MAVE – Mouvement africaine Vineyard Europe (see: #20778)
- ♦ Maventy Health International (internationally oriented national body)
- ♦ **MAVI-Group** Mathematical Views (#16603)
- ♦ MAVI / see Mathematical Views (#16603)
- ♦ MAWac / see Megacities Alliance for Water and Climate (#16697)
- ♦ **MAWAC** Megacities Alliance for Water and Climate (#16697)
- ♦ Al Mawred Al Thaqafy (#04984)
- ♦ Max Ent – International Workshop on Bayesian Inference and Maximum Entropy Methods in Science and Engineering (meeting series)
- ♦ Max Foundation (unconfirmed)
- ♦ Max Havelaar Foundation (internationally oriented national body)
- ♦ Max Planck Foundation for International Peace and the Rule of Law (internationally oriented national body)
- ♦ Max-Planck-Gesellschaft zur Förderung der Wissenschaften (internationally oriented national body)
- ♦ Max-Planck-Institut für Ausländisches und Internationales Strafrecht (internationally oriented national body)
- ♦ Max Planck Institute for Foreign and International Criminal Law (internationally oriented national body)
- ♦ Max-Planck Institute for International and Comparative Criminal Law / see Max Planck Institute for Foreign and International Criminal Law
- ♦ Max Planck Society for the Advancement of Science (internationally oriented national body)
- ♦ Max-Planck-Stiftung für Internationalen Frieden und Rechtsstaatlichkeit (internationally oriented national body)
- ♦ Mayday Rescue (unconfirmed)

♦ Mayors for Peace 16605

Pres c/o Hiroshima Peace Culture Foundation, 1-5 Nakajima-cho, Naka-ku, Hiroshima, 730-0811 Japan. T. +81822427821. Fax +81822427452. E-mail: mayorcon@pcf.city.hiroshima.jp.
URL: http://www.mayorsforpeace.org/

History 24 Jun 1982, Japan. Current title adopted in 2001 during 5th General Conference. Former names and other names: *World Conference of Mayors for Peace through Inter-city Solidarity* – former (1982 to 2001). **Aims** Through close cooperation among cities: raise international public awareness regarding the need to abolish *nuclear weapons*; contribute to the realization of lasting world peace by working to eliminate *starvation* and *poverty*, assisting *refugees*, supporting *human rights*, protecting the *environment*, and solving other problems that threaten peaceful coexistence within the human family. **Structure** General Conference (every 4 years); Secretariat located in Hiroshima (Japan); Campaign Secretariat located in Ieper (Belgium). **Languages** English, Japanese. **Staff** 7.00 FTE, paid. **Finance** Contributions of the cities of Hiroshima and Nagasaki (Japan). Budget (1 Apr 2013 – 31 Mar 2014): Yen 40,646,000. **Activities** Advocacy/lobbying/activism; events/meetings. **Events** *Quadrennial General Conference* Hiroshima (Japan) 2022, *Quadrennial General Conference* Hiroshima (Japan) 2021, *Executive Conference* Geneva (Switzerland) 2018, *Quadrennial General Conference* Nagasaki (Japan) 2017, *Executive Conference* Ieper (Belgium) 2015. **Publications** *Mayors for Peace* (annual) – newsletter. Conference proceedings in English and Japanese.
Members As of 1 May 2014, cities (6,035) in 157 countries and territories:
Afghanistan, Albania, Algeria, Andorra, Argentina, Armenia, Australia, Austria, Bangladesh, Belarus, Belgium, Benin, Bhutan, Bolivia, Bosnia-Herzegovina, Botswana, Brazil, Bulgaria, Burkina Faso, Burundi, Cambodia, Cameroon, Canada, Cape Verde, Central African Rep, Chad, Chile, China, Colombia, Congo Brazzaville, Congo DR, Costa Rica, Côte d'Ivoire, Croatia, Cuba, Cyprus, Czechia, Denmark, Djibouti, Dominica, Dominican Rep, Ecuador, Egypt, El Salvador, Eritrea, Estonia, Ethiopia, Fiji, Finland, France, Gambia, Georgia, Germany, Ghana, Greece, Greenland, Guatemala, Guinea, Guyana, Haiti, Honduras, Hungary, Iceland, India, Indonesia, Iran Islamic Rep, Iraq, Ireland, Israel, Italy, Jamaica, Japan, Jordan, Kazakhstan, Kenya, Korea Rep, Kosovo, Kyrgyzstan, Latvia, Lebanon, Lesotho, Liberia, Lithuania, Luxembourg, Madagascar, Malawi, Malaysia, Mali, Malta, Marshall Is, Mauritania, Mauritius, Mexico, Micronesia FS, Moldova, Mongolia, Morocco, Mozambique, Namibia, Nepal, Netherlands, New Zealand, Nicaragua, Niger, Nigeria, North Macedonia, Northern Cyprus, Northern Mariana Is, Norway, Pakistan, Palestine, Panama, Papua New Guinea, Paraguay, Peru, Philippines, Poland, Polynesia Fr, Portugal, Puerto Rico, Romania, Russia, Rwanda, Sao Tomé-Principe, Saudi Arabia, Senegal, Serbia, Seychelles, Sierra Leone, Slovakia, Slovenia, Solomon Is, Somalia, South Africa, South Sudan, Spain, Sri Lanka, Sweden, Switzerland, Syrian AR, Taiwan, Tajikistan, Tanzania UR, Thailand, Togo, Trinidad-Tobago, Türkiye, Uganda, UK, Ukraine, Uruguay, USA, Uzbekistan, Venezuela, Vietnam, Yemen, Zambia.
Consultative Status Consultative status granted from: *ECOSOC (#05331)* (Special). **IGO Relations** Associated with Department of Global Communications of the United Nations. **NGO Relations** Member of: *International Campaign to Abolish Nuclear Weapons (ICAN, #12426)*. Associate partner of: *World Urban Campaign (WUC, #21893)*. [2021/XF5471/**F**]

- ♦ MBAA – Master Brewers Association of the Americas (internationally oriented national body)
- ♦ MBA – Marine Biological Association (internationally oriented national body)

♦ MBA Roundtable 16606

Exec Dir 1225 LaSalle Ave, Ste 804, Minneapolis MN 55403, USA. E-mail: anne@mbaroundtable.org – info@mbaroundtable.org.
URL: http://mbaroundtable.org/

History 1995. **Aims** Inform and inspire MBA *curricular* and programmatic *innovation*. **Structure** Board of Directors, headed by President. **Finance** Members' dues. **Publications** *MBA Innovation* – electronic magazine. *The Exchange* – series. **Members** Schools (over 150). Membership countries not specified. **NGO Relations** Member of: *EFMD – The Management Development Network (#05387)*. Strategic partners include: *Graduate Management Admission Council (GMAC, #10687)*. [2020/XJ7293/**F**]

- ♦ MBB – Mediators Beyond Borders International (internationally oriented national body)
- ♦ **MBC** Euro-Mediterranean Council for Burns and Fire Disaster (#05719)
- ♦ **MBES** Mezdunarodnyj Bank Ekonomicheskogo Sotrudnicestva (#12310)
- ♦ MBF – Medical Benevolence Foundation (internationally oriented national body)
- ♦ **MBMGP** Mezdunarodnoe Bjuro po Mehanike Gornyh Porod (#12417)
- ♦ MBM / see Mont-Blanc Meetings (#16850)
- ♦ **MBM** Mont-Blanc Meetings (#16850)
- ♦ MBMSI / see MBMS International
- ♦ MBMS International (internationally oriented national body)
- ♦ MBON – Marine Biodiversity Observation Network (unconfirmed)
- ♦ MBP – International conference on Metal-Binding Peptides (meeting series)
- ♦ **MBP** Mezdunarodnoe Bjuro Prosvescenija (#12413)
- ♦ MBRGI – Mohammed Bin Rashid Al Maktoum Global Initiatives (internationally oriented national body)
- ♦ MBSHC – Mediterranean and Black Seas Hydrographic Commission (see: #13825)
- ♦ **MBW** Movement for a Better World (#16869)
- ♦ **MCAA** Marie Curie Alumni Association (#16576)
- ♦ MCAI – Maternal and Childhealth Advocacy International (internationally oriented national body)
- ♦ MCA – Mediterranean Control Association (no recent information)
- ♦ MCA – Missionary Cenacle Apostolate (religious order)
- ♦ MCANW / see Medact
- ♦ MCBI / see Marine Conservation Institute
- ♦ MCCA / see Central American Common Market (#03666)
- ♦ **MCCA** The Conference of the Methodist Church in the Caribbean and the Americas (#04629)
- ♦ MCCI – Missionarii Comboniani Cordis Jesu (religious order)
- ♦ MCC – International Symposium on Motivational and Cognitive Control (meeting series)
- ♦ MCC – Mennonite Central Committee (internationally oriented national body)
- ♦ MCC – Mercator Research Institute on Global Commons and Climate Change (internationally oriented national body)
- ♦ MCCO – Mercado Común del Caribe Oriental (inactive)
- ♦ **MCCS** Molecular and Cellular Cognition Society (#16847)
- ♦ MCDI – Medical Care Development International (internationally oriented national body)
- ♦ MCEG – Maastricht Centre for European Governance (internationally oriented national body)
- ♦ **MCEI** Marketing Communications Executives International (#16586)
- ♦ **MCE** Major Cities of Europe IT Users Group (#16551)
- ♦ **MCE** Management Centre Europe (#16561)
- ♦ MCF / see Liberation
- ♦ MCF-B (internationally oriented national body)
- ♦ MCH – Monaco Collectif Humanitaire (internationally oriented national body)
- ♦ MCIC – Macedonian Centre for International Cooperation (internationally oriented national body)
- ♦ MCIC – Manitoba Council for International Cooperation (internationally oriented national body)
- ♦ MCI – Male Contraceptive Initiative (internationally oriented national body)
- ♦ **MCI** MaterCare International (#16597)
- ♦ MCI – Mercy Corps International (internationally oriented national body)
- ♦ MCI – Microclinic International (internationally oriented national body)
- ♦ MCIS / see Munk School of Global Affairs & Public Policy, University of Toronto
- ♦ MCIS – Mountbatten Centre for International Studies (internationally oriented national body)
- ♦ McKenzie Institute Benelux (internationally oriented national body)

♦ McKenzie Institute International 16607

CEO PO Box 2026, Raumati Beach 5255, New Zealand. T. +6442996645. Fax +6442997010. E-mail: headoffice@mckenzieinstitute.org – ceo@mckenzieinstitute.org.
URL: https://mckenzieinstitute.org/

History 1982, New Zealand. **Aims** Further philosophies and treatments for *spinal disorders*, as developed by Robin McKenzie. **Structure** Board of Trustees; International Advisory Council. **Events** *International Conference in Mechanical Diagnosis and Therapy* Copenhagen (Denmark) 2015, *International extremity workshop* Paraparaumu (New Zealand) 2003.
Members Branches in 31 countries:
Argentina, Australia, Austria, Belgium, Brazil, Canada, Croatia, Czechia, Denmark, Egypt, Finland, France, Germany, Greece, Hungary, India, Italy, Japan, Luxembourg, Netherlands, New Zealand, Nigeria, Norway, Poland, Saudi Arabia, Slovakia, Slovenia, Sweden, Switzerland, UK, USA.
Regional member (1):
McKenzie Institute Benelux (MIB). [2021/XE3538/j/**E**]

- ♦ McKnight Foundation (internationally oriented national body)
- ♦ **MCLACJ** Mesa de Coordinación Latinoamericana de Comercio Justo (#16307)
- ♦ MCMA – International Conference on Monte Carlo Techniques for Medical Applications (meeting series)
- ♦ MC – The Management Centre of the Mediterranean (internationally oriented national body)
- ♦ MCM – International Conference on Monte Carlo Methods and Applications (meeting series)
- ♦ MCMJ – Mouvement du Congrès mondial de la Jeunesse (inactive)
- ♦ MCM – Maison des citoyens du monde (internationally oriented national body)
- ♦ **MCNTI** Mezdunarodnyj Centr Naucnoj i Tehniceskoj Informacii (#12514)
- ♦ MCOD / see Methodist Church Britain – World Church Office
- ♦ **MCofA** Mathematical Council of the Americas (#16600)
- ♦ MCOR / see United Methodist Committee on Relief
- ♦ **MCOS** Mezdunarodnyj Centr Obucajuscih Sistem (#12487)
- ♦ MCPC – World Conference Mass Customization, Personalization & Co-Creation (meeting series)
- ♦ MCPFE / see Ministerial Conference on the Protection of Forests in Europe (#16817)
- ♦ MCQMC – International Conference in Monte Carlo & Quasi-Monte Carlo Methods in Scientific Computing (meeting series)
- ♦ **MC** Red Mercociudades (#18721)
- ♦ MCSER – Mediterranean Center of Social and Educational Research (internationally oriented national body)
- ♦ MCS – Marine Conservation Society (internationally oriented national body)
- ♦ MC – Soeurs Missionnaires de la Consolata (religious order)
- ♦ MCTC – Golda Meir Mount Carmel International Training Centre (internationally oriented national body)
- ♦ MCTC – Multi-Country Posts and Telecommunications Training Centre, Blantyre (no recent information)
- ♦ MCWASP – Modelling of Casting, Welding and Advanced Solidification Processes Conference (meeting series)
- ♦ MCW – Miracle Corners of the World (internationally oriented national body)
- ♦ MDAC / see Validity Foundation (#20743)
- ♦ MDCE / see Maritime Development Center
- ♦ MDC – Maritime Development Center (internationally oriented national body)
- ♦ **MDC** Mint Directors Conference (#16822)
- ♦ MDF Training and Consultancy / see Management for Development Foundation
- ♦ MDF Training and Consultancy – Management for Development Foundation (internationally oriented national body)
- ♦ **MDFŽ** Mezdunarodnaja Demokraticeskaja Federacija Zenscin (#21022)
- ♦ MDG Global Watch – Millennium Development Goals Global Watch (internationally oriented national body)
- ♦ **MDI** Meeting Design Institute (#16694)
- ♦ **MDIS** Mediterranean Dental Implant Society (#16650)
- ♦ **MDM** Médecins du Monde – International (#16613)
- ♦ **MDN** Mujeres de Negro (#20987)
- ♦ MD – Ordo Patrum Excalceatorum Beatae Mariae Virginis de Mercede (religious order)
- ♦ MDPL – Movement for Disarmament, Peace and Liberty (internationally oriented national body)
- ♦ **MDP** Municipal Development Partnership for West and Central Africa (#16902)
- ♦ MDRI / see Disability Rights International

♦ MDS Alliance 16608

Secretariat c/o MDS Foundation, 4573 South Broad St, Suite 150, Yardville NJ 08620, USA. T. +16092981600. E-mail: info@mds-alliance.org.
URL: http://www.mds-alliance.org/

History Registration: 501(c)(3) organization, No/ID: EIN: 22-3283911, Start date: 2000, USA, New Jersey. **Aims** Ensure meyolodysplastic syndrome (MDS) *patients*, regardless of their age, have access to the best multi-professional care. **Structure** Leadership Group.
Members Founding members in 7 countries:
Canada, Germany, Italy, Kosovo, Spain, UK, USA.
Included in the above, 1 organization listed in this Yearbook:
Aplastic Anemia and MDS International Foundation (AA and MDSIF).
General members in 30 countries. Membership countries not specified.
NGO Relations Member of (2): *European Cancer Organisation (ECO, #06432)* (Patient Advisory Committee); *Workgroup of European Cancer Patient Advocacy Networks (WECAN, #21054).* [2023/XM4103/**C**]

- ♦ **MDS Foundation** Myelodysplastic Syndromes Foundation (#16923)
- ♦ MDS / see International Parkinson and Movement Disorder Society (#14515)
- ♦ **MDS** International Parkinson and Movement Disorder Society (#14515)
- ♦ MdS – Maison de sagesse (internationally oriented national body)
- ♦ **MDWG** Working Group of European Mint Directors for the Technical Study of the European Single Coinage System (#21059)
- ♦ MDWIT – Multinational Development of Women in Technology (internationally oriented national body)
- ♦ **MEACO** Middle East African Council of Ophthalmology (#16752)
- ♦ MEACOOP – Middle East – Africa Club of Oncology and Ocular Pathology (internationally oriented national body)
- ♦ MEACRS – Middle East Africa Cataract and refractive Surgery Society (see: #16752)
- ♦ **MEADFA** Middle East and Africa Duty Free Association (#16751)
- ♦ MEAGS – Middle East Africa Glaucoma Society (see: #16752)
- ♦ **MEAHI** Middle East Association for Health Informatics (#16753)
- ♦ **MEALA** Middle Eastern Association of Linguistic Anthropology (#16760)
- ♦ **MEA** Media Ecology Association (#16616)
- ♦ **MEA** Mesoamerican Ecotourism Alliance (#16731)
- ♦ MEAOPS – Middle East Africa Oculoplastic Society (unconfirmed)
- ♦ MEAPOSS – Middle East Africa Pediatric Ophthalmology and Strabismus Society (see: #16752)
- ♦ MEA Rugby League – Middle East Africa Rugby League (unconfirmed)
- ♦ MEASE – Middle East Association of Science Editors (no recent information)
- ♦ MEASNET / see Measuring Network of Wind Energy Institutes (#16609)
- ♦ **MEASNET** Measuring Network of Wind Energy Institutes (#16609)
- ♦ MEASOPRS – Middle East Africa Society of Ophthalmic Plastic and Reconstructive Surgery (see: #16752)
- ♦ Measuring Behavior – International Conference on Methods and Techniques in Behavioral Research (meeting series)

♦ Measuring Network of Wind Energy Institutes (MEASNET) 16609

Sec UPM-Campus de Montegancedo, Edificio CIDA, Pozuelo de Alarcón, 28223 Madrid, Spain.
URL: http://www.measnet.com/

History 1997. Founded as a co-operation of companies which are engaged in the field of wind energy. Former names and other names: *International Network for Harmonized and Recognized Measurements in Wind Energy (MEASNET)* – former. **Aims** Ensure high quality measurements, uniform interpretation of standards and recommendations, as well as interchangeability of results; establish rules and requirements which guarantee the carrying out of high quality measurements by members; enable members to perform measurements of equal quality, sufficient for mutual comparison and acceptance by the wind energy market. **Structure** Council of Members; Executive Board; Executive Chairwoman; Expert Groups. **Languages** English, German, Spanish. **Staff** 2.00 FTE, paid; 3.00 FTE, voluntary. **Finance** Sources: members' dues. **Activities** Certification/accreditation; guidance/assistance/consulting; standards/guidelines. All member countries and regions, plus Canada, India, Portugal, and Republic of Korea.

Members 29 in 9 countries:
Australia, China, Denmark, Germany, Greece, Netherlands, Spain, UK, USA. [2022.11.07/XF5819/**F**]

♦ MEATRC – Middle East Association of Training and Retreat Centres (no recent information)
♦ MEAVRS – Middle East Africa Vitreo Retinal Society (see: #16752)
♦ **MEBAA** Middle East and North Africa Business Aviation Association (#16776)
♦ **MEBFDS** Middle East Burn and Fire Disaster Society (#16754)
♦ MEBF – Mercosur – European Business Forum (internationally oriented national body)
♦ MECA – Middle East Children's Alliance (internationally oriented national body)
♦ Mécanism africain de coopération policière (#00492)
♦ Mécanisme pour l'Accord sur la facilitation des échanges (#20182)
♦ Mécanisme international appelé à exercer les fonctions résiduelles des Tribunaux pénaux (#14746)
♦ Mecanismo para el Acuerdo sobre Facilitación del Comercio (#20182)
♦ Mecanismo da União Africana para a Cooperação Policial (#00492)
♦ MECCAD – Middle East Centre for Culture and Development (internationally oriented national body)
♦ **MECC** Middle East Council of Churches (#16756)
♦ MECC – Mid-European Clay Conference (meeting series)
♦ MECERN – Medieval Central Europe Research Network (unconfirmed)
♦ MEC / see Global Health Advocates (#10400)
♦ Mechanics of Hearing (meeting series)
♦ Mechanism for International Criminal Tribunals / see International Residual Mechanism for Criminal Tribunals (#14746)
♦ MECHCOMP – International Conference on Mechanics of Composites (meeting series)
♦ Mechitaristi (religious order)
♦ Mechitarists (religious order)
♦ MECIDS – Middle East Consortium on Infectious Disease Surveillance (unconfirmed)
♦ MEC / see International Civil Servants Mutual Association (#12585)
♦ MECLA – Mercado Común Cinematografico Latinoamericano (no recent information)
♦ MECO – Conference of the Middle European Cooperation in Statistical Physics (meeting series)
♦ MECO International / see Middle East Christian Outreach
♦ **Mecomed** Middle East Medical Devices and Diagnostics Trade Association (#16772)
♦ MECO – Middle East Christian Outreach (internationally oriented national body)
♦ **MECSC** Middle East Council of Shopping Centres (#16757)
♦ MECSEA – Manufacturers of Educational and Commercial Stationery European Association (inactive)
♦ MEDAC – Mediterranean Academy of Diplomatic Studies (internationally oriented national body)
♦ **MEDAC** Mediterranean Advisory Council (#16639)
♦ Medact (internationally oriented national body)
♦ MEDAIR (internationally oriented national body)
♦ MEDAlics – Mediterranean Network for the Knowledge Economy and Innovation (internationally oriented national body)
♦ MEDA – Mennonite Economic Development Associates (internationally oriented national body)
♦ MEDA – Middle East Dietary Association (no recent information)
♦ **MEDASSET** Mediterranean Association to Save the Sea Turtles (#16647)

♦ MEDCITIES Network 16610

Réseau Medcités

SG Metropolitan Area of Barcelona, Calle 62 – no 16-18, 08040 Barcelona, Spain. E-mail: contact@medcities.org.
URL: https://medcities.org/

History 25 Nov 1991, Barcelona (Spain). Planned and launched by *United Towns Development Agency (UTDA, no recent information)* and *Mediterranean Environmental Technical Assistance Programme (METAP, inactive)*. Since 2015, a fully independent organization. **Aims** Strengthen the notion of interdependence and joint responsibility concerning *preservation* of the *environment* and *sustainable development* in the *Mediterranean* basin; strengthen the role and means of *municipalities* in the working up of local policies of protection of the environment; make decentralized cooperation programmes between its members on urban sustainable development. **Structure** General Assembly; Board; General Secretariat. **Languages** English, French, Spanish. **Staff** 7.50 FTE, paid. **Finance** Sources: members' dues. Main financing through projects. Supported by 4 partners of METAP: *European Commission (EC, #06633)*; *International Bank for Reconstruction and Development (IBRD, #12317)*; *UNDP (#20292)*. **Activities** Monitoring/evaluation. **Events** *General Assembly* Larnaca (Cyprus) 2022, *General Assembly* Barcelona (Spain) 2013, *European conference on sustainable cities and towns* Dunkerque (France) 2010, *General Assembly* Tripoli (Lebanon) 2008, *European conference on sustainable cities and towns* Aalborg (Denmark) 2004. **Publications** *Cost Recovery, Public/Private Partnerships and Financing of Local Actions* (1998); *Guidelines for Municipal Solid Waste Management in the Mediterranean Area*; *Urban Development in the Mediterranean Strategic Planning as a way of Urban Management*. Conference proceedings.
Members Mediterranean coastal cities in 18 countries and territories:
Albania, Algeria, Croatia, Cyprus, Egypt, France, Greece, Israel, Italy, Jordan, Lebanon, Libya, Morocco, Palestine, Spain, Syrian AR, Tunisia, Türkiye.
NGO Relations Member of (1): *International Federation for Sustainable Development and Fight to Poverty in the Mediterranean-Black Sea (FISPMED, #13562)*. Partner of (2): *Asociación de las Camaras de Comercio e Industria del Mediterraneo (ASCAME, #02112)*; *Conference of European Cross-border and Interregional Cities Network (CECICN, #04595)*. Participates in: *European Sustainable Cities and Towns Campaign (#08863)*.
[2023/XF3301/**F**]

♦ **MEDCOAST** Mediterranean Coastal Foundation (#16649)

♦ MedCruise 16611

SG Muelle Ribera S/N Ed Puerto Ciudad, Office 5-B, 38001 Santa Cruz de Tenerife, Spain. T. +34922533383. E-mail: secretariat@medcruise.com.
URL: http://www.medcruise.com/

History 11 Jun 1996, Rome (Italy). Former names and other names: *The Association of Mediterranean Cruise Ports (MedCruise)* – full title. **Aims** Promote the cruise industry in the Mediterranean, Black Sea, Adriatic Sea, Red Sea and Near Atlantic. **Structure** General Assembly; Board of Directors; President; Secretariat. **Languages** English. **Staff** 2.00 FTE, paid. **Finance** Sources: members' dues. **Activities** Guidance/assistance/consulting; networking/liaising; training/education. Active in all member countries. **Events** *General Assembly* Antibes (France) 2019, *General Assembly* Kusadasi (Turkey) 2019, *General Assembly* Lisbon (Portugal) 2018, *General Assembly* Valletta (Malta) 2018, *General Assembly* Toulon (France) 2017. **Publications** *MedCruise News*. Yearbook. Statistics Reports; Cruise Line Directory; MedCruise in Action.
Members Port members in 21 countries and territories:
Bulgaria, Burgas, Croatia, Cyprus, Egypt, France, Gibraltar, Greece, Israel, Italy, Malta, Monaco, Montenegro, Portugal, Romania, Russia, Slovenia, Spain, Tunisia, Türkiye, Ukraine.
Associate in 10 countries and territories:
Croatia, Cyprus, Gibraltar, Greece, Italy, Romania, Spain, Tunisia, Türkiye, Ukraine.
IGO Relations *European Commission (EC, #06633)* – DG Mare and DG Move. [2021.06.16/XM5713/**D**]

♦ MEDEA: MEDIA and LEARNING (Media and Learning Association) . . 16612

Secretariat Leuvensesteenweg 132, 3370 Roosbeek, Belgium. T. +3216284040. E-mail: info@media-and-learning.eu.
URL: http://media-and-learning.eu/

History 2012. Founded by organizations from Italy, Belgium, France, Ireland and Estonia. Registration: KBO, No/ID: BE0504.950.920, Belgium. **Aims** Promote and stimulate the use of media as a way to enhance innovation and creativity in teaching and learning across all levels of education in Europe. **Structure** General Meeting (annual); Board; Secretariat. **Languages** English. **Staff** 0.50 FTE, paid; 1.00 FTE, voluntary. **Finance** Sources: grants; members' dues; revenue from activities/projects. **Activities** Awards/prizes/competitions; events/meetings. **Events** *Conference* Leuven (Belgium) 2022, *Conference* Brussels (Belgium) 2020, *Conference* Leuven (Belgium) 2018, *Conference* Brussels (Belgium) 2014. **Publications** *Media and Learning Newsletter* (12 a year). https://media-and-learning.eu/news/.
Members Full (51) in 17 countries:
Austria, Belgium, Canada, China, Croatia, Finland, France, Germany, Ireland, Italy, Luxembourg, Netherlands, Spain, Sweden, Switzerland, UK, USA. [2021.06.09/XJ9722/**D**]

♦ **MedECC** Mediterranean Experts on Climate and Environmental Change (#16651)
♦ Médecine pour le Tiers-Monde (internationally oriented national body)
♦ Médecins pour les droits de l'homme, USA (internationally oriented national body)
♦ Médecins Internationales – ILMAV (#13186)

♦ Médecins du Monde – International (MDM) 16613

Doctors of the World – International (DOW) – Médicos del Mundo – International – Dokters van de Wereld – International

Secretariat 62 rue Marcadet, 75018 Paris, France. T. +33144921480.
Registered Office Rue Botanique 75, 1210 Brussels, Belgium.
URL: http://www.medecinsdumonde.org/

History 1981. Registration: No/ID: 0460.162.753, Start date: 30 Dec 1996, Belgium. **Aims** Promote effective access to health and a decent life for all. **Structure** International Board. **Finance** Budget (2012): euro 113 million. **Events** *Humanitarian Congress* Berlin (Germany) 2018, *Humanitarian Congress* Berlin (Germany) 2017, *Meeting* Montréal, QC (Canada) 2017, *Humanitarian Congress* Berlin (Germany) 2016, *International conference* Paris (France) 1999. **Publications** *What's up doc?* – newsletter. *Moral Report 2012*.
Members Full in 15 countries:
Argentina, Belgium, Canada, France, Germany, Greece, Japan, Luxembourg, Netherlands, Portugal, Spain, Sweden, Switzerland, UK, USA.
Consultative Status Consultative status granted from: *ECOSOC (#05331)* (General); *Council of Europe (CE, #04881)* (Participatory Status); *WHO (#20950)* (Official Relations). **IGO Relations** Participant in Fundamental Rights Platform of *European Union Agency for Fundamental Rights (FRA, #08969)*.
NGO Relations Member of:
- *Association québécoise des organismes de coopération internationale (AQOCI)*;
- *Civil Society Forum on Drugs (CSFD, #03968)*;
- *Cooperation Committee for Cambodia (CCC)*;
- *European Network for Central Africa (EurAc, #07874)*;
- *European NGO Platform Asylum and Migration (EPAM, #08051)*;
- *European Public Health Alliance (EPHA, #08297)*;
- *Fédération des employeurs ONG (FEONG)*;
- *Fédération francophone et germanophone des associations de coopération au développement (ACODEV, #09587)*;
- *Global Health Workforce Alliance (GHWA, inactive)*;
- *International Campaign to Ban Landmines – Cluster Munition Coalition (ICBL-CMC, #12427)*;
- *International Council of Voluntary Agencies (ICVA, #13092)*;
- *Platform for International Cooperation on Undocumented Migrants (PICUM, #18401)*.

Partner of: *Global Health Cluster (GHC, #10401)*. Supports: *Global Call for Action Against Poverty (GCAP, #10263)* [2020/XE4405/**E**]

♦ Médecins sans frontières / see Bureau international des Médecins sans frontières (#03366)
♦ Médecins sans vacances (internationally oriented national body)
♦ Médecins pour la survie mondiale, Canada (internationally oriented national body)
♦ MEDECOS / see International Society of Mediterranean Ecology (#15259)
♦ MEDEF International (internationally oriented national body)

♦ MEDELEC 16614

Acting SG EDF, Tour EDF, 20 Place de la Défense, 92050 Paris La Défense CEDEX, France.
URL: http://www.medelec.org/

History Set up 1992, as a "forum of exchange". Transformed into a Liaison Committee, 1997. **Aims** Play a prominent role regarding present and/or future changes within the *electricity sector* in the different countries concerned by working with international organizations and other associations in the same or similar areas of activity. **Structure** Chairman; Secretary General. **Events** *Annual Meeting* Brussels (Belgium) 2015, *Annual Meeting* Tunis (Tunisia) 2014, *Annual Meeting* Tripoli (Libya) 2013, *Annual Meeting* Amman (Jordan) 2012, *Annual Meeting* Madrid (Spain) 2011.
Members Associations (5):
Arab Union of Electricity (AUE, #01066); *Association of Power Utilities in Africa (APUA, #02867)*; *Comité Maghrébin de l'Electricité (COMELEC, #04191)*; *Union of the Electricity Industry – Eurelectric (#20379)*.
[2015/XM4256/y/**F**]

♦ **MEDEL** Magistrats européens pour la démocratie et les libertés (#16546)
♦ MedEvac Foundation International (internationally oriented national body)
♦ MEDFA / see Middle East and Africa Duty Free Association (#16751)
♦ MedGlobal (internationally oriented national body)
♦ MedGU – Mediterranean Geosciences Union (unconfirmed)
♦ Media Associates International (internationally oriented national body)
♦ Media in Cooperation and Transition (internationally oriented national body)

♦ Media Defence 16615

Registered Office 5 Chancery Lane, London, WC2A 1LG, UK. T. +442074067450. E-mail: info@mediadefence.org.
URL: http://www.mediadefence.org/

History 2008. Originating from a programme of work by *Open Society Initiative*. Former names and other names: *Media Legal Defence Initiative (MLDI)* – former. Registration: Charity Commission, No/ID: 1128789, England and Wales. **Aims** Provide legal defence to journalists, citizen journalists and independent media around the world who are under threat for their reporting. **Structure** Trustees; Secretariat. **Staff** 18.00 FTE, paid. **Finance** Supported by: *Adessium Foundation*; *Ford Foundation (#09858)*; *Luminate*; *Open Society Foundations (OSF, #17763)*. **Activities** Advocacy/lobbying/activism; capacity building; financial and/or material support; training/education. [2023.02.14/XJ9315/**F**]

♦ Media for Development International (internationally oriented national body)

♦ Media Ecology Association (MEA) 16616

Sec address not obtained.
URL: https://www.media-ecology.org/

Activities Awards/prizes/competitions; events/meetings; research/documentation. **Events** *Annual Convention* Toronto, ON (Canada) 2019, *Annual Convention* Orono, ME (USA) 2018, *Annual Convention* Moraga, CA (USA) 2017, *Annual Convention* Bologna (Italy) 2016, *Annual Convention* Denver, CO (USA) 2015.
[2020/AA0280/**C**]

♦ Media and Entertainment International (inactive)
♦ Media Focus on Africa (internationally oriented national body)

♦ Media Foundation for West Africa (MFWA) 16617

Fondation pour les Médias en Afrique de l'Ouest

Exec Dir No 28 Otele Avenue, East Legon, Accra, Ghana. T. +233302555327 – +233302955213. E-mail: info@mfwa.org.
URL: http://www.mfwa.org/

History 1997. Registration: Ghana Registrar General Department, No/ID: G. 1846/CG069472016, Start date: 20 Mar 1997, Ghana, Greater Accra. **Aims** Promote and defend the right to freedom of expression of all persons, particularly the media and human rights defenders in West Africa. **Structure** Board of Directors; Secretariat, located in Accra (Ghana). **Languages** English, French. **Staff** 20.00 FTE, paid. **Activities** Advocacy/lobbying/activism; capacity building; events/meetings; projects/programmes; research and development; research/documentation. Active in: Benin, Burkina Faso, Cape Verde, Côte d'Ivoire, Gambia, Ghana, Guinea, Guinea-Bissau, Liberia, Mali, Mauritania, Niger, Nigeria, Senegal, Sierra Leone, Togo. **Events** *Social media, fake news and elections in Africa* Accra (Ghana) 2019, *Conference* Accra (Ghana) 2018, *Forum on how regional human rights mechanisms can strengthen freedom of expression* Banjul (Gambia) 2006. **Publications** *Exile News* (12 a year); *Zongo-Giwa* (4 a year); *Media Alert West Africa* (annual). *The Law and Media Series. African Languages and Freedom of Expression*; *Freedom of Information and Civil Service Reform in Ghana*; *Legislation on Media, Speech and Expression in Ghana*; *Liberia: Human Rights Violations 1997-2002*; *Politics in the Airwaves*; *Right to Information in West Africa*; *The Face and Phases of the Ghana Police*; *The Gambia: Violations of Press Freedom by the Government of President Yahya Jammeh – 1994-2006*; *The Media in Guinea*;

Where has Aid taken Africa ? Re-Thinking Development. **Members** Membership countries not specified. **Consultative Status** Consultative status granted from: *African Commission on Human and Peoples' Rights (ACHPR, #00255)* (Observer); *ECOSOC (#05331)* (Special). **NGO Relations** Member of (5): *Africa Freedom of Information Centre (AFIC, #00175)*; *African Freedom of Expression Exchange (AFEX)*; *Global Forum for Media Development (GFMD, #10375)*; *IFEX (#11100)*; *Sudan Consortium (#20031)*. Supports (1): *International News Safety Institute (INSI, #14364)*. Hosts secretariat for: *West and Central Africa Human Rights Training Institute (WACAHRI, #20906)*. [2023.02.13/XF6942/f/F]

♦ Media Freedom Coalition (MFC) 16618

Secretariat Thomson Reuters Foundation, 5 Canada Square, Canary Wharf, London, E14 5AQ, UK. E-mail: info@mediafreedomcoalition.org.
URL: https://mediafreedomcoalition.org/

History Jul 2019. Established at Global Conference for Media Freedom. **Aims** Advocate for media freedom at home and abroad. **Structure** Executive Group; 2 rotating Co-Chairs. Secretariat. High Level Panel of Legal Experts on Media Freedom (independent advisory body). Consultative Network. *UNESCO (#20322)* participates as observer. Working Group on Media Development. **Activities** Advocacy/lobbying/activism; events/meetings; financial and/or material support; politics/policy/regulatory. **Events** *Global Conference on Media Freedom* Tallinn (Estonia) 2022.
Members Signatories to the Global Pledge on Media Freedom:
Afghanistan, Argentina, Australia, Austria, Belize, Botswana, Bulgaria, Canada, Chile, Costa Rica, Croatia, Cyprus, Czechia, Denmark, Estonia, Finland, France, Germany, Ghana, Greece, Guyana, Honduras, Iceland, Ireland, Italy, Japan, Korea Rep, Kosovo, Latvia, Lebanon, Lithuania, Luxembourg, Maldives, Montenegro, Netherlands, New Zealand, North Macedonia, Norway, Portugal, Serbia, Seychelles, Sierra Leone, Slovakia, Slovenia, Spain, Sudan, Sweden, Switzerland, UK, Ukraine, Uruguay, USA. [2022/AA2940/C*]

♦ Media Institute of Southern Africa (MISA) 16619

Institut des médias d'Afrique australe

Regional Secretariat address not obtained. T. +264242776165. E-mail: misa@misazim.co.zw.
Contact address not obtained. E-mail: info@misazambia.org.uk.
URL: http://www.misa.org/

History Officially launched, Sep 1992. **Aims** Promote free, independent and pluralistic media; promote the free flow of information and cooperation between media workers, as a principle means of nurturing *democracy* and human rights in Africa. **Structure** Regional Governing Council; Regional Secretariat. National Chapters (5): Lesotho; Malawi; Tanzania UR; Zambia; Zimbabwe. **Languages** English, Portuguese. **Staff** Regional Secretariat: 14 full-time; national chapters: over 30. **Finance** Donor funds, including from: *DANIDA*; *European Commission (EC, #06633)*; *Friedrich-Ebert-Stiftung (FES)*; *Heinrich Böll Foundation*; *Humanistisch Instituut voor Ontwikkelingssamenwerking (Hivos)*; *Norwegian Agency for Development Cooperation (Norad)*; *Swedish International Development Cooperation Agency (Sida)*; *United States Agency for International Development (USAID)*. Budget (annual): US$ 2 million. **Activities** Freedom of Expression and Access to Information; Internet Freedom/Governance; Media Freedom Monitoring; Broadcasting and ICTs; Media Support; Gender and HIV/AIDS; Legal Support. Offers: MISA Press Freedom Award. **Events** *Annual General Meeting* Blantyre (Malawi) 2007, *Forum on how regional human rights mechanisms can strengthen freedom of expression* Banjul (Gambia) 2006, *Annual General Meeting* Johannesburg (South Africa) 2006, *Media development forum for Southern Africa / Annual General Meeting* Johannesburg (South Africa) 2006, *Media development forum for Sub-Saharan Africa* Johannesburg (South Africa) 2006. **Publications** *Access to Information – Most Open and Secretive Governments in SADC* (annual); *African Media Barometer* (annual) – report; *So this is Democracy* (annual); *Southern African Media Directory* (every 2 years); *FreePress Magazine* – electronic. Annual Report; thematic research.
Members Full in 11 countries:
Angola, Botswana, Eswatini, Lesotho, Malawi, Mozambique, Namibia, South Africa, Tanzania UR, Zambia, Zimbabwe.
Consultative Status Consultative status granted from: *African Commission on Human and Peoples' Rights (ACHPR, #00255)* (Observer). **NGO Relations** Member of (6): *Africa Freedom of Information Centre (AFIC, #00175)*; *African Freedom of Expression Exchange (AFEX)*; *Coalition for an Effective African Court on Human and Peoples' Rights (African Court Coalition, #04055)*; *Freedom of Information Advocates Network (FOIAnet, #09985)*; *Gender and Media Southern Africa Network (GEMSA, #10099)*; *IFEX (#11100)*. Supports (1): *International News Safety Institute (INSI, #14364)*. [2021/XE2124/j/E]

- ♦ **Media and Learning Association** MEDEA: MEDIA and LEARNING (#16612)
- ♦ Media Legal Defence Initiative / see Media Defence (#16615)
- ♦ Media Managers / see European Federation for Managers in Technologies of Information and Communication (#07163)
- ♦ MEDIA – Mesures pour encourager le développement de l'industrie audiovisuelle (inactive)
- ♦ Media Monitoring Africa (internationally oriented national body)
- ♦ Media Monitoring Project / see Media Monitoring Africa
- ♦ MEDIA Programme (inactive)

♦ MEDIA Salles 16620

Contact c/o Agis Lombarda, Piazza Luigi di Savoia 24, 20124 Milan MI, Italy. T. +3926739781. Fax +3926690410. E-mail: infocinema@mediasalles.it.
URL: http://www.mediasalles.it/

History 1991, Rome (Italy), as an initiative of *MEDIA Programme (MEDIA, inactive)*, with the support of the Italian Government. Commenced operations in 1992. **Aims** In favour of *cinema exhibitors*, promote the *cinema* as: a service to local communities; a major means to disseminate *films*; a means to promulgate *European* films. **Structure** General Meeting; Executive Committee. **Languages** English, French, Italian. **Staff** 2.00 FTE, paid. **Finance** Co-financed by European Union's Creative Europe Programme and the Italian Government. **Activities** Training/education; events/meetings. **Publications** *DGT Online Informer* (6 a year); *European Cinema Journal* (4 a year); *European Cinema Yearbook* (annual). *White Book of the European Exhibition Industry* (1994). **Information Services** *European Cinema On-line Database* – films and companies involved in cinema from production to screen.
Members Cinema exhibition professionals; national and international organizations. Members in 15 countries:
Andorra, Austria, Belgium, Denmark, Finland, France, Germany, Hungary, Ireland, Italy, Netherlands, Norway, Portugal, Spain, Switzerland.
Included in the above, one organization listed in this Yearbook:
International Confederation of Art Cinemas (#12847). [2015/XK0502/E]

♦ Les Médias Francophones Publics (MFP) 16621

Contact Maison de la radio, M832, 116 ave du Prés Kennedy, 75016 Paris, France. E-mail: lesmediasfrancophonespublics@radiofrance.com.
URL: http://www.lesmediasfrancophones.org/

History Jan 2016. Founded on merger of *Radios francophones publiques (RFP, inactive)*, founded 1995, and *Communauté des télévisions francophones (CTF, inactive)*, founded 1964. Registration: France. **Aims** Facilitate collaboration and exchange; support French-language media; ensure that the voice of public broadcasters is heard. **Structure** Assembly; Board; Coordinating Council.
Members Full in 4 countries:
Belgium, Canada, France, Switzerland. [2021/XM5079/F]

- ♦ mediatEUr – European Forum for International Mediation and Dialogue (internationally oriented national body)
- ♦ Médiateur européen (#08084)

♦ Mediation Support Network (MSN) 16622

Secretariat c/o Center for Security Studies, ETH Zurich, Haldeneggsteig 4, IFW, 8092 Zurich ZH, Switzerland. E-mail: info@mediationsupportnetwork.net.
URL: http://www.mediationsupportnetwork.net/

History Sep 2008. **Aims** Promote and improve mediation support practices, processes and standards to address political tensions and armed conflict. **Structure** A network of organizations that support mediation in peace negotiations. **Languages** English. **Activities** Events/meetings; knowledge management/information dissemination; networking/liaising; publishing activities. **Publications** *MSN Discussion Points* (annual).
Members Organizations (25):
- *African Centre for the Constructive Resolution of Disputes (ACCORD)*;
- *Berghof Foundation*;
- *Center for Peace Mediation (CPM)*;
- *Center for Security Studies (CSS)* (Mediation Support Project);
- *Centre for Humanitarian Dialogue (The HD Centre)*;
- *Centre for Peace and Conflict Studies (CPCS, #03774)*;
- Centro de Investigacion y Educacion Popular – Programa por la Paz (CINEP);
- Clingendael Academy;
- *Conciliation Resources (CR)*;
- *Crisis Management Initiative (CMI)*;
- CSSP – Berlin Center for Integrative Mediation;
- *Folke Bernadotte Academy (FBA)*;
- *Institute for Integrated Transitions (IFIT)*;
- *Norwegian Centre for Conflict Resolution (NOREF)*;
- Ottawa Dialogue;
- *Sasakawa Peace Foundation (SPF)*;
- *Search for Common Ground (SFCG)*;
- *Servicios y Asesoria para la Paz (SERAPAZ)*;
- *Southeast Asian Conflict Studies Network (SEACSN, #19762)*;
- *Swisspeace* (Mediation Support Project);
- *The Carter Center*;
- *United Nations (UN, #20515)* (Mediation Support Unit UN MSU);
- *United States Institute of Peace (USIP)*;
- *West Africa Network for Peacebuilding (WANEP, #20878)*;
- Zimbabwe Institute (ZI).

IGO Relations UN Department of Peacekeeping Operations (DPKO) Mediation Support Unit. [2022.10.19/XJ5662/y/F]

- ♦ Mediatore Europeo (#08084)
- ♦ Mediators Beyond Borders / see Mediators Beyond Borders International
- ♦ Mediators Beyond Borders International (internationally oriented national body)
- ♦ MedicAid Africa (internationally oriented national body)
- ♦ Medical Action for Global Security / see Medact
- ♦ Medical Aid Abroad (internationally oriented national body)
- ♦ Medical Aid for Palestinians (internationally oriented national body)
- ♦ Medical Aid for the Third World (internationally oriented national body)
- ♦ Medical Ambassadors International (internationally oriented national body)
- ♦ Medical Aspects of Mental Handicap / see European Association of Intellectual Disability Medicine (#06089)
- ♦ Medical Assistance Programs / see MAP International (#16569)
- ♦ Medical Association for Chinese Medicine in Europe (inactive)
- ♦ Medical Association for the Prevention of War, Australia (internationally oriented national body)

♦ Medical Association of South East Asian Nations (MASEAN) 16623

SG c/o Singapore Medical Assn, Alumni Medical Centre, Level 2, College Road, Singapore 169850, Singapore. T. +6562231264. Fax +6562247827. E-mail: masean@sma.org.sg.
URL: http://www.masean.net/

History 1980, Penang (Malaysia). **Structure** Council. **Languages** English. **Staff** No full-time staff. **Finance** Host country pays for events. **Activities** Events/meetings. **Events** *Conference* Jakarta (Indonesia) 2020, *Meeting* Cebu City (Philippines) 2019, *Conference* Hanoi (Vietnam) 2018, *Meeting* Kuala Lumpur (Malaysia) 2017, *Conference* Pattaya (Thailand) 2016.
Members Full in 10 countries:
Brunei Darussalam, Cambodia, Indonesia, Laos, Malaysia, Myanmar, Philippines, Singapore, Thailand, Vietnam.
Consultative Status Consultative status granted from: *ASEAN (#01141)*. **NGO Relations** Collaborates with: *World Medical Association (WMA, #21646)*. [2017.06.01/XE0391/E]

- ♦ Medical Benevolence Foundation (internationally oriented national body)
- ♦ Medical Campaign Against Nuclear Weapons / see Medact
- ♦ Medical Care Development International (internationally oriented national body)
- ♦ Medical Collaboration Committee (internationally oriented national body)
- ♦ Medical Education for the Eyes of the World / see ORBIS International (#17786)
- ♦ Medical Emergency and Relief Cooperative International (internationally oriented national body)
- ♦ Medical Environmental Development with Air Assistance / see MEDAIR

♦ Medical Image Computing and Computer Assisted Intervention Society (MICCAI Society) 16624

Secretariat c/o Robarts Inst, 1151 Richmond St North, London ON N6A 5B7, Canada.
URL: http://www.miccai.org/

History 29 Jul 2004, following the activities of the earlier Medical Image Computing and Computer Assisted Intervention Conference series. Registered in the State of Minnesota (USA). **Aims** Promote, preserve and facilitate research, education and practice in the field of medical image computing and computer assisted medical interventions including biomedical imaging and robotics. **Structure** Board of Directors, including President, Secretary, Treasurer and Executive Board. **Activities** Awards/prizes/competitions; events/meetings. **Events** *International Conference* Shenzhen (China) 2019, *International Conference* Granada (Spain) 2018, *International Conference* Québec, QC (Canada) 2017, *International Conference* Istanbul (Turkey) 2016, *International Conference* Munich (Germany) 2015. **Publications** *MICCAI Newsletter*. [2018/XJ6495/C]

- ♦ Medical Imaging with Deep Learning Foundation / see MIDL Foundation
- ♦ Medical Latin American Association of Rehabilitation (#02280)
- ♦ Medical Mission Action / see MEMISA
- ♦ Medical Missionaries of Mary (religious order)
- ♦ Medical Mission Sisters (religious order)

♦ Medical Mycological Society of the Americas (MMSA) 16625

Société médicale mycologique des Amériques

Contact 7703 Floyd Curl Dr, San Antonio TX 78229, USA. T. +12105676074. Fax +12105674076.
URL: http://www.mycologicalsociety.org/

History 1966. **Aims** Encourage fellowship among members; unite all medical mycologists under a central organization that recognizes their needs and represents their interests; provide recognition of medical mycology as a flourishing and distinct division of medical *microbiology*. **Structure** General Meeting (annual). Council, composed of Officers and five Councillors. Committees. **Languages** English. **Finance** Members dues: US$ 30. **Events** *Annual General Meeting* New Orleans, LA (USA) 2015, *Annual General Meeting* San Francisco, CA (USA) 2012, *Annual General Meeting* New Orleans, LA (USA) 2011, *Annual General Meeting* San Diego, CA (USA) 2010, *Annual General Meeting* Philadelphia, PA (USA) 2009. **Publications** *MMSA Newsletter* (2 a year).
Members Individuals in 21 countries:
Argentina, Belgium, Brazil, Canada, Colombia, Ecuador, Germany, Guatemala, Honduras, India, Iran Islamic Rep, Israel, Italy, Japan, Mexico, Philippines, Puerto Rico, Switzerland, UK, USA, Venezuela.
NGO Relations Affiliated to: *International Society for Human and Animal Mycology (ISHAM, #15181)*. [2012.08.01/XD3295/D]

♦ Medical Nutrition International Industry (MNI) 16626

Exec Dir Blvd du Souverain 280, 1160 Brussels, Belgium. T. +3222302542. E-mail: secretariat@medicalnutritionindustry.com.
URL: https://medicalnutritionindustry.com/

History 2005. **Aims** Achieve better care through better nutrition, across all ages and healthcare settings. **NGO Relations** Member of (1): *European Nutrition for Health Alliance, The (ENHA, #08069)*. Cooperates with (1): *European Society for Clinical Nutrition and Metabolism (ESPEN, #08550)*. [2020/AA0933/t/F]

♦ Medical Research Support (MedicReS) 16627

World Headquarters Seyringer Strasse 1/2/288, 1210 Vienna, Austria.
USA One WTC 85th Floor, Suite 8500, New York NY 10007, USA.
URL: http://www.medicres.org/

History Founded 2007, Vienna (Austria). **Aims** Educate researchers and provoke discussion about good scientific method, statistics, ethics, publication, and education. **Structure** Scientific Board. **Staff** 10.00 FTE, paid. **Activities** Events/meetings; training/education. **Events** *International Conference on Good Biostatistical and Advanced Clinical Practice in Oncology Hematology* Vienna (Austria) 2019, *International Conference on how to Read and Write a Systematic Review Article and Meta-Analysis in Rheupatology* Vienna (Austria) 2019, *World Conference on Good Reporting, Good Reviewing and Good Publishing* Istanbul (Turkey) 2017, *Meeting* Vienna (Austria) 2017. **Members** Full (about 10,000) in 80 countries. Membership countries not specified. [2020.02.05/XM4923/**F**]

♦ Medical Retina Academy (MRA) 16628

Address not obtained.
URL: http://medicalretinaacademy.dk/

Aims Offer continued medical education in the subspecialty of medical retina diseases and diagnostics. **Structure** Steering Committee. **Activities** Events/meetings; training/education. [2021/XM7554/**D**]

- ♦ Medical Teams International (internationally oriented national body)
- ♦ Medical Tropical Fund (internationally oriented national body)

♦ Medical Users Software Exchange (MUSE) 16629

Exec Dir Ste 173, 816 W Francis Ave, Spokane WA 99205, USA. T. +12504914703. Fax +12504914773. E-mail: muse@museweb.org.
URL: http://www.museweb.org/

History 1983. **Aims** Support healthcare organizations using MEDITECH developed software and technologies. **Structure** Board of Directors, comprising Chairperson, Treasurer, Secretary and 4 Regional Directors. **Finance** Members' dues. **Activities** Events/meetings. **Events** *International conference* Vancouver, BC (Canada) 2009, *International conference* Orlando, FL (USA) 2006.
Members in 3 countries:
Canada, UK, USA. [2010/XM1726/**F**]

♦ Medical Women's International Association (MWIA) 16630

Association internationale des femmes médecins (AIFM)
SG 27 Skidmore Rd, Pleasant Valley NY 12569, USA. T. +18454717906. E-mail: secretariat@mwia.net.
URL: http://www.mwia.net/

History 1919, New York, NY (USA). Constituent Assembly 1922, Geneva (Switzerland). Statutes revised: 1956; 1966; 1987; 1998; 2004; 2019. **Aims** Offer medical women the opportunity to meet and confer on questions concerning health and well-being; develop cooperation, friendship and understanding without regard to race, religion or political views; overcome gender-related differences in health and healthcare, and inequalities in the medical profession; promote health for all with particular interest in women, health and development. **Structure** General Assembly (every 3 years); Executive Committee; Standing Finance Committee; other committees. **Languages** English. **Staff** 1.00 FTE, paid. **Finance** Sources: donations; members' dues. **Activities** Events/meetings; training/education. **Events** *International Congress* 2025, *International Congress* Taipei (Taiwan) 2022, *Central Asia Regional Congress* Mumbai (India) 2021, *Northern European Regional Congress* Pleasant Valley, NY (USA) 2021, *Western Pacific Regional Meeting* Seoul (Korea Rep) 2021. **Publications** *Update* (4 a year) – newsletter. Training manuals and modules; scientific proceedings; congress reports.
Members Affiliated: national associations of women doctors in 66 countries and territories:
Argentina, Australia, Austria, Bangladesh, Belgium, Bolivia, Bosnia-Herzegovina, Brazil, Bulgaria, Cameroon, Canada, China, Colombia, Congo Brazzaville, Czechia, Denmark, Ecuador, Egypt, Estonia, Ethiopia, Finland, France, Georgia, Germany, Ghana, Greece, Guatemala, Hong Kong, Hungary, Iceland, India, Iran Islamic Rep, Ireland, Israel, Italy, Japan, Kenya, Korea Rep, Kosovo, Mali, Mongolia, Netherlands, Nigeria, Norway, Pakistan, Panama, Peru, Philippines, Poland, Puerto Rico, Romania, Russia, Sierra Leone, Slovakia, Slovenia, South Africa, Sweden, Switzerland, Taiwan, Tanzania UR, Thailand, Uganda, UK, USA, Zambia, Zimbabwe.
Individuals: women doctors in countries where there is no national association in 48 countries and territories:
Albania, Algeria, Argentina, Armenia, Azerbaijan, Bosnia-Herzegovina, Burundi, Chad, Congo DR, Costa Rica, Croatia, Czechia, Estonia, Ethiopia, Guinea, Haiti, Indonesia, Iran Islamic Rep, Iraq, Ireland, Jordan, Kosovo, Latvia, Lithuania, Malaysia, Mexico, Montenegro, Morocco, New Zealand, Nicaragua, Pakistan, Qatar, Rwanda, Saudi Arabia, Serbia, South Africa, Spain, Sri Lanka, St Lucia, Sudan, Tonga, Tunisia, Türkiye, Ukraine, United Arab Emirates, Uzbekistan, Venezuela, Zimbabwe.
Consultative Status Consultative status granted from: *ECOSOC (#05331)* (Special); *WHO (#20950)* (Official Relations). **IGO Relations** Accredited by (1): *United Nations Office at Vienna (UNOV, #20604)*. Associated with Department of Global Communications of the United Nations. **NGO Relations** Member of (7): *Committee of NGOs on Human Rights, Geneva (#04275)*; *Conference of Non-Governmental Organizations in Consultative Relationship with the United Nations (CONGO, #04635)*; *European Women's Lobby (EWL, #09102)*; *Framework Convention Alliance (FCA, #09981)*; *Gavi – The Vaccine Alliance (Gavi, #10077)* (CSO Constituency); Kota Alliance; *PMNCH (#18410)*. Founder member of: *Council for International Organizations of Medical Sciences (CIOMS, #04905)*. [2022/XB2947/**B**]

- ♦ Medica Mondiale (internationally oriented national body)
- ♦ Medicina Alternativa / see Medicina Alternativa International (#16631)

♦ Medicina Alternativa International 16631

Chairman 28 Int'l Buddhist Centre Road, Colombo, 6, Sri Lanka. T. +94112360242. Fax +94112364148.
URL: http://www.medicina-alternativa.org/

History 1962, USSR. Founded 1962, Alma-Ata (USSR), by Anton Jayasuryia (1930-2005), at a conference sponsored by *UNICEF (#20332)* and *WHO (#20950)*. Also referred to as *Medicina Alternativa*. Part of Open International University for Complementary Medicines. Registered in accordance with the laws of Kazakhstan, Registration No: 42/LE/IN/02. **Aims** Advance the scientific study and professional practice of alternative medicines, better known as complementary medicines, and encourage its development by promoting research, laying down high standards of professional ethics, competence, conduct, education, qualifications and achievement among practitioners; promote and disseminate knowledge and philosophy of alternative medicines; encourage public interest in alternative medicines and ancillary areas of knowledge and practice. **Structure** Senate, comprising 12 members of the Board of Directors and teaching staff of qualified Doctors of Medicine under the Dean of Clinical Studies. Faculty for each discipline. **Languages** English, Sinhala. **Staff** 40 full-time, paid; 25 part-time, paid; 150 support staff. **Finance** Budget (annual): 4.7 million, to support Sir Anton Jayasuriya Memorial Hospital and Clinic. **Activities** Events/meetings; training/education. **Events** *World Congress of Integrative Medicines* Bangkok (Thailand) 2016, *World Congress of Integrated Medicines* Colombo (Sri Lanka) 2014, *World Congress of Integrated Medicines* Colombo (Sri Lanka) 2013, *World Congress* Colombo (Sri Lanka) 2011, *World congress of integrated medicines* Colombo (Sri Lanka) 2010. **Publications** Research publications; medical books. **Members** Limited to individuals who attended the first meeting where delegates from 46 countries were represented. Membership countries not specified. [2015/XF1514/v/**F**]

♦ Medicinal Cannabis Europe 16632

SG Rue Belliard 40, 1040 Brussels, Belgium. T. +3227863041. E-mail: secretariat@medicinalcannabiseurope.org.
URL: https://www.medicinalcannabiseurope.org/

History 2018. Registration: Banque-Carrefour des Entreprises, No/ID: 0744.673.552, Start date: 8 Jan 2020, Belgium; EU Transparency Register, No/ID: 377241942545-02, Start date: 5 May 2021. **Aims** Ensure patients' fair access to medicinal cannabis via the definition and establishment of an harmonized legislative framework on medicinal cannabis at European level. **Structure** Executive Board.
Members Organizations, including 2 organizations listed in this Yearbook:
European Association for Predictive, Preventive and Personalised Medicine (EPMA, #06163); *European Medical Association (EMA, #07761)*. [2021/AA1731/y/**D**]

- ♦ Medicina para el Tercer Mundo (internationally oriented national body)
- ♦ Medicine for Missions / see World Concern International (#21290)
- ♦ Medicines for all in Africa (unconfirmed)

♦ Medicines for Europe 16633

Communications Dir Rue d'Arlon 50, 1000 Brussels, Belgium. T. +3227368411. Fax +3227367438. E-mail: info@medicinesforeurope.com.
URL: http://www.medicinesforeurope.com/

History 1993. Former names and other names: *European Generics Association* – former (1993 to 7 Jul 1994); *European Generic Medicines Association (EGA)* – former (7 Jul 1994 to 10 Mar 2016); *Association européenne du médicament générique* – former (7 Jul 1994 to 10 Mar 2016); *Asociación Europea de Medicamentos Genéricos* – former (7 Jul 1994 to 10 Mar 2016); *Associação Européia de Medicamentos Genéricos* – former (7 Jul 1994 to 10 Mar 2016); *Europese Generieke Geneesmiddelen Associatie* – former (7 Jul 1994 to 10 Mar 2016). Registration: Banque-Carrefour des Entreprises, No/ID: 0449.332.209, Start date: 26 Oct 1992, Belgium; EU Transparency Register, No/ID: 48325781850-28, Start date: 16 Jun 2009. **Aims** Represent *pharmaceutical* companies supplying the largest share of medicines across Europe; act as the voice of the generic, biosimilar and value added industries. **Structure** Board; Executive. Committees. **Languages** English. **Staff** 6.00 FTE, paid. **Finance** Members' dues. **Events** *Biosimilar Medicines Conference* Brussels (Belgium) 2022, *Value Added Medicines Conference* Brussels (Belgium) 2022, *Annual Conference* Sitges (Spain) 2022, *Regulatory and Scientific Affairs Conference* Amsterdam (Netherlands) 2020, *Value Added Medicines Conference* Brussels (Belgium) 2019. **Publications** *Information – European Generic Medicines Association* (12 a year) – newsletter.
Members Companies; Affiliate; Parnter; national asscoations – full and associate. Full national associations in 11 countries:
Belgium, Denmark, France, Germany, Italy, Netherlands, Poland, Portugal, Spain, Türkiye, UK.
Associate national associations in 11 countries:
Austria, Bulgaria, Croatia, Czechia, Finland, Hungary, Ireland, Romania, Slovakia, Sweden, Switzerland.
Consultative Status Consultative status granted from: *World Intellectual Property Organization (WIPO, #21593)* (Permanent Observer Status); *WHO (#20950)* (Official Relations). **NGO Relations** Founding member of: *European Medicines Verification Organisation (EMVO, #07768)*; *International Generic and Biosimilar Medicines Association (IGBA, #13708)*. Member of: *Alliance for Safe Online Pharmacy – EU (ASOP EU, #00720)*; *European Alliance for Responsible R and D and Affordable Medicines (#05879)*; *Federation of European and International Associations Established in Belgium (FAIB, #09508)*; *Health Action International (HAI, #10868)*; *Industry4Europe (#11181)*. Stakeholder Forum of *European Network for Health Technology Assessment (EUnetHTA, #07921)*. [2022/XD3860/**D**]

♦ Medicines for Malaria Venture (MMV) 16634

Senior Director Communications PO Box 1826, Rte de Pré-Bois 20, 1215 Geneva 15, Switzerland. T. +41225550327. Fax +41227994061.
URL: http://www.mmv.org/

History 3 Nov 1999, Switzerland. Registered in accordance with Swiss Civil Code. **Aims** Reduce the burden of malaria in disease-endemic countries by discovering, developing and facilitating delivery of new, effective and affordable antimalarial *drugs*. **Structure** Board of Directors; Expert Scientific Advisory Committee; Access and Product Management Advisory Committee. **Languages** English, French. **Staff** 70.00 FTE, paid. **Finance** Funding from various organizations, including: *Bill and Melinda Gates Foundation (BMGF)*; *Department for International Development (DFID, inactive)*; *Irish Aid*; *Norwegian Agency for Development Cooperation (Norad)*; *Swiss Agency for Development and Cooperation (SDC)*; *United States Agency for International Development (USAID)*; *Wellcome Trust*; *WHO (#20950)*. Also funding from government ministries, national organizations and individual donors. **Publications** *MMV At a Glance*. Annual Report; Management Report. **Consultative Status** Consultative status granted from: *WHO (#20950)* (Official). **NGO Relations** Member of: *Global Health Technologies Coalition (GHTC)*; *PMNCH (#18410)*. Partner of: *Fight the Fakes (#09755)*. [2019/XJ4829/**F**]

- ♦ The Medicines Patent Pool / see Medicines Patent Pool (#16635)

♦ Medicines Patent Pool (MPP) 16635

Medicines Patent Pool (MPP)
Exec Dir Rue Varembé 7, 5th floor, 1202 Geneva, Switzerland. T. +41225335050. E-mail: office@medicinespatentpool.org.
URL: http://www.medicinespatentpool.org/

History 16 Jul 2010, Geneva (Switzerland). Former names and other names: *The Medicines Patent Pool (MPP)* – full title; *Medicines Patent Pool Foundation (MPPF)* – alias; *Fondation Medicines Patent Pool (MPPF)* – alias. Registration: Swiss Civil Code, Switzerland. **Aims** Increase access to, and facilitate development of, life-saving medicines for low- and middle-income countries through an innovative approach to voluntary licensing and patent pooling. **Structure** Governance Board; Expert Advisory Group (EAG); Scientific Advisory Panel (SAP); Executive Team. **Languages** English, French. **Staff** 23.00 FTE, paid. as of May 2020. **Activities** Healthcare; knowledge management/information dissemination; management of treaties and agreements; monitoring/evaluation. **Consultative Status** Associate Status (3): *Swiss Agency for Development and Cooperation (SDC)*; *Unitaid (#20493)*; *Wellcome Trust*. Consultative status granted from: *World Intellectual Property Organization (WIPO, #21593)* (Observer Status); *WHO (#20950)* (Official). **IGO Relations** Accredited by (1): *United Nations (UN, #20515)*. Cooperates with (1): *Unitaid (#20493)*. [2020.05.14/XJ8414/f/**F**]

- ♦ Medicines Patent Pool (#16635)
- ♦ Medicines Patent Pool Foundation / see Medicines Patent Pool (#16635)
- ♦ Medico International (internationally oriented national body)
- ♦ Medico-Missionarie di Maria (religious order)
- ♦ Médicos del Mundo – International (#16613)
- ♦ Medico-social Association of French-Speaking Protestants (no recent information)
- ♦ **MedicReS** Medical Research Support (#16627)
- ♦ Medicrime Covention – Council of Europe Convention on the Counterfeiting of Medical Products and Similar Crimes involving Threats to Public Health (2011 treaty)
- ♦ Medics Without Vacation (internationally oriented national body)
- ♦ Medicus Mundi Internationalis / see Medicus Mundi International – Network Health for All (#16636)
- ♦ Medicus Mundi International Network / see Medicus Mundi International – Network Health for All (#16636)

♦ Medicus Mundi International – Network Health for All (MMI) 16636

Secretariat Murbacherstrasse 34, 4013 Basel BS, Switzerland. T. +41613831811. E-mail: office@medicusmundi.org.
Geneva Office Route de Ferney 150, CP 2100, 1211 Geneva 2, Switzerland. T. +41222900806.
URL: http://www.medicusmundi.org/

History Founded 7 Nov 1964, Bensberg (Germany FR). Previously also referred to as *International Organization for Cooperation in Health Care (IOCHC)* – *Organisation internationale de coopération pour la santé (OICS)*, *Medicus Mundi Internationalis* and *Medicus Mundi International Network (MMI Network)*. Registered in accordance with the law of Germany FR, 16 Aug 1965. **Aims** Promote access to health and *health care* by supporting members' efforts; enhance the quality and effectiveness of international health cooperation through sharing know-how and joining forces. **Structure** General Assembly (annual, usually at World Health Assembly, Geneva-Switzerland); Executive Board; Secretariat, based in Basel (Switzerland). **Languages** English. **Staff** 1.00 FTE, paid. **Finance** Sources: members' dues. **Activities** Advocacy/lobbying/activism; awareness raising; knowledge management/information dissemination; networking/liaising; standards/guidelines. **Events** *Annual General Assembly* Basel (Switzerland) 2020, *Annual General Assembly* Geneva (Switzerland) 2019, *Annual General Assembly* Geneva (Switzerland) 2018, *Annual General Assembly* Geneva (Switzerland) 2017, *Annual General Assembly* Geneva (Switzerland) 2015. **Publications** *MMI Newsletter* (6-12 a year). Annual Report. Reports of technical meetings and conferences.
Members Organizations in 11 countries:
Belgium, Benin, Germany, Italy, Kenya, Netherlands, Poland, Spain, Switzerland, UK, Zimbabwe.
Included in the above, 2 organizations listed in this Yearbook:
Catholic Organization for Relief and Development (Cordaid); *Deutsches Medikamenten-Hilfswerk – action medeor*.
Consultative Status Consultative status granted from: *ECOSOC (#05331)* (Ros C); *WHO (#20950)* (Official Relations). **NGO Relations** Member of: *Geneva Global Health Hub (G2H2, #10122)*; *People's Health Movement (PHM, #18305)*. [2019.02.18/XD2310/y/**C**]

- ♦ Medienplanung für Entwicklungsländer, Mittel- und Osteuropa (#03605)
- ♦ Medieval Central Europe Research Network (unconfirmed)
- ♦ Medieval and Renaissance International Music Conference (meeting series)
- ♦ MedILS – Mediterranean Institute for Life Sciences (internationally oriented national body)
- ♦ MEDI – Marine Environmental Data Information Referral System (no recent information)
- ♦ MedINA – Mediterranean Institute for Nature and Anthropos (internationally oriented national body)
- ♦ Medio Ambiente y Desarrollo del Tercer Mundo (#05510)
- ♦ Medische Missie Aktie / see MEMISA
- ♦ Medische Missie Samenwerking / see MEMISA
- ♦ MEDITERCONGRESS – International Association of the Organizations and Congress Cities of the States Interested in the Mediterranean (inactive)
- ♦ **Mediter** Euro-Mediterranean Network for Co-operation (#05726)
- ♦ Mediterranea Foundation (internationally oriented national body)
- ♦ Mediterranean Academy / see Academy of the Mediterranean (#00041)
- ♦ Mediterranean Academy of Diplomatic Studies (internationally oriented national body)
- ♦ Mediterranean Academy of Emergency Medicine (unconfirmed)

♦ Mediterranean Academy of Forensic Sciences (MAFS) 16637

SG SIMEF, Via Nicolo' da Reggio 4, 89128 Reggio Calabria RC, Italy. T. +39965891184 – +39965891185. Fax +39965891125. E-mail: info@mafs.biz.
URL: http://www.mafs.biz/

History 14 Sep 2002, Rome (Italy). **Aims** Unite those working in the field of forensic sciences. **Structure** General Assembly (every 2 years). Board. Executive Committee, including President, Secretary and Treasurer. **Languages** English, French. **Finance** Members' dues. **Activities** Meeting activities. **Events** *Middle East Congress* Istanbul (Turkey) 2016, *IALM Intersocietal Symposium* Venice (Italy) 2016, *Biennial Congress* Reggio Calabria (Italy) 2013, *Meeting* Reggio Calabria (Italy) 2012, *Biennial Congress* Funchal (Portugal) 2011. **Publications** *MAFS Journal*.
Members in 12 countries:
Algeria, Croatia, Egypt, France, Greece, Italy, Malta, Morocco, Portugal, Spain, Tunisia, Türkiye. [2014/XM2074/**E**]

♦ Mediterranean Action Plan (MAP) 16638

Coordinator Coordinating Unit, UNEP/MEDU, Vassileos Konstantinou 48, 116 35 Athens, Greece. T. +302107273100. E-mail: unepmap@un.org.
URL: https://www.unenvironment.org/unepmap/

History Feb 1975, Barcelona (Spain). Established on adoption by Mediterranean countries and the European Community of the *Mediterranean Action Plan – Plan d'action pour la Méditerranée (PAM)*, or (full title) *Action Plan for the Protection of the Mediterranean*. Subsequently referred to as *Action Plan for the Protection of the Marine Environment and the Sustainable Development of the Coastal Areas of the Mediterranean (MAP Phase II)*. *Convention for the Protection of the Marine Environment and the Coastal Region of the Mediterranean (Barcelona Convention, 1976)*, signed 16 Feb 1976, Barcelona, entered into force in 1978, provided the legal framework. *MAP Phase II* was adopted on signature of the amendment to the Barcelona Convention, *Amendments to the Convention for the Protection of the Mediterranean Sea Against Pollution (1995)*, 10 Jun 1995, Barcelona, at Conference of Plenipotentiaries. The same conference adopted: *Amendments to the Protocol for the Prevention of Pollution of the Mediterranean Sea by Dumping from Ships and Aircraft (1995)*, amending *Protocol for the Prevention of Pollution of the Mediterranean Sea by Dumping from Ships and Aircraft (Dumping Protocol, 1976)*; *'Barcelona Resolution'*; *'Priority Field of Action'* for the period until the year 2005. Related protocols: *Protocol Concerning Cooperation in Combating Pollution of the Mediterranean Sea by Oil and other Harmful Substances in Cases of Emergency (1976)*, *Protocol Concerning Cooperation in Preventing Pollution from Ships and, in Cases of Emergency, Combating Pollution of the Mediterranean Sea (2002)*, signed Jan 2002; *Amendments to the Protocol for the Protection of the Mediterranean Sea Against Pollution from Land-based Sources and Activities (1996)*, replacing *Protocol for the Protection of the Mediterranean Sea against Pollution from Land-Based Sources and Activities (LBS Protocol, 1980)*; *Protocol Concerning Specially Protected Areas and Biological Diversity in the Mediterranean (Barcelona protocol, 1995)*, updating *Protocol Concerning Mediterranean Specially Protected Areas (1982)*; *Protocol for the Protection of the Mediterranean Sea Against Pollution Resulting from Exploration and Exploitation of the Continental Shelf and the Seabed and its Subsoil (1994)*; *Protocol on the Prevention of Pollution of the Mediterranean Sea by Transboundary Movements of Hazardous Wastes and Their Disposal (1996)* (Hazardous Wastes Protocol); *Protocol on integrated coastal zone management in the Mediterranean (ICZM Protocol)*. Also referred to as *United Nations Environment Programme Mediterranean Action Plan for the Barcelona Convention*.
Headquarters in Athens (Greece) are also referred to as *MEDU* / Mediterranean Unit, coming within the framework of *UNEP (#20299)*. Coordination was originally the responsibility of Regional Seas Programme Activity Centre – which became *UNEP Water Branch (inactive)* – and a coordination unit was set up 1980, Geneva (Switzerland). In 1982, responsibility for the Plan was transferred to *'Coordinating Unit (MAP/RCU)'*, Athens, an organizational unit of *Regional Seas Programme (#18814)* set up at the invitation of the Greek government.
Aims Coordinate activities aimed at the protection of the marine environment through a regional approach. **Structure** Governing and Subsidiary Bodies: Meeting of the Contracting Parties, with its own Bureau – *'Secretariat of the Barcelona Convention'*; National Focal Points (NFP); Mediterranean Commission for Sustainable Development (MCSD), with its own Steering Committee; Barcelona Convention Compliance Committee. Institutional set-up: MAP Coordinating Unit with its Components *MED POL – Programme for the Assessment and Control of Marine Pollution in the Mediterranean (MED POL, #16691)*; *Regional Marine Pollution Emergency Response Centre for the Mediterranean Sea (REMPEC, #18795)*; *Plan Bleu pour l'environnement et le développement en Méditerranée (Plan Bleu, #18379)* and its *Mediterranean Environment and Development Observatory (MEDO)*; *Priority Actions Programme / Regional Activity Centre (PAP/RAC, #18501)*; *Regional Activity Centre for Specially Protected Areas (RAC/SPA, #18746)*; *Regional Activity Centre for Sustainable Consumption and Production (SCP/RAC, #18747)*; *Regional Activity Centre for Information and Communication of the Barcelona Convention (INFO/RAC, #18745)*. **Languages** Arabic, English, French. **Staff** 30.00 FTE, paid. **Finance** Funded through *Mediterranean Trust Fund (MTF, #16686)*. **Activities** Advocacy/ lobbying/activism; monitoring/evaluation; politics/policy/regulatory. **Events** *Meeting of the Contracting Parties* Antalya (Turkey) 2021, *Meeting of the Contracting Parties to the Convention for the Protection of the Marine Environment and the Coastal Region of the Mediterranean and its Protocols* Naples (Italy) 2019, *SESAME : Séminaire International sur l'Eau et la Sécurité Alimentaire en Méditerranée* Montpellier (France) 2013, *Meeting on Coastal Groundwater Dependent Ecosystems in the Mediterranean* Madrid (Spain) 2011, *Meeting of the Contracting Parties* Marrakech (Morocco) 2009. **Publications** *MedWaves: MAP Magazine* (12 a year) in Arabic, English, French – e-newsletter. *MAP Technical Reports Series (MTS)*. Special publications.
Members Participating States (21):
Albania, Algeria, Bosnia-Herzegovina, Croatia, Cyprus, Egypt, France, Greece, Israel, Italy, Lebanon, Libya, Malta, Monaco, Montenegro, Morocco, Slovenia, Spain, Syrian AR, Tunisia, Türkiye.
Regional integration EU entity (1):
European Union (EU, #08967).
IGO Relations Memorandum of Understanding with: *United Nations Human Settlements Programme (UN-Habitat, #20572)*. Close relations with: *United Nations Commission on Sustainable Development (CSD, inactive)*. '100 Monuments' project cooperates in: *UNESCO Mediterranean Programme (inactive)* through Networks of Cities.
Cooperating organizations:
- *CIHEAM – International Centre for Advanced Mediterranean Agronomic Studies (CIHEAM, #03927)*;
- *Council of Europe (CE, #04881)*;
- *European Commission (EC, #06633)*;
- *FAO (#09260)*;
- *Intergovernmental Oceanographic Commission (IOC, #11496)*;
- *International Atomic Energy Agency (IAEA, #12294)*;
- *International Fund for Agricultural Development (IFAD, #13692)*;
- *International Maritime Organization (IMO, #14102)*;
- *The Mediterranean Science Commission (CIESM, #16674)*;
- *OECD (#17693)*;
- *OSPAR Commission for the Protection of the Marine Environment of the North-East Atlantic (OSPAR Commission, #17905)*;
- *Réserve internationale maritime en méditerranée occidentale (RIMMO, no recent information)*;
- *UNDP (#20292)*;
- *UNESCO (#20322)*;
- *UNIDO (#20336)*;
- *United Nations Economic Commission for Europe (UNECE, #20555)*;
- *WHO (#20950)*;
- *World Meteorological Organization (WMO, #21649)*;
- *World Tourism Organization (UNWTO, #21861)*.

Partner entitled to observe meetings: *Natura 2000 Network (see: #06633)*.
NGO Relations Member of: *International Network for Environmental Compliance and Enforcement (INECE, #14261)*. Partners entitled to observe meetings:
- *Arab Office for Youth and Environment (AOYE)*;
- *European Environmental Bureau (EEB, #06996)*;
- *Friends of the Earth International (FoEI, #10002)*;
- *Greenpeace International (#10727)*;
- *International Centre for Coastal and Ocean Policy Studies (ICCOPS)*;
- *International Centre for Coastal Resources Research (#12480)*;
- *International Juridical Organization for Environment and Development (IJO, no recent information)*;
- *International Ocean Institute (IOI, #14394)*;
- *International Petroleum Industry Environmental Conservation Association (IPIECA, #14562)*;
- *MEDCITIES Network (#16610)*;
- *Mediterranean Information Office for Environment, Culture and Sustainable Development (MIO-ECSDE, #16657)*.

Thematic organizations which may be associated with MAP general meetings or specialized activities:
- *Advisory Committee on Protection of the Sea (ACOPS, #00139)*;
- *BirdLife International (#03266)*;
- *Euro Chlor (#05659)*;
- *Fertilizers Europe (#09738)*;
- *Institut méditerranéen de l'eau (IME, #11323)*;
- *International Association of Oil and Gas Producers (IOGP, #12053)*;
- *International Council on Monuments and Sites (ICOMOS, #13049)*;
- *International Marine Centre (IMC)*;
- *MAREVIVO Associazione Ambientalista*;
- *Mediterranean Association to Save the Sea Turtles (MEDASSET, #16647)*;
- *Mediterranean Coastal Foundation (MEDCOAST, #16649)*;
- *Mediterranean Marine Bird Association (MEDMARAVIS, #16661)*;
- *The Mediterranean Wetlands Initiative (MedWet, #16688)*;
- *Network of Marine Protected Area Managers in the Mediterranean (MEDPAN, #17048)*;
- *Ricerca e Cooperazione (RC)*. [2021/XF1881/**F***]

♦ Mediterranean Advisory Council (MEDAC) 16639

Exec Sec c/o MIPAAF, Via XX Settembre 20, 00187 Rome RM, Italy. T. +39646652112. Fax +39660513259. E-mail: segreteria@med-ac.eu – info@med-ac.eu.
URL: http://en.med-ac.eu/

History Originally set up by *European Commission (EC, #06633)* Council Decision 585/2004, establishing the Regional Advisory Council; repealed by CFP Reform 1380/2013; integrated by Commission Delegated Regulation 2015/242 laying down detailed ruled on the functioning of the Advisory Councils. **Aims** Prepare opinions on *fisheries* management and socio-economic aspects in support of the fisheries sector in the Mediterranean; propose technical solutions and suggestions at the request of Member States. **Structure** General Assembly; Executive Committee; Presidency. Working Groups; Focus Groups. **Languages** Croatian, English, French, Greek, Irish Gaelic, Italian, Spanish. **Staff** 2.00 FTE, paid. **Finance** Sources: contributions; members' dues. Supported by: *European Commission (EC, #06633)*. Annual budget: 390,000 EUR. **Activities** Projects/programmes. Active in all member countries. **Events** *General Assembly* Rome (Italy) 2015.
Members Stakeholders in 8 countries:
Croatia, Cyprus, France, Greece, Italy, Malta, Slovenia, Spain.
Included in the above, 8 organizations listed in this Yearbook:
Confédération internationale de la pêche sportive (CIPS, #04562); *European Anglers Alliance (EAA, #05900)*; *European Federation of Sea Anglers (EFSA, #07211)*; *European Transport Workers' Federation (ETF, #08941)*; *European Union Fish Processors Association (#08989)*; *International Forum for Sustainable Underwater Activities (IFSUA, #13654)*; *Oceana*; *World Wide Fund for Nature (WWF, #21922)*. [2020.05.19/XJ9736/y/**E**]

♦ Mediterranean and African Society of Ultrasound (MASU) 16640

Société méditerranéenne et africaine d'ultrasonographie – Sociedad Mediterranea y Africana de Ultrasonografia – Società Mediterranea e Africana di Ultrasonografia

Pres Chair – Radiology Dept, Aga Khan Univ Hospital, Nairobi, 00100, Kenya.
SG Radiology Dept, Principe di Piemonte Hosp, 70019 Senigallia AN, Italy.

History 1986, France. Established as a non-profit scientific association. Registration: Start date: 20 Nov 1987, France. **Aims** Foster development of *medical* and *biological* ultrasound in Africa and countries bordering the Mediterranean basin; promote research activities with experts coming from different countries. **Structure** Board. **Languages** English, French, Italian, Spanish. **Staff** Voluntary. **Finance** Sources: donations; members' dues. **Activities** Events/meetings; healthcare; research and development. Organize an international scientific congress every 2 years, and international post-graduate courses in African and Middle East countries. **Events** *International Congress* Naples (Italy) 2018, *International Congress* Alexandria (Egypt) 2016, *International Congress* Tunis (Tunisia) 2014, *International Congress* Nairobi (Kenya) 2012, *International Congress* Tripoli (Libyan AJ) 2010.
Members Individuals in 19 countries:
Egypt, Ethiopia, France, Germany, Italy, Kenya, Libya, Mauritania, Nigeria, Norway, Oman, Spain, Sudan, Syrian AR, Tanzania UR, Togo, Tunisia, Uganda, Zambia.
NGO Relations Cooperates with (2): *African Society of Radiology (ASR, #00468)*; *World Federation for Ultrasound in Medicine and Biology (WFUMB, #21497)*. [2022.07.22/XF1336/v/**D**]

♦ Mediterranean Agronomic Institute of Bari (Bari MAI) 16641

Institut agronomique méditerranéen de Bari (IAM Bari) – Istituto Agronomico Mediterraneo di Bari

Contact Via Ceglie 9, 70010 Valenzano BA, Italy. T. +39804606209. Fax +39804606206. E-mail: iamdir@iamb.it.
URL: http://www.iamb.it/

History 1962, Bari (Italy). Founded in pursuance of the Agreement, 21 May 1962, setting up *CIHEAM – International Centre for Advanced Mediterranean Agronomic Studies (CIHEAM, #03927)* of which it is part. Other institutes belonging to ICAMAS: *Mediterranean Agronomic Institute of Chania (MAICh, #16642)*; *Mediterranean Agronomic Institute of Montpellier (CIHEAM Montpellier, #16643)*; *Mediterranean Agronomic Institute of Zaragoza (MAIZ, #16644)*. Also known under the acronyms *IAMB – MAIB*. **Aims** Carry out research and provide training in: land and water resource management with special reference to irrigation; integrated pest management of mediterranean fruit crops; organic farming. **Activities** Training/education; events/meetings. **Events** *International symposium on water and land management for sustainable irrigated agriculture* Adana (Turkey) 2006, *MEDPINE : international conference on conservation, regeneration and restoration of Mediterranean pines and their ecosystems* Valenzano (Italy) 2005, *Mediterranean conference on new technologies of protected cultivation* Agadir (Morocco) 2004, *International Conference* Bari (Italy) 2001, *International meeting on soil with Mediterranean type of climate* Valenzano (Italy) 2001. **Publications** *Agrometeorological Bulletin*; *Il Quaderni dello IAM*; *Mediterranean Journal of Economics, Agriculture and Environment (MEDIT)*. Information Services: Documentation centre specialized in the areas of irrigation and plant protection. Connected to *Trans-European Research and Education Networking Association (TERENA, inactive)* network. **Information Services** *Centre for the Production of Healthy Plant Material*; *Data Bank on Irrigation Projects in the Mediterranean Region*; *Documentation centre specialized in the areas of irrigation and plant protection*.
Members Full in 13 countries:
Albania, Algeria, Egypt, France, Greece, Italy, Lebanon, Malta, Morocco, Portugal, Spain, Tunisia, Türkiye.
IGO Relations Cooperates with: *Global Soil Partnership (GSP, #10608)*. **NGO Relations** Secretariat of the Mediterranean Group of: *IFOAM – Organics International (IFOAM, #11105)*. [2022/XE3981/j/**E**]

♦ Mediterranean Agronomic Institute of Chania (MAICh) 16642

Institut agronomique méditerranéen de Chania – Mesogiako Agronomiko Instituto Chanion

Dir Alsyllio Agrokipiou, PO Box 85, 731 00 Chania, Greece. T. +3028210035000. Fax +302821035001. E-mail: baouraki@maich.gr – info@maich.gr.
URL: http://www.maich.gr/

History 21 Jan 1983, Crete (Greece). 21 Jan 1983, Crete, as an organ of *CIHEAM – International Centre for Advanced Mediterranean Agronomic Studies (CIHEAM, #03927)*, on signature of an agreement between CIHEAM and the Government of Greece. Commenced operations Sep 1985; regular international programme started Sep 1986. **Aims** Contribute to *post-graduate* education, research and development of future *executives* in the *rural* sector and to *continuing education* of senior personnel in the fields of: business economics and management; geoinformation in environmental management; food quality and chemistry of natural products; horticultural genetics and biotechnology; sustainable agriculture. **Structure** Secretariat; Director. **Languages** English. **Finance** Funded by Greek Ministry of Rural Development and Food. **Activities** Training/education; events/meetings; knowledge management/information dissemination. **Events** *MEDPINE : international conference on conservation, regeneration and restoration of Mediterranean pines and their ecosystems* Chania (Greece) 2002, *Gastronomy meeting* Chania (Greece) 1994. **Publications** Books; theses; papers; conference proceedings. **Members** Not a membership organization. **IGO Relations** Member of: *International Information System for the Agricultural Sciences and Technology (AGRIS, #13848)*. **NGO Relations** Other institutes belonging to CIHEAM: *Mediterranean Agronomic Institute of Bari (Bari MAI, #16641)*; *Mediterranean Agronomic Institute of Montpellier (CIHEAM Montpellier, #16643)*; *Mediterranean Agronomic Institute of Zaragoza (MAIZ, #16644)*. Member of: *International Federation for Sustainable Development and Fight to Poverty in the Mediterranean-Black Sea (FISPMED, #13562)*; *International Society for Horticultural Science (ISHS, #15180)*. Close cooperation with several European institutions (not specified) on research topics funded through EU programmes. [2012.07.11/XE5971/j/**E**]

♦ Mediterranean Agronomic Institute of Montpellier (CIHEAM Montpellier) 16643

Institut agronomique méditerranéen de Montpellier (CIHEAM Montpellier)

Dir CIHEAM Montpellier, 3191 route de Mende, CS 43999, 34093 Montpellier CEDEX 5, France. T. +33467046000. Fax +33467542527. E-mail: contact@iamm.fr.
General Secretariat 11 rue Newton, 75116 Paris, France. T. +33153239100. E-mail: secretariat@ciheam.org.
URL: http://www.iamm.ciheam.org/

History 1962, Montpellier (France). Established within the framework of *CIHEAM – International Centre for Advanced Mediterranean Agronomic Studies (CIHEAM, #03927)*, pursuant to the agreement of 21 May 1962 setting up that body. Other institutes belonging to CIHEAM: *Mediterranean Agronomic Institute of Bari (Bari MAI, #16641)*; *Mediterranean Agronomic Institute of Chania (MAICh, #16642)*; *Mediterranean Agronomic Institute of Zaragoza (MAIZ, #16644)*. Former names and other names: *CIHEAM Montpellier* – current – now national; *CIHEAM-IAMM* – legal name; *Centre International de Hautes Etudes Agronomiques Méditerraéennes – Institut Agronomique Méditerranéen de Montpellier (CIHEAM-IAMM)* – full title; *International Center for Advanced Mediterranean Agronomic Studies – Mediterranean Agronomic Institute of Montpellier (CIHEAM-IAMM)* – full title; *CIHEAM MAIM* – former. **Aims** Offer *post-graduate* and *continuing training* to students, young professionals and senior personnel from Mediterranean and other countries; carry out research in *agro-food* and *rural development*; implement agricultural and rural development projects and programmes; participate in policy dialogue on agriculture and rural development and contribute to better understanding of agricultural and food issues. **Structure** Departments (2). **Languages** English, French. **Staff** 45.00 FTE, paid. **Finance** Sources: revenue from activities/projects. Other sources: Financed by French government contribution to CIHEAM. **Activities** Events/meetings; politics/policy/regulatory; projects/programmes; research and development; training/education. Active in all member countries. **Events** *Social embeddedness of rights and public policy* Montpellier (France) 2006, *Journées d'études* Oualidia (Morocco) 1998, *Seminar on Mediterranean forages and by-products* Montpellier (France) 1990. **Publications** *Cahiers Options méditerranéennes* – series; *Options méditerranéennes* – series; *Série A: Séminaires méditerranéens – Series A: Mediterranean Workshops*; *Série B: Etudes et recherches – Series B: Research and Analysis*. Analyses; articles; congress proceedings; handbooks; information documents; study reports; theses. Audiovisual documents.
Members Full in 13 countries:
Albania, Algeria, Egypt, France, Greece, Italy, Lebanon, Malta, Morocco, Portugal, Spain, Tunisia, Türkiye.
NGO Relations Member of (1): *Agropolis International*. Partner of (1): *Institut de Prospective économique du Monde Méditerranéen (IPEMED, #11352)*. Cooperates with (2): *Centre d'actions et de réalisations internationales (CARI)*; *Institut de recherches et d'applications des méthodes de développement (IRAM)*. Cooperates with cooperatives and producers' associations in Southern Mediterranean countries. [2023.02.14/XE3980/j/**E**]

♦ Mediterranean Agronomic Institute of Zaragoza (MAIZ) 16644

Institut agronomique méditerranéen de Zaragoza – Instituto Agronómico Mediterraneo de Zaragoza (IAMZ)

Dir Avda Montañana 1005, 50059 Saragossa, Spain. T. +34976716000. Fax +34976716001. E-mail: iamz@iamz.ciheam.org.
Contact address not obtained.
URL: http://www.iamz.ciheam.org/

History 10 Jul 1970, Saragossa (Spain). Founded under an agreement between *CIHEAM – International Centre for Advanced Mediterranean Agronomic Studies (CIHEAM, #03927)* and the Government of Spain, 10 Jul 1969. Former names and other names: *MAI of Zaragoza* – alias; *IAM de Zaragoza* – alias. **Aims** Seek solutions to problems facing Mediterranean *agriculture* by encouraging scientific and technical cooperation among the countries of the region; organize training and research programmes responding to the needs of Mediterranean agriculture. **Languages** English, French, Spanish. **Staff** 22.00 FTE, paid. **Finance** Ordinary funds provided by: Spanish government; *CIHEAM – International Centre for Advanced Mediterranean Agronomic Studies (CIHEAM, #03927)*. Other funds: *European Commission (EC, #06633)*. **Activities** Training/education; research/documentation. **Events** *Seminar on the use of geographic information systems for fisheries and aquaculture planning and management* Saragossa (Spain) 2009, *Rencontres méditerranéennes du semis direct* Saragossa (Spain) 2006, *International symposium on the challenge to sheep and goats milk sectors* Saragossa (Spain) 2004, *Seminar on mollusc production in Mediterranean countries* Saragossa (Spain) 2002, *International symposium on Loquat* Valencia (Spain) 2002. **Publications** Proceedings; reports; special numbers of the CIHEAM journal "Options Méditerranéennes"; joint publications with other institutions.
Members Covers 13 countries:
Albania, Algeria, Egypt, France, Greece, Italy, Lebanon, Malta, Morocco, Portugal, Spain, Tunisia, Türkiye.
[2020/XE3962/j/**E**]

♦ Mediterranean American International Schools / see Mediterranean Association of International Schools (#16646)

♦ Mediterranean Arbitration Council (MAC) 16645

Conseil méditerranéen de l'arbitrage (CMA)

Pres Cabinet Malouche, Galaxie Tour D, rue d'Arabie Saoudite, 1002 Tunis, Tunisia. T. +21671791793 – +21671791062. Fax +21671790513 – +21671801361.

History 23 May 1997, Tunis (Tunisia). Registered in accordance with Italian law. **Aims** Promote the arbitral culture; develop alternative dispute resolution. **Structure** Committee, including Chairman, 2 Vice-Chairmen and Secretary-General. **Languages** Arabic, English, French. **Staff** 2.50 FTE, voluntary. **Finance** Members' dues. Subventions. **Activities** Events/meetings; training/education. **Events** *Assises* Kairouan (Tunisia) 2009, *Assises* Valencia (Spain) 2008, *Mediterranean-Middle East counsel forum* Valencia (Spain) 2008, *Mediterranean-Middle East counsel forum* Rome (Italy) 2007, *Assises* Tunis (Tunisia) 2006. **Publications** *Lettre de la Présidence* (4 a year). Articles.
Members Individuals in 13 countries:
Algeria, Canada, Egypt, France, Greece, Italy, Lebanon, Malta, Morocco, Spain, Syrian AR, Tunisia, Türkiye.
NGO Relations Member of: *International Federation of Commercial Arbitration Institutions (IFCAI)*.
[2016.11.21/XD8672/**D**]

♦ Mediterranean Association for Adult Education (inactive)
♦ Mediterranean Association of Andrology (inactive)
♦ Mediterranean Association of Cardiology and Cardiac Surgery (no recent information)
♦ Mediterranean Association of Dermato-Venerology (inactive)
♦ Mediterranean Association of Environmental and Space Sciences (inactive)

♦ Mediterranean Association of International Schools (MAIS) 16646

Sec Chester College Intl School, Travesia de Montouto 2, 15894 Santiago de Compostela, La Coruña, Spain. T. +34981819160. Fax +34981819160. E-mail: info@chestercollege.org.
Exec Sec c/o American School of Madrid, Apartado 80, 28080 Madrid, Spain. T. +34917401900. Fax +34913572678. E-mail: rohale@mais-web.org.
URL: http://www.mais-web.org/

History 1981. Former names and other names: *Mediterranean American International Schools* – former. **Aims** Improve the quality of *education* in member schools; promote the professional development of faculty, administrators and school board members; serve as a liaison between member schools, host country schools, associate member organizations and other regional, professional and in-service organizations. **Languages** English. **Activities** Events/meetings; training/education. **Events** *Annual Conference* La Coruña (Spain) 2021, *Annual Conference* Tunis (Tunisia) 2020, *Annual Conference* Rome (Italy) 2019, *Annual Conference* Dubai (United Arab Emirates) 2018, *Annual Conference* Barcelona (Spain) 2015.
Members Schools (25) in 8 countries:
Cyprus, Egypt, France, Italy, Morocco, Portugal, Spain, Tunisia. [2022/XD0698/**D**]

♦ Mediterranean Association for Marine Biology and Oceanology (inactive)
♦ Mediterranean Association of Motorcycling (no recent information)
♦ Mediterranean Association of Pediatric Surgeons (inactive)
♦ Mediterranean Association for Plant Physiology (inactive)
♦ Mediterranean Association of Psychiatry (no recent information)

♦ Mediterranean Association to Save the Sea Turtles (MEDASSET) ... 16647

MEDASSET – Greece Licavitou 1(c), 106 72 Athens, Greece. T. +302103640389. Fax +302103613572.
URL: http://www.medasset.org/

History Oct 1988, by Lily Venizelos, tracing back to 1983. UK registered Charity: 1077649, Jul 1993. Greek society registered in accordance with Greek law, 1993. Company of limited liability registered in accordance with UK law, 1998: 03360065. UK registered charity: 1077649. **Aims** Halt and eventually reverse the accelerating decline of the endangered loggerhead and the critically endangered Mediterranean green turtle. **Structure** Comprises 2 independent organizations, MEDASSET-UK (international) and MEDASSET-Greece (national), both with co-incident aims. Steering Committee (MEDASSET/Greece); Trustees (MEDASSET/UK). Scientific Advisors. **Languages** English, French, Irish Gaelic. **Staff** 5.50 FTE, paid. Voluntary. **Finance** Projects co-funded by: *European Commission (EC, #06633)*, *Mediterranean Action Plan (MAP, #16638)*; *Regional Activity Centre for Specially Protected Areas (RAC/SPA, #18746)* of UNEP/MAP; other intergovernmental and nongovernmental bodies. Supplemented by fund raising, public donations and grants. **Activities** Research/documentation; training/education; networking/liaising; advocacy/lobbying/activism; awareness raising. **Publications** *Turtle-Dives* (3 a year) in Greek – newsletter. *The Mediterranean Sea – A Source of Life* in Arabic, English, Greek – environmental educational kit. Articles, brochures, posters, leaflets in English, Greek; turtle book for children in Greek; technical, research and assessment reports and papers, in English. **Information Services** *European Sea Turtle Biology and Conservation Website for Science and Education (EuroTurtle)*.
Members 'Friends of MEDASSET' individuals in 6 countries:
Greece, Ireland, Poland, Switzerland, UK, USA.
IGO Relations Cooperates with: *UNEP (#20299)*, especially *Mediterranean Action Plan (MAP, #16638)*. Permanent Action Plan partner of UNEP's Action Plan for the Conservation of Marine Mediterranean Turtles. Member of: *Standing Committee to the Bern Convention on the Conservation of European Wildlife and Natural Habitats (#19949)* at *Council of Europe (CE, #04881)*. Relevant treaties: *Convention on the Conservation of European Wildlife and Natural Habitats (Bern convention, 1979)*; *Convention for the Protection of the Marine Environment and the Coastal Region of the Mediterranean (Barcelona Convention, 1976)*. **NGO Relations** Member of: *Coastal and Marine Union – EUCC (#04072)*; *GEF CSO Network (GCN, #10087)*; *Global Islands Network (GIN, #10437)*; *International Federation for Sustainable Development and Fight to Poverty in the Mediterranean-Black Sea (FISPMED, #13562)*; *Mediterranean Information Office for Environment, Culture and Sustainable Development (MIO-ECSDE, #16657)*. Partner of: *1% for the Planet*. Also links with a number of national and international organizations active in the field. [2020/XD3109/v/**F**]

♦ Mediterranean Association for Science Advancement and Dissemination (no recent information)
♦ Mediterranean Association for Ultrasound in Obstetrics and Gynecology (no recent information)
♦ Mediterranean Badminton Confederation / see Confederation of Mediterranean Badminton (#04567)
♦ Mediterranean and Black Seas Hydrographic Commission (see: #13825)
♦ Mediterranean Burns Club / see Euro-Mediterranean Council for Burns and Fire Disaster (#05719)
♦ Mediterranean Center of Social and Educational Research (internationally oriented national body)

♦ Mediterranean Centre of Audiovisual Communication 16648

Centre Méditerranéen de la Communication Audiovisuelle (CMCA) – Centro Mediterraneo de la Comunicación Audiovisual – Mittelmeerzentrum der Audiovisuellen Kommunikation – Centro Mediterrâneo da Comunicação Audiovisual

Dir 96 la Canebière, 13001 Marseille, France. T. +33491420302. Fax +33491420183. E-mail: cmca@cmca-med.org.
URL: http://www.cmca-med.org/

History May 1986. Founded as a section of *International Radio and Television Union (#14689)*. Became independent, 1995. Functions within *UNESCO Mediterranean Programme (inactive)* as a network of *Mediterranean Media Network (no recent information)*. **Activities** Promotes Mediterranean cultural activities and cooperation: joint productions; collective and/or bilateral programme aid for creative work; research into launching of projects. Awards an annual Grand Prix – PriMed, at International Festival for Mediterranean Documentary and Current Affairs Film. **Publications** *Méditerrannée Audiovisuelle* (11 a year) – newsletter.
Members Broadcasting bodies and production companies in 13 countries and territories:
Algeria, Croatia, Egypt, France, Greece, Italy, Jordan, Morocco, Palestine, Romania, Spain, Tunisia, Türkiye.
IGO Relations *UNESCO (#20322)*. **NGO Relations** Member of: *Permanent Conference of Mediterranean Audiovisual Operators (COPEAM, #18320)*. [2020/XE1038/**E**]

♦ Mediterranean Chamber of Fine Arts / see European Cultural Network for Development Cooperation (#06869)
♦ Mediterranean Club for Burns and Fire Disaster / see Euro-Mediterranean Council for Burns and Fire Disaster (#05719)

♦ Mediterranean Coastal Foundation (MEDCOAST) 16649

Contact Kaunos Sok No 26, Dalyan, Ortaca, 48840 Mugla/Mugla, Türkiye. E-mail: medcoast@medcoast.net.
URL: http://www.medcoast.net/

History Founded early 1990's, by Middle East Technical University, Antalya (Turkey). Organized first international scientific activity in 1993. Became a recognized institution in the coastal management for the Mediterranean and the Black Sea, 2007, when adopted its current title. **Aims** Contribute to *coastal* and *marine conservation* in the *Mediterranean* and the *Black Sea* through improved coastal management practices by enhancing scientific and professional collaboration among individuals and institutes in the Mediterranean and Black Sea countries, or elsewhere, for the purpose of: (a) Producing means to improve understanding of physical, bio-chemical and ecological processes taking place in the Mediterranean and Black Sea coastal and sea environment, and their interactions with human activities; (b) Facilitating the utilization of scientific knowledge and modern management tools in achieving integrated coastal and sea management; (c) Complementing and contributing to existing efforts having similar goals. **Languages** English, Turkish. **Staff** 4.00 FTE, paid. Several voluntary. **Finance** Activities are financed on project basis by participation fees and by small donations from national and international institutions. **Activities** Events/meetings; training/education; research and development. Proposes setting up: *International MEDCOAST Centre for Coastal Management in the Mediterranean and the Black Sea (no recent information)*. **Events** *Biennial Conference* Marmaris (Turkey) 2013, *MEDCOAST : International Conference on the Mediterranean Coastal Environment* Mugla (Turkey) 2013, *MEDCOAST : International Conference on the Mediterranean Coastal Environment* Dalyan (Turkey)

2012, *Biennial Conference* Rhodes Is (Greece) 2011, *Biennial Conference* Sochi (Russia) 2009. **Publications** *Advances in Integrated Coastal Management for the Mediterranean and Black Sea* (2010); *Coastal Area Management in Turkey* (2005); *Wind and Deep Water Wave Atlas for Turkish Coast* (2002) in Turkish; *Aspects of Coastal Zone Management in the Mediterranean and Black Seas* (2000); *Journal of Ocean and Coastal Management* (1996); *Estuaries and Coastal Waters: Research and Management* (1995). Biennal Conference proceedings; other conference proceedings. Information service for Mediterranean and Black Sea countries on the topic of coastal management; directory of experts and institutions on coastal and marine issues.
Members Alumni (275) in 35 countries and territories:
Albania, Algeria, Belgium, Bosnia-Herzegovina, Bulgaria, Croatia, Egypt, Estonia, France, Georgia, Greece, Israel, Italy, Japan, Jordan, Korea Rep, Lebanon, Libya, Malta, Morocco, Netherlands, North Macedonia, Palestine, Poland, Portugal, Romania, Russia, Serbia, Slovenia, Spain, Syrian AR, Tunisia, Türkiye, UK, Ukraine.
Included in the above, 2 organizations listed in this Yearbook:
International Centre for Coastal and Ocean Policy Studies (ICCOPS); Middle East Technical University (METU).
NGO Relations Member of: *International Federation for Sustainable Development and Fight to Poverty in the Mediterranean-Black Sea (FISPMED, #13562).* [2013.06.13/XF4042/fy/F]

♦ Mediterranean College Centre for the Study of Globalization / see Centre for the Study of Globalization, Athens
♦ Mediterranean Confederation of Centres for Chelonian Conservation (inactive)
♦ Mediterranean Conference of Television and Audiovisual Operators / see Permanent Conference of Mediterranean Audiovisual Operators (#18320)
♦ Mediterranean Congress of Aesthetics (meeting series)
♦ Mediterranean Control Association (no recent information)
♦ Mediterranean Cooperative Research and Study Group on the Almond Tree / see Groupe de recherches méditerranéennes pour l'amandier – pistachier (#10770)

♦ Mediterranean Dental Implant Society (MDIS) 16650

Contact address not obtained. T. +302106437601 – +302107290963. Fax +302106423956 – +302106747369.
History 2006, following a series of congresses. **Aims** Provide implant education to the dental team to better serve patients in Mediterranean countries. **Structure** Board, comprising President, President-Elect, Vice-President, Treasurer, General Secretary and Secretariat. **Events** *Congress* Rethymnon (Greece) 2008, *Congress* Corfu (Greece) 2006, *Congress* Corfu (Greece) 2004, *Congress* Corfu (Greece) 2002. **Members** Membership countries not specified. [2008/XJ1746/E]

♦ Mediterranean Diet Foundation (internationally oriented national body)
♦ Mediterranean Dolphin Conservation / see Oceanomare-Delphis
♦ Mediterranean Energy Regulators / see Association of Mediterranean Energy Regulators (#02800)
♦ Mediterranean Engineering Schools Network (#18899)
♦ Mediterranean Entente Treaty (1887 treaty)
♦ Mediterranean Environmental Technical Assistance Programme (inactive)
♦ Mediterranean Environment and Development Observatory (internationally oriented national body)
♦ Mediterranean Environment Programme (inactive)

♦ Mediterranean Experts on Climate and Environmental Change (MedECC) 16651

Science Officer MedECC Secretariat, Plan Bleu, 16e étage Tour la Marseillaise, 2 bis, bd Euroméditerranée- Quai d'Arenc, 13002 Marseille, France.
URL: http://www.medecc.org/
History 2015. Founded in parallel of the preparation of the 21st Session of the Conference of Parties of *United Nations Framework Convention on Climate Change (UNFCCC, 1992).* **Aims** Provide sound scientific information about environmental issues of concern for the Mediterranean region. **Structure** Coordinators; Steering Committee; Secretariat. **Languages** English. **Staff** 2.00 FTE, paid. Several voluntary. **Finance** Support from: *Union for the Mediterranean (UfM, #20457)* in the framework of its Agreement with *Plan Bleu pour l'environnement et le développement en Méditerranée (Plan Bleu, #18379); Swedish International Development Cooperation Agency (Sida);* Principality of Monaco; Aix-Marseille University (France); Laboratory of Excellence OT-Med (France); Advisory Council for the Sustainable Development of Catalonia (CADS) (Spain); AIR Climat Association (France); ACTERRA Consulting (France); Métropole Aix-Marseille Provence. **Activities** Awareness raising; capacity building; events/meetings; knowledge management/information dissemination; networking/liaising; politics/policy/regulatory; publishing activities. **Events** *Atelier sur les Impacts des Changements Climatiques en Méditerranée* Montpellier (France) 2017. **Publications** MedECC (2020) Climate and Environmental Change in the Mediterranean Basin – Current Situation and Risks for the Future. First Mediterranean Assessment Report [Cramer, W., Guiot, J., Marini, K. (eds.)] Union for the Mediterranean, Plan Bleu, UNEP/MAP, Marseille, France, 632pp. ISBN: 978-2-9577416-0-1 / DOI: 10.5281/zenodo.4768833.
Members Scientists and stakeholders (over 600) in 35 countries and territories:
Albania, Algeria, Austria, Belgium, Bosnia-Herzegovina, Bulgaria, Chile, Croatia, Cyprus, Egypt, France, Germany, Greece, Iceland, Ireland, Israel, Italy, Lebanon, Malta, Monaco, Montenegro, Morocco, Pakistan, Palestine, Poland, Portugal, Saudi Arabia, Serbia, Spain, Sweden, Syrian AR, Tunisia, Türkiye, UK, USA. [2022.01.31/XM6109/v/F]

♦ Mediterranean Forest Communicators Network (unconfirmed)

♦ Mediterranean Forum of Physical and Rehabilitation Medicine (MFPRM) 16652

Pres Marmara Univ School of Medicine, Dept Physical Medicine and Rehabilitation, Pendik Ust Kaynarca, 34899 Istanbul/Istanbul, Türkiye. E-mail: gulserena@gmail.com.
URL: http://mfprm.net/
History Sep 2000, Athens (Greece), during the 3rd Mediterranean Congress on Physical and Rehabilitation Medicine. Statutes revised 24 Oct 2012 at General Assembly, Sorrento (Italy). **Aims** Be the scientific Mediterranean body for physicians working in Europe, Asia and Africa, around or in close vicinity of the Mediterranean Sea, in the fields of physical and rehabilitation medicine. **Structure** General Assembly (every 2 years at Congress); Executive Board. **Languages** English. **Staff** None. **Finance** None. **Activities** Events/meetings; training/education. **Events** *Biennial Congress* Marrakech (Morocco) 2019, *Biennial Congress* St Julian's (Malta) 2017, *Biennial Congress* Alexandria (Egypt) 2015, *Biennial Congress* Budva (Montenegro) 2013, *Biennial Congress* Sorrento (Italy) 2012. **Publications** *EUROPA MEDICOPHYSICA – the Mediterranean Journal of PRM.*
Members Full in 30 countries and territories:
Albania, Algeria, Austria, Bosnia-Herzegovina, Bulgaria, Croatia, Cyprus, Egypt, France, Greece, Hungary, Israel, Italy, Jordan, Lebanon, Malta, Moldova, Montenegro, Morocco, North Macedonia, Palestine, Portugal, Romania, Serbia, Slovenia, Spain, Sudan, Syrian AR, Tunisia, Türkiye. [2018.10.07/XF6802/F]

♦ Mediterranean Foundation of Strategic Studies (internationally oriented national body)

♦ Mediterranean Garden Society (MGS) 16653

Gen Sec Sparoza, Box 14, 190 02 Peania, Greece. Fax +302106643089. E-mail: mgssecretary@gmail.com.
URL: http://www.mediterraneangardensociety.org/
History 1994, Athens (Greece). Registered in Greece. **Aims** Further knowledge and appreciation of plants and gardens suited to the Mediterranean climate regions of the world. **Structure** Administrative Committee; Local branches (18). **Languages** English. **Staff** None. **Finance** Members' dues. Donations. **Activities** Events/meetings; research/documentation; knowledge management/information dissemination. **Events** *Annual General Meeting* Menton (France) 2014, *Annual General Meeting* Athens (Greece) 2013, *Annual General Meeting* Monterey, CA (USA) 2008, *Annual General Meeting* Athens (Greece) 2007, *Annual General Meeting* Uzès (France) 2006. **Publications** *The Mediterranean Garden* (4 a year).
Members Individuals and societies. Members in 40 countries. Membership countries not specified. International branches in 8 countries:
International branches in 8 countries:
Australia, Cyprus, Germany, Greece, Italy, Portugal, Spain, USA.
Also members in Scandinavia. Membership countries not specified. [2016.06.01/XD4222/D]

♦ Mediterranean Geosciences Union (unconfirmed)
♦ Mediterranean Group for Almond and Pistachio / see Groupe de recherches méditerranéennes pour l'amandier – pistachier (#10770)

♦ Mediterranean Group of Pesticides Research (MGPR) 16654

Pres Univ of Cagliari, Via Università 40, 09124 Cagliari, Italy. T. +39706758615. Fax +39706758612.
Treas address not obtained.
URL: http://mgpr.unica.it/
History Apr 1999, Cagliari (Italy), during 1st International Symposium on Pesticides in Food and the Environment in Mediterranean Countries. **Aims** Disseminate knowledge in all aspects of pesticide research, thus meeting demands for sustainable agricultural production in the Mediterranean region with respect to human health and environmental safety. **Structure** General Meeting; Office of the President elects President. **Languages** English, French, Italian, Spanish. **Finance** Members' dues. Grants. **Activities** Events/meetings; knowledge management/information dissemination; networking/liaising; publishing activities. **Events** *International Symposium of Pesticides in Food and the Environment in Mediterranean Countries / International Symposium* Hammamet (Tunisia) 2015, *International Symposium* Antalya (Turkey) 2013, *International Meeting* Belgrade (Serbia) 2012, *International Symposium* Thessaloniki (Greece) 2011, *International Meeting* Catania (Italy) 2010.
Members in 19 countries:
Algeria, Argentina, Brazil, Bulgaria, Cyprus, Czechia, France, Germany, Greece, Israel, Italy, Lebanon, Morocco, Portugal, Serbia, Slovakia, Spain, Tunisia, Türkiye. [2015.01.30/XF6238/F]

♦ Mediterranean Group for the Study of Diabetes (MGSD) 16655

SG Service Médecine Interne B, Hôp Lariboisière, 2 rue Ambroise-Paré, 75475 Paris CEDEX 10, France. T. +33149956565 – +33149956321. Fax +33149958212.
Pres Clinique d'endocrinologie maladies métaboliques et nutrition, 1 place Alexis Ricordeau, 44093 Nantes CEDEX 1, France. T. +33240687718. Fax +33240687805.
URL: http://www.mgsd.org/
History 1984, as a group of doctors active in Mediterranean countries. **Languages** English, French. **Activities** Working groups carry out research into: epidemiology; prenatal care; hereditary factors; education. **Events** *Congress* Barcelona (Spain) 2013, *Congress* Casablanca (Morocco) 2011, *Congress* Malta 2009, *Congress* Istanbul (Turkey) 2007, *Congress* Nice (France) 2005. **Publications** *Media News.* MGSD pocket manual; teaching slides for counsellors. **Members** Membership countries not specified. [2013/XD5641/D]

♦ Mediterranean Incontinence and Pelvic Floor Society (MIPS) 16656

Exec Dir Via S Giovanni 20, 29121 Piacenza PC, Italy. T. +39523338391. Fax +395231860018. E-mail: info@mipsnet.org.
URL: http://www.mipsnet.org/
History Inaugurated Nov 2013, Noto (Italy). **Aims** Promote, enhance and spread studies on prevention and treatment of patients affected by functional or morphological disturbances, urinary or fecal incontinence, sexual or painful pelvic floor dysfunctions related to neurological, gynecological and urological diseases with particular attention for the whole Mediterranean area. **Structure** Board of Directors; Committees. **Languages** English. **Staff** Voluntary. **Finance** Members' dues. **Activities** Events/meetings; guidance/assistance/consulting. Active in about 20 Mediterranean countries. Countries not specified. **Events** *Annual Meeting* Athens (Greece) 2021, *Annual Meeting* Barcelona (Spain) 2019, *Annual Meeting* Rome (Italy) 2018, *Annual Meeting* Valletta (Malta) 2016, *Annual Meeting* Ljubljana (Slovenia) 2015. **Members** Full in 33 countries. Membership countries not specified. **NGO Relations** Affiliate of: *European Urogynaecological Association (EUGA, #09041); International Continence Society (ICS, #12934); International Urogynecological Association (IUGA, #15835); Sociedad Iberoamericana de Neurourologia y Uroginecologia (SINUG, #19375);* national federations. [2020.01.03/XJ8682/D]

♦ Mediterranean Information Office for Environment, Culture and Sustainable Development (MIO-ECSDE) 16657

Bureau méditerranéen d'information sur l'environnement, la culture et le développement durable
Chairman 12 Kyrristou Street, 105 56 Athens, Greece. T. +302103247490 – +302103247267. Fax +302103317127. E-mail: info@mio-ecsde.org – secretariat@mio-ecsde.org.
URL: http://www.mio-ecsde.org/
History 1990. Founded as a network of NGOs, as a joint project of *European Environmental Bureau (EEB, #06996)* and the Hellenic Society for the Protection of the Environment and the Cultural Heritage (Elliniki Etairia), in close cooperation with *Arab NGO Network for Environment and Development (RAED, #01017).* Since Mar 1996 functions as a federation of Mediterranean NGOs. Registration: Greece. **Aims** Protect the natural environment (flora and fauna, biotopes, forests, coasts, natural resources, climate) and the cultural heritage (archaeological monuments, traditional settlements, cities, etc) of the entire Mediterranean region; promote sustainable development in a peaceful Mediterranean. **Structure** General Assembly; Executive Bureau; Secretariat in Athens (Greece). **Languages** English. **Staff** 10.00 FTE, paid. **Finance** Mainly financed through projects by EU, MAP/UNEP and national governments. **Activities** Monitoring/evaluation; advocacy/lobbying/activism; awareness raising; capacity building; networking/liaising; research/documentation; knowledge management/information dissemination. **Events** *Capacity building symposium on integrated water management and irrigation* Istanbul (Turkey) 2004, *European Rio plus 10 coalition annual progress conference* Brussels (Belgium) 2002, *European Rio Plus 10 Coalition annual progress conference* Brussels (Belgium) 2001, *European Rio plus 10 Coalition annual progress conference* Brussels (Belgium) 2000, *Mediterranean NGO workshop* Thessaloniki (Greece) 1997. **Publications** *Sustainable Mediterranean* (4 a year) – newsletter; *MIO-ECSDE e-News. Handbook on Methods Used in Environmental Education and Education for Sustainable Development* (2004); *The Evolution of Environmental Policies in the Mediterranean from an NGO Perspective* (2004) in English, French; *Public Participation, Environmental Information and Awareness in the Mediterranean* (2003) in English, French; *Media Kit on Fresh Water in the Mediterranean* (2002); *Planning Sustainable Regional Development: Principles, Tools and Practices – The case study of the Rhodes Island* (1999) in English, Greek; *A Guide of Successful NGO Funding* (1998); *Public Awareness: Guidelines for the Organization of Round Table Discussions* (1998) in English, French; *Agreed Positions of the Mediterranean Environmental Organizations* (1997) in English, French; *Directory of Environmental Organizations Active in the Mediterranean* (1997); *Environmental NGO Activity Kit* (1994). Workshop proceedings; brochures and leaflets.
Members Full: national and regional organizations (over 130) in 28 countries and territories:
Albania, Algeria, Belgium, Croatia, Cyprus, Egypt, France, Greece, Israel, Italy, Jordan, Lebanon, Libya, Malta, Mauritania, Montenegro, Morocco, Netherlands, North Macedonia, Pakistan, Palestine, Portugal, Slovenia, Spain, Switzerland, Syrian AR, Tunisia, Türkiye.
Included in the above, 17 organizations listed in this Yearbook:
Arab NGO Network for Environment and Development (RAED, #01017); Arab Office for Youth and Environment (AOYE); Centre régional d'intervention pour la coopération, Reggio Calabria (CRIC); Centro de Investigación y Promoción Iberoamérica-Europa (CIPIE, no recent information); Coastal and Marine Union – EUCC (#04072) (Mediterranean Centre); *Coordination of Nongovernmental Organizations for International Development Cooperation (COCIS); EcoMed 21; EcoPeace Middle East (#05325); Eco-union; Global Footprint Network (#10367); International Centre of Comparative Environmental Law (#12483); International Energy Foundation (IEF, #13273); Maghreb-Mashreq Alliance for Water (#16544); Mare Terra – Fundació Medeterrània (Mare Terra); MAREVIVO Associazione Ambientalista; Mediterranean Association to Save the Sea Turtles (MEDASSET, #16647); MEDITERRANEAN SOS Network (MEDSOS).*
Consultative Status Consultative status granted from: *ECOSOC (#05331)* (Special); *UNESCO (#20322)* (Consultative Status). **IGO Relations** Accredited to the Conference of the Parties of: *Secretariat of the United Nations Convention to Combat Desertification (Secretariat of the UNCCD, #19208).* Close collaboration with: *European Commission (EC, #06633); International Bank for Reconstruction and Development (IBRD, #12317); International Fund for Agricultural Development (IFAD, #13692); Mediterranean Action Plan (MAP, #16638); Secretariat of the Convention of Wetlands (#19200); UNDP (#20292).*
NGO Relations Member of: *Accountable Now (#00060); EDC Free Europe (#05355); EuroMed Non-Governmental Platform (#05730);* Mediterranean Technical Advisory Committee (MEDTAC) of *Global Water Partnership (GWP, #10653); Spring Alliance (inactive).* Close collaboration with:

– *Centre of Euro-Mediterranean Regions for the Environment (CERE, no recent information); Centre for International Information and Documentation, Barcelona (CIDOB Foundation); Friends of the Earth International (FoEI, #10002); International Union for Conservation of Nature and Natural Resources (IUCN, #15766); MEDCITIES Network (#16610); Mediterranean Academy of Diplomatic Studies (MEDAC); Mediterranean Marine Bird Association (MEDMARAVIS, #16661); Mediterranean NGO Network for Ecology and Sustainable Development (MED Forum, no recent information); The Mediterranean Wetlands Initiative (MedWet, #16688); Network of Marine Protected Area Managers in the Mediterranean (MEDPAN, #17048).*

Instrumental in setting up: *European Seas Environmental Cooperation (ESEC, inactive).* [2022/XF4120/y/F]

♦ Mediterranean Institute (internationally oriented national body)
♦ Mediterranean Institute (internationally oriented national body)
♦ Mediterranean Institute for Cognitive Neuroscience (internationally oriented national body)

♦ Mediterranean Institute of Fundamental Physics (MIFP) 16658

Admin Sec Via Appia Nuova 31, 00040 Marino RM, Italy. T. +39693543023. E-mail: info@mifp.eu.
Scientific Dir address not obtained.
URL: http://www.mifp.eu/

History Jul 2010. Registered in accordance with Italian law, Sep 2010. **Aims** Create a stimulating research environment; help bring together physicists of the post-Soviet scientific diaspora; promote physics in countries of the Mediterranean region. **Structure** Scientific Council. **Languages** English. **Finance** Funding from projects. **Activities** Meeting activities; research and development. **Events** *International Conference on Light-Matter Coupling in Composite Nano-Structures* Stepanakert (Armenia) 2014, *International Conference on Metamaterials and Nanophysics* Varadero (Cuba) 2014, *OECS : International Conference on Optics of Excitons in Confined Systems* Rome (Italy) 2013. **Members** Full (160) in 24 countries. Membership countries not specified. [2022/XJ8336/j/D]

♦ Mediterranean Institute of Gender Studies (internationally oriented national body)
♦ Mediterranean Institute for Life Sciences (internationally oriented national body)
♦ Mediterranean Institute of marine and terrestrial Biodiversity and Ecology (internationally oriented national body)
♦ Mediterranean Institute for Nature and Anthropos (internationally oriented national body)
♦ Mediterranean Integrated Studies at Regional And Local Scales (inactive)

♦ Mediterranean International Association of the Processing Tomato 16659

Association méditerranéenne internationale de la tomate transformée (AMITOM)

SG Chambre D'Agriculture, Site Agroparc, TSA 48449, 84912 Avignon Cedex 9, France.
URL: http://www.amitom.com/

History Statutes approved by the constitutive General Assembly, 16 May 1979, Rome; modified by several Extraordinary General Assemblies: 28 Jan 1983, Athens (Greece); 16 Jun 1986, Tel Aviv; 10 May 1990, Athens; 20 Jun 1997, Tunis (Tunisia); 26 Oct 2000, Paris (France); 20 Jun 2003, Madrid (Spain). **Aims** Establish permanent links between interprofessional or professional and cooperative representatives of the tomato processing *industry*, in order to coordinate efforts meant to safeguard their interests and improve and increase consumption of products derived from the tomato. **Structure** General Assembly (annual); Board of Directors; Executive Council; Secretary General; Commissions (3). **Languages** English, French. **Staff** 1.00 FTE, paid. **Finance** Sources: members' dues. **Activities** Knowledge management/information dissemination; research/documentation. **Events** *World Congress* San Juan (Argentina) 2020, *World Congress* Greece 2018, *World Congress* Santiago (Chile) 2016, *World Congress* Sirmione (Italy) 2014, *World congress* Estoril (Portugal) 2010. **Information Services** *Tomato News.*

Members National delegations in 9 countries:
Egypt, France, Greece, Israel, Italy, Portugal, Spain, Tunisia, Türkiye.
Associate in 7 countries:
Algeria, Hungary, Iran Islamic Rep, Malta, Russia, Syrian AR, Ukraine.

NGO Relations Member of: *International Society for Horticultural Science (ISHS, #15180); World Processing Tomato Council (WPTC, #21738).* [2020.06.23/XD5791/D]

♦ Mediterranean Landscape Charter (1993 treaty)
♦ Mediterranean League Against Thromboembolic Diseases / see European and Mediterranean League Against Thrombotic Diseases (#07771)

♦ Mediterranean League of Angiology and Vascular Surgery (MLAVS) 16660

SG KCLJ Vascular Diseases, Zaloska cesta 2, 1525 Ljubljana, Slovenia.
URL: http://www.mlavs.org/

History founded on the initiative of Panayotis Balas. **Aims** Coordinate and guide the scientific activities of angiology and vascular surgery in the Mediterranean countries. **Structure** Executive Board, comprising President, 2 Vice-Presidents, Secretary-General and Treasurer and one representative from each participating country. **Activities** Organizes annual Mediterranean Congress. Provides multicentre Mediterranean studies. **Events** *Congress* Porto (Portugal) 2021, *Congress* Ljubljana (Slovenia) 2020, *Congress* Zagreb (Croatia) 2019, *Congress* Palermo (Italy) 2018, *Congress* Aswan (Egypt) 2017. **Publications** *METLET* – official newsletter. **Members** Membership countries not specified. **NGO Relations** Joint meetings with: *International Union of Angiology (IUA, #15754); Mediterranean Blood Club (no recent information).* [2012/XD2536/D]

♦ Mediterranean Marine Bird Association (MEDMARAVIS) 16661

Association méditerranéenne pour l'avifaune marine – Asociación Mediterranea para la Avifauna Marina – Associazione Mediterranea per l'Avifauna Marina

Pres 96 via S Satta, 07041 Alghero SS, Italy. T. +3979974621. E-mail: medmaravis.info@gmail.com – medmaravis@gmail.com.
Projects Officer address not obtained. T. +393494732190.
Twitter: https://twitter.com/medmaravis

History 1984. **Aims** Conserve Mediterranean marine and coastal fauna; promote research on the importance of the seabird's role in the ecosystem; promote and manage coastal reserves and island ecosystems. **Structure** General Assembly (every 3 years); Council; Executive Board. **Languages** English, French, Italian. **Staff** 1.00 FTE, paid. Voluntary. **Activities** Training/education; awareness raising; monitoring/evaluation; research/documentation; events/meetings. **Events** *Symposium* Hammamet (Tunisia) 2015, *Symposium* Alghero (Italy) 2011, *Symposium* Vilanova (Spain) 2006, *Scientific Conference* Porto Torres (Italy) 2002, *Conference on biodiversity and hydro-carbon pollution* Porto Conte (Italy) 2001. **Publications** *MEDMARAVIS Newsletter.* Conference proceedings; case studies; manuals. **Information Services** *Coastal Geographical Information System (Coastal GIS); MEDMARAVIS Data Bank.*

Members Marine biologists, ornithologists and conservationists in 28 countries:
Albania, Algeria, Bulgaria, Croatia, Cyprus, Egypt, France, Germany, Greece, Israel, Italy, Lebanon, Libya, Malta, Montenegro, Morocco, Netherlands, Portugal, Romania, Serbia, Slovenia, Spain, Switzerland, Syrian AR, Tunisia, Türkiye, UK, Ukraine.

NGO Relations Member of: *World Seabird Union (WSU, #21774).* [2015.09.18/XD3084/D]

♦ Mediterranean Marine Pollution Assessment and Control Programme / see MED POL – Programme for the Assessment and Control of Marine Pollution in the Mediterranean (#16691)
♦ Mediterranean Maritime Arbitration Association (inactive)
♦ Mediterranean Medical Entente (no recent information)
♦ Mediterranean Medical Society (inactive)
♦ Mediterranean Medical Union (inactive)
♦ Mediterranean and Middle Eastern Endoscopic Surgery Association (#02804)
♦ Mediterranean and Middle East Gerontological and Geriatric Association (no recent information)

♦ Mediterranean Model Forest Network (MMFN) 16662

Réseau méditerranéen de Forêts Modèles (RMFM) – Red Mediterranea de Bosques Modelo (RMBM)

Secretariat Cesefor Foundation – Pol Ind Las Casas, calle C, parcela 4, 42005 Soria, Spain. T. +34975212453. Fax +34975239677. E-mail: info@medmodelforest.net – secretariat@medmodelforest.net.
URL: http://www.mmfn.info/

History 2008, Spain. Founded as a regional network of *International Model Forest Network (IMFN, #14175).* **Aims** Promote sustainability of forest landscapes. **Structure** An informal network of countries, regions and model forest associations. **Languages** English, French, Spanish. **Staff** 2.00 FTE, voluntary. **Finance** Funded by European Cooperation Projects. **Activities** Training/education; guidance/assistance/consulting; knowledge management/information dissemination; events/meetings; research/documentation. **Events** *Mediterranean Forest Week* Agadir (Morocco) 2017.

Members Participating regions/countries in 9 countries:
Algeria, Croatia, France, Greece, Italy, Morocco, Spain, Tunisia, Türkiye.

IGO Relations *AFWC/EFC/NEFC Committee on Mediterranean Forestry Questions – Silva Mediterranea (#00542).* **NGO Relations** Member of: *European Forest Institute Mediterranean Facility (EFIMED, #07298).* [2020/XJ8364/E]

♦ Mediterranean Mothers' Movement 16663

Mouvement des mères de Méditerranée

Contact 77 rue de Stalingrad, 94110 Arcueil, France. T. +33147401716.
Secretariat 18 Haldeias St, 167 77 Elliniko-Sourmena, Greece. T. +302109607676.

History 1 Nov 1994, Athens (Greece). Registered in accordance with Greek law. **Aims** Promote legal, social, economic interests of mothers, *women* in general and the *family* as an institution and socioeconomic entity; in this framework, represent women with national and international authorities, organizations and agencies. **Structure** General Assembly (annual); Executive Bureau (meets at least every 2 months), comprising President, Vice-President, Secretary-General and 2 to 5 members. **Languages** English, French, Irish Gaelic. **Staff** 4.00 FTE, voluntary. **Finance** Members' dues: euro 40. **Events** *Meeting* Athens (Greece) 2010, *Biennial meeting / Meeting* Paris (France) 2007, *Biennial meeting / Meeting* Athens (Greece) 2005, *Biennial meeting / Meeting* Paris (France) 2003, *Biennial meeting / Meeting* Athens (Greece) 2001.

Members Individuals and organizations in 15 countries:
Armenia, Belgium, Canada, Cyprus, France, Germany, Greece, Italy, Monaco, North Macedonia, Romania, Russia, Switzerland, UK, USA. [2012.07.02/XF3306/F]

♦ Mediterranean MOU – Memorandum of Understanding on Port State Control in the Mediterranean (1997 treaty)
♦ Mediterranean Music Centre, Lamia (internationally oriented national body)

♦ Mediterranean Network of Basin Organisations (MENBO) 16664

Réseau Méditerranéen des Organismes de Bassin (REMOB) – Red Mediterranea de Organismos de Cuenca (REMOC)

Permanent Tech Sec Confederación Hidrografica, Av Blasco Ibañez 48, Despacho 8942 (5a), 46010 Valencia, Spain. T. +34963938942. Fax +34961125750. E-mail: remoc1@remoc.org.
URL: http://www.remoc.org/

History 3 Nov 2002, Madrid (Spain), as a regional network of *International Network of Basin Organizations (INBO, #14235).* EU Transparency Register: 940796722614-72. **Aims** Develop lasting relations among organizations in charge of integrated *water* resources *management* in the Mediterranean region and favour exchange of experiences and expertise among them; facilitate implementation of tools suitable for institutional and financial management, for knowledge and follow up of water *resources*, for organization of data bases and for preparation of water management plans and actions programmes in the medium and long term; develop information and training programmes for local officials, for users' representatives and for different stakeholders involved in water management as well as for executives and staff of organizations in charge of water management at the river basin level; encourage the population's awareness on these issues; promote these principles in international cooperation programmes; evaluate on-going actions initiated by member organizations and disseminate their results. **Structure** General Assembly; Executive Committee; President; Permanent Technical Secretariat; Experts Committee. **Languages** English, French, Spanish. **Staff** 2.00 FTE, paid. **Finance** Supported by Júcar River Basin Authority of the Spanish Ministry of Environment, Rural and Marine Affairs. **Activities** Projects/programmes; events/meetings. **Events** *Beirut Water Week* Beirut (Lebanon) 2017, *General Assembly* St Julian's (Malta) 2017, *General Assembly* Porto (Portugal) 2011, *General Assembly* Beirut (Lebanon) 2009, *International seminar on river basin management and cooperation* Beirut (Lebanon) 2009.

Members Basin organizations; governmental administrations; bi- and multilateral cooperation agencies. Members are also considered INBO members. Permanent observers: other public organizations. Members in 17 countries:
Albania, Bosnia-Herzegovina, Cyprus, France, Greece, Israel, Italy, Jordan, Lebanon, Libya, Morocco, North Macedonia, Palestine, Portugal, Romania, Spain, Türkiye.

IGO Relations Observer status in Water Expert Group of *Union for the Mediterranean (UfM, #20457).* **NGO Relations** *Euro-Mediterranean Irrigators Community (EIC, #05723); Global Water Partnership (GWP, #10653)* Mediterranean; *Institut méditerranéen de l'eau (IME, #11323); International Federation for Sustainable Development and Fight to Poverty in the Mediterranean-Black Sea (FISPMED, #13562).* [2018/XE4434/E]

♦ Mediterranean Network of Establishments for Veterinary Education (#18871)
♦ Mediterranean Network for the Knowledge Economy and Innovation (internationally oriented national body)

♦ Mediterranean Network of Regulatory Authorities 16665

Réseau des instances de régulation méditerranéennes (RIRM)

Contact c/o Conseil supérieur de l'audiovisuel, Tour Mirabeau, 39-43 quai André-Citroën, 75739 Paris CEDEX 15, France. T. +33140583800. Fax +33140583673. E-mail: mnrasecretariat@rirm.org.
URL: http://www.rirm.org/

History 1997. **Aims** Establish a framework for discussion and exchanges of information and research on topics related to audiovisual regulation. **Events** *Plenary Assembly* Cavtat (Croatia) 2021, *Technical Committee Meeting* Rabat (Morocco) 2019, *Plenary Assembly* Barcelona (Spain) 2018, *Meeting* Lisbon (Portugal) 2012, *Annual Meeting* Morocco 2007.

Members Regulatory authorities (13) in 12 countries:
Albania, Cyprus, France, Greece, Israel, Italy, Malta, Morocco, Portugal, Serbia, Spain, Türkiye. [2007/XM2837/F]

♦ Mediterranean Network of Water Training Centers (AquaForMed) . . 16666

Réseau Méditerranéen des Centres de Formation aux Métiers de l'Eau

Technical Secretariat c/o IOW, 21 rue de Madrid, 75008 Paris, France. T. +33144908860. Fax +33140080145. E-mail: r.boyer@oieau.fr.
Presidency c/o ONEE, Post Box, Rabat Chellah, Rabat, Morocco.
URL: http://www.aquaformed.org/

History 2012, Marseille (France). Proposedat World Water Forum. Network Charter signed 19 Nov 2013, Paris (France). **Aims** Promote vocational training in the fields of water and *sanitation*. **Structure** President; Technical Secretary. **Languages** English, French. **Activities** Events/meetings; training/education. **Publications** *AQUAforMed Newsletter* (2 a year).

Members Full in 4 countries:
Algeria, France, Morocco, Tunisia.
Including in the above, 2 organizations listed in this Yearbook:
International Office for Water (IOW, #14399); Tunis International Centre for Environmental Technologies (CITET). [2015.06.04/XJ8338/F]

♦ Mediterranean Neurological Society (no recent information)

♦ Mediterranean Neuroscience Society (MNS) 16667

Gen Sec c/o Institute for Brain Research, Šalata 3, Medicinski fakultet, HR-10000 Zagreb, Croatia.
URL: https://www.medneuroscisociety.org/

History Current bylaws adopted Jun 2017. **Aims** Strengthen exchanges between mediterranean neuroscientists; promote education in the neurosciences and increase public awareness of progress made; sustain scientific, training and networking events. **Structure** General Assembly; Council; Executive Committee. *Committee on Animals in Research in the Mediterranean Area (CARMA).* **Finance** Members' dues. **Activities** Training/education; events/meetings; awards/prizes/competitions. **Events** *Conference* Dubrovnik (Croatia) 2022, *Conference* Dubrovnik (Croatia) 2021, *Conference* Marrakech (Morocco) 2019, *Conference* St Julian's (Malta) 2017, *Conference* Cagliari (Italy) 2015. **Members** Regular; Student; Affiliate. Membership countries not specified. **NGO Relations** Member of: *International Brain Research Organization (IBRO, #12392).* [2022/XM7470/D]

♦ Mediterranean Observatory for Information and Reflection (see: #18959)

♦ Mediterranean Oceanography Network for the Global Ocean Observing System (MONGOOS) 16668

Address not obtained.
URL: http://www.mongoos.eu/

History 2012, as part of *Global Ocean Observing System (GOOS, #10511)*. Comprises the previous activities of *Mediterranean Operational Oceanography Network (MOON)* and *Mediterranean Global Ocean Observing System (MedGOOS, inactive)*. **Aims** Further develop operational oceanography in the Mediterranean Sea. **Structure** Assembly; Executive Board; Bureau; Secretariat. **Events** *Meeting* Lecce (Italy) 2014, *Meeting* Madrid (Spain) 2013, *Meeting* Rome (Italy) 2012.
Members Partners in 12 countries:
Croatia, Cyprus, France, Greece, Israel, Italy, Malta, Montenegro, Morocco, Slovenia, Spain, Türkiye.
NGO Relations Cooperates with: *European Global Ocean Observing System (EuroGOOS, #07396)*; *Global Ocean Observing System for Africa (GOOS Africa, #10512)*. [2015/XJ9243/E]

♦ Mediterranean Oil Industry Group (MOIG) 16669

Dir 08 Avenue Slimen Ben Slimen, El Manar, 2092 Tunis, Tunisia. T. +21671888439. Fax +21671888439. E-mail: info.moig@planet.tn.
URL: http://www.medoilgroup.org/

History 1992, Cairo (Egypt). Officially launched on 27 Jan 2004, Tunis (Tunisia). **Aims** Strengthen members' abilities to prepare for and respond safely and effective to *oil spill* incidents; build standards and facilitate effective oil spill response partnerships; be a credible voice of the Oil and Gas Industry in the region related to oil spill preparedness and response; be proactive and share field operations experiences and best practices. **Structure** Management Committee; Permanent Secretariat based in Tunis (Tunisia). **Languages** Arabic, English, French. **Staff** 1.00 FTE, paid. **Finance** Oil and gas companies, responders, manufacturers and associations. Annual budget: 35,000 EUR. **Activities** Events/meetings; knowledge management/information dissemination; networking/liaising; training/education. **Events** *The Role of Volunteers in Pollution Response along the Coast and on the Shoreline* Hammamet (Tunisia) 2022, *Regional Workshop on Enhancing Oil Spill Preparedness and Response in the Adriatic and Mediterranean Regions* Opatija (Croatia) 2022, *Points to Consider in the Selection of Oil Spill Booms* Tunis (Tunisia) 2022, *Regional Workshop on Oil Spill Waste Management* Hammamet (Tunisia) 2021, *Tiered Preparedness for Wildlife Response in the Mediterranean Region* Tunis (Tunisia) 2021. **Publications** *MOIG Newsletter*.
Members Full in 12 countries:
Croatia, Cyprus, Denmark, Egypt, Finland, Greece, Libya, Malta, Netherlands, Tunisia, Türkiye, UK.
IGO Relations Cooperates with (2): *International Maritime Organization (IMO, #14102)*; *Regional Marine Pollution Emergency Response Centre for the Mediterranean Sea (REMPEC, #18795)*. **NGO Relations** Also links with technical partners, not specified. [2022.05.04/XF4816/t/F]

♦ Mediterranean Ombudsmen Network / see Association of Mediterranean Ombudsmen (#02802)
♦ Mediterranean Ophthalmological Society / see Mediterranean Society of Ophthalmology (#16679)
♦ Mediterranean Organization for Oncological Education and Research (inactive)

♦ Mediterranean Organization for Promotion and Science (MOPS) 16670

Address not obtained.

Aims Foster effective projects and a supportive environment for the promotion of the society's and institution's maximum potential. **Structure** Board of Trustees with members and councillors. Departments (3): Culture; Management and Governance; Science. **NGO Relations** Member of: *Euro-Mediterranean University (EMUNI, #05728)*. [2010/XJ0927/D]

♦ Mediterranean Orthodontic Integration Project (MOIP) 16671

Contact c/o SIDO, Via Gaggia 1, 20139 Milan MI, Italy. T. +39256808224. Fax +39258304804. E-mail: scientific@sido.it.
URL: http://www.sido.it/progetti_moip.asp

History Dec 2005, Cairo (Egypt). **Aims** Build a cultural bridge between the northern and southern sides of the Mediterranean; share orthodontic experiences in the different countries; facilitate the improvement both of the quality of educational programmes and the standard of patients' care. **Events** *Congress* Monte Carlo (Monaco) 2012, *Congress* Viareggio (Italy) 2010, *Congress* Venice (Italy) 2008.
Members Affiliated organizations in 17 countries:
Bulgaria, Croatia, Cyprus, Egypt, France, Greece, Israel, Italy, Lebanon, Luxembourg, Morocco, Serbia, Slovenia, Spain, Syrian AR, Tunisia, Türkiye.
Included in the above, 1 regional organization:
Arab Orthodontic Society (AOS, #01022). [2012/XJ6242/y/F]

♦ Mediterranean Phytopathological Union (MPU) 16672

Unione Fitopatologica Mediterranea

Sec-Treas Univ degli Studi, Fac di Agraria, Piazzale delle Cascine 28, 50144 Florence FI, Italy. T. +39553288279 – +39553288379. Fax +39553288273. E-mail: phymed@unifi.it.
Main Website: http://www.mpunion.eu

History 9 Jun 1962, Rome (Italy). Founded by Prof Antonio Ciccarone at first Meeting, Rome (Italy), 9 June 1962. Former names and other names: *Union phytopathlogique méditerranéenne* – former. **Aims** Disseminate and increase knowledge of phytopathology specific to the Mediterranean area considered as one *ecological* unit; establish and maintain relationships between phytopathologists and all those who are generally engaged in technical activities within the area, promoting personal contacts, collaboration and exchange of ideas and information. **Structure** Assembly of Members; Board, comprising President, Past-President, President elect, Secretary, Treasurer and 4 further members. **Languages** English. **Staff** 2.00 FTE, paid; 15.00 FTE, voluntary. **Finance** Sources: members' dues. **Activities** Events/meetings; networking/liaising; research and development; training/education. **Events** *Triennial Congress* Limassol (Cyprus) 2021, *Triennial Congress* Limassol (Cyprus) 2020, *Triennial Congress* Córdoba (Spain) 2017, *Triennial Congress* Istanbul (Turkey) 2014, *Triennial Congress* Rome (Italy) 2010. **Publications** *Phytopathologia Mediterranea* (3 a year).
Members Regular; Student. Organizations in 15 countries:
Australia, Canada, Denmark, Germany, Greece, Israel, Italy, Netherlands, New Zealand, Portugal, South Africa, Spain, Tunisia, UK, USA.
Associates in 31 countries:
Australia, Bosnia-Herzegovina, Brazil, Canada, Croatia, Denmark, Egypt, Germany, Greece, Hungary, India, Iran Islamic Rep, Iraq, Israel, Italy, Jordan, Lebanon, Malta, Morocco, Netherlands, New Zealand, Oman, Portugal, Serbia, Slovenia, South Africa, Spain, Tunisia, Türkiye, UK, USA.
IGO Relations Affiliated with (1): *European and Mediterranean Plant Protection Organization (EPPO, #07773)*. [2023.02.14/XF1273/F]

♦ Mediterranean Policy Centre (internationally oriented national body)
♦ Mediterranean Pollution Assessment and Control Programme / see MED POL – Programme for the Assessment and Control of Marine Pollution in the Mediterranean (#16691)
♦ Mediterranean Protected Areas Network / see Network of Marine Protected Area Managers in the Mediterranean (#17048)
♦ Mediterranean Regional Trust Fund for the Protection of the Mediterranean Sea Against Pollution / see Mediterranean Trust Fund (#16686)

♦ Mediterranean Sailing Union (MSU) 16673

Union méditerranéenne de voile (UMV)

SG c/o Yacht Club de Monaco, Quai Louis II, 98000 Monte Carlo, Monaco. T. +37793106300. Fax +37793508088. E-mail: ycm@yacht-club-monaco.mc.
Contact Fédération française de voile, 17 rue Henri Bocquillon, 75015 Paris, France. T. +33140603712. Fax +33140603737.
URL: http://www.ffvoile.net/umv/

History 2002. **Aims** Promote the sport of sailing in the region. **Structure** General Assembly (annual). Executive Committee, comprising President, Vice-President, Treasurer and 2 further members. **Languages** Arabic, English, French. **Finance** Members' dues. **Events** *General Assembly* 2010, *General Assembly* Monte Carlo (Monaco) 2008, *General Assembly* Almeria (Spain) 2005. **Publications** Bulletin.
Members National organizations in 13 countries:
Algeria, Croatia, Cyprus, France, Greece, Italy, Libya, Malta, Monaco, Morocco, Spain, Tunisia, Türkiye.
NGO Relations Affiliate member of: *World Sailing (#21760)*. [2010.07.29/XM2789/D]

♦ The Mediterranean Science Commission (CIESM) 16674

Commission internationale pour l'exploration scientifique de la Mer Méditerranée (CIESM) – Comisión Internacional para la Exploración Cientifica del Mar Mediterraneo

Dir Gen Villa Girasole, 16 bd de Suisse, Monte Carlo, 98000 Monte Carlo, Monaco. T. +37793303879. Fax +37792161195. E-mail: contact@ciesm.org.
URL: http://www.ciesm.org/

History 30 Mar 1910, Monaco, when present name was adopted, following recommendations, 27 Jul 1908, Geneva (Switzerland), of 9th International Geographical Congress for a proposed *Commission de la Méditerranée*. Having been delayed by World War I, the Constitutive Congress was held in Nov 1919, Madrid (Spain). Activities, again suspended during 1939-1949 by World War II, recommenced Sep 1949. Revised Statutes adopted Oct 1995; Dec 2009. Original title: *International Commission for Scientific Exploration of the Mediterranean Sea*. **Aims** Guide and coordinate development of research programmes on *marine* and *coastal environment* in the Mediterranean and in the Black Sea. **Structure** Plenary Assembly (every 3 years, at Congress); Board; Scientific Committees (6). **Languages** French. **Staff** 8.00 FTE, paid. **Finance** Members' dues (annual). **Activities** Research and development; events/meetings; knowledge management/information dissemination; guidance/assistance/consulting. **Events** *Triennial Congress* Marseille (France) 2013, *Triennial Congress* Venice (Italy) 2010, *Joint workshop to compare zooplankton ecology and methodologies between the Mediterranean and the North Atlantic* Heraklion (Greece) 2008, *World Conference on Marine Biodiversity* Valencia (Spain) 2008, *Triennial Congress* Istanbul (Turkey) 2007. **Publications** *CIESM Congress Proceedings* – series; *CIESM Science Series*; *CIESM Workshop Monographs* – series. *CIESM Atlas of Exotic Species in the Mediterranean* (2003); *CIESM Guide of Marine Institutes* (2003). Reports; atlases. **Information Services** *CIESM Bibliographic Database* – more than 6,500 titles indexed by themes, species and geographic domain.
Members Governments of 23 countries:
Algeria, Croatia, Cyprus, Egypt, France, Germany, Greece, Israel, Italy, Lebanon, Malta, Monaco, Morocco, Portugal, Romania, Russia, Slovenia, Spain, Switzerland, Syrian AR, Tunisia, Türkiye, Ukraine.
IGO Relations Relationship agreement with: *FAO (#09260)*. Observer to: *General Fisheries Commission for the Mediterranean (GFCM, #10112)*; *Intergovernmental Oceanographic Commission (IOC, #11496)*; *International Council for the Exploration of the Sea (ICES, #13021)*. Consultative Status with: *UNESCO (#20322)*. **NGO Relations** Links with a large number of organizations interested in the field, including: *International Council for Science (ICSU, inactive)*; *International Union for Conservation of Nature and Natural Resources (IUCN, #15766)*. [2020/XD1542/D*]

♦ Mediterranean Scientific Association of Environmental Protection (internationally oriented national body)
♦ Mediterranean Social Sciences Research Council (inactive)
♦ Mediterranean Society of Audiology / see Mediterranean Society of Otology and Audiology (#16680)
♦ Mediterranean Society of Chemotherapy / see Mediterranean Society of Chemotherapy and Infection (#16675)

♦ Mediterranean Society of Chemotherapy and Infection (MedSocChemI) 16675

Exec Dir 1st Klm Peanias-Markopoulou Ave, PC 19002, Peania, Greece. E-mail: z.ka@zita-congress.gr.

History 16 Oct 1976, Aci Castello (Italy), as *Mediterranean Society of Chemotherapy (ISC) – Société méditerranéenne de chimiothérapie*. Restructured under current title, 15 Nov 2013, when new statutes were adopted. Also known under the acronym *MSCI*. **Aims** Contribute to the science of chemotherapy and related fields in Mediterranean countries; ensure that production of chemotherapeutics reflects true requirements of science and clinical practice. **Structure** Board. **Activities** Events/meetings; publishing activities. **Events** *Congress* Thessaloniki (Greece) 2015, *Southeast European Conference* Thessaloniki (Greece) 2015, *Southeast European Conference* Bled (Slovenia) 2014, *Southeast European Conference* Istanbul (Turkey) 2013, *Southeast European Conference* Dubrovnik (Croatia) 2012.
Members Honorary, Active and Supporting, both individual and associate, cooperating in the development of pure or applied chemotherapy. Members in 29 countries:
Albania, Algeria, Bosnia-Herzegovina, Bulgaria, Croatia, Cyprus, Egypt, France, Greece, Israel, Italy, Jordan, Lebanon, Libya, Malta, Monaco, Montenegro, Morocco, North Macedonia, Portugal, Romania, Saudi Arabia, Serbia, Slovenia, Spain, Syrian AR, Tunisia, Türkiye, United Arab Emirates.
NGO Relations Member of: *Federation of European Societies for Chemotherapy and for Infections (FESCI, #09546)*; *International Society of Antimicrobial Chemotherapy (ISAC, #14925)*. [2017.03.10/XD0378/D]

♦ Mediterranean Society for Chronobiology (internationally oriented national body)

♦ Mediterranean Society of Coloproctology (MSCP) 16676

Société méditerranéenne de coloproctologie (SoMeCoP)

Treas Via Stazione di S Pietro 35 B, 00165 Rome RM, Italy.
URL: http://www.mscp-online.org/

History 1 Jun 1998, Rome (Italy), as *European and Mediterranean Coloproctology Association – Association européenne et méditerranéenne de coloproctologie*. **Aims** Gather into one association all surgeons and physicians from Mediterranean countries who have a special interest in coloproctology; encourage cultural exchanges among members. **Structure** Governing Council, consisting of President, Honorary President, Vice-President, Secretary, Treasurer. Committees (3): Scientific; Educational; Website and Communications. **Languages** English, French. **Staff** 15.00 FTE, paid. **Finance** Members' dues. **Activities** Events/meetings; training/education. **Events** *Biennial Congress* Thessaloniki (Greece) 2018, *Biennial Congress* Genoa (Italy) 2016, *Biennial Congress* Chioggia (Italy) 2014, *Biennial Congress* Madrid (Spain) 2012, *Congress* Thessaloniki (Greece) 2010. **Publications** *Techniques in Coloproctology* – official journal.
Members Medical doctors and scientists in 15 countries:
Albania, Algeria, Bosnia-Herzegovina, Egypt, France, Germany, Greece, Israel, Italy, Montenegro, Morocco, Serbia, Slovenia, Spain, Türkiye. [2020/XD8450/v/D]

♦ Mediterranean Society of Comparative Education (inactive)

♦ Mediterranean Society of Legal Medicine 16677

Société méditerranéenne de médecine légale (SMML)

Contact Service de Médecine Légale Univ, Farhat Harched, 4000 Sousse, Tunisia.
Gen Sec Fac de médecine de Toulouse, 37 allées Jules Guesde, 31000 Toulouse, France.

History 1976, Montpellier (France). **Languages** French. **Staff** 5.00 FTE, paid. **Activities** Knowledge management/information dissemination; events/meetings; research/documentation. **Events** *Journées Internationales* Paris (France) 2014, *Journées internationales / Biennial Meeting* Spain 2014, *Biennial Meeting* Paris (France) 2012, *Journées internationales / Biennial Meeting* Tozeur (Tunisia) 2010, *Journées internationales / Biennial Meeting* Marseille (France) 2008. **Publications** *Magazine de la société méditerranéenne de médicine légale*. Congress proceedings.
Members Individuals in 14 countries:
Algeria, Belgium, Egypt, France, Greece, Italy, Monaco, Morocco, Portugal, Romania, Serbia, Spain, Tunisia, Türkiye.
NGO Relations Instrumental in setting up: *Sevilla Working Party on Legal Medicine in Europe (no recent information)*. [2014.07.08/XD8267/D]

♦ Mediterranean Society of Lifestyle Medicine (internationally oriented national body)

♦ Mediterranean Society of Myology (MSM) 16678

Pres address not obtained.
URL: http://www.actamyologica.it/

History 4 Oct 1993, Ischia (Italy). **Aims** Unite experts in striated muscle diseases and neuromuscular disorders in the Mediterranean region; encourage research in the field. **Structure** General Meeting; Board; Executive Committee. **Languages** English. **Staff** 1.50 FTE, voluntary. **Finance** Sources: members' dues. **Activities** Events/meetings; training/education. **Events** *Congress* Uçhisar (Turkey) 2018, *Congress* Naples (Italy) 2015, *Congress* Athens (Greece) 2013, *Congress* Pisa (Italy) 2011, *Congress* Nicosia (Cyprus) 2009. **Publications** *Acta Myologica* (4 a year).

Members Founding; Active; Honorary. Individuals and organizations in 29 countries:
Albania, Algeria, Austria, Bosnia-Herzegovina, Bulgaria, Croatia, Cyprus, Egypt, France, Greece, Hungary, Israel, Italy, Jordan, Lebanon, Libya, Malta, Morocco, North Macedonia, Palestine, Portugal, Saudi Arabia, Serbia, Slovenia, Spain, Switzerland, Syrian AR, Tunisia, Türkiye. [2021.06.08/XD7396/**D**]

♦ Mediterranean Society of Ophthalmology (MSO) 16679

Société méditerranéenne d'ophtalmologie – Società Mediterranea di Oftalmologia

SG Centro Oftalmologico Bruno Lumbroso, Via A Broffero 7, 00195 Rome RM, Italy. E-mail: bruno.lumbroso@gmail.com.

History 1988, Rome (Italy). Also referred to as *Mediterranean Ophthalmological Society (MOS)*. **Aims** Coordinate efforts in countries of the Mediterranean so as to promote *continuing education*, scientific and *professional medical* exchange and support for joint research activities among countries of the Mediterranean basin. **Structure** General Assembly; Board, comprising Honorary President, 4 Vice Presidents, Past President, President and President Elect. **Languages** English, French. **Finance** Members' dues. **Events** *Congress* Algeria 2012, *Congress* Hammamet (Tunisia) 2009, *Congress* Rome (Italy) 2007, *Congress* Antalya (Turkey) 2004, *Congress* Alicante (Spain) 2002.

Members Active ophthalmologists and scientists practising in the Mediterranean area; Associate ophthalmologists and scientists from other countries. Members in 17 countries and territories:
Algeria, Bulgaria, Croatia, Egypt, France, Greece, Israel, Italy, Libya, Morocco, Palestine, Portugal, Romania, Serbia, Spain, Tunisia, Türkiye. [2016/XD7722/v/**D**]

♦ Mediterranean Society of Otology and Audiology (MSOA) 16680

Société méditerranéenne d'otologie et d'audiologie

Contact Hatay Sokak 4/8, 12 Shmuel Bait St, Kizilay, 06420 Ankara/Ankara, Türkiye. E-mail: mediotol@gmail.com.
Sec address not obtained.
URL: http://www.mediotol.org/

History 1987, Ostuni (Italy). Founded during the 1st international meeting for Mediterranean Countries. Former names and other names: *Mediterranean Society of Audiology* – former (1987). Registration: Turkey. **Aims** Investigate the science and practice of medicine, prevention, surgery and rehabilitation of *diseases* and *disorders* of the *ear* and related structures; promote the fields of otology and audiology in the Mediterranean countries; encourage the exchange of knowledge, medical education and training through lectures, meetings and symposia; promote and sponsor cooperative research among otologists, audiologists and the other professionals in the medical field in order to prevent, diagnose and treat diseases of the ear and related structures; promote friendly personal and academic relationships between all otolaryngologists in the region. **Structure** General Meeting (every 2 years). Executive Committee, including President (Chief Executive Officer), Past-President, Vice-President, Secretary, Treasurer and Academic Chairperson. **Languages** English. **Staff** None. **Finance** Sources: members' dues. **Activities** Events/meetings. **Events** *International Meeting* Ljubljana (Slovenia) 2022, *International Meeting* Ljubljana (Slovenia) 2020, *International Meeting* Israel 2018, *International Meeting* Ürgüp (Turkey) 2016, *International Meeting* Valencia (Spain) 2014. **Publications** *Journal of International Advanced Otology* (3 a year).

Members Ordinary; Honorary; Sustaining (corporate). Members in 12 countries:
Croatia, Egypt, France, Greece, Israel, Italy, Lebanon, Malta, Morocco, Spain, Tunisia, Türkiye. [2021/XD2484/**D**]

♦ Mediterranean Society of Pacing and Electrophysiology (MESPE) . . 16681

Contact Divisione di Cardiologia, Ospedaliera Riuniti, Via Giuseppe Melacrino 21, 89124 Reggio Calabria RC, Italy. T. +39965397160. Fax +39965397156. E-mail: franco.naccarella@fastwebnet.it.
Head Office Via Bruno Buozzi 22, 89100 Reggio Calabria RC, Italy.
URL: http://www.mespe.net/

Aims Promote the ethical, scientific and professional level of specialists in *cardiac* pacing and electrophysiology operating in the Mediterranean area; contribute to developing knowledge of cardiac pacing and electrophysiology and provide information; promote collaboration and exchange of scientific and professional experience of countries in the region with all national and international societies operating in this field. **Structure** General Assembly (annual). General Directive Council of 11 elected members and 2 founding members. **Finance** Free contributions; donations from public and private institutions. **Activities** Organizes meetings and scientific congresses. **Events** *Congress* Antalya (Turkey) 2014, *Congress* Malta 2007, *Congress* St Julian's (Malta) 2007, *Congress* Nice (France) 2006, *Congress* Malaga (Spain) 2005. **Members** Founding; Emeritus; Honorary; Ordinary; Associate; Institutional. Membership countries not specified. [2013/XD7557/**D**]

- ♦ Mediterranean Society of Pelvic Floor Disorders (internationally oriented national body)

♦ Mediterranean Society for Reproductive Medicine (MSRM) 16682

Address not obtained.
Pres address not obtained.
URL: http://www.medreproduction.org/

Events *Annual Congress* Barcelona (Spain) 2014, *International Meeting* Agios Nikolaos (Greece) 2013, *Annual Congress* Budva (Montenegro) 2012, *Annual Congress* Paris (France) 2011, *Annual Meeting* Florence (Italy) 2009. [2017/XM3572/**D**]

- ♦ Mediterranean Society of Therapy (inactive)
- ♦ Mediterranean Society of Tumor Marker Oncology (no recent information)
- ♦ Mediterranean Solar Council (no recent information)
- ♦ MEDITERRANEAN SOS Network (internationally oriented national body)
- ♦ Mediterranean Stroke Society (inactive)

♦ Mediterranean Studies Association (MSA) 16683

Exec Dir Box 79351, Dartmouth MA 02747, USA. T. +15089798687.
URL: http://www.mediterraneanstudies.org/

History 1994. Incorporated in the State of Massachusetts (USA). **Aims** Promote scholarly study of the Mediterranean region. **Structure** Officers: President; Past-President; Executive Director; Treasurer/Secretary. **Finance** Members' dues. **Events** *Annual Congress* Athens (Greece) 2015, *Annual Congress* Pula (Croatia) 2012, *Annual Congress* Corfu (Greece) 2011, *Annual Congress* Salamanca (Spain) 2010, *Annual Congress* Cagliari (Italy) 2009. **Publications** *Mediterranean Studies* (annual). [2015/XG9487/**D**]

- ♦ Mediterranean Study Commission / see Euro-Mediterranean Study Commission (#05727)

♦ Mediterranean Table Tennis Union (MTTU) 16684

Pres c/o FITET, Stadio Olimpico, Curva Nord, 00135 Rome RM, Italy. E-mail: antonellaflori@fitet.org – mttu@fitet.org – mttu@monaco.mc.
URL: http://www.mttu.org/

Aims Promote and stimulate table-tennis in the Mediterranean. **Structure** Executive Committee, comprising President, Deputy President, General Secretary, Treasurer and up to 6 Vice-Presidents. **Languages** Arabic, English, French. **Staff** Voluntary. **Finance** Members' dues (annual): euro 150. **Activities** Promotion plans, development and updating programmes; Mediterranean championships; seminars for coaches; women tournaments; cadet and junior tournaments.

Members Associations in 25 countries and territories:
Albania, Algeria, Bosnia-Herzegovina, Croatia, Cyprus, Egypt, France, Greece, Israel, Italy, Lebanon, Libya, Malta, Monaco, Montenegro, Morocco, Palestine, Portugal, San Marino, Serbia, Slovenia, Spain, Syrian AR, Tunisia, Türkiye.

NGO Relations Recognized by: *International Table Tennis Federation (ITTF, #15650)*. [2012.08.06/XD4772/**D**]

- ♦ Mediterranean Towns and Territories Association (no recent information)

♦ Mediterranean Travel Association (META) 16685

Contact address not obtained. T. +33442215826. Fax +33442631512.
SG address not obtained.

History 7 Dec 2005. **Aims** Ensure sustainable development and excellence of tourism professionals in the Mediterranean region. **Finance** Members' dues. **Activities** Organizes lectures and symposia. **IGO Relations** Affiliate member of: *World Tourism Organization (UNWTO, #21861)*. [2012/XM0918/**D**]

- ♦ Mediterranean Trust Fund / see Mediterranean Trust Fund (#16686)

♦ Mediterranean Trust Fund (MTF) 16686

Contact c/o Coordinating Unit, UNEP/MEDU, Vassileos Konstantinou 48, PO Box 18019, 116 10 Athens, Greece. T. +302107273123. Fax +302107253196.

History 1979. Established in accordance with Article 24 of *Convention for the Protection of the Marine Environment and the Coastal Region of the Mediterranean (Barcelona Convention, 1976)*, within the framework of *Mediterranean Action Plan (MAP, #16638)* as a fund administered by *UNEP (#20299)*. Former names and other names: *Mediterranean Regional Trust Fund for the Protection of the Mediterranean Sea Against Pollution* – full title; *Mediterranean Trust Fund* – former; *Trust Fund for the Protection of the Mediterranean Sea Against Pollution* – former; *Fonds d'affectation spéciale pour la protection de la Mer méditerranéenne contre la pollution* – former. **Finance** Sources: contributions of member/participating states. Annual budget: 5,000,000 EUR (2020). **IGO Relations** Supports: *Priority Actions Programme / Regional Activity Centre (PAP/RAC, #18501)*; *Regional Activity Centre for Specially Protected Areas (RAC/SPA, #18746)*; *Regional Marine Pollution Emergency Response Centre for the Mediterranean Sea (REMPEC, #18795)*. [2008.10.19/XF8764/f/**E***]

- ♦ Mediterranean Union of Surveyors (#20460)
- ♦ Mediterranean Union of Thoracic Pathology (inactive)

♦ Mediterranean Universities Union (UNIMED) 16687

Union des universités de la Méditerranée – Unione delle Università del Mediterraneo

Dir Corso Vittorio Emanuele II 244, 00186 Rome RM, Italy. T. +39668581430. Fax +39689290828. E-mail: unimed@uni-med.net.
URL: http://www.uni-med.net/

History Oct 1991, Rome (Italy). Founded by initiative of the *'University "Sapienza" of Rome'*. Former names and other names: *University of the Mediterranean* – former; *Université de la Méditerranée* – former. **Aims** Develop research and education in the Euro-Mediterranean area in order to contribute to scientific, cultural, social and economic cooperation. **Structure** Board of Directors; Headquarters located in Rome (Italy). Offices in Nablus (Palestine), Rabat (Morocco), Evora (Portugal). **Languages** English, French, Italian. **Staff** 20.00 FTE, paid. **Finance** Sources: members' dues. EC funding for EU projects. **Activities** Knowledge management/information dissemination; networking/liaising; research/documentation. **Events** *Arab-Euro Conference on Higher Education* Murcia (Spain) 2018, *Round Table on Higher Education in the Framework of the European Neighbourhood Policy* Brussels (Belgium) 2015, *General Assembly* Lecce (Italy) 2011, *General Assembly* Tunis (Tunisia) 2008, *International seminar* Istanbul (Turkey) 2003. **Information Services** *Study Centre Franco Rizzi*.

Members Universities (150) in 24 countries:
Albania, Algeria, Cyprus, Egypt, Finland, France, Greece, Iraq, Italy, Jordan, Kosovo, Lebanon, Libya, Mauritania, Morocco, Oman, Palestine, Portugal, Qatar, Spain, Syrian AR, Tunisia, Türkiye, Yemen.

NGO Relations Member of (5): *Association for the Documentation, Preservation and Enhancement of the Euro-Mediterranean Cultural Heritage (HERIMED, no recent information)*; *Euro-Mediterranean University (EMUNI, #05728)*; *EuroMed Permanent University Forum (EPUF, #05731)*; *Permanent Conference of Mediterranean Audiovisual Operators (COPEAM, #18320)*; *Sustainable Development Solutions Network (SDSN, #20054)*. Partner of (2): *Asociación de las Camaras de Comercio e Industria del Mediterraneo (ASCAME, #02112)*; *United Nations Academic Impact (UNAI, #20516)*. [2022.10.20/XF2630/**D**]

- ♦ Mediterranean Urological Association (no recent information)
- ♦ Mediterranean Water Charter (1992 treaty)
- ♦ Mediterranean Water Institute (#11323)
- ♦ Mediterranean Wetlands / see The Mediterranean Wetlands Initiative (#16688)

♦ The Mediterranean Wetlands Initiative (MedWet) 16688

Secretariat La Tour du Valat, Le Sambuc, 13200 Arles, France. T. +33490970678. Fax +33490972019. E-mail: info@medwet.org.
URL: https://medwet.org/

History Set up 1991, under *Convention on Wetlands of International Importance Especially as Waterfowl Habitat (Convention on Wetlands, 1971)*. Previously also referred to as *Mediterranean Wetlands*. **Aims** Ensure and support effective conservation of the functions and values of Mediterranean wetlands and sustainable use of their resources and services. **Structure** Mediterranean Wetlands Committee; Steering Group; Secretariat. Mediterranean Wetlands Observatory; MedWet Scientific and Technical Network. **Languages** Arabic, English, French. **Staff** 3.00 FTE, paid. **Finance** Members' dues. Project budgets. Secretariat financed by host country. **Activities** Knowledge management/information dissemination; capacity building; awareness raising; networking/liaising; projects/programmes. **Events** *Atelier International sur la Mise en Oeuvre de Solutions Fondées sur la Nature pour Lutter contre le Changement Climatique* Marseille (France) 2019, *Meeting* Paris (France) 2016, *Meeting* Bucharest (Romania) 2012, *Meeting* Bastia (France) 2010, *Meeting* Changwon (Korea Rep) 2009. **Publications** Surveys; strategies; reports.

Members Participating countries (28):
Albania, Algeria, Andorra, Bosnia-Herzegovina, Bulgaria, Croatia, Cyprus, Egypt, France, Greece, Israel, Italy, Jordan, Lebanon, Libya, Malta, Monaco, Montenegro, Morocco, North Macedonia, Palestine, Portugal, Serbia, Slovenia, Spain, Syrian AR, Tunisia, Türkiye.

IGO Relations Organizations and treaties involved: *Convention on the Conservation of European Wildlife and Natural Habitats (Bern convention, 1979)*; *Convention for the Protection of the Marine Environment and the Coastal Region of the Mediterranean (Barcelona Convention, 1976)*; *Council of Europe (CE, #04881)*; *European Commission (EC, #06633)*; *Global Environment Facility (GEF, #10346)*. Partner of: *Global Alliances for Water and Climate (GAfWaC, #10230)*; *Mediterranean Action Plan (MAP, #16638)*. **NGO Relations** Member of: *International Federation for Sustainable Development and Fight to Poverty in the Mediterranean-Black Sea (FISPMED, #13562)*. Partner of: *Wetlands International (#20928)*. [2021/XE2736/**E**]

- ♦ Mediterranean Women's Forum / see International Mediterranean Women's Forum (#14143)
- ♦ Mediterranean Women's Fund (internationally oriented national body)
- ♦ Mediterranean Youth Orchestra (#17788)
- ♦ Mediterraneo Senza Handicap (internationally oriented national body)
- ♦ Mediterraneo Senza Handicap Onlus / see Mediterraneo Senza Handicap

♦ Medizinische Gesellschaft für System- und Regulationsdiagnostik (EAV) 16689

International EAV Association

Manager Vökstr 36, 86150 Augsburg, Germany. T. +4982120919145. Fax +49821517428. E-mail: info@imgeav.de.
URL: http://www.eav.de/

History 1956. Former names and other names: *Internationale Medizinische Gesellschaft für Elektroakupunktur nach Dr. Voll* – former (1956); *Internationale Medizinische Gesellschaft für Elektroakupunktur nach Voll (IMGEAV)* – former. **Activities** Organizes seminars. **NGO Relations** Member of: *European Council of Doctors for Plurality in Medicine (ECPM, #06816)*. [2016/XD7209/**D**]

- ♦ Medjunarodni centar za mir (internationally oriented national body)
- ♦ **MEDMA** Middle East Drymix Mortar Association (#16759)
- ♦ **MEDMARAVIS** Mediterranean Marine Bird Association (#16661)
- ♦ Mednarodna Fakulteta za Drzbene in Poslovne Studije (internationally oriented national body)
- ♦ Mednarodna komisija za varstvo Alp / see CIPRA International (#03930)
- ♦ Mednarodna Znanstivena Konferenca Manjsin za Jutrisnjo Evropo (#14808)
- ♦ Mednarodna Zveza Splavarjev (#15691)
- ♦ Mednarodni Institut Arhivskih Znanosti Maribor / see International Institute for Archival Science of Trieste and Maribor (#13862)
- ♦ Mednarodni Institut Arhivskih Znanosti, Univerze v Maribor / see International Institute for Archival Science of Trieste and Maribor (#13862)
- ♦ Mednarodni Institut za Arhivsko Znanost Trst – Maribor (#13862)
- ♦ Mednarodni Inštitut za Bližnjevzhodne in Balkanske Študije (#13901)
- ♦ Mednarodni Znanstveni Komite za Preucevanje Alp (#14804)

- ♦ Mednarodno zdruzenje za pospesevanje inovantivnih pristopov k resevanju globalnih izzivov (#11687)
- ♦ MedNetRice Network / see FAO Inter-Regional Cooperative Research Network on Rice in the Mediterranean Climate Areas (#09263)
- ♦ MEDO – Mediterranean Environment and Development Observatory (internationally oriented national body)
- ♦ MEDPAN / see Network of Marine Protected Area Managers in the Mediterranean (#17048)
- ♦ **MEDPAN** Network of Marine Protected Area Managers in the Mediterranean (#17048)

♦ MedPharmPlast Europe (MPPE) 16690

Contact Ave de Cortenbergh 71, 1000 Brussels, Belgium. T. +3227396388.
URL: http://www.medpharmplasteurope.org/

History 2014. A sector group of *European Plastics Converters (EuPC, #08216)*. **Aims** Work and consult with European legislators to help maintain a dynamic and innovative industry; work to be the platform where companies involved in *plastics* for *medical* devices and *pharmaceutical packaging* can meet, discuss and share information at European level. **Structure** General Assembly. **Activities** Knowledge management/information dissemination; advocacy/lobbying/activism; events/meetings; monitoring/evaluation. **NGO Relations** A Sector Group of: *European Plastics Converters (EuPC, #08216).* [2022/XM7655/E]

- ♦ MED POL / see MED POL – Programme for the Assessment and Control of Marine Pollution in the Mediterranean (#16691)
- ♦ **MED POL** MED POL – Programme for the Assessment and Control of Marine Pollution in the Mediterranean (#16691)

♦ MED POL – Programme for the Assessment and Control of Marine Pollution in the Mediterranean (MED POL) 16691

Coordination MAP/RCU, MEDU-UNEP, Vassileos Konstantinou 48, PO Box 18019, 116 10 Athens, Greece. T. +302107273100. E-mail: medpol@unepmap.gr.
URL: https://www.unenvironment.org/unepmap/

History 1975. Founded within the framework of the UNEP coordinated Mediterranean Action Plan, currently *Mediterranean Action Plan (MAP, #16638)*. Phase II launched 1981; Phase III (1996-2005) launched 1-4 Jul 1996, Montpellier (France); Phase IV in 2006 on the occasion of Meetings of Contracting Parties to the *Convention for the Protection of the Marine Environment and the Coastal Region of the Mediterranean (Barcelona Convention, 1976)*. Relevant protocols: *Protocol for the Protection of the Mediterranean Sea against Pollution from Land-Based Sources and Activities (LBS Protocol, 1980)* and *Amendments to the Protocol for the Protection of the Mediterranean Sea Against Pollution from Land-based Sources and Activities (1996)*; *Protocol for the Prevention of Pollution of the Mediterranean Sea by Dumping from Ships and Aircraft (Dumping Protocol, 1976)* and *Amendments to the Protocol for the Prevention of Pollution of the Mediterranean Sea by Dumping from Ships and Aircraft (1995)*; *Protocol on the Prevention of Pollution of the Mediterranean Sea by Transboundary Movements of Hazardous Wastes and Their Disposal (1996)*. Former names and other names: *Programme for Pollution Assessment and Control in the Mediterranean Sea* – former; *Mediterranean Marine Pollution Assessment and Control Programme (MED POL)* – former; *Programme for the Assessment and Control of Pollution in the Mediterranean Sea* – former; *MED POL – Programme for the Assessment and Control of Pollution in the Mediterranean Sea* – former; *Mediterranean Pollution Assessment and Control Programme (MED POL)* – alias. **Aims** Assist Mediterranean countries in the implementation of three major protocols of the Barcelona Convention, namely the Protocol for the Protection of the Mediterranean Sea against Pollution from Land-Based Sources, the Protocol for the Prevention of Pollution in the Mediterranean Sea by Dumping from Ships and Aircraft and the Protocol on the Prevention of Pollution of the Mediterranean Sea by Transboundary Movements of Hazardous Wastes and their Disposal. **Activities** Monitoring/evaluation; projects/programmes; standards/guidelines. [2019/XK1790/E*]

- ♦ MED POL – Programme for the Assessment and Control of Pollution in the Mediterranean Sea / see MED POL – Programme for the Assessment and Control of Marine Pollution in the Mediterranean (#16691)
- ♦ **MEDRC** Middle East Desalination Research Centre (#16758)
- ♦ MedReg / see Association of Mediterranean Energy Regulators (#02800)
- ♦ **MEDREG** Association of Mediterranean Energy Regulators (#02800)
- ♦ MedRen – Medieval and Renaissance International Music Conference (meeting series)
- ♦ **MedRice Network** FAO Inter-Regional Cooperative Research Network on Rice in the Mediterranean Climate Areas (#09263)
- ♦ MedShare (internationally oriented national body)
- ♦ **MedSocChemI** Mediterranean Society of Chemotherapy and Infection (#16675)
- ♦ MEDSOS – MEDITERRANEAN SOS Network (internationally oriented national body)

♦ MedTech Europe 16692

CEO Rue Joseph II 40, 1000 Brussels, Belgium. T. +3223009643. E-mail: info@medtecheurope.org.
Events Manager address not obtained.
URL: http://www.medtecheurope.org/

History Oct 2012. Founded by *European Diagnostic Manufacturers Association (EDMA, inactive)* and *EUCOMEDC (inactive)*. Single entity set up Nov 2016. Registration: Banque-Carrefour des Entreprises, No/ID: 0508.570.208, Start date: 19 Dec 2012, Belgium; EU Transparency Register, No/ID: 433743725252-26, Start date: 26 Dec 2016. **Aims** Make innovative *medical* technology available to more people, while helping *healthcare* systems towards a sustainable path. **Structure** Board; Secretariat. **Staff** 40.00 FTE, paid. **Activities** Events/meetings; knowledge management/information dissemination; politics/policy/regulatory; training/education. **Events** *The MedTech Forum* Barcelona (Spain) 2022, *European Value-Based Procurement Conference* Brussels (Belgium) 2022, *European Medtech Forum* 2021, *European Medtech Forum* Berlin (Germany) 2020, *European Value-Based Procurement Conference* Brussels (Belgium) 2019. **Publications** *Focus on MedTech* (26 a year) – newsletter.
Members Corporate (106); Associate Corporate (7); National Assocations (49). National associations in 24 countries:
Austria, Belgium, Bulgaria, Czechia, Denmark, Finland, France, Germany, Greece, Hungary, Ireland, Italy, Netherlands, Norway, Poland, Portugal, Romania, Russia, Slovakia, Slovenia, Spain, Sweden, Switzerland, Türkiye, UK.
Included in the above, 2 organizations listed in this Yearbook:
EDANA, the voice of nonwovens (EDANA, #05353); Sterile Barrier Association (SBA, #19983).
Associate national members in 6 countries:
Germany, Hungary, Ireland, Poland, Russia, Türkiye.
Included in the above, 2 organizations listed in this Yearbook:
European Association of the Surgical Suture Industry (EASSI, #06243); Middle East Medical Devices and Diagnostics Trade Association (Mecomed, #16772).
IGO Relations *WHO (#20950)*. **NGO Relations** Member of (9): *Business and Industry Advisory Committee to the OECD (BIAC, #03385); Comité européen de normalisation (CEN, #04162)* (Associate); *Critical Raw Materials Alliance (CRM Alliance, #04959)* (Associate); *European Alliance for Cardiovascular Health (EACH, #05863); European Forum for Good Clinical Practice (EFGCP, #07313); European Institute for Innovation through Health Data (i-HD, #07561); European Policy Centre (EPC, #08240); Federation of European and International Associations Established in Belgium (FAIB, #09508); Health First Europe (HFE, #10881).* [2022/XJ9566/y/F]

- ♦ **Med-TSO** Association of the Mediterranean Transmission System Operators (#02803)
- ♦ MEDU – Mid-European Democratic Union (inactive)
- ♦ Medunarodni Centar za Podvodnu Arheologiju u Zadru (internationally oriented national body)
- ♦ Medunarodno Udruzenje za Cannabis kao Lijek / see International Association for Cannabinoid Medicines (#11754)
- ♦ MED-UOG – Mediterranean Association for Ultrasound in Obstetrics and Gynecology (no recent information)
- ♦ Medurable (internationally oriented national body)

♦ Med-Vet-Net Association (MVNA) 16693

Project Manager ANSES, 14 rue Pierre et Marie Curie, 94701 Maisons-Alfort CEDEX, France. T. +33149773868. E-mail: mvncoord@anses.fr.
URL: https://www.mvnassociation.org/

History Developed out of a European Network of Excellence, which ran Sep 2004 until Oct 2009. Former names and other names: *Association Med-Vet-Net de Recherche sur les Zoonoses* – former. Registration: RNA, No/ID: W941005117, Start date: May 2009, France. **Aims** Promote a One Health approach to combat zoonoses and antimicrobial resistance (AMR); support a healthy and sustainable food supply chain across Europe (and beyond). **Structure** Governing Board; Administration Bureau; Scientific Committee. **Activities** Events/meetings; research/documentation. **Events** *One Health EJP Annual Scientific Meeting – OHEJPASM* Copenhagen (Denmark) 2021.
Members Scientific partners (21) in 14 countries:
Austria, Belgium, Denmark, Finland, France, Germany, Ireland, Italy, Netherlands, Norway, Poland, Spain, Sweden, UK. [2021.06.16/AA1824/D]

- ♦ **MedWet** The Mediterranean Wetlands Initiative (#16688)
- ♦ MedWish International (internationally oriented national body)
- ♦ Medzinarodna Agentúra pre Prevenciu Kriminality, Trestné Pravo a Súdnictvo (internationally oriented national body)
- ♦ MEEA – Middle East Economic Association (internationally oriented national body)
- ♦ **MEEA** Middle East e-Learning Association (#16769)
- ♦ MEEDA – Middle East Eating Disorders Association (internationally oriented national body)
- ♦ Meertalig Europa (internationally oriented national body)
- ♦ Meeting for African Collaboration (meeting series)
- ♦ Meeting of Central European Presidents (meeting series)
- ♦ Meeting of the Chairmen of Latin American and Spanish Employers' Organizations (meeting series)
- ♦ Meeting of the Chief Statisticians of the Nordic Countries (meeting series)
- ♦ Meeting of Commonwealth Correctional Administrators (meeting series)

♦ Meeting Design Institute (MDI) 16694

Pres/CEO Oude Vaartstraat 43, 2300 Turnhout, Belgium. T. +3214448831. Fax +3214420661. E-mail: info@meetingsupport.org.
URL: http://www.meetingsupport.org/

History 2006. Former names and other names: *Meeting Support Institute (MSI)* – former (2006 to 2014). **Aims** Globally develop and promote the discipline of meeting design in order to improve the quality, impact and relevance of meetings and conferences. **Structure** Board, including President. **Languages** English. **Staff** 3.50 FTE, paid. Voluntary. **Finance** Members' dues. Other sources: sponsors; stand sales; catalogue sales; dinners; conferences. **Activities** Events/meetings; training/education; accreditation/certification. **Events** *FRESH Annual Conference on Designing Effective Meetings* Turnhout (Belgium) 2019, *FRESH Annual Conference on Designing Effective Meetings* Basel (Switzerland) 2018, *FRESH Annual Conference on Designing Effective Meetings* Barcelona (Spain) 2015, *FRESH Annual Conference on Designing Effective Meetings / FRESH Conference* Copenhagen (Denmark) 2014, *FRESH Annual Conference on Designing Effective Meetings / FRESH Conference* Copenhagen (Denmark) 2013. **Publications** *MDI Newsletter*; *Meetings Technology* – magazine. Catalogue; videos. **Information Services** *Knowledge Base*.
Members Companies (21) in 16 countries:
Austria, Belgium, Canada, China, Denmark, France, Germany, Italy, Netherlands, Norway, Slovakia, Spain, Sweden, Switzerland, UK, USA. [2021/XM4549/j/E]

- ♦ Meeting of Directors of Nordic Fire Prevention Associations (meeting series)
- ♦ Meeting of Directors of United Nations Training, Research and Planning Institutes (meeting series)
- ♦ Meeting of European Heart Foundations (meeting series)
- ♦ Meeting of Foreign Relations Ministers of the "Liberator's Corridor" (meeting series)
- ♦ Meeting of Foreign Relations Ministers of the Plata Basin Countries (meeting series)
- ♦ Meeting of the Group of Experts of the United Nations Programme in Public Administration and Finance / see United Nations Committee of Experts on Public Administration (#20542)
- ♦ Meeting of Heads of Nordic Exporting Organizations (meeting series)
- ♦ Meeting of Ministers of Health in the Andean Region (meeting series)
- ♦ Meeting of Ministers Responsible for the Economic Integration of Central America (meeting series)
- ♦ Meeting of Ministers Responsible for Transport in Central America (meeting series)
- ♦ Meeting of Ministers of Transport and Public Works of the Countries of the Cono Sur (meeting series)
- ♦ Meeting Planners International / see Meeting Professionals International (#16695)

♦ Meeting Professionals International (MPI) 16695

Pres and CEO Intl HQ, 2711 Lyndon B Johnson Freeway, Ste 600, Dallas TX 75234, USA. T. +19727023000. Fax +19727023070. E-mail: feedback@mpiweb.org.
Canada Office 6519-B Mississauga Rd, Mississauga ON L5N 1A6, Canada. T. +19052864807. Fax +19055677191. E-mail: emea@mpiweb.org.
URL: http://www.mpiweb.org/

History 1972, Chicago IL (USA), as *Meeting Planners International*. Present name adopted Jun 1994. **Aims** Provide innovative and relevant education, networking opportunities and business exchanges; act as a prominent voice for promotion and growth of the industry. **Structure** Board of Directors; Executive Committee. **Languages** English. **Staff** 70.00 FTE, paid. **Finance** Budget (annual): US$ 20 million. **Activities** Events/meetings; certification/accreditation; research/documentation. **Events** *World Education Congress* Las Vegas, NV (USA) 2021, *World Education Congress* Grapevine, TX (USA) 2020, *EMEC : European Meetings and Events Conference* The Hague (Netherlands) 2019, *World Education Congress* Toronto, ON (Canada) 2019, *World Education Congress* Indianapolis, IN (USA) 2018. **Publications** *TMP The Meeting Professional*.
Members Chapters (70) represent about 17,000 meeting professionals, mainly in North America, but in a total of 65 countries. Chapters in 21 countries:
Belgium, Brazil, Canada, Denmark, Finland, France, Germany, Ireland, Italy, Japan, Korea Rep, Mexico, Netherlands, Norway, Poland, Spain, Sweden, Switzerland, Türkiye, UK, USA.
IGO Relations Affiliate member of: *World Tourism Organization (UNWTO, #21861)*. **NGO Relations** Member of: *Events Industry Council (EIC, #09212); Joint Meetings Industry Council (JMIC, #16140).* [2019/XG4468/t/F]

- ♦ Meeting Support Institute / see Meeting Design Institute (#16694)
- ♦ MEEUC – Monash European and EU Centre, Melbourne (internationally oriented national body)
- ♦ ME / see European Movement International (#07825)

♦ MEF 16696

Main Office 6033 W Century Blvd, Ste 1107, Los Angeles CA 90045, USA. T. +13106422800.
URL: http://www.mef.net/

History 2001. **Aims** Develop a global federation of network, cloud and technology providers in establishing dynamic, assured, and certified services that empower enterprise digital transformation. **Structure** Board of Directors. Committees (4): Technical; Certification; Service Operations; Marketing. **Activities** Awards/prizes/competitions; certification/accreditation; training/education; events/meetings. **Events** *Carrier ethernet world congress* Madrid (Spain) 2006. **Members** Organizations (over 220). Membership countries not specified. **NGO Relations** *Small Cell Forum (#19312).* [2021/XJ8748/F]

- ♦ **MEF** Major Economies Forum on Energy and Climate (#16552)
- ♦ **MEFMA** Middle East Facility Management Association (#16763)
- ♦ **MEFMI** Macroeconomic and Financial Management Institute of Eastern and Southern Africa (#16539)
- ♦ MEF – Miners' European Federation (inactive)
- ♦ **MEFOMP** Middle East Federation of Organizations of Medical Physics (#16764)
- ♦ **MEFS** Middle East Fertility Society (#16765)

♦ Megacities Alliance for Water and Climate (MAWAC) 16697

Contact c/o UNESCO – IHP, 7 place de Fontenoy, 75007 Paris, France. E-mail: a.makarigakis@unesco.org.
URL: http://eaumega.org/

History Need to establish MAWAC identified, 2015, with a declaration signed by participants of the 1st International Conference on "Megacities Water and Global Change" (Eaumega), during 21st Conference of Parties on Climate Change, Dec 2015, Paris (France). Founders: UNESCO *International Hydrological Programme (IHP, #13826)*, ARCEAU-Idf, SIAAP and *Local Governments for Sustainability (ICLEI, #16507)*. Establishment period 2016-2018. Previously also referred to as *Megacities Alliance for Water under Climate Change (MAWac)*. Will be formally founded Dec 2020, at 2nd Conference. **Aims** Provide a platform for Megacities to share experiences and challenges, propose solutions; obtain access to technical and financial support for programmes and projects enabling them to successfully overcome the challenges of *climate change*. **Structure** Founders; Steering Committee; Secretariat. Regional alliances: Latin America and the Caribbean *MAWAC-LAC*; Asia and the Pacific *MAWAC-APAC*; Europe and North America *MAWAC-ENA*. Working Groups. **Languages** English, French, Spanish. **Staff** 9.00 FTE, paid. **Finance** Sources: donations; members' dues. Annual budget: 100,000 USD. **Activities** Events/meetings. **Events** *International Conference on Water, Megacities and Global Change* Paris (France) 2022, *International Conference on Water, Megacities and Global Change* Paris (France) 2020, *Meeting on Water, Megacities and Global Change* Paris (France) 2020. **Publications** *Water, Megacities and Global Change: Portraits of 16 Emblematic Cities of the World*.
Members Expected membership 40 megacities in 22 countries:
Argentina, Brazil, Chile, China, Colombia, Congo DR, France, India, Indonesia, Iran Islamic Rep, Japan, Malaysia, Mexico, Nigeria, Pakistan, Peru, Philippines, Thailand, Türkiye, UK, USA, Vietnam.
IGO Relations Part of: *Global Alliances for Water and Climate (GAfWaC, #10230)*. [2022/XM5940/**C**]

♦ Megacities Alliance for Water under Climate Change / see Megacities Alliance for Water and Climate (#16697)

♦ Mega-Cities Project 16698

Pres 34 Old Mountain Rd, Nyack NY 10960, USA. T. +18455983474. E-mail: janice@mega-cities.net.
URL: http://www.megacitiesproject.org/

History Aug 1986. Incorporated in the State of New York (USA), 1988. **Aims** Increase social justice, ecological sustainability, political participation and economic vitality. **Structure** Board of Directors; International Advisory Committee; Local Teams. **Languages** English, French, Portuguese, Spanish. **Staff** Voluntary. **Finance** Private foundations; government and international agencies; corporate contributions; income through consulting, research, training programmes. **Activities** Research and development; research/documentation; training/education; guidance/assistance/consulting; monitoring/evaluation; events/meetings; projects/programmes; awards/prizes/competitions. **Events** *Annual coordinators meeting* Jakarta (Indonesia) 1993. **Publications** *The Importance of Personhood: The Olympics and the Struggle for the Right to the City* (2019); *Slums: New Visions for an Enduring Global Phenomenon: Emerging Themes, Future Research and Next Steps* (2018); *FAVELA: Four Decades of Living on the Edge* (2010) by Janice Perlman; *The Dynamics of Urban Poverty in Rio de Janeiro – 1969-2005* (2008) by J Perlman; *The Myth of Marginality: Urban Poverty and Politics in Rio de Janeiro*. Articles. **Members** Not a membership organization. **IGO Relations** *ECOSOC (#05331)*; *Inter-American Development Bank (IDB, #11427)*; *International Bank for Reconstruction and Development (IBRD, #12317)* (World Bank); *OECD (#17693)*; *UNDP (#20292)*; *United Nations Human Settlements Programme (UN-Habitat, #20572)*; *United States Agency for International Development (USAID)*; *WHO (#20950)*. Associated with Department of Global Communications of the United Nations. **NGO Relations** *Ashoka – Innovators for the Public (#01248)*; *Council on Foreign Relations (CFR)*; *Ford Foundation (#09858)*; *Global Vision Corporation (#10648)*; *Henry Luce Foundation*; *Rockefeller Brothers Fund (RBF)*; *Synergos (#20082)*; *Tinker Foundation*; *W K Kellogg Foundation (WKKF)*. [2019.06.20/XF1589/**F**]

♦ MegaFlorestais 16699

Coordinator c/o RRI, 2715 M St NW, Ste 300, Washington DC 20007, USA. T. +12024703900. Fax +12029443315.
URL: http://www.megaflorestais.org/

History Established Sep 2005, Beijing (China), at a conference co-organized by *Rights and Resources Initiative (RRI, #18947)*, by leaders from Brazil, China, USA and Mexico. Full title: *MegaFlorestais – An Informal Network of Public Forest Agency Leaders*. **Aims** Advance international dialogue and exchange on transitions in *forest* governance, forest industry and the role of public forest agencies. **Structure** Co-Chairs; Secretariat, provided by *Rights and Resources Initiative (RRI, #18947)*. **Languages** Chinese, English, French, Portuguese, Spanish. **Staff** None. **Finance** Funding from members and *Rights and Resources Initiative (RRI, #18947)*. **Activities** Events/meetings; networking/liaising; publishing activities. **Events** *Annual Meeting* Vidsel (Sweden) 2018, *Annual Meeting* Vancouver, BC (Canada) 2017, *Annual Meeting* China 2016, *Annual Meeting* Cusco (Peru) 2015, *Annual Meeting* Buea (Cameroon) 2014. **Publications** *10 Years of MegaFlorestais: A Public Forest Agency Leaders' Retrospective* (2016); *Rethinking Forest Regulations: Overcoming the challenges of regulatory reform* (2016); *Public Forest Agencies in the Twenty-first Century: Driving change through transparency, tenure reform, citizen involvement and improved governance* (2014).
Members Forest government agencies of 11 countries, representing 50% of the world's forest:
Brazil, Cameroon, Canada, China, Congo DR, India, Indonesia, Mexico, Peru, Sweden, USA.
IGO Relations *FAO (#09260)*; *United Nations (UN, #20515)*. [2021/XJ7559/**F***]

♦ MegaFlorestais – An Informal Network of Public Forest Agency Leaders / see MegaFlorestais (#16699)
♦ MEGAGA – Mediterranean and Middle East Gerontological and Geriatric Association (no recent information)
♦ MEGA – Métodos Efectivos en Geometria Algebraica (meeting series)
♦ **MEGA** Middle East Gases Association (#16766)
♦ **MEGA** Middle East Gymnastics Association (#16767)
♦ MEGAT / see European Society for Alternatives to Animal Testing (#08517)
♦ MEGJR – Mitteleuropäischer Guttempler-Jugendrat (inactive)
♦ MEG – Movimento Eucaristico Giovanile (religious order)
♦ MEG Nord (meeting series)
♦ MEGRA – MittelEuropäische Gesellschaft für Regulatory Affairs (internationally oriented national body)
♦ MEHRC – Modern European History Research Centre (internationally oriented national body)
♦ Mehrsprachiges Europa (internationally oriented national body)
♦ Mehzdunarodnyj Sovet po Obshchestvennym Naukam (inactive)
♦ MEI – Media and Entertainment International (inactive)
♦ MEI – Middle East Institute, Singapore (internationally oriented national body)
♦ MEI – Middle East Institute, Washington (internationally oriented national body)
♦ **MEI** Music Encoding Initiative (#16913)
♦ MEIP – Metropolitan Environment Improvement Programme (no recent information)
♦ **MEIRA** Middle East Investor Relations Association (#16768)
♦ ME-IR / see Middle East Investor Relations Association (#16768)
♦ **MEIS** Middle European Iris Society (#16793)
♦ MEJ – Mouvement Eucharistique des Jeunes (religious order)
♦ MEJ – Movimiento Eucaristico Juvenil (religious order)
♦ MEK – Mezgosudarstvennyj Ekonomiceskij Komitet Ekonomiceskogo Sojuza (no recent information)
♦ **MEK** Mujahedin-e Khalq Organization (#16881)
♦ Mekong Committee (inactive)

♦ Mekong-Ganga Cooperation Scheme (MGC) 16700

Contact Secretary (EAST), Ministry of External Affairs, South Block, Delhi 110011, DELHI 110011, India.

History 2000, Vientiane (Lao PDR), on signature of the *Vientiane Declaration on Mekong-Ganga Cooperation* and adoption of framework and mechanism details, following an initiative of the Government of India. **Aims** Promote economic integration of the 2 subregions, with initial cooperation in tourism, culture, human resource development, transport and communications. **Structure** Working Groups (5): Tourism Cooperation; Culture Cooperation; HRD Cooperation; Transport and Communications; Action Plan. Working groups organize a meeting not more than annually. **Events** *Ministerial Meeting* Delhi (India) 2012, *Ministerial Meeting* Manila (Philippines) 2007, *Ministerial Meeting* Phnom Penh (Cambodia) 2003, *Ministerial Meeting* Hanoi (Vietnam) 2001, *Ministerial Meeting* Vientiane (Laos) 2000.
Members Signatory governments of 6 countries:
Cambodia, India, Laos, Myanmar, Thailand, Vietnam. [2012/XF6133/**F***]

♦ Mekong Institute (MI) 16701

Interim Dir 123 Khon Kaen Univ, Mittraphap Rd, Muang District, Khon Kaen, 40002, Thailand. T. +6643202411. Fax +6643343131. E-mail: information@mekonginstitute.org.
URL: http://www.mekonginstitute.org/

History Operations started 1996, following Memorandum of Understanding signed between governments of New Zealand and Thailand, 1995. MI Charter came into force, 2003, on signature of 6 governments of the Greater Mekong Subregion. Thai Cabinet approved Headquarter Agreement to recognize MI as an IGO under Thai law, Jul 2007. Officially established as an IGO, 6 Nov 2009. **Aims** Offer standard and on-demand capacity *development* programmes focusing on regional *cooperation* and *integration*. **Structure** Council. Steering Committee. Secretariat, headed by Director. National Coordinating Agencies. **Languages** English. **Staff** 68.00 FTE, paid. **Finance** Contributions from 6 GMS countries; aid from other governments, including New Zealand Foreign Affairs and Trade Aid Programs and *Swiss Agency for Development and Cooperation (SDC)*. Budget (annual): US$ 3 million. **Activities** Educational activities; policy and action research; meeting activities; consultancy services. **Publications** *Mekong Connection Newsletter* (4 a year). *MI Research Paper Series*. Annual Report.
Members Governments of 6 countries:
Cambodia, China, Laos, Myanmar, Thailand, Vietnam.
IGO Relations Development partners include: *Asian Development Bank (ADB, #01422)*; *Deutsche Gesellschaft für Internationale Zusammenarbeit (GIZ)*; *FAO (#09260)*; *MASHAV – Centre for International Cooperation*; *Mekong River Commission (MRC, #16703)*; *OECD (#17693)* Development Finance Network; *Swiss Agency for Development and Cooperation (SDC)*; *United Nations Economic and Social Commission for Asia and the Pacific (ESCAP, #20557)*. **NGO Relations** Implementing partners include: *International Institute for Trade and Development (ITD)*; *Mekong Migration Network (MMN, #16702)*; national associations. Member of: *Asia-Pacific Research and Training Network on Trade (ARTNeT, #02014)*. [2015/XJ7804/j/**E***]

♦ Mekong Migration Network (MMN) 16702

Secretariat c/o Asian Migrant Ctr, c/o Kowloon Union Church, 4 Jordan Road, Kowloon, Hong Kong. T. +85223120031. Fax +85229920111. E-mail: info@mekongmigration.org.
Chiang Mai Office PO Box 195, Chiangmai Univ, Chiang Mai, 50200, Thailand. T. +6653283259. Fax +6653283259.
URL: http://www.mekongmigration.org/

History Launched, 2003, evolving from a research project "Migration in the Mekong", initiated Sep 2001. **Aims** Promote the welfare, well-being, dignity and human rights of migrants in the Greater Mekong Subregion; build mutual support and solidarity among migrants and advocates in the region. **Structure** General Conference. Steering Committee of 7 members (one from each country, plus Coordinator). Management Committee. Secretariat.
Members Regular; Associate. Members in 5 countries:
Cambodia, China, Laos, Thailand, Vietnam.
Included in the above, 1 organization listed in this Yearbook:
Asian Migrant Centre (AMC).
IGO Relations *Mekong Institute (MI, #16701)*. **NGO Relations** Member of: *United for Foreign Domestic Workers' Rights (UFDWR, #20510)*. [2011/XJ4707/**F**]

♦ Mekong Region Law Centre (internationally oriented national body)

♦ Mekong River Commission (MRC) 16703

CEO PO Box 6101, 184 Fa Ngoum Road – Unit 18, Ban Sithane Neua – Sikhottabong District, 01000 Vientiane, Laos. T. +85621263263. Fax +85621263264. E-mail: mrcs@mrcmekong.org.
URL: http://www.mrcmekong.org/

History 5 Apr 1995, on signature of *Agreement on Cooperation for the Sustainable Development of the Mekong River Basin (1995)* by plenipotentiaries from Cambodia, Laos, Thailand and Vietnam. Replaced the former *Mekong Committee (inactive)*, set up 17 Sep 1957, Bangkok (Thailand), by the governments of Cambodia, Laos, Thailand and Vietnam, on recommendation of the then United Nations Economic Commission for Asia and the Far East (ECAFE), now *United Nations Economic and Social Commission for Asia and the Pacific (ESCAP, #20557)*, and the subsequent *Interim Committee for Coordination of Investigations of the Lower Mekong Basin (Interim Mekong Committee, inactive)*, set up Jan 1978 by Laos, Thailand and Vietnam. Currently official dialogue is held with the 2 other states of the mekong River basin, China and Myanmar. **Aims** Share benefits of common water resources, despite different national interests, and address transboundary pressures in the basin; serve as a knowledge hub that promotes regional cooperation and policy-making based on scientific evidence; provide technical assistance and develop practical tools to help its member countries make informed decisions about their development. **Structure** Council (meets annually); Joint Committee (meets 2 a year). Secretariat. Coordinating Bodies (4). **Languages** English, Laotian, Mon-Khmer languages, Thai, Vietnamese. **Staff** International and riparian. **Finance** Sources: contributions of member/participating states; government support; international organizations; members' dues. Annual budget: 16,100,000 USD. **Activities** Knowledge management/information dissemination; monitoring/evaluation; research and development; standards/guidelines. **Events** *Life on the Mekong Forum* Busan (Korea Rep) 2019, *Mekong Water Resources Data Capacity Building Project Meeting* Busan (Korea Rep) 2019, *Round Table* Busan (Korea Rep) 2019, *Seminar on Water Data Utilization and Management in the Mekong Region* Busan (Korea Rep) 2019, *Rhine-Mekong Symposium on Climate Change and its Influence on Water and Related Sectors* Koblenz (Germany) 2014. **Publications** *Catch and Culture* (3 a year). *Mekong Development*. *Basin Planning Atlas*; *Fishing Gears of the Cambodian Mekong*; *Social Atlas of the Lower Mekong Basin*. Technical Paper Series; Technical Report Series; Strategy, Plan and Procedure Series; Technical Guideline Series. Annual Report; project reports; videos; studies; CD-ROMs; maps. **Information Services** *MRC Data and Information Services Portal*.
Members Governments of 4 countries:
Cambodia, Laos, Thailand, Vietnam.
IGO Relations Cooperates with: *Asia-Pacific Fishery Commission (APFIC, #01907)*. Partner of: *Mekong Institute (MI, #16701)*. **NGO Relations** Partner of: *WorldFish (#21507)*. Member of: *Asia-Pacific Regional Space Agency Forum (APRSAF, #02010)*; *Network of Asian River Basin Organizations (NARBO, #16993)*. [2020.08.27/XE2491/**E***]

♦ MELA – Middle East Librarians Association (internationally oriented national body)
♦ **MELA** Middle East Lighting Association (#16770)
♦ Melanesian Association of Theological Schools (internationally oriented national body)

♦ Melanesian Spearhead Group (MSG) 16704

Dir Gen Private Mail Bag 051, Port Vila, Vanuatu. T. +67822913. Fax +67823142.

History 1 Sep 1994, when the *MSG Trade Agreement* entered into force. Known also as *Spearhead Group*. **Aims** Under the agreement, *trade* among the three countries is conducted free of *customs* duties in respect of tuna from the Solomon Islands, tea from Papua New Guinea and beef from Vanuatu. **Activities** The scope of cooperation is to be expanded into new area, in particular: to collaborate closely in developing a single regional framework of law and practices to regulate the forestry industry; to waive visa restrictions for all categories of visitors from the three countries; to examine, through a study, the possibility of merging the individual national airlines; to examine options for the holding of an annual Melanesian Arts Festival to promote cultural cooperation and awareness among member States as well as tourism.
Members Governments of 3 countries:
Papua New Guinea, Solomon Is, Vanuatu. [2008/XF5453/**F***]

♦ Melanoma Genetics Consortium (GenoMEL) 16705

Project Manager Epidemiology – Biostatistics Section, Leeds Inst of Molecular Medicine, St James' Univ Hosp, Leeds, LS9 7TF, UK. T. +441132066527. Fax +441132340183.
URL: http://www.genomel.org/

History 1997. **Aims** Develop and support collaborations between member groups to: identify melanoma susceptibility genes; evaluate gene-environment interactions; assess the risk of melanoma and other *cancers* related to variations in these genes. **Structure** Joint Advisory Group; Scientific Advisory Board. Chair; Vice-Chair. **Languages** Dutch, English, Spanish. **Finance** Funded by: *European Commission (EC, #06633)* – Sixth Framework Programme; US National Institutes of Health. **Events** *Meeting* Tel Aviv (Israel) 2011, *Annual genome1 meeting* Paris (France) 2008.

Members Participants in 19 countries:
Argentina, Australia, Brazil, Chile, Colombia, France, Germany, Israel, Italy, Latvia, Mexico, Netherlands, Poland, Slovenia, Spain, Sweden, UK, Uruguay, USA. [2015/XM2973/**F**]

♦ Melanoma Patient Network Europe (unconfirmed)
♦ **MELCom International** European Association of Middle East Librarians (#06121)

♦ Méliès International Festivals Federation (MIFF) 16706

Contact Rue Washington 40, 1050 Brussels, Belgium. T. +3222011713. E-mail: info@melies.org.
URL: http://www.melies.org/

History 1987. A grouping of the type *European Economic Interest Grouping (EEIG, #06960)* since 1997. Former names and other names: *European Fantastic Film Festivals Federation* – former. Registration: Banque Carrefour des Entreprises, No/ID: 0470.067.839, Start date: 8 Feb 2000, Belgium. **Aims** Promote fantastic films in Europe and throughout the world. **Structure** General Assembly (3 a year); Council. **Languages** English. **Finance** Sources: members' dues. Annual budget: 14,000 EUR. **Activities** Awards/prizes/competitions; projects/programmes.
Members Fantasy film festival organizers (29) in 19 countries:
Austria, Belgium, Brazil, Canada, Estonia, France, Germany, Italy, Korea Rep, Lebanon, Netherlands, Poland, Portugal, Slovenia, Spain, Sweden, Switzerland, UK, USA.
NGO Relations Member of: *Federation of European and International Associations Established in Belgium (FAIB, #09508).* [2022.05.10/XD5944/**D**]

♦ MELISSA – Managing the Environment Locally in Sub-Saharan Africa (no recent information)

♦ Melkite Greek Catholic Church 16707

Eglise Grecque Melkite Catholique
Sec Greek Catholic Patriarchate, PO Box 70071, Rabweh, Antelias MOUNT LEBANON, Lebanon. T. +9614413111 – +9614525655. Fax +9614418133. E-mail: secretariat@melkitepat.org.
URL: http://www.melkitepat.org/

History Founded according to the Byzantine Rite, evolved in the Church of Antioch, and reformed by St Basil and St John Chrysostom. A *'sui iuris'* church in full communion with the Roman Catholic Church. Its Patriarchal Church is spread throughout the Arab Middle East and its diaspora throughout the world. Patriarch bears the title Patriarch of Antioch and All the East, of Alexandria, and of Jerusalem, recalling the fact that all three cities still have local Eastern Christian communities whose origins date back to apostolic times. The historic loyalty of the Melkite Church to the Eastern Roman Empire and to the first 7 Ecumenical Councils is reflected in the name "Melkite", derived from the Arab word "Malki" meaning "Imperial", and appellation adopted by Chalcedonian Christians in the latter half of the 5th century. Historically and geographically distinct from the Latin Church of Rome and the Greek Orthodox Church of Antioch, it seeks to be, in the 21st century, a bridge between Western Catholics and Eastern Orthodox. **Aims** Express Christian faith through liturgical worship according to the Eastern or Byzantine Rite in accordance with the culture of the faithful and maintaining and preserving the dignity and beauty of the early Church; express faith in education through schools and college, in charitable assistance through homes for orphans, the elderly and the handicapped, hospitals for those in physical or mental distress and through relief work to displaced persons. **Structure** Holy Synod, headed by His Beatitude Patriarch Joseph Absi. Patriarchal archeparchies (3): Damascus (Syria); Jerusalem (Israel); Cairo (Egypt). Archparchies and eparchies (21). Liqaa Center, Lebanon. **Languages** Arabic, English, French, Irish Gaelic, Portuguese, Spanish. **Activities** Networking/liaising; events/meetings; training/education. **Publications** *Le Lien* (4 a year) in English, French – review.
Members About 2 million individuals in 22 countries and territories:
Argentina, Austria, Belgium, Brazil, Canada, Egypt, France, Germany, Iraq, Ireland, Israel, Italy, Kuwait, Lebanon, Mexico, New Zealand, Palestine, Sudan, Syrian AR, UK, USA, Venezuela.
NGO Relations Instrumental in setting up: *Patriarchal Order of the Holy Cross of Jerusalem.* [2018.08.20/XF5864/v/**F**]

♦ Mellemfolkeligt Samvirke (internationally oriented national body)
♦ **MELM** Middle East Lutheran Ministry (#16771)
♦ MEL – Muzika Esperanto-Ligo (no recent information)
♦ **MELODI Association** Multidisciplinary European Low Dose Initiative Association (#16882)

♦ Melody for Dialogue among Civilizations Association 16708

Contact 27 avenue Foch, 75016 Paris, France. T. +33672432644. Fax +33145450301.
New York 32W 40 St, New York NY 10018, USA. T. +12123020337. Fax +12123020337.
URL: http://www.melodydialogue.org/

History Set up 2004. **Aims** Use music as an important bridge between peoples and value its contribution to furthering a dialogue among civilizations, cultures and communities. **Structure** Honorary Council; Artistic Advisory Council; Executive Committee. **Languages** Chinese, English, French. **Staff** 4 to 20 voluntary. **Finance** Funded through projects and voluntary contributions from governments and private sectors. **Activities** Events/meetings; networking/liaising. **Events** *Africa Regional Conference on Water* Ota (Nigeria) 2011. [2018.06.15/XJ9825/**F**]

♦ Melvin Yahr International Parkinson's Disease Foundation (internationally oriented national body)
♦ **MEMAC** Marine Emergency Mutual Aid Centre (#16578)
♦ **MEMAGO** Middle East and Mediterranean Association of Gynecologic Oncologist (#16773)
♦ Membrane Science – International Conference on Membrane Science and Technology (meeting series)
♦ Membrane Society of Australasia (internationally oriented national body)
♦ **MEMBS** Middle East Molecular Biology Society (#16774)
♦ MEMDES – International Conference on Desalination using Membrane Technology (meeting series)
♦ MEMI / see Middle East Media
♦ MEMISA (internationally oriented national body)
♦ MEMO – Association internationale pour l'enseignement des langues vivantes par les méthodes modernes (inactive)
♦ Mémorandum d'accord concernant l'échange d'information sur la mise au point de systèmes de chauffage et de rafraîchissement solaires dans les bâtiments (1974 treaty)
♦ Mémorandum d'accord concernant les mesures de conservation en faveur du courlis à bec grêle (1994 treaty)
♦ Mémorandum d'accord sur les mesures de conservation pour les tortues marines de la côte atlantique de l'Afrique (1999 treaty)
♦ Mémorandum d'accord relatif à la production et au marché du blé (1942 treaty)
♦ Mémorandum d'accord relatif à un programme de vols transatlantiques par ballon (1976 treaty)
♦ Memorandum of Agreement Relating to the Production and Marketing of Wheat (1942 treaty)
♦ Memorandum of Heads of Agreement Entered at the Monetary and Economic Conference, Held in London 1933 (1933 treaty)
♦ Memorandum of Understanding Concerning the Conservation of the Manatee and Small Cetaceans of Western Africa and Macaronesia (2008 treaty)
♦ Memorandum of Understanding Concerning Conservation Measures for the Aquatic Warbler (2003 treaty)
♦ Memorandum of Understanding Concerning Conservation Measures for the Eastern Atlantic Populations of the Mediterranean Monk Seal – Monachus Monachus (2007 treaty)
♦ Memorandum of Understanding Concerning Conservation Measures for Marine Turtles of the Atlantic Coast of Africa (1999 treaty)
♦ Memorandum of Understanding Concerning Conservation Measures for the Ruddy-headed Goose – Chloephaga Rubidiceps (2006 treaty)
♦ Memorandum of Understanding Concerning Conservation Measures for the Siberian Crane, 1993 (1993 treaty)
♦ Memorandum of Understanding Concerning Conservation Measures for the Siberian Crane, 1998 (1998 treaty)
♦ Memorandum of Understanding Concerning Conservation Measures for the Slender-billed Curlew (1994 treaty)
♦ Memorandum of Understanding Concerning Conservation Measures for the West African Populations of the African Elephant – Loxodonta Africana (2005 treaty)
♦ Memorandum of Understanding Concerning the Conservation of Migratory Birds of Prey in Africa and Eurasia (2008 treaty)
♦ Memorandum of Understanding Concerning Conservation and Restoration of the Bukhara Deer (2002 treaty)
♦ Memorandum of Understanding Concerning Conservation, Restoration and Sustainable Use of the Saiga Antelope – Saiga Tatarica Tatarica (2005 treaty)
♦ Memorandum of Understanding Concerning Cooperative Information Exchange Relating to the Development of Solar Heating and Cooling Systems in Buildings (1974 treaty)
♦ Memorandum of Understanding for the Conservation of Cetaceans and Their Habitats in the Pacific Islands Region (2006 treaty)
♦ Memorandum of Understanding on the Conservation of High Andean Flamingos and Their Habitats (2008 treaty)
♦ Memorandum of Understanding on the Conservation and Management of Dugongs – Dugong Dugon – and Their Habitats Throughout Their Range (2007 treaty)
♦ Memorandum of Understanding on the Conservation and Management of Marine Turtles and Their Habitats of the Indian Ocean and South-East Asia (2001 treaty)
♦ Memorandum of Understanding on the Conservation and Management of the Middle-European Population of the Great Bustard – Otis Tarda (2000 treaty)
♦ Memorandum of Understanding on the Conservation of Southern South American Migratory Grassland Bird Species and Their Habitats (2007 treaty)
♦ Memorandum of Understanding on Port State Control in the Arab States of the Gulf (2004 treaty)

♦ Memorandum of Understanding on Port State Control in the Asia-Pacific Region (Tokyo MOU) 16709

Secretary Ascend Shimbahsi 8F, 6-19-19 Shimbashi, Minato-ku, Tokyo, 105-0004 Japan. T. +81334330621. Fax +81334330624. E-mail: secretariat@tokyo-mou.org.
URL: https://www.tokyo-mou.org/

History Set up when Memorandum was signed 1 Dec 1993, Tokyo (Japan). Effective date: 1 Apr 1994. **Aims** Establish an effective port State control regime in the Asia-Pacific region through cooperation of members and harmonization of their activities; eliminate sub-standard shipping so as to promote maritime safety; protect the *marine environment*; safeguard working and living conditions on board *ships*. **Structure** Port State Control Committee; Secretariat; *Asia-Pacific Computerized Information System (APCIS).* **Languages** English. **Staff** 4.00 FTE, paid. **Activities** Events/meetings; knowledge management/information dissemination; monitoring/evaluation; politics/policy/regulatory. **Events** *Port State Control Committee Meeting* Lima (Peru) 2022, *Technical Working Group Meeting* Lima (Peru) 2022, *Port State Control Committee Meeting* Tokyo (Japan) 2021, *Technical Working Group Meeting* Tokyo (Japan) 2021. **Publications** Annual Report.
Members Member Authorities (21):
Australia, Canada, Chile, China, Fiji, Hong Kong, Indonesia, Japan, Korea Rep, Malaysia, Marshall Is, New Zealand, Panama, Papua New Guinea, Peru, Philippines, Russia, Singapore, Thailand, Vanuatu, Vietnam.
Cooperating Member Authorities (1):
Mexico.
Observer Authorities (7):
Cambodia, Korea DPR, Macau, Samoa, Solomon Is, Tonga, USA.
Observer organizations (10):
Caribbean Memorandum of Understanding on Port State Control (Caribbean MOU, 1996); ILO (#11123); International Maritime Organization (IMO, #14102); Latin American Agreement on Port State Control of Vessels (Viña del Mar agreement, 1992); Memorandum of Understanding on Port State Control in the Arab States of the Gulf (Riyadh MOU, 2004); Memorandum of Understanding on Port State Control in the Black Sea (Black Sea MOU, 2000); Memorandum of Understanding on Port State Control in the Indian Ocean (Indian Ocean MOU, 1998); Memorandum of Understanding on Port State Control in the Mediterranean (Mediterranean MOU, 1997); Memorandum of Understanding on Port State Control in West and Central Africa (Abuja MOU, 1999); Paris Memorandum of Understanding on Port State Control (Paris MOU, 1982).
NGO Relations Observer status with (1): *Asia-Pacific Heads of Maritime Safety Agencies (APHoMSA, #01922).* [2022.11.30/XT9393/**F***]

♦ Memorandum of Understanding on Port State Control in the Black Sea (2000 treaty)
♦ Memorandum of Understanding on Port State Control in the Indian Ocean (1998 treaty)
♦ Memorandum of Understanding on Port State Control in the Mediterranean (1997 treaty)
♦ Memorandum of Understanding on Port State Control in West and Central Africa (1999 treaty)
♦ Memorandum of Understanding between the Republic of Kenya and the United Republic of Tanzania and the Republic of Uganda for Cooperation on Environment Management (1998 treaty)
♦ Memorandum of Understanding for a Trans-Atlantic Balloon Program (1976 treaty)
♦ Memorial Foundation for Jewish Culture (internationally oriented national body)
♦ Memorial Foundation of Latin America (internationally oriented national body)
♦ Mémorial de la Shoah (internationally oriented national body)
♦ Memoria Mundi – Memory of the World Programme (see: #20322)
♦ Memoria Popular Latinoamericana (internationally oriented national body)

♦ Memory Studies Association (MSA) 16710

Contact Grote Gracht 90-92, 6211 SZ Maastricht, Netherlands. E-mail: info@memorystudiesassociation.org.
URL: http://www.memorystudiesassociation.org/

History 2016, Amsterdam (Netherlands). Registration: Start date: 26 Jun 2017, Netherlands. **Aims** Become an important forum for the memory field. **Structure** Co-Presidents (3); Executive Committee. **Activities** Events/meetings. **Events** *Conference* Newcastle upon Tyne (UK) 2023, *Conference* Seoul (Korea Rep) 2022, *Conference* Warsaw (Poland) 2021, *Conference* Charlottesville, VA (USA) 2020, *Conference* Madrid (Spain) 2019. **Members** Full in 70 countries. Membership countries not specified. [2022/XM6273/**C**]

♦ Memory of the World Programme (see: #20322)
♦ MENABANK – Bank for Economic Cooperation and Development in the Middle East and North Africa (no recent information)
♦ **MENACTRIMS** Middle East North Africa Committee for Treatment and Research in Multiple Sclerosis (#16777)
♦ **MENAFATF** Middle East and North Africa Financial Action Task Force (#16779)
♦ **MENAHRA** Middle East and North Africa Harm Reduction Network (#16780)
♦ **MENALAC** Middle East and North Africa Leisure and Attractions Council (#16781)
♦ MENA – Ministère évangélique parmi les nations arabophones (internationally oriented national body)
♦ **MENANA** Middle East and North Africa Nutrition Association (#16782)

♦ MENA Private Equity Association 16711

Address not obtained.
URL: http://www.menapea.com/

Aims Support and develop the private equity and venture *capital* industry in the *Middle East* and North *Africa*. **Structure** Steering Committee.
Members Full in 6 countries:
Bahrain, Egypt, Lebanon, Qatar, Saudi Arabia, United Arab Emirates. [2014/XJ8847/**D**]

♦ **MENAP-SCI** Middle-East, North Africa and Pakistan Self-Care Industry (#16783)
♦ MENAP-SMI / see Middle-East, North Africa and Pakistan Self-Care Industry (#16783)
♦ MENAREES – Middle East and North Africa Regional Engineering Education Society (unconfirmed)
♦ MENARES – Middle East North Africa Real Estate Society (inactive)
♦ MENASO / see Middle East & North Africa Stroke Organization (#16784)
♦ **MENA Stroke** Middle East & North Africa Stroke Organization (#16784)
♦ MENATOX – Middle East and North Africa Toxicology Association (unconfirmed)
♦ **MENA Transition Fund** Middle East and North Africa Transition Fund (#16785)

♦ **MENAWCA** Middle East – North Africa Writing Centers Alliance (#16786)
♦ **MENBO** Mediterranean Network of Basin Organisations (#16664)
♦ MENCA – Ha'amota Leidud Vekidum Shmirat Hateva Bamizrach Hatichon (internationally oriented national body)
♦ MEND – Middle East Nonviolence and Democracy (internationally oriented national body)

♦ MenEngage Alliance 16712

Co-Dir 1875 K St NW, Floor 4, Washington DC 20006, USA. T. +12402735846. E-mail: info@menengage.org.
URL: http://www.menengage.org/

History 2004. Former names and other names: *MenEngage Global Alliance – boys and men for gender equality* – alias. Registration: Start date: 2017, USA, Washington DC. **Aims** Work to transform unequal power relations and patriarchal systems by transforming masculinities and working with men and boys through intersectional feminist approaches; foster joint actions in partnership with women's rights, gender- and other social justice movements. **Structure** Global Board; Regional Networks. **Languages** English, French, Spanish. **Staff** 9.00 FTE, paid. **Finance** Supported by: *Oak Foundation*; *Rädda Barnen – Save the Children Sweden*; *Swedish International Development Cooperation Agency (Sida)*; *UNDP (#20292)*. **Activities** Events/meetings. **Events** *Global Symposium Opening Event* Kigali (Rwanda) 2020, *Global Symposium* Delhi (India) 2014, *MenEngage Africa symposium* Johannesburg (South Africa) 2009, *Global symposium on engaging men and boys in gender equality* Rio de Janeiro (Brazil) 2009, *Seminar on engaging men in gender-based violence prevention in post-conflict settings* Washington, DC (USA) 2009. **Members** Civil Society organizations (over 700) and individuals across 74 countries. Membership countries not specified. [2022.03.30/XJ0761/**F**]

♦ MenEngage Global Alliance – boys and men for gender equality / see MenEngage Alliance (#16712)
♦ **MENF** Movement for a Europe of Nations and Freedom (#16870)
♦ Men Having Babies (internationally oriented national body)
♦ **MENL** Mouvement pour l'Europe des nations et des libertés (#16870)
♦ **M.E.N.** Marfan Europe Network (#16573)
♦ Men for Missions International (internationally oriented national body)
♦ Men in Movement (meeting series)
♦ La Mennais Brothers – Brothers of Christian Instruction of Ploërmel (religious order)
♦ Mennonite Brethren Mission and Service / see MBMS International
♦ Mennonite Central Committee (internationally oriented national body)
♦ Mennonite Economic Development Associates (internationally oriented national body)
♦ Mennonite Mission Network (internationally oriented national body)
♦ Mennonite Voluntary Service (internationally oriented national body)

♦ Mennonite World Conference (MWC) 16713

Conférence mennonite mondiale – Congreso Mundial Menonita – Mennonitische Weltkonferenz

Gen Sec 50 Kent Ave, Suite 206, Kitchener ON N2G 3R1, Canada. T. +15195710060. Fax +12266474224. E-mail: kitchener@mwc-cmm.org.
URL: http://www.mwc-cmm.org/

History 1925, Basel (Switzerland). Founded at 1st World Conference, as a fellowship of Mennonites and Brethren in Christ. **Aims** Provide opportunity for fellowship and communication; facilitate discussion and interaction. **Structure** Executive Committee. 5 Continental Regions: Africa; Asia and Pacific; Europe; Latin America; North America. **Languages** English, French, Spanish. **Staff** 12.00 FTE, paid. **Finance** Proceeds from conferences; individual donors. **Events** *World conference* Asunción (Paraguay) 2009, *World conference* Zimbabwe 2003, *World conference* Kolkata (India) 1997, *World conference* Winnipeg, MB (Canada) 1990, *World Conference* Strasbourg (France) 1984. **Publications** *MWC Correo* (2 a year); *MWC Courier* (2 a year); *MWC Courrier* (2 a year).

Members Membership is open to organized conferences and groups that identify themselves with the Mennonite, Brethren in Christ, or related churches. Members in 58 countries and territories:
Angola, Argentina, Austria, Belize, Bolivia, Brazil, Burkina Faso, Canada, Chile, Colombia, Congo DR, Costa Rica, Cuba, Dominican Rep, Ecuador, El Salvador, Eritrea, Ethiopia, France, Germany, Ghana, Guatemala, Honduras, Hong Kong, India, Indonesia, Italy, Jamaica, Japan, Kenya, Korea Rep, Malawi, Mexico, Mozambique, Myanmar, Nepal, Netherlands, Nicaragua, Nigeria, Panama, Paraguay, Peru, Philippines, Portugal, Puerto Rico, South Africa, Switzerland, Taiwan, Tanzania UR, Thailand, Trinidad-Tobago, Uganda, Uruguay, USA, Venezuela, Vietnam, Zambia, Zimbabwe. [2021/XF7800/**F**]

♦ Mennonitischer Freiwilligendienst (internationally oriented national body)
♦ Mennonitische Weltkonferenz (#16713)
♦ **MENOG** Middle East Network Operators Group (#16775)

♦ Mensa International 16714

Registered Address Slate Barn, Church Lane, Caythorpe, Nottingham, NG32 3EL, UK. T. +441245603550. Fax +441245603550. E-mail: enquiries@mensa.org.
URL: http://www.mensa.org

History 1946, Oxford (UK), as a UK national organization. Constitution adopted 1964. Registered as *Intermensa* in accordance with UK law, 1965. Registration: Companies House, No/ID: 00848100, Start date: 1976, England and Wales. **Aims** Promote and develop worldwide contact among members; provide resources for studies in psychology and social sciences; identify and foster *intelligence* for the benefit of humanity. **Structure** International Board of Directors, consisting of 4 Officers elected by postal ballot of all members, plus one member from each national committee. **Languages** English. **Staff** 3.00 FTE, paid. **Finance** Sources: donations; members' dues. Other sources: testing fees. **Activities** Carries out research in psychology and the social sciences; administers intelligence tests; awards scholarships to institutes of higher education; coordinates activities of Mensa organizations worldwide. *Service for Information, Guidance and Hospitality to Travellers (SIGHT)* is a network of Mensans around the world who want to meet other Mensans. **Events** *European Mensa Annual Gathering (EMAG)* Rotterdam (Netherlands) 2023, *European Mensa Annual Gathering (EMAG)* Strasbourg (France) 2022, *European Mensas Annual Gathering (EMAG)* Brno (Czechia) 2021, *European Mensas Annual Gathering (EMAG)* Brno (Czechia) 2020, *Asian Meeting* Suwon (Korea Rep) 2020. **Publications** *International Journal* (10 a year) in English; *Isolated M* (10 a year).

Members National Mensas (NM) having their own group and membership base; direct international members – individuals in countries with no NM. Individuals (100,000) whose intelligence, measured by Mensa's psychologists, is within the top 2% of the general population, in 105 countries and territories:
Albania, Argentina, Armenia, Australia, Austria, Azerbaijan, Bahamas, Bahrain, Bangladesh, Barbados, Belarus, Belgium, Belize, Bolivia, Bosnia-Herzegovina, Botswana, Brazil, Brunei Darussalam, Bulgaria, Canada, Channel Is, Chile, China, Colombia, Costa Rica, Croatia, Cuba, Cyprus, Czechia, Denmark, Dominican Rep, Ecuador, Egypt, Estonia, Finland, France, Gambia, Georgia, Germany, Ghana, Greece, Guatemala, Guinea, Hong Kong, Hungary, Iceland, India, Indonesia, Iran Islamic Rep, Ireland, Israel, Italy, Japan, Jordan, Korea Rep, Kuwait, Libya, Lithuania, Luxembourg, Madagascar, Malawi, Malaysia, Malta, Mexico, Moldova, Monaco, Mongolia, Morocco, Namibia, Nauru, Netherlands, New Zealand, North Macedonia (former Yugoslav Rep of), Norway, Pakistan, Papua New Guinea, Paraguay, Peru, Philippines, Poland, Portugal, Qatar, Romania, Russia, Saudi Arabia, Serbia, Singapore, Slovakia, Slovenia, South Africa, Spain, Sri Lanka, Sweden, Switzerland, Taiwan, Thailand, Trinidad-Tobago, Türkiye, UK, United Arab Emirates, Uruguay, USA, Venezuela, Zambia, Zimbabwe. [2020/XB2954/**B**]

♦ Menschen Hilfswerk (internationally oriented national body)
♦ Mensenbroeders / see Brothers to All Men (#03339)
♦ Mensen met een Missie (internationally oriented national body)
♦ Men's International Peace Exchange (internationally oriented national body)
♦ Men's International Professional Tennis Council (inactive)
♦ MENS – Middle East Neurosurgical Society (no recent information)
♦ Men's Resources International (internationally oriented national body)
♦ Mental Disability Advocacy Center / see Validity Foundation (#20743)
♦ Mental Disability Rights International / see Disability Rights International

♦ Mental Health Europe (MHE) 16715

Santé mentale Europe (SME)

Dir Rue de la Presse 4, 1000 Brussels, Belgium. T. +3222272708. E-mail: info@mhe-sme.org.
URL: http://www.mhe-sme.org/

History 1985, UK. Former names and other names: *European Regional Council of the World Federation for Mental Health (ERC-WFMH)* – former; *Conseil régional européen de la Fédération mondiale pour la santé mentale (CRE-FMSM)* – former; *European Regional Council of WFMH* – former; *Conseil régional européen de la FMSM* – former. Registration: Banque-Carrefour des Entreprises, No/ID: 0453.838.056, Start date: 7 Nov 1994, Belgium; EU Transparency Register, No/ID: 245350514009-47, Start date: 18 Jul 2014. **Aims** Promote positive mental health, prevent mental distress, improve care, advocate for social inclusion and protect human rights for (ex-) users of mental health services, their families and carers. **Structure** General Assembly (annual); Board; Executive Committee; Secretariat. **Languages** English, French. **Staff** 5.50 FTE, paid; 1.00 FTE, voluntary. **Finance** Sources: donations; fundraising; grants; members' dues; subsidies. **Activities** Advocacy/lobbying/activism; events/meetings; guidance/assistance/consulting; knowledge management/information dissemination. **Events** *Annual European Conference* Split (Croatia) 2012, *Annual conference / Annual European Conference* Brussels (Belgium) 2010, *Annual Conference* Aalborg (Denmark) 2008, *Annual European Conference* Aalborg (Denmark) 2008, *Annual conference / Annual European Conference* Vienna (Austria) 2007. **Publications** *Mental Health Europe Newsletter* (11 a year) in English, French, German, Spanish. *From Inclusion to Inclusion – the Way Forward to Promoting Social Inclusion of People with Mental Health Problems.* Proceedings of conferences, seminars and symposia; guidelines; reports.

Members Full; Associate; Individuals. Members in 34 countries:
Austria, Belgium, Bulgaria, Croatia, Cyprus, Czechia, Denmark, Estonia, Finland, France, Georgia, Germany, Greece, Hungary, Iceland, Ireland, Israel, Italy, Kosovo, Latvia, Lithuania, Luxembourg, Malta, Netherlands, Norway, Poland, Portugal, Romania, Slovakia, Slovenia, Spain, Sweden, Switzerland, UK.
Regional members (4):
ADHD-Europe (#00113); *European Psychiatric Nurses (HORATIO, #08291)*; *Familles du Monde (FaMiDo)*; *Santé mentale et exclusion sociale – Europa (SMES Europa, #19053)*.

Consultative Status Consultative status granted from: *Council of Europe (CE, #04881)* (Participatory Status). **NGO Relations** Member of (4): *European Alliance for Mental Health – Employment & Work (EUMH Alliance, #05875)*; *European Disability Forum (EDF, #06929)*; *European Patients' Forum (EPF, #08172)* (Associate); *European Public Health Alliance (EPHA, #08297)*. [2022/XE2345/y/**E**]

♦ Mental Health Initiative for Africans in Crisis (unconfirmed)
♦ Mental Health Social Exclusion – Europe (#19053)
♦ Mentor Foundation / see Mentor International (#16716)
♦ MENTOR Initiative (unconfirmed)

♦ Mentor International (MI) 16716

Fondation Mentor Internationale

Contact Kåkbrinken 11A, SE-111 27 Stockholm, Sweden. T. +4687891180. E-mail: info@mentorinternational.org.
URL: https://mentorinternational.org/

History 10 May 1994, Geneva (Switzerland). Founded at World Health Assembly. Former names and other names: *Youth Substance Abuse Prevention Foundation* – full title; *International Foundation Dedicated to the Prevention of Drug Abuse Among Children and Adolescents* – alias; *Mentor Foundation* – former; *Fondation Mentor* – former. Registration: Swiss Civil Code, Switzerland. **Aims** Prevent *substance abuse* and promote *health* and well-being of *children* and young people through youth empowerment. **Structure** Foundation umbrella of 4 national members and 1 regional organization. **Languages** English. **Staff** 3.00 FTE, paid. **Finance** Sources: contributions; fundraising; government support; private foundations; revenue from activities/projects. **Activities** Guidance/assistance/consulting; knowledge management/information dissemination; projects/programmes. Active in: Germany, Latvia, Lebanon, Sweden, USA. **Events** *World forum on drugs, dependencies and society* Montréal, QC (Canada) 2002, *International forum on drug abuse prevention* London (UK) 2000. **Consultative Status** Consultative status granted from: *ECOSOC (#05331)* (Special). **IGO Relations** Cooperates with (4): *UNESCO (#20322)*; *UNICEF (#20332)*; *United Nations Office on Drugs and Crime (UNODC, #20596)*; *WHO (#20950)*. **NGO Relations** Member of (2): *CIVICUS: World Alliance for Citizen Participation (#03962)*; *Vienna NGO Committee on Drugs (VNGOC, #20773)*. Links with other organizations worldwide (not specified), including: *Arab Council for Childhood and Development (ACCD, #00929)*. [2022.05.04/XF3579/f/**F**]

♦ Men of the Trees / see International Tree Foundation
♦ Menzingen Sisters – Sisters of the Holy Cross (religious order)
♦ MEOCAM – Mouvement d'étudiants de l'Organisation commune africaine et malgache (inactive)
♦ MEOC – Middle East Outreach Council (internationally oriented national body)
♦ **MEPA** Middle East Psychological Association (#16787)
♦ **MEPA** Middle East Publishers' Association (#16788)
♦ **MEPA** Mitteleuropäischen Polizeiakademie (#03711)
♦ MEPC BMCM – Baltic Maritime Coordinating Meeting (meeting series)
♦ MEPDN – Middle East Peace Dialogue Network (internationally oriented national body)
♦ MEPEI – Middle East Political and Economic Institute (internationally oriented national body)
♦ MEPLA – Memoria Popular Latinoamericana (internationally oriented national body)
♦ MEP – Mediterranean Environment Programme (inactive)
♦ MEP – Missions étrangères de Paris (religious order)
♦ MEPRA – Middle East Public Relations Association (unconfirmed)
♦ MEPSA / see Molecular and Experimental Pathology Society of Australasia

♦ MEPs against Cancer (MAC) 16717

Pres MAC Secretariat, c/o ECL, Chée de Louvain 479, 1030 Brussels, Belgium. E-mail: mac@europeancancerleagues.org.
URL: http://www.mepsagainstcancer.org/

History 22 Mar 2006, Brussels (Belgium), as an informal group. Active until end 2008, after which it was split in 2 groups, being *Forum Against Cancer Europe (FACE, inactive)* with the other relaunched under same title. **Aims** Promote action on cancer as an *EU* priority and the harnessing of European *health policy* to that end. **Structure** Secretariat provided by: *Association of European Cancer Leagues (ECL, #02500)*. **Languages** English. **Activities** Politics/policy/regulatory; events/meetings. **Members** Individuals. Membership countries not specified. [2019.08.27/XJ0528/**F**]

♦ MEPSA – Molecular and Experimental Pathology Society of Australasia (internationally oriented national body)
♦ MEPS – Maison européenne de la protection sociale, Bruxelles (internationally oriented national body)
♦ MEQA – Middle East Quality Association (no recent information)
♦ MERACON – Middle East, Eastern Europe, Central Asia and North Africa Rabies Control Network (unconfirmed)
♦ MERA – Man-Environment Research Association (internationally oriented national body)
♦ Mercado Comum do Sul (#19868)
♦ Mercado Común del Sur (#19868)
♦ Mercado Común para Africa Orientale e Austral (#04296)
♦ Mercado Común del Caribe Oriental (inactive)
♦ Mercado Común Centroamericano (#03666)
♦ Mercado Común Cinematografico Latinoamericano (no recent information)
♦ Mercantile Marine Academy / see Bangladesh Maritime Academy
♦ Mercator Education / see Mercator European Research Centre on Multilingualism and Language Learning (#16719)
♦ Mercator-Education / see Mercator European Research Centre on Multilingualism and Language Learning (#16719)

♦ Mercator European Network for Documentation and Information on Lesser-Used Languages (Mercator Media) 16718

Cynllun Mercator

Dir Dc/o Dept of Theatre/Film/Television Studies, Aberystwyth Univ, Parry Williams Bldg, Aberystwyth, SY23 3AJ, UK. T. +441970622828. E-mail: tfts@aber.ac.uk – elinhgj@gmail.com.
URL: http://www.aber.ac.uk/en/tfts/mercator/

History as part of the *Mercator Network*, set up 1987, and consisting of 3 research and documentation centres specializing in regional and minority languages within the European Union, in response to the *Kuijpers Resolution*, passed 30 Oct 1987 by *European Parliament (EP, #08146)*. Part of an activity in the World Decade for Cultural Development (1988-1997). **Aims** Act as a documentation, information and research centre on *minority languages* in countries of the European Union. **Structure** One of 3 core centres in a network coordinated by the European Commission. **Staff** 3.00 FTE, paid. **Finance** Sources: *European Commission (EC, #06633)*; University of Wales (UK). **Activities** Events/meetings; knowledge management/information dissemination; research/documentation. **Events** *International symposium* Leeuwarden (Netherlands) 2004. **Publications** *Mercator Media Forum* – journal. *Mercator Media Guide Volume 1-2-3* (1998). Information Services: Database. **NGO Relations** Close links with other Mercator core centre: *Mercator European Research Centre on Multilingualism and Language Learning (Mercator Research Centre, #16719)*. Associate member of: *Network to Promote Linguistic Diversity (NPLD, #17052)*. [2019/XF2868/**F**]

- Mercator European Network of Language Diversity Centres / see Mercator European Research Centre on Multilingualism and Language Learning (#16719)

♦ Mercator European Research Centre on Multilingualism and Language Learning (Mercator Research Centre) 16719

Project Leader c/o Fryske Akademy, PO Box 54, Ljouwert, 8900 AB Leeuwarden, Netherlands. T. +31582343063. E-mail: mercator@fryske-akademy.nl.
Street address Doelestrjitte 8, Ljouwert, 8911 DX Leeuwarden, Netherlands.
URL: http://www.mercator-research.eu/

History Founded by an initiative of *European Commission (EC, #06633)*, in response to the *Kuijpers Resolution*, passed 30 Oct 1987 by *European Parliament (EP, #08146)*. One of 4 centres within *Mercator European Network of Language Diversity Centres*, the others being: *Mercator European Network for Documentation and Information on Lesser-Used Languages (Mercator Media, #16718)*; Research Institute for Linguistics/ Hungarian Academy of Sciences in Budapest (Hungary); Mercator Stockholm (Sweden). Former names and other names: *Mercator Education* – former (1987); *Kuijpers Resolution* – former; *European Network for Information, Documentation and Research into Regional or Minority Languages in Education* – former; *European Network for Regional or Minority Languages and Education (Mercator-Education)* – former; *Réseau européen pour les langues régionales ou minoritaires et l'éducation* – former; *Mercator Research Centre* – former; *Mercator European Network of Language Diversity Centres* – former. **Aims** Acquisition and inventory, research and study, dissemination and application of knowledge in the field of language learning. **Structure** Based in Ljouwert/Leeuwarden (Netherlands), and hosted at the Fryske Akademy (Frisian Academy). **Languages** Dutch, English, French, German. **Staff** 8.00 FTE, paid. **Finance** Main sources: Province of Fryslân (Netherlands); EU related projects. **Activities** Events/meetings; knowledge management/ information dissemination; research/documentation; standards/guidelines. **Events** *Expert Seminar on Social Media and Lesser Used Languages* Leeuwarden (Netherlands) 2012, *Conference on the role of legislation in enhancing linguistic diversity* Barcelona (Spain) 2011, *Expert seminar on cultural education and civil society* Leeuwarden (Netherlands) 2011, *Languages of the wider world conference* Leeuwarden (Netherlands) 2011, *Symposium on higher education and research on multilingualism* Leeuwarden (Netherlands) 2010. **Publications** *Mercator Newsletter* (12 a year). *Regional Dossiers* – Focus on educational system in European regions that have an autochthonous lesser-used language, and on how it is embedded in this system. Books; reports; proceedings. **Information Services** *Tresoar* – Library with database of bibliographic information in the domain of bilingualism, multilingualism, minority languages, bilingual and multilingual education, language policy and learning; *Wiki on Minority Language Learning* – Complements the Mercator Regional Dossiers, and offers information on the education of minority languages that have only a (very) small place in the national education system, or none at all. **NGO Relations** Member of (2): *European Civil Society Platform for Multilingualism (ECSPM, #06569)*; *Network to Promote Linguistic Diversity (NPLD, #17052)*. Cooperates with: LEARNME/Mercator Network; *Network to Promote Linguistic Diversity (NLPD)*; organizations of European linguistic minorities. [2022.02.21/XF2275/**F**]

- **Mercator Media** Mercator European Network for Documentation and Information on Lesser-Used Languages (#16718)
- Mercator Research Centre / see Mercator European Research Centre on Multilingualism and Language Learning (#16719)
- **Mercator Research Centre** Mercator European Research Centre on Multilingualism and Language Learning (#16719)
- Mercator Research Institute on Global Commons and Climate Change (internationally oriented national body)
- Mercédaires de la Charité – Soeurs de Charité de Notre-Dame de la Merci (religious order)
- Mercédaires – Vierge Marie de la Merci (religious order)
- Mercedarians – Order of Our Lady of Mercy (religious order)
- Mercedarias de la Caridad – Hermanas de la Caridad de Nuestra Señora de las Mercedes (religious order)
- Mercedarie – Suore di Nostra Signora della Mercede (religious order)
- Mercedari Scalzi (religious order)

♦ Merchant Risk Council (MRC) 16720

Main Office 600 Stewart St, Ste 720, Seattle WA 98101, USA.
URL: http://www.merchantriskcouncil.org/

History 2000, USA. Expanded to Europe, 2010; to Asia 2021. Registration: 501(c)6, USA. **Aims** Make *commerce* safe and profitable everywhere. **Structure** Global and Regional Boards. Committees. **Activities** Events/meetings; knowledge management/information dissemination. **Events** *European Conference* Barcelona (Spain) 2023, *Congress* Las Vegas, NV (USA) 2023, *Asia Conference* Singapore (Singapore) 2022, *Congress* Las Vegas, NV (USA) 2019, *European Conference* London (UK) 2019. **Members** Companies (about 450) in over 20 countries. Membership countries not specified. [2022/XM4716/**C**]

- MERCI – Medical Emergency and Relief Cooperative International (internationally oriented national body)
- Merco Cities Network (#18721)
- **MERCOMUN** Mercado Común Centroamericano (#03666)

♦ MERCOSUL Association for the Rule of Law in International Relations 16721

Contact address not obtained. T. +551130388090. Fax +551138122495. E-mail: noadsao@ noronhaadvogados.com.br.

IGO Relations *Southern Common Market (#19868)*. [2010/XE4438/**E**]

- **MERCOSUL** Mercado Comum do Sul (#19868)
- MERCOSUR Association of Faculties of Architecture of the South (#02128)
- Mercosur Chemical Industry Council (no recent information)
- MERCOSUR Common Market Group (see: #19868)
- Mercosur EU Business Forum / see Mercosur – European Business Forum
- Mercosur – European Business Forum (internationally oriented national body)
- **MERCOSUR** Mercado Común del Sur (#19868)
- MERCOSUR Parliament (#18205)
- Mercosur Parliament (#18204)

♦ Mercosur Social Forum 16722

Contact CASLA – Casa Latino Americana, Rua João Manuel 140, Alto São Francisco, Curitiba PR, 80 510 250, Brazil. T. +554130137570.
URL: http://www.casla.com.br/

Languages Dutch, English, French, German, Portuguese, Spanish. **Events** *Forum* Curitiba (Brazil) 2008. [2009.08.06/XM3798/**F**]

- Mercy Airlift International (internationally oriented national body)
- Mercy Corps Global / see Mercy Corps International
- Mercy Corps International (internationally oriented national body)

♦ Mercy International Association (MIA) 16723

CEO 64-A Lower Baggot St, Dublin, CO. DUBLIN, Ireland. T. +35316618061. E-mail: info@ mercyinternational.ie.
URL: http://www.mercyworld.org/

History 1992, to serve the Sisters of Mercy. Registered in Ireland, Charity no: CHY 10078. **Aims** Oppose trafficking of women and children; promote sustainable development; prevent environmental degradation; respond to refugee crises; respond to natural disasters. **Structure** Board. **Languages** English. **Activities** Training/education; advocacy/lobbying/activism; events/meetings.
Members Congregations; institutes; federations. Members in 7 countries:
Australia, Canada, Ireland, New Zealand, Philippines, UK, USA.
Included in the above, 1 organization listed in this Yearbook:
Sisters of Mercy of the Americas.
IGO Relations Associated with Department of Global Communications of the United Nations. **NGO Relations** Member of: *Forum of Catholic Inspired NGOs (#09905)*; *Laudato Si' Movement (#16403)*. [2018.07.30/XM1444/**D**]

- Mercy International-USA / see Mercy-USA for Aid and Development
- Mercy Without Limits (internationally oriented national body)

♦ Mercy Ships 16724

UK Office The Lighthouse, 12 Meadway Court, Stevenage, SG1 2EF, UK. T. +441438727800. E-mail: info@mercyships.org.uk.
URL: https://www.mercyships.org.uk/

History 1978. Founded as maritime arm of *Youth with a Mission (YWAM, #22020)*; currently no longer officially associated. Registration: Charity Commission, No/ID: 1053055, England and Wales; Charity Commission, No/ID: SC039743, Scotland; 501(c)(3), USA. **Aims** Following the example of Jesus: bring hope and healing to the *poor*, alleviate human *suffering* and distress by bringing *medical* and community services to the poor, empowering them to fulfil their God-given potential. **Languages** English. **Staff** International voluntary crew from over 35 countries. **Finance** Donations; grants; gifts in-kind. **Activities** Healthcare; events/meetings. **Publications** *Onboard Magazine* (3 a year).
Members Offices in 17 countries and territories:
Australia, Canada, Denmark, Faeroe Is, France, Germany, Korea Rep, Netherlands, New Zealand, Norway, Sierra Leone, South Africa, Spain, Sweden, Switzerland, UK, USA.
IGO Relations *United States Agency for International Development (USAID)*. **NGO Relations** Member of: *Extractive Industries Transparency Initiative (EITI, #09229)*; *Partnership for Quality Medical Donations (PQMD)*. [2019.02.12/XF4557/**F**]

- Mercy-USA for Aid and Development (internationally oriented national body)
- Merenkurkun Neuvosto (#16213)
- Meridian House Foundation / see Meridian International Center
- Meridian House International / see Meridian International Center
- Meridian International Center (internationally oriented national body)
- Mérieux Foundation (internationally oriented national body)
- MERIP – Middle East Research and Information Project (internationally oriented national body)

♦ MERLIN 16725

Contact 4th Floor, 53 Parker Street, London, WC2B 5PT, UK. T. +442074398492. E-mail: info@ merlinnetwork.org.
URL: https://merlinnetwork.org/

History Former names and other names: *Merlin Network* – legal name. Registration: Companies House, No/ID: BR022218, Start date: 1 Jan 2020, England and Wales. **Aims** Provide digital music licensing for independents across the globe. **Structure** Board; Global Team; Executive Leadership. [2022/AA2364/**F**]

- Merlin Network / see MERLIN (#16725)

♦ MERLOT African Network (MAN) 16726

Chair Doctoral Program in Science/Math Education, 108 Lee Hall, Southern Univ, Baton Rouge LA 70813, USA.
URL: http://man.merlot.org/

History MERLOT stands for *Multimedia Educational Resource for Learning and Online Teaching*. **Aims** Facilitate communities of e-learning expertise and capacity building for open education, scholarship and development in Africa. **Structure** Executive Council, headed by Chair/Project Director. [2009/XM2963/**E**]

- Mer et monde (internationally oriented national body)
- **MERRCAC** Middle Eastern Regional Radioisotope Centre for the Arab Countries (#16761)
- Mershon Center / see Mershon Center for International Security Studies
- Mershon Center for Education in National Security / see Mershon Center for International Security Studies
- Mershon Center for International Security Studies (internationally oriented national body)
- Mershon Center – Programs of Research and Education in National Security, Leadership and Public Policy / see Mershon Center for International Security Studies
- Mershon Center for the Study of International Security and Public Policy / see Mershon Center for International Security Studies
- Mertz Foundation / see Mertz Gilmore Foundation
- Mertz Gilmore Foundation (internationally oriented national body)

♦ Mesa de Articulación de Asociaciones Nacionales y Redes de ONGs de América Latina y el Caribe (La Mesa de articulación) 16727

Contact Portugal 623, Oficina 4, Santiago, Santiago Metropolitan, Chile.
URL: http://www.mesadearticulacion.org/

History 2006. **Aims** Promote debate and coordination between members on issues of inclusive development, defence and promotion of human rights, as well as formulation of democracy-enhancing policies. **Structure** Central Coordination Committee. **Events** *European Union – Latin America and the Caribbean civil society forum* Madrid (Spain) 2010, *European Union – Latin America and Caribbean civil society forum* Lima (Peru) 2008.
Members Associations (16) in 11 countries:
Argentina, Bolivia, Brazil, Chile, Colombia, Guatemala, Mexico, Paraguay, Peru, Uruguay, Venezuela.
Included in the above, 2 organizations listed in this Yearbook:
Consejo de Educación de Adultos de América Latina (CEAAL, #04707); *Plataforma Interamericana de Derechos Humanos, Democracia y Desarrollo (PIDHDD, #18395)*.
IGO Relations *United Nations Non-Governmental Liaison Service (NGLS, #20591)*. **NGO Relations** Member of: *Forus (#09934)*. [2018/XJ0114/y/**D**]

- **La Mesa de articulación** Mesa de Articulación de Asociaciones Nacionales y Redes de ONGs de América Latina y el Caribe (#16727)
- Mesa de Coordinación Latinoamericana de Comercio Justo (#16307)
- MESAEP – Mediterranean Scientific Association of Environmental Protection (internationally oriented national body)

♦ MESA International 16728

Exec Dir 107 S Southgate Dr, Chandler AZ 85226, USA. T. +14808936883. Fax +14808937775. E-mail: hq@mesa.org.
URL: http://www.mesa.org/

History 1992. Former names and other names: *Manufacturing Execution Systems Association* – former; *Manufacturing Enterprise Solutions Association* – former. **Aims** Improve *operations management* capabilities through the effective application of technology solutions and best practices. **Structure** Board of Directors. Regional Groups (3): Americas; Asia-Pacific; EMEA (Europe, Middle East, Africa). **Languages** English, French, German, Russian. **Staff** 6.00 FTE, paid. **Finance** Sources: members' dues; sponsorship. Annual budget: 900,000 USD. **Activities** Events/meetings; training/education. **Events** *North American Conference* Charlotte, NC (USA) 2015. **Publications** *MESAknows* – newsletter. [2020/XN4954/**C**]

♦ MESA – Middle East Studies Association (internationally oriented national body)
♦ Mesa Redonda sobre Aceite de Palma Sostenible (#18986)
♦ Mesa Redonda Internacional para el Desarrollo de la Orientación / see International Association for Counselling (#11821)
♦ MESCE – Mediterranean Society of Comparative Education (inactive)
♦ MESC – Middle East Solidarity Council (no recent information)
♦ MESC – Middle East Studies Center, Portland (internationally oriented national body)
♦ MeSCo / see Euro-Mediterranean Study Commission (#05727)
♦ **MESEA** Society for Multi-Ethnic Studies: Europe and Americas (#19602)

♦ Mesemb Study Group (MSG) 16729

Contact Brenfield, Bolney Road, Ansty, RH17 5AW, UK. T. +441444459151. Fax +441444454061. E-mail: msg@cactus-mall.com.
URL: http://www.mesemb.org/

History 1986. **Aims** Encourage study and knowledge of plants of the family *mesembryanthemaceae*, commonly known as *living stones*. **Finance** Members' dues. Budget: about pounds8,000. **Publications** *MSG Bulletin* (4 a year).
Members Individuals in 36 countries and territories:
Australia, Austria, Belgium, Canada, China, Croatia, Czechia, Denmark, France, Germany, Hungary, India, Israel, Italy, Japan, Kenya, Malta, Mexico, Monaco, Namibia, Netherlands, New Zealand, Norway, Portugal, Russia, Serbia, Slovakia, South Africa, Spain, Sweden, Switzerland, Taiwan, Türkiye, UK, Ukraine, USA. [2015.06.01/XE3829/v/**E**]

♦ **MESGE** Middle East Society for Gynecological Endoscopy (#16789)
♦ MESIA – Middle East Solar Industry Association (internationally oriented national body)
♦ MESIC – Middle Eastern Society of Infection Control (no recent information)
♦ **MES** Mathematics Education and Society (#16604)
♦ MES – Mezgosudarstvennyj Ekologiceskij Sovet (no recent information)
♦ MESMI / see Middle-East, North Africa and Pakistan Self-Care Industry (#16783)
♦ Mesoamerican Academy of Cosmetic Surgery (internationally oriented national body)
♦ Mesoamerican Alliance of Peoples and Forests (unconfirmed)
♦ Meso-American-Caribbean Sea Hydrographic Commission (see: #13825)

♦ Meso-American and Caribbean Zoo and Aquarium Association . . . 16730

Asociación Mesoamericana y del Caribe de Zoológicos y Acuarios (AMACZOOA)
Pres Simon Bolivar Zoo, Apto 11594, San José, San José, San José, 1000, Costa Rica. T. +50622336701. Fax +50622231817. E-mail: info@fundazoo.org.
URL: http://www.amaczooa.org/

History 1988, Guatemala (Guatemala). Also referred to as *Asociación Mesoamericana de Zoologia (AMAZOO)* and as *Meso-American Zoo Association – Asociación Mesoamericana de Zoológicos*. **Aims** Support Meso-American zoos, aquaria and related institutions and their activity in conservation of Meso-American natural resources. **Structure** Board of Directors; Commissions (5). **Languages** Spanish. **Staff** 1.00 FTE, voluntary. **Finance** Members' dues. Annual budget: US$ 2,000. **Activities** Training/education; events/meetings. **Events** *Congress* Managua (Nicaragua) 2004, *Congress* Chiapas (Mexico) 2002, *Congress* San Salvador (El Salvador) 2000, *Congress* Havana (Cuba) 1998, *Congress* Guatemala (Guatemala) 1993. **Publications** *AMAZOO Bulletin* (4 a year).
Members Full in 15 countries:
Belize, Colombia, Costa Rica, Cuba, Dominican Rep, El Salvador, Guatemala, Honduras, Mexico, Nicaragua, Panama, Peru, Puerto Rico, Trinidad-Tobago, Venezuela.
NGO Relations Member of: *World Association of Zoos and Aquariums (WAZA, #21208).* [2019.04.24/XD3820/**D**]

♦ Mesoamerican Ecotourism Alliance (MEA) 16731

Dir 4076 Crystal Coart, Boulder CO 80304, USA. T. +13034403362. Fax +13034470815.
URL: http://www.travelwithmea.org/

Aims Protect wildlands of globally significant biological diversity by building local capacity through the development and promotion of sustainable tourism as a means for supporting conservation efforts in Mesoamerica. **Structure** Board of Directors, composed of representatives from each of the 20 members from 8 different countries.
Members Full in 8 countries:
Belize, El Salvador, Guatemala, Honduras, Mexico, Nicaragua, Panama, USA.
NGO Relations Member of: *Sustainable Tourism Certification Network of the Americas (STCNA, #20069).* [2015/XJ1875/**D**]

♦ Mesoamerican Reef Fund (#09835)
♦ Mesoamerican Society for Biology and Conservation (#19429)
♦ Mesoamerican Women in Resistance (unconfirmed)
♦ Meso-American Zoo Association / see Meso-American and Caribbean Zoo and Aquarium Association (#16730)
♦ Mesogiako Agronomiko Instituto Chanion (#16642)
♦ **MESOT** Middle East Society for Organ Transplantation (#16790)
♦ **MESPE** Mediterranean Society of Pacing and Electrophysiology (#16681)
♦ MESpine / see Middle East Spine Society (#16792)
♦ Messaging, Malware and Mobile Anti-Abuse Working Group (internationally oriented national body)
♦ Messianic Jewish Ministries International / see Messianic Jewish Movement International (#16732)

♦ Messianic Jewish Movement International (MJMI) 16732

Mailing Address PO Box 5846, Sun City AZ 85376-5846, USA.
URL: http://www.mjmi.org/

History 1963, USA. Founded by Manny Brotman (died 1999). Former names and other names: *Shalom Incorporated* – former (1963); *Messianic Jewish Ministries International* – alias. **Publications** *MJMI Newsletter*. Catalogue of books; tapes; videos.
Members Offices in 4 countries:
Argentina, Canada, Netherlands, USA.
NGO Relations *Grace Communion International (#10685).* [2013/XE2856/**E**]

♦ **MESS** Middle East Spine Society (#16792)
♦ **MESSM** Middle East Society for Sexual Medicine (#16791)
♦ MESTMO – Mediterranean Society of Tumor Marker Oncology (no recent information)
♦ Mesures convenues pour la conservation de la faune et de la flore de l' Antarctique (1964 treaty)
♦ Mesures pour encourager le développement de l'industrie audiovisuelle (inactive)

♦ Metabolic Syndrome Institute 16733

Contact address not obtained.
URL: http://www.metabolicsyndromeinstitute.com/

History 2003, France. Registered in accordance with French law. **Aims** Provide an international multidisciplinary approach to a worldwide public *health* problem; disseminate knowledge about the metabolic syndrome. **Structure** Executive Board; International Scientific Committee. [2016/XM4651/j/**E**]

♦ Metabolomics Society (MetSoc) 16734

Main Office c/o CT Corp System, 155 Federal St, Ste 700, Boston MA 02110, USA. E-mail: info@metabolomicssociety.org.
URL: http://www.metabolomicssociety.org/

History Mar 2004. **Aims** Promote growth and development of the field of metabolomics internationally; increase collaboration in the field. **Structure** Board of Directors. **Finance** Members' dues. **Events** *Annual Conference* Niagara Falls, ON (Canada) 2023, *Annual Conference* Valencia (Spain) 2022, *Annual Conference* 2021, *Annual Conference* Shanghai (China) 2020, *Annual Conference* The Hague (Netherlands) 2019. **Publications** *Metabolomics Journal*. **Members** Individuals (approx 1,000) in 40 countries. Membership countries not specified. **NGO Relations** Affiliated with (2): *Nordic Metabolomics Society (#17343)*; *Réseau Francophone de Métabolomique et Fluxomique (RFMF).* [2022/XM0100/**F**]

♦ META – International Conference on Metamaterials, Photonic Crystals and Plasmonics (meeting series)
♦ Metal Forming – International Conference on Metal Forming (meeting series)

♦ Metalock International Association (MIA) 16735

Secretariat Lion Court, Staunton Harold Hall, Melbourne Road, Ashby-de-la-Zouch, LE65 1RT, UK. T. +441332695081. Fax +441332695080. E-mail: enquiries@metalockinternational.org.
URL: http://www.metalockinternational.org/

History 1953. Registered in accordance with UK law: 341 3716 78. **Aims** Further development, application and marketing of the Metalock cold *cast iron repair* process. **Structure** Council of Management. **Events** *Annual Conference* Zhoushan (China) 2019, *Annual Conference* Buenos Aires (Argentina) 2018, *Annual Conference* Croatia 2017, *Annual Conference* Bali (Indonesia) 2016, *Annual Conference* Punta Cana (Dominican Rep) 2015. **Members** Companies (over 70). Membership countries not specified. [2020/XN9890/**C**]

♦ Metal Packaging Europe (MPE) 16736

Main Office Ave des Arts 41, 1040 Brussels, Belgium. E-mail: info@metalpackagingeurope.org.
URL: http://metalpackagingeurope.org/

History 2017, on merger of *Beverage Can Makers Europe (BCME, inactive)* and *European Metal Packaging (EMPAC, inactive)*. **Aims** Allow members to contribute more effectively to sustainable developments and resource efficiency, acting as a unified sector involving all parties in the chain. **Structure** Board of Directors.
Members Corporate; national associations; Associate; International Associates. Corporate in 11 countries:
Austria, Belgium, Denmark, France, Germany, Ireland, Italy, Netherlands, Switzerland, Türkiye, UK.
National associations in 10 countries:
Czechia, Denmark, France, Germany, Italy, Netherlands, Slovakia, Spain, Switzerland, UK.
Associate in 5 countries:
Belgium, Germany, Italy, Sweden, Switzerland.
Included in the above, 1 organization listed in this Yearbook:
NGO Relations *European Aluminium (#05893)*; *European Association of Producers of Steel for Packaging (#06167)*; *Fédération Européenne des Aérosols (FEA, #09557).* [2019/XJ9400/**D**]

♦ METALS FOR BUILDINGS 16737

Management c/o European Aluminium, Av de Tervuren 168, 1150 Brussels, Belgium. T. +3227756357. Fax +3227790531. E-mail: info@metalsforbuildings.eu.
URL: http://www.metalsforbuildings.eu/

History 29 Jun 2011. Full title: *European metals alliance for recyclable and sustainable buildings – METALS FOR BUILDINGS*. Registered in accordance with Belgian law, Mar 2013. **Aims** Address unique attributes of metal building products and their value for the future by including end-of-life *recycling* in all studies. **Structure** Board. **Languages** English.
Members Organizations (10):
Association européenne des métaux (EUROMETAUX, #02578); *European Aluminium (#05893)*; *European Association for Panels and Profiles (PPA-Europe, #06142)*; *European Coil Coating Association (ECCA, #06601)*; *European Copper Institute (ECI, #06796)*; *European General Galvanizers Association (EGGA, #07383)*; *European Steel Association (EUROFER, #08835)*; *Fédération des associations européennes des constructeurs de fenêtres et de façades (FAECF, #09456)*; *International Zinc Association (IZA, #15942)* (Europe); *Nickel Institute (#17133).*
NGO Relations Member of: *Construction Products Europe AISBL (#04761).* [2019.05.21/XJ7754/y/**E**]

♦ **META** Mediterranean Travel Association (#16685)
♦ METAMORPHOSE VI AISBL / see Virtual Institute for Artificial Electromagnetic Materials and Metamaterials (#20789)
♦ **METAMORPHOSE VI** Virtual Institute for Artificial Electromagnetic Materials and Metamaterials (#20789)
♦ **META** Multilingual Europe Technology Alliance (#16892)
♦ Metaplastic Breast Cancer Global Alliance (unconfirmed)
♦ METAP – Mediterranean Environmental Technical Assistance Programme (inactive)

♦ Meteoritical Society 16738

Sec US Geologocial Survey, 954 National Center, Reston VA 20192, USA. T. +17036486148.
URL: http://meteoriticalsociety.org/

History Founded 1933. **Aims** Promote research and education in planetary science with emphasis on the study of *meteorites* and other samples of extra-terrestrial materials that further our understanding of the origin and evolution of the solar system; investigate asteroids, comets, interplanetary dust, lunar samples, meteors, planets, moons, craters and other impact features, micrometeorites and tektites. **Structure** Council, comprising President, Vice President, Secretary, Treasurer, Past President and 8 Councillors. **Languages** English. **Staff** None. **Finance** Members' dues. Budget (annual): US$ 85,000. **Events** *Annual Meeting* Brussels (Belgium) 2024, *Annual Meeting* Perth, WA (Australia) 2023, *Annual Meeting* Glasgow (UK) 2022, *Annual Meeting* Chicago, IL (USA) 2021, *Annual Meeting* Glasgow (UK) 2020. **Members** Individuals (1,000 professionals and amateurs) in 47 countries. Membership countries not specified. **NGO Relations** Affiliated member of: *International Union of Geological Sciences (IUGS, #15777).* [2012.06.01/XF1534/v/**F**]

♦ Methanol Institute (internationally oriented national body)
♦ Methodist Church Britain – World Church Office (internationally oriented national body)
♦ Methodist Church Overseas Division / see Methodist Church Britain – World Church Office
♦ Methodist Church of Southern Africa (internationally oriented national body)
♦ Methodist Committee for Overseas Relief / see United Methodist Committee on Relief
♦ Methodistischer Rat für die Arbeit mit Kindern und Jugendlichen in Europa (#07788)
♦ Methodist Relief and Development Fund / see All We Can
♦ Methodist Relief Fund / see All We Can
♦ Métodos Efectivos en Geometria Algebraica (meeting series)
♦ Metre Convention (1875 treaty)
♦ **METREX** Network of European Metropolitan Regions and Areas (#17023)
♦ METRO – Maastrichts Europees Instituut voor Transnationaal Rechtswetenschappelijk Onderzoek (internationally oriented national body)
♦ **Metropolis** World Association of the Major Metropolises (#21158)
♦ Metropolitan Environment Improvement Programme (no recent information)
♦ **MetSoc** Metabolomics Society (#16734)
♦ METU – Middle East Technical University (internationally oriented national body)
♦ MEU – Communion d'églises dans trois continents / see United Evangelical Mission (#20507)
♦ **MEU** Mission évangélique unie (#20507)
♦ **MEVZA** Middle European Volleyball Zonal Association (#16794)
♦ MEWLN – Middle East Women's Leadership Network (internationally oriented national body)
♦ Mexican Association of Caribbean Studies (internationally oriented national body)
♦ Mexican Association for International Education (internationally oriented national body)
♦ Mexican International Studies Association (internationally oriented national body)
♦ Mezdunaroden Centar za Naucna i Tehniceska Informacija (#12514)
♦ Mezdunarodnaja Akademija Arhitektury (#11535)
♦ Mezdunarodnaja Associacija Ekonomiceskih Nauk (#13222)
♦ Mezdunarodnaja Associacija Fondov Mira (#12071)
♦ Mezdunarodnaja Associacija Grazdanskih Aeroportov (inactive)
♦ Mezdunarodnaja Associacija Inspekcii po Trudu (#11983)
♦ Mezdunarodnaja Associacija po Issledovaniju Problem Psihotroniki (no recent information)
♦ Mezdunarodnaja Associacija po Izuceniju Glin (#02688)
♦ Mezdunarodnaja Associacija po Izuceniju Jugo-Vostocnoj Evropy (#02693)
♦ Mezdunarodnaja Associacija Juridiceskih Nauk (#11997)
♦ Mezdunarodnaja Associacija Juristov-Demokratov (#11837)
♦ Mezdunarodnaja Associacija 'Mir cerez Kulturu' (#12070)
♦ Mezdunarodnaja Associacija Mongolovedenija (#12035)

- ♦ Mezdunarodnaja Associacija Multiplikacionnogo Kino (#02698)
- ♦ Mezdunarodnaja Associacija Politiceskoj Nauki (#14615)
- ♦ Mezdunarodnaja Associacija 'Porodnennye Goroda' (#20271)

♦ Mezdunarodnaja Associacija Prepodavatelej Russkogo Jazyka i Literatury (MAPRYAL) 16739

Association internationale des professeurs de langue et littérature russes – International Association of Teachers of Russian Language and Literature

Pres Lieutenant Schmidt Emb 11/2, Room 203, St Petersburg SANKT-PETERBURG, Russia, 199034. T. +78123329421 – +78123329423. E-mail: info@mapryal.org.
URL: http://www.mapryal.org/

History Founded 1967, Paris (France). Statutes adopted at Founding Conference, 8 Sep 1967; and modified at: 2nd General Assembly, 12 Sep 1973, Varna (Bulgaria); 4th General Assembly, 19 Aug 1979, Berlin (German DR); 5th General Assembly, 22-23 Aug 1982, Karlovy Vary (Czechoslovakia); 13 Aug 1990, Moscow (USSR); 26 Aug 1994, Regensburg (Germany). Also known under the acronym *MAPRIAL*. **Aims** Encourage the teaching and study of Russian language and literature; stimulate development of scientific methods of instruction. **Structure** General Assembly (every 4 years); Praesidium. **Languages** Russian. **Staff** 4.00 FTE, paid. **Finance** Members' dues. Sponsoring. **Activities** Research/documentation; events/meetings. **Events** *Congress* Nur-Sultan (Kazakhstan) 2019, *Congress* Granada (Spain) 2015, *Congress* Shanghai (China) 2011, *Congress* Varna (Bulgaria) 2007, *Congress* St Petersburg (Russia) 2003. **Publications** *Vestnik MAPRIAL* (periodical). *Russian Language in the Countries of the World.*

Members National groups of scholars of Russian, institutes of Slavic studies and university departments of Russian language and literature in 74 countries:
Albania, Algeria, Angola, Argentina, Australia, Austria, Belarus, Belgium, Bolivia, Brazil, Bulgaria, Canada, China, Colombia, Côte d'Ivoire, Croatia, Cuba, Czechia, Denmark, Ecuador, Egypt, Estonia, Finland, France, Georgia, Germany, Ghana, Greece, Hungary, India, Ireland, Israel, Italy, Japan, Kazakhstan, Korea DPR, Korea Rep, Kyrgyzstan, Laos, Libya, Lithuania, Madagascar, Mali, Mexico, Moldova, Mongolia, Morocco, Netherlands, New Zealand, Nigeria, Norway, Peru, Poland, Portugal, Romania, Russia, Serbia, Slovakia, Slovenia, Spain, Sri Lanka, Sudan, Sweden, Switzerland, Syrian AR, Tunisia, Uganda, UK, Ukraine, Uruguay, USA, Uzbekistan, Venezuela, Vietnam.
Individuals in 13 countries:
Argentina, Australia, Belgium, Bolivia, Bulgaria, France, Israel, Latvia, Mongolia, Morocco, South Africa, Spain, Sudan.
NGO Relations Member of: *International Federation of Language Teacher Associations (#13468).*

[2017.03.14/XD6055/**D**]

- ♦ Mezdunarodnaja Associacija Rabotnikov Prosvescenija za Vseobcsij Mir (internationally oriented national body)
- ♦ Mezdunarodnaja Associacija Sudovladelcev (inactive)
- ♦ Mezdunarodnaja Associacija po Terminologii (inactive)
- ♦ Mezdunarodnaja Associacija Universitetov (#12246)
- ♦ Mezdunarodnaja Demokraticeskaja Federacija Zenscin (#21022)
- ♦ Mezdunarodnaja Elektrotehniceskaja Komissija / see International Electrotechnical Commission (#13255)
- ♦ Mezdunarodnaja Federacija Bibliotecnyh Associacij i Ucrezdenij (#13470)
- ♦ Mezdunarodnaja Federacija Borcov Soprotivlenija (#13529)
- ♦ Mezdunarodnaja Federacija Himikov (inactive)
- ♦ Mezdunarodnaja Federacija Igry v Sahmaty po Perepiske (#12971)
- ♦ Mezdunarodnaja Federacija Pcelovodnym Obedinenij (#13370)
- ♦ Mezdunarodnaja Federacija Profsojuzov Rabotnikov Prosvescenija (#09662)
- ♦ Mezdunarodnaja Federacija Sportivnoj Akrobatiki (inactive)
- ♦ Mezdunarodnaja Federacija Torgovyh, Kontorskih, Tehniceskih Rabotnikov i Specialistov (inactive)
- ♦ Mezdunarodnaja Hristianskaja Sluzba Delu Mira / see International Christian Peace Service (#12564)
- ♦ Mezdunarodnaja Issledovatelskaja Gruppa po Svincu i Cinku (#14012)
- ♦ Mezdunarodnaja Komissija po Atmosfernomu Elektricestvu (#12665)
- ♦ Mezdunarodnaja Komissija Voennoj Istorii / see International Commission of Military History (#12705)
- ♦ Mezdunarodnaja Kommissija po Istorii Oktjabrskoj Revoljucii v Rossii / see International Commission on the History of the Russian Revolution (#12688)
- ♦ Mezdunarodnaja Kommissija po Istorii Rossiiskoj Revoljucii (#12688)
- ♦ Mezdunarodnaja Konfederacija po Izmeritelnoj Tehnike i Priborostroeniju (#14124)
- ♦ Mezdunarodnaja Korporacija Vypusknikov Sovetskih Ucebnyh Zavedenij / see International Coordination Council of Educational Institutions Alumni (#12959)
- ♦ Mezdunarodnaja Liga Trezvosti i Zdorovja (no recent information)
- ♦ Mezdunarodnaja Medicinskaja Associacija dlja Izucenija Uslovij Zizni i Zdorovija (inactive)
- ♦ Mezdunarodnaja Nepravitelstvennaja Organizacija – Korporacija INCORVUZ / see International Coordination Council of Educational Institutions Alumni (#12959)
- ♦ Mezdunarodnaja Organizacija po Kakao (#12627)
- ♦ Mezdunarodnaja Organizacija po Narodnomu Tvorcestvu (#14447)
- ♦ Mezdunarodnaja Organizacija Radiovescanija i Televidenija (inactive)
- ♦ Mezdunarodnaja Organizacija po Saharu (#15623)
- ♦ Mezdunarodnaja Organizacija po Standartizacii (#14473)
- ♦ Mezdunarodnaja Organizacija Zurnalistov (inactive)
- ♦ Mezdunarodnaja Otraslevaja Organizacija po Sotrudnicestvu v Oblasti Malotonaznoj Himiceskoj Produkcii (inactive)
- ♦ Mezdunarodnaja Registracija Grazdan Mira / see Registre des Citoyens du Monde (#18822)
- ♦ Mezdunarodnaja Sociologiceskaja Associacija (#15553)
- ♦ Mezdunarodnaja Toplivno-Energeticheskaja Associacija (#13688)
- ♦ Mezdunarodnoe Agenstvo po Atomnoj Energii (#12294)
- ♦ Mezdunarodnoe Agenstvo MSKN (#13955)
- ♦ Mezdunarodnoe Bjuro po Izuceniju Vodoplavujuscih Ptic i Vodno-Bolotnyh Ugodij (inactive)
- ♦ Mezdunarodnoe Bjuro po Mehanike Gornyh Porod (#12417)
- ♦ Mezdunarodnoe Bjuro po Molodeznomu Turizmu i Obmenam (inactive)
- ♦ Mezdunarodnoe Bjuro Prosvescenija (#12413)
- ♦ Mezdunarodnoe Dvizenie za Bratskoe Edinstvo Ras i Narodov / see Unis pour l'Equite et la Fin du Racisme (#20490)
- ♦ Mezdunarodnoe Hozjajstvennoe Obedinenie Interatomenergo (#13223)
- ♦ Mezdunarodnoe Hozjajstvennoe Obedinenie po Proizvodstvu Tehnologiceskogo Oborudovanija dlja Tekstilnoj Promyslennosti (inactive)
- ♦ Mezdunarodnoe Obedinenie Bibliotek Vyssih Tehniceskih Skol / see International Association of University Libraries (#12247)
- ♦ Mezdunarodnoe Obedinenie Profsojuzov Energetikov (inactive)
- ♦ Mezdunarodnoe Obedinenie Profsojuzov Rabotnikov Torgovli (inactive)
- ♦ Mezdunarodnoe Obedinenie Profsojuzov Trudjascihsja Metallopromyslennosti (inactive)
- ♦ Mezdunarodnoe Obedinenie Profsojuzov Trudjascihsja Neftjanoj i Rodstvennyh Otraslej Promyslennosti (inactive)
- ♦ Mezdunarodnoe Obedinenie Profsojuzov Trudjascihsja Obscestvennogo Obsluzivanija (#20191)
- ♦ Mezdunarodnoe Obedinenie Profsojuzov Trudjascihsja Piscevoj, Tabacnoj Promyslennosti, Rabotnikov Gostinnic i Rodstvennyh Otraslej (inactive)
- ♦ Mezdunarodnoe Obedinenie Profsojuzov Trudjascihsja Selskogo, Lesnogo Hozjajstva i Plantacij (inactive)
- ♦ Mezdunarodnoe Obedinenie Profsojuzov Trudjascihsja Transporta / see Trade Unions International of Transport, Fisheries and Communication (#20192)
- ♦ Mezdunarodnoe Obedinenie Trudjascihsja Profsojuzov Stroitelstva, Derevoobrabatyvajuscej Promyslennosti i Promyslennosti Stroitelnyh Materialov (#20185)
- ♦ Mezdunarodnoe Obscestvo Avtorskih Prav (no recent information)
- ♦ Mezdunarodnoe Obscestvo po Himii Zerna / see ICC – International Association for Cereal Science and Technology (#11048)
- ♦ Mezdunarodnoe Obscestvo po Hungarologii (#11948)
- ♦ Mezdunarodnoe Obscestvo Invalidov (#05097)
- ♦ Mezdunarodnoe Obscestvo po Marksejderskomu Delu (#15272)
- ♦ Mezdunarodnoe Obscestvo po Masinam dlja Ovoscevodstva, Sadovodstva i Vinogradstva (inactive)
- ♦ Mezdunarodnoe Obscestvo po Termiceskoj Obrabotke i Tehnologij Obrabotki Poverhnosti (#13443)
- ♦ Mezdunarodnoe Obscestvo po Torfu / see International Peatland Society (#14538)
- ♦ Mezdunarodnyj Bank Ekonomicheskogo Sotrudnicestva (#12310)
- ♦ Mezdunarodnyj Centr Naucnoj i Tehniceskoj Informacii (#12514)
- ♦ Mezdunarodnyj Centr Obucajuscih Sistem (#12487)
- ♦ Mezdunarodnyj Fond dlja Razvitija Fiziceskogo Vospitanija i Sporta (no recent information)
- ♦ Mezdunarodnyj Fond Spasenija Arala (#13694)
- ♦ Mezdunarodnyj Institut Mira / see International Institute for Peace (#13907)
- ♦ Mezdunarodnyj Institut Pressy (#14636)
- ♦ Mezdunarodnyj Institut Prikladnogo Sistemnogo Analiza / see International Institute for Applied Systems Analysis (#13861)
- ♦ Mezdunarodnyj Investicionnyj Bank (#13951)
- ♦ Mezdunarodnyj Komitet Byvshih Uznikov Nojergamme (#14347)
- ♦ Mezdunarodnyj Komitet Byvsih Uznikov Buhenvalda-Dora (#12749)
- ♦ Mezdunarodnyj Komitet Byvsih Uznikov Dahau (#04174)
- ♦ Mezdunarodnyj Komitet Byvsi Uznikov Osvencima (#12297)
- ♦ Mezdunarodnyj Komitet Detskih i Junoseskih Organizacij (inactive)
- ♦ Mezdunarodnyj Komitet Istoriceskih Nauk (#12777)
- ♦ Mezdunarodnyj Komitet po Izuceniju Sovetskogo Sojuza i Vostocnoj Evropy / see International Council for Central and East European Studies (#13002)
- ♦ Mezdunarodnyj Komitet po Petrologii Uglja (#12750)
- ♦ Mezdunarodnyj Kongress o Primenenii Matematik v Tehniceskih Naukah (meeting series)
- ♦ Mezdunarodnyj Kooperativnyj Alians (#12944)
- ♦ Mezdunarodnyj Koordinacionnyj Komitet po Immunologii Reprodukcii (#12958)
- ♦ Mezdunarodnyj Koordinacionnyj Sovet Associacij Aviacionno-Kosmiceskih Otraslej Promyslennosti (#12956)
- ♦ Mezdunarodnyj Naucnyj Centr Udobrenij (#03767)
- ♦ Mezdunarodnyj Postojannyj Komitet Profsojuzov Poligrafistov (inactive)
- ♦ Mezdunarodnyj Sejsmologiceskij Centr (#14830)
- ♦ Mezdunarodnyj Sojuz Aviacionnogo Strahovanija (#15750)
- ♦ Mezdunarodnyj Sojuz po Izuceniju Cetverticnogo Perioda (#15811)
- ♦ Mezdunarodnyj Sojuz Selskohozjajstvennyh Studentov / see International Association of Students in Agricultural and Related Sciences (#12191)
- ♦ Mezdunarodnyj Sojuz Studenceskih Teatrov (inactive)
- ♦ Mezdunarodnyj Sovet po Filosofii i Gumanitarnym Naukam (#13061)
- ♦ Mezdunarodnyj Sovet po Izuceniju Sovetskogo Sojuza i Vostocnoj Evropy / see International Council for Central and East European Studies (#13002)
- ♦ Mezdunarodnyj Sovet po Izuceniju Srednej i Vostocnoj Evropy (#13002)
- ♦ Mezdunarodnyj Sovet po Psenice / see International Grains Council (#13731)
- ♦ Mezdunarodnyj Sovet Sturmanov Aviakompanij (inactive)
- ♦ Mezdunarodnyj Sovet po Voprosam Pamjatnikov i Dostoprimecatelnyh Mest (#13049)
- ♦ Mezdunarodnyj Sovet po Zernu (#13731)
- ♦ Mezdunarodnyj Standartnyj Kniznyj Nomer / see International ISBN Agency (#13955)
- ♦ Mezdunarodnyj Statisticeskij Institut (#15603)
- ♦ Mezdunarodnyj Tehniceskij Komitet po Predotvrasceniju i Tuseniju Pozarov / see CTIF International Association of Fire and Rescue Services (#04979)
- ♦ Mezgosudarstvennaja Koordinacionnaja Vodohozjajstvennaja Comissija Centralnoj Azii (#15979)
- ♦ Mezgosudarstvennyj Ekologiceskij Sovet (no recent information)
- ♦ Mezgosudarstvennyj Ekonomiceskij Komitet Ekonomiceskogo Sojuza (no recent information)
- ♦ Mezgosudarstvennyj Sovet Gosudarstv Centralnoj Azii po Problemam Aralskogo Morja (inactive)
- ♦ Mezhdunarodna Fondatsia Ljudmila Zhivkova / see St Cyril and St Methodius International Foundation
- ♦ Mezhdunarodnaja Sputnikovaja Sistema Poiska i Spasanija / see International Cospas-Sarsat Programme (#12975)
- ♦ Mezhdunarodnaya Assotsiatsia – Eposy Narodov Mira (no recent information)
- ♦ Mezhdunarodnaya Assotsiatsiya Rabotnikov Agrarnykh (no recent information)
- ♦ Mezhgosudarstvennyi Bank (#15978)
- ♦ Mezhgosudarstvennyj aviacionnyj komitet (#15977)
- ♦ Mezinarodni Asociace Plavcu A Voraru (#15691)
- ♦ Mezinarodni Centr Vedeckych a Technickych Informaci (#12514)
- ♦ Mezinárodni komise pro ochranu Labe (#13249)
- ♦ Mezinarodni Komise pro Ocranu Oddry pvred Znecistenim (#13250)
- ♦ Mezinarodni Kulturni Liga (inactive)
- ♦ Mezinarodni Sdruzeni pro Psychotronicky Vyzkum (no recent information)
- ♦ Mezinarodni Svaz pro Nabozenskou Svobodu (#12130)
- ♦ Mezparlamentskaja Assambleja Gosudarstv Ucastnikov Sodruzestva Nezavissimyh Gosudarstv (#15958)
- ♦ Mezparlamentskaja Assambleja SNG / see Interparliamentary Assembly of Member Nations of the Commonwealth of Independent States (#15958)
- ♦ Mezpravitelstvennaja Komissija po Sotrudnicestvu Socialisticeskih Stran v Oblasti Vycislitelnoj Tehniki (inactive)
- ♦ Mezpravitelstvennaja Okeanograficeskaja Komissija (#11496)
- ♦ Mezrabpom – International Workers Aid, 1925 (inactive)
- ♦ Mezsovprof – International Council of Trade and Industrial Unions (inactive)
- ♦ Mezzofantibund – Union internationale des associations des langues étrangères (inactive)
- ♦ MFA Forum / see Broadband Forum (#03334)
- ♦ MFAL – Multiversidad Franciscana de América Latina (unconfirmed)
- ♦ MFA – Media Focus on Africa (internationally oriented national body)
- ♦ **MFA** Migrant Forum in Asia (#16798)
- ♦ MFAMW – Modern Free and Accepted Masons of the World (internationally oriented national body)
- ♦ MFAWP – Musicians and Fine Artists for World Peace (internationally oriented national body)
- ♦ MFBT – Miedzynarodowa Federacja Banków Terminologii (inactive)
- ♦ MFC / see International Confederation of Christian Family Movements (#12851)
- ♦ **MFC** Media Freedom Coalition (#16618)
- ♦ **MFC** Microfinance Centre (#16745)
- ♦ MFDI – Media for Development International (internationally oriented national body)
- ♦ MFE – Mouvement des fédéralistes européens (inactive)
- ♦ MFF – Investing in coastal ecosystems / see Mangroves for the Future (#16565)
- ♦ **MFF** Mangroves for the Future (#16565)
- ♦ **MFG** Madagascar Fauna and Flora Group (#16540)
- ♦ MFHR – Marangopoulos Foundation for Human Rights (internationally oriented national body)
- ♦ MFIC – Missionary Franciscan Sisters of the Immaculate Conception (religious order)
- ♦ **MFI** Malaria Foundation International (#16558)
- ♦ MFJC – Memorial Foundation for Jewish Culture (internationally oriented national body)
- ♦ MFLZ / see St Cyril and St Methodius International Foundation
- ♦ MFMI – Men for Missions International (internationally oriented national body)
- ♦ **MFM** Mouvement fédéraliste mondial (#21404)
- ♦ **MF** Mountain Forum (#16861)
- ♦ **MFN** MicroFinance Network (#16746)
- ♦ **MFO** Multinational Force and Observers (#16897)
- ♦ **MFP** Les Médias Francophones Publics (#16621)

♦ **MFPRM** Mediterranean Forum of Physical and Rehabilitation Medicine (#16652)
♦ **MFSA** Mezdunarodnyj Fond Spasenija Arala (#13694)
♦ **MFS** Multinational Finance Society (#16896)
♦ MFSN / see MicroFinance Network (#16746)
♦ MFS – Workshop on Method of Fundamental Solutions (meeting series)
♦ **MFW4A** Making Finance Work for Africa (#16555)
♦ **MFWA** Media Foundation for West Africa (#16617)
♦ **MGA** Multi-GNSS Asia (#16884)
♦ MGCA – Martial Arts Games Council of Asia (inactive)
♦ **MGC** Mekong-Ganga Cooperation Scheme (#16700)
♦ MGCY / see Children and Youth International (#03882)
♦ MGI-CPAAI / see MGI Worldwide (#16740)
♦ MGI / see International Masters Games Association (#14117)
♦ MGI / see MGI Worldwide (#16740)
♦ MGIMO – Moskovskij Gosudarstvennyj Institut Mezdunarodnyh Otnosenij (internationally oriented national body)
♦ MG – International Conference on Megagauss Magnetic Field Generation and Related Topics (meeting series)

♦ MGI Worldwide 16740

CEO IBex House, 61 Baker Street, Weybridge, KT13 8AH, UK.
URL: https://www.mgiworld.com/

History 1947. Current legal title adopted on merger with *CPA Associates International (CPAAI, inactive)*, 2020. Former names and other names: *MGI-CPAAI* – legal name (2020); *Midsnell* – former; *Midsnell Group International (MGI)* – former; *MGI Worldwide with CPAAI* – alias (2020). Registration: Company limited by guarantee, No/ID: 013238V, Isle of Man. **Aims** Bring together independent audit, accounting, tax and consulting firms. **Structure** International Committee; Global Management. Regions (8): Africa; Asia; Australasia; Europe; Latin America; Middle East and North Africa; North America; UK & Ireland. **Activities** Events/meetings; guidance/assistance/consulting. **Events** *MGI European Region Meeting* Vienna (Austria) 2022, *MGI European Region Meeting* Stockholm (Sweden) 2019. [2022/AA0760/**F**]

♦ MGI Worldwide with CPAAI / see MGI Worldwide (#16740)
♦ MgM Mine Clearance NGO / see People Against Landmines
♦ MgM – Stiftung Menschen gegen Minen (internationally oriented national body)
♦ **MGPoF** Major Groups Partnership on Forests (#16553)
♦ **MGPR** Mediterranean Group of Pesticides Research (#16654)
♦ MGSA – Modern Greek Studies Association (internationally oriented national body)
♦ **MGSD** Mediterranean Group for the Study of Diabetes (#16655)
♦ **MGS** Mediterranean Garden Society (#16653)
♦ **MGS** Movimento Giovanile Salesiano (#19039)
♦ MHAL Perspective / see Parc des trois pays – Espace ouvert sans frontières (#18195)
♦ MHA – Madonna House Apostolate (religious order)
♦ MHB – Men Having Babies (internationally oriented national body)
♦ MHC / see Health Alliance International
♦ MHD – Malteser Hilfsdienst (internationally oriented national body)
♦ **MHE** Mental Health Europe (#16715)
♦ MHI – Maventy Health International (internationally oriented national body)
♦ MHMR / see European Association for Mental Health in Intellectual Disability (#06118)
♦ MHM – Societas Missionariorum Sancti Joseph de Mill Hill (religious order)
♦ **MHRA** Modern Humanities Research Association (#16843)
♦ MIAE – Mouvement International d'Aide à l'Enfance (internationally oriented national body)
♦ MIA – Maritime Information Association (internationally oriented national body)
♦ **MIA** Mercy International Association (#16723)
♦ **MIA** Metalock International Association (#16735)
♦ **MIAMSI** Mouvement international d'apostolat des milieux sociaux indépendants (#16864)
♦ MIAP – Mouvement international d'action pour la paix (inactive)
♦ **MIASA** Mining Industry Association of Southern Africa (#16812)
♦ MIAS – Maryknoll Institute of African Studies (internationally oriented national body)
♦ MIATCO / see Food Export Association of the Midwest USA
♦ MIAZ / see International Institute for Archival Science of Trieste and Maribor (#13862)
♦ MIB – McKenzie Institute Benelux (internationally oriented national body)
♦ **MIB** Mezdunarodnyj Investicionnyj Bank (#13951)
♦ Micah / see Micah Global (#16741)

♦ Micah Global 16741

Intl Dir PO Box 381, Carlisle, CA1 9FE, UK. T. +441228231073. E-mail: info@micahglobal.org.
Intl Coordinator address not obtained.
URL: http://micahglobal.org/

History Sep 1999, Kuala Lumpur (Malaysia). Founded as *Micah Network – Réseau michée – Red Miqueas – Rede Miquéias*, by a group of leaders from Christian relief and development organizations. Previously also known as *Micah*. Merged with *Micah Challenge (inactive)* and current title adopted, Jan 2015. Registration: Charity Commission, No/ID: 1103048, Start date: 5 Apr 2004, England and Wales. **Aims** Motivate and equip a global community of *Christians* to embrace and practice integral mission. **Structure** International Board; Regional and National Coordination Groups; Secretariat. **Languages** English, French, Portuguese, Russian, Spanish. **Staff** 2.00 FTE, paid. **Finance** Members' dues. **Activities** Advocacy/lobbying/activism; training/education; networking/liaising. **Events** *Triennial Global Consultation* 2021, *Triennial Global Consultation* Tagaytay (Philippines) 2018, *Triennial Global Consultation* Lima (Peru) 2015, *Triennial Global Consultation* Thun (Switzerland) 2012. **Publications** *Micah Global Newsletter* (12 a year); *Micah Global Prayer Focus* (12 a year). M-Series books.

Members Full: implementing aid and mission organizations, colleges, local churches; Associate: networks, alliance, coalitions; Individual. Organizations (about 772) in 96 countries. Membership countries not specified.
Included in the above, 16 organizations listed in this Yearbook:
Included in the above, 16 organizations listed in this Yearbook:
African Christian Youths Development Forum (ACYDF, no recent information); Association of Evangelicals in Africa (AEA, #02587); Baptist World Aid Australia; CEDAR Fund; Feba Radio (#09283); Leprosy Mission International (TLMI, #16446); ORA International; Servants to Asia's Urban Poor; Tear; TEAR Australia; TEAR Fund; TearFund, Schweiz; Tearfund, UK; Viva Network (#20800); World Relief; World Renew.

NGO Relations Partner of: *World Evangelical Alliance (WEA, #21393).* Member of: *Restored.* Links with numerous NGOs, including: *Christian Blind Mission (CBM); Compassion International (CI, #04413); Integral (#11364); Interserve (#15974); SIL International (#19278).* [2021/XM2801/y/**F**]

♦ Micah Network / see Micah Global (#16741)
♦ MICA – Multinational Interstitial Cystitis Association (inactive)
♦ **MICCAI Society** Medical Image Computing and Computer Assisted Intervention Society (#16624)
♦ MIC – Congregatio Clericorum Marianorum ab Immaculata Conceptione Beatissimae Virginis Mariae (religious order)
♦ MICEFA – Mission Interuniversitaire de Coordination des Echanges Franco-Américains (internationally oriented national body)

♦ MICHAEL Culture Association 16742

Coordinator Rue de la Presse 4, 1000 Brussels, Belgium. T. +33631133574. E-mail: contact@michael-culture.eu.
Project Manager address not obtained.
Communication Manager address not obtained.
URL: http://www.michael-culture.eu/

History Apr 2007. MICHAEL stands for *Multilingual Inventory of Cultural Heritage in Europe*. Registration: No/ID: 0890.539.479, Start date: 3 Jul 2007, Belgium; EU Transparency Register, No/ID: 007579634856-38, Start date: 17 May 2019. **Aims** Promote and valorize European digital cultural heritage content; develop tools and services for cultural institutions and the general public; support European and national cultural policies; enhance the network of European professionals working on digital cultural heritage. **Structure** General Assembly (annual); Board of Directors. **Languages** English, French. **Activities** Advocacy/lobbying/activism; guidance/assistance/consulting; knowledge management/information dissemination; networking/liaising. **Publications** Regular publications based on Working Group topics; guidelines. **Information Services** *Multilingual Inventory of Digitized Cultural Collections Online in Europe*; *Terminology Management Platform.*

Members Formal members (13), gathering over 150 public and private institutions from 22 countries. Formal members in 10 countries:
Bulgaria, Czechia, Estonia, France, Germany, Greece, Hungary, Italy, Latvia, Poland.

NGO Relations Member of (1): *European Heritage Alliance 3.3 (#07477).* Represented on Board and Executive Committee of: *Europeana Foundation (#05839).* [2020/XM2658/**E**]

♦ Michael J Fox Foundation (internationally oriented national body)
♦ The Michael J Fox Foundation for Parkinson's Research / see Michael J Fox Foundation
♦ Michael Succow Foundation for the Protection of Nature (internationally oriented national body)
♦ Michael Succow Stiftung zum Schutz der Natur (internationally oriented national body)
♦ MIC – Meridian International Center (internationally oriented national body)
♦ MIC – Missionary Sisters of the Immaculate Conception (religious order)
♦ MIC – Missionary Sisters of the Immaculate Conception (religious order)
♦ Microalgae International Union (no recent information)
♦ Microclinic International (internationally oriented national body)

♦ Microcredit Summit Campaign 16743

Campagne du sommet du microcrédit – Campaña de la Cumbre de Microcrédito

Dir c/o RESULTS, 1101 15th St NW, Ste 1200, Washington DC 20005, USA. T. +12026379600. Fax +12024661396.
Youtube: https://www.youtube.com/channel/UCc4JUT6kvm24d5pD_moFFiA

History 4 Feb 1997, Washington DC (USA), during the Microcredit Summit. Initially a nine-year campaign. A project of *RESULTS*. **Aims** Work to ensure that 175 million of the world's *poorest* families, especially the women of those families, receive credit for self-employment and other financial and business services by the end of 2015. **Activities** carried out in line with the Millennium Development Goal on halving poverty and aim to ensure that the world's poorest families move from below US$1 a day, adjusted for purchasing power parity (PPP), to above US$1 a day, adjusted for PPP, by the end of 2015; with an average of 5 members per family this would mean that 875 million family members would be affected. Organizes: Annual Meeting; regional events. **Events** *Microcredit Summit* Abu Dhabi (United Arab Emirates) 2016, *Microcredit Summit* Mérida (Mexico) 2014, *Partnerships against Poverty Summit* Manila (Philippines) 2013, *Global Microcredit Summit* Spain 2011, *Global microcredit summit / Global Summit* Halifax, NS (Canada) 2006. **Publications** *Microcredit Summit E-News* (6 a year) – electronic newsletter; *State of the Microcredit Summit Campaign Report* (annual). **NGO Relations** Too many to list (available via website). [2016/XF5745/**F**]

♦ Microenergia – Habitat Microempresario (#16744)

♦ Microenergia – Micro Business Habitat 16744

Microenergia – Habitat Microempresario

Microenergia Secretariat Bauness 2992, 1 Piso A, 1431 Buenos Aires, Argentina. T. +541147559518 – +541147956417.
URL: http://microenergia.blogspot.com.ar/

History 2001. Registered in accordance with Argentinian law. **Aims** Increase research and action to assist territorial planning and micro enterprise clusters in search of *sustainable local* development. **Structure** Council, comprising President, Secretary, Treasurer and 2 further members. Advisory Council of 4 members. **Languages** English, Spanish. **Staff** Permanent: 6 part-time, voluntary; project: 4 voluntary. **Finance** Members' dues. Other sources: Income from activities; sales; contributions from donors. **Activities** Organizes exhibitions and training courses. Implements projects, combining housing and infrastructure to support micro-business. Participates in symposia. **Publications** Papers.

Members Individuals in 6 countries and territories:
Argentina, Colombia, El Salvador, Palestine, Rwanda, Uganda.

IGO Relations Cooperates on research projects with: *Office of the United Nations High Commissioner for Human Rights (OHCHR, #17697).* **NGO Relations** Links with national organizations. [2015/XF6614/**F**]

♦ Microfinance African Institutions Network (internationally oriented national body)

♦ Microfinance Centre (MFC) 16745

Exec Dir ul Noakowskiego 10/38, 00-666 Warsaw, Poland. T. +48226223465. Fax +48226223465. E-mail: microfinance@mfc.org.pl.
URL: http://www.mfc.org.pl/

Aims Contribute to poverty reduction and the development of human potential by promoting a socially-oriented and sustainable microfinance sector that provides adequate financial and non-financial services to a large numbers of poor families and micro-entrepreneurs. **Structure** Board of Directors. **Staff** 10.00 FTE, paid. **Finance** Supported by: *Ford Foundation (#09858); ICCO – Interchurch Organization for Development Cooperation; European Commission (EC, #06633); European Investment Bank (EIB, #07599); Oxfam Novib; Deutsche Gesellschaft für Internationale Zusammenarbeit (GIZ); The European Fund for Southeast Europe (EFSE, #07368).* **Activities** Knowledge management/information dissemination; guidance/assistance/consulting. **Events** *Annual Conference* Budva (Montenegro) 2013, *Annual Conference* Prague (Czech Rep) 2011, *Annual Conference* Astana (Kazakhstan) 2010, *Annual Conference* Belgrade (Serbia) 2009, *Annual Conference* Ulaanbaatar (Mongolia) 2008.

Members Full in 34 countries:
Albania, Armenia, Austria, Azerbaijan, Belgium, Bosnia-Herzegovina, Bulgaria, Croatia, France, Georgia, Germany, Greece, Hungary, Ireland, Kazakhstan, Kosovo, Kyrgyzstan, Luxembourg, Moldova, Mongolia, Montenegro, Netherlands, North Macedonia, Poland, Romania, Russia, Serbia, Slovakia, Switzerland, Tajikistan, UK, Ukraine, USA, Uzbekistan.
Included in the above, 6 organizations listed in this Yearbook:
European Microfinance Network (EMN, #07792); European Microfinance Platform (E-MFP, #07793); FINCA International; International Association of Investors in the Social Economy (INAISE, #11971); Mercy Corps International (MCI); Oikocredit International (Oikocredit, #17704).

NGO Relations Member of: *International Association of Investors in the Social Economy (INAISE, #11971); Small Enterprise Education and Promotion Network (SEEP); Social Performance Task Force (SPTF, #19343).* Collaborates with: *Alliance for Financial Inclusion (AFI, #00679); Consultative Group to Assist the Poor (CGAP, #04768); Habitat for Humanity International (HFHI); ICCO – Interchurch Organization for Development Cooperation.* [2020/XJ7013/y/**F**]

♦ MicroFinance Network (MFN) 16746

Réseau de microfinance – Red de MicroFinanzas

Dir Insurgentes Sur 1458, Col Actipan, 03230 Mexico City CDMX, Mexico. T. +525552767348 – +525552767251. Fax +525552767258.

History Apr 1993, Bolivia, as *Micro Financial Services Network (MFSN) – Red de Servicios Micro Financieros.* **Aims** Promote the commercial approach to microfinance among policy makers, donors and practitioners; facilitate the process of transformation of microfinance organizations into regulated financial institutions; provide network members with access to information and expertise that increases their knowledge about best practices in microfinance; improve, through the members, the lives of low-income people through the provision of credit, savings and other financial services. **Structure** Steering Committee, composed of 5 elected members representing the major geographical regions of the world. **Finance** Members' dues. Donations. **Activities** Events/meetings; networking/liaising; knowledge management/information dissemination; advocacy/lobbying/activism; financial and/or material support. **Events** *Conference* Nairobi (Kenya) 2009, *Conference* Agra (India) 2008, *Conference* Morocco 2007, *Conference* UK 2006, *Conference* Bolivia 2005. **Publications** *Challenges to Microfinance Commercialization* (2002) by Kelly Hatel and Sahra Halpern; *Current Governance Practices of Microfinance Institutions* (1998); *Moving Microfinance Forward* (1998);

Establishing a Microfinance Industry: Governance, Best Practices and Access to Capital Markets (1997) by Craig Churchill; *Key Issues in Microfinance: Supervision and Regulation, Financing Sources, Expansion of Microfinance Institutions* (1996) by Craig Churchill. Technical guides; occasional papers.
Members Organizations, financial institutions, banks (27), in 23 countries:
Bangladesh, Benin, Bolivia, Cambodia, Canada, Chile, Colombia, Dominican Rep, Egypt, Ghana, India, Indonesia, Kenya, Kyrgyzstan, Mali, Mexico, Nicaragua, Peru, Philippines, Poland, Tanzania UR, Uganda, USA.
Included in the above, 2 organizations listed in this Yearbook:
ACCION International; *Calmeadow Charitable Foundation (CCF)*.
NGO Relations Support Institutions: ACCION International; Calmeadow Charitable Foundation (CCF).
[2009/XF3304/**F**]

♦ Micro Financial Services Network / see MicroFinance Network (#16746)

♦ Microinsurance Network 16747

Exec Dir Rue Glesener 39, L-1631 Luxembourg, Luxembourg. T. +35226297825. Fax +35226297869. E-mail: info@microinsurancenetwork.org.
URL: https://microinsurancenetwork.org/

History 2002. Set up as the Working Group on Microinsurance of *Consultative Group to Assist the Poor (CGAP, #04768)*. Officially launched as a Network, 2009. Became an independent structure, 31 May 2012. Fully operational since 1 Mar 2013. Registration: Luxembourg. **Aims** Improve access to effective risk management tools in order for people of all income levels, and specially low-income consumers, to become more resilient and less vulnerable to daily and catastrophic risks; prioritise the needs, interests and well-being of beneficiaries. **Structure** General Assembly; Board of Directors; Executive Team. **Finance** Members' dues. Funded by Government of Luxembourg and grant funding. **Activities** Events/meetings; publishing activities; advocacy/lobbying/activism. **Events** *International Microinsurance Conference* Dhaka (Bangladesh) 2019, *Consultative Forum* Johannesburg (South Africa) 2019, *Consultative Forum* Panama (Panama) 2019, *Consultative Forum* Buenos Aires (Argentina) 2018, *International Microinsurance Conference* Lusaka (Zambia) 2018. **Publications** *Network Exchange* (12 a year) – newsletter; *The Landscape of Microinsurance Studies* (annual); *The State of Microinsurance* (annual) – journal. **Information Services** *World Map of Microinsurance (WMM)*.
Members Institutional; individual. Institutions include the following 13 listed in this Yearbook:
Access to Insurance Initiative (A2ii, #00051); *ADA Microfinance*; *Agence française de développement (AFD)*; *Consultative Group to Assist the Poor (CGAP, #04768)*; *Deutsche Gesellschaft für Internationale Zusammenarbeit (GIZ)*; *Federación Interamericana de Empresas de Seguros (FIDES, #09331)*; *International Actuarial Association (IAA, #11586)*; *International Fund for Agricultural Development (IFAD, #13692)*; *Swiss Agency for Development and Cooperation (SDC)*; *The World Bank Group (#21218)*; *United Nations Capital Development Fund (UNCDF, #20524)*; *Women's World Banking (WWB, #21037)*; *World Food Programme (WFP, #21510)*.
NGO Relations Instrumental in setting up (1): *Access to Insurance Initiative (A2ii, #00051)*.
[2023/XM5995/y/**F**]

♦ Micromachine Summit (meeting series)
♦ Micro and Nanotechnology Commercialization Education Foundation / see MANCEF (#16563)

♦ Micronutrient Forum 16748

Main Office 1201 Eye St NW, 10th Fl, Washington DC 20005-3915, USA. E-mail: info@micronutrientforum.org.
URL: https://micronutrientforum.org/

History 2006. Founded by *United States Agency for International Development (USAID)*, merger of *International Nutritional Anemia Consultative Group (INACG, inactive)* and *International Vitamin A Consultative Group (IVACG, inactive)*. **Aims** Serve as an internationally recognized authority, catalyst and convenor for sharing expertise, insight and experience relevant to the control of micronutrient deficiencies and their consequences worldwide. **Structure** Steering Committee of up to 15 members, including Chairman and Secretary. Secretariat. **Languages** English. **Staff** 2.00 FTE, paid. **Finance** USAID. **Activities** Sponsors, organizes and conducts international meetings of experts (annual); collaborates with international organizations in developing and establishing guidelines for public policy; provides technical guidance to implementors and policy makers through state-of-the-art publications. **Events** *Global Conference (MNF CONNECTED)* 2020, *Global Conference* Cancún (Mexico) 2016, *Global Conference* Addis Ababa (Ethiopia) 2014, *Meeting* Ankara (Turkey) 2007, *Consequences and control of micronutrient deficiencies* Istanbul (Turkey) 2007. **NGO Relations** Secretariat provided by: *International Life Sciences Institute (ILSI, #14044)*. Affiliate Affiliate Member of: *International Union of Nutritional Sciences (IUNS, #15796)*.
[2022/XM1933/**F**]

♦ Micronutrient Initiative / see Nutrition International (#17627)

♦ Micropalaeontology Society, The (TMS) 16749

Sec Aarhus Univ, Vejlsøvej 25, 8600 Silkeborg, Denmark.
Pres British Geological Survey, Nicker Hill, Keyworth, Nottingham, NG12 5GG, UK. T. +447982467403.
URL: http://tmsoc.org/

History 1970. Former names and other names: *British Micropalaeontological Group* – former (1970 to 1975); *British Micropalaeontological Society* – former (1975 to 2001). Registration: Charity Commission, No/ID: 284013, England and Wales. **Aims** Advance education in the study of micropalaeontology. **Structure** General Meeting (annual); Trustees. **Languages** English. **Staff** None. **Finance** Sources: members' dues. **Activities** Events/meetings; knowledge management/information dissemination. **Events** *Annual Conference* Bremen (Germany) 2022, *Annual Conference* Prague (Czechia) 2021, *Annual Conference* London (UK) 2020. **Publications** *Journal of Micropalaeontology*; *Newsletter of Micropalaeontology*.
Members Full in 37 countries:
Argentina, Australia, Austria, Belgium, Brazil, Canada, China, Colombia, Côte d'Ivoire, Czechia, Denmark, Finland, France, Germany, Greece, India, Ireland, Israel, Italy, Japan, Mexico, Netherlands, Norway, Poland, Portugal, Romania, Russia, Saudi Arabia, Slovakia, Spain, Sweden, Switzerland, Trinidad-Tobago, UK, Ukraine, United Arab Emirates, USA.
NGO Relations Affiliated with (4): *Collegium Palynologicum Scandinavicum (CPS, #04118)*; *International Association of Radiolarian Palaeontologists (INTERRAD, #12120)*; *International Nannoplankton Association (INA, #14208)*; *International Research Group on Ostracoda (IRGO, #14730)*. Also links with national foundations.
[2022.05.04/XM0191/**F**]

♦ Micro Rainbow International Foundation (unconfirmed)
♦ Microscopy Society of Southern Africa (internationally oriented national body)
♦ Microsoft Gezondheidszorg Gebruikers Groep Europa (#16750)

♦ Microsoft Healthcare Users Group Europe (MS-HUGe) 16750

Microsoft Gezondheidszorg Gebruikers Groep Europa

Contact Kortrijksesteenweg 214, bus 4, 9860 Sint-Martens-Latem, Belgium.

History Registered in accordance with Belgian law. **Aims** Serve as a forum for the exchange of ideas on *information systems* using Microsoft technology. **Structure** Steering Committee, including Chairman, Treasurer and Secretary. **Events** *International Conference on the Humanitarian Impact of Nuclear Weapons* Oslo (Norway) 2013, *Conference* Brussels (Belgium) 2004, *EUROREC annual conference / Conference* Berlin (Germany) 2002, *Conference* Thessaloniki (Greece) 2001, *Annual conference / Conference* Bruges (Belgium) 1999.
[2010.06.08/XE3385/**E**]

♦ MICT / see International Residual Mechanism for Criminal Tribunals (#14746)
♦ MiCT – Media in Cooperation and Transition (internationally oriented national body)
♦ **MIDADE** Mouvement international d'apostolat des enfants (#14192)
♦ **MIDADEN** Movimiento Internacional de Apostolado de los Niños (#14192)
♦ Mid-America Alliance for African Studies (internationally oriented national body)
♦ Mid-America International Agri-Trade Council / see Food Export Association of the Midwest USA
♦ **Midas** European Association of Daily Newspapers in Minority and Regional Languages (#06002)
♦ Midden-Europese Goede Tempelieren Jeugdraad (inactive)
♦ Middle Atlantic Council of Latin American Studies (internationally oriented national body)
♦ Middlebury Institute of International Studies, Monterey (internationally oriented national body)
♦ Middle East Africa Cataract and refractive Surgery Society (see: #16752)
♦ Middle East – Africa Club of Oncology and Ocular Pathology (internationally oriented national body)

♦ Middle East and Africa Duty Free Association (MEADFA) 16751

Contact Dubai Airport Free Zone Authority, West Wing 2 – Office No 2W210, PO Box 54394, Dubai, United Arab Emirates. T. +97142996663. Fax +97142996630. E-mail: info@meadfa.com.
URL: http://www.meadfa.com/

History May 2001. Former names and other names: *Middle East Duty Free Association (MEDFA)* – former (2001). **Aims** Encourage closer links between retailers and brand suppliers in the Middle East so as to facilitate growth of the industry in this region. **Structure** Board. **Activities** Training/education; events/meetings. **Events** *Conference* Dubai (United Arab Emirates) 2021, *Conference* Muscat (Oman) 2019, *Conference* Dubai (United Arab Emirates) 2018, *Conference* Beirut (Lebanon) 2017, *Conference* Dubai (United Arab Emirates) 2016.
Members Organizations (35). Membership countries not specified.
[2021/XJ1661/**D**]

♦ Middle East Africa Glaucoma Society (see: #16752)

♦ Middle East African Council of Ophthalmology (MEACO) 16752

Main Office Office No 1, 1st Floor, Cerecon Bldg No 9, Musa bin Nusair St, Olaya, PO Box 7947, Riyadh 11472, Saudi Arabia. T. +96614661085. Fax +96614661049. E-mail: info@meaco.org.
URL: http://www.meaco.org/

History 1997, Jordan, as *Pan Arab African Council of Ophthalmology (PAACO)*, by merger of *Afro-Arab Society of Ophthalmology (AASO, inactive)* and *Pan Arab Council of Ophthalmology (PACO, inactive)*, set up 1989. Current name adopted at VIII International Congress of the PAACO, 7-10 Apr 2005, Dubai (United Arab Emirates), when Iran became a member. Turkey joined in 2006. **Aims** Enhance ophthalmic training, continuing education and ophthalmic practice so as to reduce visual impairment and elevate the quality of eye care for the people of the Middle East and Africa. **Structure** Board, comprising Chairman, President, Honorary Life President, Vice President, Scientific Programme Chairman and Treasurer. **Languages** Arabic, English, French. **Staff** based in Riyadh (Saudi Arabia), Jeddah (Saudi Arabia) and Cairo (Egypt). **Activities** Organizes and sponsors biennial congress. Subspeciality societies (5): *Middle East Africa Cataract and refractive Surgery Society (MEACRS, see: #16752)*; *Middle East Africa Glaucoma Society (MEAGS, see: #16752)*; *Middle East Africa Pediatric Ophthalmology and Strabismus Society (MEAPOSS, see: #16752)*; *Middle East Africa Society of Ophthalmic Plastic and Reconstructive Surgery (MEASOPRS, see: #16752)*; *Middle East Africa Vitreo Retinal Society (MEAVRS, see: #16752)*. **Events** *WOC : World Ophthalmology Congress* Geneva (Switzerland) 2020, *Congress* Sweimeh (Jordan) 2019, *Congress* Manama (Bahrain) 2016, *Congress* Abu Dhabi (United Arab Emirates) 2012, *Congress / International Congress* Manama (Bahrain) 2009. **Publications** *Middle East African Journal of Ophthalmology (MEAJO)*.
Members Societies in 34 countries:
Algeria, Bahrain, Cameroon, Central African Rep, Congo Brazzaville, Egypt, Ethiopia, Gambia, Ghana, Iran Islamic Rep, Iraq, Jordan, Kuwait, Lebanon, Libya, Malawi, Mali, Mauritania, Morocco, Nigeria, Oman, Palestine, Qatar, Saudi Arabia, Somalia, South Africa, Sudan, Syrian AR, Tunisia, Türkiye, United Arab Emirates, Yemen, Zambia, Zimbabwe.
Included in the above, 2 organizations listed in this Yearbook:
College of Ophthalmology of Eastern Central and Southern Africa (COECSA, #04108); *Société Africaine Francophone d'Ophtalmologie (SAFO, #19453)*.
NGO Relations Recognized by: *International Council of Ophthalmology (ICO, #13057)*. Instrumental in setting up: *African Ophthalmology Council (AOC, #00402)*.
[2015/XD5982/**D**]

♦ Middle East African Oculoplastic Society (unconfirmed)
♦ Middle East Africa Pediatric Ophthalmology and Strabismus Society (see: #16752)
♦ Middle East Africa Rugby League (unconfirmed)
♦ Middle East Africa Society of Ophthalmic Plastic and Reconstructive Surgery (see: #16752)
♦ Middle East Africa Vitreo Retinal Society (see: #16752)

♦ Middle East Association for Health Informatics (MEAHI) 16753

Head Office PO Box 14665, Teheran, 1411, Iran Islamic Rep.
Pres Medical Informatics Dept, Social Security Org, Teheran, Iran Islamic Rep.
URL: http://www.meahi.org/

History 2009. **Events** *Special Topic Conference* Kuwait (Kuwait) 2015, *MEAHI Conference* Dubai (United Arab Emirates) 2013, *Conference* Beirut (Lebanon) 2010.
[2017/XJ1964/**D**]

♦ Middle East Association of Science Editors (no recent information)
♦ Middle East Association of Training and Retreat Centres (no recent information)

♦ Middle East Burn and Fire Disaster Society (MEBFDS) 16754

Pres Taskent Caddesi – 1 CADDE no 77, Bahcelievler, 06490 Ankara/Ankara, Türkiye. T. +903122127393. Fax +903122150835.

History 1987, Ankara (Turkey), by Dr Mehmet Haberal. **Aims** Conduct research, education, international scientific activities and communication in the fields of burn and fire in cooperation with scientists, researchers, other scientific *health* experts, concerned educational institutes, universities, special purpose institutes, research centres and hospitals in the specified regions. **Structure** General Assembly; Board of Directors; Board of Auditors. **Languages** English. **Finance** Members' dues. Other sources: admission fees; income from society activities; donations; grants. **Events** *Meeting* Ankara (Turkey) 2006, *Meeting* Cairo (Egypt) 2004, *Meeting* Ankara (Turkey) 2002.
Members in 7 countries:
Azerbaijan, Bulgaria, Egypt, Iran Islamic Rep, Pakistan, Türkiye, USA.
[2009.06.01/XD9431/**D**]

♦ Middle East Business Aviation Association / see Middle East and North Africa Business Aviation Association (#16776)
♦ Middle East Center, Philadelphia (internationally oriented national body)
♦ Middle East Centre for Culture and Development (internationally oriented national body)
♦ Middle East Children's Alliance (internationally oriented national body)
♦ Middle East Christian Outreach (internationally oriented national body)

♦ Middle East Committee of YMCAs 16755

Comité des UCJG du Proche orient – CVJM-Komitee für den Nahen Osten – Comité de ACJs del Medio Oriente

Liaison c/o YMCA Egypt, 72 El Gomhouria Street, Cairo, Egypt. T. +2025917360 – +2025884839. Fax +2025895092. E-mail: ymcaegypt@link.net.
URL: https://www.ymca.int/member/ymca-in-middle-east/

History within the framework of *World Alliance of Young Men's Christian Associations (YMCA, #21090)*.
[2016/XE2246/**E**]

♦ Middle East Consortium on Infectious Disease Surveillance (unconfirmed)

♦ Middle East Council of Churches (MECC) 16756

Conseil d'Eglises du Moyen-Orient (CEMO)

Head Office DEEB Building, PO Box 11-5376, Beirut, Lebanon. T. +9611353938. Fax +9611344894. E-mail: info@mecc.org.
URL: http://www.mecc.org/

History May 1974, Nicosia (Cyprus). Founded by merger of *Near East Christian Council (NECC)*, founded in 1956, and *Near East Council of Churches (NECC) – Conseil des Eglises du Proche-Orient*, set up in 1962. Expanded, 1990, by inclusion of seven Catholic churches of the Middle East. **Aims** Deepen spiritual fellowship among churches of the Middle East and unite them in word and deed as they strive to achieve unity of the churches and bear a living evangelical witness to spread the gospel of salvation and reconciliation through the Lord *Jesus Christ*, love, peace and justice throughout the region and among the people inhabiting it. **Structure** General Assembly (every 4 years); Executive Committee; General Secretariat in Beirut (Lebanon); Departments (2); Programme Units (3); Offices in Cairo (Egypt), Amman (Jordan) and Limassol (Cyprus); Liaison Offices in Arab Gulf (Dubai) and Jerusalem (Israel). **Languages** Arabic, English, French. **Activities** Networking/liaising; humanitarian/emergency aid. **Events** *General Assembly* Cyprus 2011, *General Assembly* Paphos (Cyprus) 2011, *General Assembly* Cyprus 2007, *General Assembly* Cyprus 2003, *General Assembly* Lebanon 1999. **Publications** *Al Montada News Bulletin* (4 a year) in Arabic; *Courrier oecuménique du Moyen-Orient* (4 a year) in French; *MECC News Report* (4 a year) in English. *Middle East Council of Churches: a Handbook* (revised ed 1999). Books; pamphlets.

Members Families of Churches (4) Oriental Orthodox (3), Eastern Chalcedonian Orthodox (4), Catholic (7), Evangelical Protestant (19), in 12 countries:
Algeria, Cyprus, Egypt, Iran Islamic Rep, Iraq, Israel, Jordan, Kuwait, Lebanon, Sudan, Syrian AR, Tunisia.
Included in the above, 2 listed in this Yearbook:
Greek Orthodox Patriarchate of Alexandria and All Africa (#10709); Greek Orthodox Patriarchate of Antioch and All the East (#10710).
IGO Relations Partner of: *UNHCR (#20327).* **NGO Relations** Acts as secretariat for, and charter member of: *Arab Group for Muslim-Christian Dialogue (AGMCD, see: #16756).* Also links with a number of national councils of Churches and regional ecumenical organizations (not specified). [2021/XD2971/y/**D**]

♦ Middle East Council of Shopping Centres (MECSC) 16757

CEO Unit 507 – 5th Floor, Arenco Tower, Sheikh Zhayed Road, PO Box 43972, Dubai, United Arab Emirates. T. +97143597909. Fax +97143558818.
URL: http://www.mecsc.org/
History Founded 1994. **Aims** Provide the exchange of ideas and sharing of knowledge while being a catalyst in the development of the *retail* industry in the Middle East, North Africa and beyond. **Structure** Annual General Meeting; Executive Committee; Board of Directors. **Finance** Members' dues. **Activities** Events/meetings. **Events** *Retail Congress Middle East and North Africa* Dubai (United Arab Emirates) 2019. **Publications** *MECSC Newsletter* (12 a year); *Retail People Magazine.* [2019/XM7521/**D**]

♦ Middle East Desalination Research Centre (MEDRC) 16758

Dir Bldg 3200 Al Dama Street, Al Hail North Corniche, PO Box 21, 133, Muscat, Oman. T. +96824415500. Fax +96824415541. E-mail: info@medrc.org.
URL: http://www.medrc.org/
History 1996, Muscat (Oman). **Aims** Conduct, facilitate, promote, co-ordinate and support basic and applied research in *water* desalination technology and supporting fields; raise the standard of living in the Middle East and elsewhere by cost reduction and quality improvement in the technical processes of water desalination. **Structure** Executive Board; Project Advisory Committee; Research Advisory Committee. **Languages** English. **Staff** 10.00 FTE, paid. **Finance** Supported by the Governments of Israel, Japan, Korea Rep, Netherlands, Oman, Spain, the United States, Qatar, and *European Commission (EC, #06633).* **Activities** Training/education; financial and/or material support. **Events** *EuroMed conference* Marrakech (Morocco) 2004, *EuroMed conference* Sharm el Sheikh (Egypt) 2002, *International conference on desalination strategies in South Mediterranean countries* Djerba (Tunisia) 2000. **Publications** *Watermark* – newsletter. Reports.
Members Full in 10 countries and territories:
Israel, Japan, Jordan, Korea Rep, Netherlands, Oman, Palestine, Qatar, Spain, USA. [2022/XE4569/**E**]

♦ Middle East Dietary Association (no recent information)

♦ Middle East Drymix Mortar Association (MEDMA) 16759

SG Tegernseer Landstr 26, 81541 Munich, Germany. T. +498962000232. Fax +498962009911. E-mail: info@medma.org.
History 2007, when charter was adopted. Registered in accordance with German law: VR 200628. **Aims** Promote an integrative, quality minded approach to drymix (factory made) mortars to the Middle East. **Structure** Board (Executive Committee). Executive Secretary. National Chapters; Technical Committee. **Languages** English. **Staff** 3.00 FTE, voluntary. **Finance** Members' dues. Other sources: sponsoring; events and publishing proceeds. **Activities** Events/meetings; training/education; knowledge management/ information dissemination; certification/accreditation; publishing activities. **Events** *Annual General Assembly / Annual MEDMA Conference* Dubai (United Arab Emirates) 2015, *Annual MEDMA Conference* Dubai (United Arab Emirates) 2014, *Annual MEDMA Conference* Dubai (United Arab Emirates) 2013, *Annual MEDMA Conference* Dubai (United Arab Emirates) 2012, *Annual MEDMA Conference* Dubai (United Arab Emirates) 2011. **Publications** *MEDMA Newsletter; MEDMA Technical Bulletin.*
Members Full in 6 countries:
Egypt, Jordan, Lebanon, Pakistan, Saudi Arabia, United Arab Emirates. [2015.01.14/XJ9069/**D**]

♦ Middle East Duty Free Association / see Middle East and Africa Duty Free Association (#16751)
♦ Middle East, Eastern Europe, Central Asia and North Africa Rabies Control Network (unconfirmed)
♦ Middle East Eating Disorders Association (internationally oriented national body)
♦ Middle East Economic Association (internationally oriented national body)

♦ Middle Eastern Association of Linguistic Anthropology (MEALA) ... 16760

Address not obtained.
Aims Elicit new understandings of Linguistic Anthropology, by centering research and rhetoric on Middle Eastern contexts, and the network of related fields; contribute significantly to the advanced efforts of other global societies and organizations in Linguistic Anthropology; strengthen conceptions, and interest, in Linguistic Anthropology in The Middle East, and to increasingly connect scholars working in and on Middle Eastern regions with those in other region. **Structure** Directorship; Communications; Administration; Scientific Committee. **Languages** English. **Staff** 4.00 FTE, paid; 10.00 FTE, voluntary. **Finance** Sources: contributions; fees for services; grants. **Activities** Events/meetings. **Publications** *MEALA Journal.* **NGO Relations** Constitutes *Global Network in Linguistic Anthropology*, together with *Global Council for Anthropological Linguistics (GLOCAL, #10310), Conference on Mediterranean and European Linguistic Anthropology (COMELA, #04628), South and Central American Assembly on Linguistic Anthropology (SCAALA, #19752), Conference on Oceanian Linguistic Anthropology (COOLA, #04636)* and *African Assembly of Linguistic Anthropology (AFALA, #00204).* [2020.05.01/XM8717/c/**F**]

♦ Middle Eastern Culture Center in Japan (internationally oriented national body)

♦ Middle Eastern Regional Radioisotope Centre for the Arab Countries (MERRCAC) 16761

Centre régional de radioisotopes du Moyen-Orient pour les pays arabes
Main Office 9 Ahmed El Zayat St, Dokki, Giza, 12311, Egypt. T. +2023370569 – +2023370588. Fax +2023371082. E-mail: merrcac@yahoo.com – info@merrcac.org.
URL: http://www.merrcac.org/
History Jan 1963, Cairo (Egypt), following signature, 14 Sep 1962, of an agreement by *International Atomic Energy Agency (IAEA, #12294)* and a number of Arab countries. Activities commenced and Governing Body set up, Mar 1963. **Aims** Provide research work and training courses concerning the use of *radiation* and radioisotopes in the fields of peaceful use of *atomic energy.* **Structure** General Conference; Board of Governors; Director. **Languages** Arabic. **Staff** 12.00 FTE, paid. **Finance** Member States' contributions. **Activities** Events/meetings; training/education; research and development; networking/liaising. **Publications** *Isotope and Radiation Research* (2 a year).
Members Specialists representing 14 countries:
Algeria, Egypt, Iraq, Jordan, Lebanon, Libya, Morocco, Qatar, Saudi Arabia, Sudan, Syrian AR, Tunisia, United Arab Emirates, Yemen.
IGO Relations *FAO (#09260); WHO (#20950).* [2017.06.01/XE4854/**E***]

♦ Middle Eastern Society of Infection Control (no recent information)

♦ Middle Eastern Stereotactic and Functional Neurosurgical Society (MSFNS) 16762

Contact PO Box 1502, Riyadh 11444, Saudi Arabia. T. +966504145385.
URL: http://www.msfns.org/
History Initiated Apr 2015, Dubai (United Arab Emirates). **Aims** Develop functional neurosurgical care for the benefit of *patients* and *medical* providers. **Events** *Conference* Dubai (United Arab Emirates) 2016. **NGO Relations** *Gulf Neurosurgical Society (GNS, #10836); Pan Arab Neurosurgical Society (PANS, #18151); World Society for Stereotactic and Functional Neurosurgery (WSSFN, #21812).* [2016/XM4596/**D**]

♦ Middle East Facility Management Association (MEFMA) 16763

Dir address not obtained. T. +971544254341. E-mail: info@mefma.org.
URL: http://www.mefma.org/
Aims Unify the facility management industry in the Middle East. **Structure** Board of Directors. **Activities** Research/documentation; training/education; guidance/assistance/consulting; events/meetings. **NGO Relations** Member of: *Global Facility Management Association (Global FM, #10353).* [2018/XM7523/**D**]

♦ Middle East Federation Against Cancer (inactive)
♦ Middle East Federation of Medical Physics / see Middle East Federation of Organizations of Medical Physics (#16764)

♦ Middle East Federation of Organizations of Medical Physics (MEFOMP) 16764

Pres address not obtained. T. +9613656354 – +961(97455007625. E-mail: mefomp@mefomp.org.
URL: http://mefomp.org/
History Motion of Intent for Establishing MEFOMP signed Apr 2008, Dubai (United Arab Emirates). Officially set up 2009, Munich (Germany) as a regional organization of *International Organization for Medical Physics (IOMP, #14453).* Previously also referred to as *Middle East Federation of Medical Physics.* **Aims** Promote advancement of medical physics in the region; educate and train local society members on new procedures and technologies; encourage exchange of expertise and information among societies. **Structure** Council. Executive Council, comprising President, Vice-President, Secretary-General, Treasurer and Past President. Committees (5): Nominating; Education and Training; Professional Development; Science; Publication. **Languages** Arabic, English. **Staff** Part-time, voluntary. **Activities** Organizes meetings, courses, workshops and conferences. **Events** *Meeting / Conference* Shiraz (Iran Islamic Rep) 2011, *Meeting* Munich (Germany) 2009.
Members Full; Honorary. Members in 12 countries:
Bahrain, Iran Islamic Rep, Iraq, Jordan, Kuwait, Lebanon, Oman, Qatar, Saudi Arabia, Syrian AR, United Arab Emirates, Yemen.
IGO Relations Contact with: *Arab Atomic Energy Agency (AAEA, #00901); International Atomic Energy Agency (IAEA, #12294); WHO (#20950).* **NGO Relations** Contact with: national associations. [2012.06.01/XJ5115/**E**]

♦ Middle East Fertility Society (MEFS) 16765

Exec Dir PO Box 167220, Achrafieh, Beirut, Lebanon. T. +9611612400 – +9611610400. Fax +9611610400. E-mail: info@mefs.org.
URL: http://www.mefs.org/
History 1992. Registration: Lebanon; Canada. **Aims** Improve fertility care of couples in the Arab world and Middle East through the transfer of medical knowledge and the promotion of scientific research. **Structure** Executive Committee, comprising President, President-Elect, Treasurer, Secretary, Executive Director and 5 further members. **Finance** Members' dues. **Events** *Annual Meeting* Abu Dhabi (United Arab Emirates) 2022, *Annual Meeting* Dubai (United Arab Emirates) 2021, *Annual Meeting* Beirut (Lebanon) 2020, *Annual Meeting* Cairo (Egypt) 2019, *Annual Meeting* Beirut (Lebanon) 2018. **Publications** *MEFS Newsletter, Middle East Fertility Society Journal.*
Members Individuals and organizations in 39 countries:
Algeria, Argentina, Australia, Austria, Bahrain, Belgium, Brazil, Canada, Chile, Egypt, France, Germany, Greece, India, Iran Islamic Rep, Iraq, Italy, Jordan, Kuwait, Lebanon, Libya, Mexico, Morocco, Netherlands, Nigeria, Oman, Palestine, Qatar, Saudi Arabia, Sudan, Sweden, Switzerland, Syrian AR, Tunisia, Türkiye, United Arab Emirates, USA, Venezuela, Yemen.
NGO Relations Associated with: *International Federation of Fertility Societies (IFFS, #13426).* [2022/XD9323/**D**]

♦ Middle East Gases Association (MEGA) 16766

Gen Sec Office No 6 – Dubai Assn Ctr, 2nd floor – Offices 02 Bldg in One Central, PO Box 9292, Dubai WTC Complex, Dubai, United Arab Emirates. T. +97145163030.
URL: http://www.megases.org/
History Founded 2010, Dubai (United Arab Emirates). Registered in accordance with the law of Dubai (United Arab Emirates). **Aims** Foster the exchange of technical information among members in the safe handling and use of industrial medical and food gases; work towards the highest level of safety and environmental care across the Middle East region. **Structure** Annual General Meeting; Board of Directors; Office. Technical Committee; Working Groups. **Languages** Arabic, English. **Staff** 2.00 FTE, paid. **Finance** Members' dues. **Publications** *Safety Newsletter.* Position papers; technical documents.
Members Full in 12 countries:
Bahrain, Egypt, Iraq, Jordan, Kuwait, Lebanon, Oman, Qatar, Saudi Arabia, Syrian AR, Türkiye, United Arab Emirates. [2020.01.23/XM7568/**D**]

♦ Middle East Gymnastics Association (MEGA) 16767

Chairman address not obtained.
URL: http://www.middleeastgymnasticsassociation.com/
History 2014, by gymnastics clubs in 5 countries. **Aims** Promote the protection and welfare of gymnasts, providing a training framework and overseeing the setting up and arrangement of the annual competition calendar. **Structure** Board of Governors. **Finance** Members' dues. **Publications** *MEGA Magazine.*
Members Clubs in 5 countries:
Bahrain, Jordan, Oman, Qatar, United Arab Emirates. [2017/XM4499/**D**]

♦ Middle East Institute of Japan (internationally oriented national body)
♦ Middle East Institute, Singapore (internationally oriented national body)
♦ Middle East Institute, Washington (internationally oriented national body)

♦ Middle East Investor Relations Association (MEIRA) 16768

General Manager Office 10 Level 2, The Offices 2, One Central, PO Box 9576, Dubai, United Arab Emirates. T. +97145163042. E-mail: info@meira.me.
Marketing & Events Manager address not obtained.
URL: https://meira.me/
History 1 Jul 2008, Dubai (United Arab Emirates). Previously also referred to as *Middle East Investor Relations Society (ME-IR).* **Aims** Promote best practice of investor relations in the Middle East. **Structure** Board; Executive Committee. **Languages** English. **Staff** 3.00 FTE, paid. **Activities** Training/education; accreditation/ certification; networking/liaising; events/meetings. **Events** *Annual Conference* Manama (Bahrain) 2023, *Annual Conference* Riyadh (Saudi Arabia) 2022, *Annual Conference* Dubai (United Arab Emirates) 2021, *Annual Conference* Dubai (United Arab Emirates) 2020, *Annual Conference* Dubai (United Arab Emirates) 2019. **Publications** *MEIRA Newsletter.* White paper; code of conduct. **Members** 100 in 8 countries. Membership countries not specified. [2023/XJ2274/**D**]

♦ Middle East Investor Relations Society / see Middle East Investor Relations Association (#16768)

♦ Middle East e-Learning Association (MEEA) 16769

Address not obtained.
URL: http://me-ea.org/
History Constitution adopted 2 Feb 2010. **Aims** Stimulate understanding, practice and knowledge transfer of e-learning in the region. **Structure** General Assembly. Board of Directors of 6. **IGO Relations** Partners: *Commonwealth of Learning (COL, #04346); UNESCO (#20322).* **NGO Relations** Associate member of: *International Council for Open and Distance Education (ICDE, #13056).* Partners: *EDEN Digital Learning Europe (EDEN, #05356); European Learning Industry Group (ELIG, #07674); International E-Learning Association (IELA, #13253);* national associations. [2012/XJ6302/**D**]

♦ Middle East Librarian Committee / see European Association of Middle East Librarians (#06121)
♦ Middle East Librarians Association (internationally oriented national body)

♦ Middle East Lighting Association (MELA) 16770

Dir 192 Old Bakery Str, Valletta, Malta. T. +971562740025.
URL: http://middleeastlighting.ae/
History 2012. Registered in accordance with the laws of Malta. **Aims** Support development of efficient lighting policy in the Middle East region. **Structure** Board of Directors. **Languages** Arabic, English. **Activities** Events/ meetings. **Publications** Newsletter. **NGO Relations** Member of: *Global Lighting Association (#10459).* [2017.10.11/XJ9322/**D**]

♦ Middle East Lutheran Ministry (MELM) 16771

Dir PO Box 60-307, Kanj Quarter-Jal Eddib, Beirut, Lebanon. T. +9611716272. Fax +9611724312.
URL: http://lhmlebanon.wordpress.com/

History 1950, Beirut (Lebanon), as a Lutheran Hour (LH) radio ministry; Board for Missions (BFM) joined in 1959. Presently MELM is a Christian mass media ministry to the Arab world supported by the Lutheran Hour and the Board of Missions of the Lutheran Church – Missouri Synod (LC-MS). **Aims** Proclaim the Gospel message to the Arabic speaking people – *Christians* and non-Christians – in the *Arab* world, through the different mass media and follow-up work. **Activities** Deals with several activities such as: Radio Programs, Bible Correspondence Courses, educational Christian publications, TV program, audio and video cassette ministry, production of Christian indigenous hymns, and relief work. Cooperates with local churches and church organizations where that is possible. [2015/XF1937/**F**]

♦ Middle East Media (internationally oriented national body)
♦ Middle East Media International / see Middle East Media

♦ Middle East Medical Devices and Diagnostics Trade Association (Mecomed) 16772

Main Office PO Box 35909, Dubai, United Arab Emirates. T. +971507080375. Fax +97144297265. E-mail: inna.nadelwais@mecomed.com.
URL: http://www.mecomed.com/

History 2007. **Aims** Shape the evolving environment in the Middle East into a more regulated and highly patient-centric practice arena; build and improve the industry image and perception; reduce substantially non-compliant business practice as well as other unproductive unethical market dynamics; enhance access to stakeholders, using the opportunity to positively shape the evolving environment into that of better and safer practice, as a group of companies; collaborate in critical projects with common interest. **Structure** Executive Committee. **Finance** Members' dues. **NGO Relations** Member of: *Global Medical Technology Alliance (GMTA, #10470)*; *MedTech Europe (#16692).* [2018/XJ6314/t/**D**]

♦ Middle East and Mediterranean Association of Gynecologic Oncologist (MEMAGO) 16773

Contact 19 Mayis Mah – 19 Mayis Cad, Nova Baran Center No 4 Şişli, 34360 Istanbul/Istanbul, Türkiye. T. +902123814600. Fax +902122586078. E-mail: info@memago.org.
URL: http://www.memago.org/

History 2015. **Aims** Increase awareness of gynecological cancers in the Middle East and Mediterranean; improve prevention of gynecological malignancies; carry out the evidence-based management of gynecological cancers. **Structure** Board of Directors. **Activities** Events/meetings; training/education. **Events** *Annual Congress* Tunis (Tunisia) 2022, *Annual Congress* Abu Dhabi (United Arab Emirates) 2019. [2020/AA0463/**D**]

♦ Middle East Molecular Biology Society (MEMBS) 16774

Main Office PO Box 181192, DIAC, Block 3 – 1st floor – office 113, Dubai, United Arab Emirates. T. +97144522009. Fax +97144522009. E-mail: info@membs.org.
URL: http://membs.org/

History Founded 2013. **Aims** Bring together all molecular biology- related resources from all over the world and present them to the Middle East and Arab world. **Finance** Members' dues. **Events** *Annual Conference* Amman (Jordan) 2018, *Annual Conference* Abu Dhabi (United Arab Emirates) 2017, *Annual Conference* Doha (Qatar) 2016, *Annual Conference* Istanbul (Turkey) 2015, *Annual Conference / Annual Congress* Dubai (United Arab Emirates) 2014. **Publications** *Molecular Biology* – periodical. [2019/XJ8978/**D**]

♦ Middle-East Nature Conservation Promotion Association (internationally oriented national body)

♦ Middle East Network Operators Group (MENOG) 16775

Main Office c/o RIPE NCC, PO Box 502678, Dubai Media City, Dubai, United Arab Emirates. E-mail: info@menog.org.
URL: http://www.menog.org/

Structure Coordination Team of 7. Program Committee. Chair. **Activities** Organizes meetings. **Events** *Meeting* Dubai (United Arab Emirates) 2015, *Meeting* Dubai (United Arab Emirates) 2014, *Meeting* Damascus (Syrian AR) 2011, *Meeting* Muscat (Oman) 2011, *Meeting* Istanbul (Turkey) 2010. [2016/XJ2176/**D**]

♦ Middle East Neurosurgical Society (no recent information)
♦ Middle East Nonviolence and Democracy (internationally oriented national body)

♦ Middle East and North Africa Business Aviation Association (MEBAA) 16776

Executive Chairman Tameem House, Office 2304 – Barsha Heights, PO Box 117733, Dubai, United Arab Emirates. T. +97144356670. Fax +97144574065. E-mail: info@mebaa.com.
URL: https://www.mebaa.com/

History 2006. Previously known as *Middle East Business Aviation Association.* **Aims** Achieve an effective means for communicating the concerns of Middle East and North Africa business aviation operators and suppliers to governments within the region, thereby positively influencing government response. **Structure** Board. **Finance** Members' dues. **Activities** Knowledge management/information dissemination; training/education; events/meetings; standards/guidelines; networking/liaising. **Events** *Conference* Amman (Jordan) 2021, *Conference* Amman (Jordan) 2020, *Conference* Dubai (United Arab Emirates) 2020, *Conference* Jeddah (Saudi Arabia) 2020, *Conference* Marrakech (Morocco) 2019. **Publications** *MEBAA Review.* **NGO Relations** *International Business Aviation Council (IBAC, #12418).* [2022/XM3385/**D**]

♦ Middle East North Africa Committee for Treatment and Research in Multiple Sclerosis (MENACTRIMS) 16777

Contact address not obtained. E-mail: info@menactrims.com.
URL: http://www.menactrims.com/

History Registration: Jordan. **Aims** Facilitate communication and create synergies among clinicians and scientists to promote and enhance research and improve clinical outcomes in multiple sclerosis (MS). **Structure** Council; Executive Committee; Board. **Activities** Events/meetings; awards/prizes/competitions; research/documentation. **Events** *MENACTRIMS Congress* Cairo (Egypt) 2022, *MENACTRIMS Congress* Dubai (United Arab Emirates) 2021, *MENACTRIMS Congress* Dubai (United Arab Emirates) 2019, *MENACTRIMS Congress* Dubai (United Arab Emirates) 2018, *Congress* Dubai (United Arab Emirates) 2017. [2021/XM4598/**D**]

♦ Middle East and North Africa Evaluators Network (EvalMENA) 16778

Moderator American Univ of Beirut, Environment and Sustainable Development Unit, Bliss Str, Hamra, FAFS room 308, Beirut, Lebanon.

History Set up 2009 and formalized 2011. **Aims** See that a critical mass of qualified and internationally-acknowledged evaluators, speaking a common language, has been institutionalized in the region. **Structure** Board; Technical Secretariat. **Languages** Arabic, English, French. **Staff** 1.50 FTE, paid. Others voluntary. **Finance** In-kind support, including from *International Organisation for Cooperation in Evaluation (IOCE, #14426)* and *EvalPartners (#09208)*; *UNICEF (#20332)*; *International Initiative for Impact Evaluation (3ie, #13851)*; *Islamic Corporation for the Development of the Private Sector (ICD, see: #16044)*; *UN Women (#20724)*; American University of Beirut. Budget (annual): about US$ 200,000. **Events** *General Assembly* Cairo (Egypt) 2015, *General Assembly* Amman (Jordan) 2014, *General Assembly* Amman (Jordan) 2014, *General Assembly* Beirut (Lebanon) 2012, *General Assembly* Beirut (Lebanon) 2011.
Members Voluntary Organizations for Professional Evaluation (VOPEs) in 10 countries and territories:
Algeria, Egypt, Jordan, Lebanon, Morocco, Palestine, Sudan, Syrian AR, Tunisia, Yemen.
IGO Relations *FAO (#09260)*; *ILO (#11123)*; *International Development Research Centre (IDRC, #13162)*; *International Fund for Agricultural Development (IFAD, #13692)*; *Islamic Corporation for the Development of the Private Sector (ICD, see: #16044)*; *UNICEF (#20332)*; *UN Women (#20724).* **NGO Relations** Cooperates with: *EvalPartners (#09208)*; *International Initiative for Impact Evaluation (3ie, #13851)*; *International Organisation for Cooperation in Evaluation (IOCE, #14426)*; *United Nations Evaluation Group (UNEG, #20560).* [2015.08.10/XJ9845/**F**]

♦ Middle East and North Africa Financial Action Task Force (MENAFATF) 16779

Groupe d'action financière du moyen-orient et de l'afrique du nord – (GAFIMOAN)
Contact PO Box 10881, Manama, Bahrain. T. +97317531024. Fax +97317530627. E-mail: info@menafatf.org.
URL: http://www.menafatf.org/

History 30 Nov 2004, Manama (Bahrain). Regional body of *Financial Action Task Force (FATF, #09765).* **Aims** Combat money laundering and financing of terrorism and proliferation. **Structure** President; Vice-President; Executive Secretary. **Languages** Arabic, English. **Activities** Events/meetings; knowledge management/information dissemination. **Events** *Plenary Meeting* Tunisia 2010, *Plenary Meeting* Bahrain 2009, *Plenary Meeting* Beirut (Lebanon) 2009, *Plenary Meeting* Abu Dhabi (United Arab Emirates) 2008, *Plenary Meeting* Fujairah (United Arab Emirates) 2008.
Members Governments of 19 countries and territories:
Algeria, Bahrain, Egypt, Iraq, Jordan, Kuwait, Lebanon, Libya, Mauritania, Morocco, Oman, Palestine, Qatar, Saudi Arabia, Sudan, Syrian AR, Tunisia, United Arab Emirates, Yemen.
Observers (64):
Australia, France, Somalia, Spain, UK, USA.
Observer organizations (10):
Arab Monetary Fund (AMF, #01009); *Asia/Pacific Group on Money Laundering (APG, #01921)*; *Egmont Group of Financial Intelligence Units (#05396)*; *Eurasian Group on Combating Money Laundering and Financing of Terrorism (EAG, #05608)*; Financial Action Task Force (FATF / GAFI); *Gulf Cooperation Council (GCC, #10826)*; *International Bank for Reconstruction and Development (IBRD, #12317)* (World Bank); *International Monetary Fund (IMF, #14180)*; *United Nations (UN, #20515)*; *World Customs Organization (WCO, #21350).*
IGO Relations Member of: *Asia/Pacific Group on Money Laundering (APG, #01921).* [2016.07.19/XM1037/y/**F***]

♦ Middle East and North Africa Harm Reduction Network (MENAHRA) 16780

Contact PO Box 55391, Sin El Fil, Beirut, Lebanon. E-mail: info@menahra.org.
URL: http://www.menahra.org/

History 2007. Registered in Beirut (Lebanon) under Presidential Decree number 7491. **Aims** Support, develop and advocate for harm reduction approaches in the field of drug use, HIV, public health and social exclusion by following the principles of humanity, tolerance, partnership in respect to human rights and freedoms. **Structure** General Assembly; Board of Directors; Secretariat. **Languages** Arabic, English, French. **Staff** 8.00 FTE, paid. **Finance** Main funding from: *Global Fund to Fight AIDS, Tuberculosis and Malaria (Global Fund, #10383).* **Activities** Publishing activities; projects/programmes; training/education; events/meetings; advocacy/lobbying/activism; guidance/assistance/consulting; monitoring/evaluation. **Events** *Regional Conference* Beirut (Lebanon) 2016, *Regional Conference* Beirut (Lebanon) 2013, *Regional Conference* Beirut (Lebanon) 2009. **Publications** *MENAHRA Newsletter* (12 a year). Communication guides; good practices; guidelines; operational researches; press releases; situation assessments. **Members** Organizations (22); Individuals (38). Membership countries not specified. **IGO Relations** Collaborates with many international partners, UN agencies and governments, including: *Joint United Nations Programme on HIV/AIDS (UNAIDS, #16149)*; *United Nations Office on Drugs and Crime (UNODC, #20596)*; *WHO (#20950).* [2016.06.30/XM1845/**E**]

♦ Middle East and North Africa Leisure and Attractions Council (MENALAC) 16781

Admin Dir DAC Office 207, One Central Bldg 2, Dubai World Trade Center, PO Box 9292, Dubai, United Arab Emirates. T. +97145163046. E-mail: info@menalac.org.
URL: http://www.menalac.org/

History 2016, Dubai (United Arab Emirates). Registration: Dubai Chamber, No/ID: 225492, Start date: 30 Mar 2016, United Arab Emirates, Dubai. **Aims** Bring together operators, manufacturers, suppliers, distributors, consultants, tourism boards and Government authorities on a common platform and create a harmonized code for the leisure and attractions industry within the region. **Structure** General Assembly (annual); Board of Directors. **Languages** Arabic, English. **Staff** 2.00 FTE, paid. **Finance** Sources: members' dues. **Activities** Awards/prizes/competitions; events/meetings; networking/liaising; standards/guidelines; training/education. **Publications** *MENALAC Newsletter*; *MENA Leisure Report.* **Members** Individuals. Membership countries not specified. [2022.05.18/XM7524/**D**]

♦ Middle East and North Africa Nutrition Association (MENANA) 16782

Contact Dept of Community Meidicine, Fac of Medicine, Jordan Univ of Science and Technology, PO Box 2001, Irbid, Jordan. T. +9622795668655. E-mail: imdk@just.edu.jo.
URL: http://www.iuns.org/organisations/middle-east-and-north-africa-nutrition-assoc iation-menana/
NGO Relations Affiliate Member of: *International Union of Nutritional Sciences (IUNS, #15796).* [2008/XM3544/**D**]

♦ Middle-East, North Africa and Pakistan Self-Care Industry (MENAP-SCI) 16783

Chairman c/o MINDER, Rue Beau-Séjour 11, Case postale 530, 1003 Lausanne VD, Switzerland. E-mail: contact@menap-smi.org.
URL: http://www.menap-smi.org/

History 2004. Former names and other names: *Middle East Self-Medication Industry Association (MESMI)* – former (2004); *Middle East North Africa Self Medication Industry (MENAP-SMI)* – former (2016). Registration: Switzerland. **Aims** Promote better health through responsible self-medication and personal well-being; promote a world where self-care increasingly contributes to better health and more sustainable healthcare systems. **Structure** Board of Directors. **Languages** Arabic, English, French. **Finance** Sources: meeting proceeds; members' dues. **Activities** Africa; Middle East. **Members** Companies interested in developing self-care product, device or service. Membership countries not specified. **NGO Relations** Member of (1): *Global Self-Care Federation (GSCF, #10588).* [2021.01.14/XJ4242/t/**D**]

♦ Middle East North Africa Real Estate Society (inactive)
♦ Middle East and North Africa Regional Engineering Education Society (unconfirmed)
♦ Middle East North Africa Self Medication Industry / see Middle-East, North Africa and Pakistan Self-Care Industry (#16783)

♦ Middle East & North Africa Stroke Organization (MENA Stroke) 16784

Sec address not obtained. E-mail: secretary@menastroke.org.
URL: https://menastroke.org/

History 2014. **Aims** Increase comprehensive stroke centers; decrease the rate of mortality of stroke patients; improve the level of stroke care in MENA region. **Structure** Executive Board. Core Committees. **Activities** Awards/prizes/competitions; events/meetings; training/education. **Events** *MENA Stroke Congress* Abu Dhabi (United Arab Emirates) 2022, *MENA Stroke Congress* Bahrain 2021, *MENA Stroke Congress* Cairo (Egypt) 2017, *MENA Stroke Congress* Jeddah (Saudi Arabia) 2016. **NGO Relations** Cooperates with (2): *European Stroke Organisation (ESO, #08843)*; *SITS International (#19300).* [2022/AA3286/**D**]

♦ Middle East and North Africa Toxicology Association (unconfirmed)

♦ Middle East and North Africa Transition Fund (MENA Transition Fund) 16785

Contact c/o World Bank, 1818 H St NW, Washington DC 20433, USA. E-mail: transitionfund@worldbank.org.
URL: http://www.menatransitionfund.org/

History Set up 2012 by *Deauville Partnership (#05020).* **Aims** Improve the lives of citizens in transition countries; support the transformation currently underway in several countries in the region by providing grants for technical cooperation to strengthen governance and public institutions; foster sustainable and inclusive economic growth by advancing country-led policy and institutional reforms. **Structure** Steering Committee; Implementation Support Agencies; Trustee; Coordination Unit; Roster of Experts. **Finance** Government donations. **Activities** Financial and/or material support.

Members Donor and partner countries (15):
Canada, Denmark, France, Germany, Italy, Japan, Kuwait, Netherlands, Qatar, Russia, Saudi Arabia, Türkiye, UK, United Arab Emirates, USA.
IGO Relations *The World Bank Group (#21218).* [2018/XM6832/**F***]

♦ Middle East – North Africa Writing Centers Alliance (MENAWCA) . . 16786

Contact address not obtained. E-mail: menawcaboard@gmail.com.
URL: http://menawca.org/

History Set up 2007. Current constitution adopted Feb 2013. **Aims** Foster communication among writing centers; provide a forum for concerns for writing centers in the region. **Structure** Executive Board. **Activities** Events/meetings. **Publications** *MENAWCA Newsletter.* **NGO Relations** Regional affiliate of: *International Writing Centers Association (IWCA).* [2017/XM5553/**D**]

- ♦ Middle East Optical and Optometric Association / see Eastern Mediterranean Council of Optometry (#05243)
- ♦ Middle East Outreach Council (internationally oriented national body)
- ♦ Middle East Peace Dialogue Network (internationally oriented national body)
- ♦ Middle East Political and Economic Institute (internationally oriented national body)

♦ Middle East Psychological Association (MEPA) 16787

Pres Al Hamra Business Tower 19th floor, Sharq, 13001 Kuwait, Kuwait. E-mail: president@mepa.me – info@mepa.me.
URL: http://www.mepa.me/

History Nov 2010. **Aims** Unify psychologists and other mental health practitioners in the Middle East. **Structure** Executive Committee. Committees (4): Membership; Ethics; Professional Development; Community Outreach. **Events** *Annual Conference* 2022, *Annual Conference* Kuwait (Kuwait) 2021, *Annual Conference* Kuwait (Kuwait) 2020, *Annual Conference* Kuwait (Kuwait) 2019, *International Psychology Conference* Dubai (United Arab Emirates) 2018. [2021.11.30/XM8085/**D**]

- ♦ Middle East Public Relations Association (unconfirmed)

♦ Middle East Publishers' Association (MEPA) 16788

Postal address PO Box 502038, Dubai, United Arab Emirates.
Dir Dubai Media City Office No 6, Media Business Centre, 2nd floor Bldg 2 CNN, Dubai, United Arab Emirates.
URL: http://www.arabview.com/

History Registered in accordance with the Law No 1 of 2000 of the United Arab Emirates. **Aims** Serve, promote and protect the interests of publishers in the Middle East region; unite publishers to discuss the main issues facing the industry and define practical policies that will enhance progress of the industry; ensure a secure future for the publishing industry in the region. **Structure** General Body Meeting (annual); Board of Directors; Membership Campaign Committee Meeting. **Finance** Members' dues. Sponsorship from private companies. **Activities** Events/meetings; training/education. **Publications** *MEPA's Publishers' Dirctory* (annual); *Month Bulletin*; *Weekly Newlsetter.*
Members Categories Founding; Full; Associate. Members in 15 countries and territories:
Bahrain, Egypt, Iran Islamic Rep, Iraq, Jordan, Kuwait, Lebanon, Oman, Palestine, Qatar, Saudi Arabia, Syrian AR, Türkiye, United Arab Emirates, Yemen.
NGO Relations Member of: *World Association of Newspapers and News Publishers (WAN-IFRA, #21166).* [2016/XM1299/**D**]

- ♦ Middle East Quality Association (no recent information)
- ♦ Middle East Research and Information Project (internationally oriented national body)
- ♦ Middle East Self-Medication Industry Association / see Middle-East, North Africa and Pakistan Self-Care Industry (#16783)

♦ Middle East Society for Gynecological Endoscopy (MESGE) 16789

Coordinator 16 Abd El Hamid El Abady Street, Roushdy, Alexandria, Egypt. T. +2035420102. Fax +2035420102.
URL: http://www.mesge.org/

History Launched 1 Oct 2010, Barcelona (Spain), during 19th annual meeting of *European Society for Gynaecological Endoscopy (ESGE, #08611).* **Aims** Encourage exchange of clinical experience, scientific thoughts and investigation among Middle Eastern gynaecological endoscopists and practitioners in related techniques; encourage research and evaluation of endoscopic and related techniques; recommend standards of training in the field; work as a liaison between training centres. **Structure** Executive Board; Special Interest Groups; International Advisory Board. **Languages** Arabic, English. **Staff** 4.00 FTE, paid. **Finance** Members' dues. **Activities** Events/meetings; training/education; certification/accreditation; awareness raising. **Events** *Annual Congress* Antalya (Turkey) 2015, *Annual Congress* Dubai (United Arab Emirates) 2014, *MESGE Congress* Dubai (United Arab Emirates) 2014, *Annual Congress* Antalya (Turkey) 2013. **Publications** *MESGE Newsletter* (4 a year). Updates.
Members Full in 21 countries:
Algeria, Bahrain, Cyprus, Egypt, Iran Islamic Rep, Iraq, Jordan, Kuwait, Lebanon, Libya, Morocco, Oman, Pakistan, Qatar, Saudi Arabia, Sudan, Syrian AR, Tunisia, Türkiye, United Arab Emirates, Yemen.
NGO Relations Affiliated with: *International Society for Gynecologic Endoscopy (ISGE, #15152).* [2018.08.01/XJ8685/**D**]

♦ Middle East Society for Organ Transplantation (MESOT) 16790

Sec Taskent Caddesi No 77, Kat 4, Bahcelievler, 06490 Ankara/Ankara, Türkiye. T. +903122127393. Fax +903122150835. E-mail: secretary@mesot-tx.org.
General: http://www.mesot-tx.org/

History 1987, Turkey. Registered under Swiss Law Jun 1988. Statutes most recently amended Mar 1990. **Aims** Promote and encourage education, research and cooperation in the field of organ transplantation among medical centres, countries and societies in the Middle East and Northern Africa. **Structure** General Assembly (every 2 years); Council; Committees (6). **Languages** English. **Staff** Voluntary. **Finance** Members' dues. **Activities** Events/meetings. **Events** *Biennial Congress* Istanbul (Turkey) 2014, *Biennial Congress* Abu Dhabi (United Arab Emirates) 2012, *Biennial Congress* Tunis (Tunisia) 2010, *Biennial Congress* Shiraz (Iran Islamic Rep) 2008, *Biennial Congress* Kuwait 2006. **Publications** *Clinical and Experimental Transplantation* – journal.
Members Regular; Honorary; Associate; Candidate; Supporting. Organizations in 8 countries:
Cyprus, Egypt, Iran Islamic Rep, Oman, Syrian AR, Tunisia, Türkiye, USA.
Individuals in 18 countries:
Algeria, Canada, Cyprus, Egypt, Iran Islamic Rep, Iraq, Libya, Morocco, Oman, Pakistan, Qatar, Saudi Arabia, Sudan, Syrian AR, Tunisia, Türkiye, United Arab Emirates, USA. [2022/XD2146/v/**D**]

♦ Middle East Society for Sexual Medicine (MESSM) 16791

Main Office Unit 7 Suite C, Ground Floor, 7564 Mohammed Al Azdi St, Al Murjan Dist, Jeddah 23715-3851, Saudi Arabia. E-mail: office@messm.org.
URL: http://messm.org/

History Founded Aug 2010, by a founding committee comprising a group of highly respected Sexual Medicine Specialists from the Middle East. **Aims** Encourage the highest standards of practice, education and research in the field of human sexuality; develop scientific methods for the diagnosis, prevention and treatment of conditions affecting human sexual function; promote the publication of medical and scientific literature in the field of sexual function. **Structure** Board of Directors; Executive Committee. Committees (7): Communication; Development; Financial; Prize; Public Awareness; Scholarships and Awards; Scientific. **Languages** English. **Staff** 0.50 FTE, paid. **Finance** Members' dues. **Events** *Biennial Meeting* Jeddah (Saudi Arabia) 2019, *Biennial Meeting* Abu Dhabi (United Arab Emirates) 2017, *Biennial Meeting* Hurghada (Egypt) 2015, *Biennial Meeting* Dubai (United Arab Emirates) 2013, *Biennial Meeting* Dubai (United Arab Emirates) 2011. **Publications** *MESSM Newsletter.* **Members** Full; Associate; Honorary. Membership countries not specified. [2019/XJ5294/**D**]

- ♦ Middle East Solar Industry Association (internationally oriented national body)
- ♦ Middle East Solidarity Council (no recent information)

♦ Middle East Spine Society (MESS) 16792

Sec 56 A Elkhewedi Tawfik Str, El-Mahalla El-Kubra GHARBIA, Egypt. T. +201222131154.
URL: http://www.mespine.org/

History Apr 2010, Istanbul (Turkey). Also known as *MESpine.* **Aims** Study and advance the art and science of spine *surgery* and research into the cause, prevention and cure of disease in human beings in the field of spine surgery. **Structure** Executive Committee. **Activities** Events/meetings; training/education. **Events** *Congress* Delhi (India) 2019, *Congress* Rabat (Morocco) 2017, *Meeting / International Conference* Cairo (Egypt) 2015. **Publications** *MESpine Newsletter.*
Members Full in 34 countries:
Afghanistan, Algeria, Armenia, Azerbaijan, Bahrain, Cyprus, Djibouti, Egypt, Eritrea, Georgia, Iran Islamic Rep, Iraq, Jordan, Kazakhstan, Kuwait, Kyrgyzstan, Lebanon, Libya, Mauritania, Morocco, Oman, Pakistan, Palestine, Qatar, Saudi Arabia, Somalia, Sudan, Syrian AR, Tajikistan, Tunisia, Türkiye, United Arab Emirates, Uzbekistan, Yemen. [2015/XJ9719/**D**]

- ♦ Middle East Studies Association (internationally oriented national body)
- ♦ Middle East Studies Association of North America / see Middle East Studies Association
- ♦ Middle East Studies Center, Portland (internationally oriented national body)
- ♦ Middle East Technical University (internationally oriented national body)
- ♦ Middle East Women's Leadership Network (internationally oriented national body)
- ♦ Middle East Zoo Association (no recent information)
- ♦ Middle European Good Templar Youth Council (inactive)

♦ Middle European Iris Society (MEIS) 16793

Contact Vinohradska 57, 748 01 Hlucin, Czechia.
URL: http://www.euroiris.net/

History Founded Feb 1996, Otrokovice (Czech Rep), as *Club of European Iris Society (CEIS).* Present name adopted 1997. Registered in accordance with Czech law. **Aims** Promote and popularize growing and breeding of genus irises; register and evaluate new cultivation through collaboration with botanic gardens. **Structure** General Meeting; Board. **Languages** Czech, English, Polish, Slovakian. **Staff** Voluntary. **Finance** Members' dues. Other sources: gifts; grants; income from activities; sponsors. **Activities** Events/meetings. **Publications** *MEIS Bulletin* (annual).
Members Organizations and individuals in 13 countries:
Belgium, Czechia, Estonia, France, Hungary, Lithuania, Netherlands, Poland, Romania, Slovakia, Slovenia, Ukraine, USA. [2020.03.03/XD8118/**D**]

- ♦ Middle European Organisation for Regulatory Affairs (internationally oriented national body)

♦ Middle European Volleyball Zonal Association (MEVZA) 16794

SG Sebastianplatz 3, 1030 Vienna, Austria. T. +4338631411184. E-mail: secretary@mevza.org.
URL: http://mevza.org/

History 19 Oct 2002, Schwechat (Austria). **NGO Relations** Affiliated to: *European Volleyball Confederation (#09078)*; *Fédération internationale de volleyball (FIVB, #09670).* [2020/XJ8514/**D**]

♦ Middle Powers Initiative (MPI) 16795

Chair c/o GSI, 220 East 49th Street, Suite 1B, New York NY 10017, USA. T. +16462895170. Fax +16462895171. E-mail: mpi-ny@gsinstitute.org.
URL: http://www.middlepowers.org/

History Mar 1998, a program of *Global Security Institute (GSI).* Proposals for a *Middle Power Coalition for Disarmament* date from a *Six Nation Initiative* led by *Parliamentarians for Global Action (PGA, #18208)* in the 1980s. **Aims** Work to establish a coalition of middle power countries to campaign for a realistic programme of *nuclear disarmament* and *non-proliferation.* **Publications** Briefing papers.
Members Full in 17 countries:
Brazil, Canada, Egypt, Germany, Holy See, India, Ireland, Malaysia, Mexico, Netherlands, New Zealand, Norway, Russia, Sri Lanka, Sweden, Switzerland, USA.
International citizen organizations (8):
Albert Schweitzer Institute for the Humanities; *Global Security Institute (GSI)*; *International Association of Lawyers Against Nuclear Arms (IALANA, #11994)*; *International Network of Engineers and Scientists for Global Responsibility (INES, #14260)*; *International Peace Bureau (IPB, #14535)*; *International Physicians for the Prevention of Nuclear War (IPPNW, #14578)*; *Nuclear Age Peace Foundation*; *Women's International League for Peace and Freedom (WILPF, #21024).*
NGO Relations Instrumental in setting up: *Parliamentarians for Nuclear Non-Proliferation and Disarmament (PNND, #18210).* Founding partner of: *Basel Peace Office.* Member of: *International Peace Bureau (IPB, #14535).* [2018/XF5863/y/**F**]

- ♦ Mid-European Clay Conference (meeting series)
- ♦ Mid-European Democratic Union (inactive)
- ♦ MIDL Foundation (internationally oriented national body)
- ♦ MID – Monastic Interreligious Dialogue – North America (internationally oriented national body)

♦ Mid Nordic Committee 16796

Mittnordenkommittén – Keskipohjola-Toimikunta
Main Office c/o Region Västernorrland, SE-871 85 Härnösand, Sweden.

History Set up within the framework of *Nordic Council of Ministers (NCM, #17260)* – Nordic Council of Ministers for Business, Energy and Regional Policy (MR-NER). Previously functioned within *Nordic Committee of Senior Officials for Regional Policy (EK-R / NÄRP / NERP).* **Aims** Promote sustainable development and growth in the region. **Activities** Awards/prizes/competitions; events/meetings; politics/policy/regulatory.
Members Regional county councils (4) in central regions of 3 countries:
Finland, Norway, Sweden. [2019.12.12/XK0834/**D***]

- ♦ MIDS – Madras Institute of Development Studies (internationally oriented national body)
- ♦ Midsnell / see MGI Worldwide (#16740)
- ♦ Midsnell Group International / see MGI Worldwide (#16740)
- ♦ Midwest Association for Latin American Studies (internationally oriented national body)
- ♦ **MIEC** Pax Romana, Mouvement international des étudiants catholiques (#18268)
- ♦ **MIEC** Pax Romana, Movimiento Internacional de Estudiantes Católicos (#18268)
- ♦ Miedzynarodowa Federacja Banków Terminologii (inactive)
- ♦ Miedzynarodowa Komisja Ochrony Odry przed Zanieczyszczeniem (#13250)
- ♦ Miedzynarodowa Konfederacja Europejskich Plantatorów Buraka (#12860)
- ♦ Miedzynarodowa Organizacja Terminologii Specjalistycznej (no recent information)
- ♦ Miedzynarodowa Siec Miast Dobrego Zycia / see Cittaslow (#03958)
- ♦ Miedzynarodowa Szkola Bankowosci i Finansów (internationally oriented national body)
- ♦ Miedzynarodowa Unia Monarchistyczna (no recent information)
- ♦ Miedzynarodowa Wspólnota Ekumeniczna (#13226)
- ♦ Miedzynarodowe Centrum Informacji Naukowej i Technicznej (#12514)
- ♦ Miedzynarodowe Forum Podejscia Skoncentrowanego na Osobie (meeting series)
- ♦ Miedzynarodowe Stowarzyszenie Flisaków (#15691)
- ♦ Miedzynarodowe Stowarzyszenie Motoryki Sportowej (#12178)
- ♦ Miedzynarodowe Stowarzyszenie Prawa Ochrony Srodowiska (#05503)
- ♦ Miedzynarodowe Stowarzyszenie Wolnej Mysli (#11906)
- ♦ Miedzynarodowe Towarzystwo Studiów o Otto Grossie (#12060)
- ♦ Miedzynarodowy Instytut Biologii Molekularnej i Komórkowej w Warszawie (internationally oriented national body)
- ♦ Miedzynarodowy Komitet Oswiecimski (#12297)
- ♦ Miedzynarodowy Parlament Bezpieczenstwa i Pokoju (internationally oriented national body)
- ♦ Miedzywydzialowy Instytut Medycyny Morskiej i Tropikalnej (internationally oriented national body)
- ♦ MIET Africa (internationally oriented national body)
- ♦ MIFFI – International Conference on Microbial Food and Feed Ingredients (meeting series)
- ♦ MIF / see FIM-Forum for Democratic Global Governance (#09761)
- ♦ **MIFF** Méliès International Festivals Federation (#16706)
- ♦ **MIF/IES** Mouvement international des faucons – Internationale éducative socialiste (#13327)

♦ MIF / see International Falcon Movement – Socialist Educational International (#13327)
♦ MIF – Miners' International Federation (inactive)
♦ **MIF** Multilateral Investment Fund (#16887)
♦ **MIFP** Mediterranean Institute of Fundamental Physics (#16658)
♦ **MIFRTP** Mécanisme international appelé à exercer les fonctions résiduelles des Tribunaux pénaux (#14746)
♦ **MIGA** Multilateral Investment Guarantee Agency (#16888)
♦ Mighty Earth (internationally oriented national body)
♦ MIGRAF – Association de la migration africaine (internationally oriented national body)

♦ MIGRANTE International (MI) 16797

Chairperson Episcopal Mission Center Compound, 275 E Rodriguez Sr Ave, Brgy Kalusugan, 1112 Quezon City, Philippines. T. +63270924519. Fax +63270924519. E-mail: homeoffice@migranteinternational.org – homeoffice.migrante@gmail.com.
URL: http://migranteinternational.org/

History Mar 1996, Philippines. Initiated Jan 1992 by *Asia Pacific Mission for Migrants (APMM)*. Restructured at 'founding congress', 17-20 Mar 1996, Manila (Philippines), following decision of international consultation meeting, 17-21 Dec 1995, Silang Cavite (Philippines). Former names and other names: *Alliance of Overseas Filipinos in Asia, Pacific and Middle East (MIGRANTE)* – former (Jan 1992 to Mar 1996); *MIGRANTE – International Alliance of Filipino Migrant Workers (MIGRANTE International)* – full title (Mar 1996). Registration: Security and Exchange Commission (SEC), No/ID: CN200509823, Start date: 2005, Philippines, NCR. **Aims** Uphold the dignity of Filipino migrants; promote migrants' rights against discrimination, exploitation and abuses; assert the right to organize; strengthen unity among Overseas Filipinos and organize their families; push for building a self-reliant economy to stop forced migration and work for the scrapping of government initiated labour export program; build solidarity with migrant organizations of other nationalities. **Structure** Global Council; Global Executive Committee; Secretariat, headed by the Chairperson. **Languages** English, Filipino. **Staff** 26.00 FTE, voluntary. **Finance** Sources: donations. Annual budget: 450,000 PHP. **Activities** Advocacy/lobbying/activism; events/meetings. **Events** *International Assembly of Migrants and Refugees / International Assembly of Migrants and Refugees – IAMR* Manila (Philippines) 2008, *Congress* Manila (Philippines) 1996, *International consultation meeting with the representatives of Filipino migrant organizations* Silang (Philippines) 1995. **Publications** *Tinig Migrante* (annual).
Members Organizations and individuals in 29 countries and territories:
Australia, Austria, Bahrain, Belgium, Canada, Denmark, France, Greece, Holy See, Hong Kong, Israel, Italy, Japan, Korea Rep, Kuwait, Libya, Macau, Netherlands, New Zealand, Philippines, Qatar, Saudi Arabia, Singapore, Spain, Switzerland, Taiwan, UK, United Arab Emirates, USA.
IGO Relations Partner of (1): *UNHCR (#20327)*. **NGO Relations** Member of (1): *Asia Pacific Forum on Women, Law and Development (APWLD, #01912)*. Partner of (1): *Asia Pacific Mission for Migrants (APMM)*. Instrumental in setting up (1): *International Migrants Alliance (IMA, #14161)*. [2023.02.14/XF3434/**E**]

♦ MIGRANTE – International Alliance of Filipino Migrant Workers / see MIGRANTE International (#16797)
♦ MIGRANTE International / see MIGRANTE International (#16797)
♦ MIGRANTE / see MIGRANTE International (#16797)

♦ Migrant Forum in Asia (MFA) 16798

Secretariat 25 Matiyaga Street, Central District, Diliman, 1100 Quezon City, Philippines. T. +6322779484. E-mail: mfa@mfasia.org.
URL: http://www.mfasia.org/

History 1994. **Aims** Protect and promote the rights and welfare of the migrant workers, guided by a vision of an alternative world system based on respect for human rights and dignity, social justice and gender equity, particularly for migrant workers. **Structure** General Forum (meets at General Assembly every 2 years). Executive Committee, comprising 2 representatives of each sub-region and one each from regional organizations. Secretariat. **Finance** Grants from private organizations. **Activities** Advocacy/lobbying/activism; knowledge management/information dissemination; events/meetings. **Events** *Peoples global action (PGA) on migration, development and human rights* Athens (Greece) 2009, *Peoples' global action (PGA) on migration, development and human rights* Manila (Philippines) 2008, *Regional Conference on Migration* Seoul (Korea Rep) 2004, *Regional Conference on Migration* Dhaka (Bangladesh) 2002, *Regional Conference on Migration* Jakarta (Indonesia) 2001. **Publications** *MFA Newsletter* (4 a year); *Asian Migrant Yearbook*. Training manuals.
Members Organizations (over 200) in 14 countries and territories:
Bangladesh, Cambodia, Hong Kong, India, Indonesia, Japan, Korea Rep, Malaysia, Myanmar, Nepal, Philippines, Singapore, Sri Lanka, Taiwan.
Included in the above, 1 organization listed in this Yearbook:
Asian Migrant Centre (AMC).
Consultative Status Consultative status granted from: *ECOSOC (#05331)* (Special). **IGO Relations** *Committee on Migrant Workers (CMW, #04271)*. **NGO Relations** Member of: *Asia Democracy Network (ADN, #01265)*; *Global Coalition on Migration (GCM, #10293)*; *Jubilee South – Asian Peoples' Movement on Debt and Development (JSAPMDD, #16160)*; *Women in Migration Network (WIMN, #21008)*. Supports: *Humanitarian Practice Network (HPN, #10973)*. Involved in: *Solidarity for ASEAN People's Advocacy (SAPA, #19683)*.
[2018/XF5774/**F**]

♦ Migrants Rights International (MRI) 16799

Contact CP 147, 1211 Geneva 20, Switzerland. T. +41225349313. Fax +41225349313.
Facebook: https://www.facebook.com/MigrantsRightsInternational

History Sep 1994, Cairo (Egypt), as *International Migrants Rights Watch Committee*. Current title adopted 2000. **Aims** Promote recognition and respect for the rights of all migrants and their families; advocate for universal ratification and effective implementation of the UN international convention on the protection of the rights of all migrant workers and members of their families; facilitate efforts of migrant associations and other NGOs in advocating for migrant rights; monitor trends and developments in the situation of migrants' rights and welfare. **Structure** General Assembly. Executive Council, comprising President, 2 Vice-Presidents, Secretary and Treasurer. **Finance** Sources: private foundations. **Events** *Peoples' Global Action (PGA) on Migration, Development and Human Rights* Stockholm (Sweden) 2014, *Peoples global action (PGA) on migration, development and human rights* Athens (Greece) 2009, *Peoples' global action (PGA) on migration, development and human rights* Manila (Philippines) 2008. **Publications** *Achieving Dignity: Campaigner's handbook for the migrants rights convention* (2002). **Members** Organizations, trade unions and faith-based groups. Membership countries not specified. **Consultative Status** Consultative status granted from: *ECOSOC (#05331)* (Special). **IGO Relations** Observer to: *International Organization for Migration (IOM, #14454)*. Relevant treaty: *International Convention on the Protection of the Rights of all Migrant Workers and Members of Their Families (1990)*. **NGO Relations** Member of: *Fédération des Institutions Internationales établies à Genève (FIIG, #09599)*; *International NGO Platform on the Migrant Workers' Convention (IPMWC, #14367)*.
[2019/XF6289/**F**]

♦ Migration, Asylum, Refugees Regional Initiative (MARRI) 16800

Dir MTV Building – 8th Floor, Bulevuard Goce Delcev bb, PO Box 447, 1000 Skopje, North Macedonia. T. +38923235700. Fax +38923235711. E-mail: info@marri-rc.org.mk.
URL: http://www.marri-rc.org.mk/

History 2003. Established within the context of *Stability Pact for South Eastern Europe (inactive)*, by merging the Regional Return Initiative (RRI) and the Migration and Asylum Initiative (MAI). Jul 2004, came under regional ownership as part of *South East European Cooperation Process (SEECP, #19811)*. Since 1 Jan 2008, under regional ownership of MARRI Participants. **Aims** Promote regional cooperation in the area of migration in the Western Balkans and thus, contribute to development and stability of the region. **Structure** MARRI Regional Forum of Ministers of Interior/Security (meets at least once a year); MARRI Regional Committee – High Officials at the Ministries of Foreign Affairs (meets twice a year); MARRI Regional Centre serves as Secretariat. **Languages** English. **Staff** 10.00 FTE, paid. **Finance** Sources: contributions of member/participating states; donations; revenue from activities/projects. **Activities** Awareness raising; capacity building; events/meetings; guidance/assistance/consulting; knowledge management/information dissemination; projects/programmes; training/education. Western Balkan region. **Events** *Regional Back-to-Back Meeting Asylum and Migration Management* Budva (Montenegro) 2022, *Steering Group Meeting of the PaCT Project* Budva (Montenegro) 2022, *MARRI Friends Meeting* Skopje (North Macedonia) 2022, *MARRI Permanent Working Group on Migration Statistics Meeting* Skopje (North Macedonia) 2022, *Presentation of the Analysis Report: Trends of Human Trafficking in the MARRI Participants* Skopje (North Macedonia) 2022. **Publications** *MARRI Bulletin* (2 a year) in English. *Analysis Report: Trends of Human Trafficking in the MARRI Participants* (2022) in English; *Improving the Communication and Coordination among the NRM Actors in MARRI Participants – Practical Guidance* (2022) in Albanian languages, Bosnian, English, Macedonian, Montenegrin, Serbian; *Inclusion of Survivors in the Policy Development Process and Operational Response to Trafficking in Human Beings – Practical Guidance* (2022) in Albanian, English, Macedonian, Serbian; *Analysing the influence of COVID-19 on migration in the MARRI Participants* (2021) in English; *DEVELOPING AND MONITORING NATIONAL ANTI-TRAFFICKING RESPONSE: A PRACTITIONER'S GUIDE – RAZVOJ I PRAĆENJE NACIONALNI ODGOVOR U BORBI PROTIV TRGOVINE LJUDIMA: PRAKTIČNI VODIČ – ZHVILLIMI DHE MONITORIMI I PËRGJIGJES KOMBTARE KUNDËR TRAFIKIMIT: UDHËZIM PËR PRAKTIKUESIT* (2021) in Albanian, English, Macedonian, Serbian; *Challenges in the identification and protection of vulnerable individuals and victims of gender based violence and trafficking in human beings in the context of migration crisis: Assessment Report* (2017) in English. Monographs; research papers.
Members Participating States (6):
Albania, Bosnia-Herzegovina, Kosovo, Montenegro, North Macedonia, Serbia.
IGO Relations Memorandum of Understanding with (5): *International Centre for Migration Policy Development (ICMPD, #12503)*; *International Organization for Migration (IOM, #14454)*; *Police Cooperation Convention for Southeast Europe (PCC SEE, 2006)*; *Regional Cooperation Council (RCC, #18773)*; *Southeast Europe Police Chiefs Association (SEPCA, #19824)*. Cooperates with (4): *Budapest Process (#03344)*; *Central European Initiative (CEI, #03708)*; European Union Asylum Agency; *Frontex, the European Border and Coast Guard Agency (#10005)*. [2022.10.14/XM3719/**F***]

♦ Migration Policy Group (MPG) 16801

Main Office Rue Belliard 205, Box 1, 1040 Brussels, Belgium. T. +3222305930. Fax +3222800925. E-mail: info@migpolgroup.com.
URL: http://www.migpolgroup.com/

History 1995. Registration: Banque-Carrefour des Entreprises, No/ID: 0545.923.225, Start date: 10 Feb 2014, Belgium. **Aims** Contribute innovative and effective responses to challenges posed by migration and diversity by improving policy development on mobility, migration, diversity, equality and anti-discrimination, in particular by facilitating exchanges among stakeholders. **Structure** Board. **Languages** English, French. **Staff** 13.00 FTE, paid. **Finance** Core funding from foundations; renumeration from *European Commission (EC, #06633)* and other partners. **Activities** Politics/policy/regulatory; monitoring/evaluation. **Publications** *Migration News Sheet* (12 a year); *European Journal of Migration and Law* (4 a year); *European Anti-Discrimation Law Review* (2 a year). *Immigration and Asylum Book Series*. Papers. **Members** Not a membership organization. **IGO Relations** *European Commission Against Racism and Intolerance (ECRI, see: #04881)*. Participant in Fundamental Rights Platform of: *European Union Agency for Fundamental Rights (FRA, #08969)*. **NGO Relations** Instrumental in setting up (1): *European Equality Law Network (#07004)*.
[2021/XF5955/**F**]

♦ Migration Policy Institute (internationally oriented national body)
♦ Migratory Birds of the Western Palearctic (#17712)
♦ Migratory Wildlife Network (internationally oriented national body)

♦ Migreurop 16802

Contact CICP, 21ter rue Voltaire, 75011 Paris, France. E-mail: contact@migreurop.org.
URL: http://www.migreurop.org/

History 6 Aug 2006. Registered in accordance with French law. **Aims** Promote and defend *migrants'* fundamental *rights* worldwide, especially those of people controlled, detained or under surveillance because of restrictive laws hindering the right to *mobility* and to reside in a country other than one's country of origin. **Structure** General Assembly; Board of Directors. **Languages** English, French, Italian, Spanish. **Staff** 3.00 FTE, paid. **Finance** Sources: members' dues; private foundations; sale of products. Annual budget: 200,000 EUR. **Activities** Advocacy/lobbying/activism; events/meetings. **Publications** *Atlas of Migrants in Europe: Critical Geography of Migration Policies*. Annual Report.
Members Organizations in 17 countries:
Belgium, Cyprus, Egypt, France, Germany, Italy, Lebanon, Mali, Mauritania, Morocco, Niger, Portugal, Spain, Switzerland, Tunisia, Türkiye, UK.
CIMADE; *CNCD Opération 11 11 11*; *Coordination et initiatives pour réfugiés et étrangers (CIRE)*; *Emmaüs Europe (#05444)*; *European Association for the Defence of Human Rights (AEDH, no recent information)*; *Initiatives Pour un Autre Monde (IPAM)*; *Movement Against Racism and for Friendship between Peoples (MRAP)*; *Secours catholique – Caritas France*; *Solidarité sans frontières, Berne (SOSF)*; *Spanish Commission for Refugee Assistance (CEAR)*; *Statewatch*.
NGO Relations Cooperates with: *European Alternatives (EA, #05891)*; *International Federation for Human Rights (#13452)*. [2021/XJ6892/y/**F**]

♦ MIGS – Mediterranean Institute of Gender Studies (internationally oriented national body)
♦ MIGS – Montreal Institute for Genocide and Human Rights Studies (internationally oriented national body)
♦ Miguel Agustin Pro Juarez Human Rights Center (internationally oriented national body)
♦ MIHV / see Wellshare International
♦ **MIIC** Pax Romana, Mouvement international des intellectuels catholiques (#18267)
♦ **MIIC** Pax Romana, Movimiento Internacional de Intelectuales Católicos (#18267)
♦ MIIS / see Middlebury Institute of International Studies, Monterey
♦ MIIS – Middlebury Institute of International Studies, Monterey (internationally oriented national body)

♦ MIJARC Europe 16803

Main Office Mundo-J, Rue de l'Industrie 10, 1030 Brussels, Belgium. T. +324855368474. E-mail: office@mijarc.eu.
URL: http://mijarceurope.net/

History A continental federation of *Mouvement international de la jeunesse agricole et rurale catholique (MIJARC, #16865)*. Registration: Belgium; EU Transparency Register, No/ID: 548418537340-11. **Aims** Promote sustainable agricultural, rural and international development, European citizenship, youth policies, gender equality, environmental protection, interculturality and human rights. **Structure** General Assembly; European Coordination; European Team; Secretariat. **Languages** English. **Finance** Support from: *Council of Europe (CE, #04881)* – *European Youth Foundation (EYF, #09141)*; *European Commission (EC, #06633)* – EACEA and ERASMUS; *Renovabis – Solidaritätsaktion der deutschen Katholiken mit den Menschen in Mittel- und Osteuropa*; Fondation Hippocrène. **Activities** Advocacy/lobbying/activism; meetings/events. **Publications** *Info Europe* (2 a year) – magazine. Position papers.
Members Full; Observer. Full in 10 countries:
Armenia, Belgium, Bulgaria, France, Germany, Malta, Poland, Portugal, Romania, Spain.
Observer in 3 countries:
Italy, Netherlands, North Macedonia.
NGO Relations *Conseil européen des jeunes agriculteurs (CEJA, #04689)*; *Don Bosco Youth-Net (DBYN, #05119)*; *CIDSE (CIDSE, #03926)*; *Mouvement international de la jeunesse agricole et rurale catholique (MIJARC, #16865)*; *Rural Youth Europe (#19007)*. [2020/XM6898/**D**]

♦ **MIJARC** Mouvement international de la jeunesse agricole et rurale catholique (#16865)
♦ **MIJARC** Movimiento Internacional de la Juventud Agraria y Rural Católica (#16865)
♦ MIJC – Mouvement international des juristes catholiques (inactive)
♦ MIJM – Mouvement international de jeunesse Mazdaznan (inactive)

♦ Milan Urban Food Policy Pact (MUFPP) 16804

Secretariat Piazza Duomo 19, 20121 Milan MI, Italy. E-mail: mufpp.secretariat@comune.milano.it.
URL: https://www.milanurbanfoodpolicypact.org/

History 2015, Milan (Italy). Founded as an international agreement among cities worldwide. **Aims** Support cities wishing to develop more sustainable urban food systems by fostering city to city cooperation and best practices exchange. **Structure** Assembly; Steering Committee; Secretariat. **Activities** Awards/prizes/competitions; events/meetings. **Events** *Global Forum* Rio de Janeiro (Brazil) 2022, *Global Forum* Barcelona (Spain) 2021. **Members** Cities (currently 211). Membership countries not specified. [2021/AA1750/**E**]

♦ Mildmay International (internationally oriented national body)
♦ Milieukontakt International (internationally oriented national body)
♦ Milieukontakt Oost-Europa / see Milieukontakt International
♦ Militaries' Organization for Democracy, Integration and Liberation of Latin America and the Caribbean (inactive)
♦ Military Armistice Commission in Korea / see United Nations Command Military Armistice Commission (#20529)
♦ Military and Hospitaller Order of St Lazarus of Jerusalem (religious order)
♦ Military Union of the Commonwealth of Independent States / see Collective Security Treaty Organization (#04103)
♦ Militia Immaculatae (religious order)
♦ Milizia dell'Immacolata (religious order)
♦ Milken Institute (internationally oriented national body)
♦ Millennia2025 Foundation / see Millennia2025 Women and Innovation Foundation
♦ Millennia2025 Women and Innovation Foundation (internationally oriented national body)
♦ Millennium Development Goals Global Watch (internationally oriented national body)
♦ Millennium Institute (internationally oriented national body)

♦ The Millennium Project (MP) 16805

Dir 4421 Garrison St NW, Washington DC 20016-4055, USA. T. +12026865179. Fax +12026865179.
URL: http://www.millennium-project.org/

History Founded 1996, after a 3-year feasibility study with *United Nations University (UNU, #20642)*, Smithsonian Institution, Futures Group International, and American Council for the UNU. Operated under American Council for UNU until 2007; operated under *World Federation of United Nations Associations (WFUNA, #21499)* (2007-2009). Became an independent non-profit, 2009. **Aims** Improve *thinking* about the *future* and make that thinking available through a variety of media for feedback to accumulate *wisdom* about the future for better decisions today. **Structure** Planning Committee; Board of Directors; Nodes (63) worldwide – groups of individuals and institutions that connect global and local perspectives. **Languages** Arabic, Bulgarian, Chinese, Czech, English, French, Japanese, Persian, Polish, Portuguese, Russian, Spanish. **Staff** 3.00 FTE, paid.
Finance Publication sales and subscriptions; grants and contracts from UN bodies, governments, foundations, corporations, universities, NGOs; individual donations. Past and present funders include:
- AGAHI Pakistan;
- Amir of Kuwait;
- Applied Materials;
- Azerbaijan Ministry of Communications;
- Azerbaijan State Economic University;
- Basque Government;
- Deloitte;
- Egyptian Academy of Scientific Research and Technology;
- Ford Motors;
- *Foundation for the Future (FFF, no recent information)*;
- GM;
- *International Bank for Reconstruction and Development (IBRD, #12317)*;
- Kuwait Oil Company;
- Kuwait Petroleum Corporation;
- Ministry of Education, Korea Rep;
- Motorola;
- *NATO (#16945)*;
- Pioneer Hybrid;
- *The Rockefeller Foundation (#18966)*;
- Shell International;
- South African Ministry of Finance;
- South Korean Ministry of Finance;
- *UNDP (#20292)*;
- *UNESCO (#20322)*;
- *United Nations University (UNU, #20642)*;
- US Army Environmental Policy Institute;
- US Department of Energy;
- *Woodrow Wilson International Center for Scholars (WWICS)*.

Annual budget: US$ 50,000 – 500,000.
Activities Publishing activity; research/documentation; training/education; guidance/assistance/consulting; networking/liaising; knowledge management/information dissemination. **Events** *Meeting* Washington, DC (USA) 2016, *Meeting* San Francisco, CA (USA) 2015, *Meeting* Santo Domingo (Dominican Rep) 2014, *Meeting* Baku (Azerbaijan) 2013, *Meeting* Toronto, ON (Canada) 2012. **Publications** *State of the Future* (annual) – report; *Futures Research Methodology*. Studies. **Information Services** *Global Futures Intelligence System*.
Members Country, regional and non-geographic nodes (60) representing 57 countries and the Caribbean (countries not specified) in 54 countries:
Argentina, Armenia, Australia, Azerbaijan, Belgium, Bolivia, Brazil, Bulgaria, Canada, Chile, China, Colombia, Croatia, Czechia, Dominican Rep, Egypt, El Salvador, Finland, France, Georgia, Germany, Greece, Hungary, India, Iran Islamic Rep, Israel, Italy, Japan, Kenya, Korea Rep, Kuwait, Malaysia, Mexico, Montenegro, Netherlands, Pakistan, Peru, Poland, Romania, Russia, Slovakia, Slovenia, South Africa, Spain, Sri Lanka, Tanzania UR, Tunisia, Türkiye, Uganda, UK, United Arab Emirates, Uruguay, USA, Venezuela.
Non-geographic nodes (2): Arts/Media; Cyber Node. Regional networks of nodes (2):
Regional networks of nodes (2):
European Foresight Monitoring Network (EFMN, #07295); *Red IBERoamericana de Prospectiva (RIBER)*.
[2019/XJ7114/**F**]

♦ Millennium Promise / see Millennium Promise Alliance (#16806)

♦ Millennium Promise Alliance (MPA) 16806

CEO 475 Riverside Drive, Ste 1040, New York NY 10115, USA. T. +12128702490. E-mail: info@millenniumpromise.org.
URL: http://www.millenniumpromise.org/

History 2005. Founded on the initiative of Ray Chambers and Jeffrey D Sachs. Former names and other names: *Millennium Promise* – former. Registration: 501(c)(3) non-profit, USA. **Aims** Support the achievement of the Millennium *Development* Goals, with a specific mandate to translate the world's commitment to the MDGs through the mobilization of tangible results. **Structure** Board of Directors. **Activities** Runs the *'Millennium Villages Project'*. **Consultative Status** Consultative status granted from: *ECOSOC (#05331)* (Special). **IGO Relations** Partners include: *Joint United Nations Programme on HIV/AIDS (UNAIDS, #16149)*; *World Food Programme (WFP, #21510)*. **NGO Relations** Member of (1): *American Council for Voluntary International Action (InterAction)*. Partner of (1): *Earth Institute at Columbia University*. [2020/XJ4729/**E**]

♦ Millennium Water Alliance (internationally oriented national body)
♦ Milletlerarasi Sark Tetkikleri Cemiyeti (no recent information)
♦ MILSET – Mouvement international pour le loisir scientifique et technique (internationally oriented national body)
♦ MIM / see International Management Institute, Kiev
♦ MIMC – Mahabodhi International Meditation Centre (internationally oriented national body)
♦ **MI** Mekong Institute (#16701)
♦ **MI** Mentor International (#16716)
♦ MIMETA – Centre for Culture and Development (internationally oriented national body)
♦ MI – Methanol Institute (internationally oriented national body)
♦ **MI** MIGRANTE International (#16797)
♦ MI – Militia Immaculatae (religious order)
♦ MiM – Men in Movement (meeting series)
♦ MIM – Mission of the Immaculate Mediatrix Movement (religious order)
♦ **MIM** Multilateral Initiative on Malaria (#16886)
♦ MIMO / see Moskovskij Gosudarstvennyj Institut Mezdunarodnyh Otnosenij
♦ MI – Mobility International (inactive)
♦ **MIMOSA** Machinery Information Management Open Systems Alliance (#16538)
♦ **MI** Multimedia International (#16893)
♦ Minamata Convention on Mercury (2013 treaty)
♦ MINAS / see United Nations Mine Action Service (#20585)
♦ MINC – Multilingual Internet Names Consortium (internationally oriented national body)
♦ Minda de Gunzburg Center for European Studies / see Center for European Studies, Cambridge MA
♦ Minderoo Foundation (internationally oriented national body)

♦ MindFreedom International 16807

Admin Coordinator 454 Willamette St, Ste 216, PO Box 11284, Eugene OR 97440-3484, USA. T. +15413459106. Fax +14802878833.
URL: http://www.mindfreedom.org/

History Corporate entity founded 1986; coalition set up 1990. Original title: *Support Coalition International (SCI)*. Full title: *MindFreedom International: United Action for Human Rights in Mental Health*. **Aims** Win human *rights* campaigns in *mental health*; challenge abuse by the psychiatric drug industry; support self-determination of *psychiatric* survivors and mental health consumers; promote safe, humane and effective options in mental health. **Structure** Board; International Advisory Council. **Languages** English. **Staff** 2.50 FTE, paid. **Finance** Donations and foundations. **Activities** Advocacy/lobbying/activism; knowledge management/information dissemination; events/meetings. **Events** *Choice in mental health care* New York, NY (USA) 2007. **Publications** *MindFreedom Journal*.
Members Sponsor and Affiliate groups (100) in 12 countries and territories:
Australia, Bosnia-Herzegovina, Brazil, Canada, Denmark, France, Germany, India, New Zealand, Palestine, UK, USA.
Individuals mostly people who experienced a diagnosis of a psychiatric disability in 33 countries and territories:
Australia, Bosnia-Herzegovina, Brazil, Canada, Chile, Denmark, Finland, France, Germany, Ghana, Greece, India, Ireland, Israel, Italy, Japan, Kenya, Lithuania, Netherlands, New Zealand, Norway, Pakistan, Palestine, Philippines, Romania, South Africa, Spain, Sri Lanka, Sweden, Switzerland, Thailand, UK, USA.
Consultative Status Consultative status granted from: *ECOSOC (#05331)* (Ros A). [2016.06.01/XF4176/**F**]

♦ MindFreedom International: United Action for Human Rights in Mental Health / see MindFreedom International (#16807)

♦ Mind and Life Europe (MLE) 16808

Managing Dir c/o Kuhn and Partners, Bahnhofplatz 18, 8400 Winterthur ZH, Switzerland. E-mail: office@mindandlife-europe.org.
URL: http://www.mindandlife-europe.org/

History 2008, as the European organization of *Mind and Life Institute*. Registered in accordance with Swiss Civil Code, as *Mind and Life International*. **Aims** Support and facilitate the dialogue between different branches of *science* such as neuroscience, medicine, psychology, philosophy and the *contemplative traditions* of the world. **Structure** Advisory Committee. Board. **Activities** Events/meetings; training/education; awards/prizes/competitions. [2016/XJ8584/**F**]

♦ Mind and Life Institute (internationally oriented national body)
♦ Mind and Life International / see Mind and Life Europe (#16808)

♦ MINDS International 16809

Acting Managing Dir Laimgrubengasse 10, 1060 Vienna, Austria.
Registered Address Gutleutstr 110, 60327 Frankfurt-Main, Germany.
URL: http://www.minds-international.com/

History Sep 2007. Founded following an earlier European Union co-funded project. Registration: No/ID: VR 13935, Start date: 2 Apr 2008, Germany. **Aims** Support the digital development of news agencies and the media industry in general. **Structure** General Meeting; Board of Directors. **Activities** Events/meetings. **Events** *MINDS International Conference* Sydney, NSW (Australia) 2019. **Members** News agencies. Membership countries not specified. [2020/AA0842/**F**]

♦ Mine Action Information Center (internationally oriented national body)
♦ MINEDAF – Ministers of Education and Those Responsible for Economic Planning in African Member States (meeting series)
♦ MINEDAP – Regional Conference of Ministers of Education and Those Responsible for Economic Planning in Asia and the Pacific (meeting series)
♦ MINEDARAB – Conference of Ministers of Education and Those Responsible for Economic Planning in Arab States (meeting series)
♦ MINEDEUROPE – Conference of Ministers of Education of Member States of the Europe Region (meeting series)
♦ MINEDLAC – Conference of Ministers of Education and Those Responsible for Economic Planning in Latin America and Caribbean (meeting series)
♦ Mineral Processing and Extractive Metallurgy for Mining and Recycling Innovation Association / see PROMETIA (#18538)
♦ Minerals, Metals and Materials Society (internationally oriented national body)
♦ Miners' European Federation (inactive)
♦ Miners' International Federation (inactive)
♦ Mines Advisory Group (internationally oriented national body)
♦ Mines Ministries of the Americas (no recent information)
♦ Miniature AFV Association / see Miniature Armoured Fighting Vehicle Association (#16810)
♦ Miniature AFV Collectors' Association / see Miniature Armoured Fighting Vehicle Association (#16810)

♦ Miniature Armoured Fighting Vehicle Association (MAFVA) 16810

Pres 39 The Leas, Baldock, SG7 6HZ, UK.
URL: http://www.mafva.org/

History 1965, as *Miniature AFV Collectors' Association*. Present name adopted 1969. Also referred to as *Miniature AFV Association*. **Aims** Promote interest in armoured fighting vehicles and their associated equipment; collect and disseminate information on the field. **Structure** Annual Meeting. **Languages** English. **Staff** 7.00 FTE, voluntary. **Finance** Members' dues. Sale of publications. **Events** *Annual Meeting* Duxford (UK) 2011, *Annual Meeting* Duxford (UK) 2010, *Annual Meeting* Duxford (UK) 2009, *Annual Meeting* Duxford (UK) 2008, *Annual meeting* Duxford (UK) 2007. **Publications** *Tankette* (6 a year).
Members Individuals and libraries (mostly in UK) in 71 countries and territories:
Argentina, Australia, Austria, Bahamas, Barbados, Belgium, Belize, Benin, Bermuda, Bolivia, Brazil, Canada, Chile, China, Colombia, Cyprus, Czechia, Denmark, Egypt, Finland, France, Gambia, Germany, Greece, Hong Kong, Hungary, India, Indonesia, Iraq, Ireland, Israel, Italy, Jamaica, Japan, Korea Rep, Lebanon, Luxembourg, Malaysia, Malta, Mexico, Monaco, Netherlands, New Zealand, Norway, Pakistan, Panama, Papua New Guinea, Peru, Philippines, Poland, Portugal, Romania, Russia, Serbia, Singapore, Slovakia, South Africa, Spain, Sri Lanka, St Kitts-Nevis, St Lucia, Sweden, Switzerland, Taiwan, Thailand, Türkiye, UK, Uruguay, USA, Virgin Is USA, Zimbabwe. [2018.01.25/XF4565/**F**]

♦ Minimally Invasive Robotic Association (MIRA) 16811

Exec Dir 11300 West Olympic Blvd Ste 600, Los Angeles CA 90064, USA. T. +13104243353. Fax +13104370585.
URL: http://www.mirasurgery.org/

History 2004. Also referred to as *Society of Robotic Surgery*. Previously also referred to as *Minimally Invasive Surgery Association*. **Aims** Serve as a professional surgical society dedicated to the furtherance of information relative to the field of minimally invasive robotics and the promotion of activities that will lead to the improvement of minimally invasive robotic techniques; further the study, perfection and innovation of these techniques for the purpose of improving patient care. **Structure** Officers: President; President-Elect; Vice-President; Treasurer; Secretary; Executive Director. **Languages** English. **Staff** 2.00 FTE, voluntary. **Finance** Members' dues. **Activities** Organizes robotic master classes and sessions for presentations at other minimally invasive surgical society congresses. **Events** *World congress* Athens (Greece) 2011, *World congress* San Diego, CA (USA) 2010, *World congress / Congress* Québec, QC (Canada) 2009, *Congress* Rome (Italy) 2008, *World congress* Rome (Italy) 2008. [2012/XM0337/**D**]

♦ Minimally Invasive Surgery Association / see Minimally Invasive Robotic Association (#16811)

♦ Mining Industry Association of Southern Africa (MIASA) 16812

Sec PO Box 61809, Marshalltown 2107, Johannesburg, South Africa. T. +27114987275. Fax +27118384251.
Street Address Chamber of Mines Bldg, 5 Hollard Str, Johannesburg, South Africa.
URL: http://www.miasa.org.za/
History 1998. **Structure** Chief Executives.
Members Full in 8 countries:
Botswana, Congo DR, Madagascar, Namibia, South Africa, Tanzania UR, Zambia, Zimbabwe. [2014/XJ8882/t/**D**]

♦ Mining Working Group at the UN (MWG) 16813

Contact address not obtained. E-mail: oaconnor@mercysc.org.
URL: http://miningwg.com/
Aims Advocate at and through the United Nations for human and environmental rights as related to extractive industries. **Activities** Advocacy/lobbying/activism; research/documentation.
Members Organizations, including 12 listed in this Yearbook:
Congregation of the Mission (Vincentians); Franciscans International (FI, #09982); Greek Orthodox Archdiocesan Council of America (GOAC, #10708); International Presentation Association (IPA, #14635); Medical Mission Sisters; Missionary Oblates of Mary Immaculate (OMI); Passionists International (PI, #18254); Religious of the Sacred Heart of Mary (RSHM); Society of Mary (Marianists); Temple of Understanding (ToU, #20124); UNANIMA International (#20281); VIVAT International (#20801). [2016/XM5237/y/**E**]

♦ Minipeg Research Forum (MRF) 16814

Contact address not obtained. E-mail: contact@minipigresearchforum.org.
URL: https://minipigresearchforum.org/
History 2007. **Aims** Bring together all users of Göttingen Minipigs or stakeholders having an interest in sharing knowledge and experience in the use of minipigs in biomedical research. **Structure** Scientific Steering Committee. **Activities** Events/meetings. **Events** *MRF Meeting* Vienna (Austria) 2019. **Members** Full (over 500) worlwide. Membership countries not specified. [2020/AA0372/**F**]

♦ Minipig Research Forum (MRF) 16815

Address not obtained.
URL: http://minipigresearchforum.org/
History Launched 2007. **Structure** Steering Committee. **Activities** Events/meetings. **Events** *Meeting* Dalmose (Denmark) 2022, *Meeting* Lisbon (Portugal) 2020, *Meeting* Vienna (Austria) 2019, *Meeting* Barcelona (Spain) 2018, *Meeting* Cambridge (UK) 2017. [2020/XM5425/**F**]

♦ Ministère baptiste canadien (internationally oriented national body)
♦ Ministère évangélique parmi les nations arabophones (internationally oriented national body)
♦ Ministères des mines des Amériques (no recent information)

♦ Ministerial Conference on Fisheries Cooperation Among African States Bordering the Atlantic Ocean (ATLAFCO) 16816

Conférence Ministérielle sur la Coopération Halieutique entre les Etats Africains Riverains de l'Océan Atlantique (COMHAFAT)
Secretariat No 2 Street Beni Darkoul, Ain Khalouiya, Souissi, Rabat, Morocco. T. +212530774224 – +212530774221. Fax +212530174242. E-mail: secretariat@comhafat.org – contact@comhafat.org.
URL: http://comhafat.org/
History 1989. *Regional Convention on Fisheries Cooperation among African States Bordering the Atlantic Ocean (1991)* serves as Constituent Convention. *Protocol relating to the institutional framework of ATLAFCO* adopted 15 Oct 1999, Conakry (Guinea). **Aims** Promote an effective and active cooperation between Member States for conservation and sustainable development of fisheries in the region. **Structure** Session (every 2 years); Bureau; Executive Secretariat. Networks (4): *African Association of Exporters Importers of Fishery Products – Association Africaine des Importateurs Exportateurs des Produits Halieutiques (AFIEX); African Network of Women in Fisheries Sector – Réseau Africain des Femmes de la Pêche (RAFEP); Coalition of African Maritime Training Institutions – Regroupement des établissements de formation maritime africains (REFMA); Network of Fisheries Research and Marine Sciences Institutes – Réseau des Instituts de Recherche Halieutique et des Sciences de la Mer (RAFISMER).* **Activities** Politics/policy/regulatory.
Members States (22):
Angola, Benin, Cameroon, Cape Verde, Congo Brazzaville, Congo DR, Côte d'Ivoire, Equatorial Guinea, Gabon, Gambia, Ghana, Guinea, Guinea-Bissau, Liberia, Mauritania, Morocco, Namibia, Nigeria, Sao Tomé-Principe, Senegal, Sierra Leone, Togo.
IGO Relations *FAO (#09260).* Agreement with: *INFOPECHE (#11191).* **NGO Relations** Memorandum of Understanding with: *Long Distance Advisory Council (LDAC, #16511).* [2016/XM5012/**F***]

♦ Ministerial Conference on the Protection of Forests in Europe (FOREST EUROPE) 16817

Conférence Ministérielle pour la protection des forêts en Europe – Ministerkonferenz zum Schutz der Wälder in Europa
Contact Maximilianstraße 28 B, 53111 Bonn, Germany. T. +4915111728899. E-mail: liaisonunit-bonn@foresteurope.org.
URL: http://www.foresteurope.org/
History 1990. Former names and other names: *MCPFE* – former. **Aims** Develop common strategies on how to protect and sustainably manage forests. **Structure** Ministerial Conferences; Expert Level Meetings; Round Table Meetings; Ad Hoc working groups. Organized by joint presidency of 2 countries which, with 3 support countries, comprise the General Coordinating Committee (GCC). Liaison Unit acts as service office. **Languages** English, French, Russian. **Staff** 6.00 FTE, paid. **Finance** Through a Trust Fund, which is fed with voluntary contributions of members of General Coordinating Committee. Budget varies. **Activities** Conferences adopt general declarations and resolutions which are implemented through follow-up mechanisms. *Intergovernmental Negotiating Committee for a Legally Binding Agreement on Forests in Europe (INC-Forests, inactive)* completed its worked 2014, presenting its work to an extraordinary Ministerial Conference, 2015. **Events** *Ministerial Conference on the Protection of Forests in Europe* Bratislava (Slovakia) 2021, *Expert Level Meeting* Madrid (Spain) 2015, *Extraordinary Ministerial Conference* Madrid (Spain) 2015, *Ministerial Conference* Madrid (Spain) 2015, *Expert Level Meeting* Cuenca (Spain) 2014. **Publications** Reports; documents; technical background documents.
Members Pan-European participating states (46):
Albania, Andorra, Austria, Belarus, Belgium, Bosnia-Herzegovina, Bulgaria, Croatia, Cyprus, Czechia, Denmark, Estonia, Finland, France, Georgia, Germany, Greece, Holy See, Hungary, Iceland, Ireland, Italy, Latvia, Liechtenstein, Lithuania, Luxembourg, Malta, Moldova, Monaco, Montenegro, Netherlands, North Macedonia, Norway, Poland, Portugal, Romania, Russia, Serbia, Slovakia, Slovenia, Spain, Sweden, Switzerland, Türkiye, UK, Ukraine.
Regional European participating entity (1):
European Union (EU, #08967).
Non-European observer countries (14):
Australia, Brazil, Cameroon, Canada, Chile, China, Ghana, India, Japan, Korea Rep, Malaysia, Morocco, New Zealand, USA.
IGO Relations Observers: *Bioversity International (#03262); Council of Europe (CE, #04881); European Forest Institute (EFI, #07297); European State Forest Association (EUSTAFOR, #08832); FAO (#09260); ILO (#11123); International Tropical Timber Organization (ITTO, #15737); UNEP (#20299); UNDP (#20292); United Nations Economic Commission for Europe (UNECE, #20555); United Nations Forum on Forests (UNFF, #20562); United Nations University (UNU, #20642).*
NGO Relations Observers:
- *Building and Wood Workers' International (BWI, #03355);*
- *Confederation of European Forest Owners (CEPF, #04525);*
- *Confederation of European Paper Industries (CEPI, #04529);*
- *Confédération européenne des industries du bois (CEI Bois, #04545);*
- *COPA – european farmers (COPA, #04829);*
- *European Federation of Building and Woodworkers (EFBWW, #07065);*
- *European Federation of Local Forest Communities (#07157);*
- *European Landowners' Organization (ELO, #07639);*
- *European Observatory of Mountain Forests (EOMF, #08073);*
- *Fern (#09736);*
- *Forest Stewardship Council (FSC, #09869);*
- *Greenpeace International (#10727);*
- *International Council for Game and Wildlife Conservation (#13024);*
- *International Forestry Students' Association (IFSA, #13628);*
- *International Institute for Applied Systems Analysis (IIASA, #13861);*
- *International Union for Conservation of Nature and Natural Resources (IUCN, #15766);*
- *International Union of Forest Research Organizations (IUFRO, #15774);*
- *PEFC Council (#18288);*
- *Union of European Foresters (UEF, #20387);*
- *Unión de Silvicultores del Sur de Europa (USSE, #20478);*
- *Working Group on Criteria and Indicators for the Conservation and Sustainable Management of Temperate and Boreal Forests (Montreal Process, #21058);*
- *World Wide Fund for Nature (WWF, #21922).* [2023/XF5999/c/**F***]

♦ Ministerial Conference of West and Central African States on Maritime Transport / see Maritime Organization of West and Central Africa (#16582)
♦ Ministerial Meeting of the Mediterranean Non-Aligned Countries (meeting series)
♦ Ministérios de Minas das Américas (no recent information)
♦ Ministérios de Mineria de las Américas (no recent information)
♦ Ministerkonferenz zum Schutz der Wälder in Europa (#16817)
♦ Ministers of Education and Those Responsible for Economic Planning in African Member States (meeting series)
♦ Ministers' Forum on Infrastructure Development in the Asia Pacific Region (no recent information)
♦ Minnesota Advocates for Human Rights / see Advocates for Human Rights
♦ Minnesota International Health Volunteers / see Wellshare International
♦ Minnesota Lawyers International Human Rights Committee / see Advocates for Human Rights
♦ **MINOM** Mouvement international pour une nouvelle muséologie (#16866)

♦ Minorities of Europe (MOE) 16818

Contact Legacy House, 29 Walsgrave Road, Coventry, CV2 4HE, UK. T. +442476225764. Fax +442476261679.
Registered Office 40 Stoke Row, Coventry, CV2 4JP, UK.
History 1995. UK Registered Charity: 1088601. **Aims** Support and assist cooperation, solidarity and exchange among different minority communities and *young people* in Europe. **Structure** Board. **Events** *Joint seminar on gender equality and youth participation in minority communities* Budapest (Hungary) 1999. **IGO Relations** Member of: *European Youth Centres (EYCs, #09138).* **NGO Relations** Member of: *International Interfaith Organizations Network (IION, #13945); UNITED for Intercultural Action – European Network Against Nationalism, Racism, Fascism and in Support of Migrants and Refugees (UNITED, #20511).* [2010/XN8081/**F**]

♦ Minority Dailies Association / see European Association of Daily Newspapers in Minority and Regional Languages (#06002)

♦ Minority Research Network 16819

Coordinator Erasmus School of Law, Postbus 1738, 3000 DR Rotterdam, Netherlands. T. +31104081806. E-mail: minorityresearchnetwork@gmail.com.
URL: http://www.frg.eur.nl/minorityresearchnetwork/
Aims Research and effectively address minority issues at large in an intellectually rigorous and context-sensitive manner. **Structure** International Advisory Board. **Events** *International interdisciplinary conference on socio-economic participation of minorities in relation to their rights to (respect for) identity* Rotterdam (Netherlands) 2010.
Members Individuals in 28 countries:
Australia, Austria, Bangladesh, Belgium, Canada, China, Croatia, Denmark, France, Germany, Greece, Hungary, India, Iran Islamic Rep, Israel, Italy, Kenya, Morocco, Netherlands, Norway, Serbia, Slovenia, South Africa, Spain, Switzerland, Türkiye, UK, USA.
Centres and institutions in 9 countries:
Austria, Bangladesh, Germany, Hungary, India, Italy, Netherlands, UK, USA.
Included in the above, 3 organizations listed in this Yearbook:
European Centre for Minority Issues (ECMI); Global Human Rights Defence (GHRD); Minority Rights Group International (MRG, #16820). [2011/XJ2399/y/**E**]

♦ Minority Rights Group International (MRG) 16820

Groupement pour les droits des minorités
Exec Dir 54 Commercial Street, London, E1 6LT, UK. T. +442074224200. Fax +442074224201. E-mail: minority.rights@mrgmail.org.
Dir Policy and Advocacy address not obtained.
URL: http://www.minorityrights.org/
History 1966, London (UK). Registration: Charity Commission, No/ID: 282305, UK, England and Wales. **Aims** Support minorities and indigenous peoples as they strive to maintain their rights to the lands they live on, the languages they speak, to practise their beliefs, to equal opportunities in education and employment, and full participation in public life. **Structure** International Council (meets twice a year); International Secretariat, based in London (UK); Regional Offices (2). **Languages** Arabic, English, French, Russian, Spanish, Swahili, Swedish, Turkish. **Staff** 45.00 FTE, paid; 8.00 FTE, voluntary. Staff and volunteers in about 14 countries. **Finance** Sources: donations; grants; sale of publications. Other sources: institutional funding. Recent major donors include the Ministry for Foreign Affairs of Finland, Netherlands Foreign Ministry, Royal Norwegian Ministry of Foreign Affairs, Reed Smith LLP (in kind), and the following organization: Open Society Institute. Supported by: *Baring Foundation; European Commission (EC, #06633); Irish Aid; Sigrid Rausing Trust; Swedish International Development Cooperation Agency (Sida); UNDP (#20292).* **Activities** Advocacy/lobbying/activism; events/meetings; projects/programmes; publishing activities; research/documentation; training/education. Active in all member countries. **Events** *Conférence sur la représentation des intérêts des minorités et la participation des minorités aux processus de prise de décision* Budapest (Hungary) 1999, *NGO conference* Copenhagen (Denmark) 1989. **Publications** *Minority and Indigenous Trends* (annual). Annual Review; reports on minority thematic issues or situations; online Directory; campaigning material; advocacy briefings; workshop reports; profiles; education and training material; books.
Members Partner organizations in 60 countries and territories:
Argentina, Bangladesh, Bosnia-Herzegovina, Botswana, Brazil, Bulgaria, Burundi, Cambodia, Cameroon, Central African Rep, Colombia, Congo DR, Croatia, Cyprus, Czechia, Dominican Rep, Ecuador, Ethiopia, Finland, France, Gambia, Germany, Honduras, Hungary, India, Indonesia, Iraq, Israel, Japan, Kenya, Kosovo, Kyrgyzstan, Laos, Lebanon, Malaysia, Montenegro, Nepal, Netherlands, Nicaragua, Nigeria, North Macedonia, Norway, Pakistan, Peru, Philippines, Rwanda, Senegal, Somalia, Sri Lanka, Sudan, Sweden, Switzerland, Tanzania UR, Thailand, Türkiye, Uganda, UK, Uruguay, USA, Vietnam.
Included in the above, 23 organizations listed in this Yearbook:
- *Action d'appui pour la protection des droits des minorités en Afrique centrale (AAPDMAC);*
- *AEGIS Trust;*
- *African Centre for Democracy and Human Rights Studies (ACDHRS, #00239);*
- *African Indigenous Women's Organization (AIWO, no recent information);*
- *African Initiative For Mankind Progress Organization (AIMPO);*
- *Alliance Against Genocide (AAG, #00655);*
- *Arab Association for Human Rights (HRA, no recent information);*
- *Catholic Organization for Relief and Development (Cordaid);*
- *Christian Aid;*
- *Commonwealth Human Rights Initiative (CHRI, #04340);*
- *European Roma Rights Centre (ERRC, #08401);*
- *Gandhi Peace Foundation (no recent information);*
- *Ibn Khaldoun Center for Development Studies, Cairo (ICDS);*
- *Institute of Regional Studies, Islamabad (IRS);*
- *International Alliance of the Indigenous Tribal Peoples of the Tropical Forests (IAITPTF, #11629);*
- *International Centre for Ethnic Studies (ICES, #12490);*
- *Panos Network (#18183)* (Ethiopia);
- *Raoul Wallenberg Institute of Human Rights and Humanitarian Law (RWI);*
- *Rencontre africaine pour la défense des droits de l'homme (RADDHO);*
- *South Asia Human Rights Documentation Centre (SAHRDC, #19718);*
- *South Asian Forum for Human Rights (SAFHR, no recent information);*
- *The International Movement Against All Forms of Discrimination and Racism (IMADR, #14191);*

– *World Federalist Movement – Movement for a Just World Order through a Strengthened United Nations (WFM, #21404).*
Consultative Status Consultative status granted from: *African Commission on Human and Peoples' Rights (ACHPR, #00255)* (Observer); *ECOSOC (#05331)* (Special); *UNEP (#20299)*. **IGO Relations** Accredited by (2): *International Whaling Commission (IWC, #15879)*; *United Nations Office at Vienna (UNOV, #20604)*. Associated with Department of Global Communications of the United Nations. **NGO Relations** Member of (13): *Alliance Against Genocide (AAG, #00655)*; *Child Rights International Network (CRIN, #03885)*; *Coalition of European Lobbies on Eastern African Pastoralism (CELEP, #04059)*; *European Roma Policy Coalition (ERPC, no recent information)*; *Global Partnership for the Prevention of Armed Conflict (GPPAC, #10538)*; *Human Rights and Democracy Network (HRDN, #10980)*; *International Coalition for the Responsibility to Protect (ICRtoP, #12620)*; *International Network for Economic, Social and Cultural Rights (ESCR-Net, #14255)*; *International Partnership on Religion and Sustainable Development (PaRD, #14524)*; *Minority Research Network (#16819)*; *Refugee Council (#18739)*; *Sudan Consortium (#20031)*; *World Organisation Against Torture (OMCT, #21685)*. Partner of (1): *Coalition for Religious Equality and Inclusive Development (CREID, #04067)*. Founding member of: *Consortium of Minority Resources (COMIR, no recent information)*. International Associate of: *International Dalit Solidarity Network (IDSN, #13129)*. Also links with a large number of national organizations.
[2022.10.21/XF0172/y/**F**]

♦ Minor Metals Trade Association (MMTA) 16821

General Manager 33 Queen Street, London, EC4R 1BR, UK. T. +442078330237. E-mail: admin@mmta.co.uk – executive@mmta.co.uk.
URL: https://mmta.co.uk/

History Founded 1973. Rules most recently amended and approved 28 Apr 2015. Registered in accordance with UK law. **Aims** Raise awareness of the importance of minor metals; informe on issues affecting their global trade. **Structure** Annual General Meeting; Board of Directors; Executive Team. Sub-Committees (9): Asia; Conference; Europe; Insurance Task Force; Management; Mediation and Arbitration; North America; Sustainability and Recycling; Warehousing. **Languages** English, French, German, Italian, Mandarin Chinese. **Staff** 3.00 FTE, paid. **Finance** Members' dues. Proceeds from annual conference. Annual budget: about UKpounds 300,000. **Activities** Events/meetings. Set up an EU-wide information network comprising a focal point in each member state, normally based at the competent occupational health and safety authority. Focal points set up national networks comprising all relevant national information providers, in particular social partners. Network provides information to the Agency and disseminates information from the Agency to users. Maintains network of safety and health websites in over 30 countries. **Events** *International Minor Metals Conference* Edinburgh (UK) 2019, *International Conference* Montréal, QC (Canada) 2018, *International Minor Metals Conference* Montréal, QC (Canada) 2018. **Publications** *Crucible* (12 a year) – magazine.
Members Full in 24 countries and territories:
Australia, Belgium, Canada, Chile, China, Czechia, Estonia, France, Germany, Hong Kong, India, Italy, Japan, Korea Rep, Luxembourg, Netherlands, Poland, Romania, Singapore, Sweden, Switzerland, UK, United Arab Emirates, USA.
Included in the above, 3 organizations listed in this Yearbook:
Critical Raw Materials Alliance (CRM Alliance, #04959); *International Magnesium Association (IMA, #14073)*; *Tantalum-Niobium International Study Center (T.I.C., #20095)*. [2018.09.11/XM6943/ty/**D**]

♦ Mint Directors Conference (MDC) 16822

Conférence des directeurs des monnaies – Conferencia de Directores de Ceca
Address not obtained.
History 1962, Lausanne (Switzerland), by Directors of 10 Western European Mints. Previously also referred to as *European Mint Directors' Conference* and *International Mint Directors Conference*. **Aims** Promote regular exchange of information on all *monetary* matters and related legal, economic, technical and *numismatic* questions; cooperate in the mutual study and solution of questions in these spheres. **Structure** Conference (every 2 years); Council. Executive Committee. **Languages** English, French, German. **Staff** None. **Finance** Financed autonomously. **Activities** Maintains computer-based Coin Registration Office, which acts as a clearing house for coin characteristics, helping members to plan the coins they intend to issue without danger of prejudicing or conflict with the currencies of other countries. **Events** *Biennial Conference* Seoul (Korea Rep) 2018, *Biennial Conference* Bangkok (Thailand) 2016, *Biennial Conference* Mexico City (Mexico) 2014, *Biennial Conference* Vienna (Austria) 2012, *Biennial Conference* Canberra, ACT (Australia) 2010.
Members All European mints (as defined by Conference) are eligible for membership; non-European mints may be elected, provided such mints have less than one third of the total voting power of members. Directors of official mints (33) in 30 countries:
Australia, Austria, Belgium, Brazil, Canada, China, Colombia, Denmark, Finland, France, Germany, Greece, India, Ireland, Italy, Japan, Korea Rep, Malaysia, Malta, Mexico, Netherlands, Norway, Poland, Portugal, Spain, Sweden, Switzerland, Türkiye, UK, USA. [2018/XD8145/**F**]

- ♦ Mint Directors Working Group / see Working Group of European Mint Directors for the Technical Study of the European Single Coinage System (#21059)
- ♦ MINUCI – Mission des nations unies en Côte d'Ivoire (inactive)
- ♦ MINUJUSTH – Mission des Nations Unies pour l'appui à la Justice en Haïti (inactive)
- ♦ MINUJUSTH – United Nations Mission for Justice Support in Haiti (inactive)
- ♦ MINURCAT – United Nations Mission in the Central African Republic and Chad (inactive)
- ♦ **MINURSO** Mission des Nations Unies pour l'organisation d'un referendum au Sahel occidental (#20586)
- ♦ **MINURSO** United Nations Mission for the Referendum in Western Sahara (#20586)
- ♦ **MINUSCA** Mission Multidimensionnelle Intégrée des Nations Unies pour la Stabilisation en République Centrafricaine (#20588)
- ♦ **MINUSCA** United Nations Multidimensional Integrated Stabilization Mission in the Central African Republic (#20588)
- ♦ **MINUSMA** Mission Multidimensionnelle Intégrée des Nations Unies pour la Stabilisation au Mali (#20589)
- ♦ **MINUSMA** United Nations Multidimensional Integrated Stabilization Mission in Mali (#20589)
- ♦ MINUS – Mission des Nations Unies au Soudan (inactive)
- ♦ MINUSTAH – United Nations Stabilization Mission in Haiti (inactive)
- ♦ MINUT – Mission intégrée des Nations Unies au Timor-Leste (inactive)
- ♦ MI / see Nutrition International (#17627)
- ♦ **MIO-ECSDE** Mediterranean Information Office for Environment, Culture and Sustainable Development (#16657)
- ♦ MI – Ordo Clericorum Regularium Ministrantium Infirmis (religious order)
- ♦ MIPCR – Spark M Matsunaga Institute for Peace and Conflict Resolution (internationally oriented national body)
- ♦ MIPD – Mouvement International des Parlementaires pour la Démocratie (see: #21661)
- ♦ MIPE – Men's International Peace Exchange (internationally oriented national body)

♦ MIPI Alliance 16823

Acting Managing Dir 445 Hoes Lane, Piscataway NJ 08854, USA.
URL: https://www.mipi.org

History 2003. Former names and other names: *Mobile Industry Processor Interface Alliance* – former. **Aims** Provide the hardware and software interface specifications device vendors need to create state-of-the-art, innovative mobile-connected devices while accelerating time-to-market and reducing costs. **Structure** Board of Directors. Marketing Steering Group; Technical Steering Group; Test Working Group. **Events** *Europe Meeting* Lisbon (Portugal) 2023, *Asia Meeting* Osaka (Japan) 2023, *Developers Conference* Piscataway, NJ (USA) 2020, *North America Meeting* Montréal, QC (Canada) 2019. **Members** Companies (over 300). Membership countries not specified. [2020/AA0014/**C**]

- ♦ MIPONUH – Mission de Police civile des Nations Unies en Haïti (inactive)
- ♦ MIPONUH – United Nations Civilian Police Mission in Haiti (inactive)
- ♦ **MIPS** Mediterranean Incontinence and Pelvic Floor Society (#16656)
- ♦ **MiPs** Mitochondrial Physiology Society (#16832)
- ♦ MiPsociety / see Mitochondrial Physiology Society (#16832)
- ♦ MIPTC – Men's International Professional Tennis Council (inactive)
- ♦ MIRABILIA Network – European Network of Unesco Sites (internationally oriented national body)
- ♦ Miracle Corners of the World (internationally oriented national body)

♦ MiracleFeet 16824

CEO 107 Conner Drive, Suite 230, Chapel Hill NC 27514, USA. T. +19192405572. E-mail: info@miraclefeet.org.
URL: https://www.miraclefeet.org/

History Registration: 501(c)(3) non-profit, No/ID: EIN 27-3764203, USA; Bavaria District court, No/ID: VR 204879, Start date: 7 Jun 2013, Germany, Munich; Charity Commission, No/ID: 1156868, England and Wales; Switzerland. **Aims** Increase access to proper treatment for children born with clubfoot in low- and middle-income countries through partnerships with local healthcare providers. **Structure** Board of Directors. **Activities** Healthcare. **NGO Relations** Member of (1): *Humentum (#10993)*. [2022/AA2838/**F**]

- ♦ Miracle Foundation Evangelistic Ministries / see House of Galilee International Church and Ministries
- ♦ Miraism Assocation International (#02282)
- ♦ **MIRA** Minimally Invasive Robotic Association (#16811)
- ♦ **MIRA** Mutual Images Research Association (#16918)
- ♦ MIRBIS – Moscow International Higher Business School (internationally oriented national body)
- ♦ MIR Foundation – Mission International Rescue Foundation (internationally oriented national body)
- ♦ Mir International Cooperation And Development (internationally oriented national body)
- ♦ **MIR** Mouvement international de la réconciliation (#13586)
- ♦ Mirovni inštitut (internationally oriented national body)
- ♦ MIR partenariats et développement international (internationally oriented national body)
- ♦ **MISA** Media Institute of Southern Africa (#16619)
- ♦ Misean Cara (internationally oriented national body)
- ♦ Mise en oeuvre de certaines dispositions concernant la nationalité (1969 treaty)
- ♦ MISEREOR – Bischöfliches Hilfswerk Misereor, Aktion gegen Hunger und Krankheit in der Welt (internationally oriented national body)
- ♦ Misereor Bishops' Relief Fund, Action Against Hunger and Disease in the World / see German Catholic Bishops' Organisation for Development Cooperation

♦ Misericordia International 16825

Secretariat 58 rue des Moulins, 80140 Huppy, France.
Pres en Sorbonne, 1 rue Victor Cousin, 75005 Paris, France.
URL: http://www.leedstrinity.ac.uk/departments/english/misericordia/

History 1992. **Aims** Promote the study of the *medieval* choir stalls and of profane arts in the Middle Ages, including *visual arts, music*, dance, history and literature. **Structure** President; Secretary; Editorial Staff. **Languages** English, French. **Staff** 9.00 FTE, voluntary. **Finance** Members' dues. Block foundation sponsoring. **Activities** Organizes congresses, colloquia and sessions. **Events** *International colloquium* Nijmegen (Netherlands) 2010, *International coloquium* Paris (France) 2008. **Publications** *The Profane Arts of the Middle Ages – Les Arts profanes du moyen âge* (annual). Information Services: Databases.
Members Full in 14 countries:
Austria, Belgium, Canada, France, Germany, Israel, Italy, Japan, Netherlands, New Zealand, Spain, Switzerland, UK, USA.
[2012.10.01/XF3321/**F**]

- ♦ Misión de Administración Provisional de las Naciones Unidas en Kosovo (#20343)
- ♦ Misioneras Clarisas del Santisimo Sacramento (religious order)
- ♦ Misioneras de la Doctrina Cristiana (religious order)
- ♦ Misioneras Hijas del Calvario (religious order)
- ♦ Misioneras Seculares Scalabrinianas (religious order)
- ♦ Misioneros de la Consolata (religious order)
- ♦ Misioneros de la Divina Redención (religious order)
- ♦ Misioneros del Espiritu Santo (religious order)
- ♦ Misioneros de Guadalupe (religious order)
- ♦ Misioneros Hijos del Inmaculado Corazón de Maria (religious order)
- ♦ Misioneros Javerianos de Yarumal (religious order)
- ♦ Misioneros de Mariannhill (religious order)
- ♦ Misioneros del Sagrado Corazón (religious order)
- ♦ Misión de Estabilización de las Naciones Unidas en Haiti (inactive)
- ♦ Misión de Estabilización de la Naciones Unidas en la República Democratica del Congo (#20605)
- ♦ Misión de las Naciones Unidas para la Organización del Referéndum en el Sahara Occidental (#20586)
- ♦ Misión de las Naciones Unidas en la República Democratica del Congo / see United Nations Organization Stabilization Mission in the Democratic Republic of Congo (#20605)
- ♦ Misión Vida y Familia (religious order)
- ♦ Misjonarze Sludzy Ubogich Trzeciego Swiata (religious order)
- ♦ Misjonsalliansen (internationally oriented national body)
- ♦ Mismatch Negativity conference (meeting series)
- ♦ MISNC – Multidisciplinary International Social Networks Conference (meeting series)
- ♦ Missão AMEM (#20850)
- ♦ Missão Operaria São Pedro e São Paulo (religious order)
- ♦ Missie over Grenzen (internationally oriented national body)
- ♦ Missie Zonder Grenzen / see Missie over Grenzen
- ♦ Missiezusters van het Kostbaar Bloed (religious order)

♦ Missile Technology Control Regime (MTCR) 16826

Régime de contrôle de la technologie des missiles – Trägertechnologie-Kontrollregime
Address not obtained.
URL: http://mtcr.info/

History 16 Apr 1987, by countries of *Group of Seven (G-7, #10788)*. **Aims** Limite the proliferation of missiles and missile technology. **Structure** Plenary Meeting; Rotating chairmanship; Point of Contact (POC). **Activities** Politics/policy/regulatory; events/meetings; networking/liaising; standards/guidelines. **Events** *Plenary Meeting* Dublin (Ireland) 2017, *Plenary Meeting* Busan (Korea Rep) 2016, *Plenary Meeting* Rotterdam (Netherlands) 2015, *Plenary Meeting* Oslo (Norway) 2014. **Publications** *MTCR Annex Handbook*.
Members Governments of 35 countries:
Argentina, Australia, Austria, Belgium, Brazil, Bulgaria, Canada, Czechia, Denmark, Finland, France, Germany, Greece, Hungary, Iceland, India, Ireland, Italy, Japan, Korea Rep, Luxembourg, Netherlands, New Zealand, Norway, Poland, Portugal, Russia, South Africa, Spain, Sweden, Switzerland, Türkiye, UK, Ukraine, USA.
IGO Relations *Nuclear Suppliers Group (NSG, #17621)*. [2018/XT8763/**F***]

- ♦ Missing Children Europe / see European Federation for Missing and Sexually Exploited Children (#07166)
- ♦ **Missing Children Europe** European Federation for Missing and Sexually Exploited Children (#07166)

♦ MISSIO 16827

Sec Dir Bd du Souverain 199, 1160 Brussels, Belgium. T. +3226790630. Fax +3226725569. E-mail: dir@missio.be – info@missio.be.
Registered Office Propaganda Fidei, Via di Propaganda 1/C, 00187 Rome RM, Italy. T. +39669880228.
URL: https://www.missio.org/

History Former names and other names: *Pontifical Missionary Work* – former; *Oeuvres pontificales missionnaires (OPM)* – former; *Internationales Katholische Missionswerk* – former; *Pauselijke Missiewerken* – former. **Aims** Act as a common *fund* for international solidarity to assist local *Christian* communities in the most deprived countries; assist missions in Church life, the daily life of priests, seminarists in training, health development, social training and education. **Structure** Currently comprises: *Pontifical Missionary Society for the Propagation of the Faith (Propaganda Fide)*, set up in 1822, Lyon (France), by Marie-Pauline Jaricot; *Pontifical Missionary Society of Saint Peter the Apostle (see: #16827)*, formed in 1889, Caen (France), by Stéphanie Bigard and Jeanne Bigard; *Pontificium Opus A Sancta Infantia (Enfance Missionnaire, see: #16827)*, created in 1843, Nancy (France), as *'Holy Childhood – Sainte Enfance'* and subsequently *'Pontifical Missionary Society of the Holy Childhood – Oeuvre Pontificale Missionnaire de la Sainte Enfance'*, by Mgr de Forbin-Janson, Bishop of Nancy; *Union Pontificale Missionnaire (UPM, see: #16827)*, founded in 1916, Italy, by

Paolo Manna. **Languages** Dutch, French, German. **Staff** 10.00 FTE, paid; 8.00 FTE, voluntary. **Finance** Gifts; donations; legacies. **Activities** Networking/liaising; events/meetings. **Events** *Congrès Mission* Paris (France) 2018. **Publications** *NAOMI* (5 a year) in Dutch, French; *Mission de l'Eglise* (4 a year) in French; *SUARA* (4 a year) in Dutch, French; *Tussenruimte* (4 a year) in Dutch; *SAMUEL* (7 a year) in Dutch, French; *SIMON* (7 a year) in Dutch, French.
Members Organizations in 121 countries and territories:
Algeria, Angola, Argentina, Australia, Austria, Bangladesh, Belgium, Benin, Bolivia, Bosnia-Herzegovina, Brazil, Brunei Darussalam, Burkina Faso, Burundi, Cameroon, Canada, Cape Verde, Central African Rep, Chad, Chile, Colombia, Congo Brazzaville, Congo DR, Cook Is, Costa Rica, Côte d'Ivoire, Croatia, Cuba, Curaçao, Czechia, Denmark, Dominican Rep, Ecuador, Egypt, El Salvador, Equatorial Guinea, Eritrea, Ethiopia, France, Gabon, Gambia, Germany, Ghana, Greece, Guatemala, Guinea, Guinea-Bissau, Haiti, Holy See, Honduras, Hungary, India, Indonesia, Iran Islamic Rep, Iraq, Ireland, Israel, Italy, Jamaica, Japan, Kazakhstan, Kenya, Korea Rep, Lebanon, Lesotho, Liberia, Luxembourg, Madagascar, Malawi, Malaysia, Malta, Mauritania, Mauritius, Mexico, Monaco, Morocco, Mozambique, Myanmar, Namibia, Netherlands, New Zealand, Nicaragua, Nigeria, Norway, Pakistan, Panama, Papua New Guinea, Paraguay, Peru, Philippines, Poland, Portugal, Puerto Rico, Romania, Rwanda, Scotland, Senegal, Sierra Leone, Singapore, Slovakia, Slovenia, South Africa, Spain, Sri Lanka, Sudan, Switzerland, Syrian AR, Taiwan, Tanzania UR, Thailand, Timor-Leste, Togo, Tunisia, Türkiye, Uganda, UK, Uruguay, USA, Venezuela, Zambia, Zimbabwe.
Also members in Pacific and Scandinavian countries, not specified.
NGO Relations Supports: *Catholic Media Council (CAMECO, #03605)*; *South Pacific Association of Theological Schools (SPATS, #19882).* [2017.10.11/XF3521/f/**F**]

- ♦ Mission d'administration intérimaire des Nations unies au Kosovo (#20343)
- ♦ Mission Africa (internationally oriented national body)
- ♦ Mission for the African Academy of Languages / see African Academy of Languages (#00192)
- ♦ Mission Africa Network (internationally oriented national body)

♦ Mission d'aide au développement des économies rurales afghanes (MADERA) 16828

Mission of Assistance for the Development of Rural Economies in Afghanistan
Main Office 21 ter rue Voltaire, 75011 Paris, France. T. +33143705007. Fax +33143706007. E-mail: contact@madera.asso.fr – contact@madera-asso.org.
URL: https://madera-asso.org/
History 1988. Registration: France. **Aims** Promote rehabilitation and development of rural economies destroyed by *war* in Afghanistan, focusing on agriculture, irrigation, veterinary, craft industry, forests, roads and return of *refugees*. **Finance** Sources: French government; *European Commission (EC, #06633)*; *FAO (#09260)*; *UNDP (#20292)*; *World Food Programme (WFP, #21510)*. **Activities** Intervention programmes: -Civil Engineering – road and bridge construction, rehabilitation of irrigation canals and conveyance of drinkable water. -Veterinary – vaccine fabrication and campaigns, curative veterinary care and livestock management. -Agriculture – rehabilitation of arable land, improved seed distribution and multiplication and various testing. -Forest Sector – fight against deforestation and erosion, forest management and production of forest seedlings in seedbeds. -Craft Industry – improve wool spinning and weaving techniques and diversify the types of woven products.
Members Individuals and organizations () in 7 countries:
Belgium (*), France, Germany, Italy, Norway (*), Switzerland, UK.
NGO Relations Member of: *Centre de recherche et d'information pour le développement, Paris (CRID)*; *European Network of NGOs in Afghanistan (ENNA, #07952).* [2021/XE2198/**E**]

- ♦ Missionalis Societas Sancti Pauli (religious order)
- ♦ Mission d'aménagement du fleuve Sénégal (inactive)
- ♦ Missionare, Diener der Armen der Dritten Welt (religious order)
- ♦ Missionari Ardorini – Pii Operai Catechisti Rurali (religious order)
- ♦ Missionarias do Amor Misericordioso do Coração de Jesus (religious order)
- ♦ Missionari Comboniani del Cuore di Gesù (religious order)
- ♦ Missionari della Divina Redenzione (religious order)
- ♦ Missionari Domestici di America (religious order)
- ♦ Missionarie della Carità (religious order)
- ♦ Missionarie Catechiste del Sacro Cuore (religious order)
- ♦ Missionarie Clarisse del Santissimo Sacramento (religious order)
- ♦ Missionarie Figlie del Calvario (religious order)
- ♦ Missionarie degli Infermi (religious order)
- ♦ Missionarie di Maria (religious order)
- ♦ Missionarie del Sacerdozio Regale (religious order)
- ♦ Missionarie del Sacro Cuore di Gesù (religious order)
- ♦ Missionaries of Charity (religious order)
- ♦ Missionaries of Charity Brothers (religious order)
- ♦ Missionaries of the Christian Doctrine (religious order)
- ♦ Missionaries of the Company of Mary (religious order)
- ♦ Missionarie Secolari della Passione (religious order)
- ♦ Missionarie Secolari Scalabriniane (religious order)
- ♦ Missionarie Serve dello Spirito Santo (religious order)
- ♦ Missionaries of the Holy Spirit (religious order)
- ♦ Missionaries of the Kingship of Christ (religious order)
- ♦ Missionaries of the Merciful Love of the Heart of Jesus (religious order)
- ♦ Missionaries of Our Lady of La Salette (religious order)
- ♦ Missionaries of the Sacred Heart of Jesus (religious order)
- ♦ Missionaries of the Sacred Hearts of Jesus and Mary (religious order)
- ♦ Missionaries of Scheut – Congregation of the Immaculate Heart of Mary (religious order)
- ♦ Missionaries of the Sick (religious order)
- ♦ Missionaries of St Joseph of Mexico (religious order)
- ♦ Missionari Figli del Cuore Immacolato di Maria (religious order)
- ♦ Missionarii Comboniani Cordis Jesu (religious order)
- ♦ Missionarii Dominae Nostrae a La Salette (religious order)
- ♦ Missionari dell'Immacolata Concezione (religious order)
- ♦ Missionarii Sacratissimi Cordis Jesu (religious order)
- ♦ Missionarii a Spiritu Sancto (religious order)
- ♦ Missionari di Mariannhill (religious order)
- ♦ Missionari Monfortani – Compagnia di Maria (religious order)
- ♦ Missionari di Nostra Signora de La Salette (religious order)
- ♦ Missionari Oblati di Maria Immacolata (religious order)
- ♦ Missionari degli Operai (religious order)
- ♦ Missionarios de Guadalupe (religious order)
- ♦ Missionarios Servos dos Pobres do Terceiro Mundo (religious order)
- ♦ Missionari del Preziosissimo Sangue (religious order)
- ♦ Missionari della Regalità di Nostro Signor Gesù Cristo (religious order)
- ♦ Missionari della Sacra Famiglia (religious order)
- ♦ Missionari dei Sacri Cuori di Gesù e di Maria (religious order)
- ♦ Missionari del Sacro Cuore di Gesù (religious order)
- ♦ Missionari di San Francesco di Sales d'Annecy (religious order)
- ♦ Missionari di San Giuseppe nel Messico (religious order)
- ♦ Missionari di Scheut – Congregazione del Cuore Immacolato di Maria (religious order)
- ♦ Missionari Servi dei Poveri (religious order)
- ♦ Missionari Servi della Santissima Trinità (religious order)
- ♦ Missionari dello Spirito Santo (religious order)
- ♦ Missionarissen Catechisten van het Heilig Hart (religious order)
- ♦ Missionarissen Dienaars Der Armen Van De Derde Wereld (religious order)
- ♦ Missionarissen van het Heilig Hart (religious order)
- ♦ Missionary Athletes International (internationally oriented national body)
- ♦ Missionary Brothers of St Francis of Assisi (religious order)
- ♦ Missionary Cenacle Apostolate (religious order)
- ♦ Missionary Cenacle Family (religious order)
- ♦ Missionary Childhood – Pontifical Society of the Holy Childhood (see: #16827)
- ♦ Missionary Company of the Sacred Heart (religious order)
- ♦ Missionary Daughters of Calvary (religious order)
- ♦ Missionary Enterprises / see Bright Hope International
- ♦ Missionary Family Donum Dei (religious order)
- ♦ Missionary Franciscan Sisters of the Immaculate Conception (religious order)
- ♦ Missionary Oblates of Mary Immaculate (religious order)
- ♦ Missionary Servants of the Most Blessed Trinity (religious order)
- ♦ Missionary Servants of the Most Holy Trinity (religious order)
- ♦ Missionary Servants of the Poor of the Third World (religious order)
- ♦ Missionary Service of the International Catholic Organization for Cinema and Audio-Visual / see SIGNIS Services Rome (#19274)
- ♦ Missionary Sisters of the Catholic Apostolate (religious order)
- ♦ Missionary Sisters of Christ the King (religious order)
- ♦ Missionary Sisters of the Holy Ghost (religious order)
- ♦ Missionary Sisters of the Immaculate Conception (religious order)
- ♦ Missionary Sisters of the Immaculate Conception (religious order)
- ♦ Missionary Sisters of the Immaculate Heart of Mary (religious order)
- ♦ Missionary Sisters of Mary Help of Christians (religious order)
- ♦ Missionary Sisters of the Most Sacred Heart of Jesus of Hiltrup (religious order)
- ♦ Missionary Sisters of Our Lady of Africa (religious order)
- ♦ Missionary Sisters of Our Lady of the Angels (religious order)
- ♦ Missionary Sisters of Our Lady of the Apostles (religious order)
- ♦ Missionary Sisters of Our Lady of the Holy Rosary (religious order)
- ♦ Missionary Sisters of the Precious Blood (religious order)
- ♦ Missionary Sisters of the Sacred Heart of Jesus (religious order)
- ♦ Missionary Sisters of Saint Charles Borromeo (religious order)
- ♦ Missionary Sisters Servants of the Holy Spirit (religious order)
- ♦ Missionary Sisters of the Society of Mary (religious order)
- ♦ Missionary Sisters of St Augustine (religious order)
- ♦ Missionary Sisters of St Columban (religious order)
- ♦ Missionary Sisters of St Peter Claver (religious order)
- ♦ Missionary Society of St Columban (religious order)
- ♦ Missionary Society of St Paul (religious order)
- ♦ Missionary Sons of the Immaculate Heart of Mary (religious order)
- ♦ Missionary Training Service (internationally oriented national body)
- ♦ Mission of Assistance for the Development of Rural Economies in Afghanistan (#16828)

♦ Mission Aviation Fellowship (MAF) 16829

Chair MAF International Operations Centre, Henwood, Ashford, TN24 8DH, UK. T. +441233895500. Fax +441233895570. E-mail: contact@mafint.org.
URL: https://www.mafint.org/
History 20 May 1945, UK. Founded by Christian aviators serving in World War II. National organizations cooperate with MAF International. Registration: Charity Commision, No/ID: 1058226, England and Wales. **Aims** Share God's love through aviation and technology so that isolated people are physically and spiritually transformed in Christ's name. **Structure** An international fellowship of sister organizations whose field operations are managed by *MAF International*. International Board. **Activities** Humanitarian/emergency aid. **Publications** *Flightwatch* (12 a year).
Members Independent MAF entities (" indicates part of MAF-International) in 24 countries:
Australia (*), Brazil, Canada (*), Denmark (*), Ecuador, Finland (*), France (*), Germany (*), Honduras, Indonesia, Italy (*), Korea Rep, Mexico, Netherlands (*), New Zealand (*), Norway (*), Philippines, Singapore, South Africa (*), Suriname, Sweden (*), Switzerland (*), UK (*), USA (*).
Entities operating through MAF International – " indicates in-country MAF base(s) – in 33 countries:
Angola (**), Australia (**), Bangladesh (**), Brazil, Burundi, Cambodia (**), Central African Rep, Congo DR (**), Ecuador (**), Eswatini, Guatemala, Haiti (**), Honduras, Indonesia (**), Kenya (**), Lesotho (**), Madagascar (**), Mali (**), Mexico, Mongolia (**), Mozambique (**), Namibia, Papua New Guinea, Rwanda, South Africa (**), Sudan, Suriname, Tanzania UR (**), Timor-Leste (**), Uganda (**), USA (**), Zambia, Zimbabwe.
The Learning Technologies arm operates in a number of other countries (not specified).
NGO Relations Member of: *Accord Network*; *Arbeitsgemeinschaft Evangelikaler Missionen (AEM)*; *CHS Alliance (#03911)*; *European Christian Organisations in Relief and Development (EU-CORD, #06545)*; *Global Connections.* Associate member of: *World Evangelical Alliance (WEA, #21393).* [2021/XF5009/**F**]

- ♦ Mission baptiste européenne / see EBM International (#05270)

♦ Mission Without Borders International (MWBI) 16830

Contact 711 Daily Drive, Ste 120, Camarillo CA 93010, USA. T. +18059878891. Fax +18054848378. E-mail: mwb-us@mwbi.org.
URL: http://www.mwbi.org/
History Founded 1960. **Aims** Serve the spiritual, physical, education and emotional needs of those suffering the effects of *poverty* or *oppression* without regard to their religion or ethnic background worldwide. **Structure** Sponsorship programme: *Child Rescue International (see: #16830).* **Activities** Financial and/or material support; humanitarian/emergency aid; religious activities; training/education.
Members National affiliates in 11 countries:
Australia, Belgium, Canada, Germany, Netherlands, New Zealand, Norway, South Africa, Switzerland, UK, USA.
Included in the above, 1 organization listed in this Yearbook:
Missie over Grenzen.
NGO Relations Member of: *European Evangelical Alliance (EEA, #07010).* [2017.10.10/XF6180/**F**]

- ♦ Mission Covenant Church of Norway (internationally oriented national body)
- ♦ Mission East (internationally oriented national body)
- ♦ Missionen Martyrernas Rost (#20804)
- ♦ Mission de l'envoyé de la paix mondiale (internationally oriented national body)
- ♦ Missione Operaia Pietro e Paolo (religious order)
- ♦ Mission Europa (internationally oriented national body)
- ♦ Mission évangélique internationale contre la lèpre (#16446)
- ♦ Mission évangélique unie (#20507)
- ♦ Missio Nexus (internationally oriented national body)
- ♦ Mission of the Immaculate Mediatrix Movement (religious order)
- ♦ Mission de l'Immaculée (religious order)
- ♦ Mission Inclusion (internationally oriented national body)
- ♦ Mission intégrée des Nations Unies au Timor-Leste (inactive)
- ♦ Mission International Rescue Foundation (internationally oriented national body)
- ♦ Mission Interuniversitaire de Coordination des Echanges Franco-Américains (internationally oriented national body)
- ♦ Mission laïque française (internationally oriented national body)
- ♦ Mission to Lepers in India and the East / see Leprosy Mission International (#16446)
- ♦ Mission luthérienne norvégienne (internationally oriented national body)
- ♦ Mission: Moving Mountains / see Discipling for Development
- ♦ Mission Multidimensionnelle Intégrée des Nations Unies pour la Stabilisation au Mali (#20589)
- ♦ Mission Multidimensionnelle Intégrée des Nations Unies pour la Stabilisation en République Centrafricaine (#20588)
- ♦ Missionnaires Ardorins – Pieux Ouvriers Catéchistes Ruraux (religious order)
- ♦ Missionnaires Catéchistes du Sacré-Coeur (religious order)
- ♦ Missionnaires de la Charité (religious order)

♦ Missionnaires du Christ-Roi (religious order)
♦ Missionnaires Comboniens du Coeur de Jésus (religious order)
♦ Missionnaires de la Compagnie de Marie (religious order)
♦ Missionnaires de la doctrine chrétienne (religious order)
♦ Missionnaires Fils du Coeur Immaculé de Marie (religious order)
♦ Missionnaires de l'Immaculée-Conception de Lourdes (religious order)
♦ Missionnaires des infirmes (religious order)
♦ Missionnaires de Mariannhill (religious order)
♦ Missionnaires Médicales de Marie (religious order)
♦ Missionnaires de Notre-Dame de la Salette (religious order)
♦ Missionnaires Oblats de Marie-Immaculée (religious order)
♦ Missionnaires du Précieux Sang (religious order)
♦ Missionnaires de la Royauté de Notre-Seigneur Jésus-Christ (religious order)
♦ Missionnaires du Sacré-Coeur de Jésus d'Issoudun (religious order)
♦ Missionnaires des Sacrés Coeurs de Jésus et de Marie (religious order)
♦ Missionnaires de la Sainte-Famille (religious order)
♦ Missionnaires du Saint Esprit (religious order)
♦ Missionnaires du Saint-Esprit (religious order)
♦ Missionnaires de Saint François de Sales d'Annecy (religious order)
♦ Missionnaires de Saint Joseph de Mexico (religious order)
♦ Missionnaires de Scheut – Congrégation du Coeur Immaculé de Marie (religious order)
♦ Missionnaires séculières scalabriniennes (religious order)
♦ Missionnaires Servantes du Saint-Esprit (religious order)
♦ Missionnaires Serviteurs des Pauvres (religious order)
♦ Mission des Nations Unies pour l'appui à la Justice en Haïti (inactive)
♦ Mission des nations unies en Côte d'Ivoire (inactive)
♦ Mission des Nations Unies pour l'organisation d'un referendum au Sahel occidental (#20586)
♦ Mission des Nations Unies en République Centrafricaine et au Tchad (inactive)
♦ Mission des Nations Unies en République démocratique du Congo / see United Nations Organization Stabilization Mission in the Democratic Republic of Congo (#20605)
♦ Mission des Nations Unies au Soudan (inactive)
♦ Mission des Nations Unies pour la stabilisation en Haïti (inactive)
♦ Mission d'observation des Nations Unies au Tadjikistan (inactive)
♦ Mission de l'Organisation des Nations Unies pour la Stabilisation en République démocratique du Congo (#20605)
♦ Mission of Our Lady of Bethany (religious order)
♦ Mission Ouvrière Saints Pierre et Paul (religious order)
♦ Mission Øst (internationally oriented national body)
♦ Mission de Police civile des Nations Unies en Haïti (inactive)
♦ Mission Rabies (internationally oriented national body)
♦ Mission Sahel (internationally oriented national body)
♦ Missions-Benediktinerinnen von Tutzing (religious order)
♦ Missionschwestern von Heiligen Paulus (religious order)
♦ The Mission to Seafarers (internationally oriented national body)
♦ Missions Etrangères de Bethléem en Suisse (religious order)
♦ Missions étrangères de Paris (religious order)
♦ Missions Etrangères de Scarboro (religious order)
♦ Missions Etrangères de Yarumal (religious order)

♦ Missions Europa Network 16831

Contact 452 La Monita, 102 Triq il-Bajja, Marsascala, MSK 1072, Malta. E-mail: office@missionseuropa.net.
URL: http://www.missionseuropa.net/

History Founded 2018. **Aims** Bring together like-minded Christians who want to reach Europe with the Holistic Gospel of Jesus Christ. **Structure** Leadership Team. **Languages** English. **Staff** 7.00 FTE, paid. **Finance** Annual budget: US$ 30,000. **Activities** Events/meetings. **Events** *Missions Europa Networking Conference* Malta 2022, *Missions Europa Network Conference* Malaga (Spain) 2019. [2022/XM7801/**F**]

♦ Missionsflugdienst im Pazifik (internationally oriented national body)
♦ Missionsgesellschaft Bethlehem (religious order)
♦ Missions in Norwegian Development / see Digni
♦ Missionsschwestern vom Heiligsten Herzen Jesu von Hiltrup (religious order)
♦ Missionsschwestern vom Katholischen Apostolat (religious order)
♦ Missionsschwestern vom Kostbaren Blut (religious order)
♦ Missions to Seamen / see The Mission to Seafarers
♦ Missionswerk Christus für alle Nationen (#03895)
♦ Missionszentrale der Franziskaner (internationally oriented national body)
♦ Mission to Unreached Peoples (internationally oriented national body)
♦ Mission vie et famille (religious order)
♦ Mission to the World (internationally oriented national body)
♦ MISTRALS – Mediterranean Integrated Studies at Regional And Local Scales (inactive)
♦ MIT Center for International Studies, Cambridge MA (internationally oriented national body)
♦ Miteinander Teilen (internationally oriented national body)
♦ MITF – Marin Interfaith Task Force on the Americas (internationally oriented national body)

♦ Mitochondrial Physiology Society (MiPs) 16832

Gen Sec COO Oroboros Instruments, Schöpfstrasse 18, 6020 Innsbruck, Austria.
URL: http://www.mitophysiology.org/

History Founded 2003, at 3rd Conference on Mitochondrial Physiology, as an informal grouping. Became a legal entity registered in accordance with Austrian law, 2011. Also known under the acronym *MiPsociety*. **Structure** Extended Board, consisting of Executive Committee (Chair, Co-Chair, Treasurer and 4 members), and General Secretary and 2 members. Scientific Advisory Board. **Finance** Members' dues. **Events** *Conference* Jurmala (Latvia) 2018, *Conference* Obergurgl (Austria) 2014, *Conference* Obergurgl (Austria) 2013, *Conference* Bordeaux (France) 2011, *Conference* Obergurgl (Austria) 2010. [2018/XJ6611/**E**]

♦ MitOst – Verein für Sprach- und Kulturaustausch in Mittel-, Ost- und Südosteuropa (internationally oriented national body)
♦ Mittelamerikanischer und Karibischer Gewichtheberbund (inactive)
♦ Mitteleuropa (inactive)
♦ MittelEuropäische Gesellschaft für Alternativmethoden zu Tierversuchen / see European Society for Alternatives to Animal Testing (#08517)
♦ MittelEuropäische Gesellschaft für Regulatory Affairs (internationally oriented national body)
♦ Mitteleuropäischen Polizeiakademie (#03711)
♦ Mitteleuropäischer Guttempler-Jugendrat (inactive)
♦ Mitteleuropa-Stiftung (unconfirmed)
♦ Mittelmeerzentrum der Audiovisuellen Kommunikation (#16648)
♦ Mittel-Osteuropäische Anwaltskammer (inactive)
♦ Mittnordenkommittén (#16796)
♦ MIU / see Maharishi University of Management (#16549)
♦ MIU – Microalgae International Union (no recent information)
♦ MIUSA – Mobility International USA (internationally oriented national body)
♦ Mixed Methods International Research Association (internationally oriented national body)
♦ MixEurope – Multiethnic Interaction on Xenophobia in Europe (internationally oriented national body)
♦ Miyelom Hastalari Grubu Avrupa Ag (inactive)
♦ Miznarodna Asociaciia Ukrainistiv (#12243)

♦ Mizrachi – Hapoel Hamizrachi World Organization 16833

Gen Dir 54 King George St, PO Box 7720, 90174 Jerusalem, Israel. T. +97226209000. Fax +97226257418. E-mail: info@mizrachi.org.
URL: http://www.mizrachi.org/

History 1902, Russia. 1902, Vilna (Russia). Also referred to as *World Mizrachi Movement*. **Aims** Combine active *zionism* with strict attachment to Jewish orthodoxy. **Structure** Board of Governors. **Languages** English, Hebrew. **Activities** Organizes: educational seminars throughout the branches; educational tours to Israel; Heritage Tours; leadership training; regional meetings (worldwide); Young Leadership seminars (Israel); Luncheons; Sabbath weekends; solidarity missions. **Events** *World Conference* Jerusalem (Israel) 2010, *World Conference* Jerusalem (Israel) 2008, *World Conference* Tiberias (Israel) 2007, *World Conference* Israel 2006, *World conference of Mizrachi Rabbis* 2003. **Publications** Newsletters. Conference journals.
Members Individuals (Israelis are members of National Religious Party) in 36 countries:
Argentina, Australia, Austria, Belarus, Belgium, Brazil, Canada, Chile, Colombia, Croatia, Czechia, Denmark, France, Germany, Hungary, India, Ireland, Israel, Italy, Mexico, Netherlands, New Zealand, Norway, Panama, Peru, Russia, South Africa, Spain, Sweden, Switzerland, Türkiye, UK, Ukraine, Uruguay, USA, Venezuela.
NGO Relations Associated with: *Jewish Agency for Israel (#16111)*; *World Zionist Organization (WZO, #21961)*. [2017/XE1492/**E**]

♦ MJE – Mouvement de la jeunesse européenne (inactive)
♦ MJFF – Michael J Fox Foundation (internationally oriented national body)
♦ **MJMI** Messianic Jewish Movement International (#16732)
♦ **MJS** Movimiento Juvenil Salesiano (#19039)
♦ MJ – Societas Missionariorum a Sancti Joseph (religious order)
♦ MKA / see International Co-operative Alliance (#12944)
♦ **MKA** Mezdunarodnyj Kooperativnyj Alians (#12944)
♦ **MKKIR** Mezdunarodnyj Koordinacionnyj Komitet po Immunologii Reprodukcii (#12958)
♦ MKLM / see Maryknoll Mission Association of the Faithful
♦ **MKN** Mezdunarodnyj Komitet Byvshih Uznikov Nojergamme (#14347)
♦ MKO / see Mujahedin-e Khalq Organization (#16881)
♦ **MKOL** Mezinárodní komise pro ochranu Labe (#13249)
♦ **MKOOpZ** Mezinarodni Komise pro Ocranu Oddry pvred Znecistenim (#13250)
♦ **MKOOpZ** Miedzynarodowa Komisja Ochrony Odry przed Zanieczyszczeniem (#13250)
♦ MKPP – Mezdunarodnyj Postojannyj Komitet Profsojuzov Poligrafistov (inactive)
♦ **MKVK** Mezgosudarstvennaja Koordinacionnaja Vodohozjajstvennaja Comissija Centralnoj Azii (#15979)
♦ Mladi Evropski Federalisti (#21984)
♦ Mladi Evropsti Federalisté (#21984)

♦ Mladiinfo International 16834

Contact Filip Filipovic 22, 1000 Skopje, North Macedonia. E-mail: info@mladiinfo.eu.
URL: http://mladiinfo.net/

History 2014. Founded following setting up of individual branches since 2003. Former names and other names: *Association for Education Mladiinfo International* – full title. Registration: Start date: 2014, Slovenia. **Aims** Help young people fulfil their *educational* potential as they are challenged by many educational disadvantages caused by personal, social, cultural or economic circumstances. **Structure** General Assembly; Executive Board; President. **Languages** English, Macedonian. **Staff** Skopje (North Macedonia): 9 FTE, paid; others voluntary. **Finance** Financed by various community programmes, as well as national agencies for educational programmes and mobility. Support from: *Central European Initiative (CEI, #03708)*; Erasmus+; Europe for Citizens; US Embassy; *United States Agency for International Development (USAID)*. **Activities** Knowledge management/information dissemination; guidance/assistance/consulting. Active in: Albania, Croatia, Czechia, Macedonia, Montenegro, Slovakia, Slovenia. **Publications** Handbook.
Members Full in 6 countries:
Czechia, Montenegro, North Macedonia, Slovakia.
NGO Relations Member of (1): *European Alliance for Innovation (EAI, #05872)*. [2023/XJ9310/**F**]

♦ Mladi Priatelia Europy (#21984)
♦ **MLAIC** Muzzle Loaders Associations International Committee (#16919)
♦ MLAL – Movimento Laici America Latina (internationally oriented national body)
♦ MLA – Modern Language Association of America (internationally oriented national body)
♦ **MLAVS** Mediterranean League of Angiology and Vascular Surgery (#16660)
♦ MLC – Marianist Lay Communities (see: #21334)
♦ MLDI / see Media Defence (#16615)
♦ **MLE** Mind and Life Europe (#16808)
♦ MLEU – Mouvement libéral pour l'Europe unie (inactive)
♦ Mlf – Mission laïque française (internationally oriented national body)
♦ MLFM – Movimento per la Lotta contro la Fame nel Mondo (internationally oriented national body)
♦ MLG – International Workshop on Mining and Learning with Graphs (meeting series)
♦ **ML** Monarchist League (#16848)
♦ MLTD / see European and Mediterranean League Against Thrombotic Diseases (#07771)
♦ MMA / see Bangladesh Maritime Academy
♦ MMAA – Mediterranean Maritime Arbitration Association (inactive)
♦ MMAF – Maryknoll Mission Association of the Faithful (internationally oriented national body)
♦ MMA – International Conference on Microwave Materials and their Applications (meeting series)
♦ **MMA** Multilateral Monetary Area (#16889)
♦ MMB – Sisters Mercedarian Missionaries of Bérriz (religious order)
♦ MMCS – International Conference on Mathematical Methods for Curves and Surfaces (meeting series)
♦ MMEE – Mathematical Models in Ecology and Evolution (meeting series)
♦ **MMESA** Mediterranean and Middle Eastern Endoscopic Surgery Association (#02804)
♦ MMFA – Multilayer Modular Flooring Association (internationally oriented national body)
♦ MMF Latam – Asociación Latinoamericana de Managers Musicales (unconfirmed)
♦ MMF / see Mobile & Wireless Forum (#16837)
♦ **MMFN** Mediterranean Model Forest Network (#16662)
♦ **MMI-LAC** Movimiento Mundial por la Infancia de Latinoamérica y El Caribe (#16873)
♦ **MMI** Medicus Mundi International – Network Health for All (#16636)
♦ MMI Network / see Medicus Mundi International – Network Health for All (#16636)
♦ **MMiN** International Society for Monitoring Molecules in Neuroscience (#15279)
♦ MMIRA – Mixed Methods International Research Association (internationally oriented national body)
♦ M:MM / see Discipling for Development
♦ MMM I / see Make Mothers Matter (#16554)
♦ **MMM** International Association of Margaret Morris Method (#12012)
♦ MMM – International Conference on Multiscale Materials Modeling (meeting series)
♦ MMM – International MultiMedia Modeling Conference (meeting series)
♦ MMM / see Make Mothers Matter (#16554)
♦ MMM – Mangrove Macrobenthos and Management Meeting (meeting series)
♦ MMM – Medical Missionaries of Mary (religious order)
♦ MMM / see Movement for a Better World (#16869)
♦ **MMM** Movimento per un Mondo Migliore (#16869)
♦ **MMM** Movimiento por un Mundo Mejor (#16869)
♦ **MMN** Mekong Migration Network (#16702)
♦ MMN – Mismatch Negativity conference (meeting series)
♦ MMP – International Organization of Masters, Mates and Pilots (internationally oriented national body)
♦ **MMP** Marian Movement of Priests (#16575)
♦ **MMSA** Medical Mycological Society of the Americas (#16625)
♦ MMSH – Maison méditerranéenne des sciences de l'homme (internationally oriented national body)
♦ MMS – Mediterranean Medical Society (inactive)
♦ MM – Societas de Maryknoll pro Missionibus Exteris (religious order)
♦ **MMTA** Minor Metals Trade Association (#16821)

- **MMTC** Mouvement mondial des travailleurs chrétiens (#21660)
- **MMTC** Movimiento Mundial de Trabajadores Cristianos (#21660)
- MMV – International Conference on Monitoring and Management of Visitors in Recreational and Protected Areas (meeting series)
- **MMV** Medicines for Malaria Venture (#16634)
- Mna na H-Eorpa / see Association femmes d'Europe
- MNDA – Soeurs Missionnaires de Notre-Dame des Anges (religious order)
- MNE – International Conference on Micro and Nano Engineering (meeting series)
- MNF – Multinational Peace-Keeping Force (inactive)
- **MNI** Medical Nutrition International Industry (#16626)
- **MNOAL** Movimiento de Paises No Alineados (#17146)
- MNs – International Conference on Materials and Nanomaterials (meeting series)
- **MNS** Mediterranean Neuroscience Society (#16667)
- **MNU** Matariki Network of Universities (#16596)
- MOA Foundation / see MOA International
- MOA International (internationally oriented national body)

♦ Mobey Forum 16835

Secretariat Satamaradankatu 3-B, 3rd Floor, Nordea, FI-00020 Helsinki, Finland. T. +35847503942. E-mail: mobeyforum@mobeyforum.org.
URL: http://www.mobeyforum.org/

History May 2000. **Aims** Encourage the use of *mobile technology* in *financial* services. **Structure** Board of Directors, including Chairman and Vice Chair. Executive Director. **Languages** English. **Activities** Organizes workshops (4 a year). Work plan (2006): Research and Analysis – primary focus is mobile authentication; Experience Sharing and Networking – through seminars and meetings and through cooperation with other organizations; Communication, including two tasks – (1) communication of the results of the Mobile Financial Service Business Ecosystem Analysis, and (2) increasing the Mobey Forum awareness among the biggest banks in US; Pilots and Demonstrators. **Events** *Workshop* Munich (Germany) 2001. [2013/XF6303/F]

- Mobile Air Conditioning Society Worldwide (internationally oriented national body)
- Mobile Alliance for Maternal Action (internationally oriented national body)
- MobileHCI – The International Conference Series on Human Computer Interaction with Mobile Devices and Services (meeting series)
- Mobile Industry Processor Interface Alliance / see MIPI Alliance (#16823)
- Mobile Manufacturers Forum / see Mobile & Wireless Forum (#16837)

♦ Mobile Mediterranean University of Mastology (MANOSMED) 16836

Université mobile méditerranéenne de mastologie

Pres PO Box 45500, Stavros Niarchos Avenue, Univ Hospital Ioannina, Dept Obstetrics Gynecology, Ioannina, Greece. T. +302651097238. Fax +302651007055.
URL: http://www.manosmed.net/

History 10 Mar 1992, Montpellier (France), when statutes were adopted. Original title *Mastology Association of Northern and Southern Mediterranean (MANOSMED) – Association mastologie Nord et Sud Méditerranée.* Also referred to in English as: *Association North Mediterranean Mastology*; *Mastology North Mediterranean Association.* Current title adopted 6 Feb 2006, by decision 0343018791 of French Court. Registered in accordance with French law. **Aims** Promote quality and reliable research, *diagnosis*, *treatment*, follow-up, economic and *health* problems, evaluation, *medico-legal* problems and ethical problems associated with *diseases* of the *breast.* **Structure** General Assembly (annual); Board of Administration (meets twice a year); Administrative Committee; Scientific Council. **Languages** English, French. **Staff** Full-time, voluntary. **Finance** No members' dues. No budget. **Activities** Training/education. **Events** *International Congress* Algiers (Algeria) 2012, *International Congress* Beirut (Lebanon) 2011, *International Congress* Marrakech (Morocco) 2011, *International Congress* Geneva (Switzerland) 2010, *International Congress* Tartous (Syrian AR) 2009. **Publications** *Quality in Mastology (Breast Diseases): Criteria, Control* (1997) in French; *Epidemiological Quality Criteria of Breast Cancer Mass Screening* (1996); *Quality Criteria in Pathological Anatomy* (1996); *Quality Criteria of the US Examination* (1996); *Quality Control in Mammography* (1993) in English – (1994) in French, Greek.

Members Individuals (73) in 25 countries:
Albania, Algeria, Bolivia, Colombia, Cyprus, Ecuador, Egypt, France, Germany, Greece, Italy, Lebanon, Libya, Malaysia, Mauritania, Monaco, Morocco, Oman, Portugal, Romania, Spain, Switzerland, Syrian AR, Thailand, Tunisia. [2016.06.01/XD3242/v/D]

- Mobile Virtual Network Operators / see MVNO Europe (#16920)

♦ Mobile & Wireless Forum (MWF) 16837

SG Rijvisschestraat 124, 9052 Zwijnaarde, Belgium. E-mail: enquiries@mwfai.org.
URL: https://www.mwfai.org/

History 1998. Former names and other names: *Mobile Manufacturers Forum (MMF)* – former (1998 to 2017). Registration: Belgium. **Aims** Facilitate joint funding of key research projects and cooperation on standards, regulatory issues and communications concerning the safety of wireless technology, accessibility and product integrity. **Structure** General Assembly (annual). Council. **Languages** English, French, German. **Finance** Sources: members' dues. **Events** *Mobile communications seminar* Brussels (Belgium) 2004. **Members** Manufacturing companies. Membership countries not specified. [2022/XF5993/F]

- Mobilité pour la Prosperité en Europe (#16839)

♦ MobilityData 16838

Exec Dir address not obtained. E-mail: hello@mobilitydata.org.
URL: https://mobilitydata.org/

History Initiated, 2015, as a project of the Rocky Mountain Institute. Registered in Canada, 2019, and Europe, 2021. Registration: Nonprofit, Start date: 2019, Canada. **Aims** Work towards a world where people can choose ways to travel other than driving solo, whether by walking, cycling, carpooling, or using public or on-demand transit. **Structure** Board of Directors; Executive team. **Finance** Sources: members' dues. **Events** *International Mobility Data Summit* Montréal, QC (Canada) 2022.

Members Private sector; Government & Non-Profit. Organizations include:
Development Bank of Latin America (CAF, #05055); *ODIN – Open Mobility Data in the Nordics (ODIN, #17690).* [2023/AA3186/C]

- Mobility International (inactive)
- Mobility International USA (internationally oriented national body)

♦ Mobility for Prosperity in Europe (MPE) 16839

Mobilité pour la Prosperité en Europe

Secretariat c/o ERF, Place Stephanie 6/B, 1050 Brussels, Belgium. T. +3226445877. Fax +3226475934. E-mail: info@mobilityeurope.eu.
URL: http://www.mobilityeurope.eu/

History 2005. Founded on the initiative of Ari Vatanen. Registration: Start date: 2005, France. **Aims** Promote transport systems in Europe. **Structure** General Meeting (annual); Board.

Members Members (16), including 11 organizations listed in this Yearbook:
Association des constructeurs européens de motocycles (ACEM, #02450); *Association Européenne des Concessionnaires d'Autoroutes et d'Ouvrages à Péage (ASECAP, #02559)*; *Association of European Vehicle Logistics (ECG, #02551)*; *European Automobile Manufacturers' Association (ACEA, #06300)*; *European Tyre and Rubber Manufacturers' Association (ETRMA, #08963)*; *European Union Road Federation (ERF, #09014)*; *Fédération Internationale de l'Automobile (FIA, #09613)*; *Federation of European Movers Associations (FEDEMAC, #09519)*; *International Road Transport Union (IRU, #14761)*; *Liquid Gas Europe (#16488)*; *UPEI – The voice of Europe's independent fuel suppliers (#20726).* [2016/XM1687/y/F]

- Mobility as a Service Alliance (unconfirmed)
- Mobilization Network – International Network For Early Mobilization Of Mechanically Ventilated Intensive Care Patients (unconfirmed)
- Mocidade por Cristo (#22009)

♦ Modelica Association 16840

Chair Inst of Robotics and Mechatronics, DLR Research Ctr Oberpfaffenhofen, PO Box 1116, 82230 Wessling, Germany. T. +498153282473. Fax +498153281441.
URL: http://modelica.org/

Aims Develop and promote the Modelica modelling language for modelling, simulation and programming of physical and technical systems and processes. **Structure** Board, comprising Chairperson, Vice-Chairperson, Secretary, Treasurer and 6 members. **Finance** Members' dues. **Events** *Japanese Conference* Tokyo (Japan) 2018, *International MODELICA Conference* Paris (France) 2015, *Conference* Munich (Germany) 2012, *International MODELICA Conference* Munich (Germany) 2012, *Conference* Dresden (Germany) 2011. **Publications** *Modelica Newsletter.* [2018/XJ6396/E]

- Modelling of Casting, Welding and Advanced Solidification Processes Conference (meeting series)
- Modelling in Geosciences (meeting series)

♦ Modern Asian Architecture Network (mAAN) 16841

Contact address not obtained.

History 25 Jul 2001, Macau. Preparatory meeting 22 Jul 2000, Guangzhou (China). Founded on the initiative of Dr Johannes Widodo. **Aims** Study, preserve and rehabilitate the modern architecture, townscape and civil-engineering heritages in Asia. **Structure** Executive Committee. **Events** *Symposium and students workshop* Bhopal (India) 2011, *Conference* Seoul (Korea Rep) 2011, *Conference* Singapore (Singapore) 2010, *Asian cities – legacies of modernity* Delhi (India) 2009, *International design workshop* Padang (Indonesia) 2009. **NGO Relations** Member of: *Asian Academy for Heritage Management (AAHM, #01294).* Affiliated with: *Documentation and Conservation of the Modern Movement (DOCOMOMO International, #05110).* [2009/XM0899/F]

- Modern Asia Research Centre / see Centre for Asian Studies

♦ Modern Building Alliance 16842

Exec Chair Rue Belliard 40, Box 16, 1040 Brussels, Belgium. T. +3227923039. E-mail: info@modernbuildingalliance.eu.
URL: http://www.modernbuildingalliance.eu/

History Subtitle: *Safe and sustainable construction with plastics.* **Aims** Promote greater *fire safety* across the construction *industry.* **Structure** Board. Working Groups (2): Technical; Public Affairs.

Members include 5 organizations listed in this Yearbook:
Association of Plastics Manufacturers in Europe (Plastics Europe, #02862); *European Diisocyanate and Polyol Producers Association (ISOPA, #06926)*; *European Extruded Polystyrene Insulation Board Association (EXIBA, #07019)*; *European Manufacturers of Expanded Polystyrene (EUMEPS, #07732)*; *Federation of European Rigid Polyurethane Foam Associations (PU Europe, #09538).*

NGO Relations *European Fire Safety Alliance (EuroFSA, #07258).* [2020/XM7768/y/D]

- Modern European History Research Centre (internationally oriented national body)
- Modern Free and Accepted Masons of the World (internationally oriented national body)
- Modern Greek Studies Association (internationally oriented national body)

♦ Modern Humanities Research Association (MHRA) 16843

Association d'étude des humanités modernes

Hon Sec School of Modern Languages and Cultures, Univ of Glasgow – Hetherington Bldg, Bute Gardens, Glasgow, G12 8RS, UK.
Registered Office Salisbury House, Station Road, Cambridge, CB1 2LA, UK.
URL: http://www.mhra.org.uk/

History Founded 1918, Cambridge (UK). UK Registered Charity: 1064670. **Aims** Further and encourage research and publication in the field of modern *languages* and *literatures.* **Languages** English. **Finance** Members' dues. Charity. **Publications** *Modern Language Review* (4 a year); *Slavonic and East European Review* (4 a year); *Portuguese Studies* (2 a year); *Austrian Studies* (annual); *Working papers in the Humanities* (annual) – online; *Yearbook of English Studies* (annual); *MHRA Annual Bulletin. Annual Bibliography of English Language and Literature (ABELL)* – series; *Legenda* – series; *Library of Medieval Welsh Literature* – series; *MHRA Critical Texts* – series; *Publications of the MHRA* – series. *MHRA Style Guide* (2013).

Members Institutions (110) in 15 countries:
Australia, Austria, Canada, Denmark, Germany, Ireland, Israel, Malaysia, Netherlands, New Zealand, South Africa, Sweden, Switzerland, UK, USA.

Individuals (191) in 20 countries and territories:
Australia, Austria, Belgium, Brazil, Canada, France, Germany, Hong Kong, India, Ireland, Japan, Netherlands, Portugal, Russia, Singapore, South Africa, Spain, Switzerland, UK, USA.

NGO Relations Member of: *Association of Learned and Professional Society Publishers (ALPSP, #02786).* [2018.06.01/XF1324/F]

- Modernist Studies Association (internationally oriented national body)
- Modern Language Association of America (internationally oriented national body)
- Modern Order of the Star (inactive)
- Modern Pentathlon Sudamerica / see Confederación Sudamericana de Pentatlon Moderno (#04492)

♦ MoDeST Society 16844

Secretariat Dept of Industrial Engineering, Viale delle Scienze, Bldg 6, 90128 Palermo PA, Italy. T. +399123863703. Fax +39917025020. E-mail: info@modest.org.uk.
URL: http://modest.org.uk/

History MoDeST is an acronym for: *Modification Degradation and Stabilization of Polymer.* Registration: Italy. **Aims** Promote applied research; disseminate scientific information on the modification, degradation and stabilization of polymers. **Structure** Board; Scientific Council. **Languages** English. **Staff** 4.00 FTE, paid. **Finance** Members' dues (annual). **Events** *Conference* Tokyo (Japan) 2018, *Conference* Krakow (Poland) 2016, *Conference* Portoroz (Slovenia) 2014, *Conference* Prague (Czech Rep) 2012, *Conference* Athens (Greece) 2010. [2019/XJ6988/c/E]

- Modificación al articulo 7 del Convenio interamericano sobre el servicio de radioaficionados (1988 treaty)
- Modification Degradation and Stabilization of Polymer / see MoDeST Society (#16844)
- Modification of the Police Regulations Regarding Navigation on the Rhine, the Wahal and the Lek (1923 treaty)
- Modification du règlement de police pour la navigation rhénane en ce qui concerne le Rhin, y compris le Wahal et le Lek (1923 treaty)
- Modzi Europejscy Federaliści (#21984)
- **MOE** Minorities of Europe (#16818)
- Moetzet Hapoaleot / see NA'AMAT Movement of Working Women and Volunteers
- MOGC – Maryknoll Office for Global Concern (internationally oriented national body)
- Mohammed Bin Rashid Al Maktoum Global Initiatives (internationally oriented national body)
- MoH – Mechanics of Hearing (meeting series)

♦ Mo Ibrahim Foundation 16845

Exec Dir 35 Portman Square, London, W1H 6LR, UK. E-mail: info@moibrahimfoundation.org.
Dakar Office 32 Sipres Mermoz, Dakar, Senegal. E-mail: sall.s@moibrahimfoundation.org.
URL: http://mo.ibrahim.foundation/

History Set up 2006. **Aims** Study the critical importance of governance and *leadership* in *Africa.* **Structure** Board. **Activities** Research/documentation; events/meetings; awards/prizes/competitions. **Events** *Annual Ibrahim Governance Weekend Forum* Abidjan (Côte d'Ivoire) 2019, *Annual Ibrahim Governance Weekend Forum* Kigali (Rwanda) 2018, *Annual Ibrahim Governance Weekend Forum* Marrakech (Morocco) 2017. **NGO Relations** Instrumental in setting up: *Forum de Paris sur la Paix.* [2018/XM6820/f/F]

- **MOIG** Mediterranean Oil Industry Group (#16669)
- MO – Institutum Missionariorum Opificum (religious order)
- **MOIP** Mediterranean Orthodontic Integration Project (#16671)

♦ MOKA International Foundation (FIM Group) 16846

Fondation internationale MOKA (Groupe FIM)

Contact Ave Andromède 26, 1200 Brussels, Belgium. T. +3289758897. E-mail: deshabunda@gmail.com.

Registered Office Rue Terre-Neuve 192 – 02, 1000 Brussels, Belgium.

Congo DR Office 4358 avenue du Progrès, Barumbu, BP 2032, Kinshasa 1, Congo DR.

History 1976, Hamburg (Germany FR), as *Fondation internationale Moka El-Aboubakar (FIMELA)*. Current title adopted, 2006. Registration: Belgium. **Aims** In a framework of solidarity with *African* sport and in particular with African youth: provide instruction to *orphans* and the physically *handicapped* which will assist them in becoming part of active society; assist socially maladjusted young people in understanding the value of education and responsibility which will allow them freedom of choice and ability to live up to their potential and at the same time to realize the value and dignity of human work; develop, and put at the disposal of disadvantaged youth, community services which do not discriminate on grounds of religion, race or nationality; sensitize governments, private and religious organizations and individuals to the continent's health, school, agricultural, sporting and leisure requirements; facilitate adoption of orphan children of African origin. **Structure** General Assembly (annual); Administrative Council of 7; President; Vice-President; Secretary-General; Assistant Secretary-General; Treasurer-General. Commission Secretaries; Advisers; Sections, each with its own Assembly, Council, President, Secretary and Treasurer. Includes: *Entrepreneur sans frontière (ESF, no recent information)*. **Finance** Members' dues. [2017/XF3077/f/**F**]

♦ Mokichi Okada Association International / see MOA International
♦ Mokichi Okada Cultural Services Association / see MOA International
♦ **MOK** Mezpravitelstvennaja Okeanograficeskaja Komissija (#11496)
♦ MOLEC – European Study Conference on Low Energy Molecular Collisions (meeting series)

♦ Molecular and Cellular Cognition Society (MCCS) 16847

Main Office c/o University of Iowa, Iowa City IA 52242, USA.

Pres Dept of Neurobiology, Stanford University, Fairchild D251, Stanford CA 94305-5125, USA.

URL: https://molcellcog.org/

History First meeting held in Orlando (Florida, USA), Nov 1st, 2002. **Aims** Facilitate interchanges among laboratories in the field of Molecular and Cellular Cognition. **Structure** Council of 18 members. Officers: President; Secretary; Treasurer. Branches (2): Europe; Asia. **Activities** Events/meetings. **Events** *Symposium* San Diego, CA (USA) 2022, *Asia Meeting* Seoul (Korea Rep) 2019, *Asia Meeting* Singapore (Singapore) 2017, *Annual Meeting* San Diego, CA (USA) 2013, *Annual Meeting* New Orleans, LA (USA) 2012. **NGO Relations** Member of (1): *Federation of European Neuroscience Societies (FENS, #09522)*. [2022/XM2912/**C**]

♦ Molecular and Experimental Pathology Society of Australasia (internationally oriented national body)
♦ Molecular Genetics Society of Australasia (internationally oriented national body)
♦ Moleskine Foundation (internationally oriented national body)
♦ Moleskine Foundation Onlus / see Moleskine Foundation
♦ MOMA – Mouvement pour une organisation mondiale de l'agriculture (internationally oriented national body)
♦ MOM – Stiftung Welt ohne Minen (internationally oriented national body)
♦ Món-3 – Universitaris pel Tercer Món (internationally oriented national body)
♦ Monache Carmelitane Scalze (religious order)
♦ Monaci della Regola Studita (religious order)
♦ Monaci di San Paolo Primo Eremita (religious order)
♦ Monaco Chart / see Joint IOC/IHO Guiding Committee for the General Bathymetric Chart of the Oceans (#16137)
♦ Monaco Collectif Humanitaire (internationally oriented national body)

♦ Monarchist League (ML) 16848

Chancellor PO Box 5307, Bishop's Stortford, CM23 3DZ, UK. T. +441279465551. Fax +441279466111. E-mail: enquiries@monarchyinternational.net.

URL: http://www.monarchyinternational.net/

History Founded 1943. Also referred to as *International Monarchist League*. **Aims** Support the principle of Monarchy. **Structure** Chancellor; International Council; Council Representatives. **Languages** English. **Finance** Subscriptions. **Publications** *Monarchy* (4 a year) – journal.

Members Individuals (over 1,000), represented in 38 countries and territories:
Australia, Austria, Belgium, Brazil, Bulgaria, Canada, Cyprus, Czechia, Denmark, Falklands/Malvinas, Fiji, Finland, France, Germany, Gibraltar, Hong Kong, Ireland, Italy, Kenya, Lithuania, Malaysia, Malta, Mexico, Netherlands, New Zealand, Norway, Philippines, Poland, Portugal, Russia, Saudi Arabia, South Africa, Spain, Sweden, Switzerland, UK, United Arab Emirates, USA. [2019.05.07/XF3529/v/**F**]

♦ Monarchist Union (inactive)
♦ Monash Asia Institute (internationally oriented national body)
♦ Monash European and EU Centre, Melbourne (internationally oriented national body)

♦ Monastic Interreligious Dialogue 16849

Dialogue Interreligieux Monastique (DIMMID)

SG Saint John's Abbey, PO Box 2015, Collegeville MN 56321, USA. T. +13203633921. Fax +13203633082.

Coordinator Europe Abtei Königsmünster, Postfach 1161, 59851 Meschede, Germany. T. +4929129950.

URL: http://www.dimmid.org/

History 1978. Founded within the *Aide Inter Monastères (AIM)*, when sub-committees were set up in Europe and USA, by *Benedictine Confederation*. Subcommittees merged with those set up in Australia (1991) and India/Sri Lanka (1994) under a General Secretariat for Dialogue Interreligieux Monastique/Monastic Interreligious Dialogue, 1994. Former names and other names: *Committees for Monastic Interreligious Dialogue* – alias; *Commissions pour le dialogue interreligieux monastique* – alias. **Aims** As an international Catholic monastic organization, promote and support dialogue, especially dialogue at the level of religious experience and practice, between Christian monastic men and women and followers of other religions. **Structure** Board of Directors (meets annually), consisting of Secretary General, President of *Alliance inter-monastères (AIM, #00691)*, Regional Coordinators and at least 3 Directors at large. **Languages** English, French. **Staff** None. **Finance** Sources: contributions. **Activities** Events/meetings. **Publications** *Dilatato Corde* (2 a year) – online journal. [2021.05.25/XK0475/**E**]

♦ Monastic Interreligious Dialogue – North America (internationally oriented national body)
♦ Monda Funduso de Solidareco kontraŭ la Malsato (#09836)
♦ Mondcivitana Fondajo (internationally oriented national body)
♦ Mondcivitana Respubliko (inactive)
♦ Mondcivitanner Republik (inactive)
♦ Mondcivitan Republic (inactive)
♦ MONDE-3 / see Món-3 – Universitaris pel Tercer Món
♦ Monde bilingue (#03235)
♦ Monde en harmonie (#21552)
♦ Le Monde selon les femmes (internationally oriented national body)
♦ Monde solidarité Afrique (internationally oriented national body)
♦ Mondiala de Tineret Impotriva Schimbarii Climei (inactive)
♦ Monetary Committee of the Franc Zone (#04193)
♦ Monetary Convention, 1873 (1873 treaty)
♦ Monetary Convention, 1879 (1879 treaty)
♦ Money Orders and Postal Travellers Cheques Agreement, 1979 (1979 treaty)
♦ Money Orders and Postal Travellers Cheques Agreement, 1984 (1984 treaty)
♦ **MONEYVAL** Committee of Experts on the Evaluation of Anti-Money Laundering Measures and the Financing of Terrorism (#04257)
♦ **MONGOOS** Mediterranean Oceanography Network for the Global Ocean Observing System (#16668)
♦ Moniales Bénédictines (religious order)
♦ Moniales Carmélites déchaussées (religious order)
♦ Moniales Ordinis Carmelitarum Discalceatarum (religious order)
♦ Moniales Sacramentines (religious order)
♦ Monimis Epitropi Iatron tis EK / see Standing Committee of European Doctors (#19955)
♦ **MoniQA** International Association for Monitoring and Quality Assurance in the Total Food Supply Chain (#12036)
♦ Monjes Jerónimos (religious order)
♦ Monrovia Group – Organization of Inter-African and Malagasy States (inactive)

♦ Mont-Blanc Meetings (MBM) 16850

Les Rencontres du Mont-Blanc

Contact 54 avenue de Clichy, 75018 Paris, France.

History 2005. Founded as an alternative to *World Economic Forum (WEF, #21367)* held in Davos. Current by-laws adopted Jul 2012. Former names and other names: *Mont-Blanc Meetings – – International Forum of the Social and Solidarity Entrepreneurs (MBM)* – full title; *Les Rencontres du Mont-Blanc – Forum international des dirigeants de l'économie sociale et solidaire* – full title. Registration: France. **Aims** Show that social and solidarity economy (SSE) makes another form of entrepreneurship possible, in line with an overall goal of sustainable development. **Structure** General Assembly; Board of Directors. **Languages** English, French, Spanish. **Finance** Members' dues. **Activities** Knowledge management/information dissemination; networking/liaising; projects/programmes; politics/policy/regulatory. **Events** *Meeting* Cartagena de Indias (Colombia) 2022, *Meeting* Chamonix (France) 2015, *Meeting* Chamonix (France) 2013, *Meeting* Chamonix (France) 2011, *Meeting* Chamonix (France) 2009. **Consultative Status** Consultative status granted from: *ECOSOC (#05331)* (Special). **NGO Relations** Partners include: *FMDV (#09804)*. Instrumental in setting up: *SSE International Forum (#19937)*. [2016.08.17/XJ9816/c/**F**]

♦ Mont-Blanc Meetings – – International Forum of the Social and Solidarity Entrepreneurs / see Mont-Blanc Meetings (#16850)
♦ Mont Carmel – Centre international de formation Golda Meir (internationally oriented national body)
♦ Monterey Institute of International Studies / see Middlebury Institute of International Studies, Monterey

♦ Montessori Europe 16851

Office Grünstr 23, 12555 Berlin, Germany. T. +4930214801840. E-mail: office@montessori-europe.net.

Pres Hogeschool Amsterdam, Univ of Applied Sciences, p/a Liesbos 148, 2134 SE Hoofddorp, Netherlands.

URL: http://www.montessori-europe.net/

History 2000. Current statutes adopted Oct 2016. Registered in accordance with German law. **Aims** Enable and encourage Montessori *pedagogy* at political, social and educational levels throughout Europe. **Structure** General Meeting (annual); Board; Executive Management; Advisory Councils. **Finance** Members' dues. **Activities** Research/documentation; standards/guidelines; training/education; events/meetings. **Events** *Montessori Europe Congress* Berlin (Germany) 2016. **Members** Individual; Institutional. Membership countries not specified. [2018.01.23/XM5618/**E**]

♦ Montevideo Treaty (1960 treaty)
♦ Montevideo Treaty 1980 (1980 treaty)
♦ Montfortains – Missionnaires de la Compagnie de Marie (religious order)
♦ Montfort Fathers – Missionaries of the Company of Mary (religious order)
♦ De Montfort International Centre for Sports History and Culture / see International Centre for Sports History and Culture

♦ Mont Pèlerin Society (MPS) 16852

Société du Mont-Pèlerin

Treas 313 Fletcher Hall Dept 6106, 615 McCallie Ave, Chattanooga TN 37403-2598, USA. T. +14234254118. Fax +14234255218. E-mail: mps@utc.edu.

URL: http://www.montpelerin.org/

History 1 Apr 1947, Mont Pèlerin (Switzerland). Founded 1-10 Apr 1947, Mont Pèlerin (Switzerland), at the instigation of Friedrich von Hayek, by a group of 39 economists, philosophers, jurists, historians, political scientists, literary critics and publicists, at a meeting to exchange ideas about the nature of a free society, dangers to its survival and ways and means of strengthening its intellectual support. **Aims** Bring together *economists* and others who study and promote *free-market* economies in an informal network. **Finance** Members' dues. Donations. **Activities** Events/meetings. **Events** *Special Meeting* Stanford, CA (USA) 2020, *Biennial General Meeting* Maspalomas (Spain) 2018, *Seoul Regional Meeting* Seoul (Korea Rep) 2017, *Biennial General Meeting* Miami, FL (USA) 2016, *Biennial General Meeting* Hong Kong (Hong Kong) 2014. **Members** Covers 51 countries. Membership countries not specified. [2019/XF0161/**F**]

♦ Montreal amendment – Amendment to the Montreal Protocol on Substances That Deplete the Ozone Layer, 1997 (1997 treaty)

♦ The Montreal Group (TMG) 16853

Le Groupe de Montréal

Operations Manager 5 Place Ville Marie, Ste 100, Montréal QC H3B 5E7, Canada. T. +15142231417. E-mail: secretariat@themontrealgroup.org.

URL: https://www.themontrealgroup.org/

History 2012, Montréal, QC (Canada). Registration: Canada. **Aims** Promote international cooperation, mutual learning and exchange of technical expertise among SME-focused *Development Banks*. **Structure** General Meeting (annual); Board of Directors; Secretariat. **Languages** English, French. **Staff** 3.00 FTE, paid. **Finance** Sources: members' dues. **Activities** Events/meetings; training/education. **Events** *Annual General Meeting* Riyadh (Saudi Arabia) 2022, *Annual General Meeting* Montréal, QC (Canada) 2021, *Annual General Meeting* Montréal, QC (Canada) 2020.

Members State-owned development banks of 10 countries:
Brazil, Canada, China, Finland, France, India, Italy, Malaysia, Mexico, Saudi Arabia.

NGO Relations Member of (1): *SME Finance Forum (#19323)*. [2021.09.09/XM5930/**E***]

♦ Montreal Institute for Genocide and Human Rights Studies (internationally oriented national body)
♦ Montreal International Forum / see FIM-Forum for Democratic Global Governance (#09761)
♦ **Montreal Process** Working Group on Criteria and Indicators for the Conservation and Sustainable Management of Temperate and Boreal Forests (#21058)
♦ Montreal Protocol Multilateral Fund / see Multilateral Fund for the Implementation of the Montreal Protocol (#16885)
♦ Montréal Protocol – Protocol to Amend the Convention on Offences and Certain Other Acts Committed on Board Aircraft (2014 treaty)
♦ Montreal Protocol on Substances that Deplete the Ozone Layer (1987 treaty)
♦ MONUC / see United Nations Organization Stabilization Mission in the Democratic Republic of Congo (#20605)
♦ Monumenta Europae Historica (no recent information)
♦ **MONUSCO** United Nations Organization Stabilization Mission in the Democratic Republic of Congo (#20605)
♦ MONUT – Mission d'observation des Nations Unies au Tadjikistan (inactive)
♦ MOPAN – International Conference on Multi-Organisational Partnerships, Alliances and Networks (meeting series)
♦ **MOPAN** Multilateral Organizations Performance Assessment Network (#16890)
♦ MOP – Magnetospheres of the Outer Planets (meeting series)
♦ MOPP – Missione Operaia Pietro e Paolo (religious order)
♦ MOPS International (internationally oriented national body)
♦ **MOPS** Mediterranean Organization for Promotion and Science (#16670)
♦ MOPS Outreach / see MOPS International
♦ MOPTSLHP – Mezdunarodnoe Obedinenie Profsojuzov Trudjascihsja Selskogo, Lesnogo Hozjajstva i Plantacij (inactive)
♦ MORA-Ärztegesellschaft / see International Society of Medical Doctors for Biophysical Information Therapy (#15253)

♦ Moralische Aufrüstung / see Initiatives of Change International – Caux (#11213)
♦ Moral Re-Armament / see Initiatives of Change International – Caux (#11213)

♦ Moravian Church 16854

Admin Lindegade 26, 6070 Christiansfeld, Denmark. T. +4574561420.
URL: http://www.unitasfratrum.org/

History 1475, Prague (Czech Rep), as *Unitas Fratrum* – 'Unity of the Brethren' – by followers of John Hus (died 1415). Still also referred to by original title. Church renewed 13 Aug 1727, Herrnhut (Germany). **Aims** As a protestant Christian denomination, function as part of the living Church, being aware of and participating in special gifts and tasks drawn from Jesus' life on earth. Emphasize: the word of the cross as the testimony of the Lord who was crucified for us and rose again; the word of reconciliation as God making peace with His whole creation; the word of personal union with the Saviour as the vitalizing and moulding power of the believer's life; the word of Christ-like love among one another as the fellowship of members brought about by Jesus Christ, the Head of His Church. **Structure** While recognizing the priesthood of all believers, includes bishops, presbyters, deacons and acolytes. **Publications** *The Ground of Unity* (1995) – doctrinal statement.

Members Churches in 19 provinces in 28 countries:
Antigua-Barbuda, Barbados, Canada, Congo DR, Costa Rica, Cuba, Czechia, Denmark, Dominican Rep, Estonia, Germany, Guyana, Honduras, India, Ireland, Jamaica, Netherlands, Nicaragua, South Africa, St Kitts-Nevis, Suriname, Sweden, Switzerland, Tanzania UR, Trinidad-Tobago, UK, USA, Zambia.

NGO Relations Founding member of: *World Council of Churches (WCC, #21320)*. Member of: *Oikocredit International (Oikocredit, #17704)*. [2019.02.11/XF5848/F]

♦ More and Better 16855

Secretariat c/o Terra Nuova, Viale Liegi 10, 00198 Rome RM, Italy. T. +3968070847. Fax +39680662557. E-mail: secretariat@moreandbetter.org.
URL: http://www.moreandbetter.org/

History as an international campaign. **Aims** Support and be a part of the battle to eradicate *hunger* and *poverty* through food, agriculture and rural development aid. **Structure** Coordination Committee, comprising representatives of 20 organizations.

Members Civil society organizations, networks and North/South movements, in 43 countries and territories:
Bangladesh, Belgium, Burkina Faso, Cameroon, Canada, Chile, Colombia, Congo Brazzaville, Congo DR, Ethiopia, Finland, France, Gabon, Germany, Ghana, Guatemala, Honduras, India, Indonesia, Iran Islamic Rep, Italy, Jordan, Kazakhstan, Kenya, Malawi, Malaysia, Mali, Mexico, Mozambique, Nepal, Nicaragua, Nigeria, Norway, Pakistan, Palestine, Philippines, Senegal, Sri Lanka, Tunisia, Uganda, UK, USA, Zambia.

Included in the above, 14 international organizations:
ActionAid (#00087); African Biodiversity Network (ABN, #00222); Asia Pacific Network on Food Sovereignty (APNFS, #01965); Bank Information Center (BIC); IFOAM – Organics International (IFOAM, #11105); International Federation of Agricultural Producers (IFAP, inactive); International Federation of Rural Adult Catholic Movements (#13535); La Via Campesina (#20765); Mouvement international de la jeunesse agricole et rurale catholique (MIJARC, #16865); PAN Asia and the Pacific (PANAP, #18167); West African Network of Farmers' Organizations and Agricultural Producers (#20891); World Forum of Fisher Peoples (WFFP, #21517); World Forum of Fish Harvesters and Fishworkers (WFF, #21518).

NGO Relations Secretariat hosted by: *Terra Nuova*. Cooperates with: *Alliance Against Hunger and Malnutrition (AAHM, no recent information)*. Coordinating Committee members include representatives from the following organizations listed in this Yearbook: *ActionAid (#00087); Bread for the World Institute (BFW Institute); Movimiento Agroecológico para Latinoamérica y El Caribe (MAELA, #16872); 'Terra Nuova'; La Via Campesina (#20765); West African Network of Farmers' Organizations and Agricultural Producers (#20891); World Forum of Fisher Peoples (WFFP, #21517); World Forum of Fish Harvesters and Fishworkers (WFF, #21518).* [2016/XJ0635/y/F]

♦ More in Common 16856

CEO 22bis rue des Taillandiers, 75011 Paris, France. E-mail: contact@destincommun.fr.
Berlin Office Gipsstr 3, 10119 Berlin, Germany. T. +493020459850. E-mail: deutschland@moreincommon.com.
London Office North House, 198 High Street, Tonbridge, TN9 1BE, UK. E-mail: uk@moreincommon.com.
New York Office 115 Broadway St, Floor 5, New York NY 10006, USA. E-mail: us@moreincommon.com.
URL: http://www.moreincommon.com/

History 2017. Registration: Companies House, No/ID: 10900540, Start date: 4 Aug 2017, England and Wales; RNA, No/ID: W751241689, Start date: 28 Oct 2017, France; 501(c)(3) non-profit, USA; Berlin District court, No/ID: VR 36992, Start date: 8 Nov 2018, Germany, Berlin; EU Transparency Register, No/ID: 941398343625-77, Start date: 11 Aug 2021. **Aims** Build *communities* and societies that are stronger, more united and more resilient to the increasing threats of polarization and social division. **Structure** Board of Directors. Offices in: Paris (France); Berlin (Germany); London (UK); New York NY (USA). **Activities** Research/documentation. **Publications** Reports. [2021/XM7088/F]

♦ Moremi Initiative – Moremi Initiative for Women's Leadership in Africa (internationally oriented national body)
♦ Moremi Initiative for Women's Leadership in Africa (internationally oriented national body)
♦ More Peace Less AIDS Foundation (#16594)
♦ Morgan Memorial Cooperative Industries and Stores Inc / see Goodwill Industries International
♦ MORIS – Magnetics and Optics Research International Symposium (meeting series)
♦ The Mormons / see Church of Jesus Christ of the Latter-day Saints (#03915)
♦ Moroccan Institute for International Relations (internationally oriented national body)
♦ **MOROP** Verband der Modelleisenbahner und Eisenbahnfreunde Europas (#20400)
♦ MORP – Organización de Escritores Revolucionarios (inactive)
♦ Morris E Curiel Center for International Studies, Tel Aviv (internationally oriented national body)
♦ Mortenson Center for International Library Programs (internationally oriented national body)
♦ Mortenson Center – Mortenson Center for International Library Programs (internationally oriented national body)
♦ The Morton Deutsch International Center for Cooperation and Conflict Resolution / see International Center for Cooperation and Conflict Resolution
♦ Moscow Institute of International Relations / see Moskovskij Gosudarstvennyj Institut Mezdunarodnyh Otnosenij
♦ Moscow International Higher Business School (internationally oriented national body)
♦ Moscow School of Human Rights (internationally oriented national body)
♦ Moscow State Institute of International Relations (internationally oriented national body)
♦ Moscow State University Institute of Asian and African Studies / see Institute of Asian and African Studies, Moscow State University
♦ Moselkommission (#16857)

♦ Moselle Commission 16857

Commission de la Moselle – Moselkommission

SG Franz-Ludwig-Strasse 21, 54290 Trier, Germany. T. +496519794160. E-mail: info@moselkommission.org.
URL: http://www.moselkommission.org/

History 21 Dec 1962. Established following signing of *Convention on the Canalization of the Moselle (1956)*, 27 Oct 1956. Former names and other names: *International Moselle Commission* – former; *Commission internationale de la Moselle* – former; *Internationale Moselkommission* – former. **Aims** Promote the interests of *navigation* on the international *waterway* Moselle; ensure best conditions of navigation and guarantee that proceeds remain as high as possible. **Structure** Plenary Session (2 a year); Competent Committees (4); Working Groups (2). **Languages** French, German. **Staff** 5.00 FTE, paid. **Finance** Sources: contributions of member/participating states. Annual budget: 355,000 EUR. **Activities** Politics/policy/regulatory. **Publications** *La Convention de la Moselle – 50 ans – Der Moselvertrag – 50 Jahre* (2006); *40 ans de grande navigation sur la Moselle – 40 Jahre Grossschiffahrt auf der Mosel* (2004). Booklet; flyer; brochure.

Members Governments of 3 countries:
France, Germany, Luxembourg.

NGO Relations Formal contacts with: *Association for European Inland Navigation and Waterways (VBW); European Barge Union (EBU, #06318); European Federation of Inland Ports (EFIP, #07144); Inland Navigation Europe (INE, #11216).* [2022.10.12/XJ3833/E*]

♦ MOSES – International Conference on Modelling and Optimisation of Ship Energy Systems (meeting series)
♦ Moshe Dayan Centre for Middle Eastern and African Studies (internationally oriented national body)
♦ MOSIM – International Conference on Modelling, Optimization and Simulation (meeting series)
♦ Moskovskij Gosudarstvennyj Institut Mezdunarodnyh Otnosenij (internationally oriented national body)
♦ Moskovskij Institut Mezdunarodnyh Otnosenij / see Moskovskij Gosudarstvennyj Institut Mezdunarodnyh Otnosenij
♦ **MOS** Mathematical Optimization Society (#16601)
♦ MOS / see Mediterranean Society of Ophthalmology (#16679)

♦ Most Beautiful Bays in the World Club 16858

Club des Plus Belles Baies du Monde – Club de las Bahias mas Bellas del Mundo – Clube das Mais Lindas Baias do Mundo

Gen Sec address not obtained. E-mail: contact@world-bays.com.
URL: http://www.world-bays.com/

History Founded 10 Mar 1997, Berlin (Germany). Current statutes adopted, 26 May 2011, Toubacouta (Senegal). Registered in accordance with French law. **Aims** Bring together different bays located on all continents within the Club. **Structure** General Meeting (annual); Committee. **Languages** English, French. **Finance** Members' dues. **Activities** Events/meetings. **Events** *Congress* La Baule (France) 2018, *Congress* Puerto Vallarta (Mexico) 2016, *Congress* Yeosu (Korea Rep) 2014, *Congress* Turkey 2012, *Congress* Toubacouta (Senegal) 2011.

Members Active; Founder; Benefactor; Honorary. Bays in 25 countries and territories:
Argentina, Brazil, Cambodia, Canada, Cape Verde, China, Colombia, France, Greece, Guadeloupe, India, Ireland, Korea Rep, Madagascar, Mexico, Montenegro, Morocco, Mozambique, Philippines, Portugal, South Africa, Spain, Türkiye, USA, Vietnam. [2018/XJ1372/E]

♦ **MOST** Management of Social Transformations (#16562)
♦ Motamar Al-Alam Al-Islami (#21664)
♦ Mother Child Education Foundation (internationally oriented national body)
♦ Mother Health International (internationally oriented national body)

♦ mothers2mothers (m2m) 16859

Intl Office 7441 W Sunset Blvd, Ste 205, Los Angeles CA 90046, USA. T. +13239690445. Fax +13237968152. E-mail: us@m2m.org.
South Africa Office PO Box 841, Cape Town, 8000, South Africa. T. +27214669160. Fax +27214624868. E-mail: info@m2m.org.
Europe 3 Cromwell Place, London, SW7 2JE, UK. T. +442075899254. E-mail: europe@m2m.org.
URL: http://www.m2m.org/

History 2001, Cape Town (South Africa). Registration: USA; Charity Commission, No/ID: 1119721, England and Wales. **Aims** Improve the *health* of *mothers* living with *HIV*, putting them at the heart of efforts to eliminate *paediatric AIDS*. **Publications** Annual Report. **IGO Relations** Partners and supporters include: *Canadian International Development Agency (CIDA, inactive); Global Fund to Fight AIDS, Tuberculosis and Malaria (Global Fund, #10383); UNICEF (#20332); United States Agency for International Development (USAID).* **NGO Relations** Member of (2): *Extractive Industries Transparency Initiative (EITI, #09229); PMNCH (#18410).* Partners and supporters include: *Comic Relief; EngenderHealth; Every Woman Every Child (EWEC, #09215); Skoll Foundation; Starr International Foundation (SIF).* [2019/XJ7304/F]

♦ Mothers Without Borders (internationally oriented national body)
♦ Mothers Legacy Project (internationally oriented national body)
♦ Mothers of Preschoolers / see MOPS International

♦ The Mothers' Union 16860

Chief Exec Mary Sumner House, 24 Tufton Street, London, SW1P 3RB, UK. T. +442072225533. Fax +442072229437. E-mail: mu@mothersunion.org.
URL: http://www.mothersunion.org/

History Founded 1876, UK, by Mary Sumner, as a voluntary organization to support women in their role as parents. UK Registered Charity: 240531. **Aims** Promote *Christian* care for families worldwide with a grassroots approach; work for local *communities* in activities fitting local priorities and needs; through social policy work, assist in building a just and compassionate society. Promote the well-being of families worldwide by: developing prayer and spiritual growth in families; studying and reflecting on family life and its place in society; resourcing members to take practical action to improve conditions for families, both nationally and in the communities in which they live. **Structure** General Meeting; World Wide Council; Headquarters – Mary Sumner House in London (UK) – includes Central Chapel, conference facilities and secretariat. Key Units (5): Action and Outreach; Faith and Policy; Finance and Central Services; Fundraising and Communications; Mothers' Union Enterprises – Mothers' Union trading company. **Activities** Religious activities; events/meetings; training/education; projects/programmes. **Events** *General Meeting* Nottingham (UK) 2015, *General Meeting* Belfast (UK) 2014, *General Meeting* Bath (UK) 2013, *General Meeting* Honduras 2012, *General Meeting* Llandudno (UK) 2012. **Publications** *Families First* (6 a year) – magazine; *Families Worldwide* – members' supplement. Annual Review.

Members Individuals (4 million) in 81 countries and territories:
Angola, Anguilla, Antigua-Barbuda, Argentina, Aruba, Australia, Barbados, Belgium, Belize, Botswana, Brazil, Burundi, Cameroon, Canada, Canaries, Congo Brazzaville, Congo DR, Cyprus, Dominica, Egypt, England, Eswatini, Ethiopia, Finland, France, Gambia, Germany, Ghana, Grenada, Guinea, Guyana, India, Iraq, Ireland, Isle of Man, Italy, Jamaica, Kenya, Korea Rep, Lesotho, Madagascar, Malawi, Malta, Mauritius, Montserrat, Mozambique, Myanmar, Namibia, Netherlands, New Zealand, Nigeria, Papua New Guinea, Peru, Philippines, Rwanda, Scotland, Seychelles, Sierra Leone, Solomon Is, South Africa, Spain, Sri Lanka, St Kitts-Nevis, St Lucia, St Martin, St Vincent-Grenadines, Sudan, Suriname, Switzerland, Tanzania UR, Thailand, Tonga, Trinidad-Tobago, Uganda, Uruguay, USA, Vanuatu, Wales, Zambia, Zimbabwe.

Consultative Status Consultative status granted from: *ECOSOC (#05331)* (Special). **NGO Relations** Member of: *Conference of Non-Governmental Organizations in Consultative Relationship with the United Nations (CONGO, #04635); Crisis Action (#04957); International Anglican Family Network (IAFN, see: #00827); Jubilee Research (#16158); Partnership for World Mission (PWM); Restored; We Will Speak Out (WWSO).* [2015.06.01/XF4834/v/F]

♦ Motion Picture Association (internationally oriented national body)
♦ Motion Picture Export Association / see Motion Picture Association
♦ **MOTO** Mezdunarodnoe Obscestvo po Termiceskoj Obrabotke i Tehnologij Obrabotki Poverhnosti (#13443)
♦ Motorcycle Industry in Europe (#02450)
♦ MOTS – Miedzynarodowa Organizacja Terminologii Specjalistycznej (no recent information)
♦ MOTT / see International Tree Foundation

♦ Mountain Forum (MF) 16861

Chief Dir c/o CONDESAN, Av La Molina 1895, La Molina, Lima, Peru. T. +5116189400. E-mail: condesan@condesan.org.
Twitter: https://twitter.com/Mountain_Forum

History Founded 1995, originating from events following the UN Conference on Environment and Development (UNCED), 1992, in Rio de Janeiro (Brazil), where Chapter 13 of *Global Action Plan for Environment and Development in the 21st Century (Agenda 21, inactive)* – "Fragile Ecosystems – Sustainable Mountain Development" was endorsed. Activities commenced, Jan 1996. **Aims** Promote global action toward equitable and *ecologically sustainable* mountain development through information sharing, mutual support and advocacy. **Structure** A global network of regional networks, articulated by Global Node, hosted by *Consortium for the Sustainable Development of the Andean Ecoregion (#04758)*. Nodes: *African Mountain Forum (no recent information); Asia Pacific Mountain Network (APMN, #01958); European Mountain Forum (EMF, #07824); Latin American Network on Andean Mountains (INfoAndina, #16350).* **Languages** English, French, Russian, Spanish. **Staff** 12-15, located in 6 satellite offices around the world. **Finance** Supported by: *Swiss Agency for Development and Cooperation (SDC).* **Activities** Networking/liaising; capacity building; advocacy/lobbying/activism; politics/policy/regulatory; training/education; events/meetings; knowledge management/information dissemination. **Members** Individuals (4,078). Membership countries not specified. **IGO Relations** Participating organizations include: *FAO (#09260); Inter-American Development Bank (IDB, #11427);*

International Development Research Centre (IDRC, #13162); International Fund for Agricultural Development (IFAD, #13692); Swiss Agency for Development and Cooperation (SDC); UNEP (#20299); UNESCO (#20322). **NGO Relations** Participating organizations include: *Albertine Rift Conservation Society (ARCOS, #00620); Consortium for the Sustainable Development of the Andean Ecoregion (#04758); Earth Council Alliance (ECA, inactive); Euromontana (#05737); International Centre for Alpine Environments (ICALPE, no recent information); International Centre for Integrated Mountain Development (ICIMOD, #12500); International Cultural Resources Institute, Santa Fé (ICRI, no recent information); International Mountain Laboratory (no recent information); International Potato Center (#14627); International Union for Conservation of Nature and Natural Resources (IUCN, #15766); Mountain Partnership (MP, #16862); World Agroforestry Centre (ICRAF, #21072); World Mountain People Association (WMPA, #21658).* [2017/XF3653/F]

- ♦ Mountain Gorilla and Rainforest Direct Aid (internationally oriented national body)
- ♦ Mountain Institute, The (internationally oriented national body)

♦ Mountain Partnership (MP) 16862

Partenariat de la montagne – Alianza para las Montañas

Contact FAO – Forestry Division, Viale delle Terme di Caracalla, 00153 Rome RM, Italy. E-mail: info@mountainpartnership.org.

URL: http://www.fao.org/mountain-partnership/

History 2002. Founded at the World Summit for Sustainable Development, as a Type 2 outcome. A *United Nations (UN, #20515)* voluntary alliance of partners. **Aims** Improve the lives of mountain peoples; protect mountain environments around the world. **Structure** Steering Committee; Secretariat, hosted by *FAO (#09260).* **Languages** English, French, Spanish. **Staff** 8.00 FTE, paid. **Finance** Secretariat supported by the governments of Italy and Switzerland. **Activities** Advocacy/lobbying/activism; awareness raising; capacity building; events/meetings; knowledge management/information dissemination; networking/liaising; projects/programmes. **Events** *Global Meeting* Rome (Italy) 2017, *Global Meeting* Mbale (Uganda) 2016, *Global Meeting* Erzurum (Turkey) 2013, *Global Meeting* Rio de Janeiro (Brazil) 2012, *Global Meeting* Cusco (Peru) 2004. **Publications** *Peak to Peak* (12 a year) – newsletter. *Mountain farming systems – Seeds for the future. Sustainable agricultural practices for resilient mountain livelihoods* (2021) in English; *Mountain tourism – Towards a more sustainable path* (2021) in English; *Vulnerability of mountain peoples to food insecurity: updated data and analysis of drivers* (2020) in English. Key publications; policy briefs; reports; basic documents.

Members Governments (60); IGOs (18); major groups from civil society, NGOs and the private sector (340); sub-national authorities (8). Governments of 60 countries:

Afghanistan, Algeria, Andorra, Argentina, Armenia, Austria, Bangladesh, Bhutan, Bolivia, Burundi, Cameroon, Chile, Colombia, Congo DR, Costa Rica, Cuba, Dominican Rep, Ecuador, Ethiopia, France, Georgia, Ghana, Guatemala, Guinea, India, Indonesia, Iran Islamic Rep, Italy, Jamaica, Jordan, Kenya, Kyrgyzstan, Lesotho, Liechtenstein, Madagascar, Malawi, Mexico, Monaco, Morocco, Nepal, North Macedonia, Pakistan, Papua New Guinea, Peru, Philippines, Romania, Russia, Serbia, Slovakia, Slovenia, Spain, Sri Lanka, Switzerland, Togo, Tunisia, Türkiye, Uganda, Ukraine, Venezuela, Yemen.

Intergovernmental organizations (16):

African Ministerial Conference on the Environment (AMCEN, #00374); Convention for the Protection of the Alps (Alpine convention, 1991); Convention on the Protection and Sustainable Development of the Carpathians (Carpathian convention, 2003); FAO (#09260); International Bank for Reconstruction and Development (IBRD, #12317) (World Bank); *International Centre for Integrated Mountain Development (ICIMOD, #12500); International Union for Conservation of Nature and Natural Resources (IUCN, #15766); Secretariat of the Convention on Biological Diversity (SCBD, #19197); Secretariat of the United Nations Convention to Combat Desertification (Secretariat of the UNCCD, #19208); Tropical Agriculture Research and Higher Education Center (#20246); UNDP (#20292); UNEP (#20299); UNESCO (#20322); Union for the Mediterranean (UfM, #20457); United Nations Population Fund (UNFPA, #20612); United Nations University (UNU, #20642).*

Major Groups, including 47 organizations listed in this Yearbook:

- *African Conservation Foundation (ACF);*
- *Albertine Rift Conservation Society (ARCOS, #00620);*
- *Alliance of Central Asian Mountain Communities (AGOCA, #00662);*
- *American Councils for International Education (ACTR-ACCELS);*
- *Arctic and Mountain Regions Development Institute (AMRDI);*
- *Aspen International Mountain Foundation (AIMF);*
- *Balkan Foundation for Sustainable Development (BFSD);*
- *Central-Asian Institute for Applied Geosciences (CAIAG);*
- *Centre for Development and Environment, Bern (CDE);*
- *Centre for Mountain Studies;*
- *Centro Cientifico Tropical, Costa Rica (CCT);*
- *CIHEAM – International Centre for Advanced Mediterranean Agronomic Studies (CIHEAM, #03927);*
- *CIPRA International (#03930);*
- *Consortium for the Sustainable Development of the Andean Ecoregion (#04758);*
- *Ecological Tourism in Europe (ÖTE);*
- *Euromontana (#05737);*
- *European Academy of Bozen/Bolzano (EURAC);*
- *European Association of Elected Representatives from Mountain Regions (#06021);*
- *European Mountain Forum (EMF, #07824);*
- *Ev-K2-CNR Committee (#16175);*
- *Fundación Agreste;*
- *Global Mountain Action (GMA);*
- *Global Mountain Biodiversity Assessment (GMBA, #10477);*
- *Indigenous Peoples' International Centre for Policy Research and Education (Tebtebba Foundation);*
- *International Alliance of Mountain Film (#11632);*
- *International Centre of Insect Physiology and Ecology (ICIPE, #12499);*
- *International Council for Game and Wildlife Conservation (#13024);*
- *International Livestock Research Institute (ILRI, #14062);*
- *International Potato Center (#14627);*
- *International Scientific Committee on Research in the Alps (ISCAR, #14804);*
- *International Union for Conservation of Nature and Natural Resources (IUCN, #15766);*
- *Millennium Institute;*
- *Mountain Forum (MF, #16861);*
- *Mountain Institute, The (TMI);*
- *Mountain Research Initiative (MRI, #16863);*
- *New World Hope Organization (NWHO);*
- *Positive Planet International (#18465);*
- *Practical Action (#18475);*
- *Regional Environmental Centre for Central Asia (CAREC);*
- *Regional Environmental Centre for the Caucasus (REC Caucasus, #18781);*
- *Union internationale des associations d'alpinisme (UIAA, #20420);*
- *University of Central Asia (UCA, #20698);*
- *Women Organizing for Change in Agriculture and Natural Resource Management (WOCAN);*
- *World Economic Forum (WEF, #21367);*
- *World Mountain People Association (WMPA, #21658);*
- *World Wide Fund for Nature (WWF, #21922);*
- *Yachay Wasi (#21970).*

NGO Relations Cooperates with (1): *Mountain Forum (MF, #16861).* Supports (1): *Asia Pacific Mountain Network (APMN, #01958).* Instrumental in setting up (1): *Coalition of Fragile Ecosystems (COFE).* [2022.05.10/XJ0537/y/F]

♦ Mountain Research Initiative (MRI) 16863

Exec Dir Mittelstrasse 43, 3012 Bern, Switzerland. E-mail: mri@mountainresearchinitiative.org.

URL: https://www.mountainresearchinitiative.org/

History 1 Jul 2001, Bern (Switzerland). **Aims** Promote basic and applied research to understand how drivers and processes of global change present challenges and opportunities in mountain social-ecological systems. **Structure** Governing Body is constituted by MRI Board (Chair and Co-Principle Investigators), Science Leadership Council and Executive Director; *Mountain Research Initiative (MRI, #16863);* Coordination Office. **Staff** 4.00 FTE, paid. **Finance** Sources: government support; in-kind support; international organizations; revenue from activities/projects. Supported by: Principality of Leichtenstein; SUDAC; Swiss Academy of Sciences; *Swiss Agency for Development and Cooperation (SDC);* University of Bern. **Activities** Knowledge management/information dissemination; networking/liaising; projects/programmes. **Events** *Conference on Mountains of Our Future Earth* Perth (Scotland) 2015, *Key Contact Workshop* Vienna (Austria) 2014. **Publications** *MRI Global Newsletter* (12 a year). Abstracts; articles; policy briefs; reports. **Members** Membership countries not specified. **IGO Relations** Partner of (1): *UNEP (#20299).* Participating organizations: *Global Terrestrial Observing System (GTOS, #10626); Programme on Man and the Biosphere (MAB, #18526).* Participating Organisation of: *Group on Earth Observations (GEO, #10735).* **NGO Relations** Member of (1): *Mountain Partnership (MP, #16862).* Partner of (3): *Belmont Forum (#03197); Future Earth (#10048); ISC World Data System (ISC-WDS, #16024).* [2022.10.19/XF7099/F]

- ♦ Mountbatten Centre for International Studies (internationally oriented national body)
- ♦ Mount Carmel International Training Centre for Community Development / see Golda Meir Mount Carmel International Training Centre
- ♦ Mount Sinai International Seminary (see: #21330)
- ♦ Mouvement Africain des Enfants et Jeunes Travailleurs (unconfirmed)
- ♦ Mouvement africaine Vineyard Europe (see: #20778)
- ♦ Mouvement pour une alternative non-violente (internationally oriented national body)
- ♦ Mouvement un pour cent tiers monde / see ActionAid France – Peuples Solidaires
- ♦ Mouvement pour la chambre des beaux arts de Méditerranée / see European Cultural Network for Development Cooperation (#06869)
- ♦ Mouvement des citoyens du monde (inactive)
- ♦ Mouvement du Congrès mondial de la Jeunesse (inactive)
- ♦ Mouvement contre le racisme et pour l'amitié entre les peuples (internationally oriented national body)
- ♦ Mouvement contre le racisme, l'antisémitisme et pour la paix / see Movement Against Racism and for Friendship between Peoples
- ♦ Mouvement démocratique européen pour la santé mentale (#06899)
- ♦ Mouvement pour le désarmement, la paix et la liberté (internationally oriented national body)
- ♦ Mouvement pour le développement mondial / see Global Justice Now
- ♦ Mouvement pour le développement rural en Afrique (#00447)
- ♦ Mouvement d'étudiants de l'Organisation commune africaine et malgache (inactive)
- ♦ Mouvement des étudiants pour l'unité africaine (inactive)
- ♦ Mouvement Eucharistique des Jeunes (religious order)
- ♦ Mouvement européen / see European Movement International (#07825)
- ♦ Mouvement européen du fair play (#07025)
- ♦ Mouvement européen des familles et couples binationaux / see Verband Binationaler Familien und Partnerschaften
- ♦ Mouvement européen international (#07825)
- ♦ Mouvement Europe et laïcité (internationally oriented national body)
- ♦ Mouvement pour l'Europe des nations et des libertés (#16870)
- ♦ Mouvement de l'eveil spirituel intérieur (internationally oriented national body)
- ♦ Mouvement familial chrétien / see International Confederation of Christian Family Movements (#12851)
- ♦ Mouvement des familles nouvelles (#17085)
- ♦ Mouvement fédéraliste mondial (#21404)
- ♦ Mouvement des fédéralistes européens (inactive)
- ♦ Mouvement pour la fédération des Amériques (inactive)
- ♦ Mouvement des Focolari (#09806)
- ♦ Mouvement de la Franc-maçonnerie (#16593)
- ♦ Mouvement humanité nouvelle / see New Humanity (#17088)
- ♦ Mouvement intégraliste (inactive)
- ♦ Mouvement international (inactive)
- ♦ Mouvement international d'action pour la paix (inactive)
- ♦ Mouvement International d'Aide à l'Enfance (internationally oriented national body)
- ♦ Mouvement international d'apostolat des enfants (#14192)

♦ Mouvement international d'apostolat des milieux sociaux indépendants (MIAMSI) 16864

International Movement for the Apostolate in the Independent Social Milieux – Movimiento Internacional de Apostolado en los Medios Sociales Independientes

Secretariat MIAMSI, Piazza San Calisto 16, 00153 Rome RM, Italy. T. +39669887183. E-mail: miamsi.rome@gmail.com.

URL: http://www.miamsi-rome.org/

History Founded 3 Oct 1963, when officially recognized as an international catholic organization by the Holy See. Also referred to as *International Apostolic Movement of the Independent Social Categories.* **Aims** Faithful to the inspiration of a specific apostolate (confirmed by Vatican II), link *faith* and every day life and release people from their solitude or self-imposed isolation so that dialogue becomes possible for them, thus giving them the potential of spreading the Good News. **Structure** General Assembly (every 4 years); International Bureau; Secretariat. **Languages** English, French, Spanish. **Finance** Members' dues. Other sources: grants; donations. **Activities** Religious activities; networking/liaising; projects/programmes; events/meetings. **Events** *Quadrennial General Assembly* Fortaleza (Brazil) 2012, *Quadrennial General Assembly* St Julian's (Malta) 2008, *Quadrennial General Assembly* Antananarivo (Madagascar) 2004, *Quadrennial General Assembly* Fiuggi (Italy) 2000, *Quadrennial General Assembly* Guadalajara (Mexico) 1996. **Publications** *MIAMSI Echo* (3-4 a year) in English, French, Spanish.

Members National apostolic movements (members) in 34 countries and territories:

Algeria, Argentina, Belgium, Benin, Bolivia, Brazil, Burkina Faso, Canada, Chile, Colombia, Congo DR, Ecuador, France, India, Italy, Lebanon, Madagascar, Malaysia, Mali, Malta, Mauritius, Mexico, Morocco, Niger, Paraguay, Peru, Portugal, Réunion, Seychelles, Spain, Switzerland, Uruguay, USA, Venezuela.

Associate members in 3 countries:

Costa Rica, Luxembourg, Panama.

Consultative Status Consultative status granted from: *ECOSOC (#05331)* (Special); *Council of Europe (CE, #04881)* (Participatory Status). **NGO Relations** Member of: *Crescendo Worldwide Network (#04950); Forum of Catholic Inspired NGOs (#09905); International Catholic Centre of Geneva (ICCG, #12449).* [2019/XC4169/F]

- ♦ Mouvement international ATD Quart Monde (#14193)
- ♦ Mouvement international contre toutes les formes de discriminations et le racisme (#14191)
- ♦ Mouvement international de la Croix-Rouge et du Croissant-Rouge (#14707)
- ♦ Mouvement international de cyclistes espérantistes / see International Association of Esperanto-Speaking Cyclists (#11878)
- ♦ Mouvement international des faucons / see International Falcon Movement – Socialist Educational International (#13327)
- ♦ Mouvement international des faucons – Internationale éducative socialiste (#13327)
- ♦ Mouvement international du Graal / see The Grail – International Movement of Christian Women (#10689)
- ♦ Mouvement international du Graal (#10690)

♦ Mouvement international de la jeunesse agricole et rurale catholique (MIJARC) 16865

International Movement of Catholic Agricultural and Rural Youth – Movimiento Internacional de la Juventud Agraria y Rural Católica (MIJARC) – Internationale Katholische Land- und Bauernjugendbewegung – Movimento Internacional da Juventude Agraria e Rural Católica – Movimento Internazionale della Gioventù Agricola e Rural Cattolica – Internationale Beweging van de Katholieke Landelijke Jeugd en Boerenjeugd

Pres Rue J Coosemans 53, 1030 Brussels, Belgium. T. +3227349211. Fax +3227339225. E-mail: world@mijarc.net.

URL: http://www.mijarcworld.net/

History Oct 1954, Annevoie (Belgium). Founded by the national rural Catholic movements of seven nations. Recognized as an International Catholic Organization (OIC) by the Holy See: 1966; 1985. Statutes modified: 1974, Hübingen (Germany FR); 1980, Natoye (Belgium); 1992, Olinda (Brazil); 2 Nov 1996, Chennai (India); 18 Aug 2004, Paderborn (Germany); 2012, Sri Lanka. Registration: Belgium. **Aims** Bring together Catholic and rural youth developmental organizations working on agricultural and rural youth development (economically, politically and socially) in accordance with the spirit of *Christian* fraternity and invite them to common action while respecting their autonomy; encourage new models of rural and agricultural development based on the Christian spirit; promote training and integrated education of rural youth; represent members' interests in public fora and various international institutions and organizations. **Structure** General Assembly (every 4 years); World Coordination; World Team; Secretariat. World Commissions (4): Food Sovereignty; Solidarity Economy; Women; Youth Partnership. Regions (4): Africa; Asia; *MIJARC Europe (#16803)*; Latin America. **Languages** English, French, Spanish. **Staff** 0.50 FTE, paid; 4.00 FTE, voluntary. **Finance** Sources: donations; grants; members' dues. **Activities** Advocacy/lobbying/activism; awareness raising; networking/liaising; projects/programmes; training/education. **Events** *Quadrennial General Assembly* Peru 2012, *Quadrennial General Assembly* Sri Lanka 2012, *Quadrennial General Assembly* Kampala (Uganda) 2008, *Quadrennial General Assembly* Paderborn (Germany) 2004, *Le commerce des produits agricoles et la société civile dans un mode globalisé* Brussels (Belgium) 2002. **Publications** *MIJARC-News* (2 a year) in English, French, Spanish. Congress and General Assembly reports; brochures; posters; campaign material.
Members Affiliated National Movements (39) in 39 countries and territories:
Belgium, Benin, Bolivia, Brazil, Bulgaria, Burkina Faso, Cameroon, Central African Rep, Chad, Congo Brazzaville, Dominican Rep, Ecuador, France, Germany, Guadeloupe, Guatemala, Haiti, Hungary, India, Kenya, Madagascar, Mali, Martinique, Nepal, Nicaragua, Paraguay, Peru, Philippines, Poland, Portugal, Romania, Rwanda, Senegal, Spain, Sri Lanka, Tanzania UR, Togo, Uganda, Zambia.
Consultative Status Consultative status granted from: *ECOSOC (#05331)* (Ros C); *UNESCO (#20322)* (Consultative Status); *ILO (#11123)* (Special List); *FAO (#09260)* (Special Status); *Council of Europe (CE, #04881)* (Participatory Status). **IGO Relations** Contacts with: *International Fund for Agricultural Development (IFAD, #13692)*. Member of: *European Youth Centres (EYCs, #09138)*. **NGO Relations** Member of: *Espacio Iberoamericano de Juventud (EIJ, no recent information)*; *European Youth Forum (#09140)*; *Forum of Catholic Inspired NGOs (#09905)*; *International NGO/CSO Planning Committee for Food Sovereignty (IPC, #14365)*; *La Via Campesina (#20765)*; *More and Better (#16855)*. Close cooperation with: *Alliance Against Hunger and Malnutrition (AAHM, no recent information)*. Supports: *European Citizens' Initiative Campaign (ECI Campaign, #06558)*. [2017.06.01/XB2274/**C**]

- ♦ Mouvement international de jeunesse Mazdaznan (inactive)
- ♦ Mouvement international des juristes catholiques (inactive)
- ♦ Mouvement international pour le loisir scientifique et technique (internationally oriented national body)

♦ Mouvement international pour une nouvelle muséologie (MINOM) . 16866

International Movement for a New Museology – Movimiento Internacional para una Nueva Musicologia – Movimento Internacional para una Nova Museologia

Pres address not obtained. E-mail: geral.minom@gmail.com.
URL: http://www.minom-icom.net/

History 1985, Lisbon (Portugal), during 2nd International Workshop, the movement having been planned in 1983, London (UK). **Aims** Support and develop the practice of new museology; promote social and community museology. **Structure** General Assembly (every 3 years), meeting during International Workshops; Autonomous Regional Groups; Administrative Council; Executive Council; Organizing Committee of the International Workshop. **Finance** Financed by grants and subsidies. **Activities** Events/meetings; networking/liaising. **Events** *International Conference* Brazil 2016, *International Conference* Limavady (UK) 2015, *International Conference* Havana (Cuba) 2014, *International Conference* Cape Verde 2011, *International Conference* Amsterdam (Netherlands) 2010. **Publications** *Nouvelle muséologie: une bibliographie/New Museology: A Bibliography* (1999).
Members Regional chapters in 5 countries:
Brazil, Canada, Mexico, Portugal, Spain.
Individuals (about 300) in 34 countries and territories:
Algeria, Australia, Belgium, Brazil, Canada, Cape Verde, China, Colombia, Cuba, Denmark, Finland, France, Germany, Greece, India, Israel, Italy, Japan, Korea Rep, Latvia, Lithuania, Malaysia, Mali, Mexico, Netherlands, Norway, Pakistan, Philippines, Portugal, Singapore, Spain, Sweden, UK, USA.
IGO Relations *UNESCO (#20322)*. **NGO Relations** Affiliated member of: *International Council of Museums (ICOM, #13051)*. [2022/XF2094/**F**]

- ♦ Mouvement International des Parlementaires pour la Démocratie (see: #21661)
- ♦ Mouvement international de la réconciliation (#13586)
- ♦ Mouvement international pour le service social (internationally oriented national body)
- ♦ Mouvement international pour l'Union Atlantique (inactive)
- ♦ Mouvement international pour l'union fraternelle entre les races et les peuples / see Unis pour l'Equite et la Fin du Racisme (#20490)
- ♦ Mouvement de la jeunesse pour la démocratie (#21957)
- ♦ Mouvement de la Jeunesse Dominicaine International (#13191)
- ♦ Mouvement de la jeunesse européenne (inactive)
- ♦ Mouvement des jeunesses libérales et radicales de l'Union européenne / see European Liberal Youth (#07690)
- ♦ Mouvement latinoaméricain des laïques (internationally oriented national body)
- ♦ Mouvement libéral pour l'Europe unie (inactive)
- ♦ Mouvement pour la libération et le développement / see MOVIMONDO Molisv
- ♦ Mouvement pour la lutte contre la faim dans le monde (internationally oriented national body)
- ♦ Mouvement des mères de Méditerranée (#16663)
- ♦ Mouvement pour un Monde Meilleur / see Movement for a Better World (#16869)
- ♦ Mouvement mondial pour une culture de la paix et de la non violence (see: #20322)
- ♦ Mouvement mondial des mères / see Make Mothers Matter (#16554)
- ♦ Mouvement Mondial des Mères – International / see Make Mothers Matter (#16554)
- ♦ Mouvement mondial des travailleurs chrétiens (#21660)
- ♦ Mouvement nordique de la jeunesse des partis du centre (#17232)
- ♦ Mouvement olympique (#17719)
- ♦ Mouvement pour une organisation mondiale de l'agriculture (internationally oriented national body)

♦ Mouvement de la paix 16867

French Peace Movement

Secretariat 9 rue Dulcie September, 93400 Saint-Ouen, France. T. +33140120912. E-mail: secretariat@mvtpaix.org – national@mvtpaix.org.
URL: http://www.mvtpaix.org/

History 1949. **Publications** *Planète Paix* (10 a year). **NGO Relations** Member of: *International Peace Bureau (IPB, #14535)*. [2018.07.12/XN4910/**D**]

- ♦ Mouvement de la paix intérieure (#11220)
- ♦ Mouvement panafricain de la jeunesse (inactive)
- ♦ Mouvement panafricain de libération pour l'Afrique centrale et orientale (inactive)
- ♦ Mouvement des pays non alignés (#17146)
- ♦ Mouvement raëlien international (#14690)
- ♦ Mouvement des religieux et des religieuses (religious order)
- ♦ Mouvement sacerdotal marial (#16575)
- ♦ Mouvement salésien des jeunes (#19039)
- ♦ Mouvement socialiste européen (no recent information)
- ♦ Mouvement socialiste international de formation (inactive)
- ♦ Mouvement Soufi International (religious order)
- ♦ Mouvement suisse de la paix (internationally oriented national body)
- ♦ Mouvement Thérésien d'Apostolat (religious order)
- ♦ Mouvement des travailleurs chrétiens d'Europe (#06546)
- ♦ Mouvement des travailleurs chrétiens pour l'Europe, 1949 (inactive)
- ♦ Mouvement pour l'union politique mondiale (inactive)
- ♦ Mouvement universel pour une fédération mondiale / see World Federalist Movement – Movement for a Just World Order through a Strengthened United Nations (#21404)
- ♦ Mouvement universel de la responsabilité scientifique (#20679)
- ♦ Mouvement vers une internationale chrétienne (inactive)
- ♦ Mouvement vie et travail (inactive)
- ♦ Movado sen Nomo (internationally oriented national body)
- ♦ MOVD – International Symposium for Mechanisms of Vasodilatation (meeting series)

♦ On the Move (OTM) 16868

SG Saintcetelette Square 19, 1000 Brussels, Belgium. E-mail: mobility@on-the-move.org.
URL: http://on-the-move.org/

History 2002, as a website, by *IETM – International Network for Contemporary Performing Arts (#11098)*, then still called 'Informal European Theatre Meeting'. Developed into an international non-profit, registered in accordance with Belgian law, 2004. Expanded to become *On the Move – network for cultural mobility information*, 2009. **Aims** Encourage and facilitate *cross-border mobility* and cooperation, contributing to building up a vibrant and shared European *cultural* space that is strongly connected worldwide. **Structure** General Assembly; Advisory Board; Secretariat. **Languages** English, French, Italian, Spanish. **Staff** 2.00 FTE, paid. **Finance** Supported by: French Ministry of Culture and Communication; Calouste Gulbenkian Foundation; Korea Arts Management Service; Mission of the People's Republic of China to the EU in Brussels. **Activities** Advocacy/lobbying/activism; capacity building; knowledge management/information dissemination; events/meetings; networking/liaising. **Publications** *On the Move Newsletter* (12 a year). Research dossiers; guides.
Members Organizations (37) in 22 countries. Membership countries not specified. Included in the above, 8 organizations listed in this Yearbook:
ARS BALTICA (#01114); *Asia-Europe Foundation (ASEF, #01270)*; *European Council of Artists (ECA, #06805)*; *IETM – International Network for Contemporary Performing Arts (#11098)*; *INTERARTS Foundation*; *International Federation of Actors (#13337)*; *Theatre Without Borders*; *Trans Europe Halles – A Network of Independent Cultural Centres (TEH, #20211)*. [2014.06.03/XJ5800/y/**F**]

- ♦ **MoveAbility** ICRC MoveAbility Foundation (#11087)
- ♦ Movement for the Abolition of War (internationally oriented national body)
- ♦ Movement Against Atomic Arms, for Peace by Disengagement and Disarmament / see Movement for Disarmament, Peace and Liberty
- ♦ Movement Against Racism and for Friendship between Peoples (internationally oriented national body)

♦ Movement for a Better World (MBW) 16869

Service pour un Monde Meilleur (SMM) – Movimiento por un Mundo Mejor (MMM) – Movimento per un Mondo Migliore (MMM)

SG Via Monte Altissimo 23, 00141 Rome RM, Italy. T. +3968185678. Fax +3968185678. E-mail: mondo.migliore@iol.it.
Representative to the UN address not obtained.

History 10 Feb 1952, Rome (Italy). Founded by Fr Riccardo Lombardi, following a speech by Pope Pius XII. The Holy See approved the creation of a permanent core group in 1965. Former names and other names: *Mouvement pour un Monde Meilleur (MMM)* – former. **Aims** Promote the *spirituality* of relationships and processes of *communitarian* renewal/transformation, for a *church* of communion at the service of the renewal of society in universal sister/brotherhood. **Structure** Core group constitutes an international union of persons belonging to every religious category: priests; members of religious orders and lay institutes; lay persons. **Languages** English, French, Italian, Spanish. **Staff** 345.00 FTE, paid. **Activities** Events/meetings; networking/liaising; training/education. **Events** *Latin-Europe meeting* Belgium 1989, *Canada-USA-Caribbean meeting* Montreal, QC (Canada) 1989, *Meeting* Rome (Italy) 1989, *Pan Asiatic meeting* Singapore (Singapore) 1989, *North Europe meeting* Switzerland 1989. **Publications** *Sharing* (2 a year) in English, French, Italian, Spanish. *Chiese in divenire* in Italian; *Edificarsi insieme come popolo di Dio* in Italian, Spanish – English and French private editions; *Evangelisation: the Task of Someone or the Experience of All ?* in English, French, Italian, Spanish; *Exercises for a Better World* in English, French, Italian, Spanish; *Family in Continuing Formation* in English, French, Italian, Spanish; *From a Crowd to the People of God* in English, French, Italian, Spanish; *History Challenges the Church* in English, French, Italian, Spanish; *Local Church: Communion and Structures* in English, French, Italian, Spanish; *Making Sense of Life* in English, French, Italian, Spanish; *Parish Youth Movement* in English, French, Italian, Spanish; *The Justice Whose Fruit is Peace* in English, French, Italian, Spanish.
Members Individuals in 34 countries and territories:
Argentina, Australia, Austria, Belarus, Belgium, Brazil, Burkina Faso, Cameroon, Canada, Chile, Colombia, Congo DR, Côte d'Ivoire, Czechia, Dominican Rep, Ecuador, France, India, Italy, Korea Rep, Malawi, Mexico, Papua New Guinea, Peru, Philippines, Poland, Portugal, Puerto Rico, Solomon Is, South Africa, Spain, USA, Venezuela, Zimbabwe.
Consultative Status Consultative status granted from: *ECOSOC (#05331)* (Special). [2020.04.29/XD0160/v/**F**]

- ♦ Movement of Christian Workers for Europe, 1949 (inactive)
- ♦ Movement of Colonial Freedom / see Liberation
- ♦ Movement for Disarmament, Peace and Liberty (internationally oriented national body)
- ♦ Movement Disorder Society / see International Parkinson and Movement Disorder Society (#14515)
- ♦ Movement of European Federalists (inactive)

♦ Movement for a Europe of Nations and Freedom (MENF) 16870

Mouvement pour l'Europe des nations et des libertés (MENL)

Pres Rue Wiertz 60, 1047 Brussels, Belgium.
URL: http://www.menleuropa.eu/

History 2014, succeeding *European Alliance for Freedom (EAF)*.
Members National parties of 5 countries:
Austria, Belgium, Czechia, France, Italy.
NGO Relations *Europe of Nations and Freedom Group (ENF, #09163)*. [2018/XM4323/**F**]

- ♦ Movement for the Federation of the Americas (inactive)
- ♦ Movement for the Fight Against World Hunger (internationally oriented national body)
- ♦ Movement of Non-Aligned Countries / see Coordinating Bureau of the Non-Aligned Countries (#04815)
- ♦ Movement of Non-Aligned Countries / see Non-Aligned Movement (#17146)
- ♦ Movement for a Nonviolent Alternative (internationally oriented national body)
- ♦ Movement for Peace, Disarmament and Freedom (internationally oriented national body)
- ♦ Movement for Political World Union (inactive)
- ♦ Movement of Religious Men and Women (religious order)
- ♦ Movement of Spiritual Inner Awareness (internationally oriented national body)
- ♦ Movement towards a Christian International (inactive)

♦ Movendi International 16871

Exec Dir Klara Södra Kyrkogatan 20, SE-111 50 Stockholm, Sweden. T. +46733389397. E-mail: info@movendi.ngo.
URL: https://movendi.ngo/

History Jul 1851, Utica, NY (USA). International Constitution most recently adopted Aug 2018, Sigtuna (Sweden), and Dec 2019. Former names and other names: *IOGT International* – former (2006); *International Organization of Good Templars (IOGT)* – former (1966 to 2006); *Organisation internationale des bons templiers* – former (1966 to 2006); *International Order of Good Templars* – former (1905 to 1966); *Ordre international des bons templiers* – former (1905 to 1966); *Order of Good Templars* – former (1851 to 1905). Registration: EU Transparency Register, No/ID: 100748931218-91, Start date: 16 Apr 2018. **Aims** Unite, strengthen and empower civil society to tackle alcohol and other drugs as serious obstacles to development on personal, community, societal and global level. **Structure** International World Congress (every 4 years); International Board; International Office. *International Good Templar Youth Federation (IGTYF, inactive)*, set up 8 Jul 1962, Oslo (Norway), was disbanded in 1990.From 14 Jul 1990, European IOGT youth associations

and other temperance youth associations in Europe which recognized the IOGT attitude, formed *Active – Sobriety, Friendship and Peace (inactive)*, now inactive. **Languages** English. **Staff** 6.00 FTE, paid; 3.00 FTE, voluntary. **Finance** Sources: donations; grants; members' dues. **Activities** Advocacy/lobbying/activism; awareness raising; knowledge management/information dissemination; projects/programmes. **Events** *World Congress* Stockholm (Sweden) 2022, *World Congress* Stockholm (Sweden) 2018, *World Congress* Hua Hin (Thailand) 2014, *World Congress* Fredrikstad (Norway) 2010, *Alcohol policy workshop* Kuching (Malaysia) 2008. **Publications** *Drink Revolution Update* – newsletter; *Global Alcohol Policy Round-Up* – newsletter.
Members National organizations (over 130) in 56 countries and territories:
Australia, Bangladesh, Bosnia-Herzegovina, Botswana, Burundi, Cambodia, Cameroon, Congo DR, England, Estonia, Finland, Gambia, Georgia, Germany, Ghana, Guinea-Bissau, Iceland, India, Italy, Kenya, Latvia, Lesotho, Liberia, Lithuania, Malawi, Mali, Mexico, Mongolia, Nepal, Nigeria, Norway, Pakistan, Philippines, Poland, Russia, Rwanda, Senegal, Serbia, Sierra Leone, Slovakia, Slovenia, Somalia, South Africa, South Sudan, Sri Lanka, Sweden, Switzerland, Tanzania UR, Thailand, Uganda, UK, Ukraine, USA, Vietnam, Zambia, Zimbabwe.
Consultative Status Consultative status granted from: *ECOSOC (#05331)* (Special); *WHO (#20950)* (Official Relations). **NGO Relations** Member of (5): *European Mutual-Help Network for Alcohol-Related Problems (EMNA, #07843)* (Associate member); *Geneva Global Health Hub (G2H2, #10122)*; *Global Partnership to End Violence Against Children (End Violence Against Children, #10533)*; *The NCD Alliance (NCDA, #16963)*; *Vienna NGO Committee on Drugs (VNGOC, #20773)*. Instrumental in setting up (1): *International Temperance Educational and Cultural Association (ITECA, inactive)*. [2021.07.12/XC2324/**C**]

- ♦ On the Move – network for cultural mobility information / see On the Move (#16868)
- ♦ Movimento Africa 70 / see Africa 70
- ♦ Movimento per l'Autosviluppo, l'Interscambio et la Solidarietà (internationally oriented national body)
- ♦ Movimento ed Azione dei Gesuiti Italiani per lo Sviluppo / see Movimento e Azione dei Gesuiti per lo Sviluppo
- ♦ Movimento e Azione dei Gesuiti per lo Sviluppo (internationally oriented national body)
- ♦ Movimento Eucaristico Giovanile (religious order)
- ♦ Movimento Europeo / see European Movement International (#07825)
- ♦ Movimento Europeo contra el Cancer de Mama (#05745)
- ♦ Movimento Europeo Democratico per la Salute Mentale (#06899)
- ♦ Movimento Europeo d'Opinione contro i Tumori del Seno (#05745)
- ♦ Movimento Famiglie Nuove (#17085)
- ♦ Movimento dei Focolari (#09806)
- ♦ Movimento Giovanile Salesiano (#19039)
- ♦ Movimento Internacional ao Auxilio da Infancia (internationally oriented national body)
- ♦ Movimento Internacional da Juventude Agraria e Rural Católica (#16865)
- ♦ Movimento Internacional para una Nova Museologia (#16866)
- ♦ Movimento Internazionale della Gioventù Agricola e Rurale Cattolica (#16865)
- ♦ Movimento Jovem pela Democracia (#21957)
- ♦ Movimento Laici America Latina (internationally oriented national body)
- ♦ Movimento Leigos América Latina (internationally oriented national body)
- ♦ Movimento Liberazione e Sviluppo / see MOVIMONDO Molisv
- ♦ Movimento per la Lotta contro la Fame nel Mondo (internationally oriented national body)
- ♦ Movimento per un Mondo Migliore (#16869)
- ♦ Movimento Mundial dos Trabalhadores Cristãos (#21660)
- ♦ Movimento Panafricano da Juventude (inactive)
- ♦ Movimento dei Religiosi e delle Religiose (religious order)
- ♦ Movimento Sacerdotal Mariano (#16575)
- ♦ Movimento della Sinistra Europea (no recent information)
- ♦ Movimento Sviluppo e Pace (internationally oriented national body)
- ♦ Movimento Umanità Nuova / see New Humanity (#17088)
- ♦ Movimiento Africano das Crianças e Jovens Trabalhadores (unconfirmed)

♦ Movimiento Agroecológico para Latinoamérica y El Caribe (MAELA) 16872

Latin American and Caribbean Agro-Ecological Movement

Contact address not obtained. E-mail: cafefemcafe@gmail.com – webmaela@gmail.com.
URL: https://maela.org/

History 1992, Sao Paulo (Brazil). Also referred to in English as *Latin American Agro-Ecological Movement*. **Aims** Coordinate peasant organizations of small and medium farmers, indigenous communities, landless, rural women and youth, consumers, universities and social organizations. **Structure** Assembly of delegates from 4 regions: Southern Cone; Central America/Caribbean; Amazonia; Andes. **Events** *Meeting* Colombia 1998, *Assembly* Coro (Venezuela) 1995, *Latin American conference on sustainable agriculture* Coro (Venezuela) 1995, *Meeting* Venezuela 1995, *Meeting* Sao Paulo (Brazil) 1992. **Publications** *Hoja a Hoja* (12 a year) – bulletin.
Members in 14 countries:
Argentina, Bolivia, Brazil, Chile, Colombia, Costa Rica, Ecuador, Guatemala, Honduras, Mexico, Nicaragua, Paraguay, Peru, Uruguay, Venezuela.
NGO Relations Member of: *International NGO/CSO Planning Committee for Food Sovereignty (IPC, #14365)*. Member of the Coordinating Committee of: *More and Better (#16855)*. [2019/XF2911/**F**]

- ♦ Movimiento contra el Racismo y por la Amistad entre los Pueblos (internationally oriented national body)
- ♦ Movimiento Estudiantil Cristiano / see World Student Christian Federation (#21833)
- ♦ Movimiento Eucaristico Juvenil (religious order)
- ♦ Movimiento Familiar Cristiano / see International Confederation of Christian Family Movements (#12851)
- ♦ Movimiento pro Federación Americana (inactive)
- ♦ Movimiento Internacional de Apostolado en los Medios Sociales Independientes (#16864)
- ♦ Movimiento Internacional de Apostolado de los Niños (#14192)
- ♦ Movimiento Internacional ATD Cuarto Mundo (#14193)
- ♦ Movimiento Internacional para Ayudar a la Infancia (internationally oriented national body)
- ♦ Movimiento Internacional de la Cruz Roja y de la Media Luna Roja (#14707)
- ♦ Movimiento Internacional de la Juventud Agraria y Rural Católica (#16865)
- ♦ Movimiento Internacional de Reconciliación (#13586)
- ♦ Movimiento Internacional de Recreo Scientifico y Tecnológico (internationally oriented national body)
- ♦ Movimiento Internacional para una Nueva Musicologia (#16866)
- ♦ Movimiento Juvenil para la Democracia (#21957)
- ♦ Movimiento Juvenil Dominicano Internacional (#13191)
- ♦ Movimiento Juvenil Salesiano (#19039)
- ♦ Movimiento Laicos América Latina (internationally oriented national body)
- ♦ Movimiento Liberal Europeo (inactive)
- ♦ Movimiento Mundial por los Bosques Tropicales (#21745)

♦ Movimiento Mundial por la Infancia de Latinoamérica y El Caribe (MMI-LAC) 16873

Address not obtained.
URL: http://www.movimientoporlainfancia.org/

Aims Promote, protect and defend human *rights* of children and *adolescents* in the region.
Members Permanent members (12):
Child Helpline International (CHI, #03870); *Defence for Children International (DCI, #05025)*; *End Child Prostitution, Child Pornography and Trafficking of Children for Sexual Purposes (ECPAT, #05456)*; *Inter-American Children's Institute (IACI, #11406)*; *Plan International (#18386)*; Red ANDI Internacional; *Red Latinoamericana y Caribeña por la Defensa de los Derechos de los Niños, Niñas y Adolescentes (REDLAMYC, #18705)*; *Save the Children International (#19058)*; *SOS-Kinderdorf International (#19693)*; *UNICEF (#20332)*; *World Alliance of Young Men's Christian Associations (YMCA, #21090)*; *World Vision International (WVI, #21904)*.
Observers (3):
Fondazione Marista per la Solidarietà Internazionale Onlus (#09831); *International Centre for Missing and Exploited Children (ICMEC, #12505)*; Viva, Juntos por la Niñez. [2017/XM6763/y/**F**]

- ♦ Movimiento Mundial de las Madres / see Make Mothers Matter (#16554)
- ♦ Movimiento Mundial de Trabajadores Cristianos (#21660)
- ♦ Movimiento por un Mundo Mejor (#16869)
- ♦ Movimiento de Paises No Alineados (#17146)
- ♦ Movimiento por la Paz, el Desarme y la Libertad (internationally oriented national body)
- ♦ Movimiento Sacerdotal Mariano (#16575)
- ♦ Movimiento para la Salud de los Pueblos (#18305)
- ♦ Movimiento del Sendero Interno del Alma (internationally oriented national body)
- ♦ Movimiento Siervos de los Pobres del Tercer Mundo (religious order)
- ♦ Movimiento Teresiano de Apostolado (religious order)
- ♦ Movimiento de Trabajadores Christianos de Europa (#06546)
- ♦ MOVIMONDO Molisv (internationally oriented national body)

♦ MOVING International Road Safety Association (MOVING) 16874

Association Internationale de Sécurité Routière

Pres Schumannstrasse 17, 10117 Berlin, Germany. T. +493025741670. Fax +493025741671. E-mail: info@moving-roadsafety.com.
Contact address not obtained.
URL: http://www.moving-roadsafety.com/

History Registration: Berlin District Court, No/ID: VR 31089, Start date: 13 Dec 2011, Germany, Berlin; EU Transparency Register, No/ID: 258032041139-48, Start date: 29 Jan 2021. **Aims** Promote education and accident prevention in the fields of road safety, traffic safety education and training, including associated training and testing procedures in Europe and worldwide. **Structure** General Assembly; Executive Board; Management. **Languages** English, German. **Staff** 2.00 FTE, paid. **Finance** Sources: members' dues. **Events** *General Assembly* Berlin (Germany) 2013, *General Assembly* Berlin (Germany) 2012. **Publications** *Chart of the Month* (12 a year); *German Driving School Industry Report* (every 2 years); *MOVING Newsletter*. Surveys; press releases.
Members Full; Associate; Honorary. Members in 7 countries:
Austria, Bulgaria, France, Germany, Italy, Spain, Switzerland.
IGO Relations German Federal Ministry of Transport and Digital Infrastructure. **NGO Relations** Member of (2): *European Transport Safety Council (ETSC, #08940)*; *International Commission for Driver Testing (CIECA, #12678)*. [2022.05.11/XJ7934/**D**]

- ♦ **MOVING** MOVING International Road Safety Association (#16874)
- ♦ Movin'On Sustainable Mobility Fund (internationally oriented national body)
- ♦ **MOWCA** Maritime Organization of West and Central Africa (#16582)
- ♦ Moyabi Short Wave International Centre (no recent information)
- ♦ Moynihan Institute of Global Affairs (internationally oriented national body)
- ♦ Mozambican Health Committee / see Health Alliance International
- ♦ Mozambique-Tanzania Centre for Foreign Relations / see Centre for Foreign Relations
- ♦ Mozilla Foundation (internationally oriented national body)
- ♦ MOZ – Mezdunarodnaja Organizacija Zurnalistov (inactive)

♦ MPact Global Action for Gay Men's Health and Rights (MPact) 16875

Exec Dir 4096 Piedmont Avenue, Suite 720, Oakland CA 94611, USA. T. +15108495311. E-mail: contact@mpactglobal.org.
URL: https://mpactglobal.org/

History 2006. Former names and other names: *Global Forum on MSM & HIV (MSMGF)* – former (2017). **Aims** Advocate for equitable access to effective HIV prevention, care, treatment, and support services for *gay* men and other men who have sex with men (MSM), including gay men and MSM living with HIV, while promoting their health and human rights worldwide. **Structure** Board of Directors; Steering Committee. **Staff** 10.00 FTE, paid. **Finance** Support from: Dutch Government; corporations; organizations, including: *Global Fund to Fight AIDS, Tuberculosis and Malaria (Global Fund, #10383)*; *Elton John AIDS Foundation (EJAF)*; *Humanistisch Instituut voor Ontwikkelingssamenwerking (Hivos)*; *United Nations Population Fund (UNFPA, #20612)*. **Events** *Biennial Conference* Vienna (Austria) 2010. **Members** Individuals; organizations. Membership countries not specified. **NGO Relations** Member of (2): *Council for Global Equality*; *ILGA World (International Lesbian, Gay, Bisexual, Trans and Intersex Association, #11120)*. Participates in: *HIV Young Leaders Fund (HYLF, no recent information)*. Cooperates with: *AIDS Foundation East-West (AFEW)*; *Eurasian Coalition on Male Health (ECOM, #05603)*; *Global Action for Trans Equality (GATE, #10169)*; *Global Developmental Corps (GDC)*; *Global Research and Advocacy Group (GRAG, #10569)*; *International AIDS Empowerment (IAE)*; *Islands of Southeast Asian Network on Male and Transgender Sexual Health (ISEAN, #16063)*; *Naz Foundation International*; *Share-Net International*. [2021/XJ9365/**F**]

- ♦ **MPact** MPact Global Action for Gay Men's Health and Rights (#16875)
- ♦ **MPA** Millennium Promise Alliance (#16806)
- ♦ MPA – Motion Picture Association (internationally oriented national body)
- ♦ **MPA SNG** Mezparlamentskaja Assambleja Gosudarstv Ucastnikov Sodruzestva Nezavissimyh Gosudarstv (#15958)
- ♦ MpBC Global Alliance – Metaplastic Breast Cancer Global Alliance (unconfirmed)
- ♦ MPC – Mediterranean Policy Centre (internationally oriented national body)
- ♦ **MPC** Mocidade por Cristo (#22009)
- ♦ MPDL – Movimiento por la Paz, el Desarme y la Libertad (internationally oriented national body)
- ♦ **MPE** Metal Packaging Europe (#16736)
- ♦ **MPE** Mobility for Prosperity in Europe (#16839)
- ♦ **MPE** Myeloma Patients Europe (#16924)
- ♦ MPEVH – Maison du Peuple d'Europe (internationally oriented national body)
- ♦ MPFA – Movimiento pro Federación Americana (inactive)
- ♦ MPF – Maîtresses Pieuses Filippini (religious order)
- ♦ MPF – Muslim Peace Fellowship (internationally oriented national body)
- ♦ MPFPR – Max Planck Foundation for International Peace and the Rule of Law (internationally oriented national body)
- ♦ MPFSEE / see South-Eastern Europe Brigade (#19808)
- ♦ MPG – Max-Planck-Gesellschaft zur Förderung der Wissenschaften (internationally oriented national body)
- ♦ **MPG** Migration Policy Group (#16801)
- ♦ **MPG** Music Producers Guild (#16914)
- ♦ **MPHRP** Maritime Piracy Humanitarian Response Programme (#16583)
- ♦ MPI@LHC – International Workshop on Multiple Partonic Interactions at the LHC (meeting series)
- ♦ MPI – Martin Institute for Peace Studies and Conflict Resolution (internationally oriented national body)
- ♦ **MPI** Meeting Professionals International (#16695)
- ♦ **MPI** Middle Powers Initiative (#16795)
- ♦ MPI – Migration Policy Institute (internationally oriented national body)
- ♦ MPJ – Mouvement panafricain de la jeunesse (inactive)
- ♦ MPJ – Movimento Panafricano da Juventude (inactive)
- ♦ MPK po VT – Mezpravitelstvennaja Komissija po Sotrudnicestvu Socialisticeskih Stran v Oblasti Vycislitelnoj Tehniki (inactive)
- ♦ MPLS and Frame Relay Alliance / see Broadband Forum (#03334)
- ♦ MPM / see BBC Media Action
- ♦ MPMF / see Multilateral Fund for the Implementation of the Montreal Protocol (#16885)
- ♦ **MP** The Millennium Project (#16805)
- ♦ **MP** Mountain Partnership (#16862)

♦ **MPN Advocates Network** **16876**
Contact c/o Münzgraben 6, POB 453, 3000 Bern 7, Switzerland. E-mail: mpnadvocatesnetwork@gmail.com.
URL: https://www.mpn-advocates.net/
History 2013. MPN stands for Myeloproliferative neoplasms. **Aims** Create a global network of MPN patient groups; enhance MPN patient care. **Structure** Steering Committee. Hosted by *Leukemia Patient Advocates Foundation (LePAF).* **Events** *Global Conference for MPN Patient Advocates* Lisbon (Portugal) 2019, *Global Conference for MPN Patient Advocates* Prague (Czechia) 2018, *Global Conference for MPN Patient Advocates* Frankfurt-Main (Germany) 2017, *Global Conference for MPN Patient Advocates* Belgrade (Serbia) 2016.
Members Organizations in 16 countries:
Australia, Belgium, Canada, Finland, France, Germany, Israel, Italy, Japan, Korea Rep, Netherlands, Spain, Switzerland, Thailand, UK, USA.
NGO Relations Member of (1): *Workgroup of European Cancer Patient Advocacy Networks (WECAN, #21054).* [2020/AA0354/**C**]

♦ MPNE – Melanoma Patient Network Europe (unconfirmed)
♦ **MPPE** MedPharmPlast Europe (#16690)
♦ MPPF / see Medicines Patent Pool (#16635)
♦ MPP / see Medicines Patent Pool (#16635)
♦ **MPP** Medicines Patent Pool (#16635)
♦ MPR – ICOM International Committee for Marketing and Public Relations (see: #13051)

♦ **MPS Europe** **16877**
Contact Herstallstr 35, 63739 Aschaffenburg, Germany. T. +4960214381038. Fax +496021868372. E-mail: office@mps-europe.org.
URL: http://www.mps-europe.org/
History 2016. **Aims** Gather national *Mucopolysaccharidoses* (MPS) societies and advocate for all MPS *patients* in Europe to work together collectively in the interest of the MPS community. **Structure** Advisory Board.
Members Shareholders in 12 countries:
Austria, Denmark, Germany, Hungary, Ireland, Italy, Netherlands, Serbia, Spain, Sweden, Switzerland, UK.
NGO Relations Member of: *EURORDIS – Rare Diseases Europe (#09175).* [2018/XM7447/**E**]

♦ MPS / see Mathematical Optimization Society (#16601)
♦ **MPS** Mont Pèlerin Society (#16852)
♦ MPTL – International Conference on Multimedia in Physics Teaching and Learning (meeting series)
♦ **MPU** Mediterranean Phytopathological Union (#16672)
♦ MPWU – Movement for Political World Union (inactive)
♦ MRAC – Musée royal de l'Afrique centrale (internationally oriented national body)
♦ MRA / see Initiatives of Change International – Caux (#11213)
♦ **MRA** Medical Retina Academy (#16628)
♦ MRAP – Mouvement contre le racisme et pour l'amitié entre les peuples (internationally oriented national body)
♦ **MRC** Mekong River Commission (#16703)
♦ **MRC** Merchant Risk Council (#16720)
♦ MRDF / see All We Can
♦ **MRF** Minipeg Research Forum (#16814)
♦ **MRF** Minipig Research Forum (#16815)
♦ **MRG** Minority Rights Group International (#16820)
♦ MRI Foundation – Micro Rainbow International Foundation (unconfirmed)
♦ MRI – Men's Resources International (internationally oriented national body)
♦ **MRI** Migrants Rights International (#16799)
♦ **MRI** Mountain Research Initiative (#16863)
♦ MRLC – Mekong Region Law Centre (internationally oriented national body)
♦ MR in RT Symposium (meeting series)
♦ MRS-Europe / see European Materials Research Society (#07753)
♦ **MRS** Materials Research Society (#16599)
♦ **MRU** Mano River Union (#16566)
♦ MS-13 / see Mara Salvatrucha (#16570)
♦ MS-18 / see Mara Salvatrucha (#16570)
♦ MSAACS – Mesoamerican Academy of Cosmetic Surgery (internationally oriented national body)
♦ MSAADA – Multi-Sector Architectural Assistance in Developing Africa (internationally oriented national body)
♦ MSACL – Association for Mass Spectrometry & Advances in the Clinical Lab (unconfirmed)
♦ MSA – International Congress on Multiple System Atrophy (meeting series)
♦ MSA – Malacological Society of Australasia (internationally oriented national body)
♦ **MSA** Mediterranean Studies Association (#16683)
♦ MSA – Membrane Society of Australasia (internationally oriented national body)
♦ **MSA** Memory Studies Association (#16710)
♦ MSA – Modernist Studies Association (internationally oriented national body)
♦ **MSAN** Multiport Ship Agencies Network (#16900)
♦ **MSBC** Mesoamerican Society for Biology and Conservation (#19429)
♦ MSBT – Missionary Servants of the Most Blessed Trinity (religious order)
♦ MSCI / see Mediterranean Society of Chemotherapy and Infection (#16675)
♦ MSCI – Margaret Sanger Center International (internationally oriented national body)
♦ **MSC** Marine Stewardship Council (#16580)
♦ MSC – Mediterranean Society for Chronobiology (internationally oriented national body)
♦ MSC – Missionarii Sacratissimi Cordis Jesu (religious order)
♦ MSC – Missionary Sisters of the Most Sacred Heart of Jesus of Hiltrup (religious order)
♦ MSC – Missionary Sisters of the Sacred Heart of Jesus (religious order)
♦ **MSCP** Mediterranean Society of Coloproctology (#16676)
♦ **MSC** United Nations Security Council Military Staff Committee (#20626)
♦ MSE – Mouvement socialiste européen (no recent information)
♦ MSF / see Bureau international des Médecins sans frontières (#03366)
♦ MSF – Congregatio Missionariorum a Sacra Familia (religious order)
♦ **MSF International** Bureau international des Médecins sans frontières (#03366)
♦ **MSFNS** Middle Eastern Stereotactic and Functional Neurosurgical Society (#16762)
♦ MSFS – Missionnaires de Saint François de Sales d'Annecy (religious order)
♦ **MSG** Melanesian Spearhead Group (#16704)
♦ **MSG** Mesemb Study Group (#16729)
♦ MSH – Fondation de la maison des sciences de l'homme (internationally oriented national body)
♦ MSH – Management Sciences for Health (internationally oriented national body)
♦ MSHR – Missionary Sisters of Our Lady of the Holy Rosary (religious order)
♦ **MS-HUGe** Microsoft Healthcare Users Group Europe (#16750)
♦ MSI / see MSI Reproductive Choices
♦ MSIA – Movement of Spiritual Inner Awareness (internationally oriented national body)
♦ **MSIF** Multiple Sclerosis International Federation (#16899)

♦ **MSI Global Alliance (MSI)** **16878**
Chief Executive 10 Queen Street Place, London, EC4R 1AG, UK. T. +442075837000. E-mail: enquiry@msiglobal.org.
URL: http://www.msiglobal.org/
History 1990. Founded as an alliance of independent legal and accounting firms. Former names and other names: *MSI Legal and Accounting Network Worldwide* – former. Registration: Companies House, No/ID: 02511919, England and Wales. **Aims** Provide an efficient and effective association framework that enables member firms to expand their businesses. **Structure** Board of Directors; Chief Executive; Secretariat. **Languages** English, French, German, Italian, Spanish. **Staff** 5.00 FTE, paid. **Activities** Guidance/assistance/consulting; networking/liaising. **Events** *Americas Regional Conference* 2021, *Asia Pacific Regional Conference* 2021, *Europe, Middle East and Africa Regional Conference* 2021, *International Conference* 2021, *International Conference* 2020. **Members** Independent legal and accounting firms (over 260) in over 100 countries. Membership countries not specified. **NGO Relations** Instrumental in setting up (1): *Association of International Law Firm Networks (AILFN, #02753).* [2021.05.25/XJ0705/**E**]

♦ MSI Legal and Accounting Network Worldwide / see MSI Global Alliance (#16878)
♦ MSI / see Meeting Design Institute (#16694)
♦ **MSI** MSI Global Alliance (#16878)
♦ MSI Reproductive Choices (internationally oriented national body)
♦ MSLM – Mediterranean Society of Lifestyle Medicine (internationally oriented national body)
♦ **MS** Mara Salvatrucha (#16570)
♦ MS – Mellemfolkeligt Samvirke (internationally oriented national body)
♦ MSMGF / see MPact Global Action for Gay Men's Health and Rights (#16875)
♦ MSMHC – Missionary Sisters of Mary Help of Christians (religious order)
♦ MS – Missionarii Dominae Nostrae a La Salette (religious order)
♦ MS – Mission Sahel (internationally oriented national body)
♦ **MSM** Mediterranean Society of Myology (#16678)
♦ **MSM** Movimento Sacerdotal Mariano (#16575)
♦ **MSN** Mediation Support Network (#16622)
♦ **MSOA** Mediterranean Society of Otology and Audiology (#16680)
♦ **MSO** Mediterranean Society of Ophthalmology (#16679)

♦ **MSPA** **16879**
Exec Dir 650 North Alafaya Trail, Suite 101, #780334, Orlando FL 32828-9997, USA. T. +14079196772. E-mail: inquiries@mspa-americas.org.
Founder 511 Eden Towers, Main Boulevard Gulberg, Lahore, Pakistan. T. +92425725603. Fax +92425734592. E-mail: mspa-ap@mysteryshop.org.
Europe-Africa PO Box 82276, 2508 EG The Hague, Netherlands. T. +31703587371. E-mail: europe@mysteryshop.org – info@mspa-ea.org.
URL: :
History 1 Feb 1998, Orlando, FL (USA). Former names and other names: *Mystery Shopping Providers Association (MSPA)* – former; *Mystery Shopping Professionals Association (MSPA)* – former. **Structure** Regions (3): Americas; Asia/Pacific; Europe/Africa. **Languages** English. **Activities** Events/meetings. **Events** *Annual Europe/Africa Conference* Albufeira (Portugal) 2023, *ShopperFest Conference* Pittsburgh, PA (USA) 2023, *Conference for Creating, Measuring and Enhancing the Customer Journey (CME)* New Orleans, LA (USA) 2022, *Annual Asia Pacific Conference* Phuket (Thailand) 2022, *Annual Europe/Africa Conference* Varna (Bulgaria) 2022. **Members** Companies (450). Membership countries not specified. [2021.03.18/XJ1376/t/**F**]

♦ MSPA / see MSPA (#16879)
♦ MSPFD – Mediterranean Society of Pelvic Floor Disorders (internationally oriented national body)
♦ MSPJU – Union des journalistes socialistes et progressistes de la Méditerranée (inactive)
♦ MSP – Movimento Sviluppo e Pace (internationally oriented national body)
♦ MSpS – Missionarii a Spiritu Sancto (religious order)
♦ MSPTM – Movimiento Siervos de los Pobres del Tercer Mundo (religious order)
♦ **MSRM** Mediterranean Society for Reproductive Medicine (#16682)
♦ MSSA – Microscopy Society of Southern Africa (internationally oriented national body)
♦ MSSA – Missionary Sisters of St Augustine (religious order)
♦ MSSCC – Congregatio Missionariorum a SS Cordium Jesu et Mariae (religious order)
♦ MSS – International Conference on Modulated Semiconductor Structures (meeting series)
♦ MSSP – Missionalis Societas Sancti Pauli (religious order)
♦ MSSRC – Mediterranean Social Sciences Research Council (inactive)
♦ MSSST – Congregatio Missionariorum Servorum Sanctissimae Trinitatis (religious order)
♦ MST – International Conference on Membrane Science and Technology (meeting series)
♦ MSTS – Musculoskeletal Tumor Society (internationally oriented national body)
♦ **MSU** Mediterranean Sailing Union (#16673)
♦ **MSV** Many Strong Voices (#16568)
♦ MTA – Movimiento Teresiano de Apostolado (religious order)
♦ MTA VKI – Magyar Tudomanyos Akademia Vilaggazdasagi Kutatointezet (internationally oriented national body)
♦ MTC – COMESA Metallurgical Technology Centre (inactive)
♦ **MTCE** Mouvement des travailleurs chrétiens d'Europe (#06546)
♦ MTCE – Mouvement des travailleurs chrétiens pour l'Europe, 1949 (inactive)
♦ **MTCE** Movimiento de Trabajadores Christianos de Europa (#06546)
♦ **MTCR** Missile Technology Control Regime (#16826)
♦ **MTEA** Mezdunarodnaja Toplivno-Energeticheskaja Associacija (#13688)
♦ MTEC – International Maritime and Port Technology and Development Conference (meeting series)
♦ **MTF** Mediterranean Trust Fund (#16686)
♦ MTI – Medical Teams International (internationally oriented national body)
♦ MTM / see Maison des Tiers monde et de la solidarité internationale
♦ MT – Mani Tese (internationally oriented national body)
♦ MTM SI – Maison des Tiers monde et de la solidarité internationale (internationally oriented national body)
♦ MTNS – Symposium on Mathematical Theory of Networks and Systems (meeting series)
♦ MTO / see International Peatland Society (#14538)
♦ **MTO Shahmaghsoudi** Maktab Tarighat Oveyssi Shahmaghsoudi (#16556)
♦ MTSA – International Symposium on Microwave/Terahertz Science and Applications (meeting series)
♦ MTS – Marine Technology Society (internationally oriented national body)
♦ MTS – Missionary Training Service (internationally oriented national body)
♦ MTT – Biennial Symposium on Measuring Techniques in Turbomachinery (meeting series)
♦ **MTTU** Mediterranean Table Tennis Union (#16684)
♦ **MUAC** EUROCONTROL Maastricht Upper Area Control Centre (#05670)
♦ MUA – Mediterranean Urological Association (no recent information)
♦ MU-CEL / see Macquarie University Centre for International and Environmental Law
♦ MUCE – Music Users' Council of Europe (no recent information)
♦ MU-CIEL – Macquarie University Centre for International and Environmental Law (internationally oriented national body)
♦ **MUDCA** Mujeres Demócrata Cristianas de América (#03900)
♦ **MUFPP** Milan Urban Food Policy Pact (#16804)

♦ **Muhyiddin Ibn Arabi Society** **16880**
UK Office PO Box 892, Oxford, OX2 7XL, UK. E-mail: mias.uk@ibnarabisociety.org.
USA Office 38 Miller Ave, Suite 486, Mill Valley CA 94941, USA. E-mail: mias.usa@ibnarabisociety.org.
URL: http://www.ibnarabisociety.org/
History 1977. **Aims** Promote greater understanding of the work of Ibn Arabi and his followers. **Activities** Knowledge management/information dissemination; research/documentation; events/meetings. **Events** *Annual UK symposium* Oxford (UK) 2001, *Annual USA symposium* Santa Barbara, CA (USA) 2001, *Annual UK symposium* Oxford (UK) 1996, *Annual UK symposium* UK 1995, *Annual UK symposium* Oxford (UK) 1994. **Publications** *Journal of the Muhyiddin Ibn Arabi Society* (2 a year). *Fusus al-Hikam* by Muhyiddin Ibn Arabi.
Members Individuals in 41 countries:
Australia, Austria, Bahrain, Belgium, Brazil, Canada, Chile, Denmark, Egypt, Finland, France, Germany, Ghana, Greece, India, Indonesia, Iran Islamic Rep, Ireland, Italy, Japan, Kenya, Lebanon, Luxembourg, Malaysia, Morocco, Netherlands, New Zealand, Norway, Pakistan, Qatar, Saudi Arabia, Singapore, South Africa, Spain, Sweden, Switzerland, Syrian AR, Türkiye, UK, United Arab Emirates, USA.
Branches in 1 country:
USA. [2019/XF1452/v/**F**]

♦ Mujahedin-e Khalq Organization (MEK) 16881

Address not obtained.

History in the 1960s, by young, educated Iranians, initially to counter Western influences in the regime of the Shah. Subsequently, after being left out of the new regime's power structure due to radical socialist ideology, continues to wage an armed struggle against Iran from Iraq. Also referred to by acronym *MKO* and as *'People's Mujahedin of Iran (PMOI)'*. **Aims** Use any means, political or violent, including *terrorism*, to promote a mix of *Marxism* and *Islam* through anti-Western activity and attacks on fundamentalist Islamic regimes such as that in Iran. **Structure** *'National Council of Resistance (NCR)'* or *'National Council of Resistance of Iran (NCRI)'* – set up Jul 1981, Teheran (Iran Islamic Rep), as Iran's parliament-in-exile, a political coalition comprising opposition political organizations and parties and political, cultural and social figures, specialists, artists, intellectuals, sports champions, scientists, military officers and commanders of the National Liberation Army. Militant wing: *'National Liberation Army of Iran (NLA)'*. Overseas support structure. Believed to have 15-20 bases in Iraq. **Finance** Fundraising from expatriate Iranian communities through front organizations including: *'Muslim Iranian Students Society'*. Financial and logistical support and military equipment from Government of Iraq. **Activities** World-wide campaign – mainly propaganda but occasionally violent including, Apr 1992, attacks on Iranian embassies in 13 countries and, Jun 1998, explosions in Teheran (Iran Islamic Rep) (killing 3 people) and an assassination. The NCRI is committed to political pluralism and a multi-party system and considers democracy to be the sole guarantor of progress and development; it comprises 25 committees chaired by various political groups and operated on the basis of well-developed parliamentary procedures. **Members** Several thousand members based in Iraq and sympathizers in several countries (not known).

[2010/XN7931/s/**F**]

- ♦ Pro Mujer (internationally oriented national body)
- ♦ Mujeres en la ciencia, la tecnologia y la ingenieria (#06276)
- ♦ Mujeres y Ciudades Internacional (internationally oriented national body)
- ♦ Mujeres Demócrata Cristianas de América (#03900)
- ♦ Mujeres en el Desarrollo en Europa / see WIDE+ (#20951)
- ♦ Mujeres en Empleo Informal: Globalizando y Organizando (#21003)
- ♦ Mujeres de Europa / see Association femmes d'Europe
- ♦ Mujeres por un Mundo Mejor (internationally oriented national body)
- ♦ Mujeres de Negro (#20987)
- ♦ Mujeres de Paz en el Mundo (#18283)
- ♦ Mujeres del PPE/UEDC / see EPP Women (#05516)
- ♦ Mulheres de Europa / see Association femmes d'Europe
- ♦ Mulheres no Emprego Informal: Globalizando e Organizando (#21003)
- ♦ Mulheres pela Paz ao redor do Mundo (#18283)
- ♦ Multi-Country Posts and Telecommunications Training Centre, Blantyre (no recent information)

♦ Multidisciplinary European Low Dose Initiative Association (MELODI Association) 16882

Registered Address IRSN, 31 av de la division Leclerc, BP 17, 92262 Fontenay-aux-Roses CEDEX, France. E-mail: melodi_secretariat@rivm.nl.
URL: http://www.melodi-online.eu/

History Apr 2009. Articles most recently revised Oct 2018, Rovinj (Croatia). Registration: RNA, No/ID: W921001862, Start date: 21 Jan 2011, France. **Aims** Coordinate and promote research and long term competence on effects and risks to human health associated with low-dose and low-dose rate exposures to ionizing radiation. **Structure** General Assembly; Executive Council; Secretariat. **Finance** Sources: members' dues. **Activities** Events/meetings. **Events** *Strategic Research Agenda Working Group Meeting* 2021, *Workshop* Stockholm (Sweden) 2019, *Workshop* Rovinj (Croatia) 2018, *Workshop* Paris (France) 2017, *Workshop* Oxford (UK) 2016.
Members Signatory; Subscribing; Associated; Honorary. Institutions in 18 countries:
Austria, Belgium, Bulgaria, Croatia, Czechia, Finland, France, Germany, Greece, Hungary, Italy, Netherlands, Norway, Portugal, Spain, Sweden, Switzerland, UK.
Barcelona Institute for Global Health (ISGlobal); European Association of Nuclear Medicine (EANM, #06136); European Federation of Organisations for Medical Physics (EFOMP, #07183); European Federation of Radiographer Societies (EFRS, #07203); European Society of Radiology (ESR, #08720).
NGO Relations Cooperates with (1): *European Radiation Protection Week (ERPW).* [2021/AA0940/**F**]

- ♦ Multidisciplinary International Social Networks Conference (meeting series)

♦ Multidisciplinary Joint Committee on Paediatric Urology (JCPU) 16883

Admin Coordinator KinderUrologie, UZ Gasthuisberg, Herestraat 49, 3000 Leuven, Belgium. T. +32494631046. E-mail: jcpu@espu.org.
URL: http://www.jcpu.eu/

History 2002, Leuven (Belgium), by *European Board of Paediatric Surgery (EBPS, #06369)*, *European Board of Urology (EBU, #06374)*; *European Society for Paediatric Urology (ESPU, #08688)* and *European Union of Medical Specialists (UEMS, #09001)*. **Aims** Guarantee the highest standards of care in the field of paediatric urology in Europe. **Structure** Committee, comprising President, Secretary and 5 further members. Includes: *European Academy of Paediatric Urology (EAPU, see: #16883)*. **Languages** English. **Staff** 0.50 FTE, paid; 7.00 FTE, voluntary. **Finance** Activities financed through ESPU. **Activities** Events/meetings; training/education. **NGO Relations** Reports to: Executive Bureau of UEMS. [2016.12.14/XM1083/**E**]

- ♦ Multiethnic Interaction on Xenophobia in Europe (internationally oriented national body)
- ♦ Multifibre agreement – Arrangement Regarding International Trade in Textiles (1973 treaty)

♦ Multi-GNSS Asia (MGA) 16884

Contact address not obtained. E-mail: secretariat@multignss.asia.
URL: http://www.multignss.asia/

History 2010. **Aims** Promote multi-GNSS utilization and applications in the Asia and Oceania region. **Structure** Steering Committee; Secretariat. **Events** *Annual Conference* Chiang Mai (Thailand) 2023, *Annual Conference* Phuket (Thailand) 2022, *Annual Conference* Bangkok (Thailand) 2019, *Annual Conference* Melbourne, VIC (Australia) 2018, *Annual Conference* Jakarta (Indonesia) 2017.
Members Full in 17 countries and territories:
Australia, Brunei Darussalam, China, Czechia, Germany, India, Indonesia, Italy, Japan, Korea Rep, Malaysia, Philippines, Russia, Singapore, Taiwan, Thailand, Vietnam. [2016/XM4850/**D**]

- ♦ Multilateral Agreement on Commercial Rights of Non-scheduled Air Services among the Association of South-East Asian Nations (1971 treaty)
- ♦ Multilateral Agreement on Commercial Rights of Non-scheduled Air Services in Europe (1956 treaty)
- ♦ Multilateral Agreement on Cooperation and Mutual Assistance between the National Customs Directors of Latin America, Spain and Portugal (1981 treaty)
- ♦ Multilateral Agreement on the Liberalization of International Air Transportation (2001 treaty)
- ♦ Multilateral Agreement Relating to Certificates of Airworthiness for Imported Aircraft (1960 treaty)
- ♦ Multilateral Agreement Relating to the Collection of Route Charges (1970 treaty)
- ♦ Multilateral Agreement Relating to Route Charges (1981 treaty)
- ♦ Multilateral Agreement on Search and Rescue (1973 treaty)
- ♦ Multilateral Convention for the Avoidance of Double Taxation of Copyright Royalties and Additional Protocol (1979 treaty)
- ♦ Multilateral Convention on Mutual Administrative Assistance in Tax Matters (1988 treaty)

♦ Multilateral Fund for the Implementation of the Montreal Protocol 16885

Chief Officer Ste 4100, 1000 De La Gauchetière Str West, Montréal QC H3B 4W5, Canada. T. +15142821122. Fax +15142820068. E-mail: secretariat@unmfs.org.
URL: http://www.multilateralfund.org/

History Established Jun 1990, London (UK), as *Interim Multilateral Fund*, to assist countries in meeting control measures of the *Montreal Protocol on Substances that Deplete the Ozone Layer (1987)*, signed 16 Sep 1987, Montréal QC (Canada). Confirmed as the Multilateral Fund at 4th Meeting, 1992, Copenhagen (Denmark), and replenished 1993, 1996, 1999, 2002, 2005, 2008, 2011 and 2014. Implementing agencies: *International Bank for Reconstruction and Development (IBRD, #12317); UNDP (#20292); UNEP (#20299); UNIDO (#20336)*; bilateral agencies from a number of contributing parties. Originally also referred to as: *Multilateral Fund of the Montreal Protocol*; *Montreal Protocol Multilateral Fund (MPMF)*. **Aims** Provide funds to assist developing countries Parties to the Montreal Protocol to comply with their obligations under the Montreal Protocol by phasing-out the use of ozone depleting substances (ODS) according the Protocol schedules in a collective global effort to prevent destruction of the *ozone layer*. **Structure** Meetings of the Parties to the Montreal Protocol determine policies and replenishment levels of the Multilateral Fund. Executive Committee (meets 2-3 times a year), comprising 7 representatives each from developing (Article 5) and industrialized (non-Article 5) countries manages the Fund and is assisted by the Multilateral Fund Secretariat, located in Montréal QC (Canada), whose tasks include reviewing submissions from Article 5 countries, making appropriate recommendations on project funding, monitoring implementation of projects and evaluating completed projects. **Languages** Arabic, Chinese, English, French, Russian, Spanish. **Staff** 25.00 FTE, paid. **Finance** Contributions from industrialized countries and developing countries not operating under Article 5 of the Montreal Protocol. Triennial budget: US$ 540,000,000. **Activities** Financial and/or material support; guidance/assistance/consulting; events/meetings (usually in Montréal QC, Canada). Provides developing countries with access to necessary funding and technology transfer to implement provisions of the Montreal Protocol. Countries eligible for this assistance are those with an annual per capita consumption of ODS of less than 300 grams a year, as defined in Article 5 of the Protocol. Apart from a small number of essential uses, CFCs, halons and CTC have been phased out. As of Sep 2019, 144 of 145 developing countries have phase-out plans in place to address compliance with some or all of the HCFC control measures. **Events** *Executive Committee Meeting – Part I* Montréal, QC (Canada) 2022, *Executive Committee Meeting – Part II* Montréal, QC (Canada) 2022, *Executive Committee Meeting* Montréal, QC (Canada) 2022, *Executive Committee Meeting* Montréal, QC (Canada) 2022, *Executive Committee Meeting* Montréal, QC (Canada) 2021. **Publications** Reports of Meetings of the Executive Committee; policy papers; brochure; leaflet; video; inventory of approved projects; policies, procedures, guidelines and criteria; country programme summary sheets; status of compliance of Article 5 countries.
Members As of Sep 2019, Parties (governments) to the Montreal Protocol (198):
Afghanistan, Albania, Algeria, Andorra, Angola, Antigua-Barbuda, Argentina, Armenia, Australia, Austria, Azerbaijan, Bahamas, Bahrain, Bangladesh, Barbados, Belarus, Belgium, Belize, Benin, Bhutan, Bolivia, Bosnia-Herzegovina, Botswana, Brazil, Brunei Darussalam, Bulgaria, Burkina Faso, Burundi, Cambodia, Cameroon, Canada, Cape Verde, Central African Rep, Chad, Chile, China, Colombia, Comoros, Congo Brazzaville, Congo DR, Cook Is, Costa Rica, Côte d'Ivoire, Croatia, Cuba, Cyprus, Czechia, Denmark, Djibouti, Dominica, Dominican Rep, Ecuador, Egypt, El Salvador, Equatorial Guinea, Eritrea, Estonia, Eswatini, Ethiopia, Fiji, Finland, France, Gabon, Gambia, Georgia, Germany, Ghana, Greece, Grenada, Guatemala, Guinea, Guinea-Bissau, Guyana, Haiti, Honduras, Hungary, Iceland, India, Indonesia, Iran Islamic Rep, Iraq, Ireland, Israel, Italy, Jamaica, Japan, Jordan, Kazakhstan, Kenya, Kiribati, Korea DPR, Korea Rep, Kuwait, Kyrgyzstan, Laos, Latvia, Lebanon, Lesotho, Liberia, Libya, Liechtenstein, Lithuania, Luxembourg, Madagascar, Malawi, Malaysia, Maldives, Mali, Malta, Marshall Is, Mauritania, Mauritius, Mexico, Micronesia FS, Moldova, Monaco, Mongolia, Montenegro, Morocco, Mozambique, Myanmar, Namibia, Nauru, Nepal, Netherlands, New Zealand, Nicaragua, Niger, Nigeria, Niue, North Macedonia, Northern Ireland, Norway, Oman, Pakistan, Palau, Panama, Papua New Guinea, Paraguay, Peru, Philippines, Poland, Portugal, Qatar, Romania, Russia, Rwanda, Samoa, San Marino, Sao Tomé-Principe, Saudi Arabia, Senegal, Serbia, Seychelles, Sierra Leone, Singapore, Slovakia, Slovenia, Solomon Is, Somalia, South Africa, South Sudan, Spain, Sri Lanka, St Kitts-Nevis, St Lucia, St Vincent-Grenadines, Sudan, Suriname, Sweden, Switzerland, Syrian AR, Tajikistan, Tanzania UR, Thailand, Timor-Leste, Togo, Tonga, Trinidad-Tobago, Tunisia, Türkiye, Turkmenistan, Tuvalu, Uganda, UK, Ukraine, United Arab Emirates, Uruguay, USA, Uzbekistan, Vanuatu, Venezuela, Vietnam, Yemen, Zambia, Zimbabwe.
Also included in the above, one regional integration EU entity:
European Union (EU, #08967). [2020/XF3600/f/**F***]

- ♦ Multilateral Fund of the Montreal Protocol / see Multilateral Fund for the Implementation of the Montreal Protocol (#16885)

♦ Multilateral Initiative on Malaria (MIM) 16886

Initiative multilatérale sur le paludisme

Sec Dir c/o AMANET, Commission for Science and Technology Bldg, PO Box 33207, Dar es Salaam, Tanzania UR. T. +255222700018. Fax +255222700380.

History Founded following the 1st Pan-African Malaria Conference. Previously based at: *Wellcome Trust* (1997-1999); *John E Fogarty International Center (FIC)* (1999-2001); Karolinska Institute, Stockholm, Sweden (2003-2005). Since Jan 2006, based at: *African Malaria Network Trust (AMANET, #00365)*. **Aims** Develop sustainable malaria research capacity in Africa; promote communication and cooperation between organizations and individuals concerned with malaria; ensure research findings are applied to malaria treatment and control; raise international public awareness of the problem of malaria. **Structure** Strategic Advisory Board; MIM/TDR; MIM/TDR Task Force; MR4; Secretariat. **Languages** English, French. **Staff** 9.50 FTE, paid. **Finance** Through separate multilateral mechanisms, each supporting the MIM constituents separately. Main donors include the following international organizations: *International Bank for Reconstruction and Development (IBRD, #12317)* (World Bank); *UNICEF/UNDP/World Bank/WHO Special Programme for Research and Training in Tropical Diseases (TDR, #20331)*; *Swedish International Development Cooperation Agency (Sida)* – SAREC; *WHO Regional Office for Africa (AFRO, #20943)*. Budget (annual): about US$ 4.5 million. **Activities** Includes: *'MIM-TDR'* – based at TDR (Special Programme for Research and Training in Tropical Diseases) /WHO in Geneva (Switzerland), evaluates grants and administers funding; *'MIMCom'* – communications arm; *'MR4'* – Malaria Research and Reference Reagent Resource Centre. **Events** *Pan-African Malaria Conference* Dakar (Senegal) 2018, *Pan-African Malaria Conference* Durban (South Africa) 2013, *MIM Pan-African conference on malaria* Nairobi (Kenya) 2009, *Pan-African conference on malaria* Yaoundé (Cameroon) 2005, *Pan-African conference on malaria* Arusha (Tanzania UR) 2002. **Publications** *MIM Newsletter* (2 a year). Mailing list with weekly messages.
Members MIM supported scientists in 16 countries:
Benin, Burkina Faso, Cameroon, Congo Brazzaville, Côte d'Ivoire, Ethiopia, Gabon, Ghana, Kenya, Mali, Mozambique, Nigeria, South Africa, Sudan, Tanzania UR, Uganda.
IGO Relations Partners include: *European Commission (EC, #06633)* – Poverty Diseases; *United States Agency for International Development (USAID)*; *WHO (#20950)*. **NGO Relations** Partners include: *African Malaria Network Trust (AMANET, #00365)*; *Malaria Foundation International (MFI, #16558).* [2017/XF6717/**F**]

♦ Multilateral Investment Fund (MIF) 16887

Fonds multilatéral d'investissement – Fondo Multilateral de Inversiones (FOMIN)

Main Office c/o IDB, 1300 New York Ave NW, Washington DC 20577, USA. T. +12029428211. Fax +12029428100.
URL: http://www.fomin.org/

History 11 Feb 1992, Washington DC (USA), on signature by *Inter-American Development Bank (IDB, #11427)* member countries of an establishment agreement and of an agreement appointing IDB as administrator. Both agreements became effective on 7 Jan 1993. **Aims** As a provide of technical assistance for private sector development in the Latin American and Caribbean region, pursue innovative ways to build economic opportunity by developing effective approaches to increase private investment and advance private sector development, improving the business environment, and supporting micro and small enterprises in order to support economic growth and poverty reduction in the region. **Structure** Donors' Committee. **Languages** English, French, Portuguese, Spanish. **Finance** Since its foundation, has: approved over 1,700 projects; committeed over US$ 100.5 million; mobilized a total over over US$ 200.7 million in the region. Has reached over 4 million beneficiaries. **Activities** In 2010, introduced the concept of the Access Framework, aimed at achieving greater focus and at using impact evaluation and knowledge capturing and sharing as a natural part of efforts to support innovative projects that achieve greater impact. Areas of work within the Access Framework context: *'Access to Finance'*, including microfinance, early stage equity, SME financing and financial services for low income people; *'Access to Markets and Capabilities'*, including market functioning, business capabilities and job skills; *'Access to Basic Services'*, including engaging the private sector in the provision of basic services and climate change. Operates by engaging in partnerships with local and international organizations which provide sector-specific knowledge and counterpart funding (to date exceeding US$ 100.4 million). Provides financing in the form of grants, loans, guarantees, equity and quasi-equity or any combination thereof, as well as advisory services, providing that it maintains its

essential grant-making character. Historically, approximately 65% of resources have been devoted to non-reimbursable technical assistance grants, and 35% have been used to provide loans or investments. Organizes fora, conferences and other events. **Events** *International conference on promoting entrepreneurship through equity investment* Washington, DC (USA) 1998. **Publications** *The Annual Map of Remittances in Latin America and the Caribbean. 10 Years of Innovation in Remittances*; *2010 Microfinance Americas*; *The 2010 Global Microscope on the Microfinance Business Environment*; *The 210 Infrascope: Evaluating the Environment for Public-Private Partnerships in Latin America and the Caribbean.*
Members Governments of 39 countries:
Argentina, Bahamas, Barbados, Belize, Bolivia, Brazil, Canada, Chile, China, Colombia, Costa Rica, Dominican Rep, Ecuador, El Salvador, France, Guatemala, Guyana, Haiti, Honduras, Italy, Jamaica, Japan, Korea Rep, Mexico, Netherlands, Nicaragua, Panama, Paraguay, Peru, Portugal, Spain, Suriname, Sweden, Switzerland, Trinidad-Tobago, UK, Uruguay, USA, Venezuela.
[2018/XF5287/f/**F***]

♦ Multilateral Investment Guarantee Agency (MIGA) 16888

Agence multilatérale de garantie des investissements
Exec Vice-Pres/CEO 1818 H St NW, Washington DC 20433, USA. T. +12024732503 – +12024731000. Fax +12025222630. E-mail: migainquiry@worldbank.org.
URL: http://www.miga.org/
History 12 Apr 1988, as an international organization and a member of the *The World Bank Group (#21218)*, the other members being *International Bank for Reconstruction and Development (IBRD, #12317)*, *International Development Association (IDA, #13155)*, *International Finance Corporation (IFC, #13597)* and *International Centre for Settlement of Investment Disputes (ICSID, #12515)*. As a legal entity, has its own charter (the "Convention"), share capital, financial structure, management and staff. Convention opened for signature, 11 Oct 1985, and entered into force, 12 Apr 1988. Inaugurated 8 Jun 1988; commenced operation in fiscal year 1990. A specialized agency of *United Nations (UN, #20515)* within the *United Nations System (#20635)*. World Bank organizations are part of what are often referred to as *Bretton Woods Institutions (BWIs, #03322)*. Previously also known under the French acronym *AMGI*. **Aims** Promote foreign direct investment into developing countries to support economic growth, reduce poverty, and improve people's lives through investment *insurance* covering non-commercial risks, technical assistance to promote investment opportunities and dispute resolution services. **Structure** Council of Governors, comprising one delegate and one alternate per member country. Board of Directors of 25 members. Voting power is weighted according to the share capital each director represents. **Staff** Matters dealt with through: *World Bank Group Staff Association (#21219)*. **Finance** As at 30 Jun 2014: Authorized capital base of US$ 2,018 million; subscribed capital base US$ 1,918 million. **Activities** Financial and/or material support. Online services provide information to investors on investment opportunities, business operating conditions and political risk insurance. **Events** *Seminar on encouraging investment in risky markets* Singapore (Singapore) 2009, *Special high-level meeting* New York, NY (USA) 2006, *Special high-level meeting* New York, NY (USA) 2005, *Asia-Africa business associations summit* Kuala Lumpur (Malaysia) 2000, *Le financement des investissements en Afrique* Yaoundé (Cameroon) 1999. **Publications** Electronic newsletters; studies. Information Services: Online services provide information to investors on investment opportunities, business operating conditions and political risk insurance. **Information Services** *FDI net*; *PRI-Center*.
Members Member countries, as of Dec 2014 (181):
Afghanistan, Albania, Algeria, Angola, Antigua-Barbuda, Argentina, Armenia, Australia, Austria, Azerbaijan, Bahamas, Bahrain, Bangladesh, Barbados, Belarus, Belgium, Belize, Benin, Bhutan, Bolivia, Bosnia-Herzegovina, Botswana, Brazil, Bulgaria, Burkina Faso, Burundi, Cambodia, Cameroon, Canada, Cape Verde, Central African Rep, Chad, Chile, China, Colombia, Comoros, Congo Brazzaville, Congo DR, Costa Rica, Côte d'Ivoire, Croatia, Cyprus, Czechia, Denmark, Djibouti, Dominica, Dominican Rep, Ecuador, Egypt, El Salvador, Equatorial Guinea, Eritrea, Estonia, Eswatini, Ethiopia, Fiji, Finland, France, Gabon, Gambia, Georgia, Germany, Ghana, Greece, Grenada, Guatemala, Guinea, Guinea-Bissau, Guyana, Haiti, Honduras, Hungary, Iceland, India, Indonesia, Iran Islamic Rep, Iraq, Ireland, Israel, Italy, Jamaica, Japan, Jordan, Kazakhstan, Kenya, Korea Rep, Kosovo, Kuwait, Kyrgyzstan, Laos, Latvia, Lebanon, Lesotho, Liberia, Libya, Lithuania, Luxembourg, Madagascar, Malawi, Malaysia, Maldives, Mali, Malta, Mauritania, Mauritius, Mexico, Micronesia FS, Moldova, Mongolia, Montenegro, Morocco, Mozambique, Myanmar, Namibia, Nepal, Netherlands, New Zealand, Nicaragua, Niger, Nigeria, North Macedonia, Norway, Oman, Pakistan, Palau, Panama, Papua New Guinea, Paraguay, Peru, Philippines, Poland, Portugal, Qatar, Romania, Russia, Rwanda, Samoa, Sao Tomé-Principe, Saudi Arabia, Senegal, Serbia, Seychelles, Sierra Leone, Singapore, Slovakia, Slovenia, Solomon Is, South Africa, South Sudan, Spain, Sri Lanka, St Kitts-Nevis, St Lucia, St Vincent-Grenadines, Sudan, Suriname, Sweden, Switzerland, Syrian AR, Tajikistan, Tanzania UR, Thailand, Timor-Leste, Togo, Trinidad-Tobago, Tunisia, Türkiye, Turkmenistan, Uganda, UK, Ukraine, United Arab Emirates, Uruguay, USA, Uzbekistan, Vanuatu, Venezuela, Vietnam, Yemen, Zambia, Zimbabwe.
NGO Relations Member of: *International Union of Credit and Investment Insurers (Bern Union, #15767)*. Observer member of: *Aman Union (#00763)*. Partner of: *Global Forum on Law, Justice and Development (GFLJD, #10373)*. [2017/XF1090/**F***]

♦ Multilateral Middle East Peace Process (no recent information)

♦ Multilateral Monetary Area (MMA) 16889

Address not obtained.
History 1974, as *Rand Monetary Area (RMA) – Zone monétaire du Rand*. Developed into *Common Monetary Area (CMA) – Zone monétaire commune*, 1986, with South Africa, Lesotho and Swaziland as signatories. Current title adopted, Feb 1992, when Namibia joined the monetary union. **Aims** Maintain *currencies* of members on a par with the *South African* rand.
Members Governments of 4 countries:
Eswatini, Lesotho, Namibia, South Africa. [2010/XF6517/**F***]

♦ Multilateral Organizations Performance Assessment Network (MOPAN) 16890

Address not obtained.
URL: http://www.mopanonline.org/
History 2002, by 9 donor countries. An informal network. **Aims** Assess the organizational effectiveness of multilateral organizations funded by member governments; carry out joint assessments and share information. **Structure** Secretariat rotates among members. Working groups (3): Technical; Communications; Contractual.
Members Governments of 16 countries:
Australia, Austria, Belgium, Canada, Denmark, Finland, France, Germany, Ireland, Korea Rep, Netherlands, Norway, Spain, Sweden, Switzerland, UK. [2010/XM2509/**F***]

♦ Multilateral Treaty on Free Trade and Central American Economic Integration (1958 treaty)
♦ Multilateral Treaty on Social Security (1967 treaty)

♦ Multilaw 16891

Exec Dir 125 Wood Street, London, ED2V 7AW, UK. T. +442077262211. E-mail: info@multilaw.com.
URL: https://www.multilaw.com/
History 1990. **Aims** As a network of independent law firms working together worldwide, offer the most effective way of fulfilling clients' international needs. **Structure** Board. **Events** *Global Conference* London (UK) 2022.
Members Firms in 97 countries and territories:
Angola, Anguilla, Argentina, Australia, Austria, Bahamas, Bangladesh, Belgium, Belize, Bolivia, Bosnia-Herzegovina, Brazil, Bulgaria, Cambodia, Canada, Cape Verde, Cayman Is, Chile, China, Colombia, Costa Rica, Croatia, Cyprus, Czechia, Denmark, Dominican Rep, Ecuador, Egypt, El Salvador, England, France, Germany, Greece, Guatemala, Guernsey, Honduras, Hong Kong, Hungary, India, Indonesia, Iraq, Ireland, Israel, Italy, Japan, Jersey, Kenya, Korea Rep, Laos, Luxembourg, Malaysia, Malta, Mexico, Monaco, Montenegro, Mozambique, Myanmar, Netherlands, New Zealand, Nicaragua, North Macedonia, Northern Ireland, Oman, Pakistan, Panama, Peru, Philippines, Poland, Portugal, Puerto Rico, Romania, Russia, Saudi Arabia, Serbia, Seychelles, Singapore, Slovakia, Slovenia, South Africa, Spain, Sri Lanka, St Lucia, Sweden, Switzerland, Taiwan, Tanzania UR, Thailand, Timor-Leste, Türkiye, Uganda, Ukraine, United Arab Emirates, Uruguay, USA, Venezuela, Vietnam, Virgin Is UK.
[2021.07.24/XM8857/**F**]

♦ Multilayer Modular Flooring Association (internationally oriented national body)

♦ Multilingual Europe Technology Alliance (META) 16892

Network Manager DFKI Berlin, Alt-Moabit 91c, 10559 Berlin, Germany. T. +4930238951833.
URL: http://www.meta-net.eu/
Aims Prepare an ambitious, joint international effort towards furthering Language Technology as a means towards realizing the vision of a Europe united as one single digital market and information space. **Structure** Built by *META-NET* – a Network of Excellence. **Events** *Forum* Brussels (Belgium) 2017, *Forum* Lisbon (Portugal) 2016.
Members Full (786) in 61 countries and territories:
Albania, Argentina, Australia, Austria, Belgium, Brazil, Bulgaria, Canada, China, Croatia, Cuba, Cyprus, Czechia, Denmark, Dominican Rep, Estonia, Finland, France, Georgia, Germany, Greece, Hong Kong, Hungary, Iceland, India, Indonesia, Iran Islamic Rep, Ireland, Israel, Italy, Japan, Kenya, Korea Rep, Latvia, Lithuania, Luxembourg, Malaysia, Malta, Mexico, Moldova, Morocco, Netherlands, North Macedonia, Norway, Pakistan, Poland, Portugal, Romania, Russia, Serbia, Singapore, Slovakia, Slovenia, Spain, Sweden, Switzerland, Türkiye, UK, Ukraine, USA, Vietnam.
Included in the above, 5 organizations listed in this Yearbook:
European Federation of National Institutions for Language (EFNIL, #07172); *European Patent Office (EPO, #08166)*; *European Trade Association for Business Angels, Seed Funds, and other Early Stage Market Players (EBAN, #08923)*; *Joint Research Centre (JRC, #16147)*; *Translators without Borders (#20216)*.
NGO Relations META-Net is member of: *Cracking the Language Barrier (#04942)*. [2014/XJ8957/y/**E**]

♦ Multilingual Internet Names Consortium (internationally oriented national body)
♦ Multimedia Educational Resource for Learning and Online Teaching / see MERLOT African Network (#16726)

♦ Multimedia International (MI) 16893

Address not obtained.
URL: http://www.multimedia-int.org/
History 1970, Attleboro MA (USA). **Aims** Assist, educate and challenge, through creativity and professionalism, women and men religious in all areas of the communications media; bring the media more fully into the apostolic and pastoral work of the *Church*. **Structure** General Assembly (annual). Board of Directors, consisting of President, Vice President, Secretary, Treasurer, Past President, 2 Members Executive Committee and 19 Members (including one Observer). President, Secretary, Treasurer, elected members. Sections (2): anglophone; francophone. Committees (5): Executive; Programmes; Bulletin; Special Concerns; Italian Section. **Finance** Members' dues. Other sources: services and projects; grants-in-aid. **Activities** Half or full-day sessions; continuing education; conferences, workshops and seminars in the fields of graphics, photography, journalism and media (including videos). Provides advisory and reference services and rents equipment. **Events** *Annual General Assembly* Rome (Italy) 1988, *Annual General Assembly* Rome (Italy) 1987, *Annual General Assembly* Rome (Italy) 1986. **Publications** *MI Network* (12 a year) in English; *Multimedia Bulletin* (4 a year) in English; *MI Network* (annual) in English. Special supplements and booklets on Church communications. **Members** International religious congregations (72) based in Rome. **NGO Relations** *Missionary Sisters of Our Lady of Africa (White Sisters)* is a member. [2015/XF2652/y/**F**]

♦ Multinational Advanced Postal Training School, Abidjan (no recent information)

♦ Multinational Arabidopsis Steering Committee (MASC) 16894

Coordinator Univ of Tübingen, Auf der Morgenstelle 32, 72076 Tübingen, Germany. E-mail: admin@arabidopsisresearch.org.
URL: http://www.arabidopsisresearch.org/
Aims Promote large-scale studies in Arabidopsis thaliana; strengthen international collaboration and coordination; reduce redundancy; help in guiding the community in making progress on projects that can be successful only by combined international efforts. **Structure** Chair; Co-Chair; Coordinator; Subcommittees; Country Representatives; Projects and Resources Representatives. **Activities** Events/meetings; research/documentation. **Events** *International Conference on Arabidopsis Research* Chiba (Japan) 2023, *International Conference on Arabidopsis Research* Belfast (UK) 2022, *International Conference on Arabidopsis Research* Tübingen (Germany) 2021, *International Conference on Arabidopsis Research* Seattle, WA (USA) 2020, *International Conference on Arabidopsis Research* Wuhan (China) 2019.
Members Full in 28 countries:
Argentina, Australia, Austria, Belgium, Brazil, Canada, Chile, China, Czechia, Denmark, Finland, France, Germany, Greece, Hungary, India, Ireland, Israel, Italy, Japan, Korea Rep, Netherlands, New Zealand, Spain, Sweden, Switzerland, UK, USA.
NGO Relations *International Arabidopsis Informatics Consortium (IAIC, #11664)*. [2020/XM4606/c/**E**]

♦ Multinational Association of Supportive Care in Cancer (MASCC) .. 16895

Main Office 412- 16 Industrial Parkway South, Aurora ON L4G 0R1, Canada. E-mail: mascc.office@mascc.org.
URL: https://mascc.org/
History 1990. Former names and other names: *International Conference for Supportive Care in Cancer* – former. Registration: USA. **Aims** Promote research and education in all aspects of supportive care for patients with cancer, regardless of the stage of their disease. **Structure** Board of Directors. **Languages** English. **Staff** Independent contractors; voluntary. **Activities** Training/education. **Events** *MASCC/JASCC/ISOO Annual Meeting* Nara (Japan) 2023, *International Symposium on Supportive Care in Cancer* Toronto, ON (Canada) 2022, *International Symposium on Supportive Care in Cancer* Seville (Spain) 2021, *International Symposium on Supportive Care in Cancer* Seville (Spain) 2020, *International Symposium on Supportive Care in Cancer* San Francisco, CA (USA) 2019. **Publications** *Supportive Care in Cancer* – journal. **Members** Individuals, mainly physicians and nurses, interested in supportive cancer care. Membership countries not specified. **NGO Relations** Instrumental in setting up: *Association Francophone pour les Soins Oncologiques de Support (AFSOS)*. Participates in: *Breast Health Global Initiative (BHGI, #03318)*. Liaison with: *International Society for Oral Oncology (ISOO, #15328)*. [2022/XD7411/**C**]

♦ Multinational Development of Women in Technology (internationally oriented national body)

♦ Multinational Finance Society (MFS) 16896

Admin Manager address not obtained. T. +18565596280. E-mail: mfs@mfsociety.org.
URL: http://www.mfsociety.org/
History 15 Jun 1995. **Aims** Advance and disseminate financial knowledge, philosophies, techniques and research findings pertaining to industrialized and developing countries among members of the academic and business communities. **Structure** Board of Directors. **Languages** English. **Finance** Sources: members' dues. **Activities** Awards/prizes/competitions; events/meetings. **Events** *Annual Conference* Gdansk (Poland) 2022, *Annual Conference* Limassol (Cyprus) 2020, *Annual Conference* Jerusalem (Israel) 2019, *Annual Conference* Budapest (Hungary) 2018, *Annual Conference* Bucharest (Romania) 2017. **Publications** *Multinational Finance Journal (MFJ)* (4 a year). [2017.11.15/XJ6675/**C**]

♦ Multinational Force and Observers (MFO) 16897

Sr. Operations Officer and Special Asst. to the Director General Piazza Albania 9, 00153 Rome RM, Italy. Fax +39657119444. E-mail: email@mfo.org.
URL: http://www.mfo.org/
History 3 Aug 1981. Established as an international organization by the Protocol to the Treaty of Peace, signed by the Governments of Egypt and Israel (receiving states) and witnessed by the USA. Received initial funding on 9 Sep 1981. **Aims** Supervise implementation of the *security* provisions in Annex I of the Egyptian-Israeli Treaty of Peace, dated 26 Mar 1979; employ best efforts to prevent any violation of its terms; monitor deployment of Egyptian Border Guards along the Egyptian side of the border with Gaza according to Agreed Arrangements, signed 1 Sep 2005 by Egypt and Israel, as amended 2007, 2018, and 2021; verify other agreed arrangements between the Treaty Parties. **Structure** Director General exercises authority through staff at headquarters in Rome (Italy), the Force Commander and staff in the Sinai and the Director General's Representatives and staff in Cairo (Egypt) and Israel. Sinai is largest MFO element and divided into: Headquarters; Personnel Branch; Force Protection; Operations Branch; Logistics Branch; Support Branch; Planning Branch; Information and Communications Technology Branch; Finance; Liaison Branch. Functional units include: Civilian Observer Unit; the Northern Battalion; the Southern Battalion; the Coastal Patrol Unit. Force, with personnel from 13 Troop-Contributing Nations, is supported by international direct hire civilians and Egyptian contractor personnel. **Languages** English. **Staff** 21.00 FTE, paid. **Finance** Contributions from governments of Finland, Germany, Japan, Republic of Korea, Netherlands, Norway, Sweden, and Switzerland. All other expenses shared equally among Egypt, Israel and the USA. Annual budget: 78,717,000 USD (2021). **Activities** Conflict resolution; management of treaties and agreements; monitoring/evaluation. **Publications** *Servants of Peace*.
Members Participating states (12):
Australia, Canada, Colombia, Czechia, Fiji, France, Italy, Japan, New Zealand, UK, Uruguay, USA.
Supporting state (1):
Norway. [2022.02.11/XE0178/**F***]

♦ Multinational Higher School of Telecommunications of Dakar 16898

Ecole supérieure multinationale des télécommunications de Dakar (ESMT)

Dir BP 10 000 Dakar Liberté, Dakar, Senegal. T. +2218249806. Fax +2218246890. E-mail: esmt@esmt.sn.
URL: http://www.esmt.sn/

History 1981, on the initiative of 7 West African countries and with the support of *UNDP (#20292)*. Registered in accordance with the law of Senegal. Headquarters agreement with the Government of Senegal, 1986. **Aims** Provide higher technical and commercial education in telecommunications *engineering*. **Structure** Administrative Council, comprising representatives of all member countries. Proficiency Council (advisory), comprising Director, Director of Studies, teaching staff, 2 representatives of clients and 2 representatives of trainees. **Finance** Members' dues. Assistance from: *International Telecommunication Union (ITU, #15673)*; UNDP; governments of France, Switzerland and Canada. **Activities** Training/education; events/meetings. **Events** *Forum on rural telecommunications / West African Telecommunications Conference – CTOA* Cotonou (Benin) 1999.
Members Governments of 7 countries:
Benin, Burkina Faso, Mali, Mauritania, Niger, Senegal, Togo.
IGO Relations Member of: *African and Malagasy Council for Higher Education (#00364)*. **NGO Relations** Member of: *Agence universitaire de La Francophonie (AUF, #00548)*. Memorandum of Understanding with: *Global e-Schools and Communities Initiative (GESCI)*. [2010/XE2869/**E***]

- ♦ Multinational Interstitial Cystitis Association (inactive)
- ♦ Multinational Peace Force South-Eastern Europe / see South-Eastern Europe Brigade (#19808)
- ♦ Multinational Peace-Keeping Force (inactive)
- ♦ Multinational Programming and Operational Centre / see ECA Office for North Africa (#05273)
- ♦ Multinational Stand-by Readiness Brigade for United Nations Operations (inactive)
- ♦ Multiple Association Management Institute / see AMC Institute

♦ Multiple Sclerosis International Federation (MSIF) 16899

Fédération internationale de sclérose en plaques – Federación Internacional de Esclerosis Múltiple – Internationale Bund für Multiple Sklerose

CEO Skyline House – 3rd Floor, 200 Union Street, London, SE1 0LX, UK. T. +442076201911. E-mail: info@msif.org.
URL: https://www.msif.org/

History 16 Oct 1966, Washington, DC (USA). By-Laws adopted 8 Aug 1967, London (UK). Revised: Mar 1988; Oct 1991; Sep 1993; Sep 1997. Former names and other names: *International Federation of Multiple Sclerosis Societies (IFMSS – Fédération internationale des associations de la sclérose en plaques – Internationale Vereinigung der Multiple Sklerose Gesellschaften – Federación Internacional de Sociedades contra la Esclerosis Múltiple)* – former. Registration: Start date: 1 May 1967, End date: Dec 2004, USA, Delaware; Charity Commission, No/ID: 1105321, Start date: 1 Jan 2005, England and Wales. **Aims** Eliminate multiple sclerosis and promote, stimulate and encourage scientific research into causes of and a cure for MS and related neurological diseases; educate the general public about MS, including through collecting and disseminating relevant scientific and educational information; coordinate and further the work of national MS organizations on an international level so as to encourage those affected by MS to achieve full potential as members of society by improving their quality of life; provide advice and active help in further developing voluntary national MS organizations and in formation of such organizations; aid, support and relieve persons who are in any way affected as a result of MS and related diseases, while completely involving people affected by MS. **Structure** Board of Trustees. **Languages** English, French, German, Italian, Russian, Spanish. **Staff** 9.00 FTE, paid. **Finance** Sources: contributions; members' dues. **Activities** Awards/prizes/competitions; events/meetings. **Events** *Symposium* Thessaloniki (Greece) 2005, *Central and Eastern European development seminar* Prague (Czech Rep) 2004, *Biennial meeting / General Meeting* Berlin (Germany) 2003, *Biennial meeting / General Meeting* Melbourne, VIC (Australia) 2001, *Biennial meeting / General Meeting* Basel (Switzerland) 1999. **Publications** *MS in Focus Magazine* (2 a year). *The Atlas of MS*; *The Global Economic Impact of MS*. Annual Review.
Members National associations in 42 countries:
Argentina, Australia, Austria, Belgium, Brazil, Canada, Cyprus, Czechia, Denmark, Finland, France, Germany, Greece, Hungary, Iceland, India, Iran Islamic Rep, Ireland, Israel, Italy, Japan, Korea Rep, Latvia, Luxembourg, Malta, Mexico, Netherlands, New Zealand, Norway, Poland, Portugal, Romania, Russia, Slovakia, Slovenia, Spain, Sweden, Switzerland, Türkiye, UK, Uruguay, USA.
Consultative Status Consultative status granted from: *ECOSOC (#05331)* (Roster); *WHO (#20950)* (Official Relations). **NGO Relations** Full member of: *International Alliance of Patients' Organizations (IAPO, #11633)*. In liaison with technical committees of: *International Organization for Standardization (ISO, #14473)*. Partnerships with: *Resource Alliance (#18914)*. [2020/XC1960/**C**]

- ♦ Multiple Sclerosis and Rehabilitation, Care- and Health Services in Europe / see Rehabilitation in Multiple Sclerosis (#18826)
- ♦ Multiply Christian Network (internationally oriented national body)

♦ Multiport Ship Agencies Network (MSAN) 16900

Exec Sec Minerva House, Minerva Business Park, Peterborough, PE2 6FT, UK. T. +441733232587. Fax +441733405877. E-mail: multiport@multiport.biz.
URL: http://www.multiport.org/

History 1978, Rotterdam (Netherlands). Articles adopted 29 Dec 1978; revised: 21 Dec 1982; 9 Oct 1984; 22 Sep 1992; 10 Jan 1994. Registered in accordance with Dutch law. General Secretariat relocated to London (UK) in 1995, but Association remains registered in Rotterdam. **Aims** Promote cooperation among member ship agencies; provide a worldwide network of independent ship agents who will uphold the highest standards of integrity; generate ship agency revenue for members; promote individual members through the strength of the network image. **Structure** Annual General Meeting; Board of Directors; General Secretariat based in Peterborough (UK). **Finance** Members' dues. **Activities** Events/meetings. **Events** *Meeting* London (UK) 2018, *General Meeting* Hamburg (Germany) 2010, *General Meeting* Singapore (Singapore) 2010, *General Meeting* Houston, TX (USA) 2009, *General Meeting* London (UK) 2008. **Publications** *Multiport Ship Agencies Network Directory* (annual).
Members Private and corporate enterprises operating as ship agents anywhere in the world. Members in 96 countries and territories:
Angola, Argentina, Bahamas, Bahrain, Bangladesh, Belgium, Benin, Brazil, Bulgaria, Canada, Chile, China, Colombia, Costa Rica, Côte d'Ivoire, Cuba, Cyprus, Denmark, Djibouti, Dominican Rep, Egypt, Equatorial Guinea, Estonia, Fiji, Finland, France, Gambia, Germany, Ghana, Greece, Greenland, Guatemala, Guinea, Haiti, Hong Kong, India, Indonesia, Iraq, Ireland, Italy, Jamaica, Japan, Jordan, Kenya, Kuwait, Latvia, Lebanon, Libya, Lithuania, Malaysia, Malta, Mauritania, Mauritius, Mexico, Monaco, Montenegro, Morocco, Mozambique, Namibia, Netherlands, New Zealand, Nicaragua, Nigeria, Norway, Oman, Pakistan, Palestine, Panama, Peru, Philippines, Portugal, Romania, Russia, Saudi Arabia, Senegal, Singapore, Slovenia, South Africa, Spain, Sri Lanka, Sudan, Switzerland, Syrian AR, Taiwan, Tanzania UR, Togo, Trinidad-Tobago, Tunisia, Türkiye, UK, Ukraine, United Arab Emirates, Uruguay, USA, Venezuela, Yemen.
Consultative Status Consultative status granted from: *UNCTAD (#20285)* (Special Category). [2018.06.15/XF0434/**F**]

- ♦ Multi-Purpose Women's Cooperative in Qassim / see First Multipurpose Women Cooperative in Gassim
- ♦ Multi-Sector Architectural Assistance in Developing Africa (internationally oriented national body)
- ♦ Multiversidad Franciscana de América Latina (unconfirmed)
- ♦ **MUM** Maharishi University of Management (#16549)
- ♦ Munadhamat Alwahdah Al'Ifriqyah (inactive)
- ♦ Munazzamah al-'Alamiyyah li-Hurriyat al-Thaqafah (inactive)
- ♦ Mundaneum (internationally oriented national body)
- ♦ Mundial ORT (#21698)
- ♦ Mundo en Armonia (#21552)
- ♦ **Mundo-ETF** Federación Mundo de Tecnologia del Entretenimiento y el Espectaculo (#21384)
- ♦ Mundo Maya Organization (internationally oriented national body)
- ♦ Mundo Nuevo / see Solidagro
- ♦ Mundo Real (internationally oriented national body)
- ♦ Mundo Sano (internationally oriented national body)
- ♦ Mundo Sano Foundation / see Mundo Sano
- ♦ Mundubat – Fundación Mundubat (internationally oriented national body)
- ♦ Mundubat Fundazioa (internationally oriented national body)

♦ Mundus maris 16901

Pres Av de Tervueren 3, 1040 Brussels, Belgium. E-mail: info@mundusmaris.org.
URL: https://www.mundusmaris.org/

History 2010, Brussels (Belgium). Former names and other names: *Mundus maris – Sciences and Arts for Sustainability* – full title. Registration: Banque-Carrefour des Entreprises, No/ID: 0830.328.314, Start date: 15 Oct 2010, Belgium; EU Transparency Register, No/ID: 171233439583-17, Start date: 14 Sep 2020. **Aims** Provide scientific and relevant indigenous knowledge and encourage artistic expression about the sea so as to promote its restoration, conservation and sustainable use, and further the study, understanding and respect of aquatic ecosystems and associated biological and cultural diversity. **Structure** General Assembly; Board of Directors. **Languages** English, French, German, Italian, Spanish. **Activities** Advocacy/lobbying/activism; awareness raising; capacity building; events/meetings; knowledge management/information dissemination; projects/programmes; research/documentation; training/education. [2023/AA1115/**F**]

- ♦ Mundus maris – Sciences and Arts for Sustainability / see Mundus maris (#16901)
- ♦ Municipal Development Partnership / see Municipal Development Partnership for West and Central Africa (#16902)

♦ Municipal Development Partnership for West and Central Africa (MDP) 16902

Address not obtained.
URL: http://www.pdm-net.org/

History as a joint project of *International Bank for Reconstruction and Development (IBRD, #12317)* (World Bank) and the French government. Office in Harare (Zimbabwe) set up in 1991; Office in Cotonou (Benin) set up in 1992. Developed into a programme under the title *Association de gestion du PDM (AG-PDM)*. Financial partners grew to include *Canadian International Development Agency (CIDA, inactive)*, 1995. Changed title to *Municipal Development Partnership*, 2001. Previously also referred to as: *Municipal Development Programme for Sub-Saharan Africa – Programme de développement municipal en Afrique subsaharienne (PDM)*. **Aims** Empower local authorities in the exercise of their duties in collaboration with the national association of local authorities and the central administration; support local authorities of their associations; disseminate useful and relevant information on decentralization. **Structure** General Assembly. Board of Directors; Steering Committee. Executive Secretary. **Staff** 16.00 FTE, paid. **Finance** Funded by *Canadian International Development Agency (CIDA, inactive)*, French Foreign Ministry; Swiss Cooperation; *European Commission (EC, #06633)*. **Activities** Pole for Capacity Building of Local Authorities and their Associations to offer services to the population; Pole for support of the decentralization process; Cross-cutting. **Events** *Africities Summit* Nairobi (Kenya) 2006, *International conference for integrating urban knowledge and practice* Gothenburg (Sweden) 2005, *Africities Summit* Yaoundé (Cameroon) 2003, *Africities Summit* Windhoek (Namibia) 2000, *Africacities session* Abidjan (Côte d'Ivoire) 1998. **Publications** *MDP Newsletter du PDM* (6 a year); *Revue Africaine des finances locales* (2 a year); *Etat de la decentralization danse le monde* (every 3 years). References material; guides.
Members National associations (18) in 18 countries:
Benin, Burkina Faso, Cameroon, Cape Verde, Central African Rep, Chad, Congo Brazzaville, Côte d'Ivoire, Gabon, Gambia, Ghana, Guinea, Mali, Mauritania, Niger, Nigeria, Senegal, Togo.
IGO Relations Other partners: *Communauté économique et monétaire d'Afrique centrale (CEMAC, #04374)*; *Union économique et monétaire Ouest africaine (UEMOA, #20377)*; *United Nations Human Settlements Programme (UN-Habitat, #20572)*. **NGO Relations** Other partners: *Sahel and West Africa Club (SWAC, #19034)*; *United Cities and Local Governments of Africa (UCLG Africa, #20500)*; *Programme Solidarité eau (pS-Eau, #18529)*. [2008.10.01/XF3709/**F**]

- ♦ Municipal Development Programme for Sub-Saharan Africa / see Municipal Development Partnership for West and Central Africa (#16902)

♦ Municipal Waste Europe (MWE) 16903

SG Rue d'Arlon 63, 1040 Brussels, Belgium. T. +3224001094.
URL: http://www.municipalwasteeurope.eu/

History 2008. Became an independent organization, 13 May 2009, when statutes were adopted. Registration: No/ID: 0816.952.509, Start date: 9 Jul 2009, Belgium; EU Transparency Register, No/ID: 75395701551-94, Start date: 21 Apr 2009. **Aims** Minimize the impact of waste on the environment; promote resource efficiency. **Structure** General Assembly; Board; Policy Committee; Working Groups; Secretariat, headed by Secretary-General. **Languages** English. **Staff** 2.00 FTE, paid. **Finance** Members' dues. Annual budget: about euro 200,000. **Publications** Position papers.
Members Full in 16 countries:
Austria, Belgium, Croatia, Denmark, Finland, France, Germany, Iceland, Italy, Lithuania, Netherlands, Norway, Poland, Portugal, Slovenia, Sweden.
NGO Relations Member of (1): *Circular Plastics Alliance (#03936)*. [2019.02.13/XJ4778/**D**]

- ♦ Munk Centre for International Studies, University of Toronto / see Munk School of Global Affairs & Public Policy, University of Toronto
- ♦ Munk School of Global Affairs / see Munk School of Global Affairs & Public Policy, University of Toronto
- ♦ Munk School of Global Affairs & Public Policy, University of Toronto (internationally oriented national body)
- ♦ Munk School – Munk School of Global Affairs & Public Policy, University of Toronto (internationally oriented national body)
- ♦ Al Muntada (#01055)
- ♦ MUPJ – Maryland United for Peace and Justice (internationally oriented national body)
- ♦ MUP – Mission to Unreached Peoples (internationally oriented national body)
- ♦ Murialdo World (unconfirmed)
- ♦ **MURS** Mouvement universel de la responsabilité scientifique (#20679)
- ♦ **MUSALAC** Red Latinoamericana y del Caribe para la Investigación y el Desarrollo de las Musaceas (#18389)
- ♦ MUSA – Mercy-USA for Aid and Development (internationally oriented national body)

♦ MusaNet 16904

Coordinator Parc Scientifique Agropolis II, 34397 Montpellier CEDEX 5, France. T. +33467619946. Fax +33467610334. E-mail: musanet.secretariat@gmail.com.
URL: http://www.musanet.org/

Aims Build on existing strengths in global, regional and national collections, uniting to optimize efforts to conserve, add value and promote the use and safe distribution of Musa *genetic diversity* as a foundation for further *breeding* or direct use by farmers. **Structure** Coordinating Secretariat; Expert Committee; Thematic Groups. **Activities** Research/documentation. **IGO Relations** *Bioversity International (#03262)*. [2016/XM4840/**F**]

♦ Musawah 16905

Secretariat 15 Jalan Limau Purut, Taman Bangsar, 59000 Kuala Lumpur, Malaysia. T. +60320830202 – +60320830606. Fax +60322020303. E-mail: info@musawah.org – musawah@musawah.org.
URL: http://www.musawah.org/

History Launched Feb 2009, Kuala Lumpur (Malaysia). Subtitle: *Global Movement for Equality and Justice in the Muslim Family*. **Aims** Advance *human rights* for *women* in *Muslim* contexts, in both their public and private lives. **Languages** Arabic, English, French, Indonesian. **Activities** Advocacy/lobbying/activism; knowledge management/information dissemination; capacity building; networking/liaising. **Publications** *Knowledge Building Brief*. Reports. **NGO Relations** *Committee on the Elimination of Discrimination against Women (CEDAW, #04250)*. [2020.01.23/XM8532/**F**]

♦ Musculoskeletal Tumor Society (internationally oriented national body)
♦ Musculo-Skeletal Tumor Society of North America / see Musculoskeletal Tumor Society

♦ Musculoskeletal Ultrasound Society (MUSOC) 16906

Main Office 3588 Plymouth Rd, Ste 249, Ann Arbor MI 48105, USA.
URL: http://www.musoc.com/

History Founded in the USA. **Aims** Increase ultrasound application to the musculoskeletal system. **Languages** English. **Events** *Musculoskeletal Ultrasound Conference* Toledo (Spain) 2022, *Annual Meeting* León (Mexico) 2019, *Annual Meeting* Seoul (Korea Rep) 2018, *Annual Meeting* Tel Aviv (Israel) 2017, *Annual Meeting* Ibiza (Spain) 2016. [2019/XM3425/**D**]

♦ Musée d'art des Amériques, OEA (see: #17629)
♦ Musée de l'Europe (#16907)
♦ Musée européen de la Toison d'Or / see Museum of Europe (#16907)
♦ Musée international (inactive)
♦ Musée international du sol / see ISRIC – World Soil Information (#16068)
♦ Musée Jean Monnet / see Museum of Europe (#16907)
♦ Musée royal de l'Afrique centrale (internationally oriented national body)
♦ Musée sans frontières (#16908)
♦ **MUSE** Medical Users Software Exchange (#16629)
♦ Museo Internacional de Suelos / see ISRIC – World Soil Information (#16068)
♦ Museum van Europa (#16907)

♦ Museum of Europe 16907

Musée de l'Europe – Europamuseum – Museum van Europa

Administration Rue de Suisse 29, 1060 Brussels, Belgium. T. +3225496060. Fax +3225496041.
Pres Avenue de l'Italie 35, 1050 Brussels, Belgium.
URL: http://www.expo-europe.be/

History 1997. Also referred to as *Musée Jean Monnet* and as *Musée européen de la Toison d'Or*. **Structure** Scientific Committee, comprising Director and 8 members. Financial Committee; Committee of the Founding Members. **Activities** Setting up *Museums of Europe Network*. [2011/XG3762/**E**]

♦ Museum With No Frontiers (MWNF) 16908

Musée sans frontières – Museum Ohne Grenzen

Head Office c/o Halpern – Prinz, Wasagasse 4, 1090 Vienna, Austria. E-mail: officevie@museumwnf.net – office@museumwnf.net.
Registered Office Markgraf-Rüdiger-Strasse 6, 1150 Vienna, Austria. T. +4319857560. Fax +4319857382. E-mail: msf.es@netway.at.
URL: http://www.museumwnf.org/

History 1995, Vienna (Austria). Full title: *Organisation internationale non gouvernementale pour la mise en valeur du patrimoine culturel des pays méditerranéens et autres*. Registered in accordance with Belgian law. **Aims** Make unknown and little known cultural heritage accessible and enjoyable to audiences worldwide through innovative offers in the fields of education, *culture* and *tourism*; promote mutual respect through a diversified understanding of *history*, *art* and culture conveying the local perspective of the territory and people concerned; promote international cooperation between museums, scholars and relevant small businesses. **Structure** General Assembly (annual). Council, including President, 2 Vice-Presidents and Secretary-General. **Languages** Arabic, English, French, German, Italian, Spanish. **Staff** 5.00 FTE, paid. Between 15-35 voluntary. **Finance** Members' dues (20%). Other sources: subsidies (30%); income from services and private sponsors (40%); royalties (10%). Budget (annual) – without project costs: euro 160,000. **Activities** MVNF Virtual Museum; MWNF Travel. **Publications** Books.
Members Full in 7 countries:
Egypt, Italy, Morocco, Portugal, Spain, Tunisia, Türkiye. [2018/XF6751/**F**]

♦ Museum Ohne Grenzen (#16908)

♦ Museums Association of the Caribbean (MAC) 16909

Association des Musées de la Caraïbe (MAC) – Asociación de Museos del Caribe (MAC)

Secretariat address not obtained. E-mail: secretariat@caribbeanmuseums.com.
URL: http://www.caribbeanmuseums.com/

History Nov 1989. Founded following recommendations of working group, 3-4 Dec 1987, Barbados, at a meeting organized by *Caribbean Conservation Association (CCA, #03481)* and funded by *OAS (#17629)*. Registration: INSEE, No/ID: 904531894 00015, Start date: 4 Oct 2021, France, MARTINIQUE. **Aims** Create a visible and accessible museum network for Caribbean Museums and Caribbean museum professionals in the region and the Diaspora so as to share knowledge and expertise. **Structure** General Meeting (annual); Board; Executive Committee; Special Committees. **Languages** Dutch, English, French, Papiamento, Spanish. **Staff** 0.50 FTE, paid. Voluntary. **Finance** Sources: contributions of member/participating states; fundraising; government support; grants; in-kind support; meeting proceeds; members' dues; private foundations; revenue from activities/projects; sponsorship; subsidies. Supported by: Collectivité Térritoriale de Martinique; FONDATION CLEMENT-Martinique; *International Council of Museums (ICOM, #13051)*; NATIONAL MUSEUM OF AFRICAN AMERICAN HISTORY AND CULTURE; *Smithsonian Institution*; *UNESCO (#20322)*. Annual budget: 50,000 USD (2022). **Activities** Awards/prizes/competitions; events/meetings; networking/liaising; projects/programmes; training/education. Active in all member countries. **Events** *Annual General Meeting* 2021, *Annual General Meeting* 2020, *Annual General Meeting* Fort de France (Martinique) 2019, *Annual General Meeting* Barbados 2018, *Annual General Meeting* Miami, FL (USA) 2017. **Publications** *MAC Newsletter* (4 a year). *Directory of Museums in the Caribbean* (1994). **Information Services** *MAC E-bLASTS* in English, French, Spanish.
Members Caribbean and Caribbean Diaspora Museums ,Historical and Cultural Institutions and Sites; individuals; related organizations. Members in 33 countries and territories:
Antigua-Barbuda, Barbados, Bermuda, Canada, Cayman Is, Curaçao, Dominica, Dominican Rep, Dutch Caribbean, France, Grenada, Guadeloupe, Guiana Fr, Guyana, Haiti, Jamaica, Martinique, Netherlands, Panama, Puerto Rico, St Croix Is, St Eustatius, St Kitts-Nevis, St Lucia, St Maarten, St Martin, St Vincent-Grenadines, Suriname, Trinidad-Tobago, Turks-Caicos, UK, USA, Virgin Is USA.
IGO Relations Partner of (1): *European Union – Latin America and the Caribbean Foundation (EU-LAC Foundation, #08999)*. **NGO Relations** Partner of (1): *Commonwealth Association of Museums (CAM, #04305)*. Affiliated with (1): *International Council of Museums (ICOM, #13051)*. [2022.02.17/XD2677/**D**]

♦ Museums in Oceania Project / see Pacific Island Museums Association (#17959)
♦ Pro-music (unconfirmed)

♦ Music In Africa Foundation 16910

Contact 3rd Floor, 158 Jan Smuts Avenue, Johannesburg, South Africa. T. +27101401317. Fax +27114423738. E-mail: info@musicinafrica.net.
URL: https://www.musicinafrica.net/about/music-africa-foundation/

History Founded 27 Jul 2013, Kenya. Registered in accordance with South African law. **Aims** Provide reliable and useful information promoting the African music sector and its operators. **Structure** Board. **NGO Relations** Partners include: *Goethe-Institut*; *Prince Claus Fund for Culture and Development*; *Siemens Stiftung*; *Southern African Music Rights Organizations (SAMRO, #19851)* Foundation. [2019/XM8639/f/**F**]

♦ Musica International 16911

Exec Dir c/o La Fabrique de Théâtre, 10 rue du Hohwald, 67000 Strasbourg, France. T. +33388361754. E-mail: office@musicanet.org.
URL: http://www.musicanet.org/

History 6 Feb 1998. **Aims** Develop a comprehensive database of the world's *choral music*. **Structure** General Assembly; Board. **Languages** English, French, German, Spanish. **Staff** 1.50 FTE, paid; 2.00 FTE, voluntary. **Finance** Members' dues. Other sources: donations; subscriptions. **Activities** Events/meetings. **Events** *General Assembly* Stuttgart (Germany) 2010, *General Assembly* Pomaz (Hungary) 2009.
Members Active in 25 countries:
Austria, Belgium, Canada, Congo DR, Denmark, Finland, France, Germany, Hungary, Ireland, Italy, Latvia, Luxembourg, Netherlands, New Zealand, Norway, Philippines, Slovenia, South Africa, Spain, Sweden, Switzerland, UK, USA, Venezuela. [2019.02.12/XJ0736/y/**F**]

♦ Music Business Balkan / see RUNDA (#18999)
♦ Music Climate Pact (unconfirmed)
♦ Music Council of the Three Americas (#04723)

♦ Music Crossroads 16912

Contact Square Eugene Plasky 92, 1030 Brussels, Belgium. T. +3225139774. E-mail: info@music-crossroads.net.
URL: http://www.music-crossroads.net/

History 1995. Functions as a programme of *Jeunesses Musicales International (JMI, #16110)*. Registered as a non-profit organization. **Aims** Provide music education, professional training, live performances and promotion of young talents to support development of the music education sector and the music industry in the culturally rich southern African region. **Structure** Head office in Brussels (Belgium). *Music Crossroads Academies* Academies in: Malawi; Mozambique; Zimbabwe. **Languages** English. [2019.02.04/XM4847/**E**]

♦ Music Encoding Initiative (MEI) 16913

Contact Akademie der Wissenschaften und der Literatur, Geschwister-Scholl-Str 2, 55131 Mainz, Germany. E-mail: info@music-encoding.org.
URL: http://music-encoding.org/

History 2014. **Aims** Create, promote and diffuse a semantically rich model for music notation. **Structure** Board; Technical Team. **Finance** Sources: donations; grants; members' dues. **Activities** Events/meetings; training/education. **Events** *Annual Music Encoding Conference* Medford, MA (USA) 2020, *Conference* Vienna (Austria) 2019, *Conference* College Park, MD (USA) 2018, *Conference* Montréal, QC (Canada) 2016, *Conference* Florence (Italy) 2015. **Members** Individual; Institutional. Membership countries not specified. [2020.05.12/XM6020/**F**]

♦ Musicians Against Nuclear Arms (internationally oriented national body)
♦ Musicians and Fine Artists for World Peace (internationally oriented national body)

♦ Music Producers Guild (MPG) 16914

Contact 41b Beach Road, Littlehampton, BN17 5JA, UK. T. +442032397606.
URL: http://www.mpg.org.uk/

History Founded 1995, as *Re-Pro International*, when became international, deriving from *'British Record Producers Guild'*, set up 1986. Current name adopted 1998. **Aims** Represent the needs of studio and music producers, recording, mixing and mastering engineers, programmers and remixers. **Structure** Executive Board. **Staff** Voluntary. **Finance** Members' dues. **Activities** Advocacy/lobbying/activism; awards/prizes/competitions; awareness raising; events/meetings; networking/liaising.
Members Full in 8 countries:
Austria, Belgium, Canada, Germany, South Africa, Sweden, UK, USA.
NGO Relations Instrumental in setting up: *European Sound Directors' Association (ESDA, no recent information)*. [2019.12.12/XD5872/**D**]

♦ Music Users' Council of Europe (no recent information)
♦ Musiqueurope / see Confederation of European Music Industries (#04527)
♦ Musique vivante d'aujourd'hui (#16496)
♦ Musitrad – Association internationale des musiques traditionnelles (no recent information)
♦ Muslim Aid (internationally oriented national body)
♦ Muslim Aid America / see Muslim Aid
♦ Muslim Aid Sveriges / see Muslim Aid

♦ Muslim Brotherhood 16915

Fraternité islamique – Ikhwan al-Muslimin

Address not obtained.

History 11 Apr 1929, Ismailia (Egypt), by Hasan el Banna, as a political and religious pan-Islamic association. Also spelt as *Al Ikhwan al Muslimum* and referred to as *International Moslem Brotherhood*. **Aims** Adhere strictly to *Shariah* norms: assiduous observance of *religious duties*; avoid gambling, alcohol, usury, fornication; Islamize the home; defend (by military means if necessary) *Islam* and society.
Members Sections in 6 countries:
Egypt, Iraq, Jordan, Sudan, Syrian AR, Yemen.
NGO Relations Offshoots include: Islamic Resistance Movement (HAMAS); *Hizb ut-Tahrir (HuT, #10936)*. [2009/XF5011/**F**]

♦ Muslim Council of Elders 16916

Contact address not obtained. T. +97123073777. E-mail: info@muslim-elders.com.
URL: https://muslim-elders.com/

History 18 Jul 2014. **Aims** Promote peace in the Muslim communities. **Structure** Board. **Activities** Advocacy/lobbying/activism; events/meetings; training/education. **Events** *Arab Media Convention for Human Fraternity* Abu Dhabi (United Arab Emirates) 2020. [2021/AA1575/**D**]

♦ Muslim Hands (internationally oriented national body)
♦ Muslim Peace Fellowship (internationally oriented national body)
♦ Muslims Without Borders / see United Mission for Relief & Development
♦ Muslim Women Lawyers for Human Rights (internationally oriented national body)

♦ Muslim World League (MWL) 16917

Ligue islamique mondiale – Rabita Al-Alam Al-Islami

SG PO Box 537, Makkah 21955, Saudi Arabia. T. +966125309444. Fax +966125601319. E-mail: info@themwl.org.
Street address 537 Old Jeddah Road, Makkah 21955, Saudi Arabia.
URL: https://themwl.org/

History 18 May 1962, Makkah (Saudi Arabia). Founded by an Islamic Conference, when a Constituent Council of Muslim scholars was set up. Constitution adopted 1963, officially ratified 17 Apr 1965, Makkah, at General Islamic Conference. **Aims** Present the true Islam and its tolerant principles; provide humanitarian aid; extend bridges of dialogue and cooperation with all; engage in positive openness to all cultures and civilizations; follow the path of centrism and moderation to realize the message of Islam; ward off movements calling for extremism, violence and exclusion for a world full of peace, justice and coexistence. **Structure** The Supreme Council; The World Supreme Council for Mosques; Islamic Fiqh Council; Organization of Muslim Scholars. **Languages** Arabic, English, French. **Staff** 500.00 FTE, paid. **Finance** Sources: investments. Other sources: endowments. **Activities** Events/meetings; humanitarian/emergency aid. **Events** *Conference on the Charter of Makkah* Riyadh (Saudi Arabia) 2022, *Forum On Common Values Among Religious Followers* Riyadh (Saudi Arabia) 2022, *International Conference on Initiatives for Protecting the Youth from Extremist and Violent Ideologies* Geneva (Switzerland) 2020, *Islamic World Conference* Makkah (Saudi Arabia) 2014, *International interfaith conference* Madrid (Spain) 2008. **Publications** *Journal of the MWL* (12 a year) in Arabic, English.
Members Branch Offices (17) and Islamic centers (12) in 21 countries:
Austria, Belgium, Bosnia-Herzegovina, Brazil, Comoros, Congo Brazzaville, Denmark, Indonesia, Italy, Kenya, Malaysia, Mauritania, Niger, Nigeria, Pakistan, Russia, Senegal, South Africa, Spain, Switzerland, Uganda.
Consultative Status Consultative status granted from: *ECOSOC (#05331)* (General); *UNICEF (#20332)*. **IGO Relations** Observer status with (1): *Islamic World Educational, Scientific and Cultural Organization (ICESCO, #16058)*. [2022.10.30/XC4378/**C**]

♦ Muslim World Link (internationally oriented national body)
♦ **MUSOC** Musculoskeletal Ultrasound Society (#16906)
♦ Mutagenesis and Experimental Pathology Society of Australasia / see Molecular and Experimental Pathology Society of Australasia
♦ Mutual Aid and Fraternity (internationally oriented national body)
♦ Mutual Aid Treaty, 1683 (1683 treaty)
♦ Mutual Assistance of the Latin American Government Oil Companies / see Asociación Regional de Empresas del Sector Petróleo, Gas y Biocombustibles en Latinoamérica y el Caribe (#02296)
♦ Mutual Assistance of the Latin American Oil Companies / see Asociación Regional de Empresas del Sector Petróleo, Gas y Biocombustibles en Latinoamérica y el Caribe (#02296)

♦ Mutual Images / see Mutual Images Research Association (#16918)

♦ Mutual Images Research Association (MIRA) 16918

Main Office 3 allée de l'avenir, Les Chênes, Entrée 3, 64600 Anglet, France. E-mail: mutualimages@gmail.com.
URL: https://mutualimages.org/
History 2013. Former names and other names: *Mutual Images* – legal name. Registration: RNA, No/ID: W691087048, Start date: 13 Dec 2014, France. **Structure** Board. **Activities** Events/meetings. **Events** *International Workshop* Kyoto (Japan) 2021, *International Workshop* Salford (UK) 2021, *International Workshop* Kyoto (Japan) 2020, *International Workshop* Vigo (Spain) 2019, *International Workshop* Cardiff (UK) 2018. **Publications** *Mutual Images* (annual). [2022.02.15/AA1561/**C**]

♦ Mutualism Alliance of America (#00634)
♦ MUTUELLE / see International Civil Servants Mutual Association (#12585)
♦ Mutuelle d'épargne et de crédit / see International Civil Servants Mutual Association (#12585)
♦ Muzika Esperanto-Ligo (no recent information)

♦ Muzzle Loaders Associations International Committee (MLAIC) . . . 16919

SG Bollersgasse 8, 63925 Laudenbach, Germany. E-mail: sg@mlaic.org – dsg@mlaic.org.
URL: http://mlaic.org/
History 20 Jun 1971. **Aims** Promote conservation and appreciation of *antique firearms*; promote research into the history of muzzle loading firearms. **Structure** Secretary General; Deputy Secretary General; Treasurer. **Languages** English. **Staff** Voluntary. **Activities** Sporting activities. **Publications** *MLAIC Newsletter*.
Members National associations in 28 countries:
Argentina, Australia, Austria, Belgium, Canada, Czechia, Denmark, Finland, France, Germany, Greece, Hungary, Italy, Japan, Malta, Netherlands, New Zealand, Norway, Poland, Portugal, Russia, Slovakia, South Africa, Spain, Sweden, Switzerland, UK, USA. [2020.03.06/XE4715/**D**]

♦ **MVNA** Med-Vet-Net Association (#16693)

♦ MVNO Europe 16920

Secretariat Rue de la Loi 38, 1000 Brussels, Belgium. T. +3227896623. E-mail: info@mvnoeurope.eu.
URL: http://mvnoeurope.eu/
History 2012. MVNO stands for: *Mobile Virtual Network Operators*. EU Transparency Register: 458563610807-24. **Aims** Create a more openly accessible market for all MVNOs, so as to contribute to the growth of the fast-moving mobile communication sector, ensure that consumers and business users have a wider range of diversified services to choose from and develop competition on the retail mobile market to their benefit. **Structure** Executive Committee; Secretariat. **Finance** Members' dues. [2018/XM5968/**D**]

♦ MWA – Millennium Water Alliance (internationally oriented national body)
♦ **MWBI** Mission Without Borders International (#16830)
♦ **MWC** Mennonite World Conference (#16713)
♦ **MWE** Municipal Waste Europe (#16903)
♦ MWF – Mediterranean Women's Fund (internationally oriented national body)
♦ **MWF** Mobile & Wireless Forum (#16837)
♦ **MWG** Mining Working Group at the UN (#16813)
♦ **MWIA** Medical Women's International Association (#16630)
♦ MWI – Magee Womancare International (internationally oriented national body)
♦ MWL – Mercy Without Limits (internationally oriented national body)
♦ **MWL** Muslim World League (#16917)
♦ **MWNF** Museum With No Frontiers (#16908)
♦ MWN – Materials World Network (internationally oriented national body)
♦ **MWU** Maccabi World Union (#16537)
♦ MWYC – Macedonian World Youth Congress
♦ MXY – Institutum Yarumalense pro Missionibus ad Exteras Gentes (religious order)
♦ Myanmar Actions for Mission and Evangelism (internationally oriented national body)
♦ **MYBA** MYBA The Worldwide Yachting Association (#16921)

♦ MYBA The Worldwide Yachting Association (MYBA) 16921

Gen Sec 92-120 av Eugène Donadeï, Cap Center, 06700 Saint-Laurent-du-Var, France. T. +33493318549. Fax +33493318853. E-mail: info@myba.net.
URL: http://www.myba-association.com/
History 1984. Registration: France. **Aims** Establish and maintain a high standard of professional ethics, rules and skills in charter, sales and yacht management; establish, print and distribute contractual documents specific to the profession and encourage members to promote them among professionals; encourage inter-professional exchanges and contact; provide a framework with a view to resolution of commercial conflicts. **Structure** Board; Committees (9). **Languages** English, French. **Staff** 6.00 FTE, paid.
Members Full in 21 countries and territories:
Australia, Canada, Croatia, Cyprus, France, Germany, Gibraltar, Greece, Hong Kong, Ireland, Italy, Monaco, New Zealand, Poland, Singapore, Spain, Switzerland, Türkiye, UK, USA, Virgin Is UK.
IGO Relations Also links with government organizations. [2022.06.28/XJ7237/**C**]

♦ Mycotoxin Workshop (meeting series)

♦ MyData Global 16922

General Manager address not obtained.
URL: http://mydata.org/
Aims Empower individuals by improving their *right* to self-determination regarding their personal *data*. **Structure** Board of Directors; Steering Group. **Events** *Conference* Helsinki (Finland) 2022, *Conference* Helsinki (Finland) 2019, *Conference* Helsinki (Finland) 2018, *Community Meeting* Lyon (France) 2018, *Community Meeting* Turin (Italy) 2018. **Publications** *MyData Newsletter*.
Members Organizational members in 20 countries and territories:
Australia, Austria, Bermuda, Cameroon, Denmark, Finland, France, Germany, Greece, Japan, Netherlands, Portugal, Slovakia, Slovenia, South Africa, Spain, Sweden, Switzerland, UK, USA. [2018/XM7937/**C**]

♦ MyDIO – My Drop in the Oceans (unconfirmed)
♦ My Drop in the Oceans (unconfirmed)
♦ Myelodysplastic Syndrome / see European Working Group on MDS (#09115)

♦ Myelodysplastic Syndromes Foundation (MDS Foundation) 16923

Exec Dir 4573 South Broad St, Ste 150, Yardville NJ 08620, USA. T. +16092980590. E-mail: patientliaison@mds-foundation.org.
URL: http://www.mds-foundation.org/
History Registration: USA. **Aims** Support and education patients and healthcare providers with innovative research into the fields of MDS, Acute Myeloid *Leukaemia* (AML), and related myeloid neoplasms in order to accelerate progress leading to diagnosis, control and cure of these diseases. **Structure** Board of Directors. **Finance** Members' dues. Other sources: donations; pharmaceutical support. **Activities** Training/education; research and development. **Events** *International Congress on Myelodysplastic Syndromes* 2021, *International Symposium on Myelodysplastic Syndromes* Copenhagen (Denmark) 2019, *International Symposium on Myelodysplastic Syndromes* Valencia (Spain) 2017, *International Symposium on Myelodysplastic Syndromes* Washington, DC (USA) 2015, *International Symposium on Myelodysplastic Syndromes* Berlin (Germany) 2013. **Publications** *MDS News* (2 a year). *Building Blocks of Hope* – patient resources.
Members Centres of Excellence in 37 countries and territories:
Argentina, Armenia, Australia, Austria, Belgium, Brazil, Canada, China, Czechia, Denmark, France, Germany, Greece, Hungary, India, Ireland, Israel, Italy, Japan, Korea Rep, Netherlands, Peru, Poland, Portugal, Saudi Arabia, Singapore, South Africa, Spain, Sweden, Switzerland, Taiwan, Thailand, Tunisia, Türkiye, UK, Ukraine, USA.
NGO Relations Member of (1): *Acute Leukemia Advocates Network (ALAN, #00107)*. Steering Committee member of: *MDS Alliance (#16608)*. [2018.07.27/XF6050/f/**F**]

♦ Myeloma Euronet – European Network of Myeloma Patient Groups (inactive)

♦ Myeloma Patients Europe (MPE) 16924

CEO Ave Louise 143/4, 1050 Brussels, Belgium. E-mail: info@mpeurope.org.
URL: http://www.mpeurope.org/
History 21 Oct 2011. Founded by merger of *European Network of Myeloma Patient Groups (Myeloma Euronet, inactive)* and *European Myeloma Platform (EMP, inactive)*. Registration: Banque-Carrefour des Entreprises, No/ID: 0842.182.407, Start date: 28 Dec 2011, Belgium; EU Transparency Register, No/ID: 514101642770-73, Start date: 19 May 2021. **Aims** Provide education, information and support to member groups; advocate at European, national and local levels for the best possible research and equal access treatment and care. **Structure** General Assembly; Board. **Languages** English. **Activities** Projects/programmes; events/meetings; advocacy/lobbying/activism; awareness raising; capacity building. **Events** *General Assembly* Madrid (Spain) 2016, *General Assembly* Brussels (Belgium) 2012. **Publications** factsheets; Q and A; patient guides; educational clips; videos; conference reports.
Members Myeloma patient groups (43). Full in 28 countries:
Armenia, Austria, Belgium, Croatia, Denmark, Estonia, Finland, France, Germany, Hungary, Israel, Latvia, Lithuania, Netherlands, North Macedonia, Norway, Poland, Portugal, Romania, Russia, Serbia, Slovakia, Slovenia, Spain, Sweden, Switzerland, Türkiye, UK.
Associate in 2 countries:
Czechia, Portugal.
NGO Relations Member of (6): *European Cancer Organisation (ECO, #06432)* (Patient Advisory Committee); *European Cancer Patient Coalition (ECPC, #06433)*; *European Hematology Association (EHA, #07473)* (Workgroup); *European Society for Medical Oncology (ESMO, #08648)* (Patient Advocates Working Group (ESMO PAWG)); *EURORDIS – Rare Diseases Europe (#09175)*; *Workgroup of European Cancer Patient Advocacy Networks (WECAN, #21054)*. [2021/XJ5786/**D**]

♦ MyRight – Empower People with Disabilities (internationally oriented national body)
♦ Mystery Shopping Professionals Association / see MSPA (#16879)
♦ Mystery Shopping Providers Association / see MSPA (#16879)
♦ MZF – Missionszentrale der Franziskaner (internationally oriented national body)
♦ **N3** Nordic Number theory Network (#17369)
♦ NAAA – Nordic Association of Advertising Agencies (no recent information)
♦ NAACOG / see Association of Women's Health, Obstetric and Neonatal Nurses
♦ NAAEC – North American Agreement for Environmental Cooperation (1993 treaty)
♦ NAAE / see Northern European Association for Accelerator Engineers (#17589)
♦ **NAAE** Northern European Association for Accelerator Engineers (#17589)
♦ **NAAFE** North American Association of Fisheries Economists (#17559)
♦ NAAHOLS – North American Association for the History of the Language Sciences (internationally oriented national body)
♦ NAALC – North American Agreement on Labour Cooperation (1993 treaty)
♦ NA'AMAT Movement of Working Women and Volunteers (internationally oriented national body)
♦ NAA / see NATO Parliamentary Assembly (#16946)
♦ **NAA** Nordic Acoustic Association (#17165)
♦ NAAPB / see International Association of Amusement Parks and Attractions (#11699)
♦ NAAP / see International Association of Amusement Parks and Attractions (#11699)
♦ **NAAS** Nordic Association for American Studies (#17178)
♦ NAASS – Académie arabe Nayef des sciences de sécurité / see Naif Arab University for Security Sciences (#16929)
♦ Nabakrushna Choudhury Centre for Development Studies / see Centre for Development Studies, Bhubaneswar
♦ **NABA** North American Broadcasters Association (#17561)
♦ NABC – Netherlands-African Business Council (internationally oriented national body)
♦ NABF – North American Baptist Fellowship (internationally oriented national body)
♦ **NABF** North American Boxing Federation (#17560)
♦ **NABO** North Atlantic Biocultural Organization (#17570)
♦ NABS / see Society for Freshwater Science
♦ NACACI – North American, Central American and Caribbean Islands Weightlifting Federation (inactive)
♦ **NACAC** North American, Central American and Caribbean Athletic Association (#17563)
♦ **NACACTFCA** North America, Central America and Caribbean Track and Field Coaches Association (#17558)
♦ NACADA: The Global Community for Academic Advising (internationally oriented national body)
♦ NACADA – NACADA: The Global Community for Academic Advising (internationally oriented national body)
♦ **NACA** Network of Aquaculture Centres in Asia-Pacific (#16991)
♦ NACASO – North American Council of AIDS Service Organizations (internationally oriented national body)
♦ **NACASSW** North American and Caribbean Association of Schools of Social Work (#17562)
♦ NACC / see Euro Atlantic Partnership Council (#05646)
♦ NACC' / see NATO (#16945)
♦ **NACC** Nonprofit Academic Centers Council (#17149)
♦ Nace Benelux (internationally oriented national body)
♦ **NACEE** Network of Aquaculture Centres in Central-Eastern Europe (#16992)

♦ NACE International – The Corrosion Society 16925

Main Office 15835 Park Ten Place, Houston TX 77084, USA. T. +12812286200ext210. Fax +12812286300. E-mail: firstservice@nace.org.
URL: http://www.nace.org/
History 1943, USA, as *National Association of Corrosion Engineers (NACE)*. Present name adopted 1993. **Aims** Protect people, assets and the environment from the effects of corrosion. **Structure** Board of Directors. North American areas (4): Northern; Eastern; Central; Western. Internal regions (4): East Asia/Pacific Rim; West Asia/Africa; Europe, including *Nace Benelux*; Latin America. **Activities** Conferences; training courses. **Events** *Conference* Abu Dhabi (United Arab Emirates) 2019, *International conference on environmental degradation of materials in nuclear power systems – water reactors* Boston, MA (USA) 2019, *East Asia and Pacific Area Regional Conference* Yokohama (Japan) 2019, *Annual Conference* Phoenix, AZ (USA) 2018, *Annual Conference* New Orleans, LA (USA) 2017. **Members** Individuals (20,000) in 100 countries. Membership countries not specified. **IGO Relations** Consultative status with: *International Maritime Organization (IMO, #14102)*. [2018/XN4813/**D**]

♦ NACE / see NACE International – The Corrosion Society (#16925)
♦ NACETE – North Africa Centre for Engineering and Technology Education (internationally oriented national body)
♦ **NACGF** North Atlantic Coast Guard Forum (#17571)
♦ **NACG** Nordic Alliance for Clinical Genomics (#17171)
♦ **NACHC** North America and the Caribbean Handball Confederation (#17557)
♦ Naciones Unidas (#20515)
♦ NACLA – North American Congress on Latin America (internationally oriented national body)
♦ **NAC** New Agenda Coalition (#17074)
♦ **NAC** Nordic Adoption Council (#17167)
♦ NAC – Nordic Aphasia Conference (meeting series)
♦ **NAC** North Atlantic Council (#17572)
♦ **NACP** Nordic Association for Clinical Physics (#17184)
♦ NACRA / see Rugby Americas North (#18997)
♦ **NACS** Nordic Association for Canadian Studies (#17181)
♦ **NACS** Nordic Association for China Studies (#17182)
♦ **NACS** Nordic Association for Clinical Sexology (#17185)
♦ **NACT** Nordic Association for Convulsive Therapy (#17189)
♦ NAD / see Netzwerk Afrika Deutschland
♦ Nadace pro zivé Baltské More (internationally oriented national body)

♦ Nadacia Integra (internationally oriented national body)
♦ Nadacia na Ochranu Baltického Mora (internationally oriented national body)
♦ Nadbałtyckie Centrum Kultury (internationally oriented national body)
♦ Nadi Al Bassar – Centre maghrébin de la vision, Tunis (internationally oriented national body)
♦ Nadi Al Bassar – Centre de protection du handicap visuel et de recherches appliquées à l'oeil / see Nadi Al Bassar – North African Centre for Sight and Visual Sciences, Tunis
♦ Nadi Al Bassar – North African Centre for Sight and Visual Sciences, Tunis (internationally oriented national body)
♦ NAD – Netzwerk Afrika Deutschland (internationally oriented national body)
♦ NAD – Nordic Centre for Alcohol and Drug Research (inactive)
♦ NAD – Nordiskt Center för Alkohol- och Drogforskning (inactive)
♦ NAED / see International Academies of Emergency Dispatch
♦ NAEMD / see International Academies of Emergency Dispatch
♦ **N-AERUS** Network-Association of European Researchers in Urbanisation in the South (#16996)
♦ **NAES** Nordic Association of English Studies (#17192)
♦ **NAEVG** Nordic Association for Educational and Vocational Guidance (#17191)
♦ Naevus Global (internationally oriented national body)

♦ Naevus International 16926

Coordinator address not obtained. E-mail: info@naevusinternational.com.
URL: https://www.naevusinternational.com/

History 2017. **Aims** Improve the lives of those affected by Congenital Melanocytic Naevi (CMN) worldwide. **Structure** Leader Team. Patient Advocacy Branch: *Naevus Global*. **Activities** Advocacy/lobbying/activism; events/meetings; research/documentation. **Events** *Conference* Brussels (Belgium) 2019.
[2022.06.27/AA2330/**C**]

♦ **NAEW and C** NATO Airborne Early Warning and Control Force Command (#16942)
♦ NAE World Relief Commission / see World Relief
♦ **NAFA** Nordic Anthropological Film Association (#17173)
♦ **NAFA** Nordic Association for Andrology (#17179)
♦ NAFAPA – North American Federation of Adapted Physical Activity (internationally oriented national body)
♦ **NAFC** North American Forestry Commission (#17565)
♦ **NAFEMS** International Association for the Engineering Analysis Community (#11870)
♦ NAFEO – Network of African Freedom of Expression Organizations (inactive)
♦ **NAFIA** Nordiska Arbetsgruppen för Internationella Amningsfrågor (#17470)
♦ NAF International (inactive)
♦ **NAFMDVB** North American Foot-and-Mouth Disease Vaccine Bank (#17564)
♦ NAF – NAF International (inactive)
♦ **NAF** Nordiska Administrativa Förbundet (#17477)
♦ **NAF** Nordisk Aerobiologisk Förening (#17481)
♦ NAFO – Convention on Future Multilateral Cooperation in the Northwest Atlantic Fisheries, 1978 (1978 treaty)
♦ **NAFO** Northwest Atlantic Fisheries Organization (#17606)
♦ NAFSA / see NAFSA – Association of International Educators
♦ NAFSA – Association of International Educators (internationally oriented national body)

♦ NAFTA Secretariat 16927

Secrétariat de l'ALENA – Secretariado del TLCAN

Canadian Sec 111 Sussex Drive, 5th Floor, Ottawa ON K1A 0G2, Canada. T. +13432034269. Fax +16169929392. E-mail: canada@nafta-sec-alena.org.
Mexican SG Pachuca 189, 16th floor, Condesa, Cuauhtémoc, Mexico City, Mexico, 06140 Mexico City CDMX, Mexico. T. +5257299100 ext 15010. E-mail: naftamexico@nafta-sec-alena.org.
United States Sec 1401 Constitution Ave NW, Room 2061, Washington DC 20230, USA. T. +12024825438. Fax +12024820148. E-mail: usa@nafta-sec-alena.org.

History Established Dec 1993, on signature of an agreement by Canada, Mexico and USA, to create the *North American Free Trade Area*, pursuant to Article 2002 of the *North American Free Trade Agreement (NAFTA) – Accord de libre-échange nord-américain (ALENA) – Tratado de Libre Comercio de Norteamérica (TLC)*. Had been proposed Jun 1992, the USA already having a bilateral arrangement with Mexico, signed 1987, and with Canada, signed 1988. NAFTA came into force 1 Jan 1994, on ratification by parliaments. **Aims** Administer the mechanisms specified under the NAFTA to resolve trade *disputes* between national industries and/or governments in a timely and impartial manner. **Activities** Conflict resolution; guidance/assistance/consulting. Management of treaties and agreements: *North American Agreement for Environmental Cooperation (NAAEC, 1993)*; *North American Agreement on Labour Cooperation (NAALC, 1993)*. **Events** *Meeting on biodiversity conservation* Mexico City (Mexico) 2000, *Joint conference* Austin, TX (USA) 1999, *Meeting on a regional strategy for bird conservation in North America* Mexico City (Mexico) 1998, *Transboundary environmental assessment meeting* Montréal, QC (Canada) 1998.
Members Unites 3 countries:
Canada, Mexico, USA.
[2020.08.27/XF5235/**F***]

♦ **NAFT** Nordic Association of Forensic Toxicologists (#17193)
♦ Naga International Support Centre, Amsterdam (internationally oriented national body)
♦ NAGALIM – Naga International Support Centre, Amsterdam (internationally oriented national body)
♦ Nagasaki Foundation for the Promotion of Peace (internationally oriented national body)
♦ Nagasaki Peace Institute (internationally oriented national body)
♦ NAG – Nordic Archaeobotany Group (unconfirmed)
♦ Någon att Tala med Samaritans / see Samaritans
♦ Nagoya – Kuala Lumpur Supplementary Protocol on Liability and Redress to the Cartagena Protocol on Biosafety (2010 treaty)
♦ Nagoya Protocol on Access to Genetic Resources and the Fair and Equitable Sharing of Benefits Arising from their Utilization to the Convention on Biological Diversity (2010 treaty)
♦ Nagoya Protocol – Nagoya Protocol on Access to Genetic Resources and the Fair and Equitable Sharing of Benefits Arising from their Utilization to the Convention on Biological Diversity (2010 treaty)
♦ NAHF – Northeast Asian History Foundation (internationally oriented national body)
♦ Nah- un Mittelost-Verein (internationally oriented national body)
♦ NAHP / see Nordic Offset Printing Association, The (#17373)
♦ NAHRMA – North American Human Resource Management Association (internationally oriented national body)
♦ NAID-Australasia (internationally oriented national body)

♦ NAID-Europe 16928

CEO 3030 N, 3rd St, Ste 940, Phoenix AZ 85012, USA. T. +16027886243ext2001. E-mail: info@naideurope.eu.
URL: http://naideurope.eu/

History as a standing committee of *National Association of Information Destruction (NAID)*. **Aims** Promote the information destruction industry. **Structure** Board, headed by Chair. **Events** *European Information Management Conference* Amsterdam (Netherlands) 2013, *European Regional Conference* Brussels (Belgium) 2012, *European regional conference* Budapest (Hungary) 2008. **NGO Relations** *NAID-Australasia*; *PRISM International*.
[2016/XJ4245/**E**]

♦ NAID – North American Integration and Development Center (internationally oriented national body)
♦ Naif Arab Academy for Security Sciences / see Naif Arab University for Security Sciences (#16929)

♦ Naif Arab University for Security Sciences (NAUSS) 16929

Université arabe Nayef des sciences de sécurité

Pres PO Box 6830, Riyadh 11452, Saudi Arabia. T. +96612463444. Fax +96612464713. E-mail: info@nauss.edu.sa.
URL: http://www.nauss.edu.sa/

History 4 Oct 1978, Riyadh (Saudi Arabia), as *Arab Security Studies and Training Centre (ASSTC)*, also referred to as *Arab Centre for Security Studies and Training* and *Arab Centre for Security and Training Studies*, by a decision of 2nd Meeting of the *Arab Interior Ministers' Council (AIMC, #00990)*. Became operational in 1980, and an associated entity of CAMI in 1982. Jan 1997, name changed to *Naif Arab Academy for Security Sciences (NAASS) – Académie arabe Nayef des sciences de sécurité*. **Aims** Promote and enrich studies and applied research in *security* areas, especially in *crime prevention* and *police* sciences within the context of Arab security integration; expound *Islamic* criminal *law*; upgrade training of professionals involved in crime prevention and control; establish and develop collaboration with scientific, academic and police institutions across the Arab world for the exchange of expertise and sharing of information. **Structure** Board of Directors, comprising: (1) Minister of Interior of Saudi Arabia, Chairman; (2) President of NAUSS, permanent member and Secretary General of the Board; (3) Secretary General of CAMI, permanent member; (4) 4 members selected for being notably interested in research and training in the area of crime prevention and criminal justice. Institutions (2): College of Graduate Studies, consisting of 4 departments (Criminal Justice; Police Sciences; Administrative Sciences; Social Sciences); Training College, set up 1980, consisting of 4 departments (Training Programmes; College of Forensic Sciences; Education Technologies; Security Exhibitions). Also includes Studies and Research Centre (SRC), set up 1980, consisting of 4 departments (Research and Studies; Symposia and Scientific Conventions; Publishing; Computer and Information). Scientific Departments (2): Department of International Cooperation (DIC), set up 1985; Department of Academic Affairs, set up 1997 and subdivided into Department of Admission of Registration (DAR), Statistical Division, Department of Educational Technologies, Library and Publication Division. **Finance** Arab states contributions to the annual budget of NAUSS have the same quota-ratio as their contributions as members of the League of Arab States. Other sources: gifts; unconditional donations; revenues generated by activities. **Activities** Carries out various activities to prevent crime and victimization, maintain security and peace, promote sustained development in the context of socio-economic and cultural conditions and foster justice, using cross-sectoral and interdisciplinary approach. **Events** *International Arab Forensic Science and Forensic Medicine Conference* Riyadh (Saudi Arabia) 2015, *International Arab Forensic Science and Forensic Medicine Conference / Conference* Riyadh (Saudi Arabia) 2014, *Conference on volunteer work and security in the Arab world* Riyadh (Saudi Arabia) 2000, *Meeting of the deans of security colleges, institutes and schools in the Arab countries* Riyadh (Saudi Arabia) 1998, *Symposium on legislations for combating terrorism in the Arab world* Riyadh (Saudi Arabia) 1998. **Publications** *Security and Life Magazine* (12 a year); *The Arab Journal for Security Studies and Training* (2 a year). Books; reports.
Members Governments of 21 countries and territories:
Algeria, Bahrain, Djibouti, Egypt, Iraq, Jordan, Kuwait, Lebanon, Libya, Mauritania, Morocco, Oman, Palestine, Qatar, Saudi Arabia, Somalia, Sudan, Syrian AR, Tunisia, United Arab Emirates, Yemen.
IGO Relations Close partnership with: the Bureau of *Council of Arab Ministers of Justice (no recent information)*; *League of Arab States (LAS, #16420)*. Special agreement with: *ECOSOC (#05331)*. Cooperation agreement with: *Islamic World Educational, Scientific and Cultural Organization (ICESCO, #16058)*. **NGO Relations** Member of: *Association of Arab Universities (AARU, #02374)*; *Federation of the Universities of the Islamic World (FUIW, #09710)*.
[2016/XE3945/**E***]

♦ NAIF – Nordens Akademiska Idrottsförbund (inactive)
♦ Naija Worldwide Charities (internationally oriented national body)
♦ NAIMA – North American Insulation Manufacturers Association (internationally oriented national body)
♦ **NAIMH** Nordic Association for Infant Mental Health (#17509)
♦ NAI – New Africa Initiative (no recent information)
♦ NAIN – North American Interfaith Network (internationally oriented national body)
♦ **NAI** Nordic Africa Institute (#17168)
♦ Nairobi Convention – Convention for the Protection, Management and Development of the Marine and Coastal Environment of the Eastern African Region (1985 treaty)
♦ Nairobi convention – International Convention on Mutual Administrative Assistance for the Prevention, Investigation and Repression of Customs Offences (1977 treaty)
♦ Nairobi Declaration on the Problem of Illicit Small Arms and Light Weapons in the Great Lakes Region and the Horn of Africa (2000 treaty)
♦ Nairobi International Convention on the Removal of Wrecks, 2007 (2007 treaty)
♦ Nairobi Peace Group / see NPI Africa
♦ Nairobi Secretariat / see Regional Centre on Small Arms and Light Weapons in the Great Lakes Region, the Horn of Africa and Bordering States (#18760)

♦ Nairobi Staff Union 16930

Pres PO Box 67578, Nairobi, Kenya. T. +2542621234 – +2542622706 – +2542622707. Fax +2542622755 – +2542226886-622708.
URL: http://www.unon.org/

History as *UNON Staff Union* to represent staff members of *United Nations Office at Nairobi (UNON, #20600)*. Also referred to as *United Nations Staff Union at Nairobi*. **NGO Relations** Member of: *Coordinating Committee for International Staff Unions and Associations of the United Nations System (CCISUA, #04818)*.
[2013/XE4154/**E**]

♦ Nairobi Treaty – Nairobi Treaty on the Protection of the Olympic Symbol (1981 treaty)
♦ Nairobi Treaty on the Protection of the Olympic Symbol (1981 treaty)
♦ Nairobi WRC 2007 – Nairobi International Convention on the Removal of Wrecks, 2007 (2007 treaty)
♦ NAISA – Native American and Indigenous Studies Association (internationally oriented national body)
♦ Naiset tieteen ja tekniikan aloilla (#06276)
♦ **NAJAKS** Nordic Association for Japanese and Korean Studies (#17195)
♦ NAJS – Nordic Association for the Study of Contemporary Japanese Society (internationally oriented national body)
♦ Nakshabandiya (religious order)
♦ NALACS – Netherlands Association of Latin American and Caribbean Studies (internationally oriented national body)
♦ **NALAS** Network of Associations of Local Authorities of South-East Europe (#16997)
♦ NALLD / see International Association for Language Learning Technology
♦ NALMCO – International Association of Lighting Management Companies (internationally oriented national body)
♦ **NAL** Nordic Association of Linguists (#17197)
♦ NAMA – Nordic Aeromedical Association (no recent information)

♦ Namati 16931

CEO Ste 101, 1616 P St NW, Washington DC 20036, USA. T. +12028881086. E-mail: namati@namati.org.
URL: https://namati.org/

History 2011. **Aims** Advance justice by building a movement of people who know, use and shape the laws that affect them. **Structure** Board of Directors. **Languages** English. **Staff** 100.00 FTE, paid. **Finance** US Department of State; national foundations. Supported by: *American Jewish World Service (AJWS)*; *Charles Stewart Mott Foundation*; *Department for International Development (DFID, inactive)*; *International Development Research Centre (IDRC, #13162)*; *Open Society Foundations (OSF, #17763)*; *The William and Flora Hewlett Foundation*. **Activities** Awareness raising; capacity building; guidance/assistance/consulting; networking/liaising; research/documentation; training/education. Active in: India, Kenya, Mozambique, Myanmar, Sierra Leone, USA. **Publications** *Community Paralegals and the Pursuit of Justice* (1st ed 2018) by Vivek Maru and Varun Gauri in English. **Members** Organizations (over 2,000); Individuals (over 8,000). Members in over 160 countries. Membership countries not specified. **NGO Relations** Hosts: *Global Legal Empowerment Network (#10457)*.
[2020.05.04/XJ5587/**F**]

♦ **NAM CSSTC** Non-Aligned Movement Centre for South-South Technical Cooperation (#17147)

♦ NAMED – Neglected Aspects of Motion Events Description (meeting series)
♦ **NAMES** North Africa and Middle East Science Centres Network (#17555)
♦ NAMHI / see Nordic-Baltic Association for Medical and Health Information (#17213)
♦ NAMMA – NATO Multi-Role Combat Aircraft Development and Production Management Agency (inactive)
♦ NAMMA – North America Maritime Ministry Association (internationally oriented national body)
♦ **NAMMCO** North Atlantic Marine Mammal Commission (#17573)
♦ NAMM – International Music Products Association (internationally oriented national body)
♦ **NAM** Non-Aligned Movement (#17146)
♦ NAMSO / see NATO Support and Procurement Agency (#16948)
♦ **NAM S and T Centre** Centre for Science and Technology of the Non-Aligned and Other Developing Countries (#03784)
♦ NAMU / see Nordisk Orkestermusik Union (#17525)
♦ Namur-Europe-Wallonie (internationally oriented national body)
♦ NaNA – International Conference on Networking and Network Applications (meeting series)
♦ NANAP – Non-Aligned News Agency Pool (inactive)
♦ **NA** Narcotics Anonymous (#16936)
♦ NANASO – Northern African Network of AIDS Service Organizations (see: #00272)
♦ NANBA / see North American Broadcasters Association (#17561)
♦ NANBO – North American Network of Basin Organizations (internationally oriented national body)
♦ Nancy Reynolds Bagley Foundation / see Arca Foundation
♦ Nancy Susan Reynolds Foundation / see Arca Foundation
♦ **NANDA-I** NANDA International (#16932)

♦ NANDA International (NANDA-I) 16932

Mailing Address PO Box 72, Mountain WI 54149, USA. E-mail: admin@nanda.org.
URL: http://www.nanda.org/

History 1982. Former names and other names: *North American Nursing Diagnosis Association (NANDA)* – former (1982 to 2002). **Aims** Facilitate the development, refinement, dissemination and use of standardized nursing diagnostic terminology. **Structure** Board of Directors, comprising President, President-Elect, Treasurer/Secretary, 5 Directors and Executive Director. **Languages** English. **Staff** 2.00 FTE, paid. Other contracted staff. **Finance** Sources: members' dues. Other sources: revenue from publications and other activities. **Events** *Conference* 2023, *Conference* Cancún (Mexico) 2016, *Congress* Porto (Portugal) 2014, *Congress* Porto (Portugal) 2014, *Biennial conference* Houston, TX (USA) 2012. **Publications** *International Journal of Nursing Knowledge* (4 a year); *PRONANDA: Programa de actualização em diagnósticos de enfermagem* (4 a year) in Portuguese. **Members** Full in 37 countries. Membership countries not specified. **NGO Relations** Affiliated member: *Association Francophone Européenne des Diagnostics Interventions Résultats Infirmiers (AFEDI, #02612)*; national associations. [2022/XU1068/**C**]

♦ NANDA / see NANDA International (#16932)
♦ Nando Peretti Foundation (internationally oriented national body)
♦ **NANHRI** Network of African National Human Rights Institutions (#16984)
♦ Nanmin wo Tasukerukai / see Association for Aid and Relief – Japan
♦ NANOG – North American Network Operators' Group (internationally oriented national body)
♦ NA – Nordisk Apoteksforening (inactive)

♦ Nanotechnology Industries Association (NIA) 16933

Dir Gen Avenue de Tervueren 143, 1150 Sint-Pieters-Woluwe, Belgium. T. +3228506197. E-mail: enquiries@nanotechia.org.
URL: https://nanotechia.org/

History 2005, UK. Registration: EU Transparency Register, No/ID: 33561661927-40; Belgium. **Aims** Support nanotechnology industries, regulators and policymakers, and the general public. **Structure** Board of Directors. **Activities** Research/documentation; knowledge management/information dissemination; projects/programmes; events/meetings. **Events** *International Nanotoxicology Congress* Boston, MA (USA) 2016. **Publications** *NIA Newsletter.*
Members Corporate; Associate; Affiliate. Membership countries not specified. Included in the above, one association listed in this Yearbook:
Included in the above, one association listed in this Yearbook:
International Iberian Nanotechnology Laboratory (INL).
NGO Relations Liaison Organization of: *Comité européen de normalisation (CEN, #04162).* Member of: *Industry4Europe (#11181).* [2020/XM4813/t/**D**]

♦ Nansen Center for Peace and Dialogue (NCPD) 16934

Contact Bjornstjerne Bjornsons gate 2, 2609 Lillehammer, Norway. T. +4761255500. E-mail: post@peace.no.
URL: https://www.peace.no/om-oss/

History 2010, Norway. Set up mid-1990s, via educational programme "Democracy, Human Rights and Peaceful Conflict Resolution", organized for participants from former Yugoslavia. Merged, 2010, with Norwegian Peace Center. Former names and other names: *Nansen Network in the Balkans* – former; *Nansen Dialogue Network* – alias. **Finance** Sources: contributions; government support; sponsorship. Supported by: Norwegian Foreign Ministry. **Activities** Training/education. **NGO Relations** Regional initiator of: *Global Partnership for the Prevention of Armed Conflict (GPPAC, #10538)*, initiated by *Global Partnership for the Prevention of Armed Conflict Foundation (GPPAC Foundation).* [2020/XJ3545/**F**]

♦ Nansen Committee / see Nansen Refugee Award Committee
♦ Nansen Dialogue Network / see Nansen Center for Peace and Dialogue (#16934)
♦ Nansen Environmental and Remote Sensing Center (internationally oriented national body)

♦ Nansen International Environmental and Remote Sensing Centre (NIERSC) 16935

Dir 14th Line 7, office 49, Vasilievsky Island, St Petersburg SANKT-PETERBURG, Russia, 199034. T. +78123245102 – +78123245103. Fax +78123245102. E-mail: adm@niersc.spb.ru.
URL: http://www.niersc.spb.ru/

History 1992. Full title: *Scientific Foundation "Nansen International Environmental and Remote Sensing Centre (Foundation "Nansen-Centre").* **Aims** Develop the Nansen Centre to be a significant national and international contributor to the studies of climate and environmental changes in the high northern latitudes. **Structure** General Meeting; Board of Guardians. **Languages** English, Russian. **Staff** 26.00 FTE, paid. **Activities** Research and development; events/meetings; training/education. **Publications** Monographs.
Members Organizations in 3 countries:
Germany, Norway, Russia.
Included in the above, 1 organization listed in this Yearbook:
Nansen Environmental and Remote Sensing Center (NERSC).
NGO Relations *Nansen-Zhu International Research Centre (NZC).* [2020/XJ9027/**E**]

♦ Nansen International Office for Refugees (inactive)
♦ Nansen Medal / see Nansen Refugee Award Committee
♦ Nansen Network in the Balkans / see Nansen Center for Peace and Dialogue (#16934)
♦ Nansen Refugee Award Committee (internationally oriented national body)
♦ Nansen-Zhu International Research Centre (internationally oriented national body)
♦ **NANZIBA** North American and New Zealand Institute for Bioenergetic Analysis (#17566)
♦ **NaPa** Emerging Nanopatterning Methods Consortium (#05439)
♦ NAPA – Nunani Avannarlerni Piorsarsimassutsikkut Attaveqaat (internationally oriented national body)
♦ NAPCA / see Amateo (#00765)
♦ NAPCRG – North American Primary Care Research Group (internationally oriented national body)
♦ NAPD / see International Association of Plastics Distribution
♦ **NAPE** Nordic Association for Psychiatric Epidemiology (#17201)
♦ **NAPF** North American Powerlifting Federation (#17568)
♦ NAPM / see Generic and Biosimilar Medicines of Southern Africa
♦ **NAPMA** North African Port Management Association (#17556)
♦ NAPMDD / see International Association For Premenstrual Disorders (#12098)
♦ **NAPMO** NATO Airborne Early Warning and Control Programme Management Organization (#16943)
♦ **NAP+** Network of African People Living with HIV and AIDS (#16986)
♦ NAP / see Network of Asia and Pacific Producers (#16995)
♦ NAPP / see Network of Asia and Pacific Producers (#16995)
♦ **NAPP** Network of Asia and Pacific Producers (#16995)
♦ **NAPPO** North American Plant Protection Organization (#17567)
♦ **NAPRECA** Natural Products Research Network for Eastern and Central Africa (#16956)
♦ NAPSNet / see Nautilus Peace and Security Network
♦ NAPSNet – Nautilus Peace and Security Network (internationally oriented national body)
♦ **NAPS** Network for African Peace-Builders (#16985)
♦ Naqshbandi-Haqqani tariqa (religious order)
♦ Naqshbandi Sufi Order (religious order)
♦ Naqshbandi Sufi Tariqa (religious order)
♦ **NARBO** Network of Asian River Basin Organizations (#16993)

♦ Narcotics Anonymous (NA) 16936

Narcotiques anonymes

World Service Office PO Box 9999, Van Nuys CA 91409, USA. T. +18187739999. Fax +18187000700. E-mail: info@na.org – wb@na.org – pr@na.org.
World Service Office-Europe Rue de l'Eté 48, 1050 Brussels, Belgium. T. +3226466012. Fax +3226499239.
URL: http://www.na.org/

History 1953. **Aims** Act as a community-based non-professional self-help society of addicts seeking to live drug-free and recover from the effects of addiction and to help others with similar goals to achieve them; promote the therapeutic approach of addicts supporting one another in their efforts to learn and practice a new way of living that keeps them drug-free. **Structure** World Service Conference (every 2 years) – international delegate assembly – selects members of World Board; World Service Office (headquarters) in Los Angeles CA (USA). Narcotics Anonymous (NA) groups are the basic unit; countries with a number of NA groups may form local service committees/area committees; a number of area committees may join together to create regions. **Finance** No fees or dues. **Activities** Projects/programmes; events/meetings; standards/guidelines. **Events** *World Convention* Orlando, FL (USA) 2018, *Annual Convention* Chiang Mai (Thailand) 2017, *World Convention* Rio de Janeiro (Brazil) 2015, *World Convention* Philadelphia, PA (USA) 2013, *World Convention* San Diego, CA (USA) 2011. **Publications** *Meeting By Mail* – newsletter for isolated addicts; *NA Way Magazine. Narcotics Anonymous, called The Basic Text* – basic revovery text. Handbooks; studies; guides; booklets; pamphlets. Material published in Czech, English, Danish, Dutch, French, Finnish, German, Greek, Hebrew, Hindi, Italian, Norwegian (Bokmål), Portuguese (Brazilian and Lusitanian), Spanish (Castillian), Swedish, Turkish.
Members Membership mainly in USA, but a total of 20,000 groups in 103 countries and territories:
Antigua-Barbuda, Argentina, Aruba, Australia, Austria, Bahrain, Bangladesh, Barbados, Belarus, Belgium, Belize, Bermuda, Bolivia, Brazil, Bulgaria, Canada, Chile, China, Colombia, Costa Rica, Croatia, Czechia, Denmark, Dominican Rep, Ecuador, Egypt, El Salvador, Ethiopia, Finland, France, Germany, Greece, Greenland, Grenada, Guatemala, Guyana, Haiti, Honduras, Hong Kong, Hungary, Iceland, India, Indonesia, Iran Islamic Rep, Ireland, Israel, Italy, Jamaica, Japan, Kenya, Korea Rep, Kuwait, Kyrgyzstan, Latvia, Lebanon, Liberia, Lithuania, Luxembourg, Malaysia, Maldives, Malta, Martinique, Mexico, Morocco, Mozambique, Nepal, Netherlands, New Zealand, Nicaragua, Nigeria, Northern Mariana Is, Norway, Pakistan, Panama, Paraguay, Peru, Philippines, Poland, Portugal, Russia, Samoa, Saudi Arabia, Singapore, Slovakia, Slovenia, South Africa, Spain, St Lucia, St Vincent-Grenadines, Sweden, Switzerland, Tanzania UR, Thailand, Trinidad-Tobago, Türkiye, UK, Ukraine, United Arab Emirates, Uruguay, USA, Venezuela, Virgin Is USA, Zimbabwe.
Consultative Status Consultative status granted from: *ECOSOC (#05331)* (Special). [2022/XF2953/**F**]

♦ Narcotiques anonymes (#16936)
♦ NARDA – New African Research and Development Agency (internationally oriented national body)
♦ **NARESA** Network of AIDS Researchers of Eastern and Southern Africa (#16990)
♦ **NARIC** National Academic Recognition Information Centres (#16937)
♦ Nariin Bicgiin Darga Naryn Gazar / see International Association for Mongol Studies (#12035)
♦ **NARMM** Nordic Association for Research on Men and Masculinities (#17202)
♦ **NARN** Nordic Africa Research Network (#17169)
♦ **NAR** Nordiska Afasirådet (#17174)
♦ NAR – Nordiska Akademikerrådet (inactive)
♦ **NAR** Nordisk Amatørteaterråd (#17172)
♦ Narodno-Trudovoj Sojuz (internationally oriented national body)
♦ **NARPI** Northeast Asia Regional Peacebuilding Institute (#17580)
♦ NARS – Nordic Association for Romantic Studies (internationally oriented national body)
♦ Narvik Fredssenter i Nord (internationally oriented national body)
♦ Narvik Peace Centre (internationally oriented national body)
♦ NASAA – North American Securities Administrators Association (internationally oriented national body)
♦ **NASAC** Network of African Science Academies (#16987)
♦ NASA – North Atlantic Seafood Association (inactive)
♦ Nascent Solutions (internationally oriented national body)
♦ NASCO / see North American Strategy for Competitiveness (#17569)
♦ **NASCO** North American Strategy for Competitiveness (#17569)
♦ **NASCO** North Atlantic Salmon Conservation Organization (#17574)
♦ Nasdaq Europe (inactive)
♦ NA/SDRC Tangiers / see ECA Office for North Africa (#05273)
♦ NASEAS – Nordic Association for Southeast Asian Studies (inactive)
♦ NASECODE – International Conference on the Numerical Analysis of Semiconductor Devices and Integrated Circuits (meeting series)
♦ NASEDEC – Nordic Association for the Study of Education in Developing Countries (no recent information)
♦ NASF – North Atlantic Seafood Forum (meeting series)
♦ **NASIC** Network of Academies of Sciences in Countries of Organization of Islamic Conference (#16981)
♦ Nasiriya (religious order)
♦ NASL / see North American Association of State and Provincial Lotteries
♦ NAS / see Nordic Acoustic Association (#17165)
♦ **NAS** Nordic Autophagy Society (#17211)
♦ **NAS** Nordisk Audiologisk Selskab (#17210)
♦ NASOH – North American Society for Oceanic History (internationally oriented national body)
♦ **NASOM** Nordiska Arbetarsångar- och Musikerförbundet (#17478)
♦ NASPAA – Network of Schools of Public Policy, Affairs, and Administration (internationally oriented national body)
♦ **NASPCAN** Nordic Association for Prevention of Child Abuse and Neglect (#17200)
♦ NASPL – North American Association of State and Provincial Lotteries (internationally oriented national body)
♦ NASPM / see Nordic Alliance for Clinical Genomics (#17171)
♦ NASPSPA – North American Society for Sport Psychology and Physical Activity (internationally oriented national body)
♦ NASRC / see Racing Commissioners International
♦ NASSCFL – North American Society for Seventeenth-Century French Literature (internationally oriented national body)
♦ **NASS** Nordic Association for Semiotic Studies (#17205)
♦ NASS – North American Spine Society (internationally oriented national body)
♦ NASSP – North American Society for Social Philosophy (internationally oriented national body)
♦ **NASSW** Nordic Association of Schools of Social Work (#17204)
♦ NASTT – North American Society for Trenchless Technology (internationally oriented national body)
♦ NASW – North Atlantic Native Sheep and Wool Conference (meeting series)

♦ NASYO / see Non-Aligned Students, Youth and Civil Societies Organization (#17148)
♦ **NASYO** Non-Aligned Students, Youth and Civil Societies Organization (#17148)
♦ **NATA** Network for Advancement of Transfusion Alternatives (#16982)
♦ NATAN International Humanitarian Aid / see NATAN Worldwide Disaster Relief
♦ NATAN – NATAN Worldwide Disaster Relief (internationally oriented national body)
♦ NATAN Worldwide Disaster Relief (internationally oriented national body)
♦ NATAS – North American Thermal Analysis Society (internationally oriented national body)
♦ **NATCOL** Natural Food Colours Association (#16953)
♦ NATEA – International Narcotic and Antiterrorist Enforcement Officers Association (internationally oriented national body)
♦ Natie Europa / see National-European Communitarian Party
♦ Nationaal Centrum voor Ontwikkelingssamenwerking / see Coalition of the Flemish North South Movement – 11 11 11
♦ Nationaal Europese Communautaire Partij (internationally oriented national body)

♦ National Academic Recognition Information Centres (NARIC) 16937

Contact NARIC-Flanders, Ministry of Education and Training, Hendrik Consciencegebouw Toren 2A, Koning Albert II-laan 15, 1210 Brussels, Belgium. T. +32255389581700. E-mail: naric@vlaanderen.be.
Contact NARIC of the Federation Wallonia-Brussels, Rue A Lavallée 1, 1080 Brussels, Belgium. T. +3226908747. Fax +3226908760. E-mail: equi.sup@cfwb.be.
URL: http://www.naric.be/

History 1984, by *European Commission (EC, #06633)*. Original full title: *European Community Network of the National Academic Recognition Information Centres*. Current full title: *National Academic Recognition Information Centres in the European Union*. **Aims** Strengthen exchange of information in the European Union about academic recognition and equivalence matters; offer advice and information on comparability of international qualifications and their use in education, training, professional registration and international employment. **Finance** Regular support since 1987 through *European Commission (EC, #06633)*. **Activities** Networking/liaising; training/education. **Events** *Joint Meeting* Toledo (Spain) 2012, *Joint meeting* Valletta (Malta) 2008, *Joint meeting* Bucharest (Romania) 2007, *Joint meeting* Tallinn (Estonia) 2006, *Joint meeting* Strasbourg (France) 2004. **Publications** *Catalogue of Higher Education Qualifications Recognized in Member States*; *Compendium of Existing Bilateral and Multilateral Equivalence Arrangements of the Different Member States*; *Directory of Higher Education Qualifications of EC Member States*. *Information Brochure on the NARIC Network*.
Members Information centres in 53 countries:
Albania, Andorra, Armenia, Australia, Austria, Azerbaijan, Belarus, Belgium, Bosnia-Herzegovina, Bulgaria, Canada, Croatia, Cyprus, Czechia, Denmark, Estonia, Finland, France, Georgia, Germany, Greece, Holy See, Hungary, Iceland, Ireland, Israel, Italy, Latvia, Liechtenstein, Lithuania, Luxembourg, Malta, Moldova, Monaco, Netherlands, New Zealand, North Macedonia, Norway, Poland, Portugal, Romania, Russia, San Marino, Serbia, Slovakia, Slovenia, Spain, Sweden, Switzerland, Türkiye, UK, Ukraine, USA.
IGO Relations Joint meetings with: *European Network of National Information Centres on Academic Recognition and Mobility (ENIC, #07950)*. [2019.02.12/XF0159/**F***]

♦ National Academic Recognition Information Centres in the European Union / see National Academic Recognition Information Centres (#16937)
♦ National Academies of Emergency Dispatch / see International Academies of Emergency Dispatch
♦ National Academy of Emergency Medical Dispatch / see International Academies of Emergency Dispatch
♦ National Alliance of Russian Solidarists / see Alliance of Russian Solidarists
♦ National Association of Amusement Parks / see International Association of Amusement Parks and Attractions (#11699)
♦ National Association of Amusement Parks, Pools, and Beaches / see International Association of Amusement Parks and Attractions (#11699)
♦ National Association of Casualty & Surety Agents / see Council of Insurance Agents & Brokers
♦ National Association of Corrosion Engineers / see NACE International – The Corrosion Society (#16925)
♦ National Association of Exposition Managers / see International Association of Exhibitions and Events
♦ National Association for Foreign Student Affairs / see NAFSA – Association of International Educators
♦ National Association of Holiday Inns / see IHG Owners Association (#11112)
♦ National Association of Language Lab Directors / see International Association for Language Learning Technology
♦ National Association of Lesbian and Gay Pride Coordinators / see InterPride (#15965)
♦ National Association of Pharmaceutical Manufacturers / see Generic and Biosimilar Medicines of Southern Africa
♦ National Association of Plastics Distributors / see International Association of Plastics Distribution
♦ National Association for Premenstrual Dysphoric Disorder / see International Association For Premenstrual Disorders (#12098)
♦ National Association of Rotary Clubs / see Rotary International (#18975)
♦ National Association of Round Tables of Great Britain and Ireland (internationally oriented national body)
♦ National Association of State Lotteries / see North American Association of State and Provincial Lotteries
♦ National Association of State Racing Commissioners / see Racing Commissioners International
♦ National Board for Certified Counselors (internationally oriented national body)
♦ National Boxing Association / see World Boxing Association (#21241)
♦ National Bureau of Asian Research (internationally oriented national body)
♦ National Canvas Goods Manufacturers Association / see Industrial Fabrics Association International (#11174)
♦ National Centre for Development Cooperation / see Coalition of the Flemish North South Movement – 11 11 11
♦ National Centre for Research on Europe, Christchurch (internationally oriented national body)
♦ National Centre for South Asian Studies, Clayton (internationally oriented national body)
♦ National Committee on American Foreign Policy (internationally oriented national body)
♦ National Committee for Development Education / see Nationale Commissie voor Internationale Samenwerking en Duurzame Ontwikkeling
♦ National Committee for International Cooperation and Sustainable Development (internationally oriented national body)
♦ National Conference of Standards Laboratories / see NCSL International
♦ National Contact Points for Socio-Economic Sciences and the Humanities / see Net4Society (#16976)
♦ National Council for Community Services to International Visitors / see Global Ties US
♦ National Council for Eurasian and East European Research (internationally oriented national body)
♦ National Council for International Health / see Global Health Council (#10402)
♦ National Council for International Visitors / see Global Ties US
♦ National Council for Small Business Management Development / see International Council for Small Business (#13075)
♦ National Council for Soviet and East European Research / see National Council for Eurasian and East European Research
♦ National Council for Voluntary Organizations (internationally oriented national body)
♦ National Council of Women Psychologists / see International Council of Psychologists (#13065)
♦ National Council of World Affairs Organizations / see World Affairs Councils of America
♦ National Democratic Institute / see National Democratic Institute for International Affairs
♦ National Democratic Institute for International Affairs (internationally oriented national body)
♦ National Digital Library of Theses and Dissertations / see Networked Digital Library of Theses and Dissertations (#17008)
♦ Nationale Commissie voor Internationale Samenwerking en Duurzame Ontwikkeling (internationally oriented national body)
♦ Nationale Commissie Voorlichting en Bewustwording Ontwikkelingssamenwerking / see Nationale Commissie voor Internationale Samenwerking en Duurzame Ontwikkeling
♦ National Education Telecommunications Organization – EDSAT Institute (internationally oriented national body)
♦ National Endowment for Democracy (internationally oriented national body)
♦ National Erosion Control Association / see International Erosion Control Association (#13297)
♦ Nationales Zentrum für Entwicklungsförderung / see Coalition of the Flemish North South Movement – 11 11 11
♦ Nationaleuropäische Kommunotaristische Partei (internationally oriented national body)
♦ National European Centre, Canberra / see ANU Centre for European Studies
♦ National-European Communitarian Party (internationally oriented national body)
♦ Nationality Agreement (1954 treaty)
♦ Nationally Determined Contributions / see NDC Partnership (#16964)
♦ National Microfilm Association / see Association for Intelligent Information Management (#02652)
♦ National Micrographics Association / see Association for Intelligent Information Management (#02652)

♦ National Movements and Intermediary Structures in Europe (NISE) 16938

Coordinator c/o ADVN, Lange Leemstraat 26, 2018 Antwerp, Belgium. T. +3232251837.
Administrative Coordinator address not obtained.
URL: http://nise.eu/

History Operational since 2008. Statutes signed 23 May 2012, Barcelona (Spain). Officially registered in accordance with Belgian law, 15 Feb 2013. **Aims** Facilitate the *comparative study of nationalism*; arrive at a more empirically based theory formation of nationalism. **Structure** General Assembly; Executive Board; Scientific Bodies; Scientific Council; Network; Supporting Bodies; Associated Members; Partners; Coordination Center. **Languages** English. **Staff** 2.50 FTE, paid. **Finance** Funding from: Flemish authorities; project funding; partnership contribution. **Activities** Knowledge management/information dissemination; events/meetings. **Events** *General Assembly* Amsterdam (Netherlands) 2018, *International Conference on Cultural Mobilization* Amsterdam (Netherlands) 2018, *General Assembly* Munich (Germany) 2017, *General Assembly* Prague (Czechia) 2016, *General Assembly* Swansea (UK) 2015. **Publications** *NISELetter*. *Studies on National Movements*. Monograph series; proceedings.
Members Scientific Council members (21) in 11 countries:
Austria, Belgium, Bulgaria, Czechia, France, Germany, Netherlands, North Macedonia, Russia, Spain, UK.
Network members (40) in 23 countries:
Armenia, Austria, Belgium, Bulgaria, Croatia, Czechia, Estonia, Finland, France, Germany, Hungary, Ireland, Italy, Latvia, Lithuania, Netherlands, North Macedonia, Norway, Poland, Slovakia, Spain, UK, Ukraine.
Included in the above, 5 organizations listed in this Yearbook:
Association for the Study of Ethnicity and Nationalism (ASEN); *Escarre International Centre for the Ethnic Minorities and Nations (#05535)*; *European Centre for Minority Issues (ECMI)*; *International Centre for Archival Research (ICARUS, #12477)*; *Study Platform on Interlocking Nationalisms (SPIN)*.
Associate members (9) in 8 countries:
Canada, Denmark, France, Lithuania, Moldova, Poland, Sweden, Ukraine.
Partners (8) in 6 countries:
Belgium, Finland, Netherlands, Poland, Spain, UK. [2018.08.16/XJ9104/**F**]

♦ National Newspaper Promotion Association / see International News Media Association (#14363)
♦ National Outdoor Showmen's Association / see International Association of Amusement Parks and Attractions (#11699)
♦ National Peace Academy Foundation / see National Peace Foundation
♦ National Peace Foundation (internationally oriented national body)
♦ National Peace Institute Foundation / see National Peace Foundation

♦ National Platforms' Coalition of Asia (NPCOA) 16939

Contact c/o Voluntary Action Network India, BB-5 – 1st Floor, Greater Kailash Enclave II, Delhi 110048, DELHI 110048, India. T. +911129226632 – +911129228127. Fax +911141435535. E-mail: info@vaniindia.org.
URL: http://www.ngo-asia.org/

History Started as a project on non-governmental diplomacy involving national platforms from France – *Coordination SUD* -, Brazil, Chile, Senegal and India.
Members Organizations in 8 countries:
Bangladesh, Cambodia, India, Indonesia, Japan, Nepal, Philippines, Timor-Leste.
Included in the above, 2 organizations listed in this Yearbook:
International NGO Forum on Indonesian Development (INFID, #14366); *Japanese NGO Center for International Cooperation (JANIC)*. [2012/XJ5907/y/**F**]

♦ National Programme to Prevent, Combat and Provide Humanitarian Assistance to the Victims of Natural Disasters / see Organisation internationale pour la réduction des catastrophes
♦ National Republican Institute for International Affairs / see International Republican Institute
♦ National Sanitary Supply Association / see ISSA
♦ Nationalsozialistische Weltunion (#21880)
♦ National Tent & Awning Association / see Industrial Fabrics Association International (#11174)
♦ **National Trust of Romania** Pro Patrimonio (#18264)
♦ National Union of Elevator Constructors / see International Union of Elevator Constructors
♦ National Union of Russian Youth / see Alliance of Russian Solidarists
♦ National US-Arab Chamber of Commerce (internationally oriented national body)

♦ Nation Builders International 16940

Chairman Biyem Assi, Yaoundé, Cameroon. T. +23722097270 – +23775202984.
URL: http://www.nationbuildersint.org/

History 1 Apr 2001. **Aims** Inspire human, national and global transformation and advancement through the instrument of knowledge dissemination and exchange of ideas. **Structure** Board of Directors, comprising Chairman, Vice-Chairman, Advisor, Chair Lady, Financial Secretary, Public Relations Officer, Secretary, Legal Advisor and Treasurer. Departments (15) Education; Communication; Social Affairs; Health; Agriculture; Infrastructural; Cultural Affairs; Men's Affairs; Women's Affairs; Youth Affairs; Economy and Finance; Security; International Relations; Hospitality; Sports. **Activities** Works in partnership with a wide range of network involving government and private institutions, civil society groups, international organizations and religious bodies. Organizes: Global Leadership Conference; summits. **Publications** *Nation Builder* – newsletter. [2010/XJ1906/**F**]

♦ Nation Center for Global Health and Medicine (internationally oriented national body)
♦ Nation Europa / see National-European Communitarian Party
♦ Nation Europe / see National-European Communitarian Party

♦ Nationless Worldwide Association 16941

Association anationale mondiale – Asociación Anacional Mundial – Nationsloser Weltbund – Sennacieca Asocio Tutmonda (SAT)

Contact 67 avenue Gambetta, 75020 Paris, France. T. +33953509958. E-mail: kontakto@satesperanto.org.
URL: http://www.satesperanto.org/

History 1921, Prague (Czech Rep). Registered in accordance with French law. Also referred to as *Association of Nationless Esperantist Workers*. **Aims** On a world-wide scale, use *Esperanto* as a factor of culture; develop among members a sense of *human solidarity*. **Structure** World Council, elected by referendum, composed of one Councillor per sector. Executive Committee, consisting of 8 members. **Languages** Esperanto. **Staff** Voluntary. **Finance** Members' dues. **Events** *Annual Congress* Paris (France) 2020, *Annual Congress* Barcelona (Spain) 2019, *Annual Congress* Kragujevac (Serbia) 2018, *Annual Congress* Seoul (Korea Rep) 2017, *Annual Congress* Herzberg am Harz (Germany) 2016. **Publications** *Sennaciulo* (6 a year); *Sennacieca Revuo* (annual); *SAT Yearbook*. *La Nova PIV* (2004); *Plena Ilustrita Vortaro de Esperanto Kun Suplemento* (1987).
Members Individuals in 59 countries:

Argentina, Australia, Austria, Belgium, Bosnia-Herzegovina, Brazil, Bulgaria, Canada, Chile, China, Congo DR, Croatia, Cuba, Czechia, Denmark, El Salvador, Estonia, Finland, France, Germany, Ghana, Greece, Haiti, Hungary, Iceland, India, Israel, Italy, Japan, Korea Rep, Latvia, Lithuania, Luxembourg, Madagascar, Mali, Mauritius, Mexico, Mongolia, Netherlands, New Zealand, Nigeria, North Macedonia, Norway, Poland, Portugal, Romania, Russia, Senegal, Serbia, Slovakia, Slovenia, Spain, Sweden, Switzerland, Tanzania UR, Togo, UK, Ukraine, Vietnam.
NGO Relations Associated with: *Universal Esperanto Association (UEA, #20676)*. The: *Union des travailleurs espérantistes des pays de langue française (SAT-AMIKARO, #20488)* is an affiliate. [2020/XC2970/v/**F**]

♦ Nationsloser Weltbund (#16941)
♦ Nations Unies (#20515)
♦ Nations Unies des animaux (#20497)
♦ Native American and Indigenous Studies Association (internationally oriented national body)
♦ Native Oyster Restoration Alliance (unconfirmed)
♦ NÄT – Nordiska Ämbetsmannakommittén för Transportfrågor (inactive)
♦ NATO AEW and C Programme Management Organization / see NATO Airborne Early Warning and Control Programme Management Organization (#16943)
♦ NATO Agreement on the Communication of Technical Information for Defence Purposes (1970 treaty)

♦ NATO Airborne Early Warning and Control Force Command (NAEW and C) 16942

Force aérienne de détection lointaine de l'OTAN
Headquarters Lilienthalallee 100, 52511 Geilenkirchen, Germany. T. +492451632454.
URL: http://www.e3a.nato.int/
History Established Jan 1980, as *NATO Airborne Early Warning Force Command*, following decision, Dec 1978, of NATO Defence Planning Committee. Placed within *Allied Command Operations (ACO, #00731)* of *NATO (#16945)*. Headquarters has full status as International Military Headquarters. Current name adopted, 16 Oct 1999. Headquarters relocated to NATO Airbase in Geilenkirchen (Germany), 1 Nov 2015. Complements *NATO Airborne Early Warning and Control Programme Management Organization (NAPMO, #16943)*, set up in 1978 to manage procurement aspects of *NATO Airborne Early Warning Control System (AWACS)*. **Aims** Provide an airborne early warning and control capability, trained and equipped to participate in NATO approved operations worldwide, available at graduated levels of readiness, and to support Joint Force or NRF commanders; support the integrated air defence of NATO airspace, collective defensive operations, major joint operations and crisis response operations. **Structure** Force comprises: E-3A component – 16 NATO E-3A aircraft operating from Main Operating Base (MOB) at Geilenkirchen (Germany); E-3D component – 6 UK-owned and operated E-3D aircraft, based at RAF Waddington (UK). Each aircraft is equipped with sophisticated radar systems capable of detecting aircraft at great distances over large expanses of territory. Commanded by SACEUR.
Members Participating nations (18), " – Luxembourg is a contributing nation but does not send members as part of the Force; " – the UK provides a contribution in kind of 6 E-3D aircraft:
Belgium, Canada, Czechia, Denmark, Germany, Greece, Hungary, Italy, Luxembourg (*), Netherlands, Norway, Poland, Portugal, Romania, Spain, Türkiye, UK (**), USA. [2015.10.08/XE0740/**E***]

♦ NATO Airborne Early Warning and Control Programme Management Organization (NAPMO) 16943

Headquarters c/o NAPMA, PO Box 8002, 6440 HA Brunssum, Netherlands. Fax +31455254373. E-mail: info@napma.nato.int.
Street address Rimburgerweg 30, Bldg 107, 6455 PA Brunssum, Netherlands.
URL: http://www.napma.nato.int/
History 1978, under the provisions of the 1951 Ottawa (Canada) Agreement on the Status of *NATO (#16945)*, as a NATO Production and Logistics Organization to implement the *NATO Airborne Early Warning and Control Programme (NATO AEW and C Programme)*. Also referred to as *NATO AEW and C Programme Management Organization*. Reports directly to *North Atlantic Council (NAC, #17572)*. **Structure** Board of Directors, consisting of 1 member from each participating Nation. Committees (2): Operations, Plans and Logistics (OPL); Policy and Finance (PF). Representatives of NATO Secretary General, Commander of *NATO Airborne Early Warning and Control Force Command (NAEW and C, #16942)* and other NATO bodies may attend Board and Committee meetings but have no vote. General Manager of NATO Airborne Early Warning and Control Programme Management Agency (NAPMA), Brunssum (Netherlands), is responsible for day-to-day Programme management. **Languages** English. **Staff** NAPMA and the Force Command are manned by personnel from NAPMO participating nations. **Activities** Knowledge management/information dissemination.
Members Full-member nations (17):
Belgium, Czechia, Denmark, Germany, Greece, Hungary, Italy, Luxembourg, Netherlands, Norway, Poland, Portugal, Romania, Spain, Türkiye, UK, USA.
IGO Relations *EUROCONTROL (#05667)*; *European Union (EU, #08967)*. [2018.10.16/XK2029/**E***]

♦ NATO Airborne Early Warning Force Command / see NATO Airborne Early Warning and Control Force Command (#16942)

♦ NATO Defense College (NDC) 16944

Collège de défense de l'OTAN
Commandant Via Giorgio Pelosi 1, 00143 Rome RM, Italy. T. +39650525104. Fax +39650525410. E-mail: pao@ndc.nato.int.
URL: http://www.ndc.nato.int/
History 19 Nov 1951, Paris (France). Moved to Rome (Italy), 1966. Previously directly under the Military Committee of *NATO (#16945)*. **Aims** Provide an education environment in which senior officers and officials can professionally develop at the political-strategic level and can prepare and expand their knowledge for national appointments within NATO and other multinational responsibilities. **Structure** Commandant; Dean; Director of Management; Academic Operations Division; Academic Planning and Policy Division; Research Division. **Languages** English, French. **Staff** Multinational. **Finance** Included in the NATO budget. **Activities** Training/education; research/documentation; events/meetings; networking/liaising. NDC Public Affairs Office. **Publications** *Vox Collegi* – magazine. Research papers; NDC Occasional Papers; Executives Summaries; seminar reports; monographs; essays; forum papers. **IGO Relations** Cooperates fully with the NATO *Partnership for Peace (PfP, #18240)*, Mediterranean Dialogue, Istanbul Cooperation Initiative and other partner organizations. **NGO Relations** Member of: *Anciens Association of the NATO Defense College (#00814)*; NATO Defense College Foundation; *PfP Consortium of Defence Academies and Security Studies Institutes (#18345)*. [2019.10.22/XF3091/**F***]

♦ NATO Hawk Production and Logistics Organization (no recent information)
♦ NATO Joint Civil/military Frequency Agreement (1995 treaty)
♦ NATO Maintenance and Supply Organization / see NATO Support and Procurement Agency (#16948)
♦ NATO Maintenance Supply Service System / see NATO Support and Procurement Agency (#16948)
♦ NATO Multi-Role Combat Aircraft Development and Production Management Agency (inactive)

♦ NATO – North Atlantic Treaty Organization 16945

Organisation du Traité de l'Atlantique Nord (OTAN) – Organisation des Nordatlantikvertrags
SG NATO Headquarters, Bvd Leopold III, 1110 Brussels, Belgium. T. +3227074111. Fax +3227074579. E-mail: moc@hq.nato.int – natodoc@hq.nato.int.
URL: http://www.nato.int/
History Established 4 Apr 1949, Washington DC (USA), on the basis of the *North Atlantic Treaty (1949)*, as a defensive political and military alliance of independent countries in accordance with the terms of the United Nations Charter. It provides common security for members through cooperation and consultation in political, military and economic and in scientific and other non-military fields. Also referred to as *North Atlantic Alliance*. Original signatories of the Treaty were Belgium, Canada, Denmark, France, Iceland, Italy, Luxembourg, Netherlands, Norway, Portugal, the United Kingdom and the United States of America. Greece and Turkey acceded to the Treaty in 1952 (Protocol 22 Oct 1951, London – UK); the Federal Republic of Germany in 1955 (Protocol 23 Oct 1954, Paris – France). France withdrew from the integrated military command structure in 1966 but remains a member of the Atlantic Alliance. After 1974, Greece withdrew from the integrated military command structure but rejoined Oct 1980. Spain joined NATO in 1982 (Protocol 10 Dec 1981, Brussels); Czech Rep, Hungary and Poland joined 1999; Bulgaria, Estonie, Lithuania, Romania, Slovakia and Slovenia joined 2004; Albania and Croatia joined 2009. Headquarters moved to Paris from London in Apr 1951, and to Brussels in Oct 1967. With the demise of the Warsaw Pact and the end of the Cold War, NATO began a process of fundamental transformation of its structures and policies to meet the new security challenges in Europe. This ongoing process began at the Jul 1990, London, and Nov 1991, Rome Summits, culminating in the Summit Meeting of Heads of States and Government, Jan 1994, Brussels. These changes and innovations include: a new Strategic Concept; a reduced and more flexible force structure; increased coordination and cooperation with other international institutions; active involvement in international peacekeeping operations; intensive cooperation with the countries of Central and Eastern Europe and the former Soviet Union through the establishment, 20 Dec 1991, of *'North Atlantic Cooperation Council (NACC)'*, currently, since May 1997, *Euro Atlantic Partnership Council (EAPC, #05646)*; *Treaty on Open Skies (1992)* signed 24 Mar 1992, Helsinki (Finland), between NATO and member countries of the former Warsaw Treaty Organization, which will enter into force when ratified by 20 signatory countries; agreement, Dec 1992, with Cooperation Partners to work together and consult in support of peacekeeping operations under UN or *Organization for Security and Cooperation in Europe (OSCE, #17887)* responsibility; approval of the *Partnership for Peace (PfP, #18240)* initiative, Jan 1994, and later of its Partnership Coordination Cell (PCC). Current Strategic Concept, 2010. **Aims** Safeguard the freedom and security of its members through political and military means; secure a lasting *peace* in Europe, based on common values of individual liberty, democracy, human rights and the rule of law. **Structure** *North Atlantic Council (NAC, #17572)*, established by Article 9 of the Treaty, is the principal political decision-making body within NATO and comprises an Ambassador or Permanent Representative of each member nation, supported by a national delegation. Also meets at level of Heads of State and Heads of Government or Ministers of Foreign Affairs and Ministers of Defence.
/Civilian Structure:/
'NATO Headquarters' in Brussels (Belgium), acts as political and administrative centre.
'Permanent Representatives and National Delegations'.
'International Staff (IS)':
– Private Office (PO);
– Political Affairs and Security Policy Division, comprising: NATO Liaison Office (NLO), Georgia; Office of the NATO Liaison Officer (NLO), Central Asia; *Partnership for Peace Documentation Center*;
– Operations Division, comprising: Civil Emergency Planning; *Euro-Atlantic Disaster Response Coordination Centre (EADRCC, #05644)*; NATO Situation Centre;
– Emerging Security Challenges Division, comprising Science for Peace and Security; Weapons of Mass Destruction Non-Proliferation Centre (WMDC); Defence Against Terrorism Programme of Work (DAT POW);
– Defence Policy and Planning Division, including: NATO Liaison Office (NLO), Ukraine;
– Defence Investment Division, comprising: Conference of National Armaments Directors; NATO Naval Forces Sensor and Weapons Accuracy Check Sites (FORACS); Air and Missile Defence Committee (AMDC); Aviation Committee (AVC); Munitions Safety Information Analysis Center (MSIAC);
– Public Diplomacy Division, comprising: NATO Multimedia Library; Co-sponsorship grants; NATO Information and Documentation Centre, Kiev (Ukraine); NATO Information Office, Moscow (Russia); NATO Contact Point Embassies in partner countries;
– Executive Management, comprising: Archives; Recruitment Service; NATO Internship Programme;
– NATO Office of Resources (NOR);
– NATO Office of Security (NOS);
– NATO Headquarters Consultation, Command and Control Staff;
– Office of the Financial Controller (FinCon);
– Office of the Chairman of the Senior Resource Board (SRB);
– Office of the Chairman of the Civil and Military Budget Committees (CBC/MBC);
– International Board of Auditors for NATO (IBAN);
– NATO Administrative Tribunal;
– NATO Production and Logistics Organisations (NPLO).
/Military Structure:/
'Military Committee'.
'International Military Staff':
– Plans and Policy Division;
– Operations Division;
– Intelligence Division;
– Cooperation and Regional Security Division;
– Logistics, Armaments and Resources Division;
– NATO Situation Centre;
– Financial Controller;
– NATO HQ Consultation, Control and Communications Staff;
– Partner Country Representation;
– NATO Committee on Gender Perspective (NCGP);
– NATO Military Audiovisual Working Group.
Allied Command Operations (ACO, #00731):
– *Supreme Headquarters Allied Powers Europe (SHAPE, #20039)*, Mons (Belgium);
– Headquarters *Allied Joint Force Command Brunssum (JFC Brunssum, #00734)*
– Headquarters *Allied Joint Force Command Naples (JFC Naples, #00735)*, comprising: NATO Military Liaison Office Belgrade (Serbia); NATO Headquarters Sarajevo (Bosnia-Herzegovina); NATO Headquarters Skopje (North Macedonia);
– Headquarters Allied Maritime Command, Northwood (UK), comprising: Standing NATO Maritime Groups; MARCOM Subordinate Commands; NATO Shipping Centre;
– Headquarters Allied Air Command (HQ AIRCOM), Ramstein (Germany), comprising: Combined Air Operations Centre, Torrejón de Ardoz (Spain); Combined Air Operations Centre, Uedem (Germany); Deployable Air Command and Control Centre (DACCC);
– Headquarters Allied Land Command, Izmir (Turkey);
– NATO CIS Group;
– Rapidly Deployable Corps Headquarters, comprising: *Allied Rapid Reaction Corps (ARRC, #00736)*, Gloucester (UK); *Eurocorps (#05671)*, Strasbourg (France); Multinational Corps Northeast, Szczecin (Poland); Headquarters Rapid Deployable Corps Italy; Headquarters Rapid Deployable Corps Turkey; Headquarters Rapid Deployable German-Netherlands Corps; Headquarters Rapid Deployable Corps Spain; Headquarters Rapid Deployable Corps France; Headquarters Rapid Deployable Corps Greece;
– Other Staff and Commands responsible to SACEUR, comprising: Immediate Reaction Forces (Maritime); Naval Striking and Support Forces – STRIKFORNATO; *NATO Airborne Early Warning and Control Force Command (NAEW and C, #16942).*
Allied Command Transformation (ACT, #00732):
– Headquarters Supreme Allied Commander Transformation (HQ SACT), Norfolk VA (USA);
– Joint Warfare Centre (JWC), Stavanger (Norway);
– NATO Training Group;
– NATO Joint Force Training Centre (JFTC), Bydgoszcz (Poland);
– NATO Maritime Interdiction Operational Training Center (NMIOTC), Souda Naval Base, Crete (Greece);
– NATO School, Oberammergau (Germany);
– Joint Analysis and Lessons Learned Centre, Lisbon (Portugal).
'Other NATO Command and Staff Organizations':
– Canada-US Regional Planning Group (CUSRPG);
– Combined Joint Planning Staff (CJPS), Mons (Belgium).
/Organizations and agencies/:
'Support':
– *NATO Support and Procurement Agency (NSPA, #16948)*;
'Communications and information':
– *'NATO Communications and Information Agency (NCI Agency)'*, comprising: *NATO C3 Organisation*; *NATO CIS Services Agency (NCSA)*; *NATO Consultation, Command and Control Agency (NC3A)*.
'Science and Technology (S and T)':
– *NATO Science and Technology Organization (STO)*;
– *Centre for Maritime Research and Experimentation (CMRE)*.
'NATO Standardization Office (NSO)':
– *NATO Term – The Official NATO Terminology Database.*
'Programme Offices':
– *NATO Alliance Ground Surveillance Management Agency (NAGSMA)*;
– *NATO Helicopter Design and Development Production and Logistics Management Agency (NAHEMA)*;
– *NATO Medium Extended Air Defence System Design and Development, Production and Logistics Management Agency (NAMEADSMA)*;
– *NATO Sea Sparrow Surface Missile System Office*;
– *NATO Airborne Early Warning and Control Programme Management Agency (NAPMA)*.
'Civil Emergency Planning':
– Senior Civil Emergency Planning Committee (SCEPC);
– Civil Emergency Planning Boards and Committees;
– Euro-Atlantic Disaster Response Coordination Centre (EADRCC).
'Air Traffic Management, Air Defence':

– Aviation Committee;
– *NATO Air Defence Committee (NADC)*;
– Military Committee Air Defence Study Working Group (MC-ADSWG).
'Airborn Early Warning':
– *NATO Airborne Early Warning and Control Programme Management Organization (NAPMO, #16943).*
'Electronic Warfare':
– NATO Electronic Warfare Advisory Committee (NEWAC).
'Meteorology':
– Military Committee Meteorological Group (MCMG).
'Military Oceanography':
– Military Oceanography (MILOC) Group.
'Education and Training':
– *NATO Defense College (NDC, #16944)*;
– *NATO SCHOOL Oberammergau (NSO, #16947)*;
– NATO Communications and Information Systems (NCISS) School;
– *NATO Training Group (NTG)*;
– NATO Maritime Interdiction Operational Training Center (NMIOTC).
'NATO accredited Centres of Excellence'.
'Project Steering Committees/Project Offices':
– Alliance Ground Surveillance Capability Provisional Project Office (AGS/PPO);
– Battlefield Information Collection and Exploitation System (BICES);
– NATO Continuous Acquisition and Life Cycle Support Office (CALS);
– NATO FORACS Office;
– Munitions Safety Information Analysis Center (MSIAC).

Languages English, French. **Staff** Civilian International Staff at Headquarters consists of 1,000 composed of nationals from member countries. Worldwide about 6,000 civilians work for NATO in different agencies and strategic and regional commands. International Military Staff consists of about 500, composed of military and civilian personnel from member countries. Retired civilian staff have their own organization, *Association internationale des anciens agents, retraités de l'OTAN et de leurs ayants-droits (ARO, #02665).* **Finance** Members' contributions to expenditures of the International Staff, International Military Staff and Military Committee agencies and to the common-funded elements of Peace Support Operations and Partnership for Peace activities. Civil Budget is established and executed under the supervision of the Civil Budget Committee and is primarily funded from appropriations of Ministries of Foreign Affairs. Military Budget is established and executed under the supervision of the Military Budget Committee and is mainly financed from appropriations of Ministries of Defence. **Activities** Conflict resolution; humanitarian/emergency aid; politics/policy/regulatory; networking/liaising. NATO's crisis-management operations are carried out under Article 5 of the Washington Treaty or under a UN mandate. About 18,000 military personnel are engaged in NATO missions worldwide. Currently active in Afghanistan, Kosovo -*KFOR (#16187)*, and the Mediterranean. Euro-Atlantic Partnership underpinned by 2 key mechanisms:*Euro Atlantic Partnership Council (EAPC, #05646)*; *Partnership for Peace (PfP, #18240).* Other partnerships include: NATO's Mediterranean Dialogue; Istanbul Cooperation Initiative (ICI); Partners across the globe. **Events** *Extraordinary Meeting of Ministers of Defence* Brussels (Belgium) 2022, *Extraordinary Summit* Brussels (Belgium) 2022, *Meeting of Ministers of Foreign Affairs* Brussels (Belgium) 2022, *Session* Brussels (Belgium) 2022, *Summit* Madrid (Spain) 2022. **Publications** Press releases. Information Services: E-Library comprising: Official and basic texts; Archives; Multimedia Library with over 18,000 books. **Information Services** *NATO Term* – database.

Members Governments of 29 countries:
Albania, Belgium, Bulgaria, Canada, Croatia, Czechia, Denmark, Estonia, France, Germany, Greece, Hungary, Iceland, Italy, Latvia, Lithuania, Luxembourg, Montenegro, Netherlands, Norway, Poland, Portugal, Romania, Slovakia, Slovenia, Spain, Türkiye, UK, USA.
Partner countries aspiring membership (4):
Bosnia-Herzegovina, Georgia, North Macedonia.

IGO Relations Special links with: *European Union (EU, #08967)*; *Organization for Security and Cooperation in Europe (OSCE, #17887)*; *United Nations (UN, #20515).* Links with Central and Eastern European countries and with member states of: *Commonwealth of Independent States (CIS, #04341)* through EAPC and Partnership for Peace (PfP). Supports: *African Union (AU, #00488).* **NGO Relations** *Atlantic Treaty Association (ATA, #03010)*, founded 18 Jun 1954, The Hague (Netherlands), educates and informs the public concerning aims and goals NATO. *International Committee of the Red Cross (ICRC, #12799)* annually meets with NATO Secretary-General.
[2017/XC3005/**C***]

♦ **NATO PA** NATO Parliamentary Assembly (#16946)
♦ NATO Parliamentarians' Conference / see NATO Parliamentary Assembly (#16946)

♦ NATO Parliamentary Assembly (NATO PA) 16946

Assemblée parlementaire de l'OTAN (AP OTAN)

SG Place du Petit Sablon 3, 1000 Brussels, Belgium. T. +3225132865. Fax +3225141847. E-mail: secretariat@nato-pa.int.
URL: http://www.nato-pa.int/

History 18 Jul 1955, Paris (France). Founded following first initiatives taken in 1954 by Norwegian and Canadian parliamentarians. In 1968, headquarters were transferred from Paris to Brussels (Belgium) and the Secretariat was reorganized. Support pledged by Heads of NATO Governments: in *'Declaration on Atlantic Relations'*, Jun 1974, Brussels; Jun 1987, in the Reykjavik (Iceland) Ministerial Statement; in *'An Alliance in the 21st Century'*, Apr 1999, in the Washington Summit Communiqué; in Jun 2004, in the Istanbul (Turkey) Summit Communiqué; Jul 2016, in the Warsaw (Poland) Summit Communiqué. Former names and other names: *Conference of Members of Parliament from the NATO Member Countries* – former (1955 to 1966); *Conférence des membres des Parlements des pays de l'OTAN* – former (1955 to 1966); *NATO Parliamentarians' Conference* – former (1955 to 1966); *Conférence des parlementaires de l'OTAN* – former (1955 to 1966); *North Atlantic Assembly (NAA)* – former (1966 to Jun 1999); *Assemblée de l'Atlantique Nord* – former (1966 to Jun 1999). **Aims** Foster dialogue among parliamentarians on major security issues; facilitate parliamentary awareness and understanding of Alliance policies; strengthen the transatlantic relationship; assist in development of parliamentary democracy throughout the Euro-Atlantic area; assist in development of parliamentary mechanisms, practices and 'know-how' related to democratic control of *armed forces*; contribute to making the policies of the Alliance more transparent and comprehensible to parliaments and their public. **Structure** Plenary Session (biannual). Assembly consisting of 266 parliamentarians nominated by respective parliaments (no ministers or members of governments in office). Standing Committee (Governing Body); Bureau; President. Committees (5): Defence and Security; Economics and Security; Civil Dimension of Security; Political; Science and Technology. Sub-Committees (8): Democratic Governance; NATO Partnerships; Transatlantic Relations; Transatlantic Defence and Security Cooperation; Future Security and Defence Capabilities; Transition and Development; Transatlantic Economic Relations; Technology Trends and Security. Mediterranean and Middle East Special Group; Georgia-NATO Interparliamentary Council; Ukraine-NATO Interparliamentary Council; International Secretariat. **Languages** English, French. **Staff** 28.00 FTE, paid. **Finance** Sole source: contributions of parliaments or governments of member countries in accordance with the NATO civil cost-sharing formula. **Activities** Events/meetings. **Events** *Annual Session* Lisbon (Portugal) 2021, *Annual Session* Brussels (Belgium) 2020, *Annual Session* London (UK) 2019, *Annual Session* Halifax, NS (Canada) 2018, *Annual Session* Bucharest (Romania) 2017. **Publications** Reports; recommendations.

Members Parliamentarians (266) of the 29 member countries of the North Atlantic Alliance:
Albania, Belgium, Bulgaria, Canada, Croatia, Czechia, Denmark, Estonia, France, Germany, Greece, Hungary, Iceland, Italy, Latvia, Lithuania, Luxembourg, Montenegro, Netherlands, Norway, Poland, Portugal, Romania, Slovakia, Slovenia, Spain, Türkiye, UK, USA.
Associate delegates in 12 countries:
Armenia, Austria, Azerbaijan, Bosnia-Herzegovina, Finland, Georgia, Moldova, North Macedonia, Serbia, Sweden, Switzerland, Ukraine.
Parliamentary observers in 8 countries and territories:
Australia, Egypt, Japan, Kazakhstan, Korea Rep, Kosovo, Palestine, Tunisia.
Mediterranean associate delegates in 4 countries:
Algeria, Israel, Jordan, Morocco.

IGO Relations Although completely independent of *NATO (#16945)*, constitutes a link between parliamentarians and the Alliance, acting as NATO's inter-parliamentary organization. Institutional links with: *Parliamentary Assembly of the Council of Europe (PACE, #18211). European Parliament (EP, #08146)*; *Parliamentary Assembly of the Organization for Security and Cooperation in Europe (OSCE PA, #18214).* Complements and reinforces work of: *Euro Atlantic Partnership Council (EAPC, #05646)*; *Partnership for Peace (PfP, #18240).* Regular relations with: *Parliamentary Assembly of the Mediterranean (PAM, #18212). Parliamentary Assembly of the Organization of the Black Sea Economic Cooperation (PABSEC, #18213).* Economics and Security Committee has links with: *OECD (#17693).* **NGO Relations** Partner of: *International Relations and Security Network (ISN, inactive).* Member of: *European Policy Centre (EPC, #08240).* Institutional member of: *Centre for European Policy Studies (CEPS, #03741).*
[2021/XC3004/**C**]

♦ NATO Programming Centre (inactive)
♦ NATO Research and Technology Organization (inactive)
♦ NATO School / see NATO SCHOOL Oberammergau (#16947)

♦ NATO SCHOOL Oberammergau (NSO) 16947

Public Affairs Officer Am Rainenbichl 54, 82487 Oberammergau, Germany. T. +49882294811050.
URL: https://www.natoschool.nato.int/

History Mar 1953, Germany FR. Founded following establishment of the first NATO courses in the Special Weapons Branch of the US Army Intelligence and Military Police School. Comes within the framework of *NATO (#16945)*, under *Supreme Headquarters Allied Powers Europe (SHAPE, #20039).* Special Weapons Branch became the NATO Weapons Systems Department and was placed under operational control of the Supreme Allied Commander, Europe (SACEUR) of *Allied Command Operations (ACO, #00731)*, 1966. Former names and other names: *NATO Weapons Systems School* – former (1973); *NATO School (SHAPE)* – former (1975). **Aims** Conduct education and training in support of current and developing NATO strategy, policy, doctrine and procedures. **Structure** Command Group; Academic Department; Supporting Departments. **Languages** English. **Staff** About 200 civilian and military staff from over 20 NATO and partner nations. **Finance** Funded in accordance with a bilateral agreement between the US and Germany with the majority of funds generated from student tuition fees. Facilities and logistics support provided by the German government and the United States European Command (US EUCOM). **Activities** Training/education; events/meetings. **Events** *NATO European Security Challenges and their Implication on South East European Region* Bestovje (Croatia) 2021.

Members Contributing nations (22):
Austria, Bosnia-Herzegovina, Canada, Czechia, Denmark, France, Germany, Greece, Hungary, Italy, Netherlands, Norway, Poland, Portugal, Romania, Slovakia, Slovenia, Spain, Switzerland, Türkiye, UK, USA.

IGO Relations *Centre for Security Cooperation (RACVIAC, #03785).*
[2022/XE0620/**E**]

♦ NATO Science and Technology Organization (unconfirmed)
♦ NATO Standardization Organization (inactive)

♦ NATO Support and Procurement Agency (NSPA) 16948

Agence OTAN de soutien et de'acquisition

Gen Manager Rue de la Gare 11, L-8325 Capellen, Luxembourg. T. +35230636501. Fax +352307858. E-mail: pao@nspa.nato.int.
URL: http://www.nspa.nato.int/

History May 1958, as *NATO Maintenance Supply Service System (NMSSS).* On resolution of *North Atlantic Council (NAC, #17572)*, changed into *NATO Maintenance and Supply Organization (NAMSO) – Organisation OTAN d'entretien et d'approvisionnement – NATO-Wartungs- und Versorgungsorganisation*, Oct 1964. Definition, mission, status and organization indicated in the NAMSO Charter. Certification ISO 9001: 2008; 2015. Current title adopted, 1 Apr 2015. **Aims** Provide responsive, effective and cost-efficient acquisition, including armaments procurement, logistics, operational and systems support and services to the Allies, NATO Military Authorities and partner nations, individually and collectively, in time of peace, crisis and war, so as to maximize the ability and flexibility of their armed forces, contingents, and other relevant organizations, within the guidance provided by the North Atlantic Council, to execute their core missions. **Structure** Executive body of *NATO Support and Procurement Organisation (NSPO)*, of which all 28 *NATO (#16945)* nations are members. Includes: Logistics Operations; *Central Europe Pipeline System (CEPS) Programme*; *NATO Airlift Management (NAM) Programme.* **Languages** English, French. **Staff** 1200.00 FTE, paid. **Finance** Annual budget (2016): euro 3,400 million. **Activities** Capacity building. **Events** *Meeting on ecological logistics in practice* Aberdeen (UK) 1998. **Publications** Annual Report; thematic brochures.

Members All NATO member countries. Participating nations (28):
Albania, Belgium, Bulgaria, Canada, Croatia, Czechia, Denmark, Estonia, France, Germany, Greece, Hungary, Iceland, Italy, Latvia, Lithuania, Luxembourg, Netherlands, Norway, Poland, Portugal, Romania, Slovakia, Slovenia, Spain, Türkiye, UK, USA.

IGO Relations *Allied Command Operations (ACO, #00731)*; *Supreme Headquarters Allied Powers Europe (SHAPE, #20039).*
[2017.06.01/XE3095/**E***]

♦ NATO-Wartungs- und Versorgungsorganisation / see NATO Support and Procurement Agency (#16948)

♦ NATO Watch 16949

Founder address not obtained. E-mail: info@natowatch.org.
URL: https://natowatch.org/

History 2009. **Aims** Promote a more open, transparent and accountable North Atlantic Treaty Organisation. **Activities** Events/meetings; monitoring/evaluation. **NGO Relations** Member of (2): *Freedom of Information Advocates Network (FOIAnet, #09985)*; *International Coalition for the Responsibility to Protect (ICRtoP, #12620).*
[2021.04.18/AA0975/**E**]

♦ NATO Weapons Systems School / see NATO SCHOOL Oberammergau (#16947)

♦ NATRUE 16950

Dir Rue Washington 40 – 2nd Floor, 1050 Brussels, Belgium. T. +3226132930. Fax +3226132939. E-mail: info@natrue.eu.
URL: http://www.natrue.org/

History 2007. Former names and other names: *NATRUE – The International Natural and Organic Cosmetics Association* – full title; *NATRUE – True Friends of Natural and Organic Cosmetics* – former. Registration: Banque-Carrefour des Entreprises, No/ID: 0820.350.873, Start date: 5 Nov 2009, Belgium; EU Transparency Register, No/ID: 75060586073-86, Start date: 24 Jun 2011. **Aims** Protect and promote natural and organic cosmetics to the benefit of consumers worldwide. **Structure** Membership Assembly; Board of Directors; Scientific Committee; Secretariat; Working groups. **Languages** Dutch, English, French, German, Italian, Spanish. **Staff** 5.80 FTE, paid. **Finance** Sources: fees for services; members' dues. **Activities** Events/meetings; monitoring/evaluation; standards/guidelines. **Publications** News; articles.

Members Full; Associate; Affiliate. Members in 17 countries:
Austria, Croatia, France, Germany, Greece, Hungary, Ireland, Italy, Morocco, New Zealand, Poland, Spain, Sri Lanka, Sweden, Switzerland, UK, USA.

NGO Relations Member of (5): *Comité européen de normalisation (CEN, #04162)*; *Federation of European and International Associations Established in Belgium (FAIB, #09508)*; *IFOAM Organics Europe (#11104)*; *IFOAM – Organics International (IFOAM, #11105)*; *IOAS (#16001).*
[2023.02.14/XJ1968/**D**]

♦ NATRUE – The International Natural and Organic Cosmetics Association / see NATRUE (#16950)
♦ NATRUE – True Friends of Natural and Organic Cosmetics / see NATRUE (#16950)
♦ Natura 2000 Network (see: #06633)
♦ NATURA – Forum Internacional para la Naturaleza y el Turismo (internationally oriented national body)

♦ Pro-Natura International 16951

Pres 33 avenue Duquesne, 75007 Paris, France. T. +33680610936. E-mail: pro-natura@wanadoo.fr.
URL: http://www.pronatura.org/

History 1986, Brazil, as a Brazilian NGO aiming to create protected zones of pristine forest. Became international, 1992, with headquarters in Paris (France), following *United Nations Conference on Environment and Development (UNCED)*, Rio de Janeiro (Brazil). Registered in accordance with French law; an NGO "declared of public interest in the field of environment" in Brazil. **Aims** Work on *biodiversity*, *climate change* and combating *desertification*, with a special focus on the social, economic and environmental problems facing rural communities in the *Tropics.* **Structure** Advisory Board, consisting of world authorities in the area. Executive Board, including President and Secretary-General. International management team comprising 175 specialists from all continents. Each Chapter has its own Board of Trustees and its own programme areas. **Languages** English, French, Portuguese. **Staff** Voluntary. **Finance** Income raised from corporations, bilateral and multilateral funding programmes, foundations and private donors. Budget (annual): US$ 5 million. **Activities** Projects/programmes; advocacy/lobbying/activism. **Publications** *Pro-Natura International Newsletter* (2 a year).

Members Organizations and individuals in 32 countries:
Algeria, Angola, Argentina, Australia, Belgium, Bolivia, Brazil, Canada, Côte d'Ivoire, France, Gabon, Germany, Ghana, Guatemala, Guiana Fr, Guyana, Indonesia, Italy, Laos, Madagascar, Mali, Netherlands, Niger, Nigeria, Paraguay, Peru, Senegal, South Africa, UK, USA, Vanuatu, Zambia.
NGO Relations Member of: *EarthAction (EA, #05159)*; *International Union for Conservation of Nature and Natural Resources (IUCN, #15766)*. [2017/XF3249/**F**]

♦ Natural Capital Coalition (NCC) 16952

Exec Dir c/o 1 Moorgate Place, London, EC2R 6EA, UK. E-mail: info@naturalcapitalcoalition.org.
URL: http://www.naturalcapitalcoalition.org/
History 6 Nov 2012, Singapore. TEEB stands for *The Economics of Ecosystems and Biodiversity*. United with *Social & Human Capital Coalition (inactive)* into *Capitals Coalition (#03420)*, Jan 2020. Former names and other names: *TEEB For Business Coalition* – former (2012 to 2014). **Aims** Unite the global natural capital community. **Structure** Board; Team; Advisory Panel. **Events** *International Symposium on the Natural Capital Protocol* Tokyo (Japan) 2017, *International Symposium on the Natural Capital Protocol* Tokyo (Japan) 2016, *World Forum on Natural Capital* Edinburgh (UK) 2015.
Members Business; practitioners; sustainable business initiatives; policy; associations; wider stakeholders. Members (nearly 300) include 37 organizations listed in this Yearbook:
- *African Centre for Technology Studies (ACTS, #00243)*;
- *Alliance for Water Stewardship (AWS, #00727)*;
- *Association of Chartered Certified Accountants (ACCA)*;
- *BirdLife International (#03266)*;
- *Business for Social Responsibility (BSR)*;
- *Calouste Gulbenkian Foundation*;
- *CDP (#03621)*;
- *Center for International Forestry Research (CIFOR, #03646)*;
- *Conservation Finance Alliance (CFA)*;
- *Conservation International (CI)*;
- *Convention on Biological Diversity (Biodiversity convention, 1992)*;
- *Earthmind*;
- *Earthwatch Institute (#05171)*;
- *European Commission (EC, #06633)*;
- *FAO (#09260)*;
- *Fauna & Flora International (FFI, #09277)*;
- *Fundación Global Nature*;
- *GEO Foundation (#10132)*;
- *Global Canopy (#10271)*;
- *Global Nature Fund (GNF, #10479)*;
- *Global Reporting Initiative (GRI, #10567)*;
- *Green Economy Coalition (GEC, #10717)*;
- *Inter-American Development Bank (IDB, #11427)*;
- *International Bank for Reconstruction and Development (IBRD, #12317)*;
- *International Federation of Accountants (IFAC, #13335)*;
- *International Finance Corporation (IFC, #13597)*;
- *International Union for Conservation of Nature and Natural Resources (IUCN, #15766)*;
- *The Nature Conservancy (TNC)*;
- *The Rockefeller Foundation (#18966)*;
- *The Sustainability Consortium (TSC, #20049)*;
- *UN Environment Programme World Conservation Monitoring Centre (UNEP-WCMC, #20295)*;
- *UNEP (#20299)*;
- *World Agroforestry Centre (ICRAF, #21072)*;
- *World Business Council for Sustainable Development (WBCSD, #21254)*;
- *World Resources Institute (WRI, #21753)*;
- *World Wide Fund for Nature (WWF, #21922)*.

IGO Relations *Bioversity International (#03262)*. **NGO Relations** Partner of: *Green Economy Coalition (GEC, #10717)*. Member of: *Global Commons Alliance*; *High Level Panel for a Sustainable Ocean Economy (Panel, #10917)* – Advisory Network; *Science Based Targets Network*. [2019/XJ6900/y/**C**]

♦ Natural Food Colours Association (NATCOL) 16953

SG Rond-Point Schuman 6, Boîte 5 – 5th Floor, 1040 Brussels, Belgium. E-mail: secretariat@natcol.org.
Registered Office Schaffhauserrheinweg 125, 4002 Basel BS, Switzerland.
URL: https://natcol.org/
History 26 Jan 1979. Registration: Swiss Civil Code, Switzerland; Banque-Carrefour des Entreprises, No/ID: 0696.720.514, Start date: 23 May 2018, Belgium; EU Transparency Register, No/ID: 249894348655-27, Start date: 17 Jan 2023. **Aims** Bring together views of suppliers, *food* manufacturers, scientists, legislators, academic institutions and consumers, in order to harmonize attitudes and approaches to food colouring; disseminate information on the use of natural colours in food. **Structure** General Meeting (annual); Executive Committee (meets at least twice a year); Working Groups; Secretariat. **Languages** English. **Staff** 1.50 FTE, paid. **Finance** Sources: members' dues. **Activities** Events/meetings; knowledge management/information dissemination; politics/policy/regulatory. **Events** *Annual General Meeting* Paris (France) 2016, *Annual General Meeting* Dublin (Ireland) 2015, *Annual General Meeting* Barcelona (Spain) 2014, *Annual General Meeting* Chester (UK) 2013, *Annual General Meeting* Zurich (Switzerland) 2012. **Publications** *Circular Letters* (regular).
Members Full (24) in 12 countries:
Chile, China, Denmark, France, Germany, India, Israel, Japan, Peru, Switzerland, UK, USA.
IGO Relations Observer status with (1): *Codex Alimentarius Commission (CAC, #04081)* (Committee for Food Additives (CCFA)). Cooperates with (1): *European Food Safety Authority (EFSA, #07287)*. **NGO Relations** Member of (1): *EU Specialty Food Ingredients (#09200)*. Cooperates with (1): *European Technical Caramel Association (EUTECA, #08877)*. [2023/XD7357/**D**]

♦ Natural Justice: Lawyers for Communities and the Environment (Natural Justice) 16954

Exec Dir Mercantile Bldg, 63 Hout Street, Cape Town, 8000, South Africa. T. +27214261633. Fax +27214261633. E-mail: info@naturaljustice.org.za.
URL: https://naturaljustice.org/
History 2007, Cape Town (South Africa). Founded by 2 international lawyers, Harry Jonas and Sanjay "Kabir" Bavikatte. **Aims** Enhance the collective rights of people and protect the sacred relationships that indigenous peoples and local communities have with nature. **Structure** Board. **NGO Relations** Member of (1): *Coalition for Human Rights in Development (#04061)*. [2022/AA2841/**F**]

♦ **Natural Justice** Natural Justice: Lawyers for Communities and the Environment (#16954)

♦ Natural Mineral Waters Europe (NMWE) 16955

SG Place des Barricades 1, 1000 Brussels, Belgium. T. +3228802030. Fax +3228802035. E-mail: info@nmwe.org.
PA and Office Manager address not obtained.
URL: https://naturalmineralwaterseurope.org
History Replaces *GISEM / UNESEM (inactive)*. Former names and other names: *European Federation of Bottled Waters (EFBW)* – former (2003 to 2021). Registration: Banque-Carrefour des Entreprises, No/ID: 0876.678.179, Start date: 13 Oct 2005, Belgium; EU Transparency Register, No/ID: 562370525222-50, Start date: 22 Dec 2016. **Aims** Be the voice of the European natural mineral and spring water producers. **Structure** General Assembly; Board; Executive Committee; Working Groups; Secretary General. **Languages** English. **Staff** 4.00 FTE, paid. **Finance** Annual budget: 600,000 EUR (2017). **Events** *Conference on Best in Class Deposit Return Systems (DRS) for Single-Use Beverage Packaging* Brussels (Belgium) 2019, *Meeting* Berlin (Germany) 2005.
Members Organizations (" indicates Affiliate) in 25 countries :
Austria, Belgium, Bulgaria, Croatia, Czechia, Denmark, France, Georgia (*), Germany, Greece, Hungary, Ireland, Italy, Luxembourg, Netherlands, Poland, Portugal, Romania, Serbia, Slovenia, South Africa (*), Spain, Türkiye, UK, Ukraine (*).
NGO Relations Member of (3): *Federation of European and International Associations Established in Belgium (FAIB, #09508)*; *FoodDrinkEurope (#09841)*; *International Council of Bottled Water Associations (ICBWA, #13001)*. [2021.02.23/XJ3851/**D**]

♦ Natural Products Research Network for Eastern and Central Africa (NAPRECA) 16956

Réseau de recherche des produits naturels pour l'Afrique orientale et centrale
Exec Sec Dept of Chemistry, Univ of Nairobi, PO Box 30197, Nairobi, 00100, Kenya. T. +254204451559. Fax +254204446138. E-mail: cmgina@yahoo.com – cmgina@udsm.ac.tz – napreca2019@gmail.com.
Assistant Sec/Treas address not obtained.
Twitter: https://twitter.com/naprecanetwork
History Apr 1984. Incorporated, Nov 1987, as a programme of *UNESCO (#20322)*. **Aims** Develop and promote teaching and research in the area of natural products. **Structure** Coordinating Board (meets annually). **Finance** Support from: *Deutscher Akademischer Austauschdienst (DAAD)*; UNESCO; Uppsala University (Sweden). **Activities** Scientific meetings, symposia and workshops; summer schools; training schemes, including post-graduate scholarship programme. Plans provision of analytical services in the sub-region. **Events** *Improved health and agriculture through sustainable exploration of biodiversity for drug discovery and bio-energy* Arusha (Tanzania UR) 2015, *Natural products discovery – focus on the ever increasing African health care needs* Khartoum (Sudan) 2013, *Natural products from African biodiversity* Nairobi (Kenya) 2011, *Drug discovery from African rainforest* Kinshasa (Congo DR) 2009, *Symposium* Kampala (Uganda) 2007. **Publications** *NAPRECA Newsletter* (2 a year). *NAPRECA Monograh Series* (irregular).
Members National teaching and research institutions in 10 countries:
Botswana, Congo DR, Ethiopia, Kenya, Madagascar, Rwanda, Sudan, Tanzania UR, Uganda, Zimbabwe.
NGO Relations Member of: *AFASSA (no recent information)*. [2019/XF1683/**F**]

♦ Natural Resource Governance Institute (NRGI) 16957

Acting CEO 80 Broad St, Ste 1801, New York NY 10004, USA. T. +16469299750. E-mail: nrgi@resourcegovernance.org.
UK Office 2nd Floor, 1 Knightrider Ct, London, EC4V 5BJ, UK. T. +442073322410.
URL: https://resourcegovernance.org/
History Founded 2013, on merger of Revenue Watch Institute and Natural Resource Charter. **Aims** Ensure that countries rich in oil, gas and minerals achieve sustainable, inclusive development and that people receive lasting benefits from extractives and experience reduced harms. **Structure** Board of Directors; Advisory Council; Institutional Leadership Team. **Languages** English. **Staff** 80.00 FTE, paid. **Finance** Contributions and grants from foundations, governments and international financial institutions. **Activities** Research and development; research/documentation; advocacy/lobbying/activism; capacity building; guidance/assistance/consulting; events/meetings. **Publications** Reports; briefings. **IGO Relations** *African Development Bank (ADB, #00283)*; *Inter-American Development Bank (IDB, #11427)*; *International Bank for Reconstruction and Development (IBRD, #12317)* (World Bank); *OECD (#17693)*. [2020.03.11/XM8483/**F**]

♦ Natural Resources Institute (internationally oriented national body)
♦ Natural Science Collections Alliance (internationally oriented national body)

♦ The Natural Step (TNS) 16958

Det Naturliga Steget
Contact Swedenborgsgatan 2, SE-118 48 Stockholm, Sweden. T. +4687892900.
URL: http://www.thenaturalstep.org/
History 1989, Sweden. Founded by Karl-Henrik Robèrt. Registration: No/ID: 802409-2358, Sweden. **Aims** Accelerate transition to a *sustainable* society. **Structure** National Offices (11). **Languages** Chinese, Dutch, English, Finnish, French, German, Hebrew, Italian, Portuguese, Swedish. **Activities** Awareness raising; resesarch and development; capacity building; knowledge management/information dissemination; events/meetings. **Publications** Scientific papers. **NGO Relations** Partner of: *Green Economy Coalition (GEC, #10717)*. [2021/XG3711/**F**]

♦ Nature 2000 – International – International Youth Union for the Conservation of Nature (no recent information)
♦ The Nature Conservancy (internationally oriented national body)
♦ Nature Economy and People Connected (NEPCon) / see Preferred by Nature (#18477)
♦ Nature Farming International Research and Development Centre / see International Nature Farming Research Center
♦ Nature Farming International Research Foundation / see International Nature Farming Research Center
♦ Naturefriends International (#14780)

♦ NatureNet Europe 16959

Address not obtained.
URL: http://www.natureneteurope.org/
History 7 Oct 2004, Netherlands. 7 Oct 2004, Poederoijen (Netherlands), as *EECONET Alliance*, following the signing of a memorandum of cooperation between *Coastal and Marine Union – EUCC (#04072)*, *ECNC – European Centre for Nature Conservation (#05289)* and *Eurosite (#09181)*. Present name adopted 2005. **Aims** Introduce, promote and apply new insights, innovative approaches and effective tools for *biodiversity conservation* and *sustainable* use in Europe. **Languages** English. **Staff** 15.00 FTE, paid; 1.00 FTE, voluntary. [2010/XM0913/**F**]

♦ NatureServe (internationally oriented national body)
♦ Naturfreunde Internationale (#14780)
♦ Naturfreundejugend Internationale (#15929)
♦ Det Naturliga Steget (#16958)
♦ Naturopa Network (inactive)
♦ Natuur and Milieu (internationally oriented national body)
♦ Natuurvrienden Jongeren Internationale / see International Young Nature Friends (#15929)
♦ Nätverket för Information om Utbildning i Europa (inactive)
♦ Nätverket för Regionala Lagstiftande Församlingar (#04582)
♦ **NAUA** Nordic Association of University Administrators (#17206)
♦ **NAU** Nordisk Arboretudvalg (#17491)
♦ NAU – Nordiska Unionen för Arbetsledare, Tekniska Functionärer och andra Chefer (inactive)
♦ **NAUSS** Naif Arab University for Security Sciences (#16929)
♦ Nautical Institute (internationally oriented national body)
♦ Nautilus Institute (internationally oriented national body)
♦ Nautilus Institute for Security and Sustainable Development / see Nautilus Institute

♦ Nautilus International 16960

Gen Sec The Shrubberies, 1-2 George Lane, South Woodford, London, E18 1BD, UK. T. +442089896677. Fax +442085301015. E-mail: enquiries@nautilusint.org.
URL: http://www.nautilusint.org/
History Origins traced back to 1857, when UK Mercantile Marine Service Association (MMSA) was set up. Officially created when Nautilus NL and Nautilus UK join forces, 2009. Swiss branch added, 2011. EU Transparency Register: 15174678548-65. **Aims** Be an independent and influential global *trade union* and professional organisation, giving high quality and cost-effective services to members. **Structure** Governing Council; Specialist Committees; Secretariat. Also includes *Nautilus Welfare Fund*. **Languages** Dutch, English, German. **Staff** 70.00 FTE, paid. **Finance** Members' dues. **Activities** Advocacy/lobbying/activism; awards/prizes/competitions; awareness raising; events/meetings; financial and/or material support; healthcare; publishing activities; research and development. **Publications** *Nautilus Telegraph* (12 a year).
Members Principally situated in 3 countries:
Netherlands, Switzerland, UK.
NGO Relations *European Transport Workers' Federation (ETF, #08941)*; *International Federation of Shipmasters Associations (IFSMA, #13539)*; *International Seafarers' Welfare and Assistance Network (ISWAN, #14815)*; *International Transport Workers' Federation (ITF, #15726)*. [2019.04.02/XM7050/**E**]

♦ Nautilus Pacific Research / see Nautilus Institute
♦ Nautilus Peace and Security Network (internationally oriented national body)

♦ NAUT – Nordisk Arbeidsmarkedsutvalg (inactive)
♦ Naval Agreement (1913 treaty)
♦ Naval Records Club / see International Naval Research Organization (#14221)
♦ NAVF's utredningsinstitutt / see Nordisk Institutt for Studier av Innovasjon, Forskning og Utdanning
♦ Navigators (internationally oriented national body)
♦ **NAVIGA** World Organization for Modelship Building and Modelship Sport (#21691)
♦ Naviguer pour l'Europe (#19035)
♦ **NAVT** Network of Associations of Victims of Terrorism (#16998)
♦ NAWIRA / see Rugby Americas North (#18997)
♦ **NAWMP** Network of African Women Ministers and Parliamentarians (#16988)
♦ NAYA / see World Youth Alliance – North America
♦ **NAYD** Network of African Youths for Development (#16989)
♦ Nazarene Compassionate Ministries (see: #12571)
♦ Naz Foundation International (internationally oriented national body)
♦ Naz Project / see Naz Foundation International
♦ **NBAMHI** Nordic-Baltic Association for Medical and Health Information (#17213)
♦ **NBA** Niger Basin Authority (#17134)
♦ NBA' / see World Boxing Association (#21241)
♦ **NBBC** Nordic-Baltic Bee Council (#17214)
♦ NBBR – Nordiska Blåbands- och Blåkorsrådet (inactive)
♦ NBCA – Nordic-Baltic Cardiology Alliance (unconfirmed)
♦ NBCBN / see Nile Basin Capacity Building Network for River Engineering (#17138)
♦ **NBCBN-RE** Nile Basin Capacity Building Network for River Engineering (#17138)
♦ NBCC – National Board for Certified Counselors (internationally oriented national body)
♦ NBC – Nordens Bondeorganisasjoners Centralråd (no recent information)
♦ NBC – Nordic-Baltic Conference on Biomedical Engineering and Medical Physics (meeting series)
♦ NBC – Nordic Biogas Conference (meeting series)
♦ NBC – Nordic Breastfeeding Conference (meeting series)
♦ NBDC – Nordic Baltic Drying Conference (meeting series)
♦ **NBDE** Nordic-Baltic Defence Estates (#17216)
♦ **NBD** Nile Basin Discourse (#17139)
♦ **NBF** Nordiska Betongförbundet (#17251)
♦ NBF – Nordisk Barnkirurgisk Förening (no recent information)

♦ NBIA Alliance 16961

Association International DNAI

Contact address not obtained. E-mail: info@nbiaalliance.org.
URL: http://www.nbiaalliance.org/

History Jan 2012. Former names and other names: *Neurodegeneration with Brain Iron Accumulation (NBIA)* – full title. **Aims** Bring together all NBIA lay advocacy organizations worldwide; increase awareness of NBIA; support cooperative research into NBIA disorders. **Languages** Dutch, English, French, German, Hungarian, Italian, Polish, Spanish. **Staff** Voluntary. **Finance** Sources: sponsorship. Sponsored by NBIA Disorders Association. **Activities** Knowledge management/information dissemination; research/documentation; standards/guidelines.

Members Organizations in 10 countries:
Canada, France, Germany, Hungary, Italy, Netherlands, Poland, Spain, Switzerland, USA.

NGO Relations Member of (1): *EURORDIS – Rare Diseases Europe (#09175).* [2022.02.15/XM7428/**C**]

♦ NBIA / see NBIA Alliance (#16961)
♦ **NBI** Nile Basin Initiative (#17140)
♦ **NBK** Nordisk Bispekonferance (#17498)
♦ NBM – International Conference on New Business Models (meeting series)
♦ NBM – Nordiskt Byggforskningsmöte (meeting series)
♦ NB – Nordiska Bowlingförbundet (inactive)
♦ **NBNP** Nordic-Baltic Network of Policewomen (#17218)
♦ NBO / see Housing Nordic (#10957)
♦ **NBO** Housing Nordic (#10957)
♦ **NBO** Nordiska Kooperativa och Allmännyttiga Bostadsföretags Organisation (#10957)
♦ NBR – National Bureau of Asian Research (internationally oriented national body)
♦ NBSID – Nordic-Baltic Society of Infectious Diseases (inactive)
♦ **NBS** Network for Business Sustainability (#16999)
♦ NBS – Nile Basin Society (inactive)
♦ NBTA Europe / see GBTA Europe
♦ **NBTF** Nordiska Byggnads- och Träarbetarefederationen (#17283)
♦ **NBTS** Norraena Bygginga- og Treidnadarmannasambandid (#17283)
♦ **NBU** Nordic Bridge Union (#17222)
♦ NBU – Nordiska Bankmannaunionen (inactive)
♦ **NBU** Nordisk Bueskytterunion (#17499)
♦ NCACOA / see Ostomy Association of the Americas (#17912)
♦ NC-AFM – International Conference on Non-contact Atomic Force Microscopy (meeting series)
♦ NCAFP – National Committee on American Foreign Policy (internationally oriented national body)
♦ NCAMR – Nordic Council for Arctic Medical Research (inactive)
♦ NCA – Nordic Carton Association (no recent information)
♦ NCA – Norwegian Council for Africa (internationally oriented national body)
♦ NCB – Nordic Conference on Bilingualism (meeting series)
♦ **NCB** Nordisk Copyright Bureau (#17500)

♦ NCBRS Worldwide Foundation 16962

Contact Kemp Housse, 152-160 City Road, London, EC1V 2NX, UK. E-mail: contactus@ncbrs.com.
URL: https://ncbrs-worldwide-foundation.weebly.com/

History NCBRS stands for Nicolaides-Baraitser Syndrome. Registration: Charity Commission, No/ID: 1190194, England and Wales. **Aims** Support and educate families, carers and professionals who work with them; promote awareness and understanding of the Nicolaides-Baraitser Syndrome; advocate for scientific research that increases the medical knowledge of Nicolaides-Baraitser Syndrome and best treatments. **Structure** Board. **NGO Relations** Member of (1): *Rare Diseases International (RDI, #18621).* [2022/AA2331/**F**]

♦ **NCC** Natural Capital Coalition (#16952)
♦ NCCSAS – North Carolina Consortium for South Asia Studies (internationally oriented national body)
♦ **NCCS** Nordic College of Caring Science (#17243)
♦ NCCWAVA Regional Association / see North and Central American and Caribbean Regional Association of WMA (#17575)
♦ **NCCWMA Regional Association** North and Central American and Caribbean Regional Association of WMA (#17575)

♦ The NCD Alliance (NCDA) 16963

Main Office 31-33 Ave Giuseppe Motta, 1202 Geneva, Switzerland. E-mail: info@ncdalliance.org – partnerships@ncdalliance.org.
URL: http://www.ncdalliance.org/

History May 2010. Founded by *International Diabetes Federation (IDF, #13164), World Heart Federation (WHF, #21562), Union for International Cancer Control (UICC, #20415)* and *International Union Against Tuberculosis and Lung Disease (The Union, #15752).* "NCD" derives from the phrase *Non-communicable disease.* Registration: Start date: 2017, Switzerland. **Aims** Combat the NCD *epidemic* by putting health at the centre of all policies. **Structure** Steering Group, consisting of CEOs of Founding Organizations and headed by Chair. UN Summit Partners Group; NCD Alliance Supporters. *NCD Alliance Network.* **Activities** Campaigns: Non-communicable Diseases – Join the Fight; Global NCD Framework Campaign; Global Development Campaign.

Members Civil society organizations (over 1,000) in 177 countries and territories:
Afghanistan, Albania, Algeria, Angola, Anguilla, Antigua-Barbuda, Argentina, Armenia, Aruba, Australia, Austria, Azerbaijan, Bahamas, Bahrain, Bangladesh, Barbados, Belarus, Belgium, Belize, Benin, Bermuda, Bolivia, Bosnia-Herzegovina, Botswana, Brazil, Bulgaria, Burkina Faso, Burundi, Cambodia, Cameroon, Canada, Cayman Is, Central African Rep, Chad, Chile, China, Colombia, Congo Brazzaville, Congo DR, Costa Rica, Côte d'Ivoire, Croatia, Cuba, Curaçao, Cyprus, Czechia, Denmark, Dominica, Dominican Rep, Ecuador, Egypt, El Salvador, Equatorial Guinea, Eritrea, Estonia, Ethiopia, Faeroe Is, Fiji, Finland, France, Gambia, Georgia, Germany, Ghana, Greece, Grenada, Guatemala, Guinea, Guinea-Bissau, Guyana, Haiti, Honduras, Hong Kong, Hungary, Iceland, India, Indonesia, Iran Islamic Rep, Iraq, Ireland, Israel, Italy, Jamaica, Japan, Jordan, Kazakhstan, Kenya, Korea Rep, Kuwait, Kyrgyzstan, Latvia, Lebanon, Lesotho, Libya, Lithuania, Luxembourg, Macau, Madagascar, Malawi, Malaysia, Maldives, Mali, Malta, Mauritius, Mexico, Moldova, Mongolia, Montserrat, Morocco, Mozambique, Myanmar, Namibia, Nauru, Nepal, Netherlands, New Zealand, Nicaragua, Niger, Nigeria, North Macedonia, Norway, Oman, Pakistan, Panama, Papua New Guinea, Paraguay, Peru, Philippines, Poland, Portugal, Puerto Rico, Qatar, Romania, Russia, Rwanda, Samoa, San Marino, Saudi Arabia, Senegal, Serbia, Seychelles, Singapore, Slovakia, Slovenia, South Africa, Spain, Sri Lanka, St Kitts-Nevis, St Lucia, St Maarten, Sudan, Suriname, Sweden, Switzerland, Syrian AR, Taiwan, Tanzania UR, Thailand, Togo, Tonga, Trinidad-Tobago, Tunisia, Türkiye, Uganda, UK, Ukraine, United Arab Emirates, Uruguay, USA, Uzbekistan, Vanuatu, Venezuela, Vietnam, Virgin Is UK, Yemen, Zambia, Zimbabwe.

Included in the above, 47 organizations listed in this Yearbook:
– *African Heart Network (AHN, #00336);*
– *African Oncology Institute (no recent information);*
– *African Organization for Research and Training in Cancer (AORTIC, #00405);*
– *Arab Medical Association Against Cancer (AMAAC, #01006);*
– *Asian Pacific Society of Cardiology (APSC, #01631);*
– *Asia-Pacific Heart Network (APHN, #01923);*
– *Childhood Cancer International (CCI, #03871);*
– *European Cervical Cancer Association (ECCA, #06512);*
– *European Heart Network (EHN, #07467);*
– *European Institute of Oncology, Milan (EIO);*
– *European Organisation for Research and Treatment of Cancer (EORTC, #08101);*
– *European School of Oncology (ESO, #08434);*
– *European Society for Medical Oncology (ESMO, #08648);*
– *European SocieTy for Radiotherapy and Oncology (ESTRO, #08721);*
– *European Society of Cardiology (ESC, #08536);*
– *Global Health Advocacy Incubator (GHAI);*
– *Heart Friends Around the World (HFATW, #10900);*
– *Instituto Centro Americano de la Salud (ICAS, #11328);*
– *InterAmerican Heart Foundation (IAHF, #11432);*
– *Inter-American Society of Cardiology (ISC, #11448);*
– *International Academy of Cardiovascular Sciences (IACS, #11539);*
– *International Association for Dental Research (IADR, #11838);*
– *International Council of Nurses (ICN, #13054);*
– *International Extranodal Lymphoma Study Group (IELSG);*
– *International Forum for Hypertension Control and Prevention in Africa (IFHA, #13638);*
– *International Hereditary Cancer Center;*
– *International Psycho-Oncology Society (IPOS, #14665);*
– *International Self-Monitoring Association of Oral Anticoagulated Patients (ISMAAP, #14831);*
– *International Society for Heart Research (ISHR, #15158);*
– *International Society for Holter and Noninvasive Electrocardiology (ISHNE, #15179);*
– *International Society for Nurses in Cancer Care (ISNCC, #15312);*
– *International Society of Cardiomyopathy, Myocarditis and Heart Failure (ISCMF, #14993);*
– *International Society of Cardiovascular Pharmacotherapy (ISCP, #14996);*
– *International Society on Hypertension in Blacks (ISHIB);*
– *Latin-American and Caribbean Society of Medical Oncology (#16286);*
– *Ludwig Institute for Cancer Research (LICR, #16520);*
– *Lymphoma Coalition (LC, #16535);*
– *Movendi International (#16871);*
– *Pan African Society of Cardiology (PASCAR, #18066);*
– *PATH (#18260);*
– *Pulmonary Vascular Research Institute (PVRI, #18576);*
– *Reach to Recovery International (RRI, #18625);*
– *SAARC Tuberculosis and HIV/AIDS Centre (STAC, see: #19721);*
– *Vital Strategies;*
– *World Cancer Research Fund International (WCRF);*
– *World Heart Failure Society (WHFS, #21561);*
– *World Stroke Organization (WSO, #21831).*

NGO Relations Partner of: *Every Woman Every Child (EWEC, #09215); Fight the Fakes (#09755).* [2021/XJ5872/y/**E**]

♦ **NCDA** The NCD Alliance (#16963)
♦ NCDN-CEE / see Capacity Development Network in Nutrition in Central and Eastern Europe (#03418)
♦ NCDO – Nationale Commissie voor Internationale Samenwerking en Duurzame Ontwikkeling (internationally oriented national body)
♦ NCDS / see Centre for Development Studies, Bhubaneswar
♦ **NCED** Nordic College of Equine Dentistry (#17244)
♦ NCF International / see Nurses Christian Fellowship International (#17626)
♦ **NCFI** Nurses Christian Fellowship International (#17626)
♦ **NCF** NewCities Foundation (#17080)
♦ NCF – The Next Century Foundation (internationally oriented national body)
♦ **NCF** Nordic Concrete Federation (#17251)
♦ **NCF** Nordiska Centerungdomens Förbund (#17232)
♦ NCF – Nordiska Cykelförbundet (no recent information)
♦ NCF – Nordisk Cerealist Forbund (no recent information)
♦ NCGM – Nordic Centre for Gender in Military Operations (internationally oriented national body)
♦ **NCH** Network of Concerned Historians (#17001)
♦ NCHR – Norwegian Centre for Human Rights (internationally oriented national body)
♦ NCIH / see Global Health Council (#10402)
♦ NCI / see Nordic Innovation (#17320)
♦ NCIV / see Global Ties US
♦ NCIV – Netherlands Centre for Indigenous Peoples (internationally oriented national body)
♦ **NCK** Nordiskt Centrum för Kulturarvspedagogik (#17230)
♦ NCL – International Congress on Neuronal Ceroid Lipofuscinoses (meeting series)
♦ **NCMF** Nordic Capital Markets Forum (#17226)
♦ **NCMLSG** Nordic Chronic Myeloid Leukemia Study Group (#17238)
♦ NCM – Nazarene Compassionate Ministries (see: #12571)
♦ NCM – Nordic Congress of Mathematicians (meeting series)
♦ **NCM** Nordic Council of Ministers (#17260)
♦ **NCMS** Nordic Centre for Medieval Studies (#17231)
♦ **NCM** Society for the Neural Control of Movement (#19605)
♦ **NCN** NewPOL Consortium Network (#17092)
♦ **NC** Nordic Council (#17256)
♦ NCO / see Nationale Commissie voor Internationale Samenwerking en Duurzame Ontwikkeling
♦ NCODE Flexible Learning Australasia / see Australasian Council on Open, Distance and E-Learning
♦ **NCON** Nordic Co-Operation of Ophthalmic Nurses (#17255)
♦ NCOS / see Coalition of the Flemish North South Movement – 11 11 11
♦ NCOS – Nordic Cardio-Oncology Society (unconfirmed)
♦ **NCPD** Nansen Center for Peace and Dialogue (#16934)
♦ NCP – Nationaal Europese Communautaire Partij (internationally oriented national body)
♦ NCP – National-European Communitarian Party (internationally oriented national body)
♦ **NCPN** Nordic Critical Psychology Network (#17263)
♦ NCP / see Nordic Council (#17256)
♦ NCRE – National Centre for Research on Europe, Christchurch (internationally oriented national body)
♦ NCRE – Nordic Conference of Religious Education (meeting series)
♦ NCRSG / see Inter-regional FAO-CIHEAM Network for Research and Development in Sheep and Goats (#15970)
♦ NCSAS – National Centre for South Asian Studies, Clayton (internationally oriented national body)

- ♦ **NCSC** Nordic Council of Shopping Centres (#17261)
- ♦ **NCSH** Nordic Center for Sustainable Healthcare (#17229)
- ♦ NCSL / see NCSL International
- ♦ NCSLI – NCSL International (internationally oriented national body)
- ♦ NCSL International (internationally oriented national body)
- ♦ NCS – Neurocritical Care Society (internationally oriented national body)
- ♦ NCSR – Nordic Conference for Sociology of Religion (meeting series)
- ♦ NCTN – Nordic Counter Terrorism Network (unconfirmed)
- ♦ NCTR – Nordic Conference for Professionals Working with Traumatised Refugees (meeting series)
- ♦ NCTS – Nordic Connective Tissue Society (unconfirmed)
- ♦ **NCTTCA** Northern Corridor Transit and Transport Coordination Authority (#17582)
- ♦ N-cube Network / see Nordic Number theory Network (#17369)
- ♦ **NCU** Nordic Cancer Union (#17225)
- ♦ NCVO – National Council for Voluntary Organizations (internationally oriented national body)
- ♦ NCWAO / see World Affairs Councils of America
- ♦ **NCWR** Nordic Council for Wildlife Research (#17262)
- ♦ **NCY** Nordic Centre Youth (#17232)
- ♦ NDA / see Nordic Dermatology Association (#17269)
- ♦ **NDA** Nordic Dermatology Association (#17269)
- ♦ **NDB** New Development Bank (#17081)
- ♦ NDC / see European Federation for Living (#07155)
- ♦ **NDC** NATO Defense College (#16944)

♦ NDC Partnership 16964

Communications Manager c/o WRI, 10 G St NE, Ste 800, Washington DC 20002, USA. E-mail: supportunit@ndcpartnership.org.
URL: http://ndcpartnership.org/

History Founded Nov 2016, Marrakech (Morocco), at UN Climate Change Conference COP22, in response to *Paris Agreement (2015)* and the 2030 Agenda for Sustainable Development. NDC stands for *Nationally Determined Contributions*. **Aims** Allow country and institutional members to leverage their resources and expertise to provide countries with the tools needed to implement their nationally determined contributions under the Paris Agreement and combat *climate change* to build a better future. **Structure** Co-chairs (2); Steering Committee; Support Unit hosted by *World Resources Institute (WRI, #21753)* and *United Nations Framework Convention on Climate Change – Secretariat (UNFCCC, #20564)*. **Languages** English, French, Spanish. **Staff** 30.00 FTE, paid. **Finance** Supported by governmental departments Australia, Denmark, UK, Germany, Ireland, Germany, France and Netherlands. **Activities** Capacity building; guidance/assistance/consulting; knowledge management/information dissemination.
Members Governments (85):
Antigua-Barbuda, Argentina, Armenia, Australia, Bangladesh, Belgium, Belize, Benin, Bolivia, Brazil, Burkina Faso, Burundi, Cameroon, Canada, Chad, Chile, Colombia, Congo Brazzaville, Congo DR, Costa Rica, Côte d'Ivoire, Denmark, Dominican Rep, Ecuador, El Salvador, Ethiopia, Fiji, France, Gabon, Georgia, Germany, Ghana, Grenada, Guatemala, Guinea, Guinea-Bissau, Haiti, Honduras, Indonesia, Ireland, Italy, Jamaica, Japan, Jordan, Kenya, Kyrgyzstan, Liberia, Malawi, Maldives, Mali, Marshall Is, Mexico, Mongolia, Morocco, Mozambique, Namibia, Nepal, Netherlands, New Zealand, Nigeria, Norway, Pakistan, Panama, Paraguay, Peru, Philippines, Rwanda, Sao Tomé-Principe, Seychelles, Singapore, Somalia, South Africa, Spain, St Lucia, Sweden, Togo, Tunisia, Uganda, UK, Uruguay, USA, Vanuatu, Vietnam, Zambia, Zimbabwe.
Regional entity:
European Commission (EC, #06633).
Institutions (20):
African Development Bank (ADB, #00283); *Asian Development Bank (ADB, #01422)*; *Caribbean Development Bank (CDB, #03492)*; *Commission des forêts d'Afrique centrale (COMIFAC, #04214)*; *Development Bank of Latin America (CAF, #05055)*; *East African Community (EAC, #05181)*; *European Bank for Reconstruction and Development (EBRD, #06315)*; *FAO (#09260)*; *Global Environment Facility (GEF, #10346)*; *Global Green Growth Institute (GGGI, #10392)*; *ILO (#11123)*; *Inter-American Development Bank (IDB, #11427)*; *International Renewable Energy Agency (IRENA, #14715)*; *Islamic Development Bank (IsDB, #16044)*; *Organisation of Eastern Caribbean States (OECS, #17804)*; *Pacific Community (SPC, #17942)*; *The World Bank Group (#21218)*; *UNDP (#20292)*; *UNEP (#20299)*; *United Nations Framework Convention on Climate Change – Secretariat (UNFCCC, #20564).*
Associate members (8):
Carbon Counts; *Climate Policy Initiative (CPI, #04020)*; *Global Water Partnership (GWP, #10653)*; *International Institute for Sustainable Development (IISD, #13930)*; *Local Governments for Sustainability (ICLEI, #16507)*; *SNV Netherlands Development Organisation (SNV)*; *The Nature Conservancy (TNC)*; *World Wide Fund for Nature (WWF, #21922).* [2019.02.20/XM7495/**E***]

- ♦ NDEA African Language and Area Studies Center / see African Studies Program, Bloomington
- ♦ **NDEP** Northern Dimension Environmental Partnership (#17584)
- ♦ **NDF** Nordic Development Fund (#17271)
- ♦ NdF – Nothelfergemeinschaft der Freunde (internationally oriented national body)
- ♦ **NDH** Nouveaux droits de l'homme – International (#17089)
- ♦ NDI / see National Democratic Institute for International Affairs
- ♦ NDIIA – National Democratic Institute for International Affairs (internationally oriented national body)
- ♦ NDIMA / see Africa Free Media Foundation (#00176)
- ♦ **NDI** Northern Dimension Institute (#17585)
- ♦ Ndjamena-Masawa-Djibouti Trans-Sahelian Highway Coordinating Committee (inactive)
- ♦ NDLTD / see Networked Digital Library of Theses and Dissertations (#17008)
- ♦ **NDLTD** Networked Digital Library of Theses and Dissertations (#17008)
- ♦ NDNC – International Conference on New Diamond and Nano Carbons (meeting series)
- ♦ **ND** Northern Dimension (#17583)
- ♦ **NDPC** Northern Dimension Partnership on Culture (#17586)
- ♦ **NDPHS** Northern Dimension Partnership in Public Health and Social Well-being (#17587)
- ♦ **NDPTL** Northern Dimension Partnership on Transport and Logistics (#17588)
- ♦ **NDRF** Nordic Demining Research Forum (#17267)
- ♦ **NDRI** Network of Democracy Research Institutes (#17003)
- ♦ NDS – Congrégation Notre-Dame de Sion (religious order)
- ♦ **NDS** Nordic Demographic Society (#17268)
- ♦ NDU – Nordisk Dataunion (no recent information)
- ♦ **NDU** Nordisk Dramatikerunion (#17502)
- ♦ NEAATS – North East Asia Association of Theological Schools (no recent information)
- ♦ **NEACEDT** North East Asian Centre for Environmental Data and Training (#17578)
- ♦ **NEAC** Network of European Alimentary Culture (#17012)
- ♦ **NEACSN** North East Asian Crane Site Network (#17579)
- ♦ NEADB – Northeast Asia Development Bank (unconfirmed)
- ♦ **NEAEF** Northeast Asia Economic Forum (#17577)
- ♦ **NEAFC** North-East Atlantic Fisheries Commission (#17581)
- ♦ NEAFF – Northeast Asian Forest Forum (unconfirmed)
- ♦ **NEALT** Northern European Association for Language Technology (#17590)
- ♦ NEAN / see Yonsei Northeast Asian Network
- ♦ **NEA** Nuclear Energy Agency (#17615)
- ♦ NEAPCCP / see Network of the European Associations for Person-Centred and Experiential Psychotherapy and Counselling (#17013)
- ♦ NEAPCEPC / see Network of the European Associations for Person-Centred and Experiential Psychotherapy and Counselling (#17013)
- ♦ **NEAR** Association of North East Asia Regional Governments (#02835)

♦ Near East Forestry Commission (NEFC) 16965

Commission des forêts pour le Proche-Orient (CFPO) – Comisión Forestal para el Cercano Oriente (CFCO)

Head Office FAO Regional Office for the Near East, PO Box 2223, Cairo, Egypt. T. +20233316000 – +20233316001 – +20233316007. Fax +2023745981 – +20233373419. E-mail: fao-rne@fao.org.
URL: http://www.fao.org/forestry/31112/en/

History 1953, as a regional commission of *FAO Regional Office for the Near East and North Africa (#09269)*. within the framework of *FAO (#09260)* (Article VI-1 of FAO Constitution), pursuant to resolution of regional forestry conference, 1952, Amman (Jordan). Rules of procedure adopted 1958, at 2nd session; amended: 1962; 1978; 1983. **Aims** Advise on the formulation of forest policy; review and coordinate its implementation on the regional level; exchange information and, generally through subsidiary bodies, advise on practices and action in regard to technical and economic problems. **Structure** Executive Committee, consisting of Chairman, Vice-Chairmen of Commission and Commission's subsidiary bodies, and Rapporteur. **Languages** Arabic, English, French. **Staff** 1 ad hoc; other FAO officers as required. **Finance** FAO Regular budget supports technical coordination and administration. Member countries provide logistical support. **Activities** Provided support to forestry education and public awareness of the benefits of trees and forests. Achievements include: establishment of a regional forestry and range school; development of forestry terminology in Arabic and translation of forestry literature; inclusion of forestry in curricula of agriculture schools; inclusion of broader multidisciplinary curricula in schools. Supported the Teheran Process to low-forest-cover countries (LFCCs) and development and implementation of criteria and indicators for sustainable forest management in LFCCs. **Events** *Session* Algeria 2015, *Sustainable management of forests and rangelands – towards a green economy in the Near East and North Africa region* Amman (Jordan) 2014, *Good governance of forests and rangelands – pillar of food security* Antalya (Turkey) 2012, *Forests and range – adapting to global changes for sustainable development* Hammamet (Tunisia) 2010, *Session* Khartoum (Sudan) 2008. **Publications** *The NEFC Half a Century Later: key achievements.* Books; session reports; guidelines.
Members Open to FAO Member Nations and Associate Members whose territories are situated wholly or partly in the Near East or who are responsible for the international relations of any non-self-governing territory in that region, and who desire to be considered members. Currently governmental specialists of 27 countries:
Afghanistan, Algeria, Cyprus, Egypt, Ethiopia, Iran Islamic Rep, Iraq, Jordan, Kuwait, Kyrgyzstan, Lebanon, Libya, Mauritania, Morocco, Oman, Pakistan, Qatar, Saudi Arabia, Somalia, Sudan, Syrian AR, Tajikistan, Tunisia, Türkiye, United Arab Emirates, Uzbekistan, Yemen.
Observers at sessions; representatives of 5 countries and territories:
France, Malta, Palestine, UK, USA. [2009.09.24/XE4876/**E***]

- ♦ Near East Foundation (internationally oriented national body)
- ♦ Near East and North Africa Regional Agricultural Credit Association (inactive)

♦ Near East Plant Protection Organization (NEPPO) 16966

Exec Dir Rue Oued El Makhazine No 6, 70000 Rabat, Morocco. T. +212537704810. Fax +212537708763. E-mail: hq.neppo@gmail.com.
URL: https://www.ippc.int/en/external-cooperation/regional-plant-protection-organizations/neppo/

History following a proposal 1993, within the framework of *Near East Regional Commission on Agriculture (COAG/NE, inactive)*. Agreement entered into force 9 Jan 2009. **Events** *Regional Plant Protection Organizations (RPPOs) Annual Technical Consultation* London (UK) 2022, *Regional Plant Protection Organizations (RPPOs) Annual Technical Consultation* Rome (Italy) 2021, *Regional Plant Protection Organizations (RPPOs) Annual Technical Consultation* Rome (Italy) 2020, *Regional Plant Protection Organizations (RPPOs) Annual Technical Consultation* Abuja (Nigeria) 2019, *Regional Plant Protection Organizations (RPPOs) Annual Technical Consultation* Lima (Peru) 2018.
Members Member states (11):
Algeria, Egypt, Iraq, Jordan, Libya, Malta, Morocco, Pakistan, Sudan, Syrian AR, Tunisia.
IGO Relations Since Mar 2012, serves as one of 10 Regional Plant Protection Organizations (RPPOs) of *International Plant Protection Convention, 1951 (IPPC, 1951).* [2018/XD4485/**D***]

- ♦ Near East Regional Economic and Social Policy Commission (inactive)
- ♦ Near East Relief / see Near East Foundation
- ♦ Near East School of Theology (internationally oriented national body)
- ♦ Near East South Asia Center for Strategic Studies (internationally oriented national body)

♦ Near East/South Asia Council of Overseas Schools (NESA) 16967

Contact Gravias 6, Aghia Paraskevi 153 42, Athens, Greece. T. +302106009821. Fax +302106009928. E-mail: nesa@nesacenter.org.
URL: http://www.nesacenter.org/

History Founded 1968. **Aims** Serve member schools by being the catalyst for their continuous improvement and for on-going innovation based on the best practices of American education. **Structure** Board of Directors. **Events** *Fall Leadership Conference* Abu Dhabi (United Arab Emirates) 2022, *Spring Educators Conference* Bangkok (Thailand) 2019, *Fall Leadership Conference* Athens (Greece) 2018, *Spring Educators Conference* Athens (Greece) 2018, *Fall Leadership Conference* Abu Dhabi (United Arab Emirates) 2017.
Members Schools in 32 countries:
Austria, Bangladesh, Belgium, Canada, Cyprus, Egypt, France, Greece, India, Indonesia, Iraq, Israel, Italy, Jordan, Kuwait, Lebanon, Malaysia, Nepal, Oman, Pakistan, Qatar, Saudi Arabia, Spain, Sri Lanka, Switzerland, Syrian AR, Thailand, Türkiye, UK, United Arab Emirates, USA, Yemen. [2014.09.24/XD0710/**D**]

♦ Near Field Communication Forum (NFC Forum) 16968

Contact 401 Edgewater Place, Ste 600, Wakefield MA 01880, USA. T. +17818768955. Fax +17816109864. E-mail: admin@nfc-forum.org.
URL: http://www.nfc-forum.org/

History 2004. **Aims** Advance the use of "Near Field Communication" technology by developing specifications, ensuring interoperability among devices and services, and educating the market about NFC technology. **Structure** Board of Directors. Officers: Chairman; Vice-Chairman; Secretary; Treasurer; Director. Committees (3): Special Interest Group; Technical Compliance. **Events** *Meeting* Vienna (Austria) 2016, *Meeting* Tokyo (Japan) 2014, *Meeting* Seoul (Korea Rep) 2013, *Member Meeting* Tokyo (Japan) 2012.
Members Sponsor; Principal; Associate; Implementer; Non-Profit. Members in 29 countries and territories:
Austria, Belgium, Bermuda, Canada, China, Colombia, Finland, France, Germany, Greece, Hong Kong, Hungary, India, Japan, Korea Rep, Luxembourg, Monaco, Netherlands, Norway, Portugal, Singapore, Spain, Sweden, Switzerland, Taiwan, Türkiye, UK, Ukraine, USA.
Included in the above, 1 organization listed in our Yearbook:
GSM Association (GSMA, #10813).
NGO Relations Liaison Organization of: *Comité européen de normalisation (CEN, #04162).* [2014/XJ6763/y/**F**]

- ♦ NEASPEC / see North East Asian Centre for Environmental Data and Training (#17578)
- ♦ **NEATA** North European Amateur Theatre Alliance (#17597)
- ♦ **NEAT** Network of East Asian Think-Tanks (#17005)
- ♦ NEC / see ANU Centre for European Studies
- ♦ NECC – Northern European Cathedrals Conference (meeting series)
- ♦ **NECC** North European Cybersecurity Cluster (#17598)
- ♦ **NECE** Networking European Citizenship Education (#17037)
- ♦ **NECLIME** Neogene Climate Evolution in Eurasia (#16973)
- ♦ NEC – New Europe College, Bucharest (internationally oriented national body)
- ♦ **NECS** European Network for Cinema and Media Studies (#07879)
- ♦ **NECSTouR** Network of European Regions for a Sustainable and Competitive Tourism (#17028)
- ♦ **NECTAR** Network of European CNS Transplantation and Restoration (#17015)
- ♦ **NECTAR** Network on European Communications and Transport Activity Research (#17016)
- ♦ NECTM – Northern European Conference on Travel Medicine (meeting series)
- ♦ **NEDAC** Network for the Development of Agricultural Cooperatives in Asia and the Pacific (#17004)
- ♦ Nederlands Centrum voor Inheemse Volken (internationally oriented national body)
- ♦ Nederlandse Financierings-Maatschappij voor Ontwikkelingslanden (internationally oriented national body)

- ♦ Nederlandse Ontwikkelingsorganisatie / see SNV Netherlands Development Organisation
- ♦ Nederlandse Organisatie voor Internationale Ontwikkelingssamenwerking / see Oxfam Novib
- ♦ Nederlandse Organisatie voor Internationale Samenwerking in het Hoger Onderwijs (internationally oriented national body)
- ♦ Nederlandse Overzeese Financieringsmaatschappij / see Nederlandse Financierings-Maatschappij voor Ontwikkelingslanden
- ♦ Nederlandse Taalunie (internationally oriented national body)
- ♦ Nederlandse Vereniging voor Afrika Studies (internationally oriented national body)
- ♦ Nederlandse Vereniging voor Internationaal Recht / see Royal Netherlands Society of International Law
- ♦ Nederlands Instituut voor Internationale Betrekkingen – Clingendael (internationally oriented national body)
- ♦ Nederlands Instituut voor het Nabije Oosten (internationally oriented national body)
- ♦ Nederlands Onderzoekscentrum voor het Recht in Zuid-Oost Azië en het Caraibisch Gebied / see Van Vollenhoven Institute for Law, Governance and Development
- ♦ Nederlandstalig Genootschap voor Vergelijkende Studie van Opvoeding en Onderwijs (internationally oriented national body)
- ♦ NED – National Endowment for Democracy (internationally oriented national body)
- ♦ **NEDS** Nordic Eating Disorders Society (#17273)
- ♦ NEE – Netzwerk Europäischer Eisenbahnen (internationally oriented national body)
- ♦ **NEFC** Near East Forestry Commission (#16965)
- ♦ **NEFCO** Nordic Environment Finance Corporation (#17281)
- ♦ **NEFI** Network of European Financial Institutions for SMEs (#17018)
- ♦ NEF – Near East Foundation (internationally oriented national body)
- ♦ **NEF** Network of European Foundations (#17019)
- ♦ **NEF** New Economics Foundation (#17082)
- ♦ **NEF** Next Einstein Forum (#17098)
- ♦ NEF – Nordiska Ekonomiska Forskningsrådet (inactive)
- ♦ NEF – Nordisk Elfederation (no recent information)
- ♦ Neglected Aspects of Motion Events Description (meeting series)

♦ Neglected Tropical Diseased NGO Network (NNN) 16969

Chair address not obtained. E-mail: info@ntd-ngonetwork.org.
URL: https://www.ntd-ngonetwork.org/

History Oct 2009, Accra (Ghana). **Aims** As a global forum of NGOs, work through its engagement with members to contribute to the global control, elimination and management of consequences of NTDs outlined within the internationally agreed World Health Organization NTD Roadmap. **Structure** Annual Meeting; Executive Committee; Steering Committee. Disease Specific Groups; Cross Cutting Groups; External Representation Committee; Conference Committee; Ad Hoc Task Groups. **Activities** Events/meetings; knowledge management/information dissemination; research/documentation. **Events** *Conference* Kathmandu (Nepal) 2022, *Conference* 2021, *Conference* 2020, *Conference* Liverpool (UK) 2019, *Conference* Addis Ababa (Ethiopia) 2018.

Members NGOs. Membership countries not specified. Organizations include 66 listed in this Yearbook:
- *Acción Sanitaria y Desarrollo Social (ANESVAD)*;
- AKROS;
- *American Leprosy Missions (ALM International)*;
- *Amref Health Africa (#00806)*;
- *Bureau international des Médecins sans frontières (MSF International, #03366)*;
- *CBM Global Disability Inclusion (CBM Global)*;
- *Children Without Worms (CWW, #03881)*;
- *Christian Blind Mission (CBM)*;
- *Damien Foundation – Voluntary Organization for Leprosy and TB Control (AF)*;
- *Evidence Action*;
- *FAIRMED*;
- *FHI 360*;
- *Fred Hollows Foundation*;
- *Global Alliance for Rabies Control (GARC)*;
- *Global Partnership for Zero Leprosy (#10543)*;
- Global Schistosomiasis Alliance;
- *Health and Development International (HDI)*;
- *Heart to Heart International*;
- *Helen Keller International (HKI, #10902)*;
- *IMA World Health (IMA)*;
- *INMED Partnerships for Children*;
- *International Agency for the Prevention of Blindness (IAPB, #11597)*;
- International Alliance for Global Health Dermatology;
- *International Alliance for the Control of Scabies (IACS, #11625)*;
- *International Federation of Anti-Leprosy Associations (ILEP, #13355)*;
- *International Foundation for Dermatology (IFD, #13668)*;
- *International Podoconiosis Initiative (Footwork, #14607)*;
- *International Trachoma Initiative (ITI, #15701)*;
- *Johns Hopkins University Center for Communications Programs (CCP)*;
- Kilimanjaro Center for Community Ophthalmology;
- Kongwa Trachoma Project;
- *LEPRA Health in Action (LEPRA)*;
- *Leprosy Mission International (TLMI, #16446)*;
- *Light for the World (#16474)*;
- *Lions Clubs International (LCI, #16485)*;
- *Liverpool School of Tropical Medicine (LSTM)*;
- *London School of Hygiene and Tropical Medicine (LSHTM)*;
- *Malaria Consortium*;
- Mectizan Donation Program;
- Medicines Development for Global Health;
- *MENTOR Initiative*;
- *Mundo Sano*;
- NLR – until No Leprosy Remains;
- *ORBIS International (#17786)*;
- *Organisation pour la prévention de la cécité (OPC)*;
- Partnership for Child Development, Imperial College, London;
- *Partnership for Child Development (PCD)*;
- *PATH (#18260)*;
- *RTI International*;
- *Save the Children International (#19058)*;
- *SCI Foundation*;
- *Sightsavers International (#19270)*;
- Speak up Africa;
- ST FRANCIS LEPROSY GUILD (SFLG);
- Swiss Alliance against Neglected Tropical Diseases (SANTD);
- *The Carter Center*;
- The Nala Foundation;
- The Task Force for Global Health;
- United Front Against River Blindness;
- Uniting to Combat NTDs;
- *Vétérinaires Sans Frontières International (VSF International, #20760)*;
- *Vitamin Angels*;
- *WaterAid (#20822)*;
- *World Concern International (#21290)*;
- World Scabies Program;
- *World Vision International (WVI, #21904)*. [2023.02.28/AA1031/y/**F**]

- ♦ Neglected Tropical Diseases Support Center / see Coalition for Operational Research on Neglected Tropical Diseases
- ♦ NEIAAP – New Energy Industry Association for Asia and the Pacific (internationally oriented national body)
- ♦ **NeIC** Nordic e-Infrastructure Collaboration (#17318)
- ♦ NEIDA – Network of Educational Innovation for Development in Africa (no recent information)
- ♦ Neil D Levin Graduate Institute of International Relations and Commerce (internationally oriented national body)

♦ Neil Pryde RS X Class Association 16970

Exec Sec Sulmin 3 C, 83-331 Przyjazn, Poland. T. +48503006160. E-mail: rsx.ania@gmail.com.
URL: http://www.rsxclass.com/

NGO Relations Recognized Class Association of: *World Sailing (#21760)*. [2014/XM2794/**E**]

- ♦ NEI – Nuclear Energy Institute (internationally oriented national body)
- ♦ NEI – Nutrition and Education International (internationally oriented national body)
- ♦ NELFA / see Network of European LGBTIQ Families Associations (#17021)
- ♦ **NELFA** Network of European LGBTIQ Families Associations (#17021)

♦ Nematological Society of Southern Africa (NSSA) 16971

Nematologiese Vereniging van Suidelike Afrika (NVSA)

Sec-Treas ARC-Grain Crops Inst, Private Bag X 1251, Potchefstroom, 2520, South Africa. T. +27182996379. Fax +27182947146.
Street Address c/o ARC-Grain Crops Inst, Chris Hani 114, Potchefstroom, 2520, South Africa.
Events – Organizer P/B X 11208, Nelspruit, 1200, South Africa.
URL: http://sanematodes.com/

History 1972. **Aims** Advance the science of nematology in southern Africa in both its fundamental and applied aspects. **Structure** Executive Committee. **Languages** English. **Staff** 3.50 FTE, paid. **Finance** Sources: members' dues. Annual budget: 30,000 ZAR. **Activities** Awards/prizes/competitions; events/meetings. **Events** *Symposium* Tulbagh (South Africa) 2021, *Symposium* Machadodorp (South Africa) 2019, *Symposium* South Africa 2017, *Biennial Symposium* Stellenbosch (South Africa) 2011, *Biennial Symposium* Hazyview (South Africa) 2009. **Publications** *NSSA Newsletter* (2 a year). Symposium proceedings.

Members Regular; Honorary. Individuals (148) in 15 countries:
Belgium, Benin, Botswana, Bulgaria, Cameroon, France, Ireland, Malawi, Mozambique, Netherlands, South Africa, Uganda, UK, USA, Zimbabwe.

NGO Relations Member of (1): *International Federation of Nematology Societies (IFNS, #13488)*. [2021.02.17/XD3102/v/**D**]

- ♦ Nematologiese Vereniging van Suidelike Afrika (#16971)
- ♦ NEM Initiative / see New European Media (#17083)
- ♦ **NEM Initiative** New European Media (#17083)
- ♦ **NEMO** Network of European Museum Organizations (#17024)
- ♦ NEMRA – Network for Educational and Multidisciplinary Research Africa (unconfirmed)
- ♦ Nemzetközi Kabitószer-Es Terrorellenes Tisztek Svövetsége (internationally oriented national body)
- ♦ Nemzetközi Magyarsagtudomanyi Társaság (#11948)
- ♦ Nemzetközi Szaksajto Szövetseg (inactive)
- ♦ Nemzetközi Tudomanyos és Müszaki Informaciós Központ (#12514)
- ♦ NENARACA – Near East and North Africa Regional Agricultural Credit Association (inactive)
- ♦ **NENUN** Nordic Environmental NUcleotide Network (#17280)

♦ Neobiota – European Group on Biological Invasions 16972

Pres EBD-CSIC, Avda Américo Vespucio s/n, Isla de la Cartuja, 41092 Seville, Sevilla, Spain.
Sec Messeweg 11/12, 38104 Braunschweig, Germany. T. +495312993380. Fax +495312993007.
URL: http://www.neobiota.eu/

History 1999, Berlin (Germany). **Structure** Council; Board. **Languages** English. **Staff** None. **Finance** No budget. Biennial meeting financed mostly by participants. **Activities** Events/meetings. **Events** *Conference* Tartu (Estonia) 2022, *Conference* Vodice (Croatia) 2020, *Conference* Dublin (Ireland) 2018, *Conference* Vianden (Luxembourg) 2016, *Conference* Antalya (Turkey) 2014. **Publications** *NeoBiota* – open-access journal. **IGO Relations** *European and Mediterranean Plant Protection Organization (EPPO, #07773)*. **NGO Relations** *International Union for Conservation of Nature and Natural Resources (IUCN, #15766)*. [2019.10.09/XM3990/**D**]

- ♦ Neobrain (inactive)

♦ Neogene Climate Evolution in Eurasia (NECLIME) 16973

Contact Heibelberg Ac of Sciences, ROCEEH Research Ctr, Senckenberg Research Inst, Senckenberganlage 25, 60325 Frankfurt-Main, Germany.
Contact Senckenberg Research Inst – Frankfurt-Main, Univ of Bonn, Steinmann Inst, Nussallee 8, 53115 Bonn, Germany.
URL: http://www.neclime.de/

History 1999. Founded as an open international network of geoscientists. **Aims** Work on Cenozoic paleoclimate change in Eurasia and the related evolution of ecosystems. **Structure** An open consortium of scientists. Annual Meeting; Working Groups. **Languages** English. **Staff** None. **Finance** No budget. **Activities** Events/meetings; knowledge management/information dissemination. **Events** *Conference* 2021, *Annual Meeting* St Petersburg (Russia) 2019, *Annual Meeting* Yerevan (Armenia) 2017, *Annual Meeting* Lucknow (India) 2016, *Annual Meeting* Madrid (Spain) 2015. **Publications** *NECLIME Newsletter*.

Members Individuals in 36 countries:
Armenia, Austria, Belarus, Belgium, Brazil, Bulgaria, China, Czechia, Denmark, Finland, France, Georgia, Germany, Greece, Hungary, India, Italy, Japan, Kazakhstan, Nepal, Netherlands, Norway, Poland, Portugal, Romania, Russia, Serbia, Slovakia, Spain, Sweden, Switzerland, Thailand, Türkiye, UK, Ukraine, USA. [2021/XM4670/v/**F**]

- ♦ Neoi Europei Federalistes (#21984)
- ♦ Neonatal Nursing Association of Southern Africa (internationally oriented national body)
- ♦ Neotropical Ornithological Society (#19431)
- ♦ **NEPAD** New Partnership for Africa's Development (#17091)
- ♦ **NEPC** Network of Education Policy Centers (#17010)
- ♦ NEP – Convention for Cooperation in the Protection and Sustainable Development of the Marine and Coastal Environment of the Northeast Pacific (2002 treaty)

♦ NephcEurope 16974

Founder/Pres Raaigras 12, 2411 DW Bodegraven, Netherlands. E-mail: nephceurope.foundation@gmail.com – info@nephceurope.eu.
URL: http://nephceurope.eu/nc/

History 2010. Registration: Handelsregister, No/ID: KVK 27365421, Netherlands. **Aims** Stimulate research forthe cause and cure of Nephrotic *Syndrome*. **Structure** General Board. **Staff** Voluntary. **Finance** Members' dues. **NGO Relations** Member of (2): *EURORDIS – Rare Diseases Europe (#09175)* (Associate); *Federation of European Patient Groups Affected by Renal Genetic Diseases (FEDERG, #09526)*. [2021/XJ9401/**F**]

- ♦ NephCure Kidney International (internationally oriented national body)
- ♦ **NEPPO** Near East Plant Protection Organization (#16966)
- ♦ **NEPSI** European Network on Silica (#08001)
- ♦ **NEPS** Network of European Peace Scientists (#17026)
- ♦ NER / see Near East Foundation
- ♦ **NERA** Nordic Educational Research Association (#17276)
- ♦ NERC – Nordic Early Rectal Cancer Meeting (meeting series)
- ♦ **NEREUS** Network of European Regions Using Space Technologies (#17029)
- ♦ **NERIS** European Platform on preparedness for nuclear and radiological emergency response and recovery (#08228)
- ♦ NERSC – Nansen Environmental and Remote Sensing Center (internationally oriented national body)
- ♦ NESA – Near East South Asia Center for Strategic Studies (internationally oriented national body)
- ♦ **NESA** Near East/South Asia Council of Overseas Schools (#16967)
- ♦ **NESA** New European Surgical Academy (#17084)
- ♦ NESAT – North European Symposium for Archaeological Textiles (meeting series)
- ♦ **NES** Neurootológiai és Equilibriometriai Társaság (#17072)

- ♦ **NES** Neurootological and Equilibriometric Society (#17072)
- ♦ NES – Nordic EPR Society (no recent information)
- ♦ **NES** Nordiska Ergonomisällskapet (#17480)
- ♦ **NESSI** Networked European Software and Services Initiative (#17009)
- ♦ **NESsT** Nonprofit Enterprise and Self-Sustainability Team (#17150)
- ♦ Nessuno Tocchi Caino (#10857)
- ♦ **NEST Initiative** Neural Simulation Technology Initiative (#17070)
- ♦ **Nestlé Foundation** Nestlé Foundation for the Study of Problems of Nutrition in the World (#16975)

♦ Nestlé Foundation for the Study of Problems of Nutrition in the World (Nestlé Foundation) 16975

Fondation Nestlé pour l'étude des problèmes de l'alimentation dans le monde

Dir Place de la Gare 4, Case Postale 581, 1001 Lausanne VD, Switzerland. T. +41213203351. Fax +41213203392. E-mail: nf@nestlefoundation.org.
URL: http://www.nestlefoundation.org/

History Founded 1966, Lausanne (Switzerland), by Nestlé SA, as an independent charitable trust. **Aims** Study problems of nutrition in *low-income* countries. **Structure** Council (Board of Trustees) of 5 members; Experts (2); Director. **Languages** English, French. **Finance** Capital funds. Budget (annual): Swiss Fr 2 million. **Activities** Financial and/or material support. Initiates and supports research on human nutrition in developing countries. Current research foci: nutritional problems related to energy, protein and micronutrient metabolism; interactions between nutrition and infection; effects of the diet on infant and child development. Awards study grants to collaborators of selected nutrition research institutes in low income countries. **Publications** Annual report; articles in scientific journals. **Information Services** *enLINK* – capability building tool accessible to registered users from low-income countries to bridge the digital divide in nutrition and health.
[2014/XF0112/f/**F**]

- ♦ NEST – Near East School of Theology (internationally oriented national body)
- ♦ **NeST** Network of Southern Think Tanks (#17059)
- ♦ **NESU** Nordiska Ekonomie Studerandes Union (#17479)

♦ Net4Society 16976

Coordationa Office German Aerospace Ctr, Project Management Agency, Heinrich-Konen-Str 1, 53227 Bonn, Germany.
URL: http://www.net4society.eu/

History Founded 2008, during 7th European Research Framework Programme (FP7, 2007-2013) as the network of *National Contact Points for Socio-Economic Sciences and the Humanities (SSH)*. Since Horizon 2020, composed of National Contact Points for the Societal Challenge 6 "Europe in a changing world: inclusive, innovative and reflective societies". **Finance** Funded by: *European Commission (EC, #06633)* – Horizon 2020. **Publications** *ISSUES* – online magazine; *Net4Society e-newsletter*.
Members Partners in 52 countries:
Argentina, Armenia, Austria, Azerbaijan, Belarus, Belgium, Bosnia-Herzegovina, Bulgaria, China, Croatia, Cyprus, Czechia, Denmark, Dominican Rep, Egypt, Estonia, Faeroe Is, Finland, France, Germany, Greece, Hungary, Iceland, Ireland, Israel, Italy, Kazakhstan, Korea Rep, Latvia, Lithuania, Luxembourg, Malta, Mexico, Moldova, Netherlands, North Macedonia, Norway, Poland, Portugal, Romania, Russia, Serbia, Slovakia, Slovenia, South Africa, Spain, Sweden, Switzerland, Türkiye, UK, Ukraine, Uruguay.
NGO Relations Member of: *European Alliance for the Social Sciences and Humanities (EASSH, #05885)*.
[2021/XM6598/**E**]

♦ Netball Asia 16977

Hon Treas 6 Stadium Boulevard, Singapore 397797, Singapore.
URL: http://netball.sport/inside-inf/regions-members/

History 1986, Kuala Lumpur (Malaysia), during Asian Netball Tournament and Conference, as *Asian Netball Federation (ANF)*. Subsequently changed title to *Asian Federation of Netball Associations (AFNA)*. **Aims** Foster, encourage, support and develop the game of netball in the Asian region. **Structure** Annual Meeting. Executive Committee. **Languages** English. **Finance** Members' dues: joining fee of Singapore Dollars 150; annual fee of Singapore Dollars 150. **Activities** Championships. **Events** *Annual meeting* Singapore (Singapore) 2006.
Members National organizations (13) in 13 countries and territories:
Australia, Brunei Darussalam, Hong Kong, India, Japan, Korea Rep, Malaysia, Maldives, Pakistan, Singapore, Sri Lanka, Taiwan, Thailand.
[2018/XM0683/**D**]

- ♦ NetBSD Foundation (internationally oriented national body)

♦ NET-HERITAGE (NH) 16978

Contact Italian Ministry for Cultural Heritage and Activities, V del Collegio Romano 27, 00186 Rome RM, Italy.
URL: http://www.netheritage.eu/

History as programme funded by *European Commission (EC, #06633)* in the 7th Framework Programme 2007/2013. Full title: *European Network on Research Programme Applied to the Protection of Tangible Cultural Heritage – NET-HERITAGE*. **Aims** Provide an integrated picture of the state-of-the-art of cultural heritage research in *EU* member states and at European level. **Finance** Funded by European Commission. **Information Services** *Heritage Portal*.
Members Government ministries, funding agencies and national RTD authorities of 14 countries:
Belgium, Bulgaria, France, Germany, Greece, Iceland, Italy, Latvia, Malta, Poland, Romania, Slovenia, Spain, UK.
[2012/XJ5240/**E***]

- ♦ Netherlands-African Business Council (internationally oriented national body)
- ♦ Netherlands Association of African Studies (internationally oriented national body)
- ♦ Netherlands Association for International Cultural Relations / see Dutch Centre for International Cooperation
- ♦ Netherlands Association of Latin American and Caribbean Studies (internationally oriented national body)
- ♦ Netherlands Atlantic Association (internationally oriented national body)
- ♦ Netherlands Atlantic Commission / see Netherlands Atlantic Association
- ♦ Netherlands Atlantic Committee / see Netherlands Atlantic Association
- ♦ Netherlands Centre for Indigenous Peoples (internationally oriented national body)
- ♦ Netherlands Centre for the Study of Law in South-East Asia and the Caribbean Region / see Van Vollenhoven Institute for Law, Governance and Development
- ♦ Netherlands Development Finance Company (internationally oriented national body)
- ♦ Netherlands Food Partnership (internationally oriented national body)
- ♦ Netherlands Foundation for the Advancement of Tropical Research / see WOTRO Science for Global Development
- ♦ Netherlands Foundation for International Nature Protection / see Van Tienhoven Foundation for International Nature Protection
- ♦ Netherlands Humanist Committee on Human Rights Nederlands Humanistisch Overleg Mensenrechten / see Aim for Human Rights
- ♦ Netherlands Institute of Human Rights (internationally oriented national body)
- ♦ Netherlands Institute of International Relations – Clingendael (internationally oriented national body)
- ♦ Netherlands Institute for Multiparty Democracy (internationally oriented national body)
- ♦ Netherlands Institute for the Near East (internationally oriented national body)
- ♦ Netherlands Institute for Sea Research / see Royal Netherlands Institute for Sea Research
- ♦ Netherlands International Law Association / see Royal Netherlands Society of International Law
- ♦ Netherlands Organization for International Cooperation in Higher Education (internationally oriented national body)
- ♦ Netherlands Organization for International Development Cooperation / see Oxfam Novib
- ♦ Netherlands Overseas Financing Association / see Nederlandse Financierings-Maatschappij voor Ontwikkelingslanden
- ♦ Netherlands Refugee Foundation (internationally oriented national body)
- ♦ Netherlands Universities Foundation for International Co-operation / see Netherlands Organization for International Cooperation in Higher Education

♦ NetHope 16979

Main Office 10615 Judicial Dr, Ste 402, Fairfax VA 22030, USA. T. +17033882845. E-mail: info@nethope.org.
URL: http://www.nethope.org/

History 2001. Full title: *NetHope – Wiring the Global Village*. Registration: No/ID: 20-1782011, USA. **Aims** Be a catalyst for collaboration and empower committed international *humanitarian* organizations to change the world through the power of technology, notably through improving *IT connections*. **Structure** Board of Directors. **Activities** Knowledge management/information dissemination. **Publications** *NetHope eNewsletter*.
Members International humanitarian organizations (37):
- *ACCION International*;
- *ActionAid (#00087)*;
- *Americares Foundation*;
- *Ashoka – Innovators for the Public (#01248)*;
- *CARE International (CI, #03429)*;
- *Catholic Relief Services (CRS, #03608)*;
- *ChildFund International (#03869)*;
- *Children International*;
- *Christian Aid*;
- *Compassion International (CI, #04413)*;
- *Concern Worldwide*;
- *Conservation International (CI)*;
- *FHI 360*;
- *FINCA International*;
- *Global Communities*;
- Grameen Foundation;
- *Habitat for Humanity International (HFHI)*;
- *Heifer International*;
- *International Federation of Red Cross and Red Crescent Societies (#13526)*;
- *International Rescue Committee (IRC, #14717)*;
- *Mercy Corps International (MCI)*;
- *Opportunity International (#17776)*;
- *Oxfam International (#17922)*;
- *Pact (#18016)*;
- *PATH (#18260)*;
- *Plan International (#18386)*;
- *Relief International*;
- *Save the Children International (#19058)*;
- *SOS-Kinderdorf International (#19693)*;
- *The Nature Conservancy (TNC)*;
- *Trocaire – Catholic Agency for World Development*;
- *Voluntary Service Overseas (VSO)*;
- *WaterAid (#20822)*;
- *Wildlife Conservation Society (WCS)*;
- *Winrock International*;
- *World Vision International (WVI, #21904)*;
- *World Wide Fund for Nature (WWF, #21922)*.

NGO Relations Member of (1): *Emergency Telecommunications Cluster (ETC, #05438)*. [2020/XJ2148/y/**F**]

- ♦ NetHope – Wiring the Global Village / see NetHope (#16979)
- ♦ NetIAS / see Network of European Institutes for Advanced Studies (#17020)
- ♦ **Netias** Network of European Institutes for Advanced Studies (#17020)
- ♦ Net Impact (internationally oriented national body)

♦ NETLIPSE 16980

Programme Dir AT Osborne BV, PO Box 168, 3740 AD Baarn, Netherlands. T. +31355434343. Fax +31355434344. E-mail: info@netlipse.eu.
URL: http://www.netlipse.eu/

History Set up as a research programme supported by *European Commission (EC, #06633)* 6th European Framework Programme – May 2006 until May 2008. Continued with funding from *Trans-European Transport Network (TEN-T, inactive)* – Jun 2008 until Dec 2010. Continued after 2010 with funding from public organizations. Continues as informal network. Former names and other names: *NETwork for the dissemination of knowledge on the management and organisation of Large Infrastructure ProjectS in Europe* – full title. **Aims** Positively influence Europe's *economic sustainability* by improving the successful development, delivery and operation of Large *Infrastructure* Projects (LIPs) through active and effective knowledge exchange. **Structure** Executive Board; Management Team. **Languages** English. **Staff** 2.00 FTE, paid. **Finance** Sources: contributions; in-kind support. **Activities** Events/meetings; monitoring/evaluation; research/documentation. **Events** *Network Meeting* Copenhagen (Denmark) 2022, *Network Meeting* 2021, *Network Meeting* 2021, *Network Meeting* 2020, *Network Meeting* 2020. **Publications** Research results.
Members Full in 13 countries:
Austria, Belgium, Croatia, Denmark, Finland, Germany, Italy, Netherlands, Norway, Poland, Slovakia, Sweden, UK.
[2022.05.04/XJ9637/**F**]

- ♦ NETL – Network for the Enhancement of Teaching and Learning in research-intensive universities (unconfirmed)
- ♦ NETNEP – International Nurse Education Conference (meeting series)
- ♦ **NET** Network for the European Private Sector in Tourism (#17027)
- ♦ NETO/EDSAT – National Education Telecommunications Organization – EDSAT Institute (internationally oriented national body)
- ♦ NetPra – International Conference on Internet Pragmatics (meeting series)
- ♦ **NeTROPICA** Network for Research and Training of Tropical Diseases in Central America (#17055)
- ♦ **NetSci** Network Science Society (#17056)
- ♦ NetsforLife (internationally oriented national body)
- ♦ **NETU** North European Table Tennis Union (#17599)
- ♦ **NETWAS International** Network for Water and Sanitation International (#17064)
- ♦ Netwerk voor de Ontwikkeling van Europese Programmas in Hoger Onderwijs / see Global Business Education Network (#10258)

♦ Network of Academies of Sciences in Countries of Organization of Islamic Conference (NASIC) 16981

SG Pakistan Academy of Sciences Building, 3 Constitution Avenue, Islamabad G-5/2, Pakistan. T. +92519207789. E-mail: nasicpk@yahoo.com.
URL: http://www.nasic.org.pk/

History 17 Mar 2004. **Aims** Catalyze the development of collaborative programmes among OIC member countries. **Structure** General Assembly. Executive Committee. **Activities** Research; meeting activities. **Publications** *NASIC Newsletter*. Books.
Members Academies in 18 countries and territories:
Afghanistan, Bangladesh, Bosnia-Herzegovina, Egypt, Indonesia, Iran Islamic Rep, Jordan, Kazakhstan, Malaysia, Nigeria, Pakistan, Palestine, Senegal, Sudan, Tajikistan, Tatarstan, Turkmenistan, Uganda.
Included in the above, 1 organization listed in this Yearbook:
Islamic World Academy of Sciences (IAS, #16057).
NGO Relations Member of: *InterAcademy Partnership (IAP, #11376)*. [2017/XJ7956/**F**]

♦ Network for Advancement of Transfusion Alternatives (NATA) 16982

Chair c/o Medical Education Global Solutions, 27 rue Raffet, 75016 Paris, France. T. +33144015181. Fax +33144015180. E-mail: nata.secretary@mededgs.com.
URL: http://www.nataonline.com/

History Founded Apr 1998, Graz (Austria). **Aims** As a society comprised of anesthesiologists, intensivists, surgeons, hematologists and transfusion medicine specialists, promote improved use of *blood* components and transfusion alternatives in everyday clinical practice. **Structure** Board of Directors. **Languages** English. **Activities** Organizes: Annual Symposium; regional symposia; expert meetings; e-learning; Benchmark Project. **Events** *Annual Symposium* Paris (France) 2021, *Annual Symposium* Athens (Greece) 2020, *Annual Symposium* Berlin (Germany) 2019, *Annual Symposium* Lisbon (Portugal) 2018, *Annual Symposium* Florence (Italy) 2017. **Publications** *TATM Journal*. Textbook. [2018/XM0106/**F**]

♦ Network for Advancing and Evaluating the Societal Impact of Science (AESIS) 16983

Dir Raamweg 7, 2596 HL The Hague, Netherlands. T. +31702172018. E-mail: info@aesisnet.com.
Events Manager address not obtained.
URL: https://aesisnet.com/

Aims Stimulate and demonstrate the impact of science on economy, culture and well-being. **Structure** Advisory Board. **Activities** Events/meetings. **Events** *Open Science and Societal Impact Seminar* Finland 2022. [2021/AA1722/F]

♦ Network of African Consultants (see: #00486)
♦ Network of African Countries on Local Building Materials and Technologies (no recent information)
♦ Network of African Freedom of Expression Organizations (inactive)

♦ Network of African National Human Rights Institutions (NANHRI) .. 16984

Réseau des Institutions Nationales Africaines des Droits de l'Homme (RINADH)

Office Admin 2nd Floor, CVS Plaza, Lenana Road, PO Box 74359-00200, Nairobi, 00200, Kenya. T. +2542717908 – +2542712664 – +2542717928. E-mail: info@nanhri.org.
URL: http://www.nanhri.org/

History 1996. Set up following adoption of the Yaoundé Declaration, setting up a *Coordinating Committee of African National Human Rights Institutions for the Promotion and Protection of Human Rights.* Constitution signed Oct 2007, Kigali (Rwanda), when restructured under current title. Registration: Kenya. **Aims** Support and strengthen national human rights institutions in Africa. **Structure** General Assembly; Steering Committee; Accreditation Committee; Bureau; Secretariat. **Events** *Conference* Cairo (Egypt) 2019, *Conference* Kigali (Rwanda) 2017, *Conference* Yaoundé (Cameroon) 2015, *Conference* Accra (Ghana) 2013, *Conference* Cape Town (South Africa) 2011.
Members Full in 36 countries:
Algeria, Benin, Burkina Faso, Burundi, Cameroon, Cape Verde, Central African Rep, Chad, Comoros, Congo Brazzaville, Congo DR, Côte d'Ivoire, Djibouti, Egypt, Ethiopia, Gabon, Gambia, Ghana, Guinea, Guinea-Bissau, Kenya, Liberia, Mauritania, Mauritius, Morocco, Namibia, Nigeria, Rwanda, Sierra Leone, South Africa, South Sudan, Sudan, Tanzania UR, Uganda, Zambia, Zimbabwe.
Consultative Status Consultative status granted from: *African Commission on Human and Peoples' Rights (ACHPR, #00255)* (Observer). **NGO Relations** Member of (1): *Global Alliance of National Human Rights Institutions (GANHRI, #10214).* [2020/XJ9986/F]

♦ Network for African Peace-Builders (NAPS) 16985

Coordinator PO Box 35040, Lusaka, Zambia. T. +2601223619. Fax +2601223619.

Aims Promote and support a culture of sustainable peace in Africa. **Members** Membership countries not specified. **NGO Relations** Signatory to the 'Publish What You Pay' appeal of: *Publish What You Pay Coalition (PWYP, #18573).* [2006/XF7191/F]

♦ Network of African People Living with HIV and AIDS (NAP+) 16986

Regional Coordinator PO Box 9389, Nairobi, 00200, Kenya. T. +254202734677. Fax +254202736418.
URL: http://www.rapnap.org/

History May 1994, Mombasa (Kenya). Regional network of *Global Network of People Living with HIV/AIDS (GNP+, #10494).* Constitution adopted Nov 2001. **Aims** Strengthen the quality of care for people with HIV and AIDS; empower people with the virus to influence policies on issues that affect them; help set up support groups and coordinate their activities. **Structure** Delegates Conference (every 3 years), consisting of 2 delegates per country. Management Board of 10 member, including Chairperson, Treasurer and Secretary. Executive Committee, comprising President, Treasurer and sub-regional representative. Secretariat. African sub-regions (5): North; East; West; Central; South. **Finance** Members' dues. Other sources include: donations and grants; gifts and legacies. **Events** *ICASA : international conference on AIDS and sexually transmitted infections in Africa* Nairobi (Kenya) 2003. **Members** National networks in 13 countries. Membership countries not specified. **IGO Relations** *UNDP (#20292).* **NGO Relations** Southern Region is member of: *Regional Inter-Agency Task Team on Children and AIDS in Eastern and Southern Africa (RIATT-ESA, #18791).* [2008/XF5963/F]

♦ Network of African Science Academies (NASAC) 16987

Dir PO Box 201, Karen 00502, Nairobi, Kenya. T. +254202694730. E-mail: jkado@nasaconline.org.
URL: http://www.nasaconline.org/

History 13 Dec 2001, Nairobi (Kenya), under the auspices of *African Academy of Sciences (AAS, #00193)* and *IAP – The Global Network of Science Academies (inactive).* **Aims** Provide an independent forum for African science academies to offer authoritative credible advice for policy formulation towards economic, social and cultural development. **Structure** General Assembly. Board. Secretariat. **Languages** English, French. **Staff** 4.00 FTE, paid. **Finance** Mainly funded from international funding agencies. Budget (annual): about euro 200,000. **Activities** Capacity building; education. **Events** *General Assembly* Addis Ababa (Ethiopia) 2013.
Members Academies in 18 countries:
Benin, Cameroon, Ethiopia, Ghana, Kenya, Madagascar, Mauritius, Morocco, Mozambique, Nigeria, Senegal, South Africa, Sudan, Tanzania UR, Togo, Uganda, Zambia, Zimbabwe.
Included in the above, 1 organization listed in this Yearbook:
African Academy of Sciences (AAS, #00193).
NGO Relations Regional network of: *InterAcademy Partnership (IAP, #11376).* [2014.06.01/XJ7955/y/F]

♦ Network of African Women Ministers and Parliamentarians (NAWMP) 16988

Réseau des femmes ministres africaines et parlementaires (REFAMP) – Rede das Mulheres Africanas Ministras e Parlamentares (RMAMP)

Contact REFAMP Guinée, Immeuble CNSS, avenue Tubman Rue KA 032, Commune de Kaloum, BP 527, Conakry, Guinea.

Events *Conference* Conakry (Guinea) 2000. **NGO Relations** *Femmes Africa solidarité (FAS, #09732).* [2008/XF6052/F]

♦ Network of African Youths for Development (NAYD) 16989

CEO PO Box 15422, Yaoundé, Cameroon. T. +237683350458. E-mail: help@nayd.org.
URL: http://nayd.org/

History 2006. **Aims** Empower young people with the skills, knowledge, resources and opportunities they need to implement sustainable youth-led development programmes. **Structure** General Assembly; Board of Directors; Secretariat, headed by CEO. **Languages** English, French, Portuguese. **Staff** 20.00 FTE, voluntary. **Finance** No budget. **Activities** Networking/liaising. **Publications** *INSPIRE* (4 a year) – magazine.
Members Full in 53 countries:
Algeria, Angola, Benin, Botswana, Burkina Faso, Burundi, Cameroon, Cape Verde, Central African Rep, Chad, Comoros, Congo Brazzaville, Congo DR, Côte d'Ivoire, Djibouti, Egypt, Equatorial Guinea, Eritrea, Eswatini, Ethiopia, Gambia, Ghana, Guinea, Guinea-Bissau, Kenya, Lesotho, Liberia, Libya, Madagascar, Malawi, Mali, Mauritania, Mauritius, Morocco, Mozambique, Namibia, Niger, Nigeria, Rwanda, Sao Tomé-Principe, Senegal, Seychelles, Sierra Leone, Somalia, South Africa, South Sudan, Sudan, Tanzania UR, Togo, Tunisia, Uganda, Zambia, Zimbabwe. [2023.02.15/XJ2632/F]

♦ Network of Afro-Latin American and Afro-Caribbean Women (#18722)

♦ Network of AIDS Researchers of Eastern and Southern Africa (NARESA) 16990

Réseau de recherche sur le SIDA pour l'Afrique de l'Est and australe

Address not obtained.

History Mar 1988, Nairobi (Kenya), at meeting sponsored by *International Development Research Centre (IDRC, #13162).* **Aims** Increase the effectiveness of regional AIDS research and researchers; promote research into problems related to infection with the human *immunodeficiency virus – HIV* – and other related viruses, and in any related field. **Structure** Council of Members (meets annually). Executive Committee, consisting of Chairman, Vice-Chairman, Secretary, Treasurer and 4 members-at-large. Secretariat. **Staff** 2.00 FTE, paid. **Finance** Members' dues. Grants from: Ford Foundation; International Development Research Centre (IDRC); Rockefeller Foundation. **Activities** Organizes training workshops. Links members with similar interests. Funds members' small research projects or puts them in touch with funding agencies. **Events** *Workshop / Annual General Meeting* Nairobi (Kenya) 1996, *Workshop / Annual General Meeting* Kampala (Uganda) 1995, *Workshop / Annual General Meeting* Nairobi (Kenya) 1994, *Annual General Meeting* Marrakech (Morocco) 1993. **Publications** *NARESA Newsletter* (4 a year). Monographs. Information Services: Resource centre; literature searches. **Information Services** *AIDSLINE* – database.
Members Full: AIDS researchers working in the region; Associate: AIDS researchers not working in the region; Observers: researchers who have a profession interest in AIDS. Individuals in 15 countries:
Botswana, Eswatini, Ethiopia, Kenya, Lesotho, Malawi, Mauritius, Mozambique, Rwanda, South Africa, Sudan, Tanzania UR, Uganda, Zambia, Zimbabwe.
National chapters in 3 countries:
Kenya, Tanzania UR, Uganda.
Included in the above, 8 organizations listed in this Yearbook:
ACORD – Agency for Cooperation and Research in Development (#00073); Amref Health Africa (#00806); Ford Foundation (#09858); MAP International (#16569); Society on AIDS in Africa (SAA, #19518); The Rockefeller Foundation (#18966); Trans World Radio (TWR); UNICEF (#20332).
NGO Relations Related network: *West and Central African AIDS Research Network (WCAARN, no recent information).* Member of: *Africa Capacity Alliance (ACA, #00160).* [2008/XF2561/y/F]

♦ Network of American and European Cultural Centres (#18639)

♦ Network of Aquaculture Centres in Asia-Pacific (NACA) 16991

Dir-Gen PO Box 1040, Kasetsart Post Office, Bangkok, 10903, Thailand. T. +6625611728 ext 117. Fax +6625611727. E-mail: info@enaca.org.
URL: https://enaca.org/

History 11 Jan 1990. Established on coming into force of an Agreement adopted 5-8 Jan 1988, Bangkok (Thailand), at *FAO Regional Office for Asia and the Pacific (RAP, #09266).* Former names and other names: *FAO/UNDP Network of Aquaculture Centres in Asia (ENG)* – former. **Aims** Promote sustainable aquaculture and aquatic resources management for rural development to: increase *food* production, improve *rural* income and employment, diversify farm production, and increase foreign exchange earnings and savings. **Structure** Governing Council; Technical Advisory Committee; Secretariat. **Languages** English. **Staff** 14.00 FTE, paid. **Finance** Sources: donations; fees for services; government support. Other sources: project funding. **Events** *Global Conference on Aquaculture* Shanghai (China) 2021, *Workshop on Reviewing Aquaculture Statistics Farming Classification System* Wuxi (China) 2018, *Regional Consultation on Responsible Production and Use of Feed and Feed Ingredients for Sustainable Growth of Aquaculture in Asia-Pacific* Bangkok (Thailand) 2017, *Giant Prawn Conference* Pathum Thani (Thailand) 2017, *Global conference on aquaculture* Phuket (Thailand) 2010. **Publications** *Aquaculture Asia Magazine* (4 a year); *NACA Newsletter* (4 a year); *Quarterly Aquatic Animal Health Disease Report.* All publications and podcasts open access.
Members Governments of 19 countries and territories:
Australia, Bangladesh, Cambodia, China, Hong Kong, India, Indonesia, Iran Islamic Rep, Korea DPR, Laos, Malaysia, Maldives, Myanmar, Nepal, Pakistan, Philippines, Sri Lanka, Thailand, Vietnam. [2021.08.31/XF2226/F*]

♦ Network of Aquaculture Centres in Central-Eastern Europe (NACEE) 16992

Gen Sec Anna Liget 8, Szarvas 5540, Hungary. T. +36204550279. E-mail: nacee.new@gmail.com.
URL: http://www.nacee.eu/en/

History 15 Sep 2003, St Petersburg (Russia). Official signing of founding document, 23 Nov 2004, Szarvas (Hungary). Transformed into an NGO, 26 Jan 2011. Part of: *European System of Cooperative Research Networks in Agriculture (ESCORENA, #08871).* **Aims** Facilitate the research and development sphere in Central-Eastern Europe to be an integral part of the European research area. **Structure** General Assembly (annual); Executive Board; Technical Advisory Committee; Supervisory Board. **Languages** English, Russian. **Staff** 0.50 FTE, voluntary. **Finance** Sources: members' dues; revenue from activities/projects. Annual budget: 14,500 EUR (2018). **Activities** Events/meetings; publishing activities; research/documentation; training/education. **Events** *General Assembly* Szarvas (Hungary) 2022, *Conference of Young Researchers* St Petersburg (Russia) 2021, *General Assembly* Mukachevo (Ukraine) 2019, *International Conference on Modern Technologies of Propagation and Restocking of Native Fish Species* Mukachevo (Ukraine) 2019, *H2020 TAPAS Workshop on Identified Bottlenecked in Aquaculture Governance and Licensing* St Petersburg (Russia) 2019. **Publications** Books; manuals; meeting reports.
Members Institutions (19) and individuals (20) in 10 countries:
Belarus, Bulgaria, Hungary, Kazakhstan, Latvia, Lithuania, Moldova, Poland, Russia, Ukraine.
Supporting member (1):
Network of Aquaculture Centres in Asia-Pacific (NACA, #16991).
Honorary member (1):
World Sturgeon Conservation Society (WSCS, #21835).
IGO Relations *FAO (#09260); Network of Aquaculture Centres in Asia-Pacific (NACA, #16991).* **NGO Relations** *World Sturgeon Conservation Society (WSCS, #21835).* [2022.10.21/XM0508/E]

♦ Network of Asian Producers / see Network of Asia and Pacific Producers (#16995)

♦ Network of Asian River Basin Organizations (NARBO) 16993

Secretariat Japan Water Agency, Land Axis Tower Bldg, 11-2 Shintoshin, Chuo-ku, Saitama, 330-6008 Japan. T. +81486006553. Fax +81486006509. E-mail: info@narbo.org.
URL: http://www.narbo.jp/

History Announced at 3rd World Water Forum, Mar 2003. Officially launched, Feb 2004. Charter revised: Feb 2006; Feb 2008; Nov 2010; May 2013; Feb 2017. **Aims** Strengthen capacity and effectiveness of river basin organizations (RBOs) in promoting integrated water resources management and improving water governance. **Structure** Constitutional body, comprising Chairperson, Vice-Chairperson and Secretary General; Secretariat. **Events** *General Meeting* 2010, *General Meeting* Surakarta (Indonesia) 2008, *General Meeting* Surakarta (Indonesia) 2008, *General Meeting* Jatiluhur (Indonesia) 2006, *General Meeting* Batu (Indonesia) 2004. **Publications** *NARBO Newsletter.*
Members Full in 12 countries:
Bangladesh, Cambodia, Indonesia, Japan, Korea Rep, Laos, Malaysia, Pakistan, Philippines, Sri Lanka, Thailand, Vietnam.
Regional organizations (10):
Asian Development Bank Institute (ADB Institute, #01423); Asia Pacific Association of Hydrology and Water Resources (APHW, #01843); Global Water Partnership (GWP, #10653); International Centre for Water Hazard and Risk Management (ICHARM); International Research and Training Centre on Erosion and Sedimentation (IRTCES, #14745); International Union for Conservation of Nature and Natural Resources (IUCN, #15766); International Water Management Institute (IWMI, #15867); Mekong River Commission (MRC, #16703); South Asia Network for River Basin Organizations (SASNET-RBO, no recent information); World Wide Fund for Nature (WWF, #21922). [2020.11.19/XJ0882/y/E]

♦ Network of Asia-Pacific Education and Training Institutes in Tourism (APETIT) 16994

International Affairs c/o Inst for Tourism Studies, Colina de Mong-Ha, Macau, Macau. T. +85385983036. Fax +85385061273.
URL: http://www.apetit-network.org/

History 25 Sep 1997, Teheran (Iran Islamic Rep). **Aims** Promote cooperation among tourism education, training and research institutes, national tourism organizations and tourism trade organizations in human resources development in the tourism sector in the Asia-Pacific region. **Structure** Council; Executive Committee; Rotating Secretariat. **Languages** English. **Finance** Resources through focal points. **Events** *Korea Medical Tourism Forum* Seoul (Korea Rep) 2016, *Meeting* Hong Kong (Hong Kong) 2011, *Meeting* Macau 2010. **Publications** *APETIT Newsletter.*
Members Regional; non-regional. Institutes (273) in 46 countries and territories:
Armenia, Austria, Azerbaijan, Bangladesh, Bhutan, Cambodia, China, Fiji, Guam, Hong Kong, India, Indonesia, Iran Islamic Rep, Japan, Kazakhstan, Kiribati, Korea Rep, Kyrgyzstan, Laos, Macau, Malaysia, Maldives, Mongolia, Myanmar, Nepal, New Caledonia, New Zealand, Pakistan, Papua New Guinea, Philippines, Russia, Samoa, Samoa USA, Singapore, Solomon Is, Sri Lanka, Taiwan, Tajikistan, Thailand, Timor-Leste, Tonga, Türkiye, Turkmenistan, USA, Uzbekistan, Vietnam. [2014.06.01/XF6086/F]

♦ Network of Asia and Pacific Producers (NAPP) 16995

CEO 23/2, Mallikarjuna Temple Road, Basavanagudi, Bangalore, Karnataka 560004, Bangalore KARNATAKA 560004, India. T. +918026622712.
Registered Office 3307 Tower 2, Lippo Centre, 89 Queensway, Hong Kong, Central and Western, Hong Kong.
Singapore Office 273 Thomson Road, 04-01 Novena Gardens, Singapore 307644, Singapore.
URL: http://www.fairtradenapp.org/

History 2007, as *Network of Asian Producers (NAP)*. Also referred to as *Fairtrade – Network of Asia and Pacific Producers (NAPP)* and *Fairtrade NAPP*. **Aims** Act as an organ for representation, coordination, exchange and collaboration on empowering organizations of small-scale *farmers* and farm workers in Asia within the framework of *Fairtrade* Certification. **Structure** Board.
Members Organizations in 12 countries:
Australia, Bangladesh, China, India, Indonesia, Laos, Pakistan, Papua New Guinea, Philippines, Sri Lanka, Thailand, Vietnam.
NGO Relations Regional member of: *Fairtrade International (FLO, #09240)*. [2018/XJ0832/**F**]

♦ Network-Association of European Researchers in Urbanisation in the South (N-AERUS) 16996

Réseau-association des chercheurs européens sur l'urbanisation dans les pays du Sud
Contact address not obtained. E-mail: n-aerus@n-aerus.net – naerusnetwork@gmail.com.
URL: http://www.n-aerus.net/

History Mar 1996, Brussels (Belgium). Former names and other names: *Network-Association of European Researchers in Urbanization in the South* – former. **Aims** Mobilize and develop European institutional and individual research and training capacities on *urban* issues in the South. **Structure** Coordinating Committee. **Languages** English, French, Italian, Spanish. **Staff** 2.00 FTE, paid. **Activities** Events/meetings. **Events** *Conference* Kassel (Germany) 2022, *Conference* Berlin (Germany) 2021, *Conference* Stuttgart (Germany) 2018, *Conference* Milan (Italy) 2017, *Conference* Gothenburg (Sweden) 2016. **Publications** *N-aerus Newsletter*. Conference papers. **Members** Researchers, experts, scholars and doctorate students (over 400) in over 20 countries. Membership countries not specified. [2020/XF4227/v/**F**]

♦ Network-Association of European Researchers in Urbanization in the South / see Network-Association of European Researchers in Urbanisation in the South (#16996)
♦ The Network: Associations de la communauté pour la santé par innovateurs l'éducation, le service et la recherche / see The Network: Towards Unity for Health (#17060)

♦ Network of Associations of Local Authorities of South-East Europe (NALAS) 16997

Réseau des associations de pouvoirs locaux de l'Europe du sud-est
Exec Dir Varshavska 36-A, 1000 Skopje, North Macedonia. T. +38923090818. E-mail: secretariat@nalas.eu – info@nalas.eu.
Registered Seat c/o Maison des associations, 1a, place de Orphelins, 67000 Strasbourg, France. T. +33388251939.
URL: http://www.nalas.eu/

History 2001. Founded following the 1st Forum of Cities and Regions of South-East Europe, Skopje (Macedonia), Nov 2000, organized by *Congress of Local and Regional Authorities of the Council of Europe (#04677)*. Established under the auspices of *Stability Pact for South Eastern Europe (inactive)* and *Council of Europe (CE, #04881)*. During the first years, functioned as an informal organization with regular meetings, seminars and training programmes. Secretariat set up, Mar 2007. Registration: Start date: Jul 2005, France, Strasbourg. **Aims** Promote the process of decentralization in cooperation with central governments and international organizations, considering local self-government as a key issue in the current process of transition affecting the various countries in South-East Europe. **Structure** General Assembly; Presidency; Committee of Liaison Officers/Board; Executive Bureau; Task Forces; Advisory Concilium; Networks; Secretariat. **Languages** English. **Staff** 13.00 FTE, paid. **Finance** Supported by: *Deutsche Gesellschaft für Technische Zusammenarbeit (GTZ, inactive)*; *European Commission (EC, #06633)*; *International Bank for Reconstruction and Development (IBRD, #12317)* (World Bank); *Swiss Agency for Development and Cooperation (SDC)*; UN Agencies. **Activities** Capacity building; events/meetings; knowledge management/information dissemination; politics/policy/regulatory; projects/programmes. **Events** *General Assembly* Vienna (Austria) 2017, *General Assembly* Sarajevo (Bosnia-Herzegovina) 2014, *International conference on the contribution of local and regional authorities to the water strategy of the Union for the Mediterranean* Lyon (France) 2009, *General Assembly* Tirana (Albania) 2008, *Conference on South-East Europe* Vienna (Austria) 2008. **Publications** *NALAS Digest*; *NALAS Newsletter*. Books.
Members Full (14); Associate (7). Full in 12 countries and territories:
Albania, Bosnia-Herzegovina, Bulgaria, Croatia, Kosovo, Moldova, Montenegro, North Macedonia, Romania, Serbia, Slovenia, Türkiye.
Associate include the following 3 organizations listed in this Yearbook:
Council of European Municipalities and Regions (CEMR, #04891); *Energy Cities (#05467)*; *Fondation pour l'économie et le développement durable des régions d'Europe (FEDRE, #09817)*.
IGO Relations Partner of (1): *Congress of Local and Regional Authorities of the Council of Europe (#04677)*.
NGO Relations Member of (1): *Energy Cities (#05467)*. [2022/XM2969/y/**E**]

♦ Network of Associations of Victims of Terrorism (NAVT) 16998

Dir Calle Villaamil 12, 28039 Madrid, Spain. E-mail: info@europeanvictims.com.
URL: http://www.europeanvictims.net/

History as *European Network of Victims of Terrorism (V-Net)*, following the Madrid train bombings, Mar 2004. **Aims** Stimulate trans-national cooperation between associations of victims of terrorism; enhance the representation of victims' interests at European Union level as well as the solidarity of European citizens with them; assess current aid and protection offered to victims of terrorism in the EU; gather best practices and identify gaps in the aid and protection offered to victims of terrorism. **Structure** Board. Director. **Languages** English, Spanish. **Finance** Support from *European Commission (EC, #06633)*. **Activities** Participates in European Day in Remembrance of Victims of Terrorism. Organizes seminars. **Events** *Meeting on youth dealing with terrorism and victims of terrorism* Amsterdam (Netherlands) 2012, *Meeting on the European media production on victims of terrorism* Turin (Italy) 2011, *Seminar on victims of terrorism in Europe* Lisbon (Portugal) 2010.
Members Partners in 7 countries:
France, Greece, Italy, Netherlands, Portugal, Spain, UK. [2011.06.01/XJ2278/**F**]

♦ Network di associazioni di sindrome x fragile (unconfirmed)

♦ Network for Business Sustainability (NBS) 16999

Exec Dir Ivey Business School, Western Univ, 1255 Western Road, London ON N6G 0N1, Canada. E-mail: info@nbs.net.
URL: https://www.nbs.net/

History 2005, Canada. **Aims** Build a fairer and more environmentally sound future; improve business practice by facilitating knowledge sharing across an international community of business leaders, scholars, students and policy makers. **Activities** Awards/prizes/competitions; awareness raising; events/meetings; knowledge management/information dissemination; networking/liaising; publishing activities; research and development; research/documentation; training/education. **Events** *Workshop* Cambridge, MA (USA) 2023, *Workshop* Vienna (Austria) 2021, *Workshop* Vienna (Austria) 2020, *Workshop* New York, NY (USA) 2018, *Workshop* Fontainebleau (France) 2016. [2022.06.27/AA1456/**F**]

♦ Network for Capacity Building in Integrated Water Resources Management (CAP-Net) 17000

Dir 333 Grosvenor Street, Hatfield Gardens, Block A, Pretoria, 0083, South Africa. E-mail: info@cap-net.org.
URL: http://www.cap-net.org/

History 2002 by *UNDP (#20292)* and *IHE Delft Institute for Water Education (#11110)*, within *Energy and Environment Group (see: #20292)*. **Aims** Strengthen institutional and human capacity in sustainable water management. **Languages** English, French, Spanish. **Staff** 5.00 FTE, paid. **Finance** Funded by: Dutch Ministry of Foreign Affairs; *Swedish International Development Cooperation Agency (Sida)*; *European Commission (EC, #06633)*. **Activities** Capacity building; training/education. **Publications** Training materials.
Members Autonomous international, regional and national institutions and networks. Organizations included in this Yearbook (12):
Africa Groundwater Network (AGW-NET, #00179); *Arab Water Network for Capacity Building (Awarenet, #01076)*; *Caribbean WaterNet (#03566)*; *Central American Engineering Institutions Network (REDICA, #03668)*; *Central American Water Resource Management Network (CARA, #03676)*; *Gender and Water Alliance (GWA, #10102)*; *International Waters Learning Exchange and Resource Network (IW-LEARN, #15873)*; *Nile Basin Capacity Building Network for River Engineering (NBCBN-RE, #17138)*; *Nile Capacity Building Network in Integrated Water Resources Management (Nile-IWRM Net, #17141)*; *Red Latinoamericana de Desarrollo de Capacidades para la Gestión Integrada del Agua (LA-WETnet, #18710)*; *South East Asia Regional Network for Capacity Building in IWRM (AguaJaring, #19796)*; *WaterNet (#20832)*.
NGO Relations Member of: *Global Water Operators' Partnerships Alliance (GWOPA, #10652)*; *Water and Climate Coalition (WCC, no recent information)*. Partners include: *Global Water Partnership (GWP, #10653)*. [2018.09.06/XJ2382/y/**E**]

♦ Network of Centers / see Network of Internet and Society Research Centers (#17045)
♦ Network of Children's and Juvenile Literature Documentation Centers (see: #17629)
♦ Network of Community-Oriented Educational Institutions for Health Sciences / see The Network: Towards Unity for Health (#17060)
♦ The Network: Community Partnerships for Health through Innovative Education, Service and Research / see The Network: Towards Unity for Health (#17060)

♦ Network of Concerned Historians (NCH) 17001

Contact History Dept, Univ of Groningen, PO Box 716, 9700 AS Groningen, Netherlands. Fax +31503637253.
URL: http://www.concernedhistorians.org/

History Founded 13 Oct 1995. **Aims** As a small observatory, provide a bridge between international human rights organizations campaigning for censored or persecuted historians and the global community of historians. **Structure** Network mobilized for ad-hoc campaigns. **Languages** English, French, Spanish. **Staff** Voluntary. **Finance** No budget. **Activities** Advocacy/lobbying/activism; research/documentation. **Publications** Annual Report; campaign circulars. **Members** Not a membership organization. **NGO Relations** Affiliated with: *International Students of History Association (ISHA, #15613)*; *Montreal Institute for Genocide and Human Rights Studies (MIGS)*; *Scholars at Risk (SAR)*; Science and Human Rights (SHR) Coalition of American Association for the Advancement of Science. Instrumental in setting up: *Network for Education and Academic Rights (NEAR)*. [2019/XJ5042/**F**]

♦ Network of Cord Blood Banks in Asia (AsiaCORD) 17002

Contact address not obtained. E-mail: tokikoni@ims.u-tokyo.ac.jp.
URL: http://www.asiacord.umin.jp/

History Nov 1999, Bangkok (Thailand). Current statutes adopted Apr 2013. **Aims** Spread clinical cord blood banking and transplantation with high quality. **Structure** Board. **Events** *Meeting* Kobe (Japan) 2015, *Meeting* Kobe (Japan) 2013, *Meeting* Beijing (China) 2011, *Meeting* Tokyo (Japan) 2003.
Members Full in 6 countries and territories:
China, Japan, Korea Rep, Taiwan, Thailand, Vietnam. [2020/XJ9313/**F**]

♦ Network for the Defence of Independent Media in Africa / see Africa Free Media Foundation (#00176)
♦ Network for Democracy, Human Rights and Protection of Ethnic and Religious Minorities in South Eastern Europe / see International Scientific Conference Minorities for Europe of Tomorrow (#14808)

♦ Network of Democracy Research Institutes (NDRI) 17003

Contact World Movement for Democracy, 1025 F St NW, Ste 800, Washington DC 20004-1409, USA. T. +12023789700. Fax +12023789989.
URL: https://www.ned.org/ideas/network-of-democracy-research-institutes-ndri/

History by *World Movement for Democracy (#21661)*. **Aims** Facilitate contacts among democracy scholars and activists; promote greater awareness of the diversity and vitality of democracy studies today. **Publications** *Democracy Research News*.
Members Institutes (65) in 43 countries and territories:
Albania, Argentina, Australia, Belarus, Bulgaria, Canada, Chile, Colombia, Costa Rica, Czechia, Egypt, Georgia, Germany, Ghana, Hong Kong, Hungary, India, Israel, Italy, Jordan, Korea Rep, Lebanon, Mexico, Mongolia, Montenegro, Nigeria, Pakistan, Palestine, Poland, Portugal, Romania, Russia, Serbia, Slovakia, South Africa, Spain, Sri Lanka, Taiwan, Thailand, Türkiye, UK, Ukraine, USA.
Included in the above, 12 organizations listed in this Yearbook:
Caucasian Institute for Peace, Democracy and Development (CIPDD); *Centre for Democratic Institutions (CDI)*; *Centre for the Study of Islam and Democracy (CSID)*; *Centro para la Apertura y el Desarrollo de América Latina (CADAL)*; *East Asia Institute, Seoul (EAI)*; *European Stability Initiative (ESI, #08828)*; *Human Rights Centre*; *Ibn Khaldoun Center for Development Studies, Cairo (ICDS)*; *Institute for Regional and International Studies, Sofia (IRIS)*; *International Centre for Policy Studies, Kiev (ICPS)*; *International Forum for Democratic Studies*; *Interuniversity Research Centre on Southern Europe (CIRES)*. [2013/XM2435/y/**F**]

♦ Network for the Development of Agricultural Cooperatives in Asia and the Pacific (NEDAC) 17004

Head Office c/o FAO Regional Office, 202/1 Larn Luang Rd, Klong Mahanak, Pomprabsattruphai, Bangkok, 10100, Thailand. E-mail: bangkokoffice@nedac.info – nedac@fao.org.
URL: http://www.nedac.info/

History 29 Jun 1990, Bangkok (Thailand), by *FAO (#09260)* in collaboration with *International Co-operative Alliance (ICA, #12944)* and the support of *ILO (#11123)*. **Aims** Promote ans sensitize governments on the potential of agricultural cooperatives' role in agricultural development and rural sector development; provide a forum for information exchange in the field of agricultural cooperative development in the *Asia Pacific* region. **Structure** General Assembly. Executive Committee. **Languages** English. **Staff** 2.00 FTE, paid. **Finance** Members' dues. **Activities** Events/meeings; training/education; knowledgement management/information dissemination. **Events** *General Assembly / Meeting* Bangladesh 2014, *General Assembly* Bangladesh 2013, *Meeting* India 2013, *General Assembly* Philippines 2011, *General assembly and seminar / General Assembly* Bangkok (Thailand) 2009. **Publications** Reports.
Members Full in 9 countries:
Bangladesh, China, India, Iran Islamic Rep, Japan, Nepal, Philippines, Sri Lanka, Thailand.
IGO Relations *FAO Regional Office for Asia and the Pacific (RAP, #09266)*. **NGO Relations** *International Co-operative Alliance (ICA, #12944)* Asia Pacific. [2018/XF6605/**F**]

♦ Network for the Development of Business Education Programmes / see Global Business Education Network (#10258)
♦ Network for the Development of European Programmes in Higher Education / see Global Business Education Network (#10258)
♦ NETwork for the dissemination of knowledge on the management and organisation of Large Infrastructure ProjectS in Europe / see NETLIPSE (#16980)
♦ Network of Documentation Centres for Sustainable Development and International Solidarity (internationally oriented national body)

♦ Network of East Asian Think-Tanks (NEAT) 17005

Contact RM 103, Int'l Exchange Ctre, China Foreign Affairs Univ, 24 Zhanlan Rd, 100037 Beijing, China. T. +861068322939. Fax +861068322939. E-mail: easc@cfau.edu.cn.
URL: http://www.ceac.jp/e/neat.htm

History 29 Sep 2003, Beijing (China). 29-30 Sep 2003, Beijing (China). **Aims** Integrate research resources in East Asia; promote academic exchanges; provide intellectual support for East Asian cooperation. **Events** *Country Coordinators Meeting* Quezon City (Philippines) 2021, *Country Coordinators Meeting* Quezon City (Philippines) 2021, *Country Coordinators Meeting* Jakarta (Indonesia) 2020, *Annual Conference* Tokyo (Japan) 2019, *Country Coordinators Meeting* Tokyo (Japan) 2019.
Members in 13 countries:
Brunei Darussalam, Cambodia, China, Indonesia, Japan, Korea Rep, Laos, Malaysia, Myanmar, Philippines, Singapore, Thailand, Vietnam.
NGO Relations *Asian Centre, University of the Philippines* is member. [2016/XM1174/**F**]

♦ **Network of East-West Women (NEWW)** **17006**
Dir ul Miszewskiego 17/100, 80-239 Gdansk, Poland. T. +48583443853. Fax +48583443853. E-mail: neww@neww.org.pl.
URL: http://www.neww.eu/
History Founded Jun 1991, Dubrovnik (Croatia), as an international communication and resource network supporting dialogue, informational exchange and activism among those concerned about women's situation in Central and Eastern Europe and the former Soviet Union. **Aims** Support and promote projects and activism inspired by the Statement of Principles: women's full and equal participation in the creation of a just and inclusive civil society; women's *rights* to health care, reproductive choice and control over decisions surrounding giving birth; right to be free of discrimination; right to economic justice; right to be free of violence; freedom of sexual expression and pleasure; right to be free of racial and ethnic hatred; right to full public expression of ideas. **Structure** International Council, comprising 3 officers and 16 members. Ad hoc committees. **Languages** English, Polish. **Staff** 5.00 FTE, paid; 3.00 FTE, voluntary. **Finance** Donations from international and governmental sources. Budget (annual): about euro 250,000. **Activities** Projects/programmes; training/education; events/meetings. Organizes Gender Policy Conference (every 2 years). **Events** *Gender Policy Conference* Gdansk (Poland) 2003, *Gender Policy Conference* Krakow (Poland) 2001. **Publications** *Women against Violence* (2003) by Katarzyna Kurkiewicz et al; *Women at Work* (2002) by Anna Wilkowska-Landowska; *Samorzad Kobiet Przewodnik*. Reports; conference reports. **Information Services** *NEWW On-Line* – currently 400 participants.
Members Organizations (over 80) in 28 countries and territories:
Albania, Armenia, Azerbaijan, Belarus, Bosnia-Herzegovina, Bulgaria, Canada, Croatia, Czechia, Georgia, Germany, Hungary, Kosovo, Kyrgyzstan, Latvia, Moldova, Mongolia, Montenegro, North Macedonia, Poland, Romania, Russia, Serbia, Slovakia, Spain, Tajikistan, Ukraine, USA.
Included in the above, 3 organizations listed in this Yearbook:
Association for Women's Rights in Development (AWID, #02980); *Equality Now (#05518)*; *Global Social Work Network (GSWN)*. [2016/XF4177/y/F]

♦ **Network for an Economical and Ecological Habitat (EcoSouth Network)** **17007**
Red para el Habitat Económico y Ecológico (Red EcoSur)
EcoSur Nicaragua Red EcoSur, PO Box 107, Jinotepe CARAZO, Nicaragua. T. +50525321082 – +50525320686. Fax +50525320689. E-mail: ecosur@ecosur.org.
EcoSur Ecuador Red EcoSur, PO Box 0601-1468, Riobamba, Ecuador. T. +59332940574. Fax +59332940574.
URL: http://www.ecosur.org/
History 1991, Dominican Rep. Founded at meeting of Latin American micro-concrete roofing-tile (MCR) manufacturers, rapidly spreading to other sectors. Former names and other names: *Latin American MCR Network* – former; *Red Latinoamericana de TMC* – former; *Network for an Economically and Ecologically Sustainable Habitat* – former. **Aims** Address *housing* needs of southern countries through: technology transfer of low-cost housing and construction materials; project planning for ecologically sustainable urban and rural housing interventions; develop "green" construction materials and provide knowhow transfer for them to be produced; provide scientific and technical support for the production of "lime calcined clay cement" (LC3) to cement companies. **Structure** Spanish-speaking network coordinated from Nicaragua; English-speaking network from Nicaragua. Contact office in Switzerland. **Languages** English, French, German, Spanish. **Staff** 15.00 FTE, paid; 5.00 FTE, voluntary. **Finance** Sources: donations; fees for services; fundraising; private foundations; sale of products. Annual budget: 800,000 USD (2022). **Activities** Monitoring/evaluation; projects/programmes; research and development; research/documentation; training/education. **NGO Relations** Member of (1): *Building Advisory Service and Information Network (BASIN, #03351)*. Partner of (1): *Global Network for Sustainable Housing (GNSH, #10502)*. [2023.03.06/XF6496/F]

♦ Network for an Economically and Ecologically Sustainable Habitat / see Network for an Economical and Ecological Habitat (#17007)

♦ **Networked Digital Library of Theses and Dissertations (NDLTD)** ... **17008**
Admin Assistant PO Box 6671, Christiansburg VA 24073, USA. T. +15405531856.
Exec Dir 2 E Main Street, Unit 6671, Christiansburg VA 24068, USA.
URL: http://www.ndltd.org/
History 1996, USA. Former names and other names: *National Digital Library of Theses and Dissertations (NDLTD)* – former (1996). **Aims** Promote the adoption, creation, use, dissemination and preservation of electronic theses and dissertations (ETDs). **Structure** Board of Directors; Committees; Working Groups. **Activities** Events/meetings. **Events** *International Symposium on Electronic Theses and Dissertations* Novi Sad (Serbia) 2022, *International Symposium on Electronic Theses and Dissertations* Abu Dhabi (United Arab Emirates) 2021, *International Symposium on Electronic Theses and Dissertations* Al Ain (United Arab Emirates) 2020, *International Symposium on Electronic Theses and Dissertations* Porto (Portugal) 2019, *International Symposium on Electronic Theses and Dissertations* Taipei (Taiwan) 2018. **Publications** *The Journal of Electronic Theses and Dissertations* – open access, peer-reviewed journal.
Members Institutional; Consortium; Individual. Members in 18 countries and territories:
Bangladesh, Brazil, Canada, China, Colombia, France, Germany, Hong Kong, India, Japan, Jordan, Mexico, Peru, Philippines, South Africa, Spain, UK, USA. [2022.10.21/AA1577/F]

♦ Networked and Electronic Media Initiative / see New European Media (#17083)

♦ **Networked European Software and Services Initiative (NESSI)** **17009**
Chairman c/o Nokia Technologies GmbH, Werinherstrasse 91, 81541 Munich, Germany. E-mail: office@nessi-europe.eu.
URL: http://www.nessi-europe.eu/
History 7 Sep 2005, Brussels (Belgium). Registration: EU Transparency Register, No/ID: 040237630357-81, Start date: 23 Feb 2018. **Aims** Drive data-driven innovation further and strengthen the European data economy as well as enhancing its position worldwide. **Structure** Board; Steering Committee. **Languages** English. **Staff** 0.50 FTE, paid. Several voluntary. **Finance** No formal accounts. **Activities** Research and development; events/meetings; networking/liaising. **Events** *EU-BRASIL Cooperation Consultation Workshop* Brussels (Belgium) 2014, *High-Level Meeting* Brussels (Belgium) 2014, *Meeting* Brussels (Belgium) 2014, *Software for innovation – innovation for software* Brussels (Belgium) 2014, *Workshop on Internet of Things* Brussels (Belgium) 2014. **Publications** *Strategic Research and Innovation Agenda*. Newsletters; position papers. **Members** Individuals (over 450) from industry, research and academia. Membership countries not specified.
[2018.06.01/XJ0005/E]

♦ Network of Educational Innovation for Development in Africa (no recent information)
♦ Network for Educational and Multidisciplinary Research Africa (unconfirmed)
♦ Network for Education in International Health / see TropEd (#20245)

♦ **Network of Education Policy Centers (NEPC)** **17010**
Exec Dir Martićeva ulica 72, HR-10000 Zagreb, Croatia. T. +38515587975. E-mail: nepc@edupolicy.net.
URL: https://edupolicy.net/
History 2006. Formally established 2008. **Aims** Promote flexible, participatory, evidence-based, transparent education policies reflecting open society values, which mean proactive policy initiatives as well as advocacy and monitoring activities of governments and national education systems. **Structure** General Assembly; Governing Board; Executive Director; Secretariat. **Activities** Research/documentation; knowledge management/information dissemination; training/education. **Members** Institutional (24) in 18 countries. Membership countries not specified. **NGO Relations** Member of: *SIRIUS – Policy Network on Migrant Education (SIRIUS, #19291)*. [2023/XM6570/F]

♦ Network for the Enhancement of Teaching and Learning in research-intensive universities (unconfirmed)

♦ **Network for Equity in Health in East and Southern Africa (EQUINET)** **17011**
Secretariat TARSC, Box CY2720, Causeway, Harare, HARARE, Zimbabwe. T. +2634705108. Fax +2634737220. E-mail: admin@equinetafrica.org.
URL: http://www.equinetafrica.org/
History 1998, *Network for Equity in Health in Southern Africa*. Previously also referred to as *Southern African Network on Equity in Health*. **Aims** Promote equity in health in the countries of East and Southern Africa. **Structure** Steering Committee. **Languages** English, French, Portuguese. **Activities** Events/meetings; research/documentation; training/education. **Events** *Building alliances for equity in health* Broederstroom (South Africa) 2000. **Publications** *Equinet Newsletter*. *Equinet Policy Series*. Policy resolutions; policy briefs; discussion papers; meeting reports.
Members Institutions and individuals in 16 countries:
Angola, Botswana, Congo DR, Eswatini, Kenya, Lesotho, Madagascar, Malawi, Mauritius, Mozambique, Namibia, South Africa, Tanzania UR, Uganda, Zambia, Zimbabwe.
IGO Relations Recognized by: East, Central, and Southern Africa Health Community *Southern African Development Community (SADC, #19843)*. [2014.12.27/XF5911/F]

♦ Network for Equity in Health in Southern Africa / see Network for Equity in Health in East and Southern Africa (#17011)

♦ **Network of European Alimentary Culture (NEAC)** **17012**
Netzwerk der Europäischen Esskultur
Coordinator Via Francesco Marchesiello 7, 81100 Caserta CE, Italy.
URL: http://www.neac2.eu/
Aims Encourage the emergence of a European identity in *children* by highlighting the complexity of European *food* culture. **Languages** English, French, Italian, Spanish. **Finance** Funded by: *SOCRATES Programme (inactive)*. **Activities** Organizes thematic conferences, contact seminars, youth meetings and study visits. Promotes new projects. Online databases. **Events** *Contact seminar* Barcelona (Spain) 2007, *Contact seminar* Procida (Italy) 2006, *Annual conference* Thessaloniki (Greece) 2006, *Contact seminar* Lódz (Poland) 2005, *Annual conference* Varna (Bulgaria) 2005. **Publications** *NEAC Newsletter* (every 2 months). **IGO Relations** United Nations – Division for Sustainable Development. [2011/XM1293/F]

♦ Network of the European Associations for Person-Centred Counselling and Psychotherapy / see Network of the European Associations for Person-Centred and Experiential Psychotherapy and Counselling (#17013)

♦ **Network of the European Associations for Person-Centred and Experiential Psychotherapy and Counselling (PCE Europe)** **17013**
Réseau des associations européennes pour la psychothérapie et le counselling centrés sur la personne et expérientiels – Netzwerk Europäischer Verbände für Personzentrierte und Experienzielle Psychotherapie und Beratung – Rede de Associações Europeias para Psicoterapia e Counselling Centradas na Pessoa e Experiencial
Contact c/o PCCS Books, Wyastone Business Park, Wyastone Leys, Monmouth, NP25 3SR, UK.
URL: http://www.pce-europe.org/
History Founded 27 Sep 1998, Luxembourg, as *Network of the European Associations for Person-Centred Counselling and Psychotherapy (NEAPCCP)* – *Réseau des associations européennes pour le counselling et la psychothérapie centrés sur la personne (RAECPCP)* – *Netzwerk der Europäischen Vereinigungen für Personzentrierte Beratung und Psychotherapie* – *Rede de Associações Europeias de Counselling e Psicoterapia Centradas na Pessoa (RAECPCP)*. Previously also known under the acronyms *NEAPCEPC* – *RAEPCCPE*. Statutes approved 26 Sep 1999, Athens (Greece); revised 25-26 Nov 2000, Salgótarjan (Hungary). A chapter of *World Association for Person-Centered and Experiential Psychotherapy and Counseling (WAPCEPC, #21172)*. **Aims** Further cooperation among associations and institutions in the field of psychotherapy and counselling; enhance exchange of expertise; support the legal basis of the person-centred and experiential approach. **Structure** General Assembly (every 2 years); Board. **Languages** English. **Staff** 0.50 FTE, paid. **Finance** Members' dues. Other sources: contributions; donations; conference fees; certificates. **Activities** Events/meetings; knowledge management/information dissemination; certification/accreditation. **Events** *Annual General Assembly* Prague (Czech Rep) 2014, *Annual General Assembly* Antwerp (Belgium) 2012, *Annual General Assembly* Rome (Italy) 2010, *Annual General Assembly* Szeged (Hungary) 2009, *Annual General Assembly* Norwich (UK) 2008.
Members Organizations (23) in 17 countries:
Austria, Belgium, Cyprus, Czechia, France, Germany, Greece, Hungary, Netherlands, Poland, Portugal, Romania, Russia, Slovakia, Spain, Switzerland, UK. [2018.06.18/XF5813/F]

♦ **Network of EUropean BioImage AnalystS (NEUBIAS)** **17014**
Contact IRP Barcelona, C Baldiri Reixac 10, 08028 Barcelona, Spain.
URL: http://eubias.org/NEUBIAS/
Aims Strengthen the bridge between life science, computer science and digital image processing. **Structure** Working Groups (7). **Languages** English. **Finance** Funded by: *European Cooperation in Science and Technology (COST, #06784)*. **Activities** Events/meetings; training/education; publishing activities; networking/liaising. **Events** *Annual Conference* Bordeaux (France) 2020, *Annual Conference* Luxembourg (Luxembourg) / Esch-sur-Alzette (Luxembourg) 2019, *Annual Conference* Szeged (Hungary) 2018, *Annual Conference* Oeiras (Portugal) / Lisbon (Portugal) 2017.
Members Members (over 200) from 43 COST countries:
Australia, Austria, Belarus, Belgium, Bosnia-Herzegovina, Brazil, Bulgaria, Croatia, Cyprus, Czechia, Denmark, Estonia, Finland, France, Germany, Greece, Hungary, Iceland, Ireland, Israel, Italy, Latvia, Lithuania, Luxembourg, Malta, Montenegro, Netherlands, North Macedonia, Norway, Poland, Portugal, Romania, Serbia, Singapore, Slovakia, Slovenia, Spain, Sweden, Switzerland, Türkiye, UK, Ukraine, USA. [2019.02.12/XM6158/F]

♦ **Network of European CNS Transplantation and Restoration (NECTAR)** **17015**
Pres NCBES NUI Galway, University Road, Galway, CO. GALWAY, Ireland.
URL: http://www.nectar-eu.net/
History 1990, Le Vésinet (France). **Aims** Promote transplantation and restoration in disorders of the *central nervous system*. **Structure** Board, comprising President and 6 members. **Finance** Funded by *European Commission (EC, #06633)*. **Events** *Annual Meeting* Athens (Greece) 2022, *Annual Meeting* Edinburgh (UK) 2021, *Annual Meeting* 2020, *Annual Meeting* Cardiff (UK) 2019, *Annual Meeting* Paris (France) 2018.
Members Full in 9 countries:
Austria, Denmark, France, Germany, Italy, Netherlands, Sweden, Switzerland, UK. [2014/XF4603/F]

♦ **Network on European Communications and Transport Activity Research (NECTAR)** **17016**
Chairperson c/o U-Twente, Horst Complex Z217, PO Box 217, 7500 AE Enschede, Netherlands.
URL: http://www.nectar-eu.eu/
History Nov 1985, as *ESF Network for European Communications and Transport Activities Research*, within the framework of *European Science Foundation (ESF, #08441)*; second phase from 1988-1991. Present name adopted when became independent. **Aims** Foster research, collaboration and exchange of information in the field of transport, communication and mobility among European scholars, with particular emphasis on a social science orientation towards relevant research issues. **Structure** General Assembly. Coordinating Committee, including Chair, Deputy Chair, Secretary and Treasurer. **Languages** English. **Staff** None. **Finance** Members' dues: euro 60 a year. **Activities** Organizes: conference; cluster meetings (group seminars). **Events** *NECTAR International Conference* Toronto, ON (Canada) 2022, *NECTAR International Conference* Toronto, ON (Canada) 2021, *NECTAR International Conference* Toronto, ON (Canada) 2021, *International Conference* Helsinki (Finland) 2019, *International Conference* Madrid (Spain) 2017. **Publications** *Policy Analysis of Transport Network* (2007); *New Contributions to Transportation Analysis in Europe* (1999). **Members** Individuals (over 200) in 19 countries. Membership countries not specified. [2021/XK0180/F]

♦ **Network of European Cultural Managers (ORACLE)** **17017**
Réseau d'administrateurs culturels européens
Office Av Maurice 1, 1050 Brussels, Belgium. E-mail: oraclecuturalnetwork@gmail.com.
URL: http://www.oraclecult.net/

History Founded Sep 1992. Also referred to as *Oracle Cultural Network*. Registered in accordance with Belgian law: 879 711 905. **Aims** Focus on projects of European dimensions, particularly intercultural cooperations which are of importance in modern Europe, and especially within the context of the European Union as a political construct. **Structure** General Assembly (annual); Board. **Languages** English. **Staff** 4.00 FTE, paid. **Finance** Members' dues. Supported by: *Association Marcel Hicter*. **Events** *Seminar* Copenhagen (Denmark) 2012, *Meeting* Madrid (Spain) 2011, *Meeting* Luxembourg (Luxembourg) 2010, *Meeting* Seville (Spain) 2009, *Meeting* Ljubljana (Slovenia) 2008.
Members Individuals (321) in 38 countries:
Albania, Austria, Belarus, Belgium, Bulgaria, Canada, Croatia, Czechia, Denmark, Estonia, Finland, France, Germany, Greece, Hungary, Iceland, Ireland, Italy, Latvia, Lithuania, Luxembourg, Morocco, Netherlands, North Macedonia, Norway, Poland, Portugal, Romania, Russia, Senegal, Serbia, Slovakia, Slovenia, Spain, Sweden, Switzerland, UK, Ukraine.
[2019.07.02/XF5995/F]

♦ Network of European Financial Institutions for SMEs (NEFI) 17018

Contact Rue Belliard 40, 1040 Brussels, Belgium. T. +3226451910. E-mail: nefi@nefi.eu.
URL: http://www.nefi.eu/

History 1999. Registration: EU Transparency Register, No/ID: 44013762992-64. **Aims** Maintain a permanent and constructive dialogue on SME financing issues with *European Union* institutions and with other SME-related European associations and federations; provide the EU and its institutions with expertise and advice on planning and implementing of EU-wide promotional and financing schemes; facilitate access of SMEs to both European and national financing schemes; address shortcomings in SME financial markets. **Structure** High Level Meeting; Permanent Working Group (PWG). **Languages** English. **Staff** 1.00 FTE, paid. **Finance** Members' dues. **Events** *Meeting* Berlin (Germany) 2022.
Members Specialized financial institutions (19) in 19 countries:
Austria, Bulgaria, Croatia, Czechia, Estonia, Finland, France, Germany, Hungary, Ireland, Italy, Latvia, Luxembourg, Poland, Slovakia, Slovenia, Spain, Sweden, UK. [2022/XJ0800/F]

♦ Network of European Foundations (NEF) 17019

Exec Dir Philanthropy House, Rue Royale 94, 1000 Brussels, Belgium. T. +3222352413. E-mail: info@nef-europe.org.
URL: http://www.nef-europe.org/

History 12 Jan 1977, Brussels (Belgium). Founded by *European Cultural Foundation (ECF, #06868)*. Statutes revised: 6 Nov 1997; Nov 2001; May 2015. Former names and other names: *European Cooperation Fund (ECF)* – former (1977 to 1995); *Fonds européen de coopération (FEC)* – former (1977 to 1995); *Association for Innovative Cooperation in Europe (AICE)* – former (Jan 1996 to 2001); *Network of European Foundations for Innovative Cooperation* – former (Jan 2002 to May 2010). Registration: Banque Carrefour des Entrepriss, No/ID: 0416.735.655, Start date: 12 Jan 1977, Belgium. **Aims** Realize European solidarity through philanthropy for social inclusion, international development and democracy. **Structure** General Assembly (meets at least annually); Board of Directors. **Languages** English. **Staff** 10.00 FTE, paid. **Finance** Sources: contributions. Annual budget: 3,122,823 EUR (2011). **Activities** Projects/programmes; publishing activities. Initatives include: *Alliance for Gender Equality in Europe (AGEE)*; *European Programme for Integration and Migration (EPIM, #08285)*; *Civitates (#03974)*; *European Fund for the Balkans (EFB, #07366)*; *Global Fund for Community Foundations (GFCF, #10382)*; *Ariadne – European Funders for Social Change and Human Rights (Ariadne, #01103)*. **Events** *General Assembly* Amsterdam (Netherlands) 2016, *Round table on social inclusion* The Hague (Netherlands) 1997, *Panel discussion on East and West European cultural cooperation* Brussels (Belgium) 1987. **Publications** *Alliance Magazine*; *NEF Newsletter*. *Religion and Democracy in Europe* – series. *Europe and Me* (2009); *School for Society, learning democracy in Europe* (2009); *Philanthropy in Europe* (2008); *Religion and Democracy in contemporary Europe* (2008); *Creative Europe* (2002); *Funding Europe's Solidarity* (1996). Vademecum.
Members Full: 11 organizations:
Bernard van Leer Foundation (BvLF); *Calouste Gulbenkian Foundation*; *Charles Stewart Mott Foundation*; *Company of St Paul*; *ERSTE Foundation*; *European Foundation Centre (EFC, inactive)*; *Fondation de France*; Institusjonen Fritt Ord, Norway; *King Baudouin Foundation (KBF)*; Open Society Initiative for Europe (OSIFE).
IGO Relations *European Commission (EC, #06633)*. **NGO Relations** Member of (4): *A Soul for Europe (ASF, #19697)*; *CIVICUS: World Alliance for Citizen Participation (#03962)*; *European Policy Centre (EPC, #08240)*; *Worldwide Initiatives for Grantmaker Support (WINGS, #21926)*. Instrumental in setting up (1): *ICOS (#11086)*. Previously (until their independence) provided founding structure for: *Centre for European Policy Studies (CEPS, #03741)*; *CONCORDE: Centre for Organizations and Networks for Cooperation, Research and Development in Education (no recent information)*; *East/West Parliamentary Practice Project (EWPPP, no recent information)*. [2020/XF5152/y/F]

♦ Network of European Foundations for Innovative Cooperation / see Network of European Foundations (#17019)

♦ Network of European Institutes for Advanced Studies (Netias) 17020

Contact RFIEA, 54 bd Raspail, 75006 Paris, France. E-mail: mylene.trouve@rfiea.fr.
URL: http://www.netias.science

History 2004. Founded as an informal network. **Aims** Stimulate dialogue on IAS practices and possible forms of cooperation. **Activities** Projects/programmes.
Members Institutes for Advanced Study (25) in 17 countries:
Austria, Bulgaria, Denmark, Finland, France, Germany, Hungary, Israel, Italy, Netherlands, Norway, Poland, Romania, Spain, Sweden, Switzerland, UK.
NGO Relations Member of (1): *European Alliance for the Social Sciences and Humanities (EASSH, #05885)*.
[2022.02.09/XM3992/F]

♦ Network of European LGBT Families Associations / see Network of European LGBTIQ Families Associations (#17021)

♦ Network of European LGBTIQ Families Associations (NELFA) 17021

Pres Rue du Marché au Charbon 42, 1000 Brussels, Belgium. E-mail: info@nelfa.org – secretary@nelfa.org.
URL: http://www.nelfa.org/

History 1 May 2009. Former names and other names: *Network of European LGBT Families Associations (NELFA)* – former. Registration: Banque-Carrefour des Entreprises, No/ID: 0845.937.097, Start date: 14 May 2012, Belgium; EU Transparency Register, No/ID: 248287533164-90, Start date: 12 Nov 2018. **Aims** Ensure that *children* of *lesbian, gay, bisexual, transgender, intersex* and *queer* (LGBTIQ) families in Europe enjoy the same rights as those of children in families currently recognized by law; encourage European countries to adopt *equal opportunity* policies in relation to LGBTIQ families with regard to legal, financial, educational, social and other relevant rights; ensure that LGBTIQ families can enjoy fully the EU right of freedom of movement between member states. **Structure** Board. **Languages** English. **Staff** Voluntary. **Finance** Members' dues. **Activities** Advocacy/lobbying/activism; Awareness raising; capacity building; events/meetings; guidance/assistance/consulting; networking/liaising; projects/programmes; publishing activities; training/education. **Events** *European Meeting* Lisbon (Portugal) 2015, *European Meeting* Cologne (Germany) 2014, *European Meeting* Lloret de Mar (Spain) 2012, *European Meeting* Paris (France) 2010. **Publications** *NELFA Newsletter*. Research reports; presentations.
Members Full (32) in 28 countries:
Austria, Belgium, Bosnia-Herzegovina, Bulgaria, Croatia, Denmark, Finland, France, Germany, Hungary, Iceland, Ireland, Italy, Kosovo, Malta, Montenegro, Netherlands, North Macedonia, Norway, Poland, Portugal, Russia, Serbia, Slovenia, Spain, Sweden, Switzerland, Türkiye.
Supporting (9) in 8 countries:
Albania, Czechia, Estonia, Germany, Greece, Poland, Romania, Switzerland.
Consultative Status Consultative status granted from: *Council of Europe (CE, #04881)* (Participatory Status).
NGO Relations Member of: *ILGA-Europe (#11118)*; *TGEU (#20138)*. Supporting member of: *COFACE Families Europe (#04084)*. [2020.03.03/XJ5623/D]

♦ Network of European Meteorological Services (EUMETNET) 17022

Exec Dir c/o Royal Meteorological Inst of Belgium, Ringlaan 3, 1180 Brussels, Belgium. T. +3223730518. Fax +3228909858. E-mail: info@eumetnet.eu.
URL: http://www.eumetnet.eu/

History 17 Sep 2009, Brussels (Belgium). Former names and other names: *EIG EUMETNET* – former; *GIE EUMETNET* – former. **Aims** Provide: framework for cooperation between European National Meteorological Services (NMSs) and leading expertise on weather, climate, environment and related activities; technical support; high quality data and products. **Structure** Assembly of Members (and subordinate bodies); Secretariat. **Languages** English. **Staff** 3.50 FTE, paid. **Finance** Sources: members' dues. Annual budget: 9,000,000 EUR. **Activities** Knowledge management/information dissemination; networking/liaising; projects/programmes. **Events** *European Nowcasting Conference* Brussels (Belgium) 2022, *European Nowcasting Conference* Madrid (Spain) 2019, *Short Range NWP (SRNWP) EUMETNET Meeting* Vienna (Austria) 2018, *ECAC : European Conference on Applied Climatology* Trieste (Italy) 2016, *ECAC : European Conference on Applied Climatology* Prague (Czech Rep) 2014.
Members Meteorological services in 31 countries:
Austria, Belgium, Croatia, Cyprus, Czechia, Denmark, Estonia, Finland, France, Germany, Greece, Hungary, Iceland, Ireland, Italy, Latvia, Luxembourg, Malta, Montenegro, Netherlands, North Macedonia, Norway, Poland, Portugal, Serbia, Slovakia, Slovenia, Spain, Sweden, Switzerland, UK.
Cooperation agreements with meterological services in 6 countries:
Bosnia-Herzegovina, Bulgaria, Israel, Lithuania, Moldova, Romania.
IGO Relations Cooperates with (2): *EuroGEOSS (#05685)*; *Group on Earth Observations (GEO, #10735)*.
[2022.11.07/XM0471/F]

♦ Network of European Metropolitan Regions and Areas (METREX) .. 17023

Réseau des régions et des aires métropolitaines d'Europe – Red de Regiones y Areas Metropolitanas Europeas – Netz der Europäischen Ballungs-und Grossräume – Rede de Regiões e Areas Metropolitanas Europeias – Rete delle Regioni e delle Aree Metropolitane Europee

SG Tour Part-Dieu, 129 rue Servient, 69326 Lyon, France. E-mail: info@eurometrex.org.
Head of Secretariat address not obtained.
URL: https://www.eurometrex.org/

History 13 Apr 1996, Glasgow (UK). Current statutes adopted 26 Mar 1999, Bologna (Italy). Registration: Banque Carrefour des Entreprises, Belgium. **Aims** Promote exchange of knowledge between practitioners on strategic issues of common interest; contribute the metropolitan dimension to planning at European level. **Structure** General Assembly (every 2 years); Managing Committee; Expert Groups (6); Secretariat. **Activities** Events/meetings; projects/programmes; research and development. **Events** *Conference* Nuremberg (Germany) 2021, *Conference* Riga (Latvia) 2021, *Spring Conference* Lisbon (Portugal) 2020, *Autumn Conference* Lyon (France) 2020, *Autumn Conference* Stuttgart (Germany) 2019. **NGO Relations** Cooperates with (1): *Peri-Urban Regions Platform Europe (PURPLE, #18316)*. [2023.02.13/XF6268/F]

♦ Network for European Monitoring and Development Assistance (internationally oriented national body)

♦ Network of European Museum Organizations (NEMO) 17024

SG Taubenstrasse 1, 10117 Berlin, Germany. T. +413039715661. E-mail: office@ne-mo.org.
Office Manager address not obtained.
URL: http://www.ne-mo.org/

History Statutes adopted, 1993, Italy; revised: 1995, Dublin (Ireland); 2004, Amsterdam (Netherlands). Registration: EU Transparency Register, No/ID: 435166212247-84, Start date: 12 Nov 2013. **Aims** Create an independent supranational museum network, able to match the political and administrative bodies of the *European Union* and strengthen the European cooperation among museum organizations. **Structure** Members' meeting (annual); Board; Rotating Chairmanship; Secretariat and Office follow the Chairman. **Finance** Grant from *European Commission (EC, #06633)*. **Activities** Guidance/assistance/consulting; knowledge management/information dissemination; training/education. **Events** *European Museum Conference* Rijeka (Croatia) 2020, *European Museum Conference* Tartu (Estonia) 2019, *European Museum Conference* Valletta (Malta) 2018, *European Museum Conference* Ghent (Belgium) 2017, *Annual Meeting* Dublin (Ireland) 2012. **Publications** *Nemo News* (2 a year).
Members Covers 31 countries:
Austria, Belgium, Bulgaria, Croatia, Cyprus, Czechia, Denmark, Estonia, Finland, France, Germany, Greece, Hungary, Iceland, Ireland, Italy, Latvia, Lithuania, Luxembourg, Netherlands, Norway, Poland, Portugal, Romania, Russia, Slovakia, Slovenia, Spain, Sweden, Switzerland, UK.
NGO Relations Member of (5): *Copyright for Creativity (C4C, #04832)*; *Culture Action Europe (CAE, #04981)*; *Europeana Foundation (#05839)*; *European Alliance for Culture and the Arts (#05866)*; *European Heritage Alliance 3.3 (#07477)*. [2021/XF3967/F]

♦ Network of European Neuroscience Institutes (ENINET) 17025

Coordination Office Albert-Ludwigs-Univ Freiburg, Center for Biological Systems Analysis (ZBSA), Habsburgerstr 49, 79104 Freiburg, Germany. T. +4976120397204. Fax +4976120397244.
URL: http://www.eni-net.org/

History Jan 2004, Alicante (Spain). Former names and other names: *ENI-NET Association for the Promotion of Neuroscience* – legal name. Registration: Germany. **Aims** Promote complete independent work of young neuroscience investigators. **Structure** General Assembly; Executive Board; Advisory Board; Team Leader; Young Investigators. **Languages** English. **Finance** Grant from the German Federal Ministry for Education and Research. **Activities** Events/meetings. **Events** *Annual Meeting* Vienna (Austria) 2015, *Meeting* Freiburg-Breisgau (Germany) 2014, *Meeting* Alicante (Spain) 2005.
Members Groups (54) in 23 institutes in 15 European countries and territories:
Austria, Czechia, England, France, Germany, Greece, Hungary, Italy, Netherlands, Poland, Portugal, Scotland, Spain, Sweden, Switzerland. [2016/XM0724/F]

♦ Network of European Peace Scientists (NEPS) 17026

Exec Dir c/o Politics Int Sudies, Social Sciences Building, University of Warwick, Coventry, CV4 7AL, UK. E-mail: info@europeanpeacescientists.org.
URL: http://www.europeanpeacescientists.org/

History 2003, as an informal network of scholars. Since 2011 a formal entity. **Aims** Advance peace research in Europe. **Structure** General Assembly; Steering Committee. Executive Coordinator. **Languages** English. **Staff** 1.00 FTE, paid. **Finance** Members' dues. Other sources: event proceeds; gifts, bequests and legacies; subsidies or grants. **Activities** Events/meetings; awards/prizes/competitions. **Events** *Jan Tinbergen European Peace Science Conference* London (UK) 2022, *Jan Tinbergen European Peace Science Conference* London (UK) 2021, *Jan Tinbergen European Peace Science Conference* London (UK) 2020, *Jan Tinbergen European Peace Science Conference* The Hague (Netherlands) 2019, *Jan Tinbergen European Peace Science Conference* Verona (Italy) 2018. **Publications** *NEPS Newsletter*. Working papers. **Members** Basic; Student; Supporting; Institutional. Membership countries not specified. [2020/XJ9064/F]

♦ Network of European Private Entrepreneurs in the Tourism Sector / see Network for the European Private Sector in Tourism (#17027)

♦ Network for the European Private Sector in Tourism (NET) 17027

Contact Boulevard Anspach 111, Box 4, 1000 Brussels, Belgium. T. +3225136363. Fax +3225024173.
URL: http://www.net-tourism.eu/

History Jun 1995. Previously know as *Network of European Private Entrepreneurs in the Tourism Sector*.
Aims Further the interests of private tourism entrepreneurs in Europe.
Members International organizations (8):
Confederation of National Associations of Hotels, Restaurants, Cafés and Similar Establishments in the European Union and European Economic Area (HOTREC, #04569); European Cruise Council (ECC); *European Federation of Campingsite Organisations and Holiday Park Assocations (EFCO and HPA, #07066)*; *European Federation of Rural Tourism (RuralTour, #07208)*; *European Tour Operators Association (ETOA, #08922)*; *International Association of Amusement Parks and Attractions (IAAPA, #11699)*; *International Road Transport Union (IRU, #14761)*; *The European Travel Agents' and Tour Operators' Associations (ECTAA, #08942)*.
[2011.06.15/XJ3856/y/F]

♦ Network of European Regions for a Sustainable and Competitive Tourism (NECSTouR) 17028

Director c/o Visit Flanders, Grasmarkt 61, 1000 Brussels, Belgium. E-mail: info@necstour.eu.
URL: http://www.necstour.eu/

History Nov 2007, Florence (Italy). Founded when Memorandum of Understanding was signed by 15 regions. Registration: No/ID: 0812.309.870, Start date: 16 Jun 2009, Belgium; EU Transparency Register, No/ID: 862709022846-11, Start date: 29 Jul 2016. **Aims** Develop and strengthen a framework for coordination of national and regional development and research programmes in the field of sustainable tourism. **Structure** General Assembly; Executive Committee; Committees (2); Permanent Secretariat, located in Brussels (Belgium). **Languages** English. **Staff** 3.00 FTE, paid. **Finance** Sources: members' dues. **Activities** Advocacy/lobbying/activism; events/meetings; networking/liaising; projects/programmes; research and development; training/education. **Events** *Annual General Meeting* Brussels (Belgium) 2020, *Annual General Meeting* Santa Cruz de Tenerife (Spain) 2019, *Annual General Meeting* Brussels (Belgium) 2018, *Conference on Local-Led Initiatives on Tourism and Cultural Heritage* Brussels (Belgium) 2018, *Conference on EU Financing for Innovation in Tourism* Brussels (Belgium) 2017. **Publications** *NECSTouR Newsletter* (12 a year).
Members Full (41): regional authorities in 13 countries:
Austria, Belgium, Bulgaria, Denmark, Finland, France, Ireland, Italy, Netherlands, Serbia, Spain, Sweden, UK.
Associate and Academic (35): national, European, international public/private organizations in 9 countries:
Croatia, Czechia, Finland, France, Germany, Italy, Montenegro, Spain, Switzerland.
NGO Relations Member of (2): *European Heritage Alliance 3.3 (#07477)*; *European Tourism Manifesto (#08921)*. [2022.10.19/XJ8836/y/**F**]

♦ Network of European Regions Using Space Technologies (NEREUS) 17029

SG c/o Rep of the State of Hessen, Rue Montoyer 21, 1000 Brussels, Belgium. T. +3222305775. E-mail: nereus.secretary@euroinbox.com.
URL: http://www.nereus-regions.eu/

History 28 Apr 2008. Registration: Crossroads Bank for Enterprises, No/ID: 0898.367.280, Start date: 5 Jun 2008, Belgium. **Aims** Stimulate exploitation of space technologies for the benefit of regions and their citizens; increase understanding and awareness of Europe's space systems and their potential; advocate needs of regions with respect to space uses and enhance a larger involvement of regional actors in the European Space Programmes and activities. **Structure** General Assembly (annual); Management Board. **Languages** English, French. **Staff** 2.50 FTE, paid. **Finance** Sources: members' dues. **Activities** Advocacy/lobbying/activism; events/meetings; politics/policy/regulatory; projects/programmes. **Events** *General Assembly* Brussels (Belgium) 2015, *General Assembly* Brussels (Belgium) 2014, *General Assembly* Brussels (Belgium) 2013, *Towards a smart specialization in the field of space technologies* Matera (Italy) 2012, *General Assembly* Brussels (Belgium) 2011. **Publications** *25 Uses of GMES in the NEREUS Regions*; *Applications of Space Exploration Technologies in the NEREUS Regions*; *Satellite Navigation Applications in the NEREUS Regions*; *Space Education and Training, Examples from NEREUS Regions*; *The Ever Growing Use of Copernicus across Europe's Regions*; *The Growing Use of COPERNICUS across Europe's Regions – 2nd ed*; *The Growing Use of GMES across Europe's Regions* – joint publication with Euroepan Space Agency. Position papers. Annual Report; position papers.
Members Full – regions or regional entities from EU Member States. Associate – other local authorities other than Full members, companies, corporations, associations, foundations, banks, universities, firms, private actors, stakeholders, other networks, etc. Full (25) in 9 countries:
Belgium, France, Germany, Italy, Netherlands, Poland, Portugal, Spain, UK.
Associate (40) in 8 countries:
Austria, France, Greece, Italy, Luxembourg, Portugal, Spain, UK.
NGO Relations Cooperates with (3): *Assembly of European Regions (AER, #02316)*; *Eurisy (#05625)*; *Global Satellite Operators' Association (GSOA, #10586)*. [2023/XJ2880/**E***]

♦ Network for European Social Policy Analysis (ESPAnet) 17030

Sec Swedish Inst for Social Research, Stockholm Univ, Universitetsvägen10F, SE-106 91 Stockholm, Sweden. T. +468164317. E-mail: info@espanet.org.
URL: http://www.espanet.org/

History 2002. **Aims** Facilitate exchange and cooperation between policy analysts in Europe; provide a forum of communication for the development of European social policy analysis. **Structure** Co-Chairmanship; Board; Secretariat. **Languages** English. **Staff** 0.50 FTE, voluntary. **Finance** Events financed by local organizers. **Activities** Events/meetings; politics/policy/regulatory; training/education. **Events** *Conference* Vienna (Austria) 2022, *Annual Conference* Leuven (Belgium) 2021, *Annual Conference* Leuven (Belgium) 2020, *Annual Conference* Stockholm (Sweden) 2019, *Annual Conference* Vilnius (Lithuania) 2018. **Members** Individuals (about 1,200) in about 50 countries and territories. Membership countries not specified. [2020/XF6997/**F**]

♦ Network of European Union Centres of Excellence (EUCE) 17031

Coordinator EUCE at UNC-CH, UNC-Chapel Hill, CB 3449, Chapel Hill NC 27599-3449, USA. T. +19199626765. Fax +19199625375. E-mail: euce@unc.edu.
URL: http://www.unc.edu/euce/

History 1998, by *European Commission (EC, #06633)*. **Aims** Advance the study of the European Union. **Events** *Annual Meeting* Montréal, QC (Canada) 2007. **Publications** *EUCE Newsletter* (2 a year).
Members Centres (20) in 5 countries:
Australia, Canada, Japan, New Zealand, USA.
Included in the above, 10 centres listed in this Yearbook:
American Consortium on European Union Studies (ACES, inactive); *ANU Centre for European Studies (ANUCES)*; *Center for West European Studies, Seattle WA (CWES)*; *Centre for European Studies, Ottawa (CES)*; *European Studies Center, Pittsburgh PA (CWES)*; *European Union Center of Excellence, Madison WI (ECEU)*; *Florida International University (FIU)*; *Institute for European Studies, Montréal (IES)*; *Institute of European Studies, Toronto (IES)*; *Monash European and EU Centre, Melbourne (MEEUC)*. [2007/XM2573/y/**F**]

- ♦ Network of European Voluntary Service Organisations (unconfirmed)
- ♦ Network Europeo per i Diritti degli Indigeni Australiani (internationally oriented national body)
- ♦ Network Europeo sulla Sordocecità (#06890)
- ♦ Network for the Exchange of Information between Cities and Urban Communities on Selective Waste Collection / see Association of Cities and Regions for Sustainable Resource Management (#02433)
- ♦ Network of Expertise for the Global Environment / see Global Sustainable Electricity Partnership (#10617)
- ♦ The Network Forum (unconfirmed)
- ♦ Network of Francophone Africa Women's Organizations (#18900)
- ♦ Network for a Genetic Engineered Free Latin America / see Red por una América Latina Libre de Transgénicos (#18733)

♦ Network Glia 17032

Netzwerk Glia

Pres Max Delbrück Centrum für Molekulare Medizin Berlin-Buch, Robert-Rössle-Str 10, 13125 Berlin, Germany. T. +493094063336. Fax +493094062813. E-mail: gibson@mdc-berlin.de.
URL: http://networkglia.eu/

History 2011. Also referred to as *Netzwerk Gliaforschung*. Registration: Berlin District court, No/ID: VR 30587, Start date: 6 Jun 2011, Germany, Charlottenburg. **Aims** Enhance public awareness for a defined cell type of the *brain*, the so-called *glial cells*, and for related diseases; strengthen glial cell research, especially supporting young scientists active in the field. **Structure** Board; Advisory Board. **Languages** English, German. **Staff** 0.25 FTE, paid. **Finance** Donations. **Activities** Financial and/or material support; events/meetings; training/education; awareness raising. **Events** *EUROGLIA : European Meeting on Glial Cells in Health and Disease* 2021, *EUROGLIA : European Meeting on Glial Cells in Health and Disease* Porto (Portugal) 2019, *EUROGLIA : European Meeting on Glial Cells in Health and Disease* Edinburgh (UK) 2017, *EUROGLIA : European Meeting on Glial Cells in Health and Disease / European Meeting on Glial Cells in Health and Disease* Bilbao (Spain) 2015, *EUROGLIA : European Meeting on Glial Cells in Health and Disease / European Meeting on Glial Cells in Health and Disease* Berlin (Germany) 2013. **Members** Full in 8 countries. Membership countries not specified. [2021/XJ8656/**F**]

♦ Network of Global and World History Organizations (NOGWHISTO) . 17033

Headquarters c/o Univ of Leipzig, Emil-Fuchs-Str 1, 04109 Leipzig, Germany. E-mail: headquarters@nogwhisto.org – nogwhisto@uni-leipzig.de.
URL: http://www.uni-leipzig.de/~gwhisto/

History Set up following a meeting held 2 Jul 2008, Dresden (Germany). **Aims** Connect member activities. **Structure** General Assembly. Steering Committee, including President, one or more Vice-Presidents and Treasurer. Secretariat. **Events** *General Assembly* Amsterdam (Netherlands) 2010.
Members Organizations (4):
African Network in Global History (ANGH, #00388); *Asian Association for World Historians (AAWH, #01347)*; *European Network in Universal and Global History (ENIUGH, #08029)*; *World History Association (WHA)*.
NGO Relations Affiliate member of: *International Committee of Historical Sciences (ICHS, #12777)*. [2020/XJ5058/y/**C**]

- ♦ Network Gudizzjarju Ewropeu Fil-qasam Civili u Kummercjali (#07616)
- ♦ Network on Health Expectancy and the Disability Process (unconfirmed)

♦ Network on Humanitarian Action (NOHA) 17034

Gen Sec IACS, Place Montesquieu 1/L2 08 03, 1348 Louvain-la-Neuve, Belgium. T. +3210474163. E-mail: info@nohanet.org.
Office Regus Stephanie Square Centre, Av Louise 65, Box 11, 1050 Brussels, Belgium. T. +3225357932.
URL: http://www.nohanet.org/

History 1993, by 5 European universities, jointly developed in close collaboration with DG *ECHO (inactive)* and Directorate-General for Education and Culture of the *European Commission (EC, #06633)*. Original title: *European University Network for International Humanitarian Aid Studies*. Subsequently changed title to *Network on Humanitarian Assistance (NOHA) – Réseau pour l'assistance humanitaire*. Registered in accordance with Belgian law, 2001. **Aims** Increase effectiveness and quality of humanitarian action through provision of excellence and internationally recognized education, research and training. **Structure** General Assembly; Executive Committee; Board of Directors; General Secretariat. **Languages** English, French, Spanish. **Staff** 150.00 FTE, paid. **Finance** Independently run, with support from DG Humanitarian Aid – *ECHO (inactive)*. **Activities** Training/education; events/meetings. **Events** *International meeting* Paris (France) 1995. **Publications** *Journal of International Humanitarian Action* (annual). Policy papers; research papers.
Members Full universities (12) in 12 countries:
Belgium, Denmark, France, Germany, Ireland, Italy, Lithuania, Malta, Netherlands, Poland, Spain, Sweden.
Mundus Partners universities (7) in 7 countries:
Australia, Colombia, India, Indonesia, Lebanon, South Africa, USA.
IGO Relations *European Commission (EC, #06633)*. **NGO Relations** Links with a number of NGO partners including: *Bureau international des Médecins sans frontières (MSF International, #03366)*; *Commissione Cooperazione Internazionale per lo Sviluppo (CICOPS)*; *Concern Worldwide*; *International Committee of the Red Cross (ICRC, #12799)*; *Médecins du Monde – International (MDM, #16613)*; *Oxfam International (#17922)*; *RedR International (#18729)*; *The Sphere Project (#19918)*; *Trocaire – Catholic Agency for World Development*; *Voluntary Organisations in Cooperation in Emergencies (VOICE, #20809)*. [2019/XF3389/**F**]

- ♦ Network on Humanitarian Assistance / see Network on Humanitarian Action (#17034)
- ♦ Network of Iberoamerican Antrhopologists (unconfirmed)
- ♦ Network of Iberoamerican Diplomatic Archives (#18634)

♦ Network of IFAD Supported Projects in Latin America and the Caribbean (FIDAMERICA) 17035

Address not obtained.
URL: http://www.fidamerica.cl/

History 1995, as a network of projects and institutions funded by *International Fund for Agricultural Development (IFAD, #13692)*. Implemented and organized by *Centro Latinoamericano para el Desarrollo Rural (RIMISP, #03813)*. Exists in multi-year funding and project phases. **Aims** Facilitate and increase the access of *poor rural* areas and communities in Latin America and the Caribbean to information and knowledge; strengthen the local capacities needed for the effective management of these resources. **Structure** Coordinator; 2 Consultants. **Activities** Organizes and coordinates activities which promote and facilitate communication and training processes. Projects in: Argentina; Belize (Belize); Bolivia; Brazil; Chile; Colombia; Costa Rica; Dominica; Dominican Rep; Ecuador; El Salvador; Granada; Guatemala (Guatemala); Guyana; Haiti; Honduras; Mexico; Nicaragua; Panama; Paraguay; Peru; Saint Lucia; Uruguay; Venezuela. **Publications** *Intercambios* (12 a year) – electronic. **NGO Relations** *International Forum for Development of Sustainable Land Use Systems (INFORUM, no recent information)*. [2009/XF4247/**F**]

♦ Network for Industrially Contaminated Land in Europe (NICOLE) . . . 17036

Secretariat Dutch Sino Business Promotions, Postbus 28249, 3003 KE Rotterdam, Netherlands. T. +31641374680.
URL: http://www.nicole.org/

History 1995, Hannover (Germany), following an initiative from *Conseil européen de l'industrie chimique (CEFIC, #04687)*. Initiated as a Concerted Action within *European Commission (EC, #06633)* Environment and Climate RTD Programme, Feb 1996. Self-funding since February 1999. EU Transparency Register: 228843522470-20. **Aims** Provide a European forum for dissemination and exchange of knowledge and ideas about contaminated land arising from industrial and *commercial* activities; identify research needs and promote collaborative research that will enable European *industry* to identify, assess and manage contaminated sites efficiently and cost-effectively; increase international collaboration in the field. **Structure** Steering Group, assisted by Secretariat, comprising Chairpersons, Vice-Chairs and 2 members each of the 2 Subgroups, plus an academic/researchers representative. Management Team. Subgroups (2): Industry, comprising 27 representatives from industrial companies; Service Providers, comprising 37 representatives from technology developers/service providers. Academics and researchers. **Languages** English. **Staff** Voluntary. Secretariat on a contractual basis. **Finance** Members' dues. Other sources: workshop fees for non-members; sponsoring of workshops. **Activities** Events/meetings; research/documentation; knowledge managmenet/information dissemination. **Events** *The impact of EU directives on the management of contaminated land* Sardinia (Italy) 2005, *State of the art of (ecological) risk assessment* Stockholm (Sweden) 2005, *Unlocking the barriers to the recovery of soil and the rehabilitation of contaminated land* Sofia (Bulgaria) 2004. **Publications** *NICOLE News* (annual). Meeting reports; discussion papers; training materials. **Members** Organizations and individuals (currently 115), including the academic sector/research community, research planners, non-profit making organizations, other networks and funding organizations. Membership countries not specified. [2019/XF7188/**F**]

♦ Networking European Citizenship Education (NECE) 17037

Contact Federal Agency for Civic Education, Adenauerallee 86, 53113 Bonn, Germany. T. +49228995150.
Head Project Team address not obtained. E-mail: nece-network@labconcepts.de.
URL: https://www.nece.eu/

History Set up as an initiative by the (German) Federal Agency for Civic Education (bpb). **Aims** Promote Europeanization of citizenship education; contribute to the creation of a European general public. **Structure** Advisory Board. **Activities** Events/meetings; knowledge management/information dissemination. **Events** *Conference* Brussels (Belgium) 2021, *Conference* Berlin (Germany) 2020, *Conference* Glasgow (UK) 2019, *Conference* Marseille (France) 2018, *Conference* Gdansk (Poland) 2017. **Publications** *NECE Newsletter*. **NGO Relations** No formal structure. [2021.05.20/XJ9603/c/**F**]

♦ Network for Innovation in Career Guidance and Counselling in Europe (NICE) 17038

Contact CCU-Education, Rowan Williams Court, 30 Pembroke Court, Chatham Maritime, Gillingham, ME4 4UF, UK.
URL: http://www.nice-network.eu/

History Set up as an *'ERASMUS Academic Network'*. Initial funding from the European Commission in 2009. **Aims** Contribute to the implementation of the European Lifelong Learning Programme; sustain and strengthen cooperative efforts in careers research and education. **Structure** Steering Committee. **Staff** 12.00 FTE, paid. **Finance** Maintenance (Jan 2012-Dec 2015) funded by: *European Commission (EC, #06633)*. **Activities** Standards/guidelines; networking/liaising; training/education; events/meetings. **Events** *Conference* Bratislava (Slovakia) 2015, *Conference* Canterbury (UK) 2014, *European Summit on Developing the Career Workforce of the Future* Canterbury (UK) 2014, *Conference* Istanbul (Turkey) 2013, *Conference* Jyväskylä (Finland) 2012. **Publications** *NICE Handbook*.

Members Partners in 29 countries:
Austria, Bulgaria, Cyprus, Czechia, Denmark, Estonia, Finland, France, Germany, Greece, Hungary, Iceland, Ireland, Italy, Latvia, Lithuania, Luxembourg, Netherlands, Norway, Poland, Portugal, Romania, Slovakia, Slovenia, Spain, Sweden, Switzerland, Türkiye, UK.
IGO Relations Cooperates with: *European Centre for the Development of Vocational Training (Cedefop, #06474)*; *European Commission (EC, #06633)*. **NGO Relations** Cooperates with: *European Society for Vocational Designing and Career Counseling (ESVDC, #08788)*; *International Association for Educational and Vocational Guidance (IAEVG, #11862)*. [2017/XJ6574/**E**]

♦ Network Institute for Global Democratization (internationally oriented national body)

♦ Network of Institutes and Schools of Public Administration in Central and Eastern Europe (NISPAcee) 17039

Exec Dir Polianky 5, 42, 841 01 Bratislava, Slovakia. E-mail: nispa@nispa.org.
URL: http://www.nispa.org/
History 1994. Registration: Slovakia. **Aims** Promote and strengthen the emergence of effective and democratic governance and modernization of public administration systems. **Structure** General Assembly (annual); Steering Committee. **Languages** English. **Staff** 5.00 FTE, paid. **Finance** Sources: members' dues; sponsorship. **Activities** Events/meetings; research/documentation; training/education. **Events** *Annual Conference* Belgrade (Serbia) 2023, *Annual Conference* Bucharest (Romania) 2022, *Annual Conference* Ljubljana (Slovenia) 2021, *Annual Conference* Split (Croatia) 2020, *Annual Conference* Prague (Czechia) 2019. **Publications** *NISPAcee News* (4 a year) – newsletter; *NISPAcee Journal of Public Administration and Policy* (2 a year). Annual Report; books; case studies; research reports; conference proceedings; teaching and training materials.
Members Institutional; Associate; Individual. Institutional in 24 countries:
Albania, Armenia, Azerbaijan, Belarus, Bulgaria, Croatia, Czechia, Estonia, Georgia, Hungary, Kazakhstan, Kyrgyzstan, Latvia, Lithuania, Moldova, Montenegro, North Macedonia, Poland, Romania, Russia, Serbia, Slovakia, Slovenia, Ukraine.
Associate in 5 countries:
Austria, Belgium, Netherlands, Sweden, USA.
Included in the above, 1 organization listed in this Yearbook:
European Institute of Public Administration (EIPA, #07569).
Individual (39) in 20 countries:
Albania, Austria, Belarus, Belgium, Canada, Czechia, France, Georgia, Germany, Hungary, Lithuania, Netherlands, Poland, Romania, Russia, Serbia, Slovakia, Sweden, Ukraine, USA.
IGO Relations Cooperates with (1): *United Nations Public Administration Network (UNPAN, #20615)*. **NGO Relations** Memorandum of Understanding with (1): *Asian Association for Public Administration (AAPA, #01334)*. Cooperates with (1): *European Association for Public Administration Accreditation (EAPAA, #06177)*. [2022.05.04/XF4259/y/**F**]

♦ Network of Institutes for Socioeconomic Studies of the Caribbean Basin (internationally oriented national body)
♦ Network of Institutions Dedicated to Teaching Agricultural and Rural Development Policies for Latin America and the Caribbean (#18690)
♦ Network of Institutions for the Fight Against Corruption and the Recovery of Public Ethics (see: #16294)

♦ Network of the Insular Chambers of Commerce and Industry of the European Union (INSULEUR) 17040

Réseau des Chambres de Commerce et de l'Industrie Insulaires de l'Union Européenne
Secretariat 52 Michael Livanou St, 821 00 Chios, Greece. T. +302271081670. Fax +302271081671. E-mail: insuleur.network@gmail.com – info@eoaen.com.
URL: http://www.insuleur.org/
History 1999, Basse-Terre (Guadeloupe). Founded during 4th *Conference of Chambers of Commerce and Industry of the Island Regions of the European Union*. Statutes approved May 2000. **Aims** Oversee close cooperation between insular Chambers of Commerce in the EU; promote economic and social development of islands in the EU. **Structure** General Assembly; Board of Directors; Technical Committee **Languages** English, French, Greek, Italian, Spanish. **Events** *Forum* Piraeus (Greece) 2009, *Forum* Le Port (Réunion) 2008, *Forum* Saint-Denis (Réunion) 2008, *General Assembly* Saint-Denis (Réunion) 2008, *General assembly* Gozo Is (Malta) 2007. **Publications** *INSULEUR Voice* (4 a year).
Members Chambers of Commerce of small islands in 6 countries:
France, Greece, Italy, Malta, Portugal, Spain.
IGO Relations Cooperates with (1): *European Economic and Social Committee (EESC, #06963)*. **NGO Relations** Cooperates with (8): *Association des chambres de commerce et d'industrie européennes (EUROCHAMBRES, #02423)*; Celebrate islands; *Conference of Peripheral Maritime Regions of Europe (CPMR, #04638)*; *Global Islands Network (GIN, #10437)*; Greening the Islands (GTI); Hellenic Small Islands Network (HSIN); *Observatory on Tourism in the European Islands (OTIE, #17645)*; Small Islands Organisation (SMILO). [2023.02.16/XM1879/t/**F**]

♦ Network of International Business Schools (NIBS) 17041

Registered Office Geldenaaksebaan 335, 3001 Heverlee, Belgium.
URL: https://www.nibsweb.org/
Aims Further education by uniting business schools around the world through shared ideals and resources. **Events** *Conference* London (UK) 2012, *Conference* Maastricht (Netherlands) 2011, *Conference* Bangkok (Thailand) 2010, *Conference* Antalya (Turkey) 2009, *Conference* Leuven (Belgium) 2008.
Members Schools in 29 countries:
Belgium, Brazil, Bulgaria, Canada, Chile, China, Colombia, Cyprus, Czechia, Denmark, Finland, France, Germany, Guatemala, Hungary, India, Ireland, Latvia, Mexico, Netherlands, New Zealand, Norway, Peru, Poland, Puerto Rico, Spain, Thailand, UK, USA.
NGO Relations Affiliated member of: *SPACE Network (#19899)*. [2017/XJ1626/**D**]

♦ Network of International Centres for Sustainable Development in the South / see Network of International Science and Technology Centers (#17044)
♦ Network of International Circus Exchange (unconfirmed)
♦ Network of International Development Organisations in Scotland / see Scotland's International Development Alliance

♦ Network of International Education Associations (NIEA) 17042

Exec Dir CONAHEC, Univ of Arizona, PO Box 210300, 220 W 6th St, Tucson AZ 85721-0300, USA. T. +15206217761. Fax +15206262675. E-mail: smanleyc@email.arizona.edu.
URL: http://www.ieanetwork.org/
Aims Advance internationalization of higher education; advance the global learning of post-secondary education organizations through exchange of information and dialogue, advocacy for international education, professional development, and discovery of new approaches to international education. **Structure** Council; Executive Committee. **Languages** English, French, Spanish.
Members Founding organizations (11):
Asia-Pacific Association for International Education (APAIE, #01844); *Association of International Education Administrators (AIEA)*; *Consortium for North American Higher Education Collaboration (CONAHEC, #04756)*; *European Association for International Education (EAIE, #06092)*; Foro Argentino para la Educación Internacional (FAEI); *Institute of International Education (IIE)*; *International Education Association of Australia (IEAA)*; *Japan Network for International Education (JAFSA)*; Korean Association of Foreign Student Administrators (KAFSA); *Mexican Association for International Education (AMPEI)*; *NAFSA – Association of International Educators*.
Other members (4):
Brazilian Association for International Education (FAUBAI); *Canadian Bureau for International Education (CBIE)*; *International Education Association (ISANA)*; *International Education Association of South Africa (IEASA)*. [2018.11.27/XJ1709/y/**C**]

♦ Network of International Interfaith Organizations / see International Interfaith Organizations Network (#13945)

♦ Network for International Policies and Cooperation in Education and Training (NORRAG) 17043

Exec Dir Associate Programme of the Graduate Inst of Intl and Development Studies, Rue Rothschild 20, Case Postale 1672, 1211 Geneva 1, Switzerland. T. +41229084507. E-mail: norrag@graduateinstitute.ch.
Dir address not obtained.
URL: http://www.norrag.org/
History Originally set up 1977 as a *Network of Policy Research Review and Advisory Groups on Education and Training (NORRAG)*. End 1985, first meeting of the *Northern research Review and Advisory Group*. Changed title to *Network for Policy Review Research and Advice on Education and Training*, Jul 1992. Current title adopted 2013. **Aims** Inform, challenge and influence international education and training policies and cooperation, with a specific focus on perspectives from the global South. **Structure** Management Group; Consultative Committee. **Languages** Arabic, English, French, Mandarin Chinese, Spanish. **Staff** 7.50 FTE, paid. **Finance** Sponsors; partnerships; in kind contributions for specific products. Currently funded by: *Open Society Foundations (OSF, #17763)*; *Swiss Agency for Development and Cooperation (SDC)*. **Activities** Events/meetings; training/education; politics/policy/regulatory; knowledge management/information dissemination; capacity building; guidance/assistance/consulting. **Events** *Meeting on Education and Migration* Bern (Switzerland) 2018, *Round Table* Delhi (India) 2018, *Symposium on Philanthropy in Education* Geneva (Switzerland) 2017, *Conference – The changing nature of partnership in education* Oxford (UK) 1999, *General Conference* Geneva (Switzerland) 1994. **Publications** *NORRAG Special Issue* (2 a year). *Education and Development* – book series. Policy briefs; research reports; working papers; workshop reports.
Members Individuals (over 4,900) in 172 countries and territories:
Afghanistan, Albania, Algeria, Andorra, Angola, Argentina, Armenia, Aruba, Australia, Austria, Bahamas, Bahrain, Bangladesh, Barbados, Belgium, Benin, Bhutan, Bolivia, Bosnia-Herzegovina, Botswana, Brazil, Brunei Darussalam, Bulgaria, Burkina Faso, Burundi, Cambodia, Cameroon, Canada, Cape Verde, Chad, Chile, China, Colombia, Congo Brazzaville, Congo DR, Costa Rica, Côte d'Ivoire, Croatia, Cuba, Czechia, Denmark, Dominican Rep, Ecuador, Egypt, El Salvador, Eritrea, Eswatini, Ethiopia, Fiji, Finland, France, Gabon, Gambia, Georgia, Germany, Ghana, Greece, Grenada, Guatemala, Guinea, Guinea-Bissau, Guyana, Haiti, Honduras, Hong Kong, Hungary, Iceland, India, Indonesia, Iran Islamic Rep, Iraq, Ireland, Israel, Italy, Jamaica, Japan, Jordan, Kazakhstan, Kenya, Korea DPR, Korea Rep, Kyrgyzstan, Laos, Lebanon, Lesotho, Liberia, Liechtenstein, Lithuania, Luxembourg, Madagascar, Malawi, Malaysia, Maldives, Mali, Malta, Marshall Is, Mauritania, Mauritius, Mexico, Micronesia FS, Mongolia, Montenegro, Morocco, Mozambique, Myanmar, Namibia, Nepal, Netherlands, New Zealand, Nicaragua, Niger, Nigeria, Norway, Oman, Pakistan, Palau, Palestine, Panama, Papua New Guinea, Paraguay, Peru, Philippines, Poland, Portugal, Qatar, Romania, Russia, Rwanda, Samoa, Saudi Arabia, Senegal, Serbia, Sierra Leone, Singapore, Slovakia, Solomon Is, Somalia, South Africa, South Sudan, Spain, Sri Lanka, St Kitts-Nevis, St Lucia, Sudan, Suriname, Sweden, Switzerland, Syrian AR, Taiwan, Tajikistan, Tanzania UR, Thailand, Timor-Leste, Togo, Tonga, Trinidad-Tobago, Tunisia, Türkiye, Tuvalu, Uganda, UK, Ukraine, United Arab Emirates, Uruguay, USA, Uzbekistan, Vanuatu, Venezuela, Vietnam, Yemen, Zambia, Zimbabwe.
NGO Relations Operates within a framework of similar networks, such as: *United Kingdom Forum for International Education and Training (UKFIET)*; national institutions. Member of: *Next Einstein Forum (NEF, #17098)*. [2018.09.13/XF3461/v/**F**]

♦ Network of International Science and Technology Centers 17044

Address not obtained.
URL: http://www.comsats.org/
History 4 Oct 1994, Islamabad (Pakistan). 4-5 Oct 1994, Islamabad (Pakistan), following proposal of *Consortium on Science, Technology and Innovation for the South (COSTIS, no recent information)*, 1989, and in collaboration with *UNIDO (#20336)* and *TWAS (#20270)*. Full title: *International Network of Science and Technology Centres of Excellence for Sustainable Development in the South*. Previously also referred to as *Network of International Centres for Sustainable Development in the South*. Political and financial backing from *Commission on Science and Technology for Sustainable Development in the South (COMSATS, #04239)*, set up at the same time and comprising Heads of State and Government of 21 countries. **Aims** Assist countries of the South to build and sustain a critical mass of world-class scientists and technologists in areas of frontier science and technology and environmental sciences which are of critical importance to sustainable socio-economic development; attract talent, reduce *brain-drain* and induce competent Third World scientists and technologists working abroad to return to their countries; facilitate *technology transfer* and supply to industry; assist in finding scientific solutions to complex developmental and environmental problems in the South; provide avenues for international cooperation in areas of science and technology of global concern, including *environmentally sustainable development*; provide a suitable framework for science and technology assessment and management in the South; promote joint technological ventures among members and develop strong links between them and production sectors in the South. **Structure** Coordinating Council (meets at least annually), headed by Chairperson and comprising heads of member centres or their representatives. Consultative Committee, consisting of national scientific 'focal points' of member countries, Chairman ex-officio Focal Point of host country, Secretary is COMSATS Executive Director. Technical Advisory Committee, of up to 10 members. Secretariat in Islamabad (Pakistan). **Languages** English. **Activities** Conducts: high-level training activities; basic and applied research and modelling; interdisciplinary research; scientific and technical services.
Members Centres (17) in 16 countries:
Bangladesh, Bolivia, Brazil, China, Colombia, Egypt, Ghana, Iran Islamic Rep, Jamaica, Jordan, Nigeria, Pakistan, Sudan, Syrian AR, Tanzania UR, Türkiye.
Included in the above, 4 centres listed in this Yearbook:
Centro Internacional de Fisica (CIF, #03807); *International Center for Chemical and Biological Sciences (ICCBS)*; *International Centre for Environmental and Nuclear Sciences (ICENS)*; *International Centre of Climate and Environmental Sciences (ICCES)*.
IGO Relations *UNESCO (#20322)*. [2012.08.09/XF3532/y/**F**]

♦ Network of Internet and Society Research Centers (NoC) 17045

Contact address not obtained. E-mail: contact@networkofcenters.net.
URL: http://networkofcenters.net/
History 2012. Also known as *Network of Centers* and *Global Network of Internet and Society Research Centers*. **Aims** Increase interoperability between participating centers so as to stimulate the creation of new cross-national, cross-disciplinary conversation, debate, teaching, learning, and engagement regarding the most pressing questions around new technologies, social change, and related policy and regulatory developments. **Structure** Executive Committee.
Members Founding; Participating; Affiliated. Centers in 37 countries and territories:
Argentina, Australia, Austria, Bangladesh, Belgium, Brazil, Canada, Chile, China, Denmark, Egypt, France, Germany, Hong Kong, Hungary, India, Israel, Italy, Japan, Korea Rep, Netherlands, Norway, Pakistan, Poland, Portugal, Russia, Singapore, South Africa, Spain, Sweden, Switzerland, Thailand, Tunisia, Türkiye, UK, USA, Vietnam.
Included in the above, 7 organizations listed in this Yearbook:
Arab World Internet Institute (AW2I, #01079); *Center for Global Communication Studies (CGCS)*; *Diplo Foundation*; *Global Public Policy Institute (GPPi)*; *Internet Society (ISOC, #15952)*; *Royal Institute of International Affairs (RIIA)*; *World Trade Institute (WTI, #21863)*. [2018/XM6651/y/**F**]

♦ Network for a Latin America Free of Transgenics (#18733)
♦ Network of Latin American Newspapers (#10803)

♦ Network of Latin American Women of the Fishery Sector 17046

Red Latinoamericana de las Mujeres del Sector Pesquero – Rede Latino-Americana de Mulheres do Setor Pesquero
Contact INFOPESCA, Julio Herrera y Obes 1296, Casilla de Correo 7086, Montevideo, Uruguay. T. +59829028701 – +59829028702. Fax +59829030501. E-mail: graciela.pereira@infopesca.org – infopesca@infopesca.org.
URL: http://mujeres.infopesca.org/
History Jan 2000. Also referred to as *Latin American Network of Women in Fisheries*. **Events** *Conference* Santiago de Compostela (Spain) 2018. **IGO Relations** Coordinated by: *INFOPESCA (#11192)*. [2009/XF6037/**F**]

♦ Network of Latin American Women Writers (#18649)

♦ Network of Macrouniversities of Latin America and the Caribbean . 17047

Red de Macrouniversidades públicas de América Latina y el Caribe
Main Office UNAM-UISU, Edif CIPPS-Planta Baja, Circuito Cultural, Frente a UNIVERSUM, Ciudad Universitaria, Coyoacan, 04510 Mexico City CDMX, Mexico. T. +5256221181 – +5256221182 – +5256221183. E-mail: redmacro@unam.mx – redmacroualc@gmail.com.
URL: http://www.redmacro.unam.mx/

History 14 Jun 2002, Caracas (Venezuela), on the initiative of the national universities of Mexico and Venezuela and under the auspices of *UNESCO International Institute for Higher Education in Latin America and the Caribbean (#20309)*. **Aims** Consolidate the setting up of a system of cooperation and integration. **Structure** General Assembly. Academic Executive Committee, comprising Coordinator and one representative for each of the subregions: Brazil, Caribbean, Central American, Southern Cone, Mexico, Andean Zone. President. Secretary-General. **Staff** 3.00 FTE, paid. **Events** *General Assembly* Santiago (Chile) 2020.
Members Universities (31) in 18 countries:
Argentina, Bolivia, Brazil, Colombia, Costa Rica, Cuba, Dominican Rep, Ecuador, El Salvador, Guatemala, Honduras, Mexico, Nicaragua, Panama, Paraguay, Peru, Uruguay, Venezuela.
NGO Relations Member of: *Global University Network for Innovation (GUNI, #10641)*. [2020/XM1155/**F**]

♦ Network of Marine Protected Area Managers in the Mediterranean (MEDPAN) 17048

Exec Sec 58 quai du port, 13002 Marseille, France. T. +33491523433. Fax +33491450948. E-mail: medpan@medpan.org.
URL: http://www.medpan.org/

History Oct 1990, Monaco. Founded at the initiative of *International Union for Conservation of Nature and Natural Resources (IUCN, #15766)* and *International Bank for Reconstruction and Development (IBRD, #12317)*. Became dormant, 1996. Value of the Network reaffirmed by *UNEP (#20299)* via the *'Regional Activity Center for Specially Protected Areas (RAC/SPA)'*, based in Tunis (Tunisia). Port-Cros National Park applied for new statutes, 1999. Former names and other names: *Mediterranean Protected Areas Network (MEDPAN)* – former; *Réseau des espaces protégés méditerranéens* – former. Registration: RNA, No/ID: W832001375, Start date: 1 Dec 1999, France; EU Transparency Register, No/ID: 873918940859-55, Start date: 6 Jan 2021. **Aims** Promote creation, perpetuation and operation of a Mediterranean network of marine protected areas. **Structure** General Assembly (annual); Board of Directors; Scientific Committee; Advisory Committee; Secretariat. **Languages** English, French. **Staff** 8.50 FTE, paid. **Finance** Supported by: *Fonds français pour l'environnement mondial (FFEM)*; *MAVA Foundation*; *Regional Activity Centre for Specially Protected Areas (RAC/SPA, #18746)*; Government of France (Region 'Provence/Alpes/Côte d'Azur'); Ministry of Environment (French Agency for MPAs); Prince Albert II of Monaco Foundation; Ville de Marseille. **Activities** Events/meetings. **Events** *General Assembly* Akyaka (Turkey) 2019, *General Assembly* Tirana (Albania) 2014, *General Assembly* Hyères (France) 2013, *General Assembly* Antalya (Turkey) 2012, *General Assembly* Vodice (Croatia) 2011. **Publications** *MEDPAN Newsletter*.
Members Covers 21 countries:
Albania, Algeria, Bosnia-Herzegovina, Croatia, Cyprus, Egypt, France, Greece, Israel, Italy, Lebanon, Libya, Malta, Monaco, Montenegro, Morocco, Slovenia, Spain, Syrian AR, Tunisia, Türkiye. [2020/XF4119/**F**]

♦ Network for Marine Protected Areas / see Caribbean Marine Protected Areas Management Network
♦ Network for Medicines and Development (internationally oriented national body)
♦ Network of Mediterranean Olive Oil Towns (#18868)

♦ Network of National ITS Associations (ITS Nationals) 17049

Coordinator c/o ERTICO-ITS Europe, Av Louise 326, 1050 Brussels, Belgium.
URL: http://itsnetwork.org/

History Officially launched 7 Oct 2004, London (UK). Hosted by *ERTICO ITS Europe (#05532)*. **Aims** Ensure that ITS – Intelligent *Transport* Systems – knowledge and information is transmitted to all actors at local and national levels; support ITS promotion from the ground up. **Structure** Coordination Committee; Secretariat. **Activities** Awareness raising; guidance/assistance/consulting.
Members Organizations (27) in 25 countries:
Austria, Belgium, Bulgaria, Czechia, Denmark, Estonia, Finland, France, Germany, Greece, Hungary, Ireland, Italy, Lithuania, Netherlands, Norway, Poland, Portugal, Romania, Slovenia, Spain, Sweden, Switzerland, Türkiye, UK.
[2019.12.11/XM6314/**F**]

♦ Network of Nordic Project Management Associations (NORDNET) . . 17050

Contact VSF, Engjateigur 9, 105 Reykjavik, Iceland. T. +3545532450. E-mail: vsf@vsf.is.

History 1981. **Aims** Strengthen the capability of participating national associations to develop a dynamic and competent discipline for projects, programme and portfolio management. **Structure** Board (meets biannually). **Languages** Danish, English, Finnish, Icelandic, Norwegian, Swedish. **Staff** None. **Events** *Symposium* Helsinki (Finland) 2014, *Symposium* Reykjavik (Iceland) 2013, *Symposium* Oslo (Norway) 2012, *Symposium* Stockholm (Sweden) 2011, *Symposium* Copenhagen (Denmark) 2010.
Members Full in 8 countries:
Denmark, Estonia, Finland, Iceland, Latvia, Lithuania, Norway, Sweden. [2022.10.18/XJ0626/**D**]

♦ Network of Nordic Research Libraries Associations (inactive)
♦ Network of Organizations for Development Solidarity (internationally oriented national body)
♦ Network Parlamentare per il Disarmo Nucleare (#18210)
♦ Network Performing Arts Production Workshops (meeting series)
♦ Network of Policy Research Review and Advisory Groups on Education and Training / see Network for International Policies and Cooperation in Education and Training (#17043)
♦ Network for Policy Review Research and Advice on Education and Training / see Network for International Policies and Cooperation in Education and Training (#17043)

♦ Network of the Presidents of the Supreme Judicial Courts of the European Union 17051

Réseau des présidents des cours suprêmes judiciaires de l'Union Européenne
Secretariat 5 quai de l'Horloge, 75001 Paris, France. E-mail: secretariat@networkpresidents.eu.
URL: http://www.network-presidents.eu/

History 10 Mar 2004, France. Constituent Assembly 2004, with financial support of *European Commission (EC, #06633)*. **Aims** Promote exchange of views and experience on matters concerning case law, organization and functioning of the Supreme Judicial Courts of the EU in the performance of their judicial and/or advisory functions, particularly with regard to Community Law. **Structure** Board; President; Secretary General. **Languages** English, French. **Staff** 1.50 FTE, paid. **Finance** Sources: contributions; members' dues. Supported by: *European Commission (EC, #06633)*. **Activities** Events/meetings. **Events** *Conference on the Criteria Required to Achieve Genuine Separation of Power* Tallinn (Estonia) 2017, *Biennial Colloquium* Madrid (Spain) 2016, *Biennial Colloquium* Rome (Italy) 2014, *Biennial Colloquium* Paris (France) 2012, *Conference on the Budgetary Management and Resources of the Supreme Courts* Sofia (Bulgaria) 2011. **Publications** *Network Newsletter*. **Information Services** *Common Portal of National Case Law*.
Members Presidents of the Supreme Judicial Courts of the European Union (27):
Austria, Belgium, Bulgaria, Croatia, Cyprus, Czechia, Denmark, Estonia, Finland, France, Germany, Greece, Hungary, Ireland, Italy, Latvia, Lithuania, Luxembourg, Malta, Netherlands, Poland, Portugal, Romania, Slovakia, Slovenia, Spain, Sweden.
Associate Member Presidents (3):
Liechtenstein, Norway, UK.
Observer Presidents (2):
Albania, Montenegro. [2021.05.25/XJ7878/**E**]

♦ Network for the Prevention of Food Crisis in the Sahel / see Réseau de prévention des crises alimentaires (#18905)

♦ Network to Promote Linguistic Diversity (NPLD) 17052

Admin Manager Rue de la Pépinière 1 bte 3, 1000 Brussels, Belgium. T. +32496286342. E-mail: npld@npld.eu.
URL: http://www.npld.eu/

History 2008, Cardiff (UK). Statutes adopted at inaugural General Assembly. Headquarters moved to Brussels (Belgium), 2016. Registration: Start date: Jul 2016, Belgium; EU Transparency Register, No/ID: 023293231367-63, Start date: 27 Apr 2018. **Aims** Raise awareness at European level on the vital importance of linguistic diversity; facilitate exchange of best practice among governments, policy makers, practitioners, researchers and experts from all over Europe. **Structure** General Assembly; Chair's Comittee (Board of Directors); Steering Committee. **Languages** Basque, Breton, Catalan, Cimbrian, Cornish, Corsican, Finnish, Friulian, Galician, Hungarian, Irish Gaelic, Ladin, Macedonian, Mócheno, Norwegian Nynorsk, Occitan, Sardinian, Scottish Gaelic, Sorbian languages, Welsh, Western Frisian. **Staff** 2.00 FTE, paid. **Finance** Sources: members' dues. Annual budget: 243,750 EUR (2022). **Activities** Advocacy/lobbying/activism; events/meetings; knowledge management/information dissemination; networking/liaising; projects/programmes. **Events** *General Assembly* Brussels (Belgium) 2022, *General Assembly* Palma (Spain) 2021, *Conference on the Recognition of the Cultural and Linguistic Heritage* Toulouse (France) 2019, *General Assembly* Toulouse (France) 2019, *General Assembly* Valencia (Spain) 2018. **Publications** *NPLD Newsletter*. Articles; guidelines.
Members Full – (Regional) Governments of 7 countries:
France, Ireland, Italy, Netherlands, Spain, Sweden, UK.
Associate in 12 countries and territories:
Finland, France, Greece, Italy, Netherlands, Norway, Romania, Scotland, Spain, Sweden, UK, Wales.
Included in the above, 2 organizations listed in this Yearbook:
Mercator European Network for Documentation and Information on Lesser-Used Languages (Mercator Media, #16718); *Mercator European Research Centre on Multilingualism and Language Learning (Mercator Research Centre, #16719)*.
NGO Relations Member of (1): *European Civil Society Platform for Multilingualism (ECSPM, #06569)*.
[2022.05.30/XJ9101/y/**F**]

♦ The Network for the Public Communication of Science and Technology Incorporated / see International Network on Public Communication of Science and Technology (#14311)
♦ Network of the Rectors and Deans of the Technical Universities in the Nordic and Baltic countries / see NORDTEK (#17551)

♦ Network of Reference Laboratories for Monitoring of Emerging Environmental Pollutants (NORMAN Network) 17053

Exec Sec INERIS – Direction Scientifique, Rue Jacques Taffanel – Parc Techn ALATA, 60550 Verneuil-en-Halatte, France.
URL: http://www.norman-network.net/

History Founded Sep 2005 with support from *European Commission (EC, #06633)*. Currently a permanent self-sustaining network. Registered in accordance with French law. **Aims** Enhance information exchange and collection of data on emerging environmental substances; encourage the validation and harmonization of common measurement methods and monitoring tools so that the demands of risk assessors can be better met; ensure that knowledge on emerging pollutants is maintained and developed by stimulating coordinated, interdisciplinary projects on problem-oriented research and knowledge transfer to address identified needs. **Structure** General Assembly (annual). Steering Committee, including Chairman, Treasurer and Executive Secretary. **Languages** English. **Finance** Members' dues. **Activities** Organizes: workshops; Expert Group meetings. Working Groups (4): Prioritization of Emerging Substances; Bioassays and Biomarkers in Water Quality Monitoring; Effect-directed Analysis for Hazardous Pollutant Identification; Engineered Nanoparticles. Affiliated with the *'Environmental Science Europe Journal'*, Earth Science Education Unit (ESEU). **Publications** *NORMAN Bulletin on Emerging Substances*. *NORMAN Protocol for Validation of Measurement Methods*. Position papers; workshop reports. **Information Services** *EMPODAT* – on occurrence and ecotoxicity data on emerging substances; *NORMAN EMPOMAP* – on projects, organizations and experts in emerging substances; *NORMAN MassBank* – on mass spectra of unknown or provisionally identified substances.
Members Founding; Ordinary; Associate. Founding in 16 countries:
Belgium, Czechia, Denmark, Finland, France, Germany, Italy, Netherlands, Norway, Portugal, Slovakia, Slovenia, Spain, Sweden, Switzerland, UK.
Ordinary (50) in 16 countries:
Belgium, Canada, Cyprus, Czechia, Finland, France, Germany, Italy, Netherlands, Serbia, Slovakia, Slovenia, Spain, Sweden, Switzerland, UK.
Included in the above, 3 organizations listed in this Yearbook:
Association of Plastics Manufacturers in Europe (Plastics Europe, #02862); *Euro Chlor (#05659)*; *European Centre for Ecotoxicology and Toxicology of Chemicals (ECETOC, #06477)*.
Associate (1) in one country:
France.
IGO Relations Collaboration agreement with: *Joint Research Centre (JRC, #16147)*.
[2012.07.27/XJ4618/y/**F**]

♦ Network of Regional Governments for Sustainable Development / see Regions4 Sustainable Development (#18819)

♦ Network for Religious and Traditional Peacemakers 17054

Contact c/o Finn Church Aid, PO Box 210, FI-00131 Helsinki, Finland. T. +358406213517.
Communications Coordinator address not obtained.
URL: http://www.peacemakersnetwork.org/

History Launched 2013. **Aims** Increase effectiveness of efforts towards peaceful and inclusive societies by increasing active collaboration between religious and traditional actors and other key stakeholders in conflict transformation. **Structure** Steering Group; Secretariat. **Languages** English, Finnish. **Staff** 17.00 FTE, paid. **Finance** Financial support from the Ministry for Foreign Affairs of Finland; *Finn Church Aid (FCA)*; *King Abdullah Bin Abdulaziz International Centre for Interreligious and Intercultural Dialogue (KAICIID, #16193)*; Sultanate of Oman. Other sources: in-kind contributions by several members and external funders; partnerships. **Activities** Advocacy/lobbying/activism; awareness raising; capacity building; conflict resolution; events/meetings; guidance/assistance/consulting; knowledge management/information dissemination; networking/liaising; projects/programmes; religious activities; research/documentation; training/education. Active in: Central African Rep, Kenya, Libyan AJ, Somalia, Finland. Also active in: South and Southeast Asia. Active in: Central African Rep, Finland, Libya, Somalia, South Sudan. **Publications** *Demystifying Religion in Mediation – Identifying Gaps in Training, Knowledge and Practice* (2017); *Mapping the state of play of institutional and community involvement in countering violent extremism in Kosovo* (2017); *Radicalization and Boko Haram – Perception versus Reality* (2017); *Radicalisation and al-Shabaab recruitment in Somalia* (2016); *Tradition and Faith Oriented Insider Mediators (TFIMs) in Conflict Transformation* (2016); *Reforming UN mediation through inclusion of traditional peacemakers* (2015).
Members Global and Partners (50), including 18 organizations listed in this Yearbook:
Berghof Foundation; *Center for Security Studies (CSS)*; *Centre for Humanitarian Dialogue (The HD Centre)*; *Danmission*; *Finn Church Aid (FCA)*; *Initiatives of Change International – Caux (IofC, #11213)*; *Joan B Kroc Institute for Peace and Justice (IPJ)*; *King Abdullah Bin Abdulaziz International Centre for Interreligious and Intercultural Dialogue (KAICIID, #16193)*; *Middle East Women's Leadership Network (MEWLN)*; *Norwegian Church Aid*; *Organisation of Islamic Cooperation (OIC, #17813)*; *Pax Christi – International Catholic Peace Movement (#18266)*; *Religions for Peace (RfP, #18831)*; *Salam Institute for Peace and Justice*; *Swisspeace*; *United Religions Initiative (URI, #20658)*; *United States Institute of Peace (USIP)*; *World Vision International (WVI, #21904)*.
NGO Relations Member of: *International Partnership on Religion and Sustainable Development (PaRD, #14524)*; *NGO Working Group on the Security Council (#17128)*. [2022/XM6115/y/**F**]

♦ Network for Reporting on Eastern Europe (internationally oriented national body)

♦ Network for Research and Training of Tropical Diseases in Central America (NeTROPICA) 17055

Contact PO Box 304-3000, Heredia, Heredia, Heredia, Costa Rica. T. +5062380761. Fax +5062381298.

History Feb 1998. **Aims** Assist scientists and academics in biomedical sciences in Central America that can generate sustainable scientific and educational programmes for the improvement of the living conditions in the region. **Finance** Supported by: *Swedish International Development Cooperation Agency (Sida).* **Activities** Organizes conferences and seminars. Offers fellowships. **Events** *Improving control of pathogens in the tropics* La Ceiba (Honduras) 2007, *Biennial Meeting* León (Nicaragua) 2005, *Conference / Biennial Meeting* Panama 2003, *Conference* Antigua (Guatemala) 2001, *Biennial Meeting* Guatemala (Guatemala) 2001.
Members Universities in 9 countries:
Brazil, Costa Rica, Ecuador, El Salvador, Guatemala, Honduras, Nicaragua, Panama, Sweden. [2008/XF6208/F]

♦ Network of Schools and Government Institutions in Public Affairs (see: #16294)
♦ Network of Schools of Public Policy, Affairs, and Administration (internationally oriented national body)

♦ Network Science Society (NetSci) 17056

Contact c/o Hurwit and Associates, 1150 Walnut Street, West Newton MA 02461, USA. E-mail: network.science.society@gmail.com.
URL: https://netscisociety.net/

Aims Bring under one umbrella a wide variety of researchers and stakeholders with direct interest in network science. **Structure** Board; Executive Committee. **Activities** Awards/prizes/competitions; events/meetings; training/education. **Events** *NetSci Winter Conference* Porto (Portugal) 2022, *NetSci 2022* Shanghai (China) 2022, *NetSci Conference* Bloomington, IN (USA) 2021, *NetSci Conference* Rome (Italy) 2020, *NetSci Winter Conference* Tokyo (Japan) 2020. **Publications** *NetSci Newsletter* (12 a year). [2021/AA1491/F]

♦ Network for Science and Technology Popularization in Latin America and the Caribbean 17057

Red de Popularización de la Ciencia y la Tecnologia para América Latina y el Caribe (RedPOP) – Rede de Popularização da Ciência e da Tecnologia na América Latina e no Caribe

Dir Museu da Vida, Av Brasil 4365, CEP 21040-900 Manguinhos, Rio de Janeiro RJ, 21040-900 , Brazil. T. +552138652121.
URL: http://www.redpop.org/

History 1990, Rio de Janeiro (Brazil). **Aims** Strengthen exchange and active cooperation among centres and programmes for the popularization of science and technology in Latin America and the Caribbean. **Structure** General Assembly (every 2 years); Executive Office; Advisor Committee. **Languages** English, Portuguese, Spanish. **Staff** 2.50 FTE, voluntary. **Finance** Contributions from members, national, regional and international organizations and other public and private organizations. **Activities** Training/education; knowledge management/information dissemination; research/documentation; awards/prizes/competitions; events/meetings. **Events** *Congress* Medellin (Colombia) 2015, *Meeting* Zacatecas (Mexico) 2013, *Between the global and the local* San José (Costa Rica) 2007, *Meeting* Santiago (Chile) 2006, *Meeting* Rio de Janeiro (Brazil) 2005. **Publications** *Noticias en la red* in English, Spanish – official bulletin. **Members** Formally institutionalized centres and programmes for the popularization of science and technology (over 80) in more than 15 countries in Latin America and the Caribbean. Membership countries not specified. **IGO Relations** *UNESCO Office, Montevideo – Regional Bureau for Sciences in Latin America and the Caribbean (#20314).* [2017.06.01/XF4114/F]

♦ Network of Sex Work Projects / see Global Network of Sex Work Projects (#10498)

♦ Network for Social Studies on Disaster Prevention in Latin America 17058

Réseau d'études sociales pour la prévention des catastrophes naturelles en Amérique latine – Red de Estudios Sociales en Prevención de Desastres en América Latina (LA RED)

Address not obtained.
URL: http://www.desenredando.org/

History Aug 1992, Limón (Costa Rica), at first meeting. General Coordination: *Practical Action (#18475).* **Aims** As an interinstitutional and multidisciplinary research and training network, promote and strengthen the activities of member institutions and groups. **Structure** A coordination mechanism with no formal or legal status as such. General Assembly of Members and Coordinators (every 6 months), to which Associates and Supporters are invited where appropriate, coordinates and programmes projects and activities. Following changes agreed at 6th General Meeting, Esmeraldas (Ecuador), May 1995, the Network is currently organized around 4 structures: a group of individual members, comprising founders and other invited individuals; a group of institutional coordinators, which manage projects and administer funds; a group of individual and institutional associates, which participate as researchers or practitioners in projects and activities; a group of bilateral and multilateral organization supporters, which provide financial resources, information and other services. Coordinating institutions negotiate and manage funding and contribute institutional resources for projects and activities implemented. Coordination of each project or activity is assigned to one of these institutions. Coordinators: General Coordination and Andean Region: ITDG, Lima (Peru); Coordination for North America: CIESAS, Mexico City (Mexico); Coordination for Central America and the Caribbean: FLACSO Secretaria General, San José (Costa Rica); Coordination for Brazil: Universidad Federal de Paraiba/UNCAL, Campina Grande (Brazil); Coordination for Southern Cone Countries: CENTRO, Buenos Aires (Argentina); Colombia: OSSO, Universidad del Valle, Cali (Venezuela); Canada: University of Manitoba, Disaster Research Institute, Winnipeg (Canada); Ecuador: EQUILIBRIO, Quito (Ecuador). **Finance** Institutional resources contributed by ITDG and other Coordinators constitute the local contribution to the financial structure. A number of institutions provide financial support to projects and collaboration of different kinds. **Activities** Established the first coherent comparative research program on disaster prevention and management issues in Latin America. Carries out comparative research projects in Latin America covering key disaster prevention and management issues. Organizes workshops and meetings related to specific projects, conferences, seminars, workshops and institutional presentations. Publishes and disseminates research findings. Provides information on the policies and programs of national and international organizations and raises the profile of social, economic, cultural and political issues on IDNDR agenda. **Events** *Half-Yearly General Meeting* Puerto Viejo (Costa Rica) 2002, *General Meeting* Puerto Viejo de Talamanca (Costa Rica) 2002, *General meeting / Half-Yearly General Meeting* Taboga (Panama) 1997, *General meeting / Half-Yearly General Meeting* Miami, FL (USA) 1996, *General Meeting* João Pessoa (Brazil) 1995. **Publications** *Desastres y Sociedad (Revista Semestral de la Red de Estudios Sociales en Prevención de Desastres en América Latina)* (2 a year); *Boletin de la Red de Estudios Sociales en Prevención de Desastres en América Latina* (annual). *BIBLIODES* – bibliography of social studies on disasters. Books; documents; videos. **Information Services** *Bibliographic Database on Disaster Matters.*
Members Individual Members (currently 16) in 9 countries:
Argentina, Brazil, Canada, Colombia, Costa Rica, Ecuador, Mexico, Peru, USA.
Included in the 8 Coordinators, 3 regional bodies listed in this Yearbook:
Intermediate Technology Development Group (ITDG); *Latin American Faculty of Social Sciences (#16316); Observatorio Sismológico del Sur Occidente (OSSO).*
Associates (individuals and institutions) in 7 countries:
Colombia, Costa Rica, Ecuador, El Salvador, Guatemala, Honduras, Mexico.
Supporters include 4 institutions listed in this Yearbook:
Centro de Coordinación para la Prevención de los Desastres Naturales en América Central (CEPREDENAC, #03795); Department for International Development (DFID, inactive); Emergency Aid Unit of Disaster Documentation Centre of ; *International Development Research Centre (IDRC, #13162).*
IGO Relations *OAS (#17629).* [2015/XF2761/y/F]

♦ The Network: Sociedades de la Comunidad para la Salud con Innovadores la Educación, el Servicio y la Investigación / see The Network: Towards Unity for Health (#17060)

♦ Network of Southern Think Tanks (NeST) 17059

Sec Research and Information System for Developing Countries, Core 4B – 4th Floor, India Habitat Ctr, Lodhi Road, Delhi NEW 110003, DELHI NEW 110003, India. T. +911124682176 – +911124682177 – +911124682180. Fax +911124682173 – +911124682174. E-mail: dgoffice@ris.org.in.
URL: http://southernthinktanks.org/

History Apr 2014, Mexico, at 1st High Level Meeting of *Global Partnership for Effective Development Co-operation (GPEDC, #10532).* **Aims** Provide a global platform for Southern Think-Tanks to collaboratively generate, systematize, consolidate and share knowledge on South-South Cooperation approaches in international development. **Events** *International Conference on South-South and Triangular Cooperation* Delhi (India) 2017.
Members Founding institutions in 4 countries:
Brazil, China, India, South Africa.
Included in the above, 2 organizations listed in this Yearbook:
Research and Information System for Developing Countries, India (RIS, India); South African Institute of International Affairs (SAIIA). [2016/XM5197/y/F]

♦ Network Startup Resource Center (internationally oriented national body)
♦ Network on Sustainable Food Security in Central West Africa / see Foundation for Sustainable Food Security in Central West Africa (#09975)

♦ The Network: Towards Unity for Health (The Network: TUFH) 17060

Exec Dir address not obtained. E-mail: secretariat@thenetworktufh.org.
URL: https://thenetworktufh.org/

History 1979, Kingston (Jamaica). Took over activities of *European Network for Development of Multiprofessional Education in Health Sciences (EMPE, inactive)*, 2001. Amalgamated with *'Towards Unity for Health (TUFH) Initiative'* – a WHO programme, 2002. Former names and other names: *Network of Community-Oriented Educational Institutions for Health Sciences* – former (1979 to 1999); *Réseau des établissements de formation en sciences de la santé orientés vers les besoins de la communauté* – former (1979 to 1999); *Red de Instituciones Educacionales en Ciencias de la Salud con Orientación Comunitaria* – former (1979 to 1999); *The Network: Community Partnerships for Health through Innovative Education, Service and Research* – former (1999 to 2002); *The Network: Associations de la communauté pour la santé par innovateurs l'éducation, le service et la recherche* – former (1999 to 2002); *The Network: Sociedades de la Comunidad para la Salud con Innovadores la Educación, el Servicio y la Investigación* – former (1999 to 2002). **Aims** Promote equity in health through community-oriented education, research and service. **Structure** General Assembly (annual, in conjunction with Conferences); Board of Directors; Advisory Board; Central Secretariat, headed by Executive Director. Includes student chapter: *Student Network Organization (SNO, #20014).* **Languages** English, French, Spanish. **Staff** 3.00 FTE, paid. **Finance** Sources: donations; members' dues. **Activities** Events/meetings; guidance/assistance/consulting; research/documentation; training/education. **Events** *Annual International Conference* Vancouver, BC (Canada) 2022, *Annual International Conference* Yogyakarta (Indonesia) 2021, *Annual International Conference* Mexico City (Mexico) 2020, *Annual International Conference* Darwin, NT (Australia) 2019, *Annual International Conference* Limerick (Ireland) 2018. **Publications** *Education for Health – Change in Learning and Practice* (3 a year); *TUFH Practitioner Journal* (2 a year). Books; monographs; conference reports; position papers; members' directory.
Members Individuals, groups, institutions and organizations committed to improving and maintaining health in the communities they have a mandate to serve. Members in 49 countries and territories.
Argentina, Australia, Austria, Bahrain, Bangladesh, Belgium, Bolivia, Brazil, Burundi, Cameroon, Canada, Chile, China, Colombia, Denmark, Ecuador, Egypt, France, Germany, Greece, Grenada, Hong Kong, India, Indonesia, Iraq, Israel, Italy, Jordan, Kenya, Malaysia, Mexico, Nepal, Netherlands, Nigeria, Pakistan, Philippines, South Africa, Sudan, Sweden, Switzerland, Tanzania UR, Thailand, Türkiye, Uganda, UK, United Arab Emirates, USA, Vietnam, Yemen.
Included in the above, 3 organizations listed in this Yearbook:
Aga Khan University (AKU, #00546); International Federation of Medical Students' Associations (IFMSA, #13478); International University of Africa (IUA).
Consultative Status Consultative status granted from: *WHO (#20950)* (Official Relations). **NGO Relations** Member of (1): *European Forum for Primary Care (EFPC, #07326)* (as associate member of). [2022.06.21/XF1882/y/F]

♦ **The Network: TUFH** The Network: Towards Unity for Health (#17060)

♦ Network of Universities from the Capitals of Europe (UNICA) 17061

Réseau des universités des capitales de l'Europe

Contact c/o University Foundation, Rue d'Egmont 11, 1000 Brussels, Belgium. T. +3225147800. E-mail: office@unica-network.eu.
URL: http://www.unica-network.eu/

History 24 Jan 1990, Brussels (Belgium). Founded on the initiative of Université Libre de Bruxelles. Former names and other names: *European Capitals Universities Network* – former. Registration: Crossroads Bank for Enterprises, No/ID: 0465.298.508, Start date: 11 Feb 1999, Belgium, Brussels; EU Transparency Register, No/ID: 896121848510-46, Start date: 3 Jan 2023. **Aims** Promote academic excellence, integration and cooperation between member universities throughout Europe; constitute a driving force in the development of the European higher education area; promote environmental sustainability at universities. **Structure** General Assembly; Steering Committee; International Relations Officers' Group; Working Groups. **Languages** English. **Staff** 4.00 FTE, paid. **Finance** Sources: members' dues; revenue from activities/projects. Supported by: *European Commission (EC, #06633).* **Activities** Awards/prizes/competitions; events/meetings; training/education. **Events** *General Assembly and Rectors Seminar* Dublin (Ireland) 2022, *Student Conference* Lisbon (Portugal) 2021, *General Assembly* Berlin (Germany) 2020, *General Assembly* London (UK) 2019, *EduLAB Meeting* Vienna (Austria) 2019. **Publications** *e-communication* (12 a year). UNICA Activity Report; work programme; conference proceedings.
Members Universities (53) in 36 European countries:
Albania, Austria, Belgium, Bulgaria, Croatia, Cyprus, Czechia, Denmark, Estonia, Finland, France, Germany, Greece, Hungary, Iceland, Ireland, Italy, Latvia, Lithuania, Luxembourg, Netherlands, North Macedonia, Norway, Poland, Portugal, Romania, Russia, Serbia, Slovakia, Slovenia, Spain, Sweden, Switzerland, Türkiye, UK, Ukraine.
IGO Relations Partner of (1): *OAS (#17629).* **NGO Relations** Member of (3): *Academic Cooperation Association (ACA, #00019); garagErasmus Foundation (garagErasmus, #10070); International Association of Universities (IAU, #12246).* Partner of (3): *Coimbra Group (#04089)* (of Brazilian Universities); Debating Europe; *United Nations Academic Impact (UNAI, #20516).* [2023.02.15/XF1083/F]

♦ Network on Urban Research in the European Community / see Network on Urban Research in the European Union (#17062)

♦ Network on Urban Research in the European Union (NUREC) 17062

Netzwerk für Stadtforschung in der Europäischen Union

Contact c/o Stadt Duisburg, Stabsstelle für Wahlen, Europaangelegenheiten und Informationslogistik, Bismarckplatz 1, 47198 Duisburg, Germany. T. +492032832058. Fax +492032834404.
URL: http://www.nurec.net/

History 1989, Pisa (Italy), as *Network on Urban Research in the European Community.* **Aims** Support scientific progress in comparative urban research; develop a basis for the comparability of *city* data in the European Union and beyond; enhance communication between institutions involved in urban research. **Structure** Board; Administrative Directorate in Duisburg (Germany); Scientific Directorates in Paris (France) and Milan (Italy). **Activities** Events/meetings; advice/assistance/consulting; knowledge management/information dissemination. **Publications** *International Yearbook of Large Cities Statistics. Working Papers* – series. *Atlas of Agglomerations in the European Union* – in 3 vols. Internal circulars. **Information Services** *EUROPOLIS Database; Large Cities Statistics Project Database.* **Members** Cities, other local authorities, universities, university institutes, research institutions, networks. Regular organizations from EU member countries; Associate institutions from countries outside EU. Membership countries not specified. [2014.11.12/XF3982/F]

♦ Network for the Vocational Education and Training in the Construction Sector in Europe / see REFORME (#18738)

♦ Network for Voluntary Development in Asia (NVDA) 17063

Pres Room 1022 – 10/F, Kui On House, Wo Lok Estate, Kwun Tong, Kowloon, Hong Kong. E-mail: nvda.pres@gmail.com.
URL: http://nvda-asia.org/

History 1997. **Aims** Improve local/global situations on environment, social welfare, education, culture and poverty; support local NGOs and communities for self-sufficiency, human development and empowerment; promote global friendship, understanding and solidarity among international volunteers and local people. **Structure** General Assembly (annual); Executive Committee; Secretariat. **Languages** English. **Staff** 1.00 FTE, paid. **Finance** Sources: members' dues. **Activities** Events/meetings; networking/liaising; projects/programmes; publishing activities; training/education. **Publications** *NVDA Newsletter.* Annual Report; leaflet.
Members NGOs (31) in 23 countries and territories:

Australia, Bahrain, Bangladesh, Belgium, Cambodia, China, Hong Kong, India, Indonesia, Japan, Korea Rep, Laos, Macau, Malaysia, Mongolia, Myanmar, Nepal, Philippines, Singapore, Sri Lanka, Taiwan, Thailand, Vietnam.
IGO Relations Member of: *European Youth Centres (EYCs, #09138)*. **NGO Relations** Cooperates with (2): *Alliance of European Voluntary Service Organizations (ALLIANCE, #00677)*; *Coordinating Committee for International Voluntary Service (CCIVS, #04819)*. [2020.05.29/XF6274/F]

♦ Network for Water and Sanitation International (NETWAS International) 17064

Exec Dir PO Box 15614-0053, Mbagathi, Nairobi, Kenya. T. +25420890555. Fax +25420890554. E-mail: netwas-international@netwas.org – training@netwas.org.
URL: http://www.netwas.org/
History 1986, as a regional network of *International Training Network for Water and Waste Management (ITN, no recent information)*, and under the auspices of *Amref Health Africa (#00806)*. Also sometimes referred to as *Regional Network for Water and Sanitation*. Registered in Kenya with branches in Uganda and Tanzania. **Aims** Improve *living conditions* of the *poor* in Eastern *Africa* through capacity building of the water and sanitation sector. **Structure** Executive Director. **Staff** 12 professionals: water/sanitary engineers; sociologist/ community development experts; information officers; environmentalists. **Finance** Income from training and consultancy services; mandate for networking and outreach information services supported by *Swiss Agency for Development and Cooperation (SDC)*. **Activities** Main emphasis is on management and behaviour change training through 5 programme areas: scheduled courses; tailored courses; advisory consultancy; community support and research; networking, outreach and information services. Scholarship fund (supported by SDC) provides partial assistance to needy participants. **Events** *Annual regional water and sanitation seminar* Mombasa (Kenya) 2002. **Publications** *Water and Sanitation News*. *Annotated Bibliography on Water Supply and Sanitation*; *Kenya, Water Supply and Sanitation: a Directory of Sources of Information and Documentation in Kenya*. Technical reports; meeting reports.
Members Collaborating institutions (30) in 5 countries:
Ethiopia, Kenya, Sudan, Tanzania UR, Uganda.
Associate member institutions in 8 countries:
Burkina Faso, Ghana, India, Indonesia, Netherlands, Philippines, Switzerland, Zimbabwe.
IGO Relations *UNICEF (#20332)*. **NGO Relations** Collaborates in training, consultancy and research activities with: *IRC (#16016)*; *SKAT Foundation*. [2018/XF1664/F]

♦ Network for Whaling Research / see International Network for Whaling Research (#14342)
♦ Network Women in Development Europe / see WIDE+ (#20951)

♦ Network of Women Parliamentarians of the Americas 17065

Réseau des femmes parlementaires des Amériques – Red de Mujeres Parlamentarias de las Américas – Rede de Mulheres Parlamentares das Américas
Secretariat c/o Natl Assembly of Québec, 1050 rue des Parlementaires – 4e étage, Québec QC G1A 1A3, Canada. T. +14186442888. Fax +14186431865. E-mail: feminamericas@assnat.qc.ca.
URL: http://www.feminamericas.net/
History May 1999, Antigua (Guatemala). **Aims** Encourage representation and action of women in the parliaments of the Americas; foster experience and promote solidarity among women in general; ensure both men and women parliamentarians take into consideration the rights and demands of women, from the viewpoint of respect of *human rights*, and a better distribution of wealth; support participation of women in the parliaments of the Americas. **Structure** Annual Meeting; Executive Committee. **Languages** English, French, Portuguese, Spanish. **Staff** 1.00 FTE, paid. **Finance** Contributions of member parliaments. **Activities** Politics/policy/regulatory; knowledge management/information dissemination; events/meetings. **Events** *Annual Meeting* Guanajuato (Mexico) 2015, *Annual Meeting* Asunción (Paraguay) 2014, *Annual Meeting* Brasilia (Brazil) 2013, *Annual Meeting* Asunción (Paraguay) 2012, *Consultation with Parliamentarians of the Americas* Santo Domingo (Dominican Rep) 2012. **Publications** *Marco Normative Migratorio en el Continente Americano: una Mirada desde el Género* (2015); *Access of Women to a Life Free of Violence* (2012); *Women of the Americas* (2012).
Members Parliamentary assemblies of the unitary, federal, federated and associated States, regional parliaments and interparliamentary organizations in 35 countries:
Antigua-Barbuda, Argentina, Bahamas, Barbados, Belize, Bolivia, Brazil, Canada, Chile, Colombia, Costa Rica, Cuba, Dominica, Dominican Rep, Ecuador, El Salvador, Grenada, Guatemala, Guyana, Haiti, Honduras, Jamaica, Mexico, Nicaragua, Panama, Paraguay, Peru, St Kitts-Nevis, St Lucia, St Vincent-Grenadines, Suriname, Trinidad-Tobago, Uruguay, USA, Venezuela.
NGO Relations Observer status with: *Inter-Parliamentary Union (IPU, #15961)* (through membership to Executive Committee of COPA). [2016.10.21/XF6243/F]

♦ Network of Women Sex Workers from Latin America and the Caribbean (#18731)

♦ Network for Young Nordic Neutron Scatterers (NYNNeS) 17066

Address not obtained.
Aims Enable young, active neutron scientists to establish and grow new groups; increase competence within the Nordic/Baltic region. **Activities** Awareness raising; events/meetings. **Events** *Meeting* Copenhagen (Denmark) 2018, *Meeting* Uppsala (Sweden) 2017. [2018/XM7560/c/F]

♦ Network for Young Researchers in Andrology (NYRA) 17067

Sec address not obtained.
URL: http://nyra-youngresearch.eu/
History Set up Apr 2006, Germany, as *International Network for Young Researchers in Male Fertility*. **Aims** Establish global networks between young (early stage) scientists in testicular research; promote cooperation and mutual exchange of methodologies and expertise. **Structure** Board. **Activities** Knowledge management/ information dissemination; events/meetings. **Events** *Meeting* Brussels (Belgium) 2017. **Publications** *NYRA Newsletter*. **Members** Individuals. Membership countries not specified. **NGO Relations** Member of: *International Society of Andrology (ISA, #14918)*. [2018/XM6661/v/F]

♦ Netzer Olami – International Progressive Zionist Youth Movement (Netzer Olami) 17068

Headquarters 6 Eliyahu Shamah St, Beit Shmuel, 9410806 Jerusalem, Israel. T. +97226203447. Fax +97226203525. E-mail: wupjis@wupj.org.il.
USA Office 633 Third Ave, 7th fl, New York NY 10017-6778, USA. E-mail: wupj@wupj.org.
URL: http://www.netzerolami.org/
History 1979, South Africa and Australia. **Aims** Offer opportunities to, and challenge for *young people* from Reform, Progressive, Liberal and Reconstructionist communities. **Languages** English, French, German, Hebrew, Russian, Spanish. **Staff** 7.00 FTE, paid. **Finance** Members' dues. Other sources: private grants and allocations. **Activities** Promotes: repairing the world; reform Zionism; pluralistic Judaism; Jewish unity; social justice; centrality of the state of Israel in Jewish life; equality in general and especially in Jewish life; the importance of dignity for all human beings; tolerance and respect for one another; care for the environment. Programmes include: Schnat Netzer – 10-month leadership training programme for young adults in Israel; sending long-term Schlichim to support Netzer Snifim; sending short-term Schlichim. Founded *'TaMaR – Tnuat Magshimim Reformit'* – Movement for Reform Fulfillers, 1997, aimed at young adults (18-30). Organizes: annual World Conference (always in Jerusalem, Israel); annual TaMaR Conference, always in Israel; annual Netzer Festival; Special Snifim Programmes and Visits to Israel. **Events** *Annual World Conference* Jerusalem (Israel) 2011, *Annual leadership conference / Annual World Conference* Jerusalem (Israel) 2001, *Annual leadership conference* 2000, *Annual World Conference* Jerusalem (Israel) 2000, *Annual World Conference* Jerusalem (Israel) 1999. **Publications** *Booklet on Jewish Literature*. *Jewish Library*. Curriculum handbook. Reform Zionist Activity Kit.
Members Affiliate branches and individuals in 6 countries:
Brazil, Canada, Israel, Panama, South Africa, USA.
NGO Relations Affiliated with: *ARZENU – International Federation of Reform and Progressive Religious Zionists (ARZENU, #01129)*; *World Union for Progressive Judaism (WUPJ, #21883)*. [2019/XF3725/F]

♦ **Netzer Olami** Netzer Olami – International Progressive Zionist Youth Movement (#17068)
♦ Netz der Europäischen Ballungs-und Grossräume (#17023)
♦ Netzkraft Movement ! (internationally oriented national body)
♦ Netzwerk von Abgeordneten für Nukleare Abrüstung (#18210)
♦ Netzwerk Afrika Deutschland (internationally oriented national body)
♦ Netzwerk Afrika Deutschland "Glaube und Gerechtigkeit" / see Netzwerk Afrika Deutschland
♦ Netzwerk Arbeit und Wirtschaft in den Europäischen Kirchen (#21051)
♦ Netzwerk der Europäischen Esskultur (#17012)
♦ Netzwerk der Europäischen Vereinigungen für Personzentrierte Beratung und Psychotherapie / see Network of the European Associations for Person-Centred and Experiential Psychotherapy and Counselling (#17013)
♦ Netzwerk Europäischer Eisenbahnen (internationally oriented national body)
♦ Netzwerk Europäischer Verbände für Personzentrierte und Experienzielle Psychotherapie und Beratung (#17013)
♦ Netzwerk Friedenskooperative (internationally oriented national body)
♦ Netzwerk Glia (#17032)
♦ Netzwerk Gliaforschung / see Network Glia (#17032)
♦ Netzwerk für Osteuropa-Berichterstattung (internationally oriented national body)
♦ Netzwerk der schuw-lesbischen Fussball Fanclubs Europas (internationally oriented national body)
♦ Netzwerk für Stadtforschung in der Europäischen Union (#17062)
♦ **NEUBIAS** Network of EUropean BioImage AnalystS (#17014)
♦ Neue Bachgesellschaft (#17076)
♦ Neue Kriminologische Gesellschaft / see Kriminologische Gesellschaft (#16209)
♦ **NEUMOFEDECA** Federación Centroamericana y del Caribe de Neumologia y Cirugia de Tórax (#09296)

♦ Neural Information Processing Systems Foundation (NIPS) 17069

Contact 10010 North Torrey Pines Rd, La Jolla CA 92037, USA. T. +18584531623. Fax +18585870417. E-mail: info@nips.cc.
URL: http://www.nips.cc/
Aims Foster the exchange of research on neural information processing systems in their biological, technological, mathematical, and theoretical aspects. **Structure** Board; Committees. **Activities** Events/meetings. **Events** *Neural Information Processing Systems Conference* New Orleans, LA (USA) 2022, *Conference on Neural Information Processing System (NIPS 2021)* Sydney, NSW (Australia) 2021, *Neural Information Processing Systems Conference* Vancouver, BC (Canada) 2019, *Annual Conference* Montréal, QC (Canada) 2018, *Annual Conference* Long Beach, CA (USA) 2017. [2015/XJ9682/f/F]

♦ Neural Simulation Technology Initiative (NEST Initiative) 17070

Pres Fac of Science and Technology, Norwegian Univ of Life Sciences, PO Box 5003, 1432 Ås, Norway.
URL: http://www.nest-initiative.org/
History Statutes adopted Oct 2012. Since 2012, registered in accordance with Swiss Civil Code. **Aims** Further science and research, especially in the field of simulation technology in the neurosciences. **Structure** General Assembly; Board of Directors. **Finance** Members' dues. **Events** *Conference* Ås (Norway) 2019, *Conference* Ås (Norway) 2018. [2019/XM8047/F]

♦ The Neurocritical Care / see Neurocritical Care Society
♦ Neurocritical Care Society (internationally oriented national body)
♦ Neurodegeneration with Brain Iron Accumulation / see NBIA Alliance (#16961)
♦ Neurofibromatosis Patients United / see NF Patients United (#17100)
♦ Neuro Linguistic Programming / see International Association of NLP Institutes (#12050)

♦ Neuromarketing Science and Business Association (NMSBA) 17071

Exec Dir Stalbergweg 58, 5913 BS Venlo, Netherlands. T. +31777850090. E-mail: office@ nmsba.com.
URL: http://www.nmsba.com/
History Officially launched 2 Feb 2012. **Aims** Provide professional support to neuromarketers and neuromarketing scientists around the world. **Structure** Board. Local Chairs. **Finance** Sources: members' dues. **Events** *World Forum* Los Angeles, CA (USA) 2020, *World Forum* Singapore (Singapore) 2018, *World Forum* London (UK) 2017, *World Forum* Dubai (United Arab Emirates) 2016, *World Forum* Amsterdam (Netherlands) 2012. **Publications** *Neuromarketing, Theory and Practice* – magazine.
Members Representatives in 23 countries:
Argentina, Australia, Belgium, Brazil, Canada, China, Colombia, Denmark, France, Germany, Italy, Japan, Mexico, Netherlands, Panama, Peru, Poland, Portugal, Romania, Spain, Türkiye, UK, USA. [2021/XJ5234/C]

♦ Neurootológiai és Equilibriometriai Társaság (#17072)

♦ Neurootological and Equilibriometric Society (NES) 17072

Neurootológiai és Equilibriometriai Társaság (NES)
Pres Semmelweis ORL Surgery, Szigony u 36, Budapest 1083, Hungary. Fax +3613333316.
URL: http://www.nesbasisbudapest.hu/
History 25 May 1974, Würzburg (Germany). Reestablished in Hungary, 2015. Registration: Fővárosi Törvényszék, No/ID: 01-02-0015961, Start date: 28 Aug 2015, Hungary; Start date: 20 Jun 1974, End date: 2015, Germany. **Aims** Promote clinical neurootology in practice and in the field of clinical research; inform doctors and paramedical personnel interested in neurootological diagnosis, paying special attention to tests of functional equilibrium; standardize clinical methods of research and research equipment in the field of neurootology; create functional anthropometric standards (normal values and pathological values) in the field of neurootological testing; prepare expert opinion on clinically proven neurootological malfunctions; develop selection principles for employee recruitment in the fields where functional strain particularly effects neurootological functions of the senses; enable participation, with the help of neurootological and medical viewpoints, in the development of new transport technology and other technologies, where disorientation strain occurs. **Structure** Managing Board. **Languages** English, French, German, Spanish. **Activities** Events/meetings; knowledge management/information dissemination; research and development; standards/ guidelines; training/education. **Events** *Annual Congress* Budapest (Hungary) 2022, *Annual Congress* Paphos (Cyprus) 2021, *Annual Congress* Budapest (Hungary) 2020, *Annual Congress* Tokyo (Japan) 2019, *Annual Congress* Kiev (Ukraine) 2018. **Publications** *Journal of Neurootology* in English – https://happyvertigo.com/. **Members** Medical doctors and technical experts. Membership countries not specified. [2022/XF1219/v/F]

♦ Neurosciences in Intensive Care International Symposium (meeting series)
♦ Neuros du monde (internationally oriented national body)
♦ Neurosurgical Society of Australasia (internationally oriented national body)
♦ Neurosurgical Society of East and Central Africa (no recent information)
♦ The Neurotoxicity Society / see Neurotoxicity Society (#17073)

♦ Neurotoxicity Society (NTS) 17073

Treas 3819 Jones Ferry Rd, Chapel Hill NC 27516-9381, USA.
Sec address not obtained.
URL: https://www.neurotoxicitysociety.org/
History 2001, Pucón (Chile). Founded at the *Neurotoxicity as a Mechanism for Neurodegenerative Disorders: Basic and Clinical Aspects* meeting, following discussions initiated in 1998. Former names and other names: *The Neurotoxicity Society* – full title. **Aims** Unite basic and clinical scientists in the Neurotoxicity. **Structure** Council. **Finance** Sources: members' dues. **Activities** Events/meetings; training/education. **Events** *Meeting* Punta Arenas (Chile) 2022, *Meeting* Punta Arenas (Chile) 2021, *Meeting* Florianópolis (Brazil) 2017, *Meeting* Cuenca (Spain) 2015, *Meeting* Valdivia (Chile) 2013. **NGO Relations** Cooperates with (2): *Federation of European Neuroscience Societies (FENS, #09522)*; *Society for Neuroscience (SfN)*. [2022/AA3184/C]

♦ Neutrons and Food – International Conference on Neutrons and Food (meeting series)
♦ NEVC – Nordic Equine Veterinary Conference (meeting series)
♦ Never Again International (unconfirmed)
♦ Nevin Scrimshaw International Nutrition Foundation (internationally oriented national body)
♦ NEVSO – Network of European Voluntary Service Organisations (unconfirmed)
♦ **NEVZA** Northern European Volleyball Zonal Association (#17591)

♦ New Acropolis International / see International Organization New Acropolis (#14458)
♦ New Africa Initiative (no recent information)
♦ New African Research and Development Agency (internationally oriented national body)

♦ New Agenda Coalition (NAC) 17074

Contact Department of Foreign Affairs, 80 St Stephen's Green, Dublin, CO. DUBLIN, Ireland. T. +35314780822. Fax +35314780593.

History Jun 1998, Dublin (Ireland). Address concerns related to the implementation of *Comprehensive Nuclear-Test-Ban Treaty (CTBT, 1996)*. **Aims** Work towards total elimination of nuclear weapons worldwide. **Structure** No formal constitution or permanenent secretariat; a Ministerial-level group of states.
Members Governments of 6 countries:
Brazil, Egypt, Ireland, Mexico, New Zealand, South Africa. [2018/XF5901/F*]

♦ New Alliance for Food Security and Nutrition 17075

Address not obtained.

History May 2012, by *Group of Eight (G-8, #10745)* and African leaders, with the support of *International Bank for Reconstruction and Development (IBRD, #12317)*, *African Development Bank (ADB, #00283)*, *World Food Programme (WFP, #21510)*, *International Fund for Agricultural Development (IFAD, #13692)* and *FAO (#09260)*. **Aims** Increase responsible domestic and foreign private investments in African agriculture; take innovations that can enhance agricultural productivity to scale; reduce the risk borne by vulnerable economies and communities. [2012/XJ5629/E*]

♦ New Asia Forum (internationally oriented national body)
♦ New Asia Forum towards an Asian Economic Community / see New Asia Forum

♦ New Bach Society, International Union 17076

Neue Bachgesellschaft

President Haus der Kirche, Burgstrasse 1-5, 04109 Leipzig, Germany. T. +493419601463. Fax +493412248182. E-mail: info@neue-bachgesellschaft.de.
Street Address Burgstrasse 1-5, 04109 Leipzig, Germany.
URL: http://www.neue-bachgesellschaft.de/

History 27 Jan 1900, Leipzig (Germany), succeeding *Bachgesellschaft*. Current by-laws approved 1962. **Aims** Make the complete works of *Johann Sebastian Bach* further available to the public and encourage the support of this *musical heritage* throughout the world. **Structure** Executive Committee of 6 members; Directorate of 24 members. **Languages** German. **Staff** 1.00 FTE, paid. **Finance** Members' dues. **Activities** Organizes Bach Festivals with concerts and scholarly discussions in different places (annually); discusses scholarly and practical questions which arise in connection with Bach's work; publishing activity. **Events** *General Assembly* Leipzig (Germany) 2011. **Publications** *Mitteilungsblatt* (2 a year); *Bach-Jahrbuch* (annual).
Members Individual; Married couples; Student; Corporative. Members in 31 countries:
Andorra, Argentina, Australia, Austria, Belgium, Canada, Chile, Czechia, Denmark, Finland, France, Germany, Greece, Hungary, India, Ireland, Israel, Italy, Japan, Korea Rep, Luxembourg, Netherlands, New Zealand, Norway, Poland, Russia, Spain, Sweden, Switzerland, UK, USA. [2011.08.16/XE5894/E]

♦ New Call to Peacemaking (internationally oriented national body)

♦ New Car Assessment Programme for Latin America and the Caribbean (Latin NCAP) 17077

Programa de Evaluación de Vehiculos Nuevos para América Latina y el Caribe – Programa de Avaliação de Carros Novos para América Latina e o Caribe

Contact Joaquin Nuñez 2719 Of 210, CP 11300 Montevideo, Uruguay. T. +59827158749. E-mail: secretaria@latinncap.com.
URL: http://www.latinncap.com/

History Set up 2010 as a joint initiative. Became a regular association 2014. **Aims** Provide consumers across the Latin American and Caribbean region with independent and impartial safety assessment of new cars; encourage manufacturers to improve the safety performance of the vehicles they offer for sale in the region; encourage governments across the region to apply UN vehicle crash test regulations to passenger cars. **Structure** Board of Directors; Control Board. **Finance** Major sponsors: *Inter-American Development Bank (IDB, #11427)*; Bloomberg Philanthropies; *FIA Foundation (#09742)*; *Global New Car Assessment Programme (Global NCAP, #10506)*; *International Consumer Research and Testing (ICRT, #12931)*.
Members Active in 10 countries:
Argentina, Bolivia, Brazil, Chile, Colombia, Costa Rica, Mexico, Portugal, Spain, Uruguay.
Included in the above, 3 organizations:
Federación Iberoamericana de Asociaciones de Victimas contra la Violencia Vial (FICVI, #09307); *Fédération Internationale de l'Automobile (FIA, #09613)* (Region IV); *International Consumer Research and Testing (ICRT, #12931)*. [2016/XM5015/y/F]

♦ New Car Assessment Program for Southeast Asian Countries (ASEAN NCAP) 17078

SG Malaysian Inst of Road Safety Research, Lot 125-135, Jalan TKS 1, Taman Kajang Sentral, 43000 Kajang, Selangor, Malaysia. E-mail: enquiries@aseancap.org.
URL: http://www.aseancap.org/

History Dec 2011. Founded by Malaysian Institute of Road Safety Research (MIROS) and *Global New Car Assessment Programme (Global NCAP, #10506)*. **Aims** Elevate vehicle safety standards, raise consumer awareness and thus encourage a market for safer vehicles in the region. **Structure** Steering Committee; Technical Committee; Working Groups. **Languages** English. **Staff** 5.00 FTE, paid. **Activities** Awareness raising; events/meetings; monitoring/evaluation; research/documentation. **Events** *ASEAN Automobile Safety Forum* Japan 2020, *ASEAN Automobile Safety Forum* Bali (Indonesia) 2019, *ASEAN Automobile Safety Forum* Manila (Philippines) 2017, *ASEAN Automobile Safety Forum* Ho Chi Minh City (Vietnam) 2016, *ASEAN Automobile Safety Forum* Phnom Penh (Cambodia) 2016. **Publications** Test results.
Members Organizations in 6 countries:
Cambodia, Malaysia, Philippines, Singapore, Thailand, Vietnam. [2020.05.07/XM5014/F]

♦ New Chaucer Society 17079

Exec Dir Dept of English, Washington Univ, One Brookings Drive, Box 1122, St Louis MO 63130, USA. T. +13149354407. Fax +13149359455.
URL: http://artsci.wustl.edu/~chaucer/

Aims Provide a forum for teachers and scholars of Geoffrey Chaucer and his age. **Events** *Biennial Congress* Toronto, ON (Canada) 2018, *Biennial Congress* London (UK) 2016, *Biennial Congress* Reykjavik (Iceland) 2014, *Biennial Congress* Portland, OR (USA) 2012, *Biennial Congress* Siena (Italy) 2010. **Publications** *Studies in the Age of Chaucer* (annual).
Members Individuals in 20 countries:
Australia, Belgium, Canada, Czechia, Finland, France, Germany, Ireland, Israel, Italy, Japan, Korea Rep, Netherlands, Portugal, Singapore, Spain, Switzerland, UK, USA. [2014/XE3389/E]

♦ NewCities Foundation (NCF) 17080

Exec Dir Case postale 8888, succursale Centre-ville, Bureau R-4150, Montréal QC H3C 3P8, Canada. E-mail: contact@newcities.org – manderson@newcitiesfoundation.org – contact@newcitiesfoundation.org.
Street Address Pavillon des Sciences de la gestion, bureau R-4150, 315 Rue Sainte-Catherien Est, Montréal QC H2X 3X2, Canada.
URL: http://www.newcitiesfoundation.org/

History 2010, by John Rossant. Launched 2011. Registered as a non-profit organization in Canada, Switzerland and USA. **Aims** Incubate, promote and scale urban innovations through collaborative partnerships between government, business, academia and civil society. **Structure** Members' Meeting (annual); Board of Directors; Board of Trustees. **Finance** Members' dues. **Events** *Wellbeing Cities Forum* Montréal, QC (Canada) 2019, *Summit* Montréal, QC (Canada) 2016, *Summit* Dallas, TX (USA) 2014, *The human city* Sao Paulo (Brazil) 2013, *Summit* Paris (France) 2012. **Members** Founding; Corporate; Academic and Non-Profit. Membership countries not specified. [2019/XJ7464/f/F]

♦ New Commonwealth Society (inactive)
♦ A New Course (internationally oriented national body)
♦ A New Course – Engaging Rural Women to Reduce Poverty and Environmental Degradation / see A New Course

♦ New Development Bank (NDB) 17081

Headquarters 32-36 Floors, BRICS Tower, 333 Lujiazui Ring Road, Pudong Area, 200120 Shanghai, China. E-mail: info@ndb.int.
URL: https://www.ndb.int/

History Jul 2014, Fortaleza (Brazil). Proposed 2012, New Delhi (India), at 4th *BRICS (#03325)* Summit. Established when Articles of Agreement signed July 2014; Articles entered into force July 2015. Became fully operational 27 Feb 2016. **Aims** Support infrastructure and sustainable development efforts in BRICS and other underserved, emerging economies for faster development through innovation and cutting-edge technology. **Structure** Board of Governors; Board of Directors; Senior Management. Committees. **Events** *Meeting* Shanghai (China) 2021, *Meeting* Shanghai (China) 2020, *Meeting* Cape Town (South Africa) 2019.
Members Governments (5):
Brazil, China, India, Russia, South Africa.
IGO Relations Observer status with (1): *United Nations (UN, #20515)* (General Assembly). Memorandum of Understanding with (2): *African Development Bank (ADB, #00283)*; *FAO (#09260)*. [2020/AA1016/E*]

♦ New Development Centre, Vecchiano (internationally oriented national body)
♦ NEWE / see International Instrument Users' Association – WIB

♦ New Economics Foundation (NEF) 17082

Chief Exec 10 Salamanca Place, London, SE1 7HB, UK. T. +442078206300. E-mail: info@neweconomics.org.
Head of News address not obtained.
URL: http://www.neweconomics.org/

History 1986. Grew out of *The Other Economic Summit (TOES, no recent information)* UK. Registration: Charity, No/ID: 1055254, England and Wales; EU Transparency Register, No/ID: 112607048208-13, Start date: 16 Dec 2022. **Aims** Work for a new model of wealth creation, which is human scale, socially inclusive and ecologically sustainable. undertake educational work at all levels in the development and promotion of a New Economics geared to the overall welfare of people and the planet now and in the future. **Structure** Committee of Management; Secretariat. **Languages** English. **Staff** 1.80 FTE, paid. **Finance** Sources: contributions; donations; fees for services; grants. **Activities** Events/meetings; guidance/assistance/consulting; politics/policy/regulatory; research/documentation. **Events** *International seminar* London (UK) 1994, *The other European summit* Edinburgh (UK) 1992, *Health, well-being and faith in the 21st century* London (UK) 1989. **Publications** *Radical Economics* – newspaper. Annual Review; electronic newsletter; research reports; workbooks; resource packs.
Members NEF supporters, mostly in the UK, but in a total of 28 countries and territories:
Australia, Burundi, Canada, Chile, Czechia, France, Germany, Hungary, India, Ireland, Italy, Kenya, Malaysia, Mexico, Netherlands, New Zealand, Nigeria, Norway, Philippines, Poland, Portugal, Spain, Sweden, Switzerland, Taiwan, UK, USA, Zambia.
Members also in the former USSR. Membership countries not specified.
NGO Relations Member of (2): *Jubilee Research (#16158)*; *Wellbeing Economy Alliance (WEAll, #20856)*. Cooperates with (1): *Economy for the Common Good (ECG, #05323)*. [2022/XF0548/f/F]

♦ New Education Fellowship / see World Education Fellowship (#21370)
♦ New Energy Industry Association for Asia and the Pacific (internationally oriented national body)
♦ New Energy World IG – fuel cells and hydrogen for sustainability / see Hydrogen Europe (#10998)
♦ New Energy World Industry Grouping / see Hydrogen Europe (#10998)
♦ New European Association (unconfirmed)
♦ New European Business Confederation (unconfirmed)

♦ New European Media (NEM Initiative) 17083

Secretariat Eurescom GmbH, Wieblinger Weg 19/4, 69123 Heidelberg, Germany. T. +4962219890. E-mail: contact@nem-initiative.org.
URL: http://nem-initiative.org/

History Set up as one of the European Industrial Initiatives, also known as Technology Platforms, established by relevant key European stakeholders, which address the convergence of media, communications, consumer electronics and IT as a wide opportunity for future growth. Original title: *Networked and Electronic Media Initiative (NEM Initiative)*. **Aims** Deal with connected, converging and interactive media and creative industries to drive the future of digital experience. **Structure** General Assembly (2 a year); Steering Board; Executive Group; Annual Summit. **Languages** English. **Activities** Knowledge management/information dissemination. **Events** *Summit* Heidelberg (Germany) 2021, *Summit* Heidelberg (Germany) 2020, *Summit* Zagreb (Croatia) 2019, *Summit* Madrid (Spain) 2017, *Summit* Porto (Portugal) 2016. **Publications** *NEM Vision*; *Strategic Research and Innovation Agenda*. Position papers. **Members** Relevant stakeholders world-wide. Membership countries not specified. **IGO Relations** *European Commission (EC, #06633)*. **NGO Relations** Member of: *European Alliance for Innovation (EAI, #05872)*. [2018/XJ1912/E]

♦ New European Surgical Academy (NESA) 17084

Contact Unter den Linden 21, 10117 Berlin, Germany. T. +493023910916 – +491749923614. E-mail: office@nesacademy.org.
URL: http://www.nesacademy.org/

History 29 Oct 2004, Berlin (Germany). **Aims** Increase re-evaluation of existing surgical procedures and optimizing and rationalizing where necessary; promote introduction of new surgical procedures and ideas; increase know-how sharing and transfer to countries with limited resources. **Structure** Executive Board; Advisory Board; International Board. **Activities** Events/meetings. **Events** *Days* Berlin (Germany) 2015, *NESA Days* Crete (Greece) 2014, *NESA Days* Palma (Spain) 2012, *NESA Days* Athens (Greece) 2009, *LASER FLORENCE : international congress on laser medicine* Florence (Italy) 2009. **Publications** *NESA Newsletter*. **Members** Full in 56 countries. Membership countries not specified. **IGO Relations** Cooperation agreement with: *WHO (#20950)*. **NGO Relations** Cooperation agreement with national organizations. [2021.09.07/XM2050/E]

♦ New Europe College, Bucharest (internationally oriented national body)
♦ New Europe Group (inactive)

♦ New Families Movement 17085

Mouvement des familles nouvelles – Movimento Famiglie Nuove

Secretariat Via Isonzo 64, Grottaferrata, 00046 Rome RM, Italy. T. +3969411565. Fax +3969411614. E-mail: famiglienuove@focolare.org.
URL: http://www.famiglienuove.org/

History 1967, by Chiara Lubich, as a branch of *Focolare Movement (#09806)*. A broad-based movement arising from the married *Focolarini*, married people living in their own homes but attached to Focolare communities. **Aims** Within organized groups and by personal contact: revitalize and refresh the *love* which is the foundation of each couple so as to renew unity and lead to benefits both for the education of children and for society; pay particular attention to those who *suffer* or find themselves in difficult situations – orphans, the divorced, the elderly, refugees, migrants, the handicapped, the terminally ill. **Structure** Organized in local groups linked by sharing of experience. Focolare families may move to another country to support a community developing in Focolare spirituality. Central secretariat. **Finance** Members' dues. **Activities** Functions as an aid/development agency, training centre and congress organizer. Organizes international adoptions and distance support (distance adoptions). **Events** *International conference* Rome (Italy) 1998, *European meeting of study and dialogue on the family* Bolzano (Italy) 1996, *International conference* Rome (Italy) 1993. **Members** A total of 300,000 people active in over 160 countries. Membership countries not specified. **IGO Relations** *European Commission (EC, #06633)*; *United Nations Human Settlements Programme (UN-Habitat, #20572)*; UN Secretariat for the International Year of the Family and UN Division for the Advancement of Women, New York NY (USA). [2018/XF6844/F]

♦ New Field Foundation (internationally oriented national body)

♦ New Football Federations-Board / see N.F.-Board (#17099)
♦ New Forests Fund / see New Forests Project
♦ New Forests Project (internationally oriented national body)
♦ New Forum / see Wassenaar Arrangement on Export Controls for Conventional Arms and Dual-Use Goods and Technologies (#20819)

♦ Newfrontiers 17086

Contact 21 Meadowcourt Road, Lee, London, SE3 9EU, UK. T. +442033974753. E-mail: office@newfrontierstogether.org.
URL: http://www.newfrontierstogether.org/

History Founded 1981, by Terry Virgo, as *Coastlands*. Subsequently changed title to *New Frontiers International Trust* Ltd. UK Registered Charity: 1060001. **Aims** As a worldwide family of *churches*: restore the church; promote New Testament vision and values; train leaders; make disciples of Jesus Christ; start new churches; take the *Christian* Gospel to the nations. **Languages** English. **Staff** None. **Finance** Voluntary contributions. **Activities** Training/education; events/meetings. **Events** *Conference* Brighton (UK) 1995. **Members** Churches (over 850) which have built personal relationships between leaders of the church and apostolic ministry, based in 60 countries. (not specified). **NGO Relations** Member of: *Global Connections*. [2018/XN6865/F]

♦ New Frontiers International Trust / see Newfrontiers (#17086)

♦ The New Humanitarian 17087

Dir Rue de Varembé 3, 1202 Geneva, Switzerland. T. +41225256603. E-mail: hello@thenewhumanitarian.org.
URL: https://www.thenewhumanitarian.org/

History 1995. Founded by *United Nations (UN, #20515)*, in the wake of the Rwandan genocide. Former names and other names: *IRIN News* – former (1995 to 2019). **Aims** Produce fact-based journalism from the heart of conflicts and disasters to build understanding of how to improve the lives of the millions of people affected by humanitarian crises around the world. **Structure** Board of Directors. **Finance** Sources: government support; private foundations. Further support from Australia, Belgium, Canada, Denmark, Germany, Luxembourg, Norway, Switzerland, as well as the Service de la solidarité internationale (Canton of Geneva, Switzerland), IKEA Foundation, and The Patrick J McGovern Foundation. Supported by: *Bill and Melinda Gates Foundation (BMGF)*; *David and Lucile Packard Foundation*; *Humanity United*; *Netherlands Refugee Foundation*; *Open Society Foundations (OSF, #17763)*; *Swedish International Development Cooperation Agency (Sida)*. **Activities** Events/meetings; knowledge management/information dissemination; publishing activities. **Publications** News reports; field reportage; in-depth analysis; investigations; multimedia packages; daily and weekly newsletters. **NGO Relations** Also links with national organizations. [2022.05.09/AA0048/F]

♦ New Humanity 17088

Pres Via Piave 15, Grottaferrata, 00046 Rome RM, Italy. T. +39694315635. E-mail: info@new-humanity.org.
URL: http://www.new-humanity.org/

History 1987. Founded as a broad-based movement within *Focolare Movement (#09806)*, arising from the section of Volunteers, men and women living in their own homes but totally sharing the spirituality of the Focolare. Former names and other names: *New Humanity Movement* – former; *Mouvement humanité nouvelle* – former; *Movimento Umanità Nuova* – former; *New Humanity International Association* – full title (2005). **Aims** Contribute to the creation of unity in the human family, fully respecting the individual identities of all of its members. **Structure** Headquarters in Rome (Italy); Offices in Geneva (Switzerland), New York NY (USA), Paris (France), Brussels (Belgium), Nairobi (Kenya) and Vienna (Austria). **Languages** English, Italian. **Staff** 3.00 FTE, voluntary. **Finance** Voluntary contributions from members. **Activities** Networking/liaising. **Events** *United World Week Workshop* Brussels (Belgium) 2021, *Congress* Rome (Italy) 2008, *Congress* Trento (Italy) 2005, *A society for all ages – the elderly as a resource for a united world* Rimini (Italy) 1997, *Congress* Rome (Italy) 1983. **Members** Active in over 100 countries and territories. Membership countries not specified. **Consultative Status** Consultative status granted from: *ECOSOC (#05331)* (General); *UNESCO (#20322)* (Consultative Status). **NGO Relations** Member of (1): *Forum of Catholic Inspired NGOs (#09905)*. Instrumental in setting up (2): *International Bureau of Economy and Work (inactive)*; *Youth for a United World (YUW, see: #09806)*. [2021.09.02/XF6839/E]

♦ New Humanity Group (internationally oriented national body)
♦ New Humanity International Association / see New Humanity (#17088)
♦ New Humanity Movement / see New Humanity (#17088)

♦ New Human Rights – International 17089

Nouveaux droits de l'homme – International (NDH) – Nuevos Derechos del Hombre – Nuovi Diritti dell' Uomo – Internazionale

NDH France 9 rue de Verneuil, 75007 Paris, France. T. +33147537878. E-mail: contact.ndh@gmail.com.
1NDH Head Office Combate de los Pozos 59, Piso 3 – Of 20, 1079 Buenos Aires, Argentina.
URL: http://www.ndh-france.org/

History 1977, Paris (France). **Aims** Fight for the promotion, protection and vogue of Human Rights. **Structure** High Commission. Executive Committee, comprising President, 2 Vice-Presidents, Secretary, Assistant Secretary, Treasurer and 4 members. **Finance** Members' dues. **Activities** Organizes conferences and interviews to national authorities. Maintains a library. **Publications** *Noticias* (4 a year); *Arc-en-ciel* (3 a year).
Members Organizations in 5 countries:
Argentina, Cameroon, France, Italy, Lebanon.
Consultative Status Consultative status granted from: *ECOSOC (#05331)* (Special). **IGO Relations** Associated with Department of Global Communications of the United Nations. [2018/XF4591/F]

♦ NEW-IG / see Hydrogen Europe (#10998)
♦ New Internationalist (internationally oriented national body)
♦ New Israel Fund (internationally oriented national body)
♦ New Jihad Group / see Al-Jihad (#00637)
♦ New Life International (internationally oriented national body)
♦ New Life Movement / see New Humanity Group
♦ NEW – Namur-Europe-Wallonie (internationally oriented national body)

♦ NewOpera 17090

Admin Rue Montoyer 31, 1000 Brussels, Belgium. T. +3225541200. Fax +3225541201. E-mail: newopera@newopera.org – giuseppe.rizzi@newopera.org.
URL: http://www.newopera.org/

History 1 Jan 2005, as a project running until 31 Jun 2008, following which an international non profit organization was set up. OPERA stands for *Operating Project for a European Rail Network*. Registered in accordance with Belgian law. Registration: AISBL/IVZW, Belgium. **Aims** Promote, defend and disseminate in Europe the dedicated Rail *Freight* Network Approach. **Structure** General Meeting; Management Board; Special Working Groups. **Events** *General Meeting* Brussels (Belgium) 2012, *General Meeting* Brussels (Belgium) 2011. **Members** Effective; Adherent; Sponsor; Honorary. Organizations include the following 2 listed in this Yearbook: *Community of European Railway and Infrastructure Companies (CER, #04396)*; *European Freight and Logistics Leaders Forum (F and L, #07359)*.
IGO Relations *European Commission (EC, #06633)*. [2019/XJ5631/y/E]

♦ New Partnership for African Development / see New Partnership for Africa's Development (#17091)

♦ New Partnership for Africa's Development (NEPAD) 17091

Mailing address PO Box 1234, Halfway House, Midrand, Johannesburg, 1685, South Africa.
Headquarters International Business Gateway, New Road and 6th Road, Midridge Office Park – c/o Challenger and Columbia Avenue – Block B, Midrand, Johannesburg, 1685, South Africa. T. +27112563600. Fax +27112063762. E-mail: jacintan@nepad.org – media@nepad.org.
URL: http://www.nepad.org/

History 23 Oct 2001, Nigeria, as a mandated initiative of *African Union (AU, #00488)*, on finalizing policy framework of *New Africa Initiative (NAI, no recent information)*, at a meeting of African leaders to promote trade and sound economic management. Derives from merger, finalized 3 Jul 2001, of: *Millennium Partnership for the African Recovery Programme (MAP)*, set up following decisions of Extraordinary Summit of *Organization of African Unity (OAU, inactive)*, Sep 1999, Sirte (Libyan AJ); *Omega Plan for Africa* of President Abdoulaye Wade of Senegal, OAU Summit, Jul 2000, Togo. NEPAD is sometimes referred to as *New Partnership for African Development*. *NEPAD Declaration of Good Governance* and NEPAD Plan of Action approved, 10 Jul 2002, Durban, at launch of the African Union. **Aims** Reverse Africa's economic decline and create stability and growth, with the target of more than doubling African *economic output* and sustaining those increased levels for the next 15 years; encourage funding to encourage *trade* within Africa and promote sound economic management; strengthen inter-African cooperation and *integration*; work to overcome *poverty* and achieve better *living standards* for all the peoples of Africa. Encourage African leaders to take joint responsibility for: strengthening mechanisms for *conflict prevention*, management and resolution at sub-regional and continental levels; promoting and protecting democracy and human rights; developing clear standards of accountability, transparency and participatory *governance* at national and subnational levels; building capacity of African states to set and enforce the legal framework and to maintain law and order. **Structure** Task Force for the implementation of NEPAD, set up 23 Oct 2001, Abuja (Nigeria) – Heads of State and Government Implementation Committee (meeting 3 times a year) comprises 3 states per region, including the 5 initiating states (South Africa, Nigeria, Algeria, Senegal and Egypt). Current representation: North Africa – Algeria, Egypt, Tunisia; West Africa – Nigeria, Senegal, Mali; Central Africa – Cameroon, Gabon, Sao Tomé-Principe; East Africa – Ethiopia, Mauritius, Rwanda; Southern Africa – South Africa, Botswana, Mozambique. It also includes (ex officio) Chairs of AU and its Commission. It reports annually to AU Summit. Steering Committee, composed of personal representatives of the 5 initiating Presidents, develops programme and project terms of reference and oversees Secretariat, based at *Development Bank of Southern Africa (DBSA)*. Task teams (5) identify and prepare specific projects and programmes. Includes: *African Ministers' Council on Water (AMCOW, #00376)*. **Activities** Initiatives; projects. **Events** *High Level Working Session on Banning Plastics in Africa* Addis Ababa (Ethiopia) 2019, *Session* Addis Ababa (Ethiopia) 2019, *SFSA : Science Forum South Africa* Pretoria (South Africa) 2017, *SFSA : Science Forum South Africa* Pretoria (South Africa) 2016, *SFSA : Science Forum South Africa* Pretoria (South Africa) 2015. **IGO Relations** Close relations with: *Southern African Development Community (SADC, #19843)*, especially through SADC Regional Indicative Strategic Development Plan (RISDP); *World Trade Organization (WTO, #21864)*. Formal relations with: *INFOSA (#11203)*. Observer to: *International Fund for Agricultural Development (IFAD, #13692)*; *Infrastructure Consortium for Africa (ICA, #11206)*. Involved in: *Africa Partnership Forum (APF, #00510)*; *Facilité africaine de l'eau (FAE, #09233)*. Close cooperation with: *OECD (#17693)*; *United Nations Institute for Training and Research (UNITAR, #20576)*; *United Nations System Chief Executives Board for Coordination (CEB, #20636)*. Environment Secretariat is Through AFRITACs, links with: *African Development Bank (ADB, #00283)*; *Group of Eight (G-8, #10745)*; *International Bank for Reconstruction and Development (IBRD, #12317)*; *International Monetary Fund (IMF, #14180)*; *United Nations Economic Commission for Africa (ECA, #20554)*. **NGO Relations** Cooperates with: *African Fertilizer and Agribusiness Partnership (AFAP, #00314)*; *African Technology Policy Studies Network (ATPS, #00481)*; *Association of Power Utilities in Africa (APUA, #02867)*; *International Fertilizer Development Center (IFDC, #13590)*, through Comprehensive Africa Agriculture Development Programme (CAADP); *WorldFish (#21507)*. Member of: *Forum for Agricultural Research in Africa (FARA, #09897)*; *Global Alliance for Climate-Smart Agriculture (GACSA, #10189)*. Supporting organization of: *Scaling Up Nutrition Movement (SUN Movement, #19064)*. Member of: *Réseau de prévention des crises alimentaires (RPCA, #18905)*. Cooperates with: *Association of European Parliamentarians with Africa (AWEPA, inactive)*, through Planning and Coordinating Agency (NPCA); *International Food Policy Research Institute (IFPRI, #13622)*. Instrumental in setting up: *African Institute for Mathematical Sciences (AIMS, #00342)*; *African Management Development Institutes Network (AMDIN, #00366)*. Works with: *Young Professionals for Agricultural Development (YPARD, #21996)*. [2016/XK2193/E*]

♦ New Pedagogies for Deep Learning (internationally oriented national body)
♦ New Pedagogies for Deep Learning – A Global Partnership / see New Pedagogies for Deep Learning

♦ NewPOL Consortium Network (NCN) 17092

Coordinator Jezus-Eiklaan 120, 3080 Tervuren, Belgium. T. +3227681730. Fax +3227681321.
URL: http://www.imnrc.org/

History Follows 'NewPOL' proposal for the EU 6th Framework Programme, 2002, inspired by *International Multidisciplinary Neuroscience Research Centre (IMNRC)*. **Aims** Function as a network of networks looking into an integrated understanding of *diseases* and *healing* potential in the human being explored using novel approaches to *therapy*.
Members Coordinators in 17 countries:
Belgium, Bulgaria, China, Finland, Germany, Hungary, Israel, Italy, Latvia, Malta, Romania, Russia, Serbia, Slovenia, Türkiye, Ukraine, USA. [2013/XJ3358/F]

♦ New Reality International (internationally oriented national body)
♦ New Rules for Global Finance (internationally oriented national body)
♦ New Rules for Global Finance Coalition / see New Rules for Global Finance
♦ New School of Athens (no recent information)
♦ New SIRMCE Confederation (inactive)

♦ News Media Coalition (NMC) 17093

Exec Dir Av des Arts 43, 1040 Brussels, Belgium. T. +3222311299. E-mail: andy@newsmediacoalition.org – info@newsmediacoalition.org.
URL: http://www.newsmediacoalition.org/

History Set up by *European Newspaper Publishers' Association (ENPA, #08048)*, *European Publishers Council (EPC, #08304)* and *World Association of Newspapers (WAN, inactive)*. **Aims** Focus on the threat to editorial operations, publishing and independent *journalism* from excessive control on the flow of news to the public imposed by events entities such as sports governing bodies through accreditation contracts and other means. [2019/XJ0394/F]

♦ News Media Europe (NME) 17094

Exec Dir Square de Meeûs 25, 1000 Brussels, Belgium.
URL: http://www.newsmediaeurope.eu/

History Jan 2016. Registration: Banque-Carrefour des Entreprises, No/ID: 0647.900.810, Start date: 8 Feb 2016, Belgium; EU Transparency Register, No/ID: 577812220311-81, Start date: 15 Jan 2016. **Structure** Board; Presidency. **Activities** Events/meetings; knowledge management/information dissemination. **Events** *EU Media Policy Conference* Brussels (Belgium) 2019. **Publications** Position papers.
Members Full in 14 countries and territories:
Belgium/Flemish Region, Czechia, Denmark, Estonia, Finland, Hungary, Ireland, Lithuania, Netherlands, Norway, Romania, Spain, Sweden, UK.
NGO Relations Member of (2): *Coalition for APP Fairness* (Founding); *European Advertising Standards Alliance (EASA, #05829)*. [2021/XM6742/F]

♦ News World Communications 17095

Contact c/o Washington Times, 3600 New York Ave NE, Washington DC 20002, USA. Fax +12026363000.
URL: https://www.washingtontimes.com/

History within the framework of *Holy Spirit Association for the Unification of World Christianity (HSA-UWC)*. **NGO Relations** Sponsors: *World Media Association (WMA, #21644)*. Owns: *United Press International (UPI)*. [2008/XF2720/F]

♦ New Trends in Fatigue and Fracture (meeting series)
♦ New Tribes Mission / see Ethnos360
♦ New Venture Fund (internationally oriented national body)
♦ New Vision International (internationally oriented national body)
♦ New Ways of Analyzing Variation – Asia Pacific (meeting series)
♦ New Wineskins Missionary Network (internationally oriented national body)
♦ **NEWW** Network of East-West Women (#17006)

♦ New Women for Europe (unconfirmed)
♦ New World / see Solidagro

♦ New World Academy 17096

Contact address not obtained. T. +441301703053. E-mail: iipsgp@educationaid.net.
History 1991, Washington DC (USA), by *New World Educational Foundation (no recent information)*. **Aims** Facilitate positive transformation in the *consciousness* of humankind, honouring, exemplifying and uplifting a *spiritual* standard for the millennium; nurture the planet's *transformation* by giving form to new spiritual impulses and ensuring that love, peace, justice, abundance and enlightened global cooperation finally lead to total planetary healing; facilitate and draw into the fellowship outstanding practitioners of art, science, philosophy, scholarship, exploration, statesmanship, philanthropy and well-being as *role models* for rising generations. **Structure** Global Council of 12. Officers, luminaries and honorary fellows. Field representatives (9). National/Regional Councils (currently 4, 7 under establishment). **Finance** Tithing of profits from international businesses. **Activities** Setting up "gateways" to access major populations and cultures at 13 locations worldwide, each with: a *'Fellowship Office'* for local hospitality and databank; a *'Lyceum'* to organize seminars, conferences and cultural events and to produce publications and videos; a *'Development Office'* to coordinate independent entrepreneurs and private sector businesses supporting the Academy. **Members** Founding fellows (300) – individual distinguished scholars, artists, poets, musicians, healers, ethical business leaders, educators and peace workers. Membership countries not specified. **NGO Relations** *International Institute of Peace Studies and Global Philosophy (IIPSGP, #13909).* [2013.09.25/XF2788/sv/**F**]

♦ New World Foundation (internationally oriented national body)
♦ New World Hope Organization (internationally oriented national body)
♦ New York African Studies Association (internationally oriented national body)
♦ New York Convention – Convention on the Recognition and Enforcement of Foreign Arbitral Awards (1958 treaty)

♦ New York NGO Committee on Drugs (NYNGOC) 17097

Main Office 22 West 27th St, 5th Fl, New York NY 10001, USA. E-mail: newyorkngoc@gmail.com.
URL: http://nyngoc.org/
History 1984, as a committee within *Conference of Non-Governmental Organizations in Consultative Relationship with the United Nations (CONGO, #04635)*. Previously referred to as *NGO Committee on Narcotics and Substance Abuse, New York NY*; *New York NGO Committee on Narcotics and Substance Abuse*; and as *United Nations NGO Committee on Narcotics and Substance Abuse, New York NY*. **Aims** Counter impact of substance abuse and *illicit drug trafficking* in all societies; serve as a focal point for NGOs to share information and experience, develop networks, raise issues and present views and concerns regarding *prevention* and education, demand reduction, treatment, *rehabilitation* and drug control. **Structure** Chairman, Vice-Chairman and Treasurer. **Languages** English. **Staff** Part-time, voluntary. **Finance** Members' dues (annual): US$ 15. **Activities** Cooperates with other NGO Committees, agencies and units of the United Nations System, governments and public and private organizations; encourages and supports development of interactive relationships with and between special interest groups; participates in public information briefings. Organizes: monthly meeting for NGOs on international topics; observance programme for International Day Against Drug Abuse and Illicit Trafficking. Participates in World AIDS Day and other International Day events. **Events** *International conference for NGOs in North American and English-speaking Caribbean countries* New York, NY (USA) 1994, *Meeting* New York, NY (USA) 1989. **Publications** *Substance Abuse: News and Information Exchange* (4 a year); *Comprehensive, Multidisciplinary Outline (CMO).*
Members National organizations (3) in 3 countries:
Australia, Colombia, UK.
International organizations (22), listed in this Yearbook:
– *Caritas Internationalis (CI, #03580);*
– *Christophers;*
– *Defence for Children International (DCI, #05025);*
– *Foundation for International Probation and Parole Practices (no recent information);*
– *International Advertising Association (IAA, #11590);*
– *International Alliance of Women (IAW, #11639);*
– *International Association for Volunteer Effort (IAVE, #12260);*
– *International Catholic Child Bureau (#12450);*
– *International Catholic Committee of Nurses and Medico-social Assistants (#12451);*
– *International Catholic Organizations Information Center (ICO Center);*
– *International Council of Prison Medical Services (ICPMS, no recent information);*
– *International Council of Women (ICW, #13093);*
– *International Council on Alcohol and Addictions (ICAA, #12989);*
– *International Health Awareness Network (IHAN, #13778);*
– *Lions Clubs International (LCI, #16485);*
– *Rotary International (RI, #18975);*
– *World Association of Girl Guides and Girl Scouts (WAGGGS, #21142);*
– *World Council of Churches (WCC, #21320);*
– *World Union of Catholic Women's Organisations (WUCWO, #21876);*
– *Worldview International Foundation (WIF, #21903);*
– *Zonta International (#22038).*
IGO Relations *ECOSOC (#05331); OAS (#17629).* [2016/XE1018/y/**E**]

♦ New York NGO Committee on Narcotics and Substance Abuse / see New York NGO Committee on Drugs (#17097)
♦ New Zealand Institute of International Affairs (internationally oriented national body)
♦ New Zealand Ministry of Foreign Affairs and Trade – New Zealand Aid Programme (internationally oriented national body)
♦ New Zealand's International Aid and Development Agency / see New Zealand Ministry of Foreign Affairs and Trade – New Zealand Aid Programme
♦ The Next Century Foundation (internationally oriented national body)

♦ Next Einstein Forum (NEF) 17098

Managing Dir c/o AIMS-NEI, 590 KG ST, Gasabo, Kigali, Rwanda. T. +250788315246. E-mail: info@nef.org.
URL: http://nef.org/
History Launched 2013, by *African Institute of Management Science (AIMS)* and *Robert Bosch Foundation.* **Aims** Leverage science for human development globally, by connecting *science*, society and policy in Africa and the rest of the world. **Structure** International Steering Committee; Scientific Program Committee. **Events** *Biennial Global Gathering* Nairobi (Kenya) 2020, *Biennial Global Gathering* Nairobi (Kenya) 2020, *Biennial Global Gathering* Kigali (Rwanda) 2018, *SFSA : Science Forum South Africa* Pretoria (South Africa) 2017, *SFSA : Science Forum South Africa* Pretoria (South Africa) 2016. **Publications** *NEF Newsletter.*
Members Organizations, include the following listed in this Yearbook:
African Academy of Sciences (AAS, #00193); African Centre for Technology Studies (ACTS, #00243); Association for the Development of Education in Africa (ADEA, #02471); ESMT Berlin; Forum for African Women Educationalists (FAWE, #09896); Network for International Policies and Cooperation in Education and Training (NORRAG, #17043).
IGO Relations *African Union (AU, #00488)* Commission; *International Development Research Centre (IDRC, #13162); UNESCO (#20322).* **NGO Relations** *Wellcome Trust.* [2017/XM5535/y/**F**]

♦ Next Generation Mobile Network / see NGMN Alliance (#17101)
♦ Next Generation Mobile Networks Alliance / see NGMN Alliance (#17101)
♦ Next Library (meeting series)
♦ Next Tourism Generation Alliance (unconfirmed)
♦ NEXUS (unconfirmed)
♦ NEXUS-IBA – NEXUS International Broadcasting Association (internationally oriented national body)
♦ NEXUS International Broadcasting Association (internationally oriented national body)
♦ NFA – Nordisk Förening för Allergologi (unconfirmed)
♦ NFA – Nurses for Africa (internationally oriented national body)
♦ **NFBK** Nordisk Fartygsbefälskongress (#17407)
♦ **NFB** N.F.-Board (#17099)
♦ NFBN – Nordiske Forskningsbiblioteketsforeningers Netvaerk (inactive)

♦ N.F.-Board (NFB) 17099

Headquarters c/o OMF (Pôle Administratif NF Board), BP 202, 26105 Romans-sur-Isère CEDEX, France.
URL: http://nfbwebsite.wixsite.com/nfboard/
History Apr 2003, Brussels (Belgium), as *New Football Federations-Board (NF-Board).* Registered in accordance with Belgian law. **Structure** Board. **Languages** English, French. **Activities** Networking/liaising. **Members** Football associations that are not member of FIFA. Membership countries not specified. **IGO Relations** *ECOSOC (#05331).* **NGO Relations** *Unrepresented Nations and Peoples Organization (UNPO, #20714).* [2017.11.28/XM4904/**D**]

♦ NF-Board / see N.F.-Board (#17099)
♦ **NFBO** Nordisk Forening Mot Barnemishandling og Omsorgssvikt (#17200)
♦ **NFBWW** Nordic Federation of Building and Wood Workers (#17283)
♦ **NFC Forum** Near Field Communication Forum (#16968)
♦ NFC – Nordic Femtochemistry Conference (meeting series)
♦ **NFC** Nordic Fishermen's Council (#17293)
♦ NFC – Nordiska Fiberboardindustriernas Centralförbund (inactive)
♦ NFES / see Nordic Fishermen's Council (#17293)
♦ NFF – Nordiska Fabriksarbetarefederationen (inactive)
♦ **NFF** Nordiska Frisörmästareförbundet (#17307)
♦ **Nff** Nordisk förening för folkdansforskning (#17505)
♦ **NFF** Nordisk Företagsekonomiska Förening (#17510)
♦ **NFGP ApS** Nordic Federation of General Practice ApS (#17284)
♦ NFH / see Nordic Association for Disability and Oral Health (#17190)
♦ **NFH** Nordisk Förening för Funktionshinder och Oral Hälsa (#17190)
♦ NFH – Nordisk Förening för Hematologi (no recent information)
♦ **NFI** Naturfreunde Internationale (#14780)
♦ NFI – NIDCAP Federation International (internationally oriented national body)
♦ **NFIP Movement** Nuclear-Free and Independent Pacific Movement (#17617)
♦ NFIRF / see International Nature Farming Research Center
♦ **NFJI** Naturfreundejugend Internationale (#15929)
♦ **NFKK** Nordiska Förbundet för Kyrkogårdar och Krematorier (#02418)
♦ **NFKK** Nordisk Förening för Klinisk Kemi (#17507)
♦ **NFKL** Nordisk förening för katolska läkare (#17506)
♦ NFK – Nordiska Fertilitetsklubben (inactive)
♦ NFK – Nordisk Förbund för Kvinnogymnastik (inactive)
♦ **NFKS** Nordisk Forening for Klinisk Sexologi (#17185)
♦ **NFLS** Nordiska Förbundet för Läkepedagogik och Socialterapi (#17482)
♦ NFME – Nordic Federation for Medical Education (no recent information)
♦ **NFMM** Nordisk Forening for Forskning om Menn og Maskuliniteter (#17202)
♦ NFM / see Nordic Fishermen's Council (#17293)
♦ **NFM** Nordisk Forum för Megling og Konflikthåndtering (#17513)
♦ **NFMR** Nordisk Förening för Medicinsk Radiologi (#17418)
♦ NFMU – Nordisk Federation för Medicinsk Undervisning (no recent information)
♦ **NFN** Nordic Finance Network (#17291)
♦ NF – Norsk Folkehjelp (internationally oriented national body)
♦ NFNR / see Nordic Society of Neuroradiology (#17421)
♦ **NFOG** Nordisk Förening för Obstetrik och Gynekologi (#17286)
♦ **NFOR** Nordisk Forfatter- og Oversetterråd (#17511)

♦ NF Patients United 17100

Contact Pfarrgasse 87, 1230 Vienna, Austria. E-mail: info@nf-patients.eu.
URL: https://www.nf-patients.eu/
History Former names and other names: *Neurofibromatosis Patients United (NFPU)* – full title; *NF Patients United – Global Network of Neurofibromatosis Patient Organisations* – alias. Registration: ZVR, No/ID: 1924149422, Austria.
Members Patient organizations in 12 countries:
Austria, Croatia, Denmark, Greece, Italy, Netherlands, Portugal, Russia, Spain, Switzerland, Türkiye, UK. [2021/AA1716/**F**]

♦ NF Patients United – Global Network of Neurofibromatosis Patient Organisations / see NF Patients United (#17100)
♦ NFPF / see Nordic Educational Research Association (#17276)
♦ **NFPF** Nordisk Förening för Pedagogisk Forskning (#17276)
♦ NFP – Netherlands Food Partnership (internationally oriented national body)
♦ NFP – New Forests Project (internationally oriented national body)
♦ NFP – Nordisk Förening för Pedodonti (inactive)
♦ NFPO – Nordisk Forening for Psykosocial Onkologi (no recent information)
♦ NFPU / see NF Patients United (#17100)
♦ NFPV – Nordisk Forening for Palliativ Vård (inactive)
♦ **NFR** Nordiske Fiskeres Råd (#17293)
♦ NFR – Nordisk Folke-Reso (inactive)
♦ NFR – Nordisk Förening för Rehabilitering (inactive)
♦ NFRR – Nordisk Förening av Registrerade Revisorer (inactive)
♦ NFSD – Nordic Fire & Safety Days (meeting series)
♦ NFSMH – Nordiska Föreningen för Social och Mental Hälsa (inactive)
♦ **NFS** Nordens Fackliga Samorganisation (#17158)
♦ **NFS** Nordic Fertility Society (#17288)
♦ **NFS** Nordisk Flagselskab (#17294)
♦ **NFSP** Nordiska Förbundet för Specialpedagogik (#17435)
♦ **NFSP** Nordisk Forbund for Spesialpedagogikk (#17435)
♦ NFSUN – Nordiskt Forskersymposium om Undervisning i Naturvitenskap (meeting series)
♦ **NFSU** Nordisk Förening för Spädbarns Utveckling (#17509)
♦ **NFSY** Nordisk Forbund for Studie- og Yrkesvejledning (#17191)
♦ NFTU – Nordisk Film/TV-Union (inactive)
♦ **NFTVF** Nordisk Film & TV Fond (#17503)
♦ **NFUE** Nordisk Förening för Studie- och Yrkesvägleding Nordisk Forbund for Uddannesles- og Erhvervsvejledning (#17191)
♦ NFU / see Nordic Union of Pharmaceutical Organizations (#17456)
♦ **NFU** Nordiska Finansanställdas Union (#17292)
♦ NFU – Nordiska Försäkringsmannaunionen (inactive)
♦ **NFU** Nordisk Farmaceutunion (#17456)
♦ NFU – Norsk Forening for Utviklingsforskning (internationally oriented national body)
♦ NFU – Northern Feminist University (internationally oriented national body)
♦ **NFYOG** Nordic Federation of Young Obstetricians and Gynaecologists (#17287)
♦ NGB / see Nordic Genetic Resource Centre (#17303)
♦ **NGF** Nordic Gerontological Federation (#17306)
♦ **NGF** Nordic Gerontological Federation (#17305)
♦ NGF – Nordiska Glastekniska Föreningen (inactive)
♦ N&G – International Conference on Nutrition & Growth (meeting series)
♦ **NGLS** United Nations Non-Governmental Liaison Service (#20591)

♦ NGMN Alliance 17101

Contact Grosser Hasenpfad 30, 60598 Frankfurt-Main, Germany. T. +496990749980. Fax +4969907499841. E-mail: office@ngmn.org.
URL: http://www.ngmn.org/

History Founded by world leading Mobile Network Operators. Former names and other names: *Next Generation Mobile Networks Alliance* – full title; *Next Generation Mobile Network (NGMN)* – former. Registration: UK. **Aims** Ensure the next generation network infrastructure, service platforms and devices will meet the requirements of operators and will satisfy end user demand and expectations; provide industry guidance to achieve innovative and affordable mobile telecommunication services for the end user with a particular focus on supporting 5G's full implementation, Mastering the Route to Disaggregation, Sustainability and Green Networks, and 6G; incorporate the views of all interested stakeholders in the telecommunications industry. **Structure** Board; Forum; Task Forces. **Languages** English. **Finance** Sources: members' dues. **Activities** Events/meetings; networking/liaising; projects/programmes; publishing activities. **Events** *Conference* Vancouver, BC (Canada) 2018, *Conference* Frankfurt-Main (Germany) 2016. **Members** Members (Mobile Network Operators); Contributors (vendors, software companies and other industry players); Advisors (research institutes). Membership countries not specified. **NGO Relations** Partner of (7): *European Telecommunications Standards Institute (ETSI, #08897); GSM Association (GSMA, #10813); Open Mobile Alliance (OMA, #17757); Small Cell Forum (#19312); TeleManagement Forum (TM Forum, #20123); Universal Mobile Telecommunications System Forum (UMTS Forum, inactive); Wireless World Research Forum (WWRF, #20971).* [2021.09.20/XJ8750/F]

- ♦ NGMN / see NGMN Alliance (#17101)
- ♦ NGM – Nordic Geographers Meeting (meeting series)
- ♦ NGM – Nordic Glaucoma Meeting (meeting series)
- ♦ NGO Abolition Caucus / see Abolition 2000 – Global Network to Eliminate Nuclear Weapons (#00006)
- ♦ NGO Advisory Group on Health Promotion / see Alliance for Health Promotion (#00687)
- ♦ NGO Africa 2000 Network / see Africa 2000 Plus Network, Harare (#00154)

♦ NGO Alliance on Global Concerns and Values (NGO Alliance) 17102

Address not obtained.
URL: http://ngo-connect.org/

Aims Provide enhanced opportunities for NGO participation where information sharing and pooling expertise maximizes NGO contributions and networking but with significant and important multiplier effects at the level of NGO outreach to civil society at large. **Structure** General Assembly (triennial); Board. Includes: *NGO Forum on Environment (FOE, #17125); NGO Forum on Spirituality and Values (FSV).* **Finance** Members' dues.
Members Full; Associate. Full member organizations include the following 8 listed in this Yearbook:
Brahma Kumaris World Spiritual University (BKWSU, #03311); Church of Jesus Christ of the Latter-day Saints (#03915); Foundation for Gaia (#09957); International Islamic Relief Organization (IIRO); International Network for the Prevention of Elder Abuse (INPEA, #14307); Lucis Trust (LT, #16519) (and its World Goodwill); *Mothers Legacy Project; Planetary Association for Clean Energy (PACE, #18381).*
Associate member organizations include 3 listed in this Yearbook:
EURO-MENA Human Rights Training and Education (EURO-MENA, no recent information); Institute of Global Education. [2016/XM4831/y/E]

- ♦ **NGO Alliance** NGO Alliance on Global Concerns and Values (#17102)
- ♦ **NGO BaCo** Baltic Coalition for PLWHIV (#03107)
- ♦ NGOCD / see NGO Committee for Disarmament, Geneva (#17105)
- ♦ NGO Club / see European Non-Governmental Sports Organization (#08054)
- ♦ NGO Coalition for an International Criminal Court / see Coalition for the International Criminal Court (#04062)
- ♦ NGO Committee on Ageing, Geneva (see: #04635)

♦ NGO Committee on Ageing, New York 17103

Comité des ONG s'intéressant aux personnes âgées, New York

Co-Chair PO Box 1854, New York NY 10163-1854, USA.
URL: http://www.ngocoa-ny.org/

History Founded 1977, New York NY (USA). A committee of *Conference of Non-Governmental Organizations in Consultative Relationship with the United Nations (CONGO, #04635)*, comprising NGOs having consultative status with *ECOSOC (#05331)* and concerned with problems of aging. Also referred to as *CONGO Committee on Ageing, New York.* **Aims** Encourage, facilitate and support United Nations actions related to ageing. **Structure** Executive Committee; Sub-Committees (6). No secretariat. **Languages** English. **Staff** None. **Finance** Members' dues. Donations. **Activities** Awareness raising; advocacy/lobbying/activism. **Events** *General meeting* New York, NY (USA) 2010, *Meeting on the commemoration of the 10th anniversary of the international year of older persons – toward a society for all ages* New York, NY (USA) 2009. **Publications** *Isues of Ageing and Disability: International Perspectives* (2010). Annual program reports. **Members** Representatives of NGOs, civil society and academic institutions; Students. Membership countries not specified. **IGO Relations** Cooperates with: *ILO (#11123); United Nations Programme on Ageing (inactive); WHO (#20950).* **NGO Relations** Sister committees: *NGO Committee on Ageing, Geneva (see: #04635); NGO Committee on Ageing, Vienna (see: #04635).* Cooperates with: *NGO Committee on the Family, New York NY (#17107); NGO Committee on Mental Health, New York NY (#17111); New York NGO Committee on Drugs (NYNGOC, #17097); NGO Committee on Social Development (#17115); NGO Committee on the Status of Women, New York NY (see: #04635).* [2019.02.12/XD4029/y/E]

- ♦ NGO Committee on Ageing, Vienna (see: #04635)

♦ NGO Committee on Development, Geneva 17104

Comité des ONG pour le développement à Genève

Co-Chair address not obtained.
URL: http://www.ngocongo.org/index.php?what=committees&id=25/

History 1994, under the auspices of *Conference of Non-Governmental Organizations in Consultative Relationship with the United Nations (CONGO, #04635).* **Aims** Assist and promote the work of NGOs in consultative status with ECOSOC, UNCTAD and other UN agencies in relation to ongoing work in the field of development; promote cooperation among NGOs in the Committee, with those in other CONGO committees and with NGOs from *developing countries* which have no consultative status with UN bodies; provide a forum for discussion of ideas and experience on development and for sharing information on the work of NGOs and the UN system concerning development; promote the NGO contribution to work in the field; promote links with local, national and regional NGOs working in the field and maintain a two-way communication with them. **Structure** Bureau. Officers: Chairperson; 2 Vice-Chairpersons; Secretary; Treasurer. 19 members. **Finance** Member organizations' dues. **Activities** Organizes seminars and conferences on subjects related to current social, economic and development issues with focus on human development and social justice; informs the world public about the work of the United Nations in favour of development. In the light of members' consultative status with ECOSOC, makes presentations to plenary sessions of many UN meetings. **Events** *Meeting* Geneva (Switzerland) 2010, *Committee meeting* Geneva (Switzerland) 1996, *Committee meeting* Geneva (Switzerland) 1995, *Committee meeting* Geneva (Switzerland) 1994, *Seminar on the South and the Bretton Woods institutions* Geneva (Switzerland) 1994. **Publications** Booklets; proceedings; reports; papers; minutes. **Members** Membership open to all NGOs in Consultative Status with ECOSOC. Other interested NGOs are admitted as Associate or Corresponding Members. Membership countries not specified. **NGO Relations** Sister committees: *NGO Committee on Sustainable Development, Vienna (#17119); NGO Committee on Sustainable Development, New York (#17118).* Represented on Bureau: *Women's International League for Peace and Freedom (WILPF, #21024).* [2021/XE1388/E]

- ♦ NGO Committee on Development, New York / see NGO Committee on Sustainable Development, New York (#17118)
- ♦ NGO Committee on Development, Vienna / see NGO Committee on Sustainable Development, Vienna (#17119)
- ♦ NGO Committee for Disarmament / see NGO Committee for Disarmament, Geneva (#17105)

♦ NGO Committee for Disarmament, Geneva 17105

Comité spécial des ONG pour le désarmement, Genève

Chair c/o World Council of Churches, PO Box 2100, Route de Ferney 150, 1211 Geneva, Switzerland.
URL: http://www.ngocongo.org/index.php?what=committees&id=26/

History Founded 13 Nov 1969, Geneva (Switzerland), following recommendations of *Conference of Non-Governmental Organizations in Consultative Relationship with the United Nations (CONGO, #04635)* and the work of an ad hoc committee of NGO members, as one of 2 separate committees, each referred to as *NGO Committee for Disarmament (NGOCD) – Comité des ONG pour le désarmement*, the other, *NGO Committee on Disarmament, Peace and Security, New York NY (#17106)*, based in New York NY (USA). **Aims** Promote achievement of disarmament under effective international control and support measures which may assist the realization of this aim, especially through mobilization of member organization networks and constituencies which in turn inform public opinion in certain regions; facilitate relations between NGOs interested in disarmament, international security and related problems, and the competent bodies of the United Nations system; provide a forum for the exchange of information concerning UN activities and other actions for disarmament, international security and related problems, with a view to facilitating and stimulating action and cooperation of NGOs in these fields. **Structure** An NGO committee reporting to CONGO but with independent status. **Finance** Members' dues. Grants. **Activities** Events/meetings. **Events** *Seminar on disarmament* Geneva (Switzerland) 2006.
Members International NGOs (22) whether or not members of CONGO:
- *Afro-Asian Peoples' Solidarity Organization (AAPSO, #00537);*
- *Arab Lawyers' Union (ALU, #01002);*
- *Asian Buddhist Conference for Peace (ABCP, no recent information);*
- *Conference of European Churches (CEC, #04593);*
- *Friends World Committee for Consultation (FWCC, #10004);*
- *Hungarian Peace Association;*
- *International Association of Democratic Lawyers (IADL, #11837);*
- *International Peace Bureau (IPB, #14535);*
- *Pax Christi – International Catholic Peace Movement (#18266);*
- *Pax Romana, International Catholic Movement for Intellectual and Cultural Affairs (ICMICA, #18267);*
- *Religions for Peace (RfP, #18831);*
- *Socialist International Women (SIW, #19341);*
- *The World Veterans Federation (WVF, #21900);*
- *War Resisters' International (WRI, #20818);*
- *Women's International Democratic Federation (WIDF, #21022);*
- *Women's International League for Peace and Freedom (WILPF, #21024);*
- *World Alliance of Young Men's Christian Associations (YMCA, #21090);*
- *World Council of Churches (WCC, #21320);*
- *World Federalist Movement – Movement for a Just World Order through a Strengthened United Nations (WFM, #21404);*
- *World Federation of United Nations Associations (WFUNA, #21499);*
- *World Peace Council (WPC, #21717).*

IGO Relations *ECOSOC (#05331); United Nations Disarmament Information Programme (inactive).* Associated with Department of Global Communications of the United Nations. **NGO Relations** *Franciscans International (FI, #09982); International Network of Engineers and Scientists Against Proliferation (INESAP, see: #14260); Rissho Kosei-Kai (RKK); Soka Gakkai International (SGI, #19672); Women for World Disarmament (WWD, no recent information); World Federation of Democratic Youth (WFDY, #21427).* [2018.07.30/XE4377/y/E]

♦ NGO Committee on Disarmament, Peace and Security, New York NY 17106

Pres 777 United Nations Plaza, Ste 3B, New York NY 10017, USA. T. +12126875340. Fax +12126871643.

History Jun 1969, following recommendations of *Conference of Non-Governmental Organizations in Consultative Relationship with the United Nations (CONGO, #04635)*, and the work of an ad hoc committee of NGO members, as one of 2 separate committees, each referred to as *NGO Committee on Disarmament (NGOCD) – Comité des ONG sur le désarmement*, the other, *NGO Committee for Disarmament, Geneva (#17105)*, based in Geneva. Original title: *Nongovernmental Organization Committee on Disarmament, New York NY – Comité des organisations non-gouvernementales sur le désarmement, New York NY.* **Aims** Promote achievement of general and complete disarmament under effective international control and support every measure which may assist the realization of this aim, especially through mobilization of an informed *public opinion*; consider problems of nuclear, chemical, biological *warfare*, conventional *arms* and *protection* of *human rights* in armed conflict; set up an international peace and disarmament NGO network. **Structure** An NGO committee reporting to CONGO but with independent status. **Languages** English. **Staff** 0.50 FTE, voluntary. 2-4 student interns. **Finance** Members' dues. Grants. **Activities** Holds public forums at the United Nations; organizes Spring and Fall Disarmament Week, together with sister Committee in Geneva (Switzerland). **Events** *World people's conference on peace and security* 2001, *International conference on dangers, doctrines and deterrence* Geneva (Switzerland) 2001, *Conference on nuclear disarmament at the crossroads* Geneva (Switzerland) 2000, *International conference on assuring the success of the non-proliferation treaty extension* New York, NY (USA) 1995, *Seminar* Geneva (Switzerland) 1994. **Publications** *Disarmament Times* (4 a year). Conference proceedings.
Members International NGOs (46) whether or not members of CONGO:
- *Afro-Asian Peoples' Solidarity Organization (AAPSO, #00537);*
- *Arab Lawyers' Union (ALU, #01002);*
- *Asian Buddhist Conference for Peace (ABCP, no recent information);*
- *Canadian Voice of Women for Peace (VOW);*
- *Conference of European Churches (CEC, #04593);*
- *European Confederation of Police (EuroCOP, #06719);*
- *Friends World Committee for Consultation (FWCC, #10004);*
- *Global Security Institute (GSI);*
- *Hague Appeal for Peace (HAP, #10848);*
- *Hungarian Peace Association;*
- *International Association for Volunteer Effort (IAVE, #12260);*
- *International Association of Democratic Lawyers (IADL, #11837);*
- *International Confederation of Former Prisoners of War (ICFPW, inactive);*
- *International Council of Jewish Women (ICJW, #13036);*
- *International Council of Women (ICW, #13093);*
- *International Federation of Resistance Movements (#13529);*
- *International Institute for Peace (IIP, #13907);*
- *International Network of Engineers and Scientists for Global Responsibility (INES, #14260);*
- *International Union of Socialist Youth (IUSY, #15815);*
- *Lawyers Committee on Nuclear Policy (LCNP);*
- *Muslim World League (MWL, #16917);*
- *North American Federation for Freedom and Democracy (NAFFD, no recent information);*
- *Nuclear Age Peace Foundation;*
- *Pax Christi – International Catholic Peace Movement (#18266);*
- *Pax Romana, International Catholic Movement for Intellectual and Cultural Affairs (ICMICA, #18267);*
- *Peace Action Network (PAN);*
- *Religions for Peace (RfP, #18831);*
- *Saferworld;*
- *Socialist International Women (SIW, #19341);*
- *Society for International Development (SID, #19581);*
- *Soka Gakkai International (SGI, #19672);*
- *Soviet Peace Committee (inactive);*
- *The World Veterans Federation (WVF, #21900);*
- *Union of Arab Jurists (UAJ, #20354);*
- *Union of Concerned Scientists (UCS);*
- *War and Peace Foundation;*
- *War Resisters' International (WRI, #20818);*
- *Women's International Democratic Federation (WIDF, #21022);*
- *Women's International League for Peace and Freedom (WILPF, #21024);*
- *World Alliance of Young Men's Christian Associations (YMCA, #21090);*
- *World Council of Churches (WCC, #21320);*
- *World Federalist Movement – Movement for a Just World Order through a Strengthened United Nations (WFM, #21404);*
- *World Federation of Trade Unions (WFTU, #21493);*
- *World Federation of United Nations Associations (WFUNA, #21499);*
- *World Jewish Congress (WJC, #21599);*

– *World Peace Council (WPC, #21717).*
IGO Relations *ECOSOC (#05331); United Nations Disarmament Information Programme (inactive); OPEC Fund for International Development (OFID, #17745).* Associated with Department of Global Communications of the United Nations. **NGO Relations** Member of: *NGO Working Group on the Security Council (#17128).* Represented on the Organizing Committee of: *Hague Appeal for Peace (HAP, #10848).* [2012/XE5920/y/**E**]

♦ NGO Committee on Environment / see NGO Forum on Environment (#17125)
♦ NGO Committee on the Family / see Vienna NGO Committee on the Family (#20774)

♦ NGO Committee on the Family, New York NY 17107

Co-Chair 125 Columbus Ave, New York NY 10023, USA. T. +12127340815. E-mail: ngofamilycommittee@gmail.com.
Co-Chair 1000 River Rd, Teaneck NJ 07666, USA. T. +12013272112.
URL: http://www.ngofamilyny.org/

History Set up as a committee of *Conference of Non-Governmental Organizations in Consultative Relationship with the United Nations (CONGO, #04635).* Previously referred to as *UN NGO Committee on the Family, New York NY.* **Aims** Defend *human rights* of families which are least often heard; give families a voice in shaping *policy* at the *United Nations.* **Structure** Co-Chairs (2); Treasurer; Corresponding Secretary; Recording Secretary; Members-at-Large (5). **Languages** English. **Staff** None. **Finance** Members' dues. **Activities** Events/meetings; advocacy/lobbying/activism. **Events** *Meeting on issues in post-conflict development* New York, NY (USA) 2010, *Meeting on human trafficking and families* New York, NY (USA) 2005.
Members Representatives of NGOs in 41 countries:
Armenia, Austria, Belgium, Bolivia, Brazil, Bulgaria, Burkina Faso, Canada, Central African Rep, Costa Rica, Côte d'Ivoire, Czechia, France, Germany, Ghana, Guatemala, Haiti, Honduras, Hungary, India, Ireland, Israel, Italy, Japan, Korea Rep, Madagascar, Mauritius, Netherlands, New Zealand, Peru, Philippines, Poland, Portugal, Senegal, Suriname, Switzerland, Thailand, Uganda, Ukraine, USA, Vietnam. [2017.06.01/XE2549/**E**]

♦ NGO Committee on the Family – Vienna / see Vienna NGO Committee on the Family (#20774)

♦ NGO Committee on Financing for Development, New York 17108

Chair c/o Missionary Association of Mary Immaculate, 9480 N De Mazenod Drive, Belleville IL 62223, USA. E-mail: ffdchair@ngosonffd.org – secretary@ngosonffd.org.
URL: http://www.ngosonffd.org/

History Set up as an active committee of *Conference of Non-Governmental Organizations in Consultative Relationship with the United Nations (CONGO, #04635).* **Structure** Executive Committee. **Activities** Meets on first Wednesday of each month between September and July.
Members Full; Associate. Full members including the following organizations listed in this Yearbook (28):
– *Anglican Communion (#00827)* (UN Office);
– *Baha'i International Community (#03062);*
– *Church World Service (CWS);*
– *Company of the Daughters of Charity of St Vincent de Paul (DC);*
– *Congregation of the Mission (Vincentians);*
– *Earth Rights Institute (ERI);*
– *Global 2000 – 2010 International;*
– *Institut de la Bienheureuse Vierge Marie (Dames Anglaises);*
– *International Presentation Association (IPA, #14635);*
– *International Relief Friendship Foundation (IRFF, #14713);*
– *International Union of Anthropological and Ethnological Sciences (IUAES, #15755);*
– *Medical Mission Sisters;*
– *Missionary Oblates of Mary Immaculate (OMI);*
– *Nuclear Free Pacific Network (inactive);*
– *Partnership for Global Justice;*
– *Passionists International (PI, #18254);*
– *Pax Romana, International Catholic Movement for Intellectual and Cultural Affairs (ICMICA, #18267);*
– *School Sisters of Notre Dame (SSND);*
– *Society of St Francis of Sales (Salesians of Don Bosco);*
– *Soeurs de Notre-Dame de Namur (SNDN);*
– *Soroptimist International (SI, #19686);*
– *The United Methodist Church (UMC, #20514);*
– *Unitarian Universalist Association (UUA, #20494)* (UN Office);
– *VIVAT International (#20801);*
– *Voices of African Mothers (VAM);*
– *World Association of Girl Guides and Girl Scouts (WAGGGS, #21142);*
– *World Council of Churches (WCC, #21320);*
– *World Council of the Marianist Family (WCMF, #21334).*

Associate members, including the following listed in this Yearbook (10):
European Neuropeptide Club (ENC, #08044); ICCO – Interchurch Organization for Development Cooperation; Institute of International Social Development (IISD, no recent information); International Association for Human Values (IAHV, #11947); Maryknoll Sisters of Saint Dominic; Millennium Development Goals Global Watch (MDG Global Watch); Religions for Peace (RfP, #18831); Sisters of Mercy of the Americas; Society of the Sacred Heart of Jesus (St Madeleine-Sophie Barat); Women First International Fund (#20996). [2015/XJ2168/y/**E**]

♦ NGO Committee on Freedom of Religion or Belief, Geneva (see: #04275)

♦ NGO Committee on Freedom of Religion or Belief, New York NY . . . 17109

Pres 866 UN Plaza – Ste 120, New York NY 10017, USA. T. +12128032519. Fax +12128032566. E-mail: unforb@gmail.com.
URL: http://www.unforb.org/

History Mar 1991, New York NY (USA), when formally recognized by *Conference of Non-Governmental Organizations in Consultative Relationship with the United Nations (CONGO, #04635),* as two "Sister Committees" in New York NY and Geneva (Switzerland), both chartered at the same time. New York Committee derives from a follow up on John Salzberg's "Study on the Feasibility of Developing a UN Convention on the Elimination of Intolerance and of Discrimination Based on Religion or Belief" (1989). Committee revived 25 Oct 2001. **Aims** Support initiatives against *intolerance* and *discrimination* based on religion or belief; address the relationship between enjoyment of freedom of conscience, religion or belief and other *human rights* and approaches of different religions and beliefs to human rights. **Structure** Committee meets monthly from September to May. Bureau (Executive Committee), comprises the Officers (President, Vice-President, Secretary, Treasurer) and 3 members. **Languages** English. **Staff** Voluntary. **Finance** Active members' dues, US$ 20, cover operating expenses; additional contributions for special events from special fundraising by NGOs. **Activities** Supports initiatives of "Special Rapporteur on the Elimination of Intolerance and of Discrimination Based on Religion or Belief" appointed by the then *United Nations Commission on Human Rights (inactive).* Appeals to *United Nations Human Rights Council (HRC, #20571),* which replaced *Sub-Commission on the Promotion and Protection of Human Rights (inactive)* and the Commission on Human Rights, to take appropriate action in cases of intolerance or discrimination based on religion or belief; supports and participates in conferences, consultations and other UN and NGO activities which promote tolerance and respect for different religions or beliefs. Co-sponsors annual *'Day for Freedom of Religion or Belief'* at the UN. **Events** *Meeting* New York, NY (USA) 1996. **Publications** Cooperates in developing an annual report on the worldwide situation of freedom of religion or belief; informal report on the annual Day for Freedom of Religion or Belief; brochures; minutes of meetings.
Members Representatives of 54 NGOs working in the UN community, including 33 international NGOs listed in this Yearbook:
– *Association internationale pour la défense de la liberté religieuse (AIDLR, #02681);*
– *Baha'i International Community (#03062);*
– *Baptist World Alliance (BWA, #03176);*
– *Caritas Internationalis (CI, #03580);*
– *Catholic International Education Office (#03604);*
– *Center for Global Community and World Law (CGCWL, no recent information);*
– *Christian Life Community (CLC, #03905);*
– *Church of Scientology International (CSI, #03922);*
– *Church Women United (CWU);*
– *Coordinating Board of Jewish Organizations (CBJO, #04813);*
– *General Conference of Seventh-Day Adventists (SDA, #10109);*
– *Gray Panthers Project Fund;*
– *Greek Orthodox Archdiocesan Council of America (GOAC, #10708);*
– *Humanists International (#10972);*
– *International Association for Religious Freedom (IARF, #12130);*
– *International Council of Jewish Women (ICJW, #13036);*
– *Lutheran Office for World Community;*
– *Muslim World League (MWL, #16917);*
– *Order of St Augustine (Augustinians International);*
– *Pax Christi – International Catholic Peace Movement (#18266);*
– *Pax Romana, International Catholic Movement for Intellectual and Cultural Affairs (ICMICA, #18267);*
– *Religions for Peace (RfP, #18831);*
– *Ribbon International;*
– *Salvation Army (#19041);*
– *School Sisters of Notre Dame (SSND);*
– *Share International (#19257);*
– *Sisters of Our Lady of Charity of the Good Shepherd;*
– *Soka Gakkai International (SGI, #19672);*
– *Unitarian Universalist Association (UUA, #20494);*
– *Women's Federation for World Peace International (WFWPI);*
– *Won Buddhism International;*
– *World Federation of Ukrainian Women's Organizations (WFUWO, #21496);*
– *World Peace Prayer Society.*

IGO Relations *ECOSOC (#05331).* **NGO Relations** Sister committee: *NGO Committee on Freedom of Religion or Belief, Geneva (see: #04275).* Cooperates with: *International Mahavira Jain Mission (IMJM); International Religious Foundation (IRF, no recent information); Minority Rights Group International (MRG, #16820); Movement for a Better World (MBW, #16869).* [2016/XE3149/y/**E**]

♦ NGO Committee on Housing and Shelter for the Homeless / see NGO Committee on Human Settlements (#17110)
♦ NGO Committee on Human Rights / see CONGO Committee on Human Rights (#04663)
♦ NGO Committee on Human Settlements / see Habitat International Coalition (#10845)

♦ NGO Committee on Human Settlements 17110

Chairperson 153 East 57th St – Apt 18K, New York NY 10022, USA. T. +12126447959. Fax +12126447499. E-mail: brankabalac@yahoo.com.
URL: http://www.ngochs.org/

History 1985, as *NGO Committee on Housing and Shelter for the Homeless,* as a committee within *Conference of Non-Governmental Organizations in Consultative Relationship with the United Nations (CONGO, #04635).* Subsequently referred to as *NGO Committee on Shelter and Community.* Current name adopted in 1996, in order to reflect the extensive mandate of the Habitat Agenda. **Aims** Serve as the major substantive focal point on housing and human settlements activities within the international community of NGOs and other partners in civil society organizations; promote implementation of commitments of the Conference of Human Settlements, and Agenda 21 of the Conference on the Environment and Development and relevant elements from plans of action of other United Nations conferences that promote the provision of adequate shelter for all and sustainable human settlements development in an urbanizing world. **Languages** English. **Staff** All voluntary. **Finance** Members' dues. **Activities** Organizes lectures and meetings in cooperation with UN-Habitat, governments, private sector, universities, civil society organizations and other UN agencies and international organizations. **Publications** *Newsletter* (3 a year). **Members** Membership countries not specified. **IGO Relations** Partner of: *United Nations Human Settlements Programme (UN-Habitat, #20572).* [2011.06.01/XE1644/**E**]

♦ NGO Committee on the International Decade of the World's Indigenous Peoples / see NGO Committee on the Rights of Indigenous Peoples (#17114)
♦ NGO Committee on the International Year of the World's Indigenous Peoples / see NGO Committee on the Rights of Indigenous Peoples (#17114)
♦ NGO Committee on Mental Health / see NGO Committee on Mental Health, New York NY (#17111)

♦ NGO Committee on Mental Health, New York NY 17111

Contact 777 United Nations Plaza, New York NY 10017, USA. E-mail: unngocmh@gmail.com.
URL: https://www.ngomentalhealth.org/

History as *NGO Committee on Mental Health,* as a committee within *Conference of Non-Governmental Organizations in Consultative Relationship with the United Nations (CONGO, #04635).* **Events** *Meeting* New York, NY (USA) 2004. [2020/XE2217/**E**]

♦ NGO Committee on Migration, New York 17112

Chair c/o CONGO, 777 United Nations Plaza, 6 Fl, New York NY 10017, USA. E-mail: ngomigrationcommittee@gmail.com.
URL: http://www.ngo-migration.org/

History Founded 2006, New York NY (USA), as a committee of *Conference of Non-Governmental Organizations in Consultative Relationship with the United Nations (CONGO, #04635).* **Aims** Advocate on behalf of the *human rights* of *migrants* and their families worldwide, in accordance with the UN Charter. **Structure** Executive Committee. **Languages** English. **Staff** Voluntary. **Finance** Members' dues. No annual budget. **Activities** Advocacy/lobbying/activism; events/meetings. **Events** *Meeting on issues in post-conflict development* New York, NY (USA) 2010. **Publications** Position papers; statements. **Members** NGOs (56), not specified. **IGO Relations** Links with all UN related inter-governmental bodies and organizations. [2020/XM4523/**E**]

♦ NGO Committee on Narcotic Drugs and Psychotropic Substances / see Vienna NGO Committee on Drugs (#20773)
♦ NGO Committee on Narcotics and Substance Abuse, New York NY / see New York NGO Committee on Drugs (#17097)

♦ NGO Committee on Peace, Vienna 17113

Chairmerson c/o IPPNW Austria, Schulgasse 40/17, 1180 Vienna, Austria.
URL: http://www.ngocongo.org/

History as a consultation and cooperation body of the representatives of international NGOs accredited at the United Nations Office Vienna (Austria), on the basis of their consultative status with ECOSOC. A committee of *Conference of Non-Governmental Organizations in Consultative Relationship with the United Nations (CONGO, #04635).* **Aims** Exchange information about work in peace and disarmament; cooperate with UN bodies campaigning for peace and disarmament. **Structure** Board, consisting of Chairperson, 1st and 2nd Vice-Chairperson, Secretary, Deputy-Secretary, Treasurer, Deputy-Treasurer and 6 members. **Languages** English. **Staff** None. **Finance** Members' dues. **Activities** Events/meetings; conflict resolution; knowledge management/information dissemination. **Events** *Meeting on empowering black European women and organising for leadership* Vienna (Austria) 2010, *Meeting* Vienna (Austria) 2004, *Meeting* Vienna (Austria) 2004. **Members** Representatives of 26 international NGOs participate in the work of the Committee continuously as members. Representatives of further international and national NGOs participate in certain activities on an ad hoc basis. Member NGOs not specified. **IGO Relations** Accredited by: *United Nations Office at Vienna (UNOV, #20604).* [2016.06.01/XE2219/**E**]

♦ NGO Committee on the Rights of Indigenous Peoples 17114

Chair POB 20489, New York NY 10017-0005, USA. T. +12125643329. Fax +12124316847. E-mail: indigenous.committee@gmail.com.
URL: http://www.ngocongo.org/committees/

History as *NGO Committee on the International Year of the World's Indigenous Peoples,* as a special committee focusing on indigenous issues within *Conference of Non-Governmental Organizations in Consultative Relationship with the United Nations (CONGO, #04635).* Later known as *NGO Committee on the International Decade of the World's Indigenous Peoples (NGO IDWIP).* Present name adopted, Feb 2016. **Events** *Meeting* New York, NY (USA) 2010, *Meeting* New York, NY (USA) 2010. **IGO Relations** *ECOSOC (#05331).* [2017/XE3147/**E**]

♦ NGO Committee on Shelter and Community / see NGO Committee on Human Settlements (#17110)

♦ NGO Committee on Social Development 17115

Chair c/o Baha'i Int'l Community, 866 United Nations Plz, Ste 120, New York NY 10017-1822, USA. T. +12128032500.
URL: https://ngosocdev.org/

History as a committee of *Conference of Non-Governmental Organizations in Consultative Relationship with the United Nations (CONGO, #04635).* **Aims** Impact policy formation within ECOSOC, based on the principles of the 1995 Copenhagen World Summit for Social Development; promote a people-centred development through the United Nations. **Structure** Session, always in New York NY (USA). Executive Committee; Full Committee. Officers: Chair; Vice-Chair; Secretary; Treasurer; 2 Members-at-Large. **Languages** English. **Finance** Members' dues. **Events** *Civil society forum on social integration* New York, NY (USA) 2010, *Civil society forum* New York, NY (USA) 2005, *Meeting* New York, NY (USA) 2005. **Members** Organizations (about 40). **NGO Relations** *Baha'i International Community (#03062).* [2018/XE3705/**E**]

♦ NGO Committee on Spirituality, Values and Global Concerns (CSVGC) 17116

Contact address not obtained. E-mail: csvgcinfo@gmail.com.
URL: http://www.csvgc-geneva.org/

History 30 Oct 2002. Founded as a committee of *Conference of Non-Governmental Organizations in Consultative Relationship with the United Nations (CONGO, #04635).* Takes over activities of *United Nations Spiritual Caucus*, founded 24 Oct 2001. Reactivated following dissolution in 2015. **Aims** Bring the spiritual and values dimension in all areas of the United Nations agenda and of public *policy.* **Structure** Board, comprising Chair, Vice-Chair, Secretary and Treasurer. **Languages** English, French, German, Italian. **Staff** Voluntary. **Finance** Members' dues: Swiss Fr 50. **Activities** Involved in: Proposal for United Nations Decade of Inter-Religious Dialogue and Cooperation for Peace; Sacred Natural Sites; Human Rights Council; Spiritual and ethical values; Interfaith dialogue; Indigenous values and traditions. Organizes: monthly meetings at UN; side-events at various organizations. **Events** *General Meeting* Geneva (Switzerland) 2011, *Meeting* Geneva (Switzerland) 2010, *Meeting* Geneva (Switzerland) 2010, *General Meeting* New York, NY (USA) 2010, *Week of spirituality, values and global concerns* New York, NY (USA) 2010. **Publications** Online publications.
Members NGOs in consultative status with ECOSOC and members of CONGO, including the following listed in this Yearbook (21):
- *3HO Foundation (#22046);*
- *Anglican Consultative Council (ACC, #00828);*
- *Brahma Kumaris World Spiritual University (BKWSU, #03311);*
- *CIVICUS: World Alliance for Citizen Participation (#03962);*
- *Conference of Non-Governmental Organizations in Consultative Relationship with the United Nations (CONGO, #04635);*
- *David M Kennedy Center for International Studies;*
- *European Forum of Muslim Women (EFOMW, #07321);*
- *Fondation de l'entre-connaissance (FEC);*
- *Foundation for Gaia (#09957);*
- *Institute for Planetary Synthesis (IPS, #11287);*
- *International Association for Religious Freedom (IARF, #12130);*
- *International Association of Educators for World Peace (IAEWP);*
- *International Association of Gerontology and Geriatrics (IAGG, #11920);*
- *Planetary Association for Clean Energy (PACE, #18381);*
- *Rissho Kosei-Kai (RKK);*
- *Salvation Army (#19041);*
- *Society for Psychological Study of Social Issues (SPSSI);*
- *Susila Dharma International Association (SDIA, #20048);*
- *World Federation for Mental Health (WFMH, #21455);*
- *World Student Christian Federation (WSCF, #21833);*
- *Worldwide Organization for Women (WOW).* [2020/XE4445/y/**E**]

♦ NGO Committee on the Status of Women, Geneva 17117

Pres c/o CoNGO, CP 50, 1211 Geneva 20, Switzerland. T. +41223011000. Fax +41223012020. E-mail: contact@ngocsw-geneva.ch.
URL: http://www.ngocsw-geneva.ch/

History 1973, as *Sub-Committee on the Status of Women, Geneva*; within the framework of *Conference of Non-Governmental Organizations in Consultative Relationship with the United Nations (CONGO, #04635).* Until Jan 2002 a Sub-Committee of *Committee of NGOs on Human Rights, Geneva (#04275)*, when it became a Substantive Committee of CONGO. **Aims** Work in partnership with the UN and its specialized agencies to influence *governments* to respect the commitments they have made at world conferences and through international conventions and principals; maintain a global momentum for mainstreaming *gender equality.* **Structure** Officers: President; 2 Vice-Presidents; 2 Secretaries; Treasurer. Working groups (11): ECE Working Group on Women; Employment; Environment; Girl Child; Health and Human Rights; Nutrition; Peace; Migrant and Refugee Women; Task Force on Bangwe; Task Force on Jumping the Fence; Violence Against Women. **Activities** Works to raise awareness and be sensitive to promoting gender equality and women's participation in decision making in all areas relevant to improving their lives; shares information and provides a platform where women and men come together to show how society benefits from women's equal access and opportunities to participate in policy and decision making. *'Special Project Bangwe'* concerned with promotion of peace and non violence in the region of the African Great Lakes through training in awareness raising and capacity building particularly for grassroot women. Holds joint meetings with *Vienna NGO Committee on the Status of Women (#20775)* and *NGO Committee on the Status of Women, New York NY (see: #04635)* on issues concerning gender mainstreaming and the advancement of women. **Events** *Forum* Geneva (Switzerland) 2014, *General Meeting* Geneva (Switzerland) 2009, *NGO interactive round table on the UN-ECE Beijing + 15 regional review meeting* Geneva (Switzerland) 2009, *NGO ECE forum* Geneva (Switzerland) 2004. **Publications** *Geneva Advocacy Notes.*
Members Organizations (62), including 54 organizations listed in this Yearbook:
- *All India Women's Conference (AIWC, #00737);*
- *Associated Country Women of the World (ACWW, #02338);*
- *Association for the Prevention of Torture (APT, #02869);*
- *Baha'i International Community (#03062);*
- *Brahma Kumaris World Spiritual University (BKWSU, #03311);*
- *Conference of European Churches (CEC, #04593);*
- *Education International (EI, #05371);*
- *Federation of American Women's Clubs Overseas (FAWCO, #09416);*
- *Femmes Africa solidarité (FAS, #09732);*
- *General Arab Women Federation (GAWF, no recent information);*
- *Graduate Women International (GWI, #10688);*
- *Inter-African Committee on Traditional Practices Affecting the Health of Women and Children (IAC, #11384);*
- *International Alliance of Women (IAW, #11639);*
- *International Association for Counselling (IAC, #11821);*
- *International Baby Food Action Network (IBFAN, #12305);*
- *International Council of Jewish Women (ICJW, #13036);*
- *International Council of Nurses (ICN, #13054);*
- *International Council of Women (ICW, #13093);*
- *International Council on Social Welfare (ICSW, #13076);*
- *International Federation of Business and Professional Women (BPW International, #13376);*
- *International Federation of Red Cross and Red Crescent Societies (#13526);*
- *International Federation of Settlements and Neighbourhood Centres (IFS, #13538);*
- *International Federation of Women in Legal Careers (IFWLC, #13579);*
- *International Federation of Women Lawyers (FIDA, #13578);*
- *International Inner Wheel (IIW, #13855);*
- *International Kundalini Yoga Teachers Association (IKYTA, see: #22046);*
- *International Service for Human Rights (ISHR, #14841);*
- *International Social Service (ISS, #14886);*
- *Make Mothers Matter (#16554);*
- *Organisation mondiale des anciens élèves de l'enseignement catholique (OMAEC, #17816);*
- *Pan Pacific and South East Asia Women's Association (PPSEAWA, #18186);*
- *Public Services International (PSI, #18572);*
- *Socialist International Women (SIW, #19341);*
- *Soroptimist International (SI, #19686);*
- *Terre des Hommes International Federation (TDHIF, #20133);*
- *The Lutheran World Federation (LWF, #16532);*
- *Unis pour l'Equite et la Fin du Racisme (UFER, #20490);*
- *Women's Federation for World Peace International (WFWPI);*
- *Women's International Democratic Federation (WIDF, #21022);*
- *Women's International League for Peace and Freedom (WILPF, #21024);*
- *Women's International Zionist Organization (WIZO, #21030);*
- *Women's World Summit Foundation (WWSF, #21038);*
- *World Alliance of Young Men's Christian Associations (YMCA, #21090);*
- *World Association of Girl Guides and Girl Scouts (WAGGGS, #21142);*
- *World Federation of Methodist and Uniting Church Women (WFM and UCW, #21457);*
- *World Federation of Ukrainian Women's Organizations (WFUWO, #21496);*
- *World Federation of United Nations Associations (WFUNA, #21499);*
- *World Jewish Congress (WJC, #21599);*
- *World Organisation Against Torture (OMCT, #21685);*
- *World Organization of the Scout Movement (WOSM, #21693);*
- *World Union of Catholic Women's Organisations (WUCWO, #21876);*
- *World Young Women's Christian Association (World YWCA, #21947);*
- *Zonta International (#22038).* [2016/XE2259/y/**E**]

♦ NGO Committee on the Status of Women, New York NY (see: #04635)
♦ NGO Committee on the Status of Women, Vienna / see Vienna NGO Committee on the Status of Women (#20775)
♦ NGO Committee to Stop Trafficking in Persons, Inc. / see NGO Committee to Stop Trafficking in Persons
♦ NGO Committee to Stop Trafficking in Persons (internationally oriented national body)

♦ NGO Committee on Sustainable Development, New York 17118

Co-Chair c/o Franciscans Int, 3305 Wallace Avenue, Bronx NY 10467, USA. T. +17185474604. Fax +17185474607. E-mail: ngocsdunc@gmail.com.
URL: http://ngocsd-ny.org/

History Founded as *NGO Special Committee on the Second Development Decade*, subsequently *NGO Committee on Development, New York*, in the framework of *Conference of Non-Governmental Organizations in Consultative Relationship with the United Nations (CONGO, #04635).* **Events** *Meeting on Peace Building and Education for the SDGs* New York, NY (USA) 2018. **Members** Membership not specified. [2015/XE1643/**E**]

♦ NGO Committee on Sustainable Development, Vienna 17119

Comité des ONG pour le développement à Vienne

Sec address not obtained.
URL: https://ngocsdvienna.org/

History 1994, Vienna (Austria), as a committee of *Conference of Non-Governmental Organizations in Consultative Relationship with the United Nations (CONGO, #04635).* Original title: *NGO Committee on Development, Vienna – Comité des ONG pour le développement à Vienne.* **Aims** Coordinate the work of non-governmental organizations in consultative status with the United Nations (ECOSOC) in the fields of development and North-South relations. **Structure** Board. **Languages** English. **Activities** Events/meetings.
Members Organizations (24):
- *Academic Council on the United Nations System (ACUNS, #00020);*
- *CARE International (CI, #03429);*
- *Federation of Associations of Former International Civil Servants (FAFICS, #09457);*
- *Graduate Women International (GWI, #10688);*
- *HOPE '87 – Hundreds of Original Projects for Employment;*
- *International Federation for Home Economics (IFHE, #13447);*
- *International Federation of Business and Professional Women (BPW International, #13376);*
- *International Federation of Social Workers (IFSW, #13544);*
- *International Physicians for the Prevention of Nuclear War (IPPNW, #14578);*
- *International Planned Parenthood Federation (IPPF, #14589);*
- *Pax Romana, International Catholic Movement for Intellectual and Cultural Affairs (ICMICA, #18267);*
- *SERVAS International (#19234);*
- *Socialist International Women (SIW, #19341);*
- *Society for International Development (SID, #19581);*
- Society for the Advancement of Global Understanding (VFV);
- *Soka Gakkai International (SGI, #19672);*
- *Soroptimist International (SI, #19686);*
- *Sovereign Military Order of the Temple of Jerusalem (SMOTJ);*
- *SÜDWIND – Verein für Entwicklungspolitische Bildungs- und Öffentlichkeitsarbeit;*
- *Vienna Institute for International Dialogue and Cooperation (VIDC);*
- *Women's Federation for World Peace International (WFWPI);*
- *Women's International Zionist Organization (WIZO, #21030);*
- *World Federation of United Nations Associations (WFUNA, #21499);*
- *Zonta International (#22038).*

NGO Relations Sister committees: *NGO Committee on Development, Geneva (#17104); NGO Committee on Sustainable Development, New York (#17118).* Secretariat provided by: *International Progress Organization (IPO, #14653).* [2019/XE4542/**E**]

♦ NGO Committee on UNICEF 17120

Contact UNICEF House, 3 UN Plaza, New York NY 10017, USA. T. +12123267713. Fax +12127354406. E-mail: info@ngocomunicef.org.
URL: https://ngocomunicef.org/home/about/

History Apr 1949, New York, NY (USA). Founded by 3rd Conference of International Non-Governmental Organizations held under auspices of UN Department of Public Information (DPI). Cooperative relations between the Administration of *UNICEF (#20332)* and NGOs were formalized with establishment, Jul 1949, of the *UNICEF-UNAC Advisory Committee of Non-Governmental Organizations*, consisting of 13 NGOs. In Apr 1952, UNICEF Executive Board approved the granting of consultative status to member organizations of this Committee which, at the same time, reconstituted itself under present title. Rules of procedure revised: May 1983; Apr 1986. In 1995, 186 NGOs held consultative status with UNICEF. **Aims** Advocate for the promotion and protection of children's rights in partnership with UNICEF. **Structure** Annual General Meeting of members. Board, comprising President, Deputy President and 8 member organizations, elected by postal ballot for 2-year terms, meets both in New York NY (USA) and Geneva (Switzerland). **Languages** English, French, Spanish. **Staff** None. President, Deputy President and Board members work on a voluntary basis aided by some staff from UNICEF NGO Sections in New York NY (USA) and Geneva (Switzerland). **Finance** Sources: contributions; grants; members' dues. **Activities** UNICEF grants consultative status to international NGOs that already hold consultative status with ECOSOC, based on Article 71 of UN Charter, which wish to formalize their relationship to UNICEF. These NGOs are then invited to belong to the Committee in order to undertake joint activities. The Committee has relations with both UNICEF Executive Board and its Administration. UNICEF Offices of Non-Governmental Affairs in New York NY (USA) and Geneva (Switzerland) assist in a supportive and consultative role, provide nongovernmental organizations with information on UNICEF's programmes and policy and assist in developing joint programmes at international and national levels. Reports of Committee activities are presented at annual session of UNICEF Executive Board. Working Groups of NGO representatives in New York NY and Geneva focus on: Convention on the Rights of the Child; Street Children and Children in Especially Difficult Circumstances (Children in Armed Conflicts, Exploited Children); Girls, including *NGO Working Group on Girls* and its *International Network for Girls (INfG, #14273);* Education for Girls; Values and Ethics. The Committee organizes workshops, fora, consultations and other meetings to discuss situations and make recommendations for action on behalf of children. **Events** *Children's forum* New York, NY (USA) 2002, *Conference on the implementation of Convention on the rights of the child and children in especially difficult circumstances in East Asia and Pacific Region* 1996, *Meeting on the contribution of youth to lasting peace* Geneva (Switzerland) 1994, *Annual general meeting and mini-forum* New York, NY (USA) 1994, *Conference on advancing the rights of children* Antigua (Guatemala) 1993. **Publications** Thematic publications; bibliographies; reports on meetings.
Members International NGOs (120) having consultative status with UNICEF:
- *African Association of Education for Development (ASAFED, no recent information);*
- *All India Women's Conference (AIWC, #00737);*
- *All Pakistan Women's Association (APWA);*
- *Amref Health Africa (#00806);*

- *Anti-Slavery International (#00860)*;
- *Associated Country Women of the World (ACWW, #02338)*;
- *Association Mondiale des Amis de l'Enfance (AMADE, #02808)*;
- *Baha'i International Community (#03062)*;
- *Baptist World Alliance (BWA, #03176)*;
- *Brahma Kumaris World Spiritual University (BKWSU, #03311)*;
- *CARE International (CI, #03429)*;
- *Caritas Internationalis (CI, #03580)*;
- *Catholic International Education Office (#03604)*;
- *Catholic Relief Services (CRS, #03608)*;
- *ChildFund International (#03869)*;
- *Childhood Education International (CE International)*;
- *CHILDHOPE International Alliance (inactive)*;
- *Commonwealth Medical Association (CMA, #04351)*;
- *Covenant House*;
- *Dayemi Complex Bangladesh (DCB)*;
- DCI Focal Point on Sexual Exploitation of Children;
- *Defence for Children International (DCI, #05025)*;
- *Fédération internationale des communautés éducatives (FICE-International, #09622)*;
- *Friends World Committee for Consultation (FWCC, #10004)*;
- *Graduate Women International (GWI, #10688)*;
- *Greek Orthodox Archdiocesan Council of America (GOAC, #10708)*;
- *Helen Keller International (HKI, #10902)*;
- *Humanists International (#10972)*;
- *Human Rights Watch Children's Rights Project (inactive)*;
- *Inclusion International (#11145)*;
- *International Agency for the Prevention of Blindness (IAPB, #11597)*;
- *International Association for Religious Freedom (IARF, #12130)*;
- *International Association of Educators for World Peace (IAEWP)*;
- *International Association of Logopedics and Phoniatrics (IALP, #12005)*;
- *International Association of Schools of Social Work (IASSW, #12149)*;
- *International Board on Books for Young People (IBBY, #12366)*;
- *International Catholic Child Bureau (#12450)*;
- *International Catholic Committee of Nurses and Medico-social Assistants (#12451)*;
- *International Catholic Migration Commission (ICMC, #12459)*;
- *International Centre of Films for Children and Young People (#12493)*;
- *International College of Surgeons (ICS, #12650)*;
- *International Confederation of Midwives (ICM, #12863)*;
- *International Council for Education of People with Visual Impairment (ICEVI, #13015)*;
- *International Council of Jewish Women (ICJW, #13036)*;
- *International Council of Nurses (ICN, #13054)*;
- *International Council of Voluntary Agencies (ICVA, #13092)*;
- *International Council of Women (ICW, #13093)*;
- *International Council on Jewish Social and Welfare Services (INTERCO, #13035)*;
- *International Falcon Movement – Socialist Educational International (IFM-SEI, #13327)*;
- *International Federation for Home Economics (IFHE, #13447)*;
- *International Federation of Business and Professional Women (BPW International, #13376)*;
- *International Federation of Fe y Alegria (FIFyA, #13425)*;
- *International Federation of Red Cross and Red Crescent Societies (#13526)*;
- *International Federation of Settlements and Neighbourhood Centres (IFS, #13538)*;
- *International Federation of Social Workers (IFSW, #13544)*;
- *International Federation of Women in Legal Careers (IFWLC, #13579)*;
- *International Inner Wheel (IIW, #13855)*;
- *International Institute of Rural Reconstruction (IIRR, #13921)*;
- *International League of Associations for Rheumatology (ILAR, #14016)*;
- *International Movement ATD Fourth World (#14193)*;
- *International Planned Parenthood Federation (IPPF, #14589)*;
- *International Social Service (ISS, #14886)*;
- *International Union Against Tuberculosis and Lung Disease (The Union, #15752)*;
- *International Union for Health Promotion and Education (IUHPE, #15778)*;
- *International Union of Socialist Youth (IUSY, #15815)*;
- *Junior Chamber International (JCI, #16168)*;
- *La Leche League International (LLLI, #16433)*;
- *Lions Clubs International (LCI, #16485)*;
- *Organisation mondiale des anciens élèves de l'enseignement catholique (OMAEC, #17816)*;
- *PAI (#18025)*;
- *Pan African Institute for Development (PAID, #18053)*;
- *Pan American Development Foundation (PADF, #18094)*;
- *Pan Pacific and South East Asia Women's Association (PPSEAWA, #18186)*;
- *PATH (#18260)*;
- *Pathfinder International (#18261)*;
- *Pax Christi – International Catholic Peace Movement (#18266)*;
- *Perhaps Kids Meeting Kids can make a Difference (KMK)*;
- *Plan International (#18386)*;
- *Rädda Barnen – Save the Children Sweden*;
- *Religions for Peace (RfP, #18831)*;
- *RI Global (#18948)*;
- *Rissho Kosei-Kai (RKK)*;
- *Rotary International (RI, #18975)*;
- *Salvation Army (#19041)*;
- *Save the Children Federation (SCF)*;
- *Save the Children International (#19058)*;
- *Save the Children UK (SC UK)*;
- *Society for International Development (SID, #19581)*;
- *Society for Psychological Study of Social Issues (SPSSI)*;
- *Soroptimist International (SI, #19686)*;
- *SOS-Kinderdorf International (#19693)*;
- *Susila Dharma International Association (SDIA, #20048)*;
- *Terre des Hommes International Federation (TDHIF, #20133)*;
- *Union internationale des architectes (UIA, #20419)*;
- *Unis pour l'Equite et la Fin du Racisme (UFER, #20490)*;
- *Universal Esperanto Association (UEA, #20676)*;
- *Women's International Democratic Federation (WIDF, #21022)*;
- *Women's International League for Peace and Freedom (WILPF, #21024)*;
- *World Alliance of Young Men's Christian Associations (YMCA, #21090)*;
- *World Assembly of Youth (WAY, #21113)*;
- *World Association of Girl Guides and Girl Scouts (WAGGGS, #21142)*;
- *World Confederation for Physical Therapy (WCPT, #21293)*;
- *World Council of Churches (WCC, #21320)*;
- *World Education (WE)*;
- *World Federation for Mental Health (WFMH, #21455)*;
- *World Federation of Methodist and Uniting Church Women (WFM and UCW, #21457)*;
- *World Federation of Public Health Associations (WFPHA, #21476)*;
- *World Federation of Ukrainian Women's Organizations (WFUWO, #21496)*;
- *World Federation of United Nations Associations (WFUNA, #21499)*;
- *World Information Transfer (WIT, #21583)*;
- *World Jewish Congress (WJC, #21599)*;
- *World Muslim Congress (WMC, #21664)*;
- *World Organization for Early Childhood Education (OMEP, #21689)*;
- *World Organization of Family Doctors (WONCA, #21690)*;
- *World Organization of United Cities and Local Governments (UCLG, #21695)*;
- *World Union for Progressive Judaism (WUPJ, #21883)*;
- *World Union of Catholic Women's Organisations (WUCWO, #21876)*;
- *World Vision International (WVI, #21904)*;
- *World Young Women's Christian Association (World YWCA, #21947)*;
- *Zonta International (#22038)*.

Consultative Status Consultative status granted from: *ECOSOC (#05331)* (Roster). **NGO Relations** Informal relations and communication exchange with: *International Conference of NGOs (#12883)*; *Conference of Non-Governmental Organizations in Consultative Relationship with the United Nations (CONGO, #04635)*; other groupings of non-governmental organizations. [2023/XE2973/y/**E**]

♦ NGO Committee on Youth 17121

Chair Office for Intl Affairs and Human Rights, Lutheran World Federation, Ecumenical Centre, 150 Route de Ferney, PO Box 2100, 1211 Geneva, Switzerland. T. +41227916365.
Contact CP 50, 1211 Geneva 20, Switzerland.

History New York NY (USA), as a committee of *Conference of Non-Governmental Organizations in Consultative Relationship with the United Nations (CONGO, #04635)*. Previously also been referred to as *United Nations NGO Committee on Youth*. **Aims** Serve as a space for information sharing among youth NGOs based or represented in Geneva (Switzerland) that have ECOSOC status. **Structure** Meets 6 times a year. **Languages** English. **Activities** Sponsors events in conjunction with youth organizations which have official connections at the United Nations. **Members** Large, worldwide and regional youth movements working closely with the United Nations, faith-based NGOs, political youth organizations and women's organizations. Membership countries not specified. [2016/XE1387/**E**]

♦ NGO Commonwealth Women's Network (CWN) 17122

Main Office c/o EASSI, PO Box 24965, Kampala, Uganda. T. +25641285163 – +25641285194. Fax +25641285306.

History Sep 1991. Also referred to as *Commonwealth Women's Network*. **Aims** Create and strengthen relationships among women, policy-makers and women ngos in the Commonwealth. **Events** *Meeting* Cyprus 1993. **IGO Relations** *Commonwealth Secretariat (#04362)*. **NGO Relations** Supports: *Global Call for Action Against Poverty (GCAP, #10263)*. [2016/XF6511/**F**]

♦ NGO CSTIP – NGO Committee to Stop Trafficking in Persons (internationally oriented national body)
♦ NGO CSW Vienna / see Vienna NGO Committee on the Status of Women (#20775)
♦ NGO/DPI Executive Committee / see Global NGO Executive Committee (#10507)
♦ NGO Environment Liaison Board (inactive)
♦ ngo-federatie – Vlaamse Federatie van NGO's voor Ontwikkelingssamenwerking (internationally oriented national body)
♦ NGO Forum / see NGO Forum on Cambodia (#17124)

♦ NGO Forum on ADB 17123

Exec Dir 85-A Masikap Extension, Barangay Central, Diliman, Quezon City, Philippines. T. +6324361858. Fax +6329214412. E-mail: secretariat@forum-adb.org.
URL: http://www.forum-adb.org/

History 1991, as *NGO Working Group (NWG) on the ADB*, 20 NGOs from 16 countries. Reorganized 1997. Registered in accordance with Filipino law, 2001. **Aims** Enhance the capacities of *civil society* organizations and movements in Asia *Pacific* to combat *Asian Development Bank* (ADB) policies, projects and programs that threaten people's lives, the environment and their communities. **Structure** Forum Annual Meeting (FAM). International Committee, consisting of regional representatives from: South Asia; Southeast Asia; Central Asia; Mekong Subregion; Pacific; Japan; Netherlands; Philippines. Secretariat, based in Manila (Philippines), headed by Executive Director. **Events** *Annual Symposium* Agra (India) 2016.
Members Organizations (over 250) in 31 countries and territories:
Armenia, Australia, Azerbaijan, Bangladesh, Belgium, Cambodia, China, Czechia, Germany, Hong Kong, India, Indonesia, Japan, Kazakhstan, Kyrgyzstan, Malaysia, Mongolia, Nepal, Netherlands, Norway, Pakistan, Papua New Guinea, Philippines, Sri Lanka, Tajikistan, Thailand, UK, Ukraine, USA, Uzbekistan, Vietnam.
Included in the above, 29 organizations listed in this Yearbook:
- *Asian NGO Coalition for Agrarian Reform and Rural Development (ANGOC, #01566)*;
- *Asia Pacific Network on Food Sovereignty (APNFS, #01965)*;
- *Both ENDS (#03307)*;
- *CEE Bankwatch Network (#03624)*;
- *Charles Stewart Mott Foundation*;
- *Coalition of the Flemish North South Movement – 11 11 11*;
- *Development Alternatives with Women for a New Era (DAWN, #05054)*;
- *Earth Economics*;
- *EarthRights International (ERI)*;
- *Environmental Defense Fund (EDF)*;
- *Focus on the Global South (Focus, #09807)*;
- *Ford Foundation (#09858)*;
- *Foreningen for Internasjonale Vannstudier (FIVAS)*;
- *Friends of the Earth International (FoEI, #10002)*;
- *Global Alliance for Incinerator Alternatives (GAIA, #10203)*;
- *Greenpeace International (#10727)*;
- *International Accountability Project (IAP)*;
- *International NGO Forum on Indonesian Development (INFID, #14366)*;
- *International Rivers*;
- *International South Group Network (ISGN, no recent information)*;
- *Jubilee South – Asian Peoples' Movement on Debt and Development (JSAPMDD, #16160)*;
- *NGO Forum on Cambodia (#17124)*;
- *Oxfam Australia*;
- *Oxfam GB*;
- *Sasakawa Peace Foundation (SPF)*;
- *South Asia Network on Dams, Rivers and People (SANDRP)*;
- *Southeast Asia Regional Initiatives for Community Empowerment (SEARICE, #19795)*;
- *Southeast Asia Rivers Network (SEARIN, no recent information)*;
- *Urgewald*.

IGO Relations *Asian Development Bank (ADB, #01422)*. [2015/XJ4694/y/**F**]

♦ NGO Forum on Cambodia 17124

Exec Dir 9-11 Street 476, Sk Toul Tumpung I, PO Box 2295, Phnom Penh 3, Cambodia. T. +85523214429. Fax +85523994063. E-mail: info@ngoforum.org.kh.
URL: http://www.ngoforum.org.kh/

History 1986. Moved from UK to Cambodia in 1993. Former names and other names: *Non-Governmental Organization Forum on Cambodia* – alias; *NGO Forum* – alias. Registration: Ministry of Interior, No/ID: 304 Sar Chor Nor, Start date: 7 Mar 2012, Cambodia, Phnom Penh. **Aims** Coordinate and equip members, networks of NGOs, CSOs, and other stakeholders in actively engaging in policy dialogue and advocacy to ensure equitable, inclusive and sustainable development in Cambodia. **Structure** Management Committee (as Governing Board); Coordination Committee. **Languages** English, Mon-Khmer languages. **Staff** 23.00 FTE, paid; 4.00 FTE, voluntary.
Finance Supported by:
- *ActionAid (#00087)* (Cambodia);
- *American Friends Service Committee (AFSC)*;
- *Brot für die Welt*;
- *Caritas Internationalis (CI, #03580)*;
- *Catholic Agency for Overseas Development (CAFOD)*;
- Center on Budget and Policy Priorities;
- *Development and Peace (CCODP)*;
- *DIAKONIA of Asia-Pacific (DAP, #05064)*;
- *Folkekirkens Nødhjælp (FKN)*;
- *German Catholic Bishops' Organisation for Development Cooperation (MISEREOR)*;
- *ICCO – Interchurch Organization for Development Cooperation*;
- *International Land Coalition (ILC, #13999)*;
- *International Union for Conservation of Nature and Natural Resources (IUCN, #15766)*;
- Mekong Region Land Governance;
- *Non-Timber Forest Products Exchange Programme for South and Southeast Asia (NTFP-EN, #17151)*;
- *Norwegian People's Aid (NPA)*;
- Oxfam Cambodia;
- *Oxfam GB*;
- *Oxfam Novib*;
- *Scottish Catholic International Aid Fund (SCIAF)*;
- *Trocaire – Catholic Agency for World Development*;
- *UNDP (#20292)*.

Annual budget: 1,000,000 USD (2020).
Activities Events/meetings; projects/programmes; research/documentation. **Events** *Annual General Meeting* Phnom Penh (Cambodia) 1997, *Annual general meeting* Phnom Penh (Cambodia) 1996, *Half-yearly meeting* Brussels (Belgium) 1991. **Publications** *Land and Life Newsletter*, *NGO Forum Magazine*. Annual Report; progress reports; surveys; leaflets; calendars; case studies; statements; action plans; position papers.

Members International, local and sectoral NGOs (representing Europe, North America, Australia and Japan), which have projects in Cambodia (88), including the following 33 listed in this Yearbook:
- *ActionAid (#00087)* (Cambodia);
- *ADD International*;
- *American Friends Service Committee (AFSC)*;
- *Asociación por la Paz y el Desarrollo (Paz y Desarrollo, no recent information)* (Cambodia section);
- *CARE International (CI, #03429)*;
- *Caritas Australia*;
- *Catholic Relief Services (CRS, #03608)* (Cambodia section);
- *Christian Outreach – Relief and Development (CORD)*;
- *Church World Service (CWS)*;
- *Concern Worldwide*;
- *Finn Church Aid (FCA)*;
- *Folkekirkens Nødhjaelp (FKN)*;
- *GRET*;
- *Health Poverty Action (HPA)*;
- *HelpAge International (#10904)*;
- *ICS* (Cambodia section);
- *Japan International Volunteer Centre (JVC)*;
- *Jesuit Refugee Service (JRS, #16106)* (Cambodia);
- *Maryknoll Mission Association of the Faithful (MMAF)* (Cambodia section);
- *Non-Timber Forest Products Exchange Programme for South and Southeast Asia (NTFP-EN, #17151)*;
- *Norwegian People's Aid (NPA)*;
- *Oxfam Australia*;
- *Oxfam GB*;
- *Planète Enfants & Développement*;
- *Plan International (#18386)*;
- *Save the Children Norway (Redd Barna)*;
- *Swedish NGO Centre for Development Cooperation (Forum Syd)*;
- *Swiss Interchurch Aid (EPER)*;
- *The Lutheran World Federation (LWF, #16532)* (Cambodia section);
- *Welthungerhilfe*;
- *Wildlife Alliance (#20957)*;
- *World Renew*;
- *World Vision International (WVI, #21904)* (Cambodia section).

NGO Relations Member of (1): *NGO Forum on ADB (#17123)*. Cooperates with (1): *Asian NGO Coalition for Agrarian Reform and Rural Development (ANGOC, #01566)*. [2020.12.02/XE1562/y/**E**]

♦ NGO Forum on Environment (FOE) 17125

Chair FOE NGO Alliance, Chemin de l'Etang 37, 1219 Geneva, Switzerland. E-mail: ngocoe@gmail.com.

History Set up when over 20 non-governmental organizations came together, Apr 2010, in Geneva (Switzerland), and requested the Board of the *NGO Alliance on Global Concerns and Values (NGO Alliance, #17102)* to establish a United Nations committee on the environment. Original title: *NGO Committee on Environment (CoE)*. **Aims** Further and strengthen an environmental perspective in all areas of the United Nations agenda and of public policy. **Structure** Board. **Languages** English, French. **Staff** Voluntary. **Finance** Members' dues (annual). **Activities** Politics/policy/regulatory; knowledge management/information dissemination; networking/liaising; guidance/assistance/consulting; advocacy/lobbying/activism; awareness raising; events/meetings. **Events** *Meeting* Geneva (Switzerland) 2011, *Meeting* Geneva (Switzerland) 2010.

Members Founding and current members (33):
- Al Hakim Foundation;
- *Buddha's Light International Association (BLIA, #03346)*;
- *Center for Human Rights and Environment (CEDHA)*;
- *Environmental Ambassadors for Sustainable Development (Environmental Ambassadors)*;
- *Findhorn Foundation (#09774)*;
- *Foundation for Gaia (#09957)*;
- *Global Ecovillage Network (GEN, #10331)*;
- *Graduate Women International (GWI, #10688)*;
- *Initiatives of Change International – Caux (IofC, #11213)*;
- *Institute for Planetary Synthesis (IPS, #11287)*;
- *Institute of Global Education*;
- *International Association of Gerontology and Geriatrics (IAGG, #11920)*;
- *International Council of Women (ICW, #13093)*;
- *International Federation of Business and Professional Women (BPW International, #13376)*;
- *International Islamic Relief Organization (IIRO)*;
- *Inuit Circumpolar Council (ICC, #15995)*;
- *Make Mothers Matter (#16554)*;
- North South XXI;
- *Pax Romana, International Catholic Movement for Intellectual and Cultural Affairs (ICMICA, #18267)*;
- *Planetary Association for Clean Energy (PACE, #18381)*;
- *Rencontre africaine pour la défense des droits de l'homme (RADDHO)*;
- *Soroptimist International (SI, #19686)*;
- *Sovereign Military Order of the Temple of Jerusalem (SMOTJ)*;
- *Temple of Understanding (ToU, #20124)*;
- *Tribal Link Foundation*;
- *UNESCO (#20322)* (Extea);
- *United Network of Young Peacebuilders (UNOY, #20653)*;
- *Women's International League for Peace and Freedom (WILPF, #21024)*;
- *World Association of Girl Guides and Girl Scouts (WAGGGS, #21142)*;
- *Worldwide Organization for Women (WOW)*;
- *Zonta International (#22038)*. [2016.06.01/XJ2408/y/**E**]

- ♦ NGO Group / see Child Rights Connect (#03884)
- ♦ NGO Group for the Convention on the Rights of the Child / see Child Rights Connect (#03884)
- ♦ NGO Group for the CRC / see Child Rights Connect (#03884)
- ♦ NGO Health Committee (internationally oriented national body)
- ♦ NGO for Health Promotion in Developing Countries / see Enraíza Derechos
- ♦ NGO IDWIP / see NGO Committee on the Rights of Indigenous Peoples (#17114)
- ♦ NGONET / see Choike (#03893)
- ♦ NGO Network of the Global Environment Facility / see GEF CSO Network (#10087)
- ♦ NGO Platform for the Euromed Civil Forum / see Euro-Mediterranean Foundation of Support to Human Rights Defenders (#05720)
- ♦ NGO Platform on Shipbreaking / see NGO Shipbreaking Platform (#17126)

♦ NGO Shipbreaking Platform 17126

Exec Dir Rue de la Linière 11, 1060 Brussels, Belgium. T. +3226094419. E-mail: nicola@shipbreakingplatform.org – info@shipbreakingplatform.org.
URL: http://www.shipbreakingplatform.org/

History Sep 2005, as *NGO Platform on Shipbreaking*, a global coalition of non-governmental organizations. Registered in accordance with Belgian law. EU Transparency Register: 34363287239-02. **Aims** Advance environmental, human and labour rights in the ship recycling industries. **Structure** Board. **Languages** English, French, Italian, Norwegian, Portuguese, Swedish. **Staff** 4.00 FTE, paid. **Finance** Members' dues. Additional funding. Annual budget (2016): about euro 200,000. **Activities** Advocacy/lobbying/activism; awareness raising; research/documentation. **Publications** Annual Report.

Members Organizations (18), including the following 7 listed in this Yearbook:
Basel Action Network (BAN, #03182); *Bellona Europa*; *European Federation for Transport and Environment (T and E, #07230)*; *Greenpeace International (#10727)*; *International Ban Asbestos Secretariat (IBAS)*; *International Federation for Human Rights (#13452)*; *North Sea Foundation*.

IGO Relations *Secretariat of the Basel Convention (SBC, #19196)*; *International Maritime Organization (IMO, #14102)*. **NGO Relations** Member of: *Spring Alliance (inactive)*. [2020/XJ8006/y/**E**]

- ♦ NGO Special Committee on the Second Development Decade / see NGO Committee on Sustainable Development, New York (#17118)
- ♦ NGO Sustainability (unconfirmed)

♦ NGO-UNESCO Liaison Committee 17127

Comité de liaison ONG-UNESCO

Pres Maison de l'UNESCO, 1 rue Miollis, 75732 Paris CEDEX 15, France. T. +33145683668 – +33145683667. Fax +33145683667. E-mail: comite.liaison.ong@unesco.org.
URL: http://www.ngo-unesco.net/

History Set up within the framework of *International Conference of NGOs (#12883)*, which it represents between conferences. Functions as a partnership between *UNESCO (#20322)* and non-governmental organizations. Former names and other names: *Standing Committee of NGOs* – former; *Comité permanent des ONG* – former. **Aims** Represent the collective interests of NGOs at UNESCO; implement the collective actions of NGOs; promote the achievement of the objectives set by the International Conference of NGOs, in particular through Joint Programme Commissions and Working Groups. **Structure** Conference elects Committee comprising President and representatives of 9 NGOs in official relations with UNESCO. **Languages** English, French. **Staff** None paid. **Finance** Voluntary contributions; support from *UNESCO (#20322)* and private funds. **Activities** Guidance/assistance/consulting; research/documentation; training/education. **Events** *International Forum of NGOs in Official Partnership with UNESCO* Ottawa, ON (Canada) 2022, *International Conference of Non-Governmental Organizations* Paris (France) 2022, *International Forum of NGOs in Official Partnership with UNESCO* Paris (France) 2021, *Challenging inequalities* Paris (France) 2019, *International Conference of Non-Governmental Organizations* Paris (France) 2018. **Publications** *Link/Lien* (periodical).

Members Members (2017-2018):
Catholic International Education Office (#03604); China Folklore Photographic Association; *Consejo Latinoamericano de Ciencias Sociales (CLACSO, #04718)*; *Coordinating Committee for International Voluntary Service (CCIVS, #04819)*; *Forum for African Women Educationalists (FAWE, #09896)*; *International Council of Organizations for Folklore Festivals and Folk Art (#13058)*; *International Federation of Coalitions for Cultural Diversity (IFCCD, #13394)*; *Rotary International (RI, #18975)*; *Sozopol Foundation*; *World Association of Girl Guides and Girl Scouts (WAGGGS, #21142)*.

IGO Relations *UNESCO (#20322)*. **NGO Relations** Cooperates with organizations maintaining official relations with UNESCO. Links with UNESCO joint programme commissions. [2022.10.18/XK1094/y/**E**]

- ♦ **NGOWG** NGO Working Group for Women, Peace and Security (#17129)
- ♦ NGO Working Group / see NGO Forum on ADB (#17123)

♦ NGO Working Group on the Security Council 17128

Coordinator 365 5th Ave, Suite 5203, New York NY 10016, USA. T. +12128171929. E-mail: coordinator@ngowgsc.org.
URL: http://www.ngowgsc.org/

History 1997. **Aims** Bring together NGOs for meetings with Security Council Ambassadors and high-level UN officials. **Structure** Steering Group; Secretariat. **Activities** Events/meetings.

Members Representatives of 37 NGOs:
- *Action Against Hunger (#00086)*;
- *Amnesty International (AI, #00801)*;
- *Baha'i International Community (#03062)*;
- *Bureau international des Médecins sans frontières (MSF International, #03366)*;
- *CARE International (CI, #03429)*;
- *Caritas Internationalis (CI, #03580)*;
- *Center for Civilians in Conflict (CIVIC)*;
- *Coalition for the International Criminal Court (CICC, #04062)*;
- *Crisis Action (#04957)*;
- *Franciscans International (FI, #09982)*;
- *Friedrich-Ebert-Stiftung (FES)*;
- *Global Centre for the Responsibility to Protect (GCR2P, #10277)*;
- *Global Justice Center (GJC)*;
- *Humanity and Inclusion (HI, #10975)*;
- *Human Rights Watch (HRW, #10990)*;
- *International Crisis Group (Crisis Group, #13111)*;
- *International Federation for Human Rights (#13452)*;
- *Jacob Blaustein Institute for the Advancement of Human Rights (JBI)*;
- *Lawyers Committee on Nuclear Policy (LCNP)*;
- *Lutheran Office for World Community*;
- *Mennonite Central Committee (MCC)*;
- *Network for Religious and Traditional Peacemakers (#17054)*;
- *NGO Committee on Disarmament, Peace and Security, New York NY (#17106)*;
- *NGO Working Group for Women, Peace and Security (NGOWG, #17129)*;
- *Nonviolent Peaceforce (NP, #17153)*;
- *Oxfam International (#17922)*;
- *Pax Christi – International Catholic Peace Movement (#18266)*;
- Presbyterian Church, USA;
- *Quaker United Nations Office (QUNO, #18588)*;
- *Save the Children International (#19058)*;
- *Security Council Report (SCR, #19210)*;
- *The United Methodist Church (UMC, #20514)*;
- *Watchlist on Children and Armed Conflict (Watchlist)*;
- *Women's Refugee Commission (WRC)*;
- *World Council of Churches (WCC, #21320)*;
- *World Federation of United Nations Associations (WFUNA, #21499)*. [2021.05.25/XM6113/y/**E**]

♦ NGO Working Group for Women, Peace and Security (NGOWG) 17129

Contact 777 United Nations Plaza, New York NY 10017, USA. T. +12125577298. E-mail: info@womenpeacesecurity.org.
URL: http://www.womenpeacesecurity.org/

History May 2000. **Aims** Advocate for equal and full participation of women in all efforts to create and maintain international peace and security. **Staff** 3.00 FTE, paid. **Activities** Advocacy/lobbying/activism; guidance/assistance/consulting; networking/liaising; awareness raising; monitoring/evaluation.

Members Organizations (19):
Amnesty International (AI, #00801); *CARE International (CI, #03429)*; *Catholic Organization for Relief and Development (Cordaid)*; *Center for Reproductive Rights*; Consortium on Gender, Security and Human Rights; *Global Justice Center (GJC)*; *Global Network of Women Peacebuilders (GNWP, #10503)*; *Global Partnership for the Prevention of Armed Conflict (GPPAC, #10538)*; *Human Rights Watch (HRW, #10990)*; *International Alert (#11615)*; *MADRE*; *Nobel Women's Initiative (#17144)*; *OutRight Action International*; *Oxfam International (#17922)*; *Plan International (#18386)*; *Refugees International (RI)*; *Saferworld*; *Women's International League for Peace and Freedom (WILPF, #21024)*; *Women's Refugee Commission (WRC)*.

NGO Relations Member of: *NGO Working Group on the Security Council (#17128)*. [2019.06.24/XM3631/y/**E**]

- ♦ NGPT – International Conference on Nanogenerators and Piezotronics (meeting series)
- ♦ **NGR** Nordiska Godtemplarrådet (#17483)
- ♦ NGU – Nordic Graphical Union (no recent information)
- ♦ NGU – Nordisk Grafisk Union (no recent information)

♦ NGVA Europe 17130

SG Rue d'Arlon 80, 1040 Brussels, Belgium. T. +3228944829. E-mail: info@ngva.eu.
URL: http://www.ngva.eu/

History Jan 1994. Founded, following development since 1991. Operational under current title since 2008. Former names and other names: *European Natural Gas Vehicle Association (ENGVA)* – former (1994); *NGVA Europe – Natural and Bio Gas Vehicle Association* – full title. Registration: Banque-Carrefour des Entreprises, No/ID: 0644.709.510, Start date: 21 Dec 2015, Belgium; EU Transparency Register, No/ID: 1119946481-54, Start date: 8 Oct 2008. **Aims** Defend the interests of the natural gas vehicle (NGV) related industry; drive and coordinate cooperation between the gas industry, and the vehicle and component industry, in order to have one platform for common interests and activities; serve as a link and communication channel between the industry and European decision makers to create standards, regulations and viable market conditions for bio/natural gas used as a transportation fuel. **Structure** General Meeting (annual); Board of Directors; Working Committees; Office in Brussels (Belgium). **Languages** English. **Staff** 5.00 FTE, paid. **Finance** Sources: members' dues. Other sources: participation in European projects; voluntary sponsored

contributions. **Activities** Advocacy/lobbying/activism; events/meetings; knowledge management/information dissemination; research/documentation. **Events** *Conference on Gmobility* Brussels (Belgium) 2019, *Annual Conference* Barcelona (Spain) 2017, *Regional Seminar* Helsinki (Finland) 2015, *Annual Conference* Brussels (Belgium) 2014, *Annual Conference* Gothenburg (Sweden) 2013.
Members Companies involved in distribution, pipelines, natural gas production and fuel retail; equipment suppliers; service organizations and consultants; non-profit research institutes, advocacy groups, government agencies and employees. Members (over 160) in 30 countries:
Austria, Belgium, Bosnia-Herzegovina, Bulgaria, Croatia, Czechia, Denmark, Finland, France, Germany, Greece, Hungary, Iceland, Ireland, Italy, Luxembourg, Montenegro, Netherlands, Norway, Poland, Portugal, Russia, Serbia, Slovakia, Spain, Sweden, Switzerland, Türkiye, UK, Ukraine.
IGO Relations Accredited by: *United Nations Framework Convention on Climate Change – Secretariat (UNFCCC, #20564).* **NGO Relations** Member of (2): *GasNaturally (#10074); Global Methane Initiative (GMI, #10471)* (Project Network). Cooperates with (3): *Comité européen de normalisation (CEN, #04162); Covenant of Mayors for Climate and Energy (#04939); European Automobile Manufacturers' Association (ACEA, #06300).* [2020/XD6086/**D**]

♦ NGVA Europe – Natural and Bio Gas Vehicle Association / see NGVA Europe (#17130)

♦ NGV Global 17131

Main Office PO Box 128446, Remuera, Auckland, New Zealand. T. +6495233567. E-mail: admin@ngvglobal.org.
URL: http://www.ngvglobal.org/
History 1986. Changed business name to 'NGV Global' in 2010. Former names and other names: *International Association for Natural Gas Vehicles (IANGV)* – full title. **Aims** Increase use of natural gas and biomethane for transport; facilitate efficiency, safety and durability in all areas of the industry. **Structure** General Assembly (annual); Board of Directors; Advisory Board; Technical Committee; Work Groups. **Languages** English. **Staff** 2.00 FTE, paid. **Finance** Sources: members' dues. Other sources: Educational activities. **Activities** Events/meetings; guidance/assistance/consulting; knowledge management/information dissemination; standards/guidelines. **Events** *Biennial Conference* Rotterdam (Netherlands) 2017, *Biennial Conference* Long Beach, CA (USA) 2014, *Biennial Conference* Mexico City (Mexico) 2012, *Biennial Conference* Rome (Italy) 2010, *Biennial Conference* Rio de Janeiro (Brazil) 2008. **Publications** *NGV Global Newsletter* (weekly) – electronic. Position papers; business papersj; conference updates; technology developments. Databases on NGV statistics; industry knowledgebase. **Members** Categories: Affiliated Regional and National NGV Associations; Multi-National Corporations and NGOs; Individual. Membership countries not specified. **Consultative Status** Consultative status granted from: *ECOSOC (#05331)* (Roster). **IGO Relations** Cooperates with: UN Working Party on Pollution and Energy (GRPE); UN 24th Informal Group on Gaseous Fuelled Vehicles; UN Heavy Duty Dual-Fuel Task Force. **NGO Relations** Member of: *Global Methane Initiative (GMI, #10471)* Project Network. Cooperates with: *International Organization for Standardization (ISO, #14473),* including all committee involved in NGVs. [2021/XD3580/**C**]

♦ NGVO – Nederlandstalig Genootschap voor Vergelijkende Studie van Opvoeding en Onderwijs (internationally oriented national body)
♦ NGWM – Nordic Geological Winter Meeting (meeting series)
♦ **NHA** Nordic Hunters' Alliance (#17313)
♦ **NHC** Nordic Hemophilia Council (#17311)
♦ NHC – Nordic Hydrographic Commission (see: #13825)
♦ **NHESG** Nordic Health Economists Study Group (#17309)
♦ **NHF** Nordic Handicap Federation (#17308)
♦ **NHF** Nordisk Herpetologisk Forening (#19089)
♦ **NHH** Nordic Alliance of the Hard of Hearing (#17484)
♦ NHL – Nordiske Hjerte- og Lungesykes Forbund (inactive)
♦ **NH** NET-HERITAGE (#16978)
♦ NHPLO – NATO Hawk Production and Logistics Organization (no recent information)
♦ NHRF – Norwegian Human Rights Fund (internationally oriented national body)
♦ **NHRN** Nordic Himalaya Research Network (#17312)
♦ NHR – Nordic House in Reykjavik (internationally oriented national body)
♦ NHS – Nordic History Studies (internationally oriented national body)
♦ NHS – Nordiska Handelsarbetsgivare-Föreningarnas Samarbetskommitté (inactive)
♦ **NHS** Nordiska Hörselskadades Samarbetskommittén (#17484)
♦ NHV – Nordiska högskolan för folkkälsovetenskap (inactive)
♦ Niamey Convention – African Union Convention on Cross-Border Cooperation (2014 treaty)
♦ **NIA** Nanotechnology Industries Association (#16933)
♦ NIAS-Institut nordique d'études asiatiques (#17132)
♦ NIAS / see NIAS-Nordisk Institut for Asienstudier (#17132)
♦ **NIAS** NIAS-Nordisk Institut for Asienstudier (#17132)
♦ NIAS-Nordic Institute of Asian Studies (#17132)

♦ NIAS-Nordisk Institut for Asienstudier (NIAS) 17132

NIAS-Institut nordique d'études asiatiques – NIAS-Nordic Institute of Asian Studies – NIAS-Pohjoismainen Aasiantutkimusinstituutti
Admin Oster Farimagsgade 5, 1353 Copenhagen K, Denmark. T. +4535329500. Fax +4535329504.
URL: http://nias.ku.dk/
History 8 Jun 1965, as *Scandinavian Institute of Asian Studies (SIAS) – Centralinstitut for Nordisk Asienforskning (CINA),* on acceptance by governments of Denmark, Finland, Iceland, Norway, Sweden. Commenced operations 1967. New statutes adopted: 17 Nov 1976; 1 Jan 1988; 1 Jan 1998. Subsequently changed title to *Nordic Institute of Asian Studies (NIAS) – Institut nordique d'études asiatiques – Nordisk Institut for Asienstudier (NIAS) – Pohjoismainen Aasiantutkimusinstituutti,* in 1988. Current title adopted 2005. **Aims** As a research and service institute, focus on political, economic, business, social and cultural transformations in modern Asia in their historical contexts; provide a common platform for close collaboration with communities of Asian studies scholars and students in all Nordic countries. **Structure** Board (meeting 2 times a year); Units (4); Administration. **Languages** Danish, English, Norwegian, Swedish. **Staff** 24.00 FTE, paid. **Finance** Funded by Nordic governments through *Nordic Council of Ministers (NCM, #17260)* and by members of *Nordic NIAS Council (NNC, #17368),* with Copenhagen University (Denmark) as founding partners. **Activities** Knowledge management/information dissemination; guidance/assistance/consulting; research/documentation; projects/programmes. **Events** *Sino-Nordic Women and Gender Studies Conference* Taipei (Taiwan) 2020, *Sino-Nordic Women and Gender Studies Conference* Oslo (Norway) 2017, *Conference on long peace of East Asia since 1979 and West Europe since 1945* Seoul (Korea Rep) 2009, *Symposium on oral and written traditions in Chinese fiction* Oslo (Norway) 2007, *Conference on new Asian dynamics in science, technology and innovation* Copenhagen (Denmark) 2006. **Publications** Books. Information Services: Bibliographic database. Provides: library facilities; information and documentation services. **Information Services** *NIAS Linc* – library specializing in modern Asia.
Members Academic institutions (39) in 5 countries:
Denmark, Finland, Iceland, Norway, Sweden.
NGO Relations Member of: *China-Nordic Research Center (CNARC, #03890); European Alliance for Asian Studies (#05861); European Information Network on International Relations and Area Studies (EINIRAS, #07534).* Supports and provides coordinating facilities for: *Centralasiatisk Selskab (DSCA); Eurasia Political Culture Research Network (EPCReN, no recent information); Gendering Asia Network (#10097); Nordic Association for China Studies (NACS, #17182); Nordic Association for Japanese and Korean Studies (NAJAKS, #17195); Nordic Association for South Asian Studies (NASA, no recent information); Nordic Association for Southeast Asian Studies (NASEAS, inactive); Nordic Association for the Study of Contemporary Japanese Society (NAJS); Nordic Forum for South Asia (NoFSA, #17300); Nordic Himalaya Research Network (NHRN, #17312).* Instrumental in setting up: *European Vietnam Studies Network (EUROVIET, no recent information).* Cooperates on a bilateral basis with a number of institutions in Asia, Europe, North America and Australia. [2021/XD3929/j/**E***]

♦ NIAS-Pohjoismainen Aasiantutkimusinstituutti (#17132)
♦ **NIB** Nordic Investment Bank (#17327)
♦ **NIB** Nordiska Investeringsbanken (#17327)
♦ **NIBS** Network of International Business Schools (#17041)
♦ Nicaragua and Central American Historical Institute (internationally oriented national body)
♦ NICC – Nordic Invasive Cardiology Conference (meeting series)
♦ NICCO – Nippon International Cooperation for Community Development (internationally oriented national body)
♦ Nice Agreement Concerning the International Classification of Goods and Services for the Purposes of the Registration of Marks (1957 treaty)
♦ Nicefördraget (2001 treaty)
♦ **NICE** Network for Innovation in Career Guidance and Counselling in Europe (#17038)
♦ NICE – Network of International Circus Exchange (unconfirmed)
♦ **NICE** Nordic Initiative for Corporate Economics (#17319)
♦ Nice-traktaten (2001 treaty)
♦ Nice Treaty (2001 treaty)
♦ **Nice Union** Special Union for the International Classification of Goods and Services for the Purposes of the Registration of Marks (#19913)
♦ NICIS – Neurosciences in Intensive Care International Symposium (meeting series)

♦ Nickel Institute 17133

Office Manager Rue Belliard 12, 3rd Floor, 1040 Brussels, Belgium. T. +3222903200. Fax +3222903220. E-mail: brussels@nickelinstitute.org.
Pres Bay Street 161, Suite 2700, Toronto ON M5J 2S1, Canada. T. +14165917999.
URL: http://www.nickelinstitute.org/
History 1984. Current name adopted by merger of the Nickel Development Institute (NiDI) and *Nickel Producers Environmental Research Association (NiPERA).* Registration: No/ID: 0874.267.631, Start date: 1 May 2005, Belgium; EU Transparency Register, No/ID: 77947983421-21, Start date: 8 Apr 2010. **Aims** Promote and support the proper use of nickel in appropriate applications. **Structure** Offices in: Belgium; Canada; China; Japan; USA. **Languages** English. **Staff** 41.00 FTE, paid. **Finance** Sources: members' dues. **Activities** Events/meetings; politics/policy/regulatory; research and development. **Events** *Finnish European Union Presidency Conference on Supporting a Competitive and Sustainable Battery Value Chain in the EU* Brussels (Belgium) 2019. **Publications** *Nickel Magazine* (3 a year). **Information Services** *Technical Guides* – an extensive library of technical guides for engineers and specifiers of nickel containing materials. **Members** Leading primary nickel producers (18). Membership countries not specified. **NGO Relations** Member of (6): *Association européenne des métaux (EUROMETAUX, #02578); European Committee for Surface Treatment (#06671); International Council on Mining and Metals (ICMM, #13048); METALS FOR BUILDINGS (#16737); ResponsibleSteel (#18921)* (associate); *TEAM STAINLESS (#20113).* Partner of (1): *Global Battery Alliance (GBA, #10249).* Liaison organization of: *Comité européen de normalisation (CEN, #04162).* [2022.11.10/XG6155/j/**F**]

♦ NIC – Nordic Infrastructure Conference (meeting series)
♦ NIC – Nordic Network for Intercultural Communication (internationally oriented national body)
♦ Nicolas Barré – Soeurs de l'Enfant-Jésus (religious order)
♦ Nicolas Hulot Foundation for Nature and Mankind / see Fondation pour la Nature et l'Homme
♦ **NICOLE** Network for Industrially Contaminated Land in Europe (#17036)
♦ Nicosia charter – Charter on Euro-Mediterranean Cooperation Concerning the Environment in the Mediterranean Basin (1990 treaty)
♦ NIDA / see Atlas Alliance
♦ NIDCAP Federation International (internationally oriented national body)
♦ **NIDO Europe** Nigerians in Diaspora Organisation Europe (#17135)
♦ NIDOS / see Scotland's International Development Alliance
♦ NIDPRODEV / see Leadership Initiative for Transformation and Empowerment
♦ **NIEA** Network of International Education Associations (#17042)
♦ Niederländische Sprachunion (internationally oriented national body)
♦ **NIERSC** Nansen International Environmental and Remote Sensing Centre (#16935)
♦ NIFF – Nordic Chiropractic Information Center – BatLife Nordica (unconfirmed)
♦ NIFIN / see Nordic Culture Point
♦ NIF – New Israel Fund (internationally oriented national body)
♦ NIF – Nordiska Industriarbetare Federationen (inactive)
♦ **NIFS** Nordisk Institutt for Sjørett (#17515)
♦ NIFU – Nordisk Institutt for Studier av Innovasjon, Forskning og Utdanning (internationally oriented national body)
♦ NIFU Norsk institutt for studier av forskning og utdanning / see Nordisk Institutt for Studier av Innovasjon, Forskning og Utdanning
♦ NIFU STEP / see Nordisk Institutt for Studier av Innovasjon, Forskning og Utdanning
♦ NIGD – Network Institute for Global Democratization (internationally oriented national body)

♦ Niger Basin Authority (NBA) 17134

Autorité du bassin du Niger (ABN)
Exec Sec NBA Headquarters, BP 729, Niamey, Niger. T. +22720723102. Fax +22720724208.
URL: http://www.abn.ne/
History 25 Nov 1964, Niamey (Niger). Founded in implementation of an Agreement, signed 23 Oct 1963, Niamey, by representatives of 9 States. Agreement revised: 2 Feb 1968; 15 Jun 1973. General Regulations for Navigation on the River Niger adopted at meeting of Council of Ministers, 22 Feb 1974, Niamey. Amended: 2 Feb 1968; 15 Jun 1973; 26 Jan 1979, Lagos (Nigeria). Listed name adopted, Faranah (Guinea), on signature of a new Convention. Former names and other names: *River Niger Commission* – former (25 Nov 1964 to 21 Nov 1981); *Commission du fleuve Niger (CFN)* – former (25 Nov 1964 to 21 Nov 1981). **Aims** Harmonize and coordinate national policies for development of the basin; plan development of the basin through development and execution of an "Integrated Development of the Basin"; design, achieve, exploit and maintain common infrastructures and projects; control and regulate navigation on the river, its tributaries and sub-tributaries; mobilize funds for studies and works needed for the development of the resources of the Basin. **Structure** Summit of the Heads of State and Government; Council of Ministers; Regional Steering Committee of Projects and Programs; Technical Committee of Experts; Executive Secretariat; Technical Directorate; Directorate of Administration and Finance; Basin Observatory. **Languages** English, French. **Staff** 65.00 FTE, paid. **Finance** Sources: contributions from Member States, based on a sharing formula; external assistance.
Activities cover: statistics and planning; water control and use; infrastructure; environmental control and regulation; land and agro-pastoral development. Priorities focus on: reforestation; dredging; construction of hydroelectric and multi-purpose dams, including mini-dams for rural electricity supplies and land improvements; provision of village water supplies. Integration and inter-State activities include: codifying information; regulation of river flow; improvement of water ways; energy, transport and communications.
Projects/Programmes and activities include: Niger-Hycos; Silting Control Programme in the Niger Basin; Shared Vision Process – development of a Sustainable Action Plan (SDAP), development of an Investment Programme and mobilization of investments; organizational and institutional reforms; support for integrated management of the water resources of the Niger Basin; reversing land and water degradation trends in the Niger Basin; observatory of the environment of the Niger Basin; Capacity Building of the Executive Secretariat (CIDA); financial and management capacity building for NBA; Echel EAU – IWRM tools; Development of Water Resources and Preservation of the Fragile Ecosystems of the Niger Basin. Projects/Programmes under negotiation include: River and Patrimony – reinforce water governance through networking of local riparian populations and appropriation of cultural resources – UNESCO; TwinBasin – NBA and Zambezi River Authority (ZRA); TwinBasin – CICOS and NBA; contribution of Venezuela to the actions relating to sustainable management of natural resources of the Niger Basin – UNCCD; payment of environmental services – UNDP; NigerWet Initiative – Ramsar Convention.
River Niger Basin Development Fund (no recent information), set up 1980, Conakry (Guinea), assists in financing development programmes. Maintains Centre of Hydrological Forecasting – part of the *'Hydroniger Project',* concerned with hydrological monitoring and forecasting using satellite transmission; and Documentation and Analysis Centre. Organizes regional information network; prepares regulations on navigation. Instrumental in setting up *Liptako-Gourma Integrated Development Authority (LGA, no recent information).*

Events *Ordinary session* Abuja (Nigeria) 2018, *Ordinary session* Abuja (Nigeria) 2018, *Ordinary session* Conakry (Guinea) 2017, *NBA Technical and Financial Partners Meeting* Niamey (Niger) 2017, *Extraordinary Session* Abuja (Nigeria) 2016. **Publications** *Niger Basin Authority Information Bulletin* (periodical). Bulletins on the hydrological situation (12 a year).
Members Governments of 9 countries:
Benin, Burkina Faso, Cameroon, Chad, Côte d'Ivoire, Guinea, Mali, Niger, Nigeria.
IGO Relations Memorandum of Cooperation with: *Secretariat of the Convention of Wetlands (#19200)*. Relationship agreement with: *UNIDO (#20336)*. Cooperates with: *West African Science Service Center on Climate Change and Adapted Land Use (WASCAL, #20897)*.
Partner of:
- *African Development Bank (ADB, #00283)*;
- *AGRHYMET Regional Centre (#00565)*;
- *Arab Bank for Economic Development in Africa (#00904)*;
- *Canadian International Development Agency (CIDA, inactive)*;
- *DANIDA*;
- *Deutsche Gesellschaft für Internationale Zusammenarbeit (GIZ)*;
- *Economic Community of West African States (ECOWAS, #05312)* – Water Resources Coordination Unit;
- *European Commission (EC, #06633)*;
- *Facilité africaine de l'eau (FAE, #09233)*;
- *FAO (#09260)*;
- *Fonds français pour l'environnement mondial (FFEM)*;
- *International Bank for Reconstruction and Development (IBRD, #12317)* (World Bank);
- *International Commission of the Congo-Ubangui-Sangha Basin (#12674)*;
- *Islamic Development Bank (IsDB, #16044)*;
- *Kuwait Fund for Arab Economic Development (KFAED)*;
- *Lake Chad Basin Commission (LCBC, #16220)*;
- *Liptako-Gourma Integrated Development Authority (LGA, no recent information)*;
- *OPEC Fund for International Development (OFID, #17745)*;
- *Secretariat of the United Nations Convention to Combat Desertification (Secretariat of the UNCCD, #19208)* – Venezuela Cooperation;
- *UNDP (#20292)*;
- *Union économique et monétaire Ouest africaine (UEMOA, #20377)*;
- *United Nations Economic Commission for Africa (ECA, #20554)*;
- *World Meteorological Organization (WMO, #21649)*.

NGO Relations Partner of: *BirdLife International (#03266)*; *Friedrich-Ebert-Stiftung (FES)*; *Global Water Partnership (GWP, #10653)* – West African Water Partnership; *International Secretariat for Water (ISW, #14822)*; *International Union for Conservation of Nature and Natural Resources (IUCN, #15766)*; *Kreditanstalt für Wiederaufbau (KfW)*; *Wetlands International (#20928)*; *World Wide Fund for Nature (WWF, #21922)*.
[2018/XD4526/**D***]

- ♦ Niger Delta Professionals for Development / see Leadership Initiative for Transformation and Empowerment
- ♦ Nigeria-Niger Joint Commission for Cooperation (internationally oriented national body)
- ♦ Nigerian Institute of International Affairs (internationally oriented national body)

♦ Nigerians in Diaspora Organisation Europe (NIDO Europe) 17135

Contact Nigeria High Commission, 9 Northumberland Avenue, London, WC2N 5BX, UK. T. +442079306895. E-mail: secretariat@nidoeurope.org – information@nidoeurope.org.
URL: http://www.nidoeurope.org/

History 2000. Registered in England and Wales. **Aims** Provide an umbrella to all Nigerians in Europe. **Structure** General Assembly; Board of Trustees. **Activities** Events/meetings. **Events** *AGM and Economic Development Summit* Rome (Italy) 2022, *Annual General Meeting* Lisbon (Portugal) 2017.
Members Chapters in 19 countries:
Austria, Belgium, Denmark, Finland, France, Germany, Greece, Ireland, Italy, Luxembourg, Netherlands, Poland, Russia, Spain, Sweden, Switzerland, Türkiye, UK, Ukraine. [2022/XM6439/**E**]

- ♦ Nigeria Trust Fund (internationally oriented national body)

♦ Nightingale Initiative for Global Health (NIGH World) 17136

Exec Dir 1160 Chemin d'Aylmer, Suite 108, Gatineau QC J9H 0E9, Canada. T. +18197787214. E-mail: codirector@nighvision.net.
URL: http://www.nighvision.net/

History 2006, Washington, DC (USA). Former names and other names: *NIGH USA* – former (2006 to 2008). Registration: 501(c)(3), Start date: 2006, USA; Start date: 2008, Canada. **Aims** Engage the common values and wisdom of nurses, midwives and concerned citizens; act as a catalyst for the transformation of individuals, communities and society for the achievement of a healthy world. **Structure** Board of Directors; Leadership Team. **Languages** English. **Staff** 3.00 FTE, voluntary. **Finance** Sources: donations. Annual budget: 20,000 USD. **Activities** Advocacy/lobbying/activism; events/meetings; knowledge management/information dissemination; networking/liaising. **Publications** Articles; book chapters. **Members** Not a formal membership organization. **Consultative Status** Consultative status granted from: *ECOSOC (#05331)* (Special). **NGO Relations** Member of (2): *Conference of Non-Governmental Organizations in Consultative Relationship with the United Nations (CONGO, #04635)*; *PMNCH (#18410)*. Cooperates with (3): *Commonwealth Nurses and Midwives Federation (CNMF, #04353)*; *Cooperation Canada*; *International Council of Nurses (ICN, #13054)*.
[2020.05.25/XM7246/**E**]

♦ Nightingale Mentoring Network 17137

Manager Malmö Univ, SE-206 06 Malmö, Sweden. T. +46709655510. E-mail: naktergalen@mau.se.
URL: https://nightingalementoring.mau.se/

History 2010. Initiated following programmes in Europe, the earliest one in Sweden, 1997. **Aims** Establish a European forum so as to facilitate cooperation between participants and the work with mentoring; exchange experience; improve the general quality of mentoring; provide a context elucidating cooperation between universities and local schools throughout Europe. **Structure** Board. **Languages** English. **Activities** Events/meetings; research and development. **Events** *Conference* Lillehammer (Norway) 2022, *Conference* Sweden 2021, *Conference* Malmö (Sweden) 2020, *Conference* Bodø (Norway) 2018, *Conference* Barcelona (Spain) 2017. **Publications** *Nightingale Mentoring Network Newsletter*.
Members Full in 7 countries:
Austria, Germany, Iceland, Norway, Spain, Sweden, Switzerland. [2022.05.04/XM8054/**F**]

- ♦ NIGH USA / see Nightingale Initiative for Global Health (#17136)
- ♦ **NIGH World** Nightingale Initiative for Global Health (#17136)
- ♦ NIGMI – Hydrometeorological Research Institute of Uzhydromet (internationally oriented national body)
- ♦ Nihon Chuto Gakkai (internationally oriented national body)
- ♦ Nihon Kirisuto-Kyo Kaigai Iryo-Kyoryoku Kai (internationally oriented national body)
- ♦ Nihon Kokusai Minkan Kyoryoku Kai (internationally oriented national body)
- ♦ Nihon Kokusai Mondai Kenkyu-Sho (internationally oriented national body)
- ♦ Nihon Shiryô Senmonka Oshu Kyôkai (#06095)
- ♦ NIHR / see Norwegian Centre for Human Rights
- ♦ NIIA – Nigerian Institute of International Affairs (internationally oriented national body)
- ♦ NIIS – Nordic Institute for Interoperability Solutions (internationally oriented national body)
- ♦ NIKK / see Nordic Information for Gender Knowledge (#17317)
- ♦ **NIKK** Nordic Information for Gender Knowledge (#17317)
- ♦ NILAS – Nordic Institute of Latin American Studies (internationally oriented national body)

♦ Nile Basin Capacity Building Network for River Engineering (NBCBN-RE) 17138

Manager Hydraulics Research Inst Regional Training Ctr, 13261 Delta Barrage, Cairo, Egypt. T. +20242183450. Fax +20242189539. E-mail: nbcbn-sec@nbcbn.com.
URL: http://www.nbcbn.com/

History 2002. Also known under the acronym *NBCBN*. **Aims** Through regional, multi-disciplinary and multi-stakeholder collaborative research in the Basin, contribute to sustainable solutions for integrated *water management*, achievement of Millennium Development Goals and the Nilotic water and climate dialogue. **Structure** Nodes (10). Secretariat. **Activities** Clusters (6): River Morphology Research; River Structure Research; Flood Management Research; Hydropower Research; Environmental Aspects Research; GIS and Modelling Research. **Publications** *NBCBN-RE Newsletter*.
Members Nodes in 10 countries:
Burundi, Congo DR, Egypt, Eritrea, Ethiopia, Kenya, Rwanda, Sudan, Tanzania UR, Uganda.
IGO Relations *Nile Basin Initiative (NBI, #17140)*. **NGO Relations** Member of: *Network for Capacity Building in Integrated Water Resources Management (CAP-Net, #17000)*. [2011/XJ2384/**F**]

♦ Nile Basin Discourse (NBD) 17139

Secretariat Plot 32 Nsamizi Rd, PO Box 185, Entebbe, Uganda. T. +256414322432. Fax +256414323930. E-mail: info@nilebasindiscourse.org.
URL: http://www.nilebasindiscourse.org/

History Founded 2003, with support of NB riparian states and international donors. Registered in accordance with the law of Uganda. **Aims** Promote *sustainable* and equitable *development*, management and utilization of the Nile resources, poverty reduction and cooperation in the Nile Basin. Serve as: a bottom-up communications pipeline for raising the voices of citizens and civil society up to governmental and regional levels; a top-down pipeline for educating and informing citizens and civil society on Nile issues and development projects; a horizontal pipeline between citizens and civil society organizations both within and across national borders for knowledge and capacity sharing. **Structure** General Assembly (annual); Board; Regional Secretariat located in Uganda; National Discourse Forums (NDFs). **Languages** English. **Staff** 6 FTE at Regional Secretariat; 10 FTE as National Programme Coordinators in each of the 10 Nile Basin countries. **Finance** Funded by Cooperation in International Waters in Africa (CIWA) of *International Bank for Reconstruction and Development (IBRD, #12317)* (World Bank). **Activities** Networking/liaising; advocacy/lobbying/activism; capacity building; awareness raising. **Publications** *Nile Voices*.
Members Full; Associate; Honorary. Civil society organizations (over 700) in 10 countries:
Burundi, Congo DR, Egypt, Eritrea, Ethiopia, Kenya, Rwanda, Sudan, Tanzania UR, Uganda.
IGO Relations Memorandum of Understanding with: *Intergovernmental Authority on Development (IGAD, #11472)*; *Nile Basin Initiative (NBI, #17140)*. **NGO Relations** Memorandum of Understanding with: *Global Water Partnership (GWP, #10653)*. [2016.09.02/XJ5089/**F**]

♦ Nile Basin Initiative (NBI) 17140

Initiative du bassin du Nil

Secretariat PO Box 192, Plot 12 Mpigi Road, Entebbe, Uganda. T. +256414321329 – +256414321424. Fax +256414320971. E-mail: nbisec@nilebasin.org.
URL: http://www.nilebasin.org/

History 22 Feb 1999, Dar es Salaam (Tanzania UR), by the Council of Ministers of Water Affairs of the Nile Basin states. **Aims** Work towards sustainable *socio-economic development* through the equitable utilization of, and benefit from, the common Nile basin water resources. **Structure** Nile Council of Ministers (Nile-COM), formerly Nile Council of Ministers of Water Affairs of the Nile Basin States. Supported by Technical Advisory Committee (TAC). Secretariat. Subsidiary Action Programs (SAPs) offices: Eastern Nile Technical Regional Office (ENTRO) – for *Eastern Nile Subsidiary Action Program (ENSAP)*; Nile Equatorial Lakes Subsidiary Action Program Coordination Unit (NELSAP-CU) – for *Nile Equatorial Lakes Subsidiary Action Program (NELSAP)*. **Activities** Politics/policy/regulatory. **Events** *African Great Lakes Conference* Entebbe (Uganda) 2017.
Members Governments of 10 countries:
Burundi, Congo DR, Egypt, Eritrea (Observer), Ethiopia, Kenya, Rwanda, Sudan, Tanzania UR, Uganda.
IGO Relations Partners: *African Development Bank (ADB, #00283)*; *Fonds français pour l'environnement mondial (FFEM)*; *Canadian International Development Agency (CIDA, inactive)*; *Department for International Development (DFID, inactive)*; *Deutsche Gesellschaft für Internationale Zusammenarbeit (GIZ)*; *European Union (EU, #08967)*; *International Bank for Reconstruction and Development (IBRD, #12317)*; *UNDP (#20292)*. **NGO Relations** Memorandum of Understanding with: *Nile Basin Discourse (NBD, #17139)*. Partner of: *Wetlands International (#20928)*. [2017/XF6429/**F***]

- ♦ Nile Basin Society (inactive)

♦ Nile Capacity Building Network in Integrated Water Resources Management (Nile-IWRM Net) 17141

Regional Coordinator c/o WaterTRAC, PO Box 2136, Khartoum, Sudan. T. +249912658768. Fax +249183482218.
URL: http://nileiwrm-net.org/

History Founded Mar 2005, Khartoum (Sudan). **Aims** Lead regionally driven capacity building action to enable need-responsive delivery of capacity building service in integrated water resource management by strong local institutions in the Nile Basin countries. **Structure** General Assembly; Steering Committee. Regional Secretariat. Country Chapters; Ad hoc Thematic Themes. **Languages** English. **Staff** 138.00 FTE, voluntary. 31 partner institutions. **Finance** Financed from capacity building service, international funds and partnerships. Budget: about euro 500,000. **Activities** include: capacity development; strengthening partnerships to improve water management practices; local and international knowledge management. **Publications** Case studies; training manuals.
Members Full in 10 countries:
Burundi, Congo DR, Egypt, Eritrea, Ethiopia, Kenya, Rwanda, Sudan, Tanzania UR, Uganda.
IGO Relations Support from: *Swedish International Development Cooperation Agency (Sida)*. *UNDP (#20292)*. **NGO Relations** Member of: *Network for Capacity Building in Integrated Water Resources Management (CAP-Net, #17000)*. Support from: DIGS. [2013/XJ2383/**E**]

- ♦ **Nile-IWRM Net** Nile Capacity Building Network in Integrated Water Resources Management (#17141)
- ♦ **NILS** Nordic IVF Laboratory Society (#17330)
- ♦ Nimatullahi tariqa (religious order)
- ♦ NIMD / see Netherlands Institute for Multiparty Democracy
- ♦ NIME – International Conference on New Interfaces for Musical Expression (meeting series)
- ♦ **NIME** Nordic Institute of Mission and Ecumenical Research (#17322)
- ♦ NIM – Nordic Infrastructure Managers (inactive)
- ♦ Nine Pin Association / see World Ninepin Bowling Association (#21673)
- ♦ NI – New Internationalist (internationally oriented national body)
- ♦ Niñez Integral (internationally oriented national body)
- ♦ NINO – Nederlands Instituut voor het Nabije Oosten (internationally oriented national body)
- ♦ **NI** Nonviolence International (#17152)
- ♦ Niños Alrededor del Mundo (internationally oriented national body)
- ♦ Pro Niños Pobres (internationally oriented national body)
- ♦ NIOHC – North Indian Ocean Hydrographic Commission (see: #13825)
- ♦ **NIOM** Nordiska Institutet för Odontologisk Materialprovning (#17485)
- ♦ **NIOM** Nordisk Institut for Odontologisk Materialprøvning (#17485)
- ♦ NIOZ / see Royal Netherlands Institute for Sea Research
- ♦ NIOZ – Royal Netherlands Institute for Sea Research (internationally oriented national body)
- ♦ **NIPNET** Nordic Interprofessional Network (#17326)
- ♦ Nippon Foundation (internationally oriented national body)
- ♦ Nippon International Cooperation for Community Development (internationally oriented national body)
- ♦ Nippon Kokusai Seiji Gakkai, Tokyo (internationally oriented national body)
- ♦ Nippon Oriento Gakkai (internationally oriented national body)
- ♦ **NIPS** Neural Information Processing Systems Foundation (#17069)
- ♦ NIPU – Nordic Inter-Parliamentary Union (inactive)
- ♦ NIR – Nordiska Industriläkarradet (inactive)
- ♦ **NISA** Nordic International Studies Association (#17325)
- ♦ **NISE** National Movements and Intermediary Structures in Europe (#16938)

♦ NISI MASA 17142

European Office Maison des associations du 10eme arrondissement, Bàl No 124, 206 quai de Valmy, 75010 Paris, France. E-mail: europe@nisimasa.com.
URL: http://www.nisimasa.com/

History Founded 2001. Full title: *NISI MASA – European Network of Young Cinema.* **Aims** Discover new film talents; develop cross-cultural audiovisual projects; foster *European* awareness through cinema; create a platform for discussion and collaboration for young European *filmmakers.* **Structure** Departments (4): Script; Debate; FilmLab; Network. **Languages** English, French, German. **Finance** Sources: European Project funds; structural grants. **Activities** Advocacy/lobbying/activism; events/meetings; publishing activities. **Publications** *Nisi Mazine.*

Members Full in 28 countries:
Albania, Austria, Bosnia-Herzegovina, Bulgaria, Croatia, Czechia, Denmark, Estonia, Finland, France, Germany, Greece, Italy, Kosovo, Lithuania, Luxembourg, Montenegro, Netherlands, North Macedonia, Norway, Poland, Portugal, Russia, Serbia, Slovenia, Spain, UK, Ukraine.

IGO Relations *European Commission (EC, #06633); European Youth Foundation (EYF, #09141).* **NGO Relations** *European Cultural Foundation (ECF, #06868).* [2019.06.05/XM6327/**F**]

- ♦ NISI MASA – European Network of Young Cinema / see NISI MASA (#17142)
- ♦ **NISN** Nordic Irish Studies Network (#17328)
- ♦ NIS – Nordiska Ingenjörssamfundet (inactive)
- ♦ **NISPAcee** Network of Institutes and Schools of Public Administration in Central and Eastern Europe (#17039)
- ♦ nitidae (unconfirmed)
- ♦ NIT – Institute for Tourism and Recreational Research in Northern Europe (internationally oriented national body)
- ♦ NIT – International Conference on New Information Technology (meeting series)

♦ Nitric Oxide Society (NO) 17143

Contact 2604 Elmwood Avenue, Ste 350, Rochester NY 14618, USA. E-mail: office@nitricoxidesociety.org.
URL: http://nitricoxidesociety.org/

History 1996. Incorporated in the State of California (USA). **Aims** Promote the advancement of basic and applied scientific research in all aspects of nitric oxide research; disseminate important research results to the general public concerning nitric oxide; develop and enhance the education and training of students and researchers in this field; foster interdisciplinary communication. **Structure** Board of Directors of 7. **Activities** Organizes: International Conference on the Biology, Chemistry and Therapeutic Application of Nitric Oxide. **Events** *International Conference on the Biology, Chemistry, and Therapeutic Applications of Nitric Oxide* Sendai (Japan) 2022, *International Conference on the Biology, Chemistry, and Therapeutic Applications of Nitric Oxide* Chicago, IL (USA) 2020, *International Conference on the Biology, Chemistry, and Therapeutic Applications of Nitric Oxide* Oxford (UK) 2018, *International Conference on the Biology, Chemistry and Therapeutic Application of Nitric Oxide* Cleveland, OH (USA) 2014, *International Meeting on the Role of Nitrite and Nitrate in Physiology, Pathophysiology and Therapeutics / Conference* Cleveland, OH (USA) 2014. **Publications** *Nitric Oxide Biology and Chemistry* – journal. [2013/XJ6657/**C**]

- ♦ Niue Treaty on Cooperation in Fisheries Surveillance and Law Enforcement in the South Pacific Region (treaty)
- ♦ **NIVA** Nordiska institutionen för vidareutbildning inom arbetsmiljöområdet (#17321)
- ♦ Niwano Heiwa Zaidan (internationally oriented national body)
- ♦ Niwano Peace Foundation (internationally oriented national body)
- ♦ Nizzan Sopimus (2001 treaty)
- ♦ NJAU – Nordisk Jernbane Avholdsunion (inactive)
- ♦ **NJC** Nordisk Journalistcenter (#17516)
- ♦ **NJF** Nordiska Jordbruksforskares Förening (#17486)
- ♦ **NJF** Nordiska Journalistförbundet (#17487)
- ♦ **NJF** Nordisk Jordmorforbund (#17345)
- ♦ **NJS** Forum for Nordisk Jernbane Samarbejde (#17395)
- ♦ **NJS** Nordisk Jägersamvirke (#17313)
- ♦ NJT – Nordiska Järnvägsmannaunionen (inactive)
- ♦ NJU – Nordisk Judo Union (inactive)
- ♦ NKA – Nordiska Kontaktorganet för Atomenergifrågor (inactive)
- ♦ NKB – Nordiska Kommittén för Byggbestämmelser (inactive)
- ♦ NKE – Nordiskt Kollegium för Ekologi (inactive)
- ♦ **NKF** Nordiska Konservatorsförbundet (#17188)
- ♦ **NKF** Nordiska Konstförbundet (#17176)
- ♦ **NKF** Nordisk Kökkenchef Federation (#17233)
- ♦ **NKF** Nordisk Konservatorforbund (#17188)
- ♦ NKFO – Nordisk Kollegium för Fysisk Oceanografi (inactive)
- ♦ **NKG** Nordiska Kommissionen för Geodesi (#17304)
- ♦ NKI – NephCure Kidney International (internationally oriented national body)
- ♦ NKJ / see Nordic Joint Committee for Agricultural and Food Research (#17332)
- ♦ **NKJ** Nordisk Kommitté för Jordbruks- och Matforskning (#17332)
- ♦ NKJS – Nordisk Kontaktorgan for Jord- og Skovbrugsspørgsmål (inactive)
- ♦ NKK – Nordiska Kulturkommissionen (inactive)
- ♦ NKO – Nordic Committee for Consultation in Fishery Matters (inactive)
- ♦ NKP – Nationaleuropäische Kommunotaristische Partei (internationally oriented national body)
- ♦ **NKR** Nordisk Kirkemusikråd (#17257)
- ♦ NKR / see Nordisk Tjenestemannsråd (#17538)
- ♦ **NKR** Nordkalottrådet (#17545)
- ♦ NKS – Nordiska Kvinnosaksföreningars Samorganisation (inactive)
- ♦ **NKS** Nordisk Kaktus Selskab (#17224)
- ♦ **NKS** Nordisk Kärnsäkerhetsforskning (#17517)
- ♦ NKS – Nordisk Kirkeligt Studieråd (inactive)
- ♦ **NKS** Nordisk Kommunalteknisk Samarbetskommitté (#17520)
- ♦ NKS – Nordisk Kongress i Synpedagogik (meeting series)
- ♦ NKS – Nordisk Konservativ Studienämnd (no recent information)
- ♦ **NKS** Nordisk Kontakt om Statsbyggeri (#17252)
- ♦ **NKSU** Nordens Konservativa Studentunion (#17161)
- ♦ **NKSU** Nordisk Konservator Studentunion (#17161)
- ♦ NKU – Nordisk Katolsk Udviklingshjaelp (inactive)
- ♦ **NKU** Nordisk Kennelunion (#17518)
- ♦ **NKVet** Nordisk Komité for Veterinaervitenskapelig Samarbeid (#17519)
- ♦ NKV – Nordiska Kommittén för Vägtrafiklagstiftning (inactive)
- ♦ NKV – Nordisk Komite for Vegtrafikklovgivning (inactive)
- ♦ **NKV** Nordiskt Kollegium för Viltforskning (#17262)
- ♦ **NLA** Nordic Logistics Association (#17338)
- ♦ NLC – Nordic Lung Congress (meeting series)
- ♦ **NLF** Nordisk Lichenologisk Förening (#17336)
- ♦ NLF – Nordisk Luftpostsamler Forening (inactive)
- ♦ NLKF – Nordisk Laeder Kemiker Forening (inactive)
- ♦ **NLL** Nordisk Laboratorium for Luminescensdatering (#17333)
- ♦ NLMC – Nordic Labour Market Committee (inactive)
- ♦ NLM – Norsk Luthersk Misjonssamband (internationally oriented national body)
- ♦ NLN – Nordiska Läkemedelsnämnden (inactive)
- ♦ NLP Global Body (unconfirmed)
- ♦ NLR – Nordisk Laegeråd (unconfirmed)
- ♦ NLRU – Nordens Liberale og Radikale Ungdomsforbund (no recent information)
- ♦ **NLS** Nordiska Läraerorganisationers Samråd (#17444)
- ♦ NLU – Nordisk Lastebil Union (inactive)
- ♦ **NMA** Nordic Midwives Association (#17345)
- ♦ NMCC – Nordic Memory Clinic Conference (meeting series)
- ♦ **NMC** News Media Coalition (#17093)
- ♦ NMC – Nordic Mycological Congress (meeting series)
- ♦ **NME** News Media Europe (#17094)
- ♦ NMEU – Nordic Music Education Union (inactive)
- ♦ **NMEU** Nuclear Medicine Europe (#17619)
- ♦ NMF – Nordisk Motivsamler Forbund (inactive)
- ♦ NMF / see TeleManagement Forum (#20123)
- ♦ NMKL / see Nordic-Baltic Committee on Food Analysis (#17215)
- ♦ **NMKL** Nordic-Baltic Committee on Food Analysis (#17215)
- ♦ **NML** Nordisk Medisinsk Laboratoriegruppe (#17523)
- ♦ NMM – Nordiske Meteorologmøtet (meeting series)
- ♦ **NMN** Norden Mot Narkotika (#17157)
- ♦ NM – Nordiska Samarbetskommittén för Materialforskning och- Provning (inactive)
- ♦ NMNW – No Means No Worldwide (internationally oriented national body)
- ♦ NMO – Nordic Master Painters' Organization (inactive)
- ♦ NMO – Nordisk Malermester Organisation (inactive)
- ♦ NMPU – Nordisk Musikpedagogisk Union (inactive)
- ♦ **NMR** Nordic Migration Research (#17346)
- ♦ **NMR** Nordiska Ministerrådet (#17260)
- ♦ **NMR** Nordisk Mejeriteknisk Råd (#17265)
- ♦ **NMR** Nordisk Ministerråd (#17260)
- ♦ **NMSBA** Neuromarketing Science and Business Association (#17071)
- ♦ **NMSG** Nordic Myeloma Study Group (#17347)
- ♦ NMS – Det Norske Misjonsselskap (internationally oriented national body)
- ♦ NMSSS / see NATO Support and Procurement Agency (#16948)
- ♦ NMTC – Nordic Music Therapy Conference (meeting series)
- ♦ NMU – Nordisk Musiker Union (no recent information)
- ♦ NMU – Nordisk Musikförläggerunion (no recent information)
- ♦ **NMWE** Natural Mineral Waters Europe (#16955)
- ♦ NNASA – Neonatal Nursing Association of Southern Africa (internationally oriented national body)
- ♦ **NNC** Nordic NIAS Council (#17368)
- ♦ NNC – Nordic Nutrition Conference (meeting series)
- ♦ **NNDR** Nordic Network on Disability Research (#17351)
- ♦ **NNFM** Nordic Network of Fetal Medicine (#17354)
- ♦ **NNF** Nordic Nurses' Federation (#17371)
- ♦ **NNF** Nordisk Navigasjonsforum (#17323)
- ♦ **NNGCP** Nordic Networking Group of Clinical Pharmacy (#17358)
- ♦ NNHA – Nordic Natural Horsemanship Association (inactive)
- ♦ **NNIML** Nordic Network for ICT, Media and Learning (#17357)
- ♦ NNJC – Nigeria-Niger Joint Commission for Cooperation (internationally oriented national body)
- ♦ **NNMPF** Nordisk Nettverk for Musikkpedagogikk Forskning (#17363)
- ♦ **NNN** Neglected Tropical Diseased NGO Network (#16969)
- ♦ **NNPF** Nordiskt Nätverk för Pedagogisk Filosofi (#17426)
- ♦ **NNPL** Nordic Network for research on Psychology and Law (#17364)
- ♦ **NNPS** Nordiska Neuropediatriska Sällskapet (#17367)
- ♦ **NNRME** Nordic Network for Research in Music Education (#17363)
- ♦ **NNS** Nordic Neuromodulation Society (#17366)
- ♦ NNT – International Conference on Nanoimprint and Nanoprint Technologies (meeting series)
- ♦ **NNU** Nordisk Numismatisk Union (#17370)
- ♦ **NoACM** Nordic Association for Computational Mechanics (#17187)
- ♦ NOAH International (internationally oriented national body)
- ♦ NOA – Nordic Ostomy Association (inactive)
- ♦ Noar Le'noar (#03291)
- ♦ NOAS – Norwegian Organization for Asylum Seekers (internationally oriented national body)
- ♦ **No Bases** International Network for the Abolition of Foreign Military Bases (#14225)
- ♦ Nobel Foundation (internationally oriented national body)
- ♦ Nobelstiftelsen (internationally oriented national body)

♦ Nobel Women's Initiative 17144

Main Office 261 Montreal Rd, Ste 310, Ottawa ON K1L 8C7, Canada. E-mail: info@nobelwomensinitiative.org.
URL: http://nobelwomensinitiative.org/

History 2006, by 6 Nobel Peace laureates. **Aims** Use the visibility and prestige of the Nobel prize to spotlight, amplify and promote the work of grassroots women's organizations and movements around the world; strengthen and expand feminist efforts to promote nonviolent solutions to war, violence and militarism. **NGO Relations** Member of: *Campaign to Stop Killer Robots (#03405); NGO Working Group for Women, Peace and Security (NGOWG, #17129).* Partner of: *Global Call for Climate Action (GCCA, inactive); International Campaign to Abolish Nuclear Weapons (ICAN, #12426).* [2022/XJ8319/v/**F**]

- ♦ Noble Order for Human Excellence (internationally oriented national body)

♦ NoBoMet 17145

Secretariat c/o NMi Certin, Hugo de Grootplein 1, 3314 EG Dordrecht, Netherlands. T. +31786332331.
URL: https://www.nobomet.org/

History Founded 2011, following initiation in 2010. 2010, as a *European Platform of Notified Bodies working in legal Metrology.* **Aims** Establish a platform for interagency communication in order to optimize the circumstances and conditions under which notified bodies working in legal metrology operate; make this transparent for manufacturers of measuring instruments for which conformity assessment is regulated. **Languages** English. **Finance** Members' dues. **Activities** Networking/liaising; events/meetings. **Events** *Meeting* Brussels (Belgium) 2017, *Meeting* Berlin (Germany) 2016. **Members** Notified bodies (38) working in legal metrology, including governmental agencies and private commercial organizations. Membership countries not specified. **NGO Relations** Cooperates with: *Association européenne de fabricants de compteurs d'eau et d'énergie thermique (AQUA, #02567); Comité européen des constructeurs d'instruments de pesage (CECIP, #04151); WELMEC – European Cooperation in Legal Metrology (#20857).* [2018/XJ9688/**F**]

- ♦ **NOBOS** Nordisk Møte for Barneonkologisk Sykepleie (#17524)
- ♦ Nobre Ordem Para Excelência Humana (internationally oriented national body)
- ♦ **NOCIES** Nordic Comparative and International Education Society (#17249)
- ♦ **NoC** Network of Internet and Society Research Centers (#17045)
- ♦ NOF / see Nederlandse Financierings-Maatschappij voor Ontwikkelingslanden
- ♦ NOFA – Nordisk Fagdidaktisk Konference (meeting series)
- ♦ NOFFI / see International Society of Fish and Shellfish Immunology (#15122)
- ♦ **NOF** Nordic Orthopedic Federation (#17379)
- ♦ **NOF** Nordiska Föreningen för Befrämjande af Odontologisk Undervisning och Forskning (#19070)
- ♦ NOF – Nordiska Organisationsföreningen (inactive)
- ♦ **NOF** Nordisk Odontologisk Forening (#19070)
- ♦ **NOF** Nordisk Ortopedisk Forening (#17379)
- ♦ **NOFOD** Nordic Forum for Dance Research (#17298)
- ♦ **NOFOMA** Nordic Logistics Research Network (#17339)
- ♦ **NOFOMA** Nordisk forskning om Materialadministration (#17339)
- ♦ NOFOS – Nordic Society for Forensic Odonto-Stomatology (no recent information)

- ♦ **NoFSA** Nordic Forum for South Asia (#17300)
- ♦ **NOFS** Nordens Offentliganställdas Fackliga Samorganisation (#17162)
- ♦ **NoFS** Nordic Filtration Society (#17289)
- ♦ NOFTIG – Nordisk Förening för Tillämpad Geofysik (no recent information)
- ♦ **NOGWHISTO** Network of Global and World History Organizations (#17033)
- ♦ NOHA / see Network on Humanitarian Action (#17034)
- ♦ **NOHA** Network on Humanitarian Action (#17034)
- ♦ NOHE Infancia / see Nobre Ordem Para Excelência Humana
- ♦ NOHE INTERNACIONAL – Nobre Ordem Para Excelência Humana (internationally oriented national body)
- ♦ NOHE – Noble Order for Human Excellence (internationally oriented national body)
- ♦ Noise and Vibration Emerging Methods Conference (meeting series)
- ♦ NOJFU – Nordiska Järnvägars Forsknings- och Utvecklingsråd (inactive)
- ♦ NOK – Nordic Congress of Ophthalmology (meeting series)
- ♦ **NOLAN** Nordic Latin American Research Network (#17334)
- ♦ NOLTA – International Symposium on Nonlinear Theory and its Applications (meeting series)
- ♦ NOMBA – Nordic Molecular Biology Association (no recent information)
- ♦ No Means No Worldwide (internationally oriented national body)
- ♦ **NOMESCO** Nordic Medico-Statistical Committee (#17342)
- ♦ **NOMESKO** Nordisk Medicinalstatistisk Kommitté (#17342)
- ♦ NOMS – Nordic Menopause Society (no recent information)
- ♦ NoMU / see Nordisk Orkestermusik Union (#17525)
- ♦ **NOMU** Nordisk Orkestermusik Union (#17525)
- ♦ NOMUS – Nordiska Musikkommittén (inactive)
- ♦ Non-aligned Countries Ad Hoc Group for the Solidarity Fund for Economic and Social Development (no recent information)
- ♦ Non-aligned Countries Group on Research and Information Systems / see Research and Information System for Developing Countries, India

♦ Non-Aligned Movement (NAM) 17146

Mouvement des pays non alignés – Movimiento de Paises No Alineados (MNOAL)

Correspondence Permanent Representative of the Hashemite Kingdom of Jordan to the United Nations, 866 2nd Avenue, 4th floor, New York NY 10017, USA. T. +12128329553. Fax +12128325346. E-mail: missionun@jordanmissionun.com.

History 1961, Belgrade (Yugoslavia). Sometimes referred to as *Movement of Non-Aligned Countries.* **Aims** Reaffirm and attach special importance to the following principles: *right* of the peoples who are not yet free to freedom, *self-determination* and *independence*; respect for sovereignty and territorial integrity of all states; the right of all states to equality and active participation in international affairs; the right of all sovereign nations to determine in full *freedom* the path of their internal political, economic, social and cultural *development*; the right of all peoples to the benefits of economic development and the fruits of the scientific and technological revolution; refraining from the threat or use of force; the principle of peaceful settlement of disputes. 'Basic aims of non-alignment': the pursuit of world peace and peaceful coexistence by strengthening the role of non-aligned countries within the United Nations so that it will be a more effective obstacle against all forms of aggressive action and the threat of the use of force against the freedom, independence, sovereignty and territorial integrity of any country; the fight against colonialism and racism which are a negation of human equality and dignity; the settlement of disputes by peaceful means; the ending of the arms race followed by universal disarmament; opposition to Great Power military bases and other foreign troops on the soil of other nations in the context of Great Power conflicts and colonial and racist suppression; the universality of and the stating of strengthening of the efficacy of the United Nations; the struggle for economic and mutual cooperation on the basis of equality and mutual benefit.
Structure Highest Authority is *Conference of Heads of State or Government of Non-Aligned Countries.* Chairman of the Non-Aligned Movement (Colombia for 1995-1998) is assisted by: Advisory Council; team of economic experts; Ambassadors-at-Large (4) for 4 regions (Africa, America, Europe, Asia and Middle East); Office of the Executive Assistant to the NAM Chairman; Technical Committee attached to the latter Office.
Ministerial conferences:
- *Conference of Foreign Ministers of Non-Aligned Countries*;
- *Conference of the Information Ministers of Non-Aligned Countries (COMINAC)*;
- *Ministerial Meeting of the Mediterranean Non-Aligned Countries.*

"Working Mechanism" consisting of:
- *Coordinating Bureau of the Non-Aligned Countries (#04815)*, normally meeting at United Nations Headquarters, New York NY (USA).

The Bureau coordinates joint activities aimed at implementing decisions and programmes adopted at Summit Conferences, Ministerial Conferences and other gatherings;
- *Standing Ministerial Committee for Economic Cooperation of the Non-Aligned Movement (SMC, no recent information)*;
- *Non-Aligned Movement Committee of Ministers on Imposition of Sanctions (no recent information)*;
- *Non-Aligned Movement Ministerial Committee on Methodology (no recent information)*;
- Open-ended Working Group of the Coordinating Bureau of the NAM for the Restructuring of the United Nations, including 5 Working Groups on specific issues and 5 Working/Drafting Groups to prepare NAM countries to participate in discussions on issues to be addressed by various Working Groups in the UN General Assembly;
- *Non-Aligned Committee of Nine on Palestine (no recent information)*;
- Contact Group on Cyprus;
- Task Force on Somalia;
- Task Force on Bosnia-Herzegovina.

Related bodies:
- *Centre for the Exchange of Information and Technology on Traditional Medicine (no recent information)*;
- *Group for South-South Consultation and Cooperation (no recent information)*;
- *Non-aligned Countries Ad Hoc Group for the Solidarity Fund for Economic and Social Development (no recent information)*, coordinating *Solidarity Fund for Economic and Social Development in the Non-aligned Countries (no recent information).*

Proposed body:
- *Advisory Group of Eminent Experts on Development Issues (no recent information).*

Languages Arabic, English, French, Spanish. **Staff** None, since no permanent secretariat. **Finance** Activities financed by the capacity of current Chairman and by voluntary contributions from certain members.
Activities Current special concerns include a *New World Information and Communication Order (NWICO)* and continuing imbalances and inequalities in this field. The Intergovernmental Council for Coordination of Cooperation of Non-Aligned Countries in the Field of Information and Communication aims to ensure that each non-aligned country creates the necessary material, technical and personnel conditions for cooperation this field. *Non-Aligned News Agency Pool (NANAP, inactive)* facilitates the concerted objective of member states and *Broadcasting Organizations of the Non-aligned Countries (BONAC, no recent information)* is also concerned in this arena. Work is going ahead on compiling the status of telecommunications facilities in the non-aligned countries and on encouraging bilateral and multilateral cooperation in the application of modern technology in the area of telecommunications and the mass media. *Centre for Science and Technology of the Non-Aligned and Other Developing Countries (NAM S and T Centre, #03784)* promotes cooperation and stimulates joint research and development projects and training programmes. Set up: *Non-Aligned Movement Centre for South-South Technical Cooperation (NAM CSSTC, #17147).* The following committees and groups are or were connected with the Non-Aligned Movement:
- *Non-Aligned Committee on Solidarity Fund for Southern Africa (no recent information)*;
- *Non-aligned Countries Contact Group on Cyprus (no recent information)*;
- *Non-aligned Countries Group on Education and Culture (no recent information)*;
- *Non-aligned Countries Group on Environment (no recent information)*;
- *Non-aligned Countries Group on Housing (no recent information)*;
- *Non-aligned Countries Group on Peaceful Uses of Nuclear Energy (no recent information)*;
- *Non-aligned Countries Group for Standardization, Weights, Measures and Quality Control (no recent information)*;
- *Non-aligned Countries Working Group on Disarmament and International Security (no recent information)*;
- *Non-aligned Countries Working Group for the Solidarity Fund for the Liberation of Southern Africa (no recent information)*;
- *Non-Aligned High-Level Working Group for the Restructuring of the United Nations (no recent information).*

Events *Conference of Heads of State or Government of Non-Aligned Countries* Baku (Azerbaijan) 2019, *Ministers of Health Meeting* Geneva (Switzerland) 2019, *Ministerial Conference* Baku (Azerbaijan) 2018, *Ministers of Health Meeting* Geneva (Switzerland) 2017, *Conference of Heads of State or Government of Non-Aligned Countries* Porlamar (Venezuela) 2016. **Publications** *Report of the Chairman of the Non-Aligned Movement on Activities of the Movement 1992-1995.* Information Services: *Research and Information System for Developing Countries, India (RIS, India)*; *Multisectorial Information Network (MSIN, no recent information)* – pilot scheme. **Information Services** *New International Information Centres of Non-Aligned Countries (IICNC)* – currently being set up in different continents to promote south-south cooperation.
Members Governments of 115 countries:
Afghanistan, Algeria, Angola, Bahamas, Bahrain, Bangladesh, Barbados, Belarus, Belize, Benin, Bhutan, Bolivia, Botswana, Brunei Darussalam, Burkina Faso, Burundi, Cambodia, Cameroon, Cape Verde, Central African Rep, Chad, Chile, Colombia, Comoros, Congo Brazzaville, Congo DR, Côte d'Ivoire, Cuba, Cyprus, Djibouti, Ecuador, Egypt, Equatorial Guinea, Eritrea, Eswatini, Ethiopia, Gabon, Gambia, Ghana, Grenada, Guatemala, Guinea, Guinea-Bissau, Guyana, Honduras, India, Indonesia, Iran Islamic Rep, Iraq, Jamaica, Jordan, Kenya, Korea DPR, Kuwait, Laos, Lebanon, Lesotho, Liberia, Libya, Madagascar, Malawi, Malaysia, Maldives, Mali, Malta, Mauritania, Mauritius, Mongolia, Montenegro, Morocco, Mozambique, Myanmar, Namibia, Nepal, Nicaragua, Niger, Nigeria, Oman, Pakistan, Palestine, Panama, Papua New Guinea, Peru, Philippines, Qatar, Rwanda, Sao Tomé-Principe, Saudi Arabia, Senegal, Seychelles, Sierra Leone, Singapore, Somalia, South Africa, Sri Lanka, St Lucia, Sudan, Suriname, Syrian AR, Tanzania UR, Thailand, Togo, Trinidad-Tobago, Tunisia, Turkmenistan, Uganda, United Arab Emirates, Uzbekistan, Vanuatu, Venezuela, Vietnam, Yemen, Zambia, Zimbabwe.
Countries with Observer Status (16):
Antigua-Barbuda, Armenia, Azerbaijan, Brazil, China, Costa Rica, Croatia, Dominica, Dominican Rep, El Salvador, Kazakhstan, Kyrgyzstan, Mexico, Paraguay, Ukraine, Uruguay.
Countries with Guest Statuts (26):
Australia, Austria, Bosnia-Herzegovina, Bulgaria, Canada, Czechia, Dominican Rep, Finland, Germany, Greece, Holy See, Hungary, Italy, Netherlands, New Zealand, Norway, Poland, Romania, Russia, San Marino, Slovakia, Slovenia, Spain, Sweden, Switzerland, Ukraine.
IGO Relations Close cooperation with: *Group of 77 (G-77, #10732).* Supports setting up of: *World Solidarity Fund (#21818).*
Observers at 1995 Summit:
- *League of Arab States (LAS, #16420)*;
- *Organisation of Islamic Cooperation (OIC, #17813)*;
- *United Nations (UN, #20515).*

Guests at 1995 Summit:
- *FAO (#09260)*;
- *ILO (#11123)*;
- *OAS (#17629)*;
- *UNCTAD (#20285)*;
- *UNDP (#20292)*;
- *UNESCO (#20322)*;
- *UNICEF (#20332)*;
- *UNIDO (#20336)*;
- *United Nations Committee on the Exercise of the Inalienable Rights of the Palestinian People (CEIRPP, #20539)*;
- *Special Committee on Decolonization (C-24, #19906)*;
- *WHO (#20950)*;
- *World Food Programme (WFP, #21510).*

NGO Relations Observers at 1995 Summit: *Afro-Asian Peoples' Solidarity Organization (AAPSO, #00537)*; National liberation movements. Guests at 1995 Summit; *Greenpeace International (#10727)*; *International Committee of the Red Cross (ICRC, #12799)*; *International Institute for Non-Aligned Studies (IINS, #13904)*; *Lawyers Committee on Nuclear Policy (LCNP).* [2018/XK0563/**F***]

♦ Non-Aligned Movement Centre for South-South Technical Cooperation (NAM CSSTC) 17147

Main Office NAM Centre Bldg, Jl Rendani Kav B10 No 6, Kemayoran, Jakarta 10610, Indonesia. T. +62216545321 – +62216545326. Fax +62216545325. E-mail: office@csstc.org.
URL: http://www.csstc.org/

History Proposed 1995, Bandung (Indonesia). Officially established, 1995, at 11th Summit of *Non-Aligned Movement (NAM, #17146)*, Cartagena de Indias (Colombia). Also referred to as *Centre for South South Technical Cooperation (CSSTC).* **Aims** Achieve the development goal of developing countries to attain sustained people-centered development and to enable developing countries to become equal partners in international relations. **Structure** Governing Council; Board of Directors. **Languages** English, Indonesian. **Staff** 4.00 FTE, paid. **Finance** Contributions from the government of Indonesia. **Activities** Events/meetings; networking/liaising; training/education; knowledge management/information dissemination. **Events** *International workshop on enhancing cooperation on herbal medicine* Jakarta (Indonesia) 2004. **Publications** *News List.*
Members States and territories (116):
Afghanistan, Algeria, Angola, Antigua-Barbuda, Azerbaijan, Bahamas, Bahrain, Bangladesh, Barbados, Belarus, Belize, Benin, Bhutan, Bolivia, Botswana, Brunei Darussalam, Burkina Faso, Burundi, Cambodia, Cameroon, Cape Verde, Central African Rep, Chad, Chile, Colombia, Comoros, Congo Brazzaville, Congo DR, Côte d'Ivoire, Cuba, Djibouti, Dominican Rep, Ecuador, Egypt, Equatorial Guinea, Eritrea, Eswatini, Ethiopia, Fiji, Gabon, Gambia, Ghana, Grenada, Guatemala, Guinea, Guinea-Bissau, Guyana, Haiti, Honduras, India, Indonesia, Iran Islamic Rep, Iraq, Jamaica, Jordan, Kenya, Korea DPR, Kuwait, Laos, Lebanon, Lesotho, Liberia, Libya, Madagascar, Malawi, Malaysia, Maldives, Mali, Mauritania, Mauritius, Mongolia, Morocco, Mozambique, Myanmar, Namibia, Nepal, Nicaragua, Niger, Oman, Pakistan, Palestine, Panama, Papua New Guinea, Peru, Philippines, Qatar, Rwanda, Sao Tomé-Principe, Saudi Arabia, Senegal, Seychelles, Sierra Leone, Singapore, Somalia, South Africa, St Kitts-Nevis, St Lucia, St Vincent-Grenadines, Sudan, Suriname, Tanzania UR, Thailand, Timor-Leste, Togo, Trinidad-Tobago, Tunisia, Turkmenistan, Uganda, United Arab Emirates, Uzbekistan, Vanuatu, Venezuela, Vietnam, Yemen, Zambia, Zimbabwe.
IGO Relations Partners with: *Centre on Integrated Rural Development for Asia and the Pacific (CIRDAP, #03750)*; *Colombo Plan for Cooperative Economic and Social Development in Asia and the Pacific (CPS, #04120)*; *International Institute for Democracy and Electoral Assistance (International IDEA, #13872)*; *UNDP (#20292).* [2020.01.31/XE3674/**E***]

- ♦ Non-Aligned News Agency Pool (inactive)

♦ Non-Aligned Students, Youth and Civil Societies Organization (NASYO) 17148

Organisation des jeunes, étudiants et societé civils non-alignés – Organización de los Estudiantes y Jóvenes No-Alineados

Gen Sec 140 Cocoterie Road, Port Louis, Mauritius. T. +23052543777. Fax +2302409964.
Facebook: https://m.facebook.com/nasyointernationalngo

History 30 Apr 1993, Baghdad (Iraq). Consultation started in 1975 during 1st Third World Youth Conference, Algiers (Algeria). Former names and other names: *Non-Aligned Students and Youth Organization (NASYO)* – former (30 Apr 1993); *Organisation des jeunes et étudiants non-alignés* – former (30 Apr 1993); *Organización de los Estudiantes y Jóvenes No-Alineados* – former (30 Apr 1993). **Aims** Unite students, youth and civil societies worldwide; promote the aims and objectives of the Non-Aligned Movement (NAM). **Structure** General Conference (every 5 years); Executive Committee; Geographical Zones (9); Political Zones (5); International/General Secretariat. **Languages** English. **Staff** 3.00 FTE, paid. **Finance** Sources: donations; fundraising; grants; members' dues; revenue from activities/projects. **Activities** Advocacy/lobbying/activism; events/meetings. **Events** *International Forum on the Role of Students in Defense of their People and Student's Diplomacy* Khartoum (Sudan) 2015, *General conference* Baghdad (Iraq) 1998, *Anti-imperialist youth forum* London (UK) 1997, *Meeting on the lifting of blockade on Iraqi people* London (UK) 1997, *International symposium on the role of the youth in preserving the environment* Amman (Jordan) 1996. **Publications** *NASYO Express* (12 a year); *NASYO News* (4 a year).
Members Full; associate; observer; international associate. National organizations in 100 countries:
Algeria, Angola, Argentina, Bangladesh, Belarus, Belgium, Belize, Bolivia, Botswana, Brazil, Bulgaria, Burkina Faso, Cambodia, Cape Verde, Chad, Chile, Colombia, Comoros, Costa Rica, Côte d'Ivoire, Croatia, Cuba, Cyprus, Denmark, Djibouti, Dominica, Egypt, Eritrea, Fiji, France, Gabon, Gambia, Germany, Ghana, Greece, Guatemala, Guinea, Guinea-Bissau, Hungary, India, Indonesia, Iraq, Italy, Jamaica, Japan, Jordan, Kenya, Laos, Lebanon, Lesotho, Liberia, Libya, Lithuania, Madagascar, Malawi, Malaysia, Mali, Malta, Mauritania, Mauritius, Morocco, Namibia, Nepal, Netherlands, Nicaragua, Nigeria, North Macedonia, Pakistan, Palestine, Paraguay, Peru, Philippines, Portugal, Qatar, Romania, Russia, Rwanda, Senegal, Serbia, Sierra Leone, Slovenia, Spain, Sri Lanka, St Vincent-Grenadines, Sudan, Suriname, Sweden, Syrian AR, Tonga, Tunisia, Tuvalu, Uganda, UK, Ukraine, Vanuatu, Venezuela, Vietnam, Yemen, Zambia, Zimbabwe.
Consultative Status Consultative status granted from: *ECOSOC (#05331)* (Special). **NGO Relations** Links with a number of humanitarian, environmental and human rights organizations (not specified). [2017.10.11/XD5594/**C**]

♦ Non-Aligned Students and Youth Organization / see Non-Aligned Students, Youth and Civil Societies Organization (#17148)
♦ Non c'è Pace Senza Giustizia (#17155)
♦ Non-communicable disease / see The NCD Alliance (#16963)
♦ Nongovernmental Organization Committee on Disarmament, New York NY / see NGO Committee on Disarmament, Peace and Security, New York NY (#17106)
♦ Non-Governmental Organization Forum on Cambodia / see NGO Forum on Cambodia (#17124)
♦ Non-Governmental Organizations Committee on UNICEF / see NGO Committee on UNICEF (#17120)
♦ Non-Governmental Platform for the Euro-Mediterranean Civil Forum – Plate-forme non gouvernementale EuroMed / see Euro-Mediterranean Foundation of Support to Human Rights Defenders (#05720)
♦ **NO** Nitric Oxide Society (#17143)
♦ Non Monogamies and Contemporary Intimacies Congress (meeting series)
♦ NO – Northern Optics (meeting series)

♦ Nonprofit Academic Centers Council (NACC) 17149

Exec Dir Bush School of Govt and Public Service, Texas A&M Univ, 400 Bizzell St, College Station TX 77843-4220, USA. Fax +19798622089.
Pres/Headquarters Rep address not obtained.
URL: http://www.nonprofit-academic-centers-council.org/

History 1991. Registration: 501(c)(3) organization, No/ID: EIN: 52-1974704, Start date: 1996, USA, Texas. **Aims** Promote and network centres that provide research and education in *philanthropy* and the nonprofit sector. **Structure** Board. **Staff** 1.00 FTE, paid. **Activities** Networking/liaising; standards/guidelines; events/meetings; capacity building. **Events** *Biennial Conference* Auburn, AL (USA) 2023, *Annual Member Meeting* Raleigh, NC (USA) 2022, *Annual Member Meeting* Atlanta, GA (USA) 2021. **Publications** *NACC News* (12 a year). *In Pursuit of Excellence: Indicators of Quality in Nonprofit Academic Centers* (2006). Curricular guidelines; special issues.
Members College and university affiliated centres or programmes in 6 countries:
Australia, Canada, Italy, Russia, UK, USA. [2022/XM3964/**F**]

♦ Nonprofit Enterprise and Self-Sustainability Team (NESsT) 17150

Co-CEO address not obtained. T. +1503704-9195. E-mail: nesst@nesst.org.
Co-Founder/Co-CEO address not obtained.
Global Portfolio Dir address not obtained. E-mail: rdamaschin@nesst.org.
URL: http://www.nesst.org/

History 1997. **Aims** Develop sustainable social enterprises that solve critical social problems in emerging markets. **Structure** Board of Directors. **Languages** Czech, English, Hungarian, Portuguese, Romanian, Spanish. **Staff** 44.00 FTE, paid. **Finance** Grants; fees; sales. Budget (annual): approx US$ 2 million. **Activities** Programme areas: Social enterprise development; Capacity-Building Initiatives; NESsT Venture Portfolio; NESsT Consulting; NESsT University. **Events** *Forum* Santiago (Chile) 2004, *International venture philanthropy forum* Budapest (Hungary) 2001, *Forum* Budapest (Hungary) 1999. **Publications** *NESsT News* (6 a year) in English, Spanish – online. *NESsT Case Study Series*; *NESsT Learning Series*; *NESsT Tools for Practitioners Series*. Guides.
Members Full in 10 countries:
Argentina, Brazil, Chile, Croatia, Czechia, Ecuador, Hungary, Peru, Romania, Slovakia. [2017/XF6310/**F**]

♦ Non-Profit Organisation Fenno-Ugria / see Fenno-Ugria
♦ NonProfit Organizations Knowledge Initiative (internationally oriented national body)

♦ Non-Timber Forest Products Exchange Programme for South and Southeast Asia (NTFP-EN) 17151

Exec Dir 92-A Masikap Extension, Barangay Central, Diliman, 1100 Quezon City, Philippines. T. +6329204201. Fax +6324262757. E-mail: info@ntfp.org.
URL: http://www.ntfp.org/

History Set up as an informal grouping 1998. Officially registered 2003. **Aims** Empower forest-based communities to make use of and manage forest resources in a sustainable manner. **Structure** Board of Directors, comprising President, Vice-President, Treasurer and Secretary. Secretariat, headed by Executive Director. **Finance** Support from various sponsors including: *Catholic Organization for Relief and Development (Cordaid)*; *Humanistisch Instituut voor Ontwikkelingssamenwerking (Hivos)*; *German Catholic Bishops' Organisation for Development Cooperation (MISEREOR)*. **IGO Relations** Partner of: *ASEAN Working Group on Social Forestry (AWG SF, #01247)*. **NGO Relations** Member of: *ICCA Consortium (#11041)*; *International Union for Conservation of Nature and Natural Resources (IUCN, #15766)*; *NGO Forum on Cambodia (#17124)*. [2014/XJ7125/**F**]

♦ Nonviolence International (NI) 17152

Exec Dir 4005 Wisconsin Ave, Suite 39127, Washington DC 20016, USA. T. +12022440951. E-mail: admin@nonviolenceinternational.net.
URL: http://www.nonviolenceinternational.net/

History 1989, Washington, DC (USA). Founded as a decentralized network of resource centers. Registration: Section 501(c)(3), No/ID: 52-1645787, Start date: 1 May 1989, USA, Washington DC. **Aims** Promote nonviolent action and a culture of peace; seek to reduce violence and passivity worldwide. **Structure** Resource Centers and Affiliates in: Aceh (Indonesia); Bethlehem (Palestine); Bangkok (Thailand); Kiev (Ukraine); Vancouver (Canada); New York NY (USA); Washington DC (USA). **Languages** Arabic, English, Indonesian, Russian, Tagalog, Thai. **Staff** 3.00 FTE, paid. **Activities** Awards/prizes/competitions; conflict resolution; knowledge management/information dissemination; networking/liaising; publishing activities; training/education. **Publications** Training manuals; educational curricula; pamphlets; books; films. **Consultative Status** Consultative status granted from: *ECOSOC (#05331)* (Special). **NGO Relations** Member of (6): *Control Arms (#04782)*; *EarthAction (EA, #05159)*; *International Campaign to Ban Landmines – Cluster Munition Coalition (ICBL-CMC, #12427)*; *International Coalition against Enforced Disappearances (ICAED, #12605)*; *International Peace Bureau (IPB, #14535)*; *Nonviolent Peaceforce (NP, #17153)*. Regional initiator of: *Global Partnership for the Prevention of Armed Conflict (GPPAC, #10538)*. [2022.02.08/XN6154/**F**]

♦ Nonviolent Peaceforce (NP) 17153

Exec Dir Rue de Lausanne 82, 1202 Geneva, Switzerland. T. +410225526610. E-mail: headoffice@nonviolentpeaceforce.org.
USA Office 2610 University Ave W, Ste 550, St Paul MN 55114, USA. E-mail: info@nonviolentpeaceforce.org.
URL: http://www.nonviolentpeaceforce.org/

History 2002, Brussels (Belgium). Formed at 1999 Hague Appeal for Peace. Formally launched Dec 2002 at 1st International Assembly, Delhi (India). Former names and other names: *Force non-violente de paix* – former. Registration: 501(c)(3) nonprofit organization, No/ID: EIN: 35-2197019, Start date: 2003, USA, Minnesota; Banque-Carrefour des Entreprises, No/ID: 0480.008.359, Start date: 11 Apr 2003, Belgium; RNA, No/ID: W013001326, Start date: 20 Nov 2016, France; Swiss Foundation, Switzerland. **Aims** Protect civilians in violent conflicts through unarmed strategies, build peace side by side with local communities, and advocate for the wider adoption of these approaches to safeguard human lives and dignity. **Structure** Board of Directors; Executive Director. **Languages** English, French. **Staff** 311.00 FTE, paid. **Finance** Sources: donations; government support; grants; international organizations; private foundations. Supported by: *Department for International Development (DFID, inactive)*; *Deutsche Gesellschaft für Internationale Zusammenarbeit (GIZ)*; *European Peacebuilding Liaison Office (EPLO, #08176)*; *European Union (EU, #08967)*; *GHR Foundation*; *McKnight Foundation*; *Plan International (#18386)*; *Swiss Agency for Development and Cooperation (SDC)*; *UNDP (#20292)*; *United Nations Office for the Coordination of Humanitarian Assistance to Afghanistan (UNOCHA, inactive)*; *United Nations Population Fund (UNFPA, #20612)*; *United States Agency for International Development (USAID)*; *United States Institute of Peace (USIP)*; *UN Women (#20724)*. Annual budget: 18,000,000 EUR (2021). **Activities** Advocacy/lobbying/activism; capacity building; conflict resolution; projects/programmes. Active in: Indonesia, Iraq, Myanmar, Philippines, South Sudan, Sudan, Switzerland, Ukraine, USA. **Consultative Status** Consultative status granted from: *ECOSOC (#05331)* (Special). **IGO Relations** Partner of (8): *Deutsche Gesellschaft für Internationale Zusammenarbeit (GIZ)*; *European Union (EU, #08967)*; *UNDP (#20292)*; *UNHCR (#20327)*; *United Nations Office for the Coordination of Humanitarian Assistance to Afghanistan (UNOCHA, inactive)*; *United Nations Population Fund (UNFPA, #20612)*; *United States Agency for International Development (USAID)*; *UN Women (#20724)*. **NGO Relations** Member of (9): *American Council for Voluntary International Action (InterAction)*; *CHS Alliance (#03911)*; *Conference of Non-Governmental Organizations in Consultative Relationship with the United Nations (CONGO, #04635)*; *European Peacebuilding Liaison Office (EPLO, #08176)*; *Extractive Industries Transparency Initiative (EITI, #09229)*; *Federation of European and International Associations Established in Belgium (FAIB, #09508)*; *Human Rights and Democracy Network (HRDN, #10980)*; *International Coalition for the Responsibility to Protect (ICRtoP, #12620)*; *NGO Working Group on the Security Council (#17128)*. [2022.10.21/XF6670/y/**F**]

♦ Nonviolent Radical Party / see Nonviolent Radical Party, Transnational and Transparty (#17154)

♦ Nonviolent Radical Party, Transnational and Transparty (PRNTT) ... 17154

Rome Office Via di Torre Argentina 76, 00186 Rome RM, Italy. T. +396689791. Fax +39668805396.
URL: http://www.radicalparty.org/

History 1988, as *Transnational Radical Party (TRP)* – *Parti radical transnational* – *Partito Radicale Transnazionale*. Also previously referred to as *Transnational Transparty Radical Party* and *Nonviolent Radical Party*. **Aims** As a Gandhian, *non-violent* organization, promote international political campaigns concerning: respect for human rights, particularly in non-democratic countries; promotion of democracy and freedom; anti-prohibitionist policies on drugs and against illegal trafficking in drugs; abolition of capital punishment; language rights and the use of Esperanto as the auxiliary language of international institutions; democratic reform of the United Nations. **Structure** Senate; General Council. **Languages** English, French, Italian. **Finance** Members' dues. Contributions. **Activities** Campaigned for the setting up of *International Criminal Court (ICC, #13108)*. **Events** *Joint conference* Rome (Italy) 1998, *Congress* Strasbourg (France) 1988. **Publications** *Hands Off Cain* (periodical) in English, Italian – supplement to 'Notizie Radicali'; *The New Party* (periodical) in Albanian, Croatian, Czech, English, Esperanto, French, German, Hungarian, Italian, Polish, Portuguese, Romanian, Russian, Serbian, Spanish. Pamphlets; leaflets.
Members Individual membership; radical associations. Individuals (over 50,000) in 48 countries:
Albania, Argentina, Armenia, Azerbaijan, Belarus, Belgium, Bosnia-Herzegovina, Brazil, Bulgaria, Burkina Faso, Cameroon, Canada, Congo Brazzaville, Côte d'Ivoire, Croatia, Cuba, Czechia, Estonia, France, Georgia, Hungary, India, Iran Islamic Rep, Israel, Italy, Japan, Latvia, Lithuania, Luxembourg, Moldova, Monaco, Nepal, Netherlands, Niger, North Macedonia, Poland, Portugal, Romania, Russia, Senegal, Serbia, Spain, Switzerland, Türkiye, UK, Ukraine, USA, Uzbekistan.
Consultative Status Consultative status granted from: *ECOSOC (#05331)* (General). **NGO Relations** Instrumental in setting up: *International Anti-Prohibitionist League (IAL, no recent information)*; *Hands Off Cain – Citizens' and Parliamentarians' League for the Abolition of the Death Penalty Worldwide (Hands Off Cain, #10857)*. [2010/XF1976/v/**F**]

♦ NO ONE OUT (internationally oriented national body)
♦ NOOPOLIS – Centro Internazionale di Sviluppo e Cooperazione Culturale, Roma (internationally oriented national body)
♦ Noord-Atlantisch verdrag (1949 treaty)
♦ Noordzee Conferentie (meeting series)
♦ Al Noor Institute for the Blind / see Saudi Bahraini Institute for the Blind
♦ **NOPA** Nordic Offset Printing Association, The (#17373)

♦ No Peace Without Justice (NPWJ) 17155

Non c'è Pace Senza Giustizia
Chair Via C. B. Vaccolini, 5, 00153 Rome RM, Italy. T. +39645436641. E-mail: noncepacesenzagiustizia@pec.it.
Brussels Office Rue Ducale 41, 1000 Brussels, Belgium. T. +3227810823.
URL: http://www.npwj.org/

History 1993. Founded by Emma Bonino, as a result of a campaign of *Nonviolent Radical Party, Transnational and Transparty (PRNTT, #17154)*. **Aims** Address situations where fundamental and universal principles are set aside in the name of political stability and presumed cultural incompatibility. **Structure** Board. **Languages** English, French, Italian. **Staff** 15.00 FTE, paid.
Finance Contributions. Support from international and regional organizations, various governments and public institutions and national NGOs. International organizations include:
- *Amsterdam Center for International Law (ACIL)*;
- *The Carter Center*;
- *Coalition for the International Criminal Court (CICC, #04062)*;
- *Commonwealth Secretariat (#04362)*;
- *European Commission (EC, #06633)*;
- *The European Law Students' Association (ELSA, #07660)*;
- *Forum for the Future*;
- *Freedom House*;
- *Institute for International Criminal Investigations (IICI, #11274)*;
- *International Alliance for Justice (IAJ)*;
- *International Bank for Reconstruction and Development (IBRD, #12317)* (World Bank);
- *International Crisis Group (Crisis Group, #13111)*;
- *International Institute for Democracy and Electoral Assistance (International IDEA, #13872)*;
- *IPS – Inter Press Service International Association (#16013)*;
- *Sigrid Rausing Trust*;
- *UNDP (#20292)*;
- *UNICEF (#20332)*;
- *United Nations Democracy Fund (UNDEF, #20551)*;
- *United Nations Office for Project Services (UNOPS, #20602)*;
- *United Nations Population Fund (UNFPA, #20612)*;
- *United States Agency for International Development (USAID)*.

Activities Advocacy/lobbying/activism; awareness raising; events/meetings; politics/policy/regulatory. **Events** *International Conference on Female Genital Mutilation* Madrid (Spain) 2015, *Pan-African conference on the establishment of an international criminal court* Dakar (Senegal) 1998, *Joint conference* Rome (Italy) 1998. **Publications** E-newsletter (12 a year) in English, Italian. **Members** Parliamentarians, mayors and citizens. Membership countries not specified. [2022.10.19/XF4373/v/**F**]

♦ **NOPEF** Nordiska Projektexportfonden (#17490)
♦ **NOPHO** Nordic Society for Pediatric Hematology and Oncology (#17424)
♦ NOP-HS / see Nordisk publiseringsnemnd for humanistiske og samfunnsvitenskapelige tidsskrifter (#17526)
♦ **NOP-HS** Nordisk publiseringsnemnd for humanistiske og samfunnsvitenskapelige tidsskrifter (#17526)
♦ NOP-N – Nordiska Publiceringsnämnden för Naturvetenskap (inactive)
♦ **NOPSA** Nordic Political Science Association (#17389)
♦ **NOQA** Nordic Quality Assurance Network in Higher Education (#17394)
♦ NORAD – North American Aerospace Defense Command (internationally oriented national body)
♦ Norad – Norwegian Agency for Development Cooperation (internationally oriented national body)
♦ NorAge – Nordic Society for Research in Brain Ageing (inactive)
♦ NORAM – Association of North American Operations Research Societies within IFORS (internationally oriented national body)
♦ NORA – Native Oyster Restoration Alliance (unconfirmed)
♦ Noranna Sumarhaskolinn (#17535)
♦ **NORA** Nordic Respiratory Academy (#17399)
♦ **NORA** Nordisk Atlantsamarbejde (#17209)
♦ NORBUSAM / see Organization for Nordic Children's and Youth Choirs (#17880)
♦ **NORBUSANG** Rådet för Nordiskt Barn- och Ungdomskårsamarbete (#17880)
♦ NorCast – Nordic Aluminium Casthouse Conference (meeting series)
♦ **NORCECA** Confederación Nortecentroamericana y del Caribe de Vóleibol (#17576)
♦ NORCHIP (meeting series)
♦ NORDAF – Nordiska Annonsörföreningarnas Förbund (inactive)
♦ Nordamerikanisches Luftverteidigungssystem (internationally oriented national body)
♦ **NordAN** Nordiskt Alkohol- och Narkotikapolitiskt Samarbete (#17536)
♦ NORDA – Nordiskt Samarbete om Teknisk Ackreditering (inactive)
♦ Nordatlantikvertrag (1949 treaty)

- ♦ Nordatlantiske traktat (1949 treaty)
- ♦ **Nordbåt** Nordiska Båtrådet (#17221)
- ♦ NordBatt – Nordic Battery Conference (meeting series)
- ♦ **NORDBUK** Nordic Children's and Youth Committee (#17235)
- ♦ **NordCAP** Nordic Collaboration Group for Research in Child and Adolescent Psychiatry (#17242)
- ♦ **NordCase** Nordic Casemix Centre (#17227)
- ♦ **NordCAW** Nordic Network for Communicating Animal Welfare (#17350)
- ♦ NORDCOAG – Nordic Coagulation Meeting (meeting series)
- ♦ **Nordcode** Nordic Network for Research on Communicative Product Design (#17362)
- ♦ **NORDEFCO** Nordic Defence Cooperation (#17266)
- ♦ Nordel – Organization of the Nordic Transmission System Operators (inactive)
- ♦ NordEMS – Nordic Environmental Mutagen Society (inactive)

♦ Nordenergi 17156

Assistant Rue de la Loi 227, 1040 Brussels, Belgium.
URL: http://www.nordenergi.org/

History 2005. **Aims** Further develop the *Nordic electricity* market in a European perspective; act in members' collective interests; influence national and European authorities and institutions in their decisions in order to promote a well-functioning Nordic electricity market. **Structure** Steering Group; Coordination Group; Working Groups. Chairmanship rotates between members every two years. Association holding the chairmanship is also responsible for the secretariat functions. **Languages** English. **Events** *Nordic Energy Meeting* Stockholm (Sweden) 2018.
Members Nordic associations for electricity producers, suppliers and distributors, representing over 800 market actors, in 5 countries:
Denmark, Finland, Iceland, Norway, Sweden. [2022/XM3369/**F**]

♦ Norden Mot Narkotika (NMN) 17157

Scandinavia Against Drugs

Contact address not obtained. T. +4723080550.
URL: http://nordenmotnarkotika.net/

History 1985. Previously also referred to in English as *Nordic Countries Against Drugs*. **Aims** Promote exchanges and cooperation concerning *treatment* in the Nordic countries; persuade authorities to accept their responsibility concerning the care of drug *addicts*; work for a common stand against drug abuse; work for representation on *narcotics* problems in the Nordic Council; improve dissemination of information and education concerning drugs and drug problems; coordinate all initiatives, official and private against drug abuse. **Structure** No permanent address; location changes every second year. **Finance** Members' dues. **Activities** Arranges a conference each autumn which is a forum to share experiences and information. **Events** *Annual Conference* Espoo (Finland) 1995, *Annual Conference* Helsinki (Finland) 1995, *Annual Conference* Stockholm (Sweden) 1994, *Annual conference* Reykjavik (Iceland) 1993, *Annual Conference* Oslo (Norway) 1992. **Publications** Conference papers; conference newsletter.
Members National parents' associations in the 5 Nordic countries:
Denmark, Finland, Iceland, Norway, Sweden. [2009/XF5159/**F**]

- ♦ Nordens Akademiska Idrottsförbund (inactive)
- ♦ Nordens Bondeorganisasjoners Centralråd (no recent information)

♦ Nordens Fackliga Samorganisation (NFS) 17158

Conseil des syndicats nordiques – Council of Nordic Trade Unions – Pohjolan Ammatillinen Yhteistyöjärjestö

Gen Sec c/o TCO, Linnégatan 14, SE-114 47 Stockholm, Sweden. E-mail: info@nfs.net.
URL: http://www.nfs.net/

History 1972. **Aims** Act as coordinating body for trade union confederations in the Nordic countries; promote interests of workers at the Nordic level in matters of employment, economic and industrial policy and social issues; cooperate across national boundaries to increase the ability of employees to realize their demands for work for all, social security and influence on economic and social development. **Structure** Executive Committee (meets twice a year); Steering Committee; Secretariat, headed by General Secretary; Ad-hoc Committees. **Languages** Danish, English, Finnish, Icelandic, Norwegian, Swedish. **Staff** 4.00 FTE, paid. **Finance** Members' dues. **Activities** Politics/policy/regulatory; knowledge management/information dissemination; research/documentation. **Events** *Congress / Nordisk Facklig Kongress* Oslo (Norway) 2022, *Decent Work Conference* Riga (Latvia) 2018, *The future of work – labour, just a click away?* Stockholm (Sweden) 2017, *Decent Work Conference* Tallinn (Estonia) 2016, *Kongress* Ålesund (Norway) 2012.
Members Blue- and white-collar labour confederations (16) representing 9 million workers in 7 countries and territories:
Denmark, Faeroe Is, Finland, Greenland, Iceland, Norway, Sweden.
NGO Relations Observer status with: *European Trade Union Confederation (ETUC, #08927)*; *International Trade Union Confederation (ITUC, #15708)*; *Trade Union Advisory Committee to the OECD (TUAC, #20186)*. Functions as secretariat of: *Baltic Sea Trade Union Network (BASTUN, #03151)*. Cooperates with Nordic Branch Federations. [2022/XD5936/t/**D**]

♦ Nordens Godtemplar Ungdomsråd (NORDGU) 17159

Nordic Good Templar Youth Council

Main Office Box 12825, SE-112 97 Stockholm, Sweden. E-mail: johanna.l.ahlskog@gmail.com.
URL: http://www.nordgu.net/

History as the youth organization of *Nordiska Godtemplarrådet (NGR, #17483)*. **Aims** Bring together *Nordic temperance youth* for discussions and seminars. **Events** *Congress* Brandbu (Norway) 2014. [2014/XE2461/**E**]

- ♦ Nordens Gymnastikkforbund (inactive)

♦ Nordens Husflidsforbund 17160

Nordisk Hjemstavnsforbund – Nordic Crafts Association – Association nordique pour l'économie domestique

Contact c/o Estonian Folk Art and Craft Union, Eesti Rahvakunsti ja Käsitöö Liit, Pikk 22, 10133 Tallinn, Estonia. T. +3726604772 – +3725187812. Fax +3726314075. E-mail: info@folkart.ee.

History 1927. **Events** *Conference* Oslo (Norway) 2010.
Members Full in 5 countries:
Denmark, Finland, Iceland, Norway, Sweden. [2013/XD1749/**D**]

- ♦ Nordens Husmodersförbund (no recent information)
- ♦ Nordens Hus På Faeroerne (internationally oriented national body)
- ♦ Nordens Hus i Reykjavik (internationally oriented national body)
- ♦ Nordens institut i Finland / see Nordic Culture Point
- ♦ Nordens Institut på Åland (internationally oriented national body)
- ♦ Nordens Institutt in Grønland (internationally oriented national body)

♦ Nordens Konservativa Studentunion (NKSU) 17161

Nordic Conservative Student Union – Nordisk Konservator Studentunion (NKSU)

SG c/o Box 5373, SE-102 49 Stockholm, Sweden. E-mail: alexander.fritz@fmsf.se – info@fmsf.se.
URL: https://fmsf.se/internationellt/nksu/

History Founded 1959. As of 2009 accepts members from Baltic and Northern European countries. **Aims** Encourage contact and cooperation between centre right student organizations in North European countries; work for a centre right educational policy; encourage a North European cultural understanding; cooperate with like minded international student and youth organizations. **Structure** Council. **Languages** English, Swedish. **Activities** Events/meetings. **Events** *Annual Meeting* London (UK) 2013, *Annual Meeting* Copenhagen (Denmark) 2012, *Annual Meeting* Stockholm (Sweden) 2011, *Annual Meeting* Lund (Sweden) 2009, *Annual Meeting* Tyresö (Sweden) 2008.
Members Full; Observer. Full members in 8 countries:
Denmark, Estonia, Finland, Latvia, Lithuania, Norway, Sweden, UK.
NGO Relations Member of: *International Young Democrat Union (IYDU, #15928)*. [2019/XD6954/**D**]

- ♦ Nordens Kristna Nykterhetsråd (no recent information)
- ♦ Nordens Laererinneforbund (inactive)
- ♦ Nordens Landskvinner (inactive)
- ♦ Nordens Liberale og Radikale Ungdomsforbund (no recent information)
- ♦ Nordens Livredningsforbund (inactive)

♦ Nordens Offentliganställdas Fackliga Samorganisation (NOFS) 17162

Secretariat Box 190 39, SE-104 32 Stockholm, Sweden. T. +4687284470. Fax +4687284472.
Street Address Hagagatan 2, Stockholm, Sweden.
URL: http://www.nofs.org/

History 1968. **Aims** Influence the activities of *Public Services* International and of European Federation of Public Service Unions. **Structure** Board. Secretariat.
Members Nordic trade unions (42) in 5 countries:
Denmark, Finland, Iceland, Norway, Sweden.
NGO Relations *European Federation of Public Service Unions (EPSU, #07202)*; *Public Services International (PSI, #18572)*. [2011/XJ4888/**D**]

- ♦ Nordens Resebyrå Förbund (inactive)
- ♦ Nordens Skogsägareorganisationers Förbund (inactive)
- ♦ Nordens Smalfilmforbund (inactive)
- ♦ Nordens Statstjenestemenns Samråd (no recent information)
- ♦ Nordens Största Intresseorganisation för Centrumhandel (#17261)

♦ Nordens välfärdscenter (NVC) 17163

Nordic Welfare Centre – Pohjoismainen Hyvinvointikeskus

Main Office Box 1073, SE-101 39 Stockholm, Sweden. T. +46768935726. E-mail: info@nordicwelfare.org.
URL: http://www.nordicwelfare.org/

History 1 Jan 2009, on merger of *Nordic Centre for Alcohol and Drug Research (NAD, inactive)*, *Nordiska Samarbetsorganet för Handikappfrågor (NSH, inactive)*, *Nordic Educational Programme for the Development of Social Services (inactive)* and *Nordisk Uddannelsescenter for Døvblindepersonale (NUD, inactive)*. Previously also referred to as *Nordiskt Välfärdscenter* and in English as *Nordic Centre for Welfare and Social Issues*. **Aims** Further develop and strengthen the Nordic welfare model. **Structure** Board, appointed by *Nordic Council of Ministers (NCM, #17260)*, with representatives from 5 Nordic countries. Head Office, located in Stockholm (Sweden); Office in Helsinki (Finland). **Staff** 31.00 FTE, paid. **Finance** Grants and external revenues. Budget (annual): about Swedish Kr 30 million. **Events** *Nordic Alcohol and Drug Researchers Assembly NADRA* Mariehamn (Finland) 2022, *Nordic Conference* Tampere (Finland) 2022, *Nordic Welfare Forum* Helsinki (Finland) 2021, *Seminar on Indigenous People* Helsinki (Finland) 2021, *Nordic Alcohol and Drug Researchers Assembly NADRA* Mariehamn (Finland) 2021.
Members Governments of 5 countries:
Denmark, Finland, Iceland, Norway, Sweden.
IGO Relations *Nordic Council of Ministers (NCM, #17260)*. Cooperates with: *Council of Europe (CE, #04881)*; *European Union (EU, #08967)*; *United Nations (UN, #20515)*. [2020/XM3843/**D***]

- ♦ **Nordes** Nordic Design Research (#17270)
- ♦ Nordeuropa Institute (internationally oriented national body)
- ♦ Nordeuropäisches Symposium für archäologische Textilien (meeting series)
- ♦ Nordeuropaisk Bordtennis Union (#17599)
- ♦ NorDev – Joint Nordic Development Research Conference (meeting series)
- ♦ **NORDEX** Nordisk Samarbeidskomite for Offentlig Tilsyn med Brannfarlige og Eksplosive Varer (#17247)
- ♦ **NORDFO** Nordiskt Forum för Forskning och Utvecklingsarbete inom Utbildning i Slöyd (#17537)

♦ NordForsk 17164

Head of Communications Stensberggata 25, 0170 Oslo, Norway. T. +4747614400. Fax +4722565565. E-mail: nordforsk@nordforsk.org.
Registered Address Stensberggt 27, 5th Floor, 0170 Oslo, Norway.
URL: http://www.nordforsk.org/

History 1 Jan 2005. Founded within *Nordic Council of Ministers (NCM, #17260)*. Former names and other names: *Nordic Research Board* – former. **Aims** Facilitate effective and trustful research cooperation in the Nordic Region; ensure that NordForsk funded research has the highest international quality and realizes Nordic added value. **Structure** Board (rotating Chairmanship); Secretariat located in Oslo (Norway), headed by Director. **Languages** Danish, English, Norwegian, Swedish. **Finance** on the regular budget of the Nordic Council of Ministers. **Activities** Research and development. Active in: Åland, Denmark, Faeroe Is, Finland, Greenland, Iceland, Norway, Sweden. **Events** *Digital overnight* Norway 2021, *Gender equality, Diversity and Societal Security* Oslo (Norway) 2021, *Conference on Bioethics of Clinical Innovation and Unproven Methods* Copenhagen (Denmark) 2019, *Nordic Infrastructure for Open Science (NeIC)* Copenhagen (Denmark) 2019, *Nordic Algae Symposium* Oslo (Norway) 2019. **NGO Relations** Member of (1): *ScanBalt (#19065)*. Supports (2): *Nordic Cilia and Centrosome Network (#17239)*; *Nordic Network of Narrative Studies (#17360)*. [2021.09.01/XM0903/**D**]

- ♦ Nordforsk Committee for Thermal Analysis / see Nordic Society for Thermal Analysis and Calorimetry (#17430)
- ♦ NORDFORSK – Nordiska Samarbetsorganisationen för Teknisk-Vetenskaplig Forskning (inactive)
- ♦ **NordGen** Nordic Genetic Resource Centre (#17303)
- ♦ **NORDGU** Nordens Godtemplar Ungdomsråd (#17159)
- ♦ **NORDIATRANS** Foreningen for Nordisk Dialyse og Transplantation Personale (#02827)
- ♦ Nordic Academic Sports Association (inactive)
- ♦ Nordic Academy of Management (#17510)
- ♦ Nordic Acoustical Society / see Nordic Acoustic Association (#17165)

♦ Nordic Acoustic Association (NAA) 17165

SG c/o Aeronautical Engineering, KTH Royal Inst of Technology, SE-100 44 Stockholm, Sweden. T. +4687908021.
URL: https://euracoustics.org/eaa-societies/partner-societies/nordic-acoustics-association/

History Founded 19 Jun 1954. Also referred to as *Nordic Acoustical Society*. Previously also known as *Acoustical Society of Scandinavia (ASS)* – *Nordisk Akustisk Selskap (NAS)*. **Aims** Promote development of acoustic science. **Structure** Board. **Languages** English. **Staff** Voluntary. **Finance** Members' dues. **Activities** Knowledge management/information dissemination; networking/liaising; events/meetings. **Events** *Joint Baltic-Nordic Acoustics Meeting (BNAM) & EUROREGIO Conference* Aalborg (Denmark) 2022, *Baltic-Nordic Acoustic Meeting (BNAM)* Oslo (Norway) 2021, *Baltic-Nordic Acoustic Meeting (BNAM)* Oslo (Norway) 2020, *Baltic-Nordic Acoustic Meeting* Stockholm (Sweden) 2016, *Baltic-Nordic Acoustic Meeting* Tallinn (Estonia) 2014. **Publications** Proceedings.
Members National societies in 5 countries:
Denmark, Finland, Iceland, Norway, Sweden. [2021/XD1681/**D**]

♦ Nordic Actors' Council 17166

Conseil nordique des acteurs – Nordiska Skådespelarrådet – Nordisk Skuespillerråd (NSR) – Pohjoismainen Näyttelijäneuvosto – Norraena Leikararadid

Sec Felag Islenskra Leikara, Lindargata 6, 101 Reykjavik, Iceland. T. +3545526040. Fax +3545627706.

History Founded 1936. **Aims** Ensure links among Nordic actors and *dancers*; settle questions of common interest. **Structure** An informal network of national bodies whose secretariat rotates annually. Chairmen of Nordic actors' unions meet twice a year in one of the Nordic capitals. **Languages** Danish, Finnish, Icelandic, Norwegian, Swedish. **Staff** Voluntary. **Finance** None. **Activities** Concerns: dubbing of non-Nordic films into Nordic languages; copyright and other factors involved in cable-TV transmissions from one country to another; film, theatre and television agreements and video registration/transmission of theatre and dance performances. **Events** *Half-Yearly Meeting* Reykjavik (Iceland) 2007, *Half-Yearly Meeting* Helsinki (Finland) 2006, *Half-Yearly Meeting* Oslo (Norway) 2006, *Half-Yearly Meeting* Copenhagen (Denmark) 2005, *Half-Yearly Meeting* Reykjavik (Iceland) 2005.

Members Full organizations (7) in 5 countries:
Denmark, Finland, Iceland, Norway, Sweden.
Consultative Status Consultative status granted from: *World Intellectual Property Organization (WIPO, #21593)* (Observer Status). [2014/XD0334/F]

♦ Nordic Acupuncture Society (inactive)

♦ Nordic Adoption Council (NAC) 17167

Contact DanAdopt, Pilevej 16, Sorup, 3480 Fredensborg, Denmark.
URL: http://www.nordicadoption.org/

History 1995, Copenhagen (Denmark), during the 10th Nordic Meeting. Formal organization created following cooperation initiatives dating from the 1970s. **Structure** Board of Directors. **Events** *Biennial Meeting* Gardermoen (Norway) 2015, *Biennial Meeting* Thórshavn (Faeroe Is) 2013, *Biennial Meeting* Stockholm (Sweden) 2011, *Biennial Meeting* Iceland 2009, *Meeting / Biennial Meeting* Helsinki (Finland) 2007.
Members National organizations (15) in 8 countries and territories:
Åland, Denmark, Faeroe Is, Finland, Greenland, Iceland, Norway, Sweden. [2013.07.15/XM3654/E]

♦ Nordic Adult Education Cooperation (#17504)
♦ Nordic Advisory Committee on Higher Education (inactive)
♦ Nordic Aerobiology Society (#17481)
♦ Nordic Aeromedical Association (no recent information)

♦ Nordic Africa Institute (NAI) 17168

Nordiska Afrikainstitutet – Pohjoismainen Afrikka-Instituutti

Acting Director Box 1703, SE-751 47 Uppsala, Sweden. T. +46184715200. Fax +4618562290. E-mail: nai@nai.uu.se.
URL: http://www.nai.uu.se/

History 1962, Uppsala (Sweden). Statutes registered 1964; new statutes adopted 12 Mar 1981; revised 1986; 1995; 2008; 2009. Since 1980 responsible to the Swedish Ministry of Foreign Affairs. Former names and other names: *Scandinavian Institute of African Studies (SIAS)* – former; *Institut scandinave d'études africaines* – former. **Aims** Promote research on social, political and economic developments in Africa. **Structure** Swedish public authority with a Nordic Programme and Research Council. **Languages** English, Finnish, Swedish. **Staff** 40.00 FTE, paid. **Finance** Sources: government support. Annual budget: 4,035,000,000 SEK. **Activities** Events/meetings; knowledge management/information dissemination; monitoring/evaluation; research/documentation; training/education. **Events** *Seminar on the current situation in Southern Africa* Reykjavik (Iceland) 2004, *Conference on the African Commission and the new challenges and opportunities for human rights promotion and protection in Africa* Uppsala (Sweden) 2004, *From violent conflicts to civil governance conference* Uppsala (Sweden) 2004, *International conference on looking to the future* Uppsala (Sweden) 2004, *Biennial Africa days* Uppsala (Sweden) 2003. **Publications** *Africa Now*; *NAI Policy Notes*. *Current African Issues* – series. Annual Report; monographs; collective works; research reports. **Members** Not a membership organization. [2021/XD4622/j/E]

♦ Nordic-African Foreign Ministers Meeting (meeting series)

♦ Nordic Africa Research Network (NARN) 17169

Chair Univ of Copenhagen, Centre of African Studies, Karen Blixen Plads 16, 2300 Copenhagen, Denmark. E-mail: info@narn.se.
URL: https://newsite.narn.se/

History 2015. Registration: Sweden. **Aims** Facilitate and enhance communication and cooperation between individuals and institutions in the Nordic countries working with research and/or education regarding Africa. **Structure** Board. **Languages** English. **Finance** Sources: grants; members' dues. **Activities** Events/meetings; research/documentation. **Publications** *Nordic Journal of African Studies* (4 a year) – electronic open access journal.
Members Full in 5 countries:
Denmark, Finland, Iceland, Norway, Sweden.
NGO Relations Partner of (1): *Nordic Africa Institute (NAI, #17168).* [2022.10.19/XM6351/F]

♦ Nordic Agreement on Co-operation on Upper Secondary School Education (2004 treaty)

♦ Nordic.AI 17170

Contact Ideon Science Park Beta, Scheelevägen 17, SE-223 63 Lund, Sweden. E-mail: rune@nordic-ai.com.
URL: http://nordic.ai/

Aims Gather *artificial intelligence* and machine learning *ecosystems* in Nordic countries under one umbrella. **Languages** English. **Activities** Events/meetings; monitoring/evaluation. Active in: Denmark, Estonia, Finland, Iceland, Norway, Sweden. **Events** *Conference* Copenhagen (Denmark) 2018. [2022/XM7561/D]

♦ Nordic Alcohol and Drug Policy Network (#17536)
♦ Nordic Aliens Committee / see Nordic Immigration Committee (#17315)

♦ Nordic Alliance for Clinical Genomics (NACG) 17171

Sec address not obtained. E-mail: post@nordicclinicalgenomics.org.
URL: https://nordicclinicalgenomics.org/

History Current constitution adopted 16 Nov 2017, Norway. Former names and other names: *Nordic Alliance for Sequencing and Personalized Medicine (NASPM)* – former. **Aims** Facilitate the responsible sharing of genomic data, bioinformatics tools, sequencing methods and best practices for interpretation of genomic data; enhance quality of genomic data and processes, and explore methodologies to provide assurance; understand legal barriers to the implementation of personalised medicine and to engage with key stakeholders that influence these barriers. **Structure** Steering Committee; Secretariat. **Activities** Advocacy/lobbying/activism; events/meetings; networking/liaising; research/documentation. **Events** *Workshop* Aarhus (Denmark) 2021, *Workshop* Norway 2021, *Clinical Workshop* Helsinki (Finland) 2019.
Members Members in 11 countries and territories:
Australian Capital Territory, Austria, Canada, Denmark, Finland, Germany, Iceland, Ireland, Norway, Sweden, UK. [2021.06.15/AA0514/D]

♦ Nordic Alliance of the Hard of Hearing (#17484)
♦ Nordic Alliance for Sequencing and Personalized Medicine / see Nordic Alliance for Clinical Genomics (#17171)
♦ Nordic Aluminium Casthouse Conference (meeting series)
♦ Nordic Amateur Music Co-operation Council / see Samrådet for Nordisk Amatörmusik (#19048)
♦ Nordic Amateur Music Union / see Nordisk Orkestermusik Union (#17525)

♦ Nordic Amateur Theatre Council 17172

Conseil nordique du théâtre d'amateurs – Nordisk Amatørteaterråd (NAR) – Pohjoismainen Harrastajateatterineuvosto

Secretariat c/o ATR, Box 1194, SE-721 29 Västerås, Sweden.

History 25 Nov 1967, Gothenburg (Sweden). Rules of Procedure modified at Council meetings: 22-23 Mar 1969, Voxenasen; 10 Mar 1972, Tampere (Finland); 1975, Lom (Norway); 1984, Rønne (Denmark); 1986, Reykjavik (Iceland); 1994, Tønder (Denmark). **Aims** Promote amateur theatre in Nordic countries and further collaboration with other countries. **Structure** Council (meets twice a year); Secretariat in Västerås (Sweden). **Languages** Danish, Finnish, Norwegian, Swedish. **Staff** None. **Finance** Members' dues. Other sources: grants; donations. **Activities** Awards/prizes/competitions; training/education; knowledge management/information dissemination. **Events** *Congress / Biennial Nordic Amateur Theatre Festival / Annual Congress* Harstad (Norway) 1998, *Annual Congress* Borgarnes (Iceland) 1996, *Conference on European cooperation / Annual Congress* Borgarnes (Iceland) 1996, *Annual Congress* Rønne (Denmark) / Tinder (Denmark) 1994, *International conference on theatre for elderly people* Odense (Denmark) 1993.
Members National organizations in 8 countries and territories:
Åland, Denmark, Faeroe Is, Finland, Greenland, Iceland, Norway, Sweden.
IGO Relations *Nordic Council of Ministers (NCM, #17260).* [2015.01.16/XD3175/D]

♦ Nordic Anthropological Film Association (NAFA) 17173

Gen Sec ISV/Anthropology, SVHUM D3008, UiT – The Arctic University of Norway, PO Box 6050, Langnes, 9037 Tromsø, Norway. E-mail: contact@nafafilm.org.
URL: http://nafa.uib.no/

History 1975. **Aims** Build up a video and film archive of ethnographic films, used in anthropological teaching and research; engage in online presentation and distribution of films on social and cultural diversity in the world. **Structure** General Assembly (annual); Secretary General; Assistant Secretary General; Treasurer. **Languages** Danish, English, Finnish, Icelandic, Norwegian, Swedish. **Staff** 4.00 FTE, voluntary. **Finance** Members' dues. **Activities** Knowledge management/information dissemination; events/meetings; publishing activities. **Events** *International Conference* Isafjord (Iceland) 2014, *International conference* Isafjord (Iceland) 2008, *International conference* Bergen (Norway) 2006, *International conference* Stockholm (Sweden) 2005, *International conference* Tartu (Estonia) 2004. **Publications** *NAFA-Network* (4 a year) – newsletter; *Journal of Anthropological Film*. *NAFA Book Series*.
Members Anthropological institutions in 4 countries:
Denmark, Finland, Norway, Sweden.
Individual members in 13 countries:
Australia, Bulgaria, Denmark, Finland, France, Germany, Iceland, Italy, Netherlands, Norway, Sweden, UK, USA.
IGO Relations Involved in: *International Association for the Promotion of Cooperation with Scientists from the New Independent States of the former Soviet Union (INTAS, inactive).* **NGO Relations** Member of: *World Council of Anthropological Associations (WCAA, #21317).* [2022/XD1613/D]

♦ Nordic Anthropological Research Council (inactive)
♦ Nordic Aphasia Conference (meeting series)

♦ Nordic Aphasia Council 17174

Nordiska Afasirådet (NAR) – Afasirådet i Norden

No fixed address address not obtained.

History 1994. **Structure** Board.
Members Full in 5 countries:
Denmark, Finland, Iceland, Norway, Sweden.
NGO Relations Links indicated by *Association internationale aphasie (AIA, #02668).* [2017/XD4846/D]

♦ Nordic APIs 17175

Contact Sankt Göransgatan 66, SE-112 33 Stockholm, Sweden. T. +46841073770.
URL: https://nordicapis.com/

History 2013. Registration: No/ID: 556937-4183, Sweden. **Aims** Help organizations make smarter tech decisions using APIs. **Activities** Events/meetings. **Events** *2019 Platform Summit* Stockholm (Sweden) 2019. [2020/AA0781/c/F]

♦ Nordic Arboretum Committee (#17491)
♦ Nordic Archaeobotany Group (unconfirmed)
♦ Nordic Archers' Union (#17499)
♦ Nordic Arctic Society (inactive)
♦ **Nordic ARM** Nordic Association of Rotational Moulders (#17203)

♦ Nordic Art Association 17176

Nordiska Konstförbundet (NKF) – Pohjoismainen Taideliitto (PTL)

Chair Nordisk Gästatelјé, Malongen, Nytorget 15 A, SE-116 41 Stockholm, Sweden.
URL: http://www.nkf.se/

History 1945. Statutes amended 1990. Previously referred to as *Nordic Fine Arts Federation.* **Aims** Further the interests of artists in member countries and territories; promote Nordic art by means of exhibitions, meetings, conferences and information. **Structure** General Meeting (once a year); Working Committee; Secretariat based in Oslo (Norway). **Languages** Danish, Finnish, Icelandic, Norwegian, Swedish. **Staff** 0.50 FTE, paid. **Finance** Grants from the Nordic cultural budget. **Activities** Acts as the coordinating body for visual arts in the Nordic countries. Joint conferences and exhibitions (formerly annually, now biennially), by rotation in Nordic countries. During 1995, which will be a Nordic Art Year, exhibitions will be organized in all Nordic countries; main exhibition: Autumn 1996, Copenhagen (Denmark). **Events** *Annual meeting* Helsinki (Finland) 2003, *Annual meeting / Annual Council Meeting* Finland 1995, *Annual meeting / Annual Council Meeting* Denmark 1994, *Annual Council Meeting* Åland (Finland) 1993, *Annual Council Meeting* Åland (Finland) 1993.
Members Sections in 7 countries and territories (" indicates additional section for Sami arts):
Åland, Denmark, Faeroe Is, Finland (*), Iceland, Norway, Sweden.
Contacts in 1 territory:
Greenland.
IGO Relations *Nordic Council of Ministers (NCM, #17260).* [2016/XD8197/D]

♦ Nordic Association for Accelerator Engineers / see Northern European Association for Accelerator Engineers (#17589)
♦ Nordic Association for Adult Education (#09856)
♦ Nordic Association of Advertising Agencies (no recent information)
♦ Nordic Association for Aerosol Science / see Nordic Society for Aerosol Research (#17410)
♦ Nordic Association of Agricultural Scientists (#17486)

♦ Nordic Association for Allotments 17177

Association nordique des lotissements – Nordisk Kolonihageforbund

Contact c/o Norsk Kolonihage-forbund, Hammersborg torg 3, 0179 Oslo, Norway. T. +4722110090. Fax +4722110091. E-mail: forbundet@kolonihager.no.
URL: http://www.kolonihager.no/web/

Events *Meeting / Congress* Stavanger (Norway) 2008, *Congress* Stockholm (Sweden) 1990.
Members Full in 4 countries:
Denmark, Finland, Norway, Sweden. [2015/XD1225/D]

♦ Nordic Association for American Studies (NAAS) 17178

Pres Univ of Agder, Office 111B, Universitetsveien 51, 4630 Kristiansand, Norway. T. +4791876566. E-mail: alf.t.tonnessen@uia.no.
URL: https://sites.google.com/site/naasstudies/

History 1959, Oslo (Norway). **Aims** Encourage and promote study of the *United States* in *Scandinavia*; facilitate communication and contact among Nordic Americanists. **Structure** Board. **Languages** English. **Finance** Members' dues. Contributions from Nordic foundations. **Activities** Events/meetings. **Events** *Biennial Conference* Bergen (Norway) 2019, *Biennial Conference* Odense (Denmark) 2017, *Biennial Conference* Oulu (Finland) 2015, *Biennial Conference* Karlstad (Sweden) 2013, *Biennial Conference* Oslo (Norway) 2011. **Publications** *American Studies in Scandinavia* (2 a year); *NAAS Newsletter* (2 a year).
Members National Chapters in 5 countries:
Denmark, Finland, Iceland, Norway, Sweden.
Individuals in 9 countries:
Bulgaria, Canada, Denmark, France, Iceland, Italy, Norway, Sweden, USA. [2020/XE1380/E]

♦ Nordic Association for Andrology (NAFA) 17179

Pres Centre for Andrology, M52 Karolinska Univ Hospital, SE-141 86 Huddinge, Sweden. T. +46705655406. Fax +468313691.
URL: https://www.facebook.com/NAFAweb/

History 1970. **Aims** Promote knowledge about male reporductive functions and disorders primarily in Nordic countries. **Structure** General Meeting (annual). Board (meets annually), comprising President and one National Representative from each Nordic country with at least 3 vote-entitled members. President; Vice-President; Secretary; Treasurer. **Languages** English. **Finance** Members' dues. **Activities** Scientific meetings (up to 2 a year, one at Annual General Meeting). **Events** *Annual Meeting* Tartu (Estonia) 2010, *Annual meeting* Oslo (Norway) 2007, *Annual Symposium* Malmö (Sweden) 2002, *Annual Symposium* Copenhagen (Denmark) 2001, *Annual Symposium* Kuopio (Finland) 1999.
Members Individual; Supporting (organizations). Members (about 200) in 7 countries:
Denmark, Estonia, Finland, Latvia, Lithuania, Norway, Sweden. [2017/XD2669/D]

♦ Nordic Association of Applied Geophysics (no recent information)

♦ Nordic Association for Architectural Research 17180

Nordisk Forening for Arkitekturforskning

Pres address not obtained.
URL: http://www.arkitekturforskning.net/

History Founded 1987. **Aims** Develop architectural research within different design disciplines; represent pluralist research and publish original academic contributions in the area of architecture, urban planning and landscape architecture. **Structure** Annual Meeting; Board; Working Committee; Editors-in-Chief (3). **Languages** Danish, English, Finnish, Icelandic, Norwegian, Swedish. **Staff** 7.00 FTE, paid. **Finance** Subscriptions. **Activities** Knowledge management/information dissemination; networking/liaising; events/meetings; publishing activities. **Events** *Annual Meeting and Conference* Copenhagen (Denmark) 2015, *Annual Meeting and Conference* Oulu (Finland) 2014, *Annual Meeting and Conference* Trondheim (Norway) 2013, *Annual Meeting and Conference* Alnarp (Sweden) 2012, *Annual Meeting and Conference* Aarhus (Denmark) 2011. **Publications** *Nordic Journal of Architectural Research* (2-3 a year) – online. **Members** Full (about 70) students and employed teachers and researchers. Membership open. Membership countries not specified. [2021/XD7276/**D**]

♦ Nordic Association of Campanology and Carillon (#17533)

♦ Nordic Association for Canadian Studies (NACS) 17181

Association nordique des études canadiennes (ANEC)

Pres Dept of English, Univ of Turku, FI-20014 Turku, Finland.
URL: http://www.nacs-anec.org/

History 1 May 1984, Århus (Denmark). **Aims** Promote Canadian studies at universities in Nordic countries. **Activities** Organizes seminars, conferences and symposia. **Events** *Triennial Conference* Turku (Finland) 2015, *Conference on connections and exchanges* Alta (Norway) 2014, *Triennial Conference* Aarhus (Denmark) 2011, *Triennial Conference* Aarhus (Denmark) 2011, *Triennial Conference* Trømsø (Norway) 2008.
Members Teachers, researchers and students (about 300) mainly in 6 countries:
Canada, Denmark, Finland, Iceland, Norway, Sweden.
Members also in other European countries, not specified.
NGO Relations *International Council for Canadian Studies (ICCS).* [2016.02.18/XE1382/**E**]

♦ Nordic Association for China Studies (NACS) 17182

Nordiska Föreningen för Kina-studier – Nordisk Forening for Kinastudier – Pohjoismainen Kiinan tutkimuksen seura

Chair Univ of Turku – Fac of Social Sciences, Dept of Political Science and Contemorary History, Ctr for East Asian Studies, FI-20014 Turku, Finland. T. +35823335433. Fax +35823336646.
URL: http://www.nacsorg.com/

History 1991. Previously referred to as *Nordic Association for Chinese Studies.* **Aims** Promote research and higher *education* on China within the *humanities* and *social sciences* in the Nordic region; contribute to exchange of information and contacts between researchers and students of China. **Structure** Board, consisting of 9 researchers with 9 deputies from Nordic countries. Chair; Vice-Chair; Treasurer. **Languages** Danish, English, Finnish, Icelandic, Norwegian, Swedish. **Finance** Members' dues. Other sources: *NIAS-Nordisk Institut for Asienstudier (NIAS, #17132)*; Nordic research councils and universities; foundations. **Activities** Networking/liaising; events/meetings; training/education; knowledge management/information dissemination. **Events** *Biennial Conference* Helsinki (Finland) 2021, *Biennial Conference* Bergen (Norway) 2019, *Biennial Conference* Turku (Finland) 2013, *Biennial conference* Oslo (Norway) 2011, *Biennial conference* Reykjavik (Iceland) 2009. **Publications** *China at the Turn of the 21st Century* by Jírund Buen and Björn Kjellgren.
Members Researchers, teachers and students in 5 countries:
Denmark, Finland, Iceland, Norway, Sweden.
IGO Relations *Nordic Council (NC, #17256).* [2012.06.01/XE1473/v/**E**]

♦ Nordic Association for Chinese Studies / see Nordic Association for China Studies (#17182)
♦ Nordic Association for Churchyard Culture (inactive)

♦ Nordic Association of Cleanroom Technology 17183

Nordiska Föreningen för RenhetsTeknik och Rena Rum (R3 Nordic)

Registrar's Office Ganska Företagspartner AB, Härjedalsgatan 1, SE-265 40 Åstorp, Sweden. T. +4640161080. Fax +4640161096. E-mail: info@r3nordic.org.
URL: http://r3nordic.org/

History 1970, as *Nordiska R3 Föreningen – Nordic Association for Contamination Control and Clean Rooms (R3 Nordic).* In English previously referred to as *Nordic R3 Association.* Present name adopted 2005. **Aims** Further and promote contamination control technologies. **Structure** Board. **Languages** English, Swedish. **Staff** 1.00 FTE, paid; 6.00 FTE, voluntary. **Finance** Members' dues. **Activities** Events/meetings; training/education. **Events** *Annual Symposium* Stockholm (Sweden) 2019, *Annual Symposium* Naantali (Finland) 2018, *Annual Symposium* Stockholm (Sweden) 2017, *Annual Symposium* Copenhagen (Denmark) 2016, *Annual Symposium* Lillestrøm (Norway) 2015. **Publications** *Nordic Journal for Cleanroom Technology* (4 a year).
Members in 4 countries:
Denmark, Finland, Norway, Sweden.
NGO Relations Member of: *International Confederation of Contamination Control Societies (ICCCS, #12855).* [2018.06.01/XD7673/**D**]

♦ Nordic Association for Clinical Physics (NACP) 17184

Contact c/o Strålningsfysik, Skånes universitetssjukhus, SE-205 02 Malmö, Sweden.
URL: http://www.nacp-nordisk.org/

History 1962. Inactive from 1992 to 2004, when the new Constitution was approved, Bergen (Norway). **Aims** Foster and coordinate the activities of member organizations in the field of clinical physics in all its aspects; establish relationships and collaboration where appropriate with national, regional and international societies and bodies in the fields related to clinical physics; improve standards in the field within the Nordic countries; promote Nordic cooperation and exchange of information within the field in scientific work, developments and education; recommend standards for education, training and accreditation programmes; encourage scholarships and exchange of scientific experts within appropriate fields. **Structure** General Assembly. Council (meets once a year), consisting of delegates appointed by, and preferably from the board of, each member organization. **Languages** English. **Finance** Members' dues. Other sources; gifts; subsidies and grants. **Events** *Symposium* Reykjavik (Iceland) 2021, *Symposium* Reykjavik (Iceland) 2020, *Symposium* Oslo (Norway) 2017, *Symposium* Turku (Finland) 2014, *Symposium* Aarhus (Denmark) 2008.
Members National physics societies in 5 countries:
Denmark, Finland, Iceland, Norway, Sweden. [2020/XJ0064/**D**]

♦ Nordic Association for Clinical Physiology / see Scandinavian Society of Clinical Physiology and Nuclear Medicine (#19104)

♦ Nordic Association for Clinical Sexology (NACS) 17185

Nordisk Forening for Klinisk Sexologi (NFKS)

Pres address not obtained. E-mail: info@nacs.eu.
URL: http://www.nacs.eu/

History Set up Oct 1978, Rome (Italy). First conference organized May 1979, Linköping (Sweden). Statutes adopted Sep 1999. **Aims** Promote sexual health, high professional skills and networking between sexologists in the Nordic countries. **Structure** Board, comprising President of NACS and Presidents of member associations. **Languages** English. **Activities** Offers a training programme for sexologists; delivers authorization for Nordic sexologists. **Events** *Annual Meeting* 2020, *Annual Meeting* Gothenburg (Sweden) 2019, *Annual Meeting* Turku (Finland) 2018, *Annual Meeting* Trondheim (Norway) 2017, *Annual Meeting* Tartu (Estonia) 2016.
Members Sexological associations (6) and individuals in 5 countries:
Denmark, Estonia, Finland, Iceland, Norway, Sweden. [2020/XD2311/**D**]

♦ Nordic Association for Comparative Literature (NorLit) 17186

Nordisk Förening för Litteraturvetenskap

Address not obtained.

History Former names and other names: *Nordic Association for Literary Research* – alias. **Activities** Organizes biennial international scholarly conference. **Events** *NorLit Conference* Trondheim (Norway) 2022, *NorLit Conference* Trondheim (Norway) 2021, *NorLit Conference* Copenhagen (Denmark) 2019, *Conference* Turku (Finland) 2017, *Conference* Gothenburg (Sweden) 2015. [2021/XJ1571/**D**]

♦ Nordic Association for Computational Mechanics (NoACM) 17187

Pres Dept Mathematical Sciences, NTNU, Alfred Getz vei 1, 7491 Trondheim, Norway.
URL: http://www.noacm.no/

History Oct 1988. **Aims** Stimulate and promote research and applications within computational mechanics; foster interchange of ideas among the various fields contributing to computational mechanics; provide a forum for personal contact and dissemination of knowledge in the field. **Structure** Executive Committee, comprising Chairman and 8 members. **Languages** English. **Staff** 4.00 FTE, voluntary. **Activities** *Nordic Seminar on Computational Mechanics (NSCM).* **Events** *ECCOMAS : European Congress on Computational Methods in Applied Sciences and Engineering* Oslo (Norway) 2022, *Annual Seminar* Jönköping (Sweden) 2021, *Annual Seminar* Oulu (Finland) 2019, *Annual Seminar* Umeå (Sweden) 2018, *Annual Seminar* Copenhagen (Denmark) 2017. **Publications** Seminar proceedings, short papers.
Members Full in 8 countries:
Denmark, Estonia, Finland, Iceland, Latvia, Lithuania, Norway, Sweden.
NGO Relations Member of: *European Committee on Computational Methods in Applied Sciences (ECCOMAS, #06644)*; *International Association for Computational Mechanics (IACM, #11800)*, representing Nordic interests. [2017/XD2339/v/**D**]

♦ Nordic Association of Conservators / see Nordic Association of Conservators – Restorers (#17188)

♦ Nordic Association of Conservators – Restorers 17188

Nordiska Konservatorsförbundet (NKF) – Nordisk Konservatorforbund (NKF)

Chair c/o Royal Danish Academy, Philip de Langes Allé 10, 1435 Copenhagen K, Denmark. E-mail: fo@nordiskkonservatorforbund.org.
URL: http://www.nordiskkonservatorforbund.org/

History 1951, Stockholm (Sweden). Founded as the Nordic section of *International Institute for Conservation of Historic and Artistic Works (IIC, #13871).* Former names and other names: *Nordic Association of Conservators* – alias; *Nordic Association of Restorers* – alias. **Aims** Promote collaboration between Nordic countries within the field of conservation. **Structure** Board (meets annually), headed by President. Each Nordic country has its own group, headed by President. **Languages** Danish, English, Faroese, Finnish, Icelandic, Norwegian, Swedish. **Events** *Congress* Stockholm (Sweden) 2021, *Symposium* Copenhagen (Denmark) 2019, *Congress* Reykjavik (Iceland) 2018, *Congress* Helsinki (Finland) 2015, *Congress* Oslo (Norway) 2012. **Publications** *Meddelelser om konservering* (2 a year).
Members Full national organizations in 5 countries:
Denmark, Finland, Iceland, Norway, Sweden. [2021/XD3719/**D**]

♦ Nordic Association for Contamination Control and Clean Rooms / see Nordic Association of Cleanroom Technology (#17183)

♦ Nordic Association for Convulsive Therapy (NACT) 17189

Contact address not obtained. E-mail: nactmeeting@gmail.com.
URL: http://nact.se/

History Founded Jun 2003. **Aims** Increase knowledge of Electroconvulsive Therapy (ECT) through and to the members as well as persons and organizations handling ECT in the Nordic countries. **Structure** Board. **Activities** Events/meetings; research/documentation. **Events** *Annual Meeting* Snekkersten (Denmark) 2021, *Annual Meeting* Snekkersten (Denmark) 2020, *Annual Meeting* Gjøvik (Norway) 2019, *Annual Meeting* Tallinn (Estonia) 2018, *Annual Meeting* Tampere (Finland) 2017. **NGO Relations** *European Forum for Electroconvulsive Therapy (EFFECT, #07309)*; *International Society for ECT and Neurostimulation (ISEN).* [2018/XM6520/**D**]

♦ Nordic Association for Disability and Oral Health 17190

Nordisk Förening för Funktionshinder och Oral Hälsa (NFH) – Nordisk Förening för Funktionshinder och Oral Helse

Contact Specialisttandvården, Blekingesjukhuset, SE-371 85 Karlskrona, Sweden. T. +46734471555. E-mail: kontakt@nfh-sverige.se.
Swedish Section: http://www.nfh-sverige.se/

History Founded 1974, as *Nordic Society of Odontology for the Handicapped – Société nordique d'odontologie pour les handicapés – Nordisk Förening för Handicaptandvård (NFH).* At one time referred to in English *Nordic Society of Dentistry for the Handicapped* and *Nordic Society for Disability and Oral Health.* **Languages** English, Swedish. **Staff** 6.00 FTE, voluntary. **Finance** Members' dues. Sources: congresses. **Events** *Biennial Congress* Marstrand (Sweden) 2019, *Biennial Congress* Reykjavik (Iceland) 2017, *Biennial Congress* Gothenburg (Sweden) 2015, *Biennial Congress* Gothenburg (Sweden) 2011, *Biennial Congress* Reykjavik (Iceland) 2009. **Publications** *NFH Bulletin* (2 a year).
Members Sections in 5 countries:
Denmark, Finland, Iceland, Norway, Sweden.
NGO Relations Cooperates with and meetings during meetings of *International Association for Disability and Oral Health (iADH, #11848).* [2023/XD5946/**D**]

♦ Nordic Association of the Disabled / see Nordic Handicap Federation (#17308)

♦ Nordic Association for Educational and Vocational Guidance (NAEVG) 17191

Association nordique d'orientation scolaire et professionnelle – Nordisk Förening för Studie- och Yrkesvägleding Nordisk Forbund for Uddannelses- og Erhvervsvejledning (NFUE) – Nordisk Forbund for Studie- og Yrkesvejledning (NFSY) – Pohjoismainen Ohjausalan Yhdistys/Nordisk Förening för Studie- och Yrkensvägleding (POY/NFSY) – Norraen Samtök um Nams- og Starfsradgjöf (NSNS)

Contact address not obtained.
URL: http://www.nfsy.org/

History 1953. **Aims** Strengthen professional educational and vocational guidance in Nordic countries; provide contact in terms of cooperation and information between national associations for education and vocational guidance; represent Nordic countries in international relations through representation in the IAEVG. **Structure** Board; Rotating Presidency. **Languages** Danish, English, Norwegian, Swedish. **Staff** Voluntary. **Finance** Sources: members' dues. **Activities** Events/meetings; networking/liaising. **Events** *Conference* Iceland 2010, *The impact of guidance policy making in a Nordic perspective* Lillehammer (Norway) 2004, *Conference* Thórshavn (Faeroe Is) 2002, *Conference* Grankulla (Finland) 2001, *Conference* Västerås (Sweden) 2000.
Members Full in 5 countries:
Denmark, Finland, Iceland, Norway, Sweden.
Associated members in 1 territory:
Åland. [2022/XD6128/**D**]

♦ Nordic Association for Education to a Life without Drugs (inactive)
♦ Nordic Association of Electronics Manufacturers (inactive)

♦ Nordic Association of English Studies (NAES) 17192

Contact address not obtained.

History 1980. **Aims** Advance research and study in the Nordic countries of the English language and of Anglophone literatures and societies. **Languages** English. **Events** *Triennial Conference* Kristiansand (Norway) 2016, *Triennial Conference* Oulu (Finland) 2010, *Triennial Conference* Bergen (Norway) 2007, *Triennial Conference* Aarhus (Denmark) 2004, *Triennial Conference* Aarhus (Denmark) 2004. **Publications** *Nordic Journal of English Studies.*
Members Not a membership organization. All members of English Departments at University level in the following 5 countries are entitled to participate:
Denmark, Finland, Iceland, Norway, Sweden.
NGO Relations Affiliated to: *European Society for the Study of English (ESSE, #08743).* [2013/XE1601/**E**]

♦ Nordic Association of Field Mycologists (inactive)
♦ Nordic Association of Fire Brigades (inactive)

♦ Nordic Association of Forensic Toxicologists (NAFT) 17193

Nordisk rättstoxikologisk förening

Pres Natl Board of Forensic Medicine, Dept of forensic genetics and forensic toxicology, Artillerigatan 12, SE-587 58 Linköping, Sweden. E-mail: naft.tox@gmail.com.
URL: http://naft-tox.org/

History Current statutes adopted 29 Jan 2014. Registered in accordance with Swedish law. **Aims** Promote further training of forensic toxicologists, education and research. **Structure** Annual Meeting; Board. **Activities** Events/meetings; training/education. **Events** *Annual Meeting* Reykjavik (Iceland) 2022, *Annual Meeting* Reykjavik (Iceland) 2020, *Annual Meeting* Linköping (Sweden) 2019, *Annual Meeting* Helsinki (Finland) 2018, *Annual Meeting* Trondheim (Norway) 2016.
Members Individuals in 5 countries:
Denmark, Finland, Iceland, Norway, Sweden. [2018/XM6547/D]

♦ Nordic Association of Freight Forwarders (#17543)
♦ Nordic Association for Geographic Information / see Nordic Network for Geographic Information (#17355)
♦ Nordic Association of Hairdressers / see Nordic Hairdressers' Association (#17307)
♦ Nordic Association of Heatset Printer / see Nordic Offset Printing Association, The (#17373)

♦ Nordic Association for Hydrology 17194

Société nordique d'hydrologie – Nordisk Hydrologisk Förening – Pohjoismainen Hydrologinen Yhdistys

Chair address not obtained.
URL: http://www.nhf-hydrology.org/

History 28 Aug 1970, Stockholm (Sweden). The roots of the Association go back to the organization of hydrological conferences of the Baltic Sea countries (1926-1938); the series of meetings was broken by the Second World War, and never continued as such after the war. Between 1955 and 1967, five Nordic Conferences of Hydrologists were organized on a 3-year rotational basis between the five Nordic (in sensu stricto) countries. From 1965, the International Hydrological Decade (IHD) was established under the auspices of UNESCO. A coordinating group, NUTSAM, was established between the 5 Nordic IHD committees, which identified a need for organizing a broad water-related forum for exchange of hydrological research results and professional contacts between Nordic hydrologists. Provisional statutes were drafted and discussed at the 6th Nordic Hydrological Conference in Stockholm (Sweden), 1970, which agreed to form the NHF. Statutes formally decided by the General Assembly at the following Conference, Sandefjord (Norway), 1972. **Aims** Promote cooperation in hydrological sciences and encourage their practical application in member countries. **Structure** General Assembly; Board. **Languages** Danish, English, Norwegian, Swedish. **Staff** 1.00 FTE, paid. **Finance** Members' dues. **Activities** Events/meetings; awards/prizes/competitions. **Events** *Biennial Conference* Stockholm (Sweden) 2014, *Biennial Conference* Oulu (Finland) 2012, *Biennial Conference* Riga (Latvia) 2010, *Biennial Conference* Reykjavik (Iceland) 2008, *Biennial Conference* Vejle (Denmark) 2006. **Publications** *Hydrology Research* (5 a year) – journal; *NHF Newsletter* (annual).
Members Hydrologists in 8 countries:
Denmark, Estonia, Finland, Iceland, Latvia, Lithuania, Norway, Sweden.
NGO Relations Member of: *European Geosciences Union (EGU, #07390).* [2019/XD9805/D]

♦ Nordic Association for Infant Mental Health (#17509)
♦ Nordic Association for Internal Medicine (inactive)

♦ Nordic Association for Japanese and Korean Studies (NAJAKS) ... 17195

Address not obtained.
URL: http://www.najaks.org/

History 1990. **Aims** Promote Nordic research on Japan and Korea within the *humanities* and *social sciences*; assist in establishing contacts between scholars and students in the Nordic countries and the rest of the world in the field of Japanese and Korean studies. **Structure** General Assembly; Board. **Languages** Danish, English, Norwegian, Swedish. **Staff** No regular staff. **Finance** No members' dues. Conferences financed by various foundations. **Activities** Organizes conferences. **Events** *Conference* Helsinki (Finland) 2022, *Conference* Helsinki (Finland) 2020, *Conference* Stockholm (Sweden) 2016, *Conference* Bergen (Norway) 2013, *Conference* Helsinki (Finland) 2010. **IGO Relations** *NIAS-Nordisk Institut for Asienstudier (NIAS, #17132).* **NGO Relations** Member of: *European Association for Japanese Studies (EAJS, #06096).* [2010.06.01/XE1674/E]

♦ Nordic Association of Jewelry Workers (inactive)
♦ Nordic Association of Journalists' Unions / see Nordiska Journalistförbundet (#17487)
♦ Nordic Association of Ladies' and Gentlemen's Hairdressers / see Nordic Hairdressers' Association (#17307)

♦ Nordic Association for Lexicography 17196

Nordisk Forening for Leksikografi

Contact c/o Det Norske Akademis ordbok, Grensen 3, 0159 Oslo, Norway. E-mail: nord-isk.lexikografi@gmail.com.
URL: https://www.nordisk-leksikografi.com/

History 1991, Oslo (Norway). **Aims** Promote cooperation between Nordic countries within the domain of lexicography, lexicology, language technology and linguistics; continue mutual understanding, linguistically and culturally, between Nordic countries. **Activities** Events/meetings; publishing activities. **Events** *Conference* Helsinki (Finland) 2019, *Conference* Copenhagen (Denmark) 2015, *Conference* Oslo (Norway) 2013, *Conference* Tampere (Finland) 2009, *Conference* Akureyri (Iceland) 2007. **Publications** *LexicoNordica* (annual) – 27 vols. *Normer og Regler* (1998); *Nordisk Leksikografisk Ordbok* (1997). Conference proceedings.
Members Individuals; Institutions; private enterprises. Members (250) in 8 countries and territories:
Åland, Denmark, Faeroe Is, Finland, Greenland, Iceland, Norway, Sweden.
IGO Relations *Nordic Council of Ministers (NCM, #17260).* [2020.03.25/XD3419/D]

♦ Nordic Association of Librarians (inactive)

♦ Nordic Association of Linguists (NAL) 17197

Pres c/o Inst nordiska språk, Box 527, Uppsala universitet, SE-751 20 Uppsala, Sweden.
URL: https://www.cfl.aau.dk/nordic-association-of-linguists/

History 1976, Austin, TX (USA). Operational since 1977. **Structure** Executive Committee. **Finance** Sources: members' dues. **Activities** Events/meetings. Scandinavian Conference of Linguistics; International Conference on Nordic and General Linguistics. **Events** *NGL – International Conference of Nordic and General Linguistics* Oslo (Norway) 2021, *NGL – International Conference of Nordic and General Linguistics* Oslo (Norway) 2020, *Scandinavian Conference of Linguistics (SCL26)* 2015, *NGL – International Conference of Nordic and General Linguistics* Freiburg-Breisgau (Germany) 2012, *Scandinavian conference of linguistics* Fyn (Denmark) 1998. **Publications** *Nordic Journal of Linguistics (NJL)* (3 a year). [2022/AA1833/D]

♦ Nordic Association for Literary Research / see Nordic Association for Comparative Literature (#17186)
♦ Nordic Association of Manual Medicine (inactive)

♦ Nordic Association of Marine Insurers (Cefor) 17198

Managing Dir PO Box 2550 Solli, 0202 Oslo, Norway. T. +4723086550. Fax +4722561077. E-mail: cefor@cefor.no.
Street Address Finansnaeringens Hus, Hansteens gt 2, Oslo, Norway.
URL: http://www.cefor.no/

History 15 Aug 1911, as *Central Union of Marine Underwriters – Sjíassurandírernes Centralforening (CEFOR)* by Norwegian and foreign insurance companies. Current title adopted 5 Mar 2009 to reflect pan-Nordic membership. **Aims** Strengthen and develop the basic concepts of the Nordic marine insurance market; promote members' common interests on key issues for the marine insurance industry. **Structure** General Meeting (annual). Board of Directors. Managing Director. Forums (7): Cargo; Claims; Coastal and Fishing Vessels; Energy and Offshore; Plan Revision; Statistics; Underwriting. **Events** *Annual General Meeting* Oslo (Norway) 2012, *Annual strategy meeting* Mariehamn (Finland) 2011, *Annual strategy meeting* Oslo (Norway) 2011, *Centennial conference* Oslo (Norway) 2011, *Nordic marine insurance days* Stockholm (Sweden) 2011.
Members Full in 4 countries:
Denmark, Finland, Norway, Sweden.
NGO Relations Member of: *International Maritime Statistics Forum (IMSF, #14105).* [2011/XJ2322/D]

♦ Nordic Association for Market Management (inactive)
♦ Nordic Association for Medical and Health Information / see Nordic-Baltic Association for Medical and Health Information (#17213)
♦ Nordic Association of Medical Laboratory Technologists / see Nordisk Medisinsk Laboratoriegruppe (#17523)
♦ Nordic Association on Neuro-Radiology / see Nordic Society of Neuroradiology (#17421)
♦ Nordic Association of Nurse Anaesthesiologists and Intensive Care Nurses (#17528)

♦ Nordic Association of Occupational Safety and Health (NOROSH) .. 17199

Secretariat c/o Scand J Work Environ Health, PO Box 18, FI-00032 Työterveyslaitos, Finland. T. +358304742694. Fax +35898783326. E-mail: jpar@ttl.fi.
URL: https://www.norosh.org/

History Jul 2012. Registration: Finland. **Aims** Strengthen Nordic and international cooperation in the field of occupational safety and health. **Structure** Annual General Meeting; Executive Committee. **Finance** Sources: members' dues. **Activities** Knowledge management/information dissemination; research/documentation. **Publications** *Scandinavian Journal of Work, Environment and Health.*
Members Full in 4 countries:
Denmark, Finland, Norway, Sweden.
Contributing in 2 countries:
Denmark, Sweden. [2020/AA0898/D]

♦ Nordic Association of Odontology / see Scandinavian Association for Dental Research (#19070)
♦ Nordic Association of Otolaryngology / see Scandinavian Otolaryngological Society (#19094)
♦ Nordic Association for Palliative Care (inactive)
♦ Nordic Association for Pathology and Microbiology (inactive)
♦ Nordic Association of Pedagogic Research / see Nordic Educational Research Association (#17276)
♦ Nordic Association for Pediatric Pathology (inactive)
♦ Nordic Association for Pediatric Radiology (no recent information)
♦ Nordic Association for Pedicure (inactive)
♦ Nordic Association for Pedodontics (inactive)
♦ Nordic Association for Podology (inactive)
♦ Nordic Association for Police Sports (inactive)

♦ Nordic Association for Prevention of Child Abuse and Neglect (NASPCAN) 17200

Nordisk Forening Mot Barnemishandling og Omsorgssvikt (NFBO)

Chair Norwegian Center for Violence and Traumatic Stress Studies, Gullhaugveien 1, 0484 Oslo, Norway.
Sec Roskilde police department, Skovbogade 3, 4000 Røskilde, Denmark.
URL: http://www.nfbo.org/

History 26 May 1998, Copenhagen (Denmark). Founded at a Nordic conference. Registration: Sweden. **Aims** Prevent physical, emotional and sexual abuse and neglect of children in the Nordic countries; encourage collaboration and exchange of experience in the field of child protection in the region. **Structure** Congress (every 2 years). Board (serve 4-year terms), comprising 11 ordinary members and 11 deputy members, with 2 ordinary and deputy members each from Denmark, Iceland, Norway, Sweden and Finland, and 1 ordinary and 1 deputy member representing Greenland, Faeroe Is and Åland. **Languages** Danish, English, Norwegian, Swedish. **Finance** Sources: meeting proceeds; members' dues. **Activities** Events/meetings; training/education. **Events** *Nordic Conference on Child Abuse and Neglect* Reykjavik (Iceland) 2023, *Nordic Conference on Child Abuse and Neglect* Helsinki (Finland) 2021, *Nordic Conference on Child Abuse and Neglect* Helsinki (Finland) 2020, *Nordic Conference on Child Abuse and Neglect* Thórshavn (Faeroe Is) 2018, *Congress* Stockholm (Sweden) 2016. **Publications** Newsletter (1-2 a year).
Members Professionals with an interest in child protection (study and prevention of child abuse and neglect) including lawyers, medical doctors, nurses and other health professionals, police officers, psychologists, researchers, social workers, sociologists and teachers. Individuals in 7 countries and territories:
Denmark, Faeroe Is, Finland, Greenland, Iceland, Norway, Sweden. [2022/XJ0578/v/D]

♦ Nordic Association for Psychiatric Epidemiology (NAPE) 17201

Nordisk Forening for Psykiatrisk Epidemiologi

Pres Psychiatry Dept, Univ of Oulu, FI-90014 Oulu, Finland. T. +358405237413.

History Sep 1997, Røskilde (Denmark). Takes over activities of *Nordic Planning Group for Psychiatric Epidemiological and Social-psychiatric Research.* **Aims** Promote the research of psychiatric epidemiology in the Nordic countries; stimulate cooperation in the field of psychiatric epidemiology. **Structure** General Meeting (annual). Executive Committee, comprising Chairperson, Deputy Chairperson, Treasurer, Secretary and 2 further members. **Languages** Danish, English, Norwegian, Swedish. **Finance** Members' dues. Sponsorship. **Events** *Annual meeting* Reykjavik (Iceland) 2003, *Annual meeting* Oslo (Norway) 2002, *Annual meeting* Copenhagen (Denmark) 2001, *Annual meeting* Helsinki (Finland) 2000, *Annual Meeting* Oslo (Norway) 1999. **NGO Relations** Member of: *International Federation of Psychiatric Epidemiology (IFPE, #13521).* [2010/XD8948/D]

♦ Nordic Association for Rehabilitation (inactive)
♦ Nordic Association for Research on Latin America (inactive)

♦ Nordic Association for Research on Men and Masculinities (NARMM) 17202

Nordisk Forening for Forskning om Menn og Maskuliniteter (NFMM)

Contact Reform/NORMAS, Pb 28 Sentrum, 0101 Oslo, Norway. E-mail: post@reform.no.
Contact c/o Uppsala University, Box 527, SE-751 20 Uppsala, Sweden.

History Founded 2009, Røskilde (Denmark). **Aims** Promote and disseminate knowledge on scientific research on men and masculinities, with an emphasis on research that promotes social and cultural change, equality and diversity; promote theoretical and methodological developments in the field. **Structure** Board. **Languages** Danish, English, Faroese, Icelandic, Norwegian, Swedish. **Staff** Voluntary. **Finance** Members' dues. Funding from authorities and funding agencies. **Activities** Knowledge management/information dissemination; research/documentation; networking/liaising; events/meetings. **Publications** *NORMA – International Journal for Masculinity Studies.*
Members in 5 countries:
Denmark, Finland, Iceland, Norway, Sweden. [2014.07.13/XJ6215/D]

♦ Nordic Association of Restorers / see Nordic Association of Conservators – Restorers (#17188)
♦ Nordic Association for Romantic Studies (internationally oriented national body)

♦ Nordic Association of Rotational Moulders (Nordic ARM) 17203

Contact Ekornveien 5, 3960 Stathelle, Norway. T. +4791593043. E-mail: info@nordicarm.org.
URL: http://nordicarm.org/

History 2007. **Aims** Assist the industry in setting standards and improving the quality of rotationally moulded products. **Structure** Board. **Events** *Annual Nordic ARM Conference* Stockholm (Sweden) 2019, *Annual Nordic ARM Conference* Oslo (Norway) 2018, *Annual Nordic ARM Conference* Silkeborg (Denmark) 2015, *Annual Nordic ARM Conference* Gothenburg (Sweden) 2008.
Members Full in 6 countries:
Denmark, Finland, Iceland, Norway, Sweden, UK.
NGO Relations Affiliate of: *Affiliation of Rotational Moulding Organisations (ARMO, #00149).* [2015/XJ9195/D]

♦ Nordic Association of School Librarians (#17534)

♦ Nordic Association of Schools of Social Work (NASSW) 17204

Nordisk Organisasjon for Utdanninger i Sosialt Arbeid (NOUSA)

Pres School of Social Work, Lund Univ, Box 23, SE-221 00 Lund, Sweden. T. +46462229384. Fax +46462229412.

URL: http://www.nassw.socwork.org/

History 1965, as *Nordic Committee of Schools of Social Work – Comité nordique des écoles de service social – Nordiska socialhögskolekommittén (NSHK)*. **Aims** Promote social work *education* by encouraging cooperation between Nordic universities and universities that offer education in social works; support establishment of new courses in social work in countries outside Scandinavia. **Structure** General Assembly; Chairman; Governing body of 5 elected at General Assembly (one from each Nordic country). **Languages** Danish, Icelandic, Norwegian, Swedish. **Staff** 1.00 FTE, voluntary. **Finance** Members' dues (annual): Norwegian Kr 500. **Activities** Organizes Nordic conferences and other meetings (every 2 years); stimulates Nordic cooperation between teachers and students in social work education; stimulates cooperation between teachers in Nordic and other countries working to establish and develop courses in social work; stimulates cooperation in research and professional development in social work within Nordic countries; stays informed on education politics to further quality in social work education; represents education establishments in other Nordic organizations, and such organs as may derive from these. **Events** *Nordic Social Work Conference* Reykjavik (Iceland) 2021, *Nordic Social Work Conference* Reykjavik (Iceland) 2020, *Nordic Social Work Conference* Helsinki (Finland) 2018, *Conference* Tampere (Finland) 2013, *Conference* Bodø (Norway) 2009.

Members Member schools (39) in the 6 Nordic countries and territories:
Denmark, Finland, Greenland, Iceland, Norway, Sweden.

NGO Relations Regional Committee of: *European Association of Schools of Social Work (EASSW, #06200); International Association of Schools of Social Work (IASSW, #12149).* [2018/XD3181/D]

♦ Nordic Association for Sciences in State Affairs (inactive)

♦ Nordic Association for Semiotic Studies (NASS) 17205

Contact address not obtained. E-mail: post@nordicsemiotics.org.

URL: http://nordicsemiotics.org/

History 1987, Imatra (Finland). Inactive between 2001 and 2011. Refounded 9 June 2012, Imatra (Finland). Current constitution approved 31 Aug 2012; latest amendments approved 14 June 2019, Stavanger (Norway). **Aims** Promote advancement of semiotics as an academic discipline and research domain in the Nordic countries and within the international semiotic community, fostering academic cooperation and highlighting Nordic contributions to the field. **Structure** General Assembly; Governing Board. **Languages** Danish, English, Norwegian, Swedish. **Staff** Voluntary. **Finance** Sources: members' dues. **Activities** Events/meetings. **Events** *Conference* Helsinki (Finland) 2023, *Meaning in Perception and the Senses* Vilnius (Lithuania) 2021, *Conference* Stavanger (Norway) 2019, *Conference* Kaunas (Lithuania) 2017, *Conference* Tartu (Estonia) 2015. **Publications** *Anticipation and Change – Special issue* (2021); *Anticipation and Change: The 11th Conference of the Nordic Association for Semiotic Studies (NASS XI)* (2019).

Members Full in 8 countries:
Denmark, Estonia, Finland, Iceland, Latvia, Lithuania, Norway, Sweden. [2023.02.20/XD6159/D]

♦ Nordic Association for Southeast Asian Studies (inactive)
♦ Nordic Association for the Study of Contemporary Japanese Society (internationally oriented national body)
♦ Nordic Association for the Study of Education in Developing Countries (no recent information)
♦ Nordic Association of Textile Apprentices (no recent information)
♦ Nordic Association of Tinsmiths and Plate Works (inactive)
♦ Nordic Association for Traffic Medicine (inactive)

♦ Nordic Association of University Administrators (NAUA) 17206

Association nordique des administrateurs d'université – Nordiska Universitetsadministratörssamarbetet (NUAS)

SG c/o Univ of Oslo, PB 1154 Blindern, 0318 Oslo, Norway.

URL: https://nuas.org/

History Founded 1975, as *Nordisk Kontaktudvalg for Universiteter og Higere Laereanstalter*, by *Nordic Council of Ministers (NCM, #17260)* within the framework of *Nordic Cultural Cooperation (1971)*. First Nordic seminar for university administrators, held in 1976, Røros (Norway), became an annual event. In 1982, a management group was formed, and a secretariat was set up at the University of Aarhus, where the first Chairman was located. New planning groups for different administrative areas were gradually formed. **Aims** Enhance contacts; establish networks between Nordic universities at all administrative levels. **Structure** Management Group; Planning Groups (12); Secretariat. **Languages** Danish, English, Faroese, Icelandic, Norwegian, Swedish. **Staff** 0.50 FTE, paid. **Finance** Members' dues. Seminar fees. **Activities** Events/meetings. **Events** *Facilities and Environment Conference* Joensuu (Finland) 2022, *Communication Conference* Turku (Finland) 2022, *Communication Conference* Turku (Finland) 2020, *Communication Conference* Reykjavik (Iceland) 2019, *Forum* Tromsø (Norway) 2019. **Publications** *Institutions of Higher Education in the Nordic Countries* (annual) – directory.

Members Institutions (57) in 7 countries and territories:
Denmark, Faeroe Is, Finland, Greenland, Iceland, Norway, Sweden. [2016.12.14/XE1201/D]

♦ Nordic Association of Veteran Sports Leaders (unconfirmed)

♦ Nordic Association of Vineyard Churches 17207

Vineyard Norden

Contact address not obtained.

URL: https://www.vineyardnordic.org/

History 1992. Former names and other names: *Vineyard Nordic* – alias. **Aims** Function as a *Christian evangelical* church movement.

Members Churches (approx 30) in 5 countries:
Denmark, Finland, Iceland, Norway, Sweden.

NGO Relations Member of: *Vineyard International Consortium (VIC, #20778).* [2018/XJ3626/E]

♦ Nordic Association of Violin Makers (inactive)
♦ Nordic Association of Vocational Advisers (inactive)
♦ Nordic Association for Women's Gymnastics (inactive)

♦ Nordic Association for Women's Studies and Gender Research 17208

Association nordique pour les études sur la condition féminine et la recherche sur l'égalité des sexes

Address not obtained.

History 2 Aug 1994, Turku (Finland). **Structure** Board. **Languages** Danish, Faroese, Icelandic, Norwegian, Swedish. **Events** *Triennial international interdisciplinary congress on women / Congress / Conference* Tromsø (Norway) 1999, *Conference / Congress / Conference* Oslo (Norway) 1996. **Publications** *NORA – Nordic Journal of Feminist and Gender Research.*

Members Individuals and organizations in 5 countries:
Denmark, Finland, Iceland, Norway, Sweden. [2022/XD5667/D]

♦ Nordic Atlantic Cooperation 17209

Nordisk Atlantsamarbejde (NORA)

Exec Dir Bryggjubakki 12, PO Box 259, FO-110 Thórshavn, Faeroe Is. T. +298306990. E-mail: nora@nora.fo.

URL: http://www.nora.fo/

History Established with the title *West Nordic Committee – Västnordensamarbetet*, within the framework of *Nordic Council of Ministers (NCM, #17260)* – Nordic Council of Ministers for Business, Energy and Regional Policy (MR-NER). Previously functioned within *Nordic Committee of Senior Officials for Regional Policy (EK-R / NÄRP / NERP)*. Former Finnish title *Pohjoismainen Atlantti-yhteistyö*. **Aims** Promote sustainable development by strengthening cooperation in areas where participating countries have common challenges, opportunities or interests. **Structure** Main Secretariat (Faeroe Is). Regional Secretariats (3): Iceland; Norway; Greenland. **Languages** Danish, English, Finnish, Icelandic, Norwegian, Swedish. **Staff** Main secretariat: 5; regional secretariats: 4. **Activities** Projects/programmes; networking/liaising; research/documentation; events/meetings; financial and/or material support. **Events** *Conference* Copenhagen (Denmark) 2013, *Conference* Reykjavik (Iceland) 2012, *Conference* Copenhagen (Denmark) 2011, *Conference* Reykjavik (Iceland) 2010, *Conference* Alta (Norway) 2009. **Publications** *OECD Territorial Review of the NORA Region* (2011); *Climate Change – and the North Atlantic* (2009). Annual report.

Members Representatives (3) in each of 4 countries and territories:
Faeroe Is, Greenland, Iceland, Norway. [2019.02.12/XF2741/F*]

♦ Nordic Audiological Society 17210

Nordisk Audiologisk Selskab (NAS) – Pohjoismainen Audiologian Seura – Norraenna Heyrnarfraedi Félagid – Nordisk Audiologisk Selskap – Nordiska Audiologiska Sällskapet

Pres ENT-Dept, St Olavs Hosp, Box 3250, 7005 Trondheim, Norway.

Sec Audiologopaedisk Forening, Box 34, 4130 Viby, Denmark. E-mail: pnnn@vordingborg.dk.

URL: http://www.nas.dk/

History 1960. **Aims** Organize congresses about audiological matters. **Languages** Danish, Faroese, Icelandic, Norwegian, Swedish. **Activities** Events/meetings. **Events** *Congress* Trondheim (Norway) 2016, *Tinnitus, mind and hearing, future technology in audiology* Turku (Finland) 2014, *Congress* Copenhagen (Denmark) 2010, *Quality of life with hearing loss* Reykjavik (Iceland) 2008, *Congress* Stavanger (Norway) 2006. **Publications** *International Journal of Audiology.*

Members Organizations (29) with about 105,000 members in 5 countries:
Denmark, Finland, Iceland, Norway, Sweden.

NGO Relations Joint publication with: *International Society of Audiology (ISA, #14948).* [2022/XD6829/D]

♦ Nordic Autophagy Network / see Nordic Autophagy Society (#17211)

♦ Nordic Autophagy Society (NAS) 17211

Chair/Coordinator address not obtained.

URL: http://nordicautophagy.org/

History 2011. From 2015, transitioned into a society, which was formally founded Jan 2018. Former names and other names: *Nordic Autophagy Network* – former. **Aims** Promote excellent, innovative and groundbreaking research in the field of autophagy. **Structure** Board. **Activities** Events/meetings. **Events** *Annual Conference* Denmark 2022, *Annual Conference* Tromsø (Norway) 2021, *Annual Conference* Tromsø (Norway) 2020, *Annual Conference* Utrecht (Netherlands) 2019, *Annual Conference* Riga (Latvia) 2018. [2020/AA0493/D]

♦ Nordic Back Injuries Council (inactive)

♦ Nordic and Baltic Applied Fuel Cell Technology Research Network (Nordic Fuel Cell Net) 17212

Coordinator Inst for Energy Technology, PO Box 40, 2027 Kjeller, Norway. T. +4763806360.

History A project of *Nordic Energy Research (#17278)*. **Structure** Executive Committee. Advisory Committee. **Activities** Organizes workshops. **Events** *Workshop* Stockholm (Sweden) 2006.

Members Organizations (approx 25) in 4 countries:
Denmark, Finland, Norway, Sweden.

IGO Relations *Nordic Council of Ministers (NCM, #17260).* [2007/XM2648/F]

♦ Nordic-Baltic Association for Medical and Health Information (NBAMHI) 17213

Sec Univ of Turku, Teutori Library, Lemminkaisenkatu 3-B, Turun yliopisto, FI-20014 Turku, Finland.

History 1995, as *Nordic Association for Medical and Health Information (NAMHI)*. Current title adopted 2004. **Aims** Facilitate development of and cooperation between medical and health libraries. **Structure** Board. **Languages** English. **Staff** None. **Finance** No budget. **Activities** Knowledge management/information dissemination; training/education.

Members Associations in 8 countries:
Denmark, Estonia, Finland, Iceland, Latvia, Lithuania, Norway, Sweden. [2018.10.05/XD7878/D]

♦ Nordic-Baltic Bee Council (NBBC) 17214

Contact address not obtained. E-mail: info@biodlarna.se.

Aims Promote knowledge and understanding of all aspects of beekeeping, bee science and the bee products industry. **Activities** Events/meetings. **Events** *Meeting* Oslo (Norway) 2020, *Meeting* Riga (Latvia) 2018.

Members National associations in 7 countries:
Denmark, Estonia, Finland, Latvia, Lithuania, Norway, Sweden. [2020/AA1917/D]

♦ Nordic-Baltic Cardiology Alliance (unconfirmed)

♦ Nordic-Baltic Committee on Food Analysis (NMKL) 17215

Exec Dir c/o Inst of Marine Research, PO box 1870 Nordnes, 5817 Bergen, Norway. E-mail: post@nmkl.org.

URL: https://www.nmkl.org/

History 1947. Statutes: adopted by the Governments of Denmark, Finland, Norway and Sweden; revised 1978, when Iceland became a member; revised again in 1987 and in 2000. NordVal merged into NMKL, 2007. Full name changed when Food experts from the Baltic countries Estonia, Latvia, and Lithuania joined NMKL and were incorporated at Annual Meeting, 2022. Former names and other names: *Nordic Committee on Food Analysis* – former; *Nordisk Metodikkommitté för Livsmedel (NMKL)* – former; *Nordisk Metodik Komité for Levnedsmidler* – former; *Nordisk Metodikkomité for Naeringsmidler* – former; *Pohjoismainen Elintarvikkeiden Metodiikkakomitea* – former; *Norraena Matvaelarannsóknaefndin* – former. **Aims** Select methods of analysis for food *testing* and, provided the testing is successful, release official methods in *Scandinavian* languages, in Finnish and in English; elaborate guidelines and procedures to support *quality assurance* work in analytical food *laboratories*; serve as a forum for Nordic-Baltic and international exchange of information in the field of analysis of food, feed and environmental samples. **Structure** Annual meeting; NMKL respective group meetings in Microbiology, Chemistry, Sensory and NordVal International; NMKL Board meetings. **Languages** Danish, English, Finnish, Norwegian, Swedish. **Staff** 1.50 FTE, paid. **Finance** Sources: contributions; government support; sale of publications. Funded on a governmental basis as an expert committee, through contributions from the Nordic Council of Ministers. **Activities** Events/meetings; knowledge management/information dissemination; research and development; standards/guidelines; training/education. **Events** *Annual Meeting* Seinäjoki (Finland) 2022, *Annual Meeting* Jevnaker (Norway) 2021, *Annual Meeting* Denmark 2020, *International Symposium* Oslo (Norway) 2019, *Annual meeting* Reykjavik (Iceland) 2019. **Publications** *Collection of Methods for Food Analysis* (3 a year) in English – loose-leaf; *NMKL newsletter* (3 a year) in English. Reports; procedures. Publications in English only from 2022.

Members Members consisted of national contact persons in 8 countries:
Denmark, Estonia, Finland, Iceland, Latvia, Lithuania, Norway, Sweden.

IGO Relations Observer status with (1): *Codex Alimentarius Commission (CAC, #04081).* Cooperates with (1): *Nordic Council of Ministers (NCM, #17260).* **NGO Relations** Memorandum of Understanding with (2): *AOAC INTERNATIONAL (#00863); EURACHEM (#05595).* In liaison A with technical committees of: *International Organization for Standardization (ISO, #14473).* [2022.10.17/XD4546/E*]

♦ Nordic-Baltic Conference on Biomedical Engineering and Medical Physics (meeting series)
♦ Nordic-Baltic Congress of Entomology (meeting series)
♦ Nordic – Baltic Cooperation on Plant Genetic Resources (no recent information)

♦ Nordic-Baltic Defence Estates (NBDE) 17216

Address not obtained.

History 1973. Originally a cooperation forum between organizations in Norway, Denmark and Sweden. Finland joined 1993. Current title adopted when Baltic countries (Latvia and Estonia) joined 2015. Lithuania joined 2017. Former names and other names: *Nordic Defence Estates* – former (1973 to 2015). **Events** *European Conference of Defence and the Environment (ECDE)* Stockholm (Sweden) 2019.

Members Defence management real estate organizations in 7 countries:
Denmark, Estonia, Finland, Latvia, Lithuania, Norway, Sweden.

NGO Relations Supports (1): *European Conference of Defence and the Environment (ECDE).* [2019/AA0769/F]

♦ Nordic Baltic Drying Conference (meeting series)

♦ Nordic and Baltic GeoGebra Network 17217

Chair Haskóli Islands, Stakkahlid, 105 Reykjavik, Iceland.
URL: http://nordic.geogebra.no/

History Also referred to as *Nordic GeoGebra Network*. **Aims** Share materials and exchange experiences concerning the use of *ICT* in the teaching of *mathematics* with emphasis on GeoGebra software. **Activities** Events/meetings. **Events** *Conference* Tartu (Estonia) 2019, *Conference* Copenhagen (Denmark) 2018, *Conference* Reykjavik (Iceland) 2017, *Conference* Trondheim (Norway) 2016, *Conference* Karlstad (Sweden) 2015.
Members Full in 8 countries:
Denmark, Estonia, Finland, Iceland, Latvia, Lithuania, Norway, Sweden. [2018/XM7557/c/**D**]

♦ Nordic Baltic Group on Cardiovascular Nursing and Allied Professions (unconfirmed)
♦ Nordic Baltic Group – Nordic Baltic Group on Cardiovascular Nursing and Allied Professions (unconfirmed)

♦ Nordic-Baltic Network of Policewomen (NBNP) 17218

Contact c/o Uusikaupunki Police, Välskärintie 2, FI-23500 Uusikaupunki, Finland.
URL: http://www.nbnp.ee/

History Apr 2001, Riga (Latvia). **Aims** Increase the number of policewomen in higher ranks; support the building of female networks within the police. **Structure** Board. **Languages** English. **Finance** Members' dues. Budget covers only travel expenses. **Activities** Organizes projects and conferences in human trafficking. **Events** *Conference* St Petersburg (Russia) 2010, *Conference on Pol-E-quality in diversity* Tampere (Finland) 2007.
Members in 7 countries:
Denmark, Estonia, Finland, Iceland, Latvia, Lithuania, Norway. [2021/XM3653/**F**]

♦ Nordic-Baltic Society of Infectious Diseases (inactive)
♦ Nordic Battery Conference (meeting series)

♦ Nordic Biochar Network 17219

Contact c/o SINTEF Energy Research, Kolbjørn Hejes vei 1A, 7034 Trondheim, Norway. E-mail: mail@nordicbiochar.org.
URL: https://www.nordicbiochar.org/

History 2018. Registration: Brønnøysundsregister, No/ID: 922 990 921, Start date: 2019, Norway. **Aims** Promote research and education in the field of biochar; facilitate communication and collaboration between national initiatives in the Nordic countries; promote exchange and collaboration with other national and international initiatives. **Structure** General Meeting; Board. **Activities** Awareness raising; knowledge management/information dissemination. **Events** *Nordic Biochar Conference* Stockholm (Sweden) 2019.
Members Full in 4 countries:
Denmark, Finland, Norway, Sweden. [2020/AA0761/**F**]

♦ Nordic Biogas Conference (meeting series)

♦ Nordic Biosafety Network 17220

Contact address not obtained. T. +46102052000. E-mail: nordicbiosafety@folkhalsomyndigheten.se.
URL: https://www.folkhalsomyndigheten.se/nordic-biosafety-network/

Activities Events/meetings. **Events** *Meeting* 2021, *Meeting* Helsinki (Finland) 2020, *Meeting* Oslo (Norway) 2017, *Meeting* Solna (Sweden) 2016, *Meeting* Helsinki (Finland) 2015. [2021/AA1688/**F**]

♦ Nordic Board of Amateur Musicians (#19048)
♦ Nordic Board for Periodicals in the Humanities and Social Sciences / see Nordisk publiseringsnemnd for humanistiske og samfunnsvitenskapelige tidsskrifter (#17526)

♦ Nordic Boat Council 17221

Conseil nordique des bateaux – Nordiska Båtrådet (Nordbåt)

Contact Swedish Sailing Federation, Af Pontins väg 6, SE-115 21 Stockholm, Sweden. E-mail: ssf@ssf.se.

History 1969, Gothenburg (Sweden). **Aims** Harmonize the rules and laws for pleasure crafts in Nordic countries. **Structure** Officers: President; Vice-President; Secretary General. **Languages** English, Swedish. **Staff** Voluntary. **Finance** Budget (annual): Swedish Kr 60,000. **Events** *Meeting* Helsinki (Finland) 2012, *Meeting* Denmark 2006, *Meeting* Paris (France) 2005, *Meeting* Norway 2004, *Meeting* Finland 2003.
Members Full in 5 countries:
Denmark, Finland, Iceland, Norway, Sweden.
IGO Relations Close contacts with: *Nordic Council (NC, #17256).* [2013/XD1911/t/**D**]

♦ Nordic Bookbinding Council (inactive)
♦ Nordic Bowling Association (inactive)
♦ Nordic Boxing Union (inactive)
♦ Nordic Breastfeeding Conference (meeting series)

♦ Nordic Bridge Union (NBU) 17222

Nordisk Bridge Union

Contact c/o Norsk Bridgeforbund, Sognsveien 75 A – 3rd floor, 0855 Oslo, Norway. T. +4747479400. E-mail: bridge@bridge.no.
URL: http://bridge.no/

History Founded 23 Jun 1971, Hämeenlinna (Finland), by National Bridge Federations of the Nordic countries. **Aims** Organize Nordic Bridge Championships. **Structure** Congress (every 2 years). Member organizations have one vote each. Danish Bridge Federation serves as Secretariat. **Languages** Danish, English, Norwegian, Swedish. **Staff** None. **Finance** Members' dues. **Activities** Events/meetings. Active in: the Nordic countries. **Publications** None.
Members Full in 6 countries and territories:
Denmark, Faeroe Is, Finland, Iceland, Norway, Sweden.
IGO Relations None. [2018.09.13/XF1157/**D**]

♦ Nordic Bryological Society 17223

Contact Museum of Natural History and Arch – SN, Norwegian University of Science and Technology, 7491 Trondheim, Norway.
URL: https://www.nordicbryologicalsociety.com/

History Founded 1966. **Aims** Encourage bryological research; facilitate cooperation and communication among Nordic bryologists. **Structure** Council. **Languages** English. **Staff** None. **Finance** Members' dues. **Activities** Events/meetings; projects/programmes. **Events** *Annual meeting* Lammi (Finland) 2007, *Annual meeting / Annual Meeting and Excursion* Sweden 2006, *Annual meeting / Annual Meeting and Excursion* Bulgaria 2005, *Annual Meeting and Excursion* Norway 2004, *Annual meeting* Snasavatnet (Norway) 2004. **Publications** *Lindbergia* (3 a year).
Members Members in 21 countries and territories:
Argentina, Australia, Austria, Brazil, Denmark, Finland, France, Germany, Iceland, Italy, Japan, Luxembourg, Netherlands, Norway, Portugal, Spain, Sweden, Switzerland, Taiwan, UK, USA. [2022/XD7470/**D**]

♦ Nordic Building Forum (meeting series)
♦ Nordic Building Research Meeting (meeting series)
♦ Nordic Business Association (inactive)

♦ Nordic Cacti Society 17224

Nordisk Kaktus Selskab (NKS)

Chairman Salbyvej 17, 4600 Køge, Denmark. T. +4522523208. E-mail: nordiskkaktusselskab@gmail.com.
Main Website: http://www.nordiskkaktusselskab.dk/

History 1965, Odense (Denmark). **Aims** Disseminate information on succulents; develop propagation of endangered species. **Structure** General Meeting (annual); Board. **Languages** Danish, Norwegian, Swedish. **Staff** Voluntary. **Finance** Sources: gifts, legacies; members' dues. Annual budget: 225 DKK. **Activities** Events/meetings; knowledge management/information dissemination. **Events** *General Meeting* Odense (Denmark) 2022, *General Meeting* Kíge (Denmark) 2008, *General Meeting* Grindsted (Denmark) 2007, *General Meeting* Kíge (Denmark) 2006, *General Meeting* Kalundborg (Denmark) 2005. **Publications** *Kaktus og Andre Sukkulenter* (3 a year).

Members Individuals, the majority of whom from 3 countries:
Denmark, Norway, Sweden. [2022.05.24/XD2401/v/**D**]

♦ Nordic Cancer Union (NCU) 17225

Nordisk Cancer Union

Contact Cancer Society of Finland, Unioninkatu 22, FI-00130 Helsinki, Finland. E-mail: ncu.secretariat@cancer.fi – society@cancer.fi.
URL: http://www.ncu.nu/

History 1949. **Aims** Collaborate to improve knowledge and understanding of cancer diseases, effective prevention, results of cancer treatment and rehabilitation; enhance effective application in the Nordic area. **Structure** Board (meets annually); Scientific Committee; Chairmanship and Secretariat rotate every 3 years. **Languages** Danish, English, Faroese, Icelandic, Norwegian, Swedish. **Finance** Expenses shared among member countries. **Activities** Research and development; events/meetings. **Events** *Annual Symposium* Oslo (Norway) 2006, *Annual Symposium* Helsinki (Finland) 2005, *Annual Symposium* Åland (Finland) 2004, *Annual Symposium* Åland (Finland) 2004, *Annual Symposium* Iceland 2003.
Members National cancer leagues of 6 countries and territories:
Denmark, Faeroe Is, Finland, Iceland, Norway, Sweden. [2022/XD3179/**D**]

♦ Nordic Canoe Association (inactive)
♦ Nordic Capital Conference (meeting series)

♦ Nordic Capital Markets Forum (NCMF) 17226

Secretariat c/o Mannheimer Swartling, Norrlandsgatan 21, SE-111 87 Stockholm, Sweden. T. +46709777065. E-mail: info@nordiccapitalmarketsforum.org.
URL: http://nordiccapitalmarketsforum.org/

History 24 Feb 2006, Copenhagen (Denmark). **Aims** Provide a forum for knowledge exchange between financial institutions, corporates and public institutions and their financial and legal advisers actively engaged in the Nordic debt capital markets, with particular focus on knowledge within capital market products, derivatives and structured products of relevance to the Nordic market; facilitate and strengthen professional relations between the participants in these markets. **Structure** Board of 6. [2019/XJ1648/**F**]

♦ Nordic Cardio-Oncology Society (unconfirmed)
♦ Nordic Carton Association (no recent information)

♦ Nordic Casemix Centre (NordCase) 17227

CEO Siltasaarenkatu 4, FI-00530 Helsinki, Finland. E-mail: norddrg@nordcase.org.
URL: https://www.nordcase.org/

History 2008. **Aims** Promote casemix cooperation. **Structure** Board. **Activities** Events/meetings; networking/liaising. **Events** *Nordic Casemix Conference* Copenhagen (Denmark) 2019, *Nordic Casemix Conference* Reykjavik (Iceland) 2016, *Nordic Casemix Conference* Tallinn (Estonia) 2014, *Nordic Casemix Conference* Oslo (Norway) 2012, *Nordic Casemix Conference* Helsinki (Finland) 2010.
Members Full in 5 countries:
Denmark, Finland, Iceland, Norway, Sweden. [2022/AA2366/**D**]

♦ Nordic Catalysis Society 17228

Pres Åbo Akademi, Teknisk Kemi, Biskopsgatan 8, FI-20500 Turku, Finland.
URL: http://www.nordic-catalysis.org/

History 1988, following activities begun in 1969 by the Catalysis Group at Lund University. **Structure** Board, comprising President, Vice-President, Secretary, Treasurer and 4 further members. **Activities** Organizes symposia and Summer schools. **Events** *Biennial Nordic Symposium on Catalysis Research* Espoo (Finland) 2022, *Biennial Nordic Symposium on Catalysis Research* Espoo (Finland) 2020, *Biennial Nordic Symposium on Catalysis Research* Copenhagen (Denmark) 2018, *Biennial Nordic Symposium on Catalysis Research* Lund (Sweden) 2016, *Biennial Nordic Symposium on Catalysis Research* Oslo (Norway) 2014.
Members Full in 4 countries:
Denmark, Finland, Norway, Sweden. [2013/XD4906/**D**]

♦ Nordic Catholic Development Aid (inactive)
♦ Nordic CDG Association (no recent information)
♦ Nordic Center of Excellence for Research in Water Imbalance Related Disorders (inactive)

♦ Nordic Center for Sustainable Healthcare (NCSH) 17229

Contact c/o TEM, Södra Promenaden 51, SE-211 38 Malmö, Sweden. T. +46406065580. E-mail: info@nordicshc.org.
URL: http://www.nordicshc.org/

History 2015, Lund (Sweden). Founded by Stiftelsen TEM. **Aims** Raise the status and awareness of sustainable healthcare; boost innovation and investments in sustainable healthcare; bring world class solutions and ideas to the Nordics; deliver Nordic solutions and knowledge to the world. **Structure** A networking platform. **Languages** English, Swedish. **Staff** 7.00 FTE, paid. **Finance** Sources: members' dues; revenue from activities/projects. **Activities** Events/meetings; projects/programmes. **Events** *International Conference* Sopot (Poland) 2022, *Conference* Copenhagen (Denmark) 2021, *Conference* Malmö (Sweden) 2020, *Conference on Sustainable and Smart Healthcare* Utrecht (Netherlands) 2020, *Conference* Espoo (Finland) 2019.
Members Hospitals and healthcare institutions; Universities, R and D and institutes; Companies; National agencies, TPOs and similar; NGOs, science parks, clusters and networks. Membership countries not specified. Included in the above, 3 organizations listed in this Yearbook:
Baltic Development Forum (#03111); European Health Property Network (EuHPN, #07461); Health Care Without Harm (HCWH, #10875). [2022.02.15/XM8333/y/**D**]

♦ Nordic Centre for Alcohol and Drug Research (inactive)
♦ Nordic Centre for Gender in Military Operations (internationally oriented national body)

♦ Nordic Centre of Heritage Learning and Creativity 17230

Nordiskt Centrum för Kulturarvspedagogik (NCK)

Managing Dir Box 709, SE-831 28 Östersund, Sweden. T. +46063150316. E-mail: info@nckultur.org.
URL: http://www.nckultur.org/

History 2005. Registration: No/ID: 556173-6280, Sweden. **Aims** Approach, better understand and enhance learning through heritage. **Structure** Board of Directors. **Activities** Events/meetings; research and development; training/education. **NGO Relations** Member of (2): *Culture Action Europe (CAE, #04981); Network of European Museum Organizations (NEMO, #17024).* [2022.05.11/XJ6175/**D**]

♦ Nordic Centre for Innovation / see Nordic Innovation (#17320)

♦ Nordic Centre for Medieval Studies (NCMS) 17231

Contact Univ of Bergen, PO Box 7805, 5020 Bergen, Norway. T. +4755588085. Fax +4755588090.

History Sep 2005. **Events** *International conference on new focus on retrospective methods* Bergen (Norway) 2010, *International conference on the birth of Christian life in the Nordic religion* Bergen (Norway) 2010, *Symposium on towns, guils and cultural transmission in the North, 1300-1500* Odense (Denmark) 2009, *Penitentiary texts from Uppsala conference* Stockholm (Sweden) 2008, *Conference on the spread of civilisations in a global perspective* Uppsala (Sweden) 2008.
Members in 4 countries:
Denmark, Finland, Norway, Sweden. [2008/XM3618/**E**]

♦ Nordic Centre for Welfare and Social Issues / see Nordens välfärdscenter (#17163)

♦ Nordic Centre Youth (NCY) 17232

Mouvement nordique de la jeunesse des partis du centre – Nordiska Centerungdomens Förbund (NCF)

Pres address not obtained. E-mail: rkcrtr@gmail.com.
SG address not obtained. E-mail: ncf.secretarygeneral@gmail.com.
URL: http://mittinorden.com/

History 1975, on reorganization of previous body, set up 1945. **Aims** Work in *political* field at Nordic and also European level among other political youth organizations; secure peace and peaceful development in the *Third World*; be involved in the work of centre *parties* in Nordic countries. **Structure** Congress (annual); Board; Executive Board. **Languages** Swedish. **Staff** 1.00 FTE, paid. **Finance** Members' dues. Contributions from *Nordic Council of Ministers (NCM, #17260)*. **Activities** Seminars; study journeys. **Events** *International youth consultation on social development* Copenhagen (Denmark) 1995, *Annual Congress* Sweden 1994, *Annual Congress* Sweden 1993, *Annual congress* Visby (Sweden) 1991, *Environmental seminar* Gothenburg (Sweden) 1990. **Publications** *NCY Information Letter.*
Members Full organizations (7); Observers (1). Members in 4 countries:
Finland, Iceland, Norway, Sweden.
IGO Relations Takes part in the work of: *Nordic Council (NC, #17256)*. **NGO Relations** Observer member of: *European Youth Forum (#09140)*. Umbrella organization of: *Nordic Youth Council (NYC, #17474)*.
[2015/XE1828/**E**]

♦ Nordic Chefs Association 17233
Nordisk Kökkenchef Federation (NKF) – Fédération des Chefs de Cuisine Nordique
Pres address not obtained.
Events Manager address not obtained.
URL: https://nordicchefs.com/
Aims Ensure that Nordic cuisine stays strong. **Structure** Board. **Activities** Advocacy/lobbying/activism; awards/prizes/competitions; events/meetings. **Events** *Congress* 2023, *Conference* Iceland 2021, *Congress* Stjørdal (Norway) 2021, *Conference* Finland 2017.
Members Full in 5 countries:
Denmark, Finland, Iceland, Norway, Sweden. [2021/AA2579/**D**]

♦ Nordic Chess Federation 17234
Fédération nordique des échecs – Nordisk Skakforbund
SG Källarekroken 64, SE-226 47 Lund, Sweden. T. +46406655500. Fax +46406655501.
URL: http://www.sjakk.no/nordisk/
History Founded 20 Aug 1899, Copenhagen (Denmark). **Aims** Promote chess and chess relationship between the Nordic countries. **Structure** Board. **Languages** Danish, English, Norwegian, Swedish. **Staff** Voluntary. **Finance** Members' dues. **Activities** Events/meetings. **Events** *Congress* Stavanger (Norway) 2015, *Congress* Kige (Denmark) 2013, *Congress* Reykjavik (Iceland) 2011, *Congress* Helsingør (Denmark) 2009, *Congress* Helsingør (Denmark) 2007.
Members National associations in 6 countries and territories:
Denmark, Faeroe Is, Finland, Iceland, Norway, Sweden. [2018/XD0286/**D**]

♦ Nordic Children's Film Council (inactive)

♦ Nordic Children's and Youth Committee (NORDBUK) 17235
Nordiska Ungdomskomittén (NUK) – Pohjoismaisen Nuorisoyhteistyön Komitea
Coordinator Nordisk Ministerråd, Ved Stranden 18, 1061 Copenhagen K, Denmark. T. +4529692924. E-mail: erhh@norden.org.
URL: http://www.norden.org/
History 17 Nov 1976, as a committee of *Nordic Council of Ministers (NCM, #17260)* within the framework of *Nordic Cultural Cooperation (1971)*, following a recommendation of *Nordic Council (NC, #17256)*. Implements activities of the previous *Nordic Youth Foundation (NYF, inactive)*. Originally referred to in English as *Nordic Youth Committee*. Current regulations adopted by NMR in 1996. Also referred to as *Nordic Youth Cooperation Committee – Kommittén för Nordiskt Ungdomssamarbete*. **Aims** Secure distribution of *grants* to youth organizations and free groups of young people in the Nordic countries (that work in the youth field, *funding* also being given to specific projects). **Structure** Committee; NMR Secretariat serves as secretariat. **Finance** Funding can be given as: organizational grants; project grants to organizations and free groups of young people. **Activities** Projects/programmes; financial and/or material support. **Events** *NORDBUK2 Meeting* Finland 2016, *Conference on the Nordic Countries – a Common Market for Human Trafficking* Helsinki (Finland) 2016, *Conference for young people determining the future* Inderøy (Norway) 2006, *Meeting* Copenhagen (Denmark) 2003, *Meeting* Stockholm (Sweden) 2003.
Members Covers 8 Nordic countries and territories:
Åland, Denmark, Faeroe Is, Finland, Greenland, Iceland, Norway, Sweden.
NGO Relations Funds: *Nordic Press Association (NPA, #17393)*. [2018/XE2908/**E***]

♦ Nordic Child and Youth Welfare Alliance (inactive)
♦ Nordic Chimneysweepers' Union (inactive)
♦ Nordic Chiroptera Information Center – BatLife Nordica (unconfirmed)
♦ Nordic Choir Committee / see Nordisk Korforum (#17521)

♦ Nordic Christian Democratic Youth 17236
Kristendemokratisk Ungdom i Norden (KDUN)
Contact KDU, Munkbron 1, Box 2373, SE-103 18 Stockholm, Sweden. E-mail: info@kdu.se.
History Founded 1970. **Aims** Increase, by a stronger and expanded cooperation between member organizations, Christian democratic influence, especially in *Scandinavian* politics. **Structure** Congress (annual); Praesidium. **Languages** Danish, English, Finnish, Icelandic, Norwegian, Swedish. **Activities** Politics/policy/regulatory; events/meetings. **Events** *Conference* Oslo (Norway) 2013, *Are European economical interests compatible with global solidarity ?* Helsinki (Finland) 1988, *Refugees* Denmark 1987, *Environment and energy* Nässjö (Sweden) 1987, *Seminar / Conference* Nässjö (Sweden) 1987.
Members Christian Democratic Youth parties in 4 countries and territories:
Faeroe Is, Finland, Norway, Sweden.
IGO Relations Participates in the yearly Nordic Youth Council and the *Nordic Council (NC, #17256)* sessions.
NGO Relations Umbrella organization of: *Nordic Youth Council (NYC, #17474)*. [2015.08.27/XF1834/**F**]

♦ Nordic Christian Democrats 17237
Démocrates chrétiens nordiques – Kristdemokraterna i Norden (KDN) – Kristdemokrater i Norden – Pohjola Kristillisdemokraatit
Secretariat Kristdemokraterna Box 2373, SE-103 18 Stockholm, Sweden.
URL: http://www.kristdemokraterna.se/
History 1951, Stockholm (Sweden). Founded 8 May 1964, Stockholm (Sweden), as an informal organization for talks and cooperation known as *Kristlig-Demokratiske Partiers Nordiske Samarbeidsutvalg*, having first been proposed 1951. Formalized under current title 28 Feb 1993. **Aims** Promote Christian Democracy in Nordic countries. **Structure** Rotational secretariat. **Languages** Danish, Norwegian, Swedish. **Staff** None, uses staff of presiding party. **Finance** Every country brings its own budget. **Activities** Events/meetings. **Events** *Biennial Meeting* Brussels (Belgium) 2013, *Meeting / Biennial Meeting* Oslo (Norway) 2012, *Meeting / Biennial Meeting* Oslo (Norway) 2011, *Meeting / Biennial Meeting* Helsinki (Finland) 2010, *Meeting / Biennial Meeting* Helsinki (Finland) 2009.
Members Christian democratic parties in 4 countries:
Denmark, Finland, Norway, Sweden.
IGO Relations *Nordic Council (NC, #17256)*. [2019.10.28/XD1833/**D**]

♦ Nordic Chronic Myeloid Leukemia Study Group (NCMLSG) 17238
Chairman St Olavs Hosp, Dept of Hematology, PB8250 Sluppen, 7006 Trondheim, Norway. Fax +4772571465.
URL: http://www.ncmlsg.org/
History Current bylaws adopted 1 Nov 2006. **Aims** Create a high quality group of excellence with interest in the treatment and biology of Chronic Myeloid Leukemia (CML); improve treatment and research in the Nordic countries. **Structure** Coordinating Group; Steering Group. **Activities** Research and development; guidance/assistance/support; knowledge management/information dissemination. **Events** *Spring Symposium* Helsinki (Finland) 2018.
Members Individuals in 4 countries:
Denmark, Finland, Norway, Sweden. [2018/XM7921/**D**]

♦ Nordic Cilia and Centrosome Network 17239
Coordinator Copenhagen Univ, Nirregade 10, 1017 Copenhagen, Denmark.
URL: http://nordiccilia.org/
History Aug 2010. **Structure** Steering Committee. **Finance** Supported by a grant from *NordForsk (#17164)*. **Activities** Research/documentation; training/education; events/meetings. **Events** *International Cilia Conference in Europe / International Cilia Conference* Paris (France) 2014, *Annual Meeting* Sigtuna (Sweden) 2013, *Annual Meeting* Hanko (Norway) 2012, *Annual Meeting* Kongens Lyngby (Denmark) 2011, *Annual Meeting* Lyngby (Denmark) 2011.
Members Research groups in 4 countries:
Denmark, Finland, Norway, Sweden. [2016/XM4398/**D**]

♦ **NORDIC CLL SG** Nordic CLL Study Group (#17240)

♦ Nordic CLL Study Group (NORDIC CLL SG) 17240
Contact Dept Hematology 4041, Rigshospitalet, 9 Blegdamsvej, 2100 Copenhagen, Denmark. E-mail: contact@nordic-cll.org.
URL: http://www.nordic-cll.org/
Aims Facilitate *chronic lymphocytic leukemia* (CLL) research and education in the Nordic countries. **Structure** Steering Committee. Subcommittees. **Activities** Events/meetings; research/documentation; networking/liaising. **Events** *Nordic Educational Meeting on CLL* Oslo (Norway) 2021, *Nordic Meeting* Oslo (Norway) 2020, *Nordic Meeting* Stockholm (Sweden) 2018.
Members Full in 5 countries:
Denmark, Finland, Iceland, Norway, Sweden. [2020/XM8319/**D**]

♦ Nordic Clothing Workers' Federation (inactive)

♦ Nordic Club of Paediatric Cardiologists 17241
Club nordique des cardiologues pour enfants – Nordisk Barnkardiologisk Klubb
Address not obtained.
Activities *Nordic Meeting in Pediatric Cardiology*. **Events** *Conference* Bergen (Norway) 2009, *Conference* Lund (Sweden) 2009, *Conference* Lund (Sweden) 2008, *Conference* Helsinki (Finland) 2004, *Conference* Oslo (Norway) 2003. [2010/XF0680/**F**]

♦ Nordic Coagulation Meeting (meeting series)
♦ Nordic Coffee Union (inactive)
♦ Nordic Coke Utilization Association (inactive)

♦ Nordic Collaboration Group for Research in Child and Adolescent Psychiatry (NordCAP) 17242
Contact Research Unit for Child and Adolescent Psychiatry, Psychiatric Hosp, Aalborg Univ Hosp, Milleparkvej 10, 9000 Aalborg, Denmark.
Facebook: https://www.facebook.com/nordcapresearch/
History 1986. **Aims** Enhance research and cooperation in child and adolescent psychiatry in the Nordic countries. **Structure** No permanent organization. **Languages** English. **Staff** No permanent staff. **Finance** No permanent budget. Meetings financed by participants. **Events** *Meeting* Aalborg (Denmark) 2020, *Meeting* Turku (Finland) 2018, *Meeting* Middelfart (Denmark) 2014, *Meeting* Oslo (Norway) 2011, *Meeting* Dronninglund (Denmark) 2010. **Publications** None.
Members in 5 countries:
Denmark, Finland, Iceland, Norway, Sweden.
IGO Relations None. **NGO Relations** Instrumental in setting up: *Nordic Network for Research in Affective Disorders (NNRAD, inactive)*; *Nordic Network for Research in Attention-Deficit Hyperactivity Disorder and Tourette Syndrome (inactive)*; *Nordic Network for Research in Infant Psychiatry (no recent information)*; *Nordic Network for Research in Obsessive Compulsive Disorder (no recent information)*; *Nordic Network for Treatment and Service Evaluation (no recent information)*. [2020/XE4643/c/**E**]

♦ Nordic College of Caring Science (NCCS) 17243
Sec c/o Oslomet, Fakultet for Hesevitenskap, Institutt for sykepleie og helsefremmende arbeid, Studielederområde 4, Pilestredet 32, 0800 Oslo, Norway. T. +4767236215.
URL: http://www.nccs.nu/
History Founded autumn 1981, Bergen (Norway). **Aims** Promote scientific development of Caring Science as starting point for all care; represent all Nordic healthcare researchers' interests; develop, promote and disseminate new scientific knowledge nationally and internationally. **Structure** Board; Nordic College of Caring Science Research Foundation (NCCSF), founded in 2007. **Languages** Swedish. **Finance** Members' dues. **Activities** Knowledge management/information dissemination; research/documentation; events/meetings. **Events** *Conference on Sustainable Caring for Health and Wellbeing* Vaasa (Finland) 2019, *Conference* Eskilstuna (Sweden) 2018, *Conference* Bodø (Norway) 2017, *Exploring care for human service professions* Copenhagen (Denmark) 2015, *Conference* Stockholm (Sweden) 2014. **Publications** *Scandinavian Journal of Caring Sciences* (4 a year); *NCCS Newsletter* (2 a year).
Members Individuals (about 100) in 6 countries:
Denmark, Finland, Iceland, Norway, Sweden, USA. [2019/XD0998/v/**D**]

♦ Nordic College of Equine Dentistry (NCED) 17244
Contact address not obtained. E-mail: post@nced.se.
URL: https://www.nced.se/
Aims Promote gentle care of healthy equine teeth, along with pain-free dental treatments. **Structure** Board. **Finance** Sources: members' dues. **Events** *Congress* Malmö (Sweden) 2022, *Congress* Malmö (Sweden) 2022, *Congress* Malmö (Sweden) 2020.
Members Fellows in 6 countries:
Belgium, Finland, Germany, Norway, Sweden, UK. [2022/AA2443/v/**F**]

♦ Nordic Colleges of General Practitioners / see Nordic Federation of General Practice ApS (#17284)
♦ Nordic Commission on Walking (inactive)
♦ Nordic Committee for Arboreal Questions / see Nordisk Arboretudvalg (#17491)

♦ Nordic Committee for Art History 17245
Nordisk komité for kunsthistorie
Chair address not obtained.
URL: http://www.nordik.uib.no/
History 1984. **Structure** General Assembly. **Activities** Organizes Nordic Conference for Art Historians (NORDIK). **Events** *Triennial Nordic Conference for Art Historians* Copenhagen (Denmark) 2022, *Triennial Nordic Conference for Art Historians* Copenhagen (Denmark) 2018, *Triennial Nordic Conference for Art Historians* Reykjavik (Iceland) 2015, *Triennial Nordic Conference for Art Historians* Stockholm (Sweden) 2012, *Triennial Nordic conference for art historians* Jyväskylä (Finland) 2009.
Members in 5 countries:
Denmark, Finland, Iceland, Norway, Sweden. [2014/XM1360/**E**]

♦ Nordic Committee for Biomedical Technology (inactive)
♦ Nordic Committee on Building Regulations (inactive)
♦ Nordic Committee for Consultation in Fishery Matters (inactive)

♦ Nordic Committee for Coordination of Electrical Safety Matters . . . 17246
Nordiska Kommittén för Samordning av Elektriska Säkerhetsfrågor (NSS) – Pohjoismainen Sähköturvallisuuskysymysten Yhtenäistämiskomitea
Sec NSS-Sekretariatet, c/o Norwegian Directorate for Civil Protection, PO Box 2014, 3103 Tønsberg, Norway. T. +4733412500. Fax +4733310660.
History Established 1963, on recommendation No 2/1963 issued by *Nordic Council (NC, #17256)*. Activities commenced in 1964. **Aims** Harmonize safety regulations in the field in Nordic countries. **Structure** Main Committee; Sub Committees. **Languages** Danish, English, Norwegian, Swedish. **Staff** None. **Activities** Following Recommendation No 2/1963: rationalizes safety regulations to harmonize test specifications for electrical equipment in the Nordic countries (whenever applicable, these specifications are translations of the corresponding publications issued by EC and IEC). Following NC recommendation No 7/1971 the work currently includes some other electrical safety matters which are only partially related to test specifications but nevertheless are important. **Publications** Meeting Report (annual). Recommendations.

Members National electricity authorities (20) in the 5 Nordic countries (Denmark including Faeroe Is and Greenland; Finland including Åland):
Denmark, Finland, Iceland, Norway, Sweden.
IGO Relations *Nordic Council of Ministers (NCM, #17260).* [2019.07.11/XD5795/**E***]

- ♦ Nordic Committee on Food Analysis / see Nordic-Baltic Committee on Food Analysis (#17215)
- ♦ Nordic Committee on Food Questions / see Committee of Senior Officials of the Nordic Countries, Estonia, Latvia and Lithuania in the Field of Food Issues (#04286)
- ♦ Nordic Committee of Master Shoemakers and Dealers (inactive)
- ♦ Nordic Committee on Name Research / see Nordiska Samarbetskommittén för Namnforskning (#17492)

♦ Nordic Committee for Public Inspection of Flammable and Explosive Goods 17247

Nordisk Samarbeidskomite for Offentlig Tilsyn med Brannfarlige og Eksplosive Varer (NORDEX) – Tulenarkoja ja Räjähdysaineita Valvovien Viranomaisten Pohjoismainen Yhteistyö

Contact Directorate for Civil Protection and Emergency Planning, PO Box 2014, 3101 Tønsberg, Norway. T. +4733412500. Fax +4733310660.

History 1979. **Aims** Coordinate legislation in the Nordic countries; discuss technical questions with a view to establishing common approaches; contribute to the development and exchange of knowledge and experience of interest and benefit to the supervisory authorities; report on accidents and incidents of common interest; seek to establish a joint platform within international legislative and standardizing work. **Structure** Annual Plenary Meeting. **Languages** Danish, Faroese, Icelandic, Norwegian, Swedish. **Finance** No annual budget. **Activities** Organizes: annual NORDEX Meeting; work meetings. Cooperates with Nordic meetings concerning: transport of dangerous goods; fire prevention and preparedness; gas appliances (SAMGAS); pressure vessel authorities.
Members Representatives of organizations in 6 countries and territories:
Denmark, Faeroe Is, Finland, Iceland, Norway, Sweden. [2010/XD3352/**D***]

- ♦ Nordic Committee for Road Traffic Legislation (inactive)
- ♦ Nordic Committee for Safety Research / see Nordisk Kärnsäkerhetsforskning (#17517)
- ♦ Nordic Committee of Schools of Social Work / see Nordic Association of Schools of Social Work (#17204)
- ♦ Nordic Committee of Senior Officials for Cooperation in the Building Sector (inactive)
- ♦ Nordic Committee of Senior Officials for Food Issues / see Committee of Senior Officials of the Nordic Countries, Estonia, Latvia and Lithuania in the Field of Food Issues (#04286)
- ♦ Nordic Committee of Senior Officials for Regional Policy / see Arko Cooperation
- ♦ Nordic Committee of Senior Officials for Transport Questions (inactive)
- ♦ Nordic Committee on Social Security Statistics / see Nordic Social-Statistical Committee (#17409)
- ♦ Nordic Committee for Soviet and East European Studies (inactive)

♦ Nordic Committee for Sport Libraries (NORSIB) 17248

Address not obtained.
URL: https://sites.google.com/site/norsiblibraries/home

History Statutes amended 1986 and 1987. Former names and other names: *Nordisk Samarbeidskomité fo Idrettsbibliotek* – former alias. **Aims** Promote the further development of the services of libraries and information centres at sport colleges and sport federations, as well as other sport libraries in the Nordic countries. **Structure** General Assembly; Steering Committee. **Activities** Events/meetings. **Events** *Meeting* Jyväskylä (Finland) 2021, *Meeting* Oslo (Norway) 2019, *Meeting* Copenhagen (Denmark) 2017, *Meeting* Stockholm (Sweden) 2015, *Meeting* Sogndal (Norway) 2013.
Members Full in 5 countries:
Denmark, Finland, Iceland, Norway, Sweden. [2021/AA2648/**D**]

- ♦ Nordic Committee on Sports for the Handicapped (inactive)
- ♦ Nordic Committee on Trade Procedures (inactive)
- ♦ Nordic Committee on Transplantation / see Nordic Transplant Committee (#17452)
- ♦ Nordic Committee for Veterinary Scientific Cooperation (#17519)
- ♦ Nordic Common Market (inactive)
- ♦ Nordic Communications Committee (inactive)

♦ Nordic Comparative and International Education Society (NOCIES) 17249

Association nordique d'éducation comparée et internationale

Pres NLA Univ College Bergen, Postboks 74, Campus Sandviken, 5812 Bergen, Norway. T. +4755540700. E-mail: president@nocies.org.
URL: http://www.nocies.org/

History 1992, Oslo (Norway). Re-activated in 2007, after a temporary dormant period. **Aims** Promote comparative education research amongst researchers in the Nordic and Baltic regions. **Structure** General Assembly (every 2 years); Executive Committee. **Languages** Danish, English, Faroese, Icelandic, Norwegian, Swedish. **Activities** Events/meetings. **Events** *Education and Hope in Troubled Times* 2021, *Biennial Conference* Stockholm (Sweden) 2019, *Emerging perspectives in comparative education – citizenship, multiculturalism and new technologies* Drammen (Norway) 2015, *Conference* Freiburg (Germany) 2014, *Conference* Turku (Finland) 2013. **Publications** *Nordic Journal of Comparative and International Education.* Publications by members, available on website.
Members in 5 countries:
Denmark, Finland, Iceland, Norway, Sweden. [2022.05.11/XD3775/**D**]

♦ Nordic Concert Halls 17250

Chairman c/o Musikkens Hus, Musikkens Plads 1, 9000 Aalborg, Denmark. T. +4560203110. E-mail: info@nordicconcerthalls.com.
URL: http://nordicconcerthalls.com/

History 1983. **Structure** Board.
Members Concert halls and performing arts centres (17) in 7 countries and territories:
Denmark, Faeroe Is, Greenland, Iceland, Norway, Sweden. [2020/AA1834/**F**]

♦ Nordic Concrete Federation (NCF) 17251

Fédération Nordique du Béton – Nordischer Betonverband – Nordiska Betongförbundet (NBF) – Nordisk Betonforbund – Pohjoismainen Betoniliitto – Nordisk Betongforbund – Norrajna Steinsteypussambandid

Contact c/o Norwegian Concrete Association / Tekna, Postbox 2312 Solli, 0201 Oslo, Norway. T. +4722947500. E-mail: ncf@tekna.no.
Street address Dronning Mauds gate 15, 0250 Oslo, Norway.
URL: http://www.nordicconcrete.net/

History 1978, Stockholm (Sweden). **Aims** Promote cooperation between concrete experts in Nordic countries, and thus obtain better concrete structure. **Structure** Board (meets at least annually); *Research Council of the Nordic Concrete Federation (RCNCF).* **Languages** English. **Staff** Norwegian Concrete Association (NCA) is secretariat on part-time, paid basis; others involved are voluntary. **Finance** Members' dues. **Activities** Events/meetings. **Events** *Nordic Concrete Research Symposium* Stockholm (Sweden) 2022, *Triennial Symposium* Sandefjord (Norway) 2021, *Triennial Symposium* Sandefjord (Norway) 2020, *Nordic Concrete Research Symposium.* Aalborg (Denmark) 2017, *Triennial Symposium* Reykjavik (Iceland) 2014. **Publications** *Nordic Concrete Research (NCR)* (2 a year). Workshop proceedings.
Members Federations in 5 countries:
Denmark, Finland, Iceland, Norway, Sweden. [2022/XD2982/**D**]

- ♦ Nordic Confectioners' Association (inactive)
- ♦ Nordic Confederation of Supervisors, Technicians and Other Managers (inactive)
- ♦ Nordic Conference on the Application of Scientific Methods in Archaeology (meeting series)
- ♦ Nordic Conference on Bilingualism (meeting series)
- ♦ Nordic Conference of Epidemiology and Register-Based Research (meeting series)
- ♦ Nordic Conference on Law and Information Technology (meeting series)
- ♦ Nordic Conference on Mathematical Statistics (meeting series)
- ♦ Nordic Conference in Nursing Research – Methods and Networks for the Future (meeting series)
- ♦ Nordic Conference on Plasma Spectrochemistry (meeting series)
- ♦ Nordic Conference for Professionals Working with Traumatised Refugees (meeting series)
- ♦ Nordic Conference for Psychology of Religion (meeting series)
- ♦ Nordic Conference of Rectors / see Nordic University Association (#17458)
- ♦ Nordic Conference of Religious Education (meeting series)
- ♦ Nordic Conference on Research on Violent Extremism (meeting series)
- ♦ Nordic Conference for Sociology of Religion (meeting series)
- ♦ Nordic Conference on Subject Education (meeting series)
- ♦ Nordic Conference of University Rectors / see Nordic University Association (#17458)
- ♦ Nordic Conference in Work and Rehabilitation (meeting series)
- ♦ Nordic Congress on Allergology (meeting series)
- ♦ Nordic Congress on Breast Cancer (meeting series)
- ♦ Nordic Congress of Historians (meeting series)
- ♦ Nordic Congress of Laryngectomees (meeting series)
- ♦ Nordic Congress on Life Insurance (meeting series)
- ♦ Nordic Congress in Low Vision (meeting series)
- ♦ Nordic Congress of Mathematicians (meeting series)
- ♦ Nordic Congress of Ophthalmology (meeting series)
- ♦ Nordic Connective Tissue Society (unconfirmed)
- ♦ Nordic Conservative Committee for Adult Educational Associations (no recent information)
- ♦ Nordic Conservative Student Union (#17161)
- ♦ Nordic Contact Agency for Agricultural and Forestry Affairs (inactive)
- ♦ Nordic Contact Agency for Agricultural Research / see Nordic Joint Committee for Agricultural and Food Research (#17332)
- ♦ Nordic Contact Committee for Kindergarten and Recreation Centres (inactive)

♦ Nordic Contact Concerning State Building Activities 17252

Groupe nordique pour les questions des bâtiments publiques – Nordisk Kontakt om Statsbyggeri (NKS) – Valtion Rakennustoiminnan Pohjoismainen Kontaktielin

Contact c/o DACC – Bygherreforeningen, Borgergade 111, 1300 Copenhagen K, Denmark.

History 1962, by Nordic central building authorities. **Aims** Examine common problems in state building and *property administration.* **Events** *Conference* Stockholm (Sweden) 2005, *Conference* Copenhagen (Denmark) 1980.
Members Representatives of state building authorities in 5 countries:
Denmark, Finland, Iceland, Norway, Sweden.
IGO Relations *Nordic Council of Ministers (NCM, #17260).* [2010/XD8190/**E***]

- ♦ Nordic Contact Organ for Environmental Questions (inactive)
- ♦ Nordic Convention on Social Assistance and Social Services (1994 treaty)
- ♦ Nordic Convention on Social Security (1981 treaty)
- ♦ Nordic Cooperation for Anesthesia and Intensive Care Nurses / see Nordisk Samarbeidsforum for Anestesi- og Intensivsykepleiere (#17528)

♦ Nordic Cooperation Archipelago 17253

Nordiska Skärgårdssamarbetet – Saaristoyhteistyö

Collaboration Manager Brinkasvägen 1, FI-21660 Nagu, Finland. T. +358401580555. E-mail: info@skargardssamarbetet.org.
Contact Strandgatan 7, FI-22100 Mariehamn, Finland. T. +3581814986. Fax +3581821620.
URL: http://www.skargardssamarbetet.org/

History 1978, within the framework of *Nordic Council of Ministers (NCM, #17260).* Previously a permanent organ of *Nordic Committee of Senior Officials for Regional Policy (EK-R / NÄRP / NERP).* **Aims** Promote tangible cooperation in the *Nordic* archipelagos (Finland, Sweden and Åland), focusing on *living conditions* of the resident population and demand for *recreational* facilities from the surrounding conurbations; maintain sustainable development and strengthen economic and social vital conditions for residents. **Structure** Conference (annual). Cooperation Council (meeting twice a year). Cooperation Committee. Management groups appointed for individual projects. **Languages** Swedish. **Staff** 1.00 FTE, paid. **Finance** Funding from member organizations and the Nordic Council of Ministers; also funds from various foundations for concrete projects. **Activities** Networking/liaising: events/meetings.
Members Archipelagos of 3 countries and territories:
Åland, Finland, Sweden.
IGO Relations County Governments and Regional Councils. **NGO Relations** Organizations involved in Archipelago development and environmental tasks. [2017.10.12/XK0835/**D***]

- ♦ Nordic Cooperation Body for Technical Testing / see Joint Nordic Organization for Technical Testing (#16142)

♦ Nordic Cooperation Committee for complementary and alternative Medicine (NSK) 17254

Nordisk SamarbeidsKomite for komplementaer-og alternativ medisin

Contact Turebergshuset-Turebergs, Torg 1 – 6 tr, SE-191 47 Sollentuna, Sweden. T. +468963630. Fax +4686230036.
URL: http://www.nsk-cam.org/

History 14 Mar 2000, Copenhagen (Denmark), as *Nordic Cooperation Committee for Non-conventional Medicine.* **Aims** Stimulate the use of complementary and alternative medicine within the Nordic countries.
Members Full in 5 countries:
Denmark, Finland, Iceland, Norway, Sweden.
NGO Relations Corresponding partner of: *European Coalition on Homeopathic and Anthroposophic Medicinal Products (ECHAMP, #06595).* [2016/XM1867/**D**]

- ♦ Nordic Cooperation Committee on Municipal Engineering (#17520)
- ♦ Nordic Cooperation Committee for Non-conventional Medicine / see Nordic Cooperation Committee for complementary and alternative Medicine (#17254)
- ♦ Nordic Cooperation Committee for the Poorly-Sighted (inactive)
- ♦ Nordic Cooperation Council for the Development of Mental Disorders (inactive)
- ♦ Nordic Cooperation on Disability (inactive)
- ♦ Nordic Cooperation Group for Forest Entomology (see: #17296)
- ♦ Nordic Cooperation Group for Forest Inventory (see: #17296)
- ♦ Nordic co-operation of nurses who work with children and adolescents and their families / see NoSB (#17608)

♦ Nordic Co-Operation of Ophthalmic Nurses (NCON) 17255

Chair address not obtained. T. +4646721818108. E-mail: rikkekroman@gmail.com.

Languages Danish, English, Finnish, Icelandic, Norwegian, Swedish. **Activities** Events/meetings. **Events** *Nordic meeting for Ophthalmic* Malmö (Sweden) 2022, *Nordic Congress of Ophthalmic Nursing* Malmö (Sweden) 2021, *Nordic Congress of Ophthalmic Nursing* Copenhagen (Denmark) 2018.
Members Individuals in 5 countries:
Denmark, Finland, Iceland, Norway, Sweden. [2022/XM7562/**F**]

- ♦ Nordic Cooperation Organization / see Dövas Nordiska Råd (#05126)
- ♦ Nordic Cooperative of Brick and Tilemakers' Associations (inactive)
- ♦ Nordic Cooperative Committee for Onomastic Research (#17492)
- ♦ Nordic Cooperative Organization for Applied Research (inactive)
- ♦ Nordic Copyright Bureau (#17500)
- ♦ Nordic Cosmetic Congress (meeting series)

♦ Nordic Council (NC) 17256

Conseil nordique – Consejo Nórdico – Nordiska Rådet (NR) – Nordisk Råd (NR) – Pohjoismaiden Neuvosto (PN)

SG Ved Stranden 18, 1061 Copenhagen K, Denmark. T. +4533960400. E-mail: nordisk-rad@norden.org.

URL: http://www.norden.org/

History 1952. Established by Statute drawn up by governments of Denmark, Iceland, Norway and Sweden. Finland adhered in 1955. Since 1970 the autonomous territories of the Faeroes and the Åland Islands have their own representatives on the Council and, since 1984, Greenland is also represented. The Council is sometimes referred to in English as *Nordic Council of Parliamentarians (NCP)*. It was based in Stockholm (Sweden) until Aug 1996, when it moved to Copenhagen (Denmark), where it is housed with the Secretariat of *Nordic Council of Ministers (NCM, #17260)*.

Legal Status: *Treaty of Cooperation between Denmark, Finland, Iceland, Norway and Sweden (Helsinki Treaty, 1962)*, also referred to as *'Treaty of Nordic Cooperation'*, was signed 23 Mar 1962, Helsinki (Finland), entered into force 1 Jul 1962 and revised: 13 Feb 1971; 11 Mar 1974; 15 Jun 1983; 6 May 1985; 21 Aug 1991; 18 Mar 1993. Working procedure came into force 1 Jul 1971, most recent amendments: 27 Feb 1990; 28 Feb 1991; 3 Mar 1992; 7 Nov 1993. Joint Declaration on Nordic Cooperation, Jun 1994, Corfu (Greece), indicated that Nordic countries newly members of the European Union intend to continue, in full compliance with Community law and other provisions of the *Treaty on European Union (Maastricht Treaty, 1992)*, Nordic Cooperation among themselves as well as with other countries and territories.

Prior to the setting up of the Council, *Nordic Union* or cooperation can be dated from 1397, Kalmar (Sweden), on setting up of *Kalmar Union (inactive)* when Erik of Pomerania was crowned King of Denmark, Norway and Sweden. The Kalmar Union ceased to exist in 1523, but historical cooperation continued: Sweden and Norway were united from 1815 to 1905; *Nordic Postal Union (NPU, #17391)* was set up in 1869, by a trilateral postal agreement between Denmark, Norway and Sweden and subsequently extended to include Finland and Iceland; *Scandinavian Coin Union (inactive)*, a currency union between Denmark, Norway and Sweden, existed from 1873 until 1914; *Scandinavian Interparliamentary Union (inactive)* was set up in 1908, with the help of Fredrik Bajer; Nordic inter-ministerial meetings were held between the World Wars (1918 to 1939).

Aims Instigate, monitor and accelerate the pace of Nordic *international cooperation*, rooted in the local community and based on values shared by the countries and autonomous areas forming the Nordic region; act as cooperative body of legislatures and governments of member countries in matters involving joint action and discussion of questions of common interest. **Structure** Praesidium, comprising 15 parliamentarians (at least 2 from each country). Plenary Assembly of Council (annual, open) consists of 87 members elected by and from parliaments. Each national delegation elects a chairperson and vice-chairperson from its members and has a national secretariat based in its parliament. Each member of Council (except members of the Praesidium) is assigned to one of the 4 Standing Committees, whose secretaries are a part of the Secretariat of the Praesidium. Party Groups (4). Secretariat, located in Copenhagen (Denmark). *Nordic Passport Union (#17380)* was set up in 1954, including Finland from 1958, and subsequently Iceland; and *Nordic Council of Ministers (NCM, #17260)* in 1971. Committees (6): Knowledge and Culture in the Nordic Region; Sustainable Nordic Region; Growth and Development in the Nordic Region; Welfare in the Nordic Region; Control; Election. **Languages** Danish, Finnish, Icelandic, Norwegian, Swedish. **Staff** 16.00 FTE, paid. **Finance** Member countries pay their own delegation expenses plus a proportion of the joint budget according to a formula based on their GNP.

Activities Events/meetings; politics/policy/regulatory; awards/prizes/competitions.

Management of treaties and agreements:
- *Nordic Language Convention (1981)*;
- *Agreement Concerning a Common Nordic Labour Market (1982)*;
- *Convention Concerning the Working Environment (1989)*;
- *Nordic Convention on Social Assistance and Social Services (1994)*;
- *Agreement concerning co-operation between authorities and institutions in the field of vocational rehabilitation and training for the labour market (1982)*;
- *Konvention innehållande internationellt privaträttslig bestämmelser om äktenskap, adoption och förmynderskap (1931)*;
- *Konvention angående indrivning av underhållsbidrag (1962)*;
- *Nordic public health preparedness agreement (2002)*;
- *Nordisk konvention om social trygghet (2012)*;
- *Nordic Agreement on Co-operation on Upper Secondary School Education (2004)*;
- *Agreement concluded by Denmark, Finland, Iceland, Norway and Sweden on Admission to Higher Education (1996)*;
- *Convention for the avoidance of double taxation with respect to taxes on inheritances and gifts (1989)*;
- *Agreement Concerning Cultural Cooperation (1971)*;
- *Nordic Passport Convention (1957)*;
- *Protocol Concerning the Exemption of Nationals of the Nordic Countries from the Obligation to Have a Passport or Residence Permit While Resident in a Nordic Country other than their Own (1954)*;
- *Agreement Between Denmark, Finland, Iceland, Norway and Sweden on the Implementation of Certain Provisions Concerning Nationality (2002)*;
- *Agreement between Denmark, Iceland, Norway and Sweden concerning cooperation in matters of competition (2001)*.

Events *Annual Plenary Session* Stockholm (Sweden) 2019, *Annual Plenary Session* Oslo (Norway) 2018, *Annual Plenary Session* Helsinki (Finland) 2017, *Annual Plenary Session* Copenhagen (Denmark) 2016, *December Meeting* Reykjavik (Iceland) 2016. **Publications** *Norden the Top of Europe* (12 a year) – newsletter; *Nordic News* – newsletter. Books; reports; periodicals; journals; policy birefs; strategies.

Members Parliamentarians (87) elected by legislatures of Nordic countries and autonomous territories. Members from 5 Nordic countries and 3 autonomous territories:
Åland, Denmark, Faeroe Is, Finland, Greenland, Iceland, Norway, Sweden.

IGO Relations *Baltic Assembly (BA, #03094)*; *Baltic Sea Parliamentary Conference (BSPC, #03146)*; *Benelux Inter-Parliamentary Consultative Council (Benelux Parliament, #03201)*; *Committee of Members of Parliament of EFTA Countries (EFTA CMP, #04269)*; *European Parliament (EP, #08146)*; *Nordic Culture Fund (#17264)*; *Nordic Defence Cooperation (NORDEFCO, #17266)*; *Parliamentary Assembly of the Council of Europe (PACE, #18211)*; *Standing Committee of Parliamentarians of the Arctic Region (SCPAR, #19958)*; *West Nordic Council (#20925)*. **NGO Relations** *Baltic Development Forum (#03111)*; *Danish Association for Nordic Collaboration*; *European Association for Special Education (EASE, no recent information)*; *Föreningarna Nordens Förbund (FNF, #09859)*; *Inter-Parliamentary Union (IPU, #15961)*; *Nordens Fackliga Samorganisation (NFS, #17158)*; *Nordic Youth Council (NYC, #17474)*. [2021/XD2984/**D***]

♦ Nordic Council for Alcohol Research (inactive)
♦ Nordic Council for Animal Welfare (inactive)
♦ Nordic Council for Arctic Medical Research (inactive)
♦ Nordic Council of Authors and Translators (#17511)
♦ Nordic Council for the Bakery Trade (inactive)

♦ Nordic Council of Church Music 17257

Conseil nordique pour la musique d'Eglise – Nordisk Kirkemusikråd (NKR) – Nordiska Kyrkomusikrådet

Contact DOKS 1 th, Vesterbrogade 57, 1620 Copenhagen, Denmark.

History 1957. For a while, from 1966 constituted *Singing Church (inactive)*. Also referred to as *Nordic Sacred Music Council*. **Aims** Promote cooperation between national church music organizations. **Languages** Danish, Norwegian, Swedish. **Finance** Budget (every 4 years): euro 175,000. **Events** *Quadrennial Meeting* Reykjavik (Iceland) 2021, *Quadrennial Meeting* Gothenburg (Sweden) 2016, *Quadrennial Meeting* Reykjavik (Iceland) 2012, *Quadrennial Meeting* Stavanger (Norway) 2008, *Quadrennial Meeting* Aarhus (Denmark) 2004.

Members National organizations in 5 countries:
Denmark, Finland, Iceland, Norway, Sweden. [2010/XD8127/**D**]

♦ Nordic Council for Church Studies (inactive)

♦ Nordic Council of Civil Servants Unions 17258

Nordisk Statstjenestemanns Organisasjon (NSO)

Pres ST, Box 5308, SE-102 47 Stockholm, Sweden. T. +46771555444. Fax +46771242924. E-mail: st@st.org.

History Founded 1984. **Events** *Conference* Bergen (Norway) 2007.

Members National organizations (5) in 5 countries:
Denmark, Finland, Iceland, Norway, Sweden. [2022/XM3603/**D**]

♦ Nordic Council of Deacons' Associations (inactive)
♦ Nordic Council of the Deaf (#05126)

♦ Nordic Council on Disability Policy 17259

Nordiska Handikappolitiska Rådet

Contact Nordens Välfärdscenter, Box 1073, SE-101 39 Stockholm, Sweden. T. +46854553600. E-mail: info@nordicwelfare.org.

URL: http://www.nsh.se/

History 1 Oct 1997. Advisory ad policymaking body for *Nordic Council of Ministers (NCM, #17260)*. **Structure** Council of 19 members. **IGO Relations** Supported by: *Nordiska Samarbetsorganet för Handikappfrågor (NSH, inactive)*. [2016/XD8028/**D**]

♦ Nordic Council for the Disabled (no recent information)
♦ Nordic Council for Driving Instructors (inactive)
♦ Nordic Council for Drug Research (inactive)
♦ Nordic Council for Ecology (inactive)
♦ Nordic Council of Furniture Producers (inactive)
♦ Nordic Council for the Glass and Porcelain Trade (inactive)
♦ Nordic Council of Local Government Officers / see Nordisk Tjenestemannsråd (#17538)
♦ Nordic Council of Medical Students (inactive)
♦ Nordic Council on Medicines (inactive)

♦ Nordic Council of Ministers (NCM) 17260

Conseil des ministres des pays nordiques – Consejo Nórdico de Ministros – Nordisk Ministerråd (NMR) – Nordiska Ministerrådet (NMR) – Pohjoismaiden Ministerineuvosto (PMN)

SG Ved Stranden 18, 1061 Copenhagen K, Denmark. T. +4533960200. E-mail: komm@norden.org – nmr@norden.org.

URL: http://www.norden.org/

History Established 13 Feb 1971, Copenhagen (Denmark), in an amendment to *Treaty of Cooperation between Denmark, Finland, Iceland, Norway and Sweden (Helsinki Treaty, 1962)*, signed 23 Mar 1962, and its revisions of 1971 and 1974, in order to administer cooperation among the 5 Nordic governments on the basis laid by the *Nordic Council (NC, #17256)* within the framework of Nordic Union. A permanent secretariat was set up on 18 Feb 1973, within the framework of *Nordic Cultural Cooperation (1971)*, in the secretariat of *Nordic Council of Ministers for Cultural Affairs*, Copenhagen, taking over the activities of the previous *Nordic Cultural Commissions (NKK, inactive)*; other affairs were covered by a separate secretariat in Oslo (Norway). The Cultural Cooperation Secretariat no longer exists separately, all NMR activities now coming under the same secretariat in Copenhagen. In an amendment to the Helsinki Treaty, 7 Nov 1993, the Nordic Council was given greater influence over the Nordic budget and Prime Ministers were given ultimate responsibility for Nordic Cooperation and for coordination on issues of Nordic concern. Further changes to the Treaty, 2 Jan 1996, strengthened the influence of party-groups in the Council. **Aims** Accomplish the tasks laid down by the Helsinki Treaty; examine questions of Nordic international cooperation; preserve and further develop cooperation among Nordic countries in legal, cultural, educational, social and economic fields and on communications and environment; eliminate obstacles to closer cooperation in other areas. In view of increased and deepened integration in Europe as a whole, in which Nordic cooperation is an integral part: ensure participation of Nordic countries in expanded cooperation with the rest of Europe on foreign and security policy, so as to enable Nordic countries to shape the future development of their own societies and take their share of responsibility for ensuring an order of peace and cooperation in Europe; meet future needs of Nordic countries at both Nordic and European levels by strengthening Nordic cooperation in areas of common Nordic interest and expanding political cooperation on issues related to European and regional cooperation so as to facilitate participation of Nordic countries in European Economic Area and European Union cooperation; as a priority, expand the working programme for Nordic cooperation with areas adjacent to the Nordic region.

Structure Overall responsibility for the Nordic Council of Ministers lies with the respective Prime Ministers. In practice, responsibility is delegated to the *Ministers for Nordic Cooperation (MR-SAM)* and to *Nordic Committee for Cooperation (NCC / NSK)*. Chairmanship rotates annually among member countries.

Despite generic name, consists of *'several councils'* (11):
- Nordic Council of Ministers for Labour (MR-A);
- Nordic Council of Ministers for Sustainable Growth (MR-VAEKST);
- Nordic Council of Ministers for Digitalisation 2017-2020 (MR-DIGITAL);
- Nordic Council of Ministers for Fisheries and Aquaculture, Agriculture, Food and Forestry (MR-FJLS);
- Nordic Council of Ministers for Culture (MR-K);
- Nordic Council of Ministers for Gender Equality (MR-JÄM);
- Nordic Council of Ministers for Legislative Affairs (MR-LAG);
- Nordic Council of Ministers for the Environment and Climate (MR-MK);
- Nordic Council of Ministers for Health and Social Affairs (MR-S);
- Nordic Council of Ministers for Education and Research (MR-U);
- Council of Ministers for Finance (MR-FINANS).

'Committees of Senior Officials' (15):
- *Nordic Committee of Senior Officials for Fisheries and Aquaculture, Agriculture, Food and Forestry (ÄK-FJLS Fisheries and Aquaculture / ÄK-FJLS Fiske och Vattenbruk / EK-FJLS Fiskeri og Havbrug / EK-FJLS Fiske- og Vannbruk / ÄK-FJLS, Kalastusja Vesiviljely / ÄK-FJLS Fiskveidar og Fiskeldi)*;
- *Nordic Committee for Senior Officials for Business (EK-N) – Nordiska ämbetsmannakommittén för näringspolitik (ÄK-N) – Nordisk Embedsmandskomité for Erhvervspolitik (EK-N) – Nordisk embetsmannskomité for n'ringspolitikk (EK-N) – Elinkeinopolitiikan virkamieskomitea (ÄK-N) – Norr'na emb'ttismannanefndin um atvinnustefnu (EK-N)*;
- *Nordic Committee of Senior Officials for Culture (EK-K / ÄK-K)*;
- *Nordic Committee of Senior Officials for Education & Research (EK-U) – Nordiska Ämbetsmannakommittén för Utbildning och Forskning (EK-U)*;
- *Nordic Committee of Senior Officials for Energy Policy (ÄK-NE/E)*;
- *Nordic Committee of Senior Officials for Environmental Affairs (EK-M / ÄK-MILJÖ)*;
- *Nordic Committee of Senior Officials for Finance – Nordiska Ämbetsmannakommittén för Ekonomi och Finanspolitik (ÄK-FINANS) – Nordisk Embedsmandskomité for økonomi og finanspolitik (EK-FINANS)*;
- *Nordic Committee of Senior Officials for Fisheries and Aquaculture, Agriculture, Food and Forestry (EK-FJLS Agriculture and Forestry)*;
- *Nordic Committee of Senior Officials for Gender Equality (EK-JÄM) – Nordiska Ämbetsmannakommittén för Jämställdhetsfrågor (Äk-JÄM)*;
- *Nordic Committee of Senior Officials for Labour (ÄK-A)*;
- *Nordic Committee of Senior Officials for Regional Policy (EK-R)*;
- *Nordic Committee on Health and Social Affairs*;
- *Nordic Committee of Senior Officials for Fisheries and Aquaculture, Agriculture, Food and Forestry (ÄK-FJLS Executive)*;
- *Nordic Committee of Senior Officials for Fisheries and Aquaculture, Agriculture, Food and Forestry (ÄK-FJLS Food)*;
- *Nordic Committee of Senior Officials for Legislative Affairs (ÄK-LAG)*.

Secretariat, located in Copenhagen (Denmark), consisting of Secretary General's Office and Departments: HR, Administration and Law; Communications; Culture and Resources; Growth and Climate; Knowledge and Welfare. Nordic Council of Ministers' Information Offices: Estonia; Latvia; Lithuania; Russia. Shares offices with *Nordic Council (NC, #17256)* and Nordic Culture Fund.

Instititutions and other cooperation organizations: Working Groups; Information Offices, offices and InfoPoints; Institutions; Cooperative bodies. *'Institutions'*:
- *NordForsk (#17164)*;
- *Nordic Culture Point*;
- *Nordic Energy Research (#17278)*;
- *Nordic House in the Faeroe Islands*;
- *Nordic Innovation (#17320)*;
- *Nordic Institute in Åland*;
- *Nordic School of Public Health (NHV, inactive)*;
- *Nordregio – an international research centre for regional development and planning (Nordregio, #17549)*;
- *Nordic Genetic Resource Centre (NordGen, #17303)*;
- *Nordic House in Reykjavik (NHR)*;
- *Nordic Institute for Advanced Training in Occupational Health (#17321)*;
- *Nordic Institute in Greenland (NAPA)*.

'Cooperative bodies':
- Nordic Swan Ecolabel (#17441);
- Nordic Culture Fund (#17264);
- Nordic Environment Finance Corporation (NEFCO, #17281);
- Nordisk Film & TV Fond (NFTVF, #17503);
- Nordic Forest Research Cooperation Committee (#17296);
- Nordicom (#17374);
- Nordic Information for Gender Knowledge (NIKK, #17317);
- Nordic Institute for Theoretical Physics (NORDITA, #17324);
- NIAS-Nordisk Institut for Asienstudier (NIAS, #17132);
- Nordiska Institutet för Odontologisk Materialprovning (NIOM, #17485);
- Nordisk Institutt for Sjørett (NIFS, #17515);
- Nordisk Journalistcenter (NJC, #17516);
- Nordic Medico-Statistical Committee (NOMESCO, #17342);
- Nordic Network (#17348);
- Nordiska Projektexportfonden (NOPEF, #17490);
- Nordic Social-Statistical Committee (NOSOSCO, #17409);
- Nordisk Sommeruniversitet (NSU, #17535);
- Nordic Teachers' Council (#17444);
- Nordic Volcanological Center (NordVulk, #17463);
- Nordjobb (#17544);
- Sami University of Applied Sciences;
- Council for Nordic Cooperation on Disability;
- Nordic Atlantic Cooperation (#17209);
- Nordic Development Fund (NDF, #17271);
- Nordic Joint Committee for Agricultural and Food Research (#17332).

Also functional withi NMR framework: *Mid Nordic Committee (#16796); Nordic Children's and Youth Committee (NORDBUK, #17235); Nordic Cooperation Archipelago (#17253).*
Languages Danish, Norwegian, Swedish. **Staff** 100.00 FTE, paid. **Finance** Member countries' contributions according to a scale of assessments based on each country's share of the total Nordic gross national income. Annual budget: over Danish Kr 955,000,000. Various forms of cooperation are financed directly from national budgets.
Activities Politics/policy/regulatory. Management of treaties and agreements:
- Nordic Language Convention (1981);
- Agreement Concerning a Common Nordic Labour Market (1982);
- Convention Concerning the Working Environment (1989);
- Nordic Convention on Social Assistance and Social Services (1994);
- Agreement concerning co-operation between authorities and institutions in the field of vocational rehabilitation and training for the labour market (1982);
- Konvention innehållande internationellt privaträttslig bestämmelser om äktenskap, adoption och förmynderskap (1931);
- Konvention angående indrivning av underhållsbidrag (1962);
- Nordic public health preparedness agreement (2002);
- Nordisk konvention om social trygghet (2012);
- Nordic Agreement on Co-operation on Upper Secondary School Education (2004);
- Agreement concluded by Denmark, Finland, Iceland, Norway and Sweden on Admission to Higher Education (1996);
- Convention for the avoidance of double taxation with respect to taxes on inheritances and gifts (1989);
- Agreement Concerning Cultural Cooperation (1971);
- Nordic Passport Convention (1957);
- Protocol Concerning the Exemption of Nationals of the Nordic Countries from the Obligation to Have a Passport or Residence Permit While Resident in a Nordic Country other than their Own (1954);
- Agreement Between Denmark, Finland, Iceland, Norway and Sweden on the Implementation of Certain Provisions Concerning Nationality (2002);
- Agreement between Denmark, Iceland, Norway and Sweden concerning cooperation in matters of competition (2001).

Events *Annual Forum on the EU Strategy for the Baltic Sea Region* Gdansk (Poland) 2019, *Nordic Safe Cities Conference* Helsinki (Finland) 2018, *Nordic Welfare Forum* Stockholm (Sweden) 2018, *Annual Forum on the EU Strategy for the Baltic Sea Region* Tallinn (Estonia) 2018, *Nordic Innovation Conference* Bergen (Norway) 2017. **Publications** *Analys Norden* (12 a year) in Finnish, Icelandic – newsletter; *Norden, the Top of Europe* in English, Russian – electronic newsletter; *Norden this Week* in English, Finnish, Icelandic – electronic newsletter; *Nordic Publications* in English; *Yearbook of Nordic Statistics* in English, Finnish, Swedish.
Members Governments of 8 countries and territories:
Åland, Denmark, Faeroe Is, Finland, Greenland, Iceland, Norway, Sweden.
IGO Relations
- Adjudicating Committee for the Nordic Council's Literature Prize (#00114);
- Arctic Council (#01097);
- Arctic Monitoring and Assessment Programme (AMAP, #01100);
- European Centre for Social Welfare Policy and Research (European Centre, #06500);
- International Council for the Exploration of the Sea (ICES, #13021);
- Joint Committee of the Nordic Medical Research Councils (#16125);
- Joint Nordic Organization for Lappish Culture and Reindeer Husbandry Affairs (no recent information);
- Joint Nordic Organization for Technical Testing (#16142);
- Meeting of the Chief Statisticians of the Nordic Countries;
- Nordens välfärdscenter (NVC, #17163);
- Nordic Committee for Consultation in Fishery Matters (NKO, inactive);
- Nordic Committee for Coordination of Electrical Safety Matters (#17246);
- Nordic-Baltic Committee on Food Analysis (NMKL, #17215);
- Nordic Committee for Public Inspection of Flammable and Explosive Goods (#17247);
- Nordic Contact Concerning State Building Activities (#17252);
- Nordic Immigration Committee (#17315) (not listed in official Handbook);
- Nordic Investment Bank (NIB, #17327);
- Nordic Joint Advisory Group on Refugee Policy (#17331);
- Nordic Passport Union (#17380);
- Nordic Postal Union (NPU, #17391);
- Nordic Tax Research Council (#17443);
- Nordisk Folkeoplysnings- og Voksenundervisningssamarbejde (FOVU, #17504);
- Nordisk Kärnsäkerhetsforskning (NKS, #17517);
- Nordisk Samarbeidsnaevn for Naturvidenskab (NOS-N, #17529);
- Nordiska Samarbetsrådet för Kriminologi (NSfK, #17493);
- Nordiska Tulladministrativa Rådet (NTR, #17497).
- North Atlantic Marine Mammal Commission (NAMMCO, #17573);
- United Nations Economic Commission for Europe (UNECE, #20555);
- Vision and Strategies around the Baltic Sea (VASAB, #20798);
- West-Nordic Foundation (#20926);
- WHO Regional Office for Europe (#20945).

NGO Relations
- Arctic Vocational Foundation (#01102);
- Association of European Border Regions (AEBR, #02499);
- Baltic Development Forum (#03111);
- Coalition Clean Baltic (CCB, #04053);
- Cochrane Collaboration (#04078);
- Danish Institute for Human Rights (DIHR);
- Dövas Nordiska Råd (DNR, #05126);
- Filmkontakt Nord – Nordisk Panorama Foundation (#09756);
- Föreningarna Nordens Förbund (FNF, #09859);
- Handikapporganisationernes Nordiska Råd (HNR, no recent information);
- International Society of Fish and Shellfish Immunology (ISFSI, #15122);
- Koordineringskommittén för Hydrologi i Norden (KOHYNO, no recent information);
- Nordens Fackliga Samorganisation (NFS, #17158);
- Nordic Amateur Theatre Council (#17172);
- Nordic Art Association (#17176);
- Nordic Association for the Study of Education in Developing Countries (NASEDEC, no recent information);
- Nordic Association of University Administrators (NAUA, #17206);
- Nordic Building Research Meeting (NBM);
- Nordic Cancer Union (NCU, #17225);
- Nordic Centre Youth (NCY, #17232);
- Nordic Council for Cooperation in Silvicultural Research (no recent information);
- Nordic Council for Wildlife Research (NCWR, #17262);
- Nordic Employers' Organization (no recent information);
- Nordic Federation for Medical Education (NFME, no recent information);
- Nordic Folk University (inactive);
- Nordic Geoexcursions to Iceland (no recent information);
- Nordic Housing Administration Meeting (not listed in official Handbook);
- Nordic Laboratory for Luminescence Dating (#17333);
- Nordic Molecular Biology Association (NOMBA, no recent information);
- Nordic Nurses' Federation (NNF, #17371);
- Nordic Theatres Council (#17447);
- Nordic Union Hotels, Restaurants, Catering and Tourism (NU HRCT, #17454);
- Nordic Wood Preservation Council (NWPC, #17469);
- Nordisk Institut Samarbejde (NIS, no recent information);
- Nordiska Byggforskningsorganens Samarbetsgrupp (NBS, no recent information);
- Nordiska Jordbruksforskares Förening (NJF, #17486);
- Nordiska Skogsteknologiska Rådet (NSR, no recent information);
- NORDTEL – Nordic Cooperation in the Field of Telecommunications (no recent information);
- NORDUnet (#17553);
- Saami Council (#19012);
- Samarbetsforum för Nordisk Metrologi – Mätteknik (NORMET, no recent information);
- Samarbetsnämnden för Norden-Undervisning i Utlandet (no recent information);
- Stockholm Environment Institute (SEI, #19993);
- Union of the Baltic Cities (UBC, #20366);
- World Crafts Council AISBL (WCC International, #21342). [2019.05.15/XD4238/**D***]

♦ Nordic Council of Ministers of Education and Culture (inactive)
♦ Nordic Council for Music Conservatories / see Association of Nordic Music Academies (#02830)
♦ Nordic Council of Music Research Societies (inactive)
♦ Nordic Council of Organizations of Disabled People (no recent information)
♦ Nordic Council of Paper Merchants (inactive)
♦ Nordic Council of Parliamentarians / see Nordic Council (#17256)
♦ Nordic Council of Perfumery Retailers (inactive)
♦ Nordic Council for Physical Oceanography (inactive)
♦ Nordic Council for the Professional Press (inactive)
♦ Nordic Council of Public Services Employees (#17538)
♦ Nordic Council for Railway Music (no recent information)
♦ Nordic Council for Railway Research and Development (inactive)
♦ Nordic Council for Reindeer Husbandry Research (inactive)
♦ Nordic Council for the Retail Trade (inactive)
♦ Nordic Council for Scientific Information (inactive)
♦ Nordic Council on Seed Planting for Forest Use (inactive)
♦ Nordic Council for Sheep and Goat Breeding (inactive)

♦ Nordic Council of Shopping Centres (NCSC) 17261

Nordens Största Intresseorganisation för Centrumhandel
Main Office Slödgatan 9, SE-111 57 Stockholm, Sweden. T. +4686111142. Fax +4686111299. E-mail: info@ncscnordic.org.
URL: http://ncscnordic.org/
History 1985, Helsinki (Finland). Also referred to as *Association for the Shopping Center Industry in Scandinavia.* **Aims** Create a neutral platform for benchmarking within the industry as well as between the industry and society. **Structure** Board, consisting of 4 members of each country, plus President. Executive Board, comprising President, 4 country chairs and Secretary-General. **Languages** English, Swedish. **Staff** 2.00 FTE, paid. Board, voluntary. **Finance** Members' dues. Activities. Budget (annual): Swedish Kr 13 million. **Activities** Organizes conferences, meetings and study tours; provides education. **Events** *Conference* Trondheim (Norway) 2019, *Conference* Oslo (Norway) 2018, *Seminar* Oslo (Norway) 2018, *Completely Retail Marketplace Nordics Meeting* Stockholm (Sweden) 2018, *Conference* Stavanger (Norway) 2017. **Publications** *CenterNytt* (4 a year) in Swedish – online newsletter, and newsfeed in English; *Scandinavian Market Overview* (annual) in English.
Members Companies (401) and individuals (1097) in 4 northern European countries:
Denmark, Finland, Norway, Sweden. [2018/XD6887/**D**]

♦ Nordic Council of Ski Schools (inactive)
♦ Nordic Council for Small and Medium Size Enterprises (no recent information)
♦ Nordic Council for Tax Research / see Nordic Tax Research Council (#17443)
♦ Nordic Council of the Trade, Technical and Professional Press (inactive)

♦ Nordic Council for Wildlife Research (NCWR) 17262

Conseil nordique de recherches sur la nature – Nordiskt Kollegium för Viltforskning (NKV) – Pohjoismainen Riistantutkimuskollegio
Oikos Editorial Office Oikos Editorial Offcie, Lund Univ, SE-223 62 Lund, Sweden. E-mail: me@wildlifebiology.org – info@oikosoffice.lu.se.
Chairman address not obtained.
URL: http://www.wildlifebiology.org/about-journal/nkv/
History 1971. Established under the auspices of *Nordic Council (NC, #17256).* **Aims** Promote contact and exchange among Nordic wildlife researchers; support wildlife research of common Nordic interest. **Structure** Collegium, composed of two representatives from Sweden and one from each other member country. Chairmanship rotates among countries. **Languages** Danish, English, Faroese, Icelandic, Norwegian, Swedish. **Finance** Sources: members' dues. Annual budget: 1,100,000 DKK. **Activities** Events/meetings; financial and/or material support. **Publications** *Wildlife Biology.*
Members Individuals in 4 countries:
France, Iceland, Norway, Sweden. [2021.02.17/XD4445/**D**]

♦ Nordic Council of Writers and Translators / see Nordisk Forfatter- og Oversetterråd (#17511)
♦ Nordic Counter Terrorism Network (unconfirmed)
♦ Nordic Countries Against Drugs / see Norden Mot Narkotika (#17157)
♦ Nordic Countrywomen's Organization (inactive)
♦ Nordic Crafts Association (#17160)
♦ Nordic Criminal Police Union (inactive)

♦ Nordic Critical Psychology Network (NCPN) 17263

Address not obtained.
URL: http://www.sv.uio.no/psi/english/research/network/ncpn/index.html
History An informal network of academics. [2016/XM4086/**F**]

♦ Nordic Cultural Commissions (inactive)
♦ Nordic Cultural Cooperation (1971 treaty)
♦ Nordic Cultural Fund / see Nordic Culture Fund (#17264)

♦ Nordic Culture Fund 17264

Fonds culturel nordique – Nordisk Kulturfond – Pohjoismainen Kulttuurirahasto
Contact Ved Stranden 18, 1061 Copenhagen, Denmark. T. +4533960200. E-mail: kulturfonden@norden.org.
URL: http://www.nordiskkulturfond.org/
History Oct 1966. Established by *Nordic Council (NC, #17256),* following agreement between Nordic Ministers for Culture and Education. New agreement came into force 1 Dec 1976. Comes under the secretariat of *Nordic Council of Ministers (NCM, #17260),* within the framework of *Nordic Cultural Cooperation (1971).* Former names and other names: *Nordiska Kulturfonden* – former; *Nordic Cultural Fund* – former. **Aims** Support innovative and dynamic artistic and cultural life in the Nordic Region that is diverse, accessible and of high quality. **Structure** Board. **Languages** Danish, English, Finnish, Swedish. **Staff** 5.00 FTE, paid. **Finance** Sources: contributions of member/participating states. Grants from member States on a ratio determined by Gross National Product. Annual budget: 37,000,000 DKK. **Activities** Awards/prizes/competitions; financial and/or material support; projects/programmes. **Events** *Meeting on the New Library* Helsinki (Finland) 2011, *Nordic lighthouse conference* Mariehamn (Finland) 2009, *Norden i Kongo – Kongo i Norden meeting* Espoo (Finland) 2006.
Members Representatives of 8 countries and territories:
Åland, Denmark, Faeroe Is, Finland, Greenland, Iceland, Norway, Sweden. [2020.09.03/XF4605/f/**F***]

♦ Nordic Culture Point (internationally oriented national body)
♦ Nordic Customs Cooperation Council (#17497)
♦ Nordic Customs Union (inactive)
♦ Nordic Cycling Association (no recent information)
♦ Nordic Cystic Fibrosis Association (no recent information)

♦ Nordic Dairy Technology Council 17265
Nordisk Mejeriteknisk Råd (NMR)

Contact Munkehatten 28, 5220 Odense SØ, Denmark. T. +4566124025. E-mail: info@nordicdairycongress.com.
URL: http://nordicdairycongress.com/

History 2015, as a formal collaboration, following dairy congresses having been organized since 1920. Registered in accordance with Danish law. **Structure** Steering Committee. **Activities** Events/meetings. **Events** *Nordic Dairy Congress* Copenhagen (Denmark) 2017, *Nordic Dairy Congress* Copenhagen (Denmark) 2017, *Congress* Svolvaer (Norway) 2013.
Members Full in 5 countries:
Denmark, Finland, Iceland, Norway, Sweden. [2017/XM6266/**E**]

♦ Nordic Data Union (no recent information)

♦ Nordic Defence Cooperation (NORDEFCO) 17266

Contact address not obtained. E-mail: fmn@fmn.dk.
URL: http://www.nordefco.org/

History 5 Nov 2009. Founded when NORDEFCO Memorandum of Understanding was signed. Structure established during first half 2010, when 3 parallel cooperation structures merged into one: *Nordic Coordinated Arrangement for Military Peace Support (NORDCAPS)*, set up 1997, as a successor to *NORDSAMFN*; *NORDAC* – for Armament Cooperation, set up 1990s; *NORDSUP* – for Enhanced Cooperation, set up 2008. **Aims** Strengthen participating nations' national defence; explore common synergies; facilitate efficient common solutions. **Structure** Not an organization, but a structure bringing member states together at policy and military levels in the field of Defence. Rotating Chairmanship. **Languages** English. **Staff** No staff of its own. **Finance** No budget of its own. Projects and activities financed by participating nations. **Events** *Advanced Distributed Learning Conference* Gol (Norway) 2019, *Nordic Defence Industry Seminar* Stockholm (Sweden) 2018, *Baltic Finnish Cooperation Meeting* Helsinki (Finland) 2017, *Commanders Meeting* Helsinki (Finland) 2017, *Meeting of Nordic Defence Ministers* Helsinki (Finland) 2017. **Publications** Annual Report.
Members Governments (5 – Iceland only functions at policy level):
Denmark, Finland, Iceland, Norway, Sweden. [2020/XJ8346/**F***]

♦ Nordic Defence Estates / see Nordic-Baltic Defence Estates (#17216)

♦ Nordic Demining Research Forum (NDRF) 17267

Contact address not obtained. T. +4548173898. E-mail: ole.nymann@post4.tele.dk.
URL: http://www.ndrf.dk/

Aims Stimulate research and development activities to support improvement in demining efficiency and safety. **Structure** Steering Committee. **Finance** Supported by: *Nordisk Industrifond (NI, inactive)*. **Activities** Organizes conferences, seminars and workshops. **Events** *Summer conference* Rosersberg (Sweden) 2002, *Conference* Stockholm (Sweden) 2002. **NGO Relations** *Geneva International Centre for Humanitarian Demining (GICHD)*; *Norwegian People's Aid (NPA)*; *People Against Landmines (MgM)*. [2009/XF6427/**F**]

♦ Nordic Demographic Society (NDS) 17268
Nordisk Demografisk Förening – Pohjoismaiden Väestötieteen Yhdistys – Norraent Demógrafiskt Félag

Sec c/o Statistics Norway, PO Box 8131 Dep, 0033 Oslo, Norway. T. +4721090000. Fax +4721094973.
URL: https://demografi.no/nordisk-demografisk-forening/

History 15 Aug 1968, Helsinki (Finland). Founded in connection with the 1st Nordic Demographic Symposium. Current statutes approved at General Assembly, 13 Aug 1992, Lund (Sweden). **Aims** Promote understanding of the importance of population problems and the feasibility of demographic methods in different areas of social life; stimulate interest and promote research and education in demography; promote contact among members in Nordic countries and elsewhere. **Structure** Constitutional Assembly (at least every 4 years); Board of Governors; President; Vice-President; Treasurer and Secretary are Governors representing Sweden and Norway respectively; Chairmanship rotates among national sections. **Languages** Danish, English, Finnish, Norwegian, Swedish. **Staff** Voluntary. **Finance** Members' dues. **Activities** Knowledge management/information dissemination; training/education; events/meetings. **Events** *Nordic Demographic Symposium* Oslo (Norway) 2022, *Symposium* Oslo (Norway) 2021, *Symposium* Reykjavik (Iceland) 2019, *Symposium* Turku (Finland) 2017, *Symposium* Aalborg (Denmark) 2014. **Publications** Symposia proceedings.
Members Individuals and organizations () in 10 countries:
Austria, Denmark (*), Finland (*), France, Iceland, Japan, Luxembourg, Norway (*), Sweden (*), USA. [2021/XD1821/**D**]

♦ Nordic Dermatological Association / see Nordic Dermatology Association (#17269)

♦ Nordic Dermatology Association (NDA) 17269

Main Office St Johannesgattan 22A, SE-753 12 Uppsala, Sweden. E-mail: info@nordicdermatology.com.
URL: http://www.nordicdermatology.com/

History Bylaws adopted 1910; amended 1935, 1946, 1977, 1993, 1998, 2001, 2016 and 2019. Former names and other names: *Nordiska Dermatologiska Föreningen* – former (1910); *Scandinavian Dermatological Association* – former; *Nordic Dermatological Association (NDA)* – former; *Nordisk Dermatologisk Forening* – former. **Aims** Promote the science and clinical practice of dermatology and venereology in the Nordic region; promote increased cooperation between national societies of dermatology and venereology in the region. **Structure** General Assembly; Board. **Languages** English. **Finance** Members' dues. **Activities** Events/meetings; training/education. **Events** *Nordic Congress of Dermatology and Venereology* Copenhagen (Denmark) 2022, *Nordic Congress of Dermatology and Venereology* Gothenburg (Sweden) 2019, *Nordic Congress of Dermatology and Venereology* Trondheim (Norway) 2016, *Nordic Congress of Dermatology and Venereology* Tampere (Finland) 2013, *Nordic Congress of Dermatology and Venereology* Reykjavik (Iceland) 2008. **Publications** *NDA Newsletter*, *Nordic Forum for Dermato-Venereology* – official journal.
Members Full in 5 countries:
Denmark, Finland, Iceland, Norway, Sweden. [2021/XU0197/**D**]

♦ Nordic Design Research (Nordes) 17270

Contact Aalto Univ, Dept of Design, Otaniementie 14, FI-02145 Espoo, Finland. T. +358503724428.
URL: http://www.nordes.org/

History 2005, Copenhagen (Denmark). Founded as an open network. **Structure** Board. **Activities** Events/meetings; knowledge management/information dissemination; training/education. **Events** *Conference* Kolding (Denmark) 2021, *Conference* Aalto (Finland) 2019, *Conference* Oslo (Norway) 2017, *Conference* Stockholm (Sweden) 2015, *Conference* Copenhagen (Denmark) / Malmö (Sweden) 2013. **Information Services** *Nordes Digital Archive*. [2021.09.22/XJ5416/**F**]

♦ Nordic Development Centre for Rehabilitation Technology (inactive)

♦ Nordic Development Fund (NDF) 17271
Fonds nordique de développement – Fondo Nórdico de Desarrollo – Nordiska Utvecklingsfonden – Pohjoismaiden Kehitysrahasto

Managing Director PO Box 185, FI-00171 Helsinki, Finland. T. +35810618002. Fax +358106221491. E-mail: info.ndf@ndf.fi.
URL: http://www.ndf.fi/

History 1 Feb 1989. Established Nov 1988 and commenced operations Feb 1989. Statutes revised by decision of *Nordic Council of Ministers (NCM, #17260)* : 14 January 1993; 24 August 2000; 14 September 2001; 19 January 2005; 5 May 2009. **Aims** Advance Nordic leadership in addressing climate change and development challenges through financing, knowledge and partnerships. **Structure** Control Committee; Board of Directors; Rotating Chairmanship; Managing Director. **Languages** English, Finnish, Swedish. **Staff** 19.00 FTE, paid. **Finance** NDF's capital is provided from the development cooperation budgets of the Nordic countries. The original, subscribed capital of NDF is SDR 515 million and EUR 330 million and amounts to approximately EUR 1 billion. In 2019, the subscribed capital was remitted, representing EUR 1 billion. As of end 2019, NDF's total assets are around EUR 780 million of which 81% are tied to concessional loans with long maturities. The reflow from these assets combined with NDF's liquid assets form the basis for NDF's operations. **Activities** Capacity building; financial and/or material support; projects/programmes. Lower-income countries and countries in fragile situations, including Small Island Developing States (SIDS). **Publications** *NDF Newsletter*. Annual Report; other publications.
Members Governments of 5 countries:
Denmark, Finland, Iceland, Norway, Sweden.
IGO Relations Co-financing in cooperation with: *African Development Bank Group (ADB Group, #00284)*; *Asian Development Bank (ADB, #01422)*; *Inter-American Development Bank (IDB, #11427)*; *The World Bank Group (#21218)*, *International Development Association (IDA, #13155)*. Forms the *Nordic Finance Group (#17290)* together with *Nordic Environment Finance Corporation (NEFCO, #17281)*, *Nordiska Projektexportfonden (NOPEF, #17490)* and *Nordic Investment Bank (NIB, #17327)*. **NGO Relations** Partner of (2): P4G Partnering for Green Growth and the Global Goals 2030; *Partnership on Sustainable, Low Carbon Transport Foundation (SLoCaT Foundation, #18244)*. Partner of: *Green Growth Knowledge Platform (GGKP, #10719)*.
[2020.09.07/XF0624/f/**F***]

♦ Nordic Dietetic Association (inactive)

♦ Nordic Doctoral Training in Health Sciences (NorDoc) 17272

Address not obtained.
URL: http://www.nordochealth.net/

History Founded 28 Sep 2016, Helsinki (Finland). **Aims** Initiate, facilitate and intensify collaboration among Nordic doctoral schools/faculties in all relevant fields for the benefit of Nordic doctoral candidates and their supervisors, so as to support and ensure the highest possible quality in doctoral education in health sciences. **Activities** Training/education; events/meetings. **Events** *Nordic PhD Summit* Helsinki (Finland) 2018.
Members Educational institutions in 6 countries and territories:
Denmark, Faeroe Is, Finland, Iceland, Norway, Sweden. [2019/XM7936/**F**]

♦ Nordic Documentation Centre for Mass Communication Research / see Nordicom (#17374)
♦ Nordic Dramatists Union / see Nordisk Dramatikerunion (#17502)
♦ Nordic Drinking Water Conference (meeting series)
♦ Nordic Dysmelia Confederation (no recent information)
♦ Nordic Early Rectal Cancer Meeting (meeting series)

♦ Nordic Eating Disorders Society (NEDS) 17273
Nordisk Selskap for Spiseforstyrrelser

Chair address not obtained.
URL: http://www.neds.nu/

History 1997. Previously also referred to as *Nordiska sällskapet för ätstörningar*. **Events** *Nordic Congress on Eating Disorders* Oslo (Norway) 2022, *Nordic Congress on Eating Disorders* Oslo (Norway) 2020, *Nordic Congress on Eating Disorders* Reykjavik (Iceland) 2018, *Congress* Helsinki (Finland) 2016, *Congress* Stockholm (Sweden) 2014.
Members Full in 3 countries:
Denmark, Norway, Sweden. [2021/XD7094/**D**]

♦ Nordic Eco-Labelling Board / see Nordic Swan Ecolabel (#17441)

♦ Nordic Econometric Network 17274

Contact address not obtained.
URL: http://econ.au.dk/research/other-research-entities/

History 20 Mar 2000, Uppsala (Sweden). Founded 30 Mar 2000, Uppsala (Sweden). **Aims** Support Nordic Econometric Meetings; facilitate the exchange of information and research ideas. **Structure** General Assembly; Steering Committee. **Activities** Events/meetings; training/education; knowledge management/information dissemination.
Members Full in 5 countries:
Denmark, Estonia, Finland, Norway, Sweden. [2019/XM8316/c/**F**]

♦ Nordic Economic Cattle Breeding 17275
Elevage du bétail économique des pays nordiques – Nordische Wirtschaftliche Rinderzucht – Nordisk Økonomisk Kvaegavl (NØK)

Gen Sec SE Box 254, SE-311 23 Falkenberg, Sweden.
Sec address not obtained.
URL: http://www.noek.org/

History 1948, Falkenberg (Sweden). **Aims** Promote cooperation among Nordic countries to improve economic cattle breeding. **Structure** Conference (meeting every two years); Secretary General. **Languages** Danish, Finnish, Icelandic, Norwegian, Swedish. **Staff** None. **Finance** Sources: members' dues. **Events** *Biennial Conference* Denmark 2024, *Biennial Conference* Selfoss (Iceland) 2022, *Biennial Conference* Selfoss (Iceland) 2021, *Biennial Conference* Rättvik (Sweden) 2018, *Biennial Conference* Jakobstad (Finland) 2016. **Publications** Conference proceedings.
Members Active Individuals, maximum 40 from each member country. Researchers, advisers, farmers and teachers in agricultural colleges in 5 countries:
Denmark, Finland, Iceland, Norway, Sweden. [2021/XD1859/v/**D**]

♦ Nordic Economic Research Council (inactive)
♦ Nordic Economics Students' Union (#17479)
♦ Nordic Edge (internationally oriented national body)

♦ Nordic Educational Research Association (NERA) 17276
Nordisk Förening för Pedagogisk Forskning (NFPF)

Pres c/o Univ of Iceland, Stakkahlið, 105 Reykjavik, Iceland. E-mail: nera.nfpf@gmail.com.
URL: http://www.nfpf.net/

History 1972. Former names and other names: *Nordic Association of Pedagogic Research (NFPF)* – former. **Aims** Support educational research in the Nordic countries, with specific reference to the scientific traditions that are vital. **Structure** General Assembly; Board. **Languages** Danish, English, Norwegian, Swedish. **Staff** Voluntary. **Finance** Sources: members' dues. **Activities** Awards/prizes/competitions; events/meetings. **Events** *Congress* Oslo (Norway) 2022, *Congress* Odense (Denmark) 2021, *Congress* Odense (Denmark) 2021, *Annual Congress* Turku (Finland) 2020, *Annual Congress* Uppsala (Sweden) 2019. **Publications** *Nordic Studies in Education*.
Members Full in 5 countries:
Denmark, Finland, Iceland, Norway, Sweden.
Other members in 3 countries:
Estonia, Latvia, Lithuania. [2023.02.14/XD0516/**D**]

♦ Nordic Egg Distribution Organization (inactive)
♦ Nordic Electrical Workers' Federation (no recent information)

♦ Nordic Energy Regulators (NordREG) 17277

Secretariat Swedish Energy Markets Inspectorate, Libergsgatan 6, Box 155, SE-631 03 Eskilstuna, Sweden. T. +4616162700. E-mail: internationella@ei.se.
URL: http://www.nordicenergyregulators.org/

History Founded 2002, following the signing of a Memorandum of Understanding. **Aims** Promote legal and institutional framework and conditions necessary for developing the Nordic and European electricity markets. **Structure** Board (meets 4 times a year); Chairmanship rotates annually. **Publications** Reports.
Members Full in 5 countries:
Denmark, Finland, Iceland, Norway, Sweden. [2022.05.10/XM3368/**F**]

♦ **Nordic Energy Research** **17278**
Nordisk Energiforskning – Pohjoismainen Energiantutkimus
CEO Stensberggata 25, 0170 Oslo, Norway. T. +4747614400. Fax +4722565565. E-mail: info@nordicenergy.org.
Head of Communications address not obtained.
URL: http://www.nordicenergy.org/
History 1999, by *Nordic Council of Ministers (NCM, #17260)*, as a continuation of the Nordic Energy Research Programme, set up in 1985. Previously also referred to as *Nordic Institution for Energy Research – Pohjoismainen Energiantutkimusvaliokunta.* **Aims** Contribute to promoting a Nordic research and innovation area in this areas of new energy technologies and systems relevant for the Nordic common interest; create opportunities in the Nordic region by increasing knowledge creation and competitiveness, as well as advancing good coordination and common Nordic solutions. **Structure** Board. **Languages** Danish, English, Finnish, Icelandic, Norwegian, Swedish. **Staff** 13.00 FTE, paid. **Finance** Members' dues. Basic funding from Nordic Council of Ministers with additional project funding from *European Commission (EC, #06633).* Budget (annual): about Norwegian Kr 60 million. **Activities** Research and development. **Events** *Nordic EV Summit* Oslo (Norway) 2021, *Nordic EV Summit* Oslo (Norway) 2019, *CanNord : Canada and Nordic sustainable solutions for future cities seminar* Toronto, ON (Canada) 2011, *Nordic wind power conference* Trondheim (Norway) 2010, *Nordic hydrogen conference* Oslo (Norway) 2009. **Publications** Annual Report.
Members Full in 5 countries:
Denmark, Finland, Iceland, Norway, Sweden. [2022/XE3715/**E**]

♦ **Nordic Engineer Officers' Federation** **17279**
Fédération nordique des opérateurs de machines – Nordiska Maskinbefälsfederation
Contact Maskinmestrenes Forening, Sankt Annae Plads 16, 1250 Copenhagen K, Denmark.
History 21 Feb 1919, Gothenburg (Sweden). Also known as *Nordic Engineers Federation.* **Aims** Coordinate professional, *trade union* and social matters. **Languages** Danish, Faroese, Icelandic, Norwegian, Swedish. **Activities** Organizes annual meeting (2 a year); triennial congress. **Events** *Congress* Copenhagen (Denmark) 2010, *Congress* Sweden 2007, *General Meeting* Denmark 2005, *General Meeting* Denmark 2005, *Congress* Finland 2004.
Members Engineer officers' unions and associations in 6 countries and territories:
Denmark, Faeroe Is, Finland, Iceland, Norway, Sweden. [2012.07.25/XD1956/**D**]

♦ Nordic Engineers' Association (inactive)
♦ Nordic Engineers Federation / see Nordic Engineer Officers' Federation (#17279)
♦ Nordic Engravers' Organization (inactive)
♦ Nordic Environmental Mutagen Society (inactive)

♦ **Nordic Environmental NUcleotide Network (NENUN)** **17280**
Leader c/o ENVS, Frederiksborgvej 399, 4000 Røskilde, Denmark.
URL: https://projects.au.dk/nenun/
Aims Provide a basis for a closer collaboration; foster young scientists on the use of advanced nucleotide based techniques to study microbial ecosystems in various Nordic environments. **Activities** Events/meetings; training/education. **Events** *Workshop* Uppsala (Sweden) 2019, *Workshop* Copenhagen (Denmark) 2017, *Workshop* Copenhagen (Denmark) 2017.
Members Full in 5 countries:
Denmark, Finland, Iceland, Norway, Sweden.
NGO Relations *NordForsk (#17164).* [2019/XM6280/**F**]

♦ Nordic Environmental Protection Convention (1974 treaty)

♦ **Nordic Environment Finance Corporation (NEFCO)** **17281**
Nordiska Miljöfinasieringsbolaget – Pohjoismaiden Ympäristörahoitusyhtiö
Managing Dir Fabianinkatu 34, PO Box 249, FI-00171 Helsinki, Finland. T. +3580106180630. Fax +35809630976. E-mail: info@nefco.fi.
URL: http://www.nefco.org/
History 1990, by the 5 Nordic countries, as a multilateral financial institution to support environment investments in Central and Eastern Europe. Statutes revised by decision of the *Nordic Council of Ministers (NCM, #17260)*: 13 Nov 1991; 3 Mar 1993; 9 Jan 1996; 6 Nov 1998; 9 Oct 1999. **Aims** Support the Nordic countries' efforts to increase environmental awareness in Eastern and Central Europe by providing financing to projects that reduced emissions harmful to the environment. **Structure** Board of Directors, consisting of one representative and one alternate from each member country. Observers; Control Committee; Management Committee; Managing Director. **Staff** 41.00 FTE, paid. **Finance** Initial capital: euro 113 million, contributed by member countries. Total funds valued at about euro 400 million. **Activities** Financial and/or material support through some 30 trusts funds, including: *Nordic Environmental Development Fund.* **Publications** *NEFCO Newsletter.* Annual Report.
Members Governments of 5 countries:
Denmark, Finland, Iceland, Norway, Sweden.
IGO Relations One of 4 Nordic financing institutions, the others being: *Nordic Development Fund (NDF, #17271)*; *Nordiska Projektexportfonden (NOPEF, #17490)*; *Nordic Investment Bank (NIB, #17327).* Forms the *Nordic Finance Group (#17290)* together with NIB and NDF. Accredited by: *United Nations Framework Convention on Climate Change – Secretariat (UNFCCC, #20564).* Observer to: *Arctic Council (#01097).* **NGO Relations** Member of: *Climate Technology Centre and Network (CTCN, #04023).* [2016/XF2774/e/**F***]

♦ NordicEPI – Nordic Conference of Epidemiology and Register-Based Research (meeting series)
♦ Nordic EPR Society (no recent information)
♦ Nordic Equine Veterinary Conference (meeting series)
♦ Nordic Ergonomics Society (#17480)

♦ **Nordic ESPAnet** **17282**
Contact address not obtained. E-mail: info@espanet.org.
URL: https://www.helsinki.fi/en/conferences/towards-resilient-nordic-welfare-states/nordic-espanet
History Mar 2019, Helsinki (Finland). **Aims** Promote research on welfare policy in the Nordic countries. **Structure** Board. **Activities** Events/meetings.
Members Full in 5 countries:
Denmark, Finland, Iceland, Norway, Sweden. [2020/AA0523/**F**]

♦ Nordic Ethology Association (inactive)
♦ Nordic EUS Conference (meeting series)
♦ Nordic Family Therapy Congress (meeting series)

♦ **Nordic Federation of Building and Wood Workers (NFBWW)** **17283**
Fédération nordique des travailleurs du bâtiment et du bois – Nordiska Byggnads- och Träarbetarefederationen (NBTF) – Norraena Bygginga- og Treidnadarmannasambandid (NBTS) – Pohjoismainen Rakennus- ja Puutyöväen Federaatio (PRPF)
Pres address not obtained. T. +4610601001. E-mail: nbtf@byggnads.se.
URL: http://www.nbtf.info/
History 28 Sep 1952. **Aims** Coordinate Nordic Union positions in European and global issues; exchange information regarding member unions' work at national level on issues central to the trade union movement; coordinate issues that affect cross-border work in Nordic countries. **Structure** General Assembly; Executive Committee. **Languages** English, Swedish. **Finance** Members' dues. **Activities** Events/meetings; knowledge management/information dissemination. **Events** *Triennial Congress* Bergen (Norway) 2000, *Triennial Congress* Lappeenranta (Finland) 1997, *Regional seminar on modernizing trade unions in Europe* Luxembourg (Luxembourg) 1997, *Conference on professional and managerial work in the building and wood sectors* Luxembourg (Luxembourg) 1996, *Conference on chemical hazards* Stockholm (Sweden) 1996.
Members Trade unions for building and wood-working industries and forestry workers (24), representing over 400,000 members, in 5 countries:
Denmark, Finland, Iceland, Norway, Sweden.
NGO Relations Close cooperation with: *Building and Wood Workers' International (BWI, #03355).* [2018.09.10/XD3187/**D**]

♦ Nordic Federation of Chief Cooks (no recent information)
♦ Nordic Federation of Factory Workers' Unions (inactive)
♦ Nordic Federation of Forest Owners' Associations (inactive)

♦ **Nordic Federation of General Practice ApS (NFGP ApS)** **17284**
Main Office c/o DSAM, Stockholmsgade 55, 2100 Copenhagen, Denmark. E-mail: nfgp@dsam.dk.
URL: http://www.nfgp.org/
History 2005. Continues partnership between Scandinavian Journal of Primary Health Care (SJPHC) and Nordic congresses on general practice (NKAM). Former names and other names: *Nordic Colleges of General Practitioners* – alias. **Aims** Enhance the general practitioners' role in primary health care in the Nordic countries. **Structure** General Meeting (annual). Board of 5 members, including Chairperson and Director. **Activities** Organizes *Nordic Congress on General Practice*, a congress series since 1983. **Events** *Nordic Congress of General Practice* Norway 2031, *Nordic Congress of General Practice* Denmark 2029, *Nordic Congress of General Practice* Iceland 2027, *Nordic Congress of General Practice* Sweden 2025, *Nordic Congress of General Practice* Turku (Finland) 2024. **Publications** *Scandinavian Journal of Primary Health Care* in English.
Members in 5 countries:
Denmark, Finland, Iceland, Norway, Sweden. [2020/XM2115/**D**]

♦ Nordic Federation of Journalists / see Nordiska Journalistförbundet (#17487)
♦ Nordic Federation for Medical Education (no recent information)

♦ **Nordic Federation of Public Accountants** **17285**
Nordiska Revisorsförbundet (NRF) – Nordisk Revisorforbund – Pohjoismainen Tilintarkastajaliitto – Norraena Endurskodendasambandid
SG c/o FAR, Box 6417, SE-113 82 Stockholm, Sweden.
History 4 Jan 1932, Oslo (Norway). Constitution amended: 13 May 1939, Copenhagen (Denmark); 21 Sep 1956, Stockholm (Sweden); 17 Aug 1991, Imatra (Finland); 28 Aug 1999, Kalmar (Sweden); 18 Aug 2001, Hämeenlinna (Finland); 10 Dec 2003, Brussels (Belgium). **Aims** Coordinate activities of professional accountancy bodies in the Nordic countries so as to improve their contribution to, and strengthen their influence in, international organizations; encourage the acceptance of international professional standards in the Nordic countries. **Structure** General Assembly (annual). President; Secretary. **Languages** Danish, English, Norwegian, Swedish. **Staff** 0.50 FTE, paid. **Finance** To a small extent by cash contributions to the Secretariat from member bodies (euro 80,000 a year); mainly by professional work done by member bodies and shared according to an agreed pooling system. **Activities** Organizes congresses. **Events** *General Assembly* Sweden 2008.
Members Full in 5 countries:
Denmark, Finland, Iceland, Norway, Sweden.
NGO Relations Recognized by: *International Federation of Accountants (IFAC, #13335).* [2020/XD3309/**D**]

♦ Nordic Federation for Public Administration (#17477)
♦ Nordic Federation of Societies of Obstetrics and Gynaecologists / see Nordic Federation of Societies of Obstetrics and Gynaecology (#17286)

♦ **Nordic Federation of Societies of Obstetrics and Gynaecology** **17286**
Association nordique des gynécologues et obstétriciens – Nordisk Förening för Obstetrik och Gynekologi (NFOG)
SG address not obtained.
Pres address not obtained.
URL: http://www.nfog.org/
History 29 Jun 1933, Stockholm (Sweden). Statutes amended: 1954, 1966, 1972, 1986, 1990, 2000, 2004. Legally registered in Denmark, Finland, Norway and Sweden since its foundation, and in Iceland since 1972. Former names and other names: *Nordic Federation of Societies of Obstetricians and Gynaecologists* – former; *Scandinavian Society of Obstetricians and Gynaecologists* – former. **Aims** Promote scientific and practical communications among Scandinavian gynaecologists. **Structure** General Assembly; Administrative Board (meets 2-3 times a year); Presidency rotates every 2 years. **Languages** English. **Staff** Voluntary. **Finance** Sources: members' dues. **Activities** Awards/prizes/competitions; events/meetings; training/education. **Events** *Biennial Congress* Odense (Denmark) 2018, *Biennial Congress* Helsinki (Finland) 2016, *Biennial Congress* Stockholm (Sweden) 2014, *Biennial Congress* Bergen (Norway) 2012, *Chronic Pelvic Disorders Meeting* Copenhagen (Denmark) 2011. **Publications** *Acta Obstetricia et Gynecologica Scandinavica* (periodical).
Members Individuals and organizations in 5 countries:
Denmark, Finland, Iceland, Norway, Sweden.
NGO Relations Instrumental in setting up (1): *Nordic Federation of Young Obstetricians and Gynaecologists (NFYOG, #17287).* [2021/XD3203/**D**]

♦ Nordic Federation for Special Education / see Nordic Special Needs Education Organization (#17435)
♦ Nordic Federation of Trade and Technical Press (inactive)
♦ Nordic Federation of Unions of Municipal Employees (#16204)

♦ **Nordic Federation of Young Obstetricians and Gynaecologists (NFYOG)** **17287**
Chair address not obtained.
Chair address not obtained.
URL: https://nfog.org/nfyog/
History Jun 2000, Oslo (Norway). Founded during 32rd Nordic Congress of Obstetrics and Gynaecology, organized by *Nordic Federation of Societies of Obstetrics and Gynaecology (#17286).* **Aims** Promote cooperation of trainees in gynaecology-obstetrics in the Nordic countries; advance education and specialist training in the field. **Structure** Board. **Activities** Events/meetings. **Events** *Congress* Helsinki (Finland) 2004.
Members National organizations in 5 countries:
Denmark, Finland, Iceland, Norway, Sweden. [2022/XJ4512/**D**]

♦ Nordic Femtochemistry Conference (meeting series)

♦ **Nordic Fertility Society (NFS)** **17288**
Pres Dep Obstetrics and Gynecology, Hvidovre Hospital, Copenhagen Univeristy, Kettegaard Allé 30, 2650 Hvidovre, Denmark. T. +4538625797. Fax +4538622135.
URL: http://www.nordicfs.org/
History Jan 1999, Kuusamo (Finland), following a series of meetings. **Aims** Promote cooperation and information exchange in the field of assisted *reproduction* in the Nordic countries. **Events** *Conference* Helsinki (Finland) 2022, *Conference* Helsinki (Finland) 2021, *Conference* Gothenburg (Sweden) 2019, *Conference* Nyborg (Denmark) 2017, *Conference* Reykjavik (Iceland) 2015.
Members in 5 countries:
Denmark, Finland, Iceland, Norway, Sweden. [2014/XD9120/**D**]

♦ Nordic FGC Conference (meeting series)
♦ Nordic Film and Television Society (inactive)

♦ **Nordic Filtration Society (NoFS)** **17289**
Contact c/o Industri-Textil Job AB, Box 144, SE-511 44 Kinna, Sweden. T. +4632013015. Fax +46320211245.
URL: http://www.nordicfiltrationsoc.org/
History 1 Aug 1995, Gothenburg (Sweden), as a regional chapter of *Filtration Society, The (#09757).* **Aims** Serve as a discussion forum on Nordic solid/fluid separation problems; stimulate contacts between Nordic industries, research institutes and universities. **Structure** Committee, comprising 2 Chairmen, Vice Chairman, Secretary, Treasurer and 4 further members. **Activities** Organizes *Nordic Filtration Symposium.* **Events** *Symposium* Aalborg (Denmark) 2012, *Symposium* Aalborg (Denmark) 2012, *Symposium* Lappeenranta (Finland) 2010, *Symposium* Gothenburg (Sweden) 2009, *Symposium* Copenhagen (Denmark) 2008.
[2010/XE3709/**E**]

♦ Nordic Finance Group 17290

Communications Unit Fabianinkatu 34, PO Box 249, FI-00171 Helsinki, Finland. T. +35810618001. Fax +358106180725.
URL: http://www.nib.int/

Aims Finance projects in the public and private sectors; (the Group does not negotiate any financing deals, inasmuch as this is the responsibility of the 3 international institutions). **Structure** Not an operative body and not a separate legal entity but rather an "umbrella organization" or a platform of cooperation for 3 Nordic international financing institutions in Helsinki (Finland): *Nordic Environment Finance Corporation (NEFCO, #17281)*; *Nordic Investment Bank (NIB, #17327)*; *Nordic Development Fund (NDF, #17271)*. NDF and NEFCO owned by the 5 Nordic countries (Denmark, Finland, Iceland, Norway, Sweden); NIB owned by the Nordic and Baltic countries (Baltic countries – Estonia, Latvia, Lithuania). **Finance** No budget. When the Group arranges events, the 3 international institutions are fully responsible for all arrangements and their legal implications. [2019.07.12/XF4505/y/**F***]

♦ Nordic Finance Network (NFN) 17291

Dir c/o Graduate School of Finance, Aalto Univ, School of Business, PO Box 21220, FI-00076 Aalto, Finland. T. +358403538053. E-mail: nfn@aalto.fi.
Street Address Runeberginkatu 22-24, Room G2-15 – 2nd floor, Chydenia Bldg, Helsinki, Finland.
URL: http://nfn.aalto.fi/

History Set up Mar 2006. **Aims** Increase quality and diversity of research and research training via cooperation. **Structure** Board. **Activities** Training/education; events/meetings. **Events** *Workshop* Copenhagen (Denmark) 2021, *Workshop* Oslo (Norway) 2020, *Workshop* Stockholm (Sweden) 2019, *Workshop* Lund (Sweden) 2018, *Workshop* Copenhagen (Denmark) 2017.
Members Institutions in 4 countries:
Denmark, Finland, Norway, Sweden. [2017/XM6281/**F**]

♦ Nordic Financial Unions 17292

Nordiska Finansanställdas Union (NFU)

Secretariat Box 720, SE-101 34 Stockholm, Sweden.
Street address Franzégatan 5, SE-112 51 Stockholm, Sweden.
URL: http://www.nordicfinancialunions.org/

History Set up 1 Jan 1999, by merger of *Confederation of Nordic Bank Employees' Unions (NBU, inactive)* and Confederation of *Nordic Insurance Employees Union (NFU, inactive)*. Previously referred to in English as *Confederation of the Nordic Bank, Finance and Insurance Unions*. EU Transparency Register: 4129929362-47. **Aims** Promote the interests of Nordic financial trade unions in Europe; strive to make financial sectors prosper in a way that is sustainable for employees, companies, consumers and society. **Structure** Union Council; Management Board. **Languages** English. **Staff** 3.00 FTE, paid. **Finance** Members' dues. Annual budget: about Swedish Kr 5,100,000. **Activities** Events/meetings; advocacy/lobbying/activism; politics/policy/regulatory. **Events** *Conference* Copenhagen (Denmark) 2019, *The Nordic model disrupted – a seismic shift or a natural development?* Reykjavik (Iceland) 2017, *Do you measure up?* Brussels (Belgium) 2016, *Sector Conference* Oslo (Norway) 2015, *Sector Conference* Helsinki (Finland) 2013. **Publications** Reports (2-3 a year), covering conferences or various projects.
Members National unions (7), totalling 150,000 members, in 5 countries:
Denmark, Finland, Iceland, Norway, Sweden.
IGO Relations Member unions coordinate their work towards *European Commission (EC, #06633)* and to a certain extent *European Parliament (EP, #08146)*, via NFU. **NGO Relations** Member unions are members of *UNI Global Union (#20338)* and coordinate their work towards UNI via NFU. [2019.12.12/XD8393/**D**]

♦ Nordic Fine Arts Federation / see Nordic Art Association (#17176)
♦ Nordic Fire & Safety Days (meeting series)
♦ Nordic First Aid (meeting series)

♦ Nordic Fishermen's Council (NFC) 17293

Nordiske Fiskeres Råd (NFR)

Address not obtained.
URL: http://www.norden.org/

History 1992, as *Nordic Fishermen's Environmental Secretariat (NFES) – Nordiske Fiskeres Miljøsekretariat (NFM)*. **Aims** Facilitate cooperation among fishermen's organizations in the Nordic countries; protect Nordic waters against threats to long-term survival of the fishery industry, notably marine environmental pollution and unwise exploitation of marine resources; work to achieve understanding with environmental organizations on sustainable utilization of renewable resources.
Members Fishery organizations (9) in 7 countries and territories:
Denmark, Faeroe Is, Finland, Greenland, Iceland, Norway, Sweden. [2010/XD6255/**D**]

♦ Nordic Fishermen's Environmental Secretariat / see Nordic Fishermen's Council (#17293)

♦ Nordic Flag Society 17294

Société vexillologique nordique – Nordisk Flagselskab (NFS) – Nordiska Flaggsällskapet – Pohjoismaiden Lippuseura

Pres address not obtained.
URL: http://www.nordicflagsociety.org/

History 10 Jan 1973, Copenhagen (Denmark). **Aims** Unite and inform people in the Nordic countries and elsewhere who are interested in *flags* and banners. **Structure** General Assembly (annual). **Languages** Danish, Norwegian, Swedish. **Staff** 7.00 FTE, voluntary. **Events** *Annual meeting* Helsinki (Finland) 2008, *Congress* Berlin (Germany) 2007, *Annual meeting* Gothenburg (Sweden) 2007, *Annual meeting* Copenhagen (Denmark) 2006, *Annual meeting* Oslo (Norway) 2005. **Publications** *Nordisk Flaggkontakt* (2 a year).
Members Flag manufacturers, flag enthusiasts, scientific and working people in 5 countries:
Denmark, Finland, Iceland, Norway, Sweden.
NGO Relations Member of: *Fédération internationale des associations vexillologiques (FIAV, #09611)*. [2019/XD8909/**D**]

♦ Nordic Flow Battery Network (unconfirmed)
♦ Nordic Folkecenter for Renewable Energy (internationally oriented national body)

♦ Nordic Folk High School Council 17295

Nordiska Folkhögskolerådet

Contact Nordiska Folkhögskolan, Olof Palmes väg 1, SE-442 31 Kungälv, Sweden. T. +46303206200. Fax +4630364831. E-mail: twn@ffd.dk.
URL: http://www.nordiskafolkhogskolor.com/

History 1956, Kungälv (Sweden). Founded as the umbrella organization for national associations of folk high schools. **Aims** Promote contacts among folk high school staff and students in Nordic countries; discuss matters of common interest to such schools; consult and cooperate on international issues in the field of non-formal and formal adult education. **Structure** Council, comprising 2 representatives per member association and including President and Secretary. **Languages** Danish, Norwegian, Swedish. **Finance** Sources: members' dues. Annual budget: 150,000 SEK. **Activities** Events/meetings; projects/programmes. **Events** *Meeting / Nordic Meeting* Kauniainen (Finland) 1995, *Nordic Meeting* Norway 1991, *Meeting* Norway 1989, *General Nordic meeting* 1987, *Nordic Meeting* Sweden 1987. **Publications** Books; folders; leaflets.
Members Folk high school associations, representing 400 folk high schools, in 4 countries:
Denmark, Finland, Norway, Sweden.
Associate members in 4 territories:
Åland, Faeroe Is, Greenland, Iceland.
IGO Relations *Nordic Council of Ministers (NCM, #17260)*. **NGO Relations** Member of (1): *International Council for Adult Education (ICAE, #12983)*. [2022/XD1904/**D**]

♦ Nordic Forest Economics Seminar / see Scandinavian Society of Forest Economics (#19108)

♦ Nordic Forest Research Cooperation Committee 17296

Comité de collaboration pour la recherche forestière nordique – SamNordisk Skogsforskning (SNS) – Sam Nordisk Sknovforskning (SNS) – Yhteispohjoismainen Metsäntutkimus (SNS) – Norraenar Skógarrannsóknir (SNS)

Contact c/o Jonas Rönnberg and Inga Bödeker, Southern Swedish Forest Research Centre, Swedish Univ of Agricultural Science, Box 49, SE-230 53 Alnarp, Sweden. T. +4640415179 – +4640415121.
Chairman address not obtained. T. +4687754051.
URL: http://www.nordiskskogforskning.org/

History 1972, on adoption of the first statutes. New statutes adopted 25 Mar 1980, entered into force 1 Jan 1981; present statutes adopted 19 Dec 2001. Previously also referred to as *Samarbejdsnaevnet for Nordisk Skovforskning – Pohjoismaiden Metsäntutkimuksen Yhteistyölautakunta*. Currently a permanent cooperation institution on the general budget of *Nordic Council of Ministers (NCM, #17260)*. **Aims** Promote research into the diverse functions of the forests in *sustainable* forestry, as well as advise the EK-FJLS and NMR on questions concerning forests and forest research; contribute to the socially, economically and ecologically responsible management and utilization of forests and *timber resources* in the Nordic region. **Structure** Board, consisting of 2 representatives each from Denmark, Finland, Iceland, Norway and Sweden. Representatives from the Faeroe Is, Greenland and Åland may attend meetings. Presidency and Secretariat rotates between participating countries for 4-year periods. **Languages** Danish, English, Finnish, Norwegian, Swedish. **Staff** 0.50 FTE, paid. **Activities** Cooperates in Nordic forest research, with other Nordic bodies, with adjacent areas and other international bodies. Disseminates information. Instrumental in setting up: *Nordic Virtual Centre for Advanced Research in Forest Genetics and Tree Breeding (GENECAR, no recent information)*. Acts as umbrella organization of the following specialized cooperation groups: *Nordic Network for Communication of Research Results (no recent information)*; *Northern European Network for Wood Science and Engineering (WSE, see: #17296)*; *Nordisk Arboretudvalg (NAU, #17491)*; *Nordic Cooperation Group for Forest Fertilization (no recent information)*; *Nordic Cooperation Group for Forest Inventory (see: #17296)*; *Nordic/Baltic Cooperation Group for Forest Pathology (no recent information)*; *Nordic Cooperation Group for Multiple-Use Forestry (no recent information)*; *Nordic Cooperation Group for Forest Entomology (see: #17296)*; *Nordiska Skogsteknologiska Rådet (NSR, no recent information)*; *Scandinavian Society of Forest Economics (SSFE, #19108)*; *Nordic Network on Forest Regeneration (inactive)*. **Events** *Meeting on forest pathology* Juupajoki (Finland) 2007, *Meeting* Denmark 2003. **Publications** *Scandinavian Journal of Forest Research* (6 a year) – joint publication. **Information Services** *NOLTFOX* – database, containing 12,000 long-term forest experiments in Nordic countries.
Members Governments of 5 countries:
Denmark, Finland, Iceland, Norway, Sweden.
IGO Relations Member of: *European Forest Institute (EFI, #07297)*. [2015/XD5798/**E***]

♦ Nordic Forestry Congress (meeting series)
♦ Nordic Forestry Federation (no recent information)
♦ Nordic Forestry, Veterinary and Agricultural University / see Nordic Forestry, Veterinary and Agricultural University Network (#17297)

♦ Nordic Forestry, Veterinary and Agricultural University Network (NOVA University Network) 17297

Secretariat Swedish Univ of Agricultural Sciences SLU, Almas alle 8, SE-750 07 Uppsala, Sweden. E-mail: nova@slu.se.
URL: http://www.nova-university.org/

History 24 May 1995. Established upon signature of agreement between rectors of veterinary and agricultural universities. Former names and other names: *Nordic Forestry, Veterinary and Agricultural University (NOVA)* – former. **Aims** Initiate, administer and promote active cooperation in education and research between the Nordic forestry, veterinary and agricultural universities. **Structure** Steering Group; Executive Committee; Secretariat, headed by coordinating institution. **Languages** English. **Staff** 0.10 FTE, paid. **Finance** Sources: government support; international organizations; members' dues. Annual budget: 800,000 EUR. **Activities** Knowledge management/information dissemination; training/education. Focus on joint PhD-courses. **Events** *Annual seminar* Uppsala (Sweden) 2007, *Annual Conference* Iceland 2004. **Publications** Annual Report (internal).
Members Universities/Faculties (10) in 5 countries:
Denmark, Finland, Iceland, Norway, Sweden. [2021.09.01/XF4087/**F**]

♦ Nordic Forestry, Veterinary and Agricultural University, NOVA – Baltic University Cooperation / see Baltic Forestry, Veterinary and Agricultural University Network (#03119)

♦ Nordic Forum for Dance Research (NOFOD) 17298

Nordisk Forum for Danseforskning

Chair Immolantie 50 C, FI-00780 Helsinki, Finland.
URL: http://www.nofod.org/

History Founded Oct 1990, Copenhagen (Denmark). **Aims** Bring together dance scholars and dance artists working on artistic development and research in the *art* of dance, and other dance forms. **Structure** Board, consisting of 2 representatives from each of the 5 Nordic countries. **Languages** Danish, English, Faroese, Icelandic, Norwegian, Swedish. **Staff** Voluntary. **Finance** Members' dues. **Activities** Organizes conferences and seminars; initiates and introduces new research; collaborates with scholars; distributes information and publications. **Events** *Conference* Copenhagen (Denmark) 2022, *Conference* Helsinki (Finland) 2019, *Conference* Trondheim (Norway) 2013, *Conference* Odense (Denmark) 2011, *Conference* Tampere (Finland) 2008. **Publications** *NOFOD Newsletter* (2 a year). Conference proceedings.
Members Organizations, institutions, academics, choreographers, dancers, teachers and critics (about 150) in 5 countries:
Denmark, Finland, Iceland, Norway, Sweden. [2018/XF3771/**F**]

♦ Nordic Forum for Lipid Research and Technology (Nordic Lipidforum) 17299

Sec c/o SINTEF, Borgundvegen 340, 6009 Ålesund, Norway. E-mail: secretary@lipidforum.info.
URL: https://lipidforum.info/

History 1969. Former names and other names: *Scandinavian Forum for Lipid Research and Technology (LIPIDFORUM)* – former (1969); *Nordic Forum for Science and Technology of Lipids* – former; *Nordisk Forum för Lipidforskning og- Teknologi (LIPIDFORUM)* – former. **Aims** Stimulate the establishment of a beneficial network between research institutes and industry. **Structure** Board of 10 (2 from each of the 5 Nordic countries, of which one from industry and one from universities or other institutions). Secretary General. **Finance** Sources: members' dues. Annual budget: 250,000 NOK. **Activities** Events/meetings. **Events** *Nordic Lipidforum Symposium* Ålesund (Norway) 2022, *Nordic Lipidforum Symposium* 2021, *Nordic Lipidforum Symposium* Horsens (Denmark) 2019, *Nordic Lipid Symposium / Symposium* Reykjavik (Iceland) 2015, *Nordic Lipid Symposium / Symposium* Helsinki (Finland) 2013. **Publications** *Lipidforum News* (2 a year). Booklets.
Members Personal, Institute and Company membership (450) in 14 countries:
Belgium, Canada, Denmark, Finland, France, Germany, Iceland, Ireland, Netherlands, Norway, Sweden, Switzerland, UK, USA.
NGO Relations Member of (2): *European Federation for the Science and Technology of Lipids (Euro Fed Lipid, #07210)*; *International Society for Fat Research (ISF, #15115)*. [2022.02.15/XF3012/**F**]

♦ Nordic Forum for Mediation / see Nordisk Forum for Megling og Konflikthåndtering (#17513)
♦ Nordic Forum for Mediation and Conflict Management (#17513)
♦ Nordic Forum for Science and Technology of Lipids / see Nordic Forum for Lipid Research and Technology (#17299)

♦ Nordic Forum for South Asia (NoFSA) 17300

Contact address not obtained. E-mail: nofsa-contact@ikos.uio.no.
URL: http://www.nofsa.uio.no/

History Founded mid-1990s, as Norwegian Forum for South Asia. Current title adopted 2002. **Aims** Encourage a sense of community and information sharing among people in the Nordic region with an interest in South Asia. **Structure** Board. **Activities** Knowledge management/information dissemination. **IGO Relations** *NIAS-Nordisk Institut for Asienstudier (NIAS, #17132)*. [2019/XM8490/**F**]

♦ Nordic Forum for Trauma and Emergency Radiology (NORDTER) . . . 17301

Nordiskt forum för trauma och akutradiologi Organisation

Treas Kommendörsgatan 21, SE-114 48 Stockholm, Sweden. E-mail: nordictraumarad@gmail.com.
URL: https://www.nordictraumarad.com/

History Registration: No/ID: 802413-1206, Sweden. **Aims** Act as a forum to exchange knowledge and ideas; generate educating discussions; seek cooperation with other Nordic and international organizations. **Structure** Board. **Activities** Training/education. [2020/AA0692/**F**]

- ♦ Nordic Forwarding Agents Association / see Nordiskt Speditörförbund (#17543)
- ♦ Nordic Foundation for Communication (#04381)
- ♦ The Nordic Frugal Innovation Society (unconfirmed)
- ♦ **Nordic Fuel Cell Net** Nordic and Baltic Applied Fuel Cell Technology Research Network (#17212)

♦ Nordic Galvanizers . . . 17302

Contact Danderydsvägen 146, SE-182 36 Danderyd, Sweden. T. +4684466760. Fax +4684466767. E-mail: info@nordicgalvanizers.com.
URL: http://www.nordicgalvanizers.com/

History as *Nordisk Förzinkningsförening*. **Aims** Help users of galvanized *steel* with questions regarding surface treatment, corrosion, environment, education and technology. **Activities** Performs research and development; works with environmental issues; takes part in international cooperation. **Events** *Meeting* Vaasa (Finland) 2009, *Meeting* Turku (Finland) 2006.
Members Full in 4 countries:
Denmark, Finland, Norway, Sweden.
NGO Relations Member of: *European General Galvanizers Association (EGGA, #07383).* [2016/XD6815/**D**]

- ♦ Nordic Gastroenterological Association (inactive)
- ♦ Nordic Gender Institute / see Nordic Information for Gender Knowledge (#17317)
- ♦ Nordic Gene Bank / see Nordic Genetic Resource Centre (#17303)
- ♦ Nordic Gene Bank for Agricultural and Horticultural Plants / see Nordic Genetic Resource Centre (#17303)

♦ Nordic Genetic Resource Centre (NordGen) . . . 17303

Nordisk Genresurssenter

Exec Dir PO Box 41, SE-234 56 Alnarp, Sweden. T. +4640536640. Fax +4640436650. E-mail: info@nordgen.org.
Street Address Växthusvägen 12, SE-234 56 Alnarp, Sweden.
URL: http://www.nordgen.org/

History 1 Jan 1979, Alnarp (Sweden). Founded by *Nordic Council of Ministers (NCM, #17260)* to replace corresponding national activities.1993, merged with the former *Samnordisk Planteforedling (SNP, inactive)*, (set up in 1981) so as to unite all inter-Nordic activities on plant genetic resources (PGR) in one institute. Current title adopted on merger of Nordic Gene Bank with *Nordic Gene Bank for Farm Animals* and *Nordic Council for Forest Reproductive Material*, Jan 2008. Former names and other names: *Nordic Gene Bank for Agricultural and Horticultural Plants (NGB)* – former (1 Jan 1979 to 1 Jan 1993); *Banque nordique de génétique agricole et horticole* – former (1 Jan 1979 to 1 Jan 1993); *Nordiska Genbanken för Jordbruks- och Trädgårdsväxtar (NGB)* – former (1 Jan 1979 to 1 Jan 1993); *Viljely-ja Puutarhakasvien Pohjoismainen Geenipankki* – former (1 Jan 1979 to 1 Jan 1993); *Nordic Gene Bank (NGB)* – former (1 Jan 1993 to Jan 2008); *Banque nordique de génétique* – former (1 Jan 1993 to Jan 2008); *Nordiska Genbanken (NGB)* – former (1 Jan 1993 to Jan 2008). **Aims** Preserve and record genetic variations of both wild and cultivated agricultural and horticultural materials relevant to the climatic zone of the Nordic countries; act as service institution for plant breeders and research workers; stimulate cooperation in plant breeding among Nordic countries. **Structure** Board; Technical Advisory Committee; Crop Working Groups (6). **Languages** Danish, English, Faroese, Icelandic, Norwegian, Swedish. **Staff** From all Nordic countries. **Finance** Triennial budget agreement with NMR. **Activities** Guidance/assistance/consulting; knowledge management/information dissemination; monitoring/evaluation; projects/programmes; training/education. Advises governments, in particular with respect to *Convention on Biological Diversity (Biodiversity convention, 1992)*. Project to promote plant genetic resources programme in the Baltic states. The *SADC Plant Genetic Resources Centre (SPGRC, #19024)* is a joint development project with *Southern African Development Community (SADC, #19843)*. **Events** *Annual Forest Conference* Lund (Sweden) 2022. **Publications** *Nordic Gene Bank 1979 – 1999* (1999) – pdf format; *Verksamhetsberättelse* (1999) in Danish, Norwegian, Swedish – pdf format; *Vegetable Catalogue* (1998) – pdf format; *Potatoes in the Nordic Countries* – description of old potato species in the Nordic Genebank, in all Scandinavian languages, summary in English. Catalogues; manuals. Information Services: Acts as Nordic information centre for plant genetic resources. Working groups produce a number of databases on specific topics.
Members Joint undertaking of the 5 Nordic countries:
Denmark, Finland, Iceland, Norway, Sweden.
IGO Relations Member of (1): *Global Biodiversity Information Facility (GBIF, #10250).* **NGO Relations** Instrumental in setting up (1): *Eastern Africa Plant Genetic Resources Network (EAPGREN, inactive).* [2023.02.15/XF8187/**F***]

♦ Nordic Geodetic Commission . . . 17304

Commission géodésique nordique – Nordiska Kommissionen för Geodesi (NKG)

Chair c/o Finnish Geospatial Research, NLS, Geodeetinrinne 2, FI-02430 Masala, Finland.
URL: http://www.nordicgeodeticcommission.com/

History 19 Apr 1953, Stockholm (Sweden). Statutes adopted 3 October 1986. **Aims** Promote and facilitate scientific geodetic collaboration in Nordic countries. **Structure** General Assembly (every 4 years); Praesidium (meets every year); Study Groups (meet every year). **Languages** Danish, English, Norwegian, Swedish. **Staff** Unpaid. **Finance** Grants from official and private bodies. **Events** *Quadrennial General Meeting* Helsinki (Finland) 2018, *Quadrennial General Meeting* Gothenburg (Sweden) 2014, *Quadrennial General Meeting* Sundvollen (Norway) 2010, *Quadrennial general meeting* Copenhagen (Denmark) 2006, *Quadrennial general meeting* Espoo (Finland) 2002. **Publications** Proceedings of General Assemblies.
Members National sections in 5 countries:
Denmark, Finland, Iceland, Norway, Sweden. [2020.01.01/XD2989/**D**]

- ♦ Nordic GeoGebra Network / see Nordic and Baltic GeoGebra Network (#17217)
- ♦ Nordic Geographers Meeting (meeting series)
- ♦ Nordic Geological Winter Meeting (meeting series)

♦ Nordic Gerontological Federation (NGF) . . . 17306

Nordisk Gerontologisk Forening

Sec/Treas address not obtained. T. +4550564400. E-mail: contact@ngf-geronord.se.
Pres address not obtained.
URL: https://www.ngf-geronord.se/

History 1973, Aarhus (Denmark). Umbrella organization for the gerontological and geriatric societies in the Nordic countries. **Aims** Support, develop and coordinate gerontological research, development and education in the Nordic countries. **Structure** Board; Secretariat. **Languages** Danish, English, Finnish, Norwegian, Swedish. **Finance** Sources: members' dues. **Activities** Events/meetings. **Events** *Nordic Congress of Gerontology* Stockholm (Sweden) 2024, *Biennial Congress* Odense (Denmark) 2022, *Biennial Congress* Reykjavik (Iceland) 2021, *Biennial Congress* Reykjavik (Iceland) 2020, *Biennial Congress* Oslo (Norway) 2018. **Publications** *GeroNord* (3 a year). Annual Report in English.
Members Member societies (11), grouping about 2,600 members, in 5 countries:
Denmark, Finland, Iceland, Norway, Sweden. [2023/XD4262/**D**]

♦ Nordic Gerontological Federation (NGF) . . . 17305

Sec-Treas Fac of Social Sciences and Gerontology Research Ctr, Box 100 – Tampere Univ, FI-33014 Tampere, Finland. T. +358401901647.
URL: https://www.ngf-geronord.se/

History 1974. **Aims** Support, organize and expand gerontological research, development and eduction within the Nordic countries. **Structure** Executive Committee; Scientific Committee; Secretariat. **Activities** Events/meetings. **Publications** *GeroNord.*
Members Full in 5 countries:
Denmark, Finland, Iceland, Norway, Sweden. [2020/AA0712/**D**]

- ♦ Nordic Glaucoma Meeting (meeting series)
- ♦ Nordic Goat Producers Association (inactive)
- ♦ Nordic Good Templar Council (#17483)
- ♦ Nordic Good Templar Youth Council (#17159)
- ♦ Nordic Graphical Union (no recent information)
- ♦ Nordic Grocers' Committee (inactive)
- ♦ Nordic Group of Medical Laboratory Technologists' Associations (#17523)
- ♦ Nordic Group Psychotherapy Congress (meeting series)
- ♦ Nordic Gymnastics Union (inactive)
- ♦ Nordic Gypsum Association (#17514)

♦ Nordic Hairdressers' Association . . . 17307

Association des coiffeurs nordiques – Nordischer Friseurverband – Nordiska Frisörmästareförbundet (NFF)

Pres Håndvaerkets Hus, Islands Brygge 26, 2300 Copenhagen, Denmark. T. +4563157440. Fax +4532630452.

History 1937, as *Nordic Association of Ladies' and Gentlemen's Hairdressers – Association nordique des coiffeurs pour dames et pour messieurs – Nordisk Dame og Herrefrisørmesteres Forbund.* Present name adopted 1985. Also referred to as *Nordic Hairdressing Employers Association* and as *Nordic Association of Hairdressers.* **Aims** Work for close cooperation in all relevant areas; exchange experience, views and ideas concerning pricing, legislation and general regulations, educational issues, trade literature and other matters concerning the hairdressing trade. **Structure** Board, composed of the President of each member country. **Languages** Danish, Faroese, Icelandic, Norwegian, Swedish. **Staff** 3.00 FTE, paid. **Finance** Members' dues. **Activities** Congress (every 2 years) includes Nordic Championships and rotates among member countries. **Events** *Congress* Helsinki (Finland) 2013, *Congress* Stockholm (Sweden) 2011, *Congress* Copenhagen (Denmark) 2010, *Congress* Copenhagen (Denmark) 2010, *Congress* Jönköping (Sweden) 2009.
Members National organizations of 5 countries:
Denmark, Finland, Iceland, Norway, Sweden. [2013.11.19/XD1213/**D**]

- ♦ Nordic Hairdressing Employers Association / see Nordic Hairdressers' Association (#17307)

♦ Nordic Handicap Federation (NHF) . . . 17308

Association nordique des handicapés – Nordiska Handikappförbundet

Project Coordinator Postbox 9217 Grønland, 0134 Oslo, Norway. E-mail: nhf@dhr.se – info@dhr.se.
Facebook: https://www.facebook.com/nordiskahandikappforbundet/

History 1946. Former names and other names: *Nordiska Nammden for Handikappforbundet* – alias; *Nordic Association of the Disabled* – alias. **Events** *Quadrennial meeting* Norway 2008, *Quadrennial meeting* Reykjavik (Iceland) 1996, *Quadrennial meeting* Copenhagen (Denmark) 1992, *Quadrennial meeting* Trondheim (Norway) 1988.
Members Full in 6 countries and territories:
Denmark, Faeroe Is, Finland, Iceland, Norway, Sweden.
NGO Relations Member of (1): *European Disability Forum (EDF, #06929).* [2021/XD1881/**D**]

- ♦ Nordic Handicrafts Council (inactive)

♦ Nordic Health Economists Study Group (NHESG) . . . 17309

Contact Univ of Southern Denmark, COHERE, Campusvej 55, 5230 Odense M, Denmark. E-mail: nhesg@sam.sdu.dk – nhesg@economics.gu.se.

History 1979, Lund (Sweden). **Aims** Provide a forum for contacts between health economists in the Nordic countries. **Structure** Informal structure. **Languages** Danish, English, Finnish, Icelandic, Norwegian, Swedish. **Staff** No permanent staff. **Finance** No budget. **Events** *Annual Conference* Gothenburg (Sweden) 2022, *Online Meeting* Gothenburg (Sweden) 2021, *Annual Conference* Gothenburg (Sweden) 2020, *Annual Conference* Reykjavik (Iceland) 2019, *Annual Conference* Tromsø (Norway) 2018. **Publications** None.
Members Individuals in 8 countries:
Denmark, Finland, France, Germany, Iceland, Norway, Sweden, UK. [2021/XD1912/v/**D**]

♦ Nordic Health Research and Innovation Networks (NRI-Networks) . . 17310

Project Manager Postboks 3105 Elisenberg, 0207 Oslo, Norway. T. +4745449846.

History 8 Sep 2010. **Aims** Promote health research and innovation in the Nordic region. **Structure** Board; Programme Committee; Secretariat. **Languages** English. **Staff** 3.00 FTE, paid. **Finance** Funded by partner organizations. Annual budget: 2,000,000 NOK. **Activities** Events/meetings; knowledge management/information dissemination; research and development. **Events** *Annual Conference* Oslo (Norway) 2017, *Annual Conference* Bergen (Norway) 2015, *Annual Conference* Os (Norway) 2014, *Annual Conference* Os (Norway) 2013.
Members Networks (8):
Nordic Innovation Network; Nordic Monitoring Network (NORM); Nordic NECT; Nordic Network for Nurse Research; Nordic Pediatric Network; Nordic Study Sites; Nordic Trial Alliance; NORTTH. [2017/XJ8294/**F**]

- ♦ Nordic Heart and Lung Alliance (inactive)

♦ Nordic Hemophilia Council (NHC) . . . 17311

Sec Website Editorial Board address not obtained. E-mail: info@nordichemophiliacouncil.org.
URL: http://nordichemophiliacouncil.org/

Aims As a forum of physicians responsible for the diagnosis and treatment of hemophilia, other bleeding disorders and thrombophilic disorders, standardize and improve the care of patients with the relevant conditions. **Activities** Events/meetings.
Members Full in 6 countries:
Denmark, Estonia, Finland, Iceland, Norway, Sweden. [2019/XM8465/**D**]

♦ Nordic Himalaya Research Network (NHRN) . . . 17312

Address not obtained.
URL: https://himalayanordic.wordpress.com/

History Inaugurated May 2018, Copenhagen (Denmark). **Aims** Strengthen Himalayan studies in the Nordic region; help to facilitate international collaboration. **Activities** Events/meetings. **Events** *Annual Conference* Copenhagen (Denmark) 2019, *Annual Conference* Copenhagen (Denmark) 2018. **IGO Relations** Supported by: *NIAS-Nordisk Institut for Asienstudier (NIAS, #17132).* [2019/XM8487/v/**F**]

- ♦ Nordic History Studies (internationally oriented national body)
- ♦ Nordic Home-mission Council (inactive)
- ♦ Nordic Hoofcare Association (internationally oriented national body)
- ♦ Nordic Hotel and Restaurant Association / see Nordic Union Hotels, Restaurants, Catering and Tourism (#17454)
- ♦ Nordic House in the Faeroe Islands (internationally oriented national body)
- ♦ Nordic House in Greenland / see Nordic Institute in Greenland
- ♦ Nordic House in Reykjavik (internationally oriented national body)
- ♦ Nordic Housewives Association (no recent information)
- ♦ Nordic Housing Administration Meeting (meeting series)
- ♦ Nordic Housing Companies' Organization / see Housing Nordic (#10957)
- ♦ Nordic Humour Research Network (no recent information)

♦ Nordic Hunters' Alliance (NHA) . . . 17313

Nordisk Jägersamvirke (NJS)

Main Office Molsvej 34, 8410 Rønde, Denmark. T. +4588887500. E-mail: post@jaegerne.dk.
URL: http://www.nordichunters.org/

History 1947. Previously Also known as *Nordic Hunters Association – Nordiska Jägares Samarbetsorganisation* and *Nordic Hunter's Cooperation.* EU Transparency Register: 11101757375-75. **Aims** Maintain and develop Nordic hunting traditions; contribute to game research and studies; provide information. **Events** *Meeting* Denmark 1996. **Publications** *Nordic Hunting – Securing Nature and Wildlife for Coming Generations* – brochure.

Members Full in 5 countries:
Denmark, Finland, Iceland, Norway, Sweden.
IGO Relations Observer to: *Baltic Marine Environment Protection Commission – Helsinki Commission (HELCOM, #03126)*. **NGO Relations** Member of: *International Union for Conservation of Nature and Natural Resources (IUCN, #15766)*. [2017.11.24/XH1732/**D**]

- ♦ Nordic Hunters Association / see Nordic Hunters' Alliance (#17313)
- ♦ Nordic Hunter's Cooperation / see Nordic Hunters' Alliance (#17313)
- ♦ Nordic Hydrographic Commission (see: #13825)

♦ NORDICIL 17314

Contact c/o Danske Filmskole, Theodor Christensens Plads 1, 1437 Copenhagen K, Denmark.
Aims Promote cooperation among *Nordic film schools*. **Activities** Organizes meetings and student and teacher exchanges; curriculum development. [2015/XF3063/**F**]

♦ Nordic Immigration Committee 17315

Comité nordique des étrangers – Nordiska Utlänningsutskottet – Nordisk Udlaendingeudvalg (NU) – Pohjoismainen Ulkomaalaisvaliokunta

Contact Norwegian Directorate of Immigration, PO Box 2098 Vika, 0125 Oslo, Norway. T. +4723351500. Fax +4723351501. E-mail: udi@udi.no.
History Established 12 Jul 1957, by agreement between the five Nordic countries regarding the cessation of passport control at inter-Nordic boundaries. Also referred to as *Nordic Aliens Committee*. **Aims** Act as a cooperation committee between the first instances in the immigration field in the Nordic countries; coordinate immigration control in Nordic countries and discuss questions of importance to the common passport control area. **Structure** Member states take care of all obligations related to the work of the Committee, alternating every 6 months. **Languages** Danish, Norwegian, Swedish. **Activities** Events/meetings.
Members Representatives of 5 countries:
Denmark, Finland, Iceland, Norway, Sweden.
IGO Relations *Nordic Council of Ministers (NCM, #17260)*. [2018.08.06/XD2204/**D***]

♦ Nordic immunohistochemical Quality Control (NordiQC) 17316

Contact address not obtained. E-mail: nordiqc@rn.dk.
URL: http://www.nordiqc.org/
Aims Promote the quality of immunohistochemistry and expand its clinical use by arranging schemes for immunohistochemical proficiency testing and providing examples of recommended protocols, tissue controls and other relevant information including descriptions of epitopes and technical protocol parameters. **Structure** Executive Board. **Activities** Events/meetings; training/education; monitoring/evaluation. **Events** *Workshop on Immunohistochemistry* Aalborg (Denmark) 2021, *Workshop on Immunohistochemistry* Aalborg (Denmark) 2020, *Workshop on Immunohistochemistry* Bruges (Belgium) 2018. [2021/XM7382/**D**]

- ♦ Nordic IN (#11180)
- ♦ Nordic Industrial Associations Conferences (meeting series)
- ♦ Nordic Industrial Doctors Council (inactive)
- ♦ Nordic Industry Workers' Federation (inactive)
- ♦ Nordic Information Centre for Media and Communication / see Nordicom (#17374)

♦ Nordic Information for Gender Knowledge (NIKK) 17317

Project Coordinator Göteborgs Univ – NIKK, Box 709, SE-405 30 Gothenburg, Sweden. T. +46317869203. E-mail: nikk@genus.gu.se.
Street Address Viktor Rydbergsgatan 24, SE-405 30 Gothenburg, Sweden.
URL: http://www.nikk.no/
History 1 Sep 1995, to build on and consolidate the activities of the former *Coordinator for Nordic Women's Studies*. A regional multi- and interdisciplinary research institute for the Nordic countries and autonomous territories. Original title: *Nordic Institute for Women's Studies and Gender Research – Institut nordique d'études sur la condition féminine et la recherche sur l'égalité des sexes – Instituto Nórdico en Estudios de la Mujer e Investigaciones de Género – Nordiskt Institut för Kvinno- och Könsforskning (NIKK) – Nordisk Institut for Kvinde- og Kønsforskning – Nordisk Institutt för Kvinne- og Kjønnsforskning – Pojhoismainen Naistutkimusinstituutti – Norraena Kvenna- og Kynjarannsóknastofnunin – Avannaamioqatigiit Arnanur Suiaassusersiornermulu Ilisimatusarfiat – Davviriikkalas Nisson- ja Sohkabealedutkama Instituhtta*. Until 31 Dec 2011 existed under title of *Nordisk Institutt for Kunnskap om Kjønn (NIKK) – Nordic Gender Institute*, when it was closed down by *Nordic Council of Ministers (NCM, #17260)*. Refounded under current title 2012. **Aims** Advance, initiate, coordinate and inform about women's studies and gender research both within and outside of the Nordic countries. **Structure** Board, consisting of Chair, Vice-Chair, Employee's Representative, 3 members and 6 replacement members. **Staff** 8.00 FTE, paid. **Finance** Basic funding from the *Nordic Council of Ministers (NCM, #17260)*. External funding. **Activities** Areas of activity: research; networking and cooperation; courses, seminars and conferences; information dissemination. Provides a framework for joint Nordic research programmes and projects, post-graduate courses and research training, as well as Nordic and other international exchange programmes. Runs the Nordic Research School in Interdisciplinary Gender Research. **Events** *Conference on crossroads / Conference* Oslo (Norway) 2005, *Conference on gender and visions in research policy* Helsinki (Finland) 2004, *Conference on gender in the media* Oslo (Norway) 2004, *Conference on women's movements* Reykjavik (Iceland) 2004, *Joint meeting on gender equality* Oslo (Norway) 2003. **Publications** *NIKK Magasin* (2 a year). Leaflets; brochures; reports.
Members Full in 5 countries:
Denmark, Finland, Iceland, Norway, Sweden.
IGO Relations *Nordic Council (NC, #17256)*. Involved in setting up the proposed: *European Institute for Gender Equality (EIGE, #07557)*. [2019/XE2620/**E**]

♦ Nordic e-Infrastructure Collaboration (NeIC) 17318

Dir c/o NordForsk, Stensberggata 25, 0170 Oslo, Norway. T. +4747614400.
URL: https://neic.no/
History 2003. Set up as an organizational unit under *NordForsk (#17164)*, 1 Jan 2012. **Aims** Facilitate the development and operation of high quality e-infrastructure solutions in areas of joint Nordic interest. **Structure** Board. **Staff** 16.00 FTE, paid. **Finance** Contributions from member countries plus *NordForsk (#17164)*. Budget (2013): Norwegian Kr 16.5 million. **Events** *Nordic e-Infrastructure Conference* Oslo (Norway) 2022, *Nordic e-Infrastructure Conference* Copenhagen (Denmark) 2019, *Nordic e-Infrastructure Conference* Umeå (Sweden) 2017, *Nordic e-Infrastructure Conference* Espoo (Finland) 2015, *Nordic e-Infrastructure Conference* Trondheim (Norway) 2013.
Members Full in 5 countries:
Denmark, Finland, Iceland, Norway, Sweden. [2022/XJ8558/**E**]

- ♦ Nordic Infrastructure Conference (meeting series)
- ♦ Nordic Infrastructure Managers (inactive)

♦ Nordic Initiative for Corporate Economics (NICE) 17319

Administrator Research Inst of Industrial Economics, Box 55665, SE-102 15 Stockholm, Sweden.
Co-Founder address not obtained.
Co-Founder address not obtained.
URL: https://www.nordicnice.org/
History Oct 2018, Stockholm (Sweden). **Aims** Create a forum for interaction and cross-fertilization for the various branches of economics which study the corporation, but which currently lack an organized way of interacting with and learning from each other. **Structure** Steering Committee. **Activities** Events/meetings. **Events** *Conference* Copenhagen (Denmark) 2020, *Conference* Bergen (Norway) 2019, *Conference* Stockholm (Sweden) 2018. [2019/AA0663/**F**]

♦ Nordic Innovation 17320

Nordisk Innovations

Managing Dir Stensberggt 25 – 5th Floor, 0170 Oslo, Norway. T. +4747614400. E-mail: info@nordicinnovation.org.
URL: http://www.nordicinnovation.org/
History Founded as *Nordic Innovation Centre – Nordisk Innovations Center*. Previously also referred to as *Nordic Centre for Innovation (NCI)*. Functions under the auspices of *Nordic Council of Ministers (NCM, #17260)*. Organization number: 971 516 577. **Aims** Promote cross-border trade and innovation. **Structure** Board of Directors. **Staff** 24.00 FTE, paid. **Finance** Annual budget: about Norwegian Kr 80,000,000. **Activities** *Joint Nordic Organization for Technical Testing (#16142)* has become part of NCI. **Events** *WCEF : World Circular Economy Forum* Helsinki (Finland) 2019, *Conference* Iceland 2009, *Workshop on construction products* Espoo (Finland) 2008, *Conference* Oulu (Finland) 2007, *International conference on rapid prototyping and manufacturing* Espoo (Finland) 2006. **Publications** *Innovation Quarterly* (4 a year) – bulletin.
Members in 5 countries:
Denmark, Finland, Iceland, Norway, Sweden.
NGO Relations Founding member of: *ScanBalt (#19065)*. Cooperates with: *NordForsk (#17164)*. [2019/XE3472/**E***]

- ♦ Nordic Innovation Centre / see Nordic Innovation (#17320)

♦ Nordic Institute for Advanced Training in Occupational Health 17321

Institut nordique pour la formation continue dans le domaine des conditions de travail – Nordiska institutionen för vidareutbildning inom arbetsmiljöområdet (NIVA) – Pohjoismainen työympäristöalan jatkokoulutuskeskus

Dir Topeliuksenkatu 20, FI-00250 Helsinki, Finland. T. +358400416122. E-mail: info@niva.org.
Project Manager address not obtained.
URL: http://www.niva.org/
History 1 Mar 1982. Founded by *Nordic Council of Ministers (NCM, #17260)*, as continuation of an earlier Nordic project commenced 1978. Former names and other names: *Pohjoismainen Työmpäristöalan Täydennyskoulutusinstituutti* – former. **Aims** Provide high-level training for specialists in the field of occupational health and safety. **Structure** Board of Directors set by the Ministries of the Nordic countries. **Languages** English, Finnish, Swedish. **Staff** 4.00 FTE, paid. **Finance** Nordic Council of Ministers; course fees. Annual budget: 480,000 EUR. **Activities** Training/education. **Events** *Nordic Work Environment Conference* Copenhagen (Denmark) 2022, *Nordic Work Environment Conference* Copenhagen (Denmark) 2020, *Conference on Sustainable Employability* Leuven (Belgium) 2018, *Conference on the Future of Work* Stockholm (Sweden) 2018, *Workshop on Occupational Skin Diseases* Helsinki (Finland) 2017. **Publications** Annual work programmes.
Members Ministries represented in Board of Directors:
Denmark, Finland, Iceland, Norway, Sweden. [2021.09.02/XF1037/j/**F***]

- ♦ Nordic Institute in Åland (internationally oriented national body)
- ♦ Nordic Institute of Asian Studies / see NIAS-Nordisk Institut for Asienstudier (#17132)
- ♦ Nordic Institute of Dental Materials (#17485)
- ♦ Nordic Institute in Finland / see Nordic Culture Point
- ♦ Nordic Institute in Greenland (internationally oriented national body)
- ♦ Nordic Institute of Information Technology (inactive)
- ♦ Nordic Institute for Interoperability Solutions (internationally oriented national body)
- ♦ Nordic Institute of Latin American Studies (internationally oriented national body)
- ♦ Nordic Institute for Maritime Law / see Nordisk Institutt for Sjørett (#17515)

♦ Nordic Institute of Mission and Ecumenical Research (NIME) 17322

Chairperson Centre for Mission and Global Studies, VID Specialized Univ, Misjonsmarka 12, 4024 Stavanger, Norway.
URL: http://www.missionsresearch.org/
History 1975. **Aims** Promote historical and contemporary study of *Christian* missions. **Structure** Network of scholars. **Languages** English. **Staff** 4.00 FTE, voluntary. **Finance** Annual budget: less than euro 2,000. **Events** *Annual Conference* Turku (Finland) 2007, *European missiology conference* Paris (France) 2006. **Publications** *NIME Newsletter* (occasional).
Members Institutions (21) in 5 countries:
Denmark, Finland, Iceland, Norway, Sweden.
NGO Relations Member of: *International Association for Mission Studies (IAMS, #12032)*. [2018.09.18/XM0182/j/**E**]

♦ Nordic Institute of Navigation 17323

Institut nordic de navigation – Nordisk Navigasjonsforum (NNF)

Contact address not obtained. E-mail: heidi.kuusniemi@uva.fi – borje.forssell@ntnu.no.
URL: http://www.nornav.org/
History 1983, Oslo (Norway). **Aims** Represent navigational interests in the Nordic states. **Structure** General Assembly. Board, comprising President, Secretary General, 6 members and 2 alternates. **Languages** English. **Staff** 1.00 FTE, paid. **Finance** Members' dues. Conference fees. Budget (annual) Norwegian Kr 300,000. **Activities** Up till 2008, organized international biannual conferences in the Nordic countries. **Events** *AVIGEN : international symposium on navigation in general aviation* 2004, *NORNA : Nordic conference on radionavigation* 2003, *AVIGEN : international symposium on navigation in general aviation* Bonn (Germany) 2003, *Conference on polar navigation and trafficability in Arctic and Baltic ice* Longyearbyen (Norway) 2003, *European Navigation Conference on Global Navigation Satellite Systems (GNSS-ENC)* Copenhagen (Denmark) 2002. **Publications** *European Journal of Navigation (EJN)* (3 a year) – in cooperation with Dutch, German, Polish, Portuguese and Swiss navigation institutes.
Members Individual and corporate members in 6 countries and territories:
Denmark, Faeroe Is, Finland, Iceland, Norway, Sweden.
NGO Relations Member of: *European Group of the Institutes of Navigation (EUGIN, #07424)*; *International Association of Institutes of Navigation (IAIN, #11965)*. [2019/XE3900/j/**E**]

- ♦ Nordic Institute for Studies in Innovation, Research and Education (internationally oriented national body)
- ♦ Nordic Institute for Theoretical Atomic Physics / see Nordic Institute for Theoretical Physics (#17324)

♦ Nordic Institute for Theoretical Physics (NORDITA) 17324

Institut nordique pour la physique théorique – Nordiska Institutet för Teoretisk Fysik – Nordisk Institut for Teoretisk Fysik – Nordisk Instituet for Teoretisk Fysikk – Pohjoismainen Teoreettisen Fysiikan Laitos – Norraena Stofnunin i Kennilegri Edlisfraedi

Dir AlbaNova University Centre, Nordita, Hannes Alfvéns väg 12, SE-106 91 Stockholm, Sweden. T. +46855378473. E-mail: info@nordita.org.
URL: http://www.nordita.org/
History 1 Oct 1957. Founded under the ownership of *Nordic Council of Ministers (NCM, #17260)* and located at jointly sponsored by the Governments of the 5 Niels Bohr Institute, University of Copenhagen (Denmark). Since Jan 2007, hosted jointly by KTH Royal Institute of Technology and Stockholm University. Former names and other names: *Nordic Institute for Theoretical Atomic Physics* – former (1 Oct 1957). **Aims** Carry out research and strengthen Nordic collaboration within the basic areas of theoretical physics. **Structure** Board. **Languages** English, Swedish. **Staff** 50.00 FTE, paid. **Finance** Supported by: KTH Royal Institute of Technology; *Nordic Council of Ministers (NCM, #17260)*; Swedish Research Council; Stockholm University; Uppsala University. Grants from *European Commission (EC, #06633)* and other sources support additional junior faculty and postdoctoral fellows. Annual budget: 26,000,000 SEK. **Activities** Events/meetings; research/documentation; training/education. **Events** *Nordic Network Meeting on Strings, Field and Branes* Stockholm (Sweden) 2021, *Nordic Workshop on Statistical Physics* Stockholm (Sweden) 2021, *Joint Meeting on Quantum Matter* Pohang (Korea Rep) 2020, *Nordic Network Meeting on Strings, Field and Branes* Stockholm (Sweden) 2020, *Quantum Connections Workshop* Stockholm (Sweden) 2020. **Publications** Preprint series.
Members Governments of 5 Nordic countries:
Denmark, Finland, Iceland, Norway, Sweden.
NGO Relations Member of (1): *European Physical Society (EPS, #08207)*. [2022.10.11/XD4457/j/**F***]

- ♦ Nordic Institute for Women's Studies and Gender Research / see Nordic Information for Gender Knowledge (#17317)
- ♦ Nordic Institution for Energy Research / see Nordic Energy Research (#17278)

♦ Nordic Insulation Symposium on Materials, Components and Diagnostics (meeting series)
♦ Nordic Insurance Employees Union (inactive)

♦ Nordic International Studies Association (NISA) 17325

Pres c/o NUPI, Postboks 7024, St Olavs Plass, 0130 Oslo, Norway. T. +4791848675. E-mail: ng@nupi.no.
Editor Dept of Political Science, Lund Univ, Box 52, SE-221 00 Lund, Sweden.
URL: http://www.sagepub.net/nisa/

History 27 Oct 1991, Kastrup (Denmark), at constituting conference. Inaugural conference: 18-19 Aug 1993, Oslo (Norway). **Aims** Stimulate research, advanced study and contact among academics and practitioners in the field of international studies in the Nordic countries; encourage the advancement of knowledge across disciplinary boundaries, analytical approaches, institutions and nations; promote links with research communities in other parts of the world. **Structure** Executive Committee. **Languages** Danish, English, Faroese, Icelandic, Norwegian, Swedish. **Finance** Members' dues: pounds 30/US$ 45 (full); pounds 15/US$ 23 (student). **Activities** Events/meetings; training/education; liaising/networking. **Events** *Power, vision, and order in world politics* Odense (Denmark) 2007, *CEEISA convention / Convention* Moscow (Russia) 2002, *International convention* Hong Kong (Hong Kong) 2001, *Triennial conference / Conference* Uppsala (Sweden) 1999, *Triennial conference / Conference* Helsinki (Finland) 1996. **Publications** *Cooperation and Conflict* – official journal from 27th vol.
Members Nordic scholars and foreign scholars working on Nordic issues in 9 countries:
Denmark, Estonia, Finland, Germany, Iceland, Norway, Sweden, UK, USA. [2019/XD3284/v/**D**]

♦ Nordic Inter-Parliamentary Union (inactive)

♦ Nordic Interprofessional Network (NIPNET) 17326

Head of Office c/o Gentofte Hosp, Kildegårdsvej 28, opgang 65 2 sal, 2900 Hellerup, Denmark. T. +4538669999.
Contact c/o Linköping Univ, SE-581 83 Linköping, Sweden. T. +4613286876.
URL: http://www.nipnet.org/

History 24 Aug 2001, Ålesund (Norway). **Aims** Promote interprofessional collaboration in healthcare and health and social services; promote interprofessional education as learning models to develop collaborative competences among health and social care services. **Structure** Board; Executive Group. **Events** *Conference* Reykjavik (Iceland) 2022, *Looking into the future in digitalized healthcare* Oulu (Finland) 2019, *Conference* Os (Norway) 2017, *Conference* Kolding (Denmark) 2015, *Conference* Stockholm (Sweden) 2014. **Publications** *NIPNET Newsletter.* **Members** Membership countries not specified. **NGO Relations** Member of: *Global Confederation for Interprofessional Education and Collaborative Practice (#10305).* [2020.04.29/XF7026/**F**]

♦ Nordic Invasive Cardiology Conference (meeting series)

♦ Nordic Investment Bank (NIB) 17327

Nordiska Investeringsbanken (NIB) – Den Nordiske Investeringsbank – Põhjamaade Investeerimispank – Pohjoismaiden Investointipankki – Norraeni Fjarfestingarbankinn – Ziemelu Investiciju Banka – Siaures Investiciju Bankas
Pres/CEO Fabianinkatu 34, PO Box 249, FI-00171 Helsinki, Finland. T. +35810618001. Fax +358106180723. E-mail: info@nib.int.
URL: http://www.nib.int/

History 1 Jun 1976, following signature of an international treaty, 4 Dec 1975, by the governments of Denmark, Finland, Iceland, Norway, and Sweden. Operations began in Aug 1976. Estonia, Latvia and Lithuania became members of NIB in the beginning of 2005. **Aims** Finance projects that improve productivity and benefit the environment of the Nordic and Baltic countries. **Structure** Board of Governors; Board of Directors; Control Committee of 10 members, with one member from each member country appointed by the *Nordic Council of Ministers (NCM, #17260)* and the Parliaments of Estonia, Latvia and Lithuania, respectively, and one Chairman and one Deputy Chairman, appointed by the Board of Governors. Management Committee; Departments (6); Headquarters in Helsinki (Finland). **Languages** English. **Staff** 190.00 FTE, paid. **Finance** Authorized capital stock of the Bank is subscribed by the member countries, any increase being decided upon by Bank's Board of Governors. NIB's accounts are kept in euro. Authorized capital (paid-in capital and callable capital): about euro 6,142,000. Member countries have subscribed to the authorized capital in proportion to their gross national income. Shares of capital stock are related to the GNI of member countries. About 6.82% of the subscribed authorized capital stock is paid in. Remainder of the authorized capital consists of callable capital which is subject to call if the Board of Directors deems it necessary. Total assets as of Dec 2012: euro 25,983,000. **Activities** Financial and/or material support. **Events** *Meeting* Oslo (Norway) 2012, *Annual meeting* Helsinki (Finland) 1998, *Meeting* Oslo (Norway) 1998, *Annual meeting* Helsinki (Finland) 1997, *Annual meeting* Helsinki (Finland) 1996. **Publications** *NIB Newsletter.* Annual Report; Activity Report; Environmental Bond Report; Financial Report; reports; brochures; animations; videos.
Members Governments of 8 countries:
Denmark, Estonia, Finland, Iceland, Latvia, Lithuania, Norway, Sweden.
IGO Relations Extensive cooperation with: *European Investment Bank (EIB, #07599).* Has extended loans to the following multilateral financial institutions: *Central American Bank for Economic Integration (CABEI, #03658); Development Bank of Latin America (CAF, #05055).* Forms the *Nordic Finance Group (#17290)* together with *Nordic Environment Finance Corporation (NEFCO, #17281)* and *Nordic Development Fund (NDF, #17271),* which are all three owned by the Nordic countries. Observer to: *Black Sea Trade and Development Bank (BSTDB, #03278); Joint Ministerial Committee of the Boards of Governors of the Bank and the Fund on the Transfer of Real Resources to Developing Countries (Development Committee, #16141).*
[2018.09.05/XF5791/**F***]

♦ Nordic Irish Studies Network (NISN) 17328

Communications Officer address not obtained.
URL: http://www.nordicirishstudies.org/

History 1998. **Aims** Promote and encourage the study, teaching and reporting in the Nordic countries of all aspects relating to the society and culture of the Republic of Ireland, Northern Ireland and the Irish diaspora. **Structure** General Meeting (every 2 years). Executive Committee. **Languages** English. **Staff** One. **Activities** Organizes conferences, seminars and symposia. **Events** *Conference* Turku (Finland) 2021, *Conference* Kristiansand (Norway) 2018, *Conference* Oulu (Finland) 2016, *Conference* Aalborg (Denmark) 2014, *Conference* Falun (Sweden) 2012. **Publications** *Nordic Irish Studies* – journal.
Members Individuals in 7 countries:
Denmark, Finland, Germany, Iceland, Ireland, Norway, Sweden. [2010.08.09/XD8842/**D**]

♦ Nordic ITMF Interest Group 17329

Dir Tekstiili-ja vaatetusteollisuus ry, Eteläranta 10, FI-00130 Helsinki, Finland. T. +358108301400. Fax +3589653305.
URL: http://www.finatex.fi/ [2009.08.14/XD7467/**D**]

♦ Nordic IVF Laboratory Society (NILS) 17330

Chair address not obtained.
URL: http://www.nilsivf.com/

History 1990. Current bylaws adopted Aug 2013. **Aims** Serve as a platform for Nordic laboratory professionals within the field of reproductive medicine. **Structure** Annual General Meeting; Board. **Languages** English. **Finance** Sources: members' dues. **Activities** Events/meetings. **Events** *Meeting* Finland 2021, *Meeting* Oslo (Norway) 2018.
Members Full in 4 countries:
Denmark, Finland, Norway, Sweden. [2020.06.24/XM8041/**D**]

♦ Nordic Joint Advisory Group on Refugee Policy 17331

Nordisk Samrådsgruppepåhøjt Niveau for Flygtningespørgsmål (NSHF) – Pakolaiskysymysten Pohjoismainen Neuvotteluryhmä
Contact address not obtained. T. +4533923656. Fax +4533955845. E-mail: hka@uibm.dk.

History Nov 1986. Originally also referred to in Danish as *Nordisk Samrådsgruppe for Flygtningespørgsmål (NSHF).* **Aims** Provide a forum for regular exchange of information on national and international developments as regards *asylum* and refugee issues; harmonize policy and practice of discussed refugee issues. **Structure** Political appointed Secretaries of State or high level Government Officials under the ministers responsible for immigration matters and Officials from relevant ministries. Group is chaired by member countries on an annual rotation basis and meets 3 to 4 times a year. Working groups. No permanent secretariat. **Languages** Danish, Norwegian, Swedish. **Activities** Politics/policy/regulatory; events/meetings.
Members Representatives of the 8 Nordic countries and territories:
Åland, Denmark, Faeroe Is, Finland, Greenland, Iceland, Norway, Sweden.
IGO Relations Cooperation body of *Nordic Council of Ministers (NCM, #17260).* [2011.08.24/XE1532/**E***]

♦ Nordic Joint Committee for Agricultural and Food Research 17332

Nordisk Kommitté för Jordbruks- och Matforskning (NKJ)
Contact c/o SLU, Forest Research Centre, Box 190, SE-234 22 Lomma, Sweden. E-mail: nkj@slu.se.
URL: https://nordicagriresearch.org/

History 1965, by agreement between Agricultural Research Councils in the Nordic countries. Restructured, 1987, in cooperation with *Nordic Council of Ministers (NCM, #17260).* Originally known as *Nordic Joint Committee for Agricultural Research – Institution nordique pour la coordination de la recherche agricole – Nordisk Kontaktorgan for Jordbrugsforskning (NKJ) – Maataloustutkimuksen Pohjoismainen Kontaktielin.* Also known in English as *Nordic Contact Agency for Agricultural Research* and as *Scandinavian Contact Agency for Agricultural Research.* **Aims** Promote and support cooperation on agricultural research between national research councils, or corresponding organizations. **Structure** Committee (meets at east twice a year) comprises representatives of relevant government ministries, research councils and advisory committees in the Nordic countries. Chairmanship and Secretariat rotate among member countries. **Languages** Danish, Norwegian, Swedish. **Staff** 0.50 FTE, paid. **Finance** Members' dues. Grants from national research councils and Nordic Council of Ministers (NMR). **Activities** Advises NMR on questions of research policy; submits recommendations to individual research councils on grant applications for projects accepted by the Agency; project groups carry out investigations; organizes meetings and seminars (closed). **Publications** *The Nordic Joint Commitee for Agricultural Research (NKJ) Strategy 2004 – 2006.* Annual report.
Members Government ministries and agricultural institutions in 5 countries:
Denmark, Finland, Iceland, Norway, Sweden.
NGO Relations Supports: *Nordisk Komité for Veterinaervitenskapelig Samarbeid (NKVet, #17519).*
[2021/XD5557/**E***]

♦ Nordic Joint Committee for Agricultural Research / see Nordic Joint Committee for Agricultural and Food Research (#17332)
♦ Nordic Joint Committee for the Boat Industry (inactive)
♦ Nordic Joint Committee of Commercial and Office Executives (inactive)
♦ Nordic Joint Committee of Forestry Technicians (inactive)
♦ Nordic Joint Committee for the Glass Industry (inactive)
♦ Nordic Joint Committee for Kidney Patients (inactive)
♦ Nordic Joint Committee for the Precious Metal Trade (inactive)
♦ Nordic Joint Group for Forest Nursery Questions (inactive)
♦ Nordic Joint Group for Forest Production Research (inactive)
♦ Nordic Joint Organization of Mental Hospital Personnel (inactive)
♦ Nordic Journalist Centre (#17516)
♦ Nordic Judo Union (inactive)

♦ Nordic Laboratory for Luminescence Dating 17333

Nordisk Laboratorium for Luminescensdatering (NLL)
Lab Dir Dept of Earth Sciences, Aarhus Univ – Risø DTU, 4000 Røskilde, Denmark. T. +4546775979. Fax +4546774959.

History 1979, as *Nordic Laboratory for Thermoluminescence Dating.* Became, 1989, a section of the Department of Earth Sciences of Århus University (Denmark). Also referred to as *Nordic Thermoluminescence Laboratory.* **Aims** Provide a luminescence-based dating service to *archaeologists* and *geologists,* primarily from Scandinavian countries and conduct fundamental research into luminescence dating principles and techniques. **Languages** Danish, English. **Staff** 5.00 FTE, paid. **Finance** Direct university funding; income from dating services. **Activities** Dates: glacial sediments from northern Russia and Scandinavia; aeolian sediments from Denmark, UK and Central Europe; fluvial sediments from Netherlands and Italy; colluvium from Hong Kong, Tunisia, Tanzania and Zimbabwe; archaeological material (mainly ceramics) from Scandinavia, Latin America and Tanzania. Organizes annual training courses. **Publications** Articles. [2011/XF1535/**F**]

♦ Nordic Laboratory for Thermoluminescence Dating / see Nordic Laboratory for Luminescence Dating (#17333)
♦ Nordic Labour Market Committee (inactive)
♦ Nordic Language Convention (1981 treaty)
♦ Nordic Language Council (inactive)
♦ Nordic-Latin American Association for Popular Education (no recent information)

♦ Nordic Latin American Research Network (NOLAN) 17334

Contact c/o NILAS, Stockholms universitet, Universitetsvägen 10 B, SE-106 91 Stockholm, Sweden. E-mail: info@lai.su.se.
URL: https://www.lai.su.se/research/nolan

History Former names and other names: *Nordic Network for Latin American and Caribbean Studies* – former. **Aims** Organize the biennial NOLAN conference. **Events** *CEISAL International Conference* Helsinki (Finland) 2022, *Latin American challenges in the 21st century – societies in motion* Gothenburg (Sweden) 2017, *Struggles over resources in Latin America* Helsinki (Finland) 2015, *Conference* Oslo (Norway) 2013, *Conference* Stockholm (Sweden) 2012. [2022/XM1178/**E**]

♦ Nordic Lawyers Academy 17335

Address not obtained.
URL: http://www.nordiclawyersacademy.com/

Events *Conference* Stockholm (Sweden) 2010, *Conference* Oslo (Norway) 2007, *Conference on business ethics* Copenhagen (Denmark) 2006.
Members National societies in 5 countries:
Denmark, Finland, Iceland, Norway, Sweden. [2011.09.14/XM2608/**E**]

♦ Nordic Leather Chemists Society (inactive)
♦ Nordic Liaison Committee for Atomic Energy (inactive)
♦ Nordic Liberal and Radical Youth (no recent information)

♦ Nordic Lichen Society 17336

Nordisk Lichenologisk Förening (NLF) – Nordisk Lichenologisk Forening
Sec Natural History Museum, Univ of Tartu, 40 Lai str, 51005 Tartu, Estonia.
URL: http://nhm2.uio.no/lichens/nordiclichensociety/

History 1975. **Aims** Work for increased interest in lichenology in the Nordic countries. **Structure** Board, comprising President, Vice-President, Secretary, Treasurer and 2 members-at-large. **Languages** Danish, English, Norwegian, Swedish. **Finance** Members' dues. **Activities** Biennial excursion and meeting. **Events** *Meeting* Lammi (Finland) 2007. **Publications** *Graphis Scripta* (2 a year) – journal. **Members** Individuals in 23 countries. Membership countries not specified. [2015/XD6901/**D**]

♦ Nordic Life Cycle Association (NorLCA) 17337

Secretariat LCA Center Denmark, DTU – Bldg 424, 2800 Kongens Lyngby, Denmark. T. +4539555955. Fax +4539933435.
URL: http://www.norlca.org/

History 30 Nov 2004. **Aims** Further use and, when needed, development and improvement of the life cycle disciplines. **Structure** General Meeting (annual). Board. **Languages** English. **Finance** Members' dues. **Events** *Symposium* Copenhagen (Denmark) 2012.
Members Full in 5 countries:
Denmark, Finland, Iceland, Norway, Sweden.
NGO Relations *Life Cycle Initiative (LCI, #16464).* [2014/XJ7337/**D**]

♦ **Nordic Lipidforum** Nordic Forum for Lipid Research and Technology (#17299)

♦ Nordic Logistics Association (NLA) 17338

Main Office Rue d'Arlon 55, 1040 Brussels, Belgium. E-mail: assistant1@nla.eu.
URL: http://nla.eu/

History 2012. **Aims** Act as a joint lobby-organisation for land *transport* in Brussels. **Structure** Board. **Activities** Advocacy/lobbying/activism. **Events** *Annual Meeting* Malmö (Sweden) 2021, *Annual Meeting* Copenhagen (Denmark) 2020, *Transport and Logistics Conference* Oslo (Norway) 2014. **Publications** *NLA Newsletter*.
Members Full in 3 countries:
Denmark, Norway, Sweden.
Associate in 1 country:
Finland.
IGO Relations *European Commission (EC, #06633)* – DG MOVE; *European Parliament (EP, #08146)* – Transport and Tourism Committee. **NGO Relations** Member of: *European Logistics Platform (ELP, #07711).*
[2021/XM6877/**D**]

♦ Nordic Logistics Research Network (NOFOMA) 17339

Nordisk forskning om Materialadministration (NOFOMA)
Contact address not obtained. E-mail: admin@nofoma.net.
URL: http://nofoma.net/

History 1989. **Aims** Contribute to the continuous improvement and further development of Nordic logistics research and researchers. **Activities** Organizes: Annual Conference; Nordlog Doctoral Symposium; Educators Conference; Joint-Nordic PhD Program in Logistics. **Events** *Conference* Reykjavik (Iceland) 2022, *Conference* 2021, *Conference* 2020, *Conference* Oslo (Norway) 2019, *Conference* Kolding (Denmark) 2018.
Members Researchers in 5 countries:
Denmark, Finland, Iceland, Norway, Sweden. [2018/XJ2839/**D**]

♦ Nordic Lung Congress (meeting series)
♦ Nordic Lymphology Congress (meeting series)

♦ Nordic Lymphoma Group 17340

Chairman address not obtained.
URL: http://www.nordic-lymphoma.org/

History 1987, Oslo (Norway). **Aims** Promote research into treatment, biology and epidemiology of lymphomas in the Nordic countries. **Structure** Plenary Meeting (open to members and cooperating companies); Coordinating Group; Working Groups. **Languages** English. **Staff** None. **Finance** Members' dues. Funding from pharmaceutical industry. Annual budget: euro 120,000. **Activities** Research/documentation. **Events** *Meeting* Copenhagen (Denmark) 2021, *Plenary* Stockholm (Sweden) 2014. **Publications** Clinical trials; biological studies.
Members Groups in 4 countries:
Denmark, Finland, Norway, Sweden. [2014.06.18/XD8444/**D**]

♦ Nordic Management Board (inactive)

♦ Nordic Marcé Society 17341

Sec address not obtained. E-mail: nordic.marce@gmail.com.
URL: http://nordicmarce.org/

Aims Increase the focus on research on all aspects of the mental health of women, their children and partners during childbirth. **Structure** Board. **Events** *Nordic Conference* Uppsala (Sweden) 2023, *Nordic Conference* Oslo (Norway) 2021, *Nordic Conference* Stockholm (Sweden) 2019, *Nordic Conference* Stockholm (Sweden) 2017, *Nordic Conference* Oslo (Norway) 2015. [2022/AA0762/**F**]

♦ Nordic Master Painters' Organization (inactive)
♦ Nordic Meat Industry Union (inactive)
♦ Nordic Media Days (unconfirmed)
♦ Nordic Medical Council (unconfirmed)
♦ Nordic Medical Society of Paraplegia / see Nordic Spinal Cord Society (#17436)

♦ Nordic Medico-Statistical Committee (NOMESCO) 17342

Nordisk Medicinalstatistisk Kommité (NOMESKO) – Pohjoismaiden Lääkintätilastokomitea
Secretariat Satens inst for folkesundhed, Studiestraede 6, 1455 Copenhagen K, Denmark. T. +4565507835. E-mail: nom-nos@si-folkesundhed.dk.
URL: http://nowbase.org/

History 1966, Helsinki (Finland), on the initiative of *Nordic Council (NC, #17256)*. Became a permanent body under the *Nordic Council of Ministers (NCM, #17260)* in 1978. Since 1980 a Secretariat for the Committee has been set up in Copenhagen (Denmark). **Aims** Establish comparable health statistics in Nordic countries; initiate developmental and experimental activities of relevance to the field of health statistics; keep surveillance on developments within health statistics at international level. **Structure** Plenary Session (annual); Chairmanship; Working Groups. **Languages** Danish, English, Norwegian, Swedish. **Staff** 2.00 FTE, paid. **Finance** Annual budget allocated by the Nordic Council of Ministers. **Activities** Networking/liaising. **Events** *Annual General Assembly* Oslo (Norway) 2011, *Annual General Assembly* Borgholm (Sweden) 2008, *Annual General Assembly* Sweden 2008, *Annual General Assembly* Espoo (Finland) 2007, *Annual General Assembly* Finland 2007. **Publications** *Health Statistics in the Nordic Countries* (annual).
Members Representatives appointed by the Governments of Nordic countries. Official (15) and Supplementary (6) members in 5 countries:
Denmark, Finland, Iceland, Norway, Sweden. [2020.01.09/XE8054/**E***]

♦ Nordic Meeting on Development, Stem Cells and Regeneration (meeting series)
♦ Nordic Meeting on Intermediate Energy Physics (meeting series)
♦ Nordic Meeting on Medical and Biological Engineering (meeting series)
♦ Nordic Meeting in Neuropsychology (meeting series)
♦ Nordic Meeting on Nuclear Physics (meeting series)
♦ Nordic Melanoma Meeting (meeting series)
♦ Nordic Memory Clinic Conference (meeting series)
♦ Nordic Menopause Society (no recent information)

♦ Nordic Metabolomics Society 17343

Sec address not obtained. E-mail: normetsoc@gmail.com.
URL: http://www.nordicmetsoc.org/

History 2017. Registration: No/ID: 802516-1087, Start date: May 2018, Sweden. **Aims** Promote the development of metabolomics in the Nordic region. **Structure** Board. **Activities** Events/meetings; training/education. **Events** *Nordic Metabolomics Conference* Trondheim (Norway) 2023, *Nordic Metabolomics Conference* Copenhagen (Denmark) 2022, *Nordic Metabolomics Conference* Trondheim (Norway) 2021, *Nordic Metabolomics Conference* Örebro (Sweden) 2018. **NGO Relations** Affiliated with (1): *Metabolomics Society (MetSoc, #16734).* [2021/AA0705/**D**]

♦ Nordic Metal (inactive)
♦ Nordic Meteorological Meeting (meeting series)

♦ Nordic Microscopy Society (SCANDEM) 17344

SG Univ of Jyväskylä, Dept of Biological and Environmental Science, Ambiotica C2, Ambiotica C2, FI-40500 Jyväskylä, Finland. T. +358405634422. Fax +358402602271. E-mail: secretart@scandem.org.
Events Manager address not obtained.
URL: http://www.scandem.org/

History 16 Oct 1948, Stockholm (Sweden). Former names and other names: *Scandinavian Society for Electron Microscopy (SCANDEM)* – former; *Skandinaviska Föreningen för Elektronmikroskopi* – former. **Aims** Provide an interdisciplinary forum for the presentation of papers, discussions and general exchange of knowledge on the field; collaborate with other societies at international level. **Structure** Annual Meeting, including General Assembly and Scientific Meeting; Board. **Languages** English. **Staff** Voluntary. **Finance** Sources: members' dues. **Activities** Events/meetings; training/education. **Events** *Annual Meeting* Tampere (Finland) 2022, *Annual Meeting* Oslo (Norway) 2021, *Early Career European Microscopy Congress* 2020, *Annual Meeting* Gothenburg (Sweden) 2019, *Annual Meeting* Lyngby (Denmark) 2018. **Publications** *The Growth of Electron Microscopy* (1996); *SCANDEM Circular Letter*.
Members Full (over 300), including 7 company members and 5 honorary. Members in 15 countries:
Australia, Austria, Czechia, Denmark, Estonia, Finland, France, Germany, Italy, Mexico, Netherlands, Norway, Sweden, UK, USA.
NGO Relations Affiliated with (2): *European Microscopy Society (EMS, #07795)*; *International Federation of Societies for Microscopy (IFSM, #13550).* [2021/XD6028/**D**]

♦ Nordic Midwives Association (NMA) 17345

Nordisk Jordmorforbund (NJF)
Pres Danish Midwives Assn, Jordemoderforeningen Sankt Annae Plads 30, 1250 Copenhagen K, Denmark. T. +4546953400 – +4523439433. E-mail: sek@jordemoderforeningen.dk.
Contact c/o Ljósmaedrafélag Islands, Borgartúni 6, 105 Reykjavik, Iceland. Fax +3545889239.

History 1950. **Aims** Exchange experience and raise the general standard of work in the profession; spread information on members' research through journals of member countries thereby stimulating more midwives to do research. **Structure** Board; President. **Languages** Danish, English, Faroese, Finnish, Icelandic, Norwegian, Swedish. **Staff** 0.50 FTE, voluntary. **Finance** National associations cover costs of its representatives. Additional mutual costs are shared by associations. **Activities** Events/meetings; networking/liaising. **Events** *Congress* Reykjavik (Iceland) 2019, *Midwives4ll* Gothenburg (Sweden) 2016, *Congress* Oslo (Norway) 2013, *Practice and science* Copenhagen (Denmark) 2010, *Congress* Turku (Finland) 2007. **Publications** Statements.
Members Individuals (over 11,000) in 6 countries and territories:
Denmark, Faeroe Is, Finland, Iceland, Norway, Sweden. [2021.02.17/XD1300/v/**D**]

♦ Nordic Migration Research (NMR) 17346

Chair c/o The Migration Institute of Finland, Hämeenkatu 13, FI-20500 Turku, Finland. E-mail: nordicmigrationresearch@gmail.com.
URL: http://nordicmigrationresearch.com/

History Nov 2007, Bergen (Norway). Developed out of the Nordic Migration Research Network, having been in existence since 1980s. **Aims** Stimulate and promote comparative Nordic scientific research on migration and ethnic relations. **Structure** General Assembly; Board; Secretariat. **Activities** Awareness raising; events/meetings; guidance/assistance/consulting; networking/liaising; research/documentation. **Events** *Nordic Migration Research Conference* Copenhagen (Denmark) 2022, *Nordic Migration Research Conference* Helsinki (Finland) 2021, *Nordic Migration Research Conference* Helsinki (Finland) 2020, *Nordic Migration Research Conference* Linköping (Sweden) 2018, *Nordic Migration Research Conference* Oslo (Norway) 2016. **Publications** *Nordic Journal of Migration Research (NJMR).*
Members Institutional; Individual. Members in 4 countries:
Denmark, Finland, Norway, Sweden. [2022.02.15/AA1695/**D**]

♦ Nordic Ministerial Committee for Coordination of Development Assistance (inactive)
♦ Nordic Molecular Biology Association (no recent information)
♦ Nordic Montessori Conference (meeting series)
♦ Nordic Multiple Sclerosis Council (no recent information)
♦ Nordic Music Committee (inactive)
♦ Nordic Music Education Union (inactive)
♦ Nordic Musicians' Union (no recent information)
♦ Nordic Music Publishers' Union (no recent information)
♦ Nordic Music Therapy Conference (meeting series)
♦ Nordic Mutual Emergency Assistance Agreement in Connection with Radiation Accidents (1973 treaty)
♦ Nordic Mycological Congress (meeting series)

♦ Nordic Myeloma Study Group (NMSG) 17347

Pres Dept of Medicine, Huddinge MedH H7, Unit for Hematology M54, Karolinska Universitetssjukhuset, SE-141 86 Stockholm, Sweden. T. +468735166648.
URL: http://www.nordic-myeloma.org/

History 1988. **Aims** Evaluate new therapies for patients with *myeloma*; study the mechanisms behind and the manifestations of the disease; promote the knowledge of the clinical course and the therapeutic alternatives available for patients with multiple myeloma and their relatives. **Structure** Steering Committee, comprising 2 members each from Norway, Sweden and Denmark, in addition to 15 regional coordinators. **Languages** Danish, Finnish, Icelandic, Norwegian, Swedish. **Staff** Voluntary. **Finance** Research organizations in Norway, Sweden and Denmark. Annual budget: euro 700,000. Every clinical study has separate budget of about euro 1,000,000. **Activities** Runs clinical studies; makes guidelines for the treatment of multiple myeloma. **Events** *Plenary Spring Meeting* Copenhagen (Denmark) 2022, *Plenary Spring Meeting* Copenhagen (Denmark) 2021, *Plenary Autumn Meeting* Stockholm (Sweden) 2021, *Plenary Spring Meeting* Copenhagen (Denmark) 2020, *Plenary Autumn Meeting* Stockholm (Sweden) 2020. **Publications** Studies.
Members Individuals (physicians) in 3 countries:
Denmark, Norway, Sweden. [2017/XF6855/**F**]

♦ Nordic Narcolepsy Symposium (meeting series)
♦ Nordic Narrow /16mm/ Film Society (inactive)
♦ Nordic Natural Horsemanship Association (inactive)
♦ **NORDIC NECT** Nordic Network for Early Cancer Trials (#17353)
♦ Nordic Neonatal Meeting (meeting series)

♦ Nordic Network 17348

Nordiska Nätverk – Nordiske Netvaerk – Nordiske Nettverk – Tietoa Meistä – Norraen Tengslanet – Nordurlendskt Kervi
Contact c/o FNF, Snaregade 10A – 3, 1205 Copenhagen K, Denmark. T. +4553693066.
URL: http://nordiskenet.org/

Aims Create a dynamic project, joining *civil society* with official Nordic *cooperative* bodies. **Structure** Managed by: *Föreningarna Nordens Förbund (FNF, #09859).* [2016/XM5299/**F**]

♦ Nordic Network for Adult Learning 17349

Nordiskt Nätverk för Vuxnas Lärande (NVL)
Head Coordinator VIA University College, Hedeager 2, 8200 Aarhus, Denmark. T. +4587551808. E-mail: antr@via.dk.
URL: https://nvl.org/om-nvl/in-english

History 2005. Set up as a Network within Nordic Council of Ministers for Educational and Research Issues (MR-U) of *Nordic Council of Ministers (NCM, #17260).* **Aims** Support Nordic cooperation in a LLL perspective; facilitate exchange of experience and innovations in adult learning; support development of policy and practice; disseminate Nordic expertise within priority areas like adult education competence development, validation of prior learning, digital support to learning, workplace learning, etc; support networking among adult education stakeholders. **Structure** Core Team (national coordinators, information officer, administrative staff); Thematic and Expert Networks (8-10). **Languages** Danish, English, Finnish, Icelandic, Norwegian, Swedish. **Staff** 6.50 FTE, paid. **Finance** Supported by: *Nordic Council of Ministers (NCM, #17260).* **Activities** Events/meetings; networking/liaising; training/education. Active in: Åland, Denmark, Faeroe Is, Finland, Greenland, Iceland, Norway, Sweden. **Events** *Validation of Prior Learning (VPL)* Reykjavik (Iceland) 2022, *Online and Blended Learning for Professionals/Adult Learners* Aarhus (Denmark) 2021, *Nordic Conference on Adult Learning and Sustainable Development* Aarhus (Denmark) 2020, *Nordic Conference on Adult Education and Learning* Copenhagen (Denmark) 2019, *Nordic Innovation Conference* Bergen (Norway) 2017. **Publications** *DialogWeb* (weekly) – online articles; *NVL Newsletter* (11 a year). **Members** Not a membership organization. **NGO Relations** Member of (1): *European Basic Skills Network (EBSN, #06321).*
[2022.10.21/XJ2417/**E**]

♦ Nordic Network for Communicating Animal Welfare (NordCAW) ... 17350

Manager c/o SCAW – Swedish Univ of Agricultural Sciences, SE-750 07 Uppsala, Sweden. T. +4618672251.
URL: http://www.slu.se/en/Collaborative-Centres-and-Projects/swedish- centre-for-animal-welfare-scaw/nordcaw/

History EU Transparency Register: 309768926142-64. **Aims** Facilitate communication regarding animal welfare between science, authorities, primary producers and a wider public in the Nordic countries. **Activities** Events/meetings. **Events** *260* Copenhagen (Denmark) 2017, *Seminar* Uppsala (Sweden) 2016, *Seminar* Uppsala (Sweden) 2015.
Members Full in 9 countries and territories:
Denmark, Estonia, Faeroe Is, Finland, Iceland, Latvia, Lithuania, Norway, Sweden. [2017/XM6270/**F**]

♦ Nordic Network in Development Economics (unconfirmed)

♦ Nordic Network on Disability Research (NNDR) 17351

Pres c/o NTNU, Postboks 191, 2802 Gjøvik, Norway.
URL: http://nndr.org/

History 16 Aug 1997, Frederikshavn (Denmark). **Aims** Promote and advance research and development in the field of disability in the Nordic countries. **Structure** Board of 7 members. **Finance** Members' dues; subscriptions. **Events** *NNDR Research Conference* Reykjavik (Iceland) 2023, *NNDR Research Conference* Reykjavik (Iceland) 2022, *NNDR Research Conference* Reykjavik (Iceland) 2021, *NNDR Research Conference* Copenhagen (Denmark) 2019, *NNDR Research Conference* Örebro (Sweden) 2017. **Publications** *Scandinavian Journal of Disability Research.*
Members in 5 countries:
Denmark, Finland, Iceland, Norway, Sweden. [2020/XF6753/**F**]

♦ Nordic Network for Diversity in Physics (NORNDiP) 17352

Contact address not obtained. E-mail: norndip@gmail.com.
URL: https://norndip.com/

History 2017. Founded with the idea to recreate *Nordic Network for Women in Physics (NorWIP, inactive)* (2006-2010). **Aims** Establish contacts among female physicists in the Nordic countries; increase the visibility of Nordic female physicists; develop contacts with women in physics organizations around the world. **Activities** Events/meetings; training/education. **Events** *NORNDiP 2019* Helsinki (Finland) 2019, *Conference* Stockholm (Sweden) 2018.
Members Female physicists from 4 countries:
Denmark, Finland, Norway, Sweden. [2019/AA0516/v/**F**]

♦ Nordic Network for Early Cancer Trials (NORDIC NECT) 17353

Sec ullernchausseen 64, 0379 Oslo, Norway. T. +4799293273.
Chair Ctr of Cancer Research, Herlev Hosp, 2730 Herlev, Denmark. T. +4538683868.
URL: https://nordicnect.org/

History Mar 2011. **Aims** Promote patient access to new investigational drugs and access to phase I and early phase II programs in the Nordic countries. **Activities** Events/meetings; training/education.
Members Phase I units in 4 countries:
Denmark, Finland, Norway, Sweden.
Associate member in 1 country:
Lithuania. [2020/AA1684/**F**]

♦ Nordic Network of English Speaking Schools / see Nordic Network of International Schools (#17359)

♦ Nordic Network of Fetal Medicine (NNFM) 17354

Address not obtained.
URL: https://www.nnfm.org/

Structure Steering Committee. **Activities** Events/meetings. **Events** *Annual Meeting* Stockholm (Sweden) 2022, *Annual Meeting* Stockholm (Sweden) 2021, *Annual Meeting* Trondheim (Norway) 2019, *Annual Meeting* Reykjavik (Iceland) 2018, *Annual Meeting* Helsinki (Finland) 2017.
Members Experts in 8 countries:
Denmark, Estonia, Finland, Iceland, Latvia, Lithuania, Norway, Sweden. [2020/AA0713/v/**F**]

♦ Nordic Network for Geographic Information (GI Norden) 17355

Nordisk Netvaerk for Geografisk Informasjon

SG c/o LISA Organisation, Árleyni 22, 112 Reykjavik, Iceland. E-mail: lisa@landupplysingar.is.
SG c/o Geoforum, Kalvebod Brygge 31-33, 1780 Copenhagen V, Denmark.
URL: http://ginorden.org/

History 1989. Founded as a regional organizations of AM/FM International – GIS. Restructured Jun 2013, when it became a network. Statutes approved, Apr 2013. Former names and other names: *AM/FM-GIS Nordic Region* – former; *Nordic Association for Geographic Information* – former. **Aims** Promote increased use of Geographic Information (GI) for social benefit; contribute to the utilization of competence and technology within the GI field. **Structure** Board. **Languages** English. **Staff** Voluntary. **Finance** Proceeds from events. Annual budget: less than euro 2,000. **Activities** Events/meetings; training/education; awards/prizes/competitions. **Events** *Conference* Turku (Finland) 2011, *Nordic GIS conference* Aalborg (Denmark) 2002. **Publications** Scientific papers.
Members Organizations in 5 countries:
Denmark, Finland, Iceland, Norway, Sweden. [2022/XJ9055/**F**]

♦ Nordic Network for Health Policy, Health Management, and Health Services Research 17356

Address not obtained.

Activities Events/meetings. **Events** *Workshop* Tampere (Finland) 2021, *Workshop* Helsinki (Finland) 2020, *Workshop* Copenhagen (Denmark) 2019, *Workshop* Copenhagen (Denmark) 2018. [2021/AA1690/**F**]

♦ Nordic Network for ICT, Media and Learning (NNIML) 17357

Address not obtained.

History Aug 2005, during 17th Nordic Conference on Media Studies. **Aims** Create a Nordic platform for research and development in ICT, media and learning. **Publications** *NNIML News.*
Members Individuals in 5 countries:
Denmark, Finland, Iceland, Norway, Sweden. [2007/XM3205/**F**]

♦ Nordic Networking Group of Clinical Pharmacy (NNGCP) 17358

Contact address not obtained.

History Not a registered association, but a networking group. **Aims** Create a platform where clinical pharmacists from all Nordic countries can exchange experiences and discuss challenges from everyday clinical pharmacy practice and research projects. **Events** *Meeting* Tartu (Estonia) 2015, *Meeting* Oslo (Norway) 2014, *Meeting* Gothenburg (Sweden) 2013, *Meeting* Copenhagen (Denmark) 2012, *Meeting* Reykjavik (Iceland) 2011. [2016.06.01/XJ4923/c/**F**]

♦ Nordic Network for Intercultural Communication (internationally oriented national body)

♦ Nordic Network of International Schools 17359

Sec-Treas Postbox 53, 1318 Bekkestua, Norway. T. +4767818290. Fax +4767818290. E-mail: nordicnetworkonline@gmail.com.
URL: http://www.nordicnetworkonline.net/

History 1997. Former names and other names: *Nordic Network of English Speaking Schools* – former (1997). **Aims** Enhance communication and collaboration between participants to ensure best practices in international education. **Structure** Steering Committee. **Languages** Danish, English, Norwegian, Swedish. **Events** *Annual Conference* Riga (Latvia) 2020, *Annual Conference* Copenhagen (Denmark) 2019, *Annual Conference* Gothenburg (Sweden) 2018, *Annual Conference* Oslo (Norway) 2017, *Annual Conference* Stockholm (Sweden) 2016.
Members Schools (6) in 6 countries:
Denmark, Finland, Iceland, Norway, Poland, Sweden. [2020/XJ7104/**F**]

♦ Nordic Network for Latin American and Caribbean Studies / see Nordic Latin American Research Network (#17334)
♦ Nordic Network of Leaders (#16434)

♦ Nordic Network of Narrative Studies 17360

Coordinator Dept of Comparative Literature, Tartu Univ, Ülikooli 18, 50090 Tartu, Estonia. E-mail: marina.grisakova@ut.ee.
URL: http://www.nordicnarratologynet.ut.ee/

History Feb 2007, Tartu (Estonia). **Aims** Establish a Nordic movement in narrative studies by coordinating the work of local projects and adding synergy to already established contacts; contribute to the development of high-standard research, informed by already present scientific knowledge and expertise at different not-yet connected institutions; support research training, organization of international doctoral schools and master classes; further the knowledge and understanding of narrative and inquiry into applicability of narrative studies in different branches of science and society life. **Structure** Steering Committee of 13 members, headed by Coordinator. **Languages** English. **Staff** 1.00 FTE, voluntary. **Finance** Supported by: *NordForsk (#17164).* **Activities** Organizes meetings, workshops, summer schools and conferences. **Events** *International Conference on Narration and Narratives as an Interdisciplinary Field of Study / Conference* Örebro (Sweden) 2012, *International Conference on Teaching Narrative and Teaching Through Narrative* Tampere (Finland) 2011. **Publications** Books.
Members Full in 5 countries:
Denmark, Estonia, Finland, Norway, Sweden.
NGO Relations Cooperates with: *European Narratology Network (ENN, #07853)*; *International Society for the Study of Narrative (ISSN)*; national associations. [2012.03.24/XJ5144/**D**]

♦ Nordic Network for Philosophy of Education / see Nordic Society for Philosophy of Education (#17426)

♦ Nordic Network on Recirculating Aquaculture Systems (NordicRAS) 17361

Organizer Technical Univ of Denmark, Natl Inst of Aquatic Resources, Section for Aquaculture, Nordsien Forskerpark, PO Box 101, 9850 Hirtshals, Denmark. T. +4535883216. E-mail: jtd@aqua.dtu.dk.
URL: http://www.nordicras.net/

History Formally set up Apr 2011, Hirtshals (Denmark). **Aims** Coordinate and strengthen research and development of recirculating aquaculture systems (RAS) in Nordic countries. **Structure** Steering Committee. **Events** *Workshop* Berlin (Germany) 2019, *Workshop* Aalborg (Denmark) 2017, *Workshop* Molde (Norway) 2015, *Workshop* Aalborg (Denmark) 2013, *Workshop* Helsinki (Finland) 2011.
Members Universities and research institutes; Industry; Governmental organizations; Consultancies; NGOs and others. Members in 55 countries:
Argentina, Australia, Bangladesh, Belgium, Brazil, Bulgaria, Cameroon, Canada, Chile, China, Colombia, Croatia, Denmark, Ecuador, Egypt, Estonia, Finland, France, Germany, Ghana, Greece, Iceland, India, Iran Islamic Rep, Iraq, Ireland, Israel, Japan, Kuwait, Malta, Mexico, Mozambique, Netherlands, Nigeria, Norway, Pakistan, Peru, Poland, Portugal, Puerto Rico, Romania, Saudi Arabia, Singapore, Slovenia, South Africa, Spain, Sweden, Thailand, Tunisia, Türkiye, UK, United Arab Emirates, USA, Vietnam, Zambia.
IGO Relations *Nordic Council of Ministers (NCM, #17260).* [2015/XJ9852/**F**]

♦ Nordic Network for Research on Communicative Product Design (Nordcode) 17362

Contact address not obtained.
URL: https://www.nordcode.net/

History 2000. **Aims** Support research based on theoretical approaches and developments within specific fields of design. **Activities** Events/meetings. **Events** *Annual Seminar* Espoo (Finland) 2019.
Members Universities in 4 countries:
Denmark, Finland, Norway, Sweden. [2019/AA0419/**F**]

♦ Nordic Network for Research in Music Education (NNRME) 17363

Nordisk Nettverk for Musikkpedagogikk Forskning (NNMPF)

Chairperson address not obtained.
URL: http://nnmpf.org/

History 1994. **Languages** English. **Events** *Conference* Örebro (Sweden) 2023, *Care and Compassion in Music Education Research* Jyväskylä (Finland) 2022, *Qualities in Music Education Practice and Research* Trondheim (Norway) 2021, *Conference* Copenhagen (Denmark) 2020, *Conference* Stockholm (Sweden) 2019. **Publications** *Nordic research in music education* (annual).
Members Music schools (11) in 4 countries:
Denmark, Finland, Norway, Sweden. [2023.02.13/XF7168/**F**]

♦ Nordic Network in Research on Music and Public Health (unconfirmed)

♦ Nordic Network for research on Psychology and Law (NNPL) 17364

Coordinator Postboks 1094 Blindern, 0317 Oslo, Norway. T. +4722845148.
Street Addres Room S01-23, UiO – Dept of Psychology, Fac of Social Sciences, Forskningsveien 3A, Harald Schjelderups hus, 0373 Oslo, Norway.
URL: http://www.sv.uio.no/psi/english/research/network/nnpl/

History May 2004, Gothenburg (Sweden). **Aims** Stimulate and strengthen research on psychology and law within the Nordic and Baltic region. **Structure** Executive Board. **Activities** Events/meetings; training/education. **Events** *Meeting* Reykjavik (Iceland) 2015, *Meeting* Oslo (Norway) 2014, *Meeting* Aarhus (Denmark) 2013, *Meeting* Oslo (Norway) 2011, *Meeting* Gothenburg (Sweden) 2010. [2015/XM4087/**F**]

♦ Nordic Network for Research on the Relation between Private Law and Public Law (#17539)

♦ Nordic Network for Vector-borne Diseases (NorVect) 17365

Contact address not obtained. T. +4790954723. E-mail: info@norvect.no.
URL: http://norvect.no/

Aims Build and share vital knowledge about vector-borne diseases, particularly in the fields of diagnostics and treatment. **Events** *Conference* Oslo (Norway) 2015. [2015/XM4443/**F**]

♦ Nordic Neurological Association (inactive)

♦ Nordic Neuromodulation Society (NNS) 17366

Pres address not obtained.
URL: http://nordicneuro.org/

History Sep 2004, Helsinki (Finland). A regional chapter of *International Neuromodulation Society (INS, #14354).* **Aims** Promote scientific development and awareness of neuromodulation. **Staff** 4.00 FTE, paid. **Events** *Annual Meeting* Aarhus (Denmark) 2019, *Annual Scientific Meeting* Oslo (Norway) 2017. [2022/XM6544/**D**]

♦ Nordic Neuropaediatric Society / see Nordic Neuropediatric Society (#17367)

♦ Nordic Neuropediatric Society 17367

Nordiska Neuropediatriska Sällskapet (NNPS) – Nordiska Neuropediatriska Selskapet – Nordisk Neuropediatrisk Selskap – Pohjoismainen Lastenneurologiyhdistys

Chair c/o OU HF, Postboks 4950 Nydalen, 0424 Oslo, Norway. E-mail: johan.aronsson@rjl.se – nnps@nnps.se.
URL: http://nnps.se/

History 1972, Öland (Sweden). Founded at conference, although conferences of Nordic neuropaediatricians had been held regularly since 1963. Previously also referred to in English as *Scandinavian Neuropaediatric Society* and *Nordic Neuropaediatric Society.* **Structure** Committee; Chairman. **Languages** Danish, English, Faroese, Icelandic, Norwegian, Swedish. **Staff** 4.00 FTE, voluntary. **Finance** Members' dues: Danish Kr 75. **Activities** Events/meetings. **Events** *Conference* Stockholm (Sweden) 2022, *Conference* Stockholm (Sweden) 2021, *Conference* Stockholm (Sweden) 2020, *Conference* Copenhagen (Denmark) 2018, *Conference* Helsinki (Finland) 2016.
Members Full in 5 countries:
Denmark, Finland, Iceland, Norway, Sweden. [2021/XD2416/**D**]

♦ Nordic Newspaper Publishers' Joint Board (no recent information)

♦ Nordic NIAS Council (NNC) 17368

Contact NIAS, Oster Farimagsgade 5, 1353 Copenhagen K, Denmark. T. +4535329500.
URL: http://www.nias.ku.dk/

History 1968, under the auspices of *Nordic Council of Ministers (NCM, #17260)*. **Aims** Cooperate with NIAS to develop highest level *Asian* studies in the Nordic region; promote synergy among Asia-related activities of members; support NIAS as a hub for Nordic academic activities on Asia; ensure that NIAS maintains a Nordic mandate based on cross-disciplinary studies of modern Asia. **Languages** English. **Staff** 6.00 FTE, paid. **Activities** Events/meetings; publishing activities; projects/programmes; research/documentation; knowledge management/information dissemination. **Events** *Annnual conference* Tromsø (Norway) 2018, *Annnual conference* Reykjavik (Iceland) 2009, *Annual conference* Trondheim (Norway) 2008, *Annual Conference* Höör (Sweden) 2007, *Annual Conference* Turku (Finland) 2006.
Members Full in 6 countries:
Denmark, Finland, Greenland, Iceland, Norway, Sweden.
IGO Relations Partner of: *NIAS-Nordisk Institut for Asienstudier (NIAS, #17132)*. [2019.12.13/XJ0563/**E**]

- ♦ Nordic NonStop Users' Group / see Viking NonStop User Group (#20777)
- ♦ Nordic and North European Network for the Study of Dreams (inactive)
- ♦ Nordic Nuclear Safety Research (#17517)

♦ Nordic Number theory Network (N3) 17369

Contact address not obtained. E-mail: info@n-cube.net.
URL: http://www.n-cube.net/
History Also referred to as *N-cube Network*. **Aims** Develop number theory in its various aspects, from algebraic geometry and representation theory to computational problems, analytic number theory as well as diophantine approximation, diophantine geometry, moduli spaces properties or metric properties of numbers. **Activities** Events/meetings.
Members Full in 5 countries:
Denmark, Finland, Germany, Norway, Sweden. [2019/XM8491/**F**]

♦ Nordic Numismatic Union 17370

Union numismatique nordique – Nordisk Numismatisk Union (NNU)
Editor address not obtained.
Contact Søliljevej 51, 2650 Hvidovre, Denmark.
URL: http://nnunion.net/
History 1936. **Aims** Further cooperation between national numismatic societies and scientific numismatic institutions. **Structure** General Assembly (every 3 years). **Languages** Danish, Faroese, Finnish, Icelandic, Norwegian, Swedish. **Events** *Biennial General Assembly* Helsinki (Finland) 2014, *Biennial General Assembly* Copenhagen (Denmark) 2010, *Biennial General Assembly* Stockholm (Sweden) 2007, *Biennial General Assembly* Oslo (Norway) 2005, *Biennial General Assembly* Reykjavik (Iceland) 2003. **Publications** *Nordisk Numismatisk Unions Medlemsblad* (4 a year).
Members National numismatic collections of the Nordic countries and numismatic societies and institutes in the 6 Nordic countries:
Denmark, Faeroe Is, Finland, Iceland, Norway, Sweden. [2020.03.03/XD4648/**D**]

♦ Nordic Nurses' Federation (NNF) 17371

Association des infirmières des pays du Nord – Verband Krankenschwestern im Norden – Sykepleiernes Samarbeid i Norden (SSN)
Secretariat Sankt Annae Plads 30, 1250 Copenhagen K, Denmark.
Secretariat address not obtained.
URL: https://ssn-norden.dk/en/
History 1920, Copenhagen (Denmark). Statutes adopted 1920; amended 1923, 1926, 1930, 1935, 1954, 1956, 1958, 1960, 1966, 1970, 1971, 1974, 1979, 1984, 1987, 1989, 1992, 1994, 1997, 2003, 2004, 2009. Former names and other names: *Northern Nurses' Federation* – former. **Aims** Contribute to advancement of health care in general and to improved nursing services in particular in all Nordic countries. **Structure** Board of Directors (meets 2 times a year); Secretariat; Ad-hoc Working Groups as required. **Languages** Danish, Faroese, Icelandic, Norwegian, Swedish. **Staff** 1.00 FTE, paid. **Finance** Sources: members' dues. **Activities** Events/meetings; financial and/or material support; healthcare. **Events** *Conference* Stockholm (Sweden) 2010, *Conference* Sweden 2010, *Trends and developments in Europe with an impact on health services, nursing education, nursing practice and working conditions for nurses* Denmark 2009, *Conference* Faeroe Is 2008, *Conference* Iceland 2007. **Publications** *Vård i Norden* (4 a year). *Ethical Guidelines for Nursing Research in the Nordic Countries* in Danish, English, Finnish, Icelandic, Norwegian, Swedish. Annual Report.
Members National nursing associations (6), representing over 300,000 nurses in 6 countries and territories:
Denmark, Faeroe Is, Finland, Iceland, Norway, Sweden.
IGO Relations Cooperates with (4): *Nordic Council (NC, #17256)*; *Nordic Council of Ministers (NCM, #17260)*; *WHO (#20950)*; *WHO Regional Office for Europe (#20945)*. **NGO Relations** Cooperates with (2): *International Council of Nurses (ICN, #13054)*; *Nordens Fackliga Samorganisation (NFS, #17158)*. [2020/XD3010/**D**]

- ♦ Nordic Nutrition Conference (meeting series)

♦ Nordic Oat Association 17372

Contact Hjortrongstigen 6 B, SE-271 38 Ystad, Sweden.
History Registration: No/ID: 802447-8961, Sweden. **Aims** Promote *oats* produced in Nordic countries. **Activities** Annual meeting known as 'Nordic Oat Days'. **Events** *Annual Meeting* Helsinki (Finland) 2011, *Annual meeting* Gardermoen (Norway) 2009. **Members** Membership countries not specified. [2009/XJ8147/**D**]

♦ Nordic Offset Printing Association, The (NOPA) 17373

Sec Tvätterskevägen 3, SE-112 64 Stockholm, Sweden. T. +46707166179.
URL: http://www.nopa.nu/
History Set up early 1990s. Changed title to *Nordic Association of Heatset Printer (NAHP)*, 1999. Current title adopted, 2011. Registered in accordance with Swedish law: SE 802407-1725. **Aims** Provide an exclusive meeting and networking place for leading offset printers and their suppliers, who understand the value in being updated on trends in market, product development and technology, and in exchanging ideas and experiences with colleagues and competitors in order to manage their future development. **Structure** Annual Meeting; Autumn Meeting (annual); Board. **Languages** English. **Staff** 0.20 FTE, paid. **Finance** Members' dues. Annual budget: about euro 60,000. **Activities** Events/meetings. **Events** *Annual Meeting* Stockholm (Sweden) 2020, *Autumn Meeting* Brussels (Belgium) 2019, *Annual Meeting* Stavanger (Norway) 2019, *Autumn Meeting* Brussels (Belgium) 2018, *Annual Meeting* Warsaw (Poland) 2018. **Publications** None.
Members Printing; Associated; Co-opted; Honorary. Printing in 7 countries:
Denmark, Estonia, Finland, Latvia, Lithuania, Norway, Sweden.
Associate in 6 countries:
Estonia, Finland, Germany, Netherlands, Norway, Sweden.
IGO Relations None. **NGO Relations** None. [2020.03.06/XJ9288/**D**]

- ♦ Nordic Oil and Gas Firing Union (no recent information)
- ♦ Nordic Oil Pipeline Union (no recent information)

♦ Nordicom 17374

Dir Gothenburg Univ, PO Box 713, SE-405 30 Gothenburg, Sweden. T. +46317866125. E-mail: info@nordicom.gu.se.
URL: http://www.nordicom.gu.se/
History 1 Mar 1972. Founded with the support of *Nordic Council of Ministers (NCM, #17260)*. New statutes, drawn up, 2000, by *Nordic Committee of Senior Officials for Culture*, entered into force 1 Jan 2000. Former names and other names: *Nordic Documentation Centre for Mass Communication Research* – former; *Centre de documentation nordique pour la recherche de communication en masse* – former; *Nordiska Dokumentationscentralen för Masskommunikationsforskning* – former; *Nordic Information Centre for Media and Communication* – former; *Nordisk Informationscenter for Medie- og Kommunikationsforskning (NORDICOM)* – former. **Aims** Strengthen Nordic cooperation on media and communication research; spread information on media research and development through various Nordic and international organizations as well as policy makers, media practitioners, journalists, information officers, students, teachers and others; convey knowledge and contact between Nordic and international research communities. **Structure** Scientific Advisory Board. **Languages** Danish, English, Finnish, Norwegian, Swedish. **Staff** 17.00 FTE, paid. **Finance** Financed by Nordic Council of Ministers and national ministries of culture/education. Annual budget: 15,000,000 SEK. **Activities** Events/meetings; research/documentation. **Events** *Nordic Conference for Mass Communication Research* Reykjavik (Iceland) 2021, *Nordic Conference for Mass Communication Research* Malmö (Sweden) 2019, *Nordic Conference for Mass Communication Research* Tampere (Finland) 2017, *Nordic Conference for Mass Communication Research* Copenhagen (Denmark) 2015, *Nordic Gender and Media Forum Conference* Bergen (Norway) 2014. **Publications** *European Media Policy* (3 a year) – newsletter; *Nordic Media Policy* (3 a year) – newsletter; *Nordicom Review* (2 a year) in English – refereed journal; *Nordic Journal of Media Studies* (annual) in English – refereed journal; *Scientific Anthology* (6-8 a year) in English. Books in English and Swedish. **NGO Relations** Member of (2): *euroCRIS (#05672)*; *International Association for Media and Communication Research (IAMCR, #12022)*. Operates *International Clearinghouse on Children, Youth and Media*. [2022.02.14/XE5808/**E**]

♦ Nordic Operating Room Nurses Association (NORNA) 17375

Contact c/o FORNA, Kumpulantie 3, 3 krs, FI-00520 Helsinki, Finland.
History 1993. **Events** *Congress* Bergen (Norway) 2023, *Congress* Bergen (Norway) 2020, *Congress* Stockholm (Sweden) 2018, *Congress* Copenhagen (Denmark) 2016, *Perioperative nurses in education and practice* Helsinki (Finland) 2014.
Members Full in 5 countries:
Denmark, Finland, Iceland, Norway, Sweden.
NGO Relations *European Operating Room Nurses Association (EORNA, #08087)*. [2020/XJ8821/**D**]

♦ Nordic Optical Council 17376

Conseil optique nordique – Nordisk Optiker Råd (NOR)
Contact c/o Finnish Association of Vision and Eyecare, Eteläranta 10, FI-00130 Helsinki, Finland. T. +358405422227.
History 10 Jun 1947, Bergen (Norway). Also referred to as *Scandinavian Optical Council*. **Aims** Strengthen the optical *profession*; protect professional and economic interests of opticians on the Nordic level; improve and coordinate *optometrical education* in Scandinavian countries; promote high professional standards through harmonization of the profession in the region. **Structure** Annual Meeting; Presidency (rotates every 2 years). **Languages** Danish, Faroese, Icelandic, Norwegian, Swedish. **Staff** None. **Finance** Each country pays its own costs. Shared meeting costs. **Activities** Events/meetings. **Events** *Annual Meeting* Belgrade (Serbia) 2014, *Annual Meeting* Malmö (Sweden) 2014, *Annual Meeting* Malmö (Sweden) 2013, *Annual Meeting* Copenhagen (Denmark) 2012, *Annual Meeting* Copenhagen (Denmark) 2011.
Members Full in 5 countries:
Denmark, Finland, Iceland, Norway, Sweden. [2018/XD4706/**D**]

- ♦ Nordic Orchestra Conference (meeting series)
- ♦ Nordic Organization of Customs Officials (#17540)

♦ Nordic Organization of Workers' Educational Associations (WEA in the Nordic Countries) 17377

Comité nordique d'associations pédagogiques de travailleurs – Arbetarnas Bildningsförbund i Norden (ABF Norden)
Secretariat c/o ABF Arbetarnas Bildningsförbund, Oluf Palmes Gata 9 – 5 tr, SE-111 37 Stockholm, Sweden. T. +4686135000. Fax +468215276. E-mail: info@abf.se.
History Also referred to as *Nordic Workers' Educational Associations*. Previously known as *Nordiske Arbeidernes Oplysnings Forbund (AOF i Norden)*. **Aims** Promote development of society within the ideological framework of democratic socialism through independent and voluntary popular education. **Finance** Members' dues. **Activities** Training/education; events/meetings. **Events** *Seminar on EU and employees* Helsinki (Finland) 1998, *Seminar on economic policy* Kuopio (Finland) 1998.
Members Workers' educational organizations (5) in 5 countries and territories:
Åland, Denmark, Finland, Norway, Sweden. [2018.06.01/XD4991/**D**]

- ♦ Nordic Orienteering Council (no recent information)

♦ Nordic Orthodontic Society 17378

Société nordique d'orthodontie – Nordiska Ortodontisällskapet (NOS)
Contact address not obtained. E-mail: geir@kjeveortopediskforening.no – reguleringstannlegen@yahoo.no.
Events *Congress* Bergen (Norway) 2014, *Congress* Bergen (Norway) 2014, *Congress* Oulu (Finland) 2012, *Congress* Aalborg (Denmark) 2010, *Congress* Aalborg (Denmark) 2010.
Members Full in 5 countries:
Denmark, Finland, Iceland, Norway, Sweden. [2014/XD1674/**D**]

♦ Nordic Orthopedic Federation (NOF) 17379

Nordisk Ortopedisk Forening (NOF)
Contact Parkweg 6, 5242 CA Rosmalen, Netherlands. T. +31735226004. E-mail: info@norf.org.
URL: http://www.norf.org/
History 1919. Original English title: *Scandinavian Orthopaedic Association*. Present English name adopted 10 Jun 1994. **Aims** Further orthopedic surgery within Nordic countries. **Structure** Board, consisting of President, General Secretary, Chairman of coming congress, Chairman of Acta Orthopaedica Scandinavica and Presidents of the national orthopaedic associations. **Languages** English. **Staff** 10.00 FTE, voluntary. **Finance** Membership fees: euro 8. **Activities** Organizes: biennial congress; postgraduate orthopaedic seminars, courses and workshops in the Nordic countries. **Events** *Biennial congress* Vilnius (Lithuania) 2022, *Biennial congress* Trondheim (Norway) 2020, *Biennial Congress* Reykjavik (Iceland) 2018, *Biennial Congress* Linköping (Sweden) 2016, *Biennial Congress* Helsinki (Finland) 2014. **Publications** *Acta Orthopaedica*.
Members Orthopaedic associations, grouping about 4,000 individuals, in 7 countries:
Denmark, Estonia, Finland, Iceland, Netherlands, Norway, Sweden. [2014/XD3194/**D**]

- ♦ Nordic Ostomy Association (inactive)
- ♦ Nordic Oto-Laryngological Society / see Scandinavian Otolaryngological Society (#19094)
- ♦ Nordic Packaging Association / see Scandinavian Packaging Association (#19095)
- ♦ Nordic Paediatric Federation (inactive)
- ♦ Nordic Paediatric Ophthalmic Group / see Nordic Pediatric Ophthalmology Group (#17382)
- ♦ Nordic Paediatric Orthopaedic Federation (no recent information)
- ♦ Nordic Paper History Association / see Association of Nordic Paper Historians (#02831)
- ♦ Nordic Parliamentary Committee for Freer Communications (inactive)
- ♦ Nordic Passport Convention (1957 treaty)

♦ Nordic Passport Union 17380

Union nordique des passeports
Address not obtained.
History 1 May 1958, within the framework of *Nordic Council (NC, #17256)*, on coming into force of *Nordic Passport Convention (1957)*, signed 12 Jul 1957, Copenhagen (Denmark), by governments of Denmark, Finland, Norway and Sweden. Union among Denmark, Norway and Sweden had existed since 1954. Iceland adhered later. Amendments to Convention by agreement of 27 July; Supplemented by agreements of 2 Apr 1973; 18 Sep 2000. More an idea than an organization.
Members Governments of 5 countries:
Denmark, Finland, Iceland, Norway, Sweden.
IGO Relations *Nordic Council of Ministers (NCM, #17260)*. [2006/XD0224/**F***]

♦ Nordic Patent Institute (NPI) 17381

Dir Helgeshøj Allé 81, 2630 Taastrup, Denmark. T. +4543508500. Fax +4553080008. E-mail: npi@npi.int.
URL: http://www.npi.int/
History 1 Jan 2008. **Aims** Supply international patenting and information services in close cooperation with the participating national patent offices in order to stimulate innovation in the contracting states. **Structure** Board of 3 members. Director; Vice-Director. **Languages** English. **Events** *Meeting on a World in Change* Oslo (Norway) 2011.

Members Governments of 3 countries:
Denmark, Iceland, Norway.
Consultative Status Consultative status granted from: *World Intellectual Property Organization (WIPO, #21593)* (Permanent Observer Status). **IGO Relations** Observer to Administrative Council of: *European Patent Organisation (#08167).* [2018/XJ0940/j/**D***]

♦ Nordic Peace Association (inactive)
♦ Nordic Pediatric Cardiology meeting (meeting series)

♦ Nordic Pediatric Ophthalmology Group 17383

Contact Dept of Pediatric Ophthalmology, Queen Silvia Children's Hosp, SE-416 85 Gothenburg, Sweden. E-mail: marita.gronlund@neuro.gu.se.
URL: http://seh-eye.com/npog/
Events *Biennial Meeting* Bergen (Norway) 2009, *Biennial Meeting* Helsingør (Denmark) 2007, *Biennial Meeting* Turku (Finland) 2005, *Biennial Meeting* Uppsala (Sweden) 2003, *Biennial Meeting* Tromsø (Norway) 2001. **NGO Relations** Member of: *International Pediatric Ophthalmology and Strabismus Council (IPOSC, #14544).* [2008/XM3731/**D**]

♦ Nordic Pediatric Ophthalmology Group (NPOG) 17382

Nordiske Borneoftalmologiske Gruppe – Nordisk Paediatrisk Oftalmologisk Gruppe
Address not obtained.
History Former names and other names: *Nordic Paediatric Ophthalmic Group (NPOG)* – former. **Events** *NPOG-NSA Meeting* Stockholm (Sweden) 2022, *Meeting* Copenhagen (Denmark) 2017, *Biennial Meeting* Åland (Finland) 2015, *Biennial Meeting* Gothenburg (Sweden) 2013, *Biennial Meeting* Selfoss (Iceland) 2011. **NGO Relations** *Nordic Strabismological Association (NSA, #17438).* [2022/XM0860/**D**]

♦ Nordic Peoples Travel Organization (inactive)
♦ Nordic Perfume Dealers Council (inactive)
♦ Nordic Perinatal Congress (meeting series)
♦ Nordic Pharmaceutical Laboratories Committee (inactive)

♦ Nordic PharmacoEpidemiological Network (NorPEN) 17384

Contact address not obtained. E-mail: info@norpen.org.
URL: http://www.norpen.org/
History 2008. **Aims** Facilitate research within the field of pharmacoepidemiology in the Nordic countries. **Structure** Executive Committee; Research Groups. **Languages** English. **Activities** Events/meetings; research/documentation; training/education. **Events** *Meeting* Tampere (Finland) 2022, *Meeting* Stockholm (Sweden) 2021, *Meeting* Aarhus (Denmark) 2019, *Meeting* Oslo (Norway) 2018.
Members Research groups in 5 countries:
Denmark, Finland, Iceland, Norway, Sweden. [2022.03.02/XM8042/**F**]

♦ Nordic Pharmacopoeia Council (inactive)
♦ Nordic Pharmacy Association (inactive)
♦ Nordic Photographers' Association (no recent information)
♦ Nordic Photosynthesis Congress (meeting series)

♦ Nordic Piano Technicians Association (NPTA) 17385

Contact address not obtained. E-mail: osten.haggmark@sptf.com.
URL: http://www.pianotreff.com/
History 1996. **Events** *Annual Convention* Espoo (Finland) 2013, *Annual Convention* Larvik (Norway) 2011, *Annual Convention* Espoo (Finland) 2007, *Annual Convention* Helsinki (Finland) 2007, *Annual Convention* Drammen (Norway) 2006.
Members National associations in 4 countries:
Denmark, Finland, Norway, Sweden.
NGO Relations *Rådet för Små och Mellanstora Verksamheter i Norden (no recent information).* [2012/XD7773/**D**]

♦ Nordic Planetarium Association (NPA) 17386

Pres Steno Museum, Univ of Aarhus, CF Moellers Allé 2, Building 1100, Aarhus Univ, 8000 Aarhus, Denmark.
History Founded 1984, as *Nordic Planetarium Network (NPN).* New name and status adopted 1990. **Structure** Working Groups (2): *Nordic Planetarium Management Group (NPMG); Nordic Mobile Planetarium Group (NMPG).* **Languages** English. **Activities** Organizes: meeting (every 2 year); occasional courses/seminars. **Events** *Conference* Sandnes (Norway) 2019, *Conference* Riga (Latvia) 2011, *Conference* Sandnes (Norway) 2009, *Conference* Orsa (Sweden) 2007, *Conference* Rødding (Denmark) 2005. **Publications** *NPEN* (2 a year) – electronic newsletter.
Members Institutions and individuals in 5 countries:
Denmark, Finland, Iceland, Norway, Sweden.
NGO Relations Regional member of: *International Planetarium Society (IPS, #14588).* [2012.06.01/XF1275/**D**]

♦ Nordic Planetarium Network / see Nordic Planetarium Association (#17386)
♦ Nordic Plasma – Nordic Conference on Plasma Spectrochemistry (meeting series)

♦ Nordic Plastic Pipe Association 17387

Nordiska Plaströrgruppen
Contact PO Box 55915, SE-102 16 Stockholm, Sweden. T. +46104553850.
URL: http://www.npgnordic.com/
Members Organisations in 4 countries:
Denmark, Finland, Norway, Sweden.
NGO Relations *The European Plastic Pipes and Fittings Association (TEPPFA, #08215).* [2019/XD4423/**D**]

♦ Nordic Plato Society 17388

Platonselskabet
SG c/o Chr Gorm Tortzen, Saxoinstituttet, Kobenhavns Universitet, Karen Blixens Vej 4, 2300 Copenhagen S, Denmark. E-mail: niels@bistroist.dk.
URL: http://www.platonselskabet.org/
History Founded 1971, with members from Denmark, Sweden, Finland and Norway. **Aims** Broaden the knowledge and appreciation of Plato and the intellectual legacy of antiquity in a wider sense in the Nordic countries. **Structure** Praesidium, consisting of: one member from each of the constituent countries (Denmark, Sweden, Norway, Finland, Iceland). **Languages** Danish, Finnish, Icelandic, Norwegian, Swedish. **Staff** 5.00 FTE, paid. **Finance** Members' dues (every 2 years). **Activities** Events/meetings. **Events** *Conference* Oslo (Norway) 2015, *Conference* Copenhagen (Denmark) 2013, *Conference* Lund (Sweden) 2011, *Meeting* Turku (Finland) 2007. **Publications** *Platonselskabets Skriftserie – Platonselskabets Acta* – hosted by the periodical AIGIS.
Members Scholars from 5 countries:
Denmark, Finland, Iceland, Norway, Sweden. [2015.06.07/XM0862/**F**]

♦ Nordic Plumbing Industry Association (inactive)
♦ Nordic Police Association (#17489)
♦ Nordic Police Federation / see Nordiska Polisförbundet (#17489)

♦ Nordic Political Science Association (NOPSA) 17389

Association nordique de science politique – Nordiska Förbundet för Statskunskap
Chairman Dept Political Science, Stockholm Univ, Universitetsvägen 10, SE-114 18 Stockholm, Sweden.
URL: http://www.nopsa.net/
History Dec 1975, Stockholm (Sweden). **Aims** Promote and coordinate political science research in Nordic countries. **Structure** Board (meets once or twice a year); Research Committees. **Languages** Danish, English, Norwegian, Swedish. **Staff** Variable. **Finance** Congress fees. **Activities** Research and development; training/education; events/meetings. **Events** *Triennial Congress* Reykjavik (Iceland) 2021, *Triennial Congress* Reykjavik (Iceland) 2020, *Triennial Congress* Odense (Denmark) 2017, *Triennial Congress* Gothenburg (Sweden) 2014, *Triennial Congress* Vaasa (Finland) 2011. **Publications** *Scandinavian Political Studies* (4 a year).
Members National political science associations in 5 countries:
Denmark, Finland, Iceland, Norway, Sweden.
NGO Relations Represented in: *European Consortium for Political Research (ECPR, #06762)* Executive Committee; *International Political Science Association (IPSA, #14615).* [2016.10.25/XD9175/y/**D**]

♦ Nordic POP 17390

Project Leader Univ of Copenhagen – Dept of Pharmacy, Universitetsparken 2, 2100 Copenhagen, Denmark.
Project Administrator address not obtained.
URL: https://nordicpop.ku.dk/
History Founded as a Nordic university consortium. POP stands for patient oriented products. **Aims** Provide the scientific foundation for the next generation pharmaceutical products – patient oriented products- by strengthening the use of interdisciplinary approaches within Nordic pharmaceutical sciences. **Structure** Management Team; Advisory Board. Coordinated by University of Copenhagen (Denmark). **Activities** Events/meetings; knowledge management/information dissemination. **Events** *Annual Meeting* Helsinki (Finland) 2022, *Annual Meeting* Copenhagen (Denmark) 2021, *Annual Meeting* Copenhagen (Denmark) 2020, *Annual Meeting* Oslo (Norway) 2019.
Members Partner universities in 5 countries:
Denmark, Finland, Iceland, Norway, Sweden.
Affiliated universities in 3 countries:
Estonia, Germany, Poland. [2020/AA0684/**F**]

♦ Nordic Postal Union (NPU) 17391

Union postale des pays du Nord (UPPN) – Unión Postal de los Paises del Norte – Nordischer Postverein – Nordiska Postföreningen – Nordisk Postforening – Pohjoismaiden Postiliitto
Head of Int Relations Posti Lts, PO Box 102, FI-00011 Helsinki, Finland. T. +358204511. Fax +358204514994.
History Established 1869, by trilateral postal agreement between Denmark, Norway and Sweden; extended agreement including Finland and Iceland came into force on 1 Jan 1935. Further agreement of 11 Nov 1946 adopted present title. Revised agreement, within the scope of Nordic Postal Union, came into force on 1 Jul 1991. A Restricted Union of *Universal Postal Union (UPU, #20682).* **Aims** Further postal cooperation between Nordic countries and operators in the rest of the world; improve and develop postal connections among Nordic countries; enhance views of Nordic postal operators in matters relating to activities of the UPU; facilitate cross-border operational capability. **Structure** *NORDPOST* (annual conference), in which the 5 Postal Administrations participate. Working Parties. No permanent secretariat; secretariat duties rotate among member countries in the following order: Finland, Norway, Iceland, Denmark, Sweden. **Languages** Danish, Norwegian, Swedish. **Staff** Secretariat duties provided by member operators on a rotational basis. **Finance** No budget of its own. **Activities** Events/meetings; knowledge management/information dissemination. **Events** *Annual congress / Annual Nordic Postal Congress* Lillehammer (Norway) 2002, *Annual Congress* Lappeenranta (Finland) 2001, *Annual Nordic Postal Congress* Lappeenranta (Finland) 2001, *Joint conference* Mariehamn (Finland) 2001, *Annual Nordic Postal Congress* Kenekaise (Sweden) 2000.
Members Postal public operators in 5 countries:
Denmark, Finland, Iceland, Norway, Sweden.
IGO Relations Cooperation body of: *Nordic Council of Ministers (NCM, #17260).* Links with the other Restricted Unions: *African Postal Union (APU, no recent information); Arab Permanent Postal Commission (APPC, #01025); Asian-Pacific Postal Union (APPU, #01625); Associação dos Operadores de Correios e Telecomunicações dos Paises e Territórios de Lingua Oficial Portuguesa (AICEP, #02333); Association of European Public Postal Operators (PostEurop, #02534); Baltic Postal Union (BPU, #03137); Caribbean Postal Union (CPU, #03541); Conférence européenne des administrations des postes et des télécommunications (CEPT, #04602); Conference of Posts and Telecommunications of Central Africa (#04642); Pan African Postal Union (PAPU, #18060); Postal Union of the Americas, Spain and Portugal (PUASP, #18466).* [2015.12.11/XD2994/**D***]

♦ Nordic Postmen's Union (inactive)
♦ Nordic Poultry Conference (meeting series)
♦ Nordic Poultry Science Association (inactive)

♦ Nordic Pragmatism Network (NPN) 17392

Coordinator PO Box 24, Univ of Helsinki, FI-00014 Helsinki, Finland. E-mail: info@nordprag.org.
URL: http://www.nordprag.org/
History 2006. **Aims** Bring scholars working in different fields within philosophy and related subjects together; establish contacts both inside and outside the Nordic countries. **Structure** Board. **Finance** Support from: *NordForsk (#17164).* **Events** *European Pragmatism Conference* Helsinki (Finland) 2018.
Members Full in 5 countries:
Denmark, Finland, Iceland, Norway, Sweden.
NGO Relations Member of: *European Pragmatism Association.* [2018/XM4969/**F**]

♦ Nordic Press Association (NPA) 17393

Address not obtained.
URL: https://www.nordicpress.org/
History Founded 2016. **Aims** Facilitate trainings and cooperation across the Nordic borders in progressive projects. **Structure** Executive Board. **Finance** Funded by: *Nordic Children's and Youth Committee (NORDBUK, #17235).* **Activities** Events/meetings. **Events** *Seminar* Helsinki (Finland) 2018. [2020/XM7919/**D**]

♦ Nordic Prison Officers' Union (inactive)
♦ Nordic Professional Council (inactive)
♦ Nordic Project Fund (#17490)
♦ Nordic Prosthetist and Orthotist Congress (meeting series)
♦ Nordic Psoriasis Alliance / see NORDPSO (#17548)
♦ Nordic Psychiatric Associations (unconfirmed)
♦ Nordic Psychoanalytical Association (no recent information)
♦ Nordic Psychoanalytic Congress (meeting series)
♦ Nordic public health preparedness agreement (2002 treaty)
♦ Nordic Public Services Council / see Nordisk Tjenestemannsråd (#17538)
♦ Nordic Publishers Organization (meeting series)
♦ Nordic Publishing Board in Science (inactive)

♦ Nordic Quality Assurance Network in Higher Education (NOQA) . . . 17394

Contact c/o Danish Evaluation Inst, Ostbanegade 55, No 3, 2100 Copenhagen O, Denmark. E-mail: dma@eva.dk.
URL: http://www.noqa.net/
History 2003, Bergen (Norway), following a series of annual meetings since 1992. **Aims** Create joint understanding of different Nordic viewpoints on issues related to higher education quality assurance. **Events** *Annual meeting* Norway 2008, *Annual meeting* Sweden 2007, *Annual meeting* Reykjavik (Iceland) 2006, *Annual meeting* Copenhagen (Denmark) 2005, *Annual meeting* Turku (Finland) 2004. **Publications** Reports.
Members National organizations (5) in 5 countries:
Denmark, Finland, Iceland, Norway, Sweden.
NGO Relations *European Association for Quality Assurance in Higher Education (ENQA, #06183).* [2016.06.01/XM1753/**F**]

♦ Nordic R3 Association / see Nordic Association of Cleanroom Technology (#17183)
♦ Nordic Radio Evangelistic Association (internationally oriented national body)

♦ Nordic Railway Association 17395

Forum for Nordisk Jernbane Samarbejde (NJS) – Forum för Nordiskt JärnvägsSamarbete – Forum for Nordisk Jernbanesamarbeide – Pohjoismaiden Rautatieseura
Pres NSB AS, Schweigaardsgate 23, 0190 Oslo, Norway. E-mail: arnevidarh@nsb.no.
URL: https://njs.one/om-njs/about-njs.html

History Previously referred to as *Nordisk Jernvägs Selskab*. **Activities** Organizes conferences, meetings and study-visits. **Events** *General Assembly* Oslo (Norway) 2014. **Publications** *Nordisk Järnbane Tidsskrift* (10 a year).
Members Individuals in 4 countries:
Denmark, Finland, Norway, Sweden. [2020/XD1451/D]

- ♦ Nordic Railway Temperance Union (inactive)
- ♦ **NordicRAS** Nordic Network on Recirculating Aquaculture Systems (#17361)
- ♦ Nordic Recycling Federation (inactive)
- ♦ Nordic Reflexology Network (unconfirmed)
- ♦ Nordic Registered Accountants' Association (inactive)
- ♦ Nordic Reproduction Council (inactive)
- ♦ Nordic Research Board / see NordForsk (#17164)
- ♦ Nordic Research Council for Criminology / see Nordiska Samarbetsrådet för Kriminologi (#17493)
- ♦ Nordic Research Council on European Integration Law (inactive)

♦ Nordic Research Network for Safety and Quality in Healthcare (NSQH) 17396

Address not obtained.
URL: http://www.nsqh.org/

History Founded 2008. **Aims** Promote and advance safety research concerning the health care sector in the Nordic countries; facilitate collaboration on research and application of research results among Nordic countries and among research institutions and clinical settings. **Activities** Events/meetings. **Events** *Nordic Conference on Research in Patient Safety and Quality in Healthcare* Jönköping (Sweden) 2022, *Nordic Conference on Research in Patient Safety and Quality in Healthcare* Jönköping (Sweden) 2020, *Nordic Conference on Research in Patient Safety and Quality in Healthcare* Copenhagen (Denmark) 2018, *Nordic Conference on Research in Patient Safety and Quality in Healthcare* Kuopio (Finland) 2016, *Nordic Conference on Research in Patient Safety and Quality in Healthcare* Stavanger (Norway) 2014. [2019/XM7555/c/F]

- ♦ Nordic Research Network on Special Needs Education in Mathematics (unconfirmed)

♦ Nordic Research Network on Transitions, Career and Guidance (NoRNet) 17397

Contact address not obtained.
URL: https://nornet.au.dk/

Aims Strengthen research collaboration among research environments in the Nordic countries; support international collaboration on topics important to the Nordic countries; disseminate research results, inspire international research development and increase international awareness of Nordic research on transitions, career and guidance. **Structure** Steering Committee. **Activities** Events/meetings; knowledge management/ information dissemination; research/documentation. **Events** *Conference* Bergen (Norway) 2021. **Publications** *Nordic Journal of Transitions, Careers and Guidance*. [2022/AA2567/j/F]

- ♦ Nordic research network on vocational education and training / see NORDYRK (#17554)

♦ Nordic Research School in Innovation and Entrepreneurship (NORSI) 17398

Coordinator c/o NTNU, Postboks 8900, Torgarden, 7491 Trondheim, Norway.
Coordinator c/o SSES, Saltmätargatan 9, SE-113 59 Stockholm, Sweden.
URL: https://norsi.no/

History Originally a Norwegian institute, developed into a consortium with partner institutions across the region. Former names and other names: *Norwegian Research School in Innovation (NORSI)* – former. **Aims** Enhance and strengthen the Nordic innovation and entrepreneurship research education and community. **Structure** General Assembly; Executive Committee; Management Team. **Activities** Events/meetings; training/ education. **Events** *Research Conference* Stockholm (Sweden) 2023.
Members Consortium Partner Institutions (over 30) in 5 countries:
Denmark, Finland, Iceland, Norway, Sweden. [2023/AA3304/D]

- ♦ Nordic Research Symposium on Science Education (meeting series)
- ♦ Nordic Resource Sharing, Reference and Collection Management Conference (meeting series)

♦ Nordic Respiratory Academy (NORA) 17399

Address not obtained.
URL: https://www.nora.one/

History Founded in conjunction with *Nordic Lung Congress (NLC)*, 2003, Reykjavik (Iceland), for which organization it is currently responsible. Registration: Denmark. **Aims** Foster academic respiratory medicine including respiratory allergology among scientific and medical disciplines in the Nordic countries. **Structure** General Assembly; Executive Committee. **Languages** English. **Activities** Advocacy/lobbying/activism; events/ meetings. **Events** *Nordic Lung Congress* Helsinki (Finland) 2024, *Nordic Lung Congress* Copenhagen (Denmark) 2022, *Nordic Lung Congress* Tallinn (Estonia) 2019, *Nordic Lung Congress* Visby (Sweden) 2017, *Nordic Lung Congress* Oslo (Norway) 2015. **Publications** *European Clinical Respiratory Journal*.
Members Individuals who are members of 6 national federations:
Denmark, Estonia, Finland, Iceland, Norway, Sweden. [2022/AA2519/v/E]

- ♦ Nordic Retail and Wholesale Association (internationally oriented national body)
- ♦ Nordic Revisors Congress (meeting series)

♦ Nordic Rheology Society (NRS) 17400

Det Nordiske Reologiselskap – Nordiska Reologisällskapet – Nordisk Reologiselskab – Pohjoismainen Reologiaseura – Norraena Flotfraedifélaid

Contact RWTH Aachen Univ, Inst of Physical Chemistry, Landoltweg 2, 52074 Aachen, Germany.
URL: http://nordicrheologysociety.org/

History 1991, Gothenburg (Sweden). Founded 1991 when by-laws were adopted. Derives from Swedish Society of Rheology. Revised Charter approved 1996, at annual meeting. **Aims** Promote and propagate rheology and its applications at all levels throughout the Nordic countries. **Structure** Meeting (annual, at conference); Board; Award Committee; Election Committee. **Languages** English. **Staff** None. **Finance** Sources: members' dues. **Activities** Awards/prizes/competitions; events/meetings. **Events** *Annual Conference* Reykjavik (Iceland) 2022, *Annual Conference* 2021, *Annual European Rheology Conference* 2021, *Annual Conference* 2020, *Annual Conference* Gothenburg (Sweden) 2019. **Publications** *Annual Transactions of the Nordic Rheology Society*.
Members National societies in the 5 Nordic countries:
Denmark, Finland, Iceland, Norway, Sweden.
Individuals in 17 countries:
Czechia, Denmark, Finland, France, Germany, Iceland, Iran Islamic Rep, Ireland, Italy, Norway, Russia, Spain, Sweden, Switzerland, UK, United Arab Emirates, USA.
NGO Relations Member of (2): *European Society of Rheology (ESR, #08730)*; *International Committee on Rheology (ICR, #12802)*. [2022.05.14/XD4668/D]

♦ Nordic Rheuma Council 17401

Nordisk Reuma Råd (NRR)

Contact address not obtained. T. +4722547600. Fax +4722431251.

History 1989. Former names and other names: *Nordic Rheumatism Council* – former (1989). **Aims** Seek opportunities for cooperation in the areas of treatment and rehabilitation; disseminate information and increase resources for education and scientific research on rheumatic diseases; improve cooperation between twin towns in the Nordic countries; establish and maintain contact with other relevant Nordic associations; increase influence of Nordic rheumatism associations at Nordic and international levels. **Structure** Council (meets twice a year), consisting of 2 members from each member association. Secretariat and Chairmanship rotate among member countries every 2 to 4 years. **Languages** Danish, Finnish, Icelandic, Norwegian, Swedish. **Staff** 0.50 FTE, paid. **Finance** Sources: members' dues. **Events** *Autumn meeting* Oslo (Norway) 2011.
Members Rheumatism associations in the Nordic countries. Members in 6 countries and territories:
Denmark, Faeroe Is, Finland, Iceland, Norway, Sweden. [2011.10.20/XD4833/D]

- ♦ Nordic Rheumatism Council / see Nordic Rheuma Council (#17401)

♦ Nordic Road Association 17402

Nordisk Vejforum (NVF) – Nordiskt Vägforum (NVF) – Nordisk Vegforum (NVF) – Pohjoismaiden Tie-ja Liikennefoorumi

Sec Swedish Transport Administration, SE-172 90 Sundbyberg, Sweden. E-mail: nvf@vd.dk.
URL: http://www.nvfnorden.org/

History 19 Jun 1935, Stockholm (Sweden). Founded by Nordic road and road traffic engineers. Originally referred to as *Nordic Road Association (NRA) – Association nordique de la route – Nordisk Vejteknisk Forbund – Nordiska Vägtekniska Förbundet – Nordisk Vegteknisk Forbund*. **Aims** Promote advances within the road, road traffic and road transport sector through cooperation among professionals in Nordic countries. **Structure** Board; Committees (10); Secretariat. **Languages** Danish, English, Norwegian, Swedish. **Staff** 1.00 FTE, paid. **Finance** Members' dues. Government contribution. **Activities** Events/meetings. **Events** *Via Nordica* Denmark 2024, *Via Nordica Congress* Malmö (Sweden) 2020, *Nordic Traffic Safety Forum* Lillehammer (Norway) 2019, *Nordic Traffic Safety Forum* Mariehamn (Finland) 2018, *Nordic Traffic Safety Forum* Copenhagen (Denmark) 2017.
Members National road and traffic authorities; universities; research institutions; private companies; NGOs. Members in 6 countries and territories:
Denmark, Faeroe Is, Finland, Iceland, Norway, Sweden.
NGO Relations Member of (1): *Associations and Conference Forum (AC Forum, #02909)*. Cooperates with (2): *Baltic Road Association (BRA, #03138)*; *World Road Association (PIARC, #21754)*. [2022/XD1765/D]

- ♦ Nordic Road Hauliers Union (inactive)
- ♦ Nordic Rowing Federation (#17527)
- ♦ Nordic Saami Council / see Saami Council (#19012)
- ♦ Nordic Sacred Music Council / see Nordic Council of Church Music (#17257)

♦ Nordic Safe Cities 17403

Secretariat c/o Nextstep by Bindslev, Bygmestervej 57, 2400 Copenhagen NV, Denmark. E-mail: info@nordicsafecities.org.
URL: https://nordicsafecities.org/

History Initiated 2016, by *Nordic Council of Ministers (NCM, #17260)*. Subtitle: *Light on Life*. Registered in accordance with Danish law. **Aims** Ensure safe, trustful, tolerant and resilient cities for all, while actively preventing radicalization and violent extremism. **Structure** Steering Group; Advisory Board. **Finance** Funded by: *Nordic Council of Ministers (NCM, #17260)*. **Activities** Events/meetings. **Events** *Summit* Stockholm (Sweden) 2019, *Nordic Safe Cities Conference* Helsinki (Finland) 2018, *Stop youth violence, hate speech and social exclusion in Nordic cities* Kristiansand (Norway) 2018. **Publications** *Nordic Safe Cities Newsletter* (4 a year). *The Nordic Safe Cities Guide*. Tool box. **Members** Cities (over 20); experts (over 800). Membership countries not specified. [2020.02.14/XM7927/F]

- ♦ Nordic School Managers' Meetings (meeting series)
- ♦ Nordic School of Public Health (inactive)

♦ Nordic Science Centre Association (NSCA) 17404

Nordisk Science Center Forbund (NSCF)

Chairman address not obtained. E-mail: visindasmidjan@hi.is – gudrunba@hi.is.
Contact address not obtained.
URL: http://www.nordicscience.net/

History Oct 1987, Finland. **Aims** Bring together the science centres in Scandinavia and the Baltic States; encourage cooperation and the exchange of ideas. **Structure** General Meeting; Governing Board. **Languages** English. **Activities** Awards/prizes/competitions; events/meetings. **Events** *Conference* Norrköping (Sweden) 2021, *Conference* Norrköping (Sweden) 2020, *Conference* Bergen (Norway) 2019, *Conference* Tallinn (Estonia) 2018, *Conference* Iceland 2017. **Publications** *NSCF Newsletter*.
Members Centres in 7 countries:
Denmark, Estonia, Finland, Iceland, Latvia, Norway, Sweden. [2022/AA0665/D]

- ♦ Nordic Science and Technology Studies Conference (meeting series)
- ♦ Nordic Scoliosis Society / see Nordic Spinal Deformities Society (#17437)
- ♦ Nordic Seamen's Church Council (no recent information)

♦ Nordic Seating Network 17405

Nordiske Sittenettverket – Nordisk Siddenetvaerk

Contact c/o NAV Hjelpemidler og tilrettelegging, Postboks 5 St Olavplass, 0130 Oslo, Norway.
URL: http://sitsite.socialstyrelsen.dk/

Aims Organize Nordic Seating Symposium (every 3 years). **Languages** Danish, English, Finnish, Icelandic, Norwegian, Swedish. **Activities** Organizes Nordic Seating Symposium (every 3 years). **Events** *Symposium* Copenhagen (Denmark) 2018, *Symposium* Oslo (Norway) 2015, *Triennial symposium / Symposium* Stockholm (Sweden) 2012, *Triennial symposium / Symposium* Reykjavik (Iceland) 2009, *Triennial symposium / Symposium* Copenhagen (Denmark) 2006. **Members** Worldwide. Membership countries not specified. [2019.07.04/XJ3700/F]

- ♦ Nordic Secretariat for Agricultural and Horticultural Workers (inactive)
- ♦ Nordic Semiconductor Meeting (meeting series)
- ♦ Nordic Seminar on Railway Technology (meeting series)

♦ Nordic Separation Science Society (NoSSS) 17406

Pres Vileikos St 8, LT-44404 Kaunas, Lithuania.
URL: http://nosss.vdu.lt/

History Took over activities of *Scandinavian Electrophoresis Society (inactive)*. **Aims** Promote research and education within separation sciences and their application. **Structure** General Meeting (every 2 years). Committee of 7 members, including Chairman, Vice-Chairman, Secretary and Treasurer. **Languages** English. **Finance** Members' dues. **Activities** Conducts research and education in the Separation Science field; organizes conferences, courses and summer schools. **Events** *Symposium* Djurönäset (Sweden) 2014, *Symposium* Riga (Latvia) 2011, *Symposium* Tallinn (Estonia) 2009, *Symposium* Kaunas (Lithuania) 2007, *Symposium* Copenhagen (Denmark) 2004. **Publications** *Electrophoresis* – journal.
Members in 8 countries:
Denmark, Estonia, Finland, Iceland, Latvia, Lithuania, Norway, Sweden.
NGO Relations *International Council of Electrophoresis Societies (ICES, no recent information)*. Member of: *European Society for Separation Science (EuSSS, #08732)*. Also links with national organizations active in the field. [2012.06.01/XD7899/D]

♦ Nordic Ships' Officers Congress 17407

Congrès des officiers nordiques de marine – Nordisk Navigatørkongress – Nordisk Fartygsbefälskongress (NFBK)

Contact Postboks 2000 Vika, 0125 Oslo, Norway. E-mail: oslo@sjooff.no.

History 24 Feb 1910, Stockholm (Sweden). **Activities** Events/meetings. **Events** *Meeting* Oslo (Norway) 2017, *Meeting* Gothenburg (Sweden) 2011, *Meeting* Stavanger (Norway) 2011, *Meeting* Lahti (Finland) 2010, *Meeting* Stockholm (Sweden) 2010.
Members National associations, totalling 20,000 members, in 6 countries and territories:
Denmark, Faeroe Is, Finland, Iceland, Norway, Sweden. [2017.03.15/XD2996/F]

♦ Nordic Shooting Region 17408

Union nordique de tir – Nordiska Skytteregionen

SG c/o Finnish Shooting Sport Federation, Valimotie 10, FI-00380 Helsinki, Finland. T. +358405785860.
URL: http://www.nordicshootingregion.com/

History Founded 1921, superseding *Nordic Short-Distance-Shooting Association*. Also referred to in English as *Nordic Shooting Union*. **Aims** Promote development of shooting as a *sport*; administer cooperation among member associations. **Structure** Congress (at Nordic Championships); Praesidium. **Languages** English. **Staff** 0.50 FTE, paid. **Activities** Sporting activities. **Events** *Organization development* Oslo (Norway) 1994, *Congress* Sweden 1989.
Members Full in 6 countries:
Denmark, Finland, Iceland, Norway, Sweden, UK. [2019.02.27/XD1746/D]

♦ Nordic Shooting Union / see Nordic Shooting Region (#17408)
♦ Nordic SIF – Nordic Sustainable Investment Forum (meeting series)
♦ Nordic Singer and Musician Workers Association (#17478)
♦ Nordic Singers' Association (#17532)
♦ Nordic Sleep Research and Medicine Society (no recent information)
♦ Nordic Sleep Society (unconfirmed)
♦ **NordicSMC** Nordic Sound and Music Computing Network (#17434)
♦ Nordic Smokers Guild (internationally oriented national body)
♦ Nordic Socialist Adult Education Organization (inactive)
♦ Nordic Social and Mental Health Society (inactive)
♦ Nordic Social Pharmacy and Health Services Research Conference (meeting series)

♦ Nordic Social-Statistical Committee (NOSOSCO) 17409

Comité nordique pour les statistiques sociales – Nordisk Socialstatistik Komité (NOSOSKO) – Pohjoismaiden Sosiaalitilastokomitea

Secretariat Statens inst for fulkesundhed, Studiestr'de 6, 1455 Copenhagen K, Denmark. T. +4565507835. E-mail: nom-nos@si-folkesundhed.dk.
URL: http://nowbase.org/

History 1946, following decision of the 1945 meeting of Nordic Ministers of Social Affairs. Operates as a body for cooperation in matters relating to social statistics, by virtue of a decision, 20 Dec 1978, of *Nordic Council of Ministers (NCM, #17260)*. Constituted, 1 Jan 1979, as a permanent body under NMR and Nordic Committee on Social Policy. Also referred to in English as *Nordic Committee on Social Security Statistics*. **Aims** Ensure the best possible comparability of reports on the scope and contents of social security arrangements in the Nordic countries; propose and implement development projects in the field of social statistics; prepare and coordinate publications in the field. **Structure** Composed of a maximum of 3 members and their substitutes from each country. Chairmanship rotates among member countries. **Languages** Danish, English, Norwegian, Swedish. **Staff** 2.00 FTE, paid. **Finance** Annual budget allocated by the Nordic Council of Ministers. **Activities** Networking/liaising. **Events** *Annual Session* Norway 2011, *Annual Session* Denmark 2010, *Annual Session* Iceland 2009, *Annual Session* Norway 2008, *Annual Session* Finland 2007. **Publications** *Social Protection in the Nordic Countries* (annual).
Members Representatives of 5 countries:
Denmark, Finland, Iceland, Norway, Sweden.
IGO Relations Cooperates with: *Nordic Medico-Statistical Committee (NOMESCO, #17342)*.
[2020.01.09/XE7095/**E***]

♦ Nordic Society for Aerosol Research (NOSA) 17410

Pres Dept of Chemistry, Aarhus Univ, Langelandsgate 140, 8000 Aarhus C, Denmark.
URL: http://www.nosa-aerosol.org/

History Founded 1978, as *Nordic Association for Aerosol Science*. **Aims** Promote aerosol research, interdisciplinary cooperation between members, exchange of information, international cooperation and exchange of ideas, recruitment and education of aerosol researchers. **Structure** Board. **Languages** Danish, English, Faroese, Icelandic, Norwegian, Swedish. **Events** *Annual Symposium* Sønderborg (Denmark) 2020, *Annual Symposium* Helsinki (Finland) 2018, *Annual Symposium* Lund (Sweden) 2017, *Annual Symposium* Kuopio (Finland) 2015, *Annual Symposium* Stockholm (Sweden) 2014.
Members Individuals in 19 countries:
Australia, Austria, Canada, Czechia, Denmark, Estonia, Finland, Germany, Iceland, Israel, Latvia, Lithuania, Moldova, Netherlands, Norway, Russia, Sweden, UK, USA.
NGO Relations Member of: *European Aerosol Assembly (EAA, #05836)*; *International Aerosol Research Assembly (IARA, #11593)*. [2017.10.29/XD2282/v/**D**]

♦ The Nordic Society for Aesthetics 17411

Nordiska Sällskapet för Estetik – Nordisk Selskap for Estetik – Nordisk Selskab for Aestetik – Pohjoismaiden Estetiikan Seura – Félag Norraenna Fagurfraedinga

Sec Dept of Philosophy/History/Art, Univ of Helsinki, PO Box 59, FI-00014 Helsinki, Finland. T. +358400860076.
Chair address not obtained.
URL: http://www.nsae.fi/

History 1983, Uppsala (Sweden). Refounded 2019, Helsinki (Finland). **Aims** Promote study, research, discussion and publication in aesthetics from a philosophical, psychological, sociological, historical, critical and educational point. **Structure** Board. **Events** *Annual Meeting* Paris (France) 2023, *Annual Meeting* Huddinge (Sweden) 2022, *Annual Meeting* Helsinki (Finland) 2021, *Annual Meeting* Aarhus (Denmark) 2020, *Annual Meeting* Espoo (Finland) 2019. **Publications** *The Nordic Journal of Aesthetics*. Newsletter.
Members Members in 13 countries:
China, Czechia, Denmark, Finland, Germany, Hungary, Iceland, Italy, Norway, Poland, Sweden, UK, United Arab Emirates.
NGO Relations Member of (1): *International Association for Aesthetics (IAA, #11692)*.
[2022.10.18/XM3088/**D**]

♦ Nordic Society of Allergology (unconfirmed)
♦ Nordic Society for Arctic Medicine / see Nordic Society for Circumpolar Health (#17412)
♦ Nordic Society for Campanology and Carillon / see Nordisk Selskab for Campanologi og Klokkespil (#17533)

♦ Nordic Society for Circumpolar Health (NSCH) 17412

Nordisk Sällskapet för Circumpolar Hälsa

Chair Inst of Health Sciences, PO Box 5000, Univ of Oulu, FI-90014 Oulu, Finland.
URL: http://www.oulu.fi/nsam/

History 2000, Harstad (Norway), as *Nordiska Sällskapet för Arktisk Medicin (NSAM) – Nordic Society for Arctic Medicine*, during 11th Congress of *International Union for Circumpolar Health (IUCH, #15764)*, following a proposal made, 1997, Copenhagen (Denmark), during final meeting of *Nordic Council for Arctic Medicine (NCAM, inactive)*. Present name adopted, 2010. Registered in accordance with Finnish law. **Aims** Promote and spread interest in health problems in circumpolar and related areas. **Events** *Meeting* Oulu (Finland) 2004.
NGO Relations Member of: *International Union for Circumpolar Health (IUCH, #15764)*. [2010/XJ2146/**D**]

♦ Nordic Society for Clay Research (inactive)
♦ Nordic Society of Clinical Chemistry (#17507)
♦ Nordic Society for Clinical Chemistry and Clinical Physiology / see Nordisk Förening för Klinisk Kemi (#17507)

♦ Nordic Society for Clinical Microbiology and Infectious Diseases (NSCMID) 17413

Sec c/o Aarhus Univ Hosp, Dept Infectious Diseases, Palle Juul-Jensens Bd 99, 8200 Aarhus N, Denmark.
Gen Sec address not obtained.
URL: https://nscmid.org/

History 1983. Former names and other names: *Scandinavian Society for Antimicrobial Chemotherapy (SSAC)* – former (1983). **Aims** Facilitate the acquisition and distribution of knowledge in the fields of infectious diseases and clinical microbiology. **Structure** General Meeting (annual); Board. **Languages** English. **Staff** Voluntary. **Finance** Sources: meeting proceeds; members' dues. **Activities** Events/meetings. **Events** *Annual Meeting* Örebro (Sweden) 2023, *Annual Meeting* Aalborg (Denmark) 2022, *Annual Meeting* Turku (Finland) 2021, *Annual Meeting* Stockholm (Sweden) 2020, *Annual Meeting* Trondheim (Norway) 2019.
Members Individuals (660) in 12 countries and territories:
Denmark, Faeroe Is, Finland, Germany, Iceland, Latvia, Netherlands, Norway, Spain, Sweden, UK, USA.
NGO Relations Member of (3): *European Society of Clinical Microbiology and Infectious Diseases (ESCMID, #08548)*; *Federation of European Societies for Chemotherapy and for Infections (FESCI, #09546)*; *International Society of Antimicrobial Chemotherapy (ISAC, #14925)*. [2023/XD1275/v/**D**]

♦ Nordic Society for the Conservation of Sea Mammals (inactive)
♦ Nordic Society of Dentistry for the Handicapped / see Nordic Association for Disability and Oral Health (#17190)
♦ Nordic Society for Disability and Oral Health / see Nordic Association for Disability and Oral Health (#17190)
♦ Nordic Society for Disaster Medicine (no recent information)
♦ Nordic Society of Fish Immunology / see International Society of Fish and Shellfish Immunology (#15122)
♦ Nordic Society for Forensic Odonto-Stomatology (no recent information)
♦ Nordic Society Foundation for Information about Problem Gambling (#19989)
♦ Nordic Society for Free Radical Chemistry (no recent information)

♦ Nordic Society on Gynaecological Endoscopy (NSGE) 17414

Sec Dept of Gynaecology and Obstetrics, Odense Univ Hosp, Srd Boulevard 29, 5000 Odense, Denmark.
Pres address not obtained.
URL: http://nsge.dk/

History Current statutes adopted 6 June 2019. Former names and other names: *Nordic Society on Gynaecological Endoscopy – Minimal Invasive Gynaecological Surgery* – full title. Registration: Denmark. **Aims** Be a Nordic platform for professionals dedicated to the care of women with gynaecological sickness; work for improvements in the practice of diagnosis and treatment where minimal invasive gynaecological surgery may be performed and be beneficial for women; promote and support basic and clinical research. **Structure** General Assembly; Board. **Languages** English. **Activities** Advocacy/lobbying/activism; events/meetings; research/documentation; training/education. **Events** *International Conference on Evidence Based Endoscopy and Research in Gynaecology (ICEBERG)* Amsterdam (Netherlands) 2021, *Nordic Congress on Gynaecological Endoscopy NCGE* Helsinki (Finland) 2019, *Nordic Congress on Gynaecological Endoscopy* Norefjell (Norway) 2017, *Nordic Congress on Gynaecological Endoscopy* Middelfart (Denmark) 2015.
[2020.07.16/AA0532/v/**D**]

♦ Nordic Society on Gynaecological Endoscopy – Minimal Invasive Gynaecological Surgery / see Nordic Society on Gynaecological Endoscopy (#17414)

♦ Nordic Society of Gynecological Oncology (NSGO) 17415

Nordiska Sällskapet för Gynekologisk Onkologi

Admin Dir Blegdamsvej 9, Oncology – 9431, Rigshospitalet CUH, 2100 Copenhagen, Denmark.
URL: http://www.nsgo.org/

History 1986, Oslo (Norway). **Structure** Board, comprising President, Treasurer, Secretary and 4 further members. **Events** *Annual Meeting* Helsinki (Finland) 2022, *Annual Meeting* 2021, *Annual Meeting* Oslo (Norway) 2020, *Annual Meeting* Copenhagen (Denmark) 2019, *Annual Meeting* Lund (Sweden) 2018. **Publications** *NSGO Newsletter*. **NGO Relations** *European Organisation for Research and Treatment of Cancer (EORTC, #08101)*. [2021/XD8212/**D**]

♦ Nordic Society of Hematology (no recent information)

♦ Nordic Society of Human Genetics and Precision Medicine (NSHG-PM) 17416

Contact Univ of Copenhagen, SUND, Blegdamsvej 3B, Room 1.2.14, 2200 Copenhagen, Denmark. T. +4593509163. E-mail: admin@nshg-pm.org.
Main Website: http://nshg-pm.org/

History Jun 2018, Reykjavik (Iceland). Founded following meetings organized since 2014. Former names and other names: *Nordic Society for Precision Medicine (NSPM)* – former. **Aims** Establish a Nordic framework for research into the genetics of human diseases, as well as into human evolution and population history; accelerate discovery of disease susceptibility genes and genes protecting from disease through integrated analyses using multiple large-scale datasets and a range of experimental designs. **Activities** Events/meetings; knowledge management/information dissemination. **Events** *Meeting* Helsinki (Finland) 2021, *Annual Nordic Precision Medicine Forum* Copenhagen (Denmark) 2018.
Members Full in 6 countries:
Denmark, Estonia, Finland, Iceland, Norway, Sweden. [2022.05.10/XM7545/**D**]

♦ Nordic Society of Infection Control Nurses (#17531)
♦ Nordic Society for Interarts Studies / see International Society for Intermedial Studies (#15211)
♦ Nordic Society for Intermedial Studies / see International Society for Intermedial Studies (#15211)
♦ Nordic Society for Medical and Biological Illustration (inactive)
♦ Nordic Society for Medical Humor (unconfirmed)

♦ Nordic Society for Medical Mycology (NSMM) 17417

Gen Sec Clinical Microbiology F72, Karolinska Univ Hosp, Huddinge, SE-141 86 Stockholm, Sweden. T. +4658581147. Fax +4658581125.
URL: http://www.nsmm.nu/

History 25 Aug 2003, Copenhagen (Denmark). **Aims** Encourage the practice and study of all aspects of medical mycology; facilitate, among Nordic countries, exchange of ideas, information and training pertaining to medical mycology. **Structure** General Meeting (annual); Board. **Languages** English. **Events** *Scientific Meeting* Stockholm (Sweden) 2021, *Scientific Meeting* Stockholm (Sweden) 2020, *Scientific Meeting* Helsinki (Finland) 2019, *Scientific Meeting* Oslo (Norway) 2018, *Scientific Meeting* Copenhagen (Denmark) 2017.
Members Individuals (127) in 6 countries:
Denmark, Estonia, Finland, Iceland, Norway, Sweden.
NGO Relations *European Confederation of Medical Mycology (ECMM, #06712)*; *International Society for Human and Animal Mycology (ISHAM, #15181)*. [2020.06.23/XD9325/v/**D**]

♦ Nordic Society of Medical Radiology 17418

Société nordique de la radiologie médicale – Nordisk Förening för Medicinsk Radiologi (NFMR) – Pohjoismainen Radiologiyhdistys

Pres Radiologisk afdelingen X, 3023 Rigshospitalet, Blegdamsvej 9, 2100 Copenhagen O, Denmark.
URL: http://www.nordicradiology.eu/

History 2 Jul 1919, Oslo (Norway). Former names and other names: *Scandinavian Radiological Society* – alias. **Aims** Promote periodical congresses and symposia. **Structure** Board, consisting of President appointed from the country where the next Congress is to be held, 3 other members from the same country and 2 from each of the other countries, all serving 1-year term. Secretary-General and Treasurer elected for 4-year period. **Languages** Danish, English, Finnish, Norwegian, Swedish. **Staff** 2.00 FTE, voluntary. **Finance** Budget (annual): Norwegian Kr 850,000. **Activities** Organizes: congress (annual); symposia. **Events** *Nordic Congress of Radiology and Radiography* 2023, *Biennial Congress* Helsinki (Finland) 2021, *Biennial Congress* Copenhagen (Denmark) 2019, *Biennial Congress* Reykjavik (Iceland) 2017, *Biennial Congress* Uppsala (Sweden) 2013.
Members National radiological societies in 5 countries:
Denmark, Finland, Iceland, Norway, Sweden. [2022/XD3196/**D**]

♦ Nordic Society for Metrical Studies (unconfirmed)
♦ Nordic Society for Microcirculation and Vascular Biology (inactive)

♦ Nordic Society for Middle Eastern Studies (nsmes) 17419

Sec address not obtained.
Acting Chair address not obtained. E-mail: mjrs@cas.au.dk.
URL: https://www.nsmes.org/

History Jan 1989, Uppsala (Sweden). Previously also referred in Swedish as *Nordisk Selskap for Midtaustenstudiar (NSM)*. Registration: No/ID: 39417391, Denmark. **Aims** Further cooperation among Nordic scholars of Middle Eastern studies. **Structure** Board. **Languages** English. **Staff** None. **Finance** Members' dues. **Activities** Events/meetings; training/education. **Events** *Conference* Stockholm (Sweden) 2025, *Conference* Reykjavik (Iceland) 2022, *Breaking and creating boundaries in the Middle East* Helsinki (Finland) 2019, *Triennial Conference* Odense (Denmark) 2016, *Triennial Conférence* Lund (Sweden) 2013. **Publications** *Directory of Middle Eastern Studies in the Nordic Countries*. Publications series; conference papers. **Information Services** *Nordic Monthly Bulletin on Middle Eastern Studies* – electronic.
Members Individuals (over 200) in 5 countries:
Denmark, Finland, Iceland, Norway, Sweden.
NGO Relations Part of *European Association for Middle Eastern Studies (EURAMES, #06120)*.
[2018.04.07/XD2614/v/**D**]

♦ Nordic Society of Nephrology (NSN) **17420**
Nordiske Nyredager
Congress Sec address not obtained. E-mail: birna@athygli.is.
URL: http://nsn2013.is/efni/welcome/
History Previously referred to as *Scandinavian Society of Nephrology*. **Events** *Biennial Congress* Odense (Denmark) 2022, *Biennial Congress* Turku (Finland) 2019, *Biennial Congress* Stavanger (Norway) 2015, *Biennial Congress* Reykjavik (Iceland) 2013, *Nordic Nephrology Days* Copenhagen (Denmark) 2011.
[2021/XJ4291/**D**]

♦ Nordic Society of Neuroradiology (NSNR) **17421**
Société nordique de neuroradiologie – Nordisk Forening for Neuroradiologi
Sec Vevroradiologisk Afdelning, Ullevål Universitetssykemus, 0407 Oslo, Norway. E-mail: hkpeder@gmail.com.
URL: http://www.nsnr.org/
History 1972, Bergen (Norway), as *Nordic Association on Neuro-Radiology (NFNR)*. **Languages** Danish, Faroese, Icelandic, Norwegian, Swedish. **Events** *Annual Meeting* Ålesund (Norway) 2016, *Annual Meeting* Reykjavik (Iceland) 2013, *Annual Meeting* Bornholm (Denmark) 2012, *Annual Meeting* Bologna (Italy) 2010, *Annual meeting* Iceland 2010.
Members Full in 5 countries:
Denmark, Finland, Iceland, Norway, Sweden. [2013/XD3316/**D**]

♦ Nordic Society for Oculoplastic and Reconstructive Surgery (NOSOPRS) **17422**
Address not obtained.
URL: https://www.nosoprs.com/
History 2004. **Activities** Events/meetings. **Events** *Meeting* Os (Norway) 2023, *Meeting* Os (Norway) 2021, *Meeting* Copenhagen (Denmark) 2019, *Meeting* Stockholm (Sweden) 2017, *Meetintg* Stavanger (Norway) 2013. [2022/AA2377/**D**]

♦ Nordic Society of Odontology for the Handicapped / see Nordic Association for Disability and Oral Health (#17190)

♦ Nordic Society Oikos (NSO) **17423**
Main Office Oikos Editorial Office, Geocentrum II, Sölvegatan 12, SE-223 62 Lund, Sweden. E-mail: info@nordicsocietyoikos.org – info@oikosoffice.lu.se.
URL: http://www.nordicsocietyoikos.org/
Aims Support scientific research in *ecology* and related disciplines; stimulate and enhance communication among stakeholders in ecological research in the Nordic countries and beyond. **Structure** General Assembly; Board. **Languages** English. **Staff** Voluntary. **Finance** Sources: sale of publications. **Activities** Publishing activities. **Events** *Nordic Oikos Meeting* Aarhus (Denmark) 2022, *Nordic Oikos Meeting* Reykjavik (Iceland) 2020, *Nordic Oikos Meeting* Trondheim (Norway) 2018, *Nordic Oikos Meeting* Turku (Finland) 2016, *Nordic Oikos Meeting* Stockholm (Sweden) 2014. **Publications** *ECOGRAPHY* (12 a year) – journal; *OIKOS Journal* (12 a year); *Journal of Avian Biology* (6 a year); *Nordic Journal of Botany* (6 a year); *Wildlife Biology* (6 a year). *Ecological Bulletins* – series.
Members Full in 5 countries:
Denmark, Finland, Iceland, Norway, Sweden.
NGO Relations Member of (1): *European Ecological Federation (EEF, #06956)*. [2022.05.11/XJ9353/**D**]

♦ Nordic Society for Pediatric Hematology and Oncology (NOPHO) ... **17424**
Nordisk Förening för Pediatrisk Hematologi och Onkologi
Address not obtained.
URL: http://www.nopho.org/
Structure Board; Secretariat. **Languages** English. **Activities** Events/meetings; training/education. **Events** *Annual Meeting* Tallinn (Estonia) 2024, *Annual Meeting* Lund (Sweden) 2023, *Annual Meeting* Kuopio (Finland) 2022, *Annual Meeting* Trondheim (Norway) 2021, *Annual Meeting* Trondheim (Norway) 2020.
Members Individuals in 6 countries:
Denmark, Finland, Iceland, Lithuania, Norway, Sweden. [2023/XD2662/v/**D**]

♦ Nordic Society of Pediatric Oncology Nurses (#17524)
♦ Nordic Society of Pharmacology (no recent information)
♦ Nordic Society for Phenomenology / see Nordic Society of Phenomenology (#17425)

♦ Nordic Society of Phenomenology (NoSP) **17425**
Nordisk Selskab for Faenomenologi
Pres Center for Subjectivity Research, Dept Media/Cognition/Communication, Univ of Copenhagen, Karen Blixens Plads 8, 2300 Copenhagen S, Denmark.
URL: http://nordicsocietyforphenomenology.wordpress.com/
History May 2001, Copenhagen (Denmark). Former names and other names: *Nordic Society for Phenomenology* – alias. **Aims** Further dialogue and cooperation between phenomenologists in the Nordic countries; promote scholarship, teaching, research and publication affiliated with phenomenology. **Structure** Executive Committee. **Languages** Danish, English, Finnish, French, German, Icelandic, Norwegian, Swedish. **Staff** 6.00 FTE, voluntary. **Finance** No budget. **Events** *Conference* Huddinge (Sweden) 2022, *Annual Conference* Helsinki (Finland) 2020, *Annual Conference* Copenhagen (Denmark) 2019, *Annual Conference* Gdansk (Poland) 2018, *Annual Conference* Trondheim (Norway) 2017.
Members Full (830) worldwide, but mainly in the 5 Nordic countries:
Denmark, Finland, Iceland, Norway, Sweden.
NGO Relations Member of: *Organization of Phenomenological Organizations (OPO, #17883)*.
[2020/XM1069/**D**]

♦ Nordic Society for Philosophy of Education **17426**
Nordiskt Nätverk för Pedagogisk Filosofi (NNPF)
Pres Univ of Akureyri, School of Humanities and Social Sciences, Nordurslod 2, 600 Akureyri, Iceland. T. +3544628557. Fax +3544608997.
Contact DPU, Tuborgvej 164, Bygning D lok 358, 2400 Copenhagen NV, Denmark. E-mail: sufr@dpu.dk.
URL: http://www.nfpf.net/
History 8 Mar 1997, on the initiative of Jan Bengtsson, as a network of *Nordic Educational Research Association (NERA, #17276)*. Became an independent society, 14 Mar 1998. Also referred to as *Nordic Network for Philosophy of Education*. **Aims** Foster dialogue among philosophers of education in the Nordic countries; coordinate, facilitate and support exchange of ideas, information and experiences in philosophy of education; encourage research in the field. **Structure** General Meeting. Steering Committee of up to 7 members. **Languages** English. **Events** *Annual Meeting* Reykjavik (Iceland) 2013, *Annual Meeting* Copenhagen (Denmark) 2012, *Annual congress / Annual Meeting* Jyväskylä (Finland) 2011, *Annual congress / Annual Meeting* Malmö (Sweden) 2010, *Annual Meeting* Trondheim (Norway) 2009. **Publications** *Nordic Educational Research* – journal; *Scandinavian Journal of Education Research*.
Members Individuals (156) in 5 countries:
Denmark, Finland, Iceland, Norway, Sweden.
NGO Relations Cooperates with: *International Network of Philosophers of Education (INPE, #14302)*; *Philosophy of Education Society of Australasia (PESA, #18360)*; Philosophy of Education Society of Great Britain (PESGB); Philosophy of Education Society USA (PES). [2012/XD8243/v/**D**]

♦ Nordic Society for Philosophy of Religion (NSPR) **17427**
Chairperson Faculty of Theology, Univ of Oslo, PO Box 1023, Blindern, 0315 Oslo, Norway. T. +4722850394. Fax +4722850301.
URL: http://www.tf.uio.no/nspr/
History 2007. **Aims** Gather philosophers, theologians and scholars of religion; function as a forum for conferences, workshops, doctoral courses and exchange of scholars and of information. **Structure** Board, comprising Chairperson and 6 members. **Languages** Danish, English, Faroese, Icelandic, Norwegian, Swedish. **Finance** Funded by: *NordForsk (#17164)*; *Nordic Council (NC, #17256)*. Budget (annual): Norwegian Kr 300,000. **Events** *Biennial Conference* Biri (Norway) 2019, *Biennial Conference* Oslo (Norway) 2017, *Biennial Conference* Helsinki (Finland) 2015, *Biennial Conference* Copenhagen (Denmark) 2011, *Biennial Conference* Reykjavik (Iceland) 2009. **Publications** *The Body Unbound: Philosophical Perspectives on Politics, Embodiment and Religion* (2010).
Members Full (about 170) in 10 countries:
Denmark, Estonia, Finland, Germany, Iceland, Latvia, Lithuania, Norway, Russia, Sweden.
NGO Relations Member of (1): *International Philosophy of Religion Association (IPRA)*.
[2010.06.01/XM4630/**D**]

♦ Nordic Society for Precision Medicine / see Nordic Society of Human Genetics and Precision Medicine (#17416)
♦ Nordic Society of Protistology (unconfirmed)
♦ Nordic Society for Psychosocial Oncology (no recent information)

♦ Nordic Society for Radiation Protection **17428**
Association nordique de protection contre les radiations – Nordiska Sällskapet för Strålskydd – Nordisk Selskab for Strålingsbeskyttelse (NSFS)
Sec address not obtained. E-mail: secretary@nsfs.org.
Pres address not obtained. E-mail: president@nsfs.org.
URL: http://www.nsfs.org/
History 10 Jun 1964, Stockholm (Sweden). Statutes adopted, June 1964, Stockholm; amended 19 Aug 1971, Copenhagen (Denmark); 6 Sep 1978, Visby (Sweden); 31 Aug 1990, Ronneby (Sweden); 26 Aug 1999, Skagen (Denmark); 26 Aug 2002, Åbo (Finland); 30 Aug 2005, Rättvik (Sweden). **Aims** Develop and disseminate knowledge and experience on protection against ionizing and non-ionizing radiation, including protection of workers, patients exposed for diagnostic or therapeutic purpose and members of the public. **Structure** President plus Board of 3 members from each Nordic country. Officers: President; Vice-President; Secretary; Treasurer. Presidency rotates every 4 years. **Languages** Danish, English, Finnish, Icelandic, Norwegian, Swedish. **Finance** Sources: members' dues. **Activities** Events/meetings. **Events** *Conference* Malmö (Sweden) 2023, *Conference* Espoo (Finland) 2019, *Conference* Røskilde (Denmark) 2015, *Conference* Reykjavik (Iceland) 2011, *Conference* Ålesund (Norway) 2008.
Members Ordinary; Honorary members in 5 countries:
Denmark, Finland, Iceland, Norway, Sweden. [2023.02.21/XD6058/**D**]

♦ Nordic Society of Radiographers and Radiological Technicians (inactive)
♦ Nordic Society for Research in Brain Ageing (inactive)

♦ Nordic Society for Research in Mathematics Education (NoRME) .. **17429**
Chair Stockholm Univ, Dept Mathematics and Science Education, Svante Arrhenius väg 20C, SE-106 91 Stockholm, Sweden. E-mail: norme.contact@gmail.com.
URL: http://sites.google.com/view/norme/home
History 24 Apr 2008, Copenhagen (Denmark). Founded following conferences organized since 1994. **Aims** Support the aims of member societies concerning research in mathematics education. **Structure** General Assembly (every 3 years); Board. **Activities** Events/meetings; networking/liaising. **Events** *Nordic Conference on Mathematics Education (NORMA)* Oslo (Norway) 2021, *Nordic Conference on Mathematics Education (NORMA)* Oslo (Norway) 2020, *Nordic Conference on Mathematics Education* Stockholm (Sweden) 2017. **Publications** *Nordic Studies in Mathematics Education (NOMAD)* – scientific journal. Conference proceedings.
Members Full in 8 countries:
Denmark, Estonia, Finland, Iceland, Latvia, Lithuania, Norway, Sweden. [2018.09.05/XM6500/**D**]

♦ Nordic Society for Space Research (inactive)
♦ Nordic Society of Special Subject Philately (inactive)
♦ Nordic Society for Systemic-functional Linguistics (#17508)
♦ Nordic Society for Thermal Analysis / see Nordic Society for Thermal Analysis and Calorimetry (#17430)

♦ Nordic Society for Thermal Analysis and Calorimetry (NOSTAC) ... **17430**
Sec DTU Energy, Risoe Campus, Bld 227, Frederiksborgvej 399, 4000 Røskilde, Denmark. T. +4546775722. Fax +4546775758.
History Founded Sep 1974, as *Nordic Society for Thermal Analysis (NSTA)*, also known by acronym *NOSTA*, deriving from *Nordforsk Committee for Thermal Analysis* set up within *Nordiska Samarbetsorganisationen för Teknisk-Vetenskaplig Forskning (NORDFORSK, inactive)* in 1970. **Aims** Promote contact among Nordic scientists active in the field; promote standardization of thermoanalytical methods. **Structure** Committee comprising one delegate and one substitute from each Nordic country. **Languages** Danish, English, Finnish, Norwegian. **Staff** 3.00 FTE, voluntary. **Finance** Meeting fees. Budget (annual): Danish Kr 200,000. **Activities** Events/meetings; training/education; financial and/or material support. **Events** *European Symposium on Thermal Analysis and Calorimetry* Espoo (Finland) 2014, *Symposium* Copenhagen (Denmark) 2000, *Symposium / Nordic Symposium on Thermal Analysis and Calorimetry – NSTAC* Helsinki (Finland) 1996, *Symposium / Nordic Symposium on Thermal Analysis and Calorimetry – NSTAC* Oslo (Norway) 1994, *Symposium* Stockholm (Sweden) 1992.
Members Full in 5 countries:
Denmark, Finland, Iceland, Norway, Sweden.
NGO Relations *International Confederation for Thermal Analysis and Calorimetry (ICTAC, #12871)*.
[2020/XD1662/**D**]

♦ Nordic Society for Tourism and Hospitality Research (NORTHORS) . **17431**
Sec address not obtained.
URL: http://www.northors.aau.dk/
History 1992. **Aims** Provide a platform for academic debate and development in the field of tourism and hospitality in the Nordic countries. **Structure** Board. **Languages** English. **Staff** 1.00 FTE, voluntary. **Finance** No budget. **Activities** Events/meetings. **Events** *Nordic Symposium of Tourism and Hospitality Research* Östersund (Sweden) 2023, *Nordic Symposium of Tourism and Hospitality Research* Porvoo (Finland) 2022, *Nordic Symposium of Tourism and Hospitality Research* Akureyri (Iceland) 2021, *Nordic Symposium of Tourism and Hospitality Research* Røskilde (Denmark) 2019, *Tourism implications and dilemmas* Alta (Norway) 2018. **Publications** *Scandinavian Journal of Hospitality and Tourism*. Policy and strategy documents; position papers; presentations fact sheet; video library.
Members Full in 5 countries:
Denmark, Finland, Iceland, Norway, Sweden.
IGO Relations None. [2021.03.15/XJ9391/**D**]

♦ Nordic Society of Toxicological Pathologists (inactive)

♦ Nordic Society for Veterinary Pathology **17432**
Contact Dept of Pharmacology and Pathobiology, Lab of Vet Pathology, Royal Veterinary and Agricultural Univ, Bülowsvej 17, 1870 Frederiksberg C, Denmark. T. +4535283105. Fax +4535283111.
History 1977, as *Scandinavian Society for Veterinary Pathology*. **Aims** Promote research, teaching and diagnostic competence in veterinary pathology. **Structure** President, Vice-President and country representatives elected annually at meeting. **Languages** English. **Staff** None. **Finance** Members' dues (nominal). Meetings financed by participating members and sponsorship. **Activities** Annual meeting/symposium. **Events** *Meeting and Symposium* Helsinki (Finland) 2021, *Meeting and Symposium* Copenhagen (Denmark) 2016, *Meeting and Symposium* Helsinki (Finland) 2015, *Meeting and Symposium* Tromsø (Norway) 2014, *Meeting and Symposium* Uppsala (Sweden) 2013.
Members Veterinarians engaged in research, teaching and/or diagnostic pathology in 5 countries:
Denmark (EU), Finland (EU), Iceland, Norway, Sweden (EU). [2015.01.13/XD3750/v/**D**]

♦ Nordic Sociological Association **17433**
Nordiska Sociologföreningen
Chairperson Dept of Sociology, Örebro Univ, SE-701 82 Örebro, Sweden.
Sec-Treas address not obtained.
URL: http://nordicsociologicalassociation.org/

History 1955. Former names and other names: *Scandinavian Sociological Association* – alias. **Aims** Serve as an alliance of national sociological associations in Nordic countries. **Structure** Board. **Languages** Danish, English, Norwegian, Swedish. **Staff** 1.00 FTE, paid. **Finance** Annual budget: 500,000 NOK. **Activities** Events/meetings; financial and/or material support. **Events** *Conference* Reykjavik (Iceland) 2022, *Biennial Congress* Oslo (Norway) 2021, *Biennial Congress* Oslo (Norway) 2020, *Biennial Congress* Aalborg (Denmark) 2018, *Biennial Congress* Helsinki (Finland) 2016. **Publications** *Acta Sociological* (4 a year).
Members Full in 5 countries:
Denmark, Finland, Iceland, Norway, Sweden. [2021/XD3905/**D**]

♦ Nordic Sound and Music Computing Network (NordicSMC) 17434

Project Leader AC Meyers Vaenge 15, 2450 Copenhagen, Denmark.
URL: https://nordicsmc.create.aau.dk/
Activities Events/meetings. **Events** *Nordic Sound and Music Computing Conference* Stockholm (Sweden) 2019.
Members Full in 5 countries:
Denmark, Finland, Iceland, Norway, Sweden. [2020/AA0783/**F**]

♦ Nordic Sound Symposium (meeting series)

♦ Nordic Special Needs Education Organization 17435

Nordiska Förbundet för Specialpedagogik (NFSP) – Nordisk Forbund for Spesialpedagogikk (NFSP)
Pres address not obtained. T. +3544831424. E-mail: formadur@vefurinn.is.
Sec address not obtained. T. +3544864466. E-mail: astabjork@borgarbyggd.is.
URL: http://nfsp.info/
History 1920, as *Nordiskt Hjälpskoleförbund*. Current title adopted 1959. Previously also referred to in English as *Nordic Federation for Special Education*. **Aims** Further the interests and causes of special education. **Structure** Board; Rotating Chairmanship. **Languages** Danish, English, Swedish. **Events** *Conference* Thórshavn (Faeroe Is) 2019, *Conference* Reykjavik (Iceland) 2016, *Conference / Convention* Turku (Finland) 2013, *Conference / Convention* Oslo (Norway) 2010, *Convention* Copenhagen (Denmark) 2007. **Publications** *Nordisk tidsskrift for spesialpedagogikk* (periodical).
Members Full in 6 countries and territories:
Denmark, Faeroe Is, Finland, Iceland, Norway, Sweden. [2017.01.25/XD8207/**D**]

♦ Nordic Spinal Cord Society (NoSCoS) 17436

Pres Dept of Rehabilitation Medicine, Linköping Univ Hosp, SE-581 85 Linköping, Sweden.
URL: http://noscos.org/
History Aug 1987, Finland. Former names and other names: *Nordic Medical Society of Paraplegia (SMSOP)* – former (Aug 1987). **Aims** Advance education and promote research into spinal cord injury, bringing together professionals and consumers in relevant fields with a common interest in the specialty. **Structure** Executive Committee, consisting of President, Secretary-Treasurer and member at large. Advisory Council. **Languages** Danish, English, Finnish, Icelandic, Norwegian, Swedish. **Staff** None. **Finance** Private sponsoring. **Activities** Events/meetings; training/education. **Events** *Meeting* Helsinki (Finland) 2024, *Meeting* Stockholm (Sweden) 2022, *Biennial Meeting* Copenhagen (Denmark) 2019, *Biennial Meeting* Linköping (Sweden) 2017, *Biennial Meeting* Trondheim (Norway) 2015.
Members Full in 5 countries:
Denmark, Finland, Iceland, Norway, Sweden.
Associate in 3 countries:
Estonia, Latvia, Lithuania.
NGO Relations Regional society of: *International Spinal Cord Society (ISCoS, #15581).* [2022/XD3487/**D**]

♦ Nordic Spinal Deformities Society (NSDS) 17437

Nordisk Skoliose Forening
Secretary c/o Lillebaelt Hospital, Spinecenter of Southern Denmark, Oestre Hougvej 55, 5500 Middelfart, Denmark. T. +4524453742.
Pres c/o Karolinska Univ Hosp, Orthopaedic Dept, Section for Spinal disorders, Huddinge, SE-141 86 Stockholm, Sweden. T. +46851770000 – +46736994409.
URL: http://www.nsds.dk/wm442427/
History 1974, Stockholm (Sweden), as *Nordic Scoliosis Society*. Current title adopted 1996. Also referred to as *Scandinavian Association for Scolioses* and *Nordic Spine Deformity Society*. **Aims** Promote in the Nordic countries the research and treatment of scoliosis and all diseases of the back that may lead to spinal deformity; extend collaboration between orthopaedic departments that treat scoliosis and spinal diseases. **Structure** Board, consisting of President, Secretary/Treasurer, 1 delegate from each Nordic country. **Languages** Danish, English, Norwegian, Swedish. **Staff** Voluntary. **Finance** Budget (annual): SEK 3,000 (except meetings which are paid by registration fees and exhibition fees). **Activities** Works on a spine deformity data bank. **Events** *Annual Meeting* Bergen (Norway) 2019, *Annual Meeting* Kolding (Denmark) 2018, *Annual Meeting* Stockholm (Sweden) 2017, *Annual Meeting* Naantali (Finland) 2016, *Annual Meeting* Amsterdam (Netherlands) 2015. **Publications** Abstracts.
Members Full in 5 countries:
Denmark, Finland, Iceland, Norway, Sweden. [2019/XD1217/**D**]

♦ Nordic Spine Deformity Society / see Nordic Spinal Deformities Society (#17437)
♦ Nordic Sports Committee for the Poorly-Sighted (inactive)
♦ Nordic Sports Organization for the Disabled (inactive)
♦ Nordic State Audit Seminar (meeting series)
♦ Nordic Statistical Meeting (meeting series)
♦ Nordic Steel Association (inactive)
♦ Nordic Steel Construction Conference (meeting series)
♦ Nordic STEEL – Nordic Steel Construction Conference (meeting series)

♦ Nordic Strabismological Association (NSA) 17438

Contact Haukeland Univ Hosp, Jonas Liesvvei 65, 5021 Bergen, Norway. T. +4755975000.
Events *NPOG-NSA Meeting* Stockholm (Sweden) 2022, *Meeting* Copenhagen (Denmark) 2017, *Meeting* Åland (Finland) 2015, *Meeting* Gothenburg (Sweden) 2013, *Meeting* Selfoss (Iceland) 2011. **NGO Relations** *Nordic Pediatric Ophthalmology Group (NPOG, #17382).* [2022/XM3730/**D**]

♦ Nordic Stroke Society 17439

Sec Dept of Neurology, Vilnius Univ Hosp, Santariskiu str 2, LT-08661 Vilnius, Lithuania.
Chair address not obtained.
URL: http://www.nordicstroke.org/
History 1982, *Scandinavian Society for Cerebrovascular Diseases*. Previously also referred to as *Scandinavian Association for Cerebrovascular Diseases* and *Skandinaviska Sällskapet för Cerebrovaskulära Sjukdomar*. Current title adopted, 2005. **Aims** Promote research on cerebrovascular disorders in the Scandinavian and Baltic countries with special emphasis on scientific collaboration and exchange across national borders and between professional disciplines. **Structure** General Assembly. Board, comprising Chairman, Secretary and 14 members. **Languages** English. **Staff** None. **Finance** Members' dues: euro 10 for 2 years. **Activities** Organizes biennial scientific conference. **Events** *Biennial Meeting* Tromsø (Norway) 2019, *Biennial Meeting / Meeting* Vilnius (Lithuania) 2013, *Biennial meeting / Meeting* Tallinn (Estonia) 2011, *Meeting* Finland 2009, *Biennial Meeting* Helsinki (Finland) 2009. **Members** Full (510). Membership countries not specified.
[2013.09.18/XD3219/**D**]

♦ Nordic STS Conference – Nordic Science and Technology Studies Conference (meeting series)
♦ Nordic Summer Symposium in Macroeconomics (meeting series)
♦ Nordic Summer University (#17535)
♦ Nordic Surgical Society / see Scandinavian Surgical Society (#19122)

♦ Nordic Sustainable Campus Network (NSCN) 17440

Chair Aalto Univ, PB 31000, FI-00076 Aalto, Finland. T. +358503137549. E-mail: sil@hi.is.
URL: http://nordicsustainablecampusnetwork.wordpress.com/
History Jan 2012, by higher education institutes in Finland, Sweden, Denmark, Norway and Iceland. **Aims** Support the work of sustainability experts in Nordic Higher Education Institutes (HEIs); share best practices and experiences. **Structure** Core Group. **Languages** English. **Staff** None. **Finance** Members' dues. **Activities** Events/meetings; training/education; projects/programmes. **Events** *Oslo Conference* Oslo (Norway) 2015, *Seminar* Lappeenranta (Finland) 2014, *Seminar* Espoo (Finland) 2013.
Members Higher education institutes (45) in 5 countries:
Denmark, Finland, Iceland, Norway, Sweden.
NGO Relations EAUC; *International Sustainable Campus Network (ISCN, #15635); Nordic Association of University Administrators (NAUA, #17206).* [2020.03.03/XJ7901/**D**]

♦ Nordic Sustainable Investment Forum (meeting series)

♦ Nordic Swan Ecolabel 17441

Contact address not obtained. T. +4724144600. E-mail: info@ecolabel.no.
URL: http://www.nordic-ecolabel.org/
History 1989. Founded by decision of *Nordic Council of Ministers (NCM, #17260)*. Former names and other names: *Nordic Eco-Labelling Board* – former. **Aims** Contribute to sustainable consumption and production. **Structure** Board. **Languages** Danish, English, Finnish, Icelandic, Norwegian, Swedish. **Staff** 200.00 FTE, paid. **Finance** Less than 20% public funding. **Activities** Certification/accreditation; standards/guidelines. **Publications** *Nordic Swan Ecolabel Newsletter.*
Members Full in 5 countries:
Denmark, Finland, Iceland, Norway, Sweden. [2022.05.20/XD6505/**D**]

♦ Nordic Swimming Federation / see Nordic Swimming Federations Association (#17442)

♦ Nordic Swimming Federations Association (NSF) 17442

Association des fédérations nordiques de natation – Nordisk Swimmeforbund – Nordiska Simförbundet
Main Office c/o Swedish Swimming Federation, Heliosgatan 3, SE-120 30 Stockholm, Sweden. E-mail: info@svensksimidrott.se.
URL: http://www.nordicswimmingfederation.com/
History Former names and other names: *Nordic Swimming Federation* – alias; *NSFA* – alias. **Aims** Coordinate swimming, *diving, water polo, synchronized swimming* in Nordic countries. **Languages** English. **Staff** 6.00 FTE, voluntary. **Events** *Baby Swimming Conference* Sweden 2026, *Learn to Swim Conference* Faeroe Is 2024, *Baby Swimming Conference* Norway 2024, *Nordic Baby Swim Conference* Espoo (Finland) 2022, *Learn to Swim Conference* Oslo (Norway) 2022.
Members Full in 6 countries and territories:
Denmark, Faeroe Is, Finland, Iceland, Norway, Sweden. [2023/XD1744/**D**]

♦ Nordic Symposium on Building Physics (meeting series)
♦ Nordic Symposium on Forensic Psychiatry (meeting series)
♦ Nordic Symposium on Tribology (meeting series)
♦ Nordic Table Tennis Union / see North European Table Tennis Union (#17599)
♦ Nordic TAG – Nordic Theoretical Archaeology Group (meeting series)
♦ Nordic Tandem Users' Group / see Viking NonStop User Group (#20777)

♦ Nordic Tax Research Council 17443

Conseil nordique d'études fiscales – Nordiska Skattevetenskapliga Forskningsrådet (NSFR) – Nordisk Skattevitenskapelig Forskningsråds – Pohjoismainen Verotieteellinen Tutkimusneuvosto
SG Juridiska fak – Stockholm Univ, SE-106 91 Stockholm, Sweden. T. +468161732.
URL: http://www.nsfr.se/
History 13 Apr 1973, Helsinki (Finland), by the Governments of Denmark, Finland, Norway and Sweden. Registered in Finland, 13 Feb 1974. Iceland acceded, 2002. Previously also known in English as *Nordic Council for Tax Research*. **Aims** Improve Nordic cooperation within tax research, with attention on tax issues of general Nordic interest and its relation to international taxation. **Structure** General Assembly (at least twice a year); Board. **Languages** Danish, Norwegian, Swedish. **Staff** 1.00 FTE, paid. **Finance** Ministries of Finance of member countries. **Activities** Events/meetings; awards/prizes/competitions. **Events** *Annual Seminar* Denmark 2020, *Annual Seminar* Oslo (Norway) 2019, *Annual Seminar* Stockholm (Sweden) 2018, *Annual Seminar* Porvoo (Finland) 2017, *Annual seminar* Reykjavik (Iceland) 2010. **Publications** *Nordic Tax Journal*; *Yearbook on Nordic Tax Research.*
Members Governments of 5 countries:
Denmark, Finland, Iceland, Norway, Sweden.
IGO Relations A cooperation body of: *Nordic Council of Ministers (NCM, #17260).* [2020.03.03/XD2203/**D***]

♦ Nordic Teachers' Council 17444

Conseil des syndicats nordiques des professeurs – Consejo de Sindicatos Nordicos de Profesores – Nordiska Läraerorganisationers Samråd (NLS)
SG Rautatieläisenkatu 6, FI-00520 Helsinki, Finland. E-mail: nls@oaj.fi.
URL: http://www.nls.info/
History Founded 1968. Previously referred to in English as *Council of Nordic Teachers' Associations*. **Aims** Cooperate on matters of common interest to member organizations; promote cooperation between teachers in the Nordic countries; strengthen development of cooperation between teachers in Europe and internationally. **Structure** Executive Board (meets twice a year); Rotating Presidency; Educational Commissions (5). **Languages** Danish, English, French, Norwegian, Swedish. **Staff** 2.00 FTE, paid. **Finance** Members' dues. **Events** *Science Days* Stockholm (Sweden) 2018, *Science Days* Stockholm (Sweden) 2015, *Science Days* Stockholm (Sweden) 2014.
Members Teachers' unions (17) in 7 countries and territories:
Denmark, Faeroe Is, Finland, Greenland, Iceland, Norway, Sweden.
IGO Relations *Nordic Council (NC, #17256); Nordic Council of Ministers (NCM, #17260).* **NGO Relations** *All Africa Teachers' Organization (AATO, no recent information); Education International (EI, #05371); European Trade Union Committee for Education (ETUCE, #08926); Nordens Fackliga Samorganisation (NFS, #17158).*
[2020.03.03/XD5423/**D**]

♦ Nordic Technical Accreditation (inactive)
♦ Nordic Telecommunications Association (inactive)
♦ Nordic Telecommunications Satellite Council (inactive)

♦ Nordic Telemedicine Association (NTA) 17445

Contact address not obtained. T. +4777754030.
URL: http://www.nordictelemed.org/
History Mar 1999. 2003, registered in accordance with Norwegian law. **Aims** Facilitate cooperation in the field of telemedicine and telecare between the Nordic countries and the rest of the world. **Structure** Working Group: Infrastructure within Healthnets. **Languages** English. **Finance** Members' dues. **Activities** Organizes congress and annual meeting. **Events** *Nordic congress on telemedicine / Nordic Congress on Telematic* Reykjavik (Iceland) 2010, *Nordic congress on telemedicine / Nordic Congress on Telematic* Copenhagen (Denmark) 2008, *Annual meeting / Nordic Congress on Telematic* Helsinki (Finland) 2006, *Nordic congress on telemedicine* Helsinki (Finland) 2006, *Nordic congress on telemedicine* Umeå (Sweden) 2004. **Publications** *Journal of Telemedicine and Telecare.*
Members Associations in 5 countries:
Denmark, Finland, Iceland, Norway, Sweden. [2010/XD9418/**D**]

♦ Nordic Tele Organization (no recent information)
♦ Nordic Tele Union (inactive)

♦ Nordic Television Cooperation (Nordvision) **17446**
Coopération nordique des télévisions – Nordvision (NV)
SG c/o DR, DR-Byen, Emi Holms Kanal 20, 0999 Copenhagen C, Denmark. E-mail: hrh@dr.dk.
URL: http://www.nordvision.org/
History 1959, by Directors General of four Nordic broadcasting organizations (Denmark, Finland, Norway, Sweden). Icelandic television became a member upon its establishment in 1966. Secretariat set up in 1970, changes site every 5th year. **Aims** Encourage Nordic cooperation by exchange of programmes and co-productions; facilitate reception of Finnish language programmes in Sweden and Swedish language programmes in Finland. **Structure** Director Generals' Meeting (supreme authority), assisted by Director Generals Secretariat. Nordvision Meeting, chaired by Chairman of Nordvision. Nordvision Secretariat, headed by Nordvision Secretary General. International Relations Offices. **Languages** Danish, Finnish, Norwegian, Swedish. **Staff** 3.00 FTE, paid. **Finance** Members' dues. Budget (annual): Norwegian Kr 1,5 million. **Activities** Since 1959, regular meetings of television programme editors (twice a year); divisional meetings to prepare programme collaboration details. Heads of various television output departments meet once or twice a year. Collaboration includes programme acquisition and sales. Special fund of about Swedish Kr 60 million a year is levied on cable distribution of neighbouring countries' television for the support of Nordic projects, principally co-productions. Technical Office (formed 1962) to direct broadcasts. 'Nordic Screening', annually organized by one of the member organizations, in collaboration with a number of other Nordic organizations. **Events** *Annual screening / Annual Nordic Screening* Norway 2000, *Annual screening / Annual Nordic Screening* Denmark 1999, *Annual screening / Annual Nordic Screening* Helsinki (Finland) 1998, *Annual screening / Annual Nordic Screening* Norrköping (Sweden) 1997, *Annual screening / Annual Nordic Screening* Ålesund (Norway) 1996. **Publications** *Nordvisionsstatistik* (annual); *NordvisionsNytt* (2 a month) in Danish, Norwegian, Swedish.
Members Non-commercial public service television organizations in 5 countries:
Denmark, Finland, Iceland, Norway, Sweden.
NGO Relations *European Broadcasting Union (EBU, #06404).* [2010/XD8107/**D**]

- ♦ Nordic Temperance Council (inactive)
- ♦ Nordic Textile Art (unconfirmed)
- ♦ Nordic Textile Workers Union (inactive)
- ♦ Nordic Theatre Council (no recent information)
- ♦ Nordic Theatre Managers Council / see Nordic Theatres Council (#17447)

♦ Nordic Theatres Council **17447**
Nordisk Teaterlederråd (NTLR) – Nordiska Teaterledarrådet
Contact Eerikinkatu 3 B, Eer, FI-00100 Helsinki, Finland. E-mail: info@suomenteatterit.fi.
Contact NTO, Storgt 10B, 0155 Oslo, Norway. T. +4723100992. E-mail: nto@nto.no.
History 1947, Denmark. Former names and other names: *Nordic Theatre Managers Council* – former. **Aims** Exchange information and experience to strengthen the position of theatres in Nordic countries. **Structure** Board, consisting of 2 representatives from each organization. **Languages** Danish, Finnish, Icelandic, Norwegian, Swedish. **Staff** None. **Finance** Costs paid by the national organization in chair. Expenses in relation to common arrangements or seminars paid by the various organizations. **Activities** Networking/liaising; politics/policy/regulatory; training/education. **Events** *Seminar* Thórshavn (Faeroe Is) 2002, *Actual problems of Nordic theatres and theatre artists* Malmö (Sweden) 2000, *Seminar* Tampere (Finland) 1998.
Members Theatre employers in 6 countries and territories:
Denmark, Faeroe Is, Finland, Iceland, Norway, Sweden. [2023.02.15/XD1348/**D**]

♦ Nordic Theatre Union (NTU) **17448**
Union nordique du théâtre – Nordisk Teaterunion
SG c/o Performing Arts Iceland, Tjarnargötu 12, 101 Reykjavik, Iceland. T. +3546640404.
History 1937, Stockholm (Sweden). **Aims** Strengthen and develop Nordic cooperation in the world of theatre; initiate cooperation in dealing with theatrical matters which benefit from pan-Nordic solutions; influence public bodies on pan-Nordic questions; assist theatre unions in Nordic countries having national-level problems in gaining pan-Nordic support in furthering solutions beneficial to the world of theatre; coordinate international efforts of national unions in matters of common interest. **Structure** Nordic Theatre Meeting (every 2 years); Board of 5 members. Chairman and secretariat change every 2 years. **Languages** Danish, English, Faroese, Icelandic, Norwegian, Swedish. **Staff** No permanent staff. **Finance** No budget. **Activities** Pan-Nordic manifestations and publications; prize for Nordic playwrights. **Events** *Biennial Congress* Iceland 2012, *Biennial Congress* Lund (Sweden) 2010, *Biennial Congress* Tampere (Finland) 2008, *Biennial Congress* Copenhagen (Denmark) 2006, *Biennial Congress* Oslo (Norway) 2004. **Publications** *Nordisk Teater Katalog* – online. *Drama, a Mirror – Eight Icelandic Plays*; *Drama, a Mirror – Ten Finnish Plays*; *Nordisk teaterunion – sjuttio år av samspel 1937-2008*; *Theatre Words* – in 9 languages.
Members National Theatre Unions in 6 countries and territories:
Denmark, Faeroe Is, Finland, Greenland, Iceland, Sweden.
NGO Relations Member of: *International Theatre Institute (ITI, #15683).* [2012.06.01/XD0293/**F**]

- ♦ Nordic Theoretical Archaeology Group (meeting series)
- ♦ Nordic Thermoluminescence Laboratory / see Nordic Laboratory for Luminescence Dating (#17333)

♦ Nordic Thoracic Oncology Group **17449**
Contact address not obtained.
Contact address not obtained.
URL: https://nordicthoracioncologygroup.wordpress.com/
History 1993. Registration: No/ID: 33280343, Start date: 10 Dec 2010, End date: 12 Dec 2019, Denmark. **Aims** Provide state-of-the-art lectures of contemporary issues of thoracic oncology; highlight the reseach activities and research collaboration in the collaborating Nordic countries. **Structure** Steering Committee. **Activities** Events/meetings. **Events** *Nordic Lung Cancer Symposium* Bergen (Norway) 2022, *Nordic Lung Cancer Symposium* Bergen (Norway) 2020, *Nordic Lung Cancer Symposium* Copenhagen (Denmark) 2011, *Nordic Lung Cancer Symposium* Tromsø (Norway) 2008, *Nordic Lung Cancer Symposium* Oulu (Finland) 2006. [2021/AA1804/c/**E**]

- ♦ Nordic Timber Council (inactive)

♦ Nordic Tourism Collective **17450**
Co-Founder Østerbrogade 226 st. tv, 2100 Copenhagen, Denmark.
Co-Founder address not obtained.
URL: https://www.nordictourismcollective.com/
History 2019. **Structure** Advisory Council. **Finance** Sources: members' dues. **Activities** Advocacy/lobbying/activism; guidance/assistance/consulting; networking/liaising; training/education.
Members Full in 10 countries and territories:
Denmark, Estonia, Faeroe Is, Finland, Greenland, Iceland, Latvia, Lithuania, Norway, Sweden.
NGO Relations Member of (1): *European Tourism Manifesto (#08921).* Nordic arm of: *European Tour Operators Association (ETOA, #08922).* [2020/AA0968/**F**]

- ♦ Nordic Tourist Board (no recent information)
- ♦ Nordic Trace Element Society (internationally oriented national body)

♦ Nordic Traffic Safety Academy (NTSA) **17451**
Contact address not obtained. E-mail: ntsa-group@outlook.com.
URL: https://www.ictct.net/ntsa/
History 18 May 2011, Lund (Sweden). **Aims** Promote scientific discussion within the road traffic safety society on a multidisciplinary base; strengthen the scientific aspect of road traffic safety work. **Structure** General Meeting (annual); Executive Committee. **Activities** Events/meetings. **Events** *Annual Seminar* Luleå (Sweden) 2021, *Annual Seminar* Luleå (Sweden) 2020, *Annual Seminar* Espoo (Finland) 2019, *Annual Seminar* Lund (Sweden) 2011.
Members Individuals in 12 countries:
Australia, Belgium, Denmark, Estonia, Finland, Iceland, Israel, Malaysia, Netherlands, Norway, Poland, Sweden. [2020/AA0412/v/**F**]

- ♦ Nordic Translators' Council (inactive)

♦ Nordic Transplant Committee **17452**
Sec c/o Scandiatransplant, Aarhus University Hospital, Palle Juul-Jensens Boulevard 99, 8200 Aarhus, Denmark. T. +4578455131. E-mail: scandiatransplant.office@rm.dk.
URL: http://www.scandiatransplant.org/
History Former names and other names: *Nordic Committee on Transplantation* – former. **Languages** English. **Events** *Meeting* Huddinge (Sweden) 2021, *Meeting* Stockholm (Sweden) 2020, *Meeting* Oslo (Norway) 2019, *Meeting* Tartu (Estonia) 2018. [2022/XD8134/**D**]

- ♦ Nordic Transportpolitical Network (#17542)
- ♦ Nordic Transport and Travel Committee (inactive)
- ♦ Nordic Transport Workers' Federation (#17496)
- ♦ Nordic Trans Studies Network (unconfirmed)

♦ Nordic Travel Retail Group (NTRG) **17453**
Contact Jan Hybertz Göricke, c/o Rostra Kommunikation, Svanemøllevej 58, 2900 Hellerup, Denmark. T. +4570230053. E-mail: info@nordictravelretailgroup.com.
URL: http://nordictravelretailgroup.com/
Aims Protect, promote and facilitate the Nordic and Baltic Region's duty-free and travel retail industry by providing the means to obtain the most favourable trading environment for travel-related commerce. **Structure** Board. **Activities** Events/meetings. **Events** *Annual General Meeting* Copenhagen (Denmark) 2023, *Meeting* Copenhagen (Denmark) 2017, *Annual Nordic Travel Retail Seminar* Helsinki (Finland) 2017. **Publications** *NTRG Newsletter* (weekly).
Members Full in 8 countries:
Denmark, Estonia, Finland, Iceland, Latvia, Lithuania, Norway, Sweden.
NGO Relations Member of: *European Travel Retail Confederation (ETRC, #08945).* [2017/XM6042/**D**]

- ♦ Nordic Turner Syndrome Society (inactive)
- ♦ Nordic Union of Commercial Travellers (inactive)
- ♦ Nordic Union of Dental Technicians (inactive)
- ♦ Nordic Union of Driving Schools Associations (#17541)
- ♦ Nordic Union of Food and Allied Workers' Unions (no recent information)
- ♦ Nordic Union for Health and Work (inactive)
- ♦ Nordic Union of Hotel, Café and Restaurant Workers (inactive)

♦ Nordic Union Hotels, Restaurants, Catering and Tourism (NU HRCT) **17454**
Nordisk Union Hotel, Restauration, Catering Og Turisme (NUHRCT)
Gen Sec c/o 3F, Kampmannsgade 4, 1790 Copenhagen V, Denmark. T. +4588921363 – +4588921354. E-mail: nordisk.union@3f.dk.
Sec address not obtained. T. +4528394949.
URL: https://nordichrct.org/
History 1937, as *Nordic Hotel and Restaurant Association – Association nordique des hôtels et restaurants – Nordisk Hotell- og Restaurantforbund.* **Aims** Coordinate cooperation between the five Nordic Hotel and restaurant organizations. **Structure** Management Board; Secretariat. President; Secretary General. Board, consisting of members from each country. Secretariat rotates every 2 years. **Languages** Danish, Norwegian, Swedish. **Staff** Voluntary. **Finance** By 5 national associations. Budget (annual): Swedish Kr 50,000. **Activities** include: information on hotel and restaurant industry; statistical information; credit card rapports; common contracts; common Nordic industry-political affairs and seminars. **Events** *Meeting* Savonlinna (Finland) 2006, *General Meeting* Iceland 1997, *General Meeting* Vejle (Denmark) 1994, *Conference* Imatra (Finland) 1991.
Members Unions (7) in 5 countries:
Denmark, Finland, Iceland, Norway, Sweden.
IGO Relations *Nordic Council of Ministers (NCM, #17260).* **NGO Relations** *International Hotel and Restaurant Association (IH&RA, #13813).* [2018/XD0242/**D**]

- ♦ Nordic Union of Industry (inactive)
- ♦ Nordic Union of Journalists (#17487)
- ♦ Nordic Union of Motor Schools Associations (inactive)

♦ Nordic Union of Museums **17455**
Union Nordique des Musées – Nordisk Museumsforbund
Sec Reykjaviksgade 2-4tv, 2300 Copenhagen S, Denmark. E-mail: jenmun@kk.dk.
History 1915, as *Scandinavian Union of Museums – Union scandinave des musées – Skandinavisk Museumsforbund.* **Aims** Further professional knowledge across borders of the Nordic countries. **Structure** Board. **Languages** Danish, Norwegian, Swedish. **Finance** Members' dues. **Events** *Congress* Helsinki (Finland) 2018, *New Nordic museum concept* Copenhagen (Denmark) 2015, *Congress* Stockholm (Sweden) 2013, *Congress* Faeroe Is 2010, *The great interplay – nature, culture, climate and visual arts* Longyearbyen (Norway) 2008.
Members Full in 8 countries and territories:
Åland, Denmark, Faeroe Is, Finland, Greenland, Iceland, Norway, Sweden. [2020.03.15/XD3208/**D**]

- ♦ Nordic Union for Music Educators (no recent information)
- ♦ Nordic Union for Non-Alcoholic Traffic (inactive)
- ♦ Nordic Union of Optical Wholesalers (inactive)

♦ Nordic Union of Pharmaceutical Organizations **17456**
Union nordique des pharmaciens – Nordisk Farmaceutunion (NFU)
Contact Sveriges Farmacevtförbund, Box 3215, Vasagatan 48, SE-103 64 Stockholm, Sweden.
History 1927, at first meeting. Also referred to as *Nordisk Farmaceut Union (NFU).* **Structure** Informal, based on annual meeting at which a delegation of 4 representatives from each national member association attends and elects President, normally the President of the next year's host country. **Staff** None. **Finance** No budget. **Events** *Annual meeting* Sweden 2009, *Annual meeting* Oslo (Norway) 1996, *Annual meeting* 1995, *Annual meeting* 1994.
Members National associations in 5 countries:
Denmark, Finland, Iceland, Norway, Sweden. [2011/XD1987/c/**F**]

- ♦ Nordic Union of Playwrights (#17502)
- ♦ Nordic Union of Popular Writers (inactive)
- ♦ Nordic Union of Private Schools (inactive)

♦ Nordic Union for Quaternary Research (NORDQUA) **17457**
Leader Bjerkness Ctr for Climate Research, Jahnebakken 5, 5007 Bergen, Norway. E-mail: secretariat@nordqua.org.
URL: http://www.nordqua.org/
History Proposed 1974; formally founded May 1975, Öland (Sweden). Activities faded out 1987; re-initiated Jan 2014. **Aims** Encourage broad interdisciplinary cooperation and communication among Quaternary scientists in Norden; facilitate networking between young scientists. **Structure** Steering Committee; Secretariat. **Activities** Events/meetings; networking/liaising.
Members Individuals in 5 countries:
Denmark, Finland, Iceland, Norway, Sweden. [2022/XM7496/v/**D**]

- ♦ Nordic Union of Railwaymen (inactive)
- ♦ Nordic Union of Road Construction Workers (inactive)
- ♦ Nordic Union of Telecommunication Workers (inactive)
- ♦ Nordic Union of Textile, Clothing and Leather Workers (inactive)

♦ Nordic University Association **17458**
Det Nordiska Universitetssamarbetet (NUS)
SG Assn of Swedish Higher Education Institutions (SUHF), Tryckerigatan 8, SE-111 28 Stockholm, Sweden.
Vice-Chancellor address not obtained.

History Founded 1981, as *Nordic Conference of Rectors – Nordiska Rektorskonferensen*. Previously also referred to as *Association of Nordic University Rectors' Conferences* and *Nordic Conference of University Rectors*. Previously also known under the acronym *NUA*. **Aims** Provide a forum for Nordic university rectors and channel cooperation among Nordic Rectors' conferences. **Structure** Board; Presidency rotates every 2 years. **Languages** Danish, English, Finnish, Icelandic, Norwegian, Swedish. **Staff** None. **Finance** None. **Activities** Advocacy/lobbying/activism; events/meetings; politics/policy/regulatory. **Events** *Conference* Visby (Sweden) 2019, *Conference* Helsinki (Finland) 2013, *Conference on the strategic management of internationalization in higher education / Conference* Lund (Sweden) 2011, *Conference* Reykjavik (Iceland) 2008, *Conference* Copenhagen (Denmark) 2006.
Members Rectors' conferences in 5 countries:
Denmark, Finland, Iceland, Norway, Sweden.
Observers from 3 territories:
Åland, Faeroe Is, Greenland. [2019.12.11/XD2036/cv/**F**]

♦ Nordic Urban Design Association (NUDA) 17459
Founder/Dir Sondre Ravnedalen 28, 5170 Bjirndalstrae, Norway. T. +4792048768. E-mail: haakon@nuda.no.
URL: http://www.nuda.no/
History Feb 2006. **Events** *Annual Nordic urban design conference / Conference* Bergen (Norway) 2009, *Annual Nordic urban design conference / Conference* Bergen (Norway) 2008, *Annual Nordic urban design conference* Bergen (Norway) 2007, *Annual Nordic urban design conference* Bergen (Norway) 2006. [2016/XM3605/**D**]

♦ Nordic Urban and Housing Research Network 17460
Nordisk Samarbeidsgruppe for By og Boligforskning (NSBB)
Contact Aalto Univ, Dept of Real Estate/Planning/Geoinformatics, YTK – Land Use Planning and Urban Studies Group, PO BOX 12200, FI-00076 Aalto, Finland.
History 1997. **Aims** Encourage comparative research mainly in the Nordic countries; increase interaction and exchange between Nordic researchers. **Structure** Informal network organized by Nordic/Baltic universities and research institutions. **Languages** Danish, English, Finnish, Icelandic, Norwegian, Swedish. **Staff** No permanent staff. **Finance** Conference costs covered by participation fees and sponsorship. **Activities** Events/meetings. **Events** *Annual Conference* Tallinn (Estonia) 2014, *Annual Conference* Copenhagen (Denmark) 2013, *Annual Conference* Espoo (Finland) 2012, *Annual Conference* Helsinki (Finland) 2012.
[2014.12.11/XJ6583/c/**E**]

♦ Nordic Urogynecological Association (NUGA) 17461
Nordisk Urogynekologisk Arbetsgrupp
Pres address not obtained. E-mail: runsve@ous-hf.no.
URL: http://nuga-meeting.com/
Structure Board. **Activities** Bi-annual meeting. **Events** *Biennial Meeting* Oslo (Norway) 2022, *Biennial Meeting* Oslo (Norway) 2021, *Biennial Meeting* Copenhagen (Denmark) 2019, *Biennial Meeting* Reykjavik (Iceland) 2017, *Biennial Meeting* Stockholm (Sweden) 2015. [2020/XJ8687/c/**D**]

♦ Nordic Vaccine Meeting (meeting series)
♦ Nordic Veterinarians Association for Mastitis Research and Prevention (inactive)

♦ Nordic Veterinary Acupuncture Society (NoVAS) 17462
Nordisk Veterinaer Akupunktur Selskab
Pres Norwegian Univ of Life Sciences, Fac of Veterinary Medicine and Biosciences, Dept of Companion Animal Clinical Sciences, PO Box 8146 Dep, 0033 Oslo, Norway.
Sec Lentolantie 2, FI-36220 Kangasala, Finland. T. +358405227733.
URL: http://www.novas.dk/
History 1989. **Aims** Promote excellence in the practice of veterinary acupuncture as an integral part of the total veterinary health care delivery system. **Languages** English. **Staff** 7.00 FTE, voluntary. **Finance** Members' dues. Course fees. **Activities** Events/meetings; training/education. **Events** *Annual Meeting* Aalborg (Denmark) 2016, *Annual Meeting* Helsinki (Finland) 2015, *Annual Meeting* Sundvollen (Norway) 2013, *Annual Meeting* Helsinki (Finland) 2011, *Annual Meeting* Aalborg (Denmark) 2010. **Publications** *NoVAS News* (irregular).
Members Veterinary acupuncturists (110) in 4 countries:
Denmark, Finland, Norway, Sweden.
NGO Relations A sister organization to: *International Veterinary Acupuncture Society (IVAS, #15846)*.
[2016.06.01/XD8164/**D**]

♦ Nordic Veterinary Congress (meeting series)

♦ Nordic Volcanological Center (NordVulk) 17463
Contact c/o Inst of Earth Sciences, Sturlugata 7 – Askja, 101 Reykjavik, Iceland. T. +3545254492. Fax +3545629767.
URL: http://www.norvol.hi.is/
History 11 Dec 1972, under the aegis *Nordic Council of Ministers (NCM, #17260)* within the framework of *Nordic Cultural Cooperation (1971)*. Commenced activities 1973. Also known as *Nordisk Vulkanisk Institut (NORDVOLC) – Pohjoismainen Vulkanologinen Instituutti*. Original title: *Nordic Volcanological Institute (NVI) – Institut nordique de volcanologie – Nordisk Vulkanologisk Institut (NORDVULK) – Pohjoismainen Vulkanologinen Instituutti – Norraena eldfjallastödin*. Merged with geology and geophysics sections of the Science Institute, University of Iceland into Institute of Earth Sciences, University of Iceland, 2004, when it adopted current title. **Aims** Perform volcanological research, aimed at the most important aspects of volcanology: *petrography*, *geochemistry*, *geophysics* and the history of volcanoes; provide facilities for scientists and students to study volcanism and related topics. **Structure** Board of Directors, consisting of 5 members appointed by respective ministries in the five Nordic countries. **Staff** 12.00 FTE, paid. 5 scholarships. **Finance** Financed jointly by the 5 Nordic countries. **Activities** Research and development; training/education.
Members Representatives of 5 countries:
Denmark, Finland, Iceland, Norway, Sweden. [2016/XE0569/j/**E**]

♦ Nordic Volcanological Institute / see Nordic Volcanological Center (#17463)
♦ Nordic Volleyball Conference (meeting series)
♦ Nordic Waste Water Conference (meeting series)
♦ Nordic Watchmakers' Association (no recent information)

♦ Nordic Watercolour Association 17464
Nordiska Akvarellsällskapet
Contact address not obtained.
URL: http://www.nordicwatercolour.org/
History 1989. **Aims** Promote and enhance the quality of watercolour painting; provide opportunities for the public to meet premium watercolour art; provide networking opportunities for watercolour painters in the region. **Languages** Danish, English, Norwegian, Swedish. **Publications** *Akvarellen* (4 a year) – magazine.
Members Full in 5 countries:
Denmark, Finland, Iceland, Norway, Sweden.
NGO Relations Member of: *European Confederation of Watercolour Societies (ECWS, #06726)*.
[2019.06.04/XJ5374/**D**]

♦ Nordic Water Framework Directive Conference (meeting series)

♦ Nordic Weightlifting Federation 17465
Association haltérophile nordique – Nordiska Tyngdlyftningsförbundet
Contact Øvre Alle 3, 7030 Trondheim, Norway. T. +4741525828.
Events *Congress* Akureyri (Iceland) 2013.
Members Full in 5 countries:
Denmark, Finland, Iceland, Norway, Sweden. [2017.12.07/XD1736/**D**]

♦ Nordic Welfare Centre (#17163)
♦ Nordic WFD Conference – Nordic Water Framework Directive Conference (meeting series)

♦ Nordic Wittgenstein Society (NWS) 17466
Nordiska Wittgesteinsällskapet
Chair Dept of Philosophy, Arken, Åbo Akademi, Fabriksgatan 2, FI-20500 Turku, Finland.
Sec address not obtained.
URL: http://nordicwittgensteinsociety.org/
History 28 Mar 2009. Founded by *Nordic Network for Wittgenstein Research (NNWR, inactive)*. **Aims** Promote research related to Ludwig Wittgenstein's *philosophy* and different problems and areas of philosophy inspired by his thought; provide a forum for interested Nordic research groups and individuals; strengthen and coordinate Nordic cooperation in this area. **Structure** General Assembly; Board. **Languages** Danish, English, Faroese, Icelandic, Norwegian, Swedish. **Staff** None. **Finance** No budget. **Activities** Events/meetings; training/education. **Events** *Conference* Skjolden (Norway) 2022, *Conference* Turku (Finland) 2022, *Conference* Turku (Finland) 2020, *Conference* Uppsala (Sweden) 2019, *Conference* Pardubice (Czechia) 2018. **Publications** *Nordic Wittgenstein Review*. *Nordic Wittgenstein Studies* – series.
Members Groups and individuals in 5 countries:
Denmark, Finland, Norway, Sweden, UK. [2021/XM3207/**E**]

♦ Nordic Women Against Violence 17467
Address not obtained.
History Founded 1994. **Aims** Share experiences and challenges. **Activities** Events/meetings. **Events** *Conference* Helsinki (Finland) 2018.
Members Shelters and organizations in 7 countries and territories:
Denmark, Faeroe Is, Finland, Greenland, Iceland, Norway, Sweden. [2019/XM7938/**F**]

♦ Nordic Women Mediators (NWM) 17468
Contact Laura Mitchell, PO Box 2947, 0608 Tøyen, Norway.
URL: https://nordicwomenmediators.org/
History Endorsed Apr 2015, by Nordic governments. Officially launched 27 Nov 2015, Oslo (Norway), followed by an international launch, Mar 2016, at *United Nations (UN, #20515)*. **Aims** Enable Nordic women mediators and peacebuilders to advance inclusion and meaningful participation of women in all phases of *peace* processes, so as to contribute to achieving and sustaining peace. **Structure** Annual meeting; Contact group; Operational partners; Advisory group. **Events** *Annual Meeting* Copenhagen (Denmark) 2018, *Annual Meeting* Reykjavik (Iceland) 2017, *Annual Meeting* Stockholm (Sweden) 2016.
Members Operational partners and individuals in 5 countries:
Denmark, Finland, Iceland, Norway, Sweden.
Operational partners include:
Centre for Resolution of International Conflicts (CRIC); *Crisis Management Initiative (CMI)*; *Folke Bernadotte Academy (FBA)*; *Norwegian Centre for Conflict Resolution (NOREF)*; *Peace Research Institute Oslo (PRIO)* (Centre on Gender, Peace and Security PRIO GPS Centre); *United Nations University (UNU, #20642)* (Gender Equality Studies and Training UNU-GEST). [2022/XM7564/y/**F**]

♦ Nordic Women's Association for Total Abstinence (inactive)
♦ Nordic Women's and Gender History Conference (meeting series)
♦ Nordic Women's Trade Union Committee (inactive)
♦ Nordic Wood Biorefinery Conference (meeting series)

♦ Nordic Wood Preservation Council (NWPC) 17469
Conseil nordique de la préservation du bois (CNPB) – Nordiska Träskyddsrådet (NTR) – Nordisk Traebeskyttelsesråd – Nordisk Trebeskyttelsesråd – Pohjoismaiden Puunsuojausneuvosto
SG Box 502, SE-101 30 Stockholm, Sweden. T. +4687912360.
Sec Teknologisk Institut, Tr' og Miljè, PO Box 141, 2630 Tåstrup, Denmark. T. +4572202000 – +4572202312. E-mail: nmo@teknologisk.dk.
URL: https://www.nwpc.eu/
History 9 Oct 1969. Founded following proposal adopted at 7th Nordic Research Meeting, 5 Nov 1968, Copenhagen (Denmark), and recommendation of *Nordic Council (NC, #17256)*. Administration reports to *Nordic Council of Ministers (NCM, #17260)*. Present statutes adopted 3 May 2005. Registration: EU Transparency Register, No/ID: 786474748197-95, Start date: 24 Nov 2022. **Aims** Promote development in the field of wood preservation by coordinating the contributions of individual countries. **Structure** Board of Directors; Technical Group; Secretariat. **Languages** Danish, English, Faroese, Icelandic, Norwegian, Swedish. **Finance** Member organizations. **Activities** Certification/accreditation; events/meetings; standards/guidelines. **Events** *NTR Conference* Oslo (Norway) 2022, *NTR Conference* Copenhagen (Denmark) 2018, *Congress* Hämeenlinna (Finland) 2004, *Congress* Silkeborg (Denmark) 2002, *Congress* Visby (Sweden) 2000. **Publications** *NWPC Documents*; *NWPC Informations*; *NWPC Recommendations*; *NWPC Standards*. Statistics.
Members Organizations and institutes in 5 countries:
Denmark, Finland, Iceland, Norway, Sweden.
NGO Relations *International Research Group on Wood Protection (IRG, #14733)*. [2022/XD4352/**D**]

♦ Nordic Workers' Educational Associations / see Nordic Organization of Workers' Educational Associations (#17377)
♦ Nordic Work Group of Forest Vegetation Management (no recent information)

♦ Nordic Work Group for International Breastfeeding Issues 17470
Nordiska Arbetsgruppen för Internationella Amningsfrågor (NAFIA)
Address not obtained.
History 1978. **Aims** Protect, support and promote breastfeeding, nationally and internationally. **Languages** English, Swedish. **Staff** All voluntary. **Finance** Members' dues. Other sources: donations from members and organizations; occasional project funding. **Activities** Organizes: World Breastfeeding Week; seminars; actions; meetings. Disseminates information. **Publications** *NAFIA-nytt* – newsletter. *International Baby Milk Code – Twenty Years of Experiences in Sweden 1981 – 2001*.
Members in 3 countries:
Denmark, Norway, Sweden.
NGO Relations Member of: *International Baby Food Action Network (IBFAN, #12305)*; Swedish National Breastfeeding Committee; *World Alliance for Breastfeeding Action (WABA, #21079)*; national organizations.
[2012.06.27/XN1049/**E**]

♦ Nordic Working Group on Process Control (NPC) 17471
Chair Technical University of Denmark, SØltofts Plads, Bldg 227 – room 219, 2800 Kongens Lyngby, Denmark. T. +4545252980. Fax +4545932906. E-mail: gsi@kt.dtu.dk.
URL: http://folk.ntnu.no/skoge/npc/
History 24 Oct 1994, Stockholm (Sweden). Former names and other names: *NPC Working Group* – alias. **Aims** Strengthen ties between the Nordic process control communities. **Structure** General Assembly. **Activities** Organizes 'Nordic Process Control Workshop'. Awards 'Nordic Process Control Award' to individuals who have made a lasting and significant contribution in the field of process control. **Events** *Nordic Process Control Workshop* Denmark 2032, *Nordic Process Control Workshop* Finland 2031, *Nordic Process Control Workshop* Norway 2029, *Nordic Process Control Workshop* Sweden 2028, *Nordic Process Control Workshop* Denmark 2026.
Members in 4 countries:
Denmark, Finland, Norway, Sweden. [2021/XM2757/**E**]

♦ Nordic Working Life Conference (meeting series)
♦ Nordic Workshop on Bibliometrics and Research Policy (meeting series)
♦ Nordic Workshop on Industrial Organization (meeting series)
♦ Nordic Workshop in Power System Protection and Control (meeting series)

♦ Nordic World Heritage Association 17472
Contact Christiansfeld Ctr, sister house, Noerregade 14, 6070 Christiansfeld, Denmark. E-mail: nordicworldheritage@gmail.com.
URL: https://www.nordicworldheritage.org/

History 13 Sep 2016, Selfoss (Iceland). Nordic World Heritage have met since 1995. **Aims** Aid and support the implementation of the UNESCO World Heritage Convention in the Nordic countries. **Structure** Annual Meeting; Board of Directors. **Activities** Awards/prizes/competitions; events/meetings; projects/programmes. Award donated by the City of Rauma at Nordic World Heritage Conference in 2017. Winner announced at annual Nordic World Heritage Conference and holds possession of the artwork until next year annual conference. Winner is chosen by Board at Annual Meeting of the Association. **Events** *Conference* Notodden (Norway) 2022, *Positive aspects on a global pandemic and the consequences for the World Heritage Sites* 2021, *Conference* Vestfold og Telemark (Norway) 2020, *Conference* Stockholm (Sweden) 2019, *Conference* Jelling (Denmark) 2018.
Members National World Heritage Associations or National World Heritage Groups in 5 countries:
Denmark, Finland, Iceland, Norway, Sweden.
IGO Relations *UNESCO (#20322).* [2022.03.08/AA0763/**D**]

- ♦ Nordic World Heritage Foundation (inactive)
- ♦ Nordic Wrestling Association (no recent information)

♦ Nordic Young Conservative Union (NYCU) 17473

Union nordique des jeunes conservateurs – Nordisk Ungkonservativ Union (NUU)
Contact UNR c/o FN Ungdomsförbund, Fredriksgatan 61 A-11, FI-00100 Helsinki, Finland. T. +35894542080. Fax +35897531634. E-mail: unr@pohjola-norden.fi.
History 1946. **Aims** Strengthen conservative work and thinking in the Nordic and *Baltic* countries. **Structure** Executive Committee, consisting of one member of each national organization. **Languages** Danish, English, Faroese, Finnish, Icelandic, Norwegian, Swedish. **Staff** Voluntary. **Finance** Funded by the Nordic Council of Ministers (NMR). **Activities** Youth exchanges; regional contact programmes; seminars; summer school. **Events** *Seminar* Norway 1997, *Meeting* Copenhagen (Denmark) 1996, *Seminar* Faeroe Is 1996. **Publications** *The Nordic Conservative.*
Members National organizations and individuals, totalling 50,000 individuals in all, in 10 countries and territories:
Åland, Denmark, Estonia (*), Faeroe Is, Finland, Iceland, Latvia (*), Lithuania (*), Norway, Sweden.
IGO Relations *Nordic Council (NC, #17256); Nordic Children's and Youth Committee (NORDBUK, #17235).* **NGO Relations** Regional member of: *International Young Democrat Union (IYDU, #15928).* Umbrella organization of: *Nordic Youth Council (NYC, #17474).* [2018/XD3000/**D**]

- ♦ Nordic Young Social Democrats (#09855)
- ♦ Nordic Youth Committee / see Nordic Children's and Youth Committee (#17235)
- ♦ Nordic Youth Cooperation Committee / see Nordic Children's and Youth Committee (#17235)

♦ Nordic Youth Council (NYC) 17474

Ungdomens Nordiska Råd (UNR) – Ungdommens Nordiske Råd (UNR) – Nuorten Pohjoismaiden Neuvosto – Nordurlandarad Aeskunnar
Coordinator c/o Pohjola-Nordenin Nuorisoliitto, Fredrikinkatu 61 A 11, FI-00100 Helsinki, Finland. T. +358407748107. Fax +35897531634. E-mail: unr@pohjola-norden.fi.
URL: http://www.unginorden.org/
History as an annual seminar held before the session of *Nordic Council (NC, #17256).* First session funded by Nordic Council organized 1971, Stockholm (Sweden). Became an independent organization in 2002. **Structure** Presidium, consisting of 8 representatives for the Nordic umbrella organizations, and including President. Secretariat. **Events** *Annual Session* Helsinki (Finland) 2012, *Annual Session* Copenhagen (Denmark) 2011, *Annual Session* Reykjavik (Iceland) 2010, *Annual Session* Stockholm (Sweden) 2009, *Annual Session* Espoo (Finland) 2008.
Members National youth leagues of political parties represented in the Nordic national parliaments or in the Autonomous Territories and their Nordic umbrella organizations. Members in 8 countries and territories:
Åland, Denmark, Faeroe Is, Finland, Greenland, Iceland, Norway, Sweden.
Umbrella organizations include the following 5 listed in this Yearbook:
Forbundet Nordens Socialdemokratiske Ungdom (FNSU, #09855); Nordic Centre Youth (NCY, #17232); Nordic Christian Democratic Youth (#17236); Nordic Liberal and Radical Youth (NLRU, no recent information); Nordic Young Conservative Union (NYCU, #17473).
Observer organization:
Föreningarna Nordens Ungdomsförbund (FNUF, inactive). [2011.11.30/XJ3433/y/**E**]

- ♦ Nordic Youth Foundation (inactive)
- ♦ Nordic Youth Handicap Association (inactive)

♦ Nordic Youth Orchestra 17475

Orkester Norden (ON)
Manager c/o Musikkens Hus, Musikkens Plads 1, 9000 Aalborg, Denmark. T. +4560203134. E-mail: forening@orkesternorden.com.
URL: http://www.orkesternorden.com/
History 1993, by *Föreningarna Nordens Förbund (FNF, #09859)* and the Nordic country members of *Jeunesses Musicales International (JMI, #16110)* and of *Lions Clubs International (LCI, #16485).* **Aims** Strengthen the ties between Nordic youth; develop their knowledge of Nordic *music.* **Structure** A project within Svenska Rikskonserter (Swedish Concert Institute). **Languages** English. **Staff** 2.00 FTE, paid. **Finance** Supported by: *Nordic Council of Ministers (NCM, #17260);* Nordic Investment Bank. **Activities** Annual 3-week session. Concert tours.
Members Musicians in 8 countries and territories:
Åland, Denmark, Faeroe Is, Finland, Greenland, Iceland, Norway, Sweden.
NGO Relations Member of: *European Federation of National Youth Orchestras (EFNYO, #07176).* [2015/XF3414/**F**]

♦ Nordic Youth Organization 17476

Organisation nordique des jeunes – Nordisk Samorganisajon for Ungdomsarbeid – Nordisk Samorganisation for Ungdomsarbejde (NSU)
SG Stusnäsvägen 102 c, FI-25870 Dragsfjärd, Finland. T. +358407031948. E-mail: info@nordung.org.
URL: https://www.nordung.org/
History 1946. Former names and other names: *Joint Nordic Organization for Rural Youth* – former. **Aims** Improve relations between youth organizations in Nordic countries. **Structure** General Meeting; Council. Committees (3): Culture; 4H; Rural. **Languages** Danish, Norwegian, Swedish. **Staff** 0.05 FTE, paid; 7.00 FTE, voluntary. **Finance** Members' dues. Support from: *European Commission (EC, #06633); Nordic Children's and Youth Committee (NORDBUK, #17235).* Budget (annual): Danish Kr 500,000. **Activities** Coordinates and channels information to member organizations, which organize meetings, seminars, conferences, camps, Nordic Youth Week in the name of NSU. **Events** *General Assembly* Copenhagen (Denmark) 2019, *General Meeting* Denmark 2004, *General Meeting* Sweden 2002, *General Meeting* Norway 1998, *General Meeting* Germany 1994. **Publications** *Nordisk Informasjonsbrev* (6 a year).
Members Full, youth organizations (18) in 6 countries and territories:
Denmark, Finland, Iceland, Norway, Schleswig-Holstein (Germany), Sweden. [2021/XD1769/**D**]

- ♦ Nordic Youth Research Information (inactive)
- ♦ NordILL – Nordic Resource Sharing, Reference and Collection Management Conference (meeting series)
- ♦ NORDINFO – Nordiska Samarbetsorganet för Vetenskaplig Information (inactive)
- ♦ NORDIPRO – Nordiska Handelsprocedurorganet (inactive)
- ♦ **NordiQC** Nordic immunohistochemical Quality Control (#17316)
- ♦ Nordische Föderation der Gewerkschaften der Kommunalbediensteten (#16204)
- ♦ Nordische Katholische Entwicklungshilfe (inactive)
- ♦ Nordische kulturelle zusammenarbeit (1971 treaty)
- ♦ Nordischer Betonverband (#17251)
- ♦ Nordischer Friseurverband (#17307)
- ♦ Nordischer Ministerrat für Ausbildung und Kultur (inactive)
- ♦ Nordischer Postverein (#17391)
- ♦ Nordischer Spediteurverband (#17543)
- ♦ Nordische Union für Alkoholfreien Verkehr (inactive)
- ♦ Nordische Vereinigung der Landwirtschaftsforscher (#17486)
- ♦ Nordische Wirtschaftliche Rinderzucht (#17275)

♦ Nordiska Administrativa Förbundet (NAF) 17477

Association nordique des sciences administratives – Nordic Federation for Public Administration
Main Office address not obtained. E-mail: sekretariat@nafnet.no.
URL: https://www.nafnet.no/
History 20 Sep 1918, Stockholm (Sweden). **Aims** Gather people interested in public administration within the Nordic countries; promote knowledge and understanding concerning the administrative structures of their various countries; aim towards uniformity and reform within their public administrations. **Languages** Danish, Norwegian, Swedish. **Staff** 10.00 FTE, voluntary. **Finance** Members' dues. Conference proceeds. Annual budget: Danish Kr 450,000. **Activities** Events/meetings; publishing activities. **Events** *Triennial General Meeting* Turku (Finland) 2012, *Triennial general meeting* Copenhagen (Denmark) 2006, *Triennial General Meeting* Gothenburg (Sweden) 2000, *Triennial general meeting* Gothenburg (Sweden) 2000, *Triennial general meeting* Stockholm (Sweden) 2000. **Publications** *Nordisk Administrativt Tidsskrift* (4 a year); *Administrativ Debat* (3-4 a year).
Members Independent sections in 5 countries:
Denmark, Finland, Iceland, Norway, Sweden. [2018.06.01/XD0179/**D**]

- ♦ Nordiska Afasirådet (#17174)
- ♦ Nordiska Afrikainstitutet (#17168)
- ♦ Nordiska Akademikerrådet (inactive)
- ♦ Nordiska Akvarellsällskapet (#17464)
- ♦ Nordiska Ämbetsmannakommittén för Livsmedelsfrågor / see Committee of Senior Officials of the Nordic Countries, Estonia, Latvia and Lithuania in the Field of Food Issues (#04286)
- ♦ Nordiska Ämbetsmannakommittén för Samarbete inom Byggsektorn (inactive)
- ♦ Nordiska Ämbetsmannakommittén för Transportfrågor (inactive)
- ♦ Nordiska Annonsörföreningarnas Förbund (inactive)

♦ Nordiska Arbetarsångar- och Musikerförbundet (NASOM) 17478

Nordic Singer and Musician Workers Association – Association des chanteurs et musiciens nordiques
Contact Raveien 185D, 3242 Sandefjord, Norway.
URL: http://www.nasom.nu/
History 1947, by workers' song associations.
Members Associations in 4 countries:
Denmark, Finland, Norway, Sweden.
NGO Relations *Samrådet för Nordisk Amatörmusik (SAMNAM, #19048).* [2013/XD1926/**D**]

- ♦ Nordiska Arbetsgruppen för Internationella Amningsfrågor (#17470)
- ♦ Nordiska Arboretkommittén (#17491)
- ♦ Nordiska Audiologiska Sällskapet (#17210)
- ♦ Nordiska Bageribranchens Råd (inactive)
- ♦ Nordiska Bankmannaunionen (inactive)
- ♦ Nordiska Båtrådet (#17221)
- ♦ Nordiska Beklädnadsarbetareunionen (inactive)
- ♦ Nordiska Betongförbundet (#17251)
- ♦ Nordiska Bibliotekarieförbunden (inactive)
- ♦ Nordiska Blåbands- och Blåkorsrådet (inactive)
- ♦ Nordiska Bowlingförbundet (inactive)
- ♦ Nordiska Brandförsvarsföreningen (inactive)
- ♦ Nordiska Brandförsvarsorg Direktrmöte (meeting series)
- ♦ Nordiska Byggnads- och Träarbetarefederationen (#17283)
- ♦ Nordiska CDG-föreningen (no recent information)
- ♦ Nordiska Centerungdomens Förbund (#17232)
- ♦ Nordiska Cykelförbundet (no recent information)
- ♦ Nordiska Dermatologiska Föreningen / see Nordic Dermatology Association (#17269)
- ♦ Nordiska Djurskyddsrådet (inactive)
- ♦ Nordiska Dokumentationscentralen för Masskommunikationsforskning / see Nordicom (#17374)
- ♦ Nordiska Dyslexikongressen (meeting series)

♦ Nordiska Ekonomie Studerandes Union (NESU) 17479

Nordic Economics Students' Union
Pres address not obtained. E-mail: president@nesu.net.
URL: http://www.nesu.net/
History 1947. **Aims** Assist members in improving their theoretical and practical knowledge of *business* and *economics,* while learning more about *Nordic* culture and meeting new people. **Languages** Danish, English, Finnish, Icelandic. **Staff** 3.00 FTE, paid. **Activities** Events/meetings. **Events** *Autumn Conference* Lappeenranta (Finland) 2021, *Spring Conference* Vaasa (Finland) 2021, *Spring Conference* Jyväskylä (Finland) 2020, *Autumn Conference* Oulu (Finland) 2020, *Autumn Conference* Tampere (Finland) 2019.
Members Full in 4 countries:
Denmark, Finland, Iceland, Sweden. [2021.02.20/XD6725/**D**]

- ♦ Nordiska Ekonomiska Forskningsrådet (inactive)
- ♦ Nordiska Elektronikfabrikanters Förbund (inactive)

♦ Nordiska Ergonomisällskapet (NES) 17480

Société nordique d'ergonomie – Nordic Ergonomics Society
Pres address not obtained.
URL: http://www.nordicergonomics.org/
History 1969. **Aims** Promote collaboration between member organizations and individuals in Nordic countries that have an interest in, or are working with, ergonomics and the *working environment* and facilitate Nordic collaboration in international activities; increase and promote knowledge about interaction between humans and the environment in which they live and work and facilitate the use of that knowledge in the design of environment, equipment and processes. **Structure** Executive Board; President; Treasurer. Committees; Interest Groups. **Languages** Danish, English, Finnish, Icelandic, Norwegian, Swedish. **Staff** Voluntary. **Finance** Members' dues. **Activities** Addresses current and long term issues affecting professional status and development of ergonomics, including education and practice. Organizes: conference (annual); local seminars. **Events** *Annual Conference* Kuopio (Finland) 2016, *Annual Conference* Copenhagen (Denmark) 2014, *Annual Conference* Saltsjöbaden (Sweden) 2012, *Annual Conference* Oulu (Finland) 2011, *Conference / Annual Conference* Stavanger (Norway) 2010. **Publications** Congress proceedings.
Members Organizations representing 1,368 academics, practitioners, students and individuals interested in ergonomics, in 5 countries:
Denmark, Finland, Iceland, Norway, Sweden. [2014/XD2370/**D**]

♦ Nordisk Aerobiologisk Förening (NAF) 17481

Nordic Aerobiology Society
Contact c/o Asthma-Allergy Assoc, Universitetsparken 4, 4000 Røskilde, Denmark.
URL: https://sites.google.com/site/nordicaerobiology/
History 1977, Turku (Finland). **Aims** Promote development of aerobiology and facilitate international cooperation, especially in Scandinavia. **Structure** Board, consisting of President, Vice-President, Secretary, Treasurer and 2 Contact Persons. **Finance** Members' dues. **Events** *Symposium* Riga (Latvia) 2013, *Symposium* Denmark 2009, *Symposium* Turku (Finland) 2004, *Symposium* Sjaelland (Denmark) 2001, *Symposium* Røros (Norway) 1993. **Publications** *NAF-letter* (2 a year).
Members Individuals (70) in 6 countries:
Denmark, Estonia, Finland, Iceland, Norway, Sweden.
NGO Relations *International Association for Aerobiology (IAA, #11691).* [2020/XD3269/v/**D**]

♦ Nordiska Expertkommittén för Transplantationsfrågor / see Scandiatransplant Association (#19066)
♦ Nordiska Exportfrämjande Organisationers Chefsmøte (meeting series)
♦ Nordiska Fabriksarbetarefederationen (inactive)
♦ Nordiska Fältmykologernas Förening (inactive)
♦ Nordiska Fängelsefunktionärers Union (inactive)
♦ Nordiska Fertilitetsklubben (inactive)
♦ Nordiska Fiberboardindustriernas Centralförbund (inactive)
♦ Nordiska Finansanställdas Union (#17292)
♦ Nordiska Flaggsällskapet (#17294)
♦ Nordiska Folkhögskolerådet (#17295)
♦ Nordiska Förbundet för Kyrkogårdar och Krematorier (#02418)

♦ Nordiska Förbundet för Läkepedagogik och Socialterapi (NFLS) . . . 17482

Association for Curative Education and Social Therapy in the Nordic countries

Chair address not obtained.
URL: https://nfls.nu/

Aims Develop anthroposophical curative education and social therapy. **Structure** Annual General Meeting; Board of Directors. [2022/AA2776/**F**]

♦ Nordiska Förbundet för Specialpedagogik (#17435)
♦ Nordiska Förbundet för Statskunskap (#17389)
♦ Nordiska Föreningen för Befrämjande af Odontologisk Undervisning och Forskning (#19070)
♦ Nordiska Föreningen för Kina-studier (#17182)
♦ Nordiska föreningen för lerforskning (inactive)
♦ Nordiska Föreningen för Patologi och Mikrobiologi (inactive)
♦ Nordiska Föreningen för RenhetsTeknik och Rena Rum (#17183)
♦ Nordiska Föreningen för Social och Mental Hälsa (inactive)
♦ Nordiska Föreningen för Sydöstasienstudier (inactive)
♦ Nordiska Föreningen för Tillämpad och Industriell Matematik (inactive)
♦ Nordiska Försäkringsmannaunionen (inactive)
♦ Nordiska Fredsförbund (inactive)
♦ Nordiska Frisörmästareförbundet (#17307)
♦ Nordiska Genbanken / see Nordic Genetic Resource Centre (#17303)
♦ Nordiska Genbanken för Jordbruks- och Trädgårdsväxtar / see Nordic Genetic Resource Centre (#17303)
♦ Nordiska geologiska vintermötet (meeting series)
♦ Nordiska Glastekniska Föreningen (inactive)

♦ Nordiska Godtemplarrådet (NGR) 17483

Pohjoismaiden Godtemplar-neuvosto – Nordic Good Templar Council – Conseil nordique des bons templiers

Contact Arabergsvägen 22, SE-432 96 Åskloster, Sweden. T. +46733144924.
URL: http://www.ngrnorden.se/

History 1956, Aarhus (Denmark). 1956, Århus (Denmark). Youth Council. **Structure** Board of 13, including President, Secretary and Treasurer. **Languages** Danish, Finnish, Icelandic, Norwegian, Swedish. **Staff** 13.00 FTE, paid. **Finance** Budget (annual): Swedish Kr 200,000. **Activities** Political work. Seminars. Instrumental in setting up: *Nordens Godtemplar Ungdomsråd (NORDGU, #17159)*. **Events** *Meeting* Denmark 2000, *Meeting* Boden (Sweden) 1999, *Meeting* Vaasa (Finland) 1998, *Meeting* Thórshavn (Faeroe Is) 1996, *Seminar and general assembly* Rønne (Denmark) 1987. **Publications** *NGR Newsheet* (2 a year).
Members Groups of adult Good Templars in 6 countries and territories:
Denmark, Faeroe Is, Finland, Iceland, Norway, Sweden. [2014/XD1905/**D**]

♦ Nordiska Gravörorganisationen (inactive)
♦ Nordiska Grossistförbundens Centralråd (inactive)
♦ Nordiska Handelsarbetsgivare-Föreningarnas Samarbetskommitté (inactive)
♦ Nordiska Handelsprocedurorganet (inactive)
♦ Nordiska Handicappidrottsförbundet (inactive)
♦ Nordiska Handikappförbundens Ungdom (inactive)
♦ Nordiska Handikappförbundet (#17308)
♦ Nordiska Handikappidrottskommittén (inactive)
♦ Nordiska Handikappolitiska Rådet (#17259)
♦ Nordiska Hjärt- och Lungsjukas förbund (inactive)
♦ Nordiska högskolan för folkkälsovetenskap (inactive)

♦ Nordiska Hörselskadades Samarbetskommittén (NHS) 17484

Nordic Alliance of the Hard of Hearing (NHH)

Contact c/o HLF, Brynsveien 13, box 6652 Etterstad, 0609 Oslo, Norway. T. +4741303243. E-mail: raaken@hlf.no.
Contact address not obtained.
URL: https://nhs-norden.com/

Members Full in 5 countries:
Denmark, Finland, Iceland, Norway, Sweden. [2019.06.25/XD1652/**D**]

♦ Nordiska Hovvårdsförbundet (internationally oriented national body)
♦ Nordiska Idrottskommittén för Synskadade (inactive)
♦ Nordiska Industriarbetare Federationen (inactive)
♦ Nordiska Industriläkarradet (inactive)
♦ Nordiska Ingenjörssamfundet (inactive)
♦ Nordiska Inremissionsrådet (inactive)

♦ Nordiska Institutet för Odontologisk Materialprovning (NIOM) 17485

Nordic Institute of Dental Materials – Institut nordique pour le contrôle des matériaux dentaires – Nordisk Institut for Odontologisk Materialprøvning (NIOM) – Pohjoismainen Hammasmateriaalin Koetuslaitos

Dir Sognsveien 70 A, 0855 Oslo, Norway. T. +4767512200. Fax +4767591530. E-mail: niom@niom.no.
URL: http://www.niom.no/

History 1972, by *Nordic Council (NC, #17256)*. A permanent institution on the general budget of *Nordic Council of Ministers (NCM, #17260)* until 2010. Presently a Nordic cooperative body owned by the University of Oslo and the Ministry of Health and Care Services, Norway. Previously also referred to as *Scandinavian Institute of Dental Materials*. **Aims** Promote *patient* safety. **Structure** Board. **Languages** English, Norwegian. **Staff** 25.00 FTE, paid. **Finance** Ministry of Health and Care Services; Norway Nordic Council of Ministers. Annual budget: US$ 4,000,000. **Activities** Standards/guidelines; certification/accreditation; knowledge management/ information dissemination; training/education. **Events** *Northern Lights International Symposium* Oslo (Norway) 2018, *Biological testing of dental materials, state-of-the-art* Haslum (Norway) 1990. **Publications** Research publications.
Members States (5):
Denmark, Finland, Iceland, Norway, Sweden.
NGO Relations Member of: *ORCID (#17790)*. [2017.07.03/XD2734/j/**E***]

♦ Nordiska Institutet för Sjörätt (#17515)
♦ Nordiska Institutet för Teoretisk Fysik (#17324)
♦ Nordiska institutionen för vidareutbildning inom arbetsmiljöområdet (#17321)
♦ Nordiska Investeringsbanken (#17327)
♦ Nordiska Jägares Samarbetsorganisation / see Nordic Hunters' Alliance (#17313)
♦ Nordiska Järnvägars Forsknings- och Utvecklingsråd (inactive)
♦ Nordiska Järnvägsmannaunionen (inactive)

♦ Nordiska Jordbruksforskares Förening (NJF) 17486

Association scandinave de recherches agricoles – Nordische Vereinigung der Landwirtschaftsforscher – Nordic Association of Agricultural Scientists

Address not obtained.
URL: http://www.njf.nu/

History 1918. Previously known as *Nordiske Jordbrugsforskeres Forening*. Also referred to as *Verband der Nordischen Landwirtschaftsforscher*. Since 2011, membership expanded outside Nordic countries. **Aims** Promote and develop interaction (networking) between scientists, advisors, teaching and administrators, and between agriculture, agricultural research, industry, consumers and society, particularly in member states. **Structure** Congress (every 4 years). National Associations in each country. Assembly of Delegates, consisting of Chairmen of National Associations (5) and Professional Sections (5). **Languages** English. **Staff** 1.00 FTE, paid. **Finance** Members' dues. Other sources: grants; seminar proceeds. **Activities** Arranges seminars, workshops, congress (every 4 years) and graduate courses; Specialized sections and their working parties also hold meetings. Sections (5): Plants; Animals; Environment; Economics; Technology. **Events** *Congress* Selfoss (Iceland) 2022, *Congress* Kaunas (Lithuania) 2018, *Seminar on the Role of Agriculture in Civil Defence in the Nordic- Baltic Countries* Uppsala (Sweden) 2018, *Seminar on Nordic Agrofood Expertise for Development* Helsinki (Finland) 2016, *International Conference on Localized Agri-Food Systems* Stockholm (Sweden) 2016. **Publications** *News From NJF* (4 a year) – eletronic newsletter; *NJF Report* (periodic); *Annual Report* and *Outlook*.
Members Individuals (over 1,700) in 8 countries:
Denmark, Estonia, Finland, Iceland, Latvia, Lithuania, Norway, Sweden. [2016/XD3174/v/**D**]

♦ Nordiska Journalistförbundet (NJF) 17487

Union nordique de journalistes – Nordic Union of Journalists

Gen Sec Union of Journalists in Finland, PO Box 252, FI-00531 Helsinki, Finland. T. +358405120036. Fax +3589605396.

History Founded Sep 1946, Stockholm (Sweden). Previously also referred to as *Nordic Association of Journalists' Unions – Association des unions de journalistes nordiques* and *Nordic Federation of Journalists*. **Aims** Exchange information on all professional matters; promote reciprocal economic support in situations of strike, unemployment; cooperate in influencing legislation in the Nordic countries. **Structure** Governing Body, consisting of presidents of member unions. Secretariat held by member unions in 2-year rotation. **Languages** Danish, Finnish, Norwegian, Swedish. **Staff** Provided by union holding Secretariat. **Finance** Participation in the work is covered by each union paying for itself. For common activities pro rata payment based on each union's membership. **Activities** Events/meetings; training/education; research/documentation. **Events** *Biennial Congress* Turku (Finland) 1995, *Biennial Congress* Tromsø (Norway) 1993, *Biennial Congress* Ebeltoft (Denmark) 1991, *Biennial Congress* Sandhamn (Sweden) 1989, *Biennial Congress* Mariehamn (Finland) 1987. **Publications** Reports.
Members Member unions, totalling 43,000 journalists, in 6 countries and territories:
Denmark, Faeroe Is, Finland, Iceland, Norway, Sweden.
NGO Relations Member unions are members of: *European Federation of Journalists (EFJ, #07152)*; *International Federation of Journalists (IFJ, #13462)*. [2017.11.28/XD2978/**D**]

♦ Nordiska Juristförbundens Samarbetsråd (meeting series)
♦ Nordisk Akademikerråd (inactive)
♦ Nordiska Kemistrådet (inactive)
♦ Nordiska Kommissionen för Geodesi (#17304)
♦ Nordiska Kommittén för Byggbestämmelser (inactive)
♦ Nordiska Kommittén för Kärnsäkerhetsforskning / see Nordisk Kärnsäkerhetsforskning (#17517)
♦ Nordiska Kommittén för Östeuropaforskning (inactive)
♦ Nordiska Kommittén för Samordning av Elektriska Säkerhetsfrågor (#17246)
♦ Nordiska Kommittén för Vägtrafiklagstiftning (inactive)
♦ Nordiska Kommunaltjänstemannarådet / see Nordisk Tjenestemannsråd (#17538)

♦ Nordiska kommunforskningsföreningen (Norkom) 17488

Chair address not obtained.
URL: https://www.norkom.fi/

History 2014, Finland. Conferences organized since 1992. **Structure** Board of Directors. **Languages** Danish, English, Norwegian, Norwegian Bokmål, Swedish. **Activities** Events/meetings. Active in: Denmark, Faeroe Is, Finland, Iceland, Norway, Sweden. **Events** *Annual Conference* Oslo (Norway) 2026, *Annual Conference* Gothenburg (Sweden) 2025, *Annual Conference* Turku (Finland) 2024, *Annual Conference* Odense (Denmark) 2023, *Annual Conference* Reykjavik (Iceland) 2022. [2022.06.20/AA0445/**F**]

♦ Nordiska konferensen i gruppsykoterapi (meeting series)
♦ Nordiska konferens för vårdgivare som arbetar med traumatiserade flyktingar (meeting series)
♦ Nordiska Konservatorsförbundet (#17188)
♦ Nordiska Konstförbundet (#17176)
♦ Nordiska Kontaktorganet för Atomenergifrågor (inactive)
♦ Nordiska Kontaktorganet för Fiskerifrågor (inactive)
♦ Nordiska Kooperativa och Allmännyttiga Bostadsföretags Organisation (#10957)
♦ Nordiska Kooperativa Samrådsgruppen / see Föreningarna Nordens Förbund (#09859)
♦ Nordiska Krigs-och FN-Veteranförbundet (#02834)
♦ Nordiska Kulturfonden / see Nordic Culture Fund (#17264)
♦ Nordiska Kulturkommissionen (inactive)
♦ Nordisk Akustisk Selskap / see Nordic Acoustic Association (#17165)
♦ Nordiska Kvinnoförbundet för Alkoholfrikultur (inactive)
♦ Nordiska Kvinno- och Genushistorikermötet (meeting series)
♦ Nordiska Kvinnosaksföreningars Samorganisation (inactive)
♦ Nordiska Kyrkomusikrådet (#17257)
♦ Nordiska Läkarrådet (unconfirmed)
♦ Nordiska Läkemedelsnämnden (inactive)
♦ Nordiska Läraeorganisationers Samråd (#17444)
♦ Nordiska Lärares Fredsförbund (inactive)
♦ Nordiska Latinamerikainstitutet (internationally oriented national body)
♦ Nordiska Maskinbefälsfederation (#17279)
♦ Nordisk Amatørmusikunion / see Nordisk Orkestermusik Union (#17525)
♦ Nordisk Amatørteaterråd (#17172)
♦ Nordiska Medisinrådet (inactive)
♦ Nordiska Metall (inactive)
♦ Nordiska Miljöfinasieringsbolaget (#17281)
♦ Nordiska Ministerrådet (#17260)
♦ Nordiska Multipel Skleros-Rådet (no recent information)
♦ Nordiska Musikkommittén (inactive)
♦ Nordiska Musikkvetenskapliga Sällskaparnas Råd (inactive)
♦ Nordiska Nammden for Handikappforbundet / see Nordic Handicap Federation (#17308)
♦ Nordiska Nämnden för Alkoholforskning (inactive)
♦ Nordisk Anästesiologisk Forening / see Scandinavian Society of Anaesthesiology and Intensive Care Medicine (#19101)
♦ Nordiska Nätverk (#17348)
♦ Nordiska Neuropediatriska Sällskapet (#17367)
♦ Nordiska Neuropediatriska Selskapet (#17367)
♦ Nordiska Odontologiskastudentkåerna (inactive)
♦ Nordiska Oppfinnarföreningarnes Samarbetsorganisationen (no recent information)
♦ Nordiska Optikkgrossistunioner (inactive)
♦ Nordiska Organisationsföreningen (inactive)
♦ Nordiska Orienteringsrådet (no recent information)
♦ Nordiska Ortodontisällskapet (#17378)

♦ Nordiska Översättarrådet (inactive)
♦ Nordiska Passkontrollöverenskommelsen (1957 treaty)
♦ Nordiska Plaströrgruppen (#17387)

♦ Nordiska Polisförbundet (NPF) 17489

Nordic Police Association – Association des polices nordiques

Exec Dir c/o Polisförbundet, Asemamiehenkatu 2, Box 5583, SE-114 85 Stockholm, Sweden.

History 1921. Former names and other names: *Federation of Nordic Police Unions* – alias; *Nordic Police Federation* – alias. **Events** *Meeting* Helsinki (Finland) 2017, *Meeting* Helsinki (Finland) 2002.
Members Organizations (6) in 5 countries:
Denmark (2), Finland, Iceland, Norway, Sweden. [2021/XD1958/**D**]

♦ Nordiska Polisidrottförbund (inactive)
♦ Nordiska Postföreningen (#17391)
♦ Nordiska Postmannaunionen (inactive)
♦ Nordisk Apoteksforening (inactive)

♦ Nordiska Projektexportfonden (NOPEF) 17490

Fonds nordique de projets d'exportations – Nordic Project Fund – Pohjoismaiden Projektivientirahasto

Acting Managing Dir PO Box 241, FI-00171 Helsinki, Finland. T. +35896840570. Fax +3589650113. E-mail: info@nopef.com.
Street Address Fabiansgatan 34, FI-00171 Helsinki, Finland.
URL: http://www.nopef.com/

History 1982, by *Nordic Council of Ministers (NCM, #17260)*. **Aims** Strengthen the international *competitiveness* of Nordic companies outside EU and EFTA countries by granting conditional *loans* to Nordic companies for feasibility studies and other project preparation costs of projects of Nordic interest both in the case of project exports and new project and business development. **Structure** Board with representatives of all member states. **Languages** Danish, English, Finnish, Norwegian, Swedish. **Staff** 6.00 FTE, paid. **Finance** Financed through NMR. **Activities** Grants conditional loans to Nordic companies for prefeasibility and feasibility studies of projects outside EU and EFTA countries; finances studies of general interest to Nordic industry in foreign markets; sponsors seminars and conferences; participates in project identification in cooperation with Nordic industry and regional and international institutions. **Publications** Annual Report.
Members Governments of the 5 Nordic countries:
Denmark, Finland, Iceland, Norway, Sweden.
IGO Relations One of 3 investment groups, the others being: *Nordic Environment Finance Corporation (NEFCO, #17281)*; *Nordic Development Fund (NDF, #17271)*. [2012/XF1040/f/**F***]

♦ Nordiska Publiceringskommittén för Humanistiska och Samhällsvetenskapliga Tidskrifter / see Nordisk publiseringsnemnd for humanistiske og samfunnsvitenskapelige tidsskrifter (#17526)
♦ Nordiska Publiceringsnämnden för Naturvetenskap (inactive)
♦ Nordiska R3 Föreningen / see Nordic Association of Cleanroom Technology (#17183)
♦ Nordiska Rådet (#17256)
♦ Nordiska Rådet för Antropologisk Forskning (inactive)
♦ Nordisk Arbeidsmarkedsutvalg (inactive)
♦ Nordisk Arbeidsmiljøkonvensjon (1989 treaty)
♦ Nordisk arbejdsmiljøkonvention (1989 treaty)
♦ Nordisk arbetsmiljökonvention (1989 treaty)

♦ Nordisk Arboretudvalg (NAU) 17491

Comité nordique des Arboreta – Nordiska Arboretkommittén – Nordic Arboretum Committee

Chairman Dir Arboretum Mustila, Mustilantie 55, FI-47200 Elimäki, Finland.
URL: http://www.nordicforestresearch.org/

History 1 Jun 1972, Bergen (Norway). 1-2 Jun 1972, Bergen (Norway). Comes within the framework of *Nordic Forest Research Cooperation Committee (#17296)*. Has been referred to in English as *Nordic Committee for Arboreal Questions*. **Aims** Procure new *plant* material of dendrological interest; establish registration network for *Scandinavian* collections; provide information on development of *dendrological* material; promote exchange of seed and plants between countries. **Structure** Secretariat at institute of Chairman (5-year term). No official Board. **Languages** Danish, English, Faroese, Icelandic, Norwegian, Swedish. **Staff** None. **Finance** Funded through each "mother" institute and from *Nordic Forest Research Cooperation Committee (#17296)*. **Activities** Arranges: expeditions for seed and plant collection; annual meetings; lectures; distribution of information. **Events** *Annual Meeting* Copenhagen (Denmark) 2010, *Annual Meeting* Riga (Latvia) 2009, *Annual Meeting* Oulu (Finland) 2008, *Annual meeting* Lerwick (UK) 2007, *Annual meeting* Umeå (Sweden) 2006. **Publications** Reports of expeditions. Seed lists; lecture summaries.
Members Individuals (20) in 5 countries (" includes Faeroe Is and Greenland, " includes Åland):
Denmark (*), Finland (**), Iceland, Norway, Sweden.
Affiliated membership in 4 territories:
Estonia, Latvia, Lithuania, Shetland Is. [2011.06.01/XD1740/**E**]

♦ Nordiska Reklamebyrå Förbundet (no recent information)
♦ Nordiska Rektorskonferensen / see Nordic University Association (#17458)
♦ Nordiska Reologisällskapet (#17400)
♦ Nordiska Revisorsförbundet (#17285)
♦ Nordiska Ryggmärgsskade Rådet (inactive)
♦ Nordiska Sällskapet för Arktisk Medicin / see Nordic Society for Circumpolar Health (#17412)
♦ Nordiska sällskapet för ätstörningar / see Nordic Eating Disorders Society (#17273)
♦ Nordiska Sällskapet för Estetik (#17411)
♦ Nordiska Sällskapet för Gynekologisk Onkologi (#17415)
♦ Nordiska Sällskapet för Klinisk Fysiologi / see Scandinavian Society of Clinical Physiology and Nuclear Medicine (#19104)
♦ Nordiska Sällskapet för Strålskydd (#17428)
♦ Nordiska Samarbetsgruppen för Skogproduktionsforskning (inactive)
♦ Nordiska Samarbetsgruppen för Skogsentomologi (see: #17296)
♦ Nordiska Samarbetsgruppen för Skogsgødslingsfragor (inactive)
♦ Nordiska Samarbetsgruppen för Skogsinventeringsfrågor (see: #17296)
♦ Nordiska Samarbetskommittén för Arktisk Medicinsk Forskning (inactive)
♦ Nordiska Samarbetskommittén för Materialforskning och- Provning (inactive)

♦ Nordiska Samarbetskommittén för Namnforskning (NORNA) 17492

Nordic Cooperative Committee for Onomastic Research

Pres address not obtained. E-mail: namn@sprakinstitutet.fi.
Sec address not obtained.
URL: http://www.norna.org/

History 1971. Former names and other names: *Nordic Committee on Name Research* – alias. **Aims** Advance, represent and coordinate *onomastic* sciences on a Nordic level and in an *interdisciplinary* context. **Structure** General Assembly (every 4-5 years, at Congress) elects Committee, comprising one representative from each of the Nordic countries. Secretariat, consisting of President and Secretary (who must come from the same country) and Treasurer. **Languages** Danish, Faroese, Icelandic, Norwegian, Swedish. **Finance** Grants. **Activities** Organizes symposia and congresses. **Events** *Congress* Helsinki (Finland) 2021, *Congress* Kleppe (Norway) 2016, *Symposium* Copenhagen (Denmark) 2014, *Congress* Askov (Denmark) 2012, *Symposium* Haapsalu (Estonia) 2008. **Publications** *NORNA-rapporter* – series.
Members Full (mostly in Nordic countries) in 14 countries and territories:
Belgium, Canada, Denmark, Estonia, Faeroe Is, Finland, Germany, Iceland, Netherlands, Norway, Russia, Sweden, Switzerland, UK. [2014/XE3228/**E**]

♦ Nordiska Samarbetsnämnden för Humanistisk och Samhällsvetenskaplig Forskning / see Nordisk Samarbejdsnaevn for Humanistisk og Samfundsvidenskabelig Forskning (#17530)
♦ Nordiska Samarbetsnämnden för Medicinsk Forskning (#16125)
♦ Nordiska Samarbetsorganet för Drogforskning (inactive)
♦ Nordiska Samarbetsorganet för Handikappfrågor (inactive)
♦ Nordiska Samarbetsorganet för Samespörsmål och Renskötselfrågor (no recent information)
♦ Nordiska Samarbetsorganet för Vetenskaplig Information (inactive)
♦ Nordiska Samarbetsorganisationen för Teknisk-Vetenskaplig Forskning (inactive)
♦ Nordiska Samarbetsorgan för Konditions-Idrott (inactive)

♦ Nordiska Samarbetsrådet för Kriminologi (NSfK) 17493

Conseil de coordination nordique en matière de criminologie – Scandinavian Research Council for Criminology – Nordisk Samarbetsråd for Kriminologi (NSfK) – Pohjoismaiden Kriminologinen Yhteistyöneuvosto – Nordisk Samarbejdsråd for Kriminologi (NSfK) – Norraena Sakfraedriadid

Leader of Secretariat Univ of Oslo, Dept of Criminology and Sociology of Law, Postboks 6706 St. Olavs plass, 0130 Oslo, Norway. E-mail: m.h.foshaugen@jus.uio.no.
Head of Communications address not obtained.
URL: http://www.nsfk.org/

History 1 Jan 1962, Stockholm (Sweden). Founded following recommendations made in 1961 by Nordic Ministers of Justice and in the framework of *Nordic Council of Ministers (NCM, #17260)*. Former names and other names: *Nordic Research Council for Criminology* – alias. **Aims** Initiate and conduct criminological research and further such research within member countries; assist and advise the Scandinavian governments and NMR on issues related to criminology; collect and circulate information on subjects of interest to Scandinavian criminologists. **Structure** Council, consisting of 15 members (3 from each member country). Secretariat, located in the country of the Chairperson (the Chair circulates among the Nordic countries). Working Groups. **Languages** Danish, Faroese, Icelandic, Norwegian, Swedish. **Staff** 1.00 FTE, paid. **Finance** Members' dues proportional to each country's GNP. **Activities** Initiates and coordinates comparative research in several areas of criminology, including hidden criminology, police research and victimology; awards grants (annually) to several individual Scandinavian research projects, such as studies on juvenile delinquency, minorities, white collar crime, alternatives to prison, informal and formal social control and alternative ways of settling conflicts. **Events** *Research Seminar* Halden (Norway) 2021, *Research Seminar* Halden (Norway) 2020, *Research Seminar* Helsinki (Finland) 2018, *Research Seminar* Borgarnes (Iceland) 2016, *Research Seminar* Stavern (Norway) 2015. **Publications** *NSfK Newsletter*. *Journal of Scandinavian Studies in Criminology and Crime Prevention* (2000) – together with the Nordic Council for Crime Prevention; *Scandinavian Studies in Criminology* (1965-1999). Seminar reports.
Members Full in 5 countries:
Denmark, Finland, Iceland, Norway, Sweden. [2022/XD7683/**D***]

♦ Nordiska Samarbetsutskottet för Träteknisk Forskning (inactive)
♦ Nordiska Samerådet / see Saami Council (#19012)
♦ Nordiska-Samfundet för Latinamerikaforskning (inactive)

♦ Nordiska Sekretariatet 17494

Pres address not obtained.
Facebook: https://www.facebook.com/pg/NordiskaSekretariatet/

Aims Facilitate contacts and promote a strong cooperation and raised understanding between law students in the Nordic countries. **Activities** Events/meetings. **Events** *Meeting on the General Data Protection Regulation* Bergen (Norway) 2019.
Members Law students' associations (11) in 5 countries:
Denmark, Finland, Iceland, Norway, Sweden. [2020/AA0659/**F**]

♦ Nordiska Sekretariatet för Arbetare i Jordbruk och Trädgårdsnäring (inactive)
♦ Nordiska Simförbundet (#17442)
♦ Nordiska Skådespelarrådet (#17166)
♦ Nordiska Skärgårdssamarbetet (#17253)
♦ Nordiska Skattevetenskapliga Forskningsrådet (#17443)
♦ Nordiska Skeppsteknika Mote (inactive)
♦ Nordiska Skidskolans Råd (inactive)
♦ Nordiska Skogbrukets Frö och Planträd (inactive)
♦ Nordiska Skogsekonomers Förening (#19108)
♦ Nordiska skogskongressen (meeting series)
♦ Nordiska Skorstensfejarunionen (inactive)
♦ Nordiska Skytteregionen (#17408)
♦ Nordiska socialhögskolekommittén / see Nordic Association of Schools of Social Work (#17204)
♦ Nordiska Sociologföreningen (#17433)

♦ Nordiska Socionomförbunds Samarbetskommitté (NSSK) 17495

Coordinating Committee of Nordic Associations of Social Workers

Conact c/o Akademikerförbundet SSR, Box 12800, SE-112 96 Stockholm, Sweden.

History 1970. **Aims** Promote Nordic cooperation to work for the professional and economic standards and support the development of *profession*. **Structure** Representatives (2) from each member associations meet twice a year. Chairperson and Secretary rotate every 2 years. **Finance** Members' dues. **Events** *Annual seminar* Bornholm (Denmark) 2000, *Annual seminar* Faeroe Is 1998, *Meeting* Copenhagen (Denmark) 1996, *Annual seminar* Oslo (Norway) 1996, *Annual seminar* Iceland 1994. **Publications** *Nordisk Sosialt Arbeid* (4 a year).
Members Social workers associations in 6 countries and territories:
Denmark, Faeroe Is, Finland, Iceland, Norway, Sweden.
NGO Relations Formal contacts with Nordic Groups of: *International Association of Schools of Social Work (IASSW, #12149)*; *International Council on Social Welfare (ICSW, #13076)*. All national member associations are also members of: *International Federation of Social Workers (IFSW, #13544)*. [2015/XD0321/**E**]

♦ Nordiska Sommaruniversitetet (#17535)
♦ Nordiska Språkrådet (inactive)
♦ Nordiska Stålförbundet (inactive)
♦ Nordiska Statistikermötet (meeting series)
♦ Nordiska Teaterledarrådet (#17447)
♦ Nordiska Textillärarförbundet (no recent information)
♦ Nordiska Tidningsutgivarnas Samarbetsnämnd (no recent information)
♦ Nordisk Atlantsamarbejde (#17209)
♦ Nordiska Transplantationskommittén / see Scandiatransplant Association (#19066)

♦ Nordiska Transportarbetarefederationen (NTF) 17496

Nordic Transport Workers' Federation – Fédération nordique des travailleurs du transport – Nordisk Transportarbeiderfederasjon (NTF) – Pohjoismainen Kuljetustyöntekijäinfederaatio – Norraena Flutningamannasambandiõ

Gen Sec Barnhusgatan 8, SE-111 23 Stockholm, Sweden. T. +46706330231. E-mail: ntf@nordictransport.org.
URL: http://www.nordictransport.org/

History Founded 1908, Helsingborg (Sweden), as *Scandinavian Transport Workers Federation (STF)* – *Skandinaviska Transportarbetarefederationen* – *Skandinavisk Transportarbeiderfederasjon*. Formally constituted 1 Dec 1908. **Aims** Concentrate trade union strength throughout the Nordic transport industries to combat every sort of social dumping and financial crime and to attempts to undermine collective agreements or labour law. **Structure** Congress (every 4 years); Board; Executive Council. Sections (7): Road Transport; Maritime and Fisheries; Civil Aviation; Dockers; Railway Transport; Urban Transport; Warehouse and Logistic. Secretariat based in Stockholm (Sweden). **Languages** Danish, English, Finnish, Icelandic, Norwegian, Swedish. **Staff** 3.00 FTE, paid. **Finance** Members' dues. **Activities** Advocacy/lobbying/activism. **Events** *Conference* Aalborg (Denmark) 2018, *Conference* Malmö (Sweden) 2014, *Conference* Bergen (Norway) 2010, *Assembly* Helsinki (Finland) 2008, *Conference* Helsinki (Finland) 2006.
Members National transport workers trade unions (47) organizing 400,000 transport workers, in 5 countries:
Denmark, Finland, Iceland, Norway, Sweden. [2019/XD4613/**D**]

♦ Nordiska Träskyddsrådet (#17469)

♦ Nordiska Tulladministrativa Rådet (NTR) 17497

Conseil nordique des administrations de douanes – Nordic Customs Cooperation Council – Nordisk Toldadministrativt Råd (NTR) – Pohjoismainen Tullihallintoneuvosto

Contact PO Box 512, FI-00101 Helsinki, Finland.

Street Address NTR, Finska Tullen, Semaforbron 12, FI-00520 Helsinki, Finland.

History Established 1960, by customs administrations of the 5 Nordic countries. New statutes adopted 21 Aug 2003. **Aims** Work for uniform regulations concerning customs enforcement for traffic among Nordic countries; cooperate in simplification and rationalization of customs legislation; prevent crimes against customs law; monitor international development in the customs sector. **Structure** Council (meets at least every 2 years), comprising Directors of customs administration of the 5 Nordic countries; Chairmanship rotates among members. Special working groups (meets between Council meetings); expert groups. **Languages** Danish, Norwegian, Swedish. **Staff** None. **Finance** Grants from annual budgets of national customs administrations. **Activities** Networking/liaising. **Events** *Conference* Finland 2010, *Conference* Finland 2009, *Conference* Norway 2008, *Conference* Norway 2007, *Conference* Sweden 2006.

Members Customs administrations of 5 countries:
Denmark, Finland, Iceland, Norway, Sweden. [2015.11.26/XD3093/**D***]

- ♦ Nordiska Turistrådet (no recent information)
- ♦ Nordiska Tyngdlyftningsförbundet (#17465)
- ♦ Nordisk Audiologisk Selskab (#17210)
- ♦ Nordisk Audiologisk Selskap (#17210)
- ♦ Nordiska Ungdomskomittén (#17235)
- ♦ Nordiska Unionen för Arbetsledare, Tekniska Functionärer och andra Chefer (inactive)
- ♦ Nordiska Unionen för Hotell-, Café- och Restauranganställda (inactive)
- ♦ Nordiska Unionen inom Närings- och Njutningsmedelsindustrin (no recent information)
- ♦ Nordiska Universitetsadministratörssamarbetet (#17206)
- ♦ Det Nordiska Universitetssamarbetet (#17458)
- ♦ Nordiska Upphovsrättsbyrøernas Union / see Nordisk Copyright Bureau (#17500)
- ♦ Nordiska Utlänningsutskottet (#17315)
- ♦ Nordiska Utvecklingsfonden (#17271)
- ♦ Nordiska Utvecklingsfonden för Västnorden (#20926)
- ♦ Nordiska Väg och Anläggningsarbetarunion (inactive)
- ♦ Nordiska Vägtekniska Förbundet / see Nordic Road Association (#17402)
- ♦ Nordiska Vandrarhemsorganisationernas Förbund (no recent information)
- ♦ Nordiska Wittgesteinsällskapet (#17466)
- ♦ Nordisk Barnkardiologisk Klubb (#17241)
- ♦ Nordisk Barnkirurgisk Förening (no recent information)
- ♦ Nordisk Bekledings-Arbeidersfederasjon (inactive)
- ♦ Nordisk Bekledningsarbeiderunion (inactive)
- ♦ Nordisk Betonforbund (#17251)
- ♦ Nordisk Betongforbund (#17251)
- ♦ Nordisk Bilinspektörsforbund (inactive)

♦ Nordisk Bispekonferance (NBK) 17498

Conférence épiscopale scandinave – Scandinavian Episcopal Conference – Conferentia Episcopalis Scandiae

General Secretariat Gammel Kongevej 15, Postboks 241, 1610 Copenhagen, Denmark. T. +4533556022. E-mail: nbk@katolsk.dk.

URL: http://www.nordicbishopsconference.org/

History May 1960, Bergen (Norway). Also referred to as *Scandinavian Bishops' Conference.* **Languages** English, German. **Staff** 0.50 FTE, paid. **Activities** Events/meetings. **Events** *Plenary Conference* Einsiedeln (Switzerland) 2019, *Plenary Conference* Trondheim (Norway) 2019, *Plenary Conference* Szczecin (Poland) 2018, *Plenary Conference* Hamburg (Germany) 2017, *Plenary Conference* Reykjavik (Iceland) 2017.

Members Roman Catholic bishops (7) in 5 countries:
Denmark, Finland, Iceland, Norway, Sweden.

NGO Relations Member of: *Council of European Bishops' Conferences (#04884).* [2016.06.01/XD9006/v/**D**]

- ♦ Nordisk Blikkenslagermesterforbund (inactive)
- ♦ Nordisk Bokbinderråd (inactive)
- ♦ Nordisk Bokseunion (inactive)
- ♦ Nordisk Bondeorganisations Centralråd (no recent information)
- ♦ Nordisk Bordtennis Union / see North European Table Tennis Union (#17599)
- ♦ Nordisk Bridge Union (#17222)
- ♦ Nordisk Brydeforbund (no recent information)

♦ Nordisk Bueskytterunion (NBU) 17499

Nordic Archers' Union – Union nordique de tir à l'arc

Contact address not obtained.

Aims Develop Nordic *archery.* **Structure** Loosely structured cooperative organization. **Languages** Swedish. **Staff** 3.00 FTE, voluntary. **Finance** None. **Activities** Organizes: Annual Nordic Championships on Olympic rounds for youth classes. Annual Conference. **Events** *Annual Conference* Copenhagen (Denmark) 2013. **Publications** Each country has its own magazine.

Members Full in 5 countries:
Denmark, Finland, Iceland, Norway, Sweden. [2012.07.23/XD1732/**D**]

- ♦ Nordisk Byggdag (meeting series)
- ♦ Nordisk Byggedag (meeting series)
- ♦ Nordisk Cancer Union (#17225)
- ♦ Nordisk Center for Alkohol- og Narkotikaforskning (inactive)
- ♦ Nordisk Cerealist Forbund (no recent information)
- ♦ Nordisk Chefstatistikermøde (meeting series)

♦ Nordisk Copyright Bureau (NCB) 17500

Bureau nordique des droits d'auteur – Nordic Copyright Bureau

Contact Niels Juels Gade 9-11, 1059 Copenhagen V, Denmark. T. +4533368700. Fax +4533364690. E-mail: ncb@ncb.dk.

URL: http://www.ncb.dk/

History 1915. Originally also referred to as *Nordiska Upphovsrättsbyrøernas Union.* **Aims** Serve as practical intermediary between those wanting to make recordings (producers) and those holding recording rights (copyright holders); collect royalties due and ensure payment to members at national and international level; monitor the market, including audit inspection at premises of producers in Nordic countries. **Structure** General Assembly; Board; Divisions (2); Commission. **Languages** Danish, English, Finnish, Norwegian, Swedish. **Staff** 20.00 FTE, paid. **Finance** Commission on distributed royalties. Budget (annual): Danish Kr 510 million. **Activities** Advocacy/lobbying/activism; networking/liaising.

Members Cooperating societies in 7 countries:
Denmark, Estonia, Finland, Iceland, Lithuania, Norway, Sweden.

NGO Relations Member of: *International Bureau of the Societies Administering the Rights of Mechanical Recording and Reproduction (#12416).* [2016.06.29/XD2983/**D**]

- ♦ Nordisk Dame og Herrefrisørmesteres Forbund / see Nordic Hairdressers' Association (#17307)
- ♦ Nordisk Dataunion (no recent information)

♦ Nordisk Defence Club 17501

Association des armateurs nordiques – Nordisk Skibsrederforening

Address not obtained.

URL: http://www.nordisk.org/

History 14 May 1889, Copenhagen (Denmark), by owners of steamships and sailing ships in the Northern countries. Current Statutes adopted 2008. Originally also referred to in English as *Northern Shipowners' Defence Club.* **Aims** Give legal advice to members in *shipping* matters; *insure* the cost of *litigation.* **Structure** General Meeting (annual – closed). Board, consisting of 8 members, all representing shipowners. Managing Director and Deputy Managing Director. **Languages** English. **Staff** 20 lawyers; support staff. **Finance** Members' dues. Accounts (annual): Norwegian Kr 109 million. **Events** *Annual General Meeting* Helsinki (Finland) 2012, *Annual General Meeting* Oslo (Norway) 2011, *Annual General Meeting* Bergen (Norway) 2010, *Annual General Meeting* Oslo (Norway) 2009, *Annual General Meeting* Stockholm (Sweden) 2008. **Publications** *Medlemsbladet* (2 a year); *Nordiske Domme i Sjofartsanliggender* – Northern maritime cases. Annual Report; circulars to members.

Members Shipowners with total of about 2,214 units entered, 57 million gross tons, mostly from Finland, Norway and Sweden, but also from other countries around the world. Members in 20 countries and territories:
Bahrain, Canada, Cyprus, Finland, Greece, Hong Kong, Iceland, India, Japan, Liberia, Malta, Netherlands, Norway, Panama, Philippines, Portugal, Singapore, Sweden, UK, USA.

NGO Relations *BIMCO (#03236); International Association of Independent Tanker Owners (INTERTANKO, #11959).* [2018/XF3011/v/**F**]

- ♦ Nordisk Demografisk Förening (#17268)
- ♦ Nordisk Dermatologisk Forening / see Nordic Dermatology Association (#17269)
- ♦ Nordisk Detaljhandelsråd (inactive)
- ♦ Nordisk Diakonråd (inactive)
- ♦ Nordisk dietistförening (inactive)

♦ Nordisk Dramatikerunion (NDU) 17502

Nordic Union of Playwrights

Contact Iceland Dramatists' Union, Gunnarshús, Dyngjuvegur 8, 104 Reykjavik, Iceland. E-mail: leikskald@leikskald.is.

Contact Sveriges Dramatikerförbund, Drottninggatan 85, 1tr, SE-111 60 Stockholm, Sweden. T. +468213310. Fax +4686133979. E-mail: sdf@dramatiker.se.

History 1941, by Swedish novelist and playwright Wilhelm Moberg, as an anti-fascist front. In English previously referred to as *Nordic Dramatists Union.* **Aims** Support copyright and general economic interests of playwrights in the region. **Structure** Chairmanship rotates.

Members Individuals in 5 countries:
Denmark, Finland, Iceland, Norway, Sweden. [2012/XD1263/v/**D**]

- ♦ Nordisk Dyrebeskyttelseråd (inactive)
- ♦ Nordisk Dysmeliforbund (no recent information)
- ♦ Nordiske Aegteskabskonvention (1931 treaty)
- ♦ Nordiske Arbeidernes Oplysnings Forbund / see Nordic Organization of Workers' Educational Associations (#17377)
- ♦ Nordiske Bandagist Kongres (meeting series)
- ♦ Nordiske Borneoftalmologiske Gruppe (#17382)
- ♦ Nordisk Edruskapsråd (inactive)
- ♦ Nordiske Eggomsetningsorg (inactive)
- ♦ Nordiske Fagkonferansen i Religionspsykologi (meeting series)
- ♦ Nordiske Fengselsfunksjonaerers Union (inactive)
- ♦ Nordiske Fiskeres Miljøsekretariat / see Nordic Fishermen's Council (#17293)
- ♦ Nordiske Fiskeres Råd (#17293)
- ♦ Nordiske Folkeoplysningssamarbejdsorganisationer / see Nordisk Folkeoplysnings- og Voksenundervisningssamarbejde (#17504)
- ♦ Nordiske Folkhögskolan i Genève (#19087)
- ♦ Nordiske Forening af Turner Kontaktgrupper (inactive)
- ♦ Nordiske Forleggerråd (meeting series)
- ♦ Nordiske Forskningsbiblioteketsforeningers Netvaerk (inactive)
- ♦ Nordiske Hjerte- og Lungesykes Forbund (inactive)
- ♦ Nordiske Höyre Kvinners Samarbeidsnemd (inactive)
- ♦ Nordiske Industriforbunds Fellesorgan (inactive)
- ♦ Nordiske Industriforbundskonferanser (meeting series)
- ♦ Nordiske Jepnbaldmenns Union (inactive)
- ♦ Nordiske Jernvarehandleres Permanente Komite (inactive)
- ♦ Nordiske Jordbrugsforskeres Forening / see Nordiska Jordbruksforskares Förening (#17486)
- ♦ Nordiske Kjøpmannskomité (inactive)
- ♦ Nordiske Klokkekomité / see Nordisk Selskab for Campanologi og Klokkespil (#17533)
- ♦ Nordiske Komité for Bygningsbestemmelser (inactive)
- ♦ Nordiske Kommunaltjenestemannessekretariatet / see Kommunalanställdas Nordiska Samarbete (#16204)
- ♦ Nordiske konferansen for behandlere som arbeider med traumatiserte flyktninger (meeting series)
- ♦ Nordiske Kongres i Familieterapi (meeting series)
- ♦ Nordiske Kontaktkommitteen for Barnehager og Fritidshjem (inactive)
- ♦ Nordiske Kristne Buddhistmission (religious order)
- ♦ Nordiske Laereres Fredsforbund (inactive)
- ♦ Nordisk Elfederation (no recent information)
- ♦ Nordisk Embetsmann Komité for Samarbeid innen Byggesektoren (inactive)
- ♦ Nordiske Embetsmannskomité for Transportspørgsmål (inactive)
- ♦ Nordiske Mediedager (unconfirmed)
- ♦ Nordiske Meteorologmøtet (meeting series)
- ♦ Nordiske Møbelproducenters Råd (inactive)
- ♦ Nordisk Energiforskning (#17278)
- ♦ Nordiske Nettverk (#17348)
- ♦ Nordiske Netvaerk (#17348)
- ♦ Nordiske Nyredager (#17420)
- ♦ Nordiske Oppfinnerforeningers Samarbeidsorganisasjon (no recent information)
- ♦ Nordiske Paskontroloverenskomst (1957 treaty)
- ♦ Nordiske Passkontrolloverenskomsten (1957 treaty)
- ♦ Nordiske Plantskogodlarnas Samarbetsutskott (inactive)
- ♦ Nordiske Presteforeningers Samarbeidsorgan (inactive)
- ♦ Det Nordiske Reologiselskap (#17400)
- ♦ Nordiske Revisorkongres (meeting series)
- ♦ Nordisk erhvervspædagogisk og erhvervsdidaktisk netværk / see NORDYRK (#17554)
- ♦ Nordiske Samarbejdskomite for Handels- og Kontorfunktionaerer (inactive)
- ♦ Nordiske Sittenettverket (#17405)
- ♦ Nordiske Skovkongres (meeting series)
- ♦ Nordiske Teleansattes Samarbeidsorgan (inactive)
- ♦ Nordisk Etologisk Förening (inactive)
- ♦ Nordiske Veterinaerkongress (meeting series)
- ♦ Nordisk Fagdidaktisk Konference (meeting series)
- ♦ Nordisk Fagpresseråd (inactive)
- ♦ Nordisk Farmaceut Union / see Nordic Union of Pharmaceutical Organizations (#17456)
- ♦ Nordisk Farmaceutunion (#17456)
- ♦ Nordisk Farmakologisk Selskab (no recent information)
- ♦ Nordisk Fartygsbefälskongress (#17407)
- ♦ Nordisk Federation för Medicinsk Undervisning (no recent information)

♦ **Nordisk Film & TV Fond (NFTVF)** **17503**

CEO Arbins gate 4, 0253 Oslo, Norway. T. +4764006080. E-mail: info@nftvfond.com.
URL: http://www.nordiskfilmogtvfond.com/

History 1 Jan 1990. Established by *Styringsgruppen for Nordisk Kultur- og Massemediesamarbejde (KM, inactive)*, under the aegis of *Nordic Council of Ministers (NCM, #17260)*, within the framework of *Nordic Cultural Cooperation (1971)*, on agreement between the Council and national broadcasting corporations and film institutes in the 5 Nordic countries. **Aims** Promote film and TV productions of high quality in the 5 Nordic countries (Denmark, Finland, Iceland, Norway and Sweden) by providing support for financing of feature films, TV-fiction / series and creative documentaries; finance distribution and dubbing of Nordic films inside the Nordic region and promote and initiate Industry Initiatives of professional Nordic importance. **Structure** Board. CEO. Secretariat. **Languages** Danish, English, Faroese, Icelandic, Norwegian, Swedish. **Staff** 6.00 FTE, paid. **Finance** Financed by Nordic Council of Ministers, 16 Nordic broadcasting and media companies and 5 Nordic film institutes. Annual budget: 126,000,000 NOK (2022). **Activities** Awards/prizes/competitions; events/meetings; financial and/or material support; training/education. For the events: https://nordiskfilmogtvfond.com/events **Publications** Annual Report.
Members Representatives of 5 countries:
Denmark, Finland, Iceland, Norway, Sweden. [2022.10.13/XF1035/f/**F***]

♦ Nordisk Film/TV-Union (inactive)
♦ Nordisk Flagselskab (#17294)
♦ Nordisk Flyforbund (no recent information)
♦ Nordisk Folkecenter for Vedvarende Energi (internationally oriented national body)

♦ **Nordisk Folkeoplysnings- og Voksenundervisningssamarbejde (FOVU)** **17504**

Coopération nordique en matière d'éducation des adultes – Nordic Adult Education Cooperation – Aikuiskasvatuksen ja Kansansivistystyön Pohjoismainen Yhteistyö
Address not obtained.
URL: http://www.norden.org/

History 1976, as a cooperation body of *Nordic Council of Ministers (NCM, #17260)*, based on *Nordic Cultural Cooperation (1971)* and subsequently updated. Also referred to in English as: *Steering Committee for Nordic Cooperation on Adult and General Education*; *Steering Group for Adult Education*; *Steering group for Folkeoplysning and Adult Education*. Other titles occurring in published literature: *Nordiske Folkeoplysningssamarbejdsorganisationer – Nordisk Samarbejde vedrørende Voksenundervisning og Folkeoplysning – Aikuiskasvatuksen ja Sivistystyön Pohjoismainen Yhteistyö*. **Aims** Stimulate and develop understanding of diversity and shared features of popular and adult education in the Nordic region and reinforce the Nordic dimension in an international context; advise the NMR in related matters; promote Nordic education policy development in the field. **Structure** Steering Group of 8 persons – one representative of the Ministry of Education of each Nordic country and one representative of each of 3 autonomous areas – plus a deputy for each Nordic country and (ex officio) Adviser and Secretary from NMR. Reference Group (meeting once or twice a year) comprises representatives of study associations, popular and adult education high schools, trade unions and research. Advisory working groups. **Finance** Financed by NMR. **Activities** Initiates Nordic network projects; provides financial assistance to cooperation projects, courses and conferences organized by Nordic adult education organizations and to students wishing to study in a folk high school in another Nordic country; administers temporary networks dealing with specific topics; promotes information exchange; undertakes or initiates investigations and analyses of special sectors of Nordic adult education and arranges conferences to present these themes to a wider public. Action Plan 2000-2004, based on 5-year strategy of NMR on cooperation in education, training and research, emphasizes holistic and process-oriented approaches to life-long learning and active exchange of information and experience in the field. Advisory working groups include: international contact group; evaluation group for the aid scheme; editorial council. Works on developmental and innovative efforts with the Nordic Folk Academy. **Events** *Meeting* Copenhagen (Denmark) 2005, *Meeting* Nyborg (Denmark) 2005, *Meeting* Copenhagen (Denmark) 2004, *Meeting* Copenhagen (Denmark) 2004, *Meeting* Iceland 2004. **Publications** *FOVU Dialogue* (3 a year) in Finnish; *The Golden Riches* (2 a year) in English. Reports; information material.
Members Members of the Steering Group in 8 countries and territories:
Åland, Denmark, Faeroe Is, Finland, Greenland, Iceland, Norway, Sweden. [2010/XF0428/**F***]

♦ Nordisk Folke-Reso (inactive)
♦ Nordisk Forbund for Kirkegårdskultur (inactive)
♦ Nordisk Förbund för Kvinnogymnastik (inactive)
♦ Nordisk Forbund for Markedsføring (inactive)
♦ Nordisk Forbund for Pediatrisk Patologi (inactive)
♦ Nordisk Forbund for Spesialpedagogikk (#17435)
♦ Nordisk Forbund for Studie- og Yrkesvejledning (#17191)
♦ Nordisk Förening för Allergologi (unconfirmed)
♦ Nordisk Forening for Arkitekturforskning (#17180)
♦ Nordisk Forening for Fiskeimmunologi / see International Society of Fish and Shellfish Immunology (#15122)

♦ **Nordisk förening för folkdansforskning (Nff)** **17505**

Contact Westend 13 III, 1661 Copenhagen V, Denmark.
URL: http://www.folkedansforskning.com/

History 1977. **Aims** Promote folk dance research and scholarly publications in Nordic countries. **Structure** Board. **Languages** Danish, Norwegian, Swedish. **Staff** Voluntary. **Finance** Members' dues. Fees; grants. Annual budget: Danish KR 35,000. **Activities** Events/meetings; projects/programmes; publishing activities. **Publications** *Folkdansforskning i Norden* (annual) – journal. *Norden i Dans* (2007); *Nordisk Folkedanstypologi* (1997); *Gammaldans i Norden* (1988); *Folkedanslitteratur i Norden – Ein bibliografi* (1983); *Nordisk Folkedansterminologi* (1983).
Members Individuals (about 100) in 76 countries and territories:
Denmark, Faeroe Is, Finland, Germany, Iceland, Norway, Sweden. [2016.07.09/XD1931/v/**D**]

♦ Nordisk Forening for Forskning om Menn og Maskuliniteter (#17202)
♦ Nordisk Förening för Funktionshinder och Oral Hälsa (#17190)
♦ Nordisk Forening for Funktionshinder och Oral Helse (#17190)
♦ Nordisk Förening för Fysiologi (#19097)
♦ Nordisk Förening för Fysiologisk Botanik / see Societas Physiologiae Plantarum Scandinavica (#19452)
♦ Nordisk Förening för Handicaptandvård / see Nordic Association for Disability and Oral Health (#17190)
♦ Nordisk Forening Helse og Arbete (inactive)
♦ Nordisk Förening för Hematologi (no recent information)
♦ Nordisk Forening for Invortes Medisin (inactive)

♦ **Nordisk förening för katolska läkare (NFKL)** **17506**

Association Nordique des Médecins Catholiques – Nordisk Forening for Katolske Laeger – Nordisk Forening for Katolske Leger – Norraent félag fyrir kapólska laekna
Sec Pontonjärsgatan 4, c/o Haegerstam, SE-112 22 Stockholm, Sweden.
Treas address not obtained.
URL: http://www.nfkl.org/

History 12 Mar 2005. [2011/XM8144/**D**]

♦ Nordisk Forening for Katolske Laeger (#17506)
♦ Nordisk Forening for Katolske Leger (#17506)
♦ Nordisk Forening for Kinastudier (#17182)
♦ Nordisk Förening för Klinisk Fysiologi / see Scandinavian Society of Clinical Physiology and Nuclear Medicine (#19104)

♦ **Nordisk Förening för Klinisk Kemi (NFKK)** **17507**

Société nordique de chimie clinique – Nordic Society of Clinical Chemistry
Chairman Dept of Clinical Biochemistry, Hvidovre Univ Hosp, Kettegård Alle 30, 2650 Hvidovre, Denmark. E-mail: hlj@dadlnet.dk.
URL: http://nfkk.org/

History 17 Jul 1946, Finse (Norway), as *Nordic Society for Clinical Chemistry and Clinical Physiology – Nordisk Forening for Klinisk Kjemi och Klinisk Fysiologi*. Statutes revised Jun 1984, Malmö (Sweden), when present name was adopted. Also known as *Scandinavian Society of Clinical Chemistry*. **Aims** Work for the development of clinical chemistry and for cooperation between the Nordic countries in this field. **Structure** National Societies; Board, including Chairman and Secretary. **Languages** Danish, English, Finnish, Icelandic, Norwegian, Swedish. **Finance** Each Society meets costs. **Activities** Congresses are organized in rotation. Specialized Committees and Working Groups: Nordic Biobank for Reference Samples; Nordic Reference Interval Group; Scandinavian Enzyme Committee; Scandinavian Collaboration on Testing of Laboratory Equipment for the Primary Healthcare (SKUP). **Events** *Nordic Congress of Medical Biochemistry* Reykjavik (Iceland) 2022, *Nordic Congress of Medical Biochemistry* Trondheim (Norway) 2020, *Biennial Congress* Helsinki (Finland) 2018, *Biennial Congress* Odense (Denmark) 2016, *Biennial Congress* Gothenburg (Sweden) 2014. **Publications** *Klinisk Kemi i Norden*; *Scandinavian Journal of Clinical and Laboratory Investigation*. **Information Services** *Database of Seldom Analyses (ROSAN)*.
Members Individuals (1,200) members of National Societies in 5 countries:
Denmark, Finland, Iceland, Norway, Sweden.
NGO Relations *International Federation of Clinical Chemistry and Laboratory Medicine (IFCC, #13392)*.
[2019/XD0121/**D**]

♦ Nordisk Forening for Klinisk Kjemi och Klinisk Fysiologi / see Nordisk Förening för Klinisk Kemi (#17507)
♦ Nordisk Forening for Klinisk Sexologi (#17185)
♦ Nordisk Forening for Leksikografi (#17196)
♦ Nordisk Förening för Litteraturvetenskap (#17186)
♦ Nordisk Förening för Medicinsk Radiologi (#17418)
♦ Nordisk Forening Mot Barnemishandling og Omsorgssvikt (#17200)
♦ Nordisk Forening for Neuroradiologi (#17421)
♦ Nordisk Förening för Obstetrik och Gynekologi (#17286)
♦ Nordisk Forening for Palliativ Vård (inactive)
♦ Nordisk Förening för Pedagogisk Forskning (#17276)
♦ Nordisk Förening för Pediatrisk Hematologi och Onkologi (#17424)
♦ Nordisk Förening för Pedodonti (inactive)
♦ Nordisk Förening för Podologi (inactive)
♦ Nordisk Forening for Psykiatrisk Epidemiologi (#17201)
♦ Nordisk Förening för Psykosocial Onkologi (no recent information)
♦ Nordisk Förening av Registrerade Revisorer (inactive)
♦ Nordisk Förening för Rehabilitering (inactive)
♦ Nordisk Förening för Rettssociologi (inactive)

♦ **Nordisk Forening for SFL og Socialsemiotik** **17508**

Nordisk Forening for SFL og Sosialsemiotikk – Nordisk Förening för SFL och Sociosemiotik – Pohjoismainen Systeemis-funktionaalisen Kielitieteen ja sosiosemiotiikan Yhdistys – Nordic Society for Systemic-functional Linguistics
Contact address not obtained.
URL: https://nordisksfl.org/

History 2007. **Activities** Events/meetings. **Events** *Meeting* Odense (Denmark) 2021, *Meeting* Uppsala (Sweden) 2020, *Meeting* Tønsberg (Norway) 2019, *Meeting* Aalborg (Denmark) 2018, *Nordiska Konferens om SFL och Socialsemiotik* Gothenburg (Sweden) 2017. [2021/AA0680/**D**]

♦ Nordisk Förening för SFL och Sociosemiotik (#17508)
♦ Nordisk Forening for SFL og Sosialsemiotikk (#17508)

♦ **Nordisk Förening för Spädbarns Utveckling (NFSU)** **17509**

Nordic Association for Infant Mental Health (NAIMH)
Contact address not obtained. E-mail: nfsu.org@gmail.com.
URL: http://www.nfsu.org/

History 1991.
Members Full in 3 countries:
Denmark, Norway, Sweden.
NGO Relations Member of: *World Association for Infant Mental Health (WAIMH, #21146)*.
[2020.03.18/XM8405/**D**]

♦ Nordisk Förening för Studie- och Yrkesvägleding Nordisk Forbund for Uddannesles- og Erhvervsvejledning (#17191)
♦ Nordisk Förening för Tillämpad Geofysik (no recent information)
♦ Nordisk Förening för Toxikologisk Patologi (inactive)

♦ **Nordisk Företagsekonomiska Förening (NFF)** **17510**

Nordic Academy of Management
Chair address not obtained. E-mail: rsmari@hi.is.
URL: http://www.nordicacademy.org/

History 1990. Previously also referred to as *Scandinavian Academy of Management (SAM)*. **Aims** Promote research, education and practice within *business economics* and administration in the Nordic countries. **Structure** Board (meets annually). Secretary. **Languages** Danish, English, Finnish, Norwegian, Swedish. **Staff** 1.00 FTE, paid. **Finance** Members' dues. Other sources: contributions. **Events** *Nordic energies* Vaasa (Finland) 2019, *Conference* Bodø (Norway) 2017, *Conference* Copenhagen (Denmark) 2015, *Conference* Reykjavik (Iceland) 2013, *Conference / Biennial Conference* Stockholm (Sweden) 2011. **Publications** *Scandinavian Journal of Management*.
Members in 6 countries:
Denmark, Finland, Germany, Iceland, Norway, Sweden.
NGO Relations Member of: *International Federation of Scholarly Associations of Management (IFSAM, #13536)*. [2014/XM0200/**E**]

♦ **Nordisk Forfatter- og Oversetterråd (NFOR)** **17511**

Nordic Council of Authors and Translators
Contact Strandgade 6, 1401 Copenhagen, Denmark. E-mail: danskforfatterforening@danskforfatterforening.dk.

History 1919, as *Nordisk Forfatterråd*. Also referred to as *Nordic Council of Writers and Translators*. **Languages** Danish, Norwegian, Swedish. **Finance** Meeting budget: about euro 10,000. **Activities** Events/meetings. **Events** *Annual meeting* Copenhagen (Denmark) 2006.
Members Individuals in 8 countries and territories:
Denmark, Faeroe Is, Finland, Greenland, Iceland, Lapland, Norway, Sweden. [2018.06.01/XD2007/**D**]

♦ Nordisk Forfatterråd / see Nordisk Forfatter- og Oversetterråd (#17511)
♦ Nordisk forskning om Materialadministration (#17339)
♦ Nordisk Forskningsinstitut for Maling og Trykfarver (inactive)

♦ **Nordisk Forum for Bygningskalk (Nordisk Kalkforum)** **17512**

Nordiskt Forum för Byggnadskalk – Pohjoismainen Rakennuskalkkiforum
Contact c/o Ctr for Bygningsbevaring, Raadvad 40, 2800 Kongens Lyngby, Denmark. T. +4545969990. E-mail: post@kalkforum.org.
URL: https://www.kalkforum.org/

History Statutes adopted Apr 1999; Revised 2009, 2015, 2017 and 2020. **Structure** Annual General Meeting; Board. **Finance** Sources: members' dues. **Activities** Events/meetings. **Events** *Meeting* Hamar (Norway) 2022, *Meeting* Denmark 2021, *Meeting* Stavanger (Norway) 2021.
Members Full in 4 countries:
Denmark, Finland, Norway, Sweden. [2021/AA2734/**F**]

♦ Nordisk Forum for Danseforskning (#17298)
♦ Nordisk Forum för Lipidforskning og- Teknologi / see Nordic Forum for Lipid Research and Technology (#17299)
♦ Nordisk Forum for Megling / see Nordisk Forum for Megling og Konflikthåndtering (#17513)

♦ Nordisk Forum for Megling og Konflikthåndtering (NFM) 17513

Nordic Forum for Mediation and Conflict Management

Chairman Melkeveien 45, 0779 Oslo, Norway. T. +4791719782.
URL: http://www.n-f-m.org/

History 1998, as *Nordic Forum for Mediation – Nordisk Forum for Megling.* **Aims** Promote mediation as a means of *dispute resolution.* **Structure** General Assembly (every 2 years). Board, comprising Chair, Co-Chair, Treasurers and 6 members. **Languages** Danish, English, Faroese, Icelandic, Norwegian, Swedish. **Finance** Members' dues. Other sources: project support from Nordic Ministerial Council; government and private donations. **Activities** Project: *'Nordic Map in Conflict Mediation'* – mapping reflections and experiences from mediators in the 5 Nordic countries, covering mediation in families, work places, schools, communities, in courts, victim-offender mediation and international peace mediation. Result of this project covered in a book available in Norwegian, Swedish, Finnish and English. Organizes seminars and projects. **Events** *Conference / General Assembly* Helsinki (Finland) 2006, *Conference / General Assembly* Skövde (Sweden) 2004, *Conference* Copenhagen (Denmark) 2002, *Conference* Oslo (Norway) 1999.
Members Conflict mediators in 4 countries:
Denmark, Finland, Norway, Sweden. [2009/XF7164/**F**]

♦ Nordisk Förzinkningsförening / see Nordic Galvanizers (#17302)
♦ Nordisk Fotografforbund (no recent information)
♦ Nordisk Funksjonaersammenslutning / see Service- og Tjenestebranchens Union i Norden (#19244)
♦ Nordisk Gangkommisjon (inactive)
♦ Nordisk Gastroenterologiske Forening (inactive)
♦ Nordisk Genetikerforening (no recent information)
♦ Nordisk Genresurssenter (#17303)
♦ Nordisk Geologisk Vintermøte (meeting series)
♦ Nordisk Gerontologisk Forening (#17306)

♦ Nordisk Gipspladeforening 17514

Nordic Gypsum Association

Contact c/o Confederation of Danish Industries, 1787 Copenhagen V, Denmark. T. +4533773377. Fax +4533773300. E-mail: gth@di.dk – di@di.dk.
URL: http://foreninger.di.dk/ngf/

History as *Nordisk Gipsskiveförening.*
Members Gypsum associations in 4 countries:
Denmark, Finland, Norway, Sweden. [2014/XD0957/**D**]

♦ Nordisk Gipsskiveförening / see Nordisk Gipspladeforening (#17514)
♦ Nordisk Grafisk Union (no recent information)
♦ Nordisk Grossistforbunds Sentralråd (inactive)
♦ Nordisk Gullsmedarbeiderforbund (inactive)
♦ Nordisk Handelsreisendeunion (inactive)
♦ Nordisk Handelsresandeunion (inactive)
♦ Nordisk Håndverksråd (inactive)
♦ Nordisk helseberedskapsavtale (2002 treaty)
♦ Nordisk Herpetologisk Forening (#19089)
♦ Nordisk Hjemstavnsforbund (#17160)
♦ Nordisk Hotell- og Restaurantforbund / see Nordic Union Hotels, Restaurants, Catering and Tourism (#17454)
♦ Nordisk Hovedstadskonferanse (meeting series)
♦ Nordisk Hydrologisk Förening (#17194)
♦ Nordisk Informationscenter for Medie- og Kommunikationsforskning / see Nordicom (#17374)
♦ Nordisk Innovations (#17320)
♦ Nordisk Innovations Center / see Nordic Innovation (#17320)
♦ Nordisk Inremisjonsråd (inactive)
♦ Nordisk Instituet for Teoretisk Fysikk (#17324)
♦ Nordisk Institut for Asienstudier / see NIAS-Nordisk Institut for Asienstudier (#17132)
♦ Nordisk Institut for Kvinde- og Kønsforskning / see Nordic Information for Gender Knowledge (#17317)
♦ Nordisk Institut for Odontologisk Materialprøvning (#17485)
♦ Nordisk Institut for Teoretisk Fysik (#17324)
♦ Nordisk Institutt for Informasjonsteknologi (inactive)
♦ Nordisk Institutt for Kunnskap om Kjønn / see Nordic Information for Gender Knowledge (#17317)
♦ Nordisk Institutt för Kvinne- og Kjønnsforskning / see Nordic Information for Gender Knowledge (#17317)

♦ Nordisk Institutt for Sjørett (NIFS) 17515

Institut nordique de droit maritime – Scandinavian Institute of Maritime Law – Nordiska Institutet för Sjörätt – Pohjoismainen Merioikeuden Laitos

Secretariat Postboks 6706, St Olavsplass, 0130 Oslo, Norway. T. +4722859673. Fax +4722859750.
URL: http://www.jus.uio.no/nifs/

History 1963. Statutes revised 2000. Also referred to in English as *Nordic Institute for Maritime Law.* Comes within the framework of *Nordic Cultural Cooperation (1971),* as a cooperation body of *Nordic Council of Ministers (NCM, #17260).* **Aims** Promote research and studies in the Nordic countries in maritime and *petroleum law* and other related fields; offer good working conditions to scholars and students who visit the Institute; offer scholarships to enable research fellows and students from the Nordic countries to study at the Institute; keep and develop a library of maritime and petroleum law of high standard. **Structure** Board of 5 members representing the Nordic countries; Director; Departments (2): Maritime Law; Petroleum Law. **Languages** Danish, Finnish, Icelandic, Norwegian, Swedish. **Staff** 20.00 FTE, paid. **Finance** Main financial sources: Nordic Council of Ministers; University of Oslo (Norway); sponsoring from oil companies operating in Norway. **Activities** Courses in maritime law and petroleum law. Seminars/conferences. **Events** *Conference on the Rule of Law for Oceans* Oslo (Norway) 2019, *Conference* Stockholm (Sweden) 2014, *Conference* Turku (Finland) 2012, *Conference* Hirtshals (Denmark) 1992, *Maritime law in the past, today and in the future* Visby (Sweden) 1990.
Members Full in 5 countries:
Denmark, Finland, Iceland, Norway, Sweden. [2012/XE5800/j/**E**]

♦ Nordisk Institutt for Studier av Innovasjon, Forskning og Utdanning (internationally oriented national body)
♦ Nordisk Interparlamentarisk Forbund (inactive)
♦ Nordisk Israelmisjonen / see Den Norske Israelmisjon
♦ Nordisk Jägersamvirke (#17313)
♦ Nordisk Jernbandmands Union (inactive)
♦ Nordisk Jernbane Avholdsunion (inactive)
♦ Nordisk Jernbanemusik-Råd (no recent information)
♦ Nordisk Jernvägs Selskab / see Nordic Railway Association (#17395)
♦ Nordisk Jordmorforbund (#17345)

♦ Nordisk Journalistcenter (NJC) 17516

Centre nordique pour des journalistes – Nordic Journalist Centre

Contact Helsingforsgade 6A-D, 8200 Aarhus, Denmark. T. +4520950945. E-mail: jf2@dmjx.dk.
URL: https://www.njc.dk/

History 1957, Aarhus (Denmark). Founded at recommendation of *Nordic Council (NC, #17256).* **Aims** Stimulate interest and increase knowledge among journalists concerning *current politics* and *contemporary history* of the Nordic countries; act as an inter-Nordic and international *professional* forum for Nordic, Russian and Baltic journalists; support media literacy in the digital age. **Structure** Board, consisting of media professionals from the Nordic countries and Russia. **Languages** Danish, Norwegian, Swedish. **Staff** 3.00 FTE, paid. **Finance** Sources: sponsorship. Supported by: *Nordic Council of Ministers (NCM, #17260).* **Activities** Events/meetings; networking/liaising; training/education. **NGO Relations** Member of (1): *European Journalism Training Association (EJTA, #07613).* [2020.10.19/XF0272/**F**]

♦ Nordisk Judo Union (inactive)
♦ Nordisk Kafeunion (inactive)
♦ Nordisk Kaktus Selskab (#17224)
♦ **Nordisk Kalkforum** Nordisk Forum for Bygningskalk (#17512)
♦ Nordisk Kanoforbund (inactive)
♦ Nordisk Karkirurgisk Forening (no recent information)

♦ Nordisk Kärnsäkerhetsforskning (NKS) 17517

Nordic Nuclear Safety Research – Comité nordique pour la recherche de sûreté nucléaire – Nordisk Kernesikkerhedsforskning – Nordisk Kjernesikkerhetsforskning – Norraenar Kjanöryggisrannsóknir – Pohjoismainen Ydinturvallisuustutkimus

Secretariat Box 49, 4000 Roskilde, Denmark. T. +4546774041. E-mail: nks@nks.org.
URL: http://www.nks.org/

History Established 1977, by *Nordic Liaison Committee for Atomic Energy (NKA, inactive),* as *Nordic Committee for Safety Research – Nordisk Kommité för Säkerhetsforskning – Pohjoismainen Turvallisuustutkimuksen ad Hos Ryhmä.* Also referred to as *Nordiska Kommitten för Kärnsäkerhetsforskning – Nordisk Komité for Kernesikkerhedsforskning.* Currently implements part of the former activities of NKA, which is now dormant. **Aims** Carry out joint scientific activities producing scientific reports and articles, seminars, exercises, technical reports, manuals, recommendations, and other types of reference material. **Structure** Owners; Board; Chairman; Programme Managers; Branches (2); Secretariat. **Languages** English. **Staff** None. **Events** *Status seminar* Otaniemi (Finland) 2006, *Workshop on the impact of glaciations on rock stresses, groundwater flow and hydrochemistry* Stockholm (Sweden) 1996, *Seminar* Espoo (Finland) 1993. **Publications** *NKS NewsFlashes*; *NKS NewsLetters.* NKS reports.
Members Nuclear safety authorities of 5 countries:
Denmark, Finland, Iceland, Norway, Sweden. [2017.10.13/XE4975/**E***]

♦ Nordisk Katastrofemedicinsk Førening (no recent information)
♦ Nordisk Katolsk Udviklingshjaelp (inactive)

♦ Nordisk Kennelunion (NKU) 17518

Contact Danish Kennel Klub, Parkvej 1, 2680 Solrød Strand, Denmark. T. +4556188100. E-mail: post@dkk.dk.
Members National canine organizations in 5 countries:
Denmark, Finland, Iceland, Norway, Sweden. [2013.11.18/XD1706/**D**]

♦ Nordisk Kernesikkerhedsforskning (#17517)
♦ Nordisk Kirkeligt Studieråd (inactive)
♦ Nordisk Kirkemusikråd (#17257)
♦ Nordisk Kirurgisk Förening (#19122)
♦ Nordisk Kjernesikkerhetsforskning (#17517)
♦ Nordisk Kjökkenchef Federation (no recent information)
♦ Nordisk Klubb i Handkirurgi / see Scandinavian Society for Surgery of the Hand (#19120)
♦ Nordisk Kökkenchef Federation (#17233)
♦ Nordisk Kollegium för Fysisk Oceanografi (inactive)
♦ Nordisk Kollegium for Økologi (inactive)
♦ Nordisk Kolonihageforbund (#17177)
♦ Nordisk Komite för Biomedicinsk Teknik (inactive)
♦ Nordisk Komité for Bygningsbestemmelser (inactive)
♦ Nordisk Komité for Kernesikkerhedsforskning / see Nordisk Kärnsäkerhetsforskning (#17517)
♦ Nordisk komité for kunsthistorie (#17245)
♦ Nordisk Komite for Vegtrafikklovgivning (inactive)

♦ Nordisk Komité for Veterinaervitenskapelig Samarbeid (NKVet) ... 17519

Nordic Committee for Veterinary Scientific Cooperation

Sec Livsmedelssäkerhetsverket Evira, Mustialankatu 3, FI-00790 Helsinki, Finland. T. +358207724544.
URL: http://www.nkvet.org/

History 1977. **Aims** Promote veterinary research cooperation between veterinarians and researchers in the Nordic countries. **Finance** Supported by: *Nordic Joint Committee for Agricultural and Food Research (#17332).* **Events** *Responsable use of antimicrobials in veterinary practice* Copenhagen (Denmark) 2014, *Symposium* Uppsala (Sweden) 2012, *Symposium* Reykjavik (Iceland) 2007, *Symposium* Gardermoen (Norway) 2005, *Symposium* Finland 2003. [2017/XM3413/**E**]

♦ Nordisk Kommité för Säkerhetsforskning / see Nordisk Kärnsäkerhetsforskning (#17517)
♦ Nordisk Kommittee Skomagermestre og Skohandlere (inactive)
♦ Nordisk Kommitté för Jordbruks- och Matforskning (#17332)

♦ Nordisk Kommunalteknisk Samarbetskommitté (NKS) 17520

Nordic Cooperation Committee on Municipal Engineering

Contact KTC, Kommunalteknisk Chefforening, Godthåbsvej 83, 8660 Skanderborg, Denmark. T. +4572282804. E-mail: ktc@ktc.dk.

Events *Meeting* Billund (Denmark) 2018, *Meeting* Bergen (Norway) 2014, *Meeting* Holstebro (Denmark) 2014, *Meeting* Reykjavik (Iceland) 2013, *Meeting* Stockholm (Sweden) 2013.
Members Full in 5 countries:
Denmark, Finland, Iceland, Norway, Sweden. [2022.07.18/XM3077/**E**]

♦ Nordisk Konditormesterforeningen (inactive)
♦ Nordisk konferens i familjerådslag (meeting series)
♦ Nordisk Kongress for Laryngektomerte (meeting series)
♦ Nordisk Kongress i Lymfologi (meeting series)
♦ Nordisk Kongress i Synpedagogik (meeting series)
♦ Nordisk Konservativ Studienämnd (no recent information)
♦ Nordisk Konservatorforbund (#17188)
♦ Nordisk Konservatorierâd (#02830)
♦ Nordisk Konservator Studentunion (#17161)
♦ Nordisk Kontaktorgan for Atomenergispørgsmål (inactive)
♦ Nordisk Kontaktorgan for Fiskerispørgsmål (inactive)
♦ Nordisk Kontaktorgan for Jordbrugsforskning / see Nordic Joint Committee for Agricultural and Food Research (#17332)
♦ Nordisk Kontaktorgan for Jord- og Skovbrugsspørgsmål (inactive)
♦ Nordisk Kontakt om Statsbyggeri (#17252)
♦ Nordisk Kontaktudvalg for Universiteter og Hígere Laereanstalter / see Nordic Association of University Administrators (#17206)
♦ Nordisk konvensjon om sosialhjelp og sosiale tjenester (1994 treaty)
♦ Nordisk konvensjon om trygd (2012 treaty)
♦ Nordisk Konvention om social sikring (2012 treaty)
♦ Nordisk Konvention om Socialt Bistånd och Sociala Tjänster (1994 treaty)
♦ Nordisk konvention om social trygghet (2012 treaty)

♦ **Nordisk Korforum** **17521**
Sec c/o Klintberg, Ligustervägen 5, SE-621 43 Visby, Sweden. E-mail: chairman@nordiskkorforum.org.
URL: http://nordiskkorforum.org/
History 1952. In English sometimes also referred to as *Nordic Choir Committee.* **Aims** Strengthen the role of choral music in Nordic cultural life; stimulate and emphasize Nordic music choral life; disseminate information on choral repertoire and support new compositions for choirs; initiate and organize activities for choral singers and conductors; support exchange of conductors, instructors and choirs; improve contacts between choral federations. **Structure** Board. **Languages** Danish, Finnish, Icelandic, Norwegian, Swedish. **Staff** Voluntary. **Finance** Members' dues. Other sources: Ministry of Nordic countries; sponsors. **Activities** Organizes: choral festivals; seminars. **Events** *Triennial Meeting* Uppsala (Sweden) 2007, *Triennial meeting / Triennial Festival and Meeting* Jyväskylä (Finland) 2004, *Triennial choir leaders seminar / Triennial Choir Conductor Seminar* Denmark 2002, *Triennial meeting / Triennial Festival and Meeting* Trondheim (Norway) 2001, *Triennial choir leaders seminar / Triennial Choir Conductor Seminar* Mariehamn (Finland) 1999. **Publications** *NORDKLANG Choir Repertoire.*
Members National Choral Federations from the 6 Nordic countries and territories:
Denmark, Faeroe Is, Finland, Iceland, Norway, Sweden. [2021/XD1772/**D**]

♦ Nordisk Kosmetologkongress (meeting series)
♦ Nordisk Kriminalpolitiunion (inactive)
♦ Nordisk kulturelt samarbejde (1971 treaty)
♦ Nordisk Kulturfond (#17264)
♦ Nordisk Laboratoriekomite (inactive)
♦ Nordisk Laboratorium for Luminescensdatering (#17333)
♦ Nordisk Laeder Kemiker Forening (inactive)
♦ Nordisk Laegemiddelnaevn (inactive)
♦ Nordisk Laegeråd (unconfirmed)
♦ Nordisk Lastebil Union (inactive)
♦ Nordisk Legemiddelnemnd (inactive)
♦ Nordisk Lichenologisk Förening (#17336)

♦ **Nordisk Liturgisk Netvaerk (Leitourgia)** **17522**
Chair Paavo Cajanderinkatu 7 as 13, FI-13200 Hämeenlinna, Finland.
Treas Dronningens gate 18, 8006 Bodø, Norway.
URL: http://leitourgia.org/
History Nov 2005, Oskarshamn (Sweden). **Aims** Act as a meeting place for the exchange of knowledge and reflection on the Christian faith in terms of the liturgical heritage of Christian churches and denominations. **Languages** English. **Activities** Events/meetings. **Events** *Conference* Lohja (Finland) 2022.
Members Full in 5 countries:
Denmark, Finland, Iceland, Norway, Sweden. [2022.06.03/XM8040/**F**]

♦ Nordisk Luftpostsamler Forening (inactive)
♦ Nordisk Malermester Organisation (inactive)
♦ Nordisk Medicinalstatistisk Kommité (#17342)
♦ Nordisk Medicinhistorisk Forening (no recent information)

♦ **Nordisk Medisinsk Laboratoriegruppe (NML)** **17523**
Nordic Group of Medical Laboratory Technologists' Associations
Chair address not obtained.
History Former names and other names: *Nordic Association of Medical Laboratory Technologists* – former. **Aims** Strengthen Nordic cooperation within the biomedical laboratory scientist profession; increase knowledge of the profession within the Nordic countries; support the development of the profession. **Structure** Secretariat rotates every 2 years. **Languages** English. **Events** *Conference* Sweden 2019, *Congress* Helsinki (Finland) 2017, *Congress* Reykjavik (Iceland) 2015, *Congress* Visby (Sweden) 2009, *Congress* Helsinki (Finland) 2007.
Members Full in 5 countries:
Denmark, Finland, Iceland, Norway, Sweden. [2021/XD0256/**F**]

♦ Nordisk Mejeriteknisk Råd (#17265)
♦ Nordisk Metodik Komité for Levnedsmidler / see Nordic-Baltic Committee on Food Analysis (#17215)
♦ Nordisk Metodikkomité for Naeringsmidler / see Nordic-Baltic Committee on Food Analysis (#17215)
♦ Nordisk Metodikkommitté för Livsmedel / see Nordic-Baltic Committee on Food Analysis (#17215)
♦ Nordisk Militärmedicinsk Förening (no recent information)
♦ Nordisk Ministerråd (#17260)
♦ Nordisk Ministerråd /Kultur- og Undervisningsministrene (inactive)
♦ Nordisk Mosjonskomite (inactive)
♦ Nordisk Motivsamler Forbund (inactive)

♦ **Nordisk Møte for Barneonkologisk Sykepleie (NOBOS)** **17524**
Nordic Society of Pediatric Oncology Nurses
Chairman c/o Rigshospitalet 5054, Blegdamsvej 9, 2100 Copenhagen, Denmark. E-mail: info@nobos.org.
URL: http://www.nobos.org/
Aims Coordinate and develop knowledge in clinical paediatric oncology nursing care; have free exchange of ideas and inspiration to nursing research. **Structure** Board, including Chairman and Secretary. **Languages** English. **Activities** Sub-groups (6): Adolescent; Brain Tumours; Late Effect – Long Term Following Up; Nutrition; Pain; Palliative Care. **Events** *Congress* Lund (Sweden) 2023, *Congress* Trondheim (Norway) 2021, *Congress* Trondheim (Norway) 2020, *Congress* Vilnius (Lithuania) 2018, *Congress* Reykjavik (Iceland) 2016.
Members Full in 6 countries:
Denmark, Finland, Iceland, Lithuania, Norway, Sweden. [2021.09.16/XM0026/**D**]

♦ Nordisk Museumsforbund (#17455)
♦ Nordisk Musiker Union (no recent information)
♦ Nordisk Musikförläggerunion (no recent information)
♦ Nordisk Musikpedagogisk Union (inactive)
♦ Nordisk Musik Union / see Nordisk Orkestermusik Union (#17525)
♦ Nordisk Navigasjonsforum (#17323)
♦ Nordisk Navigatørkongress (#17407)
♦ Nordisk Nettverk for Musikkpedagogikk Forskning (#17363)
♦ Nordisk Netvaerk for Geografisk Informasjon (#17355)
♦ Nordisk Neurokirurgisk Forening (#19093)
♦ Nordisk Neurologisk Förening (inactive)
♦ Nordisk Neuropediatrisk Selskap (#17367)
♦ Nordisk Numismatisk Union (#17370)
♦ Nordisk Odontologisk Forening (#19070)
♦ Nordisk Oljelednings Union (no recent information)
♦ Nordisk Optiker Råd (#17376)
♦ Nordisk Organisasjon for Utdanninger i Sosialt Arbeid (#17204)
♦ Nordisk Organ for Reindriftsforskning (inactive)
♦ Nordisk Orkester Bibliotekets Union (unconfirmed)
♦ Nordisk orkesterkonferanse (meeting series)

♦ **Nordisk Orkestermusik Union (NOMU)** **17525**
Secretariat c/o FSSMF, Hovrättsesplanaden 16, vaning 6, FI-65100 Vaasa, Finland. E-mail: formand@nordiskmusikunion.org.
URL: http://nordiskmusikunion.org/
History Founded 1949, as *Nordic Amateur Music Union – Nordisk Amatørmusikunion (NAMU)*, by associations of wind instrument orchestras in Nordic countries. 2001, name changed to *Nordisk Musik Union (NoMU).* **Aims** Strengthen and stimulate interest and participation in the Scandinavian music movement; improve the quality of music performed by amateurs; promote Scandinavian cooperation through cultural teamwork. **Structure** Executive Committee.
Members Full in 4 countries:
Denmark, Finland, Norway, Sweden.
NGO Relations *International Confederation of Music Societies (CISM, #12865).* [2017/XD4278/**D**]

♦ Nordisk Ortopedisk Forening (#17379)
♦ Nordisk Oto-Laryngologisk Forening (#19094)
♦ Nordisk Økonomisk Forskningsråd (inactive)
♦ Nordisk Økonomisk Kvaegavl (#17275)
♦ Nordisk Paediatrisk Forening (inactive)
♦ Nordisk Paediatrisk Oftalmologisk Gruppe (#17382)
♦ Nordisk Paediatrisk Ortopaedisk Federation (no recent information)
♦ Nordisk Papirhandlerråd (inactive)
♦ Nordisk Parfymehandlerråd (inactive)
♦ Nordisk Pedikyrforening (inactive)
♦ Nordisk Plastikkirurgisk Forening (#19075)
♦ Nordisk Postforening (#17391)
♦ Nordisk Privatläroverkunion (inactive)
♦ Nordisk Privatskole Union (inactive)
♦ Nordisk Publiceringsnaevn for Humanistiske og Samfundsvidenskabelige Tidsskrifter / see Nordisk publiseringsnemnd for humanistiske og samfunnsvitenskapelige tidsskrifter (#17526)

♦ **Nordisk publiseringsnemnd for humanistiske og samfunnsvitenskapelige tidsskrifter (NOP-HS)** **17526**
Contact c/o Research Council of Norway, PO Box 2700, St Hanshaugen, 0131 Oslo, Norway. T. +4722037570. E-mail: hb@forskningsradet.no – jof@forskningsradet.no.
URL: http://www.nos-hs.org/
History Founded 1 Jan 2000, on merger of *Nordic Publications Committee for Humanist Periodicals (inactive)* and *Nordic Publishing Board in Social Sciences (inactive).* A sub-committee of *Nordisk Samarbejdsnaevn for Humanistisk og Samfundsvidenskabelig Forskning (NOS-HS, #17530).* Original title: *Nordic Board for Periodicals in the Humanities and Social Sciences – Nordisk Publiceringsnaevn for Humanistiske og Samfundsvidenskabelige Tidsskrifter (NOP-HS).* Previously also referred to as *Nordiska Publiceringskommittén för Humanistiska och Samhällsvetenskapliga Tidskrifter.* **Aims** Allocate grants to Nordic *periodicals* in the *humanities* and *social sciences.* **Structure** Board. Secretariat, every 4 years rotating amongst member countries. **Languages** Danish, Faroese, Icelandic, Norwegian, Swedish. **Staff** Shared with *Nordisk Samarbejdsnaevn for Humanistisk og Samfundsvidenskabelig Forskning (NOS-HS, #17530)*: 1.5 FTE, paid. **Finance** Financed by: *Nordisk Samarbejdsnaevn for Humanistisk og Samfundsvidenskabelig Forskning (NOS-HS, #17530).* Budget (annual): euro 420,000. **Activities** Financial and/or material support.
Members National research councils in 4 countries:
Denmark, Finland, Norway, Sweden. [2014.06.01/XE4113/**E**]

♦ Nordisk Råd (#17256)
♦ Nordisk Råd for Forskning i Europaeisk Integrationsret (inactive)
♦ Nordisk Råd for Forskning i Europeisk Integrasjonsrett (inactive)
♦ Nordisk Råd for Glass- og Porselenshandel (inactive)
♦ Nordisk Råd for Saue- og Geiteavl (inactive)
♦ Nordisk rättstoxikologisk förening (#17193)
♦ Nordisk Reklamebureau Forbund (no recent information)
♦ Nordisk Reklamebyrå Forbund (no recent information)
♦ Nordisk Reologiselskab (#17400)
♦ Nordisk Reproduksjonsråd (inactive)
♦ Nordisk Reserveoffisersforbund (inactive)
♦ Nordisk Retsmedicinsk Forening (inactive)
♦ Nordisk Rettsodontologisk Forening (no recent information)
♦ Nordisk Reuma Råd (#17401)
♦ Nordisk Reumatismekomite / see Scandinavian Society for Rheumatology (#19118)
♦ Nordisk Revisorforbund (#17285)

♦ **Nordisk Roforbund (NOR)** **17527**
Nordic Rowing Federation
Pres address not obtained.
URL: http://www.nordicrowing.com/
History Founded 27 Feb 1910. **Aims** Develop competition rowing within the Nordic countries, primarily on junior levels; develop homogenous rules of racing within the Nordic countries; promote common education of umpires; empower Nordic democratic values in the International Rowing Federation. **Structure** Board. Ad hoc working groups (4): Competitive; Umpire; Coastal; Masters. **Languages** Danish, English, Finnish, Icelandic, Norwegian, Swedish. **Activities** Events/meetings. **Events** *Congress* Stockholm (Sweden) 2009, *Congress* Örkelljunga (Sweden) 2003, *Congress* Copenhagen (Denmark) 1999, *Congress* Tampere (Finland) 1997, *General Assembly* Tampere (Finland) 1987.
Members National organizations (6) in 6 countries and territories:
Denmark, Faeroe Is, Finland, Iceland, Norway, Sweden. [2017/XD1771/**D**]

♦ Nordisk Sällskapet för Circumpolar Hälsa (#17412)

♦ **Nordisk Samarbeidsforum for Anestesi- og Intensivsykepleiere (NOSAM)** **17528**
Nordic Association of Nurse Anaesthesiologists and Intensive Care Nurses
Address not obtained.
History 1970. Former names and other names: *Nordic Cooperation for Anesthesia and Intensive Care Nurses* – alias. **Events** *Nordic Congress for Anesthesia and Intensive Care Nurses (NOKIAS)* Trondheim (Norway) 2022, *Nordic Congress for Anesthesia and Intensive Care Nurses (NOKIAS)* Turku (Finland) 2016, *Congress* Stockholm (Sweden) 2007, *Congress* Stavanger (Norway) 2004.
Members Individuals in 6 countries and territories:
Denmark, Faeroe Is, Finland, Iceland, Norway, Sweden. [2022/XM1356/**D**]

♦ Nordisk Samarbeidsgruppe for By og Boligforskning (#17460)
♦ Nordisk Samarbeidskomité fo Idrettsbibliotek / see Nordic Committee for Sport Libraries (#17248)
♦ Nordisk SamarbeidsKomite for komplementaer-og alternativ medisin (#17254)
♦ Nordisk Samarbeidskomite for Offentlig Tilsyn med Brannfarlige og Eksplosive Varer (#17247)
♦ Nordisk Samarbeids-Komité for Rådgivende Ingeniørforeninger (no recent information)
♦ Nordisk Samarbeidskomite for Skogteknikere (inactive)

♦ **Nordisk Samarbeidsnaevn for Naturvidenskab (NOS-N)** **17529**
Comité de coopération des conseils nordiques de la recherche en sciences naturelles – Joint Committee of the Nordic Natural Science Research Councils – Luonnontieteellisten Tutkimusneuvostojen Pohjoismainen Yhteistyölautakunta
Director NordForsk, Stensberggata 25, 0170 Oslo, Norway. T. +4748224286. E-mail: nordforsk@nordforsk.org.
URL: http://www.nordforsk.org/
History Established Apr 1967, Turku (Finland), to complement in natural science the work of *Nordiska Samarbetsorganisationen för Teknisk-Vetenskaplig Forskning (NORDFORSK, inactive)* in applied sciences. A cooperation body set up under *Nordic Cultural Cooperation (1971).* Terms of reference revised Nov 1995, Jun 2007 and 2012. Previously also known as *Nordisk Samarbetsnemnd for Naturvitenskap.* **Aims** Encourage cooperation among natural science research councils and scientists in the region, especially so as to address scientifically challenging programmes which may be outside the limits attainable by national organizations; exchange information on national science policy and planned projects; initiate negotiations on matters in which joint action should be taken. **Structure** 2 representatives of each country. **Languages** Danish, English, Finnish, Icelandic, Norwegian, Swedish. **Staff** 0.50 FTE, paid. **Finance** Expenses borne by member councils. Annual budget: Norwegian Kr 200,000. **Activities** Knowledge management/information

dissemination; research/documentation; projects/programmes; financial and/or material support; events/meetings. **Events** *Meeting* Oslo (Norway) 2016, *Meeting* Helsinki (Finland) 2015, *Meeting* Lund (Sweden) 2015, *Meeting* Reykjavik (Iceland) 2014, *Meeting* Oslo (Norway) 2013.
Members National research councils from 5 countries:
Denmark, Finland, Iceland, Norway, Sweden.
Included in the above, 1 organization listed in this Yearbook:
NordForsk (#17164).
Associate Member (1):
Nordic Council of Ministers (NCM, #17260).
NGO Relations Instrumental in setting up: *Nordic Optical Telescope Scientific Association (NOTSA, inactive).* [2018/XD2847/y/**E***]

♦ Nordisk Samarbeidsnemnd for Naturvitenskap / see Nordisk Samarbeidsnaevn for Naturvidenskab (#17529)
♦ Nordisk Samarbeidsorgan for Vitenskapelig Informasjon (inactive)
♦ Nordisk Samarbeidsråd for Utviklingshemmede (inactive)
♦ Nordisk Samarbeiskomite for Husstellundervisning (no recent information)
♦ Nordisk Samarbejde Inden for Skoleområdet (inactive)
♦ Nordisk Samarbejde vedrørende Voksenundervisning og Folkeoplysning / see Nordisk Folkeoplysnings- og Voksenundervisningssamarbejde (#17504)
♦ Nordisk Samarbejdskomite for Husholdningsundervisning (no recent information)

♦ Nordisk Samarbejdsnaevn for Humanistisk og Samfundsvidenskabelig Forskning (NOS-HS) 17530

Comité conjoint des conseils nordiques de la recherche pour les sciences humaines et sociales – Joint Committee for Nordic Research Councils for the Humanities and the Social Sciences

Secretariat c/o Academy of Finland, Division of Social Sciences and Humanities Research, Hakaniemenranta 6, PO Box 131, FI-00531 Helsinki, Finland. T. +358295335000. E-mail: nos-hs@aka.fi.
URL: http://www.nos-hs.org/

History 2003, by merger of *Joint Committee of the Nordic Research Councils for the Humanities (inactive)* and *Joint Committee of Nordic Social Science Research Councils (inactive).* Previously also referred to as *Nordiska Samarbetsnämnden för Humanistisk och Samhällsvetenskaplig Forskning.* **Aims** Promote cooperation and information exchange between the Nordic research councils; fund Nordic research cooperation and the publishing of Nordic scientific periodicals. **Structure** Board of 10. Sub-Committee: *Nordisk publiseringsnemnd for humanistiske og samfunnsvitenskapelige tidsskrifter (NOP-HS, #17526).* Secretariat, every 4 years rotating amongst member countries. **Languages** Danish, Faroese, Icelandic, Norwegian, Swedish. **Staff** 1.50 FTE, paid. **Finance** Members' dues. Budget (annual): euro 2.5 million. **Activities** Financial and/or material support.
Members National councils in 5 countries:
Denmark, Finland, Iceland, Norway, Sweden.
NGO Relations Cooperates with: *NordForsk (#17164).* [2019/XE4681/**E**]

♦ Nordisk Samarbejdsorgan for Videnskabelig Information (inactive)
♦ Nordisk Samarbejdsråd for Kriminologi (#17493)
♦ Nordisk Samarbejdsråd for Logopedi og Foniatri (no recent information)
♦ Nordisk Samarbetskommitté för Hushås-undervisning (no recent information)
♦ Nordisk Samarbetsråd för Kriminologi (#17493)
♦ Nordisk Samfund for Campanologi / see Nordisk Selskab for Campanologi og Klokkespil (#17533)

♦ Nordisk Sammenslutning for Hygiejenesygeplejersker (NSFH) 17531

Nordic Society of Infection Control Nurses

Contact c/o Sahlgrenska Univ Hospital, Region Västra Götaland, Regionens Hus, SE-462 80 Vänersborg, Sweden.
URL: http://www.nsfh.net/

History 2003. **Events** *Conference* Helsingør (Denmark) 2022, *Conference* Trondheim (Norway) 2017, *Conference* Gothenburg (Sweden) 2014, *Conference* Vaasa (Finland) 2011, *Conference* Copenhagen (Denmark) 2007.
Members Full in 4 countries:
Denmark, Finland, Norway, Sweden. [2013/XJ5425/**D**]

♦ Nordisk Sammenslutning til Vaern for Børn og Unge (inactive)
♦ Nordisk Samorganisajon for Ungdomsarbeid (#17476)
♦ Nordisk Samorganisation för Personal vid Mentalsjukhus (inactive)
♦ Nordisk Samorganisation for Ungdomsarbejde (#17476)
♦ Nordisk Samrådsgruppe for Flygtningespørgsmål / see Nordic Joint Advisory Group on Refugee Policy (#17331)
♦ Nordisk Samrådsgruppepåhøjt Niveau for Flygtningespørgsmål (#17331)
♦ Nordisk Samvirkende Tegelforeninger (inactive)

♦ Nordisk Sangerforbund (NSF) 17532

Association nordique des chanteurs – Nordic Singers' Association

Contact Stallgränd 2 F 66, FI-00330 Helsinki, Finland.
URL: http://www.malechoirweb.com/nordisk-sangerforbund.html

History 1956. **Aims** Organize *male* voice *choirs.* **Languages** Danish, English, Norwegian, Swedish. **Staff** Voluntary. **Finance** Annual budget: about euro 1,000. **Events** *Festival* Tartu (Estonia) 2012, *Festival* Tallinn (Estonia) 2006, *Festival* Vaasa (Finland) 1996, *Congress* Trondheim (Norway) 1963, *Congress* Helsinki (Finland) 1961.
Members Organizations in 11 countries and territories:
Åland, Canada, Denmark, Estonia, Faeroe Is, Finland, Iceland, Latvia, Norway, Sweden, USA. [2018.06.13/XD1924/**D**]

♦ Nordisk Science Center Forbund (#17404)
♦ Nordisk Selskab for Aestetik (#17411)

♦ Nordisk Selskab for Campanologi og Klokkespil (NSCK) 17533

Association scandinave de campanologie et carillon – Nordic Association of Campanology and Carillon

Pres address not obtained. E-mail: info@carillon.no.
URL: http://www.nsck.org/

History 1964, Svendborg (Denmark), as *Nordiske Klokkekomité – Scandinavian Bell Committee,* at 2nd Scandinavian bell conference. Name changed to *Nordisk Samfund for Campanologi – Nordic Society for Campanology and Carillon* at 3rd conference, 1966, Valdress (Norway). Current title adopted, 1993, Løgumkloster (Denmark). **Aims** Promote interest in *bells* and *carillons* in Nordic countries. **Structure** Bell Committee (meets twice a year). **Languages** Danish, Faroese, Icelandic, Norwegian, Swedish. **Staff** 8.00 FTE, voluntary. **Finance** Members' dues. **Activities** Organizes Bell Conference (every 2-3 years). **Events** *Nordic Conference* Marstal (Denmark) / Svendborg (Denmark) 2020, *Conference* Fagernes (Norway) 2018, *Conference* Helsinki (Finland) 2007, *Conference* Sandefjord (Norway) 2004, *Conference* Västerås (Sweden) 2001. **Publications** *Acta Campanologica* (2 a year) – magazine; *Bell News* (2 a year).
Members Individuals in 5 countries:
Denmark, Finland, Iceland, Norway, Sweden.
NGO Relations Member of: *World Carillon Federation (WCF, #21260).* [2018/XD1961/v/**D**]

♦ Nordisk Selskab for Faenomenologi (#17425)
♦ Nordisk Selskab for Medicinsk og Biologisk Illustration (inactive)
♦ Nordisk Selskab for Medicinsk Humor (unconfirmed)
♦ Nordisk Selskab for Romantikstudier (internationally oriented national body)
♦ Nordisk Selskab for Strålingsbeskyttelse (#17428)
♦ Nordisk Selskap for Estetik (#17411)
♦ Nordisk Selskap for Farmakologi (no recent information)
♦ Nordisk Selskap for Interartstudier / see International Society for Intermedial Studies (#15211)
♦ Nordisk Selskap for Midtaustenstudiar / see Nordic Society for Middle Eastern Studies (#17419)
♦ Nordisk Selskap for Spiseforstyrrelser (#17273)
♦ Nordisk Siddenetvaerk (#17405)
♦ Nordisk Skakforbund (#17234)
♦ Nordisk Skattevitenskapelig Forskningsråds (#17443)
♦ Nordisk Skeppsteknisk Samarbetskommittén (inactive)
♦ Nordisk Skibsrederforening (#17501)
♦ Nordisk Skogökonomisk Seminar / see Scandinavian Society of Forest Economics (#19108)
♦ Nordisk Skogsunion (no recent information)
♦ Nordisk Sko- og Laerarbeierunion (inactive)

♦ Nordisk Skolebibliotekarforening 17534

Nordic Association of School Librarians

Sec Equatorn 12, FI-68600 Jakobstad, Finland.
Chair address not obtained.

History 1981. **Aims** Promote development, cooperation and innovation among school libraries in Nordic countries; promote and qualify literature for children and youngsters. **Structure** Board of 6. **Finance** Members' dues. Budget (annual): about euro 10,000. **Activities** Organizes biennial conference; grants Nordic award for children's literature. **Events** *Conference* Thórshavn (Faeroe Is) 2013, *Conference* Gothenburg (Sweden) 2011, *Skolbiblioteket – det osynliga barnet?* Espoo (Finland) 2009, *Conference* Røskilde (Denmark) 2007, *Conference* Iceland 2005. [2013/XM1264/**D**]

♦ Nordisk Skoleledermøde (meeting series)
♦ Nordisk Skoliose Forening (#17437)
♦ Nordisk Skuespillerråd (#17166)
♦ Nordisk Socialmedicinsk Forening (inactive)
♦ Nordisk Socialstatistik Komité (#17409)

♦ Nordisk Sommeruniversitet (NSU) 17535

Université nordique d'été – Nordic Summer University – Nordiska Sommaruniversitetet – Pohjoismainen Kesäyliopisto – Noranna Sumarhaskolinn

Contact c/o Föreningarna Nordens Förbund, Snaregade 10 A, 3 sal, 1205 Copenhagen, Denmark. E-mail: board@nsuweb.org.
URL: http://nordic.university/

History 1964. Since 1950, organizing symposia in study circles around the Nordic region, and since 2000 also the Baltic. Statutes amended: 7 Aug 1970; 7 Aug 1971; 12 Aug 1972; 9 Aug 1974; 1978; 8 Aug 1980; 28 Jul 1989; 24 Jul 1990; 30 Jul 1992; 26 Jul 1994; 30 Jul 1996. Functions as an independent private organization within the framework of *Nordic Cultural Cooperation (1971).* **Aims** Supplement professional *training* of students and broaden their academic horizon through interdisciplinary studies and by bringing together *students* and *teachers* with different academic backgrounds; further critical insight into common scientific problems, interdisciplinary problems and the relationship between science, society and culture. **Structure** General Meeting (annual); Board; Coordinators. **Finance** Sources: grants. Supported by: *Nordic Council of Ministers (NCM, #17260).* **Activities** Training/education. **Events** *Summer Session* 2020, *Summer Session* Elbiku (Estonia) 2019, *Summer Session* Fårö Is (Sweden) 2018, *Summer Session* Saulkrasti (Latvia) 2017, *Summer Session* Orivesi (Finland) 2016. **Publications** *Information fra Nordisk Sommeruniversitet* – newsletter. Books.
Members Individuals in 10 countries and territories:
Denmark, Estonia, Faeroe Is, Finland, Greenland, Iceland, Latvia, Lithuania, Norway, Sweden. [2021.05.22/XF8195/**F**]

♦ Nordisk Sømandskirkeråd (no recent information)
♦ Nordisk Sportsfiskerunion (inactive)
♦ Nordisk Sportskomite for Handikappede (inactive)
♦ Nordisk språkmøte (meeting series)
♦ Nordisk språkråd (inactive)
♦ Nordisk Sprogråd (inactive)
♦ Nordisk Srafiklaererråd (inactive)
♦ Nordisk Stålforbund (inactive)
♦ Nordisk Statstjenestemanns Organisasjon (#17258)
♦ Nordisk Strafferetskomité (inactive)
♦ Nordisk sundhedsberedskabsaftale (2002 treaty)
♦ Nordisk Swimmeforbund (#17442)

♦ Nordiskt Alkohol- och Narkotikapolitiskt Samarbete (NordAN) 17536

Nordic Alcohol and Drug Policy Network

Exec Dir Marjamaa 2, 72214 Türi, Estonia. T. +3725261884.
URL: http://www.nordan.org/

History 25 Sep 2000, Copenhagen (Denmark). Replaces *Nordiska Nykerhetsrådet.* Took over *Nordic Association for Education to a Life without Drugs (inactive).* Registration: EU Transparency Register, No/ID: 774317337944-70, Start date: 25 Apr 2020. **Aims** Reduce the consumption of alcohol and other drugs; support a restrictive alcohol and drug policy. **Structure** Assembly of Representatives (annually); Board. **Events** *Alcohol and drugs in a changing society* Helsinki (Finland) 2019, *Conference* Stockholm (Sweden) 2018, *Conference* Tallinn (Estonia) 2017, *Conference* Oslo (Norway) 2016, *Alcohol, drugs and media scene* Helsinki (Finland) 2015.
Members Organizations (90) in 10 countries and territories:
Denmark, Estonia, Faeroe Is, Finland, Greenland, Iceland, Latvia, Lithuania, Norway, Sweden.
Included in the above, 1 organization listed in this Yearbook:
Internationella Institutet för Alkoholpolitik (IIAP, no recent information).
NGO Relations Member of (1): *European Alcohol Policy Alliance (Eurocare, #05856).* [2020/XF6336/y/**F**]

♦ Nordisk Tandteknikerunion (inactive)
♦ Nordiskt Byggforskningsmöte (meeting series)
♦ Nordiskt Center för Alkohol- och Drogforskning (inactive)
♦ Nordiskt Centrum för Kulturarvspedagogik (#17230)
♦ Nordisk Teaterlaboratorium (internationally oriented national body)
♦ Nordisk Teaterlederråd (#17447)
♦ Nordisk Teater Råd (no recent information)
♦ Nordisk Teaterunion (#17448)
♦ Nordisk Tekstil-Arbeiderunion (inactive)
♦ Nordisk Tele Organisation (no recent information)
♦ Nordisk Tele Union (inactive)
♦ Nordiskt Forskersymposium om Undervisning i Naturvitenskap (meeting series)
♦ Nordiskt Forum för Byggnadskalk (#17512)

♦ Nordiskt Forum för Forskning och Utvecklingsarbete inom Utbildning i Slöyd (NORDFO) 17537

Pres Laererskoleveien 40, 3679 Notodden, Norway. T. +4735026200.
URL: http://www.nordfo.org/

History Founded 1988. **Aims** Promote cooperation among teacher educators in Nordic countries to initiate, stimulate and report research and R and D on the subjects of arts and craft, needlework and woodwork, and on *teacher education* in these subjects. **Structure** Bureau. **Languages** Danish, English, Faroese, Icelandic, Norwegian, Swedish. **Staff** All voluntary. **Finance** Budget through Nordplus: about euro 40,000. **Activities** Teacher and student mobility; PhD courses; student courses; international conference. **Events** *International Conference on Materiality and Knowledge* Notodden (Norway) 2012. **Publications** *Techne* – series.
Members Institutions in 7 countries:
Denmark, Estonia, Finland, Iceland, Latvia, Norway, Sweden. [2013.07.26/XJ6572/**F**]

♦ Nordiskt forum för trauma och akutradiologi Organisation (#17301)

- ♦ Nordiskt hälsoberedskapsavtal (2002 treaty)
- ♦ Nordiskt Hjälpskoleförbund / see Nordic Special Needs Education Organization (#17435)
- ♦ Nordisk Thoraxkirurgisk Forening (#19079)
- ♦ Nordisk Tidsskriftskomité (inactive)
- ♦ Nordiskt Institut för Kvinno- och Könsforskning / see Nordic Information for Gender Knowledge (#17317)

♦ Nordisk Tjenestemannsråd (NTR) 17538

Nordic Council of Public Services Employees

Gen Sec c/o Delta, Postbox 9202, Grønland, 0134 Oslo, Norway.
Facebook: https://www.facebook.com/ntrnorden/

History 19 Dec 1934, Copenhagen (Denmark). Former names and other names: *Nordic Council of Local Government Officers* – former (19 Dec 1934); *Secrétariat nordique des fonctionnaires des pouvoirs locaux* – former (19 Dec 1934); *Nordiska Kommunaltjänstemannarådet (NKR)* – former (19 Dec 1934); *Nordic Public Services Council* – alias. **Aims** Work for close cooperation among affiliated organizations to improve conditions for affiliated *trade union* members. **Structure** Delegate Meeting (annual). **Languages** Danish, Faroese, Finnish, Icelandic, Norwegian, Swedish. **Staff** 1.00 FTE, paid. **Finance** Members' dues. **Activities** Exchanges information and experience within the public sector about: conditions of employment and working conditions for municipal workers; society economics; labour market; trade union organizations and activities. Affiliated unions assist each other morally and economically during conflicts and within issues concerning trade union work. Provides opportunity for members of affiliated unions to have direct contact with working and organization conditions in Nordic countries through conferences, meetings and direct contact between local branches. **Events** *Conference* Svendborg (Denmark) 2014, *Conference* Røros (Norway) 2005, *Challenge for the Nordic welfare state* Oulu (Finland) 2004, *Nordic chief conference* Gothenburg (Sweden) 2003, *Conference* Thórshavn (Faeroe Is) 2003.

Members Affiliated trade unions (11), totalling 370,000 members, in 6 countries and territories:
Denmark, Faeroe Is, Finland, Iceland, Norway, Sweden.

NGO Relations *European Federation of Public Service Unions (EPSU, #07202)*; *Public Services International (PSI, #18572)*. [2020/XD2995/D]

- ♦ Nordiskt Kollegium för Ekologi (inactive)
- ♦ Nordiskt Kollegium för Viltforskning (#17262)
- ♦ Nordiskt kulturellt samarbete (1971 treaty)
- ♦ Nordiskt Nätverk för Pedagogisk Filosofi (#17426)

♦ Nordiskt Nätverk för Samspelet mellan Privat och Offentlig Rätt (PROF) 17539

Nordic Network for Research on the Relation between Private Law and Public Law

Contact Umeå Univ – Dept of Law, SE-901 87 Umeå, Sweden. T. +46907865000. Fax +46907866587. E-mail: juridik@jus.umu.se.
URL: http://www.jus.umu.se/forskning/prof/

History 2001. **Aims** Make contacts between persons working within or doing research in the areas between public and private law. **Languages** Danish, English, Faroese, Icelandic, Norwegian, Swedish. **Staff** 40.00 FTE, voluntary. **Finance** Grants from universities involved. **Events** *Nordic seminar* Tampere (Finland) 2005.

Members in 5 countries:
Denmark, Finland, Iceland, Norway, Sweden. [2012/XM0196/F]

- ♦ Nordiskt Nätverk för Vuxnas Lärande (#17349)
- ♦ Nordisk Tobakskollegium (internationally oriented national body)
- ♦ Nordisk Toldadministrativt Råd (#17497)

♦ Nordisk Tolltjenestemannsorganisasjon (NTO) 17540

Nordic Organization of Customs Officials – Organisation nordique des fonctionnaires des douanes

Communications Dir Norsk Tollerforbund, Postboks 2103 VIKA, 0125 Oslo, Norway. T. +4790591618. E-mail: post@norsktollerforbund.no.
Main Website: https://www.norsktollerforbund.no

Aims Support employees in customs and tax administrations and promote workers' rights in Nordic countries. **Languages** Danish, Faroese, Icelandic, Norwegian, Swedish. **Finance** Sources: members' dues. No budget. **Events** *Annual meeting* Paris (France) 1996, *Annual meeting* Stockholm (Sweden) 1995, *Annual meeting* Bern (Switzerland) 1994, *Annual meeting* Vejle (Denmark) 1993, *Annual meeting* Belgium 1992.

Members Unions (6) in 5 countries:
Denmark, Finland, Iceland, Norway, Sweden. [2022.05.10/XD0348/D]

- ♦ Nordiskt Organ på Provnings- och Kontrollområdet / see Joint Nordic Organization for Technical Testing (#16142)
- ♦ Nordiskt Orienteringsråd (no recent information)
- ♦ Nordiskt Råd för Rörelsehindrade (no recent information)
- ♦ Nordisk Traebeskyttelsesråd (#17469)
- ♦ Nordisk Trafikmedicinsk Forening (inactive)

♦ Nordisk Trafikskole Union (NTU) 17541

Nordic Union of Driving Schools Associations

Chairman ATL, Ryensvingen 15, 0690 Oslo, Norway.
Gen Sec address not obtained.
URL: http://www.ntu.nu/

History Set up 1947, Nordic national driving school associations. **Aims** Improve traffic safety and quality of driver education in Nordic countries through cross-border cooperation and by developing content and methods of driver education. **Structure** General Meeting (every 2 years); Board. **Languages** Danish, Norwegian, Swedish. **Staff** Voluntary. **Finance** Members' dues. **Events** *0-Vision Seminar* Stockholm (Sweden) 2015, *Nordic drivers education seminar* Helsinki (Finland) 2004, *Annual meeting* Amman (Jordan) 2003, *Nordic Drivers Education Seminar* Oslo (Norway) 2002, *Nordic drivers education seminar* Kalmar (Sweden) 2000.

Members Full in 5 countries:
Denmark, Finland, Iceland, Norway, Sweden.

NGO Relations Member of: *International Commission for Driver Testing (CIECA, #12678)*. [2015.06.25/XD0261/D]

- ♦ Nordisk Transportarbeiderfederasjon (#17496)

♦ Nordisk Transportpolitisk Nettverk (NTN) 17542

Nordic Transportpolitical Network

Address not obtained.
URL: http://www.ntn.dk/

History 1998, by regions within a joint transport corridor which links Western Scandinavia with Central European markets. Until 2000, under *INTERREG V (#15966)*. **Activities** Organizes workshops. **Events** *Conference on sustainable transport* Kristiansand (Norway) 2005, *Conference* Stavanger (Norway) 2005. **Publications** *Nyhetsbrev* – newsletter.

Members Partners (17) in 4 countries:
Denmark, Germany, Norway, Sweden.

IGO Relations *Cohesion Fund (#04087)*; *European Regional Development Fund (ERDF, #08342)*. [2010/XJ4430/F]

- ♦ Nordisk Transportteknisk Selskap (inactive)
- ♦ Nordisk Trebeskyttelsesråd (#17469)
- ♦ Nordiskt Samarbete om Teknisk Ackreditering (inactive)
- ♦ Nordiskt Seminarium i Järnvägsteknik (meeting series)
- ♦ Nordiskt Skolledarmøte (meeting series)

♦ Nordiskt Speditörförbund (NSF) 17543

Association nordique de transitaires – Nordischer Spediteurverband – Nordic Association of Freight Forwarders

SG c/o Finnish Freight Forwarders' Assc, PO Box 62, Eteläranta 10, FI-00131 Helsinki, Finland. T. +358205955065. Fax +358205955001.

History 14 May 1920. In English previously also referred to as *Nordic Forwarding Agents Association* and in French as *Association des expéditeurs des pays du Nord*. **Aims** Promote the *freight forwarding* business; encourage relations among members. **Structure** General Assembly. Board, comprising President and 2 representatives of each member association. Secretariat headed by Secretary-General. **Events** *Annual General Meeting* Finland 2012, *Congress* Helsinki (Finland) 2012, *Annual General Meeting* Tromsø (Norway) 2010, *Congress* Hamburg (Germany) 2002, *Nordic freight forwards conference / Congress* Copenhagen (Denmark) 2000.

Members Full in 4 countries:
Denmark, Finland, Norway, Sweden. [2011.06.01/XD4212/D]

- ♦ Nordiskt Utvecklingscenter för Handikapphjälpmedel (inactive)
- ♦ Nordiskt Vägforum (#17402)
- ♦ Nordiskt Välfärdscenter / see Nordens välfärdscenter (#17163)
- ♦ Nordiskt yrkespedagogiskt och yrkesdidaktiskt nätverk / see NORDYRK (#17554)
- ♦ Nordisk uddannelsesf'llesskab på det gymnasiale niveau (2004 treaty)
- ♦ Nordisk Udlaendingeudvalg (#17315)
- ♦ Nordisk Ungkonservativ Union (#17473)
- ♦ Nordisk Union for Alkoholfri Trafikk (inactive)
- ♦ Nordisk Union – Forbund innen Naerings- og Nytelsesmiddelindustrien (no recent information)
- ♦ Nordisk Union Hotel, Restauration, Catering Og Turisme (#17454)
- ♦ Nordisk Union i Kjöttbransjen (inactive)
- ♦ Nordisk Union i Kødbransjen (inactive)
- ♦ Nordisk Union för Musikutbildare (no recent information)
- ♦ Nordisk Urmakerforbund (no recent information)
- ♦ Nordisk Urogynekologisk Arbetsgrupp (#17461)
- ♦ Nordisk Urologisk Förening (#19080)
- ♦ Nordisk utbildningsgemenskap på gymnasienivå (2004 treaty)
- ♦ Nordisk utdanningsfellesskap på videregående-nivå (2004 treaty)
- ♦ Nordisk Vegforum (#17402)
- ♦ Nordisk Vegteknisk Forbund / see Nordic Road Association (#17402)
- ♦ Nordisk Vejforum (#17402)
- ♦ Nordisk Vejteknisk Forbund / see Nordic Road Association (#17402)
- ♦ Nordisk Veterinaer Akupunktur Selskab (#17462)
- ♦ Nordisk Veterinaerförening för Mastitisforskning og Bekjempelse (inactive)
- ♦ Nordisk Violinbyggareförening (inactive)
- ♦ Nordisk Volleyballkonferanse (meeting series)
- ♦ Nordisk Vulkanisk Institut / see Nordic Volcanological Center (#17463)
- ♦ Nordisk Vulkanologisk Institut / see Nordic Volcanological Center (#17463)
- ♦ Nordisk VVS-Forbund (inactive)
- ♦ Nordisk Yrkesvaegledarforbund (inactive)
- ♦ NORD-IS – Nordic Insulation Symposium on Materials, Components and Diagnostics (meeting series)
- ♦ **NORDITA** Nordic Institute for Theoretical Physics (#17324)
- ♦ NORDIWA – Nordic Waste Water Conference (meeting series)
- ♦ Nordjazz (no recent information)

♦ Nordjobb 17544

Program Manager c/o Foreningerne Nordens Forbund, Snaregade 10A, 2 sal, 1205 Copenhagen, Denmark. T. +46762345414.
URL: http://www.nordjobb.org/

History Founded Dec 1985. **Aims** Increase the mobility of *young people* on the common Nordic *labour* market; strengthen said labour market; increase the knowledge of languages and cultures in the Nordic region. **Activities** Networking/liaising.

Members Covers 8 countries and territories:
Åland, Denmark, Faeroe Is, Finland, Greenland, Iceland, Norway, Sweden.

IGO Relations *Nordic Council (NC, #17256)*; *Nordic Council of Ministers (NCM, #17260)*. [2019/XF1990/F]

- ♦ Nordkallotten Music Council (inactive)
- ♦ Nordkalott Conference (meeting series)
- ♦ Nordkalottenkonferens (meeting series)
- ♦ Nordkalottens Kulturråd (inactive)
- ♦ Nordkalottens Musikråd (inactive)

♦ Nordkalottrådet (NKR) 17545

Conseil de la calotte polaire – North Calotte Council – Pohjoiskalotin-neuvosto (PKN)

SG Regional Council of Lapland, PO Box 8056, Hallituskatu 20B, FI-96101 Rovaniemi, Finland. T. +358407118380.
URL: http://www.nordkalottradet.org/

History 1967, on an ad hoc basis. Set up on permanent basis in 1971 within the framework of *Nordic Council of Ministers (NCM, #17260)* under Nordic Cross-border Cooperation. Statutes registered 1976. **Aims** Promote cooperation in the fields of regional and *labour market policy* and in joint projects with significance for *business development* and *employment*, for social and cultural development in the North Calotte area (Nordland, Troms and Finnmark counties in Norway, Norrbotten county in Sweden and Lapland county in Finland); reduce and solve border obstacles between member states. **Structure** Council; Drafting Council; Environmental Working Groups; Border Information Offices; Secretariat. **Languages** English, Finnish, Norwegian, Swedish. **Staff** 5.00 FTE, paid. **Finance** NCM finances 30 percent through EK-R; regional financial sources. **Activities** Networking/liaising. **Events** *The demographic challenge and the attractivity of the North Calotte region* Äkäslompolo (Finland) 2010.

Members County Councils; State Provincial Offices; County Administrative Boards; County Governors; Regional Centre for Economic Development, Transport and the Environment; Chamber of Commerce; Association of Municipalities. Members in 3 countries:
Finland, Norway, Sweden. [2017.03.09/XD5790/t/E*]

♦ Nordlek Council (NORDLEK) 17546

Sec address not obtained.
URL: http://www.nordlek.org

History 26 Jun 1975, as a cooperation agreement administered by the Council. Originally also referred to as *Nordlek-Rådet*. **Aims** Promote traditional *folk culture*, particularly *folk dance* and *folk music*, in the *Nordic* countries. **Structure** Council; Board; Project Committee; Standing Committees. **Languages** Danish, Faroese, Icelandic, Norwegian, Swedish. **Staff** 0.50 FTE, paid. **Finance** Members' dues. Festival. **Activities** Events/meetings; training/education. **Events** *Meeting* Tampere (Finland) 2021, *Meeting* Falun (Sweden) 2018, *Meeting* Viborg (Denmark) 2015, *Annual Meeting* Reykjavik (Iceland) 2014, *Annual Meeting* Ilulissat (Greenland) 2013. **Publications** *Nordlek-Info* (4 a year) in Swedish.

Members Folklore organizations (21) in 8 countries and territories:
Åland, Denmark, Faeroe Is, Finland, Greenland, Iceland, Norway, Sweden. [2018/XD0318/D]

- ♦ **NORDLEK** Nordlek Council (#17546)
- ♦ Nordlek-Rådet / see Nordlek Council (#17546)
- ♦ NordMetrik – Nordic Society for Metrical Studies (unconfirmed)
- ♦ **NORDNET** Network of Nordic Project Management Associations (#17050)
- ♦ NORD – Nordiska Orienteringsrådet (no recent information)
- ♦ NORD – Nordiskt Orienteringsråd (no recent information)
- ♦ **NorDoc** Nordic Doctoral Training in Health Sciences (#17272)

♦ NordPlant 17547

Coordinator address not obtained.
Admin Coordinator address not obtained.
URL: https://www.nordplant.org/

Aims Promote education, research mobility and technological development to meet future challenges in Nordic agriculture and forestry. **Structure** Steering Committee; Executive Group. **Activities** Events/meetings; projects/programmes. **Events** *Annual Meeting* Lund (Sweden) 2022, *Annual Meeting* Tromsø (Norway) 2021, *Annual Meeting* Tromsø (Norway) 2020, *Annual Meeting* Lund (Sweden) 2019.
Members Universities (5) in 4 countries:
Denmark, Finland, Norway, Sweden. [2021/AA1810/**D**]

♦ NORDPSO 17548

Contact c/o Psoriasisförbundet, Psoriasisliitto ry, Fredrikinakatu 27 A, FI-00120 Helsinki, Finland. T. +35892511900. Fax +358925119088. E-mail: psorilinja@psori.fi.
Contact c/o Psoriasisförbundet, Bellmansgatan 30 1-tr, SE-118 47 Stockholm, Sweden. E-mail: info@pso.se.

History 1987. Former names and other names: *Nordic Psoriasis Alliance* – alias. **Aims** Carry out *psoriasis* research and assistance in the *Nordic* countries.
Members Full in 6 countries and territories:
Denmark, Faeroe Is, Finland, Iceland, Norway, Sweden.
NGO Relations *European Federation of National Psoriasis Patients Associations (EUROPSO, #07175); International Federation of Psoriasis Associations (IFPA, #13520).* [2020/XF3988/**F**]

- ♦ **NORDQUA** Nordic Union for Quaternary Research (#17457)
- ♦ Nordred (meeting series)

♦ Nordregio – an international research centre for regional development and planning (Nordregio) 17549

Dir Box 1658, SE-11186 Stockholm, Sweden. T. +4684635400 – +468(46723008857. E-mail: nordregio@nordregio.org.
URL: http://www.nordregio.se/

History Established 1 Jul 1997, Stockholm (Sweden), by decision of *Nordic Council of Ministers (NCM, #17260)*, building on the resources of, and replacing, *Nordic Institute of Regional Policy Research (NordREFO, inactive), Nordic School of Planning (inactive)* and *Nordiska Gruppen för Regional Analys (NOGRAN, inactive).* Previously came within the remit of *Nordic Committee of Senior Officials for Regional Policy (EK-R / NÄRP / NERP).* Former names and other names: *Nordregio – Nordic Centre for Spatial Development* – former. **Aims** Serve as an independent research institute on questions concerning spatial *planning* and regional *development*; integrate perspectives of physical planning and regional development with *environmental* and *sustainable* development concerns; promote a common perspective of spatial analysis, planning and policy, applying a *Nordic* and comparative *European* perspective; establish a professional environment for research and analysis on spatial planning and regional development; complement efforts of national institutes and provide direction and coordination in the field; disseminate results of research and analysis and contribute to professional discussion; assist authorities in Nordic countries with relevant data for *policy-making* decisions; constitute a meeting place/research environment for Nordic and European policy-makers and researchers. **Structure** Board, appointed by Nordic Council of Ministers, consists of 5 permanent members, one from each of the Nordic countries, 3 observers from Greenland, the Faeroe Islands and the Åland islands, and one representative chosen by personnel. Director, responsible for the institute's economy and management, reports directly to Secretary-General of Nordic Council of Ministers. **Languages** Danish, English, Estonian, Finnish, French, German, Icelandic, Lithuanian, Mandarin Chinese, Mandarin Chinese, Norwegian, Portuguese, Russian, Spanish, Swedish. **Staff** 48.00 FTE, paid. **Finance** Sources: Nordic Council of Ministers; EU (ESPON, Interreg, Horizon 2020); research contracts; consultancy. Annual budget: about Swedish Kr 50,000,000. **Activities** Research/documentation; events/meetings; networking/liaising. **Events** *Changing ruralities* Lund (Sweden) 2018, *Nordic cities, connecting the urban and the rural* Oslo (Norway) 2017, *From fossil to bio-based energy – innovation and policy for transition in Nordic Regions* Helsinki (Finland) 2016, *Forum* Helsingør (Denmark) 2015, *International conference* Nairn (UK) 2007. **Publications** *Nordregio Magazine* (6 a year); *European Journal of Spatial Development* – peer-reviewed open access academic journal. *State of the Nordic Region.* Working papers; policy briefs; reports.
Members Governments of 8 countries and territories:
Åland, Denmark, Faeroe Is, Finland, Greenland, Iceland, Norway, Sweden.
IGO Relations Cooperates with: *European Commission (EC, #06633)* and its *INTERREG V (#15966).* **NGO Relations** Cooperates with: Föreningen Norden. [2019.12.12/XE2795/**E***]

- ♦ Nordregio – Nordic Centre for Spatial Development / see Nordregio – an international research centre for regional development and planning (#17549)
- ♦ **Nordregio** Nordregio – an international research centre for regional development and planning (#17549)
- ♦ **NordREG** Nordic Energy Regulators (#17277)
- ♦ NORDROCS – Joint Nordic Meeting on Remediation of Contaminated Sites (meeting series)
- ♦ NORDROCS – NORDROCS – Joint Nordic Meeting on Remediation of Contaminated Sites (meeting series)
- ♦ NORDSAMEN – Joint Nordic Committee for Military UN Matters (inactive)
- ♦ NordScen – Nordic Centre for the Performing Arts (inactive)
- ♦ NordScen – Nordisk Center for Scenekunst (inactive)
- ♦ Nordsee-Kommission (#17604)
- ♦ NORDSTAT – Nordic Conference on Mathematical Statistics (meeting series)
- ♦ Nord-Süd-Forum / see Global Cooperation Council
- ♦ Nord-Sud XXI / see International-Lawyers.Org (#14008)
- ♦ Nord-Syd Koalitionen (internationally oriented national body)
- ♦ NORDSYMFONI – Federation of Nordic Amateur Symphony Orchestras (inactive)

♦ NORDSYNC 17550

Contact Dept of Chemistry, Univ of Oslo, PO Box 1033, Blindern, 0315 Oslo, Norway.
Contact Dept Physical Sciences, Univ of Oulu, PO Box 3000, FI-90014 Oulun Ypiopisto, Finland.

History 26 Oct 1987, Athens (Greece), as a consortium of research funding organizations (research councils) in Nordic countries being parties to the agreement of establishing NORDSYNC and representing their governments in *European Synchrotron Radiation Facility (ESRF, #08868)*, of which the Nordic share is 4%. **Aims** Facilitate *Nordic* use of European *Synchrotron* Radiation Facility. **Structure** Steering Committee, consisting of one representative of each member, representing NORDSYNC in ESRF Council. **Languages** English. **Finance** Annual contributions from NORDSYNC members to ESRF. **Activities** Appoints and nominates members of ESRF committees; supervises Nordic use of the ESRF beamlines and Nordic industrial involvement at the ESRF. **Publications** Annual Report.
Members Research councils (4) in 4 countries:
Denmark, Finland, Norway, Sweden. [2014/XD2193/**D***]

♦ NORDTEK 17551

SG address not obtained.
URL: http://nordtek.net/

History Full title: *Network of the Rectors and Deans of the Technical Universities in the Nordic and Baltic countries.* **Aims** Strengthen the advances of Engineering Sciences and their applications to our societies through cooperation. **Structure** Rectors' Meeting (annual); Board; Secretariat. **Activities** Networking/liaising; awards/prizes/competitions; events/meetings; training/education. **Events** *Conference* Reykjavik (Iceland) 2022, *Conference* Kristiansand (Norway) 2021, *Conference* Kristiansand (Norway) 2020, *Conference* Stockholm (Sweden) 2019.
Members University and university colleges in 8 countries:
Denmark, Estonia, Finland, Iceland, Latvia, Lithuania, Norway, Sweden.
NGO Relations *Association of Nordic Engineers (ANE, #02828).* [2021/XM8738/**F**]

- ♦ NORDTEL – Coopération nordique en télécommunications (no recent information)
- ♦ NORDTEL – Nordic Cooperation in the Field of Telecommunications (no recent information)
- ♦ NORDTEL – Nordisk Samarbete på Telekommunikationsområdet (no recent information)
- ♦ NORDTEL – Nordiskt Samarbeid på Telekommunikasjonsområdet (no recent information)
- ♦ NORDTEL – Pohjoismainen Teleliikenteen Yhteistyö (no recent information)

♦ NORDTERM 17552

Steering Committee Sanastokeskus, Runeberginkatu 4c B 20, FI-00100 Helsinki, Finland. T. +3584578316580. E-mail: toimisto@sanastokeskus.fi.
URL: http://www.nordterm.net/

History 1976, Stockholm (Sweden). Statutes adopted, 1987; modified, 1993; approved as amended, 1997, 2001. **Aims** Act as a *Nordic* forum and *network* in the field of *terminology.* **Structure** Assembly (meets every 2 years at Conference); Steering Committee; Presidency; Secretariat; Working Groups; Project Groups. **Languages** Danish, Faroese, Finnish, Icelandic, Kalaallisut, Norwegian, Sami languages, Swedish. **Finance** None. Project means administered separately for each project by one of the cooperating institutions. **Activities** Events/meetings; knowledge management/information dissemination; projects/programmes; training/education. **Events** *Biennial Assembly* Stockholm (Sweden) 2023, *Biennial Assembly* Helsinki (Finland) 2021, *Biennial Assembly* Copenhagen (Denmark) 2019, *Biennial Assembly* Kongsberg (Norway) 2017, *Biennial Assembly* Reykjavik (Iceland) 2015. **Publications** *Guide to Terminology* (1996); *The Science of Terminology and its Relations to Other Branches of Learning* (1992); *Vocabulary of Terminology* (1989). Conference proceedings.
Members Terminology institutions – and since 1991 also representatives of Sami language – in 5 countries:
Denmark, Finland, Iceland, Norway, Sweden.
IGO Relations Terminology Department of the: *European Commission (EC, #06633).* [2023.03.01/XD9189/**F**]

- ♦ **NORDTER** Nordic Forum for Trauma and Emergency Radiology (#17301)
- ♦ **NORDTEST** Samnordiskt Organ inom Provningsområdet (#16142)
- ♦ NORDTRIB – Nordic Symposium on Tribology (meeting series)

♦ NORDUnet 17553

Events – Conference Manager Kastruplundgade 22, 2770 Kastrup, Denmark. T. +4532462500. Fax +4545762366. E-mail: smi@nordu.net – info@nordu.net.
URL: http://www.nordu.net/

History Set up 1985, initially running as the NORDUNET Programme, (1986-1992), financed by *Nordic Council of Ministers (NCM, #17260)*, within the framework of *Nordic Cultural Cooperation (1971).* **Aims** Deliver a network integrating the National Research and Education Networks (NRENs) of the 5 Nordic countries into the global research networks and the *Internet.* **Structure** Board; Executive; Technical Team. "Shareholders": national educational and research establishments (one per country). **Activities** Networking/liaising; research and development. **Events** *Conference* Helsingør (Denmark) 2018, *Technical Workshop* Copenhagen (Denmark) 2017, *Conference* Helsinki (Finland) 2016, *Conference* Uppsala (Sweden) 2014, *Nordic e-Infrastructure Conference* Trondheim (Norway) 2013.
Members National research networks of the 5 Nordic countries:
Denmark, Finland, Iceland, Norway, Sweden.
NGO Relations Representative member of: *GÉANT Association (#10086).* Member of: *Internet Society (ISOC, #15952).* [2018.06.01/XK0479/e/**F**]

- ♦ Nordurlandahúsid i Føroyum (internationally oriented national body)
- ♦ Nordurlandarad Aeskunnar (#17474)
- ♦ Nordurlandasamningur um almannatryggingar (2012 treaty)
- ♦ Nordurlendskt Kervi (#17348)
- ♦ Nordvision (#17446)
- ♦ **Nordvision** Nordic Television Cooperation (#17446)
- ♦ NORDVOLC / see Nordic Volcanological Center (#17463)
- ♦ NORDVULK / see Nordic Volcanological Center (#17463)
- ♦ **NordVulk** Nordic Volcanological Center (#17463)

♦ NORDYRK 17554

Chair Univ of Gothenburg, Dept of Education and Special Education, Box 300, SE-405 30 Gothenburg, Sweden. T. +46317862347.
URL: http://nordyrk.net/

History Former names and other names: *Nordiskt yrkespedagogiskt och yrkesdidaktiskt nätverk* – full title; *Nordisk erhvervspædagogik og erhvervsdidaktisk netværk* – full title; *Nordic research network on vocational education and training* – full title. **Aims** Strengthen the research base of the field; promote cooperation and knowledge development on vocational issues in the Nordic countries. **Activities** Events/meetings; publishing activities. **Events** *Conference* Linköping (Sweden) 2022, *Transitions to, between and within School and Working life in Vocational Education and Training* Linköping (Sweden) 2021, *Conference* Copenhagen (Denmark) 2020, *Conference* Helsinki (Finland) 2019, *Conference* Oslo (Norway) 2018. **Publications** *Nordic Journal of Vocational Education and Training (NJVET).*
Members Full in 5 countries:
Denmark, Finland, Iceland, Norway, Sweden. [2023/AA0520/**F**]

- ♦ Norea – Nordic Radio Evangelistic Association (internationally oriented national body)
- ♦ NOREC – Norwegian Agency for Exchange Cooperation (internationally oriented national body)
- ♦ NOREF / see Norwegian Centre for Conflict Resolution
- ♦ NOREF – Norwegian Centre for Conflict Resolution (internationally oriented national body)
- ♦ NORFEIR – Nordisk Råd for Forskning i Europaeisk Integrationsret (inactive)
- ♦ NORFEIR – Nordisk Råd for Forskning i Europeisk Integrasjonsrett (inactive)
- ♦ Norfund – Norwegian Investment Fund for Developing Countries (internationally oriented national body)
- ♦ Norges Fredslag (internationally oriented national body)
- ♦ Norges Fredsråd (internationally oriented national body)
- ♦ NORIO – Nordic Workshop on Industrial Organization (meeting series)
- ♦ NORIT – Nordisk Institutt for Informasjonsteknologi (inactive)
- ♦ **Norkom** Nordiska kommunforskningsföreningen (#17488)
- ♦ **NorLCA** Nordic Life Cycle Association (#17337)
- ♦ **NorLit** Nordic Association for Comparative Literature (#17186)
- ♦ NorMac – Nordic Summer Symposium in Macroeconomics (meeting series)
- ♦ **NORMAN Network** Network of Reference Laboratories for Monitoring of Emerging Environmental Pollutants (#17053)
- ♦ Norman Paterson School of International Affairs (internationally oriented national body)
- ♦ **NoRME** Nordic Society for Research in Mathematics Education (#17429)
- ♦ NORM – International Symposium on Naturally Occurring Radioactive Material (meeting series)
- ♦ **NORNA** Nordic Operating Room Nurses Association (#17375)
- ♦ **NORNA** Nordiska Samarbetskommittén för Namnforskning (#17492)
- ♦ **NORNDiP** Nordic Network for Diversity in Physics (#17352)
- ♦ **NoRNet** Nordic Research Network on Transitions, Career and Guidance (#17397)
- ♦ **NOR** Nordisk Optiker Råd (#17376)
- ♦ NOR – Nordisk Organ for Reindriftsforskning (inactive)
- ♦ **NOR** Nordisk Roforbund (#17527)
- ♦ **NOROSH** Nordic Association of Occupational Safety and Health (#17199)
- ♦ Norourlendski Menninggargrunnurin fyri Utnordur (#20926)
- ♦ NorPeace / see Norwegian Peace Council
- ♦ **NorPEN** Nordic PharmacoEpidemiological Network (#17384)
- ♦ Norraena Byggingamalanefndin (inactive)
- ♦ Norraena Bygginga- og Treidnadarmannasambandid (#17283)
- ♦ Norraena eldfjallastödin / see Nordic Volcanological Center (#17463)
- ♦ Norraena Endurskodendasambandid (#17285)
- ♦ Norraena Flotfraedifélaid (#17400)

- ♦ Norraena Flutningamannasambandiõ (#17496)
- ♦ Norraena Húsid (internationally oriented national body)
- ♦ Norraena Kvenna- og Kynjarannsóknastofnunin / see Nordic Information for Gender Knowledge (#17317)
- ♦ Norraena Leikararadid (#17166)
- ♦ Norraena Matvaelarannsóknanefndin / see Nordic-Baltic Committee on Food Analysis (#17215)
- ♦ Norraenar Kjanöryggisrannsóknir (#17517)
- ♦ Norraenar Skógarrannsóknir (#17296)
- ♦ Norraena Sakfraediradid (#17493)
- ♦ Norraena Stofnunin i Kennilegri Edlisfraedi (#17324)
- ♦ Norraeni Fjarfestingarbankinn (#17327)
- ♦ Norraeni Tróunarsjódurinn fyrir hin Vestlaegu Nordurlönd (#20926)
- ♦ Norraenna Heyrnarfraedi Félagid (#17210)
- ♦ Norraen Samstarfsnefnd um Hússtjórnarfraeslu (no recent information)
- ♦ Norraen Samtök um Nams- og Starfsradgjöf (#17191)
- ♦ Norraent Demógrafiskt Félag (#17268)
- ♦ Norraen Tengslanet (#17348)
- ♦ Norraent félag fyrir kapólska laekna (#17506)
- ♦ Norraent Rad um Visindalegar Upplysingar (inactive)
- ♦ NORRAG / see Network for International Policies and Cooperation in Education and Training (#17043)
- ♦ **NORRAG** Network for International Policies and Cooperation in Education and Training (#17043)
- ♦ Norrajna Steinsteypussambandid (#17251)
- ♦ Norr'ni vegabréfaskodunarsamningurinn (1957 treaty)
- ♦ Norr'ni vinnuverndarsamningurinn (1989 treaty)
- ♦ Norr'nn samningur um heilbrigdisvidbúnad (2002 treaty)
- ♦ Norr'nn sattmali um félagslega adstod og félagslega pjónustu (1994 treaty)
- ♦ NORR – Nordiska Ryggmärgsskade Rådet (inactive)
- ♦ Norroena Hagrannsónaraosins (inactive)
- ♦ NORSAM Nordic Organization of Active Aging (inactive)
- ♦ NORSAM Nordiskt Samråd för Aktiv Ålderdom (inactive)
- ♦ Nor-Shipping (meeting series)
- ♦ **NORSIB** Nordic Committee for Sport Libraries (#17248)
- ♦ NORSI / see Nordic Research School in Innovation and Entrepreneurship (#17398)
- ♦ **NORSI** Nordic Research School in Innovation and Entrepreneurship (#17398)
- ♦ NorSIS / see International Society for Intermedial Studies (#15211)
- ♦ Norske Atlanterhavskomité (internationally oriented national body)
- ♦ Norske Flyktningeråd / see Norwegian Refugee Council
- ♦ Norske Menneskerettighetsfond (internationally oriented national body)
- ♦ Norske Misjonsforbund (internationally oriented national body)
- ♦ Det Norske Misjonsselskap (internationally oriented national body)
- ♦ Norske Sjømannsmisjon / see Seamen's Mission – Norwegian Church Abroad
- ♦ Norsk Folkehjelp (internationally oriented national body)
- ♦ Norsk Forening for Utviklingsforskning (internationally oriented national body)
- ♦ Norsk Luthersk Misjonssamband (internationally oriented national body)
- ♦ Norsk Misjons Bistandsnemd / see Digni
- ♦ Norsk Organisasjon for Asylsíkere (internationally oriented national body)
- ♦ Norsk Ressurssenter for Fredsbygging / see Norwegian Centre for Conflict Resolution
- ♦ Norsk senter for menneskerettigheter (internationally oriented national body)
- ♦ Norsk Sjømannsmisjon – Norsk Kirke i Utlandet / see Seamen's Mission – Norwegian Church Abroad
- ♦ Norsk Utenrikspolitisk Institutt (internationally oriented national body)
- ♦ NORSMA – Nordic Research Network on Special Needs Education in Mathematics (unconfirmed)
- ♦ Sur Norte Inversión y Desarrollo (#19881)
- ♦ North Africa Centre for Engineering and Technology Education (internationally oriented national body)

♦ North Africa and Middle East Science Centres Network (NAMES) .. 17555

Secretariat Planetarium Science Ctr, Bibliotheca Alexandrina, PO Box 138, Chatby, Alexandria, 21526, Egypt. T. +2034839999. Fax +2034820464. E-mail: namesnetwork@bibalex.org.
URL: http://www.namesnetwork.org/

History 30 Jan 2006. **Aims** Democratize science throughout the region by enhancing understanding and involvement in science among an increasingly diverse public by means of informal *education.* **Structure** General Assembly. Board of Directors, comprising President, Vice-President, Treasurer and 2 members. **Languages** Arabic, English, French. **Staff** 1.00 FTE, paid. **Finance** Members' dues. **Activities** Setting up "Islamic Inventions in Science Travelling Exhibition", targeting an audience of 9 years old upwards. Exhibition will be set up in Arabic but will also be available in English and French and will cover the most important Islamic contributions to: Medicine; Veterinary Medicine; Pharmacology and Herbal Medicine; Mathematics; Astronomy and Geography; Agriculture; Chemistry; Physics; Mechanics; Sound. It will also include a multimedia show "Golden Age of Islam" documentary. **Events** *General Assembly* Bursa (Turkey) 2014, *Science Centre World Congress* Cape Town (South Africa) 2011, *General Assembly* Khobar (Saudi Arabia) 2010, *General Assembly* Alexandria (Egypt) 2008.
Members Full; Sustaining; Honorary. Institutions in 7 countries:
Egypt, Kuwait, Morocco, Saudi Arabia, Tunisia, Türkiye, United Arab Emirates. [2015/XM2600/**E**]

- ♦ North Africa Mission / see Arab World Ministries

♦ North African Port Management Association (NAPMA) 17556

Union des administrations portuaires du Nord de l'Afrique (UAPNA)

Exec Sec 300 Lotissement Mandarona, 8A Sidi Maarouf, Casablanca, Morocco. T. +212520121314 – +212520121387. Fax +212522786102. E-mail: hassani@anp.org.ma.
Chairperson address not obtained.

History 21 Jun 1974, Alexandria (Egypt), by the *'United Nations Economic Commission for Africa (ECA)'.* Also referred to as *Port Management Association of North Africa (PMANA) – Association des administrations portuaires de l'Afrique du Nord.* Statutes adopted 17-21 Jun 1974, Alexandria (Egypt); amended 18-22 Nov 1974, Tunis (Tunisia), 15-16 Dec 1993, Casablanca (Morocco). **Aims** Improve, coordinate and standardize port operations, materials and services of members with a view to increase efficiency of their harbours in relation to ship movement and other forms of transport. **Structure** Council (meets at least annually); Ad hoc Committees; Study Groups; Headquarters in Casablanca (Morocco). **Languages** Arabic, English, French. **Staff** 4.00 FTE, voluntary. **Finance** Members' dues. **Activities** Training/education; projects/programmes; guidance/assistance/consulting. **Events** *Meeting / Council Meeting* Port Sudan (Sudan) 2015, *Meeting / Council Meeting* Tunis (Tunisia) 2014, *Meeting / Council Meeting* Nouadhibou (Mauritania) 2012, *Council Meeting* Casablanca (Morocco) 2008, *Council Meeting* Alexandria (Egypt) 2007.
Members Full national port authorities in the region; Associate port administrations or companies that exploit and offer port services and equipment for the benefit of the general public and for the transport of people and goods within a territory of a state in the region which is not a member of the United Nations Economic Commission for Africa (ECA); private port administrations or companies. National Port Authorities of 7 countries:
Algeria, Egypt, Libya, Mauritania, Morocco, Sudan, Tunisia.
IGO Relations Close working relations with: *Arab Sea Ports Federation (ASPF, #01040)*; Association des Ports Lusophones (APLOP); *Port Management Association of Eastern and Southern Africa (PMAESA, #18462)*; *Port Management Association of West and Central Africa (PMAWCA, #18463)*; *United Nations Economic Commission for Africa (ECA, #20554).* **NGO Relations** Associate Member of: *International Association of Ports and Harbors (IAPH, #12096).* [2016.10.26/XD4769/**D**]

- ♦ North African Unity and Action Front (inactive)

♦ North America and the Caribbean Handball Confederation (NACHC) 17557

Confederación Norteamérica y Caribe de Balonmano

Pres address not obtained.

History Together with *Confederación de Sur y Centro America de Balonmano (Coscabal, #04443)*, supersedes *Pan American Team Handball Federation (PATHF, inactive).* **Activities** Sporting activities.
Members Federations in 21 countries and territories:
Antigua-Barbuda, Bahamas, Barbados, Canada, Cayman Is, Cuba, Dominica, Dominican Rep, Greenland, Grenada, Guadeloupe, Haiti, Jamaica, Martinique, Mexico, Puerto Rico, St Kitts-Nevis, St Lucia, Trinidad-Tobago, USA, Virgin Is UK.
NGO Relations Member of (1): *Asociación de Confederaciones Deportivas Panamericanas (ACODEPA, #02119).* Regional federation of *International Handball Federation (IHF, #13771).* [2022/AA3095/**D**]

- ♦ North America Caribbean Rugby Association / see Rugby Americas North (#18997)

♦ North America, Central America and Caribbean Track and Field Coaches Association (NACACTFCA) 17558

Pres PO Box 4770, Carolina PR 00984-4770, USA. T. +17877625400. Fax +17872532982. E-mail: rmercado@sjs.org.
URL: http://www.nacactfca.org/

History 1990, to represent coaches of *North American, Central American and Caribbean Athletic Association (NACAC, #17563).* **Structure** Board of Directors. **Events** *Congress* San Juan (Puerto Rico) 2014, *Congress* Willemstad (Curaçao) 2013, *Congress* Nassau (Bahamas) 2012, *Congress* Mérida (Mexico) 2011, *Congress* Houston, TX (USA) 2010. [2014/XM4026/**E**]

- ♦ North America Maritime Ministry Association (internationally oriented national body)
- ♦ North American Aerospace Defense Command (internationally oriented national body)
- ♦ North American Agreement for Environmental Cooperation (1993 treaty)
- ♦ North American Agreement on Labour Cooperation (1993 treaty)
- ♦ North American Air Defence System / see North American Aerospace Defense Command
- ♦ North American Air Defense Command / see North American Aerospace Defense Command

♦ North American Association of Fisheries Economists (NAAFE) 17559

Exec Dir 226A Ballard Extension Hall, Oregon State Univ, Corvallis OR 97331, USA. T. +15417375354.
URL: https://naafe.oregonstate.edu/

History Registration: Domestic Nonprofit Corporation, USA, State of Oregon. **Aims** Facilitate communication among North American fisheries and aquaculture economists in industry, academia, government and other areas; promote dialogue between economists and others interested in fisheries and aquaculture; advance fisheries and aquaculture economics and its useful applications. **Structure** Board of Directors, comprising President, President-Elect, Treasurer and 2 further members. **Finance** Sources: members' dues. **Activities** Training/education. **Events** *Seminar* Corvallis, OR (USA) 2021, *Biennial Forum* Halifax, NS (Canada) 2019, *Biennial Forum* La Paz (Mexico) 2017, *Biennial Forum* Ketchikan, AK (USA) 2015, *Biennial Forum* St Petersburg, FL (USA) 2013.
Members in 3 countries:
Canada, Mexico, USA.
NGO Relations Secretariat provided by: *International Institute of Fisheries Economics & Trade (IIFET, #13880).* [2023.02.15/XM0274/**D**]

- ♦ North American Association for the History of the Language Sciences (internationally oriented national body)
- ♦ North American Association of State and Provincial Lotteries (internationally oriented national body)
- ♦ North American Association for the Study of Rousseau / see Rousseau Association
- ♦ North American Baptist Fellowship (internationally oriented national body)
- ♦ North American Benthological Society / see Society for Freshwater Science
- ♦ North American Board for East-West Dialogue / see Monastic Interreligious Dialogue – North America

♦ North American Boxing Federation (NABF) 17560

Pres 5255 S Decatur Blvd, Ste 110, Las Vegas NV 89118, USA. T. +17023828360.
URL: http://nabfnews.com/

History Founded 1968, as a continental boxing federation of *World Boxing Council (WBC, #21242).* **Structure** Executive; Advisory Committee. **Activities** Sporting events; meeting activities. **Events** *Annual Convention* Chicago, IL (USA) 2014.
Members Boxing federations (51) in 4 countries and territories:
Canada, Mexico, Puerto Rico, USA. [2014/XE2240/**D**]

♦ North American Broadcasters Association (NABA) 17561

Dir Gen PO Box 500, Station A, Toronto ON M5W 1E6, Canada. T. +14165989877. Fax +14165989774. E-mail: contact@nabanet.com.
URL: http://www.nabanet.com/

History 1972, as *North American National Broadcasters Association (NANBA).* **Aims** Create the opportunity for North American broadcasters to share information, identify common interests and reach consensus on issues of an international nature with a view to providing representation and leadership in global forums. **Structure** General Meeting (annual); Board of Directors; Standing Committees (6). Serves as secretariat of *World Broadcasting Unions (WBU, #21247).* **Staff** 5.00 FTE, paid. **Activities** Knowledge management/information dissemination; networking/liaising. **Events** *Annual General Meeting* Toronto, ON (Canada) 2018, *Annual General Meeting* New York, NY (USA) 2010, *Annual General Meeting* Washington, DC (USA) 2009, *Annual General Meeting* Atlanta, GA (USA) 2008, *Annual General Meeting* Mexico City (Mexico) 2007. **Publications** *NABAcaster.*
Members Full; Associate; Affiliate in 3 countries:
Canada, Mexico, USA.
Consultative Status Consultative status granted from: *UNESCO (#20322)* (Consultative Status); *World Intellectual Property Organization (WIPO, #21593)* (Permanent Observer Status). **IGO Relations** Working relations with: *International Telecommunication Union (ITU, #15673)*, especially its Radiocommunication Sector. Related union: *Arab States Broadcasting Union (ASBU, #01050).* **NGO Relations** Related unions: *African Union of Broadcasting (AUB, #00490)*; *Asia-Pacific Broadcasting Union (ABU, #01863)*; *Caribbean Broadcasting Union (CBU, #03465)*; *European Broadcasting Union (EBU, #06404)*; *International Association of Broadcasting (IAB, #11738)*; *Organización de Telecomunicaciones de Iberoamérica (OTI, #17851).* Together with related unions, organizes: *World Conference of Broadcasting Unions.* [2018/XD0185/**D**]

♦ North American and Caribbean Association of Schools of Social Work (NACASSW) 17562

Pres Univ of the West Indies, Dept Behavioural Sciences, St Augustine, Trinidad-Tobago. T. +18686622002ext85283.
Contact Renison Univ College, Univ of Waterloo, 240 Westmount Road North, Waterloo ON N2L 3G4, Canada.
URL: http://www.iassw-aiets.org/

History 1992, as *North American Regional Association of Schools of Social Work.* **Aims** Pursue social justice, social development and sustainable development through social work practice and education. **Structure** Executive Committee, comprising two representatives from each of three sub-regions: *Association of Caribbean Social Work Educators (ACSWE, #02410)*; Canadian Association for Social Work Education (CASWE); Council for Social Work Education (CSWE, USA). **Activities** Knowledge management/information dissemination; capacity building; research/documentation; networking/liaising. **Events** *General Meeting* Barbados 2003, *General Meeting* Montpellier (France) 2002, *General Meeting* Nassau (Bahamas) 2001, *General Meeting* New York, NY (USA) 2000, *General Meeting* Kingston (Jamaica) 1999. **Publications** *NACASSW Newsletter* (2 a year).
Members Schools in 9 countries:
Bahamas, Barbados, Belize, Canada, Guyana, Jamaica, Mexico, Trinidad-Tobago, USA.
Regional member (1):
University of the West Indies (UWI, #20705).
NGO Relations Regional association member of: *International Association of Schools of Social Work (IASSW, #12149).* [2018.06.01/XE2018/**E**]

♦ North American Center for Environmental Information and Communication (internationally oriented national body)

♦ North American, Central American and Caribbean Athletic Association (NACAC) 17563

Association d'athlétisme d'Amérique du Nord, d'Amérique centrale et des Caraïbes

Pres PO Box 4770, Carolina PR 00984, USA. T. +17877263586 – +17873671421 – +17876394392.
URL: http://www.athleticsnacac.org/

History 10 Dec 1986, San Juan (Puerto Rico), as the regional affiliate of *World Athletics (#21209)*. **Aims** Develop and maintain friendly and local cooperation between members for promotion and development of amateur athletics; strive to ensure no hindrance to participation of any country or individual recognized by IAAF in international athletics competition on racial, religious or political grounds; provide a forum for members to freely express concerns and seek amicable means to further development of athletics in their respective countries and throughout the area; foster transfer of technical information and material to benefit development of amateur athletics throughout the area. **Structure** Board. **Languages** English, Spanish. **Staff** 2.00 FTE, paid. **Finance** Financed by IAAF. Budget (annual): about US$ 200,000. **Activities** Sporting events; meeting activities. **Events** *Biennial Congress* Helsinki (Finland) 2005, *Biennial Congress* Santo Domingo (Dominican Rep) 2003, *Biennial Congress* Edmonton, AB (Canada) 2001, *Biennial Congress* Edmonton, AB (Canada) 2001, *Biennial Congress* Winnipeg, MB (Canada) 1999. **Publications** *NACAC Newsletter*. Congress reports.
Members National organizations in 31 countries and territories:
Anguilla, Antigua-Barbuda, Aruba, Bahamas, Barbados, Belize, Bermuda, Canada, Cayman Is, Costa Rica, Cuba, Dominica, Dominican Rep, El Salvador, Grenada, Guatemala, Haiti, Honduras, Jamaica, Mexico, Montserrat, Nicaragua, Puerto Rico, St Kitts-Nevis, St Lucia, St Vincent-Grenadines, Trinidad-Tobago, Turks-Caicos, USA, Virgin Is UK, Virgin Is USA.
NGO Relations Represented on Council of IAAF. *North America, Central America and Caribbean Track and Field Coaches Association (NACACTFCA, #17558)* acts as official coaches association. Special links with: *Asociación Panamericana de Atletismo (APA, #02284)*. [2016/XD1572/**D**]

♦ North American, Central American and Caribbean Islands Weightlifting Federation (inactive)
♦ North American Congress on Latin America (internationally oriented national body)
♦ North American Council of AIDS Service Organizations (internationally oriented national body)
♦ North American Council of Chemical Associations (no recent information)
♦ North American Diakonia / see DIAKONIA of the Americas and the Caribbean (#05063)
♦ North American Federation of Adapted Physical Activity (internationally oriented national body)
♦ North American Federation of the International College of Surgeons (see: #12650)

♦ North American Foot-and-Mouth Disease Vaccine Bank (NAFMDVB) 17564

Banque nord-américaine de vaccin de la fièvre aphteus – Banco de Vacuna de Fiebre Aftosa de América del Norte

Contact c/o PADIC, US Dept of Agriculture/APHIS/VS/NVSL/FADDL/NAFMDVB, Homeland Security, PO Box 848, Greenport NY 11944, USA.

History Established 11 Feb 1982. **Aims** In the event of an outbreak of the foot-and-mouth disease in North America, manufacture a finished vaccine and its application to susceptible species. **Structure** Shared repository between Canada, Mexico and the USA, led by the Chief Veterinary Officer (Commissioner) of each of the 3 countries. **Languages** English, French, Spanish. **Finance** Annual contributions from member countries.
Members Governments of 3 countries:
Canada, Mexico, USA. [2014.01.13/XD5500/**F***]

♦ North American Forest Commission / see North American Forestry Commission (#17565)

♦ North American Forestry Commission (NAFC) 17565

Commission des forêts pour l'Amérique du Nord – Comisión Forestal para América del Norte (CFAN)

Chair CONAFOR, Carretera a Nogales esq, Periferioc pte s/n, 5o piso, Col San Juan de Ocotan, Zapopan JAL, Mexico. T. +523337777077 – +523337777078.
URL: http://www.fs.fed.us/global/nafc/

History 1959, Rome (Italy), as a commission of *FAO (#09260)* under Article VI-1 of FAO Constitution. Also known as *North American Forest Commission*. **Aims** Advise on formulation of forestry policy; review and coordinate its implementation at a regional level; exchange information and, generally through special subsidiary bodies, advise on suitable practices and action in regard to technical problems. **Languages** English, Spanish. **Activities** Study Groups (8): Forest Tree Improvement; Fire Management; Forest Insects and Diseases; Silviculture; Multilingual Vocabulary; Forest Engineering; Atmospheric Changes; Light Frame Structures. Current major concerns: biodiversity and forest conservation; forest fire control (collection of statistics and training of personnel); special panel for "gypsy moth" policy analysis; monitoring atmospheric changes. Encourages cooperation between national forest services and transfer of technology and know-how. **Events** *Session* Campeche (Mexico) 2016, *Session* Madison, WI (USA) 2013, *Session* Québec, QC (Canada) 2012, *Session* Palenque (Mexico) 2010, *Session* San Juan (Puerto Rico) 2008. **Publications** *Forest Fire News* (periodical). *Basic Technology in Forestry Operations*; *Directory of North American Tropical Silviculturists*; *Directory of Tropical Silviculture Foresters*; *Glossary of Terms Commonly Used in Forest Genetics and Tree Improvement* in English, French, German, Portuguese, Spanish; *Light-Frame Structures Manual*; *Manual of Silvical Characteristics of Selected Tropical Tree Species*; *Multilingual Forestry and Forest Products Vocabulary*. Directories of key fire management people (updated annually).
Members Governments of 3 countries:
Canada, Mexico, USA. [2009/XE5873/**E***]

♦ North American Human Resource Management Association (internationally oriented national body)
♦ North American Insulation Manufacturers Association (internationally oriented national body)
♦ North American Integration and Development Center (internationally oriented national body)
♦ North American Interfaith Network (internationally oriented national body)
♦ North American International Trade Corridor Partnership / see North American Strategy for Competitiveness (#17569)
♦ North American National Broadcasters Association / see North American Broadcasters Association (#17561)
♦ North American Network of Basin Organizations (internationally oriented national body)
♦ North American Network Operators' Group (internationally oriented national body)

♦ North American and New Zealand Institute for Bioenergetic Analysis (NANZIBA) 17566

Address not obtained.
URL: https://www.nanziba.com/

Aims Support the growth and development of local bioenergetic institutes/societies within the region; position bioenergetics analysis as a prominent therapeutic modality within professional circles and the community at large; facilitate communication between and among local bioenergetic institutes/societies. **Activities** Events/meetings; training/education.
Members Full in 3 countries:
Canada, New Zealand, USA. [2020/XM8902/**D**]

♦ North American Nursing Diagnosis Association / see NANDA International (#16932)

♦ North American Plant Protection Organization (NAPPO) 17567

Organización Norteamericana de Protección a las Plantas – Organisation nord-américaine pour la protection des plantes

Exec Dir 1730 Varsity Drive, Ste 145, Raleigh NC 27606, USA. T. +19196174040 – +19194804761.
URL: https://www.nappo.org/

History 13 Oct 1976. Established on signature of the North American Plant Protection Agreement by representatives of the plant protection agencies of Canada, Mexico and USA. Cooperative Agreement signed 17 Oct 1989. Revised Constitution and By-Laws adopted 26 Oct 2016. A new 5-year Strategic Plan (2022-2026) endorsed by Executive Committee, 13 July 2022. Former names and other names: *Organización Norteamericana de Protección Fitosanitaria* – former. **Aims** Develop regional standards for phytosanitary measures as well as other documents and activities to protect North America from the entry, establishment and spread of regulated pests while facilitating safe agricultural trade. **Structure** Executive Committee,;Advisory and Management Committe; Industry Advisory Group; Secretariat. **Languages** English, Spanish. **Staff** 5.00 FTE, paid. **Finance** Sources: contributions of member/participating states. Annual budget: 740,000 USD. **Activities** Events/meetings; knowledge management/information dissemination; standards/guidelines. **Events** *Regional Plant Protection Organizations (RPPOs) Annual Technical Consultation* London (UK) 2022, *Annual Meeting* Raleigh, NC (USA) 2022, *Annual Meeting* Raleigh, NC (USA) 2021, *Regional Plant Protection Organizations (RPPOs) Annual Technical Consultation* Rome (Italy) 2021, *Annual Meeting* Mérida (Mexico) 2020. **Publications** *NAPPO Newsletter* (3 a year) in English, Spanish. *NAPPO Regional Standards for Phytosanitary Measures*.
Members Federal plant protection officials of 3 countries:
Canada, Mexico, USA.
IGO Relations Instrumental in setting up (1): *Grupo Interamericano de Coordinación en Sanidad Vegetal (GICSV, no recent information)*. Relationship agreement with: *FAO (#09260)*. Serves as one of 10 Regional Plant Protection Organizations (RPPOs) of *International Plant Protection Convention, 1951 (IPPC, 1951)*. [2022.10.12/XD1768/**D***]

♦ North American Powerlifting Federation (NAPF) 17568

Gen Sec PO Box 291571, Davie FL 33329-1571, USA. T. +19543844472. Fax +19543013344. E-mail: rhk@verizon.net.
URL: http://www.usapowerlifting.com/IPF-NorthAmerica/

History 2000. A regional federation of *International Powerlifting Federation (IPF, #14630)*. **Structure** Congress (annual). Executive, comprising President, Vice-President, General Secretary, Treasurer and Committee Chairmen. **Activities** Organizes championships.
Members National organizations (15) in 15 countries:
Bahamas, Canada, Costa Rica, Dominican Rep, El Salvador, Guatemala, Honduras, Jamaica, Mexico, Neth Antilles, Panama, Puerto Rico, Trinidad-Tobago, USA, Virgin Is USA. [2010/XJ4257/**D**]

♦ North American Primary Care Research Group (internationally oriented national body)
♦ North American Regional Academic Mobility Program (internationally oriented national body)
♦ North American Regional Association of Schools of Social Work / see North American and Caribbean Association of Schools of Social Work (#17562)
♦ North American Regional Broadcasting Agreement, 1937 (1937 treaty)
♦ North American Regional Broadcasting Agreement, 1950 (1950 treaty)
♦ North American Securities Administrators Association (internationally oriented national body)
♦ North American Society for Oceanic History (internationally oriented national body)
♦ North American Society for Seventeenth-Century French Literature (internationally oriented national body)
♦ North American Society for Social Philosophy (internationally oriented national body)
♦ North American Society for Sport Psychology and Physical Activity (internationally oriented national body)
♦ North American Society for Trenchless Technology (internationally oriented national body)
♦ North American Spanish Language Academy (internationally oriented national body)
♦ North American Spine Society (internationally oriented national body)

♦ North American Strategy for Competitiveness (NASCO) 17569

Exec Dir 901 Main St, Ste 4400, Dallas TX 75202, USA. T. +12147441042. Fax +12147441043.
URL: http://www.nasconetwork.com/

History 1997, as *North America's Superhighway Coalition (NASCO)*. Merged with *North American International Trade Corridor Partnership*, a former non-profit based in Mexico. Subsequently changed title to *North America's SuperCorridor Coalition*. **Aims** Support development and advocacy of an intermodal *trade* and *transportation* system between Canada, Mexico and the USA. **Structure** Board of Directors. [2015/XN8998/**D**]

♦ North American Sumo Union (internationally oriented national body)
♦ North American Thermal Analysis Society (internationally oriented national body)
♦ North American Youth Alliance / see World Youth Alliance – North America
♦ North America's SuperCorridor Coalition / see North American Strategy for Competitiveness (#17569)
♦ North America's Superhighway Coalition / see North American Strategy for Competitiveness (#17569)
♦ North America and West Indies Rugby Association / see Rugby Americas North (#18997)
♦ North Atlantic Alliance / see NATO (#16945)
♦ North Atlantic Assembly / see NATO Parliamentary Assembly (#16946)
♦ North Atlantic Bioarchaeological Organization / see North Atlantic Biocultural Organization (#17570)

♦ North Atlantic Biocultural Organization (NABO) 17570

Contact Prof Thomas H McGovern, Bioarchaeology Lab, Anthropology Dept, Hunter College CUNY, 695 Park Ave, New York NY 10021, USA. T. +12127725410. Fax +12127725423. E-mail: thomas.h.mcgovern@gmail.com.
URL: http://www.nabohome.org/

History 1992, New York NY (USA). Also referred to as *North Atlantic Bioarchaeological Organization*. **Aims** Aid scholars from a broad range of disciplines to set up wide ranging collaborative investigations of the interactions of humans, landscape, seascape and climate change in the region. **Activities** Events/meetings. **Events** *Conference* Akureyri (Iceland) 2013, *Conference* Thórshavn (Faeroe Is) 2012, *Conference on archaeological futures* Bradford (UK) 2008, *Conference on dynamics of Northern societies* Copenhagen (Denmark) 2004, *Annual Meeting* Canada 2003. **Members** Individuals in 14 countries. Membership countries not specified. [2017.03.08/XN8157/**D**]

♦ North Atlantic Coast Guard Forum (NACGF) 17571

Contact USCG Northeast, First Coast Guard District, 408 Atlantic Ave, Boston MA 02110, USA.
URL: http://www.kustwacht.nl/en/NACGF-general.html

History 2007, as a non-binding, voluntary, neither policy nor regulatory-oriented forum. **Aims** Increase cooperation among member countries on matters related to *maritime* safety and security in the region. **Structure** Chairman; Working Groups; Rotating Secretariat. **Languages** English. **Activities** Events/meetings. **Events** *Meeting* Canada 2017, *Meeting* Latvia 2016, *Meeting* Netherlands 2015, *Meeting* Canada 2014, *Meeting* Portugal 2013.
Members Governments of 20 countries:
Belgium, Canada, Denmark, Estonia, Finland, France, Germany, Iceland, Ireland, Latvia, Lithuania, Netherlands, Norway, Poland, Portugal, Russia, Spain, Sweden, UK, USA. [2019.12.11/XJ4518/**F***]

♦ North Atlantic Cooperation Council / see Euro Atlantic Partnership Council (#05646)
♦ North Atlantic Cooperation Council / see NATO (#16945)

♦ North Atlantic Council (NAC) 17572

Conseil de l'Atlantique nord

Chairman c/o NATO Headquarters, Bvd Leopold III, 1110 Brussels, Belgium. T. +3227074111. Fax +3227074579. E-mail: natodoc@hq.nato.int.
URL: http://www.nato.int/

History 4 Apr 1949, Washington DC (USA). First meeting 17 Sep 1949. Comprises permanent representatives of each country of *NATO (#16945)*, under Article 9 of the *North Atlantic Treaty (1949)*. **Structure** Permament session in Brussels (Belgium). Honorary President (one-year term, a Foreign Minister of one of the member countries); Chairman (Secretary General of NATO); Deputy-Chairman (Deputy Secretary General of NATO). Permanent Representatives. **Activities** Politics/policy/regulatory. Adopted: *NATO Joint Civil/military Frequency Agreement (1995)*, 1995. **Events** *Joint Informal Meeting on Ukraine* Brussels (Belgium) 2014, *Meeting* Brussels (Belgium) 2009, *Autumn ministerial session* Brussels (Belgium) 2001, *Special summit* Brussels (Belgium) 2001, *Ministerial meeting* Luxembourg (Luxembourg) 1998.

Members Governments of 28 countries:
Albania, Belgium, Bulgaria, Canada, Croatia, Czechia, Denmark, Estonia, France, Germany, Greece, Hungary, Iceland, Italy, Latvia, Lithuania, Luxembourg, Netherlands, Norway, Poland, Portugal, Romania, Slovakia, Slovenia, Spain, Türkiye, UK, USA.
IGO Relations *European Union (EU, #08967)*; *NATO Airborne Early Warning and Control Programme Management Organization (NAPMO, #16943)*. Together with cooperation partners, set up: *Euro Atlantic Partnership Council (EAPC, #05646)*. Instrumental in setting up: *NATO Support and Procurement Agency (NSPA, #16948)*. [2017/XK1113/**E***]

- ♦ North Atlantic Ice Patrol / see International Ice Patrol (#13832)

♦ North Atlantic Marine Mammal Commission (NAMMCO) 17573

Gen Sec Postbox 3613 Guleng, 9278 Tromsø, Norway. E-mail: nammco-sec@nammco.no.
Chair Ministry of Trade, Industry and Fisheries, POB 8090 Dep, 0032 Oslo, Norway.
URL: http://www.nammco.org/

History 7 Jul 1992. Established following an Agreement signed 9 Apr 1992, Nuuk (Greenland), between Faeroe Is, Greenland, Iceland and Norway. Inaugural meeting 11 Sep 1992, Thórshavn (Faeroe Is). **Aims** Contribute through regional consultation and cooperation to the conservation, rational management and study of marine mammals in the North Atlantic. **Structure** Council (meets annually); Committees (5); Permanent Secretariat in Tromsø (Norway). **Languages** English. **Staff** 3.00 FTE, paid; 1.00 FTE, voluntary. Internship programme. **Finance** Sources: members' dues. Annual budget: 5,500,000 NOK. **Activities** Events/meetings; knowledge management/information dissemination; monitoring/evaluation; projects/programmes; research/documentation; standards/guidelines. **Events** *Annual Meeting* Oslo (Norway) 2022, *Annual Meeting* Oslo (Norway) 2022, *Annual Meeting* Oslo (Norway) 2021, *Annual Meeting* Oslo (Norway) 2020, *Annual Meeting* Thórshavn (Faeroe Is) 2019. **Publications** *NAMMCO Scientific Publication Series*. Annual Report; workshop series; expert group meetings; conference proceedings.
Members Governments of 4 countries and territories:
Faeroe Is, Greenland, Iceland, Norway.
Observers; governments of 5 countries:
Canada, Denmark, Japan, Russia, St Lucia.
IGO Relations Exchange of observers with: *Agreement on the Conservation of Small Cetaceans of the Baltic, North East Atlantic, Irish and North Seas (ASCOBANS, 1992)*; *Arctic Council (#01097)*; *Convention on International Trade in Endangered Species of Wild Fauna and Flora (CITES, 1973)*; *FAO (#09260)*; *International Council for the Exploration of the Sea (ICES, #13021)*; *International Whaling Commission (IWC, #15879)*; *Nordic Atlantic Cooperation (#17209)*; *Nordic Council (NC, #17256)*; *Nordic Council of Ministers (NCM, #17260)*; *North Atlantic Salmon Conservation Organization (NASCO, #17574)*; *North-East Atlantic Fisheries Commission (NEAFC, #17581)*; *Northwest Atlantic Fisheries Organization (NAFO, #17606)*; *OSPAR Commission for the Protection of the Marine Environment of the North-East Atlantic (OSPAR Commission, #17905)*; **NGO Relations** Also links with national organizations. [2022.11.30/XE1846/**E***]

- ♦ North Atlantic Native Sheep and Wool Conference (meeting series)
- ♦ North Atlantic Ocean Weather Stations Agreement (1949 treaty)

♦ North Atlantic Salmon Conservation Organization (NASCO) 17574

Organisation pour la conservation du saumon de l'Atlantique Nord (OCSAN)

Address not obtained.
URL: http://www.nasco.int/

History Feb 1984, on forming of Secretariat, following *Convention for the Conservation of Salmon in the North Atlantic Ocean (1982)* of 2 Mar 1982, Reykjavik (Iceland), entered into force 1 Oct 1983. **Aims** Contribute through consultation and cooperation to conservation, restoration, enhancement and rational management of salmon stocks subject to the Convention. **Structure** Council (meets annually); Regional Commissions (3); Standing Scientific Committee; Finance and Administration Committee; *International Atlantic Salmon Research Board (IASRB, #12292)*; Secretariat. **Languages** English, French. **Staff** 4.50 FTE, paid. **Finance** Contributions from Member Parties. **Activities** Research/documentation; politics/policy/regulatory. **Events** *Annual Meeting* Edinburgh (UK) 2022, *Annual Meeting* Edinburgh (UK) 2021, *Annual Meeting* Edinburgh (UK) 2020, *Annual Meeting* Tromsø (Norway) 2019, *Annual Meeting* Portland, ME (USA) 2018. **Publications** Annual Report; basic texts; resolutions; agreements; guidelines; reports; Council and Commission papers; data and sample collections. Information Services: Databases on salmon rivers in North Atlantic.
Members Parties to the Convention in their own right – Governments of 5 countries:
Canada, Denmark (in respect of Faeroe Is and Greenland), Norway, Russia, USA.
Party to the Convention – regional integration EU entity representing governments of all EU member nations with salmon interests:
European Union (EU, #08967).
NGO Relations Observer status held by 41 NGOs, including the following organizations listed in this Yearbook: *Association internationale de défense du saumon atlantique (AIDSA)*; *Atlantic Salmon Federation (ASF)*; *Atlantic Salmon Trust (AST, #03009)*; *European Anglers Alliance (EAA, #05900)*. Instrumental in setting up: *International Atlantic Salmon Research Board*. [2020/XD5830/**D***]

- ♦ North Atlantic Seafood Association (inactive)
- ♦ North Atlantic Seafood Forum (meeting series)
- ♦ North Atlantic Treaty (1949 treaty)
- ♦ North Atlantic Treaty Organization (#16945)
- ♦ North Calotte Council (#17545)
- ♦ North Carolina Center for South Asia Studies / see North Carolina Consortium for South Asia Studies
- ♦ North Carolina Consortium for South Asia Studies (internationally oriented national body)
- ♦ North and Central America and Caribbean Ostomy Association / see Ostomy Association of the Americas (#17912)
- ♦ North and Central American Baseball Confederation (no recent information)
- ♦ North and Central American and Caribbean Football Confederation / see Confederación Norte-Centroamericana y del Caribe de Fútbol (#04465)
- ♦ North and Central American and Caribbean Regional Association of WAVA / see North and Central American and Caribbean Regional Association of WMA (#17575)

♦ North and Central American and Caribbean Regional Association of WMA (NCCWMA Regional Association) 17575

Delegate Tepetetlac 2, casa 10, Col San Miguel Xicalco, Tlalpan CP 14490, Mexico City CDMX, Mexico. T. +52555513257127 – +525554324919.
Sec Reyes Heroles 1497, Boca Del Rio, Veracruz CHIS, Mexico. T. +5212291125683. E-mail: juan-ordonez@atlemastermex.com.
URL: http://nccwma.com/index.php/home-2/

History as *North and Central American and Caribbean Regional Association of WAVA (NCCWAVA Regional Association)*, a regional body of *World Masters Athletics (WMA, #21640)*.
Members Affiliate in 31 countries:
Anguilla, Antigua-Barbuda, Bahamas, Barbados, Belize, Bermuda, Canada, Cayman Is, Costa Rica, Cuba, Dominica, Dominican Rep, El Salvador, Grenada, Guatemala, Haiti, Honduras, Jamaica, Mexico, Montserrat, Nicaragua, Panama, Puerto Rico, St Kitts-Nevis, St Lucia, St Vincent-Grenadines, Trinidad-Tobago, Turks-Caicos, USA, Virgin Is UK, Virgin Is USA. [2019.02.21/XD3692/**E**]

♦ North-Central American and Caribbean Volleyball Confederation ... 17576

Confédération Nord-centrale américaine et des Caraïbes de volley-ball – Confederación Norcentroamericana y del Caribe de Vóleibol (NORCECA)

Pres Ave 27 de Febrero Esq Maximo Gómez, Centro Olimpico Juan Pablo Duarte, Pabellón de Voleibol 3ra planta, 2706 Santo Domingo, Dominican Rep. T. +18094721222. Fax +18092273242. E-mail: norcecamanager@gmail.com – norcecapresident@hotmail.com.
URL: http://www.norceca.net/

History 1966. A confederation of *Fédération internationale de volleyball (FIVB, #09670)*. **Aims** Disseminate the *sport* of volleyball; encourage establishment of national federations and their affiliation with IVBF; organize continental *championships*. **Structure** Congress (at least every 2 years); Board of Administration (meets annually, in April); Executive Committee. Standing Commissions (7): Sport Organizing; Refereeing; Technical and Coaches; Beach Volleyball; Finance; Marketing; Medical. **Activities** Events/meetings; sporting activities. **Publications** *NORCECA's Newsletter* (regular). Competition Calendar.
Members National federations in 41countries and territories:
Anguilla, Antigua-Barbuda, Aruba, Bahamas, Barbados, Belize, Bermuda, Bonaire Is, Canada, Cayman Is, Costa Rica, Cuba, Curaçao, Dominica, Dominican Rep, El Salvador, Grenada, Guadeloupe, Guatemala, Haiti, Honduras, Jamaica, Martinique, Mexico, Montserrat, Nicaragua, Panama, Puerto Rico, Saba, St Eustatius, St Kitts-Nevis, St Lucia, St Maarten, St Martin, St Vincent-Grenadines, Suriname, Trinidad-Tobago, Turks-Caicos, USA, Virgin Is UK, Virgin Is USA.
NGO Relations Member of (1): *Asociación de Confederaciones Deportivas Panamericanas (ACODEPA, #02119)*. Formal contacts with: *International Olympic Committee (IOC, #14408)*; IVBF; National Olympic Committees of many countries. [2023/XE3784/**E**]

- ♦ North East Asia Association of Theological Schools (no recent information)
- ♦ Northeast Asia Development Bank (unconfirmed)

♦ Northeast Asia Economic Forum (NEAEF) 17577

Chairman Secretariat, 1000 Bishop St, Ste 904, Honolulu HI 96813, USA. T. +18085329677. Fax +18085328655. E-mail: admin@neaef.org.
URL: http://www.neaef.org/

History Founded 1991, Changchun (China), at a conference on Northeast Asian economic cooperation. Formalized, 1991, Tianjin (China), at a second conference. The idea for cooperation to generate dynamic new economies throughout the region first began to gain momentum with the 1988 Niigata Conference on the Sea of Japan. Despite initial progress, obstacles remained and subsequently NEAEF was created. **Aims** Provide an institutional framework for economic research, discussion, and technology exchange in Northeast Asia; serve as a networking agency to facilitate economic interaction and cooperation among concerned people and institutions in the region; promote intra-regional and inter-regional dialogue. **Structure** Annual Meeting. Board of Directors, comprising Chairman and 1 Representative from each Institutional Member. **Languages** Chinese, English, Japanese, Korean. **Staff** Paid and voluntary. **Finance** Members' donations. Government grants; contract work; contributions in kind. **Activities** Events/meetings; research/documentation. Proposes: *Northeast Asia Development Bank (NEADB)*. **Events** *Annual Conference* Incheon (Korea Rep) 2019, *Annual Conference* Sendai (Japan) 2018, *Annual International Conference* Beijing (China) / Tianjin (China) 2015, *Annual Conference* Busan (Korea Rep) 2014, *Annual International Conference* Seoul (Korea Rep) 2014. **Publications** *Regional Economic Cooperation in Northeast Asia* (annual).
Members Institutional Members committees in 4 countries:
China, Japan, Korea Rep, USA.
Invited members committees in 3 countries:
Korea DPR, Mongolia, Russia. [2016/XF3300/**F**]

- ♦ Northeast Asia Management & Economics Joint Conference (meeting series)

♦ North East Asian Centre for Environmental Data and Training (NEACEDT) 17578

Contact 7th Floor; G-Tower, 175, Art center-daero, Yeonsu-gu, Incheon 406-840, Korea Rep. E-mail: secretariat@neaspec.org.
URL: http://www.neaspec.org/

History 1996, as *Framework for Northeast Asian Subregional Programme of Environmental Cooperation (NEASPEC)* following a Meeting of Senior Officials (SOM) on Environmental Cooperation in Northeast Asia and comprising Korea DPR, Japan, Mongolia, China, Korea Rep and USSR. **Aims** Contribute to environmental protection and recovery in the Northeast Asian Subregion by coordinating the exchange of information on environmental *monitoring* and data comparability and by gathering and disseminating information on updated environmental monitoring technologies and methodologies. **Structure** Steering Committee, comprising nominated representatives from each participating country. Director; Researchers (12). **Finance** Source: government of Korea Rep. **Activities** Knowledge and expertise in monitoring and assessment of air, water, chemicals, etc. Stores, processes and analyzes information on environmental monitoring from participating countries in the subregion; communicates regularly with environmental centres within each of the Northeast Asian countries. International environmental programme for the sharing of information. Organizes training, meetings and workshops. **Publications** Reports. **IGO Relations** *United Nations Economic and Social Commission for Asia and the Pacific (ESCAP, #20557)*. [2017/XE4338/**E***]

♦ North East Asian Crane Site Network (NEACSN) 17579

Working Group Coordinator Birdlife International Tokyo, 4F TM Suidobashi Bldg, 2-14-6 Misaki-cho, Chiyoda-ku, Tokyo, 101-0061 Japan. T. +81352130461. Fax +81352130462.
URL: http://www.eaaflyway.net/

History 7 Mar 1997, Qinhuangdao (China), on the initiative of the Asia Pacific section of *Wetlands International (#20928)*. Currently a working group of *East Asian – Australasian Flyway Partnership (EAAFP, #05198)*. **Aims** Promote the *protection* and *conservation* of cranes and their habitats. **Activities** Workshops; symposia; training courses. [2019/XF6389/**F**]

- ♦ Northeast Asian Forest Forum (unconfirmed)
- ♦ Northeast Asian History Foundation (internationally oriented national body)
- ♦ Northeast Asian Network / see Yonsei Northeast Asian Network
- ♦ Northeast Asia Peace and Security Network / see Nautilus Peace and Security Network

♦ Northeast Asia Regional Peacebuilding Institute (NARPI) 17580

Administration Office 5F JoongAng Plaza, 112-2 Deokso-ri, Wabu-eup, Namyangju GYEONGGI, Korea Rep. T. +827078475010. Fax +82315779691. E-mail: admin@narpi.net.
URL: http://narpi.net/

Aims Strengthen and empower people in Northeast Asia through providing peacebuilding training and building cross-cultural networks. **Structure** Steering Committee; Administration Team. **Languages** Chinese, English, Japanese, Korean, Mongolian. **Staff** 3.00 FTE, voluntary. **Activities** Networking/liaising; training/education. **Publications** *NARPI Newsletter*. *Our Peacebuilding Story: The First Ten Years of Northeast Asia Regional Peacebuilding Institute (2011-2020)* (2022) in English. **NGO Relations** Partner of (3): *Global Partnership for the Prevention of Armed Conflict (GPPAC, #10538)*; *Mennonite Central Committee (MCC)*; *Peace Boat*. Also links with national organizations. [2023.02.15/XJ5678/j/**D**]

- ♦ Northeast Asia-United States Forum on International Policy / see Walter H Shorenstein Asia-Pacific Research Center

♦ North-East Atlantic Fisheries Commission (NEAFC) 17581

Commission des pêches de l'Atlantique Nord-Est (CPANE) – Comisión de Pesquerias del Atlantico Nordeste

Sec 44 Baker Street, London, W1U 7AL, UK. T. +442076310016. Fax +442071499950. E-mail: info@neafc.org.
URL: http://www.neafc.org/

History 18 Nov 1980. Established as successor to Commission of the same name set up 24 Jan 1959, London (UK), on signature of the *North-East Atlantic Fisheries Convention (1959)*, which came into force on 27 Jun 1963, superseding the *International Fisheries Convention*, signed 5 Apr 1946, London, which had set up *Permanent Commission of the International Fisheries Convention* of 1946. Present Convention, *Convention on Future Multilateral Cooperation in North-East Atlantic Fisheries, 1980 (1980)*, came into force 17 Mar 1982. The 1982 Convention was amended in 2004 and 2006; came into force Oct 2013. **Aims** Promote long-term conservation and optimum utilization of fishery resources of the North-East Atlantic area so as to safeguard the *marine* ecosystems in which the resources occur; encourage international cooperation and consultation with respect to these resources. **Structure** Annual Meeting, always in London (UK); Permanent Committees (2); Working Groups. **Languages** English. **Staff** 5.00 FTE, paid. **Finance** Sources: contributions of member/participating states. Annual budget: 1,900,000 GBP. **Activities** Monitoring/evaluation; politics/policy/regulatory; standards/guidelines. **Events** *Annual Meeting* London (UK) 2022, *Annual Meeting* London (UK) 2021, *Annual Meeting* London (UK) 2020, *Annual Meeting* London (UK) 2019, *Annual Meeting* London (UK) 2018. **Publications** Annual Report; scheme of control and enforcement; compliance report; meeting reports.
Members Governments of 4 countries outside the European Union (Iceland, Norway, Russian Federation and United Kingdom), together with Denmark (in respect of Faeroe Is and Greenland) and the European Union.
IGO Relations Observer status with (1): *International Council for the Exploration of the Sea (ICES, #13021)*. Memorandum of Understanding with (1): *International Maritime Organization (IMO, #14102)*. Cooperates with

(1): *FAO (#09260)*. **NGO Relations** Accredited by (1): North Atlantic Pelagic Advocacy (NAPA) Group. Observers to Annual Meeting: *Deep Sea Conservation Coalition (DSCC, #05024); Institute for Ocean Conservation Science (IOCS); Marine Stewardship Council (MSC, #16580); Seas at Risk (SAR, #19189); World Wide Fund for Nature (WWF, #21922).* [2022.10.11/XD3007/**D***]

♦ North-East Atlantic Fisheries Convention (1959 treaty)
♦ Northern African Network of AIDS Service Organizations (see: #00272)

♦ Northern Corridor Transit and Transport Coordination Authority (NCTTCA) 17582

Autorité de coordination de transit et de transport du Corridor Nord (ACTTCN)

Exec Sec P O Box 34068, Mombasa, 80118, Kenya. E-mail: ttca@ttcanc.org.
Permanent Secretariat House 1196, Links Road, Nyali, Mombasa, Kenya. T. +254733532485.
URL: http://www.ttcanc.org/

History Set up 1985, under the legal framework of the Northern Corridor Transit and Transport Agreement (NCTTA). Framework revised 2007. Original title: *Transit Transport Coordination Authority of the Northern Corridor – Autorité de coordination du transport de transit du Corridor Nord* . Subsequently changed title to: *Transit Transport Coordination Authority of the Northern Corridor (TTCA) – Autorité de coordination du transport de transit du Corridor Nord (ACTT).* **Aims** Promote harmonized transport policies and foster an efficient and cost-effective transit transport system within Member States on matters of transit and transport, customs control, documentation and procedures, as well as the development of infrastructure and facilities relating to sea ports, inland ports and waterways, roads, railways, pipelines and border posts. **Structure** Council of Ministers (meets annually); Executive Committee; Permanent Secretariat. Specialized Committees. **Languages** English, French. **Staff** 24.00 FTE, paid. **Finance** Members' direct contributions or in the form of levies collected on cargo passing through the port of Mombasa (Kenya). **Activities** Standards/guidelines; politics/policy/regulatory; events/meetings. **Events** *Regional conference on Northern corridor trade logistics* Mombasa (Kenya) 2009, *Ordinary meeting* Mombasa (Kenya) 1998, *Ordinary Meeting* Kinshasa (Zaire) 1996, *Ordinary meeting* Mombasa (Kenya) 1996, *Regional workshop* Mombasa (Kenya) 1996. **Publications** *E-Transit Monitor* – electronic newsletter; *Transit Monitor Magazine*. Annual, performance and study reports.
Members Representatives of 6 countries:
Burundi, Congo DR, Kenya, Rwanda, South Sudan, Uganda.
IGO Relations Under Lomé Conventions, links with: *European Commission (EC, #06633)*. Other major partners: *Africa Transport Policy Program (SSATP, #00527); African Development Bank (ADB, #00283); Common Market for Eastern and Southern Africa (COMESA, #04296); Communauté économique des pays des Grands Lacs (CEPGL, #04375); East African Community (EAC, #05181); Intergovernmental Authority on Development (IGAD, #11472); International Bank for Reconstruction and Development (IBRD, #12317)* (World Bank); *International Conference on the Great Lakes Region (ICGLR, #12880); Japan International Cooperation Agency (JICA); Port Management Association of Eastern and Southern Africa (PMAESA, #18462); Southern African Development Community (SADC, #19843); United Nations Economic Commission for Africa (ECA, #20554); United States Agency for International Development (USAID).* **NGO Relations** Partners include: *TradeMark East Africa (TMEA, #20183).* [2021/XF2007/**F***]

♦ Northern Council of the Deaf / see Dövas Nordiska Råd (#05126)

♦ Northern Dimension (ND) 17583

Address not obtained.
URL: http://www.northerndimension.info/

History 1999. A joint policy of 4 equal partners. Renewed ND policy launched Nov 2006, at Helsinki Summit. **Aims** Support stability, well-being and sustainable development in the region by means of practical cooperation. **Structure** Operates through 4 partnerships: *Northern Dimension Environmental Partnership (NDEP, #17584); Northern Dimension Partnership in Public Health and Social Well-being (NDPHS, #17587); Northern Dimension Partnership on Transport and Logistics (NDPTL, #17588); Northern Dimension Partnership on Culture (NDPC, #17586)* Academic partner: *Northern Dimension Institute (NDI, #17585)*. Business partner: Northern Dimension Business Council. Parliamentary component: Northern Dimension Parliamentary Forum. **Events** *Northern Dimension Parliamentary Forum* Bodø (Norway) 2019.
Members Partners (4):
Iceland, Norway, Russia.
European Union (EU, #08967).
Governments with Observer Status (2):
Canada, USA.
IGO Relations Partners: *European Bank for Reconstruction and Development (EBRD, #06315); European Investment Bank (EIB, #07599); Nordic Environment Finance Corporation (NEFCO, #17281).* [2020/AA0674/**F***]

♦ Northern Dimension Environmental Partnership (NDEP) 17584

Contact EBRD Headquarters, One Exchange Square, London, EC2A 2JN, UK. T. +442073386000. Fax +442073386848.
URL: http://www.ndep.org/

History Jul 2002, Brussels (Belgium). One of 4 partnerships within *Northern Dimension (ND, #17583)*. Mar 2001, International financial institutions (IFIs) expressed willingness to cooperate, and their cooperation, the EU's mandate and donor support led to the creation of NDEP. NDEP and NDEP Support Fund became fully operational in 2002. Implementing agencies (IFIs): *European Bank for Reconstruction and Development (EBRD, #06315); European Investment Bank (EIB, #07599); International Bank for Reconstruction and Development (IBRD, #12317)* (World Bank); *Nordic Investment Bank (NIB, #17327).* **Aims** Promote and finance environmental investments in the Baltic Sea and Barents region. **Structure** Managed by EBRD. Assembly of Contributors; Steering Group, comprising representatives from the EC, Russia and the IFIs. **Finance** Majority of funding through project finance from the IFIs and their partners. Other contributors to the fund: *European Commission (EC, #06633)*; Belgium; Canada; Denmark; Finland; France; Germany; Netherlands; Norway; Russia; Sweden; UK. **Activities** As at the end of 2005, had leveraged investments of over euro 1,500 million for environmental projects. Gathers collective expertise and know-how of the IFIs, EC and Russia; builds on the Baltic Sea Environment Programme; runs the 'Nuclear Window' programme, prioritizing the safe and secure decommissioning of Russian nuclear submarines. Grants support projects that: tackle urgent environmental infrastructure problems; require additional funding to leverage financing from international and local sources; are financially viable; involve progress monitoring and amendments to the project if necessary; have the support of the Russian government. Support Fund is designed to complement the resources provided by international financial institutions working in north-west Russia. In order to deal with nuclear waste, provides full non-refundable funding within an international cooperation framework. **Publications** *NDEP Newsletter*. **IGO Relations** Other partners include: *Canadian International Development Agency (CIDA, inactive); Department for International Development (DFID, inactive); Nordic Environment Finance Corporation (NEFCO, #17281); Swedfund – International; Swedish International Development Cooperation Agency (Sida); Teollisen Yhteistyön Rahasto (FINNFUND).* [2018/XF7096/**F***]

♦ Northern Dimension Institute (NDI) 17585

Coordinator Aalto Univ, Center for Markets in Transition, PO Box 21230, FI-00076 Aalto, Finland. T. +358505745017.
Coordinator address not obtained.
URL: http://www.northerndimension.info/contacts/northern-dimension-institute

History 2009. Academic partner in *Northern Dimension (ND, #17583)* structures. **Aims** Foster cooperation between academia, ublic sector and business actors; disseminate and promote information and expertise related to Northern Dimension among decision-makers and society at large. **Structure** Steering Group. **Languages** English. **Activities** Events/meetings; knowledge management/information dissemination; projects/programmes; research/documentation. **Events** *Climate and River Basin Management Symposium* Oulu (Finland) 2011, *Conference* Oulu (Finland) 2010.
Members Full in 11 countries:
Belarus, Cyprus, Estonia, Finland, Germany, Latvia, Lithuania, Norway, Poland, Russia, Sweden. [2019/XJ3994/j/**E**]

♦ Northern Dimension Partnership on Culture (NDPC) 17586

Sec Marijas 13/3, (Berga Bazars, Nordic Council of Ministers's Office Latvia), Riga LV-1666, Latvia. T. +37129136112. Fax +37167213233.
URL: https://www.ndpculture.org/

History One of 4 partnerships within *Northern Dimension (ND, #17583).* **Aims** Contribute to social and economic sustainable development, and innovation and diversity in the ND area by focusing on the operating conditions for cultural and creative industries. **Structure** Steering Committee. **Activities** Projects/programmes; research/documentation.
Members Member countries (9):
Denmark, Estonia, Finland, Germany, Iceland, Latvia, Lithuania, Norway, Poland.
European Union (EU, #08967). [2020/AA0675/**E***]

♦ Northern Dimension Partnership in Public Health and Social Well-being (NDPHS) 17587

Dir of Secretariat Wollmar Yxkullsgatan 23, SE-118 50 Stockholm, Sweden. E-mail: secretariat@ndphs.org.
URL: http://www.ndphs.org/

History 27 Oct 2003, Oslo (Norway). Established at a ministerial-level meeting. Proposal for the Partnership introduced 16-17 Sep 2002, Joensuu (Finland), at a high-level *Northern Dimension (ND, #17583)* Forum in Social Protection and Health, hosted by the Prime Minister of Finland. As follow-up, an international temporary working group was established, chaired by Finland's Minister of Health and Social Services, which produced a proposal outlining further details concerning the Partnership, presented for a political decision the following year. Operates in accordance with the Declaration concerning the establishment of the NDPHS (Oslo Declaration), adopted during the meeting in 2003. Since 2009, has functioned as the Coordinator for the Policy Area 'Health' in the EU Strategy for the Baltic Sea Region. Since 8 March 2022, the European Union, Iceland and Norway have suspended until further notice all activities of the Northern Dimension policy, including within the NDPHS, which involve Russia and Belarus. **Aims** Provide an inclusive cross-sectoral platform for health advocacy in Northern Europe and the Baltic Sea Region. **Structure** Partnership Annual Conference (PAC), every 2 years at ministerial level; Committee of Senior Representatives (CSR); Meetings of the Parties; Expert Groups (7); ad hoc Working Groups; Secretariat. **Languages** English. **Staff** 2.00 FTE, paid. Additional staff on project basis. Chairperson and International Technical Advisors for the Expert Groups employed, usually part-time, by appointing countries. **Finance** Sources: members' dues. Annual budget: 320,000 EUR. **Activities** Advocacy/lobbying/activism; capacity building; events/meetings; healthcare; knowledge management/information dissemination; monitoring/evaluation; networking/liaising; politics/policy/regulatory; projects/programmes. Northern Europe and the Baltic Sea Region. **Events** *Partnership Annual Conference* Warsaw (Poland) 2021, *Partnership Annual Conference* Riga (Latvia) 2019, *Partnership Annual Conference* Tallinn (Estonia) 2018, *Partnership Annual Conference* Sopot (Poland) 2016, *Partnership Annual Conference* Berlin (Germany) 2015. **Publications** *NDPHS Newsletter. Tune in Health* – podcast. Policy briefs; reports; manuscripts webinars; conference proceedings.
Members Governments of 10 countries:
Estonia, Finland, Germany, Iceland, Latvia, Lithuania, Norway, Poland, Russia, Sweden.
All activities involving Russia suspended until further notice.
International organizations (9):
Baltic Sea States Subregional Cooperation (BSSSC, #03150); Barents Euro-Arctic Council (BEAC, #03177); Council of the Baltic Sea States (CBSS, #04870); European Commission (EC, #06633); ILO (#11123); International Organization for Migration (IOM, #14454); Joint United Nations Programme on HIV/AIDS (UNAIDS, #16149); Nordic Council of Ministers (NCM, #17260); WHO (#20950).
NGO Relations Associated member of: *European Forum for Primary Care (EFPC, #07326).* [2022.10.26/XJ0995/y/**F***]

♦ Northern Dimension Partnership on Transport and Logistics (NDPTL) 17588

Dir Fabianinkatu 34, PO Box 249, FI-00171 Helsinki, Finland. E-mail: ndptl@ndptl.org.
URL: http://www.ndptl.org/

History Oct 2009. One of 4 partnerships within *Northern Dimension (ND, #17583).* **Aims** Improve, in compliance with the ecological needs of the region, major transport connections and logistics in the Northern Dimension region so as to stimulate sustainable economic growth at the local, regional and global level by focusing on a limited number of priorities that reflect both regional and national priorities in balanced way. **Structure** High Level Meeting; Steering Committee; Working Groups; Secretariat, operating as a special unit within *Nordic Investment Bank (NIB, #17327).*
Members Governments (11):
Belarus, Denmark, Estonia, Finland, Germany, Latvia, Lithuania, Norway, Poland, Russia, Sweden.
European Union (EU, #08967). [2020/AA0676/**E***]

♦ Northern European Association for Accelerator Engineers (NAAE) .. 17589

Chair Mäster Gudmunds Väg 18, SE-553 11 Jönköping, Sweden.
URL: http://www.naae.se/

History 2003, Tromsø (Norway). 2003, Tromsí (Norway), as *Nordic Association for Accelerator Engineers (NAAE).* Current title adopted 11 Nov 2016, when bylaws were also adopted. Registered in accordance with Swedish law. **Aims** Represent and promote the accelerator engineer's social and labour interests and development. **Structure** Board of Directors. **Languages** English. **Activities** Events/meetings; research/documentation. **Events** *Conference* Amsterdam (Netherlands) 2017, *Conference* Copenhagen (Denmark) 2016, *Conference* Trondheim (Norway) 2015, *Conference* Lund (Sweden) 2014, *Conference* Aarhus (Denmark) 2013. [2015/XM4460/**D**]

♦ Northern European Association for Language Technology (NEALT) . 17590

Pres c/o TILDE SIA, Vienibas gatve 75a, Riga LV-1004, Latvia.
Vice-Pres c/o Uppsala Univ, Dept of Linguistics and Philology, Box 635, SE-751 26 Uppsala, Sweden. T. +46184717860.
URL: http://omilia.uio.no/nealt/

History 2006. **Aims** Promote research and development activities in the field of language technology, including *speech* technology; promote cooperation and information exchange among related professional and technical societies; represent language technology to funding bodies and government agencies; disseminate information on language technology to the general public. **Structure** Executive Committee. **Languages** English. **Staff** None paid. **Activities** Events/meetings. **Events** *NODALIDA : Nordic Conference on Computational Linguistics* Riga (Latvia) 2021, *NODALIDA : Nordic Conference on Computational Linguistics* Turku (Finland) 2019, *NODALIDA : Nordic Conference on Computational Linguistics* Gothenburg (Sweden) 2017, *NODALIDA : Nordic Conference on Computational Linguistics / Nordic Conference on Computational Linguistics – NODALIDA* Vilnius (Lithuania) 2015, *NODALIDA : Nordic Conference on Computational Linguistics / Nordic Conference on Computational Linguistics – NODALIDA* Oslo (Norway) 2013. **Publications** *Northern European Journal of Language Technology (NEJLT). NEALT Monograph series.* Conference proceedings. [2019.06.26/XJ8303/**D**]

♦ Northern European Cathedrals Conference (meeting series)
♦ Northern European Conference on Travel Medicine (meeting series)
♦ Northern European Network for Wood Science and Engineering (see: #17296)

♦ Northern European Volleyball Zonal Association (NEVZA) 17591

SG c/o Suomen Lentopalloliitto RY, Radiokatu 20 3 fl, FI-00240 Helsinki, Finland. T. +358405565434. E-mail: office@lentopalloliitto.fi.
URL: http://nevza.com/

History 14 Jun 2003. **Aims** Strengthen friendship and cooperation between all members on all levels to develop and promote volleyball and beach volleyball. **Structure** General Assembly; Presidency; General Secretary Work Team. **Languages** English.
Members Federations in 8 countries and territories:
Denmark, England, Faeroe Is, Finland, Greenland, Iceland, Norway, Sweden.
NGO Relations Affiliated with: *European Volleyball Confederation (#09078); Fédération internationale de volleyball (FIVB, #09670).* [2016.06.01/XJ8515/**D**]

♦ Northern Federation of Advertisers' Associations (inactive)
♦ Northern Feminist University (internationally oriented national body)

♦ Northern Forum, The 17592

Exec Dir Kurashov street 24, Yakutsk SAKHA-YAKUTIA, Russia, 677000. T. +74112504450 – +74112508451. E-mail: secretariat@northernforum.org.
URL: http://www.northernforum.org/

History Nov 1991. **Aims** Improve the quality of life of northern peoples by providing northern regional leaders a means to share their knowledge and experience in addressing common challenges. **Structure** Board of Governors; Regional Coordinators Committee; Business Partners; Working Groups; Secretariat. **Languages** English, Russian. **Staff** 5.00 FTE, paid. **Finance** Members' dues. **Activities** Advocacy/lobbying/activism. **Events** *Sustainable development of the Northern regions* St Petersburg (Russia) 2019, *Northern Sustainable Development Forum* Yakutsk (Russia) 2019, *International Youth Ecological Forum* Rovaniemi (Finland) 2018, *Meeting* Rovaniemi (Finland) 2018, *General Assembly* Pyeongchang (Korea Rep) 2011. **Publications** *Monthly Secretariat Report* – internal electronic report; *Quarterly Activity Report* – electronic; *Quarterly Business Bulletin* – electronic; *Weekly Northern Regional News* – electronic.
Members Regional and national governments (13) in 4 countries:
Finland (Akureyri), Korea Rep (Gangwon Province), Russia (Krasnoyarsk Krai; Magadan Oblast; Kamchatka Krai; Primorsky Krai; Yamalo-Nenets Autonomous Okrug; Nenets Autonomous Okrug; Khanty-Mansiysk Autonomous Okrug; Sakha Rep/Yakutia; Chukotka Autonomous Okrug), USA (Alaska).
Consultative Status Consultative status granted from: *UNEP (#20299)*. **IGO Relations** Accredited by: *United Nations Framework Convention on Climate Change – Secretariat (UNFCCC, #20564)*. Observer to: *Arctic Council (#01097)*. Associated with Department of Global Communications of the United Nations.
[2022/XF6196/**F**]

♦ Northern Nurses' Federation / see Nordic Nurses' Federation (#17371)
♦ Northern Optics (meeting series)

♦ Northern Pharma Network (NPN) 17593

Contact Fac of Pharmacy – Univ of Helsinki, Viikinkaari 5 E, PO Box 56, FI-00014 Helsinki, Finland.
URL: https://www.helsinki.fi/en/faculty-of-pharmacy/research/northern-pharma-network

History 2011. **Finance** Supported by: *NordForsk (#17164)*. **Activities** Events/meetings. **Events** *Northern Pharma Network Meeting* Copenhagen (Denmark) 2020, *Northern Pharma Network Meeting* Uppsala (Sweden) 2019, *Northern Pharma Network Meeting* Odense (Denmark) 2018, *Northern Pharma Network Meeting* Tartu (Estonia) 2017, *Northern Pharma Network Meeting* Helsinki (Finland) 2016.
Members Universities in 6 countries:
Denmark, Estonia, Finland, Norway, Poland, Sweden. [2020/AA1376/**F**]

♦ Northern Research Forum (NRF) 17594

Dir Univ of Akureyri Research Centre, Borgir, Nordurslod, 600 Akureyri, Iceland. E-mail: gunnarmg@unak.is – nrf@unak.is.
URL: http://www.nrf.is/

History Idea launched Sep 1998; operations started Oct 1999. Rules of procedure adopted 2001; new rules adopted 2018. **Aims** Address critical issues and highlight opportunities faced by people living in the *Circumpolar* North, including the *Nordic* Region. **Structure** Council; secretariat. **Languages** English, Icelandic. **Staff** 1.00 FTE, paid. **Activities** Projects/programmes; events/meetings; networking/liaising; knowledge management/information dissemination; training/education. **Events** *Biennial Open Assembly* Akureyri (Iceland) 2013, *Biennial Open Assembly* Hveragerdi (Iceland) 2011, *Biennial open assembly* Hveragerdi (Iceland) 2011, *Open assembly* Oslo (Norway) / Kirkenes (Norway) 2010, *Biennial open assembly* Anchorage, AK (USA) 2008. **Publications** *The Arctic Yearbook*. Books; reports; proceedings.
Members Council members from 3 countries:
Finland, Iceland, USA. [2022/XJ1747/**F**]

♦ Northern research Review and Advisory Group / see Network for International Policies and Cooperation in Education and Training (#17043)
♦ Northern Shipowners' Defence Club / see Nordisk Defence Club (#17501)
♦ Northern Society of Allergology (inactive)

♦ Northern Sparsely Populated Areas Network (NSPA Network) 17595

Chair North Norway Office, 24 Ave Palmerston, 1000 Brussels, Belgium. E-mail: info@nspa-network.eu.
URL: http://www.nspa-network.eu/

Aims Share common circumstances and objectives; work together to raise awareness of the region in the EU institutions, influence EU policy and provide a platform for best practise. **Events** *Forum* Tromsø (Norway) 2019, *Forum* Bodø (Norway) 2014, *Forum* Oulu (Finland) 2013.
Members Regions (14) in 3 countries:
Finland, Norway, Sweden. [2022/XJ7900/**F**]

♦ Northern Triangle 17596

Address not obtained.
URL: http://www.sice.oas.org/TPD/Mex_Norte/MEX_Norte_e.asp

History Not an organization but an expression describing 3 countries of Central America united in a free trade agreement with Mexico which went into effect on 15 Mar 2001.
Members 3 countries:
El Salvador, Guatemala, Honduras. [2008/XF6879/**F***]

♦ North European Amateur Theatre Alliance (NEATA) 17597

SG c/o MAF, Undir Pisuvaria 2, PO Box 185, FO-100 Thórshavn, Faeroe Is. T. +298315624 – +298327119. E-mail: maf@maf.fo.
URL: http://www.neata.dk/

History 8 Aug 1998, Harstad (Norway). Regional centre of *International Amateur Theatre Association (AITA/IATA, #11647)*. **Aims** Promote cooperation between amateur theatres in the region. **Structure** Steering Committee. **Languages** English. **Staff** 1.00 FTE, voluntary. **Finance** Members' dues. **Activities** Events/meetings; training/education.
Members National centres in 8 countries:
Denmark, Estonia, Finland, Iceland, Latvia, Lithuania, Norway, Sweden.
Affiliate member (1) in 1 territory:
Faeroe Is. [2018/XF6357/**F**]

♦ North European Cybersecurity Cluster (NECC) 17598

CEO address not obtained.
Chair address not obtained.
URL: https://necc.network/

History Registration: EU Transparency Register, No/ID: 002481635586-11, Start date: 6 Aug 2019. **Aims** Promote information security and cybersecurity-related cooperation and collaboration in the Northern European region so as to enhance integration into the European *Digital* Single Market. **Structure** Board. **Languages** English. **Activities** Events/meetings; knowledge management/information dissemination. **Members** Full in 8 countries. Membership countries not specified. [2022/XM8551/**F**]

♦ North European Institute (internationally oriented national body)
♦ North European Institute for Tourism and Recreational Research, Kiel / see Institute for Tourism and Recreational Research in Northern Europe
♦ North European Symposium for Archaeological Textiles (meeting series)

♦ North European Table Tennis Union (NETU) 17599

Union de tennis de table de l'Europe du Nord – Nordeuropaisk Bordtennis Union

Founder address not obtained. T. +4745417912. E-mail: info@svenskbordtennis.com – bengt.paulsen@bordtennis.no.

History As *Nordic Table Tennis Union – Nordisk Bordtennis Union*. **Activities** Organizes: Nordic Championships; simultaneous Congress. **Events** *Congress* Norway 1998, *Congress* Sweden 1996, *Congress* Helsinki (Finland) 1986.
Members National associations in 10 countries and territories:
Denmark, Estonia, Faeroe Is, Finland, Greenland, Iceland, Latvia, Lithuania, Norway, Sweden.
NGO Relations Recognized by: *International Table Tennis Federation (ITTF, #15650)*. [2016/XD1709/**D**]

♦ North Indian Ocean Hydrographic Commission (see: #13825)
♦ **NORTHORS** Nordic Society for Tourism and Hospitality Research (#17431)

♦ North Pacific Anadromous Fish Commission (NPAFC) 17600

Commission des poissons anadromes du Pacifique Nord

Exec Dir 889 West Pender Street, Ste 502, Vancouver BC V6C 3B2, Canada. T. +16047755550. Fax +16047755577. E-mail: secretariat@npafc.org.
URL: http://www.npafc.org/

History 11 Feb 1992, Moscow (Russia). Established on signature by Canada, Japan, Russia and USA of *Convention for the Conservation of Anadromous Stocks in the North Pacific Ocean (1992)* which, upon exchange of ratifications, entered into force 16 Feb 1993. Korea Rep acceded to the Convention, 27 May 2003. Inaugural meeting, Feb 1993, Ottawa (Canada). Replaces *International North Pacific Fisheries Commission (INPFC, inactive)*. **Aims** Promote conservation of anadromous stocks in the North Pacific Ocean and its adjacent seas by prohibiting direct salmon *fisheries* on the high seas of the North Pacific, minimizing incidental salmon catch by other fisheries in the area and prohibiting retention onboard vessels of salmon taken as an incidental catch. **Structure** Commission, composed of 5 Contracting Parties, each appointing up to 3 representatives. Secretariat. Committees (3): Scientific Research and Statistics (CSRS); Enforcement (ENFO), Finance and Administration (F and A). CSRS Science Sub-Committee. Working Groups (4): International Year of the Salmon; Salmon Marking; Stock Assessment; Stock Identification. Plenary sessions of annual meeting open to the public; all non-public meetings closed but observers and guests may be invited. **Languages** English, Japanese, Korean, Russian. **Staff** 5.00 FTE, paid. **Finance** Sources: contributions of member/participating states. **Activities** Awards/prizes/competitions; events/meetings; research/documentation. **Events** *Annual Meeting* Busan (Korea Rep) 2023, *Annual Meeting* Vancouver, BC (Canada) 2021, *Annual Meeting* Vancouver, BC (Canada) 2020, *Annual Meeting* Portland, OR (USA) 2019, *Annual Meeting* Khabarovsk (Russia) 2018. **Publications** *NPAFC Bulletin*; *NPAFC Newsletter*. Annual Report; Statistical Yearbook; Technical Report series; special publications.
Members Governments of 5 countries:
Canada, Japan, Korea Rep, Russia, USA.
NGO Relations None. [2023/XD2788/**D***]

♦ North Pacific Fisheries Commission (NPFC) 17601

Secretariat 2F Hakuyo-Hal TUMST, 4-5-7 Konan, Minato-ku, Tokyo, 108-8477 Japan. T. +81354798717. Fax +81354798718. E-mail: executive.secretary@npfc.int – secretariat@npfc.int.
URL: https://www.npfc.int/

History 19 Jul 2015, Tokyo (Japan). Established when *Convention on the Conservation and Management of the High Seas Fisheries Resources in the North Pacific Ocean (2012)* came into force. **Aims** Ensure long-term conservation and sustainable use of fisheries resources in the Convention Area while protecting marine ecosystems of the North Pacific Ocean in which these resources occur. **Structure** Committees (3); Secretariat. **Languages** English. **Events** *Annual Meeting* Tokyo (Japan) 2022, *Annual Meeting* Tokyo (Japan) 2021, *Finance and Administration Committee Meeting* Tokyo (Japan) 2021, *Scientific Committee Meeting* Tokyo (Japan) 2021, *Technical and Compliance Committee Meeting* Tokyo (Japan) 2021. **Publications** *Yearbook*. Reports; posters; promotional material.
Members Contracting Parties (8):
Canada, China, Japan, Korea Rep, Russia, Taiwan, USA, Vanuatu.
Cooperating Non-contracting Party (1):
Panama.
IGO Relations Cooperates with (2): *North Pacific Anadromous Fish Commission (NPAFC, #17600)*; *North Pacific Marine Science Organization (PICES, #17602)*. [2022.02.15/AA0264/**D***]

♦ North Pacific Fishery Management Council (internationally oriented national body)
♦ North Pacific Fur Seal Commission (inactive)

♦ North Pacific Marine Science Organization (PICES) 17602

Organisation pour les sciences marine dans le Pacifique Nord

Exec Sec c/o Inst of Ocean Sciences, PO Box 6000, 9860 West Saanich Road, Sidney BC V8L 4B2, Canada. T. +12503636366. Fax +12503636827. E-mail: secretariat@pices.int.
URL: http://www.pices.int/

History 24 Mar 1992. Established when Convention entered into force, the Draft Convention having been approved 12 Dec 1990. Currently ratified by Canada, China, Japan, Korea Rep, Russia and USA. **Aims** Promote and coordinate marine research in the northern North Pacific and adjacent seas. **Structure** Governing Council (meets annually); Science Board; Scientific and Technical Committees; Secretariat, headed by Executive Secretary. **Languages** English. **Staff** 4.50 FTE, paid. **Finance** Contributions of Contracting Parties. **Activities** Events/meetings; knowledge management/information dissemination; monitoring/evaluation. **Events** *Annual Meeting* Busan (Korea Rep) 2022, *Annual Meeting* Qingdao (China) 2021, *Symposium on Plastics in the Arctic and Sub-Arctic Region* Reykjavik (Iceland) 2021, *Annual Meeting* Qingdao (China) 2020, *Symposium on Plastics in the Arctic and Sub-Arctic Region* Reykjavik (Iceland) 2020. **Publications** *PICES Press*. Annual Report; scientific reports; technical reports; brochures; advisory reports; special publications.
Members Countries having ratified the Convention (6):
Canada, China, Japan, Korea Rep, Russia, USA.
IGO Relations Observer status with (1): *International Council for the Exploration of the Sea (ICES, #13021)*. Memorandum of Understanding with (1): *Pacific Salmon Commission (PSC)*. Member of (1): *International Scientific Committee for Tuna and Tuna-like Species in the North Pacific Ocean (ISC, #14807)* (as Observer member of). **NGO Relations** Member of (1): *Partnership for Observation of the Global Oceans (POGO, #18239)*.
[2023.03.04/XD1596/**D***]

♦ North Pacific Research Board (internationally oriented national body)

♦ North Sea Advisory Council (NSAC) 17603

Executive Secretary Louis Braillelaan 80, 7th Floor, 2719 EK Zoetermeer, Netherlands. E-mail: admin@nsrac.org.
URL: http://www.nsrac.org/

History 1 Nov 2004. Founded by *European Commission (EC, #06633)*, following a series of meetings from 2003. Former names and other names: *North Sea Regional Advisory Council (NSRAC)* – former. Registration: No/ID: SC273169, Scotland; EU Transparency Register, No/ID: 91682404018-74. **Aims** Prepare and provide advice on the management of North Sea *fisheries* so as to promote the objectives of the Common Fisheries Policy. **Structure** General Assembly (annual); Executive Committee; Working Groups. **Languages** English. **Staff** 1.00 FTE, paid. **Finance** Sources: contributions; members' dues. Supported by: *European Commission (EC, #06633)*. **Activities** Events/meetings; guidance/assistance/consulting. Active in all member countries. **Events** *NSAC Executive Committee Forum* Zoetermeer (Netherlands) 2021, *NSAC Executive Committee Forum* Zoetermeer (Netherlands) 2020, *General Assembly* Boulogne-sur-Mer (France) 2011, *General Assembly* Boulogne-sur-Mer (France) 2011, *General Assembly* Aberdeen (UK) 2010.
Members Representatives of North Sea fisheries sector and interest groups in 8 countries:
Belgium, Denmark, France, Germany, Netherlands, Poland, Sweden, UK.
Included in the above, 9 organizations listed in this Yearbook:
ClientEarth (#03996); *European Anglers Alliance (EAA, #05900)*; *European Bureau for Conservation and Development (EBCD, #06412)*; *European Fishmeal and Fish Oil Producers (European Fishmeal, #07268)*; *European Transport Workers' Federation (ETF, #08941)*; *Oceana*; *Pew Charitable Trusts*; *Seas at Risk (SAR, #19189)*; *World Wide Fund for Nature (WWF, #21922)*.
NGO Relations AAC; *Baltic Sea Advisory Council (BSAC, #03139)*; BISAC; *Long Distance Advisory Council (LDAC, #16511)*; *Marine Aquarium Council (MAC, inactive)*; *Mediterranean Advisory Council (MEDAC, #16639)*; *North Western Waters Advisory Council (NWWAC, #17607)*; *Pelagic Advisory Council (Pelagic AC, #18289)*; *South West Waters Advisory Council (SWWAC, #19896)*. [2020.05.06/XM2606/y/**E**]

♦ North Sea Commission (NSC) 17604

Commission de la Mer du Nord – Comisión del Mar del Norte – Nordsee-Kommission – Comissão Mar do Norte – Commissione del Mar del Nord – Epitropi tis Vorias Falassas

Exec Sec c/o Region Västra Götaland, Regionens hus, SE-405 44 Gothenburg, Sweden. T. +46708756590. E-mail: nsc@crpm.org.
URL: https://cpmr-northsea.org/

History 1989, UK. Founded within the framework of *Conference of Peripheral Maritime Regions of Europe (CPMR, #04638)*. **Aims** Further partnerships between regional authorities which face the challenges and opportunities presented by the North Sea. **Structure** General Assembly (annual); Executive Committee; Thematic Groups (4); Secretariat. **Languages** English. **Finance** Members' dues. **Events** *Conference of Youth Parliaments around the North Sea* Sandnes (Norway) 2019, *North Sea Conference* Billund (Denmark) 2016, *General Assembly* Aberdeen (UK) 2014, *General Assembly* Haarlem (Netherlands) 2009, *General Assembly* Herning (Denmark) 2008. **Publications** *NSC Newsletter*. Papers; map; information leafets and booklets.
Members Regional and provincial councils in 9 countries and territories:
Belgium, Denmark, England, France, Germany, Netherlands, Norway, Scotland, Sweden.
IGO Relations Observer with: *OSPAR Commission for the Protection of the Marine Environment of the North-East Atlantic (OSPAR Commission, #17905)*. [2021/XK0533/**E**]

- ♦ North Sea Conference (meeting series)
- ♦ North Sea Foundation (internationally oriented national body)
- ♦ North Sea Hydrographic Commission (see: #13825)
- ♦ North Sea Regional Advisory Council / see North Sea Advisory Council (#17603)
- ♦ North-South Centre of the Council of Europe / see European Centre for Global Interdependence and Solidarity (#06483)
- ♦ North-South Centre / see European Centre for Global Interdependence and Solidarity (#06483)
- ♦ **North-South Centre** European Centre for Global Interdependence and Solidarity (#06483)
- ♦ North-South Centre for Technical and Cultural Interchange (inactive)
- ♦ North-South Economic and Cultural Development Agency (internationally oriented national body)
- ♦ North-South Forum / see Global Cooperation Council
- ♦ North-South Institute (internationally oriented national body)
- ♦ North-South Media Encounters (meeting series)

♦ North Star Alliance 17605

International Office Maliebaan 92, 3581 CX Utrecht, Netherlands. T. +31302343210. E-mail: info@northstar-alliance.org – communications@northstar-alliance.org.
URL: http://www.northstar-alliance.org/

History Set up 28 Sep 2006. **Aims** Provide quality *healthcare* to *mobile workers* and the communities they interact with. **Structure** Supervisory Board; Board of Directors; Office in Utrecht (Netherlands). Regions (2): Eastern; Southern Africa. **Languages** Afrikaans, Dutch, English, German, Swahili, Zulu. Xulu. **Staff** 200.00 FTE, paid. **Activities** Healthcare; networking/liaising.
Members Full in 6 countries:
Kenya, Mozambique, South Africa, Tanzania UR, Uganda, Zimbabwe.
IGO Relations *Southern African Development Community (SADC, #19843)*; *United Nations Population Fund (UNFPA, #20612)*; *United States Agency for International Development (USAID)*; *World Food Programme (WFP, #21510)*. **NGO Relations** Partners include: *AIDS Healthcare Foundation (AHF)*; *Aidsfonds*; *Amsterdam Institute for Global Health and Development (AIGHD)*; *Bureau international des Médecins sans frontières (MSF International, #03366)*; *Comfort the Children International (CTC International)*; *Elizabeth Glaser Pediatric AIDS Foundation (EGPAF)*; *FHI 360*; *Fleet Forum (#09792)*; *Management Sciences for Health (MSH)*; *Schwab Foundation for Social Entrepreneurship*; *TradeMark East Africa (TMEA, #20183)*; *Translators without Borders (#20216)*; *William J Clinton Foundation* – Clinton Global Initiative; *World Economic Forum (WEF, #21367)*. [2019.12.12/XM6757/**C**]

♦ Northwest Atlantic Fisheries Organization (NAFO) 17606

Organisation des pêches de l'Atlantique Nord-Ouest

Contact 401-1601 Lower Water Street, Halifax NS B3B 3P6, Canada. T. +19024685590. E-mail: info@nafo.int.
Main: https://www.nafo.int/

History 1 Jan 1979, Dartmouth, NS (Canada). Established on entry into force of *Convention on Future Multilateral Cooperation in the Northwest Atlantic Fisheries, 1978 (NAFO, 1978)*, which had been signed 24 Oct 1978, Ottawa (Canada), and came into force 1 Jan 1979. Successor to *International Commission for the Northwest Atlantic Fisheries (ICNAF, inactive)*, set up 3 Jul 1950, on coming into force of *International Convention for the Northwest Atlantic Fisheries (1949)*, signed 8 Feb 1949, Washington DC (USA). Amendments to the Convention approved 2007. Convention ratified 18 May 2017. **Aims** Through consultation and cooperation, contribute to the optimum utilization, rational management and conservation of the fishery resources of the Convention Area of the Northwest Atlantic Ocean; ensure the long-term conservation and sustainable use of the fishery resources in the Convention Area and, in doing so, safeguard the *marine ecosystems* in which these resources are found. **Structure** Commission, comprising the Contracting Parties and chaired by the President; Scientific Council (meets annually, plus regular and special sessions); Standing Committees (6); Secretariat. **Languages** English. **Staff** 11.00 FTE, paid. **Activities** Adopts conservation and management measures as well as a monitoring, control and surveillance scheme; plans and coordinates research work; compiles and considers results; collects and publishes fishery statistics and samples of commercially caught fish; allocates quotas. Assessment advice is based on scientific surveys of Contracting Parties, including national annual reports, scientific papers and data, fisheries statistics. Contracting Parties agree to maintain in force and implement a scheme of joint international enforcement, including reciprocal rights for boarding and inspection and for prosecution and sanctions on the basis of resulting evidence. **Events** *Annual Meeting* 2021, *Annual Meeting* Dartmouth, NS (Canada) 2020, *Annual Meeting* Bordeaux (France) 2019, *Annual Meeting* Tallinn (Estonia) 2018, *Annual Meeting* Montréal, QC (Canada) 2017. **Publications** *NAFO Conservation and Enforcement Measures* (annual); *Journal of Northwest Atlantic Fishery Science* – online. *NAFO Scientific Council Studies*. Annual Report. Meeting Proceedings; Scientific Council Reports.
Members Contracting Parties (12):
Canada, Cuba, Denmark (in respect of Faeroe Is and Greenland), France (in respect of Saint Pierre et Miquelon), Iceland, Japan, Korea Rep, Norway, Russia, UK, Ukraine, USA.
NGO Relations Observers may participate in some NAFO meetings provided they follow prescribed protocols. [2022.10.18/XC1537/y/**C***]

♦ North Western Waters Advisory Council (NWWAC) 17607

Conseil Consultatif pour les Eaux Occidentales Septentrionales – Consejo Consultivo para las Aguas Noroccidentales

Secretariat c/o Bord Iascaigh Mhara, Crofton Road, Dun Laoghaire, Dublin, CO. DUBLIN, Ireland. T. +35312144100. E-mail: nwwac@bim.ie.
URL: http://www.nwwac.org/

History 2005. Set up in accordance with *European Commission (EC, #06633)* Council Decision 2004/585/EC, setting out a common framework for Regional Advisory Councils. Former names and other names: *North Western Waters Regional Advisory Council* – former. Registration: Ireland; EU Transparency Register, No/ID: 8900132344-29. **Aims** Provide strategic advice from the stakeholders (fishing industry and civil society) to the European Commission and the Member States on sustainable fisheries management. **Structure** General Assembly; Executive Committee; Rotating Secretariat; Working Groups; Focus Groups. **Languages** English, French, Spanish. **Staff** 3.00 FTE, paid. **Finance** Supported by: *European Commission (EC, #06633)*. **Events** *General Assembly* Dublin (Ireland) 2015.
Members Stakeholders in 6 countries:
Belgium, France, Ireland, Netherlands, Spain, UK.
Included in the above, 8 organizations listed in this Yearbook:
Blue Fish Europe (#03284); *ClientEarth (#03996)*; *European Anglers Alliance (EAA, #05900)*; *European Bureau for Conservation and Development (EBCD, #06412)*; *European Transport Workers' Federation (ETF, #08941)*; *European Union Fish Processors Association (#08989)*; *International Sea Sportfishing Federation (FIPS-M, see: #04562)*; *Seas at Risk (SAR, #19189)*.
NGO Relations *Baltic Sea Advisory Council (BSAC, #03139)*; *Long Distance Advisory Council (LDAC, #16511)*; *Mediterranean Advisory Council (MEDAC, #16639)*; *North Sea Advisory Council (NSAC, #17603)*; *Pelagic Advisory Council (Pelagic AC, #18289)*; *South West Waters Advisory Council (SWWAC, #19896)*. [2021/XJ9738/y/**E**]

- ♦ North Western Waters Regional Advisory Council / see North Western Waters Advisory Council (#17607)
- ♦ North-West European Microbiological Group (inactive)
- ♦ North West Frontier Fellowship (internationally oriented national body)
- ♦ Northwest Medical Teams International / see Medical Teams International
- ♦ Northwest Pacific Action Plan / see Action Plan for Protection, Development and Management of the Marine Environment of the Northwest Pacific Region (#00092)
- ♦ Northwest Pacific Region Environmental Cooperation Center (internationally oriented national body)
- ♦ NORTIM – Nordiska Föreningen för Tillämpad och Industriell Matematik (inactive)
- ♦ **NorVect** Nordic Network for Vector-borne Diseases (#17365)
- ♦ Norwegian Agency for Development Cooperation (internationally oriented national body)
- ♦ Norwegian Agency for Exchange Cooperation (internationally oriented national body)
- ♦ Norwegian Aid to Europe / see Norwegian Refugee Council
- ♦ Norwegian Association for Development Research (internationally oriented national body)
- ♦ Norwegian Atlantic Committee (internationally oriented national body)
- ♦ Norwegian Centre for Conflict Resolution (internationally oriented national body)
- ♦ Norwegian Centre for Human Rights (internationally oriented national body)
- ♦ Norwegian Centre for International Cooperation in Higher Education (internationally oriented national body)
- ♦ Norwegian Church Aid (internationally oriented national body)
- ♦ Norwegian Church Ministry to Israel (internationally oriented national body)
- ♦ Norwegian Council for Africa (internationally oriented national body)
- ♦ Norwegian Council for Southern Africa / see Norwegian Council for Africa
- ♦ Norwegian Human Rights Fund (internationally oriented national body)
- ♦ Norwegian Institute for Human Rights / see Norwegian Centre for Human Rights
- ♦ Norwegian Institute of International Affairs (internationally oriented national body)
- ♦ Norwegian International Disability Alliance / see Atlas Alliance
- ♦ Norwegian International Folk High School Organization for 3rd World Rural Development (internationally oriented national body)
- ♦ Norwegian Investment Fund for Developing Countries (internationally oriented national body)
- ♦ Norwegian Lutheran Mission (internationally oriented national body)
- ♦ Norwegian Mission Alliance (internationally oriented national body)
- ♦ Norwegian Missionary Society (internationally oriented national body)
- ♦ Norwegian Organization for Asylum Seekers (internationally oriented national body)
- ♦ Norwegian Peace Association (internationally oriented national body)
- ♦ Norwegian Peacebuilding Resource Centre / see Norwegian Centre for Conflict Resolution
- ♦ Norwegian Peace Council (internationally oriented national body)
- ♦ Norwegian Peace Society / see Norwegian Peace Association
- ♦ Norwegian People's Aid (internationally oriented national body)
- ♦ Norwegian Refugee Council (internationally oriented national body)
- ♦ Norwegian Research School in Innovation / see Nordic Research School in Innovation and Entrepreneurship (#17398)
- ♦ Norwegian Seamen's Mission – Norwegian Church Abroad / see Seamen's Mission – Norwegian Church Abroad
- ♦ Norwegian Students' and Academics' International Assistance Fund (internationally oriented national body)
- ♦ Norwegian Volunteer Service / see Norwegian Agency for Exchange Cooperation
- ♦ NORZOAC / see Van Vollenhoven Institute for Law, Governance and Development
- ♦ NOSA / see International Association of Amusement Parks and Attractions (#11699)
- ♦ NOSALF – Nordiska-Samfundet för Latinamerikaforskning (inactive)
- ♦ NoSAMF – Nordiska Samarbetskommittén för Arktisk Medicinsk Forskning (inactive)
- ♦ **NOSAM** Nordisk Samarbeidsforum for Anestesi- og Intensivsykepleiere (#17528)
- ♦ **NOSA** Nordic Society for Aerosol Research (#17410)

♦ NoSB 17608

Contact Tollbugata 22, Postboks 456, SENTRUM, 0104 Oslo, Norway. E-mail: post@nsf.no.
URL: http://www.nsf.no/nosb/

History 1999. Former names and other names: *NoSB – Nordisk samarbeid av sykepleiere som jobber med barn og ungdom og deres familier* – full title; *Nordic co-operation of nurses who work with children and adolescents and their families* – full title. **Aims** Help spread and increase knowledge and skills and raise the level of *nurses* who work with *children* and *adolescents* and their *families*. **Activities** Events/meetings. **Events** *Listening to the children* Stockholm (Sweden) 2014, *Congress* Oslo (Norway) 2011, *Congress* Stockholm (Sweden) 1999.
Members Full in 5 countries and territories:
Denmark, Greenland, Iceland, Norway, Sweden. [2014/XJ9361/**F**]

- ♦ NoSB – Nordisk samarbeid av sykepleiere som jobber med barn og ungdom og deres familier / see NoSB (#17608)
- ♦ **NoSCoS** Nordic Spinal Cord Society (#17436)
- ♦ **NOS-HS** Nordisk Samarbejdsnaevn for Humanistisk og Samfundsvidenskabelig Forskning (#17530)
- ♦ **NOS-M** Nordiska Samarbetsnämnden för Medicinsk Forskning (#16125)
- ♦ **NOS-N** Nordisk Samarbeidsnaevn for Naturvidenskab (#17529)
- ♦ NOS – Nordiska Odontologiskastudentkåerna (inactive)
- ♦ **NOS** Nordiska Ortodontisällskapet (#17378)
- ♦ NOS – Nordiske Oppfinnerforeningers Samarbeidsorganisasjon (no recent information)
- ♦ **NOSOPRS** Nordic Society for Oculoplastic and Reconstructive Surgery (#17422)
- ♦ **NOSOSCO** Nordic Social-Statistical Committee (#17409)
- ♦ **NOSOSKO** Nordisk Socialstatistik Komité (#17409)
- ♦ Nos Petits Frères et Soeurs (internationally oriented national body)
- ♦ Nos petits orphelins / see Nuestros Pequeños Hermanos
- ♦ **NoSP** Nordic Society of Phenomenology (#17425)
- ♦ Nossal Institute for Global Health (internationally oriented national body)
- ♦ **NoSSS** Nordic Separation Science Society (#17406)
- ♦ NOSTA / see Nordic Society for Thermal Analysis and Calorimetry (#17430)
- ♦ **NOSTAC** Nordic Society for Thermal Analysis and Calorimetry (#17430)
- ♦ n-ost – Netzwerk für Osteuropa-Berichterstattung (internationally oriented national body)

♦ Notaries of Europe (CNUE) 17609

Permanent Office Ave de Cortenberg 120, 1000 Brussels, Belgium. T. +3225139529. Fax +3225139382. E-mail: info@cnue.be.
URL: http://www.cnue.eu/

History 1976, Brussels (Belgium), as *Conférence permanente des notariats de la Communauté européenne (CPNCP)*. Subsequently changed title to *Conférence des notariats de l'Union Européenne*. Adopted title *Conseil des notariats de l'Union Européenne (CNUE) – Council of the Notariats of the European Union*, 1 Jan 2006. Registered in accordance with Belgian law. EU Transparency Register: 98885666486-72. **Aims** Promote the notariat and its active contribution to any decision-making processes of the European institutions. **Structure** General Assembly; Board; Working Groups; Permanent Office, headed by Secretary General. **Events** *General Assembly* Brussels (Belgium) 2013, *Congress* Brussels (Belgium) 2012, *Conference on Clearer Patrimonial Regimes for International Couples* Brussels (Belgium) 2011, *Congress* Brussels (Belgium) 2011, *Conference on cross-border successions within the European Union* Brussels (Belgium) 2010.
Members Full in 22 countries:

Austria, Belgium, Bulgaria, Croatia, Czechia, Estonia, France, Germany, Greece, Hungary, Italy, Latvia, Lithuania, Luxembourg, Malta, Netherlands, Poland, Portugal, Romania, Slovakia, Slovenia, Spain.
Observer in 3 countries:
Montenegro, Serbia, Türkiye.
IGO Relations Recognized by: *European Commission (EC, #06633).* [2017/XE3728/**E**]

♦ Nothelfergemeinschaft der Freunde (internationally oriented national body)
♦ NoToDogMeat – World Protection for Dogs and Cats in the Meat Trade (internationally oriented national body)
♦ Notre-Dame du Bon-Conseil (religious order)
♦ Notre Dame de la Compassion de Marie (religious order)
♦ Notre Dame de la Visitation – Soeurs de Notre-Dame de la Visitation (religious order)
♦ Notre Europe / see Institut Jacques Delors
♦ Notre Europe Institut Jacques Delors / see Institut Jacques Delors
♦ Notre monde n'est pas à vendre (#17917)
♦ Not For Sale (internationally oriented national body)
♦ Not For Sale Campaign / see Not For Sale
♦ Nottingham Centre for Research on Globalisation and Economic Policy (internationally oriented national body)
♦ NOU – Nordisk Oljelednings Union (no recent information)
♦ **NOUSA** Nordisk Organisasjon for Utdanninger i Sosialt Arbeid (#17204)
♦ Nouveaux droits de l'homme – International (#17089)
♦ Nouvelle Planète (internationally oriented national body)
♦ Nouvelles Femmes pour l'Europe (unconfirmed)
♦ Nouvelle SIRMCE Confédération (inactive)
♦ NOVABA / see Baltic Forestry, Veterinary and Agricultural University Network (#03119)
♦ Novae Terrae Foundation (internationally oriented national body)
♦ NOVA / see Nordic Forestry, Veterinary and Agricultural University Network (#17297)

♦ Nova Paint Club 17610

SG Legh Road, Knutsford, WA16 8LP, UK.
URL: http://www.novapaint.org/
History 1983. **Aims** Serve as a forum for exchange of information, technology and experience between paint companies.
Members Companies in 17 countries and territories:
Argentina, Barbados, Canada, Colombia, France, Germany, Greece, Israel, Italy, Jamaica, Philippines, Portugal, Spain, Switzerland, Taiwan, UK, USA. [2022.10.19/XF4793/**F**]

♦ Novartis Foundation (internationally oriented national body)
♦ **NoVAS** Nordic Veterinary Acupuncture Society (#17462)
♦ **NOVA University Network** Nordic Forestry, Veterinary and Agricultural University Network (#17297)
♦ NOVEM – Noise and Vibration Emerging Methods Conference (meeting series)
♦ NOVIB / see Oxfam Novib
♦ Novi Most International (internationally oriented national body)

♦ NOVO Network 17611

Chairman Dept of Management Engineering, Technical Univ of Denmark, Produktionstorvet, Bygning 424, 2800 Lyngby KGS, Denmark. T. +4545256010.
URL: http://www.novo-network.dk/
History 2006. **Aims** Foster the scientific progress, knowledge and development of the working environment within *healthcare* as an integrated part of production system development. **Structure** Board. **Finance** Supported by: *Nordic Council of Ministers (NCM, #17260).* **Activities** Events/meetings. **Events** *Symposium* Helsinki (Finland) 2018.
Members Full in 5 countries:
Denmark, Finland, Iceland, Norway, Sweden. [2019/XM7941/**F**]

♦ Novussanguis / see Novus Sanguis (#17612)

♦ Novus Sanguis 17612

Contact 37 rue des Volontaires, 75725 Paris CEDEX 15, France.
History Operational launch, 14 May 2008. Also referred to as *Novussanguis.* **Aims** Develop cord *blood stem cell* research and adult stem cell research for *biotechnological*, pharmaceutical and medical purpose; educate future European research generations on *tissue engineering*, cellular therapy and regenerative medicine; create precise and unified methods, processes and protocols at European and worldwide levels and deposit patents allowing for these technologies to be applicable from the laboratory to the patient's bedside. **Members** Laboratories (about 15). Membership countries not specified. [2009/XM2945/**D**]

♦ **NOWPAP** Action Plan for Protection, Development and Management of the Marine Environment of the Northwest Pacific Region (#00092)
♦ Noyau Européen pour la Silice (#08001)
♦ NOYB – Europäisches Zentrum für digitale Rechte (#17613)

♦ NOYB – European Center for Digital Rights (NOYB) 17613

NOYB – Europäisches Zentrum für digitale Rechte (NOYB)
Registered Address Goldschlagstr 172/4/3/2, 1140 Vienna, Austria. E-mail: info@noyb.eu.
URL: https://noyb.eu/
History 12 Jun 2017, Austria. Registration: ZVR, No/ID: 1354838270, Austria; EU Transparency Register, No/ID: 488900342587-15, Start date: 11 May 2021. **Aims** Join forces with existing organizations, resources and structures to maximize the impact of GDPR, while avoiding parallel structures. **Structure** General Assembly; Executive Board; Management. **Languages** Dutch, English, French, German, Italian, Spanish. **Staff** 8.00 FTE, paid; 4.00 FTE, voluntary. **Finance** Sources: contributions; members' dues; private foundations. **Activities** Advocacy/lobbying/activism; awareness raising. Europe. **NGO Relations** Member of (1): *European Digital Rights (EDRi, #06924).* [2021.12.02/AA1758/**D**]

♦ **NOYB** NOYB – Europäisches Zentrum für digitale Rechte (#17613)
♦ **NOYB** NOYB – European Center for Digital Rights (#17613)
♦ **NØK** Nordisk Økonomisk Kvaegavl (#17275)
♦ NPAF / see National Peace Foundation
♦ **NPAFC** North Pacific Anadromous Fish Commission (#17600)
♦ **NPA** Nordic Planetarium Association (#17386)
♦ **NPA** Nordic Press Association (#17393)
♦ NPA – Norwegian Peace Association (internationally oriented national body)
♦ NPA – Norwegian People's Aid (internationally oriented national body)
♦ NPAPWS – Network Performing Arts Production Workshops (meeting series)
♦ NPA / see World Ninepin Bowling Association (#21673)
♦ NPBS – Nordic Publishing Board in Science (inactive)
♦ NPCM – Nordic Pediatric Cardiology meeting (meeting series)
♦ NPC – NATO Programming Centre (inactive)
♦ NPC – Nordic Photosynthesis Congress (meeting series)
♦ NPC – Nordic Poultry Conference (meeting series)
♦ NPC – Nordic Psychoanalytic Congress (meeting series)
♦ **NPC** Nordic Working Group on Process Control (#17471)
♦ **NPCOA** National Platforms' Coalition of Asia (#16939)
♦ NPC Working Group / see Nordic Working Group on Process Control (#17471)
♦ NPDL – New Pedagogies for Deep Learning (internationally oriented national body)
♦ NPEC – Northwest Pacific Region Environmental Cooperation Center (internationally oriented national body)
♦ **NPFC** North Pacific Fisheries Commission (#17601)
♦ NPFMC – North Pacific Fishery Management Council (internationally oriented national body)
♦ NPF – Nando Peretti Foundation (internationally oriented national body)
♦ NPF – National Peace Foundation (internationally oriented national body)
♦ **NPF** Nordiska Polisförbundet (#17489)
♦ NPFSC – North Pacific Fur Seal Commission (inactive)
♦ NPG / see NPI Africa
♦ NPH International / see Nuestros Pequeños Hermanos
♦ NPH – Nuestros Pequeños Hermanos (internationally oriented national body)
♦ NPI Africa (internationally oriented national body)
♦ NPIF / see National Peace Foundation
♦ **NPI** Nordic Patent Institute (#17381)
♦ **NPLD** Network to Promote Linguistic Diversity (#17052)
♦ NPN / see Nordic Planetarium Association (#17386)
♦ **NPN** Nordic Pragmatism Network (#17392)
♦ **NPN** Northern Pharma Network (#17593)
♦ **NP** Nonviolent Peaceforce (#17153)
♦ NPO Fenno-Ugria / see Fenno-Ugria
♦ NPOF – Nordisk Paediatrisk Ortopaedisk Federation (no recent information)
♦ NPO Global Sports Alliance / see Global Sports Alliance (#10613)
♦ NPOG / see Nordic Pediatric Ophthalmology Group (#17382)
♦ **NPOG** Nordic Pediatric Ophthalmology Group (#17382)
♦ NPOKI – NonProfit Organizations Knowledge Initiative (internationally oriented national body)
♦ NPRB – North Pacific Research Board (internationally oriented national body)
♦ NPSIA – Norman Paterson School of International Affairs (internationally oriented national body)
♦ **NPTA** Nordic Piano Technicians Association (#17385)
♦ NPT Exporters Committee / see Zangger Committee (#22030)
♦ NPT – Treaty on the Non-proliferation of Nuclear Weapons (1968 treaty)
♦ **NPU** Nordic Postal Union (#17391)
♦ NPU – Nordisk Privatskole Union (inactive)
♦ **NPWJ** No Peace Without Justice (#17155)
♦ NPY-PYY-PP Meeting – International Neuropeptide Y, Peptide YY, Pancreatic Polypeptide Meeting (meeting series)
♦ NRA / see Nordic Road Association (#17402)
♦ NRC Europe / see Norwegian Refugee Council
♦ NRC – Norwegian Refugee Council (internationally oriented national body)
♦ NRF – Nordic Recycling Federation (inactive)
♦ NRF – Nordiska Elektronikfabrikanters Förbund (inactive)
♦ NRF – Nordiska Reklamebyrå Förbundet (no recent information)
♦ **NRF** Nordiska Revisorsförbundet (#17285)
♦ NRF – Nordisk Rettsodontologisk Forening (no recent information)
♦ **NRF** Northern Research Forum (#17594)
♦ nrg4SD / see Regions4 Sustainable Development (#18819)
♦ **NRGI** Natural Resource Governance Institute (#16957)
♦ NRI – Natural Resources Institute (internationally oriented national body)
♦ **NRI-Networks** Nordic Health Research and Innovation Networks (#17310)
♦ NRI – New Reality International (internationally oriented national body)
♦ NRM – International Symposium of Functional Neuroceptor Mapping of the Living Brain (meeting series)
♦ NRN – Nordic Reflexology Network (unconfirmed)
♦ **NR** Nordiska Rådet (#17256)
♦ **NR** Nordisk Råd (#17256)
♦ **NRO** Number Resource Organization (#17625)
♦ **NRR** Nordisk Reuma Råd (#17401)
♦ **NRS** Nordic Rheology Society (#17400)
♦ NRWA – Nordic Retail and Wholesale Association (internationally oriented national body)
♦ **NSAC** North Sea Advisory Council (#17603)
♦ NSAM / see Nordic Society for Circumpolar Health (#17412)
♦ NSA – Neurosurgical Society of Australasia (internationally oriented national body)
♦ **NSA** Nordic Strabismological Association (#17438)
♦ NSAS – Nordic State Audit Seminar (meeting series)
♦ **NSBB** Nordisk Samarbeidsgruppe for By og Boligforskning (#17460)
♦ NSB – Nordic Symposium on Building Physics (meeting series)
♦ NSC / see European Centre for Global Interdependence and Solidarity (#06483)
♦ NSC Alliance – Natural Science Collections Alliance (internationally oriented national body)
♦ **NSCA** Nordic Science Centre Association (#17404)
♦ **NSCF** Nordisk Science Center Forbund (#17404)
♦ **NSCH** Nordic Society for Circumpolar Health (#17412)
♦ **NSCK** Nordisk Selskab for Campanologi og Klokkespil (#17533)
♦ **NSCMID** Nordic Society for Clinical Microbiology and Infectious Diseases (#17413)
♦ **NSCN** Nordic Sustainable Campus Network (#17440)
♦ **NSC** North Sea Commission (#17604)
♦ NSDM – Nordic Society for Disaster Medicine (no recent information)
♦ **NSDS** Nordic Spinal Deformities Society (#17437)
♦ NSFA / see Nordic Swimming Federations Association (#17442)
♦ NSFD – Nordiska Samarbetsorganet för Drogforskning (inactive)
♦ **NSFH** Nordisk Sammenslutning for Hygiejenesygeplejersker (#17531)
♦ NSF International (internationally oriented national body)
♦ **NSfK** Nordiska Samarbetsrådet för Kriminologi (#17493)
♦ **NSfK** Nordisk Samarbejdsråd for Kriminologi (#17493)
♦ **NSfK** Nordisk Samarbetsråd for Kriminologi (#17493)
♦ NSF – Nordens Skogsägareorganisationers Förbund (inactive)
♦ **NSF** Nordic Swimming Federations Association (#17442)
♦ **NSF** Nordisk Sangerforbund (#17532)
♦ **NSF** Nordiskt Speditörförbund (#17543)
♦ NSFOF – Nordic Socialist Adult Education Organization (inactive)
♦ NSFRC – Nordic Society for Free Radical Chemistry (no recent information)
♦ **NSFR** Nordiska Skattevetenskapliga Forskningsrådet (#17443)
♦ **NSFS** Nordisk Selskab for Strålingsbeskyttelse (#17428)
♦ **NSGE** Nordic Society on Gynaecological Endoscopy (#17414)
♦ NSG – Nordic Smokers Guild (internationally oriented national body)
♦ **NSG** Nuclear Suppliers Group (#17621)
♦ **NSGO** Nordic Society of Gynecological Oncology (#17415)
♦ NSHC – North Sea Hydrographic Commission (see: #13825)
♦ NSHF / see Nordic Joint Advisory Group on Refugee Policy (#17331)
♦ **NSHF** Nordisk Samrådsgruppepåhøjt Niveau for Flygtningespørgsmål (#17331)
♦ **NSHG-PM** Nordic Society of Human Genetics and Precision Medicine (#17416)
♦ NSHK / see Nordic Association of Schools of Social Work (#17204)
♦ NSH – Nordiska Samarbetsorganet för Handikappfrågor (inactive)
♦ NSI – North-South Institute (internationally oriented national body)
♦ **NSK** Nordic Cooperation Committee for complementary and alternative Medicine (#17254)
♦ NSK – Nordisk Strafferetskomité (inactive)
♦ NSLF – Nordisk Samarbejdsråd for Logopedi og Foniatri (no recent information)
♦ NSME – North-South Media Encounters (meeting series)
♦ **nsmes** Nordic Society for Middle Eastern Studies (#17419)
♦ **NSMM** Nordic Society for Medical Mycology (#17417)

♦ NSM / see Nordic Society for Middle Eastern Studies (#17419)
♦ NSM – Nordic Statistical Meeting (meeting series)
♦ NSM – Nordiska Statistikermötet (meeting series)
♦ NSMVB – Nordic Society for Microcirculation and Vascular Biology (inactive)
♦ **NSN** Nordic Society of Nephrology (#17420)
♦ **NSNR** Nordic Society of Neuroradiology (#17421)
♦ **NSNS** Norraen Samtök um Nams- og Starfsradgjöf (#17191)
♦ NSoA – New School of Athens (no recent information)
♦ **NSO** NATO SCHOOL Oberammergau (#16947)
♦ NSO – NATO Standardization Organization (inactive)
♦ **NSO** Nordic Society Oikos (#17423)
♦ **NSO** Nordisk Statstjenestemanns Organisasjon (#17258)
♦ **NSPA** NATO Support and Procurement Agency (#16948)
♦ **NSPA Network** Northern Sparsely Populated Areas Network (#17595)
♦ NSPC – Nordic Social Pharmacy and Health Services Research Conference (meeting series)
♦ NSPM / see Nordic Society of Human Genetics and Precision Medicine (#17416)
♦ **NSPR** Nordic Society for Philosophy of Religion (#17427)
♦ **NSQH** Nordic Research Network for Safety and Quality in Healthcare (#17396)
♦ NSRAC / see North Sea Advisory Council (#17603)
♦ NSRC – Network Startup Resource Center (internationally oriented national body)
♦ **NSR** Nordisk Skuespillerråd (#17166)
♦ NSRS – Nordic Sleep Research and Medicine Society (no recent information)
♦ **NSSA** Nematological Society of Southern Africa (#16971)
♦ **NSSK** Nordiska Socionomförbunds Samarbetskommitté (#17495)
♦ **NSS** Nordiska Kommittén för Samordning av Elektriska Säkerhetsfrågor (#17246)
♦ NSS – Nordisk Samarbejde Inden for Skoleområdet (inactive)
♦ NSSR – Nordic Society for Space Research (inactive)
♦ NSTA / see Nordic Society for Thermal Analysis and Calorimetry (#17430)
♦ NSTM – Nordiska Skeppsteknika Mote (inactive)
♦ NSTP – Nordic Society of Toxicological Pathologists (inactive)
♦ NSU – Nordisk Samarbeidsråd for Utviklingshemmede (inactive)
♦ **NSU** Nordisk Samorganisation for Ungdomsarbejde (#17476)
♦ **NSU** Nordisk Sommeruniversitet (#17535)
♦ NSU – Nordisk Sportsfiskerunion (inactive)
♦ NSWP / see Global Network of Sex Work Projects (#10498)
♦ **NSWP** Global Network of Sex Work Projects (#10498)
♦ NSXXI / see International-Lawyers.Org (#14008)
♦ NT2F – New Trends in Fatigue and Fracture (meeting series)
♦ **NTA** Nordic Telemedicine Association (#17445)
♦ NTA – Nordic Textile Art (unconfirmed)
♦ NTD-SC / see Coalition for Operational Research on Neglected Tropical Diseases
♦ NTES – Nordic Trace Element Society (internationally oriented national body)
♦ NTF – Nigeria Trust Fund (internationally oriented national body)
♦ NTF – Nordiska Textillärarförbundet (no recent information)
♦ **NTF** Nordiska Transportarbetarefederationen (#17496)
♦ **NTF** Nordisk Thoraxkirurgisk Forening (#19079)
♦ **NTF** Nordisk Transportarbeiderfederasjon (#17496)
♦ **NTFP-EN** Non-Timber Forest Products Exchange Programme for South and Southeast Asia (#17151)
♦ NTG – Next Tourism Generation Alliance (unconfirmed)
♦ **NTI** Nuclear Threat Initiative (#17622)
♦ NTLR – Nordisk Srafiklaererråd (inactive)
♦ **NTLR** Nordisk Teaterlederråd (#17447)
♦ NTM / see Ethnos360
♦ **NTN** Nordisk Transportpolitisk Nettverk (#17542)
♦ NT – Nordiska Turistrådet (no recent information)
♦ NTO – Nordisk Tele Organisation (no recent information)
♦ **NTO** Nordisk Tolltjenestemannsorganisasjon (#17540)
♦ **NTRG** Nordic Travel Retail Group (#17453)
♦ **NTR** Nordiska Träskyddsrådet (#17469)
♦ **NTR** Nordiska Tulladministrativa Rådet (#17497)
♦ **NTR** Nordisk Tjenestemannsråd (#17538)
♦ **NTR** Nordisk Toldadministrativt Råd (#17497)
♦ **NTSA** Nordic Traffic Safety Academy (#17451)
♦ **NTS-Asia** Consortium of Non-Traditional Security Studies in Asia (#04755)
♦ NTS Centre – Centre for Non-Traditional Security Studies (internationally oriented national body)
♦ NTS – Narodno-Trudovoj Sojuz (internationally oriented national body)
♦ **NTS** Neurotoxicity Society (#17073)
♦ NTS – Nordiska Tidningsutgivarnas Samarbetsnämnd (no recent information)
♦ NTS – Nordiske Teleansattes Samarbeidsorgan (inactive)
♦ NTS – Nordisk Transportteknisk Selskap (inactive)
♦ NTSosc / see Alliance of Russian Solidarists
♦ NTSR – Nordic Telecommunications Satellite Council (inactive)
♦ NTS Studies / see Centre for Non-Traditional Security Studies
♦ NTUG / see Viking NonStop User Group (#20777)
♦ **NTU** Nordic Theatre Union (#17448)
♦ NTU – Nordisk Tandteknikerunion (inactive)
♦ NTU – Nordisk Tele Union (inactive)
♦ **NTU** Nordisk Trafikskole Union (#17541)
♦ NUA / see Nordic University Association (#17458)
♦ **NUAS** Nordiska Universitetsadministratörssamarbetet (#17206)
♦ NUAT – Nordisk Union for Alkoholfri Trafikk (inactive)

♦ Nubian Vault Association 17614

Association Voûte Nubienne (AVN)

Dir Gen 7 rue Jean Jaures, 34190 Ganges, France. T. +33467812105.

URL: http://www.lavoutenubienne.org/

History 2000. **Aims** Reverse housing problems for many in Africa, promoting development of an adapted *housing* market via diffusion of the NV technical concept. **Structure** Board of Directors. **Languages** English, French. **Staff** Headquarters: 10; West Africa local staff: 70. **Activities** Training/education; research and development.

Members Active (30) in 5 countries:
Benin, Burkina Faso, Ghana, Mali, Senegal.

IGO Relations Accredited to the Conference of the Parties of: *Secretariat of the United Nations Convention to Combat Desertification (Secretariat of the UNCCD, #19208)*; *United Nations Framework Convention on Climate Change – Secretariat (UNFCCC, #20564)*. **NGO Relations** Member of: *Global Alliance for Buildings and Construction (GlobalABC, #10187)*; *Groupe de Travail Désertification (GTD)*; *World Alliance for Efficient Solutions*. [2019.12.13/XM5753/**F**]

♦ **NUCIS** FAO/CIHEAM Inter-Regional Cooperative Research Network on Nuts (#09258)
♦ Nuclear Age Peace Foundation (internationally oriented national body)
♦ NUCLEAR – Convention Relating to Civil Liability in the Field of Maritime Carriage of Nuclear Material (1971 treaty)

♦ Nuclear Energy Agency (NEA) 17615

Agence de l'OCDE pour l'énergie nucléaire (AEN)

Dir Gen 46 quai Alphonse Le Gallo, 92100 Boulogne-Billancourt, France. T. +33145241010. Fax +33145241110. E-mail: nea@oecd-nea.org – press@oecd-nea.org.

URL: http://www.oecd-nea.org/

History 20 Apr 1972. Founded as a semi-autonomous body taking over the activities of *European Nuclear Energy Agency (ENEA) – Agence européenne pour l'énergie nucléaire*, set up 1 Feb 1958, on coming into force of the statute adopted by *OECD (#17693)*, Dec 1957. Former names and other names: *OECD Nuclear Energy Agency* – alias. **Aims** Assist member countries in maintaining and further developing, through international cooperation, the scientific, technological and legal bases required for a safe, *environmentally* sound and economical use of nuclear energy for peaceful purposes; strive to provide authoritative assessments and forge common understandings on key issues as input to government decisions on nuclear energy policy and to broader OECD policy analyses in areas such as energy and sustainable development of low-carbon economies. **Structure** OECD Council; Steering Committee for Nuclear Energy, comprising senior representatives of all member country governments and representatives of *European Commission (EC, #06633)* and *International Atomic Energy Agency (IAEA, #12294)*. NEA Bodies (8). **Languages** English, French. **Staff** 116.00 FTE, paid. **Finance** Sources: contributions. Supplemented by voluntary contributions. Annual budget: 11,100,000 EUR (2016). **Activities** Knowledge management/information dissemination; projects/programmes; research and development. **Events** *International Conference on Nuclear Criticality Safety* Sendai (Japan) 2023, *International Conference on Geological Repositories* Helsinki (Finland) 2022, *International Conference on Geological Repositories* Helsinki (Finland) 2021, *International Workshop on Joint Utilisation of Underground Research Laboratories for Research and Development Projects* Tokyo (Japan) 2021, *Workshop on Advanced Measurement Method and Instrumentation for enhancing Severe Accident Management in an NPP addressing Emergency, Stabilization and Long-term Recovery Phases* Japan 2020. **Publications** *NEA News* (2 a year); *Nuclear Law Bulletin* (2 a year); *Nuclear Energy Data* (annual); *Uranium: Resources, Production and Demand* (every 2 years). Annual Report; policy reports; technical reports; proceedings.

Members Governments of 34 countries:
Argentina, Australia, Austria, Belgium, Bulgaria, Canada, Czechia, Denmark, Finland, France, Germany, Greece, Hungary, Iceland, Ireland, Italy, Japan, Korea Rep, Luxembourg, Mexico, Netherlands, Norway, Poland, Portugal, Romania, Russia, Slovakia, Slovenia, Spain, Sweden, Switzerland, Türkiye, UK, USA.

IGO Relations Cooperates with: IAEA. Functions as Technical Secretariat and observer member to: *Generation IV International Forum (GIF, #10115)*; *International Framework for Nuclear Energy Cooperation (IFNEC, #13681)*; Multinational Design Evaluation Programme (MDEP). [2022.02.02/XE0816/**E***]

♦ Nuclear Energy Institute (internationally oriented national body)

♦ nucleareurope 17616

Dir Av des Arts 56, 1000 Brussels, Belgium. T. +3225054595. E-mail: foratom@foratom.org – info@nucleareurope.eu.

Contact address not obtained.

URL: https://www.nucleareurope.eu/

History 12 Jul 1960, Paris (France). Current statutes adopted 30 Oct 1996, Brussels (Belgium). A trade association for the nuclear energy industry in Europe. Former names and other names: *Forum Atomique Européen* – legal name (1960); *European Atomic Forum* – former; *Europäisches Atom-Forum* – former. Registration: EU Transparency Register, No/ID: 42433582-82; Banque-Carrefour des Entreprises, No/ID: 0862.233.493, Start date: 17 Dec 2003, Belgium. **Aims** Support and promote development of nuclear energy in Europe through sustained, highly proactive and visible actions in order to ensure that a long-term EU-wide low-carbon energy strategy includes continued deployment of nuclear technologies with the ultimate aim to maintain nuclear energy's share in electricity generation. **Structure** General Assembly; Executive Board, including President. **Languages** Dutch, English, French, Romanian, Spanish. **Staff** 13.00 FTE, paid. **Finance** Sources: members' dues. **Activities** Events/meetings; knowledge management/information dissemination; networking/liaising. **Events** *Management System Event* Helsinki (Finland) 2022, *Management System Workshop* Vienna (Austria) 2016, *Technical Meeting on Stakeholder Involvement Througout the Lifecycle of Nuclear Power Plant* Vienna (Austria) 2012, *ENA : biennial European nuclear assembly* Brussels (Belgium) 2010, *Management system workshop* Vienna (Austria) 2010. **Publications** *E-bulletin* – Latest news on nuclear. Annual Report; position papers; Nuclear policy summaries.

Members National nuclear associations (15) and 2 utilities representing about 3,000 companies in 17 countries:
Belgium, Bulgaria, Czechia, Finland, France, Hungary, Italy, Netherlands, Poland, Romania, Slovakia, Slovenia, Spain, Sweden, Switzerland, UK, Ukraine.

Consultative Status Consultative status granted from: *ECOSOC (#05331)* (Ros C); *International Atomic Energy Agency (IAEA, #12294)*. **IGO Relations** Accredited by (1): *United Nations Framework Convention on Climate Change – Secretariat (UNFCCC, #20564)*. Recognized by: *European Commission (EC, #06633)*. **NGO Relations** Member of (4): *Centre for European Policy Studies (CEPS, #03741)* (as Institutional member); *European Energy Forum (EEF, #06986)* (as Associate member); *Industry4Europe (#11181)*; *Sustainable Nuclear Energy Technology Platform (SNETP, #20063)*. [2023.02.14/XD0590/**D**]

♦ Nuclear Exporters Committee / see Zangger Committee (#22030)

♦ Nuclear-Free and Independent Pacific Movement (NFIP Movement) 17617

Contact address not obtained. T. +679304649. Fax +679304755.

History 1975. **Activities** Organizes conferences. **Publications** *Pacific News Bulletin* (12 a year). **NGO Relations** Represented on the Organizing Committee of: *Hague Appeal for Peace (HAP, #10848)*. Member of: *Abolition 2000 – Global Network to Eliminate Nuclear Weapons (Abolition 2000, #00006)*; *Pacific Peace Working Group (PPWG, #17988)* is an outgrowth. [2009/XF0107/**F**]

♦ Nuclear Free Zone Local Authorities International Secretariat / see International Secretariat Committee of Nuclear Free Zone Local Authorities (#14820)

♦ Nuclear Generation II and III Association (NUGENIA) 17618

Chairman c/o EDF, Avenue des Arts 53, 1000 Brussels, Belgium. E-mail: secretariat@snetp.eu.

URL: https://snetp.eu/nugenia/

History 14 Nov 2011. Resulted from the integration process of the *Sustainable Nuclear Energy Technology Platform (SNETP, #20063)*, the NULIFE Network of Excellence and the SARNET Network of Excellence. Also includes *ENIQ Network*. **Aims** Provide a scientific and technical coordination support by initiating and monitoring international R and D projects and programmes. **Structure** General Assembly; Executive Committee; Secretariat. **Languages** English, French. **Staff** Voluntary. **Finance** Sources: members' dues. Annual budget: 200,000 EUR. **Activities** Events/meetings; knowledge management/information dissemination; research and development. **Events** *Annual Forum* Paris (France) 2019, *Annual Forum* Prague (Czechia) 2018, *General Assembly* Prague (Czechia) 2018, *Annual Forum* Amsterdam (Netherlands) 2017, *General Assembly* Amsterdam (Netherlands) 2017. **Publications** *NUGENIA Global Vision 2015*; *NUGENIA Roadmap 2013. NUGENIA VISION PAPER* (2021).

Members Full (114); Honorary 7. Members in 24 countries:
Belgium, Bulgaria, Canada, China, Croatia, Czechia, Finland, France, Germany, Hungary, Italy, Japan, Korea Rep, Netherlands, Poland, Romania, Russia, Slovakia, Slovenia, Spain, Sweden, Switzerland, UK, Ukraine. [2023.02.13/XJ8977/**E**]

♦ Nuclear Medicine Europe (NMEU) 17619

Administrator Avenue Louise 65, 4th floor, 1050 Brussels, Belgium. E-mail: admin@nmeu.org.

URL: http://nuclearmedicineeurope.eu/

History 1987. An organization of the type *European Economic Interest Grouping (EEIG, #06960)*. Former names and other names: *Association of Radiopharmaceutical producers Europe (ARPE)* – former; *Association of Radiopharmaceutical Producers and Equipment Suppliers (ARPES)* – former; *Association of Imaging Producers and Equipment Suppliers (AIPES)* – former (2001). Registration: Banque-Carrefour des Entreprises, No/ID: 0443.242.686, Start date: 19 Feb 1991, Belgium; EU Transparency Register, No/ID: 382490247809-11, Start date: 30 Sep 2022. **Aims** Foster innovation in nuclear medicine and molecular imaging; cooperate for appropriate regulations in all aspects of nuclear medicine missions; support and facilitate logistics and operations needs of our members; promote the value of nuclear medicine achievements. **Structure** General Assembly; Executive Committee; Working Groups. **Activities** Events/meetings. **Events** *Symposium* Brussels (Belgium) 2021, *Symposium* Brussels (Belgium) 2019, *Symposium* Brussels (Belgium) 2018.

Members Full in 9 countries:
Belgium, Finland, France, Germany, Hungary, Netherlands, Romania, Switzerland, UK.
Associate members in 11 countries:
Argentina, Australia, Belgium, Canada, Czechia, France, Germany, Japan, Netherlands, Poland, South Africa.
[2022/XJ9826/**D**]

♦ Nuclear Physics European Collaboration Committee (NuPECC) 17620

Scientific Sec c/o Physik-Dept E12, Technische Univ Munich, 85748 Garching, Germany. T. +498928912293 – +491728915011. Fax +498928912298.
Chair GANIL, BP 55027, 14076 Caen CEDEX 5, France. T. +33231454598. Fax +33231454586.
URL: http://www.nupecc.org/

History 1 Oct 1988. Expert Committee of *European Science Foundation (ESF, #08441)* since 1 Jan 1991. **Aims** Strengthen European collaboration in nuclear physics; define a network of complementary facilities within Europe and encourage optimization of their usage; provide a forum for discussion of provision of future facilities and instrumentation; issue recommendations on development, organization and support of European nuclear physics, and of particular projects. **Structure** Chairman elected by Committee; Scientific Secretary. **Languages** English. **Staff** 1.00 FTE, paid. **Finance** Funded by national funding agencies and institutions nominating committee members. **Activities** Events/meetings; guidance/assistance/consulting. **Events** *Meeting* Cape Town (South Africa) 2022, *Meeting* Madrid (Spain) 2022, *Meeting* Mol (Belgium) 2022, *Meeting* Liverpool (UK) 2021, *Meeting* Venice (Italy) 2021. **Publications** *Nuclear Physics News International* (4 a year). *Long Range Plans* (5th ed 2017); *NuPECC Handbook – International Access to Nuclear Physics Facilities in Europe* (6th ed 2012). Special reports; surveys; brochures.
Members Individuals (appointed by ESF Executive Council for a 3-year period) in 21 countries:
Austria, Belgium, Croatia, Czechia, Denmark, Finland, France, Germany, Greece, Hungary, Italy, Netherlands, Norway, Poland, Portugal, Romania, Slovakia, Spain, Sweden, Switzerland, UK.
Institutional (national research facilities) in 5 countries:
Belgium, France, Germany, Italy, Russia. [2022.10.19/XF5075/v/**F**]

♦ Nuclear Suppliers Group (NSG) 17621

Address not obtained.
URL: http://www.nuclearsuppliersgroup.org/

History 1975; in 1978 the *Nuclear Suppliers Guidelines* governing nuclear transfers for peaceful purposes by major nuclear supplier countries were published. These countries, previously known as *London Club – Club de Londres*, have been officially referred to under the listed title since 1993. **Aims** Facilitate the peaceful uses of nuclear energy by ensuring that nuclear and nuclear-related trade does not contribute, directly or indirectly, to the proliferation of nuclear weapons. **Structure** Plenary Meeting; Troika; Consultative Group; Information Exchange Meeting; Licensing and Enforcement Experts Meeting; Technical Experts Group; Point of Contact. **Activities** Standard/guidelines; politics/policy/regulatory; events/meetings. **Events** *Plenary Meeting* Jurmala (Latvia) 2018, *Plenary Meeting* Bern (Switzerland) 2017, *Plenary Meeting* Seoul (Korea Rep) 2016, *Plenary Meeting* Bariloche (Argentina) 2015, *Plenary Meeting* Buenos Aires (Argentina) 2014.
Members Governments of 48 countries:
Argentina, Australia, Austria, Belarus, Belgium, Brazil, Bulgaria, Canada, China, Croatia, Cyprus, Czechia, Denmark, Estonia, Finland, France, Germany, Greece, Hungary, Iceland, Ireland, Italy, Japan, Kazakhstan, Korea Rep, Latvia, Lithuania, Luxembourg, Malta, Mexico, Netherlands, New Zealand, Norway, Poland, Portugal, Romania, Russia, Serbia, Slovakia, Slovenia, South Africa, Spain, Sweden, Switzerland, Türkiye, UK, Ukraine, USA.
Observers (2):
Chair of ; *European Commission (EC, #06633)*.
IGO Relations *Australia Group (AG, #03036)*; *International Atomic Energy Agency (IAEA, #12294)*; *Missile Technology Control Regime (MTCR, #16826)*; *Wassenaar Arrangement on Export Controls for Conventional Arms and Dual-Use Goods and Technologies (Wassenaar Arrangement, #20819)*. [2021/XF5062/**F***]

♦ Nuclear Suppliers Guidelines / see Nuclear Suppliers Group (#17621)

♦ Nuclear Threat Initiative (NTI) 17622

CEO 1776 Eye Street, NW, Suite 600, Washington DC 20006, USA. T. +12022964810. Fax +12022964811. E-mail: contact@nti.org.
URL: http://www.nti.org/

History 2001, USA. Founded by Ted Turner and Sam Nunn. **Aims** Reduce the *risks* from nuclear, biological and chemical *weapons*. **Structure** Board of Directors. **Events** *Nuclear Knowledge Summit* Amsterdam (Netherlands) 2014, *International conference on nuclear disarmament* Oslo (Norway) 2008. **NGO Relations** Partner of (1): *International Partnership for Nuclear Disarmament Verification (IPNDV)*. Supports (2): *Asia-Pacific Leadership Network for Nuclear Non-Proliferation and Disarmament (APLN, #01943)*; *World Institute for Nuclear Security (WINS, #21588)*. [2020/XM8173/**F**]

♦ Núcleo de Pesquisa sobre Governança Global (internationally oriented national body)

♦ NucNet 17623

Pres Av des Arts 56 – 2nd Floor C, 1000 Brussels, Belgium. T. +3225053055. Fax +3225023902. E-mail: info@nucnet.org.
URL: http://www.nucnet.org/

History 1991. Founded within the framework of *European Nuclear Society (ENS, #08059)*. Independent since Jan 2000. **Aims** Function as an independent nuclear *news* agency, provider of information about nuclear energy, and a communications network for the *nuclear energy* industry. **Structure** Board; Central Office in Brussels (Belgium). **Languages** English, French. **Staff** 2.00 FTE, paid; 0.50 FTE, voluntary. **Finance** Sources: contributions; subscriptions. **Activities** Events/meetings; knowledge management/information dissemination; networking/liaising; publishing activities. Active in all member countries. **Publications** News (daily); newsletters; reports; interviews.
Members Nuclear executives, public communicators, consultants and journalists in 44 countries and territories:
Argentina, Armenia, Australia, Austria, Belarus, Belgium, Brazil, Bulgaria, Canada, Croatia, Czechia, Denmark, Finland, France, Germany, Hong Kong, Hungary, Israel, Italy, Japan, Jordan, Kazakhstan, Korea Rep, Lithuania, Mexico, Netherlands, Norway, Poland, Romania, Russia, Slovakia, Slovenia, South Africa, Spain, Sweden, Switzerland, Taiwan, Thailand, Türkiye, UK, Ukraine, United Arab Emirates, USA, Vietnam. [2021.08.31/XK1515/v/**F**]

♦ **NUDA** Nordic Urban Design Association (#17459)
♦ Nuestro Mundo No Esta en Venta (#17917)
♦ Nuestros Pequeños Hermanos (internationally oriented national body)
♦ Nuestros Pequeños Hermanos y Hermanas Internacional / see Nuestros Pequeños Hermanos
♦ Nueva Asociación Mundial para la Formación Hotelera y Turistica / see World Association for Hospitality and Tourism Education and Training (#21144)
♦ Nuevos Derechos del Hombre (#17089)
♦ NuFACT – International Workshop on Neutrinos from Accelerators (meeting series)
♦ NUFFIC – Nederlandse Organisatie voor Internationale Samenwerking in het Hoger Onderwijs (internationally oriented national body)
♦ Nuffield Centre for International Health and Development (internationally oriented national body)
♦ Nuffield Foundation (internationally oriented national body)

♦ Nuffield International – Nuffield Farming Scholarships Trust 17624

Sec PO Box 586, Moama NSW 2731, Australia. T. +61354800755. Fax +61354800233.
UK Office Blaston Lodge, Blaston, Market Harborough, LE16 8DB, UK.
URL: http://www.nuffieldinternational.org/

Events *Triennial conference* Adelaide, SA (Australia) 2011, *Triennial Conference* Australia 2011, *Triennial conference* Perth, WA (Australia) 2011, *Triennial Conference* Ireland 2008, *Triennial Conference* New Zealand 2005. **Consultative Status** Consultative status granted from: *UNEP (#20299)*. **NGO Relations** Member of (1): *International Agri-Food Network (IAFN, #11599)*. [2016/XM3997/**F**]

♦ **NUF** Nordisk Urologisk Förening (#19080)
♦ **NUGA** Nordic Urogynecological Association (#17461)
♦ **NUGENIA** Nuclear Generation II and III Association (#17618)
♦ **NuGO** European Nutrigenomics Organisation (#08068)
♦ NUH – Nordiskt Utvecklingscenter för Handikapphjälpmedel (inactive)
♦ **NU HRCT** Nordic Union Hotels, Restaurants, Catering and Tourism (#17454)
♦ **NUHRCT** Nordisk Union Hotel, Restauration, Catering Og Turisme (#17454)
♦ **NUK** Nordiska Ungdomskommittén (#17235)

♦ Number Resource Organization (NRO) 17625

Secretariat address not obtained. E-mail: secretariat@nro.net.
URL: http://www.nro.net/

History 24 Oct 2003, when *RIPE Network Coordination Centre (RIPE NCC, #18951)*, American Registry for Internet Numbers (ARIN), *Asian-Pacific Network Information Centre (APNIC)* and *Latin American and Caribbean Internet Address Registry (LACNIC, #16281)* signed a Memorandum of Understanding. *AFRINIC (#00533)* signed Memorandum of Understanding, 2004. **Aims** Protect the unallocated *Internet* number resource pool; promote and protect the bottom-up policy development process; act as a focal point for Internet community input into the RIR system. **Structure** Executive Council. **NGO Relations** Member of: *International Governance Forum Support Association (IGFSA, #13730)*. [2019/XJ0471/**E**]

♦ Número Internacional Normalizado para Libros / see International ISBN Agency (#13955)
♦ Numéro normalisé international du livre / see International ISBN Agency (#13955)
♦ NUMISHEET – International Conference and Workshop on Numerical Simulation of 3D Sheet Metal Forming Processes (meeting series)
♦ NUMOV – Nah- un Mittelost-Verein (internationally oriented national body)
♦ NUMU – Nordisk Union for Musikutbildare (no recent information)
♦ Nunani Avannarlerni Oqaatsinut Siunnersuisut (inactive)
♦ Nunani Avannarlerni Piorsarsimassutsikkut Attaveqaat (internationally oriented national body)
♦ Nunanut Avannarlernut Killernut Tunngatitamik Nunat Avannarliit Ineriartortitsinermut Aninggaas-aateqarfiannik (#20926)
♦ Nunat Avannarliit Killiit Siunnersuisoqatigiiffiata (#20925)
♦ **NU** Nordisk Udlaendingeudvalg (#17315)
♦ Nuorten Pohjoismaiden Neuvosto (#17474)
♦ Nuovi Diritti dell' Uomo – Internazionale (#17089)
♦ **NuPECC** Nuclear Physics European Collaboration Committee (#17620)
♦ NUPI – Norsk Utenrikspolitisk Institutt (internationally oriented national body)
♦ **NUREC** Network on Urban Research in the European Union (#17062)
♦ Nuremberg Academy – International Nuremberg Principles Academy (internationally oriented national body)
♦ Nurses for Africa (internationally oriented national body)
♦ Nurses' Association of the American College of Obstetricians and Gynecologists / see Association of Women's Health, Obstetric and Neonatal Nurses

♦ Nurses Christian Fellowship International (NCFI) 17626

Pres address not obtained.
Contact address not obtained.
URL: http://www.ncfi.org/

History 1957. Former names and other names: *NCF International* – former. Registration: Chairty Commission, No/ID: 258396, England and Wales; No/ID: 20131016427, Start date: 2013, USA, Colorado. **Aims** Encourage Christian nurses to integrate Biblical principles and Christ-centred values within clinical practice, leadership, education and research. **Structure** International Board; Executive Committee; Regional Committees (6). Includes: *International Institute of Christian Nursing (IICN)*. **Languages** English, Spanish. **Staff** 1.00 FTE, paid. **Finance** Sources: donations. **Activities** Events/meetings; networking/liaising. **Events** *Quadrennial International Conference* Lakewood, CO (USA) 2021, *Quadrennial International Conference* Denver, CO (USA) 2020, *International Nursing and Midwifery Student Conference in Spiritual Care* Copenhagen (Denmark) 2017, *Quadrennial International Conference* Tagaytay (Philippines) 2016, *International Nursing and Midwifery Student Conference in Spiritual Care* Oslo (Norway) 2015. **Publications** *Prayer Guide* (3 a year); *Christian Nurse International* (2 a year); *NCFI Cares* (24 a year); *NCFI News* (2-3 a year).
Members Full: individuals in 32 countries and territories:
Argentina, Australia, Bangladesh, Canada, Chile, Colombia, Cuba, Denmark, Ecuador, Fiji, Finland, Germany, Ghana, Haiti, Hong Kong, India, Indonesia, Japan, Korea Rep, Malaysia, Nepal, Nigeria, Norway, Pakistan, Papua New Guinea, Philippines, Singapore, Spain, Taiwan, UK, USA, Zambia. [2021.08.12/XF0733/**C**]

♦ Nuru International (internationally oriented national body)
♦ NUSACC – National US-Arab Chamber of Commerce (internationally oriented national body)
♦ NUS Global Asia Institute (internationally oriented national body)
♦ **NUS** Det Nordiska Universitetssamarbetet (#17458)
♦ Nutrition and Education International (internationally oriented national body)

♦ Nutrition International 17627

Dir 180 Elgin Street, Ste 1000, Ottawa ON K2P 2K3, Canada. T. +16137826800. Fax +16137826838. E-mail: info@nutritionintl.org.
Communications Officer address not obtained. T. +16137826808.
URL: http://www.micronutrient.org/

History Founded 1992, by: *Canadian International Development Agency (CIDA, inactive)*; *International Bank for Reconstruction and Development (IBRD, #12317)* (World Bank); *International Development Research Centre (IDRC, #13162)*; *UNDP (#20292)*; *UNICEF (#20332)*. Until 2001, operated within IDRC. Original title: *Micronutrient Initiative (MI) – Initiative pour les micronutriments – Iniciativa de Micronutrientes*. Previously also referred to in French and Spanish as *Initiative pour les micronutrients – Iniciativa para los Micronutrientes*. Current title adopted, Apr 2017. **Aims** Transform the lives of vulnerable people, especially women, adolescent girls and children, by improving their nutritional status. **Structure** Board of Directors; Executive Management Committee. Head Office in Ottawa ON (Canada); Regional Offices in Nairobi (Kenya) and Delhi (India). **Languages** English, French, Spanish. **Staff** 140.00 FTE, paid. **Finance** Funded by various donors and funding agencies in addition to government departments such as Canadian Department of Foreign Affairs, Trade and Development (DFATD). **Activities** Guidance/assistance/consulting; capacity building. Active in over 70 countries. **Events** *Congress on information technology in the advancement of nutrition in Africa* Nairobi (Kenya) 2002. **Publications** *Investigating VM Deficiency – A Challenge to Media Professionals*; *Investing in the future: A united call to action on vitamin and mineral deficiencies* in English, French; *Summary Report: Investing in the future: A united call to action on vitamin and mineral deficiencies* in Chinese, English, French; *Vitamin and Mineral Deficiency – A Challenge to the World's Food Companies*; *Vitamin and Mineral Deficiency: A global damage assessment report*; *Vitamin and Mineral Deficiency – A Global Progress Report* in English, French, Spanish; *Vitamin and Mineral Deficiency – A Partnership Drive to End Hidden Hunger in Sub-Saharan Africa*.
Members Not a membership organization. **Consultative Status** Consultative status granted from: *WHO (#20950)* (Official). **IGO Relations** Cooperates with: *Asian Development Bank (ADB, #01422)*; *Inter-American Development Bank (IDB, #11427)*; *International Bank for Reconstruction and Development (IBRD, #12317)* (World Bank); *ICDDR,B (#11051)*; *UNICEF (#20332)*; *United States Agency for International Development (USAID)*; *United States Agency for International Development (USAID)*; *World Food Programme (WFP, #21510)*. **NGO Relations** Member of (1): *Food Fortification Initiative (FFI, #09844)*. Cooperates with: *CARE International (CI, #03429)*; *Christian Blind Mission (CBM)*; Centers for Disease Control and Prevention; *Global Alliance for Improved Nutrition (GAIN, #10202)*; *Helen Keller International (HKI, #10902)*; *Iodine Global Network (IGN, #16004)*; national, regional and local governments; *Oxfam International (#17922)*; *PMNCH (#18410)*. Partner of: *1,000 Days*; *Every Woman Every Child (EWEC, #09215)*. [2019/XF4004/**F**]

♦ Nutrition Third World (internationally oriented national body)
♦ Nutrition Tiers-Monde (internationally oriented national body)
♦ **NUU** Nordisk Ungkonservativ Union (#17473)
♦ NVAS – Nederlandse Vereniging voor Afrika Studies (internationally oriented national body)
♦ **NVC** Nordens välfärdscenter (#17163)
♦ **NVDA** Network for Voluntary Development in Asia (#17063)
♦ NVF – New Venture Fund (internationally oriented national body)
♦ **NVF** Nordiskt Vägforum (#17402)
♦ **NVF** Nordisk Vegforum (#17402)

- ♦ **NVF** Nordisk Vejforum (#17402)
- ♦ NVI – New Vision International (internationally oriented national body)
- ♦ NVI / see Nordic Volcanological Center (#17463)
- ♦ **NVL** Nordiskt Nätverk för Vuxnas Lärande (#17349)
- ♦ **NV** Nordvision (#17446)
- ♦ NVOF – Nordiska Vandrarhemsorganisationernas Förbund (no recent information)
- ♦ **NVSA** Nematologiese Vereniging van Suidelike Afrika (#16971)
- ♦ NWAP-AP – New Ways of Analyzing Variation – Asia Pacific (meeting series)
- ♦ NWBC – Nordic Wood Biorefinery Conference (meeting series)
- ♦ NWB – Nordic Workshop on Bibliometrics and Research Policy (meeting series)
- ♦ NWC – Naija Worldwide Charities (internationally oriented national body)
- ♦ NWFE – New Women for Europe (unconfirmed)
- ♦ NWG on the ADB / see NGO Forum on ADB (#17123)
- ♦ NWHO – New World Hope Organization (internationally oriented national body)
- ♦ NWLC – Nordic Working Life Conference (meeting series)
- ♦ NWMN – New Wineskins Missionary Network (internationally oriented national body)
- ♦ **NWM** Nordic Women Mediators (#17468)
- ♦ NWMTI / see Medical Teams International
- ♦ **NWO EECCA** Regional Network of Water-Basin – Organizations from Eastern Europe, Caucasus and Central Asia (#18803)
- ♦ **NWPC** Nordic Wood Preservation Council (#17469)
- ♦ **NWS** Nordic Wittgenstein Society (#17466)
- ♦ **NWWAC** North Western Waters Advisory Council (#17607)
- ♦ NYASA – New York African Studies Association (internationally oriented national body)
- ♦ **NYC** Nordic Youth Council (#17474)
- ♦ **NYCU** Nordic Young Conservative Union (#17473)
- ♦ Nyéléni Europe / see European Food Sovereignty Movement (#07288)
- ♦ **NYELENI** European Food Sovereignty Movement (#07288)
- ♦ NYF – Nordic Youth Foundation (inactive)
- ♦ **NYL** Pohjola Norden Yhdistysten Liitto (#09859)
- ♦ **NYNGOC** New York NGO Committee on Drugs (#17097)
- ♦ **NYNNeS** Network for Young Nordic Neutron Scatterers (#17066)
- ♦ Nyon Arrangement (1937 treaty)
- ♦ **NYRA** Network for Young Researchers in Andrology (#17067)
- ♦ Nyresykes Nordiske Samarbeidsudvalg (inactive)
- ♦ NYRI – Nordic Youth Research Information (inactive)
- ♦ NZAID / see New Zealand Ministry of Foreign Affairs and Trade – New Zealand Aid Programme
- ♦ NZC – Nansen-Zhu International Research Centre (internationally oriented national body)
- ♦ NZE / see Coalition of the Flemish North South Movement – 11 11 11
- ♦ NZIIA – New Zealand Institute of International Affairs (internationally oriented national body)
- ♦ O2BiP – International Conference on Oxygen Binding and Sensing Proteins (meeting series)

♦ O2 Global Network (O2GN) 17628

Address not obtained.
URL: http://www.o2.org/

History 1988. Foundation set up in 1994 as an independent organization. Previously active as *O2 International*. Also referred to as *International Network for Sustainable Design*. **Aims** Promote *ecodesign*, sustainable design and design for sustainability worldwide; inform, inspire and connect people interested in sustainable design. **Structure** Foundation; Regional Hubs (Europe; India; Nordic; Switzerland; UK; USA); Local Groups; Liaisons. Board, comprising Chair, Vice-Chair and a member. **Languages** English. **Staff** 3.00 FTE, paid. **Finance** Donations. **Activities** Organizes O2 Events, meetings, lectures, green drinks, etc. **Publications** *O2 Magazine*.
Members Groups in 8 countries:
Croatia, Finland, France, Japan, Netherlands, Spain, Sweden, USA.
Liaisons (over 75) in 51 countries. Membership countries not specified. [2014.01.02/XN9640/**F**]

- ♦ **O2GN** O2 Global Network (#17628)
- ♦ O2 International / see O2 Global Network (#17628)
- ♦ O2inWines – International Association of Oxygen Management in Wine (inactive)
- ♦ O2 – Ocean Outcomes (internationally oriented national body)
- ♦ OAAA / see Oceania Athletics Association (#17651)
- ♦ OAA / see Association of Asia Pacific Airlines (#02385)
- ♦ **OAA** Oceania Athletics Association (#17651)
- ♦ **OAA** Organisation des assurances africaines (#00343)
- ♦ **OAA** Ostomy Association of the Americas (#17912)
- ♦ OAB – Organisation africaine du bois (no recent information)
- ♦ OAC / see Archives nationales d'Outre mer
- ♦ OACI – Open Air Campaigners International (internationally oriented national body)
- ♦ **OACI** Organisation de l'aviation civile internationale (#12581)
- ♦ **OACI** Organización de Aviación Civil Internacional (#12581)
- ♦ OAC – Oceania Archery Confederation (inactive)
- ♦ **OACPS** Organisation of African, Caribbean and Pacific States (#17796)
- ♦ OACT – Organisation africaine de cartographie et de télédétection (inactive)
- ♦ ÖAD / see Österreichische Austauschdienst
- ♦ ÖAD – Agentur für Internationale Bildungs- und Wissenschaftskooperation / see Österreichische Austauschdienst
- ♦ **OADA** Organisation arabe pour le développement administratif (#00893)
- ♦ OADI – Organisation arabe pour le développement industriel (inactive)
- ♦ OAD – Ordo Augustiniensium Discalceatorum (religious order)
- ♦ OADS – Organisation arabe de défense sociale contre le crime (inactive)
- ♦ OAFA – Organisation africaine des femmes autochtones (no recent information)
- ♦ **OAFCN** OLAF Anti-Fraud Communicators Network (#17714)
- ♦ **OAFCN** OLAF-Netz von Kommunikationsbeauftragten im Bereich der Betrugsbekämpfung (#17714)
- ♦ **OAFLAD** Organization of African First Ladies for Development (#17852)
- ♦ OAFLA / see Organization of African First Ladies for Development (#17852)
- ♦ OAFRESS – Organisation d'Afrique francophone pour le Renforcement des Systèmes de Santé et de la Vaccination (unconfirmed)
- ♦ **OAGS** Organisation of African Geological Surveys (#17797)
- ♦ **OAIC** Organization of African Instituted Churches (#17853)
- ♦ OAIM – Organisme arabe pour l'industrialisation militaire (inactive)
- ♦ OAI – Ocean Arks International (internationally oriented national body)
- ♦ Oak Foundation (internationally oriented national body)
- ♦ **OALY** African Liberal Youth (#00362)
- ♦ OALY-LEAD / see African Liberal Youth (#00362)
- ♦ OAMCAF – Organisation africaine et malgache du café (no recent information)
- ♦ OAMI / see European Union Intellectual Property Office (#08996)
- ♦ OAM – Organización Africana de la Madera (no recent information)
- ♦ **OANA** Organization of Asian-Pacific News Agencies (#17855)
- ♦ OA – Oblate Sisters of the Assumption (religious order)
- ♦ OA – Opus Sanctorum Angelorum (religious order)
- ♦ **OA** Overeaters Anonymous (#17919)
- ♦ OAPEC Judicial Tribunal – Judicial Tribunal of the Organization of Arab Petroleum Exporting Countries (see: #17854)
- ♦ **OAPEC** Organization of Arab Petroleum Exporting Countries (#17854)
- ♦ **OAPEN** Open Access Publishing in European Networks (#17746)
- ♦ **OAPI** Organisation africaine de la propriété intellectuelle (#00344)
- ♦ OAPI – Organización de Asociaciones de Periodistas Iberoamericanos (no recent information)
- ♦ **OAREC** Organisation africaine pour la recherche et l'enseignement sur le cancer (#00405)
- ♦ OARM – Organisation arabe des ressources minières (inactive)
- ♦ OAR – Ordo Augustinianorum Recollectorum (religious order)
- ♦ **OARSI** Osteoarthritis Research Society International (#17906)
- ♦ OASA / see Arab Administrative Development Organization (#00893)
- ♦ OASAC – Orthopedic Association of SAARC Countries (unconfirmed)
- ♦ Oasis Global (internationally oriented national body)
- ♦ Oasis International Association / see Oasis Global
- ♦ OASIS – Organization for the Advancement of Structured Information Standards (internationally oriented national body)
- ♦ OASMMECA – Organisation africaine des syndicats des mines, métaux, energie, chimie et assimilés (no recent information)

♦ OAS – Organization of American States 17629

Organisation des Etats Américains (OEA) – Organización de los Estados Americanos (OEA) – Organização dos Estados Americanos (OEA)

SG 17th Street and Constitution Ave NW, Washington DC 20006-4499, USA. T. +12023705000. Fax +12024583967.
URL: http://www.oas.org/

History 14 Apr 1890, Washington, DC (USA). Since established, April 14 has been celebrated as *Pan-American Day*. The original purpose of the Union was to ensure prompt collection and distribution of commercial information through its central office, the *Commercial Bureau of the American Republics – Bureau commercial des républiques américaines – Oficina Comercial de la Repúblicas Americanas*, in Washington DC. The 2nd International Conference of American States, 1901, Mexico City (Mexico), adopted the Protocol of Adherence of the American Republics to the conventions framed by the First Hague Peace Conference, 1899, while the name of the Commercial Bureau was changed to *International Commercial Bureau – Bureau commercial international – Oficina Comercial Internacional*. The 3rd International Conference of American States, 1906, Rio de Janeiro (Brazil), expanded the duties of the Bureau to include educational matters. At the 4th International Conference of American States, 1910, Buenos Aires (Argentina), the name of the International Commercial Bureau to *Pan American Union (PAU) – Union panaméricaine (UPA) – Unión Panamericana (UPA)*. The 5th International Conference of American States, 1923, Santiago (Chile), formalized a technique for the pacific settlement of disputes in the *Treaty to Avoid or Prevent Conflicts between the American States (Gondra Treaty, 1923)*. It also approved a resolution leading to the founding of the *Pan American Highway System (#18109)*. The International Conference of American States on Conciliation and Arbitration (a special conference), 1929, Washington DC, further strengthened the principles of arbitration and conciliation with the signing of the *General Treaty of Inter-American Arbitration (1929)* and the *General Convention of Inter-American Conciliation (1929)*. The 7th International Conference of American States, 1933, Montevideo (Uruguay), adopted the *Convention on Rights and Duties of States (1933)*, establishing the equality of states and the principle that no state has the right to intervene in the internal affairs of another. At the Inter-American Conference for Maintenance of Peace (a special conference) 1936, Buenos Aires, conventions were adopted incorporating the principle of consultation for the pacific settlement of controversies and in the event of an international war outside America that might menace the peace of the American republics. Subsequently, 3 meetings were called to devise strategy for the defence of the Western Hemisphere during World War II: 1939, Panama; 1940, Havana (Cuba); 1942, Rio de Janeiro.

Through the *Act of Chapultepec – Acta de Chapultepec*, adopted by the Inter-American Conference on the Problems of War and Peace (a special conference), 1945, Mexico City, the system of consultation was broadened; likewise, a resolution was adopted that declared in part that 'the security and solidarity of the Continent are affected to the same extent by an act of aggression against any of the American states by a non-American state, as by an act of aggression of an American state against one or more American states', and that such aggression against one or more of them would be considered aggression against them all. The meeting also created the Inter-American Economic and Social Council (CIES), superseding *Inter-American Financial and Economic Advisory Committee (inactive)*. CIES is itself currently replaced by the Inter-American Council for Integral Development (CIDI). The Inter American Conference for the Maintenance of Continental Peace and Security (a special conference), 1947, Rio de Janeiro, put into effect permanently the provisions of the Act of Chapultepec through the drawing up of the *Inter-American Treaty of Reciprocal Assistance (Rio Treaty, 1947)*. The Treaty defines the principal obligations of the signatories in the event of armed attacks against an American state or acts of aggression short of armed attack; a security zone in which the treaty is operative was drawn and the Organ of Consultation was created.

The 9th International Conference of American States, 1948, Bogota, adopted the *Charter of the Organization of American States (1948)*, and the Union of American Republics changed its name to Organization of American States, although the General Secretariat of the OAS continued to be called the Pan American Union. The International Conference of American States was renamed *Inter-American Conference – Conférence interaméricaine – Conferencia Interamericana*. The 1948 Conference also approved: *American Treaty on Pacific Settlement (Pact of Bogota, 1948)*; *American Declaration of the Rights and Duties of Man – Déclaration américaine des droits et devoirs de l'homme – Declaración Americana de los Derechos y Deberes del Hombre*; Economic Agreement of Bogota; the setting up of *Committee on Inter-American Organizations*, which studied clauses of the OAS Charter and resolutions approved by the 9th Conference with relation to Inter-American Organizations – *'Specialized Organizations'* and other entities. The 10th Inter-American Conference, 1954, Caracas (Venezuela), changed the direction and orientation of the policies and programs of the OAS by emphasizing economic, social, and cultural development. The 7th Meeting of Consultation (under the Charter), 1960, San José (Costa Rica), adopted the *Declaration of San José – Declaración de San José* that denounced all types of intervention that could endanger American solidarity. The Act of Bogota set forth measures for the social improvement and economic development of the countries within the framework of *Operation Pan America – Opération Panaméricaine – Operación Panamericana*, and laid the foundation of the *Alliance for Progress – Alliance pour le progrès – Alianza para el Progreso*. The Alliance for Progress became a reality when OAS adopted the *Charter of Punta del Este (1961)* and the *Declaration to the Peoples of America – Déclaration aux peuples d'Amérique – Declaración a los Pueblos de América*.

The 8th Meeting of Consultation (under the Rio Treaty), 1962, Punta del Este (Uruguay), approved a resolution excluding the Government of Cuba from participation in the inter-American system. The First Special Inter-American Conference, 1964, Washington DC, approved the Act of Washington that sets guidelines for the admission of new members to the Organization. The 10th Meeting of Consultation (under the Charter), 1965, Washington DC, considered the 'serious situation created by armed strife in the Dominican Republic' and created an *Inter-American Peace Force (inactive)* for that occasion. The 3rd Special Inter-American Conference, 1967, Buenos Aires, approved the Protocol of Amendments to the Charter of the OAS, known as Protocol of Buenos Aires. At a Meeting of American Chiefs of State, 1967, Punta del Este (Uruguay), the Declaration of the Presidents of America was signed, spelling out the means for the American nations to intensify inter-American cooperation. The OAS Charter, as amended by the Protocol of Buenos Aires, entered into force on 27 Feb 1970, providing the Organization with a new structure. The General Assembly replaced the Inter-American Conference and the functions previously carried out by *Inter-American Peace Committee (inactive)* were assigned to the Permanent Council of OAS, assisted by *Inter-American Committee on Peaceful Settlement (inactive)*. The first meeting of the General Assembly was held in 1971, San José, under the terms of the Charter as amended. At its 3rd regular session, 1973, Washington DC, the General Assembly created a Special Committee for the purpose of restructuring the inter-American system so that it might respond adequately to changing hemisphere and world conditions.

Treaty Concerning the Permanent Neutrality and Operation of the Panama Canal (Panama Canal Treaty, 1977) and *Protocol to the Treaty Concerning the Permanent Neutrality and Operation of the Panama Canal, 1977 (1977)*, which were signed at the OAS, entered into force on 1 Oct 1979. The *Inter-American Convention on Extradition (1981)* was approved in 1981. In its 12th regular session, 1982, Washington DC, the General Assembly ratified 24 Jul 1982 through 24 Jul 1983 as the Bicentennial Year of the Birth of the Liberator Simón Bolivar, February 18 was declared the *Day of the Women of the Americas*. 1986 was declared as the 'Inter-American Year of Peace'. At its 14th Special Session, 5 Dec 1985, Cartagena de Indias (Colombia), the General Assembly approved the *Protocol of Amendment to the Charter of the Organization of American States (Protocol of Cartagena de Indias, 1985)*, which entered into force 16 Nov 1988.

At its 21st Regular Session, Jun 1991, Santiago de Chile, the OAS General Assembly adopted the *'Santiago Commitment to Democracy and the Renewal of the Inter-American System'*, in which member states declared, among other things, their 'inescapable commitment to the defence and promotion of representative democracy and human rights in the region, within the framework of respect for the principles of self-determination and non-intervention'. At the same meeting, the General Assembly approved a resolution on *'Representative Democracy'* (AG/RES 1080), instructing OAS Secretary General to call for immediate convocation of a meeting of the Permanent Council in the event of any occurrence giving rise to sudden or irregular interruption of the democratic political institutional process or of the legitimate exercise of power by the democratically elected government in any OAS member state.
'Charter Reform': At its 16th Special Session, 14 Dec 1992, OAS General Assembly adopted the 'Protocol of Washington' containing amendments to the OAS Charter principally to incorporate provisions of AG/RES 1080 on Representative Democracy. New Article 8 bis provides that a member whose democratically elected government has been overthrown by force may be suspended from exercising the right to participate in sessions of OAS organs. Also, the eradication of extreme poverty is incorporated among essential purposes of the Organization.
At its 19th Special Session, 8 Jun 1993 in Managua (Nicaragua), the General Assembly approved the 'Protocol of Managua' of Amendments to the Charter of the Organization. The Managua Protocol entered into force on 29 Jan 1996, when ratified by two-thirds of OAS member states. It gives new impetus and approach to the promotion of cooperation in the Americas aimed at achieving integral development and eliminating extreme poverty in the Hemisphere. Under the Protocol, the Councils on Economic and Social Affairs and Education, Science and Culture are replaced by the CIDI, and other measures taken to improve the delivery of technical cooperation to the member states. Former names and other names: *International Union of American Republics* – former (1890 to 1910); *Union internationale des républiques américaines* – former (1890 to 1910); *Unión Internacional de las Repúblicas Americanas* – former (1890 to 1910); *Union of American Republics* – former (1910); *Union des républiques américaines* – former (1910); *Unión de las Repúblicas Americanas* – former (1910).
Aims Essential 'purposes':
(a) To strengthen the peace and security in the hemisphere;
(b) To promote and consolidate representative democracy, with due respect for the principle of non-intervention;
(c) To prevent possible causes of difficulties and to ensure the pacific settlement of disputes that may arise among the member states;
(d) To provide for common action on the part of those states in the event of aggression;
(e) To seek the solution of political, juridical, and economic problems that may arise among them;
(f) To promote, by cooperative action, their economic, social, and cultural development;
(g) To achieve an effective limitation of conventional weapons that will make it possible to devote the largest amount of resources to the economic and social development of the member states.
Additional purpose, approved 14 Dec 1992: To eradicate extreme poverty which constitutes an obstacle to the full democratic development of the peoples of the hemisphere.
'Principles' reaffirmed by the American States:
(a) International law is the standard of conduct of states in their reciprocal relations;
(b) International order consists essentially of respect for the personality, sovereignty, and independence of states, and the faithful fulfilment of obligations derived from treaties and other sources of international law;
(c) Good faith shall govern the relations between states;
(d) The solidarity of the American States and the high aims which are sought through it require the political organization of those states on the basis of the effective exercise of representative democracy;
(e) Every state has the right to choose, without external interference, its political, economic, and social system and to organize itself in the way best suited to it, and has the duty to abstain from intervening in the affairs of another state. Subject to the foregoing, the American States shall cooperate fully among themselves, independently of the nature of their political, economic, and social systems;
(f) The American States condemn war of aggression: victory does not give rights;
(g) An act of aggression against one American State is an act of aggression against all the other American States;
(h) Controversies of an international character arising between two or more American States shall be settled by peaceful procedures;
(i) Social justice and social security are bases of lasting peace;
(j) Economic cooperation is essential to the common welfare and prosperity of the peoples of the continent;
(k) The American States proclaim the fundamental rights of the individual without distinction as to race, nationality, creed, or sex;
(l) The spiritual unity of the continent is based on respect for the cultural values of the American countries and requires their close cooperation for the high purposes of civilization;
(m) The education of peoples should be directed toward justice, freedom, and peace.
Additional principle incorporated 14 Dec 1992: the elimination of abject poverty as an essential part of the promotion and consolidation of representative democracy and the common and shared responsibility of the American States.
At the 20th Special Session, Feb 1994, Mexico City (Mexico), the General Assembly approved 2 resolutions, one containing a 'General Policy Framework and Priorities: Partnership for Development' and the other agreeing on a 'Commitment on a Partnership for Development and Struggle to Overcome Extreme Poverty'.
At the 24th Regular Session, Jun 1994, Belém (Brazil) the Assembly adopted the 'Declaration of Belém do Para' in which Ministers of Foreign Affairs and Heads of Delegation of Member States declared: their firm commitment to strengthening the OAS as the main hemispheric forum of political consensus so that it may support the realization of member states in promoting and consolidating peace, democracy, social justice and development in accordance with the purposes and principles of the Charter; their decision to promote and deepen cooperative relations in economic, social, educational, cultural, scientific, technological and political fields; their commitment to continue and further dialogue on hemispheric security so as to consolidate and strengthen mutual confidence; their determination to continue contributing to the objective of general and complete disarmament under effective international control; their determination to strengthen regional cooperation to increase effectiveness of efforts to combat illicit use of narcotic drugs and traffic therein; their decision to cooperate in a reciprocal effort towards preventing and punishing terrorist acts, methods and practices, and development of international law in this matter; and their commitment to promote economic and social development for indigenous populations of their countries.
Structure *'General Assembly'*, the supreme organ, meets in regular annual session either in a member state or at headquarters. Special sessions may be convoked by the Permanent Council with the approval of two thirds of the member states. *Summit of the Americas* – Summit process, started 1994, is administered by *'Special Committee on Inter-American Summits Management'* and implementation of decisions monitored by *Summit Implementation Review Group (SIRG)*. *'Meeting of Consultation of Ministers of Foreign Affairs'* may be convoked either under OAS Charter to consider problems of an urgent nature of common interest to the American States, or under the Inter-American Treaty of Reciprocal Assistance to serve as Organ of Consultation in cases of armed attack or other threat to international peace and security. Meetings of Consultation may be assisted by an *'Advisory Defense Committee'*, composed of the highest military authorities of the American states.
Councils directly responsible to the General Assembly:
– *'Permanent Council'* comprises one representative of ambassadorial rank for each member state, appointed by the respective government and: takes cognizance of any matter referred to it by the General Assembly or the Meeting of Consultation of Ministers of Foreign Affairs; serves provisionally as the Organ of Consultation; keeps vigilance over the maintenance of friendly relations among member states and assists them in peaceful settlement of their disputes, for which purpose it may establish 'ad hoc' committees with membership and mandate agreed in each individual case with the consent of the parties to the dispute; acts as the Preparatory Committee of the General Assembly.
– *Inter-American Council for Integral Development (#11423)*, created 29 Jan 1996, on ratification of the Protocol of Managua (Nicaragua), replacing *Inter-American Economic and Social Council (IA-ECOSOC, inactive)* and *Inter-American Council for Education, Science and Culture (inactive)*, is the structure for implementing policies and programs to comply with the Protocol's objectives on promoting cooperation for achieving integral development and eliminating extreme poverty. CIDI includes *Inter-American Agency for Cooperation and Development (IACD, #11397)*.

Inter-American Juridical Committee (IAJC, see: #17629) – permanent headquarters in Rio de Janeiro (Brazil) – is the principal advisory juridical organ of the OAS, replacing *Inter-American Council of Jurists (inactive)*, set up by the 1948 Charter. It is composed of 11 jurists, nationals of member states, elected by OAS General Assembly for a 4-year term from candidates presented by these states and includes working groups on representative democracy, on probity and public ethics and to prepare the *'Draft American Declaration on the Rights of Indigenous Peoples'*. It holds meetings, organizes courses and seminars and undertakes studies.
Inter-American Commission on Human Rights (IACHR, #11411), created during the 5th Meeting of Consultation of Ministers of Foreign Affairs, 1959, Santiago (Chile), comprises 7 members from OAS member states, represents all countries which are members and acts on their behalf.
Corte Interamericana de Derechos Humanos (Corte IDH, #04851), established 18 Jul 1978, on coming into force of the *Inter-American Convention on Human Rights (Pact of San José de Costa Rica, 1969)* – the *'Pacto de San José'* – is headquartered in San José (Costa Rica) and comprises 7 jurists from OAS member countries; its purpose is to apply and interpret the Convention.
'General Secretariat', OAS central and permanent organ/working arm with headquarters in Washington DC (USA), carries out programs and policies decided on by General Assembly, Meetings of Consultation of Ministers of Foreign Affairs and the Councils. It is headed by the Secretary General, assisted by the Assistant Secretary. The Secretary General or his representative may participate (without vote) in all meetings of the Organization and may bring to the attention of the General Assembly or the Permanent Council any matter which in his opinion might threaten the peace and security of the Hemisphere or the development of member states. The Secretary General is represented ex officio on Board of Trustees of the Pan American Development Foundation, with which there are close links.
'Structure of the General Secretariat':
- Office of the Secretary General;
- Office of the Chief of Staff;
- Department of Legal Services;
- Summits Secretariat;
- Office of Protocol;
- Office of the Assistant Secretary General;
- Secretariat to the General Assembly, the Meeting of Consultation and the Permanent Council;
- Department of Conferences and Meetings;
- Columbus Memorial Library;
- Office of the Inspector General;
- Secretariat to the Inter-American Commission of Women;
- Secretariat to the Inter-American Commission on Human Rights;
- Secretariat to the Inter-American Telecommunications Commission;
- *Inter-American Children's Institute (IACI, #11406)*;
- Secretariat for Political Affairs;
- Department of Electoral Cooperation and Observation;
- Department of Sustainable Democracy and Special Missions;
- Department of Effective Public Management;
- Secretariat for Multi Dimensional Security;
- Executive Secretariat to the Inter-American Drug Abuse Control Commission;
- Secretariat of the Inter American Committee against Terrorism;
- Department of Public Security;
- Executive Secretariat for Integral Development (SEDI);
- Department of Human Development, Education and Employment;
- Department of Economic and Social Development;
- Department of Sustainable Development;
- Secretariat for Legal Affairs;
- Department of Legal Cooperation;
- Department of International Law;
- Secretariat to the Administrative Tribunal;
- Secretariat for External Relations;
- Department of International Affairs;
- Department of Press and Communication;
- *Art Museum of the Americas, OAS (see: #17629)*;
- Secretariat for Administration and Finance;
- Department of Human Resources;
- Department of General Services;
- Department of Financial and Administrative Management Services;
- Department of Planning and Evaluation;
- Department of Information and Technology Services;
- Department of Procurement.

'Specialized Conferences' meet to deal with special technical matters or to further inter-American cooperation in given areas. Specialized Conferences have covered a wide range of subjects: agriculture, labour – *Inter-American Conference of Ministers of Labor (no recent information)*, copyrights, private international law, economics, education, highways, ports and harbours, telecommunications, health and sanitation, natural resources, statistics, travel, child welfare, children and youth affairs, indian affairs, human rights, cultural affairs, science and technology, tourism, and trade.
'Specialized Organizations' (5), with headquarters in various cities of the Western Hemisphere:
- *Pan American Health Organization (PAHO, #18108)*, set up in 1947 and its Secretariat,
- *Pan American Sanitary Bureau (PASB, #18129)*, set up in 1902 (headquarters in Washington DC);
- *Comisión Interamericana de Mujeres (CIM, #04137)*, set up in 1928 (headquarters in Washington DC);
- *Pan American Institute of Geography and History (PAIGH, #18113)*, set up in 1928 (headquarters in Mexico City);
- *Inter-American Institute for Cooperation on Agriculture (IICA, #11434)*, set up in 1942, San José (Costa Rica).

'Other Entities' – Special commissions or agencies within the OAS, with headquarters in Washington DC, collaborate with the 3 Councils, the General Secretariat and other OAS bodies to achieve objectives of common interest:
- *Inter-American Drug Abuse Control Commission (#11429)*, formed in 1986;
- *Comisión Interamericana de Telecomunicaciones (CITEL, #04138)*, established 2 May 1923, as *'Inter-American Electrical Communication Commission'*.

Linked to OAS General Assembly:
- *Inter-American Defense Board (IADB, #11425)*, established in 1942;
- *Inter-American Defense College (IADC, #11426)*.

Languages English, French, Portuguese, Spanish. **Staff** General Secretariat staff comprise about 750 salaried personnel chosen mainly from member states, with consideration given to geographic representation. Internal personnel negotiations with *OAS Staff Association (#17631)*. *Administrative Tribunal of the Organization of American States (see: #17629)*, comprising 6 members of different nationalities, is competent to consider controversies that may arise. **Finance** Main source: quotas paid by governments of member states based on ability to pay of the respective countries and their determination to contribute in an equitable manner. Other sources: General Secretariat seeks to augment the budget through increased resources and services from non-member countries, through greater cooperation among the member states themselves, and from other possible sources. Budget (annual): about $140 million.
Activities /Policy/ – Acts as a forum for consultation and negotiation of inter-American agreements on collective and national efforts towards peacekeeping, defence of human rights, promotion and protection of democracy and economic, social, scientific, educational and cultural development.
/Operations/ – Emphasis of technical assistance is on national planning, reinforced by regional, inter-American and other multilateral cooperation. Cooperation for development is based on the groundwork of earlier OAS programs. Each member government determines its requirements and presents a National Technical Cooperation Program corresponding to its country's needs, listing specific projects ranked in order of priority. The OAS Program Budget is approved by the General Assembly.
/Applications of Representative Democracy Resolution AG/RES 1080/ – The Permanent Council examines the situation, then decides on and convenes an ad hoc meeting of the Ministers of Foreign Affairs or a special session of the General Assembly, all within a 10-day period. The Resolution has so far been applied 3 times:
– 1. *'Haiti'*: Following the coup d'Etat in Haiti and expulsion of the democratically elected President, 1991, Ministers of Foreign Affairs approved 2 resolutions, calling for: (1) full restoration of the rule of law and of constitutional order and the immediate reinstatement of President Jean-Bertrand Aristide in the exercise of his legitimate authority, and recommending diplomatic isolation of those holding power in Haiti and suspension of economic, financial and commercial ties and aid and technical cooperation other than for strictly humanitarian purposes; (2) the setting up of a civilian mission to re-establish and strengthen constitutional democracy. In May 1992, an ad hoc Meeting of Foreign Ministers again condemned the disruption of the democratic system

and called for additional measures to implement the trade embargo, increase humanitarian aid and monitor the human rights situation. They charged the OAS Secretary-General to facilitate dialogue among all Haitian sectors to bring about re-establishment of institutional democracy, to seek a peaceful resolution to the crisis and to consider bringing the situation to the attention of the UN Security Council as a means of bringing about global application of the trade embargo. Following negotiations with the de facto government, a joint OAS/UN civilian mission – *International Civilian Mission to Haiti (MICIVIH, inactive)* (mandate terminated 1999) – was sent to Haiti. UN and OAS actions to restore democratic government to Haiti are continuing.
– 2. *'Peru'*: Apr 1992, following decision of President Alberto Fujimori of Peru to disband Congress and rule by decree, an ad hoc Meeting of Foreign Ministers convened immediately, approved 2 resolutions calling for restoration of constitutional government and dispatched a special mission. President Fujimori attended a session of the ad hoc Meeting, May 1992, Bahamas, when he pledged prompt return to democratic rule. The OAS subsequently sent a number representatives to monitor the election of a Constituent Congress, 22 Nov 1992. An ad hoc Meeting of Foreign Ministers, 14 Dec 1992, reaffirmed the willingness of member states to continue cooperating to strengthen democratic institutions and absolute respect for human rights in Peru, declaring it would adjourn upon installation of the Democratic Constituent Congress. This Congress was installed, 30 Dec 1992, and OAS was invited to send observers for municipal elections scheduled on 29 Jan 1993 and for the referendum on the new Constitution in October 1993.
– 3. *'Guatemala City (Guatemala)'*: 25 May 1993, following suspension of the Constitution by the President of Guatemala; the Permanent Council met immediately, convened an ad hoc Meeting of Foreign Ministers and requested the Secretary General to carry out a fact-finding mission to Guatemala with the Foreign Ministers of Nicaragua, Uruguay and Barbados and to report their findings to an ad hoc Meeting of Foreign Ministers on 3 Jun 1993, Washington DC (USA). Following that meeting the Secretary General and other members of the mission returned to Guatemala. By the next ad hoc Meeting of Foreign Ministers, 8 Jun 1003, Managua (Nicaragua), at 23rd Regular Session of the OAS General Assembly, the Constitutional Court had declared the positions of President and Vice-President of Guatemala vacant and, in accordance with the Constitution, Congress had elected Mr Ramiro De Leon Caprio as the new President of that country. On taking note of these facts the ad hoc Meeting was adjourned.
/Trade/ – *'Trade Unit of the OAS'*, created in 1995, assists OAS member countries with matters related to trade and economic integration in the Western Hemisphere, in particular, with their efforts to establish a Free Trade Area of the Americas, or FTAA. The Unit provides technical support to member governments and prepares documents for the official FTAA Negotiating Groups providing details on the status quo of economic relationships in the region. These negotiations supersede those of *OAS Special Committee on Trade (SCT, no recent information)*, set up 1993, to promote trade liberalization and economic integration among countries of the Western hemisphere. The Special Committee has not met since 1996 and is not expected to meet again before completion of FTAA in 2005. In collaboration with a committee of donor institutions, headed by the Inter American Development Bank, an estimated US$ 7 million is being spent in 2003 on non-refundable cooperation in trade-related capacity building and sustainable development projects in Central America so as to enhance trade and improve the long-term economic well-being and development of the region as its countries embark on negotiation of *US-Central American Free Trade Agreement (CAFTA, 2004)*. OAS assistance is channelled through the Trade Unit, Inter-American Agency for Cooperation and Development (IACD) and other subsidiary bodies, and through specialized organizations.
/Institution-building and Training Activities/ – OAS has created and strengthened national and regional research institutes and educational centres. *Inter-American Program for Education (no recent information)* also includes: fellowship program and provision of expertise and equipment for a variety of projects throughout member states; *'Hemispheric Action Plan to Reduce Disasters in the Educational Sector'*. OAS Social Development and Education Unit serves as technical secretariat for the *'EDSAT-Americas Project'* of *National Education Telecommunications Organization – EDSAT Institute (NETO/EDSAT)*, which uses satellite and land technology to create a distance-education infrastructure. *Common Market of Scientific and Technological Knowledge (MERCOCYT Program, no recent information)* promotes joint use of existing resources in science in Latin American countries. Instrumental in setting up: *Red de Centros de Documentación de Literatura Infantil y Juvenil (CEDOC-LI, see: #17629)*.
/Other OAS Activities/ -
- *OAS Committee on Hemispheric Security* – first meeting Sep 2000, covers: small and light arms; confidence- and security-building measures; special security concerns of small island states and defense policies and practice; anti-personnel landmines; arms control; relations with other international and regional organizations and fora.
- *Inter-American Committee Against Terrorism (#11412)* – set up Jun 1999, to allow sharing of expertise and information on the activities of individuals, groups and movements linked to international terrorism, cooperation in tracking their methods of operation and sources of financing and development of anti-terrorism training programs.
- Mine-clearing program in Central America.
- *'Working Group on Probity and Public Ethics'*.
- *Special Committee on Civil Society Participation in OAS Activities* – set up Jun 1999.
- *ParlAmericas (#18206)* set up Mar 2001, Ottawa (Canada).
- *'Inter-American Program on the Promotion Women's Human Rights and Gender Equity and Equality'*.
- *'Developing Cooperation Mechanisms in Labor Relations in Mercosur Countries'* – project to develop expertise in mediation and alternative conflict-resolution techniques and an understanding of mediation as a vital tool in negotiating and resolving labour conflicts.
- *'OAS Caribbean Tourism Competitiveness and Sustainability Program'*, commenced 1998, including 2 projects – small hotels assistance; tourism awareness.
- *'American Cultural Capital'* – Merida (Mexico) 2000, Pereira (Colombia) 2001.
- *'Awards'*: Andres Bello Award; Bernardo A Houssay Award; Gabriela Mistral Award; Manuel Noriega Morales Award; Beca de Investigación Marcus Garvey prize (1998) commemorating the centennial of Marcus Garvey's birth; past contests, tributes and awards for the work of composers or writers for example to celebrate the 100th anniversary of Heitor Villa- Lobos' birth.

/Funds/ -
- *'OAS Emergency Relief Fund (FONDEM)'*;
- *OAS Peace Fund (#17630)*;
- *'OAS Special Fund for Democracy'* – set up Nov 2000.

/Agreements concluded under OAS auspices and not mentioned above/ -
- *Additional Protocol to the Treaties on Private International Law (1889)*;
- *Convention on the Practice of Learned Professions, 1889 (1889)*;
- *Treaty on International Civil Law, 1889 (1889)*;
- *Treaty on International Commercial Law, 1889 (1889)*;
- *Treaty on International Penal Law, 1889 (1889)*;
- *Treaty on International Procedural Law, 1889 (1889)*;
- *Treaty on Literary and Artistic Property (1889)*;
- *Treaty on Patents of Invention (1889)*;
- *Treaty on Trademarks (1889)*;
- *Convention for the Formation of Codes on Public and Private International Law (1902)*;
- *Convention on Literary and Artistic Copyright, 1902 (1902)*;
- *Convention on the Practice of Learned Professions, 1902 (1902)*;
- *Convention Relative to the Exchange of Official, Scientific, Literary and Industrial Publications (1902)*;
- *Convention Relative to the Rights of Aliens (1902)*;
- *Treaty of Arbitration for Pecuniary Claims (1902)*;
- *Treaty on Compulsory Arbitration (1902)*;
- *Treaty for the Extradition of Criminals and for Protection Against Anarchism (1902)*;
- *Treaty on Patents of Invention, Industrial Drawings and Models and Trademarks (1902)*;
- *Convention Establishing the Status of Naturalized Citizens Who Again Take up Their Residence in the Country of Their Origin (1906)*;
- *Convention on International Law (1906)*;
- *Convention on Patents of Invention, Drawings and Industrial Models, Trademarks, and Literary and Artistic Property (1906)*;
- *Convention on Pecuniary Claims, 1906 (1906)*;
- *Convention on Inventions, Patents, Designs and Industrial Models (1910)*;
- *Convention on Literary and Artistic Copyright, 1910 (1910)*;
- *Convention on Pecuniary Claims, 1910 (1910)*;
- *Convention on the Protection of Trade Marks (1910)*;
- *Agreement on Commercial Relations (1911)*;
- *Agreement on Consuls (1911)*;
- *Agreement on the History of the Liberator (1911)*;
- *Agreement on the Judicial Acts of Aliens (1911)*;
- *Agreement on Literary and Artistic Property (1911)*;
- *Agreement on Patents and Privileges of Invention (1911)*;
- *Agreement Respecting Internal Revolutions and Neutrality (1911)*;
- *Agreement Respecting the Publication of Historical Records (1911)*;
- *Agreement on Roads and Waterways (1911)*;
- *Agreement on Telegraphs (1911)*;
- *Extradition Agreement (1911)*;
- *Postal Agreement (1911)*;
- *Inter-American Convention Against Racism and all Forms of Discrimination and Intolerance* (proposed);
- *Convention for the Establishment of Free Trade, 1923 (1923)*;
- *Convention for the establishment of international commissions of inquiry (inactive)*;
- *Convention for the Establishment of Permanent Central American Commissions (1923)*;
- *Convention for the Establishment of Stations for Agricultural Experiments and Animal Industries (1923)*;
- *Convention for the Limitation of Armaments (1923)*;
- *Convention on the Practice of Liberal Professions (1923)*;
- *Convention for the Protection of Commercial, Industrial, and Agricultural Trade Marks and Commercial Names (1923)*;
- *Convention on Publicity of Customs Documents (1923)*;
- *Convention for Reciprocal Exchange of Central American Students (1923)*;
- *Convention Relative to the Preparation of Projects of Electoral Legislation (1923)*;
- *Convention for the Unification of Protective Laws for Workmen and Laborers (1923)*;
- *Convention on Uniformity of Nomenclature for the Classification of Merchandise (1923)*;
- *Extradition Convention, 1923 (1923)*;
- *Inter-American Convention on Electrical Communications (1924)*;
- *Pan American Sanitary Code (1924)*;
- *Additional Protocol to the Pan-American Sanitary Code, 1927 (1927)*;
- *Convention on Asylum, 1928 (1928)*;
- *Convention on Commercial Aviation (1928)*;
- *Convention on Consular Agents (1928)*;
- *Convention on Duties and Rights of States in the Event of Civil Strife (1928)*;
- *Convention on Maritime Neutrality (1928)*;
- *Convention on the Pan American Union (1928)*;
- *Convention on Private International Law (1928)*;
- *Convention on the Status of Aliens (1928)*;
- *Convention on Treaties (1928)*;
- *Revision of the Convention of Buenos Aires on the Protection of Literary and Artistic Copyright (1928)*;
- *General Inter-American Convention for Trade Mark and Commercial Protection (1929)*;
- *Protocol on the Inter-American Registration of Trade Marks (1929)*;
- *Protocol of Progressive Arbitration (1929)*;
- *Convention on the Regulation of Automotive Traffic (1930)*;
- *Additional Protocol to the General Convention of Inter-American Conciliation of 1929 (1933)*;
- *Convention on Extradition (1933)*;
- *Convention on Nationality (1933)*;
- *Convention on the Nationality of Women (1933)*;
- *Convention on Political Asylum, 1933 (1933)*;
- *Convention on the Teaching of History (1933)*;
- *Agreement on the Application of the Most-favored-nation Clause (1934)*;
- *Central American Extradition Convention (1934)*;
- *Treaty of Central American Fraternity (1934)*;
- *Convention for the Creation of Pan American Commercial Committees (1935)*;
- *Convention Relating to the Transit of Airplanes (1935)*;
- *Convention Relative to the Creation of a Pan American Tourist Passport and of a Transit Passport for Vehicles (1935)*;
- *Convention on the Repression of Smuggling (1935)*;
- *South American Regional Agreement on Radiocommunications, 1935 (1935)*;
- *Treaty on the Protection of Artistic and Scientific Institutions and Historic Monuments (1935)*;
- *Treaty on the Protection of Movable Property of Historic Value (1935)*;
- *Additional Protocol Relative to Non-intervention (1936)*;
- *Convention Concerning Artistic Exhibitions (1936)*;
- *Convention Concerning Facilities for Educational and Publicity Films (1936)*;
- *Convention Concerning Peaceful Orientation of Public Instruction (1936)*;
- *Convention to Coordinate, Extend and Assure the Fulfillment of the Existing Treaties between the American States (1936)*;
- *Convention on Interchange of Publications (1936)*;
- *Convention for the Maintenance, Preservation and Reestablishment of Peace (1936)*;
- *Convention on the Pan American Highway (1936)*;
- *Convention for the Promotion of Inter-American Cultural Relations, 1936 (1936)*;
- *Declaration on the Juridical Personality of Foreign Companies (1936)*;
- *Inter-American Treaty on Good Offices and Mediation (1936)*;
- *Treaty on the Prevention of Controversies (1936)*;
- *Inter-American Arrangement Concerning Radiocommunications, 1937 (1937)*;
- *Inter-American Radiocommunications Convention, 1937 (1937)*;
- *North American Regional Broadcasting Agreement, 1937 (1937)*;
- *South American Regional Agreement on Radiocommunications, 1937 (1937)*;
- *Regional Radio Convention for Central America, Panama and the Canal Zone (1938)*;
- *Convention on the Practice of Learned Professions, 1939 (1939)*;
- *Treaty on Asylum and Political Refugees (1939)*;
- *Treaty on Intellectual Property (1939)*;
- *Additional Protocol to the Treaties on Private International Law (1940)*;
- *Convention on Nature Protection and Wild Life Preservation in the Western Hemisphere (1940)*;
- *Convention on the Provisional Administration of European Colonies and Possessions in the Americas (1940)*;
- *Inter-American Radio Agreement, 1940 (1940)*;
- *Protocol on Uniformity of Powers of Attorney Which Are to be Utilized Abroad (1940)*;
- *South American Regional Agreement on Radiocommunications, 1940 (1940)*;
- *Treaty on International Civil Law, 1940 (1940)*;
- *Treaty on International Commercial Terrestrial Law (1940)*;
- *Treaty on International Penal Law, 1940 (1940)*;
- *Treaty on International Procedural Law, 1940 (1940)*;
- *Treaty on the Law of International Commercial Navigation (1940)*;
- *Protocol to the Inter-American Coffee Agreement (1941)*;
- *Convention on the Regulation of Inter-American Automotive Traffic (1943)*;
- *Inter-American Telecommunications Convention, 1945 (1945)*;
- *Inter-American Convention on the Rights of the Author in Literary, Scientific, and Artistic Works (1946)*;
- *Interim North American Regional Broadcasting Agreement (1946)*;
- *Economic Agreement of Bogota (1948)*;
- *Inter-American Convention on the Granting of Civil Rights to Women (1948)*;
- *Inter-American Convention on the Granting of Political Rights to Women (1948)*;
- *Agreement on Privileges and Immunities of the Organization of American States (1949)*;
- *North American Regional Broadcasting Agreement, 1950 (1950)*;
- *Additional Protocol to the Pan-American Sanitary Code, 1952 (1952)*;
- *Convention on Diplomatic Asylum (1954)*;
- *Convention for the Promotion of Inter-American Cultural Relations, 1954 (1954)*;
- *Convention on Territorial Asylum (1954)*;
- *Protocol to the Convention on Duties and Rights of States in the Event of Civil Strife (1957)*;
- *Agreement on the System of Central American Integrated Industries (1958)*;
- *Protocol to the Central American Agreement on Equalization of Import Charges, 1960 (1960)*;
- *Protocol of Adherence by Costa Rica to the Protocol of Managua on Equalization of Import Charges (1962)*;
- *Protocol to the Central American Agreement on Equalization of Import Charges, 1962 (1962)*;
- *Inter-American Convention on Facilitation of International Waterborne Transportation (1963)*;
- *Protocol to the Central American Agreement on Equalization of Import Charges, 1963 (1963)*;
- *Protocol to the Central American Agreement of Equalization of Import Charges (1964)*;
- *Protocol to the Central American Agreement on Equalization of Import Charges, 1965 (1965)*;
- *Special Central American Agreement on the Equalization of Import Duties on Textiles Manufactured from Rayon or from other Artificial or Synthetic Fibres (1965)*;
- *Special Protocol on Basic Grains (1965)*;
- *Protocol to the Central American Agreement on Fiscal Incentives to Industrial Development, 1966 (1966)*;
- *Protocol to the Agreement on Equalization of Import Charges and to the Agreement on the System of Central American Integrated Industries (1967)*;
- *Protocol of Amendment to the Charter of the Organization of American States (Protocol of Buenos Aires, 1967)*;
- *Agreement Concerning Postal Money Orders and Postal Travellers' Cheques, 1969 (1969)*;
- *Convention to Prevent and Punish the Acts of Terrorism Taking the Form of Crimes Against Persons and Related Extortion That Are of International Significance (1971)*;
- *Inter-American Convention on Conflict of Laws Concerning Bills of Exchange, Promissory Notes and Invoices (1975)*;
- *Inter-American Convention on Conflict of Laws Concerning Checks, 1975 (1975)*;
- *Inter-American Convention on International Commercial Arbitration (1975)*;
- *Inter-American Convention on the Legal Regime of Powers of Attorney to be Used Abroad (1975)*;
- *Inter-American Convention on Letters Rogatory (1975)*;

- *Inter-American Convention on the Taking of Evidence Abroad (1975)*;
- *Protocol of Amendment to the Inter-American Treaty of Regional Assistance (1975)*;
- *Convention on the Protection of the Archeological, Historical and Artistic of the American Nations (Convention of San Salvador, 1976)*;
- *Additional Protocol to the Inter-American Convention on Letters Rogatory (1979)*;
- *Agreement on the Adoption of the Inter-American Manual on Traffic Control Devices for Streets and Highways (Agreement of Caracas, 1979)*;
- *Inter-American Convention on Conflicts of Laws Concerning Checks, 1979 (1979)*;
- *Inter-American Convention on Conflicts of Laws Concerning Commercial Companies (1979)*;
- *Inter-American Convention on Domicile of Natural Persons in Private International Law (1979)*;
- *Inter-American Convention on Execution of Preventive Measures (1979)*;
- *Inter-American Convention on Extraterritorial Validity of Foreign Judgments and Arbitral Awards (1979)*;
- *Inter-American Convention on General Rules of Private International Law (1979)*;
- *Inter-American Convention on Proof of and Information on Foreign Law (1979)*;
- *Protocol to the Treaty Concerning the Permanent Neutrality and Operation of the Panama Canal, 1979 (1979)*;
- *Additional Protocol to the Inter-American Convention on the Taking of Evidence Abroad (1984)*;
- *Inter-American Convention on Conflict of Laws Concerning the Adoption of Minors (1984)*;
- *Inter-American Convention on Jurisdiction in the International Sphere for the Extraterritorial Validity of Foreign Judgments (1984)*;
- *Inter-American Convention on Personality and Capacity of Juridical Persons in Private International Law (1984)*;
- *Inter-American Convention to Prevent and Punish Torture (1985)*;
- *Inter-American Amateur Radio Service Convention (1987)*;
- *Additional Protocol to the American Convention on Human Rights in the Area of Economic, Social and Cultural Rights (Protocol of San Salvador, 1988)*;
- *Amendment of Article Seven of the Inter-American Amateur Radio Service Convention (1988)*;
- *Inter-American Convention on Contracts for the International Carriage of Goods by Road (1989)*;
- *Inter-American Convention on the International Return of Children (1989)*;
- *Inter-American Convention on Support Obligations (1989)*;
- *Protocol to the American Convention on Human Rights to Abolish the Death Penalty (1990)*;
- *Inter-American Convention to Facilitate Disaster Assistance (1991)*;
- *Inter-American Convention on Mutual Assistance in Criminal Matters (1992)*;
- *Protocol of Amendments to the Charter of the Organization of American States (Protocol of Washington, 1992)*;
- *Inter-American Convention on Serving Criminal Sentences Abroad (1993)*;
- *Agreement Concluded between the Governments of El Salvador, Honduras and Guatemala, the Inter-American Institute for Cooperation on Agriculture and the OAS General Secretariat Relative to an Extension for the Technical Cooperation for Execution of the Integral Development Plan for the Border Region Shared by the Three Countries (Trifinio plan, 1994)*;
- *Inter-American Convention on Forced Disappearance of Persons (1994)*;
- *Inter-American Convention on International Traffic in Minors (1994)*;
- *Inter-American Convention on the Law Applicable to International Contracts (1994)*;
- *Inter-American Convention on the Prevention, Punishment and Eradication of Violence Against Women (Convention of Belém do Para, 1994)*;
- *Optional Protocol Related to the Inter-American Convention on Mutual Assistance in Criminal Matters (1993)*;
- *Protocol of Amendment to the Charter of the Organization of American States (Protocol of Managua, 1993)*;
- *Inter-American Convention on the International Amateur Radio Permit (1995)*;
- *Inter-American Convention Against Corruption (1996)*;
- *Inter-American Convention Against the Illicit Manufacturing of and Trafficking in Firearms, Ammunition, Explosives and other Related Materials (1997)*;
- *Inter-American Convention on the Elimination of all Forms of Discrimination Against Persons with Disabilities (1999)*;
- *Inter-American Convention on Transparency in Conventional Weapons Acquisitions (1999)*;
- *Inter-American Convention Against Terrorism (2002)*.

Events *Preventing Violent Extremism – Good Practices for Engaging Youth through Sports Programs* 2020, *Workshop on Advanced Port Security Drills and Exercises* Lima (Peru) 2015, *Summit of the Americas* Panama (Panama) 2015, *Annual General Assembly* Washington, DC (USA) 2015, *Annual Americas Competitiveness Forum / Annual Meeting Americas Competitiveness Forum* Port-of-Spain (Trinidad-Tobago) 2014. **Publications** *Info'at'Citel* (12 a year) – electronically; *The Summits of the Americas Informs* (12 a year) – electronically; *Américas Magazine* (6 a year) in English, French, Spanish; *Young Americas Business Trust* (6 a year) – electronically; *Education for Democratic Values and Practices* – electronic bulletin; *El Desminado* – electronic bulletin. *Americas Alive* – film series. *The OAS: Meeting New Challenges* (1998) in English, French, Portuguese, Spanish – structure and functions of the Organization; *Business Information Sources of Latin America and the Caribbean*; *Guide to the Columbus Memorial Library*. Annual report of the Secretary General; special reports, surveys and booklets on inter-American economy, education, law, social problems, travel and other themes. **Information Services** *Columbus Memorial Library* – holdings – 300,819; periodicals – 2,670; bound volumes – 151,000; photographs – 45,000. Subjects of interest: Inter-American System; Human Rights; Democracy; Latin America; Carribean; Drugs; Trade; Sustainable Development; Women in the Americas. Special collections: United Nations and international organizations documents; official gazettes of the member countries; rare books; *Foreign Trade Information Service (SICE)* – on-line information on trade opportunities in member states; *Voice of the OAS* – short-wave radio program, some daily broadcasts being repeated by long-wave broadcasting stations throughout the Hemisphere.

Members Governments of the 35 independent countries of the Americas (" – Government of Cuba excluded from participation in the Inter-American system in 1962; suspension lifted in 2009 but has not reintegrated into the OAS):

Antigua-Barbuda, Argentina, Bahamas, Barbados, Belize, Bolivia, Brazil, Canada, Chile, Colombia, Costa Rica, Cuba (*), Dominica, Dominican Rep, Ecuador, El Salvador, Grenada, Guatemala, Guyana, Haiti, Honduras, Jamaica, Mexico, Nicaragua, Panama, Paraguay, Peru, St Kitts-Nevis, St Lucia, St Vincent-Grenadines, Suriname, Trinidad-Tobago, Uruguay, USA, Venezuela.

Permanent Observers (67):

Albania, Algeria, Angola, Armenia, Austria, Azerbaijan, Belgium, Benin, Bosnia-Herzegovina, Bulgaria, China, Croatia, Cyprus, Czechia, Denmark, Egypt, Equatorial Guinea, Estonia, Finland, France, Georgia, Germany, Ghana, Greece, Holy See, Hungary, Iceland, India, Ireland, Israel, Italy, Japan, Kazakhstan, Korea Rep, Latvia, Lebanon, Lithuania, Luxembourg, Malta, Monaco, Morocco, Netherlands, Nigeria, North Macedonia, Norway, Pakistan, Philippines, Poland, Portugal, Qatar, Romania, Russia, Saudi Arabia, Serbia, Slovakia, Slovenia, Spain, Sri Lanka, Sweden, Switzerland, Thailand, Tunisia, Türkiye, UK, Ukraine, Vanuatu, Yemen.

International Permanent Observer (1):

European Union (EU, #08967).

IGO Relations Accredited by (1): *United Nations Framework Convention on Climate Change – Secretariat (UNFCCC, #20564)*. Observer status with (2): *ECOSOC (#05331)*; *World Intellectual Property Organization (WIPO, #21593)*. Memorandum of Understanding with (1): *International Anti-Corruption Academy (IACA, #11654)*.

Observer to: *International Organization for Migration (IOM, #14454)*; General Assembly of: *United Nations (UN, #20515)*; *World Trade Organization (WTO, #21864)*. *Financial Action Task Force (FATF, #09765)* has Observer statuts. Agreements at level of governing bodies with 6 inter-American specialized organizations: PAHO; IACI; CIM; PAIGH; IAII; IICA. Formal agreement with: *UNESCO (#20322)*; *International Criminal Police Organization – INTERPOL (ICPO-INTERPOL, #13110)*. Formal agreement with: *FAO (#09260)* came into force May 1952. Cooperative agreement with: *International Institute for Democracy and Electoral Assistance (International IDEA, #13872)*. Participates as observer in the activities of: *Codex Alimentarius Commission (CAC, #04081)*. Invited to sessions of Intergovernmental Council of: *International Programme for the Development of Communication (IPDC, #14651)*. Member of: *Committee of International Development Institutions on the Environment (CIDIE, no recent information)*. Cooperative relations with:

- *ILO (#11123)*;
- *Instituto Latinoamericano de las Naciones Unidas para la Prevención del Delito y Tratamiento del Delincuente (ILANUD, #11347)*;
- *International Atomic Energy Agency (IAEA, #12294)*;
- *International Maritime Organization (IMO, #14102)*;
- *International Telecommunication Union (ITU, #15673)*;
- *UNIDO (#20336)*;
- *United Nations Economic Commission for Latin America and the Caribbean (ECLAC, #20556)*;
- *United Nations University (UNU, #20642)*;
- *World Tourism Organization (UNWTO, #21861)*.

Instrumental in setting up:

- *Caribbean Plan for Monuments and Sites (CARIMOS, no recent information)*;
- *Centro de Cooperación Regional para la Educación de Adultos en América Latina y el Caribe (CREFAL, #03794)*;
- *Centro Interamericano de Artesanias y Artes Populares (CIDAP, #03801)*;
- *Centro Interamericano de Desarrollo e Investigación Ambiental y Territorial (CIDIAT)*;
- *Centro Interamericano para el Desarrollo Regional (CINDER, no recent information)*;
- *Centro Interamericano de Etnomusicologia y Folklore (CIDEF, inactive)*, within Regional Program for Cultural Development and based at FUNDEF;
- *Comisión Interamericana de Desarrollo Social (CIDES, #04135)*;
- *Comisión Interamericana de Educación (CIE, #04136)*;
- *Inter-American Committee on Culture (no recent information)*;
- *Inter-American Committee on Ports (#11415)*;
- *Inter-American Institute of Ethnomusicology and Folklore (inactive)*;
- *Inter-American Statistical Training Centre (CIENES, no recent information)*;
- *Justice Studies Centre of the Americas (JSCA, #16171)*;
- *Pan American Center for Geographical Studies and Research (#18086)*;
- *Red Interamericana de Alto Nivel Sobre Descentralización, Gobierno Local y Participación Ciudadana (RIAD, #18691)*;
- *Simon Bolivar Inter-American Library (#19283)*.

NGO Relations Agreements with a broad range of national and international nongovernmental organizations:

- *Academia de Ciencias de América Latina (ACAL, #00010)*;
- *ADF International (#00112)*;
- *American Association of Port Authorities (AAPA, #00775)*;
- *American Film Institute (AFI)*;
- *Asociación Latinoamericana de Instituciones Financieras para el Desarrollo (ALIDE, #02233)*;
- *Association of American Chambers of Commerce in Latin America (AACCLA)*;
- *Association of Cultural Attachés from Latin American Countries, Spain and Portugal (#02462)*;
- *B'nai B'rith International (BBI, #03290)*;
- *Caribbean Hotel and Tourism Association (CHTA, #03516)*;
- *Centro Internacional de Estudios Superiores de Comunicación para América Latina (CIESPAL, #03806)*;
- *Comité Andino de Autoridades de Transporte Acuatico (CAATA, #04147)*;
- *Confederación de Organizaciones Turisticas de la América Latina (COTAL, #04466)*;
- *Confederación Sindical de Trabajadores y Trabajadoras de las Américas (CSA, #04480)*;
- *Consejo de Fundaciones Americanas de Desarrollo (SOLIDARIOS, #04712)*;
- *Cultural Foundation of the Americas (CFA)*;
- *Federación Interamericana de la Industria de la Construcción (FIIC, #09333)*;
- *Federación Internacional del Automóvil Region IV (#09337)*;
- *General Federation of Women's Clubs (GFWC)*;
- *Ibero-American Association of Chambers of Commerce (IACC, #11014)*;
- *Institutional Development and Economic Affairs Service (IDEAS, no recent information)*;
- *Inter-American Association of Sanitary and Environmental Engineering (#11400)*;
- *Inter-American Bar Association (IABA, #11401)*;
- *Inter-American Catholic Education Association (ICCE, #11403)*;
- *Inter-American College of Radiology (IACR, #11409)*;
- *Inter-American Commercial Arbitration Commission (IACAC, #11410)*;
- *Inter-American Confederation of Public Relations (#11418)*;
- *Inter-American Consular Institute (no recent information)*;
- *Inter-American Copyright Institute (ICI, #11421)*;
- *Inter-American Council of Commerce and Production (IACCP, no recent information)*;
- *Inter-American Federation of Secretaries (#11430)*;
- *Inter-American Hotel Association (IAHA, no recent information)*;
- *Inter-American Housing Union (#11433)*;
- *Inter-American Organization for Higher Education (IOHE, #11442)*;
- *Inter-American Safety Council (IASC, no recent information)*;
- *Inter-American Scout Committee (ISC, #11445)*;
- *International Association of Broadcasting (IAB, #11738)*;
- *International Association for the Exchange of Students for Technical Experience (IAESTE, #11885)*;
- *International Association of Exhibitions in Latin America (#11886)*;
- *International Association of Penal Law (IAPL, #12074)*;
- *International Association of Schools of Social Work (IASSW, #12149)*;
- *International Council for Adult Education (ICAE, #12983)*;
- *International Council on Monuments and Sites (ICOMOS, #13049)*;
- *International Council on Social Welfare (ICSW, #13076)*;
- *International Federation of Red Cross and Red Crescent Societies (#13526)*;
- *International Hotel and Restaurant Association (IH&RA, #13813)*;
- *International Literacy Association (ILA, #14057)*;
- *International Peace Institute (IPI, #14536)*;
- *International Road Federation (IRF Global, #14759)*;
- *International Social Service (ISS, #14886)*;
- *International Sweeteners Association (ISA, #15639)*;
- *International Union for Conservation of Nature and Natural Resources (IUCN, #15766)*;
- *International Union of Notaries (#15795)*;
- *Junior Chamber International (JCI, #16168)*;
- *Latin American Banking Association (#16254)*;
- *Latin American and Caribbean Alliance of YMCAs (LACA, #16264)*;
- *Latin American Confederation of Tourism Press (CLAPTUR, no recent information)*;
- *Latin American Industrialists Association (#16341)*;
- *Latin American Railways Association (#16365)*;
- *Organization of the Cooperatives of America (OCA, inactive)*;
- *Pact (#18016)*;
- *Pan American Association of Oto-Rhino-Laryngology – Head and Neck Surgery (PANAMORL, #18082)*;
- *Pan American Association of Student Loan Institutions (#18084)*;
- *Pan American Development Foundation (PADF, #18094)*;
- *Pan American Federation of Architects' Associations (#18098)*;
- *Pan American Liaison Committee of Women's Organizations (PALCO, no recent information)*;
- *Pan American Medical Women's Alliance (PAMWA, #18120)*;
- *Pan American Railway Congress Association (PARCA, #18124)*;
- *Pan American Standards Commission (#18133)*;
- *Pax Romana, International Movement of Catholic Students (IMCS, #18268)*;
- *Professional Customs Brokers Association of the Americas (#18512)*;
- *Program of Joint Studies on Latin American Economic Integration (no recent information)*;
- *RI Global (#18948)*;
- *Rizzuto Foundation (no recent information)*;
- *The Trust for the Americas (#20252)*;
- *Unión Panamericana de Asociaciones de Ingenieros (UPADI, #20469)*;
- *Universal Esperanto Association (UEA, #20676)*;
- *World Jewish Congress (WJC, #21599)*.

Accredited organization: *Centro de Derechos Humanos Miguel Agustin Pro Juarez (Centro Prodh)*. Instrumental in setting up:

- *Consejo Asesor Internacional de la Juventudes Rurales (CAJIR, no recent information)*;
- *Hemisphere Wide Inter-University Scientific and Technological Information Network (RedHUCyT, no recent information)*;
- *Inter-American Forum on Political Parties (inactive)*;
- *Inter-American Metrology System (#11440)*;
- *Inter-American Water Resources Network (IWRN, no recent information)*;
- *Red Latinoamericana de Ciencias Biológicas (RELAB, #18706)*;
- *Museums Association of the Caribbean (MAC, #16909)*.

Member of: *International Network for Environmental Compliance and Enforcement (INECE, #14261)*. Supports: *Parliamentarians for Global Action (PGA, #18208)*; *Red Latinoamericana de Quimica (RELAQ, #18718)*.

[2021/XD3030/**D***]

♦ **OASPA** Open Access Scholarly Publishers Association (#17747)

♦ OAS Peace Fund 17630

Contact c/o OAS, 1889 F St NW, Office No 646, Washington DC 20006, USA. E-mail: peacefund@oas.org.

URL: http://www.oas.org/SAP/peacefund/

History Jun 2000, Windsor ON (Canada), within *OAS (#17629)*, by Resolution 1756 (XXX-O/00). Full title: *Fund for Peace: Peaceful Settlement of Territorial Disputes*. **Aims** Strengthen OAS' capacity in peace-building and conflict resolution. **Structure** Since Sep 2008, includes *Inter-American Peace Forum*. [2012/XJ5859/f/**F***]

♦ OASRR / see African-Asian Rural Development Organization (#00203)

♦ OAS Special Committee on Trade (no recent information)

♦ OAS Staff Association 17631

Pres 1889 F St NW, Ste 694C, Washington DC 20006, USA. T. +12024586230. Fax +12024583466. E-mail: staffpres@oas.org.

URL: http://staff.oas.org/english/default.asp
History 1955, to represent staff members of *OAS (#17629)*. Also referred to as *Staff Association of the Organization of American States*. **Aims** Support, promote and defend employee compensation and *benefits*, career development, *working conditions* and the general welfare of staff members and their families, including legal problems and grievances. **Structure** Staff Committee, composed of President and 7 Committee members, Staff Representative on the Retirement and Pension Committee and alternate Representative. **Languages** English, French, Portuguese, Spanish. **Finance** Members' dues. **Events** *Broadband wireless access seminar* San Salvador (El Salvador) 2003.
Members OAS staff members in 33 countries:
Antigua-Barbuda, Argentina, Bahamas, Barbados, Belize, Bolivia, Brazil, Chile, Colombia, Costa Rica, Dominica, Dominican Rep, Ecuador, El Salvador, Grenada, Guatemala, Guyana, Haiti, Honduras, Jamaica, Mexico, Nicaragua, Panama, Paraguay, Peru, St Kitts-Nevis, St Lucia, St Vincent-Grenadines, Suriname, Trinidad-Tobago, Uruguay, USA, Venezuela.
NGO Relations Consultative Status with: *Federation of International Civil Servants' Associations (FICSA, #09603)*. [2010.06.01/XE1818/v/**E**]

- ♦ **OASTI** Observatoire Africain pour la science, la technologie et l'innovation (#00401)
- ♦ **OAT** Organisation arabe du travail (#01001)
- ♦ **OATUU** Organisation of African Trade Union Unity (#17798)
- ♦ OAU Convention Governing the Specific Aspects of Refugee Problems in Africa (1969 treaty)
- ♦ OAU Convention on the Prevention and Combating of Terrorism (1999 treaty)
- ♦ OAU Coordinating Committee on Assistance to Refugees (no recent information)
- ♦ OAU Cultural Fund (no recent information)
- ♦ OAU – Organization of African Unity (inactive)
- ♦ OAU/STRC / see African Union Scientific Technical Research Commission (#00493)
- ♦ OAU-STRC-IAPSC / see Inter-African Phytosanitary Council (#11386)
- ♦ OAVA / see Oceania Association of Master Athletes
- ♦ ÖAW-Institut für europäische Integrationsforschung / see Centre for European Integration Research
- ♦ **OAYouth** Organisation of African Youth (#17799)
- ♦ OBC / see CODE
- ♦ OBC / see FIBA Oceania (#09748)
- ♦ OBC – Oriental Bird Club (internationally oriented national body)
- ♦ OBC Transeuropa – Osservatorio balcani e caucasa transeuropa (internationally oriented national body)
- ♦ OBD – Organic Battery Days (meeting series)
- ♦ Obedinen Institut za Jadreni Izsledvanija / see Joint Institute for Nuclear Research (#16134)
- ♦ Obedinennaja Gruppa Ekspertov po Naucnym Aspektam Zagrjaznenija Morskoj Sredy / see Joint Group of Experts on the Scientific Aspects of Marine Environmental Protection (#16131)
- ♦ Obedinennaja Gruppa Ekspertov po Naucnym Aspektam Zascity Morskoj Sredy (#16131)
- ♦ Obedinennyj Institut Jadernyh Issledovanij (#16134)
- ♦ Oberster Rat der Europäischen Schulen (#03295)
- ♦ **OBESSU** Organising Bureau of European School Student Unions (#17829)
- ♦ OBF / see Oriental and Pacific Boxing Federation (#17894)
- ♦ OBF – Otto Benecke Foundation (internationally oriented national body)
- ♦ **OBFS** Organization of Biological Field Stations (#17856)
- ♦ **OBHE** The Observatory on Borderless Higher Education (#17642)
- ♦ OBI / see International Baccalaureate (#12306)
- ♦ OBI – Operation Blessing International (internationally oriented national body)
- ♦ OBiV – Ortadogu ve Balkan Incelemeleri Vakfi (internationally oriented national body)
- ♦ Objectif Sciences / see Objectif Sciences International (#17632)

♦ Objectif Sciences International (OSI) 17632

Main Office Avenue de Chamonix 7, 1207 Geneva, Switzerland. T. +41225501227. E-mail: contact-head@osi-ngo.org.
URL: http://www.osi-ngo.org/
History 1992, Geneva (Switzerland). Merged with *HORIZON Consulting* 2002. Former names and other names: *Les Scientifiques Amateurs* – former (1992 to 1995); *Les Sciences Actives* – former (1995 to 2002); *Objectif Sciences* – former (2002 to 2008). **Aims** Serve and promote *sustainable development* of human society through development of education in sciences and development of scientific research. **Structure** General Assembly; Executive Council; Scientific and Pedagogical Council; General Management; Resources Centre. **Languages** English, French. **Staff** 115.00 FTE, paid. **Finance** Members' dues. Donations. **Activities** Events/meetings. **Events** *Geneva Forum* Geneva (Switzerland) 2017, *Geneva Forum* Geneva (Switzerland) 2016, *Geneva Forum* Geneva (Switzerland) 2014. **Consultative Status** Consultative status granted from: *ECOSOC (#05331)* (Special). **IGO Relations** Member of: *International Bureau of Education (IBE, #12413)*. **NGO Relations** Member of: *American Association for the Advancement of Science (AAAS)*. [2021/XJ5194/**F**]

- ♦ Objectif Tiers-monde (internationally oriented national body)
- ♦ Objective Third World (internationally oriented national body)
- ♦ Object Management Group (internationally oriented national body)
- ♦ Objedinennyj Venskij Institut (#16150)
- ♦ OBK – Organisation pour l'aménagement et le développement du Bassin de la Rivière Kagera (no recent information)
- ♦ Oblate dell'Assunzione, Religiose Missionarie (religious order)
- ♦ Oblate di Cristo Re (religious order)
- ♦ Oblate Missionaries of Mary Immaculate (religious order)
- ♦ Oblate del Sacro Cuore di Gesù (religious order)
- ♦ Oblate del Sacro Cuore di Gesù, 1933 (religious order)
- ♦ Oblates de l'Assomption, Religieuses Missionnaires (religious order)
- ♦ Oblates Bénédictins (religious order)
- ♦ Oblates of Christ the King (religious order)
- ♦ Oblates du Coeur de Jésus (religious order)
- ♦ Oblate Sisters of the Assumption (religious order)
- ♦ Oblate Sisters of the Most Holy Redeemer (religious order)
- ♦ Oblates missionnaires de Marie Immaculée (religious order)
- ♦ Oblates of Saint Benedict (religious order)
- ♦ Oblates de Sainte-Thérèse de l'Enfant-Jésus (religious order)
- ♦ Oblates of St Francis de Sales (religious order)
- ♦ Oblates of the Virgin Mary (religious order)
- ♦ Oblati di Maria Vergine (religious order)
- ♦ Oblati di San Francesco di Sales (religious order)
- ♦ Oblati di San Giuseppe (religious order)
- ♦ Oblats de Saint-Benoît d'Albi (religious order)
- ♦ Oblats de Saint-François de Sales de Troyes (religious order)
- ♦ Oblats de la Vierge Marie (religious order)
- ♦ **OBPI** Office Benelux de la propriété intellectuelle (#03202)
- ♦ **OB-PS** Olave Baden-Powell Society (#17715)
- ♦ Obra de Cooperación Apostolica Seglar Hispanoamericana / see Obra de Cooperación Apostolica Seglar Hispanoamericana – Cristianos con el Sur
- ♦ Obra de Cooperación Apostolica Seglar Hispanoamericana – Cristianos con el Sur (internationally oriented national body)
- ♦ Obra Kolping Internacional / see KOLPING INTERNATIONAL (#16203)
- ♦ Obra de Nossa Senhora de Montligeon (religious order)
- ♦ Obra de Nuestra Señora de Montligeon (religious order)
- ♦ **OBREAL-EULARO** Observatoire des relations Union Européenne – Amérique latine (#17635)
- ♦ Obreras de la Cruz (religious order)
- ♦ OBSC / see Oceania Baseball Softball Confederation (#17652)
- ♦ Obscij Park Gruzovyh Vagonov (inactive)
- ♦ Observatoire Africain pour la science, la technologie et l'innovation (#00401)
- ♦ Observatoire des armements / CDRPC (internationally oriented national body)
- ♦ Observatoire pour la communication culturelle et audiovisuelle en méditerranée (#17643)
- ♦ Observatoire économique et statistique d'Afrique subsaharienne (#05321)
- ♦ Observatoire de l'épargne européenne (internationally oriented national body)
- ♦ Observatoire euro-méditerranéen sur la gestion des risques (internationally oriented national body)
- ♦ Observatoire européen de l'audiovisuel (#06294)
- ♦ Observatoire européen des drogues et des toxicomanies (#07820)
- ♦ Observatoire européen des éspaces multimédia (internationally oriented national body)
- ♦ l'Observatoire européen des forêts de montagne (#08073)
- ♦ Observatoire européen du logement social (#08502)
- ♦ Observatoire Européen de la Non-Discrimination et des Droits Fondamentaux (unconfirmed)
- ♦ Observatoire européen du plurilinguisme (internationally oriented national body)
- ♦ Observatoire européen des pratiques d'accès aux technologies de l'information et de la communication / see Observatoire européen des éspaces multimédia
- ♦ Observatoire Européen des Religions et de la Laïcité (internationally oriented national body)
- ♦ Observatoire européen des systèmes et des politiques de santé (#08072)
- ♦ Observatoire Européen de la Violence en Milieu Scolaire / see International Observatory of Violence in the School Environment (#14389)
- ♦ Observatoire européen de la violence scolaire / see International Observatory of Violence in the School Environment (#14389)
- ♦ Observatoire des fonctions publiques africaines (#00249)
- ♦ Observatoire français de la coopération internationale (internationally oriented national body)
- ♦ Observatoire de la Francophonie économique (internationally oriented national body)
- ♦ Observatoire International du Bonheur (internationally oriented national body)
- ♦ Observatoire international de la démocratie participative (#17640)
- ♦ Observatoire international de justice juvénile (internationally oriented national body)

♦ Observatoire international de la laïcité 17633

Pres 5 rue Le Goff, 75005 Paris, France. E-mail: observatoirelaicite@gmail.com.
URL: http://www.observatoire-laicite.org/
NGO Relations Secretariat provided by: *Mouvement Europe et laïcité*. [2010/XF6551/**F**]

- ♦ Observatoire international pour la non violence (internationally oriented national body)
- ♦ Observatoire international pour la non violence – Communes des Nations pour la Paix / see Observatoire international pour la non violence
- ♦ Observatoire International de la Violence a l'Ecole (#14389)
- ♦ Observatoire linguistique (internationally oriented national body)

♦ Observatoire méditerranéen de l'énergie (OME) 17634

Gen Dir 32 bis boulevard Haussmann, 75009 Paris, France. T. +33170169120. Fax +33170169119. E-mail: ome@ome.org.
URL: http://www.ome.org/
History 1988. Registration: Start date: 9 Oct 1991, France. **Aims** Promote regional dialogue and cooperation in the Mediterranean energy sector. **Structure** General Assembly; Executive Committee. **Activities** Training/education; events/meetings. **Events** *Seminar on the New Energy Security Risks* 2022, *Workshop on the state of art of the dialogue consumer/producer countries* Ankara (Turkey) 2004, *Réunion sur la coopération pour les interconnexions électriques dans la région méditerranéenne* Cairo (Egypt) 1991. **Publications** *La Lettre OME* (4 a year); *OME Newsletter* (4 a year).
Members Full in 12 countries:
Egypt, France, Greece, Italy, Lebanon, Libya, Morocco, Palestine, Slovenia, Spain, Tunisia, Türkiye.
IGO Relations Accredited by: *United Nations Framework Convention on Climate Change – Secretariat (UNFCCC, #20564)*. [2022/XN4461/**D**]

- ♦ Observatoire méditerranéen pour l'environnement et le développement (internationally oriented national body)
- ♦ Observatoire méditerranéen pour l'information et la réflexion – géopolitique, géoculture, géoéconomie, géoenvironnement (see: #18959)
- ♦ Observatoire permanent de la coopération française / see Observatoire français de la coopération internationale
- ♦ Observatoire PMA (#16412)

♦ Observatoire des relations Union Européenne – Amérique latine (OBREAL-EULARO) 17635

European Union – Latin America Relations Observatory – Observatorio de las Relaciones Unión Europea América Latina – Observatório das Relações União Européia – América Latina
Coordinator Univ de Barcelona, Observatorio de la Globalización, Adolf FLorensa 8, 08028 Barcelona, Spain. T. +34934034479. E-mail: info@obreal.org.
URL: http://www.obreal.org/
Aims Promote dialogue and synergies between governmental, academic and social sectors in Europe and Latin America. **Structure** General Assembly; Board of Directors. Executive Secretary. **Finance** Supported by: *European Commission (EC, #06633)*. **Events** *Europe-Latin America Bi-Regional University Association And Leadership Conference* Sao Paulo (Brazil) 2012, *General Assembly* Barcelona (Spain) 2011, *La nueva agenda de las relaciones comerciales internacionales tras el fin de la ronda de Doha* Barcelona (Spain) 2007, *International workshop* Berlin (Germany) 2006, *Seminario sobre los procesos de integracion en la encrucijada* Santiago (Chile) 2006. **Publications** *OBREAL/EULARO Newsletter*.
Members Institutions and research centres (30) in 14 countries:
Argentina, Belgium, Brazil, Chile, Colombia, France, Germany, Italy, Mexico, Peru, Poland, Portugal, Spain, UK.
Included in the above, 6 organizations listed in this Yearbook:
Andes University (ULA); *Institute for Strategic and International Studies, Lisbon (IEEI)*; *Instituto de Estudos Econômicos e Internacionais (IEEI)*; *Istituto di Studi Latinoamericani, Milano (ISLA)*; *Lateinamerika-Institut, Freie Universität Berlin (LAI)*; *Latin American Faculty of Social Sciences (#16316)*. [2012.08.08/XM2071/y/**F**]

♦ Observatoire du Sahara et du Sahel (OSS) 17636

Sahara and Sahel Observatory
Exec Secretariat Boulevard du Leader Yasser Arafat BP 31, CARTHAGE 1080 Tunis, Tunisia. T. +21671206633 – +21671206634. Fax +21671206636. E-mail: boc@oss.org.tn.
Liaison Bureau c/o UNESCO, 1 rue Miollis, 75015 Paris, France. T. +33145682876.
URL: http://www.oss-online.org/
History 1992, Paris (France), following a proposal made by François Mitterand in 1988. Established in Tunis (Tunisia), since 2000. **Aims** Work towards optimal use of resources allocated to combating *desertification* by favouring the development and capitalization of its partners' wealth of information; offer *African* states an opportunity to identify and carry out actions required for desertification control. **Structure** General Assembly (every 4 years); Executive Board; Bureau; Strategic Orientation Committee; Executive Secretariat. **Activities** Projects/programmes; awareness raising; training/education; knowledge management/information dissemination. **Events** *General assembly session* Tunis (Tunisia) 2004, *Session* Tunis (Tunisia) 2004, *Meeting* Paris (France) 1998.
Members Member States (32):
Algeria, Belgium, Benin, Burkina Faso, Cameroon, Canada, Cape Verde, Chad, Côte d'Ivoire, Djibouti, Egypt, Eritrea, Ethiopia, France, Gambia, Germany, Guinea-Bissau, Italy, Kenya, Libya, Luxembourg, Mali, Mauritania, Morocco, Niger, Nigeria, Senegal, Somalia, Sudan, Switzerland, Tunisia, Uganda.
Member Organizations (13):
Agence Panafricaine de la Grande Muraille Verte (APGMV, #00547); *Arab Maghreb Union (AMU, #01004)*; *Centre d'actions et de réalisations internationales (CARI)*; *Comité permanent inter-Etats de lutte contre la sécheresse dans le Sahel (CILSS, #04195)*; *Community of Sahel-Saharan States (CEN-SAD, #04406)*; *Environnement et développement du Tiers-monde (enda, #05510)*; *FAO (#09260)*; *Intergovernmental Authority on Development (IGAD, #11472)*; *Lake Chad Basin Commission (LCBC, #16220)*; *Regional Remote Sensing Centre for North African States (#18807)*; *Réseau Sahel Désertification (ReSaD, #18906)*; *UNESCO (#20322)*; *United Nations Convention to Combat Desertification (UNCCD, 1994)*.

IGO Relations Formal agreement with: *UNESCO (#20322)*. Accredited to the Conference of the Parties of: *Secretariat of the United Nations Convention to Combat Desertification (Secretariat of the UNCCD, #19208)*. Accredited by: *United Nations Framework Convention on Climate Change – Secretariat (UNFCCC, #20564)*. Partner of: *Group on Earth Observations (GEO, #10735)*; *International Center for Agricultural Research in the Dry Areas (ICARDA, #12466)*. **NGO Relations** Founding member of: *Global Water Solidarity (GWS, #10655)*. Member of: *World Water Council (WWC, #21908)*. Partner of: *Internationally Shared Aquifer Resources Management (ISARM, #14071)*. [2018/XN5321/y/**F***]

♦ Observatoire séismologique du Sud-Ouest (internationally oriented national body)
♦ Observatoire social européen (internationally oriented national body)

♦ Observatoire social international 17637

Pres 1 Place Samuel de Champlain, Case 2260, 92930 Paris La Défense CEDEX, France. T. +33144226568.
Headquarters Viale dell' Esperanto N71, 00144 Rome RM, Italy.
URL: http://www.observatoire-social-international.com/

History Founded 6 Dec 2000, Italy. **Aims** Create ways and means to achieve a balance between economic imperatives and new social requirements. **Languages** English, French, Spanish. **Activities** Active in: Brazil, Chile, China, Côte d'Ivoire, Morocco. **IGO Relations** Cooperates with: *International Bank for Reconstruction and Development (IBRD, #12317)*; *ILO (#11123)*; *United Nations (UN, #20515)*. **NGO Relations** Cooperates with: *SGI Europe (#19253)*; *European Trade Union Confederation (ETUC, #08927)*; *Trade Union Advisory Committee to the OECD (TUAC, #20186)*; national organizations; companies. [2017.10.11/XF6387/**F**]

♦ Observatoire du tabac en Afrique francophone (OTAF) 17638

Pres Dept of Epidemiology, Ferhat Abbas Univ of Setif, Sétif, Algeria.
Sec address not obtained. T. +22696480405.
URL: https://www.otaf.info/

History Dec 2001, Bamako (Mali). **Structure** Bureau, including President, Vice-President, Treasurer and Secretary. **Events** *Conference* Casablanca (Morocco) 2006. **Publications** *Bulletin de l'OTAF*. **NGO Relations** Member of: *Framework Convention Alliance (FCA, #09981)*. [2020/XM2780/**F**]

♦ Observatoire des technologies pour l'éducation en Europe (internationally oriented national body)
♦ Observatoire sur le Tourisme dans les Iles Européennes (#17645)
♦ Observatoire du traitement avancé du français et des langues nationales partenaires (no recent information)
♦ Observatori del Deute en la Globalització (internationally oriented national body)
♦ Observatori de Dret Europeu i Comparat / see Institute of European and Comparative Private Law

♦ Observatories and Research Facilities for European Seismology (ORFEUS) 17639

Mailing Address Seismology Div KNMI, PO Box 201, 3730 AE De Bilt, Netherlands. T. +31302206343. Fax +31302201364.
SG SED – ETH Zürich, NO FO 69.7, Sonneggstrasse 5, 8092 Zurich ZH, Switzerland.
URL: http://www.orfeus-eu.org/

History 1987. Former names and other names: *Stichting Orfeus* – legal name. Registration: No/ID: KVK 41182401, Netherlands. **Aims** Coordinate and promote digital, broadband seismology in the European-Mediterranean area. **Structure** Board of Directors. **Languages** English. **Staff** 1-4 FTE; time/project-limited contracts. **Finance** Members' dues. Other sources: annual participants' fees; international (EC) projects. **Activities** Knowledge management/information dissemination; events/meetings. **Events** *Workshop* Dublin (Ireland) 2010. **Publications** Annual Report. **Information Services** *ORFEUS Data Centre (ODC)* – on-line and off-line access to digital, broad-band waveform data from seismological stations and observatories in and around the European-Mediterranean area.
Members Earth Science Research Institutes/Observatories in 28 countries:
Austria, Azerbaijan, Belgium, Bulgaria, Czechia, Denmark, Estonia, Finland, France, Germany, Greece, Ireland, Israel, Italy, Netherlands, North Macedonia, Norway, Poland, Portugal, Romania, Serbia, Slovakia, Slovenia, Spain, Sweden, Switzerland, Türkiye, UK. [2022/XF4681/**F**]

♦ Observatori Internacional de la Democràcia Participativa (OIDP) . . . 17640

Observatoire international de la démocratie participative (OIDP) – International Observatory of Participatory Democracy

Secretariat Ajuntament de Barcelona, Dept de Participació Ciutadana, C/ Avinyó, 15 2a planta, 08002 Barcelona, Spain. T. +34933428751 – +34934815822. Fax +34933428760. E-mail: info@oidp.net.
URL: http://www.oidp.net/

History 24 Nov 2001, Barcelona (Spain). **Aims** Be open to all cities, associations, organizations and research centers interested in learning about, exchanging impressions and applying experiences of participatory democracy on a local scale with the aim of deepening the roots of democracy in municipal government. **Languages** English, French, Spanish. **Events** *Participatory cities with full rights – participatory democracy and human rights* Mexico City (Mexico) 2019, *Conference* Barcelona (Spain) 2018, *Conference* Montréal, QC (Canada) 2017, *Conference* Maputo (Mozambique) 2016, *Conference* Madrid (Spain) 2015.
Members Associates cities; collaborators organizations. Members in 28 countries:
Argentina, Belgium, Bolivia, Brazil, Bulgaria, Canada, Chile, Colombia, Costa Rica, Denmark, Dominican Rep, Ecuador, El Salvador, France, Guatemala, Honduras, Italy, Luxembourg, Mali, Mexico, Netherlands, Peru, Philippines, Portugal, Spain, Sweden, Switzerland, Uruguay.
NGO Relations Cooperates with: *World Organization of United Cities and Local Governments (UCLG, #21695)*. [2020.04.29/XF7079/**F**]

♦ Observatório Africano de Ciência, Tecnologia e Inovação (#00401)
♦ Observatorio Andino (internationally oriented national body)
♦ Observatorio Europeo de las Drogas y las Toxicomanias (#07820)
♦ Observatorio Europeo del Plurilinguismo (internationally oriented national body)
♦ Observatorio Europeo de la Violencia Escolar / see International Observatory of Violence in the School Environment (#14389)
♦ Observatório Europeu da Droga e da Toxicodependência (#07820)
♦ Observatório Europeu Plurilinguisme (internationally oriented national body)
♦ Observatorio de la Globalización (internationally oriented national body)

♦ Observatorio Iberoamericano de Seguridad Vial (OISEVI) 17641

Ibero-American Road Safety Observatory

Technical Sec address not obtained.

History Coordinate road safety strategies and initiatives at regional level. **Structure** General Assembly; Executive Committee. **Activities** Events/meetings. **Events** *General Assembly* Madrid (Spain) 2019.
Members Full in 20 countries:
Argentina, Bolivia, Brazil, Chile, Colombia, Costa Rica, Cuba, Dominican Rep, Ecuador, El Salvador, Guatemala, Honduras, Mexico, Nicaragua, Panama, Paraguay, Peru, Spain, Uruguay, Venezuela. [2016/XM5017/**F**]

♦ Observatorio Interamericano de Cerro Tololo (internationally oriented national body)
♦ Observatorio Interamericano sobre Drogas (see: #11429)
♦ Observatorio Internacional de Justicia Juvenil (internationally oriented national body)
♦ Observatorio Latinoamericano de Conflictos Ambientales, Chile (internationally oriented national body)
♦ Observatorio de las Relaciones Unión Europea América Latina (#17635)
♦ Observatório das Relações União Européia – América Latina (#17635)
♦ Observatorio Sismológico del Sur Occidente (internationally oriented national body)
♦ Observatorio de Tecnologías para la Educación en Europa (internationally oriented national body)
♦ Observatorio de Turismo en las Islas Europeas (#17645)
♦ Observatorium des Tourismus auf dem Europäischen Inseln (#17645)
♦ Observatorul European pentru Droguri si Toxicomanie (#07820)
♦ Observatorul European al Plurilvismului (internationally oriented national body)

♦ The Observatory on Borderless Higher Education (OBHE) 17642

Contact c/o Inst of Leadership and Management, JW Hinks LLP, 19 Highfield Road, Redhill, B15 3BH, UK. T. +441543266886. E-mail: jw@institutelm.com.
URL: http://www.obhe.org/

History Originally a collaborative initiative between *Association of Commonwealth Universities, The (ACU, #02440)* and Universities UK. Became part of International Graduate Insight Group (i-graduate), Aug 2010, which in turn became part of Tribal Group, Jan 2013. **Aims** Provide strategic intelligence for education leaders and policymakers attempting to navigate the opportunities and threats of borderless higher education. **Structure** Advisory Board. **Languages** English. **Staff** 4.00 FTE, paid. **Activities** Events/meetings; guidance/assistance/consulting; knowledge management/information dissemination; research and development. **Events** *Global Forum* Dubai (United Arab Emirates) 2018, *Global Forum* London (UK) 2017, *Global Forum* Albany, NY (USA) 2013, *Global Forum* Kuala Lumpur (Malaysia) 2012, *Global forum on borderless higher education* Vancouver, BC (Canada) 2011. **Publications** Analysis articles; research reports.
Members Organizational members (over 150) in 24 countries and territories:
Australia, Belgium, Canada, China, Denmark, Fiji, France, Germany, Hong Kong, India, Ireland, Italy, Japan, Malaysia, Mexico, Netherlands, New Zealand, Pakistan, Singapore, South Africa, Spain, Switzerland, UK, USA.
IGO Relations Links with multiple IGOs, not specified. [2023.02.15/XM2705/y/**F**]

♦ Observatory for Cultural and Audio-Visual Communication in the Mediterranean (OCCAM) 17643

Observatoire pour la communication culturelle et audiovisuelle en méditerranée – Osservatorio per la Comunicazione Culturale e l'Audiovisivo nel Mediterranea e nel Mondo

Pres Via Duccio di Boninsegna 21, 20145 Milan MI, Italy. T. +3928057573. E-mail: occam@occam.org.
URL: http://www.occam.org/

History Founded 1997, Milan (Italy), by *International Council of Mediterranean Cinematic Manifestations (no recent information)* and the Italian branch of *International Council for Film, Television and Audiovisual Communication (IFTC, #13022)*. Functions as a component network of *UNESCO Mediterranean Programme (inactive)*, based on *International Convention on the Recognition of Studies, Diplomas and Degrees in Higher Education in the Arab States and European States Bordering on the Mediterranean (1976)*. **Aims** Work at the service of the most disadvantaged communities by helping them to benefit from new technologies and promoting sustainable development. **Languages** English, French, Italian. **Activities** Projects/programmes; events/meetings. **Events** *Infopoverty World Conference* New York, NY (USA) 2019, *Infopoverty World Conference* New York, NY (USA) 2018, *Infopoverty world conference* New York, NY (USA) 2017, *Infopoverty World Conference* New York, NY (USA) 2016, *Infopoverty world conference* New York, NY (USA) / Rome (Italy) / Geneva (Switzerland) / Paris (France) 2007. **Consultative Status** Consultative status granted from: *ECOSOC (#05331)* (Special). [2017.03.09/XF4874/**F**]

♦ Observatory of Cultural Policies in Africa (OCPA) 17644

Contact Avda Patrice Lumumba No 850, 1o andar, PO Box 1207, Maputo, Cidade de Maputo, Mozambique. T. +25821306138. Fax +25821320304. E-mail: director@ocpanet.org – secretariat@ocpanet.org – maria.manjate011@gmail.com.
URL: http://www.ocpanet.org/

History Founded May 2002, Maputo (Mozambique), under the auspices of *African Union (AU, #00488)*, *Ford Foundation (#09858)* and *UNESCO (#20322)*. **Aims** Monitor cultural trends and national cultural policies in the region and their integration in human development strategies. **Structure** Steering Committee; Executive Committee; Technical Committee; Regional and Natonal Focal Points. **Languages** Arabic, English, French, Portuguese, Swahili. **Staff** 8.00 FTE, paid. **Finance** Funded through subventions, joint initiatives and fees from project implementation. Funds previously and currently generated from: Ford Foundation; UNESCO; Universal Forum of Cultures, Barcelona (Spain); Swiss Commission for UNESCO; *Africalia*; *African Union (AU, #00488)*; *INTERARTS Foundation*; *Organisation internationale de la Francophonie (OIF, #17809)*. Annual budget: US$ 150,000 – 200,000. **Activities** Advocacy/lobbying/activism; knowledge management/information dissemination; research/documentation; capacity building; events/meetings; guidance/assistance/consulting. **Events** *Seminar on cultural policies and local development of creative and cultural industries for the countries of West Africa* Dakar (Senegal) 2009, *Euro-African campus for cultural cooperation* Maputo (Mozambique) 2009, *Culture and development in Africa seminar* Nairobi (Kenya) 2005, *Entrepreneurship development workshop* Nairobi (Kenya) 2005, *International seminar on cultural indicators of human development in Africa* Maputo (Mozambique) 2004. **Publications** *OCPA News* – electronic. Proceedings; compendium; guidelines; articles; studies; meeting reports; books; DVD. **Members** Networks in all AU member states. **Consultative Status** Consultative status granted from: *UNESCO (#20322)* (Associate Status). **IGO Relations** Cooperates with: *Organisation of African, Caribbean and Pacific States (OACPS, #17796)* Secretariat; African Union; *Centre International de Recherche et de Documentation sur les Traditions et les Langues Africaines (CERDOTOLA, #03761)*; *Centre for Linguistic and Historical Studies by Oral Tradition (#03771)*; *East African Community (EAC, #05181)*; *Institut Régional d'Enseignement Supérieur et de Recherche en Développement Culturel (IRES-RDEC, #11355)*; *New Partnership for Africa's Development (NEPAD, #17091)*; *Organisation internationale de la Francophonie (OIF, #17809)*; UNESCO; *Union économique et monétaire Ouest africaine (UEMOA, #20377)*; *United Nations African Institute for Economic Development and Planning (#20518)*. **NGO Relations** Cooperates with: *African Academy of Languages (ACALAN, #00192)*; *Culturelink – the Network of Networks for Research and Cooperation in Cultural Development (#04982)*; Interarts Foundation, Barcelona (Spain); *ENCATC (#05452)*; *International Federation of Arts Councils and Culture Agencies (IFACCA, #13358)*; *School of African Heritage (EPA)*; *West African Museums Programme (WAMP, #20890)*. [2019.02.28/XF6440/**F**]

♦ Observatory of European and Comparative Private Law / see Institute of European and Comparative Private Law
♦ Observatory of Globalization (internationally oriented national body)
♦ Observatory on Intolerance and Discrimination against Christians – European Network (internationally oriented national body)
♦ Observatory of Technology for Education in Europe (internationally oriented national body)

♦ Observatory on Tourism in the European Islands (OTIE) 17645

Observatoire sur le Tourisme dans les Iles Européennes – Observatorio de Turismo en las Islas Europeas – Observatorium des Tourismus auf dem Europäischen Inseln – Osservatorio sul Turismo delle Isole Europee – Euroopan saarien matkailu observatorio

Pres Via Emerico Amari 38, 90139 Palermo PA, Italy. T. +39916117527. Fax +39916117527. E-mail: secretariat@otie.org – admin@otie.org – otie@mailte.it.
URL: http://www.otie.org/

History 2 Feb 2007, Palermo (Italy). **Aims** Carry out new studies and research on the islands of the European union by sharing objectives, results and policies. **Structure** General Assembly; Executive Committee; Presidency; Scientific Committee; Documentation Center; International Secretariat. **Languages** English, Italian. **Activities** Events/meetings; knowledge management/information dissemination; monitoring/evaluation; research/documentation; training/education. **Events** *International Conference on Island Tourism* Sicily (Italy) 2021, *Conference* Mytilene (Greece) 2019, *Conference* Palermo (Italy) 2018. **Publications** *Conference Abstract Book*. Reports.
Members Founder; Associate; Ordinary. Members in 3 countries:
France, Italy, Malta.
NGO Relations Member of (1): *European Tourism Manifesto (#08921)*. [2022/XM6217/**F**]

♦ Observatory on Values and Education in Humanity (internationally oriented national body)
♦ OBS – Otto Benecke Stiftung (internationally oriented national body)
♦ OCAC / see Oceania Centre for Arts, Culture and Pacific Studies (#17655)
♦ **OCACPS** Oceania Centre for Arts, Culture and Pacific Studies (#17655)
♦ OCAM – Comisión Centroamericana de Directores de Migración (no recent information)
♦ OCAM – Organisation commune africaine et mauricienne (inactive)
♦ OCA / see Oceania Canoe Association (#17654)
♦ **OCA** Oceania Canoe Association (#17654)
♦ **OCA** Olympic Council of Asia (#17718)

♦ OCA – Operation Crossroads Africa (internationally oriented national body)
♦ OCA – Organisation of Commonwealth Associations (inactive)
♦ OCA – Organización de las Cooperativas de América (inactive)
♦ OCA – Organization of the Cooperatives of America (inactive)
♦ OCAPROCE internationale – Organisation camerounaise de promotion de la coopération économique internationale (internationally oriented national body)
♦ O Carm – Ordo Fratrum Beatae Mariae Virginis de Monte Carmelo (religious order)
♦ O Cart – Ordo Cartusiensis (religious order)
♦ OCASHA / see Obra de Cooperación Apostolica Seglar Hispanoamericana – Cristianos con el Sur
♦ OCASHA – CCS – Obra de Cooperación Apostolica Seglar Hispanoamericana – Cristianos con el Sur (internationally oriented national body)
♦ OCASPE – Organización de la Administración Caribeña de Deporte y Educación Fisica (no recent information)
♦ **OCBC** Oceania Boxing Confederation (#17653)
♦ **OCCAM** Observatory for Cultural and Audio-Visual Communication in the Mediterranean (#17643)
♦ **OCCA** Oil and Colour Chemists' Association (#17707)
♦ OC – Carmelitani (religious order)
♦ **OCCAR** Organisation Conjointe de Coopération en Matière d'Armement (#17801)
♦ OCCBA – Organization of Commonwealth Caribbean Bar Associations (inactive)
♦ **OCCC** Oneworld Cockpit Crew Coalition (#17737)
♦ OCCDP / see Development and Peace
♦ OCCDP – Développement et paix (internationally oriented national body)
♦ OCCGEAC / see Organization of Coordination for the Control of Endemic Diseases in Central Africa (#17860)
♦ OCCGE – Organisation de coordination et de coopération pour la lutte contre les grandes endémies (inactive)
♦ Occupational Safety and Health Network / see ASEAN Occupational Safety and Health Network (#01215)

♦ Occupational Therapy African Region Group (OTARG) 17646

Chairperson address not obtained. E-mail: tajishuma@yahoo.com.
URL: http://www.otarg.org.za/

History 1997. **Events** *Transforming Health and Well-Being in Africa through Occupation* Windhoek (Namibia) 2021, *Giving back meaning to life – Occupational therapy at the center* Kigali (Rwanda) 2019, *Occupational therapy in Africa – changing lives positively* Accra (Ghana) 2017, *Transforming health care in Africa – a move towards occupation* Kampala (Uganda) 2015, *Promoting occupational therapy in Africa* Harare (Zimbabwe) 2013. **NGO Relations** Member of: *World Federation of Occupational Therapists (WFOT, #21468).* [2017/XE3738/**E**]

♦ Occupational Therapy Europe (OT-Europe) 17647

Registered Address Orteliuslaan 750, 3528 BB Utrecht, Netherlands. E-mail: info@oteurope.eu.
URL: https://www.oteurope.eu/

History 2011. Founded by *European Network of Occupational Therapy in Higher Education (ENOTHE, #07956)* and *Council of Occupational Therapists for the European Countries (COTEC, #04912).* Registration: EU Transparency Register, No/ID: 969465443896-79, Start date: 24 Aug 2021. **Aims** Promote and develop the delivery of occupational therapy services in Europe. **Structure** Executive Committee. **Activities** Research/documentation; training/education. **Events** *Occupational Therapy Europe Congress* Krakow (Poland) 2024.
Members Organizations (3):
Council of Occupational Therapists for the European Countries (COTEC, #04912); European Network of Occupational Therapy in Higher Education (ENOTHE, #07956); Research in Occupational Therapy and Occupational Science Foundation (ROTOS, #18860). [2021/AA2063/y/**E**]

♦ OCDC – US Overseas Cooperative Development Council (internationally oriented national body)
♦ **OCDE** Organisation de coopération et de développement économiques (#17693)
♦ OCD – Ordo Fratrum Discalceatorum Beatae Mariae Virginis de Monte Carmelo (religious order)
♦ OCDS – Ordine Secolare dei Carmelitani Scalzi (religious order)
♦ **OCEAC** Organisation de coordination pour la lutte contre les endémies en Afrique centrale (#17860)
♦ Oceana (internationally oriented national body)
♦ Ocean Arks International (internationally oriented national body)
♦ OceanCare (internationally oriented national body)
♦ The Ocean Cleanup (internationally oriented national body)
♦ Ocean Conservancy (internationally oriented national body)

♦ Ocean Data and Information Network for Africa (ODINAFRICA) 17648

Réseau d'échange de données et d'informations océaniques pour l'Afrique
Coordinator IOC Sub Commission for Africa and Adjacent Island States, UNESCO Regional Bureau for Sciences in Africa, UN Gigiri Complex Block C, PO Box 30592, Nairobi, 00100, Kenya. T. +254207621244.
URL: http://www.odinafrica.net/

History May 2000, Dakar (Senegal). **Aims** Enable IOC member states in Africa to collect oceanographic data, obtain access to ocean data and information available in other data centres, develop skills for manipulation of data and preparation of data and information products, and develop infrastructure for archival, analysis and dissemination of the data and information products. **Structure** Participating states divided into *Intergovernmental Oceanographic Commission (IOC, #11496)* Regional Subsidiary bodies. **Languages** English, French. **Staff** 3.00 FTE, paid. **Finance** Supported by: Government of Flanders; IOC. **Activities** Training/education; events/meetings. **Events** *Seminar* Maputo (Mozambique) 2013, *Symposium* Saly (Senegal) 2011, *Regional meeting* Windhoek (Namibia) 2010, *Seminar* Ostend (Belgium) 2009, *Seminar* Mombasa (Kenya) 2008. **Publications** *COSMAR News*; *WINDOW Newsletter*.
Members in 26 countries:
Algeria, Angola, Benin, Cameroon, Comoros, Congo Brazzaville, Congo DR, Côte d'Ivoire, Egypt, Gabon, Ghana, Guinea, Kenya, Madagascar, Mauritania, Mauritius, Morocco, Mozambique, Namibia, Nigeria, Senegal, Seychelles, South Africa, Tanzania UR, Togo, Tunisia. [2016.10.19/XF6702/**F**]

♦ Ocean Energy Europe (EU-OEA) 17649

CEO Renewable Energy House, Rue d'Arlon 63-65, 1040 Brussels, Belgium. T. +3224001040. Fax +3227919000. E-mail: info@oceanenergy-europe.eu.
URL: http://www.oceanenergy-europe.eu/

History 2006. Former names and other names: *European Ocean Energy Association* – full title. Registration: EU Transparency Register, No/ID: 264048311507-68; Belgium. **Aims** Improve ocean energy as a reliable energy source. **Structure** Board of Directors. **Languages** English, French, German, Italian. **Staff** 6.00 FTE, paid. **Events** *Annual Conference* Brussels (Belgium) 2016, *Annual Conference* Dublin (Ireland) 2015, *Seminar on Strategy Day and Horizon 2020* Brussels (Belgium) 2014, *What could an emerging UK tidal lagoon industry mean for Blue Energy and Growth in Europe* Brussels (Belgium) 2014, *ICOE : International Conference on Ocean Energy* Halifax, NS (Canada) 2014. **Publications** *Industry Vision Paper 2013*. **Members** Universities; research centres; institutions; companies; individuals. Membership countries not specified. **NGO Relations** Member of: *Industry4Europe (#11181).* [2020/XM3317/**D**]

♦ OCEAN / see European Ship Suppliers Organization (#08478)
♦ **OCEAN** European Ship Suppliers Organization (#08478)

♦ Ocean Facilities Exchange Group (OFEG) 17650

Contact address not obtained.
Contact address not obtained.
URL: https://www.ofeg.org/

History Feb 1996. Established when Tripartite Agreement was signed between 3 research institutes of UK, France and Germany. Netherlands joined 2002, Spain and Norway in 2006. **Aims** Maximize the overall scientific output using its state-of-the-art facilities in support of the worldwide oceanographic community. **Structure** Chair; Vice-chair; Tech chair. Includes OFEG-TECH.
Members Full in 6 countries:
France, Germany, Netherlands, Norway, Spain, UK. [2022/AA2868/**D**]

♦ The Ocean Foundation (internationally oriented national body)
♦ Ocean Futures Society (internationally oriented national body)
♦ Ocean Genome Legacy (internationally oriented national body)
♦ Oceania Amateur Athletic Association / see Oceania Athletics Association (#17651)
♦ Oceania Archery Confederation (inactive)
♦ Oceania Association of Master Athletes (internationally oriented national body)
♦ Oceania Association of Veteran Athletes / see Oceania Association of Master Athletes

♦ Oceania Athletics Association (OAA) 17651

Association d'athlétisme d'Océanie
Exec Dir 124 Varsity Parade, Varsity Lakes, Gold Coast QLD 4227, Australia. T. +61756094441.
URL: http://www.athletics-oceania.com/

History 1969, Port Moresby (Papua New Guinea), when first congress of Australasian Area Group was organized, at the instigation of *World Athletics (#21209).* Original title: *Oceania Amateur Athletic Association (OAAA) – Association d'athlétisme amateur d'Océanie.* Current title adopted Feb 2007. Registered in accordance with Australian law, Jul 2009. **Aims** Develop strong and independent Athletic Member Federations; encourage participation through promotion of sport of Athletics on all levels; develop competition at all levels from grassroots to elite; create pathways of excellence in Athletics; continue to provide education within and through the Sport of Athletics. **Structure** Congress (every 4 years); Council. **Languages** English, French. **Staff** 6.00 FTE, paid. **Finance** Grant from World Athletics. **Activities** Sporting activities; guidance/assistance/consulting; training/education; awards/prizes/competitions. **Events** *Biennial Congress* Gold Coast, QLD (Australia) 2015, *Biennial Congress* Gold Coast, QLD (Australia) 2009, *Biennial Congress* Broadbeach, QLD (Australia) 2007, *Biennial Congress* Nadi (Fiji) 2005, *Biennial Congress* Suva (Fiji) 2003.
Members IAAF members in 20 countries and territories of Oceania:
Australia, Cook Is, Fiji, Guam, Kiribati, Marshall Is, Micronesia FS, Nauru, New Zealand, Norfolk Is, Northern Mariana Is, Palau, Papua New Guinea, Polynesia Fr, Samoa, Samoa USA, Solomon Is, Tonga, Tuvalu, Vanuatu.
Associate member in 2 countries:
New Caledonia, Niue.
NGO Relations Continental Athletics Association of: *World Athletics (#21209).* Member of: *Organisation of Sports Federations of Oceania (OSFO, #17828).* [2020.03.03/XE0575/**D**]

♦ Oceania Badminton Confederation / see Badminton Oceania (#03059)

♦ Oceania Baseball Softball Confederation (WBSC Oceania) 17652

SG address not obtained. E-mail: secretarygeneral@wbscoceania.org.
URL: http://www.wbscoceania.org/

History 2017. Proposed following merge of *World Baseball Softball Confederation (WBSC, #21222),* as a merger of *Oceania Softball Confederation (inactive)* and *Baseball Confederation of Oceania (BCO, inactive).* Former names and other names: *OBSC* – alias. **Structure** Executive Board. Divisions, each headed by Executive Committe: Softball; Baseball. **Activities** Sporting activities.
Members Federations in 15 countries and territories:
Australia, Cook Is, Fiji, Guam, Marshall Is, Micronesia FS, Nauru, New Caledonia, New Zealand, Northern Mariana Is, Palau, Papua New Guinea, Samoa, Samoa USA, Solomon Is.
NGO Relations Member of (2): *Organisation of Sports Federations of Oceania (OSFO, #17828); World Baseball Softball Confederation (WBSC, #21222).* [2022/XM7778/**D**]

♦ Oceania Basketball Confederation / see FIBA Oceania (#09748)
♦ Oceania Billiards & Snooker Federation / see Asia Pacific Snooker & Billiards Federation

♦ Oceania Boxing Confederation (OCBC) 17653

Pres Sport House, Level 2 – 375, Albert Park VIC 3206, Australia. T. +61410158024. E-mail: bai@boxing.org.au.
URL: http://www.oceaniaboxing.org/home/

History Original title: *Oceania Boxing Federation.* A regional confederation of *International Boxing Association (IBA, #12385).*
Members National organizations (14) in 14 countries:
Australia, Cook Is, Fiji, Guam, Nauru, New Zealand, Niue, Papua New Guinea, Samoa, Samoa USA, Solomon Is, Tahiti Is, Tonga, Vanuatu. [2018/XD9336/**D**]

♦ Oceania Boxing Federation / see Oceania Boxing Confederation (#17653)

♦ Oceania Canoe Association (OCA) 17654

Pres address not obtained.

History Set up in 1990s. No activity between late 1990s-2006, when re-established. Former names and other names: *Oceania Canoeing Association (OCA)* – former. **Aims** Introduce the sport of canoeing to the countries of Oceania; provide pathways for talented athletes to achieve success in international events, including the Olympic Games. **Structure** Congress; Board. **Languages** English. **Staff** No paid staff. **Finance** Development funds of *International Canoe Federation (ICF, #12437).* Annual budget: US$ 20,000. **Activities** Sporting events. Active in: Australia, Cook Is, Guam, New Caledonia, New Zealand, Palau, Samoa, Tahiti Is.
Members Full in 13 countries and territories:
Australia, Cook Is, Fiji, Guam, Kiribati, New Zealand, Palau, Papua New Guinea, Samoa, Samoa USA, Tahiti Is, Tonga, Vanuatu.
Associate in 1 country:
New Caledonia.
NGO Relations Member of (2): *International Canoe Federation (ICF, #12437); Organisation of Sports Federations of Oceania (OSFO, #17828).* [2016.12.14/XM0784/**D**]

♦ Oceania Canoeing Association / see Oceania Canoe Association (#17654)
♦ Oceania Centre for Arts and Culture / see Oceania Centre for Arts, Culture and Pacific Studies (#17655)

♦ Oceania Centre for Arts, Culture and Pacific Studies (OCACPS) 17655

Dean Fac of Arts Law and Education, Private Bag, Laucala Campus, Suva, Fiji. T. +6793232332. Fax +6793231524.
Dir address not obtained. T. +6793237175.
URL: https://www.usp.ac.fj/index.php?id=8708/

History 1997, within the framework of *University of the South Pacific (USP, #20703).* Original title: *Oceania Centre for Arts and Culture (OCAC).* Since 2008, incorporated into Faculty of Arts and Law, when it merged with the Pacific Studies Program. **Aims** Combine formal academic teaching and research programmes with the creative arts. **Languages** English, French. **Staff** 20.00 FTE, paid. **Finance** Funding from *University of the South Pacific (USP, #20703).* Outside funding for special projects. **Activities** Training/education; events/meetings. **Publications** Books. **Members** USP countries. **IGO Relations** *International Information and Networking Centre for Intangible Cultural Heritage in the Asia-Pacific Region under the auspices of UNESCO (ICHCAP, #13847); Pacific Community (SPC, #17942); Secretariat of the Pacific Regional Environment Programme (SPREP, #19205); UNESCO (#20322); UNEP (#20299).* **NGO Relations** *International Council on Monuments and Sites (ICOMOS, #13049); International Union for Conservation of Nature and Natural Resources (IUCN, #15766); Pacific Island Museums Association (PIMA, #17959).* [2017.06.01/XE4698/**E**]

♦ Oceania Chondrichthyan Society (OCS) 17656

Contact c/o AIMS, PMB 3 Townsville MC, Townsville QLD 4810, Australia.
URL: http://www.oceaniasharks.org.au/

History 2005. **Aims** Promote and facilitate education, conservation and scientific study of chondrichthyan *fish*: sharks, skates, rays and chimaeras. **Structure** Council; Executive Council. **Activities** Events/meetings; awards/prizes/competitions. **Events** *Conference* Adelaide, SA (Australia) 2012, *Conference* New Caledonia 2011, *Conference* Cairns, QLD (Australia) 2010, *Conference* Fremantle, WA (Australia) 2009, *Conference* Sydney, NSW (Australia) 2008.
Members Full in 24 countries and territories:
Australia, Cook Is, Fiji, Guam, Kiribati, Marshall Is, Micronesia FS, Nauru, New Caledonia, New Zealand, Niue, Northern Mariana Is, Palau, Papua New Guinea, Pitcairn, Polynesia Fr, Samoa, Samoa USA, Solomon Is, Tokelau, Tonga, Tuvalu, Vanuatu, Wallis-Futuna. [2011/XJ2020/**D**]

♦ Oceania Comparative and International Education Society (internationally oriented national body)

♦ Oceania Confederation of Roller Sports / see World Skate Oceania

♦ Oceania Continent Handball Federation (OCHF) 17657

Secretariat PO Box 449, Avarua, Rarotonga, Avarua RAROTONGA, Cook Is.
Pres 715 route 8, Maite GU, USA. T. +16716474661. Fax +16716464233.
Facebook: https://www.facebook.com/HandballOceania/

History 1 Jul 1993. Former names and other names: *Oceania Handball Federation (OHF)* – alias. **Aims** Develop handball in Oceania. **Structure** Officers: President, Vice-President, Secretary General. Each country has 2 delegates. **Events** *Congress* Barrigada (Guam) 2014.
Members Full in 17 countries and territories:
Australia, Cook Is, Guam, Kiribati, Marshall Is, Micronesia FS, Nauru, New Caledonia, New Zealand, Northern Mariana Is, Papua New Guinea, Samoa, Samoa USA, Solomon Is, Tonga, Tuvalu, Vanuatu.
Associate member in 1 territory:
Tahiti Is.
NGO Relations Member of (2): *International Handball Federation (IHF, #13771)*; *Organisation of Sports Federations of Oceania (OSFO, #17828)*. [2022/XE2084/E]

♦ Oceania Customs Organisation (OCO) 17658

Secretariat Private Mail Bag, 84 Harris Road, Suva, Fiji. T. +6793313123. Fax +6793313126. E-mail: info@ocosec.org.
URL: http://www.ocosec.org/

History 1986, Rarotonga Is (Cook Is). Former names and other names: *Customs Heads of Administration Regional Meeting (CHARM)* – former (1986 to 1998). **Aims** Promote efficiency and effectiveness in all aspects of customs administration in Oceania, with particular emphasis on the needs of Customs Administrations in developing countries; foster harmonization, cooperation and assistance between its members on customs administration matters and ensure that their interests and concerns are projected effectively to governments, non-governmental organizations and the private sector, both within and beyond the region, so as to contribute to the economic development, security and community protection within the region. **Structure** Annual Conference. Steering Committee. Permanent Secretariat. **Languages** English. **Staff** 19.00 FTE, paid. 9 project staff. **Finance** Operation Fund (OCOOF) financed by members' dues; core budget of Secretariat funded by *Australian Aid (inactive)* and *New Zealand Ministry of Foreign Affairs and Trade – New Zealand Aid Programme*; funding for capacity building projects provided under *European Development Fund (EDF, #06914)* (EDF-10); other ad hoc funding received from other agencies for contracting the services of the Secretariat for delivery of specific activities. **Activities** Advocacy/lobbying/activism; capacity building. **Events** *Annual Conference* Nuku'alofa (Tonga) 2013, *Annual Conference* Pago Pago (Samoa USA) 2012, *Annual conference* Port Moresby (Papua New Guinea) 2011, *Annual Conference* Apia (Samoa) 2010, *Annual Conference* Port Vila (Vanuatu) 2009. **Publications** *The Quarterly News*.
Members Customs administrations in 24 countries and territories:
Australia, Cook Is, Fiji, Guam, Kiribati, Marshall Is, Micronesia FS, Nauru, New Caledonia, New Zealand, Niue, Norfolk Is, Northern Mariana Is, Palau, Papua New Guinea, Polynesia Fr, Samoa, Samoa USA, Solomon Is, Timor-Leste, Tonga, Tuvalu, Vanuatu, Wallis-Futuna.
IGO Relations Member of: *Asia/Pacific Group on Money Laundering (APG, #01921)*. [2020/XD8799/D]

♦ Oceania Cyber Security Centre (internationally oriented national body)

♦ Oceania Cycling Federation 17659

Pres 153 Prospect Road, Prospect SA 5082, Australia. T. +61883449970.

Activities Organizes championships. **NGO Relations** Continental confederation of: *Union Cycliste Internationale (UCI, #20375)*. Member of: *Organisation of Sports Federations of Oceania (OSFO, #17828)*. [2008/XM0785/D]

♦ Oceania Development Network (ODN) 17660

Chair University of the South Pacific, Private Mail Bag, Suva, Fiji.
URL: http://www.gdn-oceania.org/

Aims Provide a platform for cooperation between researchers in the region. **Structure** Executive Committee. **Activities** Organizes workshops and conferences. **Events** *Biennial Conference* Suva (Fiji) 2013, *Biennial Conference* Suva (Fiji) 2012, *Biennial Conference* Fiji 2010, *Biennial conference* Korolevu (Fiji) 2010, *Biennial conference* Apia (Samoa) 2007. **Publications** *ODN Newsletter*. **NGO Relations** Regional network of: *Global Development Network (GDN, #10318)*. [2013/XM2307/F]

♦ Oceania Fencing Confederation (OFC) 17661

President 64 Princes St, Williamstown VIC 3016, Australia. T. +61393978113. Fax +61393978113. E-mail: president@oceaniafencing.org.
Regional Development Officer 43 Edmund Avenue, Unley, Unley SA 5061, Australia. E-mail: developmentofficer@oceaniafencing.org.
Facebook: https://www.facebook.com/oceaniafencingconfederation/

History 1970, Melbourne, VIC (Australia). Reconstituted in 2002, in line with definition of the Oceania Zone of *International Olympic Committee (IOC, #14408)*. **Aims** Represent the International Fencing Federation in the Oceania zone; promote, supervise and direct all fencing activities within the Zone subject to the rules and statutes of the FIE. **Structure** Board. **Languages** English. **Staff** 0.50 FTE, paid; 8.00 FTE, voluntary. **Finance** Sources: grants. Supported by: *Fédération internationale d'escrime (FIE, #09629)*. Annual budget: 200,000 AUD (2020). **Activities** Sporting activities.
Members Countries eligible to affiliate to OFC including all countries and territories in the Pacific area, as defined by the International Olympic Committee. Currently members in 8 countries and territories:
Australia, Guam, New Caledonia, New Zealand, Papua New Guinea, Polynesia Fr, Samoa, Samoa USA.
NGO Relations Member of (1): *Organisation of Sports Federations of Oceania (OSFO, #17828)*. [2021/XJ5779/D]

♦ Oceania Football Confederation (OFC) 17662

Confédération océanienne de football

Gen Sec PO Box 62-586, Greenlane, Auckland 1546, New Zealand. T. +6495314096. Fax +6495295143. E-mail: info@oceaniafootball.com.
Street Address Ascot Office Park, Bldg B Level 2, 93-95 Ascot Ave, Remuera, Auckland 1051, New Zealand.
URL: http://www.oceaniafootball.com/

History 1966, following formal approval of *International Federation of Association Football (#13360)*. **Aims** Service and administer football in the Oceania region; use the game as a tool for social development. **Structure** Congress. Executive Committee, comprising President, Senior Vice-President, Vice-President, Treasurer, Executive Members and 2 observers. Secretariat, headed by General Secretary and comprising 9 departments: Finance; Technical; Competitions; Social Responsibility and International Relations; Logistics; Marketing; Media; Legal; Administration. **Languages** English, French. **Staff** 20-30. **Activities** Organizes competitions. **Events** *Congress* Auckland (New Zealand) 2004, *Extraordinary congress* Paris (France) 2004, *Extraordinary congress* Port Vila (Vanuatu) 2004, *Congress* Nuku'alofa (Tonga) 2002, *Congress* Apia (Samoa) 2000.
Members National associations in 11 countries and territories:
Cook Is, Fiji, New Caledonia, New Zealand, Papua New Guinea, Samoa, Samoa USA, Solomon Is, Tahiti Is, Tonga, Vanuatu.
Associate members in 3 countries and territories:
Kiribati, Niue, Tuvalu.
NGO Relations Continental confederation of: *International Federation of Association Football (#13360)*. Member of: *Organisation of Sports Federations of Oceania (OSFO, #17828)*. [2020/XD3013/D]

♦ Oceania Gymnastics Union (OGU) 17663

Contact c/o Gymnastics Australia Ltd, 3/100 Albert Road, South Melbourne, Melbourne VIC 3205, Australia. T. +61386989700. E-mail: oceaniagymnastics@gmail.com.
URL: https://oceaniagymnastics.org/

History Sep 2018. **Aims** Represent and unite the National Gymnastics Federations of the region. **Structure** Board. Committees.
Members Federations in 8 countries and territories:
Australia, Cook Is, Fiji, Guam, New Zealand, Papua New Guinea, Samoa USA, Tonga.
NGO Relations Member of (1): *Organisation of Sports Federations of Oceania (OSFO, #17828)*. [2022/AA2503/D]

♦ Oceania Handball Federation / see Oceania Continent Handball Federation (#17657)

♦ Oceania Hockey Federation 17664

Fédération de hockey d'Océanie

SG/Treas PO Box 432, Kensington Park, Adelaide SA 5068, Australia. T. +61419827115.
URL: http://www.oceaniahockey.com/

History 1984. **Aims** Promote hockey in the Oceania region. **Structure** Board; Competition Committee; Officiating Committee; Continental Development Officer. **Languages** English. **Staff** 0.80 FTE, paid. **Finance** Members' dues. Grants from *International Hockey Federation (#13802)*. **Activities** Sporting activities.
Members Hockey associations in 10 countries and territories:
Australia, Fiji, Guam, New Zealand, Papua New Guinea, Samoa, Samoa USA, Solomon Is, Tonga, Vanuatu.
NGO Relations Recognized by: *International Hockey Federation (#13802)*. Member of: *Organisation of Sports Federations of Oceania (OSFO, #17828)*. [2020.01.23/XD3371/D]

♦ Oceania Judo Union (OJU) 17665

Union Océanie de judo

Gen Sec address not obtained. T. +68987757809. E-mail: generalsecretary@oceaniajudo.com – education@oceaniajudo.org.
Pres address not obtained. E-mail: president@oceaniajudo.org.
URL: http://www.oceaniajudo.org/

History 1952. Major constitutional changes in 1992; constitutional changes 30 May 1998, Apia (Samoa) and 30 May 2002, Wellington (New Zealand). In French previously also referred to as *Union océanie de judo*. **Aims** Promote and supervise judo activities in the Oceania region; develop and spread the techniques and spirit of judo; ensure the observance of international regulations of judo in Oceania. **Structure** Congress (every 2 years). Executive Committee, comprising President, 2 Vice Presidents, Technical Director, Secretary and Treasurer. Executive of 6, elected for 4-year term. Commissions (3): Technical; Referee; Kata. **Languages** English. **Staff** Voluntary. **Finance** Subscriptions. Competition receipts; *International Olympic Committee (IOC, #14408)*; IJF (television rights). **Activities** Organizes: Oceania Championships; Oceania World Cup; South Pacific Games; OJU Composite Team; Congresses; Technical Courses (Olympic Solidarity). **Events** *Biennial Congress* Christchurch (New Zealand) 2008, *Biennial Congress* Papeete (Polynesia Fr) 2006, *Biennial Congress* Nouméa (New Caledonia) 2004, *Biennial Congress* Wellington (New Zealand) 2002, *Biennial Congress* Sydney, NSW (Australia) 2000.
Members National judo federations (limited to area defined by parallels 20 North to 50 South, and meridians 90 East to 160 East, but excluding continental Asia) in 20 countries and territories:
Australia, Cook Is, Fiji, Guam, Kiribati, Marshall Is, Nauru, New Caledonia, New Zealand, Niue, Norfolk Is, Northern Mariana Is, Palau, Papua New Guinea, Polynesia Fr, Samoa, Samoa USA, Solomon Is, Tonga, Vanuatu.
NGO Relations Continental Union of: *International Judo Federation (IJF, #13975)*. Member of: *Organisation of Sports Federations of Oceania (OSFO, #17828)*. [2018/XD0825/D]

♦ Oceania Karate Federation (see: #21608)
♦ Oceania Kurash Confederation (inactive)

♦ Oceania Mini Football Federation (OMF) 17666

Contact 144 Gregory St, Wembley WA 6014, Australia. T. +61405037857. E-mail: shoot@oceaniaminifootball.com.
URL: http://oceaniaminifootball.com/

History 2014. Regional federation of *World Minifootball Federation (WMF, #21652)*.
Members Federations in 8 countries and territories:
Australia, Cook Is, Fiji, New Caledonia, New Zealand, Papua New Guinea, Samoa USA, Solomon Is.
NGO Relations *Asian Minifootball Confederation (AMC, #01541)*; *European Minifootball Federation (EMF, #07808)*; *Confederación Panamericana de Minifutbol (CPM, #04477)*. [2015/XJ9003/D]

♦ Oceania Motorcycle Union / see FIM Oceania

♦ Oceania National Olympic Committees (ONOC) 17667

Comités nationaux olympiques d'Océanie

SG 715 Route 8, Maite GU 96910, USA. T. +16716496662. Fax +16716496662. E-mail: gnoc@teleguam.net.
Secretariat 49 Gladstone Road, GPO Box 798, Suva, Fiji. E-mail: onoc@onoc.org.fj.
URL: https://www.oceanianoc.org/

History 25 Sep 1981, Baden Baden (Germany). Founded at Constitutive General Assembly. Constitution adopted at inaugural meeting, 23 Feb 1982, Melbourne (Australia). **Aims** Develop Olympic ideals in the region; coordinate and distribute solidarity course funds. **Structure** General Assembly (annual); Executive Board; Secretariat. **Languages** English. **Staff** 3.00 FTE, paid. Plus Secretary-General. **Finance** Grant from IOC through *Olympic Solidarity (OS, #17721)*. **Activities** Knowledge management/information dissemination; projects/programmes; sporting activities; training/education. **Events** *Annual General Assembly* Brisbane, QLD (Australia) 2005, *Annual General Assembly* Palau 2004, *Annual General Assembly* Suva (Fiji) 2003, *Annual General Assembly* Port Moresby (Papua New Guinea) 2002, *Annual General Assembly* Nadi (Fiji) 2001. **Publications** *Coconut Wireless* (weekly). Annual Report.
Members National Olympic Committees (17):
Australia, Cook Is, Fiji, Guam, Kiribati, Marshall Is, Micronesia FS, Nauru, New Zealand, Palau, Papua New Guinea, Samoa, Samoa USA, Solomon Is, Tonga, Tuvalu, Vanuatu.
Associate members in 6 countries and territories:
New Caledonia, Niue, Norfolk Is, Northern Mariana Is, Tahiti Is, Wallis-Futuna.
IGO Relations Partner of (1): *University of the South Pacific (USP, #20703)*. **NGO Relations** Partner of (4): *Oceania Regional Anti-Doping Organization (ORADO, #17670)*; *Organisation of Sports Federations of Oceania (OSFO, #17828)*; *Pacific Games Council (PGC, #17951)*; *Pacific Islands News Association (PINA, #17975)*. Recognized Organization of: *International Olympic Committee (IOC, #14408)*. Continental Association of: *Association of National Olympic Committees (ANOC, #02819)*. Supports: *Badminton Oceania (BOC, #03059)*. [2022/XD1469/D]

♦ Oceanian Belt Wrestling Confederation (unconfirmed)
♦ Oceanian Federation of Kickboxing / see WKF Australia and Oceania (#20974)
♦ Oceanian Shooting Confederation / see Oceania Shooting Federation (#17674)

♦ Oceania Pocket Billiard Association (OPBA) 17668

Pres Unit 161, 36 Mountford Crs, Albury NSW, Australia.
URL: http://www.wpa-pool.com/

NGO Relations Member of: *World Pool-Billiard Association (WPA, #21733)*, through which links with *World Confederation of Billiards Sports (WCBS, #21291)*. [2018/XD7107/D]

♦ Oceania Powerlifting Federation 17669

Pres GPO Box 2322, Melbourne VIC 3001, Australia. T. +61418366416. Fax +61396704188.
Sec address not obtained.

Structure Executive. **Activities** Sporting activities.
Members National organizations in 14 countries and territories:
Australia, Cook Is, Fiji, Kiribati, Nauru, New Caledonia, New Zealand, Niue, Papua New Guinea, Polynesia Fr, Samoa, Samoa USA, Solomon Is, Tonga.
NGO Relations Member of (1): *World Powerlifting (#21735)*. [2021/XJ4254/D]

♦ Oceania RADO / see Oceania Regional Anti-Doping Organization (#17670)

♦ Oceania Regional Anti-Doping Organization (ORADO) 17670

Exec Officer Flat 8-9, Bidesi Flats, Forster St, Suva, Fiji. T. +6797732142.
URL: https://www.orado.org/

History 2005. Former names and other names: *Oceania RADO* – alias. **Aims** Promote clean sport in Oceania. **Structure** Executive Board. **Activities** Advocacy/lobbying/activism; capacity building; guidance/assistance/consulting; research/documentation; training/education.
Members Full in 16 countries and territories:
Cook Is, Fiji, Guam, Marshall Is, Micronesia FS, Nauru, New Caledonia, Palau, Papua New Guinea, Polynesia Fr, Samoa, Samoa USA, Solomon Is, Tonga, Tuvalu, Vanuatu.
IGO Relations Partner of (1): *UNESCO (#20322)*. **NGO Relations** Partner of (4): *International Olympic Committee (IOC, #14408)*; *Oceania National Olympic Committees (ONOC, #17667)*; *Pacific Games Council (PGC, #17951)*; *World Anti-Doping Agency (WADA, #21096)*. [2022/AA2498/D]

♦ Oceania Regional Powerlifting Federation (ORPF) 17671

Treas address not obtained.
SG address not obtained. E-mail: orpf.secretary.general@gmail.com.
URL: https://www.powerlifting-oceania.com/

History Aug 2018. A regional federation of *International Powerlifting Federation (IPF, #14630)*. **Structure** General Assembly; Executive.
Members National federations in 12 countries and territories:
Fiji, Kiribati, Nauru, New Caledonia, New Zealand, Niue, Papua New Guinea, Polynesia Fr, Samoa, Solomon Is, Tonga, Tuvalu.
NGO Relations Partner of (1): *Special Olympics International (SOI, #19910)*. [2022/AA2497/**D**]

♦ Oceania Rugby 17672

Contact PO Box 800, Surry Hills NSW 2010, Australia. T. +61280055662. E-mail: sarah.walker@oceaniarugby.com.
Pres address not obtained.
URL: http://oceaniarugby.com/

History 2000, as *Federation of Oceania Rugby Unions (FORU)*. **Aims** Grow rugby in Oceania through delivery of high quality and dynamic programmes and practices. **Structure** Board; Management Team. **Languages** English, French. **Staff** 10.00 FTE, paid. **Activities** Sporting activities.
Members Full (16): national rugby body in 15 countries and territories:
Australia, Cook Is, Fiji, Nauru, New Caledonia, New Zealand, Niue, Papua New Guinea, Samoa, Samoa USA, Solomon Is, Tahiti Is, Tonga, Tuvalu, Vanuatu.
Associate member in 1 territory:
Wallis-Futuna.
NGO Relations Member of (1): *Organisation of Sports Federations of Oceania (OSFO, #17828)*. Regional association of: *World Rugby (#21757)*. [2020.03.03/XD9460/**D**]

♦ Oceania Sailing Federation (OSAF) 17673

SG address not obtained. E-mail: osaf@sailing.org.au.
URL: https://www.revolutionise.com.au/osf/

Members in 11 countries and territories:
Australia, Cook Is, Fiji, Guam, New Zealand, Norfolk Is, Papua New Guinea, Samoa, Samoa USA, Tahiti Is, Vanuatu.
NGO Relations Member of (2): *Organisation of Sports Federations of Oceania (OSFO, #17828)*; *World Sailing (#21760)*. [2019/XJ6297/**D**]

♦ Oceania Shooting Federation (OSF) 17674

Hon Sec address not obtained. E-mail: oceaniasecretary@bigpond.com.
URL: http://www.oceaniashooting.org/

History 1991. Founded as a continental confederation of *International Shooting Sport Federation (ISSF, #14852)*. New constitution adopted, Jan 2019. Former names and other names: *South Pacific Shooting Region* – former; *Oceanian Shooting Confederation* – former. **Aims** Promote and guide the sound development of the shooting sport within the Oceania area; strengthen the bonds of friendship between the shooting organizations, irrespective of political, racial, physical and religious differences. **Structure** Annual General Meeting; Board. **Activities** Sporting activities.
Members National Federations in 11 countries and territories:
Australia, Fiji, Guam, New Caledonia, New Zealand, Niue, Norfolk Is, Papua New Guinea, Polynesia Fr, Samoa, Tonga.
NGO Relations Member of (1): *Organisation of Sports Federations of Oceania (OSFO, #17828)*. Affiliated with (2): *Oceania National Olympic Committees (ONOC, #17667)*; *Pacific Games Council (PGC, #17951)*. [2021/XD0246/**D**]

♦ Oceania Society for Sexual Health and HIV Medicine (unconfirmed)
♦ Oceania Softball Confederation (inactive)
♦ Oceania Sport Information Centre (internationally oriented national body)

♦ Oceania Squash Federation (OSF) 17675

Exec Officer 33 Blueberry Street, Banksia Beach, Moreton Bay Region QLD 4507, Australia. E-mail: oceaniasquash@bigpond.com.
Pres Squash New Zealand, PO Box 44039, Point Chevalier, Auckland 1246, New Zealand.
URL: http://www.oceaniasquash.org/

History Founded 13 May 1992, Auckland (New Zealand). Regional federation of: *World Squash Federation (WSF, #21826)*. **Aims** Promote and encourage growth and general welfare of the *game* of squash in the Oceania region. **Structure** General Meeting; Committee Board. **Languages** English. **Staff** 1.00 FTE, voluntary. **Finance** Members' dues. **Activities** Guidance/assistance/consulting; advocacy/lobbying/activism; events/meetings. **Events** *Strategic planning conference* Auckland (New Zealand) 2003, *Regional conference* Rarotonga Is (Cook Is) 1997.
Members Full and Associate in 10 countries and territories:
Australia, Cook Is, Fiji, Guam, New Caledonia, New Zealand, Norfolk Is, Papua New Guinea, Samoa, Tahiti Is, Vanuatu.
[2017.10.15/XD2999/**D**]

♦ Oceania Sumo Union 17676

Pres c/o ASF, PO Box 1, Stokers Siding NSW 4484, Australia.

History 1994, at World Championships in Japan. **Aims** Promote the sport of Sumo. **Languages** English. **Staff** Voluntary. **Finance** No budget. Countries mostly seek sponsorship for tournaments. **Activities** Promotes championships.
Members Full in 4 countries:
Australia, Fiji, New Zealand, Tonga. [2017/XE3864/**E**]

♦ Oceania Swimming Association 17677

Honorary Sec 180 Ocean Street, Edgecliff NSW 2027, Australia.

History 1991. **Aims** Provide competitive opportunities in aquatic *sports*, particularly in the island nations of the Oceania region. **Structure** Officers: President; Honorary Secretary; Honorary Treasurer. **Languages** English. **Activities** Sporting activities. **Events** *Championship* Samoa 2010, *Championship* Christchurch (New Zealand) 2008, *General Congress* Guam 1999.
Members National organizations in 16 countries and territories:
Australia, Cook Is, Fiji, Guam, Hawaii, Marshall Is, Micronesia FS, New Caledonia, New Zealand, Northern Mariana Is, Palau, Papua New Guinea, Samoa, Samoa USA, Tahiti Is, Vanuatu.
NGO Relations Member of: *World Aquatics (#21100)*; *Organisation of Sports Federations of Oceania (OSFO, #17828)*. [2017.03.07/XD3017/**D**]

♦ Oceania Table Tennis Federation (OTTF) 17678

Main Offic 4018/3027 The Boulevard, Carrara QLD 4211, Australia. E-mail: admin@ittfoceania.com.
URL: http://www.ittfoceania.com/

History Founded 1978. A continental federation of: *International Table Tennis Federation (ITTF, #15650)*. Constitution adopted May 1994; amended Jul 1996, Aug 1999 and Apr 2010. Also referred to as *ITTF-Oceania*. **Aims** Develop table tennis in the Oceania region. **Structure** General Meeting (biennial, during ITT-Oceania Championship); Management Committee. **Languages** English. **Staff** 0.50 FTE, paid. **Finance** Members' dues. Olympic, ITTF Development and ONOC Development funding. **Activities** Events/meetings; sporting activities. **Events** *Biennial general meeting* Polynesia Fr 2008, *Biennial general meeting* Geelong, VIC (Australia) 2006, *Biennial general meeting* Whangarei (New Zealand) 2004.
Members Associations in 24 countries and territories:
Australia, Cook Is, Fiji, Guam, Kiribati, Marshall Is, Micronesia FS, Nauru, New Caledonia, New Zealand, Niue, Norfolk Is, Northern Mariana Is, Palau, Papua New Guinea, Polynesia Fr, Samoa, Samoa USA, Solomon Is, Tokelau, Tonga, Tuvalu, Vanuatu, Wallis-Futuna.
NGO Relations Member of: *Organisation of Sports Federations of Oceania (OSFO, #17828)*. [2018/XD6740/**D**]

♦ Oceania Taekwondo Union / see World Taekwondo Oceania (#21846)

♦ Oceania Tennis Federation (OTF) 17679

Exec Member Private Bag 6060, Richmond VIC SOUTH 3121, Australia. T. +61399144050. Fax +61396502743. E-mail: itfoceania@connect.com.fj.
URL: http://www.oceaniatennis.com/

History Jan 1993, Melbourne (Australia). **Aims** Develop, promote and raise the standard of tennis throughout the Oceania region; promote cooperation between countries in the region. **Structure** General Meeting (every 2 years); Executive Committee. **Languages** English. **Staff** 1.00 FTE, paid. **Finance** Members' dues. Other sources: grants; sponsors; subsidies. Budget (annual): US$ 110,000. **Activities** Events/meetings. **Events** *General Meeting* Melbourne, VIC (Australia) 2015, *General Meeting / Executive Meeting* Fiji 2014, *General Meeting / Executive Meeting* Fiji 2013, *General Meeting* Melbourne, VIC (Australia) 2013, *Executive Meeting* Fiji 2012. **Publications** *Pacific Oceania Newsletter* (4 a year); *Hitting the Lines* (annual).
Members Full in 21 countries and territories:
Australia, Cook Is, Fiji, Guam, Kiribati, Marshall Is, Micronesia FS, Nauru, New Zealand, Norfolk Is, Northern Mariana Is, Palau, Papua New Guinea, Samoa, Samoa USA, Solomon Is, Tahiti Is, Timor-Leste, Tonga, Tuvalu, Vanuatu.
Associated in one territory:
New Caledonia.
NGO Relations Member of: *International Tennis Federation (ITF, #15676)*; *Organisation of Sports Federations of Oceania (OSFO, #17828)*. [2015.01.22/XD6249/**D**]

♦ Oceania Triathlon / see Oceania Triathlon Federation (#17680)

♦ Oceania Triathlon Federation (OTU) 17680

Pres GPO Box 4366, Sydney NSW 2001, Australia. E-mail: admin@otu.triathlon.org.
Admin address not obtained. E-mail: admin@otu.triathlon.org.
URL: http://otu.triathlon.org/

History Regional federation of *World Triathlon (#21872)*. Former names and other names: *Oceania Triathlon* – alias. **Aims** Foster and promote participation in the sport of triathlon, duathlon and aquathlon in Oceania through maintenance of friendly and loyal cooperation among members. **Languages** English. **Finance** Support from: *World Triathlon (#21872)*. **Activities** Sporting activities; events/meetings.
Members National organizations in 13 countries and territories:
Australia, Cook Is, Fiji, Guam, New Caledonia, New Zealand, Norfolk Is, Palau, Papua New Guinea, Polynesia Fr, Samoa, Solomon Is, Tonga. [2020/XM0786/**D**]

♦ Oceania University Sports Association / see FISU Oceania (#09785)

♦ Oceania Volleyball Federation 17681

Contact c/o AVF, PO Box 176, Belconnen ACT 2616, Australia.

History within *Asian Volleyball Confederation (AVC, #01779)*. **NGO Relations** Member of: *Organisation of Sports Federations of Oceania (OSFO, #17828)*. [2015/XM0787/**D**]

♦ Oceania Weightlifting Federation (OWF) 17682

Gen Sec c/o CTOS, BP 333, 98845 Nouméa, New Caledonia. E-mail: owf@bigpond.com – owf@mls.nc.
URL: http://www.oceaniaweightlifting.com/

History 1980, Melbourne, VIC (Australia). Registration: Nauru. **Aims** Promote and develop weightlifting in Oceania region. **Structure** Working Executive. **Languages** English. **Staff** 6.00 FTE, paid. **Finance** Members' dues (annual): US$ 25 per country. **Activities** Events/meetings. **Events** *Annual Congress* Brisbane, QLD (Australia) 2014, *Annual Congress* Nouméa (New Caledonia) 2014, *Annual Congress* Brisbane, QLD (Australia) 2013, *Annual Congress* Apia (Samoa) 2012, *Annual Congress* Nouméa (New Caledonia) 2011.
Members National associations in 22 countries and territories:
Australia, Cook Is, Fiji, Guam, Kiribati, Marshall Is, Micronesia FS, Nauru, New Caledonia, New Zealand, Niue, Northern Mariana Is, Palau, Papua New Guinea, Samoa, Samoa USA, Solomon Is, Tahiti Is, Tonga, Tuvalu, Vanuatu, Wallis-Futuna.
NGO Relations Continental Federation of: *International Weightlifting Federation (IWF, #15876)*. [2022/XD1549/**D**]

♦ Oceania Wrestling Federation (internationally oriented national body)
♦ Oceanic Conference on International Studies (meeting series)
♦ Oceanic Federation of Coloproctology (inactive)
♦ Oceanic Federation of Corporate Football (unconfirmed)
♦ Oceanic Preservation Society (internationally oriented national body)
♦ Oceanidas (internationally oriented national body)
♦ Ocean Lifeline (internationally oriented national body)
♦ Ocean Mammal Institute (internationally oriented national body)
♦ Ocean Navigation Congresses (inactive)
♦ Oceano Azul Foundation (internationally oriented national body)

♦ Ocean Observations Panel for Climate (OOPC) 17683

Chair IOC/UNESCO, 7 place de Fontenoy, 75732 Paris CEDEX 07, France. T. +33145684040. Fax +33145685813.
URL: http://ioc-goos-oopc.org/

History Derived from *Ocean Observing System Development Panel (OOSDP)*, set up 1990. **Languages** English. **Events** *Workshop on the South Pacific* Concepción (Chile) 2005. **NGO Relations** Member of: *Partnership for Observation of the Global Oceans (POGO, #18239)*. [2015.04.02/XE4165/**E**]

♦ Oceanographic Society of the Pacific / see Association for the Sciences of Limnology and Oceanography

♦ Oceanography Society (TOS) 17684

Exec Dir 1 Research Court, Suite 450-117, Rockville MD 20850, USA. T. +13012517708. E-mail: info@tos.org.
URL: http://www.tos.org/

History 1988, Washington, DC (USA). **Aims** Disseminate knowledge of oceanography and its application through research and education; promote communication among oceanographers; provide a constituency for consensus-building across all disciplines of the field. **Structure** Council. **Languages** English. **Staff** 1.00 FTE, paid. **Activities** Events/meetings; knowledge management/information dissemination; training/education. **Events** *Ocean Optics Conference* Norfolk, VA (USA) 2020, *Ocean Sciences Meeting* San Diego, CA (USA) 2020, *Ocean Optics Conference* Dubrovnik (Croatia) 2018, *Ocean Sciences Meeting* Portland, OR (USA) 2018, *Ocean Sciences Meeting* New Orleans, LA (USA) 2016. **Publications** *Oceanography* (4 a year). **Members** Individuals (2,300). Membership countries not specified. [2023.02.14/XN8433/**C**]

♦ Oceanomare-Delphis (internationally oriented national body)
♦ Ocean Outcomes (internationally oriented national body)

♦ Ocean Policy Institute Network in East Asian Region (OPINEAR) ... 17685

Secretariat c/o Ocean Policy Research Institute – SPF, SPF Building, 1-15-16 Toranomon, Minato-Ku, Tokyo, 105-8524 Japan. T. +81351575210. Fax +81351575230. E-mail: info@opinear.net.
URL: https://www.spf.org/opri/projects/ocean-policy/international/opinear/

History An informal network. **Aims** Provide pragmatic and efficient exchange of information and experience; conduct collaborative researches on common issues and current concerns through flexible bilateral or multilateral cooperative mechanism(s); promote capacity development. **Events** *Meeting* Tokyo (Japan) 2014, *Meeting* Singapore (Singapore) 2011, *Meeting* Seoul (Korea Rep) 2010, *Meeting* Kuala Lumpur (Malaysia) 2008, *Meeting* Tokyo (Japan) 2008.
Members Institutional (7) in 5 countries:
China, Japan, Korea Rep, Malaysia, Singapore.
Included in the above, 2 organizations listed in this Yearbook:
Center for Southeast Asian Studies-Indonesia (CSEAS-Indonesia); *Ocean Policy Research Institute (OPRI)*.
Observer (2):
Australian National Centre for Ocean Resources and Security (ANCORS); *Partnerships in Environmental Management for the Seas of East Asia (PEMSEA, #18242)*. [2014.11.13/XJ6151/jy/**F**]

♦ Ocean Policy Research Foundation / see Ocean Policy Research Institute

♦ Ocean Policy Research Institute (internationally oriented national body)

♦ Ocean Recovery Alliance (ORA) 17686

Contact 20th Fl – Central Tower, 28 Queen's Road, Central, Central and Western, Hong Kong. T. +85290203949. E-mail: info@oceanrecov.org.
URL: http://www.oceanrecov.org/

History Registered in the State of California (USA); Registered as a Charity in Hong Kong since 2011. **Aims** Create innovative solutions and collaborations to improve the health of the ocean. **Structure** Board of Directors. **Languages** English. **Activities** Projects/programmes; guidance/assistance/consulting; events/ meetings. **Publications** Reports. **Consultative Status** Consultative status granted from: *UNEP (#20299).* **IGO Relations** *Asia-Pacific Economic Cooperation (APEC, #01887); International Bank for Reconstruction and Development (IBRD, #12317)* (World Bank); *Partnerships in Environmental Management for the Seas of East Asia (PEMSEA, #18242); UNEP (#20299).* **NGO Relations** Participates in: *Global Partnership for Oceans (GPO, #10537).* [2020.03.10/XJ6778/**D**]

♦ Ocean Resources Conservation Association (inactive)
♦ Oceans 5 (internationally oriented national body)

♦ Ocean Sanctuary Alliance (OSA) 17687

Contact 400 E 67th St, New York NY 10065, USA.
Dep Exec Dir address not obtained. T. +12126302417.
URL: http://www.oceansanctuaryalliance.org/

Aims Restore and sustain the world's ocean, by securing national commitments to establish science-based *marine* sanctuaries. **Structure** Board of Directors; Board of Scientists. **Events** *Symposium on One Ocean, achieving Sustainability Through Sanctuaries* New York, NY (USA) 2015.
Members Country supporters of 14 countries:
Australia, Bahamas, Iceland, Israel, Italy, Maldives, Marshall Is, Monaco, Nauru, Netherlands, Palau, Papua New Guinea, Poland, Sweden.
Regional supporter:
European Union (EU, #08967).
Consultative Status Consultative status granted from: *ECOSOC (#05331)* (Special). [2018/XM4836/**D**]

♦ Oceans and Coastal Areas Network / see UN-OCEANS (#20711)
♦ OCEANS Network / see Organisation for Cooperation, Exchange And Networking among Students (#17802)
♦ **OCEANS** Organisation for Cooperation, Exchange And Networking among Students (#17802)
♦ Ocean Tracking Network (unconfirmed)
♦ Ocean Unite (internationally oriented national body)
♦ OCEMO – Office de Coopération Economique pour la Méditerranée et l'Orient (inactive)
♦ **OCE** Orthoptistes de la Communauté européenne (#17900)
♦ OCERINT – International Organization Center of Academic Research (internationally oriented national body)
♦ OCF – Orphans Care Federation (unconfirmed)
♦ OCGG – Oxford Council on Good Governance (internationally oriented national body)
♦ **OCHA** United Nations Office for the Coordination of Humanitarian Affairs (#20593)
♦ **OCHF** Oceania Continent Handball Federation (#17657)
♦ OCHS – Oxford Centre for Hindu Studies (internationally oriented national body)
♦ OCIA – Organic Crop Improvement Association (internationally oriented national body)
♦ OCIC Missionary Service / see SIGNIS Services Rome (#19274)
♦ OCIC – Ontario Council for International Cooperation (internationally oriented national body)
♦ OCIC – Organisation catholique internationale du cinéma et de l'audiovisuel (inactive)
♦ OCIC Servicio Misionero / see SIGNIS Services Rome (#19274)
♦ OCIES – Oceania Comparative and International Education Society (internationally oriented national body)
♦ **OCIMF** Oil Companies International Marine Forum (#17709)

♦ OC International (OCI) 17688

Address not obtained.
URL: http://www.onechallenge.org/

History 1952, as *Formosa Gospel Crusades*, also known as *Orient Crusades (Gospel Outreach).* Name changed to: *Overseas Crusades* 1956; *OC Ministries* 1979. Present name adopted 1990. **Aims** *Christian* leadership development. **Structure** African branch: *Africa Ministry Resources (AMR)*; Asia branch: OC Asia; Europe branch; Latin American branch. **Finance** Donations. Budget (annual): US$ 11.5 million. **Publications** *Church Growth Bulletin* (6 a year).
Members Full in 23 countries and territories:
Argentina, Brazil, Canada, Colombia, Eswatini, France, Germany, Greece, Guatemala, India, Indonesia, Japan, Kenya, Mexico, Mozambique, Philippines, Romania, Singapore, South Africa, Spain, Taiwan, UK, USA.
NGO Relations Member of: *European Evangelical Alliance (EEA, #07010); Global Connections.* Associate member of: *World Evangelical Alliance (WEA, #21393).* Instrumental in setting up: *Sports Ambassadors (SA).* [2017/XE3898/**E**]

♦ **OCI** OC International (#17688)
♦ **OCI** Organisation de la Coopération Islamique (#17813)
♦ OCI / see Organisation of Islamic Cooperation (#17813)
♦ OCI – Overseas Council International (internationally oriented national body)
♦ OCIPE / see Jesuit European Social Centre (#16103)
♦ OCIR – Organisation de la coopération de l'industrie des roulements à bille (inactive)
♦ OCIS – Oceanic Conference on International Studies (meeting series)
♦ OCIS – Oxford Centre for Islamic Studies (internationally oriented national body)
♦ OCist – Ordo Cisterciensis (religious order)
♦ Ockenden International (internationally oriented national body)
♦ Ockenden Venture / see Ockenden International
♦ OCLACC-AL – Asociación Católica Latinoamericana para la Radio, la Televisión y los Medios Afines (inactive)
♦ **OCLACC** Organización Católica Latinoamericana y Caribeña de Comunicación (#17833)
♦ **OCLAE** Organización Continental Latinoamericana y Caribeña de Estudiantes (#17834)
♦ OCLALAV – Organisation commune de lutte antiacridienne et de lutte antiaviaire (inactive)
♦ **OCLC** Online Computer Library Center (#17740)
♦ OCMC – Orthodox Christian Mission Center (internationally oriented national body)
♦ OCMI / see International Maritime Organization (#14102)
♦ OC Ministries / see OC International (#17688)
♦ OCMS – Oxford Centre for Mission Studies (internationally oriented national body)
♦ **OCNS** Organization for Computational Neurosciences (#17859)
♦ **OCO** Oceania Customs Organisation (#17658)
♦ **OCPA** Observatory of Cultural Policies in Africa (#17644)
♦ **OCPM** Organización de las Ciudades del Patrimonio Mundial (#17891)
♦ OCP – Old World Conference in Phonology (meeting series)
♦ OCP – Organización Cívica Panamericana (inactive)
♦ OCRBI – Organization for Cooperation in the Roller Bearings Industry (inactive)
♦ OCRS / see World Skate Oceania
♦ **OCSAN** Organisation pour la conservation du saumon de l'Atlantique Nord (#17574)
♦ OCSA – Organización de Cortes Supremas de las Américas (no recent information)
♦ OCSC – Oceania Cyber Security Centre (internationally oriented national body)
♦ OCSI – Organización de Cooperación y Solidaridad Internacional (internationally oriented national body)
♦ **OCS** Oceania Chondrichthyan Society (#17656)
♦ OCSO – Ordo Cisterciense Strictioris Observantiae (religious order)
♦ **OCS** Oriental Ceramic Society (#17892)
♦ OCTA / see Association of Overseas Countries and Territories of the European Union (#02843)
♦ **OCTA** Association of Overseas Countries and Territories of the European Union (#02843)
♦ OCT / see Association of Overseas Countries and Territories of the European Union (#02843)
♦ OCTE / see Overseas Council International
♦ OCTI / see Organisation intergouvernementale pour les transports internationaux ferroviaires (#17807)
♦ OCTPC – Organization for Cooperation of Socialist Countries in the Domain of Tele- and Postal Communications (inactive)
♦ OCTs / see Association of Overseas Countries and Territories of the European Union (#02843)
♦ OCUNA – Organisation of Commonwealth United Nations Associations (inactive)
♦ OCV / see Hand in Hand tegen Racisme
♦ **OCVV** Office communautaire des variétés végétales (#04404)
♦ OCW Consortium / see Open Education Consortium (#17751)
♦ ODA – Organization of Demographic Associates for East and Southeast Asia (inactive)
♦ **ODCA** Organización Demócrata Cristiana de América (#03899)
♦ ODCCP / see United Nations Office on Drugs and Crime (#20596)
♦ **ODECABE** Organización Deportiva Centroamericana y del Caribe (#03665)
♦ ODECA – Organización de Estados Centroamericanos (inactive)
♦ **ODEMA** Organización de Entidades Mutuales de las Américas (#17836)
♦ OdeM – Ordo Beatae Mariae Virginis de Mercede (religious order)
♦ **ODEPA** Organización Deportiva Panamericana (#18138)
♦ ODEPA / see Panam Sports Organization (#18138)
♦ **ODESUR** Organización Deportiva Sudamericana (#19708)

♦ Odette International 17689

Main Office 71 Great Peter St, London, SW1P 2BN, UK. T. +442073449227. Fax +442072357112. E-mail: info@odette.org.
URL: http://www.odette.org/

History 1 Jan 1985. Former names and other names: *Organization for Data Exchange by Teletransmission in Europe (ODETTE)* – former (1 Jan 1985); *Organisation de données échangées par télé-transmission en Europe* – former (1 Jan 1985). Registration: Companies House, No/ID: 4039150, England and Wales. **Aims** Set standards for *internet business communications*, engineering data exchange and logistics management linking *European automobile* industry businesses and their global trading partners. **Structure** Board of Directors, comprising 1 from each country. Officers: Chairman; Vice Chairman; General Manager. Main Committees (2): Logistics (LFC); Technology (TC). **Languages** English, French, German, Italian, Spanish, Swedish. **Finance** Members' dues (annual). **Activities** Develops tools and recommendations to improve flow of goods, services, product data and business information across the whole supply chain and throughout the product life-cycle. **Events** *Conference* Prague (Czechia) 2022, *Annual Conference* Lyon (France) 2014, *Annual Conference* Berlin (Germany) 2012, *Annual Conference* Stuttgart (Germany) 2012, *Annual Conference* Lyon (France) 2011. **Publications** Labels; specifications; other.
Members Full; Associate, in 12 countries:
Belgium, Czechia, France, Germany, Italy, Luxembourg, Netherlands, Romania, Spain, Sweden, Türkiye, UK.
[2021/XD8820/**E**]

♦ ODETTE / see Odette International (#17689)
♦ ODF – International Conference on Optics-photonics Design & Fabrication (meeting series)
♦ ODG / see International Development, UEA
♦ ODG – Observatori del Deute en la Globalització (internationally oriented national body)
♦ ODI Europe (unconfirmed)
♦ ODIHR / see OSCE – Office for Democratic Institutions and Human Rights (#17902)
♦ **ODINAFRICA** Ocean Data and Information Network for Africa (#17648)
♦ **ODIN** ODIN – Open Mobility Data in the Nordics (#17690)

♦ ODIN – Open Mobility Data in the Nordics (ODIN) 17690

Coordinator address not obtained.
Coordinator address not obtained.
URL: https://nordicopenmobilitydata.eu/

History Started as a project coordinated by RISE ICT Viktoria (Research Institutes of Sweden). **Aims** Accelerate and coordinate the work necessary to create a unified market within the mobility sector in the Nordics.
Members Full in 4 countries:
Denmark, Finland, Norway, Sweden.
NGO Relations Member of (1): *MobilityData (#16838).* [2022/AA3216/**F**]

♦ ODI – Open Door International: for the Economic Emancipation of the Woman Worker (no recent information)
♦ ODI – Overseas Development Institute (internationally oriented national body)
♦ **ODN** Oceania Development Network (#17660)
♦ ODN – Ordinis Dominae Nostrae (religious order)
♦ Odontological Circle of the South (inactive)
♦ Odontological Confederation of the Andean Region (inactive)

♦ Odontological Federation of Central America and Panama 17691

Fédération odontologique d'Amérique centrale et du Panama – Federación Odontológica de Centroamérica y Panama (FOCAP)

Exec Sec address not obtained.
Exec Dir address not obtained.
URL: http://www.focap.org/

History 29 Sep 1956, San Salvador (El Salvador). **Aims** Promote odontology with its scientific, ethical and cultural aspects; provide links between members; integrate odontology in the social environment. **Structure** Congress; Executive Committee. **Languages** Spanish. **Events** *Congress* Panama (Panama) 2020, *Congress* Managua (Nicaragua) 2018, *Congress* Tegucigalpa (Honduras) 2016, *Congress* San José (Costa Rica) 2015, *Biennial Congress* Panama (Panama) 2010.
Members National societies and colleges (9) in 6 countries:
Costa Rica (2), El Salvador, Guatemala (2), Honduras (2), Nicaragua, Panama.
Affiliate bodies (2) in 2 countries:
El Salvador, Honduras. [2021/XD3014/**D**]

♦ Odrudový úrad Spolecenstvi (#04404)
♦ ODSC – Oficina de Desarrollo de Seguros Cooperativos (inactive)
♦ ODSTA – Organisation démocratique syndicale des travailleurs africains (inactive)
♦ ODTÜ – Orta Dogu Teknik Üniversitesi (internationally oriented national body)
♦ **ODUCAL** Organización de Universidades Católicas de América Latina y el Caribe (#17858)
♦ ODUCAL / see Organization of Catholic Universities in Latin America and the Caribbean (#17858)
♦ ODVV – Organization for Defending Victims of Violence (internationally oriented national body)
♦ ODW – Open Data Watch (internationally oriented national body)
♦ OE / see Operation Eyesight Universal
♦ **OEACP** Organisation des Etats d'Afrique, des Caraïbes et du Pacifique (#17796)
♦ **OEACP** Organización de Estados de África, el Caribe y el Pacífico (#17796)
♦ OeAD – Österreichische Austauschdienst (internationally oriented national body)
♦ **OEAED** Organization for East Asia Economic Development (#17862)
♦ **OEA** Organisation des Etats Américains (#17629)
♦ OEA – Organisation of European Aluminium Refiners and Remelters (inactive)
♦ **OEA** Organização dos Estados Americanos (#17629)
♦ **OEA** Organización de los Estados Americanos (#17629)
♦ **OEB** Association européenne des bateliers (#08491)
♦ OEBB – Organisation européenne des bardeaux bitumés (inactive)
♦ OEBC – Organisation européenne pour la biologie cellulaire (inactive)
♦ **OEB** Office européen des brevets (#08166)

- ♦ **OECAM** Organization of European Copper Alloy Ingot Makers (#17866)
- ♦ OECC – Overseas Environment Cooperation Centre (internationally oriented national body)
- ♦ OECD anti-bribery convention – OECD Convention on Combating Bribery of Foreign Public Officials in International Business Transactions (1997 treaty)
- ♦ OECD Convention on Combating Bribery of Foreign Public Officials in International Business Transactions (1997 treaty)
- ♦ OECD Development Assistance Committee (see: #17693)

♦ OECD Development Centre 17692

Centre de développement de l'OCDE

Contact 46 quai Alphonse le Gallo, 92100 Boulogne-Billancourt, France. T. +33145248200. Fax +33144306149. E-mail: dev.contact@oecd.org – bochra.kriout@oecd.org.
Mailing Address 2 rue André-Pascal, 75775 Paris CEDEX 16, France.
URL: http://www.oecd.org/dev/

History 23 Oct 1962, Paris (France). Established as a semi-autonomous institution within *OECD (#17693)*. **Aims** Help developing countries and emerging economies find innovative policy solutions to promote sustainable growth, reduce poverty and inequalities, and improve people's lives; facilitate a policy dialogue between governments, involving public, private and philanthropic actors. **Structure** Governing Board; Director/Chief Development Economist. Although responsible to member governments, the Centre has the autonomy and scientific independence required to perform its tasks. **Languages** English, French. **Staff** 96.00 FTE, paid. **Finance** Sources: contributions of member/participating states. **Activities** Advocacy/lobbying/activism; projects/programmes. Networks: Emerging Markets Network (EMnet); Global Network of Foundations Working for Devleopment (netFWD); Development Communication (DevCom); Centre of Philanthropy. **Events** *Annual international forum on African perspectives* Paris (France) 2005, *Annual international forum on Latin American perspectives* Madrid (Spain) 2001, *Annual international forum on Latin American perspectives* Paris (France) 2000, *International forum on Asian perspectives* Paris (France) 2000, *Meeting on development and finance* Paris (France) 2000. **Publications** *Africa's Development Dynamics* (annual); *Latin American Economic Outlook* (annual); *Economic Outlook for Southeast Asia, China and India. Development Centre Policy Briefs*; *Development Centre Policy Insights*; *Development Centre Studies*; *Development Centre Working Papers*.

Members States (39):
Austria, Belgium, Brazil, Chile, Colombia, Costa Rica, Czechia, Egypt, Finland, France, Germany, Greece, Iceland, India, Indonesia, Ireland, Israel, Italy, Kenya, Korea Rep, Luxembourg, Mauritius, Mexico, Morocco, Netherlands, Norway, Peru, Poland, Portugal, Romania, Slovakia, South Africa, Spain, Sweden, Switzerland, Thailand, Türkiye, UK, Vietnam.
Regional integration EU entity (1), listed in this Yearbook:
European Union (EU, #08967).

IGO Relations Cooperates with: OECD Secretariat; UN specialized agencies; *African Development Bank (ADB, #00283)*; *Asian Development Bank (ADB, #01422)*; *Inter-American Development Bank (IDB, #11427)*; *International Bank for Reconstruction and Development (IBRD, #12317)*; *International Development Association (IDA, #13155)*; *International Monetary Fund (IMF, #14180)*. **NGO Relations** Regular contacts with some 700 development research and training institutes grouped in regional associations: *Association of Development Research and Training Institutes of Asia and the Pacific (ADIPA, inactive)*; *Council for the Development of Social Science Research in Africa (CODESRIA, #04879)*; *European Association of Development Research and Training Institutes (EADI, #06012)*; *Consejo Latinoamericano de Ciencias Sociales (CLACSO, #04718)*. Founding member of: *Global Research Consortium on Economic Structural Transformation (GReCEST)*.
[2023.02.14/XE7985/**E***]

- ♦ OECD Higher Education Programme (inactive)
- ♦ OECD-IGUS / see International Group of Experts on the Explosion Risks of Unstable Substances (#13746)
- ♦ OECD multilateral agreement on investment (inactive)
- ♦ OECD Nuclear Energy Agency / see Nuclear Energy Agency (#17615)

♦ OECD – Organisation for Economic Co-operation and Development 17693

Organisation de coopération et de développement économiques (OCDE)

SG 2 rue André Pascal, 75775 Paris CEDEX 16, France. T. +33145248200. Fax +33145248500. E-mail: webmaster@oecd.org – civilsociety@oecd.org – grs.contact@oecd.org.
URL: http://www.oecd.org/

History 30 Sep 1961, Paris (France). Established by *'Convention on the Organisation for Economic Cooperation and Development – Convention relative à l'Organisation de coopération et de développement économiques'*, signed 14 Dec 1960. Successor body to *Organization for European Economic Cooperation (OEEC, inactive)*, set up 16 Apr 1948, Paris, in connection with the *'Marshall Plan'*. **Aims** Help governments foster prosperity and fight poverty through economic growth and financial stability; help ensure that environmental implications of economic and social development are taken into account. **Structure** Council (decision-making body), comprising one representative from each member country, plus a representative of the European Commission. Executive Committee. General Secretariat, includes: International Futures Programme; Council and Executive Committee Secretariat; Directorate for Legal Affairs; Global Relations Secretariat; Internal Audit and Evaluation. Executive Directorate; Public Affairs and Communications Directorate. Departments (12): Development Co-operation Directorate; Economics Department; Directorate for Education and Skills; Directorate for Employment, Labour and Social Affairs; Centre for Entrepreneurship, SMEs and Local Development; Environment Directorate; Directorate for Financial and Enterprise Affairs; Public Governance and Territorial Development Directorate; Directorate for Science, Technology and Industry; Statistics Directorate; Centre for Tax Policy and Administration; Trade and Agriculture Directorate. Committees, working groups and expert groups (about 250 in total). Centres (4): Berlin (Germany); Mexico City (Mexico); Tokyo (Japan); Washington DC (USA). Special bodies: *Africa Partnership Forum (APF, #00510)*; *OECD Development Centre (#17692)*; *Financial Action Task Force (FATF, #09765)*; *International Energy Agency (IEA, #13270)*; *International Transport Forum (ITF, #15725)*; *Nuclear Energy Agency (NEA, #17615)*; *Sahel and West Africa Club (SWAC, #19034)*. **Languages** English, French. **Staff** 2500.00 FTE, paid. Personnel negotiations through staff associations, including: *Staff Association of the OECD (#19940)*; *International Association of Former OEEC and OECD Staff (#11904)*. *Administrative Tribunal of the Organisation for Economic Co-operation and Development (#00119)*, set up Dec 1991, works in the framework of regulations applying to staff, former officials, auxiliary staff and employees and to Council experts and consultants. **Finance** Sources: contributions of member/participating states. Annual budget: 354,000,000 EUR (2013). **Activities** Work is based on continued monitoring of events in member countries as well as outside OECD area, and includes regular projections of short and medium-term economic developments. Secretariat collects and analyzes data, after which committees discuss policy regarding this information. Council makes decisions, and then governments implement recommendations. Mutual examination by governments, multilateral surveillance and a peer review process through which the performance of individual countries is monitored by their peers, all carried out at committee-level. Representatives of the 34 OECD member countries meet in specialized committees to advance ideas and review progress in specific policy areas, such as economics, trade, science, employment, education or financial markets. Some 40,000 senior officials from national administration attend committee meetings each year to request, review and contribute to work undertaken by the OECD Secretariat. Organizes: Annual Council Meeting at Ministerial Level; Annual OECD Forum; other meetings. Instrumental in setting up: *Global Forum on Transparency and Exchange of Information for Tax Purposes (#10379)*; *OECD Development Assistance Committee (DAC, see: #17693)*; *Round Table on Sustainable Development at the OECD (see: #17693)*. **Events** *Asian Regional Round Table on Macroeconomic and Structural Policy Challenges* 2022, *Round Table on Labor Migration in Asia* Bangkok (Thailand) 2022, *Conference on Measuring Regulatory Performance* Brussels (Belgium) 2022, *Global Forum on Public Debt Management* Paris (France) 2022, *Asian Public Governance Forum* Seoul (Korea Rep) 2022. **Publications** *Going for Growth*; *OECD Economic Outlook*; *OECD Factbook*; *OECD Insights*; *OECD Observer. Better Policies Series.* OECD Economic Surveys. At-a-Glance books. **Information Services** *OECD iLibrary* – full range of OECD books, papers and statistics in PDF, WEB and XML formats, for online users at universities, governments and think tanks; *OECD Online Bookshop* – OECD books and subscriptionsn to journals and online services for individuals; *OECD Publishing* – books in the fields of economics and public affairs, including over 250 new books, 40 updated statistical databases, thousands of new staistical tables, working papers and journal arcticles each year.

Members Governments of 34 countries:
Australia, Austria, Belgium, Canada, Chile, Czechia, Denmark, Estonia, Finland, France, Germany, Greece, Hungary, Iceland, Ireland, Israel, Italy, Japan, Korea Rep, Luxembourg, Mexico, Netherlands, New Zealand, Norway, Poland, Portugal, Slovakia, Slovenia, Spain, Sweden, Switzerland, Türkiye, UK, USA.

IGO Relations
- *Asian Development Bank (ADB, #01422)*;
- *Bank for International Settlements (BIS, #03165)*;
- *Codex Alimentarius Commission (CAC, #04081)*;
- *Commonwealth Secretariat (#04362)*;
- *Convention on Biological Diversity (Biodiversity convention, 1992)*;
- *Council of Europe (CE, #04881)*;
- *ECOSOC (#05331)*;
- *EFTA (#05391)*;
- *European Bank for Reconstruction and Development (EBRD, #06315)*;
- *European Commission (EC, #06633)*;
- *European Union (EU, #08967)*;
- *FAO (#09260)*;
- *Financial Stability Board (FSB, #09770)*;
- *Group of Eight (G-8, #10745)*;
- *Group of Ten (G-10, inactive)*;
- *ILO (#11123)*;
- *Inter-American Development Bank (IDB, #11427)*;
- *International Atomic Energy Agency (IAEA, #12294)*;
- *International Bank for Reconstruction and Development (IBRD, #12317)* – World Bank;
- *International Council for the Exploration of the Sea (ICES, #13021)*;
- *International Fund for Agricultural Development (IFAD, #13692)*;
- *International Maritime Organization (IMO, #14102)*;
- *International Monetary Fund (IMF, #14180)*;
- *International Organization for Migration (IOM, #14454)*;
- *New Partnership for Africa's Development (NEPAD, #17091)*;
- *Nordic Council (NC, #17256)*;
- *OAS (#17629)*;
- *OIE – World Organisation for Animal Health (#17703)*;
- *OSPAR Commission for the Protection of the Marine Environment of the North-East Atlantic (OSPAR Commission, #17905)*;
- *Parliamentary Assembly of the Council of Europe (PACE, #18211)*;
- *Secretariat of the United Nations Convention to Combat Desertification (Secretariat of the UNCCD, #19208)*;
- *Southern Common Market (#19868)*;
- *Standing Committee to the Bern Convention on the Conservation of European Wildlife and Natural Habitats (#19949)*;
- *UNEP (#20299)*;
- *UNCTAD (#20285)*;
- *UNESCO (#20322)*;
- *UNHCR (#20327)*;
- *UNIDO (#20336)*;
- *United Nations (UN, #20515)*;
- *United Nations Conference on Environment and Development (UNCED)*;
- *United Nations Framework Convention on Climate Change (UNFCCC, 1992)*;
- *United Nations Group on the Information Society (UNGIS, #20570)*;
- *United Nations Office on Drugs and Crime (UNODC, #20596)*;
- *WHO (#20950)*;
- *World Customs Organization (WCO, #21350)*;
- *World Trade Organization (WTO, #21864)*.

NGO Relations By Decision of the Council, 13 Mar 1962, international non-governmental organisations which are deemed to be widely representative in general economic matters or in a specific economy sector can be granted consultative status enabling them to discuss subjects of common interest with a Liaison Committee chaired by Secretary-General and be consulted in a particular field by the relevant body of the Organisation. So far, this status has been granted to: *Business and Industry Advisory Committee to the OECD (BIAC, #03385)*; *International Association of Crafts and Small and Medium-Sized Enterprises (IACME, inactive)*; *Trade Union Advisory Committee to the OECD (TUAC, #20186)*. Other NGOs are regularly consulted on various aspects of OECD work programme on an ad hoc basis.
[2020/XC3023/**C***]

♦ OECD Watch 17694

Coordinator c/o SOMO, KNSM-laan 17, 1019 LA Amsterdam, Netherlands. T. +31206391291. E-mail: info@oecdwatch.org.
URL: http://www.oecdwatch.org/

History 22 Mar 2003, Amersfoort (Netherlands). **Aims** Monitor and contribute to the work of the OECD Committee on International Investment; test effectiveness of OECD Guidelines for Multinational Enterprises and its National Contact Point system as a corporate accountability tool; disseminate information to civil society groups; advise NGOs. **Structure** Coordination Committee. Hosted by: *Stichting Onderzoek Multinationale Ondernemingen (SOMO)*. **Finance** Sources include: Dutch Ministry of Foreign Affairs; *Brot für die Welt*. **Activities** Advocacy/lobbying/activism; capacity building; events/meetings; guidance/assistance/consulting; research/documentation. **Events** *Conference* Brussels (Belgium) 2007. **Publications** Quarterly case updates. Briefing papers; guidelines; submissions; NCP reviews; toolkits/guides. Information Services: Case database.

Members Organizations (over 130) in 48 countries:
Argentina, Australia, Austria, Bangladesh, Belgium, Brazil, Burkina Faso, Cambodia, Cameroon, Canada, Chile, Congo DR, Czechia, Denmark, Ecuador, Finland, France, Germany, Ghana, Guatemala, India, Indonesia, Italy, Japan, Korea Rep, Liberia, Malawi, Mali, Mexico, Netherlands, New Zealand, Norway, Pakistan, Peru, Philippines, Poland, Romania, Senegal, Slovakia, South Africa, Spain, Sweden, Switzerland, Thailand, UK, USA, Venezuela, Zambia.
Included in the above, 35 organizations listed in this Yearbook:
- *Accountability Counsel*;
- *African Law Foundation (AFRILAW)*;
- *African Resources Watch (AFREWATCH)*;
- *Alliance Sud, Swiss Alliance of Development Organisations Swissaid – Catholic Lenten Fund – Bread for All – Helvetas – Caritas – Interchurch Aid*;
- *Association africaine de défense des droits de l'homme (ASADHO)*;
- *BankTrack (#03166)*;
- *Both ENDS (#03307)*;
- *Center for Human Rights and Environment (CEDHA)*;
- *Center for International Environmental Law (CIEL)*;
- *Christian Aid*;
- *Clean Clothes Campaign (CCC, #03986)*;
- *Coordinadora Andina de Organizaciones Indígenas (CAOI, #04804)*;
- *Earthjustice*;
- *EarthRights International (ERI)*;
- *European Center for Constitutional and Human Rights (ECCHR)*;
- *European Environmental Bureau (EEB, #06996)*;
- *Fairfood International (#09237)*;
- *Forum for Kvinner og Utviklingsspørsmål (FOKUS)*;
- *Frank Bold Society*;
- *Friends of the Earth Europe (FoEE, #10001)*;
- *Global Labor Justice-International Labor Rights Forum (GLJ-ILRF)*;
- *Global Witness (GW)*;
- *International Federation for Human Rights (#13452)*;
- *International Rivers*;
- *Jus Semper Global Alliance (TJSGA)*;
- *Oxfam Australia*;
- *Oxfam Novib*;
- *Public Eye*;
- *Quaker Council for European Affairs (QCEA, #18587)*;
- *Research Group for an Alternative Economic Strategy (GRESEA)*;
- *Rights and Accountability in Development (RAID)*;
- *Sherpa*;
- *Traidcraft Exchange*;
- *Verdens Skove*;
- *Vier Pfoten International (#20776)*;
- *Wilderness Society*;
- *World Animal Protection (#21092)*;
- *World Wide Fund for Nature (WWF, #21922)*.

NGO Relations Links with NGOs worldwide, not specified.
[2022/XM3439/y/**F**]

- ♦ OECE – Organisation européenne de coopération économique (inactive)
- ♦ **OECI** Organization of European Cancer Institutes (#17865)
- ♦ OECL – Organisation européenne des industries de la conserve de légumes (inactive)
- ♦ **OECO** Organisation des Etats des Caraïbes orientales (#17804)
- ♦ **OECO** Organización de los Estados del Caribe Oriental (#17804)
- ♦ OEC – Organisation of Educational Cooperation (unconfirmed)
- ♦ OECQ / see European Organization for Quality (#08112)
- ♦ **OECS Bar Association** Organization of Eastern Caribbean Bar Associations (#17863)
- ♦ **OECS/CBU** Organisation of Eastern Caribbean States/Competitive Business Unit (#17805)
- ♦ OECS Directorate of Civil Aviation / see Eastern Caribbean Civil Aviation Authority (#05232)
- ♦ OECS/EDU / see Organisation of Eastern Caribbean States/Competitive Business Unit (#17805)
- ♦ **OECS** Organisation of Eastern Caribbean States (#17804)
- ♦ OECT – Organisation européenne du commerce de gros en textile (inactive)
- ♦ Oecumenische Ontwikkelings Coöperatie / see Oikocredit International (#17704)
- ♦ Oecumenische Vereniging van Vormingscentra in Europa (#17706)
- ♦ OEDT / see European Monitoring Centre for Drugs and Drug Addiction (#07820)
- ♦ OEEC – Organization for European Economic Cooperation (inactive)
- ♦ OEE – Observatoire de l'épargne européenne (internationally oriented national body)
- ♦ OEEPE / see European Spatial Data Research (#08806)
- ♦ **OEFM** l'Observatoire européen des forêts de montagne (#08073)
- ♦ OEF – One Earth Future Foundation (internationally oriented national body)
- ♦ OEF – Organization of Employers' Federations and Employers in Developing Countries (inactive)
- ♦ OEHE / see European Network for Ombudsmen in Higher Education (#07958)
- ♦ OEICCF – Organisation européenne des industries des confitures et conserves de fruit (inactive)
- ♦ OEICT / see European Organisation of Tomato Industries (#08104)
- ♦ OEIL-JT – Organisation européenne des unions pour l'insertion et le logement des jeunes travailleurs (no recent information)
- ♦ **OEI** Organização de Estados Ibero-americanos para a Educação, a Ciência e a Cultura (#17871)
- ♦ **OEI** Organización de Estados Iberoamericanos para la Educación, la Ciencia y la Cultura (#17871)
- ♦ OEI – Osteuropa-Institut (internationally oriented national body)
- ♦ OEIT / see European Organisation of Tomato Industries (#08104)
- ♦ OEITFL / see European Association of Fruit and Vegetable Processors (#06049)
- ♦ Oekumenische Entwicklungsgenossenschaft / see Oikocredit International (#17704)
- ♦ Oekumenischer Rat für Praktisches Christentum (inactive)
- ♦ **OEL** Gruppa Obedinennyh Evropejskih Levyh Sil (#10794)
- ♦ **OELS** Observatoire européen du logement social (#08502)
- ♦ OENDDF – Observatoire Européen de la Non-Discrimination et des Droits Fondamentaux (unconfirmed)

♦ Oenological Products and Practices (OEnoppia) 17695

Exec Dir 21-23 rue Croulebarbe, 75013 Paris, France. T. +33617855684.
URL: http://www.oenoppia.com/

History Jun 2009. **Aims** Act as a representative for all regulatory or scientific bodies implicated in considerations concerning the evolution of oenological practices. **Structure** Executive Committee. **Members** Corporate; Advisory (2), including the following listed in this Yearbook:
Confédération des Fabricants de Levure de l'Union Européenne (COFALEC, #04551).
IGO Relations Observer member of: *International Organisation of Vine and Wine (OIV, #14435).* Observer to: *Codex Alimentarius Commission (CAC, #04081).* [2019.07.24/XJ2147/y/**D**]

- ♦ **OEnoppia** Oenological Products and Practices (#17695)
- ♦ **OEPA** Onchocerciasis Elimination Program for the Americas (#17726)
- ♦ OEP – Observatoire européen du plurilinguisme (internationally oriented national body)
- ♦ **OEPP** Organisation Européenne et Méditerranéenne pour la Protection des Plantes (#07773)
- ♦ OEPTE – Organisation européenne pour la promotion du tourisme équestre (inactive)
- ♦ **OEQ** Organisation européenne pour la qualité (#08112)
- ♦ **OER Africa** Open Educational Resources Africa (#17750)
- ♦ OER – Office européen de radiodiffusion (inactive)
- ♦ OERS / see European Space Research and Technology Centre (#08802)
- ♦ **OERTC** Organisation européenne pour la recherche et le traitement du cancer (#08101)
- ♦ **OESAI** Organization of Eastern and Southern Africa Insurers (#17864)
- ♦ OESK – Osteuropaeiska Solidaritetskommittén (internationally oriented national body)
- ♦ **OESO** Organisation mondiale d'études spécialisées sur les maladies de l'oesophage (#17818)
- ♦ **OES** Organisation européenne des scieries (#08114)
- ♦ OET – Organización para Estudios Tropicales (internationally oriented national body)
- ♦ OEU / see Operation Eyesight Universal
- ♦ OEUFSJT – Organisation européenne des unions de foyers et services pour jeunes travailleurs (inactive)
- ♦ L'Oeuvre (religious order)
- ♦ Oeuvre des congrès eucharistiques internationaux / see Pontifical Committee for International Eucharistic Congresses (#18442)
- ♦ Oeuvre des écoles d'Orient / see Oeuvre d'Orient
- ♦ Oeuvre Kolping internationale / see KOLPING INTERNATIONAL (#16203)
- ♦ L'Oeuvre Léger / see Mission Inclusion
- ♦ L'Oeuvre Léger – Pour la dignité humaine au Québec et dans le monde / see Mission Inclusion
- ♦ Oeuvre Notre-Dame de Montligeon (religious order)
- ♦ Oeuvre d'Orient (internationally oriented national body)
- ♦ Oeuvre Pontificale de l'Enfance Missionnaire (see: #16827)
- ♦ Oeuvre Pontificale Missionnaire de Saint Pierre-Apôtre (see: #16827)
- ♦ Oeuvres des dames du Calvaire (religious order)
- ♦ Oeuvres Hospitalières de l'Ordre de Malte (internationally oriented national body)
- ♦ Oeuvres mir / see MIR partenariats et développement international
- ♦ Oeuvres Pontificales Missionnaire de la Propagation de la Foi (religious order)
- ♦ Oeuvres pontificales missionnaires / see MISSIO (#16827)
- ♦ Oeuvres sociales et éducatives des jésuites au Tiers-Monde (internationally oriented national body)
- ♦ OEVFVPC – Organizzazione Europea Vigili del Fuoco Volontari di Protezione Civile (internationally oriented national body)
- ♦ OEVS / see International Observatory of Violence in the School Environment (#14389)
- ♦ OFADEC – Office africain pour le développement et la coopération (internationally oriented national body)
- ♦ **OFAP** Organization of the Families of Asia and the Pacific (#17867)
- ♦ OFCA – Organisation des Fabricants de Produits Cellulosiques Alimentaires (no recent information)
- ♦ OFCI – Observatoire français de la coopération internationale (internationally oriented national body)
- ♦ **OFC** Oceania Fencing Confederation (#17661)
- ♦ **OFC** Oceania Football Confederation (#17662)
- ♦ OFCP – Oceanic Federation of Coloproctology (inactive)
- ♦ **OFEDO/UDUAL** Organización de Facultades, Escuelas y Departamentos de Odontologia de la Unión de Universidades de América Latina (#17837)
- ♦ OFE / see Euro+Med PlantBase (#05732)
- ♦ **OFEG** Ocean Facilities Exchange Group (#17650)
- ♦ OFE – Observatoire de la Francophonie économique (internationally oriented national body)
- ♦ OFE – OpenForum Europe (unconfirmed)
- ♦ Office africain pour le développement et la coopération (internationally oriented national body)
- ♦ Office allemand d'échanges universitaires (internationally oriented national body)
- ♦ Office of the Americas (internationally oriented national body)
- ♦ Office of the Americas for the Cause of Justice and Peace / see Office of the Americas
- ♦ Office du baccalauréat international / see International Baccalaureate (#12306)
- ♦ Office Benelux de la propriété intellectuelle (#03202)
- ♦ Office catholique d'information et d'initiative pour l'Europe / see Jesuit European Social Centre (#16103)
- ♦ Office central de documentation féminine (inactive)
- ♦ Office central d'entr'aide des églises (inactive)
- ♦ Office central espérantiste (inactive)
- ♦ Office central européen de police criminelle (#08239)
- ♦ Office central des institutions internationales / see Union of International Associations (#20414)
- ♦ Office central international pour le contrôle des spiritueux en Afrique (inactive)
- ♦ Office central des nationalités (inactive)
- ♦ Office central suisse d'aide aux réfugiés / see Organisation suisse d'aide aux réfugiés
- ♦ Office central des transports internationaux par chemins de fer / see Organisation intergouvernementale pour les transports internationaux ferroviaires (#17807)
- ♦ Office centroaméricain du café (inactive)
- ♦ Office communautaire des variétés végétales (#04404)
- ♦ Office de Coopération Economique pour la Méditerranée et l'Orient (inactive)
- ♦ Office for the Coordination of Humanitarian Affairs / see United Nations Office for the Coordination of Humanitarian Affairs (#20593)
- ♦ Office for Democratic Institutions and Human Rights / see OSCE – Office for Democratic Institutions and Human Rights (#17902)
- ♦ Office for Drug Control and Crime Prevention / see United Nations Office on Drugs and Crime (#20596)
- ♦ Office of Economic Cooperation for Mediterranean and Middle East (inactive)
- ♦ Office Eglantyne Jebb pour la protection de l'enfance d'origine non-européenne (inactive)
- ♦ Office Employees International Union / see Office and Professional Employees International Union
- ♦ Office eurasien des brevets (#05612)
- ♦ Office of the European Ombudsman / see European Ombudsman (#08084)
- ♦ Office européen des brevets (#08166)
- ♦ Office européen de lutte antifraude (#05906)
- ♦ Office européen de radiodiffusion (inactive)
- ♦ Office for Free Elections / see OSCE – Office for Democratic Institutions and Human Rights (#17902)
- ♦ Office de l'harmonisation dans le marché intérieur – marques, dessins et modèles / see European Union Intellectual Property Office (#08996)
- ♦ Office for Harmonization in the Internal Market – Trade Marks and Designs / see European Union Intellectual Property Office (#08996)
- ♦ Office of the High Commissioner for Refugees under the Protection of the League (inactive)

♦ Office of the High Representative in Bosnia and Herzegovina (OHR) 17696

Headquarters Emerika Bluma 1, 71000 Sarajevo, Bosnia-Herzegovina. T. +38733283500. Fax +38733283501. E-mail: sarajevo.rd@ohr.int.
URL: http://www.ohr.int/

History 14 Dec 1995, Paris (France), on signature of the *Bosnian Peace Agreement*, initiated 21 Nov 1995, Dayton OH (USA). The mandate of the High Representative is to oversee the civilian implementation of the Agreement and this mandate derives from the London (UK) Peace Implementation Conference of 8-9 Dec 1995 and Resolution 1031 of 15 Dec 1995 of *United Nations Security Council (UNSC, #20625)*. Steering Board of *Peace Implementation Council (#18279)*, set up at the same time as OHR, provides political guidance on peace implementation. **Aims** Under Annex 10 to the Peace Agreement: monitor implementation of the peace settlement; coordinate activities of *civilian* organizations and agencies; maintain close contact with the parties to the Agreement to promote their full compliance with all civilian aspects of the Agreement; facilitate the resolution of any difficulties arising in connection with civilian complementation. **Structure** Headquarters in Sarajevo (Bosnia-Herzegovina); Regional Office in Banja Luka (Bosnia-Herzegovina). **Staff** International: 15; National: 89. **Finance** Funded by PIC. Contributions: EU 54.3%; USA; 22%; Japan 10%; Russia 1.2%; Canada 3.03%; OIC 2.5%; others 6.9%. Annual budget (2016/2017) euro 5,999,000. **Activities** Monitoring/evaluation; conflict resolution. **IGO Relations** *SIGMA Programme (#19272); Organization for Security and Cooperation in Europe (OSCE, #17887).* [2017.03.22/XE3234/**E***]

- ♦ Office d'information pour le scoutisme catholique (inactive)
- ♦ Office interaméricain du café (inactive)
- ♦ Office interaméricain de radiodiffusion (inactive)
- ♦ Office of International Affairs, University of Windsor / see Windsor International, University of Windsor
- ♦ Office international du cacao et du chocolat (inactive)
- ♦ Office international du cacao, du chocolat et de la confiserie / see International Confectionery Association (#12840)
- ♦ Office international du cadastre et du régime foncier (#14398)
- ♦ Office international de chimie (inactive)
- ♦ Office international de documentation pour la chasse (inactive)
- ♦ Office international de documentation de médecine militaire (inactive)
- ♦ Office international de documentation pour la pêche (inactive)
- ♦ Office international de l'eau (#14399)
- ♦ Office International de l'Enseignement Catholique (#03604)
- ♦ Office international des épizooties / see OIE – World Organisation for Animal Health (#17703)
- ♦ Office international d'hygiène publique (inactive)
- ♦ Office international des jardins familiaux / see Fédération Internationale des Jardins Familiaux (#09641)
- ♦ Office international de médecine aéronautique (inactive)
- ♦ Office international des musées (inactive)
- ♦ Office international Nansen pour les réfugiés (inactive)
- ♦ Office international des oeuvres d'éducation populaire (inactive)
- ♦ Office international pour la protection de la nature (inactive)
- ♦ Office international du travail à domicile (inactive)
- ♦ Office international de la viande (#14125)
- ♦ Office international de la vigne et du vin / see International Organisation of Vine and Wine (#14435)
- ♦ Office international du vin / see International Organisation of Vine and Wine (#14435)
- ♦ Office mondial des statistiques du métal (#21250)
- ♦ Office des Nations Unies contre la drogue et le crime (#20596)
- ♦ Office des Nations Unies à Genève (#20597)
- ♦ Office des Nations unies à Nairobi (#20600)
- ♦ Office des Nations Unies à Vienne (#20604)
- ♦ Office notarial permanent d'échange international (see: #15795)
- ♦ Office and Professional Employees International Union (internationally oriented national body)
- ♦ Office for Project Services / see United Nations Office for Project Services (#20602)
- ♦ Office des publications de l'Union européenne (#18562)
- ♦ Office de recherche scientifique et technique outre-mer / see Institut de recherche pour le développement
- ♦ Office régional de l'OMS pour l'Asie du Sud-Est (#20946)
- ♦ Office de secours et de travaux des Nations Unies pour les réfugiés de Palestine dans le Proche-Orient (#20622)
- ♦ Office of the Special Coordinator in the Occupied Territories / see Office of the United Nations Special Coordinator for the Middle East Process (#17698)
- ♦ Office statistique des Communautés européennes / see Statistical Office of the European Union (#19974)
- ♦ Office statistique des Nations Unies (inactive)
- ♦ Office statistique de l'Union européenne (#19974)
- ♦ Office technique d'études et de coopération internationale (internationally oriented national body)

- ♦ Office for the UNESCO Representative to Brunei Darussalam, Indonesia, Malaysia, the Philippines and Timor-Leste / see UNESCO Office, Jakarta – Regional Bureau for Sciences in Asia and the Pacific (#20313)
- ♦ Office for the UNESCO Representative to Indonesia, Malaysia and the Philippines / see UNESCO Office, Jakarta – Regional Bureau for Sciences in Asia and the Pacific (#20313)
- ♦ Office for the UNESCO Representative to Indonesia, Malaysia, the Philippines and Timor-Leste / see UNESCO Office, Jakarta – Regional Bureau for Sciences in Asia and the Pacific (#20313)
- ♦ Office de l'Union Européenne pour la Propriété Intellectuelle (#08996)
- ♦ Office of the United Nations Disaster Relief Coordinator (inactive)
- ♦ Office of the United Nations Educational, Scientific and Cultural Organization in Delhi / see UNESCO Asia-Pacific Regional Bureau for Communication and Information (#20300)

♦ Office of the United Nations High Commissioner for Human Rights (OHCHR) 17697

Haut-Commissariat des Nations Unies aux droits de l'homme (HCDH) – Oficina del Alto Comisionado para los Derechos Humanos (ACNUDH)

High Commissioner Palais des Nations, Avenue de la Paix 8-14, 1211 Geneva 10, Switzerland. T. +41229179220. E-mail: infodesk@ohchr.org.
URL: http://www.ohchr.org/

History 24 Oct 1945. Established as *United Nations Centre for Human Rights (CHR, inactive)*. Re-established in current form, 15 Sep 1997, in connection with the programme for reform of the United Nations (A/51/950, para 79), when fully consolidated with the *Office of the High Commissioner for Human Rights* into a single Office based at *United Nations Office at Geneva (UNOG, #20597)*. Mandate derives from Articles 1, 13 and 55 of the Charter of the *United Nations (UN, #20515)*, from the *Vienna Declaration and Programme of Action (VDPA)* (an outcome of the World Conference on Human Rights, Jun 1993), and from UN General Assembly resolution 48/141, 20 Dec 1993, establishing the post of United Nations High Commissioner for Human Rights. **Aims** Represent the world's commitment to the promotion and protection of the full range of human rights and freedoms set out in the Universal Declaration of Human Rights. **Structure** Part of the Secretariat of the United Nations, based in Geneva (Switzerland) and an office at the United Nations headquarters in New York NY (USA), and 3 divisions: Thematic Engagement, Special Procedures and Right to Development (TESPRDD); Human Rights Council and Treaty Mechanisms (CTMD); Field Operations and Technical Cooperation (FOTCD). Headed by the High Commissioner (who is accountable to UN Secretary General) and his/her Executive Office. **Languages** Arabic, Chinese, English, French, Russian, Spanish. **Staff** 1400.00 FTE, paid. **Finance** Two thirds: voluntary contributions. Remainder: covered by UN regular budget. Annual budget: 105,600,000 USD (2019). **Activities** Guidance/assistance/consulting; monitoring/evaluation; standards/guidelines. Works to offer expertise and support to various human rights monitoring mechanisms in the UN system.

Charter-based bodies:
- *United Nations Human Rights Council (HRC, #20571)*;
- Universal Periodic Review;
- Special Procedures of the Human Rights Council;
- Human Rights Council Complain Procedure.

Treaty-based bodies:
- *Committee on the Elimination of Racial Discrimination (CERD, #04251)*;
- *United Nations Committee on Economic, Social and Cultural Rights (CESCR, #20538)*;
- *Human Rights Committee (CCPR, #10979)*;
- *Committee on the Elimination of Discrimination against Women (CEDAW, #04250)*;
- *Committee Against Torture (CAT, #04241)*;
- *Committee on the Rights of the Child (#04283)*;
- *Committee on Migrant Workers (CMW, #04271)*;
- Subcommittee on the Prevention of Torture (SPT);
- *Committee on the Rights of Persons with Disabilities (CRPD, #04284)*;
- *Committee on Enforced Disappearances (CED, #04252)*.

Relevant treaties:
- *International Convention for the Protection of all Persons from Enforced Disappearance (2006)*;
- *International Covenant on Civil and Political Rights (ICCPR, 1966)*;
- *International Convention on the Protection of the Rights of all Migrant Workers and Members of Their Families (1990)*;
- *International Convention on the Elimination of all Forms of Racial Discrimination (1965)*;
- *International Covenant on Economic, Social and Cultural Rights (ICESCR, 1966)*;
- *Convention on the Elimination of all Forms of Discrimination Against Women (CEDAW, 1979)*;
- *Convention Against Torture and other Cruel, Inhuman or Degrading Treatment or Punishment (1984)*;
- *United Nations Convention on the Rights of the Child (CRC, 1989)*;
- *Convention on the Rights of Persons with Disabilities (CRPD, 2006)*.

Events *Annual Meeting of Chairpersons of the Human Rights Treaty Bodies* New York, NY (USA) 2021, *Annual Meeting of Chairpersons of the Human Rights Treaty Bodies* 2020, *Annual Meeting of Chairpersons of the Human Rights Treaty Bodies* New York, NY (USA) 2019, *Annual Meeting of Chairpersons of the Human Rights Treaty Bodies* New York, NY (USA) 2018, *International Symposium on UN Guidance Tool on Descent-Based Discrimination* Tokyo (Japan) 2018. **Publications** Fact sheets; training and educational material; special issue papers; reference material; promotional material. **Members** Not a membership organization but field 'presences' in over 90 countries (countries not specified). **IGO Relations** Observer to: *International Organization for Migration (IOM, #14454)*. Member of: *Interagency Panel on Juvenile Justice (IPJJ, #11390)*; *United Nations Sustainable Development Group (UNSDG, #20634)*; *Inter-Agency Standing Committee (IASC, #11393)*. Cooperation agreement with: *Islamic World Educational, Scientific and Cultural Organization (ICESCO, #16058)*; *Organisation internationale de la Francophonie (OIF, #17809)*; UNESCO. Participates in: *Peace Implementation Council (#18279)*. [2022.03.01/XK1312/**E***]

♦ Office of the United Nations Special Coordinator for the Middle East Process (UNSCO) 17698

Bureau du Coordonnateur spécial des Nations Unies pour le processus de paix au Moyen-Orient

UN Special Coordinator UNSCO Government House, PO Box 490, 91004 Jerusalem, Israel. T. +97225687287. Fax +97225687289. E-mail: bakri1@un.org.
Deputy Special Coordinator address not obtained.
URL: http://www.unsco.org/

History Jun 1994, by the Secretary-General of *United Nations (UN, #20515)*, following signature, 13 Sep 1993, Washington DC (USA), by the Government of Israel and the Palestine Liberation Organization, of the Declaration of Principles on Interim Self-Government Arrangements (Oslo Accords) and the consequent need for the United Nations to create a specific mechanism to ensure effective coordination of the expanding programmes of assistance for the Palestinian people in the West Bank and Gaza Strip. Original title: *Office of the Special Coordinator in the Occupied Territories*. Mandate enhanced, Oct 1999, when it adopted current title, and became Personal Representative of the Secretary-General to the PLO and the Palestinian Authority. Full name: *Office of the UN Special Coordinator for the Middle East Peace Process and Personal Representative of the Secretary-General to the Palestine Liberation Organization and the Palestinian Authority*. Since 2002, also serves as Secretary General's envoy in the Middle East Quartet: Secretary-General of the UN, USA, *European Union (EU, #08967)* and Russia. Functions as a field office under the auspices of the Department of Political Affairs. **Aims** Mandate as of 1993: ensure the coordinated work of the United Nations system for an adequate response to the needs of the Palestinian people; mobilize financial, technical, economic and other *assistance*. Mandate expanded, 1999 to include: representation of the Secretary General by the Special Coordinator in discussions with the parties and the international community in all matters related to continuing United Nations support to the peace process; assignment of task to the Special Coordinator of establishing a unified structure in the region, with a clearly recognized focal point for the organizations contributions to the implementation of the peace agreements and with overall responsibility for making appropriate preparations in consultation with the parties to the Madrid process and the wider international community for enhancing United Nations assistance. **Structure** Front Office. Units (3): UN and Donor Coordination; Regional Affairs; Research and Communications. Elections and Legal Advisors. **Activities** Politics/policy/advisory. **Publications** *UNSCO Report on Economic and Social Conditions in the West Bank and Gaza Strip* (2 a year) – report. Monthly Security Council Briefing.

IGO Relations Close cooperation with UN bodies active in the region:
- *FAO (#09260)*;
- *ILO (#11123)*;
- *International Atomic Energy Agency (IAEA, #12294)*;
- *International Bank for Reconstruction and Development (IBRD, #12317)*;
- *International Civil Aviation Organization (ICAO, #12581)*;
- *International Fund for Agricultural Development (IFAD, #13692)*;
- *International Maritime Organization (IMO, #14102)*;
- *International Monetary Fund (IMF, #14180)*;
- *International Telecommunication Union (ITU, #15673)*;
- *International Trade Centre (ITC, #15703)*;
- *Office of the United Nations High Commissioner for Human Rights (OHCHR, #17697)*;
- *UNEP (#20299)*;
- *UNCTAD (#20285)*;
- *UNDP (#20292)*;
- *UNESCO (#20322)*;
- *UNICEF (#20332)*;
- *UNIDO (#20336)*;
- United Nations Department for Economic and Social Affairs;
- *United Nations Economic and Social Commission for Western Asia (ESCWA, #20558)*;
- *United Nations Human Settlements Programme (UN-Habitat, #20572)*;
- *United Nations Institute for Training and Research (UNITAR, #20576)*;
- *United Nations Population Fund (UNFPA, #20612)*;
- *United Nations Relief and Works Agency for Palestine Refugees in the Near East (UNRWA, #20622)*;
- *United Nations Volunteers (UNV, #20650)*;
- *Universal Postal Union (UPU, #20682)*;
- *WHO (#20950)*;
- *World Food Programme (WFP, #21510)*;
- *World Intellectual Property Organization (WIPO, #21593)*. [2016.08.26/XE3556/**E***]

- ♦ Office of the UN Special Coordinator for the Middle East Peace Process and Personal Representative of the Secretary-General to the Palestine Liberation Organization and the Palestinian Authority / see Office of the United Nations Special Coordinator for the Middle East Process (#17698)
- ♦ Office of the World Peace Envoy (internationally oriented national body)

♦ Official Monetary and Financial Institutions Forum (OMFIF) 17699

Main Office 6-9 Snow Hill, London, EC1A 2AY, UK. T. +442030085262. E-mail: secretariat@omfif.org.
URL: http://www.omfif.org/

History 2010, London (UK). Registration: EU Transparency Register, No/ID: 556946021951-27. **Aims** Focus on global policy and investment themes relating to central banks, sovereign funds, pension funds, regulators and treasuries. **Structure** Advisory Board. **Languages** English. **Activities** Events/meetings; publishing activities; research/documentation. **Events** *Round Table on Behavioural Science in Financial Policy-Making* Singapore (Singapore) 2020, *Round Table on Beijing's Tech Investment-Led Growth Path* Singapore (Singapore) 2020, *Round Table on Public Investors in the COVID-19 World* Singapore (Singapore) 2020, *Round Table on the Future of the World's Economy Flows* Singapore (Singapore) 2020, *Round Table on the Role of Social Bonds in Funding the COVID-19 Response* Singapore (Singapore) 2020. [2022.02.08/XJ9429/**F**]

- ♦ Official Portuguese-speaking African Countries (#18027)
- ♦ Offshore Group of Banking Supervisors / see Group of International Finance Centre Supervisors (#10782)
- ♦ Offshore Group of Insurance Supervisors / see Group of International Insurance Centre Supervisors (#10783)

♦ Offshore Mechanical Handling Equipment Committee (OMHEC) 17700

Contact Petroleum Safety Authority, PO Box 559, 4003 Stavanger, Norway.
URL: http://www.omhec.com/

Aims Improve safety in offshore lifting operations. **Events** *International Crane and Lifting Conference* Aberdeen (UK) 2022, *International Crane and Lifting Conference* Aberdeen (UK) 2022, *North Sea Crane and Lifting Conference* Stavanger (Norway) 2018, *North Sea Crane and Lifting Conference* Stavanger (Norway) 2013.

Members Individuals in 4 countries:
Denmark, Netherlands, Norway, UK. [2022.02.15/XM8052/**D**]

- ♦ Offshore Northern Seas Foundation (internationally oriented national body)

♦ Offshore Pollution Liability Association (OPOL) 17701

Contact Standard House, 12-13 Essex Street, London, WC2R 3AA, UK. T. +447781730766. E-mail: jacquelynn.craw@opol.org.uk – admin@opol.org.uk.
Registered office Broadgate Tower, 3rd floor, 20 Primrose St, London, EC2A 2RS, UK.
URL: http://www.opol.org.uk/

History 1974. Agreement last amended Jul 2012. **Aims** Guarantee claims to be paid expeditiously up to the maximum liability; encourage immediate remedial action; avoid complicated jurisdictional problems. **Structure** Annual Membership Meeting in London (UK). **Languages** English. **Staff** 1.00 FTE, paid. **Finance** Members' dues. Annual budget: US$ 600,000. **Events** *Annual members meeting* London (UK) 2004, *Annual members meeting* London (UK) 2003, *Annual members meeting* London (UK) 2002, *Annual members meeting* London (UK) 2001, *Annual members meeting* London (UK) 2000. **Members** Offshore exploration and production operators within the coastal states of Denmark, Faeroe Is, France, Germany, Greenland, Ireland, Isle of Man, Netherlands, Norway and UK. **NGO Relations** Formal contacts with: *International Association of Oil and Gas Producers (IOGP, #12053)*. [2017.11.23/XD3534/**D**]

- ♦ Offshore Wind Foundations Alliance (unconfirmed)
- ♦ Oficina del Alto Comisionado para los Derechos Humanos (#17697)
- ♦ Oficina del Alto Comisionado de las Naciones Unidas para los Refugiados (#20327)
- ♦ Oficina Arabe de Educación para los Estados del Golfo (#00910)
- ♦ Oficina de Armonización del Mercado Interior – Marcas, Dibujos y Modelos / see European Union Intellectual Property Office (#08996)
- ♦ Oficina del Asesor Especial para Africa (see: #20515)
- ♦ Oficina de Asuntos de Desarmede las Naciones Unidas (#20594)
- ♦ Oficina Bachillerato Internacional / see International Baccalaureate (#12306)
- ♦ Oficina Comunitaria de Variedades Vegetales (#04404)
- ♦ Oficina del Coordinador Especial para Africa y los Paises Menos Adelantados (inactive)
- ♦ Oficina del Coordinador de las Naciones Unidas para el Socorro en Casos de Desastre (inactive)
- ♦ Oficina de Desarrollo de Seguros Cooperativos (inactive)
- ♦ Oficina de Desarrollo de las Telecomunicaciones (#03358)
- ♦ Oficina de Educación Iberoamericana / see Organization of Ibero-American States for Education, Science and Culture (#17871)
- ♦ Oficina del Enviado de la Paz Mundial (internationally oriented national body)
- ♦ Oficina Estadistica de las Comunidades Europeas / see Statistical Office of the European Union (#19974)
- ♦ Oficina Estadistica de la Unión Europea (#19974)
- ♦ Oficina Europea Combinada para el Desarrollo Social / see European Community Development Network (#06679)
- ♦ Oficina Europea de Educación Popular / see European Association for the Education of Adults (#06018)
- ♦ Oficina Europea de Lucha Contra el Fraude (#05906)
- ♦ Oficina Europea del Medio Ambiente / see European Environmental Bureau (#06996)
- ♦ Oficina Intergubernamental para la Informatica (inactive)
- ♦ Oficina Internacional del Agua (#14399)
- ♦ Oficina Internacional de Antropologia Diferencial (inactive)
- ♦ Oficina Internacional del Cacao y del Chocolate (inactive)
- ♦ Oficina Internacional Católica de la Infancia (#12450)
- ♦ Oficina Internacional Contra el Alcoholism / see International Council on Alcohol and Addictions (#12989)

♦ Oficina Internacional de los Derechos de los Niños (#12412)
♦ Oficina Internacional de Educación (#12413)
♦ Oficina Internacional de la Enseñanza Católica (#03604)
♦ Oficina Internacional de Epizootias / see OIE – World Organisation for Animal Health (#17703)
♦ Oficina Internacional para la Estandardización de las Fibras Quimicas (#03369)
♦ Oficina Internacional de Mecanica de las Rocas (#12417)
♦ Oficina Internacional de la Paz (#14535)
♦ Oficina Internacional de los Textiles y las Prendas de Vestir (#15680)
♦ Oficina Internacional para el Turismo y los Intercambios de Juventud (inactive)
♦ Oficina Internacional de Turismo Social / see International Social Tourism Organisation (#14889)
♦ Oficina Mundial de los Criadores de Ganado Jersey (#21598)
♦ Oficina Mundial de Estadisticas del Metal (#21250)
♦ Oficina de las Naciones Unidas contra la Droga y el Delito (#20596)
♦ Oficina de las Naciones Unidas para la Reducción del Riesgo de Desastres (#20595)
♦ Oficina de las Naciones Unidas de Servicios para Proyectos (#20602)
♦ Oficina de las Naciones Unidas en Viena (#20604)
♦ Oficina Notarial Permanente de Intercambio Internacional (see: #15795)
♦ Oficina Permanente Internacional de la Carne (#14125)
♦ Oficina Permanente Internacional de Constructores de Automóviles / see International Organization of Motor Vehicle Manufacturers (#14455)
♦ Oficina de Preparativos para Situaciones de Emergencia y Coordinación del Socorro en Casos de Desastre / see PAHO/WHO Health Emergencies Department (#18023)
♦ Oficina Principal Regional de la UNESCO para Asia y el Pacifico / see UNESCO Asia and Pacific Regional Bureau for Education (#20301)
♦ Oficina de Propiedad Intelectual de la Unión Europea (#08996)
♦ Oficina de Publicaciones de la Unión Europea (#18562)
♦ Oficina Regional de Ciencia y Tecnologia de la UNESCO para América Latina y el Caribe / see UNESCO Office, Montevideo – Regional Bureau for Sciences in Latin America and the Caribbean (#20314)
♦ Oficina Regional de Ciencia de la UNESCO para América Latina y el Caribe (#20314)
♦ Oficina Regional de Comunicación e Información para América Latina y El Caribe (no recent information)
♦ Oficina Regional de Cultura de la UNESCO para América Latina y el Caribe (#20317)
♦ Oficina Regional de Educación de la UNESCO para América Latina y el Caribe (#20318)
♦ Oficina Regional para Europa / see FAO Regional Office for Europe and Central Asia (#09267)
♦ Oficina Regional para Europa y Asia Central (#09267)
♦ Oficina Regional de la FAO para América Latina y el Caribe (#09268)
♦ Oficina Regional de la OMS para las Américas / see Pan American Sanitary Bureau (#18129)
♦ Oficina Regional de OMS para Asia Sudoriental (#20946)
♦ Oficina Regional de la OMS para el Mediterraneo Oriental (#20944)
♦ Oficina Regional para el Pacifico Occidental de la OMS (#20947)
♦ Oficina Regional UNESCO de Educación para Africa (inactive)
♦ Oficina Regional de la UNESCO de Educación para Asia y el Pacifico / see UNESCO Asia and Pacific Regional Bureau for Education (#20301)
♦ Oficina Sanitaria Panamericana (#18129)
♦ Oficina de la UNESCO en la Havana / see UNESCO Regional Bureau for Culture for Latin America and the Caribbean (#20317)
♦ Oficina de UNESCO en Montevideo / see UNESCO Office, Montevideo – Regional Bureau for Sciences in Latin America and the Caribbean (#20314)
♦ Oficina de la UNESCO en Santiago / see UNESCO Regional Bureau for Education in Latin America and the Caribbean (#20318)
♦ Oficina en Washington para Asuntos Latinoamericanos (internationally oriented national body)
♦ Oficiul Pentru Publicatii al Uniunii Europene (#18562)
♦ **OFID** OPEC Fund for International Development (#17745)
♦ **OFIL** Organización de Farmacéuticos Ibero-Latinoamericanos (#17838)
♦ **OFI** Orangutan Foundation International (#17784)
♦ **OFI** Ornamental Fish International (#17896)
♦ Ofisi ya Uandikishaji wa Raia wa Mataifa Mbali-Mbali / see Registre des Citoyens du Monde (#18822)
♦ OFK / see WKF Australia and Oceania (#20974)
♦ OFM Cap – Ordo Fratrum Minorum Capuccinorum (religious order)
♦ OFM Conv – Ordo Fratrum Minorum Conventualium (religious order)
♦ OFM – Ordo Fratrum Minorum (religious order)
♦ **OFN** Organization for Flora Neotropica (#17868)
♦ OFPANA / see Organic Trade Association (#17795)
♦ **OFPA** Observatoire des fonctions publiques africaines (#00249)
♦ ÖFSE – Österreichische Forschungsstiftung für Entwicklungshilfe (internationally oriented national body)
♦ OFS – International Conference on Optical Fiber Sensors (meeting series)
♦ OFS – Ordine Francescano Secolare (religious order)
♦ ÖGA / see Österreichische Gesellschaft für Aussenpolitik und die Vereinten Nationen
♦ OGAVN – Österreichische Gesellschaft für Aussenpolitik und die Vereinten Nationen (internationally oriented national body)
♦ OGBS / see Group of International Finance Centre Supervisors (#10782)
♦ OGCI – Oil and Gas Climate Initiative (unconfirmed)
♦ **OGC** Open Geospatial Consortium (#17752)
♦ **OGC** UNDP Oslo Governance Centre (#20290)
♦ **OGF** Open Grid Forum (#17754)
♦ OGI – Gromadianska Initsiatyva (internationally oriented national body)
♦ OGI International – Civil Initiative International Organization (internationally oriented national body)
♦ OGIS / see Group of International Insurance Centre Supervisors (#10783)
♦ OGL – Ocean Genome Legacy (internationally oriented national body)
♦ **OG** Organization Gestosis (#17869)
♦ OGP / see International Association of Oil and Gas Producers (#12053)
♦ **OGP** Open Government Partnership (#17753)
♦ ÖGPW – Österreichische Gesellschaft für Politikwissenschaft (internationally oriented national body)
♦ **OGU** Oceania Gymnastics Union (#17663)
♦ ÖGUT – Österreichische Gesellschaft für Umwelt und Technik (internationally oriented national body)
♦ **OHADA** Organisation pour l'Harmonisation en Afrique du Droit des Affaires (#17806)
♦ OHAPEOS – Association internationale de sciences expérimentales ou d'érudition, pures et appliquées, pour un humanisme objectif (inactive)
♦ **OHBM** Organization for Human Brain Mapping (#17870)
♦ **OHCHR** Office of the United Nations High Commissioner for Human Rights (#17697)
♦ Ohdake Foundation (internationally oriented national body)
♦ OHF / see Oceania Continent Handball Federation (#17657)
♦ OHI / see Humanity and Inclusion (#10975)
♦ OHIM / see European Union Intellectual Property Office (#08996)
♦ **OHI** Organisation hydrographique internationale (#13825)
♦ OHMI / see European Union Intellectual Property Office (#08996)
♦ OH – Ordo Hospitalarius Sancti Ioannis de Deo (religious order)
♦ OHRID Institute for Economic Strategies and International Affairs (internationally oriented national body)
♦ OHRID Institute – OHRID Institute for Economic Strategies and International Affairs (internationally oriented national body)
♦ **OHR** Office of the High Representative in Bosnia and Herzegovina (#17696)
♦ **OIAC** Organisation interafricaine du café (#11383)
♦ **OIAC** Organisation pour l'interdiction des armes chimiques (#17823)
♦ **OIA** Osteopathic International Alliance (#17910)
♦ OIAPA – Organisation Internationale pour l'Avancement Politique des Africaines (unconfirmed)
♦ **OIAU** Organisation internationale pour l'aménagement des urgences (#13260)
♦ OIB – Observatoire International du Bonheur (internationally oriented national body)
♦ OIB – Orient-Institut, Beirut (internationally oriented national body)
♦ **OIBT** Organisation internationale des bois tropicaux (#15737)
♦ **OICA** Organisation internationale des constructeurs d'automobiles (#14455)
♦ OICCC / see International Confectionery Association (#12840)
♦ OICC – Office international du cacao et du chocolat (inactive)
♦ **OICC** Organization of Islamic Capitals and Cities (#17875)
♦ OICE / see European Consultants Unit (#06769)
♦ OICEM – Organisation internationale contre l'esclavage moderne (unconfirmed)
♦ OIC International / see Opportunities Industrialization Centers International (#17775)
♦ **OICI** Opportunities Industrialization Centers International (#17775)
♦ **OICI** Organización Iberoamericana de Cooperación Intermunicipal (#17839)
♦ OICMA – Organisation internationale de lutte contre le criquet migrateur africain (inactive)

♦ OIC Ministerial Standing Committee on Scientific and Technological Cooperation (COMSTECH) 17702

Comité permanent Ministériel de l'OIC pour la Coopération Scientifique et Technologique (COMSTECH)

Coordinator General 33-Constitution Avenue, Sector G-5/2, Islamabad 44000, Pakistan. T. +92519220681 – +92519220683. Fax +92519211115 – +92519220265. E-mail: comstech@comstech.org.

URL: http://www.comstech.org/

History Jan 1981, Makkah (Saudi Arabia). Established at the 3rd *Islamic Summit of Kings and Heads of States and Governments (#16053)*. A specialized committee of *Organisation of Islamic Cooperation (OIC, #17813)*. **Aims** Follow up and implement the resolutions of OIC in science in technology; study all possible means of strengthening cooperation among OIC member states and draw up programmes; submit proposals designed to increase the capability of Muslim countries in the fields of science and technology. **Structure** General Assembly; Executive Committee; General Secretariat; COMSTECH Secretariat, headed by Coordinator General. Inter-Islamic Networks: *Inter-Islamic Network on Space Sciences and Technology (ISNET, #11511)*; *Inter-Islamic Network on Water Resources Development and Management (INWRDAM, #11513)*; *Inter-Islamic Science and Technology Network on Oceanography (#11514)*; *Inter-Islamic Network on Tropical Medicine (INTROM, #11512)*; *Inter Islamic Network on Information Technology (INIT, #11508)*; *Inter-Islamic Network on Biosaline Agriculture (INBA, #11506)*; Inter-Islamic Network on Virtual Universities (CINVU); Inter-Islamic Network on Science and Technology Parks (INSTP); *Inter-Islamic Network of Nanotechnology (INN, #11509)*; *Inter-Islamic Network on Veterinary Science Research, Khartoum (INVSR)*; *Inter-Islamic Network on Environment, Khartoum (INE, inactive)*; *Inter-Islamic Network on Renewable Energy Sources (INRES, #11510)*; *Inter-Islamic Network on Genetic Engineering and Biotechnology (INOGE, #11507)*. Also includes: *Islamic World Academy of Sciences (IAS, #16057)*. **Languages** Arabic, English, French. **Staff** 73.00 FTE, paid. **Finance** Sources: contributions of member/participating states. **Activities** Awards/prizes/competitions; events/meetings; financial and/or material support; projects/programmes; research and development; training/education. **Events** *Biodiversity Conference* Amman (Jordan) 2021, *COMSTECH – QAU International Seminar* Islamabad (Pakistan) 2021, *Seminar on Light and Polymers* Islamabad (Pakistan) 2020, *Seminar on Science Advice to Governments* Islamabad (Pakistan) 2020, *Workshop on Innovation in Entrepreneurship Education* Islamabad (Pakistan) 2020. **Publications** *Proceedings: Al-Farabi Forum* (2021) by Prof Dr S Khurshid Hasanain in English; *COMSTECH Yearbook 2020* (2020) by Mr Ikram Abbasi in English; *COMSTECH Contribution to S and T Capacity Building in OIC Member States* (2015); *Goals, Priorities, and Actions for S and T in OIC Member States, 2016-25* (2015); *Urdu Translation of The Islamic World and New Century* (2014); *Directory of Active Scientists in OIC Member States* (2012); *The Impact of Climate Change on The Glaciers, Water Resources and Livelihood of Pakistan* (2010); *Leading Scientists and Engineers of OIC Member States* (2008); *Bioinformatics* (2005); *Status of Scientific Research in OIC Member States* (2005); *Science and Technology Policy for Industrialization* (2005); *World Trade Organization and OIC Member States* (2005); *Islamic Biomedical Ethics: Issues and Resources* (2004); *Energy Strategies for the OIC Member States* (2004); *COMSTECH Model Biosafety Guidelines* (2004); *Climate Change: Global and OIC Perspective* (2004); *Biotechnology: Opportunities and Challenges for OIC Member States- An Overview* (2003); *Industrial Profile of the Muslim World* (2001); *Strategy for the Development of Science and Technology in Islamic Countries* (1997); *Mineral Profile of the Muslim World* (1995); *Health and Medical Profile of the Muslim World* (1993); *Food and Agriculture Profile of the Muslim World* (1991). Information Services: COMSTECH Free Literature Search Service; electronic directory of scientists, researchers, engineers and academicians of OIC Member States.

Members Ministers in charge of Science and Technology of all 57 member countries OIC member states:
Afghanistan, Albania, Algeria, Azerbaijan, Bahrain, Bangladesh, Benin, Brunei Darussalam, Burkina Faso, Cameroon, Chad, Comoros, Côte d'Ivoire, Djibouti, Egypt, Gabon, Gambia, Guinea, Guinea-Bissau, Guyana, Indonesia, Iran Islamic Rep, Iraq, Jordan, Kazakhstan, Kuwait, Kyrgyzstan, Lebanon, Libya, Malaysia, Maldives, Mali, Mauritania, Morocco, Mozambique, Niger, Nigeria, Oman, Pakistan, Palestine, Qatar, Saudi Arabia, Senegal, Sierra Leone, Somalia, Sudan, Suriname, Syrian AR, Tajikistan, Togo, Tunisia, Türkiye, Turkmenistan, Uganda, United Arab Emirates, Uzbekistan, Yemen.
All OIC observer states (5):
Bosnia-Herzegovina, Central African Rep, Northern Cyprus, Russia, Thailand.

IGO Relations COMSTECH works in close collaboration with various Standing Committees and other organs of the OIC, Member States of the OIC and their major Scientific and Technological Institutions, in addition to some international organizations. **NGO Relations** Instrumental in setting up (1): *Federation of the Universities of the Islamic World (FUIW, #09710)*. [2021.11.15/XE5993/**E***]

♦ OICN – Organisation internationale du caoutchouc naturel (inactive)
♦ OIC – Ordo de Imitatione Christi (religious order)
♦ **OIC** Organisation internationale du café (#12630)
♦ OIC – Organisation internationale du commerce (inactive)
♦ OIC / see Organisation of Islamic Cooperation (#17813)
♦ **OIC** Organisation of Islamic Cooperation (#17813)
♦ **OICP** Organización Internacional de Ceremonial Protocolo (#14439)
♦ **OICRF** Office international du cadastre et du régime foncier (#14398)
♦ OICS / see Medicus Mundi International – Network Health for All (#16636)
♦ **OICS** Organe international de contrôle des stupéfiants (#14212)
♦ OIC Trade Centre / see Islamic Centre for Development of Trade (#16035)
♦ **OICV** Organisation internationale des commissions de valeurs (#14470)
♦ OIC / see World Trade Organization (#21864)
♦ OIDAC – European Network – Observatory on Intolerance and Discrimination against Christians – European Network (internationally oriented national body)
♦ OIDA – Ontario International Development Agency (internationally oriented national body)
♦ **OIDD** Organisation internationale de droit du développement (#13161)
♦ OIDEL / see International Organization for the Right to Education and Freedom of Education (#14468)
♦ **OIDEL** Organisation internationale pour le droit à l'éducation et la liberté d'enseignement (#14468)
♦ **OIDFA** Organisation internationale de la dentelle au fuseau et l'aiguille (#12374)
♦ OIDIF – Organisation Internationale pour le Développement Intégral de la Femme (internationally oriented national body)
♦ OIDMM – Office international de documentation de médecine militaire (inactive)
♦ OID – Observatorio Interamericano sobre Drogas (see: #11429)
♦ **OID** Organisation interaméricaine de défense (#11425)
♦ **OIDP** Observatoire international de la démocratie participative (#17640)
♦ **OIDP** Observatori Internacional de la Democràcia Participativa (#17640)
♦ ÖIE / see SÜDWIND – Verein für Entwicklungspolitische Bildungs- und Öffentlichkeitsarbeit

- ♦ **OIEA** Organismo Internacional de Energia Atómica (#12294)
- ♦ **OIEau** Office international de l'eau (#14399)
- ♦ **OIEC** Office International de l'Enseignement Catholique (#03604)
- ♦ OIEC – Organisation internationale d'échanges culturels (inactive)
- ♦ OIEC – Organization for International Economic Cooperation (inactive)
- ♦ **OIEM** Organisation internationale de l'énergie et des mines (#13274)
- ♦ **OIE** Oficina Internacional de Educación (#12413)
- ♦ OIE / see OIE – World Organisation for Animal Health (#17703)
- ♦ **OIE** Organisation internationale des employeurs (#14428)
- ♦ OIE – Organisation mondiale de la santé animale (#17703)
- ♦ **OIE** Organización Internacional de Empleadores (#14428)
- ♦ OIE – Organización Mundial de Sanidad Animal (#17703)
- ♦ **OiER** Organization for International Economic Relations (#17873)
- ♦ OIETAI – Organization for Investment, Economic and Technical Assistance of Iran (internationally oriented national body)

♦ OIE – World Organisation for Animal Health 17703

OIE – Organisation mondiale de la santé animale – OIE – Organización Mundial de Sanidad Animal

Dir Gen 12 rue de Prony, 75017 Paris, France. T. +33144151888. Fax +33142670987. E-mail: oie@oie.int.
URL: http://www.oie.int/

History Founded 1924, Paris (France), as *International Office of Epizootics – Office international des épizooties (OIE) – Oficina Internacional de Epizootias (OIE)*, by an International Agreement, an International Conference for the Study of Epizootics having been held 27 May 1921, Paris. Current title adopted, 2002, and applied from 2003 onwards. Statutes registered in *'LNTS 1/1360'*. **Aims** Ensure transparency on global animal *disease* through collection, analysis and dissemination of veterinary scientific *information*; encourage international solidarity in the control of animal diseases; safeguard world *trade* by elaborating international health *standards* for trade in *animals* and *animal products*; provide a better guarantee of *food security* and food safety; promote animal welfare through a science-based approach and improve the legal framework and resources of national *veterinary* services. **Structure** World Assembly of National Delegates from all Member Countries and Territories (meeting annually in May), always in Paris (France). Council (meeting 3 times a year). Regional Commissions (5): Europe; Africa; Americas; Asia, Far East and Oceania; Middle East. Regional Representations (5): Africa – Bamako (Mali); Americas – Buenos Aires (Argentina); Asia – Tokyo (Japan); Eastern Europe – Moscow (Russia); Middle East – Beirut (Lebanon). Sub-regional Representations (7): Europe – Brussels (Belgium); Astana (Kazakhstan); Central America – Panama (Panama); Southern Africa – Gaborone (Botswana); North Africa – Tunis (Tunisia); Eastern Africa and the Horn of Africa – Nairobi (Kenya); South East Asia – Bangkok (Thailand). Specialist Commissions (4): The Terrestrial Animal Health Standards Commission; The Scientific Commission for Animal Diseases; The Biological Standards Commissions; The Aquatic Animal Health Standards Commission. **Languages** English, French, Spanish. **Staff** 122.00 FTE, paid. The *Administrative Tribunal of the International Labour Organization (ILO Tribunal, #00118)* is competent to settle disputes linked with staff. **Finance** Sources: donations; members' dues. Other sources: inputs from national veterinary services, reference laboratories and collaborating centres. Annual budget: 31,500,000 EUR. **Activities** Advocacy/lobbying/activism; events/meetings; knowledge management/information dissemination; research/documentation; standards/guidelines. **Events** *General Session* Paris (France) 2022, *Conference* 2021, *General Session* Paris (France) 2021, *Conference* Abu Dhabi (United Arab Emirates) 2019, *Meeting for Diseases of Poultry in Asia and the Pacific Region* Sapporo (Japan) 2019. **Publications** *OIE Scientific and Technical Review* (3 a year); *World Animal Health* (annual) – online. *Aquatic Animal Health Code*; *Manual of Diagnostic Tests and Vaccines for Terrestrial Animals*; *Manual of Diagnostic Tests for Aquatic Animals*; *Terrestrial Animal Health Code*. Proceedings; joint publications; special publications.

Members Governments of 182 countries and territories:
Afghanistan, Albania, Algeria, Andorra, Angola, Argentina, Armenia, Australia, Austria, Azerbaijan, Bahamas, Bahrain, Bangladesh, Barbados, Belarus, Belgium, Belize, Benin, Bhutan, Bolivia, Bosnia-Herzegovina, Botswana, Brazil, Brunei Darussalam, Bulgaria, Burkina Faso, Burundi, Cambodia, Cameroon, Canada, Cape Verde, Central African Rep, Chad, Chile, China, Colombia, Comoros, Congo Brazzaville, Congo DR, Costa Rica, Côte d'Ivoire, Croatia, Cuba, Curaçao, Cyprus, Czechia, Denmark, Djibouti, Dominican Rep, Ecuador, Egypt, El Salvador, Equatorial Guinea, Eritrea, Estonia, Eswatini, Ethiopia, Fiji, Finland, France, Gabon, Gambia, Georgia, Germany, Ghana, Greece, Guatemala, Guinea, Guinea-Bissau, Guyana, Haiti, Honduras, Hungary, Iceland, India, Indonesia, Iran Islamic Rep, Iraq, Ireland, Israel, Italy, Jamaica, Japan, Jordan, Kazakhstan, Kenya, Korea DPR, Korea Rep, Kuwait, Kyrgyzstan, Laos, Latvia, Lebanon, Lesotho, Liberia, Libya, Liechtenstein, Lithuania, Luxembourg, Madagascar, Malawi, Malaysia, Maldives, Mali, Malta, Mauritania, Mauritius, Mexico, Micronesia FS, Moldova, Mongolia, Montenegro, Morocco, Mozambique, Myanmar, Namibia, Nepal, Netherlands, New Caledonia, New Zealand, Nicaragua, Niger, Nigeria, North Macedonia, Norway, Oman, Pakistan, Panama, Papua New Guinea, Paraguay, Peru, Philippines, Poland, Portugal, Qatar, Romania, Russia, Rwanda, San Marino, Sao Tomé-Principe, Saudi Arabia, Senegal, Serbia, Seychelles, Sierra Leone, Singapore, Slovakia, Slovenia, Somalia, South Africa, South Sudan, Spain, Sri Lanka, St Lucia, Sudan, Suriname, Sweden, Switzerland, Syrian AR, Taiwan, Tajikistan, Tanzania UR, Thailand, Timor-Leste, Togo, Trinidad-Tobago, Tunisia, Türkiye, Turkmenistan, Uganda, UK, Ukraine, United Arab Emirates, Uruguay, USA, Uzbekistan, Vanuatu, Venezuela, Vietnam, Yemen, Zambia, Zimbabwe.

IGO Relations Observer status with: *Codex Alimentarius Commission (CAC, #04081)*. Memorandum of Understanding with: *World Customs Organization (WCO, #21350)*.
NGO Relations Formal agreements with:
- *Commonwealth Veterinary Association (CVA, #04366)*;
- *Fédération Équestre Internationale (FEI, #09484)*;
- *Global Alliance of Pet Food Associations (GAPFA, #10218)*;
- *Health for Animals (#10870)*;
- *International Air Transport Association (IATA, #11614)*;
- *International Alliance for Biological Standardization (IABS, #11622)*;
- *International Council for Laboratory Animal Science (ICLAS, #13039)*;
- *International Dairy Federation (IDF, #13128)*;
- *International Egg Commission (IEC, #13245)*;
- *International Embryo Technology Society (IETS, #13257)*;
- *International Meat Secretariat (IMS, #14125)*;
- *International Poultry Council (IPC, #14628)*;
- *International Union for Conservation of Nature and Natural Resources (IUCN, #15766)*;
- *World Animal Protection (#21092)*;
- *World Association for Animal Production (WAAP, #21117)*;
- *World Association of Veterinary Laboratory Diagnosticians (WAVLD, #21205)*;
- *World Veterinary Association (WVA, #21901)*. [2018.10.04/XE2295/**B***]

- ♦ **OIFE** Osteogenesis Imperfecta Federation Europe (#17907)
- ♦ ÖIFF / see Austrian Study Centre for Peace and Conflict Resolution
- ♦ Oifig Foilseachan an Aontais Eorpaigh (#18562)
- ♦ **OIF** Organisation internationale de la Francophonie (#17809)
- ♦ OIHP – Office international d'hygiène publique (inactive)
- ♦ **OII Europe** Organisation Intersex International Europe (#17812)
- ♦ OII – Organisation Internationale des Intersexués (unconfirmed)
- ♦ OII – Orient-Institut der Deutschen Morgenländischen Gesellschaft, Istanbul (internationally oriented national body)
- ♦ oiip – Österreichisches Institut für Internationale Politik (internationally oriented national body)
- ♦ **OIJAI** Obedinennyj Institut Jadernyh Issledovanij (#16134)
- ♦ OIJJ – Observatoire international de justice juvénile (internationally oriented national body)
- ♦ OIJ – Organisation internationale des journalistes (inactive)
- ♦ OIJ – Organização Internacional dos Jornalistas (inactive)
- ♦ **OIJ** Organización Iberoamericana de Juventud (#11036)

♦ Oikocredit International (Oikocredit) 17704

Address not obtained.
URL: https://www.oikocredit.coop/

History 1975, Rotterdam (Netherlands). Former names and other names: *Ecumenical Development Cooperative Society (EDCS)* – former; *Société coopérative oecuménique pour le développement (SCOD)* – former; *Oekumenische Entwicklungsgenossenschaft* – former; *Oecumenische Ontwikkelings Coöperatie* – former. **Aims** Provide financial services and support organizations to improve the quality of life of low-income people or communities in a sustainable way. **Structure** Cooperative; Supervisory Borad; Executive Committee; Members' Council. International Support Foundation. **Languages** Dutch, English, French, German, Spanish. **Staff** 183.00 FTE, paid. **Activities** Financial and/or material support. **Events** *Meeting on Assessing the Code of Conduct and Legislative Footprints* Brussels (Belgium) 2012, *Annual General Meeting* Stockholm (Sweden) 2012, *Annual General Meeting* Brazil 2010, *Annual General Meeting* Amersfoort (Netherlands) 2009, *Annual General Meeting* India 2008. **Publications** *Oikocredit Info* (2 a year). Annual Report in English, Dutch, French, German, Spanish; Summary Annual Report in English, Dutch, French, German, Spanish; social performance report; leaflets; project sheets; prospectus. **NGO Relations** Strategic partners include: *ECLOF International (#05287)*; *ICCO – Interchurch Organization for Development Cooperation*. Relevant networks include: *African Private Equity and Venture Capital Association (AVCA, #00425)*; *Business in Development Network (BiD Network)*; *European Microfinance Platform (E-MFP, #07793)*; *Financial Inclusion Equity Council (CIEF, #09766)*; *International Association of Investors in the Social Economy (INAISE, #11971)*; *International Co-operative Alliance (ICA, #12944)*; *International Interfaith Investment Group (3iG, #13944)*; *World Fair Trade Organization (WFTO, #21396)*. [2023/XF2988/ey/**F**]

- ♦ **Oikocredit** Oikocredit International (#17704)
- ♦ Oikos – Cooperação e Desenvolvimento (internationally oriented national body)
- ♦ OIKOS – Cooperación y Desarrollo / see Oikos – Cooperação e Desenvolvimento
- ♦ OIKOS – Cooperation and Development / see Oikos – Cooperação e Desenvolvimento
- ♦ oikos – Die Umweltökonomische Studenteninitiative an der Universität St Gallen / see oikos International – students for sustainable economics and management (#17705)
- ♦ Oikos – Ecumenical Institute for Church and Development Cooperation (internationally oriented national body)
- ♦ oikos International / see oikos International – students for sustainable economics and management (#17705)
- ♦ **oikos International** oikos International – students for sustainable economics and management (#17705)
- ♦ OIKOS International Student Organization for Sustainable Economics and Management / see oikos International – students for sustainable economics and management (#17705)

♦ oikos International – students for sustainable economics and management (oikos International) 17705

Co-Pres Dufourstrasse 50, 9000 St Gallen, Switzerland. T. +4915738994014. E-mail: president@oikos-international.org – info@oikos-international.org.
Co-Pres address not obtained.
URL: https://oikos-international.org/

History 1987, St Gallen (Switzerland). Founded as a local initiative by students at the University of St Gallen. The oikos Foundation was founded in 1990 for fundraising purposes. Activities internationalized in 1998 when students in Cologne (Germany), Prague (Czech Rep), Stockholm (Sweden) and Vienna (Austria) established oikos chapters at their universities. Former names and other names: *oikos – Die Umweltökonomische Studenteninitiative an der Universität St Gallen* – former; *OIKOS International Student Organization for Sustainable Economics and Management (oikos International)* – former. Registration: Swiss Civil Code, Switzerland. **Aims** Transform economics and management *education* by empowering student change agents, raising awareness for sustainability opportunities and challenges, and building institutional support for curriculum reform. **Structure** Legislative Body of 45 members; Advisory Council; International Board; Local Chapters; remote International Management Team, based in Switzerland. **Languages** English. Local Chapters use local languages. **Staff** 5.00 FTE, paid; 2.00 FTE, voluntary. **Finance** Sources: sponsorship. **Activities** Events/meetings; networking/liaising; projects/programmes; research/documentation; training/education. **Events** *Spring Meeting* Baku (Azerbaijan) 2020, *Spring Meeting* Barcelona (Spain) 2018, *Spring Meeting* Lille (France) 2016, *Asian Meeting* Vellore (India) 2016, *Alumni Meeting* Warsaw (Poland) 2015. **Publications** Annual Report; event reports; brochure; project portfolio.

Members Local chapters (43) in 26 countries:
Austria, Azerbaijan, Belgium, Canada, China, Czechia, Denmark, Egypt, Finland, France, Georgia, Germany, India, Kenya, Morocco, Poland, Portugal, Russia, Serbia, Slovakia, Spain, Sweden, Switzerland, Türkiye, UK, USA.

NGO Relations Member of (1): *Principles for Responsible Management Education (PRME, #18500)*. [2022/XD7289/**D**]

- ♦ OIKOSNET Africa / see Association of Christian Lay Centres in Africa (#02429)

♦ Oikosnet Europe – Ecumenical Association of Academies and Laity Centres in Europe (EAALCE) 17706

Association oecuménique des centres de recherche et de rencontre en Europe – Ökumenische Vereinigung der Akademien und Laienzentren in Europa – Oecumenische Vereniging van Vormingscentra in Europa – Ekumeniska Förbundet av Konferensinstitut i Europa

Office c/o Sigtunastiftelsen, Manfred Björkquist allé 4, Box 57, SE-193 22 Sigtuna, Sweden. T. +46859258900. E-mail: office@oikosnet.eu.
Exec Sec Ecumenical/European Affairs c/o EAD, Auguststrasse 80, 10117 Berlin, Germany. T. +493028395416.
URL: http://www.oikosnet.eu/

History 1956. Former names and other names: *Ecumenical Association of Academies and Laity Centres in Europe (EAALCE)* – former (1956 to 2007). **Aims** Promote joint activities and studies, inter-disciplinary encounters and training of personnel of affiliated institutions; assist in establishment of new academies and laity centres. **Structure** Conference (annual); Board; Executive Secretary for Ecumenical and European Affairs; Office. **Languages** English. **Finance** Members' dues. **Activities** Events/meetings. **Events** *Annual Conference* Sigtuna (Sweden) 2021, *Annual Conference* Bad Boll (Germany) 2020, *Annual Conference* Turin (Italy) 2019, *Annual Conference* Chania (Greece) 2018, *Annual Conference* Flehingen (Germany) 2017. **Publications** *Communities of Hope – Lay Centres in Europe* (1993); *Ecumenical Lay Training Centres and Academies Facing the Task of Lay Training, Leadership Formation and Ecumenical Learning in the Nineties* (1991); *Directory of Ecumenical Conference Centres* (1990); *Space for Peace* (1987); *Ökumenisch Lernen* (1985).

Members Academies and lay centres (about 50) in 19 countries:
Austria, Belarus, Czechia, Finland, France, Germany, Greece, Hungary, Italy, Netherlands, Norway, Poland, Romania, Russia, Slovakia, Spain, Sweden, Switzerland, UK.

NGO Relations A regional network of: *OIKOSNET (no recent information)*. Coordinates activities with: *Conference of European Churches (CEC, #04593)*. [2022/XD5884/**D**]

- ♦ Oikos – Oecumenical Development Organization for Research, Education and Campaigns / see Oikos – Ecumenical Institute for Church and Development Cooperation
- ♦ Oikos – Oecumenische Ontwikkelingsorganisatie voor Onderzoek, Educatie en Campagnes in Nederland / see Oikos – Ecumenical Institute for Church and Development Cooperation
- ♦ Oikos – Oecumenisch Instituut Kerk en Ontwikkelingssamenwerking (internationally oriented national body)
- ♦ Oikos – Oikos – Cooperação e Desenvolvimento (internationally oriented national body)
- ♦ OILB / see International Organisation for Biological Control (#14424)
- ♦ **OILB** Organisation internationale de lutte biologique (#14424)
- ♦ Oil Change International (internationally oriented national body)

♦ Oil and Colour Chemists' Association (OCCA) 17707

Association des chimistes des peintures et vernis

Pres 4th Floor, Clayton House, 59 Piccadilly, Manchester, M1 2AQ, UK. T. +441619337280. E-mail: admin@occa.org.uk – honsec@occa.org.uk – president@occa.org.uk.
URL: http://www.occa.org.uk/

History 1918. Former names and other names: *Oil and Colour Chemists' Association – Great Britain and Commonwealth* – former (1918). Registration: Charity Commission, No/ID: 259095, England and Wales. **Aims** As a professional body, represent individuals from coating and allied sectors; provide both locally-based networking potential and a much wider interaction opportunity with members from around the world. **Structure** Council; Committees (7); Benevolent Fund Trustees; Divisions worldwide. **Finance** Sources: fees for services; meeting proceeds; members' dues; sale of publications; sponsorship. Other sources: advertising revenue; licensing revenue; investment income. **Activities** Events/meetings. **Events** *Annual General Meeting* Manchester (UK) 2021, *Annual General Meeting* Salford (UK) 2018, *Annual General Meeting* Toronto, ON (Canada) 2001, *International conference* Harrogate (UK) 2000, *Annual General Meeting* Manchester (UK) 2000. **Publications** *Surface Coatings International Journal* (6 a year). Monographs.
Members Professional (Licentiate, Associate and Fellow); Ordinary; Student; Honorary. Individuals in 26 countries:
Australia, Austria, Canada, China, Cyprus, Denmark, Egypt, Finland, France, Germany, India, Ireland, Israel, Italy, Japan, Mexico, New Zealand, Pakistan, Poland, Singapore, South Africa, Spain, Sweden, Switzerland, UK, USA.
NGO Relations Member of (1): *Coatings Societies International (CSI, #04075).* [2022.04.13/XF0226/v/F]

♦ Oil and Colour Chemists' Association – Great Britain and Commonwealth / see Oil and Colour Chemists' Association (#17707)

♦ Oil Companies' European Association for Environment, Health and Safety in Refining and Distribution (CONCAWE) 17708

Association européenne des companies pétrolières pour l'environnement, la santé et la sécurité dans le raffinage et la distribution

Dir Gen Bd du Souverain 165, 1160 Brussels, Belgium. T. +3225669160. Fax +3225669181.
URL: http://www.concawe.eu/

History Founded 1963, The Hague (Netherlands), as *Oil Companies' European Organization for Environment and Health Protection – Organisation européenne des companies pétrolières pour la protection de l'environnement et de la santé* and registered as *Stichting Concawe* under Dutch law. Originally referred to as *Oil Companies' International Study Group for Conservation of Clean Air and Water in Europe.* Name changed, 1983 to *Oil Companies' European Organization for Environmental and Health Protection.* Subsequently referred to as *Oil Companies' European Organization for Environment, Health and Safety – Organisation européenne des companies pétrolières pour l'environnement, la santé et la sécurité.* A division of *European Petroleum Refiners Association (#08194).* Registered in accordance with Belgian law, 1990. **Aims** Conduct research to provide impartial scientific information in order to: improve scientific understanding of the environmental, health, safety and performance aspects of both *petroleum* refining and the distribution and use of refined products; assist development of technically feasible and cost effective policies and legislation by EU institutions and member states; allow informed decision making and cost effective legislative compliance by members. **Structure** General Assembly (annual); Board; Scientific Committee; Management Groups and associated Special Task Forces; Secretariat located in Brussels (Belgium). **Languages** English. **Staff** 26.00 FTE, paid. **Finance** Contributions by member companies. **Activities** Research/documentation; events/meetings; training/education. **Events** *Symposium* Brussels (Belgium) 2006, *International symposium on health effects of occupational exposure to emissions from asphalt/bitumen* Dresden (Germany) 2006. **Publications** *CONCAWE Review* (2 a year). Technical reports, including regular update of worldwide motor vehicle emission regulations and fuel specifications; product dossiers. **Members** Oil companies operating in EU, Norway, Switzerland and Croatia. **IGO Relations** Observer status with (1): *OSPAR Commission for the Protection of the Marine Environment of the North-East Atlantic (OSPAR Commission, #17905).* Cooperates with (1): *United Nations Economic Commission for Europe (UNECE, #20555).* **NGO Relations** Member of (6): *Centre for European Policy Studies (CEPS, #03741); Coordinating European Council for the Development of Performance Tests for Transportation Fuels, Lubricants and Other Fluids (CEC, #04822); European Green Vehicles Initiative Association (EGVIA, #07410); European Policy Centre (EPC, #08240); European Road Transport Research Advisory Council (ERTRAC, #08396); International Petroleum Industry Environmental Conservation Association (IPIECA, #14562).* Cooperates with (7): *European Automotive Research Partners Association (EARPA, #06301); European Bitumen Association (EUROBITUME, #06348); European Council of Automotive Research and Development (EUCAR, #06806); FuelsEurope (#10014); International Association of Oil and Gas Producers (IOGP, #12053); Liquid Gas Europe (#16488); Oil Companies International Marine Forum (OCIMF, #17709).* In liaison with technical committees of: *Association technique de l'industrie européenne des lubrifiants (ATIEL, #02950); Comité européen de normalisation (CEN, #04162); International Organization for Standardization (ISO, #14473).* [2019.10.01/XD4460/D]

♦ Oil Companies' European Organization for Environmental and Health Protection / see Oil Companies' European Association for Environment, Health and Safety in Refining and Distribution (#17708)
♦ Oil Companies' European Organization for Environment and Health Protection / see Oil Companies' European Association for Environment, Health and Safety in Refining and Distribution (#17708)
♦ Oil Companies' European Organization for Environment, Health and Safety / see Oil Companies' European Association for Environment, Health and Safety in Refining and Distribution (#17708)

♦ Oil Companies International Marine Forum (OCIMF) 17709

Office Manager 29 Queen Anne's Gate, London, SW1H 9BU, UK. T. +442076541200. E-mail: enquiries@ocimf.org.
Registered Office Clarendon House, Church Street, Hamilton 5-33, Bermuda.
URL: http://www.ocimf.org/

History 8 Apr 1970, London (UK). Registration: EU Transparency Register, No/ID: 105222814108-05, Start date: 29 Jul 2014. **Aims** Lead the global marine industry in promotion of safe and environmentally responsible transportation of crude oil, oil products; petrochemicals and gas; drive the same values in management of related offshore marine operations. **Structure** General Meeting (annual); Executive Committee; Standing Committees. Secretariat. **Languages** English. **Staff** 25.00 FTE, paid. **Activities** Knowledge management/information dissemination; guidance/assistance/consulting; projects/programmes; standards/guidelines. **Events** *Offshore Vessel Inspection Database User Group Meeting* Houston, TX (USA) 2020, *Offshore Vessel Inspection Database User Group Meeting* Singapore (Singapore) 2019. **Publications** *Information Papers* – series. Annual Report; books; CDs; reports; guidelines; leaflets; joint publications with ICS, IAPH, SIGTTO.
Members Companies (112) in 40 countries:
Algeria, Angola, Australia, Austria, Brazil, Canada, Chile, China, Colombia, Denmark, Finland, France, Germany, Greece, India, Indonesia, Italy, Japan, Kuwait, Malaysia, Mexico, Nigeria, Norway, Philippines, Portugal, Qatar, Russia, Saudi Arabia, South Africa, Spain, Sudan, Sweden, Switzerland, Thailand, UK, United Arab Emirates, Uruguay, USA, Venezuela, Vietnam.
Consultative Status Consultative status granted from: *ECOSOC (#05331)* (Ros C); *International Maritime Organization (IMO, #14102).* **IGO Relations** Accredited by (1): *United Nations Office at Vienna (UNOV, #20604).* Observer status with (1): *International Oil Pollution Compensation Funds (IOPC Funds, #14402).* **NGO Relations** Supports (1): *Maritime Piracy Humanitarian Response Programme (MPHRP, #16583).* In liaison with technical committees of: *International Organization for Standardization (ISO, #14473).* Working relationship maintained on all matters of common interest with: *Advisory Committee on Protection of the Sea (ACOPS, #00139); Conseil européen de l'industrie chimique (CEFIC, #04687); CRISTAL (inactive); European Community Shipowners' Associations (ECSA, #06683); IMCA International Marine Contractors Association (IMCA, #11127); International Association of Classification Societies (IACS, #11778); International Association of Independent Tanker Owners (INTERTANKO, #11959); International Association of Oil and Gas Producers (IOGP, #12053); International Association of Ports and Harbors (IAPH, #12096); International Bunker Industry Association (IBIA, #12411); International Chamber of Shipping (ICS, #12535); International Petroleum Industry Environmental Conservation Association (IPIECA, #14562); Oil Companies' European Association for Environment, Health and Safety in Refining and Distribution (CONCAWE, #17708); PIANC (#18371); Society of International Gas Tanker and Terminal Operators (SIGTTO, #19582).* [2020/XF0436/F]

♦ Oil Companies' International Study Group for Conservation of Clean Air and Water in Europe / see Oil Companies' European Association for Environment, Health and Safety in Refining and Distribution (#17708)
♦ Oil and Gas Climate Initiative (unconfirmed)
♦ Oil & Gas Council (unconfirmed)

♦ Oil and Gas Industry Energy Access Platform (EAP) 17710

Secretariat c/o OFID, PO Box 995, 1011 Vienna, Austria. T. +431515640. Fax +4315139238.
URL: http://energyaccessplatform.org/

Aims Contribute to the achievement of the SE4ALL objective on universal energy access through the enormous potential of the industry to build upon its leadership, technology and much relevant business experience. **Structure** Secretariat. **Activities** Networking/liaising; research/documentation; knowledge management/information dissemination. **Events** *Meeting* Vienna (Austria) 2017, *Meeting* Vienna (Austria) 2017.
Members Stakeholders in the industry, including 4 organizations listed in this Yearbook:
Global LPG Partnership (GLPGP, #10461); International Gas Union (IGU, #13700); OPEC Fund for International Development (OFID, #17745); World Petroleum Council (WPC, #21722).
Observer organization:
Shell Foundation.
NGO Relations *Sustainable Energy for All (SEforALL, #20056).* [2018.03.05/XM6556/ty/F]

♦ OILPOL – International Convention for the Prevention of Pollution of the Sea by Oil (1954 treaty)

♦ Oilwatch 17711

Secretariat 30 19th Street, off Ugbowo-Lagos Road, PO Box 10577, Ugbowo, Benin City 300212, Edo, Nigeria. T. +23484236365. E-mail: contact@oilwatch.org – home@homef.org – informacion@accionecologica.org.
URL: http://www.oilwatch.org/

History Feb 1996, Quito (Ecuador), at meeting of environmental NGOs. **Aims** In view of the fragile *ecosystems* of *tropical* regions: monitor and exchange information on *petroleum* companies in these regions, including history, operational practice and social and environmental impact; provide information on the best technology available and on existing *environmental* standards. **Structure** General Assembly (every 2 years). International Steering Committee. Secretariat in Ecuador. **Publications** *Resistance Bulletin.*
Members Full in 56 countries and territories:
Angola, Argentina, Austria, Bangladesh, Belgium, Benin, Bolivia, Brazil, Burkina Faso, Cameroon, Canada, Central African Rep, Chad, Colombia, Congo Brazzaville, Congo DR, Costa Rica, Côte d'Ivoire, Cuba, Curaçao, Denmark, Ecuador, Equatorial Guinea, France, Gabon, Germany, Ghana, Guatemala, Honduras, Indonesia, Ireland, Italy, Korea Rep, Malaysia, Mexico, Myanmar, Netherlands, Nicaragua, Nigeria, Norway, Panama, Papua New Guinea, Peru, Philippines, Puerto Rico, Senegal, South Africa, Spain, Sri Lanka, Sweden, Thailand, UK, USA, Venezuela, Vietnam, Wales.
International members (2):
Greenpeace International (#10727); World Rainforest Movement (WRM, #21745). [2023/XF4342/F]

♦ **OIML** Organisation internationale de métrologie légale (#14451)
♦ **OIM** Organisation internationale pour les migrations (#14454)
♦ OIM – Organisation internationale des mineurs (no recent information)
♦ **OIM** Organización Internacional para las Migraciones (#14454)
♦ OIM – Organización Internacional de Mineros (no recent information)
♦ **OIMR** Oficina Internacional de Mecanica de las Rocas (#12417)
♦ **OIMT** Organización Internacional de las Maderas Tropicales (#15737)
♦ **OINA** Organisation internationale Nouvelle Acropole (#14458)
♦ **OI** Optimist International (#17778)
♦ **OIPA** Organisation internationale pour la protection des animaux (#17810)
♦ OIPA – Organisation internationale pour la protection des oeuvres d'art (inactive)
♦ **OIPC-INTERPOL** Organisation internationale de police criminelle – INTERPOL (#13110)
♦ **OIPC** Organisation internationale de protection civile (#12582)
♦ **OIPC** Organización Internacional de Protección Civil (#12582)
♦ **OIPEEC** Organisation internationale pour l'étude de l'endurance des cables (#14474)
♦ **OIPF** Organisation internationale de placement familial (#13663)
♦ OIP / see International Organization of Psychomotricity and Relaxation (#14465)
♦ **OIPMAs** Organisation Internationale pour les Pays les Moins Avancés (#14430)
♦ OIP – Organisation ibéroaméricaine des pilotes (no recent information)
♦ **OIP** Organisation internationale de la paléobotanique (#14459)
♦ **OIP** Organisation internationale de psychophysiologie (#14466)
♦ OIP – Organización Iberoamericana de Pilotos (no recent information)
♦ OIP – Organización Internacional de Periodistas (inactive)
♦ **OIP** Organización Internacional de Psicofisiologia (#14466)
♦ **OIPPSS** Organización Iberoamericana de Prestadores Privados de Servicios de Salud (#17841)
♦ OIPRO – Organisation internationale des preuves reliées aux ordinateurs (inactive)
♦ **OIPR** Organisation internationale de psychomotricité et de relaxation (#14465)
♦ OIPRT – Organisation internationale de la police routière et des transports (no recent information)
♦ OIRAPMM / see Ancient and Primitive Rite of Memphis-Misraïm (#00815)
♦ OIRC – Organisation internationale pour la réduction des catastrophes (internationally oriented national body)
♦ OIR – Organisation internationale pour les réfugiés (inactive)
♦ OIRP – Organisation internationale de régies publicitaires (inactive)
♦ **OIRSA** Organismo Internacional Regional de Sanidad Agropecuaria (#17830)
♦ OIRT – Organisation internationale de radiodiffusion et télévision (inactive)
♦ **OISA** Organization of the Islamic Shipowners' Association (#17876)
♦ OISCA Academy (see: #17872)
♦ OISCA College for Global Cooperation (see: #17872)
♦ **OISCA International** Organization for Industrial, Spiritual and Cultural Advancement International (#17872)

♦ Oiseaux migrateurs du paléarctique occidental (OMPO) 17712

Migratory Birds of the Western Palearctic

Contact OMPO, 59 rue Ampère, 75017 Paris, France. T. +33144010510. Fax +33144010511. E-mail: ompo@ompo.org.
URL: http://www.ompo.org/

History Founded 1987, within *International Council for Game and Wildlife Conservation (#13024).* Also referred to by initials *CIC / OMPO.* No recent information. **Aims** Promote the *hunting* of migratory birds based on wise use of natural *renewable resources,* according to rules assuring their long-term survival and based on objective and solid knowledge. **Structure** Council. Committee, comprising Chairman, 2 Vice-Chairmen, Secretary, Treasurer and 2 Acting Chairs. **Finance** Members' dues. Grants; donations; legacies; income from sales. **Events** *Annual Conference* Seoul (Korea Rep) 2005, *Global flyways conference* Edinburgh (UK) 2004, *Meeting on population status and management of migratory bird populations in Central and Eastern Europe* Odessa (Ukraine) 2003. **Consultative Status** Consultative status granted from: *Council of Europe (CE, #04881)* (Participatory Status). **IGO Relations** Observer status at: *Standing Committee to the Bern Convention on the Conservation of European Wildlife and Natural Habitats (#19949).* **NGO Relations** Member of: *International Union for Conservation of Nature and Natural Resources (IUCN, #15766).* [2012/XE3492/E]

♦ **OISEVI** Observatorio Iberoamericano de Seguridad Vial (#17641)
♦ **OIS** Organisation internationale du sucre (#15623)
♦ **OISS** Organización Iberoamericana de Seguridad Social (#11028)
♦ **OISTAT** Organisation Internationale des Scénographes, Techniciens et Architectes de Théâtre (#17811)
♦ OISTE Foundation (unconfirmed)
♦ OISTT / see Organisation Internationale des Scénographes, Techniciens et Architectes de Théâtre (#17811)
♦ OISTV / see International Union for Vacuum Science, Technique and Applications (#15826)
♦ **OITAF** Organizzazione Internazionale dei Trasporti a Fune (#14481)
♦ OIT/Cinterfor / see Centro Interamericano para el Desarrollo del Conocimiento en la Formación Profesional (#03802)
♦ **OIT/Cinterfor** Centro Interamericano para el Desarrollo del Conocimiento en la Formación Profesional (#03802)

- ♦ OIT/ETM San José – ILO Central American Multidisciplinary Technical Advisory Team (see: #11123)
- ♦ OIT-IPEC / see International Programme on the Elimination of Child Labour and Forced Labour (#14652)
- ♦ **OIT** Organisation internationale du travail (#11123)
- ♦ **OIT** Organización Internacional del Trabajo (#11123)
- ♦ **OITP** Oficina Internacional de los Textiles y las Prendas de Vestir (#15680)
- ♦ OITRA – Organización Internacional de Trabajadores de Radio y Televisión de las Américas (inactive)

♦ OITS/ European Commission for Social Tourism (CETS) 17713

Pres 2 Watteeustreet, 1000 Brussels, Belgium. T. +3222741544. Fax +3225141691. E-mail: presidente@betaniaonline.org.
Dir address not obtained.
URL: http://www.oits-isto.org/

History 8 Oct 1990, Brussels (Belgium), as *Comité européen de coordination du tourisme social*, by *International Social Tourism Organisation (ISTO, #14889)*, to replace *Comité européen de coordination du tourisme social (CECOTOS, inactive)*. Subsequently became *Conseil européen du tourisme social (CETOS)* and *BITS – Europe*, 1994. Changed name *BITS/European Union (BITS/EU) – Commission BITS Union Européenne*, 2001. **Aims** Establish a unique and qualified go-between of European institutions in the field of social tourism. **Structure** General Assembly (every 2 years, in conjunction with OITS International General Assembly since 1994). **Languages** English, French. **Activities** Knowledge management/information dissemination; research and development; projects/programmes; networking/liaising. **Events** *European Social Tourism Forum* Albufeira (Portugal) 2015, *Annual General Assembly* Sao Paulo (Brazil) 2014, *European Social Tourism Forum* Blankenberge (Belgium) 2013, *European Social Tourism Forum* St Julian's (Malta) 2011, *Seminar on helps for holidays in Europe* Strasbourg (France) 2000. **Publications** *Directory of Educational and Cultural Programs – Accommodation Network and Promotion of Youth Mobility*.
Members International organizations (98) in 15 countries:
Belgium, France, Germany, Greece, Hungary, Italy, Malta, Poland, Portugal, Russia, San Marino, Spain, Switzerland, Türkiye, UK.
NGO Relations Represents: *International Association for Social Tourism (IAST, no recent information)*. Involved in: *World Committee on Tourism Ethics (WCTE, #21287)*. Cooperation agreement with: *European Trade Union Confederation (ETUC, #08927)*. [2016.11.09/XE1657/**E**]

- ♦ **OITS** Organisation internationale du tourisme social (#14889)
- ♦ OIUCM – Open International University for Complementary Medicines (internationally oriented national body)
- ♦ **OIUDSMA** Organización Internacional de Universidades por el Desarrollo Sostenible y Medio Ambiente (#17843)
- ♦ **OIVE** Observatoire International de la Violence a l'Ecole (#14389)
- ♦ OIV / see International Organisation of Vine and Wine (#14435)
- ♦ **OIV** International Organisation of Vine and Wine (#14435)
- ♦ **OIV** Office international de la viande (#14125)
- ♦ **OIV** Organisation Internationale de la Vigne et du Vin (#14435)
- ♦ OJCE / see European Union Youth Orchestra (#09024)
- ♦ **OJCE** Orchestre des jeunes de l'Union européenne (#09024)
- ♦ OJCMPF – Organisation japonaise pour la coopération internationale en matière de planification familiale (internationally oriented national body)
- ♦ Ojcowie Paulini – Zakon Swietego Pawla Pierwszego Pustelnika (religious order)
- ♦ OJE – Zdruzenje Okoljevarstvenikov za Jedrsko Energijo (internationally oriented national body)
- ♦ **OJM** Orchestre des Jeunes de la Méditerranée (#17788)
- ♦ **OJU** Oceania Judo Union (#17665)
- ♦ OKDIA – OK-Dinghy International Association (see: #21760)
- ♦ OK-Dinghy International Association (see: #21760)
- ♦ Okeanos Foundation for the Sea (internationally oriented national body)
- ♦ Okeanos – Stiftung für das Meer (internationally oriented national body)
- ♦ OKFN / see Open Knowledge International
- ♦ Okinawa Charter on Global Information Society (2000 treaty)
- ♦ OKLC – International Conference on Organizational Learning, Knowledge and Capabilities (meeting series)
- ♦ **OKN** Open Knowledge Network (#17756)
- ♦ Öko-Ethische Internationale Union (inactive)
- ♦ Ökologischer Tourismus in Europa (internationally oriented national body)
- ♦ Ö-kommissionen (#16061)
- ♦ Ökonomische Gesellschaft zur Internationalen Förderung Wirtschaftlicher und Geistiger Werte (inactive)
- ♦ Ökumenischer Darlehensfonds / see ECLOF International (#05287)
- ♦ Ökumenischer Jugendrat in Europa (#05352)
- ♦ Ökumenischer Rat der Kirchen (#21320)
- ♦ Ökumenisches Forum Christlicher Frauen in Europa (#05347)
- ♦ Ökumenisches Netz Zentralafrika (internationally oriented national body)
- ♦ Ökumenisches Stipendienwerk / see Brot für die Welt
- ♦ Ökumenische Vereinigung der Akademien und Laienzentren in Europa (#17706)
- ♦ Ökumenische Vereinigung von Dritte-Welt-Theologen (#05344)
- ♦ **OLACEFS** Organización Latinoamericana y del Caribe de Entidades Fiscalizadoras Superiores (#17877)
- ♦ **OLACEFS** Organization of Latin American and Caribbean Supreme Audit Institutions (#17877)
- ♦ **OLACT** Organización Latino-Americana y del Caribe de Turismo (#17845)
- ♦ **OLADE** Organización Latinoamericana de Energia (#16313)
- ♦ OLADES – Organización Latino Americana de Desarrollo Secretarial (no recent information)
- ♦ ÖLAF / see Lateinamerikaforschung Austria
- ♦ OLAFABA – Organización Latinoamericana de Fabricantes de Bebidas Alcohólicas (inactive)

♦ OLAF Anti-Fraud Communicators Network (OAFCN) 17714

OLAF-Netz von Kommunikationsbeauftragten im Bereich der Betrugsbekämpfung (OAFCN)

Dir-Gen European Commission, European Anti-Fraud Office (OLAF), 1049 Brussels, Belgium. T. +3222967221. E-mail: olaf-oafcn@ec.europa.eu.
Street Address European Anti-Fraud Office, Rue Joseph II 30, 1000 Brussels, Belgium.
URL: http://ec.europa.eu/anti_fraud/olaf-oafcn/

History 2001. Founded by *European Anti-Fraud Office (#05906)*. **Aims** Prevent fraud in the European Union through a better dissemination of information and awareness-raising, with a particular focus on the new members states and candidate countries. **Activities** Events/meetings; training/education. **Events** *Meeting* Brussels (Belgium) 2023, *Meeting* Brussels (Belgium) 2022, *Meeting* Brussels (Belgium) 2021, *Meeting* Brussels (Belgium) 2020, *Meeting* Brussels (Belgium) 2018. [2023/XJ3315/**E***]

- ♦ OLAF-Netz von Kommunikationsbeauftragten im Bereich der Betrugsbekämpfung (#17714)
- ♦ **OLAF** Office européen de lutte antifraude (#05906)
- ♦ OLAMI Internacional / see Organismo Latinoamericano de Mineria (#17831)
- ♦ **OLAMI** Organismo Latinoamericano de Mineria (#17831)
- ♦ **OLA** Organización Latinoamericana de Administración (#17844)
- ♦ OLAP – Organización Latinoamericana para la Promoción de los Ciegos y Deficientes Visuales (inactive)
- ♦ OLAS – Organización Latinoamericana de Solidaridad (inactive)
- ♦ OLAS – Organization for Latin American Solidarity (inactive)

♦ Olave Baden-Powell Society (OB-PS) 17715

Contact World Bureau, Olave Ctr, 12c Lyndhurst Road, London, NW3 5PQ, UK. T. +442077941181. Fax +442074313764. E-mail: obps@wagggs.org.
URL: http://www.ob-ps.org/

History Set up to support the mission of *World Association of Girl Guides and Girl Scouts (WAGGGS, #21142)*. **Aims** Inspire generosity and sustained financial support from individuals who have knowledge and responsibility for the advancement of girls and young women through the global Girl Guide and Girl Scout Movement. **Structure** Board of Directors, including President and Vice-President. **Languages** English. **Events** *Meeting* Toronto, ON (Canada) 2019, *Meeting* Tokyo (Japan) 2018, *Meeting* London (UK) 2017, *Meeting* Pune (India) 2016, *Meeting* Tampere (Finland) 2015.
Members Full (1,402) in 59 countries and territories:
Argentina, Australia, Belgium, Botswana, Brazil, Brunei Darussalam, Canada, Cyprus, Czechia, Denmark, Ecuador, Finland, France, Germany, Ghana, Greece, Guyana, Hong Kong, Iceland, India, Indonesia, Ireland, Italy, Jamaica, Japan, Jordan, Kenya, Korea Rep, Kuwait, Lebanon, Liechtenstein, Lithuania, Madagascar, Malaysia, Maldives, Mexico, Monaco, Nepal, Netherlands, New Zealand, Nigeria, Norway, Pakistan, Palestine, Philippines, Portugal, Singapore, South Africa, Sri Lanka, Sweden, Switzerland, Taiwan, Thailand, UK, United Arab Emirates, USA, Venezuela, Zambia, Zimbabwe. [2018/XJ6644/**E**]

- ♦ OLAVU – Organización Latinoamericana del Vino y de la Uva (inactive)
- ♦ OLCA – Observatorio Latinoamericano de Conflictos Ambientales, Chile (internationally oriented national body)
- ♦ **OLCP-EA** Organisation de lutte contre le criquet pèlerin dans l'Est africain (#05042)
- ♦ Old Catholic Church Association / see International Old Catholic Bishops' Conference (#14403)
- ♦ OLDEA-EA – Open Learning and Distance Education Association of Eastern Africa (no recent information)
- ♦ **OLDEPESCA** Organización Latinoamericana de Desarrollo Pesquero (#16335)

♦ Older Women's Network – Europe (OWN Europe) 17716

Réseau européen des femmes de plus de 50 ans

Gen Sec c/o Policy Equalities Unit, Room 408, Lewisham Town Hall, Catford, London, SE6 4RU, UK.
Coordinator Via del Seraglio 8, 06073 Corciano PG, Italy. T. +39755068006. Fax +39755068006.

History Nov 1993. Registration: No/ID: 0465.303.159, Start date: 10 Jan 1999, Belgium; No/ID: KVK 09178334, Netherlands. **Aims** Promote the sharing of knowledge, skills and experience of older women across Europe in order to challenge the negative stereotypes of age, gender, race, disability and sexuality; affirm the rights and capacity of older women through self-help, social groups and political activity to contribute to policy development and change at local, national and international levels; work across cultures and generations, recognizing that age is a life-cycle issue; work with European Union institutions to ensure the older women's perspective in development of, and activity in, relevant action programmes. **Structure** Board; Coordinator. **Staff** 1.00 FTE, paid. **Finance** Members' dues. Supported by *European Commission (EC, #06633)*. **Activities** Research; debate; action. Organizes meetings. **Events** *Annual General Meeting* Italy 2001, *Annual general meeting* An Grianan (Ireland) 1995. **Publications** *OWN Newsletter* (2 a year). Bulletins.
Members Organizations in 11 countries:
Austria, Belgium, Denmark, France, Germany, Greece, Ireland, Italy, Netherlands, Spain, UK.
NGO Relations Member of: *AGE Platform Europe (#00557)*. [2011/XF3477/**F**]

- ♦ Old World Conference in Phonology (meeting series)
- ♦ OLF – Congregation Our Lady of Fidelity (religious order)

♦ Oligonucleotide Therapeutics Society (OTS) 17717

Address not obtained.
URL: http://www.oligotherapeutics.org/

History 2001, Italy. Incorporated in accordance with US law, 2004. **Aims** Foster academia and industry-based research and development of oligonucleotide therapeutics. **Structure** Board of Directors; Scientific Advisory Council. **Activities** Awards/prizes/competitions; events/meetings. **Events** *Annual Meeting* San Diego, CA (USA) 2021, *Annual Meeting* San Diego, CA (USA) 2020, *Annual Meeting* Munich (Germany) 2019, *Annual Meeting* Seattle, WA (USA) 2018, *Annual Meeting* Bordeaux (France) 2017. **Publications** *Nucleic Acid Therapeutics* – official journal. [2020/XM4846/**C**]

- ♦ Öljynpuristamoiden ja -Puhdistamoiden Liito / see FEDIOL – The EU Vegetable Oil and Proteinmeal Industry (#09718)
- ♦ OLL – Ocean Lifeline (internationally oriented national body)
- ♦ Olof Palme Institute (internationally oriented national body)
- ♦ Olof Palme International Center, Stockholm (internationally oriented national body)
- ♦ Olof Palme International Foundation (internationally oriented national body)
- ♦ Olof Palme Memorial Fund for International Understanding and Common Security (internationally oriented national body)
- ♦ Olof Palme Peace Foundation International (internationally oriented national body)
- ♦ Olof Palmes Internationella Centrum, Stockholm (internationally oriented national body)
- ♦ Olon Ulsyn Mongol Sudlalyn Holboo (#12035)
- ♦ OLPC – One Laptop per Child (internationally oriented national body)
- ♦ **OLSNE** Oñatiko Lege-Soziologiako Nazioarteko Erakundea (#17725)
- ♦ OLS – United Nations Operation Lifeline Sudan (inactive)
- ♦ Olympafrica International Foundation (#09823)

♦ Olympic Council of Asia (OCA) 17718

Conseil olympique d'Asie – Consejo Olímpico de Asia

SG PO Box 6706, 32042 Hawalli, Kuwait. T. +9655717196 – +9655734972. Fax +9655734973 – +9655726622. E-mail: info@ocasia.org.
Pres address not obtained. E-mail: president@ocasia.org.
URL: http://www.ocasia.org/

History 5 Dec 1982, Delhi (India), following Council meeting, 26 Nov 1981, of *Asian Games Federation (AGF, inactive)*, which had been set up 13 Feb 1949, Delhi, at conference of representatives of Asian countries, and whose constitution was amended 25 Aug 1972, Munich (Germany FR). OCA replaces AGF. **Aims** Promote development of Asian identity and Asian unity through *sport*; help develop in the youth of Asia those physical and moral qualities that come from fair *competition* in amateur sport, and promote international respect and goodwill among them through sport. **Structure** General Assembly (every 4 years); Executive Board. Standing Committees. **Languages** English. **Staff** 12.00 FTE, paid. **Finance** Members' fees. Government subsidies and Olympic solidarity. Budget (annual): about US$ 350,000. **Activities** Sporting activities; networking/liaising. **Events** *General Assembly* Hawalli (Kuwait) 2023, *General Assembly* Hangzhou (China) 2022, *General Assembly* Dubai (United Arab Emirates) 2021, *General Assembly* Muscat (Oman) 2020, *General Assembly* Bangkok (Thailand) 2019. **Publications** *Sportin Asia* (4 a year) – official newsletter.
Members National Olympic Committees in 44 countries and territories:
Afghanistan, Bahrain, Bangladesh, Bhutan, Brunei Darussalam, Cambodia, China, Hong Kong, India, Indonesia, Iran Islamic Rep, Iraq (suspended as member of OCA), Japan, Jordan, Kazakhstan, Korea DPR, Korea Rep, Kuwait, Kyrgyzstan, Laos, Lebanon, Macau (not recognized by IOC), Malaysia, Maldives, Mongolia, Myanmar, Nepal, Oman, Pakistan, Palestine, Philippines, Qatar, Saudi Arabia, Singapore, Sri Lanka, Syrian AR, Taiwan, Tajikistan, Thailand, Turkmenistan, United Arab Emirates, Uzbekistan, Vietnam, Yemen.
NGO Relations Partner of (2): *Asian Electronic Sports Federation (AESF, #01435)*; *Global ESports Federation (GEF, #10348)*. Continental Association of: *Association of National Olympic Committees (ANOC, #02819)*. Recognized Organization by: *International Olympic Committee (IOC, #14408)*. Grants from IOC through the intermediary of: *Olympic Solidarity (OS, #17721)*. Supports: *Generations for Peace (#10116)*. [2019/XD4467/**D**]

♦ Olympic Movement 17719

Mouvement olympique

Contact IOC, Château de Vidy, Case Postale 356, 1001 Lausanne VD, Switzerland. T. +41216216111. Fax +41216216216.
URL: https://olympics.com/ioc/olympic-movement

History Founded by Pierre de Coubertin, under the supreme authority of *International Olympic Committee (IOC, #14408)*. **Aims** Contribute to building a peaceful and better world by educating youth through sport practised without discrimination of any kind and in the Olympic spirit, which requires mutual understanding with a spirit of friendship, solidarity and fair play. **Structure** Main constituents (3): *International Olympic Committee (IOC, #14408)*; International Sports Federations (IFs); National Olympic Committees (NOCs). Also encompasses: Organising Committees of the Olympic Games (OCOGs); national associations, clubs and persons belonging to the IFs and NOCs; also includes other organisations and institutions as recognised by IOC.

Members National Olympic Committees (206):
Afghanistan, Albania, Algeria, Andorra, Angola, Antigua-Barbuda, Argentina, Armenia, Aruba, Australia, Austria, Azerbaijan, Bahamas, Bahrain, Bangladesh, Barbados, Belarus, Belgium, Belize, Benin, Bermuda, Bhutan, Bolivia, Bosnia-Herzegovina, Botswana, Brazil, Brunei Darussalam, Bulgaria, Burkina Faso, Burundi, Cambodia, Cameroon, Canada, Cape Verde, Cayman Is, Central African Rep, Chad, Chile, China, Colombia, Comoros, Congo Brazzaville, Congo DR, Cook Is, Costa Rica, Côte d'Ivoire, Croatia, Cuba, Cyprus, Czechia, Denmark, Djibouti, Dominica, Dominican Rep, Ecuador, Egypt, El Salvador, Equatorial Guinea, Eritrea, Estonia, Eswatini, Ethiopia, Fiji, Finland, France, Gabon, Gambia, Georgia, Germany, Ghana, Great Britain, Greece, Grenada, Guam, Guatemala, Guinea, Guinea-Bissau, Guyana, Haiti, Honduras, Hong Kong, Hungary, Iceland, India, Indonesia, Iran Islamic Rep, Iraq, Ireland, Israel, Italy, Jamaica, Japan, Jordan, Kazakhstan, Kenya, Kiribati, Korea DPR, Korea Rep, Kosovo, Kuwait, Kyrgyzstan, Laos, Latvia, Lebanon, Lesotho, Liberia, Libya, Liechtenstein, Lithuania, Luxembourg, Madagascar, Malawi, Malaysia, Maldives, Mali, Malta, Marshall Is, Mauritania, Mauritius, Mexico, Micronesia FS, Moldova, Monaco, Mongolia, Montenegro, Morocco, Mozambique, Myanmar, Namibia, Nauru, Nepal, Netherlands, New Zealand, Nicaragua, Niger, Nigeria, North Macedonia, Norway, Oman, Pakistan, Palau, Palestine, Panama, Papua New Guinea, Paraguay, Peru, Philippines, Poland, Portugal, Puerto Rico, Qatar, Romania, Russia (currently plays under a neutral flag), Rwanda, Samoa, Samoa USA, San Marino, Sao Tomé-Principe, Saudi Arabia, Senegal, Serbia, Seychelles, Sierra Leone, Singapore, Slovakia, Slovenia, Solomon Is, Somalia, South Africa, South Sudan, Spain, Sri Lanka, St Kitts-Nevis, St Lucia, St Vincent-Grenadines, Sudan, Suriname, Sweden, Switzerland, Syrian AR, Taiwan, Tajikistan, Tanzania UR, Thailand, Timor-Leste, Togo, Tonga, Trinidad-Tobago, Tunisia, Türkiye, Turkmenistan, Tuvalu, Uganda, Ukraine, United Arab Emirates, Uruguay, USA, Uzbekistan, Vanuatu, Venezuela, Vietnam, Virgin Is UK, Virgin Is USA, Yemen, Zambia, Zimbabwe.
International Sports Federations (40):
- *Badminton World Federation (BWF, #03060)*;
- *Fédération Équestre Internationale (FEI, #09484)*;
- *Fédération internationale de basketball (FIBA, #09614)*;
- *Fédération internationale de gymnastique (FIG, #09636)*;
- *Fédération internationale d'escrime (FIE, #09629)*;
- *Fédération Internationale de Ski (FIS, #09659)*;
- *Fédération internationale de volleyball (FIVB, #09670)*;
- *International Biathlon Union (IBU, #12336)*;
- *International Bobsleigh and Skeleton Federation (IBSF, #12375)*;
- *International Boxing Association (IBA, #12385)*;
- *International Canoe Federation (ICF, #12437)*;
- *International Federation of Association Football (#13360)*;
- *International Federation of Sport Climbing (IFSC, #13553)*;
- *International Golf Federation (IGF, #13727)*;
- *International Handball Federation (IHF, #13771)*;
- *International Hockey Federation (#13802)*;
- *International Ice Hockey Federation (IIHF, #13831)*;
- *International Judo Federation (IJF, #13975)*;
- *International Luge Federation (FIL, #14066)*;
- *International Shooting Sport Federation (ISSF, #14852)*;
- *International Skating Union (ISU, #14865)*;
- *International Ski Mountaineering Federation (ISMF, #14871)*;
- *International Surfing Association (ISA, #15630)*;
- *International Table Tennis Federation (ITTF, #15650)*;
- *International Tennis Federation (ITF, #15676)*;
- *International Weightlifting Federation (IWF, #15876)*;
- *Union Cycliste Internationale (UCI, #20375)*;
- *United World Wrestling (UWW, #20665)*;
- *World Aquatics (#21100)*;
- *World Archery (#21105)*;
- *World Athletics (#21209)*;
- *World Curling Federation (WCF, #21348)*;
- *World DanceSport Federation (WDSF, #21354)*;
- *World Penthathlon (UIPM, #21720)*;
- *World Rowing (#21756)*;
- *World Rugby (#21757)*;
- *World Sailing (#21760)*;
- *World Skate (#21786)*;
- *World Taekwondo (#21844)*;
- *World Triathlon (#21872)*.

Recognized federations (35):
- *Federación Internacional de Pelota Vasca (FIPV, #09340)*;
- *Fédération aéronautique internationale (FAI, #09397)*;
- *Fédération Internationale de l'Automobile (FIA, #09613)*;
- *Fédération Internationale de Motocyclisme (FIM, #09643)*;
- *Fédération internationale de SAMBO (FIAS, #09655)*;
- *Fédération internationale des échecs (FIDE, #09627)*;
- *Federation of International Bandy (FIB, #09601)*;
- *Federation of International Polo (FIP, #09675)*;
- *International Bowling Federation (IBF, #12384)*;
- *International Cheer Union (ICU, #12539)*;
- *International Cricket Council (ICC, #13105)*;
- *International Federation Icestocksport (IFI, #13455)*;
- *International Federation of American Football (IFAF, #13354)* (provisional);
- *International Federation of Muaythai Associations (IFMA, #13482)*;
- *International Floorball Federation (IFF, #13615)*;
- *International Korfball Federation (IKF, #13992)*;
- *International Life Saving Federation (ILS, #14040)*;
- *International Orienteering Federation (IOF, #14485)*;
- *International Racquetball Federation (IRF, #14683)*;
- *International Sumo Federation (IFS, #15624)*;
- *International Waterski and Wakeboard Federation (IWWF, #15872)*;
- *International Wushu Federation (IWUF, #15918)*;
- *Tug of War International Federation (TWIF, #20259)*;
- *Union internationale des associations d'alpinisme (UIAA, #20420)*;
- *Union internationale Motonautique (UIM, #20431)*;
- *World Association of Kickboxing Organizations (WAKO, #21151)*;
- *World Baseball Softball Confederation (WBSC, #21222)*;
- *World Bridge Federation (WBF, #21246)*;
- *World Confederation of Billiards Sports (WCBS, #21291)*;
- *World Flying Disc Federation (WFDF, #21509)*;
- *World Karate Federation (WKF, #21608)*;
- *World Lacrosse (#21616)*;
- *World Netball (WN, #21668)*;
- *World Squash Federation (WSF, #21826)*;
- *World Underwater Federation (#21873)*.

Sports on the Paris 2024 Olympic Games programme (4):
International Federation of Sport Climbing (IFSC, #13553); *International Surfing Association (ISA, #15630)*; World DanceSport Federation; *World Skate (#21786)*.
Governing Bodies (6):
Court of Arbitration for Sport (CAS, #04933); *International Committee for Fair Play (#12769)*; *International Paralympic Committee (IPC, #14512)*; *International Testing Agency (ITA, #15678)*; *World Anti-Doping Agency (WADA, #21096)*; *World Olympians Association (WOA, #21682)*.
IF Associations (4):
Alliance of Independent recognised Members of Sport (AIMS, #00690); *Association of Summer Olympic International Federations (ASOIF, #02943)*; *Association of the International Olympic Winter Sports Federations (AIOWF, #02757)*; *Association of the IOC Recognized International Sports Federations (ARISF, #02767)*.
NOC Associations (8):
Association of National Olympic Committees (ANOC, #02819); *Association of National Olympic Committees of Africa (ANOCA, #02820)*; *Central American and Caribbean Sports Organization (CACSO, #03665)*; *European Olympic Committees (EOC, #08083)*; *Oceania National Olympic Committees (ONOC, #17667)*; *Olympic Council of Asia (OCA, #17718)*; *Panam Sports Organization (Panam Sports, #18138)*; *South American Sports Organization (SASO, #19708)*.
Recognized bodies in the field of education/dissemination of the Olympic ideal/Fair Play (6):
Comité international Pierre de Coubertin (CIPC, #04184); *International Committee for Fair Play (#12769)*; *International Council for Health, Physical Education, Recreation, Sport and Dance (ICHPER-SD, #13028)*; *International Olympic Academy (IOA, #14406)*; *Panathlon International (PI, #18170)*; *Pan-Iberican Association of Olympic Academies (#18181)*.
Recognized multi-sports organizations and events / Sport for all (15):
Committee of the International Children's Games (CICG, #04264); *Commonwealth Games Federation (CGF, #04332)*; *Conseil international du sport militaire (CISM, #04695)*; *Fédération internationale Sport pour tous (FISpT, #09661)*; *International Committee of the Mediterranean Games (ICMG, #12783)*; *International Federation of Physical and Sport Education (#13510)*; *International Masters Games Association (IMGA, #14117)*; *International Police Sports Union (#14614)*; *International School Sport Federation (ISF, #14792)*; *International Sporting Federation of Catholic Schools (#15589)*; *International University Sports Federation (FISU, #15830)*; *International Workers and Amateurs in Sports Confederation (#15905)*; *International World Games Association (IWGA, #15914)*; *The Association for International Sport for All (TAFISA, #02763)*; *World Transplant Games Federation (WTGF, #21868)*.
Recognized organizations in the field of disabled sport (3):
International Committee of Sports for the Deaf (ICSD, #12805); *International Paralympic Committee (IPC, #14512)*; *Special Olympics International (SOI, #19910)*.
Recognized organizations in the field of sports medicine and sciencees (4):
European College of Sport Science (ECSS, #06616); *International Association for Non-Violent Sport (IANVS, no recent information)*; *International Council of Sport Science and Physical Education (ICSSPE, #13077)*; *International Federation of Sports Medicine (#13554)*.
Recognized organizations in the field of sports equipment and facilities (2):
Internationale Vereinigung Sport- und Freizeiteinrichtungen (IAKS, #13319); *World Federation of the Sporting Goods Industry (WFSGI, #21487)*.
Recognized organizations in the field of Media – Information (6):
Agence France Presse; *Association internationale de la presse sportive (AIPS, #02729)*; *International Association for Sports Information (IASI, #12179)*; *International Sporting Cinema and Television Federation (FICTS, #15588)*; The Associated Press; Thomson Reuters.
Other Recognized Organizations (12):
Association Internationale des Collectionneurs Olympiques (AICO, #02677); *European Non-Governmental Sports Organization (ENGSO, #08054)*; *Federazione Internazionale Cronometristi (FIC, #09717)*; *Fondation internationale Olympafrica (FINO, #09823)*; *Generations for Peace (GFP, no recent information)*; *International Olympic Truce Centre (IOTC, #14409)*; *International Society of Olympic Historians (ISOH, #15322)*; Office of the Permanent Observer for the International Committee to the United Nations; *Olympic Refuge Foundation (ORF, #17720)*; *Right to Play International (#18945)*; *World Olympians Association (WOA, #21682)*; *World Union of Olympic Cities (#21881)*. [2022/XF3401/y/F]

♦ Olympic Refuge Foundation (ORF) 17720

Contact Maison Olympique, 1007 Lausanne VD, Switzerland. E-mail: contact@olympicrefugefoundation.org.
URL: https://olympics.com/en/olympic-refuge-foundation/

History Sep 2017. Launched by *International Olympic Committee (IOC, #14408)*. **Aims** Ensure that young people affected by displacement thrive through safe sport. **Structure** Board; Executive Committee. **IGO Relations** Partner of (2): *UNHCR (#20327)*; *United Nations Population Fund (UNFPA, #20612)*. **NGO Relations** Member of (1): *Olympic Movement (#17719)*. Partner of (5): *Generations for Peace (GFP, no recent information)*; *International Olympic Committee (IOC, #14408)*; *PLAY International*; *Right to Play International (#18945)*; *Terre des hommes Foundation (Tdh Foundation, #20132)*. [2022/AA3052/f/F]

♦ Olympic Solidarity (OS) 17721

Solidarité olympique (SO) – Solidaridad Olimpica

Chairman Villa Mon Repos, Parc Mon Repos 1, CP 1374, 1005 Lausanne VD, Switzerland. T. +41216216900. Fax +41216216363.
URL: http://www.olympic.org/olympic-solidarity-commission/

History Founded 1961, as *Committee for International Olympic Aid (CIOA)*. From 1968, comprised a Commission of *International Olympic Committee (IOC, #14408)* with the same name. Merged, 1971, with 'Olympic Solidarity' project, initiated by the Permanent General Assembly of the *Association of National Olympic Committees (ANOC, #02819)* to form the IOC *Commission for Olympic Solidarity – Commission pour la solidarité olympique* or *Olympic Solidarity Commission*, which from 1971-1981 had only a consultative role but which since 1982 administers Olympic Solidarity. A Department of IOC. **Aims** Organize aid to National Olympic Committees (NOCs) recognized by IOC, particularly to those having the greatest need; promote the basic principles of the Olympic Movement; develop technical sports knowledge among athletes and coaches; improve the technical level of athletes and coaches through scholarships; train sports administrators; collaborate with the various IOC commissions as well as with the organizations and entities pursuing such objectives, particularly through Olympic education and the propagation of sport; create, where needed, simple, functional and economical sports facilities in cooperation with national or international bodies; support the organization of competitions at national, regional and continental level under the authority or patronage of the NOCs; encourage joint bilateral or multilateral cooperation programmes among NOCs; urge governments and international organizations to include sport in Official Development Assistance. **Structure** IOC Commission. **Staff** 20.00 FTE, paid. **Finance** Source: share of broadcasting rights of the Olympic Games allocated to the National Olympic Committees. **Activities** Programmes for athletes: NOC preparation programme (Olympic Winter Games, Regional and Continental Games); Olympic scholarships for athletes; Team support grants; Youth development programme. Programmes for coaches: technical courses; Scholarships for coaches; Development of national sport structure. Programmes for NOC management: NOC infrastructure; Sports administrators programme; High-level education for sports administrators; NOC management consultancy; Regional fora. Programmes Special Fields: Olympic Games participation; Sports medicine; Sport and the environment; Women and Sport; International Olympic Academy; Sport for All; Culture and Education; NOC legacy. **Events** *Meeting* Tokyo (Japan) 2018, *Regional seminar on women and sport* Auckland (New Zealand) 2005, *Symposium for women coaches* Vienna (Austria) 1990. **Publications** *Sports Administration Manual* in English, French, Spanish. Annual Report; quadrennial report; leaflet. **Members** National Olympic Committees. **NGO Relations** *Association of National Olympic Committees (ANOC, #02819)*; *Association of National Olympic Committees of Africa (ANOCA, #02820)*; *European Olympic Committees (EOC, #08083)*; *Association of Sport Performance Centres (ASPC, #02929)*; *International Olympic Academy (IOA, #14406)*; *Oceania National Olympic Committees (ONOC, #17667)*; *Oceania Sport Information Centre (OSIC)*; *Olympic Council of Asia (OCA, #17718)*; *Panam Sports Organization (Panam Sports, #18138)*. [2013.08.20/XF0281/F]

♦ Olympic Solidarity Commission / see Olympic Solidarity (#17721)
♦ Olympic Sports Federations of Oceania / see Organisation of Sports Federations of Oceania (#17828)
♦ OMA – Asociace pro Mezinarodni Otaky (internationally oriented national body)
♦ OMAEC / see Organisation mondiale des anciens élèves de l'enseignement catholique (#17816)
♦ **OMAEC** Organisation mondiale des anciens élèves de l'enseignement catholique (#17816)
♦ **OMAEP** Organisation mondiale des associations pour l'éducation prénatale (#17817)
♦ OMAI – International Symposium on Objective Measures in Auditory Implants (meeting series)
♦ **OMAINTEC** Arab Council of Operations and Maintenance (#00931)
♦ **OMAI** Organisation mondiale Agudath Israel (#00584)
♦ **OMAOC** Organisation Maritime de l'Afrique de l'Ouest et du Centre (#16582)
♦ **OMAOC** Organização Maritima da Africa do Oeste e do Centro (#16582)
♦ **OMA** Open Mobile Alliance (#17757)
♦ **OMA** Organisation mondiale de l'autisme (#21211)
♦ **OMA** Organización Mundial de Aduanas (#21350)
♦ **OMA** Organizzazione Mondiale Degli Agricoltori (#21401)
♦ **OMB** Organización Mundial de Boxeo (#21243)
♦ Ombudsman Eorpach (#08084)
♦ Ombudsman Ewropew (#08084)
♦ Ombudsmanul European (#08084)
♦ **OMCC** Organismo Mundial de Cursillos de Cristianidad (#21238)
♦ OMCI / see International Maritime Organization (#14102)
♦ **OMCL** European Network of Official Medicines Control Laboratories (#07957)
♦ **OMC** Organisation mondiale coiffure (#21550)
♦ **OMC** Organisation mondiale du commerce (#21864)

♦ **OMCT** Organizatia Mondiala a.Copiilor Talentati (#21694)
♦ OMCT/SOS Torture / see World Organisation Against Torture (#21685)
♦ **OMCT** World Organisation Against Torture (#21685)
♦ OMDA – Organisation mondiale de la diaspora africaine (unconfirmed)
♦ OMDA – Organisation mondiale des droits de l'animal (inactive)
♦ OMD – Ordo Clericorum Regularium Matris Dei (religious order)
♦ **OMD** Organisation mondiale de design (#21358)
♦ **OMD** Organisation mondiale des douanes (#21350)
♦ **OMEASE** Organisation des ministres d'éducation de l'Asie du Sud-Est (#19774)
♦ OMECA – Organisation mondiale des experts-conseils-arbitres (internationally oriented national body)
♦ OMED / see World Endoscopy Organization (#21380)
♦ Omega (religious order)
♦ **OMEM** Oficina Mundial de Estadisticas del Metal (#21250)
♦ **OME** Observatoire méditerranéen de l'énergie (#17634)
♦ **OME** Organisation mondiale de l'emballage (#21705)
♦ **OMEP** Organisation mondiale pour l'éducation préscolaire (#21689)
♦ **OMEP** Organización Mundial para la Educación Preescolar (#21689)
♦ **OMEP** Weltorganisation für Vorschulische Erziehung (#21689)
♦ **OMEP** World Organization for Early Childhood Education (#21689)
♦ OMEX – Organisation Mondiale des Experts (unconfirmed)
♦ OMF / see OMF International (#17722)
♦ **OMFIF** Official Monetary and Financial Institutions Forum (#17699)

♦ OMF International 17722

Contact Intl HQ, 2 Cluny Road, Singapore 259570, Singapore. T. +6563194550. Fax +6564722398.
URL: http://www.omf.org/

History 1865, as *China Inland Mission*, subsequently *China Inland Mission Overseas Missionary Fellowship*. Reconstituted, 1964, as *Overseas Missionary Fellowship*. Current title adopted 1993. Also referred to by initials *OMF*. **Aims** As an *interdenominational missionary* organization, glorify God by *evangelizing* the inhabitants of *East Asia*. **Structure** International Council (meets every 3-4 years); Executive Council; International Directors; Headquarters headed by General Director, based in Singapore. **Finance** Supported by interested churches and individuals. UK budget (annual): pounds5.5 million. **Events** *Central council meeting* 1995, *Consultation* 1994, *Overseas council meeting* 1993. **Publications** *East Asia's Billions* (3 a year) – magazine, UK edition. Books; prayer guides; booklets; news sheets; CD-Roms; DVDs; videos, maps. **Members** Total international membership of 1,400 individuals. Membership countries not specified. **NGO Relations** Member of: *Global Connections*. [2020/XF1328/**F**]

♦ **OMF** Oceania Mini Football Federation (#17666)
♦ OM / see Focolare Movement (#09806)
♦ **OMF** Organisation mondiale de la famille (#21399)
♦ **OMGE** Organisation mondiale de gastroentérologie (#21536)
♦ **OMGN** Oomycete Molecular Genetics Network (#17744)
♦ OMG – Object Management Group (internationally oriented national body)
♦ **OMHEC** Offshore Mechanical Handling Equipment Committee (#17700)
♦ OMHI – Organisation médicale homéopathique internationale (no recent information)
♦ OMI – Congregatio Missionariorum Oblatorum Beatae Mariae Virginis Immaculatae (religious order)
♦ OMIDELAC – Organización de Militares por la Democracia, la Integración y la Liberación de América Latina y el Caribe (inactive)
♦ OMIDOT – Organisation mondiale pour l'information sur le don d'organes ou de tissus humains (inactive)
♦ Omidyar Network (internationally oriented national body)

♦ OMiLAB 17723

Contact Lützowufer 1, 10785 Berlin, Germany. T. +493026367863. E-mail: info@omilab.org.
URL: https://www.omilab.org/

History Registration: Berlin Distric court, No/ID: HRB 193863, Start date: 23 Feb 2018, Germany. **Aims** Support an active global community for conceptual modelling that benefits from open artefacts; act as a facilitator to development of scientific methods and technologies for all those who value models; act as a platform where participants can bring in ideas related to modelling and engage in the exploration process. **Structure** Scientific Advisory Board; global network of OMiLAB nodes. **Activities** Events/meetings; knowledge management/information dissemination; research and development; research/documentation; training/education. **Publications** *Domain-Specific Conceptual Modelling* (2021) in English – book series in 2 vols.. *A Digital Innovation Environment* – brochure. [2021.12.01/AA1459/**F**]

♦ Omilos Evropaiki Ekfrassi / see European Expression
♦ OM International / see Operation Mobilisation (#17772)

♦ OM International 17724

UK Office The Quinta, Weston Rhyn, Oswestry, SY10 7LT, UK. T. +441691773388. E-mail: info@om.org.
Belgium Office Fabrieksstraat 63, 1930 Zaventem, Belgium. T. +3227207025. E-mail: personnel.be@om.org.
URL: http://www.om.org/

History Founded by George Verwer, Work started in Spain as *Send the Light*. Subsequently changed title to *Operation Mobilisation International (OM International)*, 1981. Currently only known under its acronym. **Aims** Help plant and strengthen *churches*, especially in areas of the world where Christ is least known. **Structure** Global Board. **Activities** Active in over 100 countries. [2020/XJ6849/**F**]

♦ OMI – Ocean Mammal Institute (internationally oriented national body)
♦ **OMI** Organisation maritime internationale (#14102)
♦ OMI – Organisation météorologique internationale (inactive)
♦ **OMI** Organización Maritima Internacional (#14102)
♦ OMIR – Observatoire méditerranéen pour l'information et la réflexion – géopolitique, géoculture, géoéconomie, géoenvironnement (see: #18959)
♦ OMIS – Organisation mondiale de l'image et du son (inactive)
♦ OMMA – Organización Mundial de la Medicina Alternativa (inactive)
♦ **OMM** Organisation météorologique mondiale (#21649)
♦ **OMM** Organización Meteorológica Mundial (#21649)
♦ OMM – Organización Mundo Maya (internationally oriented national body)
♦ OMMSA – Organization of Museums, Monuments and Sites of Africa (no recent information)
♦ **OMMS** Organisation Mondiale du Mouvement Scout (#21693)
♦ OMN – Organisation Mondiale de la Nature (inactive)
♦ OMN – Organización Mundial de la Naturaleza (inactive)
♦ OM – Ordo Minimorum (religious order)
♦ Omospondia Evropaion Ekdoton (#09536)
♦ Omospondias Evropaion Dimosion Liturgon (#06567)
♦ Omospondia ton Tilepikinoniakon Mihanikon tis Evropaikis Kinotitas (#09597)
♦ Omospondia Viomihagion Proton Olon ke Endiameson Proionon Artopopas ke Zaharoplastikis tis EOP / see Federation of European Manufacturers of Ingredients to the Bakery, Confectionery and Patisserie Industries (#09513)
♦ **OMPD** Organización Mundial de Personas con Discapacidad (#05097)
♦ OMPE – Organisation mondiale de la profession enseignante (inactive)
♦ **OMPH** Organisation internationale des personnes handicapées (#05097)
♦ **OMPI** Organisation mondiale de la propriété intellectuelle (#21593)
♦ **OMPI** Organización Mundial de la Propiedad Intelectual (#21593)
♦ **OMPO** Oiseaux migrateurs du paléarctique occidental (#17712)
♦ **OMPP** Organisation mondiale de la presse périodique (#17819)
♦ OMPSA – Organisation mondiale pour la promotion sociale des aveugles (inactive)
♦ Omrezje obcin – Povezanost v Alpah / see Alliance in the Alps (#00656)
♦ OMRS – Orders and Medals Research Society (internationally oriented national body)
♦ OMS / see One Mission Society
♦ OMS Bureau régional de l'Europe / see WHO Regional Office for Europe (#20945)
♦ OMS Centre panafricain pour la formation aux situations d'urgence (no recent information)
♦ OMS Centre régional pour les activités d'hygiène de l'environnement (#20942)
♦ **OMSC** Organisation mondiale pour la systémique et la cybernétique (#21686)
♦ OMSC – Overseas Ministries Study Center (internationally oriented national body)
♦ OMS initiative pour un monde sans tabac (#20949)
♦ OMS International / see One Mission Society
♦ OMSL – Organização Mundial de Software Livre (unconfirmed)
♦ OMS Oficina Regional para Europa / see WHO Regional Office for Europe (#20945)
♦ OMS – One Mission Society (internationally oriented national body)
♦ **OMS** Organisation mondiale de la santé (#20950)
♦ **OMS** Organización Mundial de la Salud (#20950)
♦ OMS Sécurité des patients (#20940)
♦ **OMTh** Organisation mondiale du thermalisme (#17820)
♦ **OMT** Organisation Mondiale du Tourisme (#21861)
♦ **OMT** Organización Mundial del Turismo (#21861)
♦ OMV / see Osteuropaverein
♦ OMV – Congregatio Oblatorum Beatae Mariae Virginis (religious order)
♦ **OMVG** Organisation pour la mise en valeur du fleuve Gambie (#17814)
♦ **OMVS** Organisation pour la mise en valeur du fleuve Sénégal (#17815)

♦ Oñati International Institute for the Sociology of Law (IISL) 17725

Institut international de sociologie juridique d'Oñati – Instituto Internacional de Sociologia Juridica de Oñati (IISJ) – Oñatiko Lege-Soziologiako Nazioarteko Erakundea (OLSNE)

Scientific Dir Avda de la Universidad nr 8, 20560 Oñati, Guipúzcoa, Spain. T. +34943783064. Fax +34943783147. E-mail: onati@iisj.es.
URL: http://www.iisj.es/

History Set up 1989, by the Basque Government and the Research Committee on Sociology of Law (RCSL) of the *International Sociological Association (ISA, #15553)*. Also referred to as *International Institute for the Sociology of Law*. **Aims** Discuss, analyse and compare research in sociology of law. **Structure** Governing Board; Committees (7). **Languages** Basque, English, French, Spanish. **Staff** 9.00 FTE, paid. **Finance** Self-financing; support from the Basque Government. **Activities** Events/meetings; training/education; knowledge management/information dissemination; publishing activities. **Events** *Too Much Litigation Workshop* Oñati (Spain) 2019, *Workshop on International Law, the United Nations Declarations of the Rights of Indigenous Peoples and Indigenous Data Sovereignty* Oñati (Spain) 2019, *Workshop on Social Control, Judicialization of Social Problems and Governance of Security in Comparative Perspectives* Oñati (Spain) 2019, *Workshop on Supporting Legal Capacity in Socio-Legal Context* Oñati (Spain) 2019, *Workshop on Youth Violence* Oñati (Spain) 2019. **Publications** *Oñati-IISL Newsletter*. *Dykinson Spanish Series*; *Hart English Series*; *Oñati Socio-Legal Series*. *Sortuz*.
Members Institutions with a scientific agreement with IISL in 33 countries and territories:
Argentina, Australia, Austria, Belgium, Brazil, Bulgaria, Canada, Chile, Colombia, Costa Rica, Denmark, Finland, France, Germany, Greece, Hungary, India, Italy, Mexico, Netherlands, Norway, Peru, Poland, Portugal, Puerto Rico, Romania, Spain, Switzerland, UK, Uruguay, USA, Vanuatu, Venezuela. [2019.03.06/XF1325/j/**F**]

♦ Oñatiko Lege-Soziologiako Nazioarteko Erakundea (#17725)
♦ Once Acre Fund (internationally oriented national body)
♦ **ONCE** Open Network for Commerce Exchange (#17758)

♦ Onchocerciasis Elimination Program for the Americas (OEPA) 17726

Programme d'élimination de l'onchocercose dans les Amériques – Programa para la Eliminación de la Oncocercosis en las Américas

Dir 14 Calle 3-51, Zona 10, Edificio Murano Center – Oficina 1401, 01010 Guatemala, Guatemala. T. +50223666106. Fax +50223666127. E-mail: oepa@oepa.net.
URL: https://www.cartercenter.org/health/river_blindness/oepa.html

History 1 Jan 1993. Established following activities initiated during the *Inter-American Conference on Onchocerciasis (IACO)*, under the mandate of *Pan American Health Organization (PAHO, #18108)* – Directing Council resolution CD34R14 (1991). **Aims** Eliminate onchocerciasis through implementation of effective, safe and locally sustainable programmes for the distribution of ivermectin in all endemic communities within the framework of a coordinated regional strategy. **Structure** Headquarters in Guatemala, includes all Ministries of Health from 6 regional endemic countries and several donors, managed by *The Carter Center*. **Languages** English, Spanish. **Staff** 10.00 FTE, paid. **Finance** Sponsors include: *Bill and Melinda Gates Foundation (BMGF)*; Carlos Slim Foundation; *The Carter Center*; Centers for Disease Control and Prevention; *Inter-American Development Bank (IDB, #11427)*; *International Bank for Reconstruction and Development (IBRD, #12317)* (World Bank); John Moores, *Lions Clubs International (LCI, #16485)*; Mectizan Donation Program (in-kind contribution); *John Merck Fund*; *Pan American Health Organization (PAHO, #18108)*; *United States Agency for International Development (USAID)*. **Activities** Research and development; knowledge management/information dissemination; events/meetings. **Events** *Conference* Mexico City (Mexico) 2014, *Conference* Quito (Ecuador) 2013, *Conference* Tuxtla Gutiérrez (Mexico) 2012, *Conference* Bogota (Colombia) 2011, *Conference* Antigua (Guatemala) 2010. **Publications** *Como vamos en coberturas de tratamiento con Mectizan ?* (2 a year) – bulletin; *Report of the Inter-American Conference on Onchocerciasis* (annual). *Guide to detecting a potential recrudescence of onchocerciasis during the posttreatmnt surveillance period: the American paradigm* (2012); *The Onchocerciasis Elimination Program for the Americas (OEPA)* (2008) by M Sauerbrey; *The Onchocerciasis Elimination Program for the Americas: a history of partnership* (1998) by J Blanks, et al.
Members Participating countries (6):
Brazil, Colombia, Ecuador, Guatemala, Mexico, Venezuela.
IGO Relations *PAHO Foundation (#18022)* (Mexico Office); *Pan American Health Organization (PAHO, #18108)* (Brazil, Colombia, Ecuador, Guatemala, Mexico and Venezuela Offices); *UNDP (#20292)* (Ecuador and Brazil Offices); *WHO (#20950)*. **NGO Relations** *Bureau international des Médecins sans frontières (MSF International, #03366)* (Brazil); *Centro Internacional de Entrenamiento e Investigaciones Médicas (CIDEIM, no recent information)*; *Light for the World (#16474)*; national organizations and universities. [2019.12.13/XE4214/**E***]

♦ Oncological Society of Central America and the Caribbean (no recent information)
♦ ONCO – Oncological Society of Central America and the Caribbean (no recent information)

♦ Oncoplastic Breast Consortium (OPBC) 17727

Address not obtained.
URL: https://www.oncoplasticbc.org/

Aims Bring safe and effective oncoplastic breast surgery to routine patient care. **Structure** National coordinators. **Activities** Events/meetings; knowledge management/information dissemination.
Members Individuals in 81 countries and territories:
Argentina, Armenia, Australia, Austria, Azerbaijan, Bahrain, Bangladesh, Belgium, Bolivia, Brazil, Bulgaria, Canada, Cayman Is, Chile, China, Colombia, Cuba, Cyprus, Czechia, Ecuador, Egypt, Estonia, Finland, France, Germany, Greece, Hong Kong, Hungary, India, Indonesia, Iran Islamic Rep, Iraq, Ireland, Israel, Italy, Japan, Jordan, Korea Rep, Lithuania, Malaysia, Malta, Mexico, Myanmar, Nepal, Netherlands, Nicaragua, North Macedonia, Norway, Pakistan, Palestine, Paraguay, Peru, Philippines, Poland, Portugal, Qatar, Romania, Russia, Saudi Arabia, Serbia, Singapore, Slovakia, Slovenia, South Africa, Spain, Sri Lanka, Sudan, Sweden, Switzerland, Taiwan, Tajikistan, Tanzania UR, Thailand, Tunisia, Türkiye, UK, Ukraine, United Arab Emirates, Uruguay, USA, Venezuela. [2021/AA2181/v/**C**]

♦ Ondernemers Zonder Grenzen (internationally oriented national body)
♦ OND – Ordre de la Compagnie de Marie Notre-Dame (religious order)
♦ ONE / see Orchestra Network for Europe (#17787)

♦ ONE 17728

UK Office Endeavour House, 189 Shaftesbury Ave, London, WC2H 8JR, UK. T. +442030196700. E-mail: enquiries@one.org.
USA Office 1299 Pennsylvania Ave, Suite 400, Washington DC 20004, USA. T. +12024952700.

URL: http://www.one.org/
History May 2004, Philadelphia PA (USA), by *Debt AIDS Trade Africa (DATA, inactive)*, *Bread for the World Institute (BFW Institute)*, CARE USA, *International Medical Corps (IMC)*, *International Rescue Committee (IRC, #14717)*, Oxfam America, Plan USA, *Save the Children Federation (SCF)*, *World Concern International (#21290)* and *World Vision International (WVI, #21904)*. Also referred to as *ONE Campaign*. Name derives from the idea of putting one percent of the USA national budget towards basic needs. DATA merged with ONE, Jan 2008. Full title: *ONE – Campaign to Make Poverty History*. EU Transparency Register: 26098317349-65. **Aims** End extreme *poverty* and preventable disease, particularly in *Africa*. **Structure** Board; Executive Management Team. Offices in (7) countries: Belgium; Canada; France; Germany; South Africa; UK; USA. Sister organization: *(RED)*. **Finance** Foundations; individuals; corporations. **Activities** Advocacy/lobbying/activism; awareness raising. **NGO Relations** Member of: *Alliance to End Hunger*, *American Council for Voluntary International Action (InterAction)*; *European Network on Debt and Development (EURODAD, #07891)*; *European Policy Centre (EPC, #08240)*; *Gavi – The Vaccine Alliance (Gavi, #10077)* CSO Constituency; *Global Coalition Against Child Pneumonia (#10290)*; *Global Open Data for Agriculture and Nutrition (GODAN, #10514)*; *InsideNGO (inactive)*; *PMNCH (#18410)*. Partner of: *1,000 Days*; *Every Woman Every Child (EWEC, #09215)*; *Global Call for Climate Action (GCCA, inactive)*; *Global Partnership for Sustainable Development Data (Data4SDGS, #10542)*; *Transparency, Accountability and Participation Network (TAP Network, #20222)*. Supports: *Global Call for Action Against Poverty (GCAP, #10263)*. [2019.06.25/XM8112/F]

♦ One Acre Fund 17729

Exec Dir 1954 First St, Ste 183, Highland Park IL 60035, USA.
URL: http://oneacrefund.org/
History 2006. **Aims** Supply financing and training to help *smallholders* grow their way out of hunger and build lasting ways to prosperity. **Structure** Governing Board; Global Directors; Field Directors. **Activities** Financial and/or material support; training/education; advocacy/lobbying/activism. **NGO Relations** Partner of: *Mastercard Foundation*. [2020/XM7114/f/F]

♦ One for All (internationally oriented national body)
♦ ONEARTH Charity Foundation (unconfirmed)
♦ One Asia Foundation / see Eurasia Foundation
♦ ONE Campaign / see ONE (#17728)
♦ ONE – Campaign to Make Poverty History / see ONE (#17728)
♦ **ONECA** Organización Negra Centroamericana (#03659)
♦ One Drop (internationally oriented national body)
♦ One Earth Future Foundation (internationally oriented national body)
♦ One Earth One World (internationally oriented national body)

♦ OneEurope 17730

Contact Sterndamm 71, 12487 Berlin, Germany. E-mail: oneeurope.team@gmail.com.
URL: http://one-europe.net/
History 2011, as a Facebook group. Registered in accordance with German law. **Aims** Raise awareness on relevant issues of Europeans; encourage *debate* on key topics; give a voice to citizens; stimulate freedom of speech in Europe; provide opportunities to Europeans build bridges and connections between cultures. **Staff** Voluntary. **Finance** Donations. **Activities** Knowledge management/information dissemination; awareness raising. **NGO Relations** *Euro Atlantic Diplomacy Society (EAD Society, #05643)*; *European Cooperative Youth Network (ECYON, #06789)*. [2018/XM4743/F]

♦ OneGeology 17731

Contact address not obtained. E-mail: onegeology@bgs.ac.uk.
URL: https://onegeology.org/
History 2008. Launched in the International Year of Planet Earth. Not a legal entity, but a non-corporate body (Consortium). **Aims** Provide access to global geoscience data via web services underpinned by commonly used geodata standards. **Structure** Operations Group; Steering Committee. **Activities** Knowledge management/information dissemination; research/documentation.
Members National surveys of 118 countries and territories:
Afghanistan, Albania, Algeria, Andorra, Argentina, Armenia, Australia, Austria, Azerbaijan, Bangladesh, Belgium, Bhutan, Bosnia-Herzegovina, Botswana, Brazil, Bulgaria, Burkina Faso, Burundi, Cambodia, Cameroon, Canada, Central African Rep, Chile, China, Colombia, Congo DR, Costa Rica, Croatia, Cuba, Cyprus, Czechia, Denmark, Djibouti, Dominican Rep, Ecuador, Egypt, Estonia, Ethiopia, Falklands/Malvinas, Finland, France, Gambia, Georgia, Germany, Ghana, Greece, Guinea, Hong Kong, Hungary, Iceland, India, Indonesia, Iran Islamic Rep, Iraq, Ireland, Israel, Italy, Jamaica, Japan, Kazakhstan, Kenya, Korea Rep, Kosovo, Laos, Latvia, Lesotho, Lithuania, Luxembourg, Macedonia, Malawi, Mali, Mexico, Mongolia, Mozambique, Myanmar, Namibia, Nepal, Netherlands, New Zealand, Nigeria, Norway, Oman, Pakistan, Papua New Guinea, Peru, Philippines, Poland, Portugal, Romania, Russia, Rwanda, Senegal, Serbia, Sierra Leone, Singapore, Slovakia, Slovenia, South Africa, Spain, Sri Lanka, Suriname, Sweden, Switzerland, Tanzania UR, Thailand, Türkiye, Uganda, UK, Ukraine, United Arab Emirates, Uruguay, USA, Uzbekistan, Vanuatu, Venezuela, Vietnam, Yemen, Zimbabwe.
NGO Relations Associated with (1): *Geoscience InfoRmation in AFrica (GIRAF)*. [2020/AA3166/F]

♦ ONE goes places / see Orchestra Network for Europe (#17787)
♦ OneHope (internationally oriented national body)
♦ One Laptop per Child (internationally oriented national body)

♦ oneM2M 17732

Secretariat c/o ETSI, 650 route des Lucioles, 06560 Valbonne, France. E-mail: onem2m_secretariat@list.onem2m.org.
Main Website: http://www.onem2m.org/
History 24 Jul 2012. Established following signature of Partnership Agreement between seven regional standards bodies: ARIB (Japan), ATIS (Americas), CCSA (China), ETSI (Europe), TIA (Americas) and TTA (S. Korea). First Technical Plenary Meeting in Nice (France), Sept 2012. First Interoperability Test event and ratification in Release 1 of oneM2M standard, 2015. Release 2 of the standard ratified in 2016 and followed by enhancements in the form of Release 2A early in 2018. Release 3 completed in 2019. Initiative on the role of Internet of Things (IoT) launched in 2021. **Aims** Develop Internet of Things (IoT) standards in order to enable interoperable, secure, and simple-to-deploy services for the IoT ecosystem; develop technical specifications for a common service layer that can be readily embedded within various hardware and software, and relied upon to connect the myriad of devices in the field with IoT application servers worldwide; attract and actively involve organizations from related business domains such as: telematics and intelligent transportation, healthcare, utilities, industrial automation, smart homes, smart cities, public safety and services, retail, agriculture etc.; ensure the global functionality of IoT systems and prevents the duplication of standardization effort by bringing together more than 200 member organizations from many diverse business domains. **Structure** Steering Committee; Technical Plenary; Working Groups; Secretariat. **Languages** English. **Staff** Secretariat staff provided by partners. **Finance** Financed by partners. **Activities** Events/meetings; publishing activities; standards/guidelines. Active in all member countries. **Events** *Interoperability Meeting* Valbonne (France) 2020, *Interoperability Meeting* Washington, DC (USA) 2018, *Interoperability Meeting* Seongnam (Korea Rep) 2017, *Interoperability Meeting* Taipei (Taiwan) 2017, *Interoperability Meeting* Kobe (Japan) 2016. **Publications** *Executive Viewpoints* – Strategic developments in the IoT marketplace, innovation and standardization.; *Technical Reports*. Standards; guidelines; tutorials; white papers. **Information Services** *oneM2M Technical Specifications*; *Ontologies used for oneM2M* – Ontologies and their OWL representations are used in oneM2M to provide syntactic and semantic interoperability between oneM2M and external systems..
Members Organizations (over 200). Partner Type 1 organizations (8) in 5 countries:
China, India, Japan, Korea Rep, USA.
Included in the above, 2 organization listed in this Yearbook:
European Telecommunications Standards Institute (ETSI, #08897); *Telecommunications Industry Association (TIA)*.
Partner Type 2 organization:
GlobalPlatform (#10551).
IGO Relations Cooperates with (1): *International Telecommunication Union (ITU, #15673)*. **NGO Relations** Partnership with national organizations. [2022.06.22/XM6155/y/C]

♦ One Mission Society (internationally oriented national body)
♦ ONE a new dimension / see Orchestra Network for Europe (#17787)
♦ One By One (internationally oriented national body)
♦ **ONE** Orchestra Network for Europe (#17787)

♦ One Percent for Development Fund (1% for Development Fund) ... 17733

Fonds un pour cent pour le développement
Main Office c/o Intl Labour Office, Room 1-40, Route des Morillons 4, 1211 Geneva 22, Switzerland. E-mail: contact@onepercentfund.net.
URL: http://www.onepercentfund.net/
History 1976. Founded by a group of United Nations staff members in Geneva (Switzerland), who decided to assign 1% of their salaries to financing small-scale development projects in health, education, water and sanitation, small-scale agriculture, small and micro enterprises and small-scale miscellaneous projects. Similar funds subsequently set up in Rome (Italy), New York NY (USA), Vienna (Austria). Since 2004, membership broadened to include all individuals. **Aims** Finance small grass-root projects in *Third World* countries and countries in transition; use various promotional activities to induce more members; develop various criteria for selecting projects and beneficiary NGOs. **Structure** General Assembly of members (twice a year). Management Committee, consisting of 16 members, meets, selects and follows projects. Fund in Geneva (Switzerland) open to all individuals, but in particular officials from all UN agencies in Geneva, CERN and IMO. Funds in New York NY (USA), London (UK), Rome (Italy) and Vienna (Austria) include only officials from UN agencies in these cities. **Languages** English, French. **Staff** 16.00 FTE, voluntary. **Finance** Sources: donations. Contributions by Fund members. Annual budget: 170,000 CHF (2021). **Activities** Finances about 7 projects (about 800 to date) every 6 months, with the maximum duration of a project being usually less than 2 years. **Publications** Articles. **Members** Staff of UN system organizations, public and private organizations in Geneva (Switzerland), as well as retirees, contributing a minimum of 1% of their salary to a common fund for development. **NGO Relations** Instrumental in setting up (1): *International Guarantee Fund (IGF, #13761)*. Links with a large number of development organizations worldwide. [2022.02.19/XF8501/f/F]

♦ One Planet Business for Biodiversity (OP2B) 17734

Contact c/o WBCSD, Avenue du Bouchet 2bis, 1209 Geneva, Switzerland. T. +41228393100.
URL: https://www.wbcsd.org/Projects/OP2B
History 23 Sep 2019, New York, NY (USA). Launched at *United Nations (UN, #20515)* Climate Action Summit. Registration: EU Transparency Register, No/ID: 254508647685-28, Start date: 20 Sep 2022. **Aims** Drive transformational systemic change and catalyze action to protect and restore cultivated and natural biodiversity within the value chains; engage institutional and financial decision-makers; develop and promote policy recommendations for the 2021 CBD COP15 framework. **Structure** Hosted by *World Business Council for Sustainable Development (WBCSD, #21254)*. **Staff** 1.00 FTE, paid. **Members** Companies (27). Membership countries not specified. [2022/AA1548/E]

♦ ONE step further / see Orchestra Network for Europe (#17787)

♦ One UN Climate Change Learning Partnership (UN CC:Learn) 17735

Partenariat d'apprentissage Unité d'action des Nations Unies en matière de changements climatiques – Asociación para el Aprendizaje sobre el Cambio Climatico de la Iniciativa Una ONU
Secretariat c/o UNITAR, Intl Environment House, Chemin des Anémones 11-13, Châtelaine, 1219 Geneva, Switzerland. E-mail: info@uncclearn.org.
URL: http://www.uncclearn.org/
History Launched 2009, Copenhagen (Denmark), at the Copenhagen Climate Change Summit. First 3-year pilot phase (2011-2013) in 5 pilot countries; 2nd 3-year phase (2014-2017) includes additional countries, new learning products and an upgraded learning platform. Former titles: *Partenariat One UN pour L'Apprentissage sur les Changements Climatiques – Iniciativa Una ONU Asociación para el Aprendizaje sobre el Cambio Climatico*. **Aims** At the global level, support knowledge sharing, promote development of common climate change learning materials and coordinate learning interventions through collaboration of UN agencies and other partners; at the national level, support countries in developing and implementing national climate change learning strategies. **Structure** Secretariat hosted by *United Nations Institute for Training and Research (UNITAR, #20576)*. Included in the One UN Climate Change Action Framework of the *United Nations System Chief Executives Board for Coordination (CEB, #20636)*. **Languages** English, French, Spanish. **Staff** 5-10 FTE, paid. **Finance** Funded by: Swiss government; UN partners. **Activities** Capacity building; events/meetings; knowledge management/information dissemination; training/education. **Events** *Annual Meeting* Geneva (Switzerland) 2018, *Annual Meeting* Bonn (Germany) 2017, *Annual Meeting* Geneva (Switzerland) 2016. **Publications** *Resource Guide for Advanced Learning on REDD+* (2017); *Resource Guide for Advanced Learning on Climate Change and Cities* (2016); *Youth Climate Dialogues: Guiding Tips to Get You All Set* (2016); *Resource Guide for Advanced Learning on Predicting and Projecting Climate Change* (2015); *Resource Guide for Advanced Learning on The Scientific Fundamentals of Climate Change* (2015); *Guidance Note for Developing a National Climate Change Learning Strategy* (2013); *Resource Guide for Advanced Learning on Integrating Climate Change in Education at Primary and Secondary Level* (2013); *Resource Guide for Advanced Learning on Understanding the Climate Change and Health Interface* (2013).
Members Partners (36):
- *Environmental Management Group (EMG, #05506)*;
- *FAO (#09260)*;
- *Global Environment Facility (GEF, #10346)*;
- *ILO (#11123)*;
- *Inter-American Development Bank (IDB, #11427)*;
- *International Bank for Reconstruction and Development (IBRD, #12317)* (World Bank);
- *International Fund for Agricultural Development (IFAD, #13692)*;
- *International Maritime Organization (IMO, #14102)*;
- *International Telecommunication Union (ITU, #15673)*;
- *Joint United Nations Programme on HIV/AIDS (UNAIDS, #16149)*;
- *UNDP (#20292)*;
- *UNEP (#20299)*;
- *UNESCO (#20322)*;
- *UNHCR (#20327)*;
- *UNICEF (#20332)*;
- *UNIDO (#20336)*;
- *United Nations Economic and Social Commission for Asia and the Pacific (ESCAP, #20557)*;
- *United Nations Economic and Social Commission for Western Asia (ESCWA, #20558)*;
- *United Nations Economic Commission for Africa (ECA, #20554)*;
- *United Nations Economic Commission for Europe (UNECE, #20555)*;
- *United Nations Framework Convention on Climate Change – Secretariat (UNFCCC, #20564)*;
- *United Nations Human Settlements Programme (UN-Habitat, #20572)*;
- *United Nations Institute for Training and Research (UNITAR, #20576)*;
- *United Nations Office for Disaster Risk Reduction (UNDRR, #20595)*;
- *United Nations Office for the Coordination of Humanitarian Affairs (OCHA, #20593)*;
- *United Nations Population Fund (UNFPA, #20612)*;
- *United Nations System Chief Executives Board for Coordination (CEB, #20636)*;
- *United Nations System Staff College (UNSSC, #20637)*;
- *United Nations University (UNU, #20642)*;
- *Universal Postal Union (UPU, #20682)*;
- *UN Women (#20724)*;
- *WHO (#20950)*;
- *World Food Programme (WFP, #21510)*;
- *World Meteorological Organization (WMO, #21649)*;
- *World Tourism Organization (UNWTO, #21861)*;
- *World Trade Organization (WTO, #21864)*. [2017.06.01/XM5078/y/F]

♦ One of Us European Federation for Life and Human Dignity (One of Us) 17736

Coordinator Office Av de l'Europe 33, 7330 Saint-Ghislain, Belgium. T. +3234645734423. E-mail: info@oneofus.eu.
URL: http://www.oneofus.eu/

History Sep 2014. Registration: EU Transparency Register, No/ID: 478454716012-16. **Aims** Work towards the unconditional recognition of the inherent and inalienable human dignity as a source of human freedoms and citizens' rights; develop a Culture of Life in Europe. **Structure** General Assembly. **Languages** English. **Activities** Awards/prizes/competitions; events/meetings. **Events** *Forum* Paris (France) 2016, *General Assembly* Madrid (Spain) 2014.
Members Full in 19 countries:
Belgium, Bulgaria, Czechia, Denmark, France, Germany, Ireland, Italy, Luxembourg, Malta, Netherlands, Poland, Portugal, Romania, Slovakia, Slovenia, Spain, Sweden, UK. [2020.03.30/XJ8960/**D**]

- ♦ **One of Us** One of Us European Federation for Life and Human Dignity (#17736)
- ♦ OneWorld Africa (see: #17738)
- ♦ One World Broadcasting Trust / see One World Media
- ♦ One World Center (internationally oriented national body)

♦ Oneworld Cockpit Crew Coalition (OCCC) 17737

Contact BALPA House, 5 Heathrow Boulevard, 278 Bath Road, West Drayton, UB7 0DQ, UK. T. +442084764000. Fax +442084764077. E-mail: webadministrator@oneworldpilots.org – balpa@balpa.org.
URL: http://www.oneworldpilots.org/
History As a coalition of pilot unions of Oneworld Alliance. **Members** Pilot unions (13), gathering 28,000 members. Membership countries not specified. [2015/XJ0785/**E**]

- ♦ One World Foundation (internationally oriented national body)
- ♦ One World Foundation of New York (internationally oriented national body)
- ♦ OneWorld Health (internationally oriented national body)
- ♦ One World Institute (internationally oriented national body)

♦ OneWorld International Foundation (OWIF) 17738

Exec Dir CAN Mezzanine, 7-14 Great Dover St, London, SE1 4YR, UK. T. +442079227844.
URL: http://oneworld.org/
History 10 Dec 1999. Founded following deliberations commencing Feb 1999. Governing body of the *OneWorld Network (OWN)*, set up at the same time, and guardian of OneWorld's vision and values. OneWorld was conceived by Peter Armstrong and Anuradha Vittachi in 1994; they set up *OneWorld Online (OWO)*, 24 Jan 1995, as an internet portal on global justice, under the aegis of the (UK) *OneWorld Broadcasting Trust (OWBT)*. Registration: Charity Commission, No/ID: 1095287, Start date: Jan 2003, England and Wales. **Aims** Promote the developing vision, values, identity and creative synergy of the OneWorld global participatory *media* network, focusing on global *justice* and innovating user-generated platforms for NGO and citizen-led *social change*; facilitate strategic and intellectual leadership for the Network; promote diversity across the Network. **Structure** International Board of Trustees, composed of one Trustee per centre. Executive Committee, consisting of Chair and 2 members. Director. International Advisers. Centres (11): Austria; Canada; Finland; Italy; Netherlands; Spain; UK; USA; *OneWorld Africa (see: #17738)*; *OneWorld Latin America (see: #17738)*; *OneWorld South Asia (OWSA, see: #17738)*. **Finance** Supported by organizations and companies, including: *Department for International Development (DFID, inactive)*; *Directorate-General for Development Cooperation (DGDC)*; *Ford Foundation (#09858)*; *Humanistisch Instituut voor Ontwikkelingssamenwerking (Hivos)*; *MacArthur Foundation*. **Activities** Publishing activities; knowledge management/information dissemination. **Events** *Annual General Meeting* Bangkok (Thailand) 2018.
Members International network of autonomous centres (12) representing over 2,000 cooperative organizations in 12 countries:
Austria, Bosnia-Herzegovina, Canada, Costa Rica, Finland, India, Italy, Netherlands, Spain, UK, USA, Zambia.
IGO Relations *Digital Opportunity Task Force (DOT Force, no recent information)*; *Water and Sanitation Programme (WSP, #20837)*. **NGO Relations** Member of: *CIVICUS: World Alliance for Citizen Participation (#03962)*; *EarthAction (EA, #05159)*; *European Partnership for Democracy (EPD, #08156)*; *Open Knowledge Network (OKN, #17756)*; *World Social Forum (WSF, #21797)*. Relations and cooperation with: *Bellanet Alliance of Social Entrepreneurs (BASE, #03196)*. Cooperation with: *Institute for Resource and Security Studies (IRSS, no recent information)*. *Women's Feature Service (WFS, #21017)* is member. Partner of: *Global Call for Climate Action (GCCA, inactive)*. [2017/XF5983/f/**F**]

- ♦ OneWorld Latin America (see: #17738)
- ♦ One World Media (internationally oriented national body)
- ♦ One World – Un seul monde / see Shared Earth
- ♦ OneWorld South Asia (see: #17738)
- ♦ One World Trust (internationally oriented national body)
- ♦ One World Volunteer Institute / see One World Institute

♦ One Young World 17739

Main Office 14 Irving Street, London, WC2H 7AF, UK. T. +442039618060. E-mail: info@oneyoungworld.com.
URL: http://www.oneyoungworld.com/
History 8 Feb 2010, London (UK). Founded on the initiative of David Jones and Kate Robinson, during Inaugural Summit. Registration: Chairty Commission, No/ID: 1147298, England and Wales; Companies House, No/ID: 06970067, England and Wales. **Aims** Connect and bring together the youngest and brightest and ensure that their concerns, opinions and solutions are heard and taken into account by those in power, whether in government, business or any other sector. **Activities** Advocacy/lobbying/activism; events/meetings. **Events** *One Young World Summit* Tokyo (Japan) 2022, *One Young World Summit* Munich (Germany) 2021, *Annual Summit* London (UK) 2019, *Annual Summit* The Hague (Netherlands) 2018, *Annual Summit* Bogota (Colombia) 2017. **NGO Relations** Partner of: *UNLEASH*. [2021/XJ2085/**F**]

- ♦ **ONF** Open Networking Foundation (#17759)
- ♦ ONG Bell International / see Bell International
- ♦ **ONG CNRJ** Organisation non Gouvernementale des Cercles Nationaux de Réflexion sur la Jeunesse (#17821)
- ♦ ONG HOPE International (internationally oriented national body)
- ♦ ONG para la Promoción de la Salud en Paises en Desarrollo / see Enraíza Derechos
- ♦ ONGs européennes pour la santé et les droits de la reproduction, la population et le développement / see Inspire – the European Partnership for Sexual and Reproductive Health and Rights (#11232)
- ♦ ONIROS/EASD / see European Association for the Study of Dreams (#06230)

♦ Online Computer Library Center (OCLC) 17740

CEO 6565 Kilgour Pl, Dublin OH 43017-3395, USA. T. +16147646000. Fax +16147646096. E-mail: oclc@oclc.org.
URL: http://www.oclc.org/
History 1967, Dublin OH (USA), as Ohio College Library Center. *Research Libraries Group (RLG, inactive)* merged into OCLC, 1 Jul 2006. **Aims** Further access to the world's information for everyone; reduce the rate of rise of library costs. **Structure** Board of Trustees. Global Council; Regional Councils. Management. **Activities** Maintains *WorldCat*, a global online public access catalogue. **Events** *Asia Pacific Regional Council Meeting* Auckland (New Zealand) 2020, *European, Middle East and Africa Regional Council Meeting* Vienna (Austria) 2020, *Asia Pacific Regional Council Meeting* Singapore (Singapore) 2019, *Asia Pacific Regional Council Meeting* Bangkok (Thailand) 2018, *Asia Pacific Regional Council Meeting* Tokyo (Japan) 2017. **Members** In 109 countries and territories. Membership countries not specified. **NGO Relations** Partner of: *American International Consortium of Academic Libraries (AMICAL, #00783)*. Member of: *ORCID (#17790)*. [2020/XJ8275/**F**]

♦ Online Progressive Engagement Network (OPEN) 17741

Exec Dir address not obtained. E-mail: hello@the-open.net.
URL: https://www.the-open.net/
History Jan 2013, USA. **Aims** Build a sustainable global movement for progressive change. **Activities** Advocacy/lobbying/activism; networking/liaising.
Members National grassroots campaigning organizations. Full in 13 countries:
Australia, Austria, Canada, Germany, Ireland, Israel, New Zealand, Poland, Romania, Sweden, Switzerland, UK, USA.
Start-ups in 5 countries:
France, Hungary, Netherlands, Serbia, South Africa. [2021/AA2659/**F**]

♦ Online Publishers Association Europe (OPA Europe) 17742

Head address not obtained.
URL: http://www.opa-europe.org/
History Mar 2003. **Aims** Advance the policies of high-quality online publishers before the advertising community, the press, government and public. **Structure** Board.
Members Companies in 8 countries:
France, Germany, Greece, Italy, Poland, Spain, Switzerland, Türkiye.
NGO Relations Partner of (1): *International News Media Association (INMA, #14363)*. [2020/XJ2872/**D**]

♦ Only Representative Organisation (ORO) 17743

Sec Fuchsstr 1, 67688 Rodenbach, Germany. T. +496374802388. Fax +496374802390. E-mail: secretary@onlyrepresentative.org.
Office Chaussée de Roodebeek 206, 1200 Brussels, Belgium. E-mail: info@onlyrepresentative.org.
URL: http://www.onlyrepresentative.org/
History 2008. Registered in accordance with Belgian law. EU Transparency Register: 92649098142-18. **Aims** Provide best practice guidance and high quality information on Only Representatives issues. **Structure** Board.
Members Companies in 12 countries:
Belgium, Bulgaria, Finland, France, Germany, Ireland, Italy, Luxembourg, Netherlands, Spain, Türkiye, UK.
IGO Relations Accredited by: *European Chemicals Agency (ECHA, #06523)*. [2017/XM5841/**D**]

- ♦ **ONOC** Oceania National Olympic Committees (#17667)
- ♦ **ONO** Organization of News Ombudsmen and Standards Editors (#17879)
- ♦ **ON** Orkester Norden (#17475)
- ♦ ONPI – Office notarial permanent d'échange international (see: #15795)
- ♦ ÖNSI – Österreichisches Nord-Süd-Institut für Entwicklungszusammenarbeit (internationally oriented national body)
- ♦ ONS – Offshore Northern Seas Foundation (internationally oriented national body)
- ♦ **ONS** Oriental Numismatic Society (#17893)
- ♦ **ONTA** Organización de Nematologos de los Trópicos Americanos (#17878)
- ♦ **ONTA** Organization of Nematologists of Tropical America (#17878)
- ♦ Ontario Council for International Cooperation (internationally oriented national body)
- ♦ Ontario International Development Agency (internationally oriented national body)
- ♦ ONT-WHO Global Observatory on Donation and Transplantation / see Global Observatory on Donation and Transplantation
- ♦ ONU-CEE Comité des transports intérieurs / see Committee on Inland Transport (#04262)
- ♦ **ONUDC** Office des Nations Unies contre la drogue et le crime (#20596)
- ♦ **ONUDD** Oficina de las Naciones Unidas contra la Droga y el Delito (#20596)
- ♦ **ONUDI** Organisation des Nations Unies pour le développement industriel (#20336)
- ♦ **ONUDI** Organización de las Naciones Unidas para el Desarrollo Industrial (#20336)
- ♦ ONU-Eau (#20723)
- ♦ ONU Femmes (#20724)
- ♦ ONU Femmes – Entité des Nations Unies pour l'égalité des sexes et l'autonomisation des femmes / see UN Women (#20724)
- ♦ **ONU-Habitat** Programme des Nations Unies pour les établissements humains (#20572)
- ♦ ONU Mujeres (#20724)
- ♦ ONU Mujeres – Entidad de las Naciones Unidad para la Igualdad de Género y el Empoderamiento de la Mujer / see UN Women (#20724)
- ♦ **ONU** Naciones Unidas (#20515)
- ♦ **ONU** Nations Unies (#20515)
- ♦ **ONUN** Office des Nations unies à Nairobi (#20600)
- ♦ ONU Nutrición (#20710)
- ♦ ONU Nutrition (#20710)
- ♦ **ONUSIDA** Programme commun des Nations unies sur le VIH/SIDA (#16149)
- ♦ **ONU-SPIDER** Plataforma de las Naciones Unidas de información obtenida desde el espacio para la gestión de desastres y la respuesta de emergencia (#20610)
- ♦ **ONUST** Organisme des Nations Unies chargé de la surveillance de la trève (#20638)
- ♦ **ONVIF** Open Network Video Interface Forum (#17760)
- ♦ Onze Kleine Weeskinderen (internationally oriented national body)
- ♦ Onze-Lieve-Vrouw van Montligeon (religious order)
- ♦ ÖNZ – Ökumenisches Netz Zentralafrika (internationally oriented national body)
- ♦ OOA – Office of the Americas (internationally oriented national body)
- ♦ **OOAS** Organisation Ouest Africaine de la santé (#20881)
- ♦ **OOAS** Organização Oest Africana da Saúde (#20881)
- ♦ **OOCUR** Organisation of Caribbean Utility Regulators (#17800)
- ♦ OOMER – Organisation oncologique méditerranéenne d'enseignement et de recherche (inactive)
- ♦ Oomoto (internationally oriented national body)

♦ Oomycete Molecular Genetics Network (OMGN) 17744

Coordinator Virginia Bioinformatics Inst, Virginia and State Univ, Washington Str, Blacksburg VA 24061-0447, USA. T. +15402317318. Fax +15402312606.
URL: http://omgn.cgrb.oregonstate.edu/
Aims Facilitate the integration of investigators into the community; further strengthen the cooperative culture of this community. **Structure** Steering Committee. **Activities** Events/meetings; training/education; research/documentation. **Events** *Annual Meeting* Brno (Czechia) 2020, *Annual Meeting* Oban (UK) 2019, *Annual Meeting* Tai'an (China) 2018, *Annual Meeting* Asilomar, CA (USA) 2017, *Annual Meeting* Malmö (Sweden) 2016. [2020/XM8890/**F**]

- ♦ **OOPC** Ocean Observations Panel for Climate (#17683)
- ♦ **OOPS** Organismo de Obras Públicas y Socorro de las Naciones Unidas para los Refugiados de Palestina en el Cercano Oriente (#20622)
- ♦ **OP2B** One Planet Business for Biodiversity (#17734)
- ♦ OPAD – Organization for Poverty Alleviation and Development (internationally oriented national body)
- ♦ **OPAEP** Organisation des pays arabes exportateurs de pétrole (#17854)
- ♦ **OPAEP** Organización de Paises Arabes Exportadores de Petróleo (#17854)
- ♦ **OPA Europe** Online Publishers Association Europe (#17742)
- ♦ OPALC – Organización de Pre-Inversión de América Latina y el Caribe (inactive)
- ♦ OPALS / see Organisation panafricaine de lutte pour la santé
- ♦ OPALS / see Organisation PanAfricaine de Lutte pour la Santé (#17822)
- ♦ OPALS – Organisation panafricaine de lutte pour la santé (internationally oriented national body)
- ♦ **OPALS** Organisation PanAfricaine de Lutte pour la Santé (#17822)
- ♦ OPAM – Opera di Promozione dell'Alfabetizzazione nel Mondo (internationally oriented national body)
- ♦ **OPANAL** Organismo para la Proscripción de las Armas Nucleares en la América Latina y el Caribe (#00554)
- ♦ OPA / see Open Partial Agreement on the Prevention of, Protection against and Organization of Relief in Major Natural and Technological Disasters (#17762)
- ♦ **OPA** Organisation de la presse africaine (#00424)
- ♦ OPAPE – Organisation panafricaine de la profession enseignante (no recent information)
- ♦ **OPAQ** Organización para la Prohibición de las Armas Quimicas (#17823)
- ♦ **OPAS** Organização Pan-Americana da Saúde (#18108)
- ♦ **OPBA** Oceania Pocket Billiard Association (#17668)
- ♦ **OPBC** Oncoplastic Breast Consortium (#17727)
- ♦ **OPBF** Oriental and Pacific Boxing Federation (#17894)
- ♦ OPCAT – Optional Protocol to the UN Convention Against Torture and other Cruel, Inhuman or Degrading Treatment or Punishment (2002 treaty)
- ♦ OPCE / see Business European Capital Cities (#03382)
- ♦ OPCF / see Observatoire français de la coopération internationale

♦ OPCMIA – Operative Plasterers and Cement Masons International Association of the United States and Canada (internationally oriented national body)
♦ OPC – Organisation pour la prévention de la cécité (internationally oriented national body)
♦ OPC – Overseas Press Club of America (internationally oriented national body)
♦ OP CRC – Optional Protocol to the Convention on the Rights of the Child on a communications procedure (2011 treaty)
♦ **OPCW** Organisation for the Prohibition of Chemical Weapons (#17823)
♦ **OP** Dominicans for Justice and Peace (#05113)
♦ OPEC Economic Commission Board (see: #17881)

♦ OPEC Fund for International Development (OFID) 17745

Fonds OPEP pour le développement international – Fondo de la OPEP para el Desarrollo Internacional

Dir-Gen PO Box 995, 1011 Vienna, Austria. T. +431515640. Fax +4315139238.
URL: https://opecfund.org/

History 1976. Established by Member States of *Organization of the Petroleum Exporting Countries (OPEC, #17881)*. Conceived at the Conference of the Sovereigns and Heads of State of OPEC Member Countries, March 1975, Algiers (Algeria). Converted to an autonomous development agency with present title in May 1980. Former names and other names: *OPEC Special Fund (OSF)* – former (1976 to 1980). **Aims** Promote cooperation between OPEC Member Countries and other developing countries as an expression of South-South solidarity; help particularly the poorer, low-income countries in pursuit of their social and economic advancement. **Structure** Ministerial Council (annual); Governing Board; Director-General. **Languages** English. **Staff** 194.00 FTE, paid. Staff from 34 countries. **Finance** Initial resources Jan 1976: about US$ 800,000,000 subsequently replenished 4 times. Last replenishment in 2011 of US$ 1,000,000,000 was a direct response to the call of OPEC member countries at the 3rd OPEC Summit to address the pressing issue of Energy Poverty as a vital tool for development. **Activities** Financial and/or material support; humanitarian/emergency aid. Active in 134 countries in: Africa; Asia; Europe; Latin America. **Events** *OPEC-ECS-OFID Annual Legal Workshop* Vienna (Austria) 2020, *Joint Symposium on Energy Poverty* Cape Town (South Africa) 2019, *OPEC-ECS-OFID Annual Legal Workshop* Vienna (Austria) 2019, *Session* Vienna (Austria) 2018, *Session* Vienna (Austria) 2018. **Publications** *OFID Quarterly* (4 a year). *OFID Pamphlet Series*. Annual Report; special publications; books; rules and procedures; financial statements.
Members Member governments (12):
Algeria, Ecuador, Gabon, Indonesia, Iran Islamic Rep, Iraq, Kuwait, Libya, Nigeria, Saudi Arabia, United Arab Emirates, Venezuela.
IGO Relations Observer status with (1): *United Nations (UN, #20515)* (General Assembly). A multilateral aid institution of *Organization of the Petroleum Exporting Countries (OPEC, #17881)*. Observer status to UN, including *ECOSOC (#05331)* and *United Nations Framework Convention on Climate Change (UNFCCC, 1992)*. Participates in the activities of: *UNCTAD (#20285)*. Member of: *International Rice Research Institute (IRRI, #14754)*. Supports and party to: *International Development Law Organization (IDLO, #13161)*. Adheres to: *Global Partnership for Effective Development Co-operation (GPEDC, #10532)*. **NGO Relations** Multilateral agency of: *Coordination Group of Arab National and Regional Development Institutions (#04826)*. Member of: *Association for Human Resources Management in International Organizations (AHRMIO, #02634)*. Partner of: *Global Forum on Law, Justice and Development (GFLJD, #10373)*. Supports: *International Partnership for Microbicides (IPM, inactive)*. [2019.08.09/XF6504/f/**F***]

♦ **OPEC** Organization of the Petroleum Exporting Countries (#17881)
♦ OPEC Special Fund / see OPEC Fund for International Development (#17745)
♦ OPEGAS – Organization of Gas Producing Countries (unconfirmed)
♦ OPEIU – Office and Professional Employees International Union (internationally oriented national body)

♦ Open Access Publishing in European Networks (OAPEN) 17746

Address not obtained.
URL: http://project.oapen.org/

History 2009. Registered as a foundation in accordance with Dutch law. **Aims** Achieve a sustainable publication model for academic books in *humanities* and *social sciences*; improve visibility and usability of high quality academic research in Europe. **Structure** Scientific Board. Consortium Board, comprising Chair and 8 members. **Publications** *OAPEN Newsletter*.
Members Partners in 13 countries:
Austria, Belgium, Canada, Denmark, Germany, Greece, Italy, Morocco, Netherlands, Norway, Spain, UK, USA.
Included in the above, 2 organizations listed in this Yearbook:
European Network for Copyright in support of Education and Science (ENCES, #07885); *IMISCOE Research Network (#11129)*.
NGO Relations Member of: *Europeana Foundation (#05839)*. [2015/XJ6283/fy/**F**]

♦ Open Access Scholarly Publishers Association (OASPA) 17747

Exec Dir Prins Willem-Alexanderhof 5, 2595 BE The Hague, Netherlands. E-mail: info@oaspa.org.
URL: http://oaspa.org/

History Nov 2008. **Aims** Represent the interests of Open Access (OA) journal and book publishers globally in all scientific, technical and scholarly disciplines. **Structure** Board. **Activities** Events/meetings. *Conference on Open Access Scholarly Publishing (COASP)*. **Events** *Online Conference on Open Access Scholarly Publishing* 2022, *Online Conference on Open Access Scholarly Publishing* 2021, *Online Conference on Open Access Scholarly Publishing* The Hague (Netherlands) 2020, *Conference* Copenhagen (Denmark) 2019, *Conference* Vienna (Austria) 2018.
Members OA professional publishing organizations; OA scientist/scholar publishers; other organizations with voting privileges; Associate. Members in 30 countries:
Australia, Brazil, Canada, Denmark, Egypt, France, Germany, Greece, Iceland, India, Italy, Japan, Malaysia, Nepal, Netherlands, New Zealand, Norway, Portugal, Qatar, Romania, Slovenia, South Africa, Spain, Sweden, Switzerland, Thailand, Uganda, UK, Ukraine, USA.
Included in the above, 2 organizations listed in this Yearbook:
International Network for the Availability of Scientific Publications (INASP, #14233); *SPARC Europe (#19902)*. [2020/XJ8231/y/**D**]

♦ Open Africa (internationally oriented national body)
♦ Open Air Campaigners International (internationally oriented national body)
♦ Open Arms (internationally oriented national body)

♦ Open City International Foundation (FOCA International) 17748

Contact 1070 H Highway 34 Ste 207, Matawan NJ 07747, USA. T. +17328171275.
Brazil Office Fua Fagundes Varela 441, Curitiba PR, CEP 82520-040, Brazil. T. +554130272828.
URL: http://www.opencityfound.org/

History First international statutes adopted in 1999, USA, following earlier national projects dating back to 1953, Italy and 1984, Brazil. **Aims** Develop projects, activities and programs for improving the quality of life and allow the harmonic integration of human beings with the economic development and the environment. **Structure** Board of Directors. **Consultative Status** Consultative status granted from: *ECOSOC (#05331)* (Special). [2010/XJ1160/t/**F**]

♦ Open Courseware Consortium / see Open Education Consortium (#17751)
♦ Open Data Watch (internationally oriented national body)
♦ Open Door International: for the Economic Emancipation of the Woman Worker (no recent information)

♦ Open Doors International 17749

Portes ouvertes international

Secretariat PO Box 47, 3840 AA Harderwijk, Netherlands. T. +31884465000. E-mail: odi-nl@od.org.
URL: http://www.opendoors.org/

History 1955. Registration: Eu Transparency Register, No/ID: 90518441599-14. **Aims** Support and strengthen *Christians* who are not free to practice their *faith* openly by providing them with *scriptures*, fellowship, training, encouragement and occasionally items such as food and clothing. **Finance** Sources: gifts, legacies. **Publications** *Open Doors*.
Members Offices in 24 countries and territories:
Australia, Austria, Brazil, Canada, Denmark, Finland, France, Germany, Hong Kong, Ireland, Italy, Korea Rep, Netherlands, New Zealand, Norway, Philippines, Poland, Romania, South Africa, Spain, Sweden, Switzerland, UK, USA.
NGO Relations Member of (3): *Forum of Bible Agencies International (#09903)*; *Fédération de missions évangéliques francophones (FMEF, #09688)*; *World Evangelical Alliance (WEA, #21393)*. Affiliated with (1): *Global Connections*. [2022/XF4398/**F**]

♦ Open Educational Resources Africa (OER Africa) 17750

Project Co-Leader PO Box 31822, Braamfontein, Johannesburg, South Africa. T. +27114032813.
Street address 14the Floor, 19 Ameshoff St, Braamfontein, Johannesburg, South Africa.
URL: http://www.oerafrica.org/

History Founded 1992, on the initiative of *'South African Institute for Distance Education (SAIDE)'* with support from *The William and Flora Hewlett Foundation*. **Aims** Collaborate with higher education institutions in African in development and use of Open Educational Resources (OER) to enhance teaching and learning. **Languages** English. **Staff** 2.50 FTE, paid. **Finance** Seed funding from: *The William and Flora Hewlett Foundation*. AgShare project funded by: *Bill and Melinda Gates Foundation (BMGF)*. Other sources: projects; partnerships. **Activities** Networking/liaising; events/meetings. **Publications** Case studies.
Members in 13 countries:
Ethiopia, Ghana, Malawi, Mozambique, Nigeria, Rwanda, South Africa, Tanzania UR, Uganda, UK, USA, Zambia, Zimbabwe.
NGO Relations Cooperates with: *African Council for Distance Education (ACDE, #00274)*; *Regional Universities Forum for Capacity Building in Agriculture (RUFORUM, #18818)*; national organizations; universities. Member of: *Open Education Consortium (#17751)*. *Regional Universities Forum for Capacity Building in Agriculture (RUFORUM, #18818)*. [2019.02.20/XJ0803/**E**]

♦ Open Education Consortium 17751

Operations Dir 60 Thoreau St, Ste 238, Concord MA 01742, USA. E-mail: feedback@oeconsortium.org.
Community Relations Manager address not obtained.
URL: http://www.oeconsortium.org/

History Set up as *Open Courseware Consortium (OCW Consortium)*. Current title adopted 2014. Full title: *Open Education Consortium – The Global Network for Open Education*. Current bylaws revised 24 Apr 2015. **Aims** Promote, support and advance openness in education around the world. **Structure** Board of Directors; Committees (9). **Finance** Support from: *The William and Flora Hewlett Foundation*. **Activities** Awareness raising; networking/liaising; advocacy/lobbying/activism; capacity building; training/education; guidance/assistance/consulting; events/meetings; awards/prizes/competitions. **Events** *Leadership Summit* Seoul (Korea Rep) 2022, *Leadership Summit* Seoul (Korea Rep) 2020, *Annual Open Education Global Conference* Delft (Netherlands) 2018, *Leadership Summit* Paris (France) 2018, *Annual Open Education Global Conference* Krakow (Poland) 2016. **Publications** Newsletter.
Members Institutional; Organizational; Associate; Corporate. Full in 49 countries and territories:
Afghanistan, Argentina, Australia, Belgium, Brazil, Canada, China, Colombia, Costa Rica, Denmark, Dominican Rep, Ecuador, Finland, France, Germany, Greece, Hong Kong, India, Indonesia, Iran Islamic Rep, Israel, Italy, Japan, Kenya, Korea Rep, Malaysia, Mexico, Mongolia, Netherlands, Nigeria, Oman, Pakistan, Palestine, Paraguay, Peru, Poland, Russia, Saudi Arabia, Serbia, Slovenia, South Africa, Spain, Sweden, Switzerland, Taiwan, Türkiye, UK, United Arab Emirates, USA, Vietnam.
Included in the above, 9 organizations listed in this Yearbook:
African Virtual University (AVU, #00496); *Commonwealth of Learning (COL, #04346)*; *Eastern Mediterranean University*; *European Association of Distance Teaching Universities (EADTU, #06016)*; *International Christian University (ICU)*; *Middle East Technical University (METU)*; *Open Educational Resources Africa (OER Africa, #17750)*; *Organisation internationale de la Francophonie (OIF, #17809)*; *Teachers Without Borders (TWB)*.
NGO Relations Associate member: *International Association for Political Science Students (IAPSS, #12095)*. [2019/XJ0557/y/**F**]

♦ Open Education Consortium – The Global Network for Open Education / see Open Education Consortium (#17751)
♦ **Open ENLoCC** European Network of Logistics Competence Centres (#07940)
♦ Open Europe (internationally oriented national body)
♦ OpenForum Europe (unconfirmed)

♦ Open Geospatial Consortium (OGC) 17752

Contact 35 Main St, Ste 5, Wayland MA 01778, USA. T. +15086555858. E-mail: info@ogc.org.
URL: https://www.ogc.org/

History 25 Sep 1994. Former names and other names: *Open GIS Consortium* – former. **Aims** Advance development and use of international standards and supporting services that promote geospatial interoperability; serve as the global forum for collaboration of geospatial data/solution providers and users. **Structure** Board of Directors; Global Advisory Council; Strategic Member Advisory Committee; Programs (4). **Languages** English. **Staff** 30.00 FTE, paid. **Finance** Sources: members' dues; revenue from activities/projects. **Activities** Events/meetings; networking/liaising; research and development; standards/guidelines. **Events** *Web Mapping Code Sprint Meeting* Brussels (Belgium) 2022, *Meeting* Banff, AB (Canada) 2019, *Meeting* Leuven (Belgium) 2019, *GeoBuiz Leaders Summit* San Francisco, CA (USA) 2019, *Meeting* Singapore (Singapore) 2019. **Publications** Abstract specifications; implementation standards; best practices; engineering reports; discussion papers; white papers; articles. **Members** As of Jan 2015, organizations (509) according to the following geographical groupings Africa (2); Asia-Pacific (86); Europe (204); Middle East (35) North America (176); South America (6). Membership countries not specified. **IGO Relations** Cooperates with (1): *United Nations Committee of Experts on Global Geospatial Information Management (UN-GGIM, #20540)*. [2021.05.18/XF4297/**F**]

♦ Open GIS Consortium / see Open Geospatial Consortium (#17752)

♦ Open Government Partnership (OGP) 17753

Alianza para el Gobierno Abierto

CEO 1110 Vermont Ave NW, Ste 500, Washington DC 20005, USA. T. +12026097859. E-mail: info@opengovpartnership.org.
URL: http://www.opengovpartnership.org/

History 20 Sep 2011. Formally launched when governments of Brazil, Indonesia, Mexico, Norway, Philippines, South African, UK and USA endorsed the *'Open Government Declaration'*. **Aims** Secure concrete commitments from governments to promote transparency, empower citizens, fight *corruption*, and harness new technologies to strengthen governance. **Structure** Steering Committee; Support Unit – Secretariat; Civil Society Engagement team; Independent Reporting Mechanism. **Finance** Grants from civil society organizations and contributions from participating governments. **Activities** Awards/prizes/competitions; events/meetings; financial and/or material support; politics/policy/regulatory. Runs the Multi-Donor Trust Fund (MDTF). **Events** *Global Summit* Seoul (Korea Rep) 2021, *Global Summit* Ottawa, ON (Canada) 2019, *Asia-Pacific Regional Meeting* Seoul (Korea Rep) 2018. **Publications** *OGP Newsletter* (12 a year) in English, Spanish; *OGP Gazette*.
Members Participating governments (75):
Afghanistan, Albania, Argentina, Armenia, Australia, Azerbaijan, Bosnia-Herzegovina, Brazil, Bulgaria, Burkina Faso, Canada, Cape Verde, Chile, Colombia, Costa Rica, Côte d'Ivoire, Croatia, Czechia, Denmark, Dominican Rep, El Salvador, Estonia, Finland, France, Georgia, Germany, Ghana, Greece, Guatemala, Honduras, Indonesia, Ireland, Israel, Italy, Jamaica, Jordan, Kenya, Korea Rep, Latvia, Liberia, Lithuania, Luxembourg, Malawi, Malta, Mexico, Moldova, Mongolia, Montenegro, Netherlands, New Zealand, Nigeria, North Macedonia, Norway, Pakistan, Panama, Papua New Guinea, Paraguay, Peru, Philippines, Romania, Serbia, Sierra Leone, Slovakia, South Africa, Spain, Sri Lanka, Sweden, Tanzania UR, Trinidad-Tobago, Tunisia, Türkiye, UK, Ukraine, Uruguay, USA.
NGO Relations Member of: *InsideNGO (inactive)*. [2021/XM5457/**F***]

♦ Open Grid Forum (OGF) 17754

Contact address not obtained. E-mail: operations@ogf.org – media@ogf.org.
URL: http://www.gridforum.org/

History 1999. Founded by merger of 'Grid Forum', *European Grid Forum (eGRID)* and *Asia-Pacific Grid*. Present name adopted upon merger with *'Enterprise Grid Alliance (EGA)'*. Former names and other names: *Global Grid Forum (GGF)* – former (1999 to 2006). **Aims** Promote and support the development, deployment and implementation of *computer* grid technologies and applications via the creation and documentation of "best practices". **Structure** General Chair; Steering Group; Working Groups; Research Groups. **Finance**

Sponsorship program, involving contributions. **Activities** Supports working groups and research groups developing common technical approaches to Grid computing. Organizes 3 meetings a year. **Events** *Meeting* Munich (Germany) 2010, *Meeting* Barcelona (Spain) 2008, *Meeting* Seoul (Korea Rep) 2005, *Meeting* 2004, *Meeting* Honolulu, HI (USA) 2004. **Publications** *GGF Newsletter* (3 a year). **Members** Individuals researchers and practitioners (over 5,000); organizations (over 300). Membership countries not specified. **NGO Relations** Collaborates with: *EGI Foundation (EGI.eu, #05395).* [2021/XF6287/**F**]

♦ Open Group 17755

Pres-CEO 548 Market St, Ste 54820, San Francisco CA 94104-5401, USA. T. +14153748280. Fax +14153748293.
URL: http://www.opengroup.org/

History 17 May 1988, as *Open Software Foundation (OSF).* **Aims** Deliver greater *business* efficiency by bringing together buyers and suppliers of information systems so as to lower time, cost and risk associated with integrating new *information technology* across an enterprise; offer organizations concerned with open information infrastructure a forum where they can share knowledge, integrate open initiatives and certify approved products and processes; achieve enterprise integration and multi-vendor interoperability. **Structure** Board. Consortia (4): X Organization Managed Consortium (X Org Tier 1, X Org Tier 2, X Org Tier 3); IBIX Managed Consortium; ICSC Managed Consortium; Active Loss Prevention Managed Consortium. Regional Chapters (9): Australia and New Zealand; Belgium and Luxembourg (Luxembourg); Germany, Netherlands, Austria and Switzerland; India; Italy and Malta; Midwest and South Atlantic USA; Japan; Portugal; United Kingdom. *Open Group Messaging Forum (see: #17755),* set up in Jan 2001, took over activities of the previous *Electronic Messaging Association (EMA, inactive).* **Activities** Certification/accreditation; research and development; events/meetings. **Events** *Conference* Sydney, NSW (Australia) 2013, *Active loss prevention forum* Amsterdam (Netherlands) 2001, *Manageability conference* Austin, TX (USA) 2001, *Mobile management forum* Berlin (Germany) 2001, *Conference on eFlow* San Jose, CA (USA) 2001.
Members Information technology organizations and companies, mainly in the USA but in a total of 16 countries:
Australia, Belgium, Canada, France, Germany, Hong Kong, Ireland, Japan, Korea Rep, Netherlands, Norway, Portugal, Slovenia, Sweden, UK, USA.
NGO Relations Member of: *Hotel Technology Next Generation (HTNG, #10952).* [2017/XF0864/**F**]

♦ Open Group Messaging Forum (see: #17755)
♦ Open International University for Complementary Medicines (internationally oriented national body)
♦ Open Knowledge Foundation / see Open Knowledge International
♦ Open Knowledge Foundation (internationally oriented national body)

♦ Open Knowledge Network (OKN) 17756

Contact c/o OneWorld International, 2nd Floor, CAN Mezzanine, 32-36 Loman St, London, SE1 0EH, UK. T. +442079227846. Fax +442079227706.
URL: http://uk.oneworld.net/article/view/112832/1/2061/

History 10 Dec 2003, Geneva (Switzerland), during World Summit on the Information Society. **Aims** Collect, share and disseminate local knowledge across Africa, Asia and the Americas. **Finance** Supported by the governments of Canada and the UK, companies. **Activities** Set up Africa Programme. **Publications** *Access Point* (4 a year).
Members Organizations (6) in 5 countries:
Canada, India, Netherlands, UK, USA.
Included in the above, 2 organizations listed in this Yearbook:
Centre for Research on Sustainable Agriculture and Rural Development (Swaminathan Research Foundation); OneWorld International Foundation (OWIF, #17738). [2010/XJ0865/y/**F**]

♦ Open Learning and Distance Education Association of Eastern Africa (no recent information)

♦ Open Mobile Alliance (OMA) 17757

General Manager 2850 Womble Rd, Ste 100, Mail Stop 300, San Diego CA 92106, USA. T. +18586230742.
URL: http://www.openmobilealliance.org/

History Jun 2002. **Aims** Promote global use of mobile technologies through the promotion of *interoperability* standards. **Activities** Events/meetings. **Events** *Technical plenary meeting* 2010, *Technical plenary meeting* 2010, *Annual General Assembly* Seoul (Korea Rep) 2010, *Technical plenary meeting* Seoul (Korea Rep) 2010, *Annual General Assembly* Los Angeles, CA (USA) 2009. **Members** Sponsor, Full, Associate, Supporter. Companies (300). Membership countries not specified. [2017/XM4568/**F**]

♦ Open Network for Commerce Exchange (ONCE) 17758

Office 711 Capital Way S, Ste 101, Olympia WA 98501, USA. T. +13603577410. Fax +13603577414. E-mail: tjw@w3net.net.
URL: http://www.connect-once.com/

History Aug 2000, as *Global Trading Web Association (GTWA).* **Aims** Facilitate and promote the growth of business-to-business electronic commerce. **Structure** Officers: Chairman; President; Secretary; Treasurer. **Finance** Members' dues. **Activities** Organizes annual and quarterly meetings, workshops and forums; sponsors annual tradeshow.
Members Companies (23) in 14 countries:
Canada, France, Germany, India, Japan, Philippines, Portugal, Singapore, Spain, Sweden, Switzerland, Thailand, UK, USA. [2013/XF6574/**F**]

♦ Open Networking Foundation (ONF) 17759

Exec Dir 1000 El Camino Real, Suite 100, Menlo Park CA 94025, USA. E-mail: info@opennetworking.org.
URL: http://www.opennetworking.org/

Aims Drive transformation of network infrastructure and carrier *business models.* **Structure** Board. **Activities** Training/education; events/meetings; certification/accreditation; projects/programmes. **NGO Relations** Member of: *Linux Foundation (#16484).* [2019/XM7800/f/**F**]

♦ Open Network Video Interface Forum (ONVIF) 17760

Exec Dir Business Operations Coordinator, 5000 Executive Parkway, Suite 302, San Ramon CA 94583, USA. T. +19252756621. Fax +19252756691. E-mail: onvif_ed@inventures.com – help@onvif.org.
URL: http://www.onvif.org/

History 2008. **Aims** Facilitate the development and use of a global open standard for the interface of network video products. **Structure** Steering Committee; Committees (3): Technical; Technical Services; Communication. **Events** *Meeting* Essen (Germany) 2010, *Meeting* Anaheim, CA (USA) 2009. **Members** Full (19); Contributing (19); User (416). Membership countries not specified. [2022/XJ4940/**F**]

♦ **OPEN** Online Progressive Engagement Network (#17741)

♦ Open Pan European Public Procurement Online (OpenPEPPOL) 17761

SG address not obtained. E-mail: info@peppol.eu.
URL: http://www.peppol.eu/

History Set up as *Pan-European Public Procurement Online (PEPPOL),* when operated under *European Commission (EC, #06633)* Competitiveness and Innovation Framework Programme. Completed and succeeded by association with current title, 1 Sep 2012. Also known as *OpenPEPPOL Association.* Registered in accordance with Belgian law, 30 Jan 2013. **Aims** Enable European businesses to easily deal electronically with any European public sector buyers in their procurement processes, thereby increasing opportunities for greater competition for government contracts and providing better value for tax payers' money. **Structure** General Assembly (annual). Managing Committee. Operating Office. Secretary General. Coordinating Communities (4): Transport Infrastructure; Post-award; eSignature and eID; Pre-award. **Finance** Members' dues. **Events** *Conference* Seoul (Korea Rep) 2010, *Conference* Oslo (Norway) 2009.
Members Full (100) in 13 countries and territories:
Austria, Denmark, France, Germany, Greece, Ireland, Italy, Netherlands, Norway, Portugal, Russia, Scotland, Sweden.
Included in the above, 1 organization listed in this Yearbook:
GS1 (#10809).
NGO Relations Liaison Organization of: *Comité européen de normalisation (CEN, #04162).* [2022/XJ1415/**E**]

♦ Open Partial Agreement on the Prevention of, Protection against and Organization of Relief in Major Natural and Technological Disasters (EUR-OPA Major Hazards Agreement) 17762

Accord partiel ouvert en matière de prévention, de protection et d'organisation des secours contre les risques naturels et technologiques majeurs (Accord EUR-OPA risques majeurs)

Exec Sec c/o Council of Europe, 67075 Strasbourg CEDEX, France. T. +33388412937 – +33388413027. Fax +33388412787. E-mail: europa.risk@coe.int – francesc.pla@coe.int.
URL: http://www.coe.int/europarisks/

History Created 20 Mar 1987, within the framework of *Council of Europe (CE, #04881),* on adoption of Resolution 87 (2) by *Committee of Ministers of the Council of Europe (#04273),* as an intergovernmental platform for cooperation in the field of major natural and technological disasters between Eastern and Central Europe, the South of the Mediterranean and Western Europe. Original title in English: *European Open Partial Agreement on Prevention of and Protection Against Major Natural and Technological Disasters (OPA).* Agreement named "Open Partial" because any State, whether a member or not of the Council of Europe, may apply to accede to it. **Aims** Reinforce and promote cooperation among member states in a multi-disciplinary context to ensure better prevention, protection and organization of relief in the event of major natural or technological disasters by calling on current resources and knowledge to ensure efficient and interdependent management of major disasters.
Structure Ministerial Meeting (every 4-5 years), is decision-making body. Committee of Permanent Correspondents and its Bureau (both meet annually). Meeting of the Directors of Specialized Euro-Mediterranean Centres (annual). Specialized Euro-Mediterranean Centres:
– Algeria – Biskra: *Euro-Mediterranean Centre for Research on Arid Areas (CRSTRA);*
– Armenia – Yerevan: *European Interregional Scientific and Educational Centre on Major Risk Management (ECRM);*
– Azerbaijan – Baku: *European Centre on Training and Formation of Local and Regional Authorities and Population in the Field of Natural and Technological Disasters (ECMHT);*
– Belgium – Brussels: *'Higher Institute of Emergency Planning (ISPU)';*
– Bulgaria – Sofia: *European Centre for Risk Prevention (ECRP, no recent information);*
– Bulgaria – -Sofia: Bulgarian National Training Centre;
– Cyprus – Nicosia: *European Centre for Disaster Awareness with the Use of Internet, Cyprus;*
– France – Bruyères-le-Châtel: *European-Mediterranean Seismological Centre (EMSC, #07774);*
– France – Biarritz: Specialized European Centre on Coastal Risks;
– France – Strasbourg: *European Centre on Geomorphological Hazards (#06482);*
– Georgia – Tbilisi: *European Centre on Geodynamic Hazards of High Dams (EC GHHD);*
– Germany – Freiburg: *Global Fire Monitoring Centre (GFMC);*
– Greece – Athens: *European Centre on Forest Fires (ECFF);*
– Greece – Athens: *European Centre on Prevention and Forecasting of Earthquakes (ECPFE, no recent information);*
– Italy – Ravello: *European University Centre for Cultural Heritage, Ravello (CUEBC);*
– Luxembourg – Walferdange: *European Centre for Geodynamics and Seismology (ECGS, #06481);*
– Malta – Valletta: *Euro-Mediterranean Centre on Insular Coastal Dynamics (ICoD, #05718);*
– Moldova – Chisinau: *European Centre for Mitigation of Natural Risks (ECMNR);*
– Morocco – Rabat: *Euro-Mediterranean Centre on Evaluation and Prevention of Seismic Risk (CEPRIS);*
– North Macedonia – Skopje: *European Centre for Vulnerability of Industrial and Lifelines Systems (ECILS, no recent information);*
– Portugal – Lisbon: *European Centre on Urban Risks (CERU);*
– Romania – Bucharest: *European Centre for Rehabilitation of Buildings (ECBR);*
– Russia – Moscow: *European Centre of New Technologies for the Management of Natural and Technological Major Hazards (ECNTRM, #06494);*
– San Marino: *European Centre for Disaster Medicine (#06475);*
– Spain – Madrid: *European Centre for Research into Techniques for Informing the Population in Emergency Situations (CEISE);*
– Turkey – Ankara: *European Natural Disasters Training Centre, Ankara (AFEM);*
– Ukraine – Kiev: *European Centre of Technological Safety (TESEC).*

Languages English, French, Russian. **Staff** 4.00 FTE, paid. **Finance** Members' dues. Budget (annual): euro 1 million. **Activities** Humanitarian/emergency aid; knowledge management/information dissemination; research/documentation; awareness raising. **Events** *Ministerial meeting / Meeting* St Petersburg (Russia) 2010, *Ministerial meeting / Meeting* Marrakech (Morocco) 2006, *Ministerial meeting / Meeting* San Marino (San Marino) 2003, *Ministerial meeting / Meeting* Bandol (France) 2002, *Ministerial meeting* Athens (Greece) / Vouliagmeni (Greece) 2000. **Publications** *Ecosystem Approach to Disaster Risk Reduction* (2013); *Facing Risks Together – 25 Years of Cooperation 1987-2010* (2012); *Ethical Principles on Disaster Risk Reduction and People's Resilience* (2011); *Lessons Learned in Psychosocial Care after Disasters* (2010).
Members Governments of 26 countries:
Albania, Algeria, Armenia, Azerbaijan, Belgium, Bosnia-Herzegovina, Bulgaria, Croatia, Cyprus, Georgia, Greece, Lebanon, Luxembourg, Malta, Moldova, Monaco, Morocco, North Macedonia, Portugal, Romania, Russia, San Marino, Serbia, Spain, Türkiye, Ukraine.
Observers (3):
France, Japan, Switzerland.
Regularly invited to attend meetings, governments of 23 countries:
Andorra, Austria, Belarus, Czechia, Denmark, Estonia, Finland, Germany, Hungary, Iceland, Ireland, Italy, Latvia, Liechtenstein, Lithuania, Montenegro, Netherlands, Norway, Poland, Slovakia, Slovenia, Sweden, UK.
IGO Relations Participants in the Agreement: *European Commission (EC, #06633); UNESCO (#20322); United Nations Office for the Coordination of Humanitarian Affairs (OCHA, #20593); WHO (#20950).* **NGO Relations** Member of (1): *Global Alliance of Disaster Research Institutes (GADRI, #10194).* [2018/XF1447/**F***]

♦ OpenPEPPOL Association / see Open Pan European Public Procurement Online (#17761)
♦ **OpenPEPPOL** Open Pan European Public Procurement Online (#17761)
♦ Open Smart Grid Protocol / see OSGP Alliance (#17903)

♦ Open Society Foundations (OSF) 17763

Dir Public Affairs Open Society Foundations, 224 West 57th St, New York NY 10019, USA. T. +12125480600. Fax +12125484600. E-mail: contact@opensocietyfoundations.org.
URL: http://www.opensocietyfoundations.org/

History Founded 1984, by investor and philanthropist George Soros, to help countries make the transition from communism. **Aims** Work to build vibrant and tolerant societies whose governments are accountable and open to participation of all people; strengthen the rule of law, respect for human rights, minorities and a diversity of opinions, democratically elected governments, and a civil society that helps keep government power in check; help shape public policies that assure greater fairness in political, legal and economic systems and safeguard fundamental rights; implement initiatives to advance justice, education, public health and independent media; build alliances across borders and continents on issues such as corruption and freedom of information. **Structure** Main offices in: New York NY (USA); Budapest (Hungary); Brussels (Belgium); London (UK); Washington DC (USA). EU Policy Arm: *Open Society European Policy Institute.* **Staff** 2000.00 FTE, paid. **Finance** Expenditures (2013) US$ 873,344,000. **Activities** Financial and/or material support. **Events** *Conference* Budapest (Hungary) 2012, *Meeting* Budapest (Hungary) 2012, *International Meeting of Families* Cali (Colombia) 2012, *Corruption conference* Budapest (Hungary) 1999, *International conference on the ratification of the statute of the international criminal court* Budapest (Hungary) 1999. **Publications** *Open Society Advances in 2010-2011; Open Society Time: Open Society Foundations Highlights, 1979-2010.* **Members** Foundations and offices in over 100 countries worldwide (not specified). **NGO Relations** Founding member and donor of: *European Roma Rights Centre (ERRC, #08401).* [2019/XF5262/f/**F**]

♦ Open Software Foundation / see Open Group (#17755)

♦ Open Source Geospatial Foundation (OSGeo) 17764

Contact 9450 SW Gemini Drive, Ste 42523, Beaverton OR 97008, USA. E-mail: info@osgeo.org.
URL: http://www.osgeo.org/

History 2006, USA. Registration: USA. **Aims** Support collaborative development of open source geospatial software and promote its widespread use. **Structure** Board of Directors; Committees. **Languages** English. **Staff** None. **Activities** Events/meetings. **Events** *FOSS4G : Annual International Conference for Free and Open Source Software for Geospatial* Florence (Italy) 2022, *FOSS4G : Annual International Conference for Free and Open Source Software for Geospatial* Busan (Korea Rep) 2019, *Annual International Conference on Free and Open Source Software for Geospatial* Dar es Salaam (Tanzania UR) 2018, *Annual International Conference on Free and Open Source Software for Geospatial* Boston, MA (USA) 2017, *FOSS4G : European Conference for Free and Open Source Software for Geospatial* Marne-la-Vallée (France) 2017. **Publications** *OSGeo Journal.*

Members Charter members in 43 countries:
Argentina, Australia, Austria, Belgium, Brazil, Canada, Chile, China, Colombia, Czechia, Denmark, Finland, France, Germany, Greece, Hungary, India, Ireland, Italy, Japan, Korea Rep, Malaysia, Mexico, Netherlands, New Zealand, Norway, Peru, Philippines, Poland, Portugal, Romania, Russia, Slovakia, Slovenia, South Africa, Spain, Sri Lanka, Switzerland, Thailand, UK, Ukraine, Uruguay, USA. [2020.05.16/XJ0041/fv/**F**]

♦ Open Source Initiative (internationally oriented national body)

♦ OpenStack Foundation 17765

Exec Dir PO Box 1903, Austin TX 78767, USA. T. +15128278633. E-mail: info@openstack.org.
URL: http://www.openstack.org/foundation/

History Founded Sep 2012. **Aims** Serve developers, users, and the entire ecosystem by providing a set of shared resources to grow the footprint of public and private OpenStack clouds, enable technology vendors targeting the platform and assist developers in producing the best cloud *software* in the industry. **Structure** Board of Directors; Committees. **Events** *Open Infra Days Nordic* Stockholm (Sweden) 2019. [2020/XM8376/f/**F**]

♦ OpenStreetMap Foundation 17766

Sec St John's Innovation Centre, Cowley Road, Cambridge, CB4 0WS, UK. E-mail: press@osmfoundation.org.
URL: https://wiki.osmfoundation.org/

History Registration: Companies House, No/ID: 05912761, Start date: 22 Aug 2006, England and Wales. **Aims** Create and provide free geographic data, such as street maps, to anyone. **Structure** Board; Advisory Board. **Events** *State of the Map Conference* Florence (Italy) 2022. [2023/AA3237/f/**F**]

♦ OpenSym – International Symposium on Open Collaboration (meeting series)

♦ Open Think Tank Network (OpenTTN) 17767

Contact address not obtained. E-mail: hello@openthinktank.org.
URL: https://www.openthinktank.org/

History 30 Jun 2017, Berlin (Germany). **Aims** Develop constructive, coherent and future-oriented policy solutions so as to foster a culture of open debate and discussions around highly relevant issues in international affairs. **Events** *Global Meeting* Vienna (Austria) 2019.
Members Think tanks (5) in 5 countries:
Austria, France, Germany, Switzerland, UK. [2020/AA0598/**F**]

♦ **OpenTTN** Open Think Tank Network (#17767)

♦ Open and User Innovation Society (OUI Society) 17768

Address not obtained.
URL: https://sites.google.com/view/oui2019

Activities Events/meetings. **Events** *Annual International Open and User Innovation Conference* Aachen (Germany) 2021, *Annual International Open and User Innovation Conference* Aachen (Germany) 2020, *Annual International Open and User Innovation Conference* Utrecht (Netherlands) 2019, *International Open and User Innovation Conference* Innsbruck (Austria) 2017. [2020/AA0492/c/**E**]

♦ Open Web Application Security Project Foundation (OWASP Foundation) 17769

Main Office 401 Edgewater Pl, Ste 600, Wakefield MA 01880, USA.
Europe Office c/o Sr Fiduciarire Cv, Steenvoordestraat 184, 9070 Destelbergen, Belgium.
URL: https://www.owasp.org/

History 1 Dec 2001. Former names and other names: *OWASP Europe* – legal name. Registration: 501(c)3, No/ID: 20-0963503, Start date: 21 Apr 2004, USA; Belgium. **Aims** Make software security visible, so that individuals and organizations are able to make informed decisions. **Structure** Board of Directors. **Activities** Projects/programmes. **Events** *Global AppSec* Dublin (Ireland) 2023, *Annual AppSec EU Security Conference* Dublin (Ireland) 2022, *Annual AppSec USA Security Conference* San Francisco, CA (USA) 2022, *Annual AppSec USA Security Conference* San Francisco, CA (USA) 2021, *Annual AppSec USA Security Conference* San Francisco, CA (USA) 2020. [2022/XM7976/f/**F**]

♦ Open Wing Alliance (unconfirmed)

♦ OpenWIS Association 17770

Registered Office Avenue Circulaire 3, 1180 Brussels, Belgium. E-mail: contact@openwis.io.
URL: http://openwis.github.io/openwis-documentation/

History Articles adopted Feb 2015. Registered in accordance with Belgian law. **Aims** Facilitate collaboration on the development, promotion and sharing of open source *software* for the exchange of global *meteorological information*. **Structure** Board; Steering Committee; Technical Committee; Project Management Committees. **Languages** English, French. **Staff** None paid. **Finance** Sources: members' dues. **Activities** Advocacy/lobbying/activism; networking/liaising.
Members Full in 4 countries:
Australia, France, Korea Rep, UK.
Strategic Partners in 2 countries:
Finland, USA.
IGO Relations *European Centre for Medium-Range Weather Forecasts (ECMWF, #06490)*; *World Meteorological Organization (WMO, #21649)*. [2018.05.18/XM6060/**C**]

♦ **OPEP** Organisation des pays exportateurs de pétrole (#17881)
♦ **OPEP** Organización de Paises Exportadores de Petróleo (#17881)
♦ Operación Sonrisa (internationally oriented national body)
♦ Opera del Divin Amore (religious order)
♦ Opera Don Guanella – Servi della Carità (religious order)

♦ Opera Europa 17771

Dir Rue Léopold 23, 1000 Brussels, Belgium. T. +3222176705. E-mail: info@opera-europa.org.
Manager address not obtained.
URL: http://www.opera-europa.org/

History Jun 2001. Founded by merger of *Eurolyrica – Association internationale de promotion de l'art lyrique (inactive)* and *European Opera Network (EON, inactive)*. **Aims** Foster a stimulating context for dynamic dialogue on topics of practical interest among members; support promotion and development of opera culture. **Structure** Board of Directors. **Languages** Dutch, English, French, German, Italian, Spanish. **Staff** 9.00 FTE, paid. **Finance** Sources: members' dues. **Activities** Events/meetings; knowledge management/information dissemination; networking/liaising; training/education. **Events** *Human Resources Forum* Helsinki (Finland) 2022, *Conference* Bergamo (Italy) 2021, *Conference* Antwerp (Belgium) 2019, *Conference* Strasbourg (France) / Karlsruhe (Germany) 2019, *Conference* Paris (France) 2018. **Publications** *Opera Europa News* (4 a year). Information Services: Maintains databases.
Members Full: organizations (over 200) in 43 countries:
Argentina, Austria, Belgium, Bulgaria, Chile, Croatia, Czechia, Denmark, Estonia, Finland, France, Georgia, Germany, Greece, Hungary, Iceland, India, Ireland, Israel, Italy, Japan, Kazakhstan, Latvia, Lithuania, Luxembourg, Malta, Monaco, Netherlands, New Zealand, Norway, Oman, Poland, Portugal, Russia, Serbia, Slovenia, Spain, Sweden, Switzerland, Tunisia, Türkiye, UK, Ukraine.
NGO Relations Member of: *Culture Action Europe (CAE, #04981)*. Associate member of: *Pearle – Live Performance Europe (#18284)*; *Réseau européen pour la sensibilisation à l'opéra et à la danse (RESEO, #18878)*. [2021.09.06/XD8862/**D**]

♦ Operaie della Croce (religious order)
♦ Opera Internazionale di Kolping / see KOLPING INTERNATIONAL (#16203)
♦ Opera Internazionale per il Personale Missionario (#14170)
♦ Opera di Maria / see Focolare Movement (#09806)
♦ Opera di Promozione dell'Alfabetizzazione nel Mondo (internationally oriented national body)
♦ OPERA RESEARCH – European Observatory on Sustainable Agriculture (unconfirmed)
♦ OPERA RESEARCH – OPERA RESEARCH – European Observatory on Sustainable Agriculture (unconfirmed)
♦ Operating Project for a European Rail Network / see NewOpera (#17090)
♦ Operational Net of Regional Cooperation of Central American Maritime Authorities (no recent information)
♦ Operation Blessing International (internationally oriented national body)
♦ Operation Brother's Keeper / see Brother's Brother Foundation
♦ Operation Crossroads Africa (internationally oriented national body)
♦ Operation Exodus (internationally oriented national body)
♦ Operation Eyesight Universal (internationally oriented national body)
♦ Operation Handicap International / see Humanity and Inclusion (#10975)
♦ Opération handicap internationale / see Humanity and Inclusion (#10975)
♦ Opération hybride de l'Union africaine et des Nations Unies au Darfour (inactive)
♦ Operation Mercy (internationally oriented national body)

♦ Operation Mobilisation 17772

International Dir 38 Orchard Road 03-00, Singapore 238836, Singapore. E-mail: info.directorsoffice@om.org.
URL: http://www.om.org/

History 1957. Also referred to as *OM International*. **Aims** Focus on *evangelism* among the least evangelized. **Activities** Networking/liaising.
Members Full in 35 countries and territories:
Argentina, Australia, Austria, Belgium, Brazil, Canada, Chile, Czechia, Denmark, Finland, France, Germany, Hong Kong, Hungary, India, Ireland, Italy, Japan, Korea Rep, Malaysia, Netherlands, New Zealand, Norway, Papua New Guinea, Philippines, Portugal, Singapore, South Africa, Spain, Sweden, Switzerland, UK, Uruguay, USA, Zimbabwe.
NGO Relations Member of: *European Evangelical Alliance (EEA, #07010)*; *Fédération de missions évangéliques francophones (FMEF, #09688)*; *Global Connections*. Associate member of: *World Evangelical Alliance (WEA, #21393)*. Support from: *Stamps for Evangelism*. [2015.01.12/XF4429/**F**]

♦ Operation Mobilisation International / see OM International (#17724)
♦ Opération des Nations Unies en Côte d'Ivoire (inactive)
♦ Operation Peace Through Unity / see Peace Through Unity
♦ Operation Rainbow (internationally oriented national body)
♦ Operation Reach All / see ORA International
♦ Operation Romanian Villages / see Operation Romanian Villages International (#17773)

♦ Operation Romanian Villages International 17773

Opération villages roumains international (OVR) – Operatiunea Satele Romanesti

Admin Ch de Jolimont 263, 7000 La Louvière, Belgium. E-mail: ovr@scarlet.be.
URL: http://www.villagesroumains.be/

History Founded 22 Dec 1988, Brussels (Belgium), as *Operation Romanian Villages – Opération villages roumains*. Officially launched 3 Feb 1989. Registered in accordance with Belgian law. **Aims** Promote the right of citizens to decide themselves on their social, political, cultural, economic, ecological and ethical environment; set up local, regional and international networks of ideas and competences permitting mutual assistance and exchange; favour, stimulate and promote in the framework of the international network initiatives and projects which participate in the global, integrated and sustainable development of villages primarily in Romania and Moldova, but also in Europe where requested. **Structure** General Assembly. International Coordination. Branches (4): Belgium; France; Moldova; Romania. Other coordination efforts in: Flanders (Belgium); Netherlands; Switzerland. **Languages** English, French, Romanian. **Staff** All voluntary. **Finance** Financed by project with national and European authorities; Budget (biennial): euro 430,000. **Activities** Advocacy/lobbying/activism; events/meetings. **Events** *General Assembly* Bogdanesti (Romania) 2014, *Congress* Brussels (Belgium) 2014, *General Assembly* Bar-le-Duc (France) 2013, *Local democracy* Timisoara (Romania) 1994. **Publications** *AllerS-RetourS* (12 a year); *La Double Flèche* – electronic newsletter. *Trait d'Union*. Books; pamphlets; studies. Information Services: Databases.
Members National coordinations, representing 2,000 individuals, in 8 countries:
Belgium, France, Germany, Luxembourg, Moldova, Netherlands, Romania, Switzerland. [2014.06.01/XF1181/**F**]

♦ Operation Smile (internationally oriented national body)
♦ Operation Smile International / see Operation Smile

♦ Operations Research Society of East Africa (ORSEA) 17774

Chair College of Humanities, Univ of Nairobi, PO Box 30197, Nairobi, Kenya.
URL: http://www.orsea.net/

History 7 Jan 2003, Ouagadougou (Burkina Faso), during African Conference on Operational Research, organized by *Association of European Operational Research Societies (EURO, #02528)*. **Aims** Foster development of operations research and decision sciences in the Eastern Africa region. **Events** *Conference* Entebbe (Uganda) 2013, *Conference* Dar es Salaam (Tanzania UR) 2009, *Conference* Nairobi (Kenya) 2008, *Conference* Entebbe (Uganda) 2006, *Conference* Dar es Salaam (Tanzania UR) 2004. **Members** Membership countries not specified. [2014/XD9368/**D**]

♦ Opération Survie au Soudan (inactive)
♦ Operation Underground Railroad (internationally oriented national body)
♦ Opération d'urgence des Nations Unies au Rwanda, Kigali (inactive)
♦ Operation USA (internationally oriented national body)
♦ Opération villages roumains / see Operation Romanian Villages International (#17773)
♦ Opération villages roumains international (#17773)
♦ Operatiunea Satele Romanesti (#17773)
♦ Operative Brewers' Guild / see International Brewers' Guild
♦ Operative Network of Regional Cooperation among Maritime Authorities of South America, Mexico, Panama and Cuba (#18725)
♦ Operative Plasterers and Cement Masons International Association of the United States and Canada (internationally oriented national body)
♦ **OPF** Organisation panafricaine des femmes (#18074)
♦ **OPGE** Organización Panamericana de Gastroenterologia (#17847)
♦ Ophtalmo sans frontières (internationally oriented national body)
♦ Ophthalmological Society of Eastern Africa (inactive)
♦ Ophthalmologist Society of the West Indies (no recent information)
♦ **OPIC** Oficina Permanente Internacional de la Carne (#14125)
♦ OPIC – Optics and Photonics International Congress (meeting series)
♦ OPIC – Overseas Private Investment Corporation (internationally oriented national body)
♦ OPIF – Orient Press International Federation (inactive)
♦ **OPINEAR** Ocean Policy Institute Network in East Asian Region (#17685)
♦ OPI – Olof Palme Institute (internationally oriented national body)
♦ OPMA – Oriented Polypropylene Film Manufacturers' Association (inactive)
♦ OPM / see MISSIO (#16827)
♦ **OPM** Organização Pan Africana Das Mulheres (#18074)
♦ **OPOL** Offshore Pollution Liability Association (#17701)
♦ **OPO** Organization of Phenomenological Organizations (#17883)
♦ OP – Orbi-Pharma (internationally oriented national body)
♦ OP – Ordo Fratrum Praedicatorum (religious order)
♦ **OPPA** Organisation des Producteurs de Pétrole Africains (#00414)
♦ OPPFI – Olof Palme Peace Foundation International (internationally oriented national body)

♦ Opportunities Industrialization Centers International (OICI) 17775

Main Office 1875 Connecticut Ave NW, 10th Fl, Washington DC 20009, USA. T. +12028466798. E-mail: info@oici.org.
URL: https://oici.org/

History 1964, Philadelphia, PA (USA). Founded by Leon H Sullivan (1922-2001), who developed the *Global Sullivan Principles*. Former names and other names: *OIC International* – alias. **Aims** Help people help themselves to improve their lives through the development of *sustainable institutions* that provide appropriate *training* and *services*. **Activities** Training/education. **Events** *African development conference* 1990, *Technical assistance conference* Lomé (Togo) 1988. **Publications** *International Voice* (periodical).

Members Headquarters () and affiliates in 18 countries:
Belize, Cameroon, Central African Rep, Côte d'Ivoire, Ethiopia, Gambia, Ghana, Guinea, Lesotho, Liberia, Niger, Nigeria, Philippines, Poland, Sierra Leone, Togo, UK, USA (*).
IGO Relations Associated with Department of Global Communications of the United Nations. **NGO Relations** Member of: *Volunteers for Economic Growth Alliance (VEGA)*. Partner of: *Helen Keller International (HKI, #10902)*. [2020/XF2490/t/F]

♦ Opportunity International 17776

Main Office 550 West Van Buren, Ste 200, Chicago IL 60607, USA. T. +13124875000. Fax +13124875642.
US Office: http://www.opportunity.org/

History Founded 1979, combining 'Opportunity Program', set up 1971, by Alfred Whittaker, with 'Maranatha Trust', set up 1976, by David Bussau. Original title: *Institute for International Development*. Registration: No/ID: 540907624, USA. **Aims** As an international *Christian development* agency, provide opportunities for people in chronic *poverty* to transform their lives by creating jobs, stimulating small business and strengthening communities among the poor; enable grassroots capitalism so that individuals, regardless of their economic status, can improve their income through hard work and *free enterprise*; stimulate individual creativity and personal responsibility by allowing each individual to choose appropriate income-generating activity. In particular, support independent, micro-business *lending* institutions that assist very poor people in starting and expanding small businesses. **Structure** 'Opportunity International' – USA, Australia, Germany, UK – together with committed organizations in Canada, France, New Zealand and Sweden, and with implementing partners, comprise the *Opportunity Network*. Board of Governors. Board of Directors of 29 members. Board of Advisors of 9 members. Women's Opportunity Fund Board of Directors. Regions: Africa; Asia; Eastern Europe; Latin America. **Activities** Projects/programmes; financial and/or material support; training/education; guidance/assistance/consulting. Assists nearly 36,000 women in 18 countries worldwide. **Publications** *Update* (4 a year) – newsletter. Annual Report.
Members Organizations (49) in 7 countries:
Australia, Canada, France, Germany, New Zealand, UK, USA.
Implementing Partners in 29 countries:
Albania, Bulgaria, Colombia, Costa Rica, Croatia, Dominican Rep, Egypt, El Salvador, Ghana, Guatemala, Honduras, India, Indonesia, Jamaica, Malaysia, Montenegro, Nicaragua, North Macedonia, Peru, Philippines, Poland, Romania, Russia, South Africa, Sri Lanka, Thailand, Uganda, Zambia, Zimbabwe.
IGO Relations Cooperates with: *UNHCR (#20327)*. **NGO Relations** Member of: *Accord Network*; *American Council for Voluntary International Action (InterAction)*; *Financial Inclusion Equity Council (CIEF, #09766)*; *Global Impact*; *InsideNGO (inactive)*; *NetHope (#16979)*; *Oikocredit International (Oikocredit, #17704)*; *Partnership for Responsible Financial Inclusion (PRFI, #18241)*. [2020/XF4555/j/F]

♦ O Praem – Candidus et Canonicus Ordo Praemonstratensis (religious order)
♦ OPRC-HNS 2000 – Protocol on Preparedness, Response and Cooperation to Pollution Incidents by Hazardous and Noxious Substances (2000 treaty)
♦ OPRC – International Convention on Oil Pollution Preparedness Response and Cooperation (1990 treaty)
♦ OPRF / see Ocean Policy Research Institute
♦ OPRI – Ocean Policy Research Institute (internationally oriented national body)
♦ OPRI-SPF / see Ocean Policy Research Institute
♦ **OPRT** Organization for the Promotion of Responsible Tuna Fisheries (#17886)
♦ OPSFA – International Symposium on Orthogonal Polynomials, Special Functions and Applications (meeting series)
♦ OPS – Oceanic Preservation Society (internationally oriented national body)
♦ **OPS** Organisation panaméricaine de la santé (#18108)
♦ **OPS** Organización Panamericana de la Salud (#18108)
♦ OPSRA – Organisation pour la paix au service de la renaissance africaine (internationally oriented national body)
♦ OPT2 – Second Optional Protocol to the International Covenant on Civil and Political Rights Aiming at the Abolition of the Death Penalty (1989 treaty)

♦ Optica 17777

CEO 2010 Mass Ave NW, Washington DC 20036, USA. T. +12022238130. Fax +12022231096. E-mail: info@optica.org.
URL: https://www.optica.org/

History 1916, USA. Founded following the activities of the Rochester Association of Applied Optics. Former names and other names: *Optical Society of America (OSA)* – legal name; *The Optical Society (OSA)* – former (2008); *Optica, the Society Advancing Optics and Photonics Worldwide (Optica)* – full title (Sep 2021). **Aims** Promote the generation, dissemination, and application of knowledge in optics and photonics. **Structure** Board of Directors; Councils; OSA Foundation Board; Executive Staff. **Activities** Advocacy/lobbying/activism; events/meetings; knowledge management/information dissemination; training/education. **Events** *Workshop on Specialty Optical Fibers and their Applications* Adelaide, SA (Australia) 2022, *Biennial International Conference on Ultrafast Phenomena* Montréal, QC (Canada) 2022, *Pacific Rim Conference on Lasers and Electro-Optics (CLEO PR)* Sapporo (Japan) 2022, *World of Photonics Congress* Mulhouse (France) 2021, *Biennial International Conference on Ultrafast Phenomena* Shanghai (China) 2020. **Publications** Journals.
Members Individuals (22,000) in 100 countries and territories. Corporate members (about 290). Sections (27); Student chapters (26) in 5 countries:
Belgium, Canada, Japan, Korea Rep, USA.
NGO Relations Member of (2): *International Commission for Optics (ICO, #12710)*; *ORCID (#17790)*. Cooperates with (2): *International Conference on Optics-photonics Design & Fabrication (ODF)*; *International Symposium on Imaging, Sensing, and Optical Memory (ISOM)*. [2022/XN8722/C]

♦ The Optical Society / see Optica (#17777)
♦ Optical Society of America / see Optica (#17777)
♦ Optica, the Society Advancing Optics and Photonics Worldwide / see Optica (#17777)
♦ Optics and Photonics International Congress (meeting series)
♦ **OPTIMA** Organization for the Phyto-Taxonomic Investigation of the Mediterranean Area (#17884)

♦ Optimist International (OI) 17778

Main Office 4494 Lindell Blvd, St Louis MO 63108, USA. T. +13143716000. Fax +13143716006.
URL: http://www.optimist.org/

History 1919, Louisville KY (USA), as *International Optimist Club*. **Aims** Foster an optimistic way of life through a network of optimists dedicated to the full development of their potential in order to provide ever-expanding service to youth, the community and the world. **Structure** International Board of Directors; 2,500 Clubs with 49 Districts and 8 Regions. **Languages** English, French. **Staff** St Louis office: 30; Montral office: 4. **Activities** Networking/liaising; financial and/or material support; events/meetings. **Events** *Annual Convention* Ottawa, ON (Canada) 2018, *Annual Convention* Albuquerque, NM (USA) 2017, *Annual Convention* Québec, QC (Canada) 2016, *Annual Convention* New Orleans, LA (USA) 2015, *Annual Convention* Las Vegas, NV (USA) 2014. **Publications** *Hotline* (6 a year) – leadership newsletter; *The Optimist* (4 a year) – magazine; *The Torch* – newsletter.
Members Membership covers 15 countries:
Bahamas, Barbados, Canada, China, France, Ghana, Jamaica, Mexico, Morocco, Nepal, Nigeria, Senegal, Thailand, Uganda, USA. [2019.10.21/XF2926/F]

♦ Optional Additional Protocol to the International Telecommunication Convention (1973 treaty)
♦ Optional Protocol Concerning the Compulsory Settlement of Disputes (1963 treaty)
♦ Optional Protocol Concerning the Suppression of Counterfeiting Currency (1929 treaty)
♦ Optional Protocol to the Convention on the Elimination of all Forms of Discrimination Against Women (1999 treaty)
♦ Optional Protocol to the Convention on the Rights of the Child on a communications procedure (2011 treaty)
♦ Optional Protocol to the Convention on the Rights of the Child on the Involvement of Children in Armed Conflict (2000 treaty)
♦ Optional Protocol to the Convention on the Rights of the Child on the Sale of Children, Child Prostitution and Child Pornography (2000 treaty)
♦ Optional Protocol to the Convention on the Rights of Persons with Disabilities (2006 treaty)
♦ Optional Protocol to the Convention on Special Missions Concerning the Compulsory Settlement of Disputes (1969 treaty)
♦ Optional Protocol to the International Covenant on Civil and Political Rights (1966 treaty)
♦ Optional Protocol to the International Covenant on Economic, Social and Cultural Rights (2008 treaty)
♦ Optional Protocol Related to the Inter-American Convention on Mutual Assistance in Criminal Matters (1993 treaty)
♦ Optional Protocol of Signature Concerning the Compulsory Settlement of Disputes (1958 treaty)
♦ Optional Protocol to the UN Convention Against Torture and other Cruel, Inhuman or Degrading Treatment or Punishment (2002 treaty)
♦ Optional Protocol to the Vienna Convention on Consular Relations Concerning Acquisition of Nationality (1963 treaty)
♦ Optional Protocol to the Vienna Convention on Consular Relations Concerning the Compulsory Settlement of Disputes (1963 treaty)
♦ Optional Protocol to the Vienna Convention on Diplomatic Relations Concerning Acquisition of Nationality (1961 treaty)
♦ Optional Protocol to the Vienna Convention on Diplomatic Relations Concerning the Compulsory Settlement of Disputes (1961 treaty)

♦ Optometristas Sirviendo a la Humanidad (OSH) 17779

Optometrists Serving Humanity
Pres Luque y Garcia Aviles, FINEC bldg Local 29, Guayaquil, Ecuador. T. +593978671796. E-mail: davaso80@gmail.com.

History Jan 2009, Ecuador. **Aims** Represent voluntary optometrists working to prevent *blindness*. **Structure** General Delegations Meeting; Governing Board; President. **Languages** Spanish. **Staff** 4.00 FTE, paid; 130.00 FTE, voluntary. **Finance** Members' dues. Other sources: events proceeds; donations from NGOs, including *Lions Clubs International (LCI, #16485)* and *Rotary International (RI, #18975)*. **Activities** Events/meetings. **Events** *Congress* Guayaquil (Ecuador) 2015, *Congress* Guayaquil (Ecuador) 2014, *Congress* Guayaquil (Ecuador) 2013, *Congress* Guayaquil (Ecuador) 2012, *Latin American meeting of blindness preventions / Congress* Lima (Peru) 2011. **Publications** *Boletin OSH* (4 a year); *Hablemos de Salud Visual* (4 a year) – magazine. *Manual Para la Evaluacion de la Agudeza Visual*; *URGENCIAS OCULARES*.
Members Full (180) in 13 countries:
Argentina, Bolivia, Brazil, Colombia, Dominican Rep, Ecuador, El Salvador, Mexico, Peru, Puerto Rico, Spain, USA, Venezuela.
IGO Relations *UNESCO (#20322)*; *WHO (#20950)*. [2019.12.11/XJ1840/F]

♦ Optometrists Serving Humanity (#17779)
♦ OPT – Optional Protocol to the International Covenant on Civil and Political Rights (1966 treaty)
♦ OPTU / see Peace Through Unity

♦ OPUS 17780

Main Office 4 quai Lices Berthelot, 84800 L'Isle-sur-la-Sorgue, France. T. +33490855115. E-mail: contact@opus.cpie84.org.
URL: https://opus.cpie84.org/

History 2014. Set up on merger of *Mediterranean Centre for the Environment (inactive)* and *Association pour la participation et l'action régionale (APARE, inactive)*. Former names and other names: *Union Association pour la Participation et l'Action Régionale – Centre Méditerranéen de l'Environnement (Union APARE-CME)* – former (2014 to 2022). Registration: France. **Aims** Promote participation of civil society and particularly the participation of young people, into the sustainable local development of territories in the Provence region as well as in the Mediterranean area. **Languages** English, French, Italian, Spanish. **Staff** 8.00 FTE, paid. **Activities** Awareness raising; training/education. Active in France. **Publications** Guides. **NGO Relations** Cooperates with French, European and Mediterranean organizations. [2022.10.20/XJ9187/E]

♦ Opus Christi Salvatoris Mundi (religious order)
♦ **Opus Dei** Prelature of the Holy Cross and Opus Dei (#18481)
♦ Opus Sanctorum Angelorum (religious order)
♦ OPV – Obscij Park Gruzovyh Vagonov (inactive)
♦ Oracle Cultural Network / see Network of European Cultural Managers (#17017)
♦ **ORACLE** Network of European Cultural Managers (#17017)
♦ **ORADO** Oceania Regional Anti-Doping Organization (#17670)
♦ ORAF / see Archbishop of Sydney's Anglican Aid
♦ ORAf / see International Trade Union Confederation – African Regional Organization (#15709)
♦ ORA International (internationally oriented national body)

♦ Oral Reconstruction Foundation (OR Foundation) 17781

Contact Margarethenstr 38, 4053 Basel BS, Switzerland. T. +41615654151. E-mail: info@orfoundation.org.
US Section 2300 Riverchase Ctr, Birmingham AL 35244, USA. T. +12059867989. E-mail: info.us@orfoundation.org.
URL: https://orfoundation.org/

History 2006. Former names and other names: *CAMLOG Foundation* – former. **Aims** Secure progress in implant *dentistry* and related fields by creating and imparting new scientific knowledge for the benefit of *patients*. **Structure** Board of Directors. Includes US Section with separate Board. **Activities** Awards/prizes/competitions; events/meetings; financial and/or material support; research/documentation; training/education. **Events** *Oral Reconstruction Symposium* Madrid (Spain) 2022, *Oral Reconstruction Symposium* Verona (Italy) 2021, *Global Symposium* New York, NY (USA) 2020, *Global Symposium* Paris (France) 2019, *Global Symposium* Rotterdam (Netherlands) 2018. [2022/XM5921/f/F]

♦ ORAN / see African Organisation for Standardisation (#00404)
♦ **Orangemen** Orange Order (#17782)

♦ Orange Order (Orangemen) 17782

Grand Lodge Schomberg House, 368 Cregagh Road, Belfast, BT6 9EY, UK. T. +442890701122. Fax +442890403700. E-mail: info@goli.org.uk.
URL: http://www.grandorangelodge.co.uk/

History 1795, Ireland, as an Irish Protestant and political society. Original title: *Orange Society*. Also referred to as *Loyal Orange Association*. **Aims** Maintain *protestantism* and the protestant succession of the *monarchy*.
Members Lodges in 8 countries:
Australia, Canada, Ghana, Great Britain, Ireland, New Zealand, Togo, USA. [2021/XF4935/F]

♦ Orange-Senqu River Commission (ORASECOM) 17783

Secretariat Private Bag X313, Pretoria, 0001, South Africa. T. +27126636826. Fax +27123367565. E-mail: lenka.thamae@orasecom.org.
Street Address Block A, 66 Corporate Park, Cnr Von Willich and Lenchen Streets, Centurion, 0163, South Africa.
URL: http://www.orasecom.org/

History Formalized by governments of Botswana, Lesotho, Namibia and South Africa on signing of Agreement for the Establishment of the Orange-Senqu Commission, 3 Nov 2000, Windhoek (Namibia). **Aims** Promote the equitable and *sustainable development* of the resources of the Orange-Senqu River. **Structure** Council; Secretariat; Task Teams.
Members Governments of 4 countries:
Botswana, Lesotho, Namibia, South Africa. [2019/XM8646/E*]

♦ Orange Society / see Orange Order (#17782)
♦ ORANG-ORANG Organization for Human / see SOCHAIR Organization (Europe) (#19331)
♦ Orangutan Foundation / see Orangutan Foundation International (#17784)

♦ Orangutan Foundation International (OFI) 17784

Pres 824 S Wellesley Ave, Los Angeles CA 90049, USA. T. +13108204962. E-mail: ofioffice@gmail.com.
URL: http://www.orangutan.org/

History 1986, by Dr Biruté Galdikas, as the USA national *'Orangutan Foundation'*. Present name adopted, 1991, when became international. **Aims** Promote *conservation* of the orangutan and its *rainforest habitat*. **Structure** Board of Trustees, comprising 9 members, including Honorary Chairperson and Director. International chapter offices (3): USA; Indonesia; Australia. **Languages** English. **Staff** 5.00 FTE, paid. **Finance** Members' dues. Other sources: grants; donations; adoption scheme; fundraising. **Activities** Actively conserves the orangutan and its rainforest habitats whilst conducting long-term research on the ecology of orangutans and other rainforest fauna and flora within their habitat. **Events** *Conference* Kuching (Malaysia) / Borneo (Malaysia) 1998, *Conference* Fullerton, CA (USA) 1994, *Conference* Jakarta (Indonesia) 1991. **Publications** *Pongo Junior Newsletter* (2 a year); *Red Ape Newsletter* (2 a year).
Members Full in 29 countries:
Australia, Austria, Belgium, Cameroon, Canada, Cyprus, Czechia, Denmark, Finland, France, Germany, Hong Kong, Indonesia, Ireland, Israel, Italy, Japan, Kenya, Malaysia, Netherlands, New Zealand, Norway, Singapore, South Africa, Spain, Sweden, Switzerland, UK, USA.
NGO Relations Member of: *Ape Alliance (#00871)*; *Species Survival Network (SSN, #19916)*. [2020/XF4883/f/F]

- ♦ Orantes de l'Assomption (religious order)
- ♦ Orantes de Marie-Médiatrice (religious order)
- ♦ **ORA** Ocean Recovery Alliance (#17686)
- ♦ ORAP / see Asia Pacific Dental Federation/Asian Pacific Regional Organization of the Fédération Dentaire Internationale (#01882)
- ♦ ORAP-FIET / see UNI Global Union – Asia and Pacific Regional Office (#20341)
- ♦ **ORASECOM** Orange-Senqu River Commission (#17783)
- ♦ Oratorian Fathers – Confederation of the Oratory of St Philip Neri (religious order)
- ♦ Oratoriani – Confederazione dell'Oratorio di San Filippo Neri (religious order)
- ♦ Oratorians – Confédération de l'Oratoire de Saint Philippe Neri (religious order)

♦ ORBICOM – International Network of UNESCO Chairs in Communication 17785

ORBICOM – Réseau international des chaires UNESCO en communication – ORBICOM – Red Internacional de las Catedras UNESCO de Comunicación

Secretariat UQAM R-5610, PO Box 8888, Downtown Station, Montréal QC H3C 3P8, Canada. T. +15149878743. Fax +15149870249. E-mail: info@orbicom.ca – orbicom@uqam.ca.
URL: http://www.orbicom.ca/

History Founded 26 May 1994, jointly by *UNESCO (#20322)* and the Université du Québec à Montréal (UQAM). Original title: *ORBICOM – Worldwide Network of UNESCO Chairs and Associates in Communications – ORBICOM – Réseau mondial des chaires UNESCO et des associés en communication – ORBICOM – Red Mundial de las Catedras UNESCO de Comunicación*. Also referred to as *ORBICOM Network – Réseau ORBICOM – Red ORBICOM*. Part of *UNITWIN/UNESCO Chairs Programme (#20669)*. **Aims** Lead the exchange and sharing of knowledge and know-how among academic, scientific, professional, industrial and governmental members and partners in a global approach to devise *strategic* broad-based plans for more *participatory* communication processes; link academic, media, corporate and government leaders in communications for exchange of information and development of shared projects; promote communications development. **Structure** General Meeting (annual); Board of Directors; Executive Committee; International Secretariat. **Languages** English, French, Spanish. **Staff** 1.50 FTE, paid. **Finance** Members' dues. Other sources: UQAM; *International Development Research Centre (IDRC, #13162)*; UNESCO; various international partnerships. Budget (annual): about US$ 300,000. **Activities** Research/documentation; training/education; publishing activity; events/meetings. **Events** *Annual Meeting* Miri (Malaysia) 2023, *Annual Meeting* Villa María (Argentina) 2022, *Annual Meeting* Madrid (Spain) 2021, *Annual Meeting* Miri (Malaysia) 2021, *Annual Meeting* Strasbourg (France) 2019. **Publications** *OrbInfo* – electronic bulletin. Research publications.
Members UNESCO chairs in communication (36) and Associate members (250) in 68 countries and territories:
Afghanistan, Algeria, Argentina, Australia, Belgium, Benin, Bolivia, Brazil, Brunei Darussalam, Bulgaria, Burkina Faso, Cambodia, Cameroon, Canada, Chile, China, Colombia, Côte d'Ivoire, Croatia, Denmark, Dominican Rep, Estonia, France, Georgia, Germany, Ghana, Greece, Guatemala, India, Indonesia, Italy, Japan, Kenya, Korea Rep, Kyrgyzstan, Laos, Lithuania, Madagascar, Malaysia, Mali, Mexico, Morocco, Namibia, Nepal, Netherlands, New Zealand, Niger, Nigeria, Pakistan, Peru, Philippines, Portugal, Puerto Rico, Russia, Senegal, Singapore, South Africa, Spain, Sweden, Switzerland, Togo, Türkiye, Uganda, UK, Uruguay, USA, Venezuela, Vietnam.
NGO Relations Member of: *Global Forum for Media Development (GFMD, #10375)*; *International Federation of Communication Associations*. [2021/XF3282/F]

- ♦ ORBICOM Network / see ORBICOM – International Network of UNESCO Chairs in Communication (#17785)
- ♦ ORBICOM – Red Internacional de las Catedras UNESCO de Comunicación (#17785)
- ♦ ORBICOM – Red Mundial de las Catedras UNESCO de Comunicación / see ORBICOM – International Network of UNESCO Chairs in Communication (#17785)
- ♦ ORBICOM – Réseau international des chaires UNESCO en communication (#17785)
- ♦ ORBICOM – Réseau mondial des chaires UNESCO et des associés en communication / see ORBICOM – International Network of UNESCO Chairs in Communication (#17785)
- ♦ ORBICOM – Worldwide Network of UNESCO Chairs and Associates in Communications / see ORBICOM – International Network of UNESCO Chairs in Communication (#17785)
- ♦ Orbi-Pharma (internationally oriented national body)

♦ ORBIS International 17786

Exec Dir/CEO 520 8th Avenue, 11th Floor, New York NY 10018-6507, USA. T. +16466745500. Fax +16466745599. E-mail: info@orbis.org.
URL: http://www.orbis.org/

History Mar 1982, Houston, TX (USA). Sub-title sometimes used: *Saving Sight Worldwide*. Former names and other names: *Medical Education for the Eyes of the World* – former; *Project ORBIS International (PO)* – alias. **Aims** Preserve and restore sight in developing countries by strengthening the capacity of local partners in their efforts to prevent and treat *blindness*. **Structure** Board of Directors. World Headquarters in New York NY (USA); Offices in: Dhaka (Bangladesh); Kunming (China); Addis Ababa (Ethiopia); Delhi (India); Hanoi (Vietnam); Hong Kong; Toronto (Canada); Dublin (Ireland); Macau; Shanghai (China); Taipei (Taiwan); London (UK). **Languages** English. **Staff** Plane staff: 24 member team including administrators, ophthalmologists, nurses, anaesthesiologists, flight mechanics, biomedical engineers and audio-visual crew. Staff at world headquarters: 67; staff at offices: 130. **Finance** Donations and gifts-in-kind from corporations, foundations, governments, individuals throughout the world. **Activities** Material and/or material support; capacity building; healthcare. **Publications** *ORBIS Observer* (annual). Annual Report. Pamphlets; brochures; photo archive; videos. **Consultative Status** Consultative status granted from: *ECOSOC (#05331)* (Ros A); *WHO (#20950)* (Official Relations). **NGO Relations** Member of (2): *InsideNGO (inactive)*; *International Coalition for Trachoma Control (ICTC, #12624)*. Instrumental in setting up (1): *VISION 2020 – The Right to Sight (inactive)*. Member of Board of Trustees: *International Agency for the Prevention of Blindness (IAPB, #11597)*. [2013/XF1419/F]

- ♦ ORBIT Association (inactive)
- ♦ ORCADES – Organisation pour la recherche, la communication et l'action en faveur d'un développement solidaire entre le Nord et le Sud (internationally oriented national body)
- ♦ **ORCA** European Organization for Caries Research (#08107)
- ♦ **ORCALC** Oficina Regional de Cultura de la UNESCO para América Latina y el Caribe (#20317)
- ♦ ORCA – Ocean Resources Conservation Association (inactive)
- ♦ Orchestra Giovanile della Comunità Europea / see European Union Youth Orchestra (#09024)
- ♦ Orchestra Giovanile dell'Unione Europea (#09024)
- ♦ Orchestra dei Giovani del Mediterraneo (#17788)

♦ Orchestra Network for Europe (ONE) 17787

Exec Dir address not obtained.
URL: http://www.orchestranetwork.eu/

History 2004. Successive periods of have been called: *ONE, ONE a new dimension, ONE step further* and (Jun 2011 – 2015) *ONE goes places*. **Finance** Support for *European Commission (EC, #06633)* – Culture Programme.
Members Orchestras (7) in 7 countries:
Bulgaria, Czechia, France, Germany, Poland, Slovakia, Slovenia. [2015/XJ9118/F]

- ♦ Orchestre des jeunes des amériques (#22022)
- ♦ Orchestre des jeunes de la Communauté européenne / see European Union Youth Orchestra (#09024)

♦ Orchestre des Jeunes de la Méditerranée (OJM) 17788

Mediterranean Youth Orchestra – Orquesta de Jóvenes del Mediterraneo – Orchestra dei Giovani del Mediterraneo – Orquestra dos Jóvens do Mediterrâneo – Orkestar Mladih Mediteranea – Akdeniz Gençler Orkestrasi

Production Manager Festival d'Aix-en-Provence, Palais de l'Ancien Archevêché, 13100 Aix-en-Provence, France. T. +33442173436.
Facebook: https://www.facebook.com/OrchestreDesJeunesDeLaMediterranee/

History 1984, by the Regional Council of Provence-Alpes-Côte d'Azur (France). **Aims** Develop musical exchanges among Mediterranean regions and countries so as to strengthen their cultural and historical ties; offer support to musical teaching and creation; assist young Mediterranean *musicians* by preparing them for their future as musicians and facilitating their entry into *professional* life. **Activities** Seminar-meetings; symphony orchestra, chamber music and oriental music workshops; international tours, seminar-meetings, international competition of symphonic music composition. **Events** *Les modes d'acquisition des langages musicaux* Aix-en-Provence (France) 1997. **Publications** *Abstracts* in Arabic, English; *Passages* in French.
Members The orchestra consists of students who have finished their studies at the main conservatories in the countries around the Mediterranean and who are seeking complimentary training of both a general and a highly specialized character. Involved countries (22):
Albania, Algeria, Andorra, Croatia, Cyprus, Egypt, France, Greece, Israel, Italy, Jordan, Lebanon, Malta, Monaco, Morocco, Portugal, Serbia, Slovenia, Spain, Syrian AR, Tunisia, Türkiye.
NGO Relations Member of: *European Federation of National Youth Orchestras (EFNYO, #07176)*. [2020/XF2453/F]

- ♦ Orchestre des jeunes de l'Union européenne (#09024)
- ♦ Orchestre philharmonique du monde (#21726)
- ♦ Orchid Project (internationally oriented national body)

♦ Orchid Society of South East Asia (OSSEA) 17789

Hon Sec Robinson Road, PO Box 2363, Singapore 904363, Singapore. Fax +6562341928.
Contact c/o ASEAN Secretariat, 70 A Jalan Sisingamangaraja, Jakarta 12110, Indonesia.
Contact c/o Maxwell Road, PO Box 2363, Singapore 9043, Singapore.
URL: http://www.ossea.org.sg/

History 1928, as a non-governmental organization within *ASEAN (#01141)*. Also referred to *ASEAN Orchid Society*. **Finance** Members' dues. **Publications** *Malayan Orchid Review* (annual). [2012/XF5567/F]

♦ ORCID 17790

Exec Dir 10411 Motor City Drive, Ste 750, Bethesda MD 20817, USA. E-mail: support@orcid.org.
URL: http://orcid.org/

History 2010. Officially launched Oct 2012. Name derives from: *Open Researcher and Contributor ID*. **Aims** Solve the name *ambiguity* problem in research and scholarly communications by creating a central registry of unique *identifiers* (ORCID IDs) for individual researchers and an open and transparent linking mechanism between these IDs and other persistent identifiers. **Structure** Board; Steering Groups; Working Groups. **Staff** 32.00 FTE, paid. **Finance** Members' dues. **Activities** Events/meetings. **Events** *Meeting* Canberra, ACT (Australia) 2016, *Meeting* Washington, DC (USA) 2016, *Joint Conference* Barcelona (Spain) 2015, *Meeting* San Francisco, CA (USA) 2015, *Meeting* Tokyo (Japan) 2014.
Members Organizations (over 1,000) in 45 countries and territories:
Australia, Austria, Belgium, Brazil, Canada, Chile, China, Colombia, Cyprus, Czechia, Denmark, Finland, France, Germany, Greece, Hungary, Iceland, India, Indonesia, Ireland, Israel, Italy, Japan, Kenya, Korea Rep, Luxembourg, Mexico, Netherlands, New Zealand, Norway, Peru, Poland, Portugal, Qatar, Saudi Arabia, Singapore, South Africa, Spain, Sweden, Switzerland, Taiwan, Türkiye, UK, United Arab Emirates, USA.
Included in the above, 18 organizations listed in this Yearbook:
- *African Academy of Sciences (AAS, #00193)*;
- *African Population and Health Research Center (APHRC, #00420)*;
- *American Association for the Advancement of Science (AAAS)*;
- *American Geophysical Union (AGU)*;
- *Andes University (ULA)*;
- *Association for Computing Machinery (ACM, #02447)*;
- *ASTM International (#02994)*;
- *CABI (#03393)*;
- *Centre de coopération internationale en recherche agronomique pour le développement (CIRAD, #03733)*;
- *Centre for International Climate and Environmental Research, Oslo (CICERO)*;
- *Commonwealth Scientific and Industrial Research Organization (CSIRO)*;
- *Electrochemical Society (ECS, #05421)*;
- *European Centre for Medium-Range Weather Forecasts (ECMWF, #06490)*;
- *European Food Safety Authority (EFSA, #07287)*;
- *European Molecular Biology Laboratory (EMBL, #07813)*;
- *European Molecular Biology Organization (EMBO, #07816)*;
- *European Organization for Nuclear Research (CERN, #08108)*;
- *European Respiratory Society (ERS, #08383)*;
- *European University Institute (EUI, #09034)*;
- *Fridtjof Nansen Institute (FNI)*;
- *GÉANT Association (#10086)*;
- *Institute of Electrical and Electronics Engineers (IEEE, #11259)*;
- *International Centre for Tropical Agriculture (#12527)*;
- *International Food Policy Research Institute (IFPRI, #13622)*;
- *International Maize and Wheat Improvement Center (#14077)*;
- *International Monetary Fund (IMF, #14180)*;
- *International School for Advanced Studies, Trieste (ISAS)*;
- *London School of Hygiene and Tropical Medicine (LSHTM)*;
- *Nansen Environmental and Remote Sensing Center (NERSC)*;
- *Nordiska Institutet för Odontologisk Materialprovning (NIOM, #17485)*;
- *Nordisk Institutt for Studier av Innovasjon, Forskning og Utdanning (NIFU)*;
- *Online Computer Library Center (OCLC, #17740)*;
- *Peace Research Institute Oslo (PRIO)*;
- *RTI International*;
- *School of Oriental and African Studies (SOAS)*;
- *SINTEF*;
- *Society for Neuroscience (SfN)*;
- *Society of Exploration Geophysicists (SEG)*;
- *UNICEF/UNDP/World Bank/WHO Special Programme for Research and Training in Tropical Diseases (TDR, #20331)*;
- *Wellcome Trust*;
- *World Agroforestry Centre (ICRAF, #21072)*.

NGO Relations Member of: *DataCite (#05011)*. [2019.02.24/XM4450/y/F]

- ♦ ORCILAC – Oficina Regional de Comunicación e Información para América Latina y El Caribe (no recent information)
- ♦ ORC – Ordo Canonicorum Regularium Sanctae Crucis (religious order)
- ♦ ORC / see Organisation for Cooperation between Railways (#17803)
- ♦ **ORCYT** Oficina Regional de Ciencia de la UNESCO para América Latina y el Caribe (#20314)
- ♦ ORCYT / see UNESCO Office, Montevideo – Regional Bureau for Sciences in Latin America and the Caribbean (#20314)
- ♦ Orden Budista Triratna / see Triratna Buddhist Community (#20243)
- ♦ Orden de los Clérigos Regulares Pobres de la Madre de Dios de las Escuelas Pias (religious order)

♦ Orden de los Clérigos Regulares Somascos (religious order)
♦ Orden Franciscana Secular (religious order)
♦ Orden de los Hermanos de Belén (religious order)
♦ Orden del Magnificat de la Madre de Dios (religious order)
♦ Orden Masónica Mixta Internacional (religious order)
♦ Orden Rosacruz (religious order)
♦ Orden de San Agustin (religious order)
♦ Orden der Schwestern vom Allerheiligsten Erlöser (religious order)
♦ Orden Seglar de los Siervos de Maria (religious order)
♦ Orden Soberana y Militar del Temple de Jerusalem (religious order)
♦ Orden Teosófica de servicio (see: #20141)

♦ Order of the Amaranth 17791

Supreme Royal Matron address not obtained. E-mail: supremesecretary@amaranth.org.
URL: http://www.amaranth.org/

History 14 Jun 1873, New York NY (USA). Comes within *Masonic Movement (#16593)*. Membership originally restricted to members of *General Grand Chapter, Order of the Eastern Star*, became independent in 1921. **Aims** Function as a social, fraternal and charitable organization for Master *Masons* and their *female* relatives. **Activities** Set up Amaranth Diabetes Foundation, 1979. Organizes annual meeting.
Members Grand courts (43) in 5 countries:
Australia, Canada, Philippines, UK, USA.
Subordinate courts in 3 countries and territories:
Hawaii, Ireland, New Zealand.
NGO Relations *International Order of Job's Daughters, Supreme Guardian Council*; *International Order of the Rainbow for Girls (IORG)*. [2022/XM0800/**F**]

♦ Order of the Annunciation (religious order)
♦ Order of the Augustinian Recollects (religious order)
♦ Order of the Basilians of St Macrina (religious order)
♦ Order of Brothers of the Blessed Virgin Mary of Mount Carmel (religious order)
♦ Order of the Canons Regular of Prémontré (religious order)
♦ Order of Cistercians (religious order)
♦ Order of Clerics Regular Poor of the Mother of God of the Pious Schools (religious order)
♦ Order of DeMolay / see DeMolay International
♦ Order of Discalced Augustinians (religious order)
♦ Order of Discalced Brothers of the Blessed Virgin Mary of Mount Carmel (religious order)
♦ Order of the Divine Redemption Missionaries (religious order)
♦ Order of Friars Minor (religious order)
♦ Order of Friars Minor Capuchin (religious order)
♦ Order of Friars Minor Conventual (religious order)
♦ Order of Good Templars / see Movendi International (#16871)
♦ Order of the Holy Cross (religious order)
♦ Order of the Holy Spirit (religious order)
♦ Order of the Imitation of Christ (religious order)
♦ Order of International Co-Freemasonry (religious order)
♦ Order of International Merit for Blood (see: #13374)
♦ Order of the King's Daughters / see International Order of the King's Daughters and Sons
♦ Order of the Knights of Columbus / see Knights of Columbus
♦ Order of Knights Templars (religious order)
♦ Order of the Magnificat of the Mother of God (religious order)
♦ Order of Minims (religious order)
♦ Order of the Most Holy Redeemer (religious order)
♦ Order of the Most Holy Saviour (religious order)
♦ Order of the Most Holy Saviour of Saint Bridget (religious order)
♦ Order of the Most Holy Saviour, Valladolid (religious order)
♦ Order of the Most Holy Trinity for the Redemption of Captives (religious order)
♦ Order of Notre Dame (religious order)
♦ Order of Our Lady of Mercy (religious order)
♦ Order of Preachers (religious order)
♦ Order of Saint Luke (religious order)
♦ Order of the Servants of Mary (religious order)
♦ Order of the Servants of the Sick (religious order)
♦ Orders and Medals Research Society (internationally oriented national body)
♦ Order of St Augustine (religious order)
♦ Order of St Basil the Great (religious order)
♦ Order of St Jerome (religious order)
♦ Order of St John (religious order)
♦ Order of St Paul the First Hermit (religious order)
♦ Order of the Visitation of the Blessed Virgin Mary (religious order)

♦ Order of World Scouts 17792

Contact Chief Commissioner, The Rectory, Church Hill, Tarrant Hinton, Blandford Forum, DT11 8JB, UK. T. +441258830764.
URL: http://www.boy-scout.net/

History 11 Nov 1911, London (UK), by Sir Francis Vane. Originally founding members in 11 countries; total reduced during the 1st World War. **Aims** Increase friendship and cooperation among member organizations; promote scouting worldwide. **Structure** General Meeting; Executive Committee; Secretariat. Officers: Grand Scoutmaster; Assistant Grand Scoutmaster; President; Vice-President; Honorary President; Chief Commissioner.
Members Organizations in 15 countries:
Argentina, Australia, Bolivia, Brazil, Chile, Dominican Rep, Ecuador, Italy, Jamaica, Mexico, Peru, Poland, UK, Ukraine, Uruguay. [2010.02.07/XF6876/**F**]

♦ Un ordinateur portable par enfant (internationally oriented national body)
♦ Ordine dei Chierici Regolari Ministri degli Infermi (religious order)
♦ Ordine dei Chierici Regolari di Somasca (religious order)
♦ Ordine Cistercense (religious order)
♦ Ordine della Compagnia di Maria Nostra Signora (religious order)
♦ Ordine Equestre del Santo Sepolcro di Gerusalemme (religious order)
♦ Ordine Francescano Frati Minori (religious order)
♦ Ordine Francescano Frati Minori Cappuccini (religious order)
♦ Ordine Francescano Frati Minori Conventuali (religious order)
♦ Ordine Francescano Secolare (religious order)
♦ Ordine dei Fratelli di Betlemme (religious order)
♦ Ordine dell'Imitazione di Cristo (religious order)
♦ Ordine del Magnificat della Madre di Dio (religious order)
♦ Ordine Massonico Misto Internazionale (religious order)
♦ Ordine Ospedaliero di San Giovanni di Dio (religious order)
♦ Ordine della Santa Croce (religious order)
♦ Ordine di Sant'Agostino (religious order)
♦ Ordine della Santissima Trinità (religious order)
♦ Ordine del Santissimo Redentore (religious order)
♦ Ordine Secolare dei Carmelitani Scalzi (religious order)
♦ Ordine Secolare dei Servi di Maria (religious order)
♦ Ordine dei Servi di Maria (religious order)
♦ Ordine Teutonico (religious order)
♦ **ORDINEX** Organisation internationale des experts (#17808)
♦ Ordinis Dominae Nostrae (religious order)
♦ Ordo Augustinianorum Recollectorum (religious order)
♦ Ordo Augustiniensium Discalceatorum (religious order)
♦ Ordo Beatae Mariae Virginis de Mercede (religious order)
♦ Ordo Canonicorum Regularium Sanctae Crucis (religious order)
♦ Ordo Cartusiensis (religious order)
♦ Ordo Cisterciense Strictioris Observantiae (religious order)
♦ Ordo Cistericensis (religious order)
♦ Ordo Clericorum Regularium Matris Dei (religious order)
♦ Ordo Clericorum Regularium Ministrantium Infirmis (religious order)
♦ Ordo Clericorum Regularium Minorum (religious order)
♦ Ordo Clericorum Regularium Pauperum Matris Dei Scholarum Piarum (religious order)
♦ Ordo Clericorum Regularium a Somascha (religious order)
♦ Ordo Clericorum Regularium vulgo Theatinorum (religious order)
♦ Ordo Franciscanus Saecularis (religious order)
♦ Ordo Fratrum Beatae Mariae Virginis de Monte Carmelo (religious order)
♦ Ordo Fratrum Discalceatorum Beatae Mariae Virginis de Monte Carmelo (religious order)
♦ Ordo Fratrum Domus Hospitalis Sanctae Mariae Teutonicorum in Jerusalem (religious order)
♦ Ordo Fratrum Minorum (religious order)
♦ Ordo Fratrum Minorum Capuccinorum (religious order)
♦ Ordo Fratrum Minorum Conventualium (religious order)
♦ Ordo Fratrum Praedicatorum (religious order)
♦ Ordo Fratrum Sancti Augustini (religious order)
♦ Ordo Fratrum Sancti Pauli Primi Eremitae (religious order)
♦ Ordo Hospitalarius Sancti Ioannis de Deo (religious order)
♦ Ordo de Imitatione Christi (religious order)
♦ Ordo Militaris Sancti Constantini Magni (religious order)
♦ Ordo dei Minimi (religious order)
♦ Ordo Minimorum (religious order)
♦ Ordo Patrum Excalceatorum Beatae Mariae Virginis de Mercede (religious order)
♦ Ordo Sanctae Crucis (religious order)
♦ Ordo Sancti Hieronymi (religious order)
♦ Ordo Sanctissimae Trinitatis (religious order)
♦ Ordo Sanctissimi Redemptoris (religious order)
♦ Ordo Sanctissimi Salvatoris (religious order)
♦ Ordo Sanctissimi Salvatoris Sanctae Birgittae (religious order)
♦ Ordo Sanctissimi Salvatoris, Valladolid (religious order)
♦ Ordo Seglar de los Carmelitas Descalzos (religious order)
♦ Ordo Servorum Mariae (religious order)
♦ Ordo Supremus Militaris Templi Hierosolymitani (religious order)
♦ Ordre des Basiliennes de Sainte Macrina (religious order)
♦ Ordre des Chartreux (religious order)
♦ Ordre Cistercien de la Stricte Observance (religious order)
♦ Ordre de Cîteaux (religious order)
♦ Ordre des Clercs Réguliers de Somasque (religious order)
♦ Ordre de la Compagnie de Marie Notre-Dame (religious order)
♦ Ordre équestre du Saint Sépulcre de Jérusalem (religious order)
♦ Ordre des Frères de Bethléem (religious order)
♦ Ordre des Frères Mineurs (religious order)
♦ Ordre des Frères Mineurs Capucins (religious order)
♦ Ordre des Frères Mineurs Conventuels (religious order)
♦ Ordre des Frères Prêcheurs (religious order)
♦ Ordre Hospitalier du Saint Esprit (religious order)
♦ Ordre hospitalier de Saint Jean de Dieu (religious order)
♦ Ordre de l'Imitation du Christ (religious order)

♦ Ordre international des anysetiers 17793

Sec 20 rue Choron, 75009 Paris, France. T. +33142253068. Fax +33145621151. E-mail: secretariat@anysetiers.com.
URL: http://www.anysetiers.org/

History 1955, as Corporation des anysetiers. Present name adopted 1968. Registered in accordance with French law. **Aims** Promote and research the use of *anise*. **Structure** General Assembly. **Events** *Annual Congress* Rotterdam (Netherlands) 2010, *Annual Congress* Vienna (Austria) 2006, *Annual Congress* Paris (France) 2005, *Annual Congress* Paris (France) 2005, *Annual Congress* Antwerp (Belgium) 2004. [2013/XM1667/**F**]

♦ Ordre international des bons templiers / see Movendi International (#16871)
♦ Ordre international pour l'éthique et la culture morale (inactive)
♦ Ordre international des experts-conseils / see Organisation internationale des experts (#17808)
♦ Ordre International du Rite Ancien et Primitif de Memphis-Misraïm / see Ancient and Primitive Rite of Memphis-Misraïm (#00815)
♦ Ordre Maçonnique International 'DELPHI' (#14112)
♦ Ordre Maçonnique mixte international 'Le Droit Humain' (religious order)
♦ Ordre du magnificat de la mère de Dieu (religious order)
♦ Ordre des Mercédaires Déchaussés (religious order)
♦ Ordre du Mérite International pour le don de Sang (see: #13374)
♦ Ordre Militaire et Hospitalier de Saint Lazare de Jérusalem (religious order)
♦ Ordre des Minimes (religious order)
♦ Ordre des Moniales du Très Saint Rédempteur (religious order)
♦ Ordre de Notre-Dame de la Merci (religious order)
♦ Ordre patriarcal de la Sainte Croix de Jérusalem (religious order)
♦ Ordre Rosicrucien – Ancien et Mystique Ordre Rosae Crucis (religious order)
♦ Ordre de Saint Augustin (religious order)
♦ Ordre de Saint-Camille de Lellis (religious order)
♦ Ordre de la Sainte Croix (religious order)
♦ Ordre Séculier du Carmel (religious order)
♦ Ordre Séculier des Carmes Déchaux (religious order)
♦ Ordre Séculier des Servites de Marie (religious order)
♦ Ordre de service théosophique (see: #20141)
♦ Ordre des Servites de Marie (religious order)
♦ Ordre des Serviteurs des Malades (religious order)
♦ Ordre Souverain Constantinien (religious order)
♦ Ordre souverain militaire hospitalier de Saint-Jean de Jérusalem, de Rhodes et de Malte (religious order)
♦ Ordre Souverain et Militaire du Temple de Jerusalem (religious order)
♦ Ordre du Temple (inactive)
♦ Ordre Teutonique (religious order)
♦ Ordre de la Très Sainte-Trinité et de la Rédemption des Captifs (religious order)
♦ Ordre des Trinitaires – Ordre de la Très Sainte-Trinité et de la Rédemption des Captifs (religious order)
♦ **OREALC/UNESCO Santiago** Oficina Regional de Educación de la UNESCO para América Latina y el Caribe (#20318)
♦ ORE / see European Regional Organization of the Fédération dentaire internationale (#08345)
♦ **ORE** Organisation régionale européenne de la FDI (#08345)

♦ ORE – Ornitologia Rondo Esperantlingva (no recent information)
♦ **ORFEUS** Observatories and Research Facilities for European Seismology (#17639)
♦ **ORF** Olympic Refuge Foundation (#17720)
♦ **OR Foundation** Oral Reconstruction Foundation (#17781)
♦ Orgalime / see Orgalim – Europe's Technology Industries (#17794)

♦ Orgalim – Europe's Technology Industries 17794

Main Office Blue Point Brussels, 5th Floor, Blvd A Reyers 80, 1030 Brussels, Belgium. T. +3222066883. E-mail: secretariat@orgalim.eu.
URL: https://orgalim.eu/

History 1947, Brussels (Belgium). Activities commenced 1954. Combined with several parallel groups, 1960. Former names and other names: *Liaison Group of the European Mechanical, Electrical, Electronic and Metalworking Industries* – former; *Liaison Group for the European Engineering Industries* – former; *Orgalime* – former (6 Nov 2019). Registration: Banque-Carrefour des Entreprises, No/ID: 0414.341.438, Start date: 12 Jul 1974, Belgium; EU Transparency Register, No/ID: 20210641335-88, Start date: 10 Mar 2009. **Aims** Provide liaison among electrical and electronic engineering, mechanical engineering and *metalworking* trade associations in Western Europe in economic, legal, technical and other matters of concern to the industries they represent. **Structure** General Assembly; Board of Directors; Presidents' Board; Permanent Secretariat; Policy Committees (3); Working Groups. **Languages** English. **Staff** 30.00 FTE, paid. **Finance** Sources: fees for services; members' dues; sale of publications. **Activities** Advocacy/lobbying/activism; knowledge management/information dissemination; research and development. **Events** *General Assembly* Brussels (Belgium) 2021, *General Assembly* Stockholm (Sweden) 2020, *Conference on Reinventing Europe's Industrial Leadership* Brussels (Belgium) 2019, *European Forum for Manufacturing* Brussels (Belgium) 2019, *General Assembly* Vilnius (Lithuania) 2018. **Publications** Annual Report. Models; guides; practical guides; position papers; international conditions; general conditions; other publications of interest to engineering industries – usually in English, French and/or German.
Members National trade organizations (34) in 22 countries:
Austria, Belgium, Bulgaria, Croatia, Denmark, Finland, France, Germany, Ireland, Italy, Latvia, Lithuania, Luxembourg, Netherlands, Norway, Poland, Portugal, Slovenia, Spain, Sweden, Switzerland, UK.
IGO Relations Recognized by: *European Commission (EC, #06633)*. Presents the industry's views to: *Council of the European Union (#04895)*; *European Parliament (EP, #08146)*. **NGO Relations** Member of (3): *European Accreditation Advisory Board (EAAB, see: #06782)*; *European Factories of the Future Research Association (EFFRA, #07023)*; *Federation of European and International Associations Established in Belgium (FAIB, #09508)*. Cooperates with (2): *BUSINESSEUROPE (#03381)*; *Council of European Employers of the Metal, Engineering and Technology-Based Industries (CEEMET, #04887)*. Works closely with about 100 European sector committees made up of national associations responsible for single product sectors (not specified).
[2022.02.16/XD2932/t/**D**]

♦ Organe international de contrôle des stupéfiants (#14212)
♦ Organic Battery Days (meeting series)
♦ Organic Crop Improvement Association (internationally oriented national body)
♦ Organic Exchange / see Textile Exchange (#20135)
♦ Organic Foods Production Association of North America / see Organic Trade Association (#17795)

♦ Organic Trade Association (OTA) 17795

Main Office 444 N Capitol St NW, Ste 445A, Washington DC 20001, USA. E-mail: info@ota.com.
URL: http://www.ota.com/

History Jun 1984, as *Organic Foods Production Association of North America (OFPANA)*. Present name adopted Sep 1994. Bylaws last revised, May 2001. **Aims** Promote and protect organic with a unifying voice that serves and engages its diverse members from farm to marketplace. **Structure** General Meeting (annual); Board of Directors; Executive Committee. **Finance** Members' dues. Tradeshow and conference proceedings. **Events** *Conference* Chicago, IL (USA) 2005, *Annual meeting* Chicago, IL (USA) 2004, *Organic conference / Annual Meeting / Conference* Chicago, IL (USA) 2004, *Annual meeting* Austin, TX (USA) 2003, *Organic conference / Annual Meeting / Conference* Austin, TX (USA) 2003. **Publications** *Organic Report Magazine* (2 a year); *Find Organic Member Directory*; *Organic Export Directory*. **NGO Relations** Member of: *Global Organic Textile Standard International Working Group (GOTS, #10515)*; *IFOAM – Organics International (IFOAM, #11105)*.
[2019.02.12/XF3830/t/**F**]

♦ Organisashon di Lingwistika Karibense (#19530)
♦ Organisasjon for de Nordiske Systemansvarlige Nettselskaper (inactive)
♦ Organisatie van de Europese Zeehavens (#08453)
♦ Organisatie der Groentenconserven-Industrieën (inactive)
♦ Organisatie van de Zeehavens van de Europese Gemeenschap / see European Sea Ports Organisation (#08453)
♦ Organisation africaine du bois (no recent information)
♦ Organisation africaine de cartographie et de télédétection (inactive)
♦ Organisation africaine pour l'étude des programmes scolaires (no recent information)
♦ Organisation africaine des femmes autochtones (no recent information)
♦ Organisation africaine des institutions supérieures de contrôle des finances publiques (#00406)
♦ Organisation africaine pour la liberté et la démocratie (no recent information)
♦ Organisation africaine et malgache du café (no recent information)
♦ Organisation Africaine de Normalisation (#00404)
♦ Organisation africaine de la propriété intellectuelle (#00344)
♦ Organisation africaine pour la recherche et l'enseignement sur le cancer (#00405)
♦ Organisation africaine des syndicats des mines, métaux, energie, chimie et assimilés (no recent information)

♦ Organisation of African, Caribbean and Pacific States (OACPS) 17796

Organisation des Etats d'Afrique, des Caraïbes et du Pacifique (OEACP) – Organización de Estados de África, el Caribe y el Pacífico (OEACP)

SG OACPS Secretariat, Waterleidingsstraat 118, Ixelles, 1050 Brussels, Belgium. T. +3227430600. Fax +3227355573. E-mail: info@acp.int – sg@acp.int.
Geneva Office Head, 37-39 Rue de Vermont, 1202 Geneva, Switzerland. T. +41227481490. Fax +41227481499.
URL: https://www.oacps.org/

History 6 Jun 1975, Georgetown, on signature of the founding text, or *Georgetown Agreement – Accord de Georgetown*, following signature, 28 Feb 1975, Lomé (Togo), of *ACP-EEC Convention (Lomé convention, 1975)* between the European Economic Community – subsequently called *European Community (inactive)* and then *European Union (EU, #08967)* – and 46 African, Caribbean and Pacific countries. The Convention succeeded two earlier Conventions, both called *Yaoundé Convention*: the first signed 20 Jul 1963 and which entered into force 1 Jul 1964; the second signed 29 Jul 1969 and which expired 31 Jan 1975. They established *Association of the European Economic Community and the African and Malagasy States (EAMA, inactive)* which, with the association between European Economic Community and the then *East African Community – 1967 (EAC, inactive)* – disintegrated in 1977 – was superseded by the new arrangement. Special agreements were concluded with 21 states belonging to the British Commonwealth in 1973, when the UK entered the EEC. *Second ACP-EEC Convention (Lomé II, 1979)* between EEC and the ACP States, signed 31 Oct 1979, Lomé, entered into force 1 Jan 1981. *Third ACP-EEC Convention (Lomé III, 1984)*, the 3rd Lomé Agreement, signed 8 Dec 1984, entered into force in May 1985, expired 28 Feb 1990. Negotiations for *Fourth ACP-EEC Convention (Lomé IV, 1989)* concluded on signature of an agreement, 15 Dec 1989, entered into force in Mar 1990 for a period of 10 years, amended 4 Nov 1995, Mauritius, following mid-term review. *ACP-EU Partnership Agreement (Cotonou agreement, 2000)*, signed 23 Jun 2000, Cotonou (Benin), will come into force when ratified. The ACP Group is also referred to as *Group of African, Caribbean and Pacific States*, as *ACP States – Etats ACP* and as *ACP Countries*. Statutes of Georgetown Agreement entered in *'UNTS/1 20345'*. **Aims** Ensure realization of the objectives of the Convention of Lomé (Togo); coordinate activities of ACP States in the application of the Convention; determine joint positions of ACP Group vis-à-vis the European Community on matters covered by the Convention; promote and strengthen existing solidarity of the ACP Group; contribute to development of greater and closer trade, economic and cultural relations among ACP States and among developing countries in general and, to this end, develop exchange of information among ACP States in the fields of trade, technology, industry and human resources; contribute to promotion of effective regional and interregional cooperation among ACP States and among developing countries in general and strengthen links between the regional organizations to which they belong; promote establishment of a new world economic order; promote and develop collective self reliance and greater and closer economic and trade relations among ACP States; work to ensure that the Lomé Convention contributes to the realization of common aspirations of developing countries.
Structure Bureau of 6 members (4 from Africa, one from the Pacific and one from the Caribbean, renewed every 6 months) directs *ACP-EU Council of Ministers (#00076)* (meeting once a year), which is assisted by *Committee of Ambassadors ACP-EC*, meeting on average 30 times a year at Brussels (Belgium) headquarters, with Chairman elected from among members of the Bureau. Also set up under the Lomé Conventions: *Centre technique de coopération agricole et rurale (CTA, inactive)*.
Permanent sub-committees of the Committee of Ambassadors (10) handle the subjects falling within the scope of the Group's objectives and relating to:
- Trade Cooperation;
- *EU Customs Union (#05579)*;
- STABEX and Mineral Products;
- *ACP Sugar Group (#00078)*;
- Financial and Technical Cooperation;
- Least Developed, Landlocked and Island Countries;
- Industrial Cooperation;
- Agricultural Cooperation;
- Intra-ACP Cooperation;
- Administration and Finance.

The sub-committees set up ad hoc working parties and expert groups within themselves as required. *ACP-EU Joint Parliamentary Assembly (#00077)*, established 8 Dec 1984, Lomé, on signature of the Lomé III Convention, took over the tasks of *'ACP-EEC Consultative Assembly – Assemblée consultative ACP-CEE'* which had been set up 31 Oct 1979, on signature of second Lomé Convention, and of *'ACP-EEC Joint Committee – Comité paritaire ACP-CEE'*, on which were 64 representatives of the European Parliament.
ACP General Secretariat in Brussels monitors implementation of the Lomé Convention, services ACP Group organs and carries out tasks at the request of the Council of Ministers and Committee of Ambassadors; it comprises 3 Divisions: Commercial Cooperation; Development Cooperation; Administration and Finance. *Programme Management Unit (PMU) – Unité de gestion de projet (UGP)*, operational from 1 Jul 2002, administers a euro 20 million programme for capacity building in ACP countries and regional economic groupings.
Languages English, French. **Finance** *European Development Fund (EDF, #06914)* is the main financial instrument of the Lomé Conventions, providing 90% of the Convention's budget, the remainder coming from from ACP member states. Total Community contributions to Lomé countries: euro 3,370.3 million, 5,512 million, 8,500 million and 12,000 million under Lomé I, II, II and IV respectively. Budget 1991-1995: euro 12,800 million.
Activities Areas of cooperation come under the following headings: Environment; Agricultural cooperation, food security and rural development (including the combating of drought and desertification); Fisheries development; Cooperation in staple commodities; Industrial development, manufacturing and transformation; Mining development; Energy development; Business development; Services development (including: objectives and principles; support services and economic development; tourism; transport, communications and informatics); Development of commerce; Cultural and social cooperation (including: taking into account of the cultural and social dimension; promotion of cultural identities and intercultural dialogue; valorization of human resources); Regional cooperation. Annex II of the Lomé Convention lists the working or processing required to be carried out on non-originating materials in order that a product can obtain originating status; textiles are covered specifically by the 1995 Mauritius amendment (Annex X). Specific commodities and resources covered by protocols of Lomé IV and its 1995 amendment are: bananas; rum; beef and veal; sugar; products within the province of the European Coal and Steel Community; forest resources (sustainable management). A new type of ACP-EU free-trade pact has been proposed by the European Commission which would stimulate economic growth among ACP states. *Economic Partnership Agreements (EPAs)* will enhance duty-free access to the EU market for exporters in ACPs and remove barriers that prevent European goods and services from entering their markets. The Programme Management Unit assists ACP countries with capacity building assistance in preparation of EPAs, including managing sub-projects in: developing specific study work and workshops aimed at developing EPA negotiating positions for ACP countries and regions; training in negotiating techniques for ACP officials; technical assistance in trade policy and consolidation of economic integration initiatives.
'Suva Declaration' and *'Suva Programme of Action'*, adopted 14 Apr 1977, led to a plan for implementation which was adopted 1980, Montego Bay, dealing with 6 major sectors and including recommendations, Nov 1979, of Nairobi (Kenya) Conference on the Development and Promotion of ACP Trade (adopted 1980) and of Bangui (Central African Rep) Charter on Maritime Transport (approved Jul 1981). Under Lomé III, stabilization of export earnings through the *STABEX System* offsets negative effects of major fluctuations in world prices for certain raw materials such as tea, coffee, cotton, groundnuts, bananas, timber and leather. The *SYSMIN System* for mining includes (repayable) assistance when production capacity falls. An additional sum is available for subsidies, special loans, risk capital and low-interest loans for development projects. Following Lomé III, areas of concern included: external debts of ACP countries; continuing decrease in prices for agricultural and mining base products and problems of access to EU markets; consequences of structural adjustments in the economies of ACP countries; creation or reinforcement of economic areas in which intra-ACP exchanges may develop. In 1987, members agreed to upgrade cooperation in technology transfer, culture and science, joint production, and development of intra-ACP enterprises; and to pursue a programme for development of transport and telecommunications links. The principal innovation of Lomé IV was aid in structural adjustment related to development objectives. A process of short-term measures of price and exchange rate stabilization was prepared by ACP countries themselves in response to the debt crisis in order to secure economic operators. The process is adapted to the particular situation in each country, having a social component and taking into account the most vulnerable social categories. Other priorities: preservation of the environment and natural resources; promotion of human rights in ACP countries; human and cultural dimensions of development programmes; health; contribution of women to development; abolition of racial, religious, cultural or social discrimination against migrant workers, students and others. Pillars of the 2000 Cotonou (Benin) Agreement are: comprehensive political dimension; participatory approaches; strengthened focus on poverty reduction; new framework for economic and trade cooperation; reform of financial cooperation.
Events *Session* Brussels (Belgium) 2020, *Symposium on South-South and Triangular Cooperation* Brussels (Belgium) 2020, *Session* Bucharest (Romania) 2019, *Heads of State and Government Summit* Nairobi (Kenya) 2019, *Session* Cotonou (Benin) 2018. **Publications** *ACP-EU Courier* (6 a year) – published jointly with EU. *Directory of ACP Technical Institutions* (1982); *Directory of ACP Universities* (1981). https://www.oacps.org/news/publications/
Members African, Caribbean and Pacific countries associated with the European Community and signatory to the Georgetown Agreement and Lomé Conventions (78, the 17 indicated with 'Y' having been associated with EU under the Yaoundé Convention. South Africa was admitted on coming into force of the revised Lomé IV convention, as indicated in a protocol signed 24 Apr 1997):
Angola, Antigua-Barbuda, Bahamas, Barbados, Belize, Benin (Y), Botswana, Burkina Faso, Burundi (Y), Cameroon (Y), Cape Verde, Central African Rep, Chad (Y), Comoros, Congo Brazzaville (Y), Congo DR (Y), Côte d'Ivoire (Y), Cuba, Djibouti, Dominica, Dominican Rep, Equatorial Guinea, Eritrea, Eswatini, Ethiopia, Fiji, Gabon (Y), Gambia, Ghana, Grenada, Guinea, Guinea-Bissau, Guyana, Haiti, Jamaica, Kenya, Kiribati, Lesotho, Liberia, Madagascar (Y), Malawi, Mali (Y), Marshall Is, Mauritania (Y), Mauritius (Y), Micronesia FS, Mozambique, Namibia, Nauru, Niger (Y), Nigeria, Palau, Papua New Guinea, Rwanda (Y), Samoa, Sao Tomé-Principe, Senegal (Y), Seychelles, Sierra Leone, Solomon Is, Somalia (Y), South Africa, St Kitts-Nevis, St Lucia, St Vincent-Grenadines, Sudan, Suriname, Tanzania UR, Togo (Y), Tonga, Trinidad-Tobago, Tuvalu, Uganda, Vanuatu, Zambia, Zimbabwe.
IGO Relations Accredited by (1): *United Nations Framework Convention on Climate Change – Secretariat (UNFCCC, #20564)*. Observer status with (7): *Committee of International Development Institutions on the Environment (CIDIE, no recent information)*; *European Union (EU, #08967)*; *Intergovernmental Group on Bananas and on Tropical Fruits (#11486)*; *International Organization for Migration (IOM, #14454)*; *UNIDO (#20336)*; *United Nations (UN, #20515)*; *World Trade Organization (WTO, #21864)*. Member of (1): *Global Facility for Disaster Reduction and Recovery (GFDRR, #10352)*. Cooperates with (1): *Organisation internationale de la*

Francophonie (OIF, #17809). Relationship agreement with: *FAO (#09260).* Special agreement with: *UNESCO (#20322); United Nations Economic Commission for Africa (ECA, #20554); ECOSOC (#05331).* Permanent observer status with: *World Intellectual Property Organization (WIPO, #21593).* Participates in the activities of: *UNCTAD (#20285).* Participates as observer in the activities of: *Codex Alimentarius Commission (CAC, #04081).* Accredited to the Conference of the Parties of: *Secretariat of the United Nations Convention to Combat Desertification (Secretariat of the UNCCD, #19208).* Negotiates with: *European Commission (EC, #06633).* Invited to sessions of Intergovernmental Council of: *International Programme for the Development of Communication (IPDC, #14651).* Adheres to: *Global Partnership for Effective Development Co-operation (GPEDC, #10532).* Close working relations with: *Agency for International Trade Information and Cooperation (AITIC, #00553).* Agricultural Commodities Programmes has links with: *Caribbean Agricultural Research and Development Institute (CARDI, #03436).* **NGO Relations** Participates in: *Global Partnership for Oceans (GPO, #10537).* [2023.02.15/XF0671/**F***]

♦ Organisation of African Geological Surveys (OAGS) 17797

Contact 280 Pretoria St, Pretoria, 1084, South Africa. E-mail: oags@geoscience.org.za.
URL: https://www.oagsafrica.org/

History 2007, South Africa. **Activities** Capacity building; events/meetings. [2021/XM5530/**D**]

♦ Organisation of African Trade Union Unity (OATUU) 17798

Organisation de l'unité syndicale africaine (OUSA)

Contact PO Box M386, Accra, Ghana. T. +233307011033. E-mail: oatuughana@gmail.com – oatuughana@yahoo.com.
SG c/o INERS-UGTA, Place du 1er Mai, Maison A Benhamouda, Algiers, Algeria. Fax +21321660969.
URL: https://oatuu.org/

History 13 Apr 1973, Addis Ababa (Ethiopia). Founded following preparatory meeting, Nov 1972, Addis Ababa, as a specialized agency of *Organization of African Unity (OAU, inactive)*, replacing *African Trade Union Confederation (ATUC, inactive)*, set up 14 Jan 1962, Dakar (Senegal), and *All African Trade Union Federation (AATUF, inactive)*, set up 31 May 1961, Casablanca (Morocco) and also referred to as *'Union syndicale des pays africains'*. Absorbed *Fédération panafricaine des syndicats des services publics (FPSSP, no recent information)*, 1974. Following dialogue with non-affiliated centres, all trade union centres in Africa became fully fledged members at First General Council, Mar 1975, Accra (Ghana). **Aims** Coordinate and guide the activities of all National Trade Unions action towards objectives defined in the Charter.
Structure Congress (every 4 years), comprising 4 delegates from each affiliated national trade union centre. General Council (annual), consisting of all the members of Executive Committee and one member representing each affiliate. Executive Committee (meets twice a year), composed of President, 7 Vice-Presidents elected from the 5 zones of OATUU in the continent and the Secretariat which comprises: Secretary-General; 2 Assistant Secretaries-General responsible for Departments under the headings: International and Organization, Press and Information, Workers' Education, Economic and Research and Documentation. Treasurer-General, responsible for Administration and Finance. Assistant Treasurer-General.
Specialized agencies (10):
- *African Organization of Mines, Metal, Energie, Chemical and Allied Trade Unions (OASMMECA, no recent information);*
- *All Africa Teachers' Organization (AATO, no recent information);*
- *Federation of African Migrant Workers in France (no recent information);*
- *Pan African Federation of Agricultural Trade Unions (PAFATU, inactive);*
- *Pan African Federation of Banks, Insurance and Financial Affairs (no recent information);*
- *Pan African Federation of Building, Construction and Woodworkers (FPTBC, no recent information);*
- *Pan African Federation of Food, Tobacco, Hotels and Allied Workers (no recent information);*
- *Pan African Federation of Petroleum and Allied Workers (FASPA, no recent information);*
- *Pan African Federation of Posts and Telecommunications Trade Unions (no recent information);*
- *Pan African Federation of Workers of Commerce (PANACOM, no recent information).*

Languages Arabic, English, French. **Staff** 26.00 FTE, paid. **Finance** Members' contributions. Other sources: subventions; fund-raising activities; gifts and legacy; services. **Activities** Organizes conferences, workshops, symposia, seminars and round tables on political and socio-economic issues for affiliated organizations. **Events** *Annual General Council* Asmara (Eritrea) 2015, *Annual General Council* Tripoli (Libyan AJ) 2008, *Annual General Council* Kisumu (Kenya) 2007, *Annual General Council* Cairo (Egypt) 2006, *Annual General Council* Khartoum (Sudan) 2005. **Publications** *Voice of African Workers* (periodical); *Information Tips* (irregular).
Members African National Trade Union Organizations (73). Trade Union Organizations in 54 countries and territories:
Algeria, Angola, Benin, Botswana, Burkina Faso, Burundi, Cameroon, Cape Verde, Central African Rep, Chad, Comoros, Congo Brazzaville, Congo DR, Côte d'Ivoire, Djibouti, Egypt, Equatorial Guinea, Eritrea, Eswatini, Ethiopia, Gabon, Gambia, Ghana, Guinea, Guinea-Bissau, Kenya, Lesotho, Liberia, Libya, Madagascar, Malawi, Mali, Mauritania, Mauritius, Morocco, Mozambique, Namibia, Niger, Nigeria, Rwanda, Sahara West, Sao Tomé-Principe, Senegal, Seychelles, Sierra Leone, Somalia, South Africa, Sudan, Tanzania UR, Togo, Tunisia, Uganda, Zambia, Zimbabwe.
Sub-regional organizations (4):
Organization of Trade Unions of Central Africa (OTUCA, no recent information); Organization of Trade Unions of West Africa (OTUWA); Southern African Trade Union Coordination Council (SATUCC, #19865); Union of Arab Maghreb Workers' Trade Unions (USTMA, no recent information).
Consultative Status Consultative status granted from: *ILO (#11123)* (Special and Regional); *FAO (#09260)* (Special Status); *UNCTAD (#20285)* (General Category). **NGO Relations** Member of: *International Centre for Trade Union Rights (ICTUR, #12525); World Social Forum (WSF, #21797).* [2019/XD0140/ty/**D**]

♦ Organisation of African Youth (OAYouth) 17799

Organizing Sec address not obtained.
Pres address not obtained.
URL: http://www.oayouth.org/

Aims Be the continental umbrella organization for all African youth, providing a platform for youth-led programmes, a forum for dialogue, and a network of future leaders. **Structure** Executive Committee. **NGO Relations** Member of: *African Coalition for Corporate Accountability (ACCA, #00252); Girls not Brides (#10154).* [2014/XJ8722/**D**]

♦ Organisation d'Afrique francophone pour le Renforcement des Systèmes de Santé et de la Vaccination (unconfirmed)
♦ Organisation afro-asiatique de coopération économique (inactive)
♦ Organisation afro-asiatique de l'habitat (inactive)
♦ Organisation afro-asiatique pour la reconstruction rurale / see African-Asian Rural Development Organization (#00203)
♦ Organisation des agences d'information d'Asie et du Pacifique (#17855)
♦ Organisation pour l'aménagement et le développement du Bassin de la Rivière Kagera (no recent information)
♦ Organisation arabe des communication par satellites (#01037)
♦ Organisation arabe de défense sociale contre le crime (inactive)
♦ Organisation arabe pour le développement administratif (#00893)
♦ Organisation Arabe du Développement Agricole (#01018)
♦ Organisation arabe pour le développement industriel (inactive)
♦ Organisation arabe des droits de l'homme (#01020)
♦ Organisation arabe pour l'éducation, la culture et la science (#01003)
♦ Organisation arabe de normalisation et de métrologie (inactive)
♦ Organisation arabe des ressources minières (inactive)
♦ Organisation arabe des sciences administratives / see Arab Administrative Development Organization (#00893)
♦ Organisation arabe des technologies de l'information et de la communication (#00982)
♦ Organisation arabe de tourisme (#01057)
♦ Organisation Arabe du Transport Aérien / see Arab Air Carriers Organization (#00896)
♦ Organisation arabe du travail (#01001)
♦ Organisation des Architectes Arabes (#00898)
♦ Organisation des arts du Commonwealth (inactive)
♦ Organisation asiatique de contrôle des parasites (inactive)
♦ Organisation asiatique des institutions supérieures de contrôle des finances publiques (#01594)
♦ Organisation de l'association islamique des armateurs (#17876)
♦ Organisation des associations d'inventeurs nordiques (no recent information)
♦ Organisation d'associations nationales d'armateurs d'Amérique latine / see Latin American Shipowners Association (#16369)
♦ Organisation d'associés démographiques pour l'Asie de l'Est et du Sud-Est (inactive)
♦ Organisation des assurances africaines (#00343)
♦ Organisation des assurances est-africaines / see Organization of Eastern and Southern Africa Insurers (#17864)
♦ Organisation de l'aviation civile internationale (#12581)
♦ Organisation du baccalauréat international / see International Baccalaureate (#12306)
♦ Organisation Benelux de la propriété intellectuelle (#03203)
♦ Organisation der Beschäftigten bei europäischen und internationalen Einrichtungen in der Bundesrepublik Deutschland (#13311)
♦ Organisation camerounaise de promotion de la coopération économique internationale (internationally oriented national body)
♦ Organisation canadienne pour l'éducation au service du développement / see CODE
♦ Organisation des capitales et villes islamiques (#17875)
♦ Organisation des Caraïbes (inactive)

♦ Organisation of Caribbean Utility Regulators (OOCUR) 17800

Chairperson c/o PUC, 106 New Garden Street, Georgetown, Guyana. T. +5922273293. Fax +5922273534. E-mail: secretariat@oocur.org.
URL: http://www.oocur.org/

History 26 Jul 2002, Ocho Rios (Jamaica). Registration: Guyana. **Aims** Assist in improvement of utility regulation; foster transparent and stable utility regulation through autonomous and independent regulators in member countries; undertake research, training and development; facilitate understanding of regulation issues and sharing of information and experience. **Structure** General Assembly; Executive Council; Secretariat. **Finance** Sources: members' dues. Supported by: *Commonwealth Telecommunications Organisation (CTO, #04365).* **Activities** Events/meetings. **Events** *Annual Conference* Anguilla 2019, *Annual Conference* Trinidad-Tobago 2017, *Annual Conference* Montego Bay (Jamaica) 2016, *World Forum on Energy Regulation (WFER)* Istanbul (Turkey) 2015, *Annual Conference* Turks-Caicos 2015.
Members Full regulatory bodies in the Caribbean. Associate non-Caribbean regulators. Full (12):
Angola, Bahamas, Barbados, Belize, Dominica, Guyana, Jamaica, St Lucia, Trinidad-Tobago, Turks-Caicos, Virgin Is UK, Virgin Is USA.
Included in the above, 1 regional body included in this Yearbook:
Eastern Caribbean Telecommunications Authority (ECTEL, #05237).
NGO Relations Member of (1): *International Confederation of Energy Regulators (ICER, #12859).* [2023/XJ4639/**D***]

♦ Organisation catholique canadienne pour le développement et la paix / see Development and Peace
♦ Organisation catholique internationale du cinéma et de l'audiovisuel (inactive)
♦ Organisation Catholique de Solidarité Internationale / see Fondation internationale pour le développement au service des coopérants et de communautés de base (#09821)
♦ Organisation centrale pour une paix durable (inactive)
♦ Organisation de la CEPGL pour l'énergie des pays de grands lacs (no recent information)
♦ Organisation chrétienne internationale des Médias (#12563)
♦ Organisation commerciale du cacao de la Communauté européenne (inactive)
♦ Organisation of Commonwealth Associations (inactive)
♦ Organisation du Commonwealth pour la science de la défense (inactive)
♦ Organisation of Commonwealth United Nations Associations (inactive)
♦ Organisation de la Communauté Européenne des ravitailleurs de navires / see European Ship Suppliers Organization (#08478)
♦ Organisation commune africaine et mauricienne (inactive)
♦ Organisation commune de lutte antiacridienne et de lutte antiaviaire (inactive)
♦ Organisation pour la communication en Afrique et de promotion de la cooperation économique internationale / see Organisation camerounaise de promotion de la coopération économique internationale
♦ Organisation de la conférence islamique / see Organisation of Islamic Cooperation (#17813)
♦ Organisation des congrès latinoaméricains d'anesthésiologie (inactive)

♦ Organisation Conjointe de Coopération en Matière d'Armement (OCCAR) 17801

Business Development Officer PO Box 2107, 53011 Bonn, Germany. T. +4922855020. Fax +492285502100. E-mail: occar.questions@occar.int.
URL: http://www.occar.int/

History Established 12 Nov 1996, Strasbourg (France), with pre-legal status, as *Organisme conjoint de coopération en matière d'armement*, by an Administrative Arrangement between Defence Ministers of France, Germany, Italy and UK. Formally established by ratification of the OCCAR Convention that came into force, 28 Jan 2001, giving OCCAR its own legal personality. Also referred to in English as *Organisation for Joint Armament Cooperation.* Joined OCCAR: Belgium in 2003; Spain in 2005. Programme Participating States (without being member states) are: Finland; Netherlands; Poland; Lithuania; Turkey; Luxembourg (via Belgium in A400M programme). **Aims** Facilitate and manage collaborative European *armament* programmes through their life cycle, as well as technology demonstrator programmes. **Structure** Board of Supervisors; Corporate Committees; Programme Boards; Programme Committees; Executive Administration. **Languages** English, French, German, Italian. **Staff** 309.00 FTE, paid. **Finance** Central Office's corporate work financed by member states; Programme Divisions and Central Office support to programmes financed by Programme Participating States. **Activities** Projects/programmes.
Members Governments of 6 countries:
Belgium, France, Germany, Italy, Spain, UK.
Non-member programme Participating States (6):
Finland, Lithuania, Luxembourg, Netherlands, Poland, Türkiye.
IGO Relations *European Air Transport Command (EATC, #05853); European Union Aviation Safety Agency (EASA, #08978); European Commission (EC, #06633); European Defence Agency (EDA, #06895); NATO Support and Procurement Agency (NSPA).* [2022/XD8586/**D***]

♦ Organisation pour la conservation du saumon de l'Atlantique Nord (#17574)
♦ Organisation consultatif juridique Afrique-Asie (#01303)
♦ Organisation continentale latinoaméricaine des étudiants / see Organización Continental Latinoamericana y Caribeña de Estudiantes (#17834)
♦ Organisation de coopération des associations nordiques des droits de la femme (inactive)
♦ Organisation pour la coopération des chemins de fer (#17803)
♦ Organisation de coopération et de développement économiques (#17693)
♦ Organisation de coopération dans le domaine des produits chimiques de petit tonnage (inactive)
♦ Organisation pour la coopération économique internationale (inactive)
♦ Organisation de coopération éducative (unconfirmed)

♦ Organisation for Cooperation, Exchange And Networking among Students (OCEANS) 17802

Pres c/o GIZ and partners, Rue de la Charité 33, 1210 Brussels, Belgium. E-mail: info@oceans-network.eu.
URL: http://www.oceans-network.eu/

History Mar 2010. Former names and other names: *OCEANS Network* – alias. **Aims** Foster exchange of international experiences, transfer of knowledge and professional development by creating a long-lasting link and access to intercultural and practical information among members from all participating countries. **Structure** Annual General Meeting. Network run by students and alumni. **Languages** English. **Finance** Funded by: *European Commission (EC, #06633).* **Activities** Events/meetings. **Events** *Annual General Meeting*

Bangkok (Thailand) 2019, *Annual General Meeting* Tallinn (Estonia) 2017, *Annual General Meeting* Berlin (Germany) 2013, *Annual General Meeting* Warsaw (Poland) 2012, *Annual General Meeting* New York, NY (USA) 2011. **Publications** *Oceans Network Newsletter*, *The Wave* – official magazine. **Members** Individuals. Membership countries not specified. [2022/XM4159/v/**E**]

- ♦ Organisation de la coopération de l'industrie des roulements à bille (inactive)
- ♦ Organisation de la Coopération Islamique (#17813)
- ♦ Organisation pour la coopération des pays socialistes dans le domaine des télécommunications et communications postales (inactive)

♦ Organisation for Cooperation between Railways (OSJD) 17803

Organisation pour la coopération des chemins de fer – Organisation für die Zusammenarbeit der Eisenbahnen (OSShD) – Organizacija Sotrudnicestva Zeleznyh Dorog (OSZD)

Chairman ul Hoza 63/67, 00-681 Warsaw, Poland. T. +48226573600. E-mail: osjd@osjd.org.pl.
Sec address not obtained.
URL: https://osjd.org/

History 28 Jun 1956, Sofia (Bulgaria). Established by decision of 1st Conference of Ministers of Transport of the Socialist Countries. Statutes approved by governments participating at the conference. Activities commenced 1 Sep 1957, following 2nd Ministerial Conference, May-Jun 1957, Beijing (China). Statutes amended: 19-22 Jun 1962, Ulaanbaatar, at 7th Ministerial Conference; 8 Jun 1993, Warsaw (Poland), at 21st session of the Ministerial Conference, when associate membership was extended to companies and organizations involved in railway activities. Latest amendments, concerning structural organization, adopted at 49th Ministerial Conference, 15-18 Jun 2021, OSJD Commitee, Warsaw, in videoconferencing mode. Former names and other names: *Organization of Railways Cooperation (ORC)* – former. **Aims** Improve standards and cooperation in implementation of railway traffic between countries of Europe and Asia, including transport of goods; improve cooperation on problems related to traffic policy and economic and ecological aspects of railway traffic. Ensure enforcement of conventions and agreements on: Agreement Concerning International Passenger Traffic (SMPS); Agreement Concerning International Freight Traffic by Railway (SMGS); International Passenger Tariff (MPT); International Transit Tariff (MTT); Uniform Transit Tariff (ETT); Rules for the Use of Freight Wagons in International Traffic (PGW); Rules for the Use of Passenger Coaches in International Traffic (PPW); agreements referring to accounting in international transport of passengers and goods and other regulations. Elaborate on general principles for standard international transport law; develop collaboration for the improvement of operation and technical specifications and for developing and updating the international transport routes and corridors; provide solutions to problems in railway transport and develop international collaboration between OSJD members. **Structure** Ministerial Conference is higher authority. *Conference of General Directors of OSJD Railways (see: #17803)* is authority for cooperation between administrations of railways. OSJD Committee (executive body), headed by Chairman and comprising specialists, including representatives of commissions and a governing authority which comprises Chairman, 2 Deputy Chairmen and Secretary. Working bodies (meeting according to Work Schedule): commissions; permanent working groups; ad hoc working groups; expert working groups; joint working groups with other international organisations. **Languages** Chinese, Russian. English and German used in international activities. **Staff** 61.00 FTE, paid. **Finance** Sources: members' dues. **Activities** Events/meetings; knowledge management/information dissemination; standards/guidelines. **Events** *International Interagency Conference on Facilitation of Border Crossing Procedures by Rail* Gdansk (Poland) 2021, *Conference of General Directors* Warsaw (Poland) 2021, *Ministerial Conference* Warsaw (Poland) 2021, *Conference of General Directors* 2020, *Ministerial Conference* Warsaw (Poland) 2020. **Publications** *OSJD Bulletin* (6 a year) in Chinese, English, Russian; *Information Guide-Book* (2 a year) in Chinese, English, German, Russian; *OSJD Activity Report* (annual) in Chinese, English, Russian; *Statistical Bulletin of OSJD Countries on Railway Transport* (annual) in Chinese, English, German, Russian.

Members Ministries of transport or governmental railway administrations of 30 countries:
Afghanistan, Albania, Azerbaijan, Belarus, Bulgaria, China, Cuba, Czechia, Estonia, Georgia, Hungary, Iran Islamic Rep, Kazakhstan, Korea DPR, Korea Rep, Kyrgyzstan, Laos, Latvia, Lithuania, Moldova, Mongolia, Poland, Romania, Russia, Slovakia, Tajikistan, Turkmenistan, Ukraine, Uzbekistan, Vietnam.
Observers (6) in 5 countries:
France, Germany, Greece, Russia, Serbia.
Affiliated enterprises (41) in 20 countries:
Armenia, Austria, Belarus, China, Czechia, Estonia, France, Germany, Hungary, Italy, Kazakhstan, Latvia, Lithuania, Mongolia, Poland, Romania, Russia, Slovakia, UK, Ukraine.

IGO Relations Special agreement with: *Organisation intergouvernementale pour les transports internationaux ferroviaires (OTIF, #17807)*. **NGO Relations** Cooperates with (3): *Comité international des transports ferroviaires (CIT, #04188)*; *European Automobile Engineers Cooperation (EAEC, #06299)*; *Fédération internationale des associations de transitaires et assimilés (FIATA, #09610)*. Joint working groups with: *International Union of Railways (#15813)*. [2023.02.15/XC3025/**C***]

- ♦ Organisation pour la coopération dans la sidérurgie (inactive)
- ♦ Organisation de coopération et de solidarité internationales (internationally oriented national body)
- ♦ Organisation coopérative nordique pour la recherche appliquée (inactive)
- ♦ Organisation des coopératives d'Amérique (inactive)
- ♦ Organisation de coordination et de coopération pour la lutte contre les grandes endémies (inactive)
- ♦ Organisation de coordination et de coopération pour la lutte contre les grandes endémies en Afrique centrale / see Organization of Coordination for the Control of Endemic Diseases in Central Africa (#17860)
- ♦ Organisation de coordination pour la lutte contre les endémies en Afrique centrale (#17860)
- ♦ Organisation cycliste européenne / see European Cyclists' Federation (#06877)
- ♦ Organisation pour défendre les victimes de violence (internationally oriented national body)
- ♦ Organisation démocrate chrétienne d'Amérique (#03899)
- ♦ Organisation démocratique syndicale des travailleurs africains (inactive)
- ♦ Organisation pour le développement global de communautés dans les pays extra-européens (internationally oriented national body)
- ♦ Organisation pour le développement rural et l'éducation rurale des Caraïbes (inactive)
- ♦ Organisation für die Zusammenarbeit der Eisenbahnen (#17803)
- ♦ Organisation für die Zusammenarbeit in der Wälzlagerindustrie (inactive)
- ♦ Organisation de données échangées par télé-transmission en Europe / see Odette International (#17689)

♦ Organisation of Eastern Caribbean States (OECS) 17804

Organisation des Etats des Caraïbes orientales (OECO) – Organización de los Estados del Caribe Oriental (OECO)

Central Secretariat Morne Fortune, PO Box 179, Castries, St Lucia. T. +17584556327. Fax +17584531628. E-mail: oecs@oecs.int – km@oecs.int.
URL: https://www.oecs.org/

History 18 Jul 1981. Established on signature of the *Treaty of Basseterre* by 7 Eastern Caribbean countries which agreed to cooperate with each other and promote unity and solidarity among Members. Following the collapse of the *West Indies Federation (inactive)* the governments of the Eastern Caribbean States created *West Indies Associated States Council of Ministers (WISA, inactive)*, in Sep 1966 and *East Caribbean Common Market (ECCM, inactive)*, in Jun 1968, prior to the signing of the Treaty of Basseterre. Establishment of the OECS is predicated on the recognition of the need of the Eastern Caribbean States for a more formal arrangement to assist with post-independence development efforts and is motivated by: a common determination to strengthen links among themselves; uniting their efforts and resources; establishing and strengthening common institutions which could serve to increase their bargaining power. A proposed sub-group, *Eastern Caribbean Islands Confederation (inactive)*, has not yet come into existence. All OECS Member State are members of *Caribbean Community (CARICOM, #03476)* and assume the same membership status in both organizations. **Aims** As a major institutional player at the regional level, assist in development of Member States by: assisting them to maximize the benefits from their collective space; facilitating their integration with the global economy; contributing to policy and programme formulation and execution in respect of national, regional and international issues and serving as a channel for bilateral and multilateral cooperation. Promote cooperation among Member States and at the regional and international levels; promote unity and solidarity among Member States and defend their sovereignty, territorial integrity and independence; seek to achieve the fullest possible harmonization of foreign policy among Member States; seek to adopt as far as possible common positions on international issues and establish and maintain wherever possible arrangements for joint overseas representation and/or common services. **Structure** Authority of Heads of Government (meets twice a year), comprising Heads of Government, is the supreme decision-making body with Chairmanship changing every year, rotating alphabetically, according to country name. Committees (4): Foreign Affairs Committee, comprising Ministers responsible for foreign affairs in their respective governments; Defence and Security Committee, comprising Ministers and Plenipotentiaries responsible for coordinating collective defence and security efforts; Economic Affairs Committee, responsible for promoting economic integration and development; Legal Affairs Committee, concerned with harmonization of the laws of Member States. Secretariat, comprising 4 Divisions. Director General (Chief Executive Officer) is responsible to the Authority for the functioning of the Secretariat and other OECS institutions. Overseas Diplomatic Missions: Brussels (Belgium), Ottawa ON (Canada), Geneva (Switzerland), Morocco. **Languages** English, French. **Staff** 163 FTE, including Diplomatic Missions. **Finance** Sources: members' dues.

Activities The agreement establishing OECS incorporates ECCM provisions, including common external tariff and free trade among member states. Particular attention is paid to intra-regional trade: all intra-OECS trade barriers were removed by 1 Jan 1988, creating a single market. Discussions continue with CARICOM on establishment of *CARICOM Single Market and Economy (CSME, #03575)*. Further, in 2001, activities of the organization have been geared towards creation of an OECS Economic Union among its Member States. Instrumental in setting up: *Eastern Caribbean Supreme Court (ECSC, #05236)*.
Secretariat carries out activities through 5 divisions:
– 1. Office of the Director General – including economic union activities; legal affairs; functional cooperation and programme management; oversees diplomatic missions; internal audit.
– 2. Economic Affairs and Regional Integration Division – trade matters; external economic negotiations; macro-economic policy; export development; statistics; tourism; agriculture and other sectoral areas.
– 3. Human and Social Division – education; health; youth development; pharmaceutical services; social policy development.
– 4. Environmental Sustainability Division – environmental management; climate change and disaster risk management; bio-diversity and eco-systems; oceans governance and fisheries; sustainable energy.

Events *OECS economic union – furthering implementation of the common tourism policy* Dominica 2014, *Regional Validation Workshop on Agro-Tourism* St Kitts-Nevis 2014, *The social sector* St Kitts-Nevis 2014, *Meeting of Ministers of Education* Antigua-Barbuda 2013, *Meeting* Brades (Montserrat) 2013. **Publications** *List of New Additions* (12 a year). *OECS Information Handbook*. Promotional brochure.

Members Full; Associate: governments of 11 States (" represents Associate members):
Anguilla (*), Antigua-Barbuda, Dominica, Grenada, Guadeloupe (*), Martinique (*), Montserrat, St Kitts-Nevis, St Lucia, St Vincent-Grenadines, Virgin Is UK (*).

IGO Relations Formal agreement with: *UNESCO (#20322)*; *FAO (#09260)*. Special agreement with: *UNIDO (#20336)*. Memorandum of Understanding with: *Agency for International Trade Information and Cooperation (AITIC, #00553)*. Under Lom Conventions, links with: *European Commission (EC, #06633)*. Observer to General Assembly of: *United Nations (UN, #20515)*. Permanent observer status with: *World Intellectual Property Organization (WIPO, #21593)*. Observer to: *Caribbean Regional Fisheries Mechanism (CRFM, #03547)*. Member of: *Caribbean Aviation Safety and Security Oversight System (CASSOS, #03462)*; *Sistema Económico Latinoamericano (SELA, #19294)*. Affiliate member of: *Caribbean Tourism Organization (CTO, #03561)*. Permanent Observer to: *ECOSOC (#05331)*. Works closely with: *Caribbean Centre for Development Administration (CARICAD, #03468)*. **NGO Relations** Founding member of: *Caribbean Digital Library Consortium (no recent information)*. Partner of: *Rainwater Partnership (no recent information)*. Participates in: *Global Island Partnership (GLISPA, #10436)*. Natural Resources Management Unit collaborates in: *Consortium of Caribbean Universities for Natural Resource Management (CCUNRM, no recent information)*. [2022/XF4346/**D***]

♦ Organisation of Eastern Caribbean States/Competitive Business Unit (OECS/CBU) 17805

Head of Unit PO Box 769, 4th Floor Financial Centre, Kennedy Ave, Roseau, Dominica. T. +17674482240. Fax +17674485554. E-mail: cbu@oecs.int.
URL: http://www.oecs.org/

History 1 Nov 1997, Dominica, as *Export Development and Agricultural Diversification Unit (EDADU)* by *Organisation of Eastern Caribbean States (OECS, #17804)*. Comprises the previous *'Agricultural Diversification Coordinating Unit (ADCU)'* and *Eastern Caribbean States Export Development Agency (ECSEDA, inactive)*. Adopted title *Organisation of Eastern Caribbean States/Export Development Unit (OECS/EDU)*, 2000. Rebranded with current title, 2014. **Aims** Act as the primary sub-regional institution of the member states for the development, promotion and expansion of exports through the mobilization of technical and financial *support* for agri-business, services and manufacturing *private sector*, play an advocacy role to member Governments and Public Sector agencies. **Structure** Head of Unit supported by Technical Specialists. **Languages** English. **Finance** Projects financed by international Donor Community, primarily: *European Union (EU, #08967)*; *Canadian International Development Agency (CIDA, inactive)*. Other projects previously also founded by: *United States Agency for International Development (USAID)*. **Activities** Guidance/assistance/consulting. **Publications** *INFOCUS – EDU News*. **Members** Members and associate members of OECS. **IGO Relations** Cooperates with: *Caribbean Development Bank (CDB, #03492)*; *Centre for the Development of Enterprise (CDE, inactive)*; *Eastern Caribbean Central Bank (ECCB, #05231)*; *European Commission (EC, #06633)*; *FAO (#09260)*; *International Trade Centre (ITC, #15703)*; *United States Agency for International Development (USAID)*. Member of: *Caribbean Community (CARICOM, #03476)*. Assisted by: *Caribbean Agricultural Research and Development Institute (CARDI, #03436)*. Partner of: *Caribbean Export Development Agency (Caribbean Export, #03501)*; *Inter-American Institute for Cooperation on Agriculture (IICA, #11434)*. **NGO Relations** Cooperates with: *Association of Eastern Caribbean Exporters (AECE, no recent information)*; *Caribbean Association of Industry and Commerce (CAIC, #03448)*; national chambers of commerce in the region; other business support organizations. [2019.12.02/XK2031/**E***]

- ♦ Organisation of Eastern Caribbean States/Export Development Unit / see Organisation of Eastern Caribbean States/Competitive Business Unit (#17805)
- ♦ Organisation for Economic Co-operation and Development (#17693)
- ♦ Organisation des éditeurs nordiques (meeting series)
- ♦ Organisation of Educational Cooperation (unconfirmed)
- ♦ Organisationen Världens ungdomar mot klimat förändringar (inactive)
- ♦ Organisation der Erdölexportierenden Länder (#17881)
- ♦ Organisation des Etats africains et malgaches (inactive)
- ♦ Organisation des Etats d'Afrique, des Caraïbes et du Pacifique (#17796)
- ♦ Organisation des Etats Américains (#17629)
- ♦ Organisation des Etats des Caraïbes orientales (#17804)
- ♦ Organisation des Etats centroaméricains (inactive)
- ♦ Organisation des Etats ibéroaméricains pour l'éducation, la science et la culture (#17871)
- ♦ Organisation pour l'étude phyto-taxonomique de la région méditerranéenne (#17884)
- ♦ Organisation d'études inter-territoires d'Afrique occidentale (inactive)
- ♦ Organisation EUREKA / see Eureka Association (#05621)
- ♦ Organisation Europäischer Hersteller von Kupfergusslegierungen (#17866)
- ♦ Organisation Europäischer Regional-Luftverkehrsgesellschaften / see European Regions Airline Association (#08347)
- ♦ Organisation of European Aluminium Refiners and Remelters (inactive)
- ♦ Organisation for European Expert Associations / see EuroExpert (#05678)
- ♦ Organisation d'Europe centrale pour les transports intérieurs (inactive)
- ♦ Organisation européenne d'affineurs d'alliages cuivreux (#17866)
- ♦ Organisation européenne pour l'agrément technique / see European Organisation for Technical Assessment (#08103)
- ♦ Organisation européenne des associations militaires / see European Organisation of Military Associations and Trade Unions (#08099)
- ♦ Organisation européenne des bardeaux bitumés (inactive)
- ♦ Organisation européenne pour la biologie cellulaire (inactive)
- ♦ Organisation européenne de biologie du développement (inactive)

- ♦ Organisation européenne de biologie moléculaire (#07816)
- ♦ Organisation européenne des brevets (#08167)
- ♦ Organisation européenne du charbon (inactive)
- ♦ Organisation européenne du commerce de gros en textile (inactive)
- ♦ Organisation européenne des compagnies d'aviation régionales / see European Regions Airline Association (#08347)
- ♦ Organisation européenne des companies pétrolières pour l'environnement, la santé et la sécurité / see Oil Companies' European Association for Environment, Health and Safety in Refining and Distribution (#17708)
- ♦ Organisation européenne des companies pétrolières pour la protection de l'environnement et de la santé / see Oil Companies' European Association for Environment, Health and Safety in Refining and Distribution (#17708)
- ♦ Organisation européenne des conseils d'entreprises en droit, audit, gestion et développement / see European Consultants Unit (#06769)
- ♦ Organisation européenne de coopération économique (inactive)
- ♦ Organisation européenne de développement régional industriel (inactive)
- ♦ Organisation européenne pour l'emballage et l'environnement (#08110)
- ♦ Organisation européenne environnementale citoyenne de normalisation / see Environmental Coalition on Standards (#05499)
- ♦ Organisation européenne pour l'équipement de l'aviation civile / see EUROCAE (#05652)
- ♦ Organisation européenne pour l'équipement électronique de l'aviation civile / see EUROCAE (#05652)
- ♦ Organisation européenne pour l'évaluation de la conformité (inactive)
- ♦ Organisation Européenne pour l'évaluation technique (#08103)
- ♦ Organisation Européenne pour l'Exploitation de Satellites Météorologiques (#08096)
- ♦ Organisation européenne de la Fédération mondiale des employés / see European Organization of the World Organization of Workers (#08116)
- ♦ Organisation européenne de l'habillement et du textile / see EURATEX – The European Apparel and Textile Confederation (#05616)
- ♦ Organisation européenne des industries des confitures et conserves de fruit (inactive)
- ♦ Organisation européenne des industries de la conserve de légumes (inactive)
- ♦ Organisation européenne des industries de la conserve de tomates / see European Organisation of Tomato Industries (#08104)
- ♦ Organisation européenne des industries de la tomate (#08104)
- ♦ Organisation Européenne des Industries Transformatrices de Fruits et Légumes (#06049)
- ♦ Organisation européenne pour l'information géographique (#08964)
- ♦ Organisation européenne pour la lutte contre les maladies circulatoires (no recent information)
- ♦ Organisation européenne des maladies rares / see EURORDIS – Rare Diseases Europe (#09175)
- ♦ Organisation européenne des mécaniciens navigants (inactive)
- ♦ Organisation Européenne et Méditerranéenne pour la Protection des Plantes (#07773)
- ♦ Organisation européenne de Mettray (#07790)
- ♦ Organisation européenne pour la mise au point et la construction des lanceurs d'engins spatiaux (inactive)
- ♦ Organisation européenne de l'organisation mondiale des travailleurs (#08116)
- ♦ Organisation européenne des ports maritimes communautaires / see European Sea Ports Organisation (#08453)
- ♦ Organisation européenne de la probation / see Confederation of European Probation (#04530)
- ♦ Organisation européenne des producteurs de mortiers / see European Mortar Industry Organization (#07822)
- ♦ Organisation européenne pour la promotion des nouvelles techniques et procédés de construction (inactive)
- ♦ Organisation européenne pour la promotion du tourisme équestre (inactive)
- ♦ Organisation européenne de la propriété agricole / see European Landowners' Organization (#07639)
- ♦ Organisation européenne de la propriété rurale (#07639)
- ♦ Organisation européenne de la protection du crédit textile (inactive)
- ♦ Organisation européenne pour la protection des droits des détenus (internationally oriented national body)
- ♦ Organisation européenne provisoire de télécommunications par satellite / see European Telecommunications Satellite Organization (#08896)
- ♦ Organisation européenne pour la qualité (#08112)
- ♦ Organisation Européenne des Radioamateurs (#08320)
- ♦ Organisation européenne pour la recherche nucléaire (#08108)
- ♦ Organisation européenne pour des recherches astronomiques dans l'hémisphère austral (#08106)
- ♦ Organisation européenne pour les recherches chimiosensorielles (#06527)
- ♦ Organisation européenne de recherches spatiales / see European Space Research and Technology Centre (#08802)
- ♦ Organisation européenne de recherches spatiales (inactive)
- ♦ Organisation européenne pour la recherche et le traitement du cancer (#08101)
- ♦ Organisation européenne des sciences de la vie (inactive)
- ♦ Organisation européenne des scieries (#08114)
- ♦ Organisation européenne pour la sécurité de la navigation aérienne / see EUROCONTROL (#05667)
- ♦ Organisation européenne de télécommunications par satellite (#08896)
- ♦ Organisation européenne des unions de foyers et services pour jeunes travailleurs (inactive)
- ♦ Organisation européenne des unions pour l'insertion et le logement des jeunes travailleurs (no recent information)
- ♦ Organisation de l'évaluation internationale du cycle de combustion nucléaire (inactive)
- ♦ Organisation des Fabricants de Produits Cellulosiques Alimentaires (no recent information)
- ♦ Organisation des facultés, écoles et départements d'odontologie de l'Union des universités de l'Amérique latine (#17837)
- ♦ Organisation faîtière du transport routier international à température dirigée / see Transfrigoroute International (#20213)
- ♦ Organisation des fédérations d'employeurs et des employeurs dans les pays en voie de développement (inactive)
- ♦ Organisation des femmes rurales nordiques (inactive)
- ♦ Organisation des femmes scientifiques du Tiers-Monde (#17890)
- ♦ Organisation ferroviaire régionale de la CEN-SAD (see: #04406)
- ♦ Organisation de Flora Europaea / see Euro+Med PlantBase (#05732)
- ♦ Organisation für Flora Europaea / see Euro+Med PlantBase (#05732)
- ♦ Organisation pour Flora Neotropica (#17868)
- ♦ Organisation du génome humain (#10968)
- ♦ Organisation gestose (#17869)

♦ Organisation pour l'Harmonisation en Afrique du Droit des Affaires (OHADA) 17806

Organization for the Harmonization of Business Law in Africa – Organización para la Armonización en Africa del Derecho Mercantil – Organização para a Harmonização em Africa do Direito dos Negócios

Permanent Sec BP 10071, Yaoundé, Cameroon. T. +23722210905 – +23722212612. Fax +23722216745. E-mail: secretariat@ohada.org.
URL: http://www.ohada.org/

History Established 17 Oct 1993, on signing of Treaty Port Louis (Mauritius); treaty revised 17 Oct 2008, Québec QC (Canada). **Aims** Promote regional integration and economic growth through: harmonization of business law of member states; promotion of arbitration as a means of settling contractual disputes; training of legal officers; research on business law. **Structure** Conference of Heads of State and of Government; Council of Ministers; Common Court of Justice and Arbitration (CCJA), in Abidjan (Côte d'Ivoire); Permanent Secretary Office in Yaoundé (Cameroon); Regional Training and Research Center for Legal Officers (ERSUMA) in Porto-Novo (Benin). **Languages** English, French, Portuguese, Spanish. **Finance** States contributions (annual). Other sources: loans concluded in conventions signed with State or international organizations; gifts; legacies. **Activities** Standards/guidelines; research/documentation; training/education; events/meetings. **Events** *African conference on international commercial law* Douala (Cameroon) 2011. **Publications** *Jurisprudence Compendium*. Official journals.

Members States (17):
Benin, Burkina Faso, Cameroon, Central African Rep, Chad, Comoros, Congo Brazzaville, Congo DR, Côte d'Ivoire, Equatorial Guinea, Gabon, Guinea, Guinea-Bissau, Mali, Niger, Senegal, Togo.

IGO Relations Partner of:
- *African Development Bank (ADB, #00283)*;
- *African Intellectual Property Organization (#00344)*;
- *African Legal Support Facility (ALSF, #00361)*;
- *African Union (AU, #00488)*;
- *Banque centrale des Etats de l'Afrique de l'Ouest (BCEAO, #03167)*;
- *Banque des Etats de l'Afrique centrale (BEAC, #03169)*;
- *Banque ouest africaine de développement (BOAD, #03170)*;
- *Commission bancaire de l'Afrique centrale (COBAC, #04204)*;
- *Communauté économique et monétaire d'Afrique centrale (CEMAC, #04374)*;
- *Economic Community of West African States (ECOWAS, #05312)*;
- *European Union (EU, #08967)*;
- *Inter-African Conference on Insurance Markets (#11385)*;
- *International Bank for Reconstruction and Development (IBRD, #12317)* (World Bank);
- *International Development Law Organization (IDLO, #13161)*;
- *International Institute for the Unification of Private Law (UNIDROIT, #13934)*;
- *International Monetary Fund (IMF, #14180)*;
- *Investment Climate Facility for Africa (ICF, #15998)*;
- *Organisation internationale de la Francophonie (OIF, #17809)*;
- *UNDP (#20292)*.

NGO Relations Partner of: *Conférence interafricaine de la prévoyance sociale (CIPRES, #04610)*.

[2020/XD7796/**D***]

- ♦ Organisation hydrographique internationale (#13825)
- ♦ Organisation d'hygiène de la Société des Nations (inactive)
- ♦ Organisation ibéroaméricaine de coopération intermunicipale (#17839)
- ♦ Organisation ibéroaméricaine des pilotes (no recent information)
- ♦ Organisation ibéroaméricaine de sécurité sociale (#11028)
- ♦ Organisation des infirmières de la Caraïbe (#03532)
- ♦ Organisation des ingénieurs-conseils des industries du Golfe (#10837)
- ♦ Organisation des institutions supérieures de contrôle des finances publiques des Caraïbes (#03536)
- ♦ Organisation des Institutions Supérieures de contrôle des finances publiques d'Europe (#08115)
- ♦ Organisation interafricaine du café (#11383)
- ♦ Organisation interafricaine pour la qualité de la vie (inactive)
- ♦ Organisation interaméricaine de défense (#11425)
- ♦ Organisation pour l'interdiction des armes chimiques (#17823)
- ♦ Organisation intergouvernementale consultative de la navigation maritime / see International Maritime Organization (#14102)
- ♦ Organisation intergouvernementale de renseignements et de conseils techniques pour la commercialisation des produits de la pêche en Asie et dans le Pacifique (#11497)

♦ Organisation intergouvernementale pour les transports internationaux ferroviaires (OTIF) 17807

Intergovernmental Organisation for International Carriage by Rail (OTIF) – Zwischenstaatliche Organisation für den Internationalen Eisenbahnverkehr (OTIF)

SG Gryphenhübeliweg 30, 3006 Bern, Switzerland. E-mail: secretary.general@otif.org.
Communications Officer address not obtained.
URL: http://www.otif.org/

History Established on coming into force of *Convention Concerning International Carriage by Rail, 1980 (COTIF, 1980)*, of 9 May 1980, when reorganization of statutory bodies dealing with CIM/CIV conventions resulted in an intergovernmental organization with a legal framework in international law. The 1st *International Convention Concerning the Carriage of Goods by Rail (CIM, 1890)* – originally called Bern Convention and later known as CIM – was signed 14 Oct 1890, came into force 1 Jan 1893 and amended in the course of several Revision Conferences (1986, 1905, 1923, 1933, 1952, 1961 and 1970). *International Convention Concerning the Carriage of Passengers and Luggage by Rail (CIV, 1924)* – known as CIV – was signed 23 Oct 1924 and came into force 1928. It was revised in ordinary Revision Conferences (1933, 1952, 1961 and 1970) together with CIM, ie *Revision of the International Conventions Concerning the Carriage of Goods by Rail and of Passengers and Luggage by Rail (CIM, CIV, 1952)*. As the original CIV Convention did not include any provisions on railway liability in the event of death or injury, *Additional Convention Relating to the Liability of the Railway for Death of and Personal Injury (1966)* was signed 26 Feb 1966 and entered into force 1 Jan 1973. The present Convention, COTIF, emerged from the 8th Revision Conference of 9 May 1980 and was signed by all member states of CIM and CIV; it came into force on 1 May 1985 and fundamentally reformed the structure of the Convention, not only setting up OTIF with a legal personality and with OCTI as its permanent Secretariat, but separating institutional provisions (which appear in the Convention proper) from rules on the Contract of Carriage. These latter appeared in two appendices: *'CIV Uniform Rules'* for the carriage of passengers and luggage; *'CIM Uniform Rules'* for the carriage of goods. Subsequent amendments to COTIF/CIV-CIM adopted by the Revision Committee, 14-21 Dec 1989, entered into force 1 Jan 1991, and those adopted on 28-31 May 1990 entered into force 1 Jun 1991. Further amendments to 'CIV Uniform Rules', to 'CIM Uniform Rules' and to the Convention proper are included in *1990 Protocol of December 20, 1990 amending the Convention concerning International Carriage by Rail – COTIF – of May 9, 1980*, entered into force 1 Nov 1996. A new version of COTIF, *Convention Concerning International Carriage by Rail, 1999 (COTIF, 1999)*, extending its application, simplifying rules and adapting them to liberalization of the international market was adopted by the 5th OTIF General Assembly, 3 Jun 1999, Vilnius (Lithuania), and entered into force, 1 Jul 2006. Statutes registered in *'LNTS 4483'*. Former names and other names: *Office central des transports internationaux par chemins de fer (OCTI)* – former (1893 to 1985).

Aims Promote, improve and facilitate international traffic by rail. **Structure** According to COTIF 1999 currently in force, functioning is ensured by the following organs: General Assembly (every 3 years); Administrative Committee (meets at least annually) represents a third of Member States and currently consists of 15 members; Secretary General, elected for a 3-year period, heads Secretariat. Committees: Revision Committee; Committee of Experts on the Transport of Dangerous Goods; Committee of Technical Experts; Rail Facilitation Committee. All committees save Administrative Committee are composed of representatives of all Member States. Secretary General performs Depositary duties and duty of Registrar to Arbitration Tribunal instituted by the Convention, prepares General Assemblies, Committee and Commissions meetings. **Languages** English, French, German. **Staff** 18.00 FTE, paid. A personnel association represents staff. The Administrative Tribunal of the Council of Europe is competent to settle disputes. **Finance** Sources: contributions of member/participating states. Contributions: 2/5 UN percentage; 3/5 length of rail network. Annual budget: 3,500,000 CHF. **Activities** Adapts international law on rail transport to new economic and technical requirements (ATMF, APTU); these Uniform Rules apply to any contract of carriage of passengers (CIV) or goods (CIM) between 2 Member States; CIM can also be applied to carriage between a Member State and a non-Member State if the parties to the contract so agree. Sets up rules for the carriage of dangerous goods (currently about half of all goods accepted for carriage) – 'Regulation concerning the International Carriage of Dangerous Goods by Rail (RID)'; RID Safety Committee has joint meetings with Group of Experts on the Carriage of Dangerous Goods of the UN Economic Commission for Europe, the latter publishing similar regulations for road carriage under *European Agreement Concerning the International Carriage of Dangerous Goods by Road (ADR, 1957)*. Both regulations have been restructured, taking into account the structure of the UN Recommendations on the Transport of Dangerous Goods (model regulations) and their application extended. Organizes Training Courses and workshops on Transport Law, Technical Interoperability and International Transport of Dangerous Goods in respect of Carriage by Rail for administrative and railway staff. Other concerns include: cooperation with

UNIDROIT in preparing for the entry into force of the Luxembourg Protocol to the *UNIDROIT Convention on International Interests in Mobile Equipment (Cape Town convention, 2001)* on matters specific to railway rolling stock; cooperation with UNECE and OSJD to establish a uniform legal system covering rail transport from the Atlantic to the Pacific; more cooperation with the European Commission and the European Rail Agency has been established concerning technical harmonization and interoperability, also with relevance to the technical appendices of COTIF 1999. Elaboration of measures for cross-border rail facilitation. **Events** *General Assembly* Bern (Switzerland) 2021, *Extraordinary General Assembly* Bern (Switzerland) 2019, *General Assembly* Bern (Switzerland) 2019, *General Assembly* Bern (Switzerland) 2018, *General Assembly* Bern (Switzerland) 2015. **Publications** *Bulletin of International Carriage by Rail* (4 a year) in English, French, German; *International Carriage of Dangerous Goods by Rail* (every 2 years) in English, French, German. Convention COTIF (including its 7 Appendices – CIV, CIM, RID, CUV, CUI, APTU, ATMF) in English, French, German; CIV and CIM list of lines of maritime and inland waterway services; CIV and CIM list of railway lines; press-releases.
Members Governments of 50 countries:
Afghanistan, Albania, Algeria, Armenia, Austria, Azerbaijan, Belgium, Bosnia-Herzegovina, Bulgaria, Croatia, Czechia, Denmark, Estonia, Finland, France, Georgia, Germany, Greece, Hungary, Iran Islamic Rep, Iraq, Ireland, Italy, Latvia, Lebanon, Liechtenstein, Lithuania, Luxembourg, Monaco, Montenegro, Morocco, Netherlands, North Macedonia, Norway, Pakistan, Poland, Portugal, Romania, Russia, Serbia, Slovakia, Slovenia, Spain, Sweden, Switzerland, Syrian AR, Tunisia, Türkiye, UK, Ukraine.
Associate Member – government of one country:
Jordan.
Regional entity:
European Union (EU, #08967).
IGO Relations Cooperates with (20): *Central Commission for the Navigation of the Rhine (CCNR, #03687); Economic Cooperation Organization (ECO, #05313); European Union Agency for Railways (#08973); European Union (EU, #08967); Gulf Cooperation Council (GCC, #10826); International Civil Aviation Organization (ICAO, #12581); International Convention on the Harmonization of Frontier Controls of Goods (1982); International Institute for the Unification of Private Law (UNIDROIT, #13934); International Maritime Organization (IMO, #14102); International Transport Forum (ITF, #15725);* National Railway Administration of China (NRA); *OECD (#17693); Organisation for Cooperation between Railways (OSJD, #17803); Organization for Security and Cooperation in Europe (OSCE, #17887); UNCTAD (#20285); United Nations Commission on International Trade Law (UNCITRAL, #20531); United Nations Committee of Experts on the Transport of Dangerous Goods and on the Globally Harmonized System of Classification and Labelling of Chemicals (Committee of Experts on TDG and GHS, #20543); United Nations Economic Commission for Europe (UNECE, #20555); World Customs Organization (WCO, #21350); World Trade Organization (WTO, #21864).* **NGO Relations** Cooperates with (4): *Cargo Rail Europe (#03431); Comité international des transports ferroviaires (CIT, #04188); International Union of Railways (#15813)* (and its regional organizations); *International Union of Wagon Keepers (#15827).*
[2022.11.30/XC0248/**C***]

- ♦ Organisation Internacional de Biofisica Pura y Aplicada / see International Union for Pure and Applied Biophysics (#15808)
- ♦ Organisation internationale de l'Afrique centrale et méridionale contre le criquet nomade (no recent information)
- ♦ Organisation internationale d'aide aux révolutionnaires (inactive)
- ♦ Organisation internationale pour l'aménagement des urgences (#13260)
- ♦ Organisation Internationale pour l'Avancement Politique des Africaines (unconfirmed)
- ♦ Organisation Internationale pour le Bambou et le Rotin (#14234)
- ♦ Organisation internationale de biosystématique des plantes (#14463)
- ♦ Organisation internationale des bois tropicaux (#15737)
- ♦ Organisation internationale des bons templiers / see Movendi International (#16871)
- ♦ Organisation internationale du cacao (#12627)
- ♦ Organisation internationale du café (#12630)
- ♦ Organisation internationale du caoutchouc naturel (inactive)
- ♦ Organisation internationale de catholiques dans les Médias / see International Christian Organisation of the Media (#12563)
- ♦ Organisation internationale de catholiques dans les Médias – Le forum mondial des professionnels et institutions dans le journalisme séculier et religieux / see International Christian Organisation of the Media (#12563)
- ♦ Organisation internationale de centralisation en médecine légale (inactive)
- ♦ Organisation internationale de classification des tapis (no recent information)
- ♦ Organisation internationale des comités pour les recherches psychiques (inactive)
- ♦ Organisation internationale du commerce / see World Trade Organization (#21864)
- ♦ Organisation internationale du commerce (inactive)
- ♦ Organisation internationale du commerce des animaux domestiques (inactive)
- ♦ Organisation internationale du commerce et de la réparation automobiles (inactive)
- ♦ Organisation internationale des commissions de valeurs (#14470)
- ♦ Organisation internationale de conservation des sols (#15560)
- ♦ Organisation internationale des constructeurs d'automobiles (#14455)
- ♦ Organisation internationale contre l'esclavage moderne (unconfirmed)
- ♦ Organisation internationale pour la coopération européenne politique et économique (inactive)
- ♦ Organisation internationale de coopération en évaluation (#14426)
- ♦ Organisation internationale de coopération pour la santé / see Medicus Mundi International – Network Health for All (#16636)
- ♦ Organisation internationale des coopératives industrielles et de services (#14429)
- ♦ Organisation Internationale des Coopératives de Production Industrielles, d'Artisanat et de Services / see International Organisation of Industrial and Service Cooperatives (#14429)
- ♦ Organisation internationale de la dentelle au fuseau et l'aiguille (#12374)
- ♦ Organisation internationale pour le développement durable (internationally oriented national body)
- ♦ Organisation Internationale pour le Développement Intégral de la Femme (internationally oriented national body)
- ♦ Organisation internationale pour le développement de la liberté d'enseignement / see International Organization for the Right to Education and Freedom of Education (#14468)
- ♦ Organisation internationale de développement des ressources indigènes (no recent information)
- ♦ Organisation internationale pour le développement rural (inactive)
- ♦ Organisation internationale de droit du développement (#13161)
- ♦ Organisation internationale pour le droit à l'éducation et la liberté d'enseignement (#14468)
- ♦ Organisation internationale d'échanges culturels (inactive)
- ♦ Organisation internationale d'écologie humaine (inactive)
- ♦ Organisation internationale économique islamique (inactive)
- ♦ Organisation internationale pour l'éducation scientifique et technique (#14469)
- ♦ Organisation internationale pour l'élimination de toute forme de discrimination raciale (#14445)
- ♦ Organisation internationale des employeurs (#14428)
- ♦ Organisation internationale des employeurs industriels / see International Organisation of Employers (#14428)
- ♦ Organisation internationale de l'énergie et des mines (#13274)
- ♦ Organisation internationale pour les energies durables (inactive)
- ♦ Organisation internationale d'épidémiologie animale / see International Society for Veterinary Epidemiology and Economics (#15540)
- ♦ Organisation internationale d'étude du développement humain (inactive)
- ♦ Organisation internationale pour l'étude de l'endurance des cables (#14474)
- ♦ Organisation internationale pour l'étude des langues anciennes par ordinateur (inactive)
- ♦ Organisation internationale d'études de la psychoanalyse (#14663)
- ♦ Organisation internationale d'études statistiques pour les maladies de l'oesophage / see Organisation mondiale d'études spécialisées sur les maladies de l'oesophage (#17818)
- ♦ Organisation internationale pour l'étude des tensions entre groupes (inactive)

♦ Organisation internationale des experts (ORDINEX) 17808

International Organization of Experts – Organización Internacional de Peritos – Internationale Expertenorganisation

International Secretariat 20 rue Bachaumont, 75002 Paris, France. E-mail: info@ordinex.net.
Head Office Rue du conseil général 6, 1205 Geneva, Switzerland.
URL: https://www.ordinex.net/

History 18 Mar 1961, Geneva (Switzerland). New Constitution adopted 10 Oct 1964, Paris (France). Former names and other names: *International Order of Experts and Consultants* – former; *Ordre international des experts-conseils* – former. Registration: Switzerland. **Aims** Meet national and international needs for expertise and advice; promote exchanges between experts and consultants same discipline and different disciplines. **Structure** General Assembly (normally annual, at least every 2 years); Administrative Council (meets twice a year) of 20 to 40 members; Executive Committee of 10; Statutory Commissions (5); Professional Sections (57); National Delegate in each country of membership. **Languages** Arabic, English, French, German, Spanish. **Staff** 1.00 FTE, paid. **Finance** Sources: donations; gifts, legacies; grants; members' dues. **Events** *General assembly / National Assembly* Paris (France) 2002, *General Assembly* Monastir (Tunisia) 2001, *Annual general assembly / National Assembly* Paris (France) 2001, *National Assembly* Paris (France) 2000, *National Assembly* Paris (France) 1999. **Publications** *Bulletin ORDINEX* (3-4 a year) – for members only.
Members Experts or consultants in any field Full; Probationary; Honorary; d'Honneur. Professional Groups. Members in 28 countries:
Algeria, Angola, Austria, Belgium, Benin, Brazil, Cameroon, Canada, Côte d'Ivoire, France, Gabon, Germany, Haiti, Iran Islamic Rep, Italy, Luxembourg, Mali, Mauritania, Monaco, Morocco, Poland, Russia, Singapore, Spain, Switzerland, Tunisia, UK, USA.
Consultative Status Consultative status granted from: *ECOSOC (#05331)* (Roster); *UNIDO (#20336)*. **IGO Relations** Cooperates with: *Council of Europe (CE, #04881)*. Recognized by: *European Commission (EC, #06633)*. Accredited by: *United Nations Office at Vienna (UNOV, #20604)*. Associated with Department of Global Communications of the United Nations. **NGO Relations** Cooperates with: *International Chamber of Commerce (ICC, #12534).*
[2019/XC2323/**C**]

- ♦ Organisation internationale des femmes sionistes (#21030)

♦ Organisation internationale de la Francophonie (OIF) 17809

SG 19-21 av Bosquet, 75007 Paris, France. T. +33144373325. Fax +33145791498. E-mail: vuth@francophonie.org.
Administrator address not obtained.
URL: https://www.francophonie.org/

History 14 Nov 1997, Hanoi (Vietnam). Established at 7th Francophone Summit, on formalization of the existence of *La Francophonie*, following formulation of the intention at the first Summit, 1986, Paris (France). Merged with *Agence intergouvernementale de La Francophonie (inactive)*, 23 Nov 2005, Antananarivo (Madagascar), finalizing the institutional restructurating. **Aims** As indicated in Article 1 of the *'Charte de la Francophonie'* – Aware of the links created among members by their sharing of the *French language* and wishing to use these links in the service of peace, cooperation and development, assist in: installing and developing *democracy*; *conflict prevention* and maintaining the rule of *law* and *human rights*; increasing dialogue among cultures and civilizations; rapprochement among peoples through mutual *understanding*; reinforcing *solidarity* through multilateral cooperative activities in order to promote economic growth.
Structure I. Institutions of La Francophonie (3):
- *Conférence au sommet des chefs d'Etat et de gouvernement des pays ayant le français en partage (Sommet de la Francophonie, #04648);*
- *Conférence ministérielle de la Francophonie (CMF, #04630);*
- *Conseil permanent de la Francophonie (CPF, #04697).*

II. Secretary-General (elected by Summit for 4-year term) acts as political spokesman and official representative of the French-speaking Community.
III. Consultative Assembly: *Assemblée parlementaire de la Francophonie (APF, #02312)*, also recognized as *'Assemblée consultative de La Francophonie'*.
IV. Direct Operators of La Francophonie (4):
- *Agence universitaire de La Francophonie (AUF, #00548);*
- *Université internationale de langue française au service du développement africain à Alexandrie d'Egypte (Université Senghor, #20691);*
- *Association Internationale des Maires et responsables des capitales et métropoles partiellement ou entièrement Francophones (AIMF, #02715);*
- *TV5Monde (TV5, #20269).*

V. Permanent Ministerial Conferences (2):
- *Conférence des ministres de l'éducation des Etats et gouvernements de la Francophonie (CONFEMEN, #04632);*
- *Conférence des ministres de la jeunesse et des sports de la Francophonie (CONFEJES, #04634).*

VI. Regional Offices (6):
- Bureau régional pour l'Afrique centrale et l'océan Indien (BRAC); Bureau régional pour l'Afrique de l'Ouest (BRAO); Bureau régional pour l'Asie et le Pacifique (BRAP); Bureau régional pour les pays de la Caraïbe (BRPC); Bureau régional pour les pays de l'Europe centrale et orientale (BRECO); Bureau régional pour l'océan Indien (BROI).

VII. Subsidiary organizations: (2):
- *Comité international des Jeux de La Francophonie (CIJF, #04178);*
- *Institut de la Francophonie pour le développement durable (IFDD, #11305).*

VIII. Permanent Representations (4):
- New York (RPNY); Geneva (RPG); European Union (RPUE); African Union (RPUA).

IX. Réseaux institutionnels de la Francophonie (RIF) – strategic partner network created 2002:
- *Conférence internationale des barreaux de tradition juridique commune (CIB, #04612);*
- *Association du notariat francophone (ANF, #02836);*
- *Association des institutions supérieures de contrôle ayant en commun l'usage du français (AISCCUF, #02647);*
- Association africaine des Hautes juridictions francophones (AAHJF);
- *Association des ombudsmans et médiateurs de la Francophonie (AOMF, #02839);*
- *Association des hautes juridictions de cassation des pays ayant en partage l'usage du Français (AHJUCAF, #02629);*
- *Association francophone des commissions nationales des droits de l'Homme (AFCNDH, #02608);*
- *Union des Conseils Economiques et Sociaux et Institutions Similaires Francophones (UCESIF);*
- *Réseau francophone des régulateurs des médias (REFRAM, #18885);*
- *Association francophone des autorités de protection des données personnelles (AFAPDP, #02606);*
- Réseau francophone de diffusion du droit (RF2D);
- *Réseau international francophone de formation policière (FRANCOPOL, #18894);*
- *Association internationale des procureurs et poursuivants francophones (AIPPF, #02730);*
- *Réseau des compétences électorales francophones (RECEF, #18869);*
- *Réseau francophone des conseils de la magistrature judiciaire (RFCMJ, #18882).*

Languages French. **Staff** 300.00 FTE, paid. **Finance** Voluntary contributions from member states to *Fonds multilatéral unique (FMU)*. Annual budget: 71,000,000 EUR (2019). **Activities** Events/meetings; politics/policy/regulatory; projects/programmes. Programmes include: *Institut de la Francophonie pour l'éducation et la formation (IFEF, #11306); Observatoire de la Francophonie économique (OFE); Institut de la Francophonie pour le développement durable (IFDD, #11305); Réseau francophone pour l'égalité femme-homme (RF-EFH, #18884).* **Events** *Sommet* Djerba (Tunisia) 2021, *Sommet* Tunis (Tunisia) 2020, *Sommet* Yerevan (Armenia) 2018, *Sommet* Antananarivo (Madagascar) 2016, *Symposium on South-South and Triangular Cooperation* Brussels (Belgium) 2016. **Publications** *La Francophonie en Brèves* (12 a year) – newsletter; *Journal de l'Agence de la Francophonie* (6 a year); *Lettre de l'assemblée parlementaire de la francophonie* (6 a year); *TV5 Info* (6 a year); *Liaison énergie-francophonie* (3 a year); *La Lettre l'Alexandrie* (2 a year). **Information Services** *Echoweb.*
Members Governments of 54 countries and territories:
Albania, Andorra, Armenia, Belgium, Belgium/Wallonia Region, Benin, Bulgaria, Burkina Faso, Burundi, Cambodia, Cameroon, Canada, Cape Verde, Central African Rep, Chad, Comoros, Congo Brazzaville, Congo DR, Côte d'Ivoire, Djibouti, Dominica, Egypt, Equatorial Guinea, France, Gabon, Greece, Guinea, Guinea-Bissau, Haiti, Laos, Lebanon, Luxembourg, Madagascar, Mali, Mauritania, Mauritius, Moldova, Monaco, Morocco, New Brunswick, Niger, North Macedonia, Québec, Romania, Rwanda, Sao Tomé-Principe, Senegal, Seychelles, St Lucia, Switzerland, Togo, Tunisia, Vanuatu, Vietnam.
Associate governments (3):
Cyprus, Ghana, Qatar.
Observer states (23):
Austria, Bosnia-Herzegovina, Costa Rica, Croatia, Czechia, Dominican Rep, Estonia, Georgia, Hungary, Kosovo, Latvia, Lithuania, Mexico, Montenegro, Mozambique, Poland, Serbia, Slovakia, Slovenia, Ukraine, United Arab Emirates, Uruguay.

IGO Relations Permanent observer status with: *World Intellectual Property Organization (WIPO, #21593)*. Observer Status at: *African Commission on Human and Peoples' Rights (ACHPR, #00255)*; *European Union (EU, #08967)*; *International Organization for Migration (IOM, #14454)*. Invited to sessions of: *International Programme for the Development of Communication (IPDC, #14651)*; Provides funding to: *African Centre for Gender (ACG)*. Memorandum of Understanding with: *Agency for International Trade Information and Cooperation (AITIC, #00553)*. Accredited to the Conference of the Parties of: *Secretariat of the United Nations Convention to Combat Desertification (Secretariat of the UNCCD, #19208)*. Accredited by: *United Nations Framework Convention on Climate Change – Secretariat (UNFCCC, #20564)*. Cooperates with: *African Development Bank (ADB, #00283)*; *European Commission (EC, #06633)*; *International Bank for Reconstruction and Development (IBRD, #12317)*; *United Nations Institute for Training and Research (UNITAR, #20576)*.
Cooperation agreement with:
- *Organisation of African, Caribbean and Pacific States (OACPS, #17796)*;
- *Arab League Educational, Cultural and Scientific Organization (ALECSO, #01003)*;
- *Association of Caribbean States (ACS, #02411)*;
- *Commonwealth Secretariat (#04362)*;
- *Community of Sahel-Saharan States (CEN-SAD, #04406)*;
- *Council of Europe (CE, #04881)*;
- *Economic Community of West African States (ECOWAS, #05312)*;
- *ECOSOC (#05331)*;
- *FAO (#09260)*;
- *ILO (#11123)*;
- *Commission de l'Océan Indien (COI, #04236)*;
- *International Institute for Democracy and Electoral Assistance (International IDEA, #13872)*;
- *Islamic World Educational, Scientific and Cultural Organization (ICESCO, #16058)*;
- *Latin Union (UL, inactive)*;
- *League of Arab States (LAS, #16420)*;
- *Office of the United Nations High Commissioner for Human Rights (OHCHR, #17697)*;
- *Organisation of Islamic Cooperation (OIC, #17813)*;
- *Organization of Ibero-American States for Education, Science and Culture (#17871)*;
- *UNCTAD (#20285)*;
- *UNDP (#20292)*;
- *UNESCO (#20322)*;
- *UNHCR (#20327)*;
- *UNICEF (#20332)*;
- *UNIDO (#20336)*;
- *United Nations (UN, #20515)*;
- *World Meteorological Organization (WMO, #21649)*.

NGO Relations As of 2020, Conférence des OING de la Francophonie (COING) accredited 127 organizations, including 57 listed in this Yearbook:
- *Fédération internationale des professeurs de français (FIPF, #09652)*;
- *European Observatory for Plurilingualism (EOP)*;
- *Vues d'Afrique*;
- *Fondation des Alliances Françaises (AF, #09814)*;
- *Réseau International des Chaires Senghor de la Francophonie (#18889)*;
- *Biennale de la langue française (BLF, #03231)*;
- *Caravane des dix mots*;
- *International PEN (#14552)*;
- *Les Anneaux de la Mémoire (#00848)*;
- *Association francophone d'amitié et de liaison (AFAL, #02605)*;
- *Association for the Prevention of Torture (APT, #02869)*;
- *International Service for Human Rights (ISHR, #14841)*;
- *ECPM*;
- *International Federation of ACATs – Action by Christians for the Abolition of Torture (#13334)*;
- *International Catholic Child Bureau (#12450)*;
- *Reporters sans frontières (RSF, #18846)*;
- *International Federation for Human Rights (#13452)*;
- *Community of Sant'Egidio*;
- *Equitas – International Centre for Human Rights Education*;
- *Action internationale pour la paix et le développement dans la région des Grands Lacs, Switzerland (AIPD-GL)*;
- *Avocats Sans Frontières (ASF, #03050)*;
- *Institut du Travail d'Afrique Centrale (ITAC)*;
- *Fédération africaine des associations nationales de parents d'élèves et étudiants (FAPE, #09398)*;
- *PAMOJA West Africa (#18031)*;
- *Groupement des retraités éducateurs sans frontières (GREF)*;
- *IECD*;
- *International Federation of Training Centres for the Promotion of Progressive Education (#13572)*;
- *VIA Don Bosco (#20766)*;
- *Federation for EDucation in Europe (FEDE, #09479)*;
- *Volontariato Internazionale per lo Sviluppo (VIS)*;
- *Comité syndical francophone de l'éducation et de la formation (CSFEF, #04198)*;
- *Village Monde*;
- *Conférence Permanente des Chambres Consulaires Africaines et Francophones (CPCCAF, #04639)*;
- *International Centre of Comparative Environmental Law (#12483)*;
- *Réseau habitat et francophonie (RHF, #18888)*;
- *Positive Planet International (#18465)*;
- *GRET*;
- *Netherlands Food Partnership (NFP)*;
- *Oeuvre d'Orient*;
- *Solidarity Water Europe (SWE)*;
- *Coordination SUD*;
- *International Association of Construction, Urbanism, and Environment and Life Style (COBATY International, #11812)*;
- *Center of Arab Women for Training and Research, Tunis (CAWTAR, #03637)*;
- *Association québécoise des organismes de coopération internationale (AQOCI)*;
- *Alliance pour la Migration, le Leadership et le Développement (AMLD)*;
- *Women in Law and Development in Africa-Afrique de l'Ouest (WiLDAF-AO, #21005)*;
- *International Movement ATD Fourth World (#14193)*;
- *Institut Afrique Monde (IAM)*;
- *Guilde européenne du raid (GER)*;
- *Association générale des intervenants retraités (AGIRabcd)*;
- *Environnement et développement du Tiers-monde (enda, #05510)*;
- *Centre d'étude et de prospective stratégique (CEPS, #03739)*;
- *Association Internationale des Technologistes Biomédicaux (ASSITEB-BIORIF, #02747)*;
- *Fédération des géomètres francophone (FGF, #09591)*;
- *Association internationale des régions francophones (AIRF, #02739)*;
- *Fédération internationale des experts-comptables francophones (FIDEF, #09630)*;
- *Réseau Africain Francophone d'Education Comparée (RAFEC, #18864)*.

Cooperation agreement with: *World Organization of the Scout Movement (WOSM, #21693)*. Partner of: *International Communications Volunteers (ICVolunteers, #12817)*. Supports: *Global Network for Good Governance (GNGG, #10490)*; *International Centre for Trade and Sustainable Development, Geneva (ICTSD, #12524)*. Works with: *Secrétariat international francophone pour l'évaluation environnementale (SIFÉE, #19201)*. Instrumental in setting up: *Centre régional francophone pour l'Europe centrale et orientale, Sofia (CREFECO, #03775)*. Instrumental in setting up and supports: *Association des ombudsmans et médiateurs de la Francophonie (AOMF, #02839)*. Member of: *International Network of Observatories in Cultural Policies (#14299)*; *World Network for Linguistic Diversity (Maaya, #21671)*. [2022/XE3879/**E***]

- ♦ Organisation internationale de l'industrie des arômes alimentaires / see International Organization of the Flavor Industry (#14446)
- ♦ Organisation internationale des institutions supérieures de contrôle des finances publiques (#14478)
- ♦ Organisation Internationale des Intersexués (unconfirmed)
- ♦ Organisation internationale islamique de secours (internationally oriented national body)
- ♦ Organisation internationale de jeunes et étudiants LGBTQ / see International Lesbian, Gay, Bisexual, Transgender, Queer and Intersex Youth and Student Organization (#14032)
- ♦ Organisation internationale de jeunes et étudiants LGBTQI (#14032)
- ♦ Organisation internationale de la jeunesse homosexuelle et lesbienne / see International Lesbian, Gay, Bisexual, Transgender, Queer and Intersex Youth and Student Organization (#14032)
- ♦ Organisation internationale des journalistes (inactive)
- ♦ Organisation internationale du jute (inactive)
- ♦ Organisation internationale de lutte biologique (#14424)
- ♦ Organisation internationale de lutte biologique contre les animaux et les plantes nuisibles / see International Organisation for Biological Control (#14424)
- ♦ Organisation internationale de lutte contre le criquet migrateur africain (inactive)
- ♦ Organisation internationale pour la lutte contre le trachoma / see International Organization Against Trachoma (#14436)
- ♦ Organisation internationale pour la lutte contre le trachome (#14436)
- ♦ Organisation internationale médicale des étudiants sur la population (inactive)
- ♦ Organisation internationale de métrologie légale (#14451)
- ♦ Organisation internationale pour les migrations (#14454)
- ♦ Organisation internationale des mineurs (no recent information)
- ♦ Organisation internationale de mycoplasmologie (#14456)
- ♦ Organisation internationale non-gouvernementale – Corporation INCORVUZ / see International Coordination Council of Educational Institutions Alumni (#12959)
- ♦ Organisation internationale non gouvernementale pour la mise en valeur du patrimoine culturel des pays méditerranéens et autres / see Museum With No Frontiers (#16908)
- ♦ Organisation internationale de normalisation (#14473)
- ♦ Organisation internationale Nouvelle Acropole (#14458)
- ♦ Organisation internationale d'odonto-stomatologie légale (#14448)
- ♦ Organisation internationale de la paléobotanique (#14459)
- ♦ Organisation internationale de parlementaires pour la santé / see International Medical Parliamentarians Organization (#14137)
- ♦ Organisation internationale hors parties Europe 2000 (inactive)
- ♦ Organisation Internationale pour les Pays les Moins Avancés (#14430)
- ♦ Organisation internationale des personnes handicapées (#05097)
- ♦ Organisation internationale de perspective mondiale (#21904)
- ♦ Organisation internationale de physique médicale (#14453)
- ♦ Organisation internationale de placement familial (#13663)
- ♦ Organisation internationale de police criminelle – INTERPOL (#13110)
- ♦ Organisation internationale de la police routière et des transports (no recent information)
- ♦ Organisation internationale des preuves reliées aux ordinateurs (inactive)
- ♦ Organisation internationale pour le progrès (#14653)
- ♦ Organisation internationale pour le progrès industriel, spirituel et culturel (#17872)

♦ Organisation internationale pour la protection des animaux (OIPA) . 17810

International Organization for Animal Protection – Internationale Organisation für den Tierschutz – Organizzazione Internazionale di Protezione Animali

Chairman c/o OIPA Italia, Via G B Brocchi 11, 20131 Milan MI, Italy. T. +3926427882. E-mail: international@oipa.org.
URL: http://www.oipa.org/

History Founded 1981. **Aims** Defend animal rights worldwide.
Members Branches in 26 countries and territories:
Argentina, Australia, Austria, Belgium, Brazil, Canada, Croatia, Czechia, Denmark, Egypt, Finland, France, Germany, Greece, Haiti, Hong Kong, Italy, Japan, Netherlands, Nigeria, Russia, Spain, Sweden, Türkiye, UK, USA.
Consultative Status Consultative status granted from: *ECOSOC (#05331)* (Special); *UNEP (#20299)*. **IGO Relations** Associated with Department of Global Communications of the United Nations. **NGO Relations** Houses secretariat of: *International Doctors – ILDAV (#13186)*. [2020/XC0139/**C**]

- ♦ Organisation internationale de protection civile (#12582)
- ♦ Organisation internationale pour la protection de l'enfance (internationally oriented national body)
- ♦ Organisation internationale pour la protection des oeuvres d'art (inactive)
- ♦ Organisation internationale de psychomotricité / see International Organization of Psychomotricity and Relaxation (#14465)
- ♦ Organisation internationale de psychomotricité et de relaxation (#14465)
- ♦ Organisation internationale de psychophysiologie (#14466)
- ♦ Organisation internationale de radiodiffusion et télévision (inactive)
- ♦ Organisation internationale pour la recherche sur les associations et l'action volontaire (inactive)
- ♦ Organisation internationale de recherche sur la cellule (#12463)
- ♦ Organisation internationale de recherche sur le cerveau (#12392)
- ♦ Organisation internationale de recherche sur les plantes succulentes (#14477)
- ♦ Organisation internationale de recherches navales (#14221)
- ♦ Organisation internationale de recherche du travail du sol (#15562)
- ♦ Organisation internationale pour la réduction des catastrophes (internationally oriented national body)
- ♦ Organisation internationale pour les réfugiés (inactive)
- ♦ Organisation internationale de régies publicitaires (inactive)

♦ Organisation Internationale des Scénographes, Techniciens et Architectes de Théâtre (OISTAT) 17811

International Organisation of Scenographers, Theatre Architects and Technicians

Exec Dir Suite L, Center for Innovation Taipei, No 1 Yumen St, Taipei 10452, Taiwan. T. +886225962294. Fax +886225981647. E-mail: headquarters@oistat.org.
URL: http://www.oistat.org/

History 1968, Prague (Czechia). Founded as *International Organization of Scenographers and Theatre Technicians (IOSTT)* – *Organisation internationale des scénographes et techniciens de théâtre (OISTT)*. Present name adopted by 7th Congress, Apr 1985, Reggio Emilia (Italy). Current statutes adopted 2011. **Aims** Stimulate exchange of ideas and innovations; promote international collaboration in professions which support live performance; promote formation of centres in each country; encourage lifelong learning among live performance practitioners; respect the integrity of all cultures and celebrate diversity as well as the similarities of those who work in support of live performances. **Structure** Congress (every 4 years); Executive Committee; Headquarters. Commissions (6); Sub-commissions (4). **Languages** English. **Staff** 4.00 FTE, paid. **Finance** Sources: members' dues; sale of publications; subsidies. Other sources: project funding. **Activities** Events/meetings. **Events** *By Candlelight Conference* Stockholm (Sweden) 2023, *By Candlelight Conference* Stockholm (Sweden) 2022, *Quadrennial Congress* 2021, *By Candlelight Conference* Stockholm (Sweden) 2021, *By Candlelight Conference* Stockholm (Sweden) 2020. **Publications** *New Theatre Words* – print and digital, in 27 languages; *OISTAT 40 Years*; *One Show, One Audience, One Single Space*; *Scenofest Catalogue*; *Technical Invention Prize Catalogue*; *Theatre Architecture Competition Catalogue*; *Understanding OISTAT-Network of Global Theatre Professionals*; *World Scenography 1975-1990*; *World Scenography 1990-2005*. Annual Report. **Information Services** *Digital Theatre Words* – in 24 languages, with online and desktop version, and mobile applications.
Members OISTAT Centres (30) in 29 countries and territories:
Austria, Belgium, Bulgaria, Canada, China, Cyprus, Czechia, Denmark, Egypt, Finland, France, Georgia, Germany, Hong Kong, Hungary, Japan, Netherlands, Philippines, Poland, Portugal, Russia, Serbia, Slovakia, Spain, Sweden, Taiwan, Türkiye, UK, USA.
Associate (23) in 15 countries and territories:
Argentina, Australia, Belgium, Brazil, China, India, Japan, Kazakhstan, Mexico, Netherlands, Philippines, Russia, Taiwan, UK, USA.
Individuals (49) in 29 countries and territories:
Australia, Bangladesh, Brazil, China, Croatia, Cuba, France, Georgia, Germany, Greece, India, Ireland, Italy, Korea Rep, Kuwait, Netherlands, New Zealand, Nigeria, Norway, Philippines, Romania, Russia, Singapore, South Africa, Spain, Taiwan, Tunisia, Türkiye, USA.
NGO Relations Member of: *International Theatre Institute (ITI, #15683)*. Cooperates with: *International Association of Theatre for Children and Young People (#12225)*; *International Association of Theatre Critics (IATC, #12226)*; *International Federation of Actors (#13337)*; *International Federation for Theatre Research (IFTR, #13570)*; *International University Theatre Association (IUTA, #15831)*; *Société internationale des bibliothèques et des musées des arts du spectacle (SIBMAS, #19475)*; *Union internationale de la marionnette (UNIMA, #20430)*. [2022/XD4904/**C**]

- ♦ Organisation internationale des scénographes et techniciens de théâtre / see Organisation Internationale des Scénographes, Techniciens et Architectes de Théâtre (#17811)
- ♦ Organisation internationale des sciences chimiques pour le développement (#14440)
- ♦ Organisation internationale pour la science et la technique du vide / see International Union for Vacuum Science, Technique and Applications (#15826)
- ♦ Organisation internationale pour les services en matière de population / see PSI (#18555)
- ♦ Organisation internationale du sucre (#15623)
- ♦ Organisation internationale des systèmes pour la surveillance des malformations congénitales / see International Clearinghouse for Birth Defects Surveillance and Research (#12594)
- ♦ Organisation internationale de télécommunications maritimes par satellites / see International Mobile Satellite Organization (#14174)
- ♦ Organisation internationale de télécommunications mobiles par satellite (#14174)
- ♦ Organisation Internationale des Télécommunications par Satellites (#15670)
- ♦ Organisation Internationale des Télécommunications Spatiales Intersputnik (#15976)
- ♦ Organisation internationale du tourisme social (#14889)
- ♦ Organisation internationale des transports à câble (#14481)
- ♦ Organisation internationale du travail (#11123)
- ♦ Organisation internationale des travailleurs de la radio et de la télévision des Amériques (inactive)
- ♦ Organisation internationale du travail – Programme international pour l'abolition du travail des enfants / see International Programme on the Elimination of Child Labour and Forced Labour (#14652)
- ♦ Organisation internationale du travail – Programme international pour l'abolition du travail des enfants et du travail forcé (#14652)
- ♦ Organisation internationale des unions de consommateurs / see Consumers International (#04773)
- ♦ Organisation Internationale de la Vigne et du Vin (#14435)
- ♦ Organisation internationale de virologie comparée (inactive)
- ♦ Organisation für Internationale Wirtschaftsbeziehungen (#17873)
- ♦ Organisation international de recherches et développement sur le caoutchouc (#14771)
- ♦ Organisation interprofessionnelle au service du transport et de la logistique à température dirigée / see Transfrigoroute International (#20213)
- ♦ Organisation interProfessionnelle des Capitales Européennes / see Business European Capital Cities (#03382)

♦ Organisation Intersex International Europe (OII Europe) 17812

Exec Dir Heidelberger Str 63/64, 12435 Berlin, Germany. E-mail: info@oiieurope.org.
URL: https://oiieurope.org/

History 10 Dec 2012, Stockholm (Sweden). Autonomous affiliate of *Organisation Internationale des Intersexués (OII)*. Registration: No/ID: VR 34983, Start date: Aug 2015, Germany, Berlin; EU Transparency Register, No/ID: 805807639961-79, Start date: 19 Oct 2020. **Aims** Work for the protection of intersex persons' human rights in Europe and Central Asia. **Structure** Steering Board; Executive Board; Staff. **Languages** English, French, German, Italian, Russian. Working language is English; materials translated into several languages. **Staff** 6.00 FTE, paid. **Finance** Sources: donations; in-kind support; private foundations. Supported by: national associations; *Sigrid Rausing Trust*. **Events** *Conference* Paris (France) 2023. **Publications** *MyIntersexStory – Personal accounts of intersex people living in Europe* (1st ed 2019) in English – With a text by intersex scholar Janik Bastien Charlebois "On our own terms and in our own words": The value of first person accounts of intersex experience. Annual Report; toolkits for parents, law and policy makers, and allies (in several languages); brochures; Good Practice Map.
Members Organizations (28) in 22 countries and territories:
Austria, Belgium, Bulgaria, Croatia, Cyprus, Finland, Flanders, France, Germany, Greece, Iceland, Ireland, Italy, Malta, Netherlands, Poland, Russia, Serbia, Sweden, Switzerland, Türkiye, UK.
NGO Relations Member of (2): *ILGA-Europe (#11118)*; *ILGA World (International Lesbian, Gay, Bisexual, Trans and Intersex Association, #11120)*. Cooperates with (1): *Heinrich Böll Foundation*. [2022.11.02/AA1144/**D**]

♦ Organisation of Islamic Cooperation (OIC) 17813

Organisation de la Coopération Islamique (OCI) – Organización de Cooperación Islamico

SG PO Box 178, Jeddah 21411, Saudi Arabia. T. +96626515222. Fax +96626512288. E-mail: bo.cabinet@oic-oci.org.
URL: http://www.oic-oci.org/

History 25 Sep 1969, Rabat (Morocco). Established at first Conference of Kings and Heads of State and Government (Islamic Summit Conference). General Secretariat established at 1st Conference of Islamic Foreign Ministers, 23-25 Mar 1970, Jeddah (Saudi Arabia); commenced operations May 1971, Jeddah. OIC Charter approved by 3rd Session of the Foreign Ministers' Conference, Mar 1972, Jeddah. Present Charter adopted at 11th Islamic Summit, 13-14 Mar 2008, Dakar (Senegal). Former names and other names: *Organization of the Islamic Conference (OIC)* – former (25 Sep 1969 to 28 Jun 2011); *Organisation de la conférence islamique (OCI)* – former (25 Sep 1969 to 28 Jun 2011); *Organización de la Conferencia Islamica* – former (25 Sep 1969 to 28 Jun 2011). **Aims** In accordance with OIC Charter: Enhance and consolidate bonds of fraternity and solidarity among member states; safeguard and protect common interests and support legitimate causes of member states and coordinate and unify their efforts in view of the challenges faced by the Islamic world in particular and the international community in general; respect the right of self-determination and non-interference in domestic affairs and respect *sovereignty*, independence and territorial integrity of each member state; ensure active participation of member states in global political, economic and social decision-making processes to secure common interests; reaffirm support for rights of peoples as stipulated in the UN Charter and international law; strengthen intra-Islamic economic and trade cooperation so as to achieve economic integration leading to establishment of an Islamic Common Market; exert efforts to achieve sustainable and comprehensive human development and economic well-being in member states; protect and defend the true image of Islam to combat defamation of Islam and encourage dialogue among civilizations and religions; enhance and develop science and technology, and encourage research and cooperation among member states.
Structure I. Bodies:
- *Islamic Summit of Kings and Heads of States and Governments (#16053)* (every 3 years), also known as *Islamic Summit Conference*;
- *Council of Foreign Ministers (CFM, see: #17813)* (annual);
- Standing Committees (4) – chaired by Kings and Heads of State and Government and set up in accordance with decisions of the Summit or on recommendation of the Council of Foreign Ministers:
- *Al-Quds Committee (#00749)*;
- *Standing Committee for Information and Cultural Affairs (COMIAC, see: #17813)*;
- *Standing Committee for Economic and Commercial Cooperation (COMCEC, #19952)*;
- *OIC Ministerial Standing Committee on Scientific and Technological Cooperation (COMSTECH, #17702)*.
- Executive Committee, comprising Chairmen of current, preceding and succeeding Islamic Summits and Councils of Foreign Ministers, host country of Headquarters of the General Secretariat plus Secretary-General (ex-officio);
- *International Islamic Court of Justice (#13958)*;
- Independent Permanent Human Rights Commission;
- Committee of Permanent Representatives;
- General Secretariat.

II. Subsidiary Organs:
- *Statistical, Economic and Social Research and Training Centre for Islamic Countries (SESRIC, #19971)*;
- *Research Centre for Islamic History, Art and Culture (IRCICA, #18852)*;
- *Islamic University of Technology (IUT, #16055)*;
- *Islamic Centre for Development of Trade (ICDT, #16035)*;
- *International Islamic Fiqh Academy (IIFA, #13960)*;
- *Islamic Solidarity Fund (ISF, #16051)*.

III. Specialized Institutions:
- *Islamic Development Bank (IsDB, #16044)*;
- *Islamic World Educational, Scientific and Cultural Organization (ICESCO, #16058)*;
- *Islamic Broadcasting Union (IBU, #16033)*;
- *Union of OIC News AGencies (UNA, #20467)*;
- *Islamic Commission for Economic, Cultural and Social Affairs (ICECSA, #16038)*;
- *Science Technology and Innovation Organization (STIO)*;
- *Islamic Organization for Food Security (IOFS)*.

IV. Affiliated Institutions:
- *Islamic Chamber of Commerce, Industry and Agriculture (ICCIA, #16036)*;
- *Organization of Islamic Capitals and Cities (OICC, #17875)*;
- *Organization of the Islamic Shipowners' Association (OISA, #17876)*;
- *Islamic Committee for International Crescent (ICIC, #16039)*;
- *Islamic Solidarity Sports Federation (ISSF, #16052)*;
- *World Federation of Arab-Islamic International Schools (inactive)*;
- *Islamic Conference Youth Forum for Dialogue and Cooperation (ICYF-DC, #16040)*;
- *International Union of Muslim Scouts (IUMS, no recent information)*;
- *General Council for Islamic Banks and Financial Institutions (CIBAFI, #10111)*;
- *Federation of Consultants from Islamic Countries (FCIC, #09476)*;
- *Islamic World Academy of Sciences (IAS, #16057)*;
- OIC Computer Emergency Response Team (OIC-CERT);
- *The Standards and Metrology Institute for Islamic Countries (SMIIC, #19947)*;
- *Islamic University in Niger (#16054)*;
- *Islamic University in Uganda (IUIU, #16056)*;
- *International Islamic University Malaysia (IIUM, #13961)*;
- OIC Media Forum (OMF);
- OIC Broadcasting Regulatory Authorities Forum (IBRAF).

V. Proposed Organization:
- *Islamic Civil Aviation Council (ICAC, inactive)*;
- *Islamic States Telecommunications Union (ISTU, inactive)*.

Languages Arabic, English, French. **Staff** 20.00 FTE, paid. **Finance** Budget of General Secretariat and Subsidiary Organs covered by member states according to national income. **Activities** Knowledge management/ information dissemination; politics/policy/regulatory; training/education. **Events** *Annual Islamic Conference of Foreign Ministers* Islamabad (Pakistan) 2022, *Annual Islamic Conference of Foreign Ministers* Niamey (Niger) 2020, *Annual Islamic Conference of Foreign Ministers* Abu Dhabi (United Arab Emirates) 2019, *Session of the Islamic Conference of Health Ministers* Abu Dhabi (United Arab Emirates) 2019, *Triennial Islamic Summit Conference* Makkah (Saudi Arabia) 2019. **Publications** *OIC Newsletter* (weekly); *OIC Journal* (4 a year); *Islamophobia Report* (annual); *OIC Daily News Bulletin*; *OIC Monthly Bulletin*. Books; Special Media Reports.
Members Open to any Muslim state on approval of application by the Conference (" indicates Founding member). Current members, 57 Muslim states:
Afghanistan (*), Albania, Algeria (*), Azerbaijan, Bahrain, Bangladesh (*), Benin, Brunei Darussalam, Burkina Faso, Cameroon, Chad (*), Comoros, Côte d'Ivoire, Djibouti, Egypt (*), Gabon, Gambia, Guinea (*), Guinea-Bissau, Guyana, Indonesia (*), Iran Islamic Rep (*), Iraq, Jordan (*), Kazakhstan, Kuwait (*), Kyrgyzstan, Lebanon (*), Libya (*), Malaysia (*), Maldives, Mali (*), Mauritania (*), Morocco (*), Mozambique, Niger (*), Nigeria, Oman, Pakistan (*), Palestine (*), Qatar, Saudi Arabia (*), Senegal (*), Sierra Leone, Somalia (*), Sudan (*), Suriname, Syrian AR (*), Tajikistan, Togo, Tunisia (*), Türkiye (*), Turkmenistan, Uganda, United Arab Emirates, Uzbekistan, Yemen (*).
Governmental observers, governments of 5 countries and territories:
Bosnia-Herzegovina, Central African Rep, Northern Cyprus, Russia, Thailand.
Muslim regional community observer:
Moro National Liberation Front of the Philippines.
IGO Relations Cooperates with:
- *Arab Common Market (ACM, no recent information)*;
- *Arab Maghreb Union (AMU, #01004)*;
- *Arab Monetary Fund (AMF, #01009)*;
- *Council of Arab Economic Unity (CAEU, #04859)*;
- *Economic Cooperation Organization (ECO, #05313)*;
- *Gulf Cooperation Council (GCC, #10826)*;
- *International Fund for Agricultural Development (IFAD, #13692)*;
- *International Programme for the Development of Communication (IPDC, #14651)*;
- *Organisation internationale de la Francophonie (OIF, #17809)*;
- *Preferential Trade Agreement for North Africa (PTA NA, no recent information)*.
- *UNCTAD (#20285)*;
- *UNIDO (#20336)*.

Observer status with: General Assembly of *United Nations (UN, #20515)*; *International Organization for Migration (IOM, #14454)*; *United Nations Committee on the Exercise of the Inalienable Rights of the Palestinian People (CEIRPP, #20539)*; *World Intellectual Property Organization (WIPO, #21593)*; *World Trade Organization (WTO, #21864)*. Memorandum of Understanding with: *King Abdullah Bin Abdulaziz International Centre for Interreligious and Intercultural Dialogue (KAICIID, #16193)*. Member of: *Intergovernmental Organizations Conference (IGO Conference, #11498)*; *Peace Implementation Council (#18279)* for Bosnia.
Instrumental in setting up:
- *Convention of the Organization of the Islamic Conference on Combating International Terrorism (1999)*;
- *Inter-Islamic Network on Biosaline Agriculture (INBA, #11506)*;
- *Inter-Islamic Network on Genetic Engineering and Biotechnology (INOGE, #11507)*;
- *Inter Islamic Network on Information Technology (INIT, #11508)*;
- *Inter-Islamic Network of Nanotechnology (INN, #11509)*;
- *Inter-Islamic Network on Renewable Energy Sources (INRES, #11510)*;
- *Inter-Islamic Network on Space Sciences and Technology (ISNET, #11511)*;
- *Inter-Islamic Network on Tropical Medicine (INTROM, #11512)*;
- *Inter-Islamic Network on Veterinary Science Research, Khartoum (INVSR)*;
- *Inter-Islamic Network on Water Resources Development and Management (INWRDAM, #11513)*;
- *Inter-Islamic Science and Technology Network on Oceanography (#11514)*;
- *Islamic Solidarity Fund for Development (ISFD, see: #16044)*;
- *Parliamentary Union of the OIC Member States (PUIC, #18220)*.

NGO Relations Observer status with: *Internet Corporation for Assigned Names and Numbers (ICANN, #15949)*. Cooperates with: *FIM-Forum for Democratic Global Governance (FIM, #09761)*. Member of: *Network for Religious and Traditional Peacemakers (#17054)*. [2022/XC4129/**C***]

- ♦ Organisation islamique afro-asiatique (inactive)
- ♦ Organisation islamique internationale (no recent information)
- ♦ Organisation japonaise pour la coopération internationale en matière de planification familiale (internationally oriented national body)
- ♦ Organisation des jeunes et étudiants non-alignés / see Non-Aligned Students, Youth and Civil Societies Organization (#17148)
- ♦ Organisation des jeunes, étudiants et societé civils non-alignés (#17148)
- ♦ Organisation des jeunes filles chrétiennes / see Girls' Brigade International (#10152)
- ♦ Organisation des jeunes socialistes de la Communauté européenne / see Young European Socialists (#21989)
- ♦ Organisation for Joint Armament Cooperation / see Organisation Conjointe de Coopération en Matière d'Armement (#17801)
- ♦ Organisation Latino-Américaine et des Caraïbes du Tourisme (#17845)
- ♦ Organisation latinoaméricaine pour le développement de la pêche (#16335)
- ♦ Organisation latinoaméricaine de l'énergie (#16313)
- ♦ Organisation latinoaméricaine des fabricants de boissons alcooliques (inactive)
- ♦ Organisation latinoaméricaine pour la promotion sociale des aveugles et des déficients visuels (inactive)
- ♦ Organisation latinoaméricaine du vin et du raisin (inactive)
- ♦ Organisation de lutte contre le criquet pèlerin dans l'Est africain (#05042)
- ♦ Organisation Maritime de l'Afrique de l'Ouest et du Centre (#16582)
- ♦ Organisation maritime internationale (#14102)
- ♦ Organisation médicale homéopathique internationale (no recent information)
- ♦ L'Organisation météorologique des Caraïbes (#03524)
- ♦ Organisation météorologique internationale (inactive)
- ♦ Organisation météorologique mondiale (#21649)
- ♦ Organisation des ministres d'éducation de l'Asie du Sud-Est (#19774)

♦ Organisation pour la mise en valeur du fleuve Gambie (OMVG) 17814

Gambia River Basin Development Organization

High Commissioner Immeuble Serign Bassirou Mbacké – Stèle Mermoz, Route de Quakam, BP 2353, CP18524 Dakar, Senegal. T. +221338592880 – +221338592840. Fax +221338642988. E-mail: omvg@omvg.sn.
URL: http://www.omvg.org/

History 30 Jun 1978. Founded by the Governments of Gambia and Senegal. Entered into force 30 Oct 1978. Guinea and Guinea-Bissau joined in 1981 and 1983 respectively. Also referred to in English as *Organization for the Development of the River Gambia.* **Aims** Coordinate rational and harmonious exploitation of the common resources of river basins of the Gambia, Kayanga/Geba and Koliba/Korubal. **Structure** Executive Secretariat; High Commission Departments (4). **Languages** English, French, Portuguese. **Staff** 47.00 FTE, paid. **Finance** Member States' contributions. Annual budget: US$ 4,300,000. **Activities** Research/documentation; guidance/assistance/consulting; research and development; projects/programmes; events/meetings. **Publications** Activity Report (4 a year); Budget (annual).
Members Governments of 4 countries:
Gambia, Guinea, Guinea-Bissau, Senegal.
IGO Relations Cooperates with: *Organisation pour la mise en valeur du fleuve Sénégal (OMVS, #17815).* [2022/XD8972/**D***]

♦ Organisation pour la mise en valeur du fleuve Sénégal (OMVS) 17815

Senegal River Development Organization
High Commissioner Rocade Fann Bel-air Cerf-volant, BP 3152, Dakar, Senegal. T. +221338598182. Fax +221338640163. E-mail: omvssphc@omvs.org.
URL: http://www.omvs.org/
History Founded 11 Mar 1972, Nouakchott (Mauritania), by Presidents of Mali, Mauritania and Senegal, to replace *Organization of Senegal Riparian States – Organisation des Etats riverains du Sénégal (OERS),* set up 2 Mar 1968, Labé, and also referred to in English as *Organization of Senegal River States.* OERS was an enlargement of a 'Comité inter-Etats' – established 26 Jul 1963, Bamako (Mali), by *Convention relative à l'aménagement du Bassin du fleuve Sénégal.* It superseded *Mission d'aménagement du fleuve Sénégal (MAS, inactive),* which was created by the French colonial administration in 1934 and which a joint organization in 1959, linking Senegal, Mauritania and Mali (the latter withdrew on independence). Current *Convention concerning the Status of the Senegal River* and *Convention establishing the Senegal River Development Organization* (adopted 13 Mar 1972) suspended the Bamako Convention of 26 Jul 1963 and the Dakar Convention of 7 Feb 1964. Convention amended: 17 Dec 1975; 21 Dec 1978; 11 Dec 1979. Also referred to in English as *Organization for the Development of the Senegal River.* **Aims** Promote cooperation among the riparian states of the Senegal *River* in the management and development of its resources. **Structure** Conference of Heads of State and Government; Council of Ministers (meeting twice a year); High Commissioner; Water Standing Commission; Infrastructure Management Agencies. **Languages** French. **Finance** Contributions from member Governments; donations; subsidies; grants. **Activities** Research and development; projects/programmes. **Events** *Session Ordinaire de la Conférence des Chefs d'Etat et de Gouvernement* Bamako (Mali) 2019, *Session Ordinaire de la Conférence des Chefs d'Etat et de Gouvernement* Conakry (Guinea) 2017, *Session Ordinaire de la Conférence des Chefs d'Etat et de Gouvernement* Conakry (Guinea) 2015, *Session Ordinaire de la Conférence des Chefs d'Etat et de Gouvernement* Nouakchott (Mauritania) 2013, *Session Ordinaire de la Conférence des Chefs d'Etat et de Gouvernement* Nouakchott (Mauritania) 2003. **Publications** *PMVS Le Journal* in French – newsletter. Studies; reports. **Information Services** *Centre de Documentation et d'Archivage de l'OMVS (CDA).*
Members Governments of 3 countries:
Mali, Mauritania, Senegal.
IGO Relations Special agreement with: *UNIDO (#20336).* Member of: *Intergovernmental Organizations Conference (IGO Conference, #11498).* [2016.09.28/XD3036/**E***]

- ♦ Organisation du Monde Islamique pour l'Education (#16058)
- ♦ Organisation mondiale de l'accordéon (inactive)
- ♦ Organisation mondiale Agudath Israel (#00584)
- ♦ Organisation mondiale des anciens et anciennes élèves de l'enseignement catholique / see Organisation mondiale des anciens élèves de l'enseignement catholique (#17816)

♦ Organisation mondiale des anciens élèves de l'enseignement catholique (OMAEC) 17816

World Organization of Former Students of Catholic Education – Organización Mundial de Antiguos Alumnos de la Educación Católica
Gen Sec Via Aurelia 476, 00165 Rome RM, Italy. E-mail: secretariogeneral@omaec.info.
Admin Office 48 Rue de Richelieu, 75001 Paris, France.
URL: http://omaec.info/
History 14 Oct 1967, Rome (Italy). Founded during 3rd Congress of the Apostolate of Laics, a study Commission having been set up following the Eucharistic Congress 1960, Munich (Germany FR). New Statutes adopted by Extraordinary General Assembly, 28 Sep 1992, Venice (Italy). Former names and other names: *Organisation mondiale des anciens et anciennes élèves de l'enseignement catholique (OMAEC)* – former; *World Organization of Former Pupils of Catholic Education* – former; *Organización Mundial de Antiguos Alumnos y Antiguas Alumnas de la Enseñanza Católica* – former. Registration: France. **Aims** Participate in affirmation and diffusion of *Evangelical* education and freedom of education, respecting different religious convictions; promote creation of world alumni congregations; serve associate organizations and encourage relationships based on understanding, mutual support and spiritual values; stimulate global commitment and cooperation of alumni, safeguarding dignity and service of the community without distinction, according to the principles of Christian education. **Structure** General Assembly (annual); Executive Council; Regional Organizations: *European Union of Former Pupils of Catholic Education (#08992);* Union Africana de Exalumnos de la Educación Católica; Union Americana de Exalumnos de la Educación Católica; Union of Alumni of Catholic Education of America (UNAEC). Former regional organizationn: *Unión Latinoamericana de Exalumnos Católicos (ULAAEC, no recent information).* **Languages** English, French, Spanish. **Staff** Voluntary. **Finance** Sources: members' dues. **Activities** Advocacy/lobbying/activism; awareness raising; knowledge management/information dissemination; religious activities. **Events** *General Assembly* Rome (Italy) 2020, *Congress* Rome (Italy) 2017, *General Assembly* Rome (Italy) 2017, *General Assembly* Paris (France) 2016, *General Assembly* Paris (France) 2014. **Publications** *Bulletin de l'OMAEC* (2 a year). Information brochures; notes; declarations.
Members Full members: national bodies open to all associations of former pupils of Catholic education in their country; international bodies (world unions or confederations) which group former students of educational establishments attached to a religious congregation or order. National associations in 18 countries:
Argentina, Cameroon, Congo Brazzaville, France, Hungary, India, Italy, Japan, Lebanon, Madagascar, Malta, Mexico, Peru, Portugal, Senegal, Spain, Thailand, Togo.
World organizations (5):
Federation of Alumni of Schools of the Tertiary Mercederian Sisters of the Child Jesus; *Union mondiale des anciens élèves Lasalliens (UMAEL, #20462); World Association of Alumnae of the Sacred Heart (#21116); World Confederation of Don Bosco Past Pupils Associations (no recent information); World Union of Jesuit Alumni and Alumnae (WUJA, #21877).*
Corresponding members in 18 countries:
Bolivia, Botswana, Chad, Congo Brazzaville, Congo DR, Côte d'Ivoire, Cuba, Dominican Rep, Ecuador, Eswatini, Guatemala, Holy See, Lesotho, Mozambique, Namibia, Panama, South Africa, Venezuela.
Included in the above, one regional organization:
European Parliament (EP, #08146).
Consultative Status Consultative status granted from: *ECOSOC (#05331)* (Special); *UNESCO (#20322)* (Consultative Status); *UNICEF (#20332).* **IGO Relations** Accredited by (1): *United Nations Office at Vienna (UNOV, #20604).* **NGO Relations** Member of (5): *Committee of NGOs on Human Rights, Geneva (#04275); Conference of Non-Governmental Organizations in Consultative Relationship with the United Nations (CONGO, #04635); Forum of Catholic Inspired NGOs (#09905); NGO Committee on the Status of Women, Geneva (#17117); NGO Committee on UNICEF (#17120).* [2021.03.03/XA4159/y/**A**]

♦ Organisation mondiale des associations pour l'éducation prénatale (OMAEP) 17817

World Organization for Prenatal Education
Pres Solomou Str 31, 106 82 Athens, Greece. E-mail: prenatalgr@hotmail.com.
Founding Pres address not obtained.
URL: http://www.omaep.com/
History 23 Oct 1991, Besançon (France). Registered in accordance with French law. **Aims** Promote prenatal education worldwide. **Structure** Executive Council, comprising President, Founding President, Vice-President, Secretary, Treasurer and one member. **Languages** French. **Staff** 7.00 FTE, voluntary. **Finance** Members' dues. Other sources: income from activities (congress, seminars). **Activities** Supports and coordinates the actions of the national associations; promotes the creation of new associations; organizes training sessions and seminars. **Events** *Congress on the prenatal experience* Parma (Italy) 2008, *World congress / Congress* Lausanne (Switzerland) 2007, *Congress* Athens (Greece) 2004, *Congress* Caracas (Venezuela) 2001, *Congress* Rome (Italy) 1998.
Members National organizations (16) in 16 countries:
Belgium, Bolivia, Bulgaria, Canada, Colombia, Congo Brazzaville, France, Germany, Greece, Italy, Latvia, Portugal, Romania, Spain, Switzerland, Venezuela.
Consultative Status Consultative status granted from: *ECOSOC (#05331)* (Special). [2017/XM0845/**D**]

- ♦ Organisation mondiale de l'autisme (#21211)
- ♦ Organisation mondiale des bouddhistes (#21501)
- ♦ Organisation mondiale du cheval arabe (#21102)
- ♦ Organisation mondiale des cités et gouvernements locaux unis (#21695)
- ♦ Organisation mondiale coiffure (#21550)
- ♦ Organisation mondiale des collèges nationaux, académies et associations académiques des généralistes et des médecins de famille / see World Organization of Family Doctors (#21690)
- ♦ Organisation mondiale du commerce (#21864)
- ♦ Organisation mondiale des congrès d'isolation acoustique thermique et acoustique (#21591)
- ♦ Organisation mondiale contre la cécité (#11597)
- ♦ Organisation mondiale contre la torture (#21685)
- ♦ Organisation mondiale de la coopération méditerranéenne pour l'énergie solaire (inactive)
- ♦ Organisation mondiale de cours chrétiens (#21238)
- ♦ Organisation mondiale de design (#21358)
- ♦ Organisation mondiale de la diaspora africaine (unconfirmed)
- ♦ Organisation mondiale des douanes (#21350)
- ♦ Organisation mondiale des droits de l'animal (inactive)
- ♦ Organisation mondiale d'éducation en matière aérospatiale (no recent information)
- ♦ Organisation mondiale pour l'éducation préscolaire (#21689)
- ♦ Organisation mondiale de l'emballage (#21705)
- ♦ Organisation mondiale d'endoscopie digestive / see World Endoscopy Organization (#21380)

♦ Organisation mondiale d'études spécialisées sur les maladies de l'oesophage (OESO) 17818

World Organization for Specialized Studies on Diseases of the Esophagus
Exec Dir 2 Bd Pershing, 75017 Paris, France. T. +33155379015. Fax +33155379040. E-mail: michele.liegeon@oeso.org.
URL: http://www.oeso.org/
History 1979, as *International Organization for Statistical Studies on Diseases of the Esophagus – Organisation internationale d'études statistiques pour les maladies de l'oesophage.* **Aims** Carry out international prospective statistical studies on epidemiology and various treatments of diseases of oesophagus. **Structure** Board of Trustees; Permanent Scientific Committee. Officers: President; Past-President; President-Elect; Vice-President; Secretary; Treasurer. Standing Committees (5): Membership and Nominating; Congresses; Finance; Research; Education and Informatics. **Finance** Members' dues. **Events** *World Conference* Vienna (Austria) 2021, *Global perspectives and novel technologies for esophageal diseases the spectrum of dysphagias* Beijing (China) 2019, *Global perspectives in esophageal diseases* Geneva (Switzerland) 2017, *The esophagiome* Monte Carlo (Monaco) 2015, *World Conference* Paris (France) 2013.
Members Individuals in 31 countries and territories:
Argentina, Austria, Belgium, Brazil, Canada, Chile, China, Ecuador, France, Germany, Greece, Hong Kong, Hungary, India, Italy, Japan, Monaco, Netherlands, Poland, Portugal, Puerto Rico, Romania, Saudi Arabia, Serbia, South Africa, Spain, Sweden, Switzerland, Türkiye, UK, USA. [2020/XD8076/v/**D**]

- ♦ Organisation Mondiale des Experts (unconfirmed)
- ♦ Organisation mondiale des experts-conseils-arbitres (internationally oriented national body)
- ♦ Organisation mondiale de la famille (#21399)
- ♦ Organisation mondiale de la famille (inactive)
- ♦ Organisation mondiale pour les familles (no recent information)
- ♦ Organisation mondiale de gastroentérologie (#21536)
- ♦ Organisation mondiale de l'image et du son (inactive)
- ♦ Organisation mondiale pour l'information sur le don d'organes ou de tissus humains (inactive)
- ♦ Organisation mondiale des jeunes contre le changement climatique (inactive)
- ♦ Organisation mondiale de la jeunesse espérantiste / see Tutmonda Esperantista Junulara Organizo (#20268)
- ♦ Organisation Mondiale de la Jeunesse Espérantophone (#20268)
- ♦ Organisation mondiale de labourage (#21731)
- ♦ Organisation mondiale des lettons libres (#18250)
- ♦ Organisation mondiale des médecins indépendants (inactive)
- ♦ Organisation mondiale de mères de tous les pays (inactive)
- ♦ Organisation mondiale de la méthode Billings d'ovulation (#21692)
- ♦ Organisation Mondiale du Mouvement Scout (#21693)
- ♦ Organisation Mondiale de la Nature (inactive)
- ♦ Organisation mondiale de navimodélisme et de sport nautique (#21691)
- ♦ Organisation mondiale des observations volcaniques (#21696)
- ♦ Organisation mondiale des orchestres d'harmonie et ensembles à vents (#21197)
- ♦ Organisation mondiale paix, assistance et secours (internationally oriented national body)
- ♦ Organisation mondiale des parlementaires contre la corruption (#10518)
- ♦ Organisation mondiale pour le potentiel humain (#11292)

♦ Organisation mondiale de la presse périodique (OMPP) 17819

World Organization of the Periodical Press (WOPP)
Pres Avenue Albert 271, 1190 Brussels, Belgium. T. +3225390369. Fax +323447098. E-mail: ompp@skynet.be.
URL: http://www.presse-periodique-monde.be/
History 1960, Brussels (Belgium). Reportedly ceased to exist on death of Dr Emile-Gaston Peeters. 2006, re-registered as an international association. Registration: Crossroads Bank for Enterprises, No/ID: 0418.715.742, Start date: 28 Jun 1978, Belgium, Brussels; Crossroads Bank for Enterprises, No/ID: 0880.195.420, Start date: 23 Mar 2006, Belgium, Brussels. **Aims** Establish permanent world-wide contact among members of the periodical press; create in all countries a national branch under the patronage of a well known representative of the press; maintain and strengthen the position and influence of the periodical press. **Activities** Events/meetings. **Events** *General Assembly* Hélécine (Belgium) 1999, *General Assembly* Namur (Belgium) 1996, *Annual General Assembly* Brussels (Belgium) 1989. **Publications** *World Periodical Press News* (4 a year). **NGO Relations** *European Institute of Ecology and Cancer (inactive); International Diplomatic Correspondents Association (inactive); International Federation of Scientific Research Societies (inactive).* [2022.10.19/XF1905/s/**F**]

- ♦ Organisation mondiale de la profession enseignante (inactive)
- ♦ Organisation mondiale pour la promotion sociale des aveugles (inactive)
- ♦ Organisation mondiale de la propriété intellectuelle (#21593)
- ♦ Organisation mondiale de la santé (#20950)
- ♦ Organisation mondiale des sourds juifs (inactive)
- ♦ Organisation mondiale pour la systémique et la cybernétique (#21686)

♦ Organisation mondiale du thermalisme (OMTh) 17820

World Hydrothermal Organization – Organización Mundial del Termalismo – Welt Organisation des Thermalismus – Organizzazione Mondiale del Termalismo

Main Office Palazzo Terme, via Vittorio Emanuele, 38056 Levico Terme TN, Italy. E-mail: info@omth.com.

URL: http://www.sithomth.com/

History 1977, Chaudfontaine (Belgium). Founded on the initiative of *Société internationale de technique hydrothermale (SITH, #19497)*, in close collaboration with: *Association européenne de médecine thermale et bioclimatologie (AEMThB, inactive)*; *Comité international interdisciplinaire de Bolzano (CIIB, no recent information)*; *Commission for Balneological Institutes of the European Socialist Countries (inactive)*; *International Society of Medical Hydrology and Climatology (ISMH, #15254)*; *Latin American Federation of Thermalism and Climatism (FLT, no recent information)*. **Aims** Promote recognition of *hydrotherapy*, climatotherapy and psammatotherapy and other natural cures in countries where these are already in existence or about to be developed; assure the rational and growing development of this curative and social activity. **Structure** General Assembly (annual). Executive Committee, consisting of President, Vice-Presidents, Secretary-General and Treasurer. **Languages** English, French, German, Italian, Japanese, Russian, Spanish. **Staff** Head office staff paid; volunteers (about 100) worldwide. **Finance** Members' dues. **Activities** Organizes: global workshops for presentation of scientific, technical and economic research; development projects. Cooperates in: congresses of founder members; post-university inter-professional courses; research centres. **Events** *Annual Congress* Brazil 2009, *Annual Congress* Cuntis (Spain) 2008, *Annual Congress* Trento (Italy) 2005, *Annual Congress* Pereira (Colombia) 2001, *Annual Congress* Marrakech (Morocco) 1994. **Publications** Congress proceedings.

Members in 23 countries:
Argentina, Austria, Belgium, Bolivia, Brazil, Bulgaria, Chile, Cuba, Czechia, France, Germany, Greece, Hungary, Ireland, Italy, Japan, Mexico, Peru, Romania, Russia, Spain, Türkiye, Venezuela.

Represented in a further 31 countries:
Albania, Algeria, Armenia, Australia, Azerbaijan, Benin, Canada, Colombia, Ecuador, Egypt, Georgia, Iran Islamic Rep, Israel, Kazakhstan, Kyrgyzstan, Lithuania, Luxembourg, Mongolia, Morocco, Panama, Paraguay, Poland, Slovakia, Switzerland, Tajikistan, Tunisia, Turkmenistan, UK, Ukraine, USA, Uzbekistan.

IGO Relations Close collaboration with: *World Tourism Organization (UNWTO, #21861)*. Contacts with: *WHO (#20950)*; *UNESCO (#20322)*; *FAO (#09260)*. [2019/XD2056/**D**]

- ♦ Organisation Mondiale du Tourisme (#21861)
- ♦ Organisation mondiale du tourisme et de l'automobile (inactive)
- ♦ Organisation mondiale des travailleurs (#21697)
- ♦ Organisation pour les musées, les monuments et les sites d'Afrique (no recent information)
- ♦ Organisation des Nations Unies pour l'alimentation et l'agriculture (#09260)
- ♦ Organisation des Nations Unies pour le développement industriel (#20336)
- ♦ Organisation des Nations Unies pour l'éducation, la science et la culture (#20322)
- ♦ Organisation naturiste espérantiste internationale (#14220)
- ♦ Organisation néerlandaise pour la coopération internationale au développement / see Oxfam Novib

♦ Organisation non Gouvernementale des Cercles Nationaux de Réflexion sur la Jeunesse (ONG CNRJ) 17821

Contact 66 av des Champs Elysées, 75008 Paris, France. T. +33890212808.

Contact address not obtained.

History 15 Mar 2011, Paris (France). Registration: No/ID: 20180015, Start date: 14 Apr 2018, France. **Aims** Work towards a *youth* capable of observing, thinking and acting on their own. **Structure** General Assembly; Presidency; Board of Directors. **Languages** English, French, German. **Staff** 10000.00 FTE, voluntary. **Finance** Sources: donations. **Activities** Advocacy/lobbying/activism; projects/programmes. **Publications** *La lettre mensuelle*; *Le speculum Universalis*. **Members** Individuals (about 10,000). Membership countries not specified. **Consultative Status** Consultative status granted from: *ECOSOC (#05331)* (Special). **NGO Relations** National organizations. [2018.09.06/XM5936/**C**]

- ♦ Organisation nord-américaine pour la protection des plantes (#17567)
- ♦ Organisation des Nordatlantikvertrags (#16945)
- ♦ Organisation nordique de coopération du personnel des instituts de santé mentale (inactive)
- ♦ Organisation nordique pour la distribution des oeufs (inactive)
- ♦ Organisation nordique des entrepreneurs peintres (inactive)
- ♦ Organisation nordique des fonctionnaires des douanes (#17540)
- ♦ Organisation nordique de graveurs (inactive)
- ♦ Organisation nordique des jeunes (#17476)
- ♦ Organisation nordique de liaison pour les pêcheurs (inactive)
- ♦ Organisation nordique des personnes âgées actives (inactive)
- ♦ Organisation nordique pour les procédés d'affaires (inactive)
- ♦ Organisation nordique des sports pour handicappés (inactive)
- ♦ Organisation nordique des voyages populaires (inactive)
- ♦ Organisation för de Nordiska Systemansvariga Nätföretagen (inactive)
- ♦ Organisation oncologique méditerranéenne d'enseignement et de recherche (inactive)
- ♦ Organisation OTAN d'entretien et d'approvisionnement / see NATO Support and Procurement Agency (#16948)
- ♦ Organisation OTAN de normalisation (inactive)
- ♦ Organisation Ouest Africaine de la santé (#20881)
- ♦ Organisation Ouest africaine de la sécurité routière (#20896)
- ♦ Organisation pour la paix au service de la renaissance africaine (internationally oriented national body)
- ♦ Organisation pour la paix et le sport (internationally oriented national body)
- ♦ Organisation Panafricaine des Agriculteurs (#18049)
- ♦ Organisation pan africaine pour le développement durable (#18057)
- ♦ Organisation panafricaine des femmes (#18074)
- ♦ Organisation panafricaine de lutte contre le SIDA / see Organisation PanAfricaine de Lutte pour la Santé (#17822)
- ♦ Organisation Pan Africaine de Lutte contre le SIDA / see Organisation panafricaine de lutte pour la santé

♦ Organisation PanAfricaine de Lutte pour la Santé (OPALS) 17822

Pan African Health Organization

Exec Dir 15/21 rue de l'Ecole de Médecine, 75006 Paris, France. T. +33145420825 – +331(33661727870. E-mail: programmes@opals.asso.fr.

URL: http://www.opals.asso.fr/

History 12 Sep 1988, Paris (France). Former names and other names: *Organisation panafricaine de lutte contre le SIDA (OPALS)* – former; *Pan African AIDS Organization* – former. Registration: France. **Aims** Work towards realization of the Millennium Development Goals, specifically reducing maternal and infant mortality in Sub-Saharan Africa and fighting against AIDS, tuberculosis, malaria and other infectious diseases; ameliorate access to care of *women* and *children* living in Sub-Saharan Africa; rehabilitate and equip *patient* care centres; train physicians and other medical personnel in the field; assist media involved in HIV prevention campaigns; establish links between African and European medical centres. **Structure** Executive Board; Administrative Office in Paris (France); on the ground themes. **Languages** English, French. **Staff** 27.00 FTE, paid. **Finance** Sources: contributions; fundraising; grants. Support from French institutions, French NGOs and United Nations Agencies. **Activities** Capacity building; guidance/assistance/consulting; training/education. **Events** *Workshop* Libreville (Gabon) 1990, *Pan-African workshop* Mbabane (Swaziland) 1988. [2021.08.31/XF0715/**F**]

- ♦ Organisation panafricaine de lutte pour la santé (internationally oriented national body)
- ♦ Organisation panafricaine de la profession enseignante (no recent information)
- ♦ Organisation panafricaine de la propriété intellectuelle (unconfirmed)
- ♦ Organisation panaméricaine de la santé (#18108)
- ♦ Organisation Patronale des Capitales Europeennes / see Business European Capital Cities (#03382)
- ♦ Organisation des pays arabes exportateurs de pétrole (#17854)
- ♦ Organisation des pays exportateurs de pétrole (#17881)
- ♦ Organisation des pêches de l'Atlantique Nord-Ouest (#17606)
- ♦ Organisation des peuples et des nations non représentés (#20714)
- ♦ Organisation des ports maritimes européens (#08453)
- ♦ Organisation de la presse africaine (#00424)
- ♦ Organisation pour la prévention de la cécité (internationally oriented national body)
- ♦ Organisation des producteurs du Commonwealth (inactive)
- ♦ Organisation des Producteurs de Pétrole Africains (#00414)

♦ Organisation for the Prohibition of Chemical Weapons (OPCW) 17823

Organisation pour l'interdiction des armes chimiques (OIAC) – Organización para la Prohibición de las Armas Quimicas (OPAQ)

Dir Gen Johan de Wittlaan 32, 2517 JR The Hague, Netherlands. T. +31704163300. Fax +31703063535. E-mail: public.affairs@opcw.org.

URL: http://www.opcw.org/

History 29 Apr 1997, The Hague (Netherlands). On entry into force of the *Convention on the Prohibition of the Development, Production, Stockpiling and Use of Chemical Weapons and on Their Destruction (CWC, 1992)*. The Convention, also referred to as *'Chemical Weapons Convention'*, was adopted by *Conference on Disarmament (CD, #04590)* on 3 Sep 1992, Geneva (Switzerland), after approval by the General Assembly of the *United Nations (UN, #20515)*; was opened for signature in Jan 1993, Paris (France); and entered into force on 29 Apr 1997. Prior to the Convention coming into force, administration was covered by *Preparatory Commission for the Organization for the Prohibition of Chemical Weapons (inactive)*. **Aims** Oversee implementation of the Chemical Weapons *Convention*; provide a forum for consultation and cooperation among states party to the Convention and for international cooperation in the peaceful uses of chemistry; provide states party to the Convention with assistance and protection against the use or threat of use of chemical weapons. **Structure** Principal organ: *Conference of States Parties of the Organization for the Prohibition of Chemical Weapons (see: #17823)*, meeting in annual session, always in The Hague (Netherlands), and in special sessions convened as necessary, comprises representatives of all member states. Executive Council comprises 41 representatives elected from among member states on a rotating basis for 2-year terms. Technical Secretariat in The Hague assists the Conference and the Executive Council, and carries out verification activities provided for in the Convention and other functions entrusted to it under the CWC or delegated to it by the Conference and Executive Council. It consists of 9 Divisions: Administration; External Relations; Inspectorate; Internal Oversight; International Cooperation and Assistance; Legal; Policy Making Organs; Strategy and Policy; Verification. *OPCW Equipment Store and Laboratory (no recent information)* inaugurated, 11 Sep 1996, Rijswijk (Netherlands). **Languages** Arabic, Chinese, English, French, Russian, Spanish. **Staff** Technical Secretariat: over 400 staff from over 80 member states, including over 100 inspectors. *Administrative Tribunal of the International Labour Organization (ILO Tribunal, #00118)* is competent to settle disputes. **Finance** Sources: contributions of member/participating states. Annual budget: 65,529,600 EUR (2018). **Activities** Chemical Weapons Convention is a comprehensive disarmament and non-proliferation treaty aiming to eliminate an entire class of weapons of mass destsruction, banning the development, production, stockpiling, acquisition, retention, transfer and use of chemical weapons, and including mechanisms for international verification of compliance. It also provides for destruction of chemical weapons and related production facilities in all States Parties to the Convention, under international supervision within a specific time-frame. Compliance is verified through a combination of detailed declaration requirements, routine inspections of declared chemical weapons and chemical industry facilities, plus short notice challenge inspections at any time, at any place under the jurisdiction or control of any party to the Convention. **Events** *States Parties Conference Session* The Hague (Netherlands) 2023, *States Parties Conference Session* The Hague (Netherlands) 2022, *States Parties Conference Session – 2nd Part* The Hague (Netherlands) 2021, *States Parties Conference Session* The Hague (Netherlands) 2021, *States Parties Conference Session – 1st Part* The Hague (Netherlands) 2020. **Publications** Annual Report; fact sheets; speeches; statements.

Members States Parties to the Convention as of 14 Sep 2018 – governments of 193 countries and territories:
Afghanistan, Albania, Algeria, Andorra, Angola, Antigua-Barbuda, Argentina, Armenia, Australia, Austria, Azerbaijan, Bahamas, Bahrain, Bangladesh, Barbados, Belarus, Belgium, Belize, Benin, Bhutan, Bolivia, Bosnia-Herzegovina, Botswana, Brazil, Brunei Darussalam, Bulgaria, Burkina Faso, Burundi, Cambodia, Cameroon, Canada, Cape Verde, Central African Rep, Chad, Chile, China, Colombia, Comoros, Congo Brazzaville, Congo DR, Cook Is, Costa Rica, Côte d'Ivoire, Croatia, Cuba, Cyprus, Czechia, Denmark, Djibouti, Dominica, Dominican Rep, Ecuador, El Salvador, Equatorial Guinea, Eritrea, Estonia, Eswatini, Ethiopia, Fiji, Finland, France, Gabon, Gambia, Georgia, Germany, Ghana, Greece, Grenada, Guatemala, Guinea, Guinea-Bissau, Guyana, Haiti, Holy See, Honduras, Hungary, Iceland, India, Indonesia, Iran Islamic Rep, Iraq, Ireland, Italy, Jamaica, Japan, Jordan, Kazakhstan, Kenya, Kiribati, Korea Rep, Kuwait, Kyrgyzstan, Laos, Latvia, Lebanon, Lesotho, Liberia, Libya, Liechtenstein, Lithuania, Luxembourg, Madagascar, Malawi, Malaysia, Maldives, Mali, Malta, Marshall Is, Mauritania, Mauritius, Mexico, Micronesia FS, Moldova, Monaco, Mongolia, Montenegro, Morocco, Mozambique, Myanmar, Namibia, Nauru, Nepal, Netherlands, New Zealand, Nicaragua, Niger, Nigeria, Niue, North Macedonia, Norway, Oman, Pakistan, Palau, Palestine, Panama, Papua New Guinea, Paraguay, Peru, Philippines, Poland, Portugal, Qatar, Romania, Russia, Rwanda, Samoa, San Marino, Sao Tomé-Principe, Saudi Arabia, Senegal, Serbia, Seychelles, Sierra Leone, Singapore, Slovakia, Slovenia, Solomon Is, Somalia, South Africa, Spain, Sri Lanka, St Kitts-Nevis, St Lucia, St Vincent-Grenadines, Sudan, Suriname, Sweden, Switzerland, Syrian AR, Tajikistan, Tanzania UR, Thailand, Timor-Leste, Togo, Tonga, Trinidad-Tobago, Tunisia, Türkiye, Turkmenistan, Tuvalu, Uganda, UK, Ukraine, United Arab Emirates, Uruguay, USA, Uzbekistan, Vanuatu, Venezuela, Vietnam, Yemen, Zambia, Zimbabwe. [2023/XB0057/**B***]

- ♦ Organisation de la propriété industrielle de l'Afrique anglophone / see African Regional Intellectual Property Organization (#00434)
- ♦ Organisation Protestante orthodoxe de film / see International Interchurch Film Organization (#13943)
- ♦ Organisation "Racisme Islamophobia Watch" (unconfirmed)
- ♦ Organisation de radiodiffusion des Etats islamiques / see Islamic Broadcasting Union (#16033)
- ♦ Organisation de recherche sur le cerveau des Caraïbes (inactive)
- ♦ Organisation pour la recherche, la communication et l'action en faveur d'un développement solidaire entre le Nord et le Sud (internationally oriented national body)
- ♦ Organisation de recherche scientifique et industrielle du Commonwealth (internationally oriented national body)
- ♦ Organisation de recherches forestières et agricoles de l'Afrique orientale (inactive)
- ♦ Organisation de recherches sur la pêche en eau douce de l'Afrique orientale (inactive)
- ♦ Organisation de recherches sur la pêche en mer pour l'Afrique orientale (inactive)
- ♦ Organisation de recherche sur la trypanosomiase en Afrique orientale (inactive)
- ♦ Organisation régionale africaine de la CISL / see International Trade Union Confederation – African Regional Organization (#15709)
- ♦ Organisation régionale africaine de communications par satellite (#18748)
- ♦ Organisation régionale africaine de normalisation / see African Organisation for Standardisation (#00404)
- ♦ Organisation régionale asiatique de formation et de développement (meeting series)
- ♦ Organisation régionale Asie Pacifique / see Asia Pacific Dental Federation/Asian Pacific Regional Organization of the Fédération Dentaire Internationale (#01882)
- ♦ Organisation Régionale des Compagnies Aériennes Arabes (#00896)
- ♦ Organisation régionale pour la conservation de l'environnement de la mer Rouge et du golfe d'Aden (#18804)
- ♦ Organisation régionale européenne de la FDI (#08345)
- ♦ Organisation régionale de la FDI pour l'Europe / see European Regional Organization of the Fédération dentaire internationale (#08345)
- ♦ Organisation régionale interaméricaine des travailleurs / see Confederación Sindical de Trabajadores y Trabajadoras de las Américas (#04480)
- ♦ Organisation régionale de l'Orient pour l'administration publique (#05249)
- ♦ Organisation régionale orientale pour l'habitation et l'urbanisme (#05248)

♦ Organisation régionale pour les pays d'Afrique du Nord et du Proche-Orient (FID NANE) 17824

Regional Organization for North Africa and Near East

Pres c/o ACML, 181-183 Ahmed Shawky Street, Roushdy, Alexandria, Egypt. T. +2035411109 – +2035411741 – +2035457352. Fax +2035411742 – +2035469470. E-mail: chairman@acml-egypt.com.
URL: http://www.acml-egypt.com/
History Oct 1996, Lisbon (Portugal), as *Commission for North Africa and Near East*, within the framework of *International Federation for Information and Documentation (FID, inactive)*. FID has ceased to exist due to lack of finance although continues to exist formally as a legal entity. **Aims** Assist *libraries* and *information centres* in *Arab* countries, Mali, Chad and Niger and provide the main tools to develop their information systems and services; contribute to the setting up of library and information centre infrastructure in the region. **Structure** Council. **Languages** Arabic, English. **Staff** 2.00 FTE, voluntary. **Finance** Donation from ACML (host organization). **Activities** Capacity building.
Members Individuals (10) representing 5 NANE sub-regions in 24 countries and territories:
Algeria, Bahrain, Chad, Djibouti, Egypt, Iraq, Jordan, Kuwait, Lebanon, Libya, Mali, Mauritania, Morocco, Niger, Oman, Palestine, Qatar, Saudi Arabia, Somalia, Sudan, Syrian AR, Tunisia, United Arab Emirates, Yemen.
NGO Relations Links with a large number of organizations active in the field (not specified).
[2014.06.23/XE2749/v/**E**]

♦ Organisation régionale pour la protection du milieu marin (#18805)
♦ Organisation régionale du tourisme pour l'Afrique australe (#18817)
♦ Organisation des Régions Unies (#20657)
♦ Organisation des relations asiatiques (inactive)
♦ Organisation pour les relations économiques internationales (#17873)
♦ Organisation pour un réseau international d'indications géographique (#17874)

♦ Organisation de la ruralité et du milieu européen (ORME) 17825

Contact address not obtained. E-mail: elo@elo.org.
URL: http://www.elo.org/
History Statutes adopted 24 Jan 1996. Registered in accordance with Belgian law. **Aims** Promote and defend the natural equilibrium of privately-owned rural areas in all aspects: agriculture, forestry, hunting, fishing, heritage, environment, mines and quarries, tourism, energy, social and socio-professional life, rural industry, outdoor sports, water, rural dwellings; establish and support organizations defending *private ownership* of the *countryside*; provide information on European *rural policy* and the management and rational utilization of *rural resources*. **Structure** General Assembly (annual). Steering/Management Committee (Council), including the Bureau which comprises President, Vice-President and 4 Directors chosen for geographical representation. **Languages** Czech, Danish, Dutch, English, Estonian, Finnish, French, German, Hungarian, Irish Gaelic, Italian, Latvian, Lithuanian, Maltese, Polish, Portuguese, Slovakian, Slovene, Spanish, Swedish. **Staff** 14.00 FTE, paid. **Finance** Members' dues. **Events** *Annual Congress* Cork (Ireland) 2004, *Annual Congress* Siracusa (Italy) 2003, *Annual Congress* Seville (Spain) 2002, *Annual Congress* Dresden (Germany) 2001, *Annual Congress* Seville (Spain) 2001. **Publications** *Countryside*. **Members** Full associations in countries of the European Union; Associate associations in other countries. Membership countries not specified. [2011.08.16/XD5688/**D**]

♦ Organisation sanitaire panaméricaine / see Pan American Health Organization (#18108)
♦ Organisation de la santé des Etats du Golfe (inactive)
♦ Organisation pour les sciences marine dans le Pacifique Nord (#17602)

♦ Organisation Scientifique et Technique Internationale de Vol à Voile (OSTIV) 17826

International Scientific and Technical Gliding Organization
Pres Inst für Strömungsmechanik, Hermann-Blenk-Strasse 37, 38108 Braunschweig, Germany. T. +4953139194251. E-mail: president@ostiv.org.
URL: http://www.ostiv.org/
History Founded 27 Jul 1948, Samedan (Switzerland), as successor to *Internationale Studienkommission für Motorlosen Flug (ISTUS, inactive)*, set up 8-10 Mar 1930, Darmstadt (Germany). Sporting activities of ISTUS were at that time taken over by *Fédération aéronautique internationale (FAI, #09397)*. Constitution adopted 3 Aug 1954, Buxton (UK); amended 12 Jun 1965, South Cerney (UK); 29 Jul 1978, Chateauroux (France); 6 Jun 1981, Paderborn (Germany FR); 2 Jul 2015, Braunschweig (Germany). **Aims** Encourage and coordinate internationally the science and technology of soaring and development and use of the sailplane in pure and applied research; improve training methods, design, construction and operation of sailplanes and accessories with a view to increasing proficiency, performance, flying qualities, safety and comfort for the benefit of soaring and *aviation* in general. **Structure** General Conference (at least every 4 years, at Congress); Board; Panels (3). Advisory body of FAI International Gliding Commission. **Languages** English. **Staff** 1.00 FTE, voluntary. **Finance** Sources: members' dues. **Activities** Awards/prizes/competitions; events/meetings; standards/guidelines; training/education. **Events** *Congress* Braunschweig (Germany) 2021, *Congress* Stendal (Germany) 2020, *Congress* Hosin (Czechia) 2018, *Congress* Benalla, VIC (Australia) 2017, *Congress* Leszno (Poland) 2014. **Publications** *Technical Soaring* (4 a year) – with reviewed OSTIV Congress papers; *OSTIV Letter*. *OSTIV Airworthiness Standards for Sailplanes* (1998); *Handbook of Meteorological Forecasting for Soaring Flight*; *Static Stability and Control of Sailplanes* by Piero Morelli.
Members Active national aero clubs (14) which are members of FAI. Scientific/Technical organizations (1) working in the aviation field and interested in furthering sciences and technologies related to soaring. Individual persons, local gliding clubs and libraries (250). Members in 33 countries:
Argentina, Australia, Austria, Belgium, Bulgaria, Canada, China, Czechia, Denmark, Finland, France, Germany, Hungary, Ireland, Italy, Japan, Lithuania, Luxembourg, Monaco, Netherlands, New Zealand, Norway, Poland, Serbia, Slovenia, South Africa, Spain, Sweden, Switzerland, Türkiye, UK, Ukraine, USA. [2019.12.23/XC2615/**C**]

♦ Organisation de la sécurité et la coopération en Europe (#17887)
♦ Organisation des services communs de l'Afrique orientale (inactive)
♦ Organisation sioniste internationale / see World Zionist Organization (#21961)
♦ Organisation sioniste mondiale (#21961)
♦ Organisation socialiste de l'Asie Pacifique (inactive)
♦ Organisation pour la solidarité d'Amérique latine (inactive)
♦ Organisation de solidarité des peuples d'Afrique, d'Asie et d'Amérique latine (#17849)
♦ Organisation de la solidarité des peuples afro-asiatiques (#00537)

♦ Organisation du Sport Africain Travailliste et Amateur (OSTA) 17827

African Workers and Amateurs Sport Organization
SG BP 4550, Nlongkak, Yaoundé, Cameroon. T. +23774443047. Fax +23722212304. E-mail: office@osta-officiel.org.
URL: https://osta-officiel.org/
History 25 Apr 2001, Banjul (Gambia). Former names and other names: *Organisation du Sport du Travail en Afrique (OSTA)* – former (2001); *African Labour Sports Organisation (ALSO)* – former (2001). **IGO Relations** Affiliated with (1): *African Union (AU, #00488)*. **NGO Relations** Member of (1): *Association of African Sports Confederations (AASC, #02360)*. Affiliated with (1): *Association of National Olympic Committees of Africa (ANOCA, #02820)*. [2021/XJ2151/**D**]

♦ Organisation sportive panaméricaine (#18138)
♦ Organisation sportive sudaméricaine (#19708)
♦ Organisation des sports d'Amérique centrale et des Caraïbes (#03665)

♦ Organisation of Sports Federations of Oceania (OSFO) 17828

Contact 48 Partridge Way, Mooroolbark VIC 3138, Australia. T. +61397271779 – +61394170022. Fax +61397275959.
URL: https://www.osfoceania.org/
History Apr 2005, Brisbane, QLD (Australia). Founded during General Assembly of *Oceania National Olympic Committees (ONOC, #17667)*. Constitution adopted 2005; most recent version adopted Mar 2019. Former names and other names: *Olympic Sports Federations of Oceania (OSFO)* – former. **Aims** Promote sport in the Pacific; protect common interests and increase cooperation among member organizations. **Structure** General Assembly (annual); Executive Committee. **Activities** Events/meetings. **Events** *General Assembly* Nadi (Fiji) 2022, *General Assembly* Suva (Fiji) 2015, *General Assembly* Guam 2014, *General Assembly* Nadi (Fiji) 2013, *General Assembly* Suva (Fiji) 2012. **Publications** *OSFO Newsletter*.
Members International organizations (30):
– *Asia-Pacific Rugby League (APRL, #02018)*;
– *Asia Pacific Snooker & Billiards Federation (APSBF)*;
– *Badminton Oceania (BOC, #03059)*;
– *Fédération Internationale de Teqball (FITEQ, #09663)*;
– *Federation of International Touch (FIT, #09680)* (Oceania);
– *FIBA Oceania (#09748)*;
– *FIM Oceania*;
– *FISU Oceania (#09785)*;
– *International Cricket Council (ICC, #13105)* (East Asia-Pacific);
– *International Waterski and Wakeboard Federation (IWWF, #15872)* (Oceania);
– *Oceania Athletics Association (OAA, #17651)*;
– *Oceania Baseball Softball Confederation (WBSC Oceania, #17652)*;
– *Oceania Canoe Association (OCA, #17654)*;
– *Oceania Continent Handball Federation (OCHF, #17657)*;
– *Oceania Cycling Federation (#17659)*;
– *Oceania Fencing Confederation (OFC, #17661)*;
– *Oceania Football Confederation (OFC, #17662)*;
– *Oceania Gymnastics Union (OGU, #17663)*;
– *Oceania Hockey Federation (#17664)*;
– *Oceania Judo Union (OJU, #17665)*;
– *Oceania Rugby (#17672)*;
– *Oceania Sailing Federation (OSAF, #17673)*;
– *Oceania Shooting Federation (OSF, #17674)*;
– *Oceania Swimming Association (#17677)*;
– *Oceania Table Tennis Federation (OTTF, #17678)*;
– *Oceania Tennis Federation (OTF, #17679)*;
– *Oceania Volleyball Federation (#17681)*;
– *Oceania Wrestling Federation*;
– *World Archery Oceania (WAO, #21109)*;
– *World Taekwondo Oceania (WTO, #21846)*.
NGO Relations Partner of (3): *Oceania National Olympic Committees (ONOC, #17667)*; *Oceania Sport Information Centre (OSIC)*; *Pacific Games Council (PGC, #17951)*. [2015/XM0782/y/**D**]

♦ Organisation du Sport du Travail en Afrique / see Organisation du Sport Africain Travailliste et Amateur (#17827)
♦ Organisation sud américaine de l'elevage du pur sang (#17850)
♦ Organisation sud-américaine de recherche sur le cerveau (inactive)
♦ Organisation suisse d'aide aux réfugiés (internationally oriented national body)
♦ Organisation technique de coopération intellectuelle (inactive)
♦ Organisation technique européenne du pneumatique et de la jante (#08962)
♦ Organisation de la télévision ibéroaméricaine / see Organización de Telecomunicaciones de Iberoamérica (#17851)
♦ Organisation territoriale des juifs (inactive)
♦ Organisation pour le timeshare en Europe / see Resort Development Organisation (#18913)
♦ Organisation du tourisme euro-méditerranéen (no recent information)
♦ Organisation touristique de l'Océan indien (no recent information)
♦ Organisation du Traité de l'Atlantique Nord (#16945)
♦ Organisation du traité central (inactive)
♦ Organisation du Traité de défense collective pour l'Asie du Sud-Est (inactive)
♦ Organisation du Traité de sécurité collective (#04103)
♦ Organisation du Traité de Varsovie (inactive)
♦ Organisation des transporteurs routiers européens (internationally oriented national body)
♦ Organisation des travailleurs de l'Afrique centrale (no recent information)
♦ Organisation des travailleurs de l'Afrique de l'Ouest (unconfirmed)
♦ Organisation de l'unité africaine (inactive)
♦ Organisation de l'unité syndicale africaine (#17798)
♦ Organisation universelle des associations d'agences de voyages (inactive)
♦ Organisation universelle pour la langue internationale interlingue (inactive)
♦ Organisation universitaire interaméricaine (#11442)
♦ Organisation des universités catholiques de l'Amérique latine / see Organization of Catholic Universities in Latin America and the Caribbean (#17858)
♦ Organisation des veuves en Afrique (no recent information)
♦ Organisation des villes arabes (#01059)
♦ Organisation des villes du patrimoine mondial (#17891)

♦ Organising Bureau of European School Student Unions (OBESSU) .. 17829

SG ad interim Rue de l'Industrie 10, 1000 Brussels, Belgium. T. +3228932414. E-mail: secretariat@obessu.org.
URL: http://www.obessu.org/
History 15 Apr 1975, Dublin (Ireland). Current statutes adopted by General Assembly, 1999, Helsinki (Finland); last revised 2015, Brussels (Belgium). Registration: EU Transparency Register, No/ID: 28818073021-14, Start date: 14 Jan 2010. **Aims** Represent the views of school students in Europe towards the different educational institutions and platforms; uphold and improve the quality and accessibility of education and educational democracy; improve conditions in secondary schools to promote greater solidarity, cooperation and understanding among school students; end discrimination and injustice where they exist within the educational system. **Structure** General Assembly (annual); Council of Members (meets annually); Executive Board; Monitoring Committee; Working Groups; Secretariat in Brussels (Belgium). **Languages** English. **Staff** 3.00 FTE, paid. **Finance** Members' dues. Other sources: *European Commission (EC, #06633)*; *European Youth Foundation (EYF, #09141)*; Maribel. **Activities** Events/meetings. **Events** *General Assembly* Brussels (Belgium) 2015, *General Assembly* Vienna (Austria) 2014, *General Assembly* Haapsalu (Estonia) 2013, *General Assembly* Copenhagen (Denmark) 2012, *General Assembly* Brussels (Belgium) 2011. **Publications** *OBESSU Newsletter* (12 a year). Publications of events; reports; brochures; leaflets; postcards; press releases; manual for school students.
Members Independent, national, representative and democratic school student organizations. Full (22) in 19 countries:
Austria, Belgium, Bosnia-Herzegovina, Czechia, Denmark, Estonia, Finland, France, Iceland, Ireland, Italy, Lithuania, Luxembourg, Romania, Serbia, Slovakia, Slovenia, Spain, Switzerland.
IGO Relations Cooperates with: *European Commission (EC, #06633)*. **NGO Relations** Member of (6): *European Students' Union (ESU, #08848)*; *European Youth Forum (#09140)*; *Generation Climate Europe (GCE, #10114)*; *Global Student Forum (GSF, #10614)*; *Lifelong Learning Platform – European Civil Society for Education (LLLP, #16466)*; *SIRIUS – Policy Network on Migrant Education (SIRIUS, #19291)*. [2021/XD9748/**E**]

♦ Organisme arabe pour l'alphabétisation et l'enseignement des adultes (inactive)
♦ Organisme arabe pour l'industrialisation militaire (inactive)
♦ Organisme Benelux de sécurité routière (no recent information)
♦ Organisme conjoint de coopération en matière d'armement / see Organisation Conjointe de Coopération en Matière d'Armement (#17801)
♦ Organisme de coordination pour le travail international de jeunesse (internationally oriented national body)
♦ Organisme européen de coordination des recherches sur le fluor et la prophylaxie de la carie dentaire / see European Organization for Caries Research (#08107)
♦ Organisme européen de recherches sur la carie (#08107)
♦ Organisme pour l'interdiction des armes nucléaires en Amérique latine / see Agency for the Prohibition of Nuclear Weapons in Latin America and the Caribbean (#00554)
♦ Organisme pour l'interdiction des armes nucléaires en Amérique latine et dans les Caraïbes (#00554)
♦ Organisme international privé pour l'avancement et l'extension des sciences et techniques agronomiques (inactive)
♦ Organisme international régional contre les maladies des plantes et des animaux (#17830)
♦ Organisme des Nations Unies chargé de la surveillance de la trève (#20638)

♦ Organisme des Nations Unies chargé de la surveillance de la trève en Palestine / see United Nations Truce Supervision Organization (#20638)
♦ Organisme nordique de contact pour les problèmes de l'environnement (inactive)
♦ Organisme nordique mixte d'éducation d'entretien (inactive)
♦ Organismo Arabe para Inversiones y Desarrollo Agricolas (#00902)
♦ Organismo Espacial Europeo (#08798)
♦ Organismo Europeu de Luta Antifraude (#05906)
♦ Organismo Internacional de Energia Atómica (#12294)
♦ Organismo Internacional para la Normalización del Rayón y las Fibras Sintéticas / see Bureau international pour la standardisation de la rayonne et des fibres synthétiques (#03369)

♦ Organismo Internacional Regional de Sanidad Agropecuaria (OIRSA) 17830

Regional International Organization for Plant Protection and Animal Health (RIOPPAH) – Organisme international régional contre les maladies des plantes et des animaux

Exec Dir Calle Ramón Belloso, Final Pasaje Isolde, Col Escalón, Aptdo Postal 61, CP 0161 San Salvador, El Salvador. T. +50322099200. Fax +5032631128. E-mail: oirsa@oirsa.org – dejecutiva@oirsa.org.
Communication Manager address not obtained. T. +50322099200ext402. E-mail: comunicaciones@oirsa.org.
URL: http://www.oirsa.org/

History 29 Oct 1953, San Salvador (El Salvador). Established by 5th Conference of Ministers of Agriculture of Central America, Mexico and Panama. Constitutive Convention ratified 15 May 1987, Guatemala (Guatemala) City. Subsequently Belize (Belize) became a member. **Aims** Coordinate among member countries improved methods of investigation, prevention, control and eradication of plant and animal diseases and of epidemics having international repercussions. **Structure** *Comité Internacional Regional de Sanidad Agropecuaria (CIRSA)* (meets annually) is the highest authority. Executive Director. Each member country appoints Technical Director on Plant and Animal Health, technical and administrative support, a Representative and an animal health and plant protection specialist. **Languages** English, Spanish. **Staff** 300.00 FTE, paid. **Finance** Sources: ordinary quota per member country; extraordinary quota for prevention of foot-and-mouth and other exotic diseases; incomes for execution of self-supporting projects. **Activities** Knowledge management/information dissemination; politics/policy/regulatory; projects/programmes; research/documentation; training/education. **Events** *Regional Plant Protection Organizations (RPPOs) Annual Technical Consultation* London (UK) 2022, *Regional Plant Protection Organizations (RPPOs) Annual Technical Consultation* Rome (Italy) 2021, *Regional Plant Protection Organizations (RPPOs) Annual Technical Consultation* Rome (Italy) 2020, *Regional Plant Protection Organizations (RPPOs) Annual Technical Consultation* Abuja (Nigeria) 2019, *Regional Plant Protection Organizations (RPPOs) Annual Technical Consultation* Lima (Peru) 2018. **Publications** *Boletín Regional del OIRSA*. Annual Report. Books; bulletins; leaflets; brochures.

Members Ministries of Agriculture of 9 countries:
Belize, Costa Rica, Dominican Rep, El Salvador, Guatemala, Honduras, Mexico, Nicaragua, Panama.

IGO Relations Observer status with (1): *World Trade Organization (WTO, #21864)*. Instrumental in setting up (1): *Grupo Interamericano de Coordinación en Sanidad Vegetal (GICSV, no recent information)*.
Relationship agreement with: *FAO (#09260)*. Formal Agreement with: *OIE – World Organisation for Animal Health (#17703)*. Serves as one of 10 Regional Plant Protection Organizations of *International Plant Protection Convention, 1951 (IPPC, 1951)*. Cooperates in related fields of interest with:
- *Andean Community (#00817)*;
- *Asia and Pacific Plant Protection Commission (APPPC, #01997)*;
- *Central American Agricultural Council (#03657)*;
- *Consejo Regional de Cooperación Agrícola de Centroamérica, México y la República Dominicana (CORECA, no recent information)*;
- *Deutsche Gesellschaft für Technische Zusammenarbeit (GTZ, inactive)*;
- *European and Mediterranean Plant Protection Organization (EPPO, #07773)*;
- *Inter-African Phytosanitary Council (AU-IAPSC, #11386)*;
- *Inter-American Development Bank (IDB, #11427)*;
- *International Atomic Energy Agency (IAEA, #12294)*;
- *International Development Association (IDA, #13155)*;
- *Pan American Foot-and-Mouth Disease Center (PAFMDC, #18106)*;
- *Pan American Health Organization (PAHO, #18108)*;
- *Secretaria Permanente del Tratado General de Integración Económica Centroamericana (SIECA, #19195)*;
- *UNDP (#20292)*;
- *WHO (#20950)*.

NGO Relations *Centro de Coordinación para la Prevención de los Desastres Naturales en América Central (CEPREDENAC, #03795)*; *International Association of Agricultural Economists (IAAE, #11695)*.
[2020/XD3154/**D***]

♦ Organismo Latinoamericano de Mineria (OLAMI) 17831

SG Av Héctor Ormachea esq Calle 7, Edificio Vera, Piso 1B – Zona de Obrajes, Casilla 730, La Paz, Bolivia. E-mail: olami.bolivia@gmail.com.
URL: http://www.olami.org.ar/

History 4 Apr 1984, Lima (Peru). Also referred to as *OLAMI Internacional*. **Structure** General Assembly. Council, including Secretary-General.

Members in 16 countries:
Argentina, Bolivia, Brazil, Chile, Colombia, Costa Rica, Cuba, Dominican Rep, Ecuador, Guatemala, Mexico, Nicaragua, Paraguay, Peru, Uruguay, Venezuela.
[2014/XD8185/**D**]

♦ Organismo Mundial de Cooperación para los Paises en Desarrollo (inactive)
♦ Organismo Mundial de Cursillos de Cristianidad (#21238)
♦ Organismo de Obras Públicas y Socorro de las Naciones Unidas para los Refugiados de Palestina en el Cercano Oriente (#20622)
♦ Organismo para la Proscripción de las Armas Nucleares en la América Latina / see Agency for the Prohibition of Nuclear Weapons in Latin America and the Caribbean (#00554)
♦ Organismo para la Proscripción de las Armas Nucleares en la América Latina y el Caribe (#00554)
♦ Organismo Sardo di Volontariato Internazionale Cristiano (internationally oriented national body)
♦ Organismo di Volontariato per la Cooperazione Internazionale – La Nostra Famiglia (internationally oriented national body)
♦ Organização das Cidades do Patrimônio Mundial / see Organization of World Heritage Cities (#17891)
♦ Organização das Cooperativas da América (inactive)
♦ Organização dos Estados Americanos (#17629)
♦ Organização de Estados Ibero-americanos para a Educação, a Ciência e a Cultura (#17871)
♦ Organização Européia da Industria de Conserva do Tomate / see European Organisation of Tomato Industries (#08104)
♦ Organização das Familias da Asia e do Pacifico (#17867)
♦ Organização para a Harmonização em Africa do Direito dos Negócios (#17806)
♦ Organização Holandesa para Cooperação Internacional de Desenvolvimento / see Oxfam Novib
♦ Organização Iberoamericana de Cooperação Inter Municipal (#17839)
♦ Organização Ibero-Americana de Pilotos (no recent information)
♦ Organização Iberoamericana de Segurança Social (#11028)
♦ Organização Internacional do Café (#12630)
♦ Organização Internacional das Comissões de Valores (#14470)
♦ Organização Internacional dos Jornalistas (inactive)
♦ Organização Latino-Americana de Administração (#17844)
♦ Organização Latino-Americana et do Caribe do Turismo (#17845)
♦ Organização Latinoamericana de Energia (#16313)
♦ Organização Maritima da Africa do Oeste e do Centro (#16582)
♦ Organização Mundial de Autismo (#21211)
♦ Organização Mundial de Jovens contra Mudança do Clima (inactive)
♦ Organização Mundial de Software Livre (unconfirmed)
♦ Organização Natural da Saúde Mundo (internationally oriented national body)
♦ Organização Oest Africana da Saúde (#20881)
♦ Organização Pan Africana Das Mulheres (#18074)
♦ Organização Pan-Africana de Propriedade Intelectual (unconfirmed)
♦ Organização Pan-Americana da Saúde (#18108)
♦ Organização do Tratado de Cooperação Amazônica (#00766)
♦ Organização Universitaria Interamericana (#11442)
♦ Organizace Fenomenologickych Organizaci (#17883)
♦ Organizacia Svet Mladych Proti Zmene Klimy (inactive)
♦ Organizacija Gestoza (#17869)
♦ Organizacija Sotrudnicestva Podsipnikovoj Promyslennosti (inactive)
♦ Organizacija Sotrudnicestva Socialisticeskih Stran v Oblasti Elektriceskoj i Poctovoj Svijazi (inactive)
♦ Organizacija Sotrudnicestva Zeleznyh Dorog (#17803)
♦ Organizacija po Sotrudnicestvu v Cernoj Metallurgii (inactive)
♦ Organizacija Varsavskogo Dogovora (inactive)
♦ Organización de la Administración Caribeña de Deporte y Educación Fisica (no recent information)
♦ Organización Africana de la Madera (no recent information)
♦ Organización Afro-Asiatica para la Reconstrucción Rural / see African-Asian Rural Development Organization (#00203)
♦ Organización Arabe de Comunicación por Satélites (#01037)
♦ Organización Arabe para la Defensa Social Contra el Crimen (inactive)
♦ Organización Arabe de Derechos Humanos (#01020)
♦ Organización Arabe para el Desarrollo Industrial (inactive)
♦ Organización Arabe para la Educación, la Cultura y la Ciencia (#01003)
♦ Organización Arabe de Recursos Mineros (inactive)
♦ Organización Arabe del Trabajo (#01001)
♦ Organización Arabe de Unificación de Normas y Metrologia (inactive)
♦ Organización para la Armonización en Africa del Derecho Mercantil (#17806)

♦ Organización de Asociaciones y Empresas de Telecomunicaciones para América Latina (TEPAL) 17832

Contact Avenida 4D y 12 de Octubre, Hato Pintado, Edificio Cable Onda, Mezzanine, Panama, Panamá, Panama PANAMá, Panama. T. +5073903419 – +5073907758. Fax +5073903429. E-mail: infotepal@tepal.org.
URL: http://www.tepal.org/home/

History Sep 1992. Registered in accordance with the law of Panama. **Structure** Board of Directors, including President, Vice-President, Treasurer and Secretary. **Languages** English, Spanish. **Staff** 1.00 FTE, paid. **Activities** Organizes events such as expos.

Members Full in 16 countries:
Argentina, Bolivia, Chile, Colombia, Costa Rica, Curaçao, Dominican Rep, Ecuador, Guatemala, Honduras, Mexico, Panama, Paraguay, Peru, Uruguay, Venezuela.

Consultative Status Consultative status granted from: *World Intellectual Property Organization (WIPO, #21593)* (Permanent Observer Status).
[2015/XJ2505/**D**]

♦ Organización de Asociaciones de Periodistas Iberoamericanos (no recent information)
♦ Organización de Aviación Civil Internacional (#12581)
♦ Organización del Bachillerato Internacional / see International Baccalaureate (#12306)
♦ Organización Católica Internacional del Cine y del Audiovisual (inactive)

♦ Organización Católica Latinoamericana y Caribeña de Comunicación (OCLACC) 17833

Exec Sec Casilla Postal 17-21-178, Alpallana E6-114 y Whimper, Quito, Ecuador. T. +59322501654. Fax +59322226839.
URL: http://signisalc.org/

History 1987. **Aims** Promote actions of service, solidarity with the excluded and promote alliances and community as the best ways to deepen development strategy; support training and professionalism of communicators; contribute to improving the quality of communication services in order to be more competitive and to better affect public opinion; foster collaboration, interchange, joint work and solidarity between members. **Structure** Executive Committee, comprising President, Vice-President and 4 Directors. **Languages** Portuguese, Spanish. **Staff** 7.00 FTE, paid; 4.00 FTE, voluntary. **Finance** Members' dues. International cooperation. Budget (annual): euro 400,000. **Events** *Congress* Porto Alegre (Brazil) 2010, *Congress* Porto Alegre (Brazil) 2009, *Congress* Loja (Ecuador) 2007, *Continental assembly* Santo Domingo (Dominican Rep) 2004, *SIGNIS Caribbean meeting* Trinidad-Tobago 2004.

Members National Associations in 18 countries:
Argentina, Bolivia, Brazil, Chile, Colombia, Costa Rica, Cuba, Dominica, Dominican Rep, Ecuador, El Salvador, Nicaragua, Panama, Paraguay, Peru, Suriname, Trinidad-Tobago, Venezuela.

NGO Relations Member of: *World Catholic Association for Communication (SIGNIS, #21264)*. Honorary member of: *Federación Latinoamericana de Facultades de Comunicación Social (FELAFACS, #09353)*. Cooperation agreement with: *World Association for Christian Communication (WACC, #21126)* (Latin America).
[2014/XD9282/**D**]

♦ Organización de las Ciudades del Patrimonio Mundial (#17891)
♦ Organización Civica Panamericana (inactive)
♦ Organización Común de Lucha Antiacridica y de Lucha Antiaviar (inactive)
♦ Organización de la Conferencia Islamica / see Organisation of Islamic Cooperation (#17813)
♦ Organización Consultiva Maritima Intergubernamental / see International Maritime Organization (#14102)

♦ Organización Continental Latinoamericana y Caribeña de Estudiantes (OCLAE) 17834

Continental Organization of Latin American and Caribbean Students

Exec Secretariat Calle 36 No 710, 9617 y 7ma, Miramar, Playa, Havana, Cuba. T. +5372033600 – +5372036496 – +5372036497. Fax +5372026168.
URL: http://oclaeamericalatina.blogspot.com/

History 11 Aug 1966, Havana (Cuba), following a series of initiatives commencing with 1st Congress of American Students, Feb 1908, Montevideo (Uruguay), and continuing with initiatives from first regional congress, 1955, Montevideo. Original title: *Latin American Continental Students Organization – Organisation continentale latinoaméricaine des étudiants – Organización Continental Latinoamericana de Estudiantes – Kontinentalnaja Organizacija Latinoamerikanskih Studentov*. **Aims** Represent and defend the interests of students and youth in the region. **Structure** *Latin American and Caribbean Congress of Students (CLAE)*; General Secretariat; Executive Secretariat; Regional Coordinators (5); Secondary Students Coordinator. **Languages** English, Spanish. **Staff** 18.00 FTE, paid. **Finance** Members' dues. Donations. **Activities** Events/meetings. **Events** *Congress* Managua (Nicaragua) 2014, *Congress* Montevideo (Uruguay) 2011, *Congress* Quito (Ecuador) 2007, *Congress* Sao Paulo (Brazil) 2005, *Congress* Guadalajara (Mexico) 2002. **Publications** *OCLAE Bulletin* (12 a year) in English, Spanish.

Members Full National student organizations (31) in 22 countries:
Argentina, Barbados, Belize, Bolivia, Brazil, Chile, Colombia, Cuba, Dominican Rep, Ecuador, El Salvador, Guatemala, Haiti, Honduras, Nicaragua, Peru, Puerto Rico, St Lucia, St Vincent-Grenadines, Trinidad-Tobago, Uruguay, Venezuela.
Associate Student organizations (8) in 4 countries:
Costa Rica, Ecuador, Guyana, Mexico.

Consultative Status Consultative status granted from: *ECOSOC (#05331)* (Special); *UNESCO (#20322)* (Consultative Status). **IGO Relations** *UNESCO Regional Bureau for Education in Latin America and the Caribbean (#20318)*. **NGO Relations** Member of (6): *Alianza Social Continental (ASC, #00635)*; *Espacio Iberoamericano de Juventud (EIJ, no recent information)*; *Foro Latinoamericano de Juventud (FLAJ, #09881)*; *Geneva Informal Meeting of International Youth Non-Governmental Organizations (GIM, no recent information)*; *Global Student Forum (GSF, #10614)*; *World Social Forum (WSF, #21797)*.
[2016.07.30/XD5381/**D**]

♦ Organización Continental Latinoamericana de Estudiantes / see Organización Continental Latinoamericana y Caribeña de Estudiantes (#17834)

♦ Organización del Convenio Andrés Bello de Integración Educativa, Cientifica, Tecnológica y Cultural (no recent information)
♦ Organización de Cooperación Educativa (unconfirmed)
♦ Organización de Cooperación Islamico (#17813)
♦ Organización de Cooperación y Solidaridad Internacional (internationally oriented national body)
♦ Organización de las Cooperativas de América (inactive)
♦ Organización de Cortes Supremas de las Américas (no recent information)
♦ Organización Cristiana internacional de los medios (#12563)
♦ Organización Demócrata Cristiana de América (#03899)
♦ Organización Deportiva Centroamericana y del Caribe (#03665)
♦ Organización Deportiva Panamericana (#18138)
♦ Organización Deportiva Panamericana de Sordos (#18093)
♦ Organización Deportiva Sudamericana (#19708)
♦ Organización Deportiva Suramericana / see South American Sports Organization (#19708)
♦ Organización Deportiva Universitaria de Centro América y el Caribe / see Organización Deportiva Universitaria Panamericana (#17835)

♦ Organización Deportiva Universitaria Panamericana (FISU América) 17835

Main Office Rua Juno 20, Sala 408, Renascença II, São Luis MA, 65075-700, Brazil.
URL: http://fisuamerica.com/

History 2007, as *Organización Deportiva Universitaria de Centro América y el Caribe*. Current title adopted 2015. Current statutes adopted, 6 Jul 2015, Korea Rep. **Structure** General Assembly; Executive Committee. **Members** Federations in 31 countries and territories:
Anguilla, Argentina, Bahamas, Barbados, Bolivia, Brazil, Canada, Chile, Colombia, Costa Rica, Cuba, Curaçao, Dominican Rep, Ecuador, El Salvador, Guatemala, Haiti, Honduras, Jamaica, Mexico, Nicaragua, Panama, Paraguay, Peru, Puerto Rico, Suriname, Trinidad-Tobago, Uruguay, USA, Venezuela, Virgin Is USA.
NGO Relations A continental federation of *International University Sports Federation (FISU, #15830)*.
[2020/XM6866/**D**]

♦ Organización de Entidades Fiscalizadoras Superiores de Africa (#00406)
♦ Organización de Entidades Fiscalizadoras Superiores de Asia (#01594)
♦ Organización de Entidades Fiscalizadoras Superiores del Caribe (#03536)
♦ Organización de Entidades Fiscalizadoras Superiores de Europa (#08115)

♦ Organización de Entidades Mutuales de las Américas (ODEMA) . . . 17836

Contact Tte Gral Perón 1379/83, C1038 ABA Buenos Aires, Argentina. T. +541143716418. E-mail: coordinacion@odema.org – info@odema.org.
URL: http://www.odema.org/

Aims Within mutual entities, promote and strengthen assistance creating conditions providing for training, exchange of experience and programmatic agreements. **Structure** Steering Committee; Supervisory Board. **Members** Full (85) in 19 countries:
Argentina, Bolivia, Brazil, Chile, Colombia, Costa Rica, Dominican Rep, Ecuador, El Salvador, Guatemala, Haiti, Honduras, Mexico, Nicaragua, Panama, Paraguay, Peru, Uruguay, USA.
Consultative Status Consultative status granted from: *ECOSOC (#05331)* (Special). **NGO Relations** Member of: *Conference of Non-Governmental Organizations in Consultative Relationship with the United Nations (CONGO, #04635)*. Participant in: *United Nations Global Compact (#20567)*. [2019/XJ5196/**D**]

♦ Organización de Escritores Revolucionarios (inactive)
♦ Organización de Estados de África, el Caribe y el Pacífico (#17796)
♦ Organización de los Estados Americanos (#17629)
♦ Organización de los Estados del Caribe Oriental (#17804)
♦ Organización de Estados Centroamericanos (inactive)
♦ Organización de Estados Iberoamericanos para la Educación, la Ciencia y la Cultura (#17871)
♦ Organización de los Estudiantes y Jóvenes No-Alineados (#17148)
♦ Organización para Estudios Tropicales (internationally oriented national body)
♦ Organización Europea de Asociaciones Militares / see European Organisation of Military Associations and Trade Unions (#08099)
♦ Organización Europea de Biologia Celular (inactive)
♦ Organización Europea de las Compañias Regionales de Aviación / see European Regions Airline Association (#08347)
♦ Organización Europea de la Federación Mundial de Empleados / see European Organization of the World Organization of Workers (#08116)
♦ Organización Europea de la FME / see European Organization of the World Organization of Workers (#08116)
♦ Organización Europea de las Industrias de la Conserva de Tomates / see European Organisation of Tomato Industries (#08104)
♦ Organización Europea de Industrias Transformadoras de Frutas y Hortalizas / see European Association of Fruit and Vegetable Processors (#06049)
♦ Organización Europea para un Mercado Audiovisual Independiente (inactive)
♦ Organización Europea de l'Organización Mundial de Trabajadores (#08116)
♦ Organización Europea para el Turismo Ecuestre (inactive)

♦ Organización de Facultades, Escuelas y Departamentos de Odontologia de la Unión de Universidades de América Latina (OFEDO/UDUAL) 17837

Organization of Faculties, Schools and Departments of Odontology of the Union of Latin American Universities – Organisation des facultés, écoles et départements d'odontologie de l'Union des universités de l'Amérique latine

Exec Sec c/o UNPHU, Av John F Kennedy 1/2, Santo Domingo, Dominican Rep. E-mail: info@ofedoudual.org.
URL: https://ofedoudual.org/

History 16 Oct 1980, Santo Domingo (Dominican Rep). Founded as a health area association of *Association of Universities of Latin America and the Caribbean (#02970)*. **Aims** Cooperate in development and progress of affiliated institutions and foster mutual knowledge through interaction; serve as coordinating body for exchange and relationship among these institutions and with other similar institutions; serve as advising and consulting centre; propose measures for coordinating teaching, academic, administrative and research organization; foster exchange of *professors, students*, researchers and graduates and of publications, studies and teaching and research materials; promote acknowledgement of and respect for university autonomy and respect for human rights and social justice; cooperate in transformation of society to benefit the majority who are still at the margin of odontology. **Structure** General Assembly (every 2 years). Board of Directors, consisting of President, 2 Vice-Presidents, 4 Members, and Executive Secretary. Executive Committee. **Finance** Members' dues: US$ 300. Budget (annual): about US$ 20,000. **Activities** Acts as advisory body for Latin American faculties of odontology concerning: curricula; under- and post-graduate dental teaching/service/research programs; workshops and seminars on dental education. **Events** *Assembly* Santo Domingo (Dominican Rep) 2019, *Conference* Bogota (Colombia) 2008, *Meeting* Bogota (Colombia) 2002, *Conference* San Salvador (El Salvador) 2002, *Biennial conference / Conference* Medellin (Colombia) 1997. **Publications** *OFEDO/UDUAL Newsletter* (4 a year). Conference, workshop, seminar reports.
Members Institutions in 22 countries:
Argentina, Bolivia, Brazil, Chile, Colombia, Costa Rica, Cuba, Dominican Rep, Ecuador, El Salvador, Guatemala, Honduras, Mexico, Nicaragua, Panama, Paraguay, Peru, Portugal, Puerto Rico, Spain, Uruguay, Venezuela.
IGO Relations *Pan American Health Organization (PAHO, #18108)*. **NGO Relations** Member of: *International Federation of Dental Educators and Associations (IFDEA, #13404)*. Set up: *Red Centroamericana de Asistentes Dentales (no recent information); Red Cientifica Latinoamericana (RCL, no recent information); Red Latinoamericana de Asistentes Dentales (no recent information)*. [2021/XD7318/**E**]

♦ Organización de Farmacéuticos Ibero-Latinoamericanos (OFIL) . . . 17838

Sec address not obtained. E-mail: venegas.catalina@gmail.com.
URL: http://ofil-internacional.org/

History Dec 1981, Spain. **Structure** Board, comprising President, Vice-President, Secretary General, Treasurer and Past President. **Activities** Education; meeting activities. **Events** *Congress* Puerto Vallarta (Mexico) 2016, *Congress* Asunción (Paraguay) 2014, *Congress* Cadiz (Spain) 2012, *Congress* Santiago (Chile) 2010, *Congress* Tegucigalpa (Honduras) 2008. **Publications** *OFIL Revista*.
Members Full in 22 countries:
Argentina, Bolivia, Brazil, Chile, Colombia, Costa Rica, Cuba, Dominican Rep, Ecuador, El Salvador, Guatemala, Honduras, Mexico, Nicaragua, Panama, Paraguay, Peru, Portugal, Puerto Rico, Spain, Uruguay, Venezuela. [2016/XJ3691/**D**]

♦ Organización de Flora Europaea / see Euro+Med PlantBase (#05732)
♦ Organización pro Flora Neotropica (#17868)
♦ Organización Gestosis (#17869)
♦ Organización del Golfo para la Asesoria Industrial (#10837)
♦ Organización Hidrografica Internacional (#13825)
♦ Organización Holandesa para la Cooperación Internacional al Desarrollo / see Oxfam Novib

♦ Organización Iberoamericana de Cooperación Intermunicipal (OICI) 17839

Organisation ibéroaméricaine de coopération intermunicipale – Ibero-American Organization of Inter-Municipal Cooperation – Organização Iberoamericana de Cooperação Inter Municipal

SG Calle Nuncio 8, 28005 Madrid, Spain. T. +34913643700. Fax +34913655482.
URL: https://www.oicies.com/

History Nov 1938, Havana (Cuba), as *Pan American Commission on Inter-Municipal Cooperation – Comisión Panamericana de Cooperación Intermunicipal*, by virtue of resolutions adopted at 5th International Conference of American States, 1923, Santiago (Chile), and at 6th International Conference of American States, 1928, Havana. Became *Inter-American Organization on Inter-Municipal Cooperation – Organización Interamericana de Cooperación Intermunicipal*, 5 May 1950, New Orleans LA (USA). New Statutes and listed name adopted at 14th Congress, 1972, Malaga (Spain), and at 16th Congress, 1977, Cartagena de Indias (Colombia). **Aims** Contribute to autonomous development of *municipalities*; promote effective incorporation of their development efforts into national development of their respective countries. **Structure** General Assembly; Regional Assembly; Executive Council; Technical Office. **Languages** Portuguese, Spanish. **Staff** Paid. **Activities** Organizes: *'Inter-American Congress of Municipalities – Congreso Iberoamericano de Municipios'*; seminars; training courses. **Events** *Biennial Congress* Cadiz (Spain) 2012, *Extraordinary congress / Biennial Congress* Lima (Peru) 2010, *Biennial Congress* Cancún (Mexico) 2008, *Biennial Congress* Mérida (Venezuela) 2004, *Extraordinary congress* Valladolid (Spain) 2004. **Publications** *Cuadernos de OICI* (4 a year).
Members Active; Founder; Honorary; Special. National associations, large municipalities, institutions and individuals in 21 countries and territories:
Argentina, Bolivia, Brazil, Chile, Colombia, Costa Rica, Dominican Rep, Ecuador, El Salvador, Guatemala, Haiti, Honduras, Mexico, Panama, Paraguay, Peru, Portugal, Puerto Rico, Spain, Uruguay, Venezuela.
IGO Relations Cooperates with: *OAS (#17629)*. [2018/XD1087/**D**]

♦ Organización Iberoamericana de Derechos de Autor (Latinautor) . . 17840

Ibero-American Copyright Organization

Pres Canelones 1122 4o piso, CP 11 000 Montevideo, Uruguay. T. +59829027866.

History Jun 1996, Buenos Aires (Argentina). **Aims** Integrate Iberoamerican repertory in systems. **Structure** Board of Directors. **Events** *Meeting* Costa Rica 2011. **Consultative Status** Consultative status granted from: *World Intellectual Property Organization (WIPO, #21593)* (Permanent Observer Status). **NGO Relations** *Confédération internationale des sociétés d'auteurs et compositeurs (CISAC, #04563)*.
[2015.01.21/XD6299/**D**]

♦ Organización Iberoamericana de Juventud (#11036)
♦ Organización Iberoamericana de Pilotos (no recent information)

♦ Organización Iberoamericana de Prestadores Privados de Servicios de Salud (OIPPSS) 17841

Ibero-American Organization of Private Health Service Providers

Contact c/o OEHSS, C/ General Perón 19, bajo B, 28020 Madrid, Spain. [2018/XD3706/**D**]

♦ Organización Iberoamericana de Seguridad Social (#11028)
♦ Organización Interamericana de Cooperación Intermunicipal / see Organización Iberoamericana de Cooperación Intermunicipal (#17839)
♦ Organización Internacional de Acabado de Tiendas (inactive)
♦ Organización Internacional del Arte Popular (#14447)
♦ Organización Internacional de Asociaciones de Consumidores / see Consumers International (#04773)
♦ Organización Internacional del Azúcar (#15623)
♦ Organización Internacional del Bambú y el Ratán (#14234)
♦ Organización Internacional del Cacao (#12627)
♦ Organización Internacional del Café (#12630)
♦ Organización internacional de católicos en los medios / see International Christian Organisation of the Media (#12563)
♦ Organización Internacional de Ceremonial Protocolo (#14439)
♦ Organización Internacional de las Ciencias Quimicas para el Desarrollo (#14440)
♦ Organización Internacional de Comercio / see World Trade Organization (#21864)
♦ Organización Internacional de Comisiones de Valores (#14470)
♦ Organización Internacional contra el Tracoma (#14436)
♦ Organización Internacional para la Cooperación en Evaluación (#14426)
♦ Organización Internacional de las Cooperativas en la Industria y los Servicios (#14429)
♦ Organización Internacional para el Derecho a la Educación y la Libertad de Enseñanza (#14468)
♦ Organización Internacional para el Desarrollo de la Libertad de Enseñanza / see International Organization for the Right to Education and Freedom of Education (#14468)
♦ Organización Internacional para la Educación Científica y Tecnológica (#14469)
♦ Organización Internacional de Empleadores (#14428)
♦ Organización Internacional de Energia y Minas (#13274)
♦ Organización Internacional de las Entidades Fiscalizadoras Superiores (#14478)
♦ Organización Internacional para el Estudio de Plantas Suculentas (#14477)
♦ Organización Internacional de Estudios de Psicoanalisis (#14663)
♦ Organización Internacional de Fisica Medica (#14453)
♦ Organización Internacional de Investigaciones Celulares (#12463)
♦ Organización Internacional de Investigaciones sobre el Cerebro (#12392)
♦ Organización Internacional para el Libro Juvenil (#12366)
♦ Organización Internacional de Lucha Biológica (#14424)
♦ Organización Internacional de las Maderas Tropicales (#15737)
♦ Organización internacional en los medios – El Foro Mundial de los Profesionales e Instituciones en el Periodismo Secular y Religioso / see International Christian Organisation of the Media (#12563)
♦ Organización Internacional de Metrologia Legal (#14451)
♦ Organización Internacional para las Migraciones (#14454)
♦ Organización Internacional de Mineros (no recent information)
♦ Organización Internacional de Mujeres Sionistas (#21030)
♦ Organización Internacional de Normalización (#14473)
♦ Organización Internacional Nueva Acrópolis (#14458)
♦ Organización Internacional de Paleobotanica (#14459)
♦ Organización Internacional de Periodistas (inactive)
♦ Organización Internacional de Peritos (#17808)
♦ Organización Internacional de Policia Criminal – INTERPOL (#13110)
♦ Organización Internacional de Protección Civil (#12582)
♦ Organización Internacional de Psicofisiologia (#14466)

- ♦ Organización Internacional de Refugiados (inactive)
- ♦ Organización Internacional de Telecomunicaciones Cósmicas Interspoutnik (#15976)
- ♦ Organización Internacional de Telecomunicaciones Maritimas por Satélite / see International Mobile Satellite Organization (#14174)
- ♦ Organización Internacional de Telecomunicaciones Móviles por Satélite (#14174)
- ♦ Organización Internacional de Telecomunicaciones por Satélite (#15670)

♦ Organización Internacional de Teletones (ORITEL) 17842

International Telethons Organization

Exec Dir PO Box 310247, Miami FL 33231-0247, USA. T. +13059079298.
URL: http://www.oritel.org/

History Aug 1998. **Aims** Improve the quality of life of people with *disabilities*; promote inclusion of people with disabilities, asserting their rights declared by the UN. **Structure** Board of Directors. **Languages** Spanish. **Staff** 1.00 FTE, paid. **Finance** Donations; contributions. **Activities** Events/meetings. **Events** *Symposium* Antigua (Guatemala) 2014, *Symposium* San José (Costa Rica) 2013, *Congress* San Juan (Puerto Rico) 2013, *Congress* Santiago (Chile) 2012.
Members Full in 12 countries:
Chile, Colombia, El Salvador, Guatemala, Honduras, Mexico, Nicaragua, Paraguay, Peru, Puerto Rico, Uruguay, USA.
IGO Relations *Inter-American Development Bank (IDB, #11427)*; *OAS (#17629)*; *Pan American Health Organization (PAHO, #18108)*. [2020.03.03/XJ6930/**D**]

- ♦ Organización Internacional de Trabajadores de Radio y Televisión de las Américas (inactive)
- ♦ Organización Internacional del Trabajo (#11123)
- ♦ Organización Internacional del Trabajo – Programa Internacional para la Erradicación del Trabajo Infantil / see International Programme on the Elimination of Child Labour and Forced Labour (#14652)
- ♦ Organización Internacional del Trabajo – Programa Internacional para la Erradicación del Trabajo Infantil y del Travajo Forzoso (#14652)
- ♦ Organización Internacional de Transportes por Cable (#14481)
- ♦ Organización Internacional de Turismo Social (#14889)

♦ Organización Internacional de Universidades por el Desarrollo Sostenible y Medio Ambiente (OIUDSMA) 17843

International Organization of Universities for Sustainable Development and Environmental Conservation

Exec Sec Dep de Botanica, Facultad de Ciencias, Univ de Granada, s/n Campus Fuentenueva, 18071 Granada, Spain. T. +34958243381. Fax +34958242899. E-mail: jrosua@ugr.es.

History 20 Nov 1995, Costa Rica. **Events** *Congress* Buenos Aires (Argentina) 2009, *Congress* Curitiba (Brazil) 2006, *Congress* Granada (Nicaragua) 2004, *Congress* Managua (Nicaragua) 2004, *Congress* Viña del Mar (Chile) 2002. [2010/XJ3601/**D**]

- ♦ Organización para la Investigación, la Comunicación y Acción a favor de un Desarrollo Solidario entre Norte y Sur (internationally oriented national body)

♦ Organización Latinoamericana de Administración (OLA) 17844

Organização Latino-Americana de Administração

Main Office Apartado 6501-1000, San José, San José, San José, Costa Rica. T. +50622530214. Fax +50622804597.
Pres address not obtained.

Events *Regional Meeting* Mendoza (Argentina) 2014, *Meeting* Lima (Peru) 2004, *Meeting* Acapulco (Mexico) 2002, *Meeting* Porto Alegre (Brazil) 2000.
Members in 10 countries:
Argentina, Bolivia, Brazil, Colombia, Ecuador, Mexico, Paraguay, Peru, Uruguay, Venezuela. [2012/XD8865/**D**]

- ♦ Organización Latinoamericana y del Caribe de Entidades Fiscalizadoras Superiores (#17877)

♦ Organización Latino-Americana y del Caribe de Turismo (OLACT) . . 17845

Organization of Latin American and Caribbean Tourism – Organisation Latino-Américaine et des Caraïbes du Tourisme – Organização Latino-Americana et do Caribe do Turismo

Admin Calle 4 4, Alvaro Obregón, 01400 Mexico City CDMX, Mexico. T. +525539756534. E-mail: info@olact.org.
URL: http://www.olact.org/

History 24 Sep 2010, Mexico City (Mexico). Founded in the context of the Americas International Tourism Fair (FITA). **Aims** Support touristic sustainable development in the region. **Structure** Advisory Board; General Secretary; Committees (4). **Languages** English, French, Portuguese, Spanish. **Staff** Voluntary. **Activities** Events/meetings; financial and/or material support; research and development; training/education. **Members** States; Sectoral members. Membership countries not specified. **IGO Relations** Ministries of Tourism in the Latinamerican and Caribbean Region. [2020.06.23/XM5507/**D**]

- ♦ Organización Latinoamericana de Desarrollo Pesquero (#16335)
- ♦ Organización Latino Americana de Desarrollo Secretarial (no recent information)
- ♦ Organización Latinoamericana de Energia (#16313)
- ♦ Organización Latinoamericana de Fabricantes de Bebidas Alcohólicas (inactive)
- ♦ Organización Latinoamericana para la Promoción de los Ciegos y Deficientes Visuales (inactive)
- ♦ Organización Latinoamericana de Solidaridad (inactive)
- ♦ Organización Latinoamericana del Vino y de la Uva (inactive)
- ♦ Organización Maritima Internacional (#14102)
- ♦ Organización Médica Homeopatica Internacional (no recent information)
- ♦ Organización Meteorológica Mundial (#21649)
- ♦ Organización de Militares por la Democracia, la Integración y la Liberación de América Latina y el Caribe (inactive)
- ♦ Organización Mundial de Aduanas (#21350)
- ♦ Organización Mundial Agudath Israel (#00584)
- ♦ Organización Mundial de Antiguos Alumnos y Antiguas Alumnas de la Enseñanza Católica / see Organisation mondiale des anciens élèves de l'enseignement catholique (#17816)
- ♦ Organización Mundial de Antiguos Alumnos de la Educación Católica (#17816)
- ♦ Organización Mundial del Autismo (#21211)
- ♦ Organización Mundial de Boxeo (#21243)
- ♦ Organización Mundial de Ciudades y Gobiernos Locales Unidos (#21695)
- ♦ Organización Mundial del Comercio (#21864)
- ♦ Organización Mundial contra la Tortura (#21685)
- ♦ Organización Mundial para la Educación Preescolar (#21689)
- ♦ Organización Mundial del Embalaje (#21705)
- ♦ Organización Mundial de Endoscopia Digestiva / see World Endoscopy Organization (#21380)
- ♦ Organización Mundial de EOD / see World EOD Foundation (#21387)
- ♦ Organización Mundial para las Familias (no recent information)
- ♦ Organización Mundial de Gastroenterologia (#21536)
- ♦ Organización Mundial de la Imagen y del Sonido (inactive)
- ♦ Organización Mundial de Jóvenes contra el Cambio Climatico (inactive)
- ♦ Organización Mundial de la Juventud Esperantista (#20268)
- ♦ Organización Mundial de la Medicina Alternativa (inactive)
- ♦ Organización Mundial del Método de la Ovulación Billings (#21692)
- ♦ Organización Mundial del Movimiento Scout (#21693)
- ♦ Organización Mundial de la Naturaleza (inactive)
- ♦ Organización Mundial del Ocio / see World Leisure Organization (#21624)
- ♦ Organización Mundial de Parlamentarias contra la Corrupción (#10518)

♦ Organización Mundial de Periodismo Turistico 17846

World Travel Journalism Organization (WTJO)

Dir Gen Avenida Corrientes, Y5900FNF Buenos Aires, Argentina. T. +541128151837. E-mail: miguelledhesma@gmail.com.
URL: https://periodismoturistico.org

History 11 Nov 2011, San Luis (Argentina). **Structure** Executive Committee. **Activities** Events/meetings. **Events** *Congreso Internacional de Periodistas y Profesionales del Turismo* Sao Paulo (Brazil) 2020, *Congreso Internacional de Periodistas y Profesionales del Turismo* Lima (Peru) 2019, *Congreso Internacional de Periodistas y Profesionales del Turismo* Sao Paulo (Brazil) 2019, *Congreso Internacional de Periodistas y Profesionales del Turismo* Puerto Iguazú (Argentina) 2018, *Congreso Internacional de Periodistas y Profesionales del Turismo* Tegucigalpa (Honduras) 2018. [2021.11.30/XM8901/**D**]

- ♦ Organización Mundial de Personas con Discapacidad (#05097)
- ♦ Organización Mundial de Profesionales de la Enseñanza (inactive)
- ♦ Organización Mundial de la Propiedad Intelectual (#21593)
- ♦ Organización Mundial de la Salud (#20950)
- ♦ Organización Mundial del Termalismo (#17820)
- ♦ Organización Mundial de Trabajadores (#21697)
- ♦ Organización Mundial del Turismo (#21861)
- ♦ Organización Mundial del Turismo y del Automóvil (inactive)
- ♦ Organización Mundo Maya (internationally oriented national body)
- ♦ Organización de las Naciones Unidas para la Agricultura y la Alimentación (#09260)
- ♦ Organización de las Naciones Unidas para el Desarrollo Industrial (#20336)
- ♦ Organización de las Naciones Unidas para la Educación, la Ciencia y la Cultura (#20322)
- ♦ Organización Natural de la Salud del Mundo (internationally oriented national body)
- ♦ Organización Negra Centroamericana (#03659)
- ♦ Organización de Nematologos de los Trópicos Americanos (#17878)
- ♦ Organización No Gubernamental Internacional – Grupo de Trabajo en Cuestiones Legales e Institucionales (#14369)
- ♦ Organización Norteamericana de Protección Fitosanitaria / see North American Plant Protection Organization (#17567)
- ♦ Organización Norteamericana de Protección a las Plantas (#17567)
- ♦ Organización de Paises Arabes Exportadores de Petróleo (#17854)
- ♦ Organización de Paises Exportadores de Gas (unconfirmed)
- ♦ Organización de Paises Exportadores de Petróleo (#17881)

♦ Organización Panamericana de Gastroenterologia (OPGE) 17847

Pan-American Gastroenterological Association – Associação Panamericana de Gastroenterologia

Contact Marcelo T de Alvear 1381, 9no de piso, C1058AUU Buenos Aires, Argentina. T. +541148169391 – +541148169396. Fax +541148126568. E-mail: secretaria@opge.org.
URL: http://opge.org/

History 22 Jul 1948, Buenos Aires (Argentina). Former names and other names: *Asociación Interamericana de Gastroenterologia (AIGE)* – former; *Inter-American Association of Gastroenterology* – former; *Associação Interamericana de Gastroenterologia* – former. **Aims** Promote development of gastroenterology in the Panamerican countries. **Structure** Plenary General Assembly (every 2 years, in conjunction with Congress); Governing Board. **Languages** English, Portuguese, Spanish. **Staff** 2.00 FTE, voluntary. **Finance** Sources: meeting proceeds; members' dues. Annual budget: 10,000 USD. **Activities** Events/meetings; financial and/or material support; networking/liaising; training/education. **Events** *Congreso Panamericano de Gastroenterología* Punta del Este (Uruguay) 2021, *Panamerican congress of digestive endoscopy* Santiago (Chile) 2008, *Panamerican congress on digestive diseases* Santiago (Chile) 2008, *Panamerican congress of digestive endoscopy* Cancún (Mexico) 2006, *Panamerican congress on digestive diseases / Panamerican Congress of Gastroenterology* Cancún (Mexico) 2006. **Publications** *Gastroenterologia Interamericana* – magazine; *Gastroenterologia y Hepatologia* – official bulletin. Congress proceedings published by national organizing society.
Members National societies and federations; specialized chapters of national societies of medicine; Founding; Honorary. Societies in 21 countries:
Argentina, Bolivia, Brazil, Canada, Chile, Colombia, Costa Rica, Cuba, Dominican Rep, Ecuador, El Salvador, Guatemala, Honduras, Mexico, Nicaragua, Panama, Paraguay, Peru, Uruguay, USA, Venezuela.
NGO Relations Regional member of: *World Gastroenterology Organisation (WGO, #21536)*.
[2021/XD1047/**D**]

- ♦ Organización Panamericana de la Salud (#18108)
- ♦ Organización de Pre-Inversión de América Latina y el Caribe (inactive)
- ♦ Organización para el Progreso Industrial, Espiritual y Cultural (#17872)
- ♦ Organización para la Prohibición de las Armas Quimicas (#17823)
- ♦ Organización Regional Africana de la CIOSL / see International Trade Union Confederation – African Regional Organization (#15709)
- ♦ Organización Regional Interamericana de la Federación Internacional de Empleados, Técnicos y Profesionales / see UNI Global Union – Americas Regional Office (#20340)
- ♦ Organización Regional Interamericana de Trabajadores / see Confederación Sindical de Trabajadores y Trabajadoras de las Américas (#04480)
- ♦ Organización Regional del Oriente para la Administración Pública (#05249)
- ♦ Organización de Regiones Unidas (#20657)
- ♦ Organización para las Relaciones Económicas Internacionales (#17873)
- ♦ Organización Sanitaria Panamericana / see Pan American Health Organization (#18108)

♦ Organización del Sector Pesquero y Acuicola del Istmo Centroamericano, Panama (OSPESCA) 17848

Organization of the Fishing and Aquaculture Sector of the Central American Isthmus

Coordinator Final Bulevar Cancilleria, Distrito El Espino, Ciudad Merliot, Antiguo Cuscatlán, 0501 La Libertad, El Salvador. T. +50322488841. Fax +50322488899. E-mail: mgonzalez@sica.int – info.ospesca@sica.int.
URL: http://www.sica.int/ospesca/

History Takes over activities of *Programa Regional de Apoyo al Desarrollo de la Pesca en el Istmo Centroamericano (PRADEPESCA, inactive)*. **Aims** Promote a coordinated and sustainable development of fishing and aquaculture as part of the process of the Central American integration. **Structure** Ministers' Council. Vice-Ministers' Committee. Commission of Directors of Fishing and Aquaculture.
[2015/XD8024/**D***]

- ♦ Organización de Sindicatos de Africa Occidental (unconfirmed)

♦ Organización de Solidaridad de los Pueblos de Africa, Asia y América Latina (OSPAAAL) 17849

Organisation de solidarité des peuples d'Afrique, d'Asie et d'Amérique latine – Organization of Solidarity of the Peoples of Africa, Asia and Latin America

SG Calle C No 670, Esq a 29, Aptds 4224 y 6130, Vedado, Havana, Cuba. T. +5378305510 – +5378305529. Fax +5378333985.
URL: http://www.ospaaal.com/

History 15 Jan 1966, Havana (Cuba), at 1st *Tricontinental Conference*. **Aims** Support the struggle of the peoples of Africa, Asia and Latin America against imperialism, colonialism and neo-colonialism, and defend their right to govern themselves according to the socio-economic system of their choice without external interference; promote solidarity of the peoples of these three continents with respect to independence, sovereignty and liberation; combat racism and all forms of discrimination; promote peaceful coexistence and development, resisting the increase in armaments (particularly nuclear arms); struggle for social development; face negative consequences and impact of neoliberal globalization. **Structure** Executive Secretariat; Departments (4); All offices and commissions in Cuba. **Languages** English, French, Spanish. **Staff** 27.00 FTE, paid. **Finance** Voluntary contributions of NGOs and others. **Activities** Events/meetings; publishing activities.

Events *International forum on NGOs of the South and the challenges of globalization* Havana (Cuba) 2000, *International meeting on legacy and validity of Che's work for the 21st century* Havana (Cuba) 1997, *Meeting* Havana (Cuba) 1996, *International meeting on crime against humanity and its impact on peace in the Western hemisphere* Havana (Cuba) 1995, *Meeting on the rights of peoples to social development* Havana (Cuba) 1994. **Publications** *Tricontinental Bulletin* (weekly) in English, Spanish; *Tricontinental Magazine* (4 a year) in English, Spanish. Posters and other publications prepared by Department of Information and Propaganda.
Members Organizations in 46 countries and territories:
Angola, Antigua-Barbuda, Argentina, Belize, Benin, Bolivia, Brazil, Cape Verde, Chile, Colombia, Congo Brazzaville, Cuba, Dominica, Dominican Rep, Egypt, El Salvador, Ghana, Guatemala, Guinea, Guinea-Bissau, Haiti, Honduras, Iraq, Japan, Kenya, Korea DPR, Laos, Martinique, Mexico, Mozambique, Namibia, Nicaragua, Nigeria, Palestine, Panama, Paraguay, Peru, Puerto Rico, Sierra Leone, South Africa, Syrian AR, Tanzania UR, Uganda, Uruguay, Venezuela, Vietnam.
Consultative Status Consultative status granted from: *ECOSOC (#05331)* (Special). **IGO Relations** *African Union (AU, #00488)*; *Non-Aligned Movement (NAM, #17146)*. **NGO Relations** Participates in consultative meetings of NGOs. [2016.07.19/XC3029/**F**]

♦ Organización de Solidaridad de Pueblos Afroasiaticos (#00537)

♦ Organización Sudamericana de Fomento del Pura Sangre de Carrera (OSAF) 17850

Organisation sud américaine de l'elevage du pur sang – South American Thoroughbred Breeding Organization

Exec Dir Rivadavia 323 – 1oA, 1642 San Isidro, Buenos Aires, Argentina. T. +541147433268. Fax +541147433268. E-mail: skoremblit@osafweb.com.ar.
URL: http://www.osafweb.com.ar/

History 1958, Sao Paulo (Brazil). 1958, San Pablo (Brazil). **Structure** Executive Council; Technical Council. **Events** *Pan American Conference* New York, NY (USA) 2015, *Annual Associate Assembly* Rio de Janeiro (Brazil) 2015.
Members Full in 11 countries:
Argentina, Brazil, Chile, Colombia, Ecuador, Mexico, Panama, Paraguay, Peru, Uruguay, Venezuela.
NGO Relations Member of: *International Federation of Horseracing Authorities (IFHA, #13449)*. [2016/XD7154/**D**]

♦ Organización de Telecomunicaciones de Iberoamérica (OTI) 17851

Main Office Av Vasco de Quiroga 2000, Col Santa Fe, Del Álvaro Obregón, 01210 Mexico City CDMX, Mexico. E-mail: contacto@otitelecom.org.
URL: https://otitelecom.org/

History 19 Mar 1971, Mexico City (Mexico). Statutes amended: 29 Mar 1973; 27 Mar 1980; 23 Mar 1990. Former names and other names: *Organización de la Televisión Iberoamericana (OTI)* – former (19 Mar 1971); *Ibero-American Television Organization* – former (19 Mar 1971); *Organisation de la télévision ibéroaméricaine* – former (19 Mar 1971); *Organización de Telecomunicaciones Iberoamericanas (OTI)* – former. **Aims** Encourage, maintain and increase relations among organizations and enterprises concerned with television and its use in developing better international understanding in *Spanish speaking* and *Portuguese speaking* countries; create operative, technical and legal means for the exchange of informational, cultural, educational and sports services. **Structure** General Assembly elects Executive Council of 11 for 2 years. **Languages** Portuguese, Spanish. **Staff** 21.00 FTE, paid. **Finance** Quota determined by number of homes with television receivers in the member-country concerned. **Activities** Daily news service via satellite; covers more than 370 annual events in the fields of sport, politics, society, economics, culture, education, etc. **Events** *Annual General Assembly* Acapulco (Mexico) 2000, *Annual General Assembly* Lisbon (Portugal) 1999, *Annual Festival* Veracruz, CHIS (Mexico) 1999, *Annual Festival* Costa Rica 1998, *Annual General Assembly* Miami, FL (USA) 1998.
Members Honorary; Full Active; Associate Active (from Spanish and Portuguese speaking countries); Adherent (from other parts of the world). Members in 21 countries:
Argentina, Bolivia, Brazil, Chile, Colombia, Costa Rica, Cuba, Ecuador, El Salvador, Guatemala, Honduras, Mexico, Nicaragua, Panama, Paraguay, Peru, Portugal, Spain, Uruguay, USA, Venezuela.
Consultative Status Consultative status granted from: *ECOSOC (#05331)* (Ros C); *UNESCO (#20322)* (Consultative Status); *World Intellectual Property Organization (WIPO, #21593)* (Permanent Observer Status).
IGO Relations Observer to: *Intergovernmental Committee of the International Convention of Rome for the Protection of Performers, Producers of Phonograms and Broadcasting Organizations (#11474)*; *Union for the International Registration of Audiovisual Works (#20444)*. Working relations with: *International Telecommunication Union (ITU, #15673)*, especially its Radiocommunication Sector. Accredited by: *United Nations Office at Vienna (UNOV, #20604)*. Related union: *Arab States Broadcasting Union (ASBU, #01050)*. Invited to sessions of Intergovernmental Council of: *International Programme for the Development of Communication (IPDC, #14651)*. **NGO Relations** Organizes: *World Conference of Broadcasting Unions*, together with related unions *Asia-Pacific Broadcasting Union (ABU, #01863)*; *Caribbean Broadcasting Union (CBU, #03465)*; *European Broadcasting Union (EBU, #06404)*; *International Association of Broadcasting (IAB, #11738)*; *North American Broadcasters Association (NABA, #17561)*; *African Union of Broadcasting (AUB, #00490)*. Member of: *World Broadcasting Unions (WBU, #21247)*. Cooperation with: International Federation of Association Football (FIFA); International Olympic Committee (IOC). [2020/XD3999/**D**]

♦ Organización de Telecomunicaciones Iberoamericanas / see Organización de Telecomunicaciones de Iberoamérica (#17851)
♦ Organización de la Televisión Iberoamericana / see Organización de Telecomunicaciones de Iberoamérica (#17851)
♦ Organización del Tratado de Cooperación Amazónica (#00766)
♦ Organización para una Red Internacional de Indicaciones Geograficas (#17874)
♦ Organización de Universidades Católicas de América Latina / see Organization of Catholic Universities in Latin America and the Caribbean (#17858)
♦ Organización de Universidades Católicas de América Latina y el Caribe (#17858)
♦ Organización Universitaria Interamericana (#11442)
♦ Organiza Societo de Internaciaj Esperanto Konferencoj (internationally oriented national body)
♦ Organizatia Mondiala a Copiilor Talentati (#21694)
♦ Organization for the Advancement of Structured Information Standards (internationally oriented national body)
♦ Organization of the African First Ladies Against HIV/AIDS / see Organization of African First Ladies for Development (#17852)

♦ Organization of African First Ladies for Development (OAFLAD) . . . 17852

Exec Sec PO Box 21291, Africa Avenue, behind Getu Commercial Centre, 1000 Addis Ababa, Ethiopia. T. +251115508069 – +251118962998. E-mail: info@oaflad.org.
Communications Officer address not obtained.
URL: https://oaflad.org/fr/

History 19 Jul 2002, Geneva (Switzerland). Founded following a series of informal meetings since 2001. Former names and other names: *Organization of the African First Ladies Against HIV/AIDS (OAFLA)* – former (2002 to 2019). **Aims** End the AIDS epidemic as a public health threat, reducing maternal and child mortality and empowering women and children through strategic partnerships in the spirit of solidarity. **Structure** General Assembly; Steering Committee; Executive Secretariat. **Languages** Arabic, English, French, Portuguese. **Activities** Advocacy/lobbying/activism; events/meetings. **Events** *Engaging men and boys for gender equality* Addis Ababa (Ethiopia) 2020, *General Assembly* Addis Ababa (Ethiopia) 2019, *General Assembly* Addis Ababa (Ethiopia) 2018, *General Assembly* Addis Ababa (Ethiopia) 2017, *General Assembly* Addis Ababa (Ethiopia) 2016. **Publications** OAFLA annual publication. **Members** Spouses of African Heads of State (32). Membership countries not specified. **IGO Relations** *African Union (AU, #00488)*; *International Planned Parenthood Federation (IPPF, #14589)*; *Joint United Nations Programme on HIV/AIDS (UNAIDS, #16149)*; *United Nations Population Fund (UNFPA, #20612)*; *WHO (#20950)*. **NGO Relations** Elizabeth Glazer Pediatric Foundation; *Every Woman Every Child (EWEC, #09215)*; *International AIDS Trust (IAT)*. [2021/XD8753/**D**]

♦ Organization of African Instituted Churches (OAIC) 17853

Contact PO Box 21736-00505, Ngong Rd, Nairobi, Kenya. T. +254203870356. E-mail: admin@oaic.org.
URL: http://www.oaic.org/

History 1978, Cairo (Egypt). **Aims** Bring African Instituted Churches together in fellowship; equip and enable them to preach the Good News of Jesus Christ in word and deed. **Structure** General Assembly. Executive Committee. General Secretary. **Events** *General Assembly* Limuru (Kenya) 1997, *General Assembly* Nairobi (Kenya) 1982. **Publications** *Our Voices, Our Lives* – electronic newsletter. **Members** Full (over 1,000). Membership countries not specified. **NGO Relations** Member of: *African Council of Religious Leaders – Religions for Peace (ACRL-RfP, #00276)*; *Joint Learning Initiative on Faith and Local Communities (JLI, #16139)*; *World Council of Churches (WCC, #21320)*. [2011/XJ2792/**D**]

♦ Organization of African Unity (inactive)
♦ Organization for Afro-Asian Peoples' Solidarity / see Afro-Asian Peoples' Solidarity Organization (#00537)
♦ Organizational Symbolism / see Standing Conference on Organizational Symbolism (#19962)
♦ Organization of American States (#17629)
♦ Organization of Arab Architects / see Arab Architects Organization (#00898)

♦ Organization of Arab Petroleum Exporting Countries (OAPEC) 17854

Organisation des pays arabes exportateurs de pétrole (OPAEP) – Organización de Paises Arabes Exportadores de Petróleo (OPAEP)

SG PO Box 20501, 13066 Safat, Kuwait. T. +96524959000. E-mail: oapec@oapecorg.org.
URL: http://www.oapecorg.org/

History 9 Jan 1968. Founded by the Governments of Saudi Arabia, Kuwait and Libya. **Aims** Coordinate efforts and encourage cooperation among member countries in the various forms of economic activity in the petroleum industry; undertake research into production and manpower requirements in Arab petroleum projects; establish a central research and documentation system. Promote and coordinate activities leading to: development of petroleum industry infrastructure in Arab countries; establishment of joint ventures in the Arab oil industry; dissemination of information on energy and economics. **Structure** Ministerial Council (meets twice a year) comprising 10 oil Ministers or comparable officials from each member country; chairmanship rotates annually. Executive Bureau (meets 3 times a year) consisting of 10 senior official (one from each member country); chairmanship rotates annually. *Judicial Tribunal of the Organization of Arab Petroleum Exporting Countries (OAPEC Judicial Tribunal, see: #17854)*, consisting of 5 judges, including Tribunal President, Vice-President and 3 members. General Secretariat, comprising Secretary General and Directors of 4 Departments: Information and Library; Finance and Administrative Affairs; Economics; Technical Affairs. The 2 latter departments comprise *Arab Centre for Energy Studies (ACES, no recent information)*. **Languages** Arabic. **Staff** 34.00 FTE, paid. **Finance** Sources: members' dues. Members contribute to the Secretariat budget in equal shares. Annual budget: 2,000,000 KWD.
Activities Organizes: Arab Energy Conference (every 4 years); Meeting of Experts from Energy Exporting and Importing Countries (every 2 years); Coordination Meeting of Environment Experts in OAPEC Countries; annual coordination meeting of OAPEC-sponsored joint ventures; specialized symposia; cooperation seminars with non-Arab countries; joint conferences, meetings and workshops; training programmes, notably through *Arab Petroleum Training Institute (APTI, no recent information)*. Presents *'OAPEC Scientific Award'* for research in the field.
Coordinates with *League of Arab States (LAS, #16420)* in the following areas:
– Participation in meetings of *High Coordination Committee for Joint Arab Action (no recent information)*;
– Monitoring progress of work on the *'Greater Arab Free Trade Area'* (GAFTA);
– Cooperation on environmental affairs, as an Observer in the meetings of *Council of Arab Ministers Responsible for the Environment (CAMRE, #04863)*;
– Unified Arab Economic Report, also in cooperation with *Arab Monetary Fund (AMF, #01009)* and *Arab Fund for Economic and Social Development (AFESD, #00965)*.
OAPEC-sponsored ventures (joint undertakings):
– *Arab Maritime Petroleum Transport Company (AMPTC, see: #17854)*;
– *Arab Shipbuilding and Repair Yard Company (ASRY, see: #17854)*;
– *Arab Petroleum Investments Corporation (APICORP, #01026)*, including –
  – *Arab Company for Detergent Chemicals (ARADET, see: #17854)*;
– *Arab Petroleum Services Company (APSCO, see: #17854)*, including –
  – *Arab Drilling and Workover Company (ADWOC, see: #17854)*,
  – *Arab Well Logging Company (AWLCO, see: #17854)*,
  – *Arab Geophysical Exploration Services Company (AGESCO, #00968)*.
Relevant treaties include: *United Nations Framework Convention on Climate Change (UNFCCC, 1992)*.
Events *Arab Energy Conference* Qatar 2023, *Annual Oxford Energy Seminar* Oxford (UK) 2021, *Annual Oxford Energy Seminar* Oxford (UK) 2019, *Quadrennial Arab Energy Conference* Marrakech (Morocco) 2018, *Annual Oxford Energy Seminar* Oxford (UK) 2017. **Publications** *Energy Resources Monitor* (4 a year) in Arabic; *Oil and Arab Cooperation* (4 a year) in Arabic – with English abstracts; *Annual Report of OAPEC Secretary-General* in Arabic, English; *OAPEC Annual Statistical Report* in Arabic, English; *OAPEC Databank* – used for statistical tables and graphs; *OAPEC Monthly Bulletin* in Arabic, English. **Information Services** *OAPEC Databank* – used for statistical tables and graphs.
Members Governments of 10 countries:
Algeria, Bahrain, Egypt, Iraq, Kuwait, Libya, Qatar, Saudi Arabia, Syrian AR, United Arab Emirates.
IGO Relations Collaborative Arab organization of: *Arab Organization for Agricultural Development (AOAD, #01018)*. Cooperation agreement with: *International Maritime Organization (IMO, #14102)*. Accredited by: *United Nations Framework Convention on Climate Change – Secretariat (UNFCCC, #20564)*. Invited to sessions of Intergovernmental Council of: *International Programme for the Development of Communication (IPDC, #14651)*. **NGO Relations** In liaison with technical committees of: *International Organization for Standardization (ISO, #14473)*. [2021.03.04/XD0064/**D***]

♦ Organization of Asian-Pacific News Agencies (OANA) 17855

Organisation des agences d'information d'Asie et du Pacifique

SG Yonhap News Agency, 25 Yulgokro 2-gil, Jongno-gu, Seoul 03143, Korea Rep. T. +8223983661. E-mail: oana_yonhap@yna.co.kr.
URL: http://www.oananews.org/

History 19 Dec 1961, Bangkok (Thailand). Founded at 1st General Assembly (when statutes were adopted), immediately following a Unesco sponsored meeting on the development of national news agencies in Asia. **Aims** Extend the areas of cooperation among the national news agencies and raise intellectual standard of the region. **Structure** General Assembly (every 3 years); Executive Board; Secretary-General. **Languages** English. **Finance** Sources: members' dues. **Activities** Awards/prizes/competitions; knowledge management/information dissemination; networking/liaising. **Events** *General Assembly* Teheran (Iran Islamic Rep) 2022, *Triennial General assembly* Seoul (Korea Rep) 2019, *Congress / General Assembly* Seoul (Korea Rep) 2010, *General Assembly* Jakarta (Indonesia) 2007, *General Assembly* Kuala Lumpur (Malaysia) 2004. **Publications** *OANA Newsletter* (4 a year).
Members News agencies (31) in 24 countries:
Afghanistan, Australia, Bangladesh, Cambodia, China, India, Indonesia, Iran Islamic Rep, Japan, Kazakhstan, Korea DPR, Korea Rep, Kyrgyzstan, Laos, Malaysia, Mongolia, Nepal, Pakistan, Philippines, Russia, Sri Lanka, Thailand, Türkiye, Vietnam.
IGO Relations *UNESCO (#20322)*. **NGO Relations** Partner of (4): *Alliance of Mediterranean News Agencies (AMAN, #00708)*; *Association of the Balkan News Agencies (ABNA, #02393)*; *European Alliance of News Agencies (EANA, #05877)*; *Fédération Atlantique des Agences de Presse Africaines (FAAPA, #09462)*. *Asia-Pacific Broadcasting Union (ABU, #01863)*; *Asian Media Information and Communication Centre (AMIC, #01536)*. [2022/XF3031/**D**]

♦ Organization of the Baltic Ports / see Baltic Ports Organization (#03136)

♦ Organization of Biological Field Stations (OBFS) 17856

Mailing Address PO Box 400327, Charlottesville VA 22904-4327, USA.
Sec 4001 Sound Hill Rd, Woodside CA 94062, USA.
URL: http://www.obfs.org/

History Proposed to set up: *International Organization of Biological Field Stations (IOBFS, no recent information).* **Aims** Advance biological sciences through field station research and teaching programmes. **Structure** Board of Directors; Executive Committee. **Staff** None. **Activities** Events/meetings. **Events** *Annual Meeting* Beaver Is, MI (USA) 2022, *Annual Meeting* Polson, MT (USA) 2021, *Annual Meeting* Polson, MT (USA) 2020, *Annual Meeting* Brussels (Belgium) 2019, *Annual Meeting* Winter Harbor, ME (USA) 2018. **Publications** *OBFS Newsletter* (2 a year).
Members Institutional; individual. Field stations (over 200) in 10 countries and territories:
Australia, Bahamas, Bermuda, Canada, Costa Rica, Dominica, Nicaragua, Panama, Puerto Rico, USA.
[2020.06.29/XD6562/**D**]

♦ Organization of Black Sea Economic Cooperation (BSEC) 17857

Permanent Int Secretariat Darüssafaka Cad, Seba Center Is Merkezi, No 45 Kat 3, Istinye, 34460 Istanbul/Istanbul, Türkiye. T. +902122296330 – +90212229633l – +902122296335. Fax +902122296336. E-mail: info@bsec-organization.org.
URL: http://www.bsec-organization.org/

History Established 25 Jun 1992, as *Black Sea Economic Cooperation – Coopération économique de la Mer Noire (CEMN)*, when Heads of State or Government of 11 States signed the Istanbul (Turkey) "Summit Declaration on Black Sea Economic Cooperation". Current name adopted, 1 May 1999, when a Charter was signed by the Heads of State or Government of the Member States, 5 Jun 1998, Yalta (Ukraine). **Aims** Ensure that the Black Sea becomes a sea of peace, stability and prosperity; promote friendly and good-neighbourly relations; develop comprehensive multilateral and bilateral economic cooperation covering various fields of activity in order to foster their economic, technological and social progress; make best use of all opportunities for enhancing the mutually advantageous economic and trade cooperation arising from the geographic proximity of member states and encourage free enterprise.
Structure Organizational structure comprises 6 components.
(i) /Intergovernmental component/: *Council of the Ministers of Foreign Affairs* of the Member States, the regular decision-making body; *'Sessional Chairman'*, rotating in alphabetical order every 6 months; *'Committee of Senior Officials'*; *'Working Groups'*; ad hoc *'Working Groups of Organizational Matters'* representing Subsidiary Bodies established by the Council; Permanent International Secretariat (PERMIS), set up 1994, headquartered in Istanbul (Turkey).
(ii) /Interparliamentary component/: *Parliamentary Assembly of the Organization of the Black Sea Economic Cooperation (PABSEC, #18213).*
(iii) /Business component/: *Organization of the Black Sea Economic Cooperation Business Council (BSEC BC)*, private sector organization, which operates through a Secretariat based in Istanbul.
(iv) /Financial component/: *Black Sea Trade and Development Bank (BSTDB, #03278)*, located in Thessaloniki (Greece).
(v) /Academic component/ or academic dimension: *International Centre for Black Sea Studies (ICBSS, #12478)*, fostering the process of cooperation among academic communities whose main purpose is the application of the achievements of science and technology to concrete fields of economic cooperation.
(vi) /Information component/: *Black Sea Economic Cooperation Centre for the Exchange of Statistical Data and Economic Information (BSECCESDEI, #03273).*
Languages English, Russian. **Staff** 24.00 FTE, paid. **Finance** Supported by all 12 Member States. **Activities** Member States agree to identify, develop and carry out projects of common interest in the following areas: agriculture; banking and finance; communications; combating crime; education; emergency; energy; environment; exchange of statistical data and information; healthcare and pharmaceutics; institutional renewal and good governance; science and technology; SMEs; tourism; trade and economic development; transport. **Events** *PromitheasNet International Scientific Conference on Energy and Climate Change* Athens (Greece) 2019, *PromitheasNet International Scientific Conference on Energy and Climate Change* Athens (Greece) 2018, *Meeting of the Ministers in Charge of Information and Communication Technologies* Baku (Azerbaijan) 2018, *Meeting* Baku (Azerbaijan) 2018, *PromitheasNet International Scientific Conference on Energy and Climate Change* Athens (Greece) 2017. **Publications** *Black Sea News. Handbook of Documents* – in 5 vols. Booklets of meetings; Brochures; statutory documents. **Information Services** *Black Sea Economic Cooperation Centre for the Exchange of Statistical Data and Economic Information* – ensures flow of statistical and economic information among Participating States.
Members Participating States (12):
Albania, Armenia, Azerbaijan, Bulgaria, Georgia, Greece, Moldova, Romania, Russia, Serbia, Türkiye, Ukraine.
Observer states (12):
Austria, Belarus, Croatia, Czechia, Egypt, Germany, Israel, Italy, Poland, Slovakia, Tunisia, USA.
Observer organizations (3):
Energy Charter Conference (#05466); European Commission (EC, #06633); International Black Sea Club (IBSC, #12358).
Sectoral Dialogue Partner states (6):
Hungary, Iran Islamic Rep, Japan, Korea Rep, Montenegro, Slovenia.
Sectoral Dialogue Partner organizations (10):
Black and Azov Seas Ports Association (BASPA, #03268); Black Sea Broadcasting Regulatory Authorities Forum (BRAF, #03272); Black Sea Region Association of Shipbuilders and Ship Repairers (BRASS, #03277); Black Sea University Network (BSUN); Commission du Danube (CD, #04210); Conference of Peripheral Maritime Regions of Europe (CPMR, #04638); International Black Sea Region Association of Shipowners (BINSA, #12359); International Network for Small and Medium Sized Enterprises (INSME, #14325); Union of Road Transport Associations in the Black Sea Economic Cooperation Region (BSEC-URTA, #20477); World Tourism Organization (UNWTO, #21861).
IGO Relations Observer status with: *ECOSOC (#05331); United Nations (UN, #20515).* Member of: Energy Charter Secretariat; *United Nations Alliance of Civilizations (UNAOC, #20520).* Memorandum of Understanding with: *Commission on the Protection of the Black Sea Against Pollution (Black Sea Commission, #04237).* Cooperates with: *Budapest Process (#03344); Central European Initiative (CEI, #03708); Committee on Sustainable Energy (#04288); OECD (#17693); Organization for Security and Cooperation in Europe (OSCE, #17887); UNIDO (#20336); United Nations Economic Commission for Europe (UNECE, #20555).* **NGO Relations** Memorandum of Understanding with: *International Road Transport Union (IRU, #14761).*
[2018/XF2514/y/**F***]

- ♦ Organization of the Black Sea Economic Cooperation Business Council (no recent information)
- ♦ Organization of Caribbean Administrators of Sport and Physical Education (no recent information)
- ♦ Organization of Catholic Universities in Latin America / see Organization of Catholic Universities in Latin America and the Caribbean (#17858)

♦ Organization of Catholic Universities in Latin America and the Caribbean 17858

Organización de Universidades Católicas de América Latina y el Caribe (ODUCAL)
Sec Av Libertador Bernardo O'Higgins 340, Of 242 – 2o piso, Santiago, Santiago Metropolitan, Chile. T. +56223541866. E-mail: oducal@uc.cl.
Pres address not obtained.
URL: http://www.oducal.uc.cl/

History 1953, Santiago (Chile), as *Organization of Catholic Universities in Latin America – Organisation des universités catholiques de l'Amérique latine – Organización de Universidades Católicas de América Latina (ODUCAL).* Regional association of *International Federation of Catholic Universities (IFCU, #13381).* Current statutes adopted, 2007. **Aims** Uphold the progress of knowledge and development of Catholic universities in Latin America and the Caribbean through promoting study of their common concerns, encouraging collaboration, and providing support for communication and cooperation amongst members. **Structure** General Assembly (every 3 years); Directive Board; Sub-Regions (4). **Languages** Portuguese, Spanish. **Staff** 2.00 FTE, paid; 2.00 FTE, voluntary. **Finance** Members' dues. Grants. **Activities** Events/meetings; training/education. **Events** *Extraordinary Assembly* Bogota (Colombia) 2020, *General Assembly* Santiago (Chile) 2018, *Annual General Assembly* Chiclayo (Peru) 2012, *Annual General Assembly* Antofagasta (Chile) 2009, *Annual General Assembly* Mexico City (Mexico) 2008.
Members Catholic universities (101) in 18 countries:
Argentina, Bolivia, Brazil, Chile, Colombia, Costa Rica, Dominican Rep, Ecuador, Guatemala, Honduras, Mexico, Nicaragua, Panama, Paraguay, Peru, Puerto Rico, Uruguay, Venezuela.
NGO Relations Cooperates with: *Consejo Episcopal Latinoamericano (CELAM, #04709).* Instrumental in setting up: *Asociación Latinoamericana de Derecho Constitucional (ALDEC, no recent information).*
[2021/XD3032/**D**]

- ♦ Organization of Central American States (inactive)
- ♦ Organization of Commonwealth Caribbean Bar Associations (inactive)

♦ Organization for Computational Neurosciences (OCNS) 17859

Main Office 2885 Sanford Ave SW, Ste 15359, Grandville MI 49418, USA. E-mail: cns@cnsorg.org.
URL: http://www.cnsorg.org/

History 2003. Registration: Start date: 11 Feb 2004, USA, California. **Aims** Create a scientific and educational forum for students, scientists, other professionals and the general public to learn about, share, contribute to, and advance the state of knowledge in computational neuroscience. **Structure** Board of Directors. **Activities** Events/meetings. **Events** *Annual Computational Neuroscience Meeting* Melbourne, VIC (Australia) 2022, *Computational Neuroscience Meeting* Grandville, MI (USA) 2021, *Annual Meeting* Barcelona (Spain) 2019, *Annual Meeting* Jeju (Korea Rep) 2016, *Annual Meeting* Prague (Czech Rep) 2015. [2021/XJ6993/**C**]

- ♦ Organization of Conventions Bureaus of Latin America and the Caribbean (no recent information)
- ♦ Organization for Cooperation in Iron and Steel Industry (inactive)
- ♦ Organization for Cooperation in the Roller Bearings Industry (inactive)
- ♦ Organization for Cooperation of Socialist Countries in the Domain of Tele- and Postal Communications (inactive)
- ♦ Organization of the Cooperatives of America (inactive)

♦ Organization of Coordination for the Control of Endemic Diseases in Central Africa 17860

Organisation de coordination pour la lutte contre les endémies en Afrique centrale (OCEAC)
SG BP 15665, Yaoundé, Cameroon. T. +23722232232. Fax +23722230061. E-mail: contact@oceac.org.
URL: http://www.oceac.org/

History Aug 1963, Yaoundé (Cameroon), by the Governments of Cameroon, Central African Republic, Chad, Congo Brazzaville and Gabon, as *Organisation de coordination et de coopération pour la lutte contre les grandes endémies en Afrique centrale (OCCGEAC)* on the initiative of Dr S P Tchoungi, Minister of Public Health of the Cameroon. Statutes adopted 8 Jul 1965, Yaoundé. Present title adopted and constitution modified, Jun 1966, Fort Lamy (currently Ndjamena). Government of Equatorial Guinea admitted Nov 1983, Brazzaville. **Aims** Constitute a regional scientific focus for public health development in Member States, a regional structure for scientific initiatives, coordinating all Member State public health activity; participate in training Member States' health personnel; provide technical support through expert missions; undertake complementary activities financed through extra-budgetary resources to obtain the interest and support of nongovernmental organizations and bilateral and multilateral aid agencies. **Structure** Administrative Council (meeting annually), comprising Health Ministers of Member States, elects President and Secretary-General. Permanent Secretariat, including Secretary-General and Technical and Scientific Director, consists of 11 doctors, an administrator, a statistical engineer and staff. Inter-State Ministerial Committee. Departments: Public Health; Information; Medical Entomology; Biology; Administrative and Financial. **Languages** English, French, Spanish. **Staff** 59.00 FTE, paid. **Finance** Member States' contribute equally. Financial aid from: French and German institutions; *WHO (#20950); WHO Regional Office for Africa (AFRO, #20943).* **Activities** Organizes training courses; coordinates and supports national programmes for the prevention and control of diseases, and education, training and applied research programmes. Negotiates assistance agreements with national and international organizations; statistical service; biennial technical conferences in Yaoundé (Cameroon) (and in alternate years elsewhere); epidemiological work groups meet in Yaoundé. *Centre inter-Etats d'enseignement supérieur de santé publique pour l'Afrique centrale (CIESPAC, no recent information)* set up, 1988, Brazzaville (Congo Brazzaville). **Events** *Technical conference* Yaoundé (Cameroon) 1994, *Meeting* Yaoundé (Cameroon) 1990, *Technical conference* Yaoundé (Cameroon) 1990, *Maladies endémo-épidémiques* Libreville (Gabon) 1988, *Working group meeting* Brazzaville (Congo Brazzaville) 1986. **Publications** *Magazine de l'OCEAC* (12 a year); *Bulletin de l'OCEAC* (4 a year). *Notes techniques.* Technical reports; conference proceedings; brochures and leaflets; CD-ROM.
Members Governments of 6 countries:
Cameroon, Central African Rep, Chad, Congo Brazzaville, Equatorial Guinea, Gabon. [2018/XD3022/**D***]

- ♦ Organization for Data Exchange by Teletransmission in Europe / see Odette International (#17689)
- ♦ Organization for Defending Victims of Violence (internationally oriented national body)

♦ Organization for Democracy and Economic Development (GUAM) . . 17861

Secretariat Sofiyivska Str 2-A, Kiev, 01001, Ukraine. T. +380442063737. Fax +380442063006. E-mail: secretariat@guam-organization.org.
URL: https://guam-organization.org/en/

History 10 Oct 1997, as *GUAM Group*, by governments of Azerbaijan, Georgia, Moldova and Ukraine. Changed title to *GUUAM Group*, Apr 1999 when Uzbekistan joined. Uzbekistan suspended membership Jun 2002 and withdrew, Apr 2005, when former title was again adopted. **Aims** Strengthen independence and *sovereignty* of former member countries of the *USSR.* **Structure** Council, working at level of Heads of State; Foreign Ministers; National Coordinators; Permanent Representatives; Secretariat, headed by Secretary General. **Events** *Summit* Yalta, Crimea (Ukraine) 2003. **Publications** *GUAM News.*
Members Governments of 4 countries:
Azerbaijan, Georgia, Moldova, Ukraine.
IGO Relations Permanent Observer to: *ECOSOC (#05331).* Observer to the General Assembly of: *United Nations (UN, #20515).* Member of: *Intergovernmental Organizations Conference (IGO Conference, #11498).*
[2021/XE4613/**E***]

- ♦ Organization of Demographic Associates for East and Southeast Asia (inactive)
- ♦ Organization for the Development of the River Gambia / see Organisation pour la mise en valeur du fleuve Gambie (#17814)
- ♦ Organization for the Development of the Senegal River / see Organisation pour la mise en valeur du fleuve Sénégal (#17815)
- ♦ Organization Earth (internationally oriented national body)

♦ Organization for East Asia Economic Development (OEAED) 17862

Contact 1-1 Johnai, Kokurakita-ku, Kitakyushu FUKUOKA, Japan. T. +81935822162. Fax +81935822176.

History Nov 1993. **Aims** Revitalize economic activities and inter-city exchanges; form new economic zones in the Yellow Sea Rim Districts; contribute to development of the East Asian Economic Zone. **Structure** General Assembly; Executive; Committees (4); Secretariat. **Languages** Chinese, Japanese, Korean. **Events** *Plenary Meeting* Incheon (Korea Rep) 2018, *Environment Working Group Meeting* Kitakyushu (Japan) 2018, *Environment Working Group Meeting* Busan (Korea Rep) 2017, *Tourism Seminar* Ulsan (Korea Rep) 2015, *Environment working Group Meeting* Seoul (Korea Rep) 2014.
Members Cities (11) in 3 countries:
China, Japan, Korea Rep. [2019.07.02/XM1816/**D**]

- ♦ Organization of Eastern Africa Insurers / see Organization of Eastern and Southern Africa Insurers (#17864)

♦ Organization of Eastern Caribbean Bar Associations (OECS Bar Association) 17863

Pres c/o Ciboney Chambers, 1 HA Blaize Street, St George's, St George, St George's ST GEORGE, Grenada.

History 21 Oct 1989, Dickenson Bay (Antigua-Barbuda), within *Eastern Caribbean Supreme Court (ECSC, #05236)*. **Aims** Represent, promote and protect the interest of the legal profession within the region; be concerned with questions of human rights and the rule of law; protect the public's rights of access to the courts and to legal representation; work for the improvement of the administration of justice; undertake any action which contributes to the protection and preservation of fundamental conditions for a well ordered society. **Structure** General Meeting (every 2 years). Council. Executive Committee, comprising President, 2 Vice-Presidents, Secretary and Treasurer. **Languages** English. **Staff** 7.00 FTE, paid. **Finance** Members' dues. **Activities** Organizes annual Law Fair.
Members Covers 9 countries and territories:
Anguilla, Antigua-Barbuda, Bahamas, Dominica, Grenada, Montserrat, St Kitts-Nevis, St Vincent-Grenadines, Virgin Is UK.
IGO Relations Close cooperation with: *Regional Judicial and Legal Services Commission (RJLSC, #18793)*.
[2012.11.29/XD8483/**D**]

♦ Organization of Eastern and Southern Africa Insurers (OESAI) 17864

Contact PO Box 58316-00200, Nairobi, Kenya. T. +254202222354. E-mail: admin@oesai.org – info@oesai.org.
Street Address 22nd Anniversary Towers, Univ Way, Nairobi, Kenya.
URL: http://www.oesai.org/
History 1973, Yaoundé (Cameroon), as *Organization of Eastern Africa Insurers – Organisation des assurances est-africaines*. **Aims** Provide a forum for promoting, expanding and developing insurance business. **Structure** Board. **Activities** Events/meetings; training/education. **Publications** *OESAI Newsletter* (12 a year).
Members Full in 18 countries:
Angola, Botswana, Côte d'Ivoire, Eritrea, Eswatini, Kenya, Malawi, Mauritius, Mozambique, Namibia, Rwanda, Seychelles, South Africa, Tanzania UR, Togo, Uganda, Zambia, Zimbabwe.
NGO Relations *African Trade Insurance Agency (ATI, #00485)*. [2019/XN0924/**D**]

- ♦ Organization of Employers' Federations and Employers in Developing Countries (inactive)
- ♦ Organization of Estonian, Latvian and Lithuanian Transmission System Operators (inactive)

♦ Organization of European Cancer Institutes (OECI) 17865

Dir c/o Fondation Universitaire, Rue d'Egmont 11, 1000 Brussels, Belgium. T. +3225413022. E-mail: oeci@oeci.eu.
Dir c/o SOS Europe, Via delle Campanule 74, 16148 Genoa GE, Italy.
URL: http://www.oeci.eu/
History 14 May 1979, Vienna (Austria). Founded at meeting of directors of European institutes. A grouping of the type *European Economic Interest Grouping (EEIG, #06960)* since 2005. Registration: Belgium; Switzerland. **Aims** Contribute to production and dissemination of knowledge in order to reduce fragmentation and increase competitiveness with the ultimate goal of finding new and better treatments, providing more comprehensive care and improving patients' quality of life through evidence-based medicine with a holistic approach. **Structure** General Assembly (annual); Executive Board; Headquarters in Brussels (Belgium). **Languages** English. **Staff** 3.00 FTE, paid. **Finance** Members' dues. Other sources: projects; public and private revenues. **Activities** Training/education; projects/programmes; certification/accreditation; standards/guidelines; knowledge management/information dissemination. **Events** *OECI Days – Annual General Assembly and Scientific Conference* Oslo (Norway) 2025, *OECI Days – Annual General Assembly and Scientific Conference* Helsinki (Finland) 2024, *OECI Days – Annual General Assembly and Scientific Conference* Paris (France) 2023, *OECI Days – Annual General Assembly and Scientific Conference* Valencia (Spain) 2022, *Joint Conference on Cancer Imaging* Oxford (UK) 2021. **Publications** *OECI Magazine*. *OECI Accreditation and Designation Manual*. Annual report; membership directory.
Members Institutes (81) in 26 countries:
Austria, Belgium, Croatia, Czechia, Denmark, Estonia, Finland, France, Germany, Hungary, Ireland, Italy, Lithuania, Netherlands, Norway, Portugal, Romania, Russia, Serbia, Slovakia, Slovenia, Spain, Sweden, Türkiye, UK, Ukraine.
NGO Relations Member of: *European Cancer Organisation (ECO, #06432)*. [2022/XD3809/**D**]

♦ Organization of European Copper Alloy Ingot Makers (OECAM) 17866

Organisation européenne d'affineurs d'alliages cuivreux – Organisation Europäischer Hersteller von Kupfergusslegierungen – Organizzazione dei Produttori Europei di Pani de Leghe di Rame
General Manager Wallstrasse 58/59, 10179 Berlin, Germany. T. +4930726207119.
URL: http://www.oecam.org/
History 1989, Venice (Italy). **Aims** Promote cooperation between copper alloy ingot makers. **Structure** Board. Officers: President; Vice-President; Treasurer. General Manager.
Members Companies in 8 countries:
Austria, France, Germany, Italy, Netherlands, Spain, Türkiye, UK. [2010.06.01/XD7153/**D**]

- ♦ Organization for European Economic Cooperation (inactive)
- ♦ Organization of European Industries Transforming Fruit and Vegetables / see European Association of Fruit and Vegetable Processors (#06049)
- ♦ Organization of European Saw-Mills / see European Organization of the Sawmill Industry (#08114)
- ♦ Organization of European Shipsuppliers / see European Ship Suppliers Organization (#08478)
- ♦ Organization européenne de la FME / see European Organization of the World Organization of Workers (#08116)
- ♦ Organization of Faculties, Schools and Departments of Odontology of the Union of Latin American Universities (#17837)

♦ Organization of the Families of Asia and the Pacific (OFAP) 17867

Organização das Familias da Asia e do Pacifico
Pres Avenida do Coronel Mesquita No 2-H, Macau, Macau. T. +85328529531. Fax +85328550224.
URL: http://www.ofapmacau.org/
History 1999, Macau. Former names and other names: *Asia and Pacific Family Organization (APFO)* – alias. **Aims** Represent families in the Asia-Pacific region at different levels; defend and fight for their interests; liaise with governments and international communities. **Structure** General Assembly. Executive Committee, comprising President, Vice-President, Secretary-General, Treasurer and members. **Events** *Reinforce the family for a better and sustainable future* Macau (Macau) 2013. **Consultative Status** Consultative status granted from: *ECOSOC (#05331)* (Special). **NGO Relations** Member of (2): *International Federation of Non-Government Organizations for the Prevention of Drug and Substance Abuse (IFNGO, #13490)*; *Vienna NGO Committee on Drugs (VNGOC, #20773)*. [2020/XJ5195/**D**]

- ♦ Organization of the Felt Industry in Europe (inactive)
- ♦ Organization of the Fishing and Aquaculture Sector of the Central American Isthmus (#17848)

♦ Organization for Flora Neotropica (OFN) 17868

Organisation pour Flora Neotropica – Organización pro Flora Neotropica
Exec Dir Inst of Systematic Botany, New York Botanical Garden, Bronx NY 10458-5126, USA. E-mail: ofn@nybg.org.
URL: https://www.nybg.org/bsci/ofn/ofn.html
History 17 Dec 1964, Sao Paulo (Brazil). Founded under the aegis of UNESCO. **Aims** Produce and publish a general and complete flora of the *tropical American* region, using services and skills of specialized *botanists* throughout the world with cooperation of botanical institutions. **Structure** Commission; Executive Board, consisting of 9 members. **Languages** English, Portuguese, Spanish. **Staff** Voluntary. **Finance** Sources: sale of publications. Other sources: grants from UNESCO. **Activities** Inventory of plant resources of the Western Hemisphere tropics. **Events** *Annual meeting* La Serena (Chile) 2010, *Annual meeting* Feira de Santana (Brazil) 2009, *Annual meeting* Puerto Maldonado (Peru) 2008, *Annual meeting* Santo Domingo (Dominican Rep) 2006, *Annual meeting* Vienna (Austria) 2005. **Publications** *Flora Neotropica* – monograph series – 82 vols to date.
Members Individuals in 36 countries and territories:
Argentina, Australia, Austria, Belgium, Bolivia, Brazil, Canada, Chile, Colombia, Costa Rica, Cuba, Denmark, Dominican Rep, Ecuador, El Salvador, Finland, France, Germany, Guiana Fr, Honduras, Japan, Mexico, Netherlands, Nicaragua, Norway, Panama, Paraguay, Peru, Puerto Rico, Spain, Suriname, Sweden, Switzerland, UK, USA, Venezuela.
IGO Relations Associated with Department of Global Communications of the United Nations.
[2020/XC4246/v/**C**]

- ♦ Organization of Gas Producing Countries (unconfirmed)

♦ Organization Gestosis (OG) 17869

Organisation gestose – Organización Gestosis – Organisation Gestose – Organizzazione per le Gestosi – Organizacija Gestoza
SG Gupte Hospital, 904 Bhandarkar Road, Pune, Maharashtra 411 004, Pune MAHARASHTRA 411 004, India.
Senior Advisor State Univ Maternity Hosp, 23 Melikishvili Str – Ap 1, 0179 Tbilisi, Georgia. T. +99532293543. Fax +99532530362.
URL: http://www.gestosis.ge/
History 1969, Basel (Switzerland). Founded at 1st International Symposium on EPH-Gestosis. The organization is acting as *Society for the Study of Pathophysiology of Pregnancy* and *International Society for Research in EPH-Gestosis*. Registration: Switzerland. **Aims** Promote the study of EPH / edema, proteinurea, hypertension/ – Gestosis pathophysiology of *pregnancy*; internationalize nomenclature and classification, both as a basis for diagnosis and therapy and as a comparative technique; standardize methods of investigation; serve as a documentation centre; foster the exchange of scientists: recommend measures for prophylaxis and treatment of EPH gestosis. **Structure** Annual Meeting (in conjunction with Congress). Steering Committee; Consulting Committee. *'Organizations Gestosis Affiliated and Sponsored Hospitals'*, comprising Chairman/President, Vice-President, Patriarch/Permanent Honorary Secretary-General, Secretary-General/Past-President and 8 members. Joint Board OG/ *International Society for the Study of Hypertension in Pregnancy (ISSHP, #15475)*. Regional Secretariats (9). **Languages** Croatian, Czech, English, French, German, Italian, Serbian, Spanish. **Staff** 0.50 FTE, paid; 1.00 FTE, voluntary. **Finance** Sources: members' dues. Annual budget: 50,000 CHF. **Activities** Attention focused on such topics as: oedema in pregnancy, proteinuria, hypertension, cytology, serum, protein. Organizes symposia and national and regional meetings; conducts workshops, discussion groups and study groups. Makes recommendations for the most modern and successful measures of prevention and treatment of EPH-Gestosis. Collects and publishes papers submitted by researchers worldwide. Publicizes findings to general public as well as to specialist individuals and organizations. **Events** *International Congress on great Obstetrical and Neonatal Syndromes* St Petersburg (Russia) 2017, *Meeting* Manila (Philippines) 2016, *Meeting* Tbilisi (Georgia) 2015, *Meeting* Tokyo (Japan) 2014, *Meeting* Athens (Greece) 2013. **Publications** *Organisation Gestosis News* (regular) in English, German; *Instruction Bulletin* (irregular) in English, German; *Organisation Gestosis Press*. Annual Congress proceedings; monographs; surveys; videos.
Members Clinics and individual scientists (obstetricians, gynaecologists, neonatologists, nephrologists, epidemiologists, pathologists, geneticists, immunologists, physiologists and health officials in the field of EPH-gestosis) – about 4,500 – in 101 countries and territories:
Algeria, Antigua-Barbuda, Argentina, Aruba, Australia, Austria, Bangladesh, Barbados, Belgium, Bolivia, Botswana, Brazil, Bulgaria, Cameroon, Canada, Chile, China, Colombia, Congo DR, Costa Rica, Côte d'Ivoire, Cuba, Curaçao, Czechia, Denmark, Dominican Rep, Ecuador, Egypt, El Salvador, Finland, France, Germany, Ghana, Greece, Guadeloupe, Guatemala, Haiti, Honduras, Hong Kong, Hungary, Iceland, India, Indonesia, Iran Islamic Rep, Iraq, Ireland, Israel, Italy, Jamaica, Japan, Jordan, Kenya, Korea Rep, Kuwait, Libya, Luxembourg, Mexico, Montenegro, Myanmar, Netherlands, New Zealand, Nicaragua, Nigeria, Norway, Pakistan, Panama, Papua New Guinea, Paraguay, Peru, Philippines, Poland, Portugal, Romania, Saudi Arabia, Senegal, Serbia, Sierra Leone, Singapore, Slovakia, South Africa, Spain, Sri Lanka, St Kitts-Nevis, St Lucia, St Vincent-Grenadines, Sudan, Sweden, Switzerland, Syrian AR, Taiwan, Tanzania UR, Thailand, Trinidad-Tobago, Tunisia, Türkiye, UK, Uruguay, USA, Venezuela, Vietnam, Zambia.
Affiliated association (1), listed in this Yearbook:
African Society of Organization Gestosis (ASOG, #00464).
IGO Relations *WHO (#20950)*. [2019/XB4165/y/**B**]

- ♦ Organization Gestosis – Society for the Study of Pathophysiology of Pregnancy / see Organization Gestosis (#17869)
- ♦ Organization for Global Development of Communities in Countries Outside Europe (internationally oriented national body)
- ♦ Organization for the Harmonization of Business Law in Africa (#17806)

♦ Organization for Human Brain Mapping (OHBM) 17870

Exec Dir 1935 County Road B2 W, Ste 165, Roseville MN 55113, USA. E-mail: info@humanbrainmapping.org.
URL: http://www.humanbrainmapping.org/
History 1997, Copenhagen (Denmark). Registration: 501(c)3, USA. **Aims** Advance understanding of the anatomical and functional organization of the human brain; provide an educational forum for the exchange of up-to-the-minute and ground breaking research across modalities exploring human brain mapping. **Structure** General Assembly; Council of 12 members. Scientific Advisory Board; Committees. **Finance** Registration fees for annual conference; corporate sponsorship. **Activities** Awards/prizes/competitions; events/meetings; training/education. **Events** *Annual Meeting* Brisbane, QLD (Australia) 2025, *Annual Meeting* Seoul (Korea Rep) 2024, *Annual Meeting* Montréal, QC (Canada) 2023, *Annual Meeting* Glasgow (UK) 2022, *Annual Meeting* Minneapolis, MN (USA) 2021. **Publications** Conference proceedings. **NGO Relations** Cooperates with (1): *International Workshop on Pattern Recognition in Neuroimaging (PRNI)*. [2022/XD6937/**D**]

- ♦ Organization of Ibero-American Journalists Associations (no recent information)

♦ Organization of Ibero-American States for Education, Science and Culture 17871

Organisation des Etats ibéroaméricains pour l'éducation, la science et la culture – Organización de Estados Iberoamericanos para la Educación, la Ciencia y la Cultura (OEI) – Organização de Estados Ibero-americanos para a Educação, a Ciência e a Cultura (OEI)
Acting SG Bravo Murillo 38, 28015 Madrid, Spain. T. +34915944382. Fax +34915943286. E-mail: oei@oei.int.
URL: http://www.oei.es/
History Oct 1949, Madrid (Spain). Founded at 1st Ibero-American Congress of Education, originally functioning as a non-governmental organization. Transformed into an inter-governmental organization at 2nd Congress, 1954, Quito (Ecuador). Statutes approved at 3rd Congress, 1957, Santo Domingo (Dominican Rep). One of 5 organizations within *Comité de Dirección Estratégica de los Organismos Iberoamericanos (CoDEI, #04149)*. Former names and other names: *Ibero-American Bureau of Education* – former; *Oficina de Educación Iberoamericana* – former. **Aims** Encourage educational, cultural and scientific cooperation in Ibero-American countries; guide and help in education, science and culture development issues. **Structure** General Assembly (every 4 years); Governing Council (every 2 years); General Secratariat, located in Madrid (Spain); Regional Offices (19). **Languages** Portuguese, Spanish. **Staff** 350.00 FTE, paid. **Finance** Sources: contributions; contributions of member/participating states; fees for services; revenue from activities/projects. **Activities** Events/meetings; publishing activities; research/documentation; training/education. Active in: Argentina, Bolivia, Brazil, Chile, Colombia, Costa Rica, Cuba, Dominican Rep, Ecuador, El Salvador, Guatemala, Honduras, Mexico, Nicaragua, Panama, Paraguay, Peru, Portugal, Spain, Uruguay. **Events** *Rectors Council Meeting* Madrid (Spain) 2019, *Iberoamerican Congress of Comparative Education* Madrid (Spain) 2014, *International Conference for the World Equilibrium* Havana (Cuba) 2013, *Seminar on Science Education* Madrid (Spain) 2012, *European Union – Latin America and the Caribbean forum of ministries of education* Madrid (Spain) 2010. **Publications** *Revista Iberamericana de Educación* (3 a year); *Revista Iberoamericana de Ciencia, Tecnologia, Sociedad e Innovación* – digital review. Books; databases. Information Services: Maintains a Centre of Documentation and Information Resources.
Members Governments of 23 countries:
Argentina, Bolivia, Brazil, Chile, Colombia, Costa Rica, Cuba, Dominican Rep, Ecuador, El Salvador, Equatorial Guinea, Guatemala, Honduras, Mexico, Nicaragua, Panama, Paraguay, Peru, Portugal, Puerto Rico, Spain, Uruguay, Venezuela.
IGO Relations Cooperates with (4): *Conferencia de Ministros de Justicia de los Países Iberoamericanos (COMJIB, #04656)*; *Ibero-American General Secretariat (#11024)*; *Ibero-American Social Security Organization (#11028)*; *Ibero-American Youth Organization (#11036)*.
Special agreements with: *UNESCO (#20322)*, 1957; *Convenio Andrés Bello de integración educativa, cientifica y cultural de América Latina y España (Convenio Andrés Bello, #04785)*, 1975; *Latin Union (UL, inactive)*, 1980; *Council of Europe (CE, #04881)*, 1982. Adheres to: *Global Partnership for Effective Development Co-operation (GPEDC, #10532)*.
Invited to sessions of Intergovernmental Council of: *International Programme for the Development of Communication (IPDC, #14651)*.
NGO Relations Member of (2): *Red de Centros Culturales de América y Europa (RCCAE, #18639)*; *Red Iberoamericana para el Aseguramiento de la Calidad en la Educación Superior (RIACES, #18657)*. Cooperates with (1): *Fundación Henry Dunant América Latina (FuHD – AL, #10024)*. [2023.02.14/XD1014/**D***]

♦ Organization for Industrial, Spiritual and Cultural Advancement International (OISCA International) 17872

Organisation internationale pour le progrès industriel, spirituel et culturel – Organización para el Progreso Industrial, Espiritual y Cultural

SG 17-5 Izumi 2-chome, Suginami-ku, Tokyo, 168-0063 Japan. T. +81333225161. Fax +81333247111. E-mail: oisca@oisca.org.
URL: http://www.oisca-international.org/

History Oct 1961, Tokyo (Japan), as *International Organization for Cultivating Human Spirit (IOCHS)*. Present name adopted Jan 1965, Tokyo. **Aims** Help elevate public consciousness to secure the well-being of current and future generations, of the earth's ecological system, and of the entire biosphere. **Structure** International Board of Directors (meets annually); International Secretariat. **Languages** English, Japanese. **Staff** 150.00 FTE, paid; 300.00 FTE, voluntary. **Finance** Members' dues. Other sources: corporate contributions; government grants; support from national/regional/international funding institutions; others. **Activities** Training/education; capacity building. **Events** *International Board of Directors Meeting* Tokyo (Japan) 2015, *Tokyo Forum* Tokyo (Japan) 2015, *Global forum on education for a sustainable future* Tokyo (Japan) 2001, *Asia Pacific youth forum* Seoul (Korea Rep) 1996, *Sacred earth gathering* Rio de Janeiro (Brazil) 1992. **Publications** *OISCA Journal* (12 a year) in Japanese. Annual Report, in English; books.
Members As of May 2012, members (over 25,000) in 35 countries and territories:
Azerbaijan, Bangladesh, Bolivia, Brazil, Cambodia, Egypt, Ethiopia, Fiji, Hong Kong, India, Indonesia, Israel, Japan, Kenya, Korea Rep, Malaysia, Mexico, Mongolia, Myanmar, Netherlands, Pakistan, Palau, Palestine, Papua New Guinea, Paraguay, Peru, Philippines, Sri Lanka, Sudan, Taiwan, Thailand, Timor-Leste, United Arab Emirates, Uruguay, USA.
Consultative Status Consultative status granted from: *ECOSOC (#05331)* (General). **IGO Relations** Accredited by: *United Nations Framework Convention on Climate Change – Secretariat (UNFCCC, #20564)*; *United Nations Office at Vienna (UNOV, #20604)*. Memorandum of Understanding with: *Secretariat of the Convention on Biological Diversity (SCBD, #19197)*. Associated with GFI, DPI and DESA of the United Nations. **NGO Relations** Coordinating institution of: *Earth Council Alliance (ECA, inactive)*. Member of: *Asia Pacific Alliance for Sexual and Reproductive Health and Rights (APA, #01825)*; *GEF CSO Network (GCN, #10087)*. Links with national institutions. Set up: May 1964, *OISCA Industrial Development Body (IDB)*, which renders technical assistance in the field of agricultural development to Asian and Pacific countries; Jul 1979, *Asian Pacific Youth Forum (APYF, #01647)*, as a regional platform for community development among youth; Apr 1982, Hamamatsu City (Japan), *OISCA Academy (see: #17872)*, a formal educational institute of 540 students; Apr 1986, Hamakita (Japan), *'OISCA Japan'* for students of all nationalities; Apr 1986, Hamakita (Japan), *OISCA College for Global Cooperation (see: #17872)* a formal education institute for students of all nationalities.
[2014.10.31/XC3024/t/**F**]

♦ Organization of Inter-African and Malagasy States (inactive)
♦ Organization for International Economic Cooperation (inactive)

♦ Organization for International Economic Relations (OiER) 17873

Organisation pour les relations économiques internationales – Organisation für Internationale Wirtschaftsbeziehungen – Organización para las Relaciones Económicas Internacionales

SG Oppolzergasse 6, Suite 9-A, 1010 Vienna, Austria. T. +4315322266. Fax +431533848499. E-mail: sg.office@oier.pro – info@oier.pro.
URL: https://www.oier.pro/

History 1947, Vienna (Austria). Former names and other names: *Donaueuropäisches Institut (IER)* – former. **Aims** Establish and foster international economic relations and business partnerships for development. **Structure** Praesidium; Board; International Council; General Secretariat. **Languages** Arabic, English, French, German, Norwegian, Russian, Swedish. **Staff** 20.00 FTE, paid. **Finance** Sources: members' dues. Other sources: Project financing. **Activities** Events/meetings. **Events** *Urban Future Global Conference* Graz (Austria) 2014, *Symposium* Budapest (Hungary) 1986, *Symposium* Vienna (Austria) 1986. **Publications** *Donaueuropäischer Informationsdienst* (12 a year); *West-Ost-Journal* (6 a year). *Global Panorama*. Occasional brochures. **Members** Businesses, governments, cities, international organizations, science institutions and financial agencies. Membership countries not specified. **Consultative Status** Consultative status granted from: *ECOSOC (#05331)* (Special); *UNIDO (#20336)*. **IGO Relations** Accredited by: *United Nations Office at Vienna (UNOV, #20604)*. Associated with Department of Global Communications of the United Nations. **NGO Relations** Participant of: *United Nations Global Compact (#20567)*. [2020/XD3609/**F**]

♦ Organization for an International Geographical Indications Network (oriGIn) 17874

Organisation pour un réseau international d'indications géographique – Organización para una Red Internacional de Indicaciones Geograficas

SG Chemin du Pavillon 2, 1218 Geneva, Switzerland. E-mail: info@origin-gi.com.
URL: http://www.origin-gi.com/

History 11 Jun 2003, Geneva (Switzerland). **Aims** Promote Geographical Indications as a tool of sustainable development as well as an instrument to protect local knowledge deeply rooted in a given territory; advocate for a more effective legal protection of GIs at national, regional and international levels. **Structure** General Assembly; Executive Committee. **Languages** English, French, Spanish. **Staff** 2.50 FTE, paid. **Activities** Advocacy/lobbying/activism; events/meetings; politics/policy/regulatory; research/documentation. **Events** *Biannual Meeting* Tbilisi (Georgia) 2019, *General Assembly* Guadalajara (Mexico) 2011, *General Assembly* Teruel (Spain) 2009. **Publications** Newsletters; manuals; advocacy letters; position papers. **Members** Associations of producers and other GI-related institutions (about 500) in 40 countries. Membership countries not specified. **Consultative Status** Consultative status granted from: *World Intellectual Property Organization (WIPO, #21593)* (Permanent Observer Status). [2023.02.15/XD9087/**D**]

♦ Organization for International Investment (internationally oriented national body)
♦ Organization Intersex International (unconfirmed)
♦ Organization for Investment, Economic and Technical Assistance of Iran (internationally oriented national body)

♦ Organization of Islamic Capitals and Cities (OICC) 17875

Organisation des capitales et villes islamiques

SG PO Box 2919, Makkah 21955, Saudi Arabia. T. +966125505195. Fax +966125505095. E-mail: webmaster@oicc.org.
General Secretariat PO Box 13621, Jeddah 21414, Saudi Arabia. T. +966126981953. Fax +966126981053.
URL: http://www.oicc.org/

History Apr 1978, Dakar (Senegal), as *Islamic Capitals Organization (ICO)*, by a decision of 9th *Council of Foreign Ministers (CFM, see: #17813)*. Began activities 30 Jan 1980. Current name adopted 1984. **Aims** In member capitals and cities: preserve identity and *heritage*; achieve and enhance *sustainable development*; establish and develop comprehensive urban norms, systems and plans that serve growth and prosperity; promote standards of development, levels of services and municipal utilities; enhance and promote capacity building programmes; consolidate cordiality, brotherhood and friendship; support and coordinate cooperation. **Structure** General Conference (every 3 years); Administrative Council; Islamic Capitals and Cities Cooperation Fund; Headquarters in Makkah Al-Mukkarramah; General Secretariat located in Jeddah. **Languages** Arabic, English, French. **Staff** 1.00 FTE, paid. **Finance** Members' dues. Other sources: investments; donations. **Activities** Events/meetings; research and documentation; training/education; awards/prizes/competitions; capacity building. **Events** *Annual Meeting / Annual Meeting of Administrative Council* Konya (Turkey) 2015, *Annual Meeting / Conference / Annual Meeting of Administrative Council* Makkah (Saudi Arabia) 2013, *Annual Meeting of Administrative Council* Doha (Qatar) 2010, *Conference* Doha (Qatar) 2010, *Annual Meeting of Administrative Council* Kazan (Russia) 2009. **Publications** *Islamic Capitals and Cities* (2 a year) in Arabic, English – also French summary. *Bukhara* in Arabic, English; *Cleanliness within the Framework of Environment Protection* in Arabic; *Housing in the Islamic City* in Arabic, English; *Khawarizm – the Forgotten Civilization between the Aral and Caspian Seas* in Arabic, English; *New Fundamentals of Naming and Numbering Streets and Districts* in Arabic, English; *Principles of Architectural Design and Urban Planning During Different Islamic Eras – Analytical Study for Cairo City*; *Principles of Architectural Design and Urban Planning During Different Islamic Eras – Analytical Study for the Capital Sanaa* in Arabic; *Road Safety and Accidents Reduction* in Arabic, English; *Symposium on Local Administration and Municipalities Systems* in Arabic; *The Islamic Methodology for the Architectural and Urban Design* in Arabic, English. **Information Services** *Fundamentals and Criteria of Classification of the Islamic Heritage Buildings and Cities and the Methods of their Preservation*; *GIS Applications in Planning and Sustainable Development*; *GIS, City Sustainability and Environment*.
Members Active; Observer; Associate, totalling 189. Active (162): capitals and cities who are members of OIC in 55 countries and territories:
Afghanistan, Albania, Algeria, Azerbaijan, Bahrain, Bangladesh, Benin, Brunei Darussalam, Burkina Faso, Cameroon, Chad, Comoros, Djibouti, Egypt, Gabon, Gambia, Guinea, Guinea-Bissau, Indonesia, Iran Islamic Rep, Iraq, Jordan, Kazakhstan, Kuwait, Kyrgyzstan, Lebanon, Libya, Malaysia, Maldives, Mali, Mauritania, Morocco, Mozambique, Niger, Nigeria, Oman, Pakistan, Palestine, Philippines, Qatar, Saudi Arabia, Senegal, Sierra Leone, Somalia, Sudan, Suriname, Syrian AR, Tajikistan, Tunisia, Türkiye, Turkmenistan, Uganda, United Arab Emirates, Uzbekistan, Yemen.
Observer (9): capitals and cities who are not members of OIC in 7 countries:
Bosnia-Herzegovina, Cyprus, Czechia, Philippines, Portugal, Russia, Spain.
Associate (18): ministries, institutions, universities and individuals in 6 countries and territories:
Egypt, Palestine, Saudi Arabia, Sudan, Syrian AR, Türkiye.
Consultative Status Consultative status granted from: *ECOSOC (#05331)* (General); *UNIDO (#20336)*; *UNICEF (#20332)*. **IGO Relations** Affiliated to: *Organisation of Islamic Cooperation (OIC, #17813)*. Accredited by: *United Nations Office at Vienna (UNOV, #20604)*. Observer member of: *Arab League Educational, Cultural and Scientific Organization (ALECSO, #01003)*; *Islamic Development Bank (IsDB, #16044)*; *Islamic World Educational, Scientific and Cultural Organization (ICESCO, #16058)*; OIC; *Research Centre for Islamic History, Art and Culture (IRCICA, #18852)*; *Statistical, Economic and Social Research and Training Centre for Islamic Countries (SESRIC, #19971)*. Cooperation agreement with: *Centre for Environment and Development for the Arab Region and Europe (CEDARE, #03738)*; IDB; *United Nations Human Settlements Programme (UN-Habitat, #20572)*. Associated with Department of Global Communications of the United Nations. **NGO Relations** Member of: *Conference of Non-Governmental Organizations in Consultative Relationship with the United Nations (CONGO, #04635)*; *Euro-Arab Cooperation Centre, Alexandria (EACC, no recent information)*; *International Council on Monuments and Sites (ICOMOS, #13049)*. Observer member of: *Islamic Chamber of Commerce, Industry and Agriculture (ICCIA, #16036)*; *Organization of the Islamic Shipowners' Association (OISA, #17876)*. Cooperation agreement with: *Arab Towns Organization (ATO, #01059)*. [2022/XE1395/**E**]

♦ Organization of the Islamic Conference / see Organisation of Islamic Cooperation (#17813)

♦ Organization of the Islamic Shipowners' Association (OISA) 17876

Organisation de l'association islamique des armateurs

Contact Shaddad Bin Awf St 20, Villa 72, Sharfiyyah District 3, PO Box 14900, Jeddah 21434, Saudi Arabia. T. +966126637882 – +966126653379. Fax +966126604920. E-mail: mail@oisaonline.com – oisa@sbm.net.sa.
URL: http://www.ipandi.club/the-club/

History Jan 1981, Makkah (Saudi Arabia), by 3rd *Islamic Summit of Kings and Heads of States and Governments (#16053)*, as an affiliated institution of *Organisation of Islamic Cooperation (OIC, #17813)*. Previously also referred to as *Islamic Shipowners' Association (ISA) – Association islamique des armateurs*. **Aims** Coordinate and unify the efforts of members in realizing cooperation among the maritime companies; protect the interests of members by providing counsel and support to them through a greater voice in international maritime affairs; establish contact between the Islamic world and other countries within an integrated maritime network; assist in drawing up a unified policy for Islamic maritime transporters; conduct studies and research in the various disciplines of maritime transport. **Structure** General Assembly (annual). Executive Committee, consisting of 14 members and a representative of the OIC Secretary-General. General Secretariat at Headquarters in Jeddah (Saudi Arabia). **Languages** Arabic, English, French. **Staff** 12.00 FTE, paid. **Finance** Members' dues (annual) and admission fees. **Activities** Provides counsel to Islamic maritime companies. Projects: *'Islamic Shipping Company'* – as Bakkah Shipping Company aims to promote shipping as the cheapest means of transportation of moving cargoes/goods/heavy commodities between Islamic states sea ports; *'Islamic Protection and Indemnity Club'* – registers vessels so they are covered for cargo/crew and contamination or loss of cargo happened on a vessel or damage sustained by/to a crew; *'Cooperative Information System (CIS)'* – exchange of relevant data and information. **Events** *General Assembly* Dubai (United Arab Emirates) 2008, *General Assembly* Dubai (United Arab Emirates) 2007, *General Assembly* Dubai (United Arab Emirates) 2006, *General Assembly* Cairo (Egypt) 2005, *General Assembly* Dubai (United Arab Emirates) 2004.
Members Membership open to all maritime transport companies engaged in international trade; similar associations registered in a member State of the OIC; companies enjoying the nationality of one of the OIC member States and owning at least 51 % of the total shares. Members in 33 countries and territories:
Bahrain, Bangladesh, Cameroon, Comoros, Djibouti, Egypt, Gambia, Guinea, Indonesia, Iran Islamic Rep, Iraq, Jordan, Kuwait, Lebanon, Libya, Malaysia, Mali, Mauritania, Morocco, Niger, Pakistan, Palestine, Qatar, Saudi Arabia, Senegal, Sierra Leone, Sudan, Suriname, Syrian AR, Tunisia, Türkiye, United Arab Emirates, Yemen.
Consultative Status Consultative status granted from: *ECOSOC (#05331)* (Ros C); *UNCTAD (#20285)* (Special Category). **IGO Relations** Links with all subsidiary, specialized and affiliated institutions of *Organisation of Islamic Cooperation (OIC, #17813)*, including: *Islamic Centre for Development of Trade (ICDT, #16035)*; *Islamic Development Bank (IsDB, #16044)*; *Islamic World Educational, Scientific and Cultural Organization (ICESCO, #16058)*; *Islamic University of Technology (IUT, #16055)*; *Statistical, Economic and Social Research and Training Centre for Islamic Countries (SESRIC, #19971)*. [2020/XD2655/**C**]

♦ Organization des Jeunes et Etudiants de l'Afrique de l'Est (internationally oriented national body)

♦ Organization of Latin American and Caribbean Supreme Audit Institutions (OLACEFS) 17877

Organización Latinoamericana y del Caribe de Entidades Fiscalizadoras Superiores (OLACEFS)

Exec Sec Contralor General de la República de Chile, Teatinos 56, 834 0521 Santiago, Santiago Metropolitan, Chile. T. +56232401158. E-mail: relacionesinternacionales@contraloria.cl.
URL: http://www.olacefs.com/

History 9 Apr 1965, Santiago (Chile). Founded at the 2nd Latin American Congress of Supreme Audit Institutions following approval by the Supreme Audit Institutions in attendance of the draft charter submitted by the Office of the Comptroller General of Chile along with a study carried out by the Office of the Comptroller General of Venezuela. Signatories to the creation of ILACIF: Argentina; Brazil; Colombia; Chile; Ecuador; El Salvador; Mexico; Nicaragua; Panama; Puerto Rico; Dominican Rep; Uruguay; Venezuela. Proposal for the creation of the institute was made during the 1st Latin American Congress of Supreme Audit Institutions, 1963. Joining later were: Peru; Bolivia; Costa Rica; Guatemala; Honduras; Paraguay; Antilles; Suriname. Changes to internal rules and organizational structure recommended by a reforming committee and approved at the special session of ILACIF's Extraordinary General Assembly, Buenos Aires (Argentina), 11 Oct 1990, when present name was adopted. Regional body of: *International Organization of Supreme Audit Institutions (INTOSAI, #14478)*. Former names and other names: *Latin American Institute of Auditing Sciences* – former; *Instituto Latinoamericano de Ciencias Fiscalizadoras (ILACIF)* – former; *Latin American and Caribbean Institute of Auditing Sciences* – alias. **Aims** Promote and conduct systematic research on the control and supervision of the management of public resources and disseminate results amongst members; organize and conduct specialization, postgraduate and training courses, as well as seminars and special events principally for staff members to carry out technical tasks relating to control and oversight; provide advisory services and technical assistance on the control and oversight of the management of public resources; compile work done in each country concerning administrative and financial organization and control, to be disseminated amongst Latin American and Caribbean nations; promote and publish written material on the control and oversight of the management of public resources; serve as liaison between the supreme audit institutions of other nations, answering queries and promoting the exchange of specialists; establish and foster a resource center principally for literature concerning the control and oversight of the management of public resources and related disciplines; maintain contact on scientific and technical matters with institutions and organizations in other parts of the world specializing in the control and oversight of the management of public resources; establish relationships with and obtain the assistance of experts on the control and oversight of the management of public resources, universities, bodies that fund development and associations for professionals; coordinate special studies requested by a government or group of governments of Latin American and Caribbean nations; organize high-level think-tanks made up of active members to analyse specific strategic issues related to supreme control and oversight; award prizes and/or offer stimulus as per the conditions laid down by the specific regulation. **Structure** General Assembly; Governing Board of 5 full members; Presidency (3-year term without re-election); Executive Secretariat and Headquarters. Committees (2): Capacity Building Committee (CBC); Special Committee to Assess the Charter and Regulations (CER). Commissions (5): Good Governance Practices (CTPBG); Citizen Participation (CPC); Environment (COMTEMA); Assessment of Performance and Performance Indicators (CEDEIR); Information and Communication Technologies (CTIC). Working Group for Public Works Audit (GTOP). **Languages** English, Portuguese, Spanish. **Finance** Sources: contributions; members' dues. Contributions from international institutions and organizations including: *Deutsche Gesellschaft für Internationale Zusammenarbeit (GIZ); Inter-American Development Bank (IDB, #11427); International Bank for Reconstruction and Development (IBRD, #12317)* (World Bank); *International Organization of Supreme Audit Institutions (INTOSAI, #14478).* **Activities** Awards/prizes/competitions; guidance/assistance/consulting; knowledge management/information dissemination; networking/liaising; research/documentation; training/education. **Events** *Annual General Assembly* Cartagena de Indias (Colombia) 2021, *Extraordinary General Assembly* Cartagena de Indias (Colombia) 2020, *Annual General Assembly* San Salvador (El Salvador) 2019, *Annual General Assembly* Buenos Aires (Argentina) 2018, *Annual General Assembly* Asunción (Paraguay) 2017. **Publications** *OLACEFS Magazine* in Spanish; *OLACEFS Newsletter* in Spanish.

Members Full (22) – Supreme Audit Institutions of the countries of Latin America and the Caribbean; Associate (28) – sub-national, state or local audit institutions, and Supreme Audit Institutions from other regions and legal entities governed by public international law that provide technical or financial support for development of the organization. Full members in 22 countries and territories:
Argentina, Belize, Bolivia, Brazil, Chile, Colombia, Costa Rica, Cuba, Curaçao, Dominican Rep, Ecuador, El Salvador, Guatemala, Honduras, Mexico, Nicaragua, Panama, Paraguay, Peru, Puerto Rico, Uruguay, Venezuela.
Associate members in 6 countries:
Argentina, Brazil, Colombia, Dominican Rep, Portugal, Spain. [2021.06.16/XD2643/**D**]

- ♦ Organization of Latin American and Caribbean Tourism (#17845)
- ♦ Organization of Latin American Congresses of Anaesthesiology (inactive)
- ♦ Organization for Latin American Solidarity (inactive)
- ♦ Organization for the Management and Development of the Kagera River Basin (no recent information)
- ♦ Organization of Manufacturers of Cellulose Products for Foodstuffs (no recent information)
- ♦ Organization mondiale de la santé naturelle (internationally oriented national body)
- ♦ Organization of Museums, Monuments and Sites of Africa (no recent information)
- ♦ Organization of National Metrological Institutions of the States of Central and Eastern Europe / see Euro-Asian Cooperation of National Metrological Institutions (#05638)

♦ Organization of Nematologists of Tropical America (ONTA) 17878

Organización de Nematologos de los Trópicos Americanos (ONTA)

Vice-Pres Florida Dept of Agriculture and Consumer Services, Div of Plant Industry, PO Box 147100, Gainesville FL 32614-7100, USA. T. +13523954755. E-mail: mlmendes@ufl.edu.
Pres Univ Privada Antenor Orrego, Av America sur 3145, Trujillo LA LIBERTAD, Peru.
URL: http://www.ontaweb.org/

History 1967, Rio Piedras (Puerto Rico). Founded as *Organization of Tropical American Nematologists (OTAN).* Registration: 501(c)(3) organization, No/ID: 30-0504991, Start date: 2009, USA. **Aims** Promote cooperation between nematologists of Latin America and the USA; disseminate knowledge of plant-parasitic, entomopathogenic-parasitic and free-living nematodes in the tropical Americas and other tropical and subtropical regions of the world; facilitate organization of scientific events dealing with tropical nematology in different countries. **Structure** Executive Committee. **Languages** English, Spanish. **Staff** Voluntary. **Finance** Members' dues. Donations. **Activities** Knowledge management/information dissemination; financial and/or material support; events/meetings. **Events** *Annual Meeting* San José (Costa Rica) 2019, *Annual Meeting* Arequipa (Peru) 2018, *Annual Meeting* Mayagüez (Puerto Rico) 2017, *Annual Meeting* Montréal, QC (Canada) 2016, *Annual Meeting* Varadero (Cuba) 2015. **Publications** *Nematropica* (2 a year) – journal; *ONTA Newsletter* (annual).

Members Regular; Sustaining. Institutions in 18 countries and territories:
Australia, Belgium, Brazil, France, Germany, Hong Kong, India, Italy, Japan, Netherlands, New Zealand, Puerto Rico, South Africa, Spain, Trinidad-Tobago, UK, USA, Venezuela.
Individuals in 43 countries and territories:
Argentina, Australia, Belgium, Bolivia, Brazil, Chile, Colombia, Costa Rica, Cuba, Dominican Rep, Ecuador, Egypt, Fiji, France, Germany, Greece, Guatemala, Hong Kong, Italy, Jamaica, Japan, Kenya, Martinique, Mexico, Netherlands, New Zealand, Nigeria, Norway, Panama, Paraguay, Peru, Portugal, Puerto Rico, South Africa, Spain, Sweden, Taiwan, Trinidad-Tobago, Türkiye, Uganda, UK, USA, Venezuela.

NGO Relations Member of: *International Federation of Nematology Societies (IFNS, #13488).* [2021/XD6985/**D**]

♦ Organization of News Ombudsmen and Standards Editors (ONO) .. 17879

Exec Dir 54 River Road West, Riverview, Sydney NSW 2066, Australia. T. +61416284743. E-mail: newsombudsmenorg@gmail.com.
URL: http://www.newsombudsmen.org/

History 1980. Registration: Section 501(c)(6), USA. **Aims** Help the journalism profession achieve and maintain high ethical standards in news reporting; establish and refine standards for the job of news ombudsman or reader representative; help in the wider establishment of the position of news ombudsman on newspapers and elsewhere in the media; provide a forum for exchanging experiences, information and ideas among its members; develop contacts with publishers, editors, press councils and other professional organizations, provide speakers for special interest groups and respond to media inquiries. **Structure** Board of Directors. **Languages** English, Spanish. **Staff** 0.20 FTE, paid; 12.00 FTE, voluntary. **Finance** Sources: members' dues. **Activities** Events/meetings; publishing activities. **Events** *Annual Conference* London (UK) 2023, *Annual Conference* Copenhagen (Denmark) 2020, *Annual Conference* New York, NY (USA) 2019, *Annual Conference* Amsterdam (Netherlands) 2018, *Annual Conference* Chennai (India) 2017. **Publications** *ONO Newsletter* (12 a year). *Handbook for News Ombudsmen*; *The Role of a News Ombudsman.*

Members Regular; associate; honorary. News ombudsmen in 23 countries:
Argentina, Australia, Belgium, Canada, Colombia, Czechia, Denmark, Estonia, Finland, Germany, India, Israel, Japan, Lithuania, Mexico, Netherlands, Portugal, South Africa, Switzerland, Türkiye, UK, USA, Zimbabwe.

NGO Relations Member of (1): *Ethical Journalism Network (EJN, #05554).* [2023.02.22/XM0506/**C**]

♦ Organization for Nordic Children's and Youth Choirs 17880

Rådet för Nordiskt Barn- och Ungdomskårsamarbete (NORBUSANG)

Sec Klostervej 32, 7620 Lemvig, Denmark. T. +4553646450. E-mail: info@norbusang.org.
URL: http://norbusang.org/

History Founded 1986. Previously also referred to as *NORBUSAM.* **Activities** Annual NORBUSANG choir festival. **Events** *Festival* Holstebro (Denmark) 2016, *Festival* Drøbak (Norway) 2008, *Festival* Gardabaer (Iceland) 2007, *Festival* Odense (Denmark) 2006, *Festival* Västerås (Sweden) 2005.

Members Choir organizations. Members in 5 countries:
Denmark, Finland, Iceland, Norway, Sweden.

NGO Relations *Samrådet for Nordisk Amatörmusik (SAMNAM, #19048).* [2016/XD8398/**D**]

- ♦ Organization of Nordic Cooperative and Municipal Housing Enterprises / see Housing Nordic (#10957)
- ♦ Organization of Nordic Cooperative and Public Utility Housing Enterprises / see Housing Nordic (#10957)
- ♦ Organization of Nordic Inventors' Associations (no recent information)
- ♦ Organization of the Nordic Transmission System Operators (inactive)
- ♦ Organization of the Oppressed on Earth / see Hezbollah Internationale (#10912)
- ♦ Organization for Peace and Appropriate Development for the Horn of Africa (internationally oriented national body)

♦ Organization of the Petroleum Exporting Countries (OPEC) 17881

Organisation des pays exportateurs de pétrole (OPEP) – Organización de Paises Exportadores de Petróleo (OPEP) – Organisation der Erdölexportierenden Länder

SG Helferstorferstrasse 17, 1010 Vienna, Austria. T. +431211120. Fax +4312164320.
Head PR Dept address not obtained. E-mail: prid@opec.org.
URL: http://www.opec.org/

History 10 Sep 1960, Baghdad (Iraq). Founded at conference of government representatives, following initiatives of Venezuela, 1949, when cooperation was established with Iran (since 1979 reconstituted as Islamic Republic of Iran), Iraq, Kuwait and Saudi Arabia; and subsequent resolutions of First Arab Petroleum Congress, 1959, Cairo (Egypt). Statutes approved at 2nd Conference, 15-21 Jan 1961, Caracas (Venezuela). In accordance with a Resolution of 8th Conference, 5-10 Apr 1965, Headquarters moved to Vienna (Austria), 1 Sep 1965. Agreement in accordance with Austrian law, 24 Jun 1965; new agreement, 18 Feb 1974. **Aims** Coordinate and unify petroleum policies of Member Countries; ensure stabilization of oil markets in order to secure an efficient, economic and regular supply of petroleum to consumers, steady income to producers and a fair return on capital for those investing in petroleum. **Structure** Conference (at least twice a year) is attended by representations of member countries, normally headed by Ministers responsible for Oil, Mines and Energy, and formulates general policy, appoints Secretary-General (3-year term) and elects Chairman of the Board of Governors. Board (meets at least twice a year) comprising one governor nominated by each member country for a 2-year term. *OPEC Economic Commission Board (see: #17881),* a specialized body operating within the framework of the Secretariat. Secretariat comprises: Office of the Secretary General; Legal Office; Research Division, including 3 Departments (Data Services; Energy Studies; Petroleum Studies); Support Services Division, including 3 Departments (Administration and IT Services; Finance and Human Resources; Public Relations and Information). Established *OPEC Fund for International Development (OFID, #17745)* as a multilateral development finance institution to promote cooperation between OPEC Member Countries and other developing countries. **Languages** English. **Staff** 139.00 FTE, paid. **Finance** Sources: contributions of member/participating states. **Activities** Guidance/assistance/consulting; knowledge management/information dissemination; monitoring/evaluation; politics/policy/regulatory; research/documentation; training/education. Monitors, forecasts and analyses development in the oil, energy and petrochemical industries and studies the evaluation of hydrocarbons and products and their non-energy uses; analyses economic and financial issues, in particular those related to international financial and monetary matters and to the international petroleum industry; financial and/or material support. **Events** *Annual Oxford Energy Seminar* Oxford (UK) 2021, *High-Level Meeting of the OPEC-China Energy Dialogue* Beijing (China) 2020, *OPEC-India Energy Dialogue High-Level Meeting* Vienna (Austria) 2020, *OPEC-Russia Energy Dialogue High-Level Meeting* Vienna (Austria) 2020, *Ordinary Conference* Vienna (Austria) 2020. **Publications** *OPEC Annual Statistical Bulletin*; *OPEC Bulletin*; *OPEC Energy Review*; *OPEC Monthly Oil Market Report*; *OPEC World Oil Outlook. I Need to Know; Who Gets What from Imported Oil?.* Annual Report; Solemn Declarations; general information booklet; OPEC Statute. Information Services: *Center for OPEC Studies (CENTROPEC, no recent information)* secures organization, promotion and diffusion of research and information programmes about OPEC and about the historic, socio-economic and cultural realities of OPEC member countries.

Members Membership open to countries with a substantial net export of crude petroleum, having fundamentally similar interests. Governments of 14 countries:
Algeria, Angola, Congo Brazzaville, Ecuador, Equatorial Guinea, Gabon, Iran Islamic Rep, Iraq, Kuwait, Libya, Nigeria, Saudi Arabia, United Arab Emirates, Venezuela.

IGO Relations Cooperates with: *ECOSOC (#05331)* under UN Resolution 1053, adopted 30 Jul 1965; *Group of 77 (G-77, #10732); UNCTAD (#20285).* Accredited by: *United Nations Framework Convention on Climate Change – Secretariat (UNFCCC, #20564).* Supports: *International Crops Research Institute for the Semi-Arid Tropics (ICRISAT, #13116).* **NGO Relations** Cooperates with: Instrumental in setting up: *Arab Oil Fund (no recent information); Joint Organisations Data Initiative (JODI, #16143).* [2022/XC3038/**C***]

♦ Organization for PhD Education in Biomedicine and Health Sciences in the European System (ORPHEUS) 17882

Pres Salata 11, HR-10000 Zagreb, Croatia. T. +38514566846. Fax +38514566843.
URL: http://www.orpheus-med.org/

History 12 Nov 2006, Dubrovnik (Croatia). **Structure** Executive Committee, including President, Vice-President, Secretary and Treasurer. **Events** *Conference on Biomedical and Health Science Doctoral Training in Europe* Lausanne (Switzerland) 2014, *European conference on phD education and health sciences* Bergen (Norway) 2012, *European conference on phD education and health sciences* Izmir (Turkey) 2011, *European conference on phD education and health sciences* Vienna (Austria) 2010, *European conference on PhD education in health sciences* Aarhus (Denmark) 2009. [2013/XM3657/**D**]

♦ Organization of Phenomenological Organizations (OPO) 17883

Organizace Fenomenologickych Organizaci

Secretariat c/o Centrum fenomenologickych badani, Jilska 1, 1 Prague, Czechia.
Contact address not obtained. E-mail: hr.sepp@web.de.

History Prague (Czech Rep). **Finance** Members' dues. **Events** *Meeting* Memphis, TN (USA) 2019, *Meeting* Segovia (Spain) 2011, *Meeting* Hong Kong (Hong Kong) 2008, *Meeting* Lima (Peru) 2005, *Meeting* Prague (Czech Rep) 2002. **Publications** *Newsletter of Phenomenology* (weekly).

Members National organizations (40) in 19 countries and territories:
Argentina, Austria, Belgium, Bulgaria, Canada, Czechia, Hong Kong, Italy, Japan, Lithuania, Peru, Poland, Portugal, Romania, Russia, Slovenia, Spain, Switzerland, USA.
Regional organizations (4):
Circulo Latinoamericano de Fenomenologia (CLAFEN, #03937); International Communicology Institute (ICI); Nordic Society of Phenomenology (NoSP, #17425); Society for Phenomenology and Media (SPM, #19618). [2017/XM1064/y/**D**]

♦ Organization for the Phyto-Taxonomic Investigation of the Mediterranean Area (OPTIMA) 17884

Organisation pour l'étude phyto-taxonomique de la région méditerranéenne

Secretariat Via Lincoln 2/A, 90133 Palermo PA, Italy. T. +3909123891209. E-mail: secr@optima-bot.org.
URL: http://www.optima-bot.org/

History Founded 1974, Geneva (Switzerland). **Aims** Stimulate and coordinate research activities, exploration, conservation and resource studies pertaining to the flora of the Mediterranean area. **Structure** General Meeting; International Board; Executive Council; Programme Committee for each OPTIMA Meeting; Commissions (13). **Languages** English, French. **Staff** None. **Finance** Members' dues. Annual budget: euro 4,000. **Activities** Events/meetings; awards/prizes/competitions. **Events** *Triennial Colloquium* Athens (Greece) 2019, *Triennial Colloquium* Montpellier (France) 2016, *Triennial Colloquium / OPTIMA Meeting* Palermo (Italy) 2013, *Triennial colloquium / OPTIMA Meeting* Antalya (Turkey) 2010, *Triennial colloquium / OPTIMA Meeting* Pisa (Italy) 2007. **Publications** *Informateur OPTIMA/OPTIMA Newsletter* in English, French – in 43 vols. *Bocconea* – in 27 vols; *Flora Mediterranea* – in 28 vols; *Med-Checklist* – in 4 vols.

Members Individuals in 47 countries:
Albania, Algeria, Armenia, Australia, Austria, Azerbaijan, Bangladesh, Belgium, Bosnia-Herzegovina, Bulgaria, Canada, Croatia, Czechia, Denmark, Egypt, Finland, France, Georgia, Germany, Greece, Iran Islamic Rep, Israel, Italy, Jordan, Libya, Malta, Mauritania, Morocco, Netherlands, Norway, Pakistan, Poland, Portugal, Russia, Saudi Arabia, Serbia, Slovakia, Slovenia, South Africa, Spain, Sweden, Switzerland, Tunisia, Türkiye, UK, Ukraine, USA.

NGO Relations Member of: *International Association of Botanical and Mycological Societies (IABMS, #11730); International Union of Biological Sciences (IUBS, #15760); International Union for Conservation of Nature and Natural Resources (IUCN, #15766).* [2019.06.27/XD6845/v/**D**]

- ♦ Organization for Poverty Alleviation and Development (internationally oriented national body)

♦ The Organization for Professionals in Regulatory Affairs (TOPRA) .. 17885

Membership Officer 6th Floor, 3 Harbour Exchange, London, E14 9GE, UK. T. +442075102560. Fax +442075372003. E-mail: info@topra.org.
Topra AISBL Blvd du Souverain 280, 1160 Brussels, Belgium.
URL: http://www.topra.org/

History 1986. Founded to respond to increasing Europeanization of the regulatory environment, the British national organization (*BIRA*) having existed since 1978. Current title adopted on merger with *BIRA.* Former names and other names: *European Society of Regulatory Affairs (ESRA)* – former (1986 to 2004). Registration: Companies House, No/ID: 01400379, Start date: 17 Nov 1978, England; Crossroads Bank for Enterprises, No/ID: 0828.280.129, Start date: 21 Jul 1979, Belgium; EU Transparency Register, No/ID: 325718122484-70, Start date: 27 Jun 2016. **Aims** Represent and promote the global healthcare regulatory profession; provide

members with top quality, relevant support with a European focus. **Structure** General Meeting (annual); Board of Directors; Advisory Council; Secretariat; Business Units (4); Special Interest Groups (4). **Languages** English, French. **Finance** Sources: members' dues. **Activities** Events/meetings; knowledge management/information dissemination; training/education. **Events** *Symposium* Vienna (Austria) 2022, *Annual Symposium* Brussels (Belgium) 2020, *Annual Symposium* Dublin (Ireland) 2019, *Annual Symposium* Stockholm (Sweden) 2018, *Annual Symposium* London (UK) 2017. **Publications** *In Touch* (12 a year) – newsletter; *Regulatory Rapporteur* (11 a year). Annual report. **Members** Full (3,000) in 50 countries. Membership countries not specified.
[2022.10.21/XD3446/tv/**D**]

♦ Organization for the Promotion of Responsible Tuna Fisheries (OPRT) 17886

Contact Sankaido Bldg, 9th floor, 1-9-13 Akasaka, Minato-ku, Tokyo, 107-0052 Japan. T. +81335686388. Fax +81335686389. E-mail: nagahata@oprt.or.jp – hitomi@oprt.or.jp.
URL: http://www.oprt.or.jp/

History 8 Dec 2000, Tokyo (Japan). **Aims** Contribute to sustainable development of tuna fisheries in compliance with international and social responsibility; ensure a stable supply of tuna products through measures to reinforce conservation and management of tuna stocks, foster healthy tuna markets and further international cooperation among fishermen. **Languages** English, Japanese. **Staff** 5.50 FTE, paid. **Finance** Members' dues. **Activities** Monitoring/evaluation; knowledge management/information dissemination. **Events** *Ordinary General Meeting* Tokyo (Japan) 2015. **Publications** *OPRT Newsletter*. Pamphlets.
Members Full: organizations of tuna longline producers; traders; distributors; consumer organizations. Supporting: individuals. Members in 15 countries and territories:
China, Cook Is, Ecuador, Indonesia, Japan, Kiribati, Korea Rep, Malaysia, Marshall Is, Micronesia FS, Philippines, Seychelles, Taiwan, Tuvalu, Vanuatu.
IGO Relations Observer at: FAO Committee of Fisheries; *Indian Ocean Tuna Commission (IOTC, #11162)*; *Inter-American Tropical Tuna Commission (IATTC, #11454)*; *International Commission for the Conservation of Atlantic Tunas (ICCAT, #12675)*; *Western and Central Pacific Fisheries Commission (WCPFC, #20912)*.
[2017.06.01/XJ3484/**D**]

- ♦ Organization for the Promotion of World Literacy (internationally oriented national body)
- ♦ Organization for the Provision of Work for Handicapped Persons / see Workability International (#21049)
- ♦ Organization Racism Islamophobia Watch (unconfirmed)
- ♦ Organization of Railways Cooperation / see Organisation for Cooperation between Railways (#17803)
- ♦ Organization for the Research, Communication and Action to further the Sustainable Development between North and South (internationally oriented national body)

♦ Organization for Security and Cooperation in Europe (OSCE) 17887

Organisation de la sécurité et la coopération en Europe (OSCE)

Contact OSCE Secretariat, Wallnerstrasse 6, 1010 Vienna, Austria. T. +436767174592. E-mail: pm@osce.org.
URL: http://www.osce.org/

History 3 Jul 1975, as a continuing series of meetings with the title *Conference on Security and Cooperation in Europe (CSCE) – Conférence sur la sécurité et la coopération en Europe (CSCE) – Konferenz für Sicherheit und Zusammenarbeit (KSZE)* to serve as a multilateral forum for dialogue and negotiation between East and West. Meeting over 2 years in Helsinki (Finland) and Geneva (Switzerland), CSCE reached agreement on the *Helsinki Final Act of the Conference on Security and Cooperation in Europe (Helsinki Accords, 1975)*, signed by Heads of State or Government of 35 states on 1 Aug 1975, a politically binding agreement, which sets out basic principles for behaviour among participating states and of governments towards citizens. Establishment followed multilateral consultations over a number of years. Institutionalized as a permanent body, 21 Nov 1990, under *Charter of Paris for a New Europe* or *Paris Charter*. Expanded and further delineated under the *Helsinki Document*, adopted Jul 1992. Current title adopted at pan-European summit, 5-6 Dec 1994, Budapest (Hungary), with effect from 1 Jan 1995. **Aims** Serve as a primary instrument for early warning, conflict prevention, crisis management and post-conflict rehabilitation; get involved in a wide range of security-related issues, arms control measures, economic and environmental activities and counter-terrorism activities; oversee democratic electoral processes, good governance and rule of law; protect human rights; help develop a free, pluralistic and independent media and build civil society; offer police training; work to prevent human trafficking; promote cooperation and dialogue between participating States, ensuring equal status and that decisions are based on consensus.
Structure *'Decision-making mechanisms'*: Summit (Meeting of Heads of State or Government). Ministerial Council (meets annually). Permanent Council (meets weekly), consisting of representatives of participating States with partner States attending as observers. *Forum for Security Cooperation (FSC)* (meets weekly, always in Vienna, Austria) with rotating chairmanship (every 4 months).
Chairmanship (annually rotating), with Chairperson-in-Office held by Foreign Minister of participating State and assisted by previous and succeeding Chairpersons, constituting the Troika. Secretary General, appointed by Ministerial Council for 3 years and serves as Chief Administrative Officer. Secretariat, headed by Secretary General, encompasses: Office of the Secretary General; Department of Management and Finance; Department of Human Resources; Prague (Czech Rep) Office; Training Section; Action against Terrorism Unit; Office of the Special Representative and Coordinator for Combating Trafficking in Human Beings; *Conflict Prevention Centre, Vienna (CPC, see: #17887)*; Office of the Coordinator of OSCE Economic and Environmental Activities; External Cooperation; Strategic Police Matters Unit; Gender Section.
'Institutions': *OSCE – Office for Democratic Institutions and Human Rights (OSCE/ODIHR, #17902)*; *OSCE High Commissioner on National Minorities (HCNM, #17901)*; Representative on Freedom of the Media.
Other structures and institutions: *Parliamentary Assembly of the Organization for Security and Cooperation in Europe (OSCE PA, #18214)*; *Court of Conciliation and Arbitration within the OSCE (OSCE Court, #04934)*; Minsk Group.
Related bodies: Joint Consultative Group; Open Skies Consultative Commission.
Languages English, French, German, Italian, Russian, Spanish. **Staff** Secretariat and Institutions – about 513. Field Operations – about 2,949. **Finance** Contributions of participating states. Annual budget (2016): euro 141,100,000.
Activities Works through political fora, field missions and institutions in the following fields: Arms control; Border management; Combating human trafficking; Combating terrorism; Conflict prevention and resolution; Economic activities; Education; Elections; Environmental activities; Gender equality; Good governance; Human rights; Media freedom and development; Military reform and cooperation; Minority rights; Policing; Roma and Sinti; Rule of law; Tolerance and non-discrimination.
Treaty on Conventional Armed Forces in Europe (CFE, 1990), signed 19 Nov 1990, Paris (France), at an OSCE meeting, is developed through *Joint Consultative Group of the Treaty on Conventional Armed Forces in Europe*, at which OSCE Members are represented by their *'OSCE Ambassadors'*. They also represent their countries in the *Open Skies Consultative Commission* for *Treaty on Open Skies (1992)*. OSCE cooperates with NATO and the WEU in European Security Architecture (ESA) initiative.
Events *Conference on Media, Terrorism and Foreign Terrorist Fighters* Bestovje (Croatia) 2021, *Meeting* Stockholm (Sweden) 2021, *Meeting* Vienna (Austria) 2021, *Meeting* Tirana (Albania) 2020, *Alliance against Trafficking in Persons Conference* Vienna (Austria) 2020. **Publications** *Highlights* – newsletter. *OSCE Handbook*. Annual Report; fact sheets.
Members Participating states (57):
Albania, Andorra, Armenia, Austria, Azerbaijan, Belarus, Belgium, Bosnia-Herzegovina, Bulgaria, Canada, Croatia, Cyprus, Czechia, Denmark, Estonia, Finland, France, Georgia, Germany, Greece, Holy See, Hungary, Iceland, Ireland, Italy, Kazakhstan, Kyrgyzstan, Latvia, Liechtenstein, Lithuania, Luxembourg, Malta, Moldova, Monaco, Mongolia, Montenegro, Netherlands, North Macedonia, Norway, Poland, Portugal, Romania, Russia, San Marino, Serbia, Slovakia, Slovenia, Spain, Sweden, Switzerland, Tajikistan, Türkiye, Turkmenistan, UK, Ukraine, USA, Uzbekistan.
Partners for cooperation (11):
Afghanistan, Algeria, Australia, Egypt, Israel, Japan, Jordan, Korea Rep, Morocco, Thailand, Tunisia.
IGO Relations Special relations with: *United Nations (UN, #20515)*; *European Commission (EC, #06633)*; *NATO (#16945)*. Cooperation with regional and sub-regional organizations:
- *Central European Initiative (CEI, #03708)*;
- *Collective Security Treaty Organization (CSTO, #04103)*;
- *Council of the Baltic Sea States (CBSS, #04870)*;
- *European Union (EU, #08967)*;
- *Organization of Black Sea Economic Cooperation (BSEC, #17857)*;
- *Organization for Democracy and Economic Development (GUAM, #17861)*;
- *South East European Cooperation Process (SEECP, #19811)*;
- *Southeast European Cooperative Initiative (SECI, #19812)*.

NGO Relations Cooperation with numerous NGOs through field missions and institutions. Important and extensive cooperation with: *International Committee of the Red Cross (ICRC, #12799)*. Academic and research institutions contact through the Section for External Cooperation and the Prague (Czech Rep) Office.
[2020/XF0947/**F***]

- ♦ Organization of Shipsuppliers in EC-Countries / see European Ship Suppliers Organization (#08478)
- ♦ Organization for Social Science Research in Eastern Africa / see Organization for Social Science Research in Eastern and Southern Africa (#17888)

♦ Organization for Social Science Research in Eastern and Southern Africa (OSSREA) 17888

Office Assistant PO Box 31971, Addis Ababa, Ethiopia. T. +251111239484. Fax +251111223921. E-mail: ossrea@ethionet.et – info@ossrea.net.
Exec Dir address not obtained.
URL: http://www.ossrea.net/

History Apr 1980, Ethiopia. Apr 1980, Nazareth (Ethiopia), on the initiative of university teachers and researchers from Eastern Africa, at inaugural conference under the auspices of *East African Universities Social Science Consultative Group (EASSCG, inactive)*, whose activities it was to replace. Original title: *Organization for Social Science Research in Eastern Africa*. Current title adopted when activities extended to Southern Africa. **Aims** Promote the development of an African research tradition; enhance policy and research interface; build capacity; undertake collaborative research and create facilities for the exchange of scholarly ideas; disseminate research outputs; promote cooperation between scientists in African and African development institutions; facilitate dialogue, cooperation and collaboration between researchers, other scholars and policy-makers in Africa. **Structure** Congress (every 3 years); Executive Committee. Headquarters in Addis Ababa (Ethiopia). **Languages** English, French, Portuguese. **Staff** 23.00 FTE, paid. **Finance** Members' dues: Full – individuals US$ 10, institutions US$ 100; Associate – individuals US$ 5, institutions US$ 50. Grants from donors, including: *Swedish International Development Cooperation Agency (Sida)*; Dutch Government; *Norwegian Agency for Development Cooperation (Norad)*; *International Development Research Centre (IDRC, #13162)*; *DANIDA*. **Activities** Events/meetings; training/education. **Events** *Triennial Congress* Dar es Salaam (Tanzania UR) 2011, *Triennial Congress* Cape Town (South Africa) 2008, *Triennial Congress* Addis Ababa (Ethiopia) 2005, *Triennial Congress* Khartoum (Sudan) 2002, *Workshop on reconstruction of war-torn communities in the Middle East, the Greater Red Sea region and Africa* Cairo (Egypt) 2001. **Publications** *OSSREA Bulletin* (3 a year); *Eastern Africa Social Science Research Review* (2 a year). *Gender Issues Research Reports* – series; *Social Science Research Abstracts* – series. *Register of Social Scientists in Eastern and Southern Africa*. Books; monographs; series of occasional papers; national workshop reports; abstracts.
Members Membership open to institutes and individual scholars in 24 Eastern and Southern African countries and territories. Current membership drawn from social scientists in 19 of the 24 eligible countries:
Angola, Botswana, Burundi, Djibouti, Eritrea, Eswatini, Ethiopia, Kenya, Lesotho, Madagascar, Malawi, Mauritius, Mozambique, Namibia, Rwanda, Seychelles, Somalia, South Africa, South Sudan, Sudan, Tanzania UR, Uganda, Zambia, Zimbabwe.
Associate members in 4 countries:
Austria, Egypt, Italy, USA.
Regional/international members (4):
African Centre for Applied Research and Training in Social Development (ACARTSOD, #00237); *African Economic Research Consortium (AERC, #00292)*; *Institute of Development Studies, Brighton (IDS)* (library of); *The Rockefeller Foundation (#18966)*.
NGO Relations Member of: *African Books Collective (ABC, #00226)*; *Globalization Studies Network (GSN, #10440)*; *International Science Council (ISC, #14796)*. Partner of: *European Association of Development Research and Training Institutes (EADI, #06012)*. Joint workshops with: *International Institute of Social Studies, The Hague (ISS)*; *Nordic Africa Institute (NAI, #17168)*. [2018/XD2238/y/**D**]

- ♦ Organization of Solidarity of the Peoples of Africa, Asia and Latin America (#17849)
- ♦ Organization of Spouses of the European Commission (internationally oriented national body)
- ♦ Organization of Supreme Courts of the Americas (no recent information)
- ♦ Organization for Testing in Europe / see European Federation of National Associations of Measurement, Testing and Analytical Laboratories (#07168)
- ♦ Organization for Timeshare in Europe / see Resort Development Organisation (#18913)
- ♦ Organization of Trade Unions of Central Africa (no recent information)
- ♦ Organization of Trade Unions of West Africa (unconfirmed)
- ♦ Organization of Tropical American Nematologists / see Organization of Nematologists of Tropical America (#17878)
- ♦ Organization for Tropical Studies (internationally oriented national body)

♦ Organization of Women in International Trade (OWIT) 17889

Sec c/o 1776 K St NW, Ste 200, Washington DC 20006, USA. E-mail: secretary@owit.org.
URL: http://www.owit.org/

History 1989, USA. **Aims** Support advancement of women in international trade and business. **Structure** Board of Directors; Executive Committee. **Languages** English. **Activities** Training/education. **Events** *Annual Conference* Monterrey (Mexico) 2008, *Annual conference / Conference* Miami, FL (USA) 2007, *Annual conference / Conference* San Francisco, CA (USA) 2006, *Annual conference / Conference* Copenhagen (Denmark) 2005, *World conference* Copenhagen (Denmark) 2005. **Members** Individuals; Chapters. Membership countries not specified. [2021/XJ4042/t/**C**]

- ♦ Organization of Women Parliamentarians from Muslim Countries (no recent information)

♦ Organization for Women in Science for the Developing World (OWSD) 17890

Organisation des femmes scientifiques du Tiers-Monde

Secretariat ICTP Campus, Adriatico Guesthouse 7th Fl, Via Grignano 9, 34151 Trieste TS, Italy. T. +3940224032l. Fax +3940220689. E-mail: owsd@owsd.net – communications@owsd.net.
URL: http://www.owsd.net/

History 20 Mar 1989, Trieste (Italy). 20-22 Mar 1989, Trieste (Italy), as *Third World Organization for Women in Science (TWOWS)*, following recommendations of the 2nd General Conference of *TWAS (#20270)*, Sep 1987, Beijing (China), and a conference organized by *Canadian International Development Agency (CIDA, inactive)* and TWAS, 3-7 Oct 1988, Trieste (Italy). Officially inaugurated, Jan 1993, Cairo (Egypt). Constitution adopted at 1st General Assembly. Present name adopted, 2010. Previously also known under the acronym *OWSDW*. **Aims** Increase participation and recognition of women in developing countries in scientific and technological research, achievements, teaching and leadership; increase their access to the socio-economic benefits of science and technology; promote participation of women scientists and technologists in the development of their countries; promote collaboration and communication among them and with the international scientific community as a whole; increase understanding of the role of science and technology in supporting women's development activities. **Structure** General Assembly (every 4-6 years); Executive Board; International Secretariat. **Languages** English. **Staff** 8.00 FTE, paid. **Finance** Sources: donations; international organizations. Other sources: Subventions. Supported by: *Carnegie Corporation of New York* (initial grant and further contributions); Elsevier Foundation (current funding); *International Development Research Centre (IDRC, #13162)* (current funding); *MacArthur Foundation* (initial grant and further contributions); *Swedish International Development Cooperation Agency (Sida)* (current funding); *Swedish International Development Cooperation Agency (Sida)* (initial grant and further contributions); *The Rockefeller Foundation (#18966)* (initial grant and further contributions); *TWAS (#20270)* (initial grant and further contributions). **Activities** Awards/prizes/competitions; events/meetings; projects/programmes; training/education. **Events** *General Assembly and International Conference* Trieste (Italy) 2021, *General Assembly and Conference* Kuwait (Kuwait) 2016, *General assembly and conference* Beijing (China) 2010, *Africa regional conference* Abuja (Nigeria) 2009, *General Conference* Durban (South Africa) 2009. **Publications** *Directory of Women Scientists* (1995). Annual Report, informational pamphlets; conference proceedings. **Information Services** *National Assessments on Gender and STI* – data collection and analysis.

Members Full; Associate; Affiliate. Over 6000 in 131 countries and territories:
Albania, Algeria, Angola, Argentina, Armenia, Australia, Azerbaijan, Bahamas, Bahrain, Bangladesh, Belgium, Benin, Bhutan, Bolivia, Botswana, Brazil, Burkina Faso, Burundi, Cambodia, Cameroon, Canada, Chad, Chile, China, Colombia, Congo Brazzaville, Congo DR, Costa Rica, Côte d'Ivoire, Cuba, Dominican Rep, Ecuador, Egypt, El Salvador, Eritrea, Eswatini, Ethiopia, Fiji, Finland, France, Gabon, Gambia, Georgia, Germany, Ghana, Greece, Guatemala, Guinea, Guyana, Haiti, Honduras, Hungary, India, Indonesia, Iran Islamic Rep, Iraq, Israel, Italy, Jamaica, Jordan, Kazakhstan, Kenya, Kuwait, Kyrgyzstan, Lebanon, Lesotho, Liberia, Libya, Madagascar, Malawi, Malaysia, Mali, Malta, Mauritania, Mauritius, Mexico, Moldova, Mongolia, Montenegro, Morocco, Mozambique, Myanmar, Namibia, Nepal, Netherlands, New Zealand, Nicaragua, Niger, Nigeria, North Macedonia, Oman, Pakistan, Palestine, Papua New Guinea, Peru, Philippines, Poland, Portugal, Romania, Rwanda, Saudi Arabia, Senegal, Serbia, Sierra Leone, Singapore, Slovakia, Slovenia, South Africa, Spain, Sri Lanka, Sudan, Sweden, Syrian AR, Tanzania UR, Thailand, Togo, Trinidad-Tobago, Tunisia, Türkiye, Uganda, UK, Ukraine, United Arab Emirates, Uruguay, USA, Uzbekistan, Venezuela, Vietnam, Yemen, Zambia, Zimbabwe.
IGO Relations Administered under: *UNESCO (#20322)*. **NGO Relations** Observer to: *InterAcademy Partnership (IAP, #11376)*. [2021/XC0076/**C**]

♦ Organization of Women Writers of Africa (internationally oriented national body)

♦ Organization of World Heritage Cities (OWHC) 17891

Organisation des villes du patrimoine mondial (OVPM) – Organización de las Ciudades del Patrimonio Mundial (OCPM)

Headquarters Maison historique Chevalier, 5, rue Cul-de-Sac, Québec QC G1K 4H6, Canada. T. +14186920000. E-mail: secretariat@ovpm.org.
URL: http://www.ovpm.org/

History 8 Sep 1993, Fez (Morocco). Former names and other names: *Réseau des villes du patrimoine mondial* – former; *World Heritage Cities Organization (WHCO)* – former; *Organização das Cidades do Patrimônio Mundial* – former. **Aims** Assist member cities adapt and improve management methods in relation to specific requirements of having a site inscribed on the UNESCO World Heritage List. **Structure** General Assembly (annual); Board of Directors; General Secretariat; Regional Secretariats (9). **Languages** Arabic, English, French, Portuguese, Spanish. **Staff** 4.00 FTE, paid. Regional coordinators and assistants: 9. **Finance** Sources: donations; grants; investments; members' dues; revenue from activities/projects. **Activities** Knowledge management/information dissemination; training/education. Works within the framework of *Convention Concerning the Protection of the World Cultural and Natural Heritage (World Heritage Convention, 1972)*. Africa and Middle East; Asia-Pacific; Central America, Caribbean and Mexico; China; Eastern and Central Europe; Euro-Asia; Northwest Europe and North America; South America; Southern Europe and Mediterranean. **Events** *World Congress* Québec, QC (Canada) 2021, *World Congress* Krakow (Poland) 2019, *World Congress* Gyeongju (Korea Rep) 2017, *Asia-Pacific Regional Conference* Gyeongju (Korea Rep) 2016, *World Congress* Arequipa (Peru) 2015. **Publications** Proceedings; recommendations.
Members World Heritage Cities recognized by UNESCO (313) in 81 countries and territories:
Albania (Berat; Gjirokastra), Algeria (Algiers; Ghardaia), Armenia (Etchmiadzin*; Yerevan*), Austria (Hallstatt; Salzburg; Vienna), Azerbaijan (Baku), Belgium (Bruges; Brussels; Namur*), Bermuda (St George), Bolivia (Potosi; Sucre), Bosnia-Herzegovina (Mostar), Brazil (Brasilia; Diamantina; Goias; Olinda; Ouro Preto; Salvador da Bahia; São Luis), Bulgaria (Nessebar), Canada (Lunenburg; Québec), Cape Verde (Cidade Velha), Chile (Valparaiso), China (Chengde; Lijiang; Macau; Ping Yao; Suzhou*), Colombia (Cartagena da Indias; Santa Cruz de Mompox), Congo DR (Kashusha*), Croatia (Dubrovnik; Split; Trogir), Cuba (Camaguey; Cienfuegos; Havana; Trinidad), Czechia (Cesky Krumlov; Holasovice; Kutna Hora; Prague; Telc; Trebic), Dominican Rep (Santo Domingo), Ecuador (Cuenca; Quito), Egypt (Cairo), Estonia (Tallinn), Ethiopia (Lamu), Finland (Rauma), France (Amiens*; Bordeaux; Carcassonne; Le Havre; Lyon; Mont-Saint-Michel; Nancy; Paris; Provins; Strasbourg), Germany (Bamberg; Berlin; Bremen; Goslar; Lubeck; Potsdam; Quedlinburg; Stralsund; Trier*; Weimar; Wismar), Greece (Corfu; Patmos; Edessa*; Rhodes), Guatemala (Antigua Guatemala), Holy See (Vatican City), Hungary (Budapest), Indonesia (Bam), Israel (Acre; Jerusalem; Tel Aviv), Italy (Assisi; Caltagirone; Capriate San Gervasio; Catania; Ferrara; Florence; Genoa; Mantua; Matera; Militello Val di Catania; Modena; Modica; Naples; Noto; Palazzolo Acreide; Pienza; Ragusa; Rome; Sabbioneta; San Gimignano; Scicli; Siena; Siracusa; Urbino; Venice; Vicenza), Japan (Kyoto; Nara; Shirakawa-Go et Gokayama), Korea Rep (Andong*), Laos (Luang Prabang), Latvia (Riga), Libya (Ghadames; Tripoli*), Lithuania (Vilnius), Luxembourg (Luxembourg), Malaysia (George Town; Melaka), Mali (Djenne; Tombuctú), Malta (Valletta), Mauritania (Chinguetti), Mexico (Campeche; Guanajuato; Mexico City; Morelia; Oaxaca; Puebla; Querétaro; San Miguel de Allende; Tlacotalpan; Zacatecas), Montenegro (Kotor), Morocco (Essaouira; Fez; Marrakech; Mazagan; Meknes; Tétouan), Mozambique (Isle de Mozambique), Nepal (Bhaktapur; Kathmandu; Patan), Netherlands (Beemster), North Macedonia (Ohrid), Norway (Bergen; Røros), Panama (Panama), Peru (Arequipa; Cusco; Lima), Philippines (Vigan), Poland (Krakow; Torun; Warsaw; Zamosc), Portugal (Angra do Heroismo; Evora; Guimarães; Porto; Sintra), Romania (Biertan; Sighisoara), Russia (Derbent; Kazan; Moscow; Novgorod; St Petersburg; Yaroslavl), San Marino, Senegal (Dakar; Is of Saint-Louis), Slovakia (Banska Stiavnica; Bardejov), Spain (Alcala de Henares; Aranjuez; Avila; Baeza; Caceres; Córdoba; Cuenca; Granada; Ibiza; Mérida; Oviedo; Salamanca; San Cristóbal de La Laguna; Santiago de Compostela; Segovia; Toledo; Ubeda), Sri Lanka (Galle; Kandy), Suriname (Paramaribo), Sweden (Karlskrona; Visby), Switzerland (Bern; Le Locle; Ville de la Chaux-Fonds), Syrian AR (Aleppo; Bosra; Damascus), Tanzania UR (Zanzibar), Tunisia (Kairouan; Monastir*; Sousse; Tunis), Türkiye (Istanbul; Safranbolu), UK (Bath; Edinburgh; Liverpool), Ukraine (Lviv), Uruguay (Colonia de Sacramento), Uzbekistan (Bukhara; Khiva; Samarkand; Shakhrisyabz), Venezuela (Coro), Vietnam (Hoi An; Hue), Yemen (Sana'a; Shibam; Zabid).
NGO Relations Member of (1): *European Heritage Alliance 3.3 (#07477)*. [2020.08.18/XD4589/**C**]

- ♦ Organizing Committee for the People's Decade of Human Rights Education / see People's Movement for Human Rights Learning (#18307)
- ♦ Organizing Society for International Conferences in Esperanto (internationally oriented national body)
- ♦ Organizzazione Europea dell'Industria delle Confetture e Conserve di Frutte (inactive)
- ♦ Organizzazione Europea delle Industrie delle Conserve di Legumi (inactive)
- ♦ Organizzazione Europea delle Industrie delle Conserve di Pomodoro / see European Organisation of Tomato Industries (#08104)
- ♦ Organizzazione Europea delle Industrie di Trasformazione di Frutta e Ortaggi / see European Association of Fruit and Vegetable Processors (#06049)
- ♦ Organizzazione Europea per la Ricerca e il Trattamento del Cancro (#08101)
- ♦ Organizzazione Europea per la Ricerca sulla Trombosi / see European Thrombosis Research Organization (#08912)
- ♦ Organizzazione Europea per il Turismo Equestre (inactive)
- ♦ Organizzazione Europea delle Unioni di Residenze e Servizi per Giovani Lavoratori (inactive)
- ♦ Organizzazione Europea Vigili del Fuoco Volontari di Protezione Civile (internationally oriented national body)
- ♦ Organizzazione per le Gestosi (#17869)
- ♦ Organizzazione Internazionale di Arredatori di Negozi (inactive)
- ♦ Organizzazione Internazionale di Protezione Animali (#17810)
- ♦ Organizzazione Internazionale per la Riconversione dei Ballerini Professionisti (no recent information)
- ♦ Organizzazione Internazionale per lo Studio della Fatica delle Funi (#14474)
- ♦ Organizzazione Internazionale dei Trasporti a Fune (#14481)
- ♦ Organizzazione Medica Omeopatica Internazionale (no recent information)
- ♦ Organizzazione Mondiale Degli Agricoltori (#21401)
- ♦ Organizzazione Mondiale per l'Autismo (#21211)
- ♦ Organizzazione Mondiale dei Giovani Contro i Cambiamenti Climatici (inactive)
- ♦ Organizzazione Mondiale delle Immagini e del Suono (inactive)
- ♦ Organizzazione Mondiale del Termalismo (#17820)
- ♦ Organizzazione Naturale di Salute del Mondo (internationally oriented national body)
- ♦ Organizzazione dei Produttori Europei di Pani de Leghe di Rame (#17866)
- ♦ Organizzazione per lo Sviluppo Globale di Comunità in Paesi Extraeuropei (internationally oriented national body)
- ♦ Organizzazione Svizzera Aiuto ai Rifugiati (internationally oriented national body)
- ♦ Organotin Environmental Programme Association (no recent information)
- ♦ Orhistra Neoleas tis Evropaikis Kinotitas / see European Union Youth Orchestra (#09024)
- ♦ ORIDP – Organizzazione Internazionale per la Riconversione dei Ballerini Professionisti (no recent information)
- ♦ Orient Airlines Association / see Association of Asia Pacific Airlines (#02385)
- ♦ Orient Airlines Research Bureau / see Association of Asia Pacific Airlines (#02385)
- ♦ Oriental Bird Club (internationally oriented national body)
- ♦ Oriental Boxing Federation / see Oriental and Pacific Boxing Federation (#17894)

♦ Oriental Ceramic Society (OCS) 17892

Admin PO Box 517, Cambridge, CB21 5BE, UK. T. +441223881328. Fax +441223881328. E-mail: ocs.london@btinternet.com.
URL: http://www.ocs-london.com/

History 1921, London (UK). UK Registered Charity: 250356. **Aims** Increase knowledge and appreciation not only of ceramics but of all the arts of Asia, providing a creative link between collectors, curators, scholars and others who share these interests. **Structure** Council; Sub-Committees. **Languages** English. **Staff** 0.50 FTE, paid. **Finance** Members' dues. **Activities** Organizes visits to collections, seminars, identification meetings, lectures and occasional exhibitions. **Publications** *OCS Newsletter* (annual); *The Transactions of the Oriental Ceramic Society* (annual).
Members National organizations in 33 countries and territories:
Australia, Austria, Belgium, Brazil, China, Denmark, Finland, France, Germany, Hong Kong, India, Indonesia, Ireland, Italy, Japan, Korea Rep (South), Malaysia, Mexico, Netherlands, New Zealand, Norway, Philippines, Russia, Singapore, South Africa, Spain, Sweden, Switzerland, Taiwan, Thailand, Türkiye, UK, USA. [2018/XD5775/**D**]

- ♦ Oriental Institute, Louvain-la-Neuve (internationally oriented national body)
- ♦ Oriental Institute, Oxford (internationally oriented national body)
- ♦ Oriental Missionary Society / see One Mission Society

♦ Oriental Numismatic Society (ONS) 17893

Société de numismatique orientale

Acting SG address not obtained.
Regional Sec Leuvensesteenweg 284 bus 3, 3200 Aarschot, Belgium.
URL: http://www.orientalnumismaticsociety.org/

History Mar 1970. **Aims** Promote research, exchange of ideas and collecting of *coins*, tokens, paper money, *currency* and *medals* of all periods from North Africa and Muslim Spain to Asia and the Far East. **Structure** Council; Regional Secretaries (6). **Languages** English, French, German. **Staff** 15.00 FTE, voluntary. **Finance** Sources: members' dues. **Activities** Events/meetings. Workshops in conjunction with *'International Numismatic Congress'* of *International Numismatic Council (INC, #14385)*. **Events** *50th Anniversary Conference* Boston, MA (USA) 2022, *European Section Meeting* Leiden (Netherlands) 2022, *North America Section Meeting* New York, NY (USA) 2022, *Annual General Meeting* Oxford (UK) 2022, *European Section meeting* Diest (Belgium) 2021. **Publications** *Journal of the Oriental Numismatic Society* (4 a year). *Information Sheets*; *Occasional Papers*.
Members Individuals (about 700) in 53 countries and territories:
Argentina, Australia, Austria, Belgium, Brazil, Canada, Channel Is, Chile, China, Czechia, Denmark, Egypt, Finland, France, Germany, Greece, Hong Kong, Iceland, India, Indonesia, Iran Islamic Rep, Ireland, Israel, Italy, Japan, Jordan, Luxembourg, Malaysia, Morocco, Netherlands, New Zealand, Nigeria, Norway, Oman, Pakistan, Poland, Portugal, Qatar, Saudi Arabia, Serbia, Singapore, Slovakia, Spain, Sri Lanka, Sweden, Switzerland, Syrian AR, Tunisia, Türkiye, UK, United Arab Emirates, USA, Yemen.
NGO Relations Member of (1): *International Numismatic Council (INC, #14385)*. [2022.02.02/XC4135/v/**C**]

♦ Oriental and Pacific Boxing Federation (OPBF) 17894

Contact c/o Japan Boxing Commission, 1-3-61 Bunkyo-ku, Tokyo, 112-8575 Japan. T. +81338166561. Fax +81338166560.
URL: http://www.opbf.jp/

History 27 Oct 1954, as *Oriental Boxing Federation (OBF)*. A continental boxing federation of *World Boxing Council (WBC, #21242)*. **Structure** Executive, comprising: President; Vice-President; Secretary-General; 2 Permanent Members.
Members Boxing federations in 13 countries and territories:
Australia, China, Guam, Hong Kong, India, Indonesia, Japan, Korea Rep, New Zealand, Papua New Guinea, Philippines, Samoa, Thailand. [2012/XE2250/**D**]

♦ Oriental Society of Aesthetic Plastic Surgery (OSAPS) 17895

Main Office Medical Plaza Ortigas, Unit 1111 – 11th Floor, San Miguel Avenue, Pasig City RIZ, Philippines. T. +6327062481.
SG 23 Mabolo St, Valle Verde 1, Pasig City RIZ, Philippines. T. +639178966411. Fax +6326716781.
Facebook: https://www.facebook.com/OSAPS-Oriental-Society-of-Aesthetic-Plastic-Surgery-1734027300142433/

History 1988, Tokyo (Japan). **Aims** Advance and develop the science and art of oriental aesthetic plastic surgery among surgeons of the highest professional integrity and who are governed by a high sense of ethical code; coordinate activities and foster and promote cooperation and understanding among surgeons practising in the field. **Structure** Executive Committee, composed of National Secretaries from each member country, and headed by Secretary-General. **Languages** English. **Staff** Part-time, mostly voluntary. **Finance** Members' dues. Congress proceeds. **Activities** Events/meetings; networking/liaising. **Events** *Biennial International Congress* Penang (Malaysia) 2020, *Biennial International Congress* Bali (Indonesia) 2018, *Biennial International Congress* Taipei (Taiwan) 2016, *Biennial International Congress* Pattaya (Thailand) 2014, *Biennial International Congress* Seoul (Korea Rep) 2012. **Publications** None.
Members Full in 13 countries and territories:
Australia, Brazil, Canada, China, Hong Kong, Indonesia, Japan, Korea Rep, Malaysia, Philippines, Taiwan, Thailand, USA.
[2020/XD7125/**D**]

- ♦ Oriental Society of Australia (internationally oriented national body)
- ♦ Oriental Studies Institute / see Oriental Institute, Louvain-la-Neuve
- ♦ Orient Crusades / see OC International (#17688)
- ♦ Oriented Polypropylene Film Manufacturers' Association (inactive)
- ♦ Oriente Foundation (internationally oriented national body)
- ♦ Orient-Institut, Beirut (internationally oriented national body)
- ♦ Orient-Institut der Deutschen Morgenländischen Gesellschaft, Istanbul (internationally oriented national body)
- ♦ Orient Institute of the German Oriental Society, Istanbul (internationally oriented national body)
- ♦ Orient-Institut in der Stiftung DGIA, Beirut / see Orient-Institut, Beirut
- ♦ Orient Press International Federation (inactive)
- ♦ **oriGIn** Organization for an International Geographical Indications Network (#17874)
- ♦ ORIT / see Confederación Sindical de Trabajadores y Trabajadoras de las Américas (#04480)
- ♦ **ORITEL** Organización Internacional de Teletones (#17842)
- ♦ Orkestar Mladih Mediteranea (#17788)
- ♦ Orkester Norden (#17475)
- ♦ **ÖRK** Ökumenischer Rat der Kirchen (#21320)
- ♦ **ORME** Organisation de la ruralité et du milieu européen (#17825)

♦ Ornamental Fish International (OFI) 17896

SG Computerweg 16, 3821 AB Amersfoort, Netherlands. T. +6582231434. E-mail: secretariat@ofish.org.
Pres address not obtained. E-mail: president@ofish.org.
URL: http://www.ofish.org/

History 1 Jun 1980, Rome (Italy). Former names and other names: *Ornamental Fish International Wholesalers Organization* – former. Registration: EU Transparency Register, No/ID: 36098352545-58, Start date: 23 Oct 2009. **Aims** Represent the ornamental aquatic industry; ensure that members' views are made known to governments and international influential bodies and institutions; raise general business and technical standards; ensure high standards of care and welfare for fish handled by members; improve standards of fish transportation; ensure members abide by OFI code of ethics; encourage importers and exporters to conduct specialist research into efficient and humane methods of transporting live fish; support, protect and further interests of the aquatic trade; protect image and interests of the industry; promote the *hobby* of fishkeeping; support conservation projects on sustainable harvesting and ethical collection methods. **Structure** Annual Meeting (odd years in Singapore (Singapore), even years in Germany); Executive Board; Board of Advisors. **Languages** English. **Staff** 1.00 FTE, paid. **Finance** Sources: members' dues; sale of products; sale of publications; sponsorship. **Activities** Awards/prizes/competitions; knowledge management/information dissemination. **Events** *Aquarama Seminar* Singapore (Singapore) 2011, *Aquarama conference* Singapore (Singapore) 2007, *Aquarama conference* Singapore (Singapore) 2003, *Meeting* Nürburg (Germany) 2002, *Aquarama conference* Singapore (Singapore) 2001. **Publications** *OFI Journal* (3 a year); *Members' Updates* (over 52 a year). Educational books.

Members Companies and other organizations in 38 countries and territories:
Australia, Austria, Belarus, Belgium, Brazil, China, Colombia, Cyprus, Czechia, Denmark, Finland, France, Germany, Hong Kong, India, Indonesia, Ireland, Israel, Italy, Japan, Kenya, Malawi, Malaysia, Netherlands, Nigeria, Norway, Peru, Russia, Singapore, Slovakia, Slovenia, Spain, Sri Lanka, Sweden, Taiwan, Thailand, UK, USA.
Included in the above, 1 organization listed in this Yearbook:
World Wide Pet Supply Association (WWPSA, no recent information).
IGO Relations Regular contacts with: *Secretariat of the Convention on International Trade in Endangered Species of Wild Fauna and Flora (CITES Secretariat, #19199).* **NGO Relations** Links with a large number of bodies, including: *Animal Transportation Association (ATA, #00844); International Air Transport Association (IATA, #11614);* (US) Marine Aquarium Council. [2021.08.31/XF3046/**F**]

- ♦ Ornamental Fish International Wholesalers Organization / see Ornamental Fish International (#17896)
- ♦ Ornithological Society of the Middle East / see Ornithological Society of the Middle East, the Caucasus and Central Asia (#17897)

♦ Ornithological Society of the Middle East, the Caucasus and Central Asia (OSME) 17897

Chair c/o The Lodge, Sandy, SG19 2DL, UK. E-mail: chairman@osme.org.
URL: http://www.osme.org/
History Founded 1978, as the successor to 'Ornithological Society of Turkey'. Original title: *Ornithological Society of the Middle East.* **Aims** Promote study of Middle Eastern, Caucasian and Central Asian ornithology and conservation of the region's birds; work with other individuals and organizations with similar objectives and pursuing charitable activities concerned with ornithology in the Middle East, Caucasus and Central Asia. **Structure** Annual General Meeting; Council. **Languages** English. **Staff** Voluntary. **Finance** Members' dues. Donations. **Activities** Financial and/or material support; projects/programmes; monitoring/evaluation; knowledge management/information dissemination; research/documentation; training/education; events/meetings. **Events** *Joint Winter Meeting* London (UK) 2015, *Annual Summer Meeting* Thetford (UK) 2015, *Annual Summer Meeting* Thetford (UK) 2015, *Annual Summer Meeting* Thetford (UK) 2014, *Annual Summer Meeting* Thetford (UK) 2013. **Publications** *Sandgrouse* (2 a year) – journal.
Members National conservation organizations in 9 countries:
Cyprus, Egypt, Iraq, Israel, Jordan, Türkiye, UK, United Arab Emirates, Uzbekistan.
Individuals in 52 countries and territories:
Armenia, Australia, Austria, Azerbaijan, Bahrain, Belgium, Bulgaria, Cambodia, Canada, Cyprus, Czechia, Denmark, Egypt, Estonia, Finland, France, Georgia, Germany, Hong Kong, Hungary, Iran Islamic Rep, Iraq, Ireland, Israel, Italy, Japan, Jordan, Kazakhstan, Kuwait, Kyrgyzstan, Lebanon, Netherlands, Norway, Oman, Palestine, Poland, Qatar, Romania, Russia, Saudi Arabia, Slovenia, Spain, Sweden, Switzerland, Syrian AR, Türkiye, Turkmenistan, UK, United Arab Emirates, USA, Uzbekistan, Yemen. [2020.01.20/XD1377/**D**]

- ♦ Ornitologia Rondo Esperantlingva (no recent information)
- ♦ **ORO** Only Representative Organisation (#17743)
- ♦ OroVerde – Die Tropenwaldstiftung (internationally oriented national body)
- ♦ OroVerde – OroVerde – Die Tropenwaldstiftung (internationally oriented national body)
- ♦ **ORPF** Oceania Regional Powerlifting Federation (#17671)

♦ Orphanet 17898

Contact INSERM US14, Rare Disease Platform, 96 rue Didot, 75014 Paris, France. T. +33156538137. Fax +33156538138. E-mail: contact.orphanet@inserm.fr.
URL: http://www.orpha.net/
History 1997, France. Founded by INSERM (French National Institute for Health and Medical Research). Became a European endeavour, 2000. **Aims** Improve the visibility of rare diseases in the fields of healthcare and research; provide high-quality information on rare diseases and expertise; contribute to generating knowledge on rare diseases. **Structure** Management Board; Steering Committee; Advisory Board. **Finance** Supported by: *European Commission (EC, #06633);* French Directorate for Health; INSERM. Annual budget: 3,000,000 EUR (2012). **Activities** Knowledge management/information dissemination; research/documentation. **Events** *European Conference on Rare Diseases and Orphan Products* Paris (France) 2022.
Members National teams in 42 countries:
Argentina, Armenia, Australia, Austria, Belgium, Bulgaria, Canada, Croatia, Cyprus, Czechia, Estonia, Finland, France, Georgia, Germany, Hungary, Ireland, Israel, Italy, Japan, Kazakhstan, Latvia, Lithuania, Luxembourg, Malta, Morocco, Netherlands, North Macedonia, Norway, Poland, Portugal, Romania, Russia, Serbia, Slovakia, Slovenia, Spain, Sweden, Switzerland, Tunisia, Türkiye, UK. [2021/XJ7386/**F**]

- ♦ Orphans Care Federation (unconfirmed)
- ♦ Orphelins Sida International (internationally oriented national body)
- ♦ **ORPHEUS** Organization for PhD Education in Biomedicine and Health Sciences in the European System (#17882)
- ♦ Orquesta de Jóvenes del Mediterraneo (#17788)
- ♦ Orquesta de Jovens das Americas (#22022)
- ♦ Orquesta Juvenil de las Américas (#22022)
- ♦ Orquestra dos Jóvens do Mediterrâneo (#17788)
- ♦ Orquestra Juvenil da Comunidade Européia / see European Union Youth Orchestra (#09024)
- ♦ Orquestra da Juventude da União Européia (#09024)
- ♦ ORSAM – Ortadogû Stratejik Arastirmalar Merkezi (internationally oriented national body)
- ♦ **ORSEA** Operations Research Society of East Africa (#17774)
- ♦ Orsoline di Gesù (religious order)
- ♦ Orsoline dell'Unione Romana (religious order)
- ♦ ORSTOM / see Institut de recherche pour le développement
- ♦ Ortadogû Stratejik Arastirmalar Merkezi (internationally oriented national body)
- ♦ Orta Dogu Teknik Üniversitesi (internationally oriented national body)
- ♦ Ortadogu ve Balkan Incelemeleri Vakfi (internationally oriented national body)
- ♦ ORTEP Association – Organotin Environmental Programme Association (no recent information)
- ♦ Orthodox Centre of the Ecumenical Patriarchate (internationally oriented national body)
- ♦ Orthodox Christian Mission Center (internationally oriented national body)
- ♦ Orthodoxon Kentron tu Ikumeniku Patriarhiu (internationally oriented national body)
- ♦ Orthodox Palestine Society (internationally oriented national body)
- ♦ Ortho Mare Nostrum – Société Internationale de Chirurgie Orthopédique de la Méditerranée (unconfirmed)
- ♦ Orthopedic Association of SAARC Countries (unconfirmed)

♦ Orthopterists' Society (OS) 17899

Exec Dir Locust Control, 125 William Webb Drive, McKellar, Canberra ACT 2617, Australia. T. +61400360200.
Pres address not obtained.
URL: http://orthsoc.org/
History 1976, San Martin de los Andes (Argentina), as *Pan American Acridological Society.* **Aims** Facilitate communication among those interested in Orthoptera in the broad sense (crickets, grasshoppers, locusts, katydids and allied insects) and related organisms; encourage collaborative research, conservation and control programmes in Orthopterology. **Structure** Officers: President; Past President; Executive Director. **Staff** No full time staff. **Finance** Members' dues. Other sources: private gifts; endowments. **Activities** Events/meetings; financial and/or material support; awards/prizes/competitions. **Events** *Quadrennial Congress* Ilhéus (Brazil) 2016, *Quadrennial Congress* Kunming (China) 2013, *Quadrennial Congress* Antalya (Turkey) 2009, *Quadrennial Congress* Canmore, AB (Canada) 2005, *Quadrennial Congress* Montpellier (France) 2001. **Publications** *Journal of Orthoptera Research; Orthopterists' Society Newsletter (Metaleptea).* Monograph series on orthopteran biodiversity.
Members Individuals (about 300) in 81 countries and territories:
Algeria, Argentina, Australia, Austria, Bangladesh, Belgium, Brazil, Bulgaria, Burkina Faso, Cameroon, Canada, Chad, Chile, China, Colombia, Croatia, Cuba, Czechia, Denmark, Dominican Rep, Egypt, Ethiopia, Finland, France, Georgia, Germany, Greece, Guatemala, Hong Kong, Hungary, India, Indonesia, Ireland, Israel, Italy, Japan, Jordan, Kazakhstan, Kenya, Korea Rep, Latvia, Libya, Lithuania, Madagascar, Mali, Mauritania, Mexico, Morocco, Netherlands, New Zealand, Nicaragua, Niger, Nigeria, Norway, Pakistan, Panama, Peru, Philippines, Poland, Portugal, Russia, Saudi Arabia, Senegal, Seychelles, Singapore, Slovakia, South Africa, Spain, Sweden, Switzerland, Syrian AR, Taiwan, Thailand, Trinidad-Tobago, Tunisia, Türkiye, UK, Uruguay, USA, Uzbekistan, Venezuela. [2018.09.05/XE3756/**E**]

♦ Orthoptistes de la Communauté européenne (OCE) 17900

Sec Gminderstr 22, 72762 Reutlingen, Germany. T. +4971219725655. Fax +4971219725657. E-mail: president@euro-orthoptics.com.
Pres address not obtained.
URL: http://www.euro-orthoptics.com/
History 20 Jan 1989. Founding countries: Italy; France; UK; West Germany. Shortly thereafter, other national organizations, including: Austria; Belgium; Denmark; Luxembourg; Netherlands; Poland; Sweden; Switzerland. **Aims** Establish the connection with member countries in view of assuring passage of information on present and future developments within the orthoptic profession in member countries; represent orthoptists in member countries to EU authorities, especially within the European Commission; disseminate suggestions and decisions made by authorities affecting the profession, as well as communicate advice and proposals to these authorities; promote among member countries coordination or working conditions and harmonization of orthoptist's training; assist member organizations when common interests are concerned, creation of an European orthoptic diploma. **Structure** General Meeting (annual); Council (meeting of all Committee members); Executive Officers. **Languages** English, French. **Staff** None. **Finance** Sources: gifts, legacies; members' dues; revenue from activities/projects. **Activities** Events/meetings; networking/liaising; research and development. **Events** *Council Meeting* Vienna (Austria) 2022, *Council Meeting* Neuchâtel (Switzerland) 2015, *Council Meeting* Valletta (Malta) 2014, *Council Meeting* Oslo (Norway) 2012, *Meeting / Council Meeting* Gdansk (Poland) 2011. **Publications** *Orthoptics in the European Union* in English, French. *OCE Code of Ethics and Principles of Professional Behaviour.* Professional survey; profile of the profession; assessment file.
Members Membership open to EU countries where individual practise is recognized in their respective countries in accordance with the modified EC General Directive 89/48. Orthoptists residing in EU member states and who have no representation on OCE may become associate members. Orthoptists in 19 countries:
Austria, Belgium, Czechia, Denmark, Finland, France, Germany, Greece, Ireland, Italy, Luxembourg, Malta, Netherlands, Norway, Poland, Portugal, Sweden, Switzerland, UK.
IGO Relations Ad-hoc contacts on specific matters. **NGO Relations** Member of (1): *International Pediatric Ophthalmology and Strabismus Council (IPOSC, #14544).* Ad-hoc contacts on specific projects. [2022.04.24/XE3940/**E**]

- ♦ ORT mondiale (#21698)
- ♦ ORT Union of Societies for the Promotion of Handicrafts and Industrial and Agricultural Work among the Jews / see World ORT (#21698)
- ♦ **ORU/FOGAR** Organisation des Régions Unies (#20657)
- ♦ **ORU/FOGAR** Organización de Regiones Unidas (#20657)
- ♦ Orville H Schell Jr Center for International Human Rights (internationally oriented national body)
- ♦ OSAA – United Nations Office of the Special Advisor on Africa (see: #20515)
- ♦ **OSAF** Oceania Sailing Federation (#17673)
- ♦ **OSAF** Organización Sudamericana de Fomento del Pura Sangre de Carrera (#17850)
- ♦ OSAN / see International Education Association
- ♦ **OSA** Ocean Sanctuary Alliance (#17687)
- ♦ OSA / see Optica (#17777)
- ♦ OSA – Ordo Fratrum Sancti Augustini (religious order)
- ♦ OSA – Oriental Society of Australia (internationally oriented national body)
- ♦ **OSAPS** Oriental Society of Aesthetic Plastic Surgery (#17895)
- ♦ OSAR – Organisation suisse d'aide aux réfugiés (internationally oriented national body)
- ♦ OSAR – Organizzazione Svizzera Aiuto ai Rifugiati (internationally oriented national body)
- ♦ OSBM – Order of the Basilians of St Macrina (religious order)
- ♦ OSCAL – United Nations Office of the Special Coordinator for Africa and the Least Developed Countries (inactive)
- ♦ Oscar A Romero: International Christian Secretariat in Solidarity with Latin America (internationally oriented national body)
- ♦ OSCAR – UK Information Service for World Mission (internationally oriented national body)
- ♦ OSCE / see Statistical Office of the European Union (#19974)
- ♦ **OSCE Court** Court of Conciliation and Arbitration within the OSCE (#04934)

♦ OSCE High Commissioner on National Minorities (HCNM) 17901

Haut Commissaire aux minorités nationales

High Commissioner PO Box 20062, 2500 EB The Hague, Netherlands. T. +31703125500. Fax +31703635910.
Street Address Prinsessegracht 22, 2514 AP The Hague, Netherlands.
URL: http://www.osce.org/hcnm/
History Established Jul 1992, Helsinki (Finland), during Summit of Conference for Security and Cooperation in Europe, currently *Organization for Security and Cooperation in Europe (OSCE, #17887).* First High Commissioner appointed Dec 1992; commenced operations Jan 1993. **Aims** Provide "early warning" and, as appropriate "early action" at the earliest possible stage in regard to tensions involving national minority issues which have not yet developed beyond an early warning stage, but, in the judgement of the High Commissioner, have the potential to develop into a conflict within the OSCE area. **Structure** Office based in The Hague (Netherlands). **Languages** English, French, German, Italian, Russian, Spanish. **Staff** 33.00 FTE, paid. **Finance** Funded by OSCE Participating States; Extra budgetary contributions. **Activities** Conflict resolution. Operating independently, impartially and confidentially of all parties involved, the High Commissioner is empowered to conduct on-site missions and to engage in preventive diplomacy at the earliest states of tension. As well as seeking to obtain first-hand information from the parties concerned, the High Commissioner also seeks to promote dialogue, confidence and cooperation between them. **Events** *Conference on OSCE Contribution to the Protection of National Minorities* Vienna (Austria) 2015. **Publications** Thematic recommendations and guidelines.
Members Participating States (57):
Albania, Andorra, Armenia, Austria, Azerbaijan, Belarus, Belgium, Bosnia-Herzegovina, Bulgaria, Canada, Croatia, Cyprus, Czechia, Denmark, Estonia, Finland, France, Georgia, Germany, Greece, Holy See, Hungary, Iceland, Ireland, Italy, Kazakhstan, Kyrgyzstan, Latvia, Liechtenstein, Lithuania, Luxembourg, Malta, Moldova, Monaco, Mongolia, Montenegro, Netherlands, North Macedonia, Norway, Poland, Portugal, Romania, Russia, San Marino, Serbia, Slovakia, Slovenia, Spain, Sweden, Switzerland, Tajikistan, Türkiye, Turkmenistan, UK, Ukraine, USA, Uzbekistan.
Asian Partners for cooperation (4):
Afghanistan, Japan, Korea Rep, Thailand.
Mediterranean partners for cooperation (6):
Algeria, Egypt, Israel, Jordan, Morocco, Tunisia. [2018/XE2753/**E***]

- ♦ **OSCE/ODIHR** OSCE – Office for Democratic Institutions and Human Rights (#17902)

♦ OSCE – Office for Democratic Institutions and Human Rights (OSCE/ODIHR) 17902

Dir Ul Miodowa 10, 00-251 Warsaw, Poland. T. +48225200600. Fax +48225200605. E-mail: office@odihr.pl.
URL: http://www.osce.org/odihr/
History 19 Nov 1990, Paris (France). Established 19-21 Nov 1990 at Conference for Security and Co-operation in Europe (CSCE) – subsequently *Organization for Security and Cooperation in Europe (OSCE, #17887)* – under *Charter of Paris for a New Europe (Paris Charter).* Former names and other names: *Office for Free Elections* – former; *Bureau pour les élections libres* – former; *CSCE – Office for Democratic Institutions and Human Rights (CSCE ODIHR)* – former; *Office for Democratic Institutions and Human Rights (ODIHR)* – alias (1992). **Aims** In the context of *security* and *cooperation* in *Europe*: promote democratic *elections*; provide assistance in consolidating democratic institutions and strengthening *civil society*; monitor and provide assistance to OSCE participating States in the implementation of OSCE human dimension commitments in areas of human rights, promoting tolerance and non-discrimination, and improving the situation of Roma and Sinti in the OSCE area. **Structure** Management; Programmatic Departments (4); OSCE Contact Point on Roma and Sinti Issues. **Languages** English, French, German, Italian, Russian, Spanish. **Staff** 180.00 FTE, paid. 10% of staff are seconded by OSCE participating States. **Finance** OSCE regular budget; voluntary contributions. Annual budget: 16,000,000 EUR. **Activities** Advocacy/lobbying/activism; events/meetings; guidance/assistance/consulting; knowledge management/information dissemination; monitoring/evaluation; politics/

policy/regulatory; training/education. **Events** *Workshop for Parliamentarians from the Balkans and South Caucasus* Bucharest (Romania) 2018, *Meeting on Torture Prevention, for National Preventive Mechanisms and Civil Society Organisations* Milan (Italy) 2018, *Annual Meeting of National Preventive Mechanisms for the OSCE Region* Vienna (Austria) 2016, *Conference on OSCE Contribution to the Protection of National Minorities* Vienna (Austria) 2015, *Annual Human Dimension Implementation Meeting* Warsaw (Poland) 2015. **Publications** Annual Report; guidelines; handbooks.

Members Participating States (57):
Albania, Andorra, Armenia, Austria, Azerbaijan, Belarus, Belgium, Bosnia-Herzegovina, Bulgaria, Canada, Croatia, Cyprus, Czechia, Denmark, Estonia, Finland, France, Georgia, Germany, Greece, Holy See, Hungary, Iceland, Ireland, Italy, Kazakhstan, Kyrgyzstan, Latvia, Liechtenstein, Lithuania, Luxembourg, Malta, Moldova, Monaco, Mongolia, Montenegro, Netherlands, North Macedonia, Norway, Poland, Portugal, Romania, Russia, San Marino, Serbia, Slovakia, Slovenia, Spain, Sweden, Switzerland, Tajikistan, Türkiye, Turkmenistan, UK, Ukraine, USA, Uzbekistan.

IGO Relations Observer status with (1): *International Holocaust Remembrance Alliance (IHRA, #13803)*. Member of (3): *Environmental Action Programme for Central and Eastern Europe (EAP, inactive)*; *European Committee on Legal Cooperation (#06655)*; *Frontex, the European Border and Coast Guard Agency (#10005)* (Consultative Forum). Cooperates with (7): *European Commission (EC, #06633)*; *International Organization for Migration (IOM, #14454)*; *Office of the United Nations High Commissioner for Human Rights (OHCHR, #17697)*; other election monitoring organizations; *Parliamentary Assembly of the Council of Europe (PACE, #18211)*; *UNDP (#20292)*; *UNHCR (#20327)*. [2021.09.03/XE3042/**E***]

- ♦ **OSCE** Organisation de la sécurité et la coopération en Europe (#17887)
- ♦ **OSCE** Organization for Security and Cooperation in Europe (#17887)
- ♦ **OSCE PA** Parliamentary Assembly of the Organization for Security and Cooperation in Europe (#18214)
- ♦ OSCE Parliamentary Assembly / see Parliamentary Assembly of the Organization for Security and Cooperation in Europe (#18214)
- ♦ OSCE Senior Council (inactive)
- ♦ OSCOM – Oslo Commission (inactive)
- ♦ **OSEAN** Osteopathic European Academic Network (#17909)
- ♦ OSEA – Ophthalmological Society of Eastern Africa (inactive)
- ♦ OSEJTM – Oeuvres sociales et éducatives des jésuites au Tiers-Monde (internationally oriented national body)
- ♦ OSE – Observatoire social européen (internationally oriented national body)
- ♦ **OSET** International Organization of Societies for Electrophysiological Technology (#14472)
- ♦ Os Europeus no Mundo (#08839)
- ♦ ÖSFK – Österreichisches Studienzentrum für Frieden und Konfliktlösung (internationally oriented national body)
- ♦ **OSF** Oceania Shooting Federation (#17674)
- ♦ **OSF** Oceania Squash Federation (#17675)
- ♦ OSFO / see Organisation of Sports Federations of Oceania (#17828)
- ♦ **OSFO** Organisation of Sports Federations of Oceania (#17828)
- ♦ OSF / see OPEC Fund for International Development (#17745)
- ♦ OSF / see Open Group (#17755)
- ♦ **OSF** Open Society Foundations (#17763)
- ♦ OSF – Ophtalmo sans frontières (internationally oriented national body)
- ♦ OSFS – Oblates of St Francis de Sales (religious order)
- ♦ **OSGeo** Open Source Geospatial Foundation (#17764)

♦ OSGP Alliance 17903

Secretariat Nieuwe Ebbingestraat 42a, 9712 NM Groningen, Netherlands. E-mail: secretariat@osgp.org.
URL: http://www.osgp.org/

History 2006. Former names and other names: *Energy Services Network Association (ESNA)* – former; *Open Smart Grid Protocol* – alias. Registration: Netherlands. **Aims** Maintain and promote adoption of the Open Smart Grid Protocol (OSGP) and infrastructure for smart grid applications towards a future proof modern smart grid. **Structure** General Meeting; Board of Directors; Executive Committee. **Languages** Dutch, English. **Activities** Events/meetings; knowledge management/information dissemination; standards/guidelines. **Events** *Annual Smart Grid Security Summit* Dubai (United Arab Emirates) 2017, *Annual Smart Grid Security Summit* Gdansk (Poland) 2016. **Publications** *OSGP Newsletter* (12 a year).

Members Companies in 19 countries:
Austria, Belgium, Denmark, Egypt, Finland, France, Germany, Japan, Korea Rep, Netherlands, Norway, Poland, Romania, Russia, Singapore, South Africa, Sweden, Türkiye, USA.

NGO Relations Technical Liaison Partner with: *European Committee for Electrotechnical Standardization (CENELEC, #06647)*. [2022.06.21/XJ4946/**C**]

- ♦ OSHNET / see ASEAN Occupational Safety and Health Network (#01215)
- ♦ Osho Commune International (see: #17904)
- ♦ Osho International – Centre for Consciousness in Organizations (see: #17904)

♦ Osho International Foundation 17904

Contact Bahhofstr 52, 8001 Zurich ZH, Switzerland. T. +4112146242. Fax +4112146203. E-mail: oshointernational@oshointernational.com.
Publishing HQ 410 Park Avenue – 15th floor, New York NY 10022, USA. T. +12122318437. Fax +12126589508.
India Office 17 Koregaon Park, Pune, Maharashtra 411001, Pune MAHARASHTRA 411001, India. T. +912066019999.
URL: http://www.osho.com/

History as *Rajneesh Foundation International*. **Aims** Promote *meditations* and meditative *therapies* developed by Osho. **Structure** *Osho Global Connections* (Pune, India) – international office for Osho meditation centres, Osho institutes and Osho information centres worldwide. **Finance** Sources include income from publications. **Activities** *Osho Commune International (OSHO, see: #17904)*, Pune (India), including meditation resort; *Osho International – Centre for Consciousness in Organizations (CCO, see: #17904)*, Pune (India); *Osho Multiversity* – centre for meditation and personal growth processes, encompassing western therapy approaches, healing arts of East and West, esoteric sciences, creative arts, centering and martial arts, tantra, zen, sufism and meditative therapy, all having meditation both at their base and as their objective. **Publications** *Osho International New York* – international publishing headquarters for for Osho's works on meditation, body-mind-spirit, philosophy, contemporary social issues, comparative religion and spirituality, including 350 books. Information Services: Music archive. **Information Services** *Osho Archive* – collection of talks. [2017/XF6507/f/**F**]

- ♦ OSHO – Osho Commune International (see: #17904)
- ♦ **OSH** Optometristas Sirviendo a la Humanidad (#17779)
- ♦ OSH – Ordo Sancti Hieronymi (religious order)
- ♦ OSIC – Oceania Sport Information Centre (internationally oriented national body)
- ♦ OSI – Congregatio Oblatorum Sancti Ioseph, Astae Pompejae (religious order)
- ♦ OSIEK – Organiza Societo de Internaciaj Esperanto Konferencoj (internationally oriented national body)
- ♦ OSI / Network Management Forum / see TeleManagement Forum (#20123)
- ♦ OS – International Conference on Open Magnetic Systems for Plasma Confinement (meeting series)
- ♦ **OSI** Objectif Sciences International (#17632)
- ♦ OSI – Open Source Initiative (internationally oriented national body)
- ♦ OSI – Orphelins Sida International (internationally oriented national body)
- ♦ OSJ – Congregation of the Oblates of St Joseph (religious order)
- ♦ **OSJD** Organisation for Cooperation between Railways (#17803)
- ♦ OSL – International Order of Saint Luke the Physician (religious order)
- ♦ OSLJ – Ordre Militaire et Hospitalier de Saint Lazare de Jérusalem (religious order)
- ♦ Oslo Commission (inactive)
- ♦ Oslo Convention – Convention for the Prevention of Marine Pollution by Dumping from Ships and Aircraft (1972 treaty)
- ♦ OSL – Order of Saint Luke (religious order)
- ♦ **OSME** Ornithological Society of the Middle East, the Caucasus and Central Asia (#17897)
- ♦ OSM – Ordo Servorum Mariae (religious order)
- ♦ **OSM** Organisation sioniste mondiale (#21961)
- ♦ OSMTH – Ordo Supremus Militaris Templi Hierosolymitani (religious order)
- ♦ OSMTJ – Orden Soberana y Militar del Temple de Jerusalem (religious order)
- ♦ **OS** Olympic Solidarity (#17721)
- ♦ **OS** Orthopterists' Society (#17899)
- ♦ **OSPAAAL** Organización de Solidaridad de los Pueblos de Africa, Asia y América Latina (#17849)
- ♦ **OSPAA** Organisation de la solidarité des peuples afro-asiatiques (#00537)
- ♦ **OSPA** Oxygenated Solvents Producers Association (#17923)
- ♦ **OSPAR Commission** OSPAR Commission for the Protection of the Marine Environment of the North-East Atlantic (#17905)

♦ OSPAR Commission for the Protection of the Marine Environment of the North-East Atlantic (OSPAR Commission) 17905

Commission OSPAR pour la protection du milieu marin de l'Atlantique du Nord-Est (Commission OSPAR)

Secretariat Victoria House, 37-63 Southampton Row, London, WC1B 4DA, UK. T. +442074305200. Fax +442072423737. E-mail: secretariat@ospar.org.
URL: http://www.ospar.org/

History 25 Mar 1998, on entry into force of *Convention for the Protection on the Marine Environment for the North-East Atlantic (OSPAR Convention, 1992)*, adopted 22 Sep 1992. The Convention incorporates and replaces: *Convention for the Prevention of Marine Pollution by Dumping from Ships and Aircraft (Oslo Convention, 1972)* of 15 Feb 1972, entered into force 6 Apr 1974, and supervised by *Oslo Commission (OSCOM, inactive)*; *Convention on the Prevention of Marine Pollution from Land-based Sources (Paris Convention, 1974)* of 4 Jun 1974, entered into force 6 May 1978, and supervised by *Paris Commission (PARCOM, inactive)*. **Aims** In accordance with the strategies and the Joint assessment and Monitoring Programme adopted in 1998 and revised in 2003: protect and conserve ecosystems and biological diversity; achieve near-background concentrations for naturally-occurring hazardous or radioactive substances and near-zero concentrations of man-made/synthetic/artificial hazardous or radioactive substances; when considering radioactive substances for the above, take into account legitimate use of the sea, technical feasibility and radiological impact on man and biota; attempt to achieve cessation of discharge, emission and loss of hazardous substances by 2020; ensure that additional concentrations of radioactive substances in the marine environment due to discharge, emission or loss are close to zero; monitor eutrophication; set environmental goals and management mechanisms for offshore oil and gas activities. **Structure** Meeting of the Commission and its 6 Committees (annually). Heads of Delegations; Committee of Chairman and Vice-Chairmen; group of linguists and jurists. Committees (6): Biodiversity; Hazardous Substances; Radioactive Substances; Eutrophication; Offshore Oil and Gas; Assessment and Monitoring. Secretariat, headed by Executive Secretary. **Languages** English, French. **Staff** 12.00 FTE, paid. **Finance** Contracting Parties contributions. Budget (2010): pounds1,139,996. **Events** *Meeting on Closing the Plastic Value Chain* Rotterdam (Netherlands) 2015, *Meeting* Barcelona (Spain) 2011, *Ministerial meeting* Bergen (Norway) 2010, *Meeting* Stockholm (Sweden) 2004, *Workshop on the environmental impact of placement of carbon dioxide in geological structures in the maritime area* Trondheim (Norway) 2004. **Publications** Conventions; annual reports; technical reports; data reports; other agreements; summary records; decisions; recommendations; overviews. All OSPAR publications are produced in English, many in French, and are available online.

Members Contracting Parties governments of 15 countries:
Belgium, Denmark, Finland, France, Germany, Iceland, Ireland, Luxembourg, Netherlands, Norway, Portugal, Spain, Sweden, Switzerland, UK.

Contracting Party – regional EU integration body (1):
European Union (EU, #08967).

IGO Relations Observers:
- *Agreement on the Conservation of Small Cetaceans of the Baltic, North East Atlantic, Irish and North Seas (ASCOBANS, 1992)*;
- *Arctic Monitoring and Assessment Programme (AMAP, #01100)*;
- *Baltic Marine Environment Protection Commission – Helsinki Commission (HELCOM, #03126)*;
- Common Wadden Sea Secretariat (CWSS);
- *Convention for the Protection of the Marine Environment and the Coastal Region of the Mediterranean (Barcelona Convention, 1976)*;
- *Cooperative Programme for Monitoring and Evaluation of the Long-range Transmission of Air Pollutants in Europe (EMEP, #04800)*;
- *European Environment Agency (EEA, #06995)*;
- *Intergovernmental Oceanographic Commission (IOC, #11496)*;
- *International Atomic Energy Agency (IAEA, #12294)*;
- *International Commission for the Protection of the Rhine (ICPR, #12721)*;
- *International Council for the Exploration of the Sea (ICES, #13021)*;
- *International Maritime Organization (IMO, #14102)*;
- *North Atlantic Marine Mammal Commission (NAMMCO, #17573)*;
- *North-East Atlantic Fisheries Commission (NEAFC, #17581)*;
- *OECD (#17693)*;
- *UNEP (#20299)*.

Memorandum of Understanding with: EEA; ICES. Secretariat administers: *Agreement for cooperation in dealing with pollution of the North Sea by oil and other harmful substances (Bonn Agreement, #00564)*. Cooperates with: *Conservation of Arctic Flora and Fauna (CAFF, #04728)*. Formal contacts with:
- *Arctic Council (#01097)*;
- *Consultative Meeting of Contracting Parties to the London Convention/Meeting of Contracting Parties to the London Protocol (#04769)*;
- *Convention on Long-range Transboundary Air Pollution (#04787)*;
- *Convention on the Prevention of Marine Pollution by Dumping of Wastes and other Matter (LDC, 1972)*;
- *European Commission (EC, #06633)*;
- *North Sea Conference*;
- *United Nations Economic Commission for Europe (UNECE, #20555)*.

NGO Relations General Observers:
- *BirdLife International (#03266)*;
- *BUSINESSEUROPE (#03381)*;
- *Conference of Peripheral Maritime Regions of Europe (CPMR, #04638)*;
- *Conseil européen de l'industrie chimique (CEFIC, #04687)*;
- *Friends of the Earth International (FoEI, #10002)*;
- *Greenpeace International (#10727)*;
- *International Association of Oil and Gas Producers (IOGP, #12053)*;
- *KIMO International (#16192)*;
- *Seas at Risk (SAR, #19189)*;
- *World Wide Fund for Nature (WWF, #21922)*.

Specialized Observers:
- *Advisory Committee on Protection of the Sea (ACOPS, #00139)*;
- *Association des organisations nationales d'entreprises de pêche de l'UE (EUROPECHE, #02841)*;
- *Central Dredging Association (CEDA, #03688)*;
- *Euro Chlor (#05659)*;
- *European Federation of Pharmaceutical Industries and Associations (EFPIA, #07191)*;
- *European Oilfield Speciality Chemicals Association (EOSCA, #08078)*;
- *Fertilizers Europe (#09738)*;
- *International Association of Ports and Harbors (IAPH, #12096)*;
- *Oil Companies' European Association for Environment, Health and Safety in Refining and Distribution (CONCAWE, #17708)*;
- *PIANC (#18371)*;
- *World Nuclear Association (WNA, #21674)*. [2014/XF4685/**F***]

- ♦ OSPAR Convention – Convention for the Protection on the Marine Environment for the North-East Atlantic (1992 treaty)
- ♦ **OSPESCA** Organización del Sector Pesquero y Acuicola del Istmo Centroamericano, Panama (#17848)
- ♦ OSPPE – Ordo Fratrum Sancti Pauli Primi Eremitae (religious order)
- ♦ OSPP – Organizacija Sotrudnicestva Podsipnikovoj Promyslennosti (inactive)
- ♦ **OSRAO** Organisation Ouest africaine de la sécurité routière (#20896)
- ♦ Osrodek Studiów Wschodnich (internationally oriented national body)

- **OSSEA** Orchid Society of South East Asia (#17789)
- Osservatorio balcani e caucasa transeuropa (internationally oriented national body)
- Osservatorio per la Comunicazione Culturale e l'Audiovisivo nel Mediterranea e nel Mondo (#17643)
- Osservatorio Europeo delle Droghe e delle Tossicodipendenze (#07820)
- Osservatorio Europeo del Plurilinguismo (internationally oriented national body)
- Osservatorio sul Turismo delle Isole Europee (#17645)
- **OSShD** Organisation für die Zusammenarbeit der Eisenbahnen (#17803)
- OSSHHM – Oceania Society for Sexual Health and HIV Medicine (unconfirmed)
- OSSM – Ordine Secolare dei Servi di Maria (religious order)
- **OSS** Observatoire du Sahara et du Sahel (#17636)
- OSSO – Observatorio Sismológico del Sur Occidente (internationally oriented national body)
- OSS – Opération Survie au Soudan (inactive)
- **OSSREA** Organization for Social Science Research in Eastern and Southern Africa (#17888)
- OSSR – Hermanas Oblatas del Santisimo Redentor (religious order)
- OSSR – Ordo Sanctissimi Redemptoris (religious order)
- OSST – Ordo Sanctissimae Trinitatis (religious order)
- OSTA / see Organisation du Sport Africain Travailliste et Amateur (#17827)
- **OSTA** Organisation du Sport Africain Travailliste et Amateur (#17827)
- Osteoarthritis Research Society / see Osteoarthritis Research Society International (#17906)

♦ Osteoarthritis Research Society International (OARSI) 17906

Main Office 1120 Route 73, Ste 200, Mount Laurel NJ 08054, USA. T. +18566424215. E-mail: info@oarsi.org.
URL: https://oarsi.org/

History 1990. Founded when taking over activities of *European Society of Osteoarthrology (ESOA, inactive)*. Former names and other names: *Osteoarthritis Research Society* – former. **Aims** Promote and encourage research in the field of osteoarthritis. **Structure** Board of Directors. Committees (5): Scientific Advisory; Publications; Membership; Corporate Development; Executive. **Languages** English. **Staff** 4.00 FTE, paid. **Finance** Members' dues: Individual – US$ 195; Associate – US$ 125; Allied Health – US$ 125; Corporate – US$ 6,000. **Events** *World Congress on Osteoarthritis* Vienna (Austria) 2024, *World Congress on Osteoarthritis* Denver, CO (USA) 2023, *World Congress on Osteoarthritis* Berlin (Germany) 2022, *World Congress* Vienna (Austria) 2020, *World Congress* Toronto, ON (Canada) 2019. **Publications** *Osteoarthritis and Cartilage* (6 a year) – journal. **Members** Regular; Associate; Industry Partners. Individuals in 48 countries. Membership countries not specified. [2022/XD7449/**B**]

♦ Osteogenesis Imperfecta Federation Europe (OIFE) 17907

Pres Schotelveldstraat 17, 2801 Heffen, Belgium. E-mail: office@oife.org.
Sec Oberdorfstr 18/1, 70794 Filderstadt, Germany. E-mail: secretary@oife.org.
URL: http://www.oife.org/

History 8 Mar 2022, Heffen (Belgium). First established 30 Sep 1993, Northampton (UK), and registered in Netherlands. Legal entity in Netherlands dissolved 1 Oct 2022 for logistical reasons and re-established in Belgium. Registration: KBO, No/ID: 0784600930, Start date: 7 Apr 2022, Belgium, Antwerp. **Aims** Increase awareness, stimulate research, and support and encourage in ways that improve the lives of people with Osteogenesis Imperfecta (OI). **Structure** General Assembly; Board. **Languages** English. **Staff** None. **Activities** Advocacy/lobbying/activism; events/meetings; knowledge management/information dissemination; networking/liaising; research/documentation. **Events** *Congress on the Latest Developments in Osteogenesis Imperfecta* Lisbon (Portugal) 2016, *General Assembly* Lisbon (Portugal) 2016, *General Assembly* Oslo (Norway) 2015, *Meeting on Soft Tissues and Soft Issues* Oslo (Norway) 2015, *General Assembly* Helsinki (Finland) 2014. **Publications** *OIFE Pass* (updated regularly) – booklet with emergency information in 22 languages; *OIFE Magazine* in English.
Members Ordinary members in 20 European countries:
Austria, Belgium, Denmark, Finland, France, Georgia, Germany, Italy, Latvia, Netherlands, Norway, Poland, Portugal, Romania, Russia, Spain, Sweden, Switzerland, UK, Ukraine.
Associate in 15 countries:
Australia, Canada, Chile, China, Ecuador, Ghana, India, Ireland, Kazakhstan, Mexico, Nigeria, Panama, Peru, South Africa, USA.
NGO Relations Member of (1): *EURORDIS – Rare Diseases Europe (#09175).* [2022.10.19/XD4701/**D**]

♦ Osteology Foundation 17908

Main Office Landenbergstrasse 35, 6002 Lucerne, Switzerland. T. +4141684444. Fax +41414926739. E-mail: info@osteology.org.
URL: http://www.osteology.org/

History Founded 2003, Switzerland, on the initiative of Dr Peter Geistlich (1926-2014). **Aims** Promote research, education and collaboration between universities and industry in the field of oral tissue regeneration with biomaterials. **Structure** Board; Executive Management Committee; Committees (3); Osteology Expert Council. **Languages** English. **Staff** 5.50 FTE, paid. **Finance** Supported by donations of founders Dr Peter Geistlich and Geistlich Pharma AG. **Activities** Events/meetings; financial and/or material support; training/education; publishing activity. **Events** *International Osteology Symposium* Barcelona (Spain) 2019, *International Osteology Symposium* Monte Carlo (Monaco) 2016, *International Symposium* Monte Carlo (Monaco) 2013, *International symposium* Cannes (France) 2011, *International Symposium* Paris (France) 2010. **Publications** *Osteology Guidelines for Oral and Maxillofacial Regeneration – Clinical Research* (2014); *Clinical Oral Implants Research – vol 23, supplement 5* (2012); *Osteology Guidelines for Oral and Maxillofacial Regeneration – Preclinical Models for Translational Research* (2011). Articles; brochures; reports. [2017/XJ0609/f/**F**]

♦ Osteopathic European Academic Network (OSEAN) 17909

Osteopathisches Europäisches Akademisches Netzwerk

Main Office Frimbergergasse 6, 1130 Vienna, Austria. T. +431879382647. Fax +431879382619. E-mail: office@osean.com.
URL: http://www.osean.com/

History 1999, Maidstone (UK). Founded on the initiative of Renzo Molinari. Registration: No/ID: 338998549, Austria, Vienna. **Aims** Develop a rigorous and standardized model of osteopathic *education* throughout Europe; ensure that osteopathic educational establishments in every country possess a comparable resource base; establish and develop common research streams; develop active scientific, academic and professional communication links so as to develop *osteopathy* as an independent, clearly identifiable entity, in its relationship with other professions in the *health care* sector; achieve academic recognition for osteopathy in all countries. **Structure** Council; Executive Committee; Permanent Secretary. Committees (2): Education; Finance. **Languages** Dutch, English, Finnish, French, German, Italian, Norwegian, Polish, Russian, Spanish, Swedish. **Staff** 2.00 FTE, paid. **Finance** Member's registration fee, reflective of the size of the institution. **Activities** Training/education; events/meetings; networking/liaising. **Events** *Open Forum for Osteopathic Education* Antwerp (Belgium) 2021, *Open Forum for Osteopathic Education* Antwerp (Belgium) 2020, *Open Forum for Osteopathic Education* Lyon (France) 2018, *Open Forum for Osteopathic Education* Vienna (Austria) 2016, *Open Forum for Osteopathic Education* Barcelona (Spain) 2014.
Members in 17 countries:
Argentina, Austria, Belgium, Canada, Croatia, Finland, France, Germany, Ireland, Italy, Netherlands, Norway, Poland, Russia, Spain, Sweden, UK.
NGO Relations Liaison Organization of: *Comité européen de normalisation (CEN, #04162).* Partner member of: *Osteopathic International Alliance (OIA, #17910).* [2020/XF2828/**F**]

♦ Osteopathic International Alliance (OIA) 17910

Sec-Treas 142 E Ontario St, 10th Floor, Chicago IL 60611, USA. T. +13122028000. Fax +13122028200. E-mail: secretariat@oialliance.org.
URL: http://www.oialliance.org/

History 2004. Inaugural conference 29-31 Jul 2005, Washington DC (USA). **Aims** Advance philosophy and practice of osteopathic medicine and osteopathy worldwide. **Structure** Board of Directors. **Languages** English. **Activities** Events/meetings. **Events** *Conference* London (UK) 2023, *Conference* Helsinki (Finland) 2022, *Conference* Rio de Janeiro (Brazil) 2021, *Conference* 2020, *Conference* Bad Nauheim (Germany) 2019.
Members Full in 7 countries:
Australia, Germany, New Zealand, Switzerland, UK, United Arab Emirates, USA.
Associate in 10 countries:
Argentina, Belgium, Brazil, Canada, France, Italy, Japan, Korea Rep, Norway, Russia.
Partner members in 17 countries:
Argentina, Australia, Austria, Belgium, Brazil, Canada, France, Germany, Italy, Japan, Korea Rep, New Zealand, Portugal, Russia, Spain, UK, USA.
Included in the above, 5 organizations listed in this Yearbook:
European Federation and Forum for Osteopathy (EFFO, #07128); European Register for Osteopathic Physicians (EROP, #08350); International Academy of Osteopathy (IAO, #11566); Osteopathic European Academic Network (OSEAN, #17909); Société Européenne de Recherche en Ostéopathie Périnatale and Pédiatrique (SEROPP).
Consultative Status Consultative status granted from: *WHO (#20950)* (Official Relations). [2023/XJ2770/**F**]

- Osteopathisches Europäisches Akademisches Netzwerk (#17909)

♦ Osteosynthesis and Trauma Care Foundation (OTC Foundation) ... 17911

General Manager Emmenholzweg 1, 4528 Zuchwil SO, Switzerland. T. +41227840142 – +4122(41794040701.
Exec Sec address not obtained. T. +41313112361. E-mail: info@otcfoundation.org.
URL: http://www.otcfoundation.org/

History Founded 4 Dec 1986, Strasbourg (France), when statutes were adopted, as *Association internationale pour l'ostéosynthèse dynamique (AIOD)*. Reorganized under current name, 2007. Also referred to with acronym *OTC Alliance* and in German as *Internationale Arbeitsgemeinschaft Dynamische Osteosynthese*. **Aims** Advance osteosynthesis and trauma care in a global network through research, education and promotion of best clinical practices. **Structure** General Assembly; Executive Board; Board of Trustees; Research Committee; Task Force Education. **Languages** English. **Staff** 1.50 FTE, paid. **Finance** Funded through annual grant budget: US$ 895,000. **Activities** Financial and/or material support; research/documentation; networking/liaising; events/meetings; training/education; events/meetings. **Events** *General Assembly* Lisbon (Portugal) 2014, *Biennial meeting* 2000, *25 ans de l'enclouage verrouillé* Strasbourg (France) 1999, *Meeting* Strasbourg (France) 1999, *Biennial Meeting* Strasbourg (France) 1998. **Publications** *OTC Foundation Newsletter* (4 a year); *Injury Supplements* (annual). Research textbooks.
Members Country chapters (19) in 18 countries and territories:
Australia, Brazil, Canada, China, Denmark, France, Germany, Greece, Hong Kong, Italy, Japan, Netherlands, New Zealand, Norway, Spain, Sweden, Switzerland, USA. [2019.12.12/XD6365/f/**D**]

- Österreichische Agentur für Internationale Mobilität und Kooperatiön in Bildung, Wissenschaft und Forschung / see Österreichische Austauschdienst
- Österreichische Austauschdienst (internationally oriented national body)
- Österreichische Forschungsstiftung für Entwicklungshilfe (internationally oriented national body)
- Österreichische Gesellschaft für Aussenpolitik und die Vereinten Nationen (internationally oriented national body)
- Österreichische Gesellschaft für Aussenpolitik und Internationale Beziehungen / see Österreichische Gesellschaft für Aussenpolitik und die Vereinten Nationen
- Österreichische Gesellschaft für Entwicklungszusammenarbeit / see Hilfswerk International
- Österreichische Gesellschaft für Politikwissenschaft (internationally oriented national body)
- Österreichische Gesellschaft für Umwelt und Technik (internationally oriented national body)
- Österreichische Liga für Menschenrechte (internationally oriented national body)
- Österreichische Organisation für Entwicklungszusammenarbeit / see HORIZONT 3000
- Österreichischer Akademischer Austauschdienst / see Österreichische Austauschdienst
- Österreichischer Austauschdienst / see Österreichische Austauschdienst
- Österreichischer Informationsdienst für Entwicklungspolitik / see SÜDWIND – Verein für Entwicklungspolitische Bildungs- und Öffentlichkeitsarbeit
- Österreichisches Institut für Europäische Rechtspolitik (internationally oriented national body)
- Österreichisches Institut für Friedenforschung und Friedenserziehung / see Austrian Study Centre for Peace and Conflict Resolution
- Österreichisches Institut für Internationale Politik (internationally oriented national body)
- Österreichisches Lateinamerika-Institut (internationally oriented national body)
- Österreichisches Nord-Süd-Institut für Entwicklungszusammenarbeit (internationally oriented national body)
- Österreichisches Studienzentrum für Frieden und Konfliktlösung (internationally oriented national body)
- Östersjöns Författar- och Översättarcentrum (#03105)
- Östersjöstiftelsen (internationally oriented national body)
- Osteuropaeiska Solidaritetskommittén (internationally oriented national body)
- Osteuropa-Institut (internationally oriented national body)
- Osteuropaverein (internationally oriented national body)
- **OSTIV** Organisation Scientifique et Technique Internationale de Vol à Voile (#17826)
- Ost-und Mitteleuropa Verein / see Osteuropaverein

♦ Ostomy Association of the Americas (OAA) 17912

Treas c/o United Ostomy Associations of America, PO Box 525, Kennebunk ME 04043-0525, USA.
Sec PMB-14 PO Box 6022, Carolina PR 00984-6022, USA. T. +7877623314. Fax +7876386175. E-mail: ostomizadospr@yahoo.com.
URL: http://www.ostomyamericas.org/

History 25 Apr 1990, as *North and Central America and Caribbean Ostomy Association (NCACOA)*. Current name adopted when merged with *South American Ostomy Association (ALADO, inactive)*, to become a regional affiliate association of *International Ostomy Association (IOA, #14491)*, following decision by the World Council, Nov 2010. **Aims** Provide an association committed to the improvement of the quality of life of ostomates in the Americas; create a society where people with ostomies and intestinal or urinary diversions are universally accepted and supported socially, economically, medically and psychologically. **Structure** Coordination Committee. **Languages** English. **Events** *Conference* Viña del Mar (Chile) 2019, *Conference* Colima (Mexico) 2009, *Conference* Puerto Real (Puerto Rico) 2007, *Conference / Meeting* Panama (Panama) 2003, *Conference / Meeting* Mexico City (Mexico) 2001.
Members Ostomy chapters in 9 countries and territories:
Bermuda, Canada, Costa Rica, Dominican Rep, Mexico, Panama, Puerto Rico, Suriname, USA.
NGO Relations Cooperates with: *Friends of Ostomates Worldwide (FOW).* [2017/XD5751/**D**]

- Ostseekonferenz für Transportsminister (meeting series)
- Ost-West-Europäisches Frauen Netzwerk / see OWEN – Mobile Academy for Gender Democracy and Promotion of Peace (#17920)
- OSU – Ursuline Sisters of Mount St Joseph (religious order)
- OSVIC – Organismo Sardo di Volontariato Internazionale Cristiano (internationally oriented national body)
- ÖSW / see Brot für die Welt
- OSWI – Ophthalmologist Society of the West Indies (no recent information)
- OSW – Osrodek Studiów Wschodnich (internationally oriented national body)
- **OSZD** Organizacija Sotrudnicestva Zeleznyh Dorog (#17803)
- OTAC – Organisation des travailleurs de l'Afrique centrale (no recent information)
- **OTAF** Observatoire du tabac en Afrique francophone (#17638)
- OTAF – Observatoire du traitement avancé du français et des langues nationales partenaires (no recent information)
- OTAN Organisation de la production de l'engin HAWK (no recent information)
- OTAN Organisation pour la recherche et la technologie (inactive)
- **OTAN** Organisation du Traité de l'Atlantique Nord (#16945)
- OTAN / see Organization of Nematologists of Tropical America (#17878)
- OTAO – Organisation des travailleurs de l'Afrique de l'Ouest (unconfirmed)

- ♦ **OTA** Organic Trade Association (#17795)
- ♦ OTA – Organisation mondiale du tourisme et de l'automobile (inactive)
- ♦ **OTARG** Occupational Therapy African Region Group (#17646)
- ♦ OTASE – Organisation du Traité de défense collective pour l'Asie du Sud-Est (inactive)
- ♦ OTB – Out of the Box International (unconfirmed)
- ♦ OTCA / see Amazon Cooperation Treaty Organization (#00766)
- ♦ OTC Alliance / see Osteosynthesis and Trauma Care Foundation (#17911)
- ♦ **OTCA** Organização do Tratado de Cooperação Amazônica (#00766)
- ♦ **OTCA** Organización del Tratado de Cooperación Amazónica (#00766)
- ♦ **OTC Foundation** Osteosynthesis and Trauma Care Foundation (#17911)
- ♦ OTECI – Office technique d'études et de coopération internationale (internationally oriented national body)
- ♦ OTEM – Organisation du tourisme euro-méditerranéen (no recent information)
- ♦ OTE – Observatoire des technologies pour l'éducation en Europe (internationally oriented national body)
- ♦ ÖTE – Ökologischer Tourismus in Europa (internationally oriented national body)
- ♦ OTE / see Resort Development Organisation (#18913)
- ♦ **OT-Europe** Occupational Therapy Europe (#17647)
- ♦ **OTF** Oceania Tennis Federation (#17679)
- ♦ Other Countries and Territories / see Association of Overseas Countries and Territories of the European Union (#02843)

♦ The Other Foundation 17913

CEO Postnet Suite 209, Private Bag X31, Saxonwold, 2132, South Africa. E-mail: info@theotherfoundation.org – admin@theotherfoundation.org.
URL: http://theotherfoundation.org/

Aims Advance equality and freedom in southern Africa with a particular focus on *sexual* orientation and *gender* identity. **Structure** Trustees. **Finance** Grant from: *Atlantic Philanthropies*. **Activities** Financial and/or material support; awards/prizes/competitions; events/meetings. **Publications** *umuntu Bulletin*. **NGO Relations** Member of: *Global Philanthropy Project (GPP, #10546)*. [2019/XM8812/f/F]

- ♦ **OTIE** Observatory on Tourism in the European Islands (#17645)
- ♦ **OTIF** Intergovernmental Organisation for International Carriage by Rail (#17807)
- ♦ **OTIF** Organisation intergouvernementale pour les transports internationaux ferroviaires (#17807)
- ♦ **OTIF** Zwischenstaatliche Organisation für den Internationalen Eisenbahnverkehr (#17807)
- ♦ OTI / see Organización de Telecomunicaciones de Iberoamérica (#17851)
- ♦ **OTI** Organización de Telecomunicaciones de Iberoamérica (#17851)
- ♦ **OTM** On the Move (#16868)
- ♦ OTM – Objectif Tiers-monde (internationally oriented national body)
- ♦ OTN – Ocean Tracking Network (unconfirmed)
- ♦ OTRE – Organisation des transporteurs routiers européens (internationally oriented national body)
- ♦ OTSA – Ottoman and Turkish Studies Association (internationally oriented national body)
- ♦ **OTSC** Organisation du Traité de sécurité collective (#04103)

♦ OTSEM Network 17914

Coordinator Univ Hamburg, Sedanstr 19, 20146 Hamburg, Germany. T. +4940428383787 – +4940428383788.
URL: http://www.otsem.uni-hamburg.de/

History 2004. **Aims** Maintain and enhance a supportive academic context for PhD scholarship holders and post doctoral scholars working in the field of *Hebrew Bible* or Old Testament studies in the Nordic and German sphere. **Structure** Steering Committee; Coordinating Committee. Coordinator. **Languages** English. **Staff** None. **Finance** Members' dues. Budget (annual): Norwegian Kr 300,000. **Events** *Meeting* London (UK) 2019, *Meeting* Helsinki (Finland) 2017, *Annual Conference* Uppsala (Sweden) 2015, *Annual Conference* Hamburg (Germany) 2014, *Annual Conference* Tartu (Estonia) 2013.
Members Professors, post doctoral scholars and PhD scholarship holders in 6 countries:
Denmark, Finland, Germany, Iceland, Norway, Sweden.
IGO Relations *Nordic Council (NC, #17256)*. [2014/XM3632/v/F]

- ♦ **OTS** Oligonucleotide Therapeutics Society (#17717)
- ♦ OTS – Organization for Tropical Studies (internationally oriented national body)
- ♦ Ottawa Convention – Convention on the Prohibition of the Use, Stockpiling, Production and Transfer of Anti-personnel Mines and on Their Destruction (1997 treaty)
- ♦ **OTTF** Oceania Table Tennis Federation (#17678)
- ♦ Otto Benecke Foundation (internationally oriented national body)
- ♦ Otto Benecke Stiftung (internationally oriented national body)
- ♦ Otto Gross Tanulmanyok Nemzetközi Tarsasaga (#12060)
- ♦ Ottoman and Turkish Studies Association (internationally oriented national body)
- ♦ OTUCA – Organization of Trade Unions of Central Africa (no recent information)
- ♦ **OTU** Oceania Triathlon Federation (#17680)
- ♦ OTUWA – Organization of Trade Unions of West Africa (unconfirmed)
- ♦ OTU / see World Taekwondo Oceania (#21846)
- ♦ OUA/CSTR / see African Union Scientific Technical Research Commission (#00493)
- ♦ OUA – Organisation de l'unité africaine (inactive)
- ♦ **OUI** Organisation universitaire interaméricaine (#11442)
- ♦ **OUI** Organização Universitaria Interamericana (#11442)
- ♦ **OUI** Organización Universitaria Interamericana (#11442)

♦ Ouishare 17915

Coordinator 12 rue Jean Jaurès, 93170 Bagnolet, France.
URL: https://www.ouishare.net/

History 2012. **Aims** Question the status quo; instigate encounters between actors from different corners of society; create forms of collaboration. **Activities** Networking/liaising; research/documentation. **Publications** *Ouishare Magazine*. **NGO Relations** Member of (1): *Wellbeing Economy Alliance (WEAll, #20856)*. [2020/AA1063/F]

- ♦ **OUI Society** Open and User Innovation Society (#17768)
- ♦ Oum Al Qura University of Niger / see Islamic University in Niger (#16054)
- ♦ **OUMSH** Olon Ulsyn Mongol Sudlalyn Holboo (#12035)

♦ Our Daily Bread Ministries 17916

Pres PO Box 2222, Grand Rapids MI 49501, USA. T. +16169742210.
Canadian Office PO Box 1622, Windsor ON N9A 6Z7, Canada.
URL: https://www.odb.org/

History 1938, as *Radio Bible Class Ministries (RBC Ministries) – RBC Radio*, by Dr M R De Haan. Present name adopted 2015. **Aims** Make the wisdom of the Bible understandable and accessible to all; encourage people of all nations to experience a personal relationship with Christ, to be more like Him and serve in a local body of His family. **Structure** Global Executive Team; Ministry Work. Offices (33): Africa; Americas; Asia-Pacific; Europe. **Languages** Afrikaans, Arabic, Chinese, Dutch, English, French, German, Greek, Hindi, Indonesian, Italian, Japanese, Malay, Mon-Khmer languages, Polish, Portuguese, Russian, Sinhala, Spanish, Tagalog, Tamil, Thai, Ukrainian, Vietnamese. Kayin. **Finance** Sources: donations; estate planning; annuities. **Activities** Religious activities; training/education. **Publications** Digital and print books; Bible studies; online courses; radio Bible-based conversations; videos. [2019.07.08/XF5947/F]

- ♦ Our Lady of Montligeon (religious order)
- ♦ Our Little Brothers and Sisters (internationally oriented national body)
- ♦ O.U.R. – Operation Underground Railroad (internationally oriented national body)

♦ Our World is Not for Sale (OWINFS) 17917

Notre monde n'est pas à vendre – Nuestro Mundo No Esta en Venta
Contact address not obtained. E-mail: owinfs@gmail.com.
URL: http://www.ourworldisnotforsale.net/

History Grew out of the international campaigns against *OECD multilateral agreement on investment (MAI, inactive)* and *World Trade Organization (WTO, #21864)*. Currently members are part of campaigns fighting trade agreements, including *African Growth and Opportunity Act (AGOA)*, *Asia-Pacific Economic Cooperation (APEC, #01887)*, *Free Trade Area of the Americas (FTAA, no recent information)* and *Puebla-Panama Plan (PPP, no recent information)*. **Aims** Fight for a *sustainable*, socially just, democratic and accountable multilateral trading system.
Members National and international organizations (216), including the following organizations listed in this Yearbook:
Asia-Pacific Research Network (APRN, #02013); Centro Internazionale Crocevia (CIC); CNCD Opération 11 11 11; CorpWatch; Development Alternatives with Women for a New Era (DAWN, #05054); Focus on the Global South (Focus, #09807); Friends of the Earth International (FoEI, #10002); Institute for Global Justice (IGJ); Institute for Global Networking, Information and Studies (IGNIS); International Gender and Trade Network (IGTN, #13707); Just World International (JWI); Mani Tese (MT); Pan American Medical Foundation (no recent information); Public Eye; Public Services International (PSI, #18572); Southern and Eastern African Trade Information and Negotiations Initiative (SEATINI, #19875); Terra Nuova; Third World Network (TWN, #20151); World Economy, Ecology and Development (WEED).
NGO Relations Instrumental in setting up: *Seattle to Brussels Network (S2B, #19190)*. Includes as European part of the network: *Seattle to Brussels Network (S2B, #19190)*. Partner of: *Arab NGO Network for Development (ANND, #01016)*. [2020/XM1857/y/F]

- ♦ OUSA / see FISU Oceania (#09785)
- ♦ **OUSA** Organisation de l'unité syndicale africaine (#17798)
- ♦ Out of the Box International (unconfirmed)
- ♦ Outlaws Motorcycle Club / see American Outlaws Association (#00788)
- ♦ Outreach Foundation of the Presbyterian Church (internationally oriented national body)
- ♦ Outreach International (internationally oriented national body)
- ♦ OutRight Action International (internationally oriented national body)
- ♦ Outstretched Hands – Organization Against Hunger and for Peoples Development / see Mani Tese

♦ Outward Bound International 17918

Exec Dir 85 Grampian Road, Aviemore, PH22 1RH, UK. T. +441479812544.
URL: http://www.outwardbound.net/

History 1941, Aberdovey (UK). *International Outward Bound Secretariat* set up in 1986. Registered in accordance with US law. **Aims** Promote and protect the good name of Outward Bound throughout the world; assist in the establishment, development and support of Outward Bound Centers able to provide safe, high quality programs that fulfil the mission. **Structure** Council; Executive Board. **Languages** English. **Staff** 0.50 FTE, paid. **Finance** Members' revenues: US$ 100 million. **Activities** Certification/accreditation; knowledge management/information dissemination; events/meetings; training/education. **Events** *International Conference* Germany 2014, *International Conference* Singapore (Singapore) 2012, *International Conference* Finland 2009, *Conference* Brunei Darussalam 2008, *International Conference* USA 2008. **Publications** *Outward Bound International Journal* – online. Essays; books.
Members Members of the Conference of Outward Bound Schools (37) in 31 countries and territories:
Belgium, Bermuda, Brazil, Brunei Darussalam, Bulgaria, Canada, Costa Rica, Croatia, Czechia, Ecuador, Finland, Germany, Hong Kong, India, Indonesia, Israel, Japan, Korea Rep, Malaysia, Mexico, Oman, Romania, Singapore, Slovakia, South Africa, Spain, Sri Lanka, Taiwan, UK, USA, Zimbabwe. [2014.06.24/XF0413/F]

- ♦ Ouvrières de la Croix (religious order)
- ♦ OVA – Organisation des veuves en Afrique (no recent information)
- ♦ **OVA** Organisation des villes arabes (#01059)
- ♦ OVCI – Organismo di Volontariato per la Cooperazione Internazionale – La Nostra Famiglia (internationally oriented national body)
- ♦ OveHum InterNational – Observatory on Values and Education in Humanity (internationally oriented national body)
- ♦ Overbrook Foundation (internationally oriented national body)

♦ Overeaters Anonymous (OA) 17919

World Service Office PO Box 44020, Rio Rancho NM 87174-4020, USA. T. +15058912664. Fax +15058914320. E-mail: info@oa.org.
URL: http://www.oa.org/

History 1960. **Aims** Provide education and support toward recovery from compulsive eating through a twelve-step programme. **Finance** Members' dues. Literature sales. **Events** *World Service Convention* Boston, MA (USA) 2016, *Triennial world service convention* Los Angeles, CA (USA) 2010, *Annual world service business conference* Albuquerque, NM (USA) 2008, *Annual world service business conference* Albuquerque, NM (USA) 2007, *Triennial world service convention* Philadelphia, PA (USA) 2007. **Publications** *Lifeline Magazine* (10 a year); *A Step Ahead* (4 a year) – online newsletter. Books; pamphlets; audio-visual; speciality items. **Members** Groups (6,500) in 80 countries and territories. Membership countries not specified. [2014.12.03/XF4847/F]

- ♦ Overeenkomst inzake de verlegging van de personencontrole naar de buitengrenzen van het Beneluxgebied (1960 treaty)
- ♦ Overeenkomst van Senningen (1996 treaty)
- ♦ Överenskommelse om gemensam nordisk arbetsmarknad (1982 treaty)
- ♦ Överenskommelse mellan Danmark, Finland, Island, Norge och Sverige om tillträde till högre utbildning (1996 treaty)
- ♦ Overenskomst om felles Nordisk Arbeidsmarked (1982 treaty)
- ♦ Overenskomst om f'lles nordisk arbejdsmarked (1982 treaty)
- ♦ Overenskomst mellem Danmark, Finland, Island, Norge og Sverige om adgang til videregående uddannelse (1996 treaty)
- ♦ Overenskomst mellem Danmark, Finland, Island, Norge og Sverige til undgåelse af dobbeltbeskatning for så vidt angår skatter af arv og gaver (1989 treaty)
- ♦ Overenskomst mellom Danmark, Finland, Island, Norge og Sverige om adgang til høyere utdanning (1996 treaty)
- ♦ Overlegcentrum voor de Vrede / see Hand in Hand tegen Racisme
- ♦ Overseas Agronomic Institute of Florence (internationally oriented national body)
- ♦ Overseas Ambassadors / see Sports Ambassadors
- ♦ Overseas Archives Centre, Aix-en-Provence / see Archives nationales d'Outre mer
- ♦ Overseas Association for College Admissions Counseling / see International Association for College Admissions Counseling
- ♦ Overseas Book Centre / see CODE
- ♦ Over-Seas Club and Patriotic League / see Royal Over-Seas League
- ♦ Overseas Council International (internationally oriented national body)
- ♦ Overseas Council for Theological Education and Missions / see Overseas Council International
- ♦ Overseas Countries and Territories / see Association of Overseas Countries and Territories of the European Union (#02843)
- ♦ Overseas Countries and Territories of the European Union Association / see Association of Overseas Countries and Territories of the European Union (#02843)
- ♦ Overseas Crusades / see OC International (#17688)
- ♦ Overseas Development Group / see International Development, UEA
- ♦ Overseas Development Institute (internationally oriented national body)
- ♦ Overseas Environment Cooperation Centre (internationally oriented national body)
- ♦ Overseas Human Resources and Industry Development Association / see Association for Overseas Technical Cooperation and Sustainable Partnerships
- ♦ Over-Seas League / see Royal Over-Seas League
- ♦ Overseas Ministries Study Center (internationally oriented national body)

- ♦ Overseas Missionary Fellowship / see OMF International (#17722)
- ♦ OVERSEAS – Organizzazione per lo Sviluppo Globale di Comunità in Paesi Extraeuropei (internationally oriented national body)
- ♦ Overseas Press Club of America (internationally oriented national body)
- ♦ Overseas Private Investment Corporation (internationally oriented national body)
- ♦ Overseas Radio and Television (internationally oriented national body)
- ♦ Overseas Service Bureau Program – Australian Volunteers Abroad / see AVI
- ♦ Overseas Service College / see Farnham Castle International Briefing and Conference Centre
- ♦ Overseas Student Advisers' Network / see International Education Association
- ♦ Oveyssi School of Sufism / see Maktab Tarighat Oveyssi Shahmaghsoudi (#16556)
- ♦ **OVPM** Organisation des villes du patrimoine mondial (#17891)
- ♦ **OVR** Opération villages roumains international (#17773)
- ♦ OWASP Europe / see Open Web Application Security Project Foundation (#17769)
- ♦ **OWASP Foundation** Open Web Application Security Project Foundation (#17769)

♦ OWEN – Mobile Academy for Gender Democracy and Promotion of Peace (OWEN) 17920

OWEN – Mobile Akademie für Geschlechterdemokratie und Friedensförderung (OWEN)

Contact Lausitzer Str 10, 10999 Berlin, Germany. T. +493061288785. E-mail: mail@owen-berlin.de.
URL: http://www.owen-berlin.de/

History 1992, following a proposal and international conference, Nov 1991, Berlin (Germany). Original title: *East-West-European Women's Network – Ost-West-Europäisches Frauen Netzwerk (OWEN).* **Aims** Promote women's *emancipation* in Eastern and Western Europe; develop effective strategies for cooperation with regard to women's *political issues*; build and consult structures of women self help groups in Eastern Europe on a local level. **Structure** Board; Managing Director. **Languages** English, German, Russian, Spanish. **Staff** 5.00 FTE, paid. **Finance** Supported by German Foreign Ministry; donations on project base. **Activities** Events/meetings; networking/liaising; training/education. **Events** *International seminar on women against discrimination, racism and xenophobia* Börnicke (Germany) 2000, *Development and development aid in EEC countries* Berlin (Germany) 1994, *German-German women conference* Nürburg (Germany) 1994, *Facism, nationalism in connection with the concept of democracy* 1993, *Workshop* Potsdam (Germany) 1992. **Publications** Handbook. Information Services: Library; infotheque.
Members Contacts with active women, women's groups, organizations and networks in 9 countries:
Armenia, Azerbaijan, Czechia, Georgia, Germany, Russia, Switzerland, UK, Ukraine. [2016.06.01/XF5372/**F**]

- ♦ OWEN – Mobile Akademie für Geschlechterdemokratie und Friedensförderung (#17920)
- ♦ OWEN / see OWEN – Mobile Academy for Gender Democracy and Promotion of Peace (#17920)
- ♦ **OWEN** OWEN – Mobile Academy for Gender Democracy and Promotion of Peace (#17920)
- ♦ **OWEN** OWEN – Mobile Akademie für Geschlechterdemokratie und Friedensförderung (#17920)
- ♦ OWFA – Offshore Wind Foundations Alliance (unconfirmed)
- ♦ **OWF** Oceania Weightlifting Federation (#17682)
- ♦ **OWHC** Organization of World Heritage Cities (#17891)
- ♦ OWH – OneWorld Health (internationally oriented national body)
- ♦ **OWIF** OneWorld International Foundation (#17738)
- ♦ **OWINFS** Our World is Not for Sale (#17917)
- ♦ **OWIT** Organization of Women in International Trade (#17889)
- ♦ OWLS / see OWLS Society (#17921)

♦ OWLS Society 17921

Gen Sec Leibniz Universitaet Hannover, Welfengarten 1, 30167 Hannover, Germany.
URL: http://www.owlssociety.org/

History Founded 13 Aug 1990, Garmisch-Partenkirchen (Germany FR). Former names and other names: *International Society on Optics Within Life Sciences (OWLS)* – full title. **Aims** Promote interaction among universities, research institutes and industry and collaboration between scientists and engineers in optics and medical, biological, environmental and cultural heritage specialists, so as to promote technological developments in optics as a means for addressing problems in these fields. **Structure** Assembly of members. Board of Directors, including President, Past-President (Vice-President), former Vice-President, Secretary General, Treasurer and Honorary President. Regional Council. Standing Committees (4): Bylaws and regulatory statutes; Finances; Technology transfer, standardization and technology assessment; Education and ethics. Secretariat in Münster (Germany). **Languages** English. **Events** *Biennial Conference* Dresden (Germany) 2022, *Biennial Conference* Dresden (Germany) 2021, *Biennial Conference* Dresden (Germany) 2020, *Biennial Conference* Rottnest Island, WA (Australia) 2018, *Biennial Conference* Mumbai (India) 2016. **Publications** *International Series on Optics Within Life Sciences.* Proceedings of conferences.
Members Individuals in 40 countries:
Argentina, Australia, Austria, Belarus, Belgium, Canada, China, Croatia, Cuba, Czechia, Finland, France, Germany, Ghana, Greece, Hungary, India, Italy, Japan, Kuwait, Libya, Malta, Mexico, Morocco, Netherlands, Pakistan, Poland, Portugal, Romania, Russia, Slovakia, South Africa, Spain, Sudan, Sweden, Switzerland, Taiwan, UK, Ukraine, USA.
IGO Relations Accredited by: *United Nations Framework Convention on Climate Change – Secretariat (UNFCCC, #20564).* **NGO Relations** Member of: *International Commission for Optics (ICO, #12710).* [2020/XC0032/v/**C**]

- ♦ **OWN Europe** Older Women's Network – Europe (#17716)
- ♦ OWPE – Office of the World Peace Envoy (internationally oriented national body)
- ♦ OWPMC – Organization of Women Parliamentarians from Muslim Countries (no recent information)
- ♦ OWSA – OneWorld South Asia (see: #17738)
- ♦ **OWSD** Organization for Women in Science for the Developing World (#17890)
- ♦ OWSDW / see Organization for Women in Science for the Developing World (#17890)
- ♦ OWT – One World Trust (internationally oriented national body)
- ♦ OWWA – Organization of Women Writers of Africa (internationally oriented national body)
- ♦ Oxfam / see Oxfam GB
- ♦ Oxfam Australia (internationally oriented national body)
- ♦ Oxfam GB (internationally oriented national body)

♦ Oxfam International 17922

Exec Dir The Atrium, Chaka Road, Kilimani, Nairobi, Kenya. T. +254202820000.
Europe Office Rue du Trône 14-16, 1000 Brussels, Belgium. T. +3222341110. E-mail: eu@oxfaminternational.org.
URL: http://www.oxfam.org/

History 1995, to work together for greater impact on the international stage to reduce poverty and injustice. Registered as a foundation in accordance with Dutch law. Previously also referred to as *Oxfam International Foundation.* Name derives from *Oxford Committee for Famine Relief*, set up 1942, Oxford (UK), and registered in accordance with UK law in 1943. From Jun 1965, became known simply as 'Oxfam'. Oxfam International Secretariat set up 1995. **Aims** Help create lasting solutions to the injustice of *poverty.* **Structure** Board, including Honorary President and Officers. Subcommittees. International Secretariat Board, comprising Executive Director, Chair of each Affiliate and International Chair. Includes: *Oxfam Trading.* **Languages** English, French, Spanish. **Staff** 77.00 FTE, paid. **Finance** Contributions from affiliate organizations. Operating budget: US$ 8.5 million. **Activities** Awareness raising; advocacy/lobbying/activism. **Events** *International workshop of women in the 21st century* Havana (Cuba) 2009. **Publications** Annual report; Strategic Plan; Research and policy papers.
Members Individual Oxfams (17) in 17 countries and territories:
Australia, Belgium, Canada, France, Germany, Hong Kong, India, Ireland, Italy, Japan, Mexico, Netherlands, New Zealand, Québec, Spain, UK, USA.
Included in the above, 4 organizations listed in this Yearbook:
INTERMON OXFAM; Oxfam Australia; Oxfam GB; Oxfam Novib.
Consultative Status Consultative status granted from: *UNCTAD (#20285)* (General); *ECOSOC (#05331)* (General). **IGO Relations** Global partner of: *United Nations Girls' Education Initiative (UNGEI, #20566).* Invited to Governing Council sessions of: *International Fund for Agricultural Development (IFAD, #13692).* **NGO Relations** Member of (16): *Accountable Now (#00060); Active Learning Network for Accountability and Performance in Humanitarian Action (ALNAP, #00101); Aspen Network of Development Entrepreneurs (ANDE, #02310); Association of Learned and Professional Society Publishers (ALPSP, #02786); Climate Action Network Europe (CAN Europe, #04001); Control Arms (#04782); EarthAction (EA, #05159); End Water Poverty (EWP, #05464); EuroMed Non-Governmental Platform (#05730); Finance Watch (#09764); Global Gender and Climate Alliance (GGCA, no recent information); International Action Network on Small Arms (IANSA, #11585); NetHope (#16979); NGO Working Group on the Security Council (#17128); Transparency, Accountability and Participation Network (TAP Network, #20222); World Benchmarking Alliance (WBA, #21228).* Supports: *Alliance for Responsible Mining (ARM, #00717); ARTICLE 19 (#01121).* American branch supports: *WorldFish (#21507).* Cooperates with: *Alliance Against Hunger and Malnutrition (AAHM, no recent information); International Civil Society Centre (#12589).* [2019/XF4447/y/**F**]

- ♦ Oxfam International Foundation / see Oxfam International (#17922)
- ♦ Oxfam Novib (internationally oriented national body)
- ♦ Oxfam Trading (internationally oriented national body)
- ♦ Oxfam UK / see Oxfam GB
- ♦ Oxfam UK and Ireland / see Oxfam GB
- ♦ Oxfam United Kingdom / see Oxfam GB
- ♦ Oxfam-Wereldwinkels (internationally oriented national body)
- ♦ Oxford Centre for Hindu Studies (internationally oriented national body)
- ♦ Oxford Centre for Islamic Studies (internationally oriented national body)
- ♦ Oxford Centre for Mission Studies (internationally oriented national body)
- ♦ Oxford Committee for Famine Relief / see Oxfam International (#17922)
- ♦ Oxford Committee for Famine Relief / see Oxfam GB
- ♦ Oxford Council on Good Governance (internationally oriented national body)
- ♦ Oxford Group / see Initiatives of Change International – Caux (#11213)
- ♦ Oxford International Centre for Publishing Studies (internationally oriented national body)
- ♦ Oxford University European Affairs Society (internationally oriented national body)

♦ Oxygenated Solvents Producers Association (OSPA) 17923

Association européenne des producteurs de solvants oxygénés

Dir Gen c/o CEFIC, Rue Belliard 40, Bte 15, 1040 Brussels, Belgium. T. +3224369300. E-mail: esig@cefic.be.
URL: http://www.glycol-ethers.eu/

History Set up as a sector group of *Conseil européen de l'industrie chimique (CEFIC, #04687).* Includes activities of the previous *European Isopropanol Producers Association (EIPPA, inactive).* **Aims** Bring together producers of oxygenated solvents in Europe; foster the perception of oxygenated solvents as valuable, eco-efficient safe solutions which serve the needs of downstream industry users as well as consumers. **Structure** General Assembly; Product Working Groups; Technical Committee. **Languages** English. **Staff** 3.00 FTE, paid. **Finance** Sources: members' dues.
Members Oxygenated solvents producers (18) in 9 countries:
Belgium, Finland, France, Germany, Italy, Netherlands, Spain, Switzerland, UK. [2022.05.04/XE3094/**E**]

- ♦ Oxygen Society / see Society for Redox Biology and Medicine (#19628)
- ♦ OZEG / see European Sea Ports Organisation (#08453)
- ♦ OZG – Ondernemers Zonder Grenzen (internationally oriented national body)
- ♦ **Ozone Secretariat** Secretariat for the Vienna Convention for the Protection of the Ozone Layer and the Montreal Protocol on Substances that Deplete the Ozone Layer (#19209)
- ♦ Ozone treaty – Vienna Convention for the Protection of the Ozone Layer (1985 treaty)
- ♦ Ø Kommission (#16061)
- ♦ Økonomiske og Sociale Udvalg / see European Economic and Social Committee (#06963)
- ♦ Økonomiske og Sociale Udvalg for de Europaeiske Faellesskaber / see European Economic and Social Committee (#06963)
- ♦ Østfold-Bohuslän Border Committee / see SvinesundKommittén
- ♦ Østfold-Bohuslän-Dalsland Committee / see SvinesundKommittén
- ♦ P3 Foundation (internationally oriented national body)
- ♦ **P3G2** Policy Parnterships Project for Genomic Governance (#18418)
- ♦ P3G / see Policy Parnterships Project for Genomic Governance (#18418)
- ♦ P3M / see Associazione Botteghe del Mondo
- ♦ P4 Agreement / see Trans-Pacific Strategic Economic Partnership (#20220)
- ♦ P4TT – Platform for Transformative Technologies (internationally oriented national body)
- ♦ PA / see Parapsychology Foundation
- ♦ PAA / see Pontifical University Antonianum
- ♦ PAAA – Pacific Asian Association for Agent-based Approach in Social Systems Sciences (internationally oriented national body)
- ♦ **PAAA** Pan African Association of Anthropologists (#18036)
- ♦ **PAAA** Pan American Aerobiology Association (#18078)
- ♦ **PAAA** Pan American Association of Anatomy (#18079)
- ♦ **PAA** Association panafricaine d'archéologie (#18035)
- ♦ PAABS / see Pan American Association for Biochemistry and Molecular Biology (#18080)
- ♦ PAACB – Pan American Aerobiology Certification Board (internationally oriented national body)
- ♦ PAACO / see Middle East African Council of Ophthalmology (#16752)
- ♦ **PAAC** Pan Arab Angiology College (#18139)
- ♦ **PAACS** Pan-African Academy of Christian Surgeons (#18033)
- ♦ **PAAFPRS** Pan Asia Academy of Facial Plastic and Reconstructive Surgery (#18159)
- ♦ PAAGS / see Pan Arab Glaucoma Society (#18145)
- ♦ PAAHS – Pan African Association on Human Settlements (inactive)
- ♦ PAALAE – Pan African Association for Literacy and Adult Education (no recent information)
- ♦ PAAL – Pan-Pacific Association of Applied Linguistics (internationally oriented national body)
- ♦ **PAAMES** Pan Asian Association of Maritime Engineering Societies (#18160)
- ♦ **PAANS** Pan African Association of Neurological Sciences (#18037)
- ♦ **PAAO** Pan-American Association of Ophthalmology (#18081)
- ♦ **PAA** Pacific Arts Association (#17928)
- ♦ **PAA** Pan-African Archaeological Association (#18035)
- ♦ **PAA** Pan Asian e-Commerce Alliance (#18162)
- ♦ PAA – Placenta Association of the Americas (internationally oriented national body)
- ♦ PAA – Population Association of America (internationally oriented national body)
- ♦ **PAARS** Pan Arab Association of Radiological Societies (#18141)
- ♦ PAAS – Pan African Association of Surgeons (no recent information)
- ♦ **PAAZA** Pan-African Association of Zoos and Aquaria (#18039)
- ♦ **PABA** Pan African Booksellers Association (#18041)
- ♦ **PABA** Pan Asian Boxing Association (#18161)
- ♦ **PABC** Confederación Panamericana de Badminton (#04467)
- ♦ **PABCON** Pan American Bowling Confederation (#18085)
- ♦ PABIN – Pan-Africa Bicycle Information Network (internationally oriented national body)
- ♦ **PABITRA** Pacific-Asia Biodiversity Transect Network (#17929)
- ♦ **PABMB** Pan American Association for Biochemistry and Molecular Biology (#18080)
- ♦ **PABPS** Pan Arab Association for Burns and Plastic Surgery (#18140)
- ♦ **PABRA** Pan-African Bean Research Alliance (#18040)
- ♦ **PABSEC** Parliamentary Assembly of the Organization of the Black Sea Economic Cooperation (#18213)
- ♦ **PABS** Pan African Burn Society (#18042)
- ♦ PACA – Pacific and Asian Communication Association (internationally oriented national body)
- ♦ PACBA – Pan African Christian Broadcast Association (inactive)
- ♦ PACB – Pan American Coffee Bureau (inactive)

♦ PacCALL 17924

Treas Room B1B19 Fac of Science, Malaysia, Jalan Broga, 43500 Semenyih, Selangor, Malaysia.
URL: https://paccall.org/

History Full title: *Pacific Association for Computer Assisted Language Learning.* **Aims** Promote the use and professional support of CALL throughout the Pacific region. **Structure** Executive Committee. **Languages** English. **Activities** Events/meetings. **Events** *Globalization and Localization in Computer-Assisted Language Learning Conference* Danang (Vietnam) 2019. **NGO Relations** *Asia-Pacific Association for Computer-Assisted Language Learning (APACALL, #01836).* [2019.02.21/XM7365/**D**]

- ♦ PAC Consortium / see Abortion and Postabortion Care Consortium (#00007)
- ♦ PACC Policy – Pan African Centre for Climate Policy (internationally oriented national body)
- ♦ PACCS / see Pan-African Academy of Christian Surgeons (#18033)
- ♦ PACCS – Pan American Cancer Cytology Society (inactive)
- ♦ Pacem in Maribus / see International Ocean Institute (#14394)
- ♦ PACE – Pan African Association of Catholic Exegetes (inactive)
- ♦ **PACE** Parliamentary Assembly of the Council of Europe (#18211)
- ♦ **PACE** Parti des citoyens européens (#18248)
- ♦ **PACE** Party of the Citizens of Europe (#18248)
- ♦ **PACE** Planetary Association for Clean Energy (#18381)
- ♦ **PaCE-SD** Pacific Centre for Environment and Sustainable Development (#17940)
- ♦ **PACFAW** Pacific Foundation for the Advancement of Women (#17950)
- ♦ Pachamama Alliance (internationally oriented national body)
- ♦ **PACHDA** Pan-Arab Congenital Heart Disease Association (#18142)
- ♦ PaC – IAGOD Commission on Paragenesis (see: #11910)
- ♦ **PACIBER** Pacific Asian Consortium for International Business Education and Research (#17930)
- ♦ Pacific Accreditation Cooperation (inactive)
- ♦ Pacific Agricultural and Forestry Policy Network (unconfirmed)
- ♦ Pacifica International Foundation (internationally oriented national body)

♦ Pacific Alliance of National Gymnastic Federations (PANGF) 17925

Alliance du Pacifique des fédérations nationales de gymnastique

Contact c/o Gymnastics Canada, 1900 Promenade City Park Dr, Ste 120, Ottawa ON K1J 1A3, Canada. T. +16137485637. Fax +16137485691.

History Jul 1981. **Aims** Develop gymnastics in the Pacific region; provide an international *competition* for nations contiguous to the Pacific Ocean. **Structure** General Assembly, consisting of member nations, President, 2 Vice-Presidents, 2 members at large and and 4 technical coordinators. **Languages** English. **Staff** Voluntary staff at office of national federation of President. **Finance** Affiliation fees of members cover the basic operation of the Alliance. Marketing and sponsorship cover the competition operational budget (biennial). **Activities** Awards/prizes/competitions. **Events** *Biennial General Assembly / Championships* Tauranga (New Zealand) 2020, *Biennial General Assembly / Championships* Medellin (Colombia) 2018, *Biennial General Assembly / Championships* Everett, WA (USA) 2016, *Biennial General Assembly / Championships* Richmond, BC (Canada) 2014, *Biennial General Assembly / Championships* Everett, WA (USA) 2012. **Publications** *PANGF Newsletter* (irregular).

Members Full in 18 countries and territories:
Australia, Canada, China, Colombia, Guatemala, Hong Kong, Indonesia, Japan, Korea Rep, Malaysia, Mexico, New Zealand, Peru, Philippines, Russia, Singapore, Taiwan, USA. [2021/XD8420/**D**]

♦ Pacific Arctic Group (PAG) 17926

Chair Polar Research Inst of China, Polar Oceanography Div, 451 Jingiao Road, Pudong, 200136 Shanghai, China. T. +862150352091. Fax +862158711663.
URL: http://pag.arcticportal.org/

Aims Identify gaps in knowledge and priority research needs across the region and implement programmes that address them; facilitate and coordinate science operations among member countries; promote and facilitate data accessibility and integrate data bases; serve as a forum for information exchange on science programmes; establish and maintain a direct link between PAG and other relevant science organizations. **Structure** Organized under *International Arctic Science Committee (IASC, #11668).* Chair and Executive Committee; Project Coordinator; Secretariat. **Languages** English. **Activities** Events/meetings; knowledge management/information dissemination; networking/liaising. **Events** *Annual Arctic Science Summit* Arkhangelsk (Russia) 2019, *Annual Arctic Science Summit* Davos (Switzerland) 2018, *Annual Arctic Science Summit* Prague (Czechia) 2017, *ISAR : International Symposium on the Arctic Research* Prague (Czechia) 2017, *Fall Meeting* Qingdao (China) 2016.

Members Founding members of 6 countries:
Canada, China, Japan, Korea Rep, Russia, USA. [2019.12.31/XM4616/**E**]

- ♦ Pacific Area Newspaper Publishers Association (inactive)

♦ Pacific Area Standards Congress (PASC) 17927

Secretariat c/o BSN, Gedung I BPPT Kebon Sirih, Jl MH Thamrin No8, Jakarta 10340, Indonesia. E-mail: pasc@bsn.go.id.
URL: http://www.pascnet.org/

History Founded 1972, Honolulu HI (USA). A specialist regional body of: *Asia-Pacific Economic Cooperation (APEC, #01887).* **Aims** Increase information exchange on international standardization activities; serve as a forum for the development of recommendations for communication to international standards bodies. **Structure** Standing Committee. **Languages** English. **Events** *Congress* 2021, *Congress* Wellington (New Zealand) 2019, *Congress* Okayama (Japan) 2018, *Congress* Vancouver, BC (Canada) 2017, *Congress* Bali (Indonesia) 2016.

Members in 22 countries and territories:
Australia, Brunei Darussalam, Canada, China, Colombia, Fiji, Hong Kong, Indonesia, Japan, Korea Rep, Malaysia, Mexico, Mongolia, New Zealand, Papua New Guinea, Philippines, Russia, Singapore, South Africa, Thailand, USA, Vietnam. [2021/XF6391/c/**F**]

- ♦ Pacific Area Travel Association / see Pacific Asia Travel Association (#17932)
- ♦ Pacific Area Travel Writers Association (internationally oriented national body)

♦ Pacific Arts Association (PAA) 17928

Association des arts du Pacifique

Pres Sainsbury RU – SCVA, Univ of East Anglia, Norwich Research Park, Norwich, NR4 7TJ, UK.
Sec address not obtained.
URL: https://pacificarts.org/

History 8 Feb 1978, Wellington (New Zealand), at 2nd International Symposium on the Arts of Oceania. **Aims** Promote study of all the arts of Oceania; make members aware of the state of all the arts in all parts of Oceania; encourage international understanding among nations involved in the arts of Oceania; promote high standards of research, interpretation and reporting; stimulate interest in teaching of courses, especially at tertiary educational level; encourage cooperation among institutions and individuals in the field; encourage high standards of conservation and preservation of the material culture in and of Oceanic arts. **Structure** Executive Committee, comprising President, 3 Vice-Presidents, Secretary, Treasurer, Editors and Associate Editors. International Advisory Committee. **Languages** English. **Staff** Voluntary. **Finance** Members' dues (annual): Professional individuals and institutions (museums, libraries, collectors, dealers) – US$ 50; Visual and performing artists, students and retired persons – US$ 35; PAA Europe – euro 10. Grants for symposia. **Activities** Organizes: triennial International Symposium; session at annual conference of College Arts Association; European annual meeting. **Events** *Europe Annual Meeting* Paris (France) 2022, *Europe Annual Meeting* Leiden (Netherlands) 2021, *Europe Annual Meeting* Basel (Switzerland) 2019, *International Symposium* Brisbane, QLD (Australia) 2019, *Europe Annual Meeting* Stuttgart (Germany) 2018. **Publications** *Pacific Arts Association Newsletter* (2 a year); *Pacific Arts – Journal of the Pacific Arts Association* (2 a year). Symposium proceedings.

Members Institutions; Individuals. Members in 37 countries and territories:
Australia, Belgium, Brazil, Canada, Cook Is, Fiji, France, Germany, Hawaii, Hungary, Israel, Italy, Japan, Kiribati, Marshall Is, Micronesia FS, Nauru, Netherlands, New Caledonia, New Zealand, Norway, Palau, Papua New Guinea, Polynesia Fr, Rapanui/Easter Is, Russia, Samoa, Samoa USA, Singapore, Solomon Is, Sweden, Switzerland, Tonga, Tuvalu, UK, USA, Vanuatu. [2022/XD8395/**D**]

- ♦ Pacific Arts Council / see Pacific Cultural Council (#17944)

♦ Pacific-Asia Biodiversity Transect Network (PABITRA) 17929

Coordinator Univ of South Australia, School of Natural and Built Sciences, GPO Box 2471, Adelaide SA 5001, Australia.
URL: http://www.herbarium.hawaii.edu/pabitra/

History Founded 1997. Comes within Division for Ecosystem Conservation in the Task Force on Biodiversity of *Pacific Science Association (PSA, #18003).* **Aims** Investigate biodiversity, *ecosystems* and *conservation* in the *tropical* Pacific Islands. **Structure** Principal Coordinator; Co-Principal Coordinators. **Languages** English. **Staff** Voluntary. **Finance** Grants. **Activities** Capacity building; events/meetings; research/documentation. **Events** *Workshop* Palau 2006. **Publications** *Biodiversity Assessment of Tropical Island Ecosystems.* Books; manuals; articles; reports. **NGO Relations** Member of: *Global Islands Network (GIN, #10437); Pacific Science Association (PSA, #18003).* [2015.08.04/XM1882/**F**]

- ♦ Pacific Asia Bridge Federation / see Asia Pacific Bridge Federation (#01862)
- ♦ Pacific-Asia Conference on Knowledge Discovery and Data Mining (meeting series)
- ♦ Pacific and Asia Conference on Korean Studies (meeting series)
- ♦ Pacific and Asia Council of Indigenous Peoples (internationally oriented national body)
- ♦ Pacific Asia Lift and Escalator Association (unconfirmed)
- ♦ Pacific and Asian American Center for Theology and Strategies, USA (internationally oriented national body)
- ♦ Pacific Asian Association for Agent-based Approach in Social Systems Sciences (internationally oriented national body)
- ♦ Pacific and Asian Communication Association (internationally oriented national body)
- ♦ Pacific Asian Congress of Municipalities (meeting series)

♦ Pacific Asian Consortium for International Business Education and Research (PACIBER) 17930

Secretariat Univ of Hawaii at Manoa, PAMI, 2404 Maile Way, A303, Honolulu HI 96822-2223, USA. T. +18089568041. Fax +18089569685.
URL: http://www.paciber.org/

History 5 Jan 1988, Honolulu HI (USA), at the initiative of *Pacific Asian Management Institute, Hawaii (PAMI).* **Aims** Advance international business education and research; provide a forum for new ideas and information exchange through faculty and students. **Structure** Executive Committee, comprising 4 elected representatives from each of the 4 regions (North America, Northeast Asia, Southeast Asia, Oceania), one elected at-large and Executive Director, heading Secretariat. University of Hawaii College of Business Administration serves as Secretariat. **Finance** Members' dues. Other sources: US Dept of Education FIPSE; contributions of University of Hawaii; contributions from administration, faculty, staff and administrators of member universities. **Activities** Joint Diploma Program; Web-Based Course Development; courses; Student exchanges and internships; annual meeting. **Events** *Annual Meeting* Seoul (Korea Rep) 2011, *Annual meeting* Queenstown (New Zealand) 2009, *Annual meeting* Hanoi (Vietnam) 2008, *Annual meeting* Kohala Coast (USA) 2007, *Annual meeting* Cebu City (Philippines) 2006. **Publications** Research Papers; Annual Progress Report; meeting minutes.

Members Schools (27) in 13 countries:
Australia, Canada, China, Hong Kong, Indonesia, Korea Rep, Malaysia, New Zealand, Philippines, Singapore, Taiwan, Thailand, USA.

Included in the above, 2 organizations listed in this Yearbook:
Asian Institute of Management (AIM, #01518); Thunderbird – The Garvin School of International Management. [2008/XF5716/**F**]

- ♦ Pacific Asian Federation of Industrial Engineering (inactive)
- ♦ Pacific Asian Management Institute, Hawaii (internationally oriented national body)

♦ Pacific and Asian Society of Minimally Invasive Spine Surgery (PASMISS) 17931

Address not obtained.
URL: http://www.doc-japan.com/pasmiss2013/welcome.html

Structure Board. **Events** *Annual Conference* Chiba (Japan) 2021, *Annual Conference* Seoul (Korea Rep) 2021, *Annual Conference* Suzhou (China) 2019, *Annual Conference* Kaohsiung (Taiwan) 2018, *Annual Conference* Sapporo (Japan) 2017. **NGO Relations** *World Society for Endoscopic, Navigated and Minimal Invasive Spine Surgery (WENMISS, inactive).* [2012/XJ1489/**E**]

- ♦ Pacific Asia Resource Centre (internationally oriented national body)
- ♦ Pacific Asia Society (internationally oriented national body)

♦ Pacific Asia Travel Association (PATA) 17932

Association de tourisme du Pacifique-Asie – Asociación Turística de la Zona del Pacifico – Verkehrsgesellschaft für den Pazifik

CEO Unit B1 – 28th Fl – Siam Piwat Tower, 989 Rama 1 Rd, Pathumwan, Bangkok, 10330, Thailand. T. +6626582000. Fax +6626582010. E-mail: communications@pata.org – membership@pata.org.
URL: http://www.pata.org/

History Jan 1951, Honolulu, HI (USA). Former names and other names: *Pacific Interim Travel Association* – former (Jan 1951 to Jan 1952); *Pacific Area Travel Association* – former (Jan 1952 to Apr 1986). Registration: USA, Hawaii. **Aims** Enhance sustainable growth, value and quality of travel and tourism to, from and within the Asia Pacific region. **Structure** Conference (annual); Board of Directors; Regional Directors; Director of Board of Relations. **Languages** English. **Staff** Headquarters (including Asia Division): 25; Americas Division: 3; Europe Division: 1; Pacific Division: 1. **Finance** Members' dues. Other sources: projects; publications; events. **Activities** Events/meetings; advocacy/lobbying/activism; awards/prizes/competitions. **Events** *PATA – GBTA APAC Travel Summit* Bangkok (Thailand) 2022, *HICAP : Annual Asia Pacific Hotel Investment Conference* Singapore (Singapore) 2022, *PATA Annual Summit (PAS)* Bangkok (Thailand) 2021, *Destination Marketing Forum* Kuching (Malaysia) 2021, *HICAP : Annual Asia Pacific Hotel Investment Conference* Singapore (Singapore) 2021. **Publications** *VE Bulletin* (12 a year); *Pacific Asia Tourism Forecasts* (annual); *PATA Annual Statistical Report* (annual); *PATA News* (52 a year); *PATA Quarterly Statistical Report.* Occasional papers; task force reports; market studies; directories.

Members Governments (138); Carriers (38); Associate Carriers (54); Travel Agents/Tour Operators (476); Hotels (266); Other Allied (251). Members in 78 countries and territories:
Australia, Azerbaijan, Bahrain, Bangladesh, Belgium, Bhutan, Brazil, Brunei Darussalam, Cambodia, Canada, Chile, China, Cook Is, Czechia, Denmark, Egypt, Fiji, Finland, France, Germany, Greece, Guam, Hong Kong, Hungary, India, Indonesia, Iran Islamic Rep, Japan, Korea DPR, Korea Rep, Laos, Latvia, Lebanon, Macau, Malaysia, Maldives, Mexico, Micronesia FS, Mongolia, Myanmar, Nepal, Netherlands, New Zealand, Nigeria, North Macedonia, Northern Mariana Is, Norway, Pakistan, Palau, Papua New Guinea, Peru, Philippines, Poland, Polynesia Fr, Romania, Russia, Samoa, Saudi Arabia, Singapore, Slovakia, South Africa, Spain, Sri Lanka, Sweden, Switzerland, Taiwan, Thailand, Timor-Leste, Tonga, Türkiye, Turkmenistan, UK, Ukraine, United Arab Emirates, USA, Uzbekistan, Vietnam.

IGO Relations Permanent observer at: *Asia-Pacific Economic Cooperation (APEC, #01887).* **NGO Relations** Member of: *Global Sustainable Tourism Council (GSTC, #10619).* Partner of: *International Institute for Peace through Tourism (IIPT).* [2022/XD3042/**D**]

- ♦ Pacific Association for Clinical Training (inactive)
- ♦ Pacific Association for Computational Linguistics (meeting series)
- ♦ Pacific Association for Computer Assisted Language Learning / see PacCALL (#17924)

♦ Pacific Association of Pediatric Surgeons (PAPS) 17933

Association des chirurgiens pédiatres du Pacifique

Sec Medical Director of 6th Floor, Children's Hospital Colorado, Anschutz Medical Campus, 13123 East 16th Ave, Aurora CO 80045, USA. E-mail: paps.secy@gmail.com.
URL: https://paps.memberclicks.net

History 1971, Los Angeles CA (USA), after preliminary meetings starting in 1967. **Aims** Foster pediatric surgery education in Pacific Rim countries. **Structure** Board. **Languages** English. **Finance** Sources: members' dues. **Events** *Annual Meeting* Aurora, CO (USA) 2021, *Annual Meeting* Christchurch (New Zealand) 2019, *Annual Meeting* Sapporo (Japan) 2018, *Annual Meeting* Seattle, WA (USA) 2017, *Annual Meeting* Kauai Is (USA) 2016. **Publications** Meeting proceedings – published in 'Journal of Pediatric Surgery'.

Members Individuals in 22 countries and territories:
Australia, Canada, Chile, China, Ecuador, Hong Kong, Indonesia, Japan, Korea Rep, Malaysia, Mexico, New Zealand, Nicaragua, Panama, Peru, Russia, Saudi Arabia, Singapore, Taiwan, Thailand, USA, Wales.
NGO Relations *World Federation of Associations of Pediatric Surgeons (WOFAPS, #21411).*
[2021/XD6870/v/**C**]

♦ Pacific Association of Quantity Surveyors (PAQS) 17934

Secretariat c/o ISM, 3rd Floor, Bangunan Jurukur, 64-66 Jalan 52/4, 46200 Petaling Jaya, Selangor, Malaysia. T. +60379551773. Fax +60379550253. E-mail: secretariat@rism.org.my.
URL: http://www.paqs.net/

Events *Annual Conference* Kuching (Malaysia) 2019, *Annual Conference* Sydney, NSW (Australia) 2018, *Annual Conference* Vancouver, BC (Canada) 2017, *Annual Conference* Christchurch (New Zealand) 2016, *Annual Conference* Yokohama (Japan) 2015. **NGO Relations** Member of: *International Cost Management Standard Coalition (ICMS Coalition, #12978).* [2016/XD6027/**D**]

♦ Pacific Association of Supreme Audit Institutions (PASAI) 17935

Chief Exec Level 1, Heards Building, 168 Parnell Road, Parnell, Auckland 1052, New Zealand. T. +6493041275. E-mail: secretariat@pasai.org.
URL: https://www.pasai.org/

History 1986. Founded as a Regional Working Group of *International Organization of Supreme Audit Institutions (INTOSAI, #14478).* Signature of Agreement and recognition of INTOSAI, at first meeting, 11 Nov 1988, Port Vila (Vanuatu). Former names and other names: *South Pacific Association of Supreme Audit Institutions (SPASAI)* – former (1986 to 2008); *Heads of Audit Offices of the South Pacific* – former (1973 to 1986). **Aims** Promote transparent, accountable, effective and efficient use of public sector resources in the Pacific; serve as a regional working group of INTOSAI, in the interest of all SAIs in the Pacific and beyond; encourage and strengthen cooperation with other SAIs, other regional working groups, organs of INTOSAI and other organizations working to improve public sector governance outcomes in the Pacific. **Structure** Congress; Governing Board; Secretariat. **Languages** English. **Staff** 9.00 FTE, paid. **Finance** Sources: grants; members' dues. **Activities** Capacity building; events/meetings; guidance/assistance/consulting; knowledge management/information dissemination; training/education. **Events** *Meeting* Auckland (New Zealand) 2021, *Meeting* Auckland (New Zealand) 2021, *Meeting* Auckland (New Zealand) 2020, *Meeting* Auckland (New Zealand) 2020, *Meeting* Auckland (New Zealand) 2020. **Publications** *PASAI Bulletin* (12 a year). Annual Report; accountability and transparency reports; cooperative audits reports; sub-regional audit support programs reports.
Members Supreme Audit Institutions (27) in 20 countries and territories (" includes New South Wales, Queensland, Victoria and Australian National Audit Office; " includes Chuuk, Kosrae, Pohnpei and Yap):
Australia (*), Cook Is, Fiji, Guam, Kiribati, Marshall Is, Micronesia FS (**), Nauru, New Caledonia, New Zealand, Northern Mariana Is, Palau, Papua New Guinea, Polynesia Fr, Samoa, Samoa USA, Solomon Is, Tonga, Tuvalu, Vanuatu.
IGO Relations Accredited by (9): *Asian Development Bank (ADB, #01422); European Union (EU, #08967); New Zealand Ministry of Foreign Affairs and Trade – New Zealand Aid Programme; Pacific Financial Technical Assistance Centre (PFTAC, #17948); Pacific Islands Forum Secretariat (#17970); The World Bank Group (#21218); UNDP (#20292); United Nations (UN, #20515); University of the South Pacific (USP, #20703).* **NGO Relations** Member of (2): *Effective Institutions Platform (EIP, #05384); International Organization of Supreme Audit Institutions (INTOSAI, #14478)* (and INTOSAI Development Initiative IDI). [2022.06.18/XD1223/**D**]

♦ Pacific Association of Technical and Vocation Education and Training (PATVET) 17936

Main Office c/o SPC, PMB, Suva, Fiji. Fax +6793397730. E-mail: patvet@spc.int.
URL: http://www.spc.int/patvet/

History Oct 2002. **Aims** Promote regional cooperation among organizations providing technical and vocation education and training in the Pacific. **Structure** General Meeting. Board, including Chairman, Secretary and Treasurer. **Events** *Meeting* Suva (Fiji) 2011, *Meeting* Samoa 2003.
Members in 12 countries:
Cook Is, Fiji, Kiribati, Nauru, Niue, Papua New Guinea, Samoa, Solomon Is, Tokelau, Tonga, Tuvalu, Vanuatu.
IGO Relations Secretariat provided by: *Pacific Community (SPC, #17942).* [2011/XM2660/**D**]

♦ Pacific Basin Consortium for Environment and Health (PBC) 17937

Main Office E-W Ctr Research Prog, 1601 East-West Rd, Honolulu HI 96848, USA. Fax +18089447399. E-mail: pbc@uq.edu.au.
URL: https://pacificbasin.org/

History 1986, Honolulu HI (USA), as *Pacific Basin Consortium for Hazardous Waste Research (PBCHW).* Subsequently changed title to *Pacific Basin Consortium for Environment and Health Sciences.* **Aims** Speed the conduct of research and its application and reduce the cost of managing hazardous waste for all members, including those at the forefront of this field. **Structure** Secretariat based at *East-West Center (EWC, #05263)*, but operates from Brisbane (Australia). **Finance** Members' dues. **Activities** Collaborative research; information exchange; training courses; professional network of experts. **Events** *Conference* Depok (Indonesia) 2015, *Joint International Conference* Gwangju (Korea Rep) 2012, *Conference* Perth, WA (Australia) 2009, *Conference* Beijing (China) 2007, *Conference* Honolulu, HI (USA) 2005. **Publications** *PBC Update* (4 a year); *Pacific Basin Consortium for Hazardous Waste Research Newsletter* (periodical).
Members Organizations located in countries either on the rim or within the basin of the Pacific Ocean; Individuals; Special Membership. Members in 23 countries and territories:
Australia, Canada, China, Denmark, Hong Kong, Hungary, India, Indonesia, Japan, Korea Rep, Malaysia, Mexico, New Zealand, Pakistan, Papua New Guinea, Peru, Philippines, Saudi Arabia, Singapore, Switzerland, Taiwan, Thailand, USA.
International organizations (2):
International Solid Waste Association (ISWA, #15567); UNEP (#20299).
NGO Relations *Asian Institute of Technology (AIT, #01519); East-West Center (EWC, #05263).*
[2017/XF0906/y/**F**]

- ♦ Pacific Basin Consortium for Environment and Health Sciences / see Pacific Basin Consortium for Environment and Health (#17937)
- ♦ Pacific Basin Consortium for Hazardous Waste Research / see Pacific Basin Consortium for Environment and Health (#17937)
- ♦ Pacific Basin Dental Association (unconfirmed)
- ♦ Pacific Basin Development Council (inactive)

♦ Pacific Basin Economic Council (PBEC) 17938

Conseil économique du bassin du Pacifique

Contact 11/F AsBAA c/o PBEC, Admiralty Center, 18 Harcourt Road, Admiralty, Hong Kong, Central and Western, Hong Kong. T. +85239753181. E-mail: info@pbec.org.
URL: https://www.pbec.org/

History 1967, as in informal organization of committees of senior business executives. First meeting: 1968, Sydney (Australia). **Aims** Foster economic relationships by building links among *business* communities across the Pacific and by promoting a spirit of regional identity and cooperation; strengthen economic and business relationships among member committees; strengthen the business enterprise system; increase *trade* and *investment* in the Pacific; generate greater economic and social progress in *developing countries* of the Pacific Basin; keep in view the need for balanced development and economic security through liberalized trade systems, broad exchange among business leaders, stable trading practices and supplies, and governmental trading policies attuned to business needs. **Structure** International General Meeting (annual). Member committees, each with Chairman and, in some cases, one or more Vice-Chairmen, and each selecting 3 members of Steering Committee. Officers: International Chairman; International Vice-Chairmen (2); International Treasurer; International Chairman Emeritus; International Secretary-General. *Pacific Forum (no recent information)*, Honolulu HI (USA), functions as International Secretariat. One secretariat per economy. **Languages** Chinese, English, Japanese, Korean, Spanish. **Staff** 6.00 FTE, paid. **Finance** Members' dues. **Activities** Serves as a liaison between business leaders and key government officials; provides advice to governments on Pacific region development issues; assists individual members in expanding their business opportunities to other Pacific markets through informal meetings with business counterparts; organizes *'Business Opportunity Tours'*, meetings, conferences, training courses and annual International General Meeting; instrumental in setting up *'Private Investment Company for Asia (PICA)'*, a multinational corporation to make and facilitate capital investment in developing countries of Asia. Member committees also have their own programmes. **Events** *Annual International General Meeting* Hong Kong (Hong Kong) 2005, *Annual International General Meeting* Hong Kong (Hong Kong) 2005, *Annual international general meeting* Beijing (China) 2004, *Annual international general meeting* Seoul (Korea Rep) 2003, *Annual international general meeting* Kuala Lumpur (Malaysia) 2002. **Publications** *PBEC Business Network* (12 a year); *IGM Executive Summary* (annual); *PBEC News Alert*; *PBEC Report*; *PBEC Survey*. Studies, policy documents and special reports.
Members Senior business executives from economies bordering the Pacific Rim and beyond. Members in 20 countries and territories:
Australia, Canada, Chile, China, Colombia, Ecuador, Hong Kong, Indonesia, Japan, Korea Rep, Malaysia, Mexico, New Zealand, Peru, Philippines, Russia, Singapore, Taiwan, Thailand, USA.
IGO Relations Partner of: *Anti-Corruption Initiative for Asia and the Pacific (#00852).* **NGO Relations** Member of: *Pacific Economic Cooperation Council (PECC, #17947).* [2020/XD4633/**E**]

- ♦ Pacific Basin Financial Management Society (inactive)

♦ Pacific Basin Medical Association (PBMA) 17939

Pres PO Box 16, Majuro Hosp, Ministry of Health, Majuro MH 96960, USA. T. +6926253399 – +6926253355 – +6926255660. E-mail: lokot22@gmail.com.
URL: https://pbma-oceanic.org/

History 1995. **Aims** Provide a network for medical practitioners to: promote high standards of medical care; encourage continuing medical education activities; support formation of local medical associations. **Structure** Officers: President; Vice-President; Secretary; Treasurer. **Languages** English. **Activities** Knowledge management/information dissemination; events/meetings; networking/liaising. **Events** *Annual Convention* Koror (Palau) 2015, *Annual Convention / Conference* Kosrae (Micronesia FS) 2013, *Annual Convention* Palau 2012, *Annual Convention / Conference* Chuuk (Micronesia FS) 2011, *Annual Convention / Conference* Yap (Micronesia FS) 2010. **Publications** *Pacific Health Dialog* – journal.
Members in 6 countries and territories:
Guam, Marshall Is, Micronesia FS, Northern Mariana Is, Palau, Samoa USA.
NGO Relations Member of: *Pacific Public Health Surveillance Network (PPHSN, #17993).* Affiliate member of: *Pacific Island Health Officers Association (PIHOA, #17958).* [2019/XD6513/**D**]

- ♦ Pacific Basin Nuclear Conference (meeting series)
- ♦ Pacific Campaign Against Sea-Launched Cruise Missiles / see Pacific Peace Working Group (#17988)
- ♦ Pacific Campaign for Disarmament and Security / see Pacific Peace Working Group (#17988)
- ♦ Pacific Campaign to Disarm the Seas / see Pacific Peace Working Group (#17988)

♦ Pacific Centre for Environment and Sustainable Development (PaCE-SD) 17940

Dir Lower Marine Campus USP, Laucala Bay Road, Suva, Fiji. E-mail: morgan.wairiu@usp.ac.fj – wainiqolo_r@usp.ac.fj – pacesd@usp.ac.fj.
URL: http://pace.usp.ac.fj/

History 2001, as a centre of the *University of the South Pacific (USP, #20703).* **Structure** Advisory Committee; Director. **Finance** Sources: Regular funding from USP; funds from consultancy and other services.
[2016.08.07/XE4695/**E**]

♦ Pacific Centre for Renewable Energy and Energy Efficiency (PCREEE) 17941

Manager MEIDECC, Sanft Bldg, Nuku'alofa, Tonga. E-mail: info@pcreee.org.
URL: http://www.pcreee.org/

History Proposed 2014, by *Pacific Community (SPC, #17942), Small Island Developing States – Island Energy for Island Life (SIDS DOCK, #19314)* and *UNIDO (#20336).* Developed 2014-2015. Inaugurated ceremony held 26 Apr 2017, Nuku-alofa (Tonga). **Aims** Improve access to modern, affordable and reliable energy services, energy security and mitigation of negative externalities of the energy system by promoting renewable energy and energy efficiency investments, markets and industries in PICTs. **Structure** Steering Committee; Secretariat, hosted by *Pacific Community (SPC, #17942).* National Focal Institutions; Thematic Hubs.
Members Partner States and Territories (22):
Cook Is, Fiji, Guam, Kiribati, Marshall Is, Micronesia FS, Nauru, New Caledonia, Niue, Northern Mariana Is, Palau, Papua New Guinea, Pitcairn, Polynesia Fr, Samoa, Samoa USA, Solomon Is, Tokelau, Tonga, Tuvalu, Vanuatu, Wallis-Futuna.
IGO Relations Core Partners: *Austrian Development Agency (ADA); Pacific Community (SPC, #17942); Small Island Developing States – Island Energy for Island Life (SIDS DOCK, #19314); UNIDO (#20336).* Cooperates with: *Caribbean Centre for Renewable Energy and Energy Efficiency (CCREEE, #03470); ECOWAS Centre for Renewable Energy and Energy Efficiency (ECREEE, #05335).* **NGO Relations** *Sustainable Energy for All (SEforALL, #20056).* [2018/XM6104/**D***]

- ♦ Pacific Charter: Southeast Asia Collective Defence Treaty (1954 treaty)
- ♦ Pacific College for Evangelism / see Alan Walker College of Evangelism (#00619)

♦ Pacific Community (SPC) 17942

Communauté du Pacifique (CPS)

Dir Gen BP D5, 98848 CEDEX Nouméa, New Caledonia. T. +687262000. Fax +687263818. E-mail: spc@spc.int.
Publisher address not obtained.
URL: http://www.spc.int/

History 6 Feb 1947, Canberra, ACT (Australia). Founded as an advisory and consultative body, following signature of *Agreement Establishing the South Pacific Commission (Canberra Agreement) – Convention créant la Commission du Pacifique Sud (Convention de Canberra)* by governments of Australia, France, the Netherlands, New Zealand, the United Kingdom and the United States. Area of activities then comprised territories lying generally South of the Equator from and including former Dutch New Guinea in the West to the French Establishments in Oceania and Pitcairn in the East. Additional agreement signed Nov 1951, Nouméa (New Caledonia), on behalf of the Participating Governments, extending the area to include Guam and the Trust Territory of the Pacific Islands. Netherlands withdrew, 31 Dec 1962, when it ceased to administer the former colony of Dutch New Guinea, now known as Irian Jaya. The following independent and self-governing Pacific States have subsequently been admitted to membership: Samoa (Oct 1965); Nauru (20 Jul 1969); Fiji (5 May 1971); Papua New Guinea (25 Sep 1975); Solomon Islands and Tuvalu (Nov 1978); Niue and Cook Islands (Oct 1980). The Commission's name was adopted at 37th Conference, 1997, Canberra, and took effect on 6 Feb 1998, when the title of the Conference became *'Conference of the Pacific Community (CPC)'*. Current legal name adopted Nov 2015, retaining the acronym SPC. Prior to 1974, Commissioners from the participating governments met in annual session, while delegates from the Pacific territories met as 'South Pacific Conference' every 3 years from 1950 to 1967, and then annually from 1967 to 1974, immediately before the Session of Commissioners, making recommendations to it. In accordance with proposals in a Memorandum of Understanding, formally signed by representatives of the 8 participating governments during the 14th South Pacific Conference, 2 Oct 1974, Rarotonga (Cook Is), the Session of Commissioners and the South Pacific Conference united to meet annually as a single body, known as *South Pacific Conference – Conférence du Pacifique Sud.* The Memorandum also provided for a Planning and Evaluation Committee and for a Committee of Representatives of Participating Governments to assist the Conference in its work. Another Memorandum of Understanding, signed by representatives of all participating governments on 20 Oct 1976, abolished the multiple voting procedure existing at that time and gave each government one vote in the Committee.
Canberra Agreement amended Jun 1980, to permit accession to the Agreement by any government whose territory is within the territorial scope of the Commission and which is either fully independent or in free association with a fully independent government, if invited to do so by all participating governments, on deposition of an instrument of accession with the Government of Australia.

The 23rd South Pacific Conference, Oct 1983, Saipan (Northern Mariana Is), wishing to modify procedures so that all governments and administrations were admitted to the Commission under equal membership, resolved that Commission members should be the following governments and administrations: American Samoa; Australia; Cook Islands; Federated States of Micronesia; Fiji; France; French Polynesia; Guam; Kiribati; Marshall Islands; Nauru; New Caledonia; New Zealand; Niue; Northern Mariana Islands; Palau; Papua New Guinea; Pitcairn Islands; Solomon Islands; New Zealand; Tonga; Tuvalu; United Kingdom (which ceased to be a member from 1 Jan 1996 but which rejoined in 1998); United States of America; Vanuatu; Wallis and Futuna; Samoa. Under these modified procedures, the Committee of Representatives of Participating Governments (CRPG) and the Planning and Evaluation Committee ceased to exist and a *Committee of Representatives of Governments and Administrations (CRGA) – Comité des représentants des gouvernements et administrations (CRGA)* was established, assuming some duties of the Conference, whose sessions were reduced to once every 2 years.
Aims Work for the well-being of Pacific people through effective and innovative application of science and knowledge, guided by a deep understanding of Pacific Island contexts and cultures. **Structure** Conference of the Pacific Community (every 2 years) is governing body with each member entitled to one vote, but usually resolved by consensus. Committee of Representatives of Governments and Administrations (CRGA) meets annually. Executive, headed by Director-General. Programs Directorate, comprising 8 Divisions: Geoscience, Energy and Maritime; Human Rights and Social Development; Fisheries, Aquaculture and Marine Ecosystems; Land Resources; Public Health; Statistics for Development; Educational Quality and Assessment Programe; Operations and Management Directorate. Regional Offices (4): Pohnpei (Federated States of Micronesia); Honiara (Solomon Is); Port Vila (Vanuatu); Nuku'alofa (Tonga). **Languages** English, French. **Staff** 700.00 FTE, paid. Nouméa (New Caledonia): 200; Suva (Fiji), together with Regional Offices in Micronesia FSM, Solomon Is, France and Vanuatu: 500. **Finance** Regular budget: contributions of member countries, assessed on an agreed formula. Voluntary contributions (extra-budgetary), representing 80% of the total budget, also provided by some member countries, other governments, various aid agencies and international organizations, and other external sources. Annual budget: 90,000,000 USD. **Activities** Awareness raising; capacity building; certification/accreditation; events/meetings; guidance/assistance/consulting; knowledge management/information dissemination; monitoring/evaluation; networking/liaising; projects/programmes; publishing activities; research and development; research/documentation; standards/guidelines; training/education. Active in: Cook Is, Fiji, Guam, Kiribati, Marshall Is, Micronesia FS, Nauru, New Caledonia, Niue, Northern Mariana Is, Palau, Papua New Guinea, Pitcairn, Polynesia Fr, Samoa, Samoa USA, Solomon Is, Tokelau, Tonga, Tuvalu, Vanuatu, Wallis-Futuna. **Events** *Conference of the Pacific Community* Port Vila (Vanuatu) 2022, *Meeting of the Committee of Representatives of Governments and Administrations* Port Vila (Vanuatu) 2022, *Biennial Conference* Nouméa (New Caledonia) 2021, *Meeting of the Committee of Representatives of Governments and Administrations* Nouméa (New Caledonia) 2021, *Meeting of the Committee of Representatives of Governments and Administrations* Nouméa (New Caledonia) / Suva (Fiji) 2020. **Publications** *Pacific Community Results Report* (annual) in English, French. Information Services: Library; interpretation and translation; computer services; audiovisual training and teaching materials.
Members Member Governments and Administrations (27):
Australia, Cook Is, Fiji, France, Guam, Kiribati, Marshall Is, Micronesia FS, Nauru, New Caledonia, New Zealand, Niue, Northern Mariana Is, Palau, Papua New Guinea, Pitcairn, Polynesia Fr, Samoa, Samoa USA, Solomon Is, Tokelau, Tonga, Tuvalu, UK, USA, Vanuatu, Wallis-Futuna.
European Union (EU, #08967).
IGO Relations Observer status with (1): *United Nations (UN, #20515)* (General Assembly).
Draft agreement signed with: *UNESCO (#20322)* in 1998. Accredited to the Conference of the Parties of: *Secretariat of the United Nations Convention to Combat Desertification (Secretariat of the UNCCD, #19208).* Relationship agreement with: *FAO (#09260).* Cooperation agreement with: *International Hydrographic Organization (IHO, #13825); International Maritime Organization (IMO, #14102).* Participates as observer in the activities of: *Codex Alimentarius Commission (CAC, #04081).* Observer member of: *Western and Central Pacific Fisheries Commission (WCPFC, #20912).* Official observer of: *Pacific Islands Law Officers' Network (PILON, #17972).* Has proposed setting up of: *South Pacific Regional Development Bank (no recent information).* Links with a large number of organizations, including:
- *Australian Centre for International Agricultural Research (ACIAR);*
- *Canadian International Development Agency (CIDA, inactive);*
- *Centre de coopération internationale en recherche agronomique pour le développement (CIRAD, #03733);*
- *Centre technique de coopération agricole et rurale (CTA, inactive);*
- *Comisión Permanente del Pacífico Sur (CPPS, #04141);*
- *Commonwealth Fund for Technical Cooperation (CFTC, #04331);*
- *Commonwealth Secretariat (#04362);*
- *Commonwealth Youth Programme (CYP, #04372);*
- *Commonwealth Youth Programme South Pacific Regional Centre (CYP-SPRC, see: #04362);*
- *European Commission (EC, #06633);*
- *European and Mediterranean Plant Protection Organization (EPPO, #07773);*
- *FAO Regional Office for Asia and the Pacific (RAP, #09266);*
- *ILO (#11123);*
- *Institut de recherche pour le développement (IRD);*
- *Institute for Research, Extension and Training in Agriculture (IRETA, #11291);*
- *Inter-American Tropical Tuna Commission (IATTC, #11454);*
- *Intergovernmental Oceanographic Commission (IOC, #11496);*
- *OIE – World Organisation for Animal Health (#17703);*
- *Pacific Cultural Council (#17944);*
- *Pacific Islands Development Program (PIDP, see: #05263);*
- *Pacific Islands Forum (#17968);*
- *Pacific Islands Forum Fisheries Agency (FFA, #17969);*
- *Pacific Islands Forum Secretariat (#17970);*
- *Pacific Islands Marine Resources Information System (PIMRIS, #17973);*
- *Secretariat of the Pacific Regional Environment Programme (SPREP, #19205);*
- *Standing Committee of the Pacific Islands Conference of Leaders (#19957);*
- *Statistical Institute for Asia and the Pacific (SIAP, #19972);*
- *UNEP (#20299);*
- *UNESCAP Pacific Operations Centre (UN/EPOC, see: #20557);*
- *UNESCO Asia and Pacific Regional Bureau for Education (#20301);*
- *UNESCO Office for the Pacific States (#20315);*
- *UNICEF (#20332);*
- *United Nations Economic and Social Commission for Asia and the Pacific (ESCAP, #20557);*
- *United Nations Population Fund (UNFPA, #20612);*
- *United States Agency for International Development (USAID);*
- *University of the South Pacific (USP, #20703);*
- *WHO (#20950);*
- *WHO Regional Office for Europe (#20945).*

NGO Relations Instrumental in setting up: *Pacific International Maritime Law Association (PIMLA, #17956); Pacific Public Health Surveillance Network (PPHSN, #17993).* Library is member of: *International Federation of Library Associations and Institutions (IFLA, #13470).* Member of: *Pacific Islands GOOS (PI-GOOS, #17971).* Participates in: *Global Partnership for Oceans (GPO, #10537).* Links with a large number of organizations, including:
- *Bureau for the Development of Research on Tropical Perennial Oil Crops (no recent information);*
- *Centre de rencontres et d'échanges internationaux du Pacifique (CREIPAC, #03778);*
- *Clean Up the World (CUW, #03992);*
- *Conferentia Episcopalis Pacifici (CEPAC, #04659);*
- *Counterpart International (FSP);*
- *International Agency for Rural Industrialization (INARI, no recent information);*
- *Oceania Customs Organisation (OCO, #17658);*
- *Pacific Agricultural Information System (PAIS, no recent information);*
- *Pacific Games Council (PGC, #17951);*
- *Pacific Island Museums Association (PIMA, #17959);*
- *Pacific Islands Maritime Association (PacMA, #17974);*
- *Pacific Islands News Association (PINA, #17975);*
- *Pacific Islands Regional Association for Distance Education (PIRADE, no recent information);*
- *Pacific Parliamentary Assembly on Population and Development (PPAPD, #17987);*
- *Pacific Plant Protection Organization (PPPO, #17989);*
- *Pacific Youth Council (Youthlink, #18013);*
- *Regional Energy Resources Information Center (RERIC, #18780);*
- *South Pacific Action Committee for Human Ecology and Environment (SPACHEE, no recent information);*
- *South Pacific Institute for Renewable Energy (SPIRE, no recent information);*
- *World Council of Churches (WCC, #21320);*
- *WorldFish (#21507).*

[2023.03.02/XD3260/**D***]

♦ Pacific Concerns Resource Centre (internationally oriented national body)

♦ Pacific Conference of Churches (PCC) 17943

Conférence des eglises du pacifique
Acting Gen Sec PO Box 208, Suva, Fiji. T. +6793311277. Fax +6793303205.
Street address 4 Thurston Street, Suva, Fiji.
URL: http://www.pcc.org.fj/
History 22 Apr 1961, Malua (Samoa USA). 22 Apr – 4 May 1961, Malua (Samoa USA), as a Continuation Committee. **Aims** Promote a spirit of *ecumenicism* among the Churches of the Pacific; help member Churches evaluate their work and plan so that their human and financial resources are used in joint action for mission; create greater awareness of the issue of justice, peace and human development facing the people and nations of the region and the world; facilitate mutual consultation; promote participation in the wider ecumenical movement; be a means for channelling help among, to and from Churches in the region in times of natural disaster or need. **Structure** General Assembly (every 5 years); Executive Committee; Secretariat. **Languages** English, French. **Staff** 10.00 FTE, paid. **Finance** Members' dues. Overseas funds. **Activities** Religious activities; advocacy/lobbying/activism; capacity building. **Events** *Quinquennial General Assembly* Auckland (New Zealand) 2018, *Quinquennial General Assembly* Honiara (Solomon Is) 2013, *Quinquennial General Assembly* Pago Pago (Samoa USA) 2007, *Quinquennial General Assembly* Rarotonga Is (Cook Is) 2002, *Quinquennial General Assembly* Tahiti Is (Polynesia Fr) 1997. **Publications** *PCC News* (4 a year). Resource Book; reports.
Members Christian churches of many denominations, including churches (32) and national councils of churches in 19 countries and territories:
Cook Is, Fiji, Kiribati, Marshall Is, Micronesia FS, Nauru, New Caledonia, New Zealand, Niue, Papua New Guinea, Pohnpei, Polynesia Fr, Samoa, Samoa USA, Solomon Is, Tonga, Tuvalu, Vanuatu, West Papua.
IGO Relations Partner of: Pacific Leadership Programme of *Australian Aid (inactive); Pacific Community (SPC, #17942).* **NGO Relations** Member of: *Pacific Islands Regional Non-governmental Organizations (PRNGO, #17978).* Instrumental in setting up: *Pacific Churches Research Centre (PCRC, no recent information).*
[2017.10.25/XD0357/y/**F**]

♦ Pacific Conference on Computer Graphics and Applications (meeting series)
♦ Pacific Congress on Marine Science and Technology International (meeting series)
♦ Pacific Council on International Policy (internationally oriented national body)
♦ Pacific Council of Structural Steel Associations (unconfirmed)
♦ Pacific Countries Ports Association / see Pacific Maritime Transport Alliance (#17982)

♦ Pacific Cultural Council 17944

Tech Support Officer c/o SPC, BP D5, Nouméa, New Caledonia. T. +687262000. Fax +687263818.
History as *South Pacific Arts Festival Council*, under the auspices of *Pacific Community (SPC, #17942)* which acts as Secretariat. Previously known as: *Council of Pacific Arts – Conseil des arts du Pacifique* and *Pacific Arts Council*. Present name adopted 2008. **Aims** Encourage awareness of a collective voice; foster protection of cultural heritage; explore and encourage creation of new dynamic arts; cultivate global awareness and appreciation of Pacific arts and cultures; promote the Pacific's traditional languages; value the wisdom of the elders; support the aspirations of youth; advocate a culture of peace through dialogue with the cultures of the Pacific; promote cultural development within the social, economic and political development of Pacific countries; encourage indigenous people of the Pacific to continue their efforts for recognition. **Structure** Council is an autonomous entity which meets normally every 2 years, subject to funding, to discuss matters pertaining to the *'Festival of Pacific Arts'*. Executive Board develops cultural goals, objectives and policies to present to the Council. **Languages** English, French. **Staff** 1.50 FTE, paid. **Events** *Quadrennial Festival of Pacific Arts* Pago Pago (Samoa USA) 2008, *Meeting / Quadrennial Festival of Pacific Arts* Koror (Palau) 2004, *Meeting* Nouméa (New Caledonia) 2002, *Meeting / Quadrennial Festival of Pacific Arts* Nouméa (New Caledonia) 2000, *Meeting* Nouméa (New Caledonia) 2000. **Publications** Meeting proceedings.
Members All countries members of SPC, plus Chile (Easter Is), Norfolk Is and Hawaii. Governments or administrations of 29 countries and territories:
Australia, Chile (Easter Is), Cook Is, Fiji, France, Guam, Hawaii, Kiribati, Marshall Is, Micronesia FS, Nauru, New Caledonia, New Zealand, Niue, Norfolk Is, Northern Mariana Is, Palau, Papua New Guinea, Pitcairn, Polynesia Fr, Samoa, Samoa USA, Solomon Is, Tokelau, Tonga, Tuvalu, USA, Vanuatu, Wallis-Futuna. [2012/XF2350/**F***]

♦ Pacific Democrat Union / see Asia Pacific Democrat Union (#01881)
♦ Pacific Dermatological Association (internationally oriented national body)
♦ Pacific Dermatologic Association / see Pacific Dermatological Association
♦ Pacific Development and Conservation Trust (internationally oriented national body)
♦ Pacific Disability Development Network (inactive)

♦ Pacific Disability Forum (PDF) 17945

CEO GPO Box 18458, Suva, Fiji. T. +6793312008. Fax +6793310469. E-mail: pdfsec@unwired.com.fj.
Manager Finance and Corporate Ground Floor, Kadavu House, Victoria Parade, Suva, Fiji.
URL: http://www.pacificdisability.org/
History 2002. Officially inaugurated, 2004. **Aims** Improve and maintain the situation of people with disabilities in Pacific Island countries and territories through collaboration with relevant stakeholders and advocacy to build and strengthen the capacity of member organizations to respond to issues affecting them. **Structure** Board. **Activities** Advocacy/lobbying/activism; capacity building; research and development. **Events** *Annual Meeting* Suva (Fiji) 2020, *Conference* Nadi (Fiji) 2019, *Conference* Apia (Samoa) 2017, *Conference* Nadi (Fiji) 2015, *Conference* Nouméa (New Caledonia) 2013.
Members Full in 17 countries and territories:
Australia, Cook Is, Fiji, Kiribati, Marshall Is, Micronesia FS, New Caledonia, New Zealand, Niue, Palau, Papua New Guinea, Samoa, Solomon Is, Tahiti Is, Tonga, Tuvalu, Vanuatu.
Associate in 12 countries and territories:
Australia, Cook Is, Fiji, Kiribati, Marshall Is, New Zealand, Papua New Guinea, Samoa USA, Solomon Is, Timor-Leste, Tonga, Tuvalu.
Consultative Status Consultative status granted from: *ECOSOC (#05331)* (Special). **IGO Relations** Partner of (2): *Pacific Islands Forum Secretariat (#17970); UN Women (#20724).* **NGO Relations** Member of (3): *International Disability Alliance (IDA, #13176); RI Global (#18948); Transparency, Accountability and Participation Network (TAP Network, #20222).* Partner of (1): *Christian Blind Mission (CBM).* Affiliated with (1): *Pacific Islands Regional Non-governmental Organizations (PRNGO, #17978).* [2021/XM8226/**D**]

♦ Pacific Disability Information Network (inactive)
♦ Pacific Disaster Center (internationally oriented national body)

♦ Pacific Early Childhood Education Research Association (PECERA) . 17946

Sec Centre for Professional Practice and Partnerships, Univ of Canterbury – Private Bag 4800, Christchurch, New Zealand. T. +6433458804.
Pres Yew Chung Education Foundation, 20 Somerset Road, Kowloon Tong, Kowloon, Hong Kong. T. +85223387106. Fax +85223046713.
URL: http://www.pecera.org/
History Constitution adopted 14 Jul 2001. **Aims** Disseminate and support research in early childhood education within the Pacific area. **Structure** Governing Board, comprising Founding President, President, Vice-President/Treasurer, Secretary and 11 members. **Events** *Annual Conference* Wellington (New Zealand) 2021, *Annual Conference* Wellington (New Zealand) 2020, *Annual Conference* Taipei (Taiwan) 2019, *Annual Conference* Kuching (Malaysia) 2018, *Annual Conference* Cebu City (Philippines) 2017. **Publications** *Asia-Pacific Journal of Research in Early Childhood Education* (2 a year).
Members Chapters in 11 countries and territories:
Australia, China, Hong Kong, Japan, Korea Rep, New Zealand, Philippines, Singapore, Taiwan, Thailand, USA.
[2016/XJ5487/**D**]

♦ **Pacific Economic Cooperation Council (PECC)** **17947**
Conseil de coopération économique du Pacifique
International Secretariat 29 Heng Mui Keng Terrace, Singapore 119620, Singapore. T. +6567379822. Fax +6567379824. E-mail: info@pecc.org.
URL: http://www.pecc.org/
History 1980. **Aims** Promote *regional* economic cooperation in the Pacific Basin. **Structure** General Meeting (every 1 or 2 years); Tripartite Group; Standing Committee; International Secretariat located in Singapore (Singapore). **Languages** English. **Finance** Members' dues. **Activities** Politics/policy/regulatory; research/documentation; events/meetings. **Events** *General Meeting* Kuala Lumpur (Malaysia) 2020, *General Meeting* Jakarta (Indonesia) 2018, *General Meeting* Hanoi (Vietnam) 2017, *Seminar on Port Management and Sustainability* Busan (Korea Rep) 2016, *General Meeting* Manila (Philippines) 2015. **Publications** *PECC LINK* (4 a year) – electronic; *State of the Region* (annual). Electronic publications; seminar reports; conference proceedings.
Members Committees in 21 countries and territories:
Australia, Brunei Darussalam, Canada, Chile, China, Colombia, Ecuador, Hong Kong, Indonesia, Japan, Korea Rep, Malaysia, Mexico, New Zealand, Peru, Philippines, Singapore, Taiwan, Thailand, USA, Vietnam.
Pacific Islands Forum (#17968).
Associate member:
France (Pacific Territories).
Institutional members (2), listed in this Yearbook:
Pacific Basin Economic Council (PBEC, #17938); Pacific Trade and Development Conference (PAFTAD, #18009).
IGO Relations Observer Status with: *Asia-Pacific Economic Cooperation (APEC, #01887).*
[2020/XF1323/y/**F**]

♦ Pacific Energy and Resources Center / see Pacific Environment
♦ Pacific Environment (internationally oriented national body)
♦ Pacific Environment and Resources Center / see Pacific Environment
♦ Pacific Federation of the International College of Surgeons (see: #12650)

♦ **Pacific Financial Technical Assistance Centre (PFTAC)** **17948**
Centre d'Assistance Technique Financière du Pacifique
Coordinator Reserve Bank Bldg, Tower 7, Pratt Street, PO Box 14877, Suva, Fiji. T. +679304866. Fax +679304045. E-mail: pftacinquires@imf.org.
URL: http://www.pftac.org/
History 1993, Suva (Fiji). Founded by *International Monetary Fund (IMF, #14180)* and *UNDP (#20292)* as the regional office to implement the Fiscal and Monetary Management Reform and Statistical Improvement Project. UNDP withdrew from project, 2001. Current funding cycle runs through Apr 2022. **Aims** Build skills and institutional capacity in member countries for effective *economic* and *financial* management that can be sustained at the national level. **Structure** Tripartite Review Committee, composed of representatives of the Executing Agency, funding agencies and participating governments. Coordinator; Advisors (4). **Languages** English. **Activities** Provides technical advice and training in public financial management, tax administration and policy, banking regulation and supervision and macroeconomic and financial statistics, largely carried out by the 4 advisors. Acts as the executing agency in the Pacific Island countries on these issues, as agreed to governments of the countries and PFTAC's donors. Organizes regional seminars and in-country workshops. **Events** *Pacific Regional Workshop on Strengthening Oversight Functions of Public Financial Management through Internal and External Audit* Honiara (Solomon Is) 2016, *Seminar* Port Moresby (Papua New Guinea) 2005. **Publications** Discussion papers on issues of regional interest.
Members Governments of 15 countries and territories:
Cook Is, Fiji, Kiribati, Marshall Is, Micronesia FS, Nauru, Niue, Palau, Papua New Guinea, Samoa, Solomon Is, Tokelau, Tonga, Tuvalu, Vanuatu.
IGO Relations Observer member of: *Asia/Pacific Group on Money Laundering (APG, #01921).*
[2020/XE4453/**E***]

♦ **Pacific Fisheries Technologists (PFT)** **17949**
Pres Osu Seafood Lab, 2001 Marine Drive, Astoria OR 97103, USA. T. +15033254531. Fax +15033252753. E-mail: surimiman1@yahoo.com.
URL: http://pftfish.net/
Structure Executive Committee, including President, Secretary and Treasurer. **Events** *Safe and sustainable seafood* Astoria, OR (USA) 2015, *Conference* Monterey, CA (USA) 2014, *Conference* Nuevo Vallarta (Mexico) 2013, *Conference* Anchorage, AK (USA) 2012, *Conference* Vancouver, BC (Canada) 2011. [2015/XJ7365/**E**]

♦ Pacific Flower Culture Promotional Conference / see World Flower Council (#21508)
♦ Pacific Forum Center for Security and International Studies (internationally oriented national body)
♦ Pacific Forum CSIS – Pacific Forum Center for Security and International Studies (internationally oriented national body)
♦ Pacific Forum Line (inactive)

♦ **Pacific Foundation for the Advancement of Women (PACFAW)** **17950**
Exec Dir 26 Pender Street, Suva, Fiji.
History 2000, Tonga. **Finance** Supported by: *European Commission (EC, #06633); Brot für die Welt.*
Members National councils in 7 countries:
Cook Is, Kiribati, Micronesia FS, Papua New Guinea, Solomon Is, Tonga, Tuvalu.
IGO Relations Partner of: *UNESCO Office, Jakarta – Regional Bureau for Sciences in Asia and the Pacific (#20313).* **NGO Relations** Part of: *Pacific Islands Regional Non-governmental Organizations (PRNGO, #17978).* Member of: *International Campaign to Ban Landmines – Cluster Munition Coalition (ICBL-CMC, #12427).*
[2009/XJ4395/f/**D**]

♦ **Pacific Games Council (PGC)** **17951**
Conseil des jeux du Pacifique
Exec Dir 139-141 Varsity Parade, Varsity Lakes QLD 4227, Australia. T. +61408536377. E-mail: pacificgamescouncil@gmail.com.
Pres GPO Box 1279, Suva, Fiji.
URL: http://www.foxsportspulse.com/assoc_page.cgi?c=2-2642-0-0-0&sID=24029/
History 1961. Founded by *Pacific Community (SPC, #17942).* Former names and other names: *South Pacific Games Council* – former; *Conseil des jeux du Pacifique Sud* – former. **Structure** General Assembly (annual); Council. Committees (3): Sports; Marketing; Audit & Finance. **Activities** Sporting activities. **Events** *Pacific Games* Honiara (Solomon Is) 2023, *Pacific Games* Apia (Samoa) 2019, *Pacific Games* Port Moresby (Papua New Guinea) 2015, *South Pacific Games* Nouméa (New Caledonia) 2011, *General Assembly* Rarotonga Is (Cook Is) 2009.
Members Associations in 22 countries and territories:
Cook Is, Fiji, Guam, Kiribati, Marshall Is, Micronesia FS, Nauru, New Caledonia, Niue, Norfolk Is, Northern Mariana Is, Palau, Papua New Guinea, Polynesia Fr, Samoa, Samoa USA, Solomon Is, Tokelau, Tonga, Tuvalu, Vanuatu, Wallis-Futuna.
Associate members in 2 countries:
Australia, New Zealand.
NGO Relations Partner of (4): *Oceania National Olympic Committees (ONOC, #17667); Oceania Regional Anti-Doping Organization (ORADO, #17670); Oceania Sport Information Centre (OSIC); Organisation of Sports Federations of Oceania (OSFO, #17828).* [2023/XF0026/**D**]

♦ Pacific Gender Climate Coalition (unconfirmed)
♦ Pacific Geoscience Centre, Sidney-Canada (internationally oriented national body)
♦ Pacific GIS and Remote Sensing Council (internationally oriented national body)
♦ Pacific Global Ocean Observing System / see Pacific Islands GOOS (#17971)
♦ PacificGOOS / see Pacific Islands GOOS (#17971)
♦ PacificGOOS Regional Alliance / see Pacific Islands GOOS (#17971)
♦ Pacific Graduate Women's Network (internationally oriented national body)
♦ Pacific Graphics – Pacific Conference on Computer Graphics and Applications (meeting series)
♦ Pacific Health Research Institute (internationally oriented national body)

♦ **Pacific History Association (PHA)** **17952**
Sec-Treas VUW History, PO Box 600, Wellington 6140, New Zealand.
URL: http://www.pacifichistoryassociation.net/
History Officially founded 11 May 1981, Noosa (Australia), after an earlier gathering of Pacific historians and other scholars, 1980, Martindale Hall (Australia). **Aims** Encourage information exchange amongst individuals, institutions and organizations interested in Pacific history and related subjects; encourage the study, discussion, writing and publishing of materials on Pacific history, on Pacific studies in general and on related matters. **Structure** Office bearers: President, Secretary/Treasurer, Newsletter Editor, Conference Convenor, 8 Executive and Co-opted Members. **Languages** English. **Staff** None. **Finance** Members' dues: Individual salaried members and institutions: Australian/New Zealand $ 20; Individual unsalaried and student members: Australian/New Zealand $ 5. **Activities** Organizes Conferences and regional workshops. **Events** *Biennial Conference* Suva (Fiji) 2021, *Biennial Conference* Suva (Fiji) 2020, *Biennial Conference* London (UK) / Cambridge (UK) 2018, *Biennial Conference* Tamuning (Guam) 2016, *Biennial Conference* Taipei (Taiwan) / Taitung (Taiwan) 2014. **Publications** *Pacific History Association Newsletter* (2-3 a year). Film guides; bibliographies; reports of workshops; conference papers; teachers guides.
Members Individual and Institutional in 30 countries and territories:
Australia, Canada, Cook Is, Denmark, Fiji, France, Germany, Hawaii, Indonesia, Japan, Kiribati, Malaysia, Marshall Is, Micronesia FS, Nauru, Netherlands, New Caledonia, New Zealand, Palau, Papua New Guinea, Philippines, Samoa, Solomon Is, Spain, Sweden, Tonga, Tuvalu, UK, USA, Vanuatu. [2016/XD0236/**D**]

♦ **Pacific Immigration Directors' Conference (PIDC)** **17953**
Secretariat PO Box, Apia 1881, Samoa. T. +68529107. E-mail: info@pidcsec.org.
URL: http://www.pidcsec.org/
History 1996. **Aims** Promote consultation and cooperation among immigration agencies within the Pacific region; enhance national immigration border; facilitate cross border travel; create national immigration agencies. **Languages** English. **Staff** 5.00 FTE, paid. **Activities** Events/meetings. **Events** *Annual Conference* Nadi (Fiji) 2018, *Annual Conference* Apia (Samoa) 2017, *Annual Conference* Majuro (Marshall Is) 2016, *Annual Conference* Apia (Samoa) 2015, *Annual Conference* Kokopo (Papua New Guinea) 2014.
Members Immigration agencies in 23 countries and territories:
Australia, Cook Is, Fiji, Guam, Kiribati, Marshall Is, Micronesia FS, Nauru, New Caledonia, New Zealand, Niue, Norfolk Is, Northern Mariana Is, Palau, Papua New Guinea, Polynesia Fr, Samoa, Samoa USA, Solomon Is, Tonga, Tuvalu, Vanuatu, Wallis-Futuna.
NGO Relations *International Air Transport Association (IATA, #11614); Oceania Customs Organisation (OCO, #17658).* [2018.06.01/XF6799/c/**F**]

♦ Pacific Indigenous Peoples' Environment Coalition (unconfirmed)
♦ The Pacific Institute / see Jonathan Napela Center for Hawaiian and Pacific Islands Studies
♦ Pacific Institute (internationally oriented national body)
♦ Pacific Institute for Resource Management (internationally oriented national body)
♦ Pacific Institute of Resource Management, Wellington (internationally oriented national body)
♦ Pacific Institute for Studies in Development, Environment and Security / see Pacific Institute
♦ Pacific Institute for Women's Health (internationally oriented national body)

♦ **Pacific Insurance Conference (PIC)** **17954**
Address not obtained.
URL: http://www.pacificinsuranceconference.org/
History 1973. Also referred to as *Pacific Insurance Congress.* Registered as a not-for-profit in Hong Kong. **Aims** Share in the free exchange of ideas and experiences concerning management, marketing and customer service in a spirit of international brotherhood. **Structure** Officers and Directors. **Events** *Conference* Hong Kong (Hong Kong) 2013, *Conference* Singapore (Singapore) 2011, *Conference* Bangkok (Thailand) 2009, *Conference* Kuala Lumpur (Malaysia) 2007, *Conference* Taipei (Taiwan) 2005. [2014/XS6060/c/**E**]

♦ Pacific Insurance Congress / see Pacific Insurance Conference (#17954)
♦ Pacific Interim Travel Association / see Pacific Asia Travel Association (#17932)

♦ **Pacific International Center for High Technology Research (PICHTR)** **17955**
Pres-CEO 1440 Kapiolani Blvd, Ste 1225, Honolulu HI 96814, USA. T. +18089439581. Fax +18089439582. E-mail: info@pichtr.org.
URL: http://www.pichtr.org/
Aims Advance an economically secure and environmentally conscious future for Hawaii and the countries of the Asia Pacific region based on sustainable technologies, systems and services. **Structure** Board of Directors of 11 members. **Events** *Conference* Suva (Fiji) 1996. **NGO Relations** Member of: *Pacific Power Association (PPA, #17991).* [2016/XE3893/**E**]

♦ **Pacific International Maritime Law Association (PIMLA)** **17956**
Pres 11f Sturges Road, Box 21734, Henderson, Auckland, New Zealand.
Contact c/o SPC Regional Maritime Prog, Private Mail Bag, Suva, Fiji. E-mail: maritime@spc.int.
URL: http://www.spc.int/maritime/
History 12 Jul 2005, Suva (Fiji), under the auspices of *Pacific Community (SPC, #17942).* Currently autonomous. **Aims** Serve as a forum for discussion on maritime legal issues in the Pacific; provide advice to regional and national governments and other organizations in enhancing the uniformity and harmonization of maritime law and practices; promote and enhance maritime capacity building; promote legal maritime interests within the region through advocacy roles and information dissemination to relevant legal counterparts in the region. **Structure** General Meeting (at least every 3 years). Executive Committee of up to 5 members, including President. **Languages** English. **Staff** 1.00 FTE, paid. **Finance** Subscriptions: Fiji $ 25. **Activities** Training/education; guidance/assistance/consulting. **Publications** Action Plan; documents.
Members Regular; associate. Members (50) in 24 countries and territories:
Australia, Cook Is, Fiji, Guam, Kiribati, Marshall Is, Micronesia FS, Nauru, New Caledonia, New Zealand, Niue, Northern Mariana Is, Palau, Papua New Guinea, Pitcairn, Polynesia Fr, Samoa, Samoa USA, Solomon Is, Tokelau, Tonga, Tuvalu, Vanuatu, Wallis-Futuna.
IGO Relations Official observer of: *Pacific Islands Law Officers' Network (PILON, #17972).* Observer status with: *Western and Central Pacific Fisheries Commission (WCPFC, #20912).* **NGO Relations** Consultative member of: *Comité maritime international (CMI, #04192).* [2018/XM1628/**D**]

♦ Pacific International Politics Conference (meeting series)
♦ Pacific Islanders' Educational Resource Centre / see Pasifika Education Centre (#18252)

♦ **Pacific Island Farmers Organisation Network (PIFON)** **17957**
Contact PO Box 9048, Nadi Airport, Nadi, Fiji. T. +6796727025. E-mail: info@pacificfarmers.com.
URL: http://www.pacificfarmers.com/
History Operating informally since 2009. Formally registered 2013. Registered in accordance with the laws of Fiji. **Aims** Make Pacific farmer organizations more vibrant, viable and sustainable organizations. **Structure** Board of Directors; Manager; Programme; Finance; Commu ications. **Finance** Members' dues. **Publications** *PIFON e-Bulletin; PIFON Newsletter.*
Members Full in 9 countries:
Cook Is, Fiji, New Caledonia, Papua New Guinea, Samoa, Solomon Is, Timor-Leste, Tonga, Vanuatu.
NGO Relations *Global Forum on Agricultural Research (GFAR, #10370).* [2019.12.11/XM4993/**F**]

♦ **Pacific Island Health Officers Association (PIHOA)** **17958**
Honolulu Office Pacific Guardian Center, Makai Tower, 733 Bishop Street, Suite 1820, Honolulu HI 96813, USA. T. +18085373131. Fax +18085376868.
Guam Office GCIC Bldg, 414 West Soledad Ave, Suite 906, Agana 96910, USA.
URL: http://www.pihoa.org/
Aims Improve health and well-being in the Pacific islands populations. **Structure** Board of Directors of 6 members. **Events** *Conference* Koror (Palau) 2015.
Members in 6 countries and territories:
Guam, Marshall Is, Micronesia FS, Northern Mariana Is, Palau, Samoa USA.
Affiliate member (1):
Pacific Basin Dental Association (PBDA).
NGO Relations Member of: *Pacific Public Health Surveillance Network (PPHSN, #17993).* [2022/XM3400/**D**]

♦ Pacific Island Museums Association (PIMA) 17959

Association des musées des îles du Pacifique

Pres Dept of Chamorro Affairs, PO Box 2950, Hagatna GU 96932, USA. T. +14754278 – +14754279. Fax +14754227. E-mail: pacificmuseums@gmail.com – pimasg@gmail.com.

Facebook: https://www.facebook.com/PACIFIC-ISLANDS-MUSEUM-ASSOCIATION-120849624593675/

History Founded 1991, as *Museums in Oceania Project*, as a project of *International Centre for the Study of the Preservation and Restoration of Cultural Property (ICCROM, #12521)*. Name change, 1993, to *Prevention in Pacific Island States (PREMO)*. Present name adopted Jul 1996. Became independent 1999, when became registered in accordance with Fiji law. Relocated Secretariat to Port Vila (Vanuatu), 2006. **Aims** Assist Pacific museums, cultural centres and peoples to preserve Pacific Island heritage. **Structure** General Assembly (annual); Executive Board; Subcommittees (3); Secretariat, headed by Secretary-General. **Languages** English, French. **Staff** 1.00 FTE, paid; 1.00 FTE, voluntary. **Finance** Sponsorships; grants; donations. Supported by companies, museums, national and international organizations. Sources include: *Australian Aid (inactive)*; ICCROM; ICOM; *New Zealand Ministry of Foreign Affairs and Trade – New Zealand Aid Programme*; *Pacific Community (SPC, #17942)*; *UNESCO Office for the Pacific States (#20315)*; *World Heritage Centre (WHC, #21566)*. **Activities** Training/education; projects/programmes. **Publications** *PIMA Newsletter* (4 a year). Electronic bulletin (occasional).

Members Institutional; Individual; Associate. Members in 24 countries and territories:
Australia, Cook Is, Fiji, Guam, Hawaii, Kiribati, Marshall Is, Micronesia FS, Nauru, New Caledonia, New Zealand, Niue, Norfolk Is, Northern Mariana Is, Palau, Papua New Guinea, Polynesia Fr, Rapanui/Easter Is, Samoa, Samoa USA, Solomon Is, Tonga, Tuvalu, Vanuatu.

NGO Relations Affiliated member of: *International Council of Museums (ICOM, #13051)*. [2020/XD6969/**D**]

- ♦ Pacific Islands Applied Geoscience Commission (inactive)
- ♦ Pacific Islands Association of Chambers of Commerce (inactive)
- ♦ Pacific Islands Association of Libraries and Archives / see Pacific Islands Association of Libraries, Archives, and Museums (#17960)

♦ Pacific Islands Association of Libraries, Archives, and Museums (PIALA) 17960

Pres PO Box 501092, Saipan MP 96950, USA. T. +16702357316. Fax +16702357550. E-mail: piala.org@gmail.com.

URL: http://piala-pacific.wix.com/piala-pacific/

History Founded 1991, as *Pacific Islands Association of Libraries and Archives*. **Aims** Enhance the quality of leadership in order to support and strengthen libraries, archives, and museums across the Pacific Islands. **Structure** Executive Board. **Languages** English. **Staff** Voluntary. **Finance** Members' dues. **Activities** Knowledge management/information dissemination; events/meetings. **Events** *Annual Conference* Barrigada (Guam) 2019, *Annual Conference* Kosrae (Micronesia FS) 2018, *Annual Conference* Pohnpei (Micronesia FS) 2017, *Annual Conference* Yap (Micronesia FS) 2016, *Annual Conference* Majuro (Marshall Is) 2015. **Publications** *Union List of Serials in Libraries in Guam and Micronesia* (every 2 years); *PIALA Newsletter* (1-2 a year). Conference proceedings.

Members Institutions (35) in 14 countries:
Australia, Fiji, Japan, Kiribati, Marshall Is, Micronesia FS, Nauru, New Zealand, Palau, Papua New Guinea, Philippines, Samoa, Singapore, USA.

Individuals (80) in 27 countries:
Australia, Canada, Fiji, Finland, France, Jamaica, Japan, Kiribati, Malaysia, Marshall Is, Micronesia FS, Nauru, Netherlands, New Zealand, Palau, Papua New Guinea, Philippines, Samoa, Singapore, Solomon Is, Sweden, Thailand, Tokelau, Tonga, Tuvalu, USA, Vanuatu.

NGO Relations Member of: *International Federation of Library Associations and Institutions (IFLA, #13470)*. [2022/XD3660/**D**]

- ♦ Pacific Islands Association of NGOs / see Pacific Islands Association of Non-Governmental Organizations (#17961)

♦ Pacific Islands Association of Non-Governmental Organizations (PIANGO) 17961

Association des ONGs des Iles du Pacifique

Exec Dir PO Box 17780, Suva, Fiji. T. +6793300060. E-mail: info@piango.org.

URL: http://www.piango.org/

History 1986. Founded at a conference of *Counterpart International (FSP)*, which acts as sponsoring agency. First Council held Aug 1991, Pago Pago (Samoa USA). Former names and other names: *Pacific Islands Association of NGOs* – alias. **Aims** Foster a strong and effective NGO and civil society sector for a just and peaceful Pacific Community. **Structure** Council; Board; Secretariat. **Languages** English, French. **Staff** 9.00 FTE, paid. **Finance** Sources: international organizations; sponsorship. Supported by: *Bread for the World Institute (BFW Institute)*; *CSO Partnership for Development Effectiveness (CPDE, #04976)*; *Forus (#09934)*; *Pacific Islands Forum Secretariat (#17970)*. **Activities** Events/meetings; standards/guidelines. **Events** *Meeting* Vanuatu 1999. **Publications** *e-Update* (12 a year); *PIANGO Link* (4 a year) – newsletter. Annual Report. Strategic Plan.

Members National Liaison Units (NLUs) grouping NGOs in 23 countries and territories:
Australia, Cook Is, Fiji, Guam, Kiribati, Marshall Is, Micronesia FS, Nauru, New Caledonia, New Zealand, Niue, Northern Mariana Is, Palau, Papua New Guinea, Polynesia Fr, Samoa, Samoa USA, Solomon Is, Tonga, Tuvalu, Vanuatu, West Papua.

Interim members:
Wallis-Futuna.

Observers in 3 countries:
Hawaii, Timor-Leste, Tokelau.

Consultative Status Consultative status granted from: *ECOSOC (#05331)* (Special). **IGO Relations** Member of (1): *Pacific Islands Development Forum (PIDF, #17967)*. Strategic relations with sponsoring agencies and: *Pacific Islands Forum Secretariat (#17970)*. **NGO Relations** Member of (3): *CSO Partnership for Development Effectiveness (CPDE, #04976)*; *Forus (#09934)*; *The Reality Of Aid (ROA, #18626)*. Part of: *Pacific Islands Regional Non-governmental Organizations (PRNGO, #17978)*. [2021.07.02/XD3083/**D**]

♦ Pacific Islands, Australia and New Zealand Electoral Administrators Network (PIANZEA) 17962

Secretariat Australian Electoral Commission, Canberra ACT 2601, Australia. E-mail: pianzea.secretariat@aec.gov.au.

URL: https://www.pianzea.org/

History 10 Oct 1997, Korolevu (Fiji). At founding meeting several Pacific countries came together to sign the Warwick Declaration which continued and maintained in the Pacific spirit this close association of Pacific electoral administrators. The declaration was initially supported by 15 countries and provides for networking, information sharing and mutual assistance. Former names and other names: *South Pacific Electoral Administrators Conference* – former; *South Pacific Electoral Administrators Network* – former. **Aims** Maintain, in the Pacific spirit, a close association of Pacific electoral administrators within an established networking arrangement to facilitate and encourage the free flow of information among member countries and to provide assistance where possible; support members by providing the information and resources needed to improve electoral administration within their constituencies; encourage continuous improvement and provision of technical assistance among members. **Structure** Secretariat is provided by the Australian Electoral Commission, with regular meetings of an advisory group comprised of representatives from member states. **Languages** English. **Staff** Support provided by the Australian Electoral Commission through the Secretariat. **Finance** Sources: government support. Funded by: Australian Department of Foreign Affairs and Trade. **Members** Electoral administrations in the Pacific region. Membership countries not specified. [2021/XF5709/**F**]

- ♦ Pacific Islands Broadcasting Association (inactive)
- ♦ Pacific Islands Business Network (internationally oriented national body)
- ♦ Pacific Islands Centre for Public Administration (unconfirmed)

♦ Pacific Islands Chapter (PICISOC) 17963

Contact address not obtained. E-mail: info@picisoc.org.

URL: http://www.picisoc.org/

History Set up 1999, during IT-PacNet. A chapter of *Internet Society (ISOC, #15952)*. **Aims** Provide impartial advise to governments and the public on *Internet*-related matters that are relevant to Pacific Island people. **Structure** General Assembly; Board. **Activities** Events/meetings. **Events** *PacINET : INET Pacific Regional Conference* Rarotonga Is (Cook Is) 2014, *PacINET : INET Pacific Regional Conference* Nuku'alofa (Tonga) 2013, *PacINET : INET Pacific Regional Conference* Suva (Fiji) 2012, *PacINET : INET Pacific Regional Conference* Port Vila (Vanuatu) 2010.

Members Full in 22 countries and territories:
Cook Is, Fiji, Guam, Kiribati, Marshall Is, Micronesia FS, Nauru, New Caledonia, New Zealand, Niue, Northern Mariana Is, Palau, Pitcairn, Polynesia Fr, Samoa, Samoa USA, Solomon Is, Tokelau, Tonga, Tuvalu, Vanuatu, Wallis-Futuna.

IGO Relations *Council of Regional Organisations of the Pacific (CROP, #04914)*. [2021/XM6975/**E**]

♦ Pacific Islands Chiefs of Police (PICP) 17964

Exec Dir 180 Molesworth Street, PO Box 3017, Wellington 6140, New Zealand. T. +6444707346. E-mail: picp.secretariat@police.govt.nz.

URL: http://www.picp.co.nz/

History 1970, Suva (Fiji). Former names and other names: *South Pacific Chiefs of Police Conference (SPCPC)* – former. **Aims** Work towards safe and secure communities for all Pacific Island countries. **Structure** Rotating Chair; Permanent Secretariat in Wellington (New Zealand). Includes: *PICP Women Advisory Network (WAN)*, set up 2003. **Languages** English, French. **Staff** 5.00 FTE, paid. **Finance** Supported by: *New Zealand Ministry of Foreign Affairs and Trade – New Zealand Aid Programme*; New Zealand Police; Australian Federal Police. **Activities** Awareness raising; knowledge management/information dissemination; networking/liaising; training/education. **Events** *Annual Conference* Nadi (Fiji) 2021, *Annual Conference* Nadi (Fiji) 2020, *Annual Conference* Pago Pago (Samoa USA) 2019, *Annual Conference* Nauru 2018, *Annual Conference* Tamuning (Guam) 2017. **Publications** Books of notes.

Members Full in 22 countries and territories:
Australia, Cook Is, Fiji, Guatemala, Kiribati, Marshall Is, Micronesia FS, Nauru, New Caledonia, New Zealand, Niue, Northern Mariana Is, Palau, Papua New Guinea, Polynesia Fr, Samoa, Samoa USA, Solomon Is, Tokelau, Tonga, Tuvalu, Vanuatu.
[2022.11.07/XF6686/**F**]

♦ Pacific Islands Climate Action Network (PICAN) 17965

Coordinator address not obtained.

URL: http://pacificclimateactionnetwork.wordpress.com/

History Regional network of *Climate Action Network (CAN, #03999)*. Registered in accordance with the laws of Tuvalu. **Aims** Unite civil society under a common voice to increase the influence and impact of their advocacy demands on Pacific island governments, leading governments to respond with more powerful and ambitious policies and action at the national and regional level. **Structure** Board. [2016/XM5332/**E**]

- ♦ Pacific Islands Conference of Leaders / see Standing Committee of the Pacific Islands Conference of Leaders (#19957)
- ♦ Pacific Islands Council for the Blind (no recent information)
- ♦ Pacific Islands Development Association / see Foundation of the Peoples of the South Pacific International (#09968)

♦ Pacific Islands Development Bank (PIDB) 17966

Pres Nanbo Guahan Bldg, 250 Route 4, Ste 205, Hagatna GU GU 96910, USA. T. +6714770047. Fax +6714770067.

URL: http://www.pacificidb.com/

History 5 Jul 1989. **Aims** Lend funds raised within and outside the Micronesian region to borrowers in member governments; attract outside investment to the region; promote commercial and economic development cooperation among member governments. **Structure** Board of Governors of 14 members; Board of Directors of 7 members; President/CEO; corporate office in Guam. **Staff** 2.00 FTE, paid. **Finance** Equity capital contributions from shareholder governments; soft loan from US Rural Development IRP programme; external sources. Budget (annual): US$ 267,000. **Activities** Lending programme; collaboration. **Events** *Annual Meeting* Chuuk (Micronesia FS) 2004, *Annual Meeting* Chuuk (Micronesia FS) 1999.

Members Full in 4 countries and territories:
Guam, Micronesia FS, Northern Mariana Is, Palau.

NGO Relations Special member of: *Association of Development Financing Institutions in the Pacific (ADFIP, #02473)*. [2014/XF4931/**F**]

♦ Pacific Islands Development Forum (PIDF) 17967

SG 56 Domain Road, PO Box 2050 – Government Buildings, Suva, Fiji. T. +6793311518 – +6793311525. Fax +6793311572. E-mail: secretariat@pidf.int.

URL: http://www.pidf.int/

History 23 Aug 2012, Nadi (Fiji). **Aims** Enable green/blue Pacific economies through inclusive strategies, multi-stakeholder governance and genuine partnerships. **Structure** Conference (every 2 years); Leaders' Summit; Members' Representative Council. National/Local Sustainable Development Boards. Secretariat. **Events** *Conference* Nadi (Fiji) 2019.

Members Governments (12):
Fiji, Kiribati, Marshall Is, Micronesia FS, Nauru, Palau, Solomon Is, Timor-Leste, Tokelau, Tonga, Tuvalu, Vanuatu.

Pacific Islands Association of Non-Governmental Organizations (PIANGO, #17961); *Pacific Islands Private Sector Organisation (PIPSO, #17977)*.

IGO Relations Observer status with (1): *United Nations (UN, #20515)* (General Assembly).
[2020/AA1017/**F***]

- ♦ Pacific Islands Development Program (see: #05263)
- ♦ Pacific Islands Forests and Trees Support Programme (inactive)

♦ Pacific Islands Forum 17968

Forum des Iles du Pacifique

SG Ratu Sukuna Road, Suva, Fiji. T. +6793312600. E-mail: info@forumsec.org.

URL: http://www.forumsec.org/

History 5 Aug 1971, Wellington (New Zealand), at first meeting, as *South Pacific Forum*, a gathering of heads of government of independent and self-governing states in the South Pacific developing a collective response to regional issues. First meeting led to a meeting of senior officials, Nov 1971, Wellington, under the title *Committee on South Pacific Trade*, which recommended the creation of a permanent Bureau to deal with trade and economic matters. This was approved at the 2nd meeting of the Forum, 1972, as 'Trade Bureau', which later became the *'South Pacific Bureau for Economic Co-operation (SPEC)'*. In 1988 this became *'South Pacific Forum Secretariat (SPFS)'*, now *Pacific Islands Forum Secretariat (#17970)*. The annual gathering of Leaders continued to be known as 'South Pacific Forum' until Oct 2000, when current title was adopted. In 2005, Leaders opened a new *'Forum Agreement'* for signature, formally establishing the Forum as an intergovernmental organization under international law. The previous legal definition of the Forum only applied to the Secretariat; the new agreement relates to the Forum's structure, purpose and functions, consistent with the Pacific Plan adopted by Leaders. **Aims** Provide an opportunity for heads of *government* to come together annually to discuss common concerns and agree on regional responses to assist national and regional priorities. **Structure** Annual Meeting of Leaders chaired on rotating basis by head of host government. Forum Officials Committee (FOC), comprising senior representatives from all member governments, acts as governing body and decides the budget and work programmes for the Forum Secretariat. **Languages** English. **Staff** 80.00 FTE, paid. **Finance** Secretariat Regular Budget (RB) funded by member governments' annual assessed contributions: Fiji $ 4.8 million in 2005. Extra Budget for the Secretariat's annual regional work programme: Fiji $ 22.2 million in 2005. **Activities** Current focus is to assist with implementation of the *Pacific Plan* to deepen regional cooperation and integration. The Plan also seeks to explore where the region might gain the most by sharing resources and aligning policies. **Events** *Annual Forum* Tuvalu 2019, *Senior Officials Meeting* Seoul (Korea Rep) 2018, *Annual Forum* Yaren (Nauru) 2018, *Annual Forum* Port Moresby (Papua New Guinea) 2015, *Annual Forum* Koror (Palau) 2014. **Publications** *Trade Forum* (6 a year); *Forum Review* (4 a year) – newsletter; *Trends and Development* (3 a year); *Forum Communique* (annual). *Directory of Aid Agencies*;

Foreign Investment Climate in South Pacific Forum Island Countries; Profile of Forum Island Countries; South Pacific Organization Coordinating Committee Handbook; South Pacific Trade Directory; Sparteca Handbook. Reports; handicraft booklets.
Members Governments of 16 countries and territories:
Australia, Cook Is, Fiji, Kiribati, Marshall Is, Micronesia FS, Nauru, New Zealand, Niue, Palau, Papua New Guinea, Samoa, Solomon Is, Tonga, Tuvalu, Vanuatu.
Observers (" Special Observer) in 4 countries and territories:
New Caledonia, Polynesia Fr, Timor-Leste (*), Tokelau.
IGO Relations Observer Status at: General Assembly of *United Nations (UN, #20515).* Observer member of: *Asia-Pacific Economic Cooperation (APEC, #01887).* Participates in the activities of: *ECOSOC (#05331).* Forum Secretary General is permanent Chair of 10 member *Council of Regional Organisations of the Pacific (CROP, #04914)*, through which the Forum links with: Fiji School of Medicine (FSchM); *Pacific Islands Development Program (PIDP, see: #05263); Pacific Islands Forum Fisheries Agency (FFA, #17969); Pacific Community (SPC, #17942); Secretariat of the Pacific Regional Environment Programme (SPREP, #19205); Pacific Tourism Organization (SPTO, #18008); University of the South Pacific (USP, #20703).*
Affiliated with:
- *Asian Development Bank (ADB, #01422);*
- *Commonwealth Fund for Technical Cooperation (CFTC, #04331);*
- *Commonwealth Secretariat (#04362);*
- *European Commission (EC, #06633);*
- *International Bank for Reconstruction and Development (IBRD, #12317);*
- *International Civil Aviation Organization (ICAO, #12581);*
- *International Monetary Fund (IMF, #14180);*
- *International Telecommunication Union (ITU, #15673);*
- *United Nations Economic and Social Commission for Asia and the Pacific (ESCAP, #20557).*

NGO Relations Encourages regional coordination of telecommunication business issues is being encouraged through: *Pacific Islands Telecommunications Association (PITA, #17979).* Member of: *Pacific Islands GOOS (PI-GOOS, #17971).* [2020/XE5377/**F***]

♦ Pacific Islands Forum Fisheries Agency (FFA) 17969

Exec Officer Barbara Hanchard, PO Box 629, Honiara, Guadalcanal, Solomon Is. T. +67721124. Fax +67723995. E-mail: penny.mautautia@ffa.int.
Street Address No1 FFA Road, West Kola'a Ridge, Honiara, Guadalcanal, Solomon Is.
URL: http://www.ffa.int/
History Aug 1977, Port Moresby (Papua New Guinea), by *Pacific Islands Forum (#17968).* Became operational Jan 1979, on signature of a convention reflecting common concern on matters of conservation and of optimum use and sovereign rights over living marine resources. Also referred to as *South Pacific Forum Fisheries Agency* and as *Forum Fisheries Agency.* **Aims** Promote and coordinate cooperation and mutual assistance among members of the South Pacific Forum in the matter of fishery policies and fishing limits; secure the maximum benefits from the living *marine resources* of the region for its peoples, particularly of member countries. **Structure** FFA functions as a consultative and advisory body and takes its direction from the Forum Fisheries Committee (FFC), which meets once a year and is composed of representatives from all FFA member countries. FFC's decisions are subsequently reviewed by SPF. **Staff** 47.00 FTE, paid. **Finance** General Fund mainly comprises contributions from member countries. Trust Fund consists of extra-budgetary funding provided by bilateral and international donors (about 85% of the overall budget). **Activities** FFA Work Programme is organized into 5 programmes: Corporate Services; Economics and Marketing; Legal; Information and Technology; Monitoring; Control and Surveillance. Multilateral treaty on fisheries with the United States concluded and signed 2 Apr 1987, Port Moresby (Papua New Guinea); renewed 1993. Also developed *Niue Treaty on Cooperation in Fisheries Surveillance and Law Enforcement in the South Pacific Region* for reciprocal and joint surveillance and enforcement in the region (opened for signature 1992). **Events** *North Pacific Fisheries Commission Meeting* Tokyo (Japan) 2019, *Meeting* Tokyo (Japan) 2007, *Meeting / Annual Meeting of the FFC* Australia 2000, *Meeting* Honolulu, HI (USA) 1999, *Meeting / Special Meeting of the FFC* Nouméa (New Caledonia) 1999. **Publications** *FFA News Digest.* Annual report. Annual work programmes. Reports.
Members Governments of 17 countries and territories:
Australia, Cook Is, Fiji, Kiribati, Marshall Is, Micronesia FS, Nauru, New Zealand, Niue, Palau, Papua New Guinea, Samoa, Solomon Is, Tokelau, Tonga, Tuvalu, Vanuatu.
IGO Relations Relationship agreement with: *FAO (#09260).* Observer member of: *Western and Central Pacific Fisheries Commission (WCPFC, #20912).* Member of: *Council of Regional Organisations of the Pacific (CROP, #04914); Pacific Islands Law Officers' Network (PILON, #17972).* Under Lomé Conventions, links with: *Standing Committee of the Pacific Islands Conference of Leaders (#19957).* **NGO Relations** Member of: *Pacific Islands GOOS (PI-GOOS, #17971).* Participates in: *Global Partnership for Oceans (GPO, #10537).* [2014/XF9594/**F***]

♦ Pacific Islands Forum Secretariat 17970

SG Forum Secretariat, Private Mail Bag, Suva, Fiji. T. +6793312600. Fax +6793220230. E-mail: media@forumsec.org – info@forumsec.org.
URL: https://www.forumsec.org/
History Sep 1972, Suva (Fiji), at 3rd Meeting of *Pacific Islands Forum (#17968)*, then known as *'Trade Bureau'*, on the recommendations of the Forum's *Committee on South Pacific Trade.* Formal agreement signed during 4th Forum Meeting, 17 Apr 1973, Apia (Samoa). Fiji, as country of Headquarters, is depository of the Agreement. Absorbed *Pacific Islands' Producers Association (PIPA, inactive)*, 1973-1974. Subsequently became *South Pacific Bureau for Economic Co-operation (SPEC) – Bureau de coopération économique du Pacifique Sud (BCEPS).* Current agreement signed 14 Jul 1980, Tarawa (Kiribati). Name changed to *South Pacific Forum Secretariat (SPFS) – Secrétariat du Forum du Pacifique du Sud* at 19th Meeting of the South Pacific Forum, 1988, Nuku'alofa (Tonga), ratification of the Agreement formalizing the name change completed by Member Governments, 23 Apr 1993. Name subsequently changed to listed title. Also referred to as *Forum Secretariat – Secrétariat du Forum.* **Aims** Encourage and promote *regional cooperation* among members; facilitate continuing cooperation and consultation among members through *trade, investments, development* and related areas; act as aid coordinating agency for regional projects; promote collaboration between relatively undeveloped island countries and more industrialized countries; further the establishment of a *free trade* area in the South Pacific region. **Structure** Official Committee as governing body. Secretariat, headed by Secretary General and one Deputy Secretary General. Divisions (4): Trade and Investment; Political and International Affairs; Development and Economic Policy; Corporate Services. **Languages** English. **Staff** 66.00 FTE, paid. **Activities** Politics/policy/regulatory; events/meetings; financial and/or material support. Management of treaties and agreements: *South Pacific Regional Trade and Economic Cooperation Agreement (SPARTECA, 1980)* – administered through *Committee on Regional Economic Issues and Trade (CREIT); Niue Treaty on Cooperation in Fisheries Surveillance and Law Enforcement in the South Pacific Region.* **Events** *Forum parliamentary assembly* Rarotonga Is (Cook Is) 2006, *Meeting on implementation and regional strategy on HIV/AIDS* 2005, *Meeting* 2005, *Tourism partnership meeting* Nadi (Fiji) 2005, *Regional workshop on services* Suva (Fiji) 2005. **Publications** *Forum Secretariat News* (4 a year). *South Pacific Forum Series. Directory of Aid Agencies; Directory of South Pacific Forum Island Countries' Products; South Pacific Organizations Coordinating Committee (SPOCC); SPARTECA* – guide for Forum Island exports to Australia and New Zealand. Secretary General's Annual Report. Handicraft booklets for Member governments; Profiles of Forum Island Countries.
Members South Pacific Forum member countries and territories (16):
Australia, Cook Is, Fiji, Kiribati, Marshall Is, Micronesia FS, Nauru, New Zealand, Niue, Palau, Papua New Guinea, Samoa, Solomon Is, Tonga, Tuvalu, Vanuatu.
IGO Relations Set up, May 1979, Sydney (Australia), the *Pacific Islands Trade and Invest (#17980)*, in cooperation with Australian government. Relationship agreement with: *FAO (#09260).* Participates in the activities of: *UNCTAD (#20285).* Cooperates with: *UNEP (#20299); United Nations Economic and Social Commission for Asia and the Pacific (ESCAP, #20557).* Accredited by: *United Nations Framework Convention on Climate Change – Secretariat (UNFCCC, #20564).* Observer member of: *Western and Central Pacific Fisheries Commission (WCPFC, #20912).* Official observer of: *Pacific Islands Law Officers' Network (PILON, #17972).* Member of: *Asia/Pacific Group on Money Laundering (APG, #01921).* Instrumental in setting up: *South Pacific Maritime Development Programme (inactive).* Under Lomé Conventions, links with: *European Commission (EC, #06633).* Adheres to: *Global Partnership for Effective Development Co-operation (GPEDC, #10532).* Cooperation with: *Asia-Pacific Telecommunity (APT, #02064).* *Council of Regional Organisations of the Pacific (CROP, #04914)*, established in the late 1980's, helps minimise duplications, particularly in administration. Through SPOCC, links with:
- *Pacific Community (SPC, #17942);*
- *Pacific Islands Development Program (PIDP, see: #05263);*
- *Pacific Islands Forum Fisheries Agency (FFA, #17969);*
- *Secretariat of the Pacific Regional Environment Programme (SPREP, #19205);*
- *Pacific Tourism Organization (SPTO, #18008);*
- *University of the South Pacific (USP, #20703).*

NGO Relations Member of: *Effective Institutions Platform (EIP, #05384); Pacific Islands Telecommunications Association (PITA, #17979).* Associate member of: *Council for Security Cooperation in the Asia Pacific (CSCAP, #04919).* Participates in: *Global Island Partnership (GLISPA, #10436); Global Partnership for Oceans (GPO, #10537).* Library is member of: *International Federation of Library Associations and Institutions (IFLA, #13470).* Supports: *Pacific Parliamentary Assembly on Population and Development (PPAPD, #17987).* [2021/XE4630/**E***]

♦ Pacific Islands – Global Ocean Observing System / see Pacific Islands GOOS (#17971)

♦ Pacific Islands GOOS (PI-GOOS) 17971

Chair c/o SPREP, PO Box 240, Apia, Samoa. T. +68521929. Fax +68520231. E-mail: sperp@sprep.org.
URL: http://www.ioc-goos.org/
History 1998, Suva (Fiji), as *Pacific Global Ocean Observing System (PacificGOOS)* at the 'Pacific Regional GOOS Capacity Building Workshop', Suva. A regional initiative within *Global Ocean Observing System (GOOS, #10511).* Full title: *Pacific Islands – Global Ocean Observing System (PI-GOOS).* Also referred to as *PacificGOOS Regional Alliance.* Present name adopted, 2002. **Aims** Assist sustainable development in Pacific Island nations by facilitating the establishment and implementation of coastal and open ocean observing programmes, and helping to improve uptake and use of the data, information and products being generated. **Structure** Steering Committee. Secretariat based at the *'South Pacific Applied Geoscience Commission (SOPAC)'*, Suva (Fiji). **Activities** Communication and Outreach; Education; Marine data and information management; Support to marine observing programmes. **Publications** Workshop reports.
Members National governments and administrations of 23 countries and territories:
Australia, Cook Is, Fiji, Guam, Kiribati, Marshall Is, Micronesia FS, Nauru, New Caledonia, New Zealand, Niue, Northern Mariana Is, Palau, Papua New Guinea, Polynesia Fr, Samoa, Samoa USA, Solomon Is, Tokelau, Tonga, Tuvalu, Vanuatu, Wallis-Futuna.
Pacific regional organizations, including the following 8 organizations listed in this Yearbook:
International Ocean Institute (IOI, #14394) (Pacific Islands); *Pacific Community (SPC, #17942); Pacific Islands Forum (#17968); Pacific Islands Forum Fisheries Agency (FFA, #17969); Pacific Tourism Organization (SPTO, #18008); Secretariat of the Pacific Regional Environment Programme (SPREP, #19205); University of the South Pacific (USP, #20703).*
External national agencies and organizations, including the following 2 organizations listed in this Yearbook:
Commonwealth Scientific and Industrial Research Organization (CSIRO); Institut de recherche pour le développement (IRD).
IGO Relations Contacts with: *Intergovernmental Oceanographic Commission (IOC, #11496); Pacific Islands Forum Secretariat (#17970).* [2015/XF6249/y/**F**]

♦ Pacific Islands Law Officers' Meeting / see Pacific Islands Law Officers' Network (#17972)

♦ Pacific Islands Law Officers' Network (PILON) 17972

Secretariat PO Box 114, Apia, Samoa.
URL: http://www.pilonsec.org/
History 1982, as *Pacific Islands Law Officers' Meeting (PILOM).* Current title adopted at 25th meeting, Feb 2007, Kiribati. **Aims** Provide a network for senior law officers in the Pacific to identify and discuss key regional law and justice issues. **Structure** Executive Committee. Independent Secretariat. **Events** *Annual Meeting* Rarotonga Is (Cook Is) 2018, *Annual Meeting* Pohnpei (Micronesia FS) 2016, *Annual Meeting* Honiara (Solomon Is) 2015, *Annual Meeting* Tarawa (Kiribati) 2014, *Annual Meeting* Nuku'alofa (Tonga) 2013.
Members Countries and territories (16):
Australia, Cook Is, Fiji, Kiribati, Marshall Is, Micronesia FS, Nauru, New Zealand, Niue, Palau, Papua New Guinea, Samoa, Solomon Is, Tonga, Tuvalu, Vanuatu.
Official observers (10):
Commonwealth Secretariat (#04362); International Committee of the Red Cross (ICRC, #12799); Pacific Community (SPC, #17942); Pacific International Maritime Law Association (PIMLA, #17956); Pacific Islands Forum Fisheries Agency (FFA, #17969); Pacific Islands Forum Secretariat (#17970); Pacific Islands Legal Information Institute (PacLII); Secretariat of the Pacific Regional Environment Programme (SPREP, #19205); United Nations Office on Drugs and Crime (UNODC, #20596); University of the South Pacific (USP, #20703). [2014/XJ1672/y/**E***]

♦ Pacific Islands Legal Information Institute (internationally oriented national body)

♦ Pacific Islands Marine Resources Information System (PIMRIS) . . . 17973

Système d'information sur les ressources marines des îles du Pacifique (SIRMIP)
Coordinator School of Marine Studies, Lower Campus, Univ of the South Pacific, Closed Mail Bag, Suva, Fiji. T. +6793232934. Fax +6793231526. E-mail: pimris@usp.ac.fj.
URL: http://www.usp.ac.fj/index.php?id=pimris
History 1989, as a joint project of: *University of the South Pacific (USP, #20703)* (where the Coordination Unit is located); *Pacific Islands Applied Geoscience Commission (SOPAC, inactive); Pacific Community (SPC, #17942); Pacific Islands Forum Fisheries Agency (FFA, #17969); Secretariat of the Pacific Regional Environment Programme (SPREP, #19205).* **Aims** Use modern technology to coordinate, collect and disseminate information on fisheries and non-living marine resources in the tropical Pacific; serve information needs of government officers in the islands of the region. **Structure** Steering Committee; *'PIMRIS Coordination Unit'*; national focal points (such as government fisheries departments). **Staff** 2.00 FTE, paid. **Finance** Supported by the French Government (for SPC's component). **Activities** On request: provides current awareness services; responds to queries on specific topics; carries out literature searches on data bases; provides or assists in acquiring documents for national focal points; assists in library organization; provides training. **Publications** *PIMRIS Newsletter* (4 a year); *SPC Special Information Bulletin* (2 a year). **Information Services** *Bibliographic Database on Marine Resources and Specific to the Pacific Islands.*
Members Pacific islands states (21):
Cook Is, Fiji, Guam, Kiribati, Marshall Is, Micronesia FS, Nauru, New Caledonia, Niue, Northern Mariana Is, Palau, Papua New Guinea, Polynesia Fr, Samoa, Samoa USA, Solomon Is, Tokelau, Tonga, Tuvalu, Vanuatu, Wallis-Futuna. [2013/XF1294/**F***]

♦ Pacific Islands Maritime Association (PacMA) 17974

Sec c/o Transport Programme, Economic Development Div, Secretariat of the Pacific Community, Private Mail Bag, Suva, Fiji. T. +6793379328 – +6793370952. Fax +6793370146. E-mail: maritime@spc.int.
URL: http://www.spc.int/edd/
History 12 Apr 1996, Suva (Fiji), at inaugural meeting, as *Association of Pacific Islands Maritime Training Institutions and Maritime Authorities (APIMTIMA).* Current title adopted, May 2003. Since 2009, includes activities of *Pacific Women in Maritime Association (PacWIMA, #18011).* Registered in accordance with the law of Fiji. **Aims** Be a united voice for the maritime sector in the Pacific; serve as a focal point for discussion of partnerships that promote a safe, secure, clean and sustainable maritime sector; establish a network of skilled resource people willing to provide advice and support to the sector; promote cooperation between maritime training institutions, authorities and the maritime sector in implementation of international uniform standards throughout the region. **Structure** General Meeting (annual); Trustees (4); Executive Committee. Secretariat/ Registered Office in Suva (Fiji). **Languages** English, French. **Staff** None. Secretariat function provided by Secretariat of the Pacific Community. **Finance** Members' dues. Other source: New Zealand overseas aid. Secretariat budget covered by *Pacific Community (SPC, #17942).* **Activities** Guidance/assistance/consulting; politics/policy/regulatory; knowledge management/information dissemination. **Events** *Annual Meeting* Nadi (Fiji) 2012, *Annual Meeting* Nadi (Fiji) 2011, *Annual Meeting* Nadi (Fiji) 2010, *Meeting / Annual Meeting* Nadi (Fiji) 2008, *Meeting / Annual Meeting* Apia (Samoa) 2007. **Publications** *Pacific Maritime Watch* (4 a year) – newsletter. Annual Report. All publications are produced by Secretariat of the Pacific Community.

Members Regular; Honorary; Associate; Observer. Maritime administrations, training institutions, maritime authorities, national shipowners associations and maritime legal personnel in 19 countries and territories:
Cook Is, Fiji, Guam, Kiribati, Marshall Is, Micronesia FS, Nauru, New Caledonia, Niue, Palau, Papua New Guinea, Polynesia Fr, Samoa, Solomon Is, Tokelau, Tonga, Tuvalu, Vanuatu, Wallis-Futuna. [2014.06.19/XD6543/**D**]

♦ Pacific Islands News Association (PINA) 17975

Secretariat 105 Amy Street, Toorak, Suva, Fiji. T. +6793315732. E-mail: pacnews1@pina.com.fj.
URL: http://www.pina.com.fj/
History 1974. Merged with *Pacific Islands Broadcasting Association (PIBA, inactive)*, Nov 2004. **Aims** Develop and maintain freedom of information and expression; raise professional standards of *journalism*; assist training in communication. **Structure** Executive Board. Permanent Secretariat, set up in 1992. **Languages** English. **Staff** 3.00 FTE, paid. **Finance** Members' dues. Subscription fees. **Activities** Events/meetings; training/education; awards/prizes/competitions; knowledge management/information dissemination. Participates in Pacific Media Assistance Scheme (PACMAS) project of *Australian Aid (inactive)*. **Events** *Pacific Media Summit* Solomon Is 2020, *Pacific Media Summit* Nuku'alofa (Tonga) 2018, *Pacific Media Summit* Koror (Palau) 2016, *Biennial Convention* Port Vila (Vanuatu) 2009, *Biennial Convention* Honiara (Solomon Is) 2007. **Publications** *Pacnews* (daily) – bulletin; *PINA Nius* – newsletter.
Members Full news media companies in the region and their representatives; Individual current and retired journalists; Associate outside the region; Supporter. Pacific Island members (" includes national affiliate) in 19 countries and territories:
Cook Is (*), Fiji (*), Kiribati, Marshall Is, Micronesia FS, Nauru, New Caledonia, Norfolk Is, Northern Mariana Is, Palau, Papua New Guinea, Polynesia Fr, Samoa (*), Samoa USA (*), Solomon Is (*), Tonga (*), Tuvalu, Vanuatu, Wallis-Futuna.
Consultative Status Consultative status granted from: *UNESCO (#20322)* (Consultative Status). **IGO Relations** Invited to sessions of Intergovernmental Council of: *International Programme for the Development of Communication (IPDC, #14651)*. Member of: *Asia-Pacific Institute for Broadcasting Development (AIBD, #01934)*. **NGO Relations** Member of: *Global Forum for Media Development (GFMD, #10375)*; *IFEX (#11100)*. Part of: *Pacific Islands Regional Non-governmental Organizations (PRNGO, #17978)*. [2022/XD0627/**D**]

♦ Pacific Islands Nutrition and Dietetic Association (inactive)

♦ Pacific Islands Political Studies Association (PIPSA) 17976

Secretariat SSGM, School of Intl/Pol/Strategic Studies, ANU College of Asia/Pacific, Australian Natl Univ, Canberra ACT 0200, Australia. E-mail: ssgm@anu.edu.au.
History 1987, Hawaii (USA). 1987, Hawaii, USA. **Aims** Foster study of politics and current affairs in the Pacific Islands; contribute to welfare of Pacific Islanders through teaching and research; encourage international interest in the region. **Structure** Management Committee. President. **Finance** Members' dues. **Activities** Produces lists of academics. Provides networking information and facilities. **Events** *Biennial Conference / Conference* Papeete (Polynesia Fr) 2014, *Conference* Apia (Samoa) 2011, *Biennial conference / Conference* Auckland (New Zealand) 2009, *Biennial conference / Conference* Port Vila (Vanuatu) 2007, *Conference* Suva (Fiji) 2005. **Publications** *PIPSA Newsletter*.
Members Individuals in 23 countries and territories:
Australia, Canada, Cook Is, Fiji, France, Guam, Indonesia, Japan, Kiribati, Marshall Is, Micronesia FS, Nauru, New Zealand, Northern Mariana Is, Palau, Papua New Guinea, Samoa, Solomon Is, Tonga, Trinidad-Tobago, Tuvalu, USA, Vanuatu.
NGO Relations Member of: *Global Islands Network (GIN, #10437)*. [2013/XD3267/v/**D**]

♦ Pacific Islands Primary Care Association (unconfirmed)

♦ Pacific Islands Private Sector Organisation (PIPSO) 17977

Programme Officer Compound, Ratu Sukuna Road, Suva, Fiji. T. +6797736301. Fax +6793305105. E-mail: info@pipso.org.fj.
URL: http://www.pipso.org.fj/
History 2007. **Aims** Be a pivotal partner in harnessing resources to bring about real growth and prosperity for the region. **Structure** Annual General Meeting; Board of Directors; Secretariat. **Events** *Pacific Women in Business Conference* Nadi (Fiji) 2012.
Members Full in 15 countries:
Cook Is, Fiji, Kiribati, Marshall Is, Micronesia FS, Nauru, New Caledonia, Niue, Palau, Papua New Guinea, Samoa, Solomon Is, Tonga, Tuvalu, Vanuatu.
IGO Relations Member of (1): *Pacific Islands Development Forum (PIDF, #17967)*. [2018/XJ6408/**D**]

♦ Pacific Islands' Producers Association (inactive)
♦ Pacific Islands Regional Association for Distance Education (no recent information)

♦ Pacific Islands Regional Non-governmental Organizations (PRNGO) 17978

Contact c/o PIANGO, PO Box 17780, Suva, Fiji. E-mail: deb.singh@yahoo.com.
URL: https://www.pasifikarising.org/prngo-alliance/
History Founded as an umbrella organization.
Members Organizations (14):
Council of Pacific Education (COPE); Fiji Women's Crisis Centre (FWCC); *Foundation of the Peoples of the South Pacific International (FSPI, #09968)*; *Greenpeace International (#10727)*; *Pacific Concerns Resource Centre (PCRC)*; *Pacific Conference of Churches (PCC, #17943)*; *Pacific Disability Forum (PDF, #17945)*; *Pacific Foundation for the Advancement of Women (PACFAW, #17950)*; *Pacific Islands Association of Non-Governmental Organizations (PIANGO, #17961)*; *Pacific Islands News Association (PINA, #17975)*; *Pacific Network on Globalization (PANG, #17984)*; *Pacific Youth Council (Youthlink, #18013)*; *South Pacific Oceania Council of Trade Unions*; *World Wide Fund for Nature (WWF, #21922)*. [2019/XJ0746/y/**E**]

♦ Pacific Islands Society of the United Kingdom and Ireland (internationally oriented national body)
♦ Pacific Islands Studies Program / see Center for Pacific Island Studies, Honolulu

♦ Pacific Islands Telecommunications Association (PITA) 17979

Manager PO Box 2027, Government Buildings, Suva, Fiji. T. +6793311638. Fax +6793308750. E-mail: pita@connect.com.fj.
Street Address 8th Floor Dominion House, Scott Street, Suva, Fiji.
URL: http://www.pita.org.fj/
History Jan 1997, Hawaii (USA), to replace the Regional Telecommunications Committee (RTC) operated by *Pacific Islands Forum Secretariat (#17970)*. **Aims** Represent the interests of small island nations in the Pacific region in the field of telecommunications; improve, promote, enhance, facilitate and provide telecommunications services in member and associate member countries. **Structure** General Meeting (annual). Officers: President; Vice-President; Executive Member; Manager. **Activities** Organizes: Annual General Meeting; Telecommunications Tradeshow; Conferences and seminars; January Members' Meeting. **Events** *Annual General Meeting* Nadi (Fiji) 2019, *Annual General Meeting* Tamuning (Guam) 2018, *Annual General Meeting* Rarotonga Is (Cook Is) 2017, *Annual General Meeting* Polynesia Fr 2016, *Annual General Meeting* Nuku'alofa (Tonga) 2015.
Members Full (37) – telecommunications entities; Associate (37) – suppliers of telecommunication equipment and/or services and regional and international organizations. Members (74) in 29 countries and territories:
Australia, Cook Is, Fiji, France, Guam, Hawaii, Israel, Kiribati, Marshall Is, Micronesia FS, Nauru, New Caledonia, New Zealand, Niue, Norfolk Is, Palau, Papua New Guinea, Polynesia Fr, Samoa, Samoa USA, Singapore, Solomon Is, Sri Lanka, Thailand, Tokelau, Tonga, Tuvalu, USA, Vanuatu.
Included in the above, 6 organizations listed in this Yearbook:
International Telecommunications Satellite Organization (ITSO, #15670); *International Telecommunication Union (ITU, #15673)*; *Pacific Telecommunications Council (PTC, #18007)*; Regional Office of South Pacific Forum Secretariat ; *SITA (#19299)* (Australian Office); South Pacific Forum Secretariat.
IGO Relations Close ties with ITU Pacific Regional Office, Thailand. Cooperation agreement with: *Commonwealth Telecommunications Organisation (CTO, #04365)*. **NGO Relations** Memorandum of Understanding with: Pacific Telecommunications Council. [2014/XD6849/y/**D**]

♦ Pacific Islands Trade and Invest 17980

Trade Commissioner PO Box 109-395, Newmarket, Auckland, New Zealand. T. +6495295165. E-mail: info@pacifictradeinvest.com.
URL: http://www.pacifictradeinvest.com/
History May 1979, Sydney (Australia), as *South Pacific Trade Commission (SPTC)*, as a trade commission within the framework of *Pacific Islands Forum (#17968)*, having been set up under the auspices of *Pacific Islands Forum Secretariat (#17970)*. Subsequent title: *Pacific Islands Trade and Investment Commission NZ (PITIC NZ)*. **Aims** Assist the Pacific Forum Island countries with marketing their products in New Zealand; encourage investment in the Pacific; promote Pacific Island tourism. **Structure** One of 4 offices of the Pacific Islands forum Secretariat, the other 3 located in Australia, Japan and China. [2011.01.13/XE0130/t/**E***]

♦ Pacific Islands Trade and Investment Commission NZ / see Pacific Islands Trade and Invest (#17980)
♦ Pacific Journalists Association (inactive)
♦ Pacific Law and Society Association (inactive)

♦ Pacific Lawyers Association 17981

Pres address not obtained.
History 2001, Auckland (New Zealand). **Aims** Provide better legal services for Pacific peoples; identify and respond to their legal needs; contribute to forming standards of legal practice; monitor legislation and promote law reform issues of particular relevance for Pacific peoples; promote the development and training of Pacific lawyers and law students. [2011/XD8713/**D**]

♦ Pacific Manuscripts Bureau (internationally oriented national body)

♦ Pacific Maritime Transport Alliance (PMTA) 17982

Secretariat Transport Programme, EDD – SPC Suva, Private Mail Bag, Suva, Fiji. T. +6793370733. Fax +6793370021. E-mail: pmta@spc.int.
URL: http://www.spc.int/edd/en/pmta/
History Founded 27 Nov 1978, Apia (Samoa), at 5th South Pacific Ports Conference, as *South Pacific Ports Association* (SPPA), when constitution was adopted. New constitution adopted and name changed to *Association of Pacific Ports (APP)* 14-17 Sep 1998, Suva (Fiji), at 25th Conference. Subsequently changed title to *Pacific Countries Ports Association (PCPA)*, 2007. Current title adopted 2010. **Aims** Promote regional cooperation, friendship and understanding among member ports and port users through mutual association, exchange of knowledge and dissemination of information useful to port administrations; promote measures to increase efficiency and safety and to facilitate harmonious development of ports in the region. **Structure** Conference (every 2 years); Executive Committee (meets annually); Sub-Committees (4): Environmental; Financial; Training; Engineering. Secretariat. **Languages** English. **Activities** Events/meetings. **Events** *Annual Conference* Apia (Samoa) 2019, *Annual Conference* Port Vila (Vanuatu) 2018, *Annual Conference* Auckland (New Zealand) 2017, *Annual Conference* Port Moresby (Papua New Guinea) 2015, *Annual Conference* Alofi (Niue) 2014. **Publications** *Pacific Maritime Watch Newsletter* (4 a year). Conference proceedings; sub-committee reports.
Members Regular port organizations, associations or other bodies (private, public or governmental) in 18 countries and territories:
Cook Is, Fiji, Kiribati, Marshall Is, Micronesia FS, Nauru, New Caledonia, Niue, Northern Mariana Is, Palau, Papua New Guinea, Polynesia Fr, Samoa, Samoa USA, Solomon Is, Tonga, Tuvalu, Vanuatu.
Associate members in 7 countries:
Australia, Canada, Fiji, New Zealand, Papua New Guinea, Samoa. [2015.01.19/XD0363/**D**]

♦ Pacific Missionary Aviation / see Pacific Mission Aviation
♦ Pacific Mission Aviation (internationally oriented national body)

♦ Pacific Neighbourhood Consortium (PNC) 17983

Secretariat PO Box 1-76 Nankang, Taipei 115, Taiwan. T. +886227898894. Fax +886227885259. E-mail: pnc@sinica.edu.tw.
URL: http://pnclink.org/
Aims Facilitate information exchange among institutions of *higher education* in the Pacific Rim through *computing* and *communications technology*. **Events** *Annual Conference* Singapore (Singapore) 2019, *Annual Conference* Taipei (Taiwan) 2014, *Annual Conference / Annual Meeting* Kyoto (Japan) 2013, *Annual Meeting* Berkeley, CA (USA) 2012, *Annual Meeting* Bangkok (Thailand) 2011. **Members** Membership countries not specified. [2014/XF7194/**F**]

♦ Pacific Network on Globalization (PANG) 17984

Contact 105 Army Street, 679, Suva, Fiji. T. +6793316722. E-mail: media@pang.org.fj.
URL: http://www.pang.org.fj/
History following a regional conference, May 2001, Fiji. **Aims** Promote *economic justice* in globalization with specific attention to: accountability and transparency in economic and trade policy processes; poverty eradication; equitable development and sustainable livelihoods; food security and environmental sustainability. **Members** Membership countries not specified. **NGO Relations** Part of: *Pacific Islands Regional Non-governmental Organizations (PRNGO, #17978)*. Partner of: *Pacific Conference of Churches (PCC, #17943)*. [2019/XJ0747/**F**]

♦ Pacific Nuclear Council (inactive)
♦ Pacific Ocean Remote Sensing Society / see International Pan Ocean Remote Sensing Conference Association (#14510)

♦ Pacific Optimization Research Activity Group (POP) 17985

Chair School of EECMS, Fac of Science and Engineering, Curtin Univ, Kent St, Perth WA 6102, Australia. T. +61892661115.
URL: http://bschool.nus.edu.sg/pop/
History Oct 2000, Hong Kong (Hong Kong). **Aims** Promote optimization research activities in the Pacific region. **Structure** Board; Working Committee. **Languages** English. **Staff** 400.00 FTE, voluntary. **Finance** No budget. **Activities** Events/meetings. **Events** *Pacific Optimization Conference* Kuala Lumpur (Malaysia) 2023, *Pacific Optimization Conference* Kuala Lumpur (Malaysia) 2021, *ICOTA : Triennial International Conference on Optimization* Hakodate (Japan) 2019, *Pacific Optimization Conference* Perth, WA (Australia) 2017, *ICOTA : Triennial International Conference on Optimization* Ulaanbaatar (Mongolia) 2016. **Publications** *Optimization Research Bridge* (4 a year) – newsletter; *Journal of Industrial and Management Optimization*; *Pacific Journal of Optimization*. *Numerical Algebra, Control and Optimization*. [2021.05.27/XE4708/**E**]

♦ Pacific Organic & Ethical Trade Community (POETCom) 17986

Coordinator c/o SPC, BP D5, 98848 Nouméa CEDEX, New Caledonia.
URL: http://www.organicpasifika.com/
Aims Grow the organic and ethical trade movement; contribute to a productive, resilient, sustainable and healthy Pacific Island region. **Structure** General Assembly; Advisory Board. Standards and Certification Committee. **Finance** Annual budget: 600,000 EUR (2019). **Activities** Capacity building; certification/accreditation; knowledge management/information dissemination; networking/liaising.
Members Full in 15 countries and territories:
Australia, Cook Is, Fiji, Kiribati, Marshall Is, New Caledonia, Niue, Palau, Papua New Guinea, Polynesia Fr, Samoa, Solomon Is, Tonga, Vanuatu, Wallis-Futuna.
IGO Relations Partner of (9): *European Union (EU, #08967)*; *FAO (#09260)*; *Global Environment Facility (GEF, #10346)* (Small Grants Scheme); *International Fund for Agricultural Development (IFAD, #13692)*; *Pacific Community (SPC, #17942)*; *Secretariat of the Pacific Regional Environment Programme (SPREP, #19205)*; *UNDP (#20292)*; *United States Agency for International Development (USAID)* (Climate Change); *University of the South Pacific (USP, #20703)*. **NGO Relations** Partner of (2): *Access Agriculture (#00047)*; *IFOAM – Organics International (IFOAM, #11105)*. [2020/AA1257/t/**D**]

♦ Pacific Parliamentary Assembly on Population and Development (PPAPD) 17987

Contact address not obtained. T. +687260178. Fax +687263818.
URL: http://www.spc.int/ppapd/index.php

History 1997, by and for Pacific Parliamentarians. **Aims** Improve the living standards, security and well-being of peoples in the Pacific by promoting practical actions by parliamentarians on population and development issues; promote good governance, transparency, accountability and sustainable development of the region's natural resources in relation to population and development; promote the interests of Pacific Island Countries in various world fora, focusing on the International Conference on Population and Development and Millennium Development Goals; encourage parliamentary and other activities aimed at facilitating population and development policies to improve the living standards, security and well-being of peoples in the Pacific. **Structure** General Assembly (at least every 2 years). Executive Committee (meets at least annually), comprising Chairperson, 3 Vice-Chairpersons and Treasurer. **Finance** Supported by: *Pacific Community (SPC, #17942)*; *United Nations Population Fund (UNFPA, #20612)*; *Pacific Islands Forum Secretariat (#17970)*; *UNDP (#20292)* – Pacific Centre; *Asian Forum of Parliamentarians on Population and Development (AFPPD, #01493)*. **Events** *Towards improved living standards and well-being of Pacific peoples* Honiara (Solomon Is) 2008.
Members in 17 countries and territories:
Australia, Cook Is, Fiji, Kiribati, Marshall Is, Micronesia FS, Nauru, New Zealand, Niue, Palau, Papua New Guinea, Samoa, Solomon Is, Tokelau, Tonga, Tuvalu, Vanuatu. [2008/XM1577/F]

♦ Pacific Path Institute (internationally oriented national body)
♦ Pacific Peacebuilding Initiatives / see Peacebuilders International

♦ Pacific Peace Working Group (PPWG) 17988

Contact 3780 Lake Road, Denman Is BC V0R 1T0, Canada. T. +12503350351. E-mail: pcdsres@telus.net.
URL: http://www.pacificpeace.net/

History Founded 1984, under the name *Pacific Campaign Against Sea-Launched Cruise Missiles*, as an outgrowth of *Nuclear-Free and Independent Pacific Movement (NFIP Movement, #17617)*. Name subsequently changed to *Pacific Campaign to Disarm the Seas*, and in 1992 to *Pacific Campaign for Disarmament and Security (PCDS)*, which served as a broad and diverse research, information and support network in the Asia-Pacific region dedicated to non-military solutions to conflict. Current name adopted, Jun 2007, when re-configured into a small, informal, decentralized working group. **Aims** Promote peace and *security* in the Asia-Pacific region; address the historical issues of concern of the PCDS. **Structure** Working Group. **Languages** English. **Staff** None. **Finance** Voluntary contributions. **Activities** Knowledge management/information dissemination.
Members Individuals in 6 countries:
Australia, Canada, Japan, Korea Rep, New Zealand, USA.
NGO Relations Member of: *International Campaign to Ban Landmines – Cluster Munition Coalition (ICBL-CMC, #12427)*. Special links with: *Peace Depot*. [2015.06.01/XF4211/v/F]

♦ Pacific Peoples' Partnership (internationally oriented national body)

♦ Pacific Plant Protection Organization (PPPO) 17989

Exec Sec c/o The Pacific Community, Land Resources Div, Private Mail Bag, Suva, Fiji. T. +6793370733. Fax +6793370021.
URL: https://www.ippc.int/en/external-cooperation/regional-plant-protection-organizations/pacificplantprotectionorganisation/

History Oct 1994. Founded by *FAO (#09260)*, under *International Plant Protection Convention, 1951 (IPPC, 1951)*. **Aims** Provide advice on phytosanitary measures in order to facilitate trade without jeopardizing the plant health status of the importing Members and countries and in particular: ensure that the views and concerns of Pacific members are adequately taken into account in the development and implementation of global phytosanitary measure; facilitate the flow of information among members and with other regional plant protection organizations; collaborate with the SPC Plant Protection Service on specific issues including pesticides and integrated pest management. **Structure** Executive Committee (elected on rotational basis every 3 years). Secretariat provided by the Land Resources Division of the *Pacific Community (SPC, #17942)*. **Languages** English, French. **Staff** Voluntary. **Finance** Supported by SPC. **Activities** Guidance/assistance/consulting; advocacy/lobbying/activism; knowledge management/information dissemination; capacity building. **Events** *Regional Plant Protection Organizations (RPPOs) Annual Technical Consultation* London (UK) 2022, *Regional Plant Protection Organizations (RPPOs) Annual Technical Consultation* Rome (Italy) 2021, *Regional Plant Protection Organizations (RPPOs) Annual Technical Consultation* Rome (Italy) 2020, *Regional Plant Protection Organizations (RPPOs) Annual Technical Consultation* Abuja (Nigeria) 2019, *Regional Plant Protection Organizations (RPPOs) Annual Technical Consultation* Lima (Peru) 2018. **Publications** *Pest Advisory* (12 a year); *Pacific Pest Info* (12 a year); *Farmer Advisory* – produced as needed; *Pest Alerts* – produced when there are incursions.
Members Pacific Island Countries and Territories (PICTS) (22) and Founding Members (4) in 26 countries and territories:
Australia, Cook Is, Fiji, France, Guam, Kiribati, Marshall Is, Micronesia FS, Nauru, New Caledonia, New Zealand, Niue, Northern Mariana Is, Palau, Papua New Guinea, Pitcairn, Polynesia Fr, Samoa, Samoa USA, Solomon Is, Tokelau, Tonga, Tuvalu, USA, Vanuatu, Wallis-Futuna.
IGO Relations Serves as one of 10 Regional Plant Protection Organizations (RPPOs) of *International Plant Protection Convention, 1951 (IPPC, 1951)*. [2020.03.08/XD4777/D*]

♦ Pacific Polymer Federation (PPF) 17990

Pres NTU-MSE, Block N 4.1, 50 Nanyang Ave, Singapore 639798, Singapore.
URL: https://pacificpolymer.org/

History 1987. **Events** *Pacific Polymer Conference* Brisbane, QLD (Australia) 2022, *Pacific Polymer Conference* Brisbane, QLD (Australia) 2021, *Pacific Polymer Conference* Singapore (Singapore) 2019, *Pacific Polymer Conference* Kauai Is (USA) 2015, *Pacific Polymer Conference* Kaohsiung (Taiwan) 2013. [2019/XD7754/D]

♦ Pacific Power Association (PPA) 17991

Exec Dir Private Mail Bag, Suva, Fiji. T. +6793306022. Fax +6793302038. E-mail: ppa@ppa.org.fj.
URL: http://www.ppa.org.fj/

History Founded 1992. **Aims** Enhance the performance of power utilities in the region through a cooperative effort by maintaining a partnership among members and national and international development partners. **Structure** Board of Directors, comprising Executive Director, Chief Executive Officer, General Managers, plus Acting Chief Executive Officers elected from Active Members and a representative elected from Allied Members. **Languages** English. **Staff** 5.00 FTE, paid. **Finance** Subscription fees; conference fees; aid from international development partners. **Activities** Organizes: Annual Conference; workshops. **Events** *Annual Conference* Kolonia (Micronesia FS) 2020, *Annual Conference* Rarotonga Is (Cook Is) 2019, *Annual Conference* Koror (Palau) 2018, *Annual Conference* Apia (Samoa) 2017, *Annual Conference* Nuku'alofa (Tonga) 2016. **Publications** *Pacific Power Magazine* (4 a year).
Members Active members in 21 countries and territories:
Chuuk, Fiji, Guam, Kiribati, Marshall Is, Micronesia FS, Nauru, Niue, Northern Mariana Is, Palau, Papua New Guinea, Pohnpei, Polynesia Fr, Samoa, Samoa USA, Solomon Is, Tonga, Tuvalu, Vanuatu, Wallis-Futuna, Yap.
Allied members in 15 countries and territories:
Australia, China, Fiji, Germany, Guatemala, Japan, Micronesia FS, New Caledonia, New Zealand, Philippines, Pohnpei, Singapore, South Africa, USA, Vanuatu.
IGO Relations Member of: *Council of Regional Organisations of the Pacific (CROP, #04914)*. [2018/XD7535/D]

♦ Pacific Preschool Council / see Pacific Pre-School Council (#17992)

♦ Pacific Pre-School Council 17992

Contact PO Box 10334, Laucala Beach Estate, Suva, Fiji. T. +16793212488.

History 1980, Suva (Fiji). Also referred to as *Pacific Preschool Council*. **Aims** Promote the development of quality early childhood services in the region. **Events** *Conference* Samoa 1995, *Conference* Vanuatu 1990, *Conference* Tonga 1987, *Conference* Fiji 1985.
Members National organizations in 12 countries:
Cook Is, Fiji, Kiribati, Marshall Is, Nauru, Niue, Samoa, Solomon Is, Tokelau, Tonga, Tuvalu, Vanuatu.
IGO Relations Close cooperation with: *University of the South Pacific (USP, #20703)*. **NGO Relations** Member of: *World Forum Foundation (#21519)*. [2010/XM1646/E]

♦ Pacific Public Health Surveillance Network (PPHSN) 17993

Réseau océanien de surveillance de la santé publique (ROSSP)

Focal Point Coordinating Body Research/Evidence/Information Progr, SPC Public Health Div, SPC, BP D5, 98848 Nouméa, New Caledonia. T. +687262000. Fax +687263818. E-mail: focalpointpphsn-cb@spc.int.
URL: http://www.pphsn.net/

History Founded 1996, Nouméa (New Caledonia), under the auspices of *Pacific Community (SPC, #17942)* and *WHO (#20950)*. Previously also referred to as *PacSurv*. **Aims** Improve public health surveillance and response in a sustainable way in the Pacific Islands. **Structure** Coordinating Body. **Languages** English, French. **Finance** Supported by Allied members and aid donors. **Activities** Monitoring/evaluation; knowledge management/information dissemination; training/education; networking/liaising; research and development. **Events** *Regional LabNet/EpiNet Meeting* Nadi (Fiji) 2015, *General Assembly* Stockholm (Sweden) 2009. **Publications** *Inform ACTION* – bulletin; *Surveillance and Communicable Disease Control*. *Pacific Outbreak Manual*; *Public Health Surveillance in the Pacific* – monograph. Guidelines; leaflet; meeting reports.
Members Core members: Ministries and Departments of Health in 22 Pacific Island countries and territories:
Cook Is, Fiji, Guam, Kiribati, Marshall Is, Micronesia FS, Nauru, New Caledonia, Niue, Northern Mariana Is, Palau, Papua New Guinea, Pitcairn, Polynesia Fr, Samoa, Samoa USA, Solomon Is, Tokelau, Tonga, Tuvalu, Vanuatu, Wallis-Futuna.
Allied members: regional training institutions, agencies, laboratories and other organizations or networks. Allied members include the following 6 organizations listed in this Yearbook:
Pacific Basin Medical Association (PBMA, #17939); *Pacific Community (SPC, #17942)*; *Pacific Island Health Officers Association (PIHOA, #17958)*; *UNICEF (#20332)*; *WHO (#20950)*. [2016.11.14/XF6559/y/F]

♦ Pacific Regional Branch of the International Council on Archives (see: #12996)
♦ Pacific Regional Environment Programme / see Secretariat of the Pacific Regional Environment Programme (#19205)

♦ Pacific Regional Science Conference Organization (PRSCO) 17994

Exec Sec c/o Dept of Architecture and Civil Engineering, Toyohashi Univ of Tech, 1-1 Tempaku, Toyohashi AICHI, 441-8580 Japan. T. +81532446963. Fax +81532446963.
URL: http://www.prsco.info/

History 1968, San Diego CA (USA), within *Regional Science Association International (RSAI, #18813)*. **Aims** Enhance and facilitate exchange of research information in the field of regional science among members; exchange this information in the Pacific Rim area. **Languages** English. **Staff** 1.00 FTE, voluntary. **Events** *Pacific Conference* Waikiki, HI (USA) 2020, *Summer Institutes* Bangkok (Thailand) 2019, *Biennial Meeting* Lima (Peru) 2018, *Biennial Conference* Tainan (Taiwan) 2017, *Biennial Meeting* Bangkok (Thailand) 2016.
Members International/regional/national organizations in 16 countries and territories:
Australia, Bangladesh, Canada, Chile, Colombia, Ecuador, India, Indonesia, Japan, Korea Rep, Malaysia, Mexico, New Zealand, Taiwan, Thailand, USA. [2020.03.11/XD7495/D]

♦ Pacific Regional Seminary (PRS) 17995

Rector Private Mail Bag, Suva, Fiji. T. +6793302224 – +6793032614. Fax +679303882. E-mail: prs@connect.com.fj.
URL: http://www.prs-fj.urbaniana.edu/

History Founded 1972, by *Conferentia Episcopalis Pacifici (CEPAC, #04659)*, as an inter-diocesan regional seminary, to which are affiliated colleges and religious congregations. Also referred to as *Pacific Regional Seminary of St Peter Chanel*. Presently affiliated to *Pontificia Universitas Urbaniana (PUU, #18454)*. Registered with Fiji Higher Education Commission as Theological School. **Aims** Provide for the spiritual, theological, pastoral and priestly formation of candidates for priesthood; provide priestly formation of candidates for the priesthood from the Pacific Islands. **Structure** Episcopal Commission; Senate. Departments (5); Affiliated Colleges (6). **Languages** English, Fijian, French. **Staff** 18.00 FTE, paid. **Finance** Student fees. Annual budget: about US$ 550,000. **Activities** Research/documentation; training/education; events/meetings. **Publications** *Annual Handbook*; *Ratio Institutionis*. Constitutions and Regulations of the Pacific Regional Seminary.
Members Membership covers 15 countries and territories:
Caroline Is, Cook Is, Fiji, Kiribati, Marshall Is, Micronesia FS, Nauru, New Caledonia, Polynesia Fr, Samoa, Samoa USA, Tahiti Is, Tonga, Vanuatu, Wallis-Futuna.
NGO Relations Member of: *South Pacific Association of Theological Schools (SPATS, #19882)*. Cooperates with: *Pacific Theological College (PTC)*. [2017.10.10/XF3826/F]

♦ Pacific Regional Seminary of St Peter Chanel / see Pacific Regional Seminary (#17995)

♦ Pacific Rim Applications and Grid Middleware Assembly (PRAGMA) 17996

Co-Chair SDSC-UCSD 0505, 9500 Gilman Dr, La Jolla CA 92093, USA.
URL: http://www.pragma-grid.net/

History 2002. **Aims** Establish sustained collaboration and advance the use of grid *technologies* in applications among a community of investigators working with leading institutions around the Pacific Rim. **Structure** Steering Committee of 18 members, headed by Chair. **Activities** Organizes workshops. Working Groups (4): Biosciences; Geosciences; Telescience; Resources and Data. **Events** *Workshop* Jeju (Korea Rep) 2019, *Workshop* Penang (Malaysia) 2018, *Workshop* Tokyo (Japan) 2018, *Workshop* Brisbane, QLD (Australia) 2017, *Workshop* Gainesville, FL (USA) 2017.
Members Institutions (34) in 15 countries and territories:
Australia, China, Hong Kong, India, Japan, Korea Rep, Malaysia, Mexico, New Zealand, Philippines, Singapore, Taiwan, Thailand, USA, Vietnam.
Included in the above, 2 institutes listed in this Yearbook:
Asia-Pacific Advanced Network (APAN, #01819); *Global Scientific Information and Computing Center (GSIC)*. [2018/XJ1324/F]

♦ Pacific Rim Association for Clinical Pharmacogenetics (no recent information)
♦ Pacific Rim Banknote Conference (meeting series)

♦ Pacific Rim College of Psychiatrists (PRCP) 17997

SG Dept of Neuropsychiatry, NTT Medical Ctr Tokyo, 5-9-22 Higashi-gotanda, Shinagawa-ku, Tokyo, 141-8625 Japan. T. +81334486508. Fax +81334486507. E-mail: info@prcp.org.
Pres Dept of Psychiatry, Fac of Medicine, Prince of Songkla Univ, Hat Yai, Songkhla, 90110, Thailand. E-mail: upichet@medicine.psu.ac.th.
URL: http://www.prcp.org/

History Founded 1980, Manila (Philippines). **Aims** Foster greater development of *mental health* services; support improvement of education and research in psychiatry through greater professional collaboration in the Asia-Pacific region. **Structure** Board of Directors; Secretariat. **Languages** English. **Activities** Events/meetings. **Events** *Biennial Scientific Meeting* Seoul (Korea Rep) 2021, *Biennial Scientific Meeting* Yangon (Myanmar) 2018, *Biennial Scientific Meeting* Kaohsiung (Taiwan) 2016, *Biennial Scientific Meeting* Vancouver, BC (Canada) 2014, *Biennial Scientific Meeting* Seoul (Korea Rep) 2012. **Publications** *Asia-Pacific Psychiatry* (4 a year) – journal.
Members Member; Member in Training; Fellow; Fellow Emeritus; Associate. Members (about 120) in 22 countries and territories:
Australia, Bangladesh, Canada, China, France, Hong Kong, India, Indonesia, Israel, Japan, Korea Rep, Malaysia, Myanmar, Nepal, New Zealand, Pakistan, Peru, Philippines, Singapore, Taiwan, Thailand, USA.
NGO Relations Member of: *World Psychiatric Association (WPA, #21741)*. [2017.01.13/XF6896/F]

♦ Pacific Rim Conference on Ceramic and Glass Technololgy (meeting series)
♦ Pacific Rim Consortium in Energy, Combustion, and the Environment (inactive)

♦ Pacific Rim Council on Urban Development (PRCUD) 17998

Exec Sec c/o USC Sol Price School of Public Policy, Univ of Southern California, Lewis Hall 312, Los Angeles CA 90089-0626, USA. T. +12138211037. Fax +12137401801. E-mail: prcud.secretariat@gmail.com.
URL: http://sites.google.com/site/prcudweb/

History Founded 1989, Los Angeles CA (USA), by a small group of professionals. **Aims** Enhance development of links among and better understanding of cities in the Pacific Rim region; encourage achievement of excellence in urban development, planning and management so as to improve their economic performance, quality of life and sustainability; provide an effective forum for professional global dialogue. **Structure** Council. Secretariat, headed by Executive Secretary. **Languages** English. **Staff** 0.50 FTE, paid; 1.50 FTE, voluntary. **Finance** Members' dues. **Activities** Events/meetings; awards/prizes/competitions. **Events** *Annual Forum* Bangkok (Thailand) 2013, *Annual Forum* Yeosu (Korea Rep) 2012, *Annual Forum* Palembang (Indonesia) 2011, *Annual Forum* Ho Chi Minh City (Vietnam) 2010, *Annual Forum* China 2009. **Publications** *PRCUD Report* (annual) – comprehensive assessment of annual professional visit; *PRCUD News Memos* (periodical). Membership directory.
Members City chapters (20) in 15 countries and territories:
Australia, Canada, Chile, China, Hong Kong, Indonesia, Japan, Korea Rep, Malaysia, Philippines, Singapore, Taiwan, Thailand, USA, Vietnam. [2016/XD4854/**D**]

♦ Pacific Rim Institute for Development and Education (internationally oriented national body)

♦ Pacific Rim International Conferences on Artificial Intelligence (PRICAI) 17999

Sec Natl Key Lab for Novel Software Technology, Nanjing Univ, Mailbox 419, 22 Hankou Rd, Nanjing, 210093 Jiangsu, China. T. +862583686268. Fax +862583866268.
Chair Inst for Integrated and Intelligent Systems, Griffith Univ, Nathan QLD 4111, Australia. T. +61737353757. Fax +61737354066.
URL: http://www.pricai.org/
History 1990, Japan. Current bylaws revised and approved 31 Aug 2010. **Aims** Create an artificial intelligence (AI) conference promoting collaborative exploitation of AI in the Pacific Rim nations. **Structure** Steering Committee. **Activities** Events/meetings; awards/prizes/competitions. **Events** *PRICAI : Pacific Rim International Conference on Artificial Intelligence* Yokohama (Japan) 2021, *PRICAI : Pacific Rim International Conference on Artificial Intelligence* Yokohama (Japan) 2020, *PRICAI : Pacific Rim International Conference on Artificial Intelligence* Cuvu (Fiji) 2019, *PRICAI : Pacific Rim International Conference on Artificial Intelligence* Nanjing (China) 2018, *PRICAI : Pacific Rim International Conference on Artificial Intelligence* Phuket (Thailand) 2016. [2015/XJ9450/c/**F**]

♦ Pacific Rim Park (PRP) 18000

Contact c/o Ilan-Lael Foundation, PO Box 1221, Julian CA 92036, USA. T. +17607653427.
URL: http://pacificrimpark.net/
History A program of Ilan-Lael Foundation. Also referred to as *Pacific Rim Park Project.* **Aims** Build friendship parks around the Pacific Rim. **Structure** Steering Committee. **Events** *Conference* Jeju (Korea Rep) 2018. [2018/XM8314/**F**]

♦ Pacific Rim Park Project / see Pacific Rim Park (#18000)

♦ Pacific Rim Real Estate Society (PRRES) 18001

Pres UTS City Campus, Bldg 6 Lvl 5, PO Box 123, Broadway Nedlands NSW 2007, Australia. Fax +61295148777.
URL: http://www.prres.net/
History 1993. **Aims** Provide a formal focus for property researchers, educators and practitioners in the Pacific-Rim region; encourage and facilitate property research and property education. **Structure** Board of Directors, including President, President Elect, Executive Director, Secretary and Treasurer. **Languages** English. **Staff** None. **Finance** Members' dues: Professional – Australian $ 110; Academic – Australian $ 110; Student – Australian $ 55. **Events** *Annual Conference* Canberra, ACT (Australia) 2020, *Annual Conference* Melbourne, VIC (Australia) 2019, *Annual Conference* Auckland (New Zealand) 2018, *Annual Conference* Sydney, NSW (Australia) 2017, *Annual Conference* Mooloolaba, QLD (Australia) 2016. **Publications** *Pacific Rim Property Research Journal (PRPRJ)* (4 a year); *PRRES Newsletter* (2 a year). Conference proceedings.
Members Individuals (150) in 10 countries and territories:
Australia, China, Fiji, Hong Kong, Indonesia, Korea Rep, Malaysia, New Zealand, Papua New Guinea, Singapore.
NGO Relations Member of: *International Real Estate Society (IRES, #14702).* Affiliated real estate societies: *African Real Estate Society (AfRES, #00428); 'American Real Estate Society'; Asian Real Estate Society (AsRES, #01680); European Real Estate Society (ERES, #08332); Latin American Real Estate Society (LARES, #16366).* [2015/XD7658/v/**D**]

♦ Pacific Rim Research Libraries Alliance (unconfirmed)
♦ Pacific Rim Society (no recent information)
♦ Pacific Rim Society for Fertility and Sterility / see Pacific Society for Reproductive Medicine (#18006)
♦ Pacific-Rim Symposium on Image and Video Technology (meeting series)

♦ Pacific Rim Vetiver Network (PRVN) 18002

Secretariat Office of the Royal Development Projects Board, 2012, Soi 36, Arun Amarin Road, Bang Yi Khan Subdistrict, Bang Phlat District, Bangkok, 10700, Thailand. T. +6624478500 ext 237. Fax +6624478543. E-mail: rdpb_vetiver@yahoo.com – foreign@rdpb.go.th.
URL: http://prvn.rdpb.go.th/
History 4 Feb 1966, Thailand. **Aims** Serve the countries of the Pacific Rim as the centre to collect, compile and disseminate information on the Vetiver System (VS). **Activities** Events/meetings; publishing activities; research/documentation; training/education.
Members National networks in 4 countries:
China, Philippines, Thailand, Vietnam.
Representatives in 16 countries and territories:
Australia, Brunei Darussalam, Cambodia, Cook Is, Fiji, Indonesia, Japan, Laos, Malaysia, New Caledonia, New Zealand, Papua New Guinea, Samoa, Taiwan, Tonga, Vanuatu. [2021.09.01/AA1330/**F**]

♦ Pacific Salmon Commission (internationally oriented national body)

♦ Pacific Science Association (PSA) 18003

Association scientifique du Pacifique – Asociación Cientifica del Pacifico
Exec Sec 1525 Bernice St, Honolulu HI 96817, USA. T. +18088484124. Fax +18088478252. E-mail: info@pacificscience.org.
Pres Research Ctr for Eco-Environmental Sciences, Chinese Academy of Sciences, 18 Shuangqing Rd, 100085 Beijing, China.
URL: http://www.pacificscience.org/
History 1920, Honolulu, HI (USA). Constitution and By-Laws adopted at 3rd Pan-Pacific Science Congress, 11 Nov 1926, Tokyo (Japan), and amended at subsequent Congresses and Inter-Congresses. Current revised statutes effective from June 2016. Former names and other names: *Wissenschaftliche Vereinigung des Pazifischen Ozeans* – former; *Tihookeanskaja Naucnaja Associacija* – former. **Aims** Facilitate interdisciplinary and international research and collaboration in the Asia-Pacific region, with a focus on key issues and problems in the region in order to engage science in the service of human needs and improve quality of life of the region's peoples and of the natural environment. **Structure** Pacific Science Council; Executive Board; Scientific Working Groups (11), including: *Pacific-Asia Biodiversity Transect Network (PABITRA, #17929)*; Permanent Secretariat. **Languages** English. **Staff** 1.50 FTE, voluntary. **Finance** Sources: members' dues. **Activities** Awards/prizes/competitions; events/meetings; publishing activities; research/documentation. **Events** *Quadrennial Congress* Shantou (China) 2021, *Quadrennial Congress* Shantou (China) 2020, *Quadrennial Congress* Taipei (Taiwan) 2016, *Human security in the Pacific* Suva (Fiji) 2013, *Quadrennial congress* Kuala Lumpur (Malaysia) 2011. **Publications** *Pacific Science.*
Members Adhering Organizations (membership by countries or appropriate areas within or bordering the Pacific Ocean or with special interests in the region, each represented by its principal scientific organization); Institutional Members (associate scientific societies and scientific institutions, including libraries); Corporate Members; Member Scientists. Members (about 600) in 32 countries and territories:
Australia, Chile, China, Cook Is, Fiji, France, Guam, Hong Kong, Indonesia, Japan, Kiribati, Korea Rep, Malaysia, Marshall Is, Nauru, New Zealand, Niue, Papua New Guinea, Philippines, Russia, Samoa, Singapore, Solomon Is, Taiwan, Thailand, Tokelau, Tonga, Tuvalu, USA, Vanuatu, Vietnam.
Consultative Status Consultative status granted from: *ECOSOC (#05331)* (Ros C). **NGO Relations** Member of: *International Science Council (ISC, #14796).* Special arrangements for cooperation with: *East-West Center (EWC, #05263); International Social Science Council (ISSC, inactive).* [2023.02.14/XD3044/**C**]

♦ Pacific Seabird Group (internationally oriented national body)
♦ Pacific Sexual and Gender Diversity Network (unconfirmed)

♦ Pacific Society of Anaesthetists 18004

Contact Dept of Anaesthesia, CWM Hospital, Box 115, Suva, Fiji. T. +6793313444. Fax +6793303232. E-mail: committeepsa@gmail.com.
History 1989. **Events** *Annual meeting* Apia (Samoa) 2007. **NGO Relations** Member of: *World Federation of Societies of Anaesthesiologists (WFSA, #21482).* [2018.06.26/XM2749/**D**]

♦ Pacific Society for Reproductive Health (PSRH) 18005

Acting Head of Secretariat 6 Claresholm Place, Mangere Bridge, Auckland 2022, New Zealand. T. +6421384451. E-mail: secretariat@psrh.org.nz – ropeti.gafa@psrh.org.nz.
Facebook: https://www.facebook.com/PSRHgroup/
History 1993. Founded following an educational meeting. Current title adopted 1997. Registration: Start date: 2008, New Zealand. **Aims** Encourage and contribute to the professional development of sexual, reproductive and neonatal health care professionals across the diversity of Pacific Island countries; advocate for the improvement of women's health in the Pacific. **Structure** Executive Committee, comprising President, Vice-President, Secretary-General, Honorary Secretary, Honorary Treasurer, Former President (ex-officio) and 3 members. **Events** *Meeting* Port Vila (Vanuatu) 2017, *Meeting* Auckland (New Zealand) 2009, *Meeting* Apia (Samoa) 2007, *Meeting* Nadi (Fiji) 2005, *Meeting* Nadi (Fiji) 2003. **Publications** *PSRH Newsletter.*
Members Full in 15 countries and territories:
Australia, Cook Is, Fiji, Kiribati, Micronesia FS, New Zealand, Niue, Palau, Papua New Guinea, Samoa, Samoa USA, Solomon Is, Tonga, Tuvalu, Vanuatu.
NGO Relations Member of: *Regional Network Supporting the HIV, Viral Hepatitis and Sexual Health Workforce in the Asia Pacific (Regional Network, #18802).* [2022/XJ3749/**D**]

♦ Pacific Society for Reproductive Medicine (PSRM) 18006

SG Dept Biomedical Science, CHA Univ, 198-1 Donggyo-dong, Pocheon GYEONGGI, Korea Rep. T. +82318817135. Fax +82318817959.
History 1996. Former names and other names: *Pacific Rim Society for Fertility and Sterility (PRSFS)* – former (1996 to 2013). **Events** *Congress* Sydney, NSW (Australia) 2023, *Congress* Sydney, NSW (Australia) 2022, *Congress* Bangkok (Thailand) 2019, *Congress* Osaka (Japan) 2017, *Congress* Seoul (Korea Rep) 2015. **Members** Membership countries not specified. **NGO Relations** *Asia-Pacific Initiative on Reproduction (ASPIRE, #01932).* [2022/XD9276/**D**]

♦ Pacific Telecommunications Council (PTC) 18007

Conseil des télécommunications du Pacifique – Consejo de Telecomunicaciones del Pacifico
CEO 914 Coolidge St, Honolulu HI 96826-3085, USA. T. +18089413789. Fax +18089444874. E-mail: info@ptc.org.
URL: http://www.ptc.org/
History 9 Jan 1980, Honolulu, HI (USA). Founded during 2nd Pacific Telecommunications Conference. Registration: USA, Hawaii. **Aims** Promote advancement of information and communication technologies (ICT) in the Pacific Rim. **Structure** Board of Governors; Standing and Ad hoc Committees. **Languages** Chinese, English, Japanese, Spanish. **Staff** 11.50 FTE, paid. **Finance** Members' dues. Other sources: conference fees; sponsorships. Annual budget: US$ 2,500,000. **Activities** Events/meetings; training/education. **Events** *Annual Conference* Honolulu, HI (USA) 2023, *Annual Conference* Honolulu, HI (USA) 2022, *Annual Conference* Honolulu, HI (USA) 2021, *Annual Conference* Honolulu, HI (USA) 2020, *Annual Conference* Honolulu, HI (USA) 2019. **Publications** *List of Non-Profit Organizations with Communication Interests in the Pacific Region* (1996); *Telecoms and the Travel Industry* (1991). Conference proceedings (annual). Annual proceedings on CD-Rom.
Members Individuals, corporations, government agencies and institutions in 40 countries and territories:
Australia, Bermuda, Brazil, Canada, China, Fiji, France, Germany, Guadeloupe, Hong Kong, India, Indonesia, Japan, Kiribati, Korea Rep, Macau, Malaysia, Marshall Is, Mexico, Micronesia FS, Mongolia, New Zealand, Niue, Palau, Papua New Guinea, Philippines, Qatar, Russia, Samoa USA, Singapore, Solomon Is, Sweden, Switzerland, Taiwan, Thailand, UK, United Arab Emirates, USA, Vanuatu, Vietnam.
NGO Relations Member of: *Pacific Islands Telecommunications Association (PITA, #17979).* [2022/XD8265/**D**]

♦ Pacific Theological College (internationally oriented national body)

♦ Pacific Tourism Organization (SPTO) 18008

Head Office Private Mail Bag, Suva, Fiji. T. +6793304177. Fax +6793301995. E-mail: tourism@spto.org.
Street Address Level 3, FNPF Place, 343-359 Victoria Parade, Suva, Fiji.
URL: http://www.spto.org/
History 1983. Established by national tourism organizations of 12 South Pacific Islands countries, a nongovernmental body within the framework of *Standing Committee of the Pacific Islands Conference of Leaders (#19957).* Became a regional intergovernmental organization in Aug 1989. Former names and other names: *Tourism Council of the South Pacific (TCSP)* – former; *South Pacific Tourism Organisation (SPTO)* – former. **Aims** Foster regional cooperation in development and promotion of tourism in the island nations of the South Pacific; strengthen resource capabilities in order to service more effectively the needs of the tourism industry of the region, both public and private sectors. **Structure** Council of Ministers (meets every 18 months); Board of Directors; Permanent Secretariat in Suva (Fiji), headed by Chief Executive and grouped into 4 Divisions (each headed by a Manager). **Languages** English. **Staff** 13.00 FTE, paid. **Finance** Sources: donations; members' dues. **Activities** Knowledge management/information dissemination; research and development. **Events** *Conference* Port Vila (Vanuatu) 2001, *South Pacific tourism conference* Polynesia Fr 1997, *Conference* Tahiti Is (Polynesia Fr) 1997, *Annual General Meeting* Suva (Fiji) 1989. **Publications** *TCSP Magazine* (4 a year). Annual report; promotional material; tourism sector views; tourism sector reviews; development plans; market research surveys; visitor surveys; statistical reports; hotel and catering training manuals; videos. **Information Services** *South Pacific Islands Computer Enquiries System (SPICE)* – includes TCSP Internet site.
Members Governments of 21 countries and territories:
China, Cook Is, Fiji, Kiribati, Marshall Is, Micronesia FS, Nauru, New Caledonia, Niue, Papua New Guinea, Polynesia Fr, Samoa, Samoa USA, Solomon Is, Timor-Leste, Tokelau, Tonga, Tuvalu, Vanuatu, Wallis-Futuna.
Rapa Nui.
IGO Relations Memorandum of Understanding with (1): *Secretariat of the Pacific Regional Environment Programme (SPREP, #19205)* (signed May 2001). Member of (1): *Council of Regional Organisations of the Pacific (CROP, #04914).* **NGO Relations** Member of (2): *Global Islands Network (GIN, #10437); Pacific Islands GOOS (PI-GOOS, #17971).* [2021.10.27/XD1008/**E***]

♦ Pacific Trade and Development Conference (PAFTAD) 18009

Secretariat Australian Natl Univ, Crawford Building 132, Lennox Crossing, Acton, Canberra ACT 2601, Australia. E-mail: paftad@gmail.com.
URL: http://paftad.org/
History 1968, Tokyo (Japan), at first conference. **Aims** Promote policy-oriented academic research and discussion of *Asia* Pacific *economic* issues; serve as an authoritative source of analysis in the Pacific by providing a forum for forward-looking dialogue on important economic and development *policy* issues. **Structure** An informal, private, academic conference series. International Steering Committee; International Secretariat; Director. **Languages** English. **Staff** 1.00 FTE, paid. **Finance** Grants from national institutes and organizations from Australia, Indonesia, Japan, Thailand and Canada. Funding from the following internationally oriented organizations: *Asia Foundation; Centre for Strategic and International Studies, Jakarta (CSIS); Ford Foundation (#09858); ISEAS – Yusof Ishak Institute (ISEAS); Pacific Basin Economic Council (PBEC, #17938); Rockefeller Brothers Fund (RBF); International Development Research Centre (IDRC, #13162).* **Activities** Research and development; networking/liaising. **Events** *Conference* Singapore (Singapore) 2015, *Conference* Hong Kong (Hong Kong) 2013, *Financial development and cooperation in Asia and the Pacific* Hong Kong (Hong Kong) 2013, *Conference* Vancouver, BC (Canada) 2012, *Conference* Beijing (China) 2010. **Publications** *PAFTAD Newsletter* (4 a year). Monographs.
Members Individuals in 19 countries and territories:

Australia, Cambodia, Canada, China, Hong Kong, India, Indonesia, Japan, Korea Rep, Malaysia, Mexico, New Zealand, Peru, Philippines, Singapore, Taiwan, Thailand, Timor-Leste, USA, Vietnam.
IGO Relations *Asia-Pacific Economic Cooperation (APEC, #01887).* **NGO Relations** *International Institute of Catechetics and Pastoral Studies (#13867).* Instrumental in setting up and close cooperation with: *Pacific Economic Cooperation Council (PECC, #17947).* [2019.12.19/XF3259/ct/**F**]

♦ Pacific Transnational Crime Network (PTCN) 18010

Team Leader Tonga Police, PO Box 1380, Nuku'alofa, Tonga.
History on the initiative of the Australian government. **Aims** Provide a proactive, transnational criminal intelligence and investigative capability to Pacific regional *law enforcement* agencies. **Finance** Funded by Australian Federal Police. **Activities** Includes: *Pacific Transnational Crime Coordination Centre (PTCCC)*, set up Jun 2004, Suva (Fiji).
Members Transnational Crime Units (TCUs) in 6 countries:
Australia, Fiji, Papua New Guinea, Samoa, Tonga, Vanuatu.
NGO Relations Memorandum with *Pacific Islands Chiefs of Police (PICP, #17964).* Member of: *Asset Recovery Interagency Network – Asia Pacific (ARIN-AP, #02320).* [2008/XM3683/**D**]

- ♦ Pacific Tsunami Warning Center (internationally oriented national body)
- ♦ Pacific tuna convention – Convention on the Conservation and Management of Highly Migratory Fish Stocks in the Western and Central Pacific Ocean (2000 treaty)
- ♦ Pacific Voice and Speech Foundation (internationally oriented national body)
- ♦ Pacific Water Association (internationally oriented national body)
- ♦ Pacific Water & Wastes Association / see Pacific Water Association
- ♦ Pacific Whale Foundation (internationally oriented national body)

♦ Pacific Women in Maritime Association (PacWIMA) 18011

Secretariat Defens Haus – Level 2, Corner Champion Parade and Hunter St, Port Moresby NCD, Papua New Guinea. T. +6753054600. E-mail: pacwima@gmail.com.
Pres National Maritime Safety Authority, PO Box 668, Port Moresby NCD, Papua New Guinea. T. +6753211244.
URL: http://www.pacwima.org/
History Feb 2005, under the auspices of *International Maritime Organization (IMO, #14102)*, through Regional Maritime Programme of *Pacific Community (SPC, #17942).* Also referred to as *WIMA.* Ceased to exist 2009, when became part of *Pacific Islands Maritime Association (PacMA, #17974).* Relaunched Apr 2016, Nuku-alofa (Tonga). **Aims** Enable the visibility of women in the maritime sector; connect, educate and inspire women and promote female maritime professionals in the Pacific. **Structure** Executive Committee. **Languages** English. **Staff** Voluntary. **Finance** Members' dues. Support from: *Pacific Community (SPC, #17942); International Maritime Organization (IMO, #14102).* **Activities** Awareness raising; capacity building; events/meetings; networking/liaising; training/education. **Events** *Inaugural Meeting* Suva (Fiji) 2005. **Publications** *PacWIMA Quarterly.* **Members** Full; Associate; Individual; Life. Membership countries not specified. **NGO Relations** *Pacific International Maritime Law Association (PIMLA, #17956); Pacific Islands Maritime Association (PacMA, #17974).* [2019/XM1629/**D**]

♦ Pacific Women's Network Against Violence Against Women 18012

Secretariat Fiji Women's Crisis Ctr, PO Box 12882, Suva, Fiji. T. +6793313300. Fax +6793313650. E-mail: fwcc@connect.com.fj.
URL: http://www.fijiwomen.com/
History 1992, Suva (Fiji). **Events** *Meeting* Fiji 2004, *Meeting* Fiji 2001. **Members** Organizations in 10 countries. Membership countries not specified. [2014.11.10/XJ4412/**F**]

- ♦ Pacific Women's Watch – New Zealand (internationally oriented national body)
- ♦ Pacific Writing Forum (internationally oriented national body)

♦ Pacific Youth Council (Youthlink) 18013

Conseil de la jeunesse océanienne
Pres Pacific Youth Resource Bureau, BP D5, CEDEX 98848 Nouméa, New Caledonia. T. +687260178. Fax +687263818. E-mail: pacificyouthcouncil@gmail.com.
URL: http://www.pacificyouthcouncil.org/
History Aug 1986. Founded by 5 countries from the South Pacific region. Ceased to exist 1990. Revival proposed during a regional youth conference in 1994. **Events** *Regional Pacific youth conference* 1998, *Regional Pacific Youth Conference* Polynesia Fr 1998, *General Assembly* Nouméa (New Caledonia) 1996.
Members Representatives of 6 countries:
Australia, Fiji, New Zealand, Papua New Guinea, Samoa, Solomon Is.
IGO Relations *Pacific Community (SPC, #17942).* **NGO Relations** Consultative Member of: *World Assembly of Youth (WAY, #21113).* Member of: *Pacific Islands Regional Non-governmental Organizations (PRNGO, #17978).* [2020/XD1434/**D**]

- ♦ Pacifika Youth (internationally oriented national body)
- ♦ PAC / see IMPACT (#11136)
- ♦ **PACIN** Pan-African Citizens Network (#18044)
- ♦ PACIP – Pacific and Asia Council of Indigenous Peoples (internationally oriented national body)
- ♦ PACJA / see Panafrican Climate Justice Alliance (#18046)
- ♦ **PACJA** Panafrican Climate Justice Alliance (#18046)

♦ Pack2Go Europe 18014

Contact Av Livingstone 13-15, 1000 Brussels, Belgium. T. +3222869496. Fax +3222869495. E-mail: ebates@pack2go-europe.com.
URL: http://www.pack2go-europe.com/
History Founded 1974, as *European Single Service Association (ESSA) – Association européenne des fabricants d'articles à usage unique.* Subsequently changed title to: *European Food Service and Packaging Association (EFPA) – Association européenne d'emballages alimentaires à usage unique – Europäischer Verband für Lebensmittelverpackungen und Einweggeschirr.* Current title adopted, 2008. Full title: *Pack2Go Europe – Europe's convenience food packaging association.* Registered in accordance with Belgian law. **Aims** Work with *packaging* and related products used in today's active lifestyles for the moments when people eat and drink on the go, including applications where food and drinks are packed or served in the packaging immediately or very shortly before consumption by the customer, as well as packaging designed to be filled on a production line but will carry and protect food or drinks that are intended to be consumed on the go. **Structure** General Assembly (twice a year); Board. **Languages** English. **Staff** 1.50 FTE, paid. **Finance** Members' dues. **Activities** Events/meetings. **Events** *Autumn Meeting* Brussels (Belgium) 2016, *Meeting* Brussels (Belgium) 2015, *Joint Meeting* London (UK) 2015, *Spring Meeting* Berlin (Germany) 2014, *Autumn Meeting* Brussels (Belgium) 2014.
Members Full (converters); Affiliate (small converters); Associate (raw material suppliers, distributors, M/C suppliers and users). Manufacturers in 12 countries:
Belgium, Finland, France, Germany, Italy, Netherlands, Poland, Spain, Sweden, Switzerland, UK, USA.
IGO Relations Recognized by: *European Commission (EC, #06633).* **NGO Relations** Member of: *European Policy Centre (EPC, #08240).* [2018.03.08/XD3252/**D**]

- ♦ Pack2Go Europe – Europe's convenience food packaging association / see Pack2Go Europe (#18014)
- ♦ Packaging and Brand Design Association of Europe / see European Brand and Packaging Design Association (#06396)
- ♦ Packaging Design Association of Europe / see European Brand and Packaging Design Association (#06396)

♦ Packaging Recovery Organization Europe (PRO-EUROPE) 18015

Managing Dir Av des Olympiades 2, 1140 Brussels, Belgium. T. +3222300067. Fax +3227346285. E-mail: info@pro-e.org.
URL: https://www.pro-e.org/
History 1995. Founded by European packaging and packaging waste recovery and recycling schemes which mainly use the 'Green Dot' trademark as a financial symbol. Registration: Banque-Carrefour des Entreprises, No/ID: 0454.492.807, Start date: 15 Feb 1995, Belgium; EU Transparency Register, No/ID: 50432033211-34, Start date: 12 Feb 2010. **Aims** Promote and protect international establishment and use of the Green Dot as the financing symbol of producer responsibility and efficient packaging waste management. **Structure** President; Managing Director. **Languages** English. **Staff** 1.00 FTE, paid. **Finance** Members' dues. **Activities** Knowledge management/information dissemination; projects/programmes. **Events** *Congress* Brussels (Belgium) 2010, *Green dot 2008 – from waste to resource management* Prague (Czech Rep) 2008, *Congress* Paris (France) 2006, *Congress* Berlin (Germany) 2004, *Congress* Madrid (Spain) 2001. **Publications** Brochures.
Members National organizations in 31 countries:
Austria, Belgium, Bosnia-Herzegovina, Bulgaria, Croatia, Cyprus, Czechia, Estonia, France, Germany, Greece, Hungary, Ireland, Israel, Latvia, Lithuania, Luxembourg, Malta, Netherlands, North Macedonia, Norway, Poland, Portugal, Romania, Serbia, Slovakia, Slovenia, Spain, Sweden, Türkiye, UK.
NGO Relations Founding Member of: *European Food Sustainable Consumption and Production Round Table (European Food SCP Roundtable, #07289).* [2019/XM3001/**D**]

- ♦ PACK – Pacific and Asia Conference on Korean Studies (meeting series)
- ♦ PacLII – Pacific Islands Legal Information Institute (internationally oriented national body)
- ♦ PACLING – Pacific Association for Computational Linguistics (meeting series)
- ♦ **PacMA** Pacific Islands Maritime Association (#17974)
- ♦ PACN – Pan Africa Chemistry Network (internationally oriented national body)
- ♦ Paco / see War Resisters' International (#20818)
- ♦ PACOM – Pacific Asian Congress of Municipalities (meeting series)
- ♦ PACON – Pacific Congress on Marine Science and Technology International (meeting series)
- ♦ PACO – Pan Arab Council of Ophthalmology (inactive)
- ♦ PAC – Pacific Accreditation Cooperation (inactive)
- ♦ **PAC** Pan-Asian Consortium of Language Teaching Societies (#18164)
- ♦ PACRIM – Pacific Rim Conference on Ceramic and Glass Technololgy (meeting series)
- ♦ **PACSA** Pan-African Composers' and Songwriters' Alliance (#18047)
- ♦ **PACSNET** Pan-African Civil Society Network (#18045)
- ♦ **PACS** Pan Arab Continence Society (#18143)
- ♦ PACSU – Commission du Pacifique Sud pour les géosciences appliquées (inactive)
- ♦ PacSurv / see Pacific Public Health Surveillance Network (#17993)

♦ Pact 18016

Pres/CEO 1140 3rd Street NE, Ste 400, Washington DC 20002, USA. T. +12024665666. Fax +12024665665. E-mail: info@pactworld.org.
URL: http://www.pactworld.org/
History 1971. Founded as a consortium of private agencies engaged in development programmes worldwide. Bylaws revised in 1992. Former names and other names: *Private Agencies Collaborating Together* – former. Registration: USA, Washington. **Aims** Work on the ground to improve the lives of those who are challenged by *poverty* and *marginalization.* **Structure** A decentralized international development organization with 3 subsidiaries: Pact Global Microfinance Fund, Pact Institute and Pact UK. Board of Directors; Headquarters in Washington DC (USA); Field Offices in Africa (13), Asia/Eurasia (7) and Latin America/Caribbean (1). **Languages** English, Mandarin Chinese. **Staff** Headquarters: about 100; worldwide: about 4,000. **Finance** Grants and contracts from: *International Bank for Reconstruction and Development (IBRD, #12317)* (World Bank); US government agencies including: *United States Agency for International Development (USAID)*; US State Department and Department of Labor; UN agencies including: *Joint United Nations Programme on HIV/AIDS (UNAIDS, #16149), UNDP (#20292), UNICEF (#20332), United Nations Office for Project Services (UNOPS, #20602)*; European bilateral organizations; foundations; corporations. **Activities** Projects/programmes; research and development; capacity building. **Events** *Meeting on financial services for the poor* Medford, MA (USA) 1991, *Workshop on managing and containing health care costs* New York, NY (USA) 1990, *Workshop on international development for US private voluntary organizations* Washington, DC (USA) 1989. **Publications** *All In* – magazine; *Inside Our Promise* – newsletter. *Measuring Pact's Mission.* Annual Report; toolkits; manuals; guides; training materials.
Members Since 1992, no longer a membership organization. Offices in 19 countries:
Colombia, Congo DR, Eswatini, Ethiopia, Kenya, Lesotho, Madagascar, Malawi, Nepal, Nigeria, Rwanda, South Africa, Tanzania UR, Thailand, Ukraine, USA, Vietnam, Zambia, Zimbabwe.
IGO Relations Has worked with IGOs including: *International Bank for Reconstruction and Development (IBRD, #12317)* (World Bank); *Joint United Nations Programme on HIV/AIDS (UNAIDS, #16149); UNDP (#20292); UNICEF (#20332); United Nations Office for Project Services (UNOPS, #20602).* **NGO Relations** *Aspen Network of Development Entrepreneurs (ANDE, #02310); CIVICUS: World Alliance for Citizen Participation (#03962)*; Coalition to End Violence Against Women and Girls Globally; *European Partnership for Responsible Minerals (EPRM, #08159); Global Battery Alliance (GBA, #10249); InsideNGO (inactive); NetHope (#16979)*; Orphans and Vulnerable Children Task Force; *Small Enterprise Education and Promotion Network (SEEP); Society for International Development (SID, #19581)*; US Global Leadership Coalition. [2021/XF1889/**F**]

- ♦ Pact of Bogota – American Treaty on Pacific Settlement (1948 treaty)
- ♦ **PACT Consortium** Postpartum Depression: Action Towards Causes and Treatment Consortium (#18470)
- ♦ Pacte de Bogota – Traité américain de règlement pacifique (1948 treaty)
- ♦ Pacte international relatif aux droits civils et politiques (1966 treaty)
- ♦ Pacte international relatif aux droits économiques, sociaux et cultures (1966 treaty)
- ♦ Pacte d'organisation de la Petite Entente (1933 treaty)
- ♦ Pacte de San José de Costa Rica – Convention interaméricaine des droits de l'homme (1969 treaty)
- ♦ Pact of Locarno – Treaty of Mutual Guarantee (1925 treaty)
- ♦ Pacto Amazónico – Tratado de Cooperación Amazónica (1978 treaty)
- ♦ Pacto de Bogota – Tratado americano des soluciones pacificas (1948 treaty)
- ♦ Pacto Mundial Consciente (unconfirmed)
- ♦ Pact of Organisation of the Little Entente (1933 treaty)
- ♦ Pacto de San José de Costa Rica – Convención interamericana de derechos humanos (1969 treaty)
- ♦ **PACTRIMS** Pan-Asian Committee for Treatment and Research in Multiple Sclerosis (#18163)
- ♦ Pact of San José de Costa Rica – Inter-American Convention on Human Rights (1969 treaty)
- ♦ PACTS – Pacific and Asian American Center for Theology and Strategies, USA (internationally oriented national body)
- ♦ **PACWA** Pan African Christian Women Alliance (#18043)
- ♦ **PacWIMA** Pacific Women in Maritime Association (#18011)
- ♦ PADA / see Organization for Peace and Appropriate Development for the Horn of Africa
- ♦ PADA Foundation – Organization for Peace and Appropriate Development for the Horn of Africa (internationally oriented national body)
- ♦ Pädagoginnen und Pädagogen für den Frieden, Germany (internationally oriented national body)
- ♦ PADEAP – Pan African Development Education and Advocacy Programme (internationally oriented national body)
- ♦ PADEC – Pan African Association for Community Development (no recent information)
- ♦ **PADEE-WHIA** World Hellenic Inter-Parliamentary Association (#21563)
- ♦ **PADF** Pan American Development Foundation (#18094)
- ♦ PADH / see Caritas Asia (#03578)
- ♦ PADIC – Patent Documentation and Information Centre (see: #00434)
- ♦ PADI International – Professional Association of Diving Instructors (internationally oriented national body)
- ♦ PADOP – International Observatory of Organization and Globalization (internationally oriented national body)
- ♦ PADRE – Partnership for Acid Drainage Remediation in Europe (see: #14168)
- ♦ Padres Basilianos (religious order)
- ♦ Padres Josefinos de Murialdo (religious order)
- ♦ Padres Maristas – Sociedad de Maria (religious order)

♦ Padre Somaschi – Ordine dei Chierici Regolari di Somasca (religious order)
♦ Padres Somascos – Orden de los Clérigos Regulares Somascos (religious order)
♦ Padri Bianchi – Società dei Missionari d'Africa (religious order)
♦ PADRIGU – Department of Peace and Development Research, Gothenburg University (internationally oriented national body)
♦ Padri Maristi – Società di Maria (religious order)
♦ Padri de Timon-David – Congregazione del Sacro Cuore di Gesù (religious order)
♦ Padri Vocazionisti – Società Divine Vocazioni (religious order)
♦ PADSG – Pan African Diabetes Study Group (no recent information)
♦ **PAEAC** Parliamentary Association for Euro-Arab Cooperation (#18217)
♦ PAECO – Parliamentary Assembly of the ECO Countries (unconfirmed)
♦ **PAEC** Pan-American Equestrian Confederation (#18097)
♦ Paediatric European Network for the Treatments of AIDS / see Paediatric European Network for the Treatments of AIDS and Infectious Diseases (#18017)

♦ Paediatric European Network for the Treatments of AIDS and Infectious Diseases (PENTA-ID) 18017

Pres c/o PENTA Foundation, Torre della Ricerca Pediatrica Corso Stati Uniti 4, 35127 Padua PD, Italy. T. +39498215447.
URL: http://penta-id.org/

History 1991, as *Paediatric European Network for the Treatments of AIDS (PENTA)*, originally as a collaboration between paediatric HIV centres in Europe. Current title adopted 2012. **Structure** Managed by *PENTA Foundation*, set up 2004, with its own Board. **Activities** Research/documentation; training/education. **Events** *General Assembly* Cape Town (South Africa) 2019, *International Workshop on HIV Pediatrics* Mexico City (Mexico) 2019, *General Assembly* Madrid (Spain) 2018, *International Workshop on HIV Pediatrics* Paris (France) 2017, *International Workshop on HIV Pediatrics* Durban (South Africa) 2016. **NGO Relations** *European Network of Paediatric Research at the European Medicines Agency (Enpr-EMA, #07963).* [2016/XM4914/**F**]

♦ Paediatric Oncology Club / see International Society of Paediatric Oncology (#15339)
♦ Paediatric Pathology Club / see Paediatric Pathology Society (#18018)

♦ Paediatric Pathology Society (PPS) 18018

Hon Sec Dept of Pathology, Southampton General Hosp, Tremona Road, Southampton, SO16 6YD, UK. T. +442381206446.
Pres Sidra Medical and Research Center, Sidra Hosp, H2M Pathology Room, 2MF 126 Qatar Foundation, PO Box 26999, Doha, Qatar.
URL: http://www.paedpath.org/

History Founded 1955, as *Paediatric Pathology Club*. Current Constitution adopted at General Assembly, 15 Sep 1989, London (UK). Currently functions as a constituent group of *International Paediatric Pathology Association (IPPA, #14498)*. Has been referred to as: *European Paediatric Pathological Society*; *European Paediatric Pathology Society*. **Aims** Promote paediatric pathology in its widest sense, embracing all disciplines of pathology. **Structure** Committee. **Languages** English. **Finance** Members' dues. Annual budget: pounds14,000. **Events** *Annual Meeting* Belgrade (Serbia) 2021, *Annual Meeting* Sheffield (UK) 2020, *Annual Meeting* Pittsburgh, PA (USA) 2019, *Annual Meeting* Paris (France) 2018, *Annual Meeting* Lisbon (Portugal) 2017. **Publications** *Paediatric Pathology Society Newsletter*, *Pediatric and Developmental Pathology* – journal. Books.
Members Individuals in 45 countries and territories:
Australia, Austria, Belarus, Belgium, Bosnia-Herzegovina, Brazil, Canada, China, Croatia, Czechia, Denmark, Estonia, Finland, France, Germany, Greece, Hong Kong, Hungary, Iceland, India, Ireland, Israel, Italy, Latvia, Malawi, Netherlands, New Zealand, North Macedonia, Norway, Poland, Portugal, Russia, Serbia, Singapore, South Africa, Spain, Sweden, Switzerland, Syrian AR, Tunisia, Türkiye, UK, United Arab Emirates, USA, Zimbabwe. [2017.10.26/XE0951/v/**D**]

♦ Paediatric Radiation Oncology Society (PROS) 18019

Pres c/o GL Events, 59 quai Rambaud – CS 80059, 69285 Lyon CEDEX 02, France. T. +33478176263. Fax +33478176257. E-mail: geraldine.bezamat@gl-events.com.
Registered Office Centre Léon Bérard, 28 rue Laennec, 69373 Lyon CEDEX 8, France.
URL: http://intpros.org/

History following a meeting on paediatric radiation oncology, Jun 2003. Officially set up, 1 Mar 2006, Lyon (France). Registered in accordance with French law. **Aims** Serve the science and art of medicine and set a worldwide standard of excellence with respect to radiation oncology aspects of the care of children and adolescents with *cancer*, provide a forum for optimal communication between radiation oncologists and exchange information with those involved in the management of pediatric and adolescent cancer; develop alternative treatments and guidelines for emerging countries. **Structure** General Assembly; Executive Committee. **Languages** English. **Finance** Sources: members' dues. **Activities** Events/meetings. **Events** *Biennial Congress* Bangkok (Thailand) 2019, *Biennial Congress* New York, NY (USA) 2017, *Biennial Congress / Congress* Ljubljana (Slovenia) 2015, *Biennial Congress* Louisville, KY (USA) 2013, *Biennial Congress* Venice (Italy) 2011. **Publications** *Red Journal – International Journal of Radiation Oncology – Biology – Physics* – official journal. Newsletter. **Members** Radiation oncologists and allied professionals (202). Membership countries not specified. [2019/XM3374/**C**]

♦ Paediatric Rheumatology European Society (PRES) 18020

Pres address not obtained.
Sec address not obtained.
URL: http://www.pres.org.uk/

History 1999. **Aims** Provide a forum for all health care professionals engaged in the care of children with rheumatic disorders, as well as researchers working on the different diseases; provide and update guidelines for best clinical practice as well as syllabi and training programmes for paediatric rheumatologists. **Structure** Council, comprising President, Secretary, Treasurer, Committee Chairs and additional members. Permanent coopted members include chairman of the Standing Paediatric Committee of *European Alliance of Associations for Rheumatology (EULAR, #05862)*. **Languages** English. **Staff** Voluntary. **Finance** Members' dues. Profits from annual scientific meetings. **Activities** Training; meeting activities. **Events** *Annual Scientific Meeting* Madrid (Spain) 2019, *Annual Scientific Meeting* Lisbon (Portugal) 2018, *Annual Scientific Meeting* Athens (Greece) 2017, *Annual Scientific Meeting* Genoa (Italy) 2016, *Annual Scientific Meeting* Belgrade (Serbia) 2014. **Publications** Guidelines.
Members Healthcare professionals in the field of paediatric rheumatology, in 33 countries:
Australia, Belgium, Bulgaria, Canada, Czechia, Denmark, Estonia, Finland, France, Germany, Greece, India, Ireland, Italy, Latvia, Lithuania, Malaysia, Netherlands, Norway, Poland, Portugal, Russia, Serbia, Singapore, Slovakia, Slovenia, Spain, Sweden, Switzerland, Türkiye, UK, Ukraine, USA.
NGO Relations Recognized by: *European Board of Paediatrics (EBP, #06368).* [2014/XD8324/v/**D**]

♦ Paediatric Surgery Postgraduate Seminars (meeting series)
♦ **PAEEB** Psychiatric Association for Eastern Europe and the Balkans (#18558)
♦ PAEF – Peace Action Education Fund (internationally oriented national body)
♦ **PAEMGS** Pan-African Environmental Mutagen and Genomic Society (#18048)
♦ PAEMS / see Pan-African Environmental Mutagen and Genomic Society (#18048)
♦ **PAE** Pain Alliance Europe (#18026)
♦ **PAEPARD** Platform for African – European Partnership on Agricultural Research for Development (#18398)
♦ PAES – Partnership for African Environmental Sustainability (internationally oriented national body)
♦ **PAFAMS** Pan American Federation of Associations of Medical Schools (#18100)
♦ **PAFA** Pan African Federation of Accountants (#18050)
♦ PAFATU – Pan African Federation of Agricultural Trade Unions (inactive)
♦ **PAFCW** Pan-African Federation of Clerical Workers (#09700)
♦ PAFETTU – Pan-African Federation of Teachers' Trade Unions (no recent information)
♦ PAFIE – Pacific Asian Federation of Industrial Engineering (inactive)
♦ PAFL – Pan American Federation of Labor (inactive)
♦ PAFMACH – Pan African Federation for Maternal and Child Health (no recent information)
♦ **PAFMDC** Pan American Foot-and-Mouth Disease Center (#18106)
♦ PAFMECA – Pan African Freedom Movement of East and Central Africa (inactive)
♦ PAFOD – Pan African Federation of the Disabled (no recent information)
♦ **PAFO** PanAfrican Farmers' Organization (#18049)
♦ **PAFOS** Pan African Federation of Oto-Rhino-Laryngological Societies (#18051)
♦ PAF – Performing Arts Forum (internationally oriented national body)
♦ PAFPNet – Pacific Agricultural and Forestry Policy Network (unconfirmed)
♦ **PAFSA** Pan Arab Federation of Societies of Anesthesia, Intensive Care and Pain Management (#18144)
♦ **PAFTAD** Pacific Trade and Development Conference (#18009)
♦ PAFTA / see Greater Arab Free-Trade Area (#10700)

♦ Pagan Federation International 18021

Coordinator Stichting PFI, Nepveulaan 103, 3705 LC Zeist, Netherlands. T. +31646156850.
General: http://www.paganfederation.org/

History Pagan Federation UK founded 1971. Pagan Federation International Foundation founded 2005. Registered in accordance with Dutch law. **Aims** Provide information on paganism; counter misconceptions about pagan, *heathen* and indigenous *religions*. **Structure** Working parties in 22 countries. **Languages** Dutch, English, French, German, Hungarian, Italian, Portuguese, Spanish, Swedish, Turkish. **Staff** 20.00 FTE, voluntary. **Finance** Donations. Annual budget: euro 2,000. **Activities** Events/meetings. **Publications** *Pagan World* – journal. Online magazine; newsletters from various PFI nations.
Members in 32 countries:
Australia, Austria, Belgium, Canada, Croatia, Czechia, Denmark, Finland, France, Germany, Hungary, Italy, Japan, Luxembourg, Malta, Mexico, Netherlands, New Zealand, Norway, Philippines, Poland, Portugal, Romania, Serbia, Slovenia, South Africa, Spain, Sweden, Switzerland, Türkiye, UK, USA. [2018.09.06/XM2885/**F**]

♦ **PAGE** Population Approach Group Europe (#18457)
♦ **PAGES** Past Global Changes (#18257)
♦ **PAGGW** Pan-African Agency of the Great Green Wall (#00547)
♦ PAGID – Pan American Group for Immunodeficiencies (internationally oriented national body)
♦ PAG – International Plant and Animal Genome Conference (meeting series)
♦ **PAG** Pacific Arctic Group (#17926)
♦ PAG-RVD / see Pan American Society for Clinical Virology
♦ **PAGS** Pan-American Glaucoma Society (#18107)
♦ **PAGS** Pan Arab Glaucoma Society (#18145)
♦ PAGS – Pelargonium and Geranium Society (internationally oriented national body)
♦ Paguosskoe Dvizenie (#18574)
♦ **PAGU** Pan American Gymnastics Union (#20471)
♦ PAHEF / see PAHO Foundation (#18022)
♦ **PAHF** Pan American Hockey Federation (#18110)

♦ PAHO Foundation 18022

Pres and CEO PO Box 27733, Washington DC 20038-7733, USA. T. +12029743416. Fax +12029743636. E-mail: info@pahef.org.
Street Address 1889 F St NW, Suite 312, Washington DC 20006, USA.
URL: http://www.pahofoundation.org/

History 1968, within *Pan American Health Organization (PAHO, #18108)*, as *Pan American Health and Education Foundation (PAHEF) – Fundación Panamericana de la Salud y Educación.* Currently an independent organzation. Registered in the state of Washington DC (USA). **Aims** Have a profound, positive impact on seemingly intractable public health problems that threaten the *health* and well being of people in *Latin America* and the *Caribbean*. **Structure** Board of Directors. **Languages** English, Spanish. [2016.06.27/XK0760/f/**F***]

♦ **PAHO** Pan American Health Organization (#18108)

♦ PAHO/WHO Health Emergencies Department (PHE) 18023

Département des urgences sanitaires OPS/OMS – Departamento de Emergencias en Salud de la OPS/OMS

Dir 9th Floor Room 910, 525 23rd St NW, Washington DC 20037-2895, USA. T. +12029743708. Fax +12029743176. E-mail: disaster@paho.org.
URL: http://www.paho.org/emergencies/

History 1977, by *Pan American Health Organization (PAHO, #18108)*, to implement *Disaster Preparedness and Mitigation in the Americas Program*, at the request of governments of the Latin America and Caribbean region. Program previously also referred to as *Emergency Preparedness and Disaster Relief Coordination Program – Programme de coordination des secours en cas d'urgence – Programa de Preparativos para Situaciones de Emergencia y Coordinación del Socorro en Casos de Desastre*. Subsequently titled: *Emergency Preparedness and Disaster Relief Coordination Office (PED) – Bureau de coordination des secours en cas d'urgence – Oficina de Preparativos para Situaciones de Emergencia y Coordinación del Socorro en Casos de Desastre.* **Aims** Reduce mortality, morbidity and societal disruption resulting from emergencies and disasters through detection, management and mitigation of high-threat pathogens, and all-hazards risk reduction, preparedness, response and early recovery activities that build resilience and use a multi-sectoral approach to contribute to health security. **Structure** Headquarters in Washington DC (USA). Subregional Offices (3): Caribbean, in Bridgetown (Barbados); Central America, in Panama (Panama); South America, in Lima (Peru). **Languages** English, French, Portuguese, Spanish. **Finance** Sources: PAHO budget; voluntary contributions, especially from *Department for International Development (DFID, inactive)*, Global Affairs Canada, Office of Foreign Disaster Assistance (OFDA) of *United States Agency for International Development (USAID)*, *Agencia Española de Cooperación Internacional para el Desarrollo (AECID)* and *Swedish International Development Cooperation Agency (Sida)*. **Activities** Humanitarian/emergency aid; monitoring/evaluation; training/education; projects/programmes; knowledge management/information dissemination. **Events** *Meeting* Santo Domingo (Dominican Rep) 1999, *International meeting on harnessing the internet for disasters and epidemies* Bogota (Colombia) 1997, *Workshop on joint civilian and military public health humanitarian assistance* Arnprior, ON (Canada) 1996, *Conference on disaster mitigation in hospitals and health care facilities* Mexico City (Mexico) 1996, *Reunion de preparativos para casos de desastres* Mexico City (Mexico) 1994. **Publications** *Disasters: Preparedness and Mitigation in the Americas* (4 a year) in English, Spanish. Reprints and translations of selected publications; technical manuals; guidelines; CD-ROMs; audiovisual training material.
Members Member Governments of PAHO (35):
Antigua-Barbuda, Argentina, Bahamas, Barbados, Belize, Bolivia, Brazil, Canada, Chile, Colombia, Costa Rica, Cuba, Dominica, Dominican Rep, Ecuador, El Salvador, Grenada, Guatemala, Guyana, Haiti, Honduras, Jamaica, Mexico, Nicaragua, Panama, Paraguay, Peru, St Kitts-Nevis, St Lucia, St Vincent-Grenadines, Suriname, Trinidad-Tobago, Uruguay, USA, Venezuela.
Associate Members (3):
France, Netherlands, UK. [2019.02.12/XE6330/**E***]

♦ PAHO/WHO Staff Association 18024

Association du personnel OPS/OMS – Asociación de Personal OPS/OMS – Associação de Pessoal OPAS/OMS

Secretariat 525 23rd St NW, Washington DC 20037, USA. T. +12029743293. Fax +12029744293. E-mail: hqstaffec@paho.org.

History 1950, Washington DC (USA), to represent staff members of *Pan American Health Organization (PAHO, #18108)* and *WHO (#20950)* stationed in Washington DC. **Aims** Represent staff; protect conditions of service; promote wellbeing and staff development; strengthen solidarity among staff. **Structure** Council (meets twice a year); Executive Committee; Local Chapters; Legal Counsel. **Languages** English, French, Spanish. **Staff** 0.50 FTE, paid. **Finance** Sources: regular contributions from members; voluntary contributions and a subsidy from PAHO. **Events** *Annual Meeting / Council Meeting* Washington, DC (USA) 2014, *Annual Meeting / Council Meeting* Costa Rica 2012, *Council Meeting* Ecuador 2009, *Council Meeting* Bolivia 2008, *Council Meeting* Nicaragua 2007. **Publications** *Executive Committee Bulletin* (12 a year).
Members Individuals in 38 countries and territories:
Antigua-Barbuda, Argentina, Bahamas, Barbados, Belize, Bermuda, Bolivia, Brazil, Canada, Chile, Colombia, Costa Rica, Cuba, Dominica, Dominican Rep, Ecuador, El Salvador, Grenada, Guatemala, Guyana, Haiti, Honduras, Jamaica, Mexico, Neth Antilles, Nicaragua, Panama, Paraguay, Peru, Puerto Rico, St Kitts-Nevis, St Lucia, St Vincent-Grenadines, Suriname, Trinidad-Tobago, Uruguay, USA, Venezuela.
NGO Relations Member of: *Federation of International Civil Servants' Associations (FICSA, #09603).* [2015.08.26/XE0229/v/**E**]

♦ PAH – Polish Humanitarian Action (internationally oriented national body)
♦ PAH – Polska Akcja Humanitarna (internationally oriented national body)

♦ PAI 18025

Pres/CEO 1300 19th St NW, Ste 200, Washington DC 20036, USA. T. +12025573400. Fax +12027284177. E-mail: info@pai.org.
URL: http://pai.org/

History May 1965, Washington, DC (USA). No longer referred to by its full title. Former names and other names: *Population Crisis Committee (PCC)* – former; *Comité de la crise démographique* – former; *Comité de la Crisis Demografica* – former; *Population Action International (PAI)* – former. **Aims** Strengthen political and financial support worldwide for population programs grounded in individual rights; commit to universal access to *family planning* and related health services and to educational and economic opportunities, especially for girls and women. **Structure** Board of Directors. **Finance** Sources: donations; gifts, legacies. Annual budget: 7,500,000 USD. **Activities** Advocacy/lobbying/activism; research/documentation. **Events** *Meeting* London (UK) 2006, *International round table on ICPD + 10* London (UK) 2004, *Seminar on antiprogestin drugs* Arlington, VA (USA) 1991. **Publications** Books; reports; guides. **Members** Not a membership organization. **Consultative Status** Consultative status granted from: *ECOSOC (#05331)* (Ros B); *ILO (#11123)* (Special List); *UNICEF (#20332)*. **IGO Relations** Consultation Status with: *United Nations Population Fund (UNFPA, #20612)*. Associated with Department of Global Communications of the United Nations. **NGO Relations** Member of (9): *American Council for Voluntary International Action (InterAction)*; *Asia Pacific Alliance for Sexual and Reproductive Health and Rights (APA, #01825)*; *Girls not Brides (#10154)*; *Global Health Council (GHC, #10402)*; *Humentum (#10993)*; *International Consortium for Emergency Contraception (ICEC, #12911)*; *PMNCH (#18410)*; *Reproductive Health Supplies Coalition (RHSC, #18847)*; *Society for International Development (SID, #19581)*. Partner of (1): *Every Woman Every Child (EWEC, #09215)*. Supports (1): *International Planned Parenthood Federation (IPPF, #14589)*. [2022/XE3960/F]

♦ PAIA – Pan American Implant Association (inactive)
♦ **PAICSAT** Pediatric Anesthesia and Intensive Care Society and Applied Technologies (#18285)
♦ PAIDA / see Asociación Panamericana de Infectologia (#02288)
♦ **PAID** Pan African Institute for Development (#18053)
♦ **PAIGH** Pan American Institute of Geography and History (#18113)
♦ **PAIMA** Pan American International Movers Association (#18114)

♦ Pain Alliance Europe (PAE) 18026

Registered Office Rue de Londres 18, 1050 Brussels, Belgium. E-mail: info@pae-eu.eu.
URL: http://www.pae-eu.eu/

History Founded alongside an initiative of members of the European Parliament (MEP) Marian Harkin with the mission "To improve the quality of life of people living with chronic pain". Statutes adopted 29 Nov 2011. Registration: Banque-Carrefour des Entreprises, No/ID: 0843.498.142, Start date: 30 Nov 2011, Belgium. **Aims** Promote awareness for chronic pain; promote a European policy on chronic pain; reduce the impact of chronic pain on the European society on all areas. **Structure** General Assembly; Board. **Languages** English. **Staff** 1.00 FTE, paid. **Finance** Sources: members' dues; revenue from activities/projects. Funding from pharmaceutical companies and partner organizations. **Activities** Events/meetings; knowledge management/ information dissemination; networking/liaising; research/documentation. **Events** *General Assembly* Brussels (Belgium) 2015, *Meeting* Brussels (Belgium) 2015, *General Assembly* Brussels (Belgium) 2014, *General Assembly* Brussels (Belgium) 2013, *General Assembly* Aachen (Germany) 2012.
Members National and regional associations (40) in 17 European countries.
Austria, Belgium, Bulgaria, Denmark, Finland, France, Germany, Greece, Ireland, Italy, Netherlands, Poland, Portugal, Romania, Spain, Sweden, UK.
Included in the above, 2 organizations listed in this Yearbook:
European Network of Fibromyalgia Associations (ENFA, #07908); *International Painful Bladder Foundation (IPBF, #14499)*.
NGO Relations Works closely with: *European Federation of Neurological Associations (EFNA, #07177)*. [2021.09.01/XJ5827/y/**D**]

♦ Du pain pour chaque enfant (internationally oriented national body)
♦ Pain pour le Monde (internationally oriented national body)
♦ Pain pour le prochain (internationally oriented national body)
♦ PAINT – Primera Asociación Internacional de Noticieros y Televisión (inactive)
♦ **PAI** Pan Africa ILGA (#18032)
♦ PAIPO – Pan-African Intellectual Property Organisation (unconfirmed)
♦ **PAIRS** Pan Arab Interventional Radiology Society (#18147)
♦ Pairti Chomhghuaillíocht na Liobralaithe agus na nDaonlathaithe don Eoraip (#00703)
♦ Pairti Daonlathach Liobralach agus Athchóiriú Eorpach / see Alliance of Liberals and Democrats for Europe Party (#00703)
♦ PAISACD – Pan-African Islamic Society for Agro-Cultural Development (inactive)

♦ Paises Africanos de Lingua Oficial Portuguesa (PALOP) 18027

Official Portuguese-speaking African Countries – Pays africains de langue officielle portugaise
Address not obtained.
Members Countries (5):
Angola, Cape Verde, Guinea-Bissau, Mozambique, Sao Tomé-Principe.
IGO Relations *Comunidade dos Paises de Lingua Portuguesa (CPLP, #04430)*. **NGO Relations** Instrumental in setting up: *Forum das ONG dos Direitos do Homem e de Criança dos PALOP (no recent information)*. [2010/XF3278/**F***]

♦ Päivähoitoalan Yhteistyötoimikunta (inactive)
♦ Paix et coopération (internationally oriented national body)
♦ Pour la paix par l'éducation / see Women's International League for Peace and Freedom (#21024)
♦ PAJU – Pan African Journalists' Union, 1961 (inactive)
♦ PAKDD – Pacific-Asia Conference on Knowledge Discovery and Data Mining (meeting series)

♦ Pakistan Development Forum (PDF) 18028

Address not obtained.
History 1960, by *International Bank for Reconstruction and Development (IBRD, #12317)* as *Aid-to-Pakistan Consortium*. Subsequently known as *Aid to Pakistan Club*. Original consortium held 92 % of Pakistan's outstanding disbursed debt at Jun 1993. **Aims** Facilitate coordination among the major providers of international assistance. **Events** *Forum* Islamabad (Pakistan) 2010, *Forum* Islamabad (Pakistan) 2007, *Forum* Islamabad (Pakistan) 2006, *Forum* Islamabad (Pakistan) 2005, *Forum* Islamabad (Pakistan) 2004.
Members Governments (6):
Canada, France, Germany, Japan, UK, USA.
International organizations (2):
Asian Development Bank (ADB, #01422); *International Bank for Reconstruction and Development (IBRD, #12317)*. [2010/XU1193/**F***]

♦ Pakistan Futuristics Foundation and Institute (internationally oriented national body)
♦ Pakistan Institute of Development Economics / see Bangladesh Institute of Development Studies
♦ Pakistan Institute of Development Economics (internationally oriented national body)
♦ The Pakistan Institute of International Affairs (internationally oriented national body)
♦ Pakistan International Peace and Human Rights Organization (internationally oriented national body)
♦ Pakolaiskysymysten Pohjoismainen Neuvotteluryhmä (#17331)
♦ Palais de la paix (internationally oriented national body)
♦ **PALA** Pan-American Lacrosse Association (#18117)
♦ PALA – Poetics and Linguistics Association (internationally oriented national body)
♦ PAL – Athens Convention Relating to the Carriage of Passengers and Their Luggage by Sea (1974 treaty)
♦ PALEA – Pacific Asia Lift and Escalator Association (unconfirmed)
♦ PALEDEC – Pan African Leadership and Entrepreneurship Development Centre (unconfirmed)

♦ Paleopathology Association 18029

Sec Dept of Archaeology, Univof Durham, South Road, Durham, DH1 1LE, UK. E-mail: paleop-ath.secretary@gmail.com.
URL: https://paleopathology-association.wildapricot.org/

History 1973. Former names and other names: *Paleopathology Club* – former. **Aims** Provide a channel of communication among workers in the field; study ancient *mummies*, *bodies* or any item that might give evidence of *disease* in former times, including ancient writings, ceramics, sculptures, mosaics, paintings and coins. **Events** *Annual Meeting* Baltimore, MD (USA) 2025, *Annual Meeting* Los Angeles, CA (USA) 2024, *Annual Meeting* Reno, NV (USA) 2023, *Annual Meeting* Denver, CO (USA) 2022, *European Meeting* Vilnius (Lithuania) 2022. **Publications** *Paleopathology Association Newsletter* (4 a year). Occasional publications; meeting abstracts.
Members Scientists (about 550), mainly in North America but in a total of in 45 countries:
Argentina, Australia, Austria, Belgium, Brazil, Bulgaria, Canada, Chile, China, Colombia, Croatia, Czechia, Denmark, Ecuador, Egypt, Estonia, France, Germany, Greece, Hungary, India, Ireland, Israel, Italy, Japan, Jordan, Lithuania, Mexico, Netherlands, New Zealand, North Macedonia, Norway, Peru, Poland, Portugal, Russia, Slovakia, South Africa, Spain, Sweden, Switzerland, Türkiye, UK, USA, Venezuela. [2022.10.24/XF5534/v/**F**]

♦ Paleopathology Club / see Paleopathology Association (#18029)
♦ Palestine Liberation Organization (internationally oriented national body)
♦ Palestinian Academic Society for the Study of International Affairs (internationally oriented national body)

♦ Pali Text Society (PTS) 18030

Office Admin Old Market Studios, 68 Old Market Street, Bristol, BS2 0EJ, UK. T. +447436534179. E-mail: info@palitextsociety.org – orders@palitext.com.
Pres/Treas address not obtained.
URL: http://www.palitext.com/

History 1881. Founded by T W Rhys Davis. **Aims** Foster and promote the study of Pali Theravada *Buddhism* texts. **Structure** General Assembly (twice a year); Regional Representatives (India, Japan, Korea Rep, New Zealand, Thailand, USA). **Languages** English, German. **Staff** 1.50 FTE, paid. **Finance** Sources: donations; members' dues; sale of publications. **Activities** Awards/prizes/competitions; publishing activities; research/ documentation. **Publications** Dictionaries; grammars; Buddhist texts in Pali and Buddhist hybrid Sanskrit or in translation.
Members Sponsoring; Ordinary primarily a corresponding membership organization. Members in 42 countries and territories:
Argentina, Australia, Austria, Bangladesh, Belgium, Brazil, Cambodia, Canada, Croatia, Denmark, Finland, France, Germany, Hong Kong, Hungary, India, Indonesia, Ireland, Israel, Italy, Japan, Jordan, Korea Rep, Luxembourg, Malaysia, Mexico, Myanmar, Nepal, Netherlands, New Zealand, Norway, Poland, Russia, Singapore, South Africa, Sri Lanka, Sweden, Switzerland, Taiwan, Thailand, UK, USA. [2022.10.19/XE3984/v/**E**]

♦ Pallottine Missionary Sisters – Missionary Sisters of the Catholic Apostolate (religious order)
♦ Pallottinerinnen – Missionsschwestern vom Katholischen Apostolat (religious order)
♦ Pallottines – Soeurs Missionnaires de l'Apostolat Catholique (religious order)
♦ Pallottini – Società dell'Apostolato Cattolico (religious order)
♦ Pallottins – Société de l'Apostolat Catholique (religious order)
♦ Palme Commission on Disarmament and Security Issues (inactive)
♦ **PALOP** Paises Africanos de Lingua Oficial Portuguesa (#18027)
♦ **PALU** Pan-African Lawyers Union (#18054)
♦ Palynological and Paleobotanical Association of Australasia (inactive)
♦ PAMA Global – Abacus and Mental Arithmetic Association (unconfirmed)
♦ PAMA Global – PAMA Global – Abacus and Mental Arithmetic Association (unconfirmed)
♦ PAMA – Pan American Medical Association (no recent information)
♦ **PAMCA** Pan-African Mosquito Control Association (#18055)
♦ **PAMDCC** Pan American Draughts and Checkers Confederation (#18095)
♦ PAME / see Protection of the Arctic Marine Environment (#18547)
♦ **PAME** Protection of the Arctic Marine Environment (#18547)
♦ **PAMESCO** Pan American Electronic Sports Confederation (#18096)
♦ PAM – International Conference on Practical Aspects of Memory (meeting series)
♦ PAMI – Pacific Asian Management Institute, Hawaii (internationally oriented national body)
♦ **PAMI** Pontificia Academia Mariana Internationalis (#18453)
♦ **PAMISS** Pan Arab Minimally Invasive Spine Society (#18149)
♦ PAM / see Mediterranean Action Plan (#16638)
♦ PAMMS – Pan-African Medical Mycology Society (inactive)
♦ PAMOJA Africa Reflect Network (internationally oriented national body)
♦ PAMOJA Afrique de l'Ouest (#18031)
♦ **Pamoja AO** PAMOJA Afrique de l'Ouest (#18031)
♦ PAMOJA – PAMOJA Africa Reflect Network (internationally oriented national body)

♦ PAMOJA West Africa 18031

PAMOJA Afrique de l'Ouest (Pamoja AO)
Coordinator 01 BP 6279, Cotonou, Benin. T. +22997476407. E-mail: contact@pamoja-west-africa.org.
Registered Office BP E 1419, Bamako, Mali.
URL: http://www.pamoja-west-africa.org/

History Registration: Start date: 19 Feb 2009, Mali. **Aims** Promote adult education and non-formal education in West Africa. **Structure** General Assembly; Board of Directors; Coordination. **Finance** Sources: members' dues. **Activities** Networking/liaising; training/education.
Members Networks in 13 countries:
Benin, Burkina Faso, Gambia, Ghana, Guinea, Guinea-Bissau, Mali, Morocco, Niger, Nigeria, Senegal, Sierra Leone, Togo.
IGO Relations Accredited by (1): *Organisation internationale de la Francophonie (OIF, #17809)*. **NGO Relations** Member of (1): *International Council for Adult Education (ICAE, #12983)*. [2021/XM7612/**F**]

♦ PAM – Pan African Movement (internationally oriented national body)
♦ **PAM** Parliamentary Assembly of the Mediterranean (#18212)
♦ **PAM** Programme alimentaire mondial (#21510)
♦ PAMS Foundation (internationally oriented national body)
♦ Pamuklu Testil Sanaylieri Birligi / see European Federation of Cotton and Allied Textiles Industries (#07093)
♦ **PAMWA** Pan American Medical Women's Alliance (#18120)
♦ **PanAAC** Pan African Agribusiness and Agro-Industry Consortium (#18034)
♦ PANABAF – Pan African Federation of Bank Employees (inactive)
♦ **PanAFITA** Pan-American Federation for Information Technology in Agriculture (#18102)
♦ Pan Africa Bible College / see Pan Africa Christian University
♦ Pan-Africa Bicycle Information Network (internationally oriented national body)
♦ Pan Africa Chemistry Network (internationally oriented national body)
♦ Pan Africa Christian University (internationally oriented national body)

♦ Pan Africa ILGA (PAI) 18032

Exec Dir 21 Village Road, Selby, Johannesburg, 2001, South Africa. T. +27113391139. E-mail: admin@panafricailga.org.
URL: http://panafricailga.org/

History A regional structure of *ILGA World (International Lesbian, Gay, Bisexual, Trans and Intersex Association, #11120)*. **Aims** Unify and strengthen LGBTIQ+ organising in Africa in order to challenge state legislation that impedes SOGIESC-related work. **Structure** Board. **Staff** 7.00 FTE, paid. **Activities** Advocacy/lobbying/ activism; events/meetings. **Events** *Regional Conference* Port Louis (Mauritius) 2023, *Regional Conference* Johannesburg (South Africa) 2021, *Regional Conference* Accra (Ghana) 2020, *Regional Conference* Gaborone (Botswana) 2018, *Regional Conference* Johannesburg (South Africa) 2016. **Publications** *Pan Africa ILGA newsletter*. **Members** African (over 150) and international (40) organizations. Membership countries not specified. [2023/AA1245/**E**]

♦ **Pan-African Academy of Christian Surgeons (PAACS)** **18033**
Exec Dir 1315 Park Ave, Palatine IL 60067, USA. T. +18475719926.
Administrator PO Box 9906, Fayetteville NC 28311-9906, USA.
URL: http://www.paacs.net/
History 1996, by missionary surgeons, as *Pan-African College of Christian Surgeons (PACCS)*. Current title adopted 2004. **Aims** Develop quality training programs in general surgery at Christian hospitals in Africa; assure a high level of professional competence among its members. **Languages** English. **Staff** 4.00 FTE, paid; 0.50 FTE, voluntary. **Finance** Voluntary donations. **Activities** Training/education. Active in: Bangladesh, Cameroon, Egypt, Ethiopia, Gabon, Kenya, Malawi, Niger, Tanzania UR. **Publications** *PAACS Bulletin* – electronic. [2016.12.15/XD8446/**D**]

♦ Pan-African Agency of the Great Green Wall (#00547)

♦ **Pan African Agribusiness and Agro-Industry Consortium (PanAAC)** **18034**
Secretariat PO Box 2542-00200, Nairobi, Kenya. T. +254202371307 – +254202679195. Fax +254202679112. E-mail: info@panaac.org.
URL: http://www.panaac.org/
History Jun 2007, Johannesburg (South Africa), and consolidated Nov 2007, Accra (Ghana). Registered in accordance with Kenyan law. **Aims** Promote sustainable agribusiness and agro-industry in Africa through enhanced productivity and competitiveness at national, regional and global levels. **Structure** General Assembly. Steering Committee, comprising Chairperson, CEO, 4 sub-regional focal point representatives, Scientific Resource person and Knowledge and Communication Officer. Chapters (4): East and Central; North; West and Central; South. Regional Secretariat, headed by CEO. **NGO Relations** Collaborates with: *African Technology Policy Studies Network (ATPS, #00481)*. Supports: *Farming First*. [2011/XJ2235/t/**D**]

♦ Pan African AIDS Organization / see Organisation PanAfricaine de Lutte pour la Santé (#17822)
♦ Pan African Anthropological Association / see Pan African Association of Anthropologists (#18036)

♦ **Pan-African Archaeological Association (PAA)** **18035**
Association panafricaine d'archéologie (PAA)
Pres address not obtained. E-mail: info@panaf.org.
URL: http://www.panafprehistory.org/en/
History Jan 1947, Nairobi (Kenya). Founded Jan 1947, (Nairobi) Kenya, on the initiative of Louis Leakey, as *Pan-African Congress on Prehistory*, which was attended by 54 delegates from 27 countries. Name changed: at 4th Congress in 1959, Leopldville (Belgian Congo), to *Pan African Congress of Prehistory and Quaternary Studies – Congrès panafricain de Préhistoire et d'études du Quaternaire*; and following the 8th Congress, Sep 1977, Nairobi, to *Pan African Association for Prehistory and Related Studies – Association panafricaine pour la préhistoire et les sciences auxilliaires*, a name under which it is still currently known. **Aims** Bring together prehistorians, palaeontologists and geologists from all over Africa; provide a forum for the exchange of information and ideas; create contacts between students, researchers and practitioners across Africa and in multiple disciplines; forge links and friendships that otherwise would not exist and to facilitate and promote inter-African collaboration. **Languages** English, French. **Events** *Congress* Zanzibar (Tanzania UR) 2022, *Congress* Rabat (Morocco) 2018, *Congress* Johannesburg (South Africa) 2014, *Congress* Dakar (Senegal) 2010, *Heritage management, eco-tourism, landscape dynamics, human evolution, trade and contact, etc* Gaborone (Botswana) 2005. **Publications** Congress Proceedings. **Members** Membership countries not specified. **NGO Relations** Cooperates with: *Society of Africanist Archaeologists (SAfA, #19517)*. [2021/XD7328/**D**]

♦ **Pan African Association of Anthropologists (PAAA)** **18036**
Association pan-africaine d'anthropologie (APA)
Pres c/o CATUC, PO Box 782, Bamenda, Cameroon.
URL: http://africananthropology.org/
History 6 Sep 1989, Yaoundé (Cameroon), on formal launching, following initial discussions at 12th International Congress of Anthropological and Ethnological Sciences, Jul 1989, Zagreb (Yugoslavia). Constitution adopted 27 Aug 1992. Sometimes referred to as *Pan African Anthropological Association*. **Aims** Promote excellence in anthropological endeavour and mobilize capacity building in the context of Africa's development; strengthen anthropological capacity, mobilize resources, stimulate research and disseminate anthropological knowledge that can have an impact on Africa's social economic and political development foster interaction among teachers and researchers in the various disciplines of anthropology; promote research and teaching of anthropology and related disciplines; coordinate regional interdisciplinary scientific research; ensure application of anthropological sciences in the search for solutions to development problems of Africa; facilitate exchange of teachers and students among teaching and research institutions. **Structure** General Assembly (every 3 years). Governing Council, comprising the Officers and 5 regional representatives. Executive Committee, comprising the Officers and one representative. Officers: President; 2 Vice Presidents; General Secretary; Deputy Secretary; Treasurer; Chairpersons of Committees (3): Research and Conferences; Public Relations; Publications and Research. Management Board. Secretariat. **Languages** English, French. **Staff** 3.00 FTE, paid; 2.00 FTE, voluntary. **Finance** Members' dues. Other sources: grants from international organizations, in particular: /First Category/ *Carnegie Corporation of New York*; *International Bank for Reconstruction and Development (IBRD, #12317)*; *International Development Research Centre (IDRC, #13162)*; *The Rockefeller Foundation (#18966)*; *UNESCO (#20322)*; *UNICEF (#20332)*; *United Nations Population Fund (UNFPA, #20612)*; *Wenner-Gren Foundations*; *WHO (#20950)*; Netherlands Embassy in Yaoundé (Cameroon). /Second Category/ African governments; local NGOs. **Activities** Organizes: annual conference; workshops; occasional meetings; training programme for junior faculty of African universities. Research networks (5): *Network of African Environmental Anthropologists (NAEA, no recent information)*; *Network of African Medical Anthropologists (NAMA, no recent information)*; *Network of African Population Anthropologists (NAPA, no recent information)*; *Network of African Students in Anthropology (NASA, no recent information)*; *Network of African Women Anthropologists (NAWA, no recent information)*. Networks organize occasional workshops and conferences on specific issues. Network training programme coordinated by *International Centre for Applied Social Science Research and Training, Yaoundé (ICASSRT, no recent information)*, which also raises funds for PAAA, implements and evaluates its programmes and presents administrative and financial reports for audit and approval before tabling at PAAA General Assembly. **Events** *Annual Conference* Yaoundé (Cameroon) 2020, *Annual conference* Cape Town (South Africa) 2006, *Annual Conference* Yaoundé (Cameroon) 2005, *Annual Conference* Accra (Ghana) 2004, *Annual Conference* Port Elizabeth (South Africa) 2003. **Publications** *PAA Newsletter* (4 a year); *African Anthropology* (2 a year) – journal. *Pan African Association of Anthropologists: Striving for Excellence* by Paul Nchoji Nkwi. Scientific papers.
Members Ordinary; Founding; Associate; Affiliate. Individuals (anthropologists) in 39 countries:
Algeria, Angola, Belgium, Benin, Botswana, Burkina Faso, Cameroon, Central African Rep, Chad, Congo Brazzaville, Congo DR, Côte d'Ivoire, Egypt, Equatorial Guinea, Eswatini, Ethiopia, Gabon, Ghana, Guinea-Bissau, Israel, Italy, Kenya, Lesotho, Liberia, Madagascar, Malawi, Mozambique, Netherlands, Niger, Nigeria, Senegal, Somalia, South Africa, Tanzania UR, Togo, Uganda, USA, Zambia, Zimbabwe.
NGO Relations Member of: *Association of Learned and Professional Society Publishers (ALPSP, #02786)*; *World Council of Anthropological Associations (WCAA, #21317)*. [2020/XD2612/**D**]

♦ Pan African Association of Artists and Intellectuals (inactive)
♦ Pan African Association of Catholic Exegetes (inactive)
♦ Pan African Association for Community Development (no recent information)
♦ Pan African Association on Human Settlements (inactive)
♦ Pan African Association for Literacy and Adult Education (no recent information)

♦ **Pan African Association of Neurological Sciences (PAANS)** **18037**
Association panafricaine des sciences neurologiques
Pres Dept of Surgery, Univ of Nairobi, Kenyatta Natl Hosp, PO Box 19676-00202, Nairobi, Kenya. E-mail: paansnairobi@gmail.com.
URL: http://www.paans.org/
History Jan 1972, Nairobi (Kenya). Founded following a Pan African Symposium on tumours. **Aims** Bring together all workers in neurosciences in Africa; collect and disseminate information on neurological, neurosurgical, psychiatric and allied disorders in Africa. **Structure** Biennial Congress; Council. **Languages** English, French. **Staff** Voluntary. **Finance** Members' dues. **Activities** Events/meetings; knowledge management/information dissemination. **Events** *Congress* Mombasa (Kenya) 2022, *Biennial Scientific and General Congress* Dar es Salaam (Tanzania UR) 2020, *Biennial Scientific and General Congress* Lomé (Togo) 2018, *Biennial Scientific and General Congress* Kampala (Uganda) 2016, *Biennial Scientific and General Congress* Grand-Bassam (Côte d'Ivoire) 2014. **Publications** *African Journal of Neurological Sciences* (4 a year).
Members Council Members; Honorary Fellows (from outside Africa); Fellows and Founding Members; Members; Associate Members, in 35 countries:
Algeria, Benin, Botswana, Burkina Faso, Burundi, Cameroon, Cape Verde, Congo DR, Côte d'Ivoire, Egypt, Ethiopia, France, Gambia, Ghana, Guinea, Kenya, Madagascar, Malawi, Mauritania, Mauritius, Morocco, Mozambique, Nigeria, Rwanda, Senegal, Sierra Leone, Somalia, South Africa, Sudan, Tanzania UR, Togo, Tunisia, Uganda, Zambia, Zimbabwe.
IGO Relations *WHO (#20950)*. [2022/XD6010/**D**]

♦ Pan African Association of Nuclear Medicine / see African Association of Nuclear Medicine (#00210)
♦ Pan-African Association of Plastic and Reconstructive Surgeons (inactive)

♦ **Pan-African Association for Port Cooperation (PAPC)** **18038**
Association pan-africaine de coopération portuaire (APCP)
Exec Sec PO Box 99209 – 80107, Mombasa, Kenya. E-mail: pmaesa@pmaesa.org.
URL: http://www.pmaesa.org/papc/
History Set up by *North African Port Management Association (NAPMA, #17556)*, *Port Management Association of Eastern and Southern Africa (PMAESA, #18462)* and *Port Management Association of West and Central Africa (PMAWCA, #18463)*, following joint seminar organized Jan 1998. **Aims** Provide a forum for cooperation on port development in Africa; ensure representation of the interests and promote the image of African ports in the world; assist in the development of African ports and improved efficiency and productivity. **Structure** Council; Board of Directors; Executive Secretariat (rotating); Committee of African Port Experts. **Languages** Arabic, English, French, Portuguese. **Events** *Conference* Mauritius 2018, *Conference* Dakar (Senegal) 2017, *Conference* Mombasa (Kenya) 2014, *Conference* Brazzaville (Congo Brazzaville) 2012, *Conference* Arusha (Tanzania UR) 2010. [2023.02.15/XD8742/**D**]

♦ Pan African Association for Prehistory and Related Studies / see Pan-African Archaeological Association (#18035)
♦ Pan African Association of Surgeons (no recent information)
♦ Pan-African Association of Women in Telecommunications and Information (no recent information)
♦ Pan African Association of Zoological Gardens, Aquaria and Botanical Gardens / see Pan-African Association of Zoos and Aquaria (#18039)

♦ **Pan-African Association of Zoos and Aquaria (PAAZA)** **18039**
Exec Dir PO Box 1586, Johannesburg, 1710, South Africa. T. +27117924567. Fax +27114766354. E-mail: executivedirector@zoosafrica.com.
Exec Office 3 Collins St, Windsor Glen, Johannesburg, 1710, South Africa.
URL: http://www.paaza.africa
History 1 Dec 1989, Pretoria (South Africa). Former names and other names: *Pan African Association of Zoological Gardens, Aquaria and Botanical Gardens* – former. **Aims** Coordinate, represent and promote the interests of African wildlife in captivity, particularly zoos and aquaria, at national, regional and international levels; promote international welfare best practice as determined by WAZA; consolidate zoo-based conservation actions, education programmes and research projects concerning fauna of the African continent; facilitate the exchange and distribution of expertise; promote professional best practice in African zoos and aquaria. **Structure** General Meeting (annual); Council; Executive Committee. Partner categories: Accredited Member; Under Construction partner; Conservation; Sanctuary; Rehab Facility; Captive Breeding; Commercial; Commercial with Animals. **Languages** English. **Finance** Sources: donations; meeting proceeds; members' dues. **Events** *Annual Conference* South Africa 2016, *Annual Conference* Durban (South Africa) 2015, *Annual Conference* Entebbe (Uganda) 2014, *Annual conference* South Africa 2007, *Annual Conference* East London (South Africa) 2006. **Publications** *PAAZA eNews* (6 a year); *PAAZAB Inventory* (annual). Conference proceedings; study books; manuals.
Members Institutional in 4 countries:
Ethiopia, Madagascar, South Africa, Uganda.
NGO Relations Member of (2): *International Zoo Educators Association (IZE, #15944)*; *World Association of Zoos and Aquariums (WAZA, #21208)*. Partner of (4): *European Association of Zoos and Aquaria (EAZA, #06283)*; *International Congress of Zookeepers (ICZ, #12902)*; *IUCN/SSC Conservation Breeding Specialist Group (CBSG)*; *Species360 (#19915)*. [2022.02.15/XD3232/**D**]

♦ **Pan-African Bean Research Alliance (PABRA)** **18040**
Contact PO Box 823-00621, Nairobi, Kenya. E-mail: ciatkenyainfo@cgiar.org.
Office PO Box 6247, Kampala, Uganda.
URL: http://www.pabra-africa.org/
History 1996. **Aims** Improve the bean crop for the benefit of Africa's rural and urban poor.
Members National agricultural research systems in 18 countries:
Angola, Burundi, Cameroon, Congo DR, Eswatini, Ethiopia, Kenya, Lesotho, Madagascar, Malawi, Mozambique, Rwanda, South Africa, Sudan, Tanzania UR, Uganda, Zambia, Zimbabwe.
Regional organizations (2):
Southern Africa Bean Research Network (SABRN, #19826).
NGO Relations *International Centre for Tropical Agriculture (#12527)*. [2021/XM2850/**F**]

♦ Pan African Bioinformatics Network for H3Africa (unconfirmed)

♦ **Pan African Booksellers Association (PABA)** **18041**
Chair c/o Moi Univ Bookshop, Box 3900, Eldoret, 30100, Kenya. T. +25453208020665 – +25453(254733712117. Fax +254532043047 – +254532043288.
History 1997. **Aims** Serve as a network for booksellers in Africa; promote and develop international cooperation within the industry. **Structure** Executive Committee, comprising Chairman, Vice-Chairman, Secretary, Treasurer and 3 members (1 ex-officio). **Languages** English, French. **Staff** None. **Finance** Members' dues (annual). Support from *Association for the Development of Education in Africa (ADEA, #02471)*. **Activities** Organizes African Booksellers Convention, annually since 1997; conducts workshops and seminars for members. Currently working on a training programme for African booksellers. **Events** *Annual African booksellers convention / Annual Convention* Dar es Salaam (Tanzania UR) 2008, *Annual African booksellers convention / Annual Convention* Dar es Salaam (Tanzania UR) 2006, *Annual African booksellers convention / Annual Convention* Lagos (Nigeria) 2005, *Regional workshop on intra Africa book trade* Accra (Ghana) 2004. **Publications** *PABA Newsletter* (4 a year).
Members Founding members in 5 countries; regular members in 25 countries:
Angola, Botswana, Cameroon, Côte d'Ivoire, Djibouti, Eritrea, Eswatini, Ethiopia, Gambia, Ghana, Guinea, Kenya, Lesotho, Malawi, Mali, Mozambique, Nigeria, Rwanda, Senegal, Sierra Leone, South Africa, Tanzania UR, Uganda, Zambia, Zimbabwe.
IGO Relations *International Bank for Reconstruction and Development (IBRD, #12317)* (World Bank). **NGO Relations** Works closely with: *African Publishers Network (APNET, #00426)*; *Book Aid International*. [2009.06.01/XD7124/**D**]

♦ **Pan African Burn Society (PABS)** **18042**
Sec Dept of Surgery, Univ Teaching Hospital, Ituku-Ozalla, Enugu, Nigeria. E-mail: africanburns@gmail.com.
URL: http://www.panafricanburns.org/
History 17 May 2004, Cape Town (South Africa). **Events** *Congress* Enugu (Nigeria) 2021, *Congress* Durban (South Africa) 2019, *Congress* Addis Ababa (Ethiopia) 2017, *Compassion and education – a new horizon for burns in Africa* Abidjan (Côte d'Ivoire) 2015, *Quality burns care in Africa – challenges and prospects* Accra (Ghana) 2013. **NGO Relations** Affiliate of: *International Society for Burn Injuries (ISBI, #14986)*. [2017/XM8247/**D**]

♦ Pan African Centre for Climate Policy (internationally oriented national body)
♦ Pan African Christian Broadcast Association (inactive)

♦ **Pan African Christian Women Alliance (PACWA)** **18043**
Alliance des Femmes Evangeliques en Afrique (AFEA)
Exec Sec PO Box 49332-00100, Nairobi, Kenya. E-mail: pacwafrica@aeafrica.org.
URL: http://www.aeafrica.org/commissions/pan.htm

History 12 Aug 1989, Nairobi (Kenya), as Commission on Women Affairs of the *Association of Evangelicals in Africa (AEA, #02587)*. **Aims** Carry the Gospel light to those who are yet to be reached; stop the tide of ungodly *secularism* and *materialism*; assert the true dignity of women as found in God's Word; inject biblical *morals* and *values* into African society through women; educate women on matters of justice, equity and socio-economic development; deliver Africa from moral decadence and ultimate collapse; foster effective cooperation of all Christian women ministries in Africa; enhance a family spirit for *evangelical* women in Africa. **Structure** PACWA Continental Council, consisting of 21 members. Executive Committee. Regions (7): West Africa Anglophone; West Africa Francophone; North Africa Anglophone; Eastern Africa Anglophone; Central Africa Francophone; Southern Africa Anglophone; the Islands. **Activities** Projects/programmes; networking/ liaising; events/meetings. **Events** *Regional conference* Mauritius 2002, *Continental Meeting* Botswana 2001, *Water information summit* Fort Lauderdale, FL (USA) 1998, *Continental conference / Continental Meeting* South Africa 1997, *Continental conference* Nairobi (Kenya) 1996. **Publications** *Christian Women and Politics*; *Our Time Has Come*.
Members Covers 34 countries:
Angola, Benin, Botswana, Burkina Faso, Burundi, Cameroon, Central African Rep, Chad, Côte d'Ivoire, Eswatini, Ethiopia, Gabon, Gambia, Ghana, Kenya, Lesotho, Liberia, Madagascar, Malawi, Mali, Mauritius, Namibia, Netherlands, Niger, Nigeria, Rwanda, South Africa, Tanzania UR, Togo, Uganda, UK, USA, Zambia, Zimbabwe.
NGO Relations Member of: *Side by Side (#19265)*. [2019/XE1582/E]

♦ Pan-African Citizens Network (PACIN) 18044

Exec Dir PO Box 21976, Nairobi, 00505, Kenya. T. +254710819046. E-mail: info@ccpau.org.
URL: http://ccpau.org/
History 2007, as *Centre for Citizens' Participation on the African Union (CCPAU)*. Current title adopted 2017. **Aims** Ensure effective civil society engagement with the African Union in the interest of the citizens of Africa. **Structure** Board; Secretariat. **Activities** Events/meetings. [2017/XM6228/F]

♦ Pan-African Civil Aviation Commission / see African Civil Aviation Commission (#00248)

♦ Pan-African Civil Society Network (PACSNET) 18045

Réseau Pan-Africain de la Société Civile (REPASC)
Pres 2nd Floor, Kano Foundation Bldg, 15 Buk Road, PO Box 14427, Kano, Nigeria. T. +23464318561. Fax +23464667394. E-mail: pacsnet2001@yahoo.co.uk.
European Pres 22 avenue Siméon Foucault, 4440 Rezé, France. E-mail: reseaupanafricainsociv@gmail.com.
URL: http://www.pacsnet.net/
History 2003. Registered in accordance with French law. **Aims** Accelerate African people's and African environment's social and economic development. **Structure** Board, headed by Funding President and European President. **Languages** English, French. **Staff** Voluntary. **Finance** Budget varies according to projects. **Activities** Strategy and Diplomacy; International Cooperation and Development; International Public Security; Good Governance and Fight against Corruption; Promotion of Peace and Human Rights. Projects in Burundi, Senegal, Rwanda, Benin, Cameroon and Congo Democratic Rep. [2012.11.19/XJ5197/F]

♦ Pan African Climate Justice Alliance / see Panafrican Climate Justice Alliance (#18046)
♦ PanAfrican Climate Justice Alliance / see Panafrican Climate Justice Alliance (#18046)

♦ Panafrican Climate Justice Alliance (PACJA) 18046

Continental Secretariat Kabarnet Road, off Ngong Road, House No J13, PO Box 51005-00200, Nairobi, Kenya. T. +254208075808. E-mail: info@pacja.org.
URL: http://www.pacja.org/
History 2008. Also referred to as *PanAfrican Climate Justice Alliance*. **Aims** Develop and promote pro-poor development and equity based positions relevant for Africa in the international *climate change* dialogue and related processes. **Structure** General Assembly; Continental Executive Committee; National Chapters; Secretariat, headed by Secretary General. **Languages** English, French. **Staff** 19.00 FTE, paid. **Finance** Members' dues. Other sources: fundraising partners; donations; grants. **Activities** Networking/liaising; events/ meetings; politics/policy/regulatory; advocacy/lobbying/activism; awards/prizes/competitions. **Publications** Policy briefs; discussion papers; magazines; statements; position papers; research work. **Members** Faith- and community-based organizations; NGO's; trusts; foundations; farmers' and pluralists' groups; other sectors. Members in 45 countries across Africa. Membership countries not specified. **Consultative Status** Consultative status granted from: *UNEP (#20299)*. **IGO Relations** Consultative Status with: *United Nations Framework Convention on Climate Change – Secretariat (UNFCCC, #20564)*. Accredited organization of: *Green Climate Fund (GCF, #10714)*; **NGO Relations** Partners include: *ACT Alliance EU (#00082)*; *Christian Aid*; *Climate Justice Now ! (CJN!, inactive)*; *Diakonia*; *Ecological Society for Eastern Africa (ESEA, #05300)*; *Finn Church Aid (FCA)*; *Jubilee South – Asian Peoples' Movement on Debt and Development (JSAPMDD, #16160)*; *Oxfam International (#17922)*; *PAI (#18025)*. Hosts: *African Coalition for Sustainable Energy and Access (ACSEA)*. [2020/XJ8943/D]

♦ Pan-African College of Christian Surgeons / see Pan-African Academy of Christian Surgeons (#18033)

♦ Pan-African Composers' and Songwriters' Alliance (PACSA) 18047

Contact PO Box 71564, Bryanston 2121, Johannesburg, South Africa. T. +27823754041.
URL: http://www.pacsa.org/
History 2010, Dakar (Senegal). **Aims** Lobby for the interests of composers and songwriters in the region. **Activities** Advocacy/lobbying/activism; awareness raising; training/education; networking/liaising.
Members Associations (35) in 29 countries:
Algeria, Angola, Benin, Burkina Faso, Cameroon, Congo Brazzaville, Côte d'Ivoire, Egypt, Guinea, Kenya, Madagascar, Malawi, Mali, Mauritius, Morocco, Mozambique, Namibia, Niger, Nigeria, Rwanda, Senegal, Seychelles, South Africa, Tanzania UR, Togo, Tunisia, Uganda, Zambia, Zimbabwe.
NGO Relations Partner of: *International Council of Music Authors (#13052) – Confédération internationale des sociétés d'auteurs et compositeurs (CISAC, #04563)*. [2018/XM6672/D]

♦ Pan-African Congress (meeting series)
♦ Pan-African Congress, 1919 (inactive)
♦ Pan-African Congress on Prehistory / see Pan-African Archaeological Association (#18035)
♦ Pan African Congress of Prehistory and Quaternary Studies / see Pan-African Archaeological Association (#18035)
♦ Pan African Conservation Network, Kenya (unconfirmed)
♦ Pan African Council for Protection of the Environment and for Development (inactive)
♦ Pan African Development Education and Advocacy Programme (internationally oriented national body)
♦ Pan African Diabetes Study Group (no recent information)
♦ Pan-African Employers' Confederation / see Business Africa (#03377)

♦ Pan-African Environmental Mutagen and Genomic Society (PAEMGS) 18048

Pres c/o AMHBI-CPUT, PO Box 1906, Bellville, Cape Town, 7530, South Africa.
History Former names and other names: *Pan African Environmental Mutagen Society (PAEMS)* – former. **Events** *International Conference* Stellenbosch (South Africa) 2021, *Conference* 2020, *Triennial Conference* Cairo (Egypt) 2017, *Triennial Conference* Cairo (Egypt) 2003, *Triennial Conference* Harare (Zimbabwe) 1999. **Members** Membership countries not specified. **NGO Relations** Member of (1): *International Association of Environmental Mutagenesis and Genomics Societies (IAEMGS, #11877)*. Cooperates with (1): *Society for Free Radical Research Africa (SFRR-Africa, #19559)*. [2021/XD7029/D]

♦ Pan African Environmental Mutagen Society / see Pan-African Environmental Mutagen and Genomic Society (#18048)
♦ Pan African Episcopal Conference (inactive)

♦ PanAfrican Farmers' Organization (PAFO) 18049

Organisation Panafricaine des Agriculteurs
Communications Officer Bibare Street KG125, House No 13, Kimironko, Kigali, Rwanda. T. +250733202069. E-mail: info@pafo-africa.org – communication@pafo-africa.org.
URL: http://pafo-africa.org/
History Oct 2010, Lilongwe (Malawi). Founded under the auspices of *African Union (AU, #00488)*. Registration: Rwanda Governance Board, No/ID: 001/RGB/19, Start date: 2019, Rwanda. **Aims** Represent the interests of African farmers and promote the development of African agriculture. **Structure** General Assembly; Board of Directors; Executive Secretariat. **Staff** 8.00 FTE, paid. **Activities** Advocacy/lobbying/activism; awareness raising; capacity building; guidance/assistance/consulting; knowledge management/information dissemination; monitoring/evaluation; projects/programmes. **Publications** *African Food Systems – Systèmes Alimentaires Africains* (2021) in English, French; *Family Farming Specificities and Land Governance Process – Spécificités de l'Agriculture Familiale et Processus de Gouvernance Foncière* (2021) in English, French; *Financing agricultural value chains to empower rural women – Financement des chaînes de valeur Agricole pour autonomiser les femmes Rurales* (2021) in English, French; *Positioning of African Farmers Organizations in the context of the AfCFTA – Positionnement des organisations paysannes africaines dans le contexte de la ZLECAf* (2021) in English, French.
Members Regional organizations (5):
Eastern African Farmers Federation (EAFF, #05223); *Plateforme Régionale des Organisations Paysannes d'Afrique Centrale (PROPAC)*; *Southern African Confederation of Agricultural Unions (SACAU, #19840)*; *Union Magrébine et Nord Africaine des Agriculteurs (UMNAGRI)*; *West African Network of Farmers' Organizations and Agricultural Producers (#20891)*.
NGO Relations Memorandum of Understanding with (1): *Alliance for a Green Revolution in Africa (AGRA, #00685)*. Member of (1): *Global Open Data for Agriculture and Nutrition (GODAN, #10514)*. [2022.02.15/XM4440/y/D]

♦ Pan African Federation of Accountants (PAFA) 18050

CEO 17 Fricker Road, Illovo, Sandton, Johannesburg, 2196, South Africa. T. +27114790602 – +27114790604. E-mail: info@pafa.org.za.
URL: http://www.pafa.org.za/
History May 2011. **Aims** Accelerate and strengthen the voice and capacity of the accountancy profession to work in the public interest; facilitate trade and enhance benefits and quality services to Africa's citizens. **Structure** Board. **Languages** English, French, Portuguese. **Staff** 5.00 FTE, paid; 1.00 FTE, voluntary. **Finance** Members' dues. **Activities** Standards/guidelines; networking/liaising; capacity building; research and development; advocacy/lobbying/activism; events/meetings. **Events** *Africa Congress of Accountants* Maputo (Mozambique) 2021, *Africa Congress of Accountants* Maputo (Mozambique) 2020, *Africa Congress of Accountants* Marrakech (Morocco) 2019, *Technical Excellence and Value Management Conference* Nairobi (Kenya) 2018, *Africa Congress of Accountants* Kampala (Uganda) 2017. **Members** Professional accountancy organizations (53) in 43 countries. Membership countries not specified. **IGO Relations** *African Union (AU, #00488)*; *Organisation pour l'Harmonisation en Afrique du Droit des Affaires (OHADA, #17806)*. **NGO Relations** *African Organisation of English-speaking Supreme Audit Institutions (AFROSAI-E, #00403)*; *Confederation of Asian and Pacific Accountants (CAPA, #04511)*; *East and Southern African Association of Accountants-General (ESAAG, #05262)*; *Fédération internationale des experts-comptables francophones (FIDEF, #09630)*; *International Federation of Accountants (IFAC, #13335)*. [2018.09.14/XJ6370/D]

♦ Pan African Federation of Agricultural and Food Workers (inactive)
♦ Pan African Federation of Agricultural Trade Unions (inactive)
♦ Pan African Federation of Associations for Persons with Mental Handicap (no recent information)
♦ Pan African Federation of Bank Employees (inactive)
♦ Pan African Federation of Banks, Insurance and Financial Affairs (no recent information)
♦ Pan African Federation of Building, Construction and Woodworkers (no recent information)
♦ Pan-African Federation of Clerical Workers (#09700)
♦ Pan African Federation of the Disabled (no recent information)
♦ Pan African Federation of Film Makers (no recent information)
♦ Pan African Federation of Food, Tobacco, Hotels and Allied Workers (no recent information)
♦ Pan African Federation of Industry Workers (no recent information)
♦ Pan African Federation of Local Government Trade Unions (inactive)
♦ Pan African Federation for Maternal and Child Health (no recent information)
♦ Pan African Federation of OAU Associations and Clubs (no recent information)

♦ Pan African Federation of Oto-Rhino-Laryngological Societies (PAFOS) 18051

Fédération panafricaine des associations d'oto-rhino-laryngologie
SG 1401 Durdoc Centre, 460 Smith Street, Durban, 4001, South Africa.
URL: https://sites.google.com/site/pafosweb/
History 1983, as a regional sub-group of *International Federation of Oto-Rhino-Laryngological Societies (IFOS, #13496)*. Statutes adopted 1989. **Aims** Promote, coordinate and unify the advancement of oto-rhino-laryngology in Africa; encourage and coordinate scientific research; represent *ORL* interests in other organizations in Africa dedicated to *prevention* and control of *diseases* and *disorders* related to ORL; train oto-rhino-laryngologists. **Structure** General Assembly (every 2 years). Executive Committee (meets every year), consisting of President, President Elect, General Secretary, Assistant Secretary and 5 other members. Pan-African Congress (every 2 years). **Finance** Members' dues. **Events** *Congress* Hammamet (Tunisia) 2019, *Conference* Abuja (Nigeria) 2017, *Congress* Luxor (Egypt) 2015, *Biennial scientific meeting* Dakar (Senegal) 1994, *Biennial scientific meeting* Cairo (Egypt) 1992.
Members National ORL societies in 5 countries:
Egypt, Ghana, Kenya, Nigeria, South Africa.
Societies waiting for registration with IFOS before becoming full PAFOS members in 9 countries:
Cameroon, Congo DR, Gabon, Malawi, Senegal, Sierra Leone, Tanzania UR, Tunisia, Uganda.
Countries and territories not having national ORL societies, grouped in Zonal Groups.
Francophone West Africa (12):
Benin, Burkina Faso, Burundi, Central African Rep, Chad, Congo Brazzaville, Côte d'Ivoire, Equatorial Guinea, Mali, Niger, Rwanda, Togo.
Anglophone West Africa (2):
Gambia, Liberia.
Portuguese and Central Africa (6):
Angola, Cape Verde, Guinea-Bissau, Mozambique, Sao Tomé-Principe, Zambia.
Southern Africa (10):
Botswana, Comoros, Eswatini, Lesotho, Madagascar, Mauritius, Namibia, Réunion, Seychelles, Zimbabwe.
North Africa (9):
Algeria, Djibouti, Ethiopia, Libya, Mauritania, Morocco, Sahara West, Somalia, Sudan. [2019/XE1274/E]

♦ Pan African Federation of Petroleum and Allied Workers (no recent information)
♦ Pan African Federation of Printers, Journalists, Cultural, Information and Allied Workers (inactive)
♦ Pan-African Federation of Teachers' Trade Unions (no recent information)
♦ Pan African Federation of Transport Workers (inactive)
♦ Pan African Federation of Workers in the Textile, Clothing and Leather Industry (no recent information)
♦ Pan African Freedom Movement of East and Central Africa (inactive)
♦ Pan African Health Organization (#17822)

♦ Pan-African Human Rights Defenders Network (AfricanDefenders) . 18052

Head of Secretariat/Coordinator Human Rights House, Plot 1853 John Kiyinji Road, Nsambya, PO Box 70356, Kampala, Uganda. E-mail: panafrica@defenddefenders.org – info@africandefenders.org.
URL: http://africandefenders.org/
History 20 Apr 2009, Johannesburg (South Africa). Founded at the All Africa Human Rights Defenders Conference (Johannesbnurg +10). **Aims** Promote and protect human rights defenders (HRDs) across the African continent. **Structure** Steering Committee; Secretariat. **Languages** Arabic, English, French, Portuguese. **Staff** 4.00 FTE, paid. **Activities** Advocacy/lobbying/activism; capacity building; research/documentation. Protection for at-risk human rights defenders. **Publications** *The State of African Human Rights Defenders 2016*.
Members Sub-regional organizations (5) covering the entire African continent:
Cairo Institute for Human Rights Studies (CIHRS, #03397); *East and Horn of Africa Human Rights Defenders Network (EHAHRD-Net, #05259)*; *Réseau des Défenseurs des Droits Humains en Afrique Centrale (REDHAC, #18870)*; *Southern African Human Rights Defenders Network (SAHRDN)*; *West African Human Rights Defenders' Network (WAHRDN, #20882)*.

IGO Relations *African Commission on Human and Peoples' Rights (ACHPR, #00255); African Court on Human and Peoples' Rights (AfCHPR, #00278); African Union (AU, #00488); United Nations (UN, #20515).* **NGO Relations** Affiliated with (1): East and Horn of Human Rights Defenders Project (DefendDefenders). [2022.05.09/XM6453/**F**]

♦ Pan African Institute for Development (PAID) 18053

Institut panafricain pour le développement (IPD) – Instituto Panafricano de Desarrollo

SG PAID Geneva Office, CP 38, Rue Varembé 3, 1211 Geneva 20, Switzerland. T. +41227336016 – +41227336017. Fax +41227330975. E-mail: sg-paid-ipd@hotmail.ch – gs@paidafrica.org.

Yaoundé Office BP 35 527, Bastos, Yaoundé, Cameroon. T. +23722208235.

URL: http://paidafrica.org/

History Founded 20 Jan 1964, Geneva (Switzerland), following initiative of Robert Vautherin, Fernand Vincent (the first Secretary-General) and Mgr Zoa at an Inter-African Colloquium, May 1962, Douala-Bassa (Cameroon). First meeting 28 Feb 1964, Geneva. Administration has been progressively transferred from non-Africans to Africans and headquarters moved from Geneva (Switzerland) to Africa. Diplomatic statute with governments of Cameroon, Burkina Faso and Zambia. Registered in accordance with Swiss Civil Code. **Aims** Maintain dual role as an international association and a training institute; further economic, social and cultural development of African countries, locally, regionally and nationally, through information, mobilization and participation of populations concerned; promote integrated, concerted, decent, *sustainable* and participatory development, stressing plurality of ways and means; assist in identification and analysis of development problems; study policy issues; provide practical *training* for *rural* development officers at all levels; train trainers, allowing maximum multiplier effect; conduct training, research and provide technical support to local, *self-help* projects. **Structure** Governing Council (meets annually); Executive Committee (meets twice a year); Management Committee; Joint Committee; General Secretariat, including Geneva Office and Yaoundé Office. Constituent Regional Institutes (5): *Institut Panafricain pour le Développement Afrique Centrale francophone (IPD-AC)*, Douala (Cameroon); *Institut Panafricain pour le Développement Afrique de l'Ouest anglophone (PAID-WA)*, Buéa (Cameroon); *Institut Panafricain pour le Développement Afrique de l'ouest et le Sahel francophone (IPD-AOS)*, Ouagadougou (Burkina Faso); *Institut Panafricain pour le Développement Afrique de l'Est et Australe anglophone (PAID-ESA)*, Kabwe (Zambia); *Institut Panafricain pour le Développement Afrique du Nord (IPD-AN)*, Salé (Morocco). Several national sections in Europe and Japan. **Languages** English, French. **Staff** 93.00 FTE, paid. Network of consultants works on a part-time basis. **Finance** Sources: projects; consultancy; research activities; bilateral programmes; grants from foundations; contributions from private and public bodies and individuals. Budget (annual): US$ 2.5 million. **Activities** Training/education; research/documentation; guidance/assistance/consulting; events/meetings. **Publications** *PAID Reports* – (annual) several series. Newsletters; magazine; articles; books.

Members National Sections and individuals, in 33 countries:
Belgium, Benin, Botswana, Burkina Faso, Burundi, Cameroon, Canada, Central African Rep, Chad, Congo DR, Côte d'Ivoire, Eswatini, Ethiopia, France, Gambia, Germany, Ghana, Kenya, Madagascar, Mali, Mauritania, Mauritius, Nigeria, Rwanda, Senegal, Sierra Leone, Switzerland, Tanzania UR, Togo, Uganda, UK, USA, Zambia.

Consultative Status Consultative status granted from: *FAO (#09260)* (Special Status); *ILO (#11123)* (Special List); *UNICEF (#20332)*.

IGO Relations Cooperates with: *United Nations African Institute for Economic Development and Planning (#20518); United Nations Economic Commission for Africa (ECA, #20554).*
Associated with Department of Global Communications of the United Nations.

NGO Relations Member of: *Association of Management Training Institutions of Eastern and Southern Africa (AMTIESA, no recent information); Fédération des Institutions Internationales établies à Genève (FIIG, #09599); NGO Committee on UNICEF (#17120).* Instrumental in setting up: *Fondation de l'Institut Panafricain pour le Développement (FIPD, #09820).* Cooperates with: *Development Innovations and Networks (#05057).* [2018.08.20/XD3046/j/**E**]

- ♦ Pan African Institute for Entrepreneurship and Community Development (internationally oriented national body)
- ♦ Pan African Institute – Pan African Institute for Entrepreneurship and Community Development (internationally oriented national body)
- ♦ Pan-African Intellectual Property Organisation (unconfirmed)
- ♦ Pan-African Islamic Society for Agro-Cultural Development (inactive)
- ♦ Pan African Journalists' Union, 1961 (inactive)
- ♦ Pan African Laity Coordination Board (#05523)
- ♦ Pan-African Lawyers' Association / see Pan-African Lawyers Union (#18054)

♦ Pan-African Lawyers Union (PALU) 18054

Communications Officer 3 Jandu Road, Corridor Area, PO Box 6065, Arusha, Tanzania UR. T. +255272543192 – +255272543194. Fax +255272543195. E-mail: secretariat@lawyersofafrica.org – info@lawyersofafrica.org.

CEO address not obtained.

URL: https://www.lawyersofafrica.org/

History 10 Sep 2002, Addis Ababa (Ethiopia). Founded when statutes and bylaws approved, following agreement on Constitution and Mission Statement, 7 Mar 2002, Addis Ababa. Former names and other names: *Pan-African Lawyers' Association* – former. Registration: Start date: Sep 2002, Ethiopia; Start date: 10 Jun 2010, Tanzania UR. **Aims** Advance the law and legal profession, rule of law, good governance, human and people's rights, and socio-economic development of the African continent. **Structure** General Assembly (at least every 3 years); Council; Executive Committee. **Languages** Arabic, English, French, Portuguese. **Staff** 10.00 FTE, paid. **Finance** Sources: donations; members' dues; sale of publications. **Activities** Events/meetings; guidance/assistance/consulting; training/education. **Events** *Annual Conference* Livingstone (Zambia) 2023, *20th Anniversary Celebrations Conference* Addis Ababa (Ethiopia) 2022, *Annual Conference* Arusha (Tanzania UR) 2022, *Annual Conference* Tunis (Tunisia) 2018, *Annual Conference* Durban (South Africa) 2017. **Publications** *Guide to Complementarity within the African Human Rights System*; *Pan African Yearbook of Law*. **Members** Regional Lawyers' Associations (5); National Lawyers' Associations (54); Individual. Membership countries not specified. **IGO Relations** Memorandum of Understanding with (1): *African Union (AU, #00488).* Member of (1): AU-ECOSOCC. **NGO Relations** Member of (3): *Coalition for an Effective African Court on Human and Peoples' Rights (African Court Coalition, #04055); International Coalition for the Responsibility to Protect (ICRtoP, #12620); International Legal Assistance Consortium (ILAC, #14025).* [2023/XD9452/**D**]

- ♦ Pan African Leadership and Entrepreneurship Development Centre (unconfirmed)
- ♦ Pan African League Against Tribalism, Sectarianism and Racism (inactive)
- ♦ Pan-African Medical Mycology Society (inactive)

♦ Pan-African Mosquito Control Association (PAMCA) 18055

Contact address not obtained. E-mail: info@pamca.org.

URL: https://pamca.org/

History 2009, Nairobi (Kenya). Founded at 5th Multilateral Initiative on Malaria (MIM) Pan African Malaria Conference. Registration: Start date: 2011, Kenya. **Aims** Provide a platform for African scientists, public health professionals and stakeholders to drive efforts towards control and elimination of mosquito borne diseases. **Structure** Board of Directors; Secretariat. **Activities** Capacity building; events/meetings; knowledge management/information dissemination; training/education. **Events** *Annual Conference* Kigali (Rwanda) 2022, *Annual Conference* Accra (Ghana) 2021, *Annual Conference* Accra (Ghana) 2020. [2020/AA0948/**D**]

- ♦ Pan African Movement (internationally oriented national body)
- ♦ Pan-African Network in Defense of Migrants' Rights (unconfirmed)

♦ Pan African Network of People with Psychosocial Disabilities (PANUSP) 18056

Contact 6 The Vines, Constantia 7806, Cape Town, South Africa. T. +27720441024. E-mail: info@panusp.org.

Facebook: https://www.facebook.com/PANPPD/

History 2005, Kampala (Uganda). Constitution officially adopted 15 Oct 2011, Cape Town (South Africa). Former names and other names: *Pan African Network of Users and Survivors of Psychiatry (PANUSP)* – former. **Aims** Represent people living with psychosocial disabilities in Africa; increase continental solidarity amongst organizations that promote and protect the rights of people with psychosocial disabilities. **Structure** Board; Secretariat. **Languages** English. **Staff** 1.00 FTE, voluntary. **Finance** No funding. **Activities** Advocacy/lobbying/activism. **Events** *Congress* Cape Town (South Africa) 2011.

Members Full in 9 countries:
Gambia, Ghana, Kenya, Malawi, Rwanda, South Africa, Tanzania UR, Uganda, Zambia.

NGO Relations Member of (1): *Africa Disability Alliance (ADA).* [2018/XJ8599/**D**]

- ♦ Pan African Network of Users and Survivors of Psychiatry / see Pan African Network of People with Psychosocial Disabilities (#18056)
- ♦ Pan-African News Agency (inactive)
- ♦ Pan African Organisation for Research and Protection of Violence on Women and Children (internationally oriented national body)

♦ Pan African Organization for Sustainable Development (POSDEV) . . 18057

Organisation pan africaine pour le développement durable

Coordinator PO Box 641, Accra North, Accra, Ghana. T. +23324677316776. E-mail: posdev@posdev.org.

URL: http://www.posdev.org/

History 1997, Sogakope (Ghana). **Aims** Build an alliance of African NGOs committed to empowerment of local grassroots movements as the driving force for attaining self-reliant sustainable development and social justice in Africa. **Structure** General Assembly (annual); Executive Committee; Permanent Secretariat headed by Coordinator. **Languages** English, French. **Staff** 5.00 FTE, paid. **Finance** Members' dues. Other sources: contributions; income from contracts; overhead and cost recovery systems with regard to facilitating programmes for member organizations; grants. **Activities** Research and development; advocacy/lobbying/activism; financial and/or material support. **Events** *General assembly* Tamale (Ghana) 2005, *General Assembly* Bamako (Mali) 2002, *General Assembly* Accra (Ghana) 2001, *Meeting* Accra (Ghana) 2001. **Publications** *POSDEV Newsletter* (4 a year).

Members Full; Associate. National organizations (11) in 9 countries:
Angola, Benin, Burkina Faso, Ghana, Mali, Niger, Sao Tomé-Principe, South Africa, Zimbabwe.
Included in the above, 2 organizations listed in this Yearbook:
African Centre for Human Development (ACHD, no recent information); Institut africain de gestion et de formation (INAGEF, no recent information).

Consultative Status Consultative status granted from: *UNCTAD (#20285)* (General). **NGO Relations** Advisory Committee member of: *Africa Liaison Program Initiative (ALPI).* Links with the Commission on the Advancement of Women of: *American Council for Voluntary International Action (InterAction).* Collaborates with: *International NGO Training and Research Centre, Oxford (INTRAC).* [2014.09.28/XD7713/**D**]

- ♦ Pan African Ornithological Congress (meeting series)

♦ Pan-African Parliament (PAP) 18058

Parliament Panafricain – Parlamento Pan-africano

Senior Media/Communications Officer 19 Richards Drive, Gallagher Estate, Midrand 1685, Johannesburg, South Africa. T. +27115455000. E-mail: info@panafricanparliament.org.

URL: https://pap.au.int

History Established following signature of a Protocol to *Treaty Establishing the African Economic Community (Abuja treaty, 1991)*, 2 Mar 2001, Sirte (Libyan AJ). An organ of *African Union (AU, #00488)*, which superseded *Organization of African Unity (OAU, inactive)* in Jul 2002. First meeting of speakers, deputy speakers, ministers, deputy ministers, ambassadors representing member states at OAU, clerks, parliamentary staff and officials from ministries responsible for foreign affairs had been held 5-17 Nov 2000, Pretoria (South Africa). Expected to function as a consultative body without legislative powers for 5 years, becoming a legislative assembly in 2007. Will come within the framework of *African Economic Community (AEC, #00290)*, which is expected to be implemented by 2025. Former names and other names: *Pan-African Parliament of the Union* – alias. **Aims** Facilitate effective implementation of policies and objectives of the OAU/AEC and, ultimately, of the African Union; promote the principles of human rights and democracy in Africa; encourage good governance, transparency and accountability in member states; familiarize the peoples of Africa with objectives and policies aimed at integration of the African Continent within the framework of the African Union; promote peace, security and stability; contribute to a more prosperous future for the peoples of Africa by promoting collective self-reliance and economic recovery; facilitate cooperation and development in Africa; strengthen solidarity and build a sense of common destiny among the peoples of Africa; facilitate cooperation among regional economic communities and their parliamentary fora. **Structure** Parliament (meeting in ordinary session at least twice a year) comprises 5 representatives of each member state, at least one of whom must be a woman, representation also reflecting the diversity of political opinions in each National Parliament or other deliberative organ. Bureau, comprising President and 4 Regional Vice-Presidents. **Languages** Arabic, English, French, Portuguese, Spanish, Swahili. **Finance** Annual budget is an integral part of the regular budget of the African Union Supported by: *African Union (AU, #00488).* Annual budget: 20,000,000 USD (2022). **Events** *APKN conference on open and learning parliaments* Midrand (South Africa) 2010, *Africa e-parliament conference* Midrand (South Africa) 2010, *Conference of African parliamentary speakers* Midrand (South Africa) 2010, *World e-parliament conference* Midrand (South Africa) 2010, *Session* Midrand (South Africa) 2009.

Members African Member States:
Algeria, Angola, Benin, Botswana, Burkina Faso, Burundi, Cameroon, Cape Verde, Central African Rep, Chad, Comoros, Congo Brazzaville, Congo DR, Côte d'Ivoire, Djibouti, Egypt, Equatorial Guinea, Eritrea, Eswatini, Ethiopia, Gabon, Gambia, Ghana, Guinea, Guinea-Bissau, Kenya, Lesotho, Liberia, Libya, Madagascar, Malawi, Mali, Mauritania, Mauritius, Morocco, Mozambique, Namibia, Niger, Nigeria, Rwanda, Sahrawi ADR, Sao Tomé-Principe, Senegal, Seychelles, Sierra Leone, Somalia, South Africa, South Sudan, Sudan, Tanzania UR, Togo, Tunisia, Uganda, Zambia, Zimbabwe.

IGO Relations Works in close cooperation with parliaments of the Regional Economic Communities and the national parliaments or other deliberative organs of member states. Agreement with: *Interparliamentary Assembly of Member Nations of the Commonwealth of Independent States (IPA CIS, #15958).* Cooperates with: *Parliamentary Assembly of the Council of Europe (PACE, #18211).* Agreement with: *Council of Europe (CE, #04881). Arab Parliament (#01023)* is observer. [2022.10.11/XF6545/**F***]

- ♦ Pan-African Parliament of the Union / see Pan-African Parliament (#18058)

♦ Pan African Pediatric Surgical Association (PAPSA) 18059

Pres PO Box 16122, Collins Street, West Victoria, Cape Town, 8007, South Africa. E-mail: info@papsa-africa.org.

URL: http://www.papsa-africa.org/

Aims Promote the practice, education and advancement of paediatric surgery in Africa; promote and maintain high clinical and ethical research standards; foster development of paediatric surgery in underprivileged areas in Africa; evaluate and carry out goal directed research; establish a forum for communication between paediatric surgeons in Africa and other parts of the world. **Structure** Board. Committees (4): Education, Scientific and Programme; Research; Standards; Finance and Fund-raising. **Activities** Events/meetings. **Events** *Scientific Meeting* 2021, *Biennial Meeting* Cairo (Egypt) 2020, *Biennial Meeting* Addis Ababa (Ethiopia) 2018, *Biennial Meeting* Lagos (Nigeria) 2016, *Biennial Meeting* Cairo (Egypt) 2014. [2022/XJ1894/**D**]

♦ Pan African Postal Union (PAPU) 18060

Union panafricaine des postes (UPAP)

SG Plot III, Block Z, Golf Course – Sekei, PO Box 6026, Arusha, Tanzania UR. T. +255272543263. Fax +255272543265. E-mail: sc@papu.co.tz – cop@papu.co.tz.

URL: http://www.upap-papu.org/

History 18 Jan 1980, following recommendations 23 June-3 Jul 1977 of Council of Ministers of the *Organization of African Unity (OAU, inactive)* and approval, 2-6 Jul 1977, Libreville (Gabon), by Conference of Heads of State and Government. Establishment approved 18-28 Jun 1980, Freetown (Sierra Leone), at 35th ordinary session of Council of Ministers of the OAU. A specialized agency of *African Union (AU, #00488)* in the postal field and a Restricted Union of *Universal Postal Union (UPU, #20682).* **Aims** Represent the interests of members at global decision-making conferences; deliver a valuable set of support services to stakeholders. **Structure** Conference of Plenipotentiaries elects Administrative Council, comprising 20 Member States, according to regional distribution, for 4-year term; Administrative and Technical Committees (4); General Secretariat. **Languages** Arabic, English, French, Portuguese, Spanish. **Staff** 2 elected; 8 professional; 15 general service. **Finance** Member States' contributions; Associate Members other funds made available to the Union with the Councils' approval. **Activities** Research and development. **Events** *Conference of Plenipotentiaries* Addis Ababa (Ethiopia) 2012, *Conference of Plenipotentiaries* Cairo (Egypt) 2008, *Conference of Plenipotentiaries* Hammamet (Tunisia) 2004, *Conference of plenipotentiaries* Malawi 2004, *Conference of plenipotentiaries* Abidjan (Côte d'Ivoire) 2000. **Publications** *PAPU News*.

Members Governments of 44 countries:

Algeria, Angola, Benin, Botswana, Burkina Faso, Burundi, Cameroon, Central African Rep, Chad, Comoros, Congo Brazzaville, Congo DR, Côte d'Ivoire, Egypt, Equatorial Guinea, Eritrea, Eswatini, Ethiopia, Gabon, Gambia, Ghana, Guinea, Kenya, Lesotho, Liberia, Libya, Madagascar, Malawi, Mali, Morocco, Mozambique, Niger, Nigeria, Senegal, Sierra Leone, Somalia, South Africa, Sudan, Tanzania UR, Togo, Tunisia, Uganda, Zambia, Zimbabwe.

IGO Relations Links with the other Restricted Unions: *African Postal Union (APU, no recent information)*; *Asian-Pacific Postal Union (APPU, #01625)*; *Associação dos Operadores de Correios e Telecomunicações dos Países e Territórios de Língua Oficial Portuguesa (AICEP, #02333)*; *Association of European Public Postal Operators (PostEurop, #02534)*; *Baltic Postal Union (BPU, #03137)*; *Caribbean Postal Union (CPU, #03541)*; *Conférence européenne des administrations des postes et des télécommunications (CEPT, #04602)*; *Conference of Posts and Telecommunications of Central Africa (#04642)*; *Nordic Postal Union (NPU, #17391)*; *Postal Union of the Americas, Spain and Portugal (PUASP, #18466)*. **NGO Relations** Member of: *European Association of Development Research and Training Institutes (EADI, #06012)*. [2019.10.25/XD4305/**D***]

♦ Pan-African Productivity Association (no recent information)

♦ Pan-African Psychology Union (PAPU) 18061

Contact PO Box 3174, Houghton, 2041, South Africa. T. +27114863322. E-mail: papu.info2018@gmail.com – panafricanpsychology@gmail.com.

Street Address PsySSA, Oakhurst Office Park, 11 St Andrews Rd, Parktown, Johannesburg, 2196, South Africa.

URL: https://www.panafricanpsychologyunion.org/

History 22 Jul 2012, Cape Town (South Africa). Constitution adopted 15 Sep 2014, Durban (South Africa). **Aims** Be a collaborative union of psychological societies and psychologists in Africa committed to scholarship and human development in our communities, countries, Africa and the World. **Structure** Assembly; Executive; Council. [2020/AA0357/**D**]

♦ Pan African Psycho-Oncology Society (no recent information)

♦ Pan-African Rabies Control Network (PARACON) 18062

Exec Dir Global Alliance for Rabies Control SA NPC, Erasmus Forum A434, Rigel Avenue, Erasmus RAND 0181, Pretoria, South Africa. T. +27124203622. Fax +27124203266.

URL: https://rabiesalliance.org/networks/paracon/

History Announced Sep 2014, through merger of *Southern and Eastern African Rabies Group (SEARG, inactive)* and *African Rabies Expert Bureau (AfroREB)*, with the support of *Global Alliance for Rabies Control (GARC)*, under which umbrella it functions. **Aims** Unify African countries and rabies control networks and promote cooperation in a One Health approach towards rabies control and elimination; create a platform to showcase countries' challenges and successes towards achieving rabies control and elimination; promote development and implementation of tools for rabies control. **Structure** General Meeting (every 3 years); Steering Committee. **Languages** English, French. **Staff** 4.00 FTE, paid. **Finance** Donations. **Activities** Events/meetings; training/education; awareness raising; guidance/assistance/consulting; networking/liaising; research and development; advocacy/lobbying/activism. **Events** *PARACON Meeting* South Africa 2018, *Inaugural PARACON meeting* Gauteng (South Africa) 2015. **Publications** *Rabid Bytes* – newsletter. *Addressing the disconnect between the estimated, reported and true rabies data: the development of a regional African rabies bulletin* (2017) by T P Scott et al; *The Formation of the Eastern Africa Rabies Network: A Sub-Regional Approach to Rabies Elimination, Tropical Medicine and Infectious Disease* (2017) by E G Pieracci et al; *The SARE tool for rabies control: Current experience in Ethiopia* (2016) by A Coetzer et al; *The Pan-African Rabies Control Network (PARACON): A unified approach to eliminating canine rabies in Africa* (2015) by T P Scott et al. Teaching material, factsheets; scientific resources; posters; articles; videos. **Information Services** *Rabies Epidemiological Bulletin*.

Members Full in 37 countries:

Angola, Benin, Botswana, Burkina Faso, Cameroon, Central African Rep, Chad, Congo Brazzaville, Congo DR, Côte d'Ivoire, Eswatini, Ethiopia, Gabon, Gambia, Ghana, Guinea, Guinea-Bissau, Kenya, Lesotho, Liberia, Madagascar, Malawi, Mali, Mozambique, Namibia, Niger, Nigeria, Rwanda, Senegal, Sierra Leone, South Africa, Sudan, Tanzania UR, Togo, Uganda, Zambia, Zimbabwe.

IGO Relations *FAO (#09260)*; *OIE – World Organisation for Animal Health (#17703)*; United States Centers for Disease Control and Prevention (US CDC); *WHO (#20950)*. **NGO Relations** Sister organizations: *Asian Rabies Control Network (ARACON)*; *Middle East, Eastern Europe, Central Asia and North Africa Rabies Control Network (MERACON)*. [2019.12.11/XJ9432/**F**]

♦ Pan-African Reconciliation Council (PARC) 18063

Conseil de reconciliation Panafricain – Panafrikanischer Versohnungsrat

Exec Dir 14/16 Abiola Street, Ketu, PO Box 9354 Marina, Lagos 101001, Nigeria. T. +2348054003843 – +234805(17098135152. Fax +16108227423. E-mail: afropax@gmail.com.

History Founded 28 Sep 1988, Lagos (Nigeria). Statutes adopted 28 Sep 1988. New constitution adopted 1 Jul 1997. Previous French title: *Conseil panafricain de la reconciliation*. **Aims** Promote peace, human rights, democracy, social justice, passive resistance to all forms of violence and oppression, emancipation of Africa and its siblings in the diaspora from the bondage of ignorance and poverty on the basis of active non-violence and self-giving love as a tool for social engineering and ultimate global order; build a social structure utilizing the resources of human ingenuity and wisdom for the benefit of all; ensure a society where no one is directly or indirectly oppressed for the benefit or pleasure of others; advocate fair and compassionate methods of treatment of offenders against society; protect, seek redress and provide welfare support for direct and indirect victims of war, natural and ecological disasters and encourage restitution and reconciliation; work towards abolition of war; help build morally disciplined homes; encourage vocational and collegial relations transcending all tribal, ethnic, creed, national or racial boundaries; promote the adversarial system of justice; uphold the truth in all facets of life. **Structure** Continental Assembly (annual). Continental Executive Committee, consisting of Secretary-General, Deputy Secretary-General, Honorary President, International Consultant, Executive Coordinator – each for West Africa, East Africa, North Africa, Central Africa, Southern Africa – Accounts Officer, Administrative Officer, Projects Officer and Information Officer. Consultative Board, acting as Steering Committee. Disciplinary Committee. Continental Secretariat in Lagos (Nigeria). **Languages** English, French. **Staff** 4.00 FTE, paid. Voluntary. **Finance** Members' dues. **Activities** Current programmes: Social and Economic Justice; Non-Violence; Refugees; Social Conflicts; Inter-Faith Activities; Youth and Women. **Events** *Meeting on laying a solid foundation for a culture of peace* Accra (Ghana) 2003, *Meeting on coping with societal chauvinism* Kaduna (Nigeria) 2003, *Meeting on a virile culture of peace for Africa and Kin in the diaspora* Lagos (Nigeria) 2003, *Meeting on global xenophobia* Freetown (Sierra Leone) 2001, *Meeting on coping with societal chauvinism* Kaduna (Nigeria) 2000. **Publications** Media resources; pamphlets; books.

Members Open to all adult Africans and blacks in diaspora. National, state or territory sections in 13 countries:

Benin, Chad, Côte d'Ivoire, Germany, Ghana, Liberia, Mauritius, New Zealand, Nigeria, Sierra Leone, Sweden, Togo, USA.

NGO Relations Represented on the Organizing Committee of: *Hague Appeal for Peace (HAP, #10848)*. Member of: *EarthAction (EA, #05159)*; *International Peace Bureau (IPB, #14535)*. Affiliate member of: *International Fellowship of Reconciliation (IFOR, #13586)*. [2012.06.01/XD3367/**F**]

♦ Pan African Sanctuary Alliance (PASA) 18064

Contact 3426 SW Arnold St, Portland OR 97219, USA. E-mail: info@pasa.org.

URL: https://pasa.org/

History 2000. Registration: USA. **Aims** Support, assist and encourage member sanctuaries in their efforts to save Africa's great apes and other primates; campaign against the threats these species face in the wild; promote the highest standards of captive animal husbandry. **Structure** Board of Directors. **Staff** Full-time, paid. **Finance** Donations. **Activities** Capacity building; networking/liaising.

Members Primate sanctuaries (23) in 13 countries:

Cameroon, Congo Brazzaville, Congo DR, Gabon, Gambia, Guinea, Kenya, Nigeria, Sierra Leone, South Africa, Uganda, USA, Zambia.

Included in the above, 1 organization listed in this Yearbook:

Jane Goodall Institute (JGI, #16089).

NGO Relations Member of (2): *Ape Alliance (#00871)*; *Species Survival Network (SSN, #19916)*. [2021.08.31/XF6673/y/**F**]

♦ Pan African Society for Agricultural Engineering (AfroAgEng) 18065

Administrative Officer 141 Cresswell Road, Pretoria, South Africa. E-mail: administrator@pasae.org.za.

URL: http://www.pasae.org.za/

History Proposed Nov 2012, South Africa, at a conference organized by *International Commission of Agricultural and Biosystems Engineering (#12661)*. **Aims** Raise awareness about the role of engineering and technological innovations in agriculture and related bio-based industries in Africa; promote curriculum reform and academic mobility among agricultural engineering programmes; facilitate information exchange on the different aspects of agricultural and bioresources engineering. **Structure** General Meeting (annual); Executive Committee. **Languages** English. **Staff** 0.50 FTE, paid. **Finance** Members' dues. Meeting proceeds. **Activities** Awards/prizes/competitions; awareness raising; capacity building; events/meetings; guidance/assistance/consulting; knowledge management/information dissemination; monitoring/evaluation; networking/liaising; projects/programmes; publishing activities; research and development; standards/guidelines; training/education. **Events** *The role of agricultural engineering in meeting the challenges of global food security* Rabat (Morocco) 2019, *Conference* Nairobi (Kenya) 2018.

Members Full in 13 countries:

Ethiopia, Ghana, Kenya, Malawi, Morocco, Mozambique, South Africa, Sudan, Tanzania UR, Uganda, UK, USA, Zimbabwe.

Included in the above, 1 organization listed in this Yearbook:

American Society of Agricultural and Biological Engineers (ASABE).

NGO Relations Member of: *International Commission of Agricultural and Biosystems Engineering (#12661)*. [2019.03.12/XM6868/**D**]

♦ Pan African Society of Cardiology (PASCAR) 18066

Société panafricaine de cardiologie (SOPAC)

Sec Dept of Medicine, Faculty of Health Sciences, University of Cape Town, Observatory 7925, Cape Town, South Africa. T. +27214066200 – +27216197. E-mail: info@pascar.org.

URL: http://www.pascar.org/

History 6 May 1981, Lagos (Nigeria), at inaugural congress. Constitution last amended at 3rd Congress, 6-11 Mar 1989, Dakar (Senegal). **Aims** Promote the prevention and treatment of cardiovascular diseases; promote the education and training of medical and paramedical personnel in cardiology, including cardiac pathology, cardiac rehabilitation, cardiovascular surgery and other related disciplines; educate the general public on cardiovascular health problems; encourage research by the formation of an African Heart Foundation which will ultimately fund and coordinate continental research activities and conferences in all aspects of cardiology. **Structure** Congress (every 2 years). Governing Council, consisting of President, 5 Regional Vice-Presidents (Western, Eastern, Southern, Central, Northern), Secretary General, Treasurer and Immediate Past President. Secretariat, headed by Secretary General. **Languages** English, French. **Staff** Voluntary. **Finance** Members' dues. Occasional support from international organizations and pharmaceuticals companies. **Activities** Works on setting up the *African Heart Foundation (no recent information)* for funding and coordinating in Africa the research activities and conferences in all aspects of cardiology. Organization of Pan African Congresses, together with congressional business meetings. Organization of seminars, workshops or other meetings on cardiovascular themes. Dissemination of up-to-date knowledge on cardiovascular diseases through its publishing activity. **Events** *Biennial Congress* Mombasa (Kenya) 2021, *Biennial Congress* Johannesburg (South Africa) 2019, *Biennial Congress* Khartoum (Sudan) 2017, *WHF African Summit on Best Practices and Access to Care* Khartoum (Sudan) 2017, *All Africa Conference on Heart Disease, Stroke and Diabetes* Balaclava (Mauritius) 2015. **Publications** *African Cardioscope* (4 a year) in English, French; *African Journal of Cardiovascular Diseases* (4 a year) in English, French.

Members Registered National or Regional Societies of Cardiology in countries that are members of OAU; Individuals engaged in cardiology, but who reside in an African country with no established Cardiac Society; Associate Members individual citizens of non-OAU countries. Members in 27 countries:

Algeria, Benin, Burundi, Cameroon, Chad, Congo Brazzaville, Congo DR, Côte d'Ivoire, Egypt, Ethiopia, Gabon, Ghana, Kenya, Liberia, Mauritania, Morocco, Niger, Nigeria, Senegal, Sierra Leone, South Africa, Tanzania UR, Togo, Uganda, USA, Zambia, Zimbabwe.

NGO Relations Formal contacts with: American Heart Association (AHA); *International Society on Hypertension in Blacks (ISHIB)*; *World Hypertension League (WHL, #21574)*. Member of: *Consortium for Non-communicable Diseases Prevention and Control in sub-Saharan Africa (CNCD-Africa, #04754)*; *The NCD Alliance (NCDA, #16963)*; *World Heart Federation (WHF, #21562)*. [2019/XD1486/**D**]

♦ Pan African Society for Musical Arts Education (PASMAE) 18067

Main Office PO Box 13552, Clubview, 0014, South Africa.

URL: http://www.pasmae.africa/

History 2000, Harare (Zimbabwe). Former names and other names: *Pan-African Society for Music Education (PASME)* – former. **Aims** Enhance and promote musical arts education throughout Africa. **Structure** Executive Committee. **Activities** Events/meetings. **Events** *Conference* Lusaka (Zambia) 2021, *Conference* Seychelles 2019, *Conference* Mbabane (Swaziland) 2017, *Conference* Mpumalanga (South Africa) 2015, *Conference* Kampala (Uganda) 2013. **Publications** *Research Studies in Music Education* – journal. Scores; titles; other publications. **NGO Relations** Member of: *African Music Council (AMC, #00379)*; [2021/XD8319/**D**]

♦ Pan-African Society for Music Education / see Pan African Society for Musical Arts Education (#18067)

♦ Pan-African Strategic and Policy Research Group (PANAFSTRAG) . . 18068

Exec Sec 302 Iju WaterW orks Road, Iju-Ishaga, Agege, Lagos, Nigeria. E-mail: panafstraginternational@yahoo.com.

URL: http://www.panafstrag.org/

History 1992, as *African Strategic and Peace Research Group*. **Aims** Carry out in-depth studies and analysis of the challenges of history and culture as a foundation for Human Security and Development in Africa; propose policy alternatives and strategies for stability and development of Africa in synergy with its diaspora. **Structure** Board of Directors; Secretariat in Nigeria. **Languages** English. **Staff** 3.00 FTE, paid. **Finance** Members' dues. Other sources: personal donations; funding from donors. **Activities** Research/documentation; events/meetings. **Events** *Joint conference on civil society, governance and integration in Africa / Conference* Addis Ababa (Ethiopia) 2005. **Publications** Newsletters. Books; monographs; occasional papers.

Members Chapters in 20 countries:

Benin, Brazil, Cameroon, Canada, Cape Verde, Côte d'Ivoire, France, Gambia, Ghana, Guinea, Guinea-Bissau, Liberia, Mali, Niger, Senegal, Sierra Leone, South Africa, Togo, UK, USA.

NGO Relations Cooperates with: *Centre for Black and African Arts and Civilization (CBAAC)*. [2014.06.01/XM0596/**F**]

♦ Pan African Students International Peace and Voluntary Services Organization (inactive)
♦ Pan African Telecommunications Network (no recent information)
♦ Pan-African Telecommunication Union (inactive)

♦ Pan African Theosophical Federation (PATF) 18069

Chairman 9 Ronean, 38 Princesses Ave, Windsor East, Johannesburg, 2194, South Africa. T. +27116787696.

URL: http://www.theosophy-inafrica.org.za/

History Founded Oct 2000, Nairobi (Kenya), at the All Africa Theosophical Convention. **Aims** Promote the theosophical way in Africa; form a nucleus of the universal brotherhood of humanity without distinction of race, creed, sex, cast or colour; encourage the study of comparative religion, philosophy and science; investigate the unexplained laws of nature and the powers latent in man. **Structure** Executive Committee. Sections (3): West African; East and Central African; Southern African. **Languages** English. **Staff** 10.00 FTE, voluntary. **Finance** Members' dues. Donations. **Events** *Meeting* Kampala (Uganda) 2009, *Southern African convention*

Cape Town (South Africa) 2008, *West African convention* Accra (Ghana) 2007, *Southern African convention* Johannesburg (South Africa) 2006, *East and Central African convention* Nairobi (Kenya) 2005. **Publications** *PATF Newsletter* (4 a year).
Members Full in 10 countries:
Cameroon, Ghana, Kenya, Liberia, Nigeria, South Africa, Tanzania UR, Uganda, Zambia, Zimbabwe.
NGO Relations Member of: *Theosophical Society (TS, #20141).* [2014.09.26/XD8736/**D**]

♦ Pan-African Thoracic Society (PATS) 18070

Administrator Nelson R Mandela School of Medicine, 719 Umbilo Road, Congella, Durban, 4013, South Africa.
URL: http://panafricanthoracic.org/
History 2003. Expected to be registered in South Africa in 2009. **Aims** Promote collaboration among people engaged in combating *respiratory* disease in African countries; meet the need for research capacity in respiratory disease in sub-Saharan Africa. **Structure** Steering Committee, comprising Chair, Secretary and 3 members. Steering Committee Advisors (3). President, Vice-Presidents and Treasurer to be elected and appointed following registration. Accounts to be held in South Africa; Secretariat to remain at Centre for Respiratory Diseases Research, Nairobi (Kenya). **Languages** English, French. **Staff** Part-time voluntary and paid. **Finance** Supported by: American Thoracic Society; *European Respiratory Society (ERS, #08383)*; French-language pulmonology societies; *International Union Against Tuberculosis and Lung Disease (The Union, #15752)*; *Federation of International Respiratory Societies*. Annual budget (dependent on donor awards): approx US$ 20,000. **Activities** Offers: *'Methods for Epidemiologic, Clinical and Operations Research (MECOR)'* training courses on – collection and interpretation of country/local specific data; understanding of research methods and skills in critical appraisal of the literature; increasing numbers of public health, academic and clinical leaders to support and facilitate research and its application to public health and health care related to respiratory diseases and critical care. Series of research training schools (2007-2012) to develop mentor partnerships between PATS-MECOR faculty and respiratory health professionals working in Africa, forming a network for support, collaborative research and advocacy. **Events** *Meeting* Cape Town (South Africa) 2006. **Publications** *African Journal of Respiratory Medicine*. MERA publications. **Members** (over 100) in more than 20 countries in all African regions. Membership countries not specified. **NGO Relations** Member of: *Federation of International Respiratory Societies*; *Framework Convention Alliance (FCA, #09981)*; *Global Coalition Against Child Pneumonia (#10290).* [2018/XM2781/**D**]

♦ Pan African Treatment Access Movement (PATAM) 18071

Coordinator 16 Fletcher Road, Mt Pleasant, Harare, HARARE, Zimbabwe. T. +2634740617.
History 22 Aug 2002, Cape Town (South Africa). **Aims** Ensure universal access to comprehensive and quality treatment, care and support for all people living with *HIV/AIDS* in Africa. **Structure** Steering Group of 7. **Languages** English, French, Portuguese. **Staff** 2.00 FTE, paid; 1.00 FTE, voluntary. **Finance** Private funding. **Activities** Campaign to end paediatric AIDS in Africa; ongoing advocacy at regional and international levels; capacity building of affiliate national-level organizations; training seminars. **Events** *Conference* Harare (Zimbabwe) 2004. **Publications** *PATAM Tree Magazine* (2 a year). **NGO Relations** Member of: *Regional Inter-Agency Task Team on Children and AIDS in Eastern and Southern Africa (RIATT-ESA, #18791)*; *Gavi – The Vaccine Alliance (Gavi, #10077)* CSO Constituency. [2011.06.01/XM0168/**F**]

- ♦ Pan-African Union of Journalists (inactive)
- ♦ Pan African Union of Science and Technology (inactive)
- ♦ Pan-African University / see Pan-Atlantic University
- ♦ Pan African University (unconfirmed)

♦ Pan African Urological Surgeons' Association (PAUSA) 18072

Pres address not obtained.
SG Hôpital General Grand Yoff, PO Box 3270, Dakar, Senegal.
URL: http://www.pausaafrica.com/
History 1992, Harare (Zimbabwe). **Aims** Promote and establish social and scientific relations among urologists from different African countries; promote initial and continued training for urologists on the continent; promote the publication of studies relevant to Africa; promote contacts among African urologists, African and international associations of urology; initiate and support research projects emanating from the practice of urology in Africa. **Structure** Officers: President, President-Elect, Secretary-General, Treasurer; Regional Representatives (5); Rotating secretariat. **Languages** English, French. **Staff** No permanent staff. **Finance** Members' dues. Congress proceeds. **Events** *Biennial Congress* Hammamet (Tunisia) 2022, *Biennial Congress* Grand-Bassam (Côte d'Ivoire) 2019, *Biennial Congress* Victoria Falls (Zimbabwe) 2017, *Biennial Congress* Kinshasa (Congo DR) 2015, *Biennial Congress* Accra (Ghana) 2013. **Publications** *African Journal of Urology*.
Members Regional associations (4):
East African Urological Association; North African Urological Association; South African Urological Association; West African Urological Association.
NGO Relations Represented on the Executive of: *International Consultation on Urological Diseases (ICUD, #12928).* [2020.03.04/XM4569/**D**]

♦ Pan African Veterinary Vaccine Center of the African Union (AU-PANVAC) 18073

Dir PO Box 1746, Debre-Zeit, Ethiopia. T. +251114338001. E-mail: aupanvac@africa-union.org.
URL: https://aupanvac.org/
History 12 Mar 2004, Debre-Zeit (Ethiopia). Launched 12 Mar 2004, Debre Zeit (Ethiopia), as a Specialized agency of *African Union (AU, #00488)*. **Aims** Promote the use of good quality vaccines and reagents for the control and eradication of animal diseases in Africa; provide international independent quality control service for veterinary vaccines produced adn imported to Africa. **Structure** Steering Committee. **Activities** Training/education; certification/accreditation; research and development. **IGO Relations** *African Union (AU, #00488)*: *Interafrican Bureau for Animal Resources (AU-IBAR, #11382).* [2019/XU2652/**E**]

- ♦ Pan African Vision for the Environment (internationally oriented national body)
- ♦ Panafrican Women Association (unconfirmed)

♦ Pan African Women's Organization (PAWO) 18074

Organisation panafricaine des femmes (OPF) – Organização Pan Africana Das Mulheres (OPM)
Pres San Marino 19, New Mucleneuk, Pretoria, 0181, South Africa. T. +27123421515. E-mail: panafpw@hotmail.com – dabellebo@hotmail.com.
URL: https://pawowomen.org/
History 31 Jul 1962, Tanzania UR. 31 Jul 1962, Dar-es-Salaam (Tanzania UR), following recommendations at conference Jul 1961, Conakry (Guinea), as *All African Women's Conference (AAWC) – Conférence des femmes africaines (CFA)*. Also known as *Conference of African Women*. Current Statutes adopted Nov 1999, Algiers (Algeria), at 8th Council. Since 2017, a Specialized Agency of *African Union (AU, #00488)*. **Aims** Unite women of African descent through the creation of a single platform that promotes an exchange of good practices and initiates joint efforts to support *human rights* and elimination of all forms of *discrimination*. **Structure** Congress (every 5 years); Council; General Secretariat; Regional Secretaries (5). **Languages** Arabic, English, French, Portuguese. **Staff** 35.00 FTE, paid. **Finance** Members' dues. Other sources: subsidies; grants; donations; proceeds from activities. **Activities** Politics/policy/regulatory; advocacy/lobbying/activism. **Events** *Congress* South Africa 2008, *Congress* South Africa 2003, *Congress* Luanda (Angola) 2002, *Meeting on PAWO's role in the establishment of a culture of peace during and after armed conflicts in Africa* Algiers (Algeria) 1999, *Regional conference on women and HIV/AIDS struggle strategies / Congress* Windhoek (Namibia) 1999. **Publications** *African Women* (4 a year) in Arabic, English, French, Portuguese.
Members Organizations in 54 countries and territories:
Algeria, Angola, Benin, Botswana, Burkina Faso, Burundi, Cameroon, Cape Verde, Central African Rep, Chad, Comoros, Congo Brazzaville, Congo DR, Côte d'Ivoire, Djibouti, Egypt, Equatorial Guinea, Eritrea, Eswatini, Ethiopia, Gabon, Gambia, Ghana, Guinea, Guinea-Bissau, Kenya, Lesotho, Liberia, Libya, Madagascar, Malawi, Mali, Mauritania, Mauritius, Morocco, Mozambique, Namibia, Niger, Nigeria, Rwanda, Sahara West, Sao Tomé-Principe, Senegal, Seychelles, Sierra Leone, Somalia, South Africa, Sudan, Tanzania UR, Togo, Tunisia, Uganda, Zambia, Zimbabwe.
Also: ANC and PAC liberation movements for South Africa.

Consultative Status Consultative status granted from: *ECOSOC (#05331)* (Special); *UNESCO (#20322)* (Consultative Status); *ILO (#11123)* (Special List). **IGO Relations** Accredited by: *United Nations Office at Vienna (UNOV, #20604)*. Associated with Department of Global Communications of the United Nations. **NGO Relations** Member of: *Conference of Non-Governmental Organizations in Consultative Relationship with the United Nations (CONGO, #04635)*; *EarthAction (EA, #05159).* [2018/XD0399/**D**]

- ♦ Pan African Workers Congress (inactive)

♦ Pan African Writers Association (PAWA) 18075

Association panafricaine des écrivains
SG PO Box C456, Cantonments, Accra, Ghana. E-mail: pawahouse@gmail.com.
PROGRAMMES OFFICER PAWA House, Roman Road, Roman Ridge, Accra, Ghana.
ACCOUNTANT address not obtained.
URL: https://panafricanwritersassociation.com/
History Nov 1989, Accra (Ghana). Founded during Constituent Congress of PAWA. **Aims** Provide a forum for all writers of Africa and those of African origin; seek and defend freedom of expression for all Africans and the material and spiritual interests of African writers and their association; promote literacy and to eradicate illiteracy in Africa; encourage inclusion of African literary works in the curriculum of educational institutions; promote African languages and the translation of African literature into African languages; promote research into recording and retrieving lost or undiscovered African heritage; promote peace and understanding in Africa and the world through literature; ensure the protection of the works of African writers through the appropriate copyright laws and agencies. **Structure** General Assembly; Council, headed by President; Secretariat, headed by Secretary General. **Languages** Arabic, English, French, Portuguese, Swahili. **Staff** 5.00 FTE, paid; 3.00 FTE, voluntary. **Finance** Annual budget: 80,000 USD. **Activities** Awards/prizes/competitions; events/meetings; financial and/or material support; projects/programmes; publishing activities; training/education. Active in all member countries. **Members** National associations of writers from 40 countries. Membership countries not specified. **NGO Relations** Member of (2): African Union Consultative Forum; International Authors Association. [2022.03.09/XD2912/**D**]

- ♦ Pan African Youth Movement (inactive)

♦ Pan African Youth Union 18076

Union panafricaine de la jeunesse (UPJ)
Main Office c/o NYCN, Nigeria Youth House, No 4 Ikot Ekpene Close, off Emeka Anyaoku St, Area 11 Garki, Abuja, Federal Capital Territory, Nigeria. T. +2348037038097.
History Nov 2003, Windhoek (Namibia). Replaces *Pan African Youth Movement (PYM, inactive)*. Headquarters in Addis Ababa (Ethiopia). **Structure** Executive Committee. **Events** *Congress* Brazzaville (Congo Brazzaville) 2008. **NGO Relations** Consultative Member of: *World Assembly of Youth (WAY, #21113).* [2010/XJ3179/**D**]

- ♦ **PAN Africa** Pesticide Action Network Africa (#18337)
- ♦ Panafrikanischer Versohnungsrat (#18063)
- ♦ **PANAFSTRAG** Pan-African Strategic and Policy Research Group (#18068)
- ♦ PANAFTEL – Pan African Telecommunications Network (no recent information)
- ♦ **PANAFTOSA** Centro Panamericano de Fiebre Aftosa (#18106)
- ♦ **PANAFUTSAL** Confederación Panamericana de Fútbol de Salón (#18112)
- ♦ Panama Canal and International Studies Institute (internationally oriented national body)
- ♦ Panama Canal Treaty – Treaty Concerning the Permanent Neutrality and Operation of the Panama Canal (1977 treaty)
- ♦ PANAMA International – International Association of Sandwich-panel Manufacturers and Associates (inactive)

♦ PanAm Aquatics 18077

Pres 154 Cinnamon Ln, San Antonio TX 78217, USA.
URL: https://www.panamaquatics.com/
History 8 Aug 1948, London (UK). Founded during Olympic Games. Former names and other names: *Unión Amateur de Natación de las Américas (UANA)* – former; *Amateur Swimming Union of the Americas (ASUA)* – former; *Unión Americana de Natación (UANA)* – former. **Aims** Develop aquatic sports in the Americas and help participants achieve individual excellence, in sport and in life. **Structure** Congress; Executive Committee. **Languages** English, Spanish. **Staff** Voluntary. **Finance** Sources: members' dues. Proceeds from Water Gala during Pan American Games. **Activities** Sporting activities. **Events** *Quadrennial Congress* Guayaquil (Ecuador) 1987, *Quadrennial Congress* Indianapolis, IN (USA) 1987, *Quadrennial Congress* Caracas (Venezuela) 1983. **Publications** *ASUA Rule Book* (every 4 years).
Members Swimming organizations and national federations in 45 countries and territories:
Anguilla, Antigua-Barbuda, Argentina, Aruba, Bahamas, Barbados, Belize, Bermuda, Bolivia, Brazil, Canada, Cayman Is, Chile, Colombia, Costa Rica, Cuba, Curaçao, Dominica, Dominican Rep, Ecuador, El Salvador, Grenada, Guatemala, Guyana, Haiti, Honduras, Jamaica, Mexico, Nicaragua, Panama, Paraguay, Peru, Puerto Rico, St Kitts-Nevis, St Lucia, St Maarten, St Vincent-Grenadines, Suriname, Trinidad-Tobago, Turks-Caicos, Uruguay, USA, Venezuela, Virgin Is UK, Virgin Is USA.
NGO Relations Member of (2): *Asociación de Confederaciones Deportivas Panamericanas (ACODEPA, #02119)*; *World Aquatics (#21100)*. Sanctioned by: *International Olympic Committee (IOC, #14408).* [2023/XD3873/**D**]

- ♦ Pan-Amazonic Social Forum (#09889)
- ♦ **PANAMDES** Pan American Deaf Sports Organization (#18093)
- ♦ Pan American Acridological Society / see Orthopterists' Society (#17899)

♦ Pan American Aerobiology Association (PAAA) 18078

Association pan-américaine d'aérobiologie (APAA) – Asociación Panamericana de Aerobiologia – Associação Panamericana de Aerobiologia
Mailing Address PO Box 714, Trumansburg NY 14886, USA. E-mail: paaaorg@gmail.com.
URL: http://www.paaa.org/
History 1988, Montréal, QC (Canada). **Aims** Promote aerobiological research and teaching in the Americas; stimulate cooperation and communication among those studying dispersal of passively airborne *microorganisms*, their identity, behaviour and survival, and their relation with immunology pathways; act as spokesman for aerobiologists' interests. **Structure** General Assembly; Executive Committee; Committees (8); Sampling Strategies Working Group. **Languages** English, French, Spanish. **Staff** 1.00 FTE, voluntary. **Finance** Annual budget: 3,000 USD. **Events** *Annual Conference* Sydney, NSW (Australia) 2014, *Annual Conference* Toronto, ON (Canada) 2013, *Annual Conference* Toronto, ON (Canada) 2013, *Annual Conference* Mérida (Mexico) 2012, *Annual Conference* San Diego, CA (USA) 2011. **Publications** *PAAA Newsletter* (2 a year).Conference proceedings published in *Aerobiologia* international journal. **Information Services** *Aerobiology Database*.
Members Members in 19 countries and territories:
Argentina, Australia, Barbados, Canada, China, Colombia, Dominican Rep, France, India, Italy, Mexico, Puerto Rico, Spain, Switzerland, Taiwan, Türkiye, UK, Uruguay, USA.
NGO Relations Acts as representative of: *International Association for Aerobiology (IAA, #11691)* in the Americas. [2022.05.11/XD3379/v/**D**]

- ♦ Pan American Aerobiology Certification Board (internationally oriented national body)
- ♦ Pan American Agricultural School 'El Zamorano' (internationally oriented national body)
- ♦ Pan American Archery Confederation / see World Archery Americas (#21106)
- ♦ Pan American Association for the Advancement of Women (inactive)

♦ Pan American Association of Anatomy (PAAA) 18079

Association panaméricaine d'anatomie – Asociación Panamericana de Anatomia – Associação Panamericana de Anatomia
Pres address not obtained. E-mail: apa.consejodirectivo@gmail.com.
URL: http://apanatomia.weebly.com/
History 28 Jul 1966, Mexico City (Mexico), at first Pan American Congress of Anatomy, following recommendations, Mar 1961, Chicago IL (USA). **Aims** Bring together *physicians* and other professionals interested in the various branches of *morphology*; stimulate development and promotion of morphology on the American continent, facilitating scientific exchange in all its aspects. **Structure** General Assembly (every 3 years). Directive Council composed of 1 Councillor and 1 Alternate for each country. Executive Committee composed

of President, Vice-President, Secretary-General, Executive Secretary and Treasurer. **Languages** English, French, Portuguese, Spanish. **Finance** Members' dues. Donations. **Activities** Sponsors and organizes Pan American Congresses of Anatomy. Scientific and cultural exchanges; guidance or teaching methods. **Events** *Triennial Congress* Ica (Peru) 2016, *Triennial Congress* Santa María Huatulco (Mexico) 2013, *Triennial Congress* Temuco (Chile) 2010, *Triennial Congress* San José (Costa Rica) 2007, *Triennial Congress* Puerto Iguazú (Argentina) / Foz do Iguaçu (Brazil) 2004. **Publications** *International Journal of Morphology.*
Members Individuals Associate and Honorary, totalling over 250 in 22 countries:
Bolivia, Brazil, Canada, Chile, Colombia, Costa Rica, Cuba, Dominican Rep, Ecuador, El Salvador, Guatemala, Haiti, Honduras, Jamaica, Mexico, Nicaragua, Panama, Paraguay, Peru, Uruguay, USA, Venezuela.
NGO Relations *International Federation of Associations of Anatomists (IFAA, #13361).*
[2017.03.13/XD4400/v/**D**]

♦ Pan American Association of Biochemical Societies / see Pan American Association for Biochemistry and Molecular Biology (#18080)

♦ Pan American Association for Biochemistry and Molecular Biology (PABMB) 18080

SG address not obtained.
Chairman address not obtained.
URL: https://www.pabmb.org/

History Mar 1975. Regional society of: *Red Latinoamericana de Ciencias Biológicas (RELAB, #18706).* Former names and other names: *Pan American Association of Biochemical Societies (PAABS)* – former; *Asociación Panamericana de Sociedades de Bioquimica* – former; *Associação Panamericana das Sociedades de Bioquimica* – former. **Aims** Promote development of biochemistry and molecular biology as well as interaction of the biochemical societies and their members on the American continent. **Structure** General Assembly; Council; Executive Committee. **Languages** English, Portuguese, Spanish. **Staff** 0.50 FTE, paid. **Finance** Sources: members' dues. Assistance from IUB. **Activities** Knowledge management/information dissemination; events/meetings; networking/liaising. **Events** *The Biochemistry Global Summit* Lisbon (Portugal) 2022, *Triennial Congress* Salta (Argentina) 2019, *Triennial Congress* Vancouver, BC (Canada) 2016, *Triennial Congress* Puerto Varas (Chile) 2013, *Triennial Congress* Aguas de Lindoia (Brazil) 2008. **Publications** *Biochemistry and Cell Biology* – journal.
Members Constituent Societies – biochemical societies and equivalent organizations in the Americas; Associated Societies; Adherent Societies – outside the continent. Constituent Societies (10) in 9 countries:
Argentina, Brazil, Canada, Chile, Mexico, Panama, Peru, Uruguay, USA (2).
Associated Societies (2) in 2 countries:
Cuba, Venezuela.
Adherent Societies (2) in 2 countries:
Portugal, Spain.
IGO Relations *OAS (#17629).* **NGO Relations** Coordinating Committees with: *Federation of Asian and Oceanian Biochemists and Molecular Biologists (FAOBMB, #09438)*; *International Union of Biochemistry and Molecular Biology (IUBMB, #15759)* (of which it is an associated member); *International Union for Pure and Applied Biophysics (IUPAB, #15808)*; *International Union of Pure and Applied Chemistry (IUPAC, #15809).*
[2022/XD7905/**D**]

♦ Pan American Association of Educational Credit Institutions / see Pan American Association of Student Loan Institutions (#18084)
♦ Pan American Association of Eye Banks (#02285)
♦ Pan American Association of Forensic Sciences (inactive)
♦ Pan-American Association of Ocular Trauma (#02293)

♦ Pan-American Association of Ophthalmology (PAAO) 18081

Association panaméricaine d'ophtalmologie – Asociación Panamericana de Oftalmologia – Associação Panamericana de Oftalmologia
Exec Dir PMB 129, 2504 W. Park Row Dr, Ste B-5, Pantego TX 76013, USA. E-mail: info@paao.org.
URL: http://www.paao.org/

History Oct 1939, Cleveland, OH (USA). Reorganized and present name adopted Dec 1945. Former names and other names: *Pan American Congress of Ophthalmology* – former (1939 to 1945). **Aims** Promote friendship and dissemination of scientific information among the profession throughout the Western Hemisphere and beyond. **Structure** Board of Directors; Executive Committee. Includes *Pan-American Ophthalmological Foundation (PAOF)*, set up 1959. **Languages** English, Portuguese, Spanish. **Staff** 2.00 FTE, paid. **Finance** Members' dues. Annual budget: US$ 500,000. **Activities** Guidance/assistance/consulting; awards/prizes/competitions. **Events** *Congress* Buenos Aires (Argentina) 2023, *Congress* Buenos Aires (Argentina) 2022, *Congress* Cancún (Mexico) 2019, *Congress* Lima (Peru) 2017, *WOC : World Ophthalmology congress* Guadalajara (Mexico) 2016. **Publications** *Vision Pan-America: The Pan-American Journal of Opthalmology* (4 a year); *PAAO Journal.*
Members Active; corresponding; member-in-training; honorary; lifetime; associate. National societies in 23 countries and territories:
Argentina, Bolivia, Brazil, Canada, Chile, Colombia, Costa Rica, Cuba, Dominican Rep, Ecuador, El Salvador, Guatemala, Haiti, Honduras, Mexico, Nicaragua, Panama, Paraguay, Peru, Puerto Rico, Uruguay, USA, Venezuela.
Also in Caribbean. Membership countries not specified. Individuals in 12 countries:
Individuals in 12 countries:
Belgium, France, Germany, Greece, Italy, Saudi Arabia, Spain, Sudan, Switzerland, Togo, Türkiye, UK.
Affiliated sub-specialty groups (19):
Asociación Latino Americana de Cirugia de Catarata, Segmento Anterior y Refractiva (ALACCSA-R, #02194); *Asociación Pan Americana de Bancos de Ojos (APABO, #02285)*; *Asociación Panamericana de Trauma Ocular (APTO, #02293)*; *Club Latinoamericano de Neuroftalmologia (CLAN, #04036)*; *Consejo Latinoamericano de Ecografia Ocular (CLEO, #04719)*; *Consejo Latinoamericano de Estrabismo (CLADE, #04720)*; *Pan-American Association for Research in Ophthalmology (#18083)*; *Pan-American Committee for the Prevention of Blindness (#18087)*; *Pan-American Cornea Society (PanCornea, #18090)*; *Pan-American Glaucoma Society (PAGS, #18107)*; *Pan-American Low Vision Society (#18119)*; *Pan-American Society of Ocular Pathology – Lorenz E Zimmerman (Zimmerman Society, #18131)*; *Pan-American Society of Ophthalmic Oncology (no recent information)*; *Sociedad de Oftalmologia Pediatrica Latinoamericana (SOPLA, #19430)*; *Sociedad Panamericana de Enfermedades Inflamatorias Oculares (SPEIO, #19432)*; *Sociedad Panamericana de Oculoplastica (SOPANOC, no recent information)*; *Sociedad Panamericana de Retinopatia del Prematuro (SPROP, #19435).*
IGO Relations Cooperates with: *OAS (#17629)*; *Pan American Health Organization (PAHO, #18108).* **NGO Relations** Instrumental in setting up: *Pan-American Glaucoma Society (PAGS, #18107)*; *Pan-American Retina and Vitreous Society (PRVS, #18126).*
[2022/XD3048/y/**D**]

♦ Pan American Association of Oto – Rhino – Laryngology and Broncho – Esophagology / see Pan American Association of Oto-Rhino-Laryngology – Head and Neck Surgery (#18082)

♦ Pan American Association of Oto-Rhino-Laryngology – Head and Neck Surgery (PANAMORL) 18082

Association panaméricaine d'oto-rhino-laryngologie – chirurgie de la tête et du cou – Asociación Panamericana de Otorrinolaringologia – Cirugia de Cabeza y Cuello
Pres Av Wheelwright 1943, 2000 Rosario, Argentina.
URL: http://www.panamorl.com.ar/

History 1946, Chicago, IL (USA). Former names and other names: *Pan American Association of Oto – Rhino – Laryngology and Broncho – Esophagology* – former (1946); *Association panaméricaine d'oto-rhino-laryngologie et de broncho-oesophagologie* – former (1946); *Asociación Panamericana de Otorrinolaringologia y Broncoesofagologia* – former (1946). **Aims** Promote the progress of oto-rhino-laryngology, and of head and neck surgery; assist union and cultural interchange among the countries of America. **Structure** General Assembly (every 2 years); Governing Council, composed of one delegate and one deputy from each country. Executive Committee, comprising President, Secretary-General, Treasurer General, 3 Vice-Presidents, 2 Secretaries, President Elect, Secretary General Elect, Treasurer and 3 Vice-Presidents Elect. **Languages** English, Portuguese, Spanish. **Staff** Voluntary. **Finance** Members dues: US$ 20 per annum. **Activities** Biennial Pan American Congresses; exchange programmes; promotes Pan American medical and cultural activities. **Events** *Pan American Congress of Otolaryngology / Congreso Panamericano de Otorrinolaringología* Punta Cana (Dominican Rep) 2024, *Pan American Congress of Otolaryngology-Head and Neck Surgery* Orlando, FL (USA) 2022, *Biennial Congress* Punta Cana (Dominican Rep) 2021, *Biennial Congress* Punta Cana (Dominican Rep) 2020, *Biennial Congress* Lima (Peru) 2018. **Publications** *Pan American Newsletter of Oto-Rhino-Laryngology – Head and Neck Surgery and Broncho.*
Members Individuals (over 2,000) in 22 countries:
Argentina, Bolivia, Brazil, Canada, Chile, Colombia, Costa Rica, Cuba, Dominican Rep, Ecuador, El Salvador, Guatemala, Honduras, Mexico, Nicaragua, Panama, Paraguay, Peru, Puerto Rico, Uruguay, USA, Venezuela.
Consultative Status Consultative status granted from: *OAS (#17629).* **IGO Relations** *WHO (#20950)*; *Pan American Health Organization (PAHO, #18108).*
[2022/XD3049/v/**D**]

♦ Pan American Association of Pediatric Surgery / see Asociación Iberoamericana de Cirugia Pediatrica (#02134)

♦ Pan-American Association for Research in Ophthalmology 18083

Chair LSU HSC Neuroscience Ctr for Excellence, 2020 Gravier St, Ste D, New Orleans LA 70112, USA. T. +15045990832. Fax +15045685801.
NGO Relations Affiliated member of: *Pan-American Association of Ophthalmology (PAAO, #18081).*
[2009/XM1746/**D**]

♦ Pan American Association of Social Medicine (inactive)

♦ Pan American Association of Student Loan Institutions 18084

Association Panaméricaine des Institutions de Crédit Éducatif – Asociación Panamericana de Instituciones de Crédito Educativo (APICE)
Exec Dir Carrera 11 No 77-20, Int 3, Bogota 110221, Bogota DC, Colombia. T. +576012179560 – +573112519362 – +573125860033. E-mail: admin@apice.org.co.
URL: http://www.apice.org.co/

History Nov 1969, Caracas (Venezuela). New statutes adopted 1994, Santafé de Bogota (Colombia); most recently revised and adopted 2009, Bogotá (Colombia). Former names and other names: *Pan American Association of Educational Credit Institutions (APICE)* – former; *Pan American Association of Student Loans (APICE)* – former. Registration: Law 14 of 1980, Start date: 18 Feb 1980, Colombia. **Aims** Encourage development of national and international systems for financing higher education students with economic participation of both public and private agencies and institutions; study and evaluate social, administrative and financial efficiency of student loan programmes; provide training for personnel from student loans institutions; promote study abroad programmes; management of educational projects. **Structure** General Assembly (annual); Board of Directors; Executive Director; Special Working Committees; *Information Network on Higher Education Studies in Latin America and the Caribbean (see: #18084).* **Languages** English, Portuguese, Spanish. **Staff** 12.00 FTE, paid; 4.00 FTE, voluntary. **Finance** Sources: contributions; fees for services; gifts, legacies; grants; investments; members' dues. Annual budget: 200,000 USD (2022). **Activities** Events/meetings; financial and/or material support; guidance/assistance/consulting; knowledge management/information dissemination; networking/liaising; research/documentation; training/education. Active in all member countries. **Events** *Pan American Conference* San José (Costa Rica) 2022, *Pan American Conference* Bogota (Colombia) 2021, *Experiences and perspectives on student loans in LAC* Bogota (Colombia) 2020, *Congress* Bogota (Colombia) 2019, *Congress* Bogota (Colombia) 2018. **Publications** *Innovations and Good Practices in Latin American Student Loans Institutions* (2020). Technical notebooks; papers; books; specialist directories; bibliographies; congress and seminar memories.
Members Founder; National; Institutional; Associate; Honorary; Individuals. Members (42) in 13 countries:
Bolivia, Brazil, Canada, Colombia, Costa Rica, Dominican Rep, Ecuador, Mexico, Panama, Paraguay, Peru, USA, Venezuela.
Included in the above, 2 organizations (2), listed in this Yearbook:
Laspau Inc.; *NAFSA – Association of International Educators.*
Consultative Status Consultative status granted from: *UNESCO (#20322)* (Consultative Status).
[2022.05.16/XD5861/**D**]

♦ Pan American Association of Student Loans / see Pan American Association of Student Loan Institutions (#18084)
♦ Pan American Association of Veterinary Medicine and Zootechnics / see Asociación Panamericana de Ciencias Veterinarias (#02287)
♦ Pan American Association of Veterinary Sciences (#02287)
♦ Panamerican Athletics Commission / see Asociación Panamericana de Atletismo (#02284)
♦ Pan American Badminton Confederation / see Confederación Panamericana de Badminton (#04467)
♦ Pan American Baseball Confederation (#04468)
♦ Pan American Basketball Confederation / see FIBA Americas (#09745)
♦ Panamerican Belt Wrestling Confederation (unconfirmed)
♦ Pan American Billiards Confederation (#04469)
♦ Panamerican Bioethics Association (no recent information)

♦ Pan American Bowling Confederation (PABCON) 18085

Chair Jardines de Moravia 19R, San José, San José, San José, Costa Rica. E-mail: presidente@acobol.org.
URL: https://panambowling.com/

History Set up as the American zone of *World Tenpin Bowling Association (WTBA, inactive).* Currently regional federation of *International Bowling Federation (IBF, #12384).* **Aims** Promote and develop bowling in the region; control and organize events; provide instruction; support and help World Bowling to gain and sustain Olympic recognition. **Structure** Presidium; Commissions. **Languages** English, Spanish. **Staff** 1.00 FTE, paid. **Finance** Members' dues. Other sources: championship proceeds.
Members Federations in 25 countries and territories:
Argentina, Aruba, Bahamas, Bermuda, Bolivia, Brazil, Canada, Chile, Colombia, Costa Rica, Curaçao, Dominican Rep, Ecuador, El Salvador, Guatemala, Honduras, Mexico, Panama, Paraguay, Peru, Puerto Rico, Uruguay, USA, Venezuela, Virgin Is USA.
NGO Relations Member of (1): *Asociación de Confederaciones Deportivas Panamericanas (ACODEPA, #02119).*
[2022/XJ0511/**D**]

♦ Pan American Cancer Cytology Society (inactive)
♦ Pan American Canoe Federation (#04471)

♦ Pan American Center for Geographical Studies and Research 18086

Centre panaméricain d'études et de recherches géographiques – Centro Panamericano de Estudios e Investigaciones Geograficas (CEPEIGE)
Mailing Address Seniergues E4-676 y Gral Telmo Paz y Miño, Ed del Inst Geografico Militar, 3er piso, Casilla 17 01 4173, 170403 Quito, Ecuador. T. +5932541200 – +59322237733. E-mail: info@cepeige.org.
URL: http://www.cepeige.org/

History 1973, Quito (Ecuador). Founded as a special unit of *Pan American Institute of Geography and History (PAIGH, #18113)* and under the auspices of the *OAS (#17629).* **Aims** Secure technical assistance to the American nations, through the training of specialists in geographical research and education, in accordance with the modern techniques and methods. **Structure** Superior Council, consisting of Secretary General of PAIGH, President of the Commission on Geography of PAIGH and President of the National Section in Ecuador of PAIGH. Academic Council, consisting of members of 4 countries designated by the Commission on Geography of PAIGH. Administrative Council, composed of the Director of CEPEIGE, President of the Advisory Committee for Financial Planning and Assessment of PAIGH and Director of Technical Cooperation Programme of PAIGH. Departments (3): Academic; Research; Administrative. **Finance** Sources: Government of Ecuador; PAIGH; other national and international organizations. Since 1975, receives OAS assistance for some programmes. **Events** *Conference* Quito (Ecuador) 1999, *International symposium on sustainable mountain development* Quito (Ecuador) 1998. **Publications** *Geografia Aplicada y Desarrollo* (2 a year). *Atlas Tematico* – serie 1 to 4. *Sintesis Informativa de Minitesis* (1988); *Geografia y Desarrollo* (1988) – Vol II; *Calidad de Vida* (1986).
Members PAIGH Member States (21):
Argentina, Belize, Bolivia, Brazil, Chile, Colombia, Costa Rica, Dominican Rep, Ecuador, El Salvador, Guatemala, Haiti, Honduras, Mexico, Nicaragua, Panama, Paraguay, Peru, Uruguay, USA, Venezuela.
[2021/XE7735/**E***]

♦ Pan American Cheer / see Pan American Federation of Cheerleading (#18101)

♦ Pan American Civic Organization (inactive)
♦ Pan American Coffee Bureau (inactive)
♦ Pan American Columbian Society (inactive)
♦ Pan American Commission on Inter-Municipal Cooperation / see Organización Iberoamericana de Cooperación Intermunicipal (#17839)

♦ Pan-American Committee for the Prevention of Blindness 18087

Chair 1301 South Bowen Rd, Ste 450, Arlington TX 76013, USA. T. +18172757553. Fax +18172753961. E-mail: info@paao.org.

Aims Offer international training programs to encourage blindness prevention at all levels. **Languages** English, Portuguese, Spanish. **Activities** Training. **NGO Relations** Affiliated member of: *Pan-American Association of Ophthalmology (PAAO, #18081).* [2013.10.04/XM1747/**D**]

♦ Pan-American Confederation of Commercial Travellers (inactive)
♦ Pan American Confederation for Highway Education (inactive)

♦ Pan American Confederation of Insurance Producers 18088

Confédération panaméricaine des assureurs – Confederación Panamericana de Productores de Seguros (COPAPROSE)

Main Office Centro Comercial Plaza Paitilla, Local 54, Piso 2, Panama, Panamá, Panama PANAMá, Panama. E-mail: copaprose@gmail.com – info@copaprose.org.

URL: https://copaprose.org/

History 3 Mar 1967. Founded during the 1st Congreso Panamericano de Productores de Seguros. **Aims** Provide information to insurance producers so the insurance profession can develop in a more competitive and efficient way, in accordance with the conditions of the global market. **Structure** General Assembly; Directive Council; Executive Council. **Languages** English, Portuguese, Spanish. **Staff** 2.00 FTE, paid. **Finance** Membership fees. **Events** *IberoAmerican Congress* Santo Domingo (Dominican Rep) 2022, *Congress* Mexico 2021, *Congress* Quito (Ecuador) 2002, *Congress* Lisbon (Portugal) 2000, *Congress* Bogota (Colombia) 1998.

Members Organizations in 20 countries:
Argentina, Bolivia, Brazil, Chile, Colombia, Costa Rica, Dominican Rep, Ecuador, El Salvador, Guatemala, Honduras, Mexico, Nicaragua, Panama, Paraguay, Peru, Portugal, Spain, Uruguay, Venezuela. [2021/XD1544/**D**]

♦ Panamerican Confederation of Mechanical and Electrical Engineering and Related Fields, San Juan 18089

Confederación Panamericana de Ingenieria Mecanica, Eléctrica y Ramas Afines (COPIMERA)

Contact address not obtained. T. +54940348867. E-mail: presidenciacopimera@gmail.com.

URL: http://www.copimerainternacional.org/

History Oct 1991, Mexico City (Mexico), during the Panamerican Congress of Mechanical and Electrical Engineering and Related Fields. **Structure** Council of 8 members. Executive Committee. **Events** *Biennial Congress* Mexico City (Mexico) 2009, *Biennial Congress* Cancún (Mexico) 2008, *Biennial Congress* Lima (Peru) 2007, *Biennial congress* Mexico City (Mexico) 2005, *Intermediate meeting* Holguin (Cuba) 2004. **NGO Relations** Collaborates with: *Unión Panamericana de Asociaciones de Ingenieros (UPADI, #20469).* [2013/XD8981/**D**]

♦ Pan-American Confederation of Mountain Sports and Climbing (#04472)
♦ Pan American Confederation for Sports for the Deaf / see Pan American Deaf Sports Organization (#18093)
♦ Pan American Confederation of Sports Medicine (no recent information)
♦ Pan-American Confederation for Suppliers of the Graphics Industry (no recent information)
♦ Pan American Congress of Journalists / see Inter American Press Association (#11444)
♦ Pan American Congress of Ophthalmology / see Pan-American Association of Ophthalmology (#18081)
♦ Pan American Congress of Physical Education (meeting series)
♦ Pan American Conservation Association (internationally oriented national body)

♦ Pan-American Cornea Society (PanCornea) 18090

Pres Clinica Pereira Gomes Oftalmologia, Rua Sabara 566 4o and cj 43 Higenôpolis, Sao Paulo SP, Brazil. T. +551132551603. Fax +551132145811.

Exec Dir address not obtained.

URL: http://www.pancornea.org/

History Original title: *Ibero-American Cornea Society – Sociedad Iberoamericana de Córnea.* **Aims** Promote exchange of technical and scientific information among ophthalmologists of the Americas specializing in cornea and external eye disease. **Structure** Board of Directors. **Languages** English, Spanish. **Activities** Events/meetings. **Members** Regular – ophthalmologists who have a minimum of 5 years practice in cornea and external disease including ocular surface and dry eye in clinical, surgical and investigational areas and who have contributed to the medical literature in the aforementioned areas in peer reviewed journals. Associate – ophthalmologists or investigators with an interest in cornea and external disease, including ocular surface and dry eye. Membership countries not specified. **NGO Relations** Member of: *Pan-American Association of Ophthalmology (PAAO, #18081).* [2017.06.01/XD6805/**D**]

♦ Pan-American Council for the Blind (inactive)

♦ Pan American Council on Education in Veterinary Science 18091

Consejo Panamericano de Educación en las Ciencias Veterinarias (COPEVET)

Pres address not obtained.

URL: http://www.panvet.org/copevet/

History Dec 1999, Lima (Peru), following an agreement between *Asociación Panamericana de Ciencias Veterinarias (PANVET, #02287)* and *Pan American Federation of University Faculties and Schools in Veterinary Sciences (#18105).* **Events** *Meeting* Mexico City (Mexico) 2003, *Meeting* Havana (Cuba) 2002, *Meeting* Santiago (Chile) 2001, *Meeting* Lima (Peru) 2000, *Meeting* Panama (Panama) 2000. [2014/XE4726/**E**]

♦ Pan American Council of Infantile Odontology (inactive)
♦ Pan American Cycle Racing Confederation / see Pan American Cycling Confederation (#18092)

♦ Pan American Cycling Confederation 18092

Confederación Panamericana de Ciclismo (COPACI)

Sec Velódromo Nacl Reinaldo Paseiro, Ave Monumental Km 4 1/2, Habana del Este, Havana, Cuba. T. +5377663776. Fax +5377664947. E-mail: panaci@enet.cu – copaci@copaci.org – sobero@inder.cu.

Dir Chief address not obtained. E-mail: prensacopaci@yahoo.es.

URL: http://www.copaci.org/en/

History 24 Sep 1922, Montevideo (Uruguay). Continental confederation of: *Union Cycliste Internationale (UCI, #20375).* Former names and other names: *Pan American Cycle Racing Confederation* – former. **Aims** Promote cycle racing in the region. **Structure** General Assembly (every 4 years); Management Committee; Commissions (14). **Languages** English, Spanish. **Staff** 4.00 FTE, paid. **Finance** Supported by: *Union Cycliste Internationale (UCI, #20375).* **Activities** Sporting activities. **Publications** *COPACI Boletin* – newsletter.

Members National organizations in 43 countries and territories:
Antigua-Barbuda, Argentina, Aruba, Bahamas, Barbados, Belize, Bermuda, Bolivia, Brazil, Canada, Cayman Is, Chile, Colombia, Costa Rica, Cuba, Curaçao, Dominica, Ecuador, El Salvador, Grenada, Guadeloupe, Guatemala, Guiana Fr, Guyana, Haiti, Honduras, Jamaica, Martinique, Mexico, Nicaragua, Panama, Paraguay, Peru, Puerto Rico, St Lucia, St Maarten, St Vincent-Grenadines, Suriname, Trinidad-Tobago, Uruguay, USA, Venezuela, Virgin Is USA.

NGO Relations Member of (1): *Asociación de Confederaciones Deportivas Panamericanas (ACODEPA, #02119).* [2023/XM1256/**D**]

♦ Pan American Dairy Federation (#09382)
♦ Panamerican Deaf Sports Confederation / see Pan American Deaf Sports Organization (#18093)

♦ Pan American Deaf Sports Organization (PANAMDES) 18093

Organización Deportiva Panamericana de Sordos

Contact address not obtained. E-mail: panamdes.america@gmail.com.

URL: http://www.panamdes.org/

History 15 Aug 1999, Havana (Cuba), as *Pan American Sports Organization of the Deaf.* Regional confederation of *International Committee of Sports for the Deaf (ICSD, #12805).* Also referred to as *Pan American Confederation for Sports for the Deaf, Pan American Sports Confederation of the Deaf* and *Panamerican Deaf Sports Confederation.* Registered in accordance with Mexican law. **Aims** Integrate the national deaf sports associations to PANAMDES; promote, direct and organize the activities programmed in the Panamerican region; represent the Panamerican sports for the deaf; develop and control deaf sports in the region; supervise the development of Panamerican deaf games and championships. **Structure** Congress (every 4 years). Executive Committee (meets annually), comprising President, Secretary/Treasurer and 3 Zone Representatives. General Secretary; Technical Delegates. **Languages** English, Spanish. **Finance** Members' dues. Other sources: contributions; donations; sponsorships; government grants. **Activities** Organizes Pan American Deaf Games and Championships. **Events** *Congress* Buenos Aires (Argentina) 2003, *Congress* 2002, *Congress* Havana (Cuba) 1999.

Members National associations (" indicates founding) in 9 countries:
Argentina (*), Brazil, Canada (*), Chile, Cuba (*), Mexico (*), Uruguay, USA (*), Venezuela (*). [2014/XD5668/**D**]

♦ Pan American Development Foundation (PADF) 18094

Fondation panaméricaine de développement – Fundación Panamericana para el Desarrollo (FUPAD)

Headquarters OAS Bldg, 1889 F St NW, 2nd Fl, Washington DC 20006, USA.

URL: http://www.padf.org/

History 21 Nov 1962, Washington DC (USA), under the auspices of the General Secretariat of the *OAS (#17629).* Registered in USA. **Aims** Improve the quality of life in Latin America and the Caribbean; promote economic and social development in these nations and reinforce democracy in the hemisphere; protect the environment and mitigation and relief of disasters. **Structure** Board of Trustees, consisting of 33 persons drawn from public and private service in USA, Latin America and the Caribbean. Officers: Chairman, Vice Chairman, President, First Vice President, Second Vice President, Executive Director, Secretary, Treasurer. **Languages** English, Portuguese, Spanish. **Staff** 17 staff in Washington DC (USA) headquarters; 80 field staff throughout the Americas. **Finance** Income derived from: United States government grants (85%); private contributions (13%); other sources (2%). Budget (annual): over US$ 22 million. **Activities** Intensification of work in the area of municipal development, as a fundamental element reinforcing democracy in the hemisphere. Projects of employment generation and support to micro-business, considered as important factors supporting economic and social growth in the countries. Projects in agroforestry and soil conservation, disaster relief, in-kind medical equipment and vocational tools, as well as special projects. **Events** *International Development Resource Exchange Forum* Miami, FL (USA) 1995, *International resource exchange forum* Miami, FL (USA) 1992, *International resource exchange forum* Miami, FL (USA) 1990, *Resource exchange forum* Bucaramanga (Colombia) 1989, *Resource exchange forum* Washington, DC (USA) 1988. **Publications** *PADF Newsletter* (2 a year). Annual report.

Members Area of responsibility OAS member countries (except Canada and USA), in 32 countries:
Antigua-Barbuda, Argentina, Bahamas, Barbados, Belize, Bolivia, Brazil, Chile, Colombia, Costa Rica, Dominica, Dominican Rep, Ecuador, El Salvador, Grenada, Guatemala, Guyana, Haiti, Honduras, Jamaica, Mexico, Nicaragua, Panama, Paraguay, Peru, St Kitts-Nevis, St Lucia, St Vincent-Grenadines, Suriname, Trinidad-Tobago, Uruguay, Venezuela.

Headquarters in:
USA.

Consultative Status Consultative status granted from: *ECOSOC (#05331)* (Ros A); *UNICEF (#20332).* **IGO Relations** *Pan American Health Organization (PAHO, #18108).* Associated with Department of Global Communications of the United Nations. **NGO Relations** Member of: *American Council for Voluntary International Action (InterAction); NGO Committee on UNICEF (#17120).* Links with a large number of organizations throughout the Caribbean and Latin America. [2020/XF3056/f/**F**]

♦ Pan American Draughts and Checkers Confederation (PAMDCC) 18095

Gen Sec Arashiweg 13, Willemstad, Curaçao.

URL: https://pamdcc.com/

Structure Board. **Activities** Awards/prizes/competitions.

Members Clubs in 14 countries and territories:
Aruba, Barbados, Bonaire Is, Brazil, Canada, Costa Rica, Curaçao, Dominican Rep, Grenada, Guadeloupe, Haiti, Suriname, Trinidad-Tobago, USA.

NGO Relations Continental federation of: *Fédération Mondiale du Jeu de Dames (FMJD, #09690).* [2020/AA1111/**D**]

♦ Pan American Electronic Sports Confederation (PAMESCO) 18096

Headquarters R Hilda Del Nero Bisquolo no 102, sala 1603-02, Jundiaí SP, 13208-703, Brazil. E-mail: contact@pamesco.org.

URL: https://pamescoesport.com/

History Registration: No/ID: 25102612000116, Brazil. **Aims** Create a standard for electronic sports; ensure that all national administrative entities promote Esports as a tool for training citizens in the professional, educational and social inclusion to have a better life. **Structure** Presidency; Board of Directors; Secretariat. Commissions; Councils; Departments.

Members Regional; National. Members in 12 countries and territories:
Argentina, Bahamas, Brazil, Colombia, Dominica, Ecuador, Guadeloupe, Jamaica, Mexico, Panama, Peru, Venezuela.
Central American and Caribbean Confederation of Esports (CACESCO); South American Esports Confederation (SAESCO).

NGO Relations Member of (2): *International Sport Network Organization (ISNO, #15592); World Esports Consortium (WESCO, #21391).* [2020/AA1092/y/**D**]

♦ Pan-American Equestrian Confederation (PAEC) 18097

SG address not obtained.

Pres address not obtained.

URL: https://paec.info/

History 2001. **Aims** Provide assistance for sustainable equestrian sports in Americas. **Structure** Board.

Members National federations in 30 countries and territories:
Antigua-Barbuda, Argentina, Barbados, Bermuda, Bolivia, Brazil, Canada, Cayman Is, Chile, Colombia, Costa Rica, Cuba, Dominica, Ecuador, El Salvador, Guatemala, Haiti, Honduras, Jamaica, Mexico, Nicaragua, Panama, Paraguay, Peru, Puerto Rico, Trinidad-Tobago, Uruguay, USA, Venezuela, Virgin Is USA.

NGO Relations Member of (1): *Asociación de Confederaciones Deportivas Panamericanas (ACODEPA, #02119).* Continental federation of: *Fédération Équestre Internationale (FEI, #09484).* [2022/AA3098/**D**]

♦ Pan American Federation of Architects' Associations 18098

Fédération panaméricaine des associations d'architectes – Federación Panamericana de Asociaciones de Arquitectos (FPAA)

Secretariat Gonzalo Ramirez 2030, 11200 Montevideo, Uruguay. T. +59824119556. Fax +59824119556. E-mail: secretaria@fpaa-arquitectos.org.

URL: http://www.fpaa-arquitectos.org/

History 1920, Montevideo (Uruguay). **Aims** Establish an active and effective link with cultural, artistic, scientific and professional purposes among architects of the Americas; maintain continuity of Panamerican Congresses of Architects; enhance the status of architects in all countries of the American Continent. **Structure** General Assembly (every 2 years); Executive Committee. Regional section: *Federation of Caribbean Associations of Architects (FCAA, #09465).* **Languages** English, French, Portuguese, Spanish. **Staff** 3.00 FTE, voluntary. **Finance** Sources: members' dues. **Activities** Events/meetings. **Events** *Pan-American Congress of Architects* Montevideo (Uruguay) 2020, *Quadrennial congress / Pan American Congress of Architecture* Maceió (Brazil) 2012, *International conference on urban development of border cities* Foz do Iguaçu (Brazil) 2009, *International conference on urban development of border cities* Foz do Iguaçu (Brazil) 2009, *Quadrennial congress / Pan American Congress of Architecture* Tegucigalpa (Honduras) 2008. **Publications** *FPAA Bulletin* (4 a year); *PanAmerican Architectura Magazine* (annual).

Members National associations in 30 countries and territories:

Argentina, Bahamas, Barbados, Bolivia, Brazil, Canada, Chile, Colombia, Costa Rica, Cuba, Dominican Rep, Ecuador, El Salvador, Guadeloupe, Guatemala, Guyana, Honduras, Jamaica, Martinique, Mexico, Nicaragua, Panama, Paraguay, Peru, Puerto Rico, Suriname, Trinidad-Tobago, Uruguay, USA, Venezuela.
Consultative Status Consultative status granted from: *OAS (#17629).* [2023.02.28/XD3057/**D**]

♦ Pan American Federation of Arts, Mass Media and Entertainment Unions (PANARTES) 18099

Federación Panamericana de Sindicatos de Artes, Medios de Comunicación y Espectaculo – Federação Panamericana de Sindicatos das Artes, Meios da Comunicação e Espectaculo

Regional Sec UNI Europa, 40 rue Joseph II, 1000 Brussels, Belgium. T. +3222345640. Fax +3222350870.
Pres c/o SAT, Quintino Bocayuva 50, CP 1181 Buenos Aires, Argentina. T. +541149837178. Fax +541149837178. E-mail: relaciones-institucionales@sal.org.ar.
URL: http://www.uniglobalunion.org/sectors/media-entertainment-arts/

History 6 Dec 1991, Silver Spring MD (USA), when Statutes were adopted, as American regional organization of *International Secretariat for Arts, Mass Media and Entertainment Trade Unions (ISETU, inactive)*, currently, since Dec 1993, *Media and Entertainment International (MEI, inactive).* **Aims** Link and coordinate *trade unions* in the sector in the Americas; further and defend their interests, those of their members and those of the arts, mass media and entertainment industry in general; develop and carry out strategies for dealing with any technological change which undermines interests of *workers* in the sector; coordinate development of cross-border representation of the sector's workers in the context of increasing regional and subregional economic integration; defend *freedom* of speech, expression, creativity and association and universal suffrage; aid and promote the expression of national, regional and subgroup *cultural* development; oppose all forms of racism, sexism, chauvinistic nationalism and other forms of discrimination. Supports: adoption of better laws and international agreements to protect *copyright* and performance rights of members; development of trade unions and other workers' organizations and their objectives of peace, work for all, equitable remuneration, social justice, equal opportunity and development of environmental policies. Represent the interests of workers in the sector and various subsectors before legislative and governmental bodies, national and international employer groups and the general public. **Structure** Congressional Assembly (supreme authority). Executive Committee, including President, First General Vice President, 2 General Vice Presidents, Treasurer, Secretary and 4 Regional Vice Presidents. Management Committee, comprising President, 3 General Vice Presidents and Treasurer plus, ex-officio, Secretary. Regional Committees (4): Region One – Argentina, Brazil, Chile, Paraguay, Uruguay; Region Two – Bolivia, Colombia, Ecuador, Peru, Venezuela; Region Three – Caribbean Islands, Central America, French Guiana, Guyana, Mexico, Panama, Surinam; Region Four – Bermuda, Canada, USA. Professional Groups (4): Broadcasting; Film Production; Writers; Advertising. Country Councils. **Languages** Aymara, Creoles and pidgins, English, French, Guarani, Nahuatl languages, Portuguese, Quechua (macrolanguage), Spanish. **Finance** Members' dues. **Activities** Provides technical assistance and professional and trade union training to affiliated unions in difficulty. Gathers and disseminates information and carries out studies. **Events** *Caribbean broadcasting workers conference* Barbados 2009, *Conference for broadcasting workers* Buenos Aires (Argentina) 2006, *General assembly* Buenos Aires (Argentina) 2006, *Caribbean regional broadcasting conference* Port-of-Spain (Trinidad-Tobago) 2005, *Film production workers conference* Santiago (Chile) 2005.
Members Affiliates (44) in 20 countries and territories of the Americas:
Argentina, Barbados, Bermuda, Bolivia, Brazil, Canada, Chile, Colombia, Ecuador, Guiana Fr, Guyana, Mexico, Panama, Paraguay, Peru, Suriname, Trinidad-Tobago, Uruguay, USA, Venezuela.
NGO Relations Agreement signed with: Latin American group of *International Federation of Musicians (#13486).* [2016/XE1912/**E**]

♦ Pan American Federation of Associations of Medical Schools (PAFAMS) 18100

Fédération panaméricaine des associations des facultés de médecine – Federación Panamericana de Asociaciones de Facultades y Escuelas de Medicina (FEPAFEM)

Pres Univ Autónoma de Guadalajara, Hosp Dr Angel Leaño, KM 5 Carretera a Testistan, 44100 Guadalajara JAL, Mexico. E-mail: rleonbor@gmail.com.
Exec Dir Manuel Lopez Cotilla 754, Colonia del Valle, 03100 Mexico City CDMX, Mexico. T. +525556879323 – +525556829482. E-mail: fepafempafams@hotmail.com.
URL: http://www.fepafempafams.org/

History 29 Nov 1962, Viña del Mar (Chile). Founded at 3rd Conference of Latin American Medical Faculties. Statutes adopted Aug 1964, Poços de Caldas (Brazil). Commenced official association with WHO, 1965. Recognized as an international body by Colombian government, 5 May 1967, and Venezuelan government, 28 Oct 1975. **Aims** Promote, improve and develop quality in medical education in the Americas. **Structure** Executive Committee; Executive Direction; Zone Directors; Assessing Council. **Languages** English, Portuguese, Spanish. **Staff** 5.00 FTE, paid. **Finance** Sources: members' dues. **Activities** Certification/accreditation; events/meetings; networking/liaising; politics/policy/regulatory; projects/programmes; research/documentation. **Events** *Pan American Conference on Medical Education* Cartagena de Indias (Colombia) 2019, *Pan American Conference on Medical Education* Cancún (Mexico) 2016, *Panamerican Conference of Medical Education* Quito (Ecuador) 2013, *Pan American conference on medical education* Buenos Aires (Argentina) 2008, *Seminario@health : seminario sobre tecnologias de la informacion aplicadas al sistema de salud* Caracas (Venezuela) 2006. **Publications** *Boletin FEPAFEM* in English, Spanish. Information Services: Documentation and information centre; databank. **Information Services** *PAFAMS Editorial Fund* – produces publications and disseminates scientific knowledge, information reports and data.
Members National Associations of Faculties/Medical Schools (14) in 13 countries:
Argentina, Bolivia, Brazil, Canada, Chile, Colombia, Costa Rica, Dominican Rep, Ecuador, Mexico, Peru, USA, Venezuela.
Individual Faculties/Medical Schools (11) in 10 countries:
Bolivia, Costa Rica, El Salvador, Guatemala, Honduras, Jamaica, Nicaragua, Panama, Paraguay, Uruguay.
IGO Relations Official relations with: *Pan American Health Organization (PAHO, #18108).* **NGO Relations** Member of (1): *World Federation for Medical Education (WFME, #21454).* [2022/XD3058/y/**D**]

♦ Pan American Federation of Cheerleading (PFC) 18101

Contact Av Canevaro 1390, Lince, 15073, Lima, Peru. T. +5112655677. E-mail: cheerperu@yahoo.com.
URL: https://panamericancheer.org/

History 2008. A continental federation of *International Federation of Cheerleading (IFC, #13386).* Former names and other names: *Pan American Cheer* – alias. **Structure** Board of Directors. **Events** *Annual Meeting* Lima (Peru) 2019. [2020/AA0995/**D**]

♦ Pan-American Federation of Consultants (#09379)
♦ Pan American Federation of Engineering Economics and Costs (no recent information)
♦ Pan American Federation of Engineering Societies / see Unión Panamericana de Asociaciones de Ingenieros (#20469)
♦ Pan American Federation of Geographical Societies / see Pan American Institute of Geography and History (#18113)
♦ Pan American Federation of Hotel, Gastronomy and Tourism Schools (#04474)
♦ Pan American Federation of Hotel and Tourism Schools / see Confederación Panamericana de Escuelas de Hoteleria, Gastronomia y Turismo (#04474)

♦ Pan-American Federation for Information Technology in Agriculture (PanAFITA) 18102

Contact c/o Univ of Florida, Dept of Agricultural and Biological Engineering, 1012 Turlington Hall, PO Box 117345, Gainesville FL 32611, USA. E-mail: fsz@ufl.edu.
URL: http://www.panfita.org/

History Jul 2003. **Aims** Promote information technology in agriculture leading to improvements in the quality of food and fiber production, the quality of life of agricultural producers and secure and sustainable food production. **Structure** General Assembly (every 2 years). Board, comprising President, President Elect, Secretary General, Treasurer and 3 further members. **Languages** English. **Staff** 5.00 FTE, voluntary. **Finance** Members' dues. **Events** *World congress on computers in agriculture (and natural resources)* Reno, NV (USA) 2009, *World conference on agricultural information and IT* Atsugi (Japan) 2008, *World congress on computers in agriculture (and natural resources)* Atsugi (Japan) 2008, *World congress on computers in agriculture (and natural resources)* Glasgow (UK) 2007, *World congress on computers in agriculture (and natural resources)* Orlando, FL (USA) 2006. **Publications** *Journal of Information Technology in Agriculture.*
Members Full in 6 countries:
Argentina, Brazil, Chile, Costa Rica, Mexico, USA.
NGO Relations Member of: *International Network for Information Technology in Agriculture (INFITA, #14287).* [2011/XM0125/**D**]

♦ Pan American Federation of Labor (inactive)

♦ Pan-American Federation For Nondestructive Testing (PANNDT) ... 18103

Contact address not obtained. E-mail: template.placeholder@gmail.com.
URL: https://www.panndt.org/

Aims Stimulate the cooperation among North, Central and South American and Caribbean countries, in every scope regarding development and use of all nondestructive testing methods. **Structure** Board of Directors; Executive Committee. **Languages** English, Spanish. **Activities** Events/meetings. **Events** *Conference* Niagara Falls, ON (Canada) 2023.
Members Full in 7 countries:
Argentina, Brazil, Canada, Colombia, Mexico, Uruguay, USA.
NGO Relations Member of (1): *International Committee on Non-Destructive Testing (ICNDT, #12793).* [2021/AA2237/**D**]

♦ Pan American Federation of Nursing Professionals 18104

Federación Panamericana de Profesionales de Enfermeria (FEPPEN)

Pres Calzada Obrero Mundial 229, Col del Valle, 03100 Mexico City CDMX, Mexico.
URL: https://www.facebook.com/FEPPENCuba/

History Founded 1970. **Structure** Executive Committee. **Publications** *Revista Panamericana de Enfermeria* (periodical).
Members Full in 19 countries and territories:
Argentina, Bolivia, Brazil, Chile, Colombia, Costa Rica, Cuba, Dominican Rep, Ecuador, El Salvador, Guatemala, Honduras, Mexico, Nicaragua, Paraguay, Peru, Puerto Rico, Uruguay, Venezuela. [2016/XD6111/**D**]

♦ Pan American Federation of Pharmacy (no recent information)

♦ Pan American Federation of University Faculties and Schools in Veterinary Sciences 18105

Federación Panamericana de Facultades y Escuelas de Ciencias Veterinarias (FPFECV)

Pres Fac de Ciencias Veterinarias – UBA, Av Chorroarin 280, C1427 CWO Buenos Aires, Argentina. E-mail: relinternacionales@fvet.uba.ar – mmiralles@fvet.uba.ar.

History 8 Oct 1992, Santiago (Chile), during XIII Congreso Panamericano de Ciencias Veterinarias. **Events** *Meeting* Lima (Peru) 2005, *Meeting* Buenos Aires (Argentina) 2004, *Meeting* Havana (Cuba) 2002, *Meeting* Panama (Panama) 2000, *Meeting* Santa Cruz (Bolivia) 1998. **NGO Relations** Together with: *Asociación Panamericana de Ciencias Veterinarias (PANVET, #02287)*, set up: *Pan American Council on Education in Veterinary Science (#18091).* [2017.06.01/XD9072/**D**]

♦ Pan American Federation for Voluntary Blood Donation (inactive)
♦ Pan American Fencing Confederation (#04475)

♦ Pan American Foot-and-Mouth Disease Center (PAFMDC) 18106

Centre panaméricain de la fièvre aphteuse – Centro Panamericano de Fiebre Aftosa (PANAFTOSA)

Dir Av Governador Leonel de Moura Brizola 7778, São Bento, Duque de Caxias RJ, 25040 002, Brazil. T. +552136619000. Fax +552136619001. E-mail: dbersot@paho.org – panaftosa@paho.org.
URL: http://www.panaftosa.org.br/

History 1951. Currently part of the Veterinary Public Health Program of *Pan American Health Organization (PAHO, #18108).* **Aims** Provide support to the foot-and-mouth disease and *zoonoses prevention*, control and eradication programmes; serve as a regional laboratory for vesicular diseases *diagnostic* and *vaccine* quality control; maintain a continental *vesicular diseases epidemiological* surveillance system; provide collaboration and coordination among countries. **Structure** Director's Office; Administration. **Staff** 100.00 FTE, paid. **Finance** Financed by PAHO regular budget and extrabudgetary funds. Budget (annual): about US$ 4.1 million. **Activities** Develops an information and epidemiological surveillance system for vesicular and zoonosis diseases; offers training programme on animal health and development research and appropriate technology. Field Services: vesicular diseases; foot-and-mouth disease; risk analysis; epidemiological surveillance system. Programmes and Services: Rabies; Brucellosis/Tuberculosis; Social Communication; International Agreements. Laboratory of Reference: Development of Biotechnology; Diagnosis of Vesicular and Differential. Acts as secretariat of *Comisión Sudamericana para la Lucha contra la Fiebre Aftosa (COSALFA, #04143).* **Events** *Meeting* Asunción (Paraguay) 2016, *Meeting* Asunción (Paraguay) 2016, *Meeting* Santiago (Chile) 2012, *Extraordinary Meeting* Rio de Janeiro (Brazil) 2010, *Meeting* Rio de Janeiro (Brazil) 2008. **Publications** *Foot-and-Mouth Disease and Vesicular Estomatitis – Epidemiological Report* (weekly); *Foot-and-Mouth Disease and Vesicular Estomatitis – Epidemiological Report* (12 a year); *Vigilancia Epidemiologica Brucelosis/Tuberculosis* (2 a year); *Vigilancia Epidemiologica de la Rabia en las Américas* (2 a year); *Boletin del Centro Panamericano de Fiebre Aftosa* (annual); *Informe Anual del Centro Panamericano de Fiebre Aftosa* (annual); *Vigilancia Epidemiológica de la Rabia en las Américas* (annual). Proceedings.
Members Member States (40):
Antigua-Barbuda, Argentina, Bahamas, Barbados, Belize, Bermuda, Bolivia, Brazil, Canada, Chile, Colombia, Costa Rica, Cuba, Dominica, Dominican Rep, Ecuador, El Salvador, France, Grenada, Guatemala, Guyana, Haiti, Honduras, Jamaica, Mexico, Netherlands, Nicaragua, Panama, Paraguay, Peru, Portugal, St Kitts-Nevis, St Lucia, St Vincent-Grenadines, Suriname, Trinidad-Tobago, UK, Uruguay, USA, Venezuela.
IGO Relations *FAO (#09260); Inter-American Development Bank (IDB, #11427); Inter-American Institute for Cooperation on Agriculture (IICA, #11434); Organismo Internacional Regional de Sanidad Agropecuaria (OIRSA, #17830).* **NGO Relations** *World Reference Laboratory for Foot and Mouth Diseases (WRLFMD).* [2018/XE8387/**E***]

♦ Pan-American Gastroenterological Association (#17847)
♦ Pan American Geographical and Historical Institute / see Pan American Institute of Geography and History (#18113)

♦ Pan-American Glaucoma Society (PAGS) 18107

Sociedad Panamericana de Glaucoma (SPAG)

Pres Shiley Eye Inst, Univ of California – San Diego, 9415 Campus Pt Drive, La Jolla CA 92093, USA. T. +18585348824. Fax +18585341625. E-mail: rweinreg@ucsd.edu.

History Apr 1975. Founded April 1975. **Aims** Promote improvement, dissemination and application of all scientific knowledge related to glaucoma in America, Spain and Portugal. **Structure** Meeting (every 2 years); Board. **Members** (207). Membership countries not specified. **NGO Relations** Member of: *Pan-American Association of Ophthalmology (PAAO, #18081); World Glaucoma Association (WGA, #21540).* [2017.12.03/XD6808/**D**]

♦ Pan American Group for Immunodeficiencies (internationally oriented national body)
♦ Pan American Group for Rapid Viral Diagnosis / see Pan American Society for Clinical Virology
♦ Pan American Gymnastics Union (#20471)
♦ Pan American Health and Education Foundation / see PAHO Foundation (#18022)

♦ Pan American Health Organization (PAHO) 18108

Organisation panaméricaine de la santé (OPS) – Organización Panamericana de la Salud (OPS) – Organização Pan-Americana da Saúde (OPAS)

Dir 525 Twenty-Third St NW, Washington DC 20037-2895, USA. T. +12029743408 – +12029743000. Fax +12029743409 – +12029743663. E-mail: director@paho.org.
USA-Mexico Border Field Office 5400 Suncrest Dr, Suite C-4, El Paso TX 79912, USA. T. +19158455950. Fax +19158454361. E-mail: mail@fep.paho.org.
URL: http://www.paho.org/

History Oct 1947, Buenos Aires (Argentina), as *Pan American Sanitary Organization – Organisation sanitaire panaméricaine – Organización Sanitaria Panamericana*, on approval of the Constitution, which was ratified 1950, Santo Domingo (Dominican Rep). Constitution amendments approved by Resolution XXXVII (1961), Resolution XXIV (1965), Resolution II (1968), Resolution I (1978) and Resolution VIII (1999). Establishment was envisaged in resolutions of the 12th Pan American Sanitary Conference. Executive organ/secretariat is *Pan American Sanitary Bureau (PASB, #18129)*, set up Jan 1902, Mexico City (Mexico), as 'International Sanitary Bureau', adopted its current title in 1923 and became Executive Organ of PAHO upon its establishment in 1947. Present name was adopted at 15th Conference, Sep-Oct 1958, San Juan (Puerto Rico). PAHO is a member of the inter-American system, being the specialized organization for health of *OAS (#17629)*. At the same time it is linked to the United Nations system through the PASB, which serves within *WHO (#20950)* as 'WHO Regional Office for the Americas'. **Aims** Ensure optimal health for peoples of the Americas; contribute to the *wellbeing* of their families and communities; lead strategic collaborative efforts among member countries and other partners to promote equity in health, combat *disease* and improve quality and length of life; encourage cooperation among the people of the Americas in charting a course to *sustainable human development*, leading to health for all and by all; work with the community to promote and protect health; collaborate with the *international community*, ministries of health, social security agencies and other government institutions, NGOs, universities, community groups and others to strengthen national and local health systems and improve health and wellbeing; defend the Americas against emerging or re-emerging dangerous infectious diseases; promote efforts leading to healthy public policies, healthy communities and health promotion, including measures to protect such high-risk groups as children, mothers, workers, indigenous peoples, the poor and the elderly. **Structure** Governing Bodies: Pan American Sanitary Conference (every 5 years), consisting delegates of Member Governments of the Organization and Participating Governments; Directing Council (convening in each of the 4 years between the Meetings of the Conference), composed of one representative from each Government; Executive Committee, comprises representatives from 9 Member Governments and including Chairman and Vice-Chairman; Subcommittee on Program, Budget and Administration (auxiliary advisory body of the Executive Committee). Executive organ: *Pan American Sanitary Bureau (PASB, #18129)*, Washington DC (USA). Meetings public, except under special circumstances. Centers (3): *Latin American and Caribbean Centre on Health Sciences Information (BIREME, #16267)*; *Latin American Center for Perinatology/ Unit of Woman and Reproductive Health (CLAP/WR, #16290)*; *Pan American Foot-and-Mouth Disease Center (PAFMDC, #18106)*. Also hosted at Secretariat: *Pharmaceutical Forum of the Americas (#18351)*. **Languages** English, French, Portuguese, Spanish. **Staff** As of 2000: 2,750 persons including 1,081 international civil servants, the remainder being nationals engaged under more flexible contracts. Negotiates through *PAHO/ WHO Staff Association (#18024)*. The *Administrative Tribunal of the International Labour Organization (ILO Tribunal, #00118)* is competent to settle disputes. **Finance** Member governments' contributions; special funds. Regular budget: about US$ 256,000,000. Nearly 90% of budget targets major strategic and programme areas, 34% of the total budget available in these areas coming from extrabudgetary sources. **Activities** Projects and programs. **Events** *Pan American Sanitary Conference* Washington, DC (USA) 2022, *Geneva Conference on Person-Centered Medicine* 2021, *Session* Washington, DC (USA) 2021, *Seminar* Washington, DC (USA) 2020, *Session* Washington, DC (USA) 2019. **Publications** *Revista Panamericana de Salud Pública – Pan American Journal of Public Health* (12 a year); *Epidemiological Bulletin* (4 a year) in English, Spanish; *Health Conditions in the Americas* (every 5 years) in English, Spanish; *Perspectives in Health* – magazine. *Charting a Future for Health in the Americas* (2002) – quadrennial report of the Director. Reports; technical publications; PAHO/WHO conference proceedings – all in Spanish, English. Information Services: Library in Washington DC (USA): includes over 50,000 volumes in public health subjects related to Americas region; maintains databases; contributes to LILACS CD-ROM; distributes WHO material.

Members Governments of 35 countries:
Antigua-Barbuda, Argentina, Bahamas, Barbados, Belize, Bolivia, Brazil, Canada, Chile, Colombia, Costa Rica, Cuba, Dominica, Dominican Rep, Ecuador, El Salvador, Grenada, Guatemala, Guyana, Haiti, Honduras, Jamaica, Mexico, Nicaragua, Panama, Paraguay, Peru, St Kitts-Nevis, St Lucia, St Vincent-Grenadines, Suriname, Trinidad-Tobago, Uruguay, USA, Venezuela.
Associate government of 4 countries and territories:
Aruba, Curaçao, Puerto Rico, St Maarten.
Participating governments (3):
France, Netherlands, UK.
Official observers (2):
Portugal, Spain.

IGO Relations Joint programme with WHO: *Latin American Cancer Research Information Project (LACRIP, no recent information)*.
Collaboration and links with:
- *Andean Cooperation in Health (CAS, no recent information)*;
- *Canadian International Development Agency (CIDA, inactive)*;
- *Caribbean Action Plan (CAR, #03432)*;
- *Caribbean Community (CARICOM, #03476)*;
- *Caribbean Development and Cooperation Committee (CDCC, inactive)*;
- *Comisión Interamericana de Mujeres (CIM, #04137)*;
- *Comisión Sudamericana para la Lucha contra la Fiebre Aftosa (COSALFA, #04143)*;
- *Commission on Genetic Resources for Food and Agriculture (CGRFA, #04215)*;
- *Consejo de Ministros de Salud de Centroamérica (COMISCA, #04722)*;
- *DANIDA*;
- *Department for International Development Cooperation*;
- *Deutsche Gesellschaft für Technische Zusammenarbeit (GTZ, inactive)*;
- *Environmental Training Network for Latin America and the Caribbean (inactive)*;
- *FAO (#09260)*;
- *Hipólito Unanue Agreement (#10921)*;
- *ILO (#11123)*;
- *Inter-American Children's Institute (IACI, #11406)*;
- *Inter-American Committee on Natural Disaster Reduction (IACNDR, #11414)*;
- *Inter-American Conference of Ministers of Labor (no recent information)*;
- *Inter-American Conference on Social Security (ICSS, #11419)*;
- *Inter-American Council for Integral Development (#11423)*;
- *Inter-American Development Bank (IDB, #11427)*;
- *Inter-American Drug Abuse Control Commission (#11429)*;
- *Inter-American Indian Institute (IAII, inactive)*;
- *Intergovernmental Commission for Chagas' Disease (no recent information)*;
- *International Atomic Energy Agency (IAEA, #12294)*;
- *International Bank for Reconstruction and Development (IBRD, #12317)*;
- *International Development Association (IDA, #13155)*;
- *International Development Research Centre (IDRC, #13162)*;
- *Latin American and Caribbean Institute for Economic and Social Planning (#16279)*;
- *Latin American Centre for Development Administration (#16294)*;
- *Latin American Faculty of Social Sciences (#16316)*;
- *Meeting of Ministers of Health in the Andean Region (REMSAA)*;
- *Norwegian Agency for Development Cooperation (Norad)*;
- *OIE – World Organisation for Animal Health (#17703)*;
- *OPEC Fund for International Development (OFID, #17745)*;
- *PAHO/WHO Health Emergencies Department (PHE, #18023)*;
- *Pan Caribbean Disaster Preparedness and Prevention Project (PCDPPP, inactive)*;
- *Pharmaceutical Procurement Service (PSS, #18354)*;
- *Organismo Internacional Regional de Sanidad Agropecuaria (OIRSA, #17830)*;
- *Regional Nursing Body, CARICOM Community (RNB, no recent information)*;
- *Secretariat of the Basel Convention (SBC, #19196)*;
- *Sistema Económico Latinoamericano (SELA, #19294)*;
- *Swedish International Development Cooperation Agency (Sida)*;
- *UNEP (#20299)*;
- *UNCTAD (#20285)*;
- *UNDP (#20292)*;
- *UNESCO (#20322)*;
- *UNESCO Regional Bureau for Culture for Latin America and the Caribbean (#20317)*;
- *UNESCO Regional Bureau for Education in Latin America and the Caribbean (#20318)*;
- *UNHCR (#20327)*;
- *UNICEF (#20332)*;
- *United Nations Economic Commission for Latin America and the Caribbean (ECLAC, #20556)*;
- *United Nations International Emergency Network (UNIENET, no recent information)*;
- *United Nations Office for Disaster Risk Reduction (UNDRR, #20595)*;
- *United Nations Population Fund (UNFPA, #20612)*;
- *United Nations University (UNU, #20642)*;
- *WHO Pan African Emergency Training Centre (PTC-Addis, no recent information)*;
- *WHO Regional Office for Europe (#20945)*;
- *World Food Programme (WFP, #21510)*.

NGO Relations Official links with: *Asociación Latinoamericana de Industrias Farmacéuticas (ALIFAR, #02232)*; *Inter-American Association of Sanitary and Environmental Engineering (#11400)*; *Inter-American College of Radiology (IACR, #11409)*; *InterAmerican Heart Foundation (IAHF, #11432)*; *International Diabetes Federation (IDF, #13164)* (North, Central and South American Regional Councils); *Latin American and Caribbean Women's Health Network (LACWHN, #16288)*; *Confederación Latinoamericana de Bioquímica Clínica (COLABIOCLI, #04454)*; *Latin American Federation of Hospitals (#16322)*; *Latin American Federation of the Pharmaceutical Industry (#16328)*; *Pan American Federation of Associations of Medical Schools (PAFAMS, #18100)*; *Pan American Federation of Nursing Professionals (#18104)*; *World Association for Sexual Health (WAS, #21187)*. Instrumental in setting up: *Red de Ciclovías Recreativas de las Américas (Red CRA, #18640)*.
[2016.09.09/XE3060/E*]

♦ Pan American Highway Confederation (inactive)
♦ Pan American Highway Finance Committee (inactive)

♦ Pan American Highway System 18109

Système panaméricain des routes – Sistema Panamericano de Carreteras

Address not obtained.

History 1923, Santiago (Chile), by a resolution approved during 5th International Conference of American States, as a network of highways in Latin America, linking most of the countries of South and Central America and USA. Currently under the aegis of *Pan American Highway Congresses (inactive)*, a specialized conference of *OAS (#17629)*. The actualization of the Pan American Highway System decided by COPACA Congress, 1984, Buenos Aires (Argentina). [2008/XF0287/F*]

♦ Pan American Hockey Federation (PAHF) 18110

Fédération panaméricaine de hockey – Federación Panamericana de Hockey

Pres Av Julio A Roca 546 C 1076 ABN, Buenos Aires, Argentina. T. +5491144748950. E-mail: president@panamhockey.org.
Hon Treas address not obtained.
URL: http://www.panamhockey.org/

History 17 Oct 1959, Greenwich, CT (USA). Continental body of: *International Hockey Federation (#13802)*. **Aims** Administer, encourage, promote and develop hockey for both men and women within the Americas at all levels (field, indoor and all current and future forms, excluding any discipline that is listed as winter or roller sport). **Structure** Congress; Board of Directors. **Languages** English, Spanish. **Staff** 2.50 FTE, paid. **Finance** Sources: grants; members' dues; revenue from activities/projects; sponsorship. Annual grant from: *International Hockey Federation (#13802)*. Annual budget: 210,000 USD. **Activities** Events/meetings; sporting activities; training/education. **Events** *Congress* Santiago (Chile) 2022, *Quadrennial Congress* Mendoza (Argentina) 2013, *Annual Meeting* Caracas (Venezuela) 1996, *Quadrennial Congress* Mar del Plata (Argentina) 1995, *Annual Meeting* San Juan (Puerto Rico) 1993. **Publications** *PAHF FUNdamental Field Hockey* (2013) in English, Spanish; *PAHF Branding Manual* (2011) in English, Spanish.

Members Full national associations in 27 countries and territories:
Argentina, Bahamas, Barbados, Bermuda, Brazil, Canada, Cayman Is, Chile, Costa Rica, Cuba, Dominican Rep, Ecuador, El Salvador, Guatemala, Guyana, Haiti, Honduras, Jamaica, Mexico, Panama, Paraguay, Peru, Puerto Rico, Trinidad-Tobago, Uruguay, USA, Venezuela.

NGO Relations Member of (4): *Asociación de Confederaciones Deportivas Panamericanas (ACODEPA, #02119)*; *Central American and Caribbean Sports Organization (CACSO, #03665)*; *Panam Sports Organization (Panam Sports, #18138)*; *South American Sports Organization (SASO, #19708)*. Maintains relations with National Olympic Committees of member nations. [2023/XD2083/D]

♦ Pan American Homeopathic Medical Congress (meeting series)

♦ Pan American and Iberian Federation of Critical Medicine and Intensive Care Societies 18111

Federación Panamericana e Ibérica de Sociedades de Medicina Crítica y Terapia Intensiva (FEPIMCTI)

Exec Sec Univ de Cartagena, Avenida del Consulado, Calle 30 No 48 – 152, Cartagena de Indias, Bolivar, Colombia. E-mail: crdc2001@gmail.com.
Pres Clínica INDISA, Avda Santa Maria 1810, Providencia, Santiago, Santiago Metropolitan, Chile. E-mail: sugarteu@gmail.com.
URL: http://www.fepimcti.org/

History 1979, Mexico City (Mexico). **Aims** Actively collaborate in the objectives and projects of WFSICCM; unify concepts regarding the field of critical care; contribute to the study and progress of critical medicine; collaborate in projects allowing the adjustment of technology to the available economic capacities; study joint plans for research and human resource training; maintain active contact with related organizations; provide incentives and support the incorporation of critical care and intensive therapy associations in those Latin American countries where there are none. **Events** *Quadrennial Congress* Porto Alegre (Brazil) 2016, *Quadrennial Congress* Madrid (Spain) 2014, *Quadrennial Congress* Punta del Este (Uruguay) 2007, *Quadrennial Congress* Cancún (Mexico) 2003, *Meeting* Sydney, NSW (Australia) 2001.

Members Organizations in 16 countries:
Argentina, Bolivia, Brazil, Chile, Colombia, Costa Rica, Ecuador, Mexico, Panama, Paraguay, Peru, Portugal, Spain, Uruguay, USA, Venezuela. [2019.02.18/XD8656/D]

♦ Pan American Implant Association (inactive)

♦ Pan American Indoor Football Confederation 18112

Confederación Panamericana de Fútbol de Salón (PANAFUTSAL)

Pres Avda Brasilia 1895 esq, Tte Frutos, 2o Piso, Casilla de Correo 2272, Asunción, Paraguay. T. +59521291907 – +59521291339. Fax +59521293031.

History 25 Sep 1990, Bogota (Colombia). Statutes adopted in 1993. Also known as *Confederación Panamericana de Futsal (CPFS)*. **Structure** Board of Directors, consisting of President, 1st Vice-President, 2nd Vice-President, 3rd Vice-President, Secretary-General, Treasurer and 3 members. **Activities** Sporting events.

Members Indoor football federations in 9 countries:
Argentina, Bolivia, Brazil, Chile, Colombia, Mexico, Paraguay, Uruguay, Venezuela.

NGO Relations *Panam Sports Organization (Panam Sports, #18138)*; *Confederación Sudamericana de Futsal (CSFS, no recent information)*; *European Futsal Association (EFA, #07371)*. Instrumental in setting up: *World Futsal Association (#21532)*. [2014/XD5666/D]

♦ Pan American Infectious Diseases Association / see Asociación Panamericana de Infectologia (#02288)
♦ Pan American Infectious Diseases Society / see Asociación Panamericana de Infectologia (#02288)

♦ Pan American Institute of Geography and History (PAIGH) 18113

Institut panaméricain de géographie et d'histoire – Instituto Panamericano de Geografía e Historia (IPGH)

SG Ex-Arzobispado 29, Col Observatorio, 11860 Mexico City CDMX, Mexico. E-mail: secretariageneral@ipgh.org – info@ipgh.org.
URL: http://www.ipgh.org/

History 7 Feb 1928, Havana (Cuba). Established by a resolution adopted at 6th International American Conference at Ministerial Level, following proposals first made in 1903. A resolution for the creation of a *Pan American Federation of Geographical Societies – Fédération panaméricaine des sociétés de géographie* had been adopted at 3rd Panamerican Scientific Congress, Lima (Peru), 1924. Statutes formally adopted at the Constituent Assembly, 1929, Mexico City (Mexico), and revised in: 1946, 1950, 1955, 1961, 1969. Agreements of specialized organization signed with *OAS (#17629)*, 12 Jan 1949 and 6 May 1974. **Aims** Encourage, coordinate and publicize *cartographical*, geographical, historical and *geophysical* studies as well as other related scientific studies of interest to the *Americas*; promote and carry out studies, work and

training in the aforementioned fields of activity; promote cooperation among organizations interested in these fields of activity in the Americas, and with related international organizations. **Structure** General Assembly (every 4 years); Directing Council (meeting annually), consists of representatives of the Governments of Member States; Commissions (4): Cartography – set up in 1941, located in Santiago (Chile); Geography – set up in 1946, located in Aguascalientes (Mexico); History – set up in 1946, located in Sao Paulo (Brazil); Geophysics – set up in 1969, located in San José (Costa Rica). General Secretariat, headed by Secretary General; Commissions (4) and Vice-President. Meeting of Officers (twice a year). **Languages** English, French, Portuguese, Spanish. **Staff** 12.00 FTE, paid. **Finance** Sources: government support. **Activities** Guidance/assistance/consulting; knowledge management/information dissemination; monitoring/evaluation; projects/programmes; research and development. **Events** *General Assembly* Quito (Ecuador) 2022, *Quadrennial General Assembly* Panama (Panama) 2017, *Meeting* Santiago (Chile) 2014, *Quadrennial General Assembly* Montevideo (Uruguay) 2013, *Quadrennial General Assembly* Quito (Ecuador) 2009. **Publications** *Antropologia Americana* (2 a year); *Revista Cartografica* (2 a year); *Revista de Historia de América* (2 a year); *Revista de Arqueologia Americana* (annual); *Revista Geográfica* (annual). **Information Services** *José Toribio Medina* – bibliographic reserve; *PAIGH Library* – about 228,548 volumes; *PAIGH Map Library.*
Members Member States (21):
Argentina, Belize, Bolivia, Brazil, Chile, Colombia, Costa Rica, Dominican Rep, Ecuador, El Salvador, Guatemala, Haiti, Honduras, Mexico, Nicaragua, Panama, Paraguay, Peru, Uruguay, USA, Venezuela.
Permanent Observers (5):
France, Israel, Jamaica, Korea Rep, Spain.
IGO Relations Cooperates with: *International Hydrographic Organization (IHO, #13825); Regional Committee of the UN on Global Geospatial Information Management for the Americas (UN-GGIM Americas, #18765).* **NGO Relations** Member of: *International Committee of Historical Sciences (ICHS, #12777); International Society for Photogrammetry and Remote Sensing (ISPRS, #15362).* [2022/XE3065/j/**E***]

- ♦ Pan-American Institute of Higher Business Studies / see IPADE Business School
- ♦ Pan American Institute of Mining Engineering and Geology (inactive)
- ♦ Pan American Institute of Naval Engineering (#11349)
- ♦ Pan American Institute on Physical Education (#11348)

♦ Pan American International Movers Association (PAIMA) 18114

Exec Dir 5201 Blue Lagoon Dr, Ste 975-B, Miami FL 33126, USA. T. +19548801085. Fax +17864974017. E-mail: tony@paimamovers.com.
URL: http://www.paimamovers.com/

Aims Provide members with the tools and exposure to increase their business within the international moving industry. **Structure** General Assembly (annual); Board of Directors. Regions (9): Canada and Mexico; USA; Central America and Caribbean; South America; Europe; Africa; Middle East; Far East; Australia and New Zealand. **Languages** English. **Staff** 1.00 FTE, paid. **Events** *Annual Convention* Toronto, ON (Canada) 2023, *Annual Convention* Seattle, WA (USA) 2022, *Annual Convention* Orlando, FL (USA) 2021, *Annual Convention* San Diego, CA (USA) 2015, *Annual Convention* Orlando, FL (USA) 2014.
Members Companies in 41 countries and territories:
Argentina, Australia, Bolivia, Brazil, Canada, Chile, China, Colombia, Costa Rica, Dominican Rep, Egypt, El Salvador, France, Germany, Guatemala, Honduras, India, Israel, Italy, Malaysia, Nepal, New Zealand, Nicaragua, Nigeria, Norway, Pakistan, Panama, Paraguay, Peru, Philippines, Puerto Rico, Singapore, South Africa, Spain, Switzerland, Thailand, UK, Uruguay, USA, Venezuela, Virgin Is USA. [2019.06.03/XD9414/**C**]

- ♦ Pan-American Judo Confederation (#04476)

♦ Pan American Judo Union (PJU) 18115

Union panaméricaine de judo – Unión Panamericana de Judo (UPJ) – União Panamericana de Judo

Pres address not obtained. T. +18099779491. Fax +18095473131. E-mail: infopju@gmail.com.
URL: http://www.pju-upj.org/

History 1952, Switzerland. *Confederación Panamericana de Judo (CPJ, #04476)* split off from PJU 2009. **Aims** Promote judo in all countries in Pan America. **Structure** Executive Committee; National federations (officially recognized by their National Olympic Committees). **Languages** English, Spanish. **Staff** 5.00 FTE, voluntary. **Finance** Quotas from TV rights. Annual budget: US$ 30,000. **Activities** Sporting activities. **Events** *Congress* Chile 1994, *Congress* Caracas (Venezuela) 1990.
Members Regional federations:
Confederación Centro y Norte Americana de Judo; *Confederación de Judo del Caribe (CJC, #04452); South American Judo Confederation (#19704).*
Federations in 43 countries and territories:
Antigua-Barbuda, Argentina, Aruba, Bahamas, Barbados, Belize, Bermuda, Bolivia, Brazil, Canada, Cayman Is, Chile, Colombia, Costa Rica, Cuba, Dominica, Dominican Rep, Ecuador, El Salvador, Grenada, Guatemala, Guyana, Haiti, Honduras, Jamaica, Mexico, Neth Antilles, Nicaragua, Panama, Paraguay, Peru, Puerto Rico, St Kitts-Nevis, St Lucia, St Maarten, St Vincent-Grenadines, Suriname, Trinidad-Tobago, Uruguay, USA, Venezuela, Virgin Is UK, Virgin Is USA.
NGO Relations Member of: *Asociación de Confederaciones Deportivas Sudamericanas (ACODESU, no recent information).* Instrumental in setting up: *Confederación Panamericana de Judo (CPJ, #04476).* [2019.02.16/XD5271/**D**]

- ♦ Panamerican Karate Federation (#09381)

♦ Pan American Kurash Union 18116

Pres Federación Boliviana de Judo, Ricardo Mujia 887, Sopocachi, La Paz, Bolivia. T. +5912411108. Fax +5912411108.
URL: http://www.kurash-ika.org/

History Continental federation of *International Kurash Association (IKA, #13993).* **Activities** Events/meetings.
Members National federations in 22 countries and territories:
Argentina, Bahamas, Barbados, Bolivia, Brazil, Canada, Chile, Colombia, Costa Rica, Dominican Rep, Ecuador, Haiti, Nicaragua, Panama, Paraguay, Peru, Puerto Rico, Suriname, Trinidad-Tobago, Uruguay, USA, Venezuela. [2015/XM0857/**D**]

♦ Pan-American Lacrosse Association (PALA) 18117

Contact address not obtained. E-mail: infopala@panamericanlacrosse.org.
URL: https://www.panamericanlacrosse.org/

History 2018. Founded under the auspices of *World Lacrosse (#21616).* **Aims** Promote and develop the sport of lacrosse across the region. **Structure** Board. **Activities** Sporting activities.
Members Members in 18 countries and territories:
Argentina, Barbados, Bermuda, Canada, Chile, Colombia, Costa Rica, Dominican Rep, Ecuador, Guatemala, Haiti, Iroquois/Haudenosaunee Nation, Jamaica, Mexico, Panama, Peru, USA, Virgin Is USA. [2021/AA1446/**D**]

- ♦ Pan American League Against Rheumatism / see Pan American League of Associations for Rheumatology (#18118)

♦ Pan American League of Associations for Rheumatology (PANLAR) 18118

Ligue panaméricaine des associations de rhumatologie – Liga Panamericana de Asociaciones de Reumatologia – Liga Panamericana de Associações de Reumatologia

Contact Wells Fargo Plaza, 333 SE 2nd Avenue, Suite 2000, Miami FL 33131, USA.
URL: http://www.panlar.org/

History 1943. Founded as a continental league of *International League of Associations for Rheumatology (ILAR, #14016).* Former names and other names: *Pan American League Against Rheumatism* – former; *Ligue panaméricaine contre le rhumatisme* – former; *Liga Panamericana contra el Reumatismo* – former; *Liga Panamericana contra o Reumatismo* – former. Registration: Swiss Civil Code, Switzerland. **Aims** Stimulate, promote and support research, prevention, treatment and rehabilitation of rheumatic conditions; foster development of rheumatology in the Americas. **Structure** General Assembly; Executive Committee. Zones: Northern; Central; Bolivian; Southern. Committees Government; Finance; Communications; Education and Science. **Languages** English, French, Portuguese, Spanish. **Finance** Sources: members' dues. **Activities** Awards/prizes/competitions; events/meetings; training/education. **Events** *Congress* Miami, FL (USA) 2020, *Congress* Quito (Ecuador) 2019, *Biennial Congress* Buenos Aires (Argentina) 2018, *Biennial Congress* Panama (Panama) 2016, *Biennial Congress* Punta del Este (Uruguay) 2014. **Publications** *PANLAR Bulletin* (4 a year).
Members National scientific or medical organizations and national community agencies. National rheumatism societies in 21 countries:
Argentina, Bolivia, Brazil, Canada, Chile, Colombia, Costa Rica, Cuba, Dominican Rep, Ecuador, El Salvador, Guatemala, Honduras, Mexico, Nicaragua, Panama, Paraguay, Peru, Uruguay, USA, Venezuela. [2020.06.22/XD2814/**D**]

♦ Pan-American Low Vision Society 18119

Sociedad Panamericana de Baja Visión

Pres address not obtained.
URL: http://www.sociedadpanamericanadebajavision.org/

History Founded 1995. **NGO Relations** Member of: *Pan-American Association of Ophthalmology (PAAO, #18081).* [2017/XD6806/**D**]

- ♦ Pan American Medical Association (no recent information)
- ♦ Pan American Medical Confederation (inactive)

♦ Pan American Medical Women's Alliance (PAMWA) 18120

Alliance panaméricaine des femmes médecins – Alianza Panamericana de Mujeres Médicas

Pres c/o SP de Pediatria, Los Geranios 151, Lince, 14, Lima, Peru.

History Founded Nov 1947, Mexico City (Mexico), on adoption of Constitution, following proposals made at Pan American Pediatrics Conference 1945, Washington DC (USA). Incorporated 1946, in the State of Ohio (USA). Present Constitution and By-Laws adopted at 16th Congress, Sep 1979, Santa Cruz (Bolivia). Also referred to as *Alianza Panamericana de Médicas.* **Aims** Bring medical women of North, South, Central America and the Caribbean area into association for mutual improvement, encouragement of their participation in all branches of medical public welfare work; exchange ideas; facilitate social and cooperative relations; assist in further education of members; forward such constructive movements as may be mutually beneficial and properly endorsed by national medical associations. **Structure** General Meeting (every 2 years); Executive Committee; Standing Committees. **Languages** English, Spanish. **Finance** Members' dues. Contributions from interested individuals. **Activities** Financial and/or material support; training/education; events/meetings. **Events** *Biennial Congress* Sao Paulo (Brazil) 2015, *Biennial Congress* Guadalajara (Mexico) 2012, *Biennial Congress* Guayaquil (Ecuador) 2010, *Biennial Congress* San Juan (Puerto Rico) 2008, *Biennial Congress* Buenos Aires (Argentina) 2006. **Publications** *PAMWA Newsletter* (1-3 a year). Proceedings of Congresses (every 2 years) in 'Journal of the American Medical Women's Association'.
Members Active; Retired; Honorary. Individual members in 19 countries and territories:
Argentina, Bolivia, Brazil, Canada, Chile, Colombia, Dominican Rep, Ecuador, El Salvador, Honduras, Mexico, Nicaragua, Panama, Paraguay, Peru, Puerto Rico, Uruguay, USA, Venezuela.
Consultative Status Consultative status granted from: *OAS (#17629).* [2015/XD3068/v/**D**]

- ♦ Pan-American Minifootball Confederation (#04477)

♦ Pan American Network for Drug Regulatory Harmonization (PANDRH) 18121

Secretariat c/o PAHO – Reginal Office for the Americas, 525 Twenty-Third St NW, Washington DC 20037-2895, USA.
URL: https://www.paho.org/en/pandrh

History 1999. An initiative of the national regulatory authorities within the Region, and *Pan American Health Organization (PAHO, #18108).* Statutes approved Dec 2015. **Aims** Strengthen the regulatory functions and systems of the countries of the Region, promoting cooperation and sharing among countries, with the Pan American Health Organization (PAHO), and with other regional and international organizations, civil society, industry associations, and academia. **Structure** Pan American Conference on Drug Regulatory Harmonization; Steering Committee; Secretariat. Technical Working Groups.
Members Governments (36):
Antigua-Barbuda, Argentina, Bahamas, Barbados, Belize, Bolivia, Brazil, Canada, Chile, Colombia, Costa Rica, Cuba, Dominica, Dominican Rep, Ecuador, El Salvador, Grenada, Guatemala, Guyana, Haiti, Honduras, Jamaica, Mexico, Montserrat, Nicaragua, Panama, Paraguay, Peru, St Kitts-Nevis, St Lucia, St Vincent-Grenadines, Suriname, Trinidad-Tobago, Uruguay, USA, Venezuela.
NGO Relations Member of (1): *International Council on Harmonisation of Technical Requirements for Registration of Pharmaceuticals for Human Use (ICH, #13027)* (Observer). [AA2021/**F***]

♦ Pan-American Network of Fish Inspection, Quality Control and Technology 18122

Secretariat c/o INFOPESCA, Julio Hererra y Obes 1296, Casilla de Correo 7086, 11200 Montevideo, Uruguay. T. +59829028701. Fax +59829030501. E-mail: infopesca@infopesca.org.
Pres Rua Cel Eurico de Souza Gomes 510, Rio de Janeiro RJ, 22620-320 RJ, Brazil. T. +552124910704.

History Dec 2006, Punta del Este (Uruguay), by merger of *Red Latinoamericana de Tecnólogos de los Productos Pesqueros (REDPESCA, inactive)* and *Pan-American Network on Fish Inspection and Quality Control (inactive).* Comes under the auspices of *FAO (#09260)* and *INFOPESCA (#11192).* **Structure** Officers: President; 3 Executive Directors. Advisory Committee of 6 members. Sections (3): Domestic Market; Fish Inspection and QC; Fish Technology. **IGO Relations** Secretariat provided by: *INFOPESCA (#11192).* [2007/XM3049/**F**]

- ♦ Pan American Nikkei Association (#02290)
- ♦ Pan American Odontological Association (inactive)
- ♦ Pan American Postal Union / see Postal Union of the Americas, Spain and Portugal (#18466)

♦ Pan American Racquetball Confederation (PARC) 18123

Confederación Panamericana de Racquetball

SG 1631 Mesa Ave, Colorado Springs CO 80906, USA. T. +17194332017.
Pres address not obtained.
URL: https://www.panamericanracquetball.com/

History 1986. **Structure** Executive Committee.
Members Federations in 35 countries and territories:
Antigua, Argentina, Aruba, Bahamas, Barbados, Belize, Bermuda, Bolivia, Brazil, Canada, Cayman Is, Chile, Colombia, Costa Rica, Cuba, Dominican Rep, Ecuador, El Salvador, Guatemala, Haiti, Honduras, Jamaica, Mexico, Nicaragua, Panama, Paraguay, Peru, Puerto Rico, St Kitts-Nevis, Trinidad-Tobago, Uruguay, USA, Venezuela, Virgin Is UK, Virgin Is USA.
NGO Relations Member of (2): *Asociación de Confederaciones Deportivas Panamericanas (ACODEPA, #02119); Asociación de Confederaciones Deportivas Sudamericanas (ACODESU, no recent information).* Affiliated with (1): *International Racquetball Federation (IRF, #14683).* [2022/XD5075/**D**]

- ♦ Pan American Railway Committee (inactive)

♦ Pan American Railway Congress Association (PARCA) 18124

Association du Congrès panaméricain des chemins de fer – Asociación del Congreso Panamericano de Ferrocarriles (ACPF) – Associação do Congresso Panamericano de Estradas de Ferro

Pres Av Dr José Maria Ramos Mejia 1302, Planta Baja, 1104 Buenos Aires, Argentina. T. +541143153445. Fax +541143123834.

History 11 Oct 1907, Buenos Aires (Argentina), as *Permanent South American Railway Congress Association – Congreso Sudamericano de Ferrocarriles – Asociación Internacional Permanent.* Panamerican character acquired and present title adopted at 4th Congress, 1941. **Aims** Promote the development and progress of railways on the American continent. **Structure** Congress (every 4 years); Permanent Commission (meets every 2 months), composed of representatives of national commissions; Executive Committee; Technical Advisory Committee. **Languages** English, Portuguese, Spanish. **Finance** Members' dues: US$ 0.30 per km of rail (US$ 2,000 minimum and US$ 25,000 maximum for Governments; US$ 1,500 minimum and 12,500 maximum for Railways); Manufacturers and Institutes US$ 500; Individuals US$ 50; Life membership US$ 5,000 unique fee. **Activities** Works with 17 National Commissions (members appointed from Government and railways): Coordinating means of transport; Standardizing accountancy, statistics and tariff systems; Maintaining track; Modernizing railway legislation; Well-being of personnel; Technical problems. Library; provides information to associated members. Annual meeting of national Commissions. **Events** *Quadrennial Congress* Buenos Aires (Argentina) 2007, *Quadrennial congress* Havana (Cuba) 2000, *Latin rail conference* Miami, FL (USA) 1996, *Quadrennial Congress* Porlamar (Venezuela) 1994, *Quadrennial congress* Porlamar (Venezuela) 1994. **Publications** *Boletin ACPF* (5 a year). Congress proceedings.
Members Born (national governments of America, state railways, railway companies); Permanent (individuals and institutions); Temporary (congress participants). Members in 20 countries:
Bolivia, Brazil, Chile, Colombia, Costa Rica, Cuba, Dominican Rep, Ecuador, El Salvador, Guatemala, Haiti, Honduras, Mexico, Nicaragua, Panama, Paraguay, Peru, Uruguay, USA, Venezuela.
Life members (non-American governments and railways) in 10 countries:
Belgium, France, Germany, Italy, Japan, Portugal, Spain, Sweden, Switzerland, UK.
Consultative Status Consultative status granted from: *OAS (#17629).* **NGO Relations** *International Union of Railways (#15813).* [2018/XD3071/**D**]

♦ Panamerican Regional Antidoping Organization / see Panamerican Regional Antidoping Organization (#18125)

♦ Panamerican Regional Antidoping Organization (PAN-RADO) 18125

Exec Manager Ciudad Deportiva Irving Saladino, Juan Diaz, Panama, Panamá, Panama PANAMá, Panama. T. +5075244698. E-mail: admin@orad-pan.org.
URL: https://www.orad-pan.org/

History Mar 2015, Panama. Former names and other names: *Panamerican Regional Antidoping Organization* – alias; *Regional Anti-Doping Organization of Central America (PAN-RADO)* – former. **Aims** Be the leading organization in the fight against doping in the ORAD-PAN member countries.
Members National organizations in 11 countries and territories: *
Belize, Bolivia, Costa Rica, El Salvador, Guatemala, Honduras, Nicaragua, Panama, Paraguay, Peru, Puerto Rico.
NGO Relations Partner of (1): *World Anti-Doping Agency (WADA, #21096).* [2023.02.16/AA2501/**D**]

♦ Pan-American Retina and Vitreous Society (PRVS) 18126

Sociedad Panamericana de Retina y Vitreo (SPRV)
Delegate Av Javier Prado Este 1010, Piso 10, San Isidro, 27, Lima, Peru. T. +5112246593. Fax +5112241603.
URL: https://spretinayvitreo.com/

History 1 Apr 2003. Founded evolving from *Grupo Latinoamericano de Angeografia Ocular, Laser y Cirurgia Vitreo-retiniana (GLADAOF)*, set up 1981, as the official Retina and Vitreous sub-specialty society affiliated to *Pan-American Association of Ophthalmology (PAAO, #18081)*. Former names and other names: *Latin American Group of Ocular Angiography, Laser and Vitreo-retinal Surgery* – former; *Grupo Latinoamericano de Angeografia Ocular, Laser y Cirurgia Vitreo-retiniana (GLADAOF)* – former. **Aims** Maintain and improve the scientific quality of the congress; publish educational material in Spanish; sponsor combined meetings with other multinational societies in the field; stimulate the scientific contribution to the literature published in Latin America; improve the academic curricula of people in Latin America. **Structure** Board of Directors. **Languages** English, Portuguese, Spanish. **Activities** Events/meetings. **Events** *Congress* Buenos Aires (Argentina) 2022, *Congress* Lima (Peru) 2010, *GLADAOF forum / Congress* Lima (Peru) 2010, *GLADAOF forum* Caracas (Venezuela) 2008, *Congress* Porlamar (Venezuela) 2008. **Publications** *Uveitis y Tumores Intraoculares: Temas Selectos* (2008); *Retina Medica: Temas Selectos* (2007). [2022/XD6804/**E**]

♦ Pan-American Rope Skipping Federation (inactive)
♦ Pan-American Rowing Confederation (#04478)

♦ Pan American Rugby Association (PARA) 18127

Asociación Panamericana de Rugby
Pres Eduardo Costa 3046, Buenos Aires, Argentina. T. +5491134401974.
History Founded 1991.
Members Founding members national federations in 11 countries:
Argentina, Bahamas, Bermuda, Brazil, Canada, Chile, Jamaica, Mexico, Trinidad-Tobago, Uruguay, USA. [2017/XD9459/**D**]

♦ Pan American Sailing Federation (PASAF) 18128

Federación Pan Americana de Vela (FEPAV)
SG address not obtained.
Pres address not obtained.
URL: https://panamsailing.org/

Aims Promote the sport of sailing in the region. **Structure** General Assembly (every 4 years); Executive Committee. **Languages** English.
Members National organizations in 29 countries and territories:
Antigua-Barbuda, Argentina, Bahamas, Barbados, Bermuda, Brazil, Canada, Cayman Is, Chile, Colombia, Cuba, Dominican Rep, Ecuador, El Salvador, Grenada, Guatemala, Jamaica, Mexico, Neth Antilles, Paraguay, Peru, Puerto Rico, St Lucia, Trinidad-Tobago, Uruguay, USA, Venezuela, Virgin Is UK, Virgin Is USA.
NGO Relations Member of (2): *Asociación de Confederaciones Deportivas Panamericanas (ACODEPA, #02119)*; *World Sailing (#21760)*. Affiliated with (1): *Panam Sports Organization (Panam Sports, #18138).* [2023/XM2787/**D**]

♦ Pan American Sanitary Bureau (PASB) 18129

Bureau sanitaire panaméricain – Oficina Sanitaria Panamericana
Head Office 525 23rd St NW, Washington DC 20037-2895, USA. T. +12029743408. Fax +12029743409. E-mail: director@paho.org.
URL: http://www.paho.org/

History Dec 1902, Washington DC (USA), as *International Sanitary Bureau – Bureau sanitaire international*, at 1st General International Convention of the American Republics. Current title adopted in 1923. On setting up of the *Pan American Sanitary Organization – Organisation sanitaire panaméricaine – Organización Sanitaria Panamericana*, 1947, PASB became Executive Organ of that body, which is currently *Pan American Health Organization (PAHO, #18108)* and is one of 6 specialized organizations of *OAS (#17629)*. At the same time, PASB is linked to the United Nations System in that it serves within *WHO (#20950)* as *WHO Regional Office for the Americas (AMRO) – Bureau régional de l'OMS pour les Amériques – Oficina Regional de la OMS para las Américas*. PASB is therefore also known as *Pan American Sanitary Bureau / WHO Regional Office for the Americas (PASB/AMRO)*. **Aims** Provide technical support and leadership to PAHO Member States as they pursue the goal of health for all and the values therein. **Structure** Executive Management: Director; Deputy Director; Assistant Director. Offices: Country and Sub-regional Coordination; Legal Counsel; Chief of Staff; Internal Oversight and Evaluation Services; Ethics Office; Ombudsman. Departments; Units; Special Program. Panamerican Centers (3): *Latin American and Caribbean Centre on Health Sciences Information (BIREME, #16267)*; *Latin American Center for Perinatology/Unit of Woman and Reproductive Health (CLAP/WR, #16290)*; *Pan American Foot-and-Mouth Disease Center (PAFMDC, #18106)*. Country Offices. **IGO Relations** Instrumental in setting up: *Institute of Nutrition of Central America and Panama (INCAP, #11285).* [2014/XE3592/**E***]

♦ Pan American Sanitary Bureau / WHO Regional Office for the Americas / see Pan American Sanitary Bureau (#18129)
♦ Pan American Sanitary Code (1924 treaty)
♦ Pan American Sanitary Organization / see Pan American Health Organization (#18108)
♦ Pan American Scientific Congress (inactive)
♦ Pan American Social Marketing Organization (internationally oriented national body)
♦ Panamerican Society of Audiology (no recent information)
♦ Pan American Society for Clinical Virology (internationally oriented national body)
♦ Pan-American Society of Contact Lens and Refraction (inactive)
♦ Panamerican Society for Dialysis and Transplantation (inactive)
♦ Panamerican Society for Infectious Diseases (#02288)
♦ Pan-American Society of Inflammatory Ocular Diseases (#19432)

♦ Pan-American Society for Neurovirology (PASNV) 18130

Sociedade Panamericana de Neurovirologia
Address not obtained.
URL: http://www.pasnv.org/

History 2000. **Aims** Understand the impact of viral infections on the nervous system in the Americas. [2012/XM0332/**D**]

♦ Pan-American Society of Ocular Pathology – Lorenz E Zimmerman (Zimmerman Society) 18131

Sociedad Panamericana de Patologia Ocular – Lorenz E Zimmerman
Pres Azcuenada 1077 – 2oB, 1115 Buenos Aires, Argentina. T. +541148232327. Fax +541148232327.
NGO Relations Member of: *Pan-American Association of Ophthalmology (PAAO, #18081).* [2015/XE3508/**E**]

♦ Pan-American Society of Ocular Trauma / see Asociación Panamericana de Trauma Ocular (#02293)
♦ Pan-American Society of Oculo-Plastics (no recent information)
♦ Pan-American Society of Ophthalmic Oncology (no recent information)
♦ Panamerican Society of Opthalmic Oncology (#19434)
♦ Panamerican Society of Phlebology and Lymphology (#19433)

♦ Pan American Society for Pigment Cell Research (PASPCR) 18132

Sec-Treas New York University School of Medicine, The Ronald O Perelman Dept of Dermatology, Smilow Research Center, 522 First Avenue, Room 401, New York NY 10016, USA.
URL: http://www.paspcr.org/

History 1988, Minneapolis MN (USA). **Aims** Support research on pigment cells. **Structure** Council, including, President, Secretary-Treasurer, President-Elect and Past-President. **Languages** English. **Staff** None. **Finance** Members' dues. **Events** *Annual Meeting* Bar Harbor, ME (USA) 2019, *Annual Meeting* Gleneden Beach, OR (USA) 2018, *Annual Meeting* Baltimore, MD (USA) 2016, *Annual Meeting* Orange, CA (USA) 2015, *Annual Meeting* Madison, WI (USA) 2013. **Publications** *PASPCR Newsletter* (4 a year); *Pigment Cell Research* – journal.
Members Individuals in 32 countries and territories:
Argentina, Australia, Belgium, Brazil, Bulgaria, Canada, China, Colombia, Denmark, France, Germany, Greece, Hong Kong, Iceland, India, Israel, Italy, Japan, Korea Rep, Mexico, Netherlands, New Zealand, Norway, Peru, Philippines, Puerto Rico, Sweden, Switzerland, Taiwan, Thailand, UK, USA.
NGO Relations Founding member of: *International Federation of Pigment Cell Societies (IFPCS, #13512).* [2016/XD6165/v/**D**]

♦ Pan-American Society of Uveitis / see Sociedad Panamericana de Enfermedades Inflamatorias Oculares (#19432)
♦ Pan American Softball Confederation / see WBSC Americas Softball (#20840)
♦ Pan American Soil Conservation Commission (inactive)
♦ Pan American Spiritist Confederation / see CEPA – Associação Espirita Internacional (#03821)
♦ Pan American Sports Committee / see Panam Sports Organization (#18138)
♦ Pan American Sports Confederation of the Deaf / see Pan American Deaf Sports Organization (#18093)
♦ Pan American Sports Organization / see Panam Sports Organization (#18138)
♦ Pan American Sports Organization of the Deaf / see Pan American Deaf Sports Organization (#18093)
♦ Panamerican Squash Federation (#09384)

♦ Pan American Standards Commission 18133

Commission panaméricaine de normalisation – Comisión Panamericana de Normas Técnicas (COPANT) – Comissão Panamericana de Normas Técnicas
Exec Sec Calle 21, Edifi Torre Lydia 8227, Piso 9 Of 907, Calacoto, La Paz, Bolivia. T. +59122774517. Fax +59122774517. E-mail: copant@copant.org.
URL: http://www.copant.org/

History Apr 1961, Montevideo (Uruguay). Statutes amended May 2008. Former names and other names: *Comité Panamericano de Normas Técnicas (CPANT)* – former (1949 to 1964); *Pan American Standards Committee* – former (1949 to 1964). **Aims** Be the reference for technical standardization and conformity assessment for the countries of the Americas for members and international peers; promote development of members. **Structure** General Assembly (annual); Executive Board; Executive Secretary; Coordinating Technical Secretariat. **Languages** English, Portuguese, Spanish. **Staff** 1.50 FTE, paid. **Finance** Members' dues. **Activities** Standards/guidelines; networking/liaising; knowledge management/information dissemination; events/meetings. **Events** *Annual General Assembly / COPANT Week* 2021, *Annual General Assembly* Mexico 2015, *Annual General Assembly* Cuba 2014, *Annual General Assembly* St Lucia 2013, *General Assembly / Annual General Assembly* Brazil 2012. **Publications** Press releases – electronic. Translations.
Members National organizations in 34 countries and territories:
Antigua-Barbuda, Argentina, Bahamas, Barbados, Belize, Bolivia, Brazil, Canada, Chile, Colombia, Costa Rica, Cuba, Dominica, Dominican Rep, Ecuador, El Salvador, Grenada, Guatemala, Guyana, Haiti, Honduras, Jamaica, Mexico, Nicaragua, Panama, Paraguay, Peru, St Kitts-Nevis, St Lucia, St Vincent-Grenadines, Suriname, Trinidad-Tobago, Uruguay, USA.
Associate institutes in 9 countries:
Australia, France, Germany, Italy, Portugal, South Africa, Spain, UK, Venezuela.
Regional organization:
Inter-American Accreditation Cooperation (IAAC, #11396).
Consultative Status Consultative status granted from: *ECOSOC (#05331)* (Ros C); *UNIDO (#20336)*. **IGO Relations** Cooperation with: *OAS (#17629)*. **NGO Relations** Member of: *Inter-American Accreditation Cooperation (IAAC, #11396)*. Memorandum of Understanding with: *Comité européen de normalisation (CEN, #04162)*; *International Electrotechnical Commission (IEC, #13255)*. Official links with: *International Organization for Standardization (ISO, #14473)*. Cooperates with: *Consejo de Armonización de Normas Electrotécnicas de las Naciones en las Américas (CANENA, #04700)*; *Inter-American Metrology System (#11440).* [2021/XD3075/y/**D**]

♦ Pan American Standards Committee / see Pan American Standards Commission (#18133)

♦ Panamerican Surety Association (PASA) 18134

Asociación Panamericana de Fianzas (APF)
Operating Office Av Santa Fe 830 – Piso 7, C1059ABP, Buenos Aires, Argentina. T. +541150328375. Fax +541150328376. E-mail: info@apfpasa.ch.
URL: http://www.apfpasa.ch/

History 29 Feb 1972, Kingston (Jamaica). As from 10th General Assembly, Oct 1988, Washington DC (USA), Association includes sureties, credit insurers and bond and credit reinsurers worldwide. Former names and other names: *Association panaméricaine de cautionnement* – former; *Associação Panamericana de Fianças e Garantias* – former. **Aims** Encourage technical cooperation and business relations among members and free discussion of issues of common interest; analyse technical principles underlying underwriting of surety bonds, guarantees and credit insurance risk promote private enterprise in underwriting of these covers; foster communication and cooperation with public and private industry-related entities and agencies; carry out educational and promotional action in connection with the industry. **Structure** Assembly; Executive Committee; Permanent or Special Committees; Operating Office, located in Buenos Aires (Argentina). **Languages** English, Spanish. **Activities** Advocacy/lobbying/activism; events/meetings; research/documentation; training/education. **Events** *General Assembly* USA 2022, *General Assembly* Praia do Forte (Brazil) 2021, *General Assembly* Praia do Forte (Brazil) 2020, *General Assenbly* Bariloche (Argentina) 2019, *General Assembly* Madrid (Spain) 2018. **Publications** Articles; proceedings of academic meetings.
Members Active private companies which underwrite surety bonds and/or credit insurance and/or reinsurance thereof. Associate companies and/or entities with majority state participation which underwrite surety bonds and/or credit insurance and/or reinsurance thereof. Members in 29 countries:
Argentina, Belgium, Bermuda, Bolivia, Brazil, Chile, China, Colombia, Costa Rica, Curaçao, Dominican Rep, Ecuador, El Salvador, France, Germany, Guatemala, Ireland, Israel, Italy, Japan, Korea Rep, Mexico, Panama, Paraguay, Peru, Switzerland, UK, USA, Venezuela.
NGO Relations Member of: *International Surety Association (ISA, #15629).* [2022/XD0481/**D**]

♦ Pan American Surf Association (PASA) 18135

Asociación Panamericana de Surf (APAS)
Pres c/o PASA HQ, Av Larco 1239 – 3B, Miraflores, L-18, Lima, Peru. E-mail: presidente@pasasurf.org – media@pasasurf.org – info@pasasurf.org.
URL: http://www.pasasurf.org/

History 29 Sep 1992, Lacanau (France). Former names and other names: *Pan American Surfing Association (PASA)* – former. **Aims** Act as the ruling and regulatory entity for the *sport* of surfing in North, Central and South America, adjacent islands and the Caribbean. **Structure** Executive Committee. **Languages** English, Spanish. **Staff** 3.00 FTE, voluntary. **Finance** Sources: grants; members' dues. Other sources: sanction fees. **Activities** Sporting activities. **Events** *Annual General Meeting* Peru 2005.
Members Full in 24 countries:
Argentina, Aruba, Bahamas, Barbados, Brazil, Canada, Chile, Colombia, Costa Rica, Dominican Rep, Ecuador, El Salvador, Guadeloupe, Guatemala, Jamaica, Mexico, Nicaragua, Panama, Peru, Puerto Rico, Trinidad-Tobago, Uruguay, USA, Venezuela.
IGO Relations None. **NGO Relations** Member of (4): *Asociación de Confederaciones Deportivas Panamericanas (ACODEPA, #02119)*; *Asociación Latinoamericana de Surfistas Profesionales (ALAS, #02270)*; *International Surfing Association (ISA, #15630)*; *Panam Sports Organization (Panam Sports, #18138).* [2023/XD4943/**D**]

♦ Pan American Surfing Association / see Pan American Surf Association (#18135)
♦ Pan American Symposium on Vasoactive Peptides and Hypertension / see Inter-American Society of Hypertension (#11449)

♦ Pan American Taekwondo Union (PATU) 18136

Union panaméricaine de taekwondo – Unión Panamericana de Taekwondo

Contact General Guadalupe Victoria 214, Zona Centro, 20000 Aguascalientes, Mexico. E-mail: info@panamericantaekwondounion.org.
URL: https://www.patutkd.org/

History 1977, Chicago, IL (USA). A regional union of *World Taekwondo (#21844)*. **Aims** Provide members everything they need to enable their member schools to train athletes to the best of their ability in both mind and body. **Structure** General Assembly; Executive Council; Executive Committee; Sub-Committees (16). **Languages** English, Spanish. **Staff** 10.00 FTE, paid. **Finance** Sources: members' dues. Other sources: WT support funds; event recognition fees; seminars; certification fees. Annual budget: 150,000 USD. **Activities** Certification/accreditation; events/meetings; sporting activities; training/education. **Events** *Meeting* Miami, FL (USA) 1999, *General Elective Assembly* Havana (Cuba) 1996. **Publications** *PATU Newsletter* (4 a year); *Directory of the PATU* (every 2 years).
Members Federations in 45 countries and territories:
Antigua-Barbuda, Argentina, Aruba, Bahamas, Barbados, Belize, Bermuda, Bolivia, Brazil, Canada, Cayman Is, Chile, Colombia, Costa Rica, Cuba, Curaçao, Dominica, Dominican Rep, Ecuador, El Salvador, Grenada, Guadeloupe, Guatemala, Guyana, Haiti, Honduras, Jamaica, Martinique, Mexico, Neth Antilles, Nicaragua, Panama, Paraguay, Peru, Puerto Rico, St Kitts-Nevis, St Lucia, St Vincent-Grenadines, Suriname, Trinidad-Tobago, Uruguay, USA, Venezuela, Virgin Is UK, Virgin Is USA.
IGO Relations Sports Ministries of PATU Member National Associations. **NGO Relations** Member of (1): *Asociación de Confederaciones Deportivas Panamericanas (ACODEPA, #02119).* [2023/XE2280/D]

♦ Panamerican Trauma Society (#19436)
♦ Pan American Triathlon Confederation / see Americas Triathlon (#00795)
♦ Pan American Union / see Inter-American Institute for Cooperation on Agriculture (#11434)
♦ Pan-American Union of Appraisal Associations (#20470)
♦ Pan American Union of Asthma and Allergy Foundations / see UNASMA – Fundación Internacional de Asma y Alergias (#20282)
♦ Pan American Union of Baptist Men (inactive)
♦ Pan American Union of Engineering Societies (#20469)
♦ Pan American Union of Karatedo Organizations / see Federación Panamericana de Karate (#09381)
♦ Pan-American Union of Mountains Associations / see Confederación Panamericana de Deportes de Montaña y Escalada (#04472)
♦ Pan American Union of Technical Experts in the Field of Economic Sciences (inactive)

♦ Pan American Weightlifting Confederation (PAWC) 18137

Confédération panaméricaine d'haltérophilie – Confederación Panamericana de Levantamiento de Pesas (PANPESAS)

Pres Av Gral Salaverry 3810, San Isidro, 15076, Lima, Peru.
URL: https://panampesas.org/

History Founded to continue activities of *Central American and Caribbean Confederation of Weightlifting (CCCLP, inactive)*, set up 1969 and formally wound up 1973. Part of *International Weightlifting Federation (IWF, #15876)*. **Aims** Have relations with Olympic Solidarity, PASO and the Organizing Committee of the Pan American Games; be responsible for and liaise with the Pan American Games organization, relative to weightlifting together with IWF. **Structure** Executive Committee. **Finance** The administrative expenses are covered by the member Federation of the President and Secretary General.
Members Federations in 35 countries and territories:
Antigua-Barbuda, Argentina, Aruba, Bahamas, Barbados, Belize, Bolivia, Brazil, Canada, Cayman Is, Chile, Colombia, Costa Rica, Cuba, Curaçao, Dominican Rep, Ecuador, El Salvador, Guatemala, Guyana, Haiti, Honduras, Jamaica, Mexico, Nicaragua, Panama, Paraguay, Peru, Puerto Rico, St Vincent-Grenadines, Suriname, Trinidad-Tobago, Uruguay, USA, Venezuela, Virgin Is USA.
NGO Relations Member of (1): *Asociación de Confederaciones Deportivas Panamericanas (ACODEPA, #02119).* [2022/XD4274/D]

♦ Pan American Women's Association (inactive)
♦ Pan American World Airways (inactive)
♦ Panamerican Wrestling on Belts Alysh Federation (unconfirmed)
♦ PANAMGRAPH – Confederación Panamericana para Proveedores de la Industria Grafica (no recent information)
♦ **PANAMORL** Pan American Association of Oto-Rhino-Laryngology – Head and Neck Surgery (#18082)

♦ Panam Sports Organization (Panam Sports) 18138

Organisation sportive panaméricaine – Organización Deportiva Panamericana (ODEPA)

SG Valentin Gomeze Farias No 51, San Rafael, DF 06470 Mexico City CDMX, Mexico. T. +525557054657. Fax +525557052275. E-mail: info@panamsports.org.
URL: https://www.panamsports.org/

History 1940, Buenos Aires (Argentina). Former names and other names: *Pan American Sports Committee* – former (1940); *Pan American Sports Organization (PASO)* – former (1955); *Organisation sportive panaméricaine* – former (1955); *Organización Deportiva Panamericana (ODEPA)* – former (1955). **Aims** Strengthen bonds of friendship and solidarity among the peoples of America; further development of the Olympic ideal in accordance with the rules and regulations of the International Olympic Committee; cooperate with and assist international federations in America duly recognized by IOC; organize and direct the *Pan American Games*; serve in the capacity of sports counsellor when requested. **Structure** Ordinary Assembly (every 4 year, before Games); Executive Committee; Commissions (15). **Languages** English, Spanish. **Finance** Members' admission and Games entry fees. Other sources: contribution by organizing Committee of next Games: grants from IOC through the intermediary of *Inter-American Investment Corporation (IIC, #11438)*. **Activities** Sporting activities. **Events** *Executive Council Meeting* Tokyo (Japan) 2018, *Pan American Games* Winnipeg, MB (Canada) 1999, *Annual general assembly / General Assembly* Mexico City (Mexico) 1998, *Annual general assembly / General Assembly* Winnipeg, MB (Canada) 1997, *Annual general assembly / General Assembly* Guatemala (Guatemala) 1996.
Members National Olympic Committees in 41 countries and territories:
Antigua-Barbuda, Argentina, Aruba, Bahamas, Barbados, Belize, Bermuda, Bolivia, Brazil, Canada, Cayman Is, Chile, Colombia, Costa Rica, Cuba, Dominica, Dominican Rep, Ecuador, El Salvador, Grenada, Guatemala, Guyana, Haiti, Honduras, Jamaica, Mexico, Nicaragua, Panama, Paraguay, Peru, Puerto Rico, St Kitts-Nevis, St Lucia, St Vincent-Grenadines, Suriname, Trinidad-Tobago, Uruguay, USA, Venezuela, Virgin Is UK, Virgin Is USA.
NGO Relations Recognized Organization by: *International Olympic Committee (IOC, #14408)*; *Olympic Movement (#17719)*. Continental Association of: *Association of National Olympic Committees (ANOC, #02819)*. Affiliated organization: *Pan American Sailing Federation (PASAF, #18128).* [2023/XD3074/D]

♦ **Panam Sports** Panam Sports Organization (#18138)
♦ PANA – Pan-African News Agency (inactive)
♦ **PANA** Physical Activity Network of the Americas (#18366)
♦ **PANAP** PAN Asia and the Pacific (#18167)
♦ Pan Arab African Council of Ophthalmology / see Middle East African Council of Ophthalmology (#16752)
♦ Pan Arab-African Glaucoma Society / see Pan Arab Glaucoma Society (#18145)

♦ Pan Arab Angiology College (PAAC) 18139

Chancellor address not obtained.
URL: http://www.paacollege.org/

History Jan 2010. **Structure** Board. **Events** *Congress* Dubai (United Arab Emirates) 2011. **Publications** *Pan Arab Angiology Journal.* **NGO Relations** Affiliated with: *Arab Association of Cardiothoracic Surgery (AACTS)*; *International Health Academy (IHA)*; *International Union of Angiology (IUA, #15754)*; *Pan Arab Vascular Surgery Association (PAVA).* [2016/XJ5345/D]

♦ Pan Arab Association for Burns and Plastic Surgery (PABPS) 18140

Contact PO Box 145, Dubai, United Arab Emirates. T. +97142699717. Fax +97142681771.
History May 1994, Tripoli (Libyan AJ). **Aims** Raise scientific standards of plastic surgery in the Arabic world; improve medical and social education related to plastic surgery. **Structure** General Assembly. Board, including President, Immediate Past President, President Elect and 2 further members. **Events** *Congress* Hammamet (Tunisia) 2013, *Congress* Tripoli (Libyan AJ) 2009, *Congress* Marrakech (Morocco) 2005, *Congress* Kuwait (Kuwait) 2002, *Congress* Amman (Jordan) 2001.
Members in 17 countries:
Algeria, Bahrain, Egypt, Iraq, Jordan, Korea Rep, Kuwait, Lebanon, Libya, Morocco, Oman, Qatar, Sudan, Syrian AR, Tunisia, United Arab Emirates, Yemen. [2013/XD7681/D]

♦ Pan Arab Association of Radiological Societies (PAARS) 18141

Association pan arabe des sociétés de radiologie

SG Fac of Medicine, Al Azhar Univ, Al Mokhaym Al Daem, Gameat Al Azhar, Nasr City, Cairo, Egypt.
Head Office PO Box 11-640, Beirut, Lebanon. T. +961161071. Fax +9611611704. E-mail: lop@cyberia.net.lb.
URL: http://www.arabrc.net/

History Sep 2004, Beirut (Lebanon). **Activities** *Arab Radiology Congress (ARC)*. **Events** *Conference* Alexandria (Egypt) 2018, *ARC : Arab Radiology Conference* Hammamet (Tunisia) 2012, *Congress* Tunisia 2012, *ARC : Arab radiology conference / Congress* Lebanon 2011, *ARC : Arab radiology conference / Congress* Jordan 2010. **Members** Societies (11). Membership countries not specified. **NGO Relations** *Pan Arab Interventional Radiology Society (PAIRS, #18147)*; *Pan-Arab NeuroRadiology Society (PANRS, #18150).* [2018/XJ8256/D]

♦ Pan-Arab Congenital Heart Disease Association (PACHDA) 18142

Pres AUBMC CHC, PO Box 11-0236, Riad El Solh, 1107 2020, Beirut, Lebanon.
URL: http://www.pachda.org/

History 4 Feb 2002, Alexandria (Egypt). **Aims** Promote and facilitate cooperation between professionals working in the field of paediatric cardiology in the Arab World and globally. **Structure** Board, comprising President, Vice-President, Secretary and 6 members. **Languages** Arabic, English. **Staff** 3.00 FTE, voluntary. **Finance** Donations. Budget (annual): about US$ 3,000. **Activities** Charity missions in Yemen, Syria and Morocco; training workshops in various Arab countries. **Members** Individuals. [2016/XM8253/v/D]

♦ Pan Arab Continence Society (PACS) 18143

Main Office 12 Boutrs Ghaly Street, Roxi 7th floor, Cairo, Egypt. E-mail: info@pacsoffice.com.
URL: http://pacsoffice.com/

History 2004. **Aims** Promote educational and awareness programmes of *urinary incontinence* and pelvic floor dysfunction. **Structure** Executive Board; Committees. **Events** *Annual Meeting* Cairo (Egypt) 2019, *Annual Meeting* Dubai (United Arab Emirates) 2018, *Annual Meeting* Dubai (United Arab Emirates) 2016, *Annual Meeting* Istanbul (Turkey) 2015, *Annual Meeting* Hurghada (Egypt) 2014. **NGO Relations** *International Continence Society (ICS, #12934).* [2018/XM2737/D]

♦ Pan Arab Council of Ophthalmology (inactive)
♦ Pan Arab Endodontic Society / see Arab Endodontic Society (#00939)
♦ Pan-Arab Federation of Neuroradiology / see Pan-Arab NeuroRadiology Society (#18150)
♦ Pan Arab Federation of Otolaryngological Societies (unconfirmed)
♦ Pan Arab Federation of Psychiatrists (no recent information)

♦ Pan Arab Federation of Societies of Anesthesia, Intensive Care and Pain Management (PAFSA) 18144

Pres Dept of Anesthesia and Surgical Critical Care, Hôtel-Dieu University Hospital, PO Box 166830 Ashrafieh, Beirut, Lebanon.
URL: http://www.pafsaco.org/

History 1990, as *Federation of Arab Societies of Anaesthesia and Intensive Care*, following the congress organizing activities of the 'Pan-Arab Scientific Committee'. **Languages** English. **Events** *Pan Arab Congress* Beirut (Lebanon) 2020, *Pan Arab Congress* Dubai (United Arab Emirates) 2018, *Pan Arab Congress* Dubai (United Arab Emirates) 2016, *Pan Arab Congress* Amman (Jordan) 2014, *Pan Arab congress* Sharjah (United Arab Emirates) 2009. **Publications** *Egyptian Journal of Anaesthesia*; *Middle East Journal of Anaesthesia.*
Members Full in 17 countries:
Algeria, Bahrain, Egypt, Iraq, Jordan, Kuwait, Lebanon, Liberia, Morocco, Oman, Qatar, Saudi Arabia, Sudan, Syrian AR, Tunisia, United Arab Emirates, Yemen. [2021/XD3395/D]

♦ Pan Arab Free Trade Area / see Greater Arab Free-Trade Area (#10700)

♦ Pan Arab Glaucoma Society (PAGS) 18145

Contact 3A Gamat El Dowal Al Arabia, Sphinix Sq, Cairo, 11553, Egypt. T. +2023477400. Fax +2023472090.
URL: http://www.paags.org/

History 1998. Previously also referred to as *Pan Arab-African Glaucoma Society (PAAGS)*. **Structure** Executive Committee, including President and Secretary. **Events** *Annual scientific meeting / Meeting* Sharm el Sheikh (Egypt) 2006, *Annual scientific meeting / Meeting* Beirut (Lebanon) 2005. **NGO Relations** Member of: *World Glaucoma Association (WGA, #21540).* [2009/XQ5455/D]

♦ Pan-Arab Hypertension Society 18146

Pres c/o Egyptian Hypertension Society, 1 ST Diwan, Garden City, Cairo, 11562, Egypt. T. +20227948877 – +20227948877. Fax +20227948879.
SG Cairo Univ – Cardiology, 25 Abdelhalim Hussien Street, Mohandecine, Cairo, 12311, Egypt. Fax +2023388348.
History 1995, Cairo (Egypt). **Structure** Board of Directors comprising President, 2 Vice-Presidents, Secretary, Assistant Secretary and Treasurer. **Languages** Arabic, English. **Staff** 5.00 FTE, paid; 4.50 FTE, voluntary. **Finance** Members' dues. Industry support. **Events** *Conference* Lebanon 2009, *Conference* Tunis (Tunisia) 2005, *Conference* Cairo (Egypt) 2003, *Conference* Abu Dhabi (United Arab Emirates) 2000, *Conference* Beirut (Lebanon) 1995.
Members Full in 13 countries:
Algeria, Bahrain, Egypt, Jordan, Kuwait, Lebanon, Morocco, Qatar, Saudi Arabia, Sudan, Tunisia, United Arab Emirates, Yemen.
IGO Relations *WHO (#20950).* [2016/XD8534/D]

♦ Pan Arab Interventional Radiology Society (PAIRS) 18147

Contact c/o Diaedu Management Consultancy, 907 Dusselforf Business Point, Al Barsha 1, Dubai, United Arab Emirates. E-mail: sara@diaedu.com – chav@diaedu.com.
URL: http://pairscongress.com/

History 2006, Dubai (United Arab Emirates), during 31st Arab Health Exhibition and Congress. **Events** *Scientific Meeting* Dubai (United Arab Emirates) 2022, *Scientific Meeting* Dubai (United Arab Emirates) 2020, *Scientific Meeting* Dubai (United Arab Emirates) 2019, *Scientific Meeting* Dubai (United Arab Emirates) 2018, *Scientific Meeting* Dubai (United Arab Emirates) 2017. **NGO Relations** *Pan Arab Association of Radiological Societies (PAARS, #18141).* [2020/XJ8251/D]

♦ Pan Arab League of Dermatology 18148

SG PO Box 94648, Riyadh 1161, Saudi Arabia.
URL: http://www.panarabderm.org/

History 1980. **Aims** Share information on different aspects of dermatology through medical lectures, workshops, conferences and visiting consultants in the Arab world. **Structure** Administrative Council; Board of Directors. General Secretariat, headed by Secretary General. **Languages** Arabic, English. **Events** *Congress* Jordan 2013, *Congress* Dubai (United Arab Emirates) 2011, *Congress* Saudi Arabia 2008, *Congress* Taiz (Yemen) 2006, *Congress* Yemen 2006. **Publications** *Journal of Pan-Arab League of Dermatologists.*
Members Full in 18 countries and territories:
Algeria, Bahrain, Egypt, Iraq, Jordan, Kuwait, Lebanon, Libya, Morocco, Oman, Palestine, Qatar, Saudi Arabia, Sudan, Syrian AR, Tunisia, United Arab Emirates, Yemen.
NGO Relations Member of: *International League of Dermatological Societies (ILDS, #14018).* [2020/XD4524/D]

♦ **Pan Arab Minimally Invasive Spine Society (PAMISS)** **18149**
Contact address not obtained. T. +96523862241. Fax +96523985165. E-mail: arshadikram@gmail.com.
URL: http://www.pamiss.com/
Aims Improve the health of patients with spinal disorders by advancing the highest quality minimally invasive spinal care for patients. **Structure** Executive Committee, comprising Chairman, Vice Chairman, Committee Chairmen, Secretary, Treasurer and Past-Chairman.
Members Individuals in 13 countries:
Côte d'Ivoire, Egypt, Germany, India, Iraq, Italy, Jordan, Kuwait, Lebanon, Qatar, Saudi Arabia, Syrian AR, UK.
[2013/XJ7206/v/**D**]

♦ **Pan-Arab NeuroRadiology Society (PANRS)** **18150**
Pres/SG Neurosciences and NeuroImaging Dept, CHU Hôtel-Dieu de France, Univ Saint Joseph, POB 16-6830, Beirut, Lebanon. Fax +9611611182.
Hon Pres Riyadh Armed Forces Hosp, PO Box 7879, Riyadh 11159, Saudi Arabia.
URL: http://www.panrs.org/
History 1994, Beirut (Lebanon), following activities initiated in May 1993. Previously also referred to as *Pan-Arab Federation of Neuroradiology.* **Aims** Advance neuroradiology in all its aspects; represent neuroradiology in the Arab world on matters of common interest. **Structure** Board, comprising Honorary President, President/Secretary General, Vice-President, Past-President, Treasurer and Historian. Council of Delegates. **Languages** Arabic, English, French. **Staff** Voluntary. **Finance** Support from companies and universities. **Events** *Arab radiological conference* Beirut (Lebanon) 2011, *Arab Radiology Conference (ARC)* Lebanon 2011, *Arab radiological conference / Arab Radiology Conference (ARC)* Jordan 2010, *Conference / Arab Radiology Conference (ARC)* Egypt 2009, *Arab radiological conference / Arab Radiology Conference (ARC)* Jordan 2007.
Members Full in 27 countries. Membership countries not specified. **NGO Relations** Member of: *World Federation of Neuroradiological Societies (WFNRS, #21463).* [2010.06.01/XG9745/**D**]

♦ **Pan Arab Neurosurgical Society (PANS)** **18151**
Head Office c/o Riyadh Armed Forces Hospital, PO Box 7897, Riyadh 11159, Saudi Arabia. T. +96614777714ext25443. Fax +96614768273.
URL: http://www.panarabneurosurgery.org.sa/
History Apr 1996, Riyadh (Saudi Arabia), following a proposal at the 10th International Congress of *World Federation of Neurosurgical Societies (WFNS, #21466),* 1993, Acapulco (Mexico). Constitution ratified 7 Dec 1996, Riyadh. **Aims** Advance neurosurgery in all its aspects; represent neurosurgery in the Arab World on matters of common interest. **Structure** General Assembly. Active Council, consisting of all active members. By-Law Council (meets at least annually), comprising 2 active executive members from each Arabian country. Executive Committee (meets at least annually) selected by the By-Law Council and comprising President, Immediate Past-President, Vice-President and President-Elect, Secretary General, Treasurer, President of Training Scientific Committee, Historian and 2 Members at Large. Committees (3): Programme Committee of the Scientific Meeting; Finance; Membership. Scientific and Special (Ad Hoc) Committees. **Languages** Arabic, English. **Finance** Members' dues (annual): Active, US$ 20; Associate, US$ 10; residents under training, US$ 5. **Activities** Knowledge management/information disseminations; standards/guidelines; events/meetings. **Events** *Dubai Spine Conference* Dubai (United Arab Emirates) 2015, *General Assembly* Abu Dhabi (United Arab Emirates) 2014, *Dubai Spine Conference* Dubai (United Arab Emirates) 2013, *Interdisciplinary World Congress on Low Back and Pelvic Pain* Dubai (United Arab Emirates) 2013, *General Assembly* Damascus (Syrian AR) 2006. **Publications** *Pan Arab Journal of Neurosurgery.*
Members Full Neurosurgical Societies; Affiliate neuroscience organizations without majority of neurosurgeons or neurologists as members. Organizations in 11 countries:
Algeria, Egypt, Iraq, Jordan, Kuwait, Lebanon, Morocco, Oman, Saudi Arabia, Syrian AR, Tunisia.
Full Neurosurgeons from countries where no Neurosurgical Society exists in 19 countries and territories:
Argentina, Australia, Bahrain, Brazil, Canada, Colombia, Ecuador, Finland, France, Germany, Libya, Mexico, Palestine, Qatar, Sudan, Sweden, United Arab Emirates, USA, Yemen.
NGO Relations Instrumental in setting up: *Arab College of Neurosurgery (#00923).* [2012/XD8204/**D**]

♦ **Pan Arab Orthopaedic Association (PAOA)** **18152**
Contact 9 Osman Ebn Affan St, Heliopolis, Cairo, Egypt. T. +2024180550. Fax +2024180550. E-mail: panarabortho@gmail.com – mdarwish424@gmail.com – fadelminia@yahoo.com.
Contact 16 Hoda Shaarawi St, Cairo, Egypt. T. +2023930013. Fax +2023930054.
URL: http://www.panarabortho.org/
History 1993. **Structure** Executive Board, comprising General Secretary, Vice-General Secretary, 3 Assistant General Secretaries, Treasurer and 2 further members. **Events** *Congress* Muscat (Oman) 2014, *Congress* Marrakech (Morocco) 2010, *Congress* Beirut (Lebanon) 2009, *Congress* Cairo (Egypt) 2004, *Congress* Bahrain 2003. **Publications** *Pan Arab Journal of Orthopaedics and Trauma.* [2017/XD4218/**D**]

♦ **Pan-Arab Osteoporosis Society (PAOS)** **18153**
Gen Sec Abtei Weg 1, 36251 Bad Hersfeld, Germany. T. +4917621249896.
Facebook: https://www.facebook.com/miedanycrd
History Apr 1997, Beit Mery (Lebanon). **Aims** Promote awareness of osteoporosis and musculockeletal related conditions among health professionals and the public in Arab countries; assist each country to establish its own society of patients; encourage research into osteoporosis. **Structure** Executive Board; Scientific Committee. **Languages** Arabic, English. **Staff** 15.00 FTE, voluntary. **Finance** Members bear their own expenses. No annual budget. **Activities** Standards/guidelines; publishing activities; training/education; events/meetings. **Events** *Congress* Beirut (Lebanon) 2018, *Congress* Amman (Jordan) 2016, *Congress* Dubai (United Arab Emirates) 2014, *Congress* Jordan 2012, *Congress* Damascus (Syrian AR) 2010. **Publications** *PAOS News Bulletin* (2 a year).
Members Organizations in 15 countries and territories:
Bahrain, Egypt, Iraq, Jordan, Kuwait, Lebanon, Libya, Morocco, Oman, Palestine, Qatar, Saudi Arabia, Syrian AR, Tunisia, United Arab Emirates.
NGO Relations Member of: *International Osteoporosis Foundation (IOF, #14490).* [2022/XD8224/**D**]

♦ Pan Arab Pediatric Neurosurgery Society (unconfirmed)
♦ Pan Arab Project for Child Development (no recent information)

♦ **Pan Arab Rhinology Society (PARS)** **18154**
Exec Sec 87 El Manial St, El Ghamrawy Station, Cairo, 62814, Egypt. T. +20216641225. E-mail: info@panarabrhinologysociety.com.
URL: http://www.panarabrhinologysociety.com/
History 2010, Cairo (Egypt). **Aims** Disseminate knowledge in the field of rhinology, sinus surgery and immunology between interested doctors in the Arab countries; encourage research work by junior doctors in the same fields. **Structure** Board. **Activities** Committees (10): Journal; Audit; Award; Foreign Relations; Information Technology; Ethics; By laws; CME; Membership; Research Grant. **Events** *Meeting* Cairo (Egypt) 2019, *Meeting* Cairo (Egypt) 2018, *Meeting* Kuwait (Kuwait) 2017, *Meeting* Manama (Bahrain) 2016, *Meeting* Riyadh (Saudi Arabia) 2015.
Members Individuals in 12 countries and territories:
Bahrain, Egypt, Jordan, Kuwait, Lebanon, Libya, Palestine, Saudi Arabia, Sudan, Syrian AR, United Arab Emirates, Yemen.
[2019/XJ5427/v/**D**]

♦ **Pan Arab Society of Andrological Sciences (PASAS)** **18155**
Sec Alexandria Univ, Fac of Medicine, Alexandria, Egypt. T. +2034214400. Fax +2034833076 – +2034833271.
History Cairo (Egypt). **Aims** Foster studies, research, and good quality practice in male reproductive health and andrological science among physicians in the Arab world. **Structure** General Assembly. Executive Council, comprising President, 2 Vice-Presidents, Secretary General, Treasurer and 11 members. Bureau, consisting of President, Secretary General and Treasurer. Regional Offices. Programme Committee. **Languages** Arabic, English. **Staff** 1.50 FTE, paid; 2.00 FTE, voluntary. **Finance** Members' dues. Grants from pharmaceutical industry. **Activities** Organizes international meetings, conferences and workshops. **Events** *Meeting* Dubai (United Arab Emirates) 2008, *Meeting* Alexandria (Egypt) 2005, *Meeting* Damascus (Syrian AR) 2003, *Meeting* Beirut (Lebanon) 2000, *Congress* Beirut (Lebanon) 1999. **Publications** *PASAS Bulletin.*
Members Organizations; Individuals. Organizations in 8 countries:
Egypt, Jordan, Kuwait, Lebanon, Saudi Arabia, Syrian AR, Tunisia, Yemen.
Individuals in 14 countries:
Algeria, Bahrain, Egypt, Jordan, Kuwait, Lebanon, Libya, Morocco, Oman, Qatar, Saudi Arabia, Syrian AR, Tunisia, Yemen.
IGO Relations *League of Arab States (LAS, #16420).* [2017/XD6337/**D**]

♦ Pan-Arab Society of Cosmetic Dermatology and Laser (no recent information)
♦ Pan Arab Society for Impotence Research and Sexual Health / see Pan Arab Society for Sexual Medicine (#18157)

♦ **Pan Arab Society for Paediatric Gastroenterology, Hepatology and Nutrition (PASPGHAN)** **18156**
Gen Sec address not obtained. E-mail: info@paspghan.com.
Sec address not obtained.
URL: https://www.paspghan.com/
History 1998, Sudan. Founded by Prof Ibrahim Fayyad. Former names and other names: *Pan-Arab Union of Pediatric Gastro-Enterology, Hepatology & Nutrition* – former. **Events** *Congress* Rabat (Morocco) 2022, *Congress* Dubai (United Arab Emirates) 2021.
Members Representatives of Arab Pediatric Gastroenterology Societies; Pediatric societies. Members in 13 countries:
Bahrain, Egypt, Jordan, Lebanon, Morocco, Palestine, Qatar, Saudi Arabia, Sudan, Syrian AR, Tunisia, United Arab Emirates, Yemen. [2022/AA2738/**D**]

♦ **Pan Arab Society for Sexual Medicine (PASSM)** **18157**
Pres 1 B Hassan Sabry St, Zamalek, Cairo, Egypt. T. +20227380644. Fax +20227380655.
URL: http://www.passm.org/
History 1999. Previously referred to as *Pan Arab Society for Impotence Research and Sexual Health (PASIR-SH).* **Aims** Encourage the highest standards of practice, education and research in the field of human sexuality in the Arab world; develop and assist in developing scientific methods for diagnosis, prevention and treatment of conditions affecting human sexual function; promote publication and encourage contributions to the medical and scientific literature in the field; deliver proper sexuality education to Arabic societies thus helping in the prevention of sexual dysfunction. **Events** *Biennial Conference* Cairo (Egypt) 2009, *Biennial conference* Dubai (United Arab Emirates) 2007. **Publications** *Health for Life*; *Sexual Health Update.*
[2011.06.01/XJ5034/**D**]

♦ Pan-Arab Union of Neurological Sciences / see Pan-Arab Union of Neurological Societies (#18158)

♦ **Pan-Arab Union of Neurological Societies (PAUNS)** **18158**
Pres Dept of Neurology, Habib Bourguiba Univ Hosp, CP-3019 Sfax, Tunisia. E-mail: info@pauns.net.
URL: http://pauns.net/
History 1975, as *Pan-Arab Union of Neurological Sciences (PAUNS).* **Aims** Progress and develop clinical and basic research in neurosciences. **Structure** Board of Directors; Council of Delegates. **Languages** Arabic, English. **Staff** 3.00 FTE, voluntary. **Finance** Members' dues. Other sources: sponsorship; donations. Annual budget: about US$ 150,000. **Activities** Events/meetings; healthcare; research and development; training/education. **Events** *Congress* Sharm el Sheikh (Egypt) 2013, *Congress* Damascus (Syrian AR) 2010, *Congress* Hammamet (Tunisia) 2007, *Congress* Jeddah (Saudi Arabia) 2005, *Congress* Cairo (Egypt) 2003. **Publications** *NeuroSciences* (periodical).
Members Full in 18 countries and territories:
Algeria, Bahrain, Egypt, Iraq, Jordan, Lebanon, Libya, Mauritania, Morocco, Oman, Palestine, Qatar, Saudi Arabia, Sudan, Syrian AR, Tunisia, United Arab Emirates, Yemen.
IGO Relations *League of Arab States (LAS, #16420).* [2018.09.28/XD8595/**D**]

♦ Pan-Arab Union of Pediatric Gastro-Enterology, Hepatology & Nutrition / see Pan Arab Society for Paediatric Gastroenterology, Hepatology and Nutrition (#18156)
♦ Pan Arab Vascular Surgery Association (unconfirmed)
♦ **PANARTES** Pan American Federation of Arts, Mass Media and Entertainment Unions (#18099)
♦ PANASCO – Pan African Students International Peace and Voluntary Services Organization (inactive)

♦ **Pan Asia Academy of Facial Plastic and Reconstructive Surgery (PAAFPRS)** **18159**
Administrative Office 18A Entertainment Bldg, 30 Queen's Road Central, Central, Central and Western, Hong Kong. T. +85225228383. Fax +85225228080. E-mail: contact@paafprs.org.
URL: http://paafprs.org/
History 2009, China. Founded during 3rd International Conference of Facial Plastic Surgery. Incorporated in accordance with Canadian law. Registration: Hong Kong. **Aims** Stimulate scientific advancement in the field of facial plastic surgery; improve the skills of those active in this practice. **Structure** Governing Council. **Events** *International Conference* Singapore (Singapore) 2023, *Congress* Kuala Lumpur (Malaysia) 2019, *Congress* Bangkok (Thailand) 2015, *Congress* Seoul (Korea Rep) 2014, *Congress* Mumbai (India) 2013.
Members Full in 15 countries and territories:
Australia, Brazil, Canada, China, Hong Kong, India, Indonesia, Japan, Korea Rep, Mexico, Philippines, Singapore, Thailand, USA, Vietnam.
NGO Relations Member of: *International Federation of Facial Plastic Surgery Societies (IFFPSS, #13422).*
[2022/XM3887/**C**]

♦ **Pan Asian Association of Maritime Engineering Societies (PAAMES)** **18160**
Dir Intl Affairs Jap Soc of Naval Architects and Ocean Engineers, 2-12-9 Shiba-daimon, Minato-ku, Tokyo, 105-0012 Japan. T. +81334382014. Fax +81334332016. E-mail: international@jasnaoe.or.jp.
URL: http://www.paames.org/
History 2004. Founded at 1st meeting. **Aims** Promote science and technology in maritime engineering; support development of maritime industry; exchange scientific information; improve the status of maritime engineers; cooperate and collaborate among member organizations. **Structure** Organizing Committee. **Activities** Events/meetings. **Events** *Advanced Maritime Engineering Conference* St Petersburg (Russia) 2021, *Advanced Maritime Engineering Conference* St Petersburg (Russia) 2020, *Advanced Maritime Engineering Conference* Busan (Korea Rep) 2018, *Advanced Maritime Engineering Conference* Hong Kong (Hong Kong) 2016, *Advanced Maritime Engineering Conference* Hangzhou (China) 2014.
Members Organizations in 7 countries and territories:
China, Hong Kong, Japan, Korea Rep, Russia, Singapore, Taiwan. [2021/XM5615/**D**]

♦ **Pan Asian Boxing Association (PABA)** **18161**
Dir PABA Main Office, 2-131 HanGangRo 2-ga, 3rd Floor 302, YongSan-gu, Seoul, Korea Rep. T. +8227901101. Fax +8227926464.
URL: http://www.pabaonline.com/
History 30 Mar 1995, Beijing (China), by *World Boxing Association (WBA, #21241).* **Structure** Executive Committee, including Honorary President, President, 2 Vice-Presidents and 2 International Commissioners. **Activities** Organizes conventions. **Events** *Annual Convention* Washington, DC (USA) 2002. **Publications** *PABA Circular Letter.*
Members Regular (30); Associate (11). Regular in 30 countries and territories:
Armenia, Australia, Belarus, China, Fiji, India, Indonesia, Kazakhstan, Korea DPR, Korea Rep, Kyrgyzstan, Macau, Moldova, Mongolia, Nepal, Netherlands, New Caledonia, New Zealand, Papua New Guinea, Philippines, Romania, Russia, Samoa, Tahiti Is, Tajikistan, Thailand, Tonga, Turkmenistan, Ukraine, Uzbekistan.
Associate in 11 countries and territories:
Argentina, Cambodia, Czechia, England, Kenya, Mexico, Solomon Is, Tanzania UR, USA, Vanuatu, Venezuela.
[2014/XD7727/**D**]

♦ **Pan Asian e-Commerce Alliance (PAA)** **18162**
Secretariat c/o Tradelink Electronic Commerce Ltd, 11/F-12/F Tower B, Regent Centre, 63 Wo Yi Hop Road, Kwai Chung, Hong Kong. T. +85221614370. Fax +85225060188.
PAA WG PMP Chair c/o Trade-Van Information Services Co, No 19-13 6F, Sanchung Road, Nankang Software Park, Taipei 115, Taiwan. T. +886237895762. Fax +886237895688.
URL: http://www.paa.net/

History Founded Jul 2000, by CrimsonLogic (Singapore), Tradelink Electronic Commerce (Hong Kong) and Trade-Van Information Service (Taiwan). **Aims** Promote and provide secure, trusted, reliable and value-adding *information technology* (IT) infrastructure and facilities to enhance seamless trade globally. **Structure** Steering Committee (meets 3 times a year); Working Groups (2); Special Task Forces; Secretariat. **Languages** English. **Activities** Networking/liaising. **Events** *Meeting* Osaka (Japan) 2018, *Meeting* Putrajaya (Malaysia) 2015, *Meeting* Jeju (Korea Rep) 2008. **Publications** Press releases.
Members Full in 11 countries and territories:
China, Hong Kong, Indonesia, Japan, Korea Rep, Macau, Malaysia, Philippines, Singapore, Taiwan, Thailand.
IGO Relations *ASEAN (#01141)*; *Asia-Pacific Economic Cooperation (APEC, #01887)*; Electronic Commerce Steering Group (ECSG). [2019/XJ0147/**D**]

♦ Pan-Asian Committee for Treatment and Research in Multiple Sclerosis (PACTRIMS) 18163

Pres Institute of Neurotherapeutics, Nishinokyo Kasuga-cho 16-44-409, Nakakyo-ku, Kyoto, 604-8453 Japan. E-mail: secretariat@pactrims.org.
URL: http://www.pactrims.org/
History 2007. **Aims** Stimulate research into the cause and treatment of multiple sclerosis (MS) and related inflammatory diseases of the central nervous system; promote an interest in and understanding of the effects of MS in the community; promote access to proven treatment for MS; represent the interests of the MS research community in the Asia Pacific region. **Structure** Central Organizing Committee. Executive Committee, comprising President/Local Organizing Committee Chairman, Vice-President/Treasurer, Secretary, 2 Deputy Secretaries and 4 members. Regional Committees (3): East Asia; Southeast Asia; Pacific. **Events** *Congress* Singapore (Singapore) 2022, *Congress* Singapore (Singapore) 2021, *Congress* Singapore (Singapore) 2020, *Congress* Singapore (Singapore) 2019, *Congress* Sydney, NSW (Australia) 2018.
Members Full in 14 countries and territories:
Australia, China, Hong Kong, India, Indonesia, Iran Islamic Rep, Japan, Korea Rep, Malaysia, New Zealand, Philippines, Singapore, Taiwan, Thailand.
NGO Relations Sister organizations: American Committee on Treatment and Research of Multiple Sclerosis (ACTRIMS); *European Committee for Treatment and Research in Multiple Sclerosis (ECTRIMS, #06673)*; *European Cooperation for Accreditation (EA, #06782)*. [2022/XJ5325/**D**]

♦ Pan-Asian Consortium of Language Teaching Societies (PAC) 18164

Contact c/o JALT, Urban Edge Bldg 5-F, 1-37-9 Taito, Taito-ku, Tokyo, 110-0016 Japan. T. +81338371630. Fax +81338371631.
URL: http://www.pac-teach.org/
History 1994. **Aims** Promote the teaching of *English* in Asia. **Events** *Conference* Tokyo (Japan) 2008, *Conference* Bangkok (Thailand) 2007, *Conference* Vladivostok (Russia) 2004, *Conference* Taipei (Taiwan) 2002, *Conference* Kitakyushu (Japan) 2001. **Publications** Conference' proceedings.
Members National organizations (7) in 7 countries:
China, Japan, Korea Rep, Philippines, Russia, Singapore, Thailand.
NGO Relations *Asian Youth Forum (AYF, #01789)*; *International Association of Teachers of English as a Foreign Language (IATEFL, #12222)*. [2008/XM3560/**F**]

♦ Pan Asian-Pacific Skin Barrier Research Society (unconfirmed)

♦ Pan-Asian Society of Sports and Physical Education 18165

Pres College of Physical Education, Suwon Univ, Wauri, Bongdam-Eup, Hwaseong GYEONGGI, Korea Rep. T. +82312202359. Fax +82312202563.
URL: http://www.isdy.net/
Aims Retrospect Western knowledge of sports and physical education on the basis of Asian wisdom. **Languages** English. **Staff** 1.00 FTE, paid. **Activities** Organizes conference. **Events** *Conference* Bolpur (India) 2014, *Congress / Conference* Cebu City (Philippines) 2013, *Conference* Manila (Philippines) 2012, *Conference* Beijing (China) 2011, *Conference* Nanchang (China) 2010. **Publications** Quarterly journal. **Members** in 67 countries. Membership countries not specified. [2013.10.08/XJ6166/**D**]

♦ Pan-Asian Urogynecologic Association (PAUGA) 18166

Address not obtained.
History 2005. **Aims** Disseminate information regarding international progress for the science of *female pelvic medicine* and *reconstructive surgery*. **Structure** Board. **Events** *Biennial Meeting* Fuzhou (China) 2010. [2014/XJ8683/**D**]

♦ PAN Asia and the Pacific (PANAP) 18167

Main Office 48 Persiaran Mutiara 1, Pusat Komersial Bandar Mutiara, Simpang Ampat,, 14120 Penang, Malaysia. E-mail: info@panap.net.
URL: http://www.panap.net/
History 1995. Founded as a regional centre of *Pesticide Action Network (PAN, #18336)*. **Aims** Create a *pesticide*-free world for global citizens while promoting *sustainable biodiversity*-based *ecological agriculture*. **Structure** Steering Council; Secretariat. **Activities** Advocacy/lobbying/activism; projects/programmes; knowledge management/information dissemination. **Members** Partner organizations (108). Membership countries not specified. **NGO Relations** Member of (3): *Asia-Pacific Research Network (APRN, #02013)*; *Coalition of Agricultural Workers International (CAWI, #04050)*; *More and Better (#16855)*. [2020/XM7500/**E**]

♦ Pan-Asia Risk and Insurance Management Association (PARIMA) 18168

Exec Dir 5 Shenton Way, UIC Bldg Suite 10-01, Singapore 068808, Singapore. E-mail: team@parima.org.
URL: http://parima.org/
History Registration: Start date: Jul 2013, Singapore. **Aims** Strengthen and enhance the culture of risk management in the region by creating opportunities for education and dialogue within the community. **Structure** Board; Executive Committee. **Finance** Partnerships. **Activities** Capacity building; certification/accreditation; events/meetings; networking/liaising; training/education. **Events** *Conference* Singapore (Singapore) 2022, *Conference* Singapore (Singapore) 2021, *Conference* Singapore (Singapore) 2020, *Conference* Kuala Lumpur (Malaysia) 2019, *Conference* Tokyo (Japan) 2018. **Publications** *Lessons Learnt in Business Interruption*; *Risk Frontiers Asia*; *Targeting a Technology Dividend in Risk Management*. **Members** Individuals (over 2,600) in 23 countries. Membership countries not specified. **NGO Relations** Member of (1): *International Federation of Risk and Insurance Management Associations (IFRIMA, #13531)*. [2023.02.20/XJ8451/**D**]

♦ Pan-Asia Securities Lending Association (PASLA) 18169

Main Office GPO Box 6383, 2 Connaught Pl, Central, Hong Kong, Central and Western, Hong Kong. E-mail: info@paslaonline.com.
URL: http://www.paslaonline.com/
History Nov 1995, following a series of conferences organized since 1992. **Structure** Executive Committee, comprising Chairman, Treasurer and 10 members. **Events** *Conference on Asian Securities Lending* Sydney, NSW (Australia) 2019, *Conference on Asian Securities Lending* Hong Kong (Hong Kong) 2018, *Conference on Asian Securities Lending* Seoul (Korea Rep) 2017, *Conference on Asian Securities Lending* Singapore (Singapore) 2016, *Conference* Hong Kong (Hong Kong) 2013. [2020/XD8666/**D**]

♦ Pan-Asia Symphony Orchestra (internationally oriented national body)
♦ Pan Asiatic Tissue Association / see Asia Pacific Association of Surgical Tissue Banking (#01854)

♦ Panathlon International (PI) 18170

Pres Villa Queirolo, Via Aurelia Ponente 1, 16035 Rapallo GE, Italy. T. +3918565295 – +3918565296. Fax +39185230513. E-mail: president@panathlon.net – info@panathlon.net.
URL: http://www.panathlon-international.org/
History 1960. Founded, uniting clubs of many nations, the first club having been created 1951, Venice (Italy). Previous statutes approved 4-5 Jun 1982, Stresa (Italy); modified 15-18 May 1986, Trieste (Italy); 4 Oct 1991, Venice (Italy); 24 Nov 2007, Antwerp (Belgium); 24 May 2014, Rapallo (Italy); 21 May 2016, Antwerp (Belgium); 15 May 2018, Florence (Italy). Current statutes approved 26 Oct 2019, Molfetta (Italy). Modelled on community service clubs. **Aims** Achieve the *sporting* ideal and establishment of its cultural and moral values as a means of development and advancement of the individual and of solidarity between individuals and peoples. **Structure** General Meeting; International Board; President's Committee; District Presidents Committee; Auditors' Committee; Constitution and Arbitration Board. National bodies: Districts; District President; District Assemblies. Local bodies: Areas; Area Governors; Area Assemblies. **Languages** English, French, German, Italian, Portuguese, Spanish. **Staff** 4.50 FTE, paid. **Finance** Sources: members' dues. **Activities** Awards/prizes/competitions; capacity building; events/meetings; research/documentation; training/education. **Events** *General Elective Meeting* Osimo (Italy) 2020, *Extraordinary General Meeting* Castellanza (Italy) 2019, *Extraordinary General Meeting* Molfetta (Italy) 2019, *Education in and through sport – Connecting values, physical literacy and wellbeing* Florence (Italy) 2018, *Extraordinary and Ordinary General Meeting* Florence (Italy) 2018. **Publications** *Panathlon International* (3 a year) in English, French, German, Italian, Portuguese, Spanish – magazine.
Members Clubs (264) in 25 countries:
Albania, Algeria, Argentina, Austria, Belgium, Bolivia, Brazil, Chile, Ecuador, France, Germany, Iran Islamic Rep, Italy, Liechtenstein, Luxembourg, Mexico, Paraguay, Peru, Portugal, Russia, San Marino, Spain, Switzerland, Togo, Uruguay.
NGO Relations Member of (3): *International Committee for Fair Play (#12769)*; *International Council of Sport Science and Physical Education (ICSSPE, #13077)*; *Olympic Movement (#17719)*. [2021/XD4243/**C**]

♦ Pan Atlantic Union (inactive)
♦ Pan-Atlantic University (internationally oriented national body)
♦ **PANCAP** Pan Caribbean Partnership against HIV and AIDS (#18171)
♦ **PanCare** Pan-European Network for Care of Survivors after Childhood and Adolescent Cancer (#18178)

♦ Pan Caribbean Partnership against HIV and AIDS (PANCAP) 18171

Secretariat CARICOM, PO Box 10827, 13-15 Area F, Plantation Turkeyen, Georgetown, Guyana. T. +5922220201 – +5922220001 – +5922220006. Fax +5922220203. E-mail: pancap@caricom.org.
URL: http://www.pancap.org/
History 14 Feb 2001, Bridgetown (Barbados). Established at Conference of Heads of Government of the Caribbean Community, within the framework of *Caribbean Community (CARICOM, #03476)*. **Aims** Advocate for HIV/AIDS issues at government and highest levels; coordinate regional response and mobilize regional and international resources; increase country-level human and financial resources to address the *epidemic*; support priority areas for action specified in the Caribbean Regional Strategic Framework. **Structure** Annual General Meeting; Regional Coordinating Mechanism (RCM) – serves as Executive Committee. Priority Areas Coordinating Committee (PACC); PANCAP Coordinating Unit (PCU) – serves as Secretariat. **Languages** English. **Staff** 13.50 FTE, paid. **Finance** Donors. **Activities** Advocacy/lobbying/activism; awards/prizes/competitions. **Events** *Annual General Meeting* Guadeloupe 2014, *Ordinary meeting* St Lucia 2009, *Regional consultation on universal access to prevention, treatment, care and support* St Lucia 2006. **Publications** *PANCAP Electronic Newsletter (e-News)*.
Members Governments of 21 countries and territories:
Anguilla, Antigua-Barbuda, Bahamas, Barbados, Belize, Bermuda, Curaçao, Dominica, Dominican Rep, Grenada, Guadeloupe, Guyana, Haiti, Jamaica, Montserrat, St Kitts-Nevis, St Lucia, St Maarten, St Vincent-Grenadines, Suriname, Trinidad-Tobago.
NGO Relations Cooperates with (1): *Caribbean Regional Network of People Living with HIV/AIDS (CRN+, #03549)*. [2021.10.26/XF6814/**E***]

♦ **PanCornea** Pan-American Cornea Society (#18090)

♦ Pancreatic Cancer Europe (PCE) 18172

Secretariat c/o RPP Group SPRL, Rue Guimard 10, 1040 Brussels, Belgium. E-mail: actionpancreaticcancer@outlook.com.
Registered Address Rue Montoyer 40, 1040 Brussels, Belgium.
URL: http://www.pancreaticcancereurope.eu/
History 2014. Former names and other names: *Pancreatic Cancer Europe – The European Multi-Stakeholder Platform on Pancreatic Cancer* – full title. Registration: Banque-Carrefour des Entreprises, No/ID: 0656.553.804, Start date: 10 Jun 2016, Belgium; EU Transparency Register, No/ID: 791220833072-74, Start date: 8 Nov 2018. **Aims** Bring together experts from all over Europe including academics, physicians, politicians, patient groups, journalists and industry with a common interest and willingness to improve care for *patients* with pancreatic cancer. **Structure** Administration Board. **Activities** Research/documentation; awareness raising; networking/liaising. **Publications** *PCE Newsletter*. **NGO Relations** Member of (2): *European Cancer Organisation (ECO, #06432)* (Patient Advisory Committee); *Workgroup of European Cancer Patient Advocacy Networks (WECAN, #21054)*. [2020/XM7474/**F**]

♦ Pancreatic Cancer Europe – The European Multi-Stakeholder Platform on Pancreatic Cancer / see Pancreatic Cancer Europe (#18172)
♦ Pandaigdigang Alyansa Para sa Batas Pangkalikasan (#05503)

♦ Pandemic Action Network (PAN) 18173

Contact address not obtained. E-mail: info@pandemicactionnetwork.org.
URL: https://pandemicactionnetwork.org/
History 2020. **Aims** Drive collective action to help bring an end to COVID-19 and ensure the world is prepared for the next pandemic. **Structure** Advisory Committee; Team. **Activities** Politics/policy/regulatory.
Members Partners include 37 organizations listed in this Yearbook:
– *ACCESS Health International (#00049)*;
– *Africa Centres for Disease Control and Prevention (Africa CDC, #00162)*;
– *African Union (AU, #00488)*;
– *Bill and Melinda Gates Foundation (BMGF)*;
– *CARE International (CI, #03429)*;
– *Eastern African Network of AIDS Service Organizations (EANNASO, see: #00272)*;
– *Fast-Track Cities (#09276)*;
– *FHI 360*;
– *Forum de Paris sur la Paix*;
– *Future Africa Forum (#10046)*;
– *Global Citizen (#10281)*;
– *Global Health Advocacy Incubator (GHAI)*;
– *Global Health Corps (GHC)*;
– *Global Health Technologies Coalition (GHTC)*;
– *Global Impact*;
– *Global Institute for Disease Elimination (GLIDE)*;
– *Global Parliamentarians Network to End Infectious Diseases (UNITE, #10526)*;
– *International Chamber of Commerce (ICC, #12534)*;
– *International Medical Corps (IMC)*;
– *Internews*;
– *Johns Hopkins Program for International Education in Gynecology and Obstetrics (JHPIEGO)*;
– *Last Mile Health*;
– *Living Goods*;
– *Management Sciences for Health (MSH)*;
– *Nuclear Threat Initiative (NTI, #17622)*;
– *ONE (#17728)*;
– *Open Government Partnership (OGP, #17753)*;
– *PATH (#18260)*;
– *PSI (#18555)*;
– *Sabin Vaccine Institute (Sabin)*;
– *Save the Children Federation (SCF)*;
– *Skoll Foundation*;
– *Task Force for Global Health (TFGH, #20098)*;
– *The Rockefeller Foundation (#18966)*;
– *United Nations Foundation (UNF, #20563)*;
– *Women Deliver (#20989)*;
– *Women in Global Health (WGH, #20998)*. [2023/AA2286/y/**F**]

♦ **PANDRH** Pan American Network for Drug Regulatory Harmonization (#18121)
♦ PanEco – Foundation for Sustainable Development Intercultural Exchange (internationally oriented national body)
♦ **Panel** High Level Panel for a Sustainable Ocean Economy (#10917)

♦ Panel of Recognised International Market Experts in Finance (P.R.I.M.E. Finance) 18174

Head of Secretariat Peace Palace, Carnegieplein 2, 2517 KJ The Hague, Netherlands. E-mail: secretary@primefinancedisputes.org.
URL: https://primefinancedisputes.org/

History Jan 2012. Registration: Netherlands. **Aims** Foster a more stable global economy and financial marketplace by reducing legal uncertainty and systemic risk, and promoting the rule of law. **Structure** Management Board; Advisory Board; Secretariat. **Activities** Conflict resolution; events/meetings; training/education. **Events** *Annual Conference* The Hague (Netherlands) 2020, *Annual Conference* The Hague (Netherlands) 2018. **Publications** *P.R.I.M.E. Finance Newsletter*. **Members** Jurisdictions (over 30). Membership countries not specified. **IGO Relations** Cooperating entities include: *Permanent Court of Arbitration (PCA, #18321)*. Observer rights with: *The Hague Conference on Private International Law (HCCH, #10850)*; *United Nations Commission on International Trade Law (UNCITRAL, #20531)*. **NGO Relations** Acknowledged by: *International Swaps and Derivatives Association (ISDA, #15638)*. Cooperating entities include: *European Judicial Training Network (EJTN, #07617)*; *International Bar Association (IBA, #12320)*.
[2020.05.17/XM7836/**F**]

♦ Pane per tutti (internationally oriented national body)
♦ Pan-Eurooppa Instituutti, Turku (internationally oriented national body)
♦ Paneuropa Union / see International Paneuropean Union (#14509)
♦ PAN Europe / see Pesticide Action Network Europe (#18338)
♦ Pan-European Ecological Network (see: #04881)

♦ Pan-European Federation of Consultants in Traditional Chinese Medicine (PEFCTCM) 18175

Fédération Pan-Européenne des Spécialistes de Médecine Traditionelle Chinoise

Contact 50 rue Jeanne d'Arc, 75013 Paris, France. E-mail: pefctcm@pefctcm.fr.
URL: http://pefctcm.fr/

History 2001. **Aims** Promote the quality of teaching, research and practice of Traditional Chinese Medicine (TCM) in Europe; promote the official integration of TCM into European medical practices; promote an authentic and high-quality Chinese medical culture in Europe. **Events** *International Congress of Traditional Medicine* Paris (France) 2005. [2021/AA2073/**D**]

♦ Pan European Federation of Regulatory Affairs Societies (inactive)
♦ Pan European Federation of TCM Societies (no recent information)
♦ Pan European ICT and eBusiness Network for SME / see European Digital SME Alliance (#06925)

♦ Pan-European Infrastructure for Ocean and Marine Data Management (SeaDataNet) 18176

Project Dir IDM/SISMER, Centre IFREMER de Brest, BP 70, 29280 Plouzané, France. T. +33298224216. Fax +33298224644.
URL: http://www.seadatanet.org/

History as in Integrated Infrastructure Initiative of the Sixth Framework Programme of *European Commission (EC, #06633)*. **Aims** Construct a standardized system for managing the large and diverse data sets collected by the oceanographic fleets and the new automatic observation systems. **Structure** Steering Committee; Project Coordination Group; Technical Task Team; Expert Advisory Board; Project Office. **Events** *Annual Plenary Meeting* Paris (France) 2010, *International conference on marine data and information systems* Paris (France) 2010. [2011/XJ2293/**E**]

♦ Pan-European Institute, Turku (internationally oriented national body)

♦ Pan-European Insurance Forum (PEIF) 18177

Sec Zurich Insurance Company Ltd, Austrasse 46, 8045 Zurich ZH, Switzerland. E-mail: peifsecretariat@zurich.com.
URL: http://www.peif.eu/

History Set up as a forum for CEOs of major European insurers. Registration: EU Transparency Register, No/ID: 03667978021-69, Start date: 8 Feb 2012. **Aims** Promote understanding and recognition of the role of the insurance business model within development of the European Union; provide members with the opportunity to discuss major policy and strategic issues affecting the insurance business in Europe and worldwide. **Structure** Rotating Chairmanship; Secretariat. **Languages** English. **Staff** 2.20 FTE, paid. Staff provided by company of Chair. **Finance** Sources: none. Members bear their own costs. **Activities** Research/documentation.
Members Full in 8 countries:
Austria, France, Germany, Italy, Netherlands, Spain, Switzerland, UK. [2020.10.22/XM4107/**F**]

♦ Pan-European Network for Care of Survivors after Childhood and Adolescent Cancer (PanCare) 18178

Communications Manager Jacobus Bellamylaan 16, 1401 AZ Bussum, Netherlands. E-mail: info@pancare.eu.
URL: http://www.pancare.eu/

History Mar 2008, Lund (Sweden). Registration: Handelsregister, No/ID: KVK 58922091, Start date: 2013, Netherlands; EU Transparency Register, No/ID: 755773342680-71, Start date: 11 May 2021. **Aims** Reduce frequency, severity and impact of late side-effects of the treatment of children and adolescents with cancer. **Structure** General Assembly; Executive Committee/Board. Committees; Groups; Taskforces. **Activities** Events/meetings; projects/programmes. **Events** *Meeting* Utrecht (Netherlands) 2021, *Meeting* Basel (Switzerland) 2019, *Meeting* Paris (France) 2018, *Meeting* Lisbon (Portugal) 2016, *Meeting* Vienna (Austria) 2015. **Publications** *PanCare Newsletter*. **NGO Relations** Partner of (2): *Childhood Cancer International Europe (CCI Europe, #03872)*; *SIOP Europe (SIOPE, #19288)*. [2021/XJ6597/**D**]

♦ Pan-European Organisation of Personal Injury Lawyers (PEOPIL) 18179

Administrator 515 Prinsengracht, 1016 HR Amsterdam, Netherlands. E-mail: admin@peopil.com.
URL: http://peopil.com/

History 1997. Registration: Handelsregister, Netherlands; EU Transparency Register, No/ID: 193897138136-26, Start date: 13 May 2020. **Aims** Support and encourage cooperation and networking of personal injury lawyers; promote access to the legal system for people suffering personal injury; promote higher standards of care and safety; promote proper and fair compensation for all personal injury cases. **Structure** Annual General Meeting; General Board; Executive Board; European Exchange Groups (7). **Languages** Dutch, English, French, German, Spanish. **Staff** 0.80 FTE, paid; 5.00 FTE, voluntary. **Finance** Sources: meeting proceeds; members' dues. **Activities** Events/meetings; networking/liaising. **Events** *Annual Conference* Malaga (Spain) 2021, *Annual Conference* Amsterdam (Netherlands) 2019, *Annual Conference* Paris (France) 2018, *Annual Conference* London (UK) 2017, *Annual Conference* Madrid (Spain) 2016. **Publications** *The Bulletin* (4 a year); *PEOPIL Newsletter* (irregular). *Fatal Accident Claims and Secondary Victims* (2005); *A Comparative Study of and Guide to: Right to Claim Full and Fair Compensation, Protection of Primary Victims, Recoverable Losses, Psychiatric Damage, Limitation Law and Harmonization* (2003).
Members Individuals (420) in 37 countries and territories:
Australia, Austria, Belgium, Brazil, Bulgaria, Canada, Croatia, Cyprus, Czechia, Denmark, England, Finland, France, Germany, Greece, Hungary, Iceland, Ireland, Israel, Italy, Malta, Netherlands, Northern Ireland, Norway, Panama, Poland, Portugal, Romania, Russia, Scotland, Serbia, Slovakia, Spain, Sweden, Switzerland, Türkiye, USA. [2023.02.14/XD7421/v/**D**]

♦ Pan-European Public Procurement Online / see Open Pan European Public Procurement Online (#17761)

♦ Pan-European Regional Council (PERC) 18180

Gen Sec International Trade Union House, Bd du Roi Albert II 5, 1210 Brussels, Belgium. T. +3222240321 – +3222240439. Fax +3222240454. E-mail: perc@ituc-csi.org.
URL: http://perc.ituc-csi.org/

History Founded 19 Mar 2007, Rome (Italy), within *International Trade Union Confederation (ITUC, #15708)*. **Aims** Promote the strategies, priorities and policies of ITUC and social development, consolidation of democracy and respect for human and *workers' rights* throughout the region. **Structure** General Assembly (at least every 4 years); Executive Committee; Secretariat, headed by Secretary-General of *European Trade Union Confederation (ETUC, #08927)*. **Languages** Bosnian, Croatian, English, Russian, Serbian. **Activities** Networking/liaising; capacity building. **Events** *Informal economy conference* Bratislava (Slovakia) 2009, *Youth conference* Brussels (Belgium) 2009, *South East European regional workshop* Kotor (Montenegro) 2009, *South-East European education meeting* Turin (Italy) 2009, *Seminar on the trade union response to the challenges of the crisis in the Baltic* Vilnius (Lithuania) 2009. **Members** National Centres affiliated to ITUC (90). Membership countries not specified. **NGO Relations** *Alter Summit*; *Eastern Partnership Civil Society Forum (EaP CSF, #05247)*. [2018.06.01/XM1592/**E**]

♦ Pan European Society for Neurology (inactive)
♦ Pan European Union / see International Paneuropean Union (#14509)
♦ Pan European Voice Conference (meeting series)
♦ PANFRICO – African Conference on the Integrated Family Planning, Nutrition and Parasite Control Project (meeting series)
♦ Pangaea Global AIDS Foundation (internationally oriented national body)
♦ Pangaea – Pangaea Global AIDS Foundation (internationally oriented national body)
♦ PANGEA Institute / see European Institute for Environmental Education, Interpretation and Training
♦ PANGEA Institute – European Institute for Environmental Education, Interpretation and Training (internationally oriented national body)
♦ **PANGF** Pacific Alliance of National Gymnastic Federations (#17925)
♦ **PANG** Pacific Network on Globalization (#17984)

♦ Pan-Iberican Association of Olympic Academies 18181

Association Panibérique des Académies Olympiques – Asociación Panibérica de Academias Olimpica (APAO)

SG Calle Arequipa 13, 28043 Madrid, Spain. T. +34913815500. Fax +34913819639. E-mail: pabgala@iies.es – academia@coe.es.
URL: http://www.coe.es/

History Founded 25 Jun 1988, as *Iberoamerican Association of Olympic Academies – Association ibéroaméricaine des académies olympiques – Asociación Iberoamericana de Academias Olimpicas (AIAO)*. Current title adopted 2002, when African National Olympic Academies joined. **Aims** Diffuse and defend fundamental principles of Olympic values using history, culture and languages as common ground. **Structure** Committee. **Languages** Portuguese, Spanish. **Staff** 3.00 FTE, voluntary. **Finance** Members' dues. Other sources: grants from Spanish Olympic Academy, Spanish Olympic Committee, IOC and official institutions. Annual budget: euro 50,000. **Activities** Events/meetings; knowledge management/information dissemination. **Events** *Biennial Congress* Cartagena de Indias (Colombia) 2016, *Biennial Congress* Lisbon (Portugal) 2014, *Extraordinary Congress* Guatemala (Guatemala) 2013, *Biennial Congress* Madrid (Spain) 2012, *Biennial Congress* Lima (Peru) 2010. **Publications** *History and Philosophy of Olympism*; *Olimpismo* by Conrado Durantez; *Origins of Olympism in Ibero-America*; *Pierre de Coubertin: Creed and Olympic Symbolism* by Conrado Durantez; *Pierre de Coubertin the Olympic Humanist*; *The Fire of Olympia* by D Conrado Durantez; *The Ideal of Pierre de Coubertin*; *The Olympic Ceremonies*; *The Panhiberican Associatin of Olympic Academies*. Congress proceedings.
Members Full in 27 countries and territories:
Andorra, Angola, Argentina, Bolivia, Brazil, Chile, Colombia, Costa Rica, Cuba, Dominican Rep, Ecuador, El Salvador, Equatorial Guinea, Guatemala, Honduras, Mexico, Mozambique, Nicaragua, Panama, Paraguay, Peru, Portugal, Puerto Rico, Sao Tomé-Principe, Spain, Uruguay, Venezuela. [2020.03.04/XD6904/**D**]

♦ PANIC – Particles and Nuclei International Conference (meeting series)
♦ PANiDMR – Pan-African Network in Defense of Migrants' Rights (unconfirmed)
♦ Pan Indian Ocean Science Association (inactive)
♦ PAN-International / see Pesticide Action Network (#18336)
♦ Pankosmion Diefnes Mitroon Politon / see Registre des Citoyens du Monde (#18822)
♦ **PANLAR** Pan American League of Associations for Rheumatology (#18118)
♦ PAN Latin America / see Red de Acción en Plaguicidas y sus Alternativas de América Latina (#18633)
♦ Pan-Latin Terminology Network (#18901)
♦ Pan para el Mundo (internationally oriented national body)
♦ Pan para el Mundo (internationally oriented national body)
♦ **PANNDT** Pan-American Federation For Nondestructive Testing (#18103)

♦ PAN-Nordic Card Association (PNC) 18182

CEO Stortorget 13 B, SE-211 22 Malmö, Sweden. T. +4640250778. E-mail: mail@pan-nordic.org.
URL: http://www.pan-nordic.org/

History Registered in accordance with Swedish law. EU Transparency Register: 23332008533-91. **Aims** Promote *payment* card solutions; work toward a single Nordic payment card market; further promote Nordic card payments interests in Europe. **Structure** General Meeting; Board of Directors; Administration.
Members Full in 4 countries:
Denmark, Finland, Norway, Sweden.
Also members in the Baltic states. Membership countries not specified.
NGO Relations Member of: *European Card Payment Association (ECPA, #06451)*. [2018.10.08/XM6236/**D**]

♦ Panos Institutes / see Panos Network (#18183)

♦ Panos Network 18183

Contact c/o Inst Panos Afrique de l'Ouest, 6 Rue Calmette, Boite Postale 21132, Dakar, Senegal. E-mail: info@panosnetwork.org.
URL: https://panosnetwork.org/about/

History May 1986, London (UK), as *Panos Institutes – Instituts Panos*. **Aims** Foster debate on under-reported, misrepresented or misunderstood *development* issues. **Structure** Council of 8 members. Network of autonomous national and regional "Panos Institutes" and country offices. /National Institutes/ (8): London (UK); Paris (France); Port-au-Prince (Haiti); Kathmandu (Nepal); Kampala (Uganda); Lusaka (Zambia); Dakar (Senegal); Vancouver (Canada). /Country Offices/ (12): Eastern Africa – Addis Ababa (Ethiopia), Khartoum (Sudan); West Africa – Bamako (Mali); Caribbean – Kingston (Jamaica), Washington DC (USA); South Asia – Karachi (Pakistan), Dhaka (Bangladesh), Delhi (India), Guwati (India), Colombo (Sri Lanka); Paris – Bujumbura (Burundi), Kinshasa (Congo DR). **Languages** English, French, Spanish. **Staff** 27.00 FTE, paid; 1.00 FTE, voluntary. **Finance** Supported by: governments of Denmark, Finland, Germany, Netherlands, Sweden, Switzerland, UK; NGOs, trusts and foundations. Donors in 2006 included: *ActionAid (#00087)*; *Catholic Organization for Relief and Development (Cordaid)*; *Comic Relief*; *DANIDA*; *Department for International Development (DFID, inactive)*; *Heinrich Böll Foundation*; *International Development Research Centre (IDRC, #13162)*; *Norwegian Agency for Development Cooperation (Norad)*; *Oxfam Novib*; *The Rockefeller Foundation (#18966)*; *Swedish International Development Cooperation Agency (Sida)*; *Swiss Agency for Development and Cooperation (SDC)*; *Trocaire – Catholic Agency for World Development*. **Activities** Knowledge management/information dissemination; events/meetings; advocacy/lobbying/activism. **Events** *Atelier sur l'étude de l'auditoire pour les radios rurales* Ouagadougou (Burkina Faso) 2001, *International media seminar* Cairo (Egypt) 1994, *International media seminar* Berlin (Germany) 1993, *Towards pluralism in the francophone African press colloquium* Paris (France) 1991, *Seminar* Khartoum (Sudan) 1988. **Publications** *Panos Features* (12 a year) – development issues; *PANOS Reports* (6 a year) – key global development issues; *Media Briefs*. Books; information dossiers; special reports. Information Services: *Centre for International ICT Policies West and Central Africa (CIPACO)*. **Information Services** *InterWorld Radio* – provides services for radio stations and broadcasters; *Panos Pictures* – documentary photographic library focusing on social, economic and political issues, with emphasis on environment and development; *Panos Radio South Asia* – capturing voices of the poor and marginalized on development issues. **Members** Not a membership organization. **Consultative Status** Consultative status granted from: *United Nations Population Fund (UNFPA, #20612)*. **IGO Relations** Consultative Status with: *ECOSOC (#05331)*. Accredited by: *United Nations Framework Convention on Climate Change – Secretariat (UNFCCC, #20564)*. Formal contacts with: *Global Information and Early Warning System on Food and Agriculture (GIEWS, #10416)*. **NGO Relations** Member of: *EarthAction (EA, #05159)*; *Environment Liaison Centre International (ELCI, no recent information)*; *Global Forum for Media Development (GFMD, #10375)*. Pano West Supports: *Southern African Network of AIDS Service Organizations (SANASO, see: #00272)*. Ethiopia National Institute is partner of: *Minority Rights Group International (MRG, #16820)*. [2019/XF2089/j/E]

- ♦ Pan Pacific Anterior Segment Society (inactive)
- ♦ Pan-Pacific Association of Applied Linguistics (internationally oriented national body)
- ♦ Pan Pacific Association of Input-Output Studies (internationally oriented national body)
- ♦ Pan Pacific Association of Private School Education (inactive)

♦ Pan-Pacific Business Association (PPBA) 18184

Pres Univ of Nebraska-Lincoln, Management Dept, 209 College of Business, Lincoln NE 68588-0491, USA. T. +14024723915. Fax +14024725855. E-mail: panpac@panpacificbusiness.org.
URL: http://www.panpacificbusiness.org/

History 1984. **Aims** Provide a forum for scholars, executives and government officials from Pacific-Rim countries to discuss important issues relating to a better quality of life in the region with emphasis on more effective utilization of human resources, technology and multilateral economic activities across borders. **Languages** English. **Staff** 4.00 FTE, voluntary. **Activities** Assists management scholars and practitioners in assessing the adaptability of various new management approaches to their own business environments, emphasizing networked organizations, e-globalization, productivity improvement, total quality management, employee empowerment, modern technology-based management systems and world-class organizations; helps business practitioners and scholars gain an understanding of the socio-cultural background of the economies and businesses in various Pacific countries; facilitates development of research and exchange of ideas for promoting international economic activities in the Pacific region; assists in establishment of export education programmes through cooperative arrangements with regional and world trade centers and bilateral and multilateral trade associations; organizes International Conference (annual). *'Service Business'* publication by Springer publishers is an affiliated journal. **Events** *Annual Conference* Seoul (Korea Rep) 2018, *Annual Conference* Lima (Peru) 2017, *Annual Conference* Miri (Malaysia) 2016, *Annual Conference* Hanoi (Vietnam) 2015, *Annual Conference* Sakai, Osaka (Japan) 2014. **Publications** *PPBA Newsletter*. Proceedings. **Members** Individuals (4,000) in 35 countries. Membership countries not specified. [2019/XD7628/v/D]

- ♦ Pan Pacific Congress of Real Estate Appraisers, Valuers and Counselors (meeting series)
- ♦ Pan-Pacific Connective Tissue Societies Symposium (meeting series)

♦ Pan Pacific Continence Society (PPCS) 18185

Pres Seoul Natl Univ Hosp, 101 Daehang-Ro Jongno-Gu, Seoul 110-744, Korea Rep. E-mail: sjo@snu.ac.kr.
SG Urology – Ansan Hospital, 123 Jeokgeum-ro, Danwon-gu, Ansan GYEONGGI 15355, Korea Rep. E-mail: kcsuro@gmail.com.
URL: http://www.ppcsoffice.org/

Events *Pan-Pacific Continence Society Meeting* Matsumoto (Japan) 2021, *Pan-Pacific Continence Society Meeting* Tokyo (Japan) 2020, *Meeting* Sydney, NSW (Australia) 2019, *Meeting* Seoul (Korea Rep) 2017, *Meeting* Taichung (Taiwan) 2014.
Members Full in 4 countries and territories:
China, Japan, Korea Rep, Taiwan. [2020/XJ1488/D]

- ♦ Pan-Pacific Implant Society / see Asia-Pacific Implant Society (#01929)
- ♦ Pan Pacific Public Relations Federation (inactive)
- ♦ Pan-Pacific Small Business Conference / see International Small Business Congress (#14875)

♦ Pan Pacific and South East Asia Women's Association (PPSEAWA) . 18186

Association des femmes du Pacifique et d'Asie du Sud-Est

Pres 9/116 Sai 2/2 Panta-ramindra Community, Panya-indra Road, Khannayo, Bangkok, 10230, Thailand. E-mail: info@ppseawa.org.
URL: http://www.ppseawa.org/

History 19 Aug 1928, Honolulu HI (USA), at 2nd Conference of Pan Pacific Women convened by *Pan Pacific Union (inactive)*, as *Pan Pacific Women's Association*. Present name adopted 28 Jan 1955, Manila (Philippines). **Aims** Strengthen the bonds of peace by fostering a better understanding and friendship among women of the Pacific and Southeast Asian areas; promote cooperation among women of these regions for study and improvement of social, economic and cultural conditions. **Structure** Conference (every 3 years); International Council. Standing Committees (3). **Languages** English. **Staff** Voluntary. **Finance** Sources: donations; members' dues. **Activities** Events/meetings; financial and/or material support; knowledge management/information dissemination. **Events** *Triennial Conference* Taipei (Taiwan) 2019, *International Mid-Term Council Meeting* Bangkok (Thailand) 2017, *International Conference* Kuala Lumpur (Malaysia) 2016, *Triennial Conference* Putrajaya (Malaysia) 2016, *Triennial Conference* Suva (Fiji) 2013. **Publications** *PPSEAWA Bulletin* (2-3 a year). Conference reports.
Members National organizations; Local groups; Individuals. Members in 17 countries and territories:
Australia, Canada, Cook Is, Fiji, Hawaii, India, Indonesia, Japan, Korea Rep, Malaysia, New Zealand, Pakistan, Samoa, Taiwan, Thailand, Tonga, USA.
Consultative Status Consultative status granted from: *ECOSOC (#05331)* (Special); *UNESCO (#20322)* (Consultative Status); *UNICEF (#20332)*. **IGO Relations** Accredited by: *United Nations Office at Vienna (UNOV, #20604)*. Associated with Department of Global Communications of the United Nations. **NGO Relations** Member of: *Geneva Global Health Hub (G2H2, #10122)*; *International Conference of NGOs (#12883)*; *Committee of NGOs on Human Rights, Geneva (#04275)*; *Conference of Non-Governmental Organizations in Consultative Relationship with the United Nations (CONGO, #04635)*; *NGO Committee on the Status of Women, Geneva (#17117)*; *NGO Committee to Stop Trafficking in Persons (NGO CSTIP)*; *NGO Committee on UNICEF (#17120)*; *Vienna NGO Committee on the Status of Women (#20775)*. Cooperative links with: *All India Women's Conference (AIWC, #00737)*; *All Pakistan Women's Association (APWA)*. [2019.12.24/XC3081/C]

♦ Pan-Pacific Surgical Association (PPSA) 18187

Association pan Pacifique de chirurgie

Contact Univ of Hawaii, John A Burns School of Medicine, 651 Ilalo St, Honolulu HI 96813, USA. T. +18085260303.
URL: http://panpacificsurgery.com/

History 1929, Honolulu HI (USA). Incorporated 5 Sep 1951, under Hawaiian law. **Aims** Facilitate exchange of medical and surgical knowledge; foster fellowship and understanding among surgeons of different specialties. **Structure** Congress (every 2 years); Board of Trustees; Council. **Languages** English. **Staff** 1.00 FTE, paid. **Finance** Members' dues; registration fees. **Activities** Operates *Living Endowment Fund*. Sponsors educational meetings and seminars. **Events** *Biennial congress* Honolulu, HI (USA) 2010, *Biennial Congress* Honolulu, HI (USA) 2008, *Biennial congress* Honolulu, HI (USA) 2006, *Biennial Congress* Honolulu, HI (USA) 2004, *Biennial Congress* Honolulu, HI (USA) 2002. **Publications** *PPSA Bulletin* (4 a year). Congress programs.
Members Regular and associate members 1,700 in 18 countries and territories:
Australia, Austria, Canada, China, Germany, Hong Kong, Indonesia, Iraq, Japan, Korea Rep, Mexico, Micronesia FS, Philippines, Saudi Arabia, Singapore, Taiwan, Thailand, UK. [2017/XD3082/D]

- ♦ Pan Pacific Suzuki Association (internationally oriented national body)

♦ Pan-Pacific Swimming Association (PPSA) 18188

Address not obtained.

History 1984. **Activities** Organizes the Pan Pacific Swimming Championship.
Members in 4 countries:
Australia, Canada, Japan, USA. [2014/XD9475/D]

- ♦ Pan Pacific Union (inactive)
- ♦ Pan Pacific Women's Association / see Pan Pacific and South East Asia Women's Association (#18186)
- ♦ **PAN** Pandemic Action Network (#18173)
- ♦ PANPA – Pacific Area Newspaper Publishers Association (inactive)
- ♦ PAN – Peace Action Network (internationally oriented national body)
- ♦ **PANPESAS** Confederación Panamericana de Levantamiento de Pesas (#18137)
- ♦ **PAN** Pesticide Action Network (#18336)
- ♦ **PAN** Planet Art Network (#18380)
- ♦ PAN and PRO EUROPE (inactive)
- ♦ PAN-RADO / see Panamerican Regional Antidoping Organization (#18125)
- ♦ **PAN-RADO** Panamerican Regional Antidoping Organization (#18125)
- ♦ **PANRS** Pan-Arab NeuroRadiology Society (#18150)
- ♦ **PANS** Pan Arab Neurosurgical Society (#18151)
- ♦ Panthera (internationally oriented national body)
- ♦ PANUSP / see Pan African Network of People with Psychosocial Disabilities (#18056)
- ♦ **PANUSP** Pan African Network of People with Psychosocial Disabilities (#18056)
- ♦ **PANVET** Asociación Panamericana de Ciencias Veterinarias (#02287)
- ♦ PAOA – Pan American Odontological Association (inactive)
- ♦ **PAOA** Pan Arab Orthopaedic Association (#18152)
- ♦ PAOC – Pan African Ornithological Congress (meeting series)
- ♦ Pão para o Mundo (internationally oriented national body)
- ♦ PAO – Planetary Activation Organization (internationally oriented national body)
- ♦ PAORP-VWC – Pan African Organisation for Research and Protection of Violence on Women and Children (internationally oriented national body)
- ♦ **PAOS** Pan-Arab Osteoporosis Society (#18153)
- ♦ PAPAIOS – Pan Pacific Association of Input-Output Studies (internationally oriented national body)
- ♦ PAPA – Pan-African Productivity Association (no recent information)
- ♦ PAPA – Parliamentarians' Alliance for Peace in Asia (unconfirmed)
- ♦ **PAPA** Phosphoric Acid and Phosphates Producers Association (#18363)
- ♦ PAPCHILD – Pan Arab Project for Child Development (no recent information)
- ♦ **PAPC** Pan-African Association for Port Cooperation (#18038)
- ♦ PAPE – Pan Pacific Association of Private School Education (inactive)
- ♦ PaPE – Phonetics and Phonology in Europe (meeting series)

♦ Paper 4 All 18189

Chairman 25 rue Michel-Ange, 75016 Paris, France.
CEO address not obtained.
URL: http://www.paper4all.org/

History 2006. UK Registered Charity: 1116888. Registered in accordance with US law: 109090026. Registered in accordance with French law: 20020080003. **Aims** Help *children* learn in better conditions in Burkina Faso; provide academic resources to improve learning conditions of children. **Languages** English, French. **Staff** 10.00 FTE, voluntary. **Finance** Donations. Budget (2014): about euro 10,000. **Activities** Financial and/or material support. Active in: Burkina Faso, Cameroon, Guinea. **IGO Relations** Burkina Faso Ministry of Education; French Embassy, Burkina Faso. [2014.06.21/XJ5000/F]

♦ Paper by Nature 18190

Contact address not obtained. E-mail: info@paperbynature.com.
Registered Address Avenue Louise 250 – Box 81, 1050 Brussels, Belgium.
URL: http://www.paperbynature.com/

History May 2008. Also referred to as *Paper by Nature Alliance*. Registered in accordance with Belgian law. **Aims** Promote environmentally friendly practices in the paper converting industry and the responsible use of paper amongst consumers. **Structure** General Assembly. Board of Directors of 4. Ethics Committee. **Languages** English. **Activities** Developed *'Paper by Nature Eco-label'*.
Members Full in 5 countries:
Belgium, Estonia, Finland, France, Sweden. [2011/XJ2395/y/D]

- ♦ Paper by Nature Alliance / see Paper by Nature (#18190)

♦ Paper and Related Industries Marketing Association (PRIMA) 18191

Association des industries du papier

Exec Dir Hauptplatz 3, 8010 Graz, Austria. T. +436643457593. Fax +433165737206.
Conference: https://www.prima-paper.com/home

History 1970, as a Component Industrial Division of *Federation of European Marketing Research Associations (FEMRA, inactive)*. Separate secretariat set up Nov 1991. Also referred to as *PRIMA – The Paper Network*. Registered in accordance with Belgian law. **Aims** Provide a forum where various representatives of the forest industry can meet and exchange views on trends and tendencies, current and future developments, products and consumer behaviour, markets and distribution, in order to improve knowledge and stimulate new ideas and initiatives. **Structure** General Assembly (annual, at PRIMA Conference); Executive Committee; Management Council. **Languages** English. **Staff** 1.00 FTE, paid. **Finance** Members' dues. **Activities** Events/meetings. **Events** *Annual Conference* Amsterdam (Netherlands) 2022, *Annual Conference* Berlin (Germany) 2019, *Annual Conference* Amsterdam (Netherlands) 2018, *Annual Conference* Berlin (Germany) 2017, *Annual Conference* Vienna (Austria) 2016. **Publications** *PRIMA Membership Directory* (annual) – online. Annual report.
Members Individual and Corporate (132) in 18 countries:
Austria, Belgium, Canada, Czechia, Denmark, Finland, France, Germany, Italy, Netherlands, Norway, Romania, Spain, Sweden, Switzerland, UK, USA. [2022/XE0937/t/D]

♦ PapiNet 18192

Address not obtained.
URL: http://www.papinet.org/

History Founded 2000. A grouping of the type *European Economic Interest Grouping (EEIG, #06960)*. **Aims** Develop, maintain and promote implementation of *electronic transaction standards* so as to facilitate exchange of information among those engaged in buying, selling or distributing forest, *paper* or *wood products*. **Structure** Executive Committee; Committees (3); Management Council. **Languages** English. **Staff** 1.00 FTE, paid; 20.00 FTE, voluntary. **Finance** Members' dues. **Activities** Knowledge management/information dissemination. [2022/XF6665/F]

- ♦ PAPNS – Pan Arab Pediatric Neurosurgery Society (unconfirmed)
- ♦ PAPOS – Pan African Psycho-Oncology Society (no recent information)
- ♦ **PAP** Pan-African Parliament (#18058)
- ♦ **PAP/RAC** Priority Actions Programme / Regional Activity Centre (#18501)
- ♦ PAPRS – Pan-African Association of Plastic and Reconstructive Surgeons (inactive)
- ♦ **PAPSA** Pan African Pediatric Surgical Association (#18059)
- ♦ PAPSBRS – Pan Asian-Pacific Skin Barrier Research Society (unconfirmed)
- ♦ **PAPS** Pacific Association of Pediatric Surgeons (#17933)
- ♦ **PAPS** Peregrinatio ad Petri Sedem (#18309)
- ♦ Päpstlicher Rat zur Förderung der Einheit der Christen (#18446)
- ♦ Päpstliches Institut für Christliche Archäologie (#18449)
- ♦ **PAPU** Pan African Postal Union (#18060)
- ♦ **PAPU** Pan-African Psychology Union (#18061)
- ♦ **PAQS** Pacific Association of Quantity Surveyors (#17934)
- ♦ Parabadminton World Federation (inactive)
- ♦ PARABERE (unconfirmed)
- ♦ **PARACON** Pan-African Rabies Control Network (#18062)
- ♦ **ParadigMS** ParadigMS Private Foundation (#18193)

♦ ParadigMS Private Foundation (ParadigMS) 18193

Contact Silversquare Europe – LAUREA, Square Meeûs 35, 1000 Brussels, Belgium. T. +32478802167.
Registered Address Rue Washington 40, 1050 Brussels, Belgium.
URL: https://paradigms.foundation/

History Registration: Banque-Carrefour des Entreprises, No/ID: 0633.545.305, Start date: 6 Jul 2015, Belgium. **Aims** Improve multiple sclerosis patient care by translating science into clinically relevant continued medical education (CME) for neurologists and residents. **Structure** Board of Directors; Executive Committee. **NGO Relations** Member of (1): *Federation of European and International Associations Established in Belgium (FAIB, #09508).* [2023/AA3232/f/**F**]

♦ Parallel CFD – International Conference on Parallel Computational Fluid Dynamics (meeting series)
♦ Parallel Corpora: Creations and Applications International Symposium (meeting series)
♦ **PARA** Pan American Rugby Association (#18127)
♦ Parapsychological Association / see Parapsychology Foundation

♦ Parapsychological Association 18194

Exec Dir PO Box 14884, Columbus OH 14884, USA. T. +16146002195.
URL: https://parapsych.org/

History 19 Jun 1957, Durham, NC (USA). Registration: 501(c)(3) non-profit, USA. **Aims** Promote scholarship and scientific inquiry into currently unexplained aspects of human experience; disseminate responsible information to the wider public and to the scientific community. **Structure** Board of Directors. **Activities** Awards/prizes/competitions; events/meetings; training/education. **Events** *Annual Convention* Paris (France) 2019. **Publications** *Journal of Parapsychology*; *Mindfield: The Bulletin of the Parapsychological Association*. **Members** Individuals. Membership countries not specified. [2020/AA0891/v/**C**]

♦ Parapsychology Foundation (internationally oriented national body)
♦ Parasitological Society of Southern Africa (internationally oriented national body)
♦ Parasitologiese Vereniging van Suidelike Afrika (internationally oriented national body)
♦ Parat der Karibik (#03482)
♦ PARBICA – Pacific Regional Branch of the International Council on Archives (see: #12996)
♦ PARC / see Program for the Advancement of Research on Conflict and Collaboration
♦ **PARCA** Pan American Railway Congress Association (#18124)
♦ Parc commun de wagons de marchandises (inactive)
♦ PARCC – Program for the Advancement of Research on Conflict and Collaboration (internationally oriented national body)
♦ Parcel Post Agreement (1911 treaty)
♦ Parcel Post Convention (1911 treaty)
♦ PARCOM – Paris Commission (inactive)
♦ PARCON – Pacific Rim Consortium in Energy, Combustion, and the Environment (inactive)
♦ PARC – Pacific Asia Resource Centre (internationally oriented national body)
♦ **PARC** Pan-African Reconciliation Council (#18063)
♦ **PARC** Pan American Racquetball Confederation (#18123)

♦ Parc des trois pays – Espace ouvert sans frontières 18195

Dreiländerpark – Offener Raum ohne Grenzen – Drielandenpark – Open Ruimte zonder Grenzen

Project Leader c/o Euregio Meuse-Rhine, Gosperstrasse 42, 4700 Eupen, Belgium. T. +3287789630. Fax +3287789633. E-mail: info@euregio-mr.eu – 3lp@euregio-mr.eu.
URL: http://www.drielandenpark.eu/

History Established Jun 1993, Maastricht (Netherlands), when officially launched as *MHAL Perspective*, to explore the possibility of founding a region comprising the transborder urban conurbations of Maastricht (Netherlands)/Heerlen (Netherlands), Hasselt (Belgium)/Genk (Belgium), Aachen (Germany)/Liège. Facilitated with the aid of *Benelux Union (#03207)*, which provided secretariat and translation facilities. Also referred to initially as *Pays sans frontières*. **Aims** Preserve and develop the (unbuilt) open area, especially the quality of the *landscape*, between and around the "MHAL cities": Maastricht (Netherlands), Hasselt (Belgium), Heerlen (Netherlands), Aachen (Germany), Liège (Belgium); formulate a development strategy for the area; translate this into specific themes and cross-border implementation projects in the field of spatial planning, sustainable agriculture, landscape and *nature* management and (eco) *tourism*. **Structure** Steering Committee; Project Group; Working Groups. **Languages** Dutch, French, German. **Staff** 0.50 FTE, paid. **Finance** Contributing partners donate euro 10,000 each: Province of Limburg (Netherlands); Flemish region (Belgium); Walloon region (Belgium); Stadt/Staedteregion Aachen/Bezirksregierung Köln (Germany). Budget (annual): about euro 50,000. **Activities** Knowledge management/information dissemination; networking/liaising.
Members Partners (9) in 4 countries and territories:
Belgium/Flemish Region, Germany, Netherlands, Wallonia.
Included in the above, 2 regional organizations:
Benelux Union (#03207); Euregio Meuse-Rhine. [2023/XF2841/**F***]

♦ **PaRD** International Partnership on Religion and Sustainable Development (#14524)
♦ PAREA – Psychedelic Access and Research European Alliance (unconfirmed)
♦ Parent Cooperative Preschools International (internationally oriented national body)

♦ Parenteral Drug Association (PDA) 18196

Pres Bethesda Towers, 4350 East West Hwy, Ste 600, Bethesda MD 20814, USA. T. +13016565900. Fax +13019860296. E-mail: info@pda.org.
PDA Europe Am Borsigturm 60, 13507 Berlin, Germany. T. +493043655080. E-mail: info-europe@pda.org.
URL: http://www.pda.org/

History 1946, USA. *PDA Foundation* created in 1997. *PDA Europe*, a subsidiary, was founded in 2006 and is registered in accordance with German law. **Aims** Advance pharmaceutical and biopharmaceutical technology internationally by promoting scientifically sound and practical technical information and education for industry and regulatory agencies. **Structure** Board; *PDA Europe*; *Foundation for Pharmaceutical Education, Training, and Research (PDA Foundation)*. **Languages** English. **Activities** Events/meetings; training/education. **Events** *Parenteral Packaging Conference* Italy 2023, *Good Aseptic Manufacturing Conference* Leipzig (Germany) 2023, *Annual Meeting* New Orleans, LA (USA) 2023, *Aseptic Processing of Biopharmaceuticals Conference* Incheon (Korea Rep) 2022, *Pharmaceutical Microbiology Conference* Washington, DC (USA) 2022. **Publications** *PDA Journal of Pharmaceutical Science and Technology*; *PDA Letter*. Annual report.
Members Chapters in 14 countries and territories:
Australia, Canada, France, India, Ireland, Israel, Italy, Japan, Korea Rep, Puerto Rico, Singapore, Taiwan, UK, USA. [2020/XM1838/**D**]

♦ Parenteral and Enteral Nutrition Society of Asia (PENSA) 18197

Contact Research Ctr for Nutrition Support, Fact of Medicine, 4th floor Dept of Nutrition Bldg, Siriraj Hosp, Plannok Rd Bangkoknoi, Bangkok, 10700, Thailand. T. +6624197740 – +6624197741. Fax +6624129841. E-mail: pensacenter@gmail.com.
URL: http://www.pensa-online.org/

History 6 May 1995, Chiang Rai (Thailand). **Aims** Foster research and development in nutritional support in Asian countries; provide a forum to address and exchange clinical experiences and scientific data in nutritional support, oriented at improvement in all patient care; propagate, by means of providing education, the awareness of physicians of the importance of nutritional support in hospitalized patients; create good relationships among international nutritional societies; perform activities concerning nutritional support for hospitalized patients without political involvement. **Structure** Scientific meeting (annual); Organizing committee; Headquarters Committee; Scientific Committee. **Languages** English. **Staff** 5 doctors, 5 councillors, 2 coordinator nurses – all part-time and voluntary. **Finance** Contributions from Organizing Committee. **Activities** Events/meetings. **Events** *Congress* Hyderabad (India) 2022, *Congress* Bangkok (Thailand) 2021, *Congress* Wan Chai (Hong Kong) 2019, *Congress* Seoul (Korea Rep) 2018, *Congress* Nagoya (Japan) 2015. **Publications** *PENSA Newsletter*.
Members Individuals interested in nutritional support and parenteral and enteral nutrition societies of all Asian countries. Full in 10 countries and territories:
China, Hong Kong, India, Indonesia, Japan, Korea Rep, Malaysia, Philippines, Taiwan, Thailand. [2019/XD6831/**D**]

♦ Parents International (IPA) 18198

Exec Dir Van Leijenberghlaan 415-1, 1082 GL Amsterdam, Netherlands. E-mail: office@parentsinternational.org – director@parentsinternational.org.
Registered Address Snip 41, 2171 KT Sassenheim, Netherlands.
URL: https://parentsinternational.org/

History Former names and other names: *Stichting International Parents Alliance (Stichting IPA)* – legal name. Registration: Handelsregister, No/ID: KVK 70900000, Netherlands. **Aims** Support parents around the world to become game-changers by helping their children to grow up happy and healthy 21st century citizens. **Structure** Board; Advisory Board. **Activities** Advocacy/lobbying/activism; capacity building; guidance/assistance/consulting; projects/programmes; research and development; training/education. **Events** *Parent Summit* Netherlands 2022, *Parent Summit* Netherlands 2021. **Consultative Status** Consultative status granted from: *Council of Europe (CE, #04881)* (Participatory Status). **NGO Relations** Member of (1): *Conference of INGOs of the Council of Europe (#04607).* [2023/AA2428/**D**]

♦ **PARIMA** Pan-Asia Risk and Insurance Management Association (#18168)
♦ Pari Mutuel Europe / see European Pari Mutuel Association (#08143)
♦ Paris, 1970 – Convention on the Means of Prohibiting and Preventing the Illicit Import, Export and Transfer of Ownership of Cultural Property (1970 treaty)
♦ **PARIS21** Partnership in Statistics for Development in the 21st Century (#18243)
♦ Paris Agreement (2015 treaty)
♦ Paris Agreement – Agreement on a Comprehensive Political Settlement of the Cambodia Conflict (1991 treaty)
♦ Paris anti-war pact – General Treaty for Renunciation of War as an Instrument of National Policy (1928 treaty)
♦ Paris Club / see Paris Club of Industrial Country Creditors (#18199)

♦ Paris Club of Industrial Country Creditors 18199

Address not obtained.
URL: http://www.clubdeparis.org/

History 1956, as an informal grouping of banks which meets from time to time. No permanent location between meetings. Also referred to as *Paris Club – Club de Paris*. **Aims** Provide a forum for debtor countries – particularly severely indebted low-income countries (SILICs) – to negotiate rescheduling of *debt* service payments or loans extended or guaranteed by governments or official agencies of participating creditor countries; help restore normal trade and project *finance* to debtor countries. **Structure** No statutes or official rules and procedures. **Activities** Meetings convened at request of debtor countries are chaired by a senior official of the French Treasury. In the framework of the Club, official creditors respond to needs of debtor countries, such as in the case of *'Multiyear rescheduling agreements (MYRAs)'*. A standard approach has evolved based on experience, precedent and the objective of equitable treatment of all creditors. Debt relief covers service on all bilateral official loans, including concessional credits and officially guaranteed export credits; previously rescheduled debt is consolidated when circumstances require. Relief is normally restricted to current maturities and typically rescheduling covers 80-100%, the consolidated portion being paid over 8-10 years with a grace period of 4-5 years. The Paris (France) Club requires that debtor countries take prompt and effective measures to address their underlying economic problems, usually demanding an IMF-supported adjustment programme that will give a country access to the upper credit tranches. Renegotiation of debt owed to commercial banks – often syndicated loans, uninsured trade or project finance – is achieved by representing the sometimes hundreds of banks by a small Advisory Committee which negotiates with the debtor country. In these cases interest cannot be rescheduled and interest arrears have to be settled before rescheduling agreements become effective. **Events** *Meeting on Bolivia* Paris (France) 1998, *Meeting* Paris (France) 1998, *Meeting* 1994. **Members** Countries of OECD and other creditor countries with similar claims. **IGO Relations** Other observers: *African Development Bank (ADB, #00283)*; *Asian Development Bank (ADB, #01422)*; *Caribbean Development Bank (CDB, #03492)*; *Inter-American Development Bank (IDB, #11427)*; *International Bank for Reconstruction and Development (IBRD, #12317)*; *UNCTAD (#20285)*. [2008/XF0591/ct/**F**]

♦ Paris Commission (inactive)
♦ Paris Convention – Convention on the Prevention of Marine Pollution from Land-based Sources (1974 treaty)
♦ Paris Convention for the Protection of Industrial Property, 1883 (1883 treaty)
♦ Paris Convention on Third Party Liability in the Field of Nuclear Energy (1960 treaty)
♦ Paris Foreign Mission Society (religious order)
♦ Paris Institute of Political Studies (internationally oriented national body)
♦ Paris Memorandum of Understanding on Port State Control (1982 treaty)
♦ Paris MOU – Paris Memorandum of Understanding on Port State Control (1982 treaty)
♦ Paris Peace Forum (internationally oriented national body)
♦ Paris Peace Forum Association / see Forum de Paris sur la Paix
♦ **Paris Union** International Union for the Protection of Industrial Property (#15805)

♦ Parkour Earth 18200

Contact 10 Queen St Place, London, EC4R 1AG, UK. E-mail: info@parkour.earth.
URL: https://parkour.earth/

History Memorandum of Association signed Jul 2017. Full title: *Parkour Earth – International Federation for Parkour/Freerunning/art du Déplacement*. Registered in accordance with UK law. **Structure** General Meeting; Board. **Languages** English, French.
Members Full in 2 countries:
New Zealand, UK.
Affiliate in 5 countries:
Australia, France, Korea Rep, Poland, South Africa.
NGO Relations Member of: *Sport Integrity Global Alliance (SIGA, #19925).* [2018/XM7092/**C**]

♦ Parkour Earth – International Federation for Parkour/Freerunning/art du Déplacement / see Parkour Earth (#18200)
♦ **PARLACEN** Parlamento Centroamericano (#18201)
♦ Parlaimint na hEorpa (#08146)
♦ Parlament Europejski (#08146)
♦ Parlament Ewropew (#08146)
♦ Parlamento Amazónico (#00767)
♦ Parlamento Andino (#00820)

♦ Parlamento Centroamericano (PARLACEN) 18201

Central American Parliament

Secretariat 12 avenida 33-04, zona 05, 01005 Guatemala, Guatemala. T. +50224244600. Fax +50224244610. E-mail: guatemala@parlacen.int.
URL: https://parlacen.int

History 1989. Founded within the framework of *Organization of Central American States (ODECA, inactive)*, currently replaced by *Central American Integration System (#03671)* in the run-up to *Central American Common Market (CACM, #03666)*. **Events** *Europe-Latin America interparliamentary conference* Lima (Peru) 2005, *Europe-Latin America interparliamentary conference* Brussels (Belgium) 2003, *Europe-Latin America interparliamentary conference* Valparaiso (Chile) 2001, *Europe-Latin America interparliamentary conference* Brussels (Belgium) 1999.
Members Representatives of 5 countries:
El Salvador, Guatemala, Honduras, Nicaragua, Panama.
IGO Relations Formal agreement with: *UNESCO (#20322)*. Observer to: *Sistema Económico Latinoamericano (SELA, #19294)*. Cooperates with: *OAS (#17629)*. Member of: *Euro-Latin American Parliamentary Assembly (EUROLAT, #05700)*. **NGO Relations** Associate member of: *Inter-Parliamentary Union (IPU, #15961)*. [2021/XF0577/**F***]

♦ Parlamento del Clima (#04019)
♦ Parlamento del Clima – Legisladores trabajando a nivel mundial para combatir el cambio climatico / see Climate Parliament (#04019)

♦ Parlamento Europeo (#08146)
♦ Parlamento Europeo, Grupo Liberal, Democratico y Reformista / see Renew Europe (#18840)
♦ Parlamento Europeo – Grupo del Partido Europeo de los Liberales, Demócratas y Reformistas / see Renew Europe (#18840)
♦ Parlamento Europeo, Gruppo Liberale e Democratico Riformatore / see Renew Europe (#18840)
♦ Parlamento Europeo – Gruppo del Partito Europeo dei Liberali, Democratici e Riformatori / see Renew Europe (#18840)
♦ Parlamento Europeu (#08146)
♦ Parlamento Europeu, Grupo Liberal, Democratico e Reformista / see Renew Europe (#18840)
♦ Parlamento Indígena y Afrodescendiente de América / see Parlamento Indígena de América (#18202)

♦ Parlamento Indígena de América (PIA) 18202

American Indigenous Parliament

Secretariat address not obtained. E-mail: mediospiagpv@gmail.com.
URL: https://www4.congreso.gob.pe/grupo_parlamentario/gp_indigena/PIA.htm

History 31 Aug 1988. Established during 2nd 'Encuentro de Legisladores Indigenas'. Former names and other names: *Parlamento Indígena y Afrodescendiente de América (PIA)* – alias. **Structure** Plenary Assembly; Board of Directors; Permanent Secretariat. Commissions (8): Education; Finance; Environment; Health; Human Rights; Law; Politics; Women. **Events** *Assembly* Mexico City (Mexico) 1999. **IGO Relations** Formal agreement with: *UNESCO (#20322).* [2022/XF6441/**F***]

♦ Parlamento Latinoamericano (PARLATINO) 18203

Parlement latinoaméricain – Latin American Parliament

Headquarters Ave Principal de Amador, Edif Parlamento Latinoamericano, Casilla 1527 Ap Zona 4, Panama, Panamá, Panama PANAMá, Panama. T. +5072019000. E-mail: info@parlatino.org.
URL: http://www.parlatino.org/

History 11 Dec 1964, Lima (Peru). Constitution adopted 18 Jul 1965, Lima. **Aims** Promote Latin American *integration* on the basis of representative democracy, social justice and human rights; encourage development of the Latin American community; combat *imperialism* and *colonialism* in Latin America; contribute to establishment of international peace, justice and security. **Structure** Assembly (annual); Executive Board; Permanent Commissions; Secretary-General. **Activities** Instrumental in setting up: *Instituto de Relaciones Europeo-Latinoamericanas (IRELA, inactive); Universidad Latinoamericana y del Caribe (ULAC, no recent information).* **Events** *Latin America and Caribbean Regional Seminar on the Sustainable Development Goals* Panama (Panama) 2016, *Europe-Latin America interparliamentary conference* Lima (Peru) 2005, *Preparatory seminar for the governmental conference on renewable energy* Santiago (Chile) 2004, *Europe-Latin America interparliamentary conference* Brussels (Belgium) 2003, *Europe-Latin America interparliamentary conference* Valparaiso (Chile) 2001.
Members Parliamentarians from 23 Latin American parliamentary democracies:
Argentina, Aruba, Bolivia, Brazil, Chile, Colombia, Costa Rica, Cuba, Curaçao, Dominican Rep, Ecuador, El Salvador, Guatemala, Honduras, Mexico, Nicaragua, Panama, Paraguay, Peru, St Maarten, Suriname, Uruguay, Venezuela.
Consultative Status Consultative status granted from: *UNCTAD (#20285)* (General Category). **IGO Relations** Instrumental in setting up: *Comunidad de Estados Latinoamericanos y Caribeños (CELAC, #04432).* Formal agreement with: *UNESCO (#20322).* Member of: *Euro-Latin American Parliamentary Assembly (EUROLAT, #05700).* Observer statuts to: *ECOSOC (#05331).* Cooperates with: *OAS (#17629).* Cooperation agreement with: *International Institute for Democracy and Electoral Assistance (International IDEA, #13872).* Agreement with: *Council of Europe (CE, #04881).* Accredited by: *United Nations Framework Convention on Climate Change – Secretariat (UNFCCC, #20564).* Observer to: *Sistema Económico Latinoamericano (SELA, #19294);* General Assembly of: *United Nations (UN, #20515).* **NGO Relations** Regular links with: *Inter-Parliamentary Union (IPU, #15961).* Member of: *Socialist International (SI, #19340).* [2022/XF2885/**F***]

♦ Parlamento do MERCOSUL (#18204)
♦ Parlamento do MERCOSUL (#18205)

♦ Parlamento de MERCOSUR (PARLASUR) 18204

Mercosur Parliament – Parlamento do MERCOSUL

Secretariat Dr Pablo de Maria 827, 11200 Montevideo, Uruguay.
URL: https://www.parlamentomercosur.org/

History 2007. **Structure** Each member country has 18 representatives.
Members Governments of 5 countries:
Argentina, Brazil, Paraguay, Uruguay, Venezuela.
IGO Relations Member of: *Euro-Latin American Parliamentary Assembly (EUROLAT, #05700).* [2021/XJ0186/**F***]

♦ Parlamento del MERCOSUR 18205

MERCOSUR Parliament – Parlamento do MERCOSUL

Administrative Sec Dr Pablo de Maria 827, CP 11200 Montevideo, Uruguay. T. +59824109797. E-mail: seccomunicacion@parlamentomercosur.org.
URL: https://www.parlamentomercosur.org/

History Proposed at XXVIIth Meeting of *Southern Common Market (#19868)* Heads of State, 17 Dec 2004, Ouro Preto (Brazil), when *Comisión Parlamentaria Conjunta del MERCOSUR (CPCM, inactive)* was instructed to write Protocol establishing the Mercosur Parliament. Protocol signed by Presidents of Argentina, Brazil, Paraguay and Uruguay, 9 Dec 2005. Officially replaced CPC at 1st session, 7 May 2007.
Members Full (5):
Argentina, Brazil, Paraguay, Uruguay, Venezuela. [2021/XJ1213/**E***]

♦ Parlamento Mondiale per la Sicurezza e la Pace (internationally oriented national body)
♦ Parlamento Mundial para Segurança e Paz (internationally oriented national body)
♦ Parlamento Mundial para Seguridad y Paz (internationally oriented national body)
♦ Parlamento Negro de las Américas (unconfirmed)
♦ Parlamento Pan-africano (#18058)
♦ Parlamentul European (#08146)
♦ Parlamentul International pentru Securitate si Pace (internationally oriented national body)

♦ ParlAmericas 18206

Dir Gen 703 – 155 Queen St, Ottawa ON K1P 6L1, Canada. T. +16139478999. E-mail: info@parlamericas.org.
URL: http://www.parlamericas.org/

History Mar 2000, Washington, DC (USA). Established when Steering Committee was created. Inaugural meeting, Mar 2001, Ottawa ON (Canada). Former names and other names: *Inter-Parliamentary Forum of the Americas (FIPA)* – former (Mar 2000 to Sep 2011); *Forum interparlementaire des Amériques* – former (Mar 2000 to Sep 2011); *Foro Interparlamentario de las Américas* – former (Mar 2000 to Sep 2011); *Fórum Interparlamentar das Américas* – former (Mar 2000 to Sep 2011). **Aims** Support members' commitment to promote parliamentary participation in the inter-American system; develop inter-parliamentary dialogue on issues of importance to the hemisphere by encouraging the sharing of experience and best practice amongst members and by working to strengthen the role of legislatures in *democratic* development; promote *harmonization* of *legislation* and hemispheric integration as instruments of sustainable and harmonious *development* in the region. **Structure** Plenary Assembly (annual); Board of Directors; Executive Committee; International Secretariat located in Ottawa (Canada); Permanent Group of Women Parliamentarians; Board Standing Committees; other working groups. **Languages** English, French, Portuguese, Spanish. **Staff** 4.00 FTE, paid. **Finance** Support from: member states; Foreign Affairs, Trade and Development Canada; international organizations. **Activities** Working Groups addressing issues such as: citizen security; trade; gender equality; fight against terrorism; poverty reduction; fiscal affairs; foreign debt; fight against drug trafficking; food security; international migration; human rights; economic and financial crisis; environment. Organizes: Plenary Assembly; meetings of the Group of Women Parliamentarians; capacity-building training and workshops for parliamentarians. **Events** *Plenary Assembly* Bogota (Colombia) 2022, *Plenary Assembly* 2021, *Plenary Assembly* 2020, *Plenary Assembly* Asunción (Paraguay) 2019, *Plenary Assembly* Victoria, BC (Canada) 2018. **Publications** *ParlAmericas Express* (4 a year) – electronic newsletter. Various Reports resulting from Plenary Assemblies, Women's Group Gatherings and parliamentary workshops. **Information Services** *News of the Americas* – online, in 4 languages.
Members National legislatures of the 35 states of the Americas:
Antigua-Barbuda, Argentina, Bahamas, Barbados, Belize, Bolivia, Brazil, Canada, Chile, Colombia, Costa Rica, Cuba, Dominica, Dominican Rep, Ecuador, El Salvador, Grenada, Guatemala, Guyana, Haiti, Honduras, Jamaica, Mexico, Nicaragua, Panama, Paraguay, Peru, St Kitts-Nevis, St Lucia, St Vincent-Grenadines, Suriname, Trinidad-Tobago, Uruguay, USA, Venezuela.
IGO Relations Memorandum of Understanding with: *OAS (#17629).* **NGO Relations** Observer status with: *Inter-Parliamentary Union (IPU, #15961).* [2022/XK2134/**F***]

♦ **PARLASUR** Parlamento de MERCOSUR (#18204)
♦ **PARLATINO** Parlamento Latinoamericano (#18203)

♦ Parlement Africain de la Société Civile (PASOCI) 18207

African Parliament of Civil Society (APCS)

Chairperson 23 BP 4466, Abidjan 23, Côte d'Ivoire. T. +2250708070824. E-mail: secretariat@parlementafricain.com.
Guinea Office: https://parlementafricain-osc.org/

History 8 Nov 2008, Accra (Ghana). **Aims** Promote democracy, human rights, correct governance and the fight against poverty. **Structure** Executive Committee. **Languages** English, French, Spanish. **Staff** 11.00 FTE, paid; 55.00 FTE, voluntary. **Finance** Sources: donations; gifts, legacies; members' dues. Annual budget: 210,000 USD. **Activities** Events/meetings. **Events** *International Conference of African NGOs members of the United Nations ECOSOC* Algiers (Algeria) 2018.
Members Full in 21 countries:
Algeria, Benin, Burkina Faso, Burundi, Cameroon, Canada, Chad, Congo Brazzaville, Congo DR, Côte d'Ivoire, France, Gabon, Ghana, Guinea, Italy, Mali, Morocco, Senegal, South Africa, Togo, USA.
Consultative Status Consultative status granted from: *ECOSOC (#05331)* (Special). **NGO Relations** Also links with national organizations. [2022.10.25/XM6334/**F**]

♦ Parlementaires pour un ordre mondial / see Parliamentarians for Global Action (#18208)
♦ Parlementair Netwerk voor Kernontwapening (#18210)
♦ Parlement andin (#00820)
♦ **Parlement Benelux** Conseil interparlementaire consultatif de Benelux (#03201)
♦ Parlement du Climat (#04019)
♦ Le Parlement du Climat – Des législateurs du monde entier combattent ensemble les changements climatiques / see Climate Parliament (#04019)
♦ Parlement européen (#08146)
♦ Parlement européen, Groupe libéral, démocratique et réformateur / see Renew Europe (#18840)
♦ Parlement européen – Groupe du Parti européen des libéraux, démocrates et réformateurs / see Renew Europe (#18840)
♦ Parlement européen des jeunes (#09145)
♦ Parlement international d'information et d'écologie (internationally oriented national body)
♦ Parlement latinoaméricain (#18203)
♦ Parlement mondial de la jeunesse pour l'eau (#21958)
♦ Parlement mondial pour la sécurité et la paix (internationally oriented national body)
♦ Parlement de l'Union du Maghreb / see Consultative Council of the Arab Maghreb Union (#04765)
♦ e-Parliament / see Climate Parliament (#04019)
♦ Parliamentarians' Alliance for Peace in Asia (unconfirmed)

♦ Parliamentarians for Global Action (PGA) 18208

Action mondiale des parlementaires – Acción Mundial de Parlamentarios

SG 44 Wall Street, Suite 903, New York NY 10005, USA. T. +12126877755. Fax +12126878409. E-mail: info@pgaction.org – sg@pgaction.org.
Senior Legal Officer Alexanderveld 5, 2585 DB The Hague, Netherlands. T. +31703604433. Fax +31703642255.
URL: http://www.pgaction.org/

History 1978, Washington, DC (USA). Founded as an international network of elected members of national Parliaments. Former names and other names: *Parliamentarians for World Order (PWO)* – former; *Parlementaires pour un ordre mondial* – former. Registration: EU Transparency Register, No/ID: 415603942670-06, Start date: 10 May 2021. **Aims** Inform and mobilize parliamentarians in all regions of the world to advocate for human rights and the rule of law, democracy, human security, non-discrimination and gender equality. **Structure** International Council; Executive Committee; Secretariat. **Languages** English, French, Spanish. **Staff** 15.00 FTE, paid. **Finance** Sources: donations; government support; members' dues; private foundations. Other sources: United Nations; governments; individual donors; support from foundations and other institutions. Core donors: *Swedish International Development Cooperation Agency (Sida); DANIDA; Charles Stewart Mott Foundation.* Donors to campaigns and programmes include: Arcus Foundation; *European Law Institute (ELI, #07658); European Union (EU, #08967)* UNSCAR; governmental departments of Canada, Estonia, Netherlands, Norway, Switzerland, Liechtenstein and USA; *Oak Foundation; Open Society Foundations (OSF, #17763); Pew Charitable Trusts;* Raymond and Elizabeth Bloch Charitable and Education Foundation; *Sigrid Rausing Trust; CRDF Global.* **Activities** Advocacy/lobbying/activism; awards/prizes/competitions; capacity building; events/meetings; guidance/assistance/consulting; knowledge management/information dissemination; monitoring/evaluation; networking/liaising; politics/policy/regulatory; projects/programmes. **Events** *Annual Forum* Praia (Cape Verde) 2019, *Annual Parliamentary Forum* Kiev (Ukraine) 2018, *Annual Parliamentary Forum* Milan (Italy) 2017, *Annual Parliamentary Forum* Rabat (Morocco) 2014, *Annual Parliamentary Forum* Bogota (Colombia) 2013. **Publications** *Women Legislators in Action – Weaving the Future Together* (4 a year) – bulletin. *Advancing the Human Rights and Inclusion of LGBTI People: A Handbook for Parliamentarians* – produced in collaboration with UNDP. Annual Report; parliamentary kit on the ICC; factsheets; handbooks; toolkits.
Members Elected national legislators (over 1,200) in 136 elected parliaments. Membership countries not specified. Regional parliaments (5):
Regional parliaments (5):
European Parliament (EP, #08146); Pan-African Parliament (PAP, #18058); Parlamento Centroamericano (PARLACEN, #18201); Parlamento Latinoamericano (PARLATINO, #18203); Parliament of the Economic Community of West African States (ECOWAS Parliament, #18221).
Observer Status Parliaments (8):
Aruba, Congo Brazzaville, Cook Is, Curaçao, Niue, Palestine, Qatar, Sudan.
Consultative Status Consultative status granted from: *ECOSOC (#05331)* (General); *UNEP (#20299).* **IGO Relations** Accredited by (1): *United Nations Office at Vienna (UNOV, #20604).* Member of (1): *International Institute for Democracy and Electoral Assistance (International IDEA, #13872).* Cooperates with (2): *Parliamentary Assembly of the Council of Europe (PACE, #18211); Parliamentary Assembly of the Organization for Security and Cooperation in Europe (OSCE PA, #18214).* Associated with Department of Global Communications of the United Nations. **NGO Relations** Partner of (1): *International Coalition for the Responsibility to Protect (ICRtoP, #12620).* Cooperates with (1): Asian Parliamentary Network on Human Rights. Represented on the Organizing Committee of: *Hague Appeal for Peace (HAP, #10848).* [2023.02.22/XF2756/**F**]

♦ Parliamentarians Network for Conflict Prevention (Parliamentarians Network) 18209

Secretariat c/o EastWest Inst, Rue de Trèves 59-61, 1040 Brussels, Belgium. T. +3227434625. Fax +3227434639. E-mail: parliamentarians@ewi.info.
URL: http://pncp.info/

History Oct 2008, Brussels (Belgium), at *European Parliament (EP, #08146)*, as an initiative of *EastWest Institute (EWI, #05264).* **Aims** Mobilize efforts towards the prevention of conflicts turning violent through diplomatic initiatives and effective collective action. **Structure** Executive Committee of 6 members. Secretariat. **Publications** *Parliamentarians Network Newsletter* (12 a year).
Members Parliamentarians in 53 countries and territories:
Afghanistan, Argentina, Australia, Austria, Azerbaijan, Bangladesh, Belgium, Bulgaria, Canada, Congo DR, Denmark, El Salvador, Estonia, Finland, France, Germany, Hungary, Iraq, Ireland, Israel, Italy, Jordan, Kenya, Kosovo, Kuwait, Latvia, Lithuania, Luxembourg, Nepal, Netherlands, Nicaragua, Nigeria, North Macedonia, Norway, Pakistan, Palestine, Philippines, Poland, Portugal, Romania, Russia, Serbia, Slovenia, Somalia, South Sudan, Spain, Sweden, Switzerland, Tanzania UR, Türkiye, UK, Ukraine, United Arab Emirates.
IGO Relations *African Development Bank (ADB, #00283); UNDP (#20292).* **NGO Relations** *Stockholm International Water Institute (SIWI).* [2018/XJ4838/**E**]

♦ **Parliamentarians Network** Parliamentarians Network for Conflict Prevention (#18209)

♦ Parliamentarians for Nuclear Non-Proliferation and Disarmament (PNND) 18210

Réseau parlementaire pour le désarmement nucléaire – Netzwerk von Abgeordneten für Nukleare Abrüstung – Network Parlamentare per il Disarmo Nucleare – Parlementair Netwerk voor Kernontwapening

Coordinator c/o Prague Vision Institute, Lipanská 4, 130 00 Prague 3, Czechia. E-mail: info@praguevision.org.
Europe Office c/o Basel Peace Office, Univ of Basel, Petersgraben 27, 4051 Basel BS, Switzerland. E-mail: info@baselpeaceoffice.org – info@pnnd.org.
UN Office c/o Global Security Institute, 866 UN Plaza, Suite 4050, New York NY 10017, USA. T. +16462895170. Fax +16462895171.
URL: http://www.pnnd.org/

History Mar 2001. Project of *Global Security Institute (GSI)* and *Middle Powers Initiative (MPI, #16795)*. Former names and other names: *Parliamentary Network for Nuclear Disarmament (PNND)* – former (2001 to 2008); *Réseau parlementaire pour le désarmement nucléaire* – former (2001 to 2008); *Netzwerk von Abgeordneten für Nukleare Abrüstung* – former (2001 to 2008); *Network Parlamentare per il Disarmo Nucleare* – former (2001 to 2008); *Parlementair Netwerk voor Kernontwapening* – former (2001 to 2008). **Aims** Engage parliamentarians in the nuclear disarmement process. **Events** *General Assembly* Prague (Czech Rep) 2015, *Prague Agenda Conference* Prague (Czech Rep) 2015, *Nuclear weapons and South Asia* Colombo (Sri Lanka) 2004, *Parliamentarians and the non-proliferation treaty* New York, NY (USA) 2004, *From nuclear dangers to cooperative security – parliamentarians and the legal imperative for nuclear disarmament* Vancouver, BC (Canada) 2003. **Publications** *PNND Update* (12 a year) – online newsletter; *PNND Notes* (annual). *Parliamentarians and Nuclear Weapons.*

Members Members of Parliament (over 500) in 38 countries:
Algeria, Argentina, Armenia, Australia, Austria, Belgium, Bolivia, Brazil, Canada, Colombia, Denmark, France, Germany, Ghana, Guyana, India, Israel, Italy, Japan, Korea Rep, Kyrgyzstan, Lithuania, Mexico, Netherlands, New Zealand, Niger, Norway, Philippines, Russia, Rwanda, South Africa, Sri Lanka, St Lucia, Sweden, Switzerland, Tanzania UR, UK, USA.

NGO Relations Founding partner of: *Basel Peace Office.* [2020/XF7034/**F**]

♦ Parliamentarians for World Order / see Parliamentarians for Global Action (#18208)
♦ Parliamentary Assembly of the Black Sea Economic Cooperation / see Parliamentary Assembly of the Organization of the Black Sea Economic Cooperation (#18213)
♦ Parliamentary Assembly of the Commonwealth of Independent States / see Interparliamentary Assembly of Member Nations of the Commonwealth of Independent States (#15958)
♦ Parliamentary Assembly of the Conference on Security and Cooperation in Europe / see Parliamentary Assembly of the Organization for Security and Cooperation in Europe (#18214)

♦ Parliamentary Assembly of the Council of Europe (PACE) 18211

Assemblée parlementaire du Conseil de l'Europe

Acting SG Council of Europe, 67075 Strasbourg CEDEX, France. T. +33388413630. Fax +33388412776.
Pres address not obtained.
URL: https://pace.coe.int/en/

History First session held 10 Aug 1949, with 2 statutory organs, the Committee of Ministers (CM) and a Consultative Assembly, which was the first international parliamentary assembly in history; not a legislative body, but a deliberative and initiating organ for political and other matters dealt with by the *Council of Europe (CE, #04881)*. **Aims** Achieve greater unity between members to safeguard and promote the ideals and principles of democracy, human rights and the rule of law in order to facilitate economic and social progress; maintain dialogue with governments, national parliaments, international organisations and civil society; set the agenda through provision of texts that filter down through law and practice to improve the lives of Europeans. **Structure** Annual Sessions divided into 4 parts (January, April, June, September/ October). Members (324) are elected or appointed by their national or federal parliaments, the numbers representing each country depend on population size. Each national delegation has an equal number of substitutes. National delegations reflect the strength of political parties in the national parliament and should include members of the under-represented sex in the same percentage as in their parliaments and at least one member of the under-represented sex is appointed as a representative. Representatives form political groups (5): *Alliance of Liberals and Democrats for Europe (ALDE, #00702)*; *European Conservatives Group (EC, #06744)*; *Group of the European People's Party (#10774)*; *Group of the Unified European Left (UEL, #10794)*; *Socialists, Democrats and Greens Group (SOC, #19342)*. Presidential Committee; Bureau of the Assembly; Joint Committee; Standing Committee; Assembly Committees (9) and sub-committees (20), as well as ad hoc committees set up by the Assembly from among its members. **Languages** English, French. Also working languages of Member States which are major contributors to CoE budget. **Staff** 85 FTE, permanent; one appointed official. **Finance** Since 2010, presents an opinion concerning its own expenditure in the form of a resolution addressed to the CM. Annual budget: euro 15,800,000. **Activities** Elects the Secretary General and Deputy Secretary General of the Council of Europe, the Secretary General of the Parliamentary Assembly and the Council of Europe Commissioner for Human Rights. Elects judges to European Court of Human Rights; maintains dialogue with Committee of Ministers of the Council of Europe; discusses and makes recommendations upon any matter within the scope of activities of the CoE and determines its own agenda; makes recommendations on any issue referred to it by the CM for opinion; makes contributions concerning execution by member states of the judgements of the European Court of Human Rights; encourages dialogue between members and non-members; provides a discussion forum for other international organizations with no parliamentary organ of their own; carries out election observation missions. Set up, 2012, the Parliamentary Project Support; Parliamentary Networks: Diaspora; Women Free from Violence; ONE in FIVE Campaign; Parliamentary Campaign to End Immigration Detention of Children; No Hate Parliamentary Alliance; PACE Anti-Corruption Platform; Terrorism: NoHateNoFear; NotinMyParliament. Prizes: The Vaclav Havel Human Rights Prize; Museum Prize; Europe Prize. **Events** *Session – First Part* Strasbourg (France) 2022, *European Conference of Presidents of Parliament* Athens (Greece) 2021, *Session – Fourth Part* Strasbourg (France) 2021, *Session – Second Part* Strasbourg (France) 2021, *Session – Third Part* Strasbourg (France) 2021. **Publications** *The Parliamentary Assembly Practice and Procedure* (11th ed 2012). Books; speeches; articles.

Members Representatives (324) and substitutes (324), elected or appointed by national or federal parliaments from among their own members, in 47 member states of the Council of Europe:
Albania, Andorra, Armenia, Austria, Azerbaijan, Belgium, Bosnia-Herzegovina, Bulgaria, Croatia, Cyprus, Czechia, Denmark, Estonia, Finland, France, Georgia, Germany, Greece, Hungary, Iceland, Ireland, Italy, Latvia, Liechtenstein, Lithuania, Luxembourg, Malta, Moldova, Monaco, Montenegro, Netherlands, North Macedonia, Norway, Poland, Portugal, Romania, Russia, San Marino, Serbia, Slovakia, Slovenia, Spain, Sweden, Switzerland, Türkiye, UK, Ukraine.

Partners for Democracy (status for institutional cooperation with parliaments of non-member states in neighbouring regions established by the Assembly in 2009):
Jordan, Kyrgyzstan, Morocco, Palestine.

Observer status in 3 countries:
Canada, Israel, Mexico.

IGO Relations Since 2005, INGOs form civil society's pillar in the CoE 'quadrilogue' with the CM, PACE and the Congress of Local and Regional Authorities. In this process they participate in intergovernmental activities and foster dialogue between members of parliament and local and regional authorities and associations confronted with challenges facing contemporary society. Cooperates with: *Benelux Inter-Parliamentary Consultative Council (Benelux Parliament, #03201)*; *European Bank for Reconstruction and Development (EBRD, #06315)*; *European Parliament (EP, #08146)*; *Interparliamentary Assembly of Member Nations of the Commonwealth of Independent States (IPA CIS, #15958)*; *Inter-Parliamentary Union (IPU, #15961)*; *NATO Parliamentary Assembly (NATO PA, #16946)*; *Pan-African Parliament (PAP, #18058)*; *Parlamento Latinoamericano (PARLATINO, #18203)*; *Parliamentary Assembly of the Organization for Security and Cooperation in Europe (OSCE PA, #18214)*; *United Nations (UN, #20515)* and its organs, including the General Assembly. Contributed to drawing up the following conventions:
– *Convention on the Conservation of European Wildlife and Natural Habitats (Bern convention, 1979)*;
– *Convention on Cybercrime (Budapest Convention, 2001)*;
– Convention on Preventing and Combatting Violence against Women and Domestic Violence;
– Convention on the Protection of Children against Sexual Exploitation and Sexual Abuse;
– *Convention for the Protection of Human Rights and Dignity of the Human Being with regard to the Application of Biology and Medicine: Convention on Human Rights and Biomedicine (1997)*;
– *Convention for the Protection of Human Rights and Fundamental Freedoms (1950)*;
– *Convention for the Protection of Individuals with Regard to Automatic Processing of Personal Data (1981)*;
– *Council of Europe Convention on Action Against Trafficking in Human Beings (2005)*;
– *European Convention on the Legal Status of Migrant Workers (1977)*;
– *European Convention for the Prevention of Torture and Inhuman or Degrading Treatment or Punishment (1987)*;
– *European Convention on Spectator Violence and Misbehaviour at Sports Events and in Particular at Football Matches (1985)*;
– *European Convention on the Suppression of Terrorism (1977)*;
– *European Convention on Transfrontier Television (1989)*;
– *European Cultural Convention (1954)*;
– *European Social Charter (1961)*;
– *Framework Convention for the Protection of National Minorities (1995)*;
– *Multilateral Convention on Mutual Administrative Assistance in Tax Matters (1988)*;
– *Nordic Council (NC, #17256)*;
– *Protocol no 6 to the Convention for the Protection of Human Rights and Fundamental Freedoms Concerning the Abolition of the Death Penalty (1983)*.

NGO Relations Cooperates with (3): *International Committee of the Red Cross (ICRC, #12799)*; *Inter-Parliamentary Union (IPU, #15961)*; *NATO Parliamentary Assembly (NATO PA, #16946)*. PACE committees develop and maintain working relations with European and international NGOs which carry out activities in the fields covered by their specific terms reference. [2021.03.02/XE8849/**F***]

♦ Parliamentary Assembly of the ECO Countries (unconfirmed)
♦ Parliamentary Assembly of the French-Speaking World (#02312)

♦ Parliamentary Assembly of the Mediterranean (PAM) 18212

Assemblée parlementaire de la Méditerranée (APM)

Regional Office Palazzo PiCo, Via Terracina 230, 80125 Naples NA, Italy. E-mail: secretariat@pam.int.
Geneva Office Chemin du Pommier 5, 1218 Le Grand-Saconnex GE, Switzerland.
URL: http://www.pam.int/

History Mar 2006. Founded to supersede *Inter-Parliamentary Conference on Security and Cooperation in the Mediterranean (CSCM, inactive)*. Inaugural meeting, 10-11 Sep 2006, Amman (Jordan). Former names and other names: *Parliamentary Assembly of Mediterranean States* – former. **Aims** Assert the centrality of the Mediterranean area and reaffirm the key role of its members in addressing their common interests and shared concerns through a forum. **Structure** Assembly; Bureau; Standing Committees (3); Special Task Forces; Ad hoc Committee; Secretariat General. **Languages** Arabic, English, French. **Finance** Members' dues. **Activities** Events/meetings. **Events** *Science policy forum for the Mediterranean region* Paris (France) 2010, *Plenary Session* Rabat (Morocco) 2010, *Annual Session* Istanbul (Turkey) 2009, *Annual Session* Monte Carlo (Monaco) 2008, *Annual Session* St Julian's (Malta) 2007. **Publications** Annual Reports; reports and resolutions; press releases; newsletters.

Members Member States (28):
Albania, Algeria, Andorra, Bosnia-Herzegovina, Croatia, Cyprus, Egypt, France, Greece, Israel, Italy, Jordan, Lebanon, Libya, Malta, Mauritania, Monaco, Montenegro, Morocco, North Macedonia, Palestine, Portugal, Romania, Serbia, Slovenia, Syrian AR, Tunisia, Türkiye.

Associate and Partner State (1):
Holy See.

Observer Members (12):
Arab Inter-Parliamentary Union (Arab IPU, #00995); *Association of Mediterranean Energy Regulators (MEDREG, #02800)*; *Comprehensive Nuclear-Test-Ban Treaty Organization (CTBTO, #04420)*; *Consultative Council of the Arab Maghreb Union (#04765)*; *Euro-Mediterranean University (EMUNI, #05728)*; *Fondazione Mediterraneo*; *League of Arab States (LAS, #16420)*; *Parliamentary Assembly of the Organization of the Black Sea Economic Cooperation (PABSEC, #18213)*; *Parliamentary Union of the OIC Member States (PUIC, #18220)*; *UNESCO (#20322)*; *Union for the Mediterranean (UfM, #20457)* (Parliamentary Assembly); *World Meteorological Organization (WMO, #21649)*.

IGO Relations Observer status with (2): *Parliamentary Union of the OIC Member States (PUIC, #18220)*; *United Nations (UN, #20515)* (General Assembly). Memorandum of Understanding with (1): *Parliamentary Assembly of the Organization of the Black Sea Economic Cooperation (PABSEC, #18213)*. Member of (1): *United Nations Alliance of Civilizations (UNAOC, #20520)*. Cooperates with (4): *International Bank for Reconstruction and Development (IBRD, #12317)*; *International Organization for Migration (IOM, #14454)*; *Organization for Security and Cooperation in Europe (OSCE, #17887)*; *Parliamentary Assembly of the Council of Europe (PACE, #18211)*. *Arab Parliament (#01023)* is observer. **NGO Relations** Observer status with (1): *Sociedad Latinoamericana de Ortopedia y Traumatología (SLAOT, #19418)*. Cooperates with (4): *Consultative Council of the Arab Maghreb Union (#04765)*; *Fondazione Mediterraneo*; *Inter-Parliamentary Union (IPU, #15961)*; *NATO Parliamentary Assembly (NATO PA, #16946)*. [2021/XJ3776/y/**F***]

♦ Parliamentary Assembly of Mediterranean States / see Parliamentary Assembly of the Mediterranean (#18212)

♦ Parliamentary Assembly of the Organization of the Black Sea Economic Cooperation (PABSEC) 18213

SG Levent Mahallesi, Levent Caddesi, Yeni Sülün Sokak No 2, 34330 Istanbul/Istanbul, Türkiye. T. +902122276070 – +902122270258. Fax +902122276080. E-mail: pabsec@pabsec.org.
URL: http://www.pabsec.org/

History 26 Feb 1993, Istanbul (Türkiye). Founded on signature of a declaration by speakers/presidents of the parliaments of 9 countries, as the interparliamentary component (parliamentary body) of *Organization of Black Sea Economic Cooperation (BSEC, #17857)*. Former names and other names: *Parliamentary Assembly of the Black Sea Economic Cooperation* – alias. **Aims** Secure understanding and adoption by the peoples of the ideals and aims of the Black Sea Economic Cooperation; provide a legal basis for economic, commercial, social, cultural and political cooperation; enact legislation for implementation of decisions taken by Heads of State; Government or Ministers of Foreign Affairs; provide assistance to national parliaments to strengthen parliamentary democracy; promote cooperation with other international and regional organizations. **Structure** General Assembly (twice a year); Bureau of the Assembly; Standing Committee; Committees (3); International Secretariat. **Languages** English, French, Russian, Turkish. **Staff** Secretariat: 9 international staff; 7 local staff. **Finance** Contributions of Participating States. **Activities** Knowledge management/information dissemination; research/documentation; politics/policy/regulatory; events/meetings. **Events** *Autumn Plenary Session* Belgrade (Serbia) 2022, *Spring Plenary Session* Russia 2022, *Spring Plenary Session* Tirana (Albania) 2018, *Autumn Plenary Session* Yerevan (Armenia) 2018, *Autumn Plenary Session* Kiev (Ukraine) 2017. **Publications** *PABSEC Bulletin* (2 a year) in English, Russian, Turkish.

Members Parliamentary representatives of 12 countries:
Albania, Armenia, Azerbaijan, Bulgaria, Georgia, Greece, Moldova, Romania, Russia, Serbia, Türkiye, Ukraine.

Observer parliaments in 6 countries:
Belarus, Egypt, France, Germany, Israel, Slovakia.

IGO Relations Cooperates with:
– *Baltic Sea Parliamentary Conference (BSPC, #03146)*;
– *Central European Initiative (CEI, #03708)* Parliamentary Assembly;
– *European Parliament (EP, #08146)*;
– *Interparliamentary Assembly of Member Nations of the Commonwealth of Independent States (IPA CIS, #15958)*;
– *NATO Parliamentary Assembly (NATO PA, #16946)*;
– *Parliamentary Assembly of the Council of Europe (PACE, #18211)*;
– *Parliamentary Assembly of the Organization for Security and Cooperation in Europe (OSCE PA, #18214)*;
– *Parliamentary Assembly of Turkic Speaking Countries (TURKPA, #18215)*;
– Parliamentary Assembly of the Union of Belarus and Russia (PAUBR);
– *Parliamentary Union of the OIC Member States (PUIC, #18220)*;
– *SEECP Parliamentary Assembly (#19212)*.

Protocol of Cooperation with: *Interparliamentary Assembly of Member Nations of the Commonwealth of Independent States (IPA CIS, #15958)*. Memorandum of Understanding with: *Parliamentary Assembly of the Mediterranean (PAM, #18212)*. Observer Status granted to: Parliamentary Dimension of *Central European Initiative (CEI, #03708)*.

NGO Relations Observer to: *Asian Parliamentary Assembly (APA, #01653).* Observer Status granted to: *Inter-Parliamentary Assembly on Orthodoxy (IAO, #15959).* Cooperates with: *Inter-Parliamentary Union (IPU, #15961); Parliamentary Network on the World Bank and International Monetary Fund (#18219).*
[2021/XF3139/y/**F***]

♦ Parliamentary Assembly of the Organization for Security and Cooperation in Europe (OSCE PA) 18214

Assemblée parlementaire de l'Organisation pour la sécurité et la coopération en Europe

SG Tordenskjoldsgade 1, 1055 Copenhagen K, Denmark. T. +4533378040. Fax +4533378030. E-mail: osce@oscepa.dk.
URL: http://www.oscepa.org/

History 2 Apr 1991, Madrid (Spain). Founded within the framework of *Organization for Security and Cooperation in Europe (OSCE, #17887)*, previously CSCE. Original title: *Parliamentary Assembly of the Conference on Security and Cooperation in Europe – Assemblée parlementaire de la Conférence sur la sécurité et la coopération en Europe.* Also referred to as *OSCE Parliamentary Assembly – Assemblée parlementaire de la OSCE*; *Parliamentary Assembly of the OSCE.* **Aims** Facilitate inter-parliamentary dialogue on OSCE related matters; support the strengthening and consolidation of *democratic* institutions in OSCE participating States; develop and promote mechanisms for *conflict prevention* and resolution; contribute to development of the institutional structures of the OSCE and of relations and cooperation among existing OSCE Institutions. **Structure** Annual Session (in July) and Winter Meeting (in February, always in Vienna, Austria) are the two main meetings. Standing Committee, comprising the Heads of the 57 National Delegations as well as Members of the Bureau. Bureau consisting of President, 9 Vice-Presidents, Officers of the 3 General Committees, and President Emeritus and Treasurer (both ex officio). General Committees (3): Political Affairs and Security; Economic Affairs, Science, Technology and Environment; Democracy, Human Rights and Humanitarian Questions. International Secretariat in Copenhagen (Denmark), headed by Secretary-General. **Languages** English, French, German, Italian, Russian, Spanish. **Staff** 19.00 FTE, paid. **Finance** Contributions from Member States. Annual budget: euro 3,100,000. **Activities** Monitoring/evaluation; events/meetings; networking/liaising; conflict resolution; capacity building. **Events** *Annual Winter Meeting* Vienna (Austria) 2023, *Annual Winter Meeting* Vienna (Austria) 2022, *Annual Session* Bucharest (Romania) 2021, *Annual Winter Meeting* Copenhagen (Denmark) 2021, *Annual Session* Vancouver, BC (Canada) 2020. **Publications** *News from Copenhagen* – newsletter. Annual Declarations. Brochures; reports.

Members Parliamentarians (323) from 58 Member Parliaments plus 2 representatives from the Holy See:
Albania, Andorra, Armenia, Austria, Azerbaijan, Belarus, Belgium, Bosnia-Herzegovina, Bulgaria, Canada, Croatia, Cyprus, Czechia, Denmark, Estonia, Finland, France, Georgia, Germany, Greece, Holy See, Hungary, Iceland, Ireland, Italy, Kazakhstan, Kyrgyzstan, Latvia, Liechtenstein, Lithuania, Luxembourg, Malta, Moldova, Monaco, Mongolia, Montenegro, Netherlands, North Macedonia, Norway, Poland, Portugal, Romania, Russia, San Marino, Serbia, Slovakia, Slovenia, Spain, Sweden, Switzerland, Tajikistan, Türkiye, Turkmenistan, UK, Ukraine, USA, Uzbekistan.
Partners for Cooperation in 11 countries:
Afghanistan, Algeria, Australia, Egypt, Israel, Japan, Jordan, Korea Rep, Morocco, Thailand, Tunisia.

IGO Relations *European Parliament (EP, #08146); Interparliamentary Assembly of Member Nations of the Commonwealth of Independent States (IPA CIS, #15958); Parliamentary Assembly of the Council of Europe (PACE, #18211).* **NGO Relations** *Inter-Parliamentary Union (IPU, #15961); NATO Parliamentary Assembly (NATO PA, #16946).* Representatives of NGOs attend Assembly meetings. The Assembly works with NGOs associated with the implementation of the Helsinki Final Act.
[2021/XF2317/**F***]

- ♦ Parliamentary Assembly of the OSCE / see Parliamentary Assembly of the Organization for Security and Cooperation in Europe (#18214)

♦ Parliamentary Assembly of Turkic Speaking Countries (TURKPA) .. 18215

SG 106 S S Akhundov str, 7 microdistr, AZ1116 Binagadi, Baku, Azerbaijan. T. +994125635835. Fax +994125635834. E-mail: info@turk-pa.org.
URL: http://turk-pa.org/

History 21 Nov 2008, Istanbul (Türkiye). Established on signing of Agreement by Heads of parliaments. Regulations, Articles of Secretariat and Baku Declaration adopted Sep 2009, Baku (Azerbaijan). **Aims** Assist in development of political dialogue; harmonize legislations and strengthen mutual activities with regard to issues relating to parliamentary cooperation on the basis of historical, cultural and language unity. **Structure** Chairmanship (rotating); Council of Assembly; Secretariat. Commissions Legal Affairs and International Relations; Social, Cultural and Humanitarian Issues; Economic Cooperation; Environment and Natural Resources. **Activities** Events/meetings. **Events** *Plenary Session* Bishkek (Kyrgyzstan) 2017, *Plenary Session* Astana (Kazakhstan) 2015, *Plenary Session* Baku (Azerbaijan) 2014, *Plenary Session* Ankara (Turkey) 2013, *Plenary Session* Bishkek (Kyrgyzstan) 2012.

Members Parliaments of 4 countries:
Azerbaijan, Kazakhstan, Kyrgyzstan, Türkiye.

IGO Relations Cooperates with: *Parliamentary Assembly of the Organization of the Black Sea Economic Cooperation (PABSEC, #18213).* **NGO Relations** Observer status with: *Inter-Parliamentary Union (IPU, #15961).*
[2020/XM6487/**F***]

♦ Parliamentary Assembly – Union for the Mediterranean (PA – UfM) 18216

Assemblée Parlementaire – Union pour la Méditerranée (AP – UpM)

Secretariat François Nègre, Eur Parliament, SQM 03 Y 007, Rue Wiertz 60, 1047 Brussels, Belgium. E-mail: francois.negre@europarl.europa.eu.
Secretariat Eur Parliament, SQM 3 Y 021, Rue Wiertz 60, 1047 Brussels, Belgium.
URL: http://www.paufm.org/

History First convened Oct 1998, Brussels (Belgium) to provide Euro-Mediterranean Partnership with a parliamentary dimension. Original title: *Euro-Mediterranean Parliamentary Forum.* Converted into *Euro-Mediterranean Parliamentary Assembly (EMPA)*, Apr 2002, Valencia (Spain). Inaugural sitting, Mar 2004, Greece. Current title adopted, Mar 2010, Amman (Jordan), at 6th Plenary Session. **Aims** Play a consultative role in UfM activities; provide impetus to the Euromed partnership. **Structure** Plenary; Presidency (rotating); Bureau. Committees (5): Political; Economic; Culture; Women's Rights; Energy, Environment and Water. **Languages** Arabic, EU languages, Hebrew, Turkish. **Staff** 2.00 FTE, paid. **Activities** Politics/policy/regulatory. Euro-Mediterranean Speakers Conference. **Events** *Plenary Session* Strasbourg (France) 2019, *Plenary Session* Cairo (Egypt) 2018, *Plenary Session* Lisbon (Portugal) 2015, *Summit of Speakers* Lisbon (Portugal) 2015, *Plenary Session* Jordan 2014.

Members Parliaments (44), consisting of 280 members, equally distributed between northern and southern shores of the Mediterranean. Parliaments of 43 governments represented:
Albania, Algeria, Austria, Belgium, Bosnia-Herzegovina, Bulgaria, Croatia, Cyprus, Czechia, Denmark, Egypt, Estonia, Finland, France, Germany, Greece, Hungary, Ireland, Israel, Italy, Jordan, Latvia, Lebanon, Lithuania, Luxembourg, Malta, Mauritania, Monaco, Montenegro, Morocco, Netherlands, Palestine, Poland, Portugal, Romania, Slovakia, Slovenia, Spain, Sweden, Syrian AR, Tunisia, Türkiye, UK.
Regional parliament:
European Parliament (EP, #08146).

IGO Relations Observer with: *International Organization for Migration (IOM, #14454).* Partner of: *European Commission (EC, #06633); Parliamentary Assembly of the Mediterranean (PAM, #18212); Parliamentary Assembly of the Organization of the Black Sea Economic Cooperation (PABSEC, #18213); Union for the Mediterranean (UfM, #20457).* **NGO Relations** Observer with: *Inter-Parliamentary Union (IPU, #15961).*
[2015.09.30/XM4183/**E***]

♦ Parliamentary Association for Euro-Arab Cooperation (PAEAC) 18217

Association parlementaire pour la coopération euro-arabe (APCEA)

Contact 24 Square de Meeûs, 5ème Etage, 1000 Brussels, Belgium. T. +3222311300. Fax +3222310646.

History 23 Mar 1974, Paris (France). **Aims** Contribute to the search for peace in the Middle East in the spirit of the United Nations resolutions; promote political, economic and cultural cooperation between Europe and the Middle East; support Euro-Arab dialogue for long-term cooperation between Europe and the Arab world and press for practical action. Particular emphasis laid on the Palestine question. **Structure** Executive Committee, consisting of 2 representatives from each member national section and 4 representatives from the section in the European Parliament. Officers: 2 co-Presidents, 3 Vice-Presidents, Treasurer and 2 Honorary Presidents. Secretariat General. **Languages** English, French. **Staff** None. **Events** *Euro-Arab parliamentary dialogue / Annual Meeting of Euro-Arab Parliamentary Dialogue (jointly with PAEAC) / Euro-Arab Parliamentary Dialogue – with the Arab Inter-Parliamentary Union* Brussels (Belgium) 2002, *Euro-Arab parliamentary dialogue* Brussels (Belgium) 2002, *Euro-Arab parliamentary dialogue / Euro-Arab Parliamentary Dialogue – with the Arab Inter-Parliamentary Union* Sanaa (Yemen) 2000, *Euro-Arab Parliamentary Dialogue – with the Arab Inter-Parliamentary Union* Rome (Italy) 1999, *Euro-Arab parliamentary dialogue* Rome (Italy) 1999.

Members Originally open to European Community countries, currently open to all Council of Europe member states. National sections, individuals (650) in national parliaments, and in European Parliament. Members in 19 countries:
Austria, Belgium, Denmark, Finland, France, Germany, Greece, Iceland, Ireland, Italy, Luxembourg, Malta, Netherlands, Norway, Portugal, Spain, Sweden, Switzerland, UK.

Consultative Status Consultative status granted from: *ECOSOC (#05331)* (Ros A). [2013.06.01/XD2745/**D**]

- ♦ Parliamentary Confederation of the Americas (#04479)
- ♦ Parliamentary Conference of the Americas / see Confederación Parlamentaria de las Américas (#04479)
- ♦ Parliamentary Conference on Cooperation in the Baltic Sea Area (meeting series)
- ♦ Parliamentary Conference on Cooperation in the Baltic Sea Region / see Baltic Sea Parliamentary Conference (#03146)
- ♦ Parliamentary Council of the European Union (no recent information)
- ♦ **Parliamentary Forum on SALW** Parliamentary Forum on Small Arms and Light Weapons (#18218)

♦ Parliamentary Forum on Small Arms and Light Weapons (Parliamentary Forum on SALW) 18218

Foro Parlamentario sobre Armas Pequeñas y Ligeras

Gen Sec Hammarby Allé 93, 4tr, SE-120 63 Stockholm, Sweden. T. +4686532543. E-mail: info@parlforum.org.
URL: http://parliamentaryforum.org/

History 1999. Officially constituted, 2002, in the Spanish Parliament. **Aims** Support parliamentarians in their work to reduce and prevent armed violence; contribute to advancement of the global disarmament agenda; provide a space for parliamentarians to meet and join forces with other stakeholders and actors. **Structure** Assembly; Board; Secretariat. **Languages** English, French, Spanish. **Finance** Donors: *Swedish International Development Cooperation Agency (Sida)*; UN Trust Facility Supporting Cooperation on Arms Regulation (UNSCAR). **Members** Parliamentarians in 80 countries. Membership countries not specified.
[2014.06.01/XJ7395/y/**F**]

- ♦ Parliamentary Group of the Party of European Socialists / see Group of the Progressive Alliance of Socialists and Democrats in the European Parliament (#10786)
- ♦ Parliamentary Network for Nuclear Disarmament / see Parliamentarians for Nuclear Non-Proliferation and Disarmament (#18210)
- ♦ Parliamentary Network on the World Bank / see Parliamentary Network on the World Bank and International Monetary Fund (#18219)

♦ Parliamentary Network on the World Bank and International Monetary Fund 18219

Head of Secretariat 66 av d'Iéna, 75116 Paris, France. T. +33140693055. Fax +33147237436.
URL: http://www.parlnet.org/

History May 2000. Founded as an informal network of individual parliamentarians. Steering Committee of 9 members elected by general assembly of the Second Annual World Bank Conference with Parliamentarians, held in London (UK) Jan 28-29 2001, to run the initiative during the following 2 years. Articles adopted and became a formal network, 7 Feb 2003. Former names and other names: *Parliamentary Network on the World Bank (PNoWB)* – former (May 2000); *Réseau parlementaire sur la Banque mondiale (RPsBm)* – former (May 2000). Registration: France. **Aims** Provide a platform for parliamentarians around the globe to advocate for increased accountability and transparency in International Financial Institutions and multilateral development financing. **Structure** General Meeting (annual, during Conference); Board of Directors; International Secretariat; Regional and country chapters. **Staff** 1.00 FTE, paid. **Finance** Biggest funders: Governments of the Netherlands and Finland. Also funding from Governments of UK, Switzerland, Greece, France, and the following organizations listed in this Yearbook: *International Monetary Fund (IMF, #14180); United Nations Foundation (UNF, #20563)*; World Bank. **Activities** Events/meetings; publishing activities; networking/liaising. **Events** *Annual Conference* Washington, DC (USA) 2015, *Annual Conference* Baku (Azerbaijan) 2013, *Annual Conference* Brussels (Belgium) 2010, *Annual Conference* Paris (France) 2008, *Annual Conference* Cape Town (South Africa) 2007. **Publications** *PN Bulletin* (12 a year); *PN Newsletter.* Briefings; research publications. **Members** Parliamentarians (over 1,000) from 140 countries. Membership countries not specified. Also Associate Membership. **IGO Relations** Works closely with: *International Bank for Reconstruction and Development (IBRD, #12317)* (World Bank); *International Monetary Fund (IMF, #14180)*; parliamentary organizations.
[2021/XF6806/**F**]

♦ Parliamentary Union of the OIC Member States (PUIC) 18220

Union parlementaire des états membres de l'OCI (UPCI)

SG 34 Pesyan Str, Corner of Moghaddas Ardabili Street, Zaferanieh, Teheran, 1986833553, Iran Islamic Rep. T. +982122418860 – +982122418861 – +982122418862. Fax +982122418858 – +982122418859. E-mail: g.s@puic.org.
Mailing Address PO Box 19395 3851, Teheran, Iran Islamic Rep.
URL: http://www.puic.org/

History 17 Jun 1999, Teheran (Iran Islamic Rep), by *Organisation of Islamic Cooperation (OIC, #17813).* Previously also known under the acronyms of *PUOICM – UPMOCI.* Former names and other names: *Islamic Inter-Parliamentary Union (IIPU)* – alias; *Parliamentary Union of the Organization of the Islamic Conference* – alias. **Aims** Introduce and disseminate principles of *Islam*; enhance and support implementation of Islamic principle of consultation in all OIC Member States; provide framework for cooperation and coordination among OIC member states parliaments in international fora and organizations; promote meeting and dialogue among OIC member and their deputies; strengthen contacts, cooperation and coordination with other parliamentary, governmental and non-governmental organizations, so as to advance common objectives; foster coordination among people worldwide in order to respect and defend human rights and humanitarian principles and establish peace, based on justice. **Structure** Conference (every 2 years). Council (meets annually), consisting of 2 members of legislative and/or consultative assemblies or similar bodies from each member of the Union. Executive Committee, comprising one member each from the delegations of previous, present and future hosts of the Conference, in addition to 6 members (2 from each Geographical group) elected by the Council. General Secretariat, headed by Secretary General. **Languages** Arabic, English, French. **Staff** 19.00 FTE, paid. **Finance** Members' dues. **Events** *Conference* Kampala (Uganda) 2010, *Council Session* Kampala (Uganda) 2010, *Council Session* Niger 2009, *Conference* Cairo (Egypt) 2008, *Council Session* Cairo (Egypt) 2008. **Publications** *PUIC Bulletin* (4 a year).

Members Parliaments of 51 OIC Member States and territories:
Afghanistan, Albania, Algeria, Azerbaijan, Bahrain, Bangladesh, Benin, Burkina Faso, Cameroon, Chad, Côte d'Ivoire, Djibouti, Egypt, Gabon, Gambia, Guinea, Guinea-Bissau, Guyana, Indonesia, Iran Islamic Rep, Iraq, Jordan, Kazakhstan, Kuwait, Kyrgyzstan, Lebanon, Libya, Malaysia, Mali, Mauritania, Morocco, Mozambique, Niger, Oman, Pakistan, Palestine, Qatar, Saudi Arabia, Senegal, Sierra Leone, Somalia, Sudan, Syrian AR, Tajikistan, Togo, Tunisia, Türkiye, Turkmenistan, Uganda, United Arab Emirates, Yemen.
Observer status granted to 14 organizations:
African Parliamentary Union (APU, #00412); African Union (AU, #00488); Arab Inter-Parliamentary Union (Arab IPU, #00995); Asian Parliamentary Assembly (APA, #01653); Consultative Council of the Arab Maghreb Union (#04765); Eurasian Economic Community (EurAsEC, inactive) (Inter-Parliamentary Assembly of); *International Committee of the Red Cross (ICRC, #12799); Inter-Parliamentary Union (IPU, #15961); League of Arab States (LAS, #16420)*; Legislative Assembly of the Turkish Republic of Northern Cyprus; OIC; *Parliamentary Assembly of the Mediterranean (PAM, #18212); Parliamentary Assembly of the Organization of the Black Sea Economic Cooperation (PABSEC, #18213).*

IGO Relations *Arab Parliament (#01023)* is observer. Cooperates with: *Islamic World Educational, Scientific and Cultural Organization (ICESCO, #16058); Parliamentary Assembly of the Organization of the Black Sea Economic Cooperation (PABSEC, #18213).*
[2021/XD7721/y/**D***]

♦ Parliamentary Union of the Organization of the Islamic Conference / see Parliamentary Union of the OIC Member States (#18220)

♦ Parliament of the Economic Community of West African States (ECOWAS Parliament) 18221

Mailing Address PMB 576, Garki, Abuja, Federal Capital Territory, Nigeria.
Street Address c/o International Conference Centre, Old Wing, Area 11, Garki, Abuja, Federal Capital Territory, Nigeria.
URL: http://www.parl.ecowas.int/

History 1990, Banjul (Gambia). Founded following a proposal as part of an agreement to rationalize subregional institutions in West Africa within the framework of *Economic Community of West African States (ECOWAS, #05312)* so that ECOWAS would eventually become the sole economic community of the West African region. Further proposed by ECOWAS Authority, 1991, Abuja. Former names and other names: *West African Parliament* – former; *Community Parliament* – former; *ECOWAS Parliament* – former. **Aims** Promote integration by serving as a forum for dialogue, consultation and consensus-building for representatives of the peoples of Western Africa. **Languages** English, French, Portuguese. **NGO Relations** Member of (1): *Inter-Parliamentary Union (IPU, #15961).* [2021/XJ4106/**F***]

♦ Parliament Panafricain (#18058)

♦ Parliament of the World's Religions (PoWR) 18222

Exec Dir 70 E Lake St, Ste 230, Chicago IL 60601, USA. T. +13126292990. E-mail: info@parliamentofreligions.org.
URL: http://www.parliamentofreligions.org/

History 27 Sep 1893, Chicago, IL (USA). Founded 1893 at World's Columbian Exposition, Chicago IL (USA). Incorporated June 1988. Former names and other names: *World Parliament of Religions* – alias; *World's Parliament of Religions* – alias; *Congrès international des religions* – alias; *Council for a Parliament of the World's Religions (CPWR)* – former. Registration: Section 501(c)(3), USA. **Aims** Cultivate harmony among the world's religious and spiritual communities and foster their engagement with the world and its guiding institutions in order to achieve a just, peaceful, and sustainable world. **Structure** Board of Trustees. **Staff** 10.00 FTE, paid. **Activities** Advocacy/lobbying/activism; awareness raising; networking/liaising; religious activities. **Events** *Parliament of the World's Religions Congress* Chicago, IL (USA) 2023, *Parliament of the World's Religions Congress* 2021, *Parliament of the World's Religions Congress* Toronto, ON (Canada) 2018, *Parliament of the world's religions congress* Salt Lake City, UT (USA) 2015, *Parliament of the World's Religions Congress* Brussels (Belgium) 2014. **Publications** *PWR Newsletter* (bi-weekly). **Consultative Status** Consultative status granted from: *UNEP (#20299).* **NGO Relations** Participates in: *United Religions Initiative (URI, #20658).* Member of: *International Interfaith Organizations Network (IION, #13945).* [2023.02.13/XE2877/**E**]

♦ Parrainage international des orphelins de guerre (inactive)
♦ PARSA – Parasitological Society of Southern Africa (internationally oriented national body)
♦ **PARSA** Pôle alpin de recherches sur les sociétés anciennes (#18412)
♦ PARSF – Pan-American Rope Skipping Federation (inactive)
♦ **PARS** Pan Arab Rhinology Society (#18154)
♦ Partage – avec les enfants du monde (internationally oriented national body)
♦ Partage avec les enfants du Tiers-monde / see Partage – avec les enfants du monde
♦ Partage – Partage – avec les enfants du monde (internationally oriented national body)
♦ Partei der Europäischen Bürger/Bürgerinnen (#18248)
♦ Partenaire libéral pour le développement (internationally oriented national body)
♦ PARTENAIRE – Partenaire libéral pour le développement (internationally oriented national body)
♦ Partenaires européens pour l'environnement (#08154)

♦ Partenalia 18223

Secretariat Rue Marie de Bourgogne 13 – 3 étage, 1050 Brussels, Belgium. T. +3227336595. E-mail: coordination@partenalia.eu – info@partenalia.eu.
URL: http://www.partenalia.eu/

History 1993. **Aims** Enhance the visibility of intermediate *local authorities* in the process of *European integration*; foster territorial cooperation and make them part of the European reality. **Structure** Political Council; Steering Group; Managing Board; Secretariat.
Members Intermediate authorities (19) and 1 observer member in 6 countries:
Belgium, Croatia, France, Italy, Romania, Spain.
IGO Relations Member of: *European Confederation of Local Intermediate Authorities (#06710).* [2016/XJ5630/**E***]

♦ Partenariat Afrique Canada / see IMPACT (#11136)
♦ Partenariat d'apprentissage Unité d'action des Nations Unies en matière de changements climatiques (#17735)
♦ Partenariat asiatique pour un développement humain / see Caritas Asia (#03578)
♦ Partenariat pour l'évaluation et la performance environnementales de l'élevage (#16500)
♦ Partenariat pour les forêts du Bassin du Congo (#04662)
♦ Partenariat International d'Action sur le Carbone (#12440)
♦ Partenariat mondial pour l'éducation (#10531)
♦ Partenariat mondial pour la prévention des conflits armés (#10538)
♦ Partenariat mondial sur les sols (#10608)
♦ Partenariat de la montagne (#16862)
♦ Partenariat One UN pour L'Apprentissage sur les Changements Climatiques / see One UN Climate Change Learning Partnership (#17735)
♦ Partenariat des OSC pour l'efficacité du développement (#04976)
♦ Partenariat pour la paix (#18240)
♦ Partenariat en politiques économiques (#18233)
♦ Partial agreement in the social and public health field (inactive)
♦ Partial Agreement on the Youth Card / see Partial Agreement on Youth Mobility Through the Youth Card (#18224)

♦ Partial Agreement on Youth Mobility Through the Youth Card 18224

Secretariat IGO Cooperation Unit, Agora Bldg – Council of Europe, Av de l'Europe, 67075 Strasbourg CEDEX, France. T. +33388412998. Fax +33388412779. E-mail: youthmobility@coe.int.
Secretariat address not obtained. E-mail: manel.sanchez@eyca.org – mail@eyca.org.
URL: http://www.coe.int/t/dg4/youth/partners/youth_card_EN.asp?

History 13 Sep 1991, between *Council of Europe (CE, #04881)* and *European Youth Card Association (EYCA, #09137).* Within the framework of *Council of Europe (CE, #04881)*, when adopted by *Committee of Ministers of the Council of Europe (#04273).* Previously known as *Partial Agreement on the Youth Card.* **Aims** Promote and facilitate mobility of *young people* in Europe through extending advantages accorded by young persons' *travel* cards systems in each country to holders of cards from other signatory countries. **Structure** Coordinating Board of the Partial Agreement on the Youth Card comprises: 8 representatives of states party to the Partial Agreement, designated by the Committee of Ministers and having national youth card organizations; 8 members of *European Youth Card Association (EYCA, #09137)*; 1 representative of the Advisory Council of *European Youth Centres (EYCs, #09138).* EYCA proposes the broad lines of the programme. Meetings assured by the Secretariat-General of the Council of Europe. **Languages** English, French. **Staff** 1.00 FTE, paid. **Finance** Members' dues. Budget (annual): euro 59,900. **Activities** Advocacy/lobbying/activism. **Events** *Seminar on Mobility Towards Inclusion* Samobor (Croatia) 2016, *European Seminar on the Role of European Youth Cards in Youth Work* Brussels (Belgium) 2015, *Seminar on the Role of European Youth Card in Implementing Youth Policies* Edinburgh (UK) 2015, *European Symposium on Mobility in the Mind* Lisbon (Portugal) 2015, *European Seminar on Inclusive Online Engagement for Young People in Europe* Strasbourg (France) 2014.
Members States party to the Agreement (21):
Andorra, Armenia, Austria, Azerbaijan, Bosnia-Herzegovina, Croatia, Cyprus, Finland, Hungary, Ireland, Luxembourg, Malta, Moldova, Montenegro, Netherlands, Portugal, San Marino, Serbia, Slovakia, Slovenia, Switzerland. [2016.06.01/XF1527/**F***]

♦ Parti de l'Alliance des Démocrates et des Libéraus pour l'Europe (#00703)
♦ Partia Porozumienia Liberalów Demokratów na rzecz Europy (#00703)
♦ Participatory Development Forum (internationally oriented national body)

♦ Participatory Ecological Land Use Management (PELUM Association) 18225

Country Coordinator PELUM-Kenya, PO Box 6123-01000, SACDEP Training Ctr Compound, Upper Hill Road next to Central Memorial Hosp, Thika, Kenya. T. +254202622674. Fax +254202622674. E-mail: pelumkenya@pelum.net.
URL: http://www.pelum.net/

History Oct 1995. **Aims** Influence agricultural and rural development policies so that it has a positive impact on the rural poor; facilitate the social capital development of smallholder farmers; develop the effectiveness of member organizations in helping the communities they work with to improve their livelihood and reduce poverty; stimulate farmer to farmer learning and inspire farmers to experiment and innovate in empowering ways; make development more effective and more equitable among, women and children, and for people infected with and by the HIV/AIDS pandemic, promoting such development by seeking greater cooperation between North and South; enhance the quality of the environment through sustainable development practices, with organic agriculture and minimal external inputs as key strategies. **Structure** General Meeting (every 3 years); Regional Board; Regional Secretariat. **Languages** English, French. **Staff** 14.00 FTE, paid. **Finance** Members' dues; funds; sales. **Activities** Events/meetings; knowledge management/information dissemination; networking/liaising. **Events** *Triennial General Meeting* Kampala (Uganda) 2014, *Triennial General Meeting* Lesotho 2011, *Triennial General Meeting* Morogoro (Tanzania UR) 2008, *Triennial General Meeting / Biennial General Meeting* Kabwe (Zambia) 2005, *Biennial General Meeting* Jinja (Uganda) 2003. **Publications** *PELUM Bulletin* (6 a year) – electronic; *Ground Up* (2 a year) – magazine. Books; policy briefs; leaflets.
Members Civil society organizations (250) in 12 countries:
Botswana, Kenya, Lesotho, Malawi, Mozambique, Namibia, Rwanda, South Africa, Tanzania UR, Uganda, Zambia, Zimbabwe.
NGO Relations Partner of (4): *Brot für die Welt*; *Comité Catholique contre la Faim et pour le Développement-Terre Solidaire (CCFD-Terre Solidaire)*; *Oxfam International (#17922)*; *Oxfam Novib.* Collaborating NGOs: *Forum for Agricultural Research in Africa (FARA, #09897)*; *West African Network of Farmers' Organizations and Agricultural Producers (#20891).* [2015/XF4652/**F**]

♦ Parti du citoyen du monde (inactive)
♦ Parti des citoyens européens (#18248)
♦ Particles in Europe (meeting series)
♦ Particles and Nuclei International Conference (meeting series)

♦ Particle Therapy Co-Operative Group (PTCOG) 18226

Sec Paul Scherrer Inst (PSI), 5232 Villigen AG, Switzerland.
Chairman MGH, 294 Washington St, Boston MA 02114, USA.
URL: https://www.ptcog.ch/

History Founded 1985. Non-profit association status since 2007. **Aims** Promote global activities in particle *radiation* therapy with the goal of improving treatment of *cancer* to the highest possible standards in radiation therapy. **Structure** General Assembly; Steering Committee; Executive Committee; Clinical and Technical Subcommittees; Regional Chapters. **Languages** English. **Staff** 1.00 FTE, paid. **Finance** Meeting registration fees; research foundations. Annual budget: about Swiss Fr 50,000. **Activities** Training/education; events/meetings. **Events** *Annual Meeting* Cincinnati, OH (USA) 2018, *Annual Meeting* Yokohama (Japan) / Chiba (Japan) 2017, *Annual Meeting* Prague (Czech Rep) 2016, *Annual Meeting / Meeting* San Diego, CA (USA) 2015, *Annual Meeting / Meeting* Shanghai (China) 2014. **Publications** *International Journal for Particle Therapy (IJPT).*
Members Individuals in 43 countries and territories:
Argentina, Australia, Austria, Belgium, Brazil, Bulgaria, Canada, Chile, China, Cuba, Czechia, Denmark, Finland, France, Germany, India, Indonesia, Iran Islamic Rep, Ireland, Israel, Italy, Japan, Korea Rep, Mexico, Netherlands, New Zealand, Norway, Poland, Portugal, Romania, Russia, Saudi Arabia, Singapore, Slovakia, Slovenia, South Africa, Spain, Sweden, Switzerland, Taiwan, Thailand, UK, USA. [2019.12.13/XJ0593/v/**E**]

♦ Parti communautaire national européen (internationally oriented national body)
♦ Parti démocrate européen (#06900)
♦ Parti démocratique des peuples d'Europe – Alliance libre européenne / see European Free Alliance (#07356)
♦ Partido Aliança dos Democratas e Liberais pela Europa (#00703)
♦ Partido de la Alianza de los Demócratas y Liberales por Europa (#00703)
♦ Partido de los Ciudadanos Europeos (#18248)
♦ Partido Comunitario Nacional-Europeo (internationally oriented national body)
♦ Partido Comunitário Nacional-Europeu (internationally oriented national body)
♦ Partido Europeo de los Liberales, Demócratas y Reformistas / see Alliance of Liberals and Democrats for Europe Party (#00703)
♦ Partido Europeu dos Liberais, Democratas e Reformistas / see Alliance of Liberals and Democrats for Europe Party (#00703)
♦ Partido Popular Europeo (#08185)
♦ Partido Popular Europeo – Federación de los Partidos Demócratas Cristianos de la Comunidad Europea / see European People's Party (#08185)
♦ Partido Popular Europeu (#08185)
♦ Partido Socialista Europeu (#18249)
♦ Partido de los Socialistas Europeos (#18249)
♦ Partidul Alianta Liberalilor si Democratilor pentru Europa (#00703)
♦ Partidul European al Liberalilor, Democratilor si Reformistilor / see Alliance of Liberals and Democrats for Europe Party (#00703)
♦ Partiet Alliansen Liberaler och Demorater för Europa (#00703)
♦ Parti européen des libéraux, démocrates et réformateurs / see Alliance of Liberals and Democrats for Europe Party (#00703)
♦ Parti Fédéraliste Européen (#07036)
♦ Partija "Eiropas Liberalu un Demokratu Apvieniba (#00703)
♦ Partij van de Alliantie van Liberalen en Democraten voor Europa (#00703)
♦ Partij van Europese Sociaaldemokraten (#18249)
♦ Parti pacifiste internationaliste (inactive)
♦ Parti populaire européen (#08185)
♦ Parti populaire européen – Fédération des partis démocrates chrétiens de la Communauté européenne / see European People's Party (#08185)
♦ Parti radical transnational / see Nonviolent Radical Party, Transnational and Transparty (#17154)
♦ Parti socialiste européen (#18249)
♦ El Partit Liberal, Demòcrata i Reformista Europeu / see Alliance of Liberals and Democrats for Europe Party (#00703)
♦ Partito dell'Alleanza dei Democratici e dei Liberali per l'Europa (#00703)
♦ Partito dei Cittadini Europei (#18248)
♦ Partito Comunitario Nazionale-Europeo (internationally oriented national body)
♦ Partito Democratico Europeo (#06900)
♦ Partito Europeo dei Liberali, Democratici e Riformatori / see Alliance of Liberals and Democrats for Europe Party (#00703)
♦ Partito Popolare Europeo (#08185)
♦ Partito Popolare Europeo – Federazione dei Partiti Democratici Cristiani della Comunità Europea / see European People's Party (#08185)
♦ Partito Radicale Transnazionale / see Nonviolent Radical Party, Transnational and Transparty (#17154)
♦ Partito del Socialismo Europeo (#18249)
♦ Partner Aid / see PartnerAid (#18227)

♦ PartnerAid 18227

Switzerland Haltmattweg 20, 4912 Aarwangen BE, Switzerland.
UK 21 Walnut Way, Amersham, HP6 5SB, UK.
URL: http://www.partneraid.ch/

History Founded 1991, Switzerland; 1992, UK; 1998; Germany as *Partner Aid International (inactive).* German association changed into a member of *World Relief.* In some offices referred to as *Partner Aid.* **Aims** Help people and communities in less developed countries to combat *poverty* and improve their living conditions. **Structure** Offices in: Switzerland; UK; USA; Netherlands. **Languages** English, German. **Staff** 200.00 FTE, paid. **Finance** Grants; donations; revenues from consultancy services and business operations. Budget (annual): about euro 2.4 million. **Activities** Projects of development cooperation and emergency assistance, in Sudan, Pakistan, Somalia, Kyrgyzstan, Yemen, Tajikistan and Tanzania. Provides education and training for holistic development. Advocacy and public awareness. **Publications** *PartnerAid News.* Annual Report. **IGO Relations** *Deutsche Gesellschaft für Internationale Zusammenarbeit (GIZ); UNDP (#20292); UNHCR (#20327); UNICEF (#20332); United States Agency for International Development (USAID); World Food Programme (WFP, #21510).* **NGO Relations** *Concern Worldwide; Centre for International Migration and Development (CIM); Dorcas (#05123); Tearfund, UK.* [2016/XJ5032/**F**]

♦ Partner Community Council (PCC EMEA) 18228

Americas Office PO Box 140759, Irving TX 75014, USA. E-mail: info@pccemea.com.
URL: http://www.pccemea.com/

History Dec 1992, London (UK), as *European Distributor Alliance Council (EuroDAC),* by Nortel networks partners. Later known as *Distributor Alliance Council EMEA (DAC EMEA).* Present name adopted following Avaya's purchase of Nortel's enterprise solutions business. **Structure** Steering Committee, including Chairperson and Sub-Committee Chairmen. Sub-Committees (4). **Events** *Fall Conference* Vienna (Austria) 2018, *Meeting* Amsterdam (Netherlands) 2015, *Spring Conference* Copenhagen (Denmark) 2012, *Fall Conference* Grand Rapids, MI (USA) 2012, *Fall conference* Porto (Portugal) 2010. [2020/XJ3382/**E**]

- ♦ Partners in Aid (internationally oriented national body)
- ♦ Partners of the Americas (internationally oriented national body)
- ♦ Partnerschaft der Bergbauregionen / see Association of Europe's Coalfield Regions (#02585)
- ♦ Partnerschaft für Erneuerbare Energien und Energieeffizienz (#18837)
- ♦ Partners for Christian Development / see Partners Worldwide
- ♦ Partners for Democratic Change / see PartnersGlobal
- ♦ Partners for Development (internationally oriented national body)
- ♦ PartnersGlobal (internationally oriented national body)
- ♦ Partners in Health (internationally oriented national body)
- ♦ Partnership for Acid Drainage Remediation in Europe (see: #14168)

♦ Partnership for Advanced Computing Europe (PRACE) 18229

Managing Dir Rue du Trône 98, 1050 Brussels, Belgium. T. +3226130922.
URL: http://www.prace-ri.eu/

History Preparatory Phase (PRACE-PP) ran 1 Jan 2008 – 30 Jun 2010; First Implementation Phase (PRACE-1IP) 1 Jul 2010 – 31 Jul 2012; Second Implementation Phase 1 Sep 2011 – 31 Aug 2013; Third Implementation Project 1 Jul 2012 – 30 Jun 2014. Fourth Implementation Phase (PRACE-4IP) 1 Feb 2015 – 30 Apr 2017. Fifth Implementation Phase (PRACE-5IP) 1 Jan 2017 – 30 Apr 2019. Sixth Implementation Phase (PRACE-6IP) 1 May 2019 – 31 Dec 2021. Registration: Banque-Carrefour des Entreprises, No/ID: 0826.890.059, Start date: 24 Jun 2010, Belgium. **Aims** Enable high impact scientific discovery and engineering research and development across all disciplines to enhance European *competitiveness* for the benefit of society; strengthen European users of High Performance Computing (HPC) in industry through various initiatives. **Structure** Council; Board of the Council; Scientific Steering Committee; Industrial Advisory Committee; Access Committee; Board of Directors. **Languages** English. **Staff** 9.00 FTE, paid. **Finance** Funded by member governments through representative organizations; contributions from: *European Union (EU, #08967).* **Activities** Events/meetings; guidance/assistance/consulting; knowledge management/information dissemination; training/education. **Events** *European HPC Summit* Porto (Portugal) 2021, *European HPC Summit* Poznań (Poland) 2019, *Digital Infrastructures for Research Conference* Lisbon (Portugal) 2018, *Scientific Conference* Ljubljana (Slovenia) 2018, *Digital Infrastructures for Research Conference* Brussels (Belgium) 2017. **Publications** *PRACE Digest* (annual) – magazine. *PRACE Scientific Case for HPC in Europe 2018-2026.* Annual Report.
Members Government organizations or legal entities representing governments; Hosting Members. Members in 26 countries:
Austria, Belgium, Bulgaria, Cyprus, Czechia, Denmark, Finland, France, Germany, Greece, Hungary, Ireland, Israel, Italy, Luxembourg, Netherlands, Norway, Poland, Portugal, Slovakia, Slovenia, Spain, Sweden, Switzerland, Türkiye, UK.
IGO Relations Cooperates with: *e-Infrastructure Reflection Group (e-IRG, #11208).* **NGO Relations** Member of: *Association of European-level Research Infrastructure Facilities (ERF-AISBL, #02518); Federation of European and International Associations Established in Belgium (FAIB, #09508).* [2022/XJ4898/**F***]

- ♦ A Partnership with Africa (internationally oriented national body)
- ♦ Partnership Africa Canada / see IMPACT (#11136)
- ♦ Partnership for African Environmental Sustainability (internationally oriented national body)

♦ Partnership for African Social and Governance Research (PASGR) . 18230

Contact I&M Bank House, 6th Floor, Second Ngong Avenue, Upper Hill, PO Box 76418, Nairobi, 00508, Kenya. T. +254202985000 – +2540731000065. E-mail: info@pasgr.org.
URL: http://www.pasgr.org/

History 2011, Nairobi (Kenya). **Aims** Enhance research excellence in governance and public policy that contributes to the overall wellbeing of women and men. **Structure** Board of Directors. **Languages** English. **Staff** 15.00 FTE, paid. **Finance** Supported by: *Carnegie Corporation of New York; Department for International Development (DFID, inactive);* Dutch Knowledge Platformon Inclusive Development (INCLUDE); *Ford Foundation (#09858); International Development Research Centre (IDRC, #13162); The William and Flora Hewlett Foundation; United Nations Foundation (UNF, #20563).* **Activities** Research and development; training/education. **Events** *Conference on Social Protection in Africa / Conference* Nairobi (Kenya) 2014. **Publications** Mapping studies; synthesis papers; policy briefs. [2023.02.14/XJ6590/**F**]

- ♦ Partnership Brokers Accreditation Scheme / see Partnership Brokers Association
- ♦ Partnership Brokers Association (internationally oriented national body)
- ♦ Partnership for Change (internationally oriented national body)
- ♦ Partnership for Child Development (internationally oriented national body)

♦ Partnership for Clean Fuels and Vehicles (PCFV) 18231

Contact UNEP, PO Box 30552, Nairobi, Kenya. T. +254207624184. Fax +254207625264. E-mail: pcfv@unep.org.
URL: http://www.unep.org/transport/pcfv/

History Launched 2002, Johannesburg (South Africa), within the framework of *UNEP (#20299).* Relaunched Oct 2012, London (UK). **Aims** Encourage countries to adopt overall clean fuel and vehicles strategies, including vehicle and fuel standards, inspection and maintenance, development of public *transport* systems – including both motorised and non-motorised options – and transportation demand management. **Staff** 9.00 FTE, paid.
Members Partners governments; International organizations; Industry; NGOs; Other. Government partners (18) of 12 countries:
Canada, China, Congo DR, Ghana, Indonesia, Kenya, Mexico, Mozambique, Netherlands, Nigeria, USA, Yemen.
Regional entity:
European Commission (EC, #06633).
Industry partners (23) include the following 9 organizations listed in this Yearbook:
African Refiners and Distributors Association (ARA, #00429); Asian Clean Fuels Association (ACFA, #01379); Association for Emissions Control by Catalyst (AECC, #02486); Association of Global Automakers; European Automobile Manufacturers' Association (ACEA, #06300); Fleet Forum (#09792); International Fuel Quality Center (IFQC, #13689); International Organization of Motor Vehicle Manufacturers (#14455); International Petroleum Industry Environmental Conservation Association (IPIECA, #14562).
Non-Governmental Organizations (19), including 9 listed in this Yearbook:
Caucasus Environmental NGO Network (CENN, #03613); CEGESTI; Centre for Environment and Development for the Arab Region and Europe (CEDARE, #03738); FIA Foundation (#09742); Global New Car Assessment Programme (Global NCAP, #10506); Observatoire du Sahara et du Sahel (OSS, #17636); Petroleum Institute of East Africa (PIEA); Regional Environmental Centre for the Caucasus (REC Caucasus, #18781); World Resources Institute (WRI, #21753).
International associations (10):
ASEAN (#01141) (Working Group); *Clean Air Asia (#03983); Comisión Centroamericana de Ambiente y Desarrollo (CCAD, #04129);* Global NCAP; *International Energy Agency (IEA, #13270); Regional Environmental Centre for Central and Eastern Europe (REC, #18782); South Asia Cooperative Environment Programme (SACEP, #19714);* UN DESA; *UNEP (#20299); World Food Programme (WFP, #21510).*
IGO Relations *ASEAN (#01141); Centre for Environment and Development for the Arab Region and Europe (CEDARE, #03738); Comisión Centroamericana de Ambiente y Desarrollo (CCAD, #04129); Regional Environmental Centre for Central and Eastern Europe (REC, #18782); South Asia Cooperative Environment Programme (SACEP, #19714);* UNDESA; *UNEP (#20299); World Food Programme (WFP, #21510).*
[2016.06.01/XJ7834/y/**E**]

- ♦ Partnership to Cut Hunger in Africa / see Partnership to Cut Hunger and Poverty in Africa
- ♦ Partnership to Cut Hunger and Poverty in Africa (internationally oriented national body)
- ♦ Partnership for Democratic Governance (inactive)

♦ Partnership for Dengue Control (PDC) 18232

Contact Fondation Mérieux, 17 rue Bourgelat, 69002 Lyon, France.
URL: http://www.controldengue.org/

History 2013. Also referred to as *PDC Foundation.* **Aims** Accelerate innovations in *vaccines,* therapeutics, vector control, *disease* surveillance and diagnostics; promote evidence-based prevention and control strategies nationally and internationally; strengthen advocacy, capacity building and networking. **Structure** Board. Hosted by *Mérieux Foundation.* **Languages** English. **Activities** Research and development; knowledge management/information dissemination; guidance/assistance/consulting; advocacy/lobbying/activism; capacity building; events/meetings. **IGO Relations** *Pan American Health Organization (PAHO, #18108); WHO (#20950).* **NGO Relations** Member of: *Global Dengue and Aedes-transmitted Diseases Consortium (GDAC, #10316).* Partners and relations include: *Bill and Melinda Gates Foundation (BMGF); Mérieux Foundation; Dengue Vaccine Initiative (DVI, #05038); Sabin Vaccine Institute (Sabin);* commercial companies.
[2020.02.14/XM5061/**F**]

- ♦ Partnership for the East Asian-Australasian Flyway / see East Asian – Australasian Flyway Partnership (#05198)

♦ Partnership for Economic Policy (PEP) 18233

Partenariat en politiques économiques

Exec Dir Duduville Campus, Kasarani, PO Box 30772-00100, Nairobi, Kenya. T. +254208632681. E-mail: info@pep-net.org – pep-nairobi@pep-net.org.
URL: https://www.pep-net.org/

History 2002. **Aims** Ensure greater participation of *local* expertise in the analysis of policy issues related to poverty, and economic and social development. **Structure** Board of Directors; Secretariat; Program Committee. **Finance** Supported by: Co-Impact; Global Affairs Canada; *International Development Research Centre (IDRC, #13162); Mastercard Foundation; The William and Flora Hewlett Foundation.* **Activities** Events/meetings; projects/programmes; research/documentation; training/education. **Events** *Annual Conference* 2022, *Conference* Manila (Philippines) 2016. **NGO Relations** Member of (1): *Global Coalition to End Child Poverty (#10292).* Instrumental in setting up (1): *South Asian Network on Economic Modeling (SANEM, #19736).* [2023/XJ5311/**F**]

- ♦ Partnership for Educational Revitalization in the Americas (internationally oriented national body)

♦ Partnership for Education and Research about Responsible Living (PERL) 18234

Project Manager Hedmark Univ College, PO Box 400, 2418 Elverum, Norway. T. +4762517636. E-mail: perl@hihm.no.
Exec Sec address not obtained. T. +4762517728.
Street Address Holsetgata 31, 2318 Hamar, Norway.
URL: http://www.perlprojects.org/

History 2003, following the activities of the 'Consumer Citizenship Network'. **Aims** Encourage people to contribute to constructive change through they way they choose to live. **Structure** Steering Group of 12 members. Core Unit, based at Elverum (Norway). Work Groups. **Finance** Grants from: Norwegian government; *European Commission (EC, #06633); UNEP (#20299);* other funders. Budget (annual): about euro 300,000. **Activities** Capacity building; events/meetings. **Events** *International Conference* Paris (France) 2015, *International Conference* Berlin (Germany) 2012, *International Conference* Istanbul (Turkey) 2011. **Publications** *PERL Newsletter. Promoting New Responses* – 5 vols to date.
Members Educators and researchers from about 140 institutions in 50 countries:
Argentina, Australia, Austria, Belgium, Brazil, Bulgaria, Burkina Faso, Canada, Chile, China, Costa Rica, Czechia, Denmark, Egypt, Estonia, Eswatini, Finland, France, Germany, Greece, Hungary, Iceland, India, Indonesia, Ireland, Italy, Japan, Kenya, Korea Rep, Latvia, Lithuania, Malta, Mexico, Nepal, Netherlands, Norway, Peru, Poland, Portugal, Romania, Senegal, Slovakia, Slovenia, South Africa, Spain, Sweden, Tanzania UR, Thailand, Türkiye, UK.
Included in the above, 3 organizations listed in this Yearbook:
Consumers International (CI, #04773); International Centre for Integrated Assessment and Sustainable Development (ICIS); UNESCO (#20322).
IGO Relations Cooperates with: *UNEP (#20299); UNESCO (#20322).* [2015/XJ4797/y/**F**]

♦ Partnership for European Environmental Research (PEER) 18235

Sec address not obtained.
Communications Coordinator address not obtained.
URL: http://www.peer.eu/

History 2001. Framework Agreement signed 25 Jun 2002, Roskilde (Denmark); renewed, 2012. **Aims** Combine forces to follow a joint strategy in environmental sciences and enhance research on ecological sustainability. **Structure** Directors Board; Secretariat; Communication Group. **Languages** English. **Activities** Events/meetings; politics/policy/regulatory; research/documentation; training/education. **Events** *Science for the Environment Conference / International Conference* Aarhus (Denmark) 2013, *Smart AgriMatics International Conference* Paris (France) 2012. **Publications** *PEER Newsletter* (3-4 a year). Reports; statements.
Members Institutions (8) in 8 countries:
Denmark, Finland, France, Germany, Italy, Netherlands, Norway, UK.
NGO Relations Cooperates with (3): *Alternet (#00756); European Network of Freshwater Research Organisations (EurAqua, #07911); European Soil Bureau (ESB, #08793).* [2023.02.15/XJ4616/**F**]

♦ Partnership of a European Group of Aeronautics and Space UniversitieS (PEGASUS) 18236

Office address not obtained. E-mail: office@pegasus-europe.org.
Registered Office c/o TU Delft, Fac of Aerospace, Kluyverweg 1, 2629 HS Delft, Netherlands.
URL: https://www.pegasus-europe.org/

History 1998, Toulouse (France). *PEGASUS Foundation* serves a legal body; Foundation Act signed, 6 Jul 2007. Former names and other names: *Stichting Partnership of a European Group of Aeronautics and Space Universities Foundation (PEGASUS Foundation)* – legal name. Registration: Netherlands. **Aims** Represent the European aerospace/aviation academic community. **Structure** Council; Board; Chairman; Working Groups. PEGASUS Foundation; PEGASUS-Industry Alliance. **Activities** Networking/liaising; training/education. **Events** *Student Conference* 2021, *Student Conference* Pisa (Italy) 2020, *Student Conference* Glasgow (UK) 2019, *Student Conference* Madrid (Spain) 2018, *Student Conference* Berlin (Germany) 2017.
Members Full; Probationary; Associate Public and/or non-profit institutions of higher education in aeronautical/aerospace engineering. Full (28) in 11 countries:
Czechia, France, Germany, Italy, Netherlands, Poland, Portugal, Slovakia, Spain, Sweden, UK.
Associate in 5 countries:
France, Lithuania, Russia, Slovakia, Ukraine. [2021.05.21/XJ8735/**F**]

♦ Partnership for European Research in Occupational Safety and Health (PEROSH) 18237

Sec c/o TNO, Sylviusweg 71, 2333 BE Leiden, Netherlands.
Main Website: https://perosh.eu/

History 7 Nov 2003, Rome (Italy). **Aims** Coordinate and cooperate on European research and development efforts in occupational safety and health. **Structure** Steering Committee (SC); Executive Committee; Scientific Steering Group (SSG); Working Groups. **Languages** Danish, Dutch, English, Finnish, French, German, Italian, Norwegian, Polish, Spanish, Swedish. **Staff** 1.00 FTE, paid. **Activities** Knowledge management/information dissemination; networking/liaising; research/documentation. **Publications** *PEROSH Newsletter*.
Members Occupational Safety and Health research institutes in 13 countries:
Austria, Denmark, Finland, France, Germany, Italy, Netherlands, Norway, Poland, Spain, Sweden, Switzerland, UK.
[2023.02.15/AA0897/**F**]

♦ Partnership for Global Justice (internationally oriented national body)
♦ Partnership International (internationally oriented national body)

♦ Partnership in International Management (PIM) 18238

Coordinator RSM Erasmus Univ, MBA Office, Bayle Bldg Room J2-38, Burgemeester Oudlaan 50, 3062 PA Rotterdam, Netherlands.
URL: http://pimnetwork.org/

History 1973, by Ecole des Hautes Etudes Commerciales (HEC), New York University (NYU), and London Business School (LBS). Governed by convenant signed 1986, Milan (Italy); revised 1994, Rotterdam (Netherlands), and 1999, Melbourne (Australia). **Aims** Facilitate the development of international cooperation among members; foster development of joint programs, students and faculty exchange, joint research and cooperation among faculty members and researchers. **Structure** Steering Committee. **Languages** English. **Staff** 0.20 FTE, paid; 13.00 FTE, voluntary. **Finance** Members' dues. Annual budget: US$ 51,200. **Activities** Events/meetings. **Events** *Annual Conference* Milan (Italy) 2020, *Annual Conference* Bangkok (Thailand) 2019, *Annual Conference* San José (Costa Rica) 2018. **Publications** *PIM Newsletter*.
Members Business schools (64) in 39 countries and territories:
Australia, Austria, Belgium, Brazil, Canada, Chile, China, Costa Rica, Czechia, Denmark, Finland, France, Germany, Hong Kong, Hungary, India, Ireland, Israel, Italy, Japan, Korea Rep, Mexico, Netherlands, New Zealand, Norway, Peru, Poland, Portugal, Russia, Singapore, South Africa, Spain, Sweden, Switzerland, Thailand, Türkiye, UK, USA, Venezuela.
IGO Relations None. **NGO Relations** None. [2020/XM5627/**F**]

♦ Partnership for Maternal, Newborn & Child Health / see PMNCH (#18410)
♦ Partnership of Mining Areas / see Association of Europe's Coalfield Regions (#02585)

♦ Partnership for Observation of the Global Oceans (POGO) 18239

Address not obtained.
URL: http://www.ocean-partners.org/

History Founded 1999, La Jolla CA (USA). UK Registered Charity: 1171692. **Aims** Promote global ocean observations; improve scientific knowledge; interpret scientific results to policy makers; enhance public awareness of oceanic issues; provide training and technology transfer with emphasis on fellowship provision in developing countries to assist researchers. **Structure** Assembly (annual); Executive Committee. **Languages** English. **Staff** 3.00 FTE, paid. **Finance** Members' dues. **Activities** Networking/liaising; capacity building; awareness raising. **Events** *Annual Meeting* Yokohama (Japan) 2016, *Annual Meeting* Hobart, TAS (Australia) 2014, *Annual Meeting / Meeting* Cape Town (South Africa) 2013, *Annual Meeting* Manoa, HI (USA) 2012, *Open science meeting for an international quiet ocean experiment* Paris (France) 2011.
Members National research institutes in 19 countries:
Australia, Belgium, Brazil, Chile, China, France, Germany, India, Ireland, Italy, Japan, Korea Rep, Mexico, Netherlands, Norway, Russia, Spain, UK, USA.
Collaborating international organizations (11):
Global Alliance of Continuous Plankton Recorder Surveys (GACS, #10191); *Global Ocean Observing System (GOOS, #10511)*; *Integrated Global Observing Strategy (IGOS, inactive)*; *Intergovernmental Oceanographic Commission (IOC, #11496)*; *International Council for Science (ICSU, inactive)*; *International Ocean Discovery Program (IODP, #14393)*; *Joint WMO-IOC Technical Commission for Oceanography and Marine Meteorology (JCOMM, #16151)*; *North Pacific Marine Science Organization (PICES, #17602)*; *Ocean Observations Panel for Climate (OOPC, #17683)*; *Scientific Committee on Oceanic Research (SCOR, #19149)*; Southern Ocean Observing System (SOOS).
NGO Relations Founding member of: *World Association of Marine Stations (WAMS, #21161)*.
[2018.06.01/XE4164/y/**E**]

♦ Partnership for Peace (PfP) 18240

Partenariat pour la paix (PPP)
Contact address not obtained. T. +3268275155. Fax +3268275196.
URL: http://www.nato.int/issues/pfp/index.html

History Jan 1994, Brussels (Belgium), when approved by Summit Meeting of Heads of State and Government of *NATO (#16945)*. A *PfP Status of Forces Agreement*, defines the legal status of NATO and Partner military forces when present on each other's territory. **Aims** Expand and intensify *political* and military *cooperation* throughout *Europe*; increase stability, diminish threats to peace and build strengthening relationships by promoting the spirit of practical cooperation and commitment to *democratic* principles; offer participating states, including Central and Eastern European countries, CIS member states and neutral European countries, the opportunity to strengthen their relations with NATO by taking part in security cooperation programmes, such as military exercises and civil emergency operations, tailored to their individual requirements and in which they increasingly have a say in planning and directing. Specific objectives: facilitate transparency in national defence planning and budgeting processes; ensure democratic control of defence forces; maintain capability and readiness to contribute to operations under the authority of the UN and/or the responsibility of the OSCE; develop cooperative military relations with NATO for the purpose of joint planning, training and exercises, in order to strengthen the ability of participating countries to undertake crisis management operations; over the longer term, develop forces better able to operate with those of the North Atlantic Alliance. **Structure** *'Political-Military Steering Committee (PMSC)'* meets as the working forum under chairmanship of NATO's Deputy Secretary General. It functions under *Euro Atlantic Partnership Council (EAPC, #05646)*, which serves as a main forum for consultation on political and conceptual issues and for exchange of experience and discussion of practical measures for cooperation, and periodically to EAPC Defence and Foreign Ministers. Partner nations designate diplomatic and military representatives to NATO headquarters. *'Partnership Coordination Cell (PCC)'* in Mons (Belgium), where SHAPE is also located, comprises permanent staff and Partner liaison teams. Partner staff elements function as international officers in NATO's International Military Staff (IMS) and its 2 Strategic Commands. Many Partners send liaison officers to permanent facilities at NATO Headquarters in Brussels (Belgium) and to the PCC. **Finance** Partners undertake to make available appropriate personnel, assets, facilities and capabilities, to fund their own participation and to share the burden of mounting exercise in which they take part. Assistance may be made available by the Alliance for Partner representatives' attendance in PfP activities. **Activities** Politics/policy/regulatory. **Events** *Geographic conference* Brussels (Belgium) 1999.
Members Membership open to EAPC states and other OSCE countries that are able and willing to contribute to the programme. Countries having signed PfP framework documents (27):
Albania, Armenia, Austria, Azerbaijan, Belarus, Bulgaria, Croatia, Estonia, Finland, Georgia, Ireland, Kazakhstan, Kyrgyzstan, Latvia, Lithuania, Moldova, North Macedonia, Romania, Russia, Slovakia, Slovenia, Sweden, Switzerland, Tajikistan, Turkmenistan, Ukraine, Uzbekistan. [2017/XF3163/**F***]

♦ Partnership for Quality Medical Donations (internationally oriented national body)

♦ Partnership for Responsible Financial Inclusion (PRFI) 18241

Secretariat c/o Ctr for Financial Inclusion at Accion, 1101 15th Str NW, Ste 400, Washington DC 20005, USA. T. +12023935113. Fax +12023935115.
URL: http://responsiblefinancialinclusion.org/

History 2011. **Aims** Advocate for responsible financial services; seek catalytic opportunities to accelerate financial access to the unserved.
Members Organizations (10):
ACCION International; Aga Khan Agency for Microfinance; *BRAC (#03310)*; CARE USA; *FINCA International*; *Grameen Foundation (GF, #10694)*; *Opportunity International (#17776)*; *Pro Mujer*; *VisionFund International (#20797)*; *Women's World Banking (WWB, #21037)*. [2017/XM6433/y/**E**]

♦ Partnerships in Environmental Management for the Seas of East Asia (PEMSEA) 18242

Secretariat PO Box 2502, 1165 Quezon City, Philippines. T. +6329292992. Fax +6324263849. E-mail: info@pemsea.org.
Street Address PEMSEA Office Bldg, DENR Compound, Visayas Avenue, Diliman, Quezon City, Philippines.
URL: http://www.pemsea.org/

History 1994. First phase (1994-1999): regional programme funded by *Global Environment Facility (GEF, #10346)*, implemented by *UNDP (#20292)* and executed by *International Maritime Organization (IMO, #14102)*, under the title *Regional Programme on Marine Pollution Prevention and Management for the East Asian Seas Region*. Second phase (1999-2008): funded by GEF, implemented by UNDP and executed by IMO, under current title. Third phase (2008-2014): with signing of the Haikou Partnership Agreement on Implementation of the Sustainable Development Strategy for the Seas of East Asia (SDS-SEA) and the Partnership Operating Arrangements (Dec 2006), transformed into regional collaborative mechanism to pursue implementation of SDS-SEA. Agreement Recognizing International Legal Personality, signed Nov 2009. Headquarters Agreement with government of Philippines ratified May 2015, by Philippine Senate, on which PEMPSEA was transformed into an IGO. Fourth phase (2014-2019): scaling up SDS-SEA Implementation. **Aims** Foster and sustain healthy and resilient oceans, coasts, communities and economies across the East Asian Seas region. **Structure** East Asian Seas (EAS) Congress (every 3 years), including Ministerial Forum. Intergovernmental and multisectoral East Asian Seas Partnership Council, currently composed of 11 Partner countries and 21 non-country Partners, and consisting of Executive Committee, Intergovernmental Session and Technical Session. Executive Committee, comprising Council Chair, Session Chairs and Secretary. PEMSEA Resource Facility provides secretarial and technical services, headed by Executive Director. **Languages** English. **Staff** 28.00 FTE, paid. **Finance** Country contributions; support from *Global Environment Facility (GEF, #10346)*; *International Bank for Reconstruction and Development (IBRD, #12317)* (World Bank); *UNEP (#20299)*. Budget variable. **Activities** Politics/policy/regulatory; guidance/assistance/consulting; knowledge management/information dissemination. **Events** *International Symposium on Marine Microplastics* Busan (Korea Rep) 2019, *International Workshop on Water Quality Monitoring* Busan (Korea Rep) 2017, *Seawater Quality Analysis Monitoring Workshop* Busan (Korea Rep) 2017, *PEMSEA Network of Local Governments (PNLG) Forum* Ansan (Korea Rep) 2016, *PEMSEA Network of Local Governments (PNLG) Forum* Shima City (Japan) 2013. **Publications** *eupdates* (12 a year); *Tropical Coasts Magazine*. *Securing the Oceans: Essays on Ocean Governance* (2008); *State of the Coasts of Batangas* (2008); *Dynamics of Integrated Coastal Management* (2007); *Manila Bay Area Environmental Atlas* (2007). Case studies; course material; manuscripts/policy briefs.
Members Country Partners (11):
Cambodia, China, Indonesia, Japan, Korea DPR, Korea Rep, Laos, Philippines, Singapore, Timor-Leste, Vietnam.
Non-Country Partners (21), including 7 organizations listed in this Yearbook:
ASEAN Centre for Biodiversity (ACB, #01149); *Global Programme of Action for the Protection of the Marine Environment from Land-Based Activities (GPA, see: #20299)*; *International Centre for the Environmental Management of Enclosed Coastal Seas (International EMECS Centre)*; *International Ocean Institute (IOI, #14394)*; *International Petroleum Industry Environmental Conservation Association (IPIECA, #14562)*; *International Union for Conservation of Nature and Natural Resources (IUCN, #15766)* (Asia Regional Office); *IOC Sub-Commission for the Western Pacific (WESTPAC, see: #11496)*; *Ocean Policy Research Institute (OPRI)*.
IGO Relations Cooperates with: *ASEAN (#01141)*; *Western and Central Pacific Fisheries Commission (WCPFC, #20912)*; Yellow Sea Large Marine Ecosystem Project. **NGO Relations** Observer to: *Ocean Policy Institute Network in East Asian Region (OPINEAR, #17685)*. Partner of: *Blue Finance (#03283)*.
[2019.02.21/XM1250/y/**E***]

♦ Partnerships in Health Information (internationally oriented national body)

♦ Partnership in Statistics for Development in the 21st Century (PARIS21) 18243

Secretariat Manager OECD/STD, 2 rue Andre Pascal, 75775 Paris CEDEX 16, France. T. +33145249051. Fax +33145249406.
Street Address 4 Quai du Point du Jour, 92100 Boulogne-Billancourt, France.
URL: http://www.paris21.org/

History Nov 1999, by *United Nations (UN, #20515)*, *European Commission (EC, #06633)*, *OECD (#17693)*, *International Monetary Fund (IMF, #14180)* and *International Bank for Reconstruction and Development (IBRD, #12317)*, in response to the UN ECOSOC resolution on the goals of the UN Conference on Development. **Aims** Develop a culture of managing for development results. **Structure** Board, comprising representatives of developing countries from each region of the world, bilateral donors, and founding institutions (UN, EC, OECD and World Bank). Executive Committee. Secretariat. **Publications** *Global Directory of Partners in Statistical Capacity Building*; *Partner Report on Support to Statistics*. [2017/XJ1178/**E***]

♦ Partnership on Sustainable, Low Carbon Transport Foundation (SLoCaT Foundation) 18244

Main Office Rue Sainte-Marie 6, 1080 Sint-Jans-Molenbeek, Belgium. E-mail: secretariat@slocatpartnership.org.
URL: http://www.slocat.net/

History Aug 2014, The Hague (Netherlands). Founded to enable, facilitate and support the SLoCat Partnership, which was set up 2009. Former names and other names: *Stichting Partnership on Sustainable, Low Carbon Transport (SLoCaT Foundation)* – legal name. Registration: Netherlands. **Aims** Promote the integration on sustainable transport in global policies on sustainable development and climate change. **Structure** Board of Directors; Secretariat. **Publications** *SLoCaT Newsletter*.
Members Organizations (over 80), including 45 listed in this Yearbook:
- *African Development Bank (ADB, #00283)*;
- *Alliance to Save Energy (ASE)*;
- *Asian Development Bank (ADB, #01422)*;
- *Association of the European Rail Supply Industry (UNIFE, #02536)*;
- *Center for Clean Air Policy (CCAP)*;
- *Clean Air Asia (#03983)*;
- *Clean Air Institute (CAI, #03985)*;
- *Climate Bonds Initiative (#04006)*;
- *Cooperation for the Continuing Development of Urban and Suburban Transportation (#04792)*;
- *Deutsche Gesellschaft für Internationale Zusammenarbeit (GIZ)*;
- *Development Bank of Latin America (CAF, #05055)*;
- *Energy and Resources Institute (TERI)*;
- *European Bank for Reconstruction and Development (EBRD, #06315)*;
- *European Cyclists' Federation (ECF, #06877)*;
- *European Institute for Sustainable Transport (EURIST)*;
- *FIA Foundation (#09742)*;
- *Global Environment Facility (GEF, #10346)*;
- *Global Infrastructure Basel Foundation (GIB Foundation, #10418)*;
- *Global Urban Development (GUD, #10643)*;
- *HealthBridge*;
- *Inter-American Development Bank (IDB, #11427)*;
- *International Association of Public Transport (#12118)*;
- *International Bank for Reconstruction and Development (IBRD, #12317)*;
- *International Energy Agency (IEA, #13270)*;
- *International Road Assessment Programme (iRAP, #14757)*;
- *International Road Federation (IRF Global, #14759)*;
- *International Transport Workers' Federation (ITF, #15726)*;
- *International Union for Conservation of Nature and Natural Resources (IUCN, #15766)*;
- *International Union of Railways (#15813)*;
- *Local Governments for Sustainability (ICLEI, #16507)*;
- *Nordic Development Fund (NDF, #17271)*;
- *Renewable Energy and Energy Efficiency Partnership (REEEP, #18837)*;
- *Stockholm Environment Institute (SEI, #19993)*;
- *Sustainable Transport Africa*;
- UN Department for Economic and Social Affairs (UN-DESA);
- *UNIDO (#20336)*;
- *United Nations Centre for Regional Development (UNCRD, #20526)*;

- *United Nations Economic and Social Commission for Asia and the Pacific (ESCAP, #20557);*
- *United Nations Economic Commission for Europe (UNECE, #20555);*
- *United Nations Human Settlements Programme (UN-Habitat, #20572);*
- *WHO (#20950);*
- *World Wide Fund for Nature (WWF, #21922);*
- *Wuppertal Institute for Climate, Environment and Energy.* [2021/XJ9723/fy/**F**]

♦ Partnership for Transparency Fund (PTF) 18245

Registered Office 1110 Vermont Avenue NW, Ste 500, Washington DC 20005, USA. T. +12406508445. E-mail: info@ptfund.org.
URL: http://ptfund.org/

History 2000. **Aims** Help citizens to fight corruption and meet citizen demand for good governance. **Structure** Board of Directors, comprising Chair, Vice-Chair, President, Treasurer, Chief Technical Officer and 6 members. Regional Coordinators for: Africa; East Asia; South Asia; Central and Eastern Europe; Latin America. **Finance** Grants. **Activities** Supports projects through small grants. **Members** Senior, experienced volunteer governance specialists retired from development institutions, NGOs and Government Agencies. Membership countries not specified. **IGO Relations** Global partner of: *Global Partnership for Social Accountability (GPSA, #10541)*. **NGO Relations** Allied partner of: *Financial Transparency Coalition (FTC, #09772)*. Supports: *Global Network for Good Governance (GNGG, #10490).* [2016/XJ4559/fv/**F**]

- ♦ Partnership for World Mission (internationally oriented national body)
- ♦ Partners of Insurance Intermediaries / see Partners of Intermediaries (#18246)

♦ Partners of Intermediaries (POI) 18246

Dir Av Albert-Elisabeth 40, 1200 Brussels, Belgium. T. +3227356048. Fax +3227321418.

History 1 Mar 2002, by *BIPAR – European Federation of Insurance Intermediaries (#03263)*. Also referred to as *Partners of Insurance Intermediaries*. Registered in accordance with Belgian law. **Aims** Offer insurance and financial intermediaries an electronic documentation, information and training centre on European and national issues related to their daily business. **Structure** General Assembly (annual); Council. **Languages** English, French. **Finance** Members' dues. **Activities** Research/documentation; events/meetings; training/education.
Members National Associations in 28 countries:
Austria, Belgium, Cyprus, Czechia, Denmark, Estonia, Finland, France, Germany, Greece, Hungary, Ireland, Italy, Lithuania, Luxembourg, Malta, Netherlands, Norway, Poland, Portugal, Romania, Russia, Slovakia, Spain, Sweden, Switzerland, Türkiye, UK. [2015.08.26/XF6858/**F**]

- ♦ Partners International (internationally oriented national body)
- ♦ Partners in Mission / see International Partners in Mission (#14526)
- ♦ Partners in Peace / see Children of the Earth
- ♦ Partners for Peace (internationally oriented national body)
- ♦ Partners in Population and Development / see Partners in Population and Development (#18247)

♦ Partners in Population and Development (PPD) 18247

Exec Dir Block-F, Plot 17/B and C, Sher-E-Bangla Nagar, Administrative Zone, Agargaon, Dhaka 1207, Bangladesh. T. +880248117938 – +880248117942. Fax +88029117817. E-mail: partners@ppdsec.org.
URL: http://www.partners-popdev.org/

History 5 Sep 1994, Cairo (Egypt). Founded as an alliance of developing countries, to do the follow up of the Program of Action of the International Conference for Population and Development. Former names and other names: *Partners in Population and Development – A South-South Initiative* – former; *Partners in Population and Development (PPD – An Intergovernmental Organization for Promoting South-South Cooperation)* – full title. **Aims** Promote South-South cooperation in the area of reproductive health, population and development issues. **Structure** Board (meets annually); Executive Committee; Secretariat located in Dhaka (Bangladesh); Africa Regional Office, Kampala (Uganda); Programme Office, Taicang (China); Liaison Office to the UN, New York NY (USA); Partners Country Coordinators (PCCs). **Languages** English, French. **Staff** 45.00 FTE, paid. **Finance** Sources: contributions of member/participating states; government support; international organizations; private foundations. **Activities** Advocacy/lobbying/activism; capacity building; events/meetings; financial and/or material support; knowledge management/information dissemination; monitoring/evaluation; research and development; research/documentation; training/education. **Events** *Nairobi Commitments and the 2030 Agenda – Taking stock and looking ahead to post COVID-19 Crisis* Dhaka (Bangladesh) 2020, *Nairobi Commitments and the 2030 Agenda – Taking stock and looking ahead to post COVID-19 Crisis* Dhaka (Bangladesh) 2020, *Nairobi Commitments and the 2030 Agenda – Taking stock and looking ahead to post COVID-19 Crisis* Dhaka (Bangladesh) 2020, *Asia Pacific Conference on Reproductive and Sexual Health and Rights* Beijing (China) 2009, *International forum on ICPD and MDGs* Yichang (China) 2004. **Publications** Annual Report; reports; declarations.
Members Governments of 27 countries:
Bangladesh, Benin, China, Colombia, Côte d'Ivoire, Egypt, Ethiopia, Gambia, Ghana, India, Indonesia, Jordan, Kenya, Mali, Mexico, Morocco, Nigeria, Pakistan, Senegal, South Africa, Sri Lanka, Thailand, Tunisia, Uganda, Vietnam, Yemen, Zimbabwe.
IGO Relations Member of (1): *Intergovernmental Organizations Conference (IGO Conference, #11498).* **NGO Relations** Member of (2): *PMNCH (#18410)*; *Reproductive Health Supplies Coalition (RHSC, #18847).* Partner of (1): *Every Woman Every Child (EWEC, #09215).* [2021.02.26/XF3019/**F***]

- ♦ Partners in Population and Development – A South-South Initiative / see Partners in Population and Development (#18247)
- ♦ Partners Worldwide (internationally oriented national body)

♦ Party of the Citizens of Europe (PACE) 18248

Parti des citoyens européens (PACE) – Partido de los Ciudadanos Europeos – Partei der Europäischen Bürger/Bürgerinnen – Partito dei Cittadini Europei

Contact c/o FAIB, Rue Washington 40, 1050 Brussels, Belgium. T. +33603622526.
Pres address not obtained.
URL: http://www.pace-europe.eu/

History 9 May 2007, Brussels (Belgium). Registered in accordance with Belgian law. **Aims** Contribute to the political integration of Europe by developing the political dialogue between citizens across the European Union. **Structure** General Assembly; Board of Administrators; President. **Languages** English, French, German, Italian, Spanish. **Staff** 0.75 FTE, paid; 5.00 FTE, voluntary. **Finance** Members' dues. Other sources: donations; proceeds from activities. **Activities** Training/education. Active in: Belgium, France, Germany, Spain. **Publications** *PACE Newsletter* – Book.
Members Full in 8 countries:
Belgium, France, Germany, Greece, Italy, Netherlands, Spain, UK. [2014.11.13/XJ8829/**F**]

♦ Party of European Socialists (PES) 18249

Parti socialiste européen (PSE) – Partido de los Socialistas Europeos – Sozialdemokratische Partei Europas – Partito del Socialismo Europeo – Partido Socialista Europeu – Partij van Europese Sociaaldemokraten – De Europaeiske Socialdemokraters Parti – De Europeiske Sosialdemokraters Parti – Euroopan Sosialidemokraattinen Puolue – Europeiska Socialdemokraters Parti

SG Rue Guimard 10, 1040 Brussels, Belgium. T. +3225489080. Fax +3222301766. E-mail: pes.secgen@pes.eu – info@pes.eu.
Pres address not obtained. E-mail: pes.president@pes.eu.
URL: http://www.pes.eu/

History Jun 1973, with the name *Confederation of the Socialist Parties in the European Community (CSPEC) – Union des partis socialistes de la Communauté européenne – Unión de los Partidos Socialistas de la Comunidad Europea – Bund der Sozialdemokratischen Parteien der Europäischen Gemeinschaft*, as successor to *Bureau of Social Democratic Parties*, set up Jan 1957, Luxembourg. Officially created at Congress, 5 Apr 1974, Luxembourg. Previously in English also referred to as *Union of Socialist Parties in the European Community*. Present name adopted Nov 1992, The Hague (Netherlands). Previously also referred to in several languages: *Parti socialiste européen (PSE) – Partido de los Socialistas Europeos – Sozialdemokratische Partei Europas – Partito del Socialismo Europeo – Partido Socialista Europeu – Partij van Europese Sociaaldemokraten – De Europaeiske Socialdemokraters Parti – De Europeiske Sosialdemokraters Parti – Euroopan Sosialidemokraattinen Puolue – Europeiska Socialdemokraters Parti.* **Aims** Strengthen the socialist and social democratic movement in the *European Union*; contribute to forming a European awareness and to expressing the political will of the citizens of the EU; define common policies for the EU and influence the decisions of European institutions; lead the European election campaign with a common strategy, visibility, manifesto and candidate to the European Commission Presidency. **Structure** Congress; Council; Leaders' Meetings; Presidency; Secretariat. **Languages** English, French. **Staff** 27.00 FTE, paid. **Finance** Affiliation dues and/or contributions from observer, associate and member parties and the Socialist Group. Other sources: *European Parliament (EP, #08146)*; contributions from associations and organizations; donations. **Activities** Politics/policy/regulatory. **Events** *Championing Equal Pay – What Are the Ways Forward?* Brussels (Belgium) 2022, *Women Annual Conference* Brussels (Belgium) 2019, *Election Congress* Madrid (Spain) 2019, *Conference on Europe in a new Era* Vienna (Austria) 2019, *Congress* Lisbon (Portugal) 2018. **Publications** Yearbook.
Members Full; Associate; Observer. Full: Socialist, Social Democratic and Labour Parties (33) in 29 countries:
Austria, Belgium, Bulgaria, Croatia, Cyprus, Czechia, Denmark, Estonia, Finland, France, Germany, Greece, Hungary, Ireland, Italy, Latvia, Lithuania, Luxembourg, Malta, Netherlands, Norway, Poland, Portugal, Romania, Slovakia, Slovenia, Spain, Sweden, UK.
Parties with associate status in 10 countries:
Albania, Bosnia-Herzegovina, Bulgaria, Iceland, Moldova, Montenegro, North Macedonia, Serbia, Switzerland, Türkiye.
Parties with observer status in 11 countries and territories:
Andorra, Armenia, Cyprus, Egypt, Georgia, Israel, Latvia, Morocco, Palestine, San Marino, Tunisia.
IGO Relations *Conference of the Regional and Local Authorities for the Eastern Partnership (CORLEAP, #04645).* **NGO Relations** Member of: *European Energy Forum (EEF, #06986)*; *European Forum for Democracy and Solidarity (EFDS, #07307)*; *European Movement International (EMI, #07825)*; *Socialist International (SI, #19340).* Consultative body: *Union of Socialist Local and Regional Representatives in Europe (USLRRE, #20479).* Instrumental in setting up: *European Senior Organization (ESO, #08465)*; *Global Progressive Forum (GPF, #10557).* Supports: *European Alliance for the Statute of the European Association (EASEA, #05886).* [2019.09.25/XE5945/**E**]

- ♦ Parvi Fratres Boni Pastoris (religious order)
- ♦ Parvum Opus Divinae Providentiae (religious order)
- ♦ **PASAF** Pan American Sailing Federation (#18128)
- ♦ **PASAI** Pacific Association of Supreme Audit Institutions (#17935)
- ♦ **PASA** Pan African Sanctuary Alliance (#18064)
- ♦ PASA – Panamerican Society of Audiology (no recent information)
- ♦ **PASA** Panamerican Surety Association (#18134)
- ♦ PASA / see Pan American Surf Association (#18135)
- ♦ **PASA** Pan American Surf Association (#18135)
- ♦ **PASAS** Pan Arab Society of Andrological Sciences (#18155)

♦ Pasaules Brivo Latviesu Apvieniba (PBLA) 18250

World Federation of Free Latvians (WFFL) – Organisation mondiale des lettons libres

Contact Lacplesa iela 29 dz 5, Riga LV-1011, Latvia. T. +37167282980. Fax +37137820176. E-mail: pbla-latvija@pbla.lv.
Contact PO Box 457, Strathfield NSW 2135, Australia. E-mail: info@laaj.org.au.
URL: http://www.pbla.lv/

History 1955, Washington, DC (USA). Recent name adopted early 1990s. Former names and other names: *Latvian Federation of the Free World* – former (1955). Registration: USA. **Aims** Unite, coordinate and assist Latvian emigrants in preserving their cultural heritage; promote and support Latvia in becoming a member of the European Union and NATO. **Publications** *Latvija Sodien.* **Members** National organizations (6). Membership countries not specified. [2015/XG5871/**D**]

- ♦ Pasaulio Lietuviu Kulturos, Mokslo ir Šietimo Centras (#16493)
- ♦ PASB/AMRO / see Pan American Sanitary Bureau (#18129)
- ♦ **PASB** Pan American Sanitary Bureau (#18129)

♦ PASCAL International Observatory 18251

CEO Univ of Glasgow, School of Education, St Andrew's Bldg, 11 Eldon Str, Glasgow, G3 6NH, UK. T. +441413301833.
Co-Dir address not obtained. T. +441413303414.
URL: http://pascalobservatory.org/

History Founded 2002, to extend the path-finding work on learning regions and cities of *OECD (#17693).* **Aims** Gather, interpret and share globally informed analyses of innovative regional development; help decision-makers narrow the gap between their region's untapped potential and aspirational goals; track global trends and identify practices that support regional development objectives that foster both measurement and accountability. **Structure** PASCAL Governing Board; PASCAL Advisory Council. Founding Centres: RMIT, Melbourne (Australia); Northern Illinois University, Dekalb IL (USA); Glasgow University, Glasgow (UK); University of South Africa, Pretoria (South Africa). **Languages** English. **Staff** None. **Finance** Grant funding from national and international agencies for generic pieces of research and/or consultancy work; consultancy work with local, regional and national governments. **Activities** Guidance/assistance/consulting; research/documentation; networking/liaising; events/meetings. **Events** *Conference* Tampere (Finland) 2022, *Conference* Suwon (Korea Rep) 2018, *Conference* Pretoria (South Africa) 2017, *Conference* Glasgow (UK) 2016, *Conference* Hong Kong (Hong Kong) 2013. **Publications** Stimulus Papers; Policy Briefs; books.
Members Network of decision-makers, academic entrepreneurs, researchers, policy analysts and locally engaged practitioners from government, higher education, non-governmental organizations and the private sector. Regional authorities and universities in 24 countries:
Australia, Belgium, Botswana, Canada, Ethiopia, Finland, France, Germany, Greece, Hungary, Iceland, Ireland, Italy, Lesotho, Malawi, Mexico, Nigeria, Norway, South Africa, Spain, Sweden, Tanzania UR, UK, USA. [2015/XJ0607/**E**]

- ♦ PASCA – Proyecto Acción SIDA de Centroamérica (internationally oriented national body)
- ♦ **PASCAR** Pan African Society of Cardiology (#18066)
- ♦ **PASC** Pacific Area Standards Congress (#17927)
- ♦ PASCV – Pan American Society for Clinical Virology (internationally oriented national body)
- ♦ **PASGR** Partnership for African Social and Governance Research (#18230)
- ♦ PASIA – Procurement and Supply Institute of Asia (unconfirmed)

♦ Pasifika Education Centre (PEC) 18252

Postal Address PO Box 22-654, Otahuhu, Auckland 1640, New Zealand. E-mail: info@pec.ac.nz.
Street Address Top Floor, Bldg 4, 17 Lambie Drive, Papatoetoe, Auckland 2014, New Zealand. T. +6492604042. Fax +6492623048.
URL: http://www.pec.ac.nz/

History 24 May 1976, as *Pacific Islanders' Educational Resource Centre.* Officially opened, 9 Sep 1978. Subsequently changed title to *PIERC Education*, 1993. Current title adopted, May 2004. **Aims** Promote life-long learning for Pacific people in the Adult and Community Education (ACE) sector; facilitate the provision of initiatives and programmes to retain Pacific culture and promote the use of Pacific languages. **Structure** Board of Trustees of 5. [2011/XE0616/**E**]

- ♦ PASIR-SH / see Pan Arab Society for Sexual Medicine (#18157)
- ♦ **PASLA** Pan-Asia Securities Lending Association (#18169)
- ♦ **PASMAE** Pan African Society for Musical Arts Education (#18067)
- ♦ PASME / see Pan African Society for Musical Arts Education (#18067)
- ♦ **PASMISS** Pacific and Asian Society of Minimally Invasive Spine Surgery (#17931)
- ♦ PASMO – Pan American Social Marketing Organization (internationally oriented national body)
- ♦ **PASNV** Pan-American Society for Neurovirology (#18130)
- ♦ **PASOCI** Parlement Africain de la Société Civile (#18207)
- ♦ PASO / see Panam Sports Organization (#18138)
- ♦ **PASOS** Policy Association for an Open Society (#18416)
- ♦ PAS – Pacific Asia Society (internationally oriented national body)
- ♦ **PASPCR** Pan American Society for Pigment Cell Research (#18132)
- ♦ **PASPGHAN** Pan Arab Society for Paediatric Gastroenterology, Hepatology and Nutrition (#18156)

♦ PASPS – International Conference on Physics and Applications of Spin Related Phenomena in Semiconductors (meeting series)
♦ PASSIA – Palestinian Academic Society for the Study of International Affairs (internationally oriented national body)

♦ Passiflora Society International (PSI) 18253

Pres address not obtained.
Sec address not obtained.
URL: http://www.passiflora.org/

History 1990. **Aims** Protect passiflora worldwide; help identify new species. **Structure** Board of Directors. **Finance** Members' dues. Budget (annual): US$ 3,000. **Activities** Functions as official registrar for all passiflora hybrids created worldwide. **Events** *Meeting* San Francisco, CA (USA) 2015, *Meeting* Cormeray (France) 2010, *Meeting* Coconut Creek, FL (USA) 2009, *Meeting* Coconut Creek, FL (USA) 2007, *Meeting* Harskamp (Netherlands) 2006. **Publications** *PSI Newsletter* (2 a year).
Members Individuals and organizations 17 in countries:
Australia, Belgium, Belize, Canada, Costa Rica, Denmark, France, Germany, Israel, Italy, Japan, Netherlands, New Zealand, Thailand, UK, USA, Venezuela. [2017/XF4189/**F**]

♦ Passionistes – Congrégation de la Passion de Jésus-Christ (religious order)
♦ Passionistes de Saint-Paul-de-la-Croix (religious order)
♦ Passionisti – Congregazione della Passione di Gesù Cristo (religious order)
♦ Passionist Nuns (religious order)
♦ Passionists – Congregation of the Passion (religious order)

♦ Passionists International (PI) 18254

Exec Dir 246 E 46th St, Apt 1F, New York NY 10017, USA. T. +13476575936. E-mail: marystrain1@mac.com – mirekl4u@gmail.com.
URL: http://www.passionistsinternational.org/

Aims Promote the work of the Passionist family, especially at the United Nations. **Consultative Status** Consultative status granted from: *ECOSOC (#05331)* (Special). **IGO Relations** Associated with Department of Global Communications of the United Nations. **NGO Relations** Member of: *Forum of Catholic Inspired NGOs (#09905)*; *Laudato Si' Movement (#16403)*; *Mining Working Group at the UN (MWG, #16813)*; *NGO Committee on Financing for Development, New York (#17108)*. [2018/XM0770/**F**]

♦ Passionist Sisters – Sisters of the Holy Cross and Passion of Our Lord Jesus Christ (religious order)
♦ Passionist Sisters of St Paul of the Cross (religious order)
♦ Passive House Institute / see International Passive House Association (#14527)

♦ Passive and Low-Energy Architecture (PLEA International) 18255

Pres c/o BLAUSTUDIO, Architect AKBW, Hauptstr 7, 83329 Waging am See, Germany. E-mail: info@plea-arch.org.
URL: http://plea-arch.org/

History 1981, Miami, FL (USA). Former names and other names: *PLEA International – Passive and Low-Energy Architecture – Sustainable Architecture and Urban Design* – full title. **Aims** Establish the highest standard of research and professionalism in building science and architecture in the interests of sustainable human settlements. **Structure** Directorate. **Languages** English. **Staff** Voluntary. **Activities** Events/meetings; guidance/assistance/consulting; publishing activities; awards/prizes/competitions. **Events** *Conference* Chile 2022, *Conference* La Coruña (Spain) 2020, *Conference* Hong Kong 2018, *Conference* Edinburgh (UK) 2017, *Conference* Los Angeles, CA (USA) 2016. **Publications** *PLEA Notes* – series. Conference proceedings.
Members Individuals in 65 countries and territories:
Algeria, Argentina, Australia, Austria, Bangladesh, Belgium, Botswana, Brazil, Bulgaria, Canada, Chile, China, Colombia, Croatia, Cyprus, Czechia, Denmark, Egypt, Finland, France, Germany, Greece, Guatemala, Hawaii, Hong Kong, Hungary, India, Iran Islamic Rep, Ireland, Israel, Italy, Japan, Jordan, Korea Rep, Lebanon, Luxembourg, Malaysia, Mexico, Morocco, Netherlands, New Zealand, Nigeria, Norway, Peru, Poland, Portugal, Romania, Russia, Saudi Arabia, Serbia, Singapore, Slovakia, Slovenia, South Africa, Spain, Sweden, Switzerland, Thailand, Türkiye, UK, United Arab Emirates, Uruguay, USA, Venezuela, Zimbabwe. [2021/XF4079/v/**F**]

♦ **PASSM** Pan Arab Society for Sexual Medicine (#18157)
♦ Pasteur Institute (internationally oriented national body)

♦ Pasteur Network 18256

International Dir Institut Pasteur, 25-28 rue du Docteur Roux, 75015 Paris, France. T. +33145688000. E-mail: reseau@pasteur.fr.
URL: https://pasteur-network.org/

History Founded by *Pasteur Institute*. New governance adopted 8 June 2021. Former names and other names: *Institut Pasteur d'outre-mer* – former (1988); *International Network of Pasteur Institutes and Associate Institutes* – former (2003); *Réseau international des instituts Pasteur et instituts associés* – former (2003); *International Network of Pasteur Institutes* – former (2003); *Réseau international des instituts Pasteur (RIIP)* – former (2011); *Institut Pasteur International Network* – former (2011). Registration: RNA, No/ID: W751209219, France. **Aims** Conduct scientific research to improve public health and education. **Structure** General Meeting; Board of Directors. Pasteur Network Foundation, sheltered at *Pasteur Institute*: Executive Committee; Management Committee. **Languages** English, French. **Activities** Capacity building; healthcare; research and development; training/education. **Events** *Fighting Emerging Threats Meeting* Seongnam (Korea Rep) 2019. **Publications** Scientific report.
Members Members (33) in 29 countries and territories:
Algeria, Belgium, Brazil, Bulgaria, Cambodia, Cameroon, Canada, Central African Rep, China, Côte d'Ivoire, France, Greece, Guadeloupe, Guiana Fr, Guinea, Hong Kong, Iran Islamic Rep, Italy, Korea Rep, Laos, Madagascar, Morocco, New Caledonia, Niger, Russia, Senegal, Tunisia, Uruguay, Vietnam.
Consultative Status Consultative status granted from: *WHO (#20950)* (Official). [2022.04.13/XJ2797/**E**]

♦ Past Global Changes (PAGES) 18257

Contact Intl Project Office, Hochschulstrasse 4, 3012 Bern, Switzerland. T. +41316315611. E-mail: pages@pages.unibe.ch.
URL: http://pastglobalchanges.org/

History 1992, as a Core Project of *International Geosphere-Biosphere Programme (IGBP, inactive)*, until end 2015. Original title: *Past Global Changes Project*. Since end 2015, functions under *Future Earth (#10048)*. **Aims** Support science aimed at understanding the Earth's past environment in order to make predictions for the future. **Structure** Scientific Steering Committee (SSC); Executive Committee (EXCOM); International Project Office (IPO) in Bern (Switzerland). **Languages** English. **Staff** 5-7. **Finance** Funded by: Chinese Academy Sciences; Swiss Academy of Sciences. **Activities** Events/meetings; research/documentation; training/education; knowledge management/information dissemination; networking/liaising. **Events** *Open Science Meeting* Agadir (Morocco) 2022, *Young Scientists Meeting* Agadir (Morocco) 2022, *Conference on the Impacts of Sea Level Rise* Utrecht (Netherlands) 2018, *Young Scientists Meeting* Huesca (Spain) 2017, *Open Science Meeting* Saragossa (Spain) 2017. **Publications** *Past Global Changes Magazine*. **Information Services** *International Paleoscience Calendar*; *PAGES People Database*; *PAGES Product Database*. **Members** Individuals (over 5,000) in 125 countries. Membership countries not specified. **NGO Relations** Member of: *International Centre for Earth Simulation (ICES Foundation)*. Partnership with: *World Climate Research Programme (WCRP, #21279)*. [2020.03.04/XK0793/**E**]

♦ Past Global Changes Project / see Past Global Changes (#18257)
♦ Pastoral and Environmental Network in the Horn of Africa (internationally oriented national body)
♦ Pastors for Peace (internationally oriented national body)
♦ Patagonia Missionary Society / see South American Mission Society (#19705)
♦ **PATAM** Pan African Treatment Access Movement (#18071)
♦ **PATA** Pacific Asia Travel Association (#17932)
♦ PATCO / see Americas Triathlon (#00795)
♦ **PatCom** Patent Committee (#18258)

♦ Patent Committee (PatCom) 18258

Pres c/o Minesoft Mtd, Boston House, Little Green, Richmond, TW9 1QE, UK. E-mail: achapman@minesoft.com.
Registered Address c/o LHIP, Suikersilo Oost 9, 1165 MS Halfweg, Netherlands. E-mail: jane@extractinfo.info.
URL: http://www.patcom.org/

History Also referred to as *Commercial Patent Services Group*. **Aims** Ensure a fair balance between the free *information services* of patent offices, commercial value-added patent information services and users' interests. **Structure** Board; Executive Council. **Languages** English. **Staff** 3.00 FTE, voluntary. **Finance** Members' dues cover secretarial services. **Activities** Events/meetings.
Members Full in 7 countries:
Austria, France, Germany, Netherlands, Spain, UK, USA.
Consultative Status Consultative status granted from: *World Intellectual Property Organization (WIPO, #21593)* (Observer Status). **IGO Relations** *European Patent Office (EPO, #08166)*. [2019/XM3771/**E**]

♦ Patent Cooperation Treaty (1970 treaty)
♦ Patent Documentation Group / see PDG (#18272)
♦ Patent Documentation and Information Centre (see: #00434)
♦ Patent Law Treaty (2000 treaty)

♦ Patent Office of Cooperation Council for the Arab States of the Gulf (GCC Patent Office) 18259

Contact PO Box 11333 340 227, Riyadh, Saudi Arabia. T. +966112551516.
URL: http://www.gccpo.org/

History Established 1992, by *Gulf Cooperation Council (GCC, #10826)*, as a regional office. **Aims** Implement law of the GCC. **Consultative Status** Consultative status granted from: *World Intellectual Property Organization (WIPO, #21593)* (Observer Status). [2019/XM8475/**E***]

♦ Paters Jozefieten (religious order)
♦ **PATF** Pan African Theosophical Federation (#18069)

♦ PATH 18260

CEO PO Box 900922, Seattle WA 98109, USA. T. +12062853500. Fax +12062856619. E-mail: info@path.org.
URL: http://www.path.org/

History 1977. Founded as *Program for the Introduction and Adaptation of Contraceptive Technology (PIACT, inactive)*. Former names and other names: *Program for Appropriate Technology in Health (PATH)* – full title. Registration: USA. **Aims** Improve the health of people around the world by advancing technologies, strengthening systems and encouraging healthy behaviours. **Structure** Board of Directors. Headquarters in Seattle WA (USA). Offices in 30 towns in 21 countries: Belgium; Cambodia; China; Côte d'Ivoire; Ethiopia; France; Ghana; India; Kenya; Nicaragua; Nigeria; Peru; Senegal; South Africa; Tanzania UR; Thailand; Uganda; Ukraine; Vietnam; USA; Zambia. **Languages** English. **Staff** 80.00 FTE, paid. **Finance** Supported by: foundations; US and other governments; multilateral agencies; corporations; individuals. **Activities** Advocacy/lobbying/activism. **Events** *Workshop on parenting disabled children* Kingston (Jamaica) 1988. **Publications** *Outlook* (4 a year) – newsletter; *Directions in Global Health* (3 a year) – newsletter; *PATH Today* (3 a year) – newsletter. e-newsletters. **Members** Not a membership organization. **Consultative Status** Consultative status granted from: *ECOSOC (#05331)* (Special); *UNICEF (#20332)*; *United Nations Population Fund (UNFPA, #20612)*; *WHO (#20950)* (Official Relations). **IGO Relations** *WHO (#20950)* designated PATH as a collaborating centre in 3 areas. Associated with Department of Global Communications of the United Nations. **NGO Relations** Member of (13): *American Council for Voluntary International Action (InterAction)*; *Coalition against Typhoid (CaT, #04049)*; *End Water Poverty (EWP, #05464)*; *Global Coalition Against Child Pneumonia (#10290)*; *InsideNGO (inactive)*; *International Consortium for Emergency Contraception (ICEC, #12911)*; *International Initiative for Impact Evaluation (3ie, #13851)*; *Neglected Tropical Diseased NGO Network (NNN, #16969)*; *NetHope (#16979)*; *NGO Committee on UNICEF (#17120)*; *PMNCH (#18410)*; *The NCD Alliance (NCDA, #16963)*; *Union for International Cancer Control (UICC, #20415)*. Member of and hosts: *Global Health Technologies Coalition (GHTC)*. Affiliate: *OneWorld Health (OWH)*. [2020/XF1034/**F**]

♦ PATH Canada / see HealthBridge
♦ **PaTHES** Philosophy and Theory of Higher Education Society (#18361)
♦ Pathfinder Fund / see Pathfinder International (#18261)

♦ Pathfinder International 18261

Headquartters 9 Galen St, Ste 217, Watertown MA 02172-4501, USA. T. +16179247200. Fax +16179243833. E-mail: information@pathfind.org.
URL: http://www.pathfind.org/

History 1957, USA, as *Pathfinder Fund*, by Clarence Gamble. Registered in accordance with USA law. **Aims** Place reproductive health services at the center; provide women, men and adolescents with a range of quality *health* services – including contraception, maternal care, HIV prevention and AIDS care and treatment; strengthen access to family planning; ensure availability of safe abortion services; advocate for sound reproductive health policies; improve the rights and lives of people. **Structure** Board of Directors of 17 members. Officers: President; Chair of the Board; Vice-Chair; Secretary; Treasurer. Chair of Head Office in Watertown MA (USA). Country Offices. **Languages** English. **Staff** 800.00 FTE, paid. **Finance** Funded by: *United States Agency for International Development (USAID)*; grants; contracts and cooperative agreements; private donors; other. **Activities** Networking/liaising; capacity building; projects/programmes. **Events** *Joint Symposium on The Belt and Road Initiative* Singapore (Singapore) 2018. **Publications** *Pathways* – newsletter. Annual Report. Technical manuals.
Members Offices in 20 countries:
Angola, Bangladesh, Bolivia, Botswana, Brazil, Egypt, Ethiopia, Ghana, India, Kenya, Mozambique, Nepal, Nigeria, Pakistan, Peru, Tanzania UR, Uganda, USA, Vietnam, Yemen.
Consultative Status Consultative status granted from: *ECOSOC (#05331)* (Special); *United Nations Population Fund (UNFPA, #20612)*. **IGO Relations** Collaborates with: *ICDDR,B (#11051)*.
NGO Relations Member of:
– *American Council for Voluntary International Action (InterAction)*; *CORE Group*; *Girls not Brides (#10154)*; *InsideNGO (inactive)*; *International Consortium for Emergency Contraception (ICEC, #12911)*; *Latin American Consortium on Emergency Contraception (LACEC, #16306)*; *NGO Committee on UNICEF (#17120)*; *NonProfit Organizations Knowledge Initiative (NPOKI)*; *PMNCH (#18410)*; *Planetary Health Alliance (PHA, #18383)*; *Abortion and Postabortion Care Consortium (APAC, #00007)*; *Reproductive Health Supplies Coalition (RHSC, #18847)*.
Supports: *Media for Development International (MFDI)*; *Parliamentarians for Global Action (PGA, #18208)*. Partner of: *Every Woman Every Child (EWEC, #09215)*. Collaborates with: *FHI 360*. [2018/XF7620/f/**F**]

♦ PathFinders Justice Initiative (internationally oriented national body)
♦ Pathologie, cytologie et développement (internationally oriented national body)
♦ Path to Peace Foundation (internationally oriented national body)

♦ Pathways To Peace (PTP) 18262

Sentiers de la paix, Les – Senderos de la Paz

Main Office PO Box 1057, Larkspur CA 94977, USA. T. +14154610500. Fax +14159250330. E-mail: info@pathwaystopeace.org.
URL: http://www.pathwaystopeace.org/

History 1962, by Avon Mattison, as an international peacebuilding, educational and consulting organization. Officially incorporated in 1983. **Aims** Foster *cooperation* amongst diverse organizations and programmes for the common purpose of building a Culture of Peace for future generations. **Structure** Executive Council, consisting of Council of Directors (including one child and/or one youth) and Coordinators of the various programmes and projects. **Staff** 8.00 FTE, voluntary. **Finance** Donations; grants. **Activities** Advocacy/lobbying/activism; events/meetings; awards/prizes/competitions. **Events** *Peace through business – the peace-building role of business in the 21st century* San Francisco, CA (USA) / Sydney, NSW (Australia) 1995. **Members** Organisations (over 4000) in 152 countries. Membership countries not specified. **Consultative Status** Consultative status granted from: *ECOSOC (#05331)* (Special); *UNICEF (#20332)*. **IGO Relations** Works with: *UNESCO (#20322)*; *UNICEF (#20332)*; *United Nations Human Settlements Programme (UN-Habitat, #20572)*. Accredited by: *United Nations Office at Geneva (UNOG, #20597)* *United Nations Office at Vienna*

(UNOV, #20604); United Nations Regional Commissions New York Office (RCNYO, #20620). Associated with Department of Global Communications of the United Nations. **NGO Relations** Member of: *CIVICUS: World Alliance for Citizen Participation (#03962); Global Movement for the Culture of Peace (GMCOP).* [2018/XF2471/**F**]

♦ Patient Classifications Systems Europe / see Patient Classification Systems International (#18263)

♦ Patient Classification Systems International (PCSI) 18263

Sec address not obtained. E-mail: secretary@pcsinternational.org.
URL: http://www.pcsinternational.org/
History 1987, Lisbon (Portugal). Former names and other names: *Patient Classifications Systems Europe (PCSE)* – former (1987); *PSI International* – alias; *PSI/I* – alias. **Aims** Work on all aspects of case-mix based classification, analysis and financing. **Structure** Executive Committee,. **Events** *International Conference* Copenhagen (Denmark) 2019, *International Conference* Sydney, NSW (Australia) 2017, *International Conference* Dublin (Ireland) 2016, *International Conference* The Hague (Netherlands) 2015, *International Conference* Doha (Qatar) 2014. [2022/XJ1518/**C**]

♦ Patient Safety Movement (internationally oriented national body)
♦ Patient Safety Programme / see WHO Patient Safety (#20940)
♦ Patients Safety and Global Support Initiative (internationally oriented national body)
♦ Patmos Foundation for World Missions (internationally oriented national body)
♦ Patmos International / see Patmos Foundation for World Missions
♦ Patres Albi – Societas Missionariorum Africae (religious order)
♦ Patriarcat grec-orthodoxe d'Alexandrie et de toute l'Afrique (#10709)
♦ Patriarcat grec-orthodoxe d'Antioche et de tout l'Orient (#10710)
♦ Il Patriarcato Anglicano (religious order)
♦ Patriarcat oecuménique de Constantinople (#05349)
♦ Patriarchal Order of the Holy Cross of Jerusalem (religious order)
♦ Patrician Brothers – Brothers of Saint Patrick (religious order)
♦ Patrimoine sans frontières (internationally oriented national body)

♦ Pro Patrimonio (National Trust of Romania) 18264

Chairman 18 Fitzhardinge Street, Manchester Square, London, W1H 6EQ, UK. T. +442074860295.
URL: http://www.propatrimonio.org/
History Founded May 2000, London (UK). **Aims** Contribute to the rescue, *restoration* and maintenance of Romania's endangered *buildings* and *lands* for the benefit of all. **Structure** Coordinating Committee. **Languages** English, French, Romanian. **Staff** 2.00 FTE, paid. Many voluntary. **Finance** Subscriptions; donations. **Activities** Advocacy/lobbying/activism; projects/programmes; training/education; events/meetings. **Publications** *Pro Patrimonio Newsletter* in English, Romanian.
Members Foundations in 4 countries:
France, Romania, UK, USA. [2019.06.25/XM0741/**F**]

♦ Patriotic Union of Kurdistan (PUK) 18265

Contact address not obtained. E-mail: pukmedianet@yahoo.com – info@pukmedia.com.
URL: http://www.pukonline.com/
History 1975.
Members Offices in 14 countries:
Belgium, Canada, France, Germany, Iran Islamic Rep, Italy, Netherlands, Russia, Spain, Sweden, Syrian AR, Türkiye, UK, USA. [2017/XE4100/**E**]

♦ Patristic Institute 'Augustinianum' (internationally oriented national body)
♦ Patronat Sud-Nord Solidaritat i Cultura (internationally oriented national body)
♦ Patrouille internationale des glaces (#13832)
♦ **PATS** Pan-African Thoracic Society (#18070)
♦ PATT – Pupils' Attitudes Toward Technology (unconfirmed)
♦ PATU – Pan-African Telecommunication Union (inactive)
♦ **PATU** Pan American Taekwondo Union (#18136)
♦ **PATVET** Pacific Association of Technical and Vocation Education and Training (#17936)
♦ PATWA – Pacific Area Travel Writers Association (internationally oriented national body)
♦ **PA – UfM** Parliamentary Assembly – Union for the Mediterranean (#18216)
♦ **PAUGA** Pan-Asian Urogynecologic Association (#18166)
♦ PAU' / see Inter-American Institute for Cooperation on Agriculture (#11434)
♦ PAUJ – Pan-African Union of Journalists (inactive)
♦ Paul Ehrlich MedChem Euro-PhD Network (unconfirmed)
♦ Paul H Nitze School of Advanced International Studies (internationally oriented national body)
♦ Pauline Fathers – Order of St Paul the First Hermit (religious order)
♦ Paulins – Pères de Saint Paul Premier Ermite (religious order)
♦ Paulista Association for Nature Protection / see AME World Ecology Foundation
♦ Paulistes (religious order)
♦ Paulist Fathers (religious order)
♦ Paulists – Paulist Fathers (religious order)
♦ Paul K Feyerabend Foundation (unconfirmed)
♦ Paulo Freire Institute (internationally oriented national body)
♦ Paulo Freire Institute for the Development of Municipal Education / see Instituto Paulo Freire
♦ Paul Reuter Fund (internationally oriented national body)
♦ PAUNS / see Pan-Arab Union of Neurological Societies (#18158)
♦ **PAUNS** Pan-Arab Union of Neurological Societies (#18158)
♦ PAU – Pan African University (unconfirmed)
♦ PAU – Pan-Atlantic University (internationally oriented national body)
♦ Paurastya Vidyapitham (internationally oriented national body)
♦ **PAUSA** Pan African Urological Surgeons' Association (#18072)
♦ Pauselijke Missiewerken / see MISSIO (#16827)
♦ Pauvres Filles des Sacrés Stigmates de Saint François d'Assise (religious order)
♦ Pauvres Frères de Saint François Séraphique (religious order)
♦ Pauvres Servantes de Jésus-Christ (religious order)
♦ Pauvres Serviteurs de la Divine Providence (religious order)
♦ Pauvres Soeurs de la Mère de Dieu (religious order)
♦ PAVA – Pan Arab Vascular Surgery Association (unconfirmed)
♦ PAVE – Pan African Vision for the Environment (internationally oriented national body)
♦ PAWA – Panafrican Women Association (unconfirmed)
♦ **PAWA** Pan African Writers Association (#18075)
♦ PAWA – Pan American Women's Association (inactive)
♦ **PAWA** Pedro Arrupe World Association (#18287)
♦ PAWC – Pan African Workers Congress (inactive)
♦ **PAWC** Pan American Weightlifting Confederation (#18137)
♦ **PAWEES** International Society of Paddy and Water Environment Engineering (#15338)
♦ **PAWI** Pentecostal Assemblies of the West Indies International (#18292)
♦ **PAWO** Pan African Women's Organization (#18074)
♦ PAWOTI – Pan-African Association of Women in Telecommunications and Information (no recent information)
♦ PAX (internationally oriented national body)
♦ Pax Christi International / see Pax Christi – International Catholic Peace Movement (#18266)

♦ Pax Christi – International Catholic Peace Movement 18266

Pax Christi, Mouvement international catholique pour la paix – Pax Christi, Movimiento Internacional Católico por la Paz
SG Rue du Progrès 323, 1030 Brussels, Belgium. T. +3225025550. Fax +3225024626. E-mail: hello@paxchristi.net.
URL: http://www.paxchristi.net/
History 13 Mar 1945. Reorganized Dec 1950. Officially consecrated as Movement of the Church, 1952. Also referred to as *Pax Christi International.* Laureate of the UNESCO Peace Prize 1983. Statutes revised Apr 2006. Registered in accordance with Belgian law. **Aims** Promote peace and nonviolence, respect of human rights, justice and reconciliation throughout the world. **Structure** World Assembly (every 5 years); General Meeting (annual); Executive Committee – Board of Directors; International Secretariat; Continental Networks; Regional Networks; Pax Christi National Sections; Pax Christi Local Groups; Affiliated organizations; Partner organizations; Strategic Alliances. Education and Youth Work for Peace, through *Pax Christi Youth and Peace Education Network (PCYF, no recent information).* **Languages** English, French, Spanish. **Staff** 7.00 FTE, paid; 5.00 FTE, voluntary. **Finance** Sections' dues. Other sources: donations, subsidies. **Activities** Conflict resolution; training/education; advocacy/lobbying/activism. **Events** *World Assembly* Hiroshima (Japan) 2021, *World Assembly* Bethlehem (Palestine) 2015, *World Assembly* Strasbourg (France) 2010, *World Assembly* Torhout (Belgium) 2007, *Interreligious dialogue seminar* Warsaw (Poland) 2005. **Publications** Newsletter, in English, French, Spanish. Books; monographs; manuals; reports; handbooks; bibliographies.
Members Global Peace Network (over 120 organizations) in 60 countries and territories:
Australia, Austria, Bangladesh, Belgium, Brazil, Burundi, Cameroon, Canada, Chad, Chile, Colombia, Congo DR, Côte d'Ivoire, Croatia, Cyprus, Dominican Rep, Egypt, El Salvador, Ethiopia, France, Germany, Guatemala, Haiti, Hungary, India, Indonesia, Ireland, Israel, Italy, Japan, Jordan, Kenya, Korea Rep, Lebanon, Liberia, Luxembourg, Mali, Mexico, Netherlands, New Zealand, Pakistan, Palestine, Peru, Philippines, Poland, Portugal, Puerto Rico, Russia, Rwanda, Slovakia, South Africa, South Sudan, Sri Lanka, Sweden, Switzerland, Taiwan, Thailand, Uganda, UK, USA.
Consultative Status Consultative status granted from: *ECOSOC (#05331)* (Special); *UNESCO (#20322)* (Consultative Status); *UNICEF (#20332); Council of Europe (CE, #04881)* (Participatory Status). **IGO Relations** Represented by: *Council of Europe (CE, #04881); UNESCO (#20322); United Nations Office at Geneva (UNOG, #20597); United Nations Office at Vienna (UNOV, #20604).* **NGO Relations** Member of: *Forum of Catholic Inspired NGOs (#09905).* Links with many coalitions and networks, including: *Alliance for Peacebuilding; Committee of Religious NGOs at the United Nations (CRNGOs, #04282); Conference of INGOs of the Council of Europe (#04607); European Network for Central Africa (EurAc, #07874); European Peacebuilding Liaison Office (EPLO, #08176); International Campaign to Abolish Nuclear Weapons (ICAN, #12426); International Peace Bureau (IPB, #14535); Mining Working Group at the UN (MWG, #16813); World Council of Churches (WCC, #21320)* – PIEF Core Group. [2020/XC3084/**F**]

♦ Pax Christi, Mouvement international catholique pour la paix (#18266)
♦ Pax Christi, Movimiento Internacional Católico por la Paz (#18266)
♦ PAX ROMANA / see Pax Romana, International Movement of Catholic Students (#18268)

♦ Pax Romana, International Catholic Movement for Intellectual and Cultural Affairs (ICMICA) 18267

Pax Romana, Mouvement international des intellectuels catholiques (MIIC) – Pax Romana, Movimiento Internacional de Intelectuales Católicos (MIIC) – Pax Romana, Internationale Bewegung der Katholischen Akademiker
Secretariat Pax Romana ICMICA/MIIC, Rue de Varembé 3 – 4th Floor, CP 161, 1211 Geneva 20, Switzerland. T. +41225701052.
URL: http://www.icmica-miic.org/
History 12 Apr 1947, Rome (Italy). Founded following 20th World Congress of the then *Pax Romana, International Secretariat for National Catholic University Federations – Pax Romana, Secrétariat international des fédérations nationales d'universitaires catholiques,* Aug 1946, Fribourg (Switzerland) when this latter organization split into two autonomous branches forming *PAX ROMANA*: ICMICA and *Pax Romana, International Movement of Catholic Students (IMCS, #18268).* Registration: Switzerland. **Aims** Promote: intercultural, interreligious and intellectual dialogue; protection of fundamental human rights for all, including socio-economic rights; critical and constructive dialogue and involvement in socio-political issues through empowerment of civil society actors and strengthening the presence of the laity in Church and Society. **Structure** Plenary Assembly (every 4 years); International Council; General Secretariat, headed by Secretary General; Regional Coordination. **Languages** English, French, Spanish. **Staff** Voluntary. **Finance** Members' dues. Other sources: donations from Friends of Pax Romana; gifts; grants; legacies. **Activities** Events/meetings. **Events** *Quadrennial Plenary Assembly* Vienna (Austria) 2012, *Quadrennial plenary assembly* Nairobi (Kenya) 2008, *International conference for the reform of international institutions* Geneva (Switzerland) 2006, *Which Europe international congress* Venice (Italy) 2006, *International congress on intercultural and interreligious dialogue* Bilbao (Spain) 2005. **Publications** Electronic Newsletter (12 a year) in English, French, Spanish. Annual Report of international secretariat; Annual Report of the Working Group on Human Rights; occasional publications.
Members Open to Catholic professionals and graduates. National titular members; corresponding members; contact groups (), in 68 countries and territories:
Argentina, Australia, Austria, Belgium, Benin (*), Bolivia, Brazil, Burkina Faso (*), Burundi (*), Cameroon (*), Canada (*), Chile, Colombia, Congo DR (*), Côte d'Ivoire (*), Croatia, Czechia, Denmark, Dominican Rep, Ecuador, Egypt, El Salvador, France, Gabon (*), Germany, Ghana, Greece (*), Hong Kong, India, Indonesia, Ireland, Italy, Japan, Kenya, Korea Rep (*), Lebanon, Luxembourg, Madagascar, Malaysia, Malta (*), Mauritius, Mexico, Netherlands, Nigeria, Peru, Philippines, Poland, Portugal, Rwanda (*), Senegal (*), Sierra Leone (*), Singapore, Slovakia, Slovenia, South Africa (*), Spain, Sri Lanka, Sweden, Switzerland, Tanzania UR, Thailand, Togo (*), Uganda, UK, Uruguay, USA, Venezuela, Zambia (*).
Specialized International Secretariats (4), listed in this Yearbook:
International Secretariat for Scientific Questions (#14821); International Society of Christian Artists (#15009); Secrétariat international des ingénieurs, des agronomes et des cadres économiques catholiques (SIIAEC, #19203); SIESC – European Federation of Christian Teachers (#19267).
Consultative Status Consultative status granted from: *African Commission on Human and Peoples' Rights (ACHPR, #00255)* (Observer); *ECOSOC (#05331)* (Special); *UNESCO (#20322)* (Associate Status); *Council of Europe (CE, #04881)* (Participatory Status); *UNEP (#20299).* **IGO Relations** Cooperates with: *UNHCR (#20327).* Accredited by: *United Nations Office at Vienna (UNOV, #20604).*
NGO Relations Founding member of: *NGO Forum on Environment (FOE, #17125).* Full member of: *NGO Committee on Financing for Development, New York (#17108).* Member of:
– *Committee of NGOs on Human Rights, Geneva (#04275);*
– *Conference of Non-Governmental Organizations in Consultative Relationship with the United Nations (CONGO, #04635);*
– *International Catholic Centre of Geneva (ICCG, #12449);*
– *International Catholic Cooperation Centre for UNESCO (CCIC, #12454);*
– *International Dalit Solidarity Network (IDSN, #13129);*
– *International Network for a Culture of Nonviolence and Peace (#14247);*
– *NGO Committee for Disarmament, Geneva (#17105);*
– *NGO Committee on Disarmament, Peace and Security, New York NY (#17106);*
– *NGO Committee on Freedom of Religion or Belief, New York NY (#17109);*
– *NGO Committee on Sustainable Development, Vienna (#17119);*
– *Vienna NGO Committee on Drugs (VNGOC, #20773);*
– *Vienna NGO Committee on the Family (#20774);*
– *World Organisation Against Torture (OMCT, #21685).*
Instrumental in setting up: *International Federation of Catholic Medical Associations (#13378); International Federation of Catholic Pharmacists (#13380). Latin American Network of Catholic Lawyers (no recent information)* is a service of the Latin American Secretariat. [2014.10.30/XB3085/y/**F**]

♦ Pax Romana, Internationale Bewegung der Katholischen Akademiker (#18267)
♦ Pax Romana, Internationale Katholische Studenten-Bewegung (#18268)

♦ Pax Romana, International Movement of Catholic Students (IMCS) . 18268

Pax Romana, Mouvement international des étudiants catholiques (MIEC) – Pax Romana, Movimiento Internacional de Estudiantes Católicos (MIEC) – Pax Romana, Internationale Katholische Studenten-Bewegung
SG 7 Impasse Reille, 75014 Paris, France. T. +33145447075.
Pres address not obtained.
URL: https://imcs-miec.com/
History 1921, Fribourg (Switzerland). Character changed from a purely student movement to a world union of Catholic university students and intellectual leaders, 12 Apr 1947, Rome (Italy), on adoption of new statutes, since which time *'PAX ROMANA'* is composed of two autonomous branches: IMCS and *Pax Romana, International Catholic Movement for Intellectual and Cultural Affairs (ICMICA, #18267).* Cooperated within *World Student Relief (WRS, inactive)* until its dissolution in 1950. Interfederal Assembly of 1978, Valladolid (Spain),

approved IMCS identity document. Former names and other names: *Pax Romana, International Secretariat for National Catholic University Federations* – former; *Pax Romana, Secrétariat international des fédérations nationales d'universitaires catholiques* – former; *PAX ROMANA* – former. Registration: Switzerland. **Aims** Provide trained Christian leaders committed to building new social structures respecting the dignity of mankind; work on liberation and development in social, economic and cultural fields; participate in the creation of, and mobilize support of the churches for world justice; participate in a critical analysis of society leading to the creation of new forms of self-determination; find ways of adapting universities to current needs of individuals and society; provide active testimony to Christian values in the intellectual, cultural and social life of society. **Structure** World Assembly (every 4 years); International Council; International Team; Regional Teams; UN Teams and Specialized Commissions; Sub-regional Coordinators; National Coordinators. **Languages** English, French, Spanish. **Staff** 3.00 FTE, paid. **Finance** Members' dues. Other sources: donations; subsidies. **Activities** Training/education; advocacy/lobbying/activism; events/meetings. **Events** *Meeting* Chennai (India) 2012, *World Assembly* Cologne (Germany) 2011, *Being a student nowadays* Szeged (Hungary) 1997, *Meeting* Nairobi (Kenya) 1996, *Meeting* Yamoussoukro (Côte d'Ivoire) 1995. **Publications** *FORUM* (annual) – magazine; *IMCS International Newsletter*. Annual Report; regional publications; proceedings of congresses and regional meetings; reports.
Members Full; correspondent. National federations in 76 countries and territories:
Australia, Austria, Bangladesh, Benin, Bolivia, Botswana, Burkina Faso, Burundi, Cameroon, Canada, Chile, Congo Brazzaville, Congo DR, Côte d'Ivoire, Croatia, Cuba, Ecuador, Egypt, England, Equatorial Guinea, Eritrea, Eswatini, Ethiopia, Germany, Ghana, Greece, Guinea, Haiti, Hong Kong, Hungary, India, Indonesia, Italy, Japan, Kenya, Korea Rep, Lebanon, Lesotho, Lithuania, Luxembourg, Macau, Madagascar, Malawi, Malaysia, Mali, Malta, Mozambique, Myanmar, Namibia, Nepal, Niger, Nigeria, Pakistan, Peru, Poland, Portugal, Romania, Rwanda, Senegal, Slovenia, South Africa, Spain, Sri Lanka, Sudan, Taiwan, Tanzania UR, Thailand, Togo, Tunisia, Uganda, Ukraine, USA, Vietnam, Wales, Zambia, Zimbabwe.
Consultative Status Consultative status granted from: *ECOSOC (#05331)* (Special); *UNESCO (#20322)* (Associate Status). **NGO Relations** Member of: *Forum of Catholic Inspired NGOs (#09905)*; *Vienna NGO Committee on Drugs (VNGOC, #20773)*. Cooperates with: International Coordination Meeting of Youth Organizations (ICMYO); *International Young Catholic Students (IYCS, #15926)*; *International Young Christian Workers (IYCW, #15927)*; *Mouvement international de la jeunesse agricole et rurale catholique (MIJARC, #16865)*; *World Council of Churches (WCC, #21320)* (youth unit); *World Student Christian Federation (WSCF, #21833)*. [2020/XB3086/**F**]

- ♦ Pax Romana, International Secretariat for National Catholic University Federations / see Pax Romana, International Movement of Catholic Students (#18268)
- ♦ Pax Romana, Mouvement international des étudiants catholiques (#18268)
- ♦ Pax Romana, Mouvement international des intellectuels catholiques (#18267)
- ♦ Pax Romana, Movimiento Internacional de Estudiantes Católicos (#18268)
- ♦ Pax Romana, Movimiento Internacional de Intelectuales Católicos (#18267)
- ♦ Pax Romana, Secrétariat international des fédérations nationales d'universitaires catholiques / see Pax Romana, International Movement of Catholic Students (#18268)
- ♦ PAX Society – Society of the Peritoneal Cavity (inactive)
- ♦ Pax World Foundation / see Pax World Service
- ♦ Pax World Service (internationally oriented national body)

♦ Payments Europe (PE) 18269

SG Avenue Marnix 23, 1000 Brussels, Belgium. T. +3222890930. E-mail: secretariat@paymentseurope.eu.
URL: https://www.paymentseurope.eu/
History Registered in accordance with Belgian law. EU Transparency Register: 795384637216-30. **Aims** Stimulate a dynamic, competitive and consumer-centric European payments landscape. **Structure** General Assembly; Board. [2020/XM8828/**D**]

- ♦ Pays africains de langue officielle portugaise (#18027)

♦ Pays africains de la Zone franc (PAZF) 18270

CFA Franc Zone
Address not obtained.
URL: http://www.izf.net/
History Not an organization; a grouping of African countries within *Zone franc (#22037)*, including those of *Communauté financière africaine (CFA, #04377)* (West Africa), Central Africa and Comoros. **Finance** From 1948 to Jan 1994 the CFA franc was fixed at 50 to 1 French franc. After several intermediate changes, from Jan 1994 this parity was fixed at 100 to 1. **Activities** Functions through: (i) full convertibility into French francs at a fixed parity; (ii) French Treasury guarantee of convertibility through establishment of "operations accounts" for each African central bank; (iii) free capital movements throughout the region; (iv) pooling of most foreign exchange reserves at the French Treasury; (v) establishment of common trade and financial policies with respect to the rest of the world. **Publications** Information Services: *Investir en Zone franc (IZF-net)* set up by *Commission de l'UEMOA (see: #20377)* and the Executive Secretariat of CEMAC on the initiative of Ministers of the Economy and Finance of the 14 countries represented at *Conférence des ministres des finances des pays de la Zone franc (#04633)*. **Information Services** *Investir en Zone franc (IZF-net)* – relayed through links with existing sites such as Centre français du commerce extérieur (CFCE) and AFP.
Members Governments of 14 countries:
Benin, Burkina Faso, Cameroon, Central African Rep, Chad, Comoros, Congo Brazzaville, Côte d'Ivoire, Equatorial Guinea, Gabon, Mali, Niger, Senegal, Togo.
Institutions of the 'Zone franc' grouping the above countries (3):
Banque centrale des Comores; *Communauté économique et monétaire d'Afrique centrale (CEMAC, #04374)*; *Union économique et monétaire Ouest africaine (UEMOA, #20377)*; *Union monétaire Ouest africaine (UMOA, inactive)*.
IGO Relations *Banque centrale des Etats de l'Afrique de l'Ouest (BCEAO, #03167)*. [2008/XF3711/y/**F***]

- ♦ Payson Center for International Development and Technology Transfer (internationally oriented national body)
- ♦ Pays sans frontières / see Parc des trois pays – Espace ouvert sans frontières (#18195)
- ♦ Pays de Visegrad / see Visegrad Group (#20794)
- ♦ PAZCI – Centro para la Paz y la Acción para la Transformación de Conflictos (unconfirmed)
- ♦ Paz y Cooperación (internationally oriented national body)
- ♦ Paz con Dignidad – Asociación de Solidaridad, Derechos Humanos y Cooperación al Desarrollo / see Asociación Paz con Dignidad
- ♦ **PAZF** Pays africains de la Zone franc (#18270)
- ♦ **+ Paz – sida Fundación** Mas Paz Menos SIDA Fundación (#16594)
- ♦ Paz y Tercer Mundo, Spain / see Fundación Mundubat
- ♦ PBA – International Symposium on Pharmaceutical and Biomedical Analysis (meeting series)
- ♦ PBA – Partnership Brokers Association (internationally oriented national body)
- ♦ PBAS / see Partnership Brokers Association
- ♦ PBC / see Confederación Panamericana de Badminton (#04467)
- ♦ PBCHW / see Pacific Basin Consortium for Environment and Health (#17937)
- ♦ **PBC** Pacific Basin Consortium for Environment and Health (#17937)
- ♦ **PBC** United Nations Peacebuilding Commission (#20606)
- ♦ PBDA – Pacific Basin Dental Association (unconfirmed)
- ♦ PBDC – Pacific Basin Development Council (inactive)
- ♦ **PBEC** Pacific Basin Economic Council (#17938)
- ♦ **PBF** United Nations Peacebuilding Fund (#20607)
- ♦ **PBIA** Public Budget International Association (#18564)
- ♦ PBI-BEO / see Protection International (#18548)
- ♦ **PBI** Peace Brigades International (#18277)
- ♦ PBI – Peacebuilders International (internationally oriented national body)
- ♦ PBI – Polar Bears International (internationally oriented national body)
- ♦ **PBI** Public Broadcasters International (#18563)
- ♦ **PBLA** Pasaules Brivo Latviesu Apvieniba (#18250)
- ♦ **PBMA** Pacific Basin Medical Association (#17939)
- ♦ PBM – International Conference on Population Balance Modelling (meeting series)
- ♦ PBM – International Conference on Population Balance Modelling (meeting series)
- ♦ PBM – Positive Birth Movement (unconfirmed)
- ♦ PBN – Plant Biologicals Network (internationally oriented national body)
- ♦ PB/RAC / see Plan Bleu pour l'environnement et le développement en Méditerranée (#18379)
- ♦ **PBSS** Pharmaceutical and BioScience Society, International (#18348)
- ♦ PBT – Pioneer Bible Translators (internationally oriented national body)
- ♦ PBVM – Union of the Sisters of the Presentation of the Blessed Virgin Mary (religious order)
- ♦ PBWF – Parabadminton World Federation (inactive)
- ♦ PCA Forum – International Forum of the Person Centered Approach (meeting series)
- ♦ **PCA** Permanent Court of Arbitration (#18321)
- ♦ PCA – Pine Chemicals Association (internationally oriented national body)
- ♦ **PCA** Presbyterian Church of Africa (#18485)
- ♦ PCAR – Peace Corps for African Renaissance (internationally oriented national body)
- ♦ **PCC EMEA** Partner Community Council (#18228)
- ♦ PCCM – Permanent Consultative Committee of the Maghreb (inactive)
- ♦ PCC NET – International Network for Patient-Centered Care (internationally oriented national body)
- ♦ **PCC** Pacific Conference of Churches (#17943)
- ♦ PCC / see PAI (#18025)
- ♦ **PCC** Permanent Committee on Cadastre in the European Union (#18319)
- ♦ **PCC** Pontificium Consilium de Cultura (#18443)
- ♦ PCC SEE – Police Cooperation Convention for Southeast Europe (2006 treaty)
- ♦ **PCC SEE Secretariat** Police Cooperation Convention for Southeast Europe Secretariat (#18415)
- ♦ **PCCS** Pontificio Consiglio delle Comunicazioni Sociali (#18447)
- ♦ **PCCS** Pontificium Consilium de Communicationibus Socialibus (#18447)
- ♦ **PCDE** Primary Care Diabetes Europe (#18495)
- ♦ PCD Europe / see Primary Care Diabetes Europe (#18495)
- ♦ PCDForum / see Living Economies Forum
- ♦ PCDNC – Pontificium Concilium pro Dialogo cum Non Credentibus (inactive)
- ♦ PCD – Partnership for Child Development (internationally oriented national body)
- ♦ PCD – Pathologie, cytologie et développement (internationally oriented national body)
- ♦ PCDS / see Pacific Peace Working Group (#17988)
- ♦ PCEA – Presbyterian Church of East Africa (internationally oriented national body)
- ♦ **PCE Europe** Network of the European Associations for Person-Centred and Experiential Psychotherapy and Counselling (#17013)
- ♦ **PCE** Pancreatic Cancer Europe (#18172)
- ♦ **PCEP** Polyolefin Circular Economy Platform (#18427)
- ♦ PCF / see Philippine Centre for Population and Development
- ♦ **PCF** Prototype Carbon Fund (#18552)
- ♦ **PCFS** People's Coalition on Food Sovereignty (#18303)
- ♦ **PCFV** Partnership for Clean Fuels and Vehicles (#18231)
- ♦ PCGIAP / see Regional Committee of United Nations Global Geospatial Information Management for Asia and the Pacific (#18766)
- ♦ PCHAlliance – Personal Connected Health Alliance (internationally oriented national body)
- ♦ PCI / see PCI Global
- ♦ PCI / see PCI Media
- ♦ PCI / see Zen Peacemakers
- ♦ PCIAOH / see International Commission on Occupational Health (#12709)

♦ PCIC Europe 18271

Sec c/o Siemens AG, Gugelstr 65, 90459 Nürburg, Germany.
URL: http://www.pcic-europe.com/
History Former names and other names: *Petroleum and Chemical Industry Committee* – former. Registration: Switzerland, Zollikofen. **Aims** Contribute to the continuous improvement of the technical competence of technicians and engineers in the field of electrical, non-electrical and safety-related items in connection with production, treatment and transport of crude-oil and related raw-materials and products, chemicals and *chemical products* and products of the *pharmaceutical* industry. **Structure** Executive Committee; Technical Programme Committee. **Events** *Petroleum and Chemistry Industry Europe Conference* London (UK) 2022, *Petroleum and Chemistry Industry Europe Conference* Nürburg (Germany) 2021, *Petroleum and Chemistry Industry Europe Conference* Copenhagen (Denmark) 2020, *Middle East Regional Conference* Abu Dhabi (United Arab Emirates) 2019, *Petroleum and Chemistry Industry Europe Conference* Paris (France) 2019. **NGO Relations** *Institute of Electrical and Electronics Engineers (IEEE, #11259)*. [2021/XJ8966/**D**]

- ♦ PC-IDEA / see Regional Committee of the UN on Global Geospatial Information Management for the Americas (#18765)
- ♦ **PCID** Pontifical Council for Interreligious Dialogue (#18444)
- ♦ PCI Global (internationally oriented national body)
- ♦ PCI Media (internationally oriented national body)
- ♦ PCI-Media Impact / see PCI Media
- ♦ **PCI** Peace Child International (#18278)
- ♦ **PCI** Powder Coating Institute (#18472)
- ♦ PCI Security Standards Council (internationally oriented national body)
- ♦ PCI SSC – PCI Security Standards Council (internationally oriented national body)
- ♦ PCJ – Sisters of the Poor Child Jesus (religious order)
- ♦ PCMA – Professional Convention Management Association (internationally oriented national body)
- ♦ **PCMG** Pharmaceutical Contract Management Group (#18350)
- ♦ PCN/CEE / see European Federation of Nurses Associations (#07180)
- ♦ **PCN** Pro Communicatio Nordica (#04381)
- ♦ **PCNE** Pharmaceutical Care Network Europe (#18349)
- ♦ PCN / see European Federation of Nurses Associations (#07180)
- ♦ PCN – Parti communautaire national européen (internationally oriented national body)
- ♦ PCN – Partido Comunitario Nacional-Europeo (internationally oriented national body)
- ♦ PCN – Partido Comunitário Nacional-Europeu (internationally oriented national body)
- ♦ PCN – Partito Comunitario Nazionale-Europeo (internationally oriented national body)
- ♦ PCN – Peace Cooperative Network (internationally oriented national body)
- ♦ PCPA / see Pacific Maritime Transport Alliance (#17982)
- ♦ **PCPCU** Pontifical Council for Promoting Christian Unity (#18446)
- ♦ PCPD – Philippine Centre for Population and Development (internationally oriented national body)
- ♦ PCPI – Parent Cooperative Preschools International (internationally oriented national body)
- ♦ **PCQVP** Publiez ce que vous payez (#18573)
- ♦ PCRC – Pacific Concerns Resource Centre (internationally oriented national body)
- ♦ **PCREEE** Pacific Centre for Renewable Energy and Energy Efficiency (#17941)
- ♦ PCR – International Organization for Peace, Care and Relief (internationally oriented national body)
- ♦ PCSE / see Patient Classification Systems International (#18263)
- ♦ **PCSI** Patient Classification Systems International (#18263)
- ♦ **PCS** Project Counselling Service (#18532)
- ♦ **PCST** International Network on Public Communication of Science and Technology (#14311)
- ♦ PCST Network / see International Network on Public Communication of Science and Technology (#14311)
- ♦ PCS / see WHO European Healthy Cities Network (#20936)
- ♦ PCT – Patent Cooperation Treaty (1970 treaty)
- ♦ **PCT Union** International Patent Cooperation Union (#14530)
- ♦ PCUWC / see Lester B Pearson United World College of the Pacific

♦ PCVC – International Foundation for Crime Prevention and Victim Care (internationally oriented national body)
♦ PCWM – Parc commun de wagons de marchandises (inactive)
♦ PCYA-AF – Promotional Council for Youth Action in Africa (unconfirmed)
♦ **PDAA** Pediatric Dentistry Association of Asia (#18286)
♦ PDA-Europe / see European Brand and Packaging Design Association (#06396)
♦ **PDA Europe** Polyurea Development Association Europe (#18428)
♦ PDA – Pan European Brand Design Association / see European Brand and Packaging Design Association (#06396)
♦ **PDA** Parenteral Drug Association (#18196)
♦ PDA – Population and Community Development Association (internationally oriented national body)
♦ **PD Burma** International Network of Political Leaders Promoting Democracy in Burma (#14305)
♦ PDCAT – International Conference on Parallel and Distributed Computing, Applications and Technologies (meeting series)
♦ PDC Foundation / see Partnership for Dengue Control (#18232)
♦ PDC – Pacific Disaster Center (internationally oriented national body)
♦ **PDC** Partnership for Dengue Control (#18232)
♦ PDCT – Pacific Development and Conservation Trust (internationally oriented national body)
♦ PDDM – Congregazione delle Pie Discepole del Divin Maestro (religious order)
♦ **PDE** Parti démocrate européen (#06900)
♦ PDF / see Global Health Europe (#10404)
♦ PD Forum – Participatory Development Forum (internationally oriented national body)
♦ **PDF** Pacific Disability Forum (#17945)
♦ **PDF** Pakistan Development Forum (#18028)
♦ PDF – Peace Development Fund (internationally oriented national body)

♦ PDG 18272

SG c/o Marius Meier, Lautengartenstrasse 7, 4052 Basel BS, Switzerland. E-mail: sg@p-d-g.org.
URL: http://www.p-d-g.org/

History 1957. Founded by 13 European oil and chemical companies. Former names and other names: *Patent Documentation Group* – former. Registration: Swiss Civil Code, Switzerland. **Aims** Enable and inspire PDG member companies to effectively advise internal customers by efficiently using patent information and adding value in a digital world. **Structure** Annual Members' Conference (AMC); Board; Working Groups; Task Forces. **Languages** English. **Staff** 0.60 FTE, paid. **Finance** Sources: members' dues. **Activities** Knowledge management/information dissemination; networking/liaising; research and development.
Members Companies based or with branches in 10 countries:
Austria, Belgium, Denmark, France, Germany, Netherlands, Spain, Sweden, Switzerland, UK.
Consultative Status Consultative status granted from: *World Intellectual Property Organization (WIPO, #21593)* (Permanent Observer Status). **IGO Relations** Member of Standing Advisory Committee on Patent Documentation and Information (SACEPO/PDI) of: *European Patent Office (EPO, #08166).* [2022.05.04/XF0131/**F**]

♦ PDG – Partnership for Democratic Governance (inactive)
♦ PDHRE-International / see People's Movement for Human Rights Learning (#18307)
♦ PDHRE / see People's Movement for Human Rights Learning (#18307)
♦ **PDHRE** People's Movement for Human Rights Learning (#18307)
♦ PDIN – Pacific Disability Information Network (inactive)
♦ PDI-POA – Protocol and Diplomacy International – Protocol Officers Association (internationally oriented national body)
♦ PDI – Population and Development International (internationally oriented national body)
♦ **PDLN** Press Database Licensing Network (#18487)
♦ PDM / see Municipal Development Partnership for West and Central Africa (#16902)
♦ PDPE-ALE / see European Free Alliance (#07356)
♦ PDT Europe (meeting series)
♦ PDU / see Asia Pacific Democrat Union (#01881)

♦ PE100+ Association 18273

Sec address not obtained.
Pres/Chairman address not obtained.
URL: http://www.pe100plus.com/

History 24 Feb 1999, by Borealis, Elenac and Solvay. **Aims** Guarantee consistent quality at the highest level in both production and usage of PE100+ pipe materials; promote the use of *polyethylene* (PE) *piping* in general; maintain focused communication towards pipe installers and end-users to promote use of PE piping. **Structure** Members Meeting (annual); Board; Advisory Board. **Languages** English. **Staff** 0.20 FTE, paid. **Finance** Sources: members' dues. Annual budget: 150,000 EUR. **Activities** Events/meetings. **Events** *Members Meeting* Brussels (Belgium) 2016, *Advisory Committee Meeting* Istanbul (Turkey) 2016, *Members Meeting* Amsterdam (Netherlands) 2015, *Advisory Committee Meeting* Krakow (Poland) 2015, *Members Meeting* Dubai (United Arab Emirates) 2014. **Publications** *PE100+ Newsletter.* **Members** Companies (11). Membership countries not specified. **NGO Relations** Member of (1): *Plastic Pipes Conference Association (PPCA, #18393).* [2015.07.16/XJ9393/**C**]

♦ Peace 2000 Institute 18274

Contact Vogasel 1, 109 Reykjavik, Iceland. T. +3544962000 – +3545571000.
London Office Lloyds Bldg, 12 Leadenhall Str, London, EC3V 1LP, UK. T. +442030266310.

History 14 Jul 1995, Reykjavik (Iceland), following 2 years of preparation, a *Peace Committee 2000* having been set up, Apr 1994, Barcelona (Spain), by *United World Foundation (UWF, inactive).* **Aims** Function as a catalyst facilitating collective action and a transition from a *war-based* to a *peaceful, balanced economy.* **Structure** *Peace 2000 Council (no recent information),* comprising representatives of member organizations. Board of Guardians, consisting of 9 independent individuals. Steering Committee for the Earth Charter, composed of 10 members. International Committee for *Media 2000.* Peace 2000 Secretariat in Reykjavik (Iceland). The planned *Peace 2000 Network (#18275)* is expected to include all Peace 2000 initiatives. **Finance** Members' dues. Sponsorship. **Activities** Developing an extensive profile of programmes to inform, educate and gain cooperation from the general public, business and industry; setting up a *'Media 2000'* campaign; setting up a *'Peace University'*; operating a dedicated Peace Aircraft for humanitarian and peace purposes; makes *'Peace 2000'* awards for excellence in media programmes emphasizing non-violence; runs *'Marketing 2000'* campaign to generate consumer awareness of the importance of world peace and responsible stewardship of the earth's resources; organizes international workshops; working towards a World Assembly, 2000, Althing (Iceland), at which world leaders would approve the *'Earth Charter'*. **Events** *Meeting / Millennium Earth Summit* Reykjavik (Iceland) 2000. **Publications** Annual Report. **Members** Individuals (about 500) and organizations (about 100). Membership countries not specified. **IGO Relations** *UNDP (#20292); UNESCO (#20322); UNHCR (#20327).* Associated with Department of Global Communications of the United Nations.
NGO Relations Member organizations and other international project alliances, of which the following are listed in this Yearbook:
– *Airline Ambassadors International (AAI);*
– *American Council for Voluntary International Action (InterAction);*
– *Bangladesh Peace and Human Rights Journalists Forum (BPHRJF, no recent information);*
– *Bureau international des Médecins sans frontières (MSF International, #03366);*
– *Campaign for a More Democratic United Nations (CAMDUN, inactive);*
– *Communications Coordination Committee for the United Nations (CCC/UN);*
– *Earthaid International Foundation, Japan (no recent information);*
– *Earthwatch Europe;*
– *European Institute for Disarmament and Development (EIDDI, no recent information);*
– *Gandhi Memorial International Foundation (GMIF, no recent information);*
– *Green Help International, Kiev (no recent information);*
– *Groupe de recherche et d'information sur la paix et la sécurité (GRIP);*
– *Hungarian Peace Association;*
– *Initiatives for International Dialogue;*
– *International Association of Educators for World Peace (IAEWP);*
– *International Association of Peace Foundations (IAPF, #12071);*
– *International Campaign to Ban Landmines (ICBL, inactive);*
– *International Gandhian Movement (IGM, no recent information);*
– *International Rescue Corps (IRC);*
– *Japan Institute of International Affairs (JIIA);*
– *New Internationalist (NI);*
– *One World Trust (OWT);*
– *Organization for Peace and Disarmament in Southern Africa (OPEDISA, no recent information);*
– *Pan-African Reconciliation Council (PARC, #18063);*
– *Peace Quest International (PQI, #18282);*
– *Peace Tribunal Foundation;*
– *Permanent Peace Movement (no recent information);*
– *SERVAS International (#19234);*
– *War and Peace Foundation;*
– *World Citizen Diplomats (no recent information);*
– *World Federation of United Nations Associations (WFUNA, #21499);*
– *World Peace Organization;*
– *Youth Action for Peace (YAP, inactive).* [2018/XE2614/j/**E**]

♦ Peace 2000 Network 18275

Contact c/o Peace 2000 Institute, Vogasel 1, 109 Reykjavik, Iceland. T. +3544962000 – +3545571000. Fax +3544962005.
Facebook: https://www.facebook.com/Earthchild/

History 1995, Iceland, on proposal of *United World Foundation (UWF, inactive),* to give a coherent structure to the *'Peace 2000'* initiatives. Draft statutes adopted 14 Jul 1995. **Aims** Advance education of the public through research into effects of violence on television and in other media; promote non-violent behaviour through responsible use of the media; promote sustainable planetary management and the conversion of military-related resources so as to address economic and social development and relief of poverty, sickness, disablement and distress; research cause, effect and means of reducing conflict between and within states; facilitate conflict resolution with the service of neutral and non-partisan peace negotiators; promote research into efficacy and maintenance of international law and development of a 'Global Charter of Civil Society'; encourage grass roots participation towards common commitment to core values able to unite all cultural, political, religious and philosophical backgrounds. **Structure** People's Assembly of adult Peace 2000 members (convened every 2 years via electronic media) and concurrent Assembly forum; *Peace 2000 Council (no recent information),* comprising representatives of Peace 2000 societies (meets at least annually); *Peace 2000 Institute (#18274)*; Guardians (9 individuals, initially appointed by UWF); Secretariat, including Executive Management Board. *Peace Ventures UK* (a commercial company supporting the humanitarian mission). **Languages** English. **Members** Peace 2000 societies of network members. [2018/XF4419/**F**]

♦ Peace Action / see Peace Action Network
♦ Peace Action Education Fund (internationally oriented national body)
♦ Peace Action Network (internationally oriented national body)
♦ **+ Peace – AIDS Foundation** More Peace Less AIDS Foundation (#16594)

♦ Peace Appeal 18276

Contact PO Box 4503, Charlottesville VA 22905, USA.
URL: https://www.peaceappeal.org/

History Founded following the proclamation of the 1997 *Appeal of the Nobel Peace Laureates for Peace and Nonviolence,* with a mandate from 5 Nobel Peace Laureates: Nelson Mandela, Desmond Tutu, F W de Klerk, Mairead Maguire and Adolfo Esquivel. Former names and other names: *Peace Appeal Foundation* – alias. **Aims** Build a culture of peace and non-violence for the children of the world. **Structure** Council; Board of Directors. [2019/AA1267/f/**F**]

♦ Peace Appeal Foundation / see Peace Appeal (#18276)
♦ Peace and Appropriate Development for the Horn of Africa / see Organization for Peace and Appropriate Development for the Horn of Africa
♦ Peace Association of Christian Scientists (inactive)
♦ Peace Boat (internationally oriented national body)

♦ Peace Brigades International (PBI) 18277

Brigades de paix internationales – Brigadas Internacionales de Paz – Internationale Friedensbrigaden

ISEC Admin Village Partenaire, Rue Fernand Bernier 15, 1060 Brussels, Belgium. T. +3225434443. E-mail: admin@peacebrigades.org.
URL: https://www.peacebrigades.org/

History Sep 1981, Canada. Founded to revitalize the activities of *World Peace Brigade (inactive),* formed in 1961. Registration: Banque-Carrefour des Entreprises, No/ID: 0884.150.149, Start date: 11 Oct 2006, Belgium; USA. **Aims** Provide protection, support and recognition to local human rights defenders who work in areas of repression and conflict. **Structure** General Assembly (every 3 years); International Council; International Secretariat; International Office; Country Groups (13). **Languages** English, Spanish. **Activities** Networking/liaising; monitoring/evaluation; knowledge management/information dissemination. Active in: Colombia, Guatemala, Honduras, Indonesia, Kenya, Mexico, Nepal. **Events** *General Assembly* Spain 2014, *General Assembly* Switzerland 2011, *Triennial general assembly / General Assembly* Hamburg (Germany) 2008, *Triennial general assembly / General Assembly* London (UK) 2005, *Triennial General Assembly* Mannenbach (Switzerland) 2001. **Publications** Annual Review; statements; reports; books; DVDs; videos.
Members PBI groups in 13 countries:
Belgium, Canada, France, Germany, Ireland, Italy, Netherlands, Norway, Spain, Sweden, Switzerland, UK, USA.
IGO Relations Associated with Department of Global Communications of the United Nations. **NGO Relations** Cooperates with wide range of NGOs at an international and national level. [2022/XF5241/**F**]

♦ Peace Builders / see SERVAS International (#19234)
♦ Peacebuilders International (internationally oriented national body)
♦ Peace Catalyst International (internationally oriented national body)
♦ Peace Center of the Theosophical Society in the Philippines / see Peace Library and Research Centre

♦ Peace Child International (PCI) 18278

Exec Dir The White House, Buntingford, SG9 9AH, UK. T. +441763274459. Fax +441763274460.
URL: http://www.peacechild.org/

History 1981, London (UK). Registered as a Charitable Trust in the UK and a not-for-profit organization in the USA. **Aims** Empower *young people* by educating them about the major *challenges* faced by their generation (making poverty history, sustainable development, combating climate change, securing human rights, pursuing the resolution of conflicts, etc) and by guiding and supporting them to take effective action to address those challenges while still young. **Structure** Network of autonomous organizations and chapters worldwide. **Languages** English, French, Spanish. **Staff** 29.00 FTE, paid. Several voluntary. **Finance** Members' dues: Full – US$ 25; Associate – US$ 10. Other sources: project grants; sales of publications; fees for training and exchange programmes. **Activities** Advocacy/lobbying/activism; awareness raising. **Events** *World Youth Congress* Conakry (Guinea) 2014, *World Youth Congress* Rio de Janeiro (Brazil) 2012, *World Youth Congress* Istanbul (Turkey) 2010, *World Youth Congress* Québec, QC (Canada) 2008, *World youth congress* Québec, QC (Canada) 2008. **Publications** *Peace Child' E-Bulletin* (4 a year). Books; pamphlets; publications written, illustrated, designed and edited by young people.
Members Full in 61 countries:
Afghanistan, Algeria, Australia, Austria, Belarus, Belgium, Benin, Bosnia-Herzegovina, Botswana, Burkina Faso, Cameroon, Chad, Congo DR, Croatia, Czechia, Denmark, Finland, France, Gambia, Germany, Ghana, Greece, Hungary, India, Indonesia, Ireland, Israel, Italy, Jordan, Kenya, Korea Rep, Latvia, Lithuania, Mali, Mauritania, Nepal, Netherlands, New Zealand, Nigeria, Norway, Pakistan, Philippines, Poland, Portugal, Russia, Senegal, Serbia, Sierra Leone, Slovenia, South Africa, Spain, Sweden, Switzerland, Tanzania UR, Thailand, Togo, Tunisia, Uganda, UK, Ukraine, Zimbabwe.
Consultative Status Consultative status granted from: *ECOSOC (#05331)* (Special); *UNEP (#20299).* **IGO Relations** Associated with Department of Global Communications of the United Nations. **NGO Relations** Member of: *EarthAction (EA, #05159).* Partner of: *Global Call for Climate Action (GCCA, inactive).* Support from: *Charities Aid Foundation of America (CAF America).* [2014.10.28/XF2364/**F**]

- ♦ Peace Coffee / see HeadWaters International
- ♦ Peace Committee of Lapland (internationally oriented national body)
- ♦ Peace Containers (internationally oriented national body)
- ♦ Peace and Cooperation (internationally oriented national body)
- ♦ Peace Cooperative Network (internationally oriented national body)
- ♦ Peace Corps (internationally oriented national body)
- ♦ Peace Corps for African Renaissance (internationally oriented national body)
- ♦ Peace Corps Institute (internationally oriented national body)
- ♦ Peace Corps of the United States of America / see Peace Corps
- ♦ Peace Council of Norway / see Norwegian Peace Council
- ♦ Peacecraft (internationally oriented national body)
- ♦ Peace and Crises Management Foundation (internationally oriented national body)
- ♦ Peace Depot (internationally oriented national body)
- ♦ Peace Development Fund (internationally oriented national body)
- ♦ Peace Direct (internationally oriented national body)
- ♦ Peace and Disarmament Committee of the Women's International Organizations (inactive)
- ♦ Peace and Disarmament Society of Kerala (internationally oriented national body)
- ♦ Peace Education Center, Columbia University (internationally oriented national body)
- ♦ Peace Education Center, Teachers College, Columbia University / see Peace Education Center, Columbia University
- ♦ Peace Education Foundation (internationally oriented national body)
- ♦ Peace Education Program of Teachers College / see Peace Education Center, Columbia University
- ♦ Peace Education Projects (internationally oriented national body)
- ♦ Peace Farm (internationally oriented national body)
- ♦ Peace History Society (internationally oriented national body)
- ♦ Peace House (internationally oriented national body)

♦ Peace Implementation Council 18279

Contact OHR SARAJEVO, Emerika Bluma 1, 71000 Sarajevo, Bosnia-Herzegovina. T. +38733283500. Fax +38733283501. E-mail: sarajevo.rd@ohr.int.
URL: http://www.ohr.int/?p=99545/

History 8 Dec 1995, London (UK). 8-9 Dec 1995, London (UK), at *'London Peace Implementation Conference'*, by signatories to the Paris (France) Agreement setting up *United Nations Mission in Bosnia and Herzegovina (UNMIBH, inactive)* and *Office of the High Representative in Bosnia and Herzegovina (OHR, #17696)*. **Structure** Council meets at ministerial level to subsume the International Conference on the Former Yugoslavia. Steering Board comprises representatives of 8 countries and 4 regional intergovernmental bodies, under the chairmanship of the High Representative; it meets monthly at the level of political directors from foreign ministries and occasionally at ministerial level and provides the High Representative with political guidance on peace implementation.
Members Governments of 43 countries (" indicates member of Steering Board):
Albania, Austria, Belgium, Bosnia-Herzegovina, Bulgaria, Canada (*), China, Croatia, Czechia, Denmark, Egypt, Finland, France (*), Germany (*), Greece, Hungary, Ireland, Italy (*), Japan (*), Jordan, Luxembourg, Malaysia, Morocco, Netherlands, North Macedonia, Norway, Oman, Pakistan, Poland, Portugal, Romania, Russia (*), Saudi Arabia, Serbia, Slovakia, Slovenia, Spain, Sweden, Switzerland, Türkiye, UK (*), Ukraine, USA (*).
%% COUNTRIES Intergovernmental members and participants (13) ('*' indicates member of Steering Board; '**' indicates represented by Turkey):
Council of Europe (CE, #04881); *European Bank for Reconstruction and Development (EBRD, #06315)*; *European Commission (EC, #06633)* (*); *European Union (EU, #08967)* (*); *International Bank for Reconstruction and Development (IBRD, #12317)*; *International Committee of the Red Cross (ICRC, #12799)*; *International Monetary Fund (IMF, #14180)*; *NATO (#16945)*; *Office of the United Nations High Commissioner for Human Rights (OHCHR, #17697)*; *Organisation of Islamic Cooperation (OIC, #17813)* (**); *Organization for Security and Cooperation in Europe (OSCE, #17887)*; Presidency of European Union *; *United Nations (UN, #20515)*.
[2018/XE3596/y/**E***]

- ♦ Peace Institute – Institute for Contemporary Social and Political Studies / see Mirovni inštitut
- ♦ Peace Institute, Ljubljana (internationally oriented national body)
- ♦ PeaceJam Foundation (internationally oriented national body)
- ♦ Peace and Justice Studies Association (internationally oriented national body)
- ♦ Peace-keeping Reserve Fund (no recent information)
- ♦ Peace Library and Research Centre (internationally oriented national body)
- ♦ Peace and Life Enhancement Initiative International (internationally oriented national body)
- ♦ Peace Without Limits – PWL – International Organization (internationally oriented national body)
- ♦ Peacemaker Circle International / see Zen Peacemakers
- ♦ Peacemaker Corps Association (internationally oriented national body)
- ♦ Peace Now (internationally oriented national body)
- ♦ Peace Now – the Israeli Peace Movement / see Peace Now
- ♦ Peace in the Oceans / see International Ocean Institute (#14394)
- ♦ Peace One Day (internationally oriented national body)

♦ Peace Operations Training Institute (POTI) 18280

Exec Dir 1309 Jamestown Rd Ste 202, Williamsburg VA 23185-3380, USA. T. +17572536933. Fax +17572536954.
URL: http://www.peaceopstraining.org/

History Registered as a Charity in the USA. **Aims** Provide globally accessible and affordable distance-learning courses on peace support, humanitarian relief, and security operations. **Structure** Board of Directors. **Languages** Arabic, English, French, Portuguese, Spanish. **Staff** 9.00 FTE, paid. **Finance** Primarily financed through grants from ministries of foreign affairs; additional funds from individual tuition and bulk enrolments. Budget (annual): about US$ 1 million. **Activities** Training/education. **Publications** *POTI Newsletter*.
[2014.07.14/XJ8473/j/**E**]

- ♦ Peace Palace (internationally oriented national body)

♦ Peace Parks Foundation 18281

CEO PO Box 12743, Die Boord, Stellenbosch, 7613, South Africa. T. +27218805100. Fax +27218801173. E-mail: ppfcomms@peaceparks.org.
Street Address 11 Termo Road, Techno Park, Stellenbosch, 7600, South Africa.
URL: http://www.peaceparks.org/

History 1 Feb 1997. Registration: South Africa. **Aims** Restore and reconnect Africa's wild spaces to create a future for humankind in harmony with nature. **Activities** Advocacy/lobbying/activism. Southern Africa. **Publications** Annual Review. **Consultative Status** Consultative status granted from: *ECOSOC (#05331)* (Special). **NGO Relations** Member of (3): *GEF CSO Network (GCN, #10087)*; *Global Rewilding Alliance (GRA, #10579)*; *International Union for Conservation of Nature and Natural Resources (IUCN, #15766)*.
[2022.10.27/XJ2996/f/**F**]

- ♦ P.E.A.C.E. – People Everywhere All Created Equal / see Global Women P.E.A.C.E. Foundation
- ♦ Peace to the Planet (internationally oriented national body)
- ♦ PeacePlayers International (internationally oriented national body)
- ♦ Peace Pledge Union (internationally oriented national body)
- ♦ **PEACE Programme** Programme for Palestinian-European-American Cooperation in Education (#18527)

♦ Peace Quest International (PQI) 18282

Samarbete för Fred – Sadarbiba Mieram

Chair Gropgränd 4, SE-753 10 Uppsala, Sweden. T. +46723261312.
URL: https://peacequestinternational.weebly.com/

History 1992, Washington, DC (USA). Former names and other names: *Cooperation for Peace (CFP)* – alias. Registration: Sweden. **Aims** Promote humanitarian interests of individuals; promote public awareness of the need to create a more emphatic, compassionate, truthful, unselfish and loving civilization. **Languages** English, Swedish.
[2020/XF4587/**F**]

- ♦ Peace Research Centre / see Richardson Institute for Peace and Conflict Studies
- ♦ Peace Research and European Security Studies (internationally oriented national body)
- ♦ Peace Research Group at the University of Konstanz (internationally oriented national body)
- ♦ Peace Research Institute Frankfurt (internationally oriented national body)
- ♦ Peace Research Institute Frankfurt-Main / see Peace Research Institute Frankfurt
- ♦ Peace Research Institute Oslo (internationally oriented national body)
- ♦ Peace Research Society – International / see Peace Science Society – International
- ♦ Peace Resource Center of San Diego (internationally oriented national body)
- ♦ Peace Resource Project (internationally oriented national body)
- ♦ Peace Revolution (internationally oriented national body)
- ♦ Peace Roundtable (internationally oriented national body)
- ♦ PEACESAT Consortium / see Consortium for International Pacific Education and Communication Experiments by Satellite (#04750)
- ♦ **PEACESAT** Consortium for International Pacific Education and Communication Experiments by Satellite (#04750)
- ♦ Peace Science Society – International (internationally oriented national body)
- ♦ Peace and Sport (internationally oriented national body)
- ♦ Peace and Sport Organization / see Peace and Sport
- ♦ Peace Studies Association of Japan (internationally oriented national body)
- ♦ Peace Studies Institute and Program in Conflict Resolution / see Manchester College Peace Studies Institute
- ♦ Peace Tax Campaign / see Conscience – the Peace Tax Campaign
- ♦ Peace and the Third World / see Fundación Mundubat
- ♦ Peace Tribunal Foundation (internationally oriented national body)
- ♦ Peace Trust (internationally oriented national body)
- ♦ Peace Union / see Peace Union of Finland
- ♦ Peace Union of Finland (internationally oriented national body)
- ♦ Peace Through Unity (internationally oriented national body)
- ♦ Peaceways / see Peaceways – Young General Assembly
- ♦ Peaceways – Young General Assembly (internationally oriented national body)
- ♦ Peace Winds (internationally oriented national body)
- ♦ Peace Winds Japan / see Peace Winds

♦ PeaceWomen Across the Globe 18283

Femmes de Paix Autour de Monde – Mujeres de Paz en el Mundo – FriendensFrauen Weltweit – Mulheres pela Paz ao redor do Mundo – Donne di Pace nel Mondo

Secretariat Maulbeerstrasse 14, 3011 Bern, Switzerland. T. +41313120240. Fax +41313120239. E-mail: info@1000peacewomen.org.
URL: http://www.1000peacewomen.org/

History Set up following the initiative "1000 Women for the Nobel Peace Prize 2005" which succeeded in nominating 1000 PeaceWomen from all over the world collectively for the Nobel Peace Prize. Registered in accordance with Swiss Civil Code. **Aims** Strengthen the influence of women in all contexts of *peace*, security and sustainability and make their work more visible. **Structure** Board of 10 members. Secretariat. Regional Coordinators for: Africa; Asia; Middle East; Europe; North America and Latin America; Oceania. **Languages** English, German, Spanish. **Finance** Private donors; public funding; foundations. **Activities** Projects in Egypt and Nepal. **Publications** *PeaceWomen Across the Global Newsletter* (2 a year). Annual Report. **NGO Relations** Member of: *Global Network of Women Peacebuilders (GNWP, #10503)*.
[2013.10.10/XJ4566/**F**]

- ♦ Peacework (internationally oriented national body)
- ♦ Peaceworkers USA (internationally oriented national body)
- ♦ Peaceworks (internationally oriented national body)
- ♦ Peace Worldwide (internationally oriented national body)
- ♦ **PEAC** Pool energétique de l'Afrique centrale (#03655)
- ♦ **PEA** Production Engineering Association (#18509)
- ♦ Pearl S Buck Foundation / see Pearl S Buck International
- ♦ Pearl S Buck International (internationally oriented national body)

♦ Pearle – Live Performance Europe 18284

Dir Square Sainctelette 19, Boîte 6, 1000 Brussels, Belgium. T. +3222036296. E-mail: info@pearle.eu.
URL: https://www.pearle.eu/

History 1991, Amsterdam (Netherlands). Former names and other names: *Pearle – Performing Arts Employers Associations League Europe* – full title; *Ligue Européenne des Associations d'employeurs du spectacle* – full title. Registration: Banque-Carrefour des Entreprises, No/ID: 0477.682.141, Start date: 13 Jun 2002, Belgium. **Aims** Establish a stable environment by supporting sustainability and promotion of Live Performance across Europe. **Structure** General Assembly (twice a year); Executive Committee; Specialist Committees. **Languages** English, French. **Staff** 2.00 FTE, paid. **Finance** Sources: grants; members' dues. **Activities** Advocacy/lobbying/activism; awards/prizes/competitions; awareness raising; capacity building; events/meetings; knowledge management/information dissemination; monitoring/evaluation; networking/liaising; projects/programmes; publishing activities; research/documentation. **Events** *Autumn Conference and General Assembly* Brussels (Belgium) 2020, *Spring Conference and General Assembly* Brussels (Belgium) 2020, *Spring Conference and General Assembly* 2019, *Autumn Conference and General Assembly* Porto (Portugal) 2019, *Autumn Conference and General Assembly* Antwerp (Belgium) 2018. **Publications** *2014-2019 EU Priorities for the Live Performance Sector*, *Impediments to mobility in the EU Live Performance Sector and Possible Solutions*; *Inventory of EU Regulations with an Impact on the Live Performance Sector*. *20 YEARS OF EUROPEAN SOCIAL DIALOGUE IN THE LIVE PERFORMANCE* in English; *Behind the Stage Final Report Publication* in English; *ON THE EUROPEAN STAGE 2019–2024 PRIORITIES FOR THE LIVE PERFORMANCE SECTOR* in English. **Information Services** *UPDATED CITES-GUIDE 'CROSSING BORDERS'* in English, French.
Members Interested representatives and established performing arts employers' associations. Full (39) in 21 countries:
Austria, Belgium, Bulgaria, Czechia, Denmark, Estonia, Finland, France, Germany, Hungary, Iceland, Netherlands, Norway, Poland, Portugal, Slovakia, Slovenia, Spain, Sweden, Switzerland, UK.
Associate in 12 countries:
Australia, Belgium, Cyprus, France, Germany, Greece, Latvia, Netherlands, Portugal, Russia, UK, USA.
Regional associations (10) include 6 organizations listed in this Yearbook:
European Circus Association (ECA, #06552); *European Early Music Network (EEMN, #06953)*; *European Festivals Association (EFA, #07242)*; *European Theatre Convention (ETC, #08905)*; *Federation for European Storytelling (FEST, #09553)*; *Opera Europa (#17771)*.
Consultative Status Consultative status granted from: *World Intellectual Property Organization (WIPO, #21593)* (Permanent Observer Status). **NGO Relations** Member of (3): *Culture Action Europe (CAE, #04981)*; *European Alliance for Culture and the Arts (#05866)*; *European Tourism Manifesto (#08921)*.
[2021.03.01/XD3607/**D**]

- ♦ Pearle – Performing Arts Employers Associations League Europe / see Pearle – Live Performance Europe (#18284)
- ♦ Pearson College UWC / see Lester B Pearson United World College of the Pacific
- ♦ PEBLDS – Council for the Pan-European Biological and Landscape Diversity Strategy (inactive)
- ♦ PEC / see Business Africa (#03377)
- ♦ **PECC** Pacific Economic Cooperation Council (#17947)
- ♦ **PECERA** Pacific Early Childhood Education Research Association (#17946)
- ♦ **PEC** Pasifika Education Centre (#18252)
- ♦ PEC – Peuple et Culture (internationally oriented national body)
- ♦ PEC – Press Emblem Campaign (internationally oriented national body)
- ♦ **Pedagogy Freinet** International Federation of Modern School Movements (#13481)
- ♦ Pedals for Progress (internationally oriented national body)
- ♦ **PED** Association transfrontalière du pôle européen de développement (#02958)

♦ **Pediatric Anesthesia and Intensive Care Society and Applied Technologies (PAICSAT)** **18285**

Contact address not obtained. E-mail: paicsat@paicsat.com.
URL: http://www.paicsat.com/

History 2011. **Structure** Executive Board. **Events** *Congress* Foggia (Italy) 2019. **Publications** *Pediatric Anesthesia and Critical Care Journal (PACCJ).* **NGO Relations** Cooperates with (1): *European Society for Computing and Technology in Anaesthesia and Intensive Care (ESCTAIC, #08564).* [2019/AA3038/**C**]

♦ Pediatric Association of Black-French-Speaking Africa / see Association des pédiatres d'Afrique noire francophone (#02854)

♦ **Pediatric Dentistry Association of Asia (PDAA)** **18286**

Pres c/o PPDSI, 5/F Medical Arts Bldg, Dr Fe Del Mundo Medical Ctr, 11 Banawe corner Cardiz St, Quezon City, Philippines.

History 10 Oct 1997. Former names and other names: *Asian Association of Paediatric Dentistry* – former. **Aims** Promote clinical and basic research in paediatric dentistry in the region; improve education in paediatric dentistry; promote cooperation and networking, particularly among paediatric dentists. **Structure** Board. **Languages** English. **Staff** 2.00 FTE, voluntary. **Events** *Conference* Suwon (Korea Rep) 2020, *Conference* Beijing (China) 2018, *Conference* Tokyo (Japan) 2016, *Challenges, innovation and future directions* Singapore (Singapore) 2014, *Conference* Bali (Indonesia) 2012.
Members in 10 countries and territories:
China, Hong Kong, Indonesia, Japan, Korea Rep, Malaysia, Philippines, Singapore, Taiwan, Thailand. [2021/XD8604/**D**]

♦ Pediatric Orthopaedic Society of North America (internationally oriented national body)
♦ Pediatric Pathology Club of North America / see Society for Pediatric Pathology
♦ PED / see PAHO/WHO Health Emergencies Department (#18023)

♦ **Pedro Arrupe World Association (PAWA)** **18287**

Association mondiale Pedro Arrupe – Asociación Mundial Pedro Arrupe

Contact c/o WUJA, Rue Jos Keup 3, L-1860 Luxembourg, Luxembourg. E-mail: info@wuja.org.
URL: http://wuja.org/pedro-arupe-foundation/presentation/

History 1986, Versailles (France). Founded within *World Union of Jesuit Alumni and Alumnae (WUJA, #21877).* Former names and other names: *Pedro Arrupe World Foundation* – former (1986 to 1992); *Fondation mondiale Pedro Arrupe* – former (1986 to 1992); *Fundación Mundial Pedro Arrupe* – former (1986 to 1992). **Aims** Promote and support commitments made by *alumni*/ae of *Jesuit* educational establishments in favour of the poor and needy, particularly *refugees*; encourage ongoing training of Jesuit alumni/ae. **Structure** Council; Executive Committee. [2021/XM0418/**E**]

♦ Pedro Arrupe World Foundation / see Pedro Arrupe World Association (#18287)
♦ Pedro Ferrandiz Foundation / see International Centre for the Documentation and Research of Basketball, Alcobendas
♦ PEEN – Pan-European Ecological Network (see: #04881)
♦ **PEE** Partenaires européens pour l'environnement (#08154)
♦ **PE** Para Equestrian (#05521)
♦ Peering Days (meeting series)
♦ **PEER** Partnership for European Environmental Research (#18235)

♦ **PEFC Council** **18288**

SG Route de l'Aéroport 10, CP 636, 1215 Geneva, Switzerland. T. +41227994540. Fax +41227994550. E-mail: info@pefc.org.
URL: http://www.pefc.org/

History 30 Jun 1999, Paris (France). Statutes most recently adopted 13 Nov 2009. Former names and other names: *PEFC Council – Programme for the Endorsement of Forest Certification* – full title; *PEFC International* – alias. Registration: Switzerland; EU Transparency Register, No/ID: 557406040297-72, Start date: 18 Nov 2020. **Aims** As the world's largest *forest certification* system, seek, through *standards*, to transform the way forests are managed globally and locally to ensure that all can enjoy the environmental, social and economic benefits that forests offer. **Structure** General Assembly (annual); Board of Directors; Secretariat headed by Secretary General. **Languages** Dutch, English, French, German, Russian, Spanish. **Staff** 15.00 FTE, paid. **Finance** Sources: members' dues. Annual budget: 4,100,000 CHF. **Activities** Certification/accreditation; events/meetings; knowledge management/information dissemination; projects/programmes; standards/guidelines. **Events** *Forest Certification Week Meeting* Würzburg (Germany) 2019, *General Assembly* Kuala Lumpur (Malaysia) 2013. **Publications** *PEFC Technical Newsletter*, *PEFC Update*; *Standards Revision Newsletter.* Annual Review; brochures; guidelines; standards; case studies.
Members National members (with endorsed national forest certification systems) in 38 countries:
Argentina, Australia, Austria, Belarus, Belgium, Brazil, Canada, Chile, China, Czechia, Denmark, Estonia, Finland, France, Gabon, Germany, Hungary, Indonesia, Ireland, Italy, Japan, Latvia, Luxembourg, Malaysia, Netherlands, New Zealand, Norway, Poland, Portugal, Russia, Slovakia, Slovenia, Spain, Sweden, Switzerland, UK, Uruguay, USA.
National members (without endorsed national forests certification systems) in 11 countries:
Bulgaria, Cameroon, Congo Brazzaville, Ghana, India, Korea Rep, Lithuania, North Macedonia, Romania, South Africa, Thailand.
International Stakeholder Members (30), including 13 organizations listed in this Yearbook:
Bioenergy Europe (#03247); Building and Wood Workers' International (BWI, #03355); Confederation of European Forest Owners (CEPF, #04525); Confederation of European Paper Industries (CEPI, #04529); European Organization of Agricultural and Rural Contractors (#08105); European Panel Federation (EPF, #08137); European Pulp Industry Sector Association (EPIS, #08305); European Timber Trade Federation (ETTF, #08915); European Tissue Symposium (ETS, #08917); International Council of Forest and Paper Associations (ICFPA, #13023); International Family Forestry Alliance (IFFA, #13329); International Technical Tropical Timber Association (ITTTA, #15668); Unión de Silvicultores del Sur de Europa (USSE, #20478).
Extraordinary: regional organizations (4):
Confédération européenne des industries du bois (CEI Bois, #04545); European Federation of Local Forest Communities (#07157); European Landowners' Organization (ELO, #07639); Union of European Foresters (UEF, #20387).
Consultative Status Consultative status granted from: *ECOSOC (#05331)* (Special). **IGO Relations** Observer status with: *Intergovernmental Negotiating Committee for a Legally Binding Agreement on Forests in Europe (INC-Forests, inactive); Ministerial Conference on the Protection of Forests in Europe (FOREST EUROPE, #16817); United Nations Framework Convention on Climate Change – Secretariat (UNFCCC, #20564).* Member of: *Congo Basin Forest Partnership (CBFP, #04662).* **NGO Relations** Cooperates with (1): *European Sustainable Tropical Timber Coalition (STTC).* Association Body Member of: *International Accreditation Forum (IAF, #11584).* Member of: *International Union for Conservation of Nature and Natural Resources (IUCN, #15766).* Associate member of: *International Family Forestry Alliance (IFFA, #13329).* Subscriber to: *ISEAL (#16026).* [2020/XD7845/y/**C**]

♦ PEFC Council – Programme for the Endorsement of Forest Certification / see PEFC Council (#18288)
♦ PEFC International / see PEFC Council (#18288)
♦ **PEFCTCM** Pan-European Federation of Consultants in Traditional Chinese Medicine (#18175)
♦ **PEF** European Pentecostal Fellowship (#08183)
♦ PEFOTS – Pan European Federation of TCM Societies (no recent information)
♦ PEF – Peace Education Foundation (internationally oriented national body)
♦ **PEF** Platform for European Fathers (#18400)
♦ PEFRAS – Pan European Federation of Regulatory Affairs Societies (inactive)
♦ **PEFY** Pentecostal European Forum for Youth Ministries (#18293)
♦ PEGASUS Foundation / see Partnership of a European Group of Aeronautics and Space UniversitieS (#18236)
♦ **PEGASUS** Partnership of a European Group of Aeronautics and Space UniversitieS (#18236)
♦ **PEGS** Groupe européen de l'industrie papetière pour les affaires sociales (#10739)
♦ **PEIF** Pan-European Insurance Forum (#18177)
♦ **PEIO** Political Economy of International Organizations (#18423)
♦ **PEI** Polar Educators International (#18411)
♦ Peipsi Center for Transboundary Cooperation (internationally oriented national body)
♦ Peipsi CTC – Peipsi Center for Transboundary Cooperation (internationally oriented national body)
♦ Peipsi Koostöör Keskus (internationally oriented national body)
♦ **Pelagic AC** Pelagic Advisory Council (#18289)

♦ **Pelagic Advisory Council (Pelagic AC)** **18289**

Assistant Sec Louis Braillelaan 80, 2719 EK Zoetermeer, Netherlands. T. +31633756324.
URL: http://www.pelagic-ac.org/

History Inaugurated 16 Aug 2005. Registered in accordance with Dutch law. **Aims** Prepare and provide advice on the management of pelagic fish stocks on behalf of the fisheries sector and other stakeholders. **Structure** General Assembly; Executive Committee. Working Groups. **Events** *General Assembly* Edinburgh (UK) 2015, *General Assembly* The Hague (Netherlands) 2014, *General Assembly* The Hague (Netherlands) 2014, *General Assembly* The Hague (Netherlands) 2013, *General Assembly* The Hague (Netherlands) 2013. **Publications** *Pelagic AC Newsletter.* **NGO Relations** *Baltic Sea Advisory Council (BSAC, #03139); Long Distance Advisory Council (LDAC, #16511); Mediterranean Advisory Council (MEDAC, #16639); North Sea Advisory Council (NSAC, #17603); North Western Waters Advisory Council (NWWAC, #17607); South West Waters Advisory Council (SWWAC, #19896).* [2018/XJ9711/**F**]

♦ Pelagic Freezer-trawler Association (unconfirmed)
♦ Pelargonium and Geranium Society (internationally oriented national body)
♦ Pelindaba Treaty – African Nuclear-weapon-free-zone Treaty (1996 treaty)
♦ **PELUM Association** Participatory Ecological Land Use Management (#18225)
♦ **PEMA** Port Equipment Manufacturers Association (#18460)
♦ PEMA – Proclamation de l'évangile par les médias en Afrique (see: #02587)
♦ Pemonton Kowantok Wacüpe Yuwanin Pataset (#03647)
♦ **PEM** Pentecostal European Mission (#18294)
♦ **PEMSEA** Partnerships in Environmental Management for the Seas of East Asia (#18242)
♦ PEN / see International PEN (#14552)
♦ PENAf – Ports Environmental Network-Africa (internationally oriented national body)

♦ **Penal Reform International (PRI)** **18290**

Exec Dir The Green House, 244-254 Cambridge Heath Road, London, E2 9DA, UK. E-mail: info@penalreform.org.
Netherlands Office Hague Humanity Hub, Fluwelen Burgwal 58, 2511 CJ The Hague, Netherlands.
URL: http://www.penalreform.org/

History 12 Nov 1989, London (UK). Registration: No/ID: 40025979, Netherlands, Groningen. **Aims** Achieve penal reform, whilst recognizing diverse cultural context, by promoting: development and implementation of international human rights instruments with regard to law enforcement, prison conditions and standards; elimination of unfair and unethical discrimination in all penal measures; abolition of the death penalty; reduction in the use of imprisonment throughout the world; use of constructive non-custodial sanctions which encourage social reintegration whilst taking account of the interests of victims. **Structure** General Meeting (annual). Board (meets annually) of at least 9 representatives. Executive Board, including Chairperson, Secretary-General, Treasurer and their deputies. Head office in UK; Offices in Russia, Georgia, Kazakhstan and Jordan. **Languages** Arabic, English, French, Russian, Spanish. **Staff** 30.00 FTE, paid. **Finance** Support from foreign affairs ministries and from government and intergovernmental bodies, including the following: Belgian Ministry of Foreign Affairs; *Center for Victims of Torture (CVT); Department for International Development (DFID, inactive)*; Development Cooperation Ireland; *European Commission (EC, #06633); European Union (EU, #08967)*; Foreign and Commonwealth Office, UK; Norwegian Mission of Rule of Law Advisors to Georgia; Open Society Institute; *Organization for Security and Cooperation in Europe (OSCE, #17887); Quaker United Nations Office (QUNO, #18588)*; Swedish Institute for Human Rights; *Swedish International Development Cooperation Agency (Sida); Swiss Agency for Development and Cooperation (SDC); UNICEF (#20332).* **Activities** Advocacy/lobbying/activism; guidance/assistance/consulting; monitoring/evaluation; events/meetings; research/documentation. **Events** *Latin American Regional Conference* Buenos Aires (Argentina) 2019, *American Regional Conference* Mérida (Mexico) 2019, *World Congress on Justice for Children* Paris (France) 2018, *High-Level Round Table on Reform of Criminal Procedure Legislation* Astana (Kazakhstan) 2014, *World Congress against the Death Penalty* Madrid (Spain) 2013. **Publications** *Penal Reform International e-Newsletter* (12 a year) in English. Regional and country-specific Together Against Torture e- newsletters (12 a year). Annual Report; manuals; information packs; reports on prison conditions; conference, seminar and workshop reports.
Members Worldwide membership (countries not specified). **Consultative Status** Consultative status granted from: *African Commission on Human and Peoples' Rights (ACHPR, #00255)* (Observer); *ECOSOC (#05331)* (Special); *Council of Europe (CE, #04881)* (Participatory Status); *African Committee of Experts on the Rights and Welfare of the Child (ACERWC, #00257)* (Observer Status). **IGO Relations** Observer status with: *African Committee of Experts on the Rights and Welfare of the Child (ACERWC, #00257); OAS (#17629).* Accredited by: *United Nations Office at Vienna (UNOV, #20604).* Member of: *Convention against Torture Initiative (CTI, #04786).* Panel member of: *Interagency Panel on Juvenile Justice (IPJJ, #11390).* Partner: *Instituto Latinoamericano de las Naciones Unidas para la Prevención del Delito y Tratamiento del Delincuente (ILANUD, #11347).*
NGO Relations Member of: *Alliance of NGOs on Crime Prevention and Criminal Justice (#00709); Conference of Eastern, Southern and Central African Heads of Correctional Services (CESCA, inactive); Global Partnership to End Violence Against Children (End Violence Against Children, #10533); Global Rights; Human Rights and Democracy Network (HRDN, #10980); World Coalition Against the Death Penalty (#21281).* Associate member of: *Altus Global Alliance (inactive).* Observer status with: *Inter-Parliamentary Union (IPU, #15961).*
Partners include:
- *Amnesty International (AI, #00801);*
- *Arab Institute for Human Rights (AIHR, #00983);*
- *Association pénitentiaire africaine (APA, no recent information);*
- *Association for the Prevention of Torture (APT, #02869);*
- *Avocats Sans Frontières (ASF, #03050);*
- *Bureau international des Médecins sans frontières (MSF International, #03366);*
- *Global Forum on Law, Justice and Development (GFLJD, #10373);*
- *Instituto Interamericano de Derechos Humanos (IIDH, #11334);*
- *International Commission of Jurists (ICJ, #12695);*
- *International Federation of ACATs – Action by Christians for the Abolition of Torture (#13334);*
- *International Federation for Human Rights (#13452).* [2022/XF1656/**F**]

♦ Pencils of Promise (internationally oriented national body)
♦ Pendaftaran Kerayatan Dunia Antarabangsa / see Registre des Citoyens du Monde (#18822)
♦ PENHA – Pastoral and Environmental Network in the Horn of Africa (internationally oriented national body)
♦ PEN Internacional (#14552)
♦ PEN International (#14552)
♦ Penny Appeal (internationally oriented national body)
♦ **PENSA** Parenteral and Enteral Nutrition Society of Asia (#18197)

♦ **PensionsEurope** **18291**

SG Rue Montoyer 23, 1000 Brussels, Belgium. T. +3222891414. E-mail: info@pensionseurope.eu.
URL: http://www.pensionseurope.eu/

History 1981. Founded to represent each EU and EFTA country's system for provision of pensions supplementary to that provided by the State. Former names and other names: *European Federation for Retirement Provision (EFRP)* – former; *Europese Federatie voor Pensioenvoorziening* – former. Registration: Banque-Carrefour des Entreprises, No/ID: 0473.016.045, Start date: 30 Mar 2000, Belgium; EU Transparency Register, No/ID: 5199259747-21, Start date: 9 Dec 2008. **Aims** Represent the interests of *workplace pensions* and promote them in Europe; support financing mechanisms; advocate partnership between state and occupational pension schemes; promote single market of occupational pensions through removal of tax hurdles and ensure that the European passport for institutions for Occupational Retirement Provision (IORP) is fully implemented; safeguard the welfare of pensioners within the *European Union* without jeopardizing competitiveness of European industry. **Structure** General Assembly (every 6 months); Board of Directors; Secretariat, headed by Secretary-General. **Languages** English. **Staff** 4.00 FTE, paid. **Finance** Sources: members' dues. Corporate and Supporter Membership: selected group of financial institutions and consultants

catering pension funds interested in activities on the workplace pension scene at a European level. **Activities** Advocacy/lobbying/activism; politics/policy/regulatory. **Events** *Conference* Brussels (Belgium) 2022, *Conference* 2021, *Conference* Brussels (Belgium) 2020, *Conference* Brussels (Belgium) 2019, *Joint Meeting* Brussels (Belgium) 2019. **Publications** Board notes; membership notes; position papers; press releases; responses; surveys.
Members National pensions associations (24) in 21 countries:
Austria, Belgium, Bulgaria, Croatia, Finland, France, Germany, Greece, Hungary, Iceland, Ireland, Italy, Luxembourg, Netherlands, Norway, Portugal, Romania, Spain, Sweden, Switzerland, UK.
IGO Relations Observer Status with: *OECD (#17693)* Private Pensions Working Party; OECD Pensions Statistics Task Force. Expert Status on: Pension Funds Business Statistics of *Statistical Office of the European Union (Eurostat, #19974)*. Represented on Consultative Panel of: *European Insurance and Occupational Pensions Authority (EIOPA, #07578)* and its Occupational Pensions Stakeholder Group (OPSG). **NGO Relations** Member of (2): *European Parliamentary Financial Services Forum (EPFSF, #08148)*; *World Pension Alliance (WPA, #21719)*. Formal contacts with: *Accountancy Europe (#00061)*; *Association Européenne des Institutions Paritaires de la Protection Sociale (AEIP, #02575)*; *BUSINESSEUROPE (#03381)*; *European Financial Reporting Advisory Group (EFRAG, #07254)*; *European Fund and Asset Management Association (EFAMA, #07365)*; *European Trade Union Confederation (ETUC, #08927)*; *Federation of European Securities Exchanges (FESE, #09542)*; *Insurance Europe (#11362)*; *Invest Europe – The Voice of Private Capital (Invest Europe, #15997)*.
[2022/XD2404/**D**]

♦ Pentagonal Conference / see Central European Initiative (#03708)
♦ Pentagonale / see Central European Initiative (#03708)
♦ Pentagonal Initiative / see Central European Initiative (#03708)
♦ Pentagon Group / see Central European Initiative (#03708)
♦ **PENTA-ID** Paediatric European Network for the Treatments of AIDS and Infectious Diseases (#18017)
♦ PENTA / see Paediatric European Network for the Treatments of AIDS and Infectious Diseases (#18017)

♦ Pentecostal Assemblies of the West Indies International (PAWI) . . . 18292

General Administrator PO Box 100, Port-of-Spain, Trinidad-Tobago. T. +18686622485. Fax +18686457719.
URL: http://www.pawi-online.org/
History 1958, Trinidad-Tobago. Founded 1958, Trinidad. Successor to the movement known as *Pentecostal Assemblies of Canada*, initiated 1910, Montserrat; formally affiliated, 1946 – 1958, as the West Indies District, with *'Pentecostal Assemblies of Canada – POAC'*. Statutes revised: 1965; 1985. Revised Constitution and Bylaws: 2006; 2010. **Aims** Establish places of worship for the propagation of the Christian faith; organize and operate schools of religious instruction and secular education; carry on missionary work; carry on charitable and philanthropic work; operate friendly societies, cooperatives and pension funds; build and operate hospitals, clinics, orphanages and homes for the aged. **Structure** *West Indies School of Theology (WIST)*, set up 1946, provides certificate, diploma and tertiary level training for ministers and church workers. **Activities** Events/meetings. **Publications** *West Indies School of Theology Yearbook – Flame Magazine*.
Members Congregations in 16 countries and territories:
Antigua-Barbuda, Bahamas, Barbados, Brazil, Canada, Dominica, Grenada, Guadeloupe, Malawi, Montenegro, St Kitts-Nevis, St Lucia, St Vincent-Grenadines, Trinidad-Tobago, USA, Venezuela.
NGO Relations Member of: *Evangelical Association of the Caribbean (EAC, #09210)*. Links with various organizations, including: *Youth with a Mission (YWAM, #22020)*.
[2016.02.01/XF4310/**F**]

♦ Pentecostal European Forum for Youth Ministries (PEFY) 18293

Contact Chaussée de Waterloo 45, 1640 St-Genesius-Rode, Belgium.
History Cooperation started 8 Jun 2003, Berlin (Germany). Developed into a more official body, 2006. Official board set up 2008. A branch of *European Pentecostal Fellowship (PEF, #08183)*. **Aims** Connect, impact and increase visibility of Pentecostal European youth through networks and youth exchange programmes. **Structure** Business Meeting (annual); Board. **Activities** Events/meetings. **Events** *Conference* Skopje (Macedonia) 2016.
[2015/XM4372/**F**]

♦ Pentecostal European Mission (PEM) 18294

Contact Waterloosesteenweg 47, 1640 St-Genesius-Rode, Belgium. E-mail: info@pem.pef.eu.
URL: http://pem.pef.eu/
History Founded 1991, Helsinki (Finland). A branch of *European Pentecostal Fellowship (PEF, #08183)*. **Aims** Serve as a coordinating body between European Pentecostal development cooperation / humanitarian and mission organizations. **Structure** Committee; Coordination Team. **Languages** English. **Staff** 2.50 FTE, paid. **Finance** Members' dues. Annual budget: euro 15,000. **Events** *Impact* Lugano (Switzerland) 2015, *Annual Meeting* Turin (Italy) 2015, *Annual Meeting* Warsaw (Poland) 2014, *Annual Meeting* Cluj-Napoca (Romania) 2013, *Impact* Palermo (Italy) 2013.
Members Full (32); Associate (9). Organizations in 23 countries:
Australia, Belarus, Belgium, Bulgaria, Croatia, Czechia, Finland, France, Germany, Hungary, Israel, Italy, Lithuania, Netherlands, Norway, Poland, Romania, Russia, Slovakia, Spain, Sweden, Switzerland, Ukraine.
[2020.02.21/XF4497/**F**]

♦ Pentecostal World Conference / see Pentecostal World Fellowship (#18295)

♦ Pentecostal World Fellowship 18295

Head Office 7777 S Lewis Ave, Tulsa OK 74171, USA. E-mail: chair@pwfellowship.org.
URL: https://www.pwfellowship.org/
History First conference for Pentecostal leaders organized, May 1947, Zurich (Switzerland). Former names and other names: *Pentecostal World Conference (PWC)* – former (1961 to May 1999). **Aims** Promote and encourage regional and continental alliances among Spirit-filled networks; promote and connect Spirit-filled leaders; speak to governments and nations when and where social justice and religious rights are compromised and/or violated for the sake of the gospel; foster world missions, support humanitarian aid and provide relief aid; serve as cooperative fellowship for Pentecostal Theological institutions to promote education and leadership training; coordinate worldwide prayer. **Structure** Advisory Committee; Executive Committee; Commissions (5); International Office. **Staff** Voluntary. **Finance** Sources: contributions; gifts, legacies. **Events** *Triennial World Pentecostal Conference* Calgary, AB (Canada) 2019, *Triennial World Pentecostal Conference* Sao Paulo (Brazil) 2016, *Triennial World Pentecostal Conference* Kuala Lumpur (Malaysia) 2013, *Triennial world conference / Triennial World Pentecostal Conference* Stockholm (Sweden) 2010, *Triennial world conference / Triennial World Pentecostal Conference* Surabaya (Indonesia) 2007.
Members National Councils, fraternal organizations, independent organizations and churches in 35 countries and territories:
Argentina, Australia, Bangladesh, Brazil, Canada, Denmark, Finland, Germany, Ghana, Haiti, Hong Kong, Hungary, India, Indonesia, Japan, Korea Rep, Liberia, Lithuania, Malaysia, Mexico, Namibia, Netherlands, Nigeria, Norway, Pakistan, Philippines, Romania, Samoa, Singapore, South Africa, Sweden, Togo, Uganda, UK, USA.
Included in the above, 4 organizations listed in this Yearbook:
European Pentecostal Fellowship (PEF, #08183); *Fida International*; *International Church of the Foursquare Gospel (ICFG)*; *International Pentecostal Holiness Church (IPHC)*.
NGO Relations Instrumental in setting up (1): *Asian Pentecostal Society (APS, #01661)*.
[2021.08.31/XF4512/y/**F**]

♦ **PEOPIL** Pan-European Organisation of Personal Injury Lawyers (#18179)

♦ Up With People (UWP) 18296

CEO 6800 Broadway, Ste 106, Denver CO 80221-2851, USA. T. +13034607100. Fax +13032254649. E-mail: tlane@upwithpeople.org – info@upwithpeople.org.
European address Stephanie Square Centre, Av Louise 65, Box 11, 1050 Brussels, Belgium. T. +3226462636.
URL: http://www.upwithpeople.org/
History 1965, Tucson AZ (USA). Incorporated 1968. Founder: J Blanton Belk. Ceased activities Dec 2000. Relaunched 2004. **Aims** Develop *human potential* in order to bring the world together through friendship and understanding by complementing traditional academic education through a combination of international *travel* with *intercultural* living, community service and *musical performance*. **Structure** Independent Board of Directors (mostly from USA); Regional Offices in Belgium and Mexico. Alumni association: *Up With People International Alumni Association (UWPIAA, #18299)*. **Languages** English. **Activities** Training/education; projects/programmes; events/meetings. **Events** *Anniversary silver conference* Denver, CO (USA) 1990. **Publications** *UWP Newsletter* (6 a year); *Upbeat Magazine* (3 a year). **Members** Alumni (over 22,000) in 131 countries. Membership countries not specified.
[2021/XF0290/**F**]

♦ People Against Landmines (internationally oriented national body)
♦ People-Centered Development Forum / see Living Economies Forum
♦ People and Culture (internationally oriented national body)
♦ People Empowering People Africa (internationally oriented national body)

♦ People for the Ethical Treatment of Animals (PETA) 18297

Pres 501 Front St, Norfolk VA 23510, USA. T. +17576227382. Fax +17576220457. E-mail: info@peta.org.
URL: http://www.peta.org/
History 1980, USA. **Aims** Establish and defend the *rights* of all animals. **Structure** Board of Directors of 3 members. Headquarters in Norfolk VA (USA). **Finance** Members' dues. Donations. Budget (annual): US$ 25 million. **Activities** Works through public education, research and investigation, legislation, special events, direct action and grassroots organizing. **Publications** *PETA's Animal Times* (4 a year) in English, German; *PETA Annual Review*. *Guide to Compassionate Living*. Books; brochures.
Members A mainly USA organization but expanding to other countries. Individuals (mostly in USA) in 23 countries and territories:
Argentina, Bahamas, Belgium, Brazil, Canada, Denmark, Dominican Rep, France, Germany, India, Israel, Italy, Japan, Mexico, Netherlands, Philippines, Puerto Rico, Spain, Sweden, Switzerland, Taiwan, Türkiye, UK.
Affiliates in 7 countries:
France, Germany, India, Netherlands, Philippines, UK, USA.
NGO Relations Member of: *International Council on Animal Protection in OECD Programmes (ICAPO, #12992)*.
[2010.09.27/XF3504/v/**F**]

♦ People First International (internationally oriented national body)
♦ People and Global Business Association (internationally oriented national body)

♦ People from Here and Elsewhere Federation 18298

Fédération des peuples d'ici et d'ailleurs (PIA)
Pres 403 rue du Bas Berri, 79230 Saint-Martin-de-Bernegoue, France. T. +33549260811. Fax +33549260811. E-mail: pia79@orange.fr.
History 29 Nov 1992, Strasbourg (France), as *Regards de peuples en Europe (RPE)*. Present name adopted Nov 1994. Registered in accordance with French law. **Aims** Prevent *exclusion*; promote *social interaction* and friendly relations between peoples from *different cultures*. **Structure** General Assembly (annual). Administrative Council (meets twice a year). Bureau, comprising President, Secretary and Treasurer. **Finance** Members' dues. **Activities** Seminars; colloquia; meetings. Training courses in areas such as in accountancy and languages. Publishing activity. Expression of solidarity with those forces that are contributing to the development of the Two-Thirds World. Support to the association sector in the form of PIA assistance to the groups of individuals wishing to form an association – this policy of assistance covers 3 different phases: (a) PIA support and assistance in the genesis of a group's project; (b) the group seeking assistance takes the initiative, and PIA's role is essentially a backup one; (c) PIA steps aside, conferring complete autonomy on the group while remaining available should difficulties arise. **Events** *Seminar* Niort (France) 2004, *Meeting / Seminar* Niort (France) 2001, *Conference / Seminar* Cluj-Napoca (Romania) 1999, *Human rights and their application* Niort (France) 1998, *Interculturality and education* Strasbourg (France) 1998. **Publications** *Peuple d'ici et d'ailleurs* (4 a year) in English, French. *Les Cahiers PIA*. Pamphlets; surveys.
Members Associations, groups and individuals in 35 countries:
Algeria, Argentina, Armenia, Belarus, Belgium, Benin, Brazil, Bulgaria, Burkina Faso, Cameroon, Canada, Chile, Congo DR, Côte d'Ivoire, Croatia, Estonia, Finland, France, Georgia, Germany, Greece, Hungary, Italy, Kenya, Luxembourg, Mali, Mongolia, Morocco, Portugal, Romania, Russia, Serbia, Spain, Türkiye, Ukraine.
[2010.07.08/XF4187/**F**]

♦ People International (internationally oriented national body)

♦ Up With People International Alumni Association (UWPIAA) 18299

Mailing Address PO Box 64434, Tucson AZ 85728, USA.
URL: http://www.uwpiaa.org/
History 1987, within the framework of *Up With People (UWP, #18296)*. **Aims** Provide a framework through which Up With People Alumni can build productive networks, participate in activities, foster mutually beneficial communication, collaboration and support among Alumni, and impact the ongoing mission of Up With People. **Structure** Board of Governors, representing all ERAs and geographies where alumni are located. **Staff** 4.00 FTE, paid. **Activities** Organizes Annual Meeting (always in Tucson AZ, USA). **Events** *Meeting* Tucson, AZ (USA) 2008, *Meeting* Tucson, AZ (USA) 2007, *Meeting* Tucson, AZ (USA) 2006, *Meeting* Tucson, AZ (USA) 2005. **Publications** *UpBeat*. **Members** 20,000 Up With People alumni worldwide. Membership countries not specified.
[2021/XE2534/**E**]

♦ PeopleLink (internationally oriented national body)
♦ People Living with HIV / see East European and Central Asian Union of PLWH (#05257)
♦ People for Medical Cooperation International (internationally oriented national body)
♦ People in Need (internationally oriented national body)
♦ People and Organisations United for Spina Bifida and Hydrocephalus / see PUSH! Global Alliance (#18580)
♦ People Organized to Stop the Rape of Imprisoned Persons / see Just Detention International
♦ People for Peace in Africa (unconfirmed)
♦ People to People Health Foundation / see Project HOPE

♦ People to People International (PTPI) 18300

World Headquarters 2405 Grand Blvd, Ste 500, Kansas City MO 64108, USA. T. +18165314701. Fax +18165617502.
LinkedIn: https://www.linkedin.com/company/people-to-people-international/
History 11 Sep 1956, USA. Founded by President Dwight D Eisenhower of the United States. Registration: Not-for-profit organization, No/ID: 501(c)(3), Start date: 31 Oct 1961, USA, Missouri. **Aims** Enhance international understanding and friendship through *educational*, *cultural* and *humanitarian* activities involving exchange of ideas and experiences directly among peoples of different countries and diverse cultures. **Structure** Includes *People to People International – Europe (PTPI Europe, #18301)*. **Languages** Dutch, English, French, German, Italian. **Staff** 5.00 FTE, voluntary. **Finance** Sources: grants; members' dues; revenue from activities/projects; sponsorship. Annual budget: 7,000 EUR (2019). **Activities** Advocacy/lobbying/activism; capacity building; events/meetings; networking/liaising. Active in: Afghanistan, Albania, Algeria, Angola, Argentina, Armenia, Aruba, Ascension Is, Australia, Austria, Bahamas, Bahrain, Bangladesh, Barbados, Belgium, Belize, Benin, Bermuda, Bhutan, Bolivia, Botswana, Brazil, British Antarctic Terr, British Indian Ocean Terr, Brunei Darussalam, Bulgaria, Burkina Faso, Burundi, Cambodia, Cameroon, Canada, Canaries, Cape Verde, Cayman Is, Central African Rep, Chad, Chile, China, Colombia, Comoros, Congo Brazzaville, Congo DR, Costa Rica, Côte d'Ivoire, Cuba, Curaçao, Czechia, Denmark, Djibouti, Dominica, Dominican Rep, Dutch Caribbean, Ecuador, Egypt, El Salvador, Ethiopia, France, Gabon, Gambia, Germany, Ghana, Guam, Guatemala, Guiana Fr, Guinea, Guyana, Haiti, Honduras, Hong Kong, India, Indonesia, Israel, Italy, Japan, Kazakhstan, Kenya, Kiribati, Korea DPR, Korea Rep, Kosovo, Kuwait, Kyrgyzstan, Lebanon, Lesotho, Liberia, Libya, Madagascar, Malawi, Malaysia, Maldives, Mali, Marshall Is, Martinique, Mauritania, Mauritius, Mayotte, Mexico, Micronesia FS, Mongolia, Montserrat, Morocco, Mozambique, Myanmar, Namibia, Nauru, Nepal, Netherlands, New Caledonia, New Zealand, Nicaragua, Niger, Nigeria, Niue, North Macedonia, Northern Mariana Is, Oman, Pakistan, Palau, Palestine, Panama, Papua New Guinea, Paraguay, Peru, Philippines, Pitcairn, Poland, Polynesia Fr, Puerto Rico, Qatar, Réunion, Romania, Russia, Rwanda, Sahara West, Sahrawi ADR, Samoa, Samoa USA, Sao Tomé-Principe, Saudi Arabia, Senegal, Seychelles, Sierra Leone, Singapore, Solomon Is, Somalia, South Africa, South Georgia, South Sudan, Sri Lanka, St Helena, St Kitts-Nevis, St Lucia, St Maarten, St Martin, St Pierre-Miquelon, St Vincent-Grenadines, Sudan, Suriname, Sweden, Switzerland, Syrian AR, Taiwan, Tajikistan, Tanzania UR, Thailand, Timor-Leste, Togo, Tokelau, Tonga, Trinidad-Tobago, Tristan da Cunha, Tunisia, Turkmenistan, Turks-Caicos, Uganda, Ukraine, United Arab Emirates, Uruguay, USA, Uzbekistan, Vanuatu, Venezuela, Vietnam, Virgin Is UK, Virgin Is USA, Yemen, Zambia, Zimbabwe. **Events** *World Conference* Seoul (Korea Rep) 2021, *World Conference* London (UK) 2017, *Americas Regional*

Conference Atlanta, GA (USA) 2015, *Asia Pacific Regional Conference* Ulaanbaatar (Mongolia) 2015, *World Conference* Tainan (Taiwan) 2014. **Members** (26,000) in 160 countries. Membership countries not specified. **Consultative Status** Consultative status granted from: *ECOSOC (#05331)* (Special). **IGO Relations** Member of: *European Youth Centres (EYCs, #09138)*. Associated with Department of Global Communications of the United Nations. **NGO Relations** Affiliated to: *Worldwide Network of the Experiment in International Living (Federation EIL, #21930)*. Member of: *Alliance for International Exchange*; *Conference of Non-Governmental Organizations in Consultative Relationship with the United Nations (CONGO, #04635)*; *UNITED for Intercultural Action – European Network Against Nationalism, Racism, Fascism and in Support of Migrants and Refugees (UNITED, #20511)* – via Estonian Branch. [2020.04.29/XF4989/**F**]

♦ People to People International – Europe (PTPI Europe) 18301

Pres Av Jules Bordet 13, 1140 Brussels, Belgium. T. +32478482023. E-mail: mail@ptpi.eu.
Dir-Gen Maison de la Francite, Rue Joseph II 18, 1000 Brussels, Belgium.
URL: https://www.ptpi.eu/

History 2 Jan 1970, Brussels (Belgium). A regional entity of *People to People International (PTPI, #18300)*. Registration: Banque Carrefour des Entreprises, No/ID: 0412.527.835, Start date: 1 Sep 1971, Belgium. **Aims** Enhance international understanding and friendship through educational, cultural, and humanitarian activities involving the exchange of ideas and experiences directly among peoples of different countries and diverse cultures. **Structure** Administrative Board; European Executive Committee (EEC Youth). **Languages** Bulgarian, English, French, German, Italian, Macedonian, Romanian, Swiss German. **Staff** 5.00 FTE, voluntary. **Finance** Sources: contributions; fees for services; fundraising; in-kind support; members' dues; private foundations; sponsorship. Supported by: Benevity. Annual budget: 1,000 EUR (2020). **Activities** Advocacy/lobbying/activism; awards/prizes/competitions; awareness raising; capacity building; events/meetings; guidance/assistance/consulting; networking/liaising; projects/programmes. **Events** *European Conference* Skopje (North Macedonia) 2021, *European Conference* Skopje (North Macedonia) 2020, *Annual European Conference* Plovdiv (Bulgaria) 2019, *European Conference* Katowice (Poland) 2018, *Annual European Conference* Yerevan (Armenia) 2017.
Members Community and Youth Chapters in 14 countries:
Armenia, Belgium, Bulgaria, Estonia, Georgia, Germany, Italy, Kosovo, Latvia, North Macedonia, Romania, Serbia, Switzerland, UK. [2021.02.08/AA1307/**E**]

♦ People in Peril (internationally oriented national body)
♦ People and Planet (internationally oriented national body)
♦ People and Plants Initiative / see People and Plants International (#18302)

♦ People and Plants International (PPI) 18302

Contact PO Box 251, Bristol VT 05443, USA. E-mail: peopleandplants@gmail.com.
URL: http://peopleandplants.org/

History 1992, as a partnership programme of *UNESCO (#20322)* and *World Wide Fund for Nature (WWF, #21922)*, with Royal Botanic Gardens Kew (UK) as an Associate. Previously a joint initiative of *Programme on Man and the Biosphere (MAB, #18526)* and WWF with the title *People and Plants Initiative*. Programme ended Dec 2004 when it became independent and adopted current title. **Aims** Support *ethno-botanists* from *developing countries* who work with local communities to: study and record use of *plant resources*; resolve conflict between *conservation* and *over-exploitation* of such resources; promote sustainable methods of *harvesting* non-cultivated plants; ensure that local communities benefit from conservation and use of plant resources. **Structure** Steering Committee of 6 members. **Finance** External funding support, including from: *Darwin Initiative*; *Department for International Development (DFID, inactive)*; *Ford Foundation (#09858)*. **Activities** Current programme areas (6): Sustainable resource management; Ethnoecology master's; Returning results; Policy development; Cultural landscapes and indigenous resource rights; Health and Habitat. **Events** *Building bridges with traditional knowledge summit* Honolulu, HI (USA) 2001. **Publications** *PPI Newsletter*. Conservations manuals; working papers; handbook modules.
Members Individuals in 11 countries:
China, Fiji, France, India, Kenya, Nepal, Pakistan, Tanzania UR, Uganda, UK, USA.
IGO Relations UNESCO. [2009/XK0537/v/**F**]

♦ People's Aid Austria (internationally oriented national body)
♦ Peoples Church of Africa (internationally oriented national body)

♦ People's Coalition on Food Sovereignty (PCFS) 18303

Global Secretariat Coordinator 143-A K-3rd St, Barangay Kamuning, 1103 Quezon City, Philippines. T. +6326646327. Fax +6329276981. E-mail: secretariat@foodsov.org.
URL: http://www.foodsov.org/

History 2001. Founded as an Asian component of the global agri-trade network on People's Food Sovereignty. Current title adopted, Nov 2004, Dhaka (Bangladesh). **Aims** Develop and promote people's food sovereignty as the alternative platform against neoliberal globalization on food and *agricultural* policies. **Structure** Global Assembly; Steering Council; Executive Committee; Regional Steering Councils (3); Regional Offices based in Bolivia, Jordan, Luxemburg and Zambia; Global Secretariat, based in Quezon City (Philippines). **Activities** Advocacy/lobbying/activism; awareness raising; capacity building; networking/liaising; politics/policy/regulatory; publishing activities; research/documentation; training/education. **Publications** *Aiding Militarism and Subversion of Agriculture* (2016).
Members 200 organizational members and networks in 53 countries. Membership countries not specified. Included in the above, 6 organizations listed in this Yearbook:
Asia Pacific Forum on Women, Law and Development (APWLD, #01912); *Asia-Pacific Research Network (APRN, #02013)*; *IBON International (#11037)*; *Pacific Asia Resource Centre (PARC)*; *Pesticide Action Network (PAN, #18336)* (Asia-Pacific); *South Asian Network for Social and Agricultural Development (SANSAD)*.
NGO Relations Member of (1): *CSO Partnership for Development Effectiveness (CPDE, #04976)*.
[2022.02.03/XJ5643/y/**C**]

♦ Peoples' Congress (internationally oriented national body)
♦ People's Decade of Human Rights Education / see People's Movement for Human Rights Learning (#18307)

♦ Peoples' Global Action Against Free Trade and the WTO (PGA) 18304

Action mondiale des peuples contre le 'libre' échange et l'OMC – Acción Global de los Pueblos contra el comercio 'libre' y la OCM – Weltweite Aktion gegen den 'Frei' handel und die WTO – Azione Globale dei Popoli contra il comercio 'libre' – Globalnye akcii chelovechestva protiv 'svobodnoy' torgovli i VTO

Contact c/o Canadian Union of Postal Workers, 377 Bank Street, Ottawa ON K2P 1Y3, Canada. Fax +16135637861. E-mail: agpweb@lists.riseup.net.
URL: https://www.nadir.org/nadir/initiativ/agp/en/

History Feb 1998, Geneva (Switzerland), at first conference. Also referred to in French as *Action mondiale des peuples (AMP)*. **Aims** Resist *free trade* through non-violent *civil disobedience* and people-oriented constructive actions. **Structure** Informal network. **Activities** Organizes counter-events for WTO meetings. **Events** *European conference* Athens (Greece) 2008, *European conference* Dijon (France) 2006, *European conference* Belgrade (Serbia-Montenegro) 2004, *Nordic meeting* Stockholm (Sweden) 2003, *European conference* Leiden (Netherlands) 2002. **Publications** *PGA Bulletin*. [2008/XF1109/**F**]

♦ People's Health Movement (PHM) 18305

Movimiento para la Salud de los Pueblos

Global Coordinator address not obtained.
URL: http://www.phmovement.org/

Aims Promote health for all by: ensuring universal access to quality *health care*, education and social services; promoting participation in formulation, implementation and evaluation of all health and social policy programmes. **Structure** Global Steering Council; Coordinating Commission; Advisory Council; Networks; Secretariat. **Activities** Events/meetings. **Events** *Assembly* Dhaka (Bangladesh) 2018, *Assembly* Cape Town (South Africa) 2012, *Assembly* Cuenca (Ecuador) 2005, *Assembly* Dhaka (Bangladesh) 2000. **Publications** *PHM Newsletter*.
Members Organizations (7):
Asian Community Health Action Network (ACHAN, #01393); *Consumers International (CI, #04773)*; Gonoshasthaya Kendra (Bangladesh); *HAI – Asia-Pacific (HAIAP, #10852)*; *International People's Health Council (IPHC)*; *Medicus Mundi International – Network Health for All (MMI, #16636)*; *Third World Network (TWN, #20151)*; *Women's Global Network for Reproductive Rights (WGNRR, #21019)*.
NGO Relations Member of (5): *ETO Consortium (ETOs, #05560)*; *Geneva Global Health Hub (G2H2, #10122)*; *International Network for Economic, Social and Cultural Rights (ESCR-Net, #14255)*; *Reproductive Health Supplies Coalition (RHSC, #18847)*; *Right to Food and Nutrition Watch Consortium (#18943)*. Supports (1): *Global Call for Action Against Poverty (GCAP, #10263)*. Together with: *Global Equity Gauge Alliance (GEGA, no recent information)* and *Medact*, set up: *Global Health Watch (GHW)*. [2020/XM1375/y/**F**]

♦ People's International League (inactive)

♦ Peoples' Movement on Climate Change (PMCC) 18306

Secretariat IBON Ctr, 114 Timog Avenue, Quezon City, METRO 1103 Manila, Philippines. T. +6329277060. Fax +6329276981.
URL: http://peoplesclimatemovement.net/

Aims Advance the People's Protocol on Climate Change as the Southern peoples' strategy and response to the climate change issue.
Members Signatories in 44 countries and territories:
Angola, Australia, Azerbaijan, Bahrain, Bangladesh, Belgium, Bolivia, Canada, China, Costa Rica, Denmark, France, Germany, Greece, Honduras, Hong Kong, India, Indonesia, Iraq, Italy, Kenya, Korea Rep, Lebanon, Malaysia, Mongolia, Morocco, Nepal, Netherlands, New Zealand, Nicaragua, Nigeria, Pakistan, Philippines, Portugal, South Africa, Sri Lanka, Sudan, Switzerland, Thailand, Uganda, UK, Ukraine, USA, Vietnam.
NGO Relations Member of: *Climate Justice Now ! (CJN!, inactive)*. [2015/XJ3223/**F**]

♦ People's Movement for Human Rights Education / see People's Movement for Human Rights Learning (#18307)

♦ People's Movement for Human Rights Learning (PDHRE) 18307

Contact City View, Room 514, 515 North La Brea Avenue, Los Angeles CA 90036, USA. T. +12125187505.
Twitter: https://twitter.com/pdhre1

History 1988, New York, NY (USA). Founded by Shulamith Koenig (1930-2021). Former names and other names: *Organizing Committee for the People's Decade of Human Rights Education (DHRE)* – former; *People's Decade of Human Rights Education (PDHRE-International)* – former; *People's Movement for Human Rights Education (PDHRE)* – former (Oct 2000). Registration: 501(c)(3) non-profit, USA. **Aims** Promote, enhance and provide learning about human rights as relevant to people's daily lives at all levels of society, that leads to action. **Structure** Board of Directors; Praesidium; International Advisory Committee; Secretariat; Regional Offices (6). **Languages** English, Spanish. **Staff** 6.00 FTE, voluntary. **Finance** Funding from: *Ford Foundation (#09858)*; Nordic governments; private foundations. Budget (annual): about US$ 100,000. **Activities** Training/education; events/meetings. **Events** *Strategy session on learning human rights as a way of life* New York, NY (USA) 2010. **Publications** Learning manuals; reports; resource packets; articles; books; videos. **Members** Endorsers, Affiliates, International Advisory Committee, local and international volunteers, members and friends in 60 countries and territories. Membership countries not specified. **Consultative Status** Consultative status granted from: *ECOSOC (#05331)* (Special). **NGO Relations** Member of: *CONGO Committee on Human Rights (#04663)*; *Habitat International Coalition (HIC, #10845)*; *International Federation for Human Rights (#13452)*; *International Institute of Human Rights – Fondation René Cassin (IIHR, #13887)*; *International Network for Economic, Social and Cultural Rights (ESCR-Net, #14255)*; *International Peace Research Association (IPRA, #14537)*; *Latin American and Caribbean Committee for the Defense of Women's Rights (#16268)*; *Servicio Paz y Justicia en América Latina (SERPAJ-AL, #19247)*. Participant of: *United Nations Global Compact (#20567)*. Supports: *Global Call for Action Against Poverty (GCAP, #10263)*.
[2018/XE1462/**F**]

♦ People's Mujahedin of Iran / see Mujahedin-e Khalq Organization (#16881)

♦ People's SAARC 18308

Secretariat PO Box 8130, 288 Gairidhara Marg, Gairidhara, Kathmandu, Nepal. T. +97714004508 – +97714004985. Fax +97714004508 – +97714443494.
URL: http://www.peoplesaarc.org/

History First proposed 1994, at a meeting held by *South Asian Forum for Human Rights (SAFHR, no recent information)*. First forum held, 1996. **Aims** Enable *non-government* voices to come together at regional level. **Structure** Regional Steering Committee; Country Group; Secretariat. **Languages** English. **Staff** 1.00 FTE, paid. **Events** *Meeting* Kathmandu (Nepal) 2014, *Meeting* Maldives 2011, *Meeting* Delhi (India) 2010, *Meeting* Colombo (Sri Lanka) 2008, *Meeting* Kathmandu (Nepal) 2007.
Members Full in 7 countries:
Afghanistan, Bangladesh, India, Maldives, Nepal, Pakistan, Sri Lanka.
IGO Relations *South Asian Association for Regional Cooperation (SAARC, #19721)*. **NGO Relations** *Asia Democracy Network (ADN, #01265)*. [2016.07.22/XJ9568/**E**]

♦ Peoples Trust for Endangered Species (internationally oriented national body)
♦ People of the United Religions Initiative / see United Religions Initiative (#20658)
♦ PEP Africa – People Empowering People Africa (internationally oriented national body)
♦ **PE** Parlamento Europeo (#08146)
♦ **PE** Parlamento Europeu (#08146)
♦ **PE** Parlement européen (#08146)
♦ **PE** Payments Europe (#18269)
♦ Pépinières Européenes de Création (internationally oriented national body)
♦ **PEP** Partnership for Economic Policy (#18233)
♦ PEPPOL / see Open Pan European Public Procurement Online (#17761)
♦ PepsiCo Foundation (internationally oriented national body)
♦ Pequena Missão para Surdos (religious order)
♦ PERA – The Innovation Network / see Pera International
♦ Pera International (internationally oriented national body)
♦ PERC / see Pacific Environment
♦ **PERC** Pan-European Regional Council (#18180)
♦ Perdana Global Peace Organization (internationally oriented national body)

♦ Peregrinatio ad Petri Sedem (PAPS) 18309

Main Office Piazza Pio XII 4, 00120 Vatican City, Vatican. T. +39669884896. Fax +39669885617. E-mail: accoglienza@peregrinatio.va.
URL: http://www.vatican.va/

History 1934, by Pope Pius IX. Designated as a Canonical Body by Pope Paul VI, 1974. Reorganized, 1975. 16 Jan 1997, new Statutes granted by Pope John Paul II. Comes within *Administrative Hierarchy of the Roman Catholic Church (#00117)*. **Aims** Assist *pilgrims* travelling to St Peter's Basilica during Holy Years; coordinate and assist pilgrims travelling to sanctuaries worldwide as part of events led by the Pope; facilitate the participation of low income persons in pilgrimages. **Structure** Board of Directors; Pastoral Council; Central Committee. [2008/XM4656/**F**]

♦ Pères Blancs – Société des Missionnaires d'Afrique (religious order)
♦ Pères Center for Peace, The (internationally oriented national body)
♦ Pères et Frères Religieux de Saint Vincent-de-Paul (religious order)
♦ Pères de Garaison – Missionnaires de l'Immaculée-Conception de Lourdes (religious order)
♦ Pères Maristes – Société de Marie (religious order)
♦ Pères de la Merci – Ordre de Notre-Dame de la Merci (religious order)
♦ Pères de Saint-Edme (religious order)
♦ Pères de Saint Paul Premier Ermite (religious order)
♦ Pères de Timon-David – Congrégation du Sacré-Coeur de Jésus (religious order)
♦ Perfect World Foundation (internationally oriented national body)
♦ Performance Management Association (unconfirmed)

♦ **Performance Review Institute (PRI)** **18310**
Main Office 161 Thorn Hill Rd, Warrendale PA 15086-7527, USA. T. +17247721616. Fax +17247721699. E-mail: priamericas@p-r-i.org – pri@p-r-i.org.
EMEA Office 1 York Street, London, W1U 6PA, UK. E-mail: priemea@p-r-i.org.
Asia Office 21F JP Tower Nagoya, 1-1-1 Meieki Nakamura-ku, Nagoya AICHI, 450-6321 Japan. E-mail: priasia@p-r-i.org.
URL: http://www.p-r-i.org/
History 1990. Founded by *SAE International*, to administer Nadcap. **Aims** Act as a global provider of customer-focused solutions designed to improve process and product quality by adding value, reducing total cost and promoting collaboration among stakeholders in industries where safety and quality are shared goals. **Structure** Board of Directors. Headquarters in Warrendale PA (USA). Offices (3): Europe – London (UK); Asia – Beijing (China) and Aichi (Japan). **Activities** Certification/accreditation; knowledge management/information dissemination; training/education. **Events** *Nadcap Meeting* London (UK) 2022, *Nadcap Meeting* Paris (France) 2019, *Nadcap Meeting* London (UK) 2018, *Nadcap Meeting* Madrid (Spain) 2016, *Nadcap Meeting* Montréal, QC (Canada) 2015. [2022/XJ9063/j/**C**]

♦ **Performance Studies International (PSI)** **18311**
Sec address not obtained. E-mail: sendto.psi@gmail.com.
URL: http://www.psi-web.org/
History 1997. **Aims** Promote communication and exchange among scholars and practitioners working in the field of performance. **Structure** Board of Directors. **Activities** Awards/prizes/competitions; events/meetings. **Events** *Annual Conference* South Africa 2023, *Annual Conference* 2022, *Annual Conference* Rijeka (Croatia) 2021, *Annual Conference* Rijeka (Croatia) 2020, *Annual Conference* Daegu (Korea Rep) 2018. **Publications** *PSI Newsletter* (2 a year).
Members Individuals and organizations in 28 countries and territories:
Australia, Austria, Brazil, Bulgaria, Canada, France, Germany, India, Japan, Korea Rep, Malta, Mexico, Netherlands, New Zealand, Nigeria, Norway, Poland, Portugal, Russia, Singapore, Slovenia, Sudan, Sweden, Switzerland, Taiwan, Türkiye, UK, USA. [2022/XN8341/**C**]

♦ Performance Studies Network (internationally oriented national body)
♦ Performing Arts Forum (internationally oriented national body)

♦ **Performing and Fine Artists for World Peace (PFAWP)** **18312**
Exec Dir PO Box 1050, Volcano HI 96785, USA. T. +18089858725. Fax +18089858725. E-mail: artpeace@hawaiiantel.net.
URL: http://www.artistsandpeace.org/
History 1986. **Aims** Support, through the arts, protection of the environment, preservation of human rights and cultural and religious rights of indigenous peoples; promote tolerance and understanding through cultural exchanges; address issues directly impacting communities at the grassroots level, such as substance abuse and addiction, crime and violence and racism. **Structure** Main programme: *Earth-Friendly Schools Hawaii-International (see: #18312)*. **Languages** English. **Staff** 2.00 FTE, voluntary. **Finance** Sources: donations. Donations from individuals, businesses, organizations and government agencies. **Activities** Events/meetings; networking/liaising. **Publications** *Message from the Misty Forest* (1st ed 2010) by HOWARD SHAPIRO and Marsha Hee. **IGO Relations** Recognized in 1987 as a Peace Messenger of *United Nations (UN, #20515)*. [2021.05.22/XF4588/**F**]

♦ Perhaps Kids Meeting Kids can make a Difference (internationally oriented national body)
♦ Periferia (internationally oriented national body)
♦ Péril-Europe / see Association for the Expansion of International Roles of the Languages of Continental Europe (#02589)
♦ **PERIL-Europe** Association pour l'expansion du rôle international des langues d'Europe continentale (#02589)
♦ Periodistas Frente a la Corrupción (internationally oriented national body)

♦ **Periodontology, Oral Surgery, Esthetic and Implant Dentistry Organization (POSEIDO)** **18313**
Contact address not obtained. E-mail: poseidorg@icloud.com.
URL: http://www.poseid.org/
History 2006. **Aims** Act as a forum for promotion of education and research in the fields of periodontal sciences, oral and cranio-maxillofacial surgery and medicine, esthetic and restorative dentistry, with a particular interest for implant dentistry, and related research. **Structure** Board of Directors, comprising Administrative and Associate Directors; Programme Directors; Study Groups. **Staff** Voluntary. **Publications** *POSEIDO* – electronic scientific journal. [2017.01.08/XJ6607/**F**]

♦ **Peripheral Nerve Society (PNS)** **18314**
Exec Dir 1935 County Road B2 W, Ste 165, Roseville MN 55113, USA. T. +19525456284. E-mail: info@pnsociety.com.
URL: http://www.pnsociety.com/
History 1994. Founded on merger of Peripheral Nerve Study Group, founded in 1974, Carville, St Gabriel LA (USA), and Peripheral Neuropathy Association, founded in 1983. Bylaws adopted, Jan 2021. **Aims** Develop and provide the best treatments for people who have peripheral nerve diseases. **Structure** Board; General Advisory Board; Standing Committee: *International Inflammatory Neuropathy Consortium (INC, see: #18314)*, set up Apr 2007. **Events** *Annual Meeting* Copenhagen (Denmark) 2023, *Annual Meeting* Miami, FL (USA) 2022, *Annual Meeting* Copenhagen (Denmark) 2021, *Annual Meeting* Minneapolis, MN (USA) 2020, *Annual Meeting* Genoa (Italy) 2019. **Publications** *Journal of the Peripheral Nervous System* – official journal. **Members** Membership countries not specified. [2022/XJ4206/**C**]

♦ Peritoneal Dialysis / see EuroPD (#05771)

♦ **Peritoneal Surface Oncology Group International (PSOGI)** **18315**
Contact 106 Irving St NW, Ste 3900, Washington DC 20010, USA. T. +12028773908. Fax +12028777287.
URL: http://www.psogi.com/
History 1998. Founded as a cooperative interaction of clinicians and scientists. **Aims** Promote research, education and innovations in patient care regarding peritoneal *metastases* worldwide; implement the transfer of basic science research and clinical research to patient care. **Structure** Executive Committee (meets twice a year). **Languages** English. **Staff** 1.00 FTE, paid. **Activities** Events/meetings. **Events** *Biennial International Conference on Peritoneal Surface Malignancies* Beijing (China) 2021, *Biennial International Conference on Peritoneal Surface Malignancies* Beijing (China) 2020, *Biennial International Workshop on Peritoneal Surface Malignancies* Paris (France) 2018, *Biennial International Workshop on Peritoneal Surface Malignancies* Washington, DC (USA) 2016, *Biennial International Workshop on Peritoneal Surface Malignancies* Amsterdam (Netherlands) 2014. **Publications** Manuscripts (about 50 a year), published in peer-reviewed literature by members of the Working Group. **Members** Clinicians and scientists interested in peritoneal carcinomatosis from gastrointestinal cancer and from gynecologic malignancy, and in peritoneal mesothelioma. Individuals in North America, Central America, South America, Europe and Asia. Membership countries not specified. **IGO Relations** None. **NGO Relations** National organizations. [2020/XM2988/**E**]

♦ **Peri-Urban Regions Platform Europe (PURPLE)** **18316**
SG Bd du Roi Albert II 15, 1210 Brussels, Belgium. T. +442085418087. E-mail: secretarygeneral@purple-eu.org – info@purple-eu.org.
URL: http://www.purple-eu.org/
History 21 Oct 2004, The Hague (Netherlands). Founded during the City and Countryside Conference. Registration: EU Transparency Register, No/ID: 11397891124-13, Start date: 11 Feb 2009; No/ID: 0639.974.227, Start date: 6 Oct 2015, Belgium. **Aims** Work for recognition of peri-urban issues in EU policy and for sustainable spatial, environmental and agricultural development in peri-urban regions. **Structure** General Assembly; Board; Working Group; Lobby Group. **Languages** English. **Staff** 0.25 FTE, paid. **Finance** Members' contributions. **Events** *Conference* Valence (France) 2014, *Conference* Poznań (Poland) 2013, *Conference* Brno (Czech Rep) 2012, *Conference* Dublin (Ireland) 2011, *General Assembly* Dublin (Ireland) 2011.
Members Regions (11) in 8 countries:
Belgium, Czechia, France, Germany, Ireland, Netherlands, Poland, UK.
NGO Relations Cooperates with: *Council of European Municipalities and Regions (CEMR, #04891)*; *Network of European Metropolitan Regions and Areas (METREX, #17023)*; *Rurality – Environment – Development (RED, #19003)*. [2020/XM0643/**F**]

♦ Perkins International (internationally oriented national body)
♦ Perl Foundation (internationally oriented national body)

♦ **Perlite Institute** **18317**
Main Office 2207 Forest Hills Drive, Harrisburg PA 17110, USA. T. +17172389723. Fax +17172389985. E-mail: info@perlite.org – office@perlite.org.
URL: http://www.perlite.org/
History 1949. Sub-title: *International Association of Perlite Producers*. **Aims** Conduct and sponsor research on physical properties of *Horticultural perlite*, perlite masonry, insulation, perlite-gypsum and perlite-portland *cement* mixes, floor fills and curtain walls, designs and specifications for perlite plaster *construction* and concrete roof decks, and fire resistance of perlite plaster and concrete construction; develop standards for quality and the application of perlite as aggregate. **Finance** Members' dues. Budget (annual): US$ 300,000 – 500,000. **Activities** Events/meetings; awards/prizes/competitions; research/documention; research and development. **Events** *Annual Meeting* Portland, OR (USA) 2016, *Annual Meeting* Barcelona (Spain) 2015, *Annual Meeting* Park City, UT (USA) 2014, *Annual Meeting* Sydney, NSW (Australia) 2013, *Annual Meeting* New Orleans, LA (USA) 2012. **Publications** *Perlite Today* (4 a year).
Members Firms, processors and applicators of perlite (mainly in USA) in 21 countries:
Argentina, Australia, Canada, Denmark, Germany, Greece, Hungary, India, Indonesia, Italy, Japan, Korea Rep, Malaysia, Netherlands, New Zealand, Norway, Philippines, Saudi Arabia, South Africa, Spain, USA. [2018/XF1334/j/**F**]

♦ **PERL** Partnership for Education and Research about Responsible Living (#18234)
♦ Permaculture Research Institute (internationally oriented national body)

♦ **Permafrost Young Researcher Network (PYRN)** **18318**
Pres Vrije Universiteit Amsterdam, Fac of Science, Earth and Climate, De Boelelaan 1081, W1N bldg, 1081 HV Amsterdam, Netherlands.
URL: http://www.pyrn.org/
History Nov 2005. Set up under the patronage of *International Permafrost Association (IPA, #14558)*. **Aims** Foster innovative collaboration; recruit, retain and promote future generations of permafrost researchers. **Structure** Council of 10 members; Executive Committee of 12 members; National Representatives (7). Hosted by: *World Association of Young Scientists (WAYS, #21207)*. **Languages** English. **Staff** Voluntary. **Activities** Research and development. Active in: Arctic; Antarctic; Alpine and mountain regions. **Publications** *PYRN Newsletter*.
Members National Committees in 20 countries:
Austria, Bulgaria, Canada, China, Czechia, Denmark, Germany, Italy, Japan, Nepal, Netherlands, New Zealand, Norway, Poland, Russia, Spain, Switzerland, UK, USA, Venezuela.
Individuals in 72 countries and territories:
Afghanistan, Algeria, Argentina, Australia, Austria, Bahrain, Bangladesh, Barbados, Belarus, Belgium, Bolivia, Brazil, Bulgaria, Canada, Chile, China, Colombia, Cyprus, Czechia, Denmark, Egypt, Eswatini, Finland, France, Germany, Hong Kong, Hungary, Iceland, India, Iran Islamic Rep, Israel, Italy, Jamaica, Japan, Kenya, Korea Rep, Malawi, Malaysia, Marshall Is, Mexico, Mongolia, Morocco, Namibia, Nepal, Netherlands, New Zealand, Nigeria, Norway, Pakistan, Philippines, Poland, Portugal, Romania, Russia, Singapore, Slovenia, South Africa, Spain, Sudan, Sweden, Switzerland, Syrian AR, Taiwan, Tunisia, Türkiye, Turkmenistan, Uganda, Ukraine, USA, Vietnam, Zambia, Zimbabwe.
NGO Relations Cooperates with (1): *Association of Polar Early Career Scientists (APECS, #02864)*. [2020/XJ5838/**F**]

♦ Permanent American Aeronautical Commission (inactive)
♦ Permanent American Aviation Commission (inactive)
♦ Permanenta Nordiska Utskottet för Livsmedelsfrågor / see Committee of Senior Officials of the Nordic Countries, Estonia, Latvia and Lithuania in the Field of Food Issues (#04286)
♦ Permanent Assembly for Human Rights (internationally oriented national body)
♦ Permanent Blind Relief War Fund / see Helen Keller International (#10902)
♦ Permanent Blind Relief War Fund for Soldiers & Sailors of the Allies / see Helen Keller International (#10902)
♦ Permanent Bureau for Arabization / see Arabization Coordination Bureau (#00999)
♦ Permanent Bureau of the International Congress of Genealogical and Heraldic Sciences (#03372)
♦ Permanent Bureau of International Sporting Federations (inactive)
♦ Permanent Central American Commission on the Eradication of the Illicit Production, Trafficking, Consumption and Use of Narcotics and Psychotropic Substances (#04130)
♦ Permanent Comité der Artsen in de EG / see Standing Committee of European Doctors (#19955)
♦ Permanent Comité van de Glasindustriën van de EEG / see Glass Alliance Europe (#10156)
♦ Permanent Comité van de Glasindustriën in Europa / see Glass Alliance Europe (#10156)
♦ Permanent Commission and International Association on Occupational Health / see International Commission on Occupational Health (#12709)
♦ Permanent Commission of the International Congresses of Home Hygiene (inactive)
♦ Permanent Commission of International Congresses of Scientific and Applied Photography (inactive)
♦ Permanent Commission of the International Fisheries Convention of 1946 (inactive)
♦ Permanent Commission of the International Sericultural Congresses / see International Sericultural Commission (#14837)
♦ Permanent Commission for the South Pacific (#04141)

♦ **Permanent Committee on Cadastre in the European Union (PCC)** . . **18319**
Comité permanent du cadastre dans l'Union européenne – Comité Permanente sobre el Catastro en la Unión Europea – Comitato Permanente del Catasto nell'Unione Europea
Contact Dirección General del Catastro, Ministerio de Hacienda y Administraciones Públicas, C/ Alcala 9, Planta Baja, 28071 Madrid, Spain. E-mail: amalia.velasco@catastro.hacienda.gob.es – pcc_secretariat@ancpi.ro.
URL: http://www.eurocadastre.org/
History 14 Oct 2002, Ispra (Italy). Established by the 15 member states of *European Union (EU, #08967)*. **Aims** Constitute a network of information on cadastre to facilitate e exchange of information, expertise and best practices; represent a privileged link between cadastral institutions and organs of the European Union and other entities requiring cadastral information to carry out their activities. **Events** *Conference and Plenary Meeting* Zagreb (Croatia) 2020, *Conference and Plenary Meeting* Bucharest (Romania) 2019, *Conference and Plenary Meeting* Helsinki (Finland) 2019, *Conference and Plenary Meeting* Sofia (Bulgaria) 2018, *Conference and Plenary Meeting* Vienna (Austria) 2018.
Members in 28 countries:
Austria, Belgium, Bulgaria, Croatia, Cyprus, Czechia, Denmark, Estonia, Finland, France, Germany, Greece, Hungary, Ireland, Italy, Latvia, Lithuania, Luxembourg, Malta, Netherlands, Poland, Portugal, Romania, Slovakia, Slovenia, Spain, Sweden, UK.
Observers (1):
EuroGeographics (#05684); Working Party on Land Administration of . [2021/XM2301/**E***]

♦ Permanent Committee on GIS Infrastructure for Asia and the Pacific / see Regional Committee of United Nations Global Geospatial Information Management for Asia and the Pacific (#18766)
♦ Permanent Committee of the International Conferences of Social Work / see International Council on Social Welfare (#13076)
♦ Permanent Committee of International Congresses of Actuaries / see International Actuarial Association (#11586)
♦ Permanent Committee for International Congresses of the Apostolate of the Laity (inactive)
♦ Permanent Committee of the International Congresses of Entomology / see Council for International Congresses of Entomology (#04900)
♦ Permanent Committee of the International Congresses of Human Genetics / see International Federation of Human Genetics Societies (#13451)
♦ Permanent Committee of International Congresses on Medical Assistance by Air (inactive)

♦ Permanent Committee of International Congresses on Neurology (inactive)
♦ Permanent Committee of the International Congresses of Philosophy (inactive)
♦ Permanent Committee of the International Congresses on School Hygiene (inactive)
♦ Permanent Committee for International Medical Congresses (inactive)
♦ Permanent Committee of International Physiological Congresses (inactive)
♦ Permanent Committee for International Veterinary Congresses (inactive)
♦ Permanent Committee of International Zoological Congresses / see International Society of Zoological Sciences (#15552)
♦ Permanent Committee of Jurists on the Unification of the Civil and Commercial Laws of America (inactive)
♦ Permanent Committee of Nurses in Liaison with EEC / see European Federation of Nurses Associations (#07180)
♦ Permanent Committee on Spatial Data Infrastructure for the Americas / see Regional Committee of the UN on Global Geospatial Information Management for the Americas (#18765)
♦ Permanent Committee for Stress Analysis / see European Association for Experimental Mechanics (#06034)
♦ Permanent Conference of Chambers of Commerce and Industry of the EEC / see Association des chambres de commerce et d'industrie européennes (#02423)
♦ Permanent Conference of International Professional Federations (inactive)
♦ Permanent Conference of Mayors of Capitals of Southeastern Europe / see Union of Central and South-Eastern European Capitals (#20372)

♦ Permanent Conference of Mediterranean Audiovisual Operators (COPEAM) 18320

Conférence permanente de l'audiovisuel méditerranéen (COPEAM)

SG Via Alberto Cadlolo 90, 00136 Rome RM, Italy. T. +390633173918. Fax +390636866626. E-mail: sgcopeam@copeam.org.
URL: http://www.copeam.org/

History Jan 1996, Cairo (Egypt). Previously functioned within *UNESCO Mediterranean Programme (inactive)* as a network of *Mediterranean Media Network (no recent information)*. Former names and other names: *Permanent Conference of Mediterranean Audiovisuals* – former; *Permanent Conference of the Televisions of the Mediterranean* – former; *Mediterranean Conference of Television and Audiovisual Operators* – former. **Aims** Promote dialogue and cultural cooperation in the Mediterranean region through involvement of major players of the audiovisual sector. **Structure** General Assembly; Steering Committee; Thematic Commissions; General Secretariat. **Languages** Arabic, English, French, Italian. **Staff** 7.00 FTE, paid. **Finance** Sources: fundraising; grants; members' dues; revenue from activities/projects. **Activities** Awards/prizes/competitions; capacity building; events/meetings; networking/liaising; projects/programmes; training/education. **Events** *Conference* Montpellier (France) 2023, *Conference* Rome (Italy) 2021, *Conference* Rome (Italy) 2020, *General Assembly* Rome (Italy) 2020, *Conference* Split (Croatia) 2019. **Publications** *COPEAM Newsletter*. Annual conference acts; project outputs.

Members Founding; Active; Associate; Benefactors. Members in 24 countries:
Albania, Algeria, Bulgaria, Croatia, Egypt, France, Greece, Italy, Jordan, Kosovo, Lebanon, Libya, Malta, Montenegro, Morocco, Palestine, Portugal, Romania, Serbia, Slovenia, Spain, Switzerland, Tunisia, Türkiye.

NGO Relations Member of (1): *International Council for Film, Television and Audiovisual Communication (IFTC, #13022)*. [2023.02.13/XK1909/y/**E**]

♦ Permanent Conference of Mediterranean Audiovisuals / see Permanent Conference of Mediterranean Audiovisual Operators (#18320)
♦ Permanent Conference for the Organization of the Universal Community of Youth for Peace (inactive)
♦ Permanent Conference of Political Parties of Latin America and the Caribbean (#04657)
♦ Permanent Conference of the Televisions of the Mediterranean / see Permanent Conference of Mediterranean Audiovisual Operators (#18320)
♦ Permanent Congress of Trade Union Unity of Latin American Workers (inactive)
♦ Permanent Consultative Committee of the Maghreb (inactive)
♦ Permanent Council of European Translators (inactive)
♦ Permanent Council of International Convention of Stresa for the Use of Appellations d'Origine and Denominations of Cheeses (no recent information)
♦ Permanent Council for International Cooperation between Composers (inactive)

♦ Permanent Court of Arbitration (PCA) 18321

Cour permanente d'arbitrage (CPA)

Head Office Peace Palace, Carnegieplein 2, 2517 KJ The Hague, Netherlands. T. +31703024165. Fax +31703024167. E-mail: bureau@pca-cpa.org.
URL: http://pca-cpa.org/

History 29 Jul 1899, The Hague (Netherlands). Established by articles 20-29 of the *Convention for the Pacific Settlements of International Conflicts, 1899 (1899)*. Maintained by Articles 41-50 of the revised *Convention for the Pacific Settlement of International Disputes, 1907 (1907)*. Headquarters at *Peace Palace*, The Hague, since 1913. **Aims** Facilitate and provide services for the resolution of *disputes* involving combinations of states, state entities, international organizations and private parties. **Structure** Administrative Council; Members of the Court; International Bureau, headed by Secretary-General. Regional offices (4): Buenos Aires, Mauritius; Singapore; Vienna. **Languages** English, French. **Staff** 50.00 FTE, paid. **Finance** Budget partially financed by Contracting Powers' contributions, according to proportions established for the Universal Postal Union.

Activities Guidance/assistance/consulting; conflict resolution. Provides registry services and administrative support to tribunals and commissions worldwide; serves as the official channel of communication, ensuring safe custody of documents in international arbitration and other dispute-resolution proceedings; administers cases under its own rules of procedure, UNCITRAL Arbitration Rules, and other rules. Cases have involved disputes between various combinations of States, international organizations, and private parties relating to various subject matters, including territorial and maritime boundaries, human rights and treaty interpretation, as well as commercial and investment disputes, including disputes arising under bilateral and multilateral investment treaties. Secretary-General is entrusted by *UNCITRAL Arbitration Rules (1976)* to designate appointing authorities and regularly requested to serve directly as appointing authority and appoint arbitrators or decide challenges to arbitrators in arbitrations under UNCITRAL arbitration rules.

Management of treaties and agreements:
- *ACP-EU Partnership Agreement (Cotonou agreement, 2000)*;
- *ASEAN Comprehensive Investment Agreement*;
- *Convention on the Conservation of Migratory Species of Wild Animals (Bonn Convention, 1979)*;
- Convention for the Establishment of Convention establishing *Convention on International Trade in Endangered Species of Wild Fauna and Flora (CITES, 1973)*;
- *Convention on the Settlement of Investment Disputes between States and Nationals of other States (1965)*;
- *Energy Charter Treaty (ECT, 1994)*;
- *European Organisation for the Exploitation of Meteorological Satellites (EUMETSAT, #08096)*;
- *Protocol to the Antarctic Treaty on Environmental Protection (1991)*;
- agreements between and with European Community and United Nations.

Events *Conference on international commercial and investment arbitration* The Hague (Netherlands) 2009, *International oil and gas conference* The Hague (Netherlands) 2009, *Conference on remedies in commercial, investment and energy arbitrations* Houston, TX (USA) 2008, *International law seminar* 2004, *International conference on environment, security and sustainable development* The Hague (Netherlands) 2004. **Publications** *PCA Award Series*; *Peace Palace Paper Series*. Annual Report. Reports; documents; summaries of awards, settlement agreements and reports; arbitrations.

Members Governments of 117 countries:
Albania, Argentina, Australia, Austria, Bahrain, Bangladesh, Belarus, Belgium, Belize, Benin, Bolivia, Brazil, Bulgaria, Burkina Faso, Cambodia, Cameroon, Canada, Chile, China, Colombia, Congo DR, Costa Rica, Croatia, Cuba, Cyprus, Czechia, Denmark, Dominican Rep, Ecuador, Egypt, El Salvador, Eritrea, Estonia, Eswatini, Ethiopia, Fiji, Finland, France, Georgia, Germany, Greece, Guatemala, Guyana, Haiti, Honduras, Hungary, Iceland, India, Iran Islamic Rep, Iraq, Ireland, Israel, Italy, Japan, Jordan, Kenya, Korea Rep, Kuwait, Kyrgyzstan, Laos, Latvia, Lebanon, Libya, Liechtenstein, Lithuania, Luxembourg, Madagascar, Malaysia, Malta, Mauritius, Mexico, Montenegro, Morocco, Netherlands, New Zealand, Nicaragua, Nigeria, North Macedonia, Norway, Pakistan, Panama, Paraguay, Peru, Philippines, Poland, Portugal, Qatar, Romania, Russia, Rwanda, Sao Tomé-Principe, Saudi Arabia, Senegal, Serbia, Singapore, Slovakia, Slovenia, South Africa, Spain, Sri Lanka, Sudan, Suriname, Sweden, Switzerland, Thailand, Togo, Türkiye, Uganda, UK, Ukraine, United Arab Emirates, Uruguay, USA, Venezuela, Vietnam, Zambia, Zimbabwe.

IGO Relations Accredited by: Conference of the Parties of *Secretariat of the United Nations Convention to Combat Desertification (Secretariat of the UNCCD, #19208)*; *United Nations Framework Convention on Climate Change – Secretariat (UNFCCC, #20564)*. Observer Status with: *Cartagena Protocol on Biosafety (2000)*; *United Nations (UN, #20515)*. **NGO Relations** Member of: *International Federation of Commercial Arbitration Institutions (IFCAI)*. [2022/XF3107/**F***]

♦ Permanent Court of International Justice (inactive)
♦ Permanente Nordiske Utvalg for Naeringsmiddelspørsmål / see Committee of Senior Officials of the Nordic Countries, Estonia, Latvia and Lithuania in the Field of Food Issues (#04286)
♦ Permanentes Internationales Komitee für das Studium der Lebensversicherungsmedizin (inactive)
♦ Permanent European Conference of Cooperatives, Mutual Societies, Associations and Foundations / see Social Economy Europe (#19335)
♦ Permanent European Conference on Probation and Aftercare / see Confederation of European Probation (#04530)
♦ Permanent Forum of the European Civil Society / see Permanent Forum of European Civil Society (#18322)

♦ Permanent Forum of European Civil Society 18322

Forum permanent de la société civile européenne – Ständiges Forum der Zivilgesellschaft

Contact address not obtained.

History Sep 1995, from an idea from Virgilio Dastoli, Secretary-General of the International *European Movement International (EMI, #07825)*, which was taken up in a call launched to NGOs and trade union organizations by the conference of the presidents of the national councils of the EM, 21 Sep 1995, Bonn (Germany). to coordinate activities in relation to the EU intergovernmental conference, 1996; subsequent agreement made this coordination permanent. Also referred to as *Permanent Forum of the European Civil Society – Forum permanent de la société civile européenne*. An organization of the type *European Economic Interest Grouping (EEIG, #06960)*. **Aims** Produce and communicate information; be a place of dialogue and reflection. Promote actions of all kinds in order to realize: an active European citizenship; a new form of governance that encourages better synergies between European institutions and civil society; a representative and participatory democracy that respects gender equality and the principles of subsidiarity and proportionality. Help coordinate, at the European level, local actions of organized civil society; reinforce the presence of civil society in Central and Eastern European countries and in the Mediterranean area. **Languages** English, French. **Staff** Voluntary. **Finance** Self-financing and donations. **Activities** Events/meetings; politics/policy/regulatory. Revision of: *Treaty on European Union (Maastricht Treaty, 1992)*. **Events** *Changeons l'Europe! Pour une Europe démocratique et solidaire* Göttingen (Germany) 1998, *Etats-Généraux de la société civile* Göttingen (Germany) 1998, *Alternative European summit* Amsterdam (Netherlands) 1997, *Europe for everybody?* Brussels (Belgium) 1996. **Publications** *The Forum's Tribune* – newsletter. Articles; press releases.

Members National, European and international organizations, including the following 6 listed in this Yearbook: *Comité européen de liaison sur les services d'intérêt général (no recent information)*; *European Citizen Action Service (ECAS, #06555)*; European Movement; *International Movement ATD Fourth World (#14193)*; *Jesuit European Social Centre (JESC, #16103)*; *Union of European Federalists, The (UEF, #20385)*.

NGO Relations Member of: *European Civic Forum (ECF, #06563)*; *Spring Alliance (inactive)*. Supports: *European Citizens' Initiative Campaign (ECI Campaign, #06558)*. [2013/XF3952/y/**F**]

♦ Permanent Forum Extreme Poverty in the World (see: #14193)
♦ Permanent Forum on Indigenous Issues / see United Nations Permanent Forum on Indigenous Issues (#20609)
♦ Permanent Forum for Leisure and recreation (#09886)
♦ Permanent Forum of the World's Indigenous People / see United Nations Permanent Forum on Indigenous Issues (#20609)
♦ Permanent Founding Committee of the Seerat Congress (inactive)
♦ Permanent Inter-American Anti-Locust Committee (inactive)
♦ Permanent Inter-American Committee on Social Security (see: #11419)

♦ Permanent Interdicasterial Commission for the Church in Eastern Europe 18323

Commission interdicastérielle permanente pour l'Eglise en Europe de l'Est – Commissione Interdicasteriale Permanente per la Chiesa in Europa Orientale

Pres Secretariat for Relations with States, 00120 Vatican City, Vatican.

History 15 Jan 1993, Rome (Italy). Founded by John-Paul II. Replaces the *Commission pontificale 'Pro Russia' – Pontificia Commissione per la Russia*, set up, 1925, by Pius XI. **Aims** Assist local *Catholic* communities to consolidate their re-establishment after decades of persecution; attend to relations of the Catholic Church with the Orthodox Church and other Eastern Churches, and promote and coordinate activities of institutions who over the long-term have assisted Catholic communities in the region. **Structure** Commission comprises: Cardinal Secretary of State (President); a Bishop as Secretary; Secretary and Under-Secretary of the Section for Relations with States; Secretaries of: *Congregation for the Clergy (#04667)*, *Congregation for Institutes of Consecrated Life and Societies of Apostolic Life (CICSAL, #04671)*, *Congregation for the Oriental Churches (CO, #04672)*. **Activities** Responsible not only for the territories of the former Soviet Union but also for other nations in Europe affected by historical circumstances resulting from atheistic communism. [2015/XE1914/**E**]

♦ Permanent International Altaistic Conference (PIAC) 18324

SG Dept of Central Eurasian Studies, Goodbody Hall 157, 1011 East Third St, Indiana University, Bloomington IN 47405-7005, USA. T. +18128552233. Fax +18128557500.
URL: http://www.indiana.edu/~jahist/

History 1957, Munich (Germany FR), at 24th International Congress of Orientalists, currently *International Congress of Asian and North African Studies (ICANAS, #12891)*. **Events** *Annual meeting / Meeting* Berlin (Germany) 2006, *Annual meeting / Meeting* Moscow (Russia) 2005, *Annual meeting / Meeting* Cambridge (UK) 2004, *Meeting* Ankara (Turkey) 2003, *Annual meeting* Istanbul (Turkey) 2003. **Publications** *PIAC Newsletter*. Proceedings.

Members Full in 34 countries and territories:
Austria, Azerbaijan, Belgium, China, Cyprus, Czechia, Denmark, Finland, France, Germany, Hong Kong, Hungary, India, Israel, Italy, Japan, Kazakhstan, Korea Rep, Kyrgyzstan, Mongolia, Netherlands, Norway, Poland, Romania, Russia, Slovakia, Sweden, Switzerland, Taiwan, Türkiye, Turkmenistan, UK, USA, Uzbekistan. [2010/XN3877/c/**F**]

♦ Permanent International Association of Navigation Congresses / see PIANC (#18371)
♦ Permanent International Association of Road Congresses / see World Road Association (#21754)
♦ Permanent International Bureau of Analytical Chemistry of Human and Animal Food (inactive)
♦ Permanent International Bureau for the Perfecting of Timekeeping in Sport (inactive)
♦ Permanent International Bureau of Secretaries of Communes (inactive)
♦ Permanent International Commission on Acetylene and Autogenous Welding / see European Industrial Gases Association (#07525)
♦ Permanent International Commission of Agricultural Associations (inactive)
♦ Permanent International Commission on Industrial Medicine / see International Commission on Occupational Health (#12709)
♦ Permanent International Commission for the Proof of Small Arms (#04227)
♦ Permanent International Commission of Studies on Sanitary Equipment (inactive)
♦ Permanent International Commission for the Study of Problems Relating to Children and the Cinema (inactive)
♦ Permanent International Commission on Viticulture (inactive)
♦ Permanent International Committee on Acetylene, Oxy-Acetylene Welding and Allied Industries / see European Industrial Gases Association (#07525)
♦ Permanent International Committee of Architects (inactive)
♦ Permanent International Committee of Carbon as a Motor Fuel (inactive)
♦ Permanent International Committee for Genetic Congresses / see International Genetics Federation (#13711)

- Permanent International Committee of Linguists (#04182)
- Permanent International Committee of Mothers (inactive)
- Permanent International Committee for Mycenaean Studies (#04181)
- Permanent International Committee for Psychical Research Congresses (inactive)

♦ Permanent International Committee for Research on the Preservation of Materials in the Marine Environment 18325

Comité international permanent pour la recherche sur la préservation des matériaux en milieu marin (COIPM)

Chairperson MAPIEM, Bât X Campus La Garde, BP 20 132, 83957 La Garde CEDEX, France.
URL: http://www.icmcf.org/

Aims Undertake cooperative research in various marine environments with different types of experts and international researchers of all disciplines. **Structure** Plenary Session (annual); Officers: Chairman and 3 Vice-Chairmen; Secretariat. **Languages** English, French. **Finance** Members' dues. **Activities** Scientific activities divided between Working Groups (currently 8): Corrosion in the marine environment; Methods of testing antifouling paints; Concrete; Surface conditions; Wood in marine environment; Pollution; Offshore; Biology. Organizes International Congresses (every 3-4 years). **Events** *International Congress on Marine Corrosion and Fouling* Toulon (France) 2016, *International Congress on Marine Corrosion and Fouling ICMCF* Singapore (Singapore) 2014, *International Congress on Marine Corrosion and Fouling* Singapore (Singapore) 2014, *International Congress on Marine Corrosion and Fouling / International Congress on Marine Corrosion and Fouling ICMCF* Seattle, WA (USA) 2012, *International Congress on Marine Corrosion and Fouling* Newcastle upon Tyne (UK) 2010.
Members Laboratories and research centres; individuals. Members in 12 countries:
Argentina, Denmark, France, Germany, Greece, Italy, Japan, Netherlands, Spain, Syrian AR, UK, USA. [2015/XE6506/**E**]

- Permanent International Committee of SIEEC / see Societas Internationalis Entomofaunistica Europae Centralis (#19444)
- Permanent International Committee for the Study of Industrial Accidents (inactive)
- Permanent International Committee for the study of Life Assurance Medicine / see International Committee for Insurance Medicine (#12780)
- Permanent and International Committee of Underground and Spatial Town Planning and Construction (inactive)
- Permanent International Conference of Private Organizations for the Protection of Migrants (inactive)
- Permanent International Council for the Exploration of the Sea / see International Council for the Exploration of the Sea (#13021)
- Permanent International Ecumenical Consultation on Religion / see Permanent International Ecumenical Consultation of Religious (#18326)

♦ Permanent International Ecumenical Consultation of Religious (PIECR) 18326

Conferenza ecumenica internazionale permanente per i religiosi

Sec Via del Velabro 19, 00186 Rome RM, Italy. T. +39669923361. Fax +39669797536.

History Founded 1980, by *International Union of Superiors General (#15820)*; *Union of Superiors General (#20484)*; and Advisory Council on the Relations of Bishops and Religious Communities in the Church of England. Activities currently suspended, 2009. Former names and other names: *Permanent International Ecumenical Consultation on Religion* – former. **Aims** Promote ecumenical dialogue between members of the consecrated life in the Roman Catholic, Anglican, Orthodox and Protestant churches. **Events** *Annual Meeting* Bose (Italy) 2011, *Annual meeting* Nafpaktos (Greece) 2008, *Annual meeting* Ostuni (Italy) 2007, *Annual meeting* Freeland (UK) 2006, *Annual Meeting* Bose (Italy) 2005. **Members** are appointed by UISG, USG, World Federation of Diaconal Associations and Diaconal Communities, Conference of Anglican Religious Orders in the Americas (CAROA) and Conference of the Leaders of Anglican Religious Communities (CLARC). Membership countries not specified. [2014.11.10/XM1391/**F**]

- Permanent International Meat Office / see International Meat Secretariat (#14125)
- Permanent Interstate Committee for Drought Control in the Sahel (#04195)
- Permanent Joint Commission of Uruguay, Paraguay and Bolivia (inactive)

♦ Permanent Joint Technical Commission for Nile Waters (PJTC) 18327

Commission technique permanente commune pour les eaux du Nil

Chairman Nile Water Sector, 13 Murad St, Giza, Egypt. Fax +2025723147 – +2025449470.
Khartoum Office address not obtained. E-mail: info@pjtcnile.com.

History 1960, Egypt. **IGO Relations** *WMO Hydrology and Water Resources Programme (HWRP, #20977)*. Working arrangement with: *World Meteorological Organization (WMO, #21649)*. [2012/XE8771/**E***]

- Permanent Liaison Committee of EU Speech and Language Therapists and Logopedists / see European Speech and Language Therapy Association (#08812)
- Permanent Liaison Committee of Organizations, Trade Unions, Associations and Unions of Journalists of European Countries (inactive)
- Permanent Mechanism for Consultation and Political Coordination (inactive)
- Permanent Nordic Committee on Food and Nutrition Policy / see Committee of Senior Officials of the Nordic Countries, Estonia, Latvia and Lithuania in the Field of Food Issues (#04286)
- Permanent Notarial International Exchange Office (see: #15795)
- Permanent Peace Movement (internationally oriented national body)

♦ Permanent Peoples' Tribunal (PPT) 18328

Tribunal Permanent des Peuples (TPP) – Tribunal Permanente de los Pueblos (TPP) – Tribunale Permanente dei Popoli (TPP)

Gen Sec Via della Dogana Vecchia 5, 00186 Rome RM, Italy. T. +3966879953. Fax +3966877774. E-mail: ppt@permanentpeoplestribunal.org.
Pres address not obtained.
URL: http://www.permanentpeoplestribunal.org/

History 24 Jun 1979, Bologna (Italy). Founded as a continuation of *Russell Tribunal II on Latin America* 1973-1976, following death of Lelio Basso and at his wish, to spread principles and research of *Fondazione Lelio e Lisli Basso – ISSOCO*, with the former *International League for the Rights and Liberation of Peoples (inactive)*. The 2nd Russell Tribunal (on Latin America) met Apr 1974, Rome (Italy); Jan 1975, Brussels (Belgium); Jan 1976, Rome. **Aims** Give recognition, visibility, and a voice to peoples suffering violations of their fundamental rights; contribute to the evolution of international law. **Structure** Presidency Committee; Secretary General. **Languages** English, French, Italian, Spanish. **Staff** 1.00 FTE, paid. **Events** *Session in Defense of the Cerrado Territories* Rome (Italy) 2021, *Session on Alleged Violations of International Law and International Humanitarian Law by the Turkish Republic and its Officials against the Kurdish People and their Organizations* Paris (France) 2018, *Session on Human Rights, Fracking and Climate Change* Rome (Italy) 2018, *Session on State Crimes Allegedly Committed in Myanmar against the Rohingyas, Kachins and Other Groups* Kuala Lumpur (Malaysia) 2017, *Opening Session on Trasnational Corporations in Southern Africa* Manzini (Swaziland) 2016.
Members Tribunal members (75) in 37 countries and territories:
Algeria, Argentina, Australia, Austria, Bangladesh, Belgium, Brazil, Cambodia, Chile, Colombia, Denmark, Ecuador, Egypt, France, Germany, Haiti, India, Ireland, Israel, Italy, Mexico, Netherlands, Nicaragua, Norway, Palestine, Peru, Portugal, Senegal, South Africa, Spain, Sweden, Switzerland, Thailand, Tunisia, UK, Uruguay, USA.
NGO Relations Links with civil society organizations, research centres, universities and NGOs. [2022.02.09/XF8212/**F**]

♦ Permanent Program Committee of the Formal Power Series and Algebraic Combinatorics (FPSAC) 18329

Co-Chair Dept of Mathematics – Univ of Washington, Office C-416 Padelford, Box 354350, Seattle WA 98195, USA.
URL: http://www.fpsac.org/

History Also referred to in French as *Séries Formelles et Combinatoire Algébrique*. **Structure** Permanent Program Committee, headed by 2 Co-Chairs. **Events** *International Conference on Formal Power Series and Algebraic Combinatorics* London (UK) 2017, *International Conference on Formal Power Series and Algebraic Combinatorics* Daejeon (Korea Rep) 2015, *International Conference on Formal Power Series and Algebraic Combinatorics / Conference* Chicago, IL (USA) 2014, *International Conference on Formal Power Series and Algebraic Combinatorics / Conference* Paris (France) 2013, *International Conference on Formal Power Series and Algebraic Combinatorics / Conference* Nagoya (Japan) 2012. [2013/XJ6659/c/**E**]

♦ Permanent Secretariat to the Agreement on the Conservation of African-Eurasian Migratory Waterbirds 18330

Exec Sec c/o UNEP/AEWA Secretariat, UN Campus, Platz der Vereinten Nationen 1, 53113 Bonn, Germany. T. +492288152413. Fax +492288152450. E-mail: aewa.secretariat@unep-aewa.org.
Main: http://www.unep-aewa.org/

History Established at 1st Meeting of Parties, Nov 1999, Cape Town (South Africa), following entry into force of *African-Eurasian Migratory /Water Bird/ Agreement (AEWA, 1995)*, an Agreement under the *Convention on the Conservation of Migratory Species of Wild Animals (Bonn Convention, 1979)*, on ratification by 7 Eurasian and 7 African countries. Agreement previously administered by *Interim Secretariat for the African-Eurasian Migratory Waterbird Agreement*, under the responsibility of the Ministry of Agriculture, Nature, Management and Fisheries of the Netherlands, set up, 8 Jan 1996, The Hague (Netherlands). Permanent Secretariat established 17 July 2000, Bonn (Germany). Integrated in *UNEP (#20299)*. **Aims** Based on the fundamental principles of the Agreement, parties shall: take measures to conserve migratory waterbirds, giving special attention to *endangered species* and to those with unfavourable status; protect endangered migratory waterbird species in the Agreement area by strict legal *protection*; ensure sustainability of any use of migratory waterbirds; identify sites and *habitats* and encourage their protection, management, rehabilitation and restoration; develop and maintain programmes to raise awareness and understanding of migratory waterbird conservation issues. **Structure** Meeting of the Parties; Standing Committee; Technical Committee. **Languages** English, French. **Staff** 11.00 FTE, paid. **Finance** Sources: donations. Assessed contributions to the AEWA Trust Fund, as well as voluntary contributions of the parties. **Activities** Events/meetings. **Events** *Meeting of the Standing Committee* Trondheim (Norway) 2013, *Meeting of the Technical Committee* Accra (Ghana) 2012, *Meeting of the parties / Meeting of Parties / Meeting of the Standing Committee* La Rochelle (France) 2012, *Meeting / Meeting of the Standing Committee* Bergen (Norway) 2011, *Meeting / Meeting of the Technical Committee* Naivasha (Kenya) 2011. **Publications** *AEWA Newsletter* (regular) in English, French – electronic. *AEWA Popular Series*; *Technical Series*. *Action Plans*; *Conservation Guidelines*; *International Implementation Priorities*; *Strategic Plan 2019-2027*. Brochures, meeting reports; conservation guidelines.
Members As of 1 Oct 2022, 83 Contracting Parties:
Albania, Algeria, Armenia, Belarus, Belgium, Benin, Botswana, Bulgaria, Burkina Faso, Burundi, Cameroon, Central African Rep, Chad, Congo Brazzaville, Côte d'Ivoire, Croatia, Cyprus, Czechia, Denmark, Djibouti, Egypt, Equatorial Guinea, Estonia, Eswatini, Ethiopia, Finland, France, Gabon, Gambia, Georgia, Germany, Ghana, Guinea, Guinea-Bissau, Hungary, Iceland, Ireland, Israel, Italy, Jordan, Kenya, Latvia, Lebanon, Libya, Lithuania, Luxembourg, Madagascar, Malawi, Mali, Mauritania, Mauritius, Moldova, Monaco, Montenegro, Morocco, Netherlands, Niger, Nigeria, North Macedonia, Norway, Portugal, Romania, Rwanda, Senegal, Serbia, Slovakia, Slovenia, South Africa, Spain, Sudan, Sweden, Switzerland, Syrian AR, Tanzania UR, Togo, Tunisia, Turkmenistan, Uganda, UK, Ukraine, Uzbekistan, Zimbabwe.
Signatory country (1):
Greece.
IGO Relations Observer status with (1): *Baltic Marine Environment Protection Commission – Helsinki Commission (HELCOM, #03126)*. [2023.02.15/XE3603/**E***]

♦ Permanent Secretariat of the Alpine Convention 18331

SG Herzog-Friedrich-Str 15, 6020 Innsbruck, Austria. T. +435125885890. E-mail: info@alpconv.org.
Branch office Viale Druso / Drususallee 1, 39100 Bolzano, Italy. T. +390471055357.
URL: https://www.alpconv.org/

History 2003. Established by a decision taken at the VII Alpine Conference of *Convention for the Protection of the Alps (Alpine convention, 1991)*, Nov 2002, Merano (Italy). **Aims** Support the bodies established by the Alpine Convention, offering professional, logistic and administrative help, and assist the countries in carrying out the actions required by the Convention and its Protocols. **Structure** Permanent Secretariat located in Innsbruck (Austria); Branch Office in Bolzano (Italy). **Languages** English, French, German, Italian, Slovene. **Activities** Awareness raising; knowledge management/information dissemination; management of treaties and agreements; projects/programmes; publishing activities. Manages the following treaties/agreements: *Convention for the Protection of the Alps (Alpine convention, 1991)*. **Publications** https://www.alpconv.org/en/home/news-publications/publications-multimedia/ [2022.10.24/AA2048/**E***]

- Permanent Secretariat of the General Treaty on Central American Economic Integration (#19195)
- Permanent Secretariat for the Multilateral Convention on Cooperation and Mutual Assistance among National Directions of Customs of Latin America, Spain and Portugal (#19194)
- Permanent Secretariat of the Pan American Congress of Physical Education (inactive)
- Permanent Secretariat of the South American Agreement on Narcotic Drugs and Psychotropic Substances (inactive)

♦ Permanent Secretariat of the World Summit of Nobel Peace Laureates 18332

Admin and Exec Office Galleria Piazza Cavalli 7b, 29121 Piacenza PC, Italy. T. +39656566159. E-mail: info@nobelpeacesummit.com.
URL: http://www.nobelpeacesummit.com/

History 2006. **Aims** Strengthen humanitarian and non-violent thinking in support of human values. **Structure** Executive Board; Executive Staff. **Activities** Events/meetings; awards/prizes/competitions; training/education. **Events** *World Summit* Seoul (Korea Rep) 2020, *World Summit* Mérida (Mexico) 2019, *World Summit* Bogota (Colombia) 2017, *World Summit* Barcelona (Spain) 2015, *World Summit* Rome (Italy) 2014. **Publications** *Being Nobel* by Livia Malcangio. **Consultative Status** Consultative status granted from: *ECOSOC (#05331)* (Special). **NGO Relations** Partners include: *International Foundation of Socio-Economic and Political Studies (Gorbachev Foundation)*; *International Peace Bureau (IPB, #14535)*; *International Physicians for the Prevention of Nuclear War (IPPNW, #14578)*; *World Centers of Compassion for Children International (WCCCI)*. [2017/XM4487/c/**E**]

♦ Permanent Service for Mean Sea Level (PSMSL) 18333

Service permanent du niveau moyen des mers

Dir Natl Oceanography Ctr, 6 Brownlow Street, Liverpool, L3 5DA, UK. T. +441517954800. Fax +441517954801. E-mail: ljr@bodc.ac.uk – psmsl@noc.ac.uk.
URL: http://www.psmsl.org/

History Set up 1933, as a permanent service of *Federation of Astronomical and Geophysical Data Analysis Services (FAGS, inactive)*. Works under the aegis of *International Association for the Physical Sciences of the Oceans (IAPSO, #12082)*. Responsible Union: *International Union of Geodesy and Geophysics (IUGG, #15776)*. **Aims** Collect, publish, analyse and interpret sea level data from the global network of tide gauges. **Finance** Support from *Intergovernmental Oceanographic Commission (IOC, #11496)* and from the UK Natural Environment Research Council. **Activities** Events/meetings; knowledge management/information dissemination; guidance/assistance/consulting. **Events** *Sea level determination conference* 2002. **Publications** Books; Annual reports; brochures; manuals; workshop reports. **NGO Relations** Member of: *Global Geodetic Observing System (GGOS, see: #11914)*. [2014.06.01/XF4059/**F**]

- Permanent Services on Fluctuations of Glaciers / see World Glacier Monitoring Service (#21539)
- Permanent South American Railway Congress Association / see Pan American Railway Congress Association (#18124)
- Permanent Southeast Pacific Commission / see Comisión Permanente del Pacifico Sur (#04141)
- Permanent Steering Committee of the Conference on Optical Chemical Sensors and Biosensors / see Europt(r)ode (#09173)
- Permanent Technical Commission for the Government of the Waters of the Danube (inactive)
- Permanent Tripartite Commission Secretariat on East African Cooperation / see East African Community (#05181)

- ♦ Permanent Way Institution (internationally oriented national body)
- ♦ Permanent Working Group of European Junior Hospital Doctors / see European Junior Doctors Association (#07620)

♦ Permits foundation 18334

Stichting Permits

Coordinator PO Box 162, Carelf van Bylandtlaan 16, 2501 AN The Hague, Netherlands. E-mail: contact@permitsfoundation.com.
URL: https://www.permitsfoundation.com/

History 2001. Registration: Handelsregister, No/ID: KVK 27199318, Netherlands; EU Transparency Register, No/ID: 111519328353-48, Start date: 15 Sep 2017. **Aims** Improve work permit regulations to make it easier for partners of expatriate staff to gain employment during an international assignment. **Structure** Board of Directors.
Members Participating countries (35):
Argentina, Australia, Austria, Belgium, Brazil, Bulgaria, Canada, Croatia, Cyprus, Czechia, Denmark, Estonia, Finland, France, Germany, Hong Kong, Hungary, Ireland, Italy, Latvia, Lithuania, Malta, Netherlands, New Zealand, Norway, Peru, Poland, Portugal, Slovakia, Slovenia, Spain, Sweden, Switzerland, UK, USA. [2021/AA1445/f/**F**]

- ♦ **PERN** Population Environment Research Network (#18459)
- ♦ **PEROSH** Partnership for European Research in Occupational Safety and Health (#18237)
- ♦ Persatuan Kajian Pelancongan ASEAN (#01239)
- ♦ Persekutuan Bolasepak Asean (#01187)
- ♦ Persekutuan Pencak Silat Antarabangsa (unconfirmed)
- ♦ **PERSGA** Regional Organization for the Conservation of the Environment of the Red Sea and Gulf of Aden (#18804)
- ♦ PERSILAT – International Pencak Silat Federation (unconfirmed)
- ♦ Personal Connected Health Alliance (internationally oriented national body)
- ♦ Personnel de réserve civil canadien pour les interventions des Nations unies / see Canadian Resource Bank for Democracy and Human Rights

♦ PERSPECTIV – Association of Historic Theatres in Europe (PERSPECTIV) 18335

PERSPECTIV – Association des théâtres historiques d'Europe – PERSPECTIV – Gesellschaft der historischen Theater Europas

Treas Villbacher Str 21, 63599 Biebergemünd, Germany. E-mail: info@perspectiv-online.org.
URL: http://www.perspectiv-online.org/

History Oct 2003. Current statutes adopted Apr 2013. Registration: No/ID: VR 32382, Germany. **Aims** Help to preserve, restore, support and promote historic theatres as part of the *cultural heritage* of Europe and the world. **Structure** General Assembly (every 2 years); Board. **Languages** English, French, German. **Finance** Sources: members' dues. Supported by: *European Commission (EC, #06633)* (Culture Programme). **Activities** Events/meetings. **Events** *By Candlelight Conference* Stockholm (Sweden) 2023, *General Assembly and Congress* Sabbioneta (Italy) 2022, *By Candlelight Conference* Stockholm (Sweden) 2022, *By Candlelight Conference* Stockholm (Sweden) 2021, *By Candlelight Conference* Stockholm (Sweden) 2020. **Publications** *The history of Europe – told by its theatres* – exhibition magazine.
Members Theatres in 16 countries:
Austria, Croatia, Czechia, Denmark, Finland, France, Germany, Italy, Malta, Norway, Poland, Russia, Spain, Sweden, Switzerland, UK.
Individuals in 2 countries:
UK, USA.
NGO Relations Member of (3): *Europa Nostra (#05767)*; *European Heritage Alliance 3.3 (#07477)*; *International Council on Monuments and Sites (ICOMOS, #13049).* [2020/XJ7970/**D**]

- ♦ PERSPECTIV – Association des théâtres historiques d'Europe (#18335)
- ♦ Perspectives Mutualisations et Convergences Europe (internationally oriented national body)
- ♦ PERSPECTIV – Gesellschaft der historischen Theater Europas (#18335)
- ♦ **PERSPECTIV** PERSPECTIV – Association of Historic Theatres in Europe (#18335)
- ♦ **PESA** Philosophy of Education Society of Australasia (#18360)
- ♦ **PES network** European network of Public Employment Services (#07979)
- ♦ **PES** Party of European Socialists (#18249)
- ♦ PESPOS – Paediatric Surgery Postgraduate Seminars (meeting series)
- ♦ Pessoas contra Minas (internationally oriented national body)
- ♦ Pestalozzi Children's Foundation (internationally oriented national body)
- ♦ Pestalozzi Children's Village / see Pestalozzi International Foundation
- ♦ Pestalozzi Children's Village Foundation / see Pestalozzi Children's Foundation
- ♦ Pestalozzi Children's Village Trust / see Pestalozzi International Foundation
- ♦ Pestalozzi International Children's Village and Development Education Centre / see Pestalozzi International Foundation
- ♦ Pestalozzi International Foundation (internationally oriented national body)
- ♦ Pestalozzi International Village Trust / see Pestalozzi International Foundation
- ♦ Pestalozzi Weltstiftung / see Pestalozzi Children's Foundation
- ♦ Pestalozzi World Foundation / see Pestalozzi Children's Foundation

♦ Pesticide Action Network (PAN) 18336

PAN Europe Rue de la Pacification 67, 1000 Brussels, Belgium. T. +3223186255. E-mail: info@pan-europe.info.
URL: http://www.pan-international.org/

History May 1982, Penang (Malaysia). Foundedfollowing a conference on global pesticide trade organized by IOCU ROAP, the Regional Office for Asia and the Pacific of *Consumers International (CI, #04773).* The international umbrella PAN – Regional Centres was incorporated in 1995: PAN UK and Pan Germany facilitate the European Region. Former names and other names: *PAN-International* – former; *Red de Acción en Plaguicidas* – former. **Aims** Persuade national governments and international agencies to develop effective pesticide policies; increase public awareness of pesticide abuse through campaigns on selected *hazardous* pesticides and *unethical* corporate marketing practices; promote alternatives to pesticide-dependent *agriculture.* **Structure** A network of NGOs, institutions and individuals being coordinated regionally: *Pesticide Action Network Africa (PAN Africa, #18337)*; *PAN Asia and the Pacific (PANAP, #18167)*; *Pesticide Action Network Europe (#18338)*; *Red de Acción en Plaguicidas y sus Alternativas de América Latina (RAP-AL, #18633)*; PAN North America. **Languages** English, French, Spanish. **Finance** Each Region is financially autonomous. **Activities** Advocacy/lobbying/activism; awareness raising; events/meetings; knowledge management/information dissemination; politics/policy/regulatory. **Events** *Conference on Belgium Moving towards Pesticide Free Towns* Brussels (Belgium) 2015, *Conference on Integrated Pest Management* Brussels (Belgium) 2012, *International meeting* 2003, *International meeting* Dakar (Senegal) 2000, *International meeting* Cuba 1997. **Publications** *Pesticide Monitor* (6 a year); *Enlace* (4 a year) in Spanish; *Pesticides News* (4 a year); *Global Pesticide Campaigner*, *Pesticides and Alternatives* in English, French. Information Services: Databases on pesticides, alternatives to pesticides for smallholder crops in tropical areas and with publications concerning health and environmental concerns with pesticides. **Members** Worldwide coalition of environment, development, consumer, trade union, religious and other groups/individuals who are opposed to the irrational spread and misuse of poisonous pesticides and who promote alternative methods of control (over 600 non-governmental organizations, institutions and individuals in over 90 countries). Membership countries not specified. **Consultative Status** Consultative status granted from: *FAO (#09260)* (Liaison Status). **IGO Relations** FAO Expert Meeting on Pesticide Management; *Group of Latin American and Caribbean States (#10784)*; *Green Climate Fund (GCF, #10714)*; *Rotterdam Convention on the Prior Informed Consent Procedure for Certain Hazardous Chemicals and Pesticides in International Trade (Rotterdam convention, 1998)*; *Stockholm Convention on Persistent Organic Pollutants (POP treaty, 2001).* Consultative status with: *European Food Safety Authority (EFSA, #07287).* **NGO Relations** Member of: *EarthAction (EA, #05159)*; *European Environmental Bureau (EEB, #06996)*; *Health and Environment Alliance (HEAL, #10879)*; *International Corporate Accountability Roundtable (ICAR, #12968)*; *International NGO/CSO Planning Committee for Food Sovereignty (IPC, #14365)*; *International Pollutants Elimination Network (IPEN, #14616)*; *People's Coalition on Food Sovereignty (PCFS, #18303)*; *Roundtable on Sustainable Palm Oil (RSPO, #18986).* Special links with founding members: *Environment Liaison Centre International (ELCI, no recent information)*; *International Coalition for Development Action (ICDA, inactive).* Signatory to Founding Statement of: *Alliance for Lobbying Transparency and Ethics Regulation (ALTER-EU, #00705).* Supports: *Global Call for Action Against Poverty (GCAP, #10263).* Regional centres individually have links with a number of international bodies; these links change regularly and are not specified. [2022.02.10/XF0481/**F**]

♦ Pesticide Action Network Africa (PAN Africa) 18337

Contact PO Box 15938, Fann, Dakar, Senegal. T. +221338254914. Fax +221338251443. E-mail: panafrica@pan-afrique.com.
URL: http://www.pan-afrique.org/

History 1995, as a regional centre of *Pesticide Action Network (PAN, #18336).* **Aims** Assist PAN groups in Africa to persuade their governments to adopt stronger controls on *pesticide* use, create awareness and teach about the *hazards* of pesticides, and work with farmers to develop and implement alternative methods of production. **Activities** Networking/liaising; advocacy/lobbying/activism; training/education; knowledge management/information dissemination. **Members** Membership countries not specified. [2019/XM7197/**E**]

♦ Pesticide Action Network Europe 18338

Main Office Rue de la Pacification 67, 1000 Brussels, Belgium. T. +3223186255. E-mail: info@pan-europe.info.
URL: http://www.pan-europe.info/

History 1987. An autonomous regional centre of *Pesticide Action Network (PAN, #18336).* Office opened in Brussels (Belgium) 2006. Former names and other names: *PAN Europe* – alias. Registration: Start date: 2003, England and Wales; Start date: 2010, Belgium; EU Transparency Register, No/ID: 15913213485-46. **Aims** Eliminate dependency on chemical *pesticides*; support safe, *sustainable* pest control methods; bring about a substantial reduction in pesticide use throughout Europe. **Structure** General Assembly; Board; Secretariat. **Languages** English. **Staff** 6.00 FTE, paid. **Finance** Sources: donations; fees for services; members' dues; private foundations. Supported by: *European Commission (EC, #06633).* **Activities** Awareness raising; events/meetings; networking/liaising; publishing activities. **Events** *Hazardous pesticides and EU Double Standards* Brussels (Belgium) 2020, *Symposium* Brussels (Belgium) 2017. **Publications** *PanE News.* Reports; policy papers; briefings; articles; factsheets.
Members Consumer, public health and environmental organizations (42) in 28 countries:
Albania, Armenia, Austria, Belgium, Bulgaria, Croatia, Denmark, Estonia, Finland, France, Germany, Greece, Ireland, Italy, Latvia, Luxembourg, Netherlands, Poland, Portugal, Romania, Serbia, Slovakia, Slovenia, Spain, Sweden, Türkiye, UK, Ukraine.
Included in the above, 3 organizations listed in this Yearbook:
ClientEarth (#03996); *GLOBAL 2000*; *Women Engage for a Common Future (WECF, #20992).* [2021.05.27/XM7320/y/**E**]

- ♦ Pet Alliance Europe (unconfirmed)
- ♦ **PETA** People for the Ethical Treatment of Animals (#18297)

♦ PET Container Recycling Europe (Petcore Europe) 18339

Secretariat Av de Broqueville 12, 1150 Brussels, Belgium. Fax +3223152488. E-mail: management@petcore-europe.org – info@petcore-europe.org.
URL: https://www.petcore-europe.org/

History 1996. Former names and other names: *PET Recycling Europe* – former; *PETCORE* – former. Registration: No/ID: 0456.829.121, Start date: 6 Dec 1994, Belgium; EU Transparency Register, No/ID: 221479213116-74, Start date: 3 Mar 2014. **Aims** Enhance the value and sustainable growth of the complete PET value chain in Europe. **Structure** Annual General Meeting; Board of Directors; Technical Committee; Working Groups. **Languages** English. **Staff** 3.50 FTE, paid. **Finance** Sources: members' dues. Annual budget: 500,000 EUR (2020). **Activities** Events/meetings; knowledge management/information dissemination; networking/liaising; projects/programmes. **Events** *Annual Conference* Brussels (Belgium) 2022, *Depolymerization Forum* Brussels (Belgium) 2022, *Recotrace – Recording, Tracing and Database* Brussels (Belgium) 2022, *Reuse in Focus, Challenges and Opportunities for the PET Industry* Brussels (Belgium) 2022, *Tray Circularity Evaluation Platform (TCEP)* Brussels (Belgium) 2022.
Members Industry sector associations and individual companies. Membership countries not specified.
Associations (4):
European Plastics Converters (EuPC, #08216); *Forum PET Europe*; *PET EUROPE – Producers' Association (#18340)*; *Plastics Recyclers Europe (PRE, #18394).*
NGO Relations Member of (1): *Circular Plastics Alliance (#03936).* [2022/XD3891/**D**]

- ♦ PETCORE / see PET Container Recycling Europe (#18339)
- ♦ **Petcore Europe** PET Container Recycling Europe (#18339)
- ♦ Peter Hesse Foundation – Solidarity in Partnership for One World (internationally oriented national body)
- ♦ Peter-Hesse-Stiftung – Partnerschaft mit der Dritten Welt / see Peter Hesse Foundation – Solidarity in Partnership for One World
- ♦ Peter-Hesse-Stiftung – Solidarität in Partnerschaft für eine Welt (internationally oriented national body)
- ♦ Peterson Institute for International Economics, Washington (internationally oriented national body)

♦ PET EUROPE – Producers' Association 18340

SG Rue Théodore de Cuyper 100, 1200 Brussels, Belgium. E-mail: info@pet-europe.org.
URL: https://www.pet-europe.org/

History 2010. Former names and other names: *The Committee of PET Manufacturers in Europe (CPME)* – full title; *PET Manufacturers in Europe (CPME)* – former (2010). Registration: Banque-Carrefour des Entreprises, Belgium; EU Transparency Register, No/ID: 73204818098-04. **Aims** Ensure the European PET industry is sustainable and can develop and grow by focusing on stakeholder needs. **Languages** English. **Activities** Advocacy/lobbying/activism; awareness raising; knowledge management/information dissemination; monitoring/evaluation; networking/liaising; politics/policy/regulatory; research and development; research/documentation. **Publications** Position papers.
Members Full in 9 countries:
Belgium, Germany, Greece, Italy, Lithuania, Netherlands, Poland, Spain, UK.
Associate in 4 countries:
Belgium, Netherlands, Portugal, Spain.
NGO Relations Member of (1): *PET Container Recycling Europe (Petcore Europe, #18339).* [2023/XM5745/**D**]

- ♦ Petites Iles en Méditerranée Initiative (internationally oriented national body)
- ♦ Petites Missionnaires de la Charité (religious order)
- ♦ Petites Servantes du Coeur de Jésus (religious order)
- ♦ Petites Soeurs de l'Assomption (religious order)
- ♦ Petites Soeurs Dominicaines (religious order)
- ♦ Petites Soeurs de Jésus de Charles de Foucauld (religious order)
- ♦ Petites Soeurs de la Miséricorde (religious order)
- ♦ Petites Soeurs des Pauvres (religious order)
- ♦ Petites Soeurs du Sacré-Coeur de Charles de Foucauld (religious order)
- ♦ Petites Soeurs de la Sainte Enfance (religious order)
- ♦ Petites Soeurs de la Sainte-Famille (religious order)
- ♦ Petites Soeurs de la Sainte Famille de Vérone (religious order)
- ♦ Petites Soeurs de Saint François d'Assise (religious order)
- ♦ Petites Soeurs de Saint Joseph (religious order)
- ♦ Petites Soeurs des Vieillards Abandonnés (religious order)
- ♦ Petit Mission pour les Sourds (religious order)
- ♦ Petits Frères de la Croix (religious order)
- ♦ Petits Frères de Jésus du Père de Foucauld (religious order)
- ♦ Petits Frères de Marie – Frères Maristes des Ecoles (religious order)
- ♦ PET Manufacturers in Europe / see PET EUROPE – Producers' Association (#18340)
- ♦ PetPower – Pet Alliance Europe (unconfirmed)

- PETRAD – International Programme for Petroleum Management and Administration (internationally oriented national body)
- PET Recycling Europe / see PET Container Recycling Europe (#18339)

Petrochemical Feedstock Association 18341

Contact 3 Kingfisher Court, Bowesfield Park, Stockton-on-Tees, TS18 3EX, UK.
Registered Office Avenue Louise 287, Boîte 6, 1050 Brussels, Belgium.

History 1990. Registration: No/ID: 0446.657.977, Belgium. **Aims** Provide a forum for producers, consumers and traders concerned with *hydrocarbons* for petrochemical *products*; contribute to exchange of ideas and discussion on supply and use of base materials for petrochemical products in *Europe* and the world, and to research on their manufacture, marketing and use. **Structure** General Meeting (annual); Executive Committee. Membership limited to two from any company. **Languages** English. **Staff** 1.00 FTE, paid. **Finance** Members' dues. **Events** *Annual General Meeting* London (UK) 1997, *Spring seminar* Madrid (Spain) 1997, *Spring seminar* Budapest (Hungary) 1996, *Annual general meeting* London (UK) 1996, *Annual General Meeting* London (UK) 1995.
Members Individuals in 21 countries:
Algeria, Austria, Belgium, Cyprus, Finland, France, Germany, Greece, Hungary, India, Italy, Japan, Kuwait, Netherlands, Norway, Saudi Arabia, Spain, Sweden, Switzerland, UK, USA.
NGO Relations Reciprocal invitations with meetings of: *Petrochemical Feedstock Association of the Americas (PFAA).* [2016/XD3324/v/**D**]

- Petrochemical Feedstock Association of the Americas (internationally oriented national body)

Petrochemicals Europe 18342

Exec Dir Rue Belliard 40 – bte 15, 1040 Brussels, Belgium. T. +32496087485. E-mail: csu@cefic.be – info@petrochemistry.eu.
URL: http://www.petrochemistry.eu/

History Feb 1985. Founded as a major group of *Conseil européen de l'industrie chimique (CEFIC, #04687).* Currently an industry sector of CEFIC. Former names and other names: *Association of Petrochemicals Producers in Europe (APPE)* – former; *Association des producteurs de produits pétrochimiques en Europe* – former. **Aims** Promote the best possible environmental, social and economic conditions to develop and maintain a healthy petrochemical industry in Europe. **Structure** General Assembly (annual); Board; Products and Sector Groups (about 20), including: *Acrylonitrile Producers' Association (see: #04687); European Ethylene Producers Committee (EEPC, #07008).* **Languages** English, French. **Staff** 11.00 FTE, paid. **Activities** Awareness raising; events/meetings; research/documentation. **Information Services** *Industrial Statistics data base.* **Members** Petrochemical producers (about 90) manufacturing ethylene and propylene from steam cracking and/or other olefins, and/or aromatics for chemical use, and/or major first stage petrochemical derivatives (excluding polymer) in Europe. Membership countries not specified. **NGO Relations** Cooperates with (1): *Association of Plastics Manufacturers in Europe (Plastics Europe, #02862).* [2022.11.03/XD8230/**E**]

- Petroleum and Chemical Industry Committee / see PCIC Europe (#18271)
- Petroleum Institute of East Africa (unconfirmed)

Petroleum Philatelic Society International (Petrophil) 18343

Pres 251 Dartmouth Ave, Fair Haven NJ 07704, USA. E-mail: president@ppsi.org.uk – editor@ppsi.org.uk.
Vice Pres address not obtained.
URL: http://www.ppsi.org.uk/

History 1974. **Aims** Advance the philately of *oil, natural gas* and *petrochemical industries.* **Languages** English. **Publications** *Petro-Philatelist* (4 a year) – journal. *Petroleum Stamps of the World (PSW)* – catalogue.
Members Individuals (mostly in USA) in 43 countries and territories:
Albania, Algeria, Argentina, Austria, Belgium, Bermuda, Bolivia, Brazil, Canada, Chile, China, Colombia, Congo Brazzaville, Denmark, Egypt, Finland, France, Gabon, Germany, Hong Kong, Hungary, Indonesia, Israel, Japan, Liberia, Malaysia, Mexico, Netherlands, Norway, Paraguay, Peru, Poland, Qatar, Romania, Saudi Arabia, Serbia, Singapore, Sweden, Switzerland, Taiwan, Uruguay, USA, Venezuela. [2021.08.31/XF2939/**F**]

- PetroPhase – International Conference on Petroleum Phase Behavior and Fouling (meeting series)
- **Petrophil** Petroleum Philatelic Society International (#18343)

PET Sheet Europe 18344

Contact Avenue de Cortenbergh 71, 1000 Brussels, Belgium. T. +3227324124. E-mail: info@eupc.org.
URL: http://www.petsheeteurope.eu/

History 2016. Subtitle: *European PET film and sheet producers.* **Aims** Study and discuss scientific, technical, economic, regulatory and institutional matter that contribute to the creation of a good trading and investment environment for PET sheet producers. **Structure** Board. **Activities** Standards/guidelines; advocacy/lobbying/activism; monitoring/evaluation; research and development. **NGO Relations** A Sector Group of: *European Plastics Converters (EuPC, #08216).* [2018/XM7656/**E**]

- PETS – Privacy Enhancing Technologies Symposium (meeting series)
- Peuple et Culture (internationally oriented national body)
- Peuples solidaires / see ActionAid France – Peuples Solidaires
- PEVOC – Pan European Voice Conference (meeting series)
- Pew Center on Global Climate Change (internationally oriented national body)
- Pew Charitable Trusts (internationally oriented national body)
- Pew Institute for Ocean Sciences / see Institute for Ocean Conservation Science
- PFAA – Petrochemical Feedstock Association of the Americas (internationally oriented national body)
- PF ADS / see Sustainable, Innovative and United Agriculture and Food Network
- PFAFW – Pan African Federation of Agricultural and Food Workers (inactive)
- PFA – Pelagic Freezer-trawler Association (unconfirmed)
- **PFA** Pierre Fauchard Academy (#18372)
- PFA – Press Foundation of Asia (inactive)
- **PFAWP** Performing and Fine Artists for World Peace (#18312)
- **PFBC** Partenariat pour les forêts du Bassin du Congo (#04662)
- **PFC** Pan American Federation of Cheerleading (#18101)
- PfC – Partnership for Change (internationally oriented national body)
- PFC – Periodistas Frente a la Corrupción (internationally oriented national body)
- PFD – Partners for Development (internationally oriented national body)
- PFE – Platform Fortress Europe (inactive)
- PFF – Presbyterian Frontier Fellowship (internationally oriented national body)
- PFI / see Society of Police Futurists International
- PFI – Pakistan Futuristics Foundation and Institute (internationally oriented national body)
- PFI – Paulo Freire Institute (internationally oriented national body)
- PFI – People First International (internationally oriented national body)
- **PFI** Prison Fellowship International (#18503)
- PFL – Pacific Forum Line (inactive)
- PF – Parapsychology Foundation (internationally oriented national body)

PfP Consortium of Defence Academies and Security Studies Institutes 18345

Exec Dir Sheridan Kaserne, Gernackerstrasse 2, 82467 Garmisch-Partenkirchen, Germany. T. +4988217502708. E-mail: pfpconsortium@marshallcenter.org.
URL: http://www.pfp-consortium.org/

History Founded 1998, Zurich (Switzerland), by US Secretary of State William Cohen and German Defense Minister Volker Rühe, at Defense Ministers' Session of *Euro Atlantic Partnership Council (EAPC, #05646).* Endorsed Apr 1999 during NATO Summit, Washington DC (USA). 'PfP' derives from 'Partnership for Peace'. **Aims** Strengthen partner nations' capacity to assess, prevent and address common transnational threats and challenges in the spirit of the Partnership for Peace Program, recognizing that a sustainable strengthening of the security and defense sector effectively contributes to common stability. **Structure** Senior Advisory Council; Consortium Steering Committee; Working/Study Groups (8); Editorial Board. **Languages** English. **Staff** Consortium operations staff at: *George C Marshall European Centre for Security Studies, Garmisch Partenkirchen (GCMC).* **Finance** Financed by governments of Austria, Switzerland and USA, and by *NATO (#16945).* Contributions in kind by partner organizations and nations. Annual budget: over US$ 1,000,000. **Activities** Events/meetings; training/education; knowledge management/information dissemination. **Events** *Annual Conference* Bucharest (Romania) 2014, *Annual Conference* Tbilisi (Georgia) 2012, *Annual Conference* Garmisch-Partenkirchen (Germany) 2011, *Annual Conference* Warsaw (Poland) 2010, *Annual Conference* Munich (Germany) 2009. **Publications** *Connections* (4 a year) in English, Russian – journal. Annual Report; policy papers; background papers; conference proceedings.
Members Stakeholder members (8):
Austria, Bulgaria, Canada, Germany, Poland, Sweden, Switzerland, USA.
Rotating member:
Denmark. [2019.12.13/XE4372/y/**E**]

- **PfP** Partnership for Peace (#18240)
- PFP / see Primary Food Processors (#18496)
- **PFP** Primary Food Processors (#18496)
- PFSA – Prayer Fellowship for South Asia (internationally oriented national body)
- **PFTAC** Pacific Financial Technical Assistance Centre (#17948)
- **PFT** Pacific Fisheries Technologists (#17949)
- **PGA** Parliamentarians for Global Action (#18208)
- **PGA** Peoples' Global Action Against Free Trade and the WTO (#18304)
- **PGAs of Europe** Professional Golfers' Associations of Europe, The (#18513)
- P and GBA – People and Global Business Association (internationally oriented national body)
- **PGC** Pacific Games Council (#17951)
- PGC – Pacific Geoscience Centre, Sidney-Canada (internationally oriented national body)
- **PGDIS** Preimplantation Genetic Diagnosis International Society (#18480)
- PGEC / see Pharmaceutical Group of the European Union (#18352)
- **PGEU** Pharmaceutical Group of the European Union (#18352)
- PGLF – Preparing Global Leaders Foundation (internationally oriented national body)
- PGM – International Conference on Probabilistic Graphical Models (meeting series)
- PGRSC – Pacific GIS and Remote Sensing Council (internationally oriented national body)
- PGS-I – Polisportive Giovanili Salesiane – Internationale (internationally oriented national body)
- PGS – Physicians for Global Survival, Canada (internationally oriented national body)
- PGWNet – Pacific Graduate Women's Network (internationally oriented national body)
- PHAB International Federation (inactive)
- PHA Europe – European pulmonary hypertension association / see Pulmonary Hypertension Association Europe (#18575)
- PHA Europe / see Pulmonary Hypertension Association Europe (#18575)
- **PHA Europe** Pulmonary Hypertension Association Europe (#18575)
- **PHA** Pacific History Association (#17952)
- **PHA** Planetary Health Alliance (#18383)
- PHAP / see Professionals in Humanitarian Assistance and Protection (#18515)
- **PHAP** Professionals in Humanitarian Assistance and Protection (#18515)
- PHA – Project Hope for Africa (internationally oriented national body)

Pharmabiotic Research Institute (PRI) 18346

Sec 1 quai Vallière, 11100 Narbonne, France. E-mail: contact@pharmabiotic.org.
URL: https://www.pharmabiotic.org/

History Registration: France; EU Transparency Register, No/ID: 897994636209-21, Start date: 14 Oct 2019. **Aims** Make microbiotic medicinal products a therapeutic reality in Europe. **Structure** Board of Directors. **Finance** Sources: members' dues. **Events** *Pharmabiotics* Lyon (France) 2022, *Pharmabiotics* Paris (France) 2021. **Members** Research institutes; Partnering members; Incubator members; Regulatory members. Membership countries not specified. [2022/AA2717/**D**]

Pharmaceutical BFS International Operators Association (BFS IOA) 18347

Contact c/o MELITEK, Hartvig Jensensvej 1, 4840 Nørre Alslev, Denmark. T. +4570250255. Fax +4570250277. E-mail: bfs@melitek.com.
URL: http://www.bfsioa.org/

History Founded 1988, as an interest group of pharmaceutical and associated companies actively involved in BFS processing. **Aims** Provide members with an opportunity to exchange ideas and opinions, and to formulate agreement on operating standards relating to blow-fill-seal (BFS) technology; provide a forum to speak with a unified voice to machine manufacturers, commercial suppliers and regulatory bodies. **Structure** General Meeting (annual). **Finance** Subscriptions; sponsors. **Activities** Events/meetings. **Events** *Asia-Pacific Meeting* Bangkok (Thailand) 2019, *European Meeting* Stockholm (Sweden) 2019, *European Meeting* Colmar (France) 2018, *Asia-Pacific Meeting* Tashkent (Uzbekistan) 2018, *Asia-Pacific Meeting* Melbourne, VIC (Australia) 2017. **Publications** *BFS Newsletter.*
Members Companies (over 80) in 23 countries:
Australia, Bangladesh, Belgium, Czechia, Denmark, Finland, France, Germany, India, Ireland, Italy, Japan, Kenya, Malaysia, Norway, Puerto Rico, Saudi Arabia, South Africa, Sweden, Switzerland, UK, United Arab Emirates, USA. [2018.10.08/XM0027/**D**]

Pharmaceutical and BioScience Society, International (PBSS) 18348

President PO Box 2342, San Francisco CA SOUTH 94083-2342, USA. E-mail: info@pbss.org.
URL: https://www.pbss.org/aspx/homeSF.aspx

Aims Promote the exchange of scientific ideas while providing educational and growth opportunities in the fields of pharmaceutical / life science related disciplines. **Structure** Governing Board. **Events** *Korea Workshop* Daejeon (Korea Rep) 2020, *Korea Workshop* Daejeon (Korea Rep) 2019, *Korea Workshop* Daejeon (Korea Rep) 2019, *Korea Workshop* Daejeon (Korea Rep) 2019, *Korea Workshop* Daejeon (Korea Rep) 2018.
Members Organizations (5) in 3 countries:
Canada, Korea Rep, USA. [2023/XM8298/**D**]

Pharmaceutical Care Network Europe (PCNE) 18349

Professional Sec Margrietlaan 1, 9471 CT Zuidlaren, Netherlands. T. +31504029095. E-mail: info@pcne.org.
Chairman Univ of Leiden Medical Centre, Albinusdreef 2, 2333 ZA Leiden, Netherlands.
URL: http://www.pcne.org/

History 1994, Lisbon (Portugal). Registered in accordance with Dutch law, 2001. **Aims** Offer a communication platform for researchers in the field of pharmaceutical care in Europe and beyond; coordinate pharmaceutical care research. **Structure** General Assembly (Association); Board. **Languages** English. **Staff** 0.10 FTE, paid. **Finance** Annual budget for secretariat: euro 3,000. **Activities** Events/meetings. **Events** *Symposium* Lisbon (Portugal) 2022, *Biennial Conference* Zuidlaren (Netherlands) 2021, *Symposium* Egmond aan Zee (Netherlands) 2020, *Biennial Conference* Egmond aan Zee (Netherlands) 2019, *Symposium* Fuengirola (Spain) 2018. **Publications** *PCNE Newsletter* (4 a year).
Members Individuals and scientific university or university-related departments in 31 countries:
Australia, Belgium, Bosnia-Herzegovina, Bulgaria, Croatia, Czechia, Denmark, Finland, Germany, Hungary, Ireland, Italy, Jordan, Kosovo, Malta, Moldova, Netherlands, Nigeria, Norway, Peru, Poland, Portugal, Qatar, Serbia, Slovenia, Spain, Sweden, Switzerland, UK, Ukraine, USA.
NGO Relations Cooperates with: *European Society of Clinical Pharmacy (ESCP, #08551); International Pharmaceutical Federation (#14566).* Links with universities and private research organizations. [2019.12.11/XF5779/**F**]

Pharmaceutical Contract Management Group (PCMG) 18350

Admin Office Chester House, 68 Chestergate, Macclesfield, SK11 6DY, UK. T. +441625664546. Fax +441625664510. E-mail: admin@pcmg.org.uk.
URL: http://www.pcmg.org.uk/

History 1994. Registration: Companies House, No/ID: 07166604, England and Wales. **Aims** Foster a consistent, professional approach to managing R and D outsourcing and thereby establish recognition of the role of outsourcing management in the pharmaceutical industry; generate standards for the management of pharmaceutical R and D outsourcing and provide a forum for the exchange of ideas to achieve this; develop the skills of pharmaceutical R and D outsourcing and contracting professionals. **Structure** Voluntary Committee. **Finance** Members' dues. **Activities** Events/meetings; training/education; standards/guidelines; networking/liaising. **Events** *Annual Conference* Krakow (Poland) 2022, *Annual Conference* Palma (Spain) 2021, *Annual Conference* Krakow (Poland) 2020, *Annual Conference* Sitges (Spain) 2019, *Annual Conference* Valletta (Malta) 2018. **Publications** *PCMG Newsletter*. **Members** Individuals; Corporate; Associate. Membership countries not specified. **NGO Relations** *European CRO Federation (EUCROF, #06863)*. [2021/XM6285/D]

♦ Pharmaceutical Forum of the Americas 18351

Foro Farmacéutico de las Américas (FFA)

Permanent Contact PAHO/OPS, 525 23rd St NW, Washington DC 20037-2895, USA. T. +12029743229. Fax +12029743610. E-mail: forofarm@paho.org.
Pres address not obtained.
URL: http://www1.paho.org/english/ad/ths/ev/ffa-home.htm

History 1999, Santiago (Chile), as part of *Pan American Health Organization (PAHO, #18108)*. **Aims** Improve the health of people in the Americas through actions involving pharmacists participation; encourage and support a dialogue and cooperation among all national and regional pharmaceutical associations in the region of the Americas; develop and enhance pharmacy practice; encourage implementation of pharmacy practice projects by all national and regional pharmaceutical associations; integrate appropriate PAHO/WHO policies into undergraduate, postgraduate and continuing education programmes; formulate policy statements on health issues. **Structure** Plenary Session (annual), allowing each member association 2 representatives but with only one vote, elects Executive Committee, comprising President, 3 Vice-Presidents, Treasurer and 2 Directors, serving 2-year terms. Executive Secretariat located in PAHO/WHO Headquarters in Washington DC (USA), headed by Professional Secretary. **Languages** English, Spanish. **Finance** Members' dues. **Activities** Projects.

Members National Pharmaceutical association and councils and regional federations in 15 countries:
Argentina, Bolivia, Brazil, Chile, Colombia, Costa Rica, Dominican Rep, Ecuador, Honduras, Mexico, Paraguay, Peru, Uruguay, USA, Venezuela.

Included in the above, 5 regional organizations listed in this Yearbook:
Caribbean Association of Pharmacists (CAP, #03458); *Federación Farmacéutica Centroamericana y del Caribe (FFCC, #09301)*; *Federación Farmacéutica Sudamericana (FEFAS, #09302)*; *Federación Panamericana de Farmacia (FEPAFAR, no recent information)*; *International Pharmaceutical Federation (#14566)*.

NGO Relations Observer to: *EuroPharm Forum (inactive)*. [2011/XF6250/y/F]

♦ Pharmaceutical Group of the European Community / see Pharmaceutical Group of the European Union (#18352)

♦ Pharmaceutical Group of the European Union (PGEU) 18352

Groupement pharmaceutique de l'Union européenne (GPUE) – Zusammenschluss der Apotheker der Europäischen Union – Gruppo Farmaceutico dell'Unione Europea – Groepering van Apotekers van de Europese Unie

SG Rue du Luxembourg 19, 1000 Brussels, Belgium. T. +3222380818. E-mail: pharmacy@pgeu.eu.
URL: http://www.pgeu.eu/

History 29 May 1959, Frankfurt-Main (Germany). Former names and other names: *Pharmaceutical Group of the European Community (PGEC)* – former; *Groupement pharmaceutique de la Communauté européenne (GPCE)* – former (1959); *Zusammenschluss der Apotheker der Europäischen Gemeinschaft* – former (1959); *Gruppo Farmaceutico della Comunità Europea* – former (1959); *Groep van Apotekers van de Europese Gemeenschap* – former (1959). Registration: No/ID: 0468.971.838, Start date: 13 Jan 2000, Belgium; EU Transparency Register, No/ID: 00086317186-42, Start date: 18 Nov 2011. **Aims** Promote and develop cooperation in Community Pharmacy among European nations; advocate for the contribution community pharmacists make to health systems and to public health through provision of health services and promotion of rational and appropriate use of medicines; ensure that the Group's vision of Community Pharmacy is reflected in EU policy and legislative developments. **Structure** General Assembly (2 a year); Executive Committee/Management Board; Working Groups. **Languages** English, French. **Staff** 5.00 FTE, paid. **Finance** Sources: members' dues; revenue from activities/projects. **Activities** Advocacy/lobbying/activism; events/meetings; politics/policy/regulatory. **Events** *General Assembly* Marbella (Spain) 2018, *General Assembly* London (UK) 2017, *Conference on the State of Health in the EU* Brussels (Belgium) 2016, *General Assembly* Dublin (Ireland) 2015, *Meeting* Vienna (Austria) 2014. **Publications** Annual Report; position papers; facts and figures; white papers.

Members National organizations. Ordinary members in 26 countries:
Austria, Belgium, Bulgaria, Croatia, Cyprus, Czechia, Denmark, Estonia, Finland, France, Germany, Greece, Hungary, Ireland, Italy, Latvia, Luxembourg, Malta, Netherlands, Poland, Portugal, Romania, Slovakia, Slovenia, Spain, Sweden.

Observers in 6 countries:
Kosovo, North Macedonia, Norway, Serbia, Türkiye, UK.

NGO Relations Observer status with (2): *Alliance for Safe Online Pharmacy – EU (ASOP EU, #00720)*; *European Health professionals Competent Authorities (EurHeCA, #07460)*. Member of (5): *European Forum for Primary Care (EFPC, #07326)*; *European Medicines Verification Organisation (EMVO, #07768)*; *European Nutrition for Health Alliance, The (ENHA, #08069)*; *Federation of European and International Associations Established in Belgium (FAIB, #09508)*; *International Pharmaceutical Federation (#14566)*. Participating organization of: *European Alliance for Personalised Medicine (EAPM, #05878)*. Endorses: *Steering Group on Influenza Vaccination (#19980)*. [2023.02.14/XE3883/E]

♦ Pharmaceutical Inspection Co-operation Scheme (PIC/S) 18353

Secretariat 14 rue du Roveray, 1207 Geneva, Switzerland. T. +41227389216. E-mail: info@picscheme.org.
URL: https://picscheme.org/

History 1995. Established as an extension to *Convention for the Mutual Recognition of Inspections in Respect of the Manufacture of Pharmaceutical Products (PIC, 1970)*. A non-binding, informal co-operative arrangement between Regulatory Authorities in the field of Good Manufacturing Practice (GMP) of medicinal products for human or veterinary use. Between 1971-2003, no distinct legal identity with Secretariat provided by *European Fair Trade Association (EFTA, #07026)*. Became independent with its own Secretaria, 1 Jan 2004. Registration: Registre du Commerce, No/ID: CH-660-9587004-3, Start date: 11 Nov 2004, Switzerland, Geneva. **Aims** Lead the international development, implementation and maintenance of harmonized Good Manufacturing Practice (GMP) standards and quality systems of inspectorates in the field of medicinal products. **Structure** Committee; Executive Bureau; Secretariat. Sub-committees (7). **Activities** Events/meetings; monitoring/evaluation; networking/liaising; standards/guidelines; training/education.

Members Participating Authorities in 50 countries and territories:
Argentina, Australia, Austria, Belgium, Brazil, Canada, Croatia, Cyprus, Czechia, Denmark, Estonia, Finland, France, Germany, Greece, Hong Kong, Hungary, Iceland, Indonesia, Iran Islamic Rep, Ireland, Israel, Italy, Japan, Korea Rep, Latvia, Liechtenstein, Lithuania, Malaysia, Malta, Mexico, Netherlands, New Zealand, Norway, Poland, Portugal, Romania, Singapore, Slovakia, Slovenia, South Africa, Spain, Sweden, Switzerland, Taiwan, Thailand, Türkiye, UK, Ukraine, USA.

NGO Relations Partner of (1): *International Coalition of Medicines Regulatory Authorities (ICMRA, #12616)*. [2022/AA2678/E]

♦ Pharmaceutical Procurement Service (PSS) 18354

Main Office PO Box 3093, Castries, St Lucia. T. +17584525058. Fax +17584530227. E-mail: pps@oecs.org.
URL: http://www.oecs.org/pps-about

History 1986, by *Organisation of Eastern Caribbean States (OECS, #17804)*. Full title: *Eastern Caribbean Drug Service (ECDS) – Pharmaceutical Procurement Service (PPS) – Service pharmaceutique des Caraïbes orientales (SPCO)*. **Aims** Assist Participating States in developing policies and programmes leading to more efficient utilization of *health* sector resources through improvement, procurement, management and use of pharmaceuticals and *medical* supplies. **Structure** Policy Board, consisting of OECS Ministers of Health, and assisted by Technical Advisory Committee (Tenders and Formulary and Therapeutics Sub-Committees). Director General OECS; Managing Director. **Languages** English. **Staff** 12.00 FTE, paid. **Finance** Funded by OECS countries participating in the scheme. The *Eastern Caribbean Central Bank (ECCB, #05231)* is the payments agent for pharmaceuticals and medical supplies purchased through PPS. **Activities** Manages international tendering contracting and procurement process for pharmaceuticals and medical supplies for Participating States; pools pharmaceutical and medical supply needs of the Participating States for international tendering and solicits tenders for supply of such items to Participating States; evaluates tenders from suppliers for the supply of pharmaceuticals and medical supplies to Participating States; monitors individual purchase orders; manages on behalf of Participating States, a range of quality assurance activities respecting pharmaceuticals and medical supplies; develops in-country management practices which result in reduction of unit costs of pharmaceuticals and medical supplies; facilitates an exchange of professional ideas, news and drug information targeted at prescribers and pharmacists, through the organisation of training and continuing education programmes; provides a vehicle for strengthening professional networks and improving the professional competence of health workers and other government employees concerned with the provision of Health Services in the Participating States; provides training and assistance to Participating States in formulary development and techniques for improving the management of Ministry of Health Supply Systems. **Publications** *PPS Bulletin*; *PPS Regional Formulary and Therapeutics Manual*.

Members Governments of 9 countries and territories:
Anguilla, Antigua-Barbuda, Dominica, Grenada, Montserrat, St Kitts-Nevis, St Lucia, St Vincent-Grenadines, Virgin Is UK.

IGO Relations *Pan American Health Organization (PAHO, #18108)*; *United States Agency for International Development (USAID)*. [2014.01.16/XF2009/F*]

♦ Pharmaceutical Security Institute (PSI) 18355

Main Office 8100 Boone Blvd, Ste 220, Vienna VA 22182, USA. T. +17038480160. Fax +17038480164. E-mail: psi@psi-inc.org.
URL: http://www.psi-inc.org/

History 2002, Washington, DC (USA). Founded by Security Directors from 14 major pharmaceutical companies. **Aims** Protect public *health*; share information on the *counterfeiting* of pharmaceuticals; initiate *enforcement* actions through appropriate authorities. **Structure** Offices in: Singapore; Sweden; USA. **Members** Pharmaceutical manufacturing companies (26). Membership countries not specified. **NGO Relations** Partner of: *Fight the Fakes (#09755)*. [2020/XM3833/j/F]

♦ Pharmaceutical Solid State Research Cluster (PSSRC) 18356

Contact address not obtained. E-mail: contact@pssrc.org.
URL: http://www.pssrc.org/

History 2006, San Antonio, TX (USA). **Aims** Initiate and foster collaborative research between members in all areas of the pharmaceutical solid state field. **Structure** Steering Board. **Activities** Events/meetings; research/documentation. **Events** *Annual Symposium* Helsinki (Finland) 2022, *Annual Symposium* Helsinki (Finland) 2021, *Annual Symposium* Helsinki (Finland) 2020.

Members Individuals from 10 countries:
Austria, Belgium, Denmark, Finland, France, Germany, New Zealand, Portugal, Slovenia, UK. [2021/AA1694/v/F]

♦ Pharmaceutical Trade Marks Group (PTMG) 18357

Sec Tillingbourne House, 115 Gregories Road, Beaconsfield, JP9 1HZ, UK.
Registered Office 100 New Bridge Street, London, EC4V 6JA, UK.
URL: http://www.ptmg.org/

History 25 Sep 1970, Surbiton (UK). Legal structure updated, 2002. Registered in accordance with UK law: 4432263. **Aims** Enable members to meet at regular intervals to consider problems of mutual interest. **Structure** General Meeting (annual, at Spring Conference). **Languages** English. **Activities** Events/meetings; training/education. **Events** *Autumn Conference* Berlin (Germany) 2019, *Spring Conference* Rome (Italy) 2019, *Autumn Conference* Dubrovnik (Croatia) 2018, *Spring Conference* Porto (Portugal) 2018, *Autumn Conference* Toronto, ON (Canada) 2017. **Members** Full in 100 countries. Membership countries not specified. [2019.02.12/XJ8293/t/F]

♦ Pharmaceutical Users Software Exchange / see PHUSE (#18365)
♦ PHD Foundation (internationally oriented national body)
♦ PHD Foundation – Peace, Health and Human Development / see PHD Foundation
♦ pHealth – International Conference on Wearable, Micro and Nano Technologies for Personalized Health (meeting series)
♦ PHEA – Plastics Heritage European Association (unconfirmed)
♦ Phelps Stokes (internationally oriented national body)
♦ Phelps Stokes Fund / see Phelps Stokes
♦ **PHE** PAHO/WHO Health Emergencies Department (#18023)
♦ PHESA – Public Health Evidence South Asia (unconfirmed)
♦ Ph Eur Commission / see European Pharmacopoeia Commission (#08198)
♦ Phi Delta Phi International Legal Fraternity (internationally oriented national body)
♦ Philalethes Society (internationally oriented national body)

♦ Philanthropy Europe Association (Philea) 18358

Events Manager Philanthropy House, Rue Royale 94, 1000 Brussels, Belgium. T. +3225128938. E-mail: info@philea.eu.
URL: https://philea.eu/

History Dec 2021. Created on merger of *European Foundation Centre (EFC, inactive)* and *DAFNE (inactive)*. **Aims** Harness the multidimensional potential of European philanthropy. **Activities** Events/meetings. **Events** *Philea Forum* Sibenik (Croatia) 2023, *Forum* Barcelona (Spain) 2022, *PEXforum* Istanbul (Türkiye) 2022.

Members Organizations in 34 countries:
Austria, Belgium, Bosnia-Herzegovina, Bulgaria, Chile, Croatia, Cyprus, Czechia, Denmark, Estonia, Finland, France, Georgia, Germany, Greece, Ireland, Italy, Latvia, Liechtenstein, Luxembourg, Netherlands, Norway, Poland, Portugal, Senegal, Serbia, Slovakia, Spain, Sweden, Switzerland, Türkiye, UK, Ukraine, USA.

- *Adessium Foundation*;
- *Adriano Olivetti Foundation*;
- *Aga Khan Foundation (AKF, #00545)*;
- *Barrow Cadbury Trust*;
- *Bertelsmann Foundation*;
- *Bill and Melinda Gates Foundation (BMGF)*;
- *Calouste Gulbenkian Foundation*;
- *Charities Aid Foundation (CAF)*;
- *Charles Stewart Mott Foundation*;
- *Conrad N Hilton Foundation (CNHF)*;
- *ERSTE Foundation*;
- *Essl Foundation*;
- *European Climate Foundation (ECF, #06574)*;
- *European Cultural Foundation (ECF, #06868)*;
- *Europe Foundation (EPF, #09158)*;
- *Europska zaklada za filantropiju i drusveni razvoj*;
- *Evens Foundation (EF)*;
- *Fondation Charles Léopold Mayer pour le progrès de l'homme (FPH, #09815)*;
- *Fondation de France*;
- *Ford Foundation (#09858)*;
- *Freudenberg Foundation*;
- *Fundação Luso-Americana para o Desenvolvimento (FLAD)*;
- *Fundação Oriente, Lisboa*;
- *Fundación ONCE para América Latina (FOAL)*;
- *German Marshall Fund of the United States (GMF)*;
- *International Renaissance Foundation (IRF)*;
- *Jacobs Foundation (JF, #16084)*;
- *Joseph Rowntree Charitable Trust*;
- *King Baudouin Foundation (KBF)*;
- *Körber Stiftung*;
- *Learning for Well-being Foundation (L4WB, #16431)*;
- *Mama Cash (#16560)*;
- *MAVA Foundation*;

- *Oak Foundation*;
- *Open Society Foundations (OSF, #17763)*;
- *Pew Charitable Trusts*;
- *Porticus*;
- *Prince Claus Fund for Culture and Development*;
- *Robert Bosch Foundation*;
- *Rockefeller Brothers Fund (RBF)*;
- *Stiftung Mercator*;
- *TrustAfrica (#20251)*;
- *Trust for Mutual Understanding*;
- *Unidea – UniCredit Foundation*;
- *Volkswagen Foundation*;
- *Wellcome Trust*.

NGO Relations Member of (2): *European Charities' Committee on Value-Added Tax (ECCVAT, #06519)*; *Global NPO Coalition on FATF (#10508)*. [2023/AA2702/**D**]

♦ Philanthropy without Frontiers, Canada (internationally oriented national body)
♦ Philanthropy Impact (internationally oriented national body)
♦ Philanthropy Leadership Network (unconfirmed)

♦ Philanthropy Workshop (TPW) 18359

CEO 110 East 25th St, New York NY 10010, USA. T. +16467901587. E-mail: info@tpw.org.
URL: http://www.tpw.org/

History Founded 1995, New York NY (USA), as an offshoot of *The Rockefeller Foundation (#18966)*. Institute of Philanthropy, set up 1 Jan 2000, London (UK) and TPW West, set up 1 Jan 2001, merged into TPW, 2014. **Aims** Inspire, transform and catalyze a network of effective philanthropists as a means to a more just, sustainable and enriching world. **Structure** Chairman; Trustees. **Languages** English. **Staff** 9.00 FTE, paid. **Finance** Grants; donations; earned income. **Activities** Networking/liaising; events/meetings; projects/programmes. **Publications** *The State of UK Charity Boards* (2011) – Think Philanthropy Papers. **Members** Membership countries not specified. **NGO Relations** *The William and Flora Hewlett Foundation*; *The Rockefeller Foundation (#18966)*. [2016.12.22/XM7094/**F**]

♦ Philatelic Esperanto League (#05545)
♦ **Philea** Philanthropy Europe Association (#18358)
♦ PHILIA – Association of Multiethnic Cities of Southeast Europe (no recent information)
♦ Philippine Centre for Population and Development (internationally oriented national body)
♦ Philip Stephenson Foundation (internationally oriented national body)
♦ Philosophers and Historians for Peace / see European Philosophers for Peace
♦ Philosophers for Peace / see European Philosophers for Peace
♦ Philosophical Issues in Psychiatry (meeting series)
♦ Philosophical Society of Southern Africa (internationally oriented national body)
♦ Philosophical Society for the Study of Sport / see International Association for the Philosophy of Sport (#12078)

♦ Philosophy of Education Society of Australasia (PESA) 18360

Sec address not obtained. E-mail: secretary@pesa.org.au.
URL: http://www.pesa.org.au/

History 1969, Sydney, NSW (Australia). Registration: No/ID: 57432755082, Start date: 2005, Australia, Western Australia. **Aims** Engage with philosophical questions related to education, teaching and learning. **Structure** Annual General Assembly and Conference. **Languages** English. **Staff** Voluntary. **Finance** Sources: members' dues. **Events** *Annual Conference* Sydney, NSW (Australia) 2020, *Annual Conference* Hong Kong (Hong Kong) 2019, *Annual Conference* Rotorua (New Zealand) 2018, *Annual Conference* Newcastle, NSW (Australia) 2017, *Annual Conference* Korolevu (Fiji) 2016. **Publications** *ACCESS: Contemporary Issues in Education* – Online, open access academic journal. *Educational Philosophy and Theory*. Journals.
Members Full in 11 countries and territories:
Australia, China, Hong Kong, Korea Rep, New Zealand, Papua New Guinea, Singapore, South Africa, Taiwan, UK, USA.
[2021.06.21/XD0150/**D**]

♦ Philosophy and Theory of Higher Education Society (PaTHES) 18361

Chair Aarhus Univ, Ctr for Teaching Development and Digital Media, Bldg 1483 – Office 626, Jens Chr Skous Vej 4 6, 8000 Aarhus C, Denmark. T. +4520467019.
Sec address not obtained.
URL: https://pathes.org/

History Feb 2018. Registration: Denmark. **Aims** Form and promote an effective worldwide community of scholars and academics developing philosophy and social theory; engage in educational, social, and societal matters and activities around the future of universities and higher education. **Structure** General Assembly; Board. **Finance** Sources: members' dues. **Activities** Advocacy/lobbying/activism; events/meetings. **Events** *PHEC – Philosophy and Theory of Higher Education Conference* Uppsala (Sweden) 2022, *PHEC – Philosophy and Theory of Higher Education Conference* 2021, *PHEC – Philosophy and Theory of Higher Education Conference* Uppsala (Sweden) 2020, *Conference* Leuven (Belgium) 2019, *Conference* London (UK) 2018. **Publications** *Quarterly Community Forum* (4 a year); *Journal of Philosophy and Theory in Higher Education*. **Members** Individual; Associate. Membership countries not specified. [2022/XM7063/**C**]

♦ PHIN – Pro-Hope International (internationally oriented national body)
♦ PHI – Partnerships in Health Information (internationally oriented national body)
♦ PHI – Post-Polio Health International (internationally oriented national body)
♦ **PHI** Programa Hidrológico Internacional (#13826)
♦ **PHI** Programme hydrologique international (#13826)

♦ Phiren Amenca 18362

Contact Krúdy utca 2, fsz 7, Budapest 1088, Hungary. E-mail: info@phirenamenca.eu.
URL: http://phirenamenca.eu/

History Founded 2012, continuing an initiative started Sep 2000. Full title: *Phiren Amenca – Roma-Gadje Dialogue through Service (RGDTS)*. Also referred to as *Phiren Amenca International Network*. Registered in accordance with Belgian law. **Aims** Create opportunities for non-formal education, dialogue and engagement, in order to challenge stereotypes and *racism*. **Languages** English. **Staff** 3.00 FTE, paid; 5.00 FTE, voluntary. **Finance** *Council of Europe (CE, #04881)*; *European Commission (EC, #06633)*; *ICCO – Interchurch Organization for Development Cooperation*; private funding. **Activities** Events/meetings; training/education; standards/guidelines. **Publications** *European Boogie Man Complex – Challenging Antigypsyism through Non-formal Education*.
Members Organizations in 12 countries:
Albania, Austria, Denmark, France, Germany, Hungary, Italy, Netherlands, Romania, Slovakia, Spain, Ukraine.
IGO Relations *Council of Europe (CE, #04881)* Youth Department – Roma Youth Action Plan. **NGO Relations** Partner of: *Armenian General Benevolent Union (AGBU, #01110)*; *ERGO Network (#05531)*; *European Union of Jewish Students (EUJS, #08997)*; *Youth of European Nationalities (YEN, #22013)*. [2017.10.24/XJ8832/**F**]

♦ Phiren Amenca International Network / see Phiren Amenca (#18362)
♦ Phiren Amenca – Roma-Gadje Dialogue through Service / see Phiren Amenca (#18362)
♦ PHJC – Poor Handmaids of Jesus Christ (religious order)
♦ **PHM** People's Health Movement (#18305)
♦ phmsociety – Prognostics and Health Management Society (internationally oriented national body)
♦ Phoenician International Research Center (unconfirmed)
♦ Phonetics and Phonology in Europe (meeting series)
♦ Phonetic Teachers' Association / see International Phonetic Association (#14573)
♦ Phonology in the Nordic Countries (meeting series)

♦ Phosphoric Acid and Phosphates Producers Association (PAPA) . . . 18363

Sector Group Manager c/o CEFIC, Rue Belliard 40, Box 15, 1040 Brussels, Belgium. T. +3224369468. E-mail: map@cefic.be.
URL: http://www.cefic.org/

History A sector group of *Conseil européen de l'industrie chimique (CEFIC, #04687)*.
Members Companies (3) in 3 countries:
Belgium, France, Germany. [2021/XJ5959/**E**]

♦ Phosphorus, Inorganic and Nitrogen Flame Retardants Association (pinfa) 18364

Dir c/o CEFIC, Rue Belliard 40, 1040 Brussels, Belgium. T. +3224269414. E-mail: pinfa@cefic.be.
URL: http://www.pinfa.eu/

History A Sector Group within *Conseil européen de l'industrie chimique (CEFIC, #04687)*. **Aims** Support fire safety through innovative, reliable and sustainable fire performance solutions, using products based on phosphorus, nitrogen and inorganic compounds. **Structure** General Assembly; Board; Working Groups. **Languages** English. **Publications** *pinfa Newsletter*. Brochures; factsheets.
Members Non-halogenated flame retardants manufacturers and users (20) in 8 countries:
France, Germany, Italy, Netherlands, Sweden, Switzerland, UK, USA. [2020/XJ5751/**E**]

♦ PHOS – Platform Handicap en Ontwikkelingssamenwerking (internationally oriented national body)
♦ Photo International (inactive)
♦ **PHPCI** Public Health Palliative Care International (#18565)
♦ PHP – Presbyterian Hunger Program (internationally oriented national body)
♦ PHR-Israel – Physicians for Human Rights, Israel (internationally oriented national body)
♦ PHR-USA – Physicians for Human Rights, USA (internationally oriented national body)
♦ PHS – Peace History Society (internationally oriented national body)

♦ PHUSE 18365

Office Kent Innovation Centre, Millennium Way, Broadstairs, CT10 2QQ, UK. T. +441843609600. Fax +441843265850. E-mail: office@phuse.eu.
URL: https://www.phuse.eu/

History 2005, Heidelberg (Germany). Set up as a conference. Former names and other names: *Pharmaceutical Users Software Exchange* – full title. Registration: Companies House, No/ID: 05422297, England and Wales. **Aims** Discuss topics encompassing the work of data managers, biostatisticians, statistical programmers and e-clinical IT professionals. **Structure** Board. **Languages** English. **Activities** Events/meetings. **Events** *Annual Conference* Amsterdam (Netherlands) 2019, *Annual Conference* Barcelona (Spain) 2016, *Annual Computational Science Symposium (CSS)* Silver Spring, MD (USA) 2015, *Annual Conference* Vienna (Austria) 2015, *Annual PhUSE Conference* London (UK) 2014. **Publications** *Pharmaceutical Programming*. Blogs; news mailings. [2020.10.15/XJ9021/**F**]

♦ Physical Activity Network of the Americas (PANA) 18366

Red de Actividad Fisica de las Americas (RAFA)

General Coordination CELAFISCS, Rua Heloisa Pamplona 279, sala 31, CEP 09520-320, Bairro Fundação, Sao Paulo SP, 09520 320, Brazil. T. +551142298980. Fax +551142299643. E-mail: matsudo.celafiscs@gmail.com – celafiscs.secretaria@gmail.com.
URL: http://www.rafapana.org/

History 2000, Sao Paulo (Brazil). **Aims** As a "network of national networks" integrating members of public and private institutions, improve, recover, maintain or promote good *health* and quality of life among the Americas through regular physical activity practice (PA). **Structure** Executive Committee; President; Working Committees. **Languages** Spanish. **Events** *Annual Meeting* Montevideo (Uruguay) 2013, *Annual Conference* Medellin (Colombia) 2010, *Annual Conference* Sao Paulo (Brazil) 2009, *Annual Conference* San José (Costa Rica) 2008, *Annual Conference* Santiago (Chile) 2007. **Publications** *Rafa News*. Handbooks; statements.
Members Networks in 21 countries and territories:
Argentina, Aruba, Bolivia, Brazil, Canada, Chile, Colombia, Costa Rica, Cuba, Dominican Rep, Ecuador, El Salvador, Guatemala, Mexico, Panama, Paraguay, Peru, Puerto Rico, Uruguay, USA, Venezuela.
NGO Relations Regional network of: *Agita Mundo Network (#00560)*. [2018.06.01/XJ0658/**F**]

♦ Physical Security Interoperability Alliance (PSIA) 18367

Exec Dir 65 Washington St, Ste 170, Santa Clara CA 95050, USA. T. +16509386945. Fax +14082539938. E-mail: dmaguire@psialliance.org – info@psialliance.org.
URL: http://www.psialliance.org/

History Feb 2008. Incorporated Mar 2009. **Aims** Develop standards relevant to networked physical security technology. **Structure** Board of Directors. **Members** Companies. Membership countries not specified. [2014/XJ4945/**C**]

♦ Physicians for Global Survival, Canada (internationally oriented national body)
♦ Physicians for Human Rights, Israel (internationally oriented national body)
♦ Physicians for Human Rights, USA (internationally oriented national body)
♦ Physicians for Peace (internationally oriented national body)

♦ Physics of Membrane Processes (PMP) 18368

Chair address not obtained. E-mail: info@physicsofmembranes.org.
URL: https://physicsofmembranes.org/

Structure Working Group. **Activities** Events/meetings. **Events** *International Symposium on Physics of Membrane Processes* Rennes (France) 2021. [2021/AA1630/**F**]

♦ Physiological Association / see Société de Physiologie (#19509)
♦ Physiology and Biochemistry Society of Southern Africa / see Physiology Society of Southern Africa
♦ Physiology Society of Southern Africa (internationally oriented national body)
♦ Phytobiomes Alliance / see International Alliance for Phytobiomes Research (#11634)
♦ Phytochemical Group / see Phytochemical Society of Europe (#18370)
♦ Phytochemical Society / see Phytochemical Society of Europe (#18370)

♦ Phytochemical Society of Asia (PSA) 18369

SG PPSKTM, Universiti Kebangsaan Malaysia, 43600 UKM Bangi, Kuala Lumpur, Malaysia. T. +60389215445. E-mail: kiamco65@gmail.com – kiam@ukm.edu.my.
URL: http://phytochemsoc-asia.com/

History Founded 24 Aug 2007, Kuala Lumpur (Malaysia) during 12th Asian Chemical Congress, organized by *Federation of Asian Chemical Societies (FACS, #09431)*. **Aims** Promote the growth and advancement in research of natural products from flora and fauna of the region; educate and enlighten the public on matters related to natural products; actively promote collaborative research between scientists within the region and encourage collaboration with scientists from outside the region. **Structure** Council, including President, Vice-President, Secretary-General and Honorary Treasurer. **Languages** English. **Activities** Events/meetings; training/education; networking/liaising; knowledge management/information dissemination. **Events** *International Symposium on Natural Products for the Future* Tokushima (Japan) 2016, *Symposium* Tokushima (Japan) 2015, *Inaugural general meeting* Kuala Lumpur (Malaysia) 2007, *Malaysian international symposium on analytical sciences* Kuala Lumpur (Malaysia) 2007. **Members** (775). Membership countries not specified. [2015.11.18/XM2299/**D**]

♦ Phytochemical Society of Europe (PSE) 18370

Société Phytochimique d'Europe

Pres address not obtained.
Gen Sec address not obtained.
URL: https://new.phytochemicalsociety.org

History 1957, Cambridge (UK). Founded as an informal group of chemists and biologists interested in the phenolic constituents of plants. Expanded to form a group,1964, Leeds (UK), at 7th Annual Meeting. Former names and other names: *Plant Phenolics Group* – former (1957 to 1964); *Phytochemical Group* – former (1964 to 1967); *Phytochemical Society* – former (1967 to 6 Jan 1977). **Aims** Serve all those with an interest in the chemistry and biochemistry of plants and in applications of such knowledge in industry and agriculture. **Structure** General Meeting (annual); Executive Committee. **Languages** English. **Staff** 8.00 FTE, voluntary. **Finance** Sources: grants; members' dues. **Activities** Awards/prizes/competitions; events/meetings. **Events** *PSE Trends in Natural Products Research* Kolymbari (Greece) 2022, *International Congress on Natural Products Research* San Francisco, CA (USA) 2020, *Euroindoamerican Natural Products Meeting* Madrid (Spain) 2018, *Joint Natural Products Conference* Copenhagen (Denmark) 2016, *EIAMNP : Euroindoamerican Natural Products Meeting* Madrid (Spain) 2016. **Publications** *Phytochemistry* – journal; *Phytochemistry Letters*; *Phytochemistry Reviews* – journal. Proceedings.
Members Individuals (343) in 68 countries:

Argentina, Armenia, Australia, Austria, Belgium, Botswana, Brazil, Bulgaria, Canada, China, Colombia, Costa Rica, Czechia, Denmark, Dominican Rep, Ecuador, Ethiopia, Finland, France, Germany, Ghana, Greece, Guinea, Hungary, Iceland, India, Indonesia, Iran Islamic Rep, Ireland, Israel, Italy, Japan, Jordan, Kenya, Korea Rep, Kuwait, Libya, Malaysia, Mexico, Netherlands, New Zealand, Nigeria, Norway, Pakistan, Palestine, Panama, Peru, Poland, Portugal, Russia, Rwanda, Saudi Arabia, Serbia, Sierra Leone, Singapore, Slovenia, South Africa, Spain, Sri Lanka, Sudan, Sweden, Switzerland, Thailand, Trinidad-Tobago, Türkiye, UK, Uruguay, USA. [2022.05.19/XD2707/v/**D**]

♦ Phyto-sanitary Convention for Africa (1967 treaty)
♦ Phyto-sanitary Convention for Africa South of the Sahara (1954 treaty)
♦ **PhytoTrade Africa** Southern African Natural Products Trade Association (#19852)
♦ PI / see Sail For Ethics
♦ PIACC – Pacific Islands Association of Chambers of Commerce (inactive)
♦ **PIAC** Permanent International Altaistic Conference (#18324)
♦ **PIAC** Pontificio Istituto di Archeologia Cristiana (#18449)
♦ **PIA** Fédération des peuples d'ici et d'ailleurs (#18298)
♦ **PIALA** Pacific Islands Association of Libraries, Archives, and Museums (#17960)

♦ PIANC 18371

SG Bât Graaf de Ferraris – 8th floor, Bd du Roi Albert II 20, Box 3, 1000 Brussels, Belgium. T. +3225537161. E-mail: secretary.general@pianc.org – info@pianc.org.
Pres address not obtained. E-mail: president@pianc.org.
URL: https://www.pianc.org/

History 1894, The Hague (Netherlands). Founded following amalgamation of *Inland Navigation Congresses (inactive)*, set up 1885, Brussels (Belgium), and *Ocean Navigation Congresses (inactive)*, formed 1889. Former names and other names: *Permanent International Association of Navigation Congresses* – former; *Association internationale permanente des congrès de navigation* – former; *Asociación Internacional Permanente de los Congresos de Navegación* – former; *International Ständiger Verband für Schiffahrtkongresse* – former; *International Navigation Association (PIANC)* – former; *Association internationale de navigation (AIPCN)* – former; *Asociación Internacional de Navegación* – former; *Internationaler Verband für Schiffahrt* – former; *PIANC – Navigation, Ports, Waterways* – former; *PIANC – Navigation, ports, voies navigables* – former; *PIANC – The World Association for Waterborne Transport Infrastructure* – full title; *PIANC – Association mondiale pour des infrastructures de transport maritime et fluviales* – full title. Registration: Banque-Carrefour des Entreprises, No/ID: 0408.287.945, Start date: 23 Mar 1923, Belgium; EU Transparency Register, No/ID: 399880022485-82, Start date: 28 Jun 2016. **Aims** Promote maintenance and operation of inland and maritime *navigation* by fostering progress in the planning, design, construction, improvement, maintenance and operation of inland and maritime *waterways* and *ports* and of coastal areas, for general use in industrialized and industrializing countries, including fisheries and sport and pleasure navigation; take responsibility for, and play a major role in, development of global waterborne transportation; function as an international forum for analysis and discussion of all aspects of waterborne transport, including policy, management, design, economics, integration with other transport modes, technology, safety and environment; contribute to integrated management of navigable water systems; provide assistance and advice to countries in transition; promote a comprehensive network of international navigation and port professionals and other stakeholders; enhance navigational function of waterways, ports and coastal zones, achieving sustainable development through balancing environmental and economic interests. **Structure** Annual General Assembly (AGA); Council (meets twice a year); Executive Committee (ExCom); Commissions (8); Temporary Study Commissions and Technical Working Groups. **Languages** English, French. **Finance** Sources: members' dues; sale of publications; subsidies. **Activities** Awards/prizes/competitions; events/meetings; research/documentation. **Events** *World Congress* Cape Town (South Africa) 2024, *International Conference on Coastal and Port Engineering in Developing Countries* Manila (Philippines) 2022, *International Smart Rivers Conference* Nanjing (China) 2022, *Australasian Coasts and Ports Conference* Christchurch (New Zealand) 2021, *International Smart Rivers Conference* Nanjing (China) 2021. **Publications** *Sailing Ahead* – newsletter. Yearbook; congress proceedings; technical reports.

Members Qualifying national governments; regional governments of a national state; intergovernmental organizations; river commissions; corporate (societies, companies, harbour and other boards, chambers of commerce, laboratories, libraries); individuals; students. Members in 70 countries and territories (" indicates Qualifying Member):
Algeria, Argentina (*), Australia (*), Austria (*), Belgium (*), Brazil (*), Canada (*), Chile, China (*), Colombia (*), Croatia, Cyprus, Czechia (*), Denmark (*), Dominica, Dominican Rep, Egypt, Faeroe Is, Finland (*), France (*), Germany (*), Greece, Hong Kong, Iceland (*), India (*), Iran Islamic Rep, Ireland, Israel, Italy (*), Japan (*), Korea Rep (*), Lebanon, Luxembourg, Malaysia, Malta, Mauritius, Mexico, Monaco (*), Morocco (*), Namibia, Netherlands (*), New Zealand, Nigeria, Norway (*), Paraguay, Peru (*), Portugal (*), Romania (*), Russia, Saudi Arabia, Senegal, Serbia, Slovakia, Solomon Is, South Africa (*), Spain (*), Sri Lanka, Sweden (*), Switzerland (*), Taiwan, Tanzania UR, Thailand, Trinidad-Tobago, Tunisia, Türkiye, UK (*), United Arab Emirates, Uruguay, USA (*), Venezuela.
Included in the above, one intergovernmental river commission listed in this Yearbook:
Central Commission for the Navigation of the Rhine (CCNR, #03687).
National sections in 24 countries:
Argentina, Australia, Austria, Belgium, Colombia, Denmark, Finland, France, Germany, India, Italy, Japan, Korea Rep, Netherlands, Norway, Poland, Portugal, Serbia, South Africa, Spain, Sweden, Switzerland, UK, USA.

Consultative Status Consultative status granted from: *ECOSOC (#05331)* (Ros A); *UNCTAD (#20285)* (Special Category). **IGO Relations** Observer to: *OSPAR Commission for the Protection of the Marine Environment of the North-East Atlantic (OSPAR Commission, #17905)*. Cooperates with: *Consultative Meeting of Contracting Parties to the London Convention/Meeting of Contracting Parties to the London Protocol (#04769)*. Accredited by: *United Nations Office at Vienna (UNOV, #20604)*. **NGO Relations** Member of (2): *International Water-Related Associations' Liaison Committee (IWALC, #15869)*; *World Water Council (WWC, #21908)*. In liaison with technical committees of: *International Organization for Standardization (ISO, #14473)*. *European Boating Industry (EBI, #06377)* is member of Navigation Task Group on Water Framework Directive and Marine Strategy Directive. [2023/XB3111/y/**B**]

♦ PIANC – Association mondiale pour des infrastructures de transport maritime et fluviales / see PIANC (#18371)
♦ PIANC – Navigation, ports, voies navigables / see PIANC (#18371)
♦ PIANC – Navigation, Ports, Waterways / see PIANC (#18371)
♦ PIANC – The World Association for Waterborne Transport Infrastructure / see PIANC (#18371)
♦ **PIANGO** Pacific Islands Association of Non-Governmental Organizations (#17961)
♦ Pianobygger-Fagforbundenes Europeiske Union (#20391)
♦ **PIANZEA** Pacific Islands, Australia and New Zealand Electoral Administrators Network (#17962)
♦ PIA / see Parlamento Indígena de América (#18202)
♦ **PIA** Parlamento Indígena de América (#18202)
♦ **PIA** Presse internationale des assurances (#13938)
♦ PIA – Private Investors for Africa (unconfirmed)
♦ **PIARC** World Road Association (#21754)
♦ Piaristes – Clercs Réguliers Pauvres de la Mère de Dieu des Ecoles Pies (religious order)
♦ Piarist Fathers – Order of Clerics Regular Poor of the Mother of God of the Pious Schools (religious order)
♦ Pia Sociedade Filhas de São Paulo (religious order)
♦ Pia Sociedad de Hijas de San Pablo (religious order)
♦ Pia Società delle Figlie di Santo Paolo (religious order)
♦ Pia Unione in Suffragio dei Defunti sotto il Patrocinio di S Nicola da Tolentino (religious order)
♦ PIBAC – Permanent International Bureau of Analytical Chemistry of Human and Animal Food (inactive)
♦ PIBA – Pacific Islands Broadcasting Association (inactive)
♦ PIBN – Pacific Islands Business Network (internationally oriented national body)
♦ **PICAN** Pacific Islands Climate Action Network (#17965)
♦ PICA – Permanent International Commission of Agricultural Associations (inactive)
♦ Piccola Compagnia di Maria (religious order)
♦ Piccola Missione per i Sordomuti (religious order)
♦ Piccola Opera della Divina Provvidenza (religious order)
♦ Piccola Opera della Redenzione (religious order)
♦ Piccole Apostoli della Redenzione (religious order)
♦ Piccole Sorelle dei Poveri (religious order)
♦ Piccole Sorelle di San Francesco (religious order)
♦ Piccole Suore degli Anziani Abbandonati (religious order)
♦ Piccole Suore dell'Assunzione (religious order)
♦ Piccole Suore Missionarie della Carità (religious order)
♦ Piccole Suore della Sacra Famiglia (religious order)
♦ Piccoli Fratelli del Buon Pastore (religious order)
♦ Piccoli Fratelli di Gesù (religious order)
♦ Piccoli Fratelli di Maria – Fratelli Maristi delle Scuole (religious order)
♦ PIC – Convention for the Mutual Recognition of Inspections in Respect of the Manufacture of Pharmaceutical Products (1970 treaty)
♦ **PICES** North Pacific Marine Science Organization (#17602)
♦ PICGC / see International Genetics Federation (#13711)
♦ **PICG** Programa Internacional de Ciencias de la Tierra (#13715)
♦ **PICG** Programme international de géoscience (#13715)
♦ **PICHTR** Pacific International Center for High Technology Research (#17955)
♦ **PICISOC** Pacific Islands Chapter (#17963)
♦ Picker Institute Europe (internationally oriented national body)
♦ PICL / see Standing Committee of the Pacific Islands Conference of Leaders (#19957)
♦ P and I Clubs / see International Group of P and I Clubs (#13751)
♦ PICM – Permanent International Committee of Mothers (inactive)
♦ **PIC** Pacific Insurance Conference (#17954)
♦ PICPA – Pacific Islands Centre for Public Administration (unconfirmed)
♦ **PICP** Pacific Islands Chiefs of Police (#17964)
♦ Picpuciens – Congrégation des Sacrés-Coeurs de Jésus et de Marie (religious order)
♦ Picpus – Congregazione dei Sacri Cuori (religious order)
♦ Picpus Sisters (religious order)
♦ **PIC/S** Pharmaceutical Inspection Co-operation Scheme (#18353)
♦ Picture and Sound World Organization (inactive)
♦ **PICUM** Platform for International Cooperation on Undocumented Migrants (#18401)
♦ PIDA / see Foundation of the Peoples of the South Pacific International (#09968)
♦ **PIDB** Pacific Islands Development Bank (#17966)
♦ **PIDC** Pacific Immigration Directors' Conference (#17953)
♦ PIDCP – Pacte international relatif aux droits civils et politiques (1966 treaty)
♦ **PIDC** Programa Internacional para el Desarrollo de la Comunicación (#14651)
♦ **PIDC** Programme international pour le développement de la communication (#14651)
♦ PIDE / see Bangladesh Institute of Development Studies
♦ PIDE – Pakistan Institute of Development Economics (internationally oriented national body)
♦ PIDESC – Pacte international relatif aux droits économiques, sociaux et cultures (1966 treaty)
♦ **PIDF** Pacific Islands Development Forum (#17967)
♦ **PIDHDD** Plataforma Interamericana de Derechos Humanos, Democracia y Desarrollo (#18395)
♦ PIDP – Pacific Islands Development Program (see: #05263)
♦ PIEA – Petroleum Institute of East Africa (unconfirmed)
♦ PIECA / see Asociación de Universidades Privadas de Centroamérica y Panama (#02306)
♦ **PIECR** Permanent International Ecumenical Consultation of Religious (#18326)
♦ PIEE – UNESCO-PNUE Programme international d'éducation relative à l'environnement (inactive)
♦ PiE – Particles in Europe (meeting series)
♦ Pierce Butler Jr, Foundation for Education in World Law / see Fund for Peace
♦ PIERC Education / see Pasifika Education Centre (#18252)

♦ Pierre Fauchard Academy (PFA) 18372

Exec Dir 41 East 400 North, Ste 546, Logan UT 84321-4020, USA. T. +14352139089. Fax +14352139136.
Pres 3900 Frey Road, Suite 100, Kennesaw GA 30144, USA. E-mail: kstoc@aol.com.
URL: http://www.fauchard.org/

History 1936. An international dental honour organization. **Aims** Elevate the character, education and professional ability of dentists by making available to them dental literature representing developments and opinions in *dentistry*. **Structure** Management Committee. Standing Committees (10): Executive; Membership; Budget and Finance; Nominating; Constitution and By-Laws; Publicity; Awards; Past Presidents; International Advisory; Special Projects. Autonomous Sections (7): USA; Asia; Australia; Canada; Europe; Japan; Latin America. **Events** *Meeting* Seoul (Korea Rep) 2019, *Annual Meeting* Seoul (Korea Rep) 2017, *Symposium* Busan (Korea Rep) 2015, *Annual Meeting* Washington, DC (USA) 2015, *Annual Meeting* San Antonio, TX (USA) 2014. **Members** Fellows (about 8,200) in 105 sections worldwide. Membership countries not specified. **NGO Relations** Affiliate member of: *FDI – World Dental Federation (#09281)*. [2015/XM4028/**E**]

♦ Pierre Richet Institute (no recent information)
♦ Pierre Robin Europe (unconfirmed)
♦ **PIESA** Power Institute for East and Southern Africa (#18474)
♦ Pieuse Société des Filles de Saint Paul (religious order)
♦ Pieux Ouvriers Catéchistes Ruraux (religious order)
♦ **PIFON** Pacific Island Farmers Organisation Network (#17957)
♦ PIFS – Program on International Financial Systems (internationally oriented national body)
♦ PIF/TSP – Pacific Islands Forests and Trees Support Programme (inactive)
♦ PI-GOOS / see Pacific Islands GOOS (#17971)
♦ **PI-GOOS** Pacific Islands GOOS (#17971)
♦ **PIHOA** Pacific Island Health Officers Association (#17958)
♦ PIH – Partners in Health (internationally oriented national body)
♦ PIIA – The Pakistan Institute of International Affairs (internationally oriented national body)
♦ PIIA – Polish Institute of International Affairs (internationally oriented national body)
♦ PIIE – Peterson Institute for International Economics, Washington (internationally oriented national body)
♦ P and I / see International Group of P and I Clubs (#13751)
♦ Pii Operai Catechisti Rurali (religious order)
♦ PIIPA – Public Interest Intellectual Property Advisors (internationally oriented national body)
♦ PIIRS – Princeton Institute for International and Regional Studies (internationally oriented national body)
♦ PIK – Potsdam Institute for Climate Impact Research (internationally oriented national body)
♦ Pilgrim Africa (internationally oriented national body)
♦ PILI / see Global Network for Public Interest Law
♦ PILnet – Global Network for Public Interest Law (internationally oriented national body)
♦ PILOM / see Pacific Islands Law Officers' Network (#17972)
♦ **PILON** Pacific Islands Law Officers' Network (#17972)
♦ Pilot Club International / see Pilot International
♦ Piloten zonder Grenzen, België (internationally oriented national body)
♦ Piloten Zonder Grenzen, Nederland (internationally oriented national body)
♦ Pilot International (internationally oriented national body)
♦ Pilotprojekt der Volkswagenstiftung: Kriegsverbrecherprozesse gegen Deutsche und Japaner / see International Research and Documentation Centre for War Crimes Trials
♦ Pilots Without Borders, Netherlands (internationally oriented national body)
♦ PILPG – Public International Law and Policy Group (internationally oriented national body)
♦ **PIMA** Pacific Island Museums Association (#17959)
♦ PIMED – Association pour une information médicale éthique et le développement (inactive)
♦ **PIME** Pontificium Institutum pro Missionibus Exteris (#18450)
♦ PIM Initiative – Petites Iles en Méditerranée Initiative (internationally oriented national body)

♦ PIM Initiative – Small Islands Initiative (internationally oriented national body)
♦ PIM / see International Ocean Institute (#14394)
♦ PIM / see International Partners in Mission (#14526)
♦ **PIMLA** Pacific International Maritime Law Association (#17956)
♦ **PIM** Partnership in International Management (#18238)
♦ **PIMRIS** Pacific Islands Marine Resources Information System (#17973)
♦ **PIMS** Pontificio Istituto di Musica Sacra (#18455)
♦ **PINA** Pacific Islands News Association (#17975)
♦ Pinay Circle / see Le Cercle (#03826)
♦ PINDA – Pacific Islands Nutrition and Dietetic Association (inactive)
♦ Pine Chemicals Association (internationally oriented national body)
♦ **PI-Net** Postgraduates International Network (#18468)
♦ **pinfa** Phosphorus, Inorganic and Nitrogen Flame Retardants Association (#18364)
♦ PIN – People in Need (internationally oriented national body)
♦ PIN / see Skin Inflammation and Psoriasis International Network (#19308)
♦ PIN-SME / see European Digital SME Alliance (#06925)
♦ **PIOB** Public Interest Oversight Board (#18566)
♦ PIOG – Parrainage international des orphelins de guerre (inactive)
♦ Pioneer Bible Translators (internationally oriented national body)
♦ Pioneers International (internationally oriented national body)
♦ Pioneers UK (internationally oriented national body)
♦ PIOSA – Pan Indian Ocean Science Association (inactive)
♦ Pious Congregation of St Joseph (religious order)
♦ Pious Society of the Daughters of St Paul (religious order)
♦ Pious Union of Our Mother of Good Counsel (religious order)
♦ Pious Union of St Nicholas for the Holy Souls (religious order)
♦ **PI** Panathlon International (#18170)
♦ PIPA – Pacific Islands' Producers Association (inactive)
♦ PI – Partnership International (internationally oriented national body)
♦ **PI** Passionists International (#18254)
♦ PIPCA – Pacific Islands Primary Care Association (unconfirmed)
♦ PIPC – Pacific International Politics Conference (meeting series)
♦ Pipeline Research Council International (internationally oriented national body)
♦ PI – People International (internationally oriented national body)
♦ PI – Photo International (inactive)
♦ PIPHRO – Pakistan International Peace and Human Rights Organization (internationally oriented national body)
♦ PI – Population Institute (internationally oriented national body)
♦ **PI** Privacy International (#18504)
♦ **PI** Protection International (#18548)
♦ **PIPSA** Pacific Islands Political Studies Association (#17976)
♦ **PIPSO** Pacific Islands Private Sector Organisation (#17977)

♦ Piracy Reporting Centre, Kuala Lumpur 18373

Contact c/o ICC IMB – Asia Regional Office, PO Box 12559, 50782 Kuala Lumpur, Malaysia. T. +60320785763. Fax +60320785769. E-mail: imbkl@icc-ccs.org – piracy@icc-ccs.org.
URL: http://www.icc-ccs.org/

History 1 Oct 1992. Founded the support of *International Maritime Organization (IMO, #14102)* and *International Mobile Satellite Organization (IMSO, #14174)*, also known as INMARSAT, following a meeting convened by the ICC-IMB. Previously also referred to as *Regional Piracy Centre, Kuala Lumpur (RPC) – IMB Piracy Reporting Centre (IMB PRC)*. Specialized division of *International Chamber of Commerce (ICC, #12534)*. Secretariat at *International Maritime Bureau (IMB, #14097)*. **Aims** Act as a focal point in combating all types of *maritime fraud*, criles, *malpractice* and piracy; prevent piracy through information sharing; provide assistance during and following piracy attacks; cooperate with relevant *law enforcement* agencies and navies. **Finance** Sources: contributions. **Activities** Events/meetings; guidance/assistance/consulting; knowledge management/information dissemination. **Events** *International meeting on piracy and phantom ships* Kuala Lumpur (Malaysia) 2001. **Publications** *Piracy and Armed Robbery Against Ships* (4 a year). Annual Report; special reports; weekly reports; warnings/alerts. **Members** IMB Membership. **IGO Relations** Observer status with (2): *International Criminal Police Organization – INTERPOL (ICPO-INTERPOL, #13110)*; *International Maritime Organization (IMO, #14102)*. Cooperates with (1): *World Customs Organization (WCO, #21350)*. **NGO Relations** Cooperates with international maritime organizations. [2020.11.17/XE0582/**E**]

♦ PIRADE – Pacific Islands Regional Association for Distance Education (no recent information)

♦ Pirate Parties International (PPI) 18374

Contact BST-Avocats, Bd des Tranchées 4, 1205 Geneva, Switzerland. E-mail: board@pp-international.net.
URL: http://pp-international.net/

History 2010, Brussels (Belgium). Registration: Banque-Carrefour des Entreprises, No/ID: 0845.017.775, Start date: 4 Apr 2012, Belgium; Swiss Civil Code, Start date: 2016, Switzerland. **Aims** Establish, support, promote and maintain communication and cooperation between pirate parties around the world. **Structure** General Assembly; Board. **Languages** English. **Staff** 27.00 FTE, voluntary. **Finance** Sources: members' dues. **Activities** Events/meetings. **Events** *General Assembly* 2022, *General Assembly* 2022, *General Assembly* 2021, *General Assembly* 2020, *General Assembly* 2020. **Publications** Documents; reports.
Members Ordinary; Observer; Supporting. Ordinary in 37 countries and territories:
Austria, Belarus, Belgium, Bosnia-Herzegovina, Brazil, Bulgaria, Catalunya, Croatia, Czechia, Estonia, Finland, France, Germany, Greece, Hungary, Israel, Italy, Japan, Kazakhstan, Korea Rep, Latvia, Luxembourg, Morocco, Netherlands, New Zealand, Norway, Poland, Portugal, Romania, Russia, Slovakia, Slovenia, Spain, Switzerland, Tunisia, Türkiye, Ukraine.
Observer in 7 countries:
Austria, France, Germany, Iceland, Spain, Sweden, USA.
Consultative Status Consultative status granted from: *ECOSOC (#05331)* (Special). **IGO Relations** *World Trade Organization (WTO, #21864)*. [2022/XM7255/**C**]

♦ PIRC – Phoenician International Research Center (unconfirmed)
♦ Pirinioetako Ian Elkartea (#21057)
♦ PIRM – Pacific Institute for Resource Management (internationally oriented national body)
♦ PIRM – Pacific Institute of Resource Management, Wellington (internationally oriented national body)
♦ **PIR** Public Interest Registry (#18567)
♦ **PISAI** Pontificio Istituto di Studi Arabi e d'Islamistica (#18448)
♦ **PISC** Programme international sur la sécurité des substances chimiques (#14650)
♦ PISM – Polski Instytut Spraw Miedzynarodowych (internationally oriented national body)
♦ PISUKI – Pacific Islands Society of the United Kingdom and Ireland (internationally oriented national body)
♦ **PITA** Pacific Islands Telecommunications Association (#17979)
♦ PITIC NZ / see Pacific Islands Trade and Invest (#17980)

♦ Pituitary Society (PS) 18375

Contact 8700 Beverly Blvd, Room 2051, Los Angeles CA 90048, USA. T. +13109889486. E-mail: info@pituitarysociety.org.
URL: http://www.pituitarysociety.org/

Aims Advance global education and treatment of pituitary *disease*. **Structure** Board of Directors; Executive Committee. **Activities** Events/meetings; training/education. **Events** *International Pituitary Congress* Los Angeles, CA (USA) 2021, *International Pituitary Congress* New Orleans, LA (USA) 2019, *International Pituitary Congress* Orlando, FL (USA) 2017, *International Pituitary Congress* San Diego, CA (USA) 2015, *International Pituitary Congress* San Francisco, CA (USA) 2013. **Publications** *Pituitary* – journal. [2020/XM5063/**C**]

♦ Pius X Secular Institute 18376

Institut séculier Pie X – Instituto Secular Pio X

Dir-Gen CP 87731, Succ Charlesbourg, Québec QC G1G 5W6, Canada. T. +14186265882. Fax +14186265882. E-mail: info@ispx.org.
URL: http://www.ispx.org/

History Founded 1939, Manchester NH (USA). **Aims** Spread the *Gospel*, especially among poor, working class individuals, and those who are farthest from the *faith*. **Structure** General Assembly (meets every 5 years); General Council. **Languages** English, French, Spanish. **Staff** Elected and voluntary. **Finance** Members' contributions. **Events** *Quadrennial General Assembly* Charlesbourg, QC (Canada) 2005, *Quadrennial General Assembly* Charlesbourg, QC (Canada) 2001, *General Assembly* Charlesbourg, QC (Canada) 1997, *General Assembly* Charlesbourg, QC (Canada) 1995, *General Assembly* Québec, QC (Canada) 1989.
Members Consecrated and Associate in 6 countries:
Canada, Colombia, Guatemala, Spain, USA, Venezuela. [2016.07.24/XE0900/j/**F**]

♦ PIVAC – International Conference on Progress in Vaccination Against Cancer (meeting series)
♦ PIWH – Pacific Institute for Women's Health (internationally oriented national body)
♦ PIXE – International Conference on Particle Induced X-ray Emission (meeting series)
♦ PJA – Pacific Journalists Association (inactive)
♦ **PJC** Pan-American Judo Confederation (#04476)
♦ PJI – PathFinders Justice Initiative (internationally oriented national body)
♦ PJSA – Peace and Justice Studies Association (internationally oriented national body)
♦ **PJTC** Permanent Joint Technical Commission for Nile Waters (#18327)
♦ **PJU** Pan American Judo Union (#18115)
♦ **PKF** Panamerican Karate Federation (#09381)
♦ **PKN** Pohjoiskalotin-neuvosto (#17545)
♦ Placenta Association of the Americas (internationally oriented national body)
♦ PLAC – Programa Latinoamericano del Carbono (see: #05055)

♦ Plain Ink 18377

Head Office Via Giacomo Zanella 54/56, 20133 Milan MI, Italy.
Registered Office Via Eugenio Curiel 63, 20050 Mezzago MB, Italy.

History Registration: Italy. **Aims** Through *storytelling*, help people gain new skills, increase *literacy* levels and engage communities around the world in finding their own solutions. **Structure** Board of 6. [2020/XJ5783/**F**]

♦ Plain Language Association International (PLAIN) 18378

Pres c/o Language Council of Norway, Postboks 1573, Vika, 0118 Oslo, Norway. E-mail: info@plainlanguagenetwork.org.
URL: http://plainlanguagenetwork.org/

History 1993, Canada, as *Plain Language Network*. 2008, incorporated as a nonprofit in accordance with Canadian law. **Aims** Increase public awareness of plain language as a means of making communications from government, business, industry, the professions (including the medical, legal, information management, education and communications professions), and community organizations accessible internally and to a broad, public audience. **Structure** Board of Directors, comprising President, Vice-President, Treasurer, Secretary, Web Manager, Forum Coordinator, Conference Coordinator and 3 members. Executive Committee. **Events** *Biennial Conference* Oslo (Norway) 2019, *Biennial Conference* Graz (Austria) 2017, *Biennial Conference* Dublin (Ireland) 2015, *Biennial Conference* Vancouver, BC (Canada) 2013, *Biennial Conference* Stockholm (Sweden) 2011.
Members Individuals and organizations in 16 countries:
Australia, Canada, Denmark, Estonia, Finland, France, Germany, Malaysia, Mexico, New Zealand, Norway, Portugal, South Africa, Sweden, UK, USA. [2019/XJ8068/**C**]

♦ Plain Language Network / see Plain Language Association International (#18378)
♦ **PLAIN** Plain Language Association International (#18378)
♦ Plan / see Plan International (#18386)
♦ Plan de Acción para la Protección del Medio Marino y Areas Costeras del Pacifico Sudeste (#00095)
♦ Plan d'action pour la Méditerranée / see Mediterranean Action Plan (#16638)

♦ Plan Bleu pour l'environnement et le développement en Méditerranée (Plan Bleu) 18379

Dir Tour la Marseillaise, 2 bis bd Euroméditerranée, Quai d'Arenc, 13002 Marseille, France. T. +33643082023. E-mail: planbleu@planbleu.org.
URL: http://www.planbleu.org/

History 1977. Founded as a regional activity centre of the Mediterranean Action Plan, currently *Mediterranean Action Plan (MAP, #16638)* of *UNEP (#20299)*, to implement the work of MAP's *Blue Plan (BP)*. Former names and other names: *Plan Bleu Regional Activity Centre (PB/RAC)* – alias; *Blue Plan – Regional Activity Centre for the Mediterranean (BP/RAC)* – former; *Plan bleu pour la Méditerranée – Centre d'activités régionales (CAR/PB)* – former. Registration: Start date: 12 Apr 1985, France. **Aims** Develop regional cooperation so as to set up and make available a fund of knowledge intended to facilitate the implementation of sustained environmentally-friendly development; produce prospective analyses of the environment and development; act as a Mediterranean observatory for sustainable development. **Structure** General Assembly; Bureau. Set up and maintains *Mediterranean Environment and Development Observatory (MEDO)*. **Finance** Funding by 21 riparian states and *European Commission (EC, #06633)*. Annual budget: 2,800,000 EUR. **Activities** Knowledge management/information dissemination; research/documentation. **Events** *Atelier International sur la Mise en Oeuvre de Solutions Fondées sur la Nature pour Lutter contre le Changement Climatique* Marseille (France) 2019, *Mediterranean Forest Week* Agadir (Morocco) 2017, *SESAME : Séminaire International sur l'Eau et la Sécurité Alimentaire en Méditerranée* Montpellier (France) 2013, *Mediterranean forest week* Avignon (France) 2011, *Mediterranean forest week* Istanbul (Turkey) 2010. **Publications** *Blue Plan Paper* – series; *Blue Plans Notes* – series. *State of the Environment Report*. Technical Reports; papers; books. **IGO Relations** Participates in the work of: *United Nations Economic Commission for Europe (UNECE, #20555)*. **NGO Relations** Member of (5): *European Forest Institute Mediterranean Facility (EFIMED, #07298)*; *Global Water Partnership (GWP, #10653)* (Mediterranean Technical Advisory Committee (MEDTAC)); *Green Industry Platform (GIP, #10722)*; *International Office for Water (IOW, #14399)* (Associate); *World Water Council (WWC, #21908)*. Partner of (1): *Institut de Prospective économique du Monde Méditerranéen (IPEMED, #11352)*. [2022.11.30/XK1605/**E***]

♦ Plan bleu pour la Méditerranée – Centre d'activités régionales / see Plan Bleu pour l'environnement et le développement en Méditerranée (#18379)
♦ **Plan Bleu** Plan Bleu pour l'environnement et le développement en Méditerranée (#18379)
♦ Plan Bleu Regional Activity Centre / see Plan Bleu pour l'environnement et le développement en Méditerranée (#18379)
♦ Plan Børnefonden (internationally oriented national body)
♦ Plan de Colombo pour la coopération économique et sociale en Asie et dans le Pacifique (#04120)
♦ Plan de Escuelas Asociadas en la Educación para la Cooperación Internacional y la Paz / see UNESCO Associated Schools Project Network (#20302)
♦ Plan de Escuelas Asociadas de la UNESCO / see UNESCO Associated Schools Project Network (#20302)
♦ Plan de Escuelas Asociadas de la UNESCO para el Fomento de la Educación por la Paz, los Derechos Humanos, la Democracia y la Comprensión Internacional / see UNESCO Associated Schools Project Network (#20302)
♦ Planet Aid (internationally oriented national body)
♦ Planetarische Vereinigung für Saubere Energie (#18381)

♦ Planet Art Network (PAN) 18380

Red de Arte Planetaria (RAP)

Contact c/o Foundation for the Law of Time, Box 156, Ashland OR 97520, USA. T. +15414880714. Fax +15414880714. E-mail: info@lawoftime.org.
URL: http://www.lawoftime.org/

Aims Promote the Thirteen Moon 28-day calendar and the law of time, including the biosphere-noosphere transition and Universal Peace through Culture, and a new 13:20 revolution based on love, art and synchronicity. **Finance** Autonomous world movement. **Activities** Celebrates the annual 'Day Out of Time – Planetary Peace through Culture Festival', every 25 July; distributes educational materials (many available online). Some nodes also host ongoing educational seminars, classes and art projects, and create sustainable peace gardens. **Publications** *Cosmic History Chronicles*.
Members Nodes and study groups in 46 countries:
Argentina, Australia, Austria, Belgium, Brazil, Bulgaria, Canada, Chile, Colombia, Costa Rica, Croatia, Cuba, Czechia, Dominican Rep, Ecuador, Finland, France, Germany, Greece, Guatemala, Hungary, Ireland, Israel, Italy, Japan, Kenya, Mexico, Netherlands, New Zealand, Norway, Paraguay, Peru, Philippines, Poland, Portugal, Russia, Senegal, Serbia, South Africa, Spain, Sweden, Switzerland, UK, Uruguay, USA, Venezuela. [2013.08.12/XN4001/F]

♦ Planetary Activation Organization (internationally oriented national body)

♦ Planetary Association for Clean Energy (PACE) 18381

Société planétaire pour l'assainissement de l'énergie – Planetarische Vereinigung für Saubere Energie

Pres 100 Bronson Avenue, Ste 1001, Ottawa ON K1R 6G8, Canada. T. +16132366265. Fax +16132355876. E-mail: paceincnet@gmail.com.
URL: http://pacenet.homestead.com/

History Jun 1975, Ottawa, ON (Canada). Founded under the guidance of the Hon Senator Chesley W Carter, then Chairperson of the Senate's Standing Committee on Health, Welfare and Science as well as member of the Senate Special Committee on Science Policy. Registration: Start date: 1979, Canada. **Aims** Facilitate discovery, research, development, demonstration and evaluation of clean energy. **Structure** Informal international network of researchers, whether specialist or multidisciplinary. 'Stewardship of clean energy technology humanitarian strategies with UN and NGOs'. **Languages** English, French, Spanish. **Staff** 10.00 FTE, voluntary. **Finance** Sources: donations; fees for services; members' dues; sale of publications. Annual budget: 50,000 CAD (2020). **Activities** Guidance/assistance/consulting; research and development; standards/guidelines. **Events** *International symposium on new energy* Denver, CO (USA) 1996, *International symposium on new energy* Denver, CO (USA) 1994, *International symposium on non-conventional energy technologies* Hull, ON (Canada) 1987. **Publications** *Planetary Association for Clean Energy Newsletter* (irregular). Books; presentations; electronic documentation; archival materials. **Information Services** *Digital Archive Project* – Special research library..
Members Individual; Corporate; Community. Members in 58 countries and territories:
Argentina, Australia, Austria, Belgium, Brazil, Cameroon, Canada, Chile, China, Colombia, Congo DR, Costa Rica, Côte d'Ivoire, Czechia, Denmark, Finland, France, Germany, Greece, Hong Kong, Hungary, India, Ireland, Israel, Italy, Japan, Korea Rep, Liberia, Madagascar, Malaysia, Mexico, Namibia, Netherlands, New Zealand, Nigeria, Norway, Pakistan, Philippines, Poland, Portugal, Romania, Russia, Serbia, Singapore, Slovakia, Slovenia, South Africa, Spain, Sweden, Switzerland, Taiwan, Togo, Tunisia, Türkiye, UK, Uruguay, USA, Venezuela.
Consultative Status Consultative status granted from: *ECOSOC (#05331)* (Special). **IGO Relations** Associated with Department of Global Communications of the United Nations. **NGO Relations** Member of (2): *NGO Alliance on Global Concerns and Values (NGO Alliance, #17102)*; *NGO Forum on Environment (FOE, #17125)*. [2022/XE3992/F]

♦ Planetary Collegium 18382

Pres Fac of Technology, School of Art and Media, Univ of Plymouth, Portland Square, Plymouth, PL4 8AA, UK. T. +441752600600.
URL: http://www.z-node.net/

History 1 May 2003, Plymouth (UK). 1 May 2003, PLymouth (UK), building on the work of Centre of Advanced Inquiry in the Interactive Arts (CAiiA). **Aims** Produce new knowledge in the context of the arts, with special reference to *technoetic* research and to advances in science and technology. **Structure** Board, including Chair. **Events** *Annual International Research Conference* Lisbon (Portugal) 2011, *Annual International Research Conference* Trondheim (Norway) 2010, *Conference* Munich (Germany) 2009, *Reviewing the future – vision, innovation, emergence* Montréal, QC (Canada) 2007, *International research conference* Plymouth (UK) 2006. **Members** Honorary; Academic. [2015/XM2321/F]

♦ Planetary Health Alliance (PHA) 18383

Dir 665 Huntington Ave, Bldg 1 Rm 1312, Boston MA 02115, USA. T. +16179982626. E-mail: pha@harvard.edu.
URL: https://www.planetaryhealthalliance.org/

History 2016. Founded with the support of *The Rockefeller Foundation (#18966)*. **Aims** Understand and address global environmental change and its health impacts. **Structure** Steering Committee; Secretariat. **Activities** Events/meetings; projects/programmes. **Events** *Planetary Health Annual Meeting* Boston, MA (USA) 2022, *Annual Meeting* Sao Paulo (Brazil) 2021, *Annual Meeting* Stanford, CA (USA) 2019.
Members Academic institutions in 19 countries and territories:
Australia, Azerbaijan, Brazil, Canada, Cyprus, Denmark, Ghana, Hong Kong, Israel, Italy, Japan, Kenya, Korea Rep, Norway, Spain, Thailand, Uganda, UK, USA.
Included in the above, 2 organizations listed in this Yearbook:
United Nations University (UNU, #20642); *University of the West Indies (UWI, #20705)*.
NGOs include 12 organizations listed in this Yearbook:
Caribbean College of Family Physicians (CCFP, #03474); *Child Family Health International (CFHI)*; *Consortium of Universities for Global Health (CUGH)*; *EcoHealth Alliance*; *Global Health Group International (GHGI)*; *Health Care Without Harm (HCWH, #10875)*; *International Federation of Medical Students' Associations (IFMSA, #13478)*; *Mediterranean Society of Lifestyle Medicine (MSLM)*; *Pathfinder International (#18261)*; *United Nations Foundation (UNF, #20563)*; *World Federation of Public Health Associations (WFPHA, #21476)*; *World Obesity (#21678)*.
Research institutions include 5 organizations listed in this Yearbook:
African Population and Health Research Center (APHRC, #00420); *Bioversity International (#03262)*; *Center for International Forestry Research (CIFOR, #03646)*; *ICDDR,B (#11051)*; *Pasteur Institute*. [2022/XM8982/y/D]

♦ Planetary Movement Limited (internationally oriented national body)
♦ Planetary Security Initiative (internationally oriented national body)
♦ Planetary Society (internationally oriented national body)
♦ The Planet Earth Institute / see Earth Science Matters Foundation (#05169)
♦ Planète Enfants & Développement (internationally oriented national body)

♦ PLANET'ERE 18384

General Secretariat c/o AQPERE, Collège de Rosemont, 6400 16 Avenue, Montréal QC H1X 259 QC, Canada. T. +15143761065. Fax +15143761905. E-mail: infoplanetere@crosemont.qc.ca.
URL: http://www.planetere.org/

History Founded 24 Nov 2001, on an informal basis. Founding Assembly, 15 Apr 2005, Paris (France). Full title: *PLANET'ERE – Réseau francophone des acteurs de l'éducation à l'environnement*. Also written as: *Planèt'ERE*. **Aims** Encourage development and promotion of education on environmental issues. **Structure** General Assembly. Administrative Council of 26 members. Executive Board, comprising President, Secretary-General, Treasurer and Communications Officer. Thematic Commissions (5): Financing; Youth; Research; Statutes; Partnerships. **Languages** French. **Activities** Events/meetings. **Events** *International Conference* Montréal, QC (Canada) 2020, *International Conference* Montréal, QC (Canada) 2020, *Forum* Montréal, QC (Canada) 2017, *Forum* Marrakech (Morocco) 2013, *Forum* Yaoundé (Cameroon) 2010. **Publications** Online bulletin. [2020/XJ0584/C]

♦ PLANET'ERE – Réseau francophone des acteurs de l'éducation à l'environnement / see PLANET'ERE (#18384)
♦ Planète urgence (internationally oriented national body)
♦ PlaNet Finance / see Positive Planet International (#18465)

♦ Planetree International 18385

Office Coordinator address not obtained.
URL: https://planetree.org/

History 1978. **Aims** Empower staff with opportunities and responsibilities to personalize care and services – promoting continuity, consistency, accountability, and partnership with each patient and their loved ones. **Structure** Board of Directors. Offices (6). **Activities** Certification/accreditation; events/meetings; guidance/assistance/consulting. **Events** *International Conference on Person-Centered Care* Baltimore, MD (USA) 2022. **Publications** *The Putting Patients First Field Guide*. **NGO Relations** Member of (1): *International Society for Quality in Health Care (ISQua, #15405)*. [2022/AA2865/C]

♦ Planet Savers / see Defensores do Planeta
♦ Planet Society (see: #20322)
♦ **PlaNet** Student Planning Network (#20015)
♦ Planet Water (unconfirmed)
♦ Planetwork (internationally oriented national body)
♦ Planetworkshops (meeting series)

♦ Plan International 18386

Headquarters Dukes Court, Block A, Duke Street, Woking, GU21 5BH, UK. T. +441483755155. Fax +441483756505.
EU Office Galerie Ravenstein 27/4, 1000 Brussels, Belgium.
Registered Address 228 East 45th St, 15th Fl, New York NY 10017, USA.
URL: http://www.plan-international.org/

History 1937. Founded by British journalist John Langdon-Davies and refugee worker Eric Muggeridge. Former names and other names: *Foster Parents Plan International* – former; *Plan de parrainage international* – former; *PLAN International* – former; *Plan* – former; *Childreach* – former. Registration: EU Transparency Register, No/ID: 83357751766-93, Start date: 27 May 2009. **Aims** Advocate for, promote and value child rights; create opportunities for meaningful child participation. **Structure** International Board of Directors; International Headquarters; Regional Offices; country offices; national organizations. **Languages** English, French, Spanish. **Staff** 7500.00 FTE, paid; 60000.00 FTE, voluntary. **Finance** Child sponsorship; grants; project sponsorship; appeals; bequests; gifts sales; investment income. **Activities** Advocacy/lobbying/activism. **Events** *Asia Pacific Youth Symposium* Incheon (Korea Rep) 2020, *Global Girls Summit* Brussels (Belgium) 2018, *Global Girls'Summit* Paris (France) 2017, *Meeting on Promoting Child Rights to end Child Poverty* Brussels (Belgium) 2014, *Global youth enterprise conference* Washington, DC (USA) 2009. **Publications** Annual report; information/press packs.
Members National organizations in 17 countries:
Australia, Belgium, Canada, Denmark, Finland, France, Germany, Ireland, Japan, Korea Rep, Netherlands, Norway, Spain, Sweden, Switzerland, UK, USA.
Programmes/Programme Offices in 48 countries:
Albania, Bangladesh, Benin, Bolivia, Brazil, Burkina Faso, Cambodia, Cameroon, China, Colombia, Dominican Rep, Ecuador, Egypt, El Salvador, Ethiopia, Ghana, Guatemala, Guinea, Guinea-Bissau, Haiti, Honduras, India, Indonesia, Kenya, Laos, Liberia, Malawi, Mali, Mozambique, Nepal, Nicaragua, Niger, Pakistan, Paraguay, Peru, Philippines, Senegal, Sierra Leone, Sri Lanka, Sudan, Tanzania UR, Thailand, Timor-Leste, Togo, Uganda, Vietnam, Zambia, Zimbabwe.
Consultative Status Consultative status granted from: *ECOSOC (#05331)* (General); *UNICEF (#20332)*; *African Committee of Experts on the Rights and Welfare of the Child (ACERWC, #00257)* (Observer Status); *UNESCO (#20322)* (Consultative Status). **IGO Relations** Accredited by: *United Nations Office at Vienna (UNOV, #20604)*. Global partner of: *United Nations Girls' Education Initiative (UNGEI, #20566)*. *United Nations Volunteers (UNV, #20650)*. Collaborates with: *ICDDR,B (#11051)*. Associated with Department of Global Communications of the United Nations.
NGO Relations Full member of: *British Overseas NGO's for Development (BOND)*. Belgian Section member of: *Fédération francophone et germanophone des associations de coopération au développement (ACODEV, #09587)*. Member of the Advisory Committee of: *Making Cents International*. Member of:
- *Accountable Now (#00060)*;
- *Alliance for Child Protection in Humanitarian Action (The Alliance, #00667)*;
- *Child Rights Connect (#03884)*;
- *Child Rights International Network (CRIN, #03885)*;
- *CHS Alliance (#03911)*;
- *Communicating with Disaster Affected Communities Network (CDAC Network, #04379)*;
- *Confédération européenne des ong d'urgence et de développement (CONCORD, #04547)*;
- *Consortium for Street Children (CSC)*;
- *Cooperation Committee for Cambodia (CCC)*;
- *CORE Group*;
- *Council for Education in the Commonwealth (CEC)*;
- *Early Childhood Development Action Network (ECDAN, #05155)*;
- *Emergency Telecommunications Cluster (ETC, #05438)*;
- *End Water Poverty (EWP, #05464)*;
- *Girls not Brides (#10154)*;
- *Gavi – The Vaccine Alliance (Gavi, #10077)* CSO Constituency;
- *Global Campaign for Education (GCE, #10264)*;
- *Global Education Cluster (#10333)*;
- *Global Impact*;
- *End Corporal Punishment (#05457)*;
- *Global Partnership for Sustainable Development Data (Data4SDGS, #10542)*;
- *Global WASH Cluster (GWC, #10651)*;
- *Human Rights and Democracy Network (HRDN, #10980)*;
- *Inter-agency Network for Education in Emergencies (INEE, #11387)*;
- *International Coalition for the Optional Protocol to the Convention on the Rights of the Child on a Communications Procedure (Ratify OP3CRC, #12617)*;
- *International Council of Voluntary Agencies (ICVA, #13092)*;
- *International Disability and Development Consortium (IDDC, #13177)*;
- *Keeping Children Safe*;
- *Movimiento Mundial por la Infancia de Latinoamérica y El Caribe (MMI-LAC, #16873)*;
- *National Council for Voluntary Organizations (NCVO)*;
- *NetHope (#16979)*;
- *NGO Forum on Cambodia (#17124)*;
- *NGO Working Group for Women, Peace and Security (NGOWG, #17129)*;
- *PMNCH (#18410)*;
- *Saskatchewan Council for International Cooperation (SCIC)*;
- *Start Network (#19969)*;
- *Sustainable Sanitation Alliance (SuSanA, #20066)*;
- *Think Global – Development Education Association (DEA)*;
- *Transparency, Accountability and Participation Network (TAP Network, #20222)*;
- *Verband Entwicklungspolitik und Humanitäre Hilfe e.V. (VENRO)*.

Participates in: *Global Partnership on Children with Disabilities (GPcwd, #10529)*. Supporting organization of: *Scaling Up Nutrition Movement (SUN Movement, #19064)*. Stakeholder in: *Child and Youth Finance International (CYFI, inactive)*. Shareholder in: *International Civil Society Centre (#12589)*. On the Board of Directors of: *NGO Committee on UNICEF (#17120)*, working with the NGO Nutrition Working Group and NGO Working Group on the Rights of Children; *The Sphere Project (#19918)*. Signatory to INGO Accountability Charter. Supports: *Africare (#00516)*; *Asia-Pacific Regional Network for Early Childhood (ARNEC, #02009)*; *Campaña Latinoamericana por el Derecho a la Educación (CLADE, #03407)*; *End Child Prostitution, Child Pornography and Trafficking of Children for Sexual Purposes (ECPAT, #05456)*; *Global Call for Action Against Poverty (GCAP, #10263)*; *International Development Enterprises (IDE, #13156)*; *International Crops Research Institute for the Semi-Arid Tropics (ICRISAT, #13116)*; *Media for Development International (MFDI)*; *World Young Women's Christian Association (World YWCA, #21947)*. Partner of: *Action for Global Health (AfGH, #00090)*; *Adventist Development and Relief Agency International (ADRA, #00131)*; *Global Call for Climate Action (GCCA, inactive)*; *Helen Keller International (HKI, #10902)*; *Movement of Spiritual Inner Awareness (MSIA)*. Netherlands national office instrumental in setting up: *African Child Policy Forum (ACPF, #00246)*. [2017/XF0138/F]

♦ Plan Nagua (internationally oriented national body)

♦ PLANNORD Network (PLANNORD) 18387

Contact address not obtained.
URL: https://www.en.plan.aau.dk/networks/plannord

History An open platform. **Aims** Act as a forum for networking and exchange of knowledge concerning spatial planning. **Activities** Events/meetings; training/education. **Events** *Biennial Nordic Planning Research Symposium* Aalborg (Denmark) 2022, *Biennial Nordic Planning Research Symposium* Drøbak (Norway) 2019, *Biennial Nordic Planning Research Symposium* Finland 2017, *Biennial Nordic Planning Research Symposium* Stockholm (Sweden) 2015.
Members Research institutions and planning authorities and companies. Members in 5 countries:
Denmark, Finland, Iceland, Norway, Sweden. [2019/AA0677/**F**]

♦ **PLANNORD** PLANNORD Network (#18387)
♦ Plan de parrainage international / see Plan International (#18386)

♦ Planta Europa 18388

Chair ArtDatabanken SLU, Swedish Species Information Centre, Bäcklösavägen 10, PO Box 7007, SE-750 07 Uppsala, Sweden. T. +4618673414.
Dir Planta Europa Foundation, Laan van Meerdervoort 1030, 2564 AW The Hague, Netherlands. T. +3163748672.
URL: https://www.plantaeuropa.com/

History Proposal made, 1993, by Plantlife to Bern Convention Plant Expert Meeting for conference to discuss pan-European collaboration for plant conservation. Ministry of Environment (France) hosted first Planta Europa conference in 1995, Hyères (France). In 1996, draft constitution of Planta Europa agreed. Formerly the European programme for *Plantlife International* (2000-2009). Original title: *International Network of Administrations and Research Organisms Involved in the Plant Conservation in Europe (Planta Europa).* Registered in accordance with Dutch law. **Aims** Protect and conserve wild plants and *fungi* and their habitats in Europe. **Structure** Steering Committee; Secretariat hosted by ArtDataBanken, Uppsala (Sweden). **Finance** Members' dues. **Events** *Planta-Europa : European Conference on the Conservation of Wild Plants* Paris (France) 2020, *Planta-Europa : European Conference on the Conservation of Wild Plants* Kiev (Ukraine) 2017, *Planta-Europa : European Conference on the Conservation of Wild Plants* Kolymbari (Greece) 2014, *Planta-Europa : European conference on the conservation of wild plants / Conference* Krakow (Poland) 2011, *Planta-Europa : European conference on the conservation of wild plants / Conference* Cluj-Napoca (Romania) 2007. **Publications** *Declaration of Crete* (2014); *Declaration of Krakow* (2011); *Important Plant Areas in Central and Eastern Europe: Priority Sites for Plant Conservation* (2005); *Mid-Term Review* (2005); *Planta Europa Critical Targets 2005-2007* (2005); *European Strategy for Plant Conservation* (2002); *The European Strategy for Plant Conservation 2008-2014.*
Members National organizations and private persons (86) in 37 countries (not specified). Affiliated members International Organizations (2):
Affiliated members International Organizations (2):
European Committee of Conservation of Bryophytes (ECCB); *European Council for the Conservation of Fungi (ECCF, #06811).* [2014.11.04/XF5929/y/**F**]

♦ Plantain and Banana Research and Development Network for Latin America and the Caribbean 18389

Red Latinoamericana y del Caribe para la Investigación y el Desarrollo de las Musaceas (MUSALAC)
Contact Bioversity Intl, c/o CATIE, Cartago, Turrialba, Turrialba, 7170, Costa Rica. T. +5065562431. Fax +5065562431. E-mail: bioversity-costarica@cgiar.org.
URL: http://banana-networks.org/musalac/

History 1987, as INIBAP *Latin America and the Caribbean Network (LACNET).* 6 Jun 2000, Cartagena de Indias (Colombia), relaunched with current title. Coordinated by *Bioversity International (#03262).* **Events** *Congress* Corupá (Brazil) 2015, *Congress* Armenia (Colombia) 2013, *Congress* Piura (Peru) 2011, *Congreso internacional sobre manejo de la Sigatoka negra en banano y platano* San José (Costa Rica) 2005. **Publications** *Boletin MUSALAC.*
Members National organizations in 16 countries:
Argentina, Bolivia, Brazil, Colombia, Costa Rica, Cuba, Dominican Rep, Ecuador, Guatemala, Honduras, Mexico, Nicaragua, Panama, Peru, Puerto Rico, Venezuela.
Regional organization:
Centre de coopération internationale en recherche agronomique pour le développement (CIRAD, #03733). [2018/XM0131/y/**F**]

♦ Plantation Workers' International Federation (inactive)
♦ Plant Biologicals Network (internationally oriented national body)
♦ **Plant ETP** European Technology Platform 'Plants for the Future' (#08890)
♦ Plantlife International (internationally oriented national body)
♦ Plant Phenolics Group / see Phytochemical Society of Europe (#18370)

♦ Plant-for-the-Planet Foundation 18390

Contact Am Bahnhof 1, 82449 Uffing am Staffelsee, Germany. T. +4988089345. Fax +4988089346. E-mail: info@plant-for-the-planet.org.
URL: http://www.plant-for-the-planet.org/

History 31 Jan 2010. Initiative set up in Germany, 2007. Former names and other names: *Trees for Climate Justice* – alias. **Aims** Fight the climate crisis by planting trees around the world. **Structure** Bureau. **Languages** English, German, Portuguese, Spanish. **Activities** Awareness raising; capacity building; events/meetings; projects/programmes; training/education. **Publications** *Wunderpflanze gegen Klimakrise entdeckt: Der Baum!: Warum wir für unser Überleben pflanzen müssen!* (1st ed 2019) by Felix Finkbeiner in German; *Everything Would Be Alright*; *Tree by Tree.* **IGO Relations** Accredited by (2): *United Nations Convention to Combat Desertification (UNCCD, 1994)*; *United Nations Framework Convention on Climate Change (UNFCCC, 1992). UNEP (#20299).* **NGO Relations** Member of (2): AFR 100; *Community Action in Europe Network (CAN, inactive).* Member of: *Global Call for Climate Action (GCCA, inactive)*; Klima-Allianz. [2020.07.01/XJ5606/f/**F**]

♦ Plant Protection Agreement for the Asia and Pacific Region (1956 treaty)
♦ Plant Protection Committee for the South-East Asia and Pacific Region / see Asia and Pacific Plant Protection Commission (#01997)
♦ Plant With Purpose (internationally oriented national body)
♦ Plant Research International (internationally oriented national body)

♦ Plant Resources of South-East Asia (PROSEA Association) 18391

Director Jalan Ir H Juanda 18, Bogor 16122, Indonesia. T. +622518322859. Fax +622518370934. E-mail: info@proseanet.org.
URL: http://www.proseanet.org/

History 1990, Bogor (Indonesia), as a foundation in accordance with Indonesian law. Originally an initiative started when Wageningen Agricultural University (Netherlands) conducted a feasibility study for establishing an international network (1985-1986); followed by Preparatory Phase (1987-1990). having been operational as a project since 1985. Functioning based on a set of agreements between PROSEA Foundation and 5 participating institutions in Europe and Southeast Asia. Restructured as an association, 20 Jun 2007, Jakarta (Indonesia). Also referred to as *Association of Plant Resources in South East Asia.* **Aims** Promote the sustainable use of plant resources in the South East Asia region; document and make available the existing information on plant resources in South-East Asia for education, extension work, research and industry as well as for end users. **Structure** Board of Trustees, comprising Chairman, Vice-Chairman and 5 members. Management, consisting of Director, Secretary and Treasurer. Supervisors (2). **Languages** English. **Staff** 1.50 FTE, paid; 10.00 FTE, voluntary. **Finance** Principal financial support derived from voluntary contributions and fellowships provided by governments, institutions and individuals, based on regular estimates of budgetary requirements. **Activities** Establishment and operation of databases; research activity, to make existing knowledge accessible, to disseminate it and to facilitate its use in agriculture, horticulture, forestry, botany, industry and other disciplines; publishing activity; sponsorship, support and organization of conferences, workshops, seminars and other meetings; plant conservation campaign; compilation of encyclopaedia of Indonesian mango tree. **Events** *Seminar on medicinal, aromatic and cosmetic plants* Bogor (Indonesia) 2004, *International Workshop* Wageningen (Netherlands) 2003, *International workshop* Bogor (Indonesia) 1999, *International Workshop* Bogor (Indonesia) 1994, *International Workshop* Jakarta (Indonesia) 1989. **Publications** *PROSEA Newsletter. Plant Resources of Southeast Asia* – series. *Multi Volume Handbook on Discrete Commodities* – 19 vols to date. Encyclopedia. Monographs; bibliographies; reports; manuals; CD-ROMs. **Information Services** *PROSEA Databank* – containing 7 databases: BASELIST, CATALOG, PREPHASE, ORGANYM, PERSONYM, TEXTFILE, PHOTFILE.
Members Offices (" indicates Liaison Office) in 6 countries:
Indonesia, Malaysia, Netherlands (*), Philippines, Thailand, Vietnam.
IGO Relations Participating institutions: *CABI (#03393)*; *International Tropical Timber Organization (ITTO, #15737)*; *UNDP (#20292).* **NGO Relations** Participating institutions: *Center for International Forestry Research (CIFOR, #03646)*; *World Agroforestry Centre (ICRAF, #21072).* Supports: national foundations. [2012.06.01/XF1187/**D**]

♦ **PLA** Private Libraries Association (#18505)
♦ **PlasEnSys** European Plastic Energy Storage Systems Association (#08212)
♦ PlasFuelSys / see European Plastic Energy Storage Systems Association (#08212)

♦ Plasma Protein Therapeutics Association (PPTA) 18392

Pres/CEO c/o Headquarters, 147 Old Solomons Island Rd, Ste 100, Annapolis MD 21401, USA. T. +12027893100. Fax +14102632298.
Dir Europe c/o Bd Brand Whitlock 114 – Box 4, 1200 Brussels, Belgium. T. +3227055811. Fax +3227055820.
URL: http://www.pptaglobal.org/

History 1992. European division set up, Jan 1994, Brussels (Belgium), with title *European Association of the Plasma Products Industry (EAPPI).* Current title adopted when EAPPI and IPPIA merged, 2000. Merged with American Blood Resources Association (ABRA), 2002. Former names and other names: *International Plasma Products Industry Association (IPPIA)* – former. **Aims** Promote the availability of and access to safe and effective plasma protein therapeutics for all patients in the world. **Structure** Boards of Directors (4): Global; Europe; North America; Source. **Languages** English, French. **Staff** 30.00 FTE, paid. **Finance** Members' dues. **Activities** Advocacy/lobbying/activism; events/meetings; politics/policy/regulatory; standards/guidelines. **Events** *Global Plasma Summit* Annapolis, MD (USA) 2020, *Congress* Berlin (Germany) 2020, *Congress* Amsterdam (Netherlands) 2019, *Congress* Budapest (Hungary) 2018, *Congress* Prague (Czechia) 2017. **Publications** *The Source* (4 a year). **Members** produce about 80% of the plasma protein therapies used in the USA and more than 60% worldwide. Membership countries not specified. **NGO Relations** Member of (1): *EU Health Coalition.* [2021/XD4930/**D**]

♦ PLASTEUROFILM – European Federation of Plastic Films Producers (inactive)
♦ PLASTEUROPAC – European Association of Plastic Packaging Manufacturers (inactive)
♦ Plastic Change (internationally oriented national body)
♦ Plasticity Forum (meeting series)
♦ Plasticity – Plasticity Forum (meeting series)

♦ Plastic Pipes Conference Association (PPCA) 18393

Vice Chair / Treas 3 Kneeton Park, Middleton, DL10 6SB, UK.
Events – Conference Organizer address not obtained.
URL: http://www.plasticpipesconference.com/

Aims Organize and run the series of Plastic Pipes Conferences on behalf of the international plastics pipes industry. **Structure** Board. **Events** *Plastic Pipes Conference* Lake Buena Vista, FL (USA) 2023, *Plastic Pipes Conference* Amsterdam (Netherlands) 2021, *Plastic Pipes Conference* Amsterdam (Netherlands) 2020, *Plastic Pipes Conference* Las Vegas, NV (USA) 2018, *Plastic Pipes Conference* Berlin (Germany) 2016.
Members Organizations (3):
PE100+ Association (#18273); Plastic Pipe Institute; *The European Plastic Pipes and Fittings Association (TEPPFA, #08215).* [2022/XJ9395/cy/**E**]

♦ Plastic Pollution Coalition (unconfirmed)
♦ **Plastics Europe** Association of Plastics Manufacturers in Europe (#02862)
♦ Plastics Heritage European Association (unconfirmed)
♦ Plastic Soup Foundation (internationally oriented national body)

♦ Plastics Recyclers Europe (PRE) 18394

Pres Avenue de Broqueville 12, 1150 Brussels, Belgium. T. +3223152460. E-mail: info@plasticsrecyclers.eu.
URL: http://www.plasticsrecyclers.eu/

History 1996. Former names and other names: *European Plastics Recyclers (EuPR)* – former; *Association européenne des recycleurs de plastiques* – former. Registration: Banque-Carrefour des Entreprises, No/ID: 0465.304.050, Start date: 10 Jan 1999, Belgium; EU Transparency Register, No/ID: 00162715418-92, Start date: 4 Mar 2011. **Aims** Promote plastics recycling and create conditions that enable profitable and sustainable business; represent and defend the plastics recycling industry vis-à-vis the European institutions; develop and promote the use of harmonized European standards for recycled plastics. **Structure** Management Committee. Working Groups (7). **Activities** Advocacy/lobbying/activism; events/meetings. **Events** *Annual Meeting* 2021, *General Assembly* Brussels (Belgium) 2021, *Annual Meeting* 2020, *Annual Meeting* Brussels (Belgium) 2019, *Annual Meeting* Cascais (Portugal) 2018. **Members** Companies and associated organizations, all together representing 80% of the recycling capacity in Europe. Membership countries not specified. **NGO Relations** Member of (5): *Circular Plastics Alliance (#03936)*; *Industry4Europe (#11181)*; *PET Container Recycling Europe (Petcore Europe, #18339)*; *Reloop Platform (Reloop, #18835)*; *Styrenics Circular Solutions (SCS, #20022).* [2022/XD5945/**D**]

♦ Plataforma Interamericana de Derechos Humanos, Democracia y Desarrollo (PIDHDD) 18395

Regional Coordinator Avda 6 de Diciembre N26-158y Av Orellana, Piso 1 Oficina 1-A, Edificio FAMER, Quito, Ecuador. T. +59322553161. E-mail: coordinacionregionalpidhdd@gmail.com – pidhddecuador@gmail.com.

History Nov 1992, Villa de Leiva (Colombia). Nov 1992, Villa de Leyva (Colombia). **Aims** Promote information, exchange, formation and elaboration of proposals and monitoring of human rights, as well as economic, social and cultural rights on national and international levels; develop a culture and conscience of rights and peace with justice in society, as well as an ample political and social consensus around the integrality of human rights, democracy and development. **Structure** Assembly (every 2 years). Regional Coordination Committee (elected by the Assembly), comprising representatives of National Chapters and of CEEAL. Regional Technical Secretariat and Regional Coordination Committee change seat every 2 years (currently in Brazil, 2002-2005). **Activities** *'Conceptual Production'* – conceptual, methodical and instrumental document production on human rights, democracy and development. *'Public Action'* – campaigns and investigative actions, education, diffusion and mobilization. Instrumental in setting up: *Observatorio Control Interamericano de los Derechos de los Migrantes (OCIM, no recent information).* **Events** *Euro-Latin American and Caribbean civil society forum / European – Latin American – Caribbean Civil Society Forum* Patzcuaro (Mexico) 2004. **Publications** *Los Derechos Humanos Económicos, Sociales y Culturales* – series. *Un Guia para la Acción.* Information bulletins; notebooks.
Members National Chapters in 12 countries:
Argentina, Bolivia, Brazil, Chile, Colombia, Cuba, Ecuador, El Salvador, Haiti, Paraguay, Peru, Venezuela.
One regional member, listed in this Yearbook:
Consejo de Educación de Adultos de América Latina (CEAAL, #04707).
NGO Relations Delegate of International Council of: *World Social Forum (WSF, #21797).* Cooperates with: *Diakonia*; *Ford Foundation (#09858)*; *Humanistisch Instituut voor Ontwikkelingssamenwerking (Hivos)*; *International Network for Economic, Social and Cultural Rights (ESCR-Net, #14255)*; *Oxfam Novib.* Close links with: *ActionAid (#00087)*; *Habitat International Coalition (HIC, #10845)*; *Ibis – Denmark*; *Consejo Latinoamericano de Ciencias Sociales (CLACSO, #04718)*; *Social Watch (#19350).* Supports: *Global Call for Action Against Poverty (GCAP, #10263).* Member of: *Alianza Social Continental (ASC, #00635)*; *ETO Consortium (ETOs, #05560)*; *Right to Food and Nutrition Watch Consortium (#18943)*; *Mesa de Articulación de Asociaciones Nacionales y Redes de ONGs de América Latina y el Caribe (La Mesa de articulación, #16727).* [2015/XJ3097/**F**]

♦ Plataforma Internacional de Bioenergia (#12347)
♦ Plataforma Internacional ONG para la Convención sobre Trabajadores Migratorios (#14367)
♦ Plataforma de las Naciones Unidas de información obtenida desde el espacio para la gestión de desastres y la respuesta de emergencia (#20610)
♦ Plataforma Ruralter (#19004)

- ♦ Plate-forme pour des agricultures durables et solidaires / see Sustainable, Innovative and United Agriculture and Food Network
- ♦ Plateforme euro-med jeunesse (inactive)
- ♦ Plateforme européenne des femmes scientifiques (#08235)
- ♦ Plate-forme européenne des instances de régulation de l'audiovisuel (#08229)
- ♦ Plate-forme européenne des personnes agées / see AGE Platform Europe (#00557)
- ♦ Plateforme internationale sur la bioénergie (#12347)
- ♦ Plateforme internationale contre l'isolation (#14598)
- ♦ Plate-forme internationale des ong sur la Convention pour les travailleurs migrants (#14367)
- ♦ Plateforme internationale sur le sport et le développement (internationally oriented national body)
- ♦ Plate-forme non gouvernementale EuroMed (#05730)
- ♦ Plate-forme des ONG européennes du secteur social / see Social Platform (#19344)
- ♦ Plateforme de Protection des Lanceurs d'Alerte en Afrique (#18402)
- ♦ Plateforme Régionale des Organisations Paysannes d'Afrique Centrale (unconfirmed)
- ♦ Plate-forme ruralter (#19004)
- ♦ Plate-forme sociale (#19344)
- ♦ Plateforme de la Société Civile pour la Consolidation de la Paix et le Renforcement de l'Etat (#03970)

♦ Plateforme Universitaire de Recherche sur L'Islam en Europe et au Liban (PLURIEL) 18396

University Platform for Research on Islam in Europe and Lebanon

Contact address not obtained. T. +33472325052. E-mail: pluriel@univ-catholyon.fr.
URL: http://pluriel.fuce.eu/

History Set up by *European Federation of Catholic Universities (#07070)* for *International Federation of Catholic Universities (IFCU, #13381).* **Aims** Promote the link between researchers on Islam and the Muslim-Christian dialogue, in connection with Eastern Christians; foster interaction between academics, social actors and economic organizations. **Structure** Coordination Team. **Activities** Events/meetings. **Events** *Congrès International – Phase 2* Beirut (Lebanon) 2022, *Congrès International – Phase 1* Beirut (Lebanon) 2021, *Congrès International* Beirut (Lebanon) 2020, *Congrès International* Rome (Italy) 2018, *Congrès International* Lyon (France) 2016. **Publications** *PLURIEL Newsletter.*
Members Full in 8 countries:
Austria, Canada, Egypt, France, Germany, Italy, Lebanon, Spain. [2017/XM6022/**F**]

- ♦ PLATE – Product Lifetimes and The Environment (meeting series)

♦ PLATFORMA 18397

Secretariat c/o CEMR, Square de Meeûs 1, 1000 Brussels, Belgium. T. +3222650930. E-mail: platforma@ccre-cemr.org.
Main Website: https://platforma-dev.eu/

History Nov 2008. Officially launched on the occasion of the European Development Days in Strasbourg. Financially supported by the European Commission since 2009. Framework Partnership Agreement (FPA) with the European Commission, through the Directorate General for International Partnerships (DG INTPA, former Directorate General for Cooperation and Development DG DEVCO) signed in 2015; renewed 2022. Former names and other names: *PLATFORMA – The European voice of Local and Regional authorities for development* – former; *La voix européenne des Autorités Locals et Régionales pour le développement* – former; *La voz europea de las autoridades Locales y Regionales para el desarrollo* – former; *PLATFORMA – Local & Regional International Action* – full title; *PLATFORMA – Action internationale locale et régionale* – full title; *PLATFORMA – Acción internacional local i regional* – full title. **Aims** Boost European local and regional governments' contribution to EU development cooperation policies and international frameworks. **Structure** Secretariat hosted by Council of European Municipalities and Regions (CEMR). **Languages** English, French. **Activities** Advocacy/lobbying/activism; awards/prizes/competitions; awareness raising; knowledge management/information dissemination; monitoring/evaluation; networking/liaising; politics/policy/regulatory; publishing activities; training/education. **Members** Towns, regions and their national, EU and global associations active in city-to-city and region-to-region development cooperation. Membership countries not specified. **IGO Relations** Framework Partnership Agreement with: *European Commission (EC, #06633).* **NGO Relations** Framework Partnership Agreement with: *Association Internationale des Maires et responsables des capitales et métropoles partiellement ou entièrement Francophones (AIMF, #02715); Commonwealth Local Government Forum (CLGF, #04348); World Organization of United Cities and Local Governments (UCLG, #21695); United Cities and Local Governments of Africa (UCLG Africa, #20500).* Hosted by: *Council of European Municipalities and Regions (CEMR, #04891).* Member of: *Global Taskforce of Local and Regional Governments (Global Taskforce, #10622).* [2022.10.27/XM5802/**E**]

- ♦ PLATFORMA – Acción internacional local i regional / see PLATFORMA (#18397)
- ♦ PLATFORMA – Action internationale locale et régionale / see PLATFORMA (#18397)
- ♦ PLATFORMA – The European voice of Local and Regional authorities for development / see PLATFORMA (#18397)

♦ Platform for African – European Partnership on Agricultural Research for Development (PAEPARD) 18398

Exec Dir c/o FARA Secretariat, PMB CT 173 Cantonments, Accra, Ghana. T. +233217772823 – +23321779421. Fax +23321773676.
Chairperson address not obtained. E-mail: ckagiso@yahoo.com.
URL: http://paepard.blogspot.com/

History as a partnership between *European Forum on Agricultural Research for Development (EFARD, #07302), Forum for Agricultural Research in Africa (FARA, #09897), Advisory Committee on Science and Technology for Development (ACSTD, inactive)* and *European Commission (EC, #06633).* **Aims** Strengthen African ARD stakeholders' capacity to participate in European-led development initiatives for Africa; create more responsive development programs for Africa; mobilize resources for priority projects that combine African and European institutional and financial resources for mutually advantageous projects.
Members Partners (4):
AGRINATURA (#00578); European Commission (EC, #06633); European Forum on Agricultural Research for Development (EFARD, #07302); Forum for Agricultural Research in Africa (FARA, #09897). [2020/XJ0492/y/**F**]

- ♦ PLATFORMA – Local & Regional International Action / see PLATFORMA (#18397)

♦ Platform for Better Oral Health in Europe 18399

Secretariat Rue Montoyer 47, 1000 Brussels, Belgium. T. +3226459852. E-mail: secretariat@oralhealthplatform.eu – info@oralhealthplatform.eu.
URL: http://www.oralhealthplatform.eu/

History Set up by: *Association for Dental Education in Europe (ADEE, #02467), Council of European Chief Dental Officers (CECDO, #04885)* and *European Association of Dental Public Health (EADPH, #06007),* with support of *European Dental Hygienists Federation (EDHF, #06903).* EU Transparency Register: 685410422002-19. **Aims** Improve oral health; enhance cost-effective prevention of oral diseases in Europe.
Members Full (4):
Association for Dental Education in Europe (ADEE, #02467); Council of European Chief Dental Officers (CECDO, #04885); European Association of Dental Public Health (EADPH, #06007); International Dental Hygienists Federation (IDHF).
Associate members include 7 organizations listed in this Yearbook:
European Academy of Paediatric Dentistry (EAPD, #05810); European Association for Oral Medicine (EAOM, #06137); European College of Gerodontology (ECG, #06610); European Dental Hygienists Federation (EDHF, #06903); European Federation of Periodontology (EFP, #07190); European Organization for Caries Research (ORCA, #08107); International Association for Dental Research (IADR, #11838) (Pan European Region). [2017.06.01/XM4192/y/**F**]

- ♦ Platform for Collaboration in Distance Education in Europe / see EDEN Digital Learning Europe (#05356)
- ♦ Platform for Communication Rights / see Centre for Communication Rights (#03732)
- ♦ Platform for Cooperation / see Centre for Communication Rights (#03732)
- ♦ Platform for Cooperation on Democratization of Communication / see Centre for Communication Rights (#03732)
- ♦ Platform Disability and Development Cooperation (internationally oriented national body)

♦ Platform for European Fathers (PEF) 18400

Sec Jacob Cabeliaustraat 17, 3554 VH Utrecht, Netherlands. T. +31302383636. E-mail: secretary@europeanfathers.eu.
URL: http://europeanfathers.wordpress.com/

History 27 Jun 2011, Brussels (Belgium), at *European Parliament (EP, #08146).* Registered in accordance with Belgian law. **Aims** Monitor community law and family and work policies; campaign for equal parenting and acknowledgement of the role and significance of involved fathers and responsible fatherhood for children in EU laws and policies. **Structure** Committee, including Chair, Vice-Chair and Secretary.
Members Father organizations (22) in 13 countries:
Austria, Belgium, France, Germany, Greece, Hungary, Iceland, Ireland, Netherlands, Portugal, Spain, Switzerland, UK. [2012/XJ5658/**F**]

- ♦ Platform of European Social NGOs / see Social Platform (#19344)
- ♦ The platform of the European Societies in Information and Communication Sciences and Technologies / see European Forum for ICST (#07316)
- ♦ Platform Fortress Europe (inactive)
- ♦ Platform Handicap en Ontwikkelingssamenwerking (internationally oriented national body)

♦ Platform for International Cooperation on Undocumented Migrants (PICUM) 18401

Main Office Rue du Congrès 37-41, post box 5, 1000 Brussels, Belgium. T. +3222101780. Fax +3222101789. E-mail: info@picum.org.
URL: http://www.picum.org/

History Founded Oct 2001; launched 1998; office opened in Nov 2000. Registration: EU Transparency Register, No/ID: 19093363838-48; Belgium. **Aims** Promote respect for *human rights* of undocumented migrants within *Europe.* **Structure** General Assembly (annual); Executive Committee; Secretariat. **Languages** English. **Staff** 8.00 FTE, paid. **Finance** Donations. **Activities** Research/documentation; networking/liaising. **Events** *Annual General Assembly* Brussels (Belgium) 2016, *Conference on undocumented migrants and the Stockholm programme* Brussels (Belgium) 2010, *General Assembly* Brussels (Belgium) 2008, *General Assembly* Brussels (Belgium) 2007, *General Assembly* Brussels (Belgium) 2006. **Publications** *PICUM Quarterly* (4 a year); *PICUM Bulletin* (irregular). Annual Report; policy briefs; reports; position papers; conference and workshop reports.
Members Individuals; Platform Members (organizations). Members in 31 countries:
Austria, Belgium, Croatia, Cyprus, Czechia, Denmark, Estonia, Finland, France, Georgia, Germany, Greece, Ireland, Israel, Italy, Kazakhstan, Luxembourg, Malta, Morocco, Nepal, Netherlands, Nigeria, Norway, Pakistan, Poland, Portugal, Romania, Spain, Sweden, Switzerland, UK.
Included in the above, 10 organizations listed in this Yearbook:
Anti-Slavery International (#00860); European AIDS Treatment Group (EATG, #05850); European Network of Migrant Women (ENoMW, #07947); International Catholic Migration Commission (ICMC, #12459) (Europe); *Jesuit Refugee Service (JRS, #16106)* (Europe); *La Strada International (LSI, #20002); Médecins du Monde – International (MDM, #16613); Pax Christi – International Catholic Peace Movement (#18266); UNITED for Intercultural Action – European Network Against Nationalism, Racism, Fascism and in Support of Migrants and Refugees (UNITED, #20511).*
Consultative Status Consultative status granted from: *Council of Europe (CE, #04881)* (Participatory Status); *ECOSOC (#05331)* (Special). **IGO Relations** Cooperates with: *European Union Agency for Fundamental Rights (FRA, #08969).* Member of: Consultative Forum of *Frontex, the European Border and Coast Guard Agency (#10005).* **NGO Relations** Member of: *Ending Violence Against Migrants (EVAM); EU Alliance for a democratic, social and sustainable European Semester (EU Semester Alliance, #05565); European Anti-Poverty Network (EAPN, #05908); European NGO Platform Asylum and Migration (EPAM, #08051); European Platform for Migrant Workers' Rights (EPMWR, #08225); Global Coalition on Migration (GCM, #10293); Human Rights and Democracy Network (HRDN, #10980); Migrants Rights International (MRI, #16799); Social Platform (#19344); Women in Migration Network (WIMN, #21008).* [2021/XF6790/y/**F**]

♦ Platform to Protect Whistleblowers in Africa (PPLAAF) 18402

Plateforme de Protection des Lanceurs d'Alerte en Afrique

Contact address not obtained. T. +27105002322. E-mail: info@pplaaf.org.
URL: https://www.pplaaf.org/

Aims Defend whistleblowers, as well as strategically litigate and advocate on their behalf where their disclosures speak to the public interest of African citizens. **Structure** Management; Advisory Board. **Activities** Guidance/assistance/consulting; advocacy/lobbying/activism; research/documentation. **NGO Relations** Partners include: *Africa Freedom of Information Centre (AFIC, #00175); Economic Justice Network for Churches in Eastern and Southern Africa (EJN, #05317); Health of Mother Earth Foundation (HOMEF); International Consortium of Investigative Journalists (ICIJ); Ligue Africaine des Blogueurs et Cyber-activistes pour la Démocratie (AFRICTIVISTES, #16476); Sherpa;* Tax Justice Network-Africa (TJN-A, #20101). [2019/XM8843/**F**]

- ♦ Platform for Sustainable and United Agriculture / see Sustainable, Innovative and United Agriculture and Food Network
- ♦ Platform for Transformative Technologies (internationally oriented national body)
- ♦ Platonselskabet (#17388)
- ♦ Plattform Zivile Konfliktbearbeitung (internationally oriented national body)
- ♦ Plattform ZKB / see German Platform for Peaceful Conflict Management

♦ Play for Change 18403

Registered Address Suite LG, 11 St James's Place, London, SW1A 1NP, UK. E-mail: info@playforchange.org.
URL: http://www.playforchange.org/

History Founded 2010. Since 2013, a Registered Charity in England and Wales: 1152390. **Aims** Enhance life opportunities for under-privileged *children* by using the powerful values of *sport.* **Structure** Board of Directors. **Activities** Sporting activities; events/meetings; training/education; projects/programmes. [2020.03.12/XM7375/**F**]

- ♦ Play Fair Europe (no recent information)

♦ Play the Game 18404

International Dir Frederiksgade 78B 2, 8000 Aarhus C, Denmark. T. +4532661030. E-mail: info@playthegame.org.
Events – Conference Manager address not obtained.
URL: http://www.playthegame.org/

History 1 Jan 2004, Copenhagen (Denmark). Founded by 3 sports organizations in Denmark in close cooperation with: *International Federation of Journalists (IFJ, #13462).* As of 1 Jan 2011, part of Danish Institute for Sport Studies. **Aims** Raise ethical standards and promote democracy, transparency and freedom of expression in world sport. **Structure** Board. Organized by Danish Institute for Sports Studies (Idan). **Languages** English. **Staff** 6.00 FTE, paid. **Finance** Funded by Danish Ministry of Culture. **Activities** Events/meetings; training/education. **Events** *World conference* Denmark 2022, *World Conference* Colorado Springs, CO (USA) 2019, *World Conference* Eindhoven (Netherlands) 2017, *World Conference* Aarhus (Denmark) 2015, *World Conference* Aarhus (Denmark) 2013. **Publications** Newsletter; news stories; background articles. **IGO Relations** Member of (1): *Enlarged Partial Agreement on Sport (EPAS, #05487).* [2022.11.10/XJ2191/**D**]

- ♦ PLAY International (internationally oriented national body)
- ♦ PLAY SOCCER Nonprofit International (internationally oriented national body)
- ♦ PLC – SADC Parliamentary Leadership Centre (internationally oriented national body)
- ♦ PLDA – Professional Lighting Designers' Association (inactive)
- ♦ **PLEA International** Passive and Low-Energy Architecture (#18255)

♦ PLEA International – Passive and Low-Energy Architecture – Sustainable Architecture and Urban Design / see Passive and Low-Energy Architecture (#18255)
♦ PLEII – Peace and Life Enhancement Initiative International (internationally oriented national body)
♦ Plenty / see Plenty International (#18405)

♦ Plenty International 18405

Main Office PO Box 394, Summertown TN 38483, USA. T. +19319644323. E-mail: info@plenty.org.
URL: http://www.plenty.org/

History 1974, as a nonprofit relief and development organization. Evolved from a vision of the essential oneness of people through the activity of *The Farm*, a new-age spiritual community of 1,000 people. Workers are drawn from among residents of Farm communities around the world. Formerly known as *'Plenty'* and as *'Plenty-USA'*. Registered US 501c3 nonprofit corporation. **Aims** Help protect and share the world's abundance and knowledge for the benefit of all. **Languages** English, Spanish. **Staff** 4.00 FTE, paid. **Finance** Grants; individual donations. **Activities** Humanitarian/emergency aid; capacity building. Active in: Africa; Caribbean; Central America; USA. **Events** *International conference on desalination strategies in South Mediterranean countries* Djerba (Tunisia) 2000. **Publications** *Plenty Bulletin* (2 a year). Books.
Members Network of organizations in 2 countries:
Belize, USA. [2019.02.14/XF5497/**F**]

♦ Plenty-USA / see Plenty International (#18405)

♦ PLMA International Council 18406

Contact Strawinskylaan 671, 1077 XX Amsterdam, Netherlands. T. +31205753032. Fax +31205753093. E-mail: info@plma.nl.
URL: http://www.plmainternational.com/

History US *Private Label Manufacturers Association* having existed since 1979. **Events** *Annual Conference* Amsterdam (Netherlands) 2020, *Annual Conference* Amsterdam (Netherlands) 2019, *Annual Conference* Amsterdam (Netherlands) 2018, *Annual Conference* Amsterdam (Netherlands) 2017, *Annual Conference* Amsterdam (Netherlands) 2016. [2014/XN1635/y/**E**]

♦ PLN / see European Prison Litigation Network (#08277)
♦ PLN – Philanthropy Leadership Network (unconfirmed)
♦ PLO – Palestine Liberation Organization (internationally oriented national body)
♦ **PLPR** International Academic Association on Planning, Law and Property Rights (#11531)
♦ **PLQP** Publiquen Lo Que Pagan (#18573)

♦ PLR International 18407

Coordinator address not obtained.
URL: http://www.plrinternational.com/

History Founded 1995, as an informal network. Previously known as *International Public Lending Right Network (International PLR Network)*. Present name adopted 2016. **Aims** Promote international awareness of Public Lending Rights and inform the PLR community of events, developments and news from around the world. **Structure** Steering Committee; Coordinator. **Languages** English. **Staff** 1.00 FTE, paid. **Finance** Funding from: *International Federation of Reproduction Rights Organizations (IFRRO, #13527)*. No annual budget. **Activities** Events/meetings; guidance/assistance/consulting; awareness raising. **Events** *Conference* Paris (France) 2017, *Conference* The Hague (Netherlands) 2015, *Conference* Dublin (Ireland) 2013, *Conference* Brussels (Belgium) 2011, *Biennial conference / Conference* Lisbon (Portugal) 2009. **Publications** Conference proceedings. **Members** No formal membership. [2018.09.05/XJ1392/**F**]

♦ PLSA – Pacific Law and Society Association (inactive)
♦ PLS – Pour la Solidarité (internationally oriented national body)
♦ PLT – Patent Law Treaty (2000 treaty)
♦ Plumbing Brass Institute / see Plumbing Manufacturers International
♦ Plumbing Manufacturers Institute / see Plumbing Manufacturers International
♦ Plumbing Manufacturers International (internationally oriented national body)
♦ **PLURIEL** Plateforme Universitaire de Recherche sur L'Islam en Europe et au Liban (#18396)
♦ Plurilingual Europe (internationally oriented national body)
♦ PLUS Coalition (internationally oriented national body)
♦ Plus Europe Association (internationally oriented national body)

♦ Plymouth Brethren 18408

Contact 100 Wharf Rd, Ermington, Sydney NSW 2115, Australia. T. +611300780858 – +611300780857.
UK Contact Albacore Meeting Room, Beckenham Hill Road, London, BR3 1TH, UK. T. +442083917620. Fax +442083917621.
URL: http://www.plymouthbrethrenchristianchurch.org/

History 1829, on formation of first permanent meetings, following spontaneous springing up of independent gatherings in response to growing dissatisfaction within the Anglican Church. Became a worldwide fellowship as members emigrated and set up congregations in the Americas, Africa, Australia and New Zealand. **Aims** Meet together in a fellowship based on the teachings of the New Testament and centred on the celebration of the Lord's Supper (Holy Communion); focus on the individual's direct relationship with God and the emphasis this places on personal *responsibility*. **Members** Membership countries not specified. [2019/XU0186/**F**]

♦ PMA / see Pacific Mission Aviation
♦ **PMAC** Port Management Association of the Caribbean (#18461)
♦ PMAEA / see Port Management Association of Eastern and Southern Africa (#18462)
♦ **PMAESA** Port Management Association of Eastern and Southern Africa (#18462)
♦ PMAF – Protection mondiale des animaux de ferme (internationally oriented national body)
♦ PMANA / see North African Port Management Association (#17556)
♦ PMA – Pacific Mission Aviation (internationally oriented national body)
♦ PMA – Performance Management Association (unconfirmed)
♦ **PMA** Programa Mundial de Alimentos (#21510)

♦ PMAPS International Society 18409

Conference Secretariat Istanbul Technical Univ, Dept of Electrical Engineering, Maslak, 34469 Istanbul/Istanbul, Türkiye. T. +902122856759. Fax +902122856700. E-mail: pmaps2012@itu.edu.tr.
URL: http://www.pmaps2012.itu.edu.tr/

History 1986, as *International Council on Probabilistic Methods Applied to Power Systems (PMAPS)*. Current title adopted following 5th PMAPS Conference, 1997, Vancouver BC (Canada). **Events** *PMAPS Conference* Istanbul (Turkey) 2012, *PMAPS Conference* Singapore (Singapore) 2010, *PMAPS Conference* Rincón (Puerto Rico) 2008, *PMAPS Conference* Stockholm (Sweden) 2006, *PMAPS Conference* Ames, IA (USA) 2004. [2013/XJ6448/c/**E**]

♦ PMAPS / see PMAPS International Society (#18409)
♦ **PMA** Public Media Alliance (#18568)
♦ **PMAWCA** Port Management Association of West and Central Africa (#18463)
♦ PMB – Pacific Manuscripts Bureau (internationally oriented national body)
♦ **PMCC** Peoples' Movement on Climate Change (#18306)
♦ PMC-Europe – Perspectives Mutualisations et Convergences Europe (internationally oriented national body)
♦ PMC / see Integrated Marketing Communications Council of Europe (#11369)
♦ PMC International – People for Medical Cooperation International (internationally oriented national body)
♦ PMC – Pacto Mundial Consciente (unconfirmed)
♦ PMC – Petites Missionnaires de la Charité (religious order)
♦ PMDA / see Centre for Heritage Development in Africa (#03748)
♦ **PME** International Group for the Psychology of Mathematics Education (#13753)
♦ PME – Societas pro Missionibus Exteris Provinciae Quebecensis (religious order)
♦ **PMF** Project Mind Foundation (#18535)
♦ PMI / see Plumbing Manufacturers International
♦ **PMIC** Programa Mundial de Investigaciones Climaticas (#21279)
♦ PMI – Plumbing Manufacturers International (internationally oriented national body)
♦ **PMI** Presse musicale internationale (#18488)
♦ **PMI** Project Management Institute (#18534)
♦ **PMJE** Parlement mondial de la jeunesse pour l'eau (#21958)

♦ PMNCH 18410

Exec Dir c/o WHO, Av Appia 20, 1211 Geneva 27, Switzerland. T. +41227915895. E-mail: pmnch@who.int.
URL: https://pmnch.who.int

History Sep 2005. Founded when *Partnership for Safe Motherhood and Newborn Health (inactive)*, *Healthy Newborn Partnership* and *Child Survival Partnership* merged. **Aims** Mobilize, align and amplify the voices of partners to advocate for women's, children's and adolescents' health and well-being, particularly the most vulnerable. **Structure** Board; Committees; Secretariat, administered within *WHO (#20950)*. **Languages** English. **Staff** 20.00 FTE, paid. **Activities** Advocacy/lobbying/activism; knowledge management/information dissemination. **Events** *1.8 Billion Campaign – Launch Event Meeting* 2022, *Protect the Promise: Equal Access and Opportunity for Every Woman, Child and Adolescent* Berlin (Germany) 2022, *Annual Accountability Breakfast Summit* 2021. **Publications** *PMNCH 2021-2025 Strategy* (2021).
Members Partners (over 1,000) including 190 organizations listed in this Yearbook:
– *ABANTU for Development (#00003)*;
– *ACTION (#00085)*;
– *Action Against Hunger (#00086)*;
– *African Relief in Action (ARIA International)*;
– *African Youth Safe Abortion Alliance (AYOSA, #00508)*;
– *Africa Youth for Peace and Development (AYPAD)*;
– *Aga Khan Development Network (AKDN, #00544)*;
– *Aga Khan University (AKU, #00546)*;
– *Amref Health Africa (#00806)*;
– *Association Internationale des Technologistes Biomédicaux (ASSITEB-BIORIF, #02747)*;
– *Barcelona Institute for Global Health (ISGlobal)*;
– *BCARE International*;
– *Bill and Melinda Gates Foundation (BMGF)*;
– *Blumont International*;
– *BRAC (#03310)*;
– *Canadian Association Global Health (CAGH)*;
– *Caring and Living As Neighbours (CLAN)*;
– *Catholic Medical Mission Board (CMMB)*;
– *Chamber of Computer Logistics People Worldwide (CCLP Worldwide, #03847)*;
– *Childbirth Survival International (CSI)*;
– *Childhood and Early Parenting Principles (CEPPs, #03873)*;
– *Children's HeartLink (CHL)*;
– *Children's Investment Fund Foundation (CIFF)*;
– *Commonwealth Association of Paediatric Gastroenterology and Nutrition (CAPGAN, #04306)*;
– *Commonwealth Secretariat (#04362)*;
– *Concern Worldwide*;
– *CORE Group*;
– *Council of International Neonatal Nurses (COINN, #04904)*;
– *CUAMM – Medici con l'Africa*;
– *Curamericas*;
– *Department for International Development (DFID, inactive)*;
– *Deutsche Stiftung Weltbevölkerung (DSW)*;
– *Development Media International (DMI)*;
– *East, Central and Southern African Health Community (ECSA-HC, #05216)*;
– *Elizabeth Glaser Pediatric AIDS Foundation (EGPAF)*;
– *Enfants du Monde (EdM)*;
– *EngenderHealth*;
– *European Commission (EC, #06633)*;
– *European Foundation for the Care of Newborn Infants (EFCNI, #07344)*;
– *European Youth Network on Sexual and Reproductive Rights (YouAct, #09144)*;
– *Evangelize China Fellowship (ECF)*;
– *Fédération Internationale de Gynécologie et d'Obstétrique (FIGO, #09638)*;
– *Federation of Asia-Oceania Perinatal Societies (FAOPS, #09452)*;
– *FHI 360*;
– *Free World Foundation (FWF)*;
– *Frontline AIDS (#10007)*;
– *Future Generations*;
– *Gavi – The Vaccine Alliance (Gavi, #10077)*;
– *GBCHealth*;
– *Gesellschaft für Tropenpädiatrie und Internationale Kindergesundheit (GTP)*;
– *Global Alliance to Prevent Prematurity and Stillbirth (GAPPS)*;
– *Global Fund to Fight AIDS, Tuberculosis and Malaria (Global Fund, #10383)*;
– *Global Future*;
– *Global Health Council (GHC, #10402)*;
– *Global Health Next Generation Network (GHNGN, no recent information)*;
– *Global Health Promise*;
– *Global Health Visions (GHV)*;
– *Global Movement for Children (GMFC, inactive)*;
– *Global Network for Perinatal and Reproductive Health (GNPRH, #10495)*;
– *Global Network for Women's and Children's health Research*;
– *Global Organization for Maternal and Child Health (Go-MCH)*;
– *Global Youth Coalition Against Cancer (GYCC)*;
– *GoodBirth Network (#10678)*;
– *GSM Association (GSMA, #10813)*;
– *Health Alliance International (HAI)*;
– *Health and Development International (HDI)*;
– *HealthNet TPO*;
– *HealthRight International*;
– *Helen Keller International (HKI, #10902)*;
– *Humanity and Inclusion (HI, #10975)*;
– *Human Rights Watch (HRW, #10990)*;
– *Hunger Project (#10994)*;
– *Ibis Reproductive Health*;
– *ICDDR,B (#11051)*;
– *IDA Foundation (#11091)*;
– *ILO (#11123)*;
– *IMA World Health (IMA)*;
– *Institute of Tropical Medicine Antwerp (IMT)*;
– *Intergovernment Institution for the use of Micro-Algae Spirulina against Malnutrition (IIMSAM, #11504)*;
– *International Baby Food Action Network (IBFAN, #12305)*;
– *International Bank for Reconstruction and Development (IBRD, #12317)* (World Bank);
– *International Center for Research on Women (ICRW)*;
– *International Centre for Reproductive Health (ICRH)*;
– *International Child Health Group (ICHG)*;
– *International Children's Center (ICC)*;
– *International Committee for Rehabilitation Aid to Afghanistan (ICRAA)*;
– *International Confederation of Midwives (ICM, #12863)*;
– *International Council of Nurses (ICN, #13054)*;
– *International Diabetes Federation (IDF, #13164)*;
– *International Federation for Spina Bifida and Hydrocephalus (IF SBH, #13552)*;
– *International Federation of Pharmaceutical Wholesalers (IFPW, #13506)*;
– *International Federation of Red Cross and Red Crescent Societies (#13526)*;
– *International Food Policy Research Institute (IFPRI, #13622)*;
– *International Foundation for Mother and Child Health (IFMCH)*;
– *International Institute for Health Care Professionals (IIHCP)*;
– *International Institute for Population Sciences (IIPS, #13911)*;
– *International Lactation Consultant Association (ILCA)*;
– *International Maternal and Child Health Foundation Canada (IMCHF)*;

- *International Medical Equipment Collaborative (IMEC);*
- *International Pediatric Association (IPA, #14541);*
- *International Pharmaceutical Federation (#14566);*
- *International Pharmaceutical Students' Federation (IPSF, #14568);*
- *International Planned Parenthood Federation (IPPF, #14589);*
- *International Society for the Study of Hypertension in Pregnancy (ISSHP, #15475);*
- *International Society of Ultrasound in Obstetrics and Gynaecology (ISUOG, #15527);*
- *International Stillbirth Alliance (ISA, #15608);*
- *International Union Against Tuberculosis and Lung Disease (The Union, #15752);*
- *International Youth Alliance for Family Planning (IYAFP, #15931);*
- *Inter-Parliamentary Union (IPU, #15961);*
- *IntraHealth International;*
- *Iodine Global Network (IGN, #16004);*
- *IPAS (#16010);*
- *Japanese Organization for International Cooperation in Family Planning (JOICFP);*
- *Japan International Cooperation Agency (JICA);*
- *Johns Hopkins Program for International Education in Gynecology and Obstetrics (JHPIEGO);*
- *Joint United Nations Programme on HIV/AIDS (UNAIDS, #16149);*
- *Korea International Cooperation Agency (KOICA);*
- *La Leche League International (LLLI, #16433);*
- *Liverpool School of Tropical Medicine (LSTM)* (Centre for Maternal and Newborn Health);
- *London School of Hygiene and Tropical Medicine (LSHTM);*
- *MacArthur Foundation;*
- *Management Sciences for Health (MSH);*
- *Maternal and Childhealth Advocacy International (MCAI);*
- *Maternity Worldwide;*
- *Medical Women's International Association (MWIA, #16630);*
- *Medicines for Malaria Venture (MMV, #16634);*
- *Medicus Mundi International – Network Health for All (MMI, #16636);*
- *MEMISA;*
- *Mother Health International;*
- *mothers2mothers (m2m, #16859);*
- *MSI Reproductive Choices;*
- *Nightingale Initiative for Global Health (NIGH World, #17136);*
- *Norwegian Agency for Development Cooperation (Norad);*
- *Nutrition International (#17627);*
- *ONE (#17728);*
- *Orchid Project;*
- *PAI (#18025);*
- *Pan African Development Education and Advocacy Programme (PADEAP);*
- *Partners in Health (PIH);*
- *Partners in Population and Development (PPD, #18247);*
- *PATH (#18260);*
- *Pathfinder International (#18261);*
- *PCI Global;*
- *Peace and Life Enhancement Initiative International (PLEII);*
- *Plan International (#18386)* (Asia);
- *Population Council (#18458);*
- *Population Reference Bureau (PRB);*
- *Project HOPE;*
- *Promundo;*
- *PRONTO International;*
- *PSI (#18555);*
- *RESULTS;*
- *Results for Development (R4D, #18923);*
- *Riders for Health II (#18940);*
- *Rotary International (RI, #18975);*
- *Royal Academy of Science International Trust (RASIT);*
- *RTI International;*
- *Save the Children Federation (SCF);*
- *Save the Children UK (SC UK);*
- *Save the Mothers (STM, #19059);*
- *Save Visions Africa (SVA);*
- *SickKids International (SKI);*
- *SIMAVI;*
- *South Asian Society on Atherosclerosis and Thrombosis (SASAT, #19741);*
- *SRHR Africa Trust (SAT, #19934);*
- *SurfAid international (SAI, #20040);*
- *Swedish Organization for Global Health (SOGH);*
- *Synergies Africaines contre le SIDA et les Souffrances (Synergies Africaines, #20081);*
- *Task Force for Global Health (TFGH, #20098);*
- *The Children's Project International (TCPI);*
- *Together for Girls;*
- *UCL Institute for Global Health (IGH);*
- *UNICEF (#20332);*
- *United Nations Foundation (UNF, #20563);*
- *United Nations Office for Project Services (UNOPS, #20602);*
- *United Nations Population Fund (UNFPA, #20612);*
- *United States Agency for International Development (USAID);*
- *WaterAid (#20822);*
- *Wellbeing Foundation Africa (ABFA);*
- *Wellshare International;*
- *White Ribbon Alliance for Safe Motherhood (WRA, #20934);*
- *WHO (#20950);*
- *Women and Health Alliance International (WAHA, #21001);*
- *Women Deliver (#20989);*
- *World Congress of Muslim Philanthropists (WCMP, #21308);*
- *World Connect;*
- *World Federation of Societies of Anaesthesiologists (WFSA, #21482);*
- *World Vision International (WVI, #21904);*
- *World Young Women's Christian Association (World YWCA, #21947);*
- *Youth Peer Education Network (Y-PEER).*

NGO Relations Observer status with (1): *Inter-Parliamentary Union (IPU, #15961).* Partner of (2): *Every Woman Every Child (EWEC, #09215); Healthy Newborn Network (HNN, #10894).* [2022.10.19/XM3774/y/**E**]

♦ **PMN** Pohjoismaiden Ministerineuvosto (#17260)
♦ PMOI' / see Mujahedin-e Khalq Organization (#16881)
♦ **PMP** Physics of Membrane Processes (#18368)
♦ **PMRC** Programme mondial de recherches sur le climat (#21279)
♦ PM – Sisters of the Presentation of Mary (religious order)
♦ PMSS – Programa MERCOSUR Social y Solidario (unconfirmed)
♦ **PMTA** Pacific Maritime Transport Alliance (#17982)
♦ PMU Interlife (internationally oriented national body)
♦ PMWB – Project Managers Without Borders (internationally oriented national body)
♦ **PNC** Pacific Neighbourhood Consortium (#17983)
♦ PNC – Pacific Nuclear Council (inactive)
♦ **PNC** PAN-Nordic Card Association (#18182)
♦ **PNEUROP** European Committee of Manufacturers of Compressors, Vacuum Pumps and Pneumatic Tools (#06657)
♦ **PNIRS** PsychoNeuroImmunology Research Society (#18560)
♦ PNND / see Parliamentarians for Nuclear Non-Proliferation and Disarmament (#18210)
♦ **PNND** Parliamentarians for Nuclear Non-Proliferation and Disarmament (#18210)
♦ PNoWB / see Parliamentary Network on the World Bank and International Monetary Fund (#18219)
♦ PN – Peace Now (internationally oriented national body)
♦ PNP – Pro Niños Pobres (internationally oriented national body)
♦ **PN** Pohjoismaiden Neuvosto (#17256)
♦ **PNS** Peripheral Nerve Society (#18314)
♦ PNUCID – Programme des Nations Unies pour le contrôle international de la drogue (inactive)
♦ PNUD/Banco Mundial/OMS Programa Especial de Investigaciones y Enseñanzas sobre Enfermedades Tropicales / see UNICEF/UNDP/World Bank/WHO Special Programme for Research and Training in Tropical Diseases (#20331)
♦ PNUD/Banque mondiale/OMS Programme spécial de recherche et de formation concernant les maladies tropicales / see UNICEF/UNDP/World Bank/WHO Special Programme for Research and Training in Tropical Diseases (#20331)
♦ **PNUD** Programa de las Naciones Unidas para el Desarrollo (#20292)
♦ **PNUD** Programme des Nations Unies pour le développement (#20292)
♦ **PNUE** Programme des Nations Unies pour l'environnement (#20299)
♦ PNUFID – Programa de las Naciones Unidas para la Fiscalización Internacional de las Drogas (inactive)
♦ **PNUMA** Programa de las Naciones Unidas para el Medio Ambiente (#20299)
♦ PNUN / see Committee of Senior Officials of the Nordic Countries, Estonia, Latvia and Lithuania in the Field of Food Issues (#04286)
♦ **POAC** Port and Ocean Engineering under Arctic Conditions International Committee (#18464)
♦ POA – Pulse of Asia (unconfirmed)
♦ POC – Postal Operations Council (see: #20682)
♦ POCR – Congregatio Piorum Operariorum Catechistarum Ruralium (religious order)
♦ **POED** Partenariat des OSC pour l'efficacité du développement (#04976)
♦ Poe Studies Association (internationally oriented national body)
♦ **POETCom** Pacific Organic & Ethical Trade Community (#17986)
♦ Poetics and Linguistics Association (internationally oriented national body)
♦ Pogodba o Ustavi za Evropo (2004 treaty)
♦ **POGO** Partnership for Observation of the Global Oceans (#18239)
♦ Pohjoiskalotin-neuvosto (#17545)
♦ Pohjoismaiden Estetiikan Seura (#17411)
♦ Pohjoismaiden Godtemplar-neuvosto (#17483)
♦ Pohjoismaiden Investointipankki (#17327)
♦ Pohjoismaiden Kehitysrahasto (#17271)
♦ Pohjoismaiden kielineuvosto (inactive)
♦ Pohjoismaiden Kriminologinen Yhteistyöneuvosto (#17493)
♦ Pohjoismaiden Lääkintätilastokomitea (#17342)
♦ Pohjoismaiden Lippuseura (#17294)
♦ Pohjoismaiden Metsäntutkimuksen Yhteistyölautakunta / see Nordic Forest Research Cooperation Committee (#17296)
♦ Pohjoismaiden Ministerineuvosto (#17260)
♦ Pohjoismaiden Ministerineuvosto /Kulttuuri- ja Opetusministerit (inactive)
♦ Pohjoismaiden Neuvosto (#17256)
♦ Pohjoismaiden Neuvoston Kirjallisuuspalkinnon Arvostelulautakunta (#00114)
♦ Pohjoismaiden Painiliitto (no recent information)
♦ Pohjoismaiden Postiliitto (#17391)
♦ Pohjoismaiden Projektivientirahasto (#17490)
♦ Pohjoismaiden Puunsuojausneuvosto (#17469)
♦ Pohjoismaiden Rautatieläisten Unioni (inactive)
♦ Pohjoismaiden Rautatieseura (#17395)
♦ Pohjoismaiden Saamelaisneuvosto / see Saami Council (#19012)
♦ Pohjoismaiden Sosiaalitilastokomitea (#17409)
♦ Pohjoismaiden Suomen Instituutti / see Nordic Culture Point
♦ Pohjoismaiden Taloudellinen Tutkimuksneuvosto (inactive)
♦ Pohjoismaiden Teollisuustyöntekijät (#11180)
♦ Pohjoismaiden Terveydenhuoltoalankorkeakoulu (inactive)
♦ Pohjoismaiden Tie-ja Liikennefoorumi (#17402)
♦ Pohjoismaiden Työmarkkinatoimikunta (inactive)
♦ Pohjoismaiden Väestötieteen Yhdistys (#17268)
♦ Pohjoismaiden Ympäristörahoitusyhtiö (#17281)
♦ Pohjoismainen Aasiantutkimusinstituutti / see NIAS-Nordisk Institut for Asienstudier (#17132)
♦ Pohjoismainen Afrikka-Instituutti (#17168)
♦ Pohjoismainen Atlantti-yhteistyö / see Nordic Atlantic Cooperation (#17209)
♦ Pohjoismainen Atomienergiayhdyselin (inactive)
♦ Pohjoismainen Audiologian Seura (#17210)
♦ Pohjoismainen avioliittokonventio (1931 treaty)
♦ Pohjoismainen Betoniliitto (#17251)
♦ Pohjoismainen Elintarvikeasiain Virkamieskomitea / see Committee of Senior Officials of the Nordic Countries, Estonia, Latvia and Lithuania in the Field of Food Issues (#04286)
♦ Pohjoismainen Elintarvikkeiden Metodiikkakomitea / see Nordic-Baltic Committee on Food Analysis (#17215)
♦ Pohjoismainen Elintensiirtokomitea / see Scandiatransplant Association (#19066)
♦ Pohjoismainen Energiantutkimus (#17278)
♦ Pohjoismainen Energiantutkimusvaliokunta / see Nordic Energy Research (#17278)
♦ Pohjoismainen Hammasmateriaalin Koetuslaitos (#17485)
♦ Pohjoismainen Harrastajateatterineuvosto (#17172)
♦ Pohjoismainen Hydrologinen Yhdistys (#17194)
♦ Pohjoismainen Hyvinvointikeskus (#17163)
♦ Pohjoismainen Kesäyliopisto (#17535)
♦ Pohjoismainen Kiinan tutkimuksen seura (#17182)
♦ Pohjoismainen Kuljetustyöntekijäinfederaatio (#17496)
♦ Pohjoismainen Kulttuurirahasto (#17264)
♦ Pohjoismainen Kultuuripiste (internationally oriented national body)
♦ Pohjoismainen kultuuriyhteistyö (1971 treaty)
♦ Pohjoismainen Lääkeainelautakunta (inactive)
♦ Pohjoismainen Lastenneurologiyhdistys (#17367)
♦ Pohjoismainen Latinalaisen Amerikan Tutkimusyhdistys (inactive)
♦ Pohjoismainen Luonnontieteiden Julkaisulautakunta (inactive)
♦ Pohjoismainen Mainostoimistojen Liitto (no recent information)
♦ Pohjoismainen Merioikeuden Laitos (#17515)
♦ Pohjoismainen metsäkongressi (meeting series)
♦ Pohjoismainen Musiikkikomitea (inactive)
♦ Pohjoismainen Musiikkipedagoginen Unioni (inactive)
♦ Pohjoismainen Näyttelijäneuvosto (#17166)
♦ Pohjoismainen Ohjausalan Yhdistys/Nordisk Förening för Studie- och Yrkensvägleding (#17191)
♦ Pohjoismainen Päihdetutkimuskeskus (inactive)
♦ Pohjoismainen passintarkastussopimus (1957 treaty)
♦ Pohjoismainen Poronhoidontutkimuselin (inactive)
♦ Pohjoismainen Radiologiyhdistys (#17418)
♦ Pohjoismainen Rakennusalan Virkamieskomitea (inactive)
♦ Pohjoismainen Rakennus- ja Puutyöväen Federaatio (#17283)
♦ Pohjoismainen Rakennuskalkkiforum (#17512)
♦ Pohjoismainen Rakentamismääräyskomitea (inactive)
♦ Pohjoismainen Rautatieläisten Raittiusliitto (inactive)
♦ Pohjoismainen Rekennustutkimuskokous (meeting series)
♦ Pohjoismainen Reologiaseura (#17400)
♦ Pohjoismainen Riistantutkimuskollegio (#17262)
♦ Pohjoismainen Rikosoikeuskomitea (inactive)

♦ Pohjoismainen Sähköturvallisuuskysymysten Yhtenäistämiskomitea (#17246)
♦ Pohjoismainen sosiaalipalvelusopimus (1994 treaty)
♦ Pohjoismainen sosiaaliturvasopimus (2012 treaty)
♦ Pohjoismainen Suupatologian ja Suulääketieteen Yhdistys (#19303)
♦ Pohjoismainen Systeemis-funktionaalisen Kielitieteen ja sosiosemiotiikan Yhdistys (#17508)
♦ Pohjoismainen Taideliitto (#17176)
♦ Pohjoismainen Teoreettisen Fysiikan Laitos (#17324)
♦ Pohjoismainen Tieliikennelainsäädäntökomitea (inactive)
♦ Pohjoismainen Tilastopäällikkökokous (meeting series)
♦ Pohjoismainen Tilintarkastajaliitto (#17285)
♦ Pohjoismainen Tullihallintoneuvosto (#17497)
♦ Pohjoismainen Turvallisuustutkimuksen ad Hos Ryhmä / see Nordisk Kärnsäkerhetsforskning (#17517)
♦ Pohjoismainen Työmpäristöalan Täydennyskoulutusinstituutti / see Nordic Institute for Advanced Training in Occupational Health (#17321)
♦ Pohjoismainen työympäristöalan jatkokoulutuskeskus (#17321)
♦ Pohjoismainen Ulkomaalaisvaliokunta (#17315)
♦ Pohjoismainen Vammaisasiain Yhteistyölin (inactive)
♦ Pohjoismainen Verotieteellinen Tutkimusneuvosto (#17443)
♦ Pohjoismainen Vulkanologinen Instituutti / see Nordic Volcanological Center (#17463)
♦ Pohjoismainen Ydinturvallisuustutkimus (#17517)
♦ Pohjoismainen Yhteistyö Teknisen Akkreditoinnin Alalla (inactive)
♦ Pohjoismaisen Kehitysapuprojektien Hallitus (inactive)
♦ Pohjoismaisen Nuorisoyhteistyön Komitea (#17235)
♦ Pohjoismaiset Rakennuspäivät (meeting series)
♦ Pohjoismaisten Kantaverkkoyritysten Yhteistyöelin (inactive)
♦ Pohjola Kristillisdemokraatit (#17237)
♦ Pohjolan Ammatillinen Yhteistyöjärjestö (#17158)
♦ Pohjola Norden Yhdistysten Liitto (#09859)
♦ Pohjolan Talo Reykjavikissä (internationally oriented national body)
♦ Point of Peace Foundation (internationally oriented national body)
♦ **POI** Partners of Intermediaries (#18246)
♦ POI – Preventive Oncology International (internationally oriented national body)
♦ Poisson – International Conference on Poisson Geometry (meeting series)
♦ Pöjhamaade Investeerimispank (#17327)
♦ Pojhoismainen Naistutkimusinstituutti / see Nordic Information for Gender Knowledge (#17317)
♦ **POLA** Presidents of Law Associations in Asia (#18486)
♦ Polar Bears International (internationally oriented national body)

♦ Polar Educators International (PEI) 18411

Pres address not obtained. E-mail: polareducators@gmail.com.
URL: http://www.polareducator.org/

History 2012. Founded following the International Polar Year Conference "From Knowledge to Action", Montréal QC (Canada). **Aims** Connect polar education, research, indigenous knowledge and the global community; provide a deeper understanding of current polar sciences to a global audience. **Structure** Council; Executive Committee; Working Groups. **Languages** English. **Staff** 5.00 FTE, voluntary. **Activities** Events/meetings; training/education. **Publications** *Polar News.* **NGO Relations** Memorandum of Understanding with (1): *Association of Polar Early Career Scientists (APECS, #02864).* Partner of (2): *International Arctic Science Committee (IASC, #11668); Scientific Committee on Antarctic Research (SCAR, #19147).*
[2022.10.31/XM5559/**C**]

♦ Pôle Afrique / see Institut français de recherche en Afrique

♦ Pôle alpin de recherches sur les sociétés anciennes (PARSA) 18412

Dir Université Pierre Mendès-France (UPMF), Bureau B19, BP 47, 38040 Grenoble CEDEX 9, France. T. +33476827385. Fax +33476827356.

History 1992. **Aims** Increase transborder university cooperation; promote student exchange among members. **Events** *Colloquium* Turin (Italy) 2008, *Colloquium* Paris (France) 2007, *Colloquium* Geneva (Switzerland) 2005, *Colloquium* Barcelona (Spain) 2004, *Colloquium* Toulouse (France) 2003.
Members in 4 countries:
France, Italy, Spain, Switzerland.
NGO Relations Member of: *Fédération internationale des associations d'études classiques (FIEC, #09607).*
[2011/XJ4011/**F**]

♦ Pôle européen de développement Athus-Longwy-Rodange / see Association transfrontalière du pôle européen de développement (#02958)
♦ Pôle européen des trois frontières / see Association transfrontalière du pôle européen de développement (#02958)

♦ Pôle régional de recherche appliquée au développement des systèmes agricoles d'Afrique Centrale (PRASAC) 18413

Gen Manager BP 764, Ndjamena, Chad. T. +23522527024. Fax +23522527877. E-mail: daoud@prasac-cemac.org – djimadam@yahoo.fr – prasac_dg@yahoo.fr.
URL: http://www.prasac-cemac.org/

History Established Sep 1997, with the support of *West and Central African Council for Agricultural Research and Development (WECARD, #20907).* Currently also an institution of *Communauté économique et monétaire d'Afrique centrale (CEMAC, #04374).* **Aims** Foster sub-regional cooperation so as to strengthen the institutional and scientific capacity of national agricultural research. **Structure** General Management; One Focal Point per country, headed by a National Delegate. **Languages** English, French. **Staff** 16.00 FTE, paid. **Finance** Funded by CEMAC. **Activities** Research/documentation; capacity building; events/meetings. **Publications** Atlas; texts; research studies; colloquia proceedings; chapters.
Members Governments of 6 countries:
Cameroon, Central African Rep, Chad, Congo Brazzaville, Equatorial Guinea, Gabon.
IGO Relations Supports: *Centre Africain de Recherches sur Bananiers et Plantains (CARBAP, #03725).*
[2021/XJ2673/**E***]

♦ Pole Sports & Arts World Federation (POSA) 18414

Contact address not obtained. E-mail: contact@posaworld.org.
URL: https://www.posaworld.org/

Aims Unite, regulate, organize, lead, and develop the practice and competition of pole sport and pole art around the world. **Activities** Advocacy/lobbying/activism; sporting activities; training/education.
Members Federations in 29 countries:
Armenia, Belarus, Brazil, Canada, Czechia, Finland, France, Georgia, Greece, Haiti, Hungary, India, Israel, Italy, Korea Rep, Malta, Mexico, Monaco, Poland, Romania, Russia, Slovakia, Spain, Switzerland, Trinidad-Tobago, UK, Ukraine, USA, Uzbekistan.
NGO Relations Member of (2): *International Sport Network Organization (ISNO, #15592); World Heavy Events Association (WHEA).*
[2020/AA1089/**D**]

♦ Pôle universitaire Euclide (#05575)
♦ Police Convention (1920 treaty)
♦ Police Cooperation Convention for Southeast Europe (2006 treaty)

♦ Police Cooperation Convention for Southeast Europe Secretariat (PCC SEE Secretariat) 18415

Head Gospodinjska ulica 8, 1000 Ljubljana, Slovenia. T. +38615609300. Fax +38615609303. E-mail: info@pccseesecretariat.si.
URL: http://www.pccseesecretariat.si/

History 17 Jul 2008, Vienna (Austria), by decision of the Committee of Ministers of *Police Cooperation Convention for Southeast Europe (PCC SEE, 2006).* Became operational 1 Sep 2008. **Aims** Assist and support the Contracting Parties in implementing and applying the provisions of the PCC SEE. **Structure** Technical Expert Body hosted by DCAF. **Languages** Albanian, Bosnian, Bulgarian, English, German, Hungarian, Irish Gaelic, Macedonian, Romanian, Serbian, Slovene. Moldovan. **Staff** National secondments of Contracting Parties and DCAF employees. **Finance** Sources: *Geneva Centre for Security Sector Governance (DCAF, #10121);* Swiss Government; *European Commission (EC, #06633).* Annual contributions of Contracting Parties (according to MoU), seconding Contracting Parties. **Activities** Networking/liaising; financial and/or material support; meeting activities. **Events** *Meeting* Kranj (Slovenia) 2010, *Meeting* Sofia (Bulgaria) 2010, *Meeting* Brussels (Belgium) 2009, *Meeting* Vienna (Austria) 2008.
Members Contracting Parties (11):
Albania, Austria, Bosnia-Herzegovina, Bulgaria, Hungary, Moldova, Montenegro, North Macedonia, Romania, Serbia, Slovenia.
[2017.03.10/XJ2477/**E***]

♦ Police Futurists International / see Society of Police Futurists International

♦ Policy Association for an Open Society (PASOS) 18416

Exec Dir Zitna 608/27, 110 00 Prague 1, Czechia. T. +420773072321.
URL: http://pasos.org/

History Set up Dec 2003. Registered in accordance with Czech law, 16 Sep 2004. **Aims** Promote and protect democracy, human rights and open society values – including the rule of law, good governance, and economic and social development. **Structure** General Assembly; Board of Directors; Advisory Council; Secretariat. **Activities** Knowledge management/information dissemination; events/meetings. **Publications** Annual Report. Policy briefs; guides; booklets.
Members Organizations. Full in 22 countries:
Albania, Armenia, Azerbaijan, Belarus, Bosnia-Herzegovina, Bulgaria, Czechia, Estonia, Georgia, Hungary, Kosovo, Kyrgyzstan, Latvia, Moldova, Montenegro, North Macedonia, Poland, Romania, Serbia, Slovakia, Slovenia, Ukraine.
Included in the above, 8 organizations listed in this Yearbook:
Analytical Centre on Globalization and Regional Cooperation (ACGRC); Caucasian Institute for Peace, Democracy and Development (CIPDD); Central and Eastern European University Network (CEEUN); European Institute Foundation, Sofia; Institut pro evropskou politiku (EUROPEUM); International Centre for Human Development (ICHD); International Centre for Policy Studies, Kiev (ICPS); Mirovni inštitut.
Associate in 11 countries:
Azerbaijan, Bosnia-Herzegovina, Bulgaria, Czechia, Georgia, Italy, Kazakhstan, Romania, Russia, Türkiye, UK.
Included in the above, 3 organizations listed in this Yearbook:
European Council on Foreign Relations (ECFR, #06821); Global Political Trends Center (GPoT); International Centre for Minority Studies and Intercultural Relations (IMIR, #12504).
NGO Relations Member of: *Eastern Partnership Civil Society Forum (EaP CSF, #05247).* [2020/XM4820/y/**D**]

♦ Policy Center for Roma and Minorities (internationally oriented national body)

♦ Policy Network 18417

Contact 11 Tufton Street, 3rd Floor, London, SW1P 3QB, UK. T. +442073402200. Fax +442073402211.
URL: https://policynetwork.org/

History 1997, as *International Network for Progressive Governance – Internationella Nätverket för Progressiv Politik.* **Events** *Summit* London (UK) 2006, *Summit* Johannesburg (South Africa) 2005, *Summit* Budapest (Hungary) 2004, *Summit* London (UK) 2003, *Summit* London (UK) 2003. **Members** Social Democrats. Membership countries not specified. [2018/XF6330/**F***]

♦ Policy Parnterships Project for Genomic Governance (P3G2) 18418

Projet de Partenariats sur les Politiques de Gouvernance en Génomique

Contact McGill – Genome Quebec Innovation Ctr, 740 Dr Penfield Ave, Ste 5104, Montréal QC H3A 0G1, Canada. T. +15143981618. E-mail: secretariat@p3g2.org.
URL: http://p3g2.org/

History 2003, Montréal, QC (Canada). Founded as an international consortium. Phase II started 2012. From 2004 to 2019 structured as a not-for-profit corporation; from 2019 comes within McGill University's Centre of Genomics and Policy. Former names and other names: *Public Population Project in Genomics (P3G)* – former (2003 to 2017). **Aims** Develop and support policy, ethical and governance frameworks of biobanks, genomic research databases and other similar health and social research infrastructures so as to optimize cross-border access and use. **Structure** Secretariat; General Assembly; Board of Directors; Steering Committee; International Working Groups. **Languages** English, French. **Activities** Events/meeting. **Events** *Annual general meeting / Annual Meeting* Montréal, QC (Canada) 2010, *Meeting* Brussels (Belgium) 2009, *Annual General Meeting* Luxembourg (Luxembourg) 2009, *Annual general meeting / Annual Meeting* Barcelona (Spain) 2008, *Annual general meeting / Annual Meeting* Montréal, QC (Canada) 2007. **Members** Individuals and not-for-profit organizations. Charter, Associate and Individual. Members in over 45 countries. Membership countries not specified. [2021/XM4638/**F**]

♦ Policy Studies Organization (internationally oriented national body)

♦ POLIS 18419

Acting Gen Sec Rue du Trône 98, 1050 Brussels, Belgium. T. +3225005675. Fax +3225005680. E-mail: polis@polisnetwork.eu.
URL: http://www.polisnetwork.eu/

History 1989. Former names and other names: *Promoting Operational Links with Integrated Services (POLIS)* – former; *European Cities and Regions Networking for New Transport Solutions* – former; *Réseau de villes et de régions européennes pour de nouvelles solutions de transport* – former; *Europäische Stadt und Regionen Arbeiten an Neuen Verkehrslösungen* – former; *European Cities and Regions Networking for Innovative Transport Solutions* – full title. Registration: Banque-Carrefour des Entreprises, Belgium; EU Transparency Register, No/ID: 27284005223-47. **Aims** Foster cooperation across *Europe* on common local and regional *transport* and *mobility* issues; increase awareness of European transport *policies* and programmes at *local* level; build up expertise and stimulate exchange of experience on innovative transport policies, technologies and funding; investigate and promote new solutions to transport problems and improve transport management; communicate the transport needs and priorities of cities and regions. **Structure** General Assembly; Management Committee; Secretariat. **Languages** English. **Staff** 18.00 FTE, paid. **Finance** Sources: members' dues. **Activities** Advocacy/lobbying/activism; awareness raising; events/meetings; knowledge management/information dissemination; networking/liaising; politics/policy/regulatory; research/documentation. **Events** *Annual POLIS Conference* Brussels (Belgium) 2022, *Urban Air Mobility: Preparing for (very) near future* Brussels (Belgium) 2022, *Annual POLIS Conference* Gothenburg (Sweden) 2021, *Annual POLIS Conference* Netherlands 2020, *Annual POLIS Conference* Brussels (Belgium) 2019. **Publications** *POLIS Public Newsletter* (4 a year); *Thinking Cities* (2 a year); *InfoPolis* (24 a year) – members' newsletter.
Members Full (cities, towns, regions and regional organizations with the character of local authorities and having a democratically elected government, local public transport corporations) in 17 countries:
Belgium, Czechia, Denmark, Estonia, France, Germany, Greece, Hungary, Ireland, Italy, Netherlands, Norway, Portugal, Romania, Spain, Sweden, UK.
Associate (bodies eligible for full membership and outside bodies with related interests) in 7 countries:
Brazil, Czechia, France, Greece, Israel, Netherlands, UK.
NGO Relations Member of (1): *European Road Transport Research Advisory Council (ERTRAC, #08396).*
[2021.09.02/XF1446/**F**]

♦ Polish Humanitarian Action (internationally oriented national body)
♦ Polish Institute of International Affairs (internationally oriented national body)
♦ Polish Institute of International Economic Relations / see Polish Institute of International Affairs

♦ Polish-Scandinavian Research Institute (IPS) 18420

Polsk-Skandinavisk Forskningsinstitut – Instytut Polsko-Skandynawski

Pres Østerbrogade 230, II th, 2100 Copenhagen Ø, Denmark. T. +4539299826.
Sec Sponholzstr 38, 12159 Berlin, Germany.

History 3 Oct 1985. **Aims** Initiate and support scientific studies of relations between Poland and Scandinavian countries, with reference to their history. **Structure** General Assembly; Board. **Languages** Danish, Faroese, Icelandic, Norwegian, Polish, Swedish. **Staff** 2.00 FTE, voluntary. 2 voluntary. **Finance** Donations. **Activities** Networking/liaising; events/meetings; awards/prizes/competitions; research/documentation; publishing activities. **Events** *Conference* Gdansk (Poland) 2017, *Conference* Gdansk (Poland) 2015, *Conference* Lund (Sweden) 2005. **Publications** *History of the Institute 1985-2019.* Annual Report; conference volumes; monographs; essays.
Members Ordinary (14); Corresponding (9). Individuals in 6 countries:
Denmark, Estonia, Germany, Norway, Poland, Sweden. [2019.12.12/XN6935/jv/**D**]

♦ POLIS – Institute for Politics and International Studies (internationally oriented national body)

♦ Polis – International Network in Environmental Education (INEE) 18421

Polis – Réseau international en éducation à l'environnement (RIEE)

Coordinator PO Box 4, Siros, 841 00 Ermoúpolis, Greece. T. +30281087804. Fax +30281087840. E-mail: polis.eenet@gmail.com.
URL: https://polis-inee.org/

History May 1994, with the assistance of *Fondation Charles Léopold Mayer pour le progrès de l'homme (FPH, #09815).* Originally referred to in French as *Réseau européen d'éducation à l'environnement.* **Aims** Promote the work of people and organizations active in the field of environmental education by the exchange if their experience; promote international collaboration on mutual aid for the members' actions as educators. **Finance** During 1997: *European Commission (EC, #06633)* through DG22; Government of Greece. During 1998-1999: FPH. **Activities** Organizes meetings and training sessions. **Publications** *Dialogues for Environmental Education* in English, French, Greek – bulletin. Books. **Information Services** *Dialogues for the Progress of Humanity* – created by FPH.
Members Organizations () and individuals in 60 countries:
Algeria, Argentina, Australia, Bahamas, Belgium, Brazil, Burkina Faso, Burundi, Canada, Chile (*), China, Congo Brazzaville, Congo DR, Côte d'Ivoire, Croatia, Cuba, Denmark (*), Ecuador, Egypt, Fiji, Finland, France (*), Gambia, Germany, Ghana, Greece, Guinea, India, Indonesia, Ireland, Italy (*), Japan, Kenya, Lebanon, Madagascar, Malta, Mauritius, Mexico, Morocco, Namibia, Nepal, Netherlands, New Zealand, Philippines, Portugal, Senegal, Singapore, Slovenia, South Africa, Spain (*), Sri Lanka, Switzerland, Tanzania UR, Thailand, Togo, Uganda, UK (*), USA, Venezuela, Zimbabwe.
NGO Relations Member of: *Alliance for a Responsible and United World (inactive).* [2016/XF3779/**F**]

♦ Polisportive Giovanili Salesiane – Internationale (internationally oriented national body)
♦ Polis – Réseau international en éducation à l'environnement (#18421)
♦ Political Agreement (1922 treaty)

♦ Political Ecology Network (POLLEN) 18422

Secretariat Dept of Food and Resources Economics, Univ of Copenhagen, Rolighedsvej 23, 1958 Frederiksberg C, Denmark. E-mail: politicalecologynetwork@gmail.com.
URL: https://politicalecologynetwork.org/

History Founded 2015, by a group of European 'nodes'. Developed into a global network. **Aims** Be the umbrella organization for political ecology research and conversations; enable and facilitate cross-fertilization of information about political ecology research, literature, and relevant funding opportunities among the nodes; encourage and strengthen political ecology work, both within and outside academia; find ways to engage with activist, civil society and political groups and work to bring these groups into discussion with the network. **Structure** Secretariat. **Languages** English. **Staff** Voluntary. **Activities** Events/meetings; knowledge management/information dissemination; networking/liaising. **Events** *Biennial Conference* Frederiksberg (Denmark) 2020, *Biennial Conference* Oslo (Norway) 2018, *Biennial Conference* Wageningen (Netherlands) 2016. **Publications** *POLLEN Newsletter.* [2020.01.20/XM8060/**F**]

♦ Political Economy of International Organizations (PEIO) 18423

Contact Univ of Heidelberg, Alfred-Weber-Inst for Economics, Bergheimer Str 58, 69115 Heidelberg, Germany. T. +496221542921. E-mail: conference@peio.me.
URL: http://www.peio.me/

History Founded 2008. **Aims** Bring together economists, political scientists and other scholars to discuss political-economy issues related to any international organization. **Structure** Informal structure, with organizing Board responsible for annual conference. **Languages** English. **Finance** Annual budget: euro 30,000. **Activities** Events/meetings. **Events** *Annual Conference* Oxford (UK) 2022, *Annual Conference* Vancouver, BC (Canada) 2020, *Annual Conference* Salzburg (Austria) 2019, *Annual Conference* Madison, WI (USA) 2018, *Annual Conference* Bern (Switzerland) 2017. **Publications** *Review of International Organizations.* [2019.12.13/XJ2636/c/**E**]

♦ Political Science and International Relations Institute, Bogota (internationally oriented national body)
♦ Politique de coopération des organisations non-gouvernementales / see Verband Entwicklungspolitik und Humanitäre Hilfe e.V.

♦ Politzer Society 18424

Sec Dept Otolaryngology, Medical College of Wisconsin, 9200 W Wisconsin Ave, Milwaukee WI 53226, USA. E-mail: info@politzersociety.org.
URL: http://www.politzersociety.org/

History 1978. Former names and other names: *Politzer Society – The International Society for Otologic Surgery and Science* – full title; *International Society for Otological Surgery* – former. **Aims** Advance clinical and basic science knowledge of otologic surgery and related fields. **Structure** Board of Directors, including President, President-Elect, Secretary, Treasurer and Program Committee Chairman. **Languages** English. **Staff** 12.00 FTE, paid. **Finance** Meeting registrations; commercial company donations. **Activities** Organizes: biennial meeting; satellite meetings. **Events** *Meeting* Sao Paulo (Brazil) 2022, *Meeting* Warsaw (Poland) 2019, *Meeting* Las Palmas de Gran Canaria (Spain) 2018, *Meeting* Niigata (Japan) 2015, *Meeting* Antalya (Turkey) 2013. [2021/XD5746/**D**]

♦ Politzer Society – The International Society for Otologic Surgery and Science / see Politzer Society (#18424)
♦ Pollen Education (internationally oriented national body)
♦ **POLLEN** Political Ecology Network (#18422)
♦ Polska Akcja Humanitarna (internationally oriented national body)
♦ Polski Instytut Spraw Miedzynarodowych (internationally oriented national body)
♦ Polsk-Skandinavisk Forskningsinstitut (#18420)
♦ POLY-CHAR – International Polymer Characterization Forum (meeting series)
♦ POLYCHAR – World Forum on Advanced Materials (meeting series)
♦ Polyglot Conference (meeting series)
♦ POLYMER BLENDS – European Symposium on Polymer Blends (meeting series)
♦ Polymer Network Club / see Polymer Networks Group (#18425)

♦ Polymer Networks Group 18425

Contact Dep of Chemistry, Univ of Cyprus, 75 Kallipoleos Ave, PO Box 20537, CY-1678 Nicosia, Cyprus. T. +35799583332. Fax +35722892801. E-mail: info@polymernetworksgroup.org.
URL: http://www.polymernetworksgroup.org/

History Oct 1975, as *Polymer Network Club.* Present name adopted 1977. **Aims** Promote international contacts and the stimulation of research in the field of polymer networks. **Events** *Biennial International Conference* Rome (Italy) 2022, *Biennial International Conference* Potomac, MD (USA) 2020, *Biennial International Conference* Prague (Czechia) 2018, *Biennial International Conference* Stockholm (Sweden) 2016, *Biennial International Conference* Tokyo (Japan) 2014. [2018/XM2300/**F**]

♦ Polymer Processing Society (PPS) 18426

Sec Natl Technical Univ of Athens, School Mining Eng and Metallurgy, Zografou, 157 80 Athens, Greece. T. +302107722163. Fax +302107722251.
Pres address not obtained.
URL: http://www.tpps.org/

History Mar 1985, Akron, OH (USA). Former names and other names: *International Polymer Processing Society* – former. Registration: 501(c)(6) organization, No/ID: EIN: 34-1470253, Start date: 1987, USA. **Aims** Foster scientific understanding and technical innovation in polymer processing. **Structure** Executive Committee. **Languages** English. **Staff** Voluntary. **Finance** Sources: meeting proceeds; members' dues. Annual budget: 50,000 USD. **Events** *International Conference* Cartagena de Indias (Colombia) 2024, *International Conference* St Gallen (Switzerland) 2023, *International Conference* Fukuoka (Japan) 2022, *International Conference* Fukuoka (Japan) 2021, *International Conference* Montréal, QC (Canada) 2021. **Publications** *International Polymer Processing* (5 a year). *Progress in Polymer Processing.*
Members Full in 45 countries and territories:
Algeria, Australia, Austria, Belgium, Brazil, Canada, China, Cyprus, Czechia, Denmark, Finland, France, Germany, Greece, Hong Kong, Hungary, India, Iran Islamic Rep, Ireland, Israel, Italy, Japan, Korea Rep, Kuwait, Mexico, Netherlands, New Zealand, Norway, Poland, Portugal, Romania, Russia, Saudi Arabia, Singapore, Slovakia, South Africa, Spain, Sweden, Switzerland, Taiwan, Thailand, Türkiye, UK, USA. [2022.10.11/XD7649/**B**]

♦ Polyolefin Circular Economy Platform (PCEP) 18427

SG Avenue des Arts 6-9, 1210 Brussels, Belgium. E-mail: info@pcep.eu.
URL: https://pcep.eu/

History Registration: Banque-Carrefour des Entreprises, No/ID: 0737.397.463, Start date: 20 Oct 2019, Belgium; EU Transparency Register, No/ID: 096637338526-53, Start date: 11 Jun 2020. **Aims** Design out waste; keep maximum products and material in use for as long as possible; recycle products into high-quality new raw material. **Structure** Steering Board. **Events** *Annual Conference* 2021. **NGO Relations** Partner of (1): *European Coalition for Chemical Recycling.* [2021/AA2025/**F**]

♦ PolyStyreneLoop Cooperative (unconfirmed)

♦ Polyurea Development Association Europe (PDA Europe) 18428

Pres Av de Tervuren 188A, 1150 Brussels, Belgium. T. +3227611611. E-mail: info@pda-europe.org.
URL: http://www.pda-europe.org/

History Registration: Banque-Carrefour des Entreprises, No/ID: 0889.832.270, Start date: 4 Jun 2007. **Aims** Pursue the interests of the European polyurea industry; promote exchange of ideas for development of highest standards and operating efficiency with the European polyurea industry; develop methods for improving conditions and advancing best interests of the industry; support and promote equality opportunity within the industry. **Structure** Board of Directors; Committees (4). **Events** *Annual Conference* Orlando, FL (USA) 2021, *Annual Conference* Brussels (Belgium) 2020, *Annual Conference* Brussels (Belgium) 2019, *Annual Conference* London (UK) 2017, *Annual Conference* Berlin (Germany) 2015.
Members Companies in 31 countries:
Belgium, Brazil, China, Colombia, Cyprus, Czechia, Denmark, Estonia, Finland, France, Germany, Greece, Hungary, Italy, Korea Rep, Latvia, Netherlands, North Macedonia, Norway, Portugal, Romania, Saudi Arabia, Slovakia, South Africa, Spain, Sweden, Switzerland, Türkiye, UK, United Arab Emirates, USA. [2020/XJ6256/**D**]

♦ POMBE – International Fission Yeast Meeting (meeting series)
♦ POMED – Project on Middle East Democracy (internationally oriented national body)
♦ Pomoc Kosciolowi w Potrzebie (#00587)
♦ Pomoc Pronasledovane Cirkvi (#20804)
♦ **Pompidou Group** Co-operation Group to Combat Drug Abuse and Illicit Trafficking in Drugs (#04796)
♦ Pompiers sans frontières (#09779)
♦ POMS – Production and Operations Management Society (internationally oriented national body)

♦ The Pond: Philosophy Of Science Around the Mediterranean (POND) 18429

Address not obtained.
URL: https://pondposmed.wordpress.com/

History First meeting organized 2016. **Structure** Steering Committee. **Activities** Events/meetings. **Events** *Conference* Lisbon (Portugal) 2018.
Members Individuals in 14 countries:
Albania, Bulgaria, Cyprus, France, Greece, Israel, Italy, Lebanon, Malta, Portugal, Serbia, Spain, Tunisia, Türkiye. [2018/XM7962/**F**]

♦ **POND** The Pond: Philosophy Of Science Around the Mediterranean (#18429)

♦ Pontifical Academy Cultorum Martyrum 18430

Pontificia Accademia Cultorum Martyrum

Gen Sec Via Napoleone III 1, 00185 Rome RM, Italy. T. +39064455833. E-mail: cultorum.martyrum@org.va.
Headquarters Piazza Protomartiri Romani, 00120 Vatican City, Vatican.
Main Website: https://www.vatican.va/roman_curia/pontifical_academies/cult-martyrum/index_it.htm

History 2 Feb 1879, Holy See. Founded by Mariano Armellini, Orazio Marucchi, Adolfo Hytreck and Enrico Stevenson, scholars of sacred antiquity. Statutes revised and approved, 1995. Since then, elevated by Pope John Paul II to the rank of Pontifical Academy. Coordinated by *Pontifical Council for Culture (#18443).* Former names and other names: *Collegium Cultorum Martyrum* – former (1879 to 1994). **Aims** Promote the cult of the Holy Martyrs, as well as the history of the Witnesses of the Faith and the monuments connected to them since the firts centuries of Christianity. **Structure** Magister; Sacerdos; Ab Epistulis; Procurator; Arcarius; Consiglieri; Sodali e Associati. **Languages** Italian. **Activities** Active in: Holy See, Italy. [2022.06.14/XM4664/**F**]

♦ Pontifical Academy of the Immaculate Conception 18431

Pontificia Accademia dell'Immacolata

Vice-Pres c/o PCCS, Via della Conciliazione 5, 00120 Vatican City, Vatican.
Sec Via del Serafico 1, 00142 Rome RM, Italy.
URL: http://www.vatican.va/

History 1835, Rome (Italy). Comes within *Administrative Hierarchy of the Roman Catholic Church (#00117).* [2008/XM4662/**F**]

♦ Pontifical Academy for Life 18432

Académie pontificale pour la vie – Pontificia Accademia per la Vita – Pontificia Academia pro Vita

Communications Manager Via della Conciliazione 1, 00193 Rome RM, Italy. T. +39669895200. Fax +39669882014. E-mail: pressoffice@pav.va.
Events Manager address not obtained.
URL: http://www.academyforlife.va/

History Founded 11 Feb 1994, when statute was defined by motu proprio *Vitae Mysterium* of Pope John-Paul II. Comes within the *Administrative Hierarchy of the Roman Catholic Church (#00117).* **Aims** Promote and defend *human life,* especially regarding *bioethics* as it impinges on *Christian morality.* **Structure** General Assembly; Board of Directors; Central Office. **Activities** Events/meetings; publishing activities. **Events** *Assembly* Vatican City (Vatican) 2023, *Assemblée générale* Vatican City (Vatican) 2019, *Assemblée générale* Vatican City (Vatican) 2018, *Assemblée générale* Rome (Italy) 2017, *Assemblée générale* Vatican City (Vatican) 2016. **Publications** *Public Health in Global Perspective – Pandemic, Bioethics, Future* (1st 2023) – Proceedings of XXVII General Assembly 2021 -; *Etica Teologica della Vita – Theological Ethics of Life* (2nd 2022) in English, French, Italian, Spanish – Atti del Seminario di studio promosso dalla Pontificia Accademia per la Vita; *Pandemic and Universal Brotherhood – Pandemia e Fraternità Universale* (1st 2022) in English, Italian – Notes on the COVID19 Emergency; *The Cloning Prohibition in the International Debate* (2003); *Animal and Vegetable Biotechnology: New Frontiers and New Responsibilities* (1999); *Evangelium Vitae of Pope Giovanni Paolo II* (1995). Proceedings of General Assembly; workshop proceedings.
Members Categories: Ordinary; Correspondant; Young; Honorary. Academicians (160) in 38 countries:
Argentina, Australia, Austria, Belgium, Bolivia, Brazil, Burkina Faso, Canada, Chile, Colombia, Congo DR, Cuba, Czechia, Egypt, France, Germany, Greece, Hungary, India, Israel, Italy, Japan, Korea Rep, Malaysia, Malta, Mexico, Peru, Philippines, Poland, Portugal, Spain, Sweden, Tunisia, UK, Ukraine, Uruguay, USA, Venezuela.
NGO Relations Cooperates with: scientific medical societies; universities. [2023.02.14/XE2114/v/**E**]

♦ Pontifical Academy of the New Lincei / see Pontifical Academy of Sciences (#18433)

♦ Pontifical Academy of Sciences 18433

Académie pontificale des sciences – Pontificia Accademia delle Scienze – Pontificia Academia Scientarium

Head Office Casina Pio IV, 00120 Vatican City, Vatican. T. +39669883195. Fax +39669885218. E-mail: pas@pas.va.
URL: http://www.casinapioiv.va/

History 1603, as *Academy of the Lincei*; restored, 1847, as *Pontifical Academy of the New Lincei*; reorganized, and present name adopted, 1936. Comes within the *Administrative Hierarchy of the Roman Catholic Church (#00117)*. **Aims** Promote progress of *mathematical, physical* and *natural sciences* and the study of *epistemological problems*; keep the *Church* informed of scientific advances; provide a forum to give a moral dimension to scientific work. **Structure** Plenary Session (every 2 years, Vatican City) of Catholic and non-Catholic scientists (80, including 25 Nobel Prize Winners), elected for life, without discrimination as to religion or race. Working Groups; Study Weeks. **Languages** English, French, German, Italian, Spanish. **Staff** 2.00 FTE, paid. **Activities** Events/meetings; training/education; awards/prizes/competitions. **Events** *Plenary session* Vatican City (Vatican) 2006, *Plenary Session* Vatican City (Vatican) 2004, *Plenary Session* Vatican City (Vatican) 2003, *Plenary session* Vatican City (Vatican) 2002, *Plenary session* Vatican City (Vatican) 1998. **Publications** Proceedings; commentaries; articles; guides.
Members Individuals in 24 countries and territories:
Argentina, Australia, Austria, Belgium, Brazil, Canada, Chile, China, France, Germany, Ghana, Holy See, India, Israel, Italy, Japan, Poland, Russia, Spain, Sweden, Switzerland, Taiwan, UK, USA.
NGO Relations Sponsored the setting up of: *Academia de Ciencias de América Latina (ACAL, #00010)*; *TWAS (#20270)*. Close coordination with: *Pontifical Council for Culture (#18443)*. [2017.03.09/XF3272/v/**E**]

♦ Pontifical Academy of Social Sciences 18434

Académie pontificale des sciences sociales – Pontificia Accademia delle Scienze Sociali – Pontificia Academia Scientiarum Socialium

Pres Casina Pio IV, 00120 Vatican City, Vatican. T. +39669881441. Fax +39669885218. E-mail: pass@pass.va.
URL: http://www.pass.va/

History Founded 1994, activities being coordinated by *Pontifical Council for Justice and Peace (inactive)* within the *Administrative Hierarchy of the Roman Catholic Church (#00117)*. **Aims** Promote study and progress of social, *economic, political* and *juridical* sciences, thus offering the *Church* the elements which she can use in the study and development of her *social doctrine*. **Structure** Academy comprises President and 20-40 members; Foundation of the Academy has a Council of 7 members. **Languages** English, French, German, Italian, Spanish. **Finance** Financial support from "Foundation for the Promotion of the Social Sciences", located in Vaduz (Liechtenstein). Other sources: donations; gifts. **Activities** Events/meetings; training/education; research/documentation; publishing activities. **Events** *Plenary Session* Vatican City (Vatican) 2010, *Plenary Session* Vatican City (Vatican) 2009, *Plenary Session* Vatican City (Vatican) 2008, *Plenary Session* Vatican City (Vatican) 2007, *Plenary Session* Vatican City (Vatican) 2006. **Publications** Proceedings (Acta).
Members Individuals in 17 countries:
Argentina, Austria, Belgium, Canada, China, Czechia, France, Germany, Italy, Japan, Mexico, Norway, Philippines, South Africa; Spain, UK, USA.
NGO Relations *Pontifical Council for Culture (#18443)*. [2017.03.09/XF2723/v/**E**]

♦ Pontifical Academy of St Thomas Aquinas 18435

Pontificia Accademia di San Tommaso d'Aquino

Sec c/o Casina Pio IV, 00120 Vatican City, Vatican. T. +39669881441. Fax +39669885218. E-mail: past@past.va.
URL: http://www.past.va/

History Founded 15 Oct 1879, by Pope Leo XII. 1904, status confirmed by Pope Pius X. Activities expanded by Pope Benedict XV, 1914. 1934, absorbed *Academy of Catholic Religion*. 28 Jan 1999, reformed by Pope John Paul II. Also referred to as *Pontifical Academy of St Thomas Aquinas and Catholic Religion*. Comes within *Administrative Hierarchy of the Roman Catholic Church (#00117)*.
Members Ordinary (53); Honorary (22); Emeritus (16). Members in 13 countries and territories:
Argentina, Austria, Belgium, Chile, France, Germany, Holy See, Italy, Mexico, Spain, Switzerland, USA, Venezuela.
[2014.11.25/XM4661/**F**]

♦ Pontifical Academy of St Thomas Aquinas and Catholic Religion / see Pontifical Academy of St Thomas Aquinas (#18435)

♦ Pontifical Athenaeum Antonianum / see Pontifical University Antonianum

♦ Pontifical Biblical Commission 18436

Commission biblique pontificale – Pontificia Commissione Biblica – Pontificia Commissio Biblica

Main Office Piazza del Sant'Uffizio, 00193 Rome RM, Italy. T. +39669884846 – +39669883736. E-mail: vati419@cfaith.va.
URL: http://vatican.va/roman_curia/congregations/cfaith/pcb_index.htm

History 30 Oct 1902, by Leo XIII, as *Commissio Pontificia de Re Biblica*; completely restructured 27 Jun 1971, by Pope Paul VI. Assists *Congregation for the Doctrine of the Faith (#04669)* within the framework of the *Administrative Hierarchy of the Roman Catholic Church (#00117)*. **Structure** Headed by Cardinal Prefect of the Congregation for the Doctrine of the Faith. [2018/XF4771/**E**]

♦ Pontifical Biblical Institute 18437

Institut biblique pontifical – Pontificio Istituto Biblico – Pontificium Institutum Biblicum de Urbe

SG Via della Pilotta 25, 00187 Rome RM, Italy. T. +396695266179 – +396695261. Fax +396695266211. E-mail: pibsegr@biblico.it.
Jerusalem 3 P E Botta Str, PO Box 497, 91004 Jerusalem, Israel. T. +97226252843. Fax +97226241203. E-mail: admipib@gmail.com.
URL: http://www.biblico.it/

History 1909, Rome (Italy). Founded by Pope Pius X and entrusted by him to the *Society of Jesus (SJ)*. Maintains *Pontifical Biblical Institute of Jerusalem*, set up in 1927, as a branch of the Roman Institute. **Aims** Promote scriptural studies. **Languages** English, Italian. **Finance** Sources: donations; fees for services. **Activities** Certification/accreditation; training/education. **Publications** *Biblica* (4 a year); *Orientalia* (3 a year); *Acta Pontificii Instituti Biblici* (annual); *Elenchus of Biblica* (annual). Analecta Biblica / Dissertationes; Analecta Biblica / Studia; Analecta Orientalia; Bible in Dialogue; Biblica et Orientalia; Studia Pohl; Subsidia Biblica. **NGO Relations** Member of (1): *International Federation of Catholic Universities (IFCU, #13381)*.
[2023/XF4835/j/**F**]

♦ Pontifical Commission for Authentic Interpretation of the Code of Canon Law / see Pontifical Council for Legislative Texts (#18445)

♦ Pontifical Commission for the Cultural Heritage of the Church / see Pontifical Commission for the Cultural Patrimony of the Church (#18438)

♦ Pontifical Commission for the Cultural Patrimony of the Church ... 18438

Commission pontificale pour les biens culturels de l'Eglise – Pontificia Commissio de Bonis Culturalibus Ecclesiae

Pres Via della Conciliazione 5-7, 00120 Vatican City, Vatican. T. +39669885640. Fax +39669884621.
URL: http://www.vatican.va/roman_curia/index.htm

History 28 Jun 1988, by Pope John-Paul II, as *Commission pontificale pour la conservation du patrimoine artistique et historique de l'Eglise – Pontificia Commissione per la Conservazione del Patrimonio Artistico e Storico*. Subsequently referred to as *Pontifical Commission for the Cultural Heritage of the Church*. Originally attached to *Congregation for the Clergy (#04667)*, as an organism of the Holy See and within the *Administrative Hierarchy of the Roman Catholic Church (#00117)*. Current title adopted when it was made independent by Papal 'Motu Proprio', 25 Mar 1993. **Aims** Care for and conserve the *artistic* and *historic* heritage created by the *Catholic* Church worldwide, in particular: (i) *art* – paintings, architecture, sculpture, *museums* of Christian art; (ii) Church *archives*; (iii) ecclesiastical *libraries*. **Structure** Structured according to geographical sectors corresponding to the various main languages of the world. Group of consultants. **Languages** English, Italian, Spanish. **Staff** 1.00 FTE, paid. **Finance** Financed by Holy See. **Activities** Direct contact with Episcopal Commissions for the Cultural Heritage in each nation and with local Commissions for the Cultural Heritage in each diocese. **Publications** Proceedings. **IGO Relations** Formal contacts with: *Council of Europe (CE, #04881)*; *International Centre for the Study of the Preservation and Restoration of Cultural Property (ICCROM, #12521)*; *UNESCO (#20322)*. **NGO Relations** Formal contacts with: *International Council on Monuments and Sites (ICOMOS, #13049)*; *International Council of Museums (ICOM, #13051)*. President is also President of: *Pontifical Commission for Sacred Archeology (#18441)*. President is also member of: Pontifical Congregation for Catholic Education; *Pontifical Council for Promoting Christian Unity (PCPCU, #18446)*; Pontifical Council for Promoting New Evangelization. [2011.06.01/XE1851/v/**E**]

♦ Pontifical Commission for Didactic and Religious Motion Pictures / see Pontifical Council for Social Communications (#18447)

♦ Pontifical Commission "Ecclesia Dei" 18439

Commission pontificale "Ecclesia Dei"

Pres Piazza della Città Leonina, 00193 Rome RM, Italy. T. +39668307088. E-mail: cdf@cfaith.va.
URL: http://www.vatican.va/roman_curia/pontifical_commissions/ecclsdei/

Structure Cardinal Prefect of *Congregation for the Doctrine of the Faith (#04669)* acts as President. Secretary; 5 Cardinal members; assistants. Group of "permanent experts", composed of representatives of the dicasteries concerned, offers advice and expertise. **Activities** Regularizes canonical situation of a certain number of religious communities of a traditionalist nature which already exist but without recognition on the part of the Church by giving them a canonical form corresponding to their charism. Moreover, an ecclesial integration has been found for a number of traditionalist priests who had not been incardinated. Collaborates with local bishops with a view to satisfying groups of faithful linked to the Latin liturgical tradition which request a regular celebration of the Holy Mass in keeping with the 1962 rite in their dioceses.
Members Groups in 11 countries:
Argentina, Australia, Austria, Canada, Chile, France, Germany, Italy, Switzerland, UK, USA. [2012/XE2302/**E**]

♦ Pontifical Commission for Educational and Religious Cinematography / see Pontifical Council for Social Communications (#18447)

♦ Pontifical Commission for Latin America 18440

Commission pontificale pour l'Amérique latine – Pontificia Comisión para América Latina – Pontificia Commissione per l'America Latina – Pontificia Commissio pro America Latina

Sec of Vice Pres Palazzo San Paolo, 4th floor, Via della Conciliazione 1, 00120 Vatican City, Vatican. E-mail: pcal@latinamer.va.
URL: http://www.vatican.va/roman_curia/congregations/cbishops/pcal/

History 21 apr 1958, by Pius XII. Restructured, 18 Jun 1988, by Pope John-Paul II with the Motu Proprio 'Decessores Nostri'. Comes within *Administrative Hierarchy of the Roman Catholic Church (#00117)*. **Aims** Study the fundamental problems of the *Catholic* way of life in Latin America. **Structure** President and Vice-President, assisted by 32 Councillors and 13 members who are Cardinals or Bishops selected within Roman Curia or Latin American episcopate. **Events** *Plenary Assembly* Rome (Italy) 2011, *Plenary Assembly* Vatican City (Vatican) 2007, *General Session* Vatican City (Vatican) 1993, *Plenary Meeting* Vatican City (Vatican) 1993, *Latin American congress* Bogota (Colombia) 1990.
Members Individuals in 19 countries:
Argentina, Bolivia, Brazil, Canada, Chile, Cuba, Dominican Rep, Ecuador, El Salvador, Germany, Guatemala, Holy See, Honduras, Mexico, Nicaragua, Panama, Peru, Spain, USA. [2009/XF9144/v/**E**]

♦ Pontifical Commission for the Media of Social Communication / see Pontifical Council for Social Communications (#18447)

♦ Pontifical Commission for Motion Pictures / see Pontifical Council for Social Communications (#18447)

♦ Pontifical Commission for Motion Pictures, Radio and Television / see Pontifical Council for Social Communications (#18447)

♦ Pontifical Commission for Sacred Archeology 18441

Commission pontificale d'archéologie sacrée – Pontificia Commissione di Archeologia Sacra

Pres address not obtained. T. +39669893811. Fax +39669887368 – +39669887165. E-mail: cultura@cultura.va.
URL: http://www.vatican.va/roman_curia/pontifical_commissions/

History Founded 6 Jan 1852, by Pope Pius IX, within the framework of *Administrative Hierarchy of the Roman Catholic Church (#00117)*. **Aims** Provide protection, *conservation* and care for ancient sacred burial grounds and *catacombs*. **Structure** President; Secretary; Archeological Superintendent; Officials. **Languages** Italian. **Staff** 10.00 FTE, paid. **Finance** No budget. **Activities** Protection, conservation and care is currently aimed at early Christian catacombs found in and around the city of Rome, in Italy and throughout the Mediterranean basin. *Pontifical Institute of Christian Archaeology (#18449)*, set up in 1925, Rome, by Pope Pius XI, acts as research and training centre for the Commission and for the 'Pontificia Accademia Romana di Archeologia'. **Publications** *Rivista di Archeologia Cristiana* – with the Pontifical Institute. **NGO Relations** President is also President of: *Pontifical Commission for the Cultural Patrimony of the Church (#18438)*.
[2013.06.13/XE2301/v/**E**]

♦ Pontifical Committee for International Eucharistic Congresses 18442

Comité pontifical pour les congrès eucharistiques internationaux – Pontificio Comitato per i Congressi Eucaristici Internazionali – Pontificius Comitatus Eucharisticis Internationalibus Conventibus Provehendis

Sec Piazza San Calisto 16, 00120 Vatican City, Vatican. T. +39669887366. Fax +39669887154. E-mail: eucharistcongress@org.va.
Pres address not obtained.
URL: http://www.congressieucaristici.va/

History 1881, Lille (France). Founded at 1st International Eucharistic Congress. Formerly: *Oeuvre des congrès eucharistiques internationaux*. **Aims** Make ever better known, loved and served, Our Lord *Jesus Christ* in the Eucharistic Mystery, as centre of the life of the *Church* and of its mission for the salvation of the world. **Structure** Pontifical Commission: President, appointed by the Holy Father; the other members, appointed by the Holy Father, who elect the Vice-President from among their own number. **Languages** French, German, Italian, Spanish. **Staff** 5.00 FTE, paid. **Finance** Expenses relative to the preparation and celebration of the Congress sustained by the Local Committee. Ordinary expenses sustained by Amministrazione Patrimonio Sede Apostolica (APSA). **Activities** International Eucharistic Congresses (usually celebrated every 4 years); national eucharistic congresses worldwide. **Events** *Quadrennial Congress* Quito (Ecuador) 2024, *Quadrennial Congress* Budapest (Hungary) 2021, *Quadrennial Congress* Budapest (Hungary) 2020, *Quadrennial Congress* Cebu City (Philippines) 2016, *Quadrennial congress* Dublin (Ireland) 2012.
Members National Committees and National Delegates in 159 countries and territories:
Afghanistan, Albania, Algeria, Angola, Argentina, Australia, Austria, Bahrain, Bangladesh, Belarus, Belgium, Benin, Bhutan, Bolivia, Bosnia-Herzegovina, Botswana, Brazil, Brunei Darussalam, Bulgaria, Burkina Faso, Burundi, Cambodia, Cameroon, Canada, Cape Verde, Central African Rep, Chad, Chile, China, Colombia, Congo Brazzaville, Congo DR, Costa Rica, Côte d'Ivoire, Croatia, Cuba, Cyprus, Czechia, Denmark, Dominica, Dominican Rep, Ecuador, Egypt, El Salvador, Equatorial Guinea, Estonia, Ethiopia, Fiji, Finland, France, Gabon, Germany, Ghana, Greece, Grenada, Guatemala, Guinea, Guinea-Bissau, Guyana, Haiti, Holy See, Honduras, Hong Kong, Hungary, Iceland, India, Indonesia, Iran Islamic Rep, Iraq, Ireland, Israel, Italy, Japan, Jordan, Kazakhstan, Kenya, Kiribati, Korea DPR, Korea Rep, Kuwait, Kyrgyzstan, Laos, Latvia, Lebanon, Lesotho, Liberia, Liechtenstein, Lithuania, Luxembourg, Madagascar, Malawi, Malaysia, Mali, Malta, Marshall Is, Mauritania, Mauritius, Mexico, Micronesia FS, Morocco, Mozambique, Myanmar, Namibia, Nauru, Netherlands, New Zealand, Nicaragua, Niger, Nigeria, Norway, Pakistan, Palau, Palestine, Panama, Papua New Guinea, Paraguay, Peru, Philippines, Poland, Portugal, Puerto Rico, Romania, Russia, Rwanda, Samoa, Sao Tomé-Principe, Senegal, Seychelles, Sierra Leone, Singapore, Slovakia, Slovenia, Solomon Is, Somalia, South Africa, Spain, Sri Lanka, Sudan, Switzerland, Syrian AR, Taiwan, Tanzania UR, Thailand, Togo, Tonga, Trinidad-Tobago, Tunisia, Türkiye, Tuvalu, Uganda, UK, Ukraine, Uruguay, USA, Vanuatu, Venezuela, Vietnam, Zambia, Zimbabwe.
[2023/XF3975/**F**]

♦ Pontifical Council for Culture 18443

Conseil pontifical de la culture – Pontificio Consejo de la Cultura – Pontificium Consilium de Cultura (PCC) – Pontificio Consiglio della Cultura

Secretariat Via della Conciliazione 5, 00120 Vatican City, Vatican. T. +39669893811. Fax +39669887368 – +39669887165. E-mail: cultura@cultura.va.
URL: http://www.cultura.va/

History 25 Mar 1993. Founded as a dicastery of the Roman Curia, uniting the previous Pontifical Council of the same name, set up 20 May 1982, with *Pontificium Concilium pro Dialogo cum Non Credentibus (PCDNC, inactive)*, created 9 Apr 1965, by Pope Paul VI, as *'Secretariatus pro Non Credentibus'*. Part of the *Administrative Hierarchy of the Roman Catholic Church (#00117)*. **Aims** Witness to the Church's pastoral concern concerning the gap between faith and cultures; study unbelief and religious indifference, inquiring into the causes and consequences in different cultures; support the Church's evangelization of cultures and inculturation of the Gospel; promote initiatives of dialogue between faith and culture, as well as a dialogue with those who do not believe in God, whenever these show themselves open to sincere cooperation. **Structure** Plenary Session (always in Vatican City). Sections (2): *'Faith and Culture'* which pursues activities previously carried out by the 1982 Pontifical Council for Culture; *'Dialogue with Cultures'* which pursues the activities previously carried out by the Pontifical Council for Dialogue with Non-Believers. Presided over by a Cardinal or Archbishop, assisted by Secretary and Under-Secretary. Members and Consultors in various countries, nominated by the Pope. **Languages** English, French, German, Italian, Portuguese, Spanish. **Staff** 19.00 FTE, paid. **Finance** Directly from the Vatican. **Activities** Organizes: study conferences; seminars; research; intercultural dialogue; annual ceremony for Pontifical Academies whose activities are coordinated by Pontifical Council for Culture, when the Pope awards a prize to a young student, an artist or institution. Engages in a series of continental meetings, aimed at gathering information. **Events** *Plenary Assembly* Rome (Italy) 2008, *Rencontre des responsables des centres culturels catholiques du Bassin Méditerranéen* Sarajevo (Bosnia-Herzegovina) 2005, *Plenary Assembly* Vatican City (Vatican) 2004, *Conference on the presence and absence of Christians in art* Spydeberg (Norway) 2002, *Plenary assembly* Vatican City (Vatican) 1999. **Publications** *Cultures and Faith* (3 a year) in English, French, Italian, Spanish. *International Directory of Catholic Cultural Centres* (4th ed 2006).
Members Individuals in 42 countries:
Argentina, Australia, Austria, Bangladesh, Belgium, Benin, Burkina Faso, Cameroon, Canada, Chile, China, Colombia, Congo DR, Cuba, Estonia, France, Germany, Guatemala, Holy See, Hungary, India, Indonesia, Ireland, Italy, Japan, Luxembourg, Mexico, Myanmar, Netherlands, Panama, Peru, Philippines, Poland, Portugal, Senegal, Slovenia, Spain, Sri Lanka, Tanzania UR, UK, USA, Venezuela.
IGO Relations *Council of Europe (CE, #04881)* (Culture Committee); *UNESCO (#20322)*. **NGO Relations** Contacts with and coordination of activities with: *Illustrious Pontifical Academy of Fine Arts and Letters of the Virtuosi of the Pantheon (#11121)*; *Pontifical Academy of Sciences (#18433)*; *Pontifical Academy of Social Sciences (#18434)*; *Pontificia Academia Mariana Internationalis (PAMI, #18453)*; Pontifical Academy of Saint Thomas of Aquinas; Pontifical Academy of Theology; Pontifical "Cultorum Martyrum" Academy; Pontifical Roman Archaeological Academy. [2021/XE3800/v/E]

♦ Pontifical Council for Dialogue with Non-Believers (inactive)
♦ Pontifical Council for the Interpretation of Legislative Texts / see Pontifical Council for Legislative Texts (#18445)

♦ Pontifical Council for Interreligious Dialogue (PCID) 18444

Conseil pontifical pour le dialogue interreligieux – Pontificio Consiglio per il Dialogo Interreligioso – Pontificium Consilium pro Dialogo inter Religiones

Pres Via della Conciliazione 5, 00120 Vatican City, Vatican. T. +39669884321. Fax +39669884494. E-mail: dialogo@interrel.va.
URL: http://www.pcinterreligious.org/

History 19 May 1964, as *Secretariat for Non-Christians*, within the framework of *Administrative Hierarchy of the Roman Catholic Church (#00117)*. Current name adopted, 1988. **Aims** Deepen mutual understanding and respect between *Catholics* and followers of other *religious* traditions; encourage study of *religions*; promote friendly relations with other *believers*. **Structure** President; Secretary; Under-Secretary; Officials for Islam, Asia, Africa and New Religious Movements. **Events** *International Conference on the Religions and the Sustainable Development Goals (SDGs)* Vatican City (Vatican) 2019, *Catholic and Muslim cooperation in promoting justice in the contemporary world* Rome (Italy) 2012, *Colloquium* Teheran (Iran Islamic Rep) 2010, *Annual meeting* Rome (Italy) 2009, *Faith and reason in christianity and islam* Vatican City (Vatican) 2008. **Publications** *Pro Dialogo* (3 a year). **NGO Relations** Instrumental in setting up: *Monastic Interreligious Dialogue – North America (MID)*. [2019/XF1183/v/E]

♦ Pontifical Council for Legislative Texts 18445

Conseil pontifical pour les textes législatifs – Pontificio Consiglio per i Testi Legislativi – Pontificium Consilium de Legum Textibus

Pres Palazzo delle Congregazioni, Piazza Pio XII 10, 00193 Rome RM, Italy. T. +39669884008. Fax +39669884710. E-mail: vati495@legtxt.va.
Sec address not obtained.
URL: http://www.vatican.va/roman_curia/pontifical_councils/intrptxt/index_it.htm

History 2 Jan 1984, by Pope John-Paul II, as *Pontifical Commission for Authentic Interpretation of the Code of Canon Law*, with competence to interpret the provisions of the Code of Canon Law, promulgated 25 Jan 1983, and other universal laws of the Latin Church. Derives from an earlier *Pontifical Commission for Authentic Interpretation of the Canon Law*, created on 15 Sep 1917 by Pope Benedict XV, for authentic interpretation of the previous Code of Canon Law, promulgated 27 May 1917; this Commission continued until establishment of the *Pontifical Council for the Revision of the Code of Canon Law* by Pope John XXIII on 28 Mar 1963, with the task of revising the Code of Pope Benedict XV in the light of decrees of the Second Vatican Council. A related body, *Pontifical Commission for the Interpretation of the Decrees of the Second Vatican Council*, was set up on 11 Jul 1967, by Pope Paul VI. The competence of the latter Commission was subsequently extended to include the interpretation of all documents issued by the Holy See for execution of Conciliar decrees. The current Commission replaces both the 1963 and the 1967 Commission.
The Apostolic Constitution *'Pastor Bonus'*, 28 Jun 1988, expanded the competence of the Commission and changed its title to *Pontifical Council for the Interpretation of Legislative Texts – Conseil pontifical pour l'interprétation des textes législatifs – Pontificio Consiglio per l'Interpretazione dei Testi Legislativi – Pontificium Consilium de Legum Textibus Interpretandis*. The function of the Dicastery was further expanded on promulgation of the *'Codex Canonem Ecclesiarum Orientalium (CCEO)'*, 18 Oct 1990, and suppression by Pope John Paul II of the *Pontifical Commission for the Revision of the Code of Eastern Canon Law* – established by Pope Paul VI, 10 Jun 1972 – following completion of its work. The Council now also has the task of interpreting the CCEO and all the common laws of the Eastern Catholic Churches. It functions as part of the *Administrative Hierarchy of the Roman Catholic Church (#00117)*.
Aims Interpret the universal laws of the Catholic Church, including the Code of Canon Law and the Code of Canons of the Eastern Catholic Churches. **Structure** President; Secretary; Under-Secretary; Members (17); Staff Officials (7); Consultors (48). **Languages** English, French, German, Italian, Latin, Portuguese, Spanish. **Staff** 10.00 FTE, paid. **Activities** Competencies: *'Authentic interpretation'*, confirmed by Pontifical authority, of the universal laws of the Church – laws that pertain to all of the Latin Church and laws common to the Eastern Catholic Churches; *'Technical-juridical assistance'* to the other Dicasteries of the Roman Curia in preparation or revision of general normative documents such as General Decrees, Instructions and Directories, and in the study of specific disciplinary problems; *'Examination from a juridical perspective'* of the general decrees of episcopal bodies such as Episcopal Conferences and Particular Councils; *'Judgement concerning conformity'* of particular laws and general decrees issued by legislators below the level of the supreme authority with the universal laws of the Church. **Events** *Meeting* Vatican City (Vatican) 2008. **Publications** *Communicationes* (2 a year).
Members Individuals in 10 countries and territories:
Colombia, Germany, Hungary, India, Italy, Lebanon, Poland, Spain, Ukraine, USA.
Consultors in 24 countries and territories:
Argentina, Australia, Austria, Belgium, Canada, Chile, Egypt, France, Germany, Greece, Hungary, India, Israel, Italy, Lebanon, New Zealand, Poland, Portugal, Slovakia, Spain, Taiwan, UK, Ukraine, USA. [2013.07.23/XF1076/v/E]

♦ Pontifical Council for the Media of Social Communication / see Pontifical Council for Social Communications (#18447)

♦ Pontifical Council for Promoting Christian Unity (PCPCU) 18446

Conseil pontifical pour la promotion de l'unité des chrétiens – Pontificio Consejo para la Promoción de la Unidad de los Cristianos – Pontificio Consiglio per la Promozione dell'Unità dei Cristiani – Päpstlicher Rat zur Förderung der Einheit der Christen – Pontificium Consilium ad Unitatem Christianorum Fovendam

Main Office Via della Conciliazione 5, 00193 Rome RM, Italy. E-mail: office@christianunity.va.
URL: http://www.christianunity.va/

History 5 Jun 1960. Founded within the framework of *Administrative Hierarchy of the Roman Catholic Church (#00117)*. Confirmed, 3 Jan 1966. Former names and other names: *Secretariat for Promoting Christian Unity (SPCU)* – former (5 Jun 1960 to 28 Jun 1988); *Secrétariat pour l'unité des chrétiens (SPUC)* – former (5 Jun 1960 to 28 Jun 1988); *Secretariado para la Unión de los Cristianos (SPUC)* – former (5 Jun 1960 to 28 Jun 1988); *Secretariatus ad Christianorum Unitatem Fovendam* – former (5 Jun 1960 to 28 Jun 1988). **Aims** Further Christian unity through dialogue on international level; stimulate the *ecumenical* engagement of the Roman Catholic Church on all levels. **Structure** International body of 30 members (Cardinals and Bishops), assisted by internationally chosen experts. **Staff** 20.00 FTE, paid. **Finance** Financed by the Holy See. **Events** *Meeting* Salzburg (Austria) 2009, *Meeting* Bern (Switzerland) 2008, *Plenary Assembly* Vatican City (Vatican) 2008, *Meeting* Würzburg (Germany) 2008, *Meeting* Würzburg (Germany) 2007. **Publications** *Information Service* (4 a year) in English, French – bulletin.
NGO Relations Sponsors, together with:
– the Assyrian Church of the East, *Joint Committee for Theological Dialogue Between the Catholic Church and the Assyrian Church of the East*;
– the Malankara Jacobite Syrian Orthodox Church, *Joint International Commission for Dialogue between the Roman Catholic Church and the Malankara Jacobite Syrian Orthodox Church (no recent information)*;
– the Malankara Orthodox Syrian Church, *Joint International Commission for Dialogue between the Roman Catholic Church and the Malankara Orthodox Syrian Church (no recent information)*;
– the Oriental Orthodox Churches, *Joint International Commission for Theological Dialogue between the Catholic Church and the Oriental Orthodox Churches (#16136)*;
– the *The Lutheran World Federation (LWF, #16532)*, *Lutheran-Roman Catholic Commission on Unity (#16531)*;
– *World Methodist Council (WMC, #21650)*, *International Joint Commission for Dialogue between the World Methodist Council and the Vatican (#13972)*.
– *Disciples Ecumenical Consultative Council (DECC, #05100)*, *'Roman Catholic/Disciples of Christ Dialogue'*;
– *Joint International Commission for Dialogue between the Roman Catholic Church and the Coptic Orthodox Church (no recent information)*;
– some leaders of the Evangelical Movement.
Also responsible for: *Commission for Religious Relations with the Jews (#04238)*; *International Catholic-Jewish Liaison Committee (ILC, #12458)*. Represented on the Board of: *Catholic Biblical Federation (CBF, #03600)*, to whom it has granted liaison status. Cooperates with *World Council of Churches (WCC, #21320)* through *Joint Working Group between the Roman Catholic Church and the World Council of Churches (JWG, #16152)*. [2020/XF0800/v/E]

♦ Pontifical Council for Social Communications 18447

Conseil pontifical pour les communications sociales – Pontificio Consiglio delle Comunicazioni Sociali (PCCS) – Pontificium Consilium de Communicationibus Socialibus (PCCS)

Contact Via della Conciliazione 5, 00120 Vatican City, Vatican. T. +39669891800. Fax +39669891840.
Pres address not obtained.
URL: http://www.pccs.va/

History 1948, Vatican City, as *Pontifical Commission for Educational and Religious Cinematography* or *Pontifical Commission for Didactic and Religious Motion Pictures*, within the framework of *Administrative Hierarchy of the Roman Catholic Church (#00117)*. Constitution approved 17 Sep 1948. Replaced, 1 Jan 1952, by *Pontifical Commission for Motion Pictures*, which was further extended to become, 16 Dec 1954, *Pontifical Commission for Motion Pictures, Radio and Television*, and, 4 Dec 1964, following recommendations of Vatican Council II, *Pontifical Commission for the Media of Social Communication*. Subsequently name changed to: *Pontifical Council for the Media of Social Communication*. Present name adopted 1989. Established as permanent office of the Holy See, 22 Feb 1959. **Aims** Study *pastoral* problems related to the *media*; execute norms and arrangements established by Papal authority in the field; administer the Vatican Film Library and Audiovisual Service – which authorizes *television*, *film*, photographic and *radio* work in the Vatican; promote *Catholic* communications activity in the world; coordinate worldwide telecasts of papal ceremonies. **Events** *Plenary Assembly* Vatican City (Vatican) 2011, *Plenary Assembly* Vatican City (Vatican) 2009, *Plenary Assembly* Vatican City (Vatican) 2007, *Plenary Assembly* Vatican City (Vatican) 2006, *Plenary Assembly* Vatican City (Vatican) 2004. **Publications** *Bulletin du CPCS* (annual); *Social Communications Directory* (annual). **NGO Relations** Member of: *Catholic Media Council (CAMECO, #03605)*. Instrumental in setting up: *Red Informatica de la Iglesia en América Latina (RIIAL, #18689)*. [2014/XF9363/v/E]

♦ Pontifical Institute for Arabic and Islamic Studies 18448

Institut pontifical d'études arabes et d'islamologie (IPEA) – Pontificio Istituto di Studi Arabi e d'Islamistica (PISAI)

Rector Viale di Trastevere 89, 00153 Rome RM, Italy. T. +39658392611. Fax +3965882595. E-mail: info@pisai.it.
URL: http://www.pisai.it/

History 1926, Manouba (Tunisia), by *Society of Missionaries of Africa (White Fathers)*. Name changed, 1931, to *Institut des belles lettres arabes (IBLA)*. Became, 19 Mar 1960, *Institut pontifical d'études orientales*. When the office was transferred to Rome (Italy), 1964, received the name of *Institut pontifical d'études arabes – Pontificio Istituto di Studi Arabi*. Present title officially adopted 5 Mar 1988. **Aims** Train students from an intellectual and spiritual point of view in the specific theological and cultural aspects of Islam so as to equip them to undertake informed dialogue with Muslims in academic, civil and religious-pastoral settings. **Languages** Arabic, English, French, Italian. **Staff** 4.00 FTE, paid. **Activities** Training/education; knowledge management/information dissemination; events/meetings. **Events** *Conference on Rahma – Muslim and Christian Studies in Mercy* Rome (Italy) 2016, *Conference on Studying and Understanding the Religion of the Other* Rome (Italy) 2015, *Colloquium* Rome (Italy) 1997, *Colloquium* Rome (Italy) 1995, *Colloquium* Grottaferrata (Italy) 1993. **Publications** *Encounter* (10 a year) in English – journal; *Etudes Arabes* (annual) in English, French, Italian – monograph; *Islamochristiana* (annual) in Arabic, English, French – journal. *Studi Arabo-Islamici del PISAI*. [2017.07.25/XF8993/j/F]

♦ Pontifical Institute of Christian Archaeology 18449

Institut pontifical d'archéologie chrétienne – Pontificio Istituto di Archeologia Cristiana (PIAC) – Päpstliches Institut für Christliche Archäologie

Rector Via Napoleone III 1, 00185 Rome RM, Italy. T. +3964465574. Fax +3964469197. E-mail: piac.rettore@piac.it – piac.segretario@piac.it – segreteria@piac.it.
URL: http://www.piac.it/

History 11 Dec 1925, Rome (Italy), by Pope Pius XI. **Languages** English, French, German, Italian, Spanish. **Staff** 1.00 FTE, paid. **Finance** By Holy See. **Activities** Training/education; awards/prizes/competitions; research/documentation; events/meetings. **Events** *International Congress of Christian Archaeology* Utrecht (Netherlands) / Nijmegen (Netherlands) 2018, *International Congress of Christian Archaeology* Rome (Italy) 2013, *International congress* Rome (Italy) 2013, *International congress / International Congress of Christian Archaeology* Toledo (Spain) 2008, *International congress / International Congress of Christian Archaeology* Vienna (Austria) 1999. **Publications** *Rivista di Archeologia Cristiana* (annual). *Monumenti dell'Antichità Cristiana – Prima Serie* – in 2 vols; *Monumenti dell'Antichità Cristiana – Seconda Serie* – in 20 vols. *Inscriptiones Christianae Urbis Romee* – collection, in 10 vols; *Rome Sotterranea Cristiana* – collection, in 9 vols; *Studi di Antichità Cristiana* – collection, in 62 vols; *Sussidi allo Studio delle Antichità Cristiane* – collection, in 20 vols.
Members Individuals, institutes and governments. Members in 32 countries:
Algeria, Argentina, Austria, Belgium, Bosnia-Herzegovina, Brazil, Canada, Croatia, Cyprus, Finland, France, Germany, Greece, Holy See, Hungary, India, Ireland, Japan, Jordan, Lebanon, Malta, Netherlands, Poland, Romania, Slovenia, Spain, Sri Lanka, Switzerland, Tunisia, Türkiye, UK, USA.
NGO Relations Acts as research and training centre for: *Pontifical Commission for Sacred Archeology (#18441)*; *Pontificia Accademia Romana di Archeologia*. Provides permanent base for: *Comitato Promotore Permanente dei Congressi Internazionali di Archeologia Cristiana*. Member of: *Associazione Internazionale di Archeologia Classica (AIAC, #02988)*; *International Union of Institutes of Archaeology, History and Art History in Rome (#15782)*. [2019.06.25/XF5162/j/E]

♦ Pontifical Institute for Foreign Missions 18450

Pontificio Istituto Missioni Estere – Pontificio Instituto das Missões Estrangeiras – Pontificium Institutum pro Missionibus Exteris (PIME)

Superior Gen Via Monte Rosa 81, 20149 Milan MI, Italy. T. +392438201. Fax +39243822699. E-mail: pimegeneral@pime.org.
URL: http://www.pime.org/

History 23 May 1926, Rome (Italy). Established by merger of *'Seminario Lombardo per le Missioni Estere'*, set up in 1850, and *'Pontificio Seminario dei Santi Apostoli Pietro e Paolo di Roma'*, set up in 1874. **Aims** Conduct *missionary* activity and, in particular, the *evangelization* of peoples and groups of people who are not yet *Christians*. **Structure** Depends directly on the *Congregation for the Evangelization of Peoples (CEP, #04670)*. Internal authority exercised by General Assembly, by the Superior General with his Council, by Regional and Delegate Superiors, assisted by their respective Councils. The Institute is divided into Circumscriptions and their respective local communities. **Languages** English, Italian, Portuguese. **Finance** Sources: donations; gifts, legacies; investments; revenue from activities/projects. **Publications** *Mondo e Missione* (10 a year); *Mundo e Missão* (10 a year) in Portuguese; *Mission World* (6 a year) in English; *Asianews*.
Members Individuals (399), in 31 communities, in 19 countries and territories:
Algeria, Bangladesh, Brazil, Cambodia, Cameroon, Chad, Côte d'Ivoire, Guinea-Bissau, Hong Kong, India, Italy, Japan, Mexico, Myanmar, Papua New Guinea, Philippines, Thailand, Tunisia, USA. [2022.05.04/XR9815/j/**F**]

- ♦ Pontifical Institute of Oriental Studies / see Pontifical Oriental Institute (#18451)
- ♦ Pontifical Institute of the Religious Teachers Filippini (religious order)
- ♦ Pontifical Institute of Sacred Music (#18455)
- ♦ Pontifical Marian International Academy (#18453)
- ♦ Pontifical Missionary Society for the Propagation of the Faith (religious order)
- ♦ Pontifical Missionary Society of Saint Peter the Apostle (see: #16827)
- ♦ Pontifical Missionary Union (see: #16827)
- ♦ Pontifical Missionary Work / see MISSIO (#16827)

♦ Pontifical Oriental Institute 18451

Institut pontifical oriental – Pontificio Istituto Orientale – Pontificium Institutum Orientale

Contact Piazza Santa Maria Maggiore 7, 00185 Rome RM, Italy. T. +39064474170. Fax +39064465576. E-mail: press@orientale.it – segreteria@orientale.it – rettorato@orientale.it.
URL: http://www.orientale.it

History 15 Oct 1917, Rome (Italy). Founded by Benedict XV, and entrusted to *Society of Jesus (SJ)* in 1922, the Institute, under the title of *Pontifical Institute of Oriental Studies – Pontificio Istituto per gli Studi Orientali – Pontificium Institutum Orientalium Studiorum* was set up separately in 1926 by Pius XI. **Aims** Study Eastern churches, *Catholic* and non-Catholic, *Byzantine* and non-Byzantine; impart knowledge both by teaching and by publication of writings dealing with the Christian East, thereby disclosing to priests and laymen of the Latin church the ecclesiastical treasures of the East and expanding the knowledge of oriental people, Catholics and non-Catholics, about their own rites and churches; foster a better understanding between the Eastern and Western churches in the hope of an eventual reunion. **Activities** Offers three-year courses open to clerics and laity (whether Catholic or not), leading to academic degrees in 'Oriental Ecclesiastical Sciences and Canon Law'. Maintains a library of 300,000 volumes. **Publications** *Orientalia Christiana Periodica* (2 a year). *Orientalia Christiana* – series; *Orientalia Christiana Analecta* – series. *Anaphorae Syriacae* – collection; *Concilium Florentinum* – collection; *Kanonika* – collection. [2023.02.14/XF9225/j/**F**]

- ♦ Pontifical Oriental Institute of Religious Studies (internationally oriented national body)
- ♦ Pontifical Roman Theological Academy / see Pontifical Theological Academy (#18452)
- ♦ Pontifical Society of the Holy Childhood (see: #16827)

♦ Pontifical Theological Academy 18452

Pontificia Accademia di Teologia – Pontificia Academia Theologica – Pontificia Academia Theologiae

Sec Via della Conciliazione 5, 00120 Vatican City, Vatican. E-mail: path.segr@gmail.com.
Registered Office Piazza della Cancelleria 1, 00120 Vatican City, Vatican.
URL: http://www.vatican.va/roman_curia/pontifical_academies/

History 1695, as *Pontifical Roman Theological Academy – Pontificiae Academiae Theologicae Romanae*, also referred to as *Roman Theological Pontifical Academy*. New statutes given and mission expanded under Pope Pius XII. Comes within *Administrative Hierarchy of the Roman Catholic Church (#00117)*. **Activities** *Forum Internazionale PATH*. **Publications** *PATH* (annual). [2012/XM4660/**F**]

- ♦ Pontifical University Antonianum (internationally oriented national body)
- ♦ Pontifical Urbaniana University (#18454)

♦ Pontificia Academia Mariana Internationalis (PAMI) 18453

Académie pontificale mariale internationale – Pontificia Accademia Mariana Internazionale – Pontifical Marian International Academy

Secretariat Via Merulana 124, 00185 Rome RM, Italy. T. +39670373235. Fax +39670373234.
URL: http://www.pami.info/

History 1946, Rome (Italy). Pontifical status conferred by John XXIII, 8 Dec 1959. Statutes definitively approved by Paul VI, 6 Jul 1964. Renewed by Pope John-Paul II, 12 Jan 1997. **Aims** Foster both speculative and historo-critical scientific studies concerning the Blessed *Virgin Mary*; promote publication of *Mariological* historical and devotional collections. **Structure** Under the authority of the Holy See and the *Pontifical Council for Culture (#18443)*. Directed by Council, consisting of President, Secretary, Treasurer and a least 6 other members. **Finance** Voluntary contributions from honorary and benefactor members. **Events** *International Mariological and Marian Congress* Le Puy-en-Velay (France) 2004, *International Mariological and Marian Congress* Rome (Italy) 2000, *Mary and the mystery of the Saint Trinity* Rome (Italy) 2000, *Congress / International Mariological and Marian Congress* Czestochowa (Poland) 1996, *International Mariological and Marian Congress* Huelva (Spain) 1992. **Publications** *PAMI Scientific Collections* – 7 to date. Congress proceedings.
Members Ordinary (maximum 80); Associate (Corresponding, Honorary, Benefactors). Individuals in 44 countries and territories:
Argentina, Australia, Austria, Belgium, Brazil, Canada, Colombia, Costa Rica, Croatia, Dominican Rep, Ecuador, Egypt, Ethiopia, France, Germany, Haiti, Holy See, India, Indonesia, Ireland, Israel, Italy, Kenya, Lebanon, Malta, Mexico, Netherlands, Pakistan, Peru, Philippines, Poland, Portugal, Puerto Rico, South Africa, Spain, Switzerland, Syrian AR, Taiwan, Tanzania UR, Türkiye, Uganda, UK, USA, Venezuela.
NGO Relations *Internationaler Mariologischer Arbeitskreis Kevelaer (IMAK, no recent information).* [2013/XF9746/v/**F**]

- ♦ Pontificia Academia Scientarium (#18433)
- ♦ Pontificia Academia Scientiarum Socialium (#18434)
- ♦ Pontificia Academia Theologiae (#18452)
- ♦ Pontificia Academia Theologica (#18452)
- ♦ Pontificia Academia pro Vita (#18432)
- ♦ Pontificia Accademia Cultorum Martyrum (#18430)
- ♦ Pontificia Accademia dell'Immacolata (#18431)
- ♦ Pontificia Accademia Mariana Internazionale (#18453)
- ♦ Pontificia Accademia di San Tommaso d'Aquino (#18435)
- ♦ Pontificia Accademia delle Scienze (#18433)
- ♦ Pontificia Accademia delle Scienze Sociali (#18434)
- ♦ Pontificia Accademia di Teologia (#18452)
- ♦ Pontificia Accademia per la Vita (#18432)
- ♦ Pontificia Comisión para América Latina (#18440)
- ♦ Pontificia Commissio pro America Latina (#18440)
- ♦ Pontificia Commissio Biblica (#18436)
- ♦ Pontificia Commissio de Bonis Culturalibus Ecclesiae (#18438)
- ♦ Pontificia Commissione per l'America Latina (#18440)
- ♦ Pontificia Commissione di Archeologia Sacra (#18441)
- ♦ Pontificia Commissione Biblica (#18436)
- ♦ Pontificia Commissione per la Conservazione del Patrimonio Artistico e Storico / see Pontifical Commission for the Cultural Patrimony of the Church (#18438)
- ♦ Pontificiae Academiae Theologicae Romanae / see Pontifical Theological Academy (#18452)
- ♦ Pontificia Insigne Accademia di Belle Arti e Lettere dei Virtuosi al Pantheon (#11121)
- ♦ Pontificia Studiorum Universitas Salesiana (#19038)
- ♦ Pontificia Università Antonianum (internationally oriented national body)

♦ Pontificia Universitas Urbaniana (PUU) 18454

Pontifical Urbaniana University

SG Via Urbano VIII/16, 00165 Rome RM, Italy. T. +39669889656. Fax +39669881871.
URL: http://www.urbaniana.edu/

History 1 Aug 1627, Rome (Italy), as Collegio Urbano, by Pope Urban VIII. Became a Pontifical University with current name, 1 Oct 1962, by the Motu Proprio 'Fidei Propagandae' of Pope John XXIII. Originally 2 Faculties: Theology; Philosophy. Comes within *Congregation for the Evangelization of Peoples (CEP, #04670)*. **Aims** Prepare priests, religious men and women and lay people for the *missions*. **Structure** Faculties (4); Institute Councils (3); Committees (4); Commissions (4). **Languages** Italian. **Staff** 161 professors; 40 non-teaching staff. **Publications** *Annales* (annual); *Bibliographia Missionaria* – journal; *Euntes Docente* – journal; *IUS Missionale* – journal. *Chiesa, Missione e Culture* – collections; *Ricerche* – collections; *Studia* – monographs; *Subsidia* – textbooks.
Members Organization (1):
Conferenza Rettori delle Università Pontificie Romane (CRUPR). [2018.06.19/XM2039/y/**F**]

- ♦ Pontificio Ateneo Antonianum / see Pontifical University Antonianum
- ♦ Pontificio Ateneo Salesiano / see Salesian Pontifical University (#19038)
- ♦ Pontificio Comitato per i Congressi Eucaristici Internazionali (#18442)
- ♦ Pontificio Consejo de la Cultura (#18443)
- ♦ Pontificio Consejo para la Promoción de la Unidad de los Cristianos (#18446)
- ♦ Pontificio Consiglio delle Comunicazioni Sociali (#18447)
- ♦ Pontificio Consiglio della Cultura (#18443)
- ♦ Pontificio Consiglio per il Dialogo Interreligioso (#18444)
- ♦ Pontificio Consiglio per il Dialogo con i Non-Credenti (inactive)
- ♦ Pontificio Consiglio per l'Interpretazione dei Testi Legislativi / see Pontifical Council for Legislative Texts (#18445)
- ♦ Pontificio Consiglio per la Promozione dell'Unità dei Cristiani (#18446)
- ♦ Pontificio Consiglio per i Testi Legislativi (#18445)
- ♦ Pontificio Instituto das Missões Estrangeiras (#18450)
- ♦ Pontificio Istituto di Archeologia Cristiana (#18449)
- ♦ Pontificio Istituto Biblico (#18437)
- ♦ Pontificio Istituto Missioni Estere (#18450)

♦ Pontificio Istituto di Musica Sacra (PIMS) 18455

Institut pontifical de musique sacrée – Pontifical Institute of Sacred Music – Pontificium Institutum Musicae Sacrae

Sec Via di Torre Rossa 21, 00165 Rome RM, Italy. T. +3966638792. Fax +39666018432. E-mail: pims@musicasacra.va.
URL: http://www.musicasacra.va/

History 1910, Rome (Italy). Founded by Pius X; inaugurated 3 Jan 1911. Present name adopted when included among Pontifical universities and faculties and received right to grant academic degrees. Former names and other names: *Scuola Superiore di Musica Sacra* – former. **Aims** Teach and promote disciplines of sacred music, including Gregorian chant, sacred composition, organ, musicology, choral music, singing teaching, piano and didactic singing. **Languages** Italian. **Staff** 3.00 FTE, paid. **Finance** Annual budget: 334,000 EUR. **Activities** Events/meetings; training/education. **Events** *Anniversary of foundation* Rome (Italy) 1986. **Publications** *DIALETTICA E PARADIGMI DEL SACRO IN MUSICA – Canto gregoriano, polifonia e strumenti musicali* (2021) by Prof Gilberto Sessantini; *GRADUALE NOVUM – Commentario* (2020) by Prof Johannes Berchmans Goschl; *OFFICINA GREGORIANA – Accompagnamenti organistici, sviluppi polifonici, brani improntati a timbri modali e composizioni* (2020) by Prof Theo Flury and Fr Gennaro M. Becchimanzi; *Guida Accademica; Il Neuma e il Modo* by Alberto Turco; *Iniziazione al Canto Gregoriano* by Alberto Turco; *Nella mente del notatore* by Fulvio Rampi – Alessandro De Lillo. [2022.02.09/XF4833/y/**F**]

- ♦ Pontificio Istituto Orientale (#18451)
- ♦ Pontificio Istituto di Studi Arabi / see Pontifical Institute for Arabic and Islamic Studies (#18448)
- ♦ Pontificio Istituto di Studi Arabi e d'Islamistica (#18448)
- ♦ Pontificio Istituto per gli Studi Orientali / see Pontifical Oriental Institute (#18451)
- ♦ Pontificium Athenaeum Salesianum / see Salesian Pontifical University (#19038)
- ♦ Pontificium Concilium pro Dialogo cum Non Credentibus (inactive)
- ♦ Pontificium Consilium de Communicationibus Socialibus (#18447)
- ♦ Pontificium Consilium de Cultura (#18443)
- ♦ Pontificium Consilium pro Dialogo inter Religiones (#18444)
- ♦ Pontificium Consilium de Legum Textibus (#18445)
- ♦ Pontificium Consilium de Legum Textibus Interpretandis / see Pontifical Council for Legislative Texts (#18445)
- ♦ Pontificium Consilium ad Unitatem Christianorum Fovendam (#18446)
- ♦ Pontificium Institutum Altioris Latinitatis / see Salesian Pontifical University (#19038)
- ♦ Pontificium Institutum Biblicum de Urbe (#18437)
- ♦ Pontificium Institutum pro Missionibus Exteris (#18450)
- ♦ Pontificium Institutum Musicae Sacrae (#18455)
- ♦ Pontificium Institutum Orientale (#18451)
- ♦ Pontificium Institutum Orientalium Studiorum / see Pontifical Oriental Institute (#18451)
- ♦ Pontificium Opus A Sancta Infantia (see: #16827)
- ♦ Pontificius Comitatus Eucharisticis Internationalibus Conventibus Provehendis (#18442)
- ♦ Ponts pour la paix (internationally oriented national body)
- ♦ Le pont avec le Sud / see Brücke-Le pont
- ♦ Pool des agences de presse des pays non-alignés (inactive)
- ♦ Pool de Agencias de Prensa de los Paises No Alineados (inactive)
- ♦ Pool energétique de l'Afrique centrale (#03655)
- ♦ PO / see ORBIS International (#17786)
- ♦ For Poor Children (internationally oriented national body)
- ♦ Poor Handmaids of Jesus Christ (religious order)
- ♦ Poor Servants of Divine Providence (religious order)
- ♦ Poor Servants of the Mother of God (religious order)
- ♦ **POP** Pacific Optimization Research Activity Group (#17985)
- ♦ PoP – Pencils of Promise (internationally oriented national body)
- ♦ POP protocol – Protocol to the Convention on Long Range Transboundary Air Pollution on Persistent Organic Pollutants (1998 treaty)
- ♦ POP treaty – Stockholm Convention on Persistent Organic Pollutants (2001 treaty)
- ♦ Popular Coalition to Eradicate Hunger and Poverty / see International Land Coalition (#13999)
- ♦ Popular Communication Center of Latin America (internationally oriented national body)

♦ Popular Education Coordinated Regional Program 18456

Programme régional coordonné d'éducation populaire – Programa Regional Coordinado de Educación Popular (ALFORJA)

Address not obtained.
URL: http://www.redalforja.net/

History May 1981. **Aims** Strengthen and improve the resources of all member centers; contribute to the reflection on, and the analysis and systematization of various aspects of popular education; provide an exchange of information on the educational experiences in all the seven countries involved. **Languages** Spanish. **Staff** 1.50 FTE, paid. Plus personnel in each member center.

Members Centers – non-governmental organizations – (7) in 7 countries:
Costa Rica, El Salvador, Guatemala, Honduras, Mexico, Nicaragua, Panama.
NGO Relations Member of: *Consejo de Educación de Adultos de América Latina (CEAAL, #04707).* [2017/XF1152/**F**]

♦ Population Action International / see PAI (#18025)

♦ Population Approach Group Europe (PAGE) 18457

Contact Registered Office, 1 Somerset Road, London, W13 9PD, UK. E-mail: rs@page-meeting.org.
URL: http://www.page-meeting.org/
History 1992, Basel (Switzerland). Registered in accordance with UK law. **Aims** Promote *data analysis* using the population approach. **Languages** English. **Staff** All voluntary. **Finance** Participant registration fees. **Activities** Research/documentation; events/meetings. **Events** *Annual Meeting* Stockholm (Sweden) 2019, *Annual Meeting* Lisbon (Portugal) 2016, *Annual Meeting* Hersonissos (Greece) 2015, *Annual Meeting* Alicante (Spain) 2014, *Annual Meeting* Glasgow (UK) 2013. **Publications** *PAGE Journal.* **Members** Not a membership organization. [2015.03.19/XF6758/c/**F**]

♦ Population Association of America (internationally oriented national body)
♦ Population Centre Foundation / see Philippine Centre for Population and Development
♦ Population Communications International / see PCI Media
♦ Population and Community Development Association (internationally oriented national body)
♦ Population Connection (internationally oriented national body)

♦ Population Council 18458

Conseil de la population – Consejo de Población
Headquarters 1 Dag Hammarskjold Plaza, New York NY 10017, USA. T. +12123390500. Fax +12127556052. E-mail: pubinfo@popcouncil.org – publications@popcouncil.org.
URL: http://www.popcouncil.org/
History Founded Nov 1952. **Aims** Conduct research to address critical health and development issues; work to stop the spread of *HIV*, provide more *reproductive* choices, and ensure that young people lead full and productive lives. **Structure** Board of Trustees; Executive Team; Programmatic Directors; Country Directors. **Languages** Arabic, English, French, Spanish, Swahili. **Staff** 540.00 FTE, paid. Staff from 30 countries. **Finance** Sources: governments; multilateral organizations; foundations; individuals. **Activities** Research and development; projects/programmes; healthcare; knowledge management/information dissemination. **Events** *International seminar on potential and actual contributions of behavioural change to curbing the spread of HIV* Entebbe (Uganda) 2008, *Seminar on antiprogestin drugs* Arlington, VA (USA) 1991, *International conference on family planning and the health of women and children* Nairobi (Kenya) 1987. **Publications** *Population and Development Review* (4 a year); *Studies in Family Planning* (4 a year). Books; reports; articles; briefs; working papers; newsletters; toolkits. **Members** Not a membership organization. **Consultative Status** Consultative status granted from: *ECOSOC (#05331)* (Special); *FAO (#09260)* (Special Status); *ILO (#11123)* (Special List); *WHO (#20950)* (Official Relations); *UNICEF (#20332)*. **IGO Relations** Maintains relations with: *Joint United Nations Programme on HIV/AIDS (UNAIDS, #16149); United Nations Population Fund (UNFPA, #20612).* Accredited by: *United Nations Office at Vienna (UNOV, #20604).* **NGO Relations** Representative partnerships and participation: *Girls not Brides (#10154); Global Health Technologies Coalition (GHTC); InsideNGO (inactive); Inter-Agency Task Team on Children affected by AIDS (IATT, #11394); International Consortium for Emergency Contraception (ICEC, #12911); Latin American Consortium on Emergency Contraception (LACEC, #16306); PMNCH (#18410); Abortion and Postabortion Care Consortium (APAC, #00007); Reproductive Health Supplies Coalition (RHSC, #18847).* Associate member of: *International Initiative for Impact Evaluation (3ie, #13851).* Partner of: *Every Woman Every Child (EWEC, #09215); Social Aspects of HIV/AIDS Research Alliance (SAHARA).* Stakeholder in: *Child and Youth Finance International (CYFI, inactive).* Supports: *DKT International.* Instrumental in setting up: *African Population and Health Research Center (APHRC, #00420); Association for Population / Family Planning Libraries and Information Centers – International (APLIC International); International Contraceptive Access Foundation (ICA Foundation, #12936).* Collaborates with: *FHI 360.* [2018.09.05/XF1868/**F**]

♦ Population Crisis Committee / see PAI (#18025)
♦ Population and Development International (internationally oriented national body)

♦ Population Environment Research Network (PERN) 18459

Co-coordinator c/o CIESIN, Columbia Univ, 61 Route 9W, PO Box 1000, Palisades NY 10964, USA. E-mail: pernadmin@ciesin.columbia.edu.
Co-coordinator address not obtained.
URL: http://www.populationenvironmentresearch.org/
History 2001. Founded by *International Union for the Scientific Study of Population (IUSSP, #15814)*, as an Internet-based network. **Aims** Facilitate scientific analysis and dialogue about population-environment relationships. **Structure** Scientific Committee; co-Coordinators. **Languages** English. **Staff** 5.00 FTE, paid. **Finance** Sources: donations; in-kind support. Initial funding from *MacArthur Foundation.* Support from the NASA Socioeconomic Data and Applications Center (SEDAC), managed by *Center for International Earth Science Information Network (CIESIN)* at Columbia University. **Activities** Events/meetings; knowledge management/information dissemination; networking/liaising; publishing activities. **Events** *The Habitability Concept in the Field of Population-Environment Studies* 2023, *The Demography of Sustainable Human Wellbeing* 2022, *Refugee and Internally Displaced Populations, Environmental Impacts and Climate Risks* 2021. **Publications** Articles. **Information Services** *eLibrary.* **Members** Individuals (about 2,100) in 137 countries. Membership countries not specified. [2023.02.28/XJ1855/**E**]

♦ Population Information Program / see Johns Hopkins University Center for Communications Programs
♦ Population Institute (internationally oriented national body)
♦ Population Reference Bureau (internationally oriented national body)
♦ Population Services Europe / see MSI Reproductive Choices
♦ Population Services International / see PSI (#18555)
♦ **POQP** Publique o que Paga (#18573)
♦ Portable Sanitation Association International (internationally oriented national body)
♦ Portable Sanitation Europe (internationally oriented national body)
♦ Portal Regional para la Transferencia de Tecnología y la Acción frente al Cambio Climático en América Latina y el Caribe (#18786)

♦ Port Equipment Manufacturers Association (PEMA) 18460

Head of Administration 15-17 St Cross St, London, EC1N 8UW, UK. T. +447766228958 – +447766(442034093100.
Registered Office p/a EIA, Rue d'Arenberg 44, 1000 Brussels, Belgium.
URL: http://www.pema.org/
History Founded 2004. Constitution revised 2008. Registered in accordance with Belgian law. **Aims** Provide a forum and public voice for the global port equipment and technology sectors, reflecting their critical role in enabling safe, secure, sustainable and productive ports and thereby supporting world *maritime* trade; foster good relations within communities represented and with other industry organizations; contribute to best practice initiatives. **Structure** General Assembly and Members Meeting (annual, in February); Members and Guests Autumn Meeting (annual, usually in October/November); Board of Directors. **Languages** English. **Staff** 3.00 FTE, paid. **Finance** Members' dues. **Activities** Networking/liaising; awareness raising; knowledge management/information dissemination; standard/guidelines; monitoring/evaluation; events/meetings; training/education. **Events** *Annual General Meeting* London (UK) 2020, *Annual General Meeting* Amsterdam (Netherlands) 2019, *Autumn Members Meeting* Marseille (France) 2019, *Annual General Meeting* Bilbao (Spain) 2018, *Autumn Members Meeting* Hong Kong (Hong Kong) 2018. **Members** Membership is open to suppliers of port equipment, providers of technology that supports port handling operations, and consultants in the fields of port and equipment design. Companies (over 80). Membership countries not specified. [2019.07.03/XM3319/**D**]

♦ Portes ouvertes international (#17749)
♦ Porticus (internationally oriented national body)
♦ Porticus Global / see Porticus

♦ PORTIUS – International and EU Port Law Centre (internationally oriented national body)

♦ Port Management Association of the Caribbean (PMAC) 18461

Exec Sec PO Box 929 GPO, Bridgetown, St Michael, Bridgetown ST MICHAEL, Barbados. T. +12464346505. Fax +12464301450.
URL: http://pmac-ports.com/
History 26 Jun 1998, Antigua (Antigua-Barbuda). Founded 26 Jun 1998, Antigua, as a successor to *Port Management Association of the Eastern Caribbean (PMAEC)*, established 16 May 1988. **Aims** Improve proficiency of member ports and quality of services offered to their users, specifically through facilitation of relevant training and development, and the sharing of experience, information and ideas, as well as advocacy and representation at multilateral levels. **Structure** Annual General Meeting; Council of Members; Executive Committee. **Languages** English. **Staff** 1.50 FTE, paid. **Finance** Members' dues. **Events** *General Meeting* Miami, FL (USA) 2019, *General Meeting* Ocho Rios (Jamaica) 2018, *General Meeting* Cayman Is 2017, *General Meeting* Grand Cayman Is (Cayman Is) 2016, *General Meeting* Suriname 2015. **Publications** *Portside Caribbean* (4 a year).
Members Ports (19) in 18 countries and territories:
Anguilla, Antigua-Barbuda, Barbados, Bermuda, Cayman Is, Curaçao, Guiana Fr, Jamaica, Martinique, Montserrat, St Kitts-Nevis, St Lucia, St Maarten, St Martin, St Vincent-Grenadines, Suriname, Turks-Caicos, Virgin Is UK.
Associate: organizations (26) in 13 countries and territories:
Barbados, Canada, Denmark, France, Guadeloupe, Jamaica, Martinique, Mexico, Netherlands, Suriname, UK, USA, Virgin Is UK. [2019.12.12/XJ0984/**D**]

♦ Port Management Association of Eastern Africa / see Port Management Association of Eastern and Southern Africa (#18462)

♦ Port Management Association of Eastern and Southern Africa (PMAESA) 18462

Association de gestion des ports de l'Afrique de l'Est et australe (AGPAEA)
Contact PO Box 99209, Mombasa, Kenya. T. +254202381184. E-mail: pmaesa@pmaesa.org.
Street address KPA Bldg Asset No 480038, Kaunda Ave, Kizingo Estate, Mombasa, Kenya.
URL: http://www.pmaesa.org/
History 16 Apr 1973, Mombasa (Kenya). Established following initiatives arising from meeting of African Ministers responsible for Transport, Feb 1971, Tunis (Tunisia). Former names and other names: *Port Management Association of Eastern Africa (PMAEA)* – former; *Association d'Afrique de l'Est pour la gestion portuaire* – former. **Aims** Offer a framework for exchange of information and ideas among members; create an environment where members can interface in the port, transport and trade arenas. **Structure** Council (meets at least annually), consisting of all members (quorum is over 50 percent); Board (meets annually before Council), comprising Chairman, 2 Vice-Chairmen, Treasurer, 2 members, and ex-officio Immediate Past Chairman and Chairman of the Cruise Indian Ocean Association; Secretariat, headed by Secretary General; Committees, Study Groups and subsidiary organs. **Languages** English, French. **Staff** 5.00 FTE, paid. **Finance** Sources: members' dues. Annual budget: 250,000 USD. **Activities** Events/meetings; research/documentation. **Events** *Meeting* Mauritius 2018, *Raising the profile of landlinked countries in the maritime and logistics sectors* Livingstone (Zambia) 2017, *Meeting* Walvis Bay (Namibia) 2011, *Pan African ports conference* Abuja (Nigeria) 2006, *Annual meeting* Sudan 2006. **Publications** Annual Activity Report.
Members Full Port Authorities/Governments in 21 countries and territories:
Angola, Burundi, Comoros, Djibouti, Eritrea, Ethiopia, Kenya, Madagascar, Malawi, Mauritius, Mozambique, Namibia, Réunion, Rwanda, Seychelles, Somalia, South Africa, Sudan, Tanzania UR, Zambia, Zimbabwe.
Associate members port-related industries in 4 countries:
Djibouti, Kenya, Mauritius, Tanzania UR.
IGO Relations Cooperates with (1): *International Maritime Organization (IMO, #14102).* **NGO Relations** Instrumental in setting up (1): *Pan-African Association for Port Cooperation (PAPC, #18038).* [2023.02.15/XD4382/**D***]

♦ Port Management Association of North Africa / see North African Port Management Association (#17556)

♦ Port Management Association of West and Central Africa (PMAWCA) 18463

Association de gestion des ports de l'Afrique de l'Ouest et du Centre (AGPAOC)
SG 12 Park Lane, Box 1113, Apapa, Lagos, Nigeria. T. +23417755571 – +23417737609. E-mail: pmawca_agpaoc@yahoo.com – secretariat@agpaoc-pmawca.org.
URL: http://agpaoc-pmawca.org/
History 13 Oct 1972, Freetown (Sierra Leone), at a meeting under the auspices of *United Nations Economic Commission for Africa (ECA, #20554)*, as a specialized agency of *Maritime Organization of West and Central Africa (MOWCA, #16582).* **Aims** Contribute towards improvement, coordination and harmonization of port and harbor activities, services and infrastructure in the region. **Structure** Council (meets annually); Board of Directors; Technical Committees (4); Secretariat. **Languages** English, French, Portuguese. **Staff** 8.00 FTE, paid. **Finance** Members' contributions. Annual budget: about US$ 300,000. **Activities** Events/meetings; training/education. **Events** *African Ports Environment and Sustainability Conference* Pointe Noire (Congo Brazzaville) 2020, *Pan African ports conference* Abuja (Nigeria) 2006, *Annual Council Meeting* Luanda (Angola) 2002, *Pan African ports conference* Abidjan (Côte d'Ivoire) 2001, *Annual council meeting / Annual Meeting* Lomé (Togo) 2001. **Publications** *PMAWCA Newsletter* (2 a year); *Naval* (every 2 years); *West and Central African Harbour Guide* (every 2 years). Information Handbook; proceedings; reports; information brochures.
Members Regular port authorities (24); Associate maritime related companies (6). Members in 20 countries:
Angola, Benin, Cameroon, Cape Verde, Congo Brazzaville, Congo DR, Côte d'Ivoire, Equatorial Guinea, Gabon, Gambia, Ghana, Guinea, Guinea-Bissau, Liberia, Mauritania, Nigeria, Sao Tomé-Principe, Senegal, Sierra Leone, Togo.
IGO Relations *Union of African Shippers' Councils (UASC, #20348)* participates in activities. Cooperation agreement with: *International Hydrographic Organization (IHO, #13825); International Maritime Organization (IMO, #14102).* **NGO Relations** African Port Conference Series, organized jointly with: *North African Port Management Association (NAPMA, #17556); Pan-African Association for Port Cooperation (PAPC, #18038).* [2018.10.09/XD3960/**E***]

♦ Port and Ocean Engineering under Arctic Conditions International Committee (POAC) 18464

SG Canadian Hydraulics Centre, M-32, National Research Council, Ottawa ON OT K1A 0R6, Canada. T. +16139937695.
URL: http://www.poac.com/
History Founded 1971. **Aims** Improve knowledge of ice-related problems by having scientists, technologists and design and development engineers discuss and exchange ideas on relevant topics. **Events** *Congress* Moscow (Russia) 2021, *Port and ocean engineering under Arctic conditions* Delft (Netherlands) 2019, *Congress* Busan (Korea Rep) 2017, *Congress* Trondheim (Norway) 2015, *Congress* Helsinki (Finland) 2013. [2020/XF5183/**F**]

♦ Ports Environmental Network-Africa (internationally oriented national body)
♦ Portugal-Africa Foundation (internationally oriented national body)
♦ Portuguese Institute for International Relations and Security (internationally oriented national body)
♦ Portuguese League for Development (internationally oriented national body)
♦ Portuguese Refugee Council (internationally oriented national body)
♦ **POSA** Pole Sports & Arts World Federation (#18414)
♦ **POSDEV** Pan African Organization for Sustainable Development (#18057)
♦ **POSEIDO** Periodontology, Oral Surgery, Esthetic and Implant Dentistry Organization (#18313)
♦ **PoSF** Pompiers sans frontières (#09779)
♦ Positive Birth Movement (unconfirmed)
♦ Positive Futures Network (internationally oriented national body)

♦ **Positive Planet International** **18465**

Registered Office 1 place Victor Hugo, 92400 Courbevoie, France. T. +33141252700. E-mail: contact@positiveplanet.ngo.
URL: http://positiveplanetinternational.org/

History 5 Oct 1998. Former names and other names: *PlaNet Finance* – former. Registration: SIREN, No/ID: 421020033, France; RNA, No/ID: W931004024, France. **Aims** Prevent the emergence and persistence of precarious situations in less advanced countries. **Structure** Board of Directors. Bureaux (7): Paris (France); Johannesburg (South Africa); Antananarivo (Madagascar); Dubai (United Arab Emirates); Cairo (Egypt); Dakar (Senegal); Abidjan (Côte d'Ivoire). Affiliated Bureaux (5): Milan (Italy); Geneva (Switzerland); New York NY (USA); London (UK); Tokyo (Japan). **Languages** English, French. **Staff** 100.00 FTE, paid. **Finance** Funded by: private companies; public funds; individual donors; investors. Annual budget: euro 4,016,000,000. **Activities** Projects/programmes. **Events** *Dubai microfinance forum* Dubai (United Arab Emirates) 2006, *Forum des microentrepreneurs* Parakou (Benin) 2006, *Conférence sur les villes et la microfinance* Antananarivo (Madagascar) 2005, *Conférence sur la microfinance contre la pauvreté en Argentine* Buenos Aires (Argentina) 2005, *Forum des solidarités nord-sud* Marseille (France) 2005. **Publications** Annual activities report. **Members** Not a membership organization. **Consultative Status** Consultative status granted from: *ECOSOC (#05331)* (Special). **IGO Relations** Accredited by (1): *Organisation internationale de la Francophonie (OIF, #17809)*. **NGO Relations** Member of (1): *Coordination SUD*. [2022/XF4711/**F**]

♦ Poslanecky Klub Evropské Lidové Strany – Krest'anskych Demokrat (#10775)
♦ Poslanecky Klub Evrópske l'Udovej Strany – Krest'anskych Demokratov (#10775)
♦ Poslanska Skupina Evropske Ljudske Stranke – Krscanskih Demokratov (#10775)
♦ Poslovna sola Bled / see IEDC – Bled School of Management
♦ POSNA – Pediatric Orthopaedic Society of North America (internationally oriented national body)
♦ Posner Center for International Development (internationally oriented national body)
♦ Posner Center – Posner Center for International Development (internationally oriented national body)
♦ POSRIP / see Just Detention International
♦ Postabortion Care Consortium / see Abortion and Postabortion Care Consortium (#00007)
♦ Postal Agreement (1911 treaty)
♦ Postal Operations Council (see: #20682)
♦ Postal Parcels Agreement (1979 treaty)
♦ Postal Parcels Agreement, 1984 (1984 treaty)
♦ Postal Payment Service Agreement (1999 treaty)
♦ Postal Union of the Americas and Spain / see Postal Union of the Americas, Spain and Portugal (#18466)

♦ **Postal Union of the Americas, Spain and Portugal (PUASP)** **18466**

Union postale des Amériques, de l'Espagne et du Portugal – Unión Postal de las Américas, España y Portugal (UPAEP)

SG Calle Cebollati 1468/1470, 11100 Montevideo, Uruguay. T. +59824000070 – +59824100070. E-mail: secretaria@upaep.int.
URL: http://www.upaep.int/

History 1911, Montevideo (Uruguay). Established during 1st South American Postal Congress, by representatives of Argentina, Bolivia, Brazil, Chile, Colombia, Ecuador, Paraguay, Peru, Uruguay and Venezuela. Name changed, 1921, Buenos Aires (Argentina), when nine additional countries: Costa-Rica, Cuba, Dominican Rep, El Salvador, Guatemala (Guatemala), Mexico, Nicaragua, Panama and USA, became members. Honduras and Spain were incorporated as members at next congress, 1926, Mexico City (Mexico). Suriname became a member 1 Jan 1978. Name changed, 1931, Madrid (Spain) (when Canada and Haiti also adhered to the Union). Name changed, 1991, when Portugal adhered to the Union. Last Convention and Agreements signed 15 Sep 1995, Mexico City. A Restricted Union of *Universal Postal Union (UPU, #20682)*. Statutes registered in *'LNTS 1/3023'*. Former names and other names: *Union of South American Posts* – former (1911 to 1921); *Union des postes sud-américaines* – former (1911 to 1921); *Unión de los Correos Sudamericanos* – former (1911 to 1921); *Pan American Postal Union* – former (1921 to 1931); *Union postale panaméricaine* – former (1921 to 1931); *Unión Postal Panamericana* – former (1921 to 1931); *Postal Union of the Americas and Spain (PUAS)* – former (1931 to 1991); *Union postale des Amériques et de l'Espagne (UPAE)* – former (1931 to 1991); *Unión Postal de las Américas y España* – former (1931 to 1991). **Aims** Be the Regional Intergovernmental Organization leader in the transformation of the postal sector that contributes significantly to the sustainable economic and social development of its member countries and territories; promote strengthening of regulation, and reform and technical cooperation for the transformation and sustainable development of the postal sector, which ensures access to quality services in member countries and territories, as well as consensus for the Union integration. **Structure** Congress (every 4 years); General Secretariat (Montevideo); Consultative and Executive Council (meets annually); Management Committee (meets twice a year). **Languages** English, Portuguese, Spanish. **Staff** 32.00 FTE, paid. **Finance** Sources: members' dues. **Activities** Capacity building; events/meetings; knowledge management/information dissemination; networking/liaising; research and development. **Events** *Congress* Willemstad (Curaçao) 2021, *Congress* Mexico City (Mexico) 2017, *Congress* Havana (Cuba) 2013, *Congress* Santiago (Chile) 2009, *Congress* Montevideo (Uruguay) 2007. **Publications** Acts; documents of Consultative and Executive Council; seminar and workshop documents; plans of studies.
Members Governments of 28 countries and territories:
Argentina, Aruba, Bolivia, Brazil, Canada, Chile, Colombia, Costa Rica, Cuba, Curaçao, Dominican Rep, Ecuador, El Salvador, Guatemala, Haiti, Honduras, Mexico, Nicaragua, Panama, Paraguay, Peru, Portugal, Spain, St Maarten, Suriname, Uruguay, USA, Venezuela.
IGO Relations
- *African Postal Union (APU, no recent information);*
- *Arab Permanent Postal Commission (APPC, #01025);*
- *Asian-Pacific Postal Union (APPU, #01625);*
- *Associação dos Operadores de Correios e Telecomunicações dos Países e Territórios de Língua Oficial Portuguesa (AICEP, #02333);*
- *Association of European Public Postal Operators (PostEurop, #02534);*
- *Baltic Postal Union (BPU, #03137);*
- *Caribbean Postal Union (CPU, #03541);*
- *Conférence européenne des administrations des postes et des télécommunications (CEPT, #04602);*
- *Conference of Posts and Telecommunications of Central Africa (#04642);*
- *International Trade Centre (ITC, #15703);*
- *Nordic Postal Union (NPU, #17391);*
- *Pan African Postal Union (PAPU, #18060);*
- *Regional Commonwealth in the Field of Communications (RCC, #18767);*
- *Secretaría Permanente del Convenio Multilateral sobre Cooperación y Asistencia Mutua entre las Direcciones Nacionales de Aduanas de América Latina, España y Portugal (COMALEP, #19194);*
- *Southern Common Market (#19868);*
- *UNDP (#20292);*
- *United Nations Regional Centre for Peace, Disarmament and Development in Latin America and the Caribbean (UNLIREC, #20618);*
- *Universal Postal Union (UPU, #20682).*
- *Latin American Integration Association (LAIA, #16343);*
- *OAS (#17629).*

NGO Relations *International Post Corporation (IPC, #14624).* [2021.10.25/XD3137/**D***]

♦ Postal Union of EurAsia (inactive)

♦ **Postal Union for the Mediterranean (PUMed)** **18467**

Secretariat c/o MaltaPost, pcl, 305 Triq Hal Qormi, Marsa, MTP 1001, Malta. T. +35625961262. Fax +35679468703. E-mail: rabela@maltapost.com – info@euromed-postal.org.
URL: http://www.euromed-postal.org/

History 15 Mar 2011. Restricted Union of *Universal Postal Union (UPU, #20682)*. **Aims** Develop, promote and protect the collective interests of member countries while increasing their revenues and improving quality of services provided. **Structure** General Assembly; Board of Directors; Administrators; Secretary General. **Languages** Arabic, English, French. **Activities** Awards/prizes/competitions; events/meetings.
Members Postal unions in 21 countries and territories:
Albania, Algeria, Croatia, Cyprus, Egypt, France, Greece, Italy, Jordan, Lebanon, Libya, Malta, Mauritania, Monaco, Montenegro, Morocco, Portugal, Slovenia, Spain, Tunisia, Türkiye. [2022/XM4929/**E**]

♦ **PostEurop** Association of European Public Postal Operators (#02534)
♦ Post-Graduate Network in Administration and Public Policy (see: #16294)

♦ **Postgraduates International Network (PI-Net)** **18468**

Pres Kossuth L tér 9 III/1, Budapest 1055, Hungary.
URL: http://www.pi-network.info/

History 25 Oct 1997, Budapest (Hungary), at 1st international conference. Registered in accordance with Hungarian law, 2001. **Aims** Encourage international cooperation between postgraduate student associations; facilitate communication within international postgraduate community. **Structure** Board, comprising President, General Secretary and 4 Vice-Presidents. Technical Working Groups (4): Constitution; Founding; Membership Expansion; Web Page and Public Relation. **Languages** English, French, German. **Events** *Conference* Budapest (Hungary) 2012, *Conference* Budapest (Hungary) 2011.
Members Organizations (9) in 9 countries:
France, Germany, Hungary, Ireland, Italy, Norway, Slovenia, Switzerland, USA.
Supporting organizations (6) in 6 countries and territories:
Australia, Canada, Hong Kong, Netherlands, New Zealand, UK.
International supporting organizations (2):
European Association for the Advancement of Science and Technology (EUROSCIENCE, #05927); UNESCO (#20322). [2015/XF5990/y/**F**]

♦ **PostgreSQL Europe** **18469**

Registered Office Carpeaux Diem, 13 rue du square carpeaux, 75018 Paris, France. E-mail: board@postgresql.eu.
URL: http://www.postgresql.eu/

History Registration: France. **Aims** Promote and suport deployment and development of the open-source *software* PostgreSQL and its derivatives (and related projects) in Europe. **Structure** General Assembly; Board of Directors; Executive Committee. **Activities** Events/meetings. **Events** *Nordic PGDay* Helsinki (Finland) 2022, *Nordic PGDay* 2021, *Nordic PG Day Meeting* Copenhagen (Denmark) 2019. [2021/XM7964/**D**]

♦ Postojannyj Kongress Profsojuznogo Edinstva Trudjascihsja Latinskoj Ameriki (inactive)

♦ **Postpartum Depression: Action Towards Causes and Treatment Consortium (PACT Consortium)** **18470**

Contact address not obtained. E-mail: pact.questions@med.unc.edu.
URL: https://www.momgenesfightppd.org/

Aims Understand the interaction of genes and environment to predict which women are at risk of postpartum depression (PPD). **Activities** Research and development.
Members Researchers in 5 countries:
Australia, Canada, Denmark, Sweden, USA.
NGO Relations Member of: *Global Alliance for Maternal Mental Health (GAMMH, #10208).* [2019/XM8737/v/**F**]

♦ Postpartum Support, International (internationally oriented national body)
♦ Post-Polio Health International (internationally oriented national body)
♦ Postverwaltung der Vereinten Nationen (#20613)
♦ **POTI** Peace Operations Training Institute (#18280)
♦ Potsdam Institute for Climate Impact Research (internationally oriented national body)
♦ Potsdam-Institut für Klimafolgenforschung (internationally oriented national body)

♦ **Poultry Veterinary Study Group of the EU (PVSG EU)** **18471**

Address not obtained.
URL: http://pvsgeu.org/

History Current constitution revised Nov 2007 and again May 2011. **Aims** Share practical experience and information regarding the sanitary situation in poultry and avian species of each country; develop and maintain the scientific knowledge of members; place a network of technical experts and alarm on disease outbreaks; provide a friendly environment for free information exchange. **Structure** Committee, including President, 2 Vice-Presidents, Treasurer and Secretary. **Languages** English. **Activities** Organizes biannual meetings. **Events** *Spring Meeting* Copenhagen (Denmark) 2015, *Spring Meeting / Meeting* Netherlands 2014, *Winter Meeting* Switzerland 2014, *Spring Meeting / Meeting* Lithuania 2013, *Winter Meeting / Meeting* Spain 2013.
Members Full (not over 100); honorary; observer. Individuals in 19 countries:
Austria, Belgium, Denmark, Finland, France, Germany, Greece, Hungary, Ireland, Italy, Lithuania, Netherlands, Norway, Poland, Portugal, Spain, Sweden, Switzerland, UK. [2013/XJ2420/**E**]

♦ Povere Ancelle di Gesù Cristo (religious order)
♦ Povere Ancelle della Madre di Dio (religious order)
♦ Povere Figlie delle Sante Stigmate di Santo Francesco d'Assisi (religious order)
♦ Povezanost v Alpah (#00656)
♦ Povezanost v Alpah – Omrezje Obcin / see Alliance in the Alps (#00656)

♦ **Powder Coating Institute (PCI)** **18472**

Exec Dir PO Box 110578, Lakeland FL 34211-0578, USA. T. +19413731830.
URL: http://www.powdercoating.org/

History 1 May 1981. **Aims** Promote the use of powder coating technology. **Structure** Executive Committee. Board of Directors. Committees (7): Finance; Industry Communications; Trade Show; Technical; Membership; Custom Coaters; Raw Materials Suppliers. Executive Director manages day-to-day activities. **Activities** Events/meetings; training/education; knowledge management/information dissemination. **Events** *Meeting* Indianapolis, IN (USA) 2002. **Publications** *PCI Newsletter*, *Powder Coated Tough* – magazine. *Powder Coating – The Complete Finisher's Handbook*. **Members** Companies (mostly in Canada, Mexico, USA). Membership countries not specified. [2015.08.26/XE3503/**E**]

♦ POWER / see POWER International
♦ POWER – Ability not Disability / see POWER International
♦ e-to-the-power-of-five / see European Business Council for a Sustainable Energy Future (#06417)

♦ **Powering Past Coal Alliance (PPCA)** **18473**

Communications Manager Dept for Business/Energy/Industrial Strategy, 1 Victoria Str, London, SW1H 0ET, UK. T. +442072155000. E-mail: secretariat@poweringpastcoal.org.
Programme Advisor address not obtained.
URL: https://poweringpastcoal.org/

History Launched Nov 2017, Bonn (Germany), by governments of UK and Canada. **Aims** Move the world from burning coal to *cleaner power* sources. **Events** *PPCA Global Summit* London (UK) 2021.
Members Partner countries and states (27) in 21 countries:
Alberta, Angola, Austria, Belgium, British Columbia, Canada (as country), Costa Rica, Denmark, El Salvador, Fiji, Finland, France, Italy, Luxembourg, Marshall Is, Mexico, Netherlands, New Zealand, Niue, Ontario, Portugal, Québec, Switzerland, UK, USA (States of Oregon and Washington). [2022/XM6239/**C***]

♦ **Power Institute for East and Southern Africa (PIESA)** **18474**

Exec Dir PO Box 868, Ferndale, 2160, South Africa. T. +27117891384. Fax +27117891385.
Street Address 359 Pretoria Str, 1st Floor – Fern Isle Bldg, Randburg, South Africa.
URL: http://www.piesa.com/

History 28 Feb 1998. **Aims** Improve electrification in East and Southern Africa through sharing of information, research, technology, skills and experiences for the benefit of customers and suppliers in the electricity distribution industry. **Structure** Board of Directors, comprising Chairman, Executive Director and 9 members. **Languages** English. **Staff** 2.00 FTE, paid. **Finance** Members' dues: full – US$ 6,000; corporate affiliate – US$ 1,500; individual affiliate – US$ 800. **Activities** Technical Working Groups (4): Electrification; Non-Technical Loss Reduction; Environment Management; Standardization. Organizes: conferences; meetings; training courses. **Publications** *PIESA Newsletter* (4 a year).
Members Full in 9 countries:
Congo DR, Kenya, Lesotho, Malawi, South Africa, Tanzania UR, Uganda, Zambia, Zimbabwe.
IGO Relations *New Partnership for Africa's Development (NEPAD, #17091).* **NGO Relations** Affiliate member of: *African Electrotechnical Standardization Commission (AFSEC, #00295).* [2015/XJ2231/j/**D**]

- ♦ POWER International (internationally oriented national body)
- ♦ POWER International – breaking the poverty and disability cycle / see POWER International
- ♦ POWER – International Limb Project / see POWER International
- ♦ POW Europe / see Protect Our Winters Europe (#18549)
- ♦ **POW** Protect Our Winters Europe (#18549)
- ♦ **PoWR** Parliament of the World's Religions (#18222)
- ♦ Powszechne Biale Bractwo (#20684)
- ♦ **POY/NFSY** Pohjoismainen Ohjausalan Yhdistys/Nordisk Förening för Studie- och Yrkensvägleding (#17191)
- ♦ Pöytäkirjan virallinen norjankielinen teksti on julkaistu Suomen asetuskokoelman sopimussarjan ruotsinkielisen painoksen vastaavassa numerossa (1954 treaty)
- ♦ PPAA – Palynological and Paleobotanical Association of Australasia (inactive)
- ♦ **PPA-Europe** European Association for Panels and Profiles (#06142)
- ♦ PPAF – Public-Private Alliance Foundation (internationally oriented national body)
- ♦ **PPA** Pacific Power Association (#17991)
- ♦ **PPAPD** Pacific Parliamentary Assembly on Population and Development (#17987)
- ♦ PPA – People for Peace in Africa (unconfirmed)
- ♦ **PPBA** Pan-Pacific Business Association (#18184)
- ♦ PPBI / see Peacebuilders International
- ♦ PPC/AP / see Asia and Pacific Plant Protection Commission (#01997)
- ♦ **PPCA** Plastic Pipes Conference Association (#18393)
- ♦ **PPCA** Powering Past Coal Alliance (#18473)
- ♦ PPCSEAPR / see Asia and Pacific Plant Protection Commission (#01997)
- ♦ **PPCS** Pan Pacific Continence Society (#18185)
- ♦ PPD – An Intergovernmental Organization for Promoting South-South Cooperation / see Partners in Population and Development (#18247)
- ♦ **PPD** Partners in Population and Development (#18247)
- ♦ **PPE** Groupe du Parti Populaire Européen – Démocrates-chrétiens (#10775)
- ♦ **PPE** Grúpa Phairti an Phobail Eorpaigh – Na Daonlathaithe Criostaí (#10775)
- ♦ **PPE** Grupo del Partido Popular Europeo – Demócrata-Cristianos (#10775)
- ♦ **PPE** Grupo do Partido Popular Europeu – Democratas-Cristãos (#10775)
- ♦ **PPE** Gruppo del Partito Popolare Europeo – Democratici Cristiano (#10775)
- ♦ **PPE** Grupp tal-Partit Popolari Ewropew – Dokristjani (#10775)
- ♦ **PPE** Grupul Partidului Popular European – Crestin Democrat (#10775)
- ♦ **PPE** Partido Popular Europeo (#08185)
- ♦ **PPE** Partido Popular Europeu (#08185)
- ♦ **PPE** Parti populaire européen (#08185)
- ♦ **PPE** Partito Popolare Europeo (#08185)
- ♦ PPEPPD – Properties and Phase Equilibria for Product and Process Design (meeting series)
- ♦ **PPF** Pacific Polymer Federation (#17990)
- ♦ PPF – Pädagoginnen und Pädagogen für den Frieden, Germany (internationally oriented national body)
- ♦ PPG – Preinsulated Pipe Group (no recent information)
- ♦ **PPHSN** Pacific Public Health Surveillance Network (#17993)
- ♦ **PPIAF** Public-Private Infrastructure Advisory Facility (#18569)
- ♦ **PPID** International Bar Association – Public and Professional Interest Division (#12321)
- ♦ PPI – PeacePlayers International (internationally oriented national body)
- ♦ **PPI** People and Plants International (#18302)
- ♦ **PPI** Pirate Parties International (#18374)
- ♦ PPIS / see Asia-Pacific Implant Society (#01929)
- ♦ **PPLAAF** Platform to Protect Whistleblowers in Africa (#18402)
- ♦ PPL/IR Europe (internationally oriented national body)
- ♦ PPM – Permanent Peace Movement (internationally oriented national body)
- ♦ PPOWP / see Psychologists for Peace
- ♦ **PPPC** Pulp and Paper Products Council (#18577)
- ♦ PPPHW / see Global Handwashing Partnership (#10396)
- ♦ **PPPO** Pacific Plant Protection Organization (#17989)
- ♦ PPP – Pacific Peoples' Partnership (internationally oriented national body)
- ♦ **PPP** Partenariat pour la paix (#18240)
- ♦ PPPRF – Pan Pacific Public Relations Federation (inactive)
- ♦ PPP – World Association of Probiotics, Prebiotics, Postbiotics in Pediatrics (unconfirmed)
- ♦ **PPSA** Pan-Pacific Surgical Association (#18187)
- ♦ PPSA – Pan Pacific Suzuki Association (internationally oriented national body)
- ♦ **PPSA** Pan-Pacific Swimming Association (#18188)
- ♦ **PPSEAWA** Pan Pacific and South East Asia Women's Association (#18186)
- ♦ **PPS** Paediatric Pathology Society (#18018)
- ♦ PPS / see Pharmaceutical Procurement Service (#18354)
- ♦ **PPS** Polymer Processing Society (#18426)
- ♦ **PPS** Purine and Pyrimidine Society (#18579)
- ♦ **PPTA** Plasma Protein Therapeutics Association (#18392)
- ♦ **PPT** Permanent Peoples' Tribunal (#18328)
- ♦ PPU – Peace Pledge Union (internationally oriented national body)
- ♦ **PPWG** Pacific Peace Working Group (#17988)
- ♦ PPWM – Saint Peter and Saint Paul's Workers' Mission (religious order)
- ♦ **PQI** Peace Quest International (#18282)
- ♦ PQMD – Partnership for Quality Medical Donations (internationally oriented national body)
- ♦ **PRACE** Partnership for Advanced Computing Europe (#18229)
- ♦ Pracovné Spolocenstvo Podunajskych Krajin (#21056)
- ♦ Pracovni Spolecenstvi Podunajskych Zemi (#21056)
- ♦ PRACP – Pacific Rim Association for Clinical Pharmacogenetics (no recent information)
- ♦ PRACTICA Foundation (internationally oriented national body)

♦ Practical Action 18475

Chief Exec The Robbins Bldg, 25 Albert Str, Rugby, CV21 2SD, UK. T. +441926634400. Fax +441926634401. E-mail: enquiries@practicalaction.org.uk.
URL: http://www.practicalaction.org/

History May 1965, London (UK). Founded by Dr E F Schumacher, as a primarily UK body. Former names and other names: *Intermediate Technology Development Group (ITDG)* – former; *IT International* – former. Registration: Charity Commission, No/ID: 247257, England and Wales; EU Transparency Register, No/ID: 13386822830-30, Start date: 17 Dec 2009. **Aims** Ensure a secure, fulfilling and dignified way of life to people in poverty by increasing grassroots access to *appropriate technology*, information and knowledge; provide technical assistance to *Third World* small and micro enterprises. Concerns: diffusion of technology; environmental sustainability of small-scale industries; factors influencing development of technological capacity of small-scale producers. **Structure** Board of Trustees. Includes 2 wholly owned subsidiaries: Practical Action Consultants; Practical Action Publishing. Technical Enquiry Unit. **Staff** 250.00 FTE, paid. **Finance** Main source: *Department for International Development (DFID, inactive)*. Other sources: groups and organizations, including *European Commission (EC, #06633)*. **Activities** Projects/programmes; guidance/assistance/consulting. **Events** *Séminaire international sur la chaux et les autres ciments alternatifs* Stoneleigh (UK) 1991. **Publications** *Appropriate Technology Journal* (4 a year); *Waterlines Journal* (4 a year); *Boiling Point* (3 a year); *Small Enterprise Development Journal* (3 a year); *Books by Post* (annual). Annual Report. **Members** Offices in 8 countries:
Bangladesh, Kenya, Nepal, Peru, Sri Lanka, Sudan, UK (Head Office), Zimbabwe.

Consultative Status Consultative status granted from: *ECOSOC (#05331)* (Ros A); *FAO (#09260)* (Liaison Status); *UNEP (#20299)*. **IGO Relations** Accredited organization of: *Green Climate Fund (GCF, #10714)*. **NGO Relations** Full member of: *British Overseas NGO's for Development (BOND)*. Member of: *Climate Action Network Europe (CAN Europe, #04001)*; *Coalition of European Lobbies on Eastern African Pastoralism (CELEP, #04059)*; *Global Call for Climate Action (GCCA, inactive)*; *Global Open Data for Agriculture and Nutrition (GODAN, #10514)*; *InsideNGO (inactive)*; *International NGO/CSO Planning Committee for Food Sovereignty (IPC, #14365)*; *Mountain Partnership (MP, #16862)*. Support from: *Charities Aid Foundation of America (CAF America)*. Coordinates: *Network for Social Studies on Disaster Prevention in Latin America (#17058)*. Endorses: *Ban Terminator Campaign (#03172)*. Partner of: *Energy 4 Impact (#05465)*; *Sustainable Energy for All (SEforALL, #20056)*; *World Urban Campaign (WUC, #21893)*. Collaborates with: *African Technology Policy Studies Network (ATPS, #00481)*; *International Network of Resource Centers on Urban Agriculture and Food Security (RUAF Foundation, #14319)*. [2021/XF5044/**F**]

♦ Practitioners' Network for European Development Cooperation . . . 18476

Coordinator Square de Meeûs 38-40, 1000 Brussels, Belgium. T. +3224016811. E-mail: info@dev-practitioners.eu.
URL: http://www.dev-practitioners.eu/

History 2007. Founded as an informal open-platform. **Aims** Achieve coherence within the EU *donor* community; benefit from the wide diversity of organizations, so as to make of plurality the mainspring of innovation. **Structure** General Assembly; Steering Committee; Troika; Presidency; Working Groups; Task Forces. **Languages** English, French. **Staff** 1 consultant. **Activities** Events/meetings; projects/programmes. **Events** *Annual Meeting* Brussels (Belgium) 2016, *Annual Meeting* Paris (France) 2015, *Annual Meeting* Berlin (Germany) 2013, *Annual Meeting* Luxembourg (Luxembourg) 2012, *Annual Meeting* London (UK) 2011. **Members** Agencies (22) including the following 15 international organizations listed in this Yearbook:
Agence française de développement (AFD); *Agencia Española de Cooperación Internacional para el Desarrollo (AECID)*; *Austrian Development Agency (ADA)*; *BC Council for International Cooperation (BCCIC)*; *Czech Development Agency (CzDA)*; *DANIDA*; *Deutsche Gesellschaft für Internationale Zusammenarbeit (GIZ)*; *Enabel*; *Fundación Internacional y para Iberoamérica de Administración y Politicas Públicas (FIIAPP, #10030)*; *Goethe-Institut*; *Kreditanstalt für Wiederaufbau (KfW)*; *Luxembourg Agency for Development Cooperation (LUXDEV)*; *Slovak Agency for International Development Cooperation (SAIDC)* (SlovakAid); *SNV Netherlands Development Organisation (SNV)*; *Swedish International Development Cooperation Agency (Sida)*.
Observer (2):
ESTDEV; *European Commission (EC, #06633)* (Development and Cooperation – EuropeAid).
[2022.11.10/XJ3340/y/**F**]

- ♦ PRADS – International Symposium on Practical Design of Ships and other Floating Designs (meeting series)
- ♦ **PRAGMA** Pacific Rim Applications and Grid Middleware Assembly (#17996)
- ♦ Prague Institute for Global Urban Development / see Global Urban Development (#10643)
- ♦ Prague Society for International Cooperation (internationally oriented national body)
- ♦ Prajapita Brahma Kumaris Ishwariya Vishwa Vidyalaya (#03311)
- ♦ **PRASAC** Pôle régional de recherche appliquée au développement des systèmes agricoles d'Afrique Centrale (#18413)
- ♦ **PRAT** Prehistoric Rock Art Trails (#18478)
- ♦ **PRAWA** Prisoners Rehabilitation and Welfare Action (#18502)
- ♦ Praxis Peace Institute (internationally oriented national body)
- ♦ **Praxity** Global Alliance of Independent Firms (#10204)
- ♦ Prayer Fellowship for South Asia (internationally oriented national body)
- ♦ PRBC – Pacific Rim Banknote Conference (meeting series)
- ♦ PRB – Population Reference Bureau (internationally oriented national body)
- ♦ PRCI – Pipeline Research Council International (internationally oriented national body)
- ♦ **PRCM** Programme régional de Conservation de la zone Côtière et Marine en Afrique de l'Ouest (#18528)
- ♦ **PRCP** Pacific Rim College of Psychiatrists (#17997)
- ♦ **PRCUD** Pacific Rim Council on Urban Development (#17998)
- ♦ PRDD – Programme du Réseau du développement durable – PNUD (no recent information)
- ♦ PRD / see International Association of Parkinsonism and Related Disorders (#12068)
- ♦ PRDS – Programa Red de Desarrollo Sostenible – PNUD (no recent information)
- ♦ Preachers' Help International (internationally oriented national body)
- ♦ PREAL – Partnership for Educational Revitalization in the Americas (internationally oriented national body)
- ♦ **PREBIC** Preterm Birth International Collaborative (#18490)
- ♦ **PRE** Fédération européenne des fabricants de produits réfractaires (#08339)
- ♦ Preferential Trade Area for Eastern and Southern African States (inactive)

♦ Preferred by Nature 18477

Exec Dir Skindergade 23 – 3, 1159 Copenhagen, Denmark. E-mail: info@preferredbynature.org.
URL: https://www.preferredbynature.org/

History 1994. Former names and other names: *Nature Economy and People Connected (NEPCon)* – former (1994 to 1 Oct 2020). **Aims** Work to support farmers, foresters, businesses, NGOs and governments to support better land management and business practices that benefit people, nature and the climate. **Structure** Board of Directors; Executive Director; Works and Impartiality Committee; Divisions (5). 28 Registered Offices across Africa, Americas, Asia and Europe. **Staff** 300.00 FTE, paid. Staff in over 40 countries. **Activities** Awareness raising; capacity building; certification/accreditation; guidance/assistance/consulting; knowledge management/information dissemination; monitoring/evaluation; projects/programmes; standards/guidelines; training/education. **Publications** *Newsletter / Update*. **NGO Relations** Accredited by (2): *Assurance Services International (ASI, #02993)*; *Sustainable Agriculture Network (SAN, #20052)*. Member of (4): *Forest Stewardship Council (FSC, #09869)*; *Global Sustainable Tourism Council (GSTC, #10619)*; *Rainforest Alliance*; *Tropical Forest Alliance (TFA, #20249)*. Subscriber to: *ISEAL (#16026)*. [2022.06.07/XM8965/**F**]

♦ Prehistoric Rock Art Trails (PRAT) 18478

Caminos de Arte Rupestre Prehistórico (CARP)

Headquarters C/ Luis Riera Vega 2, 39012 Santander, Cantabria, Spain. T. +34942321283. Fax +3400000000. E-mail: info@prehistour.eu.
URL: http://www.prehistour.eu/

History 19 Nov 2007, Madrid (Spain). Registration: Registro Nacional de Asociaciones (RNA), No/ID: 590799, End date: 27 May 2008, Spain. **Aims** Promote study, conservation and dissemination of the first art evidences in Council of Europe states; consolidate Prehistoric Rock Art Europe as a high-quality destination in cultural *tourism*. **Structure** General Assembly (annual); Board of Directors; Technical Staff; Experts Committee. **Languages** English, French, Spanish. **Staff** 2.00 FTE, paid. **Finance** Sources: contributions; members' dues. **Activities** Events/meetings; projects/programmes; research and development.
Members Full (24); Collaborating (18). Partner institutions in 7 countries:
Azerbaijan, France, Ireland, Italy, Norway, Portugal, Spain. [2021.05.26/XJ5962/**E**]

♦ Pre-hospital Stroke Treatment Organization (PRESTO) 18479

Main Office 5841 Cedar Lake Rd, Ste 204, Minneapolis MN 55416, USA. E-mail: connect@prestomsu.org.
URL: https://www.prestomsu.org/

History 2016. **Aims** Improve stroke outcomes through research and education supporting the appropriate proliferation and distribution of Mobile Stroke Units (MSU) and other pre-hospital technology and services. **Structure** Board of Directors; Executive Committee. Working Groups. **Events** *Mid-Year Meeting* Lyon (France) 2022. [2022/AA3113/**C**]

♦ Preimplantation Genetic Diagnosis International Society (PGDIS) . . 18480

Exec Dir 2910 MacArthur Blvd, Northbrook IL 60062, USA. T. +18474001515. Fax +18474001516. E-mail: mail@rgipgd.com.
URL: http://www.pgdis.org

History Oct 2002. Founded following 4th International Symposium on Preimplantation Genetics, 10-13 Apr 2002, Limassol (Cyprus), Inaugurated during 5th International Symposium on Preimplantation Genetics, 5-7 Jun 2003, Antalya (Turkey). **Aims** Collect and distribute information on the progress of centres involved in preimplantation genetics diagnosis (PGD); promote implementation of accurate PGD technology available in the field. **Structure** Annual Meeting; Officers (5); Directors (8); Committees (9). **Languages** English. **Staff** Voluntary. **Finance** Sources: members' dues. **Activities** Events/meetings; research and development; training/education. **Events** *International Conference on Preimplantation Genetic Diagnosis* Berlin (Germany) 2022, *International Conference on Preimplantation Genetic Diagnosis* Berlin (Germany) 2021, *International Conference on Preimplantation Genetic Diagnosis* Geneva (Switzerland) 2019, *International Conference on Preimplantation Genetic Diagnosis* Bangkok (Thailand) 2018, *International Conference on Preimplantation Genetic Diagnosis* Valencia (Spain) 2017. **Publications** *Reproductive BioMedicine Online.*
Members Individuals in 39 countries:
Argentina, Australia, Austria, Azerbaijan, Belgium, Brazil, Bulgaria, Canada, Chile, China, Cyprus, Czechia, Egypt, Finland, France, Georgia, Germany, Greece, Hungary, India, Indonesia, Israel, Italy, Japan, Jordan, Kuwait, Mexico, Netherlands, Nigeria, Norway, Russia, Singapore, Spain, Sweden, Thailand, Türkiye, UK, Ukraine, USA. [2021.09.07/XJ3788/v/**D**]

♦ Preinsulated Pipe Group (no recent information)
♦ Preinvestment Organization for Latin America and the Caribbean (inactive)
♦ Preis Europäische Frauen (#20993)

♦ Prelature of the Holy Cross and Opus Dei (Opus Dei) 18481

Prelature de la Sainte-Croix et Opus Dei
Prelate Titular Bishop of Cilibia, Viale Bruno Buozzi 73, 00197 Rome RM, Italy. T. +396808961. E-mail: international@opusdei.org – info@opusdei.org.
URL: http://www.opusdei.org/
History 2 Oct 1928, Madrid (Spain), by Saint Josemaria Escriva de Balaguer. Received pontifical approvals in 1947 and 1950. Erected as a personal Prelature in the Catholic Church by Pope John-Paul II, 28 Nov 1982. **Aims** Spread, at every level of society, an increased awareness of the universal call to *holiness* and *apostolate*, in the exercise of one's work and in the fulfilment of the ordinary duties of a *Christian*. **Structure** Opus Dei is a Personal Prelature of the Catholic Church of international scope. Consists of an ecclesiastical circumscription, made up of a Prelate, the clergy incardinated in the Prelature, and lay persons – men and women, single and married, of every social condition – who freely incorporate themselves. Also includes Cooperators (some of whom are not Catholics) who are not incorporated into the Prelature. Intrinsically united to Opus Dei is the *Priestly Society of the Holy Cross (inactive)*, for priests of the secular clergy. **Publications** *Romana* (2 a year).
Members 90,502 (among them 2,073 priests) in 69 countries and territories where Opus Dei activities have been formally set up:
Argentina, Australia, Austria, Belgium, Bolivia, Brazil, Cameroon, Canada, Chile, Colombia, Congo DR, Costa Rica, Côte d'Ivoire, Croatia, Czechia, Dominican Rep, Ecuador, El Salvador, Estonia, Finland, France, Germany, Guatemala, Honduras, Hong Kong, Hungary, India, Indonesia, Ireland, Israel, Italy, Japan, Kazakhstan, Kenya, Korea Rep, Latvia, Lebanon, Lithuania, Macau, Malaysia, Mexico, Netherlands, New Zealand, Nicaragua, Nigeria, Panama, Paraguay, Peru, Philippines, Poland, Portugal, Puerto Rico, Romania, Russia, Singapore, Slovakia, Slovenia, South Africa, Spain, Sri Lanka, Sweden, Switzerland, Taiwan, Trinidad-Tobago, Uganda, UK, Uruguay, USA, Venezuela. [2016.11.22/XF3805/**F**]

♦ Prelature de la Sainte-Croix et Opus Dei (#18481)
♦ Premier accord de compensation monétaire multilatérale (1947 treaty)
♦ Première association internationale de la presse filmée et télévisée (inactive)
♦ Première Eglise du Christ, Scientiste (#09782)
♦ Première Urgence Internationale (internationally oriented national body)
♦ Premio Donne d'Europa (#20993)
♦ Premio Mujeres de Europa (#20993)
♦ Prêmio Mulheres da Europa (#20993)
♦ Premonstratensians – Order of the Canons Regular of Prémontré (religious order)
♦ Prémontrés – Chanoines Réguliers de Prémontré (religious order)
♦ PREMO / see Pacific Island Museums Association (#17959)
♦ Prensa Internacional de Seguros (#13938)

♦ Preparatory Commission for the Comprehensive Nuclear-Test-Ban Treaty Organization (CTBTO) 18482

Commission préparatoire de l'Organisation du traité d'interdiction complète des essais nucléaires
Contact Vienna International Centre, PO Box 1200, 1400 Vienna, Austria. T. +431260306200. Fax +431260305823. E-mail: info@ctbto.org.
URL: http://www.ctbto.org/
History 19 Nov 1996. Originated from formal negotiations on the *Comprehensive Nuclear-Test-Ban Treaty (CTBT, 1996)* from 1994 to 1996. An autonomous organization linked to *United Nations (UN, #20515)* under a relationship agreement. Headquarters in Vienna (Austria). **Aims** Advance entry into force of the CTBT, which bans all nuclear explosions in all environments, by promoting signatures and ratifications; ensure the build-up of a global verification regime capable of detecting nuclear explosions underground, underwater and in the atmosphere. **Structure** Preparatory Commission (PrepCom), composed of all States Signatories. Secretariat. Executive Secretary. Working Groups (2): Administration and Budget; Verification. Advisory Group. **Languages** English. **Staff** As of Feb 2021: about 289 Staff. The *Administrative Tribunal of the International Labour Organization (ILO Tribunal, #00118)* is competent to settle disputes. **Finance** Sources: contributions of member/participating states; international organizations. Annual budget: 130,000,000 USD. **Activities** Events/meetings; politics/policy/regulatory. **Events** *CTBT: Science and Technology conference series (SnT2023)* Vienna (Austria) 2023, *Session* Vienna (Austria) 2021, *Session* Vienna (Austria) 2021, *Session* Vienna (Austria) 2021, *Session* Vienna (Austria) 2021. **Publications** *CTBTO Spectrum* (annual) – magazine. Annual Report; information booklets; other information materials, including video-audio materials and animations. **Members** As of 22 Feb 2021,185 states had signed the Treaty, of which 170 had also ratified. Membership countries not specified. **IGO Relations** Agreement regulating relations with *United Nations (UN, #20515)* entered into force on 15 Jun 2000. UN Secretary-General is the Treaty's Depositary, a situation that contravenes the Treaty's provisions may be brought to the UN's attention (Article V); *International Court of Justice (ICJ, #13098)* may be requested to give an advisory opinion (Article VI). Agreements with: *Agency for the Prohibition of Nuclear Weapons in Latin America and the Caribbean (#00554)*, 18 Sep 2002; *Association of Caribbean States (ACS, #02411)*, 7 Mar 2005; *European Centre for Medium-Range Weather Forecasts (ECMWF, #06490)*, 24 Jun 2003; *UNDP (#20292)*, 7 Dec 2000; *World Meteorological Organization (WMO, #21649)*, 23 May 2003; *UNESCO (#20322)*, 3 Feb 2010; *International Computing Centre (ICC, #12839)*, 17 May 2010. Observer organizations: *International Telecommunication Union (ITU, #15673)*; *International Atomic Energy Agency (IAEA, #12294)*; *League of Arab States (LAS, #16420)*; *Organisation for the Prohibition of Chemical Weapons (OPCW, #17823)*; United Nations; *WHO (#20950)*; WMO. Relations with numerous scientific and academic institutions involved in the four CTBT verification technologies (ie, seismic, hydro-acoustic, infrasound and radionuclide monitoring) and collaborates with civil society in the field of non-proliferation and disarmament. [2021.03.02/XE3237/**E***]

♦ PREPARE Network 18483

Contact Prof Aida Szilagyi, CNPCD Madrid 22, 307140 Timisoara, Romania. E-mail: prepare-net@prepare-net.com.
URL: http://www.prepare.dk/
History 1989. Full title: *Preventive Environmental Protection Approaches in Europe (PREPARE)*. **Aims** Promote sustainable consumption and production (SCP); set SCP agenda by proactively addressing new challenges and implementing new, innovative solutions. **Structure** Core Group (CG); Preparatory Committee (PC); Thematic Groups (TGs). **Languages** English. **Staff** 2.00 FTE, paid. **Finance** Members'dues. **Activities** Knowledge management/information dissemination; projects/programmes; events/meetings. **Events** *Workshop* Bregenz (Austria) 2012, *Workshop* Barcelona (Spain) 2009, *Annual Conference* Graz (Austria) 2006, *ERSCP : European round table on sustainable consumption and production* Bilbao (Spain) 2004.
Members Full; Associate. Full in 14 countries:
Austria, Belgium, Bulgaria, Czechia, Denmark, Greece, Lithuania, Netherlands, Poland, Portugal, Romania, Slovenia, Spain, Türkiye.
Associate in 4 countries:
Croatia, Hungary, North Macedonia, Serbia.
IGO Relations *UNIDO (#20336)*. **NGO Relations** Partner of (1): *European Roundtable on Sustainable Consumption and Production Society (ERSCP Society, #08408).* [2019.07.15/XJ3106/**F**]

♦ PREPARE – Partnership for Rural Europe 18484

SG Chaussée Saint-Pierre 260, 1040 Brussels, Belgium. T. +37126468620.
Pres address not obtained.
URL: http://www.preparenetwork.org/
History Became operational 1998. Registered as a legal entity, 2016. **Aims** Strengthen civil society; promote multi-national exchange between those who are involved (individuals or organisations) in rural development anywhere in Europe. **Languages** English. **Finance** Members' dues. **Activities** Events/meetings; training/education; networking/liaising. **Events** *Gathering* Korce (Albania) 2016, *Gathering* Slovenia 2009, *Gathering* Poland 2007, *Gathering* Czech Rep 2006, *Gathering* Lithuania 2005. **Publications** *Prepare News.*
Members Partners in 17 countries:
Albania, Bosnia-Herzegovina, Croatia, Czechia, Estonia, Finland, Hungary, Kosovo, Latvia, Lithuania, Montenegro, North Macedonia, Poland, Serbia, Slovakia, Slovenia, Sweden.
International partners (2):
European Council for the Village and Small Town (ECOVAST, #06848); *Forum synergies.* [2019.06.19/XM1580/y/**F**]

♦ PREPARE / see PREPARE Network (#18483)
♦ Preparing Global Leaders Foundation (internationally oriented national body)
♦ **PRE** Plastics Recyclers Europe (#18394)
♦ PrePreg Network (unconfirmed)
♦ **PRERICO** ICOMOS International Scientific Committee on Places of Religion and Ritual (#11079)

♦ Presbyterian Church of Africa (PCA) 18485

SG Box 72 Nyanga, Cape Town, 7755, South Africa.
URL: http://www.presbyterianchurchofafrica.co.za/
History 1898, as an all black Church. In 1973, the general synod of PCA accepted that there was no scriptural ground for remaining exclusively black, and decided that the independent community should not remain isolated from other parts of the body of Christ. **Aims** Belong to the whole people of *God*, though keeping its own charismatic gifts.
Members Presbyteries (8) in 3 countries:
Malawi, South Africa (6), Zimbabwe.
NGO Relations Member of: *Oikocredit International (Oikocredit, #17704)*; *South African Council of Churches (SACC, #19699)*; *World Communion of Reformed Churches (WCRC, #21289)*; *World Council of Churches (WCC, #21320).* [2009/XF5135/**F**]

♦ Presbyterian Church of East Africa (internationally oriented national body)
♦ Presbyterian Frontier Fellowship (internationally oriented national body)
♦ Presbyterian Hunger Program (internationally oriented national body)
♦ Presbyterian World Service and Development (internationally oriented national body)
♦ PRES – Conference on Process Integration for Energy Saving and Pollution Reduction (meeting series)
♦ Présence et vie (religious order)
♦ Presentation Brothers (religious order)

♦ Presidents of Law Associations in Asia (POLA) 18486

Contact Intl Affairs Div Korean Bar Assc, 18F 124 Teheran-ro, Gangnam-gu, Seoul 135784, Korea Rep. T. +82220877782. Fax +82234762770. E-mail: council@malaysianbar.org.my.
URL: http://www.polanet.org/
History 1990, Tokyo (Japan). Former names and other names: *Conference of the Presidents of Bar Associations in Asia* – former (1990). **Aims** Provide a forum for leaders of bar associations across the Asia-Pacific region to exchange ideas and information, collaborate on issues of mutual interest and promote friendship. **Structure** A conference series; not an organization. **Languages** English. **Finance** Expenses of annual conference covered by host country. **Activities** Knowledge management/information dissemination; networking/liaising; events/meetings. **Events** *Conference* Kuala Lumpur (Malaysia) 2023, *Conference* Seoul (Korea Rep) 2021, *Conference* Seoul (Korea Rep) 2020, *Conference* Kunming (China) 2019, *Conference* Canberra, ACT (Australia) 2018. **Publications** Members publish annual country, territorial or regional reports.
Members Full in 25 countries and territories:
Australia, Bangladesh, Cambodia, China, Fiji, Hong Kong, India, Indonesia, Israel, Japan, Korea Rep, Laos, Macau, Malaysia, Mongolia, Myanmar, Nepal, New Zealand, Pakistan, Philippines, Singapore, Sri Lanka, Taiwan, Thailand, Vietnam.
Observers (4):
International Bar Association (IBA, #12320); *Inter-Pacific Bar Association (IPBA, #15957)*; *LAWASIA – Law Association for Asia and the Pacific (#16406)*; *Union Internationale des Avocats (UIA, #20422).* [2022/XS0267/cy/**E**]

♦ Presiding Bishop's Fund for World Relief / see Episcopal Relief and Development
♦ **PRES** Paediatric Rheumatology European Society (#18020)
♦ Press Congress of the World (inactive)

♦ Press Database Licensing Network (PDLN) 18487

SG c/o NLA media access, 16-18 New Bridge Street, London, EC4V 6AG, UK. E-mail: pdlninfo@nla.co.uk.
URL: http://www.pdln.info/
History Nov 2008, Brussels (Belgium). Previously registered in accordance with Belgian law; now registered under UK law. **Aims** Protect and promote the interest of publishers in the digital age in relation to press cutting and media monitoring services. **Structure** Executive Board. **Languages** English. **Staff** None paid. **Finance** Members' dues. Annual budget: about euro 30,000. **Events** *Conference* Madrid (Spain) 2014, *Conference* Stockholm (Sweden) 2013, *Conference* Dublin (Ireland) 2012, *Conference* Lisbon (Portugal) 2011, *Conference* Copenhagen (Denmark) 2010. **Publications** *PDLN Newsletter* (every 10 weeks).
Members Full in 23 countries:
Australia, Austria, Belgium, Denmark, Finland, France, Germany, Greece, Ireland, Italy, Japan, Korea Rep, Netherlands, New Zealand, Norway, Poland, Portugal, South Africa, Spain, Sweden, Switzerland, UK, USA.
NGO Relations Member of: *International Federation of Reproduction Rights Organizations (IFRRO, #13527).* [2019/XJ7455/**F**]

♦ Presse internationale des assurances (#13938)
♦ Press Emblem Campaign (internationally oriented national body)
♦ Press emblème campagne (internationally oriented national body)

♦ Presse musicale internationale (PMI) 18488

International Music Critics
Pres address not obtained.
URL: http://www.musicalpress.org/
History 30 Jan 1986, Cannes (France), at 20th MIDEM, as *European Musical Press Association – Association européenne de la presse musicale*. **Aims** Unite *professional* critics of serious music in all countries. **Structure** General Assembly (annual); President; Bureau, composed of 4 Vice-Presidents and Treasurer; Secretariat General. **Languages** English, French. **Staff** 0.50 FTE, paid. **Finance** Members' dues. Subventions. **Activities** Awards (with SACD) annual prize for video dance. **Events** *General Assembly* Orange (France) 2003, *General Assembly* Bonn (Germany) 2002, *General Assembly* Colmar (France) 2001, *General Assembly* Saint-Jean-de-Luz (France) 2000, *General Assembly* Reims (France) 1999. **Publications** *La Lettre de la PMI.*
Members Individual critics (200) in 17 countries:
Argentina, Austria, Belgium, Canada, Egypt, France, Germany, Italy, Japan, Netherlands, Poland, Romania, Russia, Spain, Sweden, Switzerland, USA.
NGO Relations Joint activities with: *Société des auteurs et compositeurs dramatiques (SACD).* [2016/XD6710/v/**D**]

♦ Press Foundation of Asia (inactive)

♦ Pressothèque de langue française 18489

Secretariat 3 Cité Bergère, 75009 Paris, France. T. +33147700280. Fax +33148242632. E-mail: union@presse-francophone.org.
URL: http://www.presse-francophone.org/

History 1950, Paris (France), as a documentation centre of *Union internationale de la presse francophone (UPF, #20435)*. **Aims** Make available for consultation almost 1,500 *newspapers, magazines* and bulletins published wholly or partially in the French language, from over 70 countries. **Languages** French. **Staff** 7.00 FTE, paid. **Finance** Budget (annual): euro 500,000. **Events** *Meeting* Rabat (Morocco) 2010, *Meeting* Yaoundé (Cameroon) 2009, *Meeting* Montréal, QC (Canada) 2008, *Meeting* Abidjan (Côte d'Ivoire) 2007, *Meeting* Bucharest (Romania) 2006. **Publications** *La gazette de la presse francophone* (6 a year).
Members Individuals in 91 countries and territories:
Albania, Algeria, Andorra, Angola, Argentina, Armenia, Austria, Azerbaijan, Belgium, Bolivia, Bosnia-Herzegovina, Brazil, Bulgaria, Burundi, Cambodia, Cameroon, Canada, Cape Verde, Central African Rep, Chad, Chile, Comoros, Congo Brazzaville, Congo DR, Côte d'Ivoire, Croatia, Czechia, Denmark, Djibouti, Egypt, Equatorial Guinea, Estonia, Finland, France, Gabon, Georgia, Germany, Greece, Guinea, Guinea-Bissau, Haiti, Hong Kong, Hungary, India, Iraq, Ireland, Israel, Italy, Jordan, Laos, Lebanon, Liechtenstein, Lithuania, Luxembourg, Madagascar, Mali, Mauritania, Mauritius, Mexico, Moldova, Monaco, Montenegro, Morocco, Netherlands, Niger, Nigeria, North Macedonia, Palestine, Portugal, Qatar, Romania, Russia, Rwanda, Saudi Arabia, Senegal, Serbia, Seychelles, Singapore, Slovenia, Spain, Switzerland, Thailand, Togo, Tunisia, Türkiye, UK, Ukraine, United Arab Emirates, USA, Vanuatu, Vietnam.
IGO Relations *European Commission (EC, #06633); Organisation internationale de la Francophonie (OIF, #17809); Parliamentary Assembly of the Council of Europe (PACE, #18211); UNESCO (#20322).*
[2011.08.04/XF9001/v/F]

- ♦ **PRESTO** Pre-hospital Stroke Treatment Organization (#18479)
- ♦ Prestressed Concrete Association of Central America and Panama (inactive)

♦ Preterm Birth International Collaborative (PREBIC) 18490

Contact 150 Dorset Street, Unit 240-245, South Burlington VT 05403, USA.
URL: http://www.prebicglobal.org/
History Workshops organized since 2003. **Aims** Optimize *newborn* health and long-term development for *mothers* and *children*. **Structure** Board of Directors; Executive Council. Branches (4): Australasia; Europe; South America/Africa; North America. Working Groups (7). **Activities** Events/meetings; research/documentation. **Events** *Global Annual Meeting* South Burlington, VT (USA) 2021, *Annual Scientific Meeting* Guangzhou (China) 2018, *Australasia Branch Symposium* Seoul (Korea Rep) 2018, *Annual Scientific Meeting* Galveston, TX (USA) 2017, *Annual Scientific Meeting* Florence (Italy) 2016. **NGO Relations** *Every Woman Every Child (EWEC, #09215).*
[2019/XM5153/C]

- ♦ Preti del Sacro Cuore di Gesù di Bétharram (religious order)
- ♦ Prêtres de la Doctrine Chrétienne (religious order)
- ♦ Prêtres du Sacré-Coeur de Jésus (religious order)
- ♦ Prêtres du Sacré-Coeur de Jésus de Bétharram (religious order)
- ♦ Prêtres de Saint Basil (religious order)
- ♦ Prêtres de Sainte Marie de Tinchebray (religious order)
- ♦ Prêtres des Saints Stigmates de Notre Seigneur Jésus Christ (religious order)

♦ Preventing Overdiagnosis Board 18491

Contact address not obtained. E-mail: info@preventingoverdiagnosis.net.
URL: http://www.preventingoverdiagnosis.net/
Aims Develop strategies to sustain the international scientific conferences. **Structure** Board; Scientific Committee; Advisory Board; Junior Researcher Committee; Local Organizing Committee. **Activities** Events/meetings. **Events** *International Preventing Overdiagnosis Conference* Calgary, AB (Canada) 2022, *International Preventing Overdiagnosis Conference* Sydney, NSW (Australia) 2019, *International Preventing Overdiagnosis Conference* Copenhagen (Denmark) 2018, *International Preventing Overdiagnosis Conference* Québec, QC (Canada) 2017, *International Preventing Overdiagnosis Conference* Barcelona (Spain) 2016.
[2022/XM6298/c/E]

♦ Prevention of Honey Bee COlony LOSSes (COLOSS) 18492

Contact c/o Inst of Bee Health, Univ of Bern, Schwarzenburgstr 161, 3003 Bern, Switzerland. E-mail: coloss.network@gmail.com.
URL: http://www.coloss.org/
History Also referred to as *COLOSS – honey bee research association*. Current statutes approved 28 Sep 2013. Registered in accordance with Swiss Civil Code. **Aims** Improve the well-being of bees at a global level. **Structure** General Assembly; Executive Committee. Working Groups. **Finance** Sources: donations; grants; meeting proceeds; members' dues. **Activities** Monitoring/evaluation; projects/programmes. **Events** *Conference* Montréal, QC (Canada) 2019, *Conference* Ghent (Belgium) 2018, *Conference* Athens (Greece) 2017, *Conference* Cluj-Napoca (Romania) 2016. **Publications** Newsletter; conference proceedings.
Members Individuals in 65 countries:
Algeria, Argentina, Armenia, Australia, Austria, Belgium, Benin, Bolivia, Brazil, Canada, Central African Rep, Chile, China, Colombia, Croatia, Czechia, Egypt, Ethiopia, France, Germany, Greece, Guatemala, Hungary, India, Iran Islamic Rep, Ireland, Israel, Italy, Jordan, Libya, Lithuania, Malaysia, Malta, Mexico, Netherlands, New Zealand, Nigeria, North Macedonia, Norway, Oman, Pakistan, Peru, Poland, Portugal, Romania, Russia, Rwanda, Saudi Arabia, Serbia, Slovakia, Slovenia, South Africa, Spain, Sudan, Sweden, Switzerland, Thailand, Türkiye, Uganda, UK, Ukraine, Uruguay, USA, Vietnam, Yemen.
NGO Relations *International Bee Research Association (IBRA, #12330).*
[2019/XM4724/v/B]

- ♦ Prevention in Pacific Island States / see Pacific Island Museums Association (#17959)

♦ La Prévention Routière Internationale (PRI) 18493

International Road Safety Organisation – Internationale Verkehrssicherheitsorganisation
Pres c/o CNPAC, Avenue Al Araar, Hay Riyad, 10000 Rabat, Morocco. T. +212537712201. Fax +212537716953. E-mail: secretariat@lapri.info – contact@lapri.info.
URL: http://www.lapri.info/
History 9 Jul 1957, Bonn (Germany). Established by representatives of European countries. Current statutes adopted 24 Jun 1977, Paris (France); modified Jun 1989, Luxembourg; 21 Jun 2000, Bled (Slovenia); 15 Jun 2007, Lisbon (Portugal). Former names and other names: *Commission de liaison des associations et organismes de prévention routière* – former (9 Jul 1957 to 2 Jan 1959). **Aims** Encourage cooperation among national organizations for road *accident* prevention; stimulate establishment of such civil society organizations in countries where they do not yet exist; promote effective action to reduce the number of road *traffic* victims; facilitate exchange of knowledge, experience, developments, best practice and worse cases among members and between members and other stakeholders in the field; advocate safe mobility for everyone, especially vulnerable road users, young people and in developing countries and countries in transition; raise awareness for road safety. **Structure** General Meeting (annual). Presidency, consisting of President and maximum 3 Vice-Presidents, Chairpersons of Regional Groups and Coordinator of Special Committees. Secretariat located in Eemnes (Netherlands). **Languages** English, French, German. **Staff** 1.00 FTE, paid. **Finance** Sources: members' dues. **Activities** (Co)-organizes: World Congress (every 4 years); Road Safety Forum (annual); regional conferences; seminars; workshops. Sets up traineeships and road safety courses for members; distributes declarations, resolutions and press releases; lobbying activities. Various members are signatories of the EU Charter. Core business of members includes: education for school children; road safety campaigns and communication; advocacy; active involvement of citizens; volunteers and civil society. **Events** *World Congress* St Catharines, ON (Canada) 2021, *World Congress* Montréal, QC (Canada) 2020, *International conference on Road Safety* Paris (France) 2018, *World Congress* Gammarth (Tunisia) 2017, *International Conference on Pedestrian and Cyclist Safety* Kiev (Ukraine) 2013. **Publications** *PRI News* (4 a year). *Manual for Voluntary Work (VAMOS); Strategic Road Safety Plans (Code of Good Practice).* Annual Report; white books; manuals; studies; proceedings, declarations and recommendations of World Congresses, international symposia and other events.
Members (a) Active: national organizations for the prevention of road crashes; (b) Associated: university institutes, specialized research centres and other institutions interested in the aims of PRI; (c) Affiliated: commercial and industrial entities and other societies interested in the aims of PRI; (d) Individual; (e) Honorary. Active members in 39 countries and territories:
Argentina, Bahrain, Belgium, Benin, China, Croatia, Czechia, Egypt, France, Gabon, Germany, Hungary, Italy, Japan, Jordan, Korea Rep, Lebanon, Luxembourg, Madagascar, Morocco, Netherlands, Nigeria, North Macedonia, Oman, Poland, Portugal, Romania, Saudi Arabia, Serbia, Slovenia, South Africa, Spain, Srpska, Sweden, Switzerland, Syrian AR, Tunisia, Ukraine, United Arab Emirates.
Included in the above, 1 organization listed in this Yearbook:
Global Road Safety Partnership (GRSP, #10581).
IGO Relations Accredited by (1): *United Nations Office at Vienna (UNOV, #20604).* Member of (1): United Nations Road Safety Collaboration (UNRSC). Consultative status with: *International Transport Forum (ITF, #15725); United Nations (UN, #20515).* Official relations with: *European Commission (EC, #06633)* (Directorate-General Transport); *WHO (#20950).* Signatory to: *European Road Safety Charter.* **NGO Relations** Member of: Global Alliance of NGOs for Road Safety. Partnership with: *Association for Safe International Road Travel (ASIRT); European Association for Injury Prevention and Safety Promotion (EuroSafe, #06083); European Federation of Road Traffic Victims (#07207); FIA Foundation (#09742); Global Road Safety Partnership (GRSP, #10581); International Federation of Senior Police Officers (IFSPO, no recent information); International Road Federation (IRF Global, #14759); International Union of Professional Drivers (#15802); World Road Association (PIARC, #21754).*
[2021/XC2377/B]

- ♦ Preventive Environmental Protection Approaches in Europe / see PREPARE Network (#18483)
- ♦ Preventive Oncology International (internationally oriented national body)
- ♦ **PRFI** Partnership for Responsible Financial Inclusion (#18241)
- ♦ PRIA – Society for Participatory Research in Asia (internationally oriented national body)
- ♦ PRI Association / see Principles for Responsible Investment Initiative (#18499)
- ♦ **PRICAI** Pacific Rim International Conferences on Artificial Intelligence (#17999)
- ♦ PRIDE – Pacific Rim Institute for Development and Education (internationally oriented national body)
- ♦ Priesterbruderschaft St Pius X (#18494)
- ♦ Priestly Fraternity of Saint Peter (religious order)

♦ Priestly Society of Saint Pius X (SSPX) 18494

Fraternité sacerdotale internationale Saint-Pie X (FSSPX) – Priesterbruderschaft St Pius X
Information Office Assocn Civiroma, 33 rue Galande, 75005 Paris, France. E-mail: secretariat@dici.org.
URL: http://www.fsspx.org/
History 1970, Fribourg (Switzerland), as *International Sacerdotal Brotherhood Saint Pius X – Fraternité sacerdotale internationale Saint-Pie X*, by Archbishop Marcel Lefebve. **Aims** Train *Catholic priests* in priestly seminaries. **Structure** Superior General, 2 General Assistants, Secretary General, General Bursar; District Superiors (by countries); Rectors of Seminaries. **Finance** Financed by gifts of benefactors. **Events** *Biennial general chapter* Riddes (Switzerland) 1994, *Christopher Columbus, glory of the Americas* Buenos Aires (Argentina) 1992. **Publications** *Mitteilungsblatt* (12 a year) in German; *Fideliter* (6 a year) – in France; *The Angelus* (6 a year) – in USA; *Jesus Christus* (periodical) – in Argentina. Maintains a Library (50,000 books).
Members Priests (590); movements and associations, in 28 countries:
Argentina, Australia, Austria, Belgium, Canada, Chile, Colombia, Dominican Rep, France, Gabon, Germany, Guatemala, India, Ireland, Italy, Mexico, Netherlands, New Zealand, Philippines, Poland, Portugal, South Africa, Spain, Sri Lanka, Switzerland, UK, USA, Zimbabwe.
Included in the above, 3 organizations listed in this Yearbook:
Mouvement Eucharistique des Jeunes (MEJ); Séminaire international Saint-Pie X (no recent information); Third Order of the Society of St Pius X.
Priestly seminaries in 6 countries:
Argentina, Australia, France, Germany, Switzerland, USA.
[2014.11.04/XF1381/y/F]

- ♦ Priest Missionaries of the Kingship of Christ (religious order)
- ♦ Priests of the Sacred Heart of Jesus (religious order)
- ♦ Prieuré de Sion (religious order)
- ♦ PRIF / see Peace Research Institute Frankfurt
- ♦ PRIF – Peace Research Institute Frankfurt (internationally oriented national body)
- ♦ **PRI Initiative** Principles for Responsible Investment Initiative (#18499)
- ♦ Prijs Vrouwen van Europa (#20993)
- ♦ Primafamed-Ghent University – International Centre for Primary Health Care and Family Medicine (internationally oriented national body)
- ♦ PRIMA – International Conference on Principles and Practice of Multi-Agent Systems (meeting series)
- ♦ PRIMA – The Paper Network / see Paper and Related Industries Marketing Association (#18191)
- ♦ **PRIMA** Paper and Related Industries Marketing Association (#18191)

♦ Primary Care Diabetes Europe (PCDE) 18495

Operational Manager Aronskelk 31, 7392 AM Twello, Netherlands. T. +31648546892. E-mail: secretary@pcdeurope.org.
Chair address not obtained.
Registered Seat Bredestraat 79, 2180 Ekeren, Belgium.
URL: http://www.pcdeurope.org/
History Founded according to objectives of Saint Vincent Declaration (1989) of *International Diabetes Federation (IDF, #13164)* and *WHO (#20950)*. First meeting 1996, Lisbon (Portugal). Became independent in 2000. Former names and other names: *St Vincent Declaration Primary Care Diabetes Group* – former (1996 to 2001); *PCD Europe* – alias. Registration: Banque Carrefour des Entreprises, No/ID: 0871.319.821, Start date: 10 Jan 2005, Belgium; EU Transparency Register, No/ID: 450577821932-74, Start date: 25 May 2016. **Aims** Provide a focal point for primary care clinicians and their patients; promote high standards of care for people living with diabetes throughout Europe. **Structure** General Assembly. Executive Committee, including Chairman, Honorary General Secretary and Honorary Treasurer. **Languages** English. **Staff** 1.00 FTE, paid. **Finance** Sources: publication proceeds; sponsorships; grants from the industry. **Activities** Cooperates with other organizations in groups and on studies and projects. Database of researchers' expertise in sports engineering; database of over 7,000 sports-related references and papers. **Events** *International Conference* Barcelona (Spain) 2022, *International Conference* Barcelona (Spain) 2020, *International Conference* Barcelona (Spain) 2018, *International Conference* Barcelona (Spain) 2016, *International Conference / Conference* Barcelona (Spain) 2012. **Publications** *Primary Care Diabetes* – journal; *Primary Care Diabetes Journal.* Information Services: Maintains an online Knowledge Resource Centre. **Information Services** *MEDLINE.*
Members Individuals (about 4,200) in 46 countries:
Albania, Armenia, Austria, Azerbaijan, Belarus, Belgium, Bosnia-Herzegovina, Croatia, Czechia, Denmark, Egypt, Estonia, Finland, Georgia, Germany, Greece, Hungary, Iceland, Ireland, Israel, Italy, Jordan, Kazakhstan, Kyrgyzstan, Latvia, Lithuania, Luxembourg, Malta, Monaco, Netherlands, North Macedonia, Norway, Poland, Portugal, Romania, Russia, Slovakia, Slovenia, Spain, Sweden, Switzerland, Tajikistan, Türkiye, UK, Ukraine, Uzbekistan.
NGO Relations Member of (4): *European Alliance for Diabetes Research (EURADIA, #05868); European Coalition for Diabetes (ECD, #06592); European Forum for Primary Care (EFPC, #07326); European Foundation for the Study of Diabetes (EFSD, #07351).* Sister organization: *Foundation of European Nurses in Diabetes (FEND, #09953).* Special Interest Group of: *European Society of General Practice/Family Medicine (WONCA Europe, #08609).* Close relations with: *European Association for the Study of Diabetes (EASD, #06228); European General Practice Research Network (EGPRN, #07384); European Primary Care Cardiovascular Society (EPCCS, #08273); International Diabetes Federation (IDF, #13164)* – Europe; *World Organization of Family Doctors (WONCA, #21690).*
[2020/XM2298/D]

♦ Primary Food Processors (PFP) 18496

Main Office Avenue de Tervueren 168, Boîte 12, 1050 Brussels, Belgium. E-mail: info@pfp-eu.org.
URL: http://www.pfp-eu.org/
History Former names and other names: *Association of the Primary Food Processors of the EU (PFP)* – former. Registration: EU Transparency Register, No/ID: 71338036982-24. **Aims** Represent the European primary food processing industries' interests, at the level of both European and international institutions. **Structure** Board of Directors; Committee of Associations' Managers. **Events** *Forum* Brussels (Belgium) 2022, *Forum* 2021, *Forum* 2020, *Forum on Availability of Raw Materials in the Context of Current and Future EU Policies* Brussels (Belgium) 2018, *General Assembly* Brussels (Belgium) 2017.
Members Organizations (6):
Comité européen des fabricants de sucre (CEFS, #04159); European Cocoa Association (ECA, #06599); European Flour Millers' Association (#07272); European Vegetable Protein Association (EUVEPRO, #09047); FEDIOL – The EU Vegetable Oil and Proteinmeal Industry (#09718); Starch Europe (#19966).
NGO Relations Member of: Advisory Group on the Food Chain and Animal and Plant Health; *European Bioeconomy Alliance (EUBA, #06334); European Food Sustainable Consumption and Production Round Table (European Food SCP Roundtable, #07289); Industry4Europe (#11181).*
[2022/XJ2205/y/E]

♦ Primary Tungsten Association (inactive)

♦ Primates Meeting of the Anglican Communion 18497

SG St Andrew's House, 16 Tavistock Crescent, London, W11, UK. E-mail: aco@anglicancommunion.org.
Chairman Archbishop of Canterbury, Lambeth Palace, London, SE1 7JU, UK.
URL: http://www.anglicancommunion.org/structures/instruments-of-communion/ primates- meeting.aspx/

History 1978, within the framework of *Anglican Communion (#00827)*, on recommendation of *Lambeth Conference of Bishops of the Anglican Communion (#16224)*. First met 1979. **Aims** Meet for leisurely thought, prayer and deep consultation on theological, social and international issues. **Structure** Primates of the autonomous churches of the Communion meet every year or every 2 years. Moderators of the United Churches are members of the meeting. **Events** *Meeting* Canterbury (UK) 2016, *Meeting* Dublin (Ireland) 2011, *Meeting* Alexandria (Egypt) 2009, *Meeting* Dar es Salaam (Tanzania UR) 2007, *Meeting* Tanzania UR 2007. **Publications** *Anglican World* (4 a year) – magazine.
Members Primates of the 38 autonomous Churches of the Anglican Communion. National churches of 24 countries and territories:
Australia, Brazil, Burundi, Canada, Congo DR, England, Hong Kong, Ireland, Japan, Kenya, Korea Rep, Mexico, Myanmar, Nigeria, Papua New Guinea, Philippines, Portugal, Rwanda, Scotland, Sudan, Tanzania UR, Uganda, USA, Wales.
Provincial Churches (11):
Anglican Church in Aotearoa, New Zealand and Polynesia (#00823); Anglican Church of Southern Africa (ACSA, #00826); Anglican Church of the Province of the Indian Ocean (#00824); Church in the Province of the West Indies (CPWI, #03921); Church of the Province of Central Africa (#03917); Church of the Province of Melanesia (#03918); Church of the Province of South East Asia (#03919); Church of the Province of West Africa (CPWA, #03920); Episcopal Church in Jerusalem and the Middle East (#05513); Iglesia Anglicana de la Region Central de América (IARCA, #11108); The Anglican Church of South America (#00825).
United Churches (union of Anglicans with Christians of other traditions) in 3 countries:
Bangladesh, India (2), Pakistan. [2016.06.29/XF5110/cy/**F**]

♦ Primate's World Relief and Development Fund (internationally oriented national body)
♦ Primate's World Relief Fund / see Primate's World Relief and Development Fund
♦ PRIME (internationally oriented national body)
♦ PRIME ALLIANCE (unconfirmed)
♦ PRIME – European Association of Public Relations and Communications Students (no recent information)
♦ **P.R.I.M.E. Finance** Panel of Recognised International Market Experts in Finance (#18174)

♦ PrimeGlobal 18498

Main Office 3235 Satellite Blvd, Bldg 400 – Ste 300, Duluth GA 30096, USA. T. +16784177730 ext300. Fax +16789993959. E-mail: info@primeglobal.net.
URL: http://www.primeglobal.net/

History 2011. Founded as a result of merger between *IGAF Polaris (inactive)* and *Fidunion International*. Registration: USA, Delaware. **Aims** Coordinate *communication* among independent member *accountancy firms* of autonomous regional members. **Structure** Autonomous regions (4): North America; Europe; Asia Pacific; Latin America and the Caribbean. **Languages** English, French, Spanish. **Staff** 13.50 FTE, paid. **Finance** Members' dues. **Activities** Events/meetings. **Events** *EMEA Regional Conference* Cape Town (South Africa) 2020, *Nordic Baltic Countries Meeting* Oslo (Norway) 2020, *EMEA Benelux Conference* Bruges (Belgium) 2018, *EMEA Regional Conference* Madrid (Spain) 2018, *World Conference* Paris (France) 2015.
Members Firms (over 300) in 85 countries and territories:
Afghanistan, Argentina, Aruba, Australia, Austria, Bangladesh, Belgium, Belize, Bolivia, Brazil, Bulgaria, Canada, Chile, China, Colombia, Costa Rica, Croatia, Cyprus, Czechia, Denmark, Dominica, Dominican Rep, Ecuador, Egypt, El Salvador, Finland, France, Germany, Gibraltar, Greece, Guatemala, Honduras, Hong Kong, India, Indonesia, Ireland, Israel, Italy, Japan, Jersey, Jordan, Kenya, Korea Rep, Kuwait, Lebanon, Luxembourg, Malaysia, Malta, Mauritius, Mexico, Morocco, Mozambique, Netherlands, New Zealand, Nigeria, Norway, Pakistan, Palestine, Panama, Peru, Philippines, Poland, Portugal, Puerto Rico, Romania, Russia, Saudi Arabia, Singapore, Slovenia, South Africa, Spain, Sweden, Switzerland, Taiwan, Thailand, Tunisia, Türkiye, Uganda, UK, Ukraine, United Arab Emirates, Uruguay, USA, Venezuela, Vietnam. [2021/XJ7558/**F**]

♦ PRIME – International Peace Research Institute, Meiji Gakuin University (internationally oriented national body)
♦ Prime Ministers Meetings / see Commonwealth Heads of Government Meeting (#04337)
♦ PRIME Partnerships in International Medical Education / see PRIME
♦ Primera Asociación Internacional de Noticieros y Televisión (inactive)
♦ Prince Abdul Mohsin Bin Jalawi Centre for Research and Islamic Studies, Sharjah (unconfirmed)
♦ Prince Alwaleed Bin Talal Center for Muslim-Christian Understanding (internationally oriented national body)
♦ Prince Alwaleed Bin Talal Centre of Islamic Studies (internationally oriented national body)
♦ Prince Bernhard Centre for International Nature Conservation (internationally oriented national body)
♦ Prince Claus Fund for Culture and Development (internationally oriented national body)
♦ Prince Leopold Institute of Tropical Medicine / see Institute of Tropical Medicine Antwerp
♦ Princeton Institute for International and Regional Studies (internationally oriented national body)
♦ Princeton School of Public and International Affairs (internationally oriented national body)
♦ Prince of Wales's Corporate Leaders Group / see CLG Europe
♦ Prince of Wales's EU Corporate Leaders Group on Climate Change (EU CLG) / see CLG Europe
♦ Principes pour le contrôle des établissements des banques à l'étranger (1983 treaty)
♦ Principes pour l'investissement responsable (#18499)
♦ Principles Governing the Use by States of Artificial Earth Satellites for International Direct Television Broadcasting (1982 treaty)
♦ Principles Relating to Remote Sensing of the Earth from Outer Space (1986 treaty)
♦ Principles Relevant to the Use of Nuclear Power Sources in Outer Space (1992 treaty)

♦ Principles for Responsible Investment Initiative (PRI Initiative) 18499

Principes pour l'investissement responsable (Initiative PRI)

Main Office 5th Floor, 25 Camperdown Street, London, E1 8DZ, UK. T. +442037143220. E-mail: info@unpri.org.
URL: http://www.unpri.org/

History 2005, when convened, and launched in 2006, on the initiative of *United Nations (UN, #20515)* Secretary General, and coordinated by *UNEP (#20299)* Finance Initiative and *United Nations Global Compact (#20567)*. Also referred to as *PRI Association*. Registered in accordance with UK law: 7207947. **Aims** As a network of international investors, backed by the United Nations, work together to put the six Principles for Responsible Investment into practice. **Structure** PRI Signatures; Board of 16 representatives; Advisory Board; Secretariat, managed by PRI Secretariat. **Activities** Knowledge management/information dissemination. **Events** *Annual Conference* 2021, *Annual Conference* Tokyo (Japan) 2020, *Annual Academic Conference* Paris (France) 2019, *Annual Conference* Paris (France) 2019, *ESG Forum* Singapore (Singapore) 2019.
Members Signatories: asset owners; investment managers; professional service partners. Signatories in 53 countries and territories:
Argentina, Australia, Austria, Barbados, Belgium, Brazil, Canada, Cayman Is, China, Colombia, Denmark, Ecuador, Estonia, Finland, France, Germany, Hong Kong, Iceland, India, Indonesia, Ireland, Israel, Italy, Japan, Korea Rep, Latvia, Liechtenstein, Lithuania, Luxembourg, Malaysia, Mauritius, Mexico, Netherlands, New Zealand, Nigeria, Norway, Pakistan, Poland, Portugal, Puerto Rico, Singapore, Slovakia, South Africa, Spain, St Vincent-Grenadines, Sweden, Switzerland, Thailand, Türkiye, UK, United Arab Emirates, USA, Vietnam.
Included in the above, 1 organization listed in this Yearbook:
Global Sustain.
NGO Relations Member of (1): *World Benchmarking Alliance (WBA, #21228).* [2020/XJ1312/**E**]

♦ Principles for Responsible Management Education (PRME) 18500

Head Foundation for the Global Compact, 685 3rd Ave, 12th Floor, New York NY 10017, USA. T. +12129071349. E-mail: prmesecretariat@unprme.org – info@unprme.org.
Coordinator address not obtained.
URL: http://www.unprme.org/

History 2007. Founded as an initiative. Drafting process co-convened by *United Nations Global Compact (#20567)*, *AACSB International – Association to Advance Collegiate Schools of Business*, Aspen Institute Business and Society Program, European Academy of Business in Society (EABIS) – currently *Academy of Business in Society (ABIS, #00032)*, *Globally Responsible Leadership Initiative (GRLI, #10462)* and *Net Impact*. **Aims** Inspire and champion responsible management education, research and thought leadership globally. **Structure** Steering Committee, comprising: *United Nations Global Compact (#20567); AACSB International – Association to Advance Collegiate Schools of Business; EFMD – The Management Development Network (#05387); Association of MBAs (AMBA, #02795); CEEMAN – International Association for Management Development in Dynamic Societies (CEEMAN, #03625); Association of African Business Schools (AABS, #02351); Latin American Council of Business Schools (#16308); Accreditation Council for Business Schools and Programs (ACBSP)*; Russian Association of Business Education (RABE); *Academy of Business in Society (ABIS, #00032); Globally Responsible Leadership Initiative (GRLI, #10462)*. Advisory Committee; Secretariat at *Foundation for the Global Compact*. Working Groups. **Languages** English, German, Spanish. **Staff** 4.50 FTE, paid. 1 intern. **Finance** Steering Committee contributions; administrative service fee contributions from PRME signatories; individual project funding. Sponsors include: *Bertelsmann Foundation*. **Activities** Events/meetings; knowledge management/information dissemination. **Events** *Global Forum* New York, NY (USA) 2021, *Global Forum* New York, NY (USA) 2020, *Global Forum* New York, NY (USA) 2017, *Middle East and North Africa Regional Forum* Casablanca (Morocco) 2014, *Asian Forum* Kuala Lumpur (Malaysia) 2014. **Publications** Books; reports.
Members Academic institutions (540) in 81 countries and territories:
Albania, Argentina, Australia, Austria, Bangladesh, Belarus, Belgium, Brazil, Bulgaria, Canada, Chile, China, Colombia, Costa Rica, Croatia, Czechia, Denmark, Dominica, Dominican Rep, Ecuador, Egypt, Finland, France, Georgia, Germany, Greece, Hungary, Iceland, India, Indonesia, Ireland, Italy, Japan, Jordan, Kazakhstan, Kenya, Korea Rep, Kosovo, Kyrgyzstan, Latvia, Lebanon, Lithuania, Malaysia, Mexico, Monaco, Morocco, Namibia, Netherlands, New Zealand, Nigeria, Norway, Pakistan, Panama, Paraguay, Peru, Philippines, Poland, Portugal, Romania, Russia, Rwanda, Saudi Arabia, Serbia, Singapore, Slovenia, South Africa, Spain, Sri Lanka, Sweden, Switzerland, Tanzania UR, Thailand, Trinidad-Tobago, Türkiye, Uganda, UK, Ukraine, United Arab Emirates, USA, Venezuela, Vietnam.
Included in the above, 14 organizations listed in this Yearbook:
CEMS – The Global Alliance in Management Education (#03635); China-Europe International Business School (CEIBS, #03888); ESCP Europe Business School (#05536); INSEAD (#11228); International Association of Jesuit Business Schools (IAJBS, #11974); International Culture University (ICU); International Management Institute, St Petersburg (IMISP); International University of Monaco; IPADE Business School; Keio University Global Research Institute (KGRI); Latin American Quality Institute (LAQI, #16364); oikos International – students for sustainable economics and management (oikos International, #17705); Sociedade Latino Americana de Coaching (SLAC); World Learning.
NGO Relations Partner of: *UNLEASH*. *International Humanistic Management Association (IHMA)* serves as Working Group. [2022/XJ2424/y/**E**]

♦ Principles for the Supervision of Banks' Foreign Establishments (1983 treaty)
♦ Prins Leopold Instituut voor Tropische Geneeskunde (internationally oriented national body)
♦ PRIO / see Peace Research Institute Oslo
♦ PRIO – Peace Research Institute Oslo (internationally oriented national body)

♦ Priority Actions Programme / Regional Activity Centre (PAP/RAC) . 18501

Centre d'activités régionales du programme d'actions prioritaires (CAR/PAP)

Dir Kraj Sv Ivana 11, HR-21000 Split, Croatia. T. +38521340470. Fax +38521340490. E-mail: paprac@paprac.org.
URL: http://paprac.org/

History 1977. Founded within the framework of *Mediterranean Action Plan (MAP, #16638)* to assist the countries of the Region in dealing with priority environmental issues. **Aims** Support Mediterranean countries on their path towards sustainable coastal development. **Structure** Executive Board; Focal Points; Headquarters based in Split (Croatia). **Languages** English, French. **Staff** 10.00 FTE, paid. **Finance** Supported by: *Mediterranean Trust Fund (MTF, #16686)*. **Activities** Awareness raising; capacity building; guidance/assistance/consulting; projects/programmes; training/education. Coordinates the implementation of the Protocol on Integrated Coastal Zone Management (ICZM) of the Barcelona Convention for the Protection of the Mediterranean Sea and Coast. **Publications** Reports; guidelines; manuals; plans; strategies; compendiums.
Members Governments of 21 countries:
Albania, Algeria, Bosnia-Herzegovina, Croatia, Cyprus, Egypt, France, Greece, Israel, Italy, Lebanon, Libya, Malta, Monaco, Montenegro, Morocco, Slovenia, Spain, Syrian AR, Tunisia, Türkiye.
Intergovernmental organization:
European Union (EU, #08967).
IGO Relations Cooperates with (6): *European Commission (EC, #06633); European Environment Agency (EEA, #06995); Intergovernmental Oceanographic Commission (IOC, #11496); International Bank for Reconstruction and Development (IBRD, #12317)* (World Bank); *OECD (#17693)* (Environment Directorate); *Union for the Mediterranean (UfM, #20457)*. **NGO Relations** Cooperates with (1): *Conference of Peripheral Maritime Regions of Europe (CPMR, #04638).* [2021.10.26/XK1791/**E***]

♦ **PRI** Penal Reform International (#18290)
♦ **PRI** Performance Review Institute (#18310)
♦ PRI – Permaculture Research Institute (internationally oriented national body)
♦ **PRI** Pharmabiotic Research Institute (#18346)
♦ PRI – Plant Research International (internationally oriented national body)
♦ **PRI** La Prévention Routière Internationale (#18493)
♦ Prisma (internationally oriented national body)
♦ PRISM International (internationally oriented national body)

♦ Prisoners Rehabilitation and Welfare Action (PRAWA) 18502

Exec Dir 104 Upper Chime Avenue, New Haven, Enugu, Nigeria. T. +2341048486057.
URL: http://www.prawa.org/

History 16 Dec 1994. **Aims** Promote the development of humane criminal *justice* and penal systems in African nations. **Activities** *'Alternative to Violence Project in West Africa'* established in 1998. **Members** Membership countries not specified. **IGO Relations** Observer to: *African Commission on Human and Peoples' Rights (ACHPR, #00255)*. **NGO Relations** Member of: *African Security Sector Network (ASSN, #00453); African Correctional Services Association (ACSA, #00269)*. Hosted 10th International Conference on Penal Abolition (ICOPA X) of *International Circle of Penal Abolitionists (ICOPA, #12574).* [2010/XJ8217/**F**]

♦ Prison Fellowship International (PFI) 18503

Fraternité internationale des prisons – Confraternidad Carcelaria Internacional (CCI)

CEO PO Box 17434, Washington DC 20041, USA. T. +17034810000. Fax +17034810003. E-mail: info@pfi.org.
Europe Office Heinrich-Längerer-Str 27, 71229 Leonberg, Germany.
Singapore Office Tanglin Post Office, PO Box 216, Singapore 912408, Singapore.
URL: http://www.pfi.org/

History 1979, Washington DC (USA). **Aims** Encourage and assist the Church in prisons and in the community, in its ministry to prisoners, ex-prisoners, victims and their families; promote *restorative justice*; act as a *Christian* movement of reconciliation and restoration in the *criminal* justice system, thereby proclaiming and demonstrating the redemptive power and transforming love of Jesus Christ for all people. **Structure** International Council; Board of Directors; Executive Committee; Regional offices (4). **Languages** English, French, Russian, Spanish. **Staff** 300.00 FTE, paid; 100000.00 FTE, voluntary. **Activities** Advocacy/lobbying/activism; training/education. **Events** *European Summit* Amsterdam (Netherlands) 2014, *Triennial International Convocation* Toronto, ON (Canada) 2011, *Quadrennial convocation / Triennial International Convocation* Toronto, ON (Canada) 2007, *Triennial International Convocation* Toronto, ON (Canada) 2003, *Quadrennial convocation / Triennial International Convocation* Sofia (Bulgaria) 1999. **Publications** *Global Link* (6 a year). Annual Report.
Members Chartered: national prison fellowship organizations in 121 countries and territories:

Albania, Angola, Antigua-Barbuda, Argentina, Armenia, Australia, Bahamas, Bangladesh, Barbados, Belarus, Belize, Benin, Bermuda, Bolivia, Botswana, Brazil, Bulgaria, Burkina Faso, Burundi, Cambodia, Cameroon, Canada, Cayman Is, Central African Rep, Chile, Colombia, Congo DR, Costa Rica, Côte d'Ivoire, Curaçao, Czechia, Dominica, Ecuador, El Salvador, England, Estonia, Eswatini, Ethiopia, Fiji, Finland, France, Gambia, Georgia, Germany, Ghana, Guam, Guatemala, Guernsey, Guinea, Guinea-Bissau, Guyana, Haiti, Honduras, Hungary, India, Israel, Italy, Jamaica, Kazakhstan, Kenya, Kyrgyzstan, Latvia, Lebanon, Lesotho, Liberia, Madagascar, Malawi, Malaysia, Mali, Malta, Mauritius, Mexico, Moldova, Mongolia, Mozambique, Namibia, Nepal, Netherlands, New Zealand, Nicaragua, Niger, Nigeria, Northern Ireland, Northern Mariana Is, Norway, Pakistan, Panama, Papua New Guinea, Peru, Philippines, Poland, Portugal, Puerto Rico, Romania, Russia, Rwanda, Scotland, Senegal, Sierra Leone, Singapore, Slovakia, Solomon Is, South Africa, Spain, Sri Lanka, St Vincent-Grenadines, Suriname, Switzerland, Togo, Tonga, Trinidad-Tobago, Uganda, Ukraine, Uruguay, USA, Venezuela, Virgin Is UK, Virgin Is USA, Wales, Zambia, Zimbabwe.
Consultative Status Consultative status granted from: *ECOSOC (#05331)* (Special). **IGO Relations** Accredited by: *United Nations Office at Vienna (UNOV, #20604)*. Associated with Department of Global Communications of the United Nations. **NGO Relations** Member of: *Alliance of NGOs on Crime Prevention and Criminal Justice (#00709)*; *Association of Evangelicals in Africa (AEA, #02587)*. [2017.06.01/XF1346/F]

- ♦ Prison Litigation Network / see European Prison Litigation Network (#08277)
- ♦ Prisonniers Sans Frontières (internationally oriented national body)
- ♦ Privacy Enhancing Technologies Symposium (meeting series)

♦ Privacy International (PI) 18504

Exec Dir 62 Britton Street, Clerkenwell, London, EC1M 5UY, UK. T. +442034224321. E-mail: press@privacyinternational.org.
URL: https://www.privacyinternational.org/

History 1990. Former names and other names: *World Organization for the Protection of Privacy* – alias. Registration: Charity Commission, No/ID: 1147471, England and Wales; EU Transparency Register, No/ID: 78180074927-85, Start date: 10 Jan 2011. **Aims** Protect democracy, defend people's dignity, and demand accountability from institutions who breach public trust. **Structure** Board of Trustees. **Finance** Sources: donations; grants; meeting proceeds; sale of publications. **Activities** Events/meetings; knowledge management/information dissemination; monitoring/evaluation. **Events** *Half-yearly meeting* Sydney, NSW (Australia) 1992. **Publications** Annual report on privacy violations.
Members Working group of 120 private experts (academics, advocates, data protection experts, political scientists, journalists, the judiciary, lawyers, computer professionals, FOI experts, some government officials); human rights organizations. Members in 35 countries and territories:
Argentina, Australia, Austria, Belgium, Canada, Chile, Costa Rica, Czechia, Denmark, Egypt, France, Germany, Haiti, Hong Kong, Hungary, India, Israel, Japan, Kenya, Netherlands, New Zealand, Nigeria, Norway, Panama, Philippines, Serbia-Montenegro, South Africa, Spain, Sweden, Switzerland, Thailand, UK, USA, Zambia, Zimbabwe.
Members also in the former USSR; countries not specified.
IGO Relations *Council of Europe (CE, #04881)*. Participant in Fundamental Rights Platform of: *European Union Agency for Fundamental Rights (FRA, #08969)*. **NGO Relations** Member of: *IFEX (#11100)*. Signatory to Founding Statement of: *Alliance for Lobbying Transparency and Ethics Regulation (ALTER-EU, #00705)*. [2023/XF2262/F]

- ♦ Private Agencies Collaborating Together / see Pact (#18016)
- ♦ Private Committees, Associations and Organizations for the Safeguarding of Venice / see Association of International Private Committees for the Safeguarding of Venice (#02758)
- ♦ Private International Agency for the Advancement and Development of Agronomical Sciences and Techniques (inactive)
- ♦ Private Investors for Africa (unconfirmed)
- ♦ Private Label Manufacturers Association / see PLMA International Council (#18406)

♦ Private Libraries Association (PLA) 18505

Association des bibliothèques privées
Hon Membership Sec 29 Eden Drive, Hull, HU8 8JQ, UK.
Registered address Ravelston, South View Road, Pinner, HA5 3YD, UK.
URL: http://www.plabooks.org/

History 1957. Registered in accordance with UK law. **Aims** Serve as an international society of *book collectors*. **Structure** Committee. **Languages** English. **Staff** Voluntary. **Finance** Members' dues. **Publications** *PLA Newsletter* (4 a year); *The Private Library* (4 a year); *Private Press Books* (annual). Exchange list; Members' Handbook; books on book collecting.
Members Individuals (500) and libraries (85) in 27 countries and territories:
Argentina, Australia, Belgium, Canada, China, Denmark, Finland, France, Germany, Greenland, Hong Kong, Iceland, India, Ireland, Israel, Italy, Japan, Latvia, Malta, Mexico, Monaco, Netherlands, New Zealand, Singapore, South Africa, UK, USA. [2019.12.18/XD3141/D]

- ♦ Private Pilot License / see PPL/IR Europe
- ♦ Prix Femmes d'Europe (#20993)
- ♦ Prix Jeunesse (internationally oriented national body)
- ♦ Prix Jeunesse Foundation / see Prix Jeunesse
- ♦ Prix jeunesse international / see Prix Jeunesse
- ♦ **PRME** Principles for Responsible Management Education (#18500)
- ♦ **PRMIA** Professional Risk Managers' International Association (#18514)
- ♦ PRMVS / see Instituto Internacional en Conservación y Manejo en Vida Silvestre (#11336)
- ♦ **PRNGO** Pacific Islands Regional Non-governmental Organizations (#17978)
- ♦ PRNI – International Workshop on Pattern Recognition in Neuroimaging (meeting series)
- ♦ PRN – Productivity Research Network (unconfirmed)
- ♦ **PRNTT** Nonviolent Radical Party, Transnational and Transparty (#17154)

♦ ProAct 18506

Dir Les Deux Cèdres, Avenue Alfred-Cortot 7D, 1260 Nyon VD, Switzerland. T. +41223625384. Fax +41223625385. E-mail: info@proactnetwork.org.
URL: http://proactnetwork.org/

History Also referred to as *ProAct Network*. **Aims** Help vulnerable communities improve resilience to disasters, *climate change*, and humanitarian *crises* through sustainable environmental management. **Events** *COHAB : international conference on health and biodiversity* Galway (Ireland) 2008. **IGO Relations** Partners include: *Global Resource Information Database (GRID, #10578)*; *UNHCR (#20327)*; *United Nations Office for Disaster Risk Reduction (UNDRR, #20595)*. **NGO Relations** Partners include: *CARE International (CI, #03429)*; *Global Shelter Cluster (GSC, #10594)*; *International Union for Conservation of Nature and Natural Resources (IUCN, #15766)*; *Norwegian Refugee Council (NRC)*; *World Wide Fund for Nature (WWF, #21922)*. [2018/XJ0668/F]

- ♦ Proactiva Open Arms / see Open Arms
- ♦ ProAct Network / see ProAct (#18506)
- ♦ PROAP / see UNESCO Asia and Pacific Regional Bureau for Education (#20301)
- ♦ Probe International (internationally oriented national body)
- ♦ PROBIDAD (internationally oriented national body)
- ♦ Problemnaja Komissija Mnogostoronnego Sotrudnicestva Akademii Nauk Socialisticeskih Stran – Ekonomika i Politika Razvivajuscihsja Stran (inactive)
- ♦ **PRO CARTON** Association of European Cartonboard and Carton Manufacturers (#02502)
- ♦ **Proceso de Montreal** Grupo de Trabajo sobre Criterios e Indicadores para la Conservación y el Manejo Sustentable de los Bosques Templados y Boreales (#21058)
- ♦ Process Systems Engineering Conference (meeting series)
- ♦ **le Processus de Montréal** Groupe de travail sur les critères et les indicateurs de la conservation et de l'aménagement durable des forêts des régions tempérées et boréales (#21058)
- ♦ Procès-verbal concernant les règles de la guerre sous-marine prévues par la parties IV du Traité de Londres (1936 treaty)
- ♦ Procès-verbal Relating to the Rules of Submarine Warfare Set Forth in Part IV of the Treaty of London (1936 treaty)
- ♦ PROCICARIBE – Caribbean Agricultural Science and Technology Networking System (no recent information)
- ♦ **PROCISUR** Programa Cooperativo para el Desarrollo Tecnológico Agroalimentario y Agroindustrial del Cono Sur (#18522)
- ♦ PROCITROPICOS / see Programa Cooperative de Investigación, Desarrollo e Innovación Agricolo para los Trópicos Suramericanos (#18521)
- ♦ **PROCITROPICOS** Programa Cooperative de Investigación, Desarrollo e Innovación Agricolo para los Trópicos Suramericanos (#18521)
- ♦ Proclade Internacional (#18507)
- ♦ Proclade International (#18507)

♦ PROCLADE Internazionale Onlus 18507

Proclade International – Proclade Internacional
Main Office Via Sacro Cuore di Maria 5, 00197 Rome RM, Italy. T. +39680910011. E-mail: projects.proclade@gmail.com – procmis@cmfgen.org.
URL: http://www.procladeint.org/

History Set up 2006, as a foundation, as the missionary and solidarity arm of *Missionary Sons of the Immaculate Heart of Mary (Claretians)*. Registered in accordance with Italian law. **Aims** Assist, together with Claretian counterparts, in development of the most disadvantaged peoples, in promotion of their human well-being, integral development of individuals, solidity of communities, justice and peace. **Structure** Administration Council; Board of Directors. **Activities** Training/education; healthcare; advocacy/lobbying/activism. **Consultative Status** Consultative status granted from: *ECOSOC (#05331)* (Special). [2019.06.26/XM8139/f/F]

- ♦ Proclamation de l'évangile par les médias en Afrique (see: #02587)
- ♦ ProCor (internationally oriented national body)
- ♦ Procurement and Supply Institute of Asia (unconfirmed)
- ♦ PRODEVA / see Terre sans frontières
- ♦ PRODOCS – Progetto Domani – Cultura e Solidarietà (internationally oriented national body)
- ♦ Prodotti Terzo Mondo / see Associazione Botteghe del Mondo

♦ Producer Responsibility Organisations Packaging Alliance (PROsPA) 18508

Contact address not obtained. E-mail: info@prospalliance.org.
URL: https://prospalliance.org/

Aims Advocate for the full implementation and enforcement of EU waste legislation already in effect and support further improvements and targets.
Members Full in countries:
Austria, France, Germany, Ireland, Poland, Portugal, UK.
NGO Relations Member of (1): *Circular Plastics Alliance (#03936)*. [2020/AA2949/D]

♦ Production Engineering Association (PEA) 18509

Network Manager c/o OTM Consulting, Great Burgh, Yew Tree Bottom Road, Epsom, KT18 5XT, UK. T. +441372631950.
URL: http://www.peajip.com/

History 1991. **Aims** Promote industry improvements in *hydrocarbon* production technology; function as an authoritative and coherent voice on the industry's needs in the field; provide a forum for member companies to share information and learn from each other's experiences as well as discussing new technology needs and applications. **Structure** Committee, comprising Chairman, Vice-Chairman and 4 members plus Secretariat. **Languages** English. **Finance** Subscription funded. **Activities** Events/meetings; knowledge management/information dissemination. **Events** *Technical Forum* Copenhagen (Denmark) 2002, *Technical Forum* Reading (UK) 2002, *Main meeting* Stavanger (Norway) 2002, *Technical Forum* Stavanger (Norway) 2002, *Technical Forum* Stavanger (Norway) 2002.
Members Europe-based international oil companies (over 20) in 12 countries:
Austria, Canada, Denmark, France, Germany, Ireland, Italy, Netherlands, Norway, Spain, Switzerland, UK. [2018/XD6551/D]

- ♦ Production and Operations Management Society (internationally oriented national body)
- ♦ Productivity Research Network (unconfirmed)
- ♦ Product Lifetimes and The Environment (meeting series)
- ♦ Product Safety Enforcement Forum of Europe / see Product Safety Forum of Europe (#18510)

♦ Product Safety Forum of Europe (PROSAFE) 18510

Main Office Av des Arts 41, 1040 Brussels, Belgium. T. +3228080996 – +3228080997. E-mail: info@prosafe.org.
URL: http://www.prosafe.org/

History 11 Mar 1991, Amsterdam (Netherlands), by the now defunct *European Consumer Safety Association (ECOSA, inactive)*, as an informal grouping of European non-food product safety law enforcement practitioners. Original title: *Product Safety Enforcement Forum of Europe*. **Aims** Facilitate cooperation between market surveillance officers to improve product and service safety. **Structure** General Assembly (biannual); Board; Executive Director. **Languages** English. **Staff** 3.00 FTE, paid. **Finance** Co-funding for Joint Market Surveillance Actions from: *European Commission (EC, #06633)*. **Activities** Research and development; knowledge management/information dissemination; events/meetings. **Events** *Meeting* Edinburgh (UK) 1998, *Meeting* Stockholm (Sweden) 1997, *Meeting* Vienna (Austria) 1997, *Meeting* 1996, *Meeting* Brussels (Belgium) 1996. **Publications** *Best Practice Techniques in Market Surveillance*.
Members As of 2014, members in 37 countries:
Albania, Austria, Belgium, Bosnia-Herzegovina, Bulgaria, Cyprus, Czechia, Denmark, Estonia, Finland, France, Germany, Greece, Hungary, Iceland, Ireland, Italy, Latvia, Lithuania, Luxembourg, Malta, Montenegro, Netherlands, North Macedonia, Norway, Poland, Portugal, Romania, Slovakia, Slovenia, Spain, Sweden, Switzerland, Türkiye, UK, Ukraine. [2018/XF1454/F]

♦ Product and Systems Internationalisation (P and SI) 18511

Sec senbarila GmbH, Töginger Str 237, 84453 Mühldorf-Inn, Germany. T. +4986311853137. Fax +4986311853179. E-mail: contact@iwips.org.
URL: http://iwips.org/

History 2002, Austin TX (USA), as a not-for-profit corporation. **Structure** Executive Committee, comprising President, Vice-President, Treasurer, Secretary and Publicity Chair. Board. **Activities** Organizes *International Workshop on Internationalisation of Products and Systems (IWIPS)*. **Events** *IWIPS: International Workshop on Internationalisation of Products and Systems / IWIPS Workshop* Bangalore (India) 2012, *IWIPS : international workshop on internationalisation of products and systems / IWIPS Workshop* Kuching (Malaysia) 2011, *IWIPS : international workshop on internationalisation of products and systems / IWIPS Workshop* London (UK) 2010, *IWIPS : international workshop on internationalisation of products and systems / IWIPS Workshop* Mérida (Mexico) 2007, *IWIPS Workshop* Amsterdam (Netherlands) 2005. **Publications** Proceedings. [2012/XJ4865/ce/E]

- ♦ Produits du Tiers-monde / see Associazione Botteghe del Mondo
- ♦ Proekt Modeli Novogo Mirovogo Porjadka (#21684)
- ♦ **PROE** Programme régional océanien de l'environnement (#19205)
- ♦ **PRO-EUROPE** Packaging Recovery Organization Europe (#18015)
- ♦ **PROFEL** European Association of Fruit and Vegetable Processors (#06049)
- ♦ PROFES – International Conference on on Product-Focused Software Process Improvement (meeting series)
- ♦ Professional Association of Diving Instructors (internationally oriented national body)
- ♦ Professional Association of Natural Rubber in Africa (no recent information)
- ♦ Professional Billiards Players' Association / see World Professional Billiards and Snooker Association (#21740)
- ♦ Professional Boardsailors Association / see Professional Windsurfers Association
- ♦ Professional Convention Management Association (internationally oriented national body)

♦ Professional Customs Brokers Association of the Americas 18512

Asociación de Agentes Profesionales de Aduana de las Américas (ASAPRA)

SG Zabala 1425/37, Montevideo, Uruguay. T. +59829165612. Fax +59829165612. E-mail: info@asapra.com.

URL: http://www.asapra.com/

History Founded 27 Nov 1969, as *Asociación Americana de Profesionales de Aduana (ASAPRA)*. Previously also referred to in English as *Latin American Customs Brokers and Forwarders Association.* **Aims** Unite the chambers, federations, associations and unions of agents, brokers and/or customs brokers of America, Spain and Portugal. **Structure** General Assembly; Directorate. **Languages** English, Portuguese, Spanish. **Events** *Assembly* Barcelona (Spain) 2018, *Assembly* Julian Dolio (Dominican Rep) 2007, *Congress* Santa Cruz (Bolivia) 2006, *General Assembly* Santa Cruz (Bolivia) 2006, *General Assembly* Mexico City (Mexico) 2005.

Members National organizations in 21 countries:

Argentina, Bolivia, Brazil, Chile, Colombia, Costa Rica, Dominican Rep, Ecuador, El Salvador, Guatemala, Honduras, Mexico, Nicaragua, Panama, Paraguay, Peru, Portugal, Spain, Uruguay, USA, Venezuela.

NGO Relations Cooperates with: *Confédération internationale des agents en douanes (CONFIAD, #04559); International Federation of Customs Brokers Associations (IFCBA, #13400).* [2019.12.13/XD9037/t/**D**]

♦ Professional Golfers' Associations of Europe, The (PGAs of Europe) 18513

Contact Hunters lodge, The Belfry, Tamworth Road, Wishaw, B76 9PS, UK. T. +441675475822. Fax +441675470615. E-mail: info@pgae.com.

URL: http://www.pgae.com/

History 1990. Registered in accordance with UK law, 1992. **Aims** Advance golf, golfers and the golf profession across Europe. **Structure** General Meeting (annual); Board. **Languages** English. **Staff** 4.00 FTE, paid. **Finance** Members' dues. Other sources: licensing agreements; sponsorship. **Activities** Sporting activities; training/education; capacity building. **Events** *Annual Congress* Antalya (Turkey) 2016, *Annual Congress* Antalya (Turkey) 2015, *Annual Congress* Antalya (Turkey) 2014, *Annual Congress* Portugal 2011, *Annual Congress* Portugal 2010. **Publications** *International Golf Pro News* (12 a year) – magazine; *The PGAs of Europe Annual Review: Working Together.*

Members National PGAs (36) with a collective membership of over 21,000 golf professionals in 35 countries and territories:

Austria, Belgium, Bulgaria, Canada, Croatia, Czechia, Denmark, England, Estonia, Finland, France, Germany, Greece, Hong Kong, Hungary, Iceland, Ireland, Israel, Italy, Lithuania, Malta, Netherlands, Norway, Poland, Portugal, Russia, Scotland, Slovakia, Slovenia, South Africa, Spain, Sweden, Switzerland, Türkiye, Wales.

NGO Relations Supports: *GEO Foundation (#10132).* [2016.06.01/XD0395/**D**]

- ♦ Professional Group of Industrial Pharmacists of Europe / see European Industrial Pharmacist Group (#07530)
- ♦ Professional Lighting Designers' Association (inactive)
- ♦ Professional Practice, Education and Leadership (unconfirmed)
- ♦ Professional Records and Information Services Management / see PRISM International

♦ Professional Risk Managers' International Association (PRMIA) ... 18514

Contact 1700 Cannon Rd, Suite 200, Northfield MN 55057, USA. E-mail: support@prmia.org.

URL: http://www.prmia.org/

History 2002. **Aims** Promote, develop and share professional risk management practices globally. **Structure** Board of Directors. **Activities** Training/education; events/meetings; networking/liaising; knowledge management/information dissemination. **Publications** *Intelligent Risk; Professional Risk Manager Handbook.*

Members Individuals (50,000). Membership countries not specified. [2019.12.20/XM0059/t/**D**]

- ♦ Professional Secretaries International / see International Association of Administrative Professionals

♦ Professionals in Humanitarian Assistance and Protection (PHAP) .. 18515

Main Office Av de la Chasse 133, 1040 Brussels, Belgium. T. +3228887274. E-mail: admin@phap.org.

Exec Dir 87 rue de Montbrillant, 1202 Geneva, Switzerland. T. +41225180458.

Registered Address 40 rue Washington, 1050 Brussels, Belgium.

URL: http://www.phap.org/

History 2010, Brussels (Belgium). Founded taking over activities of *International Association for Humanitarian Policy and Conflict Research (HPCR International, inactive).* Former names and other names: *International Association of Professionals in Humanitarian Assistance and Protection (PHAP)* – alias. Registration: Belgium. **Aims** Enhance the capacity of the global humanitarian community to respond effectively and professionally to current and future crises by focusing on concrete, practical measures to enhance the availability, experiences, skills, competences, professional networks, and both formal and informal support structures, of humanitarian personnel at all levels, and in all parts of the system. **Structure** Board of Directors. **Staff** 4.00 FTE, paid. **Activities** Capacity building; events/meetings; guidance/assistance/consulting; training/education. **Events** *Panel Discussion on the Future of Integrating Humanitarian Action into Multilateral Operation* Brussels (Belgium) 2012. **Members** Individuals. Membership countries not specified. **NGO Relations** Member of (1): *Federation of European and International Associations Established in Belgium (FAIB, #09508).* [2021/XJ4607/t/**F**]

♦ Professional Society of Genetic Counselors in Asia (PSGCA) 18516

Contact address not obtained.

URL: https://www.psgca.org/

History 16 Sep 2015, Hanoi (Vietnam). Founded as a special interest group of *Asia Pacific Society of Human Genetics (APSHG, #02038).* **Aims** Promote quality genetic counseling services in the region. **Activities** Events/meetings; research/documentation; training/education. [2020/AA0197/**E**]

♦ Professional Squash Association (PSA) 18517

Main Office 46 The Calls, Leeds, LS2 7EY, UK. T. +441138591000. E-mail: office@psaworldtour.com.

London Office c/o Centenary House, The Queens Club, Palliser Road, London, W14 9EQ, UK.

URL: http://www.psaworldtour.com/

History 1973, Birmingham (UK). Merged with *World Professional Squash Association (WPSA, inactive)* of North America, 1 Jan 1993. Former names and other names: *International Squash Players Association (ISPA)* – former (1973 to 1993). Registration: Private Limited Company by guarantee, No/ID: 02748136, Start date: 11 Sep 1992, England. **Aims** Promote men's professional squash worldwide; formulate and maintain high standards to govern the conduct of members and their relations with each other and with the public; defend the interests of *tournament* players. **Structure** Board of Directors. **Languages** English. **Staff** 4.50 FTE, paid. **Finance** Sources: members' dues. Annual budget: 300,000 GBP. **Activities** Services all major squash tournaments world-wide. **Events** *Annual General Meeting* New York, NY (USA) 2002, *Annual World Open Championship* Cairo (Egypt) 1999, *Annual World Open Championship* Qatar 1998, *Annual World Open Championship* Kuala Lumpur (Malaysia) 1997, *Annual World Open Championship* Karachi (Pakistan) 1996. **Publications** Press releases to newspapers and magazines.

Members Full; Provisional; Past Player. Leading professional squash players (343) in 44 countries and territories:

Argentina, Australia, Austria, Belgium, Bermuda, Brazil, Canada, Chile, Colombia, Costa Rica, Denmark, Egypt, England, Finland, France, Germany, Greece, Guyana, Hong Kong, Iran Islamic Rep, Ireland, Israel, Italy, Japan, Jordan, Luxembourg, Malaysia, Mexico, Netherlands, New Zealand, Norway, Pakistan, Paraguay, Portugal, Scotland, Singapore, South Africa, Spain, Sweden, Switzerland, Taiwan, Uruguay, USA, Wales.

NGO Relations *Women's Squash Association (WSA, #21034).* Affiliate member of: *World Squash Federation (WSF, #21826).* [2020/XD6180/**C**]

♦ Professional Tennis Coaches Association (PTCA) 18518

Pres Route de Bettembourg 20, Kockelscheuer, L-1899 Roeser, Luxembourg. T. +352472285. Fax +352482287. E-mail: danjo@pt.lu.

URL: http://www.ptcatennis.net/

History 2011, Paris (France), by world class ATP and WTA Coaches during French Open Tournament. Current statutes adopted, 27 May 2012, Paris (France). Registered in accordance with Luxembourg law. **Aims** Create an advocacy platform, intended to promote the professional, intellectual and friendly relationships between international coaches, physiotherapists and individuals in medical professions related to sports. **Structure** General Assembly. Executive Board. Includes PTCA Academy. **Finance** Members' dues. **Members** Ordinary; Affiliated. Membership countries not specified. [2014/XJ8317/v/**E**]

- ♦ Professional Travel Bloggers Association (internationally oriented national body)
- ♦ Professional Windsurfers Association (internationally oriented national body)
- ♦ Professional Women of the Eurasia in Pest Management (unconfirmed)

♦ Professional Yachting Association (PYA) 18519

Head Office 23 rue du Général d'Andréossy, 06600 Antibes, France. T. +33493349116. E-mail: info@pya.org.

URL: http://www.pya.org/

History 1991. Registration: EU Transparency Register, No/ID: 01788508225-66, Start date: 1 Mar 2012. **Aims** Represent the interests of professional yacht crew around the world. **Structure** Annual General Meeting; Council. **Activities** Certification/accreditation; events/meetings. **NGO Relations** Affiliated with (6): *Association of Yacht Support Services (AYSS, #02986); International Association of Maritime Institutions (IAMI, #12015); International Superyacht Society (ISS, #15627); MYBA The Worldwide Yachting Association (MYBA, #16921); Superyacht Builders Association (SYBAss, #20037); World Association of Chefs Societies (WACS, #21124).* [2022.10.13/XM5838/t/**C**]

♦ Professors World Peace Academy (PWPA) 18520

Académie des professeurs pour la paix mondiale (APPM)

SG 3600 Labore Rd, Ste 1, St Paul MN 55110, USA. T. +16516443087. Fax +16516440997. E-mail: gordon@pwpa.org.

General: http://www.pwpa.org/

History May 1973, Seoul (Korea Rep). Founded by *International Cultural Foundation (ICF, no recent information)*, under the auspices of *Holy Spirit Association for the Unification of World Christianity (HSA-UWC)* which was founded by the late Rev Sun Myung Moon. Former names and other names: *World Peace Academy* – alias; *Académie pour la paix mondiale* – alias; *PWPA International* – alias. **Aims** Formulate new ideas and methods of realizing a viable world order; engender hope and practical strategies for a better world by developing future scenarios for a better society; provide an international developmental vehicle for members of the academic community to advance the cause of world peace; promote global values and the highest standards of academic excellence. **Structure** Board of Directors; National Chapters; international and interdisciplinary scholars and scientists. **Languages** English. **Finance** Sources: donations; sale of publications. **Activities** Awards/prizes/competitions; events/meetings; networking/liaising. **Events** *International congress* Seoul (Korea Rep) 2002, *International conference on world peace* Bangkok (Thailand) 2000, *International congress* Seoul (Korea Rep) 2000, *International congress* Washington, DC (USA) 1997, *International congress* Seoul (Korea Rep) 1995. **Publications** *International Journal on World Peace* (4 a year). Books in the following fields: liberal democratic societies; peace studies; Asian studies; European studies; Middle East studies; African studies.

Members Chapters in 102 countries and territories:

Afghanistan, Argentina, Armenia, Australia, Bahamas, Bahrain, Bangladesh, Barbados, Benin, Bolivia, Botswana, Brazil, Bulgaria, Burkina Faso, Cameroon, Canada, Chile, Colombia, Congo DR, Costa Rica, Côte d'Ivoire, Croatia, Cyprus, Czechia, Denmark, Dominican Rep, Ecuador, Egypt, El Salvador, Eswatini, Finland, France, Gabon, Gambia, Germany, Ghana, Greece, Guatemala, Guinea, Guyana, Haiti, Honduras, Hong Kong, Hungary, Iceland, India, Indonesia, Israel, Italy, Jamaica, Japan, Jordan, Kenya, Korea Rep, Lebanon, Liberia, Lithuania, Malawi, Malaysia, Mexico, Morocco, Namibia, Nepal, Netherlands, New Zealand, Nicaragua, Nigeria, Norway, Pakistan, Panama, Paraguay, Peru, Philippines, Poland, Portugal, Romania, Russia, Senegal, Sierra Leone, Singapore, Somalia, South Africa, Spain, Sri Lanka, Sudan, Suriname, Sweden, Switzerland, Taiwan, Thailand, Togo, Tunisia, Türkiye, Uganda, UK, Ukraine, Uruguay, USA, Venezuela, Yemen, Zambia, Zimbabwe.

Affiliated organizations in 3 countries and territories:

Singapore, Taiwan, USA.

NGO Relations Instrumental in setting up (1): *World University Federation (see: #18520).* [2021.05.18/XF0207/**F**]

- ♦ Profintern – International Council of Red Trade Unions (inactive)
- ♦ PROFMEX – Consortium for Research on Mexico (internationally oriented national body)
- ♦ **PROF** Nordiskt Nätverk för Samspelet mellan Privat och Offentlig Rätt (#17539)
- ♦ **PROFOR** Program on Forests (#18525)
- ♦ Profugo (internationally oriented national body)
- ♦ ProGEO / see International Association for the Conservation of the Geological Heritage (#11810)
- ♦ **ProGEO** International Association for the Conservation of the Geological Heritage (#11810)
- ♦ Progetto Domani – Cultura e Solidarietà (internationally oriented national body)
- ♦ Progetto dei Modelli del'Ordine Mondiale (#21684)
- ♦ Prognostics and Health Management Society (internationally oriented national body)
- ♦ Programa de Agua y Saneamienta (#20837)
- ♦ Programa de Aplicaciones Meterotológicas de la OMM (see: #21649)
- ♦ Programa de Avaliação de Carros Novos para América Latina e o Caribe (#17077)
- ♦ Programa de Becas de la UNESCO (see: #20322)
- ♦ Programa de Biotecnologia para Entrenamiento de Posgrado en Ciencias Biológicas / see Red Latinoamericana de Ciencias Biológicas (#18706)

♦ Programa Cooperative de Investigación, Desarrollo e Innovación Agricolo para los Trópicos Suramericanos (PROCITROPICOS) 18521

Exec Sec SHIS QI 01 – Conjunto 01, Casa 20, Lago Sul, CP 02995, Brasilia DF, 71605-010, Brazil. T. +55613652907 – +55613652908. Fax +55613655093. E-mail: procitropicos@procitropicos.org.br.

URL: http://www.procitropicos.org.br/

History 1992, following an agreement between the national agricultural research institutes of 8 Amazonian countries and *Inter-American Institute for Cooperation on Agriculture (IICA, #11434).* New Agreement of Technical Cooperation to execute 2nd phase of the Cooperative Programme (1998-2001), signed by 7 Amazonian countries and IICA in 1998; extended (2002-2005); 3rd phase (2006-2009); extended (2010-2014). Original title: *Cooperative Program on Research and Technology Transfer for the South American Tropics – Programa Cooperativo de Investigación y Transferencia de Tecnologia Agropecuaria para los Trópicos Suramericanos (PROCITROPICOS).* **Aims** Articulate, coordinate and promote the generation and transfer of *agricultural* technology through reciprocal technical cooperation among countries of the region. **Structure** Executive Committee; Executive Secretariat, headed by Executive Secretary. **Finance** Sources include: *Deutsche Gesellschaft für Technische Zusammenarbeit (GTZ, inactive); International Bank for Reconstruction and Development (IBRD, #12317); Inter-American Development Bank (IDB, #11427); Fondo Regional de Tecnologia Agropecuaria (FONTAGRO, #09834)* (IDB and IICA). **Activities** Capacity building; knowledge management/information dissemination. **Events** *Seminar on palma aceitera* Belém (Brazil) 2000, *Seminar on development of the continental aquaculture in the Amazone Region* Manaus (Brazil) 2000. **Publications** *Procitropicos News* (4 a year) in English, Spanish. Annual Report.

Members National institutions in 7 countries:

Bolivia, Brazil, Colombia, Ecuador, Peru, Suriname, Venezuela.

IGO Relations Close cooperation/joint activities with: *Programa Cooperativo de Investigación y Transferencia de Tecnologia Agropecuaria para la Subregión Andina (PROCIANDINO, no recent information); Programa Cooperativo para el Desarrollo Tecnológico Agroalimentario y Agroindustrial del Cono Sur (PROCISUR, #18522).* **NGO Relations** Member of: *Global Forum on Agricultural Research (GFAR, #10370).* Close cooperation/joint activities with: *Center for International Forestry Research (CIFOR, #03646); International Centre for Tropical Agriculture (#12527); International Service for National Agricultural Research (ISNAR, inactive).* [2019/XE3608/**E***]

♦ Programa Cooperativo para el Desarrollo Tecnológico Agroalimentario y Agroindustrial del Cono Sur (PROCISUR) 18522

Cooperative Program for the Development of Agricultural Technology in the Southern Cone

Exec Sec Edif Mercosur, Luis P Piera 1992, Piso 3, Casilla de Correo 1217, 11-100 Montevideo, Uruguay. T. +59824101676. Fax +59824101778. E-mail: sejecutiva@procisur.org.uy – emilio.ruz@procisur.org.uy.

Admin Office c/o IICA, Apartado Postal 55, San José, Coronado, 2200, Costa Rica. T. +5062290222. Fax +5062294741.

URL: http://www.procisur.org.uy/

History 1980, as *Programa Cooperativo para el Desarrollo Tecnológico Agropecuario del Cono Sur*, following a technical cooperation agreement between *Inter-American Institute for Cooperation on Agriculture (IICA, #11434)* and countries in the region. Previously also referred to in English as *Cooperative Program for the Agri-Food and Agro-Industrial Technological Development of the Southern Cone*. **Aims** Provide answers to the technological demands of member countries, in order to increase internal and external competitiveness of the farming and agro-industrial sector. **Structure** Executive Committee. **Publications** *DIALOGO* – series; *DOCUMENTOS* – series; *Proyecto Global* – series. Paper series.
Members Government institutions in 6 countries:
Argentina, Bolivia, Brazil, Chile, Paraguay, Uruguay.
IGO Relations Joint activities with: *Programa Cooperative de Investigación, Desarrollo e Innovación Agricolo para los Trópicos Suramericanos (PROCITROPICOS, #18521)*. **NGO Relations** Member of: *Global Forum on Agricultural Research (GFAR, #10370)*. [2014/XE3528/**E***]

♦ Programa Cooperativo para el Desarrollo Tecnológico Agropecuario del Cono Sur / see Programa Cooperativo para el Desarrollo Tecnológico Agroalimentario y Agroindustrial del Cono Sur (#18522)
♦ Programa Cooperativo Europeo de Recursos Fitogenéticos (#06787)
♦ Programa Cooperativo Europeo para Redes de Recursos Fitogenéticos / see European Cooperative Programme for Plant Genetic Resources (#06787)
♦ Programa Cooperativo de Investigación y Transferencia de Tecnologia Agropecuaria para los Trópicos Suramericanos / see Programa Cooperative de Investigación, Desarrollo e Innovación Agricolo para los Trópicos Suramericanos (#18521)
♦ Programa Cooperativo Regional para el Desarrollo Tecnológico de la Caficultura en Centroamérica, República Dominica y Jamaica (#18775)
♦ Program for the Advancement of Research on Conflict and Collaboration (internationally oriented national body)
♦ Programa para la Eliminación de la Oncocercosis en las Américas (#17726)

♦ Programa para el Estudio Regional del Fenómeno El Niño en el Pacifico Sudeste (ERFEN) 18523

Programme for the Regional Study of the El Niño Phenomenon in the Southeastern Pacific
Contact c/o CPPS, Avenida Carlos Julio Arosemena, Km 3, Complejo Alban Borja, edificio Classic, piso 2, Guayaquil, Ecuador. T. +59342221202 – +59342221203. E-mail: sgeneral@cpps-int.org.
History 13 Dec 1976, Callao (Peru). 13-17 Dec 1976, Callao (Peru), as an ad hoc group within the framework of *Comisión Permanente del Pacifico Sur (CPPS, #04141)*, following recommendations of a Workshop, 4-12 Dec 1974, Guayaquil (Ecuador). Other sponsoring organizations: *FAO (#09260)*; *Intergovernmental Oceanographic Commission (IOC, #11496)*; *World Meteorological Organization (WMO, #21649)*. 1st Session: 16-20 Oct 1978, Lima (Peru). Protocol signed, 6 Nov 1992, by the representatives of the governments of Chile, Colombia, Ecuador and Peru. Original title *Joint IOC/WMO/CPPS Working Group on the Investigation of El Niño – Groupe de travail mixte COI/OMM/CPPS pour l'étude du phénomène El Niño – Grupo Mixto de Trabajo COI-OMM-CPPS sobre las Investigaciones relativas a El Niño*. **Aims** As a multi-disciplinary programme, promote regional research into the 'El Niño' phenomenon from the standpoint of meteorology, physical and chemical oceanography, marine and fish biology, so as to improve forecasting capacity and reduce constraints facing such forecasting and thus mitigate the detrimental effects and properly benefit from positive effects. **Structure** Executive and Coordinating Unit (UEC-EFREN); Regional Scientific Committee (CCR-EFREN), integrated by experts from the region; National Committees (CN-EFREN); Specialized Institutions (IE-EFREN). **Languages** Spanish. **Staff** 2.00 FTE, paid. **Finance** Contributions from member countries. **Activities** Carries out global and regional investigations and services relevant to: *Global Ocean Observing System (GOOS, #10511)*; *IOC Group of Experts on the Global Sea-Level Observing System (GLOSS, see: #11496)*; World Ocean Circulation Experiment. Encourages member states to set up and maintain information on national oceanographic and meteorological data sources, to develop information systems for transmission of data and to establish stations and/or telecommunications procedures for reception and transmission of data. **Events** *Session* Lima (Peru) 2008, *Session* Guayaquil (Ecuador) 2007, *Meeting* Lima (Peru) 2007, *Session* Bogota (Colombia) 2006, *Session* Bogota (Colombia) 2006. **Publications** *Boletin de Alerta Climatico – BAC* (12 a year); *Boletin sobre el Estudio del Fenomeno El Niño, ERFEN* (4 a year).
Members Full in 4 countries:
Chile, Colombia, Ecuador, Peru.
IGO Relations *UNESCO (#20322)*; *IOC Sub-Commission for the Caribbean and Adjacent Regions (IOCARIBE, #16003)*; *Joint WMO-IOC Technical Commission for Oceanography and Marine Meteorology (JCOMM, #16151)*. [2014/XF2863/**F***]

♦ Programa de Evaluación de Vehiculos Nuevos para América Latina y el Caribe (#17077)
♦ Programa de Hidrologia y Recursos Hidricos de la OMM (#20977)
♦ Programa Hidrológico Internacional (#13826)
♦ Programa sobre el Hombre y la Biósfera (#18526)

♦ Programa Iberoamericano de Ciencia y Tecnologia para el Desarrollo (CYTED) 18524

Ibero-American Programme of Science and Technology for Development
SG Amaniel 4, 28015 Madrid, Spain. T. +34915316387. Fax +34915227845. E-mail: sgral@cyted.org.
Communications Dir address not obtained.
URL: http://www.cyted.org/
History 1984, as a programme of 'Comisión Interministerial de Ciencia y Tecnologia' (Spain). Became a programme of Ibero-American Summit of Chiefs of State and Government, 1995. **Aims** Contribute to harmonious development of the Ibero-American region by establishing mechanisms for cooperation among research groups at universities, R and D centres and innovative companies so as to allow the results of scientific and technological *research* to be transferred to systems of production and to social policies; cooperate with other initiatives so as to optimize resources and facilitate scientific and technological research in the region; act as a bridge for cooperation between Latin America and the European Union. **Structure** /Institutional/: General Assembly (annual), comprising Signatory Bodies responsible for scientific policy in each member country, designated by national governments, responsible in each country for management of the Programme at national level. Technical Steering Committee (meets twice a year), comprising one delegate from each Signatory Body (National Organizations for Science and Technology), Secretary General (non-voting), delegates from International Observer Organisms (BID, CEPAL, CAB, ORCYT, OEI, OEA – non-voting) and (by invitation) the International Coordinators of Sub-Programmes. /Functional/: Sub-Programmes (18), each comprising a strategic theme for economic and social development and headed by an International Coordinator. *Proyectos de Innovación IBEROEKA (IBEROEKA, see: #18524)* (by analogy with the EUREKA Programme) – comprises innovative projects to promote cooperation in research and technological development between industrial companies and research centres. /International General Secretariat/: linking institutional and functional components and carrying out global management and coordination. **Languages** Portuguese, Spanish. **Staff** 10.00 FTE, paid. **Finance** Co-financed by the Government of Spain (at least 50%) and participating countries. Budget (annual): US$ 6 million.
Activities Science and technology framework divided into Thematic Areas, in which Sub-Programmes are located. Sub-programmes are divided into Research Projects and Thematic Networks. Other cooperation is conducted through IBEROEKA, through the IBEROEKA Innovative Projects.
'Thematic Areas':
- Science and Technology Application Policies;
- Agriculture, Livestock/Herding, and Fisheries;
- Health;
- Habitat;
- Energy;
- Industrial Development Promotion;
- Information Society;
- Environment;
- Biotechnology.

'Sub-Programmes':
- II Aquaculture;
- III Biotechnology;
- IV Biomass as Source of Chemicals and Energy;
- V Catalysis and Adsorbents;
- VI New Sources and Conservation of Energy.
- VII Applied Electronics and Informatics;
- VIII Materials Technology;
- IX Micro-electronics;
- X Chemicals for Pharmaceuticals;
- XI Treatment and Preservation of Foodstuffs;
- XII Biological Diversity;
- XIII Mineral Technology;
- XIV Technology of Social Interest Housing (HABYTED);
- XV Corrosion and Environmental Impact of Materials;
- XVI Management of Research and Technology Development;
- XVII Usage and Management of Water Resources;
- XVIII Technology of Forecasting and Evaluating Natural Disasters;
- XIX Agricultural Technology.

As of 2003, the Programme has 55 Research Projects and 47 Thematic Networks, and has generated 45 new IBEROEKA Innovative Projects. The participation of researchers, scientists and technicians is estimated around 10,000.
Events *International Workshop* Madrid (Spain) 2015, *International congress of geomatics* Havana (Cuba) 2009, *Virtual Educa : international conference on education, training and new technologies* São José dos Campos (Brazil) 2007, *International seminar CYTED-XVII* Buenos Aires (Argentina) 2005, *International symposium on frontiers in biomedical polymers* Granada (Spain) 2005. **Publications** *Boletin CYTED* (4 a year) in Spanish; *Memoria del Programa CYTED* (annual). Proceedings. Sub-Programmes, Research Projects and Thematic Networks have their own publications.
Members Signatory Bodies representing governments of 21 countries:
Argentina, Bolivia, Brazil, Chile, Colombia, Costa Rica, Cuba, Dominican Rep, Ecuador, El Salvador, Guatemala, Honduras, Mexico, Nicaragua, Panama, Paraguay, Peru, Portugal, Spain, Uruguay, Venezuela.
IGO Relations Observers: Secretariat of *Convenio Andrés Bello de integración educativa, cientifica y cultural de América Latina y España (Convenio Andrés Bello, #04785)*; *Inter-American Development Bank (IDB, #11427)*; *OAS (#17629)*; *Organization of Ibero-American States for Education, Science and Culture (#17871)*; *UNESCO (#20322)*; *UNESCO Office, Montevideo – Regional Bureau for Sciences in Latin America and the Caribbean (#20314)*; *United Nations Economic Commission for Latin America and the Caribbean (ECLAC, #20556)*. Member of: *Global Biodiversity Information Facility (GBIF, #10250)*. [2021/XF1426/**F***]

♦ Programa Internacional de Ciencias de la Tierra (#13715)
♦ Programa Internacional de Correlación Geológica / see International Geoscience Programme (#13715)
♦ Programa Internacional para el Desarrollo de la Comunicación (#14651)
♦ Programa de Investigación y Desarrollo de la OMM (see: #21649)
♦ Programa Latinoamericano del Carbono (see: #05055)
♦ Programa MERCOSUR Social y Solidario (unconfirmed)
♦ Programa Mundial de Alimentos (#21510)
♦ Programa Mundial de Evaluación de los Recursos Hidricos (#21907)
♦ Programa Mundial de Investigaciones Climaticas (#21279)
♦ Programa Mundial de las Naciones Unidas Contra el Blanqueo de Dinero (#20568)
♦ Programa de las Naciones Unidas para el Desarrollo (#20292)
♦ Programa de las Naciones Unidas para la Fiscalización Internacional de las Drogas (inactive)
♦ Programa de Naciones Unidas de Información Desarme (inactive)
♦ Programa de las Naciones Unidas para el Medio Ambiente (#20299)
♦ Program on the Analysis and Resolution of Conflicts / see Program for the Advancement of Research on Conflict and Collaboration
♦ Program for Appropriate Technology in Health / see PATH (#18260)
♦ Programa de Preparativos para Situaciones de Emergencia y Coordinación del Socorro en Casos de Desastre / see PAHO/WHO Health Emergencies Department (#18023)
♦ Programa de Promoción de la Reforma Educativa en América Latina y el Caribe (internationally oriented national body)
♦ Programa Red de Desarrollo Sostenible – PNUD (no recent information)
♦ Programa Regional Coordinado de Educación Popular (#18456)
♦ Programa Regional en Manejo de Vida Silvestre para Mesoamérica y el Caribe / see Instituto Internacional en Conservación y Manejo en Vida Silvestre (#11336)
♦ Programa de la Sociedad de la Información para América Latina y el Caribe (inactive)

♦ Program on Forests (PROFOR) 18525

Manager 1818 H St NW, Washington DC 20433, USA. T. +12024581692. Fax +12025223307.
URL: http://www.profor.info/
History 1997. **Aims** Support in-depth analysis, innovative processes and knowledge-sharing and dialogue, in the belief that sound forest policy can lead to better outcomes on issues ranging from livelihoods and financing, to illegal logging, biodiversity and climate change. **Structure** Secretariat housed by *International Bank for Reconstruction and Development (IBRD, #12317)* (World Bank). **Finance** Supported by: *Department for International Development (DFID, inactive)*; *Swiss Agency for Development and Cooperation (SDC)*; *European Union (EU, #08967)*; governmental departments of Germany, Finland, Japan, Italy and Netherlands; *International Bank for Reconstruction and Development (IBRD, #12317)*. **NGO Relations** Partner of: *Global Partnership on Forest and Landscape Restoration (GPFLR, #10535)*. [2017/XM5818/**F**]

♦ Program on International Financial Systems (internationally oriented national body)
♦ Program for International Training in Health / see IntraHealth International
♦ Programa Europeo sobre Recursos Genéticos Forestales (#07296)
♦ Programme d'action mondial pour la protection du milieu marin contre la pollution due aux activités terrestres (see: #20299)
♦ Programme africain de lutte contre l'onchocercose (no recent information)
♦ Programme alimentaire mondial (#21510)
♦ Programme des applications de la météorologie de l'OMM (see: #21649)
♦ Programme for the Assessment and Control of Pollution in the Mediterranean Sea / see MED POL – Programme for the Assessment and Control of Marine Pollution in the Mediterranean (#16691)
♦ Programme d'assistance des Nations Unies aux fins de l'enseignement, de l'étude, de la diffusion et d'une compréhension plus large du droit international (#20614)
♦ Programme d'assistance technique pour l'environnement en Méditerranée (inactive)
♦ Programme de biotechnologie en Amérique latine et dans les Caraïbes (see: #20642)
♦ Programme de bourses Robert S McNamara (internationally oriented national body)
♦ Programme de bourses de l'UNESCO (see: #20322)
♦ Programme du Commonwealth pour la jeunesse (#04372)
♦ Programme commun des Nations unies sur le VIH/SIDA (#16149)
♦ Programme concerté de surveillance continue et d'évaluation du transport à longue distance des polluants atmosphériques en Europe (#04800)
♦ Programme coopératif sur l'environnement pour l'Asie du Sud (#19714)
♦ Programme coopératif européen de réseaux sur les ressources phytogénétiques des cultures / see European Cooperative Programme for Plant Genetic Resources (#06787)
♦ Programme coopératif européen sur les ressources phytogénétiques (#06787)
♦ Programme de coordination des secours en cas d'urgence / see PAHO/WHO Health Emergencies Department (#18023)
♦ Programme de développement des compétences techniques en Asie et dans le Pacifique (no recent information)
♦ Programme de développement municipal en Afrique subsaharienne / see Municipal Development Partnership for West and Central Africa (#16902)
♦ Programme pour l'eau et l'assainissement (#20837)
♦ Programme d'éducation pour tous en Asie et dans le Pacifique (#02002)
♦ Programme d'élimination de l'onchocercose dans les Amériques (#17726)

- ♦ Programme d'enseignement et de formation des Nations Unies pour l'Afrique australe (inactive)
- ♦ Programme européen pour l'évaluation d'automobiles neuves / see European New Car Assessment Programme (#08046)
- ♦ Programme européen pour les ressources génétiques forestières (#07296)
- ♦ Programme du Golfe arabe pour les organisations de développement des Nations Unies (#00971)
- ♦ Programme sur l'Homme et la biosphère (#18526)
- ♦ Programme d'hydrologie et de mise en valeur des ressources en eau de l'OMM (#20977)
- ♦ Programme hydrologique international (#13826)
- ♦ Programme d'information des Nations Unies sur le désarmement (inactive)
- ♦ Programme d'information sur la population / see Johns Hopkins University Center for Communications Programs
- ♦ Programme d'innovation éducative pour le développement dans les Etats arabes (inactive)
- ♦ Programme international de corrélation géologique / see International Geoscience Programme (#13715)
- ♦ Programme international pour le développement de la communication (#14651)
- ♦ Programme international de géoscience (#13715)
- ♦ Programme international de recherche sur la santé, le rayonnement solaire ultraviolet et les modifications de l'environnement (#14740)
- ♦ Programme international sur la sécurité des substances chimiques (#14650)

♦ Programme on Man and the Biosphere (MAB) 18526

Programme sur l'Homme et la biosphère – Programa sobre el Hombre y la Biósfera

Headquarters Director Div of Ecological and Earth Sciences – UNESCO, 7 place de Fontenoy, 75007 Paris, France. T. +33145680788 – +33145680805. E-mail: s.taheri@unesco.org – mab@unesco.org.
URL: http://www.unesco.org/mab/

History Nov 1971, Paris (France). Established within the framework of *UNESCO (#20322)*, following approval of the draft programme, 1970, by 16th Session of UNESCO General Conference, and arising from *International Biological Programme (IBP)*, 1964-1974. **Aims** Within the natural and social sciences, develop a basis for sustainable use and conservation of biological diversity and for improvement of the global relationship between people and their environment; encourage interdisciplinary research, demonstration and training in natural resource management; by this means, contribute to a better understanding of the environment, including global change, and to greater involvement science and scientists in policy development concerning wise use of biological diversity; set up an international network of sites (biosphere reserves) for research, monitoring, training and information exchange; associate environmental protection with sustainable land use development. **Structure** *International Coordinating Council of the Programme on Man and the Biosphere – Conseil international de coordination du Programme sur l'Homme et la biosphère – Consejo Internacional de Coordinación del Programa sobre el Hombre y la Biósfera* (meets every 2 years) comprising 34 members elected by UNESCO General Conference; meetings attended by observers from non-member states, other UN agencies and nongovernmental organizations. Bureau, consisting of Chairman and 5 Vice-Chairmen. International Secretariat provided by UNESCO Division of Ecological Sciences. Regional Coordination Groups and Research Panels. National Committees (145). *Advisory Committee on Biosphere Reserves* appointed by UNESCO, Oct 1991. **Languages** Arabic, Chinese, English, French, Russian, Spanish. **Staff** 30.00 FTE, paid. **Finance** Regular budget of UNESCO; funds-in-trust granted by member states; extra-budgetary funds from other sources.

Activities Develops the basis within the natural and social sciences for the rational and sustainable use and conservation of the resources of the biosphere and for the improvement of the overall relationship between people and their environment. Regional networks: Assists in implementing: *Global Action Plan for Environment and Development in the 21st Century (Agenda 21, inactive)*; environmental goals of *New Partnership for Africa's Development (NEPAD, #17091)*; *Convention on Biological Diversity (Biodiversity convention, 1992)*; *Convention on Wetlands of International Importance Especially as Waterfowl Habitat (Convention on Wetlands, 1971)*; *Convention on International Trade in Endangered Species of Wild Fauna and Flora (CITES, 1973)*. In particular, cooperates in conservation of the natural heritage in biosphere reserves and sites inscribed on the World Heritage List under *Convention Concerning the Protection of the World Cultural and Natural Heritage (World Heritage Convention, 1972)*. Instrumental in setting up: *World Network of Biosphere Reserves (WNBR, #21669)*.

Regional networks:
- *South and Central Asia MAB Network (SACAM Network, no recent information)*;
- *AfriMAB Network (#00532)*;
- *ArabMAB Network (no recent information)*;
- *Southeast Asian Biosphere Reserve Network (SeaBRnet, #19759)*;
- *East Asian Biosphere Reserve Network (EABRN, #05199)*;
- *EuroMAB (#05708)*;
- *Red Iberoamericana de Comités MAB y Reservas de la Biósfera (IberoMAB, #18661)*;
- *Red del Atlantico Este de Reservas de Biósfera (REDBIOS, #18635)*.

Ecosystem-specific networks: Mountains; *World Network of Island and Coastal Biosphere Reserves*; Tropical forests; Drylands; Urban areas; Savannahs; gro-ecosystems.

Events *Session* Paris (France) 2019, *Workshop on Sustainable Development for Biosphere Reserve* Jeju (Korea Rep) 2016, *Session* Paris (France) 2015, *International Conference on Botanists of the Twenty-first Century* Paris (France) 2014, *Global Workshop on Long-Term Observatories of Mountain Social-Ecological Systems* Reno, NV (USA) 2014. **Publications** *MAB Report Series (Green Reports)*. *UNESCO-SCOPE Policy Briefs*. State-of-the-art reports; biosphere reserve maps and brochures, Biosphere reserve technical notes; reports of working groups; audiovisual series; video-cassettes; films. Information Services: Via UNESCO-MABnet: Directory of MAB National Committees and contacts; World Network of Biosphere Reserves; MAB's thematic and regional networks; collaborative scientific programmes, such as GTOS; UNESCO Cousteau Ecotechnie Programme; MAB Young Scientists Awards; South-South Cooperation in the Humid Tropics; major MAB publications. **Information Services** *Man and the Biosphere* – database; *UNESCO-MABnet on the Internet* – electronic clearing house for information exchange and scientific networking for countries involved in MAB.

Members National Committees or MAB Focal Points in 149 countries:
Afghanistan, Albania, Algeria, Angola, Argentina, Armenia, Australia, Austria, Azerbaijan, Bahrain, Bangladesh, Barbados, Belarus, Belgium, Benin, Bolivia, Brazil, Bulgaria, Burkina Faso, Burundi, Cameroon, Canada, Cape Verde, Central African Rep, Chad, Chile, China, Colombia, Congo Brazzaville, Congo DR, Costa Rica, Côte d'Ivoire, Croatia, Cuba, Cyprus, Czechia, Denmark, Dominica, Dominican Rep, Ecuador, Egypt, Estonia, Ethiopia, Finland, France, Gabon, Gambia, Georgia, Germany, Ghana, Greece, Guinea, Guinea-Bissau, Guyana, Hungary, Iceland, India, Indonesia, Iran Islamic Rep, Iraq, Israel, Italy, Jamaica, Japan, Jordan, Kazakhstan, Kenya, Kiribati, Korea DPR, Korea Rep, Kuwait, Kyrgyzstan, Latvia, Lebanon, Libya, Lithuania, Madagascar, Malaysia, Maldives, Mali, Malta, Marshall Is, Mauritania, Mauritius, Mexico, Moldova, Mongolia, Montenegro, Morocco, Mozambique, Myanmar, Nepal, Netherlands, New Zealand, Niger, Nigeria, North Macedonia, Norway, Oman, Pakistan, Panama, Papua New Guinea, Paraguay, Peru, Philippines, Poland, Portugal, Romania, Russia, Rwanda, Samoa, Saudi Arabia, Senegal, Serbia, Sierra Leone, Slovakia, Slovenia, South Africa, Spain, Sri Lanka, St Kitts-Nevis, St Lucia, Sudan, Suriname, Sweden, Switzerland, Syrian AR, Tajikistan, Tanzania UR, Thailand, Togo, Trinidad-Tobago, Tunisia, Türkiye, Turkmenistan, Tuvalu, Uganda, UK, Ukraine, United Arab Emirates, Uruguay, USA, Uzbekistan, Vanuatu, Venezuela, Vietnam, Yemen, Zambia, Zimbabwe.

IGO Relations Close cooperation with: *FAO (#09260)*; *UNEP (#20299)*; *WHO (#20950)*; *World Meteorological Organization (WMO, #21649)*. Also cooperates with: *Asian Development Bank (ADB, #01422)*; *International Bank for Reconstruction and Development (IBRD, #12317)* (World Bank); *UNESCO Office, Jakarta – Regional Bureau for Sciences in Asia and the Pacific (#20313)*; *United Nations University (UNU, #20642)*. Partner of: *International Center for Agricultural Research in the Dry Areas (ICARDA, #12466)*. **NGO Relations** Memorandum of Understanding with: *Botanic Gardens Conservation International (BGCI, #03306)*. Participates in: *Mountain Research Initiative (MRI, #16863)*. Instrumental in setting up: *Archipelago (no recent information)*; *DIVERSITAS in Western Pacific and Asia (DIWPA Network, #05105)*; *People and Plants International (PPI, #18302)*. [2020.08.27/XE4356/**F***]

- ♦ Programme méditerranée de l'Unesco (inactive)
- ♦ Programme mondial pour l'évaluation des ressources en eau (#21907)
- ♦ Programme mondial des nations unies contre le blanchiment de l'argent (#20568)
- ♦ Programme mondial de recherches sur le climat (#21279)
- ♦ Programme des musées de l'Afrique de l'Ouest (#20890)
- ♦ Programme for Museum Development in Africa / see Centre for Heritage Development in Africa (#03748)
- ♦ Programme national de prévention de lutte et d'assistance humanitaire aux victimes des catastrophes naturelles / see Organisation internationale pour la réduction des catastrophes
- ♦ Programme des Nations Unies pour le contrôle international de la drogue (inactive)
- ♦ Programme des Nations Unies pour le développement (#20292)
- ♦ Programme des Nations Unies pour l'environnement (#20299)
- ♦ Programme des Nations Unies pour les établissements humains (#20572)
- ♦ Programme des nations unies pour l'exploitation de l'information d'origine spatiale aux fins de gestion des catastrophes et des interventions d'urgence (#20610)
- ♦ Programme de l'OCDE sur l'enseignement supérieur (inactive)
- ♦ Programme OMS tabac ou santé / see WHO Tobacco Free Initiative (#20949)
- ♦ Programme for Palestinian-European Academic Cooperation in Education / see Programme for Palestinian-European-American Cooperation in Education (#18527)

♦ Programme for Palestinian-European-American Cooperation in Education (PEACE Programme) 18527

Contact address not obtained. T. +33145684107. E-mail: peace.programme@unesco.org.
URL: http://www.peace-programme.org/

History 1 Nov 1991, Jerusalem (Israel), as *Programme for Palestinian-European Academic Cooperation in Education*, at a meeting of presidents of 12 European universities and their colleagues from 6 Palestinian universities. Sub-title: *International University Network for Cooperation with Palestinian Higher Education Institutions – Réseau universitaire international pour la coopération avec les institutions palestiniennes d'enseignement supérieur.* Previously functioned as a component network of *UNESCO Mediterranean Programme (inactive)*, based on *International Convention on the Recognition of Studies, Diplomas and Degrees in Higher Education in the Arab States and European States Bordering on the Mediterranean (1976)*. Currently functions as a component network of *UNITWIN/UNESCO Chairs Programme (#20669)* – UNESCO Chair Programme. **Aims** Promote international cooperation with Palestinian universities; extend support to their institutional and staff development, and enhancement of the quality of their academic programmes. **Structure** General Assembly (every 2 years). Steering Committee (meets twice a year), consisting of Chairperson, Vice-Chairperson, Secretary General, Treasurer and 6 other members. PEACE Programme Office at UNESCO in Paris (France). **Languages** Arabic, English, French. **Staff** 2.00 FTE, paid. **Finance** Members' dues. Other sources: allocations from *Anna Lindh Euro-Mediterranean Foundation for the Dialogue between Cultures (Anna Lindh Foundation, #00847)*, *Arab Gulf Programme for United Nations Development Organizations (AGFUND, #00971)*, *Association of Arab and European Universities (AEUA, #02373)*, *Association of Commonwealth Universities, The (ACU, #02440)*, *Association of Southeast Asian Institutions of Higher Learning (ASAIHL, #02920)*, *Coimbra Group (#04089)*, *European Commission (EC, #06633)*, *European University Association (EUA, #09027)*, *International Association of Universities (IAU, #12246)*, *International Council for Open and Distance Education (ICDE, #13056)*, *International Federation of Catholic Universities (IFCU, #13381)*, *UNESCO (#20322)*; allocations from governments in support of Palestinian higher education; scholarships and grants from member institutions for Palestinian students and young academics. **Activities** Areas of action include: scholarships to Palestinian students and young academics for them to pursue post-graduate studies abroad; exchange of teachers and researchers as staff development at Palestinian universities; academic programmes at Palestinian universities through bilateral and multilateral agreements and through consortia of member universities. **Events** *Conference* Barcelona (Spain) 2010, *General Assembly* Paris (France) 2007, *International conference on research development in Palestinian universities / Conference* Paris (France) 2007, *Conference* Bethlehem (Palestine) 2005, *Conference* Paris (France) 2001. **Publications** Proceedings.

Members Universities (62) in 15 countries and territories:
Belgium, Canada, Denmark, France, Italy, Malta, Netherlands, Norway, Palestine, Portugal, Spain, Sweden, Switzerland, UK, USA.

NGO Relations *Community of Mediterranean Universities (CMU, #04403)* is member. Member of: *Euro-Mediterranean University (EMUNI, #05728).* [2012/XF2415/y/**F**]

- ♦ Programme for Pollution Assessment and Control in the Mediterranean Sea / see MED POL – Programme for the Assessment and Control of Marine Pollution in the Mediterranean (#16691)
- ♦ Programme de recherche et de développement de l'OMM (see: #21649)
- ♦ Programme de recherches atmosphériques globales (inactive)

♦ Programme régional de Conservation de la zone Côtière et Marine en Afrique de l'Ouest (PRCM) 18528

Regional Marine and Coastal Conservation Programme for West Africa

Contact Unité de Coordination, S/C UICN Mauritanie, Avenue Charles De Gaulle, Nouakchott, Mauritania. T. +2225290977. Fax +2225241869. E-mail: prcm@iucn.org.
URL: http://www.prcmarine.org/

History An initiative of *International Union for Conservation of Nature and Natural Resources (IUCN, #15766)*, *World Wide Fund for Nature (WWF, #21922)*, *Wetlands International (#20928)* and *Fondation internationale du Banc d'Arguin (FIBA)*, in partnership with: *Sub-Regional Fisheries Commission (SRFC, #20026)*. Phase II: 2008-2012. **Aims** Coordinate efforts made by institutions and private individuals to preserve the littoral of coastal countries in the sub-region. **Structure** Regional Forum; Steering Committee; Coordination Unit; Scientific and Technical Advisory Committee. **Activities** Programme covers: Cape Verde, Gambia, Guinea, Guinea Bissau, Mauritania, Senegal, and Sierra Leone. [2016/XJ5901/**E**]

- ♦ Programme régional coordonné d'éducation populaire (#18456)
- ♦ Programme régional océanien de l'environnement (#19205)
- ♦ Programme for the Regional Study of the El Niño Phenomenon in the Southeastern Pacific (#18523)
- ♦ Programme du Réseau du développement durable – PNUD (no recent information)

♦ Programme Solidarité eau (pS-Eau) 18529

Water Solidarity Network

Dir 32 rue Le Peletier, 75009 Paris, France. T. +33153349120. Fax +33153349121. E-mail: pseau@pseau.org.
Admin Sec address not obtained.
URL: http://www.pseau.org/

History Jun 1984, as *Water Network – Solidarité eau – Wasser Solidarität – Acqua Solidarità*, by resolution of *Council of the European Union (#04895)* meeting, as Ministers of the Environment. Also referred to in English as *Water Solidarity Programme (Water-Sp)*. **Aims** Cooperate with developing countries in areas of water and health, agriculture and environment; allow European actors to bring effective aid to local enterprises hampered by lack of technical and financial means. **Structure** Board of Directors; Executive Secretariat, headed by Director. Officers: President; Vice-President; Secretary; Treasurer. **Languages** English, French, Spanish. **Staff** 12.00 FTE, paid. **Finance** Mostly financed by French Ministries. Budget (annual): euro 1.4 million. **Activities** Rather than providing funds itself, puts those requiring assistance with a project in touch with those willing to give assistance. Sub-programmes by sector. Services: information and promotion of decentralized cooperation initiatives in the field of water; help with finding partners and with setting up projects; preparation of priority action proposals; concerted action and discussion for the production of reference documents in the field of water; suggested framework of activity enabling greater consistency and durability of activities. **Events** *General Assembly* 2001. **Publications** *La lettre du programme Solidarité eau* (4 a year). *Cahiers du pS-Eau*. Technical notebooks; background papers.

Members Mainly French membership, but members in 34 countries and territories:
Argentina, Belgium, Benin, Brazil, Burkina Faso, Cambodia, Cameroon, Chad, Colombia, Comoros, Congo Brazzaville, Côte d'Ivoire, Ecuador, France, Germany, Guinea, Guinea-Bissau, Haiti, Italy, Kenya, Laos, Madagascar, Mali, Mauritania, Morocco, Netherlands, Niger, Palestine, Senegal, Spain, Sweden, Switzerland, Togo, Tunisia.

IGO Relations Accredited to the Conference of the Parties of: *Secretariat of the United Nations Convention to Combat Desertification (Secretariat of the UNCCD, #19208)*. Partner of: *Global Alliances for Water and Climate (GAfWaC, #10230)*. **NGO Relations** Founding member of: *Global Water Solidarity (GWS, #10655)*. Member of: *Groupe de Travail Désertification (GTD).* [2013.06.01/XF5349/**F**]

- ♦ Programme Villes-santé / see WHO European Healthy Cities Network (#20936)

♦ Progressive Alliance for Freedom, Justice and Solidarity (Progressive Alliance) 18530

Global Coordinator Willy-Brandt-Haus, Wilhelmstr 141, 10963 Berlin, Germany. T. +493025991329. E-mail: contact@progressive-alliance.info.
URL: https://progressive-alliance.info/

History 2013, Leipzig (Germany). **Aims** Make the 21st century a century of democratic, social and ecological progress. **Structure** Steering Committee; Board. **Languages** English, French, Spanish. **Events** *Asia's Social Democratic New Deal for Peace, Democracy, Recovery, Sustainability* Kuala Lumpur (Malaysia) 2022, *Convention* Stockholm (Sweden) 2019, *Convention* Berlin (Germany) 2017.
Members Political parties in 92 countries and territories:
Algeria, Argentina, Australia, Austria, Bahrain, Belarus, Belgium, Bolivia, Bosnia-Herzegovina, Brazil, Bulgaria, Burkina Faso, Cameroon, Canada, Central African Rep, Chile, Congo Brazzaville, Congo DR, Costa Rica, Côte d'Ivoire, Croatia, Cyprus, Czechia, Denmark, Dominican Rep, Egypt, Equatorial Guinea, Eritrea, Eswatini, Finland, France, Georgia, Germany, Ghana, Greece, Guinea, Hungary, India, Indonesia, Iran Islamic Rep, Iraq, Ireland, Israel, Italy, Jordan, Kenya, Latvia, Lebanon, Lithuania, Luxembourg, Malaysia, Mauritania, Mauritius, Mexico, Moldova, Mongolia, Montenegro, Morocco, Myanmar, Nepal, Netherlands, New Zealand, Nicaragua, Niger, North Macedonia, Norway, Palestine, Paraguay, Philippines, Poland, Portugal, Romania, Sahara West, Sao Tomé-Principe, Senegal, Serbia, Slovakia, Slovenia, Spain, St Lucia, Sweden, Switzerland, Syrian AR, Tanzania UR, Timor-Leste, Tunisia, Türkiye, UK, Uruguay, USA, Yemen, Zimbabwe.
Associated partners include 16 organizations listed in this Yearbook:
Arab Social Democratic Forum (ASDF); *Central and Eastern European Network for Gender Issues (CEE Gender Network, #03695)*; *European Forum for Democracy and Solidarity (EFDS, #07307)*; *Foundation Max van der Stoel (FMS)*; *Friedrich-Ebert-Stiftung (FES)*; *Global Progressive Forum (GPF, #10557)*; *Group of the Progressive Alliance of Socialists and Democrats in the European Parliament (S and D, #10786)*; *International Trade Union Confederation (ITUC, #15708)*; *International Union of Socialist Youth (IUSY, #15815)*; *Olof Palme International Center, Stockholm*; *Party of European Socialists (PES, #18249)*; *Social Democracy in Asia (SocDem Asia, #19334)*; *Socialist International Women (SIW, #19341)*; *Socialists, Democrats and Greens Group (SOC, #19342)*; *SOLIDAR (#19680)*; *Young European Socialists (YES, #21989)*. [2023/AA0764/y/**C**]

- ♦ **Progressive Alliance** Progressive Alliance for Freedom, Justice and Solidarity (#18530)
- ♦ PRO Human Rights Organization CLG / see SOCHAIR Organization (Europe) (#19331)
- ♦ **PROI** Public Relations Organisation International (#18570)
- ♦ PROI Worldwide / see Public Relations Organisation International (#18570)

♦ Project Aladdin 18531

Projet Aladin – Projekt Aladin – Projesi Aladdin
Exec Dir 8 rue de Prague, 75012 Paris, France. T. +33143072576. Fax +33143077327. E-mail: info@projectaladdin.org.
URL: http://www.projetaladin.org/

History Mar 2009. Launched under the patronage of *UNESCO (#20322)*. **Aims** Promote greater mutual knowledge among peoples of different cultures and religions, particularly Jews and Muslims, so as to bring about changes in attitudes and perceptions and develop a culture of peace and tolerance. **Structure** Board of Directors; Executive Committee; Advisory Board. **Finance** Sources: donations; grants. **Activities** Events/meetings; knowledge management/information dissemination. **Consultative Status** Consultative status granted from: *UNESCO (#20322)* (Consultative Status). [2022/AA0002/**F**]

- ♦ Project AWARE Foundation (internationally oriented national body)
- ♦ Project Concern, Inc / see PCI Global
- ♦ Project Concern International / see PCI Global

♦ Project Counselling Service (PCS) 18532

Consejeria en Proyectos
Administration 11 Avenida 14 – 80 Zona 10, Guatemala, Guatemala. T. +50223632928. Fax +50223632928.
Denmark Borgergade 10/2, 1300 Copenhagen K, Denmark. T. +4533735000. Fax +4533328448.
URL: http://www.pcslatin.org/

History 1979, as a consortium of European and Canadian NGOs working in Latin America. Previously referred to as *Consejeria en Proyectos para Refugiados Latinoamericanos (CPRL)*. **Aims** Strengthen the capacities of *refugee* and *displaced* populations and those affected by other forms of uprootedness to enhance their autonomous, democratic and intercultural organizational processes and incorporate a gender perspective to further their work on the promotion and defence of *human rights*, understood holistically. **Structure** Board of Directors, comprising member agencies, including Inter Pares, Danish Refugee Council and Swiss Interchurch Aid-Heks. Secretariat in Lima (Peru). Offices in Bogota (Colombia) and Guatemala (Guatemala). **Finance** Member agencies form Board of Directors. Additional financing from member governments and others, including: *Canadian International Development Agency (CIDA, inactive)*; *Catholic Agency for Overseas Development (CAFOD)*; *Christian Aid*; *ICCO – Interchurch Organization for Development Cooperation*; *Norwegian Human Rights Fund (NHRF)*; *Oxfam GB*; *Primate's World Relief and Development Fund (PWRDF)*; *Swiss Agency for Development and Cooperation (SDC)*. **Activities** Advocacy/lobbying/activism. **Publications** Annual Report; internal reports; conference proceedings.
Members Regional organizations (2):
Inter Pares; *Swiss Interchurch Aid (EPER)*.
NGO Relations . [2016/XE2974/y/**E**]

- ♦ PROJECT C.U.R.E. (internationally oriented national body)
- ♦ PROJECT C.U.R.E. – Commission on Urgent Relief and Equipment / see PROJECT C.U.R.E.
- ♦ Project ECHELON / see ECHELON Network (#05282)

♦ Project Gaia 18533

Exec Dir PO Box 4190, Gettysburg PA 17325, USA. T. +17173345594. E-mail: info@projectgaia.com.
URL: http://projectgaia.com/

History Incorporated in Ethiopia, 2005; incorporated in the US, 2007. Registration: USA. **Aims** Eradicate *energy poverty* by increasing access to sustainable cooking fuels, especially simple alcohols, ethanol and methanol, and liquid biofuels. **Structure** Board of Directors. **Languages** English, French. **Staff** 60.00 FTE, paid. **Finance** Sources: donations; grants; private foundations. **Activities** Awareness raising; capacity building; financial and/or material support; guidance/assistance/consulting; humanitarian/emergency aid; knowledge management/information dissemination; networking/liaising; projects/programmes.
Members Full in 3 countries:
Ethiopia, Kenya, Nigeria.
IGO Relations Accredited by (1): *Green Climate Fund (GCF, #10714)*. Implementing partner of: *UNHCR (#20327)*. [2022.02.15/XM5278/**F**]

- ♦ Project Group for Technical Development Cooperation (internationally oriented national body)
- ♦ Project Harmony (internationally oriented national body)
- ♦ Project HOPE (internationally oriented national body)
- ♦ Project Hope for Africa (internationally oriented national body)
- ♦ Project-Hope International / see Pro-Hope International
- ♦ Project Lighthawk / see Lighthawk

♦ Project Management Institute (PMI) 18534

Main Office 14 Campus Blvd, Newtown Square PA 19073-3299, USA. T. +16103564600. Fax +16103564647. E-mail: customercare@pmi.org – customercare.emea@pmi.org.
URL: http://www.pmi.org/

History 1969. **Aims** Advance the state-of-the-art in the management of projects. **Structure** Board of Directors, comprising Chair, Vice-Chair, Secretary-Treasurer and 12 Directors-at-large. Local chapters, including *PMI Benelux Chapter*, Beveren (Belgium); Specific Interest Groups; Colleges. *PMI Educational Foundation (PMIEF)*. **Activities** Events/meetings; certification/accreditation; research/documentation; standards/guidelines. **Events** *Global Summit* Las Vegas, NV (USA) 2022, *Eastern European Conference* St Petersburg (Russia) 2021, *Meeting* Abu Dhabi (United Arab Emirates) 2019, *Global congress* Dublin (Ireland) 2019, *Meeting* Vienna (Austria) 2019. **Publications** *PMI Today* (12 a year) – newsletter; *PM Network* (12 a year) – magazine; *Project Management Journal* (4 a year). *Project Management Institute Research Series*. *A Guide to the Project Management Body of Knowledge (PMBOK Guide)*. Books; training tools; resources. **Members** Individuals (over 60,000) and organizations (299) in 106 countries. Membership countries not specified. **NGO Relations** Member of: *EFMD – The Management Development Network (#05387)*. [2022/XE3493/j/**E**]

- ♦ Project Managers Without Borders (internationally oriented national body)
- ♦ Project on Middle East Democracy (internationally oriented national body)

♦ Project Mind Foundation (PMF) 18535

Keren Mivtsa Mochin
Contact address not obtained. T. +97226240280. Fax +97226221860. E-mail: info@project-mind.org.
URL: http://project-mind.org/

History 1993. Registration: No/ID: 58-027-560-0, Start date: 1995, Israel. **Aims** Render science more effective through a higher, more potent form of creativity – accelerated thought; free the human spirit from the crushing illusion of materialism by using the transformative genius, latent in all humans, to eliminate real and addictive lack; discover science as the ultimate spiritual endeavour in which the whole body must become an instrument of creative vision serving holistic, restriction-eliminating, abundance-generating, spirit-liberating, physical world transformation. **Structure** Charter Members: Chairman/Executive Director; Secretary General; Public Relations; Treasurer; Comptroller; Consultants (4) – biological sciences, tradition, media and history, consciousness research. Executive Committee. Tasks Committee. Advisory Board. Esoteric, mesoteric and exoteric circles. **Finance** Donations. **Activities** Currently building a higher creativity "mind tank" facility for scientists as candidates for accelerated thought, expected to house up to 36 scientists at a time plus staff. **Events** *Meeting / Conference* Cheltenham (UK) 1999. **Publications** *Project Mind: the Conscious Conquest of Man and Matter through Accelerated Thought*. Brochures; essays.
Members Associates (individuals) (58) in 15 countries:
Australia, Canada, Colombia, Ecuador, France, India, Israel, Malaysia, Mexico, Netherlands, Pakistan, Portugal, Spain, UK, USA. [2021/XF4012/fv/**F**]

- ♦ Project ORBIS International / see ORBIS International (#17786)
- ♦ Project Planning Centre for Developing Countries / see Bradford Centre for International Development
- ♦ Project Ploughshares (internationally oriented national body)
- ♦ Project Solidarity (internationally oriented national body)
- ♦ Project Survival Pacific (internationally oriented national body)
- ♦ Project Towards the Creation of a Spiritual Forum for World Peace at the United Nations (internationally oriented national body)
- ♦ Project Trust (internationally oriented national body)
- ♦ Project WET Foundation (internationally oriented national body)
- ♦ Project WET – Water Education for Teachers / see Project WET Foundation
- ♦ Projekt Aladin (#18531)
- ♦ Projektgroep voor Technische Ontwikkelingssamenwerking (internationally oriented national body)
- ♦ Projektgruppe Friedensforschung Konstanz (internationally oriented national body)
- ♦ Projektpartnerschaft Dritte Welt / see Aktion Eine Welt
- ♦ Projektstyregruppen for Fiskeimmunologi / see International Society of Fish and Shellfish Immunology (#15122)
- ♦ Projesi Aladdin (#18531)
- ♦ Projet Aladin (#18531)
- ♦ Projet de collaboration internationale entre bibliothèques théologiques / see European Theological Libraries (#08906)
- ♦ Projet faim (#10994)
- ♦ Projet GRAM-Kivu / see Vision GRAM-International
- ♦ **Projet HEREIN** Réseau européen d'information sur les politiques du patrimoine culturel (#07533)
- ♦ Projet international de l'Association pour la stérilisation volontaire / see EngenderHealth
- ♦ Projet des modèles de l'ordre mondial (#21684)
- ♦ Projeto Planeta Azul (internationally oriented national body)
- ♦ Projet de Partenariats sur les Politiques de Gouvernance en Génomique (#18418)
- ♦ Projet planète bleue (internationally oriented national body)
- ♦ Projet sur la radiodiffusion télévisuelle numérique / see DVB Project (#05147)
- ♦ Projet régional pour l'Asie de coopération intéressant l'irradiation des denrées alimentaires (inactive)
- ♦ Projet de réhydratation (internationally oriented national body)
- ♦ Projet pour la survie des grands singes (#10699)

♦ Proliferation Security Initiative (PSI) 18536

Address not obtained.
URL: http://www.state.gov/t/isn/c10390.htm

History 31 May 2003, by US President George W Bush. **Aims** Interdict transfer of banned weapons and weapons technology; focusing on combating proliferation of nuclear, chemical and biological weapons and materials. **Events** *Regional workshop* Busan (Korea Rep) 2010, *Meeting* Singapore (Singapore) 2006.
Members Governments of 17 countries:
Australia, Canada, Denmark, France, Germany, Italy, Japan, Netherlands, Norway, Poland, Portugal, Russia, Singapore, Spain, Türkiye, UK, USA. [2016/XM3089/**F***]

♦ PROLINNOVA 18537

Secretariat c/o KIT, Mauritskade 63, 1092 AD Amsterdam, Netherlands.
Secretariat address not obtained.
URL: http://www.prolinnova.net/

History Dec 1999, Rambouillet (France). Launched facilitated by *ETC* and supported by *Global Forum on Agricultural Research (GFAR, #10370)*, NGO Committee of *CGIAR System Organization (CGIAR, #03843)* and French Ministry of Foreign Affairs. Functions as a decentralized programme. Full title: *PROLINNOVA – PROmoting Local INNOVAtion in ecologically-oriented agriculture and natural and natural resource management*. **Aims** Promote mainstream agricultural development and research approaches building on local innovation and participatory innovation development towards ecologically oriented *agriculture* and *natural resource* management (NRM). **Structure** National Steering Committee per country or region, International Support Team. **Finance** Core donors: *Global Forum on Agricultural Research (GFAR, #10370)*; Dutch Ministry of Foreign Affairs; *The Rockefeller Foundation (#18966)*. Activity-based donors include: *ActionAid (#00087)*; *CGIAR System Organization (CGIAR, #03843)*; *Centre technique de coopération agricole et rurale (CTA, inactive)*; *International Fund for Agricultural Development (IFAD, #13692)*; *German Catholic Bishops' Organisation for Development Cooperation (MISEREOR)*; *McKnight Foundation*.
Members Regional or country platforms in 20 countries:
Bolivia, Cambodia, Cameroon, Ecuador, Ethiopia, Ghana, India, Kenya, Mali, Mozambique, Nepal, Niger, Nigeria, Peru, Philippines, Senegal, South Africa, Sudan, Tanzania UR, Uganda.
NGO Relations *International Institute of Rural Reconstruction (IIRR, #13921)* is part of International Support Team. Cooperates with: *Global Forum on Agricultural Research (GFAR, #10370)*. [2016/XJ5094/**E**]

- ♦ PROLINNOVA – PROmoting Local INNOVAtion in ecologically-oriented agriculture and natural and natural resource management / see PROLINNOVA (#18537)
- ♦ ProLiteracy Worldwide (internationally oriented national body)
- ♦ PromaxBDA (internationally oriented national body)
- ♦ Promax International / see PromaxBDA
- ♦ **PROMECAFE** Programa Cooperativo Regional para el Desarrollo Tecnológico de la Caficultura en Centroamérica, República Dominica y Jamaica (#18775)

♦ PROMETIA 18538

Secretariat c/o LGI Consulting, Square de Meeûs 38/40, 1000 Brussels, Belgium. E-mail: contact@prometia.eu.
URL: http://prometia.eu/

History 2014. Full title: *Mineral Processing and Extractive Metallurgy for Mining and Recycling Innovation Association (PROMETIA)*. Registered in accordance with Belgian law. **Aims** Promote innovation in *mineral* processing and extractive *metallurgy* for *mining* and *recycling* of raw materials. **Structure** General Assembly; Executive Committee; Technical Secretariat. Scientific Board; Pilot Board. **Languages** English. **Staff** None paid. **Finance** Members' dues. **Activities** Research/documentation; knowledge management/information dissemination; guidance/assistance/consulting; events/meetings. **Events** *Scientific Seminar* Barcelona (Spain) 2022, *Scientific Seminar* Seville (Spain) 2021, *Scientific Seminar* Brussels (Belgium) 2020, *Scientific Seminar* Kristiansand (Norway) 2019, *Scientific Seminar* Berlin (Germany) 2018. **Publications** *PROMETIA Newsletter* (3 a year). Books; reports.

Members Full; Associate; Permanent Observer. Members in 16 countries:
Australia, Belgium, Brazil, Finland, France, Germany, Greece, Italy, Netherlands, Norway, Poland, Portugal, Spain, Sweden, UK, USA.
IGO Relations *European Institute of Innovation and Technology (EIT, #07562)* – RawMaterials.
[2017.06.20/XM6061/**D**]

♦ PROMETRA International 18539

Pres BP 6134 Dakar-Etoile, Dakar, Senegal. T. +221338322850. Fax +221338325749. E-mail: prometra@prometra.org.
URL: http://www.prometra.org/
History Also referred to as *Association for the Promotion of Traditional Medicine International*. **Aims** Preserve and promote *African traditional medicine*, culture and indigenous science through research, education, advocacy and traditional medical practice. **Structure** Chapters (26). **Activities** Organizes Annual Meeting, always in Dakar (Senegal). **Events** *International conference on traditional medicine* Minneapolis, MN (USA) 2005, *International conference on traditional medicine* Dakar (Senegal) 2004. **Publications** *Medecine Verte* (4 a year) in English, French. Books; studies; guides.
Members Chapters in 26 countries and territories:
Benin, Burkina Faso, Cameroon, Central African Rep, Congo DR, Côte d'Ivoire, France, Gabon, Ghana, Guadeloupe, Guiana Fr, Guinea, Guinea-Bissau, Haiti, Kenya, Mali, Martinique, Mozambique, New Caledonia, Nigeria, Senegal, South Africa, Spain, Togo, Uganda, USA.
IGO Relations Partners: *African Intellectual Property Organization (#00344)*; *UNDP (#20292)*; *United States Agency for International Development (USAID)*; *WHO (#20950)*; *WHO Regional Office for Africa (AFRO, #20943)*; *World Intellectual Property Organization (WIPO, #21593)*. **NGO Relations** Partners: *Environnement et développement du Tiers-monde (enda, #05510)*; *Global Health Council (GHC, #10402)*; *Oxfam Novib*; national organizations. [2019/XM0167/**F**]

♦ PROMITHEASNET 18540

Contact address not obtained. T. +302107275732 – +302107275809. Fax +302107275858. E-mail: promitheas@kepa.uoa.gr.
URL: http://www.promitheasnet.kepa.uoa.gr/
History Full title: *PROMITHEASNET – The Energy and Climate Change Policy Network*. **Activities** Events/meetings; training/education; research/documentation. **Events** *PromitheasNet International Scientific Conference on Energy and Climate Change* Athens (Greece) 2019, *PromitheasNet International Scientific Conference on Energy and Climate Change* Athens (Greece) 2018, *PromitheasNet International Scientific Conference on Energy and Climate Change* Athens (Greece) 2017, *PromitheasNet International Scientific Conference on Energy and Climate Change* Athens (Greece) 2016. **Publications** *Euro-Asian Journal of Sustainable Energy Development Policy* (2 a year).
Members Research centres (26) in 16 countries:
Albania, Armenia, Azerbaijan, Bulgaria, Georgia, Greece, Kazakhstan, Kyrgyzstan, Moldova, Romania, Russia, Serbia, Tajikistan, Türkiye, Ukraine, Uzbekistan. [2017/XM6083/**F**]

- ♦ PROMITHEASNET – The Energy and Climate Change Policy Network / see PROMITHEASNET (#18540)
- ♦ Promoción del Control de la Tuberculosis Internacionalmente / see ACTION (#00085)

♦ Promoting Earth Science for Society (YES Network) 18541

Sec 36-38 Rue Joseph II, 1000 Brussels, Belgium.
URL: http://www.networkyes.net/
History Founded as a result of the UN International Year of Planet Earth (IYPE). Launched, Feb 2008. Previously also referred to as *Young Earth Scientists for Society (YES)*. **Aims** Link early-career geoscientists through scientific research and interdisciplinary networking; provide resources for professional development to prepare early-career geoscientists for geoscience careers and to help prepare them to serve as key leaders and advisors on the intersections between environmental sustainability, geo-resource exploration, and quality of human life issues. **Structure** Executive Board. Support Teams. National Representatives of the Chapters; Regional Representatives; Organizational Representatives; Advisors. **Languages** English. **Activities** Advocacy/lobbying/activism; events/meetings; training/education. **Events** *World Congress* Berlin (Germany) 2019, *International YES Congress* Iran Islamic Rep 2017, *International YES Congress* Tanzania UR 2014, *International YES Congress* Tanzania UR 2014, *Africa Symposium* Addis Ababa (Ethiopia) 2013. **Publications** *Yes Network Bulletin*; *YES Network Newsletter*.
Members National Representatives from 47 countries:
Argentina, Australia, Azerbaijan, Bangladesh, Botswana, Cameroon, Canada, Chile, China, Côte d'Ivoire, Cuba, Czechia, Denmark, Egypt, Eritrea, Ethiopia, Gabon, Germany, Ghana, India, Italy, Madagascar, Malawi, Malaysia, Mongolia, Morocco, Mozambique, Namibia, Netherlands, Nigeria, Pakistan, Peru, Portugal, Russia, Senegal, South Africa, Sri Lanka, Switzerland, Tanzania UR, Tunisia, Uganda, UK, Uruguay, USA, Uzbekistan, Yemen, Zambia.
IGO Relations Patronage from *UNESCO (#20322)*. **NGO Relations** Affiliate member of: *International Union of Geodesy and Geophysics (IUGG, #15776)*. Affiliated with: *International Union of Geological Sciences (IUGS, #15777)*. Partner of: *Earth Science Matters Foundation (ESM, #05169)*. [2020/XJ0571/v/**E**]

- ♦ Promoting Operational Links with Integrated Services / see POLIS (#18419)
- ♦ Promoting the Rights of Persons with Disabilities in the Digital Age / see Global Initiative for Inclusive Information and Communication Technologies (#10425)
- ♦ Promotional Council for Youth Action in Africa (unconfirmed)
- ♦ Promotional Framework for Occupational Safety and Health Convention (2006 treaty)
- ♦ Promotional Marketing Council of Europe / see Integrated Marketing Communications Council of Europe (#11369)
- ♦ Promotion of Education and Information Activities for the Advancement of Space Technology and its Applications in Europe / see Eurisy (#05625)
- ♦ Promotion of Global Education and Research / see EDU (#05363)
- ♦ Promotion de la lutte contre la tuberculose au plan international / see ACTION (#00085)
- ♦ Promovere – Association mondiale pour la promotion culturelle (inactive)
- ♦ PROMPTEX – Fédération européenne pour la promotion des marchés publics – textiles et cuir (inactive)
- ♦ Promundo (internationally oriented national body)
- ♦ PRONAPLUCAN' / see Organisation internationale pour la réduction des catastrophes
- ♦ PRONTO International (internationally oriented national body)
- ♦ PROPAC – Plateforme Régionale des Organisations Paysannes d'Afrique Centrale (unconfirmed)
- ♦ Propaganda Fide – Oeuvres Pontificale Missionnaire de la Propagation de la Foi (religious order)
- ♦ De Propaganda Fide / see Congregation for the Evangelization of Peoples (#04670)
- ♦ PROPARCO – Société de promotion et de participations pour la coopération économique, Paris (internationally oriented national body)
- ♦ ProPEL – Professional Practice, Education and Leadership (unconfirmed)
- ♦ Properties and Phase Equilibria for Product and Process Design (meeting series)
- ♦ ProPoor (internationally oriented national body)
- ♦ Met and Props – International Conference on Metrology and Properties of Engineering Surfaces (meeting series)
- ♦ **PROSAFE** Product Safety Forum of Europe (#18510)

♦ Prosalud Inter Americana Foundation (PSIA) 18542

Pres c/o Richard Herrmann Esq Grant, Herrmann Schwartz and Klinger LLP, 675 3rd Avenue New York, New York NY 1017-5704, USA. T. +12126821800.
History 2003. **Aims** Encourage a preventive culture with regards to *reproductive health* contributing to a responsible, healthy and risk-free *sexuality*, through different educational approaches. **Structure** Country offices in: Bolivia, Chile, Ecuador, Peru, Venezuela. **Languages** English, Spanish. **Staff** 40.00 FTE, paid; 3.00 FTE, voluntary. **Finance** Donations: US$ 750,000. **NGO Relations** Member of: *International Consortium for Emergency Contraception (ICEC, #12911)*; *Latin American Consortium on Emergency Contraception (LACEC, #16306)*; *Reproductive Health Supplies Coalition (RHSC, #18847)*. [2013.08.21/XJ7163/f/**F**]

- ♦ PROSALUS / see Enraíza Derechos
- ♦ **PROSEA Association** Plant Resources of South-East Asia (#18391)

♦ PRO SILVA 18543

Pres Poitschach 2, Llanafan, 9560 Feldkirchen in Kärnten, Austria. T. +436644416214. E-mail: president@prosilva.org.
URL: http://www.prosilvaeurope.org/
History 1989, Yugoslavia. Former names and other names: *Association of European Foresters Practicing Management which Follows Natural Processes* – full title; *Union européenne de forestiers aux conceptions de gestion proche de la nature* – full title; *Verband der Naturnah Dekenden Forstleute in Europe* – full title; *PRO SILVA Europe* – alias. **Aims** Promote *forest* management strategies which optimize the maintenance, *conservation* and utilization of forest *ecosystems* in such a way that the ecological and socio-economic functions are sustainable and profitable; advocates general approach to management which includes market and non-market objectives and takes the whole forest ecosystem into consideration; promote forestry according to principles which serve biodiversity in general and species diversity in particular. **Structure** Delegate Assembly; Board. **Languages** English, French, German. **Staff** 0.50 FTE, paid; 4.00 FTE, voluntary. **Finance** Sources: members' dues. **Events** *Annual Meeting* Luxembourg (Luxembourg) 2022, *Annual Meeting* Luxembourg (Luxembourg) 2021, *Annual Meeting* Radlje ob Dravi (Slovenia) 2019, *Annual Meeting* Weimar (Germany) 2018, *Annual Meeting* Sibiu (Romania) 2017. **Publications** Newsletter; articles. Information Services: Website provides links to exemplary forests.
Members in 26 countries:
Albania, Austria, Belgium, Bulgaria, Croatia, Czechia, Denmark, Estonia, Finland, France, Germany, Hungary, Ireland, Italy, Luxembourg, Netherlands, Norway, Poland, Portugal, Romania, Slovakia, Slovenia, Spain, Switzerland, UK, USA.
[2020/XD7261/**D**]

- ♦ PRO SILVA Europe / see PRO SILVA (#18543)
- ♦ **PROS** Paediatric Radiation Oncology Society (#18019)
- ♦ **PROsPA** Producer Responsibility Organisations Packaging Alliance (#18508)

♦ Prospective 2100 18544

Pres 59 rue Saint-André-des-Arts, 75006 Paris, France.
URL: http://www.2100.org/
History Jun 1996, Paris (France), as an association. *Fondation 2100*, set up 15 Dec 2016, gradually taking over activities of the association. Registered in accordance with French law. **Aims** In view of the cognitive revolution arising from technological change, in particular *microelectronics* and man-biosphere relations: provide a permanent forum for decision-making issuing from *future studies*; carry out interdisciplinary study for the 21st century; pre-empt social crisis by timely response to true needs of mankind and nature; elaborate on proposals for infrastructure programmes. **Structure** Scientific Committee; Bureau. **Languages** English, French, Spanish. **Staff** 2.00 FTE, paid. **Finance** Voluntary contributions; expertise contracts. **Activities** Training/education; events/meetings; research/documentation. **Events** *Space technology to prevent major risks* Paris (France) 2000.
Members Individuals (about 250) in 20 countries:
Algeria, Belgium, Brazil, Burkina Faso, Cameroon, Canada, Colombia, France, Germany, India, Japan, Mexico, Monaco, Morocco, Peru, Russia, Switzerland, UK, Ukraine, USA. [2019/XF4762/v/**F**]

- ♦ Prospective internationale / see Sail For Ethics

♦ Prospera – International Network of Women's Funds (INWF) 18545

Exec Dir Tlaxcala No 178 dep 402 O, Col Condesa Del Cuauhtémoc, 06170 Mexico City CDMX, Mexico. T. +5215554098657. E-mail: info@prospera-inwf.org.
Main Office 123 Slater St, Ottawa ON K19 5H2, Canada. T. +16132362664 ext 230.
URL: http://www.prospera-inwf.org/
History Activities started 1998. Officially set up 2000. Registration: EU Transparency Register, No/ID: 908150137027-18. **Aims** Link women's funds to promote philanthropy with a feminist perspective; expand resources available to women's rights organizations worldwide by providing grants to seed, support and strengthen these organizations. **Structure** Board. **Languages** English. **Activities** Capacity building; networking/liaising; awareness raising. **Events** *Biennial Meeting / Biennial Conference* Johannesburg (South Africa) 2012, *Biennial Conference* Mongolia 2010, *Biennial Conference* South Africa 2008, *Biennial Conference* Ukraine 2006, *Biennial Conference* Rio de Janeiro (Brazil) 2004.
Members Funds (38) in 33 countries and territories:
Argentina, Bangladesh, Bolivia, Brazil, Bulgaria, Chile, Colombia, Congo Brazzaville, Croatia, Czechia, France, Georgia, Germany, Ghana, Hong Kong, India, Kenya, Korea Rep, Mexico, Mongolia, Nepal, Netherlands, Nicaragua, Peru, Serbia, Slovakia, South Africa, Spain, Sri Lanka, Tanzania UR, UK, Ukraine, USA.
Included in the above, 7 funds listed in this Yearbook:
African Women's Development Fund (AWDF, #00504); *Central American Women's Fund (#03677)*; *Ecumenical Women's Initiative (EWI, #05351)*; *Global Fund for Women (GFW, #10384)*; *Mediterranean Women's Fund (MWF)*; *Urgent Action Fund for Women's Human Rights (UAF)*; *Women's Fund Asia (#21018)*.
NGO Relations Member of: *Association for Women's Rights in Development (AWID, #02980)*; *Worldwide Initiatives for Grantmaker Support (WINGS, #21926)*. [2020/XM2820/y/**F**]

- ♦ Prosper Ménière Society (internationally oriented national body)
- ♦ Prospero World (internationally oriented national body)
- ♦ Prospero World Charitable Trust / see Prospero World
- ♦ ProSTEP / see ProSTEP iViP Association
- ♦ ProSTEP Association for the Advancement of International Product Data Standards / see ProSTEP iViP Association
- ♦ ProSTEP iViP Association (internationally oriented national body)
- ♦ Prosthetic and Orthotic Worldwide Education and Relief / see POWER International
- ♦ **PROSUL** Fórum para o Progresso e Desenvolvimento da América do Sul (#09888)
- ♦ **PROSUR** Foro para el Progreso y Desarrollo de América del Sur (#09888)

♦ ProtectDefenders.eu 18546

Head Secretariat FIDDH, Rue de la Loi 81A, 1040 Brussels, Belgium. E-mail: contact@protectdefenders.eu.
URL: https://protectdefenders.eu/
History Acts as the *European Union (EU, #08967)* Human Rights Defenders mechanism. **Aims** Potect defenders at high risk and facing the most difficult situations worldwide. **Structure** Board with rotating Chairmanship among 4 members: *Front Line Defenders (FLD, #10008)*; *Reporters sans frontières (RSF, #18846)*; *World Organisation Against Torture (OMCT, #21685)*; *International Federation for Human Rights (#13452)*. Secretariat. **Activities** Advocacy/lobbying/activism; awareness raising; financial and/or material support; guidance/assistance/consulting; monitoring/evaluation; training/education.
Members A consortium of 12 NGOs in the field of human rights:
Asian Forum for Human Rights and Development (FORUM-ASIA, #01491); *DefendDefenders (#05026)*; *Euro-Mediterranean Foundation of Support to Human Rights Defenders (EMHRF, #05720)*; *Front Line Defenders (FLD, #10008)*; *ILGA World (International Lesbian, Gay, Bisexual, Trans and Intersex Association, #11120)*; *International Federation for Human Rights (#13452)*; *International Network for Economic, Social and Cultural Rights (ESCR-Net, #14255)*; *Peace Brigades International (PBI, #18277)*; *Protection International (PI, #18548)*; *Reporters sans frontières (RSF, #18846)*; *Urgent Action Fund for Women's Human Rights (UAF)*; *World Organisation Against Torture (OMCT, #21685)*. [2022/AA2844/y/**E**]

- ♦ Protection Against Accidents / Dockers, 1932 (1932 treaty)

♦ Protection of the Arctic Marine Environment (PAME) 18547

Exec Sec Intl Secretariat, Borgir, Nordurslod, 600 Akureyri, Iceland. T. +3544611355. E-mail: olga@pame.is – pame@pame.is.
URL: http://www.pame.is/
History Sep 1993, Nuuk (Greenland). Established as a programme of *Arctic Environmental Protection Strategy (AEPS, inactive)*; currently functions under the auspices of *Arctic Council (#01097)*. Former names and other names: *Arctic Council – Protection Arctic Marine Environment* – alias; *Arctic Council Working Group on Protection of the Arctic Marine Environment (PAME)* – alias. **Aims** Take preventative and other measures directly or through competent international organizations regarding *prevention* of marine *pollution* in the Arctic; aware that Arctic populations are very exposed to environmental *contaminants*, strengthen

regional capacity building with respect to priority pollution sources, especially in Russia. **Structure** Chairman. Secretariat located in Akureyri (Iceland). **Finance** Voluntary contributions from Member States. **Activities** currently focus on: conducting a comprehensive and integrated Arctic marine shipping assessment; assessing existing measures for port reception facilities for ship-generated waste and cargo residues and developing harmonized guidelines for consideration by States; contributing to the *'Arctic Council Assessment of Potential Impacts of Oil and Gas'*. In the Arctic: responding to the *'Arctic Climate Impact Assessment (ACIA)'* findings and recommendations; compiling an inventory of ecosystem-based projects and initiating the identification of Large Marine Ecosystems in the Arctic and indicators of ecosystem health and ecosystem objectives; organizing a workshop to encourage implementation of the *'Arctic Council Offshore Oil and Gas Guidelines (2002)'*; advancing implementation of *Regional Programme of Action for the Protection of the Arctic Marine Environment from Land-based Activities (RPA, #18806)*; and assessing the need to further develop and update its scope; developing a communication plan to support understanding and involvement in implementing the Arctic Marine Strategic Plan. **Events** *Meeting* 2022, *Arctic Shipping Best Practice Information Forum Meeting* 2021, *Meeting* 2021, *Arctic Shipping Best Practice Information Forum Meeting* 2020, *Meeting* 2020. **Publications** Reports; guidelines.
Members Full in 10 countries and territories:
Canada, Denmark, Faeroe Is, Finland, Greenland, Iceland, Norway, Russia, Sweden, USA.
IGO Relations Memorandum of Understanding with (1): *Arctic Regional Hydrographic Commission (ARHC, #01101)*. Cooperates with other working groups within Arctic Council: *Arctic Monitoring and Assessment Programme (AMAP, #01100)*; *Conservation of Arctic Flora and Fauna (CAFF, #04728)*; *Emergency, Prevention, Preparedness and Response (EPPR, #05437)*; *Working Group on Sustainable Development (SDWG, #21061)*.
[2019/XK1390/**E***]

♦ Protection International (PI) 18548

Exec Dir Rue de la Linière 11, 1060 Brussels, Belgium. T. +3226094405. Fax +3225361982. E-mail: contactpi@protectioninternational.org.
URL: https://www.protectioninternational.org/
History 26 Jul 2007, Belgium. Set up as EU Bureau of *Peace Brigades International (PBI, #18277)* (PBI-BEO). Former names and other names: *European Bureau of Peace Brigades International (PBI-BEO)* – former. Registration: Banque-Carrefour des Entreprises, No/ID: 0465.152.711, Start date: 24 Dec 1998, Belgium. **Aims** Promote a world in which fundamental human rights and fundamental freedoms are universally recognized and respected by all, and where everyone has the right to defend these rights and freedoms without fear of threats and attack; support human rights defenders (HRDs) through comprehensive protection programmes that enable them to manage their protection effectively, allow those that protect them to fulfill their obligations, and convince other individuals and institutions with a stake in the protection of human rights defenders to maximise their positive contribution. **Structure** Decentralized governance composed of independent Regional Protection Hubs in Africa, Europe, Latin America and South-East Asia. **Languages** English, French, Spanish. **Staff** 90.00 FTE, paid. **Activities** Capacity building; guidance/assistance/consulting; projects/programmes; training/education. Active in: Brazil, Colombia, Congo DR, El Salvador, Guatemala, Honduras, Indonesia, Kenya, Thailand. **Publications** Annual Report; protection manuals; videos; defenders tools; policy makers tools. More details on: https://www.protectioninternational.org/en/#resources **Information Services** *Focus Observatory* in English – On-line platform to monitor , analyze and promote good practices in policy developments for protecting human rights defenders. **NGO Relations** Member of (4): *EU-LAT Network (#05585)*; *European Network for Central Africa (EurAc, #07874)*; *Human Rights and Democracy Network (HRDN, #10980)*; *ProtectDefenders.eu (#18546)*. Cooperates with (1): *Coalition for Human Rights in Development (#04061)*.
[2022.07.27/XJ0937/**F**]

♦ Protection mondiale des animaux de ferme (internationally oriented national body)

♦ Protect Our Winters Europe (POW) 18549

Contact Pembaurstraße 14, 6020 Innsbruck, Austria. E-mail: hello@protectourwinters.eu.
Contact address not obtained.
Vice-Pres address not obtained.
URL: https://protectourwinters.eu/
History 2020, Austria. Founded following pro snowboarder Jeremy Jones' observation that more and more resorts were closing due to lack of snow. Extended from a kernel of an idea into a worldwide network, with first European chapter starting in 2013, Norway. Chapters also present outside Europe, in Canada, Australia, New Zealand and Japan. Former names and other names: *POW Europe* – alias. Registration: No/ID: 1094440070, Austria; EU Transparency Register, No/ID: 771110337973-66, Start date: 28 Apr 2020. **Aims** Help passionate outdoor people protect the lifestyles and places they love from climate change; as a community of athletes, scientists, creatives, and business leaders, advance non-partisan policies that protect our world today and for future generations. **Structure** Network of 9 national chapters in Europe. **Languages** English. **Staff** 3.00 FTE, paid; 2.00 FTE, voluntary. **Activities** Advocacy/lobbying/activism; awareness raising; capacity building; events/meetings; projects/programmes; sporting activities; training/education. Active in all member countries.
Members Chapters in 9 countries:
Austria, Finland, France, Germany, Italy, Norway, Sweden, Switzerland, UK.
NGO Relations Member of (1): *Climate Action Network Europe (CAN Europe, #04001)*.
[2022.03.26/AA0057/**F**]

♦ Protein Society 18550

Exec Dir 18336 Soledad Canyon Rd, PO Box 1217, Santa Clarita CA 91386, USA. T. +18443776834. E-mail: staff@proteinsociety.org.
Dir of Events address not obtained.
URL: http://www.proteinsociety.org/
History 1986. **Aims** Provide international forums to facilitate communication, cooperation and collaboration with respect to all aspects of the study of proteins. **Structure** Executive Council. Committees (6): Finance; Nominating; Education; Membership; Publication; Mentoring. **Activities** Events/meetings. **Events** *Symposium* Boston, MA (USA) 2023, *Symposium* San Francisco, CA (USA) 2022, *Symposium* 2021, *World Conference on Protein Science (2020 WCPS)* Sapporo (Japan) 2020, *Symposium* Seattle, WA (USA) 2019. **Publications** *Protein Science* (12 a year) – journal. **Members** Scientists from industry and academia involved in all aspects of protein sciences, including emerging fields of proteomics, bioinformatics, structural biology and computational biology pertaining to proteins at the molecular and cellular level, from all levels of career advancement, undergraduate through Emeritus. Members in 52 countries (not specified).
[2021/XW0192/**D**]

♦ Proteoglycans – International Conference on Proteoglycans (meeting series)

♦ ProTerra Foundation 18551

Contact Jan Steenlaan 5A, 3723 BS Bilthoven, Netherlands. T. +31683292852. E-mail: info@proterrafoundation.org.
URL: http://www.proterrafoundation.org/
History 2012, Netherlands. Registration: EU Transparency Register, No/ID: 903449238027-58, Start date: 5 May 2020. **Aims** Encourage all businesses to contribute to the protection of biodiversity by switching to sustainable production, conserve natural resources and ensure that local communities are treated with dignity and respect. **Structure** Board of Directors; Stakeholders Council; Certification and Standard Committee. **Languages** English, French, German, Italian, Portuguese. **Activities** Awareness raising; certification/accreditation; events/meetings; politics/policy/regulatory; projects/programmes; research and development; standards/guidelines; training/education. **Publications** *Newsletter*. Consolidated reports.
Members Networks in 42 countries and territories:
Argentina, Austria, Belgium, Belize, Brazil, Canada, Colombia, Costa Rica, Dominican Rep, Egypt, Eswatini, Finland, France, Germany, Guadeloupe, Guyana, Hungary, India, Italy, Malawi, Mexico, Mozambique, Netherlands, Nicaragua, Norway, Paraguay, Peru, Philippines, Poland, Portugal, Romania, Russia, South Africa, Spain, Switzerland, Thailand, UK, Ukraine, United Arab Emirates, Uruguay, USA, Zimbabwe.
Associate members in 4 countries:
Austria, Belgium, Germany, UK.
NGO Relations Active exchange with NGOs.
[2022.05.04/XM6457/f/**F**]

♦ Protestant Institute for Interdisciplinary Research (internationally oriented national body)
♦ Protestantischer Weltverband (inactive)
♦ Protestant Liaison Board for World Mission / see Association of Protestant Churches and Missions in Germany
♦ Protestantse Solidariteit (internationally oriented national body)
♦ Protestant Union (inactive)
♦ Protocol of 1973 to the International Convention Relating to Intervention of the High Seas in Cases of Oil Pollution Casualties (1973 treaty)
♦ Protocol of 1978 Relating to the International Convention for the Safety of Life at Sea, 1974 (1978 treaty)
♦ Protocol to the 1979 Convention on Long-range Transboundary Air Pollution to Abate Acidification, Eutrophication and Ground-level Ozone (1999 treaty)
♦ Protocol to the 1979 Convention on Long Range Transboundary Air Pollution Concerning the Control of Emissions of Volatile Organic Compounds on Their Transboundary Fluxes (1991 treaty)
♦ Protocol to the 1979 Convention on Long Range Transboundary Air Pollution Concerning the Control of Nitrogen Oxides Emissions or Their Transboundary Fluxes (1988 treaty)
♦ Protocol to the 1979 Convention on Long Range Transboundary Air Pollution on Further Reduction of Sulphur Emissions (1994 treaty)
♦ Protocol to the 1979 Convention on Long Range Transboundary Air Pollution on Long-term Financing of the Cooperative Programme for Monitoring and Evaluation of the Long-range Transmission of Air-pollutants in Europe (1984 treaty)
♦ Protocol to the 1979 Convention on Long Range Transboundary Air Pollution on the Reduction of Sulphur Emissions or Their Transboundary Fluxes by at Least 30 per Cent (1985 treaty)
♦ Protocol of 1988 Relating to the International Convention for the Safety of Life at Sea (1988 treaty)
♦ Protocol of 1996 to the Convention on Limitation of Liability for Maritime Claims (1996 treaty)
♦ Protocol de 1996 relatif à la Convention sur la limitation de la responsabilité en matière de créances maritimes (1996 treaty)
♦ Protocol of 1997 to Amend the International Convention for the Prevention of Pollution from Ships, 1973, as Modified by the Protocol of 1978 Relating Thereto (1997 treaty)
♦ Protocol 1 Annexed to the Universal Copyright Convention Concerning the Application of That Convention to the Works of Stateless Persons and Refugees, 1952 (1952 treaty)
♦ Protocol 1 Annexed to the Universal Copyright Convention Concerning the Application of That Convention to Works of Stateless Persons and Refugees, 1971 (1971 treaty)
♦ Protocol of 2005 to the Convention for the Suppression of Unlawful Acts against the Safety of Maritime Navigation (2005 treaty)
♦ Protocol of 2005 to the Protocol for the Suppression of Unlawful Acts against the Safety of Fixed Platforms Located on the Continental Shelf (2005 treaty)
♦ Protocol of 2010 to Amend the International Convention of Liability and Compensation for Damage in Connection with the Carriage of Hazardous and Noxious Substances by Sea (2010 treaty)
♦ Protocol 2 Annexed to the Universal Copyright Convention, Concerning the Application of That Convention to the Works of Certain International Organizations, 1952 (1952 treaty)
♦ Protocol 2 Annexed to the Universal Copyright Convention Concerning the Application of That Convention to the Works of Certain International Organizations, 1971 (1971 treaty)
♦ Protocol 3 Annexed to the Universal Copyright Convention (1952 treaty)
♦ Protocol on the Abolition of Controls and Formalities at Internal Benelux Frontiers, and the Abolition of Barriers to Free Movement (treaty)
♦ Protocol Additional to the Convention for the Protection of the Rhine from Pollution by Chlorides (1991 treaty)
♦ Protocol Additional to the Geneva Conventions of 12 August 1949 and Relating to the Protection of Victims of International Armed Conflicts (1977 treaty)
♦ Protocol of Adherence by Costa Rica to the Protocol of Managua on Equalization of Import Charges (1962 treaty)
♦ Protocol Against the Illicit Manufacturing of and Trafficking in Firearms, Their Parts and Components and Ammunition (2001 treaty)
♦ Protocol Against the Smuggling of Migrants by Land, Sea and Air (2000 treaty)
♦ Protocol to the Agreement Concerning the International Deposit of Industrial Design (1975 treaty)
♦ Protocol Agreement on the Conservation of Common Natural Resources (1982 treaty)
♦ Protocol to the Agreement on Equalization of Import Charges and to the Agreement on the System of Central American Integrated Industries (1967 treaty)
♦ Protocol to the Agreement on the Importation of Educational, Scientific and Cultural Materials (1976 treaty)
♦ Protocol to the Agreement on the Régime for Central American Integration Industries (1963 treaty)
♦ Protocol to the Agreement on the System of Central American Integrated Industries, 1963 (1963 treaty)
♦ Protocol to the Agreement on the System of Central American Integrated Industries, 1965 (1965 treaty)
♦ Protocol to Amend the 1910 Convention for the Unification of Certain Rules of Law Relating to Assistance and Salvage at Sea (1967 treaty)
♦ Protocol to Amend the 1924 International Convention for the Unification of Certain Rules of Law Relating to Bills of Lading (1968 treaty)
♦ Protocol to Amend the Convention of 31 January 1963 Supplementary to the Paris Convention of 29 July 1960 on Third Party Liability in the Field of Nuclear Energy, as Amended by the Additional Protocol of 28 January 1964 and by the Protocol of 16 November 1982 (2001 treaty)
♦ Protocol to Amend the Convention of 31st January 1963 Supplementary to the Paris Convention of 29th July 1960 on Third Party Liability in the Field of Nuclear Energy, as Amended by the Additional Protocol of 28th January 1964 (1982 treaty)
♦ Protocol to Amend the Convention on Damage Caused by Foreign Aircraft to Third Parties on the Surface (1978 treaty)
♦ Protocol to Amend the Convention on Offences and Certain Other Acts Committed on Board Aircraft (2014 treaty)
♦ Protocol to Amend the Convention for the Suppression of the Circulation of and Traffic in Obscene Publications (1947 treaty)
♦ Protocol to Amend the Convention for the Suppression of the Traffic in Women and Children (1947 treaty)
♦ Protocol to Amend the Convention on Third Party Liability in the Field of Nuclear Energy of 29 July 1960, as Amended by the Additional Protocol of 28 January 1964 and by the Protocol of 16 November 1982 (2004 treaty)
♦ Protocol to Amend the Convention on Third Party Liability in the Field of Nuclear Energy of 29th July 1960, as Amended by the Additional Protocol of 28th January 1964 (1982 treaty)
♦ Protocol to Amend the Convention for the Unification of Certain Rules Relating to International Carriage by Air (1955 treaty)
♦ Protocol to Amend the Convention for the Unification of Certain Rules Relating to International Carriage by Air Signed Warsaw on 12 October 1929 as Amended by the Protocol Done at The Hague on 28 September 1955 (1971 treaty)
♦ Protocol to Amend the Convention on Wetlands of International Importance Especially as Waterfowl Habitat (1982 treaty)
♦ Protocol amending the Additional Protocol to the Convention on the Transfer of Sentenced Persons (2017 treaty)
♦ Protocol Amending of the Additional Protocol to the "Eurocontrol" International Convention Relating to Cooperation for the Safety of Air Navigation, 1981 (1981 treaty)
♦ Protocol Amending the Agreement on the Protection of the Salmon in the Baltic Sea (1972 treaty)
♦ Protocol Amending the Agreements, Conventions and Protocols on Narcotic Drugs (1946 treaty)
♦ Protocol Amending the Agreement for the Suppression of the Circulation of Obscene Publications (1949 treaty)
♦ Protocol Amending Article 1-a, Article 14-1 and Article 14-3b of the European Agreement of 30 September 1957 Concerning the International Carriage of Dangerous Goods by Road (1993 treaty)

♦ Protocol Amending the Benelux Convention on the Hunting and Protection of Birds (1977 treaty)
♦ Protocol amending the Benelux Convention on the Hunting and Protection of Birds, 2016 (2016 treaty)
♦ Protocol Amending the Convention on the Canalization of the Moselle (1974 treaty)
♦ Protocol Amending the Convention on the Limitation Period in the International Sale of Goods (1980 treaty)
♦ Protocol amending the Convention on Mutual Administrative Assistance in Tax Matters (2010 treaty)
♦ Protocol Amending the Convention for the Prevention of Marine Pollution by Dumping from Ships and Aircraft (1983 treaty)
♦ Protocol Amending the Convention for the Prevention of Marine Pollution from Land-based Sources, Kuwait (1990 treaty)
♦ Protocol Amending the Convention for the Prevention of Marine Pollution from Land-based Sources, Paris (1986 treaty)
♦ Protocol amending the Convention for the Protection of Individuals with regard to Automatic Processing of Personal Data (2018 treaty)
♦ Protocol Amending the Convention on the Reduction of Cases of Multiple Nationality and Military Obligations in Cases of Multiples Nationality (1977 treaty)
♦ Protocol Amending the European Agreement Concerning the International Carriage of Dangerous Goods by Rail (1975 treaty)
♦ Protocol Amending the European Agreement on the Restriction of the Use of Certain Detergents in Washing and Cleaning Products (1983 treaty)
♦ Protocol Amending the European Convention on the Suppression of Terrorism (2003 treaty)
♦ Protocol Amending the European Convention on Transfrontier Television (1998 treaty)
♦ Protocol amending the European Landscape Convention (2016 treaty)
♦ Protocol Amending the European Social Charter (1991 treaty)
♦ Protocol Amending the International Agreement for the Suppression of the White Slave Traffic (1949 treaty)
♦ Protocol Amending the International Convention for the Conservation of Atlantic Tunas, 1984 (1984 treaty)
♦ Protocol Amending the International Convention for the Conservation of Atlantic Tunas, 1992 (1992 treaty)
♦ Protocol Amending the International Convention for the High Seas Fisheries of the North Pacific Ocean (1978 treaty)
♦ Protocol Amending the International Convention Relating to Economic Statistics (1948 treaty)
♦ Protocol Amending the International Convention Relating to the Limitation of the Liability of Owners of Sea-going Ships (1979 treaty)
♦ Protocol Amending the International Convention for the Unification of Certain Rules Relating to Bills of Lading (1979 treaty)
♦ Protocol Amending the Single Convention on Narcotic Drugs (1972 treaty)
♦ Protocol Amending the Slavery Convention (1953 treaty)
♦ Protocol to Amend the International Convention on Civil Liability for Oil Pollution Damage, 1984 (1984 treaty)
♦ Protocol for the Amendment of the 1956 Agreement on the Joint Financing of Certain Air Navigation Services in Greenland and the Faeroe Islands (1982 treaty)
♦ Protocol for the Amendment of the 1956 Agreement on the Joint Financing of Certain Air Navigation Services in Iceland (1982 treaty)
♦ Protocol for the Amendment of the Additional Protocol to the "Eurocontrol" International Convention Relating to Cooperation for the Safety of Air Navigation, 1978 (1978 treaty)
♦ Protocol of Amendment to the Charter of the Organization of American States (1985 treaty)
♦ Protocol of Amendment to the Charter of the Organization of American States (1967 treaty)
♦ Protocol of Amendment to the Charter of the Organization of American States (1993 treaty)
♦ Protocol to an Amendment to the Convention on International Civil Aviation – Final Clause, Russian Text (1977 treaty)
♦ Protocol of Amendment to the Convention on the Nomenclature for the Classification of Goods in Customs Tariffs (1955 treaty)
♦ Protocol of Amendment to the European Convention for the Protection of Animals Kept for Farming Purposes (1992 treaty)
♦ Protocol of Amendment to the European Convention for the Protection of Vertebrate Animals Used for Experimental and other Scientific Purposes (1998 treaty)
♦ Protocol of Amendment to the Inter-American Treaty of Reciprocal Assistance (1975 treaty)
♦ Protocol of Amendment to the Inter-American Treaty of Regional Assistance (1975 treaty)
♦ Protocol of Amendments to the Charter of the Organization of American States (1992 treaty)
♦ Protocol to Amend the Vienna Convention on Civil Liability for Nuclear Damage (1997 treaty)
♦ Protocol to the American Convention on Human Rights to Abolish the Death Penalty (1990 treaty)
♦ Protocol to the Antarctic Treaty on Environmental Protection (1991 treaty)
♦ Protocol on Arbitration Clauses (1923 treaty)
♦ Protocol to the Athens Convention Relating to the Carriage of Passengers and Their Luggage by Sea, 1976 (1976 treaty)
♦ Protocol to the Athens Convention Relating to the Carriage of Passengers and Their Luggage by Sea, 1990 (1990 treaty)
♦ Protocol to the Athens Convention Relating to the Carriage of Passengers and Their Luggage by Sea, 2002 (2002 treaty)
♦ Protocol on the Authentic Quadrilingual Text of the Convention on International Civil Aviation, Chicago 1944 (1977 treaty)
♦ Protocol on the Authentic Quinquelingual Text of the Convention on International Civil Aviation, Chicago 1944 (1995 treaty)
♦ Protocol on the Authentic Six-language Text of the Convention on International Civil Aviation, Chicago 1944 (1998 treaty)
♦ Protocol on the Authentic Trilingual Text of the Convention on International Civil Aviation (1968 treaty)
♦ Protocol to the Belgo-Luxembourg-Netherlands Customs Convention, Signed at London on 5 Sep 1944 (1947 treaty)
♦ Protocol Bringing under International Control Drugs Outside the Scope of the Convention of 13 July 1931 (1948 treaty)
♦ Protocol of Buenos Aires – Protocol of Amendment to the Charter of the Organization of American States (1967 treaty)
♦ Protocol of Cartagena de Indias – Protocol of Amendment to the Charter of the Organization of American States (1985 treaty)
♦ Protocol to the Central American Agreement of Equalization of Import Charges (1964 treaty)
♦ Protocol to the Central American Agreement on Equalization of Import Charges, 1959 (1959 treaty)
♦ Protocol to the Central American Agreement on Equalization of Import Charges, 1960 (1960 treaty)
♦ Protocol to the Central American Agreement on Equalization of Import Charges, 1962 (1962 treaty)
♦ Protocol to the Central American Agreement on Equalization of Import Charges, 1963 (1963 treaty)
♦ Protocol to the Central American Agreement on Equalization of Import Charges, 1965 (1965 treaty)
♦ Protocol to the Central American Agreement on Fiscal Incentives to Industrial Development, 1966 (1966 treaty)
♦ Protocol on Civil Liability and Compensation for Damage Caused by the Transboundary Effects of Industrial Accidents on Transboundary Waters (2003 treaty)
♦ Protocol Concerning the Abolition of Passports for Travel (1952 treaty)
♦ Protocol Concerning the Adhesion of States Not Represented at the Fourth Conference on Private International Law, to the Convention of July 17 1905, Relating to the Conflicts of Laws with Regard to the Effects of Marriage (1923 treaty)
♦ Protocol Concerning the Adhesion of States Not Represented at the Fourth Conference on Private International Law to the Convention of July 17 1905, Relating to Deprivation of Civil Rights and Similar Measures of Protection (1923 treaty)
♦ Protocol Concerning the Adhesion of States Not Represented at the Third Conference on Private International Law to the Convention of June 12 1902, Regulating the Guardianship of Minors (1923 treaty)
♦ Protocol Concerning the Adhesion of States Not Represented at the Third Conference on Private International Law to the Convention of June 12 1902, Relating to the Settlement of the Conflict of Laws Concerning Marriage (1923 treaty)
♦ Protocol Concerning the Adhesion of States Not Represented at the Third Conference on Private International Law to the Convention of June 12 1902, Relating to the Settlement of the Conflicts of Laws and Jurisdictions as Regards Divorce and Separation (1923 treaty)
♦ Protocol Concerning Commercial Policy (1953 treaty)
♦ Protocol Concerning Cooperation in Combating Marine Pollution in Cases of Emergency in the Eastern African Region (1985 treaty)
♦ Protocol Concerning Cooperation in Combating Oil Spills in the Wider Caribbean Region (1983 treaty)
♦ Protocol Concerning Cooperation in Combating Pollution in Cases of Emergency (1981 treaty)
♦ Protocol Concerning Cooperation in Combating Pollution Emergencies in the South Pacific Region (1986 treaty)
♦ Protocol Concerning Cooperation in Combating Pollution of the Mediterranean Sea by Oil and other Harmful Substances in Cases of Emergency (1976 treaty)
♦ Protocol Concerning Cooperation in Preventing Pollution from Ships and, in Cases of Emergency, Combating Pollution of the Mediterranean Sea (2002 treaty)
♦ Protocol Concerning the Co-ordination of Economic and Social Policies (1953 treaty)
♦ Protocol Concerning Countries or Territories at Present Occupied (1949 treaty)
♦ Protocol Concerning the Exchange of Commodities (1950 treaty)
♦ Protocol Concerning the Exemption of Nationals of the Nordic Countries from the Obligation to Have a Passport or Residence Permit While Resident in a Nordic Country other than their Own (1954 treaty)
♦ Protocol Concerning Marine Pollution Resulting from Exploration and Exploitation of the Continental Shelf (1989 treaty)
♦ Protocol Concerning Mediterranean Specially Protected Areas (1982 treaty)
♦ Protocol Concerning Mutual Assistance in the Conduct of Legal Proceedings (1957 treaty)
♦ Protocol Concerning National Treatment in the Award of Public Works Contracts and the Purchase of Goods (1956 treaty)
♦ Protocol Concerning Pollution from Land-based Sources and Activities (1999 treaty)
♦ Protocol Concerning Protected Areas and Wild Fauna and Flora in the Eastern African Region (1985 treaty)
♦ Protocol Concerning Regional Cooperation in Combating Pollution by Oil and other Harmful Substances in Case of Emergency (1982 treaty)
♦ Protocol Concerning Regional Cooperation in Combating Pollution by Oil and other Harmful Substances in Cases of Emergency (1978 treaty)
♦ Protocol Concerning Specially Protected Areas and Biological Diversity in the Mediterranean (1995 treaty)
♦ Protocol Concerning Specially Protected Areas and Wildlife to the Convention for the Protection and Development of the Marine Environment of the Wider Caribbean Region (1990 treaty)
♦ Protocol to the Conference of the States Parties to the Convention on Fishing and Conservation of Living Resources in the Baltic Sea and the Belts (1982 treaty)
♦ Protocol for the Conservation and Management of Protected Marine and Coastal Areas of the Southeast Pacific (1989 treaty)
♦ Protocol on the Control of Marine Transboundary Movements and Disposal of Hazardous Wastes (1998 treaty)
♦ Protocol to the Convention concerning night work of women (1990 treaty)
♦ Protocol to the Convention on the Contract for the International Carriage of Goods by Road (1978 treaty)
♦ Protocol to the Convention on the Contract for the International Carriage of Passengers and Luggage by Inland Waterways (1978 treaty)
♦ Protocol to the Convention on the Contract for the International Carriage of Passengers and Luggage by Road (1978 treaty)
♦ Protocol to the Convention on Duties and Rights of States in the Event of Civil Strife (1957 treaty)
♦ Protocol to the Convention on the Elaboration of a European Pharmacopoeia (1989 treaty)
♦ Protocol to the Convention on Insider Trading (1989 treaty)
♦ Protocol to the Convention on International Interests in Mobile Equipment on Matters Specific to Aircraft Equipment (2001 treaty)
♦ Protocol to the Convention on International Interests in Mobile Equipment on Matters Specific to Space Assets (2012 treaty)
♦ Protocol to the Convention on Long-range Transboundary Air Pollution on Heavy Metals (1998 treaty)
♦ Protocol to the Convention on Long Range Transboundary Air Pollution on Persistent Organic Pollutants (1998 treaty)
♦ Protocol a la Convention de l'OUA sur la prévention et la lutte contre le terrorisme (2004 treaty)
♦ Protocol to the Convention for the Protection of Human Rights and Fundamental Freedoms (1952 treaty)
♦ Protocol to the Convention Relating to the Limitation of Liability of Owners of Inland Navigation Vessels (1978 treaty)
♦ Protocol on Cooperation in Combating Pollution of the Black Sea Marine Environment by Oil and other Harmful Substances in Emergency Situations (1992 treaty)
♦ Protocol and Diplomacy International – Protocol Officers Association (internationally oriented national body)
♦ Protocole de 1978 relatif à la Convention internationale de 1974 pour la sauvegarde de la vie humaine en mer (1978 treaty)
♦ Protocole de 1988 relatif à la Convention internationale pour la sauvegarde de la vie humaine en mer (1988 treaty)
♦ Protocole de 1996 à la Convention de 1972 sur la prévention de la pollution des mers résultant de l' immersion de déchets (1996 treaty)
♦ Protocole de 1997 relatif à la Convention internationale pour la prévention de la pollution par les navires (1997 treaty)
♦ Protocole à l'Accord centroaméricain relatif aux stimulants fiscaux du développement industriel, 1966 (1966 treaty)
♦ Protocole d' accord concernant la conservation des ressources naturelles communes (1982 treaty)
♦ Protocole à l'Accord pour l'importation d'objets de caractère éducatif, scientifique et culturel (1976 treaty)
♦ Protocole D'accord entre les Pays Producteurs de Café de la Zone Franc (1960 treaty)
♦ Protocole additionnel à l'Accord concernant la coopération régionale dans la lutte contre la pollution par les hydrocarbones et autres substances nuisibles dans le Pacifique du Sud-Est (1983 treaty)
♦ Protocole additionnel à l'Accord européen sur l'échange de réactifs pour la détermination des groupes tissulaires (1976 treaty)
♦ Protocole additionnel à l'Accord européen relatif à l'échange des réactifs pour la détermination des groupes sanguins (1983 treaty)
♦ Protocole additionnel à l'Accord européen relatif à l'échange de substances thérapeutiques d'origine humaine (1983 treaty)
♦ Protocole additionnel à l'Accord européen sur la transmission des demandes d'assistance judiciaire (2001 treaty)
♦ Protocole additionnel à l'Accord général sur les privilèges et immunités du Conseil de l'Europe (1952 treaty)
♦ Protocole additionnel à l'Accord pour l'importation temporaire en franchise de douane, à titre de prêt gratuit et à des fins diagnostiques ou thérapeutiques, de matériel médico-chirurgical et de laboratoire destiné aux établissements sanitaires (1983 treaty)

♦ Protocole additionnel à l'accord intérimaire européen concernant les régimes de sécurité sociale relatifs à la vieillesse, à l'invalidité et aux survivants (1953 treaty)
♦ Protocole additionnel à l'Accord intérimaire européen concernant la sécurité sociale à l'exclusion des régimes relatifs à la vieillesse, à l'invalidité et aux survivants (1953 treaty)
♦ Protocole additionnel à la Charte européenne de l'autonomie locale sur le droit de participer aux affaires des collectivités locales (2009 treaty)
♦ Protocole additionnel à la charte sociale européenne, 1988 (1988 treaty)
♦ Protocole additionnel à la Charte sociale européenne prévoyant un système de réclamations collectives (1995 treaty)
♦ Protocole additionnel à la Convention du 31 janvier 1963 complémentaire à la Convention de Paris du 29 juillet 1960 sur la responsabilité civile dans le domaine de l' énergie nucléaire (1964 treaty)
♦ Protocole additionnel à la Convention américaine relative aux droits de l'homme traitant des droits économiques, sociaux et culturels (1988 treaty)
♦ Protocole additionnel à la Convention-cadre européenne sur la coopération transfrontalière des collectivités ou autorités territoriales (1995 treaty)
♦ Protocole additionnel à la Convention du Conseil de l'Europe pour la prévention du terrorisme (2015 treaty)
♦ Protocole additionnel à la Convention contre le dopage (2002 treaty)
♦ Protocole additionnel à la Convention sur la cybercriminalité, relatif à l'incrimination d'actes de nature raciste et xénophobe commis par le biais de systèmes informatiques (2003 treaty)
♦ Protocole additionnel à la Convention sur les droits de l'homme et la biomédecine, relatif à la recherche biomédicale (2005 treaty)
♦ Protocole additionnel à la Convention sur les Droits de l'Homme et la biomédecine relatif aux tests génétiques à des fins médicales (2008 treaty)
♦ Protocole additionnel à la Convention sur les droits de l'homme et la biomédecine relatif à la transplantation d'organes et de tissus d'origine humaine (2002 treaty)
♦ Protocole additionnel à la Convention européenne d'assistance sociale et médicale (1953 treaty)
♦ Protocole additionnel à la Convention européenne dans le domaine de l'information sur le droit étranger (1978 treaty)
♦ Protocole additionnel à la Convention européenne d'entraide judiciaire en matière pénale (1978 treaty)
♦ Protocole additionnel à la Convention européenne d'extradition (1975 treaty)
♦ Protocole additionnel à la Convention européenne sur l'immunité des Etats (1972 treaty)
♦ Protocole additionnel à la Convention européenne sur la protection des animaux en transport international (1979 treaty)
♦ Protocole additionnel à la Convention européenne relative à l'équivalence des diplômes donnant accès aux établissements universitaires (1964 treaty)
♦ Protocole additionnel à la Convention sur les facilités douanières en faveur du tourisme relatif à l'importation de documents et matériel de propagande touristique (1954 treaty)
♦ Protocole additionnel à la Convention générale de conciliation interaméricaine de 1929 (1933 treaty)
♦ Protocole additionnel à la Convention pénale sur la corruption (2003 treaty)
♦ Protocole additionnel à la Convention pour la protection des personnes à l'égard du traitement automatisé des données à caractère personnel, concernant les autorités de contrôle et les flux transfrontières de données (2001 treaty)
♦ Protocole additionnel à la Convention sur la réduction des cas de pluralité de nationalités et sur les obligations militaires en cas de pluralité de nationalités (1977 treaty)
♦ Protocole additionnel à la Convention sur le régime des voies navigables d'intérêt international (1921 treaty)
♦ Protocole additionnel à la Convention relative à la protection du Rhin contre la pollution par les chlorures (1991 treaty)
♦ Protocole additionnel à la Convention sur la responsabilité civile dans le domaine de l' énergie nucléaire (1964 treaty)
♦ Protocole additionnel à la Convention de sauvegarde des droits de l'homme et de la dignité de l'être humain à l'égard des applications de la biologie et de la médecine, portant interdiction du clonage d'êtres humains (1998 treaty)
♦ Protocole additionnel à la Convention de sauvegarde des droits de l'homme et des libertés fondamentales (1952 treaty)
♦ Protocole additionnel aux Conventions de Genève du 12 août 1949 relatif à la protection des victimes des conflits armés internationaux (1977 treaty)
♦ Protocole additionnel à la Convention sur le transfèrement des personnes condamnées (1997 treaty)
♦ Protocole additionnel facultatif à la Convention internationale des télécommunications (1973 treaty)
♦ Protocole additionnel II aux quatre Conventions de Genève relatif à la protection des victimes des conflits armés non internationaux (1977 treaty)
♦ Protocole additionnel de Nagoya – Kuala Lumpur sur la responsabilité et la réparation relatif au Protocole de Cartagena sur la prévention des risques biotechnologiques (2010 treaty)
♦ Protocole additionnel au Protocole à l'Arrangement européen pour la protection des émissions de télévision (1983 treaty)
♦ Protocole additionnel au Protocole à l'Arrangement européen pour la protection des émissions de télévision, 1974 (1974 treaty)
♦ Protocole additionnel relatif au Code sanitaire panaméricain, 1927 (1927 treaty)
♦ Protocole additionnel relatif au Code sanitaire panaméricain, 1952 (1952 treaty)
♦ Protocole additionnel relatif à la non-intervention (1936 treaty)
♦ Protocole D'adhésion de la Principauté de Monaco à la Convention sur la Protection des Alpes (1994 treaty)
♦ Protocole adicional à Convenção americana sobre direitos humanos em matéria de direitos econômicos, sociais e culturais (1988 treaty)
♦ Protocole amendant les accords, conventions et protocoles sur les stupéfiants (1946 treaty)
♦ Protocole amendant l'Arrangement relatif à la répression de la circulation des publications obscènes (1949 treaty)
♦ Protocole amendant la Convention relative à l'esclavage (1953 treaty)
♦ Protocole amendant la Convention pour la répression de la circulation et du trafic des publications obscènes (1947 treaty)
♦ Protocole amendant la Convention pour la répression de la traite des femmes et des enfants (1947 treaty)
♦ Protocole d'amendement à la Convention concernant l'assistance administrative mutuelle en matière fiscale (2010 treaty)
♦ Protocole d'amendement à la Convention européenne sur la protection des animaux dans les élevages (1992 treaty)
♦ Protocole d'amendement à la Convention européenne sur la protection des animaux vertébrés utilisés à des fins expérimentales ou à d'autres fins scientifiques (1998 treaty)
♦ Protocole d'amendement de la convention pour la prévention de la marine d'origine tellurique, Kuwait (1990 treaty)
♦ Protocole d'amendement de la convention pour la prévention de la pollution marine d' origine tellurique, Paris (1986 treaty)
♦ Protocole d'amendements de la Charte de l'Organisation des Etats américains (1985 treaty)
♦ Protocole annexe 1 à la Convention universelle sur le droit d'auteur, 1971 (1971 treaty)
♦ Protocole annexe 1 à la Convention universelle sur le droit d'auteur concernant la protection des oeuvres des personnes apatrides et des réfugiés, 1952 (1952 treaty)
♦ Protocole annexe 2 à la Convention universelle sur le droit d'auteur, 1971 (1971 treaty)
♦ Protocole annexe 2 à la Convention universelle sur le droit d'auteur concernant l'application de la Convention aux oeuvres de certaines organisations internationales, 1952 (1952 treaty)
♦ Protocole annexe 3 à la Convention universelle sur le droit d'auteur (1952 treaty)
♦ Protocole D'application de la Convention Alpine de 1991 dans le Domaine de L' Energie (1998 treaty)
♦ Protocole d'application de la Convention alpine de 1991 dans la domaine des forêts de montagne (1996 treaty)
♦ Protocole de L'application de la Convention Alpine de 1991 dans le Domaine de la Protection des Sols (1998 treaty)
♦ Protocole D'application de la Convention Alpine de 1991 dans le Domaine du Tourisme (1998 treaty)
♦ Protocole d' application de la Convention alpine dans le domaine de l' agriculture de montagne (1994 treaty)
♦ Protocole d'application de la Convention alpine dans le domaine de l'aménagement du territoire et du développement durable (1994 treaty)
♦ Protocole d' application de la Convention alpine dans le domaine de la protection de la nature et de l' entretien des paysages (1994 treaty)
♦ Protocole d'application de la convention alpine dans le domaine des transports (2000 treaty)
♦ Protocole d'arbitrage progressif (1929 treaty)
♦ Protocole à l'Arrangement européen pour la protection des émissions de télévision (1965 treaty)
♦ Protocole de Bâle sur la responsabilité et l'indemnisation en cas de dommages résultant de mouvements transfrontières et de l'élimination de déchets dangereux (1999 treaty)
♦ Protocole de Cartagena de Indias – Protocole d'amendements de la Charte de l'Organisation des Etats américains (1985 treaty)
♦ Protocole de Cartagena sur la prévention des risques biotechnologiques relatif à la Convention sur la diversité biologique (2000 treaty)
♦ Protocole de la Charte de l'énergie sur l' efficacité énergétique et les aspects environnementaux connexes (1994 treaty)
♦ Protocole au Code européen de sécurité sociale (1964 treaty)
♦ Protocole commun relatif à l'application de la Convention de Vienne et de la Convention de Paris (1988 treaty)
♦ Protocole comportant une déclaration sur la personnalité juridique des sociétés étrangères (1936 treaty)
♦ Protocole concernant l'adhésion des Etats non représentés à la Quatrième conférence du 17 juillet 1905, relative à l'interdiction et aux mesures de protection analogues (1923 treaty)
♦ Protocole concernant l'adhésion des Etats non représentés à la Troisième conférence de droit international privé, à la Convention du 12 Juin 1902, relative au règlement des conflits de lois et de juridictions en matière de divorce et de séparation de corps (1923 treaty)
♦ Protocole concernant l'adhésion des Etats non représentés à la Troisième conférence de droit international privé à la Convention du 12 juin 1902, relative au règlement des conflits de lois en matière de mariage (1923 treaty)
♦ Protocole concernant l'adhésion des Etats non représentés à la troisième Conférence de droit international privé, à la Convention du 12 juin 1902 relative au règlement de la tutelle des mineurs (1923 treaty)
♦ Protocole concernant un amendement à la Convention relative à l'aviation civile internationale, article 45 (1954 treaty)
♦ Protocole concernant un amendement à la Convention relative à l'aviation civile internationale, article 48a (1962 treaty)
♦ Protocole concernant un amendement à la Convention relative à l'aviation civile internationale, article 56 (1989 treaty)
♦ Protocole concernant un amendement à la Convention relative à l'aviation internationale, article 3bis (1984 treaty)
♦ Protocole concernant un amendement à la Convention relative à l'aviation internationale, article 50a (1990 treaty)
♦ Protocole concernant un amendement à la Convention relative à l'aviation internationale, article 56 (1971 treaty)
♦ Protocole concernant un amendement à la Convention relative à l' aviation internationale, article 83bis (1980 treaty)
♦ Protocole concernant un amendement à la Convention relative à l'aviation internationale, article 93bis (1947 treaty)
♦ Protocole concernant un amendement à la Convention relative à l'aviation internationale, articles 48a, 49e, 61 (1954 treaty)
♦ Protocole concernant la compétence judiciaire et l'exécution des décisions en matière civile et commerciale (1971 treaty)
♦ Protocole concernant la conservation et la gestion des aires marines protégées du Pacifique du Sud-Est (1989 treaty)
♦ Protocole concernant l'entraide judiciaire (1957 treaty)
♦ Protocole concernant la pollution marine causée par l' exploration et à l' exploitation du plateau continental (1989 treaty)
♦ Protocole concernant la prohibition d'emploi à la guerre de gaz asphyxiants, toxiques ou similaires et de moyens bactériologiques (1925 treaty)
♦ Protocole concernant la protection du Pacifique du Sud-Est contre la pollution radioactive (1989 treaty)
♦ Protocole concernant le renouvellement de la Convention géodésique baltique (1936 treaty)
♦ Protocole concernant le texte authentique quinquélingue de la Convention relative à l'aviation civile internationale, Chicago 1944 (1995 treaty)
♦ Protocole concernant le texte authentique trilingue de la Convention relative à l'aviation civile internationale (1968 treaty)
♦ Protocole concernant le traitement national en matière d'adjudications de travaux et d'achats de marchandises (1956 treaty)
♦ Protocole contre la fabrication et le trafic illicites d'armes à feu, de leurs pièces, éléments et munitions (2001 treaty)
♦ Protocole contre le trafic illicite de migrants par terre, air et mer (2000 treaty)
♦ Protocole à la Convention de 1979 sur la pollution atmosphérique transfrontière à longue distance, relatif à la réduction de l'acidification, de l'eutrophisation et de l'ozone troposphérique (1999 treaty)
♦ Protocole de la Convention d'Athènes relative au transport par mer de passagers et leurs bagages, 1976 (1976 treaty)
♦ Protocole de la Convention d'Athènes relative au transport par mer de passagers et leurs bagages, 1990 (1990 treaty)
♦ Protocole de la Convention d'Athènes relative au transport par mer de passagers et leurs bagages, 2002 (2002 treaty)
♦ Protocole à la Convention sur les devoirs et les droits des états en cas de luttes civiles (1957 treaty)
♦ Protocole à la Convention douanière belgo-luxembourgeoise-néerlandaise, signée à Londres le 5 septembre 1944 (1947 treaty)
♦ Protocole à la Convention européenne sur les fonctions consulaires relatif aux fonctions consulaires en matière d'aviation civile (1967 treaty)
♦ Protocole à la Convention européenne sur les fonctions consulaires relatif à la protection des réfugiés (1967 treaty)
♦ Protocole à la Convention européenne de sécurité sociale (1994 treaty)
♦ Protocole à la Convention internationale pour la réglementation de la chasse à la baleine (1956 treaty)
♦ Protocole de la Convention internationale sur la responsabilité civile pour les dommages dus à la pollution par les hydrocarbure, 1976 (1976 treaty)
♦ Protocole à la Convention sur les opérations financières des "initiés" (1989 treaty)
♦ Protocole à la Convention sur la pollution atmosphérique à longue distance relatif à une nouvelle réduction des émissions de soufre (1994 treaty)
♦ Protocole à la Convention sur la pollution atmosphérique transfrontière à longue distance de 1979, relatif à la lutte contre les émissions des composés organiques volatils ou leurs flux transfrontières (1991 treaty)

♦ Protocole à la Convention sur la pollution atmosphérique transfrontière à longue distance de 1979, relatif à la lutte contre les émissions d'oxydes d'azote ou de leurs flux transfrontières (1988 treaty)
♦ Protocole à la Convention sur la pollution atmosphérique transfrontière à longue distance, relatif au financement à long terme du programme concerté de surveillance continue et d'évaluation du transport à longue distance des polluants atmosphériques en Europe (1984 treaty)
♦ Protocole à la Convention sur la pollution atmosphérique transfrontière à longue distance, relatif aux métaux lourds (1998 treaty)
♦ Protocole à la Convention sur la pollution atmosphérique transfrontière à longue distance, relatif aux pollutants organiques persistants (1998 treaty)
♦ Protocole à la Convention sur la pollution atmosphérique transfrontière à longue distance relatif à la réduction des émissions de soufre ou de leurs flux transfrontières d'au moins 30 pour cent (1985 treaty)
♦ Protocole à la Convention relative au contrat de transport international de marchandises par route (1978 treaty)
♦ Protocole à la Convention relative au contrat de transport international de marchandises par route (1978 treaty)
♦ Protocole à la Convention relative à l'élaboration d'une pharmacopée européenne (1989 treaty)
♦ Protocole à la Convention relative au régime des industries centroaméricaines d'intégration économique (1963 treaty)
♦ Protocole de coopération dans les interventions d' urgence contre les incidents générateurs de pollution dans la région du Pacifique Sud (1986 treaty)
♦ Protocole sur l'eau at la santé à la Convention de 1992 sur la protection et l'utilisation des cours d'eau transfrontières et des lacs internationaux (1999 treaty)
♦ Protocole pour éliminer le commerce illicite des produits du tabac (2012 treaty)
♦ Protocole sur les emménagements à bord des navires à passagers qui effectuent des transports spéciaux (1973 treaty)
♦ Protocole sur l'enregistrement interaméricain des marques de fabrique (1929 treaty)
♦ Protocole pour l'établissement d'un nouveau tarif des droits d'entrée (1958 treaty)
♦ Protocole facultatif concernant la répression du faux monnayage (1929 treaty)
♦ Protocole facultatif à la Convention sur l'élimination de toutes les formes de discrimination à l'égard des femmes (1999 treaty)
♦ Protocole facultatif à la Convention relative aux droits de l'enfant et concernant la participation des enfants aux conflits armés (2000 treaty)
♦ Protocole facultatif à la Convention relative aux droits de l'enfant, concernant la vente d'enfants, la prostitution des enfants et la pornographie mettant en scène des enfants (2000 treaty)
♦ Protocole facultatif se rapportant au Pacte international relatif aux droits civils et politiques (1966 treaty)
♦ Protocole Facultatif se Rapportant au Pacte International Relatif aux Droits Économiques, Sociaux et Culturels (2008 treaty)
♦ Protocole I à la Convention pour l' interdiction de la pêche au filet maillant dérivant de grande dimension dans le Pacifique Sud (1990 treaty)
♦ Protocole II à la Convention pour l' interdiction de la pêche au filet maillant dérivant de grande dimension dans le Pacifique Sud (1990 treaty)
♦ Protocole sur l'intervention en haute mer en cas de pollution par des substances autres que les hydrocarbures (1973 treaty)
♦ Protocol to Eliminate Illicit Trade in Tobacco Products (2012 treaty)
♦ Protocole sur les marques routières (1973 treaty)
♦ Protocol Embodying a Declaration Concerning the Juridical Personality of Foreign Companies (1936 treaty)
♦ Protocole mettant fin aux arrangements de Bruxelles pour l'unification de la formule des médicaments héroïques (1952 treaty)
♦ Protocole Modifiant La Convention Benelux en matière de chasse et de protection des oiseaux (2016 treaty)
♦ Protocole modifiant la Convention Benelux en matière de chasse et de protection des oiseaux (1977 treaty)
♦ Protocole modifiant la Convention internationale concernant les pêcheries hauturières de l' Océan Pacifique Nord (1978 treaty)
♦ Protocole modifiant la Convention internationale concernant les statistiques économiques (1948 treaty)
♦ Protocole modifiant la Convention internationale sur la responsabilité civile por les dommages dus à la pollution par les hydrocarbures, 1984 (1984 treaty)
♦ Protocole modifiant la Convention pour la prévention de la pollution marine par les opérations d'immersion effectuées par les navires et aéronefs (1983 treaty)
♦ Protocole de Montréal relatif à des substances qui appauvrissent la couche d'ozone (1987 treaty)
♦ Protocole no 10 à la Convention de sauvegarde des droits de l'homme et les libertés fondamentales (1992 treaty)
♦ Protocole no 11 à la Convention de sauvegarde des droits de l'homme et les libertés fondamentales (1994 treaty)
♦ Protocole no 12 à la Convention de sauvegarde des droits de l'homme et les libertés fondamentales (2000 treaty)
♦ Protocole no 13 à la Convention de sauvegarde des droits de l'homme et des libertés fondamentales, relatif à l'abolition de la peine de mort en toutes circonstances (2002 treaty)
♦ Protocole no 14bis à la Convention de sauvegarde des Droits de l'Homme et des Libertés fondamentales (inactive)
♦ Protocole no 14 à la Convention de sauvegarde des droits de l'homme et des libertés fondamentales, amendant le système de contrôle de la convention (2004 treaty)
♦ Protocole no 15 portant amendement à la Convention de sauvegarde des Droits de l'Homme et des Libertés fondamentales (2013 treaty)
♦ Protocole no 16 à la Convention de sauvegarde des Droits de l'Homme et des Libertés fondamentales (2013 treaty)
♦ Protocole no 1 à la Convention européenne pour la prévention de la torture et des peines ou traitements inhumains ou dégradants (1993 treaty)
♦ Protocole no 2 à la Convention-cadre européenne sur la coopération transfrontalière des collectivités ou autorités territoriales relatif à la coopération interterritoriale (1998 treaty)
♦ Protocole no 2 à la Convention européenne pour la prévention de la torture et des peines ou traitements inhumains ou dégradants (1993 treaty)
♦ Protocole no 2 à la Convention de sauvegarde des droits de l'homme et des libertés fondamentales (1963 treaty)
♦ Protocole no 3 à la Convention-cadre européenne sur la coopération transfrontalière des collectivités ou autorités territoriales relatif aux Groupements eurorégionaux de coopération – GEC (2009 treaty)
♦ Protocole no 3 à la Convention de sauvegarde des droits de l'homme et des libertés fondamentales, modifiant les articles 29, 30 et 34 de la Convention (1963 treaty)
♦ Protocole no 4 à la Convention de sauvegarde des droits de l'homme et des libertés fondamentales, reconnaissant certains droits et libertés autres que ceux figurant déjà dans la Convention et dans le premier Protocole additionnel à la Convention (1963 treaty)
♦ Protocole no 5 à la Convention de sauvegarde des droits de l'homme et des libertés fondamentales (1966 treaty)
♦ Protocole no 6 à la Convention de sauvegarde des droits de l'homme et des libertés fondamentales concernant l'abolition de la peine de mort (1983 treaty)
♦ Protocole no 7 à la Convention de sauvegarde des droits de l'homme et des libertés fondamentales (1984 treaty)
♦ Protocole no 8 à la Convention de sauvegarde des droits de l'homme et des libertés fondamentales (1985 treaty)
♦ Protocole no 9 à la Convention de sauvegarde des droits de l'homme et des libertés fondamentales (1990 treaty)
♦ Protocole plaçant sous contrôle international certaines drogues non visées par la Convention du 13 juillet 1931 (1948 treaty)
♦ Protocole portant amendement à l'Accord européen sur le limitation de l'emploi de certains détergents dans les produits de lavage et de nettoyage (1983 treaty)
♦ Protocole portant amendement de l'Accord européen relatif au transport international des marchandises dangereuses par route (1975 treaty)
♦ Protocole portant amendement de l'Accord sur la protection du saumon dans la mer Baltique (1972 treaty)
♦ Protocole portant amendement des articles 1-a, 14-1 et 14-3b de l'accord européen du 30 septembre 1957 relatif au transport international des marchandises dangereuses par route (1993 treaty)
♦ Protocole portant amendement à la Charte sociale européenne (1991 treaty)
♦ Protocole portant amendement à la Convention européenne pour la répression du terrorisme (2003 treaty)
♦ Protocole portant amendement à la Convention internationale sur la responsabilité civile pour des dommages dus à la pollution par les hydrocarbures (1992 treaty)
♦ Protocole portant amendement à la Convention relative à l'aviation civile internationale, article 50a (1971 treaty)
♦ Protocole portant amendement à la Convention relative à l'aviation civile internationale, article 50a (1974 treaty)
♦ Protocole portant amendement à la Convention relative à l'aviation civile internationale, article 50a (1961 treaty)
♦ Protocole portant amendement à la Convention au sujet de la canalisation de la Moselle (1974 treaty)
♦ Protocole portant amendement à la Convention unique sur les stupéfiants (1972 treaty)
♦ Protocole portant modification de la Convention du 29 juillet 1960 sur la responsabilité civile dans le domaine de l' énergie nucléaire, amendée par le protocole additionnel du 28 janvier 1964 (1982 treaty)
♦ Protocole portant modification de la convention du 29 juillet 1960 sur la responsabilité civile dans le domaine de l'énergie nucléaire, amendée par le protocole additionnel du 28 janvier 1964 et par le protocole du 16 novembre 1982 (2004 treaty)
♦ Protocole portant modification de la Convention du 31 janvier 1963 complémentaire à la Convention de Paris du 29 juillet 1960 sur la responsabilité civile dans le domaine de l' énergie nucléaire, amendée par le protocole additionnel du 28 janvier 1964 (1982 treaty)
♦ Protocole portant modification de la convention du 31 janvier 1963 complémentaire à la convention de Paris du 29 juillet 1960 sur la responsabilité civile dans le domaine de l'énergie nucléaire, amendée par le protocole additionnel du 28 janvier 1964 et par le protocole du 16 novembre 1982 (2001 treaty)
♦ Protocole portant modification de la Convention internationale sur la limitation de la responsabilité des propriétaires de navires de mer (1979 treaty)
♦ Protocole portant modification de la Convention internationale pour l'unification de certaines règles en matière de connaissement (1968 treaty)
♦ Protocole portant modification de la Convention internationale pour l'unification de certaines règles en matière de connaissement (1979 treaty)
♦ Protocole portant modification à la Convention sur la réduction des cas de pluralité des nationalités et sur les obligations militaires en cas de pluralité de nationalités (1977 treaty)
♦ Protocole portant modification de la Convention pour l'unification de certaines règles relatives au transport aérien international (1955 treaty)
♦ Protocole sur la prévention de la pollution de la région du Pacifique Sud résultant de l' immersion des déchets (1986 treaty)
♦ Protocole prorogeant la durée de la Convention sanitaire internationale de 1944 (1946 treaty)
♦ Protocole prorogeant la durée de la Convention sanitaire internationale pour la navigation aérienne (1946 treaty)
♦ Protocole pour la protection des biens culturels en cas de conflit armé (1954 treaty)
♦ Protocole sur la protection de l'environnement dans l'Antarctique (1991 treaty)
♦ Protocole de rectification à la Convention sur la nomenclature pour la classification des marchandises dans les tarifs douaniers (1955 treaty)
♦ Protocole pour la réglementation de la chasse à la baleine (1945 treaty)
♦ Protocole relatif aux aires spécialement protégées et à la diversité biologique en Méditerranée (1995 treaty)
♦ Protocole relatif aux aires spécialement protégées de la Méditerranée (1982 treaty)
♦ Protocole relatif à l'Arrangement de Madrid concernant l'enregistrement international des marques (1989 treaty)
♦ Protocole relatif à un cas d'apatride (1930 treaty)
♦ Protocole relatif à certaines concessions accordées dans l'Empire ottoman et déclaration (1923 treaty)
♦ Protocole relatif aux clauses d'arbitrage (1923 treaty)
♦ Protocole relatif à la coopération en matière de lutte contre les déversements d' hydrocarbures dans la région des Caraïbes (1983 treaty)
♦ Protocole relatif à la coopération en matière de lutte contre la pollution en cas de situation critique (1981 treaty)
♦ Protocole relatif à la coopération en matière de lutte contre la pollution de la mer Méditerranée par les hydrocarbures et autres substances nuisibles en cas de situation critique (1976 treaty)
♦ Protocole relatif à la coopération en matière de lutte contre la pollution des mers en cas de situation critique (1985 treaty)
♦ Protocole relatif à la coopération en matière de prévention de la pollution par les navires et, en cas de situation critique, de lutte contre la pollution de la Méditerranée (2002 treaty)
♦ Protocole relatif à la coopération régionale en matière de lutte contre la pollution par les hydrocarbures et autres substances nuisibles en cas de situation critique (1978 treaty)
♦ Protocole relatif aux échanges commerciaux (1950 treaty)
♦ Protocole relatif aux marins réfugiés (1973 treaty)
♦ Protocole relatif aux mesures à prendre contre le mouvement anarchiste (1904 treaty)
♦ Protocole relatif aux obligations militaires dans certains cas de double nationalité (1930 treaty)
♦ Protocole relatif à la politique commerciale (1953 treaty)
♦ Protocole relatif à la pollution due à des sources et activités terrestres (1999 treaty)
♦ Protocole relatif à la prévention de la pollution de la mer Méditerranée par les mouvements transfrontières de déchets dangereux et leur élimination (1996 treaty)
♦ Protocole relatif à la protection de la mer Méditerranée contre la pollution résultant de l'exploration et de l'exploitation du plateau continental, du fond de la mer et de son sous-sol (1994 treaty)
♦ Protocole relatif à la protection du Pacifique Sud contre la pollution d'origine tellurique (1983 treaty)
♦ Protocole relatif au statut des réfugiés (1967 treaty)
♦ Protocole relatif à la suppression des passeports pour les voyages (1952 treaty)
♦ Protocole relatif au Territoire de Karagatch, ainsi qu'aux Iles de Imbros et Ténédos (1923 treaty)
♦ Protocole relatif aux zones protégées ainsi qu' à la faune et la flore sauvages dans la région de l' Afrique orientale (1985 treaty)
♦ Protocole sur la responsabilité civile et l'indemnisation en cas de dommages causés par les effets transfrontières d'accidents industriels sur les eaux transfrontières (2003 treaty)
♦ Protocole de signature facultative concernant le règlement obligatoire des différends (1958 treaty)
♦ Protocole de signature facultative à la Convention de Vienne sur les relations consulaires, concernant l'acquisition de la nationalité (1963 treaty)
♦ Protocole de signature facultative à la Convention de Vienne sur les relations consulaires, concernant le règlement obligatoire des différends (1963 treaty)

- ♦ Protocole de signature facultative à la Convention de Vienne sur les relations diplomatiques, concernant l'acquisition de la nationalité (1961 treaty)
- ♦ Protocole de signature facultative à la Convention de Vienne sur les relations diplomatiques, concernant le règlement obligatoire des différends (1961 treaty)
- ♦ Protocole spécial sur les céréales de base (1965 treaty)
- ♦ Protocole au sujet de l'adhésion des Etats non représentés à la Quatrième conférence de droit international privé, à la Convention du 17 juillet 1905, concernant les conflits de lois relatifs aux effets du mariage (1923 treaty)
- ♦ Protocole au Traité concernant la neutralité permanente et le fonctionnement du canal de Panama, 1977 (1977 treaty)
- ♦ Protocole au Traité général d'intégration économique de l'Amérique centrale – dispositions d'urgence en vue du maintien de la balance des paiements, 1968 (1968 treaty)
- ♦ Protocole au traité instituant la Communauté économique africaine, relatif à la libre circulation des personnes, au droit de résidence et au droit d'établissement (2018 treaty)
- ♦ Protocole aux traités concernant la délimitation du plateau continental sous la Mer du Nord (1971 treaty)
- ♦ Protocole sur l'uniformité des procurations destinées à être employées à l'extérieur (1940 treaty)
- ♦ Protocol to the European Agreement on the Protection of Television Broadcasts (1965 treaty)
- ♦ Protocol to the European Agreement on Social Security Schemes Relating to Old Age, Invalidity and Survivors (1953 treaty)
- ♦ Protocol to the European Code of Social Security (1964 treaty)
- ♦ Protocol to the European Convention on Consular Functions Concerning the Protection of Refugees (1967 treaty)
- ♦ Protocol to the European Convention on Consular Functions Relating to Consular Functions in Respect of Civil Aircraft (1967 treaty)
- ♦ Protocol to the European Convention on the Equivalence of Diplomas Leading to Admission to Universities (1964 treaty)
- ♦ Protocol to the European Convention on the Protection of the Audiovisual Heritage, on the Protection of Television Productions (2001 treaty)
- ♦ Protocol to the European Convention on Social and Medical Assistance (1953 treaty)
- ♦ Protocol to the European Convention on Social Security (1994 treaty)
- ♦ Protocol to the European Interim Agreement on Social Security other Than Schemes for Old Age, Invalidity and Survivors (1953 treaty)
- ♦ Protocole visant à limiter et à réglementer la culture du pavot, ainsi que la production, le commerce international, le commerce de gros et l'emploi de l'opium (1953 treaty)
- ♦ Protocole visant à prévenir, réprimer et punir la traite des personnes, en particulier des femmes et des enfants (2000 treaty)
- ♦ Protocole en vue d'amender la Convention relative aux zones humides d'importance internationale particulièrement comme habitats de la sauvagine (1982 treaty)
- ♦ Protocol for Extending the Period of Validity of the Convention on the Declaration of Death of Missing Persons (1957 treaty)
- ♦ Protocole sur les zones et la vie sauvage spécialement protégées à la Convention pour la protection et la mise en valeur du milieu marin de la région des Caraïbes (1990 treaty)
- ♦ Protocol facultatif se rapportant à la Convention contre la torture et autres peines ou traitements cruels, inhumains ou dégradants (2002 treaty)
- ♦ Protocol to the General Agreement on Privileges and Immunities of the Council of Europe (1952 treaty)
- ♦ Protocol to the General Treaty of Central American Economic Integration, 1993 (1993 treaty)
- ♦ Protocol to the General Treaty of Central American Economic Integration – Central American Uniform Customs Code (1963 treaty)
- ♦ Protocol to the General Treaty of Central American Economic Integration – Emergency Measures to Protect the Balance of Payments, 1968 (1968 treaty)
- ♦ Protocol to the General Treaty of Central American Economic Integration – Emergency Measures to Protect the Balance of Payments, 1973 (1973 treaty)
- ♦ Protocol to the General Treaty of Central American Economic Integration – List of Merchandise Subject to Temporary Exceptions to the Free Trade between Costa Rica and Each of the other Member States (1962 treaty)
- ♦ Protocol houdende wijziging van het verdrag van 29 juli 1960 inzake wettelijke aansprakelijkheid op het gebied van de kernenergie, zoals gewijzigd bij het aanvullend protocol van 28 januari 1964 en bij het protocol van 16 november 1982 (2004 treaty)
- ♦ Protocol houdende wijziging van het verdrag van 31 januari 1963 tot aanvulling van het verdrag van Parijs van 29 juli 1960 inzake wettelijke aansprakelijkheid op het gebied van de kernenergie, zoals gewijzigd bij het aanvullend protocol van 28 januari 1964 en bij het protocol van 16 november 1982 (2001 treaty)
- ♦ Protocol I to the Convention for the Prohibition of Fishing with Long Driftnets in the South Pacific (1990 treaty)
- ♦ Protocol II Additional to the Four 1949 Geneva Conventions Relating to the Protection of Victims of Non-international Armed Conflicts (1977 treaty)
- ♦ Protocol II to the Convention for the Prohibition of Fishing with Long Driftnets in the South Pacific (1990 treaty)
- ♦ Protocol for the Implementation of the Alpine Convention in the Field of Mountain Agriculture (1994 treaty)
- ♦ Protocol for the Implementation of the Alpine Convention in the Field of Mountain Forests (1996 treaty)
- ♦ Protocol for the Implementation of the Alpine Convention in the Field of Nature Protection and Landscape Conservation (1994 treaty)
- ♦ Protocol for the Implementation of the Alpine Convention in the Field of Town and Country Planning and Sustainable Development (1994 treaty)
- ♦ Protocol for the Implementation of the Alpine Convention in the Field of Transport (2000 treaty)
- ♦ Protocol instituant une commission de conciliation et de bons offices chargée de rechercher la solution des différends qui naîtraient enter Etats parties à la Convention concernant la lutte contre la discrimination dans le domaine de l'enseignement (1962 treaty)
- ♦ Protocol Instituting a Conciliation and Good Offices Commission to be Responsible for Seeking the Settlement of Any Disputes Which May Arise between States Parties to the Convention Against Discrimination in Education (1962 treaty)
- ♦ Protocol Instituting a New Schedule of Import Duties (1958 treaty)
- ♦ Protocol on Integrated Coastal Zone Management in the Mediterranean (2008 treaty)
- ♦ Protocol to the Inter-American Coffee Agreement (1941 treaty)
- ♦ Protocol on the Inter-American Registration of Trade Marks (1929 treaty)
- ♦ Protocol to the International Convention on Civil Liability for Oil Pollution Damage, 1976 (1976 treaty)
- ♦ Protocol to the International Convention on Civil Liability for Oil Pollution Damage, 1992 (1992 treaty)
- ♦ Protocol to the International Convention for the Regulation of Whaling (1956 treaty)
- ♦ Protocol inzake samenwerking bij de voorkoming van verontreiniging door schepen en bij de bestrijding van de verontreiniging van de Middellandse Zee in noodsituaties (2002 treaty)
- ♦ Protocol I – Protocol Additional to the Geneva Conventions of 12 August 1949 and Relating to the Protection of Victims of International Armed Conflicts (1977 treaty)
- ♦ Protocol on the Law Applicable to Maintenance Obligations (2007 treaty)
- ♦ Protocol for Limiting and Regulating the Cultivation of the Poppy Plant, the Production Of, International and Wholesale Trade In, and Use of Opium (1953 treaty)
- ♦ Protocollo addizionale all'Accordo europeo concernente lo scambio dei reagenti per la determinazione dei gruppi sanguigni (1983 treaty)
- ♦ Protocollo addizionale all'Accordo europeo concernente lo scambio di sostanze terapeutiche d'origine umana (1983 treaty)
- ♦ Protocollo addizionale all'Accordo europeo sullo scambio di reattivi per la determinazione dei gruppi tissulari (1976 treaty)
- ♦ Protocollo addizionale all'Accordo europeo sulla trasmissione delle domande di assistenza giudiziaria (2001 treaty)
- ♦ Protocollo addizionale all'Accordo per l'importazione temporanea in franchigia doganale, come prestito gratuito e a scopi diagnostici o terapeutici, di materiale medico-chirurgico e di laboratorio, destinato agli istituti sanitari (1983 treaty)
- ♦ Protocollo addizionale all' Accordo provvisorio europeo concernente la sicurezza sociale con esclusione dei regimi relativi alla vecchiaia, l'invalidità ed i superstiti (1953 treaty)
- ♦ Protocollo addizionale all' Accordo provvisorio europeo su i regimi di sicurezza sociale relativi all'anzianità, l'invalidità ed i superstiti (1953 treaty)
- ♦ Protocollo addizionale alla Carta sociale europea, 1988 (1988 treaty)
- ♦ Protocollo addizionale alla Carta sociale europea su un sistema di reclamo collettivo (1995 treaty)
- ♦ Protocollo addizionale alla Convenzione contro il doping (2002 treaty)
- ♦ Protocollo addizionale alla Convenzione sulla criminalità informatica, relativo all'incriminazione di atti di natura razzista e xenofobica commessi a mezzo di sistemi informatici (2003 treaty)
- ♦ Protocollo addizionale alla Convenzione sulla diminuzione dei casi di doppia nazionalità e sugli obblighi militari in caso di doppia nazionalità (1977 treaty)
- ♦ Protocollo addizionale alla Convenzione sui diritti dell'uomo e la biomedicina, relativo alla ricerca biomedica (2005 treaty)
- ♦ Protocollo addizionale alla Convenzione europea di assistenza giudiziaria in materia penale (1978 treaty)
- ♦ Protocollo addizionale alla Convenzione europea di assistenza sociale et medica (1953 treaty)
- ♦ Protocollo addizionale alla Convenzione europea nel campo dell'informazione sul diritto estero (1978 treaty)
- ♦ Protocollo addizionale alla Convenzione europea sulla protezione degli animali nel trasporto internazionale (1979 treaty)
- ♦ Protocollo addizionale alla Convenzione europea relativa all'equipollenza dei diplomi per l'ammissione alle università (1964 treaty)
- ♦ Protocollo addizionale alla Convenzione penale sulla corruzione (2003 treaty)
- ♦ Protocollo addizionale alla Convenzione sulla protezione delle persone rispetto al trattamento automatizzato dei dati a carattere personale, concernente le autorità di controllo ed i flussi transfrontalieri (2001 treaty)
- ♦ Protocollo addizionale alla Convenzione-quadro europea sulla cooperazione transfrontaliera delle collettività o autorità territoriali (1995 treaty)
- ♦ Protocollo addizionale alla Convenzione per la salvaguardia dei diritti dell'uomo e delle libertà fondamentali (1952 treaty)
- ♦ Protocollo addizionale alla Convenzione sul trasferimento delle persone condannate (1997 treaty)
- ♦ Protocollo addizionale al Protocollo all'Accordo europeo per la protezione delle emissioni televisive (1983 treaty)
- ♦ Protocollo addizionale al Protocollo all'Accordo europeo per la protezione delle emissioni televisive (1974 treaty)
- ♦ Protocollo aggiuntivo alla Convenzione europea di estradizione (1975 treaty)
- ♦ Protocollo all'Accordo europeo per la protezione delle emissioni televisive (1965 treaty)
- ♦ Protocollo all'Accordo generale su i privilegi e le immunità del Consiglio d'Europa (1952 treaty)
- ♦ Protocollo al Codice europeo di sicurezza sociale (1964 treaty)
- ♦ Protocollo alla Convenzione concernente l'elaborazione di una farmacopea europea (1989 treaty)
- ♦ Protocollo alla Convenzione europea sulle funzioni consolari relativo alle funzioni consolari in materia d'aviazione civile (1967 treaty)
- ♦ Protocollo alla Convenzione europea sulle funzioni consolari relativo alla protezione dei rifugiati (1967 treaty)
- ♦ Protocollo alla Convenzione europea di sicurezza sociale (1994 treaty)
- ♦ Protocollo alla Convenzione sull'insider trading (1989 treaty)
- ♦ Protocollo di emendamento all'Accordo europeo sulla limitazione dell'impiego di taluni detersivi nei prodotti di lavatura e pulitura (1983 treaty)
- ♦ Protocollo di emendamento alla Carta sociale europea (1991 treaty)
- ♦ Protocollo di emendamento alla Convenzione europea sulla protezione degli animali negli allevamenti (1992 treaty)
- ♦ Protocollo di emendamento alla Convenzione europea sulla protezione degli animali vertebrati utilizzati a fini sperimentali o ad altri fini scientifici (1998 treaty)
- ♦ Protocollo di emendamento alla Convenzione europea per la repressione del terrorismo (2003 treaty)
- ♦ Protocollo di emendamento alla Convenzione europea sulla televisione transfrontaliera (1998 treaty)
- ♦ Protocollo emendativo della convenzione del 29 luglio 1960 sulla responsabilità civile nel campo dell'energia nucleare, emendata dal protocollo addizionale del 28 gennaio 1964 e dal protocollo del 16 novembre 1982 (2004 treaty)
- ♦ Protocollo emendativo della convenzione del 31 gennaio 1963 complementare alla convenzione di Parigi del 29 luglio 1960 sulla responsabilità civile nel campo dell'energia nucleare, emendata dal protocollo addizionale del 28 gennaio 1964 e dal protocollo del 16 novembre 1982 (2001 treaty)
- ♦ Protocollo d'intesa per l'applicazione dell'Accordo europeo per la concessione di cure mediche alle persone in soggiorno temporaneo, con annesso (1988 treaty)
- ♦ Protocollo di modifica alla Convenzione sulla diminuzione dei casi di doppia nazionalità e sugli obblighi militari in caso di doppia nazionalità (1977 treaty)
- ♦ Protocollo no 10 alla Convenzione per la salvaguardia dei diritti dell'uomo e delle libertà fondamentali (1992 treaty)
- ♦ Protocollo no 11 alla Convenzione per la salvaguardia dei diritti dell'uomo e delle libertà fondamentali, che ristruttura il meccanismo di controllo istituito dalla convenzione (1994 treaty)
- ♦ Protocollo no 12 alla Convenzione per la salvaguardia dei diritti dell'uomo e delle libertà fondamentali (2000 treaty)
- ♦ Protocollo no 13 alla Convenzione per la salvaguardia dei diritti dell'uomo e delle libertà fondamentali relativo all'abolizione delle pena di morte in ogni circostanza (2002 treaty)
- ♦ Protocollo no 14 alla Convenzione per la salvaguardia dei diritti dell'uomo e delle libertà fondamentali, il quale emenda il sistema di controllo della convenzione (2004 treaty)
- ♦ Protocollo no 1 alla Convenzione europea per la prevenzione della tortura e delle pene o trattamenti inumani o degradanti (1993 treaty)
- ♦ Protocollo no 2 alla Convenzione europea per la prevenzione della tortura e delle pene o trattamenti inumani o degradanti (1993 treaty)
- ♦ Protocollo no 2 alla Convenzione-quadro europea sulla cooperazione transfrontaliera delle collettività o autorità territoriali sulla cooperazione interterritoriale (1998 treaty)
- ♦ Protocollo no 2 alla Convenzione per la salvaguardia dei diritti dell'uomo e della libertà fondamentali, per l'attribuzione alla Corte europea dei diritti dell'uomo della competenza ad esprimere pareri consultivi (1963 treaty)
- ♦ Protocollo no 3 alla Convenzione per la salvaguardia dei diritti dell'uomo e della libertà fondamentali, che modifica gli articoli 29, 30 e 34 della convenzione (1963 treaty)
- ♦ Protocollo no 4 alla Convenzione per la salvaguardia dei diritti dell'uomo e della libertà fondamentali, che riconosce ulteriori diritti e libertà fondamentali rispetto a quelli già garantiti dalla convenzione e dal primo protocollo addizionale alla convenzione (1963 treaty)
- ♦ Protocollo no 5 alla Convenzione per la salvaguardia dei diritti dell'uomo e della libertà fondamentali, che modifica gli articoli 22 e 40 della convenzione (1966 treaty)
- ♦ Protocollo no 6 alla Convenzione per la salvaguardia dei diritti dell'uomo e delle libertà fondamentali sull'abolizione delle pena di morte (1983 treaty)
- ♦ Protocollo no 7 alla Convenzione per la salvaguardia dei diritti dell'uomo e delle libertà fondamentali (1984 treaty)
- ♦ Protocollo no 8 alla Convenzione per la salvaguardia dei diritti dell'uomo e delle libertà fondamentali (1985 treaty)

- ♦ Protocollo no 9 alla Convenzione per la salvaguardia dei diritti dell'uomo e delle libertà fondamentali (1990 treaty)
- ♦ Protocollo relativo alla cooperazione in materia di prevenzione dell'inquinamento provocato dalle navi e, in caso di situazione critica, di lotta contro l'inquinamento del Mare Mediterraneo (2002 treaty)
- ♦ Protocol to the Madrid Agreement Concerning the International Registration of Marks (1989 treaty)
- ♦ Protocol of Managua / see Inter-American Council for Integral Development (#11423)
- ♦ Protocol of Managua – Protocol of Amendment to the Charter of the Organization of American States (1993 treaty)
- ♦ Protocol no 10 to the Convention for the Protection of Human Rights and Fundamental Freedoms (1992 treaty)
- ♦ Protocol no 11 to the Convention for the Protection of Human Rights and Fundamental Freedoms (1994 treaty)
- ♦ Protocol no 12 to the Convention for the Protection of Human Rights and Fundamental Freedoms (2000 treaty)
- ♦ Protocol no 13 to the Convention for the Protection of Human Rights and Fundamental Freedoms, Concerning the Abolition of the Death Penalty in all Circumstances (2002 treaty)
- ♦ Protocol No 14bis to the Convention for the Protection of Human Rights and Fundamental Freedoms (inactive)
- ♦ Protocol no 14 to the Convention for the Protection of Human Rights and Fundamental Freedoms, Amending the Control System of the Convention (2004 treaty)
- ♦ Protocol No 15 amending the Convention for the Protection of Human Rights and Fundamental Freedoms (2013 treaty)
- ♦ Protocol No 16 to the Convention for the Protection of Human Rights and Fundamental Freedoms (2013 treaty)
- ♦ Protocol no 1 to the European Convention for the Prevention of Torture and Inhuman or Degrading Treatment or Punishment (1993 treaty)
- ♦ Protocol no 2 to the Convention for the Protection of Human Rights and Fundamental Freedoms, conferring upon the European Court of Human Rights competence to give advisory opinions (1963 treaty)
- ♦ Protocol no 2 to the European Convention for the Prevention of Torture and Inhuman or Degrading Treatment or Punishment (1993 treaty)
- ♦ Protocol no 2 to the European Outline Convention on Transfrontier Coöperation between Territorial Communities or Authorities Concerning Interterritorial Cooperation (1998 treaty)
- ♦ Protocol no 3 to the Convention for the Protection of Human Rights and Fundamental Freedoms, amending Articles 29, 30 and 34 of the Convention (1963 treaty)
- ♦ Protocol No 3 to the European Outline Convention on Transfrontier Co-operation between Territorial Communities or Authorities concerning Euroregional Co-operation Groupings – ECGs (2009 treaty)
- ♦ Protocol no 4 to the Convention for Protection of Human Rights and Fundamental Freedoms, securing certain rights and freedoms other than those already included in the Convention and in the first Protocol thereto (1963 treaty)
- ♦ Protocol No. 5 to the Convention for the Protection of Human Rights and Fundamental Freedoms, amending Articles 22 and 40 of the Convention (1966 treaty)
- ♦ Protocol no 6 to the Convention for the Protection of Human Rights and Fundamental Freedoms Concerning the Abolition of the Death Penalty (1983 treaty)
- ♦ Protocol No 7 to the Convention for the Protection of Human Rights and Fundamental Freedoms (1984 treaty)
- ♦ Protocol no 8 to the Convention for the Protection of Human Rights and Fundamental Freedoms (1985 treaty)
- ♦ Protocol no 9 to the Convention for the Protection of Human Rights and Fundamental Freedoms (1990 treaty)
- ♦ Protocolo de 1978 relativo al Convenio internacional para la seguridad de la vida humana en el mar, 1974, en su forma enmendada (1978 treaty)
- ♦ Protocolo de 1996 relative al Convenio sobre limitación de la responsabilidad nacida de reclamaciones de derecho maritimo (1996 treaty)
- ♦ Protocolo de 1997 relativo al Convenio internacional para prevenir la contaminación por los buques (1997 treaty)
- ♦ Protocolo al Acuerdo para la importación de objectos a caracter educativo, cientifico y cultural (1976 treaty)
- ♦ Protocolo adicional ao Código Sanitario Pan-Americano, 1927 (1927 treaty)
- ♦ Protocolo adicional ao Código Sanitario Pan-Americano, 1952 (1952 treaty)
- ♦ Protocolo adicional al Código Sanitario Panamericano, 1927 (1927 treaty)
- ♦ Protocolo adicional al Código Sanitario Panamericano, 1952 (1952 treaty)
- ♦ Protocolo adicional à Convenção geral de conciliação Interamericana de 1929 (1933 treaty)
- ♦ Protocolo adicional a la Convención americana sobre derechos humanos en materia de derechos económicos, sociales y culturales (1988 treaty)
- ♦ Protocolo adicional a la Convención sobre facilidades aduaneras para el turismo relativo a la importación de documentos y de material de propaganda turistica (1954 treaty)
- ♦ Protocolo adicional a la Convención general de conciliación Interamericana de 1929 (1933 treaty)
- ♦ Protocolo adicional a la Convención interamericana sobre exhortos y cartas rogatorias (1979 treaty)
- ♦ Protocolo adicional a la Convención interamericana sobre recepción de pruebas en el extranjero (1984 treaty)
- ♦ Protocolo adicional relativo à não-intervenção (1936 treaty)
- ♦ Protocolo adicional relativo a non intervención (1936 treaty)
- ♦ Protocolo ao Tradado que Estabelece a Comunidade Económica Africana em Matéria de Livre Circulação de Pessoas, Direito de Residência e Direito de Estabelecimento (2018 treaty)
- ♦ Protocolo de arbitraje progresivo (1929 treaty)
- ♦ Protocolo de arbitramento progressivo (1929 treaty)
- ♦ Protocol to the OAU Convention on the Prevention and Combating of Terrorism (2004 treaty)
- ♦ Protocolo de Cartagena das Indias – Protocolo de Reforma da Carta da Organização dos Estados Americanos (1985 treaty)
- ♦ Protocolo de Cartagena de Indias – Protocolo de Reforma a la Carta de la Organización de los Estados Americanos (1985 treaty)
- ♦ Protocolo complementario del Acuerdo sobre la cooperación regional para el combate contra la contaminación del Pacifico Sudeste por hidrocarburos y otras sustancias nocivas (1983 treaty)
- ♦ Protocolo Contra el Trafico Ilicito de Migrantes por Tierra, Mar y Aire (2000 treaty)
- ♦ Protocolo à Convenção da OUA sobre a Prevenção e o Combate ao Terrorismo (2004 treaty)
- ♦ Protocolo a la Convención americana sobre derechos humanos relativos a la abolición de la pena de muerte (1990 treaty)
- ♦ Protocolo a la Convención sobre deberes y derechos de los estados en los casos de luchas civiles (1957 treaty)
- ♦ Protocolo al Convenio centroamericano de incentivos fiscales al desarrollo industrial, 1966 (1966 treaty)
- ♦ Protocolo al Convenio sobre el régimen de industrias centroamericanas de integración (1963 treaty)
- ♦ Protocolo sobre cooperación para combatir en situación de emergencia la contaminación del Mar Méditerraneo causada por hidrocarburos y otras sustancias perjudiciales (1976 treaty)
- ♦ Protocolo sobre cooperación para prevenir la contaminación por los buques y, en situaciones de emergencia, combatir la contaminación del mar Mediterraneo (2002 treaty)
- ♦ Protocolo para la eliminación del comercio ilicito de productos de tabaco (2012 treaty)
- ♦ Protocolo sobre espacios habitables en los buques de pasaje que prestan servicios especiales (1973 treaty)
- ♦ Protocolo Facultativo à Convenção contra a tortura e outors tratamentos ou peñas cruéis, desumanos ou degradantes (2002 treaty)
- ♦ Protocolo facultativo de la Convención contra la tortura y otros tratos o peñas crueles, inhumanos o degradantes (2002 treaty)
- ♦ Protocolo facultativo de la Convención sobre los derechos del Niño relativo a la participación de niños en los conflictos armados (2000 treaty)
- ♦ Protocolo Facultativo del Pacto Internacional de Derechos Economicos, Sociales y Culturales (2008 treaty)
- ♦ Protocolo facultativo relativo a la Convención interamericana sobre asistencia mutua en materia penal (1993 treaty)
- ♦ Protocolo de Guatemala – Protocolo al Tratado general de integración económica centroamericana (1993 treaty)
- ♦ Protocolo de Integración Educativa y Reconocimiento de Certificados, Titulos y Estudios de Nivel Primario y Medio no Técnico (1994 treaty)
- ♦ Protocolo de Managua – Protocolo de Reforma a la Carta de la Organización de los Estados Americanos (1993 treaty)
- ♦ Protocolo para la protección del Pacifico Sudeste contra la contaminación proveniente de fuentes terrestres (1983 treaty)
- ♦ Protocolo que enmienda el Convenio internacional sobre responsabilidad civil nacida de daños debidos a contaminación por hidrocarburos, 1984 (1984 treaty)
- ♦ Protocolo que modifica el convenio de 29 de julio de 1960 sobre la responsabilidad civil en materia de energia nuclear, modificado por el protocolo adicional de 28 de enero de 1964 y por el protocolo de 16 de noviembre de 1982 (2004 treaty)
- ♦ Protocolo que modifica el convenio de 31 de enero de 1963 complementario al convenio de Paris de 29 de julio de 1960 sobre la responsabilidad civil en materia de energia nuclear, modificado por el protocolo adicional de 28 de enero de 1964 y por el protocolo de 16 de noviembre de 1982 (2001 treaty)
- ♦ Protocolo de Reforma da Carta da Organização dos Estados Americanos (1985 treaty)
- ♦ Protocolo de Reforma a la Carta de la Organización de los Estados Americanos (1985 treaty)
- ♦ Protocolo de reforma a la Carta de la Organización de los Estados Americanos (1967 treaty)
- ♦ Protocolo de Reforma a la Carta de la Organización de los Estados Americanos (1993 treaty)
- ♦ Protocolo de Reforma a la Carta de la Organización de los Estados Americanos (1992 treaty)
- ♦ Protocolo de reforma al Tratado interamericano de asistencia reciproca (1975 treaty)
- ♦ Protocolo sobre el registro Interamericano de marcas de fabrica (1929 treaty)
- ♦ Protocolo sobre o registro Interamericano de marcas de fabrica (1929 treaty)
- ♦ Protocolo relativo a las clausulas de arbitraje (1923 treaty)
- ♦ Protocolo relativo a la contaminación procedente de fuentes y actividades terrestres (1999 treaty)
- ♦ Protocolo relativo al Convenio internacional sobre responsabilidad civil nacida de daños debidos a contaminación por hidrocarburos, 1976 (1976 treaty)
- ♦ Protocolo relativo a la intervención en alta mar en casos de contaminación por sustancias distintas de los hidrocarburos (1973 treaty)
- ♦ Protocolo relativo a substancias que apobrecen la capa de ozone (1987 treaty)
- ♦ Protocolo relativo a una enmienda al Convenio sobre aviación civil internacional, articulo 3bis (1984 treaty)
- ♦ Protocolo relativo a una enmienda al Convenio sobre aviación civil internacional, articulo 45 (1954 treaty)
- ♦ Protocolo relativo a una enmienda al Convenio sobre aviación civil internacional, articulo 48a (1962 treaty)
- ♦ Protocolo relativo a una enmienda al Convenio sobre aviación civil internacional, articulo 50a (1974 treaty)
- ♦ Protocolo relativo a una enmienda al Convenio sobre aviación civil internacional, articulo 50a (1961 treaty)
- ♦ Protocolo relativo a una enmienda al Convenio sobre aviación civil internacional, articulo 50a (1971 treaty)
- ♦ Protocolo relativo a una enmienda al Convenio sobre aviación civil internacional, articulo 50a (1990 treaty)
- ♦ Protocolo relativo a una enmienda al Convenio sobre aviación civil internacional, articulo 56 (1989 treaty)
- ♦ Protocolo relativo a una enmienda al Convenio sobre aviación civil internacional, articulo 56 (1971 treaty)
- ♦ Protocolo relativo a una enmienda al Convenio sobre aviación civil internacional, articulo 83bis (1980 treaty)
- ♦ Protocolo relativo a una enmienda al Convenio sobre aviación civil internacional, articulo 93bis (1947 treaty)
- ♦ Protocolo relativo a una enmienda al Convenio sobre aviación civil internacional, articulos 48a, 49e, 61 (1954 treaty)
- ♦ Protocolo de Tegucigalpa (1991 treaty)
- ♦ Protocolo al Tratado general de integración económica centroamericana (1993 treaty)
- ♦ Protocolo al Tratado general de Integración económica centroamericana, medidas de emergencia de defensa de la balanza de pagos, 1968 (1968 treaty)
- ♦ Protocolo sobre uniformidade do regime legal das procurações (1940 treaty)
- ♦ Protocolo sobre uniformidad del régimen legal de los poderes (1940 treaty)
- ♦ Protocolo de Washington – Protocolo de Reforma a la Carta de la Organización de los Estados Americanos (1992 treaty)
- ♦ Protocol on Patents and Industrial Designs within the Framework of ARIPO (1982 treaty)
- ♦ Protocol on Pollutant Release and Transfer Registers (2003 treaty)
- ♦ Protocol portant amendement à la Convention européenne sur la télévision transfrontière (1998 treaty)
- ♦ Protocol on Preparedness, Response and Cooperation to Pollution Incidents by Hazardous and Noxious Substances (2000 treaty)
- ♦ Protocol for the Prevention of Pollution of the Mediterranean Sea by Dumping from Ships and Aircraft (1976 treaty)
- ♦ Protocol on the Prevention of Pollution of the Mediterranean Sea by Transboundary Movements of Hazardous Wastes and Their Disposal (1996 treaty)
- ♦ Protocol for the Prevention of Pollution of the South Pacific Region by Dumping (1986 treaty)
- ♦ Protocol on the Prevention, Reduction and Control of Land-based Sources and Activities (1999 treaty)
- ♦ Protocol to Prevent, Suppress and Punish Trafficking in Persons, Especially Women and Children (2000 treaty)
- ♦ Protocol on the Privileges and Immunities of the International Seabed Authority (1998 treaty)
- ♦ Protocol of Progressive Arbitration (1929 treaty)
- ♦ Protocol for the Prohibition of the Use in War of Asphyxiating, Poisonous or other Gases, and of Bacteriological Methods of Warfare (1925 treaty)
- ♦ Protocol to Prolong the International Sanitary Convention, 1944 (1946 treaty)
- ♦ Protocol to Prolong the International Sanitary Convention for Aerial Navigation (1946 treaty)
- ♦ Protocol on the Protection of the Black Sea Marine Environment Against Pollution by Dumping (1992 treaty)
- ♦ Protocol on Protection of the Black Sea Marine Environment Against Pollution from Land-based Sources (1992 treaty)
- ♦ Protocol for the Protection of Cultural Property in the Event of Armed Conflict (1954 treaty)
- ♦ Protocol for the Protection of the Mediterranean Sea against Pollution from Land-Based Sources and Activities (1980 treaty)
- ♦ Protocol for the Protection of the Mediterranean Sea Against Pollution Resulting from Exploration and Exploitation of the Continental Shelf and the Seabed and its Subsoil (1994 treaty)
- ♦ Protocol for the Protection of the Southeast Pacific Against Pollution from Land-based Sources (1983 treaty)
- ♦ Protocol for the Protection of the South East Pacific Against Radioactive Contamination (1989 treaty)
- ♦ Protocol Regarding the Renewal of the Baltic Geodetic Convention (1936 treaty)
- ♦ Protocol for the Regulation of Whaling (1945 treaty)

- Protocol relatif à la coopération régionale en matière de lutte contre la pollution par les hydrocarbures et autres substances nuisibles en cas de situation critique (1982 treaty)
- Protocol Relating to an Amendment to the Convention on International Civil Aviation, Article 3bis (1984 treaty)
- Protocol Relating to an Amendment to the Convention on International Civil Aviation, Article 45 (1954 treaty)
- Protocol Relating to an Amendment of the Convention on International Civil Aviation, Article 48a (1962 treaty)
- Protocol Relating to an Amendment to the Convention on International Civil Aviation, Article 50a (1971 treaty)
- Protocol Relating to an Amendment to the Convention on International Civil Aviation, Article 50a (1961 treaty)
- Protocol Relating to an Amendment to the Convention on International Civil Aviation, Article 50a (1974 treaty)
- Protocol Relating to an Amendment to the Convention of International Civil Aviation, Article 50a (1990 treaty)
- Protocol Relating to an Amendment to the Convention on International Civil Aviation, Article 56 (1989 treaty)
- Protocol Relating to an Amendment to the Convention on International Civil Aviation, Article 56 (1971 treaty)
- Protocol Relating to an Amendment to the Convention on International Civil Aviation, Article 83bis (1980 treaty)
- Protocol Relating to an Amendment to the Convention on International Civil Aviation, Article 93bis (1947 treaty)
- Protocol Relating to an Amendment to the Convention on International Civil Aviation, Articles 48a, 49e, 61 (1954 treaty)
- Protocol Relating to an Amendment to the Convention on International Civil Aviation – Final Clause, Arabic Text (1995 treaty)
- Protocol Relating to an Amendment to the Convention on International Civil Aviation – Final Clause, Chinese Text (1998 treaty)
- Protocol Relating to a Certain Case of Statelessness (1930 treaty)
- Protocol Relating to Certain Concessions Granted in the Ottoman Empire and Declaration (1923 treaty)
- Protocol Relating to the International Convention on Load Lines (1988 treaty)
- Protocol Relating to Intervention on the High Seas in Cases of Marine Pollution by Substances other Than Oil (1973 treaty)
- Protocol Relating to the Karagatch Territory and the Islands of Imbros and Tenedos (1923 treaty)
- Protocol Relating to Military Obligations in Certain Cases of Double Nationality (1930 treaty)
- Protocol Relating to Refugee Seamen (1973 treaty)
- Protocol Relating to the Status of Refugees (1967 treaty)
- Protocol Relating to Trade Negotiations among Developing Countries (1971 treaty)
- Protocol Relative to the Abolition of the System of Foreign Settlements at Chosen (1913 treaty)
- Protocol Respecting Measures to be Taken Against the Anarchist Movement (1904 treaty)
- Protocol on Road Markings (1973 treaty)
- Protocol on Road Signs and Signals (1949 treaty)
- Protocol of San Salvador – Additional Protocol to the American Convention on Human Rights in the Area of Economic, Social and Cultural Rights (1988 treaty)
- Protocol on Shared Watercourse Systems in the Southern African Development Community Region (1995 treaty)
- Protocol on Space Requirements for Special Trade Passenger Ships (1973 treaty)
- Protocol on Strategic Environmental Assessment (2003 treaty)
- Protocol Supplementary to the Convention for the Suppression of Unlawful Seizure of Aircraft (2010 treaty)
- Protocol for the Suppression of Unlawful Acts Against the Safety of Fixed Platforms Located on the Continental Shelf (1988 treaty)
- Protocol for the Suppression of Unlawful Acts of Violence at Airports Serving International Civil Aviation (1988 treaty)
- Protocol of Tegucigalpa (1991 treaty)
- Protocol for the Termination of the Brussels Agreements for the Unification of Pharmacopoeial Formulas for Potent Drugs (1952 treaty)
- Protocol tot Wijziging van de Benelux-Overeenkomst op het Gebied van de Jacht en de Vogelbescherming (2016 treaty)
- Protocol to the Treaties Concerning the Delimitation of the Continental Shelf under the North Sea (1971 treaty)
- Protocol to the Treaty Concerning the Permanent Neutrality and Operation of the Panama Canal, 1977 (1977 treaty)
- Protocol to the Treaty Concerning the Permanent Neutrality and Operation of the Panama Canal, 1979 (1979 treaty)
- Protocol to the Treaty Establishing the African Economic Community Relating to Free Movement of Persons, Right of Residence and Right of Establishment (2018 treaty)
- Protocol on Uniformity of Powers of Attorney Which Are to be Utilized Abroad (1940 treaty)
- Protocol of Washington – Protocol of Amendments to the Charter of the Organization of American States (1992 treaty)
- Protocol on Water and Health to the 1992 Convention on the Protection and Use of Transboundary Watercourses and International Lakes (1999 treaty)
- Protocol on Wildlife Conservation and Law Enforcement (1999 treaty)
- Protodikio ton Evropaikon Kinotiton (inactive)
- Protokoll zur änderung des Europäischen abkommens über die beschränkung der verwendung bestimmter detergenzien in wasch- und reinigungsmitteln (1983 treaty)
- Protokoll zur änderung der Europäischen sozialcharta (1991 treaty)
- Protokoll zur änderung des Europäischen übereinkommens zur bekämpfung des terrorismus (2003 treaty)
- Protokoll zur änderung des übereinkommens über die verringerung der mehrstaatigkeit und über die wehrpflicht von mehrstaatern (1977 treaty)
- Protokoll zur änderung des Übereinkommens vom 20 dezember 1962 über den schutz des lachsbestandes in der ostsee (1972 treaty)
- Protokoll zur änderung des übereinkommens vom 29 juli 1960 über die haftung gegenüber dritten auf dem gebiet der kernenergie in der fassung des zusatzprotokolls vom 28 januar 1964 und des protokolls vom 16 november 1982 (2004 treaty)
- Protokoll zur änderung des zusatzübereinkommens vom 31 januar 1963 zum Pariser übereinkommens vom 29 juli 1960 über die haftung gegenüber dritten auf dem gebiet der kernenergie in der fassung des zusatzprotokolls vom 28 januar 1964 und des protokolls vom 16 november 1982 (2001 treaty)
- Protokoll angående befrielse för nordiska medborgare från att under uppehåll i annat nordiskt land än hemlandet innehava pass och uppehållstillstånd (1954 treaty)
- Protokoll zu dem Europäischen abkommen zum schutz von fernsehsendungen (1965 treaty)
- Protokoll zum Europäischen abkommen über soziale sicherheit (1994 treaty)
- Protokoll zur Europäischen ordnung der sozialen sicherheit (1964 treaty)
- Protokoll zu dem Europäischen übereinkommen über konsularische aufgaben betreffend die zivilluftfahrt (1967 treaty)
- Protokoll zu dem Europäischen übereinkommen über konsularische aufgaben betreffend den schutz der flüchtlinge (1967 treaty)
- Protokoll om fritakelse for statsborgere i Norge, Danmark, Finland og Sverige fra å inneha pass og oppholdstillatelse under opphold i annet nordisk land enn hjemlandet (1954 treaty)
- Protokoll nr 10 zur Konvention zum schutze der menschenrechte und grundfreiheiten (1992 treaty)
- Protokoll Nr 11 zur Konvention zum schutze der menschenrechte und grundfreiheiten, über die umgestaltung des durch die konvention eingeführten kontrollmechanismus (1994 treaty)
- Protokoll nr 12 zur Konvention zum schutze der menschenrechte und grundfreiheiten (2000 treaty)
- Protokoll nr 13 zur Konvention zum schutze der menschenrechte und grundfreiheiten bezüglich der abschaffung der todesstrafe unter allen umständen (2002 treaty)
- Protokoll nr 14 zur Konvention zum schutze der menschenrechte und grundfreiheiten über die änderung des kontrollsystems der konvention (2004 treaty)
- Protokoll nr 1 zu dem Europäischen übereinkommen zur verhütung von folter und unmenschlicher oder erniedrigender behandlung oder strafe (1993 treaty)
- Protokoll Nr 2 zum Europäischen rahmenübereinkommen über die grenzüberschreitende zusammenarbeit zwischen gebietskörperschaften in bezug auf die interterritoriale zusammenarbeit (1998 treaty)
- Protokoll nr 2 zu dem Europäischen übereinkommen zur verhütung von folter und unmenschlicher oder erniedrigender behandlung oder strafe (1993 treaty)
- Protokoll nr 2 zur Konvention zum schutze der menschenrechte und grundfreiheiten, durch das dem Europäischen gerichtshof für menschenrechte die zuständigkeit zur erstattung von gutachten übertragen wird (1963 treaty)
- Protokoll nr 3 zur Konvention zum schutze der menschenrechte und grundfreiheiten, durch das die artikel 29, 30 und 34 der konvention geändert werden (1963 treaty)
- Protokoll nr 4 zur Konvention zum schutze der menschenrechte und grundfreiheiten, durch das gewisse rechte und freiheiten gewährleistet werden, die nicht bereits in der konvention oder im ersten zusatzprotokoll enthalten sind (1963 treaty)
- Protokoll nr 5 zur Konvention zum schutze der menschenrechte und grundfreiheiten, durch das die artikel 22 und 40 der konvention geändert werden (1966 treaty)
- Protokoll nr 6 zur Konvention zum schutze der menschenrechte und grundfreiheiten über die abschaffung der todesstrafe (1983 treaty)
- Protokoll nr 7 zur Konvention zum schutze der menschenrechte und grundfreiheiten (1984 treaty)
- Protokoll nr 8 zur Konvention zum schutze der menschenrechte und grundfreiheiten (1985 treaty)
- Protokoll nr 9 zur Konvention zum schutze der menschenrechte und grundfreiheiten (1990 treaty)
- Protokoll zum Übereinkommen über die ausarbeitung eines Europäischen arzneibuches (1989 treaty)
- Protokoll zum übereinkommen über insidergeschäfte (1989 treaty)
- Protokol über die zusammenarbeit bei der vermeidung der verschmutzung durch schiffe und bei der bekämpfung der verschmutzung des Mittelmeers in notfällen (2002 treaty)
- Protokol vedrørende fritagelse for nordiske medborgere for at v're i besiddelse af pas og opholdstilladelse under ophold i andet nordisk land end hjemlandet (1954 treaty)
- Protolang Conference (meeting series)
- PROTOS – Projektgroep voor Technische Ontwikkelingssamenwerking (internationally oriented national body)
- Protostars and Planets (meeting series)

♦ Prototype Carbon Fund (PCF) 18552

Contact World Bank, 1818 H St NW, Washington DC 20433, USA.
URL: http://prototypecarbonfund.org/

History 20 Jul 1999, by *International Bank for Reconstruction and Development (IBRD, #12317)*. Became operational Apr 2000. **Aims** Show how project-based *greenhouse gas emissions* reduction transactions can promote and contribute to sustainable development and lower the cost of compliance with the Kyoto Protocol. **Events** *South East Asia forum on greenhouse gas mitigation, market mechanisms and sustainable development* Manila (Philippines) 2003. **Publications** Annual report.
Members Governments of 6 countries:
Canada, Finland, Japan, Netherlands, Norway, Sweden.
Companies (17) in 8 countries:
Belgium, Finland, France, Germany, Japan, Netherlands, Norway, UK. [2008/XF6759/f/**F***]

♦ Proutist Universal (PROUT) 18553

Global Office Platanvej 30, 1810 Frederiksberg, Denmark. E-mail: contact@prout-global.org.
URL: https://prout.info/

History 1975. Founded based on the economic theory developed in 1959 by Prabhat Ranjan Sarkar. The word "Prout" derives from the phrase "Progressive Utilization Theory". **Aims** Promote *Progressive* Utilization Theory (PROUT), integrating *economic democracy* and *spiritual values*. By means of this theory, change the world through: education and social services; economic decentralization; regional self-sufficiency; individual leadership and communication skills; spirituality. **Finance** Sources: sale of publications; individual and institutional contributions; seminar fees. Budget (annual): US$ 550,000. **Events** *Convention / Annual Global PROUT Convention* Sao Paulo (Brazil) 1995, *Convention / Annual Global PROUT Convention* Delhi (India) 1994, *Convention / Annual Global PROUT Convention* Sydney, NSW (Australia) 1993, *Convention / Annual Global PROUT Convention* Washington, DC (USA) 1992, *Convention / Annual Global PROUT Convention* Accra (Ghana) 1991. **Publications** *PROUT Weekly* (weekly); *PROUT Post* (12 a year); *PROUT Journal* (4 a year); *Tara Magazine* (4 a year) – journal of the women's Prout movement; *PROUT Times*. Books by Prabhat Rainjan Sarkar and Ravi Batra. Handbooks; guides; booklets. Information services available on-line through EcoNet or APC networks.
Members Individual membership covers 94 countries and territories:
Andorra, Argentina, Australia, Austria, Bangladesh, Barbados, Belgium, Belize, Bolivia, Brazil, Bulgaria, Burkina Faso, Cameroon, Canada, Chile, China, Colombia, Congo Brazzaville, Congo DR, Cyprus, Czechia, Denmark, Dominican Rep, Ecuador, Egypt, El Salvador, Ethiopia, Fiji, Finland, France, Germany, Ghana, Greece, Guatemala, Guyana, Haiti, Hong Kong, Hungary, Iceland, India, Indonesia, Ireland, Israel, Italy, Jamaica, Japan, Jordan, Kenya, Korea Rep, Kuwait, Lebanon, Liberia, Luxembourg, Malaysia, Mali, Mexico, Mozambique, Namibia, Nepal, Netherlands, New Zealand, Nicaragua, Norway, Pakistan, Papua New Guinea, Paraguay, Peru, Philippines, Poland, Portugal, Romania, Samoa, Saudi Arabia, Serbia, Singapore, Slovakia, South Africa, Spain, Sri Lanka, St Vincent-Grenadines, Sweden, Switzerland, Taiwan, Tanzania UR, Thailand, Togo, Trinidad-Tobago, UK, United Arab Emirates, Uruguay, USA, Venezuela, Zambia, Zimbabwe.
IGO Relations Associated with Department of Global Communications of the United Nations. **NGO Relations** Maintains: *Peoples' News Agency (PNA, no recent information)*; *Prout Research Institute (no recent information)*; *Women Proutists (WP, no recent information)*; *Universal Proutist Farmers Federation (no recent information)*; *Universal Proutist Intellectual Federation (no recent information)*; *Universal Proutist Labor Federation (UPLF, no recent information)*; *Universal Proutist Student Federation (no recent information)*; *Universal Proutist Youth Federation (UPYF, no recent information)*. [2021/XF1541/v/**F**]

- **PROUT** Proutist Universal (#18553)
- Provansa Eklesiastikan'ny Ranomasimbe Indiana (#00824)
- Provedor de Justiça Europeu (#08084)

♦ ProVeg International 18554

Headquarters 1380 Monroe St NW, Ste 222, Washington DC 20010, USA. E-mail: info.us@proveg.com.
URL: http://proveg.com/

History Registration: 501(c)3, No/ID: 46-303 8496, USA. **Aims** Reduce the global consumption of animals by 50% by 2040 through a *vegan lifestyle*. **Activities** Awareness raising; advocacy/lobbying/activism. **Consultative Status** Consultative status granted from: *UNEP (#20299)*. [2022/XM6850/**F**]

- Providential Union of Officials of the European Union / see AFILIATYS (#00151)
- Provident and Insurance Group of International Officials (#10764)
- Province ecclésiastique de l'Océan indien (#00824)
- Provisional Agreement Respecting the Whangpoo Conservancy (1912 treaty)
- Provisional Arrangement Concerning the Status of Refugees Coming from Germany (1936 treaty)
- Provisional Committee of the All Africa Church Conference / see All Africa Conference of Churches (#00640)
- Provisional European Telecommunications Satellite Organization / see European Telecommunications Satellite Organization (#08896)
- Provisional Intergovernmental Committee for the Movement of Migrants from Europe / see International Organization for Migration (#14454)

- ♦ Provisional International Crystallographic Committee / see International Union of Crystallography (#15768)
- ♦ Provisional Understanding Regarding Deep Seabed Matters (1984 treaty)
- ♦ Provisional World Parliament (see: #21313)
- ♦ Provisions for a Unit of Account and Adjustment of Limitations of Liability (1982 treaty)
- ♦ ProvSec – International Conference on Provable Security (meeting series)
- ♦ Proyecto Acción SIDA de Centroamérica (internationally oriented national body)
- ♦ Proyecto Centro Americano de Energia Solar (internationally oriented national body)
- ♦ Proyecto de Ciudades Saludables / see WHO European Healthy Cities Network (#20936)
- ♦ Proyecto Hambre (#10994)
- ♦ Proyecto de Modelos de Orden Mundial (#21684)
- ♦ Proyecto Planeta Azul (internationally oriented national body)
- ♦ Proyecto para Potenciar los Recursos del Artista Latinoamericano (internationally oriented national body)
- ♦ Proyecto de la Rehidratación (internationally oriented national body)
- ♦ Proyectos de Innovación IBEROEKA (see: #18524)
- ♦ Proyecto Solidario (internationally oriented national body)
- ♦ **PRPF** Pohjoismainen Rakennus- ja Puutyöväen Federaatio (#17283)
- ♦ **PRP** Pacific Rim Park (#18000)
- ♦ PRP – Peace Resource Project (internationally oriented national body)
- ♦ PRRC – Al-Awda – Palestine Right to Return Coalition (internationally oriented national body)
- ♦ **PRRES** Pacific Rim Real Estate Society (#18001)
- ♦ PRRLA – Pacific Rim Research Libraries Alliance (unconfirmed)
- ♦ **PRSCO** Pacific Regional Science Conference Organization (#17994)
- ♦ PRSF – Prisonniers Sans Frontières (internationally oriented national body)
- ♦ PRSFS / see Pacific Society for Reproductive Medicine (#18006)
- ♦ **PRS** Pacific Regional Seminary (#17995)
- ♦ PRS – Pacific Rim Society (no recent information)
- ♦ Pruth International Union for the Control of Navigation on the Danube (inactive)
- ♦ **PRVN** Pacific Rim Vetiver Network (#18002)
- ♦ **PRVS** Pan-American Retina and Vitreous Society (#18126)
- ♦ PSA / see African Regional Centre for Space Science and Technology Education – English (#00431)
- ♦ PSAI – Portable Sanitation Association International (internationally oriented national body)
- ♦ PSAJ – Peace Studies Association of Japan (internationally oriented national body)
- ♦ **PSA** Pacific Science Association (#18003)
- ♦ PSA – Petites Soeurs de l'Assomption (religious order)
- ♦ **PSA** Phytochemical Society of Asia (#18369)
- ♦ PSA – Poe Studies Association (internationally oriented national body)
- ♦ **PSA** Professional Squash Association (#18517)
- ♦ PSAS – International Conference on Precision Physics of Simple Atomic Systems (meeting series)
- ♦ PSBI – Pearl S Buck International (internationally oriented national body)
- ♦ **PSCC** Trade Unions' Portuguese Speaking Countries Community (#04431)
- ♦ PSCE / see Public Safety Communication Europe (#18571)
- ♦ PSCE Forum / see Public Safety Communication Europe (#18571)
- ♦ **PSC Europe** Public Safety Communication Europe (#18571)
- ♦ PSC – Pacific Salmon Commission (internationally oriented national body)
- ♦ PSDP – Petites Soeurs des Pauvres (religious order)
- ♦ PSDP – Piccole Sorelle dei Poveri (religious order)
- ♦ PSDT – Panamerican Society for Dialysis and Transplantation (inactive)
- ♦ **pS-Eau** Programme Solidarité eau (#18529)
- ♦ **PSE** Parti socialiste européen (#18249)
- ♦ PSE / see Party of European Socialists (#18249)
- ♦ **PSE** Phytochemical Society of Europe (#18370)
- ♦ PSE – Portable Sanitation Europe (internationally oriented national body)
- ♦ PSE – Process Systems Engineering Conference (meeting series)
- ♦ PSE – Pyramid Society Europe (internationally oriented national body)
- ♦ Pseudoxanthoma Elasticum International (internationally oriented national body)
- ♦ PSFG / see World Glacier Monitoring Service (#21539)
- ♦ PSF – Patrimoine sans frontières (internationally oriented national body)
- ♦ PSF – Plastic Soup Foundation (internationally oriented national body)
- ♦ **PSGCA** Professional Society of Genetic Counselors in Asia (#18516)
- ♦ PSGDN – Pacific Sexual and Gender Diversity Network (unconfirmed)
- ♦ PSG – Pacific Seabird Group (internationally oriented national body)
- ♦ PSGSI – Patients Safety and Global Support Initiative (internationally oriented national body)
- ♦ PSI / see International Association of Administrative Professionals

♦ PSI 18555

Pres/CEO 1120 19th St NW, Ste 600, Washington DC 20036, USA. T. +12027850072. Fax +12027850120. E-mail: info@psi.org.
Europe Office Herengracht 124-128, 1015 BT Amsterdam, Netherlands.
Africa Office 28 Whitefield Place, School Lane, Westlands, PO Box 14355-00800, Nairobi, Kenya.
URL: http://www.psi.org/

History 1970, USA. Founded by Tim Black (1937-2014) and Phil Harvey (1938-). Currently only known under its acronym. Former names and other names: *Population Services International (PSI)* – former; *Organisation internationale pour les services en matière de population* – former. Registration: 501(c)3, No/ID: 56-0942853, USA. **Aims** Help people in developing countries live healthier lives and plan the families they desire. improve *health* by focusing on serious challenges like lack of family planning, *HIV* and *AIDS*, barriers to maternal health, and the greatest threats to children under five, including malaria, diarrhea, pneumonia and malnutrition. **Structure** Board of Directors. A decentralized network with headquarters in Washington DC (USA) and affiliates in over 50 countries. **Staff** 8900.00 FTE, paid. **Finance** Funding by: governments of USA, UK, Germany and Netherlands; *Global Fund to Fight AIDS, Tuberculosis and Malaria (Global Fund, #10383)*; UN agencies; private foundations; corporations; individuals. Annual budget (2015): US$ 652,776,127,000,000. **Activities** Advocacy/lobbying/activism; projects/programmes. **Events** *Annual international harm reduction conferences / International Conference on the Reduction of Drug Related Harm* Bangkok (Thailand) 2009. **Publications** *Report* (2 a year). **Members** Offices and Affiliates in over 50 countries and territories. Membership countries not specified. **NGO Relations** Collaborates with: *FHI 360*. Member of: *Alliance for Malaria Prevention (AMP, #00706)*; *Global Coalition Against Child Pneumonia (#10290)*; *Global WASH Cluster (GWC, #10651)*; *InsideNGO (inactive)*; *International Consortium for Emergency Contraception (ICEC, #12911)*; *International Initiative for Impact Evaluation (3ie, #13851)*; *NonProfit Organizations Knowledge Initiative (NPOKI)*; *PMNCH (#18410)*; *Reproductive Health Supplies Coalition (RHSC, #18847)*. Partner of: *1,000 Days*; *Every Woman Every Child (EWEC, #09215)*; *Sanitation and Water for All (SWA, #19051)*. Instrumental in setting up: *Pan American Social Marketing Organization (PASMO)*. Links include: *Bixby Center for Global Reproductive Health*; *EngenderHealth*; *Global Health Council (GHC, #10402)*; *International Planned Parenthood Federation (IPPF, #14589)*; *Johns Hopkins University Center for Communications Programs (CCP)*; *Management Sciences for Health (MSH)*; *PATH (#18260)*; *Pathfinder International (#18261)*; *PAI (#18025)*; *Population Council (#18458)*; *Southern African Network of AIDS Service Organizations (SANASO, see: #00272)*. [2020/XN5031/**F**]

♦ PSI Alliance 18556

Contact c/o Luther Pendragon Brussels, Rue d'Arlon 40, 1000 Brussels, Belgium. T. +3222350534.
URL: http://www.psialliance.eu/

Aims Encourage the public sector to maintain a *trading* environment that is fair and equitable, in particular in relation to the licensing and re-use of public sector information (PSI). **Structure** Members Meeting; Board. **Activities** Organizes Annual Conference. **Events** *Annual Conference* Brussels (Belgium) 2010, *Conference / Annual Conference* Brussels (Belgium) 2009, *Members Meeting* Paris (France) 2009, *Conference / Annual Conference* Brussels (Belgium) 2008.
Members Private sector companies and associations in 12 countries:
Austria, Belgium, Finland, France, Germany, Italy, Latvia, Netherlands, Slovakia, Spain, Sweden, UK. [2015/XJ0322/**F**]

- ♦ **PSIA** Physical Security Interoperability Alliance (#18367)
- ♦ **PSIA** Prosalud Inter Americana Foundation (#18542)
- ♦ PSIFUT – Sociedad Internacional de Psicólogos para el Futbol (unconfirmed)
- ♦ PSI/I / see Patient Classification Systems International (#18263)
- ♦ PSI International / see Patient Classification Systems International (#18263)
- ♦ **Psi-k** Euro-Network for Electronic Structure Calculations (#05740)
- ♦ PSILPH – International Symposium on Plant-Soil Interactions at Low PH (meeting series)
- ♦ **PSI** Passiflora Society International (#18253)
- ♦ **PSI** Performance Studies International (#18311)
- ♦ **PSI** Pharmaceutical Security Institute (#18355)
- ♦ PSI – Planetary Security Initiative (internationally oriented national body)
- ♦ PSI – Postpartum Support, International (internationally oriented national body)
- ♦ **P and SI** Product and Systems Internationalisation (#18511)
- ♦ **PSI** Proliferation Security Initiative (#18536)
- ♦ **PSI** Public Services International (#18572)
- ♦ PSIVT – Pacific-Rim Symposium on Image and Video Technology (meeting series)
- ♦ PS Loop – PolyStyreneLoop Cooperative (unconfirmed)
- ♦ PSM – Congregatio Presbyterorum a Sancta Maria de Tinchebray (religious order)
- ♦ PSMdC – Piccole Suore Missionarie della Carità (religious order)
- ♦ **PSMSL** Permanent Service for Mean Sea Level (#18333)
- ♦ PSNI – PLAY SOCCER Nonprofit International (internationally oriented national body)
- ♦ PSN – Performance Studies Network (internationally oriented national body)
- ♦ **PSOGI** Peritoneal Surface Oncology Group International (#18315)
- ♦ PSO – Policy Studies Organization (internationally oriented national body)
- ♦ Psoriasis Asia Pacific (unconfirmed)
- ♦ Psoriasis International Network / see Skin Inflammation and Psoriasis International Network (#19308)
- ♦ **PS** Pituitary Society (#18375)
- ♦ PS – Planetary Society (internationally oriented national body)
- ♦ PS – Planet Society (see: #20322)
- ♦ PSP – Project Survival Pacific (internationally oriented national body)
- ♦ **PSRH** Pacific Society for Reproductive Health (#18005)
- ♦ **PSRM** Pacific Society for Reproductive Medicine (#18006)
- ♦ PSSA – Philosophical Society of Southern Africa (internationally oriented national body)
- ♦ PSSA – Physiology Society of Southern Africa (internationally oriented national body)
- ♦ PSSAT – Pusat Studi Sosial Asia Tenggara (internationally oriented national body)
- ♦ PSSCA – Pacific Council of Structural Steel Associations (unconfirmed)
- ♦ PSSF – Istituto delle Piccole Suore della Sacra Famiglia (religious order)
- ♦ PSSF – Little Sisters of the Holy Family (religious order)
- ♦ PSSI – Peace Science Society – International (internationally oriented national body)
- ♦ **PSS** Pharmaceutical Procurement Service (#18354)
- ♦ **PSSRC** Pharmaceutical Solid State Research Cluster (#18356)
- ♦ PSSS / see International Association for the Philosophy of Sport (#12078)
- ♦ PSS – Societas Presbyterorum a Sancto Sulpitio (religious order)
- ♦ PST – International Conference on Privacy, Security and Trust (meeting series)
- ♦ PSWO – Picture and Sound World Organization (inactive)
- ♦ PsyArt – International Conference on Psychology and the Arts (meeting series)
- ♦ Psychedelic Access and Research European Alliance (unconfirmed)

♦ PsychedelicsEurope 18557

SG Boulevard Charlemagne 27A, 1000 Brussels, Belgium. E-mail: info@psychedelicseurope.org.
URL: https://www.psychedelicseurope.org/

History Registration: Banque-Carrefour des Entreprises, No/ID: 0768.929.094, Start date: 31 May 2021, Belgium; EU Transparency Register, No/ID: 302850543434-74, Start date: 6 Jul 2021. **Aims** Support establishment of the EU-wide regulatory framework that promotes medicinal use of psychedelic substances to the benefit of patients, stimulates research, harmonizes rules on the market and secures safe and predictable environment for companies and entrepreneurs in Europe. **Structure** Scientific Committee; Secretariat. [2021/AA1931/**D**]

♦ Psychiatric Association for Eastern Europe and the Balkans (PAEEB) 18558

Pres Inst of Mental Health, Palmoticeva 37, Belgrade, PAK 11000, Serbia. T. +381113238160. Fax +381113231333.
URL: http://paeeb.com/

History 2005. Registered in accordance with Greek law. **Structure** General Assembly; Executive Committee. Standing Committees; Task Forces. **Events** *Eastern European Psychiatric Congress* Athens (Greece) 2015, *Eastern European Psychiatric Congress* Belgrade (Serbia) 2012, *Eastern European Psychiatric Congress* Moscow (Russia) 2009, *Eastern European Psychiatric Congress* Thessaloniki (Greece) 2007. **NGO Relations** Affiliate member of: *World Psychiatric Association (WPA, #21741)*. Voting member of: *World Federation for Mental Health (WFMH, #21455)*. [2016/XM4787/**D**]

- ♦ Psychoanalytical Association of Latin America (#09386)
- ♦ Psychogeriatrics International / see International Psychogeriatric Association (#14664)

♦ Psychological Warfare Society 18559

Editor address not obtained.
URL: http://www.psywarsoc.org/

History 1958, as *Psywar Society*. **Aims** Bring together collectors and historians interested in aerial propaganda. **Finance** Members' dues. **Publications** *The Falling Leaf* (4 a year). Catalogues of aerial propaganda leaflets.
Members Societies in 15 countries:
Australia, Austria, Belgium, Canada, France, Germany, Italy, Japan, Korea Rep, Netherlands, Singapore, Spain, Switzerland, UK, USA. [2012/XD4314/**F**]

- ♦ Psychologists for Peace (internationally oriented national body)
- ♦ Psychologists for the Prevention of War / see Psychologists for Peace
- ♦ Psychologists for the Promotion of World Peace / see Psychologists for Peace

♦ PsychoNeuroImmunology Research Society (PNIRS) 18560

Exec Dir 1123 Comanche Path, Bandera TX 78003-4212, USA. T. +18307969393. Fax +18307969394. E-mail: pnirs@pnirs.org.
URL: http://www.pnirs.org/

History Apr 1993. Incorporated in the State of Pennsylvania. **Aims** Promote study of interrelationships among behavioural, neural, endocrine and immune processes; encourage collaborations among immunologists, neuroscientists, clinicians, health psychologists and behavioural neuroscientists. **Finance** Members' dues. **Activities** Awards/prizes/competitions; events/meetings; training/education. **Events** *Annual Meeting* Boulder, CO (USA) 2023, *Annual Meeting* 2021, *Annual Meeting* Berlin (Germany) 2019, *Annual Meeting* Seattle, WA (USA) 2015, *Annual Meeting* Philadelphia, PA (USA) 2014. **Publications** *Brain, Behavior and Immunity* (8 a year).
Members Individuals in 21 countries and territories:
Australia, Austria, Belgium, Canada, China, France, Germany, Greece, India, Israel, Italy, Japan, Korea Rep, Mexico, Netherlands, Russia, Spain, Switzerland, Taiwan, UK, USA. [2022/XJ3111/**D**]

- ♦ Psychosocial Rehabilitation International / see World Association for Psychosocial Rehabilitation (#21178)
- ♦ Psywar Society / see Psychological Warfare Society (#18559)
- ♦ PTA – Agreement on ASEAN Preferential Trading Arrangements (1977 treaty)
- ♦ PTA Bank / see Trade and Development Bank (#20181)
- ♦ PTA Leather Institute / see Africa Leather and Leather Products Institute (#00185)

♦ PTA Leather and Leather Products Institute / see Africa Leather and Leather Products Institute (#00185)
♦ PTA – Preferential Trade Area for Eastern and Southern African States (inactive)
♦ PTA – Primary Tungsten Association (inactive)

♦ PTA Reinsurance Company (ZEP-RE) 18561

Compagnie de réassurance de la Zone d'échanges préférentiels

Managing Dir PO Box 42769, Nairobi, 00100, Kenya. T. +254202738221. Fax +254202738444. E-mail: mail@zep-re.com.
URL: http://www.zep-re.com/

History 21 Nov 1990, Mbabane (Eswatini). Established by an Agreement of Heads of State and Government of the COMESA region. Operations began, Jan 1993, as an institution of *Preferential Trade Area for Eastern and Southern African States (PTA, inactive).* From 8 Dec 1994, an institution of *Common Market for Eastern and Southern Africa (COMESA, #04296).* Former names and other names: *COMESA Reinsurance Company* – alias; *Common Market Reinsurance Company* – alias; *Compagnie de réassurance de la ZEP-RE* – alias. **Aims** Foster the development of the insurance and reinsurance industry in the PTA sub-region; promote the growth of national, sub-regional and regional underwriting and retention capacity; support sub-regional economic development. **Structure** General Assembly; Board of Directors. Committees (3): Audit; Investment; Human Resource. **Finance** Authorized shared capital: US$ 27,280,000, 50% of which is payable and the balance is callable. **Activities** Provides reinsurance services to insurance and reinsurance companies within and outside the COMESA region. **Events** *Annual General Assembly* Maputo (Mozambique) 2005, *Reinsurance seminar* Nairobi (Kenya) 2005, *Annual General Assembly* Kigali (Rwanda) 2004, *Annual General Assembly* Lusaka (Zambia) 1999, *Annual General Assembly* Nairobi (Kenya) 1998.
Members States, members of COMESA, that have signed the agreement. Governments of 19 countries:
Burundi, Comoros, Congo DR, Djibouti, Egypt, Eritrea, Eswatini, Ethiopia, Kenya, Libya, Madagascar, Malawi, Mauritius, Rwanda, Seychelles, Sudan, Uganda, Zambia, Zimbabwe.
IGO Relations Member of (1): *Trade and Development Bank (TDB, #20181).* Formal contacts with: *African Trade Insurance Agency (ATI, #00485)*; COMESA Secretariat. **NGO Relations** Contacts with international reinsurance companies. [2020/XF3052/e/**F***]

♦ PTBA – Professional Travel Bloggers Association (internationally oriented national body)
♦ PTC-Addis – WHO Pan African Emergency Training Centre (no recent information)
♦ **PTCA** Professional Tennis Coaches Association (#18518)
♦ **PTC** International Association 'Peace through Culture' (#12070)
♦ **PTCN** Pacific Transnational Crime Network (#18010)
♦ **PTCOG** Particle Therapy Co-Operative Group (#18226)
♦ **PTC** Pacific Telecommunications Council (#18007)
♦ PTC – Pacific Theological College (internationally oriented national body)
♦ **PTC** WMO/ESCAP Panel on Tropical Cyclones (#20976)
♦ PTES – Peoples Trust for Endangered Species (internationally oriented national body)
♦ **PTF** Partnership for Transparency Fund (#18245)
♦ **PTID Society** International Society for the Prevention of Tobacco Induced Diseases (#15387)
♦ **PTL** Pohjoismainen Taideliitto (#17176)
♦ **PTMG** Pharmaceutical Trade Marks Group (#18357)
♦ PTM-mundubat / see Fundación Mundubat
♦ **PTPI Europe** People to People International – Europe (#18301)
♦ **PTPI** People to People International (#18300)
♦ **PTP** Pathways To Peace (#18262)
♦ **PTS** Pali Text Society (#18030)
♦ PTU – Peace Through Unity (internationally oriented national body)
♦ PTWC – Pacific Tsunami Warning Center (internationally oriented national body)
♦ PUAS / see Postal Union of the Americas, Spain and Portugal (#18466)
♦ **PUASP** Postal Union of the Americas, Spain and Portugal (#18466)

♦ Publications Office of the European Union (Publications Office) ... 18562

Office des publications de l'Union européenne – Oficina de Publicaciones de la Unión Europea – Amt für Veröffentlichungen der Europäischen Union – Serviço das Publicações da União Europeia – Ufficio delle Pubblicazioni dell'Unione Europea – Bureau voor publicaties van de Europese Unie – Europeiska unionens publikationsbyrå – Den Europ'iske Unions Publikationskontor – Euroopan unionin julkaisutoimisto – Oifig Foilseachan an Aontais Eorpaigh – Urad pro Publikace Evropské unie – Urad pre vydavanie Publikacii Európskej únie – Az Európai Unió Kiadóhivatala – Urzad Publikacji Unii Europejskiej – Urad za Publikacije Evropske unije – Euroopa Liidu Väljaannete Talitus – Eiropas Savienības Publikaciju birojs – Europos Sajungos leidiniu biuras – Ured za publikacije Europske unije – Oficiul Pentru Publicatii al Uniunii Europene

Dir Gen Rue Mercier 2, L-2985 Luxembourg, Luxembourg. E-mail: info@publications.europa.eu.
Main: http://publications.europa.eu/

History Established 1969, by interinstitutional agreement as the official publisher of all the institutions of the *European Communities (EC, inactive)* and now of the *European Union (EU, #08967).* Commission Current mandate by Decision 2009/496/EC, Euratom. **Aims** Publish the publications of the institutions of the European Union. **Structure** Management Committee, comprising representatives of *European Parliament (EP, #08146), Council of the European Union (#04895), European Commission (EC, #06633), Court of Justice of the European Union (CJEU, #04938), European Court of Auditors (#06854), European Economic and Social Committee (EESC, #06963), European Committee of the Regions (CoR, #06665)* and *European Central Bank (ECB, #06466)* (Observer). Directorates (4): Resource and Logistics; Core Business Services; Official Journals and Publications Production; Dissemination and Reuse. **Languages** EU languages. **Staff** 595.00 FTE, paid. **Finance** Administrative budget (2016): euro 123,750,000. **Activities** Publishing activities; knowledge management/information dissemination. **Events** *Forum des éditeurs de l'Union Européenne* Brussels (Belgium) 1999, *Forum des éditeurs de l'Union Européenne* Frankfurt-Main (Germany) 1999. **Publications** *Official Journal of the European Union.* General EU publications. **Information Services** *CORDIS*; *EU Bookshop*; *EU Open Data Portal*; *EUR-Lex*; *TED – Tenders Electronic Daily.* **IGO Relations** Official publisher for institutions of the European Union, including the following: *European Committee of the Regions (CoR, #06665)*; *Council of the European Union (#04895)*; *Court of Justice of the European Union (CJEU, #04938)*; *European Central Bank (ECB, #06466)*; *European Commission (EC, #06633)*; *European Court of Auditors (#06854)*; *European Economic and Social Committee (EESC, #06963)*; *European Parliament (EP, #08146)*; all other European agencies. **NGO Relations** Member of: *The Bridge – Forum Dialogue*; *Eurolib (#05703)*; *International DOI Foundation (IDF, #13188).* Provides secretariat for: *Global Network of Tolerance Education Centres (no recent information).* [2017.03.30/XE9782/**E***]

♦ **Publications Office** Publications Office of the European Union (#18562)

♦ Public Broadcasters International (PBI) 18563

SG Rm 613, Higashi-kan, NHK Broadcasting Center, Tokyo, 150-8001 Japan.
URL: http://www.publicbroadcastersinternational.org/

History 1990. **Aims** Establish and sustain a network for the discussion of goals, ideas and experience, for information exchange, and for the support of values common to all public broadcasters. **Structure** Steering Committee. **Languages** English. **Staff** 1.00 FTE, voluntary. Host of conference provides staff. **Finance** Members' dues. **Events** *Annual Conference* Tokyo (Japan) 2022, *Annual Conference* Helsinki (Finland) 2019, *Annual Conference* Seoul (Korea Rep) 2018, *Annual Conference* Sinaia (Romania) 2017, *Annual Conference* Montréal, QC (Canada) 2016. **Publications** Annual Report. **Members** Permanent Public Service Media or State broadcasters; Associate. Membership countries not specified. **IGO Relations** *Asia-Pacific Institute for Broadcasting Development (AIBD, #01934).* **NGO Relations** *Asia-Pacific Broadcasting Union (ABU, #01863)*; *Public Media Alliance (PMA, #18568)*; *European Broadcasting Union (EBU, #06404)*; *International Radio and Television Union (#14689).* [2015.06.01/XS0323/c/**E**]

♦ Public Budget International Association (PBIA) 18564

Association internationale du budget public – Asociación Internacional de Presupuesto Público (ASIP) – Associação Internacional de Orçamento Público

Exec Sec Avenida Belgrano 1370, Piso 5, C1093AAO Buenos Aires, Argentina. T. +541143812139 – +541143819386. Fax +541143812139. E-mail: info@asip.org.ar.
URL: http://www.asip.org.ar/

History May 1973, Santiago (Chile), as *Inter-American and Iberian Public Budget Association – Asociación Interamericana y Ibérica de Presupuesto Público.* Also known as *Inter-American Public Budget Association.* **Aims** As a technical organization, study, analyse, research and publish topics related to public finance. **Structure** Board of Directors; Deliberative Board; Executive Secretariat based in Buenos Aires (Argentina) and headed by Executive Secretary; Regional offices (3). **Finance** Financing from Public Budget Directorates and National Associations of member countries. **Activities** Events/meetings; training/education; awards/prizes/competitions; research/documentation. **Events** *Annual seminar* Madrid (Spain) 2010, *Annual seminar* San José (Costa Rica) 2004, *Annual seminar* Havana (Cuba) 2003, *International conference on fiscal policy and budgetary management in times of the increasing globalization* Lima (Peru) 2003, *Annual seminar* Ixtapan de la Sal (Mexico) 2002. **Publications** *ASIP Newsletter* (6 a year) in English, Spanish; *International Journal of Public Budget* (4 a year) in English, Spanish. Research papers. **Members** Associations and individuals Founding; Active; Adherent; Honorary. National Budget and Financial Administration Associations (7). Membership countries not specified. **IGO Relations** Agreement with: *Agencia Española de Cooperación Internacional para el Desarrollo (AECID).* [2020.03.04/XD7374/**D**]

♦ Public Expenditure Network / see Caribbean Public Finance Association (#03543)
♦ Public Eye (internationally oriented national body)
♦ Public Health Evidence South Asia (unconfirmed)

♦ Public Health Palliative Care International (PHPCI) 18565

Contact address not obtained. E-mail: info@phpci.org.
URL: https://www.phpci.org/

History Apr 2013, Limerick (Ireland). Inaugurated during 3rd International Conference on Public Health and Palliative Care. **Aims** Promote practice learning and professional support; facilitate local and international communication between members around the world in their individual attempts at embedding a public health approach to the practice of palliative care. **Structure** Annual General Meeting; Council. **Activities** Events/meetings. **Events** *International Public Health and Palliative Care Conference* Bruges (Belgium) 2022, *International Public Health and Palliative Care Conference* Sydney, NSW (Australia) 2019, *International Public Health and Palliative Care Conference* Ottawa, ON (Canada) 2017, *International Public Health and Palliative Care Conference* Bristol (UK) 2015, *International Public Health and Palliative Care Conference* Limerick (Ireland) 2013. **Publications** *Palliative Care & Social Practice.* [2022.06.25/AA0825/**C**]

♦ Public Interest Intellectual Property Advisors (internationally oriented national body)
♦ Public Interest Law Initiative / see Global Network for Public Interest Law
♦ Public Interest Law Institute / see Global Network for Public Interest Law

♦ Public Interest Oversight Board (PIOB) 18566

SG C/ Oquendo 12, 28006 Madrid, Spain. T. +34917820528. Fax +34917824887. E-mail: info@ipiob.org.
Chair address not obtained.
URL: http://www.ipiob.org/

History Constitution adopted Feb 2005. A global independent oversight board and collaborative effort by *International Federation of Accountants (IFAC, #13335)* and the international financial regulatory community. **Aims** Improve the quality and public interest focus of international standards formulated by *Standard* Setting Boards supported by the International Federation of *Accountants* in the areas of audit and assurance and ethics. **Structure** Board (meets 4 times a year); Secretary-General; Secretariat. Oversees: *International Auditing and Assurance Standards Board (IAASB, #12296)*; *International Ethics Standards Board for Accountants (IESBA, #13306).* **Staff** 5.00 FTE, paid. **Events** *Meeting* Madrid (Spain) 2014. **Publications** *Quarterly Updates* (4 a year). Annual Public Report. [2020.06.16/XJ7859/**E**]

♦ Public Interest Registry (PIR) 18567

Contact 1775 Wiehle Ave, Ste 100, Reston VA 20190, USA. T. +17038895778. Fax +17038895779. E-mail: info@pir.org.
URL: http://www.pir.org/

History 2002, by *Internet Society (ISOC, #15952).* **Aims** Be an exemplary domain name registry and industry through leader providing a trusted digital identity and helping educate those who dedicate themselves to improving the world. **Structure** Board of Directors; Advisory Council. **Publications** *Advocate Policy Newsletter*, *State of 'dot' ORG Industry Newsletter.* [2019.02.11/XG9876/**F**]

♦ Public International Law and Policy Group (internationally oriented national body)
♦ Publicitaires sans frontières (unconfirmed)
♦ Publicitarios sin Fronteras (unconfirmed)
♦ Public Library Association of Latin America and the Caribbean (no recent information)

♦ Public Media Alliance (PMA) 18568

CEO Room Arts 1-80 DEV, Univ of East Anglia, Norwich, NR4 7TJ, UK. T. +441603592335. E-mail: info@publicmediaalliance.org.
URL: http://publicmediaalliance.org/

History Feb 1945, London (UK). Arose from collaboration during World War II between Commonwealth countries, with a view to continuing that cooperation and exchange. *Commonwealth Broadcasting Secretariat* set up Dec 1963, London, following 5th Conference, Jun 1963, Montréal/Toronto. Former names and other names: *Commonwealth Broadcasting Conference* – former (Feb 1945 to 1974); *Commonwealth Broadcasting Association (CBA)* – former (1974 to 2014); *Association de radiodiffusion du Commonwealth* – former (1974 to 2014). **Aims** Create, with its members, the leading forum for exchange of knowledge to support Public Service Broadcasting/Media and the principles of free and independent media worldwide. **Structure** General Conference (every 2 years); Executive Committee; Secretariat headed by Secretary-General. **Languages** English. **Staff** 5.00 FTE, paid. **Finance** Sources: members' dues. Other sources: Project funding. **Activities** Advocacy/lobbying/activism; events/meetings; knowledge management/information dissemination; training/education. **Events** *Biennial General Conference* Kingston (Jamaica) 2018, *Biennial General Conference* Montréal, QC (Canada) 2016, *Biennial General Conference* Glasgow (UK) 2014, *Biennial General Conference* Brisbane, QLD (Australia) 2012, *Biennial general conference* Johannesburg (South Africa) 2010. **Publications** *Inform* – journal (2012). Research publications. **Information Services** *PSM Weekly.*
Members Full; Affiliate. Public media organizations and like media operations in 35 countries and territories:
Australia, Bahamas, Bangladesh, Barbados, Botswana, Brunei Darussalam, Cameroon, Canada, Cayman Is, Eswatini, Germany, Ghana, Gibraltar, Grenada, Guyana, Jamaica, Kenya, Lesotho, Malawi, Mauritius, Montserrat, Mozambique, Namibia, New Zealand, Nigeria, Rwanda, Seychelles, Solomon Is, South Africa, St Vincent-Grenadines, Tanzania UR, Tonga, Trinidad-Tobago, UK, USA.
Included in the above, 5 organizations listed in this Yearbook:
African Union of Broadcasting (AUB, #00490); *Caribbean Broadcasting Corporation (CBC)*; *Caribbean Broadcasting Union (CBU, #03465)*; *International Academy of Television Arts and Sciences (IATAS)*; *Southern African Broadcasting Association (SABA, #19837).*
IGO Relations Partner with: *UNESCO (#20322).* Associated with Department of Global Communications of the United Nations. **NGO Relations** Member of (1): *Ethical Journalism Network (EJN, #05554).* Instrumental in setting up: *Commonwealth Human Rights Initiative (CHRI, #04340).* [2019.05.07/XC0363/y/**C**]

♦ Public Population Project in Genomics / see Policy Parnterships Project for Genomic Governance (#18418)
♦ Public-Private Alliance Foundation (internationally oriented national body)

♦ Public-Private Infrastructure Advisory Facility (PPIAF) 18569

Program Manager World Bank Group, Mail Stop Number MC6-614, 1818 H St NW, Washington DC 20433, USA. T. +12024584727.
URL: http://www.ppiaf.org/

History 1999, as a joint initiative of the Governments of UK and Japan; in close cooperation with *The World Bank Group (#21218)*. Formally launched Jul 1999. Initially launched for a 3-year-period only. A multi-donor program owned and directed by participating donors. **Aims** Help eliminate poverty and achieve sustainable development by facilitating private investment in infrastructure. **Structure** Program Council, consisting of participating donors. Technical Advisory Panel. Program Management Unit. Regional Coordination Offices. **Finance** Donors: *Asian Development Bank (ADB, #01422)*; *Australian Aid (inactive)*; *European Bank for Reconstruction and Development (EBRD, #06315)*; *Agence française de développement (AFD)*; *International Finance Corporation (IFC, #13597)*; Millennium Challenge Corporation; *Swedish International Development Cooperation Agency (Sida)*; *Department for International Development (DFID, inactive)*; *United States Agency for International Development (USAID)*; *International Bank for Reconstruction and Development (IBRD, #12317)*; Finance ministries of Austria, Germany, Italy, Japan, Netherlands and Switzerland. **Activities** Channels technical assistance to governments in developing countries on strategies and measures to tap the full potential of private sector involvement in infrastructure; identifies, disseminates and promotes best practices on matters related to private sector involvement in infrastructure in developing countries. **Publications** Annual Report. Brochures. **IGO Relations** *African Legal Support Facility (ALSF, #00361)*; *Asian Development Bank Institute (ADB Institute, #01423)*. [2015/XJ5316/**F***]

♦ Public-Private Partnerships for the Urban Environment / see Sustainable Project Management- Public-Private Partnerships for the Urban Environment (#20064)

♦ Public Relations Organisation International (PROI) 18570

Main Office 125 S Wacker Dr, Ste 2600, Chicago IL 60606, USA. E-mail: information@proi.com.
URL: http://www.proi.com/

History 1970, Europe. Former names and other names: *PROI Worldwide* – alias. **Structure** International Management Board, comprising President, Chair, 6 Regional Vice-Presidents (2 per region: Europe, Middle and Africa; Americas; Asia-Pacific). **Events** *Summit* Dubrovnik (Croatia) 2022, *Europe, Middle East and Africa Regional Meeting* Brussels (Belgium) 2015, *Meeting on measuring PR in the digital age workshop* Singapore (Singapore) 2010, *Meeting* Vienna (Austria) 2009.
Members Partners in 36 countries and territories:
Argentina, Australia, Austria, Bahrain, Belgium, Brazil, Bulgaria, Canada, China, Denmark, Egypt, Finland, France, Germany, India, Italy, Japan, Korea Rep, Kuwait, Malta, Mexico, Netherlands, Oman, Portugal, Qatar, Saudi Arabia, Singapore, Slovakia, Spain, Sweden, Switzerland, Taiwan, Türkiye, UK, United Arab Emirates, USA. [2022/XJ1354/**C**]

♦ Public Safety Communication Europe (PSC Europe) 18571

Secretariat Rue des Deux Eglises 39, 1000 Brussels, Belgium. T. +3227380763. Fax +3227380764. E-mail: secretariat@psc-europe.eu.
URL: http://www.psc-europe.eu/

History Also known under the acronyms *PSCE* and *PSCE Forum*. **Aims** Foster, by consensus building, excellence in the development and use of public safety communications and information management systems; improve the provision of public safety services and the safety of the citizens of Europe and the rest of the world. **Structure** General Assembly. Board, including at least President, Vice-President, Treasurer and Relation and Communication Officer. Advisory Board. Committees (3): Users; Industrials; Researchers. Secretariat, headed by Secretary-General. **Activities** Working Groups (8): Authority to Citizen Communications; Broadband Trends and Challenges; Human Factors – ETD in PSCE; Operational Interoperability Challenges; Open Safety and Security Architecture Framework (OSSAF); SHARPS; Spectrum Harmonization Initiative; Terminology. **Events** *Winter Conference* Brussels (Belgium) 2022, *Conference* Salzburg (Austria) 2022, *Conference* Brussels (Belgium) 2021, *Conference* Lancaster (UK) 2019, *Conference* Paris (France) 2019. **Publications** *Flash News*; *PSCE Newsletter*. Factsheets. [2022/XJ2140/**F**]

♦ Public Services International (PSI) 18572

Internationale des Services Publics (ISP) – Internacional de Servicios Públicos (ISP) – Internationale der Öffentlichen Dienste (IÖD) – Internationalen för Stats- och Kommunalsanställda (ISKA)

Gen Sec 45 av Voltaire, BP 9, 01211 Ferney-Voltaire CEDEX, France. T. +33450406464. Fax +33450407320. E-mail: edith.rojas@world-psi.org.
Main: https://publicservices.international/

History 25 Aug 1907. Merged, 10 Aug 1935, with *International Federation of Civil Servants (inactive)*, formed 15 May 1925, to become *International Federation of Unions of Employees in Public and Civil Services – Confédération internationale des fédérations de fonctionnaires et du personnel des services publics*. Current Constitution adopted 3 Nov 2017. Former names and other names: *International Federation of Municipal Employees* – former (1907 to 1935); *Fédération internationale des employés municipaux* – former (1907 to 1935); *International Federation of Unions of Employees in Public and Civil Services* – former (1935 to 1958); *Confédération internationale des fédérations de fonctionnaires et du personnel des services publics* – former (1935 to 1958). **Aims** Champion *human rights*; advocate for *social justice*; promote *universal access* to quality public services. **Structure** World Congress (every 5 years); Executive Board (annual); Steering Committee (annual); World Women's Committee (annual); Secretariat; Regional Executive Committees (3) (annual); In Europe, PSI merged its European Regional Organization with *European Federation of Public Service Unions (EPSU, #07202)*, which is part of European Trade Union Confederation (ETUC). **Languages** English, French, German, Japanese, Spanish, Swedish. **Staff** 70.00 FTE, paid. **Finance** Sources: members' dues. **Activities** Events/meetings; guidance/assistance/consulting; knowledge management/information dissemination; politics/policy/regulatory. **Events** *Quinquennial Congress* Geneva (Switzerland) 2023, *Asia Pacific Regional Strategy Meeting on Trade Justice* Singapore (Singapore) 2018, *Quinquennial Congress* Geneva (Switzerland) 2017, *Asia Pacific Womens Committee Meeting* Singapore (Singapore) 2017, *Quinquennial Congress* Durban (South Africa) 2012. **Publications** Annual Report in English/French/Spanish; meeting/conference papers; manuals; handbooks; policy papers; research papers.
Members Trade unions and professional associations, totalling over 30 million members. Affiliated unions (717) in 154 countries and territories:
Albania, Algeria, Angola, Anguilla, Antigua-Barbuda, Argentina, Armenia, Aruba, Australia, Austria, Azerbaijan, Bahamas, Bahrain, Bangladesh, Barbados, Belarus, Belgium, Belize, Benin, Bermuda, Bolivia, Bosnia-Herzegovina, Botswana, Brazil, Bulgaria, Burkina Faso, Burundi, Cambodia, Cameroon, Canada, Central African Rep, Chad, Chile, Colombia, Congo DR, Cook Is, Costa Rica, Côte d'Ivoire, Croatia, Curaçao, Cyprus, Czechia, Denmark, Dominica, Dominican Rep, Ecuador, Egypt, El Salvador, Estonia, Eswatini, Fiji, Finland, France, Georgia, Germany, Ghana, Greece, Grenada, Guatemala, Guinea, Guyana, Haiti, Honduras, Hong Kong, Hungary, Iceland, India, Indonesia, Iraq, Ireland, Israel, Italy, Jamaica, Japan, Jordan, Kazakhstan, Kenya, Korea Rep, Kosovo, Kuwait, Kyrgyzstan, Latvia, Lebanon, Lesotho, Liberia, Lithuania, Luxembourg, Macau, Malawi, Malaysia, Mali, Malta, Mauritius, Mexico, Moldova, Mongolia, Montenegro, Montserrat, Morocco, Mozambique, Namibia, Nepal, Netherlands, New Zealand, Nicaragua, Niger, Nigeria, North Macedonia, Norway, Pakistan, Palestine, Panama, Papua New Guinea, Paraguay, Peru, Philippines, Portugal, Romania, Russia, Rwanda, Samoa, Senegal, Serbia, Sierra Leone, Singapore, Slovakia, Slovenia, South Africa, Spain, Sri Lanka, St Lucia, St Maarten, St Vincent-Grenadines, Sweden, Switzerland, Taiwan, Tajikistan, Tanzania UR, Thailand, Togo, Tonga, Trinidad-Tobago, Tunisia, Türkiye, Uganda, UK, Ukraine, Uruguay, USA, Vanuatu, Venezuela, Yemen, Zambia, Zimbabwe.
Included in the above 1 organization listed in this yearbook:
Union Syndicale Fédérale (USF, #20485).
Consultative Status Consultative status granted from: *ECOSOC (#05331)* (Special); *UNCTAD (#20285)* (General Category); *WHO (#20950)* (Official Relations). **IGO Relations** Member of (1): UN Secretary General's Advisory Board on Water. Cooperates with (1): *UN-Water (#20723)*. Associated with Department of Global Communications of the United Nations. **NGO Relations** Member of (13): *Conference of Non-Governmental Organizations in Consultative Relationship with the United Nations (CONGO, #04635)*; *Geneva Global Health Hub (G2H2, #10122)*; *Global Campaign for Education (GCE, #10264)*; *Global Campaign for Ratification of the Convention on the Rights of Migrant Workers (#10267)*; *Global Health Workforce Alliance (GHWA, inactive)*; *Global Labour University (GLU, #10448)*; *Global Union Federations (GUF, #10638)*; *ILGA World (International Lesbian, Gay, Bisexual, Trans and Intersex Association, #11120)*; *International NGO Platform on the Migrant Workers' Convention (IPMWC, #14367)*; *NGO Committee on the Status of Women, Geneva (#17117)*; *Our World is Not for Sale (OWINFS, #17917)*; *UNCAC Coalition (#20283)*; *Women in Migration Network (WIMN, #21008)*. Cooperates with (1): *World Medical Association (WMA, #21646)*. Supports (1): *Global Call for Action Against Poverty (GCAP, #10263)*. [2022.12.05/XB2374/y/**B**]

♦ Publiez ce que vous payez (#18573)
♦ Publiquen Lo Que Pagan (#18573)
♦ Publique o que Paga (#18573)
♦ Publishers Alliance (inactive)
♦ Publishers and Booksellers Association of ASEAN / see ASEAN Book Publishers Association (#01145)
♦ Publish What You Fund (internationally oriented national body)
♦ Publish What You Fund – The Global Campaign for Aid Transparency / see Publish What You Fund

♦ Publish What You Pay Coalition (PWYP) 18573

Publiez ce que vous payez (PCQVP) – Publiquen Lo Que Pagan (PLQP) – Publique o que Paga (POQP)

Communications Dir The Office Group, 201 Borough High Street, London, SE1 1JA, UK. T. +442030967715. E-mail: info@pwyp.org.
URL: https://www.pwyp.org/

History Founded by *Open Society Foundations (OSF, #17763)*, *Catholic Agency for Overseas Development (CAFOD)*, *Global Witness (GW)*, *Save the Children UK (SC UK)*, *Transparency International (TI, #20223)* and *Oxfam GB*. UK Registered Charity: 1170959. Registration: Charity Commission, No/ID: 1170959, England and Wales; Companies House, No/ID: 9533183, England and Wales. **Aims** Advocate for transparency and *accountability* in the *gas*, *oil* and *mining* industry so that revenues form the basis for development and improve the lives of citizens in resource-rich countries. **Structure** Global Assembly; Global Council; Global Steering Committee; Board. Secretariat. **Events** *Making Transparency Possible Conference* Oslo (Norway) 2020, *Making Transparency Possible Conference* Oslo (Norway) 2019. **Publications** Electronic newsletter (every 2 weeks). **Members** Coalitions in 41 countries (not specified); member organizations (over 800) in 26 countries (not specified).
NGO Relations Signatories to the 'Publish What You Pay' appeal, national and international organizations (84), including the following organizations listed in this Yearbook:
- *Acçao para o Desenvolvimento Pesquisa e Cooperação Internacional, Angola (ADPCI, no recent information)*;
- *Africa Centre for Constitutional Development, Nigeria (no recent information)*;
- *African Oil Policy Initiative Group (AOPIG, no recent information)*;
- *Amnesty International (AI, #00801)*;
- *Association for the Taxation of Financial Transactions for the Aid of Citizens (#02947)*;
- *Campaign Against Arms Trade (CAAT)*;
- *Catholic Relief Services (CRS, #03608)*;
- *CEE Bankwatch Network (#03624)*;
- *Center for Economic and Social Rights (CESR)*;
- *Christian Aid*;
- *Concern for Development Initiatives in Africa (ForDIA)*;
- *Friends of the Earth International (FoEI, #10002)*;
- *Human Rights Watch (HRW, #10990)*;
- *IMPACT (#11136)*;
- *INTERMON OXFAM*;
- *International Federation for Human Rights (#13452)*;
- *Medico International*;
- *Network for African Peace-Builders (NAPS, #16985)*;
- *Oxfam International (#17922)*;
- *Oxfam Novib*;
- *Public Eye*;
- *Save the Children International (#19058)*;
- *Scottish Catholic International Aid Fund (SCIAF)*;
- *Secours catholique – Caritas France*;
- *Sherpa*;
- *SOLIDAR (#19680)*;
- *Tearfund, UK*;
- *West African NGO Network (WANGONeT)*.

Partner of: *Actions for Genuine Democratic Alternatives (AGENDA, #00097)*. [2022/XG9468/**F**]

♦ PUEA – Postal Union of EurAsia (inactive)
♦ Puebla Process / see Regional Conference on Migration (#18769)
♦ Pueblito Canada (internationally oriented national body)
♦ Pueblos Hermanos (internationally oriented national body)
♦ Puentes para la Paz (internationally oriented national body)
♦ **PU Europe** Federation of European Rigid Polyurethane Foam Associations (#09538)
♦ PUF – Millennia2025 Women and Innovation Foundation (internationally oriented national body)

♦ Pugwash Conferences on Science and World Affairs 18574

Conférences Pugwash sur la science et les problèmes internationaux – Paguosskoe Dvizenie

Rome Office Via della Lungara 10, 00165 Rome RM, Italy. T. +393334566661.
Geneva Office 7bis Avenue de la Paix, 2d Floor, 1202 Geneva, Switzerland. T. +41229073667.
URL: http://www.pugwash.org/

History 7 Jul 1957, Pugwash, NS (Canada). 7-10 Jul 1957, Pugwash (Canada), during 1st Conference. Membership enlarged at 3rd Conference, 14-20 Sep 1958, Kitzbühel/Vienna (Austria). Awarded Nobel Peace Prize in 1995. **Aims** Bring together influential scholars and public figures concerned with reducing the danger of armed conflict and seeking cooperative solutions for global problems. Organize international conferences of scientists to discuss: problems which have arisen as a result of the progress of science, and in particular dangers to mankind from the development of weapons of mass destruction; problems of disarmament; international scientific collaboration; aid to developing countries. **Structure** Quinquennial Conference elects Council (26 members); Executive Council; President; Secretary-General. Small permanent offices in Geneva (Switzerland), London (UK) and Rome (Italy); National Pugwash Groups. *International School on Disarmament and Research on Conflicts (ISODARCO)* functions as Italian Group. **Languages** English. **Staff** 2.00 FTE, paid. Voluntary. **Finance** Grants from Foundations, Academies of Science and individuals. **Activities** Participants meet in private as individuals to exchange views and explore alternative approaches to arms control and tension reduction. Insights from Pugwash discussions tend to penetrate quickly to the appropriate levels of official policy-making. Pugwash Conferences, Symposia and Workshops. Workshop series: science, media and world affairs; conventional forces in Europe; non-military dimensions of global security; foreign debts and international stability; security and cooperation in the South Atlantic; nuclear forces; chemical and biological weapon. Projects: Desirability and Feasibility of a Nuclear-Weapon-Free World; Conversion of Military Research and Development to Civilian Uses; Monitoring Implementation of Chemical and Biological Weapons Treaties. Pugwash-SIPRI Thiodiglycol Project with *Stockholm International Peace Research Institute (SIPRI, #19994)*. **Events** *Annual Conference* Nagasaki (Japan) 2015, *Annual Conference* Istanbul (Turkey) 2013, *Annual Conference* Berlin (Germany) 2011, *Annual Conference* The Hague (Netherlands) 2009, *Annual Conference* Bari (Italy) 2007. **Publications** *Pugwash Newsletter* (4 a year). *Annals of Pugwash* – series. *War No More* (2003); *A Nuclear Weapon-Free World: Steps Along the Way* (2000); *Ending War: The Force of Reason* (1999); *Nuclear Energy: Promise or Peril* (1999); *Remember Your Humanity* (1999); *A World at the Crossroads: New Conflicts, New Solutions* (1994); *A Nuclear-Weapon-Free World: Desirable ? Feasible ?* (1993) – in English, (1994) in Russian, (1995) in Arabic/Chinese; *Verification: Monitoring Disarmament* (1991); *Nuclear Non-Proliferation and the Non-Proliferation Treaty* (1990) by M P Fry et al; *Scientists in the Quest for Peace: A History of the Pugwash Conferences* (1972) by J Rotblat. Pugwash monographs; conference proceedings.
Members National Pugwash Groups and individuals in 70 countries:
Algeria, Argentina, Australia, Austria, Azerbaijan, Bangladesh, Belarus, Belgium, Bosnia-Herzegovina, Brazil, Bulgaria, Canada, Chile, China, Costa Rica, Croatia, Cuba, Czechia, Denmark, Egypt, Estonia, Finland, France, Georgia, Germany, Ghana, Greece, Hungary, India, Iran Islamic Rep, Ireland, Israel, Italy, Japan, Jordan, Kazakhstan, Kenya, Korea Rep, Latvia, Lebanon, Malta, Mexico, Nepal, Netherlands, New Zealand, Nigeria, Norway, Pakistan, Peru, Philippines, Poland, Portugal, Romania, Russia, Serbia, Sierra Leone, Slovakia, Slovenia, South Africa, Spain, Sudan, Sweden, Switzerland, Thailand, Türkiye, UK, Ukraine, USA, Zambia, Zimbabwe.
Consultative Status Consultative status granted from: *ECOSOC (#05331)* (Special). **IGO Relations** Accredited by: *United Nations Office at Vienna (UNOV, #20604)*. Associated with Department of Global Communications of the United Nations. **NGO Relations** Member of: *Campaign to Stop Killer Robots (#03405)*; *Fédération des Institutions Internationales établies à Genève (FIIG, #09599)*. Represented on the Organizing Committee of: *Hague Appeal for Peace (HAP, #10848)*. Invited to participate in the work of: *Commission mondiale d'éthique des connaissances scientifiques et des technologies de l'UNESCO (COMEST, #04235)*. Instrumental in setting up: *International Student/Young Pugwash (ISYP, #15614)*. Joint conferences with: *International Colloquium on Conflict and Aggression (#12653)*. [2018/XE3148/**F**]

♦ **PUIC** Parliamentary Union of the OIC Member States (#18220)

♦ PUKO / see Federación Panamericana de Karate (#09381)
♦ **PUK** Patriotic Union of Kurdistan (#18265)
♦ Pulitzer Center on Crisis Reporting (internationally oriented national body)

♦ Pulmonary Hypertension Association Europe (PHA Europe) 18575

Europäische Arbeitsgruppe für Lungenhochdruck
Contact Mooslackengasse 17, 1190 Vienna, Austria. E-mail: info@phaeurope.org.
URL: http://www.phaeurope.org/

History 2003. Former names and other names: *Pulmonary Hypertension Association Europe – europäische Arbeitsgruppe für Lungehochdruck (PHA Europe)* – full title; *PHA Europe – European pulmonary hypertension association* – full title. Registration: No/ID: 070826881, Austria; EU Transparency Register, No/ID: 432824341542-09, Start date: 15 Mar 2021. **Aims** Advocate for better healthcare and quality of life for patients; advance general education and awareness of pulmonary hypertension; support setting up of national patient associations. **Structure** General Assembly (annual); Board of Directors; Executive Committee; Scientific Board. **Languages** English. **Staff** 4.00 FTE, paid. **Finance** Sources: members' dues. Annual budget: 900,000 EUR. **Activities** Advocacy/lobbying/activism; awareness raising; capacity building; training/education; knowledge management/information dissemination; events/meetings. **Events** *Annual PH European Conference* Castelldefels (Spain) 2019, *Annual Conference* Barcelona (Spain) 2017, *Annual Conference* Barcelona (Spain) 2016, *Annual Conference* Barcelona (Spain) 2015, *Annual Conference* Barcelona (Spain) 2014. **Publications** *Mariposa News* (2 a year). Journal.
Members Affiliates in 33 countries:
Austria, Belarus, Belgium, Bosnia-Herzegovina, Bulgaria, Croatia, Czechia, Denmark, Finland, France, Germany, Greece, Hungary, Ireland, Israel, Italy, Latvia, Lithuania, Netherlands, North Macedonia, Norway, Poland, Portugal, Romania, Russia, Serbia, Slovakia, Slovenia, Spain, Sweden, Switzerland, Türkiye, Ukraine.
NGO Relations Member of: *EURORDIS – Rare Diseases Europe (#09175)*; *European Patients' Forum (EPF, #08172)*; *European Public Health Alliance (EPHA, #08297)*. [2020/XM1566/**D**]

♦ Pulmonary Hypertension Association Europe – europäische Arbeitsgruppe für Lungehochdruck / see Pulmonary Hypertension Association Europe (#18575)

♦ Pulmonary Vascular Research Institute (PVRI) 18576

Chief Exec 33 St George's Place, Canterbury, CT1 1UT, UK. T. +441227787972. E-mail: admin@pvrinstitute.org.
URL: https://pvrinstitute.org/

History Founded 2007. A UK Registered Charity: 1127115. **Aims** Reduce the global burden of pulmonary vascular disease (PVD) within 10 years. **Structure** Board of Trustees; Sub-Committees; Task Forces. **Languages** English. **Staff** 4.00 FTE, paid. **Staff** Several voluntary. **Finance** Sources: grants; members' dues; sponsorship. Other sources: registration fees. **Activities** Events/meetings; networking/liaising; research and development; training/education. **Events** *Annual World Congress on Pulmonary Vascular Disease* Athens (Greece) 2022, *Pulmonary Hypertension Meeting* Cairo (Egypt) 2020, *Annual World Congress on Pulmonary Vascular Disease* Lima (Peru) 2020, *Annual World Congress on Pulmonary Vascular Disease* Barcelona (Spain) 2019, *Annual Pulmonary Hypertension Conference* Dubai (United Arab Emirates) 2018. **Publications** *Pulmonary Circulation* – journal. **Members** Individuals (about 6,300) in 103 countries. Membership countries not specified. **NGO Relations** Member of: *The NCD Alliance (NCDA, #16963)*; *World Heart Federation (WHF, #21562)*. [2020.02.18/XM8081/**C**]

♦ Pulp Chemicals Association / see Pine Chemicals Association

♦ Pulp and Paper Products Council (PPPC) 18577

Head Office 1200 Ave McGill College, Ste 1000, Montréal QC H3B 4G7, Canada. T. +15148618828. Fax +15148664863. E-mail: general@pppc.org.
China Office Suite 2483 Level 24, Tower 3 China Central Place, 77 Jianguo Road, Chaoyang District, 100025 Beijing, China.
European Office Av Louise 250, 1050 Brussels, Belgium.
URL: http://www.pppc.org

History A Participating Industry Sector of *Confederation of European Paper Industries (CEPI, #04529)*. **Aims** Be the industry reference and principal source of information on the global pulp and graphic paper markets. **Languages** Chinese, English, French, German, Spanish. **Staff** 25.00 FTE, paid. **Activities** Events/meetings. **Events** *International paper week* Montréal, QC (Canada) 2002, *International paper week* Montréal, QC (Canada) 2001. **Members** Product associations serving an international membership in the pulp and paper industry. Membership countries not specified. [2017.10.11/XM7405/**F**]

♦ Pulse of Asia (unconfirmed)
♦ **PUMed** Postal Union for the Mediterranean (#18467)
♦ PUOICM / see Parliamentary Union of the OIC Member States (#18220)
♦ Pupils' Attitudes Toward Technology (unconfirmed)
♦ **PUPOL** Academic Network Public and Political Leadership (#00021)
♦ Puppeteers Without Borders (internationally oriented national body)

♦ Pure Earth 18578

CEO 475 Riverside Dr, Ste 860, New York NY 10115, USA. T. +12128703490. E-mail: info@pureearth.org.
URL: https://www.pureearth.org/

History 1999. Former names and other names: *Blacksmith Institute* – former. **Aims** Save and improve lives, particularly lives of children in poor communities, by reducing disease-causing *pollution*, particularly of lead and mercury. **Structure** Board; Leadership Council; Technical Advisory Board. **Publications** Annual report. **Consultative Status** Consultative status granted from: *ECOSOC (#05331)* (Special); *UNEP (#20299)*. **NGO Relations** Member of (1): *Climate and Clean Air Coalition (CCAC, #04010)*. Partner of (1): *Global Battery Alliance (GBA, #10249)*. [2023.02.13/XM3216/j/**F**]

♦ Pure Water for the World (internationally oriented national body)
♦ Purine Club (internationally oriented national body)

♦ Purine and Pyrimidine Society (PPS) 18579

Sec Lab Medical Oncology, Vu Univ Medical Center, De Boelelaan 1117, 1081 HV Amsterdam, Netherlands.
URL: http://www.ppsociety.org/

History Founded 1987, Switzerland, as *European Society for the Study of Purine and Pyrimidine Metabolism in Man (ESSPPMM)*, during the 1st European Symposium on Purine and Pyrimidine Metabolism in Man. Statutes adopted Jan 1988. Present name adopted, 2003, when *International Symposium on Purine Metabolism (inactive)* started being organized by PPS. Registered in accordance with Dutch law. **Aims** Improve diagnosis, treatment and understanding of inherited and acquired purine and pyrimidine disorders; extend knowledge of the importance of normal purine and pyrimidine metabolism in man; apply this knowledge to diagnose and treat patients with diseases such as in the cardiovascular system, cancer, immunology, rheumatology, inflammatory diseases, parasite infections and viral infections. **Structure** General Assembly (every 2 years); Scientific Committee; Executive Committee. **Languages** English. **Staff** None. **Finance** Members' dues. **Activities** Events/meetings. **Events** *International Symposium* Lyon (France) 2019, *International Symposium* Gdansk (Poland) 2017, *International Symposium* New York, NY (USA) 2015, *International Symposium* Madrid (Spain) 2013, *International Symposium* Tokyo (Japan) 2011. **Publications** *Nucleosides, Nucleotides and Nucleic Acids*. **Members** Full; Student; Corporate; Honorary. Membership, in principle, open to all countries worldwide. Membership countries not specified. [2018.10.11/XD8126/**D**]

♦ **PURPLE** Peri-Urban Regions Platform Europe (#18316)
♦ Pusat Studi Sosial Asia Tenggara (internationally oriented national body)

♦ PUSH! Global Alliance 18580

Address not obtained.
URL: http://www.pu-sh.org/

History Former names and other names: *People and Organisations United for Spina Bifida and Hydrocephalus* – full title. **Aims** Unite organizations as the global voice, to accelerate spina bifida and hydrocephalus prevention, and to realize optimal care and a better quality of life for those affected. **Structure** Steering Committee; Executive Committee.

Members Private and public organizations in healthcare, research, academia and patient advocacy. Included 3 organizations listed in this Yearbook:
Cure International; *Food Fortification Initiative (FFI, #09844)*; *International Federation for Spina Bifida and Hydrocephalus (IF SBH, #13552)*. [2017/AA1171/y/**C**]

♦ PUST – Pan African Union of Science and Technology (inactive)
♦ Putri Bunda Hati Kudus (religious order)
♦ Putting Poverty in the Past / see P3 Foundation
♦ **PUU** Pontificia Universitas Urbaniana (#18454)

♦ PVC4Cables 18581

Contact Av de Cortenbergh 71, 1000 Brussels, Belgium. T. +323295105. E-mail: info@pvc4cables.org.
URL: http://www.pvc4cables.org/

History A value chain platform of *European Council of Vinyl Manufacturers (ECVM, #06849)*. **Aims** Proactively engage in promoting *PVC cables*, highlighting their contribution to *sustainable* development and to the circular economy, as well as their numerous technical and functional benefits for final users and consumers. **Events** *PVC4Cables Conference* Bologna (Italy) 2022. **NGO Relations** Partners include: *European Stabiliser Producers Association (ESPA, #08827)*. [2022/XM7354/**E**]

♦ PVC4Pipes 18582

Contact Av de Cortenbergh 71, 1000 Brussels, Belgium. E-mail: info@pvc4pipes.com.
URL: http://www.pvc4pipes.com/

History 2003, Brussels (Belgium). A value chain platform of *European Council of Vinyl Manufacturers (ECVM, #06849)*. **Aims** Develop and promote *sustainable PVC* piping systems in the global market. **Languages** English. **Activities** Advocacy/lobbying/activism; awareness raising; guidance/assistance/consulting; knowledge management/information dissemination; management of treaties and agreements; projects/programmes; publishing activities; research/documentation; training/education. **Events** *Piping Systems for Utilities – Resilient, Efficient and Sustainable* Italy 2021.
Members Resin Producers, Pipes Producers, Additive Suppliers, Machinery Producers; Associations; Communication Bodies; Institutes. Associations include 1 organization listed in this Yearbook:
European Council of Vinyl Manufacturers (ECVM, #06849).
NGO Relations Cooperates with (1): *Plastic Pipes Conference Association (PPCA, #18393)*. [2021.05.25/XJ9394/y/**E**]

♦ PVCMed Alliance 18583

Contact Avenue de Cortenbergh 71, 1000 Brussels, Belgium. E-mail: info@pvcmed.org.
URL: http://pvcmed.org/

History A value chain platform of: *European Council of Vinyl Manufacturers (ECVM, #06849)*. EU Transparency Register: 794691133516-55. **Aims** Provide a focal point for communication with all stakeholdes involved – healthcare professionals and managers, medical device companies, regulators and the general public – about *PVC*-based *healthcare* applications. [2018/XM7353/**E**]

♦ PV CYCLE Association (unconfirmed)
♦ PVDD – Pour un vrai développement durable (internationally oriented national body)
♦ PVF – Pro Victimis Foundation (internationally oriented national body)
♦ **PVRI** Pulmonary Vascular Research Institute (#18576)
♦ PVSEC – International Photovoltaic Science and Engineering Conference (meeting series)
♦ PVSF – Pacific Voice and Speech Foundation (internationally oriented national body)
♦ **PVSG EU** Poultry Veterinary Study Group of the EU (#18471)
♦ PWA – Pacific Water Association (internationally oriented national body)
♦ PWA – Professional Windsurfers Association (internationally oriented national body)
♦ PWC / see Pentecostal World Fellowship (#18295)
♦ PWF / see Pax World Service
♦ PWI – Permanent Way Institution (internationally oriented national body)
♦ PWJ / see Peace Winds
♦ PWL – Peace Without Limits – PWL – International Organization (internationally oriented national body)
♦ PWM – Partnership for World Mission (internationally oriented national body)

♦ PWN Global – Professional Women's Network (PWN Global) 18584

Global 128 rue La Boétie, 75008 Paris, France. T. +33970446262. E-mail: rebecca.fountain@pwnglobal.net – contact@pwnglobal.net.
URL: http://www.pwnglobal.net/

History 1996, Paris (France), as *European Professional Women's Network (European PWN)*. Registered in accordance with French law: 487 942 583. EU Transparency Register: 967400137517-43. **Aims** Promote professional progress of women through their career; increase sustainable and innovative professional career paths; encourage companies to recognize the necessity of diverse management approaches; raise visibility of European women in business. **Structure** Federation Board; City Networks Boards. **Finance** Members' dues. **Activities** Events/meetings; networking/liaising; knowledge management/information dissemination. **Events** *Annual General Meeting* Amsterdam (Netherlands) 2014, *Annual General Meeting* Madrid (Spain) 2011, *Conference* Madrid (Spain) 2011. **Publications** *European PWN Newsletter* (12 a year). *Women 'at' Work* – series.
Members City networks in 20 countries:
Austria, Belgium, Brazil, Bulgaria, Croatia, Denmark, France, Germany, Ireland, Italy, Netherlands, Norway, Poland, Portugal, Romania, Spain, Sweden, Switzerland, Türkiye, UK. [2020/XM1656/t/**F**]

♦ **PWN Global** PWN Global – Professional Women's Network (#18584)
♦ PWO / see Parliamentarians for Global Action (#18208)
♦ PWPA International / see Professors World Peace Academy (#18520)
♦ **PWPA** Professors World Peace Academy (#18520)
♦ PWRDF – Primate's World Relief and Development Fund (internationally oriented national body)
♦ PWS and D – Presbyterian World Service and Development (internationally oriented national body)
♦ PWS – Pax World Service (internationally oriented national body)
♦ PWWA / see Pacific Water Association
♦ PWW-NZ – Pacific Women's Watch – New Zealand (internationally oriented national body)
♦ PWW – Pure Water for the World (internationally oriented national body)
♦ **PWYP** Publish What You Pay Coalition (#18573)
♦ PXE International – Pseudoxanthoma Elasticum International (internationally oriented national body)
♦ **PYA** Professional Yachting Association (#18519)
♦ PYM – Pan African Youth Movement (inactive)

♦ Pyramide Europe 18585

SG Pyramide Norden, DJfotograferne, Gammel Strand 46, 1202 Copenhagen K, Denmark.
Registered Address Walter-Gropius-Allee 1, 68519 Viernheim, Germany.

History 1989. A grouping of the type *European Economic Interest Grouping (EEIG, #06960)*. Registration: Companies House, No/ID: 04913658, Start date: 2003, End date: 2021, England and Wales; Hesse District court, No/ID: HRB 96109, Start date: 2016, Germany, Darmstadt. **Aims** Create an environment where *photographers* and other visual *artists* can continue to be *creative* in a market that is open and fair. **Languages** English, French. **Staff** Voluntary. **Finance** Funds provided from national member organizations.
Members Full in 12 countries:
Denmark, Finland, France, Germany, Greece, Iceland, Ireland, Italy, Netherlands, Spain, Sweden, UK.
NGO Relations Member of (2): *International Authors Forum (IAF, #12298)*; *International Federation of Reproduction Rights Organizations (IFRRO, #13527)*. [2020/XJ7456/**F**]

♦ Pyramid Society Europe (internationally oriented national body)
♦ **PYRN** Permafrost Young Researcher Network (#18318)
♦ Pyro – International Symposium on Analytical and Applied Pyrolysis (meeting series)
♦ PYXERA Global (internationally oriented national body)

♦ PZG Nederland – Piloten Zonder Grenzen, Nederland (internationally oriented national body)
♦ PZKB / see German Platform for Peaceful Conflict Management
♦ PZK – Plattform Zivile Konfliktbearbeitung (internationally oriented national body)
♦ Qaddafi International Foundation for Charity Associations / see Gaddafi International Charity and Development Foundation
♦ Qadiriya (religious order)
♦ Al Qaeda / see Al-Qa'ida (#00748)
♦ QAHE – International Association for Quality Assurance in Higher Education (internationally oriented national body)
♦ Qa'idat al-Jihad / see Al-Qa'ida (#00748)
♦ **QA-Islamic** Association of Quality Assurance Agencies of the Islamic World (#02882)
♦ Qandil / see Swedish Development Aid Organization
♦ **QCEA** Quaker Council for European Affairs (#18587)
♦ QCIR / see Centre for International and Defence Policy, Kingston ON
♦ QCMC – International Conference on Quantum Communication, Measurement and Computing (meeting series)
♦ QCMS – QSAR, Cheminformatics and Modeling Society (unconfirmed)
♦ QCRYPT – Conference on Quantum Cryptography (meeting series)
♦ QD – International Conference on Quantum Dots (meeting series)
♦ QEC-ERAN / see Local Urban Development European Network (#16508)
♦ QEST – International Conference on Quantitative Evaluation of Systems (meeting series)
♦ QEW – Quaker Earthcare Witness (internationally oriented national body)
♦ QFF – Queer Football Fanclubs (internationally oriented national body)
♦ QIF / see Mission Africa
♦ QIPC – Quantum Information Processing and Communication (meeting series)
♦ **QI** Quota International (#18596)
♦ QIRT – International Conference on Quantitative InfraRed Thermography (meeting series)
♦ **QJF** Quality Juice Foundation (#18592)
♦ **QMEA** Quali Middle East Association (#18591)
♦ QMOD – International Quality Management and Organisational Development Conference (meeting series)
♦ QMSKI – International Workshop on Quantitative Musculoskeletal Imaging (meeting series)
♦ QNP – International Conference on Quarks and Nuclear Physics (meeting series)
♦ Il-Qorti Ewropea Ta' l-Awdituri (#06854)
♦ Il-Qorti tal-Gustizzja tal-Komunitajiet Ewropej / see Court of Justice of the European Union (#04938)
♦ QPN / see Quaker Peace Network West Africa
♦ QPNWA – Quaker Peace Network West Africa (internationally oriented national body)
♦ QPSW – Quaker Peace and Social Witness (see: #10004)
♦ QR – International Workshop on Qualitative Reasoning (meeting series)
♦ QRS – International Workshop on Quantum Reactive Scattering (meeting series)
♦ QSAR, Cheminformatics and Modeling Society (unconfirmed)
♦ QSAR – International Workshop on (Quantitative) Structure-Activity Relationships in Environmental and Health Sciences (meeting series)
♦ QSCC – Quadrilateral Symposium on Coordination Chemistry (meeting series)
♦ QSIP – Quantum Structure Infrared Photodetectors Conference (meeting series)
♦ QTD – Conference on Quantum Thermodynamics (meeting series)
♦ QTS – International Symposium Quantum Theory and Symmetries (meeting series)
♦ **Quad Group** Quadrilateral Group of Industrialized Economies (#18586)
♦ Quadragonale / see Central European Initiative (#03708)

♦ Quadrilateral Group of Industrialized Economies (Quad Group) 18586

Address not obtained.
Members Trade Ministers of 3 countries:
Canada, Japan, USA.
Trade ministers of 1 regional grouping:
European Union (EU, #08967). [2010/XF3562/t/**F***]

♦ Quadrilateral Initiative / see Central European Initiative (#03708)
♦ Quadrilateral Symposium on Coordination Chemistry (meeting series)
♦ Quadripartite Agreement (1972 treaty)
♦ Quadripartite Commission (no recent information)
♦ Quadruple Alliance, 1666 (1666 treaty)
♦ Quadruple Alliance Treaty, 1745 (1745 treaty)
♦ Quadruple Alliance Treaty, 1834 (1834 treaty)
♦ Quadruple Alliance Treaty, 1840 (1840 treaty)
♦ Qua Iboe Fellowship / see Mission Africa

♦ Quaker Council for European Affairs (QCEA) 18587

Conseil quaker pour les affaires européennes – Quäkerrat für Europäische Angelegenheiten
Representative Quaker House, Square Ambiorix 50, 1000 Brussels, Belgium. T. +3222304935. Fax +3222306370. E-mail: office@qcea.org.
URL: http://www.qcea.org/
History Founded 31 Mar 1979, Brussels (Belgium). International administration of Quaker organizations is through *Friends World Committee for Consultation (FWCC, #10004)* within the general framework of *Religious Society of Friends (Quakers, #18834)*, with QCEA independent of FWCC. Registration: EU Transparency Register, No/ID: 3960234639-24; AISBL/IVZW, No/ID: 0420.346.728, Belgium. **Aims** Promote Quaker *values* in the European context; express a Quaker vision in matters of peace, human rights, sustainability, economic justice and democratic accountability; act as a centre for networks of Quakers and others sympathetic to Quaker values working at European level; provide information to Quakers and others sympathetic to Quaker values to enable informed, active and timely participation in decision-making processes. **Structure** Council (meets twice a year in Brussels). Committees (3), reporting to the Council: Bureau; Finance; Nominations. Provides secretariat for: *Europe and Middle East Young Friends (EMEYF, #09162).* **Languages** Dutch, English, French, German. **Staff** 2.50 FTE, paid. 2 paid internships. **Finance** Donations from: individuals; Quaker bodies; charitable trusts, including *Joseph Rowntree Charitable Trust.* Budget (annual): about euro 300,000. **Activities** Research/documentation; advocacy/lobbying/activism; events/meetings. **Events** *Peace Education Conference* London (UK) 2021, *Biennial Week-End Conference* Brussels (Belgium) 2015, *Biennial Week-End Conference* Brussels (Belgium) 2013, *Biennial Week-End Conference* Brussels (Belgium) 2010, *Biennial Week-End Conference* Brussels (Belgium) 2008. **Publications** *Around Europe* (6 a year). Annual Report; reports; surveys; studies; briefing papers.
Members European Quaker Organizations (14); Founder Members (8); Co-opted (3). Member organizations and supporters in 27 countries and territories:
Austria, Belgium, Bulgaria, Croatia, Czechia, Denmark, Estonia, Finland, France, Georgia, Germany, Greece, Hungary, Ireland, Italy, Latvia, Lebanon, Lithuania, Luxembourg, Netherlands, Norway, Palestine, Russia, Spain, Sweden, Switzerland, UK.
Consultative Status Consultative status granted from: *Council of Europe (CE, #04881)* (Participatory Status).
NGO Relations Member of: *European Peacebuilding Liaison Office (EPLO, #08176); European NGO Platform Asylum and Migration (EPAM, #08051); Human Rights and Democracy Network (HRDN, #10980); OECD Watch (#17694).* [2020/XD6231/**D**]

♦ Quaker Earthcare Witness (internationally oriented national body)
♦ Quaker Network for the Prevention of Violent Conflict (unconfirmed)
♦ Quaker Peace Network West Africa (internationally oriented national body)
♦ Quaker Peace and Social Witness (see: #10004)
♦ Quäkerrat für Europäische Angelegenheiten (#18587)
♦ Quakers Friends Church / see Religious Society of Friends (#18834)
♦ **Quäkers** Religiöse Gesellschaft der Freunde (#18834)
♦ **Quakers** Religious Society of Friends (#18834)

♦ Quaker United Nations Office (QUNO) 18588

Bureau Quaker auprès des Nations Unies
Dir Av du Mervelet 13, 1209 Geneva, Switzerland. T. +41227484800. Fax +41227484819. E-mail: quno@quno.ch.
Dir & Quaker UN Rep 777 UN Plaza, New York NY 10017, USA. T. +12126822745. Fax +12129830034. E-mail: qunony@afsc.org.
URL: https://quno.org/
History 1926, Geneva (Switzerland). Founded as Geneva Office, with the title *International Quaker Centre – Centre Quaker international*, also referred to as *Friends International Centre.* Current centre, also referred to as *Quaker UN Office*, founded 1947. Administered jointly by *Quaker Peace and Social Witness (QPSW, see: #10004)* of Britain Yearly Meeting and by *Friends World Committee for Consultation (FWCC, #10004)* within the general framework of *Religious Society of Friends (Quakers, #18834).* New York Office founded 1947; administered jointly by American Friends Service Committee (AFSC) and FWCC. **Aims** Represent Quakers worldwide to the UN and other IGOs in Geneva (Switzerland) and New York NY (USA) on key *peace* and *justice* concerns. **Structure** Comprises two offices relating to separate Quaker UN Committees. Geneva office comprises representatives of Quaker Peace and Social Witness and FWCC; New York office comprises representatives of AFSC and FWCC. Both offices have accreditation with the UN via FWCC. **Languages** English. **Staff** Geneva (Switzerland): 9; New York NY (USA): 6. **Finance** Sources: contributions; government support; grants; private foundations. **Activities** Advocacy/lobbying/activism; events/meetings; knowledge management/information dissemination; networking/liaising. **Events** *International conference on child soldiers* Amman (Jordan) 2001. **Publications** *QUNO Geneva Reporter* (4 a year) – newsletter; *In and Around the UN* – QUNO New York newsletter. Annual Report. Annual reports on the UN Human Rights Council; various studies and publications in the areas of human rights, peace building, economic justice.
Members Worldwide members through FWCC. Membership countries not specified. **NGO Relations** Member of (5): *Fédération des Institutions Internationales établies à Genève (FIIG, #09599); Geneva Forum; Geneva Peacebuilding Platform (GPP); International Action Network on Small Arms (IANSA, #11585); NGO Working Group on the Security Council (#17128).* [2022.02.02/XE3630/**E**]

♦ Quaker UN Office / see Quaker United Nations Office (#18588)

♦ QUALANOD 18589

Secretariat c/o ARCO Association Management AG, Tödistr 42, 8002 Zurich ZH, Switzerland. E-mail: info@qualanod.net.
URL: http://www.qualanod.net/
History 1974. Founded by *European association for Surface Treatment on Aluminium (ESTAL, #06242)* and *European Wrought Aluminium Association (EWAA, inactive).* QUALANOD stands for: *Quality Label for Sulphuric Acid-Based Anodizing of Aluminium.* **Aims** Maintain and promote the quality of *anodised* aluminium and its *alloys* for *architectural* applications. **Structure** Chairman. Secretariat. **Languages** English. [2020.05.29/XM2908/**E**]

♦ QUALICOAT 18590

Acting Managing Dir Tödistrasse 48, 8002 Zurich ZH, Switzerland. T. +41445159841. E-mail: info@qualicoat.net.
URL: http://www.qualicoat.net/
History 1986. Former names and other names: *Association of Quality Control in the Lacquering, Painting and Coating Industry* – alias. Registration: Swiss Civil Code, No/ID: SCESp0130, Switzerland. **Aims** Maintain and promote the quality of coating on aluminium and its alloys for architectural applications. **Structure** Executive Committee, headed by Chairman; Secretariat; Committees; Working Groups. **Languages** English. **Staff** 4.00 FTE, paid. **Activities** Certification/accreditation; monitoring/evaluation; research and development; standards/guidelines. **Publications** *QUALICOAT News.*
Members Full in 64 countries and territories:
Albania, Algeria, Argentina, Australia, Austria, Bahrain, Belarus, Belgium, Bosnia-Herzegovina, Brazil, Bulgaria, Chile, China, Colombia, Croatia, Cyprus, Czechia, Egypt, England, France, Germany, Greece, Hungary, India, Indonesia, Ireland, Israel, Italy, Japan, Kazakhstan, Kuwait, Latvia, Lebanon, Lithuania, Malaysia, Mauritius, Mexico, Morocco, Netherlands, Oman, Peru, Poland, Portugal, Qatar, Réunion, Romania, Russia, Saudi Arabia, Serbia, Slovakia, South Africa, Spain, Sri Lanka, Sweden, Switzerland, Thailand, Tunisia, Türkiye, UK, Ukraine, United Arab Emirates, USA, Uzbekistan, Vietnam.
NGO Relations Liaises with: *International Organization for Standardization (ISO, #14473).* Associate member of: *Fédération des associations européennes des constructeurs de fenêtres et de façades (FAECF, #09456).* [2021.02.17/XM2907/t/**D**]

♦ Quali Middle East Association (QMEA) 18591

Gen Sec c/o Dubai Association Centre, Office No 207 (16), Level 2, Bldg 2 at One Central, Dubai World Trade Centre, PO Box 23070, Dubai, United Arab Emirates. T. +97145163052. E-mail: admin@qualimiddleeast.com.
URL: http://www.qualimiddleeast.com/
History Nov 2006. Registration: Dubai Association Centre, No/ID: 225591, Start date: 13 Aug 2017, United Arab Emirates, Dubai. **Aims** Provide and promote established *quality standards* and best practices to obtain a high quality *coating* on *aluminium* and aluminium surfaces; promote quality labels in the region; advance technical interests of members both nationally and internationally. **Structure** General Assembly; Board of Directors; Committee; Secretariat. **Languages** English. **Staff** 1.00 FTE, paid. **Activities** Events/meetings; training/education.
Members Full in 9 countries:
Bahrain, Egypt, Jordan, Kuwait, Oman, Qatar, Saudi Arabia, Syrian AR, United Arab Emirates.
Provisional license to establish quality standards in 6 countries:
Bangladesh, Bhutan, India, Nepal, Pakistan, Sri Lanka. [2022.02.15/XM7567/**D**]

♦ Quality Juice Foundation (QJF) 18592

Contct Am Hahnenbusch 14 b, 55268 Nieder-Olm, Germany. T. +49613692280. Fax +496136922810.
URL: http://www.qualityjuice.org/
History 2009. Registered in accordance with German law. **Aims** Promote the quality and safety of fruit juices and of fair competition for fruit drinks; promote in cooperation with the public and private sector public healthcare, fair competition and consumer protection. **Structure** Executive Committee; Advisory Board. **Finance** Original assets: euro 25,000. Since 2009, assumed assets of *SGF International (#19252).* Additional sources: donations. **Activities** Events/meetings; training/education; advocacy/lobbying/activism; awards/prizes/competitions; research/documentation. [2017/XM6016/f/**F**]

♦ Quality Label for Sulphuric Acid-Based Anodizing of Aluminium / see QUALANOD (#18589)
♦ Quantum Information Processing and Communication (meeting series)
♦ Quantum Structure Infrared Photodetectors Conference (meeting series)
♦ Quark Confinement and the Hadron Spectrum (meeting series)
♦ Quark Matter – International Conference on Ultra-relativistic Nucleus-Nucleus Collisions (meeting series)
♦ Quarry Managers' Association / see The Institute of Quarrying (#11290)

♦ Quartet Group 18593

Quatuor pour le Moyen-Orient
Address not obtained.
History 2002, by representatives from *United Nations (UN, #20515), European Union (EU, #08967)*, Russia and the United States. Also referred to as *Quartet on the Middle East, Diplomatic Quartet* and *Madrid Quartet.* **Aims** Promote a just, comprehensive and lasting settlement of the *Middle East* conflict. [2011/XF6755/**F***]

♦ Quartet on the Middle East / see Quartet Group (#18593)
♦ Quartiers en crise / see Local Urban Development European Network (#16508)
♦ Quartiers en Crise – European Regeneration Areas Network / see Local Urban Development European Network (#16508)
♦ Quarto Protocollo addizionale all'Accordo generale su i privilegi e le immunità del Consiglio d'Europa (1961 treaty)
♦ Quatrième convention ACP-CEE (1989 treaty)
♦ Quatrième internationale (inactive)

- ♦ Quatrième protocole additionnel à l'Accord général sur les privilèges et immunités du Conseil de l'Europe (1961 treaty)
- ♦ Quatrième Protocole additionnel à la Convention européenne d'extradition (2012 treaty)
- ♦ Quatuor pour le Moyen-Orient (#18593)
- ♦ Québec Center for International Relations / see École supérieure d'études internationales
- ♦ Québec National and International Commercial Arbitration Centre (internationally oriented national body)
- ♦ Queen Helen's International Association (#02740)
- ♦ Queen's Centre for International Relations / see Centre for International and Defence Policy, Kingston ON
- ♦ Queens World Network (internationally oriented national body)
- ♦ Queer Football Fanclubs (internationally oriented national body)
- ♦ Quest International / see Lions Quest (#16486)

♦ Quest International Users Group 18594

Exec Dir 2365 Harrodsburg Rd, Ste A-325, Lexington KY 40504, USA. T. +18592264307. Fax +18592264321. E-mail: questdirect@questdirect.org.
URL: http://www.questdirect.org/

History 1995. **Aims** Serve as a platform for users of Oracle's PeopleSoft, JD Edwards and Oracle Utilities *software* applications. **Activities** Organizes: regional conferences and meetings; training events. **Events** *Asia conference* Singapore (Singapore) 2003. **Members** Individuals (about 50,000) in 90 user groups worldwide, countries not specified. [2014/XJ8206/**E**]

- ♦ Quest for Peace (internationally oriented national body)

♦ Questscope 18595

Contact 71-75 Shelton Street, London, WC2H 2JQ, UK. T. +442034224321. E-mail: infous@questscope.org.
Middle East PO Box 910729, Amman 11191, Jordan. T. +96264618951. Fax +96264618952.
USA 615 1st Avenue NE, Suite 500, Minneapolis MN 55413, USA. T. +16126076472.
URL: http://www.questscope.org/

Aims Work with individuals, communities, local organizations and international partners to produce social, educational, and entrepreneurial *opportunities* for *marginalized youth*. **Structure** Board of Directors; International Council. **Activities** Training/education; projects/programmes; capacity building; advocacy/lobbying/activism. [2017/XM5006/**F**]

- ♦ **QuIC** European Quantum Industry Consortium (#08315)
- ♦ Quincy Jones Listen Up Foundation (internationally oriented national body)
- ♦ Quinoa (internationally oriented national body)
- ♦ Quinto protocollo addizionale all'Accordo generale su i privilegi e le immunità del Consiglio d'Europa (1990 treaty)
- ♦ Quisper (unconfirmed)
- ♦ QUITEL – Congreso Internacional de Quimicos Teóricos de Expresión Latina (meeting series)
- ♦ **Quito Protocol** Association of South American Electoral Organizations (#02919)
- ♦ **QUNO** Quaker United Nations Office (#18588)
- ♦ Quota Club International / see Quota International (#18596)

♦ Quota International (QI) 18596

Main Office 1420 21st St NW, Washington DC 20036, USA. T. +12023319694. Fax +12023314395. E-mail: staff@quota.org.
South Pacific Office PO Box 205, Margate QLD 4019, Australia.
URL: http://www.quotainternational.org/

History 1919, as *Quota Club International*. **Aims** Create a worldwide network of friendship through service; unite *business executives* and *professionals* for service to others. **Structure** Areas (6); Districts (40); Local clubs (280). **Languages** English. **Staff** 5.00 FTE, paid. **Finance** Budget (annual): US$ 800,000. **Activities** Offers services to deaf, hard-of-hearing and speech-impaired individuals, as well as to disadvantaged women and children. Committees (4): Community service; Disadvantaged women and children; Hearing and speech; World service. Operates *We Share Foundation* charitable foundation. **Events** *Biennial Meeting* Gold Coast, QLD (Australia) 2016, *Biennial Meeting / Annual Meeting* Cincinnati, OH (USA) 2014, *Biennial Meeting / Annual Meeting* Honolulu, HI (USA) 2012, *Biennial Meeting / Annual Meeting* Vancouver, BC (Canada) 2010, *Annual meeting* San Jose, CA (USA) 2008. **Publications** *Quotarian* (annual) – magazine. Brochures.
Members Local clubs (330) in 14 countries and territories:
Aruba, Australia, Canada, Curaçao, Fiji, India, Indonesia, Malaysia, Netherlands, New Zealand, Philippines, Singapore, Suriname, USA.
Consultative Status Consultative status granted from: *ECOSOC (#05331)* (Ros A). [2018/XD5360/**F**]

- ♦ QWN – Queens World Network (internationally oriented national body)
- ♦ **R20** Regions of Climate Action (#18820)

♦ r3.0 18597

Officer Manager Alexanderstr 7, 10178 Berlin, Germany. E-mail: hello@r3-0.org.
URL: https://www.r3-0.org/

History Founded as a non-profit platform. Former names and other names: *Redesign – Resilience – Regeneration (r3.0)* – full title. **Aims** Promote Redesign for Resilience and Regeneration; crowdsource open recommendations for necessary transformations across diverse fields and sectors, in response to the ecological and social collapses humanity is experiencing, so as to achieve a thriving, regenerative and distributive economy and society. **Structure** Steering Board; Operations Team. **Activities** Events/meetings; guidance/assistance/consulting; knowledge management/information dissemination; networking/liaising. **Events** *International Conference* Berlin (Germany) 2020, *International Conference* Rotterdam (Netherlands) 2019, *International Conference* Amsterdam (Netherlands) 2018, *International Conference* Amsterdam (Netherlands) 2017, *International Conference* Berlin (Germany) 2015. **Publications** *r3.0 Newsletter*. **NGO Relations** Member of (1): *Wellbeing Economy Alliance (WEAll, #20856)*. [AA1064/**F**]

- ♦ R3 Nordic / see Nordic Association of Cleanroom Technology (#17183)
- ♦ **R3 Nordic** Nordiska Föreningen för RenhetsTeknik och Rena Rum (#17183)
- ♦ R4A / see Renewable Energy Solutions for Africa
- ♦ R4D / see Results for Development (#18923)
- ♦ **R4D** Results for Development (#18923)
- ♦ Raad van de Afrikaanse Gemeenschappen in België en in Europa / see Conseil des communautés africaines en Europe/Belgique
- ♦ Raad van de Afrikaanse Gemeenschappen in België, Vlaanderen and in Europa / see Conseil des communautés africaines en Europe/Belgique
- ♦ Raad van de Afrikaanse Gemeenschappen in Europe/Vlaanderen (internationally oriented national body)
- ♦ Raad der Amerikaanse Ontwikkelingsstichtingen (#04712)
- ♦ Raad van Bestuur van de Europese Scholen (#03295)
- ♦ Raad van de Europese Gemeenschappen / see Council of the European Union (#04895)
- ♦ Raad der Europese Gemeenten / see Council of European Municipalities and Regions (#04891)
- ♦ Raad der Europese Gemeenten en Regios (#04891)
- ♦ Raad van de Europese Unie (#04895)
- ♦ Raadgevende Interparlementaire Beneluxraad (#03201)
- ♦ **RaAM** Researching and Applying Metaphor International Association (#18856)
- ♦ **RAA** Rheumatism Association of ASEAN (#18935)

♦ Rabbinical Centre of Europe (RCE) 18598

Contact Rue du Cornet 22, 1040 Brussels, Belgium. T. +3228082753. Fax +3227919259.
URL: https://rce.eu.com/

History Founded 2000. **Aims** Enlarge the scope of spiritual opportunities in Europe and support the sacred work of European Rabbis. **Structure** Rabbinical Council. **Events** *General Assembly* Budapest (Hungary) 2014. **NGO Relations** *European Jewish Association (EJA, #07608)*. [2020/XG8308/**E**]

- ♦ Rabies in the Americas (meeting series)

♦ Rabies in Asia Foundation (RIA) 18599

Pres Kempegowda Inst of Medical Sciences, Bangalore, Karnataka 560 070, Bangalore KARNATAKA 560 070, India. Fax +918026712798.
URL: http://rabiesinasia.org/

History Apr 2006, India. Registered in accordance with Indian law. **Aims** Work for the elimination of rabies from Asia. **Structure** Chapters (9); Headquarters in Bangalore (India). **Activities** Organizes scientific programmes and conferences. **Events** *Conference* Bangkok (Thailand) 2013, *Conference* Colombo (Sri Lanka) 2011, *Conference* Hanoi (Vietnam) 2009, *Conference* Bangalore (India) 2007. **Publications** Reports; DVD. [2013.07.19/XM8264/f/**F**]

- ♦ Rabita Al-Alam Al-Islami (#16917)
- ♦ Rabotna Obstnost Dunavski Strani (#21056)
- ♦ RAB – Regional Advisory Board in Agriculture (meeting series)
- ♦ **RACAL** Red Latinoamericana para el Análisis de la Calidad Ambiental en América Latina (#18701)
- ♦ Race & Equality – International Institute on Race, Equality, and Human Rights (unconfirmed)
- ♦ Race for Water Foundation (internationally oriented national body)
- ♦ Racing Commissioners International (internationally oriented national body)
- ♦ **RAC/SPA** Regional Activity Centre for Specially Protected Areas (#18746)
- ♦ RACS – Royal Australasian College of Surgeons (internationally oriented national body)
- ♦ **RACVIAC** Centre for Security Cooperation (#03785)
- ♦ Rada Europesjka (#06801)
- ♦ Rada Európskej Unie (#04895)
- ♦ Rada Evropské Unie (#04895)
- ♦ RAD-AID International (internationally oriented national body)
- ♦ RADAR / see International Network on Family Poultry Development (#14267)
- ♦ Rada Unii Europejskiej (#04895)
- ♦ **RADC** Réseau africain de droit constitutionnel (#00384)
- ♦ Rädda Barnen – Save the Children Sweden (internationally oriented national body)
- ♦ RADDHO – Rencontre africaine pour la défense des droits de l'homme (internationally oriented national body)
- ♦ **RADECS Association** RADECS Association for Radiations, Effects on Components and Systems (#18600)

♦ RADECS Association for Radiations, Effects on Components and Systems (RADECS Association) 18600

Registered Office Montpellier Electronics Ctr, Box 083 – Univ Montpellier II, 34095 Montpellier CEDEX 05, France. E-mail: contact@radecs-association.net.
URL: http://www.radecs-association.net/

History 1992. Conference series founded following 1987 IEEE Nuclear & Space Radiation Effects Conference, Snowmass CO (USA). Registration: France. **Aims** Promote scientific fundamental and applied research, primarily in the field of radiation and its effect on materials, components and systems, but also in all relevant fields. **Structure** General Meeting. Board of Administration, including President, Vice-President and Treasurer. **Events** *RADiation Effects on Components and Systems (RADECS)* Venice (Italy) 2022, *RADiation Effects on Components and Systems (RADECS)* Vienna (Austria) 2021, *Conference* Vannes (France) 2020, *Conference* Montpellier (France) 2019, *Conference* Copenhagen (Denmark) 2018. **Members** Membership countries not specified. **NGO Relations** *Institute of Electrical and Electronics Engineers (IEEE, #11259)*. [2021/XJ6942/**E**]

- ♦ **RADE** Rotaria Amikaro de Esperanto (#18973)
- ♦ Rådet for Den Europaeske Union (#04895)
- ♦ Rådet for de Europaeiske Faellesskaber / see Council of the European Union (#04895)
- ♦ Rådet för Europas Kommuner och Regioner (#04891)
- ♦ Rådet för Föreningar i Europa / see European Council for Non-Profit Organizations (#06834)
- ♦ Rådet för Nordiskt Barn- och Ungdomskårsamarbete (#17880)
- ♦ Rådet för Små och Mellanstora Verksamheter i Norden (no recent information)
- ♦ Rådgivningsgruppen för Nordiskt Samarbete inom Högre Utbildning (inactive)
- ♦ RADHORT – Réseau africain pour le développement de l'horticulture (no recent information)
- ♦ Radiant.Earth / see Radiant Earth Foundation
- ♦ Radiant Earth Foundation (internationally oriented national body)
- ♦ Radiation Commission of International Union of Geodesy and Geophysics / see International Radiation Commission (#14684)
- ♦ Radiation Effects Research Foundation (internationally oriented national body)

♦ Radio Amateur Satellite Corporation (AMSAT) 18601

Société de communication par satellite pour radio-amateurs

Manager 10605 Concord St, Ste 304, Kensington MD 20895, USA. T. +13018224376.
Pres address not obtained.
URL: http://www.amsat.org/

History 3 Mar 1969, Washington DC (USA). Registered in the District of Columbia (USA). **Aims** Provide satellites that can be used for amateur radio communication and experimentation by suitably equipped amateur radio stations throughout the world on a non-discriminatory basis; encourage development of skills and the advancement of specialized knowledge in the art and practice of amateur radio *communications* and *space science*; foster international goodwill and cooperation through joint experimentation and study, and through wide participation in these activities on a noncommercial basis by radio amateurs of the world; facilitate communications by means of amateur satellites in times of emergency; encourage the more effective and expanded use of the higher frequency amateur bands. **Structure** Postal ballot of members determines Board of Directors who elect Corporate Officers. **Finance** Members' dues. **Activities** Has been responsible for satellite projects involving over 6,000 satellite users in more than 100 countries. These include: (a) extensive modifications, testing, launch arrangements, licensing and data collection for *'Australis-OSCAR 5'* satellite, built by students at Melbourne (Australia) University in Australia and launched by NASA Jan 1970. (b) Spacecraft design, fabrication, testing, launch arrangements, licensing, and operation of *'AMSAT-OSCAR 6'*, first of a series of amateur satellites, which served for nearly 5 years following launch by NASA in 1972. (c) *'AMSAT-OSCAR 7'*, amateur communications satellite launched by NASA in Nov 1974. (d) Construction by AMSAT groups of 2 transponders for *'AMSAT-OSCAR 8'*, amateur satellite launched by NASA, Mar 1978. (e) Currently involved in 'Phase III' project, a new series of satellites designed for long-lifetime operation in high-altitude synchronous, circular or elliptical orbits, which commenced 16 Jun 1983 with the launching of *'AMSAT-OSCAR 10'*, providing emergency communications resource for public services and for transmitting educational material; this provides a new band comparable to the 20-meters and reliable inter-continental contacts. *'AMSAT-OSCAR 13'* launched, 15 Jun 1988, by Arianespace (no more operational). AMSAT prepares documentation on amateur satellites for international and national organizations; arranges and presents papers for technical, professional and amateur meetings; reviews and advises on curriculum material on the use of amateur satellite terminals in schools for instruction in the physical sciences. AMSAT launched, 21 Jun 1990, four MicroSats which provide voice, CW and packet bulletin board style communications to amateur radio operators worldwide. AMSAT-OSCA 16, built by volunteers in Colorado, is the orbiting packet radio bulletin board. LO-17, built by AMSAT-Argentina, provides real-time packet, CW, and voice communications capabilities. Weber State University's WO-18 is an orbiting 'test bed' providing amateur radio operators an opportunity to follow experiments undertaken by University students as well as downloading and displaying pictures taken by this spacecraft. **Events** *Space Symposium* Dayton, OH (USA) 2015, *Space symposium* San Francisco, CA (USA) 2006, *Space symposium* Lafayette, LA (USA) 2005, *Space symposium* Washington, DC (USA) 2004, *Space symposium* Vicksburg, MS (USA) 1998. **Publications** *The AMSAT Journal* (6 a year).
Members Societies; Individuals. Members in 63 countries and territories:
Argentina, Australia, Austria, Barbados, Belgium, Bermuda, Bolivia, Botswana, Brazil, Canada, Cayman Is, Chile, Colombia, Cuba, Denmark, Dominica, Dominican Rep, Ecuador, Finland, France, Gabon, Germany, Greece, Grenada, Guatemala, Haiti, Honduras, Hong Kong, Hungary, India, Indonesia, Ireland, Israel, Italy, Jamaica, Japan, Kenya, Lebanon, Malaysia, Mexico, Namibia, Netherlands, New Caledonia, New Zealand, Norway, Philippines, Portugal, Puerto Rico, Romania, Saudi Arabia, Serbia, South Africa, Spain, Sri Lanka, Sweden, Switzerland, Thailand, Trinidad-Tobago, UK, USA, Venezuela, Zambia, Zimbabwe. [2015/XF4009/**F**]

♦ Radio Benevolencija Foundation (internationally oriented national body)
♦ Radio Bible Class Ministries / see Our Daily Bread Ministries (#17916)
♦ RADIOCARBON – International Radiocarbon Conference (meeting series)
♦ Radio France internationale (internationally oriented national body)
♦ Radio Free Asia (internationally oriented national body)
♦ Radio Free Europe/Radio Liberty (internationally oriented national body)
♦ Radio Frequency Identification / see International RFID Business Association (#14751)
♦ Radio Internacional Feminista (internationally oriented national body)
♦ Radiolähetysjärjestö Sanansaattajat (internationally oriented national body)

♦ Radiological Society of SAARC Countries (RSSC) 18602

Gen Sec Nepal Medical Assn Bldg, Siddhi Sadan, Exhibition Road, PO Box 189, Kathmandu, Nepal. T. +97714225860. Fax +97714225300.
URL: http://saarcradiology.org/

History Recognized by *South Asian Association for Regional Cooperation (SAARC, #19721)*. **Aims** Monitor and coordinate implementation of programmes and policies pertaining to radiological science in the region. **Events** *Congress* Islamabad (Pakistan) 2013, *Congress* Dharan (Nepal) 2012, *Congress* India 2010, *Congress* Sri Lanka 2009, *Congress* Pakistan 2008. [2013/XJ0477/**D**]

♦ Radiology Association of French-Speaking Africa (no recent information)
♦ Radio Mission The Messengers (internationally oriented national body)
♦ Radionavigation Intergovernmental Council of the CIS / see Radionavigation Interstate Council of the CIS (#18603)

♦ Radionavigation Interstate Council of the CIS 18603

Chairman State Military Industrial Committee, Republic of Belarus, 115 Nezavisimosti Ave, 220114 Minsk, Belarus. T. +81072809100. E-mail: gvpk01@mail.belpak.by.
Contact Bolshoy Trekhsvyatitelsky per 2, Moscow MOSKVA, Russia, 109028. T. +74956262501. Fax +74956262883. E-mail: internavigation@rgcc.ru.
URL: http://www.internavigation.ru/

History 22 Jan 1993, Minsk (Belarus), as *Radionavigation Intergovernmental Council of the CIS*, by Resolution of the Heads of Governments of member states of the *Commonwealth of Independent States (CIS, #04341)*. Regulations validated by Resolution of the Heads of Governments of CIS, Apr 1994. **Aims** Promote development and cooperated application of radionavigation systems and aids to fulfil target missions by various users; provide information support for *safety* systems for all *transport* modes. **Structure** Council (meets twice a year), comprising plenipotentiaries of CIS states (one from each state); Council Chairman elected in turn from Council members for one year, with possible prolongation. Council's activities are supported by the Internavigation Research and Technical Centre (RTC), a state establishment of Russia; RTC Director is the standing Deputy Chairman of the Council with deliberative vote. **Finance** Annual fees of the Commonwealth States for implementation of the Intergovernmental Radionavigation Programme. **Activities** Politics/policy/regulatory. **Events** *Meeting* Moscow (Russia) 2014, *International radionavigation conference / International Conference* Moscow (Russia) 2000, *International conference* Moscow (Russia) 1999, *International conference* Moscow (Russia) 1997, *International conference* Moscow (Russia) 1995. **Publications** *Navigation News* – journal. Conference proceedings.
Members Governments of CIS Member States (11):
Armenia, Azerbaijan, Belarus, Georgia, Kazakhstan, Kyrgyzstan, Moldova, Russia, Tajikistan, Ukraine, Uzbekistan.
IGO Relations Cooperates with: *European Commission (EC, #06633)*; *EUROCONTROL (#05667)*; *European Space Agency (ESA, #08798)*; *International Mobile Satellite Organization (IMSO, #14174)*. **NGO Relations** Formal contacts with: *International Association of Marine Aids to Navigation and Lighthouse Authorities (IALA, #12013)*. [2014/XE2456/**E***]

♦ Radio Regulations (1979 treaty)
♦ Radios Rurales Internationales (#09274)
♦ Radio Technical Commission for Aeronautics (internationally oriented national body)
♦ Radio Technical Commission for Marine Service / see Radio Technical Commission for Maritime Services
♦ Radio Technical Commission for Maritime Services (internationally oriented national body)
♦ Radio and Telecommunications Terminal Equipment Compliance Association / see R and TTE Compliance Association (#18994)
♦ Radiotelegraph convention – International Wireless Telegraph Convention (1906 treaty)
♦ Radio Vaticana – Vatican News (internationally oriented national body)

♦ Radio Veritas Asia 18604

General Manager Buick Street, Fairview Park, PO Box 2642, 1166 Quezon City, Philippines. T. +6329390011 – +6329390012 – +6329390014. Fax +6329381940. E-mail: rveritas-asia@rveritas-asia.org.
URL: http://www.rveritas-asia.org/

History Founded 11 Apr 1969. Previously also referred to in French as *Radio Veritas Asie*. **Aims** Proclaim the message of God's love to the peoples of Asia, by producing human development and Catholic evangelization programs in cooperation with recognized production centers and transmitting these programs via shortwave and related means of electronic media. **Structure** Board of Trustees. **Publications** *UPLINK* (4 a year) – newsletter. *Kapisanan ng mga Brodkaster Ng Pilipinas*.
Members Individuals in 10 countries:
Bangladesh, Cambodia, India, Myanmar, Pakistan, Philippines, Sri Lanka, Taiwan, Thailand, Vietnam.
NGO Relations Member of (2): *Conference of International Broadcasters' Audience Research Services (CIBAR, #04611)*; *World Catholic Association for Communication (SIGNIS, #21264)*. [2014.11.10/XF4999/v/**F**]

♦ Radio Veritas Asie / see Radio Veritas Asia (#18604)
♦ Radio Worldwide (internationally oriented national body)
♦ **RADI** Red de Archivos Diplomaticos Latinoamericanos (#18634)
♦ **RADI** Réseau africain pour le développement intégré (#00390)
♦ RADISCON – Regional Animal Disease Surveillance and Control Network (inactive)
♦ **RADLA** Reunión Anual de Dermatólogos Latinoamericanos (#18929)
♦ **RADLD** Raising Awareness of Developmental Language Disorder (#18616)
♦ Radna Zajednica Alpe-Jadran / see Alps-Adriatic-Alliance (#00747)
♦ Radna Zajednica Podunavskih Regija (#21056)
♦ Radna Zajednica Podunavskih Zemalja (#21056)
♦ Radna Zajednica Pokrajina, Zupanija Regija i Republika Istocnoalpskog Podrucja / see Alps-Adriatic-Alliance (#00747)
♦ RADO-CAM / see Panamerican Regional Antidoping Organization (#18125)
♦ Radstock Ministries (internationally oriented national body)

♦ RadTech Asia Organization 18605

Sec RadTech China, Room 413, North Anhua Bldg, Cherry Blossoms West Street 8, Chaoyang District, 100029 Beijing, China. T. +861064415732. Fax +861064415715. E-mail: radtechconf@126.com.
URL: http://www.radtechasia.org/

History 1997, by RadTech Japan and RadTech China, as one of the *RadTech International* organizations. **Aims** Promote development and applications of UV/EB curing technology by providing a collaborative platform, in particular gain economical, environmental and social benefits. **Structure** Committee, comprising Honorary President, President, 2 Vice-Presidents and 2 Executive Secretaries. **Events** *International Conference* Tsukuba (Japan) 2022, *International Conference* Hangzhou (China) 2019, *International Conference on Radiation Curing in Asia* Tokyo (Japan) 2016, *Conference* Shanghai (China) 2013.
Members Full in 6 countries:
Australia, China, India, Japan, Korea Rep, Malaysia. [2019/XJ7344/**D**]

♦ RadTech Europe (RTE) 18606

Europe Office PO Box 85612, 2508 CH The Hague, Netherlands. T. +31703123920. Fax +31703636348. E-mail: mail@radtech-europe.com.
Registered Office c/o LAM, Laan Copes van Cattenburch 79, 2585 EW The Hague, Netherlands.
URL: http://www.radtech-europe.com/

History 1988. Full title: *European Association for the Advancement of Radiation Curing by UV, EB and Laser Beams*. Has also been referred to as *European Association on Radiation*. Statutes adopted 18 Dec 1989, Brussels (Belgium) and Fribourg (Switzerland). Most recent statutes: 18 Jan 2007, Paris (France). Registered in accordance with Belgian law. EU Transparency Register: 562924737652-63. **Aims** Act as a forum and source of education and information for those involved in use of instant *polymerization* of *monomer* and *oligomer* blends using ultraviolet (UV) and electron beam (EB) *ionising radiation* or who supply *chemicals*, equipment or other materials to such users; develop and disseminate procedures and data on safe equipment operation and materials handling, testing and quality control. **Structure** General Assembly (annual). Management Committee (meets at least twice a year), consisting of President, 1-2 Vice-Presidents, Honorary Treasurer, Honorary Secretary and Committee Chairpersons. Executive Secretary. Marketing Committee. Working Groups (2): Powder Coating; Graphic Arts. **Languages** English. **Staff** 1.50 FTE, paid. **Finance** Members' dues: individual euro 200; affiliate euro 200. **Activities** Organizes conferences, seminars, exhibitions and technical information. Makes Paul Dufour and Innovation awards. **Events** *RadTech Europe Conference* Basel (Switzerland) 2013, *RadTech Europe Conference* Basel (Switzerland) 2011, *RADTECH Asia : conference on radiation curing* Yokohama (Japan) 2011, *RadTech Europe Conference* Nice (France) 2009, *Annual General Assembly* Prague (Czech Rep) 2008. **Publications** *RadTech News* (3 a year) – magazine. Brochures; conference proceedings.
Members Categories I – suppliers of raw materials and chemicals; II – suppliers of equipment, formulators and consultants; III – end users of UV/EB material; IV – individual employees of any of the above; V – affiliates (sister RadTech associations, non-commercial, academic). Companies (140); Individual and academic members (160). Members (" indicates individuals but not companies) in 26 countries:
Australia, Austria, Belgium, Denmark, Finland, France, Germany, Iran Islamic Rep, Ireland, Israel, Italy, Japan (*), Liechtenstein (*), Luxembourg (*), Netherlands, New Zealand, Norway, Russia, Spain, Sweden, Switzerland, Taiwan, Thailand, Türkiye, UK, USA.
NGO Relations 'Sister' associations: *RadTech International* (organizer of RadTech North America); 'RadTech Japan' (organizer of RadTech Asia). Supporter of Declaration of on Paper Recovery, maintained by *European Paper Recycling Council (EPRC, #08139)*. [2019/XE1485/**E**]

♦ RadTech International (internationally oriented national body)
♦ RadTech International North America / see RadTech International
♦ RAECPCP / see Network of the European Associations for Person-Centred and Experiential Psychotherapy and Counselling (#17013)
♦ **RAED** Arab NGO Network for Environment and Development (#01017)
♦ Raelian Religion / see International Raelian Movement (#14690)
♦ RAEPCCPE / see Network of the European Associations for Person-Centred and Experiential Psychotherapy and Counselling (#17013)
♦ **RAERESA** Regional Association of Energy Regulators for Eastern and Southern Africa (#18751)
♦ RAFAD Foundation (#09827)
♦ **RAFA** Red de Actividad Fisica de las Americas (#18366)
♦ **RAFEC** Réseau Africain Francophone d'Education Comparée (#18864)
♦ RAFI / see Action Group on Erosion, Technology and Concentration (#00091)
♦ **RAFM** Réseau africain de Forêts Modèles (#00377)
♦ RAF – Regional Arab Federation of Associations for Voluntary Fertility Control (inactive)
♦ Rafto Foundation (internationally oriented national body)
♦ Rafto Foundation for Human Rights / see Rafto Foundation
♦ **RAF-VIH** Réseau africain des formations sur le VIH et le SIDA (#18863)
♦ RAFWA – Refugees Aid for West Africa (internationally oriented national body)
♦ **RAGA** Secretaria de la Regional de Arquitectos del Grupo Andino (#18816)
♦ Raggruppamento delle Associazioni degli Industriali del Mais de Paesi della CEE / see Euromaisiers (#05709)
♦ Raggruppamento Europeo delle Associazioni dei Commercianti di Prodotti Dietetici (no recent information)
♦ Raggruppamento dei Produttori di Piastrelle di Ceramica del Mercato Comune / see European Ceramic Tile Manufacturers' Federation (#06508)
♦ RAG – Réseau action globale (internationally oriented national body)
♦ Rahmaniya (religious order)
♦ Rahmenkonvention des Europarates über den wert des kulturerbes für die gesellschaft (2005 treaty)
♦ Rahmenübereinkommen zum schutz nationaler minderheiten (1995 treaty)
♦ **RAHM** Réseau Africain d'Histoire Mondiale (#00388)
♦ Rahvusvaheline Kaitseuuringute Keskus (internationally oriented national body)
♦ RAIAL / see International Action Network on Small Arms (#11585)
♦ RAID – Rights and Accountability in Development (internationally oriented national body)

♦ Rail Forum Europe (RFE) 18607

Main Office Ave des Arts 53, 1000 Brussels, Belgium. T. +3226422329. E-mail: info@rail-forum.eu.
URL: http://www.rail-forum.eu/

History 16 Feb 2011. Founded to replace *European Rail Circle (ERC, inactive)*. Registration: Belgium. **Aims** Bring together EU decision-makers and the rail sector to achieve a better understanding of rail-related issues. **Structure** General Assembly; Managing Board; Advisory Committee; Secretariat, headed by Executive Secretary. **Languages** English. **Activities** Events/meetings; knowledge management/information dissemination. **Events** *Conference on new Competition Perspectives for Passengers in European Railways* Brussels (Belgium) 2018, *Conference on Track Access Charging and the Competitiveness of European Rail Freights* Brussels (Belgium) 2016.
Members Full Members of European Parliament. Associate corporate bodies and associations. Associations include the following 9 listed in this Yearbook:
Association of the European Rail Supply Industry (UNIFE, #02536); *Community of European Railway and Infrastructure Companies (CER, #04396)*; *European Federation of Railway Trackworks Contractors (EFRTC, #07205)*; *European Passengers' Federation (EPF, #08162)*; *European Rail Freight Association (ERFA, #08323)*; *International Association of Public Transport (#12118)*; *International Union for Combined Road – Rail Transport (UIRR, #15765)*; *International Union of Railways (#15813)*; *International Union of Wagon Keepers (#15827)*. [2021/XJ6810/y/**F**]

♦ RailNetEurope (RNE) 18608

SG Joint Office, Jakov-Lind-Straße 5, Austria Campus 3, 1020 Vienna, Austria. T. +431907627200. E-mail: mailbox@rne.eu.
URL: http://www.rne.eu/

History Jan 2004. Registration: Zentrales Vereinsregister, No/ID: 533991259, Start date: 2 Jan 2004, Austria, Vienna; EU Transparency Register, No/ID: 316132422919-70, Start date: 3 Aug 2016. **Aims** Enable fast, easy access to European *rail*; increase the quality and efficiency of European rail; harmonize conditions and procedures in the field of international rail infrastructure management for the benefit of the entire rail industry across Europe. **Structure** General Assembly; Managing Board; Joint Office; High Level Groups; Working Groups. **Languages** English. **Staff** 50.00 FTE, paid. **Finance** Sources: members' dues. Supported by: *European Union (EU, #08967)*. **Activities** Capacity building; events/meetings; training/education. **Events** *General Assembly* Vienna (Austria) 2022, *General Assembly* Vienna (Austria) 2022, *General Assembly* Vienna (Austria) 2020, *Rail Freight Day Meeting* Vienna (Austria) 2020, *General Assembly* Vienna (Austria) 2019. **Publications** Annual Report; glossary; technical guidelines; handbooks; brochures.
Members Full (38) in 29 countries:
Austria, Belgium, Bosnia-Herzegovina, Bulgaria, Croatia, Czechia, Denmark, Finland, France, Germany, Greece, Hungary, Italy, Latvia, Lithuania, Luxembourg, Netherlands, North Macedonia, Norway, Poland, Portugal, Romania, Serbia, Slovakia, Slovenia, Spain, Sweden, Switzerland, UK.
Associate (11): Rail Freight Corridors across Europe. [2023.02.14/XM1302/**D**]

- ♦ **RAILPOL** European Network of Railway Police Forces (#07981)
- ♦ Railway Children (internationally oriented national body)
- ♦ Railway Convention (1912 treaty)
- ♦ Railwaymen's International Games Union (inactive)

♦ Railway Transport Committee of the Maghreb 18609

Comité des transports ferroviaires du Maghreb (CTFM)

Permanent Sec 21-23 Boulevard Mohammed V, Algiers, Algeria. T. +21321634066 – +21321711510 ext2622. Fax +21321633298 – +21321633934.

History Established 8 Apr 1964, Algiers (Algeria). Structure amended 11 Nov 1965, Marrakech (Morocco), under the aegis of *Commission maghrébine des transports et communications (CMTC, inactive)*, which was in its turn a dependent body of *Permanent Consultative Committee of the Maghreb (PCCM, inactive)*. **Aims** Study questions concerning unification and improvement of operating conditions of member networks; coordinate and initiate susceptible actions that may ameliorate and develop the railway transport in the Maghreb countries; unify and improve the exploitation conditions of the Maghrebian nets; adapt in commun the general techniques and economic arrangements relating to the coordination and the harmonization of the railway transports in the Maghrebian countries and that concern the used equipments, the exploitation rules, training and personnel management; research and set a Maghrebian *speedy train* (TVGM) linking Tripoli (Libyan AJ) to Casablanca via Algeria and Tunisia in the parallel of the improvement of the Transmaghreb prestations. **Structure** Committee of Directors-General (meeting twice a year). *Central Office for Maghrebian Compensation (BCCM, no recent information)*. Office of Wagons. Permanent Secretary. Committees (5). Rotating Presidency (annual). **Languages** Arabic, French. **Finance** Members' contributions. **Activities** Committees (5): Transport and Commercial; Material and Traction; Supplying; Social and Human Resources; Working on the Maghrebian High Speed Train (TGVM). **Events** *Meeting* Tripoli (Libyan AJ) 2009, *World symposium on railroads* Libyan AJ 2000, *Meeting* Rabat (Morocco) 2000, *Meeting* Rabat (Morocco) 2000, *European congress on the future of rail transport in Maghreb countries* Tripoli (Libyan AJ) 1999.

Members Contracting Networks national railway companies of 5 countries:
Algeria, Libya, Mauritania, Morocco, Tunisia. [2014/XE0658/**E***]

♦ Rail Working Group (RWG) 18610

Office c/o Howard Rosen Solicitors, Baarerstr 96, PO Box 7262, 6302 Zug, Switzerland. T. +41417602888. Fax +41417602909. E-mail: info@railworkinggroup.org.
URL: https://www.railworkinggroup.org/

History Established at the request of *International Institute for the Unification of Private Law (UNIDROIT, #13934)* to represent the position of the rail industry relating to adopting and implementation of *Luxembourg Protocol to the Convention on International Interests in Mobile Equipment on Matters Specific to Railway Rolling Stock (Luxembourg Protocol, 2007)* to *UNIDROIT Convention on International Interests in Mobile Equipment (Cape Town convention, 2001)*. Articles adopted 4 Sep 2008; amended 16 Mar 2016. Registration: Swiss Civil Code, Switzerland. **Aims** Work with the rail industry, government and government agencies to raise awareness of the proposed Rail Protocol and promote its adoption in a form that will encourage greater and more cost-effective *financing* by the private sector of capital investment in railway *rolling stock*. **Structure** Management Committee. **Finance** Members' dues. [2023/XM7342/**E**]

♦ Rainbow Cities Network (RCN) 18611

Dir Volgersweg 58, 30175 Hannover, Germany. T. +4917661416602. E-mail: info@rainbowcities.com.
URL: https://www.rainbowcities.com/

History Founded by the cities of Amsterdam (Netherlands), Barcelona (Spain), Cologne (Germany) and Turin (Italy), as an informal network. Registration: EU Transparency Register, No/ID: 152657543865-54, Start date: 23 Aug 2021. **Aims** Protect and support LGBTI citizens. **Structure** Board; Coordinator. **Activities** Events/meetings; knowledge management/information dissemination; networking/liaising.

Members Cities in 18 countries:
Austria (Linz; Vienna), Belgium (Bruges; Brussels Capital Region; Ghent; Leuven; Ostende), Brazil (São Paulo), Denmark (Aarhus), Finland (Helsinki), France (Bordeaux; Paris), Germany (Berlin; Cologne; Frankfurt; Hamburg; Hannover; Heidelberg; Mannheim; Munich; Nuremberg; Wiesbaden), Iceland (Reykjavik), Ireland (Cork), Luxembourg (Esch-sur-Alzette), Mexico (Mexico City), Montenegro (Kotor), Netherlands (Amsterdam; Rotterdam), Norway (Bergen; Oslo), Slovenia (Ljubljana), Spain (Barcelona), Switzerland (Bern; Geneva; Zurich), Taiwan (New Taipei City; Taipei). [2022/AA2061/**F**]

- ♦ Rainbow Currency Foundation / see YEM Foundation (#21974)

♦ Rainbow Family of Living Light (Rainbow Family) 18612

Contact address not obtained. E-mail: rob@welcomehome.org.
URL: http://www.welcomehome.org/rainbow.html

History A community of volunteers interested in *non-violence* and *alternative lifestyles*. **Structure** No formal structure. **Activities** Events/meetings. **Members** Mainly North American membership. [2020.05.12/XJ3021/**F**]

- ♦ **Rainbow Family** Rainbow Family of Living Light (#18612)

♦ Rainbow Rose 18613

Contact Löwelstrasse 18, 1010 Vienna, Austria. E-mail: contact@rainbowrose.eu.
URL: http://rainbowrose.eu/

History A political LGBTI organization in the framework of *Party of European Socialists (PES, #18249)* family since 2006. Statutes and procedures officially adopted 2013, Brussels (Belgium); modified 2016, Paris (France); 2018, Vienna (Austria); 2022, Maastricht (Netherlands). Registration: Start date: 2018, Austria; End date: 2018, France; EU Transparency Register, No/ID: 258962912667-77. **Aims** Create a strong *LGBTI* Social Democratic network in each *EU* Member State; create and implement LGBTI sensitive political agenda within the PES family; support LGBTI political initiatives in Council of Europe member states, with a special focus on countries with hostile environments for LGBTI people; build networks and cooperate with national, European and global LGBTI organizations to achieve the *equality* legally and socially for all LGBTI European citizens. **Structure** General Assembly; Board. **Languages** Dutch, English, French, German, Spanish. **Staff** 9.00 FTE, voluntary. **Activities** Events/meetings.

Members Structures in 16 countries and territories:
Belgium/Flemish Region, Belgium/Wallonia Region, Denmark, Estonia, Finland, France, Germany, Ireland, Lithuania, Luxembourg, Netherlands, Norway, Spain, Sweden, Switzerland, Türkiye.
Non-affiliated members in 8 countries and territories:
Czechia, Italy, Latvia, Malta, Northern Ireland, Portugal, Romania, Slovenia. [2022.10.19/XM6857/**E**]

♦ Rainforest Action Network (RAN) 18614

Exec Dir 425 Bush St Ste 300, San Francisco CA 94108, USA. E-mail: answers@ran.org.
URL: http://www.ran.org/

History Nov 1985, at conference called to draft a plan of action. Subsequently merged with *People of the Earth (POE, inactive)*. **Aims** Protect tropical rain forests and support the rights of indigenous peoples; campaign through direct action, from letter writing to boycotting of goods; inform the public on how they can assist in rain forest preservation; cooperate with other environmental and human rights organizations on major campaigns to protect rain forests. **Structure** Executive Director; Managing Director; Development Director; Media Director. Board of Directors, consisting of 11 members. Board of Advisors, comprising 6 members. **Staff** Program staff – 11; support staff – 8; interns. **Finance** Sources: membership – 65%; foundations and donations – 35%; special events – 10%. **Activities** Works through: negotiation to resolve problems; public pressure; direct action, such as letter writing campaigns, boycotts, consumer campaigns, demonstrations and selective bans; grassroots organizing in USA; building coalitions and collaborating with other environmental, scientific and grassroots groups; conducting research; supporting economic alternatives; spearheading public education and media outreach projects and small grants to groups in tropical countries. Organizes: Protect-an-Acre Program; Rainforest Action Groups (RAGs); Education Outreach Program; World Rainforest Week; Old Growth Forest; Campaign, Campaign for a Sane Economy. **Publications** *Action Alert* (6 a year); *World Rainforest Report* (2 a year). Annual Report; fact sheets; campaign study. Information Services: International information clearinghouse.

Members Individuals (37,000). Affiliates organizations and groups (150). Membership covers 74 countries and territories:
Andorra, Argentina, Australia, Austria, Bangladesh, Barbados, Belgium, Belize, Bolivia, Brazil, Cameroon, Canada, Chile, Colombia, Costa Rica, Denmark, Dominica, Dominican Rep, Ecuador, Finland, France, Gabon, Germany, Ghana, Greece, Guatemala, Guyana, Honduras, Hong Kong, Hungary, India, Indonesia, Ireland, Israel, Italy, Jamaica, Japan, Kenya, Korea Rep, Malaysia, Mexico, Monaco, Nepal, Netherlands, New Zealand, Nicaragua, Nigeria, Norway, Pakistan, Panama, Papua New Guinea, Peru, Philippines, Poland, Portugal, Samoa, Saudi Arabia, Serbia, Sierra Leone, Singapore, South Africa, Spain, Sri Lanka, Sweden, Switzerland, Taiwan, Tanzania UR, Thailand, Togo, Uganda, Uruguay, USA, Venezuela.

IGO Relations *International Tropical Timber Organization (ITTO, #15737)*. **NGO Relations** Member of: *Advocacy Network for Africa (ADNA)*; *Climate Justice Now ! (CJN!, inactive)*; *Environmental Paper Network (EPN, #05507)*; *EarthAction (EA, #05159)*; *Environment Liaison Centre International (ELCI, no recent information)*; *Forest Stewardship Council (FSC, #09869)*; *Global Call for Climate Action (GCCA, inactive)*; *Taiga Rescue Network (TRN, inactive)*. Affiliate member of: *Friends of the Earth International (FoEI, #10002)*. Member of Steering Committee of: *World Bank Bonds Boycott (WBBB, no recent information)*. Partner of: *Wetlands International (#20928)*. Contacts with: *African NGOs Environment Network (ANEN, no recent information)*; *Earth Island Institute (EII)*; *Forest Movement Europe (FME, #09864)*; *Japan Tropical Forest Action Network (JATAN)*; *Netherlands Centre for Indigenous Peoples (NCIV)*; *Probe International*; *Rainforest Information Centre (RIC)*; *World Rainforest Movement (WRM, #21745)*. [2015/XF1912/**F**]

- ♦ Rainforest Alliance (internationally oriented national body)
- ♦ Rainforest Concern (internationally oriented national body)

♦ Rainforest Foundation International (RFI) 18615

Dir – UK Office 233a Kentish Town Road, London, NW5 2JT, UK. T. +442074851093. Fax +442074850315. E-mail: rainforestuk@rainforestuk.com.
URL: http://www.rainforestfoundationuk.org/

History 1989. **Aims** Support indigenous people and traditional populations of the rainforest in their efforts to protect their environment and fulfil their rights by assisting them in: securing and controlling natural resources and managing these resources in ways that do not harm their environment, violate their culture or compromise their future; developing means to protect their individual and collective rights and obtain, shape and control basic services from the state. **Structure** Fund operates through 3 autonomous organizations. **Languages** English, French, Norwegian. **Staff** UK – 13; USA – 4; Norway – 6. **Finance** Grants; events; donations from individuals and individuals; legacies. **Activities** Overseas project work in support for forest peoples in 20 countries. **Publications** Annual Report.

Members Autonomous organizations in 3 countries:
Rainforest Foundation UK (RFUK); *Rainforest Foundation US*; *Regnskogfondet (RFN)*.
Partners in 2 countries:
Brazil, Japan.

Consultative Status Consultative status granted from: *ECOSOC (#05331)* (Special). **IGO Relations** Associated with Department of Global Communications of the United Nations. **NGO Relations** Member of: *EarthAction (EA, #05159)*. [2015/XF6170/f/**F**]

- ♦ Rainforest Foundation Norway (internationally oriented national body)
- ♦ Rainforest Foundation UK (internationally oriented national body)
- ♦ Rainforest Foundation US (internationally oriented national body)
- ♦ Rainforest Fund (internationally oriented national body)
- ♦ Rainforest Information Centre (internationally oriented national body)
- ♦ Rainforest Project Foundation (internationally oriented national body)
- ♦ Rainforest Trust (internationally oriented national body)
- ♦ RAIN – Rainwater Harvesting Implementation Network (internationally oriented national body)
- ♦ Rainwater Harvesting Implementation Network (internationally oriented national body)
- ♦ RAIPON – Russian Association of Indigenous Peoples of the North (internationally oriented national body)
- ♦ **RAI** Red Andina de Información (#00819)
- ♦ **RAI** Regional Anti-Corruption Initiative (#18750)
- ♦ RAI – Rencontre assyriologique internationale (meeting series)
- ♦ RAISE – Reproductive Health Access, Information and Services in Emergencies (internationally oriented national body)

♦ Raising Awareness of Developmental Language Disorder (RADLD) . 18616

Contact address not obtained. E-mail: hello@radld.org.
URL: https://radld.org/

History Former names and other names: *Raising Awareness of Language Learning Impairments (RALLI)* – former. **Aims** Increase awareness of Developmental Language Disorder (DLD); disseminate evidence-based information and signpost to further reliable resources; develop a global network of people advocating in their local context. **Structure** International Committee. [2020/AA1143/v/**F**]

- ♦ Raising Awareness of Language Learning Impairments / see Raising Awareness of Developmental Language Disorder (#18616)

♦ Raising the Floor 18617

CEO Route de Ferney 150, 1218 Le Grand-Saconnex GE, Switzerland. E-mail: info@raisingthefloor.org.
URL: https://www.raisingthefloor.org/

History 2010. **Aims** Advance social equity through digital inclusion. **Structure** Divisions (3): International (Switzerland); US; Europe (Belgium). **Activities** Guidance/assistance/consulting; research and development; training/education. **NGO Relations** Member of (1): *Global Alliance of Assistive Technology Organizations (GAATO, #10185)*. [2022.02.15/AA2108/**C**]

- ♦ **RAIST** Réseau africain d'institutions scientifiques et techniques (#00395)
- ♦ **RAIU** Réserve alimentaire internationale d'urgence (#13259)
- ♦ S Rajaratnam School of International Studies (internationally oriented national body)
- ♦ Rajneesh Foundation International / see Osho International Foundation (#17904)
- ♦ Raleigh International (internationally oriented national body)
- ♦ RALLI / see Raising Awareness of Developmental Language Disorder (#18616)
- ♦ **RALLT** Red por una América Latina Libre de Transgénicos (#18733)
- ♦ Ralph Bunche Institute for International Studies (internationally oriented national body)
- ♦ Ralph Bunche Institute on the United Nations / see Ralph Bunche Institute for International Studies
- ♦ Ralph J Bunche International Affairs Center (internationally oriented national body)
- ♦ Ramakrishna Math (religious order)
- ♦ Ramakrishna Mission
- ♦ RAMiCS – International Conference on Relational and Algebraic Methods in Computer Science (meeting series)
- ♦ **RAMICS** Research Association on Monetary Innovation and Community and Complementary Currency Systems (#18851)
- ♦ RAMI – International Congress on Rapid Methods and Automation in Microbiology and Immunology (meeting series)
- ♦ RAMOGE agreement – Agreement Concerning the Protection of the Waters of the Mediterranean Shores (1976 treaty)
- ♦ RAMOGE Commission / see Accord RAMOGE (#00057)
- ♦ RAMP – North American Regional Academic Mobility Program (internationally oriented national body)
- ♦ RAM – Rare Advocacy Movement (unconfirmed)
- ♦ Ramsar Convention Bureau / see Secretariat of the Convention of Wetlands (#19200)
- ♦ **RAMSES** Robotic Assisted Microsurgical and Endoscopic Society (#18962)
- ♦ RAND Center for Asia Pacific Policy (internationally oriented national body)
- ♦ RAND Center for Middle East Public Policy (internationally oriented national body)
- ♦ RAND Center for Russia and Eurasia (internationally oriented national body)
- ♦ RAND Corporation (internationally oriented national body)
- ♦ RAND Europe (internationally oriented national body)
- ♦ RAND International Security and Defense Policy Center (internationally oriented national body)

- ♦ Rand Monetary Area / see Multilateral Monetary Area (#16889)
- ♦ Randonneurs européens / see Brevets Randonneurs Mondiaux (#03323)
- ♦ Randonneurs mondiaux / see Brevets Randonneurs Mondiaux (#03323)
- ♦ RANESA – Resource Accounting Network for Eastern and Southern Africa (internationally oriented national body)
- ♦ Ranfurly Library Service / see Book Aid International
- ♦ **RANN** Réseau Art Nouveau Network (#18867)
- ♦ **RAN** Rainforest Action Network (#18614)
- ♦ **RAN** Rugby Americas North (#18997)
- ♦ RANZCR – Royal Australian and New Zealand College of Radiologists (internationally oriented national body)
- ♦ **RAOB** Réseau africain des organismes de bassin (#00381)
- ♦ RAOS – Royal Academy of Overseas Sciences (internationally oriented national body)

♦ Raoul Follereau International Union 18618

Union internationale Raoul Follereau

Main Office 31 rue de Dantzig, 75015 Paris, France. T. +33153689898. Fax +33148562222. E-mail: follereau@raoul-follereau.org – legs@raoul-follereau.org.
URL: http://www.raoul-follereau.org/

History 10 Oct 1971, Paris (France), as *International Association of the Raoul Follereau Foundations – Association internationale des fondations Raoul Follereau (AIFRF) – Internationale Vereinigung der Stiftungen Raoul Follereau – Associazione Internazionale delle Fondazioni Raoul Follereau*. Present name adopted 28 Sep 1991, Viviers (France). Registered in accordance with French law. **Aims** Maintain and promote the work inspired by the initiatives of Raoul Follereau in the campaign against *leprosy*. **Structure** General Assembly (every 2 years). Board (meets twice a year), consisting of 6 co-opted founding members and 4 members elected by the General Assembly. **Finance** Members' dues. Grants from Association française Raoul Follereau. **Activities** Supports creation of national associations in developing countries through mutual communication and dispersion of information. Provides national members with publicity material for International Leprosy Day. Encourages cross-cultural links between member associations. **Events** *African Summit on Neglected Tropical Diseases* Cotonou (Benin) 2009, *Biennial General Assembly* Viviers (France) 1991, *Biennial general assembly and congress* Paris (France) 1989.
Members Founder; Full; Delegate; Honorary. Individuals and associations in 24 countries:
Benin, Burkina Faso, Cameroon, Canada, Chad, Congo Brazzaville, Côte d'Ivoire, France, Greece, Guinea, India, Madagascar, Mali, Malta, Mauritania, Mauritius, Niger, Poland, Portugal, Senegal, Spain, Switzerland, Togo, UK.
IGO Relations *UNESCO (#20322).* [2020/XE4889/**E**]

- ♦ Raoul Wallenberg Centre for Human Rights (internationally oriented national body)
- ♦ Raoul Wallenberg Institute of Human Rights and Humanitarian Law (internationally oriented national body)
- ♦ Raoul Wallenberg Institutet for Manskliga Rattigheter och Humanitar Ratt (internationally oriented national body)
- ♦ **RAP 21** African Press Network for the 21st Century (#00423)
- ♦ RAPA / see FAO Regional Office for Asia and the Pacific (#09266)
- ♦ **RAPAC** Réseau des aires protégées d'Afrique centrale (#03656)
- ♦ **RAP-AL** Red de Acción en Plaguicidas y sus Alternativas de América Latina (#18633)
- ♦ **RAP** FAO Regional Office for Asia and the Pacific (#09266)
- ♦ Raphaelsverein / see Raphaelswerk
- ♦ Raphaelswerk (internationally oriented national body)
- ♦ Raphaels-Werk – Dienst am Menschen unterwegs / see Raphaelswerk
- ♦ Rapid Manufacturing Platform / see European Technology Platform in Additive Manufacturing (#08886)
- ♦ RAPON / see Russian Association of Indigenous Peoples of the North
- ♦ **RAPPANE** Réseau africain pour la prévention et la protection contre l'abus et la négligence de l'enfant (#00393)
- ♦ **RAPP** Réseau Africain des Personnels des Parlements (#18865)
- ♦ **RAP** Red de Arte Planetaria (#18380)
- ♦ RAP – Regulatory Assistance Project (internationally oriented national body)

♦ Raptor Research Foundation (RRF) 18619

Pres 1640 Oriole Lane NW, Olympia WA 98502-4342, USA. T. +13609437394. Fax +13609437394.
URL: http://raptorresearchfoundation.org/

History 11 Feb 1966. **Aims** Stimulate dissemination of information concerning raptorial birds worldwide; promote better public understanding and appreciation of the value of birds of prey. **Structure** Board of Directors of 12 members. Officers: President; Vice President; Secretary; Treasurer. Standing Committees (9): Awards; Conferences; Conservation; Development; Education; Membership; Nominations; Resolutions; Scientific Program. **Finance** Members' dues. Donations. **Events** *Conference* Fort Collins, CO (USA) 2019, *Conference* Skukuza (South Africa) 2018, *Conference* Salt Lake City, UT (USA) 2017, *Conference* Cape May, NJ (USA) 2016, *Conference* Sacramento, CA (USA) 2015. **Publications** *Journal of Reptor Research*; *Raptor Research Reports*; *WINGSPAN* – newsletter. [2014/XD7479/f/**F**]

- ♦ Rare (internationally oriented national body)
- ♦ Rare Advocacy Movement (unconfirmed)

♦ Rare Cancers Europe (RCE) 18620

Secretariat c/o ESMO, Via Luigi Taddei 4, 6962 Viganello, Switzerland. T. +41919731925. Fax +41919731918. E-mail: rarecancerseurope@esmo.org.
URL: http://www.rarecancerseurope.org/

History Set up as a partnership of cooperating organizations. **Aims** Place the issue of rare cancers firmly on the European policy agenda; identify and promote appropriate solutions; exchange best practice. **Events** *Conference* Brussels (Belgium) 2012.
Members Participating organizations, include the following 17 organizations listed in this Yearbook:
Association of European Cancer Leagues (ECL, #02500); *CML Advocacy Network (#04040)*; *European Cancer Patient Coalition (ECPC, #06433)*; *European Institute of Oncology, Milan (EIO)*; *European LAM Federation*; *European Oncology Nursing Society (EONS, #08086)*; *European Organisation for Research and Treatment of Cancer (EORTC, #08101)*; *European School of Oncology (ESO, #08434)*; *European Society for Medical Oncology (ESMO, #08648)*; *European Society of Pathology (ESP, #08689)*; *European Society of Surgical Oncology (ESSO, #08753)*; *EURORDIS – Rare Diseases Europe (#09175)*; *International Brain Tumour Alliance (IBTA, #12393)*; *International Kidney Cancer Coalition (IKCC, #13983)*; *Sarcoma Patients EuroNet (SPAEN, #19054)*; *SIOP Europe (SIOPE, #19288)*; *World Sarcoma Network (WSN, #21763).* [2018/XJ6432/y/**F**]

- ♦ Rare Center for Tropical Bird Conservation / see Rare
- ♦ Rare Center for Tropical Conservation / see Rare

♦ Rare Diseases International (RDI) 18621

Exec Dir 96 rue Didot, 75014 Paris, France. E-mail: comms@rarediseasesint.org.
URL: http://www.rarediseasesinternational.org/

History 28 May 2015, Madrid (Spain). Instigated by *EURORDIS – Rare Diseases Europe (#09175)*. Current bylaws adopted 10 Jan 2017. **Aims** United, expand and reinforce the rare diseases movement of patient organisations and *patient* advocates; put rare diseases on the agenda of international organizations and multilateral institutions, and on the national agenda of countries worldwide; strengthen rare disease patient groups capacity to act at local, national, regional and global levels and to interact with other rare disease groups. **Structure** Annual Meeting; Council. Committees (2): Finance and Sustainability; Advocacy. Working Groups. Hosted by *EURORDIS – Rare Diseases Europe (#09175)*. **Finance** Sources: members' dues. **Activities** Advocacy/lobbying/activism; capacity building; events/meetings. **Events** *Annual Meeting* 2021, *Annual Meeting* 2020, *Annual Meeting* New York, NY (USA) 2019, *Annual Meeting* Vienna (Austria) 2018, *Annual Meeting* Barcelona (Spain) 2017. **Publications** *RDI Newsletter* (12 a year).
Members Full; Associate. Full in 33 countries and territories:
Argentina, Australia, Austria, Belgium, Brazil, Canada, China, Colombia, Croatia, Cyprus, France, Germany, Greece, Hong Kong, India, Iran Islamic Rep, Israel, Japan, Malaysia, Mexico, Netherlands, New Zealand, Norway, Palestine, Romania, Russia, Serbia, South Africa, Spain, Sweden, Switzerland, UK, USA.
- *Alianza Iberoamericana de Enfermedades Raras o Poco Frecuentes (ALIBER, #00630)*;
- *Asia Pacific Alliance for Rare Disease Organisations (APARDO, #01824)*;
- *CDH International*;
- *CMTC-OVM*;
- *Cutis Laxa Internationale (CLI)*;
- *DEBRA International (#05021)*;
- *Ehlers-Danlos Society*;
- *Esophageal ATresia Global Support Groups (EAT, #05540)*;
- *EURORDIS – Rare Diseases Europe (#09175)*;
- *Fabry International Network (FIN, #09231)*;
- *Federation of European Patient Groups Affected by Renal Genetic Diseases (FEDERG, #09526)*;
- *Global Alliance of Sickle Cell Disease Organizations (GASCDO, #10227)*;
- *International Federation for Spina Bifida and Hydrocephalus (IF SBH, #13552)*;
- *International Gaucher Alliance (IGA, #13701)*;
- *International Niemann-Pick Disease Alliance (INPDA, #14371)*;
- *International Patient Organization for Primary Immunodeficiencies (IPOPI, #14533)*;
- *International Prader-Willi Syndrome Organisation (IPWSO, #14633)*;
- *Leukemia Patient Advocates Foundation (LePAF)*;
- *Naevus Global*;
- *NCBRS Worldwide Foundation (#16962)*;
- *Retina International (RI, #18926)*;
- *Sociedad Latina de Hipertensión Pulmonar (SLHP, #19388)*;
- *Thalassaemia International Federation (#20139)*;
- *World Alliance of Pituitary Organizations (WAPO, #21087)*;
- *World Duchenne Organization (WDO, #21366)*;
- *World Federation of Hemophilia (WFH, #21437).*

Associate in 12 countries:
Argentina, Botswana, China, Cyprus, France, Ghana, Kenya, Philippines, Portugal, Spain, UK, Zimbabwe.
International Alliance of Dermatology Patient Organizations (IAPDO, #11626). [2022/XM7435/y/**E**]

- ♦ Rare Earth Research Conference (meeting series)
- ♦ RA – Religious of the Assumption (religious order)
- ♦ RARE – Rare Animal Relief Effort / see Rare
- ♦ **RA** Resilience Alliance (#18911)

♦ Rare Skin Diseases Network 18622

Contact c/o Fondation René Touraine, Hôp Necker, 149 rue de Sèvres, 75015 Paris, France.
URL: https://www.frt-rareskin.org/

History 2003. Founded by Fondation René Touraine. Former names and other names: *Genodermatoses & Rare Skin Disorders in Mediterranean* – former (2003 to 2011); *Genodermatoses & Rare Skin Disorders Network* – former (2011 to 2020). **Aims** Improve patient care in the field of severe and rare genetic skin diseases at national, European and international level. **Structure** Scientific Committee. **Languages** English, French. **Activities** Awards/prizes/competitions; awareness raising; events/meetings; knowledge management/information dissemination; networking/liaising; projects/programmes; training/education. [2021.06.09/XM8720/**F**]

- ♦ **RASCOM** Regional African Satellite Communications Organization (#18748)
- ♦ **RASC** Royal Agricultural Society of the Commonwealth (#18987)
- ♦ **RASEF** Réseau africain pour le soutien à l'entrepreneuriat féminin (#00397)
- ♦ RASIT – Royal Academy of Science International Trust (internationally oriented national body)
- ♦ **RASMA** Réseau africain de statistique mathématique et ses applications (#18866)
- ♦ RASPAF – Réseau d'associations de santé publique d'Afrique francophone (inactive)
- ♦ **RAS** Red de Agricultura Sostenible (#20052)
- ♦ RAS – Regional Asia-Pacific Secretariat for Rehabilitation of Survivors of Organized Violence (inactive)
- ♦ RAS – Royal African Society (internationally oriented national body)
- ♦ Rassemblement mondial contre le racisme / see International League Against Racism and Antisemitism (#14014)
- ♦ Rat der Amerikanischen Entwicklungsstiftungen (#04712)
- ♦ Rat der Europäischen Bischofskonferenzen (#04884)
- ♦ Rat der Europäischen Gemeinschaften / see Council of the European Union (#04895)
- ♦ Rat der Europäischen Handelsföderationen (inactive)
- ♦ Rat der Europäischen Nationalkomitees der Jugendverbände (inactive)
- ♦ Rat der Europäischen Union (#04895)
- ♦ Rat der Europäischen Zahnärzte (#04886)
- ♦ Rat für Gegenseitige Wirtschaftshilfe (inactive)
- ♦ Rat der Gemeinden Europas / see Council of European Municipalities and Regions (#04891)
- ♦ Rat der Gemeinden und Regionen Europas (#04891)
- ♦ **Ratify OP3CRC** International Coalition for the Optional Protocol to the Convention on the Rights of the Child on a Communications Procedure (#12617)
- ♦ **RATIN** Regional Agricultural Trade Intelligence Network (#18749)
- ♦ Rat Lutherischer Kirchen in Zentralamerika und Panama (inactive)
- ♦ RATN / see Africa Capacity Alliance (#00160)
- ♦ Rat der Regionen Europas / see Assembly of European Regions (#02316)
- ♦ Rauhan-ja konfliktintutkimuskeskus (internationally oriented national body)
- ♦ Ravi Zacharias International Ministries (internationally oriented national body)
- ♦ Raymond Lemaire International Centre for the Conservation of Historic Towns and Buildings (internationally oriented national body)
- ♦ Rayonnement français et réalités internationales / see Association Réalités et Relations Internationales
- ♦ RBA – Responsible Business Alliance (internationally oriented national body)
- ♦ RBC Ministries / see Our Daily Bread Ministries (#17916)
- ♦ RBC Radio / see Our Daily Bread Ministries (#17916)
- ♦ RBF – Risk, Finance and Banking Society (internationally oriented national body)
- ♦ RBF – Rockefeller Brothers Fund (internationally oriented national body)
- ♦ **RBM** Roll Back Malaria Partnership (#18968)
- ♦ RBWC – Reinventing Bretton Woods Committee (unconfirmed)
- ♦ RCAKL / see Kuala Lumpur Regional Centre for Arbitration (#16210)

♦ RCAR 18623

SG 515 Christie Avenue, Selkirk MB R1A 0W1, Canada. E-mail: rcarorg@hotmail.com.
URL: http://www.rcar.org/

History 1972. Former names and other names: *Research Committee for Automobile Repairs* – former (1972 to 1995); *Research Council for Automobile Repairs (RCAR)* – former (1995 to 2013). **Aims** Provide a forum to exchange information on research findings and strategies for implementation on automotive *design*, repair, and vehicle and road *safety*. **Events** *Annual Conference* Madrid (Spain) 2018, *Annual Conference* Seoul (Korea Rep) 2016, *Annual Conference* Stratford-upon-Avon (UK) 2015, *Annual Conference* Cartagena de Indias (Colombia) 2014, *Annual Conference* Kuala Lumpur (Malaysia) 2013. **Publications** *RCAR Newsletter* (3 a year).
Members Full in 19 countries:
Argentina, Australia, Brazil, China, Colombia, Finland, France, Germany, Italy, Japan, Korea Rep, Malaysia, Mexico, Norway, Spain, Sweden, Switzerland, UK, USA. [2022/XJ5428/**C**]

- ♦ RCA – Reformed Church in America (internationally oriented national body)
- ♦ **RCA** Regional Cooperative Agreement for Research, Development and Training Related to Nuclear Science and Technology in Asia (#18774)
- ♦ RCA – Rencontre de collaboration africaine (meeting series)
- ♦ **RCA** Resuscitation Council of Asia (#18924)
- ♦ RCB – Regional Centre for Biotechnology Training and Education, India (internationally oriented national body)

- ♦ **RCCAE** Red de Centros Culturales de América y Europa (#18639)
- ♦ RCCA / see Institut Régional d'Enseignement Supérieur et de Recherche en Développement Culturel (#11355)
- ♦ RCCDC / see Centre for International Cooperation and Development
- ♦ RCC – East European Engineering Organizations (no recent information)
- ♦ **RCC** Regional Commonwealth in the Field of Communications (#18767)
- ♦ **RCC** Regional Cooperation Council (#18773)
- ♦ RCD – Regional Cooperation for Development (inactive)
- ♦ **RCEL** Royal Commonwealth Ex-Services League (#18989)
- ♦ **RCEP** Regional Center for Educational Planning (#18752)
- ♦ **RCEP** Regional Comprehensive Economic Partnership (#18768)
- ♦ RCEP-UNESCO / see Regional Center for Educational Planning (#18752)
- ♦ **RCE** Rabbinical Centre of Europe (#18598)
- ♦ **RCE** Rare Cancers Europe (#18620)
- ♦ RCE – Religious of Christian Education (religious order)
- ♦ RCE – Renaissance des cités d'Europe (internationally oriented national body)
- ♦ RC Foundation / see YEM Foundation (#21974)
- ♦ **RCF** Roberto Cimetta Fund (#09837)
- ♦ RCF / see YEM Foundation (#21974)
- ♦ RCGG – Research Centre for Global Governance (internationally oriented national body)
- ♦ RCI – Congregatio Rogationistarum a Corde Iesu (religious order)
- ♦ **RCIDT** Red/Consejo Iberoamericano de Donación y Trasplante (#18642)
- ♦ RCIE – Research Center for International Economics (internationally oriented national body)
- ♦ RCI – Racing Commissioners International (internationally oriented national body)
- ♦ **RCI** Red Cartagena de Ingenieria (#03590)
- ♦ RCIVS / see International Forum for Volunteering in Development (#13659)
- ♦ RCJ – Rogationistes du Coeur de Jésus (religious order)
- ♦ **RCMA** Religious Conference Management Association (#18832)
- ♦ RCMNS – Regional Committee on Mediterranean Neogene Stratigraphy (internationally oriented national body)
- ♦ **RCMRD** Regional Centre for Mapping of Resources for Development (#18757)
- ♦ **RCM** Red Cultural Mercosur (#18644)
- ♦ **RCM** Regional Conference on Migration (#18769)
- ♦ **RCNF** Robert Carr civil society Networks Fund (#18956)
- ♦ RCN J&D – RCN Justice et Démocratie (internationally oriented national body)
- ♦ RCN Justice et Démocratie (internationally oriented national body)
- ♦ **RCN** Rainbow Cities Network (#18611)
- ♦ RCNUWC – UWC Red Cross Nordic (internationally oriented national body)
- ♦ **RCNYO** United Nations Regional Commissions New York Office (#20620)
- ♦ RCOA – Refugee Council of Australia (internationally oriented national body)
- ♦ RCPA – Royal College of Pathologists of Australasia (internationally oriented national body)
- ♦ RCP / see European Prison Litigation Network (#08277)
- ♦ **RCQE** Regional Center of Quality and Excellence in Education (#18753)
- ♦ **RCREEE** Regional Center for Renewable Energy and Energy Efficiency (#18754)
- ♦ **RCRF** Rei Cretariae Romanae Fautores (#18827)
- ♦ RC – Ricerca e Cooperazione (internationally oriented national body)
- ♦ RCSA – Resuscitation Council of Southern Africa (internationally oriented national body)
- ♦ RCSB / see Sightsavers International (#19270)
- ♦ **RCS** Royal Commonwealth Society (#18990)
- ♦ RCSSMRS / see Regional Centre for Mapping of Resources for Development (#18757)
- ♦ RCSS – Regional Centre for Strategic Studies, Colombo (internationally oriented national body)
- ♦ RCT / see DIGNITY – Danish Institute Against Torture
- ♦ RCTT / see Asian and Pacific Centre for Transfer of Technology (#01603)
- ♦ RCTWS – Regional Centre for Training and Water Studies of Arid and Semiarid Zones, Cairo (internationally oriented national body)
- ♦ **RCUWM** Regional Centre on Urban Water Management, Teheran (#18761)
- ♦ RDA – Internationaler Bustouristik Verband (internationally oriented national body)
- ♦ **RDA** Research Data Alliance (#18853)
- ♦ **RDC Netwerk** Europese Documentatiecentra (#06937)
- ♦ **RDE** Association Radiodays Europe (#02883)
- ♦ RDF Global – Rural Development Foundation Global (internationally oriented national body)
- ♦ RDI / see Landesa – Rural Development Institute
- ♦ **RDI** Rare Diseases International (#18621)
- ♦ RDJA – Recherches et documentation juridiques africaines (internationally oriented national body)
- ♦ **RDO** Resort Development Organisation (#18913)
- ♦ RdR – Rettet den Regenwald (internationally oriented national body)
- ♦ RDTC – Regional Dermatology Training Centre (internationally oriented national body)
- ♦ RE100 (unconfirmed)
- ♦ **REAAA** Road Engineering Association of Asia and Australasia (#18955)
- ♦ ReachAcross (internationally oriented national body)

♦ REACH ALLIANCE 18624

Exec Dir address not obtained. T. +351211377504. E-mail: team@reach-alliance.org.
URL: http://www.reach-alliance.org/

History Proposed 2016; founded early 2017, by Foundation Alliance of Civilizations. Full title: *REACH ALLIANCE – Global Network*. **Aims** Empower community growth through active learning and through activities, initiatives and projects of collaborative *intercultural* dialogue in a contribution to global peace, development, environment and security. **Structure** General Meeting. **Activities** Awareness raising; networking/liaising.
Members Full in 11 countries:
Azerbaijan, Egypt, Greece, Italy, Jordan, Lebanon, Mexico, North Macedonia, Portugal, Serbia, Spain.
IGO Relations *United Nations Alliance of Civilizations (UNAOC, #20520).* [2018/XM7796/**E**]

- ♦ REACH ALLIANCE – Global Network / see REACH ALLIANCE (#18624)
- ♦ Reach Alternatives (internationally oriented national body)
- ♦ Reach Beyond (internationally oriented national body)
- ♦ Reach the Children (internationally oriented national body)
- ♦ Reach Out to Asia (internationally oriented national body)

♦ Reach to Recovery International (RRI) 18625

Contact 7905 Springway Rd, Towson MD 21204, USA. T. +14105835885. E-mail: info@reachtorecoveryinternational.org.
URL: https://www.reachtorecoveryinternational.org/

History 1952. Founded as a US organization. Included Europe as of 1974. Became a programme of *Union for International Cancer Control (UICC, #20415)*, 1994, and developed into a full member, 2009. Registration: 501(c)3, Start date: 2017, USA, Maryland. **Aims** Improve the quality of life of women facing *breast cancer* and their families. **Structure** Board of Directors; Officers. **Languages** English. **Staff** Voluntary. **Finance** Sources: donations; meeting proceeds. **Activities** Events/meetings; networking/liaising; training/education. **Events** *International Conference* Prague (Czechia) 2019, *Meeting* Paris (France) 2016, *International Conference* Beijing (China) 2015, *International Conference* Cape Town (South Africa) 2013, *International Conference* Taipei (Taiwan) 2011. **Publications** *Bloom* (2 a year) – e-newsletter/magazine.
Members Organizations holding full membership in 20 countries and territories:
Australia, Austria, Belgium, China, Eswatini, Hong Kong, Indonesia, Israel, Kenya, Malaysia, Mauritius, New Zealand, Norway, Portugal, South Africa, Tanzania UR, UK, Ukraine, USA, Zambia.
NGO Relations Member of (3): *The NCD Alliance (NCDA, #16963); Union for International Cancer Control (UICC, #20415); World Patients Alliance (WPA).* [2022/XJ5873/**E**]

- ♦ **ReAct** Action on Antibiotic Resistance (#00089)
- ♦ READ Global (internationally oriented national body)
- ♦ Reading and Writing Foundation (internationally oriented national body)
- ♦ READI – Red Euro-Arabe de ONG para el Desarrollo y la Integración (internationally oriented national body)
- ♦ Real Colegio Seminario de San Buenaventura de Mérida / see Andes University
- ♦ Real Collegio Asiatico / see University Institute of Oriental Studies
- ♦ Real Instituto Elcano de Estudios Internacionales y Estratégicos (internationally oriented national body)
- ♦ **Realiter** Réseau panlatin de terminologie (#18901)
- ♦ Réalités européennes du présent (internationally oriented national body)

♦ The Reality Of Aid (ROA) 18626

Secretariat 3rd Floor, IBON Center, 114 Timog Avenue, 1103 Quezon City, Philippines. T. +6329277001 – +6329277060. Fax +6329276891. E-mail: secretariat@realityofaid.org.
URL: http://www.realityofaid.org/

History Set up within IBON Foundation (Philippines). **Aims** Contribute to more effective international aid and development cooperation strategies to eliminate *poverty*, based on principles of *North/South* solidarity and equity. **Structure** International Coordinating Committee, including Chairperson and Vice-Chairperson, plus CSO representatives from different regions and Global Secretariat Coordinator. **Languages** English. **Staff** 2.00 FTE, paid. **Finance** Contributions from INGO members; funds on per activity basis. **Events** *Global Assembly* Paris (France) 2017. **Publications** *Reality Check* – official newsletter. Biennial Report.
Members Organizations (187) in 75 countries and territories:
Angola, Argentina, Australia, Austria, Bangladesh, Belgium, Benin, Bolivia, Brazil, Burundi, Cambodia, Cameroon, Canada, Chile, China, Colombia, Congo DR, Costa Rica, Côte d'Ivoire, Cuba, Denmark, Dominican Rep, Ecuador, El Salvador, Fiji, Finland, France, Germany, Ghana, Guatemala, Honduras, Hong Kong, India, Indonesia, Ireland, Italy, Japan, Kenya, Korea Rep, Kyrgyzstan, Lebanon, Malawi, Malaysia, Mexico, Mozambique, Nepal, Netherlands, New Zealand, Nicaragua, Nigeria, Norway, Pakistan, Panama, Paraguay, Peru, Philippines, Portugal, Senegal, South Africa, Spain, Sri Lanka, Sweden, Switzerland, Tajikistan, Tanzania UR, Thailand, Timor-Leste, Uganda, UK, Uruguay, USA, Venezuela, Vietnam, Zambia, Zimbabwe.
Included in the above, 48 international organizations listed in this Yearbook:
- *Africa Leadership Forum (ALF, #00183);*
- *African Forum and Network on Debt and Development (AFRODAD, #00321);*
- *African Network for Environment and Economic Justice (ANEEJ);*
- *Alliance Sud, Swiss Alliance of Development Organisations Swissaid – Catholic Lenten Fund – Bread for All – Helvetas – Caritas – Interchurch Aid;*
- *American Council for Voluntary International Action (InterAction);*
- *Andean Center of Popular Action (CAAP);*
- *Arab NGO Network for Development (ANND, #01016);*
- *Asia Pacific Mission for Migrants (APMM);*
- *Asociación Latinoamericana de Organizaciones de Promoción (ALOP, inactive);*
- *Australian Council for International Development (ACFID);*
- *Austrian Research Foundation for Development Cooperation (ÖFSE);*
- *British Overseas NGO's for Development (BOND);*
- *Center for Development Studies and Promotion (DESCO);*
- *Centre for Economic Governance and AIDS in Africa (CEGAA);*
- *Centro di Studi di Politica Internazionale (CeSPI);*
- *Christian Blind Mission (CBM);*
- *Coalition of the Flemish North South Movement – 11 11 11;*
- *Concern Worldwide;*
- *Cooperation Canada;*
- *Coordination SUD;*
- *Council for International Development (CID);*
- *Diakonia;*
- *Economic Justice Network for Churches in Eastern and Southern Africa (EJN, #05317);*
- *ECOWAS Network on Debt and Development (ECONDAD, #05336);*
- *European Network on Debt and Development (EURODAD, #07891);*
- *Europe External Programme with Africa (EEPA, #09155);*
- *Forum for Development and Environment (ForUM);*
- *Foundation for Grassroots Initiatives in Africa (GrassRootsAfrica);*
- *GLOBAL RESPONSIBILITY – Austrian Platform for Development and Humanitarian Aid;*
- *Ibis – Denmark;*
- *Institute of Development Studies, Harare (IDS);*
- *Inter-American Cooperative Institute (ICI, #11420);*
- *INTERMON OXFAM;*
- *International NGO Forum on Indonesian Development (INFID, #14366);*
- *Japanese NGO Center for International Cooperation (JANIC);*
- *Japan International Volunteer Centre (JVC);*
- *Mellemfolkeligt Samvirke (MS);*
- *Oxfam Novib;*
- *Pacific Asia Resource Centre (PARC);*
- *Pacific Islands Association of Non-Governmental Organizations (PIANGO, #17961);*
- *Red Latinoamericana sobre Deuda, Desarrollo y Derechos (LATINDADD, #18711);*
- *South Asian Network for Social and Agricultural Development (SANSAD);*
- *Southern African Centre for the Constructive Resolution of Disputes (SACCORD);*
- *Suomalaiset Kehitysjärjestöt (Fingo);*
- *Swedish NGO Centre for Development Cooperation (Forum Syd);*
- *Terre des Hommes International Federation (TDHIF, #20133)* (German Section);
- *Third World Network (TWN, #20151);*
- *Universidad CLAEH (#20688).*

Consultative Status Consultative status granted from: *ECOSOC (#05331)* (Special). **NGO Relations** Hosted and coordinated by: *IBON International (#11037).* Member of: *Effective Institutions Platform (EIP, #05384).* [2020/XM1990/y/**F**]

- ♦ Reall (internationally oriented national body)
- ♦ Real Options – International Conference on Real Options (meeting series)
- ♦ REALs – Reach Alternatives (internationally oriented national body)
- ♦ REAP – Regional Environmental Assessment Programme (inactive)
- ♦ REARB / see African Network of Research on Storage Insects (#00394)
- ♦ **REARIS** Réseau africain de recherche sur les insectes des stocks (#00394)
- ♦ Réarmement moral / see Initiatives of Change International – Caux (#11213)
- ♦ Rearme Moral / see Initiatives of Change International – Caux (#11213)
- ♦ Reason Partnership (internationally oriented national body)
- ♦ Rebirth of European Cities (internationally oriented national body)
- ♦ **ReCAAP ISC** Regional Cooperation Agreement on Combating Piracy and Armed Robbery against Ships in Asia – Information Sharing Centre (#18771)
- ♦ **RECAN** Regional European and Central Asian ALARA Network (#18784)
- ♦ **RECA** Réseau de recherche caféière en Afrique (#00253)
- ♦ **REC Caucasus** Regional Environmental Centre for the Caucasus (#18781)
- ♦ **RECEF** Réseau des compétences électorales francophones (#18869)
- ♦ Recent Progress in Graphene and Two-dimensional Materials Research Conference (meeting series)
- ♦ **RECEP-ENELC** European Network of Local and Regional Authorities for the Implementation of the European Landscape Convention (#07939)
- ♦ **RECEVIN** Réseau Européen des Villes du Vin (#18881)
- ♦ RECFAM – Research and Counselling Foundation for African Migrants (internationally oriented national body)

♦ RECHARGE 18627

Secretariat Ave de Tervueren 168, Box 3, 1150 Brussels, Belgium. T. +3227770567. Fax +3227770565. E-mail: recharge@rechargebatteries.org.
Dir Gen address not obtained. E-mail: jpwiaux@rechargebatteries.org.
Chair c/o SAFT, Rue Sadi Carnot 12, 93170 Bagnolet, France.
URL: http://www.rechargebatteries.org/

History 1998. Registration: Banque-Carrefour des Entreprises, No/ID: 0874.269.017, Start date: 28 Oct 2004, Belgium; EU Transparency Register, No/ID: 673674011803-02, Start date: 5 Sep 2013. **Aims** Promote the value of *rechargeable* batteries; represent the interests of all members in the chain of *battery* life. **Languages** English. **Staff** 3.00 FTE, paid. **Events** *Battery Conference* Seoul (Korea Rep) 2016.
Members Companies and associations (26) in 7 countries:
Belgium, France, Germany, Netherlands, Switzerland, UK, USA.
Included in the above, 2 organizations listed in this Yearbook:
European Power Tool Association (EPTA, #08264); International Cadmium Association (ICdA, #12424).
IGO Relations Involved in: *United Nations Committee of Experts on the Transport of Dangerous Goods and on the Globally Harmonized System of Classification and Labelling of Chemicals (Committee of Experts on TDG and GHS, #20543).* **NGO Relations** Member of: *Association européenne des métaux (EUROMETAUX, #02578); European Green Vehicles Initiative Association (EGVIA, #07410); Federation of European and International Associations Established in Belgium (FAIB, #09508); Industry4Europe (#11181).* [2020/XM1468/**F**]

♦ Recherche et développement des cultures vivrières dans les zones semi-arides (#19226)
♦ Recherche et Etudes en Politique Internationale (internationally oriented national body)
♦ Recherches et documentation juridiques africaines (internationally oriented national body)
♦ Rechnungshof der Europäischen Gemeinschaften / see European Court of Auditors (#06854)
♦ **RECIF** Réseau d'épidémiologie clinique international francophone (#09992)
♦ Reciprocal Enforcement of Judgements Agreement (1952 treaty)
♦ **RECIT** Réseau européen des centres internationaux de traducteurs littéraires (#18873)
♦ **RECJ** Réseau européen des conseils de la justice (#07886)
♦ RECLA / see Red Universitaria de Educación Continua de Latinoamérica y Europa (#18734)
♦ **RECLA** Red Universitaria de Educación Continua de Latinoamérica y Europa (#18734)
♦ **RECOFI** Regional Commission for Fisheries (#18763)

♦ RECOFTC – The Center for People and Forests (RECOFTC) 18628

Exec Dir PO Box 1111, Kasetsart Post Office, Phahonyothin Rd, Bangkok, 10903, Thailand. T. +6629405700 ext 1200. Fax +6625614880 – +6625620960. E-mail: info@recoftc.org.
URL: http://www.recoftc.org/

History 1987, Bangkok (Thailand). Founded within *Asia-Pacific Agroforestry Network (APAN, inactive).* First building inaugurated 1991. Became independent in 2000. Former names and other names: *Forests, Trees and People Programme in Asia (FTPP)* – former (1987); *Regional Community Forestry Training Centre* – former; *Regional Community Forestry Training Centre for Asia and the Pacific* – former. **Aims** Develop and support learning processes that enhance community forestry development in *Asia*; support capacity building and change processes that enhance the effectiveness of organizations involved in community forestry; support development of effective institutional arrangements for improved forest governance. **Structure** Board of Trustees; Executive Committee. **Finance** Grants; revenue from activities. Funding partners include: *Swedish International Development Cooperation Agency (Sida); Swiss Agency for Development and Cooperation (SDC); Japan International Cooperation Agency (JICA).* **Activities** Capacity building; training/education; financial and/or material support. **Events** *FORTROP : international conference on tropical forestry change in a changing world* Bangkok (Thailand) 2008, *International seminar on cultivating forests / International Seminar* Bangkok (Thailand) 1998. **Publications** *Asia-Pacific Community Forestry Newsletter.* Annual Report; reports of regional seminars; Community forestry case studies and trainers guidelines; working papers. **Members** Membership countries not specified. **IGO Relations** Memorandum of Understanding with: *South Asia Cooperative Environment Programme (SACEP, #19714).* Close cooperation with: *Asian Forest Cooperation Organization (AFoCO, #01489).* **NGO Relations** Member of: *Global Gender and Climate Alliance (GGCA, no recent information); International Union for Conservation of Nature and Natural Resources (IUCN, #15766).* Instrumental in setting up and partner of: *Rights and Resources Initiative (RRI, #18947).* [2022/XF3137/**E**]

♦ **RECOFTC** RECOFTC – The Center for People and Forests (#18628)
♦ RECOMB – International Conference on Research in Computational Molecular Biology (meeting series)
♦ **ReCOMed** Réseau des Cités Oléicoles de la Méditerranée (#18868)
♦ Recommendation Complémentaire à la Convention Concernant la Sécurité dans L'utilisation des Produits Chimiques au Travail (1990 treaty)
♦ Recommendation Complémentaire à la Convention Concernant le Travail de Nuit (1990 treaty)
♦ RECOM mreža pomirenja (unconfirmed)
♦ RECOM Reconciliation Network (unconfirmed)
♦ RECOM – Regional Commission for the Determination of Facts about War Crimes and Other Serious Violations of Human Rights Committed on the Territory of the Former SFRY from January 1, 1991 to December 31, 2001 (unconfirmed)

♦ Reconstructing Women International (RWI) 18629

Co-Founder c/o Stiftungszentrum, Widenmayerstr 10, 80538 Munich, Germany.
URL: https://www.reconstructingwomen.org/

History 2007. Founded by Dr Marita Eisenmann-Klein and Dr Constance Neuhann-Lorenz. Former names and other names: *WomenforWomen Reconstructive Surgery* – former. **Aims** Address the medical needs of women and young girls who have suffered disfiguring and disabling injuries and trauma, working to restore them physically and helping them to return to happy and productive lives. **Structure** Leadership Team. **Activities** Healthcare; training/education. India, Pakistan, Bangladesh, Haiti, East Africa. [2018/AA1926/**F**]

♦ Recording-Media Industry Association of Europe (inactive)
♦ Records and Information Management Professionals Australasia (internationally oriented national body)
♦ Records Management Association of Australasia / see Records and Information Management Professionals Australasia

♦ Recourse 18630

Co-Dir Kraijenhoffstr 137A, 1018 RG Amsterdam, Netherlands. T. +31614820789.
Co-Dir Address not obtained.
URL: https://www.re-course.org/

History Former names and other names: *Stichting Re-course International* – legal name; *Bank Information Center Europe* – former. Registration: Handelsregister, No/ID: KVK 64363635, Start date: 17 Dec 2019, Netherlands. **Aims** Make finance accountable to people and planet. **Structure** Board of Directors. **Activities** Advocacy/lobbying/activism; guidance/assistance/consulting; networking/liaising; research/documentation. **NGO Relations** Member of (1): *European Network on Debt and Development (EURODAD, #07891).* Partner of (1): *Arab Watch Coalition (AWC, #01074).* [2022/AA2843/f/**F**]

♦ **RECOWA** Regional Episcopal Conference of West Africa (#18783)
♦ **RECPJ** Red Europea de Consejos del Poder Judicial (#07886)
♦ **RECPnet** Global Network for Resource Efficient and Cleaner Production (#10497)
♦ Recreational Scuba Training Council / see World Recreational Scuba Training Council (#21747)
♦ **REC** Regional Environmental Centre for Central and Eastern Europe (#18782)
♦ **RECR** Réseau européen pour une consommation responsable (#07994)
♦ RECSA / see Regional Centre on Small Arms and Light Weapons in the Great Lakes Region, the Horn of Africa and Bordering States (#18760)
♦ **RECSA** Regional Centre on Small Arms and Light Weapons in the Great Lakes Region, the Horn of Africa and Bordering States (#18760)
♦ RECSEA-PGR – Regional Cooperation in Southeast Asia on Plant Genetic Resources (inactive)
♦ RECS Energy Certificate Association / see RECS International (#18631)

♦ RECS International 18631

SG Achter de Tolbrug 151, 5211 SM 's Hertogenbosch, Netherlands. E-mail: secretariat@recs.org.
Registered Address Utrechtseweg 310/H02, 6812 AR Arnhem, Netherlands. T. +31268200396.
URL: http://www.recs.org/

History 2000. Systems test phase, 2001-2002. Since 2003, fully operational. Changed status from foundation to association in 2004. Former names and other names: *Renewable Energy Certificate System International (RECS International)* – former; *RECS Energy Certificate Association* – alias. Registration: Handelsregister, No/ID: KVK 59468025, Start date: 2011, Netherlands; Banque-Carrefour des Entreprises, End date: 2010, Belgium; EU Transparency Register, No/ID: 358492746482-66, Start date: 10 May 2022. **Aims** Create an open and transparent demand-driven renewable energy market, facilitated by commonly accepted and harmonized tracking systems. **Structure** General Meeting; Board; Working Groups; Secretariat. **Languages** English. **Staff** 3.00 FTE, paid. **Finance** Sources: members' dues. **Activities** Advocacy/lobbying/activism; certification/accreditation; events/meetings; projects/programmes; standards/guidelines. **Events** *General Meeting* Brussels (Belgium) 2022, *General Meeting* Amsterdam (Netherlands) 2021, *General Meeting* Amsterdam (Netherlands) 2020, *General Meeting* Amsterdam (Netherlands) 2019, *General Meeting* Amsterdam (Netherlands) 2018. **Publications** *RECS Newsletter.*
Members Renewable energy producers, traders, suppliers and brokers (about 200) trading in renewable energy certificates, in 22 countries:
Austria, Belgium, Denmark, Estonia, Finland, France, Germany, Greece, Iceland, Italy, Luxembourg, Netherlands, Norway, Poland, Portugal, Slovakia, Slovenia, South Africa, Spain, Sweden, Switzerland, UK.
NGO Relations Partner of (5): *Association of Issuing Bodies (AIB, #02768); European Federation of Energy Traders (EFET, #07108); International REC Standard Foundation (I-REC Standard, #14705); RE100; RE-Source Platform (RE-Source, #18916).* [2022/XJ0806/**F**]

♦ **RECSO** Regional Clean Sea Organization (#18762)
♦ RECTAS / see African Regional Institute for Geospatial Information Science and Technology (#00433)

♦ Rectors' Conference of the Universities of the Adriatic Universities (AARC) 18632

Pres Univ na Primorskem, Titov trg 4, 6000 Koper, Slovenia.
URL: http://www.alps-adriatic.net/

History 1979. **Aims** Promote dialogue among higher educational institutions of the Alps Adriatic regions in the field of education, scientific research and didactics. **Structure** Scientific Committee. **Activities** Training/education; awards/prizes/competitions. **Events** *Annual Conference* Koper (Slovenia) 2016, *Annual Conference* Klagenfurt am Wörthersee (Austria) 2015, *Annual Conference* Zagreb (Croatia) 2012.
Members Universities in 9 countries:
Albania, Austria, Bosnia-Herzegovina, Croatia, Germany, Hungary, Italy, Serbia, Slovenia. [2016.11.17/XJ2228/**D**]

♦ RED / see Latin America Network of Assisted Reproduction (#16315)
♦ (RED) (internationally oriented national body)
♦ Red académica internacional "Estudios Organizacionales en América Latina, el Caribe e Iberoamécia" (unconfirmed)
♦ Red ACA / see Red Latinoamericana sobre Deuda, Desarrollo y Derechos (#18711)
♦ Red de Acción en Plaguicidas / see Pesticide Action Network (#18336)

♦ Red de Acción en Plaguicidas y sus Alternativas de América Latina (RAP-AL) 18633

Contact Alonso de Ovalle 1618, oficina A, Santiago, Santiago Metropolitan, Chile. T. +5626997375. E-mail: rap-al@terra.cl – secretaria@rapa.cl – malenarozas@terra.cl.
URL: http://www.rap-al.org/

History Set up Jun 1983. Since 1995, a a regional centre of *Pesticide Action Network (PAN, #18336)* and also referred to as *PAN Latin America.* **Aims** Assist PAN groups in Latin America to persuade their governments to adopt stronger controls on *pesticide* use, create awareness and teach about the *hazards* of pesticides and work with farmers to develop and implement alternative methods of production. **Finance** Members' dues. **Activities** Advocacy/lobbying/activism. **Members** Organizations (17). Membership countries not specified. [2018/XM7491/**E**]

♦ Rédacteurs-en-chef européens de publications relatives aux sciences de la vie (inactive)
♦ Red de Actividad Fisica de las Americas (#18366)
♦ Red ACYM / see América Cooperativa y Mutual (#00773)
♦ Red Africana de Bosques Modelo (#00377)
♦ Red Africana para el Desarrollo de la Horticultura (no recent information)
♦ Red de Agricultura Sostenible / see Social Agriculture Network (#19333)
♦ Red de Agricultura Sostenible (#20052)
♦ **Red AMEC** América Cooperativa y Mutual (#00773)
♦ Red Americana y Caribeña de Ecologia Social (#16283)
♦ Red Americana de Investigación en Información y Comunicación / see Communication Policy Research Latin America (#04382)
♦ Red de las Américas sobre Nacionalidad y Apartridia (unconfirmed)
♦ Red ANA – Red de las Américas sobre Nacionalidad y Apartridia (unconfirmed)
♦ Red Andina de Información (#00819)
♦ Red Andina de la Seda (inactive)
♦ REDAPP – Red de Postgrados en Administración y Politicas Públicas (see: #16294)

♦ Red de Archivos Diplomaticos Latinoamericanos (RADI) 18634

Network of Iberoamerican Diplomatic Archives

Main Office Secretaria de Relaciones Exteriores de México, Ricardo Flores Magón 2, Edif Triangular Nivel 2, ala B, Col Guerrero, Alcaldia Cuauhtémoc, 06300 Mexico City CDMX, Mexico. T. +525536865100 ext 4609. E-mail: unidad.tecnica@archivosiberoamericanos.org – solivo@sre.gob.mx.
URL: http://archivosiberoamericanos.org/

History 1997. **Aims** Promote cooperation in the organization, administration, conservation and use of archival systems of the Ibero-American Ministries of Foreign Affairs. **Structure** Intergovernmental Council; Presidency; Technical Unit. **Languages** Portuguese, Spanish. **Finance** Government funding. **Activities** Awards/prizes/competitions; capacity building; events/meetings; knowledge management/information dissemination. **Events** *Annual Meeting* Mexico City (Mexico) 2020, *Annual Meeting* Santo Domingo (Dominican Rep) 2019, *Annual Meeting* Lisbon (Portugal) 2018, *Annual Meeting* Mexico City (Mexico) 2017, *Annual Meeting* Bogota (Colombia) 2016. **Publications** *Los documentos cuentan nuestra historia. A propósito del bicentenario de la cancillería del Perú* (2021) in Spanish – Ministerio de Relaciones Exteriores del Perú; Gestión Documental y Archivos. *El exilio brasileño en México durante la dictadura militar 1964-1979* (2018) by Daniela Morales Muñoz; *El Sistema Institucional de Archivos: Por qué? Para qué?* (2016) by Aida Luz Mendoza; *Servicios Basicos de los Archivos Diplomaticos Iberoamericanos* (2011) by José Antonio Ramirez De León; *Politicas y sistemas de archivos* (2010) by José Maria Jardim.
Members Archives of 16 countries:
Argentina, Bolivia, Chile, Colombia, Cuba, Dominican Rep, Ecuador, El Salvador, Honduras, Mexico, Panama, Paraguay, Peru, Portugal, Spain, Uruguay.
NGO Relations APOYOnline. [2021.09.06/XF6588/**F***]

♦ Red de las Areas Protegidas del Africa Central (#03656)
♦ Red de Arte Planetaria (#18380)
♦ Red Asiatica de Instituciones de Formación e Investigación en Planificación de la Educación (#01561)

♦ Red del Atlantico Este de Reservas de Biósfera (REDBIOS) 18635

Réseau est atlantique de réserves de biosphère – REDBIOS Network

Contact UNESCO, Div of Ecological and Earth Sciences, 7 Place Fontenoy, 75007 Paris CEDEX 15, France. T. +33145680887. E-mail: m.cardenas@unesco.org.
URL: http://www.unesco.org/mab/networks.shtml

History 11 Apr 1999, Agadir (Morocco), within the framework of *Programme on Man and the Biosphere (MAB, #18526)*, to fulfil the interregional mandate of *Integrated Biodiversity Strategies for Islands and Coastal Regions (IBSICA Project, inactive).* Formerly known as *Réseau est atlantique de réserves de biosphère.* **Aims** Within the framework of the IBSICA Project mandate, give particular attention in the East Atlantic region to countries having or planning biosphere reserves on islands and/or coastal zones and to countries having

signed the Biodiversity Convention. **Languages** Members express themselves in their own languages. **Events** *Meeting* Madeira (Portugal) 2012, *Meeting* Fuerteventura Is (Spain) 2011, *Meeting* Las Palmas de Gran Canaria (Spain) 2011, *Meeting* Horta (Portugal) 2009, *Meeting* El Hierro Is (Spain) 2006. **Publications** Brochures; research reports; papers.
Members Reserves in 8 countries and territories:
Azores, Canaries, Cape Verde, Guinea-Bissau, Madeira, Mauritania, Morocco, Senegal. [2018.06.26/XF5964/**F***]

♦ Red de Autoridades en Medicamentos de Iberoamérica (Red EAMI) . 18636

Rede das Autoridades em Medicamentos dos Países Ibero-americanos
Address not obtained.
URL: https://www.redeami.net/
History Feb 1997. Founded at 1st Meeting of Competent Authorities on Medicines in Ibero-American Countries. **Structure** Secretariat. **Activities** Events/meetings. **Events** *Meeting* Lisbon (Portugal) 2018, *Meeting* Varadero (Cuba) / Havana (Cuba) 2016, *Meeting* San Salvador (El Salvador) 2014, *Meeting* Santiago (Chile) 2012, *Meeting* Madrid (Spain) 2010.
Members Medicine agencies or directorates in 22 countries:
Andorra, Argentina, Bolivia, Brazil, Chile, Colombia, Costa Rica, Cuba, Dominican Rep, Ecuador, El Salvador, Guatemala, Honduras, Mexico, Nicaragua, Panama, Paraguay, Peru, Portugal, Spain, Uruguay, Venezuela.
IGO Relations Listed in the Registro de Redes Iberoamericano, held by *Ibero-American General Secretariat (#11024).* [2021/AA1239/**F**]

- ♦ Red Barnet (internationally oriented national body)
- ♦ Red de Biodiversidad de los Pueblos Indigenas (#11164)
- ♦ Redbioética / see Red Latinoamericana y del Caribe de Bioética (#18702)
- ♦ **REDBIOETICA** Red Latinoamericana y del Caribe de Bioética (#18702)
- ♦ REDBIO International Foundation
- ♦ REDBIOS Network (#18635)
- ♦ **REDBIOS** Red del Atlantico Este de Reservas de Biósfera (#18635)
- ♦ Red de Bolsas Agropecuarias de las Américas (see: #11434)

♦ Red de Bosques Andinos 18637

Contact Calle German Aleman E12-28 y Juan Ramirez (Batan Baj), Quito, Ecuador. T. +59322469072 – +59322469073.
URL: http://www.condesan.org/redbosques/
History 2011. **Aims** Promote research in Andean forest ecosystems. **Finance** Supported by: *Consortium for the Sustainable Development of the Andean Ecoregion (#04758); Deutsche Gesellschaft für Internationale Zusammenarbeit (GIZ); Swiss Agency for Development and Cooperation (SDC).*
Members Individuals in 6 countries:
Argentina, Colombia, Ecuador, Germany, Peru, USA.
Included in the above, 3 organizations listed in this Yearbook:
Consortium for the Sustainable Development of the Andean Ecoregion (#04758); Deutsche Gesellschaft für Internationale Zusammenarbeit (GIZ); Swiss Agency for Development and Cooperation (SDC).
[2015/XM4190/y/**F**]

- ♦ REDCAMIF – Red Centroamericana y del Caribe de Microfinanzas (unconfirmed)
- ♦ **REDCAPA** Red de Instituciones Vinculadas a la Capacitación en Economia y Politicas Agricolas en América Latina y el Caribe (#18690)
- ♦ Red Caribeña de Investigadores/Clinicos sobre la Drepanocitosis y las Talas (#03529)
- ♦ Red del Caribe de Sanidad Animal (#03440)
- ♦ Red Cartagena de Ingenieria (#03590)

♦ Red Centroamericana de Acción del Agua 18638

Freshwater Action Network – Central America (FANCA)
Regional Coordinator c/o ARCA, PO Box 1852-2050 Sur del Higuerón, San Pedro, San José, San José, San José, Costa Rica. T. +50622806516. Fax +50622801530. E-mail: jmorapo@arca.co.cr – fancaregional@gmail.com.
Facebook: https://www.facebook.com/pages/category/Community/Red-Centroamericana-de-Acci%C3%B3n-del-Agua-110711092315626/
Structure Hosted by: *Asociación Regional Centroamericana para el Agua el Ambiente (ARCA, no recent information).*
Members National associations in 6 countries:
Costa Rica, El Salvador, Guatemala, Honduras, Nicaragua, Panama.
Included in the above, 2 organizations listed in this Yearbook:
Asociación Centroamericana para la Economia, la Salud y el Ambiente (ACEPESA); Asociación Regional Centroamericana para el Agua el Ambiente (ARCA, no recent information).
NGO Relations Member of: *Alianza por el Agua (no recent information); The Butterfly Effect (BE, #03389).* Partner of: *Sanitation and Water for All (SWA, #19051).* [2020/XJ5182/y/**D**]

- ♦ Red Centroamericana y del Caribe de Microfinanzas (unconfirmed)
- ♦ Red Centroamericana de Instituciones Vinculadas de Ingenieria / see Central American Engineering Institutions Network (#03668)
- ♦ Red Centroamericana de Manejo de Recursos Hidricos (#03676)

♦ Red de Centros Culturales de América y Europa (RCCAE) 18639

Network of American and European Cultural Centres
Exec Sec UCA – Centro Cultural, Av Alicia Moreau de Justo 1500, Edif San Alberto Magno, Buenos Aires, Argentina.
URL: http://www.rccae.com/
History 2002. **Events** *Meeting* Genoa (Italy) 2009, *Meeting* Maracaibo (Venezuela) 2008, *Meeting* Lima (Peru) 2007, *Meeting* Berlin (Germany) 2006, *Meeting* Santiago (Chile) 2005.
Members Centres in 24 countries:
Argentina, Austria, Bolivia, Brazil, Chile, Colombia, Costa Rica, Cuba, Dominican Rep, Ecuador, France, Germany, Italy, Mexico, Panama, Paraguay, Peru, Portugal, Spain, Switzerland, UK, Uruguay, USA, Venezuela.
Included in the above, 11 organizations listed in this Yearbook:
Andean Institute of Popular Arts (IADAP, no recent information); Casa de las Américas; Centro Cultural Iberoamericano 'Casa de América', Madrid; Convenio Andrés Bello de integración educativa, cientifica y cultural de América Latina y España (Convenio Andrés Bello, #04785); Ibero-Amerikanisches Institut Preussischer Kulturbesitz (IAI); Institut Català de Cooperació Iberoamericana (ICCI); Instituto Latinoamericano de Museos (ILAM); International Integration Institute of the Andrés Bello Convention (#13940); Memorial Foundation of Latin America; Organization of Ibero-American States for Education, Science and Culture (#17871); Österreichisches Lateinamerika-Institut (LAI). [2011/XJ0837/y/**F**]

- ♦ Red de Centros de Documentación de Literatura Infantil y Juvenil (see: #17629)
- ♦ Red de Centros de Estudio de América Latina y el Caribe sobre Asia Pacifico (internationally oriented national body)
- ♦ Red de Certificación en Turismo Sostenible de las Américas (#20069)

♦ Red de Ciclovias Recreativas de las Américas (Red CRA) 18640

Technical Secretary General Holley 186 of G, Santiago, Santiago Metropolitan, Chile. T. +5622340668.
URL: http://www.cicloviasrecreativas.org/
History 13 Nov 2005, Bogota (Colombia). as *Ciclovias Unidas de las Américas (CUA)* by 16 organizations and one individual: Instituto Municipal de Urbanismo Pereira Passos (Brazil); Instituto Distrital para la Recreación y el Deporte (Colombia); Ciudad Humana (Colombia); Jaime Ortiz Mariño (Colombia); Instituto para el Deporte y la Recreación (Colombia); GEOMAS (Chile); Centers for Disease Control and Prevention (USA); Chicago Land Bicycle Federation (USA); *Pan American Health Organization (PAHO, #18108)* – Non-communicable Diseases Unit (USA); Municipalidad de Guatemala (Guatemala); Ciudades Publicas (Mexico); Centro Mexicano de Derecho Ambiental (Mexico); Fundación Biciacción (Ecuador); Instituto Peruano del Deporte de San Borja (Peru); Municipalidad de San Borja (Peru); Instituto Autónomo de Circulación y Transito (Venezuela); Municipalidad de Chacao, Caracas (Venezuela). **Aims** Promote across cities in the Americas the temporary closure of certain streets to motorized traffic in order to form safe routes where *pedestrians* and *cyclists* can play, sport, walk or participate in recreational activities. **Structure** Any governmental institutions, non-governmental organizations, civil associations, university departments, private corporations or individuals willing to promote open street programmes (ciclovias recreativas) in the Americas are eligible for membership. **Languages** English, Spanish. **Finance** Supported by: *Pan American Health Organization (PAHO, #18108);* Center for Disease Control and Prevention (USA). **Activities** Organizes international seminars and workshops. **Events** *International seminar* Mexico City (Mexico) 2010, *International seminar* Caracas (Venezuela) 2009, *International seminar* Quito (Ecuador) 2008, *International seminar* Bogota (Colombia) 2005. **Publications** *Ciclovia Recreativa: Implementation and Advocacy Manual* (2009) by Olga Sarmiento. **Members** Membership countries not specified. **NGO Relations** Works with national non-governmental organizations in the Americas. [2018/XJ0752/**F**]

- ♦ **RedCLARA** Cooperación Latino Americana de Redes Avanzadas (#04790)

♦ Red Cochrane Iberoamericana 18641

Iberoamerican Cochrane Network (IbCN)
Contact Centro Cochrane Iberoamericano, Hospital de la Santa Creu i Sant Pau, Pavelló 18 – Planta 0, Sant Antoni Maria Claret 167, 08025 Barcelona, Spain. T. +34935537814. Fax +34935537809. E-mail: cochrane@cochrane.es.
URL: http://www.es.cochrane.org/es/red-cochrane-iberoamericana/
History Founded 2000. **Aims** Create a network of institutions and people committed to the objectives of the Cochrane Collaboration in Spain and South America; help local professionals make well-informed decisions about *healthcare* by preparing, maintaining and ensuring accessibility of systematic reviews of the effects of healthcare interventions. **Structure** Coordinated by: *Centro Cochrane Iberoamericano (CCIb).* Regional Branches (5). **Languages** English, Spanish. **Staff** 25.00 FTE, paid. **Finance** Support from member institutions. **Activities** Training/education; knowledge management/information dissemination. **Events** *Meeting / Annual Meeting* Montevideo (Uruguay) 2015, *Meeting / Annual Meeting* Panama (Panama) 2014, *Meeting / Annual Meeting* Monterrey (Mexico) 2013, *Annual Meeting* Lima (Peru) 2012, *Annual Meeting* Madrid (Spain) 2011. **Publications** *Boletin Cochrane Iberoamérica* – electronic bulletin.
Members Coordinating (28); Associated (42) universities, hospitals; governmental bodies. Centres in 17 countries:
Argentina, Bolivia, Chile, Colombia, Costa Rica, Cuba, Ecuador, El Salvador, Guatemala, Mexico, Panama, Paraguay, Peru, Portugal, Spain, Uruguay, Venezuela. [2016.12.16/XM2744/**F**]

- ♦ Red de Conocimiento para el Desarrollo (internationally oriented national body)

♦ Red/Consejo Iberoamericano de Donación y Trasplante (RCIDT) . . . 18642

Iberoamerican Network/Council on Donation and Transplantation
Contact c/o ONT, C/ Sinesio Delgado 6-8, Pabellón 3, 28029 Madrid, Spain.
URL: http://www.transplant-observatory.org/iberoamericano/
History 14 Oct 2005, Salamanca (Spain). Founded during *VII Conferencia Iberoamericana de Ministras y Ministros de Salud / Iberoamerican Conference of Health Ministers.* **Structure** Committee. **Events** *Meeting* 2020, *Meeting* Havana (Cuba) 2019, *Meeting* Buenos Aires (Argentina) 2017, *Meeting* Havana (Cuba) 2008, *Meeting* Santiago (Chile) 2007. **Publications** *RCIDT Newsletter.*
Members Full in 20 countries:
Argentina, Bolivia, Brazil, Chile, Colombia, Costa Rica, Cuba, Dominica, Ecuador, El Salvador, Honduras, Mexico, Nicaragua, Panama, Paraguay, Peru, Portugal, Spain, Uruguay, Venezuela.
IGO Relations Listed in the Registro de Redes Iberoamericano, held by *Ibero-American General Secretariat (#11024).* **NGO Relations** Participates in: *Global Observatory on Donation and Transplantation (GODT).* [2020/XJ2223/**D**]

- ♦ Red de Cooperación Tecnica entre Laboratorios de Investigación y Diagnóstico Veterinario (see: #09268)
- ♦ Red Cooperativa Europea de Investigación del Olivo (#15969)
- ♦ **Red CRA** Red de Ciclovias Recreativas de las Américas (#18640)
- ♦ Red Cross / see Anarchist Black Cross Network (#00812)
- ♦ Red Cross / EU Liaison Bureau / see Red Cross EU Office (#18643)

♦ Red Cross EU Office 18643

Bureau Croix-Rouge auprès de l'UE
Dir Rue de Trèves 59-61, 1040 Brussels, Belgium. T. +3222350680. Fax +3222305464. E-mail: infoboard@redcross.eu.
URL: http://redcross.eu/
History 1983. Founded by Red Cross national societies of European Union countries. Former names and other names: *Red Cross / EU Liaison Bureau* – former; *Bureau de liaison Croix-Rouge / UE* – former. **Aims** Represent Red Cross National Societies in the EU, as well as Norway, and the International Federation of Red Cross and Red Crescent Societies (IFRC) before the institutions of the European Union; increase the influence of the Red Cross on EU policies that have an impact on the interests of vulnerable people; provide support to members by sharing information, building partnerships and facilitating access to EU funding. **Structure** Annual Meeting, comprising Secretary General or Presidents of Red Cross National Societies of the EU and *International Federation of Red Cross and Red Crescent Societies (#13526).* Red Cross EU Office, headed by Director. Coordination Group. **Languages** English. **Finance** IFRC and Red Cross National Societies. Annual budget: 800,000 EUR. **Activities** Events/meetings; guidance/assistance/consulting; knowledge management/information dissemination. **Events** *Conference on Social Care in Times of Crisis* Brussels (Belgium) 2012, *Rencontre entre jeunes d'Europe* Paris (France) 1987.
Members Red Cross Societies in 28 countries:
Austria, Belgium, Bulgaria, Croatia, Cyprus, Czechia, Denmark, Estonia, Finland, France, Germany, Greece, Hungary, Ireland, Italy, Latvia, Lithuania, Luxembourg, Malta, Netherlands, Norway, Poland, Portugal, Romania, Slovakia, Slovenia, Spain, Sweden.
International organization (1), listed in this Yearbook:
IFRC.
IGO Relations Member of Consultative Forum of *Frontex, the European Border and Coast Guard Agency (#10005).* **NGO Relations** Red Cross networks the Office is a member of: *European Council on Refugees and Exiles (ECRE, #06839);* European Legal Support Group; *European Network for Psychosocial Support (ENPS, #07978); European Network on Volunteer Development (ENDOV, #08032); European Public Support Group (EPSG); European Reference Centre for First Aid Education (EREH);* IFRC Reference Centre on Psychosocial Support; *Platform for European Red Cross Cooperation on Refugees, Asylum-seekers and Migrants (PERCO, no recent information); Red Cross and Red Crescent Network against Trafficking in Human Beings (no recent information);* Reference Centre on Volunteering; *Social Services Europe (#19347).* [2022.05.13/XE2446/**E**]

- ♦ Red Cross Nordic United World College / see UWC Red Cross Nordic
- ♦ Red Cross Red Crescent Climate Centre (internationally oriented national body)
- ♦ Red Cross and Red Crescent European Group for First Aid Education / see First Aid Education European Network (#09781)
- ♦ Red Cross and Red Crescent Youth (see: #13526)

♦ Red Cultural Mercosur (RCM) 18644

Rede Cultural Mercosul
Exec Sec address not obtained. T. +541143746551. E-mail: info@redculturalmercosur.org.
URL: http://www.redculturalmercosur.org/
History 1998. **Aims** Boost geographical and cultural interaction in the region, understanding of artistic creation and implementation of socio-cultural projects as a fundamental factor of integration. **Structure** Executive Council, comprising President and 7 National Coordinators. **Events** *Meeting* Buenos Aires (Argentina) 2007.
Members Full in 7 countries:
Argentina, Bolivia, Brazil, Chile, Paraguay, Uruguay, Venezuela.
NGO Relations Member of: *ORION (inactive).* [2011/XJ4649/**D**]

- ♦ REDD+ / see United Nations Collaborative Programme on Reducing Emissions from Deforestation and Forest Degradation in Developing Countries (#20528)

♦ Redd Barna – Save the Children Norway / see Save the Children Norway
♦ Redd Barna – Save the Children Norway (internationally oriented national body)

♦ Red de Desarrollo Territorial de América Latina y El Caribe (Red Dete) 18645

General Coordinator address not obtained.
URL: http://red-dete.org/

History Registered in accordance with Spanish law, 22 Jun 2007. **Structure** Assembly; Coordinating Committee; Scientific Committee. **Events** *Assembly* San José (Costa Rica) 2012. **Publications** *Desarrollo y Territorio* – review.
Members Full in 12 countries:
Argentina, Bolivia, Brazil, Chile, Dominican Rep, Ecuador, Hungary, Italy, Mexico, Peru, Spain, Uruguay. [2019/XJ6972/F]

♦ **Red-DESC** Red Internacional para los Derechos Económicos, Sociales y Culturales (#14255)
♦ **Red Dete** Red de Desarrollo Territorial de América Latina y El Caribe (#18645)
♦ Red Docente de América Latina y El Caribe (#20110)
♦ Rede Africana de Editores (#00426)
♦ Rede Africana de Juristas Constitucionalistas (#00384)
♦ Rede Africano do Sector da Segurança (#00453)
♦ REDEALAP – Red de Centros de Estudio de América Latina y el Caribe sobre Asia Pacifico (internationally oriented national body)
♦ Rede Americana de Pesquisa em Informação e Comunicação / see Communication Policy Research Latin America (#04382)
♦ **RedEAmérica** Red Interamericana de Fundaciones y Acciones Empresariales para el Desarrollo de Base (#18693)
♦ Rede das Américas sobre Nacionalidade e Apatridia (unconfirmed)
♦ **Red EAMI** Red de Autoridades en Medicamentos de Iberoamérica (#18636)
♦ Rede das Areas Prategidas da Africa Central (#03656)
♦ Rede de Associações Europeias de Counselling e Psicoterapia Centradas na Pessoa / see Network of the European Associations for Person-Centred and Experiential Psychotherapy and Counselling (#17013)
♦ Rede de Associações Europeias pela Psicoterapia e Counselling Centradas na Pessoa e Experiencial (#17013)
♦ Rede das Autoridades em Medicamentos dos Países Ibero-americanos (#18636)
♦ REDECOM / see Communication Policy Research Latin America (#04382)
♦ **Red EcoSur** Red para el Habitat Económico y Ecológico (#17007)
♦ Rede Cultural Mercosul (#18644)
♦ Red de Editores del Caribe (#03546)
♦ Red de Educación Continua de Latinoamérica y Europa / see Red Universitaria de Educación Continua de Latinoamérica y Europa (#18734)

♦ Red de Educación Matematica de América Central y El Caribe (REDUMATE) 18646

Mathematics Education Network for Central America and the Caribbean – Rede de Educação Matematica da América Central e do Caribe

Dir Casa 155 Condominio Barlovento, Concepcion, San José, San José, San José, 30305, Costa Rica. T. +50687201371.
URL: https://www.redumate.org

History Aug 2012, San José (Costa Rica). Founded during the International Seminar on Capacity Building in Mathematics and Mathematics Education (Capacity and Networking Project), held between August 6 and 17, 2012 in San José, Costa Rica, sponsored by *International Commission on Mathematical Instruction (ICMI, #12700)*. **Aims** Strengthen mathematics education within the Central American and Caribbean region. **Structure** International Council; Steering Committee; National Representatives; REDUMATE Community. **Languages** Portuguese, Spanish. **Staff** 30.00 FTE, voluntary. **Activities** Capacity building; events/meetings; networking/liaising; research and development; training/education. **Events** *Congreso de Educación Matematica de América Central y El Caribe* San José (Costa Rica) 2021, *Congreso de Educación Matematica de América Central y El Caribe* Cali (Colombia) 2017, *Congreso de Educación Matematica de América Central y El Caribe* Santo Domingo (Dominican Rep) 2013. **Publications** Reports.
Members Individuals (about 50) in 16 countries and territories:
Brazil, Chile, Colombia, Costa Rica, Cuba, Dominican Rep, El Salvador, Guatemala, Honduras, Mexico, Nicaragua, Panama, Puerto Rico, Spain, USA, Venezuela.
IGO Relations Ministry of Public Education, Costa Rica. [2023.02.13/XM5586/F]

♦ Red de Educación Popular entre Mujeres / see Red de Educación Popular entre Mujeres de América Latina y el Caribe (#18647)

♦ Red de Educación Popular entre Mujeres de América Latina y el Caribe (REPEM LAC) 18647

Main Office Av Arce 2132, Edificio Illampu, Piso 1 Oficina A, La Paz, Bolivia. E-mail: repemenvio@repem.org.
URL: http://www.repem.org/

History 1981, in the framework of *Consejo de Educación de Adultos de América Latina (CEAAL, #04707)*, as *Women's Network of the Council for Adult Education in Latin America – Red de Mujeres del Consejo de Educación de Adultos de América Latina (REPEM)*. Autonomous status within CEAAL since 1988. Also referred to in Spanish as *Red de Educación Popular entre Mujeres*. **Aims** Support the *grass roots* women's movement; coordinate NGOs and individuals in countries of the region; promote collective action, projects, efforts and hopes in the search for *equality* and peace; facilitate the shaping of popular education methodology and technology from a *feminist* perspective. **Structure** General Assembly. Continental coordination, consisting of President, Vice-President, Secretary, Treasurer, General Coordinator and subregional coordinators (3) for: Central America and the Caribbean; Andean Subregion; Brazil and the Southern Cone. **Finance** Budget (annual): US$ 80,000. **Activities** Fields of work: training; leadership; systematization of educational programmes; communication; solidarity; exchanges. **Events** *Regional conference in Latin America and the Caribbean on literacy* Mexico City (Mexico) 2008, *Feminist popular education in Latin America* Fusagasuga (Colombia) 1992, *Atelier sur le leadership des femmes en Amérique centrale* Guatemala (Guatemala) 1990, *Atelier sur le rôle des femmes dans la construction de la démocratie* Paraguay 1990, *Atelier sur le leadership des femmes dans la construction de la démocratie en Amérique latine* Quito (Ecuador) 1990. **Publications** *Tejiendo Nuestra Red* (2 a year). Occasional publications.
Members Covers 20 countries:
Argentina, Bolivia, Brazil, Chile, Colombia, Costa Rica, Cuba, Dominican Rep, Ecuador, El Salvador, Guatemala, Haiti, Mexico, Nicaragua, Panama, Paraguay, Peru, Puerto Rico, Uruguay, Venezuela.
Consultative Status Consultative status granted from: *ECOSOC (#05331)* (Special). **NGO Relations** Member of: *Feminist Articulation Marcosur (FAM, #09730)*; *Global Campaign for Education (GCE, #10264)*; *World Social Forum (WSF, #21797)*. Regional member of: *International Council for Adult Education (ICAE, #12983)*. Supports: *Global Call for Action Against Poverty (GCAP, #10263)*. [2020/XF1246/F]

♦ Red Educación y Sólidaridad (#05374)
♦ Rede Ecumênica Latino Americana de Missiologas (#16312)
♦ Rede de Educação Matematica da América Central e do Caribe (#18646)
♦ Red een Kind (internationally oriented national body)
♦ Rede Eurodesk (#05675)
♦ Rede Européia de Ação Social (#08499)
♦ Rede Europeia de Associações da Síndrome do X Frágil (unconfirmed)
♦ Rede Europeia de Cidades do Vinho (#18881)
♦ Rede Européia Direito e Sociedade (#07937)
♦ A Rede Europeia Dos Grupos de Doentes Afectados do Mieloma Múltiplo (inactive)
♦ Rede de Gestão da Defesa e da Segurança da Africa Austral (inactive)
♦ Rede Global da OMS de Cidades e Comunidades Amigas das Pessoas Idosas (#20937)
♦ Rede Ibérica de Entidades Transfronteiriças (internationally oriented national body)
♦ Rede Ibero-Americana de Direito Sanitario (#18663)
♦ Rede Ibero-Americana de Terminologia (#18685)
♦ Rede de Informação sobre Educação na Europa (inactive)
♦ Rede de Informação Tecnológica Latinoamericana (see: #19294)
♦ Rede de Informações Interamericana sobre a Biodiversidade / see Inter-American Biodiversity Information Network (#11402)
♦ Rede de Innovação Educativa para Desenvolvimento em Africa (no recent information)
♦ Rede de Innovações para a América Latina e o Caribe (#16275)
♦ Rede Interamericana de Informação a Biodiversidad (#11402)
♦ Rede de Intercâmbio dos Parlamentos da América Latina e do Caribe (#18696)
♦ Rede Interinstitucional para a Educação em Situações de Emergência (#11387)
♦ Rede Internacional de Cidades onde Viver é Facil / see Cittaslow (#03958)
♦ Rede Internacional de Motricidade Humana (unconfirmed)
♦ Rede Internacional para as Pequeñas e Médias Empresas (#14325)
♦ Rede Jesuita Africana contra a SIDA (#00348)
♦ Rede Judiciaria Europeia em Matéria Civil e Comercial (#07616)
♦ Rede Latino-Americana e Caribenha de Mulheres Negras (internationally oriented national body)
♦ Rede Latinoamericana de Ciencias Biológicas (#18706)
♦ Rede Latino-Americana de Juizes (#18714)
♦ Rede Latino-Americana de Mulheres do Setor Pesquiero (#17046)
♦ Rede Latinoamericana de Nanotecnologia e Sociedada (#16349)
♦ Rede Latino-Americana para a Prevenção do Genocidio e Atrocidades Massivas (#18716)
♦ Rede Latinoamericana de Psoriase (#18717)
♦ Rede Latino-americana de Reprodução Assistida (#16315)
♦ Rede Miquéias / see Micah Global (#16741)
♦ RedEmprendia (unconfirmed)
♦ Rédemptoristes – Congrégation du Très Saint Rédempteur (religious order)
♦ Redemptoristines – Order of the Most Holy Redeemer (religious order)
♦ Redemptorists – Congregation of the Most Holy Redeemer (religious order)
♦ Rede das Mulheres Africanas Ministras e Parlamentares (#16988)
♦ Rede de Mulheres Parlamentares das Américas (#17065)
♦ Red de Entidades para el Desarrollo Solidario (internationally oriented national body)
♦ Redentoristi – Congregazione del Santissimo Redentore (religious order)
♦ Rede Panlatina de Terminologia (#18901)
♦ Rede Panlatina de Terminoloxia (#18901)
♦ Rede de Pesquisa-Ação das Américas (#00096)
♦ Rede de Popularização da Ciência e da Tecnologia na América Latina e no Caribe (#17057)
♦ Rede de Regiões e Áreas Metropolitanas Europeias (#17023)

♦ Rede Regional da Sociedade Civil para a Segurança Alimentar e Nutricional na CPLP (REDSAN-CPLP) 18648

Secretariat c/o ACTUAR, INOPOL – Escola Superior Agraria de Coimbra, Quita Agricola – Bencanta, 3045-601 Coimbra, Portugal. T. +351961585638. E-mail: geral@redsan-cplp.org.
URL: http://www.redsan-cplp.org/

Activities Networking/liaising; research/documentation; training/education; knowledge management/information dissemination; advocacy/lobbying/activism. **Events** *Forum* Sao Tomé-Principe 2015.
Members Civil society organizations (about 400). National networks in 8 countries:
Angola, Brazil, Cape Verde, Guinea-Bissau, Mozambique, Portugal, Sao Tomé-Principe, Timor-Leste.
IGO Relations *Comunidade dos Paises de Lingua Portuguesa (CPLP, #04430)*. **NGO Relations** Member of: *Right to Food and Nutrition Watch Consortium (#18943)*. Regional partner of: *International Food Security Network (IFSN, #13623)*. [2015/XM4253/F]

♦ Red de Escritoras Latinoamericanas (RELAT) 18649

Network of Latin American Women Writers

Pres Av Higienopolis 968, Ap 43-B, Sao Paulo SP, 01238-000, Brazil.

History Oct 1998. **Aims** Help women in Latin America develop a stronger public voice. **Structure** Board of Directors; Steering Committee.
Members Individuals (23) in 7 countries:
Argentina, Brazil, Chile, Colombia, Peru, Puerto Rico, Venezuela.
NGO Relations *World Association of Women Journalists and Writers (#21206)*. [2010/XF6666/F]

♦ Red de Escuelas e Institutos Gubernamentales en Asuntos Públicos (see: #16294)
♦ Redesign – Resilience – Regeneration / see r3.0 (#18597)
♦ Rede Sindical Internacional de Solidariedade e Lutas (unconfirmed)
♦ Rede de Solidariedade Asia Pacifico (internationally oriented national body)
♦ REDES – Red de Entidades para el Desarrollo Solidario (internationally oriented national body)
♦ Red de Estudios Sociales en Prevención de Desastres en América Latina (#17058)

♦ Red de Estudios Visuales Latinoamericanos (ReVLaT) 18650

Contact address not obtained. E-mail: redevalt@gmail.com.
URL: https://www.revlat.com/

Aims Promote critical analysis of images and visuality practices. **Events** *International Meeting* Madrid (Spain) 2019, *International Meeting* Seville (Spain) 2017, *International Meeting* Querétaro (Mexico) 2015, *International Meeting* Pachuca de Soto (Mexico) 2014, *International Meeting* Morelia (Mexico) 2013. **Publications** *Artefacto Visual – Revista de Estudios Visuales Latinoamericanos*; *ReVLaT Newsletter*. [2020/AA0553/D]

♦ Rede de Terminologia / see Red Iberoamericana de Terminologia (#18685)

♦ redEtis 18651

Contact Agüero 2071, C1425EHS Buenos Aires, Argentina. E-mail: contacto@iiep.unesco.org.

History as a project of *International Institute for Educational Planning (IIEP, #13874)*. Full title: *Educación, Trabajo Inserción Social, América Latina (redEtis)*. **Aims** Identify main research and intervention trends in the field and strengthen the dissemination of knowledge; evaluate programmes and policies establishing links among education, work and social insertion; promote training and the strengthening of members' skills in planning, implementing and evaluating programmes and projects; promote interaction among actors and institutions and facilitate generation of local and regional networks. **Structure** Secretariat at *Instituto de Desarrollo Económico y Social (IDES)*. **Activities** Knowledge production; evaluation; training. **Publications** Newsletter. [2009/XJ0444/E]

♦ **RedETSA** Red de Evaluación de Tecnologias en Salud de las Américas (#18655)
♦ Red EU-LAT (#05585)
♦ Red EU-LAT – Red de Incidencia Europa – Latinoamérica / see EU-LAT Network (#05585)
♦ Red Euro-Arabe de ONG para el Desarrollo y la Integración (internationally oriented national body)
♦ Red Eurodesk (#05675)
♦ Red Eurolatinoamericana de Analisis de Trabajo y Sindicalismo (unconfirmed)
♦ Red Europea de Acción Social (#08499)
♦ Red Europea de la Chromosoma 11 (#06547)
♦ Red Europea de la Chromosoma 11Q / see European Chromosome 11 Network (#06547)
♦ Red Europea de Ciudades Digitales (#07893)
♦ Red Europea de Ciudades del Vino (#18881)
♦ Red Europea de Consejos del Poder Judicial (#07886)
♦ Red Europea contra el Nacionalismo, el Racismo, el Fascismo y por el Apoyo de los Refugiados y Emigrantes (#20511)
♦ Red Europea para las Derechas Australianas Indigenas (internationally oriented national body)
♦ Red Europea Derecho y Sociedad (#07937)

- Red Europea de Desarrollo Rural (#07995)
- Red Europea para Deuda y Desarrollo (#07891)
- Red Europea de Grupos de Ayuda para Pacientes con Mieloma (inactive)
- Red Europea Iglesia por la Libertad (#07878)

♦ Red Europea de Información y Documentación sobre América Latina (REDIAL) 18652

European Network for Information and Documentation on Latin America – Réseau européen d'information et de documentation sur l'Amérique latine (REDIAL)

Sec c/o AECID, Biblioteca Hispanica, Avda Reyes Católicos 4, 28040 Madrid, Spain. T. +34915838175 – +34915838164. E-mail: redredial@gmail.com.
URL: https://rediceisal.hypotheses.org/

History 1 Dec 1989, France. Founded in Bordeaux (France) and Saint Emilion (France) (simultaneously), at the Founding Assembly. Registration: Start date: 2012, Spain; France; Banque-Carrefour des Entreprises, No/ID: 0442.182.616, Start date: 12 Dec 1990, Belgium. **Aims** Offer an information system specialized in European humanities and social science research on Latin America. **Structure** General Assembly; Directorate. **Languages** Portuguese, Spanish. **Events** *General Assembly* Helsinki (Finland) 2022, *Assembly* 2021, *International Colloquim of Young Researchers in Hispano-American Literature* Madrid (Spain) 2016, *General Assembly* London (UK) 2011. **Publications** *Anuario Americanista Europeo* – journal.
Members Institutions in 6 countries:
France, Germany, Netherlands, Russia, Spain, Sweden.
NGO Relations Partner of (1): *Consejo Latinoamericano de Ciencias Sociales (CLACSO, #04718)*. Cooperates with (2): *Consejo Europeo de Investigaciones Sociales de América Latina (CEISAL, #04710)*; *Sistema Regional de Información en Linea para Revistas Científicas de América Latina, el Caribe, España y Portugal (Latindex, #19297)*. [2022.05.04/XF3351/y/F]

♦ Red Europea de Institutos de la Familia (REDIF) 18653

Réseau européen des instituts de la famille – European Family Institutes Network

Pres c/Sant Gervasi de Cassoles 88-90, 08022 Barcelona, Spain. E-mail: carlespt@fvb.cat.
URL: http://www.redif.org/

History 16 Dec 1995, a sectorial group of *International Federation of Catholic Universities (IFCU, #13381)*. Previously also referred to as *Red Europea de Institutos Familiares – Rete Europea degli Istituti della Famiglia*. **Aims** Promote scientific research on matters related to the family; activate real discussions on challenges of familial politics and the rights of the family. **Structure** Assembly; Council; President. **Languages** English, French, Italian. **Finance** Members' dues. **Activities** Research/documentation; events/meetings. **Events** *International Congress* Madrid (Spain) 2013, *International congress / Annual Meeting* Barcelona (Spain) 2007, *International congress / Annual Meeting* Louvain-la-Neuve (Belgium) 2006, *International congress / Annual Meeting* Madrid (Spain) 2005, *International congress / Annual Meeting* Milan (Italy) 2004. **Publications** *Familia* – magazine; *Revue du REDIF*. *Familia e Interculturalidad*; *Familia y Cultura*; *Familia y Transmisión*. Books; periodicals.
Members Full in 4 countries:
Belgium, France, Italy, Spain. [2016.06.01/XF6067/F]

- Red Europea de Institutos Familiares / see Red Europea de Institutos de la Familia (#18653)

♦ Red Europea y Latinoamericana de Escuelas Sistémicas (Red RELATES) 18654

Address not obtained.
URL: http://redrelates.com/

History Jul 2005, Guadalajara (Mexico). **Aims** Disseminate Systemic Family Therapy throught the Spanish-speaking world. **Structure** Board of Directors. **Activities** Certification/accreditation; events/meetings. **Events** *International Congress* Bogota (Colombia) 2022, *International Meeting* Lisbon (Portugal) 2017. **Publications** *Boletin Terapia Familiar*; *Revista REDES*.
Members Full in 12 countries:
Argentina, Brazil, Chile, Colombia, Costa Rica, Dominican Rep, Ecuador, Italy, Mexico, Peru, Portugal, Spain.
Adhering members in 5 countries:
Brazil, Colombia, Portugal, Uruguay, USA. [2022/XJ9058/D]

- Red Europea de Microfinanzas (#07792)
- Red Europea de Mujeres Policias (#07970)
- Red Europea para la Sordoceguera (#06890)
- Red Europea de Voluntarios Mayores / see European Network of Older-Volunteer Organizations

♦ Red de Evaluación de Tecnologias en Salud de las Américas (RedETSA) 18655

Health Technology Assessment Network of the Americas

Address not obtained.
URL: http://redetsa.org/

History Launched Jun 2011, Rio de Janeiro (Brazil). **Structure** Executive Committee.
Members Ministries of health; regulatory authorities; health technology assessment agencies; collaborating centres of PAHO/WHO; research and education institutions. Members in 15 countries:
Argentina, Bolivia, Brazil, Canada, Chile, Colombia, Costa Rica, Cuba, Ecuador, El Salvador, Mexico, Panama, Paraguay, Peru, Uruguay.
IGO Relations *Pan American Health Organization (PAHO, #18108)*. **NGO Relations** *international HealthTech-Scan (i-HTS, #13784)*. [2017/XM5807/F]

- Red Feminista Latinoamericana y del Caribe contra la Violencia Doméstica y Sexual (#16277)
- Red Feminista Latinoamericana y del Caribe por una vida sin violencia contra las mujeres / see Latin American and Caribbean Feminist Network Against Domestic and Sexual Violence (#16277)

♦ Red de Fondos Ambientales de Latinoamérica y el Caribe (RedLAC) 18656

Latin American and Caribbean Network of Environmental Funds

Coordinator 12 Calle Oriente 27 A, Colonia Utila, CP 1501 Santa Tecla, La Libertad, El Salvador. T. +50322492900. E-mail: info@redlac.org.
URL: http://www.redlac.org/

History 1999. **Aims** Promote the interrelationships of environmental funds in Latin America and the Caribbean, through capacity building and knowledge management initiatives that contribute to to *biodiversity conservation* and sustainable development. **Structure** Assembly. **Events** *Assembly* Mérida (Mexico) 2019, *Assembly* Santa Cruz (Bolivia) 2018, *Assembly* Punta Cana (Dominican Rep) 2017.
Members Organizations (27) in 19 countries:
Antigua-Barbuda, Belize, Bolivia, Brazil, Chile, Colombia, Costa Rica, Dominican Rep, Ecuador, El Salvador, Guyana, Honduras, Jamaica, Mexico, Panama, Paraguay, Peru, St Lucia, Suriname.
Included in the above, 2 organizations listed in this Yearbook:
Caribbean Biodiversity Fund (CBF); *Fondo para el Sistema Arrecifal Mesoamericano (Fondo SAM, #09835)*. [2022.02.08/XM7581/y/F]

- Red de Formación Ambiental para América Latina y del Caribe (inactive)
- Red para la Formación Profesional en el Sector de la Construcción en Europa / see REFORME (#18738)
- Red Global de Acción Juvenil (internationally oriented national body)
- Red Global para la Innovación Bancaria en Microfinanzas (#10482)
- Red Global de Monitores Electorales Nacionales (#10487)
- Red Global de Organizaciones de la Sociedad Civil para la Reducción de Desastres (#10485)
- Red Global de Periodismo de Investigación (#10433)
- Red Global para la Trimembración Social (#10501)
- Red de Gobiernos Regionales por un Desarrollo Sostenible / see Regions4 Sustainable Development (#18819)
- Red para el Habitat Económico y Ecológico (#17007)
- REDHAC Réseau des Défenseurs des Droits Humains en Afrique Centrale (#18870)
- REDIAL Red Europea de Información y Documentación sobre América Latina (#18652)
- REDIAL Réseau européen d'information et de documentation sur l'Amérique latine (#18652)
- REDIAP – Red Latinoamericana de Documentación e Información en Administración Pública (see: #16294)
- Red Ibérica de Entidades Transfronterizas (internationally oriented national body)
- Red Iberoamericana para la Acreditación de la Calidad de la Educación Superior / see Red Iberoamericana para el Aseguramiento de la Calidad en la Educación Superior (#18657)

♦ Red Iberoamericana para el Aseguramiento de la Calidad en la Educación Superior (RIACES) 18657

Sec c/o ANEAES, Yegros No 930 entre Manuel Dominguez y Teniente Fariña Yegros, Asunción, Paraguay. T. +59521494940. E-mail: altogua@gmail.com – secretariaejecutiva@riaces.org – presidencia@riaces.org.
URL: http://riaces.org/

History May 2003, Buenos Aires (Argentina), as *Red Iberoamericana para la Acreditación de la Calidad de la Educación Superior*. **Aims** Improve *harmonization* and quality of higher education in the region. **Structure** General Assembly; Executive Committee. **Events** *General Assembly* Cartagena de Indias (Colombia) 2022, *General Assembly* Madrid (Spain) 2019, *General Assembly* Managua (Nicaragua) 2018, *International Conference on Diversity, Quality and Improvement* Santiago (Chile) 2018, *General Assembly* Asunción (Paraguay) 2015.
Members Full in 15 countries:
Bolivia, Brazil, Chile, Colombia, Costa Rica, Cuba, Dominican Rep, El Salvador, Mexico, Nicaragua, Panama, Paraguay, Spain, Uruguay, Venezuela.
Regional organizations (6):
Agencia Centroamericana de Acreditación de Programas de Arquitectura y de Ingenieria (ACAAI, #00549); *Centro Interuniversitario de Desarrollo (CINDA, #03809)*; *Confederación Universitaria Centroamericana (CSUCA, #04497)*; *Consejo Centroamericano de Acreditación de la Educación Superior (CCA, #04703)*; *Organization of Ibero-American States for Education, Science and Culture (#17871)*; *UNESCO International Institute for Higher Education in Latin America and the Caribbean (#20309)*.
NGO Relations Regional member of: *International Network of Quality Assurance Agencies in Higher Education (INQAAHE, #14312)*. [2022/XM3015/y/F]

♦ Red Iberoamericana de Asociaciones de Adultos Mayores (RIAAM) 18658

Iberoamerican Network of Senior Citizens Associations

Pres C/Juan de Olias 24 (Entrada por Gabriel Diéz), 28020 Madrid, Spain. T. +34914561750 – +34914252698. Fax +34914561755. E-mail: magonlam@yahoo.es.

History 1996, Havana (Cuba). Registered in accordance with Spanish law. **Aims** Promote, facilitate and organize the associative movement of senior citizens so as to improve their quality of life. **Structure** General Assembly; Board of Directors, comprising President, Vice-President, Secretary, Treasurer and members. **Events** *Follow-up meeting to the 2nd world assembly on ageing on old people facing associationism / General Assembly* Cartagena de Indias (Colombia) 2006, *Congress* Chile 2004. **Publications** *RIAAM Newseltter* (2 a year).
Members Organizations in 21 countries:
Argentina, Bolivia, Brazil, Chile, Colombia, Costa Rica, Cuba, Dominican Rep, Ecuador, El Salvador, Guatemala, Honduras, Mexico, Nicaragua, Panama, Paraguay, Peru, Portugal, Spain, Uruguay, Venezuela.
IGO Relations *Red Intergubernamental Iberoamericana de Cooperación Técnica para el Desarrollo de Politicas de Atención a personas con Discapacidad y Adultos Mayores (RIICOTEC, #18697)*. [2009/XF6946/F]

- Red Iberoamericana Bioinformatica (inactive)

♦ Red Iberoamericana de Bosques Modelo (RLABM) 18659

Ibero-American Model Forest Network (IAMFN)

General Manager CATIE, 7170 Cartago, Cartago, Turrialba, Turrialba, 30501, Costa Rica. T. +50625582318. E-mail: redlatinbosquesmodelo@gmail.com – info@bosquesmodelo.net.
Pres address not obtained.
URL: http://www.bosquesmodelo.net/

History 2002. Founded as a regional network of *International Model Forest Network (IMFN, #14175)* and based at *Tropical Agriculture Research and Higher Education Center (#20246)*. Former names and other names: *Latin America and Caribbean Model Forest Network (LAC-Net)* – former; *Réseau ibéro-américain de Fôrets Modèles (RIAFM)* – former. **Aims** Promote cooperation among Model Forests, institutions, organizations and countries to contribute to sustainable territorial management of the forest landscape, which contributes to sustainable human development. **Structure** Board of Directors; Secretariat. **Languages** English, Portuguese, Spanish. **Publications** *Model Forest Experiences*. Annual Report; planning strategies; proceedings; research reports; standards.
Members Sites (34) in 15 countries:
Argentina, Bolivia, Brazil, Chile, Colombia, Costa Rica, Cuba, Dominican Rep, Ecuador, Guatemala, Honduras, Paraguay, Peru, Puerto Rico, Spain.
IGO Relations Listed in the Registro de Redes Iberoamericano, held by *Ibero-American General Secretariat (#11024)*. **NGO Relations** Member of (1): *International Model Forest Network (IMFN, #14175)*. [2020/XJ8366/F]

- Red Iberoamericana y del Caribe de Restauración Ecológica (inactive)

♦ Red Iberoamericana de Ciclo de Vida 18660

Chair address not obtained.
URL: http://rediberoamericanadeciclodevida.wordpress.com/

History Set up as the regional programme of *Life Cycle Initiative (LCI, #16464)*. **Structure** Executive Committee.
Members National committees in 9 countries:
Argentina, Brazil, Chile, Costa Rica, Cuba, Mexico, Peru, Portugal, Spain. [2013/XJ7339/E]

♦ Red Iberoamericana de Comités MAB y Reservas de la Biósfera (IberoMAB) 18661

Ibero-American Network of Biosphere Reserves and MAB Committees

Contact Div of Ecological and Earth Sciences, UNESCO, 1 rue Miollis, 75732 Paris CEDEX 15, France. T. +33145684146. Fax +33145685804.
URL: http://www.unesco.org/new/es/natural-sciences/environment/ecological-sciences/man-and-biosphere-programme/networks/iberomab/

History 1993, within the framework of *Programme on Man and the Biosphere (MAB, #18526)*. Also referred to as *Red Iberoamericana de Comités y Reservas de la Biósfere*. **Aims** Strengthen the MAB Programme in Latin American countries, Spain and Portugal, notably by consolidating their MAB National Committees and cooperative links and promoting the creation of new biosphere reserves. **Events** *Meeting* Tumbes (Peru) 2011, *Meeting* Puerto Morelos (Mexico) 2010, *Meeting* Quintana Roo, CHIS (Mexico) 2010, *Meeting* San Salvador (El Salvador) 2009, *Meeting* Madrid (Spain) 2008. [2019/XF4521/F]

- Red Iberoamericana de Comités y Reservas de la Biósfere / see Red Iberoamericana de Comités MAB y Reservas de la Biósfera (#18661)

♦ Red Iberoamericana de Cooperación Jurídica Internacional (IberRed) 18662

Secretariat Paseo de Recoletos, 8 Primera Planta, 28001 Madrid, Spain. T. +34915753624. Fax +34914351972. E-mail: secretaria.general@iberred.org.
URL: https://www.iberred.org/

History 27 Oct 2004. Founded by *Conferencia de Ministros de Justicia de los Países Iberoamericanos (COMJIB, #04656)*, *Inter-American Juridical Committee (IAJC, see: #17629)* and *Asociación Iberoamericana de Ministerios Públicos (AIAMP, #02149)*.
Members Central authorities and contact points from ministries of justice, public prosecutors' offices and judicial powers. Members in 22 countries:

Andorra, Argentina, Bolivia, Brazil, Chile, Colombia, Costa Rica, Cuba, Dominican Rep, Ecuador, El Salvador, Guatemala, Honduras, Mexico, Nicaragua, Panama, Paraguay, Peru, Portugal, Spain, Uruguay, Venezuela.
IGO Relations Listed in the Registro de Redes Iberoamericano, held by *Ibero-American General Secretariat (#11024).* [2020/AA1241/**F**]

♦ Red Iberoamericana de Derecho Sanitario 18663

Rede Ibero-Americana de Direito Sanitario

Contact CEDSABIO ISALUD, Venezuela 931 847 758, C1095AAS Buenos Aires, Argentina.
Contact address not obtained. E-mail: cayon_j@cantabria.es.

History Apr 2011, Buenos Aires (Argentina). **Structure** Executive Council. **Languages** Portuguese, Spanish. **Staff** 1.00 FTE, paid. Others voluntary. **Finance** No direct financing. **Activities** Active in: most Iberoamerican countries. **Events** *Congress* Bogota (Colombia) 2015, *Congress* San José (Costa Rica) 2014, *Congress* Brasilia (Brazil) 2013, *Congress* Seville (Spain) 2012, *Congress* Buenos Aires (Argentina) 2011. **Publications** *Cadernos Ibero-Americanos de Direito Sanitario* in Portuguese, Spanish.
Members Full in 15 countries:
Argentina, Brazil, Chile, Colombia, Costa Rica, Cuba, Ecuador, El Salvador, Guatemala, Mexico, Peru, Portugal, Spain, Uruguay, Venezuela.
IGO Relations *Pan American Health Organization (PAHO, #18108).* [2016/XJ9714/**D**]

♦ Red Iberoamericana de Docencia e Investigación en Celulosa y Papel (RIADICYP) 18664

Ibero-American Network for Teaching and Research on Pulp and Paper

Scientific Coordinator Programa de Celulosia y Papel – PROCYP, Inst de Materiales de Misiones – IMAM, Félix de Azara 1552, 3300 Posadas, Argentina. T. +543764422198. Fax +543764422198.
URL: http://www.riadicyp.org/

History Set up 2000, following first CIADICYP Congress. **Aims** Enhance dialogue and cooperation; promote initiatives and international research projects; strengthen research in lignocellulosic materials, pulp, paper and recycling. **Structure** Standing Committee; Advisory Group. **Languages** English, Portuguese, Spanish. **Staff** 2.00 FTE, voluntary. **Finance** Members' dues (annual). **Activities** Networking/liaising; financial and/or material support; events/meetings. **Events** *Congress* Turku (Finland) 2016, *International Symposium on Lignocellulosic Materials* Concepción (Chile) 2015, *Congress / Ibero-American Congress on pulp and Paper Research – CIADICYP* Medellin (Colombia) 2014, *International Symposium on Lignocellulosic Materials* Puerto Iguazú (Argentina) 2013, *Congress / Ibero-American Congress on pulp and Paper Research – CIADICYP* Sao Paulo (Brazil) 2012. **Publications** *RIADICYP Newsletter* (12 a year). *Panorama de la Industria de Celulosa y Papel en Ibero-América* (2008); *Red Ibero-Americana de Celulosa y Papel – CYTED* (2008).
Members Individuals (156) from 33 institutions in 15 countries:
Argentina, Brazil, Chile, Colombia, Cuba, El Salvador, Finland, Mexico, Peru, Portugal, Spain, Türkiye, Uruguay, USA, Venezuela. [2015.09.04/XJ6991/**D**]

♦ Red Iberoamericana de Estudios Internacionales (RIBEI) 18665

Secretariat C/ Principe de Vergara 51, 28006 Madrid, Spain. T. +34917816781.
URL: http://www.ribei.org/

History 18 Nov 2010. **Structure** General Assembly; Board of Directors. **Activities** Events/meetings. **Events** *International Conference* Lisbon (Portugal) 2018, *International Conference* Buenos Aires (Argentina) 2017, *International Conference* Bogota (Colombia) 2016, *International Conference* Santo Domingo (Dominican Rep) 2015, *International Conference* Sao Paulo (Brazil) 2014. **Publications** *Boletin RIBEI.*
Members Associations (45) in 16 countries. Membership countries not specified. Included in the above, 4 organizations listed in this Yearbook:
Included in the above, 4 organizations listed in this Yearbook:
Global Foundation for Democracy and Development (GFDD); Instituto Complutense de Estudios Internacionales (ICEI); Instituto de Estudios Politicos y Relaciones Internacionales, Bogota (IEPRI); Latin American Faculty of Social Sciences (#16316).
IGO Relations Listed in the Registro de Redes Iberoamericano, held by *Ibero-American General Secretariat (#11024).* [2018/XM7966/y/**F**]

♦ Red Ibero-Americana de Evaluación y Decisión Multicriterio / see Red Iberoamericana de Evaluación y Decisión Multicriterio (#18666)

♦ Red Iberoamericana de Evaluación y Decisión Multicriterio (RED-M) 18666

Exec Sec c/o Facultad de Ingenieria y Ciencias UDP, Av Ejército 441, 8370190 Santiago, Santiago Metropolitan, Chile.
Contact Periférico Nte 799, 45100 Zapopan JAL, Mexico. E-mail: laura.plazola@redudg.udg.mx.
URL: http://www.redmsociety.org/

History Also referred to as *Red Ibero-Americana de Evaluación y Decisión Multicriterio (RED-M).* **Structure** General Assembly. **Languages** English, Portuguese, Spanish. **Staff** 1.00 FTE, paid. **Events** *Meeting* Bahia Blanca (Argentina) 2015, *Meeting* Monterrey (Mexico) 2014, *Meeting* Concepción (Chile) 2013, *Meeting* Sao Paulo (Brazil) 2011, *Meeting* Zapopan (Mexico) 2009. **Members** Full in more than 16 countries of Iberoamerica. Membership countries not specified. **NGO Relations** *Eureka Iberoamérica (no recent information); Latin-Iberian-American Association of Operations Research Societies (#16398).* [2016/XJ1123/**F**]

♦ Red Iberoamericana de Garantias (REGAR) 18667

Ibero-American Guarantees Network

Contact address not obtained. E-mail: redegarantias@gmail.com.
URL: http://www.redegarantias.com/

History 25 Sep 1998, Burgos (Spain). **Structure** General Assembly; Executive Board; Secretary General. **Events** *Forum* Argentina 2012, *Foro Iberoamericano de sistemas de garantia* Buenos Aires (Argentina) 2012, *Foro Iberoamericano de sistemas de garantia / Forum* San José (Costa Rica) 2011, *Foro Iberoamericano de sistemas de garantia / Forum* Mexico City (Mexico) 2010, *Foro Iberoamericano de sistemas de garantia / Forum* Lisbon (Portugal) 2009. **Publications** *REGAR Boletin.* **IGO Relations** Listed in the Registro de Redes Iberoamericano, held by *Ibero-American General Secretariat (#11024).* [2012/XJ1393/**F**]

♦ Red Iberoamericana de Hipercolesterolemia Familiar 18668

Iberoamerican Network of Family Hypercholesterolemia

Contact C/ General Alvarez de Castro 14, 1o-E, 28010 Madrid, Spain. E-mail: info@colesterolfamiliar.org.
URL: http://www.colesterolfamiliar.org/red-iberoamericana/

History 22 Aug 2013, Montevideo (Uruguay). Former names and other names: *Asociación de la Red Iberoamericana de Hipercolesterolemia Familiar* – legal name. **Structure** Board of Directors. **Events** *Symposium* Lisbon (Portugal) 2018, *Meeting* Madrid (Spain) 2014.
Members Full in 10 countries:
Argentina, Brazil, Chile, Colombia, Cuba, Mexico, Portugal, Spain, Uruguay, Venezuela. [2020/XM7953/**D**]

♦ Red Iberoamericana de Indicadores de Ciencia y Tecnologia / see Ibéro-American and Inter-American Network of Science and Technology Indicators (#11025)
♦ Red Iberoamericana e Interamericana de Indicadores de Ciencia y Tecnologia (#11025)

♦ Red Iberoamericana de Investigación en Transporte Aéreo (RIDITA) 18669

Iberoamerican Air Transportation Research Society

Contact Inst de Geografia, Fac Filosofia y Letras, Univ Buenos Aires, Puan 480 4o piso, C1406CQJ Buenos Aires, Argentina. T. +541144320606. Fax +541144320606.
URL: http://www.ridita.org/

History 14 Nov 2007, Buenos Aires (Argentina). **Structure** General Assembly. Board of Directors, comprising President, Vice-President, Secretary General and 3 members. **Events** *Air transportation sustainability – technological, operational, economic, social and environemntal strategies* Covilhã (Portugal) 2019, *Congress* Santiago (Chile) 2017, *Congress* Barcelona (Spain) 2015, *Congress* La Plata (Argentina) 2013, *Congress* Madrid (Spain) 2011.
Members Individuals in 11 countries:
Argentina, Brazil, Chile, Cuba, Ecuador, El Salvador, France, Mexico, Peru, Portugal, Spain. [2018/XJ5193/v/**F**]

♦ Red Iberoamericana de Investigadores sobre Globalización y Territorio (RII) 18670

Hispano-American Network of Researchers in Globalization and Territory

Contact Paseo Tollocan 1402 Poniente, Ciudad Universitaria, CP 50110, Toluca MEX, Mexico. T. +527222831516 – +527222145351. E-mail: seminariorii@gmail.com.
Main Website: https://seminariorii.uaemex.mx/index.html

History Mar 1994, Pereira (Colombia). Related initiatives developed after an international seminar on "the geographical consequences of social and economic transformations resulting from the increasing internationalization of capital and the scientific-technical revolution", organized by the Latin American and Caribbean Institute for Economic and Social Planning (ILPES) of the United Nations and the Institute for Urban Studies (Instituto de Estudios Urbanos IEU) from the Pontificia Universidad Católica de Chile, Aug 1989, Santiago de Chile (Chile). Organization established after the international seminar on the impact of the process of economic opening, State reform, and productive restructuring on territories, 22-24 March 1994, Pereira (Colombia). **Aims** Foster and coordinate research on geographical transformations caused by the advancement of restructuring and globalization processes. **Structure** Scientific Committees (every 2 years, with international seminar); General Coordination; Assistant Coordination; Thematic Bodies. **Languages** Portuguese, Spanish. **Staff** Voluntary. **Finance** Sources: contributions. **Activities** Events/meetings; projects/programmes. Active in all member countries. **Events** *International Seminar* Blumenau (Brazil) 2020, *International Seminar* Monterrey (Mexico) 2016, *International Seminar* Salvador (Brazil) 2014, *International Seminar* Belo Horizonte (Brazil) 2012, *International seminar* Mendoza (Argentina) 2010. **Publications** *EURE* – review. *Globalización y territorio. Impactos y perspectivas.* (1998) by Carlos A de Mattos and Daniel Hiernaux et al – Founding book published by the Pontificia Universidad Católica de Chile and Fondo de Cultura Económica (Mexico).
Members Researchers (+1000) from institutions (100) in 23 countries:
Argentina, Austria, Bolivia, Brazil, Canada, Chile, Colombia, Cuba, Ecuador, France, Germany, Guatemala, Italy, Mexico, Netherlands, Nicaragua, Peru, Poland, Spain, UK, Uruguay, USA, Venezuela.
NGO Relations Instrumental in setting up (1): *Red Iberoamericana de Postgrados sobre Politica y Estudios Territoriales (RIPPET, #18680).* [2022.05.04/XF6055/**F**]

♦ Red Iberoamericana de Investigadores "Kant: Ética, Política y Sociedad (RIKEPS) 18671

Coordinator address not obtained. E-mail: kantrikeps@gmail.com.
URL: https://kantrikeps.es/

Aims Coordinate and increase contemporary research and academic mobility and exchange in Latin America on Kant's ethical and political thought, with special attention to the scope and limits of his contemporaneity. **Finance** Supported by: *Asociación Universitaria Iberoamericana de Postgrado (AUIP, #02307).* **Activities** Events/meetings. **Events** *Congress* Madrid (Spain) 2019. **Publications** *Con-textos Kantianos – International Journal of Philosophy.*
Members Researchers from 20 universities in 11 countries:
Argentina, Brazil, Chile, Colombia, Ecuador, Mexico, Peru, Portugal, Spain, Uruguay, Venezuela. [2022.11.10/AA0584/v/**F**]

♦ Red Iberoamericana de Juventud Indigena y Afrodescendiente (REJINA) 18672

SG address not obtained. T. +445215542951219. E-mail: revistaiguanazul@gmail.com.
Contact address not obtained. E-mail: redrejina@hotmail.com.
URL: http://redrejina.wordpress.com/

Structure Coordinators (4) in the following areas: General Indigenous (2); African Descent (2).
Members Full in 14 countries:
Bolivia, Brazil, Colombia, Costa Rica, Dominican Rep, Ecuador, Guatemala, Mexico, Panama, Paraguay, Peru, Spain, Uruguay, Venezuela.
NGO Relations Member of: *Espacio Iberoamericano de Juventud (EIJ, no recent information).* [2012/XJ1718/**D**]

♦ Red Iberoamericana de Luz 18673

Latin American Light Network

Address not obtained.
URL: http://rediberoamericanadeluz.blogspot.be/

History Feb 1998. An informal network. **Aims** Reunite ties between people in the co-creation of a society that is based on new *paradigms* and whose harmonious forms are articulated in its multiple facets. **Events** *Meeting* Santiago (Chile) 2005, *Meeting* Chapadmalal (Argentina) 2004, *Meeting* Buga (Colombia) 2003, *Meeting* Caracas (Venezuela) 2002, *Meeting* San José (Costa Rica) 2001. [2015/XM0302/**F**]

♦ Red Iberoamericana de Mercadotecnia en Salud (RIMS) 18674

Ibero American Network Marketing in Health

SG Escuela Nacional de Salue Pública, Calle I Esquina Linea, Vedado, Municipio Plaza de la Revolución, Havana, Cuba. E-mail: nerysl@infomed.sld.cu.
Pres DACS-UJAT, Av Gregorio Méndez Magaña 2838-A, Col Tamulté, 86150 Villahermosa TAB, Mexico. T. +52993358150ext6313 – +52993358150ext6300. E-mail: heberto_priego@hotmail.com.
URL: http://www.rims.org.mx/

History 25 Feb 2002, Villahermosa (Mexico). Registered in accordance with Mexican law. **Aims** Promote knowledge and study of health management and health care marketing. **Structure** General Assembly; Board of Directors; Executive Secretary; Commissions (6). **Languages** Portuguese, Spanish. **Staff** 3.00 FTE, paid. **Finance** Members' dues. Other sources: proceeds from events; collaborative agreements. **Activities** Knowledge management/information dissemination; capacity building; training/education. **Events** *Annual Convention* Quito (Ecuador) 2017, *Annual Convention* Bogota (Colombia) 2016, *Annual Convention* Villahermosa (Mexico) 2015, *Annual Convention / Convention – Symposium* Chiclayo (Peru) 2014, *Annual Convention / Convention – Symposium* Santiago (Chile) 2013. **Publications** *Mercadotecnia y empoderamiento social de la salud* (2019); *Mercadotecnia, innovación y tecnologias en salud* (2018); *Marketing en la promoción y la profesionalización de la salud* (2018); *Enfoque social de la mercadotecnia sanitaria* (2017); *Mercadotecnia y calidad en salud* (2017). Guidelines; educational materials.
Members in 17 countries:
Argentina, Bolivia, Brazil, Chile, Colombia, Costa Rica, Cuba, Ecuador, Guatemala, Mexico, Nicaragua, Panama, Paraguay, Peru, Portugal, Spain, Uruguay.
NGO Relations Cooperates with: universities; national and international organizations, not specified. [2019.12.13/XM4018/**D**]

♦ Red Iberoamericana de Migraciones Profesionales de Salud (RIMPS) 18675

General Coordinator address not obtained.
Technical Sec address not obtained.

Structure Assembly; Technical Advisory Committee; Technical Secretariat. **Members** Ministries of health. Membership countries not specified. **IGO Relations** Listed in the Registro de Redes Iberoamericano, held by *Ibero-American General Secretariat (#11024).* [2018/AA1243/**F***]

♦ Red Iberoamericana Ministerial de Aprendizaje e Investigación en Salud (RIMAIS) 18676

Secretariat Ministerio de Salud – RIMAIS, Aptdo Postal 10123-1000, San José, San José, San José, Costa Rica. T. +50622216258. Fax +50622216258.
URL: http://www.rimais.net/

History 2005, Salamanca (Spain). Founded on the initiative of Costa Rica during the XV Cumbre Iberoamericana de Jefes del Gobierno. **Aims** Strengthen the capacities of Ministries of Health so they can promote education and research about public health. **Structure** Executive Committee.
Members Participating governments (19):
Argentina, Bolivia, Brazil, Chile, Colombia, Costa Rica, Cuba, Dominican Rep, Ecuador, El Salvador, Guatemala, Honduras, Mexico, Panama, Paraguay, Peru, Portugal, Spain, Uruguay.
IGO Relations Listed in the Registro de Redes Iberoamericano, held by *Ibero-American General Secretariat (#11024).* [2020/XM4021/**F***]

♦ Red Iberoamericana de Oficinas de Cambio Climático (RIOCC) 18677

Address not obtained.
URL: http://www.lariocc.net/
History Oct 2004, Cascais (Portugal), during 4th Ibero-American Forum of Ministers for the Environment. **Events** *Annual meeting* Madrid (Spain) 2009, *Annual meeting* Cartagena de Indias (Colombia) 2008, *Annual meeting* Cartagena de Indias (Colombia) 2007, *Annual meeting* Santa Cruz (Bolivia) 2006, *Annual meeting* Antigua (Guatemala) 2005.
Members Governments (21):
Argentina, Bolivia, Brazil, Chile, Colombia, Costa Rica, Cuba, Dominican Rep, Ecuador, El Salvador, Guatemala, Honduras, Mexico, Nicaragua, Panama, Paraguay, Peru, Portugal, Spain, Uruguay, Venezuela. [2020/XJ1715/**D***]

♦ Red Iberoamericana de Organismos y Organizaciones contra la Discriminación (RIOOD) 18678

Sec Dante No 14, Col Anzures Alcadía de Miguel Hidalgo, 11590 Mexico City CDMX, Mexico. T. +525552621490 ext 5316. E-mail: secretariatecnica@redriood.org.
URL: http://redriood.org/
History 24 Sep 2007, Mexico City (Mexico). **Structure** General Assembly; Presidency; Technical Secretariat. **Events** *Ordinary Meeting* Mexico City (Mexico) 2019, *Ordinary Meeting* Cartagena de Indias (Colombia) 2018, *Ordinary Meeting* Santa Cruz (Bolivia) 2017, *Extraordinary Meeting* Buenos Aires (Argentina) 2016, *Ordinary Meeting* Guatemala (Guatemala) 2015.
Members Governmental (25) and non-governmental (22) organizations; academic institutions (3); regional and international organizations (6). Members in 17 countries:
Argentina, Bolivia, Brazil, Chile, Colombia, Costa Rica, Ecuador, El Salvador, Guatemala, Honduras, Mexico, Nicaragua, Panama, Paraguay, Peru, Portugal, Spain.
Andean Community (#00817); *Asociación Internacional de Lesbianas, Gays, Bisexuales, Trans e Intersex para América Latina y el Caribe (ILGALAC, #02166)*; *Fondo para el Desarrollo de los Pueblos Indígenas de América Latina y el Caribe (FILAC, #09832).* [2020/AA1244/y/**F**]

♦ Red Iberoamericana de Organizaciones No Gubernamentales Especializadas en Drogodependencias / see Red Iberoamericana de Organizaciones no Gubernamentales que Trabajan en Drogodependencias (#18679)
♦ Red Iberoamericana de Organizaciones No Gubernamentales de Personas con Discapacidad y sus Familias (#16354)

♦ Red Iberoamericana de Organizaciones no Gubernamentales que Trabajan en Drogodependencias (RIOD) 18679

Ibero-American Network of Nongovernmental Organizations working on Drug Addiction
Coordinator Avda Brasil 17 Entreplanta, 28020 Madrid, Spain. T. +34695807199. E-mail: riod@riod.org.
URL: http://www.riod.org/
History May 1999. Founded on the initiative of the Spanish Government and *Agencia Española de Cooperación Internacional para el Desarrollo (AECID).* Former names and other names: *Red Iberoamericana de Organizaciones No Gubernamentales Especializadas en Drogodependencias* – alias. **Structure** General Assembly; Board of Directors; Geographical Nodes: Andean, Central America and the Caribbean, Southern Cone, Spain; Permanent Consultative Council; Commissions; Technical Secretariat. **Events** *Seminario Iberoamericano sobre Drogas y Cooperación* Madrid (Spain) 2020, *Seminario Iberoamericano sobre Drogas y Cooperación* Madrid (Spain) 2018.
Members Nongovernmental organizations (58) in 18 countries. Membership countries not specified. Honorary Members (2):
Honorary Members (2):
Delegación del gobierno de España para el Plan Nacional sobre Drogas; *Inter-American Drug Abuse Control Commission (#11429).*
Consultative Status Consultative status granted from: *ECOSOC (#05331)* (Special). **IGO Relations** Listed in the Registro de Redes Iberoamericano, held by *Ibero-American General Secretariat (#11024).* [2020/XF6203/**F**]

♦ Red Iberoamericana de Politicas Integrales para los Mayores y Discapacidad / see Red Intergubernamental Iberoamericana de Cooperación Técnica para el Desarrollo de Politicas de Atención a personas con Discapacidad y Adultos Mayores (#18697)

♦ Red Iberoamericana de Postgrados sobre Politica y Estudios Territoriales (RIPPET) 18680

Ibero-American Network of Postgraduate Programmes on Territorial Policies and Studies
SG c/o RII, Paseo Tollocan 1402 Poniente, Ciudad Universitaria, 50110 Toluca MEX, Mexico. E-mail: contacto@seminariorii.com.
URL: http://cebem.org/?page_id=670
History 1996. Founded within the framework of *Red Iberoamericana de Investigadores sobre Globalización y Territorio (RII, #18670).* **Aims** Promote improved exchange, coordination and cooperation between postgraduates in the area of politics and territorial studies in the South Cone and Mexico. **Events** *Encuentro de Posgrados Iberoamericanos sobre Desarrollo y Políticas Territoriales* Cuenca (Ecuador) 2018, *Encuentro de Posgrados Iberoamericanos sobre Desarrollo y Políticas Territoriales* Mendoza (Argentina) 2016, *Encuentro de Postgrados Iberoamericanos Sobre Desarrollo y Políticas Territoriales* Monterrey (Mexico) 2013, *Encuentro de Postgrados Iberoamericanos Sobre Desarrollo y Políticas Territoriales* Toluca (Mexico) 2011, *Encuentro extraordinario de Postgrados en Políticas y Estudios Territoriales* Mendoza (Argentina) 2010. [2018/XM3649/**D**]

♦ Red IBERoamericana de Prospectiva (unconfirmed)

♦ Red Iberoamericana de Protección de Datos (RIPD) 18681

Iberoamerican Network on Data Protection
Contact c/o Agencia Española de Protección de Datos, C/ Jorge Juan 6, 28001 Madrid, Spain. T. +34913996301. E-mail: secretaria.ripd@agpd.es.
URL: http://www.redipd.org/
History Jun 2003, Antigua (Guatemala). Founded during Ibero-American Symposium on Data Protection (EIPD). **Aims** Foster, maintain and strengthen a close and constant exchange of information, experiences and knowledge among Ibero-American countries, through dialogue and collaboration in issues related to personal data protection. **Structure** General Assembly (annual, at Ibero-American Symposium). Executive Committee, comprising Presidency and 4 members. Secretariat. **Languages** English, Portuguese, Spanish. **Staff** 1.00 FTE, paid. **Finance** Public budget. **Events** *Meeting* Punta del Este (Uruguay) 2012, *Meeting* Antigua (Guatemala) 2011, *Meeting* Cartagena de Indias (Colombia) 2011, *Meeting* Mexico City (Mexico) 2011, *Meeting* Mexico City (Mexico) 2010.
Members Full in 22 countries:
Andorra, Argentina, Bolivia, Brazil, Chile, Colombia, Costa Rica, Dominican Rep, Ecuador, El Salvador, Guatemala, Haiti, Honduras, Mexico, Nicaragua, Panama, Paraguay, Peru, Portugal, Spain, Uruguay, Venezuela.
IGO Relations Listed in the Registro de Redes Iberoamericano, held by *Ibero-American General Secretariat (#11024).* [2020/XJ0818/**F**]

♦ Red Iberoamericana de Revistas de Comunicación y Cultura 18682

Ibero-American Network of Communications and Cultural Journals
Tech Sec UNLP Fac de Periodismo, Alicia Moreau de Justo 550, Buenos Aires, Argentina. E-mail: fsaintout@perio.unlp.edu.ar.
URL: http://www.revistasdecomunicacion.org/
History 1982, Sao Paulo (Brazil) during I Encuentro de Revistas. [2008/XF1047/**F**]

♦ Red Iberoamericana de Salud y Medioambiente (Red ISMA) 18683

Coordination c/o CSIC, Lab de Toxicologia Ambiental, Serrano 115bis, 28006 Madrid, Spain. T. +34917452500ext955120. E-mail: red.isma@gmail.com.
URL: http://www.redisma.org/
History 2009. **Activities** Training/education; events/meetings.
Members Full in 11 countries:
Argentina, Bolivia, Chile, Colombia, Costa Rica, Cuba, Mexico, Peru, Portugal, Spain, Venezuela.
NGO Relations *Red Iberoamericana de Toxicologia y Seguridad Quimica (RITSQ, #18686).* [2015/XM4122/**D**]

♦ Red Iberoamericana de Sistemas de Información Geografica (REDISIG) 18684

Exec Pres c/o UEx Fac Fil y Letras, Av Universidad s/n, 10003 Caceres, Badajoz, Spain. E-mail: info@redisig.org.
URL: http://www.redisig.org/
History Founded 29 Sep 2017, Cuenca (Ecuador), on merger of *Sociedad Iberoamericana de Sistemas de Información Geografica (SIBSIG, inactive)* and *Conferencia Iberoamericana de Sistemas de Información Geografica (CONFIBSIG).* **Aims** Generate scientific production in theory, methodology and application of spatial analysis with geographic information systems in the Ibero-American context. **Activities** Events/meetings. **Events** *CONFIBSIG : Iberoamerican Conference on Geographic Information Systems* Brazil 2029, *CONFIBSIG : Iberoamerican Conference on Geographic Information Systems* Mexico 2027, *CONFIBSIG : Iberoamerican Conference on Geographic Information Systems* Costa Rica 2025, *CONFIBSIG : Iberoamerican Conference on Geographic Information Systems* Caceres (Spain) 2023, *CONFIBSIG : Iberoamerican Conference on Geographic Information Systems* Caceres (Spain) 2021.
Members Universities in 8 countries:
Argentina, Brazil, Chile, Costa Rica, Ecuador, Mexico, Puerto Rico, Spain. [2019/XM8783/**F**]

♦ Red Iberoamericana de Terminologia (RITerm) 18685

Réseau ibéro-américain de terminologie – Rede Ibero-Americana de Terminologia – Xarxa Iberoamericana de Terminologia
Sec c/o Centro de Enseñanza de Lenguas Extranjeras, UNAM, Ciudad Universitaria Escolar, Coyoacan, Mexico City CDMX, Mexico. T. +525556220650. E-mail: marisela.colin@cele.unam.mx.
Headquarters Universidad Autónoma de Manizales, Grupo de Investigación CITERM, Manizales, Caldas, Colombia. E-mail: riterm.secretaria@gmail.com.
URL: http://www.ufrgs.br/riterm/esp/index.html/
History 1987, Caracas (Venezuela), by *International Information Centre for Terminology (INFOTERM, #13846)* and *Latin Union (UL, inactive).* Previously also known as *Red de Terminologia – Réseau de terminologie – Rede de Terminologia.* **Aims** Establish a cooperation channel between members to consolidate terminologies in countries where Catalan, Portuguese or Spanish is spoken. **Structure** General Assembly (every 2 years); Executive Committee. **Languages** Catalan, Portuguese, Spanish. **Staff** 5.00 FTE, voluntary. **Finance** Members' dues. **Activities** Events/meetings; training/education; publishing activities; knowledge management/ information dissemination; networking/liaising. **Events** *Simposio iberoamericano de terminologia* Sao Paulo (Brazil) 2016, *Simposio iberoamericano de terminologia* Santiago (Chile) 2014, *Simposio iberoamericano de terminologia* Alicante (Spain) 2012, *Simposio iberoamericano de terminologia* Buenos Aires (Argentina) 2010, *Simposio iberoamericano de terminologia* Lima (Peru) 2008. **Publications** *Debate Terminológico* (annual) – review.
Members Individuals in 11 countries:
Argentina, Belgium, Brazil, Cuba, France, Mexico, Peru, Portugal, Spain, Uruguay, Venezuela.
Institutional members in 14 countries:
Argentina, Brazil, Canada, Chile, Colombia, Cuba, France, Mexico, Paraguay, Peru, Portugal, Spain, USA, Venezuela.
NGO Relations In liaison with technical committees of: *International Organization for Standardization (ISO, #14473).* [2016.06.01/XF5153/**F**]

♦ Red Iberoamericana de Toxicologia y Seguridad Quimica (RITSQ) .. 18686

Coordination Lab de Genotoxicologia y Mutagénesis Ambiental, Inst Ciencias Agrarias CSIC, C/ Serrano 115 Dpdo, 28006 Madrid, Spain. T. +34917452500ext955120. Fax +34915640800.
URL: http://www.ritsq.org/
History 2006. **Events** *Meeting* Barcelona (Spain) 2010, *Meeting* Montréal, QC (Canada) 2007.
Members Full in 12 countries:
Argentina, Bolivia, Brazil, Chile, Colombia, Costa Rica, Mexico, Peru, Portugal, Spain, Uruguay, Venezuela.
NGO Relations *Red Iberoamericana de Salud y Medioambiente (Red ISMA, #18683).* [2017.12.13/XM4121/**D**]

♦ Red Iberoamericana de Trabajo con las Familias 18687

Contact Av Belgrano 687 – 8 Of 33, CABA, Buenos Aires, Argentina. T. +541143432706 – +541143344844.
URL: http://www.rediberoamericanadetrabajoconfamilias.org/
History Founded Jan 1994, Valparaiso (Chile), following 2nd Iberoamerican Conference on Families which gathered together 500 participants from two continents. **Aims** Improve the quality of life of families and of each individual comprising a family. **Structure** Executive Committee. **Languages** English, Portuguese, Spanish. **Staff** 5.00 FTE, paid; 15.00 FTE, voluntary. **Finance** Members' dues. Other sources: events; capacity courses; donations; contributions. **Activities** Events/meetings; projects/programmes. **Events** *Conference* Puno (Peru) 2021, *Conference* Bogota (Colombia) 2020, *Conference* Madrid (Spain) 2015, *Conference* Buenos Aires (Argentina) 2009, *Conference* Mexico City (Mexico) 2007. **Publications** *La Familia, Realidad Social en Proceso de Cambio*; *Revista CUHSO Universidad Católica de Temuco Chile*; *Revista Latinoamericana de Familia Universidad de Caldas Manizales Colombia.*
Members Individuals (118) in 12 countries and territories:
Argentina, Brazil, Chile, Colombia, Guatemala, Mexico, Panama, Peru, Puerto Rico, Spain, Uruguay, Venezuela.
NGO Relations *World Organisation for Families (Familis WOF, no recent information)*; national organizations and universities. [2019.07.25/XF4746/v/**F**]

♦ Red Iberoamericana de Universidades Promotoras de la Salud (RIUPS) 18688

Coordinator address not obtained.
History 6 Oct 2007. **Events** *General Assembly* Puerto Rico 2013, *General Assembly* San José (Costa Rica) 2011. **Publications** *RIUPS Bulletin.* [2012/XJ5875/**D**]

♦ REDICA / see Central American Engineering Institutions Network (#03668)
♦ **REDICA** Central American Engineering Institutions Network (#03668)
♦ **REDIF** Red Europea de Institutos de la Familia (#18653)
♦ **ReDi** International Society for the Research and Study of Diaconia and Christian Social Practice (#15424)
♦ REDILPES (see: #16279)
♦ Red Infojuve de la UNESCO / see INFOYOUTH – Worldwide Information Network on Youth Related Issues (#11204)
♦ Red de Información sobre la Educación en Europa (inactive)
♦ Red de Información Interamericana sobre Diversidad Biológica / see Inter-American Biodiversity Information Network (#11402)
♦ Red de Información Tecnológica Latinoamericana (see: #19294)
♦ Red de Información Tercer Mundo (internationally oriented national body)

♦ Red Informatica de la Iglesia en América Latina (RIIAL) 18689

Digital Network of the Church in Latin America
Coordinator PCCS, Via della Conciliazione 5, 00120 Vatican City, Vatican. T. +39669891800. Fax +39669891840.
URL: http://www.riial.org/
History 1987, by *Consejo Episcopal Latinoamericano (CELAM, #04709)* and *Pontifical Council for Social Communications (#18447).* **Aims** Provide a forum for cooperation, communion and sharing of communication services in the Catholic Church, especially in the field of mission and evangelization. **Structure** Committee. Coordinator; Vice-Coordinator. **Languages** Portuguese, Spanish. **Events** *Continental Meeting* Santiago (Chile) 2011, *Continental Meeting* Bogota (Colombia) 2009. **Publications** *Cultura Digital en América Latina – Investigación InterUniversitaria Educación y Evangelización* (2012); *Todos Online* (2005); *El Rostro Humano de la Cultura Digital* (2000). [2012.08.28/XM0277/**F**]

♦ Red Informatica Internacional sobre Blanqueo de Dinero (#14181)
♦ Red de Innovaciones Educativas para América Latina y el Caribe (#16275)
♦ Red de Instituciones de Combate a la Corrupción y Rescate de la Etica Pública (see: #16294)
♦ Red de Instituciones Educacionales en Ciencias de la Salud con Orientación Comunitaria / see The Network: Towards Unity for Health (#17060)
♦ Red de Instituciones Nacionales para la Promoción y Protección de los Derechos Humanos del Continente Americano (unconfirmed)

♦ Red de Instituciones Vinculadas a la Capacitación en Economia y Politicas Agricolas en América Latina y el Caribe (REDCAPA) 18690

Network of Institutions Dedicated to Teaching Agricultural and Rural Development Policies for Latin America and the Caribbean

Dir Avenida Presidente Vargas 417, 8 piso, Centro, Rio de Janeiro RJ, 20071-003, Brazil.

History 1993. **Aims** Contribute to the progress of education and research in the field of *agricultural* economy and policies and *rural* and *environmental* development of the region, strengthen the institutional development and promote cooperation on national and international level between its members. **Structure** General Assembly (every 2 years). Management Board, consisting of 9 members. Executive Secretariat, comprising 5 members. **Finance** Members' dues. **Publications** *CartaRed* – newsletter; *Politicas Agricolas* – scientific review. *Cuadernos de Politicas Agricolas* – series.

Members Full; Associate; Honorary; Supporting. Members in 12 countries:
Colombia, Costa Rica, Cuba, Ecuador, El Salvador, Honduras, Mexico, Nicaragua, Peru, Trinidad-Tobago, USA, Venezuela.
[2010/XF3866/F]

♦ Red de Institutos de Investigación Económica y Social de la Cuenca del Caribe (internationally oriented national body)
♦ Red Interagencial para Educación en Situaciones de Emergencias (#11387)
♦ Red Interamericana de Academias de Ciencias (#11441)

♦ Red Interamericana de Alto Nivel Sobre Descentralización, Gobierno Local y Participación Ciudadana (RIAD) 18691

High-Level Inter-American Network on Decentralization, Local Government and Citizen Participation

Coordinator c/o OAS – Unit for Promotion of Democracy, 1889 F St NW, GSB 6665, Washington DC 20006, USA. T. +12024583879 – +12024583000. Fax +12024586250 – +12024586482.
URL: http://www.oas.org/

History 31 Jul 2001, La Paz (Bolivia), within *OAS (#17629)*. **Aims** Link high level officials and experts from ministries and government agencies responsible for decentralization, strengthening regional and municipal administrations and civil society participation, in order to: enhance exchange of skills, information and experience at the highest government level within the framework of the OAS; develop general and strategic guidelines as a reference point for development and application of public policies to strengthen and guarantee continuity of the decentralization process – local government and citizen participation; provide follow-up and systematic support for implementing mandates of Summits of Heads of State and Government of the Americas in this area; promote activities with international, institutional and/or private organizations, so as to enable financing and cooperation for networks of experts, subregional and national forums, electronic and virtual links, horizontal technical advisory services, training courses and seminars, research and publications. **Structure** Inter-American meeting of Ministers and High Level Authorities Responsible for Policies on Decentralization, Local Government and Citizen Participation at the Municipal Level. Chair; Vice-Chair; 4 Subregional Vice-Chairs. Technical Secretariat provided by OAS General Secretariat's Unit for Promotion of Democracy and comprising Executive Coordinator of the Unit, Coordinator of Strategic Programs for Democratic Strengthening of UPD/OAS, Senior Specialist of UPD/OAS and Coordinator of RIAD Technical Secretariat.

Activities *'Initial Work Areas'* defined by the Declaration of La Paz (Bolivia): public policies on strengthening decentralization, regional and municipal administrations, citizen participation and civil society, also incorporating a gender perspective; constitutional and legal framework governing relations among various levels of government; transfering of responsibility from central to local level, including funding options and means of strengthening technical capabilities and their impact on democratic governance; opportunities and mechanisms for citizen participation at the regional, municipal and community levels, including policies and strategies for promoting them.
'Guidelines and Priorities' established by Mexico City (Mexico) Plan of Action, and based on initial work areas, include: a long-term approach to decentralization policies, oriented to reduction of regional socio-economic disparities, to strengthening of capacity to combat poverty and to promoting favourable local conditions for sustainable and environmental economic and social development; cooperative intergovernmental relations providing political agreement based on increased cooperation among different levels or orders of government and civil society; preferential support for countries less advanced in developing decentralization; professionalization of local public services and provision of continuity in design and orchestration of development strategies in regional and local government, within the framework of effective modernization processes at state level.

Events *Meeting of ministers and high officials responsible for decentralization policies, local government and citizen participation* Mexico City (Mexico) 2003, *Working meeting* Cancún (Mexico) 2002. **IGO Relations** *Development Bank of Latin America (CAF, #05055)*; *Inter-American Development Bank (IDB, #11427)*; *International Bank for Reconstruction and Development (IBRD, #12317)* (World Bank); *United Nations Economic Commission for Latin America and the Caribbean (ECLAC, #20556)*. [2010/XF6777/F*]

♦ Red Interamericana de Citricos (#11407)
♦ Red Interamericana de Competitividad (#11416)

♦ Red Interamericana para la Democracia (RID) 18692

Inter-American Democracy Network (IADN)

Contact Av Libertador 184, piso 9o "C", AB01001, Ciudad A, Buenos Aires, Argentina. T. +541143132701.

History 1995. Original founding organizations (6): Partners of the Americas (USA); Corporación Participa (Chile); Asociación Conciencia and Poder Cuidadano Foundation (Argentina); Instituto de Investigación y Autoformación Politica (Guatemala); Political Science Department of the Universidad de los Andes (Colombia). **Aims** Strengthen democracy by encouraging responsible *citizen* participation and supporting implementation of mechanisms and laws that guarantee this participation; promote citizens' understanding of their democratic rights and responsibilities so that they can be effectively utilized at the community level; foster collaboration among *civil society* organizations, national and local governments and regional democratic leaders; strengthen members' technical and institutional capacities and finance strategic projects. **Structure** Executive Secretariat. **Languages** English, Spanish. **Finance** Members' dues. International funds. **Activities** Areas of expertise: Transparency and Anti-Corruption; Hemispheric Processes; Decentralization and Local Government Strengthening; Civic Responsibility; Political Parties; Citizen Deliberation. Services include: *'INFORID'* – America Civic News Agency providing information about the activities conducted by Inter-American Democracy Network member non-governmental organizations to the mass media throughout the continent; *'Virtual Training Campus (VTC)'* – access to virtual discussion fora, on-line library, calendar of events and *'Latin American Citizen Participation Index (LACPI)'*, which is a study evaluating fields, levels and motivation of citizen participation in each of the analysed countries. **Events** *Civil society regional forum* Mexico City (Mexico) 2003. **Publications** *InfoRID* (daily).

Members Organizations (over 350) in 23 countries and territories:
Argentina, Bolivia, Brazil, Canada, Chile, Colombia, Costa Rica, Dominican Rep, Ecuador, El Salvador, Grenada, Guatemala, Haiti, Honduras, Jamaica, Mexico, Nicaragua, Paraguay, Peru, Puerto Rico, Uruguay, USA, Venezuela.

IGO Relations Participates on consulting rounds of: *Inter-American Development Bank (IDB, #11427)*. **NGO Relations** Member of: *Democracy Users' Network (DUN, no recent information)*. Associated to: *CIVICUS: World Alliance for Citizen Participation (#03962)*. Agreement to support the Latin America Democratic Development Index with: *Konrad Adenauer Foundation (KAF)*. [2009.06.01/XF7113/F]

♦ Red Interamericana de Fundaciones y Acciones Empresariales para el Desarrollo de Base (RedEAmérica) 18693

Exec Dir Calle 72 No 9-55 Oficina 602, Edificio Santiago de Chile, Bogota, Bogota DC, Colombia. T. +5713100379 – +5713461774. E-mail: direccionejecutiva@redeamerica.org – comunicaciones@redeamerica.org.
URL: http://www.redeamerica.org/

History Sep 2002. **Aims** Provide leadership, management and know-how in the field of *poverty* reduction; make *grassroots* development central to development strategies in the Americas. **Structure** General Assembly (annual); Council; Secretariat.

Members Foundations (52) in 12 countries:
Argentina, Bolivia, Brazil, Chile, Colombia, Dominican Rep, Ecuador, Mexico, Peru, Uruguay, USA, Venezuela.
Included in the above, 1 organization listed in this Yearbook:
Inter-American Foundation (IAF, #11431). [2017/XJ3801/F]

♦ Red Interamericana de Información sobre Biodiversidad (#11402)

♦ Red Interamericana de Laboratorios de Analisis de Alimentos (RILAA) 18694

Inter-American Network of Food Analysis Laboratories (INFAL)

Contact Av Governador Leonel de Moura Brizola 7778, Duque de Caxias, Rio de Janeiro RJ, 25040-004, Brazil. E-mail: rilaa@paho.org.
URL: http://rilaa.net/

History Founded 12 Dec 1997. Previously also referred to in English as *Inter-American Food Laboratory Network*. **Aims** Achieve methodological harmonization of food analysis laboratories; promote implementation of equivalent quality management systems in INFAL laboratories; strengthen technical and scientific cooperation among countries involved. **Structure** Assembly; Executive Committee; Technical Groups; National Networks; Ex-officio Secretariat. **Languages** English, Spanish. **Staff** 10.50 FTE, paid. **Finance** General operations funded by: *Pan American Health Organization (PAHO, #18108)*. **Activities** Events/meetings; training/education; guidance/assistance/consulting. **Events** *General Assembly* Santo Domingo (Dominican Rep) 2018, *General Assembly* Panama (Panama) 2016, *Assembly* Guayaquil (Ecuador) 2012, *Assembly* Brasilia (Brazil) 2010, *Assembly* Panama (Panama) 2008. **Publications** *RILAA News*. Technical notes; checklists; CD-ROMs.

Members Laboratories (170). Full (63) in 30 countries and territories:
Argentina, Aruba, Barbados, Belize, Bolivia, Brazil, Canada, Chile, Colombia, Costa Rica, Cuba, Dominica, Dominican Rep, Ecuador, El Salvador, Guatemala, Guyana, Honduras, Mexico, Nicaragua, Panama, Paraguay, Peru, St Kitts-Nevis, St Lucia, St Vincent-Grenadines, Suriname, Uruguay, USA, Venezuela.
Member laboratories (91) through national networks (12) in 10 countries:
Argentina, Bolivia, Brazil, Chile, Cuba, Dominican Rep, Mexico, Peru, Uruguay, Venezuela. [2017.10.23/XF6026/F]

♦ Red Interamericana para el Mejoramiento de la Calidad Ambiental (no recent information)
♦ Red Interamericana de Protección Social (#11447)
♦ Red Interamericana de Refugios (unconfirmed)
♦ Red Interamericana de Salud y Vivienda / see Red Interamericana de Vivienda Saludable (#18695)

♦ Red Interamericana de Vivienda Saludable (Red VIVSALUD) 18695

Interamerican Network for Healthful Housing

Contact CEPIS, Los Pinos 251, Urbanización Camacho, La Molina, 12, Lima, Peru. T. +5114371077. Fax +5114378289.

History 1995, within *Pan American Health Organization (PAHO, #18108)*. Also referred to as *Red Interamericana de Salud y Vivienda*. **Aims** Represent the interests of members; complement and reinforce national capacities through links and cooperation. **Events** *Inter-American congress of environmental health* Havana (Cuba) 2005.

Members in 13 countries:
Argentina, Bolivia, Brazil, Chile, Cuba, Ecuador, El Salvador, Haiti, Mexico, Nicaragua, Peru, USA, Venezuela.
[2019/XM0146/F]

♦ Red de Intercambio de los Parlamentos de América Latina y El Caribe (RIPALC) 18696

Exchange Network of Parliaments of Latin America and The Caribbean (ENPLAC) – Rede de Intercâmbio dos Parlamentos da América Latina e do Caribe

Secretariat Praça dos Três Poderes, Ed Câmara dos Deputados, Anexo II Cedi, Brasilia DF, 70 160-900, Brazil. E-mail: ripalc@camara.gov.br.
URL: http://www.ripalc.org/

History Proposed Jan 2011, Valparaiso (Chile). Network presented and approved at meeting of *Association of Secretaries General of Parliaments (ASGP, #02911)*, Apr 2011, Panama. **Aims** Promote the exchange of information, knowledge and good practices among parliament administrations of countries in Latin America and the Caribbean. **Structure** Council of Secretaries General. Executive Committee. Conference of the Correspondents. Secretariat Director. **Languages** English, Portuguese, Spanish. **Staff** Part-time. **Finance** No direct funds. **Activities** Meeting activities; education. **Publications** Reports.

Members National and regional parliaments of 18 houses in 15 countries:
Barbados, Belize, Brazil, Chile, Colombia, Ecuador, El Salvador, Guyana, Nicaragua, Panama, Paraguay, St Vincent-Grenadines, Suriname, Trinidad-Tobago, Uruguay. [2014.04.10/XJ7891/F*]

♦ Red Intercontinental de Promoción de la Economia Social y Solidaria (#11463)

♦ Red Intergubernamental Iberoamericana de Cooperación Técnica para el Desarrollo de Politicas de Atención a personas con Discapacidad y Adultos Mayores (RIICOTEC) 18697

Iberoamerican Intergovernmental Network for Technical Cooperation

Contact c/o IMSERSO, Avda de la Ilustración s/n, c/v a Ginzo de Limia 58, 28029 Madrid, Spain. T. +34917033831. Fax +34917033880. E-mail: secretariaejecutiva.riicotec@imserso.es.
URL: http://www.riicotec.org/

History 1991, Madrid (Spain). Former names and other names: *Red Iberoamericana de Politicas Integrales para los Mayores y Discapacidad* – alias. **Structure** Board; Executive Secretary; Regional Representatives (4). **Events** *General Assembly* Montevideo (Uruguay) 2014, *Conference / General Assembly* Valencia (Spain) 2007, *Follow-up meeting to the 2nd world assembly on ageing on old people facing associationism / General Assembly* Cartagena de Indias (Colombia) 2006, *Conference / General Assembly* Natal (Brazil) 2005, *Conference / General Assembly* Acapulco (Mexico) 2003.

Members Governmental agencies in 21 countries:
Argentina, Bolivia, Brazil, Chile, Colombia, Costa Rica, Cuba, Dominican Rep, Ecuador, El Salvador, Guatemala, Honduras, Mexico, Nicaragua, Panama, Paraguay, Peru, Portugal, Spain, Uruguay, Venezuela.

IGO Relations Listed in the Registro de Redes Iberoamericano, held by *Ibero-American General Secretariat (#11024)*. [2020/XF5739/F*]

♦ Red Interinstitucional sobre la Mujer y la Igualdad entre los Géneros (#11388)
♦ Red Internacional de Bosques Modelo (#14175)
♦ Red Internacional de Centros de Capacitación en Agua (#14341)
♦ Red Internacional para los Derechos Económicos, Sociales y Culturales (#14255)
♦ Red Internacional de Derechos Humanos (#18891)
♦ Red Internacional de Derechos Humanos I Europa (#14286)
♦ Red Internacional para el Desarrollo Aves Caseras de Familia (#14267)

♦ Red Internacional de Escritores por la Tierra (TIER) 18698

Managing Dir C/ Francoli 56-58, 43006 Tarragona, Spain. T. +34977551300. E-mail: riet@mare-terra.org.
URL: http://redescritoresporlatierra.org/

History 2005. **Aims** Strengthen society based on socio-environmental balance, so as to eradicate extreme poverty and hunger, guarantee access to education and health, promote gender equity and the autonomy of women, social justice, sustainable development and the conservation of earth. **Languages** Catalan, English, Spanish. **Activities** Events/meetings. **Publications** Books; articles. **Members** Individuals. Membership countries not specified. **NGO Relations** *Mare Terra – Fundació Medeterrània (Mare Terra).*
[2020.03.11/XM8752/v/E]

- ♦ Red Internacional de Foresteria Analoga (#11650)
- ♦ Red Internacional de Género y Comercio (#13707)
- ♦ Red Internacional de Grupos pro Alimentación Infantil (#12305)
- ♦ Red Internacional pro Hospitales sin Fumar / see Anti-Smoking International Alliance (#00861)
- ♦ Red Internacional de Investigadores en Turismo, Cooperación y Desarrollo (#14318)
- ♦ Red Internacional de Jóvenes Perodistas (#14346)
- ♦ Red Internacional de Metodologia de Investigación de Sistemas de Producción / see Centro Latinoamericano para el Desarrollo Rural (#03813)
- ♦ Red Internacional de Motricidad Humana (unconfirmed)
- ♦ Red Internacional de Mujeres contra el Tabaco (#14343)
- ♦ Red Internacional "Mujeres y Mineria" (#15895)
- ♦ Red Internacional de Municipios por la calidad de vida / see Cittaslow (#03958)
- ♦ Red Internacional de Organismos de Cuenca (#14235)
- ♦ Red Internacional para las Pequeñas y Medianas Empresas (#14325)
- ♦ Red Internacional de Politicas Culturales (#14246)
- ♦ Red Internacional para la Promoción del Voluntariado en Europa / see Volonteurope (#20807)
- ♦ Red de Investigación Acción de América (#00096)
- ♦ Red de Investigación Internacional sobre la Desertificación (#02823)
- ♦ **REDISIG** Red Iberoamericana de Sistemas de Información Geografica (#18684)
- ♦ **Red ISMA** Red Iberoamericana de Salud y Medioambiente (#18683)
- ♦ Red Judicial Europea en Materia Civil y Mercantil (#07616)
- ♦ Red de Justicia Fiscal de América Latina y el Caribe (unconfirmed)
- ♦ Red Kidlink / see Kidlink Association (#16189)
- ♦ REDLAB – Red de Cooperación Tecnica entre Laboratorios de Investigación y Diagnóstico Veterinario (see: #09268)
- ♦ **RedLACES** Red Americana y Caribeña de Ecologia Social (#16283)
- ♦ **REDLAC** Latin American and Caribbean Youth Network for Sexual and Reproductive Health and Rights (#16289)
- ♦ **RedLAC** Red de Fondos Ambientales de Latinoamérica y el Caribe (#18656)
- ♦ Red Lacre – Red Latinoamericana de Recicladores (unconfirmed)
- ♦ **REDLACTRANS** Red de Latinoamérica y El Caribe de Personas Trans (#18699)
- ♦ **RedLad** Red Latinoamericana y del Caribe para la Democracia (#18704)
- ♦ RedLAES / see Latin American and Caribbean Network for Social Ecology (#16283)
- ♦ **REDLAJ** Red Latinoamericana de Jueces (#18714)
- ♦ **RED LA+** Latin American Network of People Living with HIV/AIDS (#16355)
- ♦ **REDLAMYC** Red Latinoamericana y Caribeña por la Defensa de los Derechos de los Niños, Niñas y Adolescentes (#18705)
- ♦ **REDLARA** Red Latinoamericana de Reproducción Asistida (#16315)
- ♦ **REDLAR** Red Latinoamericana Contra Represas y por los Rios, sus Comunidades y el Agua (#18709)
- ♦ **Red LASES** Red Latinoamericana de Socio-Economia Solidaria (#18720)

♦ Red de Latinoamérica y El Caribe de Personas Trans (REDLAC-TRANS) 18699

Latin America and the Caribbean Network of TRANS People

Regional Secretariat Maipu N 464 8VO Of 806 Caba, C1006ACC Buenos Aires, Argentina. T. +541150326335. E-mail: info@redlactrans.org.
URL: http://redlactrans.org/

History 17 Oct 2004. Founded by 4 NGOs in Argentina, Brazil, Mexico and Chile. **Aims** Secure the *human rights* of transgender people of Latin America and the Caribbean, particularly in the fields of health, education, employment and justice. **Structure** Executive Commission. **Languages** Portuguese, Spanish. **Activities** Advocacy/lobbying/activism; capacity building; networking/liaising.
Members Organizations in 22 countries:
Argentina, Bahamas, Barbados, Belize, Bolivia, Brazil, Chile, Colombia, Costa Rica, Dominican Rep, Ecuador, El Salvador, Guatemala, Honduras, Jamaica, Mexico, Nicaragua, Panama, Paraguay, Peru, Suriname, Uruguay.
NGO Relations Member of (1): *Robert Carr civil society Networks Fund (RCNF, #18956).* Cooperates with (1): *Horizontal Technical Cooperation Group of Latin America and the Caribbean on HIV/AIDS (HTGC, #10945).*
[2021.02.19/XM3592/D]

- ♦ Red Latinoamericana de Abogados de Impacto (inactive)

♦ Red Latinoamericana de Acogimiento Familiar (RELAF) 18700

Latin American Foster Care Network

Project Leader Plaza Independencia 1376, 8vo Piso, 11100 Montevideo, Uruguay. E-mail: info@relaf.org.
Technican Support Office 158 25 de Mayo 158, Office 22, 1002 Buenos Aires, Argentina. T. +541143427672. E-mail: info@relaf.org.
URL: http://www.relaf.org/

History 2003, as a branch of *International Foster Care Organization (IFCO, #13663).* Since 2009, an independent charity. **Aims** Create and strengthen the active network of regional stakeholders in order to contribute to de-institutionalization processes of children and adolescents and to prevention of separation of origin families and their communities; promote family-based care in Latin America to achieve the right to community and family-based care. **Structure** Board; Consultative Council; Technical Team. **Languages** English, French, Portuguese, Spanish. **Staff** 8.50 FTE, paid. **Finance** Financed mainly through cooperation agreements with *UNICEF (#20332), Save the Children International (#19058)* and *Hope and Homes for Children.* Additional funding through fundraising. **Activities** Projects/programmes; events/meetings; training/education. **Publications** *RELAF Newsletter.* Manuals; handbooks; guides. **Members** Full in most Latin American countries. Membership countries not specified. **IGO Relations** Partners include: *Inter-American Commission on Human Rights (IACHR, #11411); UNICEF (#20332).* **NGO Relations** Partners include: *Hope and Homes for Children; International Social Service (ISS, #14886); Red Latinoamericana y Caribeña por la Defensa de los Derechos de los Niños, Niñas y Adolescentes (REDLAMYC, #18705); Save the Children International (#19058).* Member of: *Child Rights Connect (#03884).*
[2020/XJ9780/F]

♦ Red Latinoamericana para el Análisis de la Calidad Ambiental en América Latina (RACAL) 18701

Contact address not obtained. T. +50625114505. E-mail: info@redracal.org.
Pres Lab de Analises de Residuos de Pesticidas, Depto Quimica – UFSM, Prédio 17, 2° Andar LARP, Santa Maria RS, 97105-900, Brazil.
URL: https://www.redracal.org/

History 1990. Functions as regional branch of *International Association of Environmental Analytical Chemistry (IAEAC, #11876).* **Aims** Promote studies in the area of the environment, so as to enrich and update knowledge related to environmental, health and microbiological issues. **Structure** Executive Board. **Activities** Events/meetings. **Events** *Latin American Symposium on Environmental Analytical Chemistry (LASEAC)* Bento Gonçalves (Brazil) 2019, *Latin American Symposium on Environmental Analytical Chemistry (LASEAC)* La Serena (Chile) 2018, *Latin American Symposium on Environmental Analytical Chemistry (LASEAC)* Manizales (Colombia) 2017, *Latin American Symposium on Environmental Analytical Chemistry (LASEAC)* Cochabamba (Bolivia) 2015, *Latin American Symposium on Environmental Analytical Chemistry (LASEAC)* Puebla (Mexico) 2013.
Members Professionals in 10 countries:
Argentina, Brazil, Chile, Colombia, Costa Rica, Ecuador, Guatemala, Honduras, Mexico, Uruguay. [2019/AA1263/F]

- ♦ Red Latinoamericana de Botanica (#16362)
- ♦ Red Latinoamericana de Cambio Climatico (#04002)

♦ Red Latinoamericana y del Caribe de Bioética (REDBIOETICA) 18702

Contact c/o ORCYT, Dr Luis P Piera 1992, 2o piso, 11200 Montevideo, Uruguay. T. +59824132075. Fax +59824132094. E-mail: info@redbioetica.com.ar – redbioeticaunesco@gmail.com.
URL: https://redbioetica.com.ar/

History 2 May 2003, Cancún (Mexico). Also referred to as *Redbioética.* **Structure** Plenary. Council, comprising President, Vice-President, Executive Secretary, Executive Coordinator and 11 Councillors. **Publications** *Revista Redbioética.* **IGO Relations** *UNESCO (#20322).* Secretariat at: *UNESCO Office, Montevideo – Regional Bureau for Sciences in Latin America and the Caribbean (#20314).* [2019/XJ4821/E]

♦ Red Latinoamericana y del Caribe para la Conservación de los Murciélagos (RELCOM) 18703

Latin American and Caribbean Network for the Conservation of Bats

General Coordinator address not obtained.

History Aug 2007. Current statutes adopted 2011. **Aims** Ensure the persistence of healthy and viable bat species and populations in Latin America; ensure that their importance is known and appreciated. **Structure** Board. **Activities** Advocacy/lobbying/activism; events/meetings; training/education. **Events** *Latin American and Caribbean Triennial Bat Congress* Mérida (Mexico) 2022, *Latin American and Caribbean Triennial Bat Congress* Mérida (Mexico) 2020, *Latin American and Caribbean Triennial Bat Congress* San Salvador (El Salvador) 2017, *Latin American and Caribbean Triennial Bat Congress* Quito (Ecuador) 2014. **Publications** *Boletín de la Red Latinoamericana y del Caribe para la Conservación de los Murciélagos* in Spanish.
Members Full in 24 countries and territories:
Argentina, Aruba, Bolivia, Bonaire Is, Brazil, Chile, Colombia, Costa Rica, Cuba, Curaçao, Dominican Rep, Ecuador, El Salvador, Guatemala, Honduras, Mexico, Nicaragua, Panama, Paraguay, Peru, Puerto Rico, Trinidad-Tobago, Uruguay, Venezuela.
[2020/AA0394/D]

- ♦ Red Latinoamericana y del Caribe contra la Explotación Sexual de Mujeres, Niñas y Niños / see Coalition Against Trafficking in Women – Latin America (#04048)

♦ Red Latinoamericana y del Caribe para la Democracia (RedLad) . . . 18704

Latin American and Caribbean Network for Democracy

Secretariat Calle 69 no 4-68, Of 202 Edif XUE, Bogota 110231, Bogota DC, Colombia. E-mail: comunicaciones@redlad.org – secretariado@redlad.org.
URL: http://www.redlad.org/

History 2008, Massachusetts (USA). 2008, in the State of Massachusetts (USA). EU Transparency Register: 496874434912-19. **Aims** Provide support and solidarity to individuals and groups in situations where democracy is in danger. **Structure** Coordination Board, comprising General Coordinator, 3 Sub-Coordinators and Executive Director. Sub-Region Coordination Board, divided in: Mexico and Central America; Andean; South; Caribbean; North America; Special Regions. Permanent Secretariat located in Costa Rica. **Finance** Donations from organizations, *National Endowment for Democracy (NED),* and governments of Canada (National Endowment for Democracy) and Taiwan. **Activities** Initiates causes and complaints of violations of human rights; reports acts of unconstitutional and undemocratic actions; serves as a permanent observatory in each of the countries of the region in terms of democracy and human rights; monitors fundamental freedoms; publicizes human rights violations; organizes meetings; monitors elections. Themes: World Movement for Democracy (WMD); Council for a Community of Democracies (CCD); Indigenous Peoples and Movements and Afrodescendents; Gender Issues; Youth Movement; Research and Training; Inter Institutional Affairs. **Events** *Assembly* Tegucigalpa (Honduras) 2013, *Assembly* Rosario (Argentina) 2011. **Publications** *RedLad Newsletter* (4 a year). Press releases.
Members Organizations (250) in 22 countries:
Argentina, Bolivia, Brazil, Canada, Chile, Colombia, Cuba, Dominican Rep, Ecuador, El Salvador, Guatemala, Haiti, Honduras, Mexico, Nicaragua, Panama, Paraguay, Peru, Switzerland, Uruguay, USA, Venezuela.
IGO Relations Member of: Civil Society Forum of *OAS (#17629).* **NGO Relations** Formal contact with: *Council for a Community of Democracies (CCD); World Movement for Democracy (#21661).* [2022/XJ1960/E]

- ♦ Red Latinoamericana y del Caribe para la Investigación y el Desarrollo de las Musaceas (#18389)
- ♦ Red Latinoamericana y Caribeña contra la Explotación Sexual de Mujeres y Niñas / see Coalition Against Trafficking in Women – Latin America (#04048)

♦ Red Latinoamericana y Caribeña por la Defensa de los Derechos de los Niños, Niñas y Adolescentes (REDLAMYC) 18705

Latin-American and Caribbean Network to Defend the Rights of Children and Adolescents

Exec Sec Av México Coyoacan 350, Col General Anaya, Delegación Benito Juarez, Distrito Federal, 03340 Mexico City CDMX, Mexico. T. +525556016278. E-mail: info@redlamyc.org.
URL: http://www.redlamyc.info/

History Jun 2000, New York NY (USA), during First Substantive Session of the Preparatory Committee, by NGOs and NGO Networks participating in the preparatory process for the Special Session for Children of the General Assembly of the United Nations. Subsequently extended to allow full participation of organized civil society of the region in: the Special Session for Children; follow up of commitments undertaken in the resulting document; guaranteeing full validity of children and adolescents' rights within the framework of *United Nations Convention on the Rights of the Child (CRC, 1989).* **Structure** Executive Secretary. Sub-Regions (3), each with Coordinator: Andean; Central American and Caribbean; Southern Cone / Brazil. Coordination Teams. **Languages** Spanish. **Staff** 2.00 FTE, paid. **Finance** Support from NGOs and international agencies (not specified). No fixed annual budget. **Activities** Projects/programmes; events/meetings. **Events** *Annual Assembly* Santiago (Chile) 2015, *Annual Assembly* Mexico 2014, *Congress on the Rights of Children and Adolescents* Puebla (Mexico) 2014, *Congress on the Rights of Children and Adolescents* Barcelona (Spain) 2007. **Publications** *La Convención en un Lenguaje Amigable.* Studies; documents.
Members Organizations in 19 countries:
Argentina, Bolivia, Brazil, Chile, Colombia, Costa Rica, Cuba, Dominican Rep, Ecuador, El Salvador, Guatemala, Honduras, Mexico, Nicaragua, Panama, Paraguay, Peru, Uruguay, Venezuela.
NGO Relations Member of: *Child Rights Connect (#03884); International Coalition for the Optional Protocol to the Convention on the Rights of the Child on a Communications Procedure (Ratify OP3CRC, #12617); Movimiento Mundial por la Infancia de Latinoamérica y El Caribe (MMI-LAC, #16873).*
[2015.07.22/XJ4343/F]

- ♦ Red Latinoamericana y Caribeña de Jóvenes por los Derechos Sexuales y Reproductivos (#16289)
- ♦ Red Latinoamericana de Centros y Programas de Escritura (unconfirmed)

♦ Red Latinoamericana de Ciencias Biológicas (RELAB) 18706

Latin American Network of Biological Sciences – Réseau latinoaméricain de sciences biologiques – Rede Latinoamericana de Ciencias Biológicas

Regional Coordinator Univ Nacl Autonoma de Mexico, Inst de Fisiologia Celular, Dept de Bioquimica y Biologia Estructural, Apartado Postal 70-242, CP 04500 Mexico City CDMX, Mexico. T. +525556225631. Fax +525556225630.
Pres Asesor Relaciones Internacionales Univ de Chile, Avda Independencia 102 7 / 3er / piso / Sector E, 8380453 Santiago, Santiago Metropolitan, Chile. T. +5629786255. Fax +5627376320.
Contact address not obtained.
URL: http://relab.biologia.ucr.ac.cr/

History 1975. Founded at the initiative of scientists from the region with the signature of the UNDP/UNESCO project RLA/75/047 by the Governments of Bolivia, Chile, Colombia, Ecuador and Peru. Former names and other names: *Programa de Biotecnologia para Entrenamiento de Posgrado en Ciencias Biológicas* – former. **Aims** Accelerate scientific and technological development of participating countries in the field of basic biological sciences; promote scientific research in biological problems related to development and well-being of peoples of the region; stimulate technical cooperation among participating countries through collaboration of biologists in their endeavours of research and training. **Structure** Regional Executive Council (REC); National Committees (NC); Regional Directive Council (CDR); President and Regional Coordinator. Regional biological societies (5): *Asociación Latinoamericana de Genética (ALAG, #02225); Latin American Association* *of Pharmacology (LAP, #16249); Latin American Association of Physiological Sciences (#16250); Asociación Latinoamericana de Botanica (ALB, #02187); Pan American Association for Biochemistry and Molecular Biology (PABMB, #18080).* **Languages** Portuguese, Spanish. **Staff** 4.00 FTE, voluntary. **Finance** Sources: members' dues. Other sources: activities partially supported by contributions from *UNESCO (#20322); International Council for Science (ICSU, inactive); UNU Programme for Biotechnology in Latin America and the Caribbean (UNU/BIOLAC, see: #20642); InterAmerican Network of Academies of Science (IANAS, #11441)*; national institutions in member countries. No fixed budget. **Activities** Events/meetings; networking/liaising; training/education. **Events** *Symposium* Panama (Panama) 2015, *Symposium* Montevideo (Uruguay) 2013, *Symposium* Santiago (Chile) 2011, *Symposium* Cuernavaca (Mexico) 2009, *Workshop on molecular biology of viral diseases* Punta del Este (Uruguay) 2009. **Publications** *Boletin RELAB* (2 a year). *El Financiamiento de la Investigación en Ciencias Biológicas en América Latina* (1993); *La Formación, Retención y Recuperación de Recursos Humanos en Ciencias Biológicas para América Latina* (1992); *La Biologia como Instrumento de Desarrollo para América Latina* (1990); *Bioquimica en América del Sur y España: Directorio de Investigadores en Bioquimica.* Proceedings.

Members Membership open to all Latin American and Caribbean countries and to regional associations and societies in the field of biological sciences. Governments and scientific communities of 12 countries:
Argentina, Bolivia, Brazil, Chile, Colombia, Costa Rica, Cuba, Honduras, Mexico, Panama, Peru, Venezuela.

IGO Relations Permanent Observers: *International Centre for Genetic Engineering and Biotechnology (ICGEB, #12494); OAS (#17629); UNESCO (#20322).* **NGO Relations** Permanent Observer: *International Council for Science (ICSU, inactive).* [2022/XF2820/F]

♦ Red Latinoamericana de Comercialización Comunitaria (RELACC) . 18707

Latin American Network for Community Marketing

Exec Dir Av Rumichaca S26-365, y Moro Moro, Quito, Ecuador. T. +59322670925 – +59322674776. E-mail: info@relacc-la.org.
URL: http://www.relacc-la.org/

History 1991. **Aims** Contribute to building a just and fraternal society by strengthening the organizations participating in the network through common *marketing.* **Structure** General Assembly; Executive Secretariat; National Coordinations. **Finance** Members' dues. Grants. **Events** *Instrumentos financieros y comercializacion comunitaria* Quito (Ecuador) 1996, *Continental meeting / Latin American Meeting* Quito (Ecuador) 1995, *Latin American Meeting* Quito (Ecuador) 1991. **Publications** *RELACC Relata* (periodical). Meeting reports.

Members Participating organizations in 17 countries:
Argentina, Bolivia, Brazil, Chile, Colombia, Costa Rica, Ecuador, El Salvador, Guatemala, Honduras, Mexico, Nicaragua, Panama, Paraguay, Peru, Uruguay, Venezuela.

NGO Relations Institutional member of: *Society for International Development (SID, #19581).* Also member of: *World Fair Trade Organization (WFTO, #21396).* [2019/XF2644/F]

♦ Red Latinoamericana de Composición de Alimentos (LATINFOODS) 18708

Pres University of Bio Bio, Avda. Collao 1202, Casilla 5-C, 405 1381 Concepción, Bio Bío, Chile.
Vice-Pres address not obtained.
URL: http://latinfoods.inta.cl/

History as the Latin American arm of *International Network of Food Data Systems (INFOODS, #14271).* **Structure** Assembly; Executive Committee; Subregional centres (2): MESOCARIBEFOODS; SAFOODS. **Publications** *Circular.*

Members Full in 19 countries:
Argentina, Bolivia, Brazil, Chile, Colombia, Costa Rica, Cuba, Dominican Rep, Ecuador, El Salvador, Guatemala, Honduras, Mexico, Nicaragua, Panama, Paraguay, Peru, Uruguay, Venezuela. [2022.02.15/XJ4990/E]

♦ Red Latinoamericana Contra el Libre Comercio (internationally oriented national body)

♦ Red Latinoamericana Contra Represas y por los Rios, sus Comunidades y el Agua (REDLAR) 18709

Latin American Network for Rivers, River Communities and Water

Contact address not obtained. E-mail: redlar.org@gmail.com.

History 2002, Guatemala. **Events** *Meeting* Guatemala 2013, *Meeting* El Salvador 2007, *Meeting* Guatemala 2005, *Meeting* El Salvador 2004, *Meeting* Honduras 2003.

Members in 12 countries:
Argentina, Brazil, Chile, Colombia, Costa Rica, Ecuador, El Salvador, Honduras, Mexico, Nicaragua, Panama, Uruguay. [2016/XM2686/F]

♦ Red Latinoamericana de Cooperación Técnica en Parques Nacionales, otras Areas Protegidas, Flora y Fauna Silvestres (#20117)
♦ Red Latinoamericana de Coordinación y Promoción de Tecnologia Apropiada (inactive)

♦ Red Latinoamericana de Desarrollo de Capacidades para la Gestión Integrada del Agua (LA-WETnet) 18710

Contact Billinghurst 470, Planta Alta, Oficina 16, San Isidro, B1642BDJ Buenos Aires, Argentina. T. +541147233948. Fax +541147233948. E-mail: mschreider@gmail.com – parismarta@gmail.com.
URL: https://lawetnet.org/

Aims Acts as focal point for regional *capacity building* activities in the field of integrated *water resources* management in Latin America. **Structure** General Assembly. Steering Committee. **Publications** *LA-WETnet Newsletter.*

Members Full in 12 countries:
Argentina, Bolivia, Brazil, Colombia, Costa Rica, Ecuador, Guatemala, Honduras, Mexico, Peru, Uruguay, Venezuela.

NGO Relations Member of: *Network for Capacity Building in Integrated Water Resources Management (CAP-Net, #17000).* [2020/XJ2390/F]

♦ Red Latinoamericana sobre Desarrollo Sostenible de Montañas (#16350)

♦ Red Latinoamericana sobre Deuda, Desarrollo y Derechos (LATINDADD) 18711

Latin American Network on Debt, Development and Rights

Co-Pres Calle Daniel Olaechea 175, Jesús Maria, Lima, Peru. T. +5112076856. Fax +5112076840. E-mail: latindadd@latindadd.org.
Co-Pres address not obtained.
URL: http://www.latindadd.org/

History Founded as *Estrategia Andina, Centroamericana y Amazónica (Red ACA)*, by organizations from Bolivia, Brazil, Peru, Ecuador, Honduras, Colombia and Nicaragua. Current title adopted in 2005. **Aims** Promote a new international financial architecture based on respect for human rights; promote tax justice which through progressive growth to new levels in tax collection and public spending. **Structure** General Assembly (annual); Presidency; Board. Working Groups (5); Headquarters in Lima (Peru). **Languages** Spanish. **Staff** 9.00 FTE, paid. **Activities** Advocacy/lobbying/activism; knowledge management/information dissemination; training/education; research/documentation. **Events** *Conference* Lima (Peru) 2014, *Civil society forum* Doha (Qatar) 2008. **Publications** *Economia Critica.*

Members (21) in 12 countries:
Argentina, Bolivia, Brazil, Colombia, Costa Rica, Ecuador, El Salvador, Guatemala, Honduras, Mexico, Nicaragua, Peru.

NGO Relations Member of: *The Reality Of Aid (ROA, #18626); Red de Justicia Fiscal de América Latina y el Caribe; Tax Justice Network (TJN, #20100).* Cooperates with: *European Network on Debt and Development (EURODAD, #07891); Financial Transparency Coalition (FTC, #09772).* [2016.10.26/XM3621/D]

♦ Red Latinoamericana de Documentación e Información en Administración Pública (see: #16294)
♦ Red Latinoamericana de Educación y Capacitación en Recursos Hidricos (#16393)
♦ Red Latinoamericana para la Educación y la Capacitación en Tecnologia Nuclear (#16353)

♦ Red Latinoamericana para Educación e Investigación en Derechos Humanos (RedLEIDH) 18712

Latin American Human Rights Education and Research Network

Contact c/o CERLAC, York Univ, 800 Kaneff Tower, 4700 Keele St, North York ON M3J 1P3, Canada. T. +14167365237. Fax +14167365737.

History 2004, by *Centre for Research on Latin America and the Caribbean (CERLAC).* **Aims** Promote human rights education, applied research and capacity-building in the region. **Structure** Board of Directors. Project Coordinator; Technical Coordinator. **Staff** 2.00 FTE, paid. **Finance** Grant from: *Canadian International Development Agency (CIDA, inactive).* **NGO Relations** Founding partners include: *Instituto Interamericano de Derechos Humanos (IIDH, #11334); Latin American Institute for and Alternative Society and an Alternative Law (ILSA).* [2014.02.07/XM1927/F]

♦ Red Latinoamericana de Epidemiologia Clinica (#16298)
♦ Red Latinoamericana de Estudios de Traducción e Interpretación (unconfirmed)

♦ Red Latinoamericana de Información Teologica (RLIT) 18713

Latin American Theological Information Network

Coordinator Instituto Teológico, Beato Roque Gonzalez 2049, Casilla 336, 3360 Oberá, Argentina. T. +543755421863. Fax +543755421863.
URL: http://www.ibiblio.org/rlit/

History 1994. Previously also referred to as *Theological Libraries of Latin America (LATIN).* **Aims** Encourage research and diffusion of theological information in Latin America; promote inter-library cooperation among Latin American theological institutions. **Structure** Coordinating Group. **Events** *Biennial Conference* Buenos Aires (Argentina) 2006, *Biennial Conference* Havana (Cuba) 2002, *Biennial Conference* Quito (Ecuador) 2000, *Biennial Conference* La Paz (Bolivia) 1998, *Biennial Conference* San José (Costa Rica) 1996. **Publications** *Boletin del Bibliotecario Teologico Latinoamericano.*

Members in 11 countries:
Bolivia, Brazil, Colombia, Costa Rica, Cuba, Ecuador, Guatemala, Honduras, Mexico, Nicaragua, USA.

NGO Relations *European Theological Libraries (#08906).* [2010/XF6248/F]

♦ Red Latinoamericana de Jueces (REDLAJ) 18714

Latin-American Network of Judges – Rede Latino-Americana de Juizes

Secretariat C/ Antônio de Albuquerque 1159, 1o Piso, Barrio de Lourdes, Belo Horizonte MG, 30112-011, Brazil. Fax +553121040995. E-mail: contacto@red-laj.net.
URL: https://www.red-laj.net/

History 24 Nov 2006, Barcelona (Spain). **Aims** Bring together Latin American judges to develop mechanisms for judicial cooperation and integration based on a framework of trust and collective intelligence. **Structure** Officers: President; Vice-President; 4 Vice-Presidents (Financial; Institutional Relations; Higher Studies and Research; Human Rights) Regional Vice-Presidents (South America; Central America, Caribbean and Mexico) and Secretary-General. **Languages** Portuguese, Spanish. **Activities** Develops activities for judicial cooperation between the judiciary and directly between judges. Promotes conferences, courses and exchange of judicial authorities. **Events** *Congress* Madrid (Spain) 2014, *Congress* Lima (Peru) 2011, *Congress* Cartagena de Indias (Colombia) 2010, *Congress* Fortaleza (Brazil) 2009, *Congress* Santiago (Chile) 2008. **Members** Judges (over 500) in 19 countries. Membership countries not specified. **NGO Relations** Founding member of: *Escuela Judicial de América Latina (EJAL, #05537).* [2021/XM3674/F]

♦ Red Latinoamericana de Lombricultura (unconfirmed)

♦ Red Latinoamericana de Maestrias en Derechos y Politicas Sociales de Infancia y Adolescencia (RMI) 18715

Latin American Network of Masters in Children's Rights

Contact address not obtained. E-mail: info@redmaestrias.org.
URL: http://www.redmaestriasinfancia.org/

History 2002, by Latin-American universities and *Rädda Barnen – Save the Children Sweden.*

Members Organizations in 5 countries:
Bolivia, Colombia, Ecuador, Nicaragua, Peru.

NGO Relations Cooperates with: *Children's Rights European Academic Network (CREAN, #03878).* [2012/XJ1082/E]

♦ Red Latinoamericana de las Mujeres del Sector Pesquero (#17046)
♦ Red Latinoamericana Mujeres Transformando la Economia (#16395)
♦ Red Latinoamericana de Nanotecnologia y Sociedad (#16349)
♦ Red Latinoamericana de Organizaciones de Cuenca (#16351)
♦ Red Latinoamericana de Portales Educativos (unconfirmed)

♦ Red Latinoamericana para la Prevención del Genocidio y Atrocidades Masivas (La RED) 18716

Latin American Network for Genocide and Mass Atrocity Prevention – Rede Latino-Americana para a Prevenção do Genocidio e Atrocidades Massivas

Sec Inst Auschwitz para la Paz y la Reconciliación, 2 West 45th St, Ste 1602, New York NY 10036, USA. T. +12125752605. Fax +12125752654.
URL: http://redlatinoamericana.org/

History Launched Mar 2012, as an initiative led by the governments of Argentina and Brazil. **Aims** Provide a regional forum to implement national and regional initiatives aimed at preventing genocide. **Structure** Technical Secretariat hosted by *Auschwitz Institute for the Prevention of Genocide and Mass Atrocities.* **Activities** Training/education; capacity building.

Members Representatives of state institutions from 17 countries:
Argentina, Brazil, Chile, Colombia, Costa Rica, Dominican Rep, Ecuador, El Salvador, Guatemala, Honduras, Mexico, Nicaragua, Panama, Paraguay, Peru, Uruguay, Venezuela. [2017/XM4971/F]

♦ Red Latinoamericana de Productores Independientes de Arte Contemporaneo / see Red de Promotores Culturales de Latinoamérica y el Caribe (#18727)

♦ Red Latinoamericana de Psoriasis (LATINAPSO) 18717

Rede Latinoamericana de Psoriase

Contact c/o AEPSO, Av de Mayo Nro 749, Piso 8 – Dpto 42, Buenos Aires, Argentina. E-mail: contacto@latinapso.org.
URL: http://www.latinapso.org/

Events *Meeting* Buenos Aires (Argentina) 2010.

Members Full in 7 countries:
Argentina, Brazil, Panama, Peru, Puerto Rico, Uruguay, Venezuela. [2019/XJ2327/D]

♦ Red Latinoamericana de Quimica (RELAQ) 18718

Latin American Chemical Network (LAChIN)

Coordinator CINVESTAV, Av Instituto Politécnico Nacional 2508, Col San Pedro Zacatenco, CP 07360, 07360 Mexico City CDMX, Mexico. E-mail: mexicayolt@relaq.mx.
URL: http://www.relaq.mx/

History 1995, Mexico. Proposed by *'Academia Mexicana de Ciencias – Mexican Academy of Sciences'.* **Aims** Disseminate chemical information, its geographical location and means of access; promote exchange of information between countries of the region; establish and strengthen links between scientific-academic systems and the *industrial* sector. **Languages** Spanish. **Finance** Supported by: Academia Mexicana de Ciencias; *OAS (#17629)*; Centro de Investigación y de Estudios Avanzados. **Events** *International congress on chemistry and chemical engineering* Havana (Cuba) 2004. **Publications** Information Services: Maintains database. [2017.03.15/XF5291/F]

♦ Red Latinoamericana de Recicladores (unconfirmed)
♦ Red Latinoamericana de Reproducción Asistida (#16315)

♦ Red Latinoamericana de Servicios de Extensión Rural (RELASER) . . 18719

Exec Sec Andrés de Fuenzalida 17, Oficina 22, Providencia, 751 0077 Santiago, Santiago Metropolitan, Chile. T. +56222359466. E-mail: secretariat@relaser.org.
URL: http://www.relaser.org/

History Oct 2010, Santiago (Chile). Founded by *Global Forum for Rural Advisory Services (GFRAS, #10378).* **Structure** Executive Committee; Executive Secretariat. **Finance** Annual budget: 240,000 USD.

Members Individual; Institutional.
Deutsche Gesellschaft für Internationale Zusammenarbeit (GIZ); FAO (#09260); Inter-American Institute for Cooperation on Agriculture (IICA, #11434).

NGO Relations Partner of (1): *Access Agriculture (#00047).* [2020/AA1258/F]

♦ Red Latinoamericana de Socio-Economia Solidaria (Red LASES) .. 18720
Réseau latinoaméricain de socio-economie solidaire

Contact Fac Ciencias Económicas UBA, Avenida Córdoba 2122, 1120 AAQ Buenos Aires, Argentina.
URL: http://redlases.org/

History 4 Dec 1999, Buenos Aires (Argentina).
Members in 14 countries:
Argentina, Bolivia, Brazil, Chile, Colombia, Costa Rica, Ecuador, El Salvador, Honduras, Mexico, Paraguay, Peru, Uruguay, Venezuela.
NGO Relations Member of: *Intercontinental Network for the Promotion of the Social Solidarity Economy (INPSSE, #11463).* [2012/XM1899/F]

- ♦ Red Latinoamericana de TMC / see Network for an Economical and Ecological Habitat (#17007)
- ♦ **RedLEIDH** Red Latinoamericana para Educación e Investigación en Derechos Humanos (#18712)
- ♦ Red Liberal de América Latina (unconfirmed)
- ♦ Red de Macrouniversidades públicas de América Latina y el Caribe (#17047)
- ♦ Red-MAMLa – Red de Mujeres de Autoridades Maritimas de Latinoamérica (unconfirmed)
- ♦ Red MC / see Red Mercociudades (#18721)
- ♦ Red Mediterranea de Bosques Modelo (#16662)
- ♦ Red Mediterranea de Comunicadores Forestales (unconfirmed)
- ♦ Red Mediterranea de Organismos de Cuenca (#16664)

♦ Red Mercociudades (MC) 18721
Merco Cities Network

Tech Secretariat Luis Piera 1992, Edif Mercosur, 11200 Montevideo, Uruguay. T. +59824136624. E-mail: comunicastpm@mercociudades.org.
URL: http://www.mercociudades.org/

History 7 Mar 1995, Asunción (Paraguay). Known also under the initials *Red MC.* **Aims** Strengthen integration to ensure development of cities and welfare in South America. **Structure** Secretariat rotates. **Languages** Portuguese, Spanish. **Finance** Members cities' contributions. **Events** *Seminar on opportunities to finance Southern Cone cities* Santiago (Chile) 2001, *International seminar of cultural policy* Rio de Janeiro (Brazil) 2000.
Members in 10 countries:
Argentina, Bolivia, Brazil, Chile, Colombia, Ecuador, Paraguay, Peru, Uruguay, Venezuela.
NGO Relations Member of: *Global Taskforce of Local and Regional Governments (Global Taskforce, #10622).* [2019.02.20/XF5715/F]

- ♦ Red de MicroFinanzas (#16746)
- ♦ Red Miqueas / see Micah Global (#16741)
- ♦ RED-M / see Red Iberoamericana de Evaluación y Decisión Multicriterio (#18666)
- ♦ **RED-M** Red Iberoamericana de Evaluación y Decisión Multicriterio (#18666)

♦ Red de Mujeres Afrolatinoamericanas y Afrocaribeñas y la Diaspora 18722
Network of Afro-Latin American and Afro-Caribbean Women

Contact address not obtained. T. +50522442223. Fax +50522442223. E-mail: comuni@mujeresafro.org.
URL: http://www.mujeresafro.org/

NGO Relations *Latin American and Caribbean Feminist Network Against Domestic and Sexual Violence (#16277).* [2015/XF6510/F]

- ♦ Red de Mujeres de Autoridades Maritimas de Latinoamérica (unconfirmed)
- ♦ Red de Mujeres del Consejo de Educación de Adultos de América Latina / see Red de Educación Popular entre Mujeres de América Latina y el Caribe (#18647)

♦ Red de Mujeres Latinoamericanas y del Caribe en Gestion de Organizaciones (Women in Management) 18723
REDWIM Network

Address not obtained.
URL: http://www.wim-network.org/

History Jan 1998. Established following a training, 1997, organized by *Swedish International Development Cooperation Agency (Sida).* Former names and other names: *WIM Network* – former. **Aims** Enhance the capabilities and opportunities of women in organizational management through provision of training and management consulting with a focus on gender. **Structure** Management Team. **Events** *International Meeting* Cali (Colombia) 2019. **NGO Relations** Member of (1): *International Organisation for Cooperation in Evaluation (IOCE, #14426).* [2014/XJ8542/F]

- ♦ Red de Mujeres Parlamentarias de las Américas (#17065)
- ♦ Red de Mujeres Trabajadoras Sexuales de Latinoamérica y El Caribe / see Red de Trabajadoras Sexuales de América Latina y el Caribe (#18731)
- ♦ Red Mundial de las Ciudades Portuarias (#02751)
- ♦ Red Mundial Crescendo (#04950)
- ♦ Red Mundial de Emisoras de Televisión Indígena (#21580)
- ♦ Red Mundial de Mujeres por los Derechos Reproductivos (#21019)
- ♦ Red Mundial de la OMS de Ciudades y Comunidades Amigables con las Personas Mayores (#20937)
- ♦ Red Mundial de Personas con VIH y SIDA (#10494)
- ♦ Red Mundial de Reservas de la Biosfera (#21669)
- ♦ RED NOSES Clowndoctors / see Red Noses Clowndoctors International (#18724)

♦ Red Noses Clowndoctors International (RNI) 18724
CEO Wattgasse 48, 1170 Vienna, Austria. T. +431318031311. E-mail: smile@rednoses.eu.
External Relations Manager address not obtained.
URL: http://www.rednoses.eu/

History 1994, Austria. Former names and other names: *RED NOSES Clowndoctors* – former (1994 to 2003). Registration: Republik Österreich Firmenbuch, No/ID: 5863473, Start date: 1 May 2003, Austria. **Aims** Bring humour and laughter to people in need of joy through the art and philosophy of professional clowning; help people discover and rediscover moments of happiness, especially in times and places of crisis and hardship; contribute to a healthier and more humane world. **Structure** Managing Board; Advisory Board; Board of Experts; Medical Advisory Board; Humour Ambassadors. **Languages** Arabic, Danish, English, French, German, Italian, Romanian, Spanish. **Staff** 600.00 FTE, paid. **Finance** Sources: donations; fundraising; grants. Annual budget: 20,000,000 EUR. **Activities** Advocacy/lobbying/activism; awareness raising; capacity building; certification/accreditation; events/meetings; guidance/assistance/consulting; healthcare; humanitarian/emergency aid; monitoring/evaluation; networking/liaising; research/documentation; training/education. Europe & Middle East. **Events** *Healthcare Clowning International Meeting* Netherlands 2021, *Healthcare Clowning International Meeting* Vienna (Austria) 2018. **Publications** Articles.
Members Organizations in 11 countries and territories:
Austria, Croatia, Czechia, Germany, Hungary, Jordan, Lithuania, Palestine, Poland, Slovakia, Slovenia.
NGO Relations Member of (1): *World Patients Alliance (WPA).* [2023/XM7988/F]

- ♦ Red de Objectores Latinoamericanos (inactive)
- ♦ **RéDoc** Réseau international d'écoles doctorales en sociologie/sciences sociales (#18892)
- ♦ Red Operativa de Cooperación Regional de Autoridades Maritimas – Central América (no recent information)

♦ Red Operativa de Cooperación Regional de Autoridades Maritimas de Sudamérica, México, Panama y Cuba (ROCRAM) 18725
Operative Network of Regional Cooperation among Maritime Authorities of South America, Mexico, Panama and Cuba

SG Diretoria de Portos e Costas, Rua Teófilo Otoni 04 – Centro, Rio de Janeiro RJ, CEP 20090-080, Brazil. T. +52138705193 – +52138705194. Fax +52138702134.
URL: http://www.rocram.net/

History 1983, Santiago (Chile), in the framework of *International Maritime Organization (IMO, #14102).* **Aims** Provide a system of cooperation among Latin American Maritime Authorities for the exchange of experience and best practices with a view to the effective implementation of the conventions and other instruments of the IMO. **Structure** Meeting of Maritime Authorities (every 2 years). Network Secretariat or Office of Secretary General, *SECROCRAM,* is the executive body of ROCRAM and rotates every 2 years between Maritime Authorities who are Network members. **Languages** Portuguese, Spanish. **Finance** Supported by such organizations as: IMO; *UNDP (#20292); United Nations Economic Commission for Latin America and the Caribbean (ECLAC, #20556).* **Activities** Under a Memorandum of Understanding with IMO, organizes regional training activities on maritime safety, marine environment protection, facilitation of international maritime traffic and maritime legislation. **Events** *Regional Workshop for Latin-American Countries to Implement and Ratify Treaties Dealing with Liability and Compensation* Buenos Aires (Argentina) 2018, *Biennial Meeting* Porlamar (Venezuela) 2000, *Biennial Meeting* Cartagena de Indias (Colombia) 1998, *Biennial Meeting* Guayaquil (Ecuador) 1997, *Extraordinary Meeting* London (UK) 1997.
Members Maritime Authorities of 13 countries:
Argentina, Bolivia, Brazil, Chile, Colombia, Cuba, Ecuador, Mexico, Panama, Paraguay, Peru, Uruguay, Venezuela.
IGO Relations Instrumental in setting up: *Operational Net of Regional Cooperation of Central American Maritime Authorities (ROCRAM-CA, no recent information).* [2010/XF3868/F*]

- ♦ Red ORBICOM / see ORBICOM – International Network of UNESCO Chairs in Communication (#17785)
- ♦ Red de Organizaciones de Cuenca de America del Norte (internationally oriented national body)
- ♦ Red de Organizaciones de X frágil (unconfirmed)
- ♦ Red Pacifico Asiatica del Corazón (#01923)

♦ Red Panda Network (RPN) 18726
Contact 494 W 10th Ave, Suite 7, Eugene OR 97401, USA. T. +18778542391. E-mail: info@redpandanetwork.org.
URL: http://www.redpandanetwork.org/

History 2007. A US 501(c)3 not-for-profit organization: EIN 26-1103671. **Aims** Ensure the survival of wild red pandas; preserve their habitat for future generations to study, experience and enjoy. **Structure** Board of Directors. **Activities** Research/documentation; training/education; advocacy/lobbying/activism. **NGO Relations** Member of: *International Union for Conservation of Nature and Natural Resources (IUCN, #15766).* Partners include: *European Association of Zoos and Aquaria (EAZA, #06283); Fondation Segré; International Centre for Integrated Mountain Development (ICIMOD, #12500); Mountain Institute, The (TMI); Rainforest Trust; World Association of Zoos and Aquariums (WAZA, #21208); World Wide Fund for Nature (WWF, #21922).* [2019.03.11/XM6795/F]

- ♦ Red Panlatina de Terminologia (#18901)
- ♦ **REDPARQUES** Red Latinoamericana de Cooperación Técnica en Parques Nacionales, otras Areas Protegidas, Flora y Fauna Silvestres (#20117)
- ♦ Red PLENTY – Alternativa Solidaria: Intercambio con Pueblos Indigenas / see alterNativa – Intercanvi amb Pobles Indigenes
- ♦ **RedPOP** Red de Popularización de la Ciencia y la Tecnologia para América Latina y el Caribe (#17057)
- ♦ Red de Popularización de la Ciencia y la Tecnologia para América Latina y el Caribe (#17057)
- ♦ Red de Postgrados en Administración y Politicas Públicas (see: #16294)

♦ Red de Promotores Culturales de Latinoamérica y el Caribe (La Red) 18727
Contact c/o Redlat Colombia, Calle 36 No 21-10, Piso 2, Bogota, Bogota DC, Colombia. Fax +5718050166. E-mail: info@redlat.org.
URL: http://www.redlat.org/

History 1991, as *Latin American Network of Independent Presenters of Contemporary Art – Red Latinoamericana de Productores Independientes de Arte Contemporaneo (La Red).* **Aims** Promote recognition of contemporary arts in Latin America; encourage exchange among artists dedicated to development of new forms and non-mainstream concepts in contemporary theatre, dance, performance and music. **Events** *Meeting / Annual Meeting* Caracas (Venezuela) 2006, *Annual Meeting* San Juan (Puerto Rico) 1998, *Annual meeting* La Paz (Bolivia) 1997.
Members Theatres, festivals and cultural centres (20) in 19 countries:
Argentina, Bolivia, Brazil, Chile, Colombia, Costa Rica, Cuba, Ecuador, El Salvador, Guatemala, Mexico, Nicaragua, Paraguay, Peru, Puerto Rico, Trinidad-Tobago, Uruguay, USA, Venezuela.
Included in the above, 1 organization listed in this Yearbook:
Centro Latinoamericano de Danza, Caracas (no recent information).
NGO Relations *The Rockefeller Foundation (#18966).* [2008/XF3598/F]

- ♦ Red de Radio Rural de los Paises en Desarrollo / see Farm Radio International (#09274)
- ♦ **La RED** Red Latinoamericana para la Prevención del Genocidio y Atrocidades Masivas (#18716)
- ♦ La Red / see Red de Promotores Culturales de Latinoamérica y el Caribe (#18727)
- ♦ **La Red** Red de Promotores Culturales de Latinoamérica y el Caribe (#18727)

♦ Red Regional de Organizaciones Civiles para las Migraciones (RROCM) 18728
Technical Secretariat REDNAM Costa Rica, San Pedro, Los Yoses, Oficentro Casa Alameda Of 7, San José, San José, San José, 1353-2050, Costa Rica. T. +50622808968. Fax +50622340182. E-mail: stcidehumrrocm@gmail.com – cidehum@gmail.com.
URL: http://www.rrocm.org/

History 1996. **Aims** Strive for protection, defense and promotion of human rights of migrants, refugees and their families, in places of origin, transit and destination, from a comprehensive and multidisciplinary perspective. **Structure** General Assembly; Executive Committee; Technical Secretariat; Working Groups. **Languages** English, French, Spanish. **Finance** Support from: *Alianza para las Migraciones en Centroamérica y México (CAMMINA); European Union (EU, #08967); Trocaire – Catholic Agency for World Development.*
Members Full in 11 countries:
Belize, Canada, Costa Rica, Dominican Rep, El Salvador, Guatemala, Honduras, Mexico, Nicaragua, Panama, USA.
Included in the above, 2 organizations listed in this Yearbook:
Centro Internacional para los Derechos Humanos de los Migrantes (CIDEHUM); Instituto Centroamericano de Estudios Sociales y Desarrollo (INCEDES, #11327).
IGO Relations *Regional Conference on Migration (RCM, #18769).* [2015/XJ8890/y/F]

- ♦ Red de Regiones y Areas Metropolitanas Europeas (#17023)
- ♦ Red Reino Unido-América Latina de Filosofía Política Analítica (unconfirmed)
- ♦ **Red RELATES** Red Europea y Latinoamericana de Escuelas Sistémicas (#18654)
- ♦ RED REOALCeI – Red académica internacional "Estudios Organizacionales en América Latina, el Caribe e Iberoamécia" (unconfirmed)
- ♦ REDRESS (internationally oriented national body)
- ♦ The Redress Trust / see REDRESS

♦ RedR International 18729
International Coordinator Lower Beer, Uplowman, Tiverton, EX16 7PF, UK. T. +441884821239.
Registered Office Ch de la Vigne-Noire 3, 1290 Versoix GE, Switzerland.
URL: http://www.redr.org/

History 1980, Basingstoke (UK). Founded by Peter Guthrie. Former names and other names: *Register of Engineers for Disaster Relief (RedR)* – former; *Registered Engineers for Disaster Relief* – alias. Registration: Swiss Civil Code, Start date: 1993. **Aims** Relieve suffering in *disasters* by selecting, training and providing effective relief personnel to *humanitarian* relief agencies world-wide. **Structure** General Assembly; Board of Directors; International Director/Coordinator. **Languages** English, French. **Staff** 1.00 FTE, paid. **Finance** Members' dues. **Activities** Humanitarian/emergency aid; knowledge management/information dissemination; training/education. **Events** *General Assembly* Amman (Jordan) 2022, *General Assembly* London (UK) 2008, *Annual General Assembly* Kuala Lumpur (Malaysia) 2007, *Emergency Personnel Network annual conference* Geneva (Switzerland) 2006, *Annual General Assembly* Sydney, NSW (Australia) 2006. **Publications** *Engineering in Emergencies – A Practical Guide for Relief Workers* (2001) – manual. Information Services: Provides technical advice and information.

Members Member organisations in 6 countries:
Australia, India, Indonesia, Malaysia, UK, USA.
IGO Relations *UNHCR (#20327).* **NGO Relations** Member of: *Inter-agency Network for Education in Emergencies (INEE, #11387).* On Governing Board of: *The Sphere Project (#19918). Water, Engineering and Development Centre (WEDC).* [2022.10.18/XF4586/**F**]

- ♦ **REDR** Red Europea de Desarrollo Rural (#07995)
- ♦ RedR / see RedR International (#18729)
- ♦ **REDR** Réseau européen de développement rural (#07995)
- ♦ **RED** Ruralité – Environnement – Développement (#19003)
- ♦ **RED** Rurality – Environment – Development (#19003)
- ♦ Red de Salud (see: #15807)
- ♦ Red de Salud de las Mujeres Latinoamericanas y del Caribe (#16288)
- ♦ **REDSAN-CPLP** Rede Regional da Sociedade Civil para a Segurança Alimentar e Nutricional na CPLP (#18648)
- ♦ Red Sea Conference (meeting series)
- ♦ Red Sea Mission Team / see ReachAcross
- ♦ Red Sea Team International / see ReachAcross
- ♦ Red de Seguimiento, Evaluación y Sistematización de América Latine y el Caribe (unconfirmed)

♦ Red de Seguridad y Defensa de América Latina (RESDAL) 18730

Security and Defense Network of Latin America

Exec Sec Av Corrientes 1785 – 5oj, 1042 Buenos Aires, Argentina. T. +541143713822. Fax +541143715522. E-mail: secretaria@resdal.org.
URL: http://www.resdal.org/

History 2001. **Aims** Promote the institutionalization of state security and defence functions within a framework of democracy, by strengthening *civilian* capacities. **Structure** Board. Executive Secretariat, based in Buenos Aires (Argentina). **Languages** English, Spanish. **Staff** 5.00 FTE, paid. **Activities** Knowledge management/information dissemination; research and development; financial and/or material support; training/education. **Events** *Conference of ministers of defense of the Americas* Quito (Ecuador) 2004, *Conference of ministers of defense of the Americas* Santiago (Chile) 2002, *Conference of ministers of defense of the Americas* Manaus (Brazil) 2000, *Conference of ministers of defense of the Americas* Cartagena de Indias (Colombia) 1998, *Conference of ministers of defense of the Americas* Bariloche (Argentina) 1996. **Publications** *Military Justice: between the reform and the permanence* (2010); *Women in the Armed and Police Forces: resolution 1325 and peace operations in Latin America* (2009, 2010); *Comparative Atlas of Defence in Latin America* (2005, 2007, 2008, 2010); *The Defence Budget in Latin America: the importance of transparency and Tools for an independent monitoring* (2004); *Parliamant and Defence in Latin America: the role of the committees* – in 2 vols, 2004, 2009.
Members Full (over 280) in 26 countries:
Argentina, Bolivia, Brazil, Canada, Chile, Colombia, Costa Rica, Cuba, Dominican Rep, Ecuador, El Salvador, Germany, Guatemala, Honduras, Mexico, Netherlands, Nicaragua, Paraguay, Peru, Portugal, Puerto Rico, Spain, Uruguay, USA, Venezuela.
IGO Relations Cooperates with: *Latin American Faculty of Social Sciences (#16316).* **NGO Relations** Member of: *Global Network of Women Peacebuilders (GNWP, #10503).* [2016/XF7122/**F**]

- ♦ Red de Servicios e Información en el Sector de la Construcción (#03351)
- ♦ Red de Servicios Micro Financieros / see MicroFinance Network (#16746)
- ♦ Red Sindical Internacional de Solidaridad y de Luchas (unconfirmed)
- ♦ Red de los Sistemas Nacionales de Inversión Pública de América Latina y el Caribe (unconfirmed)
- ♦ RedSNIP – Red de los Sistemas Nacionales de Inversión Pública de América Latina y el Caribe (unconfirmed)
- ♦ Red de la Sociedad Civil SUN (#20035)
- ♦ **REDS** Réseau européen droit et société (#07937)
- ♦ Red T (internationally oriented national body)
- ♦ Red de Terminologia / see Red Iberoamericana de Terminologia (#18685)
- ♦ Red T – Protecting Translators and Interpreters Worldwide / see Red T

♦ Red de Trabajadoras Sexuales de América Latina y el Caribe (REDTRASEX) 18731

Network of Women Sex Workers from Latin America and the Caribbean

Main Office Remedios de Escalada de San Martin 666, Lanus, Buenos Aires, Argentina. E-mail: secejecutiva@redtrasex.org.
URL: http://www.redtrasex.org/

History 1997. Also referred to as *Red de Mujeres Trabajadoras Sexuales de Latinoamérica y El Caribe.* **Aims** Promote and defend recognition of Women Sex Workers' (WSWs) *human rights* across Latin America and the Caribbean, with a focus on their labour rights and economic independence; achieve legal change on discriminatory norms and policies, and increase participation in decision-making spaces in order to raise visibility of WSWs'issues. **Structure** General Assembly (every 4 years); Board of Directors. Executive Secretariat, located in Buenos Aires (Argentina). **Languages** English, Spanish. **Staff** 1.00 FTE, paid. **Finance** Support from: *Deutsche Gesellschaft für Internationale Zusammenarbeit (GIZ); Frontline AIDS (#10007); Global Fund to Fight AIDS, Tuberculosis and Malaria (Global Fund, #10383); Global Fund for Women (GFW, #10384); Joint United Nations Programme on HIV/AIDS (UNAIDS, #16149); Mama Cash (#16560); Robert Carr civil society Networks Fund (RCNF, #18956); United Nations Population Fund (UNFPA, #20612).* Other sources: Spanish and Dutch Union Confederations; national and provincial HIV programmes; national women's program. **Activities** Advocacy/lobbying/activism; politics/policy/regulatory; awareness raising; monitoring/evaluation; research/documentation; training/education; publishing activities; guidance/assistance/consulting; capacity building. **Publications** *Manifesto on the Right to Sex Work and Women's Equality* (2018); *10 Years of Action* (2011). Manuals and guides; policy statements; audios and videos; research outcomes.
Members WSWs-led organizations in 14 countries:
Argentina, Brazil, Chile, Colombia, Costa Rica, Dominican Rep, El Salvador, Guatemala, Honduras, Mexico, Nicaragua, Panama, Paraguay, Peru.
IGO Relations Member of: *Horizontal Technical Cooperation Group of Latin America and the Caribbean on HIV/AIDS (HTGC, #10945); UN Women (#20724)*'s Civil Society Advisory Group for Latin America and the Caribbean. [2020.03.04/XM3593/**D**]

♦ Red de Transparencia y Acceso a la Información (RTA) 18732

Secretariat address not obtained. E-mail: secretariaejecutiva@cplt.cl – president.rta@inai.org.mx.
URL: https://redrta.org/

History 2011. Founded with the support of *International Bank for Reconstruction and Development (IBRD, #12317)* – World Bank and 5 countries. **Aims** Create a space for the exchange of experiences, dialogues and good practices in access to information and transparency so as to support the implementation and scope of these rights in the region.
Members Full in 16 countries:
Argentina, Bolivia, Brazil, Chile, Dominican Rep, Ecuador, El Salvador, Guatemala, Honduras, Mexico, Panama, Paraguay, Peru, Portugal, Spain, Uruguay.
Adherent members (4):
Fundación Internacional y para Iberoamérica de Administración y Politicas Públicas (FIIAPP, #10030); International Bank for Reconstruction and Development (IBRD, #12317); OAS (#17629); Red Federal de Transparencia y Acceso a la Información Pública, Argentina. [2022/AA2867/**D**]

- ♦ **REDTRASEX** Red de Trabajadoras Sexuales de América Latina y el Caribe (#18731)
- ♦ **Red ULAM** Union Latinoamericana de Mujeres (#20452)
- ♦ **REDUMATE** Red de Educación Matemática de América Central y El Caribe (#18646)

♦ Red por una América Latina Libre de Transgénicos (RALLT) 18733

Network for a Latin America Free of Transgenics

Secretariat c/o Acción Ecológica, Alejandro de Valdez N24 33 y Av La Gasca, Quito, Ecuador. E-mail: ebravo@rallt.org.
URL: http://www.rallt.org/

History 1999. Also referred to as *Network for a Genetic Engineered Free Latin America.* **Publications** *Boletin de la RALLT.* **NGO Relations** Endorses: *Ban Terminator Campaign (#03172).* [2007/XM1331/**F**]

- ♦ Red UNESCO de Bibliotecas Asociadas (#20311)
- ♦ Red UNIAL – Universo Audiovisual del Niño Latinoamericano (internationally oriented national body)
- ♦ Red Universitaria de Educación Continua de América Latina y el Caribe / see Red Universitaria de Educación Continua de Latinoamérica y Europa (#18734)

♦ Red Universitaria de Educación Continua de Latinoamérica y Europa (RECLA) 18734

Latin American and European Network of University Continuing Education

Contact Av Cra 9 No 132 – 28 Piso 3, Bogota, Bogota DC, Colombia. T. +573125844678. E-mail: secretaria@recla.org.
URL: http://www.recla.org/

History Bogota (Colombia). Statutes adopted Dec 1997. Former names and other names: *Red Universitaria de Educación Continua de América Latina y el Caribe (RECLA)* – former; *Latin American and Caribbean Network of University Continuing Education* – former; *Red de Educación Continua de Latinoamérica y Europa* – alias. **Aims** Promote development and growth of continuing education so as to obtain the highest standards of academic and administrative quality; contribute to development of a fairer and more balanced society. **Structure** Directive Committee. **Languages** English, Portuguese, Spanish. **Staff** 3.00 FTE, paid. **Finance** Sources: members' dues. **Activities** Events/meetings; training/education. **Events** *General Assembly* Guadalajara (Mexico) 2015, *General Assembly* Cartagena de Indias (Colombia) 2014, *General Assembly* Valencia (Spain) 2013, *General Assembly* Córdoba (Argentina) 2012, *General Assembly* San José (Costa Rica) 2011. **Publications** *REtos y CLAves de la Educación Continua.*
Members Individuals and universities in 17 countries:
Argentina, Bolivia, Brazil, Chile, Colombia, Costa Rica, Dominican Rep, El Salvador, Guatemala, Mexico, Nicaragua, Peru, Portugal, Puerto Rico, Spain, Uruguay, USA.
NGO Relations Partner of (1): *Asociación Universitaria Iberoamericana de Postgrado (AUIP, #02307).* [2022.02.08/XF4627/**F**]

- ♦ Red VIDA – Red Vigilancia Interamericana para la Defensa y Derecho al Agua (unconfirmed)
- ♦ Red Vigilancia Interamericana para la Defensa y Derecho al Agua (unconfirmed)
- ♦ **Red VIVSALUD** Red Interamericana de Vivienda Saludable (#18695)
- ♦ REDWG Monitoring Committee Secretariat – Regional Economic Development Working Group Monitoring Committee Secretariat (no recent information)
- ♦ REDWIM Network (#18723)
- ♦ Reebok Foundation / see Reebok Human Rights Foundation
- ♦ Reebok Human Rights Foundation (internationally oriented national body)
- ♦ REECA – Renewable Energy and Environmental Conservation Association in Developing Countries (inactive)
- ♦ Reed Midem (internationally oriented national body)
- ♦ Reed Midem Organization / see Reed Midem
- ♦ Rééducateurs Solidaires (internationally oriented national body)
- ♦ **REEEP** Renewable Energy and Energy Efficiency Partnership (#18837)
- ♦ REE / see The Federation of International Employers (#09644)
- ♦ **REEF** Roundtable for Europe's Energy Future (#18980)
- ♦ Reef-World Foundation (internationally oriented national body)
- ♦ REEI – Russian and East European Institute, Bloomington IN (internationally oriented national body)
- ♦ REELC / see European Society of Comparative Literature (#08561)
- ♦ **REEN** Research in Engineering Education Network (#18854)
- ♦ REESAO – Réseau pour l'excellence de l'enseignement supérieur en Afrique de l'Ouest (unconfirmed)
- ♦ REES – Center for Russian and East European Studies, Pittsburgh PA (internationally oriented national body)
- ♦ **REEV-Med** Réseau des établissements d'enseignement vétérinaire de la Méditerranée (#18871)
- ♦ REF / see RESULTS
- ♦ REFACOF – Réseau des Femmes Africaines pour la Gestion Communautaire des forêts (unconfirmed)
- ♦ **REFAMP** Réseau des femmes ministres africaines et parlementaires (#16988)
- ♦ REFCES – Réseau européen pour le perfectionnement du personnel de l'enseignement supérieur (inactive)
- ♦ **REFIPS** Réseau francophone international pour la promotion de la santé (#18883)
- ♦ **REFJ** Réseau européen de formation judiciaire (#07617)
- ♦ Reflective Insulation Manufacturers Association / see Reflective Insulation Manufacturers Association International (#18735)

♦ Reflective Insulation Manufacturers Association International (RIMA-I) 18735

Exec Dir PO Box 14174, Lenexa KS 66285, USA. T. +17854247115. E-mail: rima@rima.net.
URL: http://www.rimainternational.org/

History Founded 1978, as *Reflective Insulation Manufacturers Association (RIMA).* Current title adopted Apr 2008. Also known as *RIMA International.* **Aims** Develop and grow the reflective insulation, radiant barrier, interior radiation control coating (IRCC) and reflective fabric industries; be a reliable source of accurate and reliable information for building professionals and consumers alike; develop and work with building codes and other agencies and government entities to ensure reflectives are included and properly represented. **Structure** Board of Directors. **Staff** 1.00 FTE, paid. **Finance** Sources: members' dues. **Events** *Bi-Annual Membership Meetings* Orlando, FL (USA) 2024, *Bi-Annual Membership Meetings* Philadelphia, PA (USA) 2024, *Conference* Milan (Italy) 2023, *Bi-Annual Membership Meetings* Tampa, FL (USA) 2023, *Bi-Annual Membership Meetings* Washington, DC (USA) 2023. **Publications** *RIMA Newsletter.*
Members Manufacturers; Associate; Distributors. Manufacturers in 9 countries:
Argentina, Australia, Canada, Costa Rica, France, India, Korea Rep, Malaysia, USA.
Associate in 3 countries:
Canada, India, USA.
Distributors in 3 countries:
Japan, Norway, USA. [2019/XJ4953/**C**]

♦ Reflexology in Europe Network (RiEN) 18736

Sec Bovenover 59, 1025 Amsterdam, Netherlands. E-mail: sec.rien@gmail.com.
URL: http://www.reflexeurope.org/

History 1992. **Aims** Serve as a forum for the exchange of ideas, information and experience. **Structure** Board, comprising Chairman, Treasurer and Secretary. **Finance** Members' dues. **Activities** Working Groups (3): Brussels; Education; Research. **Events** *Annual General Meeting* Amsterdam (Netherlands) 2017, *Conference* Brussels (Belgium) 2016, *Conference* Funchal (Portugal) 2014, *Conference* Athens (Greece) 2013, *Conference* Echternach (Luxembourg) 2012. **Publications** *RiEN Newsletter.*
Members Full organizations; friend individuals. Members in 19 countries:
Belgium, Denmark, Estonia, France, Germany, Greece, Iceland, Ireland, Italy, Luxembourg, Netherlands, Norway, Poland, Portugal, Slovenia, Spain, Sweden, Switzerland, UK.
Included in the above, 1 organization listed in this Yearbook:
International Institute of Reflexology, Walkley (IIR). [2014/XM1685/**F**]

- ♦ **REFORC** Reformation Research Consortium (#18737)

♦ Reformation Research Consortium (REFORC) 18737

Contact Stichting Refor500, Hendric Stevinstraat 5, 3841 KB Harderwijk, Netherlands. E-mail: info@reforc.com.
URL: https://reforc.com/

History A department of Refo 500 Foundation (Netherlands). **Aims** Strengthen interdisciplinary research on Early Modern Christianity. **Structure** General Assembly; Board; Presidency; Secretariat. **Activities** Events/meetings; networking/liaising; research/documentation. **Events** *Annual Conference on Early Modern Christianity* Palermo (Italy) 2024, *Annual REFORC Conference on Early Modern Christianity* Berlin (Germany) 2022, *Annual Conference on Early Modern Christianity* Budapest (Hungary) 2021, *Annual RefoRC Conference* Lutherstadt Wittenberg (Germany) 2017, *Annual RefoRC Conference* Copenhagen (Denmark) 2016.
Members Institutions; Societies; Individuals. Members in 6 countries:
Belgium, Denmark, Germany, Romania, Switzerland, USA. [2021/AA2179/**C**]

♦ RE.FORM.E / see REFORME (#18738)

♦ REFORME 18738

Contact c/o FLC ASTURIAS, L'Alto'l Caleyu 2, 33170 Ribera de Arriba, Murcia, Spain. T. +34985928800. E-mail: reforme@flc.es.
URL: http://www.reforme.org/

History 1986. Full title: *Network for the Vocational Education and Training in the Construction Sector in Europe – Réseau pour la Formation Professionnelle dans le Secteur de la Construction en Europe – Red para la Formación Profesional en el Sector de la Construcción en Europa.* Also known by acronym *RE.FORM.E.* **Aims** Favour professionalization of young people, professionals and trainers, mainly in the fields of: *restoration* of *architectural heritage*; new *construction.* **Activities** Training/education; events/meetings. **Events** *Summit* Lecce (Italy) 2012, *Summit* Gijón (Spain) 2008, *Summit* Lisbon (Portugal) 2003, *Summit* Avignon (France) 1999, *Summit* Tilburg (Netherlands) 1996.
Members Organizations (11) in 9 countries:
Belgium, Finland, France, Germany, Italy, Portugal, Spain, Sweden, Switzerland. [2015/XJ9050/**F**]

♦ Reformed Church in Africa (internationally oriented national body)
♦ Reformed Church in America (internationally oriented national body)
♦ Reformed Presbyterian Global Alliance / see RP Global Alliance (#18993)
♦ **REFORMED** Regroupement Européen pour la FOrmation et la Reconnaissance des MEDecines non-conventionnelles (#18824)
♦ Reformierter Weltbund (inactive)
♦ **REFRAM** Réseau francophone des régulateurs des médias (#18885)
♦ **RÉF** Réseau international de Recherche en éducation et en formation (#18896)
♦ The Refrigeration Research Foundation / see World Food Logistics Organization
♦ RéFRI – Réseau Francophone de recherche sur l'intersexuation (unconfirmed)
♦ REFSQ – International Working Conference on Requirements Engineering: Foundation for Software Quality (meeting series)
♦ Refugee Children of the World (internationally oriented national body)

♦ Refugee Council 18739

Main Office PO Box 68614, London, E15 9DQ, UK. T. +442073466700. E-mail: marketing@refugeecouncil.org.uk.
URL: http://www.refugeecouncil.org.uk/

History 1951, as *British Refugee Council.* Registered in accordance with British law. UK Registered Charity: 1014576. **Aims** Make the UK a welcoming place of safety for people who seek refuge from *persecution* and *human rights* abuses abroad. **Structure** Board of Trustees. **Activities** Guidance/assistance/consulting; networking/liaising; training/education. **Events** *Annual General Meeting* London (UK) 1997, *Child care conference* London (UK) 1997, *Annual sixth-form conference* UK 1994, *International conference on elderly refugees* Noordwijkerhout (Netherlands) 1988. **Publications** Annual Report; briefings; reports; policy papers.
Members Full and Associate. National and international organizations (78), mainly based in the UK and including 12 organizations listed in this Yearbook:
Africa Educational Trust; Airey Neave Trust; Amnesty International (AI, #00801); International Tamil Refugee Network (no recent information); Jesuit Refugee Service (JRS, #16106); Joint Council for the Welfare of Immigrants (JCWI); Methodist Church Britain – World Church Office; Minority Rights Group International (MRG, #16820); Oxfam GB; Quaker Peace and Social Witness (QPSW, see: #10004); Refugee Studies Centre, Oxford (RSC); UK Council for International Student Affairs (UKCISA).
IGO Relations *International Organization for Migration (IOM, #14454); UNHCR (#20327).* Contacts with: *European Commission (EC, #06633).* **NGO Relations** Member of: *Crisis Action (#04957); Think Global – Development Education Association (DEA); European Council on Refugees and Exiles (ECRE, #06839); National Council for Voluntary Organizations (NCVO).* [2018.07.24/XF4991/y/**F**]

♦ Refugee Council of Australia (internationally oriented national body)
♦ Refugee Documentation Project / see Centre for Refugee Studies, York
♦ Refugee Education Sponsorship Program: Enhancing Communities Together / see Refugee Education Sponsorship Program International
♦ Refugee Education Sponsorship Program International (internationally oriented national body)
♦ Refugee Empowerment International (internationally oriented national body)
♦ Refugee Hub Europe (unconfirmed)

♦ Refugee and Migrant Education Network (RME Network) 18740

Pres address not obtained. E-mail: info@rmenetwork.org.
URL: https://rmenetwork.org/

History Founded following a conference organized by Being the Blessing Foundation and *International Federation of Catholic Universities (IFCU, #13381)*, Nov 2017. **Aims** Foster and expand education of refugees and migrants, as well as on human mobility. **Activities** Events/meetings; research/documentation; training/education. **Events** *International Conference* Rome (Italy) 2022.
Members Universities, NGOs and not-for-profit organizations (over 40) in 15 countries:
Argentina, Australia, Brazil, Chile, France, Germany, Holy See, India, Italy, Lebanon, Poland, Portugal, Spain, Ukraine, USA.
Caritas Internationalis (CI, #03580); International Federation of Catholic Universities (IFCU, #13381); Jesuit Refugee Service (JRS, #16106); Jesuit Worldwide Learning (JWS, #16108); NATAN Worldwide Disaster Relief (NATAN); Pax Romana, International Movement of Catholic Students (IMCS, #18268); Scalabrini International Migration Institute (SIMI, #19062). [2022/AA2999/**F**]

♦ Refugee Relief International (internationally oriented national body)
♦ Refugees Aid for West Africa (internationally oriented national body)
♦ Refugees International (internationally oriented national body)
♦ Refugees International Japan / see Refugee Empowerment International
♦ Refugee Studies Centre, Oxford (internationally oriented national body)
♦ Refugee Studies Programme, Oxford / see Refugee Studies Centre, Oxford

♦ Refugee Working Group (RWG) 18741

Contact address not obtained. T. +16139440563. Fax +16139441200.
URL: http://www.international.gc.ca/name-anmo/peace_process-processus_paix/

History 1992, Moscow (Russia), as a follow-up to the Madrid Process, launched in 1991, as one of 5 Working Groups to address the refugee issue. **Aims** Within the framework of the multilateral track of *Middle East* peace *negotiations*, deal with the sensitive question of Palestinian refugees; improve the current *living conditions* of refugees and displaced persons without prejudice to their rights and future status; ease and extend access to family reunification; support the process of achieving a viable and comprehensive solution to the refugee issue. **Structure** Plenary Session of 45 delegations. Chaired by Canada. Other countries, referred to as "shepherds", coordinate specific aspects to be discussed. USA and Russia are co-sponsors of the multilateral track and key participants in working groups. Co-organizers: *European Community (inactive)*; Japan. **Activities** Provides a forum for dialogue among the regional parties on refugee issues. Projects include: "Survey of Living Conditions among Palestinians in Gaza, West Bank and Arab Jerusalem". **IGO Relations** *United Nations Relief and Works Agency for Palestine Refugees in the Near East (UNRWA, #20622).* [2013/XE4532/**E***]

♦ Refugee Year 89/90 / see International Refugee Trust
♦ REFUTS – Réseau Européen de Formation Universitaire en Travail Social (unconfirmed)
♦ Regards de peuples en Europe / see People from Here and Elsewhere Federation (#18298)
♦ **REGAR** Red Iberoamericana de Garantias (#18667)
♦ REGATEC – International Conference on Renewable Energy Gas Technology (meeting series)
♦ **REGATTA** Regional Gateway for Technology Transfer and Climate Change Action (#18786)
♦ REG / see Council of European Municipalities and Regions (#04891)
♦ Regeaua Europeana a Pacientilor cu Mielom (inactive)

♦ ReGeneration 2030 18742

Gen Sec Ålandsvägen 35, AX-22100 Mariehamn, Finland. E-mail: info@regeneration2030.org.
URL: https://www.regeneration2030.org/

History Former names and other names: *The ReGeneration 2030 Foundation* – full title; *Stiftelsen ReGeneration 2030 sr* – full title. Registration: Finland. **Aims** Bring together activists aged 15-30 from across the region to share knowledge and strategize to fight climate collapse and build a sustainable future for all. **Structure** Secretariat; Working Groups. **Languages** English. Region-specific meetings in relevant languages. **Staff** 1.50 FTE, paid; 10.00 FTE, voluntary. **Finance** Annual budget: 200,000 EUR (2022). **Activities** Advocacy/lobbying/activism; awareness raising; events/meetings; knowledge management/information dissemination; networking/liaising; projects/programmes; training/education. Active in: Denmark, Estonia, Finland, Germany, Iceland, Latvia, Lithuania, Norway, Sweden. **Events** *ReGeneration2030 Week Meeting* Mariehamn (Finland) 2021, *Summit* Finland 2020, *Summit* Mariehamn (Finland) 2019, *Summit* Mariehamn (Finland) 2018. [2022.05.10/AA0430/**F**]

♦ The ReGeneration 2030 Foundation / see ReGeneration 2030 (#18742)

♦ Regeneration International 18743

Contact c/o OCA, 6771 South Silver Hill Dr, Finland MN 55603, USA. E-mail: info@regenerationinternational.org.
URL: http://regenerationinternational.org/

History 2015. Registered in accordance with USA law. **Aims** Build a global network of farmers, scientists, businesses, activists, educators, journalists, governments and consumers who will promote and put into practice regenerative *agriculture* and land-use practices that: provide abundant, nutritious food; revive local economies; rebuild soil fertility and *biodiversity*; and restore climate stability by returning carbon to the soil, through the natural process of photosynthesis. **Structure** Steering Committee. **Activities** Advocacy/lobbying/activism. [2018/XM6343/**F**]

♦ Pro Regenwald (internationally oriented national body)
♦ Reggio Terzo Mondo (internationally oriented national body)
♦ Régime de contrôle de la technologie des missiles (#16826)
♦ REGIMEN – Réseau d'études sur la globalisation, la gouvernance internationale et les mutations de l'état et des nations (internationally oriented national body)
♦ Régimes d'écoulement déterminés à partir de données internationales expérimentales et de réseaux (see: #13826)
♦ Régiók Európai Bizottsága (#06665)
♦ Regionaal Informatiecentrum van de Verenigde Naties (#20621)

♦ Regional Academy of Maritime Science and Technology 18744

Académie Régionale des Sciences et Techniques de la Mer d'Abidjan

Managing Dir BP V 158, Niangon-Lokoa, Côte d'Ivoire. T. +22523460808 – +22523460809. Fax +22523460811.

History Founded as a regional academy of *Maritime Organization of West and Central Africa (MOWCA, #16582).* Also referred to as *Abidjan Regional Maritime Academy.* **Aims** Promote and provide training in *francophone West* and *Central Africa.* **Structure** Sister organization working in anglophone African countries: *Regional Maritime University, Accra (RMU, #18796).* **Languages** French. **Activities** Training/education. Organizes courses and training for francophone West and Central African states.
Members Representatives of 15 countries:
Benin, Burkina Faso, Cameroon, Central African Rep, Chad, Congo Brazzaville, Congo DR, Côte d'Ivoire, Gabon, Guinea, Mali, Mauritania, Niger, Senegal, Togo.
IGO Relations Contacts with the Directorate General for Development (VIII) of: *European Commission (EC, #06633).* [2014.01.16/XF1845/**F***]

♦ Regional Activity Centre for Environment Remote Sensing / see Regional Activity Centre for Information and Communication of the Barcelona Convention (#18745)
♦ Regional Activity Centre for Information and Communication / see Regional Activity Centre for Information and Communication of the Barcelona Convention (#18745)

♦ Regional Activity Centre for Information and Communication of the Barcelona Convention (INFO/RAC) 18745

Centre d'Activités Régionales pour l'Information et la Communication de la Convention de Barcelone (INFO/CAR)

Dir c/o ISPRA, Via Vitaliano Brancati 48, 00144 Rome RM, Italy. E-mail: info@info-rac.org.
URL: http://www.info-rac.org/

History 1993, Palermo (Italy). Founded within the framework of the *Mediterranean Action Plan (MAP, #16638).* Transformed into centre under current title, 2005, by decision of 14th Meeting of the Contracting Parties. Former names and other names: *Regional Activity Centre for Environment Remote Sensing (ERS/RAC)* – former; *Centre d'activités régionales de télédétection appliquée à l'environnement (CAR/TDE)* – former; *ERS/RAC* – former; *Centre d'activités régionales pour la télédétection en matière d'environnement (CAR/TDE)* – former; *Regional Activity Centre for Information and Communication (INFO/RAC)* – former; *Centre d'activités régionales de télédétection appliquée à l'environnement* – former. **Aims** Provide adequate information and communication services and infrastructure technologies on public participation of Barcelona Convention (Article 15) and on reporting (Article 26) related to the issue for the protection of the Mediterranean marine and coastal environment, setting the obligations "to prevent, abate, combat and to the fullest extent possible eliminate pollution of the Mediterranean Sea Area" and "to protect and enhance the marine environment in that area so as to contribute towards its sustainable development". **Structure** Units (3): Coordinating; Information and Communication Technology; Communication, Education and Dissemination. **Languages** English, French, Italian. **Finance** UNEP/MAP biennial Programme of Work; project agreements; Italian government financial support; in-kind and financial contribution from ISPRA. **Activities** Awareness raising; knowledge management/information dissemination; research and development; training/education. **IGO Relations** *European Commission (EC, #06633); European Environment Agency (EEA, #06995); FAO (#09260); Global Environment Facility (GEF, #10346); Regional Seas Programme (#18814).* [2020/XG5439/**E***]

♦ Regional Activity Centre for Specially Protected Areas (RAC/SPA) 18746

Centre d'Activités Régionales pour les Aires Spécialement Protégées (CAR/ASP)

Dir Bld du Leader Yasser Arafat, BP 337, 1080 Tunis, Tunisia. T. +21671206485 – +21671206649. Fax +21671206490. E-mail: car-asp@spa-rac.org – director@spa-rac.org.
URL: http://www.rac-spa.org/

History 1985, Tunis (Tunisia). Founded following meeting of Mediterranean governments, 1980, Athens (Greece). Set up at the invitation of the Government of Tunisia, as a regional activity centre of *Mediterranean Action Plan (MAP, #16638)* to implement *Protocol Concerning Mediterranean Specially Protected Areas (1982),* which came into force Mar 1986, and was replaced by *Protocol Concerning Specially Protected Areas and Biological Diversity in the Mediterranean (Barcelona protocol, 1995).* **Aims** Contribute to the implementation of the Protocol concerning Specially Protected Areas and Biological Diversity in the Mediterranean (SPA/BD Protocol). **Languages** Arabic, English, French. **Staff** 16.00 FTE, paid. **Finance** Supported by: *Mediterranean Trust Fund (MTF, #16686)*; In-Kind contribution from Tunisia, international donors; bilateral cooperation. **Activities** Capacity building; guidance/assistance/consulting; monitoring/evaluation; research/documentation. **Publications** *Speciality Protected Areas in the Mediterranean: Assessment and Perspectives* (2010); *Impact of Climate Change on Marine and Coastal Biodiversity in the Mediterranean Sea: Current State of Knowledge* (2010); *Speciality Protected Areas of Mediterranean Importance: SPAMIs* (2010); *The Mediterranean Sea Biodiversity: State of the Ecosystems, Pressures, Impacts and Future Priorities* (2010); *Synthesis of National Overviews on Vulnerability and Impacts of Climate Change on Marine and Coastal Biological Diversity in the Mediterranean Region* (2009); *Impact of Climate Change on Biodiversity in the Mediterranean Sea* (2008); *Economic Aspects of Marine Protected Areas (MPAs)* (2006); *Guidelines for the Establishment and Management of Mediterranean Marine and Coastal Protected Areas* (2006); *Reference List of Marine Habitat Types for the Selection of Sites to be included in the National Inventories of Natural Sites of Conservation Interest* (2006); *The SPA/BD Protocol* (1995); *Action Programme for the Conservation of the Biological Diversity*

in the Mediterranean Region (SAP BIO); MED NATURE II; Protected Areas in the Mediterranean – from Geneva 1982 to Barcelona 1995. Technical reports; sub-regional and other reports; action plans; posters; guidelines; handbooks; training courses and books; conference proceedings; leaflets; CD-ROMs. **NGO Relations** Supports (1): *Network of Marine Protected Area Managers in the Mediterranean (MEDPAN, #17048).*
[2023/XK1608/**E***]

♦ Regional Activity Centre for Sustainable Consumption and Production (SCP/RAC) 18747

Centre d'Activités Régionales pour la Consommation et la Production Durables – Centro de Actividad Regional para el Consumo y la Producción Sostenibles

Administration Sant Pau Recinte Modernista, Pavelló de Nostra Senyora de la Mercè, Carrer de Sant Antoni Maria Claret 167, 08025 Barcelona, Spain. T. +34934151112. Fax +34932370286.
Communications Officer address not obtained.
Communications Officer address not obtained.
URL: http://www.cprac.org/

History Jun 1995. Founded within the framework of the *Mediterranean Action Plan (MAP, #16638).* Since 2009, also a regional centre for *Stockholm Convention on Persistent Organic Pollutants (POP treaty, 2001).* Former names and other names: *Centre for Environmentally Clean Technology (CT/RAC)* – former; *Centre for Environmentally Clean Production* – former; *Centro d'Iniciatives per a la Producció Neta* – former; *CP/RAC* – former. **Aims** Promote cleaner production techniques and eco-efficiency among *Mediterranean* companies. **Languages** Catalan, English, French, Spanish. **Staff** 21.00 FTE, paid. **Finance** provided by the Catalan Ministry of the Environment, for activities in Catalonia, and by the Spanish Ministry for the Environment for activities in the Mediterranean region. **Activities** Capacity building; events/meetings; research/documentation; training/education. **Publications** *SCP News* – electronic; *SCP/RAC Annual Technical Publication.* Brochures. Information Services: Technology databases in textile, pulp and paper and metal sectors. **Information Services** *Database of Mediterranean Experts on Pollution Prevention.*

Members Focal Points of governments in 21 Mediterranean countries:
Albania, Algeria, Bosnia-Herzegovina, Croatia, Cyprus, Egypt, France, Greece, Israel, Italy, Lebanon, Libya, Malta, Monaco, Morocco, Serbia, Slovenia, Spain, Syrian AR, Tunisia, Türkiye.
Intergovernmental organization:
European Union (EU, #08967).
NGO Relations Memorandum of Understanding with (1): *Asociación de las Camaras de Comercio e Industria del Mediterraneo (ASCAME, #02112).* [2020/XK1779/**E***]

♦ Regional Advisory Board in Agriculture (meeting series)

♦ Regional African Satellite Communications Organization (RASCOM) 18748

Organisation régionale africaine de communications par satellite

CEO 2 Avenue Thomasset, Abidjan 01, Côte d'Ivoire. T. +2252720257373 – +2252720257354. Fax +2252720223676. E-mail: rascomps@rascom.org – info@rascom.org.
URL: http://www.rascom.org/

History May 1992. Founded by African Ministers in charge of telecommunications. Operational since Nov 1993. Legal instruments (3): Convention, which established the organization and defines its legal entity; Operating Agreement, which deals with the operating principles; Non Signatory Shareholders Agreement for participation of equity in RASCOM investment programme by private African or non African and international organizations. Former names and other names: *Regional African Satellite Communication System for the Development of Africa* – former. **Aims** Provide an efficient and economical means of telecommunications, including requirements for transmission of sound and television broadcasting, to all areas in African countries, using a regional African satellite system, complemented by any other appropriate technology, which shall be integrated in the existing and/or planned national networks with a view to fostering development of African countries. **Structure** Basic organs (3): *'Assembly of Parties'*, the highest organ, consists of representatives of all African governments who are Parties to RASCOM; *'Board of Directors'* comprises representatives of Signatories or Groups of Signatories and Non-Signatories holding the largest 15 shares in RASCOM and regional representatives from 5 regions of Africa, elected by the Assembly of Parties; *'Executive Organ'* is headed by the Director General, who is responsible for the implementing decisions of the Board of Directors. **Languages** English, French. **Staff** 5.00 FTE, paid. **Finance** Feasibility study co-financed by contributions from UNDP, ITU, UNESCO, Italy, Germany and a technical assistance grant of ADB. **Activities** Advocacy/lobbying/activism; awareness raising; research and development. **Events** *Assembly of Parties* Dakar (Senegal) 2016, *Assembly of Parties* Abidjan (Côte d'Ivoire) 2013, *Assembly of Parties* Harare (Zimbabwe) 2011, *Assembly of Parties* Banjul (Gambia) 2009, *Assembly of parties* Khartoum (Sudan) 2007. **Publications** *RASCOM Newsletter.*

Members 45 African countries:
Algeria, Angola, Benin, Burkina Faso, Burundi, Cameroon, Cape Verde, Central African Rep, Chad, Comoros, Congo Brazzaville, Congo DR, Côte d'Ivoire, Djibouti, Egypt, Eritrea, Eswatini, Ethiopia, Gabon, Gambia, Ghana, Guinea, Guinea-Bissau, Kenya, Lesotho, Liberia, Libya, Malawi, Mali, Mauritania, Mauritius, Mozambique, Namibia, Niger, Nigeria, Senegal, Sierra Leone, South Africa, Sudan, Tanzania UR, Togo, Tunisia, Uganda, Zambia, Zimbabwe.
1 African Financial Institution and 1 African Organization (not specified).
IGO Relations Supervising agency: *International Telecommunication Union (ITU, #15673).*
[2022.10.25/XF2197/**F***]

♦ Regional African Satellite Communication System for the Development of Africa / see Regional African Satellite Communications Organization (#18748)
♦ Regional Agreement on Access to Information, Public Participation and Justice in Environmental Matters in Latin America and the Caribbean (2018 treaty)
♦ Regional Agreement on the Temporary Importation of Vehicles by Highway (1956 treaty)
♦ Regional Agreement on the Transboundary Movement of Hazardous Wastes (1992 treaty)

♦ Regional Agricultural Trade Intelligence Network (RATIN) 18749

Contact Lavington, Mbaazi Avenue off Kingara Road, PO Box 218, Nairobi, 00606, Kenya. T. +254733444035. E-mail: ratin@eagc.org.
URL: http://www.ratin.net/

History 2 Feb 2004, Nairobi (Kenya). **Aims** Strengthen food security and enhance economic growth in East Africa. **Events** *International meeting on emerging diseases and surveillance* Vienna (Austria) 2007. **Publications** *Food Trade Bulletin for East Africa.* **IGO Relations** Organizations involved: *Famine Early Warning System Network (FEWS NET); United States Agency for International Development (USAID).*
[2021/XJ3165/**F**]

♦ Regional AIDS Training Network / see Africa Capacity Alliance (#00160)
♦ Regional Animal Disease Surveillance and Control Network (inactive)
♦ Regional Animal Production and Health Commission for Asia, the Far East and the South-West Pacific / see Animal Production and Health Commission for Asia and the Pacific (#00839)

♦ Regional Anti-Corruption Initiative (RAI) 18750

Secretariat Fra Andjela Zvizdovica 1, B/7, 71000 Sarajevo, Bosnia-Herzegovina. T. +38733296327. Fax +38733296329. E-mail: info@rai-see.org.
URL: http://www.rai-see.org/

History Feb 2000, Sarajevo (Bosnia-Herzegovina). Current title adopted, Podgorica (Montenegro), when *Stability Pact for South Eastern Europe (inactive)* transformed into *Regional Cooperation Council (RCC, #18773).* Former names and other names: *Stability Pact Anti-corruption Initiative (SPAI)* – former (2000 to 2007). **Aims** Acts as a regional process through which governments of the region, local and international civil society organizations, bilateral aid agencies, and international organizations combine their efforts to help curb corruption in South Eastern Europe (SEE). **Structure** Steering Group, comprising high level representative; Secretariat. **Languages** English. **Finance** Members' dues (annual), secured by signing the Memorandum of Understanding concerning Cooperation in Fighting Corruption through the South-Eastern European Anticorruption Initiative (Article 2). **Activities** Awareness raising; capacity building; networking/liaising; projects/programmes. Activities are limited to the area of anti-corruption. **Events** *Strengthening Integrity in the Security Sector* Zagreb County (Croatia) 2021, *Regional Workshop on Integrity and Professional Standards in Law Enforcement* Bucharest (Romania) 2017. **Publications** *RAI Newsletter.* Reports.

Members Countries (9):
Albania, Bosnia-Herzegovina, Bulgaria, Croatia, Moldova, Montenegro, North Macedonia, Romania, Serbia.
Observers (3):
Georgia, Poland, Slovenia.
IGO Relations Memorandum of Understanding with (1): *Regional Cooperation Council (RCC, #18773).*
[2021.10.26/XJ2475/**F***]

♦ Regional Anti-Doping Organization of Central America / see Panamerican Regional Antidoping Organization (#18125)
♦ Regional Arab Federation of Associations for Voluntary Fertility Control (inactive)
♦ Regional Arms Control Verification and Implementation Assistance Centre / see Centre for Security Cooperation (#03785)
♦ Regional Asia-Pacific Secretariat for Rehabilitation of Survivors of Organized Violence (inactive)
♦ Regional Assistance Treaty on Food Emergencies (treaty)

♦ Regional Association of Energy Regulators for Eastern and Southern Africa (RAERESA) 18751

SG COMESA Centre, Ben Bella Road, PO Box 30051, Lusaka 10101, Zambia. T. +260211230768. Fax +260211227107.
URL: https://www.comesa.int/regional-association-of-energy-regulators-for-eastern-and-southern-africa/

History 16 Mar 2009. Officially launched at *Common Market for Eastern and Southern Africa (COMESA, #04296).* **Aims** Promote energy regulation and protect consumer welfare within the COMESA region thereby facilitating regional integration of the energy markets in the COMESA region. **Structure** Plenary; Executive Committee; Portfolio Committees; Secretariat. **Languages** Arabic, English, French. **Staff** 6.00 FTE, paid. **Finance** Sources: international organizations; members' dues. Supported by: *African Development Bank (ADB, #00283); Common Market for Eastern and Southern Africa (COMESA, #04296); European Union (EU, #08967); United States Agency for International Development (USAID).* Annual budget: 1,700,000 USD. **Activities** Capacity building; events/meetings; knowledge management/information dissemination. Active in: Eastern and Southern Africa. **Events** *Annual General Meeting* 2022, *Annual General Meeting* 2021, *Annual General Meeting* Addis Ababa (Ethiopia) 2020, *Annual General Meeting* Khartoum (Sudan) 2018, *Annual General Meeting* Lusaka (Zambia) 2017. **Publications** Reports; guidelines.

Members Full: Energy Regulators in 13 countries:
Burundi, Egypt, Ethiopia, Kenya, Madagascar, Malawi, Mauritius, Rwanda, Seychelles, Sudan, Uganda, Zambia, Zimbabwe.
Associate: countries where no independent energy regulator has been established. Associate in 7 countries:
Comoros, Congo DR, Djibouti, Eritrea, Libya, Somalia, Tunisia.
Observers in 1 countries:
Eswatini.
IGO Relations Links with Regional Economic Communities (RECs) in Africa and beyond, and their associations of energy regulators such as: *European Union (EU, #08967); United States Agency for International Development (USAID).* **NGO Relations** Member of (1): *International Confederation of Energy Regulators (ICER, #12859).*
[2022/XJ2866/**E***]

♦ Regional Association on Forced Migrations (no recent information)
♦ Regional Association of Oil, Gas and Biofuels Sector Companies in Latin America and the Caribbean (#02296)
♦ Regional Association of Oil and Natural Gas Companies in Latin America and the Caribbean / see Asociación Regional de Empresas del Sector Petróleo, Gas y Biocombustibles en Latinoamérica y el Caribe (#02296)
♦ Regional Branch for Central Africa of the International Council on Archives (see: #12996)
♦ Regional Bureau for European Scientific Cooperation / see UNESCO Office in Venice – UNESCO Regional Bureau for Science and Culture in Europe (#20316)

♦ Regional Center for Educational Planning (RCEP) 18752

Dir Sharjah University City, PO Box 68855, University City, Sharjah, United Arab Emirates. T. +971065055333. Fax +971065455004 – +971065455005. E-mail: mahra.hilal@rcep-unesco.ae – info@rcep-unesco.ae.
URL: http://www.rcepunesco.ae/EN/

History Established by an agreement, signed 17 Oct 2003, between the government of the United Arab Emirates and *UNESCO (#20322),* preceded by a request submitted by the UAE delegation to the 31st UNESCO General Conference. Agreement ratified in 2004. Officially inaugurated, 14 Nov 2007. Agreement renewed: 7 May 2008; 2012 for the period 2012-2015, based on Resolution 390/C 2009. Also referred to as *RCEP-UNESCO.* **Aims** Build national and regional capacity for modern educational planning by targeting senior officials and technical staff of ministries of education, local level education offices and other ministries directly related to the education sector. **Structure** Governing Board; Consultation Board. Departments (3): Training; Educational Researches and Consultation; Resources Management and Supportive Services. **Languages** Arabic, English. **Staff** 11.00 FTE, paid. **Finance** Part of United Arab Emirates Ministry of Education (UAE MOE) budget, allocated by the Ministry of Finance. **Activities** Training/education; guidance/assistance/consulting; knowledge management/information dissemination; events/meetings; awareness raising; capacity building. **Publications** *Capacity Development in Educational Planning and Management: learning from successes and failures; Education Orivatization: Causes, consequence, and planning implications; Global Perspective on Teacher Learning: improving policy and practice; Monitoring Educational Achievements; Quantitative Research.* **Information Services** *MS Dynamic CRM; MS Dynamic GP; SharePoint LMS; SharePoint Portal; Sonic Foundery MediaSite; Teamviewer Cooperate; WebEx Events.*

Members Governments (6):
Bahrain, Kuwait, Oman, Qatar, Saudi Arabia, United Arab Emirates.
International organizations (2):
International Institute for Educational Planning (IIEP, #13874); UNESCO (#20322). [2014.12.14/XJ5116/**E***]

♦ Regional Center of Quality and Excellence in Education (RCQE) . . . 18753

Dir Gen PO Box 94966, Riyadh 11614, Saudi Arabia. T. +966115629700. Fax +966115629700. E-mail: r.alyousef@rcqe.org.
URL: http://www.rcqe.org/

History Set up by agreement between government of Kingdom of Saudi Arabia and *UNESCO (#20322).* Current agreement valid as of Oct 2014. A Category II centre under the auspices of UNESCO. **Aims** Provide and facilitate training and consultation in areas of quality, academic *accreditation,* excellence of institutions and educational organizations across the *Arab World* countries, as a hub of expertise in the field of educational quality. **Structure** Governing Board; Consultative Committee. **Languages** Arabic, English. **Staff** 15.00 FTE, paid. **Finance** Financed by Kingdom of Saudi Arabia. **Activities** Training/education; research/documentation; events/meetings; knowledge management/information dissemination. **Members** Not a membership organization. **IGO Relations** *Centre international pour l'éducation des filles et des femmes en Afrique de l'Union Africaine (UA/CIEFFA, #03752); International Bureau of Education (IBE, #12413); International Institute for Educational Planning (IIEP, #13874); Regional Center for Educational Planning (RCEP, #18752).* **NGO Relations** *Asia-Pacific Centre of Education for International Understanding (APCEIU);* International Centre for Higher Education Innovation; International Mother Language Institute (IMLI); *South Asian Centre for Teacher Development (SACTD); Southeast Asian Center for Lifelong Learning for Sustainable Development (SEA-CLLSD); UNESCO International Research and Training Centre for Rural Education (INRULED).*
[2019.02.25/XJ9384/**E**]

♦ Regional Center for Renewable Energy and Energy Efficiency (RCREEE) 18754

Centre Régional pour les Énergies Renouvelables et le Efficacité Énergétique

Exec Dir Hydro Power Bldg – 7th Floor, Block 11 – Piece 15, Mesla District, Ard El Gofl, Nasr City, Cairo, Egypt. T. +20224154755. Fax +20224154661.
URL: http://www.rcreee.org/

History Set up following signing of Cairo Declaration, Jun 2008, by delegates and representatives of 10 Arab countries. Acquired legal status, Aug 2010. **Aims** Enable and increase adoption of renewable energy and energy efficiency practices in the *Arab* region; initiate and lead clean energy policy dialogues, strategies, technologies and capacity development in order to increase Arab states' share of tomorrow's energy. **Structure** Board of Trustees; Executive Committee; Focal Points; Secretariat. **Languages** Arabic, English, French. **Staff** 30.00 FTE, paid. **Finance** Member State contributions; governments grants from Germany – *Deutsche Gesellschaft für Internationale Zusammenarbeit (GIZ)*, Denmark – *DANIDA* and Egypt – New and Renewable Energy Authority. Also financing through selected fee-for-service contracts. **Activities** Research/documentation; capacity building; guidance/assistance/consulting. **Publications** *RCREEE Newsletter*. Annual Report; studies; assessments.
Members Governments (17):
Algeria, Bahrain, Djibouti, Egypt, Iraq, Jordan, Kuwait, Lebanon, Libya, Mauritania, Morocco, Palestine, Somalia, Sudan, Syrian AR, Tunisia, Yemen.
IGO Relations Memorandum of Understanding with: *African Energy Commission (AFREC, #00298)*; Global Women's Network for Energy Transition (GWNET); *International Renewable Energy Agency (IRENA, #14715)*; *Islamic Development Bank (IsDB, #16044)*. Collaborates with: *European Bank for Reconstruction and Development (EBRD, #06315)*; *International Energy Agency (IEA, #13270)*; *League of Arab States (LAS, #16420)*; *UNEP (#20299)*; *UNIDO (#20336)*; *United Nations Economic and Social Commission for Western Asia (ESCWA, #20558)*; *The World Bank Group (#21218)*. **NGO Relations** *Nederlandse Financierings-Maatschappij voor Ontwikkelingslanden (FMO).* [2019.02.25/XM6151/**D***]

♦ Regional Center for Seismology for South America (#03818)
♦ Regional Centre for Adult Education (no recent information)

♦ Regional Centre on Agrarian Reform and Rural Development for the Near East 18755

Centre régional de la réforme agraire et de développement rural au Proche-Orient (CARDNE)
Chief Exec PO Box 851840, Amman 11185, Jordan. T. +96265924348 – +96265934708. E-mail: cardne@cardne.org.
URL: http://www.cardne.org/
History Established Sep 1983, following a *FAO (#09260)* sponsored meeting of representatives and observers from 18 Near Eastern states. Agreement establishing CARDNE came into effect in 1987. **Aims** Assist national action and stimulate and promote regional cooperation relating to agrarian reform and rural development; improve production, income and living conditions of small-scale farmers, pastoral nomads and other needy rural groups; integrate rural people in the development process and promote their involvement in the social, economic and cultural life of their communities; serve member states by providing consultative services and technical support, fostering the exchange of ideas and experience and encouraging collaborative activities. **Structure** Governing Council, consisting of all member states (meets every 2 years). Executive Committee of 5 members (meets annually). Officers: Director; Deputy Director; Programme Officer; Section Officer and Section and Services Employees. **Languages** Arabic, English. **Staff** 8.00 FTE, paid. **Finance** Contributions by governments according to UN rates. **Activities** Events/meetings; guidance/assistance/consulting; knowledge management/information dissemination; networking/liaising; research/documentation; training/education. **Publications** *The Region* (4 a year) – newsletter. Annual Report.
Members Governments of 10 countries:
Egypt, Iraq, Jordan, Lebanon, Mauritania, Morocco, Sudan, Syrian AR, Tunisia, Yemen.
Observer (1):
Palestine.
IGO Relations Signed agreements and memorandum of understanding with international and regional organizations, including: *Arab Centre for the Studies of Arid Zones and Dry Lands (ACSAD, #00918)*; *Arab Organization for Agricultural Development (AOAD, #01018)*; *CIHEAM – International Centre for Advanced Mediterranean Agronomic Studies (CIHEAM, #03927)*; FAO; *Inter-Islamic Network on Water Resources Development and Management (INWRDAM, #11513)*; *International Center for Agricultural Research in the Dry Areas (ICARDA, #12466)*; *United Nations Economic and Social Commission for Western Asia (ESCWA, #20558)*. Observer to: *International Fund for Agricultural Development (IFAD, #13692).* [2017.06.01/XE3888/**E***]

♦ Regional Centre for Arbitration Kuala Lumpur / see Kuala Lumpur Regional Centre for Arbitration (#16210)
♦ Regional Centre for Biotechnology Training and Education, India (internationally oriented national body)
♦ Regional Centre for Cultural Action / see Institut Régional d'Enseignement Supérieur et de Recherche en Développement Culturel (#11355)
♦ Regional Centre for Environmental Health Activities / see WHO Regional Centre for Environmental Health Activities (#20942)

♦ Regional Centre for International Commercial Arbitration, Lagos (LRCICA) 18756

Dir 2A Ozumba Mbadiwe Ave, Victoria Island, Lagos 50565, Nigeria. E-mail: info@rcical.org.
Facebook: https://www.facebook.com/rcicalagos/
History by *Asian-African Legal Consultative Organization (AALCO, #01303)*. **Aims** Settle commercial *disputes* arising out of international transactions by arbitration and other Alternative Dispute Resolution (ADR) methods expeditiously and under a fair procedure in a less costly manner to litigation; encourage parties to settle their disputes in the region where the investment was made or in the place of performance of the contact (under an international transaction), where it is a country within Sub-Sahara region, so that recourse to arbitration outside the region would be less desirable. **Structure** Director/CEO; Units (2). **Finance** Internally generated revenue; annual grants from the Host Government of Nigeria. Annual budget: about US$ 2,850,000. **Activities** Conflict resolution; events/meetings; training/education; capacity building. **IGO Relations** Reciprocal agreement with: *International Centre for Settlement of Investment Disputes (ICSID, #12515)*. **NGO Relations** Cooperation agreement with: *Chartered Institute of Arbitrators (CIArb).* [2020/XE3116/**E***]

♦ Regional Centre for Issuing Scientific and Technical Documentation for Latin America and the Caribbean (internationally oriented national body)
♦ Regional Centre for the Living Arts in Africa (internationally oriented national body)
♦ Regional Centre for Low-Cost Water Supply and Sanitation / see Water and Sanitation for Africa (#20836)

♦ Regional Centre for Mapping of Resources for Development (RCMRD) 18757

Dir-Gen Kasarani Road, Off Thika Road, PO Box 632-00618, Nairobi, 00618, Kenya. T. +254202680722 – +254202680748. Fax +254202680747. E-mail: rcmrd@rcmrd.org – website@rcmrd.org.
Communications Manager address not obtained.
URL: http://www.rcmrd.org/
History Mar 1975. Commenced operations, pursuant to resolution passed at first United Nations Regional Cartographic Conference for Africa, 1963, Nairobi (Kenya), and to recommendations of a meeting of experts on joint centres for specialized services in surveying and mapping, 30 Jun – 3 Jul 1965, Addis Ababa (Ethiopia). Works under the auspices of *United Nations Economic Commission for Africa (ECA, #20554)* and *African Union (AU, #00488)* – originally *Organization of African Unity (OAU, inactive)*. Former names and other names: *Regional Centre for Services in Surveying, Mapping and Remote Sensing (RCSSMRS)* – former; *Centre régional de topographie, cartographie et télédétection* – former. **Aims** Strengthen Member States' and stakeholders' capacity through generation, application and dissemination of geo-information and allied technologies for sustainable development. **Structure** Conference of Ministers (every 2 years); Governing Council (GC) (meets annually). **Languages** English. **Staff** 100.00 FTE, paid. **Finance** Sources: contributions of member/participating states; donations; grants; in-kind support; international organizations; revenue from activities/projects. Supported by: *Alliance for a Green Revolution in Africa (AGRA, #00685)*; *Deutsche Gesellschaft für Internationale Zusammenarbeit (GIZ)*; *United States Agency for International Development (USAID)*. **Activities** Capacity building; events/meetings; guidance/assistance/consulting; knowledge management/information dissemination; research and development; research/documentation; training/education. **Events** *International Conference* Nairobi (Kenya) 2022, *International Conference* 2021, *Annual Conference* Nairobi (Kenya) 2019, *Annual Conference* Nairobi (Kenya) 2018, *Annual Conference* Nairobi (Kenya) 2017. **Publications** *RCMRD Newsletter* (4 a year); *Earth Resources Mapping in Africa* (2 a year). *Strategic Plan 2019-2022*. Annual Report; calendars; project reports; posters; videos; conference reports.
Members Contracting member states (20):
Botswana, Burundi, Comoros, Eswatini, Ethiopia, Kenya, Lesotho, Malawi, Mauritius, Namibia, Rwanda, Seychelles, Somalia, South Africa, South Sudan, Sudan, Tanzania UR, Uganda, Zambia, Zimbabwe.
States participating in the activities of the Centre (6):
Angola, Congo DR, Djibouti, Eritrea, Madagascar, Mozambique.
IGO Relations Contacts with:
- *African Centre of Meteorological Applications for Development (ACMAD, #00242)*;
- *African Development Bank (ADB, #00283)*;
- *African Development Bank Group (ADB Group, #00284)*;
- *African Minerals and Geosciences Centre (AMGC, #00373)*;
- *African Organisation for Standardisation (ARSO, #00404)*;
- *African Regional Institute for Geospatial Information Science and Technology (AFRIGIST, #00433)*;
- *Eastern and Southern African Management Institute (ESAMI, #05254)*;
- *Famine Early Warning System Network (FEWS NET)*;
- *Group on Earth Observations (GEO, #10735)*;
- *Intergovernmental Authority on Development (IGAD, #11472)*;
- *International Civil Aviation Organization (ICAO, #12581)*;
- *International Livestock Research Institute (ILRI, #14062)*;
- *Secretariat of the United Nations Convention to Combat Desertification (Secretariat of the UNCCD, #19208)*;
- *Swedish International Development Cooperation Agency (Sida)*;
- *UNEP (#20299)*;
- *UNESCO (#20322)*;
- *United Nations Human Settlements Programme (UN-Habitat, #20572)*;
- *United States Agency for International Development (USAID).*

NGO Relations Member of: *Global Land Tool Network (GLTN, #10452)*; *International Society for Photogrammetry and Remote Sensing (ISPRS, #15362)*. Affiliate member of: *International Cartographic Association (ICA, #12446).* [2022/XE0071/**E***]

♦ Regional Centre for the Promotion of Books in Latin America and the Caribbean 18758

Centre régional pour la promotion du livre en Amérique latine et dans les Caraïbes – Centro Regional para el Fomento del Libro en América Latina y el Caribe (CERLALC) – Centro Regional para o Fomento do Livro na América Latina e o Caribe
Main Office Calle 70 – No 9-52, Apartado 57348, Bogota, Bogota DC, Colombia. T. +5715402071. Fax +5715416398. E-mail: cerlalc@cerlalc.org.
URL: http://www.cerlalc.org/
History Apr 1971, Bogota (Colombia). Established under an International Cooperation Agreement between *UNESCO (#20322)* and the Government of Colombia, as an integral part of a UNESCO programme for the establishment of similar centres in other regions (Karachi, Tokyo (Japan), Yaoundé). Agreement approved by the Colombian Government, Dec 1971; new Agreement approved by he Columbian Government, Nov 1986. A UNESCO Category II Centre. **Aims** Instigate the formulation of national policies on books and *reading* aimed at improving the production, dissemination and distribution of books in Latin America and the Caribbean; promote measures to develop and coordinate the book market in this region as a step towards forming a common book market; support national book and reading promotion activities; conduct or support research on reading habits, levels and interest; carry out studies on the best strategies for promoting reading; promote training courses for people working in the field; advise and help strengthen public and school *libraries*; provide general and technical information on all stages of creating, printing and distributing books and on reading and *copyright* laws, by carrying out studies and compiling and distributing statistics, information and documentation on production, distribution, marketing and demand for books. **Structure** Council, consisting of representatives from Colombia (as organization headquarters), member states and UNESCO, elects Executive Committee from among its members. Centre Director, assisted by Secretary General and Technical and Administrative Deputy Secretaries. **Languages** Portuguese, Spanish. **Finance** Sources: Government of Colombia; UNESCO; Governments of other Member States. **Activities** Encourages and supports initiatives of Latin America and Caribbean nations and promotes cooperation and exchange between them. Activities based on the following main areas: (i) Cooperation with governments through technical assistance services. (ii) Copyright and literary property: provides consulting services designed to help update national laws on this subject and help adapt laws to existing international agreements. (iii) Human resources training, including audio-visual courses for librarians, booksellers, book illustrators and designers. (iv) Support for studies on: national profiles on book production; taxes and duties on books and the materials used to make them: cost structure of the printing industry; training needs; development of school and public libraries; university publishing organizations; government publications; reading habits and reader behaviour. (v) Support for public and school libraries, emphasizing staff training, in particular to work with governments to improve their public and school library programmes. (vi) Promotion and support for programmes to stimulate reading. (vii) Publications, including teaching materials. (viii) Regional Information Service on Books, Reading and Copyright, gathering statistical information on book production, translation, adaptation and marketing in Latin America and the Caribbean, and publishing geographical and topical directories, and an up-to-date record of current legislation on copyright and literary property and on government policies. Identifies and distributes information on courses and seminars, on research in progress and on public and school library programmes, systems and networks functioning in the region. **Events** *Reading 2013 Congress* Havana (Cuba) 2013, *Reading 2011 congress* Havana (Cuba) 2011, *Reading 2009 congress* Havana (Cuba) 2009, *Congrès des libraires d'Amérique latine* Bogota (Colombia) 2007, *Reading 2007 congress* Havana (Cuba) 2007. **Publications** *Correo de Bibliotecas Públicas Iberoamericanas* – electronic bulletin; *Libro al Dia* – electronic newsletter; *RedPlanes* – electronic bulletin. *Pensar el Libro*. Series of monographs; document series on seminars organized by the Centre; reading and education series to provide support for reading campaigns; manuals on book publishing and other training materials.
Members Governments of 21 countries:
Argentina, Bolivia, Brazil, Chile, Colombia, Costa Rica, Cuba, Dominican Rep, Ecuador, El Salvador, Guatemala, Honduras, Mexico, Nicaragua, Panama, Paraguay, Peru, Portugal, Spain, Uruguay, Venezuela.
Consultative Status Consultative status granted from: *World Intellectual Property Organization (WIPO, #21593)* (Observer Status). [2021/XE0145/**E***]

♦ Regional Centre for the Safeguarding of Intangible Cultural Heritage in Africa (unconfirmed)
♦ Regional Centre for the Safeguarding of Intangible Cultural Heritage in South-Eastern Europe under the auspices of UNESCO / see Regional Centre for the Safeguarding of the Intangible Cultural Heritage in South-Eastern Europe under the auspices of UNESCO (#18759)

♦ Regional Centre for the Safeguarding of the Intangible Cultural Heritage in South-Eastern Europe under the auspices of UNESCO 18759

Contact zh k Iztok 7, Lachezar Stanchev Str, 1797 Sofia, Bulgaria. T. +35924442103. E-mail: office@unesco-centerbg.org.
URL: http://www.unesco-centerbg.org/
History Became a *UNESCO (#20322)* Category II Centre, Oct 2009; Agreement between UNESCO and government of Bulgaria signed 25 Oct 2010, Paris (France). Officially inaugurated 20 Feb 2012, Sofia (Bulgaria). Agreement between UNESCO and Government of Bulgaria concerning continuation of the Regional Centre signed 10 Nov 2017, Paris (France). Registered in accordance with Bulgarian law. Former names and other names: *Regional Centre for the Safeguarding of Intangible Cultural Heritage in South-Eastern Europe under the auspices of UNESCO* – former. **Aims** Promote the: Convention for the Safeguarding of Intangible Cultural Heritage and contribute to its implementation in the South-Eastern European (SEE) sub-region; increase the participation of communities, groups and individuals in safeguarding the Intangible Cultural Heritage (ICH) in SEE countries; enhance the capacity of UNESCO's SEE Member States in the safeguarding of ICH; coordinate, exchange and disseminate information regarding the safeguarding of ICH in the sub-region; foster regional and international cooperation for the safeguarding of ICH. **Structure** General Assembly (annual); Executive Board; Executive Director; Secretariat. **Languages** Bulgarian, English. **Staff** 6.00 FTE,

paid. **Finance** Government of Bulgaria provides all resources, amounting to at least the equivalent of euro 200,000. **Activities** Capacity building; events/meetings; knowledge management/information dissemination; awareness raising; publishing activities. **Events** *Annual Coordination Meeting* Shiraz (Iran Islamic Rep) 2017. **Publications** *Living Heritage* (2 a year) – magazine; *Regional Centre Sofia Newsletter* – online. *Between the Visible and the Invisible: the Intangible Cultural Heritage and the Museum*; *Masterpieces of Intangible Cultural Heritage in South-East Europe*; *The contribution of UNESCO Member States of South-East Europe to the Implementation of the Convention for the Safeguarding of the Intangible Cultural Heritage*.
Members Full in 16 countries:
Albania, Armenia, Bosnia-Herzegovina, Bulgaria, Croatia, Cyprus, Georgia, Greece, Moldova, Montenegro, North Macedonia, Romania, Serbia, Slovenia, Türkiye, Ukraine.
IGO Relations *International Information and Networking Centre for Intangible Cultural Heritage in the Asia-Pacific Region under the auspices of UNESCO (ICHCAP, #13847)*; *International Research Centre for Intangible Cultural Heritage in the Asia-Pacific Region under the Auspices of UNESCO (IRCI, #14721)*. **NGO Relations** *Centro Regional para la Salvaguardia del Patrimonio Cultural Inmaterial de América Latina (CRESPIAL, #03817)*; *International Training Center for Intangible Cultural Heritage in the Asia-Pacific Region under the auspices of UNESCO (CRIHAP, #15716)*; *Regional Centre for the Safeguarding of Intangible Cultural Heritage in Africa*; *Regional Research Centre for Safeguarding Intangible Cultural Heritage in West and Central Asia (Tehran ICH Centre, #18808)*. [2019.04.15/XM6092/**E**]

- ♦ Regional Centre for Services in Surveying, Mapping and Remote Sensing / see Regional Centre for Mapping of Resources for Development (#18757)
- ♦ Regional Centre on Small Arms and Light Weapons / see Regional Centre on Small Arms and Light Weapons in the Great Lakes Region, the Horn of Africa and Bordering States (#18760)

♦ Regional Centre on Small Arms and Light Weapons in the Great Lakes Region, the Horn of Africa and Bordering States (RECSA) 18760

Centre régional sur les armes légères et de petit calibre dans la région des Grands Lacs, la corne de l'Afrique et les États limitrophes

Exec Sec 7th Floor Timau Plaza, Argwings kodhek road, Timau lane, Nairobi, 00200, Kenya. T. +254203877456 – +254203876023. Fax +254203877397. E-mail: info@recsasec.org.
URL: http://www.recsasec.org/

History 2005, Nairobi (Kenya). Started out as *Nairobi Secretariat*, set up 2000, to coordinate implementation of *Nairobi Declaration on the Problem of Illicit Small Arms and Light Weapons in the Great Lakes Region and the Horn of Africa (2000)* and the Nairobi Protocol on the Prevention, Control and Management of Small Arms and Light Weapons in the Great Lakes Region, the Horn of Africa and Bordering States. Former names and other names: *Regional Centre on Small Arms and Light Weapons (RECSA)* – former; *Nairobi Secretariat* – former (2000). **Aims** Coordinate action against small arms and light weapons proliferation in the Great Lakes Region, the Horn of Africa and Bordering States. **Structure** Council of Ministers; Technical Advisory Committee; Secretariat. **Languages** Arabic, English, French. **Finance** Sources: contributions of member/participating states; donations. **Activities** Awareness raising; capacity building; management of treaties and agreements; monitoring/evaluation; projects/programmes; research and development; research/documentation. **Publications** *Nairobi Protocol* in Arabic, English, French. Annual Report; reports; guidelines; Conducted Researches.
Members Governments of 15 countries:
Burundi, Central African Rep, Congo Brazzaville, Congo DR, Djibouti, Eritrea, Ethiopia, Kenya, Rwanda, Seychelles, Somalia, South Sudan, Sudan, Tanzania UR, Uganda.
IGO Relations Observer status with (1): *United Nations (UN, #20515)* (General Assembly). **NGO Relations** Member of (1): *International Partnership on Religion and Sustainable Development (PaRD, #14524)*. [2022.11.01/XM2250/**E***]

- ♦ Regional Centre for Space Science and Technology Education for Western Asia (see: #04277)
- ♦ Regional Centre for Strategic Studies, Colombo (internationally oriented national body)
- ♦ Regional Centre for Technology Transfer / see Asian and Pacific Centre for Transfer of Technology (#01603)
- ♦ Regional Centre for Training in Aerospace Surveys / see African Regional Institute for Geospatial Information Science and Technology (#00433)
- ♦ Regional Centre for Training Research and Post-Graduate Study in Tropical Biology / see Southeast Asian Regional Centre for Tropical Biology (#19782)
- ♦ Regional Centre for Training and Water Studies of Arid and Semiarid Zones, Cairo (internationally oriented national body)
- ♦ Regional Centre on Urban Water Management (internationally oriented national body)

♦ Regional Centre on Urban Water Management, Teheran (RCUWM) . 18761

Dir No 120 Khoramshahr St, Teheran, 1553713511, Iran Islamic Rep. T. +982188754936. Fax +982188741230. E-mail: info@rcuwm.org.ir.

History Feb 2002, Teheran (Iran Islamic Rep), under the auspices of *UNESCO (#20322)*. **Aims** Generate and provide scientific and technical information on urban water management issues in the region; promote research on urban water management issues through regional cooperative arrangements; undertake capacity building and awareness raising activities at institutional and professional levels; enhance cooperation with international institutions in order to advance knowledge in the field. **Structure** Board; Secretariat. **Activities** Organizes workshops. **Events** *International workshop on groundwater for emergency situations* Teheran (Iran Islamic Rep) 2006. **Publications** *Dialogue on Drops* – newsletter.
Members Governments of 10 countries:
Bangladesh, Egypt, Germany, India, Iran Islamic Rep, Kuwait, Lebanon, Oman, Syrian AR, Tajikistan.
International organizations (4):
IHE Delft Institute for Water Education (#11110); *International Water Academy (TIWA, no recent information)*; *International Water Association (IWA, #15865)*; UNESCO.
NGO Relations Member of: *Water and Development Information for Arid Lands Global Network (G-WADI, #20826)*. [2009/XM1324/y/**E***]

♦ Regional Clean Sea Organization (RECSO) 18762

Chairman Amim, City Tower 1, Office no 304, Sheikh Zayed Road, PO Box 58142, Dubai, United Arab Emirates. T. +97143314443. Fax +97143311933. E-mail: info@recso1972.com.
URL: http://www.recso.org/

History Founded 1972, by 13 oil companies. **Aims** Protect the regional seas and *environment* from oil *pollution* emanating from operations, shipping and other related activities of members in the region. **Structure** Operators Committee; Executive Committee; Technical Secretariat; Technical Committee. **Activities** Capacity building; advocacy/lobbying/activism; guidance/assistance/consulting; events/meetings; training/education; monitoring/evaluation. **Events** *EnviroSpill Conference* Abu Dhabi (United Arab Emirates) 2019, *EnviroSpill Conference* Abu Dhabi (United Arab Emirates) 2018, *EnviroSpill Conference* Abu Dhabi (United Arab Emirates) 2017, *Annual Meeting* Dubai (United Arab Emirates) 2016, *Offshore Arabia Biennial Conference* Dubai (United Arab Emirates) 2014. **Publications** *Offshore Arabia* – magazine.
Members Companies. Full (8) in 6 countries:
Bahrain, Kuwait, Oman, Qatar, Saudi Arabia, United Arab Emirates.
Associate (5) in 1 country:
Saudi Arabia. [2017.08.06/XM1215/**D**]

- ♦ Regional Commission for the Determination of Facts about War Crimes and Other Serious Violations of Human Rights Committed on the Territory of the Former SFRY from January 1, 1991 to December 31, 2001 (unconfirmed)

♦ Regional Commission for Fisheries (RECOFI) 18763

Sec FAO RNE, 11 Al Eslah El Zerai Str, Dokki, PO Box 2223, Cairo, Egypt. T. +20233316000ext2818. Fax +20233495981.
URL: http://www.fao.org/fishery/rfb/recofi/en/

History Established on the basis of Resolution 1/117 adopted by the Council at its 117th Session. Comes within the framework of *FAO (#09260)*. Replaces in terms of geographical area the former *'Committee for the Development and Management of Fisheries Resources of the Gulfs'*, a subsidiary body of the *Indian Ocean Fishery Commission (IOFC, inactive)*, abolished by Resolution 116/1 of the Council, Jun 1999. Regional Commission of *FAO Regional Office for the Near East and North Africa (#09269)*. **Aims** Promote development, conservation, rational management and best utilization of living marine resources, as well as the sustainable development of aquaculture in the Indo-Pacific region. **Structure** Commission; Secretariat. Working Groups (2): Fisheries Management; Aquaculture. **Languages** Arabic, English. **Finance** Contributions from members (annual): US$ 5,000. **Activities** Research/documentation; research and development; knowledge management/information dissemination. **Events** *Session* Muscat (Oman) 2015, *Session* Teheran (Iran Islamic Rep) 2013, *Session* Rome (Italy) 2011, *Session* Dubai (United Arab Emirates) 2009, *Session* Riyadh (Saudi Arabia) 2007.
Members Open to all Members and Associate Member of FAO that are coastal members or Associated Members situated mainly or partly within the area; Member Nations or Associate Members whose vessels are engaged in fishing in the area; regional economic integration organizations of which any Member Nation referred to above is a Member to which that Member Nation has transferred competence over matters within the purview of the Agreement establishing the Commission. Governments of 8 countries:
Bahrain, Iran Islamic Rep, Iraq, Kuwait, Oman, Qatar, Saudi Arabia, United Arab Emirates.
Observers (8) of which 5 are listed in this Yearbook:
Arab Federation of Fish Producers (AFFP, #00945); *Arab Organization for Agricultural Development (AOAD, #01018)*; *Gulf Cooperation Council (GCC, #10826)* (Secretaries); *Regional Organization for the Protection of the Marine Environment (ROPME, #18805)*; *WorldFish (#21507)*. [2019/XM0774/y/**E***]

♦ Regional Commission for Power Integration 18764

Comisión de Integración Energética Regional (CIER) – Comissão de Integração Energética Regional (CIER)

Secretariat Blvr Gral Artigas 1040, 11300 Montevideo, Uruguay. T. +59827090611 – +59827095359. Fax +59827083193. E-mail: secier@cier.org.uy.
URL: http://www.cier.org.uy/

History Jul 1964, Montevideo (Uruguay), on the initiative of the electrical authorities of Uruguay. Original title: *Commission of Regional Electrical Integration – Commission d'intégration électrique régionale – Comisión de Integración Eléctrica Regional – Comissão de Integração Elétrica Regional*. Current Statutes adopted 22 Nov 1990, Buenos Aires (Argentina). **Aims** Promote and encourage integration of regional electrical sectors and their markets in South America, in order to achieve: greater efficiency of electric power companies in member countries; systematic interchange of information and personnel at all levels; technical cooperation and assistance; regional approach to project studies, with the possibility of establishing international electrical interconnections; orientation and coordination of studies and analysis; preparation of general purchasing procedures and technical specifications emphasizing regional acceptance; utilization of regional technical personnel for projects and studies. **Structure** Central Committee (meets annually), consisting of up to 3 representatives of each National Committee and chaired by President. Board, composed of President and Vice-Presidents. General Secretariat, headed by Executive Director. National Committees. Business areas (5). **Languages** Portuguese, Spanish. **Staff** 10.00 FTE, paid. **Finance** Contributions by National Committees. **Activities** Studies and analyses specific problems, leading to the drawing up of a working programme undertaken by Business Areas (5): Generation; Transmission; Commercialization; Distribution; Corporate Areas. Other subjects are specially considered on International Seminars about different and current subjects. Current priorities are adopted through high executives to assimilate changes due to privatization; modifying national committee structure to assist relationships between electrical utilities and the Commission; reorganizing technical committees and creating new ones. **Events** *International Congress of System Operation and Energy Markets* Medellin (Colombia) 2013, *International congress on environment and energy industry* Argentina 2007, *International congress on work on electric tension and security of transmission and distribution of electricty* Argentina 2007, *Seminario internacional sobre el manejo de activos y el mantenimiento en la transmision* Brasilia (Brazil) 2007, *Congress* Cartagena de Indias (Colombia) 2007. **Publications** *CIER Magazine* (4 a year); *CIER's Regional Electric Atlas* – periodical. Technical books; statistical leaflets. **Information Services** *ACTAS Database*; *HERA Database*; *ZEUS Database*.
Members Electrical power enterprises in 10 countries:
Argentina, Bolivia, Brazil, Chile, Colombia, Ecuador, Paraguay, Peru, Uruguay, Venezuela.
Associate Members (5) in 5 countries:
Canada, France, Mexico, Portugal, Spain. [2017/XD4042/**D**]

- ♦ Regional Committee of Animal Health (no recent information)
- ♦ Regional Committee of the Convention on the Recognition of Studies, Diplomas and Degrees concerning Higher Education in the States belonging to the Europe Region (inactive)
- ♦ Regional Committee on Hydraulic Resources of Water Resources Committee of the Central American Isthmus (#04196)
- ♦ Regional Committee on Mediterranean Neogene Stratigraphy (internationally oriented national body)

♦ Regional Committee of the UN on Global Geospatial Information Management for the Americas (UN-GGIM Americas) 18765

Comité Regional de las Naciones Unidas sobre la Gestión Global de Información Geoespacial para las Américas

Exec Sec National Geographical and Environmental Information Subsystem, INEGI, Av Héroe de Nacozari Sur 2301, Jardines del Parque, 20270 Aguascalientes, Mexico. T. +524494624743.
URL: http://www.un-ggim-americas.org/

History Established 29 Feb 2000, pursuant to Resolution 3 of 6th *United Nations Regional Cartographic Conference for the Americas (UNRCCA)*, Jun 1997, New York NY (USA), as *Permanent Committee on Spatial Data Infrastructure for the Americas (PC-IDEA) – Comité Permanente para la Infrastructura de Datos Geoespaciales de las Américas (CP-IDEA)*. Operates under purview of UNRCCA. Restructured under current title, 23 Aug 2013, New York NY (USA), in accordance with Resolution 7, adopted at 10th UN Regional Cartographic Conference for the Americas. **Aims** Maximize economic, social and environmental benefits derived from use of geospatial information through knowledge transfer and exchange of experiences and technologies between countries, based on common standards, which would allow establishment of the Geospatial Data Infrastructure of the Americas. **Structure** General Assembly; Board of Directors; Working Groups (3); Work Lines (5). **Languages** English, Spanish. **Staff** Voluntary. **Finance** No annual budget. **Activities** Knowledge management/information dissemination; research/documentation; standards/guidelines; networking/liaising; capacity building; events/meetings. **Events** *Meeting* Mexico City (Mexico) 2014, *Meeting* New York, NY (USA) 2013, *Meeting* Rio de Janeiro (Brazil) 2012, *Meeting* Rio de Janeiro (Brazil) 2011, *Meeting* Seoul (Korea Rep) 2011. **Publications** Newsletter. Annual Report; articles.
Members Governments (36):
Antigua-Barbuda, Argentina, Bahamas, Barbados, Belize, Bolivia, Brazil, Canada, Chile, Colombia, Costa Rica, Cuba, Dominica, Dominican Rep, Ecuador, El Salvador, Grenada, Guatemala, Guyana, Haiti, Honduras, Jamaica, Mexico, Nicaragua, Panama, Paraguay, Peru, St Kitts-Nevis, St Lucia, St Maarten, St Vincent-Grenadines, Suriname, Trinidad-Tobago, Uruguay, USA, Venezuela.
IGO Relations Cooperates with: *United Nations Committee of Experts on Global Geospatial Information Management (UN-GGIM, #20540)* and its regional bodies (N-GGIM Asia-Pacific, UN-GGIM Arab States, UN-GGIM Europa, UN-GGIM Africa). **NGO Relations** Cooperates with: *International Organization for Standardization (ISO, #14473)*. Sistema de Referencia Geocéntrico para Las Américas (SIRGAS); *Asociación Sudamericana de Estudios Geopolíticos e Internacionales, Montevideo (GEOSUR, no recent information)*. [2019.12.11/XE4729/**E***]

♦ Regional Committee of United Nations Global Geospatial Information Management for Asia and the Pacific (UN-GGIM-AP) 18766

Secretariat c/o UN ESCAP, The United Nations Bldg, Rajadamnern Nok Avenue, Bangkok, 10200, Thailand. T. +6622881456. Fax +6622883012. E-mail: un-ggim-ap@un.org.
Pres Geoscience Australia, GPO Box 378, Canberra ACT 2601, Australia. E-mail: un-ggim-ap.australia@ga.gov.au.
URL: http://www.un-ggim-ap.org/

History 12 Jul 1995, Kuala Lumpur (Malaysia). Established on recommendations of 13th *United Nations Regional Cartographic Conference for Asia and the Pacific (UNRCC-AP)*, 9-18 May 1994, Beijing (China). Comes within the framework of *United Nations (UN, #20515)*. Original title: *Permanent Committee on GIS Infrastructure for Asia and the Pacific (PCGIAP)*. Current title adopted 2012, Bangkok (Thailand), pursuant to resolution 8 of 19th UNRCC-AP. Current statutes amended 1 Nov 2012. Operates under purview of UNRCC-AP. **Aims** Identify regional issues relevant to geospatial information management and take necessary actions on them for the furtherance of the discussions in UNRCC-AP, and thus contribute to the discussions in the UNCE-GGIM so that the economic, social and environmental benefits of geospatial information will be maximized in Asia and the Pacific region. **Structure** Plenary Meeting (annual); Executive Board, comprising 4 officers and 6 members. Working Groups (4): Geodetic Reference Frame; Disaster Risk Management; Regional SDI; Cadastre and Land Management. **Languages** English. **Finance** By each members' national government. **Activities** Events/meetings. **Events** *Plenary Meeting* Indonesia 2021, *Plenary Meeting* Indonesia 2020, *Plenary Meeting* Canberra, ACT (Australia) 2019, *Plenary Meeting* Deqing (China) 2018, *Plenary Meeting* Kumamoto (Japan) 2017.

Members Directorates of national surveying and mapping organizations (NMOs) and national geospatial information authorities (NGIAs) of 56 countries and territories:
Afghanistan, Armenia, Australia, Azerbaijan, Bangladesh, Bhutan, Brunei Darussalam, Cambodia, China, Cook Is, Fiji, Guam, Hong Kong, India, Indonesia, Iran Islamic Rep, Japan, Kazakhstan, Kiribati, Korea DPR, Korea Rep, Kyrgyzstan, Laos, Macau, Malaysia, Maldives, Marshall Is, Micronesia FS, Mongolia, Myanmar, Nauru, Nepal, New Caledonia, New Zealand, Niue, Northern Mariana Is, Pakistan, Palau, Papua New Guinea, Philippines, Polynesia Fr, Russia, Samoa, Samoa USA, Singapore, Solomon Is, Sri Lanka, Tajikistan, Thailand, Timor-Leste, Tonga, Turkmenistan, Tuvalu, Uzbekistan, Vanuatu, Vietnam.
[2022/XE3281/E*]

♦ Regional Commonwealth in the Field of Communications (RCC) . . . 18767

Communauté régionale des postes et télécommunications (CRPT)

Dir Gen 3 Avangardnaya Str, Moscow MOSKVA, Russia, 125493. T. +74956927134. E-mail: ecrcc@rcc.org.ru.
Deputy Dir Gen address not obtained.
URL: http://www.rcc.org.ru/

History 17 Dec 1991. Established on signature of an agreement by heads of postal and telecommunications administrations of member countries. A Restricted Union of *Universal Postal Union (UPU, #20682)* and a regional union of *International Telecommunication Union (ITU, #15673)*. **Aims** Coordinate activities relating to provision of communication services; harmonize development of communication networks and facilities; work out principles to govern scientific and tariff policy, vocational training and the work of educational communications institutions. **Structure** Board (meets twice a year); Executive Committee. **Languages** Russian. **Staff** 22.00 FTE, paid; 22.00 FTE, voluntary. **Finance** Sources: members' dues. Annual budget: 41,000,000 RUB (2021). **Activities** Priority directions of the Commonwealth activities include: development of ICT-based communication systems; new services for the customers; protection of common interests of the communications administrations at international organizations and their organs. Works to expand mutually beneficial cooperation between the RCC communications administrations in development of communications and information and communication technologies. Coordinates communications administrations interaction in the sphere of: scientific and technical policy; spectrum management; creation of a single postal space in the CIS territory; economic policy issues related to tariffs for communication services and settlements; personnel training; interaction with ITU, UPU and other international organizations; information sharing. Organizes conferences and seminars together with ITU and UPU. **Events** *Session* Ashgabat (Turkmenistan) 1994. **Publications** *Elektrosviaz* (12 a year); *Postal Communication – Facilities and Technologies* (12 a year); *Vestnik Sviazi* (12 a year); *RCC News*; *Statistical Yearbook*.

Members Communications Administrations of 12 countries:
Armenia, Azerbaijan, Belarus, Georgia, Kazakhstan, Kyrgyzstan, Moldova, Russia, Tajikistan, Turkmenistan, Ukraine, Uzbekistan.
Observers in 5 countries:
Afghanistan, Bulgaria, Latvia, Lithuania, Slovenia.
Also included in the above, 3 organizations listed in this Yearbook:
European Telecommunications Satellite Organization (EUTELSAT IGO, #08896); *International Mobile Satellite Organization (IMSO, #14174)*; *Intersputnik International Organization of Space Communications (#15976)*.
[2022/XF2918/D*]

- ♦ Regional Community Forestry Training Centre / see RECOFTC – The Center for People and Forests (#18628)
- ♦ Regional Community Forestry Training Centre for Asia and the Pacific / see RECOFTC – The Center for People and Forests (#18628)

♦ Regional Comprehensive Economic Partnership (RCEP) 18768

Address not obtained.
URL: https://asean.org/?static_post=rcep-regional-comprehensive-economic-partnership

History Aug 2012, Economic Ministers endorsed Guiding Principles and Objectives for Negotiating RCEP. Negotiations launched Nov 2012. **Aims** Achieve a modern, comprehensive, high-quality, and mutually beneficial economic partnership agreement among the ASEAN Member States and ASEAN's FTA partners. **Structure** Ministerial Meeting and Intersessional Ministerial Meeting. **Activities** Politics/policy/regulatory. **Events** *Ministerial Meeting* Bangkok (Thailand) 2019, *Ministerial Meeting* Bangkok (Thailand) 2019, *Summit* Bangkok (Thailand) 2019, *Meeting* Melbourne, VIC (Australia) 2019, *Meeting* Zhengzhou (China) 2019.

Members Member States (16):
Australia, Brunei Darussalam, Cambodia, China, India, Indonesia, Japan, Korea Rep, Laos, Malaysia, Myanmar, New Zealand, Philippines, Singapore, Thailand, Vietnam.
Included in the above, 1 organization:
ASEAN (#01141).
[2018/XM6823/E*]

- ♦ Regional Conference on the Integration of Women into the Economic and Social Development of Latin America and the Caribbean / see Regional Conference on Women in Latin America and the Caribbean (#18770)
- ♦ Regional Conference on International Voluntary Service / see International Forum for Volunteering in Development (#13659)

♦ Regional Conference on Migration (RCM) 18769

Conferencia Regional sobre Migración (CRM)

Exec Secretariat Sabana Business Ctr – 7th Floor, San José, San José, San José, 1222050, Costa Rica. T. +50640523403 – +50688511009. E-mail: crmst@iom.int.
URL: https://crmsv.org

History Feb 1996. Established as a result of the Tuxtla II Presidential Summit. Former names and other names: *Puebla Process* – alias. **Aims** Create a forum for frank and honest discussion on regional migration issues, leading to greater regional coordination and cooperation; undertake regional efforts to protect human rights of migrants and strengthen the integrity of each member state's immigration laws, borders, and national security, as well as to strengthen the links between migration and development. **Structure** Meeting of Vice-Ministers; Presidency Pro-Tempore; Regional Consultation Group on Migration (RCGM); Working Groups; Executive Secretariat. **Languages** English, Spanish. **Staff** 3.00 FTE, paid. **Activities** Events/meetings; guidance/assistance/consulting; networking/liaising; politics/policy/regulatory; training/education. **Events** *Meeting* San Salvador (El Salvador) 2022, *Meeting* Ciudad de México (Mexico) 2021, *Meeting* San José (Costa Rica) 2020, *Meeting* Guatemala (Guatemala) 2019, *Meeting* Panama (Panama) 2018. **Publications** Guidelines; mechanisms; protocols; proceedings.

Members Governments (11):
Belize, Canada, Costa Rica, Dominican Rep, El Salvador, Guatemala, Honduras, Mexico, Nicaragua, Panama, USA.
Countries with Observer status (5):
Argentina, Colombia, Ecuador, Jamaica, Peru.
Regional and international observer organizations:
Central American Integration System (#03671); *Ibero-American General Secretariat (#11024)*; *ILO (#11123)*; *Inter-American Commission on Human Rights (IACHR, #11411)*; *International Committee of the Red Cross (ICRC, #12799)*; *International Organization for Migration (IOM, #14454)*; Special Rapporteur on Human Rights of Migrants of the United Nations Organization; *UNDP (#20292)*; *UNHCR (#20327)*; *UNICEF (#20332)*; *United Nations Economic Commission for Latin America and the Caribbean (ECLAC, #20556)*; *United Nations Office on Drugs and Crime (UNODC, #20596)*; *United Nations Population Fund (UNFPA, #20612)*.

IGO Relations *United Nations (UN, #20515)*. **NGO Relations** *Red Regional de Organizaciones Civiles para las Migraciones (RROCM, #18728)*.
[2023.02.17/XM5884/E*]

- ♦ Regional Conference of Ministers of Education and Those Responsible for Economic Planning in Asia and the Pacific (meeting series)

♦ Regional Conference on Women in Latin America and the Caribbean 18770

Conférence régionale sur les femmes de l'Amérique Latine et des Caraïbes – Conferencia Regional sobre la Mujer de América Latina y el Caribe

Contact c/o CEPAL, Casilla 179 D, Santiago, Santiago Metropolitan, Chile. T. +5622102565. Fax +5622081946 – +5622080252. E-mail: dag@cepal.org.
URL: http://www.eclac.org/mujer/

History 1977, as a subsidiary permanent body of *United Nations Economic Commission for Latin America and the Caribbean (ECLAC, #20556)*. Original title: *Regional Conference on the Integration of Women into the Economic and Social Development of Latin America and the Caribbean – Conférence régionale sur l'intégration de la femme au développement économique et sociale de l'Amérique latine et des Caraïbes – Conferencia Regional para la Integración de la Mujer en el Desarrollo Económico y Social de América Latina y el Caribe*. Present name adopted at 7th Meeting, Nov 1997, Santiago (Chile). **Aims** Determine regional and sub-regional priorities for technical assistance; support *United Nations* bodies operating in the region so they can meet such needs; make recommendations to governments and to ECLAC based on studies carried out by the secretariat on implementing agreements adopted by UN regional conferences; review and periodically appraise the activities of ECLAC and other UN agencies in compliance with the Programme for the Decade of Women; in particular, draw up recommendations for regional conferences on women to be held before World Conferences; periodically evaluate the accomplishment of the Regional Plan of Action (1977), Regional Programme of Action for the Women of Latin America and the Caribbean (1995-2001) and Regional Gender Agenda commitments; provide a forum for exchange of information to facilitate mutual coordination and support of programmes for integration of women into economic and social development at various levels and to permit countries in the region to share experience. **Structure** Conference is held every 3 years. Presiding Officers of the Regional Conference (meeting twice a year) are elected by member states; they remain in office until the next Conference and link governments and ECLAC secretariat in the field of gender oriented policies. **Languages** English, Spanish. **Finance** Regular budget of ECLAC. **Activities** Research/documentation; events/meetings. **Events** *Regional Conference* Santo Domingo (Dominican Rep) 2013, *Regional Conference* Brasilia (Brazil) 2010, *Regional Conference* Mexico 2004, *Regional conference* Mexico City (Mexico) 2004, *Regional conference* Lima (Peru) 2000. **Publications** *Mujer y Desarrollo*. Various documents and publications published by ECLAC. Information Services: ECLAC Library.

Members As for ECLAC, governments of 46 countries:
Antigua-Barbuda, Argentina, Bahamas, Barbados, Belize, Bolivia, Brazil, Canada, Chile, Colombia, Costa Rica, Cuba, Dominica, Dominican Rep, Ecuador, El Salvador, France, Germany, Grenada, Guatemala, Guyana, Haiti, Honduras, Italy, Jamaica, Japan, Korea Rep, Mexico, Netherlands, Nicaragua, Norway, Panama, Paraguay, Peru, Portugal, Spain, St Kitts-Nevis, St Lucia, St Vincent-Grenadines, Suriname, Trinidad-Tobago, Türkiye, UK, Uruguay, USA, Venezuela.
Associate members (13):
Anguilla, Aruba, Bermuda, Cayman Is, Curaçao, Guadeloupe, Martinique, Montserrat, Puerto Rico, St Maarten, Turks-Caicos, Virgin Is UK, Virgin Is USA.

IGO Relations *Caribbean Community (CARICOM, #03476)*; *Comisión Interamericana de Mujeres (CIM, #04137)*; *Inter-American Development Bank (IDB, #11427)*; *International Organization for Migration (IOM, #14454)*; *Latin American Faculty of Social Sciences (#16316)*; *OAS (#17629)*; *UN Women (#20724)*; *UNDP (#20292)*; *United Nations Population Fund (UNFPA, #20612)*; *UNICEF (#20332)*; *UNHCR (#20327)*; *Office of the United Nations High Commissioner for Human Rights (OHCHR, #17697)*; *World Food Programme (WFP, #21510)*; *ILO (#11123)*; *FAO (#09260)*; *UNESCO (#20322)*; *WHO (#20950)*; *Pan American Health Organization (PAHO, #18108)*; *International Organization for Migration (IOM, #14454)*; *Development Bank of Latin America (CAF, #05055)*. **NGO Relations** Formal contacts with: *Instituto Interamericano de Derechos Humanos (IIDH, #11334)*; organizations listed as having consultative status with ECOSOC (not specified); civil society gender networks.
[2019.02.25/XF2175/c/F*]

- ♦ Regional Convention on Fisheries Cooperation among African States Bordering the Atlantic Ocean (1991 treaty)
- ♦ Regional Convention for the Management and Conservation of the Natural Forest Ecosystems and the Development of Forest Plantations (1993 treaty)
- ♦ Regional Convention on the Recognition of Studies, Certificates, Diplomas, Degrees and other Academic Qualifications in Higher Education in the African States (1981 treaty)
- ♦ Regional Convention on the Recognition of Studies, Diplomas and Degrees in Higher Education in Asia and the Pacific (1983 treaty)
- ♦ Regional Convention on the Recognition of Studies, Diplomas and Degrees in Higher Education in Latin America and the Caribbean (1974 treaty)
- ♦ Regional Convention on the Recognition of Titles, Studies and Diplomas (1911 treaty)

♦ Regional Cooperation Agreement on Combating Piracy and Armed Robbery against Ships in Asia – Information Sharing Centre (ReCAAP ISC) 18771

Exec Dir Infinite Studios, 21 Media Circle, No 05-04, Singapore 138562, Singapore. T. +6563763063. Fax +6563763066. E-mail: secretariat@recaap.org – info@recaap.org.
URL: http://www.recaap.org/

History Agreement finalized 11 Nov 2004, Tokyo (Japan); came into force 4 Sep 2006. Information Sharing Centre set up under the Agreement and officially launched 29 Nov 2006, Singapore (Singapore). Formally accorded as international organization status 30 Jan 2007. **Aims** Promote and enhance cooperation against piracy and armed robbery against ships in Asia. **Structure** Governing Council (meeting at least annually), consisting of one representative from each Contracting Party; Focal Point Senior Officers' Meeting (annual); Executive Director. **Languages** English. **Staff** 16.00 FTE, paid. **Finance** Voluntary contributions from: Host State financing and support; Contracting Parties; International organizations and other entities. **Activities** Knowledge management/information dissemination; capacity building; networking/liaising; events/meetings. **Events** *Nautical Forum* Singapore (Singapore) 2021, *Annual Governing Council Meeting* Singapore (Singapore) 2020, *Nautical Forum* Singapore (Singapore) 2020, *Annual Governing Council Meeting* Singapore (Singapore) 2019, *Piracy and Sea Robbery Conference* Singapore (Singapore) 2019. **Publications** Reports.

Members Contracting parties (20):
Australia, Bangladesh, Brunei Darussalam, Cambodia, China, Denmark, India, Japan, Korea Rep, Laos, Myanmar, Netherlands, Norway, Philippines, Singapore, Sri Lanka, Thailand, UK, USA, Vietnam.

IGO Relations Agreement of cooperation with: *International Maritime Organization (IMO, #14102)*. **NGO Relations** Memorandum of Understanding with: *Asian Shipowners Association (ASA, #01697)*; *BIMCO (#03236)*. Observer of: *Asia-Pacific Heads of Maritime Safety Agencies (APHoMSA, #01922)*.
[2020/XJ1610/E*]

♦ Regional Cooperation Agreement for the Promotion of Nuclear Science and Technology in Latin America and the Caribbean (ARCAL Agreement) 18772

Acuerdo Regional de Cooperación para la Promoción de la Ciencia y Tecnologia Nucleares en América Latina y el Caribe (ARCAL)

Coordination c/o IAEA, PO Box 100, 1400 Vienna, Austria. T. +43126000. Fax +43126007. E-mail: official.mail@iaea.org.
URL: https://www.iaea.org/news/3363/

History 1984, as *Regional Cooperative Arrangements for the Promotion of Nuclear Science and Technology in Latin America* on signature of an agreement by member countries. Current title adopted, 25 Sep 1998, when intergovernmental agreement was approved by the Board of Governors and *International Atomic Energy Agency (IAEA, #12294)* and opened for signature. Agreement entered into force, 5 Sep 2005. **Aims** Promote, foster, coordinate and implement cooperation activities for training, research, development and applications of nuclear science and technology in Latin America and the Caribbean region; target projects in the priority areas of human health, food and agriculture, energy and industry, environment and radiation protection, intensifying collaboration on the specific shared needs of members. **Structure** Board of Representatives; Technical Coordination Board. President; Vice-President; Secretary. **Languages** English, Spanish. **Staff** None. **Finance** Funding through IAEA Technical Cooperation Fund, extra budgetary contributions and financial and in-kind contributions of Member States. **Activities** Programme (as of Nov 2009): 33 active projects. **Events** *Joint Final Coordination Meeting on Improving Agricultural Production Systems Through Resource Use Efficiency* Havana (Cuba) 2017, *Meeting on nuclear cooperation* Havana (Cuba) 2003, *Technical coordination meeting* Mendoza (Argentina) 2000, *Meeting of representatives* Vienna (Austria) 1999, *Regional congress* Cusco (Peru) 1995.

Members Signatories to the ARCAL Agreement, 19 countries as of Sep 2009:
Argentina, Bolivia, Brazil, Chile, Colombia, Costa Rica, Cuba, Dominican Rep, Ecuador, El Salvador, Guatemala, Haiti, Mexico, Nicaragua, Panama, Paraguay, Peru, Uruguay, Venezuela.
Associate Member (1):
Spain. [2018/XF3074/**F***]

♦ Regional Cooperation Center for Adult Education in Latin America and the Caribbean (#03794)

♦ Regional Cooperation Council (RCC) 18773

Conseil de coopération régionale

SG Trg Bosne i Hercegovine 1/V, 71000 Sarajevo, Bosnia-Herzegovina. T. +38733561700. Fax +38733561701. E-mail: rcc@rcc.int.
URL: http://www.rcc.int/

History 27 Feb 2008. Established as successor to *Stability Pact for South Eastern Europe (inactive)*. Operational arm of *South East European Cooperation Process (SEECP, #19811)*. Since 1 Jan 2010 *South-Eastern European Health Network (SEE Health Network, #19807)* takes care of regional cooperation for health and development. **Aims** Promote mutual cooperation and European and Euro-Atlantic integration of South East Europe so as to inspire development in the region to the benefit of its people. **Structure** Annual Meeting, held back-to-back with the SEECP Summit. Board of 28. Secretariat in Sarajevo (Bosnia-Herzegovina); Liaison Office in Brussels (Belgium). **Languages** English. **Staff** 38 full-time, paid (Sarajevo: 32; Brussels: 6); 1 part-time, paid. **Finance** Contributions from: RCC members in South East Europe (1/3); other RCC members (1/3); *European Commission (EC, #06633)* (1/3). Budget (annual): euro 3 million. **Activities** Politics/policy/regulatory. **Events** *Conference on Media, Terrorism and Foreign Terrorist Fighters* Bestovje (Croatia) 2021, *South-East European parliamentarians workshop* Sarajevo (Bosnia-Herzegovina) 2008. **Publications** *RCC Newsletter* (12 a year) – electronic; *RCC Factsheet* (periodical); *RCC Flyer* (periodical). *2011-2013 Strategy and Work Programme* (2010). Annual Report.

Members Participating states (32):
Albania, Austria, Bosnia-Herzegovina, Bulgaria, Canada, Croatia, Czechia, Denmark, Finland, France, Germany, Greece, Hungary, Ireland, Italy, Kosovo, Latvia, Moldova, Montenegro, North Macedonia, Norway, Poland, Romania, Serbia, Slovakia, Slovenia, Spain, Sweden, Switzerland, Türkiye, UK, USA.
Also 14 member organizations:
Council of Europe (CE, #04881); Council of Europe Development Bank (CEB, #04897); European Bank for Reconstruction and Development (EBRD, #06315); European Investment Bank (EIB, #07599); European Union (EU, #08967) (represented by representative of the High Representative of the Union for Foreign Affairs and Security Policy and a representative of European Commission); *International Bank for Reconstruction and Development (IBRD, #12317)* (World Bank); *International Organization for Migration (IOM, #14454); NATO (#16945); OECD (#17693); Organization for Security and Cooperation in Europe (OSCE, #17887); Southeast European Cooperative Initiative (SECI, #19812); UNDP (#20292); United Nations Economic Commission for Europe (UNECE, #20555); United Nations (UN, #20515).*

IGO Relations Represented in: *Education Reform Initiative of South Eastern Europe (ERI SEE, #05372)*. Cooperates with: *International Centre for Promotion of Enterprises (ICPE, #12509)*. Memorandum of Understanding with: *Regional Anti-Corruption Initiative (RAI, #18750)*. **NGO Relations** Member of: *Centre for European Policy Studies (CEPS, #03741); European Policy Centre (EPC, #08240)*. Cooperates with: *European Association for Local Democracy (ALDA, #06110); Center for Democracy and Reconciliation in Southeast Europe (CDRSEE, #03639); European Centre for Peace and Development (ECPD, #06496); European Stability Initiative (ESI, #08828); Friedrich-Ebert-Stiftung (FES); Heinrich Böll Foundation; King Baudouin Foundation (KBF); Konrad Adenauer Foundation (KAF).* [2021/XM3681/y/**F***]

♦ Regional Cooperation for Development (inactive)
♦ Regional Cooperation in Southeast Asia on Plant Genetic Resources (inactive)
♦ Regional Cooperative Agreement for Research, Development and Training Related to Nuclear Science and Technology (1972 treaty)

♦ Regional Cooperative Agreement for Research, Development and Training Related to Nuclear Science and Technology in Asia (RCA) 18774

Dir c/o Korea Atomic Energy Research Institute, Daedeok-daero 989-111, Yuseong-gu, Daejeon 34057, Korea Rep. T. +82428682778 – +82428688584. Fax +82428641626. E-mail: rcaro@rcaro.org.
URL: http://www.rcaro.org/

History 1972, initially for 5 years. Current (7th) agreement commenced Jun 2002, for a further period of 5 years. **Aims** Promote and coordinate cooperative research, development and training projects in the field of nuclear science and technology. **Structure** Regional office in Taejon (Korea Rep). **Finance** Secretariat and "seed funding": *International Atomic Energy Agency (IAEA, #12294)*. Projects 2002-2007: *UNDP (#20292)*; IAEA; governments of Australia, Japan, China, Malaysia and the Philippines. **Activities** Projects and priorities determined by member states. Current programme: Energy; Development of TCDC in Asia and the Pacific; Research reactor utilization; Strengthening of nuclear medicine in RCA member states; Nuclear material applications; Radiation sterilization of tissue grafts; UNDP 'Environmentally sound technologies'; Strengthening of radiation protection infrastructure; Improvement of cancer therapy (Phase II); Enhancement of genetic diversity in rice; Irradiation for safety/phytosanitary measures; Animal reproduction and nutrition; Industrial application of isotopes for radiation technology. Organizes regional events related to current projects. **Events** *RAS1022 Mid-Term Review Meeting* Seoul (Korea Rep) 2020, *Workshop on Diagnosis of Cardiovascular and Pulmonary Disease* Seoul (Korea Rep) 2019, *Working Group for Coordination of the RCA Medium-Term Strategy Meeting* Seoul (Korea Rep) / Busan (Korea Rep) 2019, *Regional Meeting of National RCA Representatives* Busan (Korea Rep) 2018, *Research Project Kickoff Meeting* Jeju (Korea Rep) 2018. **Publications** Annual report.

Members Signatories to the agreement (17 countries):
Australia, Bangladesh, China, India, Indonesia, Japan, Korea Rep, Malaysia, Mongolia, Myanmar, New Zealand, Pakistan, Philippines, Singapore, Sri Lanka, Thailand, Vietnam. [2020/XF2528/**F***]

♦ Regional Cooperative Arrangements for the Promotion of Nuclear Science and Technology in Latin America / see Regional Cooperation Agreement for the Promotion of Nuclear Science and Technology in Latin America and the Caribbean (#18772)

♦ Regional Cooperative Program for the Technological Development and Modernization of Coffee Cultivation in Central America, Panama, Dominican Rep and Jamaica 18775

Programa Cooperativo Regional para el Desarrollo Tecnológico de la Caficultura en Centroamérica, República Dominica y Jamaica (PROMECAFE)

Exec Sec c/o IICA Guatemala, 7 avenida 14-44 zona 9, Edif La Galeria, cuarto piso, Oficina 402, Apdo Postal 1815, 01901 Guatemala, Guatemala. T. +50223865902. Fax +50223865923.
URL: https://promecafe.net/

History in the framework of *Inter-American Institute for Cooperation on Agriculture (IICA, #11434)*. **Aims** Connect producing countries, research institutions and international cooperation to join efforts in making coffee production a long-term sustainable activity. **Languages** English, Spanish. **Finance** Members' dues. **Activities** Events/meetings.

Members Full in 9 countries:
Costa Rica, Dominican Rep, El Salvador, Guatemala, Honduras, Jamaica, Mexico, Nicaragua, Panama. [2019.10.10/XJ4235/**E***]

♦ Regional Coordination of Economic and Social Research (#04812)
♦ Regional Coordination of Economic and Social Research on Central America and Caribbean / see Coordinadora Regional de Investigaciones Económicas y Sociales (#04812)
♦ Regional Council for Adult Education and Literacy in Africa (no recent information)

♦ Regional Council on Human Rights in Asia 18776

SG c/o Free Legal Assistance Group, Room 116 Alumni Center Annex, Magsaysay Avenue, UP Campus, Diliman, Quezon City, Philippines. Fax +6329205132. E-mail: flag@flag.com.ph.

History Founded 18 Feb 1982, Manila (Philippines), at founding meeting, the creation of the Council having been discussed in Penang (Malaysia), 2 Dec 1981. *Declaration of the Basic Duties of ASEAN Peoples and Governments* adopted by 1st General Assembly, 9 Dec 1983, Jakarta (Indonesia). **Aims** Adopt and disseminate a Regional Declaration of Human Rights that reflects the culture, values, and aspirations of the people of the region and seek the support of the people of the region for that Declaration; promote respect for individual and collective civil, political, social, economic and cultural human rights; receive petitions and complaints and assist in redressing violations of these rights; encourage governments of the region to ratify or concur in the International Conventions on Human Rights; undertake studies and research. **Activities** Advocacy/lobbying/activism. **Events** *General assembly* Bangkok (Thailand) 1988.

Members Civil rights leaders in 5 countries:
Indonesia, Malaysia, Philippines, Singapore, Thailand.

Consultative Status Consultative status granted from: *ECOSOC (#05331)* (Ros A). **IGO Relations** Accredited by: *United Nations Office at Vienna (UNOV, #20604)*. Associated with Department of Global Communications of the United Nations. **NGO Relations** Member of: *World Organisation Against Torture (OMCT, #21685).* [2016/XD0040/v/**F**]

♦ Regional Council for Planning (#04725)
♦ Regional Council for Public Savings and Financial Markets (#04698)
♦ Regional Cultural Action Centre / see Institut Régional d'Enseignement Supérieur et de Recherche en Développement Culturel (#11355)
♦ Regional Dermatology Training Centre (internationally oriented national body)

♦ Regional Dialogue on the Information Society 18777

Dialogo Regional sobre la Sociedad de la Información (DIRSI)

Coordinator c/o Inst de Estudio Peruanos, Horacio Urteaga 694, 11, Lima, Peru. T. +5113326194 ext219. Fax +5113326173.
URL: http://www.dirsi.net/

History 2004, Montevideo (Uruguay). Formally set up 2005, Rio de Janeiro (Brazil). **Aims** Create knowledge and stimulate discussion to support the development of policies that enable the effective participation of Latin America's poor and marginalized communities in emerging information societies and economies. **Structure** Management Team. **Languages** English, Spanish. **Staff** 4.00 FTE, paid. **Activities** Events/meetings. **IGO Relations** *International Development Research Centre (IDRC, #13162)*. **NGO Relations** Member of: *Alliance for Affordable Internet (A4AI, #00651).* [2016.06.27/XJ4816/**F**]

♦ Regional Disaster Information Center for Latin America and the Caribbean 18778

Centro Regional de Información sobre Desastres para América Latina y el Caribe (CRID)

Contact address not obtained. T. +50622484600. Fax +50622484600.
Facebook: https://www.facebook.com/CRIDlac/

History 1990, by *Pan American Health Organization (PAHO, #18108)*. Since 1994, a multi-agency project of *United Nations Office for Disaster Risk Reduction (UNDRR, #20595)*, PAHO, *International Federation of Red Cross and Red Crescent Societies (#13526), Centro de Coordinación para la Prevención de los Desastres Naturales en América Central (CEPREDENAC, #03795)*; regional office of *Bureau international des Médecins sans frontières (MSF International, #03366)*, and the National Emergency Commission (CNE) of Costa Rica. **Aims** Promote a culture of disaster risk reduction (DRR) in the nations of Latin America and the Caribbean, by means of analysis, systematization and diffusion of information on risk management, promotion and strengthening of information centres, a cooperative effort with key players and an opportune and efficient response to user's requirements and those of players working within the milieu of DRR; improve access to disaster-related information for technicians working in different institutions and the general population through the use of computers and the Internet; contribute to creating a culture of disaster risk reduction using these technologies. **Structure** Part of the *'Foundation for the Coordination of Information Resources in Disaster Preparedness (FUNDACRID)'*. Headquarters based in San José (Costa Rica). Departments (5): General Direction; Information Management; Technologies; Communication; Finances and Administration. **Languages** English, French, Spanish. **Staff** 7.00 FTE, paid. **Activities** Serves as one of the largest reference centres with over 18,000 full text specific documents freely accessible by users; improves disaster information gathering, processing and dissemination; provides information services on all aspects of disaster reduction to a large base of users in Latin America and the Caribbean; strengthens local and national capacities for the creation and maintenance of disaster information centres; develops information products for users and partners; promotes the use of IT in disaster information management and dissemination. Has developed a network of 14 information centres in Central America and South America that provide information about disasters and risk management. **Publications** Collection of catalogues about tools and information resources for disaster preparedness (1st ed 2009, 2nd ed 2010). Information Services: Website on education and disaster reduction, created in 2009 and periodically updated. **IGO Relations** Other partners: *UNESCO (#20322); UNICEF (#20332)*. **NGO Relations** Other partner: US National Library of Medicine (NLM). [2018/XE3341/**E**]

♦ Regional Documentation Centre on Oral Traditions / see Centre for Linguistic and Historical Studies by Oral Tradition (#03771)
♦ Regional East European and Mediterranean Countries ALARA Network / see Regional European and Central Asian ALARA Network (#18784)
♦ Regional Economic Development Working Group Monitoring Committee Secretariat (no recent information)

♦ Regional Electricity Regulators Association of Southern Africa (RERA) 18779

Exec Sec Bonsec Heights, No 6 Feld Street, Office No 3, PO Box 23029, Windhoek, Namibia. T. +26461221720. Fax +26461223176. E-mail: secretariat@rerasadc.com.

History Jul 2002, by *Southern African Development Community (SADC, #19843)*, in terms of SADC Protocol on Energy (1996), SADC Energy Cooperation Policy and Strategy (1996), SADC Energy Section Action Plan (1997), SADC Energy Activity Plan (2000) and in pursuit of the initiative of *New Partnership for Africa's Development (NEPAD, #17091)* and *African Energy Commission (AFREC, #00298)*. Officially launched 26 Sep 2002, Windhoek (Namibia). Registered in accordance with the law of Namibia, 3 Oct 2003. **Aims** Facilitate harmonization of regulatory policies, legislation, standards and practices; be a platform for effective cooperation among energy regulators within the SADC region. **Structure** Plenary (annual). Executive Committee. Portfolio Committees (3): Capacity Building; Facilitation; Regulatory Cooperation. Secretariat, headed by Executive Secretary. **Finance** Support from: *United States Agency for International Development (USAID)*. **Events** *Annual Conference* Johannesburg (South Africa) 2010.

Members Electricity supply industry regulators of SADC countries, limited to one regulator per country. Members in 9 countries:
Angola, Lesotho, Malawi, Mozambique, Namibia, South Africa, Tanzania UR, Zambia, Zimbabwe.

IGO Relations Invited to meetings of: *Regional Association of Energy Regulators for Eastern and Southern Africa (RAERESA, #18751)*. **NGO Relations** Member of: *International Confederation of Energy Regulators (ICER, #12859)*. Invited to meetings of: *African Forum for Utility Regulators (AFUR, #00324).* [2011/XJ2864/**E**]

♦ Regional Energy Resources Information Center (RERIC) 18780

Centre régional d'information sur les ressources d'énergie

Dir c/o Asian Institute of Technology, PO Box 4, Klong Luang, Pathum Thani, 12120, Thailand. T. +6625245413 – +6625246216. Fax +6625245439 – +6625162126. E-mail: mithulan@ait.ac.th – enreric@ait.ac.th.

URL: http://www.rericjournal.ait.ac.th/
History May 1978, Bangkok (Thailand), with the name *Renewable Energy Resources Information Center*, as a specialized information centre of *Asian Institute of Technology (AIT, #01519)*, coming within the remit of *AIT Library*. Present name adopted 1 Jan 1988. **Aims** Act as a specialized information centre for *renewable energy* – solar, biomass, wind, small scale hydropower – and for energy conservation and energy planning R and D projects: promote energy efficient and *environmentally sound* technology; establish contacts and cooperate with existing centres, organizations and individuals active in the field on a world-wide basis, so as to avoid duplication of effort and seek collaboration in meeting the information needs of *developing countries*. **Languages** English. **Staff** 5.00 FTE, paid. **Finance** Members' dues. Support from: AIT; own income. **Activities** Fields of specialization: *'biomass energy'*: biogas, alcohol, fuelwood, charcoal, producer gas, biomass energy farms; *'solar energy'*: solar radiation, solar collectors, solar energy conversion, solar energy storage, solar drying, solar heating and cooling, solar power plants, solar water pumps; *'wind energy'*: irrigation, electric power generation, heating and cooling; *'small-scale hydropower'*; *'energy conservation'*; *'energy planning'*. **Events** *Seminar on new and renewable energy* Hanoi (Vietnam) 1989. **Publications** *EE – Energy and Environment News* (4 a year); *International Energy Journal* (4 a year). *AIT Research Reports*. Occasional publications including: do-it-yourself booklets; directories; monographs; conference proceedings; theses; internal sources of information, including reports of research work carried out by AIT postgraduate and doctoral students and specialists. Information Services: Provides information to both developing and industrialized countries. **Information Services** *RERIC Database* – about 11,500 records on publications related to energy and renewable energy resources available at AIT.
Members Individual; Institutional. Members (145) in 41 countries and territories:
Australia, Bangladesh, Belgium, Botswana, Brazil, Canada, China, Costa Rica, Dominica, Fiji, France, Germany, Hong Kong, India, Indonesia, Israel, Italy, Japan, Malaysia, Morocco, Nepal, Netherlands, New Caledonia, Norway, Pakistan, Papua New Guinea, Philippines, Portugal, Saudi Arabia, Seychelles, Singapore, South Africa, Sri Lanka, Sweden, Switzerland, Thailand, Trinidad-Tobago, Uganda, UK, USA, Venezuela.
International and regional institutional members (16):
Abdus Salam International Centre for Theoretical Physics (ICTP, #00005); *Asian Development Bank (ADB, #01422)*; Asian Institute of Technology (AIT); *Australian Aid (inactive)*; *Commonwealth Science Council (CSC, #04361)*; *Commonwealth Scientific and Industrial Research Organization (CSIRO)*; *East-West Center (EWC, #05263)*; *European Cooperative Research Network on Sustainable Rural Environmental and Energy (SREN, see: #08871)*; *FAO Regional Office for Asia and the Pacific (RAP, #09266)*; *International Development Research Centre (IDRC, #13162)*; *International Research Center for Energy and Economic Development (ICEED)*; *Pacific Community (SPC, #17942)*; *Regional Centre for Energy, Heat and Mass Transfer for Asia and Pacific (RCEHMT, no recent information)*; *UNIDO (#20336)*; *United States Agency for International Development (USAID)*; *University of the South Pacific (USP, #20703)*.
NGO Relations Member of: *Asian and Pacific Energy-Environment Planning Network (APENPLAN, no recent information)*; *International Network for Sustainable Energy (INFORSE, #14331)*. [2010/XE0042/y/**E**]

♦ Regional English Language Centre / see SEAMEO Regional Language Centre (#19181)
♦ Regional Environmental Assessment Programme (inactive)

♦ Regional Environmental Centre for the Caucasus (REC Caucasus) . 18781

Exec Dir 76C Chavchavadze Ave, 3rd floor, 0179 Tbilisi, Georgia. T. +9953222253649 – +9953222253648. Fax +995322916352. E-mail: info@rec-caucasus.org.
URL: http://www.rec-caucasus.org/
History Mar 2000, following signature of founding document (charter) signed by the Governments of Armenia, Azerbaijan, Georgia and European Union in Sep 1999, within the framework of the "Environment for Europe Process". **Aims** Assist South Caucasus states in solving environmental problems; support in building civil society through promotion of public participation in the decision-making process, development of free exchange of information and encouragement of cooperation at national and regional levels among NGOs, governments, businesses, local communities and all other stakeholders. **Structure** Board of Directors; International Advisory Council; Executive Body. **Languages** Armenian, Azerbaijani, English, Georgian, Russian. **Staff** 21.00 FTE, paid. **Finance** Based on grant and service contracts. Donors include: Eurasian Partnership Foundation; *European Commission (EC, #06633)*; *Global Environment Facility (GEF, #10346)*; *Organization for Security and Cooperation in Europe (OSCE, #17887)*; *United States Agency for International Development (USAID)*; governments of Germany, Liechtenstein, Netherlands, Norway. **Activities** Projects/programmes; networking/liaising; training/education; events/meetings; knowledge management/information dissemination; capacity building. **Events** *Annual International Conference* Shindisi (Georgia) 2006, *Annual International Conference* Tbilisi (Georgia) 2005, *Annual International Conference* Tbilisi (Georgia) 2004, *Annual International Conference* Tbilisi (Georgia) 2003, *Annual International Conference* Tbilisi (Georgia) 2002. **Publications** Annual Report; directories; brochures.
Members Governments of 3 countries:
Armenia, Azerbaijan, Georgia.
International organization:
European Union (EU, #08967).
IGO Relations Accredited to the Conference of the Parties of: *Secretariat of the United Nations Convention to Combat Desertification (Secretariat of the UNCCD, #19208)*. Accredited by: *UNEP (#20299)*. **NGO Relations** Member of: *GEF CSO Network (GCN, #10087)*; *Mountain Partnership (MP, #16862)*.
[2017.06.01/XM3545/y/**E***]

♦ Regional Environmental Centre for Central Asia (internationally oriented national body)

♦ Regional Environmental Centre for Central and Eastern Europe (REC) 18782

Centre régional pour l'environnement en Europe centrale et en Europe de l'Est
Exec Dir Ady Endre ut 9-11, Szentendre 2000, Hungary. T. +3626504000. Fax +3626311294.
URL: http://www.rec.org/
History 6 Sep 1990, Budapest (Hungary). Signing of the International Agreement on the Legal Status of REC, 13 Jul 2011. **Aims** Contribute to transparency, sustainability and European integration, implementing projects that build resilience to climate change, promote clean energy solutions, champion sustainable mobility and strengthen environmental governance. **Activities** Networking/liaising; knowledge management/information dissemination; financial and/or material support. **Events** *Workshop on Promoting Transboundary Water Cooperation in the Middle East and Northern Africa Region on the Basis of the Water Convention* Budapest (Hungary) 2015, *Meeting* Szentendre (Hungary) 2012, *Local government climate change leadership summit* Copenhagen (Denmark) 2009, *Regional workshop on the phase-out of lead in gasoline* Burgas (Bulgaria) 1997, *Environmental media workshop* Szentendre (Hungary) 1997. **Publications** *Green Horizon* (4 a year) in English. *NGO Directory*. Annual Report; surveys; assessment results; workshop proceedings. **Information Services** *Business Information Service (BIS)* – information and research services to encourage business and industry to adopt sustainable development practices in Central and Eastern Europe and to help build local capacity to solve environmental problems consistent with sustainable development principles.
Members Local Offices and beneficiary countries (17):
Albania, Bosnia-Herzegovina, Bulgaria, Croatia, Czechia, Estonia, Hungary, Latvia, Lithuania, Montenegro, North Macedonia, Poland, Romania, Serbia, Slovakia, Slovenia, Türkiye.
IGO Relations Accredited to the Conference of the Parties of: *Secretariat of the United Nations Convention to Combat Desertification (Secretariat of the UNCCD, #19208)*. Observer to: *Intergovernmental Negotiating Committee for a Legally Binding Agreement on Forests in Europe (INC-Forests, inactive)*. Accredited by: *United Nations Framework Convention on Climate Change – Secretariat (UNFCCC, #20564)*. Member of: *International Commission for the Protection of the Danube River (ICPDR, #12720)*. **NGO Relations** Member of: *Bellagio Forum for Sustainable Development (BFSD, no recent information)*; *British Overseas NGO's for Development (BOND)*; *Climate and Clean Air Coalition (CCAC, #04010)*; *Dinaric Arc Initiative (DAI, no recent information)*; *Global Health and Environment Library Network (GELNET, no recent information)*; *International Network for Environmental Compliance and Enforcement (INECE, #14261)*; *International Network for Sustainable Energy (INFORSE, #14331)*. Partner of: *Partnership for Clean Fuels and Vehicles (PCFV, #18231)*.
[2018.06.22/XE1435/**E***]

♦ Regionale Organisation der FDI für Europa / see European Regional Organization of the Fédération dentaire internationale (#08345)

♦ Regional Episcopal Conference of French-Speaking West Africa (inactive)
♦ Regional Episcopal Conference of North Africa (#04605)

♦ Regional Episcopal Conference of West Africa (RECOWA) 18783

Conférence épiscopale régionale de l'Afrique de l'Ouest (CERAO)
SG PO Box 12135, Garki, Abuja, Federal Capital Territory, Nigeria. T. +22587535379. E-mail: info@recowacerao.org.
Pres address not obtained.
URL: https://recowacerao.org/
History 2007, Abuja (Nigeria). Replaced *Conférence épiscopale régionale de l'Afrique de l'Ouest francophone (CERAO, inactive)* and *Association of Episcopal Conferences of Anglophone West Africa (AECAWA, inactive)*, both which continued to operate until 1 Sep 2009. Former names and other names: *Association of the Episcopal Conferences of West Africa (AECOWA)* – former. **Aims** Enhance the Church's mission in the region; maintain and foster relations between the constituent episcopal conferences and establish close relations between the episcopal conferences. **Structure** Commissions (8): Seminaries, Clergy and Religious; Justice, Peace and Development; Laity and Family; Inter-Religious Dialogue and Ecumenism; Catechises, Catholic Education and Culture; Social communications; Liturgy, Theology and Biblical Apostolate; Mission and Migration. **Languages** English, French, Portuguese. **Staff** 12.00 FTE, paid. **Finance** Sources: members' dues. **Activities** Networking/liaising; religious activities. **Events** *Assembly* Yamoussoukro (Côte d'Ivoire) 2012, *Assembly* Banjul (Gambia) 2009, *Assembly* Abuja (Nigeria) 2007.
Members in 16 countries:
Benin, Burkina Faso, Cape Verde, Côte d'Ivoire, Gambia, Ghana, Guinea, Guinea-Bissau, Liberia, Mali, Mauritania, Niger, Nigeria, Senegal, Sierra Leone, Togo.
Consultative Status Consultative status granted from: *African Commission on Human and Peoples' Rights (ACHPR, #00255)* (Observer). **IGO Relations** Observer status with (1): *Economic Community of West African States (ECOWAS, #05312)*. **NGO Relations** Member of (1): *Symposium of Episcopal Conferences of Africa and Madagascar (SECAM, #20077)*. [2020/XM3475/**D**]

♦ Regionales Informationszentrum der Vereinten Nationen (#20621)

♦ Regional European and Central Asian ALARA Network (RECAN) . . . 18784

Contact c/o IAEA, Dept of Nuclear Safety and Security, PO Box 100, Wagramer Strasse 5, 1400 Vienna, Austria. T. +431260022713. Fax +43126007.
Contact EKOTEH Ltd, Vladimira Ruzdjaka 21, HR-10000 Zagreb, Croatia.
History 2001, as *Regional East European and Mediterranean Countries ALARA Network (REMAN)*, to replace *Central Eastern European ALARA Network (CEEAN, inactive)*. Present name adopted 2005. **Activities** Organizes workshops. [2010/XM1875/**F**]

♦ Regional Federation of Health Informatics Societies in Latin America and the Caribbean / see International Medical Informatics Association for Latin America and the Caribbean (#14135)

♦ Regional Fisheries Committee for the Gulf of Guinea 18785

Comité régional des pêches du Golfe de Guinée (COREP)
Contact c/o MINEF, BP 8224, Libreville, Gabon.
URL: http://www.fao.org/fishery/rfb/corep
History 1984. Convention signed 21 Jun 1984. **Aims** Be informed about the situation of *fisheries* in the region covered by the Convention and gather all data referring to *fishing* resources; coordinate the fishery policies of the member states in the region. **Events** *Extraordinary session* Brazzaville (Congo Brazzaville) 2009, *Ordinary session* Brazzaville (Congo Brazzaville) 2008.
Members Representatives from 7 countries:
Angola, Cameroon, Congo Brazzaville, Congo DR, Equatorial Guinea, Gabon, Sao Tomé-Principe.
IGO Relations *Fishery Committee for the Eastern Central Atlantic (CECAF, #09784)*. [2009/XF1064/**E***]

♦ Regional Fund for Agricultural Technology (#09834)

♦ Regional Gateway for Technology Transfer and Climate Change Action (REGATTA) 18786

Portal Regional para la Transferencia de Tecnología y la Acción frente al Cambio Climático en América Latina y el Caribe
Secretariat UNEP, Clayton City of of Knowledge, Bldg 103, Morse Avenue, Ancón, Panama, Panamá, Panama PANAMÁ, Panama. T. +5073053100. Fax +5073053105. E-mail: regatta@unep.org.
URL: http://www.climatechange-regatta.org/
History Set up as the regional node of *Global Adaptation Network (GAN, #10170)*. Launched Jul 2012. **Aims** Strengthen capacity and knowledge sharing of climate change technologies and experiences for adaptation and mitigation in *Latin America* and the *Caribbean*. **Finance** Supported by governments of Spain, Norway and Sweden. **Activities** Seminars, workshops and policy dialogues. **IGO Relations** Partners include: *Inter-American Development Bank (IDB, #11427)*; *Latin American Energy Organization (#16313)*; *University of the West Indies (UWI, #20705)*. **NGO Relations** Partners include: *International Centre for Tropical Agriculture (#12527)*; *UNEP Copenhagen Climate Centre (#20296)*. [2020/XJ7850/**F**]

♦ Regional Gene Bank for Plant Genetic Resources / see SADC Plant Genetic Resources Centre (#19024)
♦ Regional Heads of Government Meeting (meeting series)
♦ Regional HIV and AIDS Behaviour Change Communication Network / see African Network for Strategic Communication in Health and Development (#00396)

♦ Regional Humid Tropics Hydrology and Water Resources Centre for South East Asia and the Pacific (HTC) 18787

Dir c/o HTC Kuala Lumpur, Dept of Irrigation, No 2 Jalan Ledang, Off Jalan Duta, 50480 Kuala Lumpur, Malaysia. T. +60320958700. Fax +60320953366. E-mail: htckl@water.gov.my.
Sec address not obtained.
URL: http://htckl.water.gov.my/
History 17 Apr 1996, Kuala Lumpur (Malaysia). Established upon approval of Malaysia Cabinet Paper. Memorandum of Agreement signed between Government of Malaysia and *UNESCO (#20322)*, 28 Oct 1999. Founded as one of the UNESCO Category 2 Water Centre, to achieve the 2030 Agenda of the Sustainable Development Goals. Former names and other names: *Humid Tropics Centre Kuala Lumpur (HTC KL)* – alias. **Aims** Promote a conducive atmosphere for collaboration among countries in the regions of Southeast Asia and the Pacific through technology and information exchange, education and science; increase scientific and technological knowledge about hydrologic cycle, thus increasing our capacity to better manage and develop our water resources in a holistic manner. **Structure** Coordination Committee (meets annually) oversees programmes and activities and comprises Chairman, Secretary, representatives from National Committee for IHP, UNESCO of Southeast Asia and the Pacific, UNESCO, intergovernmental organizations and observers. Secretariat operated by staff of the Department of Irrigation and Drainage Malaysia in Kuala Lumpur (Malaysia). **Finance** Sources: donations. Other sources: governments of Japan and Germany; corporate organizations. Supported by: *UNESCO (#20322)*. **Activities** Events/meetings; knowledge management/information dissemination; projects/programmes; publishing activities; research and development; training/education. Deals with UNESCO regarding various activities in the region undertaken by the National Committees of International Hydrological Programme.
Members Governments of 20 countries and territories:
Australia, Cambodia, China, Fiji, Indonesia, Japan, Kiribati, Korea DPR, Korea Rep, Laos, Malaysia, New Zealand, Niue, Papua New Guinea, Philippines, Samoa USA, Solomon Is, Thailand, Tonga, Vietnam.
IGO Relations Cooperates with (3): *International Hydrological Programme (IHP, #13826)*; *UNESCO Office, Jakarta – Regional Bureau for Sciences in Asia and the Pacific (#20313)*; *Water Center for the Humid Tropics of Latin America and the Caribbean (#20824)*. [2022/XE3625/**E***]

♦ Regional Information Network / see Regional Information System (#18788)
♦ Regional Information Service Centre for Southeast Asia on Appropriate Technology (internationally oriented national body)

♦ Regional Information System 18788

Sistema Regional de Información (SIRI)

Coordinator c/o OREALC, Calle Enrique Delpiano 2058, Plaza Pedro de Valdivia, Casilla 127, Providencia, 7511019 Santiago, Santiago Metropolitan, Chile. T. +5626551050. Fax +5626551046. E-mail: santiago@unesco.org.

History 1985, Santiago (Chile). Established within the framework of *Major Project in the Field of Education in Latin America and the Caribbean (inactive)* of *UNESCO Regional Bureau for Education in Latin America and the Caribbean (#20318)*. Became independent on termination of PROMEDLAC, Mar 2001. Former names and other names: *Regional Information Network* – former; *Sistema Regional de Información del Proyecto Principal (SIRI)* – former. **Aims** In cooperation with UNESCO Institute for Statistics, contribute to the collection, use and dissemination of *educational information* in the *Latin American* and *Caribbean* region, in the framework of international cooperation for development; support the Regional Project of Education; develop new patterns of data analysis which permit examination of educational policies adopted by countries from a regional perspective; contribute to improve production and analytical capabilities of statistics and indicators systems in the field of education in the countries of the region. **Structure** Focal points in the Ministries of Education of member countries. **Finance** Contributions from *UNESCO (#20322)*. Ad hoc grants from: *Convenio Andrés Bello de integración educativa, científica y cultural de América Latina y España (Convenio Andrés Bello, #04785)*; *Ford Foundation (#09858)*; *Inter-American Development Bank (IDB, #11427)*; *International Bank for Reconstruction and Development (IBRD, #12317)* (World Bank); *United States Agency for International Development (USAID)*. **Activities** Organizes: workshops for statistical officers; workshops on information-related subjects, such as production and use of information for policy-making and evaluation; studies aimed at improving the use of information. **Publications** Studies on statistical systems and indicators in the field of education.

Members Governments of 35 countries and territories:
Antigua-Barbuda, Argentina, Aruba, Bahamas, Barbados, Belize, Bolivia, Brazil, Chile, Colombia, Costa Rica, Cuba, Dominica, Dominican Rep, Ecuador, El Salvador, Grenada, Guatemala, Guyana, Haiti, Honduras, Jamaica, Mexico, Neth Antilles, Nicaragua, Panama, Paraguay, Peru, St Kitts-Nevis, St Lucia, St Vincent-Grenadines, Suriname, Trinidad-Tobago, Uruguay, Venezuela.

NGO Relations Access to regional education studies through: *Information Network on Education for Latin America (no recent information)*. [2011/XK0192/**E***]

♦ Regional Information Technology and Software Engineering Centre (RITSEC) 18789

Secretariat 11-A Hassan Sabry St, Zamalek, Cairo, 11211, Egypt. T. +20227391300 – +20227361779. Fax +20227360955 – +2020959.

URL: https://www.riti.org/

History Also referred to by French initials *CERIST*. **Aims** Help accelerate socio-economic development of the Arab region and support its readiness for the global knowledge-based economy. **Languages** Arabic, English. **Activities** Conducts/contributes to national and regional events; catalyzes the socio-economic development of the region through intelligent utilization of ICT; initiates, encourages and promote human resource development and transfer of knowledge and experience within the region; supports development of the information and communication infrastructure, resources and value added services. **Events** *Resumed regular session* Rome (Italy) 2006. **IGO Relations** Cooperates with: *Islamic World Educational, Scientific and Cultural Organization (ICESCO, #16058)*. **NGO Relations** *Regional Institute for Informatics and Telecommunications (IRSIT, no recent information)*. Member of: *EuroMed Permanent University Forum (EPUF, #05731)*. [2010.09.16/XE3453/**E**]

- ♦ Regional Institute of Higher Education and Development / see SEAMEO Regional Centre for Higher Education and Development (#19174)
- ♦ Regional Institute of Higher Education and Research in Cultural Development (#11355)
- ♦ Regional Institute for Population Studies (no recent information)
- ♦ Regional Institute for Training and Research in Statistics for the Near East / see Arab Institute for Training and Research in Statistics (#00987)

♦ Regional Integrated Multi-Hazard Early Warning System for Africa and Asia (RIMES) 18790

Operational Office AIT, PO Box 4, Klong Luang, Pathum Thani, 12120, Thailand. E-mail: rimes@rimes.int.

Street Address 2nd Floor, Outreach Bldg – AIT campus, 58 Moo 9 Paholyothin Rd, Klong Nueng, Klong Luang, Pathum Thani, 12120, Thailand. T. +6625245901.

Contact address not obtained. T. +9603323084. Fax +9603341797. E-mail: admin@meteorology.gov.mv.

URL: https://www.rimes.int/

History 30 Apr 2009. Evolved from the efforts of countries in Africa and Asia, in the aftermath of the 2004 Indian Ocean tsunami. Evolved from the proposal by Royal Thai Government to the Special ASEAN Leaders' Meeting, 6 Jan 2005, and subsequently to the Phuket Ministerial Meeting on Tsunami Early Warning Arrangement, 28-29 Jan 2005. Registered with *United Nations (UN, #20515)*, 1 July 2009. **Structure** Council, composed of heads of National Meteorological and Hydrological Services and national scientific and technical agencies. Executive Board; Advisory Committee; Program Unit; Secretariat. Operates from its regional warning centre located at campus of *Asian Institute of Technology (AIT, #01519)*, Pathumthani (Thailand). **Activities** Knowledge management/information dissemination; research/documentation; training/education. **IGO Relations** Partner of (9): *DANIDA*; *European Centre for Medium-Range Weather Forecasts (ECMWF, #06490)*; *FAO (#09260)*; *International Center for Agricultural Research in the Dry Areas (ICARDA, #12466)*; *UNDP (#20292)*; *UNEP (#20299)*; *United Nations Economic and Social Commission for Asia and the Pacific (ESCAP, #20557)*; *United States Agency for International Development (USAID)*; *World Meteorological Organization (WMO, #21649)*. [2022/AA3008/**F***]

♦ Regional Inter-Agency Task Team on Children and AIDS in Eastern and Southern Africa (RIATT-ESA) 18791

Contact c/o REPSSI, 266 West Ave, Unit 2, Waterfront Office Park, Randburg, 2194, South Africa. T. +27119985820. E-mail: riattesamanagement@repssi.org.

URL: http://www.riatt-esa.org/

History 2006. Also referred to as *Eastern and Southern Africa Regional Inter Agency Task Team on Children and AIDS (RIATT-ESA)*. **Aims** Support the UN General Assembly Special Session declaration of commitment to universal access for children to prevention, care, treatment and support in the context of *HIV* and AIDS, through a multi-sectoral joint response within the eastern and southern African region. **Structure** Steering Committee. **Events** *Psychosocial Support Forum (PSS Forum)* Windhoek (Namibia) 2019.

Members Partners: Academic institutions (6); Bilateral donor agencies (5); Civil society organizations (23); Grant-Making Trust (1); Humanitarian aid organization (1): Multilateral agencies (2); Regional economic cluster (1). Partners include 30 organizations listed in this Yearbook:
- *African Child Policy Forum (ACPF, #00246)*;
- *African Network for Care of Children Affected by HIV/AIDS (ANECCA, #00382)*;
- *Africa Platform for Social Protection (APSP, #00514)*;
- *Australian Aid (inactive)*;
- *CARE International (CI, #03429)*;
- *Disability HIV and AIDS Trust (DHAT, #05094)*;
- *Eastern African Network of AIDS Service Organizations (EANNASO, see: #00272)*;
- *Frontline AIDS (#10007)*;
- *HelpAge International (#10904)*;
- *Hope Worldwide*;
- *Inter-Agency Task Team on Children affected by AIDS (IATT, #11394)*;
- *International Federation of Red Cross and Red Crescent Societies (#13526)*;
- *International Network for Caregiving Children (INCC)*;
- *Irish Aid*;
- *Media Monitoring Africa*;
- *MIET Africa*;
- *Network of African People Living with HIV and AIDS (NAP+, #16986)* (Southern Africa Region NAPSAR);
- *Norwegian Agency for Development Cooperation (Norad)*;
- *Pan African Treatment Access Movement (PATAM, #18071)*;
- *REPSSI (#18848)*;
- *Restless Development*;
- *Save the Children Federation (SCF)*;
- *Southern Africa HIV/AIDS Information Dissemination Service (SAfAIDS, #19831)*;
- *Southern African Development Community (SADC, #19843)*;
- *SRHR Africa Trust (SAT, #19934)*;
- *Swedish International Development Cooperation Agency (Sida)*;
- *Swiss Agency for Development and Cooperation (SDC)*;
- *UNICEF (#20332)*;
- *Voluntary Service Overseas (VSO)*;
- *World Vision International (WVI, #21904)*. [2020/XJ7262/y/**E**]

- ♦ Regional International Organization for Plant Protection and Animal Health (#17830)
- ♦ Regional Inter-University Council (inactive)

♦ Regional Islamic Da'wah Council of Southeast Asia and the Pacific (RISEAP) 18792

Conseil régional islamique Da'wah de l'Asie du Sud-Est et du Pacifique – Majlis Da'wah Islamiah Serantau Asia Tenggara dan Pasifik

SG Mohamad Marzuki Mohamad Omar, PERKIM Building, Jalan Sultan Azlan Shah, 51200 Kuala Lumpur, Malaysia. T. +60340428166 – +60340412417. Fax +60340410655. E-mail: webmaster@riseap.org.

URL: http://riseap.org/

History 11 Nov 1980, Kuala Lumpur (Malaysia), at Inaugural Conference, as a result of a regional Islamic Conference, Jan 1980, Kuala Lumpur. Also referred to as *South-East Asia and Pacific Region Islamic Dawah Council*. **Aims** Bring together the Muslim-minority countries in East Asia and the Pacific in order to pursue collective ambitions and remain fired with enthusiasm of the Islamic cause. **Structure** General Assembly (every 2 years); Executive Committee; Secretariat based in Kuala Lumpur (Malaysia), headed by Secretary-General. **Languages** Arabic, Chinese, English, Malay. **Staff** 9.00 FTE, paid. **Finance** Funded by the Government of Malaysia and the State of Sarawak. Annual budget: US$ 300,000. **Activities** Training/education; projects/programmes; guidance/assistance/consulting; events/meetings. **Events** *Biennial General Assembly* Bangkok (Thailand) 2019, *Biennial General Assembly* Singapore (Singapore) 2017, *Forum* Bangkok (Thailand) 2013, *Biennial General Assembly* Bogor (Indonesia) 2007, *Biennial General Assembly* Kuching (Malaysia) 1999. **Publications** *Al Nahdah* (3 a year). Occasional religious booklets and literature.

Members Ordinary: Muslim organizations (49) in 20 countries and territories:
Australia, Cambodia, Fiji, Hong Kong, Indonesia, Japan, Korea Rep, Macau, Malaysia, Myanmar, New Caledonia, New Zealand, Papua New Guinea, Philippines, Samoa, Singapore, Taiwan, Thailand, Tonga, Vanuatu.
Associate: Muslim organizations (3) in 3 countries:
Maldives, Sri Lanka, Vietnam. [2018.06.01/XD3136/**D**]

♦ Regional Judicial and Legal Services Commission (RJLSC) 18793

Contact c/o Caribbean Court of Justice, 134 Henry Street, PO Box 1768, Port-of-Spain, Trinidad-Tobago. E-mail: rjlsc@rjlsc.org.

URL: https://ccj.org/about-the-ccj/rjlsc-2/

History 14 Feb 2001. Established in accordance to Article V(1) of the Agreement Establishing *Caribbean Court of Justice (CCJ, #03486)*, executed by the Heads of Government of *Caribbean Community (CARICOM, #03476)*. Entered into force, 23 Jul 2003, by virtue of the deposit of Instruments of Ratification or Accession in accordance with Article XXXIV, by three Member States of the Caribbean Community. **Aims** Be a modern and effective administrative system exemplifying the best practices in support of the CCJ discharging a fair and efficient system of justice; ensure that the financial and human resources management of the Court and Commission is efficient, equitable and progressive; cultivate an environment conducive to the development of professionalism, work ethics, managerial competence and job satisfaction. **Structure** Commission composed of the President of the Court who is also the Chairman of the Commission; two persons nominated jointly by the Organisation of the Commonwealth Caribbean Bar Association (OCCBA) and the Organisation of Eastern Caribbean States (OECS) Bar Association; one chairman of the Judicial Services Commission of a contracting state selected in rotation in the English alphabetical order for a period of three years; the Chairman of a Public Service Commission of a contracting state selected in rotation in the reverse English alphabetical order for a period of three years; two persons from civil society nominated jointly by the Secretary-General of the Caribbean Community and the Director General of the OECS for a period of three years following consultations with regional non-governmental organisations; two distinguished jurists nominated jointly by the Dean of the Faculty of Law of the University of the West Indies, the Deans of the Faculties of Law of any of the contracting states and the Chairman of the Council of Legal Education; and two persons nominated jointly by the Bar or Law Associations of the Contracting Parties. **Languages** English. **Staff** 4.00 FTE, paid. **Finance** CCJ Trust Fund was developed to ensure financial independence of the Caribbean Court of Justice from political interference. The Fund was established with US$ 100,000,000 from contributions of Member States of Caricom. The fund was then turned over to trustees to finance expenditures of the Court (remuneration of judges and other employees, operation of the court) in perpetuity. The CCJ Trust Fund also finances expenditure of the Regional Judicial and Legal Services Commission. **Activities** Politics/policy/regulatory. The main functions of the Commission are set out in Article V.3(1) of the Agreement. This Article provides that: "The Commission shall have responsibility for: making appointments to the office of Judge of the Court, other than that of President making appointments of those officials and employees referred to in Article XXVII and for determining the salaries and allowances to be paid to such officials and employees; the determination of the terms and conditions of service of officials and employees; and the termination of appointments in accordance with the provisions of the Agreement." **Publications** Annual Report.

Members Member States and Territories (15):
Antigua-Barbuda, Bahamas, Barbados, Belize, Dominica, Grenada, Guyana, Haiti, Jamaica, Montserrat, St Kitts-Nevis, St Lucia, St Vincent-Grenadines, Suriname, Trinidad-Tobago.

IGO Relations Represented on the Commission: *University of the West Indies (UWI, #20705)*. Also represented on the Commissions of: Community Secretariat; Heads of Government of Member States of CARICOM; Judicial Services; Public Service. **NGO Relations** Represented on the Commission: *Organization of Commonwealth Caribbean Bar Associations (OCCBA, inactive)*; *Organization of Eastern Caribbean Bar Associations (OECS Bar Association, #17863)*; Regional Bar or Law Associations. [2022.10.18/XE4193/**E***]

- ♦ Regional Library of Medicine / see Latin American and Caribbean Centre on Health Sciences Information (#16267)
- ♦ Regional Marine and Coastal Conservation Programme for West Africa (#18528)

♦ Regional Marine Pollution Emergency Information and Training Centre – Wider Caribbean (REMPEITC-Carib) 18794

Dir Ministry of Traffic, Seru Mahuma z/n, Aviation-Meteorology Bldg, Willemstad, Curaçao. T. +59998684612. Fax +59998684996. E-mail: rempeitc@racrempeitc.org.

URL: http://www.racrempeitc.org/

History Dec 1994. Established on a provisional basis, by decision, at 7th Intergovernmental Meeting of the Action Plan and the Fourth Meeting of the Contracting Parties of the Cartagena Convention and Protocols, and the 4th Meeting of *Convention for the Protection and Development of the Marine Environment of the Wider Caribbean Region (Cartagena Convention, 1983)* and protocols. Establishment follows requests in the early nineties by the Regional Island States and Territories that *International Maritime Organization (IMO, #14102)* support and establish a regional centre to achieve the goal of oil spill preparedness and to promote cooperation, training and exercises. It was also requested, Mar 1994, Curaçao, during the IMO/IPIECA Conference, to consolidate the then 10-year existence of the IMO Consultant on oil pollution preparedness in Puerto Rico, and to have a Regional Maritime Pollution Emergency Information and Training Center for the Wider Caribbean Region. enhance and promote direct regional cooperation in reference to *International Convention on Oil Pollution Preparedness Response and Cooperation (OPRC, 1990)*. Centre opened, 15 Jun 1995, within the framework of *Caribbean Environment Programme (CEP, #03497)*, coming within *UNEP (#20299)*, and with the support of the governments of Neth Antilles, Netherlands and USA. Hosted by the government of Curaçao. **Aims** Assist countries in the Wider Caribbean Region to prevent and respond to pollution in the marine environment. **Structure** *'MOU Partner Meeting'*. Steering Committee of Partners to the Memorandum of Understanding. Senior Consultants (2); expert consultants on marine environment, port safety and security; regional training instructors. **Languages** Dutch, English, French, Spanish. **Staff** 4.00

FTE, paid. Staffed by subject matter experts voluntarily seconded by states signatory to the Cartagena Convention of 1993. **Finance** Supported by MOU Partners and USA and France for expert secondment. Budget (annual): about US$ 380,000. **Activities** Capacity building; networking/liaising; guidance/assistance/consulting; training/education; awareness raising. Coordinates response resources for emergencies; assists in establishing a legal response framework. **Events** *Workshop on Oil Spill Preparedness for the Wider Caribbean* Cartagena de Indias (Colombia) 2017. **Publications** *RAC REMPEITC News. Status of Contingency Planning for the Caribbean Islands and Territories* (2015) – revised; *Oil Spills: How Caribbean disaster managers can prepare and respond* (2012). Brochure.
Members Governments of 28 countries:
Antigua-Barbuda, Bahamas, Barbados, Belize, Colombia, Costa Rica, Cuba, Dominica, Dominican Rep, France, Grenada, Guatemala, Guyana, Haiti, Honduras, Jamaica, Mexico, Netherlands, Nicaragua, Panama, St Kitts-Nevis, St Lucia, St Vincent-Grenadines, Suriname, Trinidad-Tobago, UK, USA, Venezuela.
IGO Relations Memorandum of Understanding between: *Caribbean Action Plan (CAR, #03432); International Maritime Organization (IMO, #14102); UNEP (#20299).* [2022/XE3347/E*]

♦ Regional Marine Pollution Emergency Response Centre for the Mediterranean Sea (REMPEC) 18795

Centre régional méditerranéen pour l'intervention d'urgence contre la pollution marine accidentelle

Head of Office Sa Maison Hill, Floriana, FRN 1613, Malta. T. +35621337296 – +35621337297 – +35621337298. Fax +35621339951. E-mail: rempec@rempec.org.
URL: http://www.rempec.org/
History Dec 1976, Malta. Established by conference of plenipotentiaries of 16 coastal states of the Mediterranean, 1976, Barcelona (Spain). Operated by *International Maritime Organization (IMO, #14102)* within the framework of *Mediterranean Action Plan (MAP, #16638)* Phase II – in the *Regional Seas Programme (#18814)*. Former names and other names: *Regional Oil Combating Centre for the Mediterranean Sea (ROCC)* – former; *Centre régional méditerranéen de lutte contre la pollution par les hydrocarbures* – former. **Aims** Strengthen capacity of coastal States in the Mediterranean; facilitate cooperation in preventing pollution from ships; combating marine pollution caused by major marine pollution incidents. **Structure** Administered by *International Maritime Organization (IMO, #14102)* in cooperation with *Mediterranean Action Plan (MAP, #16638)*. National Focal Points. **Languages** English, French. **Staff** 6.00 FTE, paid. Staff recruited by *International Maritime Organization (IMO, #14102)*. **Finance** Contributions deposited by coastal States in *Mediterranean Trust Fund (MTF, #16686)*. Additional voluntary contributions from EU countries and the French oil industry; other external funds from the IMO ITCP for executing projects. **Activities** Capacity building; events/meetings; guidance/assistance/consulting; knowledge management/information dissemination; networking/liaising; training/education. **Events** *Meeting of the Focal Points* San Gwann (Malta) 2021, *Regional Workshop on Response to Potential Spill Incidents Involving Hazardous and Noxious Substances* Valletta (Malta) 2018, *Workshop on Regional Response Capacity and Coordination for Major Oil Spill in the Mediterranean Sea* Athens (Greece) 2013, *Regional workshop on places of refuge* Barcelona (Spain) 2006, *Meeting* Malta 2003. **Publications** Technical papers, training materials, documents, studies and reports; proceedings. **Information Services** *Guidelines and Tools; Mediterranean Integrated GIS on Marine Pollution Risk Assessmemnt and Response (MEDGIS-MAAR); Regional Information System (RIS)* – on prevention of, preparedness for and response to marine pollution from ships.
Members Governments of 21 Mediterranean countries:
Albania, Algeria, Bosnia-Herzegovina, Croatia, Cyprus, Egypt, France, Greece, Israel, Italy, Lebanon, Libya, Malta, Monaco, Montenegro, Morocco, Slovenia, Spain, Syrian AR, Tunisia, Türkiye.
Regional EU integration entity (1):
European Union (EU, #08967).
IGO Relations Observer status with (3): *Agreement for cooperation in dealing with pollution of the North Sea by oil and other harmful substances (Bonn Agreement, #00564); Council for Mediterranean Countries (MEDA, no recent information); International Oil Pollution Compensation Funds (IOPC Funds, #14402).* Partner of (2): *European Commission (EC, #06633); European Space Agency (ESA, #08798).* **NGO Relations** Partner of (7): *Centre of Documentation, Research and Experimentation on Accidental Water Pollution (CEDRE); Conseil européen de l'industrie chimique (CEFIC, #04687); International Association of Independent Tanker Owners (INTERTANKO, #11959); International Petroleum Industry Environmental Conservation Association (IPIECA, #14562); ITOPF Ltd (#16073); Mediterranean Oil Industry Group (MOIG, #16669); World Wide Fund for Nature (WWF, #21922).* Also links with national organizations. [2022.03.29/XE5479/E*]

♦ The Regional Maritime Academy, Accra / see Regional Maritime University, Accra (#18796)

♦ Regional Maritime University, Accra (RMU) 18796

Dir of Finance Nungua, PO Box 1115, Accra, Ghana. T. +2337127712775 – +233712343 – +233718225. E-mail: registrar@rmu.edu.gh.
URL: http://www.rmu.edu.gh/
History 26 May 1983, by MINCONMAR, currently *Maritime Organization of West and Central Africa (MOWCA, #16582)*, on completion of transformation from the (national) Ghana Nautical College, set up 1957. Original title: */The/ Regional Maritime Academy, Accra (RMA) – Académie maritime régionale d'Accra.* Founding members: Cameroon; Gambia; Ghana; Liberia; Sierra Leone. Set up with the assistance of *UNDP (#20292), International Maritime Organization (IMO, #14102)* and governments of Norway and Egypt. Upgraded into a university, Oct 2007. Former names and other names: *The Regional Maritime Academy, Accra (RMA)* – former; *Académie maritime régionale d'Accra* – former. **Aims** Develop maritime *industry* in the sub-region and beyond, through capacity building of the highest international standard; offer educational programmes relevant to modern trends and challenges of the industry and related fields; ensure availability of all IMO 'Standard of Training, Certification and Watchkeeping for Seafarers (STCW95)' mandatory training programmes. **Structure** University in Ghana serves anglophone countries while sister academy, *Regional Academy of Maritime Science and Technology (#18744)*, Côte d'Ivoire, serves francophone countries. Board of Governors comprises: ministers of maritime affairs of founding member countries; Secretary General of MOWCA; University Rector; Students' Representative. Rector serves as Chief Executive and is responsible for day-to-day management. Educational departments (6): Nautical Studies; Marine Engineering; Marine Electricals and Electronics; Maritime Studies; Maritime Safety; Information Communication and Technology. **Languages** English, French. **Staff** Qualified teaching staff. **Finance** Members' dues. Other sources: income from student fees, short course programmes, and donations. **Activities** Programmes: academic, including BSc Marine Engineering, BSc Electrical/Electronic Engineering, BSc Ports and Shipping Administration, BSc Nautical Science, BSc Computer Engineering, Master of Arts in Ports and Shipping Administration, Diploma in Ports and Shipping Management and Marine Engine Mechanic. Organizes courses and training, including IMO Model Short Courses, for residential and non-residential students from Ghana, countries of West and Central Africa, Ethiopia and some East African countries. Since Dec 2004, granted Institutional Accreditation by National Accreditation Board, Ghana, National Commission on Higher Education, Liberia, and Department of State for Education, Gambia. Participates in international events.
Members Governments of 5 countries:
Cameroon, Gambia, Ghana, Liberia, Sierra Leone.
NGO Relations Member of: *Association of African Maritime Training Institutes (AAMTI, no recent information). Swedish NGO Centre for Development Cooperation (Forum Syd)* is member. [2018/XF1562/E*]

♦ Regional Model Forest Network – Asia (RMFN-Asia) 18797

Contact address not obtained.
URL: https://rmfnasia.org/
History Mar 2010. Founded as a regional network of *International Model Forest Network (IMFN, #14175)*. **Aims** Enhance Asia's forests and other ecosystem services at the landscape level to sustainably meet stakeholder needs and values. **Structure** Advisory Committee; Office. [2020/AA1240/F]

♦ Regional Network of Agricultural Policy Research Institutes (ReNAPRI) 18798

Exec Dir c/o IAPRI, 26A Middleway Road, Postnet Box 99 Kabulonga, Lusaka 10100, Zambia. E-mail: info@renapi.org.
URL: http://www.renapri.org/
History 16 Nov 2012. Registration: Start date: 31 Oct 2014, Zambia. **Aims** Play an active role in transforming Africa's agricultural sector by developing the capacity of national agricultural policy research Institutes in the continent, strengthening and nurturing dynamic collaboration, towards providing objective and innovative policy advice to national, regional and continental level stakeholders, through effective outreach. **Structure** Executive Board; Secretariat. **Activities** Events/meetings; research/documentation. **Events** *Stakeholders Conference* Accra (Ghana) 2021, *Stakeholder Conference* Lilongwe (Malawi) 2020, *Stakeholder Conference* Kampala (Uganda) 2019.
Members Institutes in 11 countries:
Congo DR, Ghana, Kenya, Malawi, Mozambique, Namibia, South Africa, Tanzania UR, Uganda, Zambia, Zimbabwe.
IGO Relations Partner of (3): *Alliance for Commodity Trade in Eastern and Southern Africa (ACTESA, #00668); Centre for Coordination of Agricultural Research and Development for Southern Africa (CCARDESA, #03736); FAO (#09260).* **NGO Relations** Partner of (1): *Food, Agriculture and Natural Resources Policy Analysis Network (FANRPAN, #09839).* [2021/AA2229/j/F]

♦ Regional Network for the Chemistry of Natural Products in Southeast Asia (inactive)
♦ Regional Network for the Exchange of Information and Experience in Science and Technology in Asia and the Pacific (inactive)

♦ Regional Network of Local Authorities for the Management of Human Settlements (CITYNET) 18799

Réseau régional des autorités locales pour les établissements humains

SG 38 Jongno, Jongno-gu, Seoul 110-110, Korea Rep. T. +8227230639. Fax +8227230640. E-mail: info@citynet-ap.org.
URL: http://www.citynet-ap.org/
History Set up 1987, with the support of *United Nations Economic and Social Commission for Asia and the Pacific (ESCAP, #20557), UNDP (#20292), United Nations Human Settlements Programme (UN-Habitat, #20572)* and 27 members, following 1st Regional Congress of Local Authorities for the Development of Human Settlements in the Asia Pacific, 1982, Yokohama (Japan). Charter adopted, 1989, at Shanghai (China) Congress. Secretariat set up in Yokohama (Japan), 1992. Also referred to as *Regional Network of Local Authorities for the Management of Human Settlements in Asia and the Pacific.* Relocated from Yokohama (Japan) to Seoul (Korea Rep), 2013. **Aims** Connect local governments and urban stakeholders to champion sustainable cities in Asia and the Pacific. **Structure** General Assembly (every 4 years). Executive Committee. Secretariat. **Languages** English, Korean. **Staff** 9.00 FTE, paid. **Finance** Members' dues. Host city subsidy. **Activities** Capacity building; training/education; meeting activities; networking/liaising; knowledge management/information dissemination. **Events** *Congress* Kuala Lumpur (Malaysia) 2022, *Changing Face of Urban Tourism Post COVID: Asian Experience* Seoul (Korea Rep) 2021, *Localizing Urban Eco-Solutions Workshop* Seoul (Korea Rep) 2021, *Post-Pandemic Urban Recovery-Smart Health Solutions – Asian Perspective* Seoul (Korea Rep) 2021, *Workshop for Indonesian Cities* Seoul (Korea Rep) 2021. **Publications** *Newsletter* (12 a year) – electronic; *CityVoices* – magazine. Annual Report.
Members Full (81) city authorities in Asia and the Pacific region. Associate (42) NGOs (26), national-level organizations (12) and development agencies (2) within the region, and one city in Europe, one corporation. Members in 23 countries and territories:
Australia, Bangladesh, Bhutan, Cambodia, China, Fiji, France, India, Indonesia, Iran Islamic Rep, Japan, Korea Rep, Malaysia, Mongolia, Myanmar, Nepal, Pakistan, Philippines, Singapore, Sri Lanka, Taiwan, Thailand, Vietnam.
Included in the above, 3 international or regional non-governmental organizations listed in this Yearbook:
Asian Coalition for Housing Rights (ACHR, #01381); Yokohama Association for International Communications and Exchanges (YOKE); Youth for Unity and Voluntary Action (YUVA).
Consultative Status Consultative status granted from: *ECOSOC (#05331)* (Special). [2022/XF1792/y/F]

♦ Regional Network of Local Authorities for the Management of Human Settlements in Asia and the Pacific / see Regional Network of Local Authorities for the Management of Human Settlements (#18799)
♦ Regional Network for Microbiology in Southeast Asia / see UNESCO Regional Network for Microbiology and Microbial Biotechnology in Southeast Asia (#20319)

♦ Regional Network Office for Urban Safety (RNUS) 18800

Coordinator School of Engineering and Technology – AIT, Room N-201 North Academic Bldg, 58 Moo 9 Paholyothin Rd, Klong Luang, Pathum Thani, 12120, Thailand. T. +6625246418. Fax +6625245565. E-mail: rnus@ait.ac.th.
URL: http://www.set.ait.ac.th/rnus/
History Oct 2002. **Aims** Develop innovative technologies such as numerical models and geospatial technologies for managing urban infrastructures, mitigating urban disaster risk and environmental problems and adopting climate change for sustainable development in Asian cities and the Mekong River basin. **Structure** Jointly operated by the School of Engineering and Technology (SET), *Asian Institute of Technology (AIT, #01519)* and *International Centre for Urban Safety Engineering (ICUS)*, Institute of Industrial Science at the University of Tokyo. **Languages** English, Japanese, Thai. **Activities** *'Research'* – (1) Urban earthquake disaster mitigation engineering, including: e-strategy for urban safety and disaster reduction; universal disaster environment simulator; lifeline earthquake engineering; (2) Construction material management, including: maintenance management of concrete structure; modelling of concrete structures based on risk evaluation; development of simulation tool for evaluating environmental actions on concrete structures; (3) Remote sensing and GIS, including: satellite observation network in Asia for disaster and environment monitoring; development of spatial data analysis method for urban safety issues; development of satellite remote sensing data receiving, visualization and distribution on WWW; (4) Urban traffic management, including: traffic control and operation; transportation demand management; human traffic behaviour analysis; intelligent transport systems. Serves as a regional hub of researchers and research centres; transfer information and technical know-how. Organizes: International Symposium on New Technologies for Urban Safety of Mega-Cities in Asia; seminars; workshops; conferences. **Events** *Symposium* Chiang Mai (Thailand) 2011, *Symposium* Kobe (Japan) 2010. **Publications** Symposium and conference proceedings; technical reports; newsletters. [2011.09.09/XM0048/F]

♦ **Regional Network** Regional Network Supporting the HIV, Viral Hepatitis and Sexual Health Workforce in the Asia Pacific (#18802)

♦ Regional Network for Research, Surveillance and Control of Asian Schistosomiasis (RNSA) 18801

Chairman Natl Inst of Parasitic Diseases, Chinese Cntr for Disease Control and Prevention, 207 Rui Jin Er Rd, 200025 Shanghai, China. T. +862154653507. Fax +862154653512.
Co-Chairman Research Inst for Tropical Medicine, Dept of Health Compound, FILINVEST Corporate City, Alabang, 1781 Muntinlupa City METRO MANILA, Philippines. T. +6328097599 – +6328072628. Fax +6328422245.
URL: http://www.rnas.org.cn/
History Sep 1998, Wuxi (China). Activities started, 1999, Shanghai (China), with the support of *UNICEF/UNDP/World Bank/WHO Special Programme for Research and Training in Tropical Diseases (TDR, #20331).* **Aims** Strengthen communication, cooperation and coordination among scientists and control authorities concerned with schistosomiasis japonica. **Events** *Annual Workshop* Danang (Vietnam) 2019, *Annual Workshop* Daegu (Korea Rep) 2018, *Annual Workshop* Manila (Philippines) 2015, *Annual Workshop* Bogor (Indonesia) 2014, *Annual Workshop* Khon Kaen (Thailand) 2013. **Publications** *RNAS Newsletter.*
Members in 6 countries:
Cambodia, China, Indonesia, Laos, Malaysia, Philippines. [2018/XM0828/F]

♦ Regional Network on Southern European Societies (see: #08790)

♦ Regional Network Supporting the HIV, Viral Hepatitis and Sexual Health Workforce in the Asia Pacific (Regional Network) 18802

Contact c/o ASHM, Locked Mail Bag 5057, Darlinghurst NSW 1300, Australia. T. +61282040700. Fax +61292122382. E-mail: regionalnetwork@ashm.org.au.
URL: https://www.ashm.org.au/international/regional-network/

History 2008. **Aims** Share knowledge and best practice in the field of workforce professional development in the HIV, viral hepatitis and sexual health areas. **Structure** Managed by *Australasian Society for HIV, Viral Hepatitis and Sexual Health Medicine (ASHM)*. **Languages** English. **Staff** 38.00 FTE, paid. **Finance** Small grants; self-funding; pro bono members' contributions. **Activities** Events/meetings. **Events** *International Workshop on HIV Pediatrics* Mexico City (Mexico) 2019, *International Workshop on HIV Pediatrics* Paris (France) 2017, *Assembly* Bangkok (Thailand) 2016, *International Workshop on HIV Pediatrics* Durban (South Africa) 2016, *International Workshop on HIV Pediatrics* Vancouver, BC (Canada) 2015.
Members Full in 18 countries and territories:
Australia, Cambodia, Fiji, Hong Kong, India, Indonesia, Japan, Laos, Malaysia, Myanmar, Papua New Guinea, Philippines, Singapore, Sri Lanka, Taiwan, Thailand, Timor-Leste, Vietnam.
Included in the above, 4 organizations listed in this Yearbook:
Australasian Society for HIV, Viral Hepatitis and Sexual Health Medicine (ASHM); International Union against Sexually Transmitted Infections (IUSTI, #15751); Oceania Society for Sexual Health and HIV Medicine (OSSHHM); Pacific Society for Reproductive Health (PSRH, #18005).
IGO Relations *Joint United Nations Programme on HIV/AIDS (UNAIDS, #16149); WHO Regional Office for the Western Pacific (WPRO, #20947); WHO Regional Office for South-East Asia (SEARO, #20946).* **NGO Relations** *Asia Pacific Coalition on Male Sexual Health (APCOM, #01872); Australasian Society for HIV, Viral Hepatitis and Sexual Health Medicine (ASHM); International Union against Sexually Transmitted Infections (IUSTI, #15751); Oceania Society for Sexual Health and HIV Medicine (OSSHHM); Pacific Society for Reproductive Health (PSRH, #18005).* [2016.09.08/XM4942/y/**F**]

♦ Regional Network of Water-Basin – Organizations from Eastern Europe, Caucasus and Central Asia (NWO EECCA) 18803

Secretariat c/o SIC-ICWC, 11 Karasu-4, Tashkent, Uzbekistan, 100187. E-mail: dukh@icwc-aral.uz.
URL: http://www.eecca-water.net/
History 2010, Moscow (Russia), as a regional network of *International Network of Basin Organizations (INBO, #14235).* **Aims** Develop integrated *water resources management* and create conditions for comprehensive and environmentally friendly rational use of water and reclaimed land. **Structure** Convention; Board of Directors, headed by President; Secretariat, based in Tashkent (Uzbekistan). **Languages** English, Russian. **Events** *International Conference on the Challenges of River Basin Management in Context of Climate Change* Moscow (Russia) 2017, *Convention* Moscow (Russia) 2010. **Publications** *CAWATER Info.* Scientific papers.
Members Full in 12 countries:
Armenia, Azerbaijan, Belarus, Georgia, Kazakhstan, Kyrgyzstan, Moldova, Russia, Tajikistan, Turkmenistan, Ukraine, Uzbekistan. [2017/XJ4913/**E**]

- ♦ Regional Network for Water and Sanitation / see Network for Water and Sanitation International (#17064)
- ♦ Regional Nursing Body, CARICOM Community (no recent information)
- ♦ Regional Observatory on Financing Culture in East-Central Europe (internationally oriented national body)
- ♦ Regional Office for Education in Latin America and the Caribbean – UNESCO / see UNESCO Regional Bureau for Education in Latin America and the Caribbean (#20318)
- ♦ Regional Office for Science and Technology for the Arab States / see UNESCO Office, Cairo – Regional Bureau for Sciences in the Arab States (#20312)
- ♦ Regional Oil Combating Centre for the Mediterranean Sea / see Regional Marine Pollution Emergency Response Centre for the Mediterranean Sea (#18795)
- ♦ Regional Organization of Arab Airlines / see Arab Air Carriers Organization (#00896)

♦ Regional Organization for the Conservation of the Environment of the Red Sea and Gulf of Aden (PERSGA) 18804

Organisation régionale pour la conservation de l'environnement de la mer Rouge et du golfe d'Aden
SG 7th Floor, PME Bldg, Hael Street, Rwais district, PO Box 53662, Jeddah 21583, Saudi Arabia. T. +966124238855. E-mail: persga@persga.org.
URL: http://www.persga.org/
History Sep 1995, Cairo (Egypt), on signature of the *'Cairo Declaration'* by representatives of member states, having been envisaged in *Convention for the Conservation of the Red Sea and Gulf of Aden Environment (Jeddah convention, 1982)*, 14 Feb 1982, Jeddah, under the umbrella of *League of Arab States (LAS, #16420).* An independent regional organization, succeeding the *Red Sea and Gulf of Aden Environment Programme (PERSGA, inactive)* of *Arab League Educational, Cultural and Scientific Organization (ALECSO, #01003).* **Aims** Promote activities that safeguard the coastal and marine environments and support sustainable development in the countries of the Red Sea and Gulf of Aden (Yemen) region. **Structure** Council (meets annually); Secretariat. **Languages** Arabic, English. **Finance** Members states' contributions. Projects also funded by international organizations, such as *Global Environment Facility (GEF, #10346)* and *Islamic Development Bank (IsDB, #16044).* **Activities** Events/meetings; training/education. **Events** *Regional Workshop on the Implementation of the London Protocol and Particularly Sensitive Sea Areas* Jeddah (Saudi Arabia) 2015, *Sea to sea regional forum* Cairo (Egypt) 2005, *Regional workshop on marine safety information dissemination* Oman 2000, *Sea to sea regional forum / Regional Conference* Jeddah (Saudi Arabia) 1995. **Publications** *Al Sanbouk* (4 a year) in Arabic, English – newsletter. Technical Series; Workshop Report Series.
Members Membership countries (7):
Djibouti, Egypt, Jordan, Saudi Arabia, Somalia, Sudan, Yemen.
IGO Relations Cooperation agreement with: *International Maritime Organization (IMO, #14102); Islamic World Educational, Scientific and Cultural Organization (ICESCO, #16058).* Partner of: *International Coral Reef Initiative (ICRI, #12965).* **NGO Relations** Partner of: *WorldFish (#21507).* [2019.02.12/XE1269/**E***]

- ♦ Regional Organization for North Africa and Near East (#17824)

♦ Regional Organization for the Protection of the Marine Environment (ROPME) 18805

Organisation régionale pour la protection du milieu marin
Coordinator PO Box 26388, 13124 Safat, Kuwait. T. +96522093939. Fax +96524861668. E-mail: ropme@ropme.org.
URL: http://www.ropme.org/
History Established on deposition of 5 instruments of ratification to *Kuwait Regional Convention for Cooperation on the Protection on the Marine Environment from Pollution (1978)* (1978) and under the auspices of *UNEP (#20299).* Interim Secretariat, inaugurated 7 Jul 1980, Kuwait, and in force until 31 Dec 1981, formulated and administered work programme together with *UNEP Water Branch (inactive).* **Aims** Protect and develop the marine environment and *coastal* areas as designated in the Kuwait Convention and its protocols. **Structure** Council; Executive Committee (EXCOM); Senior Executives Steering Committee (SESCOM) (meets once a year); ROPME Secretariat, established Jan 1982; Judicial Commission. Departments (4): Programmes; Protocols; Administration and Finance; Environmental Awareness. Includes: *Marine Emergency Mutual Aid Centre (MEMAC, #16578)*, established 1982. **Languages** Arabic, English, Persian. **Staff** 40.00 FTE, paid. **Finance** Sources: contributions of member/participating states. Annual budget: 1,000,000 KWD. **Activities** Awareness raising; events/meetings; knowledge management/information dissemination; management of treaties and agreements; monitoring/evaluation; research/documentation; standards/guidelines; training/education. Manages the following treaties/agreements: *Convention on Biological Diversity (Biodiversity convention, 1992); International Convention on Oil Pollution Preparedness Response and Cooperation (OPRC, 1990); Protocol Concerning Cooperation in Combating Pollution of the Mediterranean Sea by Oil and other Harmful Substances in Cases of Emergency (1976); Protocol Concerning Marine Pollution Resulting from Exploration and Exploitation of the Continental Shelf (1989); Protocol on the Control of Marine Transboundary Movements and Disposal of Hazardous Wastes (1998).* **Events** *Workshop of Technical Support Group on Blue Carbon Inventory in the ROPME Sea Area* Muscat (Oman) 2020, *Meeting on the Report of the Workshop on Coastal Habitat Conservation and Rehabilitation in the ROPME Sea Area* Kuwait (Kuwait) 2019, *Workshop of Technical Support Group on Marine Climate Change Risk Assessment* Muscat (Oman) 2019, *Workshop of the Regional Task Force on Marine Climate Change Strategy for the ROPME Sea Area* Muscat (Oman) 2019, *Meeting of the Regional Task Force on Marine Biodiversity Strategy for the ROPME Sea Area* Tokyo (Japan) 2018. **Publications** *ROPME Newsletter* (4 a year) in Arabic, Persian; *Sea KAPS* (occasional) in English – special issues of ROPME Newsletter. *Technical Report and Monograph Series on ROPME Oceanographic Cruise* (2006). *Manual for Investigating Marine Mortality Incidents in the ROPME Sea Area* (2007); *Regional Report of the State of the Marine Environment Report (SOMER)* (2003, 2013); *Atlas – ROPME Region from Space* (2000); *Integrated Coastal Areas Management* (2000) – guidelines for the ROPME Region; *Manual of Oceanographic Observations and Pollutant Analyses Methods (MOOPAM)* (1999, 2010); *Protocol on the Control of Marine Transboundary Movements and Disposal of Hazardous Wastes and Other Wastes* (1998); *Use of Oil Spill Chemicals in the ROPME Sea Area* (1998); *Protocol for the Protection of the Marine Environment against Pollution from Land-Based Sources* (1990); *Protocol concerning Marine Pollution resulting from Exploration and Exploitation of the Continental Shelf* (1989); *Convention for Cooperation on the Protection of the Marine Environment from Pollution* (1978); *Protocol concerning Regional Cooperation in Combating Pollution by Oil and other Harmful Substances in Cases of Emergency* (1978); *Marine Environment Protection Legislation Guide; Marine Pollution Combat Directory; Oil Pollution Combating Equipment Guide; Oil Spill Response Safety Guide; Guidelines for the Preparation of National Report on the State of the Marine Environment Report; Regional Manual for Compensation Claims; Regional Oil Spill Damage Assessment Guidelines; Development of a Protocol concerning the Conservation of Biological Diversity and the Establishment of Protected Areas* – draft; *The Environmental Catastrophy in Kuwait; Oil Spill Incidents in ROPME Sea Area (1965-2002).* Monograph series; workshop reports; LBA Technical Guidelines; technical reports.
Members Governments of countries surrounding the seas in question (8):
Bahrain, Iran Islamic Rep, Iraq, Kuwait, Oman, Qatar, Saudi Arabia, United Arab Emirates.
IGO Relations Cooperates with: *International Coral Reef Initiative (ICRI, #12965); International Maritime Organization (IMO, #14102).* Observer status with: *ROPME Sea Area Hydrographic Commission (RSAHC, #18971); Regional Commission for Fisheries (RECOFI, #18763).* [2021.09.05/XD0319/**D***]

- ♦ Regional Piracy Centre, Kuala Lumpur / see Piracy Reporting Centre, Kuala Lumpur (#18373)
- ♦ Regional Post-Graduate Training School on Integrated Management of Tropical Forests and Lands (internationally oriented national body)
- ♦ Regional Post-Graduate Training School on Integrated Tropical Forest Management / see Ecole régionale post-universitaire d'aménagement et de gestion intégrés des forêts et territoires tropicaux
- ♦ Regional Powers Network (internationally oriented national body)
- ♦ Regional Pre-School Child Development Centre / see Caribbean Child Development Centre

♦ Regional Programme of Action for the Protection of the Arctic Marine Environment from Land-based Activities (RPA) 18806

Contact Ministry of Foreign Affairs, POBox 8114 Dep, 0032 Oslo, Norway. T. +4722243600 – +4722243428. Fax +4722249580. E-mail: kkl@mfa.no.
URL: http://www.arctic-council.org/
History 18 Sep 1998, under the auspices of *Arctic Council (#01097).* Implemented and developed by *Protection of the Arctic Marine Environment (PAME, #18547).* **Aims** Address global and regional commitments; strengthen regional cooperation and capacity building, particularly in relation to addressing regional priority *pollution* sources found in the Russian Federation. **Activities** Major concerns include: *Global Programme of Action for the Protection of the Marine Environment from Land-Based Activities (GPA, see: #20299);* 'UNEP negotiations on Persistent Organic Pollutants (POPs)'; UNECE LRTAP – *Convention on Long-range Transboundary Air Pollution (#04787).* **IGO Relations** *UNEP (#20299); United Nations Economic Commission for Europe (UNECE, #20555); Regional Seas Programme (#18814).* [2022/XE3700/**E***]

- ♦ Regional Programme on Marine Pollution Prevention and Management for the East Asian Seas Region / see Partnerships in Environmental Management for the Seas of East Asia (#18242)
- ♦ Regional Psychological Support Initiative / see REPSSI (#18848)
- ♦ Regional Radio Convention for Central America, Panama and the Canal Zone (1938 treaty)

♦ Regional Remote Sensing Centre for North African States 18807

Centre Régional de Télédétection des Etats de l'Afrique du nord (CRTEAN)
Dir Gen 18 Rue Moussa Ibn Nousair, El Menzah, 1004 Tunis, Tunisia. T. +21671236575 – +21671237466. Fax +21671238882. E-mail: dg.crtean@crtean.intl.tn.
URL: http://www.crtean.org.tn/
History 6 Oct 1990. Established following signing of the Constitutive Act of the 6 party member countries of North Africa. Previously a regional organization of *African Organization of Cartography and Remote Sensing (AOCRS, inactive).* **Aims** Encourage institutions in Member States to use remote sensing techniques and upstream systems in the areas of sustainable development and scientific research. **Structure** Board of Directors; Scientific Council. **Languages** Arabic, English, French. **Staff** 5.00 FTE, paid. **Finance** Member state contributions. Other sources: member partners admitted to the Centre; proceeds of scientific advice; operational costs for regional projects; donations. **Activities** Capacity building; training/education; events/meetings; projects/programmes; research/documentation; guidance/assistance/consulting. Projects areas include: food security; desertification; cadastral; water scarcity; maritime surveillance; space law for countries in the region. **Events** *TeanGeo – International Conference on Advanced Geospatial Science and Technology* Tunis (Tunisia) 2021, *TeanGeo – International Conference on Advanced Geospatial Science and Technology* Tunis (Tunisia) 2018, *TeanGeo – International Conference on Advanced Geospatial Science and Technology* Tunis (Tunisia) 2016, *Seminar* Tunis (Tunisia) 2008, *Remote sensing and space sciences* Tunis (Tunisia) 2007. **Publications** *Journal of Science Space Technologies* – court specialized regional scientific journal, in collaboration with FARSRC.
Members Member countries (7):
Algeria, Egypt, Libya, Mauritania, Morocco, Sudan, Tunisia.
Associate States (4):
Mali, Senegal, Syrian AR, Yemen.
Associate organizations in 3 countries:
Belgium, France, Libya.
Included in the above, 5 organizations listed in this Yearbook:
African Organization of Cartography and Remote Sensing (AOCRS, inactive); Arab League Educational, Cultural and Scientific Organization (ALECSO, #01003); Arab Maghreb Union (AMU, #01004); Arab Water Council (AWC, #01075); Federation of Arab Scientific Research Councils (FASRC, no recent information).
IGO Relations Cooperates with: *African Organization of Cartography and Remote Sensing (AOCRS, inactive); FAO (#09260); League of Arab States (LAS, #16420); Observatoire du Sahara et du Sahel (OSS, #17636); UNDP (#20292); UNESCO (#20322); United Nations Economic Commission for Africa (ECA, #20554); United Nations Office for Outer Space Affairs (UNOOSA, #20601).* Consultative status with: *Committee on the Peaceful Uses of Outer Space (COPUOS, #04277).* Member of: *Observatoire du Sahara et du Sahel (OSS, #17636).* Partner of: *Group on Earth Observations (GEO, #10735).* Also links with national specialized institutions in remote sensing and GIS matter of member states. **NGO Relations** Member of: *International Society for Photogrammetry and Remote Sensing (ISPRS, #15362).* [2021/XE2678/y/**E***]

- ♦ Regional Remote Sensing Centre, Ouagadougou (inactive)

♦ Regional Research Centre for Safeguarding Intangible Cultural Heritage in West and Central Asia (Tehran ICH Centre) 18808

Contact No 31 Mohana Alley, Taghavi St, Ferdowsi St, ZIP Fund 111553693, Teheran, 1145686314, Iran Islamic Rep. T. +982166170174 – +982166171336 – +982166170180. Fax +982166170160.
URL: http://www.tichct.org/
History 28 Apr 2010, on Agreement between Government of Iran Islamic Rep and *UNESCO (#20322).* Full title: *Regional Research Centre for Safeguarding Intangible Cultural Heritage in West and Central Asia – Under the Auspices of UNESCO.* A UNESCO Category II Centre. **Structure** Governing Council; Executive Board.
Members Full in 10 countries:
Armenia, Iran Islamic Rep, Iraq, Kazakhstan, Kyrgyzstan, Lebanon, Pakistan, Palestine, Tajikistan, Türkiye. [2017/XM6093/**E**]

- ♦ Regional Research Centre for Safeguarding Intangible Cultural Heritage in West and Central Asia – Under the Auspices of UNESCO / see Regional Research Centre for Safeguarding Intangible Cultural Heritage in West and Central Asia (#18808)
- ♦ Regional Research Network / see Latin American and Caribbean Research Network (#16284)

♦ Regional School for Aerial Navigation and Management 18809

Ecole régionale de la navigation aérienne et du management (ERNAM)

Contact BP 8001, Route de l'Aéroport Léopold Sédar Senghor, Dakar, Senegal. T. +221338207104. Fax +221338204569. E-mail: ernamavsec@sentoo.sn.

Contact c/o ASECNA Direction Générale, 32-38 Avenue Jean Jaurès, BP 3144, Dakar, Senegal. T. +221338496600. Fax +221338234654.

URL: http://www.asecna.aero/

History 1960, as *Ecole régionale de la navigation aérienne et de la météorologie*. A training centre of *Agency for the Safety of Aerial Navigation in Africa and Madagascar (#00556)*. [2015/XE2556/E*]

♦ Regional School of Public Administration (ReSPA) 18810

Dir Branelovica, 81410 Danilovgrad, Montenegro. T. +38220817200. Fax +38220817238.

URL: http://www.respaweb.eu/

History Initially formulated following Jun 2003 Thessaloniki Agenda. Phase 1 started 1 Nov 2006. Phase 2 formally launched Sep 2010. Fully self-managed since 1 oct 2011. **Aims** Help governments in the *Western Balkans* region develop better public administration, public services and overall governance systems for their citizens and businesses; prepare them for membership of the European Union. **Structure** Governing Board; Committees (2); Advisory Board; Secretariat. **Languages** English. **Staff** 15.00 FTE, paid. **Finance** Members dues. Activities financed by: *European Commission (EC, #06633)*. Administration financed by member states' equal contribution of euro 150,000 a year. Annual budget: euro 2,000,000. **Activities** Politics/policy/regulatory; research/documentation; training/education; knowledge management/information dissemination; networking/liaising; advocacy/lobbying/activism; events/meetings. **Publications** Studies; policy recommendations; conference proceedings; analytical papers; videos.

Members Governments (5):

Albania, Bosnia-Herzegovina, Montenegro, North Macedonia, Serbia.

IGO Relations Partner institutions: *European Commission (EC, #06633)*; *European Institute of Public Administration (EIPA, #07569)*; *OECD (#17693)*; *SIGMA Programme (#19272)*; *United Nations Public Administration Network (UNPAN, #20615)*. **NGO Relations** Partner institutions: *College of Europe (#04105)*; *Network of Institutes and Schools of Public Administration in Central and Eastern Europe (NISPAcee, #17039)*. [2018.09.05/XJ1179/E*]

♦ Regional School of Sanitary Engineering and Hydraulic Resources . 18811

Escuela Regional de Ingenieria Sanitaria y Recursos Hidraulicos (ERIS)

Dir Fac de Ingenieria, Univ de San Carlos de Guatemala, Edificio ERIS – Area de Prefabricados de Ingenieria, Ciudad Universitaria – Zona 12, 01012 Guatemala, Guatemala. T. +50224189136 – +50224189140 – +50224198150. E-mail: pcsaravia@yahoo.com.

URL: http://sitios.ingenieria.usac.edu.gt/eris

History Founded 1965. Former title in Spanish: *Escuela Regional de Ingenieria Sanitaria (ERIS)*. Part of Universidad de San Carlos de Guatemala (Univ de SCdG). **Aims** Provide advanced education (theory, practical with research activities) according to the progress of science and technology, taking into account the needs and resources of the Central American region. **Structure** Director; Coordination. **Languages** Spanish. **Staff** 16.00 FTE, paid. **Finance** Supported by: *Deutscher Akademischer Austauschdienst (DAAD)*; University of San Carlos. **Activities** Training/education. Active in Central America. **Publications** *Water, Sanitation and Environment* (annual) – magazine. **IGO Relations** *Pan American Health Organization (PAHO, #18108)*; *UNESCO (#20322)*. **NGO Relations** *Confederación Universitaria Centroamericana (CSUCA, #04497)*; *Inter-American Association of Sanitary and Environmental Engineering (#11400)*. [2015.09.19/XE1531/E]

♦ Regional Schools and Colleges Permaculture Programme (ReSCOPE Programme) 18812

Facilitator PO Box 30833, Lusaka 10101, Zambia. E-mail: rescope@seedingschools.org.

Chair address not obtained.

URL: https://www.seedingschools.org/

History 19 Dec 2006, Lusaka (Zambia). Registration: No/ID: RNGO/101/0553/16, Start date: 17 Mar 2016, Zambia; Start date: 2007, Malawi. **Aims** Promote the sharing of experiences by partners who are committed to assisting schools and colleges to demonstrate sustainable land use with a view of enhancing healthy environments in and out of school. **Structure** Board; Secretariat; headed by General Coordinator. **Activities** Advocacy/lobbying/activism; capacity building; financial and/or material support. **Publications** *ReSCOPE Newsletter*.

Members Chapters in 5 countries:

Kenya, Malawi, Uganda, Zambia, Zimbabwe.

NGO Relations Member of (1): *Alliance for Food Sovereignty in Africa (AFSA, #00680)*. [2020/AA1176/F]

♦ Regional Science Association / see Regional Science Association International (#18813)

♦ Regional Science Association International (RSAI) 18813

Exec Sec Univ of Azores, Office 155-156, Rua Capitao Joao D'Avila, 9700-042 Angra do Heroismo, Portugal. E-mail: rsai@apdr.pt.

URL: http://www.regionalscience.org/

History 1954. Former names and other names: *Regional Science Association (RSA)* – former. Registration: Charity Commission, No/ID: 1112654, Start date: 6 Jan 2006, End date: 28 Jan 2013, England and Wales. **Aims** Advance for the benefit of the public, regional analysis and related spatial and areal studies. **Structure** Council. Sections: *European Regional Science Association (ERSA, #08346)*; Regional Science Association of the Americas (RSAmericas); *Pacific Regional Science Conference Organization (PRSCO, #17994)*. **Languages** English. **Staff** None. **Finance** Sources: sale of publications. Annual budget: 113,000 EUR (2019). **Activities** Awards/prizes/competitions; events/meetings; training/education. **Events** *World Congress* Marrakech (Morocco) 2021, *World Congress* Marrakech (Morocco) 2020, *World Congress* Goa (India) 2018, *World Congress* Istanbul (Turkey) 2016, *Meeting* Okayama (Japan) 2015. **Publications** *Papers in Regional Science* – journal; *Regional Science Policy and Practice* – journal.

Members in 34 countries and territories:

Australia, Austria, Belgium, Brazil, Canada, Chile, Croatia, Denmark, Finland, France, Germany, Greece, India, Ireland, Israel, Italy, Japan, Korea Rep, Malaysia, Mexico, Netherlands, New Zealand, Norway, Portugal, Romania, Russia, Slovakia, Spain, Sweden, Taiwan, Türkiye, UK, USA, Venezuela. [2021/XD1288/F]

♦ Regional Seas Action Plan for the Wider Caribbean / see Caribbean Action Plan (#03432)

♦ Regional Seas Programme 18814

Coordinator UNEP, PO Box 30552, Room T-108, Nairobi, Kenya. T. +254207624033 – +254207624544. Fax +254207624618.

URL: https://www.unep.org/explore-topics/oceans-seas/what-we-do/regional-seas-programme

History 1974, within the framework of *UNEP (#20299)*. Also referred to as *UNEP Regional Seas Programme*. At first coordinated by *'Oceans and Coastal Areas Programme Activity Centre (OCAPAC)'*, subsequently *UNEP Water Branch (inactive)*. Currently coordinated by UNEP Division for Environmental Policy Implementation. **Aims** Address the accelerating degradation of oceans and coastal areas through sustainable management and use of marine and coastal environments, by engaging neighbouring countries in comprehensive and specific action to protect their shared marine environment; coordinate conventions and action plans to establish a comprehensive strategy and framework for protecting the natural environment and promoting sustainable development. **Structure** Since Jun 1998, secretariats and coordinating units of the regional programmes have held annual meetings to monitor progress and set the stage for their continued work. Programme coordinated by staff from an office located in UNEP Headquarters in Nairobi (Kenya), within the UNEP Division of Environmental Policy Implementation. Regional Coordinating Unit manages work of Regional Seas Programmes, and is aided by Regional Activity Centres. **Languages** English, French, Spanish. **Staff** 6.00 FTE, paid. **Finance** through environment fund and trust funds.

Activities Regional Seas Action Plans are adopted by member governments. They outline the strategy and substance of the programme based on the particular environmental challenges and socio-economic and political situation in each region and normally include: environmental assessment, management and legislation; institutional and financial arrangements. Currently over 140 countries participate in 13 Regional Programmes: Black Sea; Wider Caribbean; East Africa; South East Asia; ROPME Sea Area; Mediterranean; North-East Pacific; North-West Pacific; Red Sea and Gulf of Aden (Yemen); South Asia; South-East Pacific; South Pacific; West and Central Africa. In addition, there are 5 partner programmes for the Antarctic, Arctic, Baltic Sea, Caspian Sea and North-East Atlantic Regions.

Regional Seas Conventions and Action Plans aim to: act as a platform for the regional implementation of Multilateral Environmental Agreements (MEAs) and global programmes and initiatives; increase both regional and inter-regional collaboration by promoting horizontal ties among the Regional Seas Programmes and partner programmes, strengthening their cooperation with international organizations, and forging new partnerships. Major concerns and priorities: marine litter; land-based sources of marine pollution; ship-generated marine pollution; increased urbanization and coastal development; conservation and management of marine and coastal ecosystems; Integrated Coastal Area Management (ICAM); Integrated Coastal Area and River Basin Management (ICARM); over-exploitation and depletion of living marine resources; monitoring, reporting and assessment of the marine environment.

/Regional Seas Conventions and Action Plans Administered by UNEP/

- *Convention for the Protection of the Marine Environment and the Coastal Region of the Mediterranean (Barcelona Convention, 1976)* and *Amendments to the Convention for the Protection of the Mediterranean Sea Against Pollution (1995)*. Protocols: *Protocol for the Prevention of Pollution of the Mediterranean Sea by Dumping from Ships and Aircraft (Dumping Protocol, 1976)* – amended by *Amendments to the Protocol for the Prevention of Pollution of the Mediterranean Sea by Dumping from Ships and Aircraft (1995)*; *Protocol Concerning Cooperation in Preventing Pollution from Ships and, in Cases of Emergency, Combating Pollution of the Mediterranean Sea (2002)* – which replaces *Protocol Concerning Cooperation in Combating Pollution of the Mediterranean Sea by Oil and other Harmful Substances in Cases of Emergency (1976)*; *Protocol for the Protection of the Mediterranean Sea against Pollution from Land-Based Sources and Activities (LBS Protocol, 1980)* – amended by *Amendments to the Protocol for the Protection of the Mediterranean Sea Against Pollution from Land-based Sources and Activities (1996)*; *Protocol Concerning Specially Protected Areas and Biological Diversity in the Mediterranean (Barcelona protocol, 1995)* – replaces *Protocol Concerning Mediterranean Specially Protected Areas (1982)*; *Protocol for the Protection of the Mediterranean Sea Against Pollution Resulting from Exploration and Exploitation of the Continental Shelf and the Seabed and its Subsoil (1994)*; *Protocol on the Prevention of Pollution of the Mediterranean Sea by Transboundary Movements of Hazardous Wastes and Their Disposal (1996)*; *Protocol on Integrated Coastal Zone Management in the Mediterranean (ICZM Protocol, 2008)*. Action Plan: *Mediterranean Action Plan (MAP, #16638)*.
- *Convention for Cooperation in the Protection and Development of the Marine and Coastal Environment of the West and Central African Region (Abidjan convention, 1981)*. Protocol: *Protocol Concerning Cooperation in Combating Pollution in Cases of Emergency (1981)*. Action Plan: *West and Central African Action Plan (WACAF, no recent information)*.
- *Convention for the Protection and Development of the Marine Environment of the Wider Caribbean Region (Cartagena Convention, 1983)*. Protocols: *Protocol Concerning Cooperation in Combating Oil Spills in the Wider Caribbean Region (1983)*; *Protocol Concerning Specially Protected Areas and Wildlife to the Convention for the Protection and Development of the Marine Environment of the Wider Caribbean Region (1990)*; *Protocol Concerning Pollution from Land-based Sources and Activities (1999)*. Action Plan: *Caribbean Action Plan (CAR, #03432)*. Relevant organization: *Regional Marine Pollution Emergency Information and Training Centre – Wider Caribbean (REMPEITC-Carib, #18794)*.
- *Convention for the Protection, Management and Development of the Marine and Coastal Environment of the Eastern African Region (Nairobi Convention, 1985)*.Protocols: *Protocol Concerning Protected Areas and Wild Fauna and Flora in the Eastern African Region (1985)*; *Protocol Concerning Cooperation in Combating Marine Pollution in Cases of Emergency in the Eastern African Region (1985)*. Action Plan: *Eastern African Action Plan (EAF, no recent information)*.
- *Action Plan for Protection, Development and Management of the Marine Environment of the Northwest Pacific Region (NOWPAP, #00092)*.
- *Action Plan for the Protection and Development of the Marine Environment and Coastal Areas of the East Asian Region (EAS, #00093)*.

/Regional Seas Conventions and Action Plans Facilitated by UNEP/

- *Convention for Cooperation in the Protection and Sustainable Development of the Marine and Coastal Environment of the Northeast Pacific (NEP, 2002)*. Action Plan: *Plan of Action for Cooperation in the Protection and Sustainable Development of the Marine and Coastal Environment of the Northeast Pacific (no recent information)*. Relevant organization: *Comisión Centroamericana de Transporte Maritimo (COCATRAM, #04131)*.
- *Kuwait Regional Convention for Cooperation on the Protection on the Marine Environment from Pollution (1978)*. Protocols: *Protocol Concerning Regional Cooperation in Combating Pollution by Oil and other Harmful Substances in Cases of Emergency (1978)*; *Protocol Concerning Marine Pollution Resulting from Exploration and Exploitation of the Continental Shelf (1989)*; *Protocol Amending the Convention for the Prevention of Marine Pollution from Land-based Sources, Kuwait (1990)*; *Protocol on the Control of Marine Transboundary Movements and Disposal of Hazardous Wastes (1998)*. Action Plan: *Kuwait Action Plan (KAP, no recent information)*.
- *Convention for the Protection of the Marine Environment and Coastal Area of the Southeast Pacific (Lima Convention, 1981)*. Protocols: *Protocol for the Protection of the Southeast Pacific Against Pollution from Land-based Sources (1983)*; *Complementary Protocol to the Agreement on Regional Cooperation in Combating Pollution of the Southeast Pacific by Hydrocarbons and other Harmful Substances (1983)*; *Protocol for the Protection of the South East Pacific Against Radioactive Contamination (1989)*; *Protocol for the Conservation and Management of Protected Marine and Coastal Areas of the Southeast Pacific (1989)*. Action Plan: *Action Plan for the Protection of the Marine Environment and Coastal Areas in the South East Pacific (SE/PCF, #00095)*. Relevant organization: *Comisión Permanente del Pacifico Sur (CPPS, #04141)*.
- *Convention for the Conservation of the Red Sea and Gulf of Aden Environment (Jeddah convention, 1982)*. Protocol: *Protocol Concerning Regional Cooperation in Combating Pollution by Oil and other Harmful Substances in Case of Emergency (1982)*. Action Plan: *Regional Organization for the Conservation of the Environment of the Red Sea and Gulf of Aden (PERSGA, #18804)*.
- *Convention for the Protection of the Natural Resources and Environment of the South Pacific Region (SPREP convention, 1986)*. Relevant organization: *Secretariat of the Pacific Regional Environment Programme (SPREP, #19205)*.
- *Convention on the Protection of the Black Sea Against Pollution (Bucharest convention, 1992)*. Protocols: *Protocol on Cooperation in Combating Pollution of the Black Sea Marine Environment by Oil and other Harmful Substances in Emergency Situations (1992)*; *Protocol on the Protection of the Black Sea Marine Environment Against Pollution by Dumping (1992)*; *Protocol on Protection of the Black Sea Marine Environment Against Pollution from Land-based Sources (1992)*. Action Plan: *Black Sea Action Plan (BSAP, no recent information)*.
- *Action Plan for the Protection and Management of the South Asia Seas Region (SASP, #00094)*. Relevant organization: *South Asia Cooperative Environment Programme (SACEP, #19714)*.

/Regional Seas Conventions and Action Plans of Independent Partners/

- *Convention on the Protection of the Marine Environment of the Baltic Sea Area (Helsinki Convention, 1974, 1974)*, *Convention on the Protection of the Marine Environment of the Baltic Sea Area, 1992 (Helsinki Convention, 1992, 1992)* and *Convention on the Protection of the Marine Environment of the Baltic Sea Area, 1999 (Helsinki Convention, 1999, 1999)*.
- *Convention for the Protection on the Marine Environment for the North-East Atlantic (OSPAR Convention, 1992)*. Relevant organization: *OSPAR Commission for the Protection of the Marine Environment of the North-East Atlantic (OSPAR Commission, #17905)*.
- *Framework Convention for the Protection of the Marine Environment of the Caspian Sea (Tehran Convention, 2003)*.
- *Regional Programme of Action for the Protection of the Arctic Marine Environment from Land-based Activities (RPA, #18806)*.

Events *Global Meeting* Seychelles 2022, *Global meeting of the regional seas conventions and action plans* Busan (Korea Rep) 2011, *Global meeting of the regional seas conventions and action plans* Bergen (Norway) 2010, *Workshop on the joint work programme on marine and coastal invasive alien species* Montréal, QC (Canada) 2005, *Global meeting of the regional seas conventions and action plans* Nairobi (Kenya) 2003. **Publications** *Regional Seas Reports and Studies* – series. Directories and biliographies; reference methods for marine pollution studies; technical bulletins for marine pollution studies; meeting reports; brochures; leaflets.

Members Not a membership organization.

IGO Relations Partners:

- *FAO (#09260)*;
- *Global Programme of Action for the Protection of the Marine Environment from Land-Based Activities (GPA, see: #20299)*;
- *Intergovernmental Oceanographic Commission (IOC, #11496)*;
- *International Atomic Energy Agency (IAEA, #12294)*;
- *International Maritime Organization (IMO, #14102)*;
- *UNDP (#20292)*;
- UNEP Divisions (various).

Inter-agency cooperative initiatives – inter-agency cooperation has been instrumental to development and implementation of the Regional Seas Action Plans and Conventions. Among such initiatives:

- Global Assessment of the State of the Marine Environment (GMA) programme of UNEP;
- *Global Environment Facility (GEF, #10346)*;
- *Global Ocean Observing System (GOOS, #10511)*;
- *Global Plan of Action for the Conservation, Management and Utilization of Marine Mammals (Marine Mammal Action Plan, inactive)*;
- *Global Terrestrial Observing System (GTOS, #10626)*;
- *International Coral Reef Action Network (ICRAN, #12964)*;
- *International Coral Reef Initiative (ICRI, #12965)*.

Global Conventions and MEAs:

- *Agreement for the Implementation of the Provisions of the United Nations Convention on the Law of the Sea Relating to the Conservation and Management of Straddling Fish Stocks and Highly Migratory Fish Stocks (1995)*;
- *Convention on Biological Diversity (Biodiversity convention, 1992)*;
- *Convention Concerning the Protection of the World Cultural and Natural Heritage (World Heritage Convention, 1972)*;
- *Convention on the Conservation of Migratory Species of Wild Animals (Bonn Convention, 1979)*;
- *Basel Convention on the Control of Transboundary Movements of Hazardous Wastes and Their Disposal (UNCRTD, 1989)*;
- *Convention on International Trade in Endangered Species of Wild Fauna and Flora (CITES, 1973)*;
- *Convention on the Prevention of Marine Pollution by Dumping of Wastes and other Matter (LDC, 1972)*;
- *Convention on Wetlands of International Importance Especially as Waterfowl Habitat (Convention on Wetlands, 1971)*;

- Convention for the Establishment of
- *Inter-American Tropical Tuna Commission (IATTC, #11454)*;
- *International Convention for the Regulation of Whaling (1946)*;
- Marine Mammal Action Plan;
- *United Nations Convention on the Law of the Sea (UNCLOS, 1982)*;
- *United Nations Framework Convention on Climate Change (UNFCCC, 1992)*.

Regional agreements:
- *African Convention on the Conservation of Nature and Natural Resources (1968)*;
- *Convention on the Conservation of Antarctic Marine Living Resources (CCAMLR, 1980)*;
- *Convention for the Conservation of Antarctic Seals (CCAS, 1972)*;
- *Convention on the Conservation of European Wildlife and Natural Habitats (Bern convention, 1979)*;
- *Convention for the Prohibition of Fishing with Long Driftnets in the South Pacific (1989)*;
- *Protocol to the Antarctic Treaty on Environmental Protection (1991)*.

National agreements: Australian Whale Protection Act; Marine Mammal Protection Act of the United States.
Regional organizations – in several of the regional seas, regional organizations double as secretariats and implementing agencies for their respective Regional Seas programme, including:
- *Caribbean Environment Programme (CEP, #03497)*;
- *Caspian Environment Programme (CEP, #03596)*;
- *Commission for the Conservation of Antarctic Marine Living Resources (CCAMLR, #04206)*;
- *Protection of the Arctic Marine Environment (PAME, #18547)*;
- *Regional Organization for the Protection of the Marine Environment (ROPME, #18805)*.

NGO Relations Inter-agency cooperative initiatives: *Global Coral Reef Monitoring Network (GCRMN, #10306)*. Other organizations involved in the Programme: *International Union for Conservation of Nature and Natural Resources (IUCN, #15766)*; *World Wide Fund for Nature (WWF, #21922)*. [2022/XF4234/F*]

♦ Regional Seas Trust Fund for the Eastern African Region
♦ Regional Secretariat of Catholic Education for Africa and Madagascar / see Association of Catholic Education for Africa and Madagascar (#02415)
♦ Regional Secretariat for Gender, Science and Technology in Southeast Asia and the Pacific (see: #20313)

♦ Regional Secretariat for Parliamentary Cooperation in South-East Europe (RSPC SEE) 18815

Head 1 Aleksandar I Square, 1169 Sofia, Bulgaria. T. +35929878038.
URL: http://www.rspcsee.org/

History Jul 1996, Sofia (Bulgaria). Established during a meeting of the Ministers of Foreign Affairs of South-East European countries, which decided to start a long-term process of multilateral cooperation among participating states in the following 4 fields: strengthening stability, security and good-neighbourly relations; economic development; humanitarian, social and cultural issues; justice, combat against organized crime, illicit drug and arms trafficking, and terrorism. **Structure** Coordinates *South East European Cooperation Process (SEECP, #19811)* and *SEECP Parliamentary Assembly (#19212)*. **Events** *How can parliaments meet the challenge of the EU acquis communautaire parliamentary seminar* Sofia (Bulgaria) 2009, *Parliamentary workshop on food safety legislation and its enforcement* Sofia (Bulgaria) 2009, *Parliamentary seminar for Western Balkan parliaments* Brussels (Belgium) 2008, *Regional workshop on strengthening of the institutional framework of the parliamentary cooperation in South East Europe* Chisinau (Moldova) 2008, *South-East European parliamentarians workshop* Sarajevo (Bosnia-Herzegovina) 2008. **IGO Relations** *Regional Cooperation Council (RCC, #18773)*. [2021/XM3812/E*]

♦ Regional Secretary of the Andean Region Architects 18816

Secrétaire régional des architectes de la région andine – Secretaria de la Regional de Arquitectos del Grupo Andino (RAGA)

Address not obtained.
Pres Sociedad Colombiana de Arquitectos, Carrera 6 No 26b-85, Piso 11, Bogota, Bogota DC, Colombia. T. +5713509922. Fax +5713509994. E-mail: delegado.internacional@sca-pn.org – proyect-sya@hotmail.com.

History 7 Apr 1980, as part of *Pan American Federation of Architects' Associations (#18098)*. **Aims** Integrate architects of the Region for sharing experiences. **Structure** Board; Secretary-General. **Languages** Spanish. **Events** *Meeting* Chiclayo (Peru) 1999, *Convention / Meeting* San Cristobal, BO (Venezuela) 1997, *Convention / Meeting* San Andrés (Colombia) 1995, *Convention / Meeting* Machala (Ecuador) 1994, *Convention / Meeting* Sucre (Bolivia) 1993. **Publications** *RAGA Bulletin* (3 a year); *RAGA Magazine*.
Members Ordinary; Extraordinary. Individuals in 5 countries:
Bolivia, Colombia, Ecuador, Peru, Venezuela.
NGO Relations *Union internationale des architectes (UIA, #20419)*. [2019.11.29/XE8973/v/E]

♦ Regional Studies Association (internationally oriented national body)
♦ Regional Study Centre for Resistance and Adaptation to Drought (see: #20907)

♦ Regional Tourism Organisation of Southern Africa (RETOSA) 18817

Organisation régionale du tourisme pour l'Afrique australe

Contact PO Box 7381, Halfway House, Midrand, 1685, South Africa.
Street address Unit C39 Lond Creek, Waterfall Park, Midrand, South Africa.
URL: http://www.retosa.co.za/

History 1997, by *Southern African Development Community (SADC, #19843)*, on signature of a Charter. Replaces *Southern Africa Regional Tourism Council (SARTOC, inactive)*. **Aims** Develop tourism effective marketing of the region in collaboration with the public and private sector. **Structure** Board, consisting of 1 representative of the public and private sector each, of each SADC Member State. **Languages** English, French, Portuguese. **Staff** 7.00 FTE, paid. **Finance** Members' dues. Cooperative partner funding; programme generated funds. **Activities** Encourages and facilitates movement and flow of tourists into and within the region; develops, coordinates and facilitates marketing and promotion of tourism of the region; encourages, facilitates and monitors quality of service in tourism and accommodation facilities; encourages and promotes consistency in the quality and maintenance of standards and grading of tourism and accommodation facilities in the region. **Publications** *Essence of Africa* – tourism directory; *Southern Africa Tourism News*.
Members Full in 15 countries:
Angola, Botswana, Congo DR, Eswatini, Lesotho, Madagascar, Malawi, Mauritius, Mozambique, Namibia, Seychelles, South Africa, Tanzania UR, Zambia, Zimbabwe.
Organizations in 5 countries:
Australia, France, Germany, UK, USA.
NGO Relations Member of: *Sustainable Tourism Certification Alliance Africa (STCAA, #20068)*. [2019/XD7613/D]

♦ Regional Training and Resource Centre in Early Childhood Care and Education for Asia / see SEED Institute (#19215)
♦ Regional Trust Fund for the Implementation of the Action Plan for the Caribbean Environment Programme (see: #20299)
♦ Regional United Nations Information Centre for Western Europe / see United Nations Regional Information Centre for Western Europe (#20621)
♦ Regional Unit of Technical Assistance (#20333)

♦ Regional Universities Forum for Capacity Building in Agriculture (RUFORUM) 18818

Exec Sec RUFORUM Secretariat, Plot 151/155 Garden Hill, Makerere Univ Main Campus, PO Box 16811, Wandegeya, Kampala, Uganda. T. +256417713300. E-mail: secretariat@ruforum.org.
URL: http://www.ruforum.org/

Aims Promote integration of university research, training and outreach into national and regional research for development. **Structure** General Meeting (annual); Board of Trustees; International Advisory Panel; Technical Committee. **Languages** Arabic, English, French, Portuguese. **Staff** 32.00 FTE, paid. **Activities** Research and development; training/education; advocacy/lobbying/activism; capacity building. **Events** *Annual General Meeting* Cape Coast (Ghana) 2019, *Annual General Meeting* Nairobi (Kenya) 2018, *Biennial Conference* Nairobi (Kenya) 2018, *Annual General Meeting* Lilongwe (Malawi) 2017, *Annual General Meeting* Cape Town (South Africa) 2016. **Publications** *RUFORUM Newsletter* (12 a year). Annual Report; books; briefing papers; policy briefs; brochures; fact sheets; case studies; articles; conference and workshop proceedings; consultancy reports; articles; research briefs.
Members Universities (66) in 25 countries:
Benin, Botswana, Burundi, Congo DR, Egypt, Ethiopia, Ghana, Kenya, Lesotho, Madagascar, Malawi, Mali, Mauritius, Mozambique, Namibia, Nigeria, Rwanda, Senegal, South Africa, South Sudan, Sudan, Tanzania UR, Uganda, Zambia, Zimbabwe.
NGO Relations Partner of: *Mastercard Foundation*. Member of: *Global Confederation of Higher Education Associations for Agriculture and Life Sciences (GCHERA, #10304)*. [2017.08.18/XM3266/F]

♦ Regional Vocational Training Information System (#19296)
♦ Regional Water Centre for Arid and Semi-Arid Regions of Latin America and the Caribbean (internationally oriented national body)
♦ Regional Wildlife Management Program for Meso-America and the Caribbean / see Instituto Internacional en Conservación y Manejo en Vida Silvestre (#11336)
♦ **Regions4** Regions4 Sustainable Development (#18819)

♦ Regions4 Sustainable Development (Regions4) 18819

Secretariat Chaussée d'Alsemberg 999, 1180 Brussels, Belgium. E-mail: info@regions4.org.
URL: https://www.regions4.org/

History 2002, Johannesburg (South Africa). Founded during World Summit of *United Nations Commission on Sustainable Development (CSD, inactive)*. Former names and other names: *Network of Regional Governments for Sustainable Development (nrg4SD)* – former; *Réseau des Gouvernements Régionaux pour le Développement Durable* – former; *Red de Gobiernos Regionales por un Desarrollo Sostenible* – former. Registration: EU Transparency Register, No/ID: 713195539225-67, Start date: 17 Aug 2020. **Aims** Empower regional governments by enabling the strongest connections inside and outside the network and translating them into impactful action; promote sustainable development at subnational level worldwide; seek wider recognition at international level of the important role played by subnational governments towards the realization of the global agendas; contribute to the elaboration and implementation of responsible, ambitious and coherent territorial policies, tools and resources which are adapted to the subnational level; encourage expertise, knowledge exchange, partnerships and projects among regional governments. **Structure** General Assembly (annual); Steering Committee (meets twice a year). Secretariat, headed by Secretary-General. **Languages** English, French, Spanish. **Staff** 6.00 FTE, paid. **Finance** Sources: contributions; members' dues. **Activities** Advocacy/lobbying/activism; awareness raising; capacity building; monitoring/evaluation; projects/programmes. **Events** *General Assembly* Barcelona (Spain) 2016, *Conference* Rio de Janeiro (Brazil) 2012, *General Assembly* Rio de Janeiro (Brazil) 2012, *Conference* Québec, QC (Canada) 2011, *General Assembly* Québec, QC (Canada) 2011. **Publications** *RegionsAdapt Report* (annual); *SDGs at the subnational Level: Regional Governments in the Voluntary National Reviews. Global Challenges, Regional Solutions: The Regions for Biodiversity Learning Platform, Two Years of Lessons Learned*; *Localizing the SDGs: Regional Governments Paving the Way*; *Subnational Governments Achievements towards the Aichi Biodiversity Target 9 and SDG target 15-8*.
Members Full: regional governments and networks of regional governments. Associate: interested organizations. Members in 20 countries:
Belgium, Benin, Brazil, Burkina Faso, Canada, Côte d'Ivoire, Ecuador, France, Ghana, Indonesia, Italy, Kenya, Mexico, Morocco, Senegal, Spain, Sri Lanka, Uganda, UK, Uruguay.
Consultative Status Consultative status granted from: *UNEP (#20299)*. **IGO Relations** Accredited to: *Convention on Biological Diversity (Biodiversity convention, 1992)*; Department of Economic and Social Affairs (UN DESA) of: *United Nations (UN, #20515)*; *UNDP (#20292)*; *UNEP (#20299)*; *United Nations Framework Convention on Climate Change – Secretariat (UNFCCC, #20564)*. Cooperates with: *European Committee of the Regions (CoR, #06665)*; *European Commission (EC, #06633)*. **NGO Relations** Organizing partner of: *Local Governments for Sustainability (ICLEI, #16507)*; *World Organization of United Cities and Local Governments (UCLG, #21695)*. Partners with: Basque Center for Climate Change (BC3); *CDP (#03621)*. [2020.05.05/XM0315/F]

♦ Regions of Climate Action (R20) 18820

Exec Dir Chemin de Balexert 7-9, Vernier, 1219 Geneva, Switzerland. T. +41227556545. Fax +41227556549. E-mail: secretariat@regions20.org.
Dir 1223 Wilshire Blvd, Ste 776, Santa Monica CA 90403, USA. T. +13106640300. Fax +13106640305. E-mail: khaddad@regions20.org.
URL: http://regions20.org/

History Founded by Governor Arnold Schwarzenegger and other global leaders in cooperation with *United Nations (UN, #20515)*. Charter signed 10 Nov 2010. Registration: EU Transparency Register, No/ID: 115848728203-28, Start date: 1 Sep 2017. **Aims** Help sub-national governments around the world to develop low-carbon and climate resilient economic *development* projects. **Structure** Governing Board; Executive Committee; Board of Partners. Offices: Geneva (Switzerland); Santa Monica CA (USA); Mexico; Brazil; China; Indonesia (2); Austria; Algeria; Saudi Arabia; Senegal; South Africa. **Staff** 24.00 FTE, paid. **Events** *Austrian World Summit* Vienna (Austria) 2021, *Austrian World Summit* Vienna (Austria) 2020, *R20 Austrian World Summit* Vienna (Austria) 2019, *Austrian World Summit* Vienna (Austria) 2018, *Austrian World Summit* Vienna (Austria) 2017.
Members Subnational and local governments (over 560) from 24 countries:
Algeria, Austria, Brazil, Burkina Faso, Canada, China, Croatia, Ecuador, France, India, Korea Rep, Mali, Mexico, Morocco, Netherlands, Nigeria, Peru, Philippines, Portugal, Romania, Rwanda, Senegal, Ukraine, USA.
Affiliate members include 3 organizations listed in this Yearbook:
Assembly of European Regions (AER, #02316); *Association of North East Asia Regional Governments (NEAR, #02835)*; *World Association of the Major Metropolises (Metropolis, #21158)*.
IGO Relations *International Solar Alliance (ISA, #15563)*; *UNEP (#20299)* (Accredited status). **NGO Relations** Member of: *Cities Climate Finance Leadership Alliance (CCFLA, #03952)*. Founding member of: *Global Alliance for Smart Cities in Africa (GASCA)*. [2019/XJ8801/C*]

♦ Regions for Health Network (RHN) 18821

Coordinator c/o WHO European Office Health and Development, Ospedale SS Giovanni e Paolo, Castello 6777, 30122 Venice VE, Italy. T. +39412793865. Fax +39412793869. E-mail: eurorhn@who.int.
URL: http://www.euro.who.int/rhn

History 1992, within *WHO (#20950)*. **Aims** Improve health and well-being through prioritizing equity, developing strategic delivery alliances and fostering good governance. **Structure** General Meeting (annual); Regional Ministerial Forum (every 2 years); Steering Committee, consisting of representatives from 5 of the regions (by rotation) and a WHO focal point for the network; Secretariat outsourced by WHO and (temporarily) run on a rotational basis. **Languages** English. **Finance** Members' dues. Other sources: WHO regular budget. **Activities** Projects/programmes; healthcare; training/education; events/meetings; research/documentation; capacity building; publishing activities. **Events** *Annual Conference* Kaunas (Lithuania) 2016, *Annual Conference* Milan (Italy) 2015, *Annual Conference* Milan (Italy) 2014, *Annual Conference* Cardiff (UK) 2013, *Annual Conference* St Petersburg (Russia) 2012. **Publications** Annual report; conference reports; training modules; cqse studies; policy papers.
Members Regions (42) in 26 countries:
Austria, Belgium, Bulgaria, Canada, Croatia, Czechia, Estonia, Germany, Hungary, Israel, Italy, Kazakhstan, Lithuania, Moldova, Netherlands, Norway, Portugal, Romania, San Marino, Slovakia, Slovenia, Spain, Sweden, Switzerland, Turkmenistan, UK.
IGO Relations Focal Point provided by: *WHO Regional Office for Europe (#20945)*. [2019.10.15/XF4142/F]

♦ Registered Engineers for Disaster Relief / see RedR International (#18729)
♦ Register of Engineers for Disaster Relief / see RedR International (#18729)
♦ Register för Världsmedborgare (#18822)
♦ Register van Wereldburgers (#18822)
♦ Registo dos Cidadões do Mundo (#18822)
♦ Registo Internacional dos Cidadões do Mundo / see Registre des Citoyens du Monde (#18822)

♦ Registre des Citoyens du Monde (RICM) 18822

Registry of World Citizens (IRWC) – Registro de los Ciudadanos del Mundo – Weltbürger-Register – Registo dos Cidadões do Mundo – Registro dei Cittadini del Mondo – Register van Wereldburgers – Register för Världsmedborgare – Rejester Obywateli – Rejstrik Obcanu Sveta – Vilagpolgarok Nemzetközi Nyilvantartasi Könyve – Registrolibro de la Mondcivitanoj

Pres 66 bd Vincent Auriol, 75013 Paris, France. T. +33241784775. E-mail: registre.cdm@gmail.com.
URL: http://www.recim.org/cdm/

History 27 Jul 1949, Paris (France). Reorganized 1952, under the moral guaranty of the now defunct *World Council for the Peoples World Convention (CMACP, inactive)*. Former names and other names: *International Registry of World Citizens (IRWC)* – former; *Registre international des citoyens du monde (RICM)* – former; *Registro Internacional de los Ciudadanos del Mundo* – former; *Internationales Weltbürger-Register* – former; *Registo Internacional dos Cidadões do Mundo* – former; *Mezdunarodnaja Registracija Grazdan Mira* – former; *Registro Internazionale dei Cittadini del Mondo* – former; *Internationaal Register van Wereldburgers* – former; *Internationell Registrering för Världsmedborgare* – former; *Ubhaliso Lwabantu Belizwe Jukelele* – former; *Pendaftaran Kerayatan Dunia Antarabangsa* – former; *Ofisi ya Uandikishaji wa Raia wa Mataifa Mbali-Mbali* – former; *Urzad Miedzy Narodowy Obywateli Swiata* – former; *Kungiyar Sada Zumunci Tsakanin Al'ummar Kasasha, Duniya* – former; *Internacia Registrolibro de la Civitanoj del Mondo* – former; *Pankosmion Diefnes Mitroon Politon* – former; *Tabulae Orbis Terrarum Civium* – former. Registration: France. **Aims** Become an instrument for encouraging, focusing and measuring the growth of public opinion in favour of world unity and in support of a People's World Convention, through the issuing of 'World Citizen Identity Cards', implying the right to vote for a direct representation to the Convention, to those who are prepared to recognize their responsibilities as members of the world community. **Structure** General Assembly (annual); Federal Council (annual). **Languages** English, Esperanto, French. **Staff** 105.00 FTE, voluntary. **Finance** Sources: contributions; sale of products. **Activities** Awareness raising; events/meetings; training/education. **Events** *General Assembly* Paris (France) 2000, *Biennial General Assembly* San Francisco, CA (USA) 1995, *General assembly / Biennial General Assembly* Paris (France) 1992, *General assembly / Biennial General Assembly* Geneva (Switzerland) 1990, *General assembly / Biennial General Assembly* Paris (France) 1988. **Publications** *IRWC Information Bulletin* in Dutch, English, Esperanto, French, German, Spanish; *RECIM Info* – newsletter. *Mundialist Studies* (1988). Books.
Members Registration centres in 14 countries:
Australia, Belgium, Benin, Burkina Faso, Cameroon, Canada, Congo DR, France, Japan, Madagascar, Mali, Senegal, Togo, USA.
Individuals (World Citizens): pver 13000. Membership countries not specified. [2021/XF2409/**F**]

- ♦ Registre international des citoyens du monde / see Registre des Citoyens du Monde (#18822)
- ♦ Registro dei Cittadini del Mondo (#18822)
- ♦ Registro de los Ciudadanos del Mundo (#18822)
- ♦ Registro Internacional de los Ciudadanos del Mundo / see Registre des Citoyens du Monde (#18822)
- ♦ Registro Internazionale dei Cittadini del Mondo / see Registre des Citoyens du Monde (#18822)
- ♦ Registrolibro de la Mondcivitanoj (#18822)
- ♦ Registry of World Citizens (#18822)
- ♦ Reglamento para las faenas de caza maritima en las aguas del Pacifico Sur (1952 treaty)
- ♦ Reglamento internacional para prevenir los abordajes en el mar (1960 treaty)
- ♦ Reglamento de radiocomunicaciones (1979 treaty)
- ♦ Reglamento sanitario internacional, 1969 (1969 treaty)
- ♦ Reglamento de las telecomunicaciones internacionales (1988 treaty)
- ♦ Reglamento telegrafico, reglamento telefónico (1973 treaty)
- ♦ Reglas de la CNUDCI en materia de arbitraje (1976 treaty)
- ♦ Reglas uniformes relativas a clausulas contractuales estipulando que una suma convenida es debida en caso de no ejecución (1983 treaty)

♦ REGLEG 18823

Contact address not obtained. E-mail: info@regleg.eu.
URL: http://www.regleg.eu/

History 15 Nov 2001, Liège (Belgium), as a political network and not a formal association. Also referred to as *Conference of Presidents of Regions with Legislative Power*. **Aims** Raise the level of *democratic* participation from legislative regions in *EU* affairs. **Structure** Annual Conference. Coordination Committee, consisting of 1-4 Regions. **Events** *Annual Conference* Turin (Italy) 2009, *Annual Conference* Brussels (Belgium) 2008, *Annual Conference* Barcelona (Spain) 2007, *Annual Conference* Cardiff (UK) 2006, *Annual Conference* Munich (Germany) 2005.
Members Regions (73) in 8 countries:
Austria, Belgium, Finland, Germany, Italy, Portugal, Spain, UK.
IGO Relations Agreement with: *Council of Europe (CE, #04881)*. Cooperates with: *European Committee of the Regions (CoR, #06665)*. [2009/XJ0808/**E***]

- ♦ Règlement d'arbitrage et de conciliation pour les conflits internationaux entre deux parties dont l'une seulement est un Etat (1962 treaty)
- ♦ Réglementation de la pêche dans les eaux du Pacifique Sud (1952 treaty)
- ♦ Règlement d'introduction des instances et règlement d'arbitrage (1968 treaty)
- ♦ Règlement of Navigation and Police Applicable to the Danube between Galatz and the Mouths (1911 treaty)
- ♦ Règlement no 1 relatif à la nomenclature concernant les maladies et causes de décès (1948 treaty)
- ♦ Règlement relatif à la délivrance des patentes de bateliers du Rhin du 14 décembre 1922 (1925 treaty)
- ♦ Règlement relatif à la nomenclature concernant les maladies et causes de décès (1949 treaty)
- ♦ Règlement sanitaire international, 1951 (1951 treaty)
- ♦ Règlement sanitaire international, 1969 (1969 treaty)
- ♦ Règlement des télécommunications (1979 treaty)
- ♦ Règlement des télécommunications internationales (1988 treaty)
- ♦ Règlement télégraphique, règlement téléphonique (1973 treaty)
- ♦ Règles de la CNUDCI en matière d'arbitrage (1976 treaty)
- ♦ Règles internationales pour prévenir les abordages en mer, 1960 (1960 treaty)
- ♦ Règles uniformes relatives aux clauses contractuelles stipulant qu'une somme convenue est due en cas de défaut d'exécution (1983 treaty)
- ♦ Regnskogfondet (internationally oriented national body)
- ♦ Regnum Christi (internationally oriented national body)
- ♦ **REGPEP Society** International Regulatory Peptide Society (#14711)
- ♦ **REG** Respiratory Effectiveness Group (#18918)

♦ Regroupement Européen pour la FOrmation et la Reconnaissance des MEDecines non-conventionnelles (REFORMED) 18824

Founder/Pres 8 rue Palouzié, 93400 Saint-Ouen, France. T. +33687625486.
Registered Office Rue de Quesval, Spontin 2 Map box A, 5530 Yvoir, Belgium.
URL: http://reformed-eu.org/

History 2004. Formalized when statutes were adopted, 27 Mar 2007. Registration: Banque-Carrefour des Entreprises, No/ID: 0890.128.121, Start date: 18 Jun 2007. **Aims** Harmonize knowledge between medicine and non-medicine practitioner in the sector of the non-conventional medicine by branches to get good practice and recognition in the sector. **Languages** English, French. **Activities** Certification/accreditation; events/meetings. **Events** *International Symposium* Brussels (Belgium) 2017.
Members Full in 11 countries:
Algeria, Belgium, France, Germany, Greece, Italy, Japan, Morocco, Romania, Spain, Switzerland.
NGO Relations Member of (1): *Federation of European and International Associations Established in Belgium (FAIB, #09508)*. [2021/XJ8833/**F**]

- ♦ Regroupement des missionnaires laïques / see Réseau Entraide Solidarité Monde
- ♦ Regular Academic Conferences for Administration in Europe / see Association Europa
- ♦ **REGULATEL** Foro Latinoamericano de Entes Reguladores de Telecomunicaciones (#09880)
- ♦ Regulations Concerning the Granting of Rhine Navigation Certificates of December 14 1922 (1925 treaty)
- ♦ Regulations for Maritime Hunting Operations in the Waters of the South Pacific (1952 treaty)
- ♦ Regulations no 1 Regarding Nomenclature of Diseases and Causes of Death (1948 treaty)
- ♦ Regulations Regarding Nomenclature with Respect to Diseases and Causes of Death (1949 treaty)
- ♦ Regulatory Assistance Project (internationally oriented national body)
- ♦ Rehabilitación Internacional / see RI Global (#18948)
- ♦ Rehabilitation Gazette / see Post-Polio Health International
- ♦ Réhabilitation internationale / see RI Global (#18948)

♦ Rehabilitation International – European Communities Association (RI-ECA) 18825

SG 866 United Nations Plaza, Office 422, New York NY 10017, USA. T. +12124201500. Fax +12125050871. E-mail: info@riglobal.org.
URL: http://www.riglobal.org/

History 18 Nov 1988, Madrid (Spain), within the framework of *RI Global (#18948)*, when officially formed, after some years of informal existence, to carry out RI work in the countries of the European Communities. Statutes latest amended: 2000. Registered in accordance with Belgian law. **Aims** Promote rehabilitation of people with *disabilities*; participate in the elaboration of a European policy for people with disabilities and ensure access to equal participation of disabled people with regard to all activities promoted by the *European Union*. **Structure** General Assembly. Administrative Council. Executive Committee. Officers: President; Vice-President; Secretary; Treasurer. **Finance** Members' dues. Other sources: EC subsidies; co-financement for specific activities. **Activities** Organizes and coordinates collaboration and serves as a link between national RI associations and EC/EU institutions; organizes conferences and seminars at the European Union level. **Events** *Annual General Assembly* Beirut (Lebanon) 2001, *Annual General Assembly* Budapest (Hungary) 2000, *Annual General Assembly* London (UK) 1999, *Annual General Assembly* Jerusalem (Israel) 1998, *Annual General Assembly* Netherlands 1997. **Publications** *RI-ECA News* (4 a year).
Members Full national organizations, members of RI; Associate governmental and charitable bodies collaborating with RI national organizations. Members in the 15 European Union countries:
Austria, Belgium, Denmark, Finland, France, Germany, Greece, Ireland, Italy, Luxembourg, Netherlands, Portugal, Spain, Sweden, UK.
Observer members associate in 2 countries:
Iceland, Norway. [2020/XE1667/**E**]

♦ Rehabilitation in Multiple Sclerosis (RIMS) 18826

Pres RIMS iVZW, Tervuursevest 101 box 1501, 3001 Leuven, Belgium. E-mail: secretariat@eurims.org.
URL: http://www.eurims.org/

History Founded 1991, Milan (Italy). Subtitle: *European Network for Best Practice and Research*. Previously referred to as *Multiple Sclerosis and Rehabilitation, Care- and Health Services in Europe (MARCH)*. Registered under Belgian law: BE871838770. **Aims** Enhance activity, participation and autonomy of people with *Multiple Sclerosis* by developing and advocating evidence-based rehabilitation. **Structure** Executive Board. **Languages** English. **Staff** 0.40 FTE, paid. **Finance** Members' dues. **Activities** Advocacy/lobbying/activism; healthcare; events/meetings; training/education; projects/programmes; financial and/or material support. **Events** *Annual Meeting* Amsterdam (Netherlands) 2018, *Annual Meeting* Barcelona (Spain) 2017, *Annual Meeting* London (UK) 2016, *Annual Meeting* Milan (Italy) 2015, *Annual Meeting* Brighton (UK) 2014.
Members Organizations in 21 countries:
Austria, Belgium, Denmark, Estonia, Finland, France, Germany, Greece, Hungary, Ireland, Italy, Luxembourg, Netherlands, Norway, Poland, Portugal, Slovenia, Spain, Sweden, Switzerland, UK.
NGO Relations Working relations with: *European Multiple Sclerosis Platform (EMSP, #07833)*.
[2018.02.13/XE3555/**E**]

- ♦ Rehabilitation and Research Centre for Torture Victims / see DIGNITY – Danish Institute Against Torture
- ♦ Rehabiliterings- og Forskningscentret for Torturofre / see DIGNITY – Danish Institute Against Torture
- ♦ RehabiMed (internationally oriented national body)
- ♦ RehabWeek (meeting series)
- ♦ REH – Rencontre européenne humaine (inactive)
- ♦ REHVA / see Federation of European Heating, Ventilation and Air-Conditioning Associations (#09507)
- ♦ **REHVA** Federation of European Heating, Ventilation and Air-Conditioning Associations (#09507)
- ♦ Rehydration Project (internationally oriented national body)

♦ Rei Cretariae Romanae Fautores (RCRF) 18827

Société des archéologues de la céramique romaine – Association of Roman Ceramic Archaeologists

Treas Dipto Civiltà e Forme del Sapere, via dei Mille 19, 56126 Pisa PI, Italy. E-mail: treasurer@fautores.org.
Pres Narodni Muzej, Trg Republike 1a, Belgrade, PAK 11000, Serbia. E-mail: president@fautores.org.
URL: https://fautores.org/

History 2 Aug 1957, Brugg (Switzerland), as *Rei Cretariae Romanae Fautores ubique Consistentes*. Title abbreviated 1958, Arezzo (Italy). **Aims** Promote study of all categories of Roman ceramic. **Structure** General Meeting (every 2 years); Executive Committee. **Languages** English, French, German, Italian, Spanish. **Staff** 5.00 FTE, voluntary. **Finance** Sources: members' dues. Other sources: Grants from institutions for publications. **Activities** Events/meetings; knowledge management/information dissemination; networking/liaising; publishing activities; research/documentation. **Events** *Biennial Congress* Leiden (Netherlands) 2024, *Biennial Congress* Athens (Greece) 2022, *Biennial Congress* Athens (Greece) 2020, *Biennial Congress* Cluj-Napoca (Romania) 2018, *Biennial Congress* Lisbon (Portugal) 2016. **Publications** *Acta RCRF* (regular); *Communicationes* (regular); *Supplementa* (irregular).
Members Individuals (about 325); Institutions (about 100) in 30 countries:
Albania, Australia, Austria, Belgium, Bulgaria, Canada, Croatia, Czechia, Denmark, France, Germany, Greece, Hungary, Israel, Italy, Liechtenstein, Netherlands, Poland, Portugal, Romania, Russia, Serbia, Slovakia, Slovenia, Spain, Switzerland, Türkiye, UK, Ukraine, USA. [2021/XD3156/**C**]

- ♦ Rei Cretariae Romanae Fautores ubique Consistentes / see Rei Cretariae Romanae Fautores (#18827)
- ♦ REIGAP – Red de Escuelas e Institutos Gubernamentales en Asuntos Públicos (see: #16294)

♦ Reiki Alliance 18828

Sec address not obtained. E-mail: info@reikialliance.com.
URL: http://www.reikialliance.com/

History 1983. **Aims** Support member teachers of the *Usui System* of *Reiki Healing*. **Structure** International Board. **Staff** 8.00 FTE, paid. **Finance** Members' dues. Other sources: donations; mail order sales. **Events** *Annual Conference* Copenhagen (Denmark) 2005, *Annual Conference* Gersfeld (Germany) 2002, *Annual Conference* Cancún (Mexico) 2001, *Annual Conference* Retie (Belgium) 2000, *Annual Conference* Navasota, TX (USA) 1999. **Publications** *Member Newsletter* (3 a year). *Reiki Alliance Student Book*.
Members Individuals (750) in 40 countries and territories:
Argentina, Australia, Austria, Belgium, Brazil, Canada, Chile, China, Colombia, Croatia, Czechia, Denmark, Finland, France, Germany, Greece, Guadeloupe, India, Ireland, Israel, Italy, Kazakhstan, Liechtenstein, Mexico, Netherlands, New Zealand, Norway, Peru, Poland, Portugal, Russia, Spain, Suriname, Sweden, Switzerland, Trinidad-Tobago, UK, Uruguay, USA.
[2020/XF0857/v/**F**]

- ♦ REINA – Rencontres internationales sur l'environnement et la nature (meeting series)
- ♦ **REIN** Réseau Européen pour l'Insertion Sociale et Professionnelle de Personnes Défavorisées (#18874)
- ♦ Re-Pro International / see Music Producers Guild (#16914)
- ♦ Reinventing Bretton Woods Committee (unconfirmed)
- ♦ REI – Refugee Empowerment International (internationally oriented national body)
- ♦ **REIRPR** Réseau européen interdisciplinaire de recherche sur psychologie et réanimation (#18876)
- ♦ REISSE / see European Network of Sport Education (#08012)
- ♦ REISS / see European Network of Sport Education (#08012)

♦ Rejection of Sins and Exodus 18829

Takfir Wa al-Hijra

Address not obtained.

History Some sources suggest the group was founded early 1970s, Egypt, by Mustafa Shukri. Other sources say group grew out of the al-Zawahiri faction of the early 1980s split Egyptian Islamic Jihad (EIJ). An Islamic terrorist organization. Also referred to as *Martyrs for Morocco*. Linked with murder of Dutch film maker Theo van Gogh, Nov 2004. **Members** Individuals throughout the Arab and Muslim world. Also cells in Europe. Membership countries not specified. **NGO Relations** Related organization: *Al-Qa'ida (#00748)*.
[2008/XM0479/s/**F**]

♦ Rejester Obywateli (#18822)
♦ **REJINA** Red Iberoamericana de Juventud Indigena y Afrodescendiente (#18672)
♦ **R-E-J** Réseau express jeunes (#22017)
♦ Rejstrik Obcanu Sveta (#18822)
♦ Rekenkamer van de Europese Gemeenschappen / see European Court of Auditors (#06854)
♦ **RELAB** Red Latinoamericana de Ciencias Biológicas (#18706)
♦ **RELACC** Red Latinoamericana de Comercialización Comunitaria (#18707)
♦ ReLAC – Red de Seguimiento, Evaluación y Sistematización de América Latine y el Caribe (unconfirmed)
♦ RELAETI – Red Latinoamericana de Estudios de Traducción e Interpretación (unconfirmed)
♦ **RELAF** Red Latinoamericana de Acogimiento Familiar (#18700)

♦ Relais et Châteaux 18830

Pres 58-60 rue de Prony, 75017 Paris, France. T. +33145729000. E-mail: president@relaischateaux.com – rc-paris@relaischateaux.com.
URL: http://www.relaischateaux.com/

History 1975, France, by merger of 'Châteaux hotels', *International Association of 'Country Relays' (inactive)* and 'Relais gourmands'. Registered in accordance with French law of 1901. **Aims** Further the cultural and economic stature of members; *market* independent *hotels* and *restaurants* around the world. **Structure** Board of Directors, comprising International President, 1st Vice-President, Vice-President, Vice-President in Charge of Grand Chefs, Secretary General, Deputy Secretary General, Treasurer, Deputy Treasurer, 2 members of the bureau and 17 members. Offices in: Berlin (Germany); Barcelona (Spain); Milan (Italy); Tokyo (Japan). Houses in: Paris (France); London (UK); New York NY (USA). **Languages** English, French, German, Italian, Spanish. **Staff** 49.00 FTE, paid. **Events** *Congress* London (UK) 2019, *Congress* Madrid (Spain) 2017, *Congress* Tokyo (Japan) 2016, *Congress* Paris (France) 2014, *Congress* Berlin (Germany) 2013. **Publications** *Relais and Chateaux International Guide* in English, French, German, Italian, Spanish.
Members Hotels and restaurants (about 500) in 50 countries and territories:
Argentina, Australia, Austria, Barbados, Belgium, Brazil, Canada, China, Denmark, Ecuador, France, Germany, Greece, Indonesia, Ireland, Israel, Italy, Japan, Korea Rep, Lebanon, Liechtenstein, Lithuania, Luxembourg, Madagascar, Malta, Mauritius, Mexico, Morocco, Namibia, Netherlands, New Zealand, Norway, Poland, Polynesia Fr, Portugal, Puerto Rico, Seychelles, Slovenia, South Africa, Spain, St Kitts-Nevis, Switzerland, Tanzania UR, Türkiye, UK, United Arab Emirates, Uruguay, USA, Virgin Is USA, Zimbabwe. [2013/XF5997/**F**]

♦ RELAMA-UMALCA / see Unión Matematica de América Latina y el Caribe (#20456)
♦ **RELAMI** Rede Ecumênica Latino Americana de Missiologas (#16312)
♦ **ReLANS** Red Latinoamericana de Nanotecnologia y Sociedad (#16349)
♦ **RELAQ** Red Latinoamericana de Quimica (#18718)
♦ **RELASER** Red Latinoamericana de Servicios de Extensión Rural (#18719)
♦ **RELAT** Red de Escritoras Latinoamericanas (#18649)
♦ RELATS – Red Eurolatinoamericana de Analisis de Trabajo y Sindicalismo (unconfirmed)
♦ RELC / see SEAMEO Regional Language Centre (#19181)
♦ **RELCOM** Red Latinoamericana y del Caribe para la Conservación de los Murciélagos (#18703)
♦ Release International (internationally oriented national body)
♦ RELIAL – Red Liberal de América Latina (unconfirmed)
♦ Relief Inter-Committee for Refugees of Central Europe (inactive)
♦ Relief International (internationally oriented national body)
♦ Relief and Rehabilitation Network / see Humanitarian Practice Network (#10973)
♦ Religieuses Adoratrices du Très Précieux Sang de Notre-Seigneur Jésus Christ de l'Union de Saint-Hyacinthe (religious order)
♦ Religieuses de l'Assomption (religious order)
♦ Religieuses de Bethléem (religious order)
♦ Religieuses de la Compagnie de Sainte-Ursule (religious order)
♦ Religieuses de l'Enfant-Jésus de Lille (religious order)
♦ Religieuses Hospitalières de Saint-Joseph (religious order)
♦ Religieuses de Jésus-Marie (religious order)
♦ Religieuses de Nazareth (religious order)
♦ Religieuses de Notre-Dame des Missions (religious order)
♦ Religieuses de la Providence de Lisieux (religious order)
♦ Religieuses du Sacré-Coeur de Marie (religious order)
♦ Religieuses de Sainte-Clotilde (religious order)
♦ Religieuses de la Sainte-Union des Sacrés-Coeurs (religious order)
♦ Religieuses de Saint François d'Assise de Lyon (religious order)
♦ Religieuses du Saint-Sacrement de Valence (religious order)
♦ Religieux de Notre-Dame de Sion (religious order)
♦ Religieux de Saint Vincent de Paul (religious order)
♦ Religion raëlienne / see International Raelian Movement (#14690)

♦ Religions for Peace (RfP) 18831

SG 777 UN Plaza, New York NY 10017, USA. T. +12126872163. Fax +12129830566. E-mail: info@rfp.org – rfpsgoffice@rfp.org.
URL: https://rfp.org/

History 16 Oct 1970, Kyoto (Japan). Founded during 1st World Conference on Religion and Peace, on the initiative of American, Japanese and Indian religious leaders, following consolidation of separate national movements meeting in 1969, Istanbul (Turkey). Former names and other names: *World Conference of Religions for Peace* – former; *Conférence mondiale des religions pour la paix* – former; *Conferencia Mundial de la Religión por la Paz* – former; *Weltkonferenz der Religionen für den Frieden* – former; *World Conference on Religion and Peace* – former; *WCRP* – former. **Aims** Advance common action among the world's religious communities for peace. **Structure** World Assembly (every 5 years); World Council; Executive Committee; Regional Councils and Groups; *Global Women of Faith Network*; *Global Religious Youth Network*; Secretariat. Regional networks include: *African Council of Religious Leaders – Religions for Peace (ACRL-RfP, #00276)*; *Asian Conference of Religions for Peace (ACRP, #01400)*; *European Council of Religious Leaders – Religions for Peace (ECRL, #06840)*. Regional offices (4) in: USA; Japan; Australia; Switzerland. **Languages** English. **Staff** 30.00 FTE, paid. **Finance** Sources: contributions. **Activities** Events/meetings. **Events** *Conference of the World Council of Religious Leaders on Faith and Diplomacy: Generations in Dialogue* Lindau (Germany) 2021, *Assembly on Women, Faith, and Diplomacy* Lindau (Germany) 2020, *World Assembly* Lindau (Germany) 2019, *Special Session* Tokyo (Japan) 2016, *World Assembly* Vienna (Austria) 2013. **Publications** Reports; brochures.
Members Institutions and individuals, representing major religions, in 111 countries:
Albania, Algeria, Argentina, Armenia, Australia, Austria, Bahamas, Bangladesh, Barbados, Belarus, Belgium, Benin, Bolivia, Bosnia-Herzegovina, Botswana, Brazil, Burundi, Cambodia, Cameroon, Canada, Chile, China, Colombia, Congo Brazzaville, Congo DR, Costa Rica, Croatia, Cyprus, Czechia, Denmark, Dominican Rep, Ecuador, Egypt, El Salvador, Estonia, Fiji, Finland, France, Gambia, Georgia, Germany, Ghana, Greece, Guatemala, Haiti, Hungary, India, Indonesia, Iran Islamic Rep, Iraq, Ireland, Israel, Italy, Japan, Jordan, Kazakhstan, Kenya, Korea DPR, Korea Rep, Lesotho, Libya, Lithuania, Luxembourg, Madagascar, Malawi, Malaysia, Mali, Malta, Mauritius, Mexico, Mongolia, Morocco, Myanmar, Namibia, Nepal, Netherlands, New Zealand, Nigeria, Norway, Pakistan, Peru, Philippines, Poland, Portugal, Romania, Russia, Rwanda, Samoa, Saudi Arabia, Senegal, Serbia, Sierra Leone, Singapore, South Africa, Spain, Sri Lanka, Sweden, Syrian AR, Thailand, Trinidad-Tobago, Tunisia, Türkiye, Uganda, UK, Ukraine, USA, Uzbekistan, Venezuela, Vietnam, Zambia, Zimbabwe.
Observer Missions in 2 countries:
Holy See, Switzerland.
Consultative Status Consultative status granted from: *ECOSOC (#05331)* (General); *UNESCO (#20322)* (Consultative Status); *UNICEF (#20332)*. **IGO Relations** Memorandum of Understanding with (1): *King Abdullah Bin Abdulaziz International Centre for Interreligious and Intercultural Dialogue (KAICIID, #16193)*. Cooperates with (1): *Islamic World Educational, Scientific and Cultural Organization (ICESCO, #16058)*. Associated with Department of Global Communications of the United Nations.
NGO Relations Member of (14): *American Council for Voluntary International Action (InterAction)*; *Committee of Religious NGOs at the United Nations (CRNGOs, #04282)*; *Conference of Non-Governmental Organizations in Consultative Relationship with the United Nations (CONGO, #04635)*; *European Network on Religion and Belief (ENORB, #07985)*; *Fédération des Institutions Internationales établies à Genève (FIIG, #09599)*; *Global Call for Climate Action (GCCA, inactive)*; *International Campaign to Ban Landmines – Cluster Munition Coalition (ICBL-CMC, #12427)*; *International Interfaith Organizations Network (IION, #13945)*; *International Partnership on Religion and Sustainable Development (PaRD, #14524)*; *Joint Learning Initiative on Faith and Local Communities (JLI, #16139)*; *Network for Religious and Traditional Peacemakers (#17054)*; *NGO Committee on Financing for Development, New York (#17108)*; *NGO Committee on Freedom of Religion or Belief, New York NY (#17109)*; *NGO Committee on UNICEF (#17120)*. Partner of (1): *International Campaign to Abolish Nuclear Weapons (ICAN, #12426)*.
Cooperates with (25):
- *Baha'i International Community (#03062)*;
- *CARE International (CI, #03429)*;
- *Catholic Foreign Missionary Society of America (Maryknoll Fathers)*;
- *Conference of European Churches (CEC, #04593)*;
- *G20 Interfaith Forum Association (IF20, #10055)*;
- *General Board of Church and Society of the United Methodist Church (GBCS)*;
- *Greek Orthodox Archdiocesan Council of America (GOAC, #10708)*;
- *International Association for Religious Freedom (IARF, #12130)*;
- *International Catholic Child Bureau (#12450)*;
- *International Federation of ACATs – Action by Christians for the Abolition of Torture (#13334)*;
- *International Fellowship of Reconciliation (IFOR, #13586)*;
- *International Mahavira Jain Mission (IMJM)*;
- *Muslim World League (MWL, #16917)*;
- *NGO Committee for Disarmament, Geneva (#17105)*;
- *NGO Committee on Disarmament, Peace and Security, New York NY (#17106)*;
- *Pax Christi – International Catholic Peace Movement (#18266)*;
- *Rabita Council International (Rasbak, no recent information)*;
- *Rissho Kosei-Kai (RKK)*;
- *Temple of Understanding (ToU, #20124)*;
- *The Lutheran World Federation (LWF, #16532)*;
- *The Rockefeller Foundation (#18966)*;
- *Unitarian Universalist Association (UUA, #20494)*;
- *Wainwright House*;
- *World Muslim Congress (WMC, #21664)*;
- *World Union for Progressive Judaism (WUPJ, #21883)*.

Supports (1): *Global Call for Action Against Poverty (GCAP, #10263)*. [2022.05.03/XD4008/**F**]

♦ Religions for Peace Asia / see Asian Conference of Religions for Peace (#01400)
♦ Religiosas Dominicas de Santa Catalina de Siena (religious order)
♦ Religiosas Filipenses Misioneras de Enseñanza (religious order)
♦ Religiosas de Maria Inmaculada (religious order)
♦ Religiosas Sacramentinas de Bérgamo (religious order)
♦ Religiosas do Sagrado Coração de Maria (religious order)
♦ Religiosas del Verbo Encarnado y del Santisimo Sacramento (religious order)
♦ Religiose dell'Assunzione (religious order)
♦ Religiose della Compagnia di Santa Orsola (religious order)
♦ Religiose Filippine Missionarie dell'Insegnamento (religious order)
♦ Religiöse Gesellschaft der Freunde (#18834)
♦ Religiose di Gesù-Maria (religious order)
♦ Religiose di Maria Immacolata (religious order)
♦ Religiose di Nazareth (religious order)
♦ Religiöser Menschheitsbund (inactive)
♦ Religiose del Sacro Cuore di Maria (religious order)
♦ Religiosi di Santo Vincenzo de Paoli, Padri e Fratelli (religious order)
♦ Religious of the Assumption (religious order)
♦ Religious Centre for Information and Analysis of Comics / see International Christian Centre for Research on Information about and Analysis of the Strip Cartoon (#12557)
♦ Religious of Christian Education (religious order)

♦ Religious Conference Management Association (RCMA) 18832

Exec Dir 7702 Woodland Drive, Ste 120, Indianapolis IN 46278, USA. T. +13176321888. Fax +13176327909. E-mail: dhochstetler@rcmaweb.org.
URL: https://www.myrcma.org/

History 1972. **Aims** Provide a forum for international membership to: gain increased insights into the arts and sciences of religious meeting planning and management; keep abreast of the latest developments in the field; expand the breadth and scope of knowledge essential to success. **Events** *Annual World Conference* Sacramento, CA (USA) 2014, *Annual World Conference / Annual Conference* Minneapolis, MN (USA) 2013, *Annual World Conference / Annual Conference* Kansas City, MO (USA) 2012, *Annual world conference / Annual Conference* Tampa, FL (USA) 2011, *Annual world conference* Fort Worth, TX (USA) 2010. **Publications** *RCMA Highlights* (daily) – during each Conference and Exposition; *Who's Who in Religious Conference Management* (annual); *Religious Conference Manager* – magazine.
Members Individuals in 17 countries and territories:
Aruba, Bahamas, Barbados, Belgium, Bermuda, Brazil, Canada, Ethiopia, Germany, Greece, Israel, Jamaica, Netherlands, South Africa, Türkiye, UK, USA.
NGO Relations Member of: *Events Industry Council (EIC, #09212)*. [2021/XF2931/v/**F**]

♦ Religious in Europe Networking Against Trafficking and Exploitation (RENATE) 18833

Registered Address Pastoor de Kroonstraat 349, 5211 XJ 's Hertogenbosch, Netherlands. E-mail: renatenetwork@gmail.com – communications@renate-europe.net.
URL: http://www.renate-europe.net/

History 's Hertogenbosch (Netherlands). Founded Den Bosch (Netherlands). Registration: No/ID: KVK 17271216, Netherlands. **Aims** Respond in the light of Gospel values to the issue of trafficking of women, children and men. **Structure** General Assembly; Core Group; Board. **Staff** 4.00 FTE, paid. **Publications** *RENATE Newsletter*.
Members Networks (136). Membership countries not specified. Included in the above, 48 organizations listed in this Yearbook:
Included in the above, 48 organizations listed in this Yearbook:
- *Adorers of the Blood of Christ (ASC Sisters)*;
- *Anti-Slavery International (#00860)*;
- *Caritas Internationalis (CI, #03580)*;
- *Carmelitane Missionarie (CM)*;
- *Comboni Missionary Sisters (CMS)*;
- *Company of the Daughters of Charity of St Vincent de Paul (DC)*;
- *Confederation of the Oratory of St Philip Neri (Oratorian Fathers)*;
- *Council of Europe (CE, #04881)*;
- *Daughters of Mary and Joseph (DMJ)*;
- *Daughters of Mary Help of Christians (Salesian Sisters)*;
- *End Child Prostitution, Child Pornography and Trafficking of Children for Sexual Purposes (ECPAT, #05456)*;
- *Franciscan Missionaries of Mary (FMM)*;
- *Free the Slaves*;
- *Handmaids of the Sacred Heart of Jesus (ACJ)*;
- *ILO (#11123)*;
- *Institut de la Bienheureuse Vierge Marie (Dames Anglaises)*;
- *International Criminal Police Organization – INTERPOL (ICPO-INTERPOL, #13110)*;
- *International Union of Superiors General (#15820)*;
- *Jesuit Refugee Service (JRS, #16106)*;
- *Medical Missionaries of Mary (MMM)*;
- *Missionarie Serve dello Spirito Santo (SSpS)*;
- *Missionary Sisters of Our Lady of Africa (White Sisters)*;
- *Missionary Sisters of Our Lady of the Apostles*;
- *Missionary Sisters of St Columban (SSC)*;
- *Not For Sale*;
- *Oblate Sisters of the Most Holy Redeemer (OSSR)*;

- *OECD (#17693)*;
- *Organization for Security and Cooperation in Europe (OSCE, #17887)*;
- *Salvation Army (#19041)*;
- *Save the Children International (#19058)*;
- *School Sisters of Notre Dame (SSND)*;
- *Sisters of Charity of St Jeanne-Antide Thouret*;
- *Sisters of Mercy of the Holy Cross (Kreuzschwestern von Ingenbohl)*;
- *Sisters of St Joseph of Annecy*;
- *Sisters of the Divine Savior (SDS)*;
- *Sisters of the Holy Cross and Passion of Our Lord Jesus Christ (Passionist Sisters)*;
- *Sisters of the Holy Family of Bordeaux*;
- *Sisters of the Sacred Heart of Jesus (SSCJ)*;
- *Sisters of the Sacred Hearts of Jesus and Mary (SHJM)*;
- *Soeurs Missionnaires de la Consolata (MC)*;
- *Solidarity With Women in Distress (SOLWODI)*;
- *Talitha Kum – International Network against Trafficking in Persons (Talitha Kum, #20090)*;
- *UNANIMA International (#20281)*;
- *UNICEF (#20332)*;
- *Unio Conferentiarum Europae Superiorum Maiorum (UCESM, #20344)*;
- *Union of the Sisters of the Presentation of the Blessed Virgin Mary (PBVM)*;
- *United Nations Office on Drugs and Crime (UNODC, #20596)*;
- *Ursuline Sisters of Mount St Joseph (OSU)*.

Consultative Status Consultative status granted from: *Council of Europe (CE, #04881)* (Participatory Status). [2023/XM8892/y/**F**]

♦ Religious of the Holy Union of the Sacred Hearts (religious order)
♦ Religious Hospitallers of St Joseph (religious order)
♦ Religious of Jesus-Mary (religious order)
♦ Religious of Nazareth (religious order)
♦ Religious of the Sacred Heart of Mary (religious order)
♦ Religious of Sion (religious order)

♦ Religious Society of Friends (Quakers) 18834

Société religieuse des amis – Sociedad Religiosa de los Amigos – Religiöse Gesellschaft der Freunde (Quäkers)

Exec Dir Friends Publishing Corporation, 1216 Arch St No 2D, Philadelphia PA 19107, USA. T. +12155638629.

URL: http://www.quaker.org/

History 1652, UK. Founded mid 17th century by George Fox, among others, as a radical protestant group favouring pacifism and social reform. International administration is carried out by *Friends World Committee for Consultation (FWCC, #10004)*. Former names and other names: *Society of Friends* – former; *Quakers Friends Church* – former. **Structure** Not a formal structure; each country has its own 'Religious Society of Friends'. **Events** *Meeting* Exeter (UK) 1986. **NGO Relations** Other organizations coming under the Quaker umbrella include: *American Friends Service Committee (AFSC)*; *Canadian Friends Service Committee (CFSC)*; *Europe and Middle East Young Friends (EMEYF, #09162)*; *Evangelical Friends Church, International (EFCI, no recent information)*; Friends General Conference (FGC); *Friends Peace Center (CAP)*; *Friends Peace Teams (FPT)*; *Friends United Meeting (FUM)*; *Quaker Council for European Affairs (QCEA, #18587)*; *Quaker Peace and Social Witness (QPSW, see: #10004)*; *Quaker United Nations Office (QUNO, #18588)*; *Right Sharing of World Resources (RSWR)*; *Wider Quaker Fellowship (WQF, see: #10004)*. [2022.02.08/XF5814/**F**]

♦ Religious Teachers Filippini (religious order)
♦ Religious Youth Service
♦ **RELOB** Réseau latino-américain des organismes de bassin (#16351)
♦ **RELOC** Red Latinoamericana de Organizaciones de Cuenca (#16351)
♦ Reloop Platform / see Reloop Platform (#18835)

♦ Reloop Platform (Reloop) 18835

CEO Rés Palace, Rue de La Loi 155, Bte 97, 1040 Brussels, Belgium.

URL: http://reloopplatform.eu/

History Former names and other names: *Reloop Platform* – former. Registration: Belgium. **Aims** Bring together industry, government and NGOs to form a network for advances in policy that create enabling system conditions for circular *economy*. **Languages** English, French. **Staff** 5.00 FTE, paid. **Finance** Members' dues. Other sources: programme partners; project sponsors; in-kind contributions; general donors. **Activities** Knowledge management/information dissemination; networking/liaising; events/meetings. **Events** *Conference on Best in Class Deposit Return Systems (DRS) for Single-Use Beverage Packaging* Brussels (Belgium) 2019. **Publications** Position papers; factsheets; reports; videos.

Members Organizations in 20 countries. Membership countries not specified. Included in the above, 6 organizations listed in this Yearbook:

Included in the above, 6 organizations listed in this Yearbook:

Association européenne des associations du commerce de gros de bière et boissons des pays de l'Europe (CEGROBB, #02555); *European Reconditioners of Industrial Packaging (#08333)*; *Marine Conservation Society (MCS)*; *Plastic Soup Foundation (PSF)*; *Plastics Recyclers Europe (PRE, #18394)*; *Waste Free Oceans (WFO, #20820)*.

NGO Relations Partner of: *Association of Cities and Regions for Sustainable Resource Management (ACR+, #02433)*. [2021/XM6452/**F**]

♦ **Reloop** Reloop Platform (#18835)
♦ RELPE – Red Latinoamericana de Portales Educativos (unconfirmed)
♦ **REMADEL** Réseau maghrebin d'associations de développement local en milieu rural (#18898)
♦ REMAN / see Regional European and Central Asian ALARA Network (#18784)
♦ Remanufacturing Industries Council International / see Remanufacturing Institute
♦ Remanufacturing Institute (internationally oriented national body)
♦ **REMA** Réseau Européen de la Musique Ancienne (#06953)
♦ REMAR International (internationally oriented national body)
♦ Remarque Institute, New York (internationally oriented national body)
♦ REMDH / see EuroMed Rights (#05733)
♦ REMECAB – Reunión de Ministros de Educación del Convenio Andrés Bello (meeting series)
♦ ReMeD – Réseau médicaments et développement (internationally oriented national body)
♦ **REMEP** Rome Euro-Mediterranean Energy Platform (#18969)
♦ **REMIFOR** Réseau euro-méditerranéen d'information et de formation pour la gestion des risques (#18872)
♦ REM – International Network of Mechatronics Universities (unconfirmed)
♦ REMISIS – Réseau d'information sur les migrations internationales (internationally oriented national body)
♦ RemitFund (unconfirmed)
♦ REMITRAN – Reunión de Ministros de Transporte de Centroamérica (meeting series)
♦ **REMOB** Réseau Méditerranéen des Organismes de Bassin (#16664)
♦ **REMOC** Red Mediterranea de Organismos de Cuenca (#16664)
♦ Remote Sensing and Photogrammetry Association of Australasia (inactive)
♦ **REMPEC** Regional Marine Pollution Emergency Response Centre for the Mediterranean Sea (#18795)
♦ **REMPEITC-Carib** Regional Marine Pollution Emergency Information and Training Centre – Wider Caribbean (#18794)
♦ **REM** Red Europea de Microfinanzas (#07792)
♦ **REM** Réseau Européen de la Microfinance (#07792)
♦ REMSAA – Reunión de Ministros de Salud del Area Andina (meeting series)
♦ **REMTE** Red Latinoamericana Mujeres Transformando la Economia (#16395)

♦ REN21 18836

Exec Dir c/o UN Environment Programme, Building VII, 1 rue Miollis, 75015 Paris, France. T. +33144374263. Fax +33144371474. E-mail: secretariat@ren21.net.

URL: http://www.ren21.net/

History Jun 2005, Copenhagen (Denmark). Established following the International Renewable Energy Conference, 2004, Bonn (Germany). Former names and other names: *Renewable Energy Policy Network for the 21st Century* – full title. **Aims** Promote renewable energy to meet the needs of both industrialized and developing countries that are driven by climate change, energy security, development and poverty alleviation. **Structure** General Assembly (every 3 years); Steering Committee; Bureau; Secretariat. **Languages** English, French, German, Spanish. **Staff** 9.00 FTE, paid. **Activities** Awareness raising; events/meetings; knowledge management/information dissemination; networking/liaising; research and development. **Events** *IREC : International Renewable Energy Conference* Seoul (Korea Rep) 2019, *IREC : International Renewable Energy Conference* Mexico City (Mexico) 2017, *IREC : International Renewable Energy Conference* Cape Town (South Africa) 2015, *IREC : International Renewable Energy Conference* Abu Dhabi (United Arab Emirates) 2013, *IREC : International Renewable Energy Conference* Delhi (India) 2010. **Publications** *REN21 Newsletter* (4 a year) in English. *Global Futures Reports*; *Regional Status Reports* – Asia and the Pacific; Southern African; Middle East and North Africa; West Africa; East Africa; India; China; UNECE countries; *Renewables Global Status Report*; *Renewables in Cities Global Status Report*. *Renewables Interactive Map*. Thematic Reports; papers. **Consultative Status** Consultative status granted from: *UNEP (#20299)*. **IGO Relations** Organizations involved: *European Commission (EC, #06633)*; *Global Environment Facility (GEF, #10346)*; *International Energy Agency (IEA, #13270)*; *International Renewable Energy Agency (IRENA, #14715)*; *UNDP (#20292)*; *UNEP (#20299)*. Accredited organization of: *Green Climate Fund (GCF, #10714)*. **NGO Relations** Organizations involved: *AFREPREN/FWD (#00153)*; *Energy and Resources Institute (TERI)*; *Global Wind Energy Council (GWEC, #10656)*; *Greenpeace International (#10727)*; industry and finance groups; *International Renewable Energy Alliance (Ren Alliance, #14716)*; national organizations; *United Nations Foundation (UNF, #20563)*; *World Wide Fund for Nature (WWF, #21922)*; *World Wind Energy Association (WWEA, #21937)*. Member of: *Climate Knowledge Brokers (CKB, #04016)*; *Climate Technology Centre and Network (CTCN, #04023)*; *LEDS Global Partnership (LEDS GP, #16435)*. Partner of: *Sustainable Energy for All (SEforALL, #20056)*. [2020.09.26/XM1915/**F**]

♦ Renaissance des cités d'Europe (internationally oriented national body)
♦ Renaissance Universal (internationally oriented national body)
♦ **Ren Alliance** International Renewable Energy Alliance (#14716)
♦ Renal Society of Australasia (internationally oriented national body)
♦ **ReNAPRI** Regional Network of Agricultural Policy Research Institutes (#18798)
♦ **RENATE** Religious in Europe Networking Against Trafficking and Exploitation (#18833)
♦ reNature Foundation (internationally oriented national body)
♦ Rencontre africaine pour la défense des droits de l'homme (internationally oriented national body)
♦ Rencontre assyriologique internationale (meeting series)
♦ Rencontre de collaboration africaine (meeting series)
♦ Rencontre européenne humaine (inactive)
♦ Rencontre d'évêques des plus grandes villes d'Europe (meeting series)
♦ Rencontre internationale du génie chimique et de la biotechnologie (meeting series)
♦ les Rencontres africa (meeting series)
♦ Les Rencontres / see European Cities and Regions for Culture (#06554)
♦ Rencontres européennes de drama (internationally oriented national body)
♦ Rencontres Francophones Transport-Mobilité (meeting series)
♦ Rencontres internationales des assureurs défense / see Legal Protection International (#16440)
♦ Rencontres internationales sur l'environnement et la nature (meeting series)
♦ Rencontres internationales des Jeunes Chercheurs en patrimoine (meeting series)
♦ Rencontres médias Nord-Sud (meeting series)
♦ Les Rencontres du Mont-Blanc (#16850)
♦ Les Rencontres du Mont-Blanc – Forum international des dirigeants de l'économie sociale et solidaire / see Mont-Blanc Meetings (#16850)
♦ Rencontres philosophiques de l'UNESCO (meeting series)
♦ **RENEB** Running the European Network of Biological and retrospective Physical dosimetry (#19000)
♦ RenéCassin / see René Cassin
♦ René Cassin (internationally oriented national body)
♦ Renewable Energy Certificate System International / see RECS International (#18631)

♦ Renewable Energy and Energy Efficiency Partnership (REEEP) 18837

Asociación para las Energias Renovables y el Ahorro Energético – Partnerschaft für Erneuerbare Energien und Energieeffizienz

Contact Vienna International Centre, Room D-1861, Wagramer Strasse 5, 1400 Vienna, Austria. T. +431260263425. E-mail: info@reeep.org.

URL: http://www.reeep.org/

History Aug 2002, Johannesburg (South Africa). Founded during the World Summit on Sustainable Development. **Aims** Accelerate markets for clean energy in order to generate prosperity while avoiding and/or reducing CO2 emissions. **Structure** Headquarters located in Vienna (Austria). **Languages** English, French, German. **Staff** 25.00 FTE, paid. **Finance** Sources: contributions; government support. Since 2002, largely supported by: governments of Australia, Austria, Canada, Germany, Ireland, Italy, Japan, Netherlands, New Zealand, Norway, Spain, Sweden, UK and USA; private sector contributions. Supported by: *European Commission (EC, #06633)*. **Activities** Financial and/or material support; guidance/assistance/consulting; knowledge management/information dissemination; monitoring/evaluation; projects/programmes. **Events** *Asia Forum for Climate and Clean Energy Financing* Singapore (Singapore) 2018, *Project Implementers Meeting* Vienna (Austria) 2013, *Annual Gentech World Asia Conference* Singapore (Singapore) 2012, *Annual LNG Outlook Asia Conference* Singapore (Singapore) 2012, *Utility Revenue and Customer Management World Asia Conference* Singapore (Singapore) 2012. **Publications** Annual Report; audit reports; project profiles.

Members Partner organizations (over 300) – NGOs, academic institutions, industry associations, businesses; governments; governmental agencies. Governments of 46 countries and territories:

Angola, Argentina, Australia, Austria, Bolivia, Brazil, Canada, Chile, Croatia, Finland, France, Germany, Ghana, Guatemala, Hong Kong, Hungary, Iceland, Indonesia, Ireland, Italy, Japan, Korea Rep, Kyrgyzstan, Mexico, Nepal, Netherlands, New Zealand, Norway, Philippines, Romania, Senegal, Singapore, Slovakia, Solomon Is, South Africa, Spain, Sri Lanka, St Lucia, Switzerland, Tonga, Tunisia, Tuvalu, UK, USA, Vanuatu, Yemen.

Governmental agencies in 11 countries and territories:

China, Czechia, India, Morocco, Nepal, Nigeria, Palestine, Peru, Uganda, UK, Ukraine.

IGO Relations Cooperates with (2): *International Renewable Energy Agency (IRENA, #14715)*; *UNIDO (#20336)*. **NGO Relations** Member of (3): *Climate Knowledge Brokers (CKB, #04016)*; *Climate Technology Centre and Network (CTCN, #04023)*; *LEDS Global Partnership (LEDS GP, #16435)*. Partner of (3): *Green Growth Knowledge Platform (GGKP, #10719)*; *Partnership on Sustainable, Low Carbon Transport Foundation (SLoCaT Foundation, #18244)*; *Sustainable Energy for All (SEforALL, #20056)*. Cooperates with (2): *Energy 4 Impact (#05465)*; *SolarAid*. [2021.09.10/XJ3087/**F**]

♦ Renewable Energy and Environmental Conservation Association in Developing Countries (inactive)
♦ Renewable Energy and Environment Group / see GERES
♦ Renewable Energy, Environment and Solidarity Group / see GERES
♦ Renewable Energy Group / see GERES
♦ Renewable Energy Policy Network for the 21st Century / see REN21 (#18836)
♦ Renewable Energy Resources Information Center / see Regional Energy Resources Information Center (#18780)
♦ Renewable Energy Solutions for Africa (internationally oriented national body)
♦ Renewable Energy Sources Cooperative / see European Federation of Citizen Energy Cooperatives (#07077)
♦ Renewable Futures (meeting series)

♦ **Renewable Hydrogen Coalition** **18838**

Dir Rue Belliard 40, 1040 Brussels, Belgium. E-mail: info@renewableh2.eu.
URL: https://renewableh2.eu

History Founded by *SolarPower Europe (#19676)* and *WindEurope (#20965)* following the 'Choose Renewable Hydrogen campaign'. **Aims** Promote the critical role of renewable hydrogen to deliver the EU's long-term decarbonisation goals. **Events** *Renewable Hydrogen Summit* Brussels (Belgium) 2022. [2022/AA3071/**D**]

♦ **Renewables Grid Initiative (RGI)** **18839**

Contact Krausenstr 8, 10117 Berlin, Germany. T. +4930767719450. Fax +4930767719459. E-mail: info@renewables-grid.eu.
URL: http://www.renewables-grid.eu/

History Launched Jul 2009. Registered in accordance with German law. **Aims** Promote transparent, environmentally sensitive grid development to enable the further steady growth of renewable *energy* and the energy transition. **Structure** Members Assembly; Board; Secretariat; CEO. **Languages** English, German, Italian. **Staff** 14.00 FTE, paid. **Finance** Members' dues. Funding from: Mercator Foundation; *European Climate Foundation (ECF, #06574)*; TSO project grants; operating grant from LIFE NGO – *European Commission (EC, #06633)* – DG Environment. **Activities** Events/meetings; awards/prizes/competitions; training/education. **Events** *emPOWER – The Energy Transition Summit* Brussels (Belgium) 2020. **Publications** *RGI Newsletter*. Position papers; reports; brochures; declarations.
Members Transmission System Operators (TSOs) in 10 countries:
Belgium, Croatia, France, Germany, Ireland, Italy, Netherlands, Norway, Spain, Switzerland.
NGOs include 3 organizations listed in this Yearbook:
BirdLife International (#03266); *Climate Action Network Europe (CAN Europe, #04001)*; *World Wide Fund for Nature (WWF, #21922)*.
IGO Relations *European Commission (EC, #06633)* – DG Environment; *International Renewable Energy Agency (IRENA, #14715)*. **NGO Relations** *European Network of Transmission System Operators for Electricity (ENTSO-E, #08026)*; *WindEurope (#20965)*. [2018.01.25/XM6251/y/**F**]

♦ Renew the Earth (internationally oriented national body)

♦ **Renew Europe** **18840**

SG Rue Wiertz 60, 1047 Brussels, Belgium. T. +3222842111. Fax +3222302485. E-mail: reneweuropegroup@europarl.europa.eu.
Strasbourg Office Allée de Printemps, BIP 1024, 67070 Strasbourg, France. T. +33388174001. Fax +33388176929.
URL: https://reneweuropegroup.eu/

History 20 Jun 1953. Initially one of the founding political groups of the then *'Common Assembly of the European Coal and Steel Community'*, now *European Parliament (EP, #08146)*. Former names and other names: *European Parliament Liberal, Democratic and Reform Group (LDR)* – former (20 Jun 1953 to 1976); *Parlement européen, Groupe libéral, démocratique et réformateur* – former (20 Jun 1953 to 1976); *Parlamento Europeo, Grupo Liberal, Democratico y Reformista* – former (20 Jun 1953 to 1976); *Europäisches Parlament, Liberale und Demokratische Fraktion* – former (20 Jun 1953 to 1976); *Parlamento Europeu, Grupo Liberal, Democratico e Reformista* – former (20 Jun 1953 to 1976); *Parlamento Europeo, Gruppo Liberale e Democratico Riformatore* – former (20 Jun 1953 to 1976); *Europees Parlement, Liberale en Democratische Fractie* – former (20 Jun 1953 to 1976); *Europa-Parlamentet, Liberale og Demokratiske Gruppe* – former (20 Jun 1953 to 1976); *European Parliament – European Liberal, Democrat and Reform Party Group (ELDR Group)* – former (1976 to 2004); *Parlement européen – Groupe du Parti européen des libéraux, démocrates et réformateurs (Groupe ELDR)* – former (1976 to 2004); *Parlamento Europeo – Grupo del Partido Europeo de los Liberales, Demócratas y Reformistas* – former (1976 to 2004); *Europäisches Parlament – Fraktion der Europäischen Liberalen, Demokratischen und Reform Partei* – former (1976 to 2004); *Parlamento Europeo – Gruppo del Partito Europeo dei Liberali, Democratici e Riformatori* – former (1976 to 2004); *Europees Parlement – Fractie van de Partij van Europese Liberalen en Democraten* – former (1976 to 2004); *Europa-Parlamentet – Europeiska Liberale Demokratiska och Reformistiska Partigruppen* – former (1976 to 2004); *Europa-Parlamentet – Det Europaeiske Liberale og Demokratiske Partis Gruppe* – former (1976 to 2004); *Evropaiko Kinovulio – Euroopan Liberaali-ja Demokraattipouleen Ryhmä* – former (1976 to 2004); *Alliance of Liberals and Democrats for Europe (ALDE Group)* – former (2004 to 2019); *Alliance des démocrates et des libéraux pour l'Europe (ACDE)* – former (2004 to 2019); *Alianza de los Demócratas y Liberales por Europa* – former (2004 to 2019); *Fraktion der Allianz der Liberalen und Demokraten für Europa* – former (2004 to 2019); *Grupo da Aliança dos Democratas e Liberais pela Europa* – former (2004 to 2019); *Gruppo dell'Alleanza dei Democratici e dei Liberali per l'Europa* – former (2004 to 2019); *Alliantie van Liberalen en Democraten voor Europa Fractie* – former (2004 to 2019); *Gruppen Alliansen Liberaler och Demokrater för Europa* – former (2004 to 2019); *Gruppen Alliancen af Liberale og Demokrater for Europa* – former (2004 to 2019); *Euroopan liberaalidemokraattien Liiton Ryhmä* – former (2004 to 2019); *Skupina Aliance Liberalu a Demokratu pro Evropu* – former (2004 to 2019); *Skupina Aliancie Liberalov a Demokratov za Európu* – former (2004 to 2019); *Liberalisok és Demokratak Szövetsége Európáért Képviselocsoport* – former (2004 to 2019); *Grupa Porozumienia Liberałów i Demokratów na rzecz Europy* – former (2004 to 2019); *Skupina Zaveznistva Liberalcev in Demokratov za Evropo* – former (2004 to 2019); *Euroopa Demokraatide ja Liberaalide liidu Fraktsioon* – former (2004 to 2019); *Eiropas Liberalu un Demokratu Apvienibas Grupa* – former (2004 to 2019); *Liberalu ir Demokratu Aljanso uz Europa Frakcija* – former (2004 to 2019); *Grupp ta'l- Alleanza tal-Liberali u d-Demokratici ghall-Ewropa* – former (2004 to 2019). **Aims** Promote European values of democracy, the rule of law and fundamental rights; invest in a sustainable environment; promote economic growth as well as a united Europe as a response to the various contemporary issues. **Languages** Bulgarian, Croatian, Czech, Danish, Dutch, English, Estonian, Finnish, French, German, Hungarian, Irish Gaelic, Italian, Latvian, Lithuanian, Romanian, Slovakian, Slovene, Spanish, Swedish. **Staff** 143.00 FTE, paid. **Finance** Supported by: *European Parliament (EP, #08146)*. **Activities** Events/meetings; politics/policy/regulatory. **Events** *Congress* Brussels (Belgium) 1997, *European liberal conference* Brussels (Belgium) 1997, *East European conference* Bucharest (Romania) 1997, *Joint conference* Prague (Czechoslovakia) 1992. **Publications** *Renew Europe Policy Papers* – Renew Europe has issued a series of policy papers to show what they stand for:. **Information Services** *Renew Europe latest updates*.
Members Members of the European Parliament (98) representing liberal, centrist, democratic and reformist political parties in 22 countries:
Austria, Belgium, Bulgaria, Croatia, Czechia, Denmark, Estonia, Finland, France, Germany, Hungary, Ireland, Italy, Latvia, Lithuania, Luxembourg, Netherlands, Romania, Slovakia, Slovenia, Spain, Sweden. [2021.09.09/XF2706/v/**F**]

♦ **Renew Europe – Committee of the Regions (Renew Europe)** **18841**

SG c/o Commmittee of the Regions, Rue Belliard 101, 1040 Brussels, Belgium. T. +3222822059. Fax +3222822331. E-mail: renew-europe@cor.europa.eu.
URL: https://reneweurope-cor.eu/

History 1998. Founded within *European Committee of the Regions (CoR, #06665)*. Former names and other names: *European Liberal Democrat and Reform Party (ELDR)* – former (1998 to 2005); *Alliance of Liberals and Democrats for Europe – Committee of the Regions (ALDE-CoR)* – former (2005 to 26 Jun 2019). **Aims** Ensure that the European Union develops legislation in as decentralized a manner as possible, communicating with and listening to Europe's citizens in a systematic way. **Structure** Bureau; Coordinators; Secretariat.
Members Individuals in 28 countries:
Austria, Belgium, Bulgaria, Croatia, Cyprus, Czechia, Denmark, Estonia, Finland, France, Germany, Greece, Hungary, Ireland, Italy, Latvia, Lithuania, Luxembourg, Malta, Netherlands, Poland, Portugal, Romania, Slovakia, Slovenia, Spain, Sweden, UK. [2022/XM4739/v/**E**]

♦ **Renew Europe** Renew Europe – Committee of the Regions (#18841)
♦ RENEW International (internationally oriented national body)

♦ **Renju International Federation (RIF)** **18842**

Pres address not obtained. E-mail: web@renju.net.
SG address not obtained.
URL: http://www.renju.net/

History 8 Aug 1988, Stockholm (Sweden). **Structure** General Assembly; Central Committee. Commissions. **Activities** Sporting activities. **Events** *World Championship* Tallinn (Estonia) 1995, *World Championship* Arjeplog (Sweden) 1993, *World Championship* Moscow (Russia) 1991, *World Championship* Kyoto (Japan) 1989.

Members Full in 7 countries:
Canada, China, Czechia, Estonia, Finland, Greece, Japan, Korea Rep, Latvia, Macau, Poland, Russia, Sweden, Taipei, Türkiye, Uzbekistan. [2021/XD5469/**C**]

♦ Renovabis – Solidaritätsaktion der deutschen Katholiken mit den Menschen in Mittel- und Osteuropa (internationally oriented national body)
♦ Renovabis – Solidarity initiative of the German Catholics with the people in Central and Eastern Europe (internationally oriented national body)
♦ Rensselaerville Institute (internationally oriented national body)
♦ Reorganized Church of Jesus Christ of Latter Day Saints / see Community of Christ (#04392)
♦ **REPAOC** Réseau des Plate-formes nationales d'ONG d'Afrique de l'Ouest et du Centre (#18902)
♦ **REPAO** Réseau sur les Politiques de Pêche en Afrique de l'Ouest (#18904)
♦ **REPASC** Réseau Pan-Africain de la Société Civile (#18045)
♦ REPC / see European Crime Prevention Network (#06858)
♦ REPEAF – Repositioning Peace in Africa (internationally oriented national body)
♦ **REPEM LAC** Red de Educación Popular entre Mujeres de América Latina y el Caribe (#18647)
♦ REPEM / see Red de Educación Popular entre Mujeres de América Latina y el Caribe (#18647)

♦ **Repercussion Group** **18843**

Contact c/o Head for Change, Applecross House, Chepstow Road, Newport, NP18 2JP, UK.
URL: https://www.repercussiongroup.com/

Aims Promote person-centered, ethical and transparent research on trauma-induced brain injury. [2022/AA2974/v/**C**]

♦ **Répertoire international d'iconographie musicale (RIdIM)** **18844**

International Repertory of Musical Iconography – Internationales Repertorium der Musikikonographie

Pres RIdIM International Centre, Badergasse 9, 8001 Zurich ZH, Switzerland.
Sec address not obtained.
URL: http://www.ridim.org/

History 1971. Also referred to as *International Inventory of Musical Iconography*. Sponsored by: *International Association of Music Libraries, Archives and Documentation Centres (IAML, #12042)*; *International Council of Museums (ICOM, #13051)*; *International Musicological Society (IMS, #14201)*. **Aims** Develop methods, means and research centres for classification, cataloguing, reproduction and study of iconographical material related to music, dance and the dramatic arts; assist performers, historians, librarians, students, instrument makers, record manufacturers and book publishers to make the fullest use of visual materials for scholarly and practical purposes. **Structure** General Assembly; Council; Executive Board; Working and Advisory Commissions. **Languages** English, French, German, Italian, Spanish. **Activities** Research/documentation; projects/programmes; events/meetings. **Events** *Annual Meeting* Prague (Czechia) 2021, *Annual Meeting* Prague (Czechia) 2020, *Annual Meeting* Hobart, TAS (Australia) 2019, *Annual Meeting* Canterbury (UK) 2018, *Annual Meeting* Athens (Greece) 2017. **Publications** *Imago Musicae* (annual); *RIdIM Newsletter*. *RIdIM/RCMI Inventories of Music Iconography* – series. Central catalogue of authors/artists available for public use.
Members National committees in 21 countries:
Australia, Austria, Belgium, Canada, Croatia, Czechia, Denmark, France, Germany, Hungary, Iran Islamic Rep, Ireland, Italy, Japan, Mexico, Netherlands, Slovakia, Sweden, Switzerland, UK, USA. [2019.06.30/XF2608/**F**]

♦ **Répertoire International de Littérature Musicale (RILM)** **18845**

International Repertory of Musical Literature – Internationales Repertorium der Musikliteratur

Exec Dir RILM Int'l Center / CUNY, Ste 3108, 365 Fifth Ave, New York NY 10016-4309, USA. T. +12128171990. Fax +12128171569. E-mail: info@rilm.org.
URL: http://www.rilm.org/

History 1966. Founded under the joint sponsorship of *International Association of Music Libraries, Archives and Documentation Centres (IAML, #12042)* and *International Musicological Society (IMS, #14201)*. As of 2007, third sponsoring society: *International Council for Traditional Music (ICTM, #13087)*. Former names and other names: *RILM* – alias; *RILM Abstracts of Music Literature* – former alias. Registration: 501(c)3, USA. **Aims** Document the world's knowledge about all musical traditions, and to make this knowledge accessible to research and performance communities worldwide via digital collections and advanced tools; include the music scholarship of all countries, in all languages, and across all disciplinary and cultural boundaries, thereby fostering research in the arts, humanities, sciences and social sciences. **Structure** Commission Internationale Mixte; national committees. **Languages** English. Over 140 other languages. **Staff** 45.00 FTE, paid; 250.00 FTE, voluntary. **Finance** Sources: subscriptions. **Events** *Global Digital Music Studies Conference* New York, NY (USA) 2023, *Annual Meeting* Antwerp (Belgium) 2014, *Annual Meeting* Shanghai (China) 2013, *Annual Meeting* Rome (Italy) 2012, *Annual Meeting* Rome (Italy) 2012. **Publications** *RILM Perspectives* – series; *RILM Retrospectives* – series. *How to Write About Music*. *MGG Online*; *RILM Abstracts of Music Literature*; *RILM Music Encyclopedias*.
Members National Committees in 49 countries and territories:
Australia, Austria, Belgium, Brazil, Canada, China, Colombia, Croatia, Cuba, Cyprus, Czechia, Denmark, Estonia, Finland, France, Germany, Greece, Guatemala, Hong Kong, Hungary, Iceland, Ireland, Israel, Italy, Japan, Korea Rep, Latvia, Lithuania, Malaysia, Malta, Mexico, Netherlands, New Zealand, North Macedonia, Norway, Poland, Portugal, Serbia, Slovakia, Slovenia, South Africa, Spain, Sweden, Switzerland, Taiwan, Türkiye, UK, USA, Venezuela. [2022.10.11/XF2612/**F**]

♦ Répertoire international de la presse musicale (internationally oriented national body)
♦ Répertoire international des sources musicales (#13949)
♦ REPICA – Reunión de Empresas Portuarias de Centroamerica (meeting series)
♦ REPI – Recherche et Etudes en Politique Internationale (internationally oriented national body)
♦ REPM – International Workshop on Rare-Earth Permanent Magnets and their Applications (meeting series)
♦ **REPONGAC** Réseau des Plateformes des ONG de l'Afrique Centrale (#18903)
♦ Réponse Optimale au Consommateur / see ECR Community (#05340)
♦ Reporters Without Borders (#18846)

♦ **Reporters sans frontières (RSF)** **18846**

Reporters Without Borders

Dir-Gen CS 90247, 75083 Paris Cedex 02, 75083 Paris, France. T. +33144838484. Fax +33145231151. E-mail: secretariat@rsf.org.
URL: http://www.rsf.org/

History Jun 1985, Montpellier (France). Former names and other names: *Reporters sans frontières – international* – former. Registration: France. **Aims** Defend and promote freedom, independence and pluralism of journalism worldwide. **Structure** Offices; Sections. **Languages** Arabic, Chinese, English, French, Persian, Spanish. **Staff** 45.00 FTE, paid. A network of 130 Correspondents. **Finance** Sources: donations; grants; meeting proceeds; revenue from activities/projects; sale of publications. **Activities** Advocacy/lobbying/activism; awards/prizes/competitions; financial and/or material support; networking/liaising. **Events** *DW Global Media forum* Bonn (Germany) 2008. **Publications** *100 Photos for Press Freedom – 100 photos pour la liberté de la presse* (3 a year); *The Press Freedom Round-up*; *The World Press Freedom Index*. Thematic reports.
Members Partner organizations (17). Corresponding individuals (over 120) in 78 countries and territories:
Algeria, Angola, Australia, Austria, Bangladesh, Belgium, Benin, Bolivia, Bosnia-Herzegovina, Bulgaria, Burkina Faso, Burundi, Cameroon, Canada, Cape Verde, Central African Rep, Chad, Chile, Colombia, Comoros, Congo Brazzaville, Congo DR, Côte d'Ivoire, Croatia, Cyprus, Czechia, Denmark, Egypt, Equatorial Guinea, France, Gabon, Germany, Ghana, Greece, Haiti, Hungary, India, Israel, Italy, Japan, Kenya, Lithuania, Luxembourg, Madagascar, Mali, Mauritania, Mauritius, Mexico, Montenegro, Morocco, Namibia, Nepal, Netherlands, Niger, Nigeria, Pakistan, Peru, Poland, Portugal, Romania, Russia, Rwanda, Senegal, Serbia, Sierra Leone, South Africa, Spain, Sri Lanka, Sweden, Switzerland, Taiwan, Togo, Tunisia, Türkiye, UK, Uruguay, USA, Venezuela.
Consultative Status Consultative status granted from: *ECOSOC (#05331)* (Special); *UNESCO (#20322)* (Consultative Status); *Council of Europe (CE, #04881)* (Participatory Status); *African Commission on Human and Peoples' Rights (ACHPR, #00255)* (Observer). **IGO Relations** Accredited by: *United Nations Office at Vienna (UNOV, #20604)*; *Organisation internationale de la Francophonie (OIF, #17809)*. Invited to sessions of Intergovernmental Council of: *International Programme for the Development of Communication (IPDC, #14651)*. **NGO Relations** Member of (3): *Ethical Journalism Network (EJN, #05554)*; *International Campaign to Ban Landmines – Cluster Munition Coalition (ICBL-CMC, #12427)*; *ProtectDefenders.eu (#18546)*. Participates in: *IFEX (#11100)*. Supports: *International News Safety Institute (INSI, #14364)*. [2020.05.04/XF5485/**F**]

- Reporters sans frontières – international / see Reporters sans frontières (#18846)
- Repositioning Peace in Africa (internationally oriented national body)
- REP – Réalités européennes du présent (internationally oriented national body)
- Representatives of European Heating and Ventilation Associations / see Federation of European Heating, Ventilation and Air-Conditioning Associations (#09507)
- Reprieve (internationally oriented national body)
- Reproductive Health Access, Information and Services in Emergencies (internationally oriented national body)

♦ Reproductive Health Supplies Coalition (RHSC) 18847

Secretariat Rue Marie-Thérèse 21, 1000 Brussels, Belgium. T. +3222100220. Fax +3222193363. E-mail: secretariat@rhsupplies.org.
URL: http://www.rhsupplies.org/

History 2004. **Aims** Ensuring that all people in low- and middle-income countries can access and use *affordable*, high-quality supplies to ensure their better reproductive health. **Structure** General Membership Meeting. Executive Committee, comprising Chair, Coalition Director and 12 members. **Staff** 14.00 FTE, paid. **Finance** Grant from: *Bill and Melinda Gates Foundation (BMGF)*. **Events** *Annual Membership Meeting* Kathmandu (Nepal) 2019, *Annual Membership Meeting* Brussels (Belgium) 2018, *Annual Membership Meeting* Dakar (Senegal) 2017, *Annual Membership Meeting* Seattle, WA (USA) 2016, *Annual Membership Meeting* Oslo (Norway) 2015. **Publications** *RHSC Newsletter*.

Members Governmental organizations (31); Commerce and Industry members (45); Foundations and Institutions of Higher Learning (20); Technical Support Agencies and Partnerships (75); Civil Society organizations (74). Governmental agencies of 20 countries:
China, Denmark, Dominican Rep, Ethiopia, France, Germany, Ghana, Mauritania, Mexico, Netherlands, Nicaragua, Nigeria, Norway, Senegal, Spain, Tanzania UR, UK, Uruguay, USA, Zambia.
Included in the above, 12 (inter)governmental agencies:
Department for International Development (DFID, inactive); *East African Community (EAC, #05181)*; *European Commission (EC, #06633)*; *Global Fund to Fight AIDS, Tuberculosis and Malaria (Global Fund, #10383)*; *International Bank for Reconstruction and Development (IBRD, #12317)*; *Norwegian Agency for Development Cooperation (Norad)*; *Partners in Population and Development (PPD, #18247)*; *United Nations Office for Project Services (UNOPS, #20602)*; *United Nations Population Fund (UNFPA, #20612)*; *United States Agency for International Development (USAID)*; *West African Health Organization (WAHO, #20881)*; *WHO (#20950)* (Essential Drugs Management).
Commerce and Industry partner include 2 organizations listed in this Yearbook:
International Contraceptive Access Foundation (ICA Foundation, #12936); *Prosalud Inter Americana Foundation (PSIA, #18542)*.
Foundations and institutions include 6 organizations listed in this Yearbook:
Bill and Melinda Gates Foundation (BMGF); *Bixby Center for Global Reproductive Health*; *International Centre for Reproductive Health (ICRH)*; *MacArthur Foundation*; *The William and Flora Hewlett Foundation*; *United Nations Foundation (UNF, #20563)*.
Technical support agencies include 21 organizations listed in this Yearbook:
- *Asia Pacific Alliance for Sexual and Reproductive Health and Rights (APA, #01825)*;
- *Christian Connections for International Health (CCIH)*;
- *DKT International*;
- *EngenderHealth*;
- *European Parliamentary Forum for Sexual & Reproductive Rights (EPF, #08149)*;
- *FHI 360*;
- *Ibis Reproductive Health*;
- *Inter-American Development Bank (IDB, #11427)*;
- *International Consortium for Emergency Contraception (ICEC, #12911)*;
- *International Council on the Management of Population Programs (ICOMP, #13043)*;
- *IntraHealth International*;
- *IPAS (#16010)*;
- *Johns Hopkins Program for International Education in Gynecology and Obstetrics (JHPIEGO)*;
- *Latin American Consortium on Emergency Contraception (LACEC, #16306)*;
- *MSI Reproductive Choices*;
- *Pan American Social Marketing Organization (PASMO)*;
- *PATH (#18260)*;
- *Pathfinder International (#18261)*;
- *People's Health Movement (PHM, #18305)*;
- *Population Council (#18458)*;
- *PSI (#18555)*.

Civil Society organizations include 19 organizations listed in this Yearbook:
Advocates for Youth, Washington DC; *African Institute for Development Policy Research and Dialogue (AFIDEP)*; *African Woman and Child Features Service (AWC)*; *Catholics for Choice (#03609)*; *Center for Health and Gender Equity (CHANGE)*; *Consortio Latinoamericano Contra el Aborto Inseguro (CLACAI, #04733)*; *Days for Girls International (DfGI)*; *Federación Latinoamericana de Sociedades de Obstetricia y Ginecologia (FLASOG, #09372)*; *Fédération Internationale de Gynécologie et d'Obstétrique (FIGO, #09638)*; *Global Hope Mobilization (GLOHOMO)*; *HAI Africa (#10851)*; *International Partnership for Microbicides (IPM, inactive)*; *International Planned Parenthood Federation (IPPF, #14589)*; *Latin American and Caribbean Women's Health Network (LACWHN, #16288)*; *PAI (#18025)*; *Rutgers (#19011)*; *Women and Health Alliance International (WAHA, #21001)*; *World Health Partners (WHP)*; *Youth Coalition (YCSRR, #22011)*.
NGO Relations Secretariat provided by: *PATH (#18260)*. Partner of: *Every Woman Every Child (EWEC, #09215)*. [2020/XM3114/y/**B**]

♦ REPSSI 18848

Secretariat PO Box 23076, Randburg West, Johannesburg, 2167, South Africa. T. +27119985820. E-mail: info@repssi.org – south@repssi.org.
URL: http://www.repssi.org/

History REPSSI derives from: *Regional Psychological Support Initiative*. **Aims** Lessen the devastating social and emotional – *psychosocial* – impact of poverty, conflict, HIV and AIDS among *children* and *youth* across East and Southern *Africa*. **Structure** Board of Directors (regional); Boards of Directors for each sub-region. **Finance** Funding from various partners including: *Swiss Agency for Development and Cooperation (SDC)*; *Swedish International Development Cooperation Agency (Sida)*; *Norwegian Agency for Development Cooperation (Norad)*; *Novartis Foundation*; *Comic Relief*; *Australian Aid (inactive)*; *UNICEF (#20332)* – ESARO; *United States Agency for International Development (USAID)*. **Events** *Psychosocial Support Forum (PSS Forum)* Windhoek (Namibia) 2019. **Consultative Status** Consultative status granted from: *African Committee of Experts on the Rights and Welfare of the Child (ACERWC, #00257)* (Observer Status). **NGO Relations** Member of: *Global Partnership to End Violence Against Children (End Violence Against Children, #10533)*; *Inter-Agency Task Team on Children affected by AIDS (IATT, #11394)*; *Regional Inter-Agency Task Team on Children and AIDS in Eastern and Southern Africa (RIATT-ESA, #18791)*. [2020/XJ7265/**D**]

- REPT / see European Network for Smoking and Tobacco Prevention (#08002)
- République des citoyens du monde (inactive)
- Requirements and Technical Concepts for Aviation / see Radio Technical Commission for Aeronautics
- **RERA** Regional Electricity Regulators Association of Southern Africa (#18779)
- RERC – Rare Earth Research Conference (meeting series)
- **RE** Rethinking Economics (#18925)
- RERF – Radiation Effects Research Foundation (internationally oriented national body)
- **RERFT** Réseau européen de recherche forestière tropicale (#08950)
- **RERIC** Regional Energy Resources Information Center (#18780)
- **RERIES** Réseau européen de recherche et d'innovation dans l'enseignement supérieur (#18877)
- **RERIS** Réseaux d'études des relations internationales sportives (#18909)
- RERT – Réseau européen des registres testamentaires (unconfirmed)
- RES4Africa – Renewable Energy Solutions for Africa (internationally oriented national body)
- RESADOC – Réseau sahélien d'information et de documentation scientifiques et techniques (no recent information)
- **ReSaD** Réseau Sahel Désertification (#18906)
- RESAPSI – Réseau Africain des Praticiens Assurant la Prise en Charge Médicale des Personnes Vivant avec le VIH/SIDA (unconfirmed)
- **ReSA** Research Software Alliance (#18862)
- RES ARTIS – Association internationale de centres de résidences d'artistes / see Worldwide Network of Artists Residencies (#21928)
- RES ARTIS – International Association of Residential Arts Centres / see Worldwide Network of Artists Residencies (#21928)
- **Res Artis** Worldwide Network of Artists Residencies (#21928)

♦ RESCALED (European Movement for Detention Houses) 18849

Exec Dir Pleinlaan 5, 1050 Brussels, Belgium. E-mail: info@rescaled.org.
Coordinator address not obtained.
Coordinator address not obtained.
URL: https://www.rescaled.org/

History Registration: Banque-Carrefour des Entreprises, No/ID: 0773.345.762, Start date: 20 May 2021, Belgium; EU Transparency Register, No/ID: 935703346110-06, Start date: 12 Apr 2022. **Aims** Support the use of detention houses instead of large prison institutions. **Structure** Board; Teams; Partners. **Languages** English. **Activities** Advocacy/lobbying/activism; awareness raising; knowledge management/information dissemination; networking/liaising; politics/policy/regulatory.
Members Partners in 7 countries:
Belgium, Czechia, France, Malta, Netherlands, Norway, Portugal. [2022.05.17/AA2625/**F**]

- REScoop 20-20-20 / see European Federation of Citizen Energy Cooperatives (#07077)
- **REScoop.eu** European Federation of Citizen Energy Cooperatives (#07077)
- **ReSCOPE Programme** Regional Schools and Colleges Permaculture Programme (#18812)
- Rescue the Rainforest (internationally oriented national body)

♦ Rescue Swimmers Association (EURORSA) 18850

Sec address not obtained. E-mail: info@eurorsa.com.
URL: https://www.eurorsa.com/

History Registration: Finland. **Aims** Enable SAR aircrew, who are working full-time as helicopter rescue swimmers, mutual and general benefits related to practicing the profession, improving cooperation between members, and improving the general conditions of the occupation. **Structure** Board. **Activities** Awards/prizes/competitions; events/meetings. **Events** *Rescue Swimmer Meeting* Cascais (Portugal) 2020, *Rescue Swimmer Meeting* Reykjavik (Iceland) 2018, *Rescue Swimmer Meeting* La Spezia (Italy) 2016, *Rescue Swimmer Meeting* Gijón (Spain) 2014, *Rescue Swimmer Meeting* Aalborg (Denmark) 2012. **Publications** *Rescue Swimmer*.
Members SAR operators in 18 countries:
Australia, Cyprus, Denmark, Estonia, Finland, France, Greece, Iceland, Ireland, Italy, Latvia, Netherlands, Norway, Poland, Portugal, Spain, Sweden, UK. [2022/AA2522/**D**]

- **RESDAL** Red de Seguridad y Defensa de América Latina (#18730)
- Research and Action Group for Rural Development in the Third World (internationally oriented national body)
- Research and Applications for Alternative Financing for Development / see Fondation RAFAD – Recherches et applications de financements alternatifs au développement (#09827)
- Research Association for International Agrarian and Economic Development, Heidelberg (internationally oriented national body)

♦ Research Association on Monetary Innovation and Community and Complementary Currency Systems (RAMICS) 18851

Association de recherche sur les innovations monétaires et les systèmes de monnaies complémentaires

Registered Address UMR Triangle / Inst des sciences de l'homme, 14 av Berthelot, 69007 Lyon, France. E-mail: contact@ramics.org.
URL: https://ramics.org/

History 29 Nov 2015, Salvador (Brazil). Created following a series of three academic conferences in 2011, 2013, the last one held on 29 Oct 2015, Salvador da Bahia (Brazil). Constitution amended in 2017, Barcelona (Spain); 2019, Tahayama-Hida (Japan). Registration: RNA, No/ID: W691089492, Start date: 2015, France. **Aims** Promote academic research on diverse monetary and social exchange systems. **Structure** General Assembly (annual); Management Committee. **Languages** English, French. **Finance** Sources: members' dues. **Activities** Events/meetings; research/documentation. **Events** *Conference* Sofia (Bulgaria) 2022, *Conference* Takayama (Japan) 2019. **Publications** *International Journal of Community Research (IJCCR)*. [2022.06.21/AA0093/**C**]

- Research Association for Planning and Building in Developing Countries (internationally oriented national body)
- Research Association for Planning and Building in the Third World / see Research Association for Planning and Building in Developing Countries
- Research Center for International Economics (internationally oriented national body)
- Research Centre of Applied Economy (internationally oriented national body)
- Research Centre for Cooperation with Developing Countries / see Centre for International Cooperation and Development
- Research Centre on Development and International Relations (internationally oriented national body)
- Research Centre for East European Studies (internationally oriented national body)
- Research Centre for Global Governance (internationally oriented national body)
- Research Centre for International Agrarian Development, Heidelberg / see Forschungsstelle für Internationale Agrar- und Wirtschaftsentwicklung, Heidelberg
- Research Centre for International Agrarian and Economic Development, Heidelberg / see Forschungsstelle für Internationale Agrar- und Wirtschaftsentwicklung, Heidelberg
- Research Centre for International Law / see Lauterpacht Centre for International Law

♦ Research Centre for Islamic History, Art and Culture (IRCICA) 18852

Centre de recherches sur l'histoire, l'art et la culture islamiques

Dir Gen Alemdar Caddesi No 15, Babiali Girisi, Cagaloglu – Fatih, 34110 Istanbul/Istanbul, Türkiye. T. +902124020000. Fax +902122584365. E-mail: ircica@ircica.org.
URL: http://www.ircica.org/

History 1978, Dakar (Senegal). Founded as a subsidiary body of *Organisation of Islamic Cooperation (OIC, #17813)*, on adoption of Statute by 9th *Council of Foreign Ministers (CFM, see: #17813)*, following decision of 7th Conference, May 1976. First programme approved May 1980, Islamabad (Pakistan), at 11th Islamic Conference; first Governing Council appointed 1981, Baghdad (Iraq), at 12th Islamic Conference. **Aims** Promote better understanding of Islam, its *civilization* and Muslim cultures by acting as focal point and meeting place for scholars, researchers, historians, intellectuals and artists from member countries and worldwide in the field of research on the Islamic legacy; create conditions for close cooperation among researchers and research institutions of member countries; take measures and establish incentive programmes to promote excellence in research into arts, and architectural and cultural heritage. **Structure** *Islamic Commission for Economic, Cultural and Social Affairs (ICECSA, #16038)* acts as General Assembly. Governing Board; Executive Committee; General Directorate, headed by Director General. **Languages** Arabic, English, French. **Staff** 55.00 FTE, paid. **Finance** Contributions of OIC Member States. **Activities** Events/meetings; knowledge management/information dissemination. **Events** *Congress* Amman (Jordan) 2013, *Congress* Kuwait (Kuwait) 2013, *Congress* Zanzibar (Tanzania UR) 2013, *International Congress on China and the Muslim World / Congress* Beijing (China) 2012, *International Congress on Islamic Civilization in the Volga-Ural Region* Kazan (Russia) 2012. **Publications** *IRCICA Newsletter* (3 a year) in Arabic, English, French; *IRCICA Journal*. *The West and Islam – Towards a Dialogue* – lecture series. *History of Ottoman Astrology Literature* (2011); *Sullam al wusul ila Tabaqat al-Fuhul* (2010) by Katip Chalabi; *Tatar History and Civilization* (2010); *Globalisation and Images of the Other Challenges and New Perspectives for History Teaching in Europe* (2009); *World Bibliography of Translations of the Holy Qur'an in Manuscript Form II – Translations in Urdu* (2009); *History of the Literature of Medical Sciences during the Ottoman Period* (2009); *Qur'an facsimile edition* (2009) – Cairo copy; *Qur'an – facsimile edition* (2008) – Istanbul copy; *Religious Values and the Rise of Science in*

Europe (2005); *Cultural Contacts in Building a Universal Civilization: Islamic Contributions* (2005); *A Culture of Peaceful Coexistence: Early Islamic and Ottoman Turkish Examples* (2004); *History of Military Art and Science Literature during the Ottoman Period* (2004); *Sana'l Bark Al-Shami* (2004); *Creativity and Crafts in the Muslim World* (2004); *Koca Sinan Pasa'nin Telhisleri* (2004); *Islamic Monuments of Cairo in the Ottoman Period* (2003); *The Diwany-Jaly Diwani-Riq'a Mashqs* (2003); *Traces of Turkish Culture in Egypt – Turkish Words in Egyptian Popular Language* (2003); *L'enseignement Islamique en Afrique Francophone: Les Medersas de la République du Mali* (2003); *Mathematicians, Astronomers, and Other Scholars of Islamic Civilization and Their Works (7th-19th C)* (2003); *History of Music Literature During the Ottoman Period* (2002); *Traditional Carpets and Kilims in the Muslim World: Past, Present and Future Prospects* (2002); *Egypt as viewed in the 19th Century* (2001); *World Bibliography of Translations of the Holy Qur'an in Manuscript Form* (2000); *On the History of Arab Countries During the Ottoman Period* (2000); *History of Geographical Literature During the Ottoman Period* (2000); *Islamic Swords and Swordsmiths* (2000); *History of Ottoman State and Civilization* (1999); *La Civilisation Islamique en Afrique de l'Ouest* (1999); *The West and Islam – Towards a Dialogue* (1999); *Erzurum in Gravures and Old Photographs* (1998); *Islamic Civilization in the Malay World* (1997); *Curtains of the Haramein Sharifein* (1997); *The Advent of Islam in Korea – A Historical Account* (1997); *History of Ottoman Astronomy Literature* (1997); *Old Bridge (Stari Most) in Mostar* (1995); *Population of Bosnia in the Ottoman Period: A Historical Overview* (1994); *Islamic Architecture in Bosnia and Herzegovina* (1994); *Islamic Art Terms* (1994); *Transfer of Modern Science and Technology to the Muslim World* (1992); *Research in Islamic Civilization – Outlook for the Coming Decade* (1992); *Arab-Turkish Relations* (1991-1993); *Cultural Dimensions of Development in OIC Member States* (1991); *The Art of Calligraphy in the Islamic Heritage* (1990-1996); *Ottoman Architecture in Albania* (1990); *Kitab al-Hiyal* (1990) by Banu Musa bin Shakir; *Turkish Art and Architecture* (1987); *Ottoman Scientific and Professional Associations* (1987); *Ottoman Archives* (1986) – also on CD-Rom; *World Bibliography of Translations of the Meaning of the Holy Qur'an – Printed Translations 1515-1980* (1986); *Annotated Bibliography of Turkish Literature of Chemistry* (1985); *L'Enseignement arabo-islamique au Sénégal* (1985); *Ottoman Yearbooks Salnames and Nevsals* (1982) – also on CD-Rom; *Muslim Pious Foundations and Real Estates in Palestine* (1982) – also on CD-Rom. Catalogues; directories; studies; albums; surveys; international symposia and seminar proceedings; video cassettes. Specialized digital reference library; documentation and information facility.
Members Governments of 59 countries and territories:
Afghanistan, Albania, Algeria, Azerbaijan, Bahrain, Bangladesh, Benin, Brunei Darussalam, Burkina Faso, Cameroon, Chad, Comoros, Côte d'Ivoire, Djibouti, Egypt, Gabon, Gambia, Guinea, Guinea-Bissau, Guyana, Indonesia, Iran Islamic Rep, Iraq, Jordan, Kazakhstan, Kuwait, Kyrgyzstan, Lebanon, Libya, Malaysia, Maldives, Mali, Mauritania, Morocco, Mozambique, Niger, Nigeria, Oman, Pakistan, Palestine, Qatar, Russia, Saudi Arabia, Senegal, Sierra Leone, Somalia, Sudan, Suriname, Syrian AR, Tajikistan, Thailand, Togo, Tunisia, Türkiye, Turkmenistan, Uganda, United Arab Emirates, Uzbekistan, Yemen.
Observer governments (5):
Bosnia-Herzegovina, Central African Rep, Northern Cyprus, Russia, Thailand.
IGO Relations Memorandum of Understanding with (5): *Arab League Educational, Cultural and Scientific Organization (ALECSO, #01003)*; *Islamic World Educational, Scientific and Cultural Organization (ICESCO, #16058)*; *UNDP (#20292)*; *UNESCO (#20322)*; *World Heritage Centre (WHC, #21566)*. Member of (1): *United Nations Alliance of Civilizations (UNAOC, #20520)*. Works closely with: *ECO Cultural Institute (ECI, #05292)*; *Parliamentary Union of the OIC Member States (PUIC, #18220)*; *Statistical, Economic and Social Research and Training Centre for Islamic Countries (SESRIC, #19971)*; national associations. **NGO Relations** Member of (1): *Inter-University Centre for Advanced Studies (IUC, #15986)*. [2023.02.14/XE1000/**E***]

- ♦ Research Centre on Social and Economic Development in Southern Asia (inactive)
- ♦ Research Centre for Turkestan and Azerbaijan (internationally oriented national body)
- ♦ Research Centre on World Economy / see Centre on World Economy Studies
- ♦ Research Committee for Automobile Repairs / see RCAR (#18623)
- ♦ Research Consortium for School Health and Nutrition (unconfirmed)
- ♦ Research Consortium for SHN – Research Consortium for School Health and Nutrition (unconfirmed)
- ♦ Research Council for Automobile Repairs / see RCAR (#18623)
- ♦ Research and Counselling Foundation for African Migrants (internationally oriented national body)

♦ Research Data Alliance (RDA) 18853

SG RDA Foundation, Bd Louis Schmidt 24, 1040 Brussels, Belgium. E-mail: enquiries@rd-alliance.org.
URL: http://www.rd-alliance.org/
History 2013, Gothenburg (Sweden). Launched as a community-driven organization by the *European Commission (EC, #06633)*, US Government's National Science Foundation, National Institute of Standards and Technology (USA) and Australian Government's Department of Innovation. Registration: Charity, No/ID: 1162762, Start date: 21 Jul 2015, England and Wales; Banque-Carrefour des Entreprises, No/ID: 0745.917.132, Start date: 9 Apr 2020, Belgium; EU Transparency Register, No/ID: 597317423088-24, Start date: 23 Aug 2016. **Aims** Develop infrastructure and community activities to reduce the social and technical barriers to data sharing and re-use; promote acceleration of data driven innovation and discovery worldwide. **Structure** Plenary (twice a year in different places around the world); Council; Technical Advisory Board; Organisational Advisory Board; Secretariat. **Languages** English. **Staff** 2.00 FTE, paid. **Finance** Infrastructure supported by the following regions and organizations: *'Australia'* – Supported by the Australian Commonwealth Government through the Australian National Data Service, supported by the National Collaborative Research Infrastructure Strategy Program and the Education Investment Fund (EIF) Super Science; *'Europe (RDA EU)'* – Supported by the *European Commission (EC, #06633)* through the RDA Europe projects funded under the 7th and Horizon 2020 Framework Programmes; *'United States (RDA/US)'* – Supported at Rensselaer Polytechnic Institute (RPI) by the National Science Foundation, the National Institute of Standards and Technology, the Alfred P Sloan Foundation and the *MacArthur Foundation*. **Activities** Knowledge management/information dissemination; networking/liaising; research and development. **Events** *Plenary Meeting* Edinburgh (UK) 2021, *Plenary Meeting* Costa Rica 2020, *Plenary Meeting* Melbourne, VIC (Australia) 2020, *Plenary Meeting* Helsinki (Finland) 2019, *Plenary Meeting* Philadelphia, PA (USA) 2019. **Publications** *The Data Harvest Report – Sharing Data For Knowledge, Jobs And Growth* (2014); *The Research Data Alliance: globally co-ordinated action against barriers to data publishing and sharing* (2014). *RDA COVID-19 Recommendations and Guidelines for Data Sharing* (2020). ERCIM News special theme Scientific Data Sharing and Re-use (2015). **Members** Organizations (52); Affiliates (12); Individuals (over 11,000). Members across 145 countries. Membership countries not specified. **IGO Relations** Partner of (1): *Group on Earth Observations (GEO, #10735)*. **NGO Relations** Member of (1): *ISC World Data System (ISC-WDS, #16024)*. Signatory to agreement of *Coalition for Advancing Research Assessment (CoARA, #04045)*.
[2021.06.17/XJ6804/**C**]

♦ Research in Engineering Education Network (REEN) 18854

Address not obtained.
URL: https://www.reen.co/
Aims Provide an independent, international and inclusive forum to advance scholarly discourse on research in Engineering Education. **Structure** Governing Board. **Activities** Awards/prizes/competitions; events/meetings.
[2020/AA0045/**F**]

- ♦ Research Group for an Alternative Economic Strategy (internationally oriented national body)

♦ Research Group on Collaborative Spaces (RGCS) 18855

Contact address not obtained. E-mail: collaborativespaces@gmail.com.
URL: http://rgcs-owee.org/
History Nov 2014. **Aims** Transform jointly academic and entrepreneurial work practices through the research method: Open Walked Event-Based Experimentations (OWEE). **Structure** Board. **Activities** Events/meetings. **Events** *International Symposium* Lyon (France) 2020, *International Symposium* Milan (Italy) 2020, *International Symposium* Barcelona (Spain) 2019, *International Symposium* London (UK) 2018, *International Symposium* Paris (France) 2016.
Members Autonomous chapters in 15 countries:
Brazil, Canada, Estonia, France, Germany, Italy, Japan, Netherlands, Norway, Portugal, Singapore, Spain, Thailand, UK, USA.
[2021/AA1598/**F**]

- ♦ Research Group for the Study of African Arachnids / see African Arachnological Society (#00202)
- ♦ Research Group on Transnational Crime / see Joint Research Centre on Transnational Crime
- ♦ Research Group on Weed Control / see European Weed Research Society (#09089)
- ♦ Research ICT Africa Network (internationally oriented national body)
- ♦ Research and Information Center for Asian Studies (internationally oriented national body)
- ♦ Research and Information System for Developing Countries, India (internationally oriented national body)
- ♦ Research and Information System for the Non-Aligned and Other Developing Countries, India / see Research and Information System for Developing Countries, India

♦ Researching and Applying Metaphor International Association (RaAM) 18856

Chair Frankland Bldg, Univ of Birmingham, Edgbaston, Birmingham, B15 2TT, UK. E-mail: chair@raam.org.uk.
URL: http://www.raam.org.uk/
History 12 Apr 2006, Leeds (UK). Founded during 6th RaAM Conference. Registration: Charity Commission, No/ID: 1119686, England and Wales. **Aims** Advance the study of metaphor for public benefit, with a commitment to the application of metaphor research to real world issues. **Activities** Events/meetings. **Events** *RaAM Conference* Bialystok (Poland) 2022, *RaAM Conference* Vilnius (Lithuania) 2021, *RaAM Conference* Hamar (Norway) 2020, *Metaphor across contexts and domains – from description to application* Hong Kong (Hong Kong) 2018, *Metaphor in the arts, in media and communication* Berlin (Germany) 2016. **Members** Individuals. Membership countries not specified. [2022.10.27/XJ8098/**D**]

- ♦ Research Initiative for Wheat Improvement / see Wheat Initiative (#20931)
- ♦ Research Institute for Asia and the Pacific, Sydney (internationally oriented national body)
- ♦ Research Institute for Association and Nonprofit Management (internationally oriented national body)
- ♦ Research Institute for Cancer of the Digestive System / see European Institute of Tele-Surgery
- ♦ Research Institute on Contemporary Southeast Asia (internationally oriented national body)
- ♦ Research Institute for European Affairs, Vienna / see Europe Institute, Vienna
- ♦ Research Institute for European and American Studies (internationally oriented national body)
- ♦ Research Institute for European Studies / see Research Institute for European and American Studies
- ♦ Research Institute for Inner Asian Studies / see Sinor Research Institute for Inner Asian Studies
- ♦ Research Institute of Innovative Technology for the Earth (internationally oriented national body)
- ♦ Research Institute for International Politics and Security / see Stiftung Wissenschaft und Politik
- ♦ Research Institute on the Mediterranean Economy, Naples / see Istituto di Studi sul Mediterraneo
- ♦ Research Institute on the Non-Violent Resolution of Conflicts (internationally oriented national body)

♦ Research Institute of Organic Agriculture 18857

Institut de recherche de l'agriculture biologique – Forschungsinstitut für biologischen Landbau (FiBL) – Istituti di ricerca dell'agricoltura biologica
Europe Office Rue de la Presse 4, 1000 Brussels, Belgium. T. +3222271122. E-mail: info.europe@fibl.org.
Contact Ackerstr 113, Postfach 219, 5070 Frick AG, Switzerland. T. +41628657272. Fax +41626857273. E-mail: info.suisse@fibl.org.
URL: http://www.fibl.org/
History 1973. **Aims** Advance cutting-edge science in the field of organic agriculture. **Structure** Consists of different centres: FiBL Switzerland; FiBL Germany; FiBL Austria; FiBL Team France and FiBL-Team Suisse Romande; *FiBL Europe*. **Languages** English, French, German. **Staff** 165.00 FTE, paid. 40-50 voluntary. **Activities** Knowledge management/information dissemination. **Events** *Conference on Organic Agriculture Sciences* Eisenstadt (Austria) 2018, *ABIM : annual biocontrol industry meeting* Lucerne (Switzerland) 2006. **NGO Relations** Subscriber to: *ISEAL (#16026)*. [2021/XM6079/j/**F**]

- ♦ Research Institute for Peace and Security, Tokyo (internationally oriented national body)
- ♦ Research Institute for Questions concerning the Danube Region / see Institut für den Donauraum und Mitteleuropa
- ♦ Research Institute for Southeast Asia, Marseille (internationally oriented national body)
- ♦ Research Institute of Southeast Asia, Nagasaki / see Institute of South-East Asian Studies, Nagasaki
- ♦ Research Institute for Spirituality and Health (internationally oriented national body)
- ♦ Research Institute for Subtropics, Okinawa (internationally oriented national body)
- ♦ Research Institute of Tropical Medicine (internationally oriented national body)

♦ Research in International Economics and Finance Network (RIEF) . 18858

Contact CEPII, 113 rue de Grenelle, 75007 Paris, France.
URL: https://sites.google.com/site/riefnetwork/
History 2004. **Aims** Reinforce scientific collaboration and contacts between European research centres working on international economics. **Structure** Scientific Committee. **Activities** Annual Doctoral meeting; occasional conference. **Events** *Meeting* Zurich (Switzerland) 2014, *Biennial Conference* Rome (Italy) 2007, *Conference* Rome (Italy) 2007, *Conference / Biennial Conference* Paris (France) 2004. [2015/XM3172/**F**]

- ♦ Research Network "European Cultures in Business and Corporate Communication" / see Europäische Kulturen in der Wirtschaftskommunikation (#05754)
- ♦ Research Network on International Governance, Globalization and the Transformations of the State (internationally oriented national body)

♦ Research Network for Schistosomiasis in Africa (RNSA) 18859

Coordinator Copperbelt Univ – School of Medicine, PO Box 71191, Ndola, Zambia. T. +260212618511. E-mail: vickapasa@gmail.com – vicsale@zamtel.zm.
History Mar 2004, Geneva (Switzerland). **Aims** Improve quality of schistosomiasis operational and basic research relevant to effective control strategies Africa. **Structure** Advisory Committee; Secretariats (2). **Languages** English, French. **Staff** 4.00 FTE, paid. **Finance** Funded by special programme on Research and Training in Tropical Diseases and Danish Bilharziasis Laboratory. Budget (annual): US$ 7,500. **Activities** Events/meetings. **Events** *Meeting* Lusaka (Zambia) 2008, *Meeting* Bamako (Mali) 2007, *Meeting* Lusaka (Zambia) 2006, *Meeting* Mombasa (Kenya) 2005. **Publications** *RNSA News*.
Members Full in 15 countries:
Belgium, Denmark, Ghana, Kenya, Madagascar, Malawi, Mozambique, Nigeria, Switzerland, Tanzania UR, Uganda, UK, USA, Zambia, Zimbabwe.
IGO Relations Partners: *UNICEF/UNDP/World Bank/WHO Special Programme for Research and Training in Tropical Diseases (TDR, #20331)*; national organizations. **NGO Relations** Partners: *Bill and Melinda Gates Foundation (BMGF)*; national institutes. [2015.06.01/XM0827/**F**]

♦ Research in Occupational Therapy and Occupational Science Foundation (ROTOS) 18860

Registered Address Orteliuslaan 750, 3528 BB Utrecht, Netherlands.
Sec address not obtained.
URL: https://www.rotosfoundation.eu/
History 2020. Active as a committee since 2016. Registration: Handelsregister, No/ID: KVK 77629779, Start date: 11 Mar 2020, Netherlands. **Aims** Grow the research connectivity among the European occupational therapy and occupational science community. **Structure** Board. **Events** *Occupational Therapy Europe Congress* Krakow (Poland) 2024. **NGO Relations** A branch of *Occupational Therapy Europe (OT-Europe, #17647)*. [2021/AA2062/f/**F**]

- ♦ Research Policy Institute, Lund (internationally oriented national body)
- ♦ Research School of Asian, African and Amerindian Studies (internationally oriented national body)
- ♦ Research School CNWS – Research School of Asian, African and Amerindian Studies (internationally oriented national body)
- ♦ Research School of Pacific and Asian Studies, Canberra (internationally oriented national body)
- ♦ Research School of Pacific Studies / see Research School of Pacific and Asian Studies, Canberra
- ♦ Research School for Resource Studies for Development (internationally oriented national body)

♦ **Research Society for Victorian Periodicals (RSVP)** **18861**
Société de recherches sur les périodiques de l'époque victorienne
Pres Liverpool John Moores Univ, John Foster Bldg, 98 Mount Pleasant, Liverpool, L35 2UZ, UK. E-mail: president@rs4vp.org.
Sec English Dept Knorr 107, Pacific Lutheran Univ, Tacoma WA 98447, USA. E-mail: secretary@rs4vp.org.
URL: http://www.rs4vp.org/
History 1969. While the central focus of the society is on Great Britain and Ireland, it also deals with the press in other parts of the English-speaking world. Constitution most recently amended 15 Sep 2006. **Aims** Explore the richly diverse world of the 19th-century press, both magazines and newspapers. **Structure** Board of Directors; Planning Committee; Finance Committee. **Languages** English. **Finance** Sources: members' dues; sale of publications. **Activities** Awards/prizes/competitions; events/meetings; financial and/or material support; networking/liaising. **Events** *Conference* Philadelphia, PA (USA) 2021, *Conference* Philadelphia, PA (USA) 2020, *Conference* Brighton (UK) 2019, *Conference* Victoria, BC (Canada) 2018, *Conference* Freiburg-Breisgau (Germany) 2017. **Publications** *Victorian Periodicals Review (VPR)* (4 a year). Bibliographies; directories.
Members Students in 14 countries:
Australia, Canada, France, Germany, Ireland, Italy, Japan, Netherlands, New Zealand, South Africa, Spain, Sweden, UK, USA.
[2018.06.01/XN3259/**C**]

♦ **Research Software Alliance (ReSA)** **18862**
Dir address not obtained.
URL: https://www.researchsoft.org/
Aims Bring research software communities together to collaborate on the advancement of the research software ecosystem. **Structure** Steering Committee. **NGO Relations** Signatory to agreement of *Coalition for Advancing Research Assessment (CoARA, #04045).* [2022/AA3083/**C**]

♦ Research and technological Exchange Group / see GRET
♦ Research Triangle Institute / see RTI International
♦ Réseau académique de droit pénal européen (#06860)
♦ Réseau d'action européen pour les bananes (#06310)
♦ Réseau action globale (internationally oriented national body)
♦ Réseau d'action international sur les armes légères / see International Action Network on Small Arms (#11585)
♦ Réseau d'administrateurs culturels européens (#17017)
♦ Réseau Africain de Campagne pour l'Education pour Tous (#00302)
♦ Réseau africain pour le développement de l'aviculture en milieu rurale / see International Network on Family Poultry Development (#14267)
♦ Réseau africain pour le développement de l'horticulture (no recent information)
♦ Réseau africain pour le développement intégré (#00390)
♦ Réseau africain de droit constitutionnel (#00384)
♦ Réseau Africain d'épidémiologie de terrain (#00315)
♦ Réseau africain de Forêts Modèles (#00377)

♦ **Réseau africain des formations sur le VIH et le SIDA (RAF-VIH)** **18863**
Contact Kadiogo, 01 BP 909, Ouagadougou 01, Burkina Faso. T. +22650300053 – +22670295416.
URL: http://www.raf-vih.net/
Aims Improve the overall medical and psycho-social care of people living with AIDS or HIV in sub-Saharan Africa. **Structure** General Assembly; Committee. **Staff** 6.00 FTE, paid. **Finance** Support from: *Deutsche Gesellschaft für Internationale Zusammenarbeit (GIZ)* Backup; ESTHER; *Joint United Nations Programme on HIV/AIDS (UNAIDS, #16149)*; Sidaction; *UNDP (#20292)*; *WHO (#20950).* **Activities** Organizes courses and training.
Members Full in 8 countries:
Benin, Burkina Faso, Burundi, Cameroon, Côte d'Ivoire, Mali, Niger, Senegal.
IGO Relations Partner of: *Deutsche Gesellschaft für Internationale Zusammenarbeit (GIZ)* Backup; *Joint United Nations Programme on HIV/AIDS (UNAIDS, #16149)*; *UNDP (#20292)*; *United Nations Population Fund (UNFPA, #20612)*; *West African Health Organization (WAHO, #20881)*; *WHO (#20950).* [2013.09.24/XJ1239/**F**]

♦ **Réseau Africain Francophone d'Education Comparée (RAFEC)** **18864**
Contact address not obtained. E-mail: inforafec@rafec.org.
URL: http://www.rafec.org/
History 12 Jan 2011, Koudougou (Burkina Faso). **Structure** General Assembly; Board. **Events** *Colloquium* Niger 2015, *Colloquium* Yaoundé (Cameroon) 2013.
Members Full in 9 countries:
Benin, Burkina Faso, Cameroon, Chad, Gabon, Madagascar, Niger, Senegal, Togo.
IGO Relations Accredited by (1): *Organisation internationale de la Francophonie (OIF, #17809).*
[2019/XM4281/**F**]

♦ Réseau Africain pour la Geo-Education (#00387)
♦ Réseau Africain d'Histoire Mondiale (#00388)
♦ Réseau africain d'institutions scientifiques et techniques (#00395)
♦ Réseau africain de microfinance (#00189)
♦ Réseau africain des organismes de bassin (#00381)

♦ **Réseau Africain des Personnels des Parlements (RAPP)** **18865**
Sec address not obtained. T. +22520208294. Fax +22520209629.
URL: https://www.rappafrik.org/
History Sep 1995, Porto-Novo (Benin). Statutes adopted Sep 2016. **Aims** Build the capacity of member parliaments; contribute to the professional training of parliamentary staff; be a focal point for inter-parliamentary cooperation; create the conditions for a sustainable and efficient parliamentary administration. **Structure** General Assembly; Executive Committee; Standing Committees; Secretariat.
Members Individuals in 15 countries:
Benin, Burkina Faso, Central African Rep, Chad, Congo Brazzaville, Congo DR, Côte d'Ivoire, Gabon, Guinea, Madagascar, Mali, Morocco, Niger, Senegal, Togo. [2019/AA2211/v/**F**]

♦ Réseau Africain des Praticiens Assurant la Prise en Charge Médicale des Personnes Vivant avec le VIH/SIDA (unconfirmed)
♦ Réseau africain pour la presse du 21ème siècle (#00423)
♦ Réseau africain pour la prévention et la protection contre l'abus et la négligence de l'enfant (#00393)
♦ Réseau africain de recherche sur les bruches / see African Network of Research on Storage Insects (#00394)
♦ Réseau africain de recherche et développement pour l'exploitation industrielle des plantes médicinales (inactive)
♦ Réseau africain de recherche sur les insectes des stocks (#00394)
♦ Réseau africain du secteur de la sécurité (#00453)
♦ Réseau africain de la société civile sur l'eau et l'assainissement (#00250)
♦ Réseau africain pour le soutien à l'entrepreneuriat féminin (#00397)

♦ **Réseau africain de statistique mathématique et ses applications (RASMA)** **18866**
African Network of Mathematical Statistics and its Applications (ANMSA)
Pres Univ de Masuku, Franceville, Gabon.
URL: http://www.rasma-net.org/
History 16 Jan 2008, Franceville (Gabon). **Structure** General Assembly. Executive Bureau, comprising President, Vice-President, Secretary General and Treasurer. **Activities** Organizes workshops. **Members** Individuals. Membership countries not specified. **NGO Relations** *Southern Africa Bean Research Network (SABRN, #19826).* [2010/XM3930/**D**]

♦ Réseau AfriMAB (#00532)
♦ Réseau Afrique 2000 / see Africa 2000 Plus Network, Harare (#00154)
♦ Réseau afro-asiatique pour le développement de l'aviculture en milieu rurale / see International Network on Family Poultry Development (#14267)
♦ Réseau d'agriculture durable / see Social Agriculture Network (#19333)
♦ Réseau des aires protégées d'Afrique centrale (#03656)
♦ Réseau des Amériques sur la Nationalité et l'Apatridie (unconfirmed)
♦ Réseau arabe des ONG pour l'environnement et le développement (#01017)
♦ Réseau Art Nouveau / see Réseau Art Nouveau Network (#18867)

♦ **Réseau Art Nouveau Network (RANN)** **18867**
Coordinator Rue de la Grande Ile 11, 1000 Brussels, Belgium. E-mail: info@artnouveau-net.eu.
Communication address not obtained.
Main Website: http://www.artnouveau-net.eu/
History 1999. Former names and other names: *Art Nouveau Network* – former; *Réseau Art Nouveau* – former. Registration: Banque-Carrefour des Entreprises, No/ID: 0888.903.347, Start date: 22 Oct 2006, Belgium. **Aims** Keep researchers and professionals informed, and make the general public aware of the cultural significance and European dimension of the Art Nouveau heritage. **Structure** Board; Secretariat. **Languages** English, French. **Staff** 2.00 FTE, paid. **Finance** Sources: members' dues; revenue from activities/projects; subsidies. Supported by: *European Commission (EC, #06633).* **Activities** Events/meetings; projects/programmes. **Events** *Colloque International sur les Intérieurs d'Epoque Art Nouveau* Brussels (Belgium) 2019, *Multilateral Exchange Seminar* Helsinki (Finland) 2013. **Publications** *Art Nouveau Network Newsletter. A strange world – Metamorphosis and Hybridization in Art Nouveau and Symbolism* (2013) – catalogue. Educational booklets; proceedings.
Members Cities in 15 countries:
Austria, Belgium, Cuba, France, Germany, Hungary, Italy, Latvia, Norway, Portugal, Romania, Serbia, Slovenia, Spain, Switzerland.
NGO Relations Member of (2): *European Heritage Alliance 3.3 (#07477)*; *European Institute of Cultural Routes (EICR).* [2022.02.09/XJ8590/**F**]

♦ Réseau asiatique pour l'habitat (#01381)
♦ Réseau asiatique d'institutions de formation et de recherche en planification de l'éducation (#01561)
♦ Réseau Asie / see Institute of Asian Worlds
♦ Réseau asien d'enseignement de la physique (#01664)
♦ Réseau de l'Asie du Sud-Est sur la microbiologie / see UNESCO Regional Network for Microbiology and Microbial Biotechnology in Southeast Asia (#20319)
♦ Réseau pour l'assistance humanitaire / see Network on Humanitarian Action (#17034)
♦ Réseau-association des chercheurs européens sur l'urbanisation dans les pays du Sud (#16996)
♦ Réseau des associations européennes pour le counselling et la psychothérapie centrés sur la personne / see Network of the European Associations for Person-Centred and Experiential Psychotherapy and Counselling (#17013)
♦ Réseau des associations européennes pour la psychothérapie et le counselling centrés sur la personne et expérientiels (#17013)
♦ Réseau des associations francophones de science politique (unconfirmed)
♦ Réseau des associations de la jeunesse pour les nations unies (#20652)
♦ Réseau des associations de pouvoirs locaux de l'Europe du sud-est (#16997)
♦ Réseau d'associations de santé publique d'Afrique francophone (inactive)
♦ Réseau Caraïbéen des Chercheurs/Cliniciens sur la Drépanocytose et les Thalassemies (#03529)
♦ Réseau caraïbéen de santé animale (#03440)
♦ Réseau Carthagène d'Ingénierie (#03590)
♦ **Réseau CDE** Centres de documentation européenne (#06937)
♦ Réseau des centres européens des consommateurs (#06770)
♦ Réseau des centres francophones de formation au journalisme / see Théophraste Network (#20140)
♦ Réseau des Chambres de Commerce et de l'Industrie Insulaires de l'Union Européenne (#17040)

♦ **Réseau des Cités Oléicoles de la Méditerranée (ReCOMed)** **18868**
Network of Mediterranean Olive Oil Towns
Permanent Secretariat c/o Azienda Speciale "PromImperia", CCIAA Imperia, Via T Schiva 29, 18100 Imperia IM, Italy. T. +39183793280. Fax +39183274816.
History Founded 18 Nov 2011, at 1st Mediterranean Diet Forum. Successor to *Fédération euroméditerranéenne des municipalités oléicoles (FEMO, inactive).* Registered in accordance with Italian law. **Aims** Preserve and optimize the history of olive cultivation and production of olive oil, so as to maintain its origin and the typical qualities of local production. **Structure** General Assembly; Board of Directors. **Languages** English. **Staff** 1.00 FTE, paid. **Finance** Members' quota; COI and EU projects. **Activities** Knowledge management/information dissemination. **Events** *General Assembly / Mediterranean Diet Forum* Milan (Italy) 2015, *Mediterranean Diet Forum* Milan (Italy) 2015, *Mediterranean Diet Forum* Imperia (Italy) 2014, *General Assembly* Kalamata (Greece) / Koroni (Greece) 2014, *Mediterranean Diet Forum* Imperia (Italy) 2013. **Publications** Forum proceedings.
Members Full in 13 countries:
Albania, Croatia, Greece, Israel, Italy, Lebanon, Montenegro, Morocco, Portugal, Slovenia, Spain, Tunisia, Türkiye.
[2015.06.01/XJ8738/**F**]

♦ Réseau citoyens / see RCN Justice et Démocratie
♦ Réseau des citoyens d'Europe / see RCN Justice et Démocratie
♦ Réseau des collèges de traducteurs littéraires en Europe / see Réseau européen des centres internationaux de traducteurs littéraires (#18873)
♦ Réseau de communes – Alliance dans les Alpes / see Alliance in the Alps (#00656)
♦ Réseau de communes alpines / see Alliance in the Alps (#00656)
♦ Réseau Communicateurs Forestiers Méditerranéen (unconfirmed)

♦ **Réseau des compétences électorales francophones (RECEF)** **18869**
Secretariat 1045 avenue Wilfrid-Pelletier, Bureau 200, Québec QC G1W 0C6, Canada. T. +14185280422. E-mail: recef@electionsquebec.qc.ca.
URL: https://recef.org/
History 2011, Québec (Canada). **Aims** Promote the regular conduct of free, fair and transparent elections. **Structure** General Assembly; Bureau. **Events** *Assemblée Générale* Québec, QC (Canada) 2021, *Assemblée Générale* Québec, QC (Canada) 2020, *Assemblée Générale* Sinaia (Romania) 2019, *Assemblée Générale* Antananarivo (Madagascar) 2018, *Assemblée Générale Extraordinaire* Praia (Cape Verde) 2017.
Members Full in 31 countries and territories:
Belgium, Benin, Burkina Faso, Burundi, Cameroon, Canada, Cape Verde, Central African Rep, Chad, Comoros, Congo DR, Côte d'Ivoire, Djibouti, France, Gabon, Guinea, Guinea-Bissau, Haiti, Madagascar, Mali, Mauritania, Mauritius, Moldova, Niger, Québec, Romania, Rwanda, Sao Tomé-Principe, Senegal, Togo, Tunisia.
IGO Relations Partner of (1): *Organisation internationale de la Francophonie (OIF, #17809).*
[2023/AA2320/**F**]

♦ Réseau Contentieux Pénitentiaire / see European Prison Litigation Network (#08277)
♦ Réseau coopératif européen de recherche sur l'olivier (#15969)
♦ Réseau coopératif interrégional de la FAO de recherche sur le riz en climat méditerranéen (#09263)
♦ Réseau coopératif inter-universitaire de formation et de perfectionnement du personnel d'enseignement supérieur (no recent information)
♦ Réseau culturel européen de coopération au développement (#06869)
♦ Réseau pour la Défense and la Gestion de la Sécurité de l'Afrique Australe (inactive)

♦ **Réseau des Défenseurs des Droits Humains en Afrique Centrale (REDHAC)** **18870**
Exec Dir BP 2863, Douala, Cameroon. T. +237233426404 – +237695848653.
URL: http://www.redhac.org/

History Founded Apr 2007, Kigali (Rwanda). Current constitution adopted 9 Jul 2010, Douala (Cameroon). Registered in accordance with the law of Cameroon. **Aims** Ensure and protection those fighting for human rights in Central Africa. **Structure** General Assembly (every 4 years); Board of Directors of 7 members; Advisory Board; Permanent Secretariat. **Languages** French. **Staff** 5.00 FTE, paid. **Finance** Funded by *National Endowment for Democracy (NED)*. **Activities** Advocacy/lobbying/activism; networking/liaising; capacity building; monitoring/evaluation; guidance/assistance/consulting; events/meetings. **Publications** *Reporting Severe Human Rights Violations in Central Africa* (2015); *Human Rights and the States of Central Africa: Defensers situations and democratic perspectives for the 21st century* (2014).
Members Full in 8 countries:
Cameroon, Central African Rep, Chad, Congo Brazzaville, Congo DR, Equatorial Guinea, Gabon, Sao Tomé-Principe.
Consultative Status Consultative status granted from: *African Commission on Human and Peoples' Rights (ACHPR, #00255)* (Observer). **NGO Relations** Sub-regional member of: *Pan-African Human Rights Defenders Network (AfricanDefenders, #18052).* [2016.08.05/XJ6701/**D**]

- ♦ **Réseau-DESC** Réseau international pour les droits économiques, sociaux et culturels (#14255)
- ♦ Réseau sur la dette et le développement d'ECOWAS (#05336)
- ♦ Réseau pour le développement de programmes européens en enseignement supérieur / see Global Business Education Network (#10258)
- ♦ Réseau dialogues pour le progrès de l'humanité / see Dialogues, propositions, histoires pour une citoyenneté mondiale (#05067)
- ♦ Réseau DPH / see Dialogues, propositions, histoires pour une citoyenneté mondiale (#05067)
- ♦ Réseau d'échange de données et d'informations océaniques pour l'Afrique (#17648)
- ♦ Réseau écologique paneuropéen (see: #04881)
- ♦ Réseau des éditeurs africains (#00426)
- ♦ Réseau Education et Solidarité (#05374)
- ♦ Réseau éleveurs-environnement dans la corne de l'Afrique (internationally oriented national body)
- ♦ Réseau émeraude (see: #19949)
- ♦ Réseau Entraide Solidarité Monde (internationally oriented national body)
- ♦ Réseau d'épidémiologie clinique international francophone (#09992)
- ♦ Réseau des espaces protégés méditerranéens / see Network of Marine Protected Area Managers in the Mediterranean (#17048)
- ♦ Réseau sur les espèces forestières envahissantes en Afrique (#09863)
- ♦ Réseau Espérance de Vie en Santé (unconfirmed)
- ♦ Réseau est atlantique de réserves de biosphère (#18635)

♦ Réseau des établissements d'enseignement vétérinaire de la Méditerranée (REEV-Med) 18871

Mediterranean Network of Establishments for Veterinary Education

President OIE Sub-Regional Representation North Africa, 17 Avenue of Africa, El Menzah V, 2091 Tunis, Tunisia. T. +21671237400. Fax +21671237339. E-mail: rsr.afriquedunord@oie.int.
Main Website: http://www.reev-med.org/

History Sep 2012, Rabat (Morocco). Process initiated Oct 2010, Paris (France). Registration: France. **Structure** General Assemlbly; Executive Committee. **Events** *General Assembly* 2021, *General Assembly* Hammamet (Tunisia) 2014, *General Assembly* Rabat (Morocco) 2012.
Members Full in 12 countries:
Algeria, Bosnia-Herzegovina, Egypt, France, Greece, Italy, Morocco, North Macedonia, Serbia, Slovenia, Tunisia, Türkiye.
IGO Relations *OIE – World Organisation for Animal Health (#17703).* **NGO Relations** *European Association of Establishments for Veterinary Education (EAEVE, #06031).* [2020.05.27/XM4251/**F**]

- ♦ Réseau des établissements de formation en sciences de la santé orientés vers les besoins de la communauté / see The Network: Towards Unity for Health (#17060)
- ♦ Réseau d'études sur la globalisation, la gouvernance internationale et les mutations de l'état et des nations (internationally oriented national body)
- ♦ Réseau d'études sur la politique technologique en Afrique (#00481)
- ♦ Réseau d'études sociales pour la prévention des catastrophes naturelles en Amérique latine (#17058)
- ♦ Réseau d'étude des systèmes de production en Afrique de l'Ouest (#20880)
- ♦ Réseau des étudiants africains en nutrition (#00330)
- ♦ Réseau étudiants universitaire pour la santé sociale et internationale (internationally oriented national body)
- ♦ Réseau Eurodesk (#05675)
- ♦ Réseau Euro-méditerranéen de bassins représentatifs et expérimentaux / see European Network of Experimental and Representative Basins (#07905)
- ♦ Réseau euro-méditerranéen des droits de l'humains / see EuroMed Rights (#05733)

♦ Réseau euro-méditerranéen d'information et de formation pour la gestion des risques (REMIFOR) 18872

Pres c/o ESA Headquarters, 8-10 rue Mario Nikis, 75738 Paris CEDEX 15, France. T. +33153697654. Fax +331536975.
Contact 247 rue Jean Aicard, 83300 Draguignan, France. T. +33494501275. Fax +33494687703.
[2008/XJ4107/**F**]

- ♦ Réseau européen d'action sociale (#08499)
- ♦ Réseau européen pour l'Afrique centrale (#07874)
- ♦ Réseau européen des associations de lutte contre la pauvreté et l'exclusion sociale / see European Anti-Poverty Network (#05908)
- ♦ Réseau européen des associations de professeurs de géographie (#06054)
- ♦ Réseau européen des associations X fragile (unconfirmed)
- ♦ Réseau Européen des Autorités Compétentes Médicales (#07944)
- ♦ Réseau européen de bassins représentatifs et expérimentaux (#07905)
- ♦ Réseau européen des centres culturels (#07888)
- ♦ Réseau européen des centres culturels – monuments historiques / see European Network of Cultural Centres in Historic Monuments
- ♦ Réseau européen des centres culturels de rencontre / see European Network of Cultural Centres in Historic Monuments
- ♦ Réseau européen des centres européens d'entreprise et d'innovation (#06420)
- ♦ Réseau européen des centres de formation d'administrateurs culturels / see ENCATC (#05452)
- ♦ Réseau européen de centres d'information du spectacle vivant (#07933)

♦ Réseau européen des centres internationaux de traducteurs littéraires (RECIT) 18873

European Network of Literary Translation Centres

Sec c/o British Centre for Literary Translation, Univ of East Anglia, Norwich Research Park, Norwich, NR4 7TJ, UK. T. +441603592785. E-mail: bclt@uea.ac.uk.
Pres address not obtained.
URL: http://www.re-cit.org/

History 21 Sep 1991. Founded on ratification of 'Charte de Procida' by heads of European colleges of literary translators, the first college having been set up, 1980, Straelen (Germany FR). Former names and other names: *Réseau européen des collèges de traducteurs littéraires* – alias; *Réseau des collèges de traducteurs littéraires en Europe* – alias. **Aims** As a network of European literary translation centres, offer residencies for translators and organize public events bringing together writers, translators and audiences internationally. **Activities** Events/meetings. **Events** *Assises* Arles (France) 2003.
Members Organizations in 12 countries:
Belgium, Bulgaria, France, Germany, Hungary, Ireland, Italy, Latvia, Netherlands, Sweden, Switzerland, UK.
Included in the above, 3 organizations listed in this Yearbook:
Baltic Centre for Writers and Translators (BCWT, #03105); Collège international des traducteurs littéraires (CITL); Europäisches Übersetzer-Kollegium (EÜK). [2022.05.04/XF3968/y/**F**]

- ♦ Réseau européen des centres nationaux d'information sur la reconnaissance et la mobilité académiques (#07950)
- ♦ Réseau européen du chromosome 11 (#06547)
- ♦ Réseau européen du chromosome 11Q / see European Chromosome 11 Network (#06547)
- ♦ Réseau européen du coeur (#07467)
- ♦ Réseau européen des collèges de traducteurs littéraires / see Réseau européen des centres internationaux de traducteurs littéraires (#18873)
- ♦ Réseau européen des conseils de l'éducation (#07898)
- ♦ Réseau européen des conseils de la justice (#07886)
- ♦ Réseau européen pour une consommation responsable (#07994)
- ♦ Réseau européen contre le nationalisme, le racisme, le fascisme et pour le soutien des réfugiés et des migrants (#20511)
- ♦ Réseau européen contre le racisme (#07862)
- ♦ Réseau européen de développement rural (#07995)
- ♦ Réseau européen des directeurs d'écoles d'architecture (#07918)
- ♦ Réseau européen droit et société (#07937)
- ♦ Réseau européen de l'économie solidaire et du développement local (#07895)
- ♦ Réseau européen d'éducation à l'environnement / see Polis – International Network in Environmental Education (#18421)
- ♦ Réseau Européen pour l'Égalité des Langues (#07647)
- ♦ Réseau Européen Église et liberté (#07878)
- ♦ Réseau européen EMES / see EMES International Research Network (#05440)
- ♦ Réseau européen des employeurs / see The Federation of International Employers (#09644)
- ♦ Réseau européen d'enseignement à distance / see EDEN Digital Learning Europe (#05356)
- ♦ Réseau européen pour l'enseignement des sciences nucléaires (#08057)
- ♦ Réseau européen des établissements scolaires attachés à la promotion de la santé / see Schools for Health in Europe network foundation (#19133)
- ♦ Réseau Européen d'Etudes Littéraires Comparées / see European Society of Comparative Literature (#08561)
- ♦ Réseau européen d'études utilitaristes (internationally oriented national body)
- ♦ Réseau européen des femmes de plus de 50 ans (#17716)
- ♦ Réseau européen des femmes dans la police (#07970)
- ♦ Réseau européen femmes et sport (#09104)
- ♦ Réseau européen en formation continue universitaire (#09030)
- ♦ Réseau européen de formation judiciaire (#07617)
- ♦ Réseau Européen de Formation Universitaire en Travail Social (unconfirmed)
- ♦ Réseau européen de groupes de de patients atteints du myélome multiple (inactive)
- ♦ Réseau européen hôpitaux sans tabac / see ENSH-Global Network for Tobacco Free Health Care Services (#05490)
- ♦ Réseau européen pour l'inclusion et l'action sociale locale (#07707)
- ♦ Réseau européen d'information et de documentation sur l'Amérique latine (#18652)
- ♦ Réseau européen d'information sur les politiques du patrimoine culturel (#07533)

♦ Réseau Européen pour l'Insertion Sociale et Professionnelle de Personnes Défavorisées (REIN) 18874

European Network for the Insertion of Disfavoured People

Exec Manager Eichenallee 5, 59514 Welver, Germany. T. +492384941457. Fax +492384941458.
Registered Office MAI, Rue Washington 40, 1050 Brussels, Belgium.
URL: http://www.rein-network.org/

History 1993. Registration: Banque-Carrefour des Entreprises, No/ID: 0471.929.942, Start date: 25 May 2000, Belgium. **Aims** Support, evaluate and document European social cooperation; identify, develop and increase methods of labour market integration; train trainers in a European perspective; compare and analyse social enterprises; support communication and exchange on all social and technical levels; mainstream and disseminate best practice models; support network(ing) projects. **Structure** General Assembly (twice a year); Steering Committee. **Languages** English, French, Spanish. **Staff** Voluntary. **Finance** Members' dues. Budget (2012): euro 30,000. **Activities** Research/documentation; training/education; networking/liaising; events/meetings. **Events** *Half-Yearly General Assembly* Cognac (France) 2013, *Half-Yearly General Assembly* Lódz (Poland) 2013, *Half-Yearly General Assembly* Welver (Germany) 2013, *Half-Yearly General Assembly* Lódz (Poland) 2012, *Half-Yearly General Assembly* Marburg (Germany) 2012.
Members Organizations in 9 countries:
Belgium, Bulgaria, France, Germany, Hungary, Italy, Poland, Portugal, Spain.
NGO Relations Member of: *Federation of European and International Associations Established in Belgium (FAIB, #09508).* Cooperates with: *East-West-Network Europe (EWNE, #05265).* [2018/XF7207/**F**]

- ♦ Réseau européen des institutions de formation pour les collectivités territoriales (#08023)
- ♦ Réseau européen des institutions en sciences du sport pour l'éducation et pour l'emploi / see European Network of Sport Education (#08012)
- ♦ Réseau européen des instituts de la famille (#18653)

♦ Réseau européen d'instituts de formation d'enseignants (Assocation Comenius) 18875

European network of teacher training institutes (Comenius Association)

Sec Pädagogische Hochschule Schwäbish Gmünd, Akademisches Auslandsamt, Oberbettringer Str 200, 73525 Schwäbisch Gmünd, Germany. T. +497171983225. Fax +497171983388.
Registered Office Haute Ecole Léonard de Vinci – ENCBW, Place de l'Alma 2, 1200 Brussels, Belgium.
URL: http://www.associationcomenius.org/

History Founded 20 Feb 1993. Registered in accordance with Belgian law. **Aims** Promote internationalization in education within the different partner institutions. **Structure** General Assembly; Board of Management. **Finance** Members' dues.
Members Full in 17 countries:
Austria, Belgium, Czechia, Denmark, France, Germany, Hungary, Ireland, Italy, Lithuania, Netherlands, Norway, Portugal, Spain, Sweden, Switzerland, UK. [2020/XM8881/**F**]

- ♦ Réseau européen des instituts de sciences du sport / see European Network of Sport Education (#08012)

♦ Réseau européen interdisciplinaire de recherche sur psychologie et réanimation (REIRPR) 18876

Contact 4 rue de Provence, 67540 Ostwald, France. T. +33388663141. Fax +33388663141.
URL: http://reirpr.chez-alice.fr/

History 5 Feb 1990, Strasbourg (France). Founded 5-6 Feb 1990, Strasbourg (France). Registered in accordance with French law. **Aims** Promote dissemination of information in the fields of *psychology* and *resuscitation*, particularly of psychological and human *risks* involved, and of work and experience in the field; promote relevant research and its application in health care organizations. **Languages** French. **Staff** 4.00 FTE, voluntary. **Finance** Members' dues. Other sources: colloquium fees; publications; subventions. **Activities** Organizes: colloquia; workshops. **Events** *Journées annuelles* Strasbourg (France) 2000, *Journées annuelles* Strasbourg (France) 1999, *Journées annuelles* Strasbourg (France) 1998, *Journées annuelles* Strasbourg (France) 1997, *Journées annuelles* Strasbourg (France) 1996. **Publications** *Cahiers du réseau*; *Les Cahiers du Reseau Psychologie et Réanimation* – magazine. *L'Enfant Réanimé – Clinique de la Rupture et du Lien* (2007); *Réanimation, coma: Soin psychique et vécu du patient* (2006) by M Grosclaude; *En réanimation: ombres et clartés* (1996) by M Grosclaude et al; *Réanimation, coma: à la recherche du sujet inconscient* (1996) by M Grosclaude. Colloquium proceedings. **Information Services** *Système MEDLINE*; *Système PASCAL*.
Members Based in France, but members in 4 countries:
Belgium, France, Italy, Switzerland. [2012.07.16/XF2886/**F**]

- ♦ Réseau européen des laboratoires officiels de contrôle des médicaments (#07957)

- ♦ Réseau européen pour les langues régionales ou minoritaires et l'éducation / see Mercator European Research Centre on Multilingualism and Language Learning (#16719)
- ♦ Réseau Européen de la Microfinance (#07792)
- ♦ Réseau Européen de la Musique Ancienne (#06953)
- ♦ Réseau européen des organisations de femmes de la pêche et de l'aquaculture (#08035)
- ♦ Réseau Européen du Patrimoine des Jardins (#07378)
- ♦ Réseau européen pour le perfectionnement du personnel de l'enseignement supérieur (inactive)
- ♦ Réseau européen de police aéronautique et de service de sécurité frontalière (#07866)
- ♦ Réseau européen de prévention de la criminalité / see European Crime Prevention Network (#06858)
- ♦ Réseau européen pour la prévention du tabagisme / see European Network for Smoking and Tobacco Prevention (#08002)
- ♦ Réseau européen de la promotion de la santé dans les écoles / see Schools for Health in Europe network foundation (#19133)
- ♦ Réseau européen de psychologie du travail et des organisations (#07960)
- ♦ Réseau européen de recherche forestière tropicale (#08950)

♦ Réseau européen de recherche et d'innovation dans l'enseignement supérieur (RERIES) 18877

European Network for Research and Innovation in Higher Education

Contact Univ Cath Louvain, UNESCO Chair of University Teaching and Learning, Place C Mercier 10, 1348 Louvain-la-Neuve, Belgium.

URL: http://www.uclouvain.be/chaire-pedagogie-universitaire.html

History Regional network of *Global University Network for Innovation (GUNI, #10641)*. **Aims** Contribute to the enhancement of the relevance and quality of higher education on the basis of its research and development activities, its reflection and expertise, and international cooperation based on true partnership. **Structure** General Assembly. Executive Committee, comprising President, 2 Vice-Presidents and General Rapporteur. **Languages** English, French. **Members** Regular UNESCO Chairs of Higher Education. Institutions universities; centres; faculties; departments. Members in Europe and North America. Membership countries not specified. **IGO Relations** *UNESCO (#20322)*; *United Nations University (UNU, #20642)*. [2011.06.01/XM0275/**E**]

- ♦ Réseau européen de recherche sur l'insertion des jeunes (#08377)
- ♦ Réseau européen pour la recherche sur le logement (#07924)
- ♦ Réseau européen de recherche pour les PME / see European Network for Social and Economic Research (#08005)
- ♦ Réseau européen de recherche social et économique (#08005)
- ♦ Réseau européen des registres testamentaires (unconfirmed)
- ♦ Réseau européen des responsables des politiques d'évaluation des systèmes éducatifs (#07971)
- ♦ Réseau européen de science politique (#05339)

♦ Réseau européen pour la sensibilisation à l'opéra et à la danse (RESEO) 18878

European Network for Opera and Dance Education

Main Office Rue Léopold 23, 1000 Brussels, Belgium. T. +3222176817. E-mail: reseo@reseo.org.

URL: http://www.reseo.org/

History Mar 1996, *European Network of Education Departments in Opera Houses – Réseau européen des services éducatifs des maisons d'opéra*. Registered in accordance with Belgian law. **Aims** Act as a forum for exchange of information, experience and ideas about opera and dance education; advocate for development of cultural education in Europe; develop research, practice and dissemination of the practice of opera and dance education; promote productions for young audiences and other target groups. **Structure** General Assembly (annual); Steering Committee. **Languages** English, French. **Staff** 1.00 FTE, paid. **Finance** Members' dues. Support from: *European Commission (EC, #06633)*; sponsors; income from activities. **Activities** Training/education; advocacy/lobbying/activism; events/meetings. **Events** *Conference* Bristol (UK) 2016, *Conference* Paris (France) 2016, *Conference* Como (Italy) 2015, *Conference* Lisbon (Portugal) 2015, *All aboard* Glasgow (UK) 2014. **Publications** *RESEO* (6 a year) in English, French – newsletter. Research studies; thematic publications.

Members Companies (84) in 25 countries:
Australia, Austria, Belgium, Bulgaria, Chile, Denmark, Estonia, Finland, France, Germany, Ireland, Italy, Lithuania, Montenegro, Netherlands, Norway, Poland, Portugal, Romania, Russia, Serbia, Spain, Sweden, Switzerland, UK.
Individuals (7) in 5 countries:
Belgium, France, Germany, Switzerland, UK.

IGO Relations Partner: European Commission (DG Education and Culture). *European Economic and Social Committee (EESC, #06963)*. **NGO Relations** Member of Executive Committee and ordinary member of: *Culture Action Europe (CAE, #04981)*. Member of: *European Alliance for Culture and the Arts (#05866)*. Formal contact with: *Opera Europa (#17771)*. [2016/XF4820/**F**]

- ♦ Réseau européen des services éducatifs des maisons d'opéra / see Réseau européen pour la sensibilisation à l'opéra et à la danse (#18878)
- ♦ Réseau européen 'Services et espace / see European Network for REsearch on SERvices (#07992)
- ♦ Réseau européen de sources d'information sur les aliments (#07285)
- ♦ Réseau européen pour les sourds-aveugles (#06890)
- ♦ Réseau européen de soutien psychologique / see European Network for Psychosocial Support (#07978)
- ♦ Réseau européen pour le soutien psychosocial (#07978)
- ♦ Réseau européen du sprinkleur anti-incendie (#07262)
- ♦ Réseau européen du textile (#08903)

♦ Réseau européen – Théâtre contemporain pour le jeune public (ARCHIPEL) 18879

Contemporary Theatre for Young Audiences

Contact Théâtre Nouvelle Génération, 23 rue de Bourgogne, 69009 Lyon, France. T. +33472531510. Fax +33452531519. E-mail: renseignements@tng-lyon.fr.

Aims Constitute an alternative international forum aiming at the elaboration and promotion of new artistic and professional productions; encourage an awareness of contemporary theatre by drawing new audiences; support through concrete collective actions, all professional initiatives aiming at the increase of permanent theatres or centres for young audiences. **Activities** Produces analytical evaluations, both quantitative and qualitative, on the nature and the impact of new forms of creation, on the evolving tastes and behaviour of youthful spectators, on the technical and economic conditions of the different modes of production and distribution, on the prominent role played by established theatres and distribution centres (cultural centres, festivals, etc) and on the improvements of the artistic quality of stage productions; engages, finances and coordinates desirable initiatives (publication activities, organization of seminars, national and international symposia, etc) to introduce the groups' activities to theatre professionals and other persons in charge of cultural development in various countries in order to reach the broadest public possible. **Members** Individuals. Membership countries not specified. [2008/XF3966/v/**F**]

- ♦ Réseau européen de la transfusion sanguine (#08024)
- ♦ Réseau européen des universités du troisième âge / see Association internationale des universités du troisième âge (#02749)
- ♦ Réseau Européen du Vieillissement (#05841)
- ♦ Réseau européen des villes numériques (#07893)

♦ Réseau Européen des Villes and Régions de l'Économie Sociale (REVES) 18880

European Network of Cities and Regions for the Social Economy

SG Bvd Charlemagne 74, 1000 Brussels, Belgium. T. +3222308810. Fax +3222304618. E-mail: office@revesnetwork.eu.

URL: http://www.revesnetwork.eu/

History Oct 1996, Östersund (Sweden). Oct 1996, Ostersund (Sweden). Registered in accordance with Belgian law. EU Transparency Register: 67482205645-83. **Aims** Create stable partnerships between local authorities and social economy actors with a view to promote common policies for sustainable local development and social inclusion; promote Territorial Social Responsibility (TSR, copyright). **Structure** General Assembly; Board of Directors; Presidency Committee. **Languages** English, French. **Staff** 5.00 FTE, paid. **Finance** Members' dues. Other sources: projects and services. **Activities** Advocacy/lobbying/activism; events/meetings; awards/prizes/competitions. **Events** *Annual Meeting* Darfo Boario Terme (Italy) 2014, *Conference* Brussels (Belgium) 2005, *Public procurement, social clauses, gender balanced policies – different aspects of the territorial social responsibility approach* Kokkola (Finland) 2005, *New Approaches in the fight against social exclusion* Messina (Italy) 2005, *Conference* Italy 2000. **Publications** *REVES Newsletter*. Guides; guidelines; articles; CD-Roms.

Members Cities; local authorities; social economy organizations. Members in 18 countries:
Austria, Belgium, Bulgaria, Croatia, Denmark, Finland, France, Germany, Greece, Hungary, Ireland, Italy, Morocco, Poland, Slovakia, Spain, Sweden, UK.
Regional organization (1):
Confédération européenne des coopératives de travail associé, des coopératives sociales et des entreprises sociales et participatives (CECOP, #04541).

IGO Relations Formal links with: *European Committee of the Regions (CoR, #06665)*. Member of: Local Economic and Employment Development Committee (LEED) Programme of *OECD (#17693)*. Cooperates with: *UNDP (#20292)*. **NGO Relations** Member of: *Spring Alliance (inactive)*. [2017/XF5808/**F**]

♦ Réseau Européen des Villes du Vin (RECEVIN) 18881

European Network of Wine Cities – Red Europea de Ciudades del Vino – Rede Europeia de Cidades do Vinho – Rette Europea delle Città del Vino

General Secretariat Plaça de l'Agora 1, 08720 Vilafranca del Penedès, Barcelona, Spain. T. +34938180137. Fax +34938171979. E-mail: recevin@recevin.eu.

Pres Via Annunziata, Palazzo Mosti, 82100 Benevento BN, Italy.

URL: http://www.recevin.eu/

History Began operations 1995. Formally set up 19 Nov 1999, Strasbourg (France). Former names and other names: *European Network of Wine Growing Towns* – alias; *European Association of Wine Cities* – alias. Registration: France. **Aims** Improve *living standards* of inhabitants of wine-growing towns through: promotion of "wine culture"; tourism; town planning; architectonic and rural heritage; social and historic heritage; employment; training. **Structure** General Assembly (annual); Board of Directors; Presidency; General Secretariat. **Languages** English, French, Spanish. **Staff** Part-time. **Finance** Members' dues (annual): euro 500. **Activities** Awards/prizes/competitions; training/education; knowledge management/information dissemination; advocacy/lobbying/activism. **Events** *General Assembly* Jerez de la Frontera (Spain) 2014, *General Assembly* Marsala (Italy) 2014, *General Assembly* Marsala (Italy) 2013, *General Assembly* Palmela (Portugal) 2012, *General Assembly* Logroño (Spain) 2011. **Publications** *Virtual Recevin Newsletter* (12 a year). *European Wine-Growing Cities Guide* (1999) in Italian, Spanish; *European Paper on Wine Tourism*; *The Vademecum on European Wine Tourism*. Reports; leaflets.

Members Wine-producing cities (71) in 9 countries of the European Union:
Austria, France, Germany, Greece, Hungary, Italy, Portugal, Slovenia, Spain.

NGO Relations Cooperates with: *Assembly of European Wine Regions (AREV, #02317)*; *Comité européen des entreprises vins (CEEV, #04157)*; *Wine in Moderation (WIM, #20967)*; national associations. [2020/XF5891/**F**]

- ♦ Réseau d'Europe occidentale sur le travail, le chômage et les Eglises / see Work and Economy Research Network in the European Churches (#21051)
- ♦ Réseau des Evaluateurs Environnementaux (#05502)
- ♦ Réseau express jeunes (#22017)
- ♦ Réseau FAO-CIHEAM de recherches coopératives sur les ovins et les caprins / see Inter-regional FAO-CIHEAM Network for Research and Development in Sheep and Goats (#15970)
- ♦ Réseau femise (#09731)
- ♦ Réseau des femmes africaines pour le développement et la communication (#00503)
- ♦ Réseau des Femmes Africaines pour la Gestion Communautaire des forêts (unconfirmed)
- ♦ Réseau des femmes ministres africaines et parlementaires (#16988)
- ♦ Réseau des femmes parlementaires des Amériques (#17065)
- ♦ Réseau foi et justice Afrique-Europe (#00171)
- ♦ Réseau foi et justice Europe – Afrique / see Africa-Europe Faith and Justice Network (#00171)
- ♦ Réseau de formation sur l'environnement en Amérique latine et des Caraïbes (inactive)
- ♦ Réseau pour la Formation Professionnelle dans le Secteur de la Construction en Europe / see REFORME (#18738)
- ♦ Réseau Français de Métabolomique et Fluxomique / see Réseau Francophone de Métabolomique et Fluxomique

♦ Réseau francophone des conseils de la magistrature judiciaire (RFCMJ) 18882

Registered Address 300 boulevard Jean-Lesage, bureau RC-01, Québec QC G1K 8K6, Canada. E-mail: inforeseau@cm.gouv.qc.ca.

URL: https://rfcmj.com/

Aims Promote cooperation through exchange of information, experience and knowledge. **Structure** General Assembly; Presidency; Bureau; General Secretariat.

Members Full in 22 countries and territories:
Andorra, Belgium, Benin, Burkina Faso, Canada, Central African Rep, Congo DR, Egypt, France, Gabon, Guinea, Haiti, Lebanon, Madagascar, Mali, Mauritania, Monaco, Morocco, Québec, Senegal, Togo, Tunisia.
Observer:
Organisation internationale de la Francophonie (OIF, #17809).

IGO Relations Partner of (1): *Organisation internationale de la Francophonie (OIF, #17809)*. [2021/AA2321/**F**]

- ♦ Réseau francophone de formation et de recherche sur la classification internationale du fonctionnement, du handicap et de la santé / see Groupe International Francophone pour la Formation aux Classifications du Handicap (#10749)

♦ Réseau francophone international pour la promotion de la santé (REFIPS) 18883

Sec 5455 Avenue de Gaspé, Bur 200, Montréal QC H2T 3B3, Canada. T. +15149371227. E-mail: coordination@refips.org.

Main Website: http://www.refips.org/

History 1992, Montréal, QC (Canada). Registration: Canada, Québec. **Aims** Reinforce health promotion in francophone countries through exchange and dissemination of competences and best practices. **Structure** General Assembly; Council. **Languages** French. **Activities** Events/meetings; training/education. All Francophone countries. **Events** *Séminaire* Bordeaux (France) 2007. **Publications** *Planifier pour mieux agir* (3rd ed 2020) by Lise Renaud in French; *25 ans d'histoire: les retombées de la Charte d'Ottawa pour la promotion de la santé dan divers pays francophones* (2012) in French; *Guide d'implantation de l'approche de la Santé dans Toutes les Politiques au palier local* by Alexis Jacques-Brisson and Louise St-Pierre in French; *Guide pratique Intervenir en promotion de la santé à l'aide de l'approche écologique* (2nd ed) by Lise Renaud and Ginette Lafontaine in French. *Glossaire des principaux concepts liés à l'équité en santé* (2022) in French; *Mesures environnementales pour améliorer la sécurité des piétons* (2022) in French; *Recueil des outils proposés dans le guide pratique Plaidoyer pour la santé* (2022); *Plaidoyer pour la santé: Un guide pratique* (2021) in French; *Renforcer les capacités d'adaptation des individus et des communautés en contexte de pandémie : le rôle clé du sentiment de cohérence* (2020) in French. **Members** Individuals (about 1,500). Membership countries not specified. [2022.06.30/XJ1522/**C**]

♦ Réseau francophone pour l'égalité femme-homme (RF-EFH) 18884

Coordinator Rue 2 x 207 Ngor Diarama, BP 7295, 12500 Dakar, Senegal. T. +221338201102.

URL: https://rf-efh.org/

History Oct 2013. Founded by *Organisation internationale de la Francophonie (OIF, #17809)*. **Aims** Federate the actions and expertise of Francophone INGOs and CSOs in contributing to the promotion of gender equality and women's empowerment in the countries of the Francophonie, in terms of reflection, advocacy and mobilisation within the Francosphone sphere and on the international scene. **Structure** General Assembly; Coordination. Thematic Groups.
Members Founding members include 9 organizations listed in this Yearbook:
African Women's Development and Communication Network (FEMNET, #00503); Aide et Action International Afrique (#00589); Association of African Women for Research and Development (AAWORD, #02362); Center of Arab Women for Training and Research, Tunis (CAWTAR, #03637); Environnement et développement du Tiers-monde (enda, #05510); Forum for African Women Educationalists (FAWE, #09896); International Federation for Human Rights (#13452); The World According to Women; Women in Law and Development in Africa-Afrique de l'Ouest (WiLDAF-AO, #21005).
Members include 3 organizations listed in this Yearbook:
Canadian Centre for International Studies and Cooperation (CECI); Inter-African Committee on Traditional Practices Affecting the Health of Women and Children (IAC, #11384); Réseau des Organisations Féminines d'Afrique Francophone (ROFAF, #18900).
Observers.
IGO Relations Partner of (3): *Economic Community of West African States (ECOWAS, #05312); Organisation internationale de la Francophonie (OIF, #17809); TV5Monde (TV5, #20269).* **NGO Relations** Partner of (3): *Agence universitaire de La Francophonie (AUF, #00548); Assemblée parlementaire de la Francophonie (APF, #02312); Association Internationale des Maires et responsables des capitales et métropoles partiellement ou entièrement Francophones (AIMF, #02715).* [2023/AA2316/y/**F**]

♦ Réseau Francophone de Métabolomique et Fluxomique (internationally oriented national body)
♦ Réseau Francophone de recherche sur l'intersexuation (unconfirmed)

♦ Réseau francophone des régulateurs des médias (REFRAM) 18885

Address not obtained.
URL: https://www.refram.org/
History 1 Jul 2007, Ouagadougou (Burkina Faso). Founded with the support of *Organisation internationale de la Francophonie (OIF, #17809)*. **Aims** Consolidate the rule of law, democracy and human rights. **Structure** President; Secretariat.
Members Members (30) in 30 countries:
Albania, Belgium, Benin, Bulgaria, Burkina Faso, Burundi, Cameroon, Canada, Central African Rep, Chad, Comoros, Congo Brazzaville, Congo DR, Côte d'Ivoire, Djibouti, France, Gabon, Guinea, Lebanon, Luxembourg, Mali, Mauritania, Moldova, Morocco, Niger, Romania, Senegal, Switzerland, Togo, Tunisia.
Observer:
Organisation internationale de la Francophonie (OIF, #17809). [2022/AA2318/**F**]

♦ Réseau francophone de la régulation des télécommunications (FRATEL) 18886

Executive Secretariat 7 square Max Hymans, 75730 Paris CEDEX 15, France. T. +33140477228. E-mail: fratel@fratel.org.
URL: http://www.fratel.org/
History 28 Oct 2003, Bamako (Mali). Set up 28 oct 2003, Bamako (Mali), following symposium held Jun 2002, Paris (France), which resulted in a final "Declaration". **Aims** Establish and strengthen collaboration. **Structure** Coordinating Committee; Executive Secretariat. **Languages** French. **Staff** 0.70 FTE, paid. **Finance** No budget. Members are responsible for their own expenses. **Activities** Networking/liaising; knowledge management/information dissemination; training/education; events/meetings. **Events** *Réunion Annuelle* Paris (France) 2020, *Séminaire* Paris (France) 2020, *Réunion Annuelle* Bucharest (Romania) 2019, *Séminaire* Douala (Cameroon) 2019, *Réunion Annuelle* Paris (France) 2018. **Publications** Reports.
Members Telecommunication regulators of 48 countries and territories:
Albania, Algeria, Belgium, Benin, Bulgaria, Burkina Faso, Burundi, Cambodia, Cameroon, Canada, Cape Verde, Central African Rep, Chad, Comoros, Congo Brazzaville, Congo DR, Côte d'Ivoire, Djibouti, Dominican Rep, Egypt, Gabon, Guinea, Guinea-Bissau, Haiti, Laos, Lebanon, Luxembourg, Madagascar, Mali, Mauritania, Mauritius, Moldova, Monaco, Morocco, New Caledonia, Niger, Poland, Polynesia Fr, Romania, Rwanda, Senegal, Seychelles, St Lucia, Switzerland, Thailand, Togo, Tunisia, Vietnam.
IGO Relations *European Commission (EC, #06633); International Telecommunication Union (ITU, #15673); Organisation internationale de la Francophonie (OIF, #17809).* [2017.07.19/XM5907/**F***]

♦ Réseau francophone des sciences vasculaires (RFSV) 18887

Pres Clinique du Parisis, 15 avenue de la Libération, 95240 Cormeilles-en-Parisis, France. T. +33139317480.
Events *Journées internationales francophones d'angéiologie* Paris (France) 2007, *Journées internationales francophones d'angéiologie* Paris (France) 2006, *Journées internationales francophones d'angéiologie* Paris (France) 2003. **Members** Membership countries not specified. [2010/XF6988/**F**]

♦ Réseau Francophone des Villes Amies des Aînés (internationally oriented national body)
♦ Réseau des geoparks européens (#07389)
♦ Réseau global sur la gestion des ressources en eau en zones arides et semi-arides (#20826)
♦ Réseau des Gouvernements Régionaux pour le Développement Durable / see Regions4 Sustainable Development (#18819)

♦ Réseau habitat et francophonie (RHF) 18888

SG 14 rue Lord Byron, 75384 Paris CEDEX 08, France. T. +33140755083 – +33140755077. Fax +33140755056. E-mail: rhf@habitatfrancophonie.org.
URL: http://www.habitatfrancophonie.org/
History 4 Dec 1987, Paris (France), as *Association des organismes d'habitat social pour le développement d'un réseau international de coopération.* Present name adopted 15 Nov 1996, Montpellier (France). Registered in accordance with French law. **Aims** Develop an international cooperative network among organizations dealing with *social housing* for sharing of know-how and links; defend principles and the application of the right to housing in order to allow access to suitable housing and accessible price for people and families with modest incomes; take an active part in the blossoming of the francophonie in the world; help to break professional or linguistic isolation; act as a place of exchanges and reflection; facilitate twinning among members and promote joint activities. **Structure** General Assembly (annual); Council; Bureau. **Languages** French. **Staff** 2.00 FTE, paid. **Finance** Members' dues. Subsidies. **Activities** Events/meetings; advocacy/lobbying/activism. **Events** *International Conference* Saint-Denis (Réunion) 2016, *International Conference* Rabat (Morocco) 2015, *International Conference* Arras (France) 2014, *International Conference* Gatineau, QC (Canada) 2013, *International Conference* Liège (Belgium) 2012. **Publications** *Revue Habitat et Francophonie – Spécial Réunion* (2016). Annual Report; conference proceedings.
Members Honorary; active. Organizations and companies in 15 countries:
Belgium, Cameroon, Canada, Central African Rep, Congo Brazzaville, Congo DR, Côte d'Ivoire, France, Gabon, Madagascar, Mali, Mauritania, Morocco, Senegal, Tunisia.
IGO Relations "Consultative Status" with: *United Nations Human Settlements Programme (UN-Habitat, #20572).* Formal arrangement with: *European Commission (EC, #06633).* **NGO Relations** Member of: *European Housing Forum (EHF, #07504).* [2016.06.17/XF5778/**F**]

♦ Réseau ibéro-américain de Fôrets Modèles / see Red Iberoamericana de Bosques Modelo (#18659)
♦ Réseau ibéro-américain de terminologie (#18685)
♦ Réseau Infojeunesse de l'UNESCO / see INFOYOUTH – Worldwide Information Network on Youth Related Issues (#11204)
♦ Réseau d'information pour l'Asie et le Pacifique sur les plantes médicinales et aromatiques (no recent information)
♦ Réseau d'information sur la biodiversité inter-américaine / see Inter-American Biodiversity Information Network (#11402)
♦ Réseau d'information, documentation et conseil en bâtiment / see Building Advisory Service and Information Network (#03351)
♦ Réseau d'information sur l'éducation en Europe (inactive)
♦ Réseau d'information sur les migrations internationales (internationally oriented national body)
♦ Réseau d'information des terres arides de l'Afrique de l'est (#01105)
♦ Réseau d'information Tiers-monde (internationally oriented national body)
♦ Réseau d'information Tiers-Monde des centres de documentation pour le développement (internationally oriented national body)
♦ Réseau informel régional des organisations non gouvernementales des Nations Unies (#20573)
♦ Réseau d'innovation éducative pour le développement en Afrique (no recent information)
♦ Réseau des instances africaines de régulation de la communication (#00259)
♦ Réseau des instances de régulation méditerranéennes (#16665)
♦ Réseau des Institutions Nationales Africaines des Droits de l'Homme (#16984)
♦ Réseau pour l'Intégration des Femmes des Organisations Non Gouvernementales et Associations Africaines (unconfirmed)
♦ Réseau inter-agences pour l'éducation en situations d'urgence (#11387)
♦ Réseau interaméricain de protection de l'environnement (no recent information)
♦ Réseau intercontinental de promotion de l'économie sociale et solidaire (#11463)
♦ Réseau interinstitutions pour les femmes et l'égalité des sexes (#11388)
♦ Réseau inter-islamique d'agriculture biosaline (#11506)
♦ Réseau inter-islamique pour l'energie renouvelable (#11510)
♦ Réseau inter-islamique de génie génétique et de la biotechnologie (#11507)
♦ Réseau inter-islamique de science et technologie de l'océanographie (#11514)
♦ Réseau inter-islamique de la technologie informatique (#11508)
♦ Réseau international d'accès aux publications scientifiques (#14233)
♦ Réseau international des amis de la terre / see Friends of the Earth International (#10002)
♦ Réseau international pour l'analyse des réseaux sociaux (#14326)
♦ Réseau international des centres de formations aux métiers de l'eau (#14341)

♦ Réseau International des Chaires Senghor de la Francophonie 18889

SG Chaire Senghor de l'Univ Jean Moulin Lyon 3, Inst Intl pour la Francophonie (2IF), 1C avenue des Frères Lumière – CS 78242, 69372 Lyon CEDEX 08, France.
URL: https://www.chaires-senghor.com/
History Registration: RNA, No/ID: W691092241, Start date: 2017, France. **Aims** Network the francophone territories so as to train in the institutional Francophonie; observe and work independently on the Francophonie. **Structure** Bureau.
Members Senghor chairs in 14 countries:
Armenia, Cameroon, Canada, Egypt, France, Gabon, Italy, Lebanon, Morocco, Romania, Senegal, Türkiye, USA, Vietnam.
IGO Relations Accredited by (1): *Organisation internationale de la Francophonie (OIF, #17809).* [2022/AA2371/**F**]

♦ Réseau international des Cités des métiers 18890

Cités des métiers International Network
International Coordinator Cité des Sciences et de l'Industrie, 30 avenue Corentin-Cariou, 75930 Paris CEDEX 19, France. E-mail: info@reseaucitesdesmetiers.com.
SG address not obtained.
URL: https://www.reseaucitesdesmetiers.org/
History 18 Oct 2001, France. Current statutes adopted 31 Mar 2016. Registration: RNA, No/ID: W751151640, Start date: 1 Aug 2017, France. **Structure** General Assembly; Executive Committee; Permanent Assembly of Managers; Strategic Council. **Publications** *Cités des métiers International Network NewsLetter.* **NGO Relations** Member of (1): *Lifelong Learning Platform – European Civil Society for Education (LLLP, #16466).* [2021/XM6572/**F**]

♦ Réseau international de la concurrence (#12832)
♦ Réseau international de contrôle de la commercialisation / see International Consumer Protection and Enforcement Network (#12930)
♦ Réseau international de contrôle et de protection des consommateurs (#12930)
♦ Réseau international de droit de l'environnement (#05504)
♦ Réseau international pour les droits des aborigènes australiens (internationally oriented national body)
♦ Réseau international pour les droits économiques, sociaux et culturels (#14255)

♦ Réseau International des Droits Humains (RIDH) 18891

International Network of Human Rights (INHR) – Red Internacional de Derechos Humanos (RIDH)
Dir Rue Gardiol 8, Case Postale 158, 1218 Le Grand-Saconnex GE, Switzerland. T. +41227322189. E-mail: info@ridh.org.
URL: http://ridh.org/
History Jun 2008. **Structure** General Assembly; Executive Committee. Includes: *International Network of Human Rights | Europe (RIDHE, #14286).* **Activities** Advocacy/lobbying/activism; knowledge management/information dissemination; research/documentation; training/education.
Members Full in 9 countries:
Argentina, Chile, Colombia, Guatemala, Guyana, Mexico, Nicaragua, Uruguay, Venezuela.
Consultative Status Consultative status granted from: *ECOSOC (#05331)* (Special). [2022/XJ9936/**F**]

♦ Réseau International des Droits Humains | Europe (#14286)

♦ Réseau international d'écoles doctorales en sociologie/sciences sociales (RéDoc) 18892

Pres Univ de Namur, Rue de Bruxelles 61, 5000 Namur, Belgium. E-mail: coordination.redoc@aislf.org.
URL: https://aislf.org/redoc-presentation
History Founded by *Association internationale des sociologues de langue française (AISLF, #02744)*, with the aid of *Agence universitaire de La Francophonie (AUF, #00548).* **Aims** Encourage doctoral training in sociology/social science in francophone countries. **Structure** Scientific Committee. Secretariat. **Languages** French. **Staff** 0.50 FTE, paid; 4.00 FTE, voluntary. **Finance** Financed by participating universities and by *Agence universitaire de La Francophonie (AUF, #00548).* Budget (annual): about US$ 50,000. **Activities** Organizes: training sessions; annual summer university with one of the member doctoral schools. **Events** *Summer University* Brussels (Belgium) 2014, *Summer University* Aix-en-Provence (France) 2013, *Summer University* Tunis (Tunisia) 2012, *Summer University* Montréal, QC (Canada) 2011, *Summer University* Lausanne (Switzerland) 2010.
Members Universities in 16 countries:
Belgium, Bulgaria, Cameroon, Canada, Congo Brazzaville, Congo DR, France, Gabon, Greece, Lebanon, Madagascar, Morocco, Senegal, Switzerland, Tunisia, Türkiye. [2022/XJ1867/**E**]

♦ Réseau internationale pour le développement de l'aviculture familiale (#14267)
♦ Réseau International de l'Enseignement Protestant (internationally oriented national body)
♦ Réseau international des femmes contre le tabac (#14344)
♦ Réseau International de Foresterie Analogue (#11650)
♦ Réseau international de Forêts Modèles (#14175)
♦ Réseau international de formation et de recherche en éducation permanente / see Réseau international de Recherche en éducation et en formation (#18896)
♦ Réseau international des formations aux métiers de la forêt (#05375)
♦ Réseau international francophone d'aménagement linguistique (inactive)

♦ Réseau international francophone des établissements de formation de formateurs (RIFEFF) 18893

Coordinator Fac des sciences de l'éducation, Univ de Montréal, CP 6128, Succursale Centre-ville, Montréal QC H3C 3J7, Canada. E-mail: info@rifeff.org.
URL: http://www.rifeff.org/

History 2003. Institutional network member of *Agence universitaire de La Francophonie (AUF, #00548).* Provisionally registered in accordance with Canadian law. **Aims** Promote cooperation and solidarity between francophone institutions working for the training of trainers, so as to contribute to the improvement of the quality of education and professionalization of education. **Structure** General Assembly; Board; Executive Office. **Languages** French. **Staff** 12.00 FTE, voluntary. **Finance** Members' dues. Subsidies from public and private sector, including *Agence universitaire de La Francophonie (AUF, #00548)*; donations. Budget (annual): euro 100,000. **Activities** Training/education; knowledge management/information dissemination; monitoring/evaluation; networking/liaising; politics/policy/regulatory; projects/programmes; publishing activities; research and development; events/meetings. Active in member countries. **Events** *Colloquium* Oran (Algeria) 2019, *Colloquium* Cergy-Pontoise (France) 2018, *Colloquium* Patras (Greece) 2015, *Colloquium* Hanoi (Vietnam) 2013, *Colloquium* Beirut (Lebanon) 2011. **Publications** *Bulletin de liaison.*
Members Institutions (95) in 38 countries:
Algeria, Armenia, Belgium, Benin, Burkina Faso, Burundi, Cameroon, Canada, Central African Rep, Chad, Colombia, Comoros, Congo Brazzaville, Congo DR, Côte d'Ivoire, Djibouti, France, Gabon, Greece, Guinea, Haiti, Jordan, Lebanon, Madagascar, Mali, Mauritania, Mauritius, Morocco, New Caledonia, Niger, Poland, Romania, Russia, Senegal, Switzerland, Togo, Tunisia, Vietnam.
Included in the above, 1 organization listed in this Yearbook:
Beirut Arab University (BAU). [2019/XM1551/E]

♦ Réseau international francophone de formation policière (FRANCOPOL) 18894

Secretariat 1701 rue Parthenais, Montréal QC H2K 3S7, Canada. T. +15145963220. Fax +15145906885. E-mail: info@francopol.org.
URL: http://www.francopol.org/
History Officially set up 8 Sep 2008, Québec QC (Canada). **Aims** Promote sharing of best practices, as well as research in the field of police training and expertise. **Structure** General Assembly; International Bureau; Executive Committee; Council of Elders; Secretariat. **Events** *Congrès International* Montréal, QC (Canada) 2021, *Congrès International* Montréal, QC (Canada) 2020, *Congrès International* Dakar (Senegal) 2018, *Congrès International* Montreux (Switzerland) 2015, *Congrès International* Mons (Belgium) 2013.
Members Organizations in 23 countries:
Belgium, Benin, Burkina Faso, Burundi, Cameroon, Canada, Cape Verde, Côte d'Ivoire, Egypt, France, Gabon, Guinea, Haiti, Luxembourg, Mali, Mauritania, Monaco, Niger, Senegal, Spain, Switzerland, Togo, USA. [2022/XJ4875/F]

♦ Réseau international francophone pour la responsabilité sociale en santé (RIFRESS) 18895

SG address not obtained. E-mail: secretariat@rifress.org.
URL: https://rifress.org/
History 2018. **Aims** Bring together academic institutions related to the training of future health care providers to define their social responsibility. **Structure** General Assembly; Board of Directors; General Secretariat. Scientific Committee. **Activities** Advocacy/lobbying/activism; events/meetings; networking/liaising; research/documentation; training/education. **Events** *Congrès International* Brussels (Belgium) 2022. **Publications** *RIFRESS Bulletin* in French. [2022/AA2830/C]

- ♦ Réseau international des groupes d'action pour l'alimentation infantile (#12305)
- ♦ Réseau international pour les hôpitaux sans tabac / see Anti-Smoking International Alliance (#00861)
- ♦ Réseau international d'information sur le blanchiment de l'argent (#14181)
- ♦ Réseau international d'information chimique (#12542)
- ♦ Réseau international d'information concernant l'enseignement des sciences et de la technologie (inactive)
- ♦ Réseau international des instituts Pasteur / see Pasteur Network (#18256)
- ♦ Réseau international des instituts Pasteur et instituts associés / see Pasteur Network (#18256)
- ♦ Réseau international de jeunes chercheurs en histoire de l'intégration européenne (#14739)
- ♦ Réseau international de jeunes journalistes (#14346)
- ♦ Réseau international de journalisme d'investigation (#10433)
- ♦ Réseau international des journaux de rue / see International Network of Street Papers (#14330)
- ♦ Réseau International des Juristes Africanistes (unconfirmed)
- ♦ Réseau international d'organisations d'entraide et de lutte contre le SIDA / see ICASO (#11040)
- ♦ Réseau international des organismes de bassin (#14235)
- ♦ Réseau international des organismes de promotion de la qualité en enseignement supérieur (#14312)
- ♦ Réseau international pour les petites et moyennes entreprises (#14325)
- ♦ Réseau International pour la Planification et l'Amélioration de la Qualité et la Sécurité dans les systèmes de santé en Afrique (#14304)
- ♦ Réseau international sur la politique culturelle (#14246)
- ♦ Réseau international pour la promotion du volontariat / see Volonteurope (#20807)

♦ Réseau international de Recherche en éducation et en formation (RÉF) 18896

International Education and Training Research Network
Address not obtained.
URL: http://refmontreal2015.com/
History 1989, taking the shape of meetings and gatherings for French-speaking education professionals. Previously referred to as *Réseau international de formation et de recherche en éducation permanente (RIFRED).* **Aims** Highlight diversity and complementarity of research and practice in education and training; facilitate, intensify and promote connections between individuals and entities concerned by education and research training (researchers, teachers, decision-makers); promote international cooperation in the area of education and training by means of the *French language.* **Structure** Informal structure. Network coordinated by the unit responsible for the upcoming meeting. **Finance** Meetings are self-financed. **Activities** Events/meetings. **Events** *Meeting* Montréal, QC (Canada) 2015, *Meeting* Louvain-la-Neuve (Belgium) 2011, *Meeting* Sherbrooke, QC (Canada) 2007, *Meeting* Geneva (Switzerland) 2003, *Meeting* Toulouse (France) 1998. **Publications** Studies; proceedings.
Members Individuals in 4 countries:
Belgium, Canada, France, Switzerland. [2016/XF3503/v/F]

- ♦ Réseau international de recherche en tourisme polaire (#14608)
- ♦ Réseau international de systèmes de données sur l'alimentation (#14271)
- ♦ Réseau international de terminologie (#14332)
- ♦ Réseau international de travailleurs sociaux de rue (internationally oriented national body)
- ♦ Réseau International des Universités Libres (unconfirmed)
- ♦ Réseau international pour l'usage rationnel des médicaments (#14313)
- ♦ Réseau international des villes du bien vivre / see Cittaslow (#03958)
- ♦ Réseau islamique de développement et de gestion des ressources hydrauliques (#11513)
- ♦ Réseau jésuite africain contre le SIDA (#00348)
- ♦ Réseau de Jeunes Catholiques pour un Environnement durable en Afrique (#03611)
- ♦ Réseau des Jeunes Entrepreneurs pour l'Emergence de l'Afrique (internationally oriented national body)
- ♦ Réseau judiciaire européen (#07615)
- ♦ Réseau judiciaire européen en matière civile et commerciale (#07616)
- ♦ Réseau kidlink / see Kidlink Association (#16189)
- ♦ Réseau latinoaméricain de botanique (#16362)
- ♦ Réseau latinoaméricaine d'action climatique (#04002)
- ♦ Réseau latinoaméricain pour l'information technologique (see: #19294)
- ♦ Réseau latino-américain des organismes de bassin (#16351)
- ♦ Réseau latinoaméricain de sciences biologiques (#18706)
- ♦ Réseau latinoaméricain de socio-economie solidaire (#18720)
- ♦ Réseau pour l'excellence de l'enseignement supérieur en Afrique de l'Ouest (unconfirmed)

♦ Réseau Lexicologie, Terminologie, Traduction (Réseau LTT) 18897

Registered Office ULB – Centre de recherche Tradital, Rue Joseph Hazard 34, 1180 Brussels, Belgium. E-mail: contact@reseau-ltt.net.
URL: https://www.reseau-ltt.net/
History A research network of *Agence universitaire de La Francophonie (AUF, #00548)* until 2010, when it became an international association. Registration: Banque-Carrefour des Entreprises, No/ID: 0841.715.025, Start date: 12 Dec 2011, Belgium. **Aims** Support and promote research, publication and training in the network's fields of competence by providing technological support to cope with human, social, political and economic developments; ensure the production of reference tools in general and specialized languages. **Structure** General Assembly; Board of Directors; Bureau.
Members Full in 12 countries:
Belgium, Canada, France, Italy, Lebanon, Morocco, Portugal, Rwanda, Senegal, Slovakia, Spain, Tunisia.
NGO Relations Cooperates with (1): *European Association for Terminology (EAFT, #06252).* [2022/AA2918/F]

- ♦ Réseau LGBTQI francophone international (unconfirmed)
- ♦ Réseau liberal africain (#00187)
- ♦ **Réseau LTT** Réseau Lexicologie, Terminologie, Traduction (#18897)

♦ Réseau maghrebin d'associations de développement local en milieu rural (REMADEL) 18898

Exec Sec 4 rue Er-Rachidia, 4100 Médenine, Tunisia. T. +21698455520. Fax +21675649866. E-mail: remadel_maghreb@yahoo.fr.
URL: http://www.remadel.org/
History 2 Apr 2008. **Aims** Promote global Maghreb development on a local level. **Structure** Coordination Committee; Executive Secretariat. **Languages** French. **Staff** None paid. **Finance** No budget. **Activities** Active in North Africa.
Members Full in 4 countries:
Algeria, Mauritania, Morocco, Tunisia. [2021.05.23/XM4995/F]

- ♦ Réseau Medcités (#16610)
- ♦ Réseau médicaments et développement (internationally oriented national body)
- ♦ Réseau Méditerranéen des Centres de Formation aux Métiers de l'Eau (#16666)

♦ Réseau méditerranéen des écoles d'ingénieurs (RMEI) 18899

Mediterranean Engineering Schools Network
Gen Delegate Ecole Centrale Marseille, Technopôle Château-Gombert, 38 rue Joliot Curie, 13451 Marseille CEDEX 20, France. T. +33491054509. E-mail: secretariat@rmei.info.
URL: http://www.rmei.info/
History Jun 1997, Marseille (France). Registration: RNA, No/ID: W133005365, Start date: 25 Apr 2007, France. **Aims** Give students a positive image of higher education and research in the Mediterranean countries. **Structure** President. Colleges, including *Réseau méditerranéen des écoles de management (RMEM, inactive).* Working Groups (3). **Languages** English, French. **Staff** 2.00 FTE, paid. **Activities** Training/education; awareness raising; networking/liaising; capacity building. **Events** *General Assembly* Marseille (France) 2021, *General Assembly* Monastir (Tunisia) / Sousse (Tunisia) 2020, *General assembly* Rome (Italy) 2019, *General Assembly* Marrakech (Morocco) 2018, *General assembly* Barcelona (Spain) 2017.
Members Institutes, schools and universities (100) in 16 countries:
Algeria, Armenia, Egypt, France, Greece, Israel, Italy, Jordan, Lebanon, Libya, Montenegro, Morocco, Spain, Syrian AR, Tunisia, Türkiye.
Included in the above, 2 organizations listed in this Yearbook:
Community of Mediterranean Universities (CMU, #04403); Université de la Méditerranée, Marseille.
NGO Relations Member of (1): *Engineering Association of Mediterranean Countries (EAMC, #05480).* [2020/XM2327/y/F]

- ♦ Réseau méditerranéen de Forêts Modèles (#16662)
- ♦ Réseau Méditerranéen des Organismes de Bassin (#16664)
- ♦ Réseau michée / see Micah Global (#16741)
- ♦ Réseau de microfinance (#16746)
- ♦ Réseau mondial d'alerte et d'action en cas d'épidémie (#10521)
- ♦ Réseau mondial Crescendo (#04950)
- ♦ Réseau mondial pour la diversité linguistique (#21671)
- ♦ Réseau mondial des femmes pour les droits sur la reproduction (#21019)
- ♦ Réseau mondial pour l'innovation dans l'enseignement supérieur (#10641)
- ♦ Réseau de la Mondialisation du Droit (internationally oriented national body)
- ♦ Réseau mondial d'observateurs nationaux des élections (#10487)
- ♦ Réseau Mondial de l'OMS des Villes et Communautés Amies des Aînés (#20937)
- ♦ Réseau mondial des Organisations de la Société civile pour la réduction des catastrophes (#10485)
- ♦ Réseau mondial de réserves de biosphère (#21669)
- ♦ Réseau mondial pour la triarticulation sociale (#10501)
- ♦ Réseau océanien de surveillance de la santé publique (#17993)
- ♦ Réseau Océan Mondial (#21681)
- ♦ Réseau ORBICOM / see ORBICOM – International Network of UNESCO Chairs in Communication (#17785)
- ♦ Réseau des organisations de bassin d'Amérique du Nord (internationally oriented national body)

♦ Réseau des Organisations Féminines d'Afrique Francophone (ROFAF) 18900

Network of Francophone Africa Women's Organizations
Founder/Exec Dir Quartier Attiégou, Boulevard du Zio, Angle Rues 238 et 393 No12, 03 BP 30888, Lomé, Togo. T. +22822615858 – +22822615856. E-mail: rofaf@rofaf.org.
URL: http://www.rofaf.org/
History 28 Jul 2006. Registered in accordance with the law of Togo. **Aims** Mobilize financial resources for women's rights work in Francophone Africa. **Structure** Executive Management. **Languages** French. **Staff** 12.00 FTE, paid. **Finance** Donations; private sources. **Activities** Knowledge management/information dissemination; capacity building; financial and/or material support; advocacy/lobbying; activism. Active in: Benin, Burundi, Congo DR, Côte d'Ivoire, Mali, Niger, Senegal, Togo. **Publications** *ROFAF News* (6 a year); *Tribune* (2 a year) – newsletter.
Members Organizations (over 130) in 17 countries:
Benin, Burkina Faso, Burundi, Cameroon, Central African Rep, Chad, Congo Brazzaville, Congo DR, Côte d'Ivoire, Gabon, Guinea, Mali, Mauritania, Niger, Rwanda, Senegal, Togo.
Consultative Status Consultative status granted from: *ECOSOC (#05331)* (Special). **IGO Relations** *Economic Community of West African States (ECOWAS, #05312); Organisation internationale de la Francophonie (OIF, #17809); Union économique et monétaire Ouest africaine (UEMOA, #20377).* **NGO Relations** Partners include: *African Women's Development Fund (AWDF, #00504); Association for Women's Rights in Development (AWID, #02980); Global Fund for Women (GFW, #10384); Mama Cash (#16560); Oxfam Novib.* [2017.03.09/XJ9935/F]

- ♦ Réseau des organisations paysannes et des producteurs agricoles de l'Afrique de l'Ouest (#20891)
- ♦ Réseau des Organisations de Solidarité Internationale Côte d'Ivoire (internationally oriented national body)
- ♦ Réseau Ouest Africain des Défenseurs des Droits Humains (#20882)
- ♦ Réseau ouest africain pour la sécurité et la gouvernance démocratique (#20892)
- ♦ Réseau de l'ouest et du centre de l'Afrique recherche opérationnelle (inactive)
- ♦ Réseau Pan-Africain de la Société Civile (#18045)
- ♦ Réseau panafricain de télécommunications (no recent information)
- ♦ Réseau Panafrican pour la Défense des Droits des Migrants (unconfirmed)

♦ Réseau panlatin de terminologie (Realiter) 18901

Pan-Latin Terminology Network – Red Panlatina de Terminologia – Rede Panlatina de Terminologia – Rede Panlatina de Terminoloxia – Rete Panlatina di Terminologia – Reteaua Panlatina de Terminologie – Xarxa Panllatina de Terminologia

SG Largo Gemelli 1, 20123 Milan MI, Italy. T. +39272345724. Fax +39272345731. E-mail: realiter@unicatt.it.
URL: http://www.realiter.net/

History Dec 1993, Paris (France). **Aims** Support common language policies for *neo-latin languages*; promote neo-latin terminologies; study specialized terminologies and promote diachronic and synchronic researches in neo-latin languages. **Structure** General Assembly; Executive Committee; Secretariat; Working Groups. **Languages** Catalan, French, Galician, Italian, Portuguese, Romanian, Spanish. **Staff** 4.00 FTE, paid. **Finance** Sources: Délégation générale à la langue française et aux langues de France; Osservatorio di Terminologia e Politiche Linguistiche (OPTL – Università Cattolica del Sacro Cuore); Associazione Italiana per la Terminologia. Annual budget: about euro 12,000. **Activities** Events/meetings; publishing activities. **Events** *Plenary Meeting* Brussels (Belgium) 2015, *Plenary Meeting* Bucharest (Romania) 2014, *Plenary Meeting* Paris (France) 2013, *Plenary Meeting* Milan (Italy) 2012, *Plenary Meeting* Québec, QC (Canada) 2011. **Publications** Lexicons; glossaries; proceedings.

Members Individuals and organizations in 16 countries:
Argentina, Belgium, Brazil, Canada, Chile, Colombia, Cuba, France, Italy, Mexico, Moldova, Peru, Portugal, Romania, Spain, Switzerland.

NGO Relations In liaison with technical committees of: *International Organization for Standardization (ISO, #14473).* [2019.12.11/XF6928/y/**F**]

- ♦ Réseau parlementaire sur la Banque mondiale / see Parliamentary Network on the World Bank and International Monetary Fund (#18219)
- ♦ Réseau parlementaire pour le désarmement nucléaire (#18210)
- ♦ Réseau des Petits États insulaires en développement (#19315)
- ♦ Réseau Pharmaceutique Oecuménique (#05350)

♦ Réseau des Plate-formes nationales d'ONG d'Afrique de l'Ouest et du Centre (REPAOC) 18902

Secretariat Liberté VI Extension, Immeuble Soda Marième – 4ème étage, BP 47485 Liberté, Dakar, Senegal. T. +221338277646 – +22133(221772333387. E-mail: guy@repaoc.org – info@repaoc.org.
URL: http://www.repaoc.org/

History Current statutes approved 19 Feb 2007, Nairobi (Kenya). Registered in accordance with Senegalese law. **Aims** Work collectively in the fight against poverty and promotion of human rights at regional and international level in the context of increasing inequality North-South but also South-South. **Structure** General Assembly; Board of Directors; Executive Office; Permanent Secretariat. **Languages** English, French. **Staff** 4.00 FTE, paid. **Finance** Financed through projects with: *European Exiled Journalists (no recent information); Gavi – The Vaccine Alliance (Gavi, #10077).* Annual subsidy from *Coordination SUD*. Annual budget: euro 75,000. **Activities** Projects/programmes. **Publications** Reports; studies.

Members NGOs in 15 countries:
Benin, Burkina Faso, Cape Verde, Côte d'Ivoire, Gambia, Ghana, Guinea, Guinea-Bissau, Liberia, Mali, Niger, Nigeria, Senegal, Sierra Leone, Togo.

Consultative Status Consultative status granted from: *ECOSOC (#05331)* (Special). **IGO Relations** *African Union (AU, #00488); ECOSOC (#05331).* **NGO Relations** Member of: *Civil Society Platform for Peacebuilding and Statebuilding (CSPPS, #03970);* Consultative Group of Civil Society of *UHC2030 (#20277); Gavi – The Vaccine Alliance (Gavi, #10077)* CSO Constituency; *Forus (#09934).* Partners with: *Organisation d'Afrique francophone pour le Renforcement des Systèmes de Santé et de la Vaccination (OAFRESS); Réseau des Plateformes des ONG de l'Afrique Centrale (REPONGAC, #18903).* Cooperates with: *Confédération européenne des ong d'urgence et de développement (CONCORD, #04547).* [2019.12.12/XJ5906/**F**]

♦ Réseau des Plateformes des ONG de l'Afrique Centrale (REPONGAC) 18903

Address not obtained.
URL: http://www.repongac.org/

History 27 Mar 2008, Brazzaville (Congo Brazzaville). **Structure** General Assembly.

Members NGOs in 6 countries:
Angola, Central African Rep, Chad, Congo Brazzaville, Congo DR, Rwanda.

NGO Relations Member of: *Forus (#09934).* Partners with: *Coordination SUD; Réseau des Plate-formes nationales d'ONG d'Afrique de l'Ouest et du Centre (REPAOC, #18902).* [2012/XJ5905/**F**]

♦ Réseau sur les Politiques de Pêche en Afrique de l'Ouest (REPAO) . 18904

Exec Sec Sicap Liberté IV villa No 5000, BP 47076 Liberté, Dakar, Senegal. T. +221338252787. Fax +221338252799. E-mail: repao@orange.sn.
URL: http://repao.org/

History 2005. **Structure** General Assembly. Board of Directors of 7. Executive Secretariat. [2017/XJ4803/**F**]

- ♦ Réseau des présidents des cours suprêmes judiciaires de l'Union Européenne (#17051)

♦ Réseau de prévention des crises alimentaires (RPCA) 18905

Food Crisis Prevention Network

Admin c/o CSAO/OCDE, 2 rue André-Pascal, 75775 Paris CEDEX 16, France. T. +33145248281. Fax +33144306238.
URL: http://www.food-security.net/

History Founded Jan 1985, Nouakchott (Mauritania), on the initiative of *Sahel and West Africa Club (SWAC, #19034)* and *Comité permanent inter-Etats de lutte contre la sécheresse dans le Sahel (CILSS, #04195)*, under the original title: *Network for the Prevention of Food Crisis in the Sahel – Réseau de prévention des crises alimentaires dans le Sahel. Food Aid Charter – Charte de l'aide alimentaire* adopted by member states of Club de Sahel and CILSS and approved, 10 Feb 1990, Guinea-Bissau, by summit of CILSS Heads of State. Charter for food crises prevention and management adopted 17 Nov 2011, Conakry (Guinea) by *Economic Community of West African States (ECOWAS, #05312)* member states, Chad and Mauritania, and approved by ECOWAS Ordinary Heads of States and Government Summit, Feb 2012, Abuja (Nigeria). **Aims** Offer an open platform for consultation, coordination, dialogue, analysis and action around food and nutritional security issues in the Sahel and West Africa. **Structure** Under the political leadership of *Economic Community of West African States (ECOWAS, #05312)* and *Union économique et monétaire Ouest africaine (UEMOA, #20377).* Co-facilitated by: *Sahel and West Africa Club (SWAC, #19034)* Secretariat and *Comité permanent inter-Etats de lutte contre la sécheresse dans le Sahel (CILSS, #04195).* **Languages** English, French. **Staff** No independent staff; staff through SWAC and CILSS Secretariats: 4 FTE. **Finance** Annual budget: about euro 110,000. **Activities** Events/meetings; knowledge management/information dissemination; advocacy/lobbying/activism; politics/policy/regulatory. **Events** *Annual Meeting* Banjul (Gambia) 2018, *Annual Meeting* Cotonou (Benin) 2017, *Annual Meeting* Abuja (Nigeria) 2016, *Annual Meeting* Dakar (Senegal) 2015, *Special Session* Milan (Italy) 2015. **Publications** *RPCA News* (4 a year); *RPCA Policy Note (NAD)* (annual). *La Prévention de Crises Alimentaires au Sahel: 10 Ans d'Expériences d'une Action Menée en Réseau, 1985-1995* (1997). Conference proceedings; policy recommendations.

Members Food security actors in 27 countries:
Belgium, Benin, Burkina Faso, Canada, Cape Verde, Chad, Côte d'Ivoire, France, Gambia, Germany, Ghana, Guinea, Guinea-Bissau, Italy, Liberia, Luxembourg, Mali, Mauritania, Netherlands, Niger, Nigeria, Senegal, Sierra Leone, Spain, Switzerland, Togo, USA.

Included in the above, 17 organizations listed in this Yearbook:
Action Against Hunger (#00086); Afrique verte; Comité permanent inter-Etats de lutte contre la sécheresse dans le Sahel (CILSS, #04195); ECHO (inactive); Economic Community of West African States (ECOWAS, #05312); European Union (EU, #08967) (DEVCO); *Famine Early Warning System Network (FEWS NET); FAO (#09260); Intergovernmental Authority on Development (IGAD, #11472); New Partnership for Africa's Development (NEPAD, #17091); Oxfam International (#17922); Sahel and West Africa Club (SWAC, #19034); Union économique et monétaire Ouest africaine (UEMOA, #20377); United Nations Office for the Coordination of Humanitarian Affairs (OCHA, #20593); West African Network of Farmers' Organizations and Agricultural Producers (#20891); World Food Programme (WFP, #21510).* [2019.12.12/XF4781/y/**F**]

- ♦ Réseau de prévention des crises alimentaires dans le Sahel / see Réseau de prévention des crises alimentaires (#18905)
- ♦ Réseau de quaker pour l'empêchement de conflit violent (unconfirmed)
- ♦ Réseau pour la Qualité de l'Environnement en Afrique Sub-Saharienne (internationally oriented national body)
- ♦ Réseau de radio rurale des pays en développement / see Farm Radio International (#09274)
- ♦ Réseau de Recherche Appliquée en Équité, Santé et Développement (#00880)
- ♦ Réseau de recherche caféière en Afrique (#00253)
- ♦ Réseau de recherche en éducation pour l'Afrique de l'Ouest et centrale (#05368)
- ♦ Réseau de recherche forestière en Afrique subsaharienne (#09866)
- ♦ Reseau pour la recherche internationale sur la desertification (#02823)
- ♦ Réseau de recherche des produits naturels pour l'Afrique orientale et centrale (#16956)
- ♦ Réseau de recherche SADAOC / see Foundation for Sustainable Food Security in Central West Africa (#09975)
- ♦ Réseau de recherche sur le SIDA pour l'Afrique de l'Est and australe (#16990)
- ♦ Réseau régional des autorités locales pour les établissements humains (#18799)
- ♦ Réseau régional pour l'échange d'information et d'expérience en science et technologie en Asie et dans le Pacifique (inactive)
- ♦ Réseau des régions et des aires métropolitaines d'Europe (#17023)
- ♦ Réseau de réserves de biosphère d'Asie de l'Est (#05199)
- ♦ Réseau SADAOC / see Foundation for Sustainable Food Security in Central West Africa (#09975)

♦ Réseau Sahel Désertification (ReSaD) 18906

Burkina Faso Omer Ouedraogo, SPONG, Point focal ReSaD, Ouagadougou 01, Burkina Faso. T. +22670924814.
France Adeline Derkimba, GTD, 12 rue de Courreau, 34380 Viols-le-Fort, France. T. +33467556118.
URL: http://www.resad-sahel.org/

History 2010, Montpellier (France). **Structure** Fight against desertification.

Members Full in 4 countries:
Burkina Faso, France, Mali, Niger.

IGO Relations Partners include: *Agence française de développement (AFD); European Union (EU, #08967); Global Mechanism (GM, #10468); Observatoire du Sahara et du Sahel (OSS, #17636).* **NGO Relations** Partners include: *Drynet (#05140).* [2018/XM6845/**F**]

- ♦ Réseau sahélien d'information et de documentation scientifiques et techniques (no recent information)
- ♦ Réseau sanitaire pour les femmes d'Amérique latine et de Caraïbes (#16288)
- ♦ Réseau de sécurité alimentaire durable en Afrique de l'Ouest centrale / see Foundation for Sustainable Food Security in Central West Africa (#09975)
- ♦ Réseau de services consultatifs et d'information pour le secteur de la construction (#03351)
- ♦ Réseau Sésame / see Réseau VERTECH CITY (#18908)
- ♦ Réseau SESAME Network – International Network of Cities / see Réseau VERTECH CITY (#18908)
- ♦ Réseau social européen (#08505)
- ♦ Réseau de la société civile SUN (#20035)
- ♦ Réseau des solutions pour le développement durable des Nations-unies (#20054)
- ♦ Réseau sud-est asiatique pour un système d'information géologique (#19778)
- ♦ Réseau Syndical International de Solidarité et de Luttes (unconfirmed)
- ♦ Réseau de terminologie / see Red Iberoamericana de Terminologia (#18685)
- ♦ Réseau Théophraste (#20140)
- ♦ Réseau travail et économie dans les Eglises européennes (#21051)
- ♦ Réseau UNESCO de bibliothèques associées (#20311)
- ♦ Réseau UNITWIN / see UNITWIN/UNESCO Chairs Programme (#20669)
- ♦ Réseau universitaire européen en sciences du sport / see European Network of Sport Education (#08012)
- ♦ Réseau universitaire international pour la coopération avec les institutions palestiniennes d'enseignement supérieur / see Programme for Palestinian-European-American Cooperation in Education (#18527)
- ♦ Réseau universitaire international de Genève (internationally oriented national body)
- ♦ Réseau universitaires-chercheurs (internationally oriented national body)

♦ Réseau Universitaire et Scientifique Euro-Méditerranéen sur le Genre et les Femmes (RUSEMEG) 18907

Contact 51 rue des Dominicaines, 13001 Marseille, France. T. +33491911489. E-mail: rus.euromed.gender@gmail.com.
URL: http://rusemeg.blogspot.be/

History Dec 2012. Registered in accordance with French law. **Structure** General Assembly; Board of Directors; Scientific Council.

Members Full in 5 countries:
Algeria, France, Morocco, Spain, Tunisia.

NGO Relations Founding member of: *Euro-Mediterranean Women's Foundation (#05729).* [2016/XM5077/f/**F**]

- ♦ Réseau des universités des capitales de l'Europe (#17061)
- ♦ Réseau VERTECH / see Réseau VERTECH CITY (#18908)

♦ Réseau VERTECH CITY 18908

VERTECH CITY Network

Contact CRI Namur Capitale, La Bourse, Place d'Armes 1, 5000 Namur, Belgium. T. +3281241133. E-mail: reseauvertech@namur.be.
Main Website: https://www.vertechcity.com/

History 31 Jul 1992. Relaunched 2012. Former names and other names: *Sesame Network* – former; *Réseau Sésame* – former; *Réseau SESAME Network – International Network of Cities* – former; *Réseau VERTECH* – former; *VERTECH CITY* – former. **Aims** Search for global and sustainable energy solutions. **Structure** Administrators from each member city. **Languages** English, French. **Activities** Training/education. **Events** *Colloquium* Lafayette, LA (USA) 2017, *Colloquium* Namur (Belgium) 2016, *Colloquium* Victoriaville, QC (Canada) 2014, *Conference* Poitiers (France) / La Rochelle (France) 2013, *Conference* Lafayette, LA (USA) 2012.

Members 4 cities in 4 countries:
Belgium (Namur), Canada (Victoriaville QC), France (Poitiers), USA (Lafayette LA). [2020.10.13/XF5281/**F**]

- ♦ Réseau des villes du patrimoine mondial / see Organization of World Heritage Cities (#17891)
- ♦ Réseau de villes et de régions européennes pour de nouvelles solutions de transport / see POLIS (#18419)
- ♦ Réseau WAGNE – Wagon africain de gestion de nouvelles électroniques (see: #12575)

♦ Réseaux d'études des relations internationales sportives (RERIS) . 18909

Contact address not obtained. E-mail: reris.network@gmail.com.

Activities Advocacy/lobbying/activism; events/meetings; knowledge management/information dissemination; networking/liaising.

Members Individuals in 11 countries:
Australia, France, Germany, Italy, Poland, Portugal, Spain, Sweden, Switzerland, UK, USA. [2020/AA0427/**F**]

♦ Réseaux ferroviaires Européens Développement social et Solidarité dans les Gares (Gare Européenne et Solidarité) 18910

Secretariat c/o NRIC, Mariya Luiza 10, 1233 Sofia, Bulgaria. E-mail: office@rail-infra.bg.
Co-Pres Ferrovie dello Stato Italiane, Direzione Centrale Comunicazione Esterna di Gruppo, Piazza della Croce Rossa 1, 00161 Rome RM, Italy.
URL: http://www.garesolidaire.net/

History Set up, 29 Oct 2008, Rome (Italy), on signing the European Charter for development of social initiatives in stations. **Aims** Create a large network – integrating *railway* companies, public authorities and third sector organizations and enterprises – that operates with a common methodology to take action on social issues in stations, firstly favouring the exchange of knowledge and best practice amongst partners. **Structure** Steering Committee; Co-Presidents (2). **Languages** English, French. **Staff** Part-time. **Finance** No dedicated budget. **Activities** Politics/policy/regulatory. Active in: Belgium, Bulgaria, France, Italy, Luxembourg, Poland. **Events** *CODIR Conference* Milan (Italy) 2015, *Meeting* Rome (Italy) 2015.
Members Signatories in 12 countries:
Belgium, Bulgaria, Czechia, Denmark, France, Italy, Luxembourg, Norway, Poland, Romania, Slovenia, Sweden.
[2017/XJ9116/F]

- ♦ Réseaux IP européens Network Coordination Centre / see RIPE Network Coordination Centre (#18951)
- ♦ **RESEO** Réseau européen pour la sensibilisation à l'opéra et à la danse (#18878)
- ♦ RESER / see European Network for REsearch on SERvices (#07992)
- ♦ **RESER** European Network for REsearch on SERvices (#07992)
- ♦ Reserva Alimentaria Internacional de Emergencia (#13259)
- ♦ Réserve alimentaire internationale d'urgence (#13259)
- ♦ Réserve internationale maritime en méditerranée occidentale (no recent information)
- ♦ Resettlement Fund for National Refugees and Over-Population in Europe / see Council of Europe Development Bank (#04897)
- ♦ RESGEST – Regional Secretariat for Gender, Science and Technology in Southeast Asia and the Pacific (see: #20313)
- ♦ Résidence Palace – Centre de presse international (internationally oriented national body)
- ♦ Residence Palace – Internationaal Perscentrum (internationally oriented national body)
- ♦ Residence Palace – Internationales Pressezentrum (internationally oriented national body)
- ♦ Residence Palace – International Press Centre (internationally oriented national body)
- ♦ Residence Palace – IPC – Residence Palace – International Press Centre (internationally oriented national body)
- ♦ Residenze Universitarie Internazionali / see Rui Foundation

♦ Resilience Alliance (RA) 18911

Exec Dir Biology Dept, Acadia Univ, Wolfville NS B4P 2R6, Canada. T. +19025851287. Fax +19025851059. E-mail: editor@resalliance.org.
URL: http://www.resalliance.org/

History Founded 1999. Registered in accordance with USA law. **Aims** Facilitate collaboration across disciplines to explore the dynamics of *social-ecological systems*; develop a body of knowledge encompassing key concepts of resilience, adaptability and transformability, and providing a foundation for *sustainable development* policy and practice. **Structure** Board of Directors; Board of Science. **Activities** International conference (triennial). **Events** *Resilience International Science and Policy Conference* Stockholm (Sweden) 2017, *Resilience International Science and Policy Conference* Montpellier (France) 2014, *Resilience international science and policy conference* Stockholm (Sweden) 2008.
Members Organizations (16) in 9 countries:
Australia, Canada, France, Kenya, Netherlands, South Africa, Sweden, UK, USA.
Included in the above, 4 organizations listed in this Yearbook:
Beijer Institute – International Institute of Ecological Economics; *Centre de coopération internationale en recherche agronomique pour le développement (CIRAD, #03733)*; *Commonwealth Scientific and Industrial Research Organization (CSIRO)*; *Stockholm Environment Institute (SEI, #19993)*.
NGO Relations *Integrated Assessment Society, The (TIAS, #11367)*. [2016/XM3240/y/F]

♦ Resilience Measurement Evidence and Learning Community of Practice (RMEL CoP) 18912

Contact c/o Global Resilience Partnership, Stockholm Resilience Centre, Stockholm Univ, Kräftriket 2B, SE-106 91 Stockholm, Sweden. E-mail: info@globalresiliencepartnership.org.
URL: https://www.globalresiliencepartnership.org/resource/resilience-measurement-evidence-and-learning-community-or-practice/

History 2016. Jan 2021, integrated into the Resilience Knowledge Coalition, hosted by *Global Resilience Partnership (GRP, #10577)*. **Aims** Create a more cohesive field of diverse actors collaborating to improve resilience measurement concepts, approaches, and methods and to increase capacities to use them; strengthen evidence of what works to increase the ability of individuals, communities, and systems to be more resilient; influence decision-making and *sustainable* development practice, policy, and investments across diverse sectors and geographies. **Structure** Conference; Steering Committee; Secretariat. **Activities** Awards/prizes/competitions; events/meetings. **Events** *Resilience Measurement, Evidence and Learning Conference* New Orleans, LA (USA) 2018. **Members** Scientists, specialists, advisors, programmes and influencers (over 200). Membership countries not specified. [2022/XM6959/v/F]

- ♦ Resilient Futures International (internationally oriented national body)
- ♦ **RESILIO** Association Internationale pour la Promotion et a la Diffusion de la Recherche sur la Résilience (#12108)
- ♦ **RESILIO** International Association for the Promotion and Dissemination of Research on Resilience (#12108)
- ♦ RESM – Réseau Entraide Solidarité Monde (internationally oriented national body)
- ♦ RESO-Femmes International (unconfirmed)
- ♦ Résolution sur les Minorités Linguistiques et Culturelles dans la Communauté Européenne (1994 treaty)
- ♦ Résolution recommandant la création d'un nouveau chemin de fer intercontinental (1902 treaty)
- ♦ Resolution Recommending the Construction of New Intercontinental Railways (1902 treaty)
- ♦ Resolution Relative to Customs (1902 treaty)
- ♦ Résolution relative aux douanes (1902 treaty)
- ♦ Résolution relative aux méthodes facilitant le commerce international (1902 treaty)
- ♦ Resolution Relative to Methods of Facilitating International Trade (1902 treaty)
- ♦ Résolution relative à la police sanitaire, 1902 (1902 treaty)
- ♦ Resolution Relative to Sanitary Police, 1902 (1902 treaty)
- ♦ Resolution Relative to Sanitary Police, 1906 (1906 treaty)
- ♦ Resolution Relative to Statistics (1902 treaty)
- ♦ Résolution relative aux statistiques (1902 treaty)
- ♦ Resolution Relative to Steamer Communications (1910 treaty)
- ♦ Resolution Respecting Censuses (1910 treaty)
- ♦ Resolution Respecting Commercial Statistics (1910 treaty)
- ♦ Resolution Respecting the Construction of a Pan-American Railway (1910 treaty)
- ♦ Resolution Respecting Consular Documents (1910 treaty)
- ♦ Resolution Respecting the Development of Commercial Relations (1906 treaty)
- ♦ Resolution Respecting the Exchange of Professors and Students (1910 treaty)
- ♦ Resolution Respecting Sanitary Police (1910 treaty)
- ♦ Resolutions Adopted by the Allied Economic Conference (1916 treaty)
- ♦ Resolutions of the Sanitary Convention (1902 treaty)
- ♦ RESOLVE (internationally oriented national body)
- ♦ Resolve to Save Lives (internationally oriented national body)

♦ Resort Development Organisation (RDO) 18913

Main Office 4th Fl, 3 More London Riverside, London, SE1 2AQ, UK. E-mail: info@rdo.org.
URL: http://www.rdo.org/

History 1998. Former names and other names: *European Timeshare Federation (ETF)* – former (1998); *Fédération européenne de timeshare* – former (1998); *Organization for Timeshare in Europe (OTE)* – former (1998 to Nov 2011); *Organisation pour le timeshare en Europe* – former (1998 to Nov 2011); *The Timeshare Council* – former (Jun 1990). Registration: Belgium; UK, Jersey. **Aims** Be the recognized voice for the *timeshare* and shared ownership industry. **Structure** Board; Legislative Council. **Languages** English, Spanish. **Staff** 4.00 FTE, paid. **Finance** Members' dues. **Activities** Advocacy/lobbying/activism; events/meetings; networking/liaising; training/education; research/documentation; conflict resolution; politics/policy/regulatory. **Events** *Conference* Vilamoura (Portugal) 2020, *Conference* Marbella (Spain) 2019, *Conference* London (UK) 2018, *Conference* Las Palmas de Gran Canaria (Spain) 2013, *Conference* Marbella (Spain) 2011. **Publications** Weekly news feed and monthly members only newsletter. **Members** Full: companies and other businesses established in Europe and directly engaged in the resort development industry. Associate: companies providing specialist services to the industry. International affiliate: companies operating outside Europe but otherwise eligible for membership. Membership countries not specified. [2021/XD5555/D]

- ♦ Resource Accounting Network for Eastern and Southern Africa (internationally oriented national body)
- ♦ Resource Africa (internationally oriented national body)

♦ Resource Alliance 18914

Head Office Eagle House, 163 City Rd, London, EC1V 1NR, UK. T. +442039185294. E-mail: contact@resource-alliance.org.
URL: http://www.resource-alliance.org/

History 1981, USA. Permanent secretariat established 1991, London (UK). *International Fund Raising Workshops*, set up 1992, formalizes UK operations. Former names and other names: *International Fund Raising Group (IFRG)* – former (1981 to 2000). Registration: Charity Commission, No/ID: 1099889, England and Wales; USA, New Jersey. **Aims** Promote a strong, independent and self-sufficient *voluntary* sector in all nations, based on broad domestic popular support; help voluntary organizations develop such support by providing training in ethical and professional fund raising; provide a forum for fund raisers to meet, exchange ideas and learn from each other. **Structure** Board of 8-12 members; regional organizations; country representatives. **Staff** 10.00 FTE, paid. **Finance** Members' dues. Other sources: grants from funding partners; donations. **Activities** Participates in a programme with donor agencies to provide training in 6 regions of the developing world (South America; East Africa; Southern Africa; South Asia; South East Asia; Central and Eastern Europe); holds International Fund Raising Congress (annually, in Netherlands) and Hemispheric Congress on Fund Raising; organizes regional workshops and seminars worldwide. **Events** *International Fundraising Congress* Leeuwenhorst (Netherlands) 2022, *International Fundraising Congress* Noordwijkerhout (Netherlands) 2019, *International Fundraising Congress* Noordwijkerhout (Netherlands) 2018, *International Fundraising Congress* Bangkok (Thailand) 2017, *International Fundraising Congress* Noordwijkerhout (Netherlands) 2017. **Publications** *Global Connections* (6 a year) – e-mail newsletter; *Worldwide Fundraiser's Handbook*.
Members Board and Advisory Board members in 21 countries:
Argentina, Bosnia-Herzegovina, Brazil, Canada, Costa Rica, Czechia, Hungary, India, Kenya, Korea Rep, Mexico, Peru, Singapore, Slovakia, Sweden, Tanzania UR, Uganda, UK, Ukraine, USA, Zimbabwe.
IGO Relations Partners: *Asian Development Bank (ADB, #01422)*; *European Commission (EC, #06633)*; *Swedish International Development Cooperation Agency (Sida)*.
NGO Relations Partners:
- *ActionAid (#00087)*;
- *Charities Aid Foundation (CAF)*;
- *ChildFund International (#03869)*;
- *Christian Aid*;
- *Citi Foundation*;
- *Folkekirkens Nødhjaelp (FKN)*;
- *Ford Foundation (#09858)*;
- *Greenpeace International (#10727)*;
- *International Federation of Red Cross and Red Crescent Societies (#13526)*;
- *Multiple Sclerosis International Federation (MSIF, #16899)*;
- *Oxfam GB*;
- *Plan International (#18386)*;
- *Sightsavers International (#19270)*;
- *Strømme Foundation (SF)*;
- *World Wide Fund for Nature (WWF, #21922)*. [2022/XF3601/F]

- ♦ The Resource Centre / see Environment and Development Resource Centre
- ♦ Resource Centre on Urban Agriculture and Forestry / see International Network of Resource Centers on Urban Agriculture and Food Security (#14319)
- ♦ RE-Source – European platform for corporate renewable energy sourcing / see RE-Source Platform (#18916)

♦ Resource Foundation 18915

Pres/CEO 500 Seventh Avenue, 8th Floor, New York NY 10018, USA. T. +12126756170.
URL: http://www.resourcefnd.org/

History 1987, USA. **Aims** Support and empower private *development* organizations in *Latin America* to address local needs; assist individual and institutional donors to maximize the impact of their philanthropy. **Structure** Board of Directors, comprising Director Emeritus and 21 Directors. **Staff** 7.00 FTE, paid. **Finance** Members dues. Other sources: individual donors; foundation grants; corporate support. **Activities** Offers tailored services to corporate, foundation and individual donors. Programme areas: Affordable Housing; Capacity Building; Cultural Programmes; Disaster Relief; Education and Job Skills; Environment; Health Care and HIV/AIDS; Microenterprise; Potable Water and Sanitation; Sustainable Agriculture.
Members Affiliated organizations (41) in 17 countries; Associated organizations (157) in 27 countries and territories:
Argentina, Bolivia, Brazil, Cayman Is, Chile, Colombia, Costa Rica, Dominica, Dominican Rep, Ecuador, El Salvador, Grenada, Guatemala, Guyana, Haiti, Honduras, Jamaica, Mexico, Nicaragua, Panama, Paraguay, Peru, St Lucia, Suriname, Trinidad-Tobago, Uruguay, Venezuela.
NGO Relations Collaborates with organizations in the USA and Europe, as well as over 198 local development organizations throughout Latin America and the Caribbean. [2019/XM4556/f/F]

♦ RE-Source Platform (RE-Source) 18916

Contact address not obtained. E-mail: info@resource-platform.eu.
URL: https://resource-platform.eu/

History Jun 2017, Brussels (Belgium). Founded by *SolarPower Europe (#19676)*, *WindEurope (#20965)*, *RE100* and *World Business Council for Sustainable Development (WBCSD, #21254)*. Former names and other names: *RE-Source – European platform for corporate renewable energy sourcing* – full title. **Aims** Remove regulatory and administrative barriers to corporate renewable energy procurement in Europe in support of the EU's climate and energy goals. **Structure** Steering Committee. **Finance** Supported by: *European Commission (EC, #06633)*; *IRENA Coalition for Action (#16018)*. **Events** *RE-Source* Amsterdam (Netherlands) 2022, *RE-Source* Amsterdam (Netherlands) 2021.
Members Founding organizations (4):
RE100; *SolarPower Europe (#19676)*; *WindEurope (#20965)*; *World Business Council for Sustainable Development (WBCSD, #21254)*.
NGO Relations Partner of (7): *Association of Issuing Bodies (AIB, #02768)*; *Conseil européen de l'industrie chimique (CEFIC, #04687)*; *EKOenergy (#05412)*; *European Federation of Energy Traders (EFET, #07108)*; *RECS International (#18631)*; *Union of the Electricity Industry – Eurelectric (#20379)*; *We Mean Business*. [2022/AA2824/y/F]

- ♦ Resource Renewal Institute (internationally oriented national body)
- ♦ **RE-Source** RE-Source Platform (#18916)
- ♦ Resources for the Future (internationally oriented national body)
- ♦ **RESPAO** Réseau d'étude des systèmes de production en Afrique de l'Ouest (#20880)
- ♦ **ReSPA** Regional School of Public Administration (#18810)
- ♦ RESPECT / see Refugee Education Sponsorship Program International

♦ RESPECT 18917

Contact Eerste Weteringsplantsoen 2c, 1017 SJ Amsterdam, Netherlands. Fax +31205287236.
URL: http://www.respectnetworkeu.org/

History 1998, as a network of migrant domestic workers. Also referred to as *RESPECT Network*. RESPECT stands for *Rights – Equality – Solidarity – Power – Europe Cooperation Today !*. **Aims** Improve the social, economic and legal position of the growing number of *migrant workers* who work in the private *domestic* sphere as *cleaners* and/or *carers*.

Members Full in 10 countries:
Belgium, Cyprus, France, Germany, Greece, Ireland, Netherlands, Spain, Switzerland, UK.
IGO Relations Participant in Fundamental Rights Platform of: *European Union Agency for Fundamental Rights (FRA, #08969).* [2012/XJ6207/**F**]

♦ RESPECT International – Refugee Education Sponsorship Program International (internationally oriented national body)
♦ RESPECT Network / see RESPECT (#18917)
♦ RESPECT Refugiados (internationally oriented national body)
♦ RESPECT Refugiados Europe / see RESPECT Refugiados

♦ Respiratory Effectiveness Group (REG) 18918

CEO Unit 14B, E-space North, 181 Wisbech Road, Littleport, Ely, CB6 1RA, UK. E-mail: enquiries@regresearchnetwork.org.
URL: https://www.regresearchnetwork.org/
Aims Transform respiratory patient care by maximizing/exploiting/utilis-zing real-life research and evidence. **Activities** Events/meetings; knowledge management/information dissemination; research/documentation. **Events** *REG Summit* Barcelona (Spain) 2021, *REG Summit* Barcelona (Spain) 2020, *REG Summit* Athens (Greece) 2019, *REG Summit* Amsterdam (Netherlands) 2018, *REG Summit* London (UK) 2017. [2022/AA1753/**F**]

♦ Respiratory Syncytial Virus Network Foundation (ReSViNET Foundation) 18919

Sec Broederplein 41-43, 3703 CD Zeist, Netherlands. E-mail: info@resvinet.org.
URL: http://www.resvinet.org/
History Inception of the network, 14 Jan 2014, Utrecht (Netherlands). Officially launched as a foundation Feb 2018. Registration: Start date: Feb 2018, Netherlands. **Aims** Support performance of high quality research; improve knowledge of RSV epidemiology; develop safe and effective therapeutic and preventive interventions. **Structure** Board of Directors; Scientific Advisory Board. **Languages** English. **Staff** 23.00 FTE, paid. **Finance** Until feb 2018, part of Julius Clinical. Currently independent. **Activities** Events/meetings; research/documentation. **Events** *Meeting* Lisbon (Portugal) 2023, *Meeting* Zeist (Netherlands) 2021, *Meeting* Accra (Ghana) 2019, *Meeting* Amsterdam (Netherlands) 2017, *Meeting* Malaga (Spain) 2017. **Publications** Books; brochures.
Members Full in 15 countries:
Argentina, Australia, Brazil, Canada, Finland, France, Germany, Greece, Italy, Japan, Netherlands, South Africa, Spain, UK, USA. [2023/XM6848/f/**F**]

♦ Responding to Climate Change (unconfirmed)
♦ Responsible Business Alliance (internationally oriented national body)
♦ Responsible Fashion Series (meeting series)
♦ Responsible Finance Forum (meeting series)

♦ Responsible Jewellery Council (RJC) 18920

Exec Dir Quality House, 5-9 Quality Court, London, WC2A 1HP, UK. T. +442073210992. E-mail: info@responsiblejewellery.com.
URL: http://www.responsiblejewellery.com/
History 2005. Former names and other names: *Council for Responsible Jewellery Practices* – legal name. Registration: Companies House, No/ID: 05449042, Start date: 11 May 2005, England. **Aims** Advance responsible ethical, social and environmental practices, which respect human rights, throughout the diamond, gold and platinum metals jewellery supply chain, from mine to retail. **Structure** General Meeting (annual); Board of Directors; Executive Committee. **Languages** English. **Staff** 6.00 FTE, paid. **Finance** Sources: members' dues. **Activities** Certification/accreditation.
Members Companies (over 270). Membership countries not specified. Included in the above, one organizations listed in this Yearbook:
Included in the above, one organizations listed in this Yearbook:
World Gold Council (WGC, #21541).
NGO Relations Member of (1): *ISEAL (#16026).* Partner of (1): *United Nations Global Compact (#20567).* [2020/XJ2186/y/**C**]

♦ Responsible Minerals Initiative (internationally oriented national body)
♦ Responsible Mining Assurance Initiative / see Initiative for Responsible Mining Assurance (#11212)
♦ Responsible Society / see Family Education Trust

♦ ResponsibleSteel 18921

Communications Dir PKF Newcastle Pty Limited, 755 Hunter Street, Newcastle NSW 2302, Australia.
URL: https://www.responsiblesteel.org/
History Founded as a membership-led programme. **Aims** Ensure businesses and consumers can be confident that the steel they use has been sourced and produced responsibly at every stage. **Structure** Board of Directors; Secretariat. **Finance** Sources: contributions; donations; members' dues. **Activities** Certification/accreditation; events/meetings; standards/guidelines; training/education.
Members Civil Society and Social/Environmental Organizations, including:
CDP (#03621); Climate Group (#04013); Fauna & Flora International (FFI, #09277); IndustriALL Global Union (IndustriALL, #11177); International Union for Conservation of Nature and Natural Resources (IUCN, #15766); Mighty Earth; We Mean Business.
Business Members:
Associate members, including:
Climate Bonds Initiative (#04006); Cobalt Institute (CI, #04076); Energy and Resources Institute (TERI); European General Galvanizers Association (EGGA, #07383); European Outdoor Group (EOG, #08122); Initiative for Responsible Mining Assurance (IRMA, #11212); International Manganese Institute (IMnI, #14083); International Tin Association (#15692); International Zinc Association (IZA, #15942); Nickel Institute (#17133); Pacific Institute. [2021/AA1030/y/**F**]

♦ **RESP** Réseau européen pour le soutien psychosocial (#07978)
♦ **RESR** Rete europea per lo sviluppo rurale (#07995)
♦ RES – Russian and Euroasian Security Network (internationally oriented national body)

♦ Restauradores Sin Fronteras (A-RSF) 18922

SG Ctr Cultural Pablo Iglesias, Avda Baunata 18 – 1a Planta, 28701 San Sebastian de los Reyes, Madrid, Spain. T. +34916588990ext336. E-mail: info@a-rsf.org.
URL: http://www.a-rsf.org/
History 1999. Registered in accordance with Spanish law. **Aims** Conduct activities that socially and economically benefit the peoples of the *poorest* countries, using cultural *heritage* as a tool for *sustainable development.* **Structure** International Council. Board of Directors, comprising President, Vice-President, Secretary-General and 2 members. **Finance** Support from: *Agencia Española de Cooperación Internacional para el Desarrollo (AECID)*; autonomous regions; foundations; etc. **Publications** *A-RSF Newsletter.*
Members Groups in 7 countries:
Colombia, Costa Rica, Mexico, Peru, Portugal, Spain, Venezuela. [2012/XJ5249/**F**]

♦ Restless Development (internationally oriented national body)
♦ Restorative Justice for All International Institute (internationally oriented national body)
♦ Restored (internationally oriented national body)
♦ RESULTS (internationally oriented national body)

♦ Results for Development (R4D) 18923

Acting Managing Dir 1111 19th St NW, Ste 700, Washington DC 20036, USA. T. +12024705711. E-mail: info@r4d.org – info@r4d.org.
URL: https://r4d.org/
History 2008. Former names and other names: *Results for Development Institute (R4D)* – former. **Aims** Unlock solutions to development challenges that prevent people in low- and middle-income countries from realizing their full potential. **Structure** Board of Directors; Leadership Team. **NGO Relations** Member of (5): *Early Childhood Development Action Network (ECDAN, #05155); Global Health Technologies Coalition (GHTC); Global Innovation Exchange (The Exchange, inactive); Humentum (#10993); PMNCH (#18410).* [2022/XJ7318/j/**C**]

♦ Results for Development Institute / see Results for Development (#18923)
♦ RESULTS Educational Fund / see RESULTS
♦ ReSurge International (internationally oriented national body)
♦ Resurrectionists – Congregation of the Resurrection of our Lord Jesus Christ (religious order)

♦ Resuscitation Council of Asia (RCA) 18924

Chairman Blk A Level 6, Natl Heart Ctr, 226 Outram Road, Singapore 169039, Singapore.
URL: http://resuscitationcouncil.asia/
History Founded 17 Jul 2005, Aichi (Japan). **Aims** Preserve life by improving standards of resuscitation and the chain of survival in Asia; coordinate activities of Asian organizations with an interest in resuscitation medicine. **Structure** General Assembly; Council. **Finance** Members' dues. **Events** *Conference* Taipei (Taiwan) 2021, *General Assembly* Taipei (Taiwan) 2014.
Members Active; Associate; Honorary; Patron. Members in 7 countries and territories:
Hong Kong, Japan, Korea Rep, Philippines, Singapore, Taiwan, Thailand.
NGO Relations Member of: *International Liaison Committee on Resuscitation (ILCOR, #14036).* [2021/XJ5006/**D**]

♦ Resuscitation Council of Southern Africa (internationally oriented national body)
♦ **ReSViNET Foundation** Respiratory Syncytial Virus Network Foundation (#18919)
♦ Retail Industry Leaders Association (internationally oriented national body)
♦ RE TE – Associazione di tecnici per la solidarietà e cooperazione internazionale (internationally oriented national body)
♦ Reteaua Panlatina de Terminologie (#18901)
♦ Rete di Comuni – Alleanza nelle Alpi / see Alliance in the Alps (#00656)
♦ Rete Europea d'Azione Sociale (#08499)
♦ Rete Europea delle Città Digitali (#07893)
♦ Rete Europea Diritto e Società (#07937)
♦ Rete Europea di Gruppi di Assistenza per Pazienti Affetti da Mieloma Multiplo (inactive)
♦ Rete Europea degli Istituti della Famiglia / see Red Europea de Institutos de la Familia (#18653)
♦ Rete European Dei Volontari Anziani / see European Network of Older-Volunteer Organizations
♦ Rete europea per lo sviluppo rurale (#07995)
♦ Rete Giudiziaria Europea in Materia Civile e Commerciale (#07616)
♦ Rete di Informazione sull'Istruzione in Europa (inactive)
♦ Rete Internazionale di Giornali di Strada / see International Network of Street Papers (#14330)
♦ Rete internazionale per le Piccole e Medie Imprese (#14325)
♦ Rete Internazionale per la Promozione del Volontariato in Europa / see Volonteurope (#20807)
♦ Rete Internazionale delle Religiose Contro il Traffico di Persone (unconfirmed)
♦ Rete Mediterranea di Comunicatori Forestali (unconfirmed)
♦ Rete Panlatina di Terminologia (#18901)
♦ Rete delle Regioni e delle Aree Metropolitane Europee (#17023)
♦ Rete Sindicale Internazionale di Solidarieta e di Lotta (unconfirmed)

♦ Rethinking Economics (RE) 18925

Co-Dir 22a Beswick St, Manchester, M4 7HR, UK. T. +447512307123. E-mail: info@rethinkeconomics.org.
URL: https://www.rethinkeconomics.org/
History 2011, UK. Former names and other names: *Rethinking Economics Network* – alias; *Rethinking Economics International* – legal name. Registration: Charity Commission, No/ID: 1158972, Start date: 2015, England and Wales. **Aims** As an international network of students, academics and professionals, build a better economics in society and the classroom. **Structure** Members' Council; Trustee Board. **Events** *International Gathering* Chaussy (France) 2022.
Members Groups in 45 countries:
Argentina, Australia, Austria, Bangladesh, Belgium, Brazil, Canada, Chile, Colombia, Denmark, Ecuador, Finland, France, Germany, Greece, India, Indonesia, Ireland, Israel, Malta, Mexico, Namibia, Netherlands, New Zealand, Nigeria, Norway, Pakistan, Peru, Philippines, Poland, Portugal, Singapore, South Africa, Spain, Sri Lanka, Sweden, Switzerland, Trinidad-Tobago, Tunisia, Türkiye, Uganda, UK, USA, Vietnam, Zambia. [2022/AA2654/**F**]

♦ Rethinking Economics International / see Rethinking Economics (#18925)
♦ Rethinking Economics Network / see Rethinking Economics (#18925)
♦ Retina Europe Youth (no recent information)

♦ Retina International (RI) 18926

Pres Ausstellungsstrasse 36, 8005 Zurich ZH, Switzerland. T. +41444441077. Fax +41444441070. E-mail: info@retina-international.org.
CEO 7 Ely Pl, Dublin, 2, CO. DUBLIN, D02 TW98, Ireland. T. +35316789004.
URL: http://www.retina-international.org/
History 1978, London (UK). Current statutes revised Oct 2006, Rio de Janeiro (Brazil). Former names and other names: *International Retinitis Pigmentosa Association (IRPA)* – former. **Aims** Promote the search for a treatment for Retinitis Pigmentosa (RP), Usher Syndrome, Macular Degeneration and allied retinal dystrophies. **Structure** General Assembly; Management Committee; Scientific and Medical Advisory Board. **Languages** English. **Staff** 6.00 FTE, voluntary. **Finance** Sources: members' dues. **Activities** Awareness raising; knowledge management/information dissemination; research/documentation. **Events** *Congress* Reykjavik (Iceland) 2022, *Congress* Reykjavik (Iceland) 2020, *Congress* Auckland (New Zealand) 2018, *Congress* Taipei (Taiwan) 2016, *Congress / International Congress* Paris (France) 2014.
Members Full; Candidate; Interested Group. Full in 22 countries and territories:
Australia, Brazil, Canada, Finland, France, Germany, Iceland, Ireland, Israel, Italy, Japan, Netherlands, New Zealand, Norway, Pakistan, South Africa, Spain, Sweden, Switzerland, Taiwan, UK, USA.
IGO Relations *European Commission (EC, #06633).* **NGO Relations** Member of (2): *Asian Cities Against Drugs (ASCAD); Rare Diseases International (RDI, #18621).* [2021/XD2219/**C**]

♦ RET International 18927

CEO Rue de Saint-jean 34, 1203 Geneva, Switzerland. T. +41227750522. E-mail: info@theret.org.
URL: http://theret.org/
History 2000, Geneva (Switzerland). Former names and other names: *Foundation for the Refugee Education Trust* – former. **Aims** Alleviate suffering and catalyze sustainable development in crises, conflicts and fragile contexts, by providing a broad diversity of programmes to protect and build the resilience of youth, women and girls. **Structure** Board; Advisory Board; Headquarters located in Geneva (Switzerland); Administrative Centres (LAC Bureau, EMEAA Bureau); Country Offices. **Staff** 550 – 1300 Field Staff **Finance** Sources: contributions; donations; government support; private foundations. Supported by: UN agencies. **Activities** Awareness raising; capacity building; humanitarian/emergency aid; projects/programmes; training/education. RET has implemented projects in 34 countries within Africa, Asia, Europe, Latin America and the Caribbean, the Middle East and Asia. **Publications** *RET Newsletter.* **Consultative Status** Consultative status granted from: *ECOSOC (#05331)* (Special). **NGO Relations** Member of (7): *Alliance for Child Protection in Humanitarian Action (The Alliance, #00667)*; G-7 Global Task Force; Global Alliance for Disaster Risk Reduction & Resilience in the Education Sector (GADRRRES); *Global Refugee Leaders Forum*; *Inter-agency Network for Education in Emergencies (INEE, #11387)*; *International Council of Voluntary Agencies (ICVA, #13092)*; Youth Compact in Humanitarian Action. [2022.11.09/XM6399/**F**]

♦ Retired Generals and Admirals for Peace and Disarmament / see Strategies for Peace (#20008)
♦ **RETOSA** Regional Tourism Organisation of Southern Africa (#18817)
♦ **RETRAC** SEAMEO Regional Training Centre, Ho Chi Minh City (#19183)
♦ Retrak (internationally oriented national body)
♦ **RET** Réseau européen du textile (#08903)
♦ RETROPATH – International Workshop on Retroviral Pathogenesis (meeting series)
♦ Rette Europea delle Città del Vino (#18881)
♦ Rettet den Regenwald (internationally oriented national body)

♦ Rett Syndrome Europe (RSE) 18928

Address not obtained.
URL: http://www.rettsyndrome.eu/

History Registered in accordance with Luxembourg law. Previously referred to as *European Association for Rett Syndrome (EARS)*. **Aims** Represent the interests of people with Rett syndrome and their families. **Structure** General Assembly (annual). Board, comprising President, Secretary, Treasurer and 2 further members. **Finance** Members' dues. **Events** *European Rett Syndrome Conference* Tampere (Finland) 2019, *European Rett Syndrome Conference* Berlin (Germany) 2017, *European Rett Syndrome Conference* Maastricht (Netherlands) 2013, *Meeting* London (UK) 2012, *Meeting* Paris (France) 2011.
Members in 28 countries:
Austria, Belgium, Bosnia-Herzegovina, Bulgaria, Croatia, Czechia, Denmark, Estonia, Finland, France, Germany, Greece, Hungary, Italy, Lithuania, Malta, Netherlands, Norway, Poland, Portugal, Russia, Serbia, Slovakia, Spain, Sweden, Switzerland, Türkiye, UK.
NGO Relations Member of: *EURORDIS – Rare Diseases Europe (#09175).* [2013/XE4732/**E**]

- ♦ Returned Volunteer Action (internationally oriented national body)
- ♦ "Return & Restitution" Intergovernmental Committee / see Intergovernmental Committee for Promoting the Return of Cultural Property to its Countries of Origin or its Restitution in case of Illicit Appropriation (#11476)
- ♦ Reunião Inter-Regional dos Bispos da Africa Austral (#15971)

♦ Reunión Anual de Dermatólogos Latinoamericanos (RADLA) 18929

Coordinator Brazil address not obtained.
Coordinator Argentina address not obtained.
URL: http://www.radla.org/

History 27 Oct 1972, Buenos Aires (Argentina). **Structure** Council of Delegates, including President and Former Presidents of Annual Meetings. Executive Committee, including Chairman, Vice-President, Treasurer, Secretary General and Scientific Secretary. **Events** *Annual Meeting* Asunción (Paraguay) 2021, *Annual Meeting* Buenos Aires (Argentina) 2019, *Annual Meeting* Cancún (Mexico) 2018, *Annual Meeting* Lima (Peru) 2015, *Annual Meeting* Santiago (Chile) 2014. **Publications** *Boletin RADLA*.
Members Full in 12 countries:
Argentina, Bolivia, Brazil, Chile, Colombia, Dominican Rep, Ecuador, Mexico, Paraguay, Peru, Uruguay, Venezuela.
[2014/XJ6759/c/**E**]

- ♦ Réunion centroaméricaine des directeurs de l'aéronautique civile (meeting series)
- ♦ Reunión Centroamericana de Directores de Aeronautica Civil (meeting series)
- ♦ Réunion des chefs des organisations nordiques d'export (meeting series)
- ♦ Réunion commune des ministres de l'économie et des travaux publics des pays d'Amérique centrale (meeting series)
- ♦ Reunión Conjunta de Ministros de Economia y Obras Públicas de Centroamérica (meeting series)
- ♦ Réunion des directeurs d'associations de sapeurs-pompiers nordiques (meeting series)
- ♦ Reunión de Empresas Portuarias de Centroamerica (meeting series)
- ♦ Réunion d'étude sur la construction nordique (meeting series)
- ♦ Réunion internationale des écrivains (meeting series)

♦ Réunion internationale des laboratoires d'essais et de recherches sur les matériaux et les constructions (RILEM) 18930

International Union of Laboratories and Experts in Construction Materials, Systems and Structures

Gen Sec 4 ave du Recteur Poincaré, 75016 Paris, France. T. +33142246446. Fax +33970295120. E-mail: dg@rilem.net.
URL: http://www.rilem.net/

History Founded 20 Jun 1947, Paris (France). Previously referred in English as *International Union of Testing and Research Laboratories for Materials and Structures*. Registered in accordance with Swiss law. **Aims** Contribute to the progress of *construction* sciences, techniques and industries, essentially by means of communication it fosters between research and practice; develop the knowledge of properties of materials and performance of structures, at defining the means for their assessment under laboratory and service conditions, and at unifying measurement and testing methods used with this objective. **Structure** General Council (annual); Bureau. Standing Committees (3); Regional groups (3); Technical Committees (40). **Languages** English, French. **Staff** 3.00 FTE, paid. **Finance** Sources: members' dues. **Activities** Events/meetings; knowledge management/information dissemination; research and development; training/education. **Events** *International Conference on Bio-Based Building Materials* Vienna (Austria) 2023, *Annual Week Meeting* Kyoto (Japan) 2022, *International Congress on Materials and Structural Stability* Rabat (Morocco) 2022, *International Conference on Bio-Based Building Materials* Barcelona (Spain) 2021, *Annual Week Meeting* Mérida (Mexico) 2021. **Publications** *Materials and Structures – Matériaux et constructions* (10 a year) in English, French; *RILEM Directory of Technical Committees*; *RILEM Members' Directory*; *RILEM Technical Letters* – open-access journal. *RILEM Bookseries*. *RILEM Recommendations for Testing Methods*; *RILEM Technical Recommendations*. Technical and state-of-the-art reports. *RILEM Publications*, a publishing subsidiary, ensures publication of: symposium, workshop and seminar proceedings. **Members** Corporate and individual memberships in over 70 countries. Membership countries not specified. **NGO Relations** Member of: Association Française de Génie Civil; *ASTM International (#02994)*. Founding member of: *Liaison Committee of International Associations of Civil Engineering (#16453)* and member of its *Joint Committee on Structural Safety (JCSS, #16126)*, together with *European Convention for Constructional Steelwork (ECCS, #06779)*; *Fédération internationale du béton (FIB, #09615)*; *International Association for Bridge and Structural Engineering (IABSE, #11737)*; *International Association for Shell and Spatial Structures (IASS, #12162)*; *International Council for Research and Innovation in Building and Construction (CIB, #13069)*. [2021/XB2784/**B**]

- ♦ Réunion inter-régionale des évêques de l'Afrique australe / see Inter-Regional Meeting of Bishops of Southern Africa (#15971)
- ♦ Reunión de Jefes de Organismos Nacionales Encargados de Combatir el Trafico Ilicito de Drogas (meeting series)
- ♦ Reunión Ministerial Institucionalizada UE-Grupo de Rio (inactive)
- ♦ Réunion des ministres des finances du Commonwealth (meeting series)
- ♦ Réunion des ministres responsables de l'intégration et du développement de l'Amérique centrale (meeting series)
- ♦ Reunión de Ministros de Educación del Convenio Andrés Bello (meeting series)
- ♦ Reunión de Ministros de Obras Públicas y de Transportes de los Paises de l Cono Sur (meeting series)
- ♦ Reunión de Ministros Responsables de le Integración y Desarrollo de Centroamérica (meeting series)
- ♦ Reunión de Ministros de Salud del Area Andina (meeting series)
- ♦ Reunión de Ministros de Transporte de Centroamérica (meeting series)
- ♦ Réunion des présidents d'Europe centrale (meeting series)
- ♦ Réunion régionale centroaméricaine des chemins de fer (meeting series)
- ♦ Réunions Bilderberg (#03234)
- ♦ Réunions internationales des architectes (inactive)
- ♦ Réunions nordiques des directeurs d'écoles (meeting series)
- ♦ Reunión Zonal Centroamérica de Ferrocarriles (meeting series)

♦ Re-Use and Recycling European Union Social Enterprises (RREUSE) 18931

Dir Rue d'Edimbourg 26, 1050 Brussels, Belgium. T. +3228944614. E-mail: info@rreuse.org.
URL: http://www.rreuse.org/

History 2001. Registration: No/ID: 0474.728.985, Start date: 26 Feb 2001, Belgium; EU Transparency Register, No/ID: 05052317999-60, Start date: 16 Feb 2012. **Aims** Represent and promote European social enterprises active in different fields of re-use and recycling of end-of-life products; coordinate and strengthen collaboration between them; promote sustainable development in the aspects of social employment, environment and economic activity. **Structure** General Assembly (annual); Board of Directors. **Languages** English. **Staff** 1.50 FTE, paid. **Finance** Sources: members' dues. Supported by: *European Commission (EC, #06633)*. **Activities** Advocacy/lobbying/activism; projects/programmes. **Events** *Annual Conference* Vienna (Austria) 2022, *Annual Conference* 2021, *International Conference on the Role of Social & Solidarity Enterprises in the Circular Economy / Conferencia Internacional sobre el Rol de las Entidades Sociales y Solidarias en la Economía Circular* Pamplona (Spain) 2019, *International RREUSE Conference* Nijmegen (Netherlands) 2018, *International Conference on the Role of Social Enterprise in a Circular Economy* Charleroi (Belgium) 2017.
Members Companies and organizations in 19 countries:
Austria, Belgium, Bosnia-Herzegovina, Croatia, Finland, France, Germany, Greece, Hungary, Ireland, Italy, Netherlands, Poland, Romania, Slovenia, Spain, Sweden, UK, USA.
Included in the above, 1 organization listed in this Yearbook:
Emmaüs Europe (#05444).
NGO Relations Member of: *Environmental Coalition on Standards (ECOS, #05499)*; *Resource and Waste Chain Forum (RWCF, no recent information)*; *Spring Alliance (inactive)*. Associate member of: *Social Platform (#19344)*. [2020/XD8299/**D**]

- ♦ REUSSI – Réseau étudiants universitaire pour la santé sociale et internationale (internationally oriented national body)
- ♦ REVES – Réseau Espérance de Vie en Santé (unconfirmed)
- ♦ **REVES** Réseau Européen des Villes and Régions de l'Économie Sociale (#18880)
- ♦ Revisão da Convenção de Buenos Aires sobre a proteção à propriedade literaria e artistica (1928 treaty)
- ♦ Revised African Convention on the Conservation of Nature and Natural Resources (2017 treaty)
- ♦ Revised General Act for the Pacific Settlement of International Disputes (1949 treaty)
- ♦ Revised General Arrangements to Borrow (1962 treaty)
- ♦ Revised Protocol on Shared Watercourses (2000 treaty)
- ♦ Revision of Agreement of Madrid of 14 Apr 1891 Concerning International Registration of Commercial and Industrial Trade Marks (1911 treaty)
- ♦ Revision of Agreement of Madrid of 14 Apr 1891 for the Prevention of False Indications of Origin on Goods (1911 treaty)
- ♦ Révision de l'Arrangement concernant l'enregistrement international des marques de fabrique ou de commerce (1911 treaty)
- ♦ Révision de l'Arrangement concernant la répression des fausses indications de provenance sur les marchandises (1911 treaty)
- ♦ Revisión de la Convención de Buenos Aires sobre protección a la propiedad literaria y artistica (1928 treaty)
- ♦ Revision of the Convention of Buenos Aires on the Protection of Literary and Artistic Copyright (1928 treaty)
- ♦ Révision de la Convention de Buenos Aires pour la protection de la propriété littéraire et artistique (1928 treaty)
- ♦ Revision of the International Conventions Concerning the Carriage of Goods by Rail and of Passengers and Luggage by Rail (1952 treaty)

♦ Revival Fellowship 18932

Contact address not obtained. E-mail: webmaster@trf.org.au.
URL: http://www.trf.org.au/

History Australia. **Events** *Convention* Perth, WA (Australia) 2008, *Convention* Brisbane, QLD (Australia) 2006, *Convention* Perth, WA (Australia) 2005. **Publications** *Revival Times* (annual).
Members in 17 countries:
Australia, Brazil, Canada, China, Czechia, Fiji, France, Hungary, Netherlands, New Zealand, Papua New Guinea, Singapore, South Africa, Thailand, UK, USA, Zimbabwe. [2008/XF4027/s/**F**]

- ♦ **ReVLaT** Red de Estudios Visuales Latinoamericanos (#18650)
- ♦ REV Ocean (internationally oriented national body)
- ♦ Revolutionary Justice Organization / see Hezbollah Internationale (#10912)
- ♦ Re:wild (internationally oriented national body)

♦ Rewilding Europe 18933

Exec Dir Toernooiveld 1, 6525 ED Nijmegen, Netherlands. E-mail: info@rewildingeurope.com.
URL: http://www.rewildingeurope.com/

History 2011, Netherlands. Initiated by *World Wide Fund for Nature (WWF, #21922)* Netherlands, ARK Nature, Wild Wonders of Europe and Conservation Capital. Registration: Handelsregister, Start date: 28 Jun 2011, Netherlands; EU Transparency Register, No/ID: 203835118406-89, Start date: 3 Aug 2015. **Aims** Apply rewilding principles, models and toolsto deliver measurable, demonstrable, and sustained benefits for nature and people. **Structure** Executive Board; Supervisory Board; Management Team; Central Team; Landscape Teams. **Languages** English. **Staff** 25.00 FTE, paid; 10.00 FTE, voluntary. **Finance** Sources: contributions; international organizations; investments. Annual budget: 2,000,000 EUR. **Activities** Awareness raising; capacity building; events/meetings; financial and/or material support; guidance/assistance/consulting; knowledge management/information dissemination; networking/liaising; projects/programmes; publishing activities; training/education. **Publications** Annual Review; brochures; policy briefs; species publications; practical guides; scientific reports; factsheets.
Members Full (12) in countries:
Bulgaria, Croatia, Germany, Italy, Moldova, Netherlands, Poland, Portugal, Romania, Spain, Sweden, Ukraine.
NGO Relations Member of (3): *European Habitats Forum (EHF, #07443)*; *Global Rewilding Alliance (GRA, #10579)*; *International Union for Conservation of Nature and Natural Resources (IUCN, #15766)*.
[2022.05.06/XJ4615/**F**]

- ♦ ReX and GG – Conference on Recrystallization and Grain Growth (meeting series)
- ♦ REY – Retina Europe Youth (no recent information)
- ♦ RFA – Radio Free Asia (internationally oriented national body)
- ♦ **RFCMJ** Réseau francophone des conseils de la magistrature judiciaire (#18882)
- ♦ **RF-EFH** Réseau francophone pour l'égalité femme-homme (#18884)
- ♦ **RFE** Rail Forum Europe (#18607)
- ♦ RFE/RL – Radio Free Europe/Radio Liberty (internationally oriented national body)
- ♦ RFF-CMCC European Institute on Economics and the Environment (internationally oriented national body)
- ♦ RFF – Resources for the Future (internationally oriented national body)
- ♦ RFF – Responsible Finance Forum (meeting series)
- ♦ RFH / see Riders for Health II (#18940)
- ♦ RFI / see Reason Partnership
- ♦ **RFIDba** International RFID Business Association (#14751)
- ♦ RFI – Radio France internationale (internationally oriented national body)
- ♦ **RFI** Rainforest Foundation International (#18615)
- ♦ RFI – Resilient Futures International (internationally oriented national body)
- ♦ RFK Center / see Robert F Kennedy Human Rights
- ♦ RFMF – Réseau Francophone de Métabolomique et Fluxomique (internationally oriented national body)
- ♦ RFN – Rainforest Foundation Norway (internationally oriented national body)
- ♦ **RfP** Religions for Peace (#18831)
- ♦ RF – Renewable Futures (meeting series)
- ♦ **RF** Rome Foundation (#18970)
- ♦ **RFSV** Réseau francophone des sciences vasculaires (#18887)
- ♦ RFTM – Rencontres Francophones Transport-Mobilité (meeting series)
- ♦ RFUK – Rainforest Foundation UK (internationally oriented national body)
- ♦ RFUND – Rainforest Fund (internationally oriented national body)
- ♦ RFVAA – Réseau Francophone des Villes Amies des Aînés (internationally oriented national body)
- ♦ RGA / see Tropical Growers' Association (#20250)
- ♦ RGC – International Rosaceae Genomics Conference (meeting series)
- ♦ **RGCS** Research Group on Collaborative Spaces (#18855)
- ♦ RGDTS / see Phiren Amenca (#18362)

♦ RGE / see Council of European Municipalities and Regions (#04891)
♦ **RGI** Renewables Grid Initiative (#18839)
♦ **RGRE** Rat der Gemeinden und Regionen Europas (#04891)
♦ RGS' / see Royal Geographical Society – with the Institute of British Geographers
♦ RGS-IBG – Royal Geographical Society – with the Institute of British Geographers (internationally oriented national body)
♦ RGW – Rat für Gegenseitige Wirtschaftshilfe (inactive)
♦ **RHC-Platform** European Technology Platform on Renewable Heating and Cooling (#08891)

♦ Rhetoric Society of Europe (RSE) 18934

Pres Klein Dalenstraat 32, 3020 Herent, Belgium. E-mail: info@rhetoricsocietyeurope.eu.
Communications Officer address not obtained.
URL: https://rhetoricsocietyeurope.eu/

History Originates in 1st Rhetoric in Society conference, 2006, Aalborg (Denmark). Current constitution adopted Jan 2013, Copenhagen (Denmark). Registration: No/ID: 0701.633.959, Start date: 21 Aug 2018, Belgium. **Aims** Promote and advance the research, study and teaching of rhetoric in Europe; facilitate professional cooperation between its members. **Structure** General Assembly; Executive Board; Advisory Board. **Languages** English. **Finance** Sources: members' dues. **Activities** Events/meetings; knowledge management/information dissemination; research/documentation. **Events** *Rhetoric in Society Conference* Tübingen (Germany) 2023, *RSE Virtual Gathering* Tübingen (Germany) 2021, *Rhetoric in Society Conference* Tübingen (Germany) 2021, *Rhetoric in Society Conference* Ghent (Belgium) 2019, *Rhetoric in Society Conference* Norwich (UK) 2017. [2021/AA0623/**D**]

♦ Rheumatism Association of ASEAN (RAA) 18935

Secretariat Philippine Rheumatology Assn, Rm 1408 – 14/F North Tower, Cathedral Heights Bldg Complex, St Luke Medical Ctr, E Rodriguez Sr Avenue, 1112 Quezon City, Philippines.

History 1984, Manila (Philippines). Constitution and by-laws adopted 20 Jan 1984, Bangkok (Thailand). Previously referred to as *Rheumatology Association of ASEAN*. **Aims** Stimulate and promote the development of awareness, knowledge and the means of prevention, *treatment*, *rehabilitation* and relief of rheumatic *diseases*. **Structure** General Assembly (every 2 years). Officers: President, Immediate Past President, Senior Vice-President, Vice-Presidents, Secretary-General and Treasurer. Executive Committee, consisting of President, Immediate Past President, Senior Vice-President, Secretary-General and Treasurer. Executive Secretariat. **Events** *Congress / Biennial Congress* Manila (Philippines) 1998, *Biennial Congress* Singapore (Singapore) 1993, *Biennial Congress* Bangkok (Thailand) 1991, *Biennial Congress* Manila (Philippines) 1989. **Publications** *Rheumatism Association of ASEAN Newsletter*.
Members National organizations in 5 countries:
Indonesia, Malaysia, Philippines, Singapore, Thailand.
Consultative Status Consultative status granted from: *ASEAN (#01141)*. **NGO Relations** *Asia Pacific League of Associations for Rheumatology (APLAR, #01945)*. [2015/XE1337/**E**]

♦ Rheumatology Association of ASEAN / see Rheumatism Association of ASEAN (#18935)
♦ **RHF** Réseau habitat et francophonie (#18888)
♦ Rhineland-Westphalia Foreign Affairs Society (internationally oriented national body)
♦ Rhine Union of Chambers of Commerce / see Union of European Chambers of Commerce for Transport (#20384)
♦ Rhinology Research Forum in Asia (meeting series)

♦ Rhinoplasty Society of Europe 18936

Admin Dir Vallstedter Weg 114 A, 38268 Lengede, Germany. T. +495344915948. Fax +495344915949. E-mail: rhinoplasty.europe@gmail.com.
URL: http://www.rhinoplastysociety.eu/

History May 2011, Stuttgart (Germany). **Aims** Stimulate open exchange of innovative ideas and techniques concerning plastic, reconstructive and aesthetic rhinoplasty. **Structure** Board of Directors. **Events** *Annual Meeting* Stuttgart (Germany) 2019, *Annual Meeting* Bergamo (Italy) 2018, *Annual Meeting* Moscow (Russia) 2017, *Annual Meeting* Paris (France) 2016, *Annual Meeting* Stuttgart (Germany) 2015.
Members Individuals in 36 countries:
Armenia, Austria, Azerbaijan, Belgium, Brazil, Chile, Cyprus, Czechia, Egypt, France, Germany, Greece, Iran Islamic Rep, Iraq, Ireland, Israel, Italy, Jordan, Kosovo, Kuwait, Latvia, Luxembourg, Malta, Netherlands, Norway, Poland, Romania, Russia, Saudi Arabia, Singapore, South Africa, Spain, Switzerland, Türkiye, UK, USA. [2015/XJ9146/v/**D**]

♦ **RHN** Regions for Health Network (#18821)
♦ Rhodes-Livingstone Institute for Social Research / see Institute of Economic and Social Research
♦ Rhodes Trust (internationally oriented national body)
♦ **RHSC** Reproductive Health Supplies Coalition (#18847)
♦ **RIAAM** Red Iberoamericana de Asociaciones de Adultos Mayores (#18658)
♦ **RIACES** Red Iberoamericana para el Aseguramiento de la Calidad en la Educación Superior (#18657)
♦ **RIAC** Red Interamericana de Citricos (#11407)
♦ **RIAC** Red Interamericana de Competitividad (#11416)
♦ RIACRE – Red Iberoamericana y del Caribe de Restauración Ecológica (inactive)
♦ RIAC – Russian International Affairs Council (internationally oriented national body)
♦ RIAD-IALEX / see Legal Protection International (#16440)
♦ **RIADICYP** Red Iberoamericana de Docencia e Investigación en Celulosa y Papel (#18664)
♦ **RIADIS** Red Iberoamericana de Organizaciones No Gubernamentales de Personas con Discapacidad y sus Familias (#16354)
♦ RIAD / see Legal Protection International (#16440)
♦ **RIAD** Red Interamericana de Alto Nivel Sobre Descentralización, Gobierno Local y Participación Ciudadana (#18691)
♦ RIAE – Recording-Media Industry Association of Europe (inactive)
♦ RIAFM / see Red Iberoamericana de Bosques Modelo (#18659)
♦ RIAP – Research Institute for Asia and the Pacific, Sydney (internationally oriented national body)
♦ **RIA** Rabies in Asia Foundation (#18599)
♦ **RIARC** Réseau des instances africaines de régulation de la communication (#00259)
♦ RIA – Research ICT Africa Network (internationally oriented national body)
♦ RIA – Réunions internationales des architectes (inactive)
♦ RIATT-ESA / see Regional Inter-Agency Task Team on Children and AIDS in Eastern and Southern Africa (#18791)
♦ **RIATT-ESA** Regional Inter-Agency Task Team on Children and AIDS in Eastern and Southern Africa (#18791)
♦ Ribbon International (internationally oriented national body)
♦ **RIBEI** Red Iberoamericana de Estudios Internacionales (#18665)
♦ RIBER – Red IBERoamericana de Prospectiva (unconfirmed)
♦ **RIBM** Red Internacional de Bosques Modelo (#14175)
♦ RIB – Red Iberoamericana Bioinformatica (inactive)
♦ RICA – Red Interamericana para el Mejoramiento de la Calidad Ambiental (no recent information)
♦ RICAS – Research and Information Center for Asian Studies (internationally oriented national body)
♦ **RICCA** Red Internacional de Centros de Capacitación en Agua (#14341)
♦ RICC / see International Consumer Protection and Enforcement Network (#12930)
♦ Ricerca e Cooperazione (internationally oriented national body)

♦ Rice-Wheat Consortium for the Indo-Gangetic Plains (RWC) 18937

Address not obtained.

History 1994, within *CGIAR System Organization (CGIAR, #03843)*. Dormant for several years, but since 2012 in the process of being revived. **Aims** Strengthen existing linkages and partnerships with national research programmes, other international centres, advanced institutions and the private sector working in the region to develop and deploy more efficient, productive and sustainable technologies for the diverse rice-wheat production systems of the Indo-Gangetic Plains so as to produce more food at less cost and improve livelihoods of those involved with agriculture and as a consequence to decrease poverty. **Structure** Regional Steering Committee (RSC), consisting of the Chief Executives of the NARS and the Convening Center, promotes integration of national and regional efforts; RSC may invite resource persons to participate at meetings if required. Regional Technical Coordination Committee (RTCC) consists of one senior representative (Coordinator) from each of the four NARS, one representative each of IRRI, CIMMYT, IIMI, ICRISAT, CIP, and Cornell University staff assigned to rice-wheat activities in the region and the Facilitator; RTCC may invite other resource persons to participate. Facilitation Unit. **Languages** English. **Staff** 20.00 FTE, paid. **Finance** Numerous sources, varying with the nature of the activity. Important funding sources include: special projects financed by donor and development institutions; externally aided national projects (eg, World Bank loan funds managed by NARIs); core resources of participating NARIs; core resources of participating International Centers. **Activities** Focuses on 4 research themes: tillage and crop establishment; integrated nutrient management; integrated water management; system ecology/integrated pest management. Crop improvement research, socioeconomics and policy analysis are treated as overarching issues that affect all 4 research themes. Responsibility for each theme rests with specific international research centres, universities and advanced research institutions. National management committees coordinate research at the national and site levels. **Events** *World congress on conservation agriculture* Delhi (India) 2009, *OSCAR final workshop* Delhi (India) 2006.
Members Full in 4 countries:
Bangladesh, India, Nepal, Pakistan.
Associate member (1):
China. [2012/XF5555/**F**]

♦ **RICFME** Réseau international des centres de formations aux métiers de l'eau (#14341)
♦ Richardson Institute for Peace and Conflict Studies (internationally oriented national body)
♦ Richardson Institute for Peace Studies / see Richardson Institute for Peace and Conflict Studies
♦ Richard Wagner Verband International (#12261)

♦ Richelieu International (RI) 18938

Contact 301, promenade Moodie, bureau 400, Ottawa ON K2H 9C4, Canada. T. +18002676525. E-mail: international@richelieu.org.
URL: http://richelieu.org/

History 21 Feb 1944, Ottawa, ON (Canada). Established to promote the social and cultural needs of the francophone population of Canada. Expanded in order to respond to needs of French communities worldwide. *Fondation Richelieu International* set up 1977. Former names and other names: *Société Richelieu* – former (1944 to 1971). **Aims** Promote *francophonie* at local, national and international levels. **Structure** General Assembly (annual); Board of Directors; Regions (12); Clubs. **Languages** French. **Finance** Sources: members' dues. **Activities** Events/meetings; humanitarian/emergency aid; networking/liaising. **Events** *Assemblée générale* Ottawa, ON (Canada) 2020, *Congrès Annuel et Assemblée Générale* Ottawa, ON (Canada) 2019, *Congrès Annuel et Assemblée Générale* Montréal, QC (Canada) 2018, *Congrès Annuel et Assemblée Générale* Montmagny, QC (Canada) 2017, *Congrès Annuel et Assemblée Générale* Saguenay, QC (Canada) 2016.
Members Individuals (2,500) and Clubs (130) in 5 countries:
Canada, Côte d'Ivoire, France, Haiti, USA.
NGO Relations Member of (1): *Forum francophone des affaires (FFA, #09916)*. Cooperates with (1): *Assemblée parlementaire de la Francophonie (APF, #02312)*. [2020.11.16/XF8203/**E**]

♦ **RICHIE Association** International Research Network of Young Historians of European Integration (#14739)
♦ Richmond Fellowship International / see Reason Partnership
♦ RICI / see Remanufacturing Institute
♦ Ricky Martin Foundation (internationally oriented national body)
♦ RICM / see Registre des Citoyens du Monde (#18822)
♦ **RICM** Registre des Citoyens du Monde (#18822)
♦ RICOREP – Red de Instituciones de Combate a la Corrupción y Rescate de la Etica Pública (see: #16294)
♦ **RICPC** Réseau international de contrôle et de protection des consommateurs (#12930)
♦ RIC – Rainforest Information Centre (internationally oriented national body)

♦ RICS Europe 18939

Regional Managing Dir, Europe Rue Ducale 67, 1000 Brussels, Belgium. T. +3227331019. Fax +3227429748. E-mail: ricseurope@rics.org.
URL: http://www.rics.org/

History 15 Oct 1993, Paris (France). Founded as *European Society of Chartered Surveyors*. Currently functions as European headquarters of *Royal Institution of Chartered Surveyors (RICS, #18991)*, London (UK). Based in Brussels (Belgium). Registration: EU Transparency Register, No/ID: 12309911354-39, Start date: 12 Mar 2009. **Aims** As part of RICS, facilitate promotion of the chartered *surveying profession* in continental Europe and exchange of experience and information in the *property* sector; facilitate training, qualification and mutual recognition; establish Europe-wide *standards* of professional practice and codes of conduct; support and promote development of the property and *construction* professions for the benefit of all living or working within Europe. **Structure** Offices in: Brussels (Belgium); Budapest (Hungary); Frankfurt-Main (Germany); Lisbon (Portugal); Milan (Italy); Moscow (Russia); Nicosia (Cyprus); Paris (France); Stockholm (Sweden); Voorburg (Netherlands). **Languages** Dutch, English, French, German, Hungarian, Italian, Portuguese, Russian, Spanish, Swedish. **Staff** 50.00 FTE, paid. **Finance** Members' dues. **Activities** Events/meetings. **Events** *Meeting* Brussels (Belgium) 2010, *Meeting* Brussels (Belgium) 2010, *Meeting* Brussels (Belgium) 2010, *Meeting* Lisbon (Portugal) 2010, *Meeting* Brussels (Belgium) 2009.
Members National groups in 24 countries:
Austria, Belgium, Cyprus, Czechia, Denmark, Estonia, Finland, France, Germany, Greece, Hungary, Italy, Latvia, Lithuania, Luxembourg, Netherlands, Poland, Portugal, Romania, Russia, Spain, Sweden, Switzerland, Türkiye. [2020/XD3565/**E**]

♦ **RICS** Royal Institution of Chartered Surveyors (#18991)
♦ RIC – Union internationale des voitures et fourgons (inactive)
♦ **RICYT** Red Iberoamericana e Interamericana de Indicadores de Ciencia y Tecnologia (#11025)
♦ **RIDAF** Red Internacional para el Desarrollo Aves Caseras de Familia (#14267)
♦ **RIDAF** Réseau internationale pour le développement de l'aviculture familiale (#14267)
♦ RIDE AFRICA – Human Rights and Democracy Link Africa (internationally oriented national body)
♦ Riders / see Riders for Health II (#18940)
♦ Riders for Health / see Riders for Health II (#18940)

♦ Riders for Health II 18940

Registered Address The law office of William Francis Xavier Becker, 3007 Viburnum Place, Olney MD 20832, USA. E-mail: info@riders.org.
UK Office Eagle House, 28 Billing Road, Northampton, NN1 5AJ, UK.
URL: https://www.riders.org/

History 1986. Former names and other names: *Riders for Health (RFH)* – trading name; *Riders* – trading name. Registration: 501(c)3, No/ID: 98-0225419, USA; Charity, No/ID: 1054565, Start date: 27 Mar 1996, End date: Jul 2018, England and Wales. **Aims** Raise awareness of transport needs in the developing world; manage fleets of two- and four-wheeled vehicles for health delivery in Africa; build capacity in Africa through training and systems development. **Structure** Autonomous organization with Boards of Trustees in each country. Management Council, comprising Programme Directors of each country. **Finance** Sources: donations; government support; grants; international organizations; revenue from activities/projects. Programmes largely funded by service contracts with local governments in partnerships with multinational organizations. Additional support through income from events, donations and grants from Europe and the USA. **Activities** Advocacy/lobbying/activism; healthcare; monitoring/evaluation; training/education.
Members National organizations in 7 countries:
Gambia, Lesotho, Liberia, Malawi, Nigeria, UK, USA.
NGO Relations Member of (2): *Philanthropy Impact*; *PMNCH (#18410)*. Associate member of: *British Overseas NGO's for Development (BOND)*; *Fédération Internationale de Motocyclisme (FIM, #09643)*. [2022.11.10/XF6822/**F**]

♦ **RIDHE** International Network of Human Rights | Europe (#14286)

- ♦ **RIDHE** Réseau International des Droits Humains I Europe (#14286)
- ♦ **RIDH** Red Internacional de Derechos Humanos (#18891)
- ♦ **RIDH** Réseau International des Droits Humains (#18891)
- ♦ **RIdIM** Répertoire international d'iconographie musicale (#18844)
- ♦ **RIDITA** Red Iberoamericana de Investigación en Transporte Aéreo (#18669)
- ♦ RIDPA – Rural Integrated Development Program of Africa (internationally oriented national body)
- ♦ **RID** Red Interamericana para la Democracia (#18692)
- ♦ RIEAS – Research Institute for European and American Studies (internationally oriented national body)
- ♦ **RI-ECA** Rehabilitation International – European Communities Association (#18825)
- ♦ **RIEE** Polis – Réseau international en éducation à l'environnement (#18421)
- ♦ **RIEF** Research in International Economics and Finance Network (#18858)
- ♦ **RiEN** Reflexology in Europe Network (#18736)
- ♦ RIEP – Réseau International de l'Enseignement Protestant (internationally oriented national body)
- ♦ RIES / see Research Institute for European and American Studies
- ♦ RIET – Red Ibérica de Entidades Transfronterizas (internationally oriented national body)
- ♦ Rifa'iya (religious order)
- ♦ RIFAL – Réseau international francophone d'aménagement linguistique (inactive)
- ♦ **RIFA** Réseau International de Foresterie Analogue (#11650)
- ♦ **RIFEFF** Réseau international francophone des établissements de formation de formateurs (#18893)
- ♦ RIFIAS / see Sinor Research Institute for Inner Asian Studies
- ♦ **RIFM** Réseau international de Forêts Modèles (#14175)
- ♦ RIFONGA – Réseau pour l'Intégration des Femmes des Organisations Non Gouvernementales et Associations Africaines (unconfirmed)
- ♦ RIF – Radio Internacional Feminista (internationally oriented national body)
- ♦ RIFRED / see Réseau international de Recherche en éducation et en formation (#18896)
- ♦ **RIF** Renju International Federation (#18842)
- ♦ **RIFRESS** Réseau international francophone pour la responsabilité sociale en santé (#18895)
- ♦ Riga International School of Economics and Business Administration (internationally oriented national body)

♦ Right to Die Europe (RtDE) 18941

Sec Mermansstraat 17, 2300 Turnhout, Belgium. E-mail: secretariat@rtde.eu.
Pres Transvaal 13, 1865 AK Bergen aan Zee, Netherlands. E-mail: as@rtde.eu.
URL: http://www.rtde.eu/

History 1993. Founded as a division of *World Federation of Right to Die Societies (WFRtDS, #21477)*. Constitution revised Oct 2003; modified Nov 2010; amended as agreed Sep 2011. Formally known as *European Federation of Right to Die Societies – Europese Federatie van de Right to Die Societies.* **Aims** Strengthen the movement in Europe for choice in dying; encourage formation of societies in those countries without them; share knowledge and expertise of members societies with other societies; represent at the appropriate European organizations the interests of those who wish to have a choice in dying; oppose those who wish to deny self-determination at the end of life; campaign for legal recognition of living wills; seek social acceptance and legal recognition in Europe of self-determination in dying. **Structure** Board of Directors. **Languages** Danish, Dutch, English, French, German, Italian, Spanish. **Staff** None. **Finance** Members' dues. Donations. Development Fund to finance projects. **Activities** Networking/liaising; events/meetings. **Events** *Conference of Delegates* Brussels (Belgium) 2017, *Conference of Delegates* Berlin (Germany) 2015, *Interim Meeting of Delegates* Chicago, IL (USA) 2014, *Conference of Delegates* Rome (Italy) 2013, *Interim Meeting of Delegates* Zurich (Switzerland) 2012.
Members Societies (39) in 19 countries:
Austria, Belgium, Denmark, Finland, France, Germany, Iceland, Ireland, Israel, Italy, Luxembourg, Netherlands, Norway, Poland, Portugal, Spain, Sweden, Switzerland, UK.
Consultative Status Consultative status granted from: *Council of Europe (CE, #04881)* (Participatory Status). **IGO Relations** *Office of the United Nations High Commissioner for Human Rights (OHCHR, #17697).* [2021/XJ4901/E]

♦ Right to Education Initiative (RTE) 18942

Exec Dir c/o ActionAid Intl, 33-39 Bowling Green Lane, London, EC1R 0BJ, UK. E-mail: info@right-to-education.org.
URL: http://www.right-to-education.org/

History 2000. Founded by 1st UN Special Rapporteur on the Right to Education, Katarina Tomasevski. Relaunched 2008, as a collaborative initiative. Former names and other names: *Right to Education Project* – former. Registration: Charity Commission, No/ID: 1173115, Start date: May 2017, England and Wales. **Aims** Promote education as a human right, making international and national law accessible to everybody. **Structure** Executive Board. **Languages** Arabic, English, French, Spanish. **Staff** 3.60 FTE, paid. **Finance** Sources: donations; private foundations. Annual budget: 250,000 GBP (2020). **Activities** Advocacy/lobbying/activism; awareness raising; capacity building; events/meetings; knowledge management/information dissemination; research/documentation. **Publications** *RTE e-bulletin* (12 a year). Annual Report. **NGO Relations** Member of (3): *Inter-agency Network for Education in Emergencies (INEE, #11387)*; *International Network for Economic, Social and Cultural Rights (ESCR-Net, #14255)*; Privatization in Education and Human Rights Consortium (PEHRC). Supports (1): *End Corporal Punishment (#05457).* [2021.06.09/XJ7691/F]

- ♦ Right to Education Project / see Right to Education Initiative (#18942)
- ♦ Right to Energy – SOS Future (internationally oriented national body)

♦ Right to Food and Nutrition Watch Consortium 18943

Secretariat c/o FIAN International, Willy-Brandt-Platz 5, 69115 Heidelberg, Germany. T. +4962216530030. Fax +4962216530033.

History Launched 24 Jun 2013, as *Global Network for the Right to Food and Nutrition.* **Aims** Publish the annual *'Right to Food and Nutrition Watch'*.
Members International organizations (22):
- African Network on the Right to Food (ANoRF);
- *Brot für die Welt*;
- *Centro Internazionale Crocevia (CIC)*;
- *Ecumenical Advocacy Alliance (EAA, inactive)*;
- *FIAN International (#09743)*;
- *Folkekirkens Nødhjaelp (FKN)*;
- *Habitat International Coalition (HIC, #10845)*;
- *ICCO – Interchurch Organization for Development Cooperation*;
- *International Baby Food Action Network (IBFAN, #12305)*;
- *International Indian Treaty Council (IITC, #13836)*;
- Observatory – Economic, Social and Cultural Rights (ODESC);
- Pakistan Fisherfolk Forum (PFF);
- *People's Health Movement (PHM, #18305)*;
- *Plataforma Interamericana de Derechos Humanos, Democracia y Desarrollo (PIDHDD, #18395)*;
- *Rede Regional da Sociedade Civil para a Segurança Alimentar e Nutricional na CPLP (REDSAN-CPLP, #18648)*;
- *Society for International Development (SID, #19581)*;
- *Swiss Interchurch Aid (EPER)*;
- *Terra Nuova*;
- US Food Sovereignty Alliance (USFSA);
- *World Alliance for Breastfeeding Action (WABA, #21079)*;
- *World Alliance of Mobile Indigenous Peoples (WAMIP)*;
- *World Organisation Against Torture (OMCT, #21685).* [2015/XJ9389/y/F]

- ♦ Right Livelihood Award Foundation / see Right Livelihood Foundation (#18944)

♦ Right Livelihood Foundation 18944

Exec Dir Stockholmsvägen 23, SE-122 62 Enskede, Sweden. T. +4687020340. E-mail: info@rightlivelihood.org.
Dir Geneva Office Maison de la Paix, Chemin Eugène-Rigot 2E, Building 5, 1202 Geneva, Switzerland.
URL: https://www.rightlivelihood.org/

History 1980, Isle of Man. Former names and other names: *Right Livelihood Award Foundation* – legal name. Registration: Charity foundation, Sweden. **Aims** Promote scientific research, education, public understanding and practical activities which: contribute to a global ecological balance; are aimed at eliminating material and spiritual *poverty*; contribute to lasting peace and justice in the world. **Structure** Board of Trustees; International Jury; Advisory Board; Head Office in Stockholm (Sweden); Office in Geneva. **Languages** English, French, German, Spanish, Swedish. **Staff** 20.00 FTE, paid. **Finance** Sources: donations; fundraising. Annual budget: 55,000,000 SEK (2022). **Activities** Awards/prizes/competitions; capacity building; publishing activities. **Events** *Regional Conference / Conference* Cairo (Egypt) 2014, *Regional Conference / Conference* Bogota (Colombia) 2013, *Conference* Bonn (Germany) 2010, *International conference on energy, resources and peace* Berlin (Germany) / Osnabrück (Germany) 2007, *Annual seminar* Stockholm (Sweden) 2007. **Publications** *Backstage Heroes – Alternative Nobel Prize Laureates* (2012) by Katharina Mouratidi; *Vorbilder* (2008) by Jürgen Streich; *Der Alternative Nobelpreis* (2005) by Jürgen Streich; *Die Alternative, Wege und Weltbild des Alternativen Nobelpreises* (2003) by Gesko V Lüpke in German; *Pioneers of Change* (1993) by Jeremy Seabrook; *A New World Order, Grassroots Movements for Global Change* (1992) by Paul Ekins in English; *Vivir Ligeramente sobre la Tierra* (1992) in Spanish; *Projekte der Hoffnung* (1990) by J von Uexkull and Bernd Dost in German; *Vi och vår jord* (1989) in Swedish; *Il Premio Nobel Alternativo* (1988) by J von Uexkull in Italian; *People and Planet* (1987) in English; *Der Alternative Nobelpreis* (1986) by J von Uexkull in German. **Members** Not a membership organization. **Consultative Status** Consultative status granted from: *ECOSOC (#05331)* (Special). **NGO Relations** Maintains partnerships with numerous NGOs. [2022.10.19/XF1899/t/F]

♦ Right to Play International 18945

CEO 18 King St East, Suite 14, Toronto ON M5C 1C4, Canada. T. +14162030190. E-mail: info@righttoplay.com.
URL: http://www.righttoplay.com/

History Evolved from a fundraising organization *Olympic Aid*, set up 2000. **Aims** Improve the lives of children in some of the most disadvantaged areas of the world by using the power of sport and play for development, health and peace. **Structure** Board. **Consultative Status** Consultative status granted from: *ECOSOC (#05331)* (Special). **NGO Relations** Recognized by: *International Olympic Committee (IOC, #14408)*. Member of: *Girls not Brides (#10154)*; *Inter-agency Network for Education in Emergencies (INEE, #11387).* [2019/XJ1231/E]

- ♦ Rights and Accountability in Development (internationally oriented national body)
- ♦ Rights – Equality – Solidarity – Power – Europe Cooperation Today ! / see RESPECT (#18917)
- ♦ Right Sharing of World Resources (internationally oriented national body)

♦ Rights and Humanity 18946

Contact address not obtained. E-mail: jhausermann@gmail.com – info@rightsandhumanity.org.
URL: http://www.rightsandhumanity.org/

History 10 Dec 1986, on the initiative of Julia Häusermann. Sub-title: *International Movement for the Promotion and Realization of Human Rights and Responsibilities.* Constitution adopted 1 Aug 1986. Registered in accordance with Swiss law. UK Registered Charity: 1001555. **Aims** Promote economic and social justice and human development for all, through respect for human rights and the observance of responsibilities at all levels of international and national governance and society, so that all people may live in dignity and achieve their full potential in a just and compassionate world. **Structure** International Board of Trustees; Management Board; President; UK Trustees. Global Strategy Group. **Staff** Secretariat staff; interns. **Finance** Members' dues. Other sources: donations; consultancy fees. Budget (annual): about pounds250,000. **Activities** Undertakes research to identify causes of economic and social injustice and promotes practical strategies for action based on respect of human rights and the principles of humanity; promotes development of human rights theory and law in order that they adequately address the needs of real people; facilitates bridge-building between people of different faiths, cultures and professions in order to develop common strategies to promote equity and social justice for all; promotes constitutional protection of human rights and integration into national law of international obligations; articulates the human rights framework for policy-making and identifies measures necessary to ensure implementation of human rights at all levels; develops global consensus concerning good practice guidelines to shape law, policy, and action to ensure respect for human rights at all levels; promotes integration of human rights norms and principles of humanity in international and national policy-making by participating in and contributing to the conclusions of relevant UN conferences and other international meetings; conducts education and training in human rights and responsibilities for government officials, and the professional and educational spheres; carries out projects in partnership with local NGO's both in the UK and abroad. Established *'Human Rights and Development Forum'* in the UK. **Events** *Global Leaders Congress* Liverpool (UK) 2011, *Table ronde sur les droits de l'homme et les politiques culturelles dans l'Europe en transformation / Meeting* Helsinki (Finland) 1993. **Publications** Books; reports; papers; statements; excerpts; proposals; analyses; newsletters. **Members** in 52 countries. Membership countries not specified. **IGO Relations** *Commonwealth Secretariat (#04362)*; *UNHCR (#20327)*; *WHO (#20950)* Comprehensive Programme. **NGO Relations** Instrumental in setting up: *Human Rights Caucus (no recent information)*; *Human Rights Centre, Krakow (no recent information).* [2019/XF2981/F]

- ♦ Rights International (internationally oriented national body)
- ♦ Rights International, The Center for International Human Rights Law / see Rights International

♦ Rights and Resources Initiative (RRI) 18947

Initiative pour les Droits et Ressources – Iniciativa para los Derechos y Recursos
Contact 2715 M St NW, Suite 300, Washington DC 20007, USA. T. +12024703900. Fax +12029443315. E-mail: info@rightsandresources.org.
URL: http://www.rightsandresources.org/

History 2005, by *Asociación Coordinadora Indígena y Campesina de Agroforestería Comunitaria (ACICAFOC, #02120)*, *Center for International Forestry Research (CIFOR, #03646)*, *Forest Trends (#09870)*, *'Foundation for People and Community Development'* (Papua New Guinea), *International Union for Conservation of Nature and Natural Resources (IUCN, #15766)* and *RECOFTC – The Center for People and Forests (RECOFTC, #18628).* **Aims** Support local communities' and *indigenous* peoples' struggles against *poverty* and *marginalization* by promoting greater global commitment and action towards policy, market and legal reforms that secure their rights to own, control and benefit from natural resources, especially land and *forests*; encourage transformation of forest economy so that business reflects local development agendas and support local livelihoods. **Structure** Board of Directors; Fellows (13). **Languages** English, French, Hindi, Indonesian, Nepali, Spanish. **Staff** 31.00 FTE, paid. **Finance** Rights and Resources Group (RRG) manages finances. **Activities** Networking/liaising; monitoring/evaluation; projects/programmes; politics/policy/regulatory; research and development. **Events** *Dialogue on Forests, Governance and Climate Change* Bogota (Colombia) 2013, *Global Conference on Community Participatory Mapping of Indigenous People's Territories* Samosir Is (Indonesia) 2013, *RRI Dialogue on Forests, Governance and Climate Change* Yaoundé (Cameroon) 2013, *Annual Workshop on Rethinking Forest Regulations* Missoula, MT (USA) 2012. **Publications** *Annual Narrative Report*; *RRI Quarterly Update*; *Tenure Trends.*
Members Partners (15), including the following 6 organizations listed in this Yearbook:
Forest Trends (#09870); *HELVETAS Swiss Intercooperation*; *Indigenous Peoples' International Centre for Policy Research and Education (Tebtebba Foundation)*; *International Forestry and Resources Institutions (IFRI)*; *RECOFTC – The Center for People and Forests (RECOFTC, #18628)*; *World Agroforestry Centre (ICRAF, #21072).*
IGO Relations Provides secretariat for: *MegaFlorestais (#16699).* **NGO Relations** Charter member of: *Global Landscapes Forum (GLF, #10451).* [2019.10.31/XJ2972/y/F]

♦ RI Global 18948

SG 866 United Nations Plaza, Office 422, New York NY 10017, USA. T. +12124201500. Fax +12125050871. E-mail: info@riglobal.org.
URL: http://www.riglobal.org/

History 1922, Elyria, OH (USA). Constitution most recently amended, 19 Jun 2004, Oslo (Norway). Former names and other names: *International Society for Crippled Children* – former; *Société internationale d'assistance aux enfants estropiés* – former; *International Society for the Welfare of Cripples* – former; *Société internationale pour la protection des invalides* – former; *International Society for Rehabilitation of the Disabled (ISRD)* – former; *RI – Rehabilitation International* – former; *Réhabilitation internationale* – former; *Rehabilitación Internacional* – former. Registration: Start date: 1929, USA. **Aims** Advance the rights and

inclusion of persons with *disabilities* worldwide. **Structure** Assembly (annual), consisting of representatives designated by Affiliated National Organizations and by International Member Organizations. Each country of membership is represented by a National Secretary, agreed among Affiliated National Organizations if more than one per country, and appointed by the Assembly where there is no National Affiliate. Board of Directors; Executive Committee. Regional Committees (7): Africa; Arab; Asia and the Pacific; Caribbean; Europe; Latin America; North America. International Secretariat in New York NY (USA), headed by Secretary General. Autonomous EU organization, *Rehabilitation International – European Communities Association (RI-ECA, #18825)*, based in Nemours (France). Working Commissions (7): Work and Employment; Education; Technology and Accessibility *ICTA*; Health and Function; Policy and Service; Social; Leisure, Recreation and Physical Activities. **Languages** English. **Staff** 5.00 FTE, paid. **Finance** Sources: contributions; grants; members' dues. **Activities** Advocacy/lobbying/activism; events/meetings; guidance/assistance/consulting; networking/liaising; politics/policy/regulatory. Actively supports: *Convention on the Rights of Persons with Disabilities (CRPD, 2006)*; *Convention Concerning Vocational Rehabilitation and Employment (1983)*. **Events** *Rehabilitation World Congress* Aarhus (Denmark) 2021, *Rehabilitation World Congress* Aarhus (Denmark) 2020, *Rehabilitation World Congress* Edinburgh (UK) 2016, *Annual General Assembly* Warsaw (Poland) 2014, *Quadrennial World Congress* Incheon (Korea Rep) 2012. **Publications** *International Journal of Rehabilitation Research* (4 a year); *One-in-Ten* (4 a year) – newsletter on childhood disability in developing countries; *International Rehabilitation Review* (3 a year); *Rehabilitación: Prevención y Integración* (2 a year) in Spanish. Congress/conference proceedings; books; studies; pamphlets; resolutions; catalogue of audiovisual materials for public education and training (1998); resource kit; videos. **Information Services** *Rehabilitation International Information Services* – information distributed regularly from New York NY to more than 150 countries. **Members** Organizations involved in disability prevention and rehabilitation service development. National secretaries and member organizations in 79 countries and territories:
Afghanistan, Angola, Australia, Austria, Bahrain, Bangladesh, Belgium, Bhutan, Brazil, Burkina Faso, Burundi, Cambodia, Cameroon, Canada, China, Colombia, Congo DR, Czechia, Denmark, Ethiopia, Finland, Gambia, Germany, Ghana, Greece, Hong Kong, Hungary, Iceland, India, Indonesia, Iraq, Ireland, Israel, Italy, Japan, Jordan, Kenya, Korea Rep, Kuwait, Lebanon, Lithuania, Luxembourg, Malaysia, Mexico, Moldova, Mongolia, Nepal, New Zealand, Nigeria, Norway, Oman, Pakistan, Palestine, Poland, Qatar, Saudi Arabia, Seychelles, Sierra Leone, Slovakia, Slovenia, South Africa, Spain, Sri Lanka, Sudan, Sweden, Switzerland, Syrian AR, Taiwan, Tanzania UR, Thailand, Timor-Leste, Tunisia, Uganda, UK, United Arab Emirates, USA, Vietnam, Yemen, Zimbabwe.
Included in the above, 1 organization listed in this Yearbook:
Fédération Africaine des Professionnels de la Réadaptation (FATO, #09399).
International Member Organizations (4):
Goodwill Industries International (GII); *International Society for Augmentative and Alternative Communication (ISAAC, #14949)*; *Norwegian People's Aid (NPA)*; *Pacific Disability Forum (PDF, #17945).*
Consultative Status Consultative status granted from: *ECOSOC (#05331)* (Special); *ILO (#11123)* (Special List); *UNICEF (#20332)*; *Council of Europe (CE, #04881)* (Participatory Status). **IGO Relations** Accredited by (1): *United Nations Office at Vienna (UNOV, #20604)*. Official relations with: *UNESCO (#20322)*; *European Commission (EC, #06633)*; *OAS (#17629)*. Associated with Department of Global Communications of the United Nations. **NGO Relations** Member of (5): *All Africa Leprosy, Tuberculosis and Rehabilitation Training Centre (ALERT, #00642)*; *Conference of Non-Governmental Organizations in Consultative Relationship with the United Nations (CONGO, #04635)*; *End Corporal Punishment (#05457)*; *New World Hope Organization (NWHO)*; *NGO Committee on UNICEF (#17120)*. Participates in: *Global Partnership on Children with Disabilities (GPcwd, #10529).* [2021/XA2501/y/**A**]

♦ Rigoberta Menchú Tum Foundation (internationally oriented national body)

♦ RIGPA 18949

International Office Lerab Ling, L'Engayresque, 34650 Roqueredonde, France. T. +33467884600. Fax +33467884601. E-mail: lerab.ling@rigpa.org.
Rigpa UK 330 Caledonian Road, London, N1 1BB, UK. T. +442077000185. Fax +442076096068. E-mail: enquiries@rigpa.org.uk.
URL: http://www.rigpa.org/
History by Dilgo Khyentse Rinpoche. **Aims** Function as an international *network* of *Buddhist meditation* centres and groups. **Publications** *RIGPA Journal* (occasional).
Members Centres and groups in 11 countries:
Australia, Belgium, Canada, France, Germany, India, Ireland, Netherlands, Switzerland, UK, USA. [2018/XF6009/**F**]

♦ **RIHED** SEAMEO Regional Centre for Higher Education and Development (#19174)
♦ **RIIAL** Red Informatica de la Iglesia en América Latina (#18689)
♦ RIIA – Royal Institute of International Affairs (internationally oriented national body)
♦ **RIICOTEC** Red Intergubernamental Iberoamericana de Cooperación Técnica para el Desarrollo de Políticas de Atención a personas con Discapacidad y Adultos Mayores (#18697)
♦ RIIP / see Pasteur Network (#18256)
♦ RIIR / see Egmont Institute
♦ **RII** Red Iberoamericana de Investigadores sobre Globalización y Territorio (#18670)
♦ **RIITA** Robotics, Informatics, and Intelligent control Technology Association (#18963)
♦ RIJ / see Refugee Empowerment International
♦ RIJA – Réseau International des Juristes Africanistes (unconfirmed)
♦ **RIKEPS** Red Iberoamericana de Investigadores "Kant: Ética, Política y Sociedad (#18671)
♦ Rikolto (internationally oriented national body)
♦ **RILAA** Red Interamericana de Laboratorios de Analisis de Alimentos (#18694)
♦ RILA – Retail Industry Leaders Association (internationally oriented national body)
♦ **RILEM** Réunion internationale des laboratoires d'essais et de recherches sur les matériaux et les constructions (#18930)
♦ RILM / see Répertoire International de Littérature Musicale (#18845)
♦ RILM Abstracts of Music Literature / see Répertoire International de Littérature Musicale (#18845)
♦ **RILM** Répertoire International de Littérature Musicale (#18845)
♦ RIMA International / see Reflective Insulation Manufacturers Association International (#18735)
♦ **RIMA-I** Reflective Insulation Manufacturers Association International (#18735)
♦ **RIMAIS** Red Iberoamericana Ministerial de Aprendizaje e Investigación en Salud (#18676)
♦ RIMA / see Reflective Insulation Manufacturers Association International (#18735)
♦ RIME / see Istituto di Studi sul Mediterraneo
♦ **RIMES** Regional Integrated Multi-Hazard Early Warning System for Africa and Asia (#18790)
♦ RIMISP / see Centro Latinoamericano para el Desarrollo Rural (#03813)
♦ **RIMISP** Centro Latinoamericano para el Desarrollo Rural (#03813)
♦ RIMMO – Réserve internationale maritime en méditerranée occidentale (no recent information)
♦ **RIMM** Red Internacional "Mujeres y Mineria" (#15895)
♦ RIMPA – Records and Information Management Professionals Australasia (internationally oriented national body)
♦ **RIMPS** Red Iberoamericana de Migraciones Profesionales de Salud (#18675)
♦ Rimskij Klub (#04038)
♦ **RIMS** Red Iberoamericana de Mercadotecnia en Salud (#18674)
♦ **RIMS** Rehabilitation in Multiple Sclerosis (#18826)
♦ RIMS – Risk and Insurance Management Society (internationally oriented national body)
♦ **RINADH** Réseau des Institutions Nationales Africaines des Droits de l'Homme (#16984)
♦ RINA – Royal Institution of Naval Architects (internationally oriented national body)
♦ RINDHCA – Red de Instituciones Nacionales para la Promoción y Protección de los Derechos Humanos del Continente Americano (unconfirmed)

♦ Ring14 International 18950

Headquarters Via Lusenti 1/1, 42121 Reggio Emilia RE, Italy. T. +39522421037. Fax +39522421037. E-mail: info@ring14.org.
Pres address not obtained. T. +17654916910.
Registered Office Via Santa Maria alla Porta 2, 20123 Milan MI, Italy.
URL: http://www.ring14.org/
History Founded May 2002, Reggio Emilia (Italy) as an Italian organization. International network founded 2014. Registered in accordance with Italian law. **Aims** Support and promote, on an international level, medical and scientific *research* regarding the *syndrome* of *Chromosome 14*; carry out free assistance, support, direction and aid to affected *children* and their families. **Structure** Board of Directors; Scientific Advisory Board. **Finance** Members' dues. Other sources: donations; fundraising. **Activities** Healthcare; knowledge management/information dissemination; research and development; events/meetings.
Members Organizations in 7 countries:
Belgium, France, Italy, Netherlands, Spain, UK, USA.
NGO Relations Member of: *EURORDIS – Rare Diseases Europe (#09175).* [2018/XM7451/**F**]

♦ Rinoceros (internationally oriented national body)
♦ RINORD – Consulting Engineers in the Nordic Countries (no recent information)
♦ Rio Abierto Foundation (internationally oriented national body)
♦ **RIOB** Réseau international des organismes de bassin (#14235)
♦ **RIOCC** Red Iberoamericana de Oficinas de Cambio Climático (#18677)
♦ **RIOD** Red Iberoamericana de Organizaciones no Gubernamentales que Trabajan en Drogodependencias (#18679)
♦ Rio Group – Permanent Mechanism for Consultation and Political Coordination (inactive)
♦ **RIOOD** Red Iberoamericana de Organismos y Organizaciones contra la Discriminación (#18678)
♦ **RIOPPAH** Regional International Organization for Plant Protection and Animal Health (#17830)
♦ Rio Treaty – Inter-American Treaty of Reciprocal Assistance (1947 treaty)
♦ Rio treaty – Protocol of Amendment to the Inter-American Treaty of Reciprocal Assistance (1975 treaty)
♦ Rio+twenties / see Children and Youth International (#03882)
♦ **RIPALC** Red de Intercambio de los Parlamentos de América Latina y El Caribe (#18696)
♦ **RIPAQS** Réseau International pour la Planification et l'Amélioration de la Qualité et la Sécurité dans les systèmes de santé en Afrique (#14304)
♦ **RIPC** Réseau international sur la politique culturelle (#14246)
♦ **RIPD** Red Iberoamericana de Protección de Datos (#18681)
♦ RIPE NCC / see RIPE Network Coordination Centre (#18951)
♦ **RIPE NCC** RIPE Network Coordination Centre (#18951)

♦ RIPE Network Coordination Centre (RIPE NCC) 18951

Mailing Address PO Box 10096, 1001 EB Amsterdam, Netherlands. T. +31205354444. Fax +31205354445.
URL: http://www.ripe.net/
History 1992. Founded as a service of *Trans-European Research and Education Networking Association (TERENA, inactive)* (formerly *Réseaux associés pour la recherche européenne (RARE, inactive)* to serve as secretariat to the RIPE community and as Regional Internet Registry (RIR). Established as a separate, non-profit association under current title, 1 Jan 1998. Former names and other names: *Réseaux IP européens Network Coordination Centre (RIPE NCC)* – former (1992 to 1 Jan 1998). Registration: Netherlands. **Aims** Serve the needs of the RIPE community; ensure fair *distribution* of *Internet* number resources in the RIPE NCC service region (Europe, Middle East and parts Central Asia); facilitate the stable and reliable operation of the Internet. **Structure** General Meeting (twice a year); Executive Board. Divisions (13): Software Engineering; Communications; Customer Services; RIPE Database; Finance; Facilities, Administration, Reception (FAR); Global Information Infrastructure (GII); Human Resources; IT; Policy Development Office; Registration Services; Research and Development (R and D); Training Services; Web Services. **Languages** English. **Staff** 13.00 FTE, paid. **Activities** Guidance/assistance/consulting; knowledge management/information dissemination; training/education. **Events** *Meeting* Amsterdam (Netherlands) 2021, *Meeting* Amsterdam (Netherlands) 2020, *Meeting* Amsterdam (Netherlands) 2020, *Meeting* Rotterdam (Netherlands) 2019, *Meeting* Marseille (France) 2018. **Publications** *Member Update* – newsletter. Annual and Financial Report; organizational information brochures. **Information Services** *Global Information Infrastructure (GII)*; *RIPE Atlas*; *RIPELabs*; *RIPEstat*.
Members As of Dec 2014: Local Internet Registries (LIRs) (23,500) in 240 countries and territories:
Afghanistan, Åland, Albania, Algeria, Andorra, Angola, Anguilla, Antigua-Barbuda, Argentina, Armenia, Aruba, Australia, Austria, Azerbaijan, Bahamas, Bahrain, Bangladesh, Barbados, Belarus, Belgium, Belize, Benin, Bermuda, Bhutan, Bolivia, Bosnia-Herzegovina, Botswana, Brazil, British Indian Ocean Terr, Brunei Darussalam, Bulgaria, Burkina Faso, Burundi, Cambodia, Cameroon, Canada, Cape Verde, Cayman Is, Central African Rep, Chad, Chile, China, Christmas Is, Cocos-Keeling Is, Colombia, Comoros, Congo Brazzaville, Congo DR, Cook Is, Costa Rica, Côte d'Ivoire, Croatia, Cuba, Cyprus, Czechia, Denmark, Djibouti, Dominica, Dominican Rep, Ecuador, Egypt, El Salvador, Equatorial Guinea, Eritrea, Estonia, Eswatini, Ethiopia, Faeroe Is, Falklands/Malvinas, Fiji, Finland, France, French Southern and Antarctic Terr, Gabon, Gambia, Georgia, Germany, Ghana, Gibraltar, Greece, Greenland, Grenada, Guadeloupe, Guam, Guatemala, Guernsey, Guiana Fr, Guinea, Guinea-Bissau, Guyana, Haiti, Heard Is, Holy See, Honduras, Hong Kong, Hungary, Iceland, India, Indonesia, Iran Islamic Rep, Iraq, Ireland, Isle of Man, Israel, Italy, Jamaica, Japan, Jersey, Jordan, Kazakhstan, Kenya, Kiribati, Korea DPR, Korea Rep, Kuwait, Kyrgyzstan, Laos, Latvia, Lebanon, Lesotho, Liberia, Libya, Liechtenstein, Lithuania, Luxembourg, Macau, Madagascar, Malawi, Malaysia, Maldives, Mali, Malta, Marshall Is, Martinique, Mauritania, Mauritius, Mayotte, McDonald Is, Mexico, Micronesia FS, Moldova, Monaco, Mongolia, Montenegro, Montserrat, Morocco, Mozambique, Namibia, Nauru, Nepal, Netherlands, New Caledonia, New Zealand, Nicaragua, Niger, Nigeria, Niue, Norfolk Is, North Macedonia, Northern Mariana Is, Norway, Oman, Pakistan, Palau, Palestine, Panama, Papua New Guinea, Paraguay, Peru, Philippines, Pitcairn, Poland, Polynesia Fr, Portugal, Puerto Rico, Qatar, Réunion, Romania, Russia, Rwanda, Sahara West, Samoa, Samoa USA, San Marino, Sao Tomé-Principe, Saudi Arabia, Senegal, Serbia, Seychelles, Sierra Leone, Singapore, Slovakia, Slovenia, Solomon Is, Somalia, South Africa, South Georgia, Spain, Sri Lanka, St Helena, St Kitts-Nevis, St Lucia, St Pierre-Miquelon, St Vincent-Grenadines, Sudan, Suriname, Sweden, Switzerland, Syrian AR, Taiwan, Tajikistan, Tanzania UR, Timor-Leste, Togo, Tokelau, Tonga, Trinidad-Tobago, Tunisia, Türkiye, Turkmenistan, Turks-Caicos, Tuvalu, Uganda, UK, Ukraine, United Arab Emirates, Uruguay, USA, Uzbekistan, Vanuatu, Venezuela, Vietnam, Virgin Is UK, Virgin Is USA, Wallis-Futuna, Yemen, Zambia, Zimbabwe.
Note: Not all territories listed by RIPE NCC are listed above.
Consultative Status Consultative status granted from: *ECOSOC (#05331)* (Special). **NGO Relations** Observer of: *Alliance for Safe Online Pharmacy – EU (ASOP EU, #00720)*. Cooperates with: *Internet (#15948)*. Member of: *Number Resource Organization (NRO, #17625).* [2021/XF3837/**F**]

♦ RIPESS Europe – Economy Solidarity Europe (RIPESS Europe) 18952

Delegate General Rue de Moulin 1, L-4251 Esch-sur-Alzette, Luxembourg. T. +352621236255. E-mail: info@ripess.eu.
General Coordinator address not obtained.
URL: https://ripess.eu/en/
History 2011, Barcelona (Spain). Set up as a continental federation of *Intercontinental Network for the Promotion of the Social Solidarity Economy (INPSSE, #11463)*. Registration: Mémorial C, No/ID: F0008943, Start date: 19 Dec 2011, Luxembourg, Esch-sur-Alzette. **Aims** Exchange practices; commit to common activities to broaden and improve visibility of social and solidarity *economics*. **Structure** General Meeting; Coordination Committee; Coordination Bureau. **Languages** English, French. **Staff** 0.50 FTE, paid. **Finance** Members' dues. Support from: *Fondation Charles Léopold Mayer pour le progrès de l'homme (FPH, #09815)*. **Activities** Events/meetings; networking/liaising. **Events** *General Assembly* Wroclaw (Poland) 2022, *General Assembly* Paris (France) 2021, *General Assembly* Esch-sur-Alzette (Luxembourg) 2020, *General Assembly* Lyon (France) 2019, *General Assembly* Zagreb (Croatia) 2018. **Publications** *RIPESSS EUROPE Newsletter*.
Members Full in 19 countries:
Belgium, Bulgaria, Croatia, Czechia, Finland, France, Germany, Greece, Hungary, Italy, Latvia, Luxembourg, North Macedonia, Poland, Portugal, Romania, Spain, Switzerland, UK.
Included in the above, 4 organizations listed in this Yearbook:
Autre Terre (#03044); *European Institute for Solidarity based Economy (#07572)*; *European Inter-Network of Ethical and Responsible Initiatives (#07593)*; *International Association of Investors in the Social Economy (INAISE, #11971).* [2022/XJ8665/y/**E**]

♦ **RIPESS Europe** RIPESS Europe – Economy Solidarity Europe (#18952)
♦ **RIPESS** Réseau intercontinental de promotion de l'économie sociale et solidaire (#11463)
♦ RIPM – Répertoire international de la presse musicale (internationally oriented national body)
♦ **RIPPET** Red Iberoamericana de Postgrados sobre Política y Estudios Territoriales (#18680)
♦ **RIPSO** Red Interamericana de Protección Social (#11447)
♦ RIPS – Regional Institute for Population Studies (no recent information)
♦ RI – Refugees International (internationally oriented national body)
♦ RI – Rehabilitation International / see RI Global (#18948)

♦ RIRE – Red Interamericana de Refugios (unconfirmed)
♦ **RI** Retina International (#18926)
♦ **RI** Richelieu International (#18938)
♦ RI – Rights International (internationally oriented national body)
♦ **RIRM** Réseau des instances de régulation méditerranéennes (#16665)
♦ RI – Rodale Institute (internationally oriented national body)
♦ **RI** Rotary International (#18975)
♦ **RIRTP** Réseau international de recherche en tourisme polaire (#14608)
♦ RISA – Russian International Studies Association (internationally oriented national body)
♦ Rise Against Hunger (internationally oriented national body)
♦ **RISEAP** Regional Islamic Da'wah Council of Southeast Asia and the Pacific (#18792)
♦ RISE-AT – Regional Information Service Centre for Southeast Asia on Appropriate Technology (internationally oriented national body)
♦ RISEBA – Riga International School of Economics and Business Administration (internationally oriented national body)
♦ **RISE Foundation** Rural Investment Support for Europe Foundation (#19002)
♦ RISH – Research Institute for Spirituality and Health (internationally oriented national body)
♦ RIS, India – Research and Information System for Developing Countries, India (internationally oriented national body)
♦ Rising Tide / see Rising Tide International (#18953)
♦ Rising Tide Coalition / see Rising Tide International (#18953)
♦ Rising Tide Coalition for Climate Justice / see Rising Tide International (#18953)

♦ Rising Tide International 18953

Contact c/o London Action Resource Centre, 62 Fieldgate Street, London, E1 1ES, UK. E-mail: info@risingtide.org.uk.
URL: https://www.risingtidenorthamerica.org/

History 2000, Netherlands. Founded to oppose COP6 climate talks. Former names and other names: *Rising Tide Coalition* – former; *Rising Tide Coalition for Climate Justice* – former; *Rising Tide* – former. **Members** Membership countries not specified. [2022.10.18/XF6615/**F**]

♦ RISI – Rossijskij Institut Strategiceskih Issledovanij (internationally oriented national body)
♦ Risk, Finance and Banking Society (internationally oriented national body)
♦ Risk and Insurance Management Society (internationally oriented national body)
♦ Risk Management Institution of Australasia (internationally oriented national body)
♦ **RISM** Répertoire international des sources musicales (#13949)
♦ RIS – Research Institute for Subtropics, Okinawa (internationally oriented national body)
♦ Rissho Kosei-Kai (internationally oriented national body)
♦ RISS – Russia's Institute for Strategic Studies (internationally oriented national body)
♦ Risurrezionisti – Congregazione della Risurrezione di Nostro Signore Gesù Cristo (religious order)
♦ **RITA-Afrique de l'est** Réseau d'information des terres arides de l'Afrique de l'est (#01105)
♦ RITA – Rabies in the Americas (meeting series)
♦ Rite ancien et primitif de Memphis-Misraïm (#00815)
♦ RITE – Research Institute of Innovative Technology for the Earth (internationally oriented national body)
♦ **RITerm** Red Iberoamericana de Terminologia (#18685)
♦ RITIMO – Réseau d'information Tiers-Monde des centres de documentation pour le développement (internationally oriented national body)
♦ RITLA – Red de Información Tecnológica Latinoamericana (see: #19294)
♦ RITM – Research Institute of Tropical Medicine (internationally oriented national body)
♦ **RITSEC** Regional Information Technology and Software Engineering Centre (#18789)
♦ **RITSQ** Red Iberoamericana de Toxicologia y Seguridad Quimica (#18686)
♦ Ritsumeikan Asia Pacific University (internationally oriented national body)
♦ Ritterorden vom Heiligen Grab zu Jerusalem (religious order)
♦ RIUL – Réseau International des Universités Libres (unconfirmed)
♦ Riunione delle Opere per l'Aiuto alle Chiese Orientali (see: #04672)
♦ **RIUPS** Red Iberoamericana de Universidades Promotoras de la Salud (#18688)
♦ River Basin Initiative (no recent information)
♦ River Cleanup (internationally oriented national body)
♦ River Niger Commission / see Niger Basin Authority (#17134)
♦ River Plate Basin System / see Comité Intergubernamental Coordinador de los Paises de la Cuenca del Plata (#04172)
♦ Rivers without Boundaries (unconfirmed)
♦ RiverWatch (internationally oriented national body)
♦ RiverWatch – Society for the Protection of Rivers / see RiverWatch
♦ RIV – Union internationale des wagons (inactive)
♦ **RIWA** Association of River Water Companies (#02895)
♦ Riyad Convention on Cooperation in Civil, Commercial and Criminal Matters (1983 treaty)
♦ Riyadh MOU – Memorandum of Understanding on Port State Control in the Arab States of the Gulf (2004 treaty)
♦ RJ4All – Restorative Justice for All International Institute (internationally oriented national body)
♦ **RJC** Responsible Jewellery Council (#18920)
♦ RJEEA – Réseau des Jeunes Entrepreneurs pour l'Emergence de l'Afrique (internationally oriented national body)
♦ **RJE** Réseau judiciaire européen (#07615)
♦ Rjeti i Muzeve të Ballkanit (#03080)
♦ **RJLSC** Regional Judicial and Legal Services Commission (#18793)
♦ RJM – Religious of Jesus-Mary (religious order)
♦ RKK – Rissho Kosei-Kai (internationally oriented national body)
♦ **RLABM** Red Iberoamericana de Bosques Modelo (#18659)
♦ RLAI – Red Latinoamericana de Abogados de Impacto (inactive)
♦ **RLB** Red Latinoamericana de Botanica (#16362)
♦ RLCPE – Red Latinoamericana de Centros y Programas de Escritura (unconfirmed)
♦ RLEF / see European Rugby League (#08411)
♦ RLICC – Raymond Lemaire International Centre for the Conservation of Historic Towns and Buildings (internationally oriented national body)
♦ **RLIT** Red Latinoamericana de Información Teologica (#18713)
♦ RLL / see Groupe de coordination pour l'épidémiologie et l'enregistrement du cancer dans les pays de langue latine (#10737)
♦ RLR – Congregation of La Retraite (religious order)
♦ RLS – Rosa Luxemburg Stiftung (internationally oriented national body)
♦ **RLSS** Royal Life Saving Society (#18992)
♦ RMAA / see Records and Information Management Professionals Australasia
♦ RMAI / see Initiative for Responsible Mining Assurance (#11212)
♦ RMA – International Recording Musicians Association (internationally oriented national body)
♦ **RMAMP** Rede das Mulheres Africanas Ministras e Parlamentares (#16988)
♦ RMA / see Regional Maritime University, Accra (#18796)
♦ RMA – Zone monétaire du Rand / see Multilateral Monetary Area (#16889)
♦ **RMBM** Red Mediterranea de Bosques Modelo (#16662)
♦ RM / see Brevets Randonneurs Mondiaux (#03323)
♦ **RMEI** Réseau méditerranéen des écoles d'ingénieurs (#18899)
♦ **RMEL CoP** Resilience Measurement Evidence and Learning Community of Practice (#18912)
♦ **RME Network** Refugee and Migrant Education Network (#18740)
♦ RMF / see GoodWeave International (#10681)
♦ **RMFM** Réseau méditerranéen de Forêts Modèles (#16662)
♦ **RMFN-Asia** Regional Model Forest Network – Asia (#18797)
♦ RMF – Ricky Martin Foundation (internationally oriented national body)
♦ RMIA – Risk Management Institution of Australasia (internationally oriented national body)
♦ **RMIES** Réseau mondial pour l'innovation dans l'enseignement supérieur (#10641)
♦ RMI / see GoodWeave International (#10681)
♦ **RMI** Red Latinoamericana de Maestrias en Derechos y Politicas Sociales de Infancia y Adolescencia (#18715)
♦ RMI – Responsible Minerals Initiative (internationally oriented national body)
♦ RML / see Réseau Entraide Solidarité Monde
♦ RMNS – Rencontres médias Nord-Sud (meeting series)
♦ RMO – WMO Resource Mobilization Office (see: #21649)
♦ RM Platform / see European Technology Platform in Additive Manufacturing (#08886)
♦ **RMU** Regional Maritime University, Accra (#18796)

♦ RNA Society 18954

CEO 7918 Jones Branch Dr, Ste 300, McLean VA 22102, USA. T. +13016347166. E-mail: rna@rnasociety.org – secretary@rnasociety.org – ceo@rnasociety.org.
URL: http://www.rnasociety.org/

History 1993. Current articles adopted 28 Jun 1995. **Aims** Facilitate sharing and dissemination of experimental results and emerging concepts in *ribonucleic acid* research in the broadest sense, from the ribosome to the spliceosome, from RNA viruses to catalytic RNAs, and from long noncoding RNAs to micro RNAs; represent polecular, evolutionary and structural biology, biochemistry, biomedical sciences, chemistry, genetics and virology as they relate to questions of the structure and function of RNA and of ribonucleoprotein assemblies. **Structure** Elected Officials: President, President-Elect or Past-President, Directors; Officers: CEO, CFO, Secretary; Standing Committees. **Activities** Awards/prizes/competitions; awareness raising; events/meetings; networking/liaising; publishing activities; research and development; research/documentation; training/education. **Events** *Annual Meeting* Boulder, CO (USA) 2022, *Annual Meeting* 2021, *Annual Meeting* McLean, VA (USA) 2020, *Annual Meeting* Krakow (Poland) 2019, *Annual Meeting* Berkeley, CA (USA) 2018. **Publications** *RNA* (12 a year) – peer-reviewed journal; *RNA Society Newsletter*. *An Imperfect Account of the Founding of the RNA Society* (2005) by Dr Olke Uhlenbeck. **Members** Individuals (over 3,200). Membership countries not specified. [2022.02.02/XJ6483/**C**]

♦ RNA Stability Conference (meeting series)
♦ RNB – Regional Nursing Body, CARICOM Community (no recent information)
♦ RNDM – Religieuses de Notre-Dame des Missions (religious order)
♦ **RNE** RailNetEurope (#18608)
♦ **RNI** Red Noses Clowndoctors International (#18724)
♦ **RNSA** Regional Network for Research, Surveillance and Control of Asian Schistosomiasis (#18801)
♦ **RNSA** Research Network for Schistosomiasis in Africa (#18859)
♦ **RNUS** Regional Network Office for Urban Safety (#18800)
♦ ROACO – Riunione delle Opere per l'Aiuto alle Chiese Orientali (see: #04672)
♦ **ROADDH** Réseau Ouest Africain des Défenseurs des Droits Humains (#20882)

♦ Road Engineering Association of Asia and Australasia (REAAA) ... 18955

Association d'ingénierie routière d'Asie et d'Australasie

Exec Sec 46B Jalan Bola Tampar 13/14, Section 13, 40100 Shah Alam, Selangor, Malaysia. T. +60355136380 – +60355246380. Fax +60355136390.
URL: http://www.reaaa.net/

History 15 Jun 1973, Kuala Lumpur (Malaysia). Also referred to as *Association des ingénieurs de la route d'Asie et d'Australasie*. **Aims** Promote the science and practice of road engineering and related professions in the Asia Pacific region though developing professional and commercial links within and between countries in the region. **Structure** General Meeting (held in conjunction with the Conference); Council; Executive Secretary. **Languages** English. **Staff** 2.00 FTE, paid. **Finance** Members' dues. Entrance fees. **Activities** Events/meetings; training/education; knowledge management/information dissemination; awards/prizes/competitions. **Events** *Conference* Manila (Philippines) 2021, *International Seminar and Workshop on Safer Roads by Infrastructure Design and Operation* Kuala Lumpur (Malaysia) 2019, *International Seminar on Towards Advanced Technology and Material in Bridge Engineering* Kuala Lumpur (Malaysia) 2019, *International Seminar on Disaster and Risk Management for Roads* Hanoi (Vietnam) 2018, *Roads for better living* Bali (Indonesia) 2017. **Publications** *REAAA Journal*; *REAAA Newsletter*. Information Services: Index of related literature and articles.

Members Life; Associate; Institutional; Honorary; Ordinary; Affiliate. Individuals (over 1,400) in 28 countries and territories:
Australia, Bangladesh, Brunei Darussalam, Denmark, France, Hong Kong, India, Indonesia, Iran Islamic Rep, Japan, Korea Rep, Malaysia, Nepal, New Zealand, Pakistan, Papua New Guinea, Philippines, Seychelles, Singapore, Spain, Sri Lanka, Sweden, Switzerland, Taiwan, Thailand, UK, United Arab Emirates, USA.
Local chapters in 6 countries:
Australia, Brunei Darussalam, Korea Rep, Malaysia, New Zealand, Philippines.
NGO Relations Affiliated to: *International Road Federation (IRF Global, #14759).* [2019.07.04/XD6515/**D**]

♦ **ROADPOL** European Roads Policing Network (#08395)
♦ Road Safety on Five Continents (meeting series)
♦ Road Scholar – Elderhostel (internationally oriented national body)
♦ **ROA** The Reality Of Aid (#18626)
♦ ROASE / see West Africa Election Observers Network (#20865)
♦ ROBAN – Réseau des organisations de bassin d'Amérique du Nord (internationally oriented national body)
♦ Robert Bosch Foundation (internationally oriented national body)
♦ Robert Bosch Stiftung (internationally oriented national body)

♦ Robert Carr civil society Networks Fund (RCNF) 18956

Secretariat Condensatorweg 54, 1014 AX Amsterdam, Netherlands. T. +31206262669. Fax +31206275221. E-mail: secretariat@robertcarrfund.org.
URL: http://www.robertcarrfund.org/

History Also know as *Robert Carr Fund for civil society networks*. **Aims** Support civil society networks in addressing critical factors for scaling up access to *HIV* prevention, treatment, care and support. **Structure** International Steering Committee (ISC); Program Advisory Panel (PAP); Fund Management Agency (FMA). **Languages** Dutch, English, Russian. **Staff** 5.00 FTE, paid. **Finance** Support from: BMGF; *Department for International Development (DFID, inactive)*; *Global Fund to Fight AIDS, Tuberculosis and Malaria (Global Fund, #10383)*; *Norwegian Agency for Development Cooperation (Norad)*; PEPFAR. **Activities** Capacity building; healthcare; networking/liaising; knowledge management/information dissemination. **Events** *Meeting* Amsterdam (Netherlands) 2019, *Meeting* Amsterdam (Netherlands) 2018, *Rights, Resources and Resilience Asia Pacific Summit* Bangkok (Thailand) 2017.

Members Networks and consortia of networks (18), including the following 6 organizations listed in this Yearbook:
Asia and Pacific Transgender Network (APTN, #02069); *Caribbean Vulnerable Communities Coalition (CVC, #03565)*; *Coordination of Action Research on AIDS and Mobility – Asia (CARAM Asia)*; *International Community of Women Living with HIV/AIDS (ICW, #12826)*; *International Network of Religious Leaders Living with or Personally Affected by HIV and AIDS (INERELA+, #14315)*; *Red de Latinoamérica y El Caribe de Personas Trans (REDLACTRANS, #18699)*.
NGO Relations Supports: *World Young Women's Christian Association (World YWCA, #21947)*. Links with civil society networks that are active in the HIV response. [2022/XM4148/f/**F**]

♦ Robert Carr Fund for civil society networks / see Robert Carr civil society Networks Fund (#18956)
♦ Robert F Kennedy Center for Justice and Human Rights / see Robert F Kennedy Human Rights
♦ Robert F Kennedy Human Rights (internationally oriented national body)
♦ Robert F Kennedy Memorial Center for Human Rights / see Robert F Kennedy Human Rights
♦ Robert S McNamara Fellowships Program (internationally oriented national body)

♦ Roberto Cimetta Fund (#09837)
♦ Robert and Renée Belfer Center for Science and International Affairs / see Belfer Center for Science and International Affairs
♦ Robert Schuman Centre for Advanced Studies (see: #09034)
♦ Robert Schuman Foundation (internationally oriented national body)

♦ Robert Schuman Foundation for Cooperation among Christian Democrats in Europe (RSF) 18957

Contact address not obtained. T. +3222843025. Fax +3222846950. E-mail: epp-schuman@europarl.europa.eu.
URL: http://www.schumanfoundation.eu/

History 18 Oct 1989. **Aims** Promote training of young people; provide political education; strengthen democracy and pluralism worldwide. **Structure** Executive Committee, comprising 7 members. **Events** *Annual CIS conference* Kiev (Ukraine) 1999, *Annual CIS conference* St Petersburg (Russia) 1998. [2013/XF3422/f/**F**]

♦ Robert Schuman Institute for Developing Democracy in Central and Eastern Europe (RSI) 18958

Robert Schuman Intézet a Közép-Kelet Európai Demokraciak Fejlödéséért Egyesület

Dir Alkotas u 5, Budapest 1123, Hungary. T. +3612020000. Fax +3612018985. E-mail: office@schuman-institute.eu.
URL: https://schuman-institute.eu/

History 31 Oct 1995, Budapest (Hungary). Replaced *Christian Democratic Academy for Central and Eastern Europe (inactive)*, founded 1991. Registration: EU Transparency Register, No/ID: 50962829391-94, Start date: 22 Aug 2012. **Aims** As a European educational centre for politicians and parties belonging to the political family of the European People's Party (EPP): fulfil, under the auspices of the EPP and in the spirit of Robert Schuman, the idea of United Europe; spread European values; support and promote democracy and civil society in countries inside and outside the European Union. **Structure** General Assembly/Members' Meeting (annual); International Board; Supervisory Board; Secretariat. **Languages** English. **Staff** 6.00 FTE, paid. **Finance** Members' dues; donations. Main supporters: *European People's Party (EPP, #08185)*; *Robert Schuman Foundation* – Luxembourg. **Activities** Politics/policy/regulatory; training/education; events/meetings. **Publications** *RSI Newsletter*. Books; booklets; conference proceedings.

Members Partner organizations in 21 countries:
Armenia, Austria, Belgium, Bosnia-Herzegovina, Czechia, Estonia, France, Germany, Greece, Hungary, Italy, Netherlands, North Macedonia, Norway, Romania, Serbia, Slovakia, Slovenia, Spain, Sweden, Ukraine.
European organizations (7):
European Centre for Workers' Questions (#06505); *European Democrat Students (EDS, #06901)*; *European People's Party (EPP, #08185)*; *European Seniors' Union (ESU, #08466)*; *European Union of Christian Democratic Workers (EUCDW, #08981)*; *Robert Schuman Foundation* (Luxembourg); *Youth of the European People's Party (YEPP, #22014)*.

IGO Relations Cooperates with: *European Parliament (EP, #08146)* (EPP Group). **NGO Relations** Cooperates with: *Eduardo Frei Foundation*; *European Democrat Students (EDS, #06901)*; *Hanns Seidel Foundation*; *International Republican Institute (IRI)*; *Konrad Adenauer Foundation (KAF)*; Kós Karoly Foundation; *Kristdemokratiskt Internationellt Center (KIC)*; *Wilfried Martens Centre for European Studies (Martens Centre, #20962)*; *EPP Women (#05516)*; *Youth of the European People's Party (YEPP, #22014)*; national organizations. [2022/XE2800/jy/**E**]

♦ Robert Schuman Institute for Europe (IRSE) 18959

Institut Robert Schuman pour l'Europe (IRSE)

SG 2 rue Robert Schuman, 57160 Scy-Chazelles, France. T. +33387601015. Fax +33387601471. E-mail: info@institut-robert-schuman.eu.
URL: http://www.institut-robert-schuman.eu/

History 9 May 1982. Statutes adopted 25 Sep 1982, Chantilly (France). Statutes modified: 27 Nov 1988; 22 Dec 2001; 27 Mar 2004. Registration: France. **Aims** Promote the work of Robert Schuman; increase awareness among Europeans of the intrinsic unity underlying their diverse cultures; replace nationalist antagonism by European *cooperation*; promote *peace* through cooperating regional communities. **Structure** General Assembly (at least annually); Council; Board. Antennae: *Conseil pour la paix et la réconciliation entre les peuples*, which makes the award *'Etoile de l'Europe pour la paix et la réconciliation entre les peuples'* to honour individual contributions promoting Europe; *Observatoire méditerranéen pour l'information et la réflexion – géopolitique, géoculture, géoéconomie, géoenvironnement (OMIR, see: #18959)*. **Languages** English, French, German. **Staff** 6.00 FTE, voluntary. **Finance** Sources: government support; meeting proceeds; members' dues; revenue from activities/projects; sponsorship. **Activities** Events/meetings. **Events** *International Conference* Paris (France) 2012, *International Conference* Paris (France) 2011, *Alumni conference* Budapest (Hungary) 2010, *Conférence internationale pour célébrer le 60ème anniversaire de la Déclaration de Robert Schuman, le 9 mai 1950 / International Conference* Paris (France) 2010, *Annual statutory general assembly* Moulins-lès-Metz (France) 2009. **Publications** *La construction européenne: une oeuvre de paix* (2014); *Europe – Islam – Droits de l'Homme* (2013); *L'Europe d'aujourd'hui, l'Europe du futur* (2011); *Europe-Cultures* – collection – 19 vols to date.

Members Founder; Active (individuals and corporate bodies); 'Membres d'honneur'. Organizations in 5 countries:
Congo Brazzaville, France, Italy, Luxembourg, Switzerland.
Individuals in 24 countries:
Algeria, Austria, Belgium, Cameroon, Canada, Congo Brazzaville, Denmark, France, Georgia, Germany, Greece, Holy See, Ireland, Italy, Kazakhstan, Luxembourg, Morocco, Portugal, Russia, Spain, Switzerland, Tunisia, Turkmenistan, UK.
Adhering European bodies (7):
Association Robert Schuman (#02896); Bureau européen d'études et de recherches de synergie; *Centre d'étude et de prospective stratégique (CEPS, #03739)*; *Centre Robert Schuman*; *Istituto di Studi Europei 'Alcide de Gasperi' (ISE)*; Journal du Parlement – Les dépêches de Brazzaville; *Religions for Peace (RfP, #18831)* (French section).

Consultative Status Consultative status granted from: *Council of Europe (CE, #04881)* (Participatory Status). **NGO Relations** Member of (3): *Conference of INGOs of the Council of Europe (#04607)*; *European Movement International (EMI, #07825)*; *Permanent Forum of European Civil Society (#18322)*. [2022.11.05/XE0848/jy/**E**]

♦ Robert Schuman Intézet a Közép-Kelet Európai Demokraciak Fejlödéséért Egyesület (#18958)
♦ Robert Triffin International (internationally oriented national body)
♦ Robin Hood Tax Network / see Stamp Out Poverty

♦ RoboCup Federation 18960

Operational Headquarters 1900 Embarcadero Rd, Suite 101, Palo Alto CA 94303, USA. E-mail: april.robocup@gmail.com.
Pres Univ of Texas at Austin, Dept of Computer Science, 2317 Speedway, Stop D9500, Austin TX 78712, USA.
URL: http://www.robocup.org/

History 1997. Registration: Swiss Civil Code, Switzerland. **Aims** Promote robotics and AI research by using competitions as a vehicle. **Structure** Board of Trustees; Internal Advisory Board; Regional Committees; Organizing Committees; Technical Committees. **Activities** Awards/prizes/competitions; events/meetings. **Events** *RoboCup 2021 Worldwide Symposium* 2021, *International Symposium* Bordeaux (France) 2021, *International Symposium* Bordeaux (France) 2020, *International Symposium* Sydney, NSW (Australia) 2019, *Asia Pacific Symposium* Kish (Iran Islamic Rep) 2018. [2021.09.09/XJ7006/**C**]

♦ Robot Framework Foundation 18961

Chairman address not obtained. E-mail: robotframework-foundation@googlegroups.com.
Sec address not obtained.
URL: https://robotframework.org/foundation/

Aims Foster the growth of Robot Framework. **Finance** Members' dues. **Activities** Advocacy/lobbying/activism. **Events** *Conference* Helsinki (Finland) 2018. **Members** Companies. Membership countries not specified. [2020/XM7916/f/**F**]

♦ Robotic Assisted Microsurgical and Endoscopic Society (RAMSES) 18962

Contact 15548 W Colonial Drive, Winter Garden, Clermont FL 34787, USA. T. +19737691020. Fax +18479603862. E-mail: sijo@avantconciergeurol.com.
URL: http://www.ramsesrobotics.com/

History 15 Feb 2010. **Aims** Further the development and application of robotic assisted microsurgical tools and platforms for enhanced surgical and *patient* outcomes. **Structure** Board of Directors; Managing Board; Executive Advisory Board. **Activities** Events/meetings. **Events** *Annual Symposium* Orlando, FL (USA) 2022, *Annual Symposium* Sao Paulo (Brazil) 2019, *Annual Symposium* Cartagena de Indias (Colombia) 2018, *Annual Symposium* Maastricht (Netherlands) 2017, *Annual Symposium* Istanbul (Turkey) 2016. [2022/XM7484/**C**]

♦ Robotics, Informatics, and Intelligent control Technology Association (RIITA) 18963

Chair Rajamangala University of Technology Thanyaburi, 39 Moo1, Klong 6, Khlong Luang, Pathum Thani, 12110, Thailand.

Aims Propose empirical research that tests, extends or builds business management theory and contributes to management practice. **Structure** Committee. **Events** *Conference* Bangkok (Thailand) 2022, *Conference* Bangkok (Thailand) 2018. **Publications** *JAMIC Journal*. [2022/XM8071/**C**]

♦ Robotics: Science and Systems Foundation (RSS Foundation) 18964

Contact address not obtained. E-mail: rssconfboard@gmail.com.
URL: https://www.roboticsfoundation.org

History The governing body behind the Robotics: Science and Systems (RSS) conference. **Structure** Foundation Board; Advisory Board. **Activities** Awards/prizes/competitions; events/meetings. **Events** *Robotics: Science and Systems* Daegu (Korea Rep) 2023, *Robotics: Science and Systems* New York, NY (USA) 2022, *Robotics: Science and Systems* 2021, *Robotics: Science and Systems* 2020, *Robotics: Science and Systems* Freiburg-Breisgau (Germany) 2019. [2023/XS1412/c/**E**]

♦ ROCAN – Red de Organizaciones de Cuenca de America del Norte (internationally oriented national body)
♦ **ROCARE** Réseau de recherche en éducation pour l'Afrique de l'Ouest et centrale (#05368)
♦ ROCARO – Réseau de l'ouest et du centre de l'Afrique recherche opérationnelle (inactive)
♦ ROCC / see Regional Marine Pollution Emergency Response Centre for the Mediterranean Sea (#18795)
♦ RocDyn – International Conference on Rock Dynamics and Applications (meeting series)

♦ A Rocha International 18965

Main Office 89 Worship Street, London, EC2A 2BF, UK.
URL: http://www.arocha.org/

History Founded Dec 1983, as *A Rocha Trust – Christians in Conservation*. UK Registered Charity: 1136041. Company Registration No: 6852417. EU Transparency Register: 371263033273-46. **Aims** Put into practice the *biblical* call to *care* for all creation; preserve *biological diversity* through practical *conservation* projects based on careful fieldwork. **Structure** Council of Reference; International Trustees; International Team; National Organizations; National Committees. **Languages** English. **Staff** 120.00 FTE, paid. **Finance** Financial support from trust, individuals, churches and organizations. **Activities** Research/documentation; training/education; knowledge management/information dissemination. **Publications** *A Rocha International News* (2 a year). Annual Review.

Members Organizations and projects in 20 countries:
Brazil, Bulgaria, Canada, Czechia, Finland, France, Ghana, India, Kenya, Lebanon, Netherlands, New Zealand, Nigeria, Peru, Portugal, South Africa, Switzerland, Uganda, UK, USA.

NGO Relations Member of: *European Habitats Forum (EHF, #07443)*; *Eurosite (#09181)*; *Global Connections*; *International Union for Conservation of Nature and Natural Resources (IUCN, #15766)*. [2018/XF4231/**F**]

♦ A Rocha Trust – Christians in Conservation / see A Rocha International (#18965)
♦ Rockefeller Brothers Fund (internationally oriented national body)

♦ The Rockefeller Foundation 18966

Main Office 420 Fifth Avenue, New York NY 10018, USA. T. +12128698500. Fax +12127643468.
URL: https://www.rockefellerfoundation.org/

History 1913. Registration: EU Transparency Register, No/ID: 496082445811-18, Start date: 15 Mar 2022. **Aims** Promote *well-being* of humanity by addressing the root causes of serious problems; expand opportunities for poor and vulnerable people; help ensure that the benefits of globalization are shared more equitably. **Structure** Board of Trustees, consisting of Chair and 16 members. **Finance** Budget (annual): US$ 147 million.

Activities Makes grants according to programme themes and cross-themes, each theme and cross-theme having a programme strategy. Grants are organized into categories – by theme, cross-theme, regional programmes and special programmes (which includes Global Philanthropy, Next Generation Leadership, Population and the Cairo (Egypt) Agenda, Communication for Social Change and Other Grants). Programmes include:

– *'Creativity and Culture'* to give full expression to creative impulses of individuals and communities in order to enhance the well-being of societies and better equip them to interact in a globalized world. Programme supports: preservation and renewal of the cultural heritage of people excluded from the benefits of globalization; strengthening civil society and free flow of ideas through initiatives in the humanities and religion; creation and presentation of new work in media and performing arts that promotes cultural diversity, innovation and understanding across cultures.
– *'Food Security'* to improve food security of the rural poor through generation of agricultural technologies, institutions and policies that will provide sustainable livelihoods in areas of sub-Saharan Africa and Asia bypassed by the Green Revolution. Work areas include: development of improved crop varieties for Africa and Asia; enhancement soil productivity in Africa; improvement of efficiency and equity of markets to raise the income of poor farmers in Africa; generation of international public goods that can help developing countries better serve poor farmers.
– *'Health Equity'* to advance global health equity by pursuing reduction of avoidable and unfair differences in the health status of populations. Work areas include: acceleration of development of and access to vaccines and medicines for diseases of the poor by creating public/private partnerships to overcome the lack of commercial interest in these products; development of appropriately skilled human resources and better management of information to improve health care in developed countries; rising to the challenge of AIDS through development of preventive technologies and accelerating access to care and mobilizing greater resources within the foundation community.
– *'Working Communities'* to transform poor urban neighbourhoods into working communities – safe, healthy and effective neighbourhoods – by increasing the amount and quality of employment, improving the quality of all urban schools and increasing the influence and voice of the poor and excluded in political decisions that affect their lives. Work areas include: research on consequences of economic, technological and demographic trends on the structure of work and their impact on the least skilled and research into the structural components of racial and ethnic exclusion and their implications for democracy; national initiatives that support community development corporations or city-specific initiatives to increase the scale and impact of reform in poor school districts; research to improve the employment access and advancement opportunities, the quality of education for poor and limited English-speaking children and innovative locally based projects that increase voice and participation of poor and excluded people.
– *'Global Inclusion'* to help broaden the benefits and reduce the negative impacts of globalization on vulnerable communities, families and individuals around the world. Supports work on key policy issues at the regional and global level under the following objectives: to foster inclusive, global dialogues about the uptake of plant biotechnology; to support the emergence of fairer, development-oriented intellectual-property policies; to examine the impact of science and technology on poor people; to better understand the changing dynamics of North American transnational communities, particularly financial remittances; to support knowledge building and new practices aimed at increasing pro-poor philanthropic investments globally; to inform global approaches to conflict prevention and management.
– *'Special Programme/Assets and Capacities'* includes:
– /Communication for Social Change/ – to enhance the effectiveness of development initiatives that focus on improving the lives of poor and excluded people by fostering innovative, sustainable and empowering communication approaches aimed at engendering positive social change.
– /Bellagio Study and Conference Center/ – located in Italy, offers 1-month stays for 15 residents at a time from February to mid-December in any discipline or field and coming from any country who expect a publication, exhibition, performance or other concrete product to result. Offers interdisciplinary, intercultural networking through the convening of small working groups of policy-makers, practitioners, scholars, scientists, artists and others.
– /Program Venture Experiment (ProVenEx)/ – seeks to catalyze private-sector investments in areas that will benefit poor and excluded people.
– *'Regional Programmes'* includes:
– /Africa Regional Program/ – to contribute to the revitalization of the African continent by building the required human and institutional capacity and providing critical information that will promote effective policies and programmes to improve the lives and livelihoods of the poor.

– /Southeast Asia Regional Program/ – focuses on the uneven economic development and cultural tensions in the Greater Mekong Sub-Region and the resulting inequities among its diverse population.
Events *All Africa Postharvest Congress* Addis Ababa (Ethiopia) 2019, *International Fundraising Congress* Bangkok (Thailand) 2017, *All Africa Postharvest Congress* Nairobi (Kenya) 2017, *Social Good Summit* New York, NY (USA) 2017, *Asia-Pacific urban forum* Bangkok (Thailand) 2011. **Publications** Annual Report; reports. **Consultative Status** Consultative status granted from: *ECOSOC (#05331)* (Special). **IGO Relations** Accredited by: *United Nations Framework Convention on Climate Change – Secretariat (UNFCCC, #20564)*. Associated with Department of Global Communications of the United Nations. **NGO Relations** Member of: *Africa Grantmakers' Affinity Group (AGAG)*; *Aspen Network of Development Entrepreneurs (ANDE, #02310)*; *Global Network of Foundations Working for Development (netFWD)*; *International Working Group on Education (IWGE, #15909)*. Together with: *Bill and Melinda Gates Foundation (BMGF)*, instrumental in setting up: *Alliance for a Green Revolution in Africa (AGRA, #00685)*. Funds grant programmes of a large number of international and national organizations worldwide (not specified). [2020/XF1885/f/F]

- ♦ Rockefeller Philanthropy Advisors (internationally oriented national body)
- ♦ ROCRAM-CA – Red Operativa de Cooperación Regional de Autoridades Maritimas – Central América (no recent information)
- ♦ **ROCRAM** Red Operativa de Cooperación Regional de Autoridades Maritimas de Sudamérica, México, Panama y Cuba (#18725)
- ♦ Rodale Institute (internationally oriented national body)
- ♦ Rodale International / see Rodale Institute
- ♦ Rodens et Spatium – International Conference on Rodent Biology (meeting series)
- ♦ ROEAP / see UNESCO Asia and Pacific Regional Bureau for Education (#20301)
- ♦ Roerich Foundation pro Pace, Arte, Scientia et Labore (inactive)
- ♦ **ROFAF** Réseau des Organisations Féminines d'Afrique Francophone (#18900)
- ♦ Rogano Meeting (meeting series)
- ♦ Rogationistes du Coeur de Jésus (religious order)
- ♦ Rogazionisti del Cuore di Gesù (religious order)
- ♦ Roger Scruton Legacy Foundation (internationally oriented national body)
- ♦ Roger Thayer Stone Center for Latin American Studies / see Stone Center for Latin American Studies, New Orleans

♦ ROKPA INTERNATIONAL 18967

Gen Manager Böcklinstr 27, 8032 Zurich ZH, Switzerland. T. +41442626888. E-mail: info@rokpa.org.
URL: http://www.rokpa.org/

History 1980. Registration: Swiss Civil Code, Switzerland. **Aims** Help where humanitarian aid is exceptionally difficult, but desperately needed, primarily in the areas of education, medicine and food/living costs. **Structure** Executive Board. An umbrella organization for offices in 15 countries. **Languages** English, German. **Staff** 4.10 FTE, paid; 20.00 FTE, voluntary. **Finance** Sources: donations. Annual budget: 1,500,000 CHF (2021). **Activities** Humanitarian/emergency aid; projects/programmes; training/education. Active in Tibetan areas of China and Nepal. **Publications** *ROKPA Times* (3 a year).
Members Represented in 15 countries:
Austria, Canada, Cantabria, Germany, India, Ireland, Italy, Nepal, Netherlands, Poland, South Africa, Spain, UK, USA, Zimbabwe.
Consultative Status Consultative status granted from: *ECOSOC (#05331)* (Special). **IGO Relations** None. **NGO Relations** Partner of (1): *NGO Alliance on Global Concerns and Values (NGO Alliance, #17102)*. [2021.10.26/XJ9877/F]

- ♦ Rolf Institute of Structural Integration (internationally oriented national body)

♦ Roll Back Malaria Partnership (RBM) 18968

Exec Dir c/o WHO, Avenue Appia 20, 1211 Geneva 27, Switzerland. T. +41227913735. E-mail: menthona@who.int – inforbm@who.int.
URL: http://www.rollbackmalaria.org/

History 1998, by *WHO (#20950)*, *UNICEF (#20332)*, *UNDP (#20292)* and *International Bank for Reconstruction and Development (IBRD, #12317)*. **Aims** Provide a coordinated global approach to fighting malaria. **Structure** Board of 21 members, comprising 8 representatives from malaria endemic countries, 3 representatives from OECD donor countries, 4 representatives from multilateral development partners, a representative from research and academia, 2 representatives from NGOs and 2 representatives from private sector. Secretariat. **Events** *Meeting on Humanitarian Challenges in Africa* Yokohama (Japan) 2013.
Members Organizations included in this Yearbook:
Global Fund to Fight AIDS, Tuberculosis and Malaria (Global Fund, #10383); *Unitaid (#20493)*.
NGO Relations Partner of: *Fight the Fakes (#09755)*. [2014/XM1992/y/E]

- ♦ RollerSoccer International Federation / see Federation International Football Skating (#09671)
- ♦ ROL – Red de Objectores Latinoamericanos (inactive)
- ♦ Roman Catholic/Lutheran Joint Commission / see Lutheran-Roman Catholic Commission on Unity (#16531)
- ♦ Roman Catholic / World Methodist International Commission / see International Joint Commission for Dialogue between the World Methodist Council and the Vatican (#13972)
- ♦ Roman Congregation of Saint Dominic (religious order)
- ♦ Romanian Center for European Policies (internationally oriented national body)
- ♦ Romanian Centre for Studies on Globalization (internationally oriented national body)
- ♦ Romanian Institute of International Studies – Nicolae Titulescu (internationally oriented national body)
- ♦ Romani International Union / see International Romani Union (#14765)
- ♦ Romani Unia (#14765)
- ♦ Romani Union / see International Romani Union (#14765)
- ♦ Romani World Union / see International Romani Union (#14765)
- ♦ Romanorum juxta mare pharmacopolum collegium (#19508)
- ♦ Roman Theological Pontifical Academy / see Pontifical Theological Academy (#18452)
- ♦ Rome Convention – International Convention for the Protection of Performers, Producers of Phonograms and Broadcasting Organizations (1961 treaty)

♦ Rome Euro-Mediterranean Energy Platform (REMEP) 18969

Address not obtained.
URL: http://www.remep.org/

History 2003, at Euro-Mediterranean Energy Ministers Conference. Declaration of Intent signed 2 Dec 2003, Rome (Italy). **Aims** Provide technical support to ensure the timely implementation of the resolutions made by Ministers regarding the Euro-Mediterranean energy cooperation; enhance the effectiveness of the initiatives promoted by the Euro-Mediterranean Energy Forum; collaborate with and provide logistical support to MEDREG (Mediterranean Working Group on Electricity and Natural Gas Regulation); further develop the Euro-Mediterranean Energy Partnership and dialogue between the EU and the Mediterranean partner countries in the energy area.
Members Governments (18):
Algeria, Austria, Belgium, Bulgaria, Cyprus, Egypt, France, Hungary, Israel, Italy, Jordan, Lebanon, Morocco, Palestine, Romania, Spain, Tunisia, Türkiye.
Regional entity:
European Union (EU, #08967).
NGO Relations *Association of Mediterranean Energy Regulators (MEDREG, #02800)*. [2010/XJ1236/E*]

♦ Rome Foundation (RF) 18970

Pres PO Box 6524, Raleigh NC 27628, USA. T. +19195379461. Fax +19199007646. E-mail: mpickard@theromefoundation.org.
URL: http://www.romecriteria.org/

History Registered in accordance with USA law. **Aims** Advance the treatment of functional *gastrointestinal* disorders through the support of programmes developing research and educational information. [2015/XM4052/f/F]

- ♦ ROMRIECA – Reunión de Ministros Responsables de le Integración y Desarrollo de Centroamérica (meeting series)
- ♦ Rómulo Gallegos Center for Latin American Studies (internationally oriented national body)
- ♦ Rooftops Canada (internationally oriented national body)
- ♦ Room to Read (internationally oriented national body)
- ♦ Roosevelt Institute (internationally oriented national body)
- ♦ Root Capital (internationally oriented national body)
- ♦ Rooting – International Symposium on Root Development (meeting series)
- ♦ Roots of Peace (internationally oriented national body)
- ♦ **ROPME** Regional Organization for the Protection of the Marine Environment (#18805)

♦ ROPME Sea Area Hydrographic Commission (RSAHC) 18971

Commission hydrographique de la zone maritime ROPME (CHZMR)

Chair Oman National Hydrographic Office, Royal Navy of Oman, Bait Al Falaj PO Box 113, 100, Muscat, Oman. E-mail: nhooman@omantel.net.om.
URL: http://www.iho.int/

History Oct 2000, Teheran (Iran Islamic Rep), as a Hydrographic Commission of *International Hydrographic Organization (IHO, #13825)*. Statutes adopted 10 Oct 2000; amended 3 May 2006. **Events** *Meeting* Kuwait 2013, *Meeting* Riyadh (Saudi Arabia) 2013, *Meeting* Muscat (Oman) 2011, *Meeting* Monte Carlo (Monaco) 2009, *Meeting* Teheran (Iran Islamic Rep) 2006.
Members Governments (8):
Bahrain, Iran Islamic Rep, Kuwait, Oman, Pakistan, Qatar, Saudi Arabia, United Arab Emirates.
Associate members (2).
Observers (2):
UK, USA. [2012/XJ5156/E*]

- ♦ **ROPPA** Réseau des organisations paysannes et des producteurs agricoles de l'Afrique de l'Ouest (#20891)
- ♦ Rosa Luxemburg Foundation (internationally oriented national body)
- ♦ Rosa Luxemburg Stiftung (internationally oriented national body)
- ♦ Rosenkranzbruderschaft (religious order)
- ♦ Rosenthal Institute for Holocaust Studies (internationally oriented national body)
- ♦ La ROSE – La Route du Sel et de l'Espoir (internationally oriented national body)
- ♦ ROSI Côte d'Ivoire – Réseau des Organisations de Solidarité Internationale Côte d'Ivoire (internationally oriented national body)

♦ Rosicrucian Fellowship, The (TRF) 18972

Contact 2222 Mission Ave, Oceanside CA 92049, USA. T. +17607576600. Fax +17607213806. E-mail: trfcorporate@gmail.com.
URL: http://www.rosicrucianfellowship.org/

History Founded 8 Aug 1909, Seattle WA (USA). Purchase of the land to be used to build international headquarters, 3 May 1911, Oceanside CA (USA); dedication, 28 Oct 1911, Oceanside CA. **Aims** Educate those pioneering souls who are spiritually awakened and sincerely seeking the truth and the light; teach the esoteric *Christian* message of the *gospel* of the coming Age of Aquarius; heal the sick using a spiritual method based on the mystical knowledge of the stars. **Structure** Board of Trustees; Executive Council; Ecclesiastical Council. Departments (6): Business Office; Grounds and Maintenance; Education; Computer; Healing; Esoteric. **Languages** English, French, German, Italian, Portuguese, Spanish. **Staff** All voluntary. **Finance** Donations; sale of books and other publications. **Activities** Religious activities; events/meetings; knowledge management/information dissemination. **Events** *Western wisdom workshop* Oceanside, CA (USA) 2003. **Publications** Books; booklets; pamphlets; CDs; DVDs.
Members Individuals in 83 countries and territories:
Algeria, Angola, Antigua-Barbuda, Argentina, Australia, Austria, Belgium, Benin, Bolivia, Brazil, Bulgaria, Burkina Faso, Cameroon, Canada, Chile, Colombia, Congo Brazzaville, Congo DR, Costa Rica, Côte d'Ivoire, Croatia, Cuba, Cyprus, Czechia, Denmark, Dominica, Dominican Rep, Ecuador, Egypt, El Salvador, Ethiopia, Finland, France, Gabon, Germany, Ghana, Greece, Guatemala, Guinea, Guinea-Bissau, Guyana, Haiti, Hong Kong, Ireland, Israel, Italy, Jamaica, Japan, Kenya, Lebanon, Liberia, Luxembourg, Madagascar, Mexico, Morocco, Netherlands, New Zealand, Nicaragua, Nigeria, Panama, Paraguay, Peru, Philippines, Poland, Portugal, Puerto Rico, Romania, Rwanda, Senegal, South Africa, Spain, Sri Lanka, Sweden, Switzerland, Togo, Trinidad-Tobago, Tunisia, Uganda, UK, Uruguay, USA, Venezuela, Zambia. [2016.06.21/XF6200/F]

- ♦ Rosicrucian Order, Ancient and Mystical Order Rosae Crucis (religious order)
- ♦ ROSL – Royal Over-Seas League (internationally oriented national body)
- ♦ Rosminiani – Istituto della Carità (religious order)
- ♦ Rosminians – Institute of Charity (religious order)
- ♦ Rosminian Sisters of Providence (religious order)
- ♦ Rossijskij Fond Mira (internationally oriented national body)
- ♦ Rossijskij Institut Strategiceskih Issledovanij (internationally oriented national body)
- ♦ **ROSSP** Réseau océanien de surveillance de la santé publique (#17993)
- ♦ ROSTAS / see UNESCO Office, Cairo – Regional Bureau for Sciences in the Arab States (#20312)
- ♦ **ROSTAS** UNESCO Office, Cairo – Regional Bureau for Sciences in the Arab States (#20312)
- ♦ ROSTA – UNESCO Office, Nairobi – Regional Bureau for Sciences in Africa (inactive)
- ♦ ROSTE / see UNESCO Office in Venice – UNESCO Regional Bureau for Science and Culture in Europe (#20316)
- ♦ ROSTLAC / see UNESCO Office, Montevideo – Regional Bureau for Sciences in Latin America and the Caribbean (#20314)
- ♦ ROSTSCA / see UNESCO Asia-Pacific Regional Bureau for Communication and Information (#20300)
- ♦ ROSTSEA / see UNESCO Office, Jakarta – Regional Bureau for Sciences in Asia and the Pacific (#20313)
- ♦ ROTA – Reach Out to Asia (internationally oriented national body)

♦ Rotaria Amikaro de Esperanto (RADE) 18973

Amicale rotarienne internationale des espérantistes – International Esperanto Fellowship of Rotarians

Pres address not obtained.
URL: http://rade.fontoj.net/

History 1928. Founded by English and French Rotarians. Reorganized after World War II. Former names and other names: *World Rotary Fellowship of Esperantists* – alias. **Aims** Develop friendship and service in Rotary thanks to Esperanto; encourage the use of Esperanto in Rotary clubs. **Structure** Steering Committee. **Languages** Bulgarian, English, Esperanto, French, Italian, Portuguese. **Finance** None. **Activities** Events/meetings. **Events** *Esperanto World Congress* Reykjavik (Iceland) 2013, *Esperanto World Congress* Hanoi (Vietnam) 2012, *Esperanto World Congress* Copenhagen (Denmark) 2010, *Meeting / Esperanto World Congress* Bialystok (Poland) 2009, *Meeting / Rotary International Convention* Birmingham (UK) 2009. **Publications** *RADE Informilo* (4 a year). *Rotary International ADVANCER*. Information letter.
Members Individuals in 28 countries and territories:
Argentina, Australia, Belgium, Brazil, Bulgaria, Canada, Egypt, France, Germany, Guiana Fr, India, Italy, Japan, Lithuania, Mexico, Netherlands, New Zealand, Nigeria, Norway, Peru, Portugal, Samoa, Slovakia, South Africa, Sweden, Ukraine, USA, Venezuela.
NGO Relations Cooperates with: *Universal Esperanto Association (UEA, #20676)*. [2018.01.22/XE8493/v/E]

- ♦ Rotariens pour les Nations Unies (internationally oriented national body)
- ♦ Rotarios amigos de las Naciones Unidas (internationally oriented national body)

♦ Rotary Foundation of Rotary International 18974

Fondation Rotary – Fundación Rotaria – Fundação Rotaria

Contact One Rotary Center, 1560 Sherman Avenue, Evanston IL 60201, USA.
URL: https://www.rotary.org/en/about-rotary/rotary-foundation

History 1917, as an endowment fund, by *Rotary International (RI, #18975)*. Formally established 1928. **Aims** Support the efforts of Rotary International to achieve international understanding and peace and further friendly relations through international humanitarian, educational and cultural exchange programmes. **Finance** Sources: grants; investments; bequests; voluntary contributions from Rotary members and friends of Rotary. Total contributions (2052-2006): US$ 111.9 million.

Activities Provides humanitarian grants to improve the quality of life throughout the world; supports international ambassadors of good will through educational awards to university students and teachers and through international exchanges of business and professional people. Awards and grants are made in conjunction with Rotary club and district international service activities; applications for funding must be initiated by a Rotary club or district.
– *'PolioPlus Programme'*: top priority programme, Rotary has committed over US$ 334 million to support international health organizations in their aim of eradicating polio by 2005.
– *'Humanitarian programmes'*:
– *'Matching Grants'*: grants up to US$ 50,000 for humanitarian projects sponsored and partially funded by Rotary clubs or districts in 2 or more countries.
– *'Health, Hunger and Humanity (3-H) Program'*: awards grants of US$ 100,000-500,000 over 1-3 years for large-scale, international humanitarian projects emphasizing self-help and improve health, alleviate hunger and enhance human and social development.
– *'Carl P Miller Discovery Grants'*: covers travel and related expenses for Rotarians exploring and planning new international service projects.
– *'Grants for Rotary Volunteers'*: subsidizes expenses of Rotarians, Foundation alumni and Rotaractors who volunteer their services in another country. Established *'Rotary Centres for International Studies in Peace and Conflict Resolution'*.
'Educational Programmes'.
Events *Multi-Districts 3310, 3330, 3340, 3350, 3360 Conference* Bangkok (Thailand) 2017, *International meeting* Lille (France) 2005. **Publications** Annual report; newsletters; brochures. **IGO Relations** Cooperates with: *UNICEF (#20332)*; *WHO (#20950)*. **NGO Relations** Member of: *Global Impact*. Supports: *PROJECT C.U.R.E.*. [2018/XF7993/f/F]

♦ Rotary International (RI) 18975

Gen Sec One Rotary Center, 1560 Sherman Ave, Evanston IL 60201-3698, USA. T. +18478663000. Fax +18478668237. E-mail: ers@rotary.org.
URL: http://www.rotary.org/

History 23 Feb 1905, Chicago, IL (USA). Former names and other names: *International Association of Rotary Clubs* – former (1912 to 1922); *National Association of Rotary Clubs* – former (23 Feb 1905 to 1912). Registration: Start date: 30 Jan 1911, USA, Illinois. **Aims** As an organization of business and professional *leaders* united worldwide, provide *humanitarian* service, encourage high ethical standards in all vocations and help build goodwill and peace in the world. Main objective is service – in the community, in the workplace and throughout the world. **Structure** Convention (annual), open to Rotary members, their guests and the media. International Board of Directors and over 530 District Governors. Committees appointed by President. Autonomous Rotary Clubs operating under Rotary International Constitution and By-Laws. Membership by invitation. *Rotary Foundation of Rotary International (#18974)*. Global Networking Groups: Rotary Fellowships; Rotarian Action Groups. **Languages** English, French, German, Italian, Japanese, Korean, Portuguese, Spanish, Swedish. **Staff** About 610 paid, of whom 484 work at the World Headquarters, Evanston IL (USA). **Finance** Members' dues. Investments. **Activities** Networking/liaising; financial and/or material support; humanitarian/emergency aid. **Events** *Annual Convention* Calgary, AB (Canada) 2025, *Annual Convention* Singapore (Singapore) 2024, *Annual Convention* Melbourne, VIC (Australia) 2023, *Annual Convention* Houston, TX (USA) 2022, *Presidential Conference* Gyeongju (Korea Rep) 2021. **Publications** *The Rotarian* (12 a year) in English. Regional magazines of 'The Rotarian' and 'Rotary World'. Proceedings of annual convention.
Members Rotary clubs (32,000) with a total membership of 1.2 million representing a cross-section of the community's business and professional men and women. Members in 204 countries and territories:
Afghanistan, Åland, Albania, Algeria, Andorra, Angola, Anguilla, Antigua-Barbuda, Argentina, Armenia, Aruba, Australia, Austria, Azerbaijan, Bahamas, Bahrain, Bangladesh, Barbados, Belarus, Belgium, Belize, Benin, Bermuda, Bolivia, Bosnia-Herzegovina, Botswana, Brazil, Brunei Darussalam, Bulgaria, Burkina Faso, Burundi, Cambodia, Cameroon, Canada, Cape Verde, Cayman Is, Central African Rep, Chad, Channel Is, Chile, China, Colombia, Comoros, Congo Brazzaville, Congo DR, Cook Is, Costa Rica, Côte d'Ivoire, Croatia, Cyprus, Czechia, Denmark, Djibouti, Dominica, Dominican Rep, Ecuador, Egypt, El Salvador, England, Equatorial Guinea, Eritrea, Estonia, Eswatini, Ethiopia, Faeroe Is, Fiji, Finland, France, Gabon, Gambia, Georgia, Germany, Ghana, Gibraltar, Greece, Greenland, Grenada, Guam, Guatemala, Guiana Fr, Guinea, Guinea-Bissau, Guyana, Haiti, Honduras, Hong Kong, Hungary, Iceland, India, Indonesia, Ireland, Isle of Man, Israel, Italy, Jamaica, Japan, Jordan, Kazakhstan, Kenya, Korea Rep, Kosovo, Kyrgyzstan, Laos, Latvia, Lebanon, Lesotho, Liberia, Liechtenstein, Lithuania, Luxembourg, Macau, Madagascar, Malawi, Malaysia, Mali, Malta, Mauritania, Mauritius, Mayotte, Mexico, Micronesia FS, Moldova, Monaco, Mongolia, Montenegro, Montserrat, Morocco, Mozambique, Namibia, Nepal, Netherlands, New Caledonia, New Zealand, Nicaragua, Niger, Nigeria, Norfolk Is, North Macedonia, Northern Ireland, Northern Mariana Is, Norway, Pakistan, Palau, Panama, Papua New Guinea, Paraguay, Peru, Philippines, Poland, Polynesia Fr, Portugal, Puerto Rico, Réunion, Romania, Russia, Rwanda, Samoa, Samoa USA, San Marino, Sao Tomé-Principe, Scotland, Senegal, Serbia, Seychelles, Sierra Leone, Singapore, Slovakia, Slovenia, Solomon Is, South Africa, Spain, Sri Lanka, St Kitts-Nevis, St Lucia, St Pierre-Miquelon, St Vincent-Grenadines, Sudan, Suriname, Sweden, Switzerland, Taiwan, Tajikistan, Tanzania UR, Thailand, Timor-Leste, Togo, Tonga, Trinidad-Tobago, Tunisia, Türkiye, Turks-Caicos, Uganda, Ukraine, United Arab Emirates, Uruguay, USA, Vanuatu, Venezuela, Virgin Is UK, Virgin Is USA, Wales, Zambia, Zimbabwe.
Also members in the West Indies (membership countries not specified) and in Antarctica.
Consultative Status Consultative status granted from: *ECOSOC (#05331)* (General); *UNESCO (#20322)* (Associate Status); *FAO (#09260)* (Liaison Status); *WHO (#20950)* (Official Relations); *UNICEF (#20332)*; *Council of Europe (CE, #04881)* (Participatory Status); *UNEP (#20299)*. **IGO Relations** Observer status with: *OAS (#17629)*; *United Nations Human Settlements Programme (UN-Habitat, #20572)*. Accredited by: United Nations Headquarters in New York; *United Nations Office at Geneva (UNOG, #20597)*; *United Nations Office at Vienna (UNOV, #20604)*. Associated with Department of Global Communications of the United Nations. **NGO Relations** Member of: *Conference of Non-Governmental Organizations in Consultative Relationship with the United Nations (CONGO, #04635)*; *Global NGO Executive Committee (GNEC, #10507)*; *Global Polio Eradication Initiative (GPEI, #10553)*; *NGO Committee on Human Settlements (#17110)*; *NGO Committee on Sustainable Development, New York (#17118)*; *NGO-UNESCO Liaison Committee (#17127)*; *NGO Committee on UNICEF (#17120)*; *New York NGO Committee on Drugs (NYNGOC, #17097)*; *Vienna NGO Committee on Drugs (VNGOC, #20773)*. [2021/XF3164/F]

♦ Rotary Yoneyama Memorial Foundation (internationally oriented national body)
♦ Rothamsted International (internationally oriented national body)

♦ Roth Williams International Society of Orthodontists (RWISO) 18976

Main Office PO Box 1820, Los Gatos CA 95031, USA. T. +14083370901. Fax +14085219191. E-mail: info@rwiso.org.
URL: http://www.rwiso.org/

History Named after Dr Ron Roth (1933-2005) and Dr Robert Williams. **Aims** Advance worldwide excellence in orthodontics from a foundation of functional occlusion and aesthetics. **Structure** Council. Board of Directors, including President, President Elect, Vice-President, Immediate Past President, Treasurer and Executive Director. **Events** *Annual Meeting* Orlando, FL (USA) 2016, *Annual Meeting* Fort Lauderdale, FL (USA) 2015, *Annual Meeting* Miami, FL (USA) 2014, *Annual Meeting* Sao Paulo (Brazil) 2013, *Annual Meeting* Washington, DC (USA) 2013.
Members Teaching centres in 9 countries:
Argentina, Brazil, Chile, Italy, Japan, Korea Rep, Spain, Uruguay, USA. [2016/XM3242/E]

♦ Rotman International Centre for Pension Management (ICPM) 18977

Main Office 411 Richmond Street East, Suite 200, Toronto ON M5A 3S5, Canada. T. +14169254153. E-mail: icpm@icpmnetwork.com.
URL: http://www.icpmnetwork.com/

History May 2005. **Aims** Focus on fostering long-term investing, strengthening governance of pension investments, and improving design and governance of pension schemes. **Structure** Board of Directors; Research Committee. **Activities** Events/meetings; publishing activities; research/documentation; training/education. **Events** *Discussion Forum* Montréal, QC (Canada) 2023, *Discussion Forum* Toronto, ON (Canada) 2022, *Discussion Forum* Washington, DC (USA) 2022, *Discussion Forum* 2021, *Discussion Forum* 2021. **Publications** *Rotman International Journal of Pension Management*. Annual Report. **Members** Research Partners, each making a financial commitment of about Canadian $ 30,000 to further pension research, as well as to fund the organization and execution of the Discussion Forums. Membership countries not specified. [2023.02.13/XJ1795/E]

♦ **ROTOS** Research in Occupational Therapy and Occupational Science Foundation (#18860)
♦ Rotterdam Convention on the Prior Informed Consent Procedure for Certain Hazardous Chemicals and Pesticides in International Trade (1998 treaty)
♦ Rotterdam convention – Rotterdam Convention on the Prior Informed Consent Procedure for Certain Hazardous Chemicals and Pesticides in International Trade (1998 treaty)
♦ Rotterdam Rules – United Nations Convention on Contracts for the International Carriage of Goods Wholly or Partly by Sea (2008 treaty)
♦ Rouble Zone (no recent information)
♦ Rouedad Europa evit Kevatalded ar Yezhoù (#07647)

♦ Round Square 18978

CEO First Floor, Morgan House, Madeira Walk, Windsor, SL4 1EP, UK.
URL: http://www.roundsquare.org/

History 1966. Registration: UK Registered Charity, No/ID: 327117, England and Wales; Companies House, No/ID: 02011514, England and Wales. **Aims** Promote *learning* built around six IDEALS: internationalism; democracy; environmentalism; adventure; leadership; service. **Structure** Board of Trustees. **Languages** English. **Staff** 17.00 FTE, paid. **Finance** Members' dues. Students and member schools for specific projects. **Activities** Awards/prizes/competitions; events/meetings; knowledge management/information dissemination; networking/liaising; projects/programmes; research/documentation; training/education. **Events** *Regents Conference* Bangkok (Thailand) 2018, *Global Conference* Montréal, QC (Canada) / Toronto, ON (Canada) / Ottawa, ON (Canada) 2018, *International Conference* Singapore (Singapore) 2015, *Peace be with you* Bhopal (India) / Madaba (India) 2014, *Conference* India 2014.
Members Schools (over 190) in 44 countries and territories:
Argentina, Armenia, Australia, Bangladesh, Bermuda, Canada, Cayman Is, Chile, China, Colombia, Denmark, France, Germany, Ghana, Hong Kong, India, Indonesia, Japan, Jordan, Kenya, Korea Rep, Malaysia, Mexico, Mongolia, Morocco, Namibia, Nepal, New Zealand, Oman, Pakistan, Peru, Romania, Rwanda, Singapore, South Africa, Spain, Switzerland, Tanzania UR, Thailand, Türkiye, UK, United Arab Emirates, USA, Vietnam. [2020/XJ6931/F]

♦ Round Table Arabian Gulf (RTAG) 18979

Pres PO Box 26073, Manama, Bahrain. T. +97317564755. Fax +97317564929. E-mail: artagsec@gmail.com.
URL: http://www.rtag.info

History 1981, as *Association of Round Tables in the Arabian Gulf (ARTAG)*, within the framework of *Round Table International (RTI, #18982)*. **Events** *Annual General Meeting* Bahrain 2008, *Annual General Meeting* Bahrain 2006, *Annual General Meeting* Dubai (United Arab Emirates) 2005.
Members Round Tables in 4 countries:
Bahrain, Kuwait, Saudi Arabia, United Arab Emirates.
NGO Relations Member of: *World Council of Service Clubs (WOCO, no recent information)*. [2015/XE2309/E]

♦ Roundtable of European Energy Industrialists / see Roundtable for Europe's Energy Future (#18980)

♦ Roundtable for Europe's Energy Future (REEF) 18980

CEO Norway House, Rue Archimède 17 – 1st floor, 1000 Brussels, Belgium.
Secretariat Statnett, Nydalen Allé 33, 0484 Oslo, Norway. T. +4797487884.
URL: https://www.energy-roundtable.eu/

History 2011. Former names and other names: *Roundtable of European Energy Industrialists* – former. Registration: EU Transparency Register, No/ID: 101903316808-95, Start date: 8 Apr 2015. **Aims** Contribute to the development of an interconnected European grid with empowered markets and consumers. **Activities** Events/meetings. **Events** *Annual Meeting* Berlin (Germany) 2014. **Publications** Position papers. [2023.03.03/XM5673/F]

♦ The Round Table Foundation (TRTF) 18981

Pres/CEO address not obtained. E-mail: centralmaildesk@trtf.eu.
URL: http://www.trtf.eu/

History Informally active since 1982; incorporated as a foundation, 1992. **Aims** Promote *learning* and *teaching*, interdisciplinary science and research, support *academia* and intercultural understanding, and aid the young. **Structure** Chapters: Ethics and Philosophy; *European Magnetic Resonance Forum Foundation (EMRF Foundation, #07724)*; Humanitarian Aid; Pro Academia Prize. **Languages** English. **Finance** Privately funded. **Activities** Training/education; research/documentation; knowledge management/information dissemination; events/meetings; awards/prizes/competitions. **Members** Individuals (by invitation only). Membership countries not specified. [2021/XM5241/f/F]

♦ Round Table International (RTI) 18982

Table ronde internationale
Sec address not obtained. E-mail: secretary@rtinternational.org.
Public Relations Officer address not obtained.
URL: http://www.round-table.org/

History 1927, Norwich (UK). Originally a UK national organization. International organization founded 1948. Merged, 1961, with *'World Council of Young Men's Service Clubs – Conseil mondial des clubs d'entraide de jeunes gens'*, currently *World Council of Service Clubs (WOCO, no recent information)*, which had been set up Oct 1946, Sacramento CO (USA). Currently one of several organizations constituting WOCO, members of which are also members of WOCO although no longer governed by WOCO. Refounded 1991. Former names and other names: *Table ronde internationale* – former. **Aims** Bring together young men between 18-40 years of age to challenge, inspire and learn from each other to make a positive impact at home, work and in the community. **Structure** General Meeting (annual); International Board. Regions (5): CEE – Central and Eastern Europe; NEAR – Northern Europe and Americas; SEM – Southern Europe and Mediterranean; ASPA – Asia Pacific; AMI – Africa, Middle East and Indian Ocean. Includes: *Round Table Arabian Gulf (RTAG, #18979)*; *Round Table Central Africa (RTCA, no recent information)*; *Association of Round Tables in Eastern Africa (ARTEA, #02898)*; *Round Table Southern Africa (RTSA, #18984)*. **Languages** English. **Staff** Voluntary. **Finance** Annual budget: 145,000 EUR (2022). **Activities** Awareness raising; financial and/or material support; networking/liaising. **Events** *Annual General Meeting* Copenhagen (Denmark) 2022, *Meeting* Marrakech (Morocco) 2022, *Central European Tablers Meeting* Bielefeld (Germany) 2021, *Euromeeting* Bryne (Norway) 2018, *Asia Pacific Meeting* Singapore (Singapore) 2018.
Members Active Round Tables in 66 countries and territories:
Australia, Austria, Bahrain, Bangladesh, Belgium, Bermuda, Botswana, Brazil, Bulgaria, Canada, Cyprus, Czechia, Denmark, Estonia, Ethiopia, Finland, France, Germany, Gibraltar, Greece, Hong Kong, Hungary, Iceland, India, Ireland, Israel, Italy, Kenya, Latvia, Lesotho, Lithuania, Luxembourg, Madagascar, Malawi, Malaysia, Malta, Mauritius, Moldova, Monaco, Morocco, Nepal, Netherlands, New Zealand, Nigeria, Norway, Philippines, Poland, Portugal, Romania, Russia, San Marino, Senegal, Seychelles, Singapore, Slovakia, Sri Lanka, Suriname, Sweden, Switzerland, Trinidad-Tobago, Tunisia, Türkiye, UK, USA, Zambia, Zimbabwe.
NGO Relations Cooperates with (4): *41 International (#22047)*; *AGORA Club International (#00563)*; *Ladies Circle International (LCI, #16217)*; *Tangent Club International (TCI, #20094)*. [2022/XE2022/E]

♦ Round Table on Responsible Soy Association (RTRS) 18983

Exec Dir Utoquai 29/31, 8008 Zurich ZH, Switzerland. E-mail: info@responsiblesoy.org.
Communications Officer address not obtained.
URL: http://www.responsiblesoy.org/

History 2006, Switzerland. The original Organizational Committee was made up of Grupo Amaggi, *Catholic Organization for Relief and Development (Cordaid)*, COOP, *World Wide Fund for Nature (WWF, #21922)*, Fetrauf-Sul and Unilever. **Aims** Promote growth on production, trade and use of responsible soy through cooperation with actors in and relevant to the soy value chain from production to consumption in an open dialogue with stakeholders including producers, suppliers, manufacturers, retailers, financial institutions, civil society organizations and other relevant actors. **Structure** General Assembly; Executive Board; Secretariat based in Argentina. **Languages** English, Portuguese, Spanish. **Staff** 8.00 FTE, paid. **Finance** Sources: members' dues. Other sources: RTRS Credits Supporting Responsible Soy purchase fees; special funding from other organizations for specific projects. **Activities** Active in: Argentina, Belgium, Bolivia, Brazil, Canada, China, Denmark, Finland, France, Germany, India, Italy, Netherlands, Norway, Paraguay, Singapore, South Africa, Sweden, Switzerland, UK, Uruguay, USA. **Events** *International Conference* Cologne (Germany) 2022, *International Conference* Utrecht (Netherlands) 2019, *International Conference* Lille (France) 2018, *International Conference* Lille (France) 2017, *International Conference* Brasilia (Brazil) 2016.
Members Members in 34 countries and territories:

Argentina, Australia, Austria, Belgium, Bolivia, Brazil, Canada, Chile, China, Colombia, Denmark, Ecuador, Estonia, Finland, France, Germany, India, Ireland, Italy, Japan, Netherlands, Norway, Paraguay, Peru, Portugal, Singapore, South Africa, Spain, Sweden, Switzerland, Taiwan, UK, Uruguay, USA.
European Vegetable Protein Association (EUVEPRO, #09047); Fédération européenne des fabricants d'aliments composés pour animaux (FEFAC, #09566); FEDIOL – The EU Vegetable Oil and Proteinmeal Industry (#09718); World Wide Fund for Nature (WWF, #21922).
NGO Relations Member of (1): *HCV Network Ltd (HCV Network, #10865).* Partner of (1): *Wetlands International (#20928).* Subscriber to: *ISEAL (#16026).* [2023.02.16/XJ0466/**C**]

♦ Round Table Southern Africa (RTSA) 18984
Tafelrondes Suidelike Afrika (TRSA)
Branding Officer PO Box 401, Kenton-on-Sea, 6191, South Africa. E-mail: branding@roundtable.co.za.
URL: http://www.roundtable.co.za/
History 1951, as *Association of Round Tables in Southern Africa (ARTSA) – Vereniging van Tafelrondes in Suidelike Afrika*, within the framework of *Round Table International (RTI, #18982).* **Aims** Promote social networking and fellowship among young professional men; quicken individual interest in everything affecting public welfare; promote understanding among peoples of different cultural, language and political backgrounds.
Members Round Tables (143) in 2 countries:
Namibia, South Africa. [2016.07.07/XE4570/**E**]

♦ Roundtable on Sustainable Biofuels / see Roundtable on Sustainable Biomaterials (#18985)

♦ Roundtable on Sustainable Biomaterials (RSB) 18985
Exec Dir Impact Hub Geneva, Rue Fendt 1, 1201 Geneva, Switzerland. T. +41225349050. E-mail: info@rsb.org.
URL: http://www.rsb.org/
History Former title: *Roundtable on Sustainable Biofuels (RSB).* **Aims** Provide tools and solutions that mitigate business risk and contribute to achieving UN Sustainable Development Goals and has the world's most trusted, peer-reviewed global certification standard for sustainable biomaterials, biofuels and biomass production. **Structure** Board of Directors; Member Chambers; Secretariat; Expert Groups. **Languages** English, French. **Staff** 7.00 FTE, paid. **Activities** Standards/guidelines; certification/accreditation; guidance/assistance/consulting; knowledge management/information dissemination; networking/liaising; projects/programmes; monitoring/evaluation.
Members Companies and organizations in 32 countries and territories:
Australia, Belgium, Brazil, Canada, China, Denmark, Finland, France, Germany, Hong Kong, India, Italy, Japan, Kenya, Luxembourg, Malaysia, Mexico, Nepal, Netherlands, New Zealand, Norway, Philippines, Qatar, Singapore, South Africa, Sweden, Switzerland, Tanzania UR, Thailand, UK, United Arab Emirates, USA.
Included in the above, 5 organizations listed in this Yearbook:
FAO (#09260); International Air Transport Association (IATA, #11614); International Petroleum Industry Environmental Conservation Association (IPIECA, #14562); UNEP (#20299); World Wide Fund for Nature (WWF, #21922).
NGO Relations Partner of: *Wetlands International (#20928).* [2018.09.05/XJ6088/y/**F**]

♦ Round Table on Sustainable Development at the OECD (see: #17693)

♦ Roundtable on Sustainable Palm Oil (RSPO) 18986
Table rond huile de palme durable – Mesa Redonda sobre Aceite de Palma Sostenible – Runder Tisch für Nachhaltiges Palmöl
CEO Unit 13A-1 Level 13A, Menara Eitqa, No 3 Jalan Bangsar Utama 1, 59000 Kuala Lumpur, Malaysia. T. +6023021500. Fax +6023021542.
URL: http://www.rspo.org/
History 8 Apr 2004, Zurich (Switzerland). An Organizing Committee was set to organize 1st Roundtable, Kuala Lumpur (Malaysia), 2003. Registration: Switzerland. **Aims** Advance production, procurement, finance and use of sustainable palm oil products. **Structure** General Assembly; Board of Governors; Standing Committees; Working Groups; Task Forces; Secretariat. **Events** *Meeting* Bangkok (Thailand) 2019, *Meeting* Kota Kinabalu (Malaysia) 2018, *Meeting* Bangkok (Thailand) 2016, *European Meeting* Milan (Italy) 2016, *Meeting* Kuala Lumpur (Malaysia) 2015.
Members Ordinary Palm oil growers, processors and traders; consumer goods manufacturers; retailers; banks; ngos. Affiliate national and international ngos; individuals. Members (over 4000) in 73 countries and territories:
Argentina, Australia, Austria, Belgium, Brazil, Bulgaria, Canada, China, Colombia, Côte d'Ivoire, Croatia, Cyprus, Czechia, Denmark, Ecuador, Egypt, Estonia, Finland, France, Germany, Ghana, Greece, Honduras, Hong Kong, Hungary, India, Indonesia, Ireland, Isle of Man, Israel, Italy, Japan, Jordan, Kenya, Korea Rep, Latvia, Liechtenstein, Lithuania, Luxembourg, Malaysia, Mexico, Monaco, Netherlands, New Zealand, Nigeria, Panama, Papua New Guinea, Peru, Philippines, Poland, Portugal, Puerto Rico, Romania, Russia, Saudi Arabia, Serbia, Singapore, Slovakia, Slovenia, South Africa, Spain, Sri Lanka, Sweden, Switzerland, Taiwan, Thailand, Türkiye, Uganda, Ukraine, United Arab Emirates, USA, Vietnam, Virgin Is UK.
Included in the above, 8 organizations listed in this Yearbook:
Centre de coopération internationale en recherche agronomique pour le développement (CIRAD, #03733); FEDIOL – The EU Vegetable Oil and Proteinmeal Industry (#09718); Global Environment Centre (GEC); International Institute for Land Reclamation and Improvement (Alterra-ILRI, inactive); Oxfam GB; Pesticide Action Network (PAN, #18336); Save the Orangutan (#19060); World Wide Fund for Nature (WWF, #21922).
NGO Relations Member of (2): *HCV Network Ltd (HCV Network, #10865); ISEAL (#16026).* Supports (1): *Wetlands International (#20928).* Participant of: *United Nations Global Compact (#20567).* [2022/XM0564/y/**F**]

♦ Rousseau Association (internationally oriented national body)
♦ Route européenne del Modernisme (#01125)
♦ La Route du Sel et de l'Espoir (internationally oriented national body)
♦ **Rowe Fund** Leo S Rowe Pan American Fund (#16445)
♦ Royal Aal al-Bayt Institute for Islamic Thought (internationally oriented national body)
♦ Royal Academy of Colonial Sciences / see Royal Academy of Overseas Sciences
♦ Royal Academy for Islamic Civilization Research / see Royal Aal al-Bayt Institute for Islamic Thought
♦ Royal Academy of Overseas Sciences (internationally oriented national body)
♦ Royal Academy of Science International Trust (internationally oriented national body)
♦ Royal African Society (internationally oriented national body)

♦ Royal Agricultural Society of the Commonwealth (RASC) 18987
Société royale de l'agriculture du Commonwealth
Hon Sec c/o RNAA, Norfolk Showground, Dereham Road, Norwich, NR5 0TT, UK. T. +447919958895. E-mail: info@therasc.com.
Registered Office 1 King's Arms Yard, London, EC2R 7AF, UK.
URL: https://www.therasc.com/
History 1957, UK. UK Registered Charity: 1101337. Registration: Charity Commission, No/ID: 1101337, England and Wales. **Aims** Promote interchange and development of knowledge and experience in the science and practice of sustainable agriculture, forestry, fishing and the rural environment, particularly in developing areas, working with and through the leading agricultural and show societies of all commonwealth countries; encourage higher standards of sustainable agriculture and the rural economy through farmers' organization; educate the general public and especially consumers in the interests of the agricultural community; help agricultural societies learn and gain strength from each other through cooperation and exchanges. **Structure** Officers: President; Deputy President; Chairman; Honorary Secretary; Honorary Press Officer; Honorary Treasurer. **Languages** English. **Staff** 2.00 FTE, voluntary. **Finance** Members' dues. Sponsorship. **Activities** Organizes conferences and seminars. **Events** *Commonwealth Agriculture Conference* Cape Town (South Africa) 2022, *Commonwealth Agriculture Conference* Norwich (UK) 2020, *Agriculture at the crossroads – bridging the rural-urban divide* Edmonton, AB (Canada) 2018, *Agriculture at the crossroads – bridging the rural-urban divide* Singapore (Singapore) 2016, *Biennial Conference* Brisbane, QLD (Australia) 2014. **Publications** *RASC Newsletter* (4 a year). Conference reports.
Members National agricultural societies (51) in 21 Commonwealth countries:
Australia, Botswana, Cameroon, Canada, Cyprus, Falklands/Malvinas, India, Jamaica, Kenya, Malawi, Mauritius, New Zealand, Pakistan, Papua New Guinea, Singapore, South Africa, Tanzania UR, Trinidad-Tobago, Uganda, UK, Zambia. [2020/XF4139/**F**]

♦ Royal Asiatic College / see University Institute of Oriental Studies

♦ Royal Asiatic Society of Great Britain and Ireland 18988
Dir 14 Stephenson Way, London, NW1 2HD, UK. T. +442073884539. Fax +442073919429. E-mail: info@royalasiaticsociety.org.
URL: https://royalasiaticsociety.org/
History 1823, London (UK). **Structure** Associate Societies. **Finance** Budget (annual): approx pounds170,000. **Publications** *Journal of the Royal Asiatic Society* (4 a year).
Members Headquarters (UK) and branches (4). Members in 14 countries:
Bangladesh, France, Germany, Hong Kong, India, Iran Islamic Rep, Italy, Japan, Korea Rep, Malaysia, Pakistan, Sri Lanka, UK, USA. [2022/XE2336/**E**]

♦ Royal Australasian College of Surgeons (internationally oriented national body)
♦ Royal Australian and New Zealand College of Radiologists (internationally oriented national body)
♦ Royal Belgian Colonial Institute / see Royal Academy of Overseas Sciences
♦ Royal Central Asian Society / see Royal Society for Asian Affairs
♦ Royal College of Pathologists of Australasia (internationally oriented national body)
♦ Royal Colonial Institute / see Royal Commonwealth Society (#18990)

♦ Royal Commonwealth Ex-Services League (RCEL) 18989
SG Haig House, 199 Borough High Street, London, SE1 1AA, UK. T. +442032072413. Fax +442032072115.
URL: http://www.commonwealthveterans.org.uk/
History 1921. Former names and other names: *British Empire Service League* – former; *British Commonwealth Ex-Services League (BCEL)* – former; *Ligue des anciens des armées du Commonwealth britannique* – former; *Commonwealth Ex-Services League (CEL)* – former (2002 to 2003); *Ligue des anciens des armées du Commonwealth* – former (2002 to 2003). Registration: Charity Commission, No/ID: 1174874, England and Wales. **Aims** Ensure that no Commonwealth ex-service man or woman who served the British Crown, or widow, shall be without help if in need. **Structure** Conference (every 5 years); Commonwealth Council; Executive Committee; Secretariat. **Languages** English. **Staff** 3.00 FTE, paid. **Finance** Sources: members' dues. Members and fundraising contribute to a Welfare Fund. **Activities** Events/meetings. **Events** *Conference* Malta 2012, *Conference* Ghana 2008, *Conference* Ottawa, ON (Canada) 2005, *Triennial Conference* Ottawa, ON (Canada) 2005, *Triennial conference / Conference* London (UK) 2002. **Publications** *Veterans Charter.* Quadrennial conference report; annual report; accounts.
Members Organizations of Commonwealth ex-servicemen and women (57, representing 10 million ex-servicemen and women) in 48 countries and territories:
Antigua-Barbuda, Australia, Bahamas, Bangladesh, Barbados, Belize, Bermuda, Botswana, Cameroon, Canada, Cayman Is, Cyprus, Dominica, Eswatini, Fiji, Gambia, Ghana, Grenada, Guyana, Hong Kong, India, Jamaica, Kenya, Lesotho, Malawi, Malaysia, Malta, Mauritius, Montserrat, Myanmar, Namibia, New Zealand, Nigeria, Pakistan, Scotland, Seychelles, Sierra Leone, South Africa, Sri Lanka, St Lucia, St Vincent-Grenadines, Tanzania UR, Trinidad-Tobago, Turks-Caicos, Uganda, UK, Zambia, Zimbabwe. [2022/XC0197/**F**]

♦ Royal Commonwealth Society (RCS) 18990
Dir Commonwealth House, 55-58 Pall Mall, London, SW1Y 5JH, UK. T. +442037274300. E-mail: info@thercs.org.
URL: http://www.thercs.org/
History Founded 1868, as *Colonial Society*; name changed, 1870, to *Colonial Institute*; received Royal Charter, 1882, as *Royal Colonial Institute.* Name changed, 1927, to *Royal Empire Society.* Present name adopted in 1958. **Aims** Promote knowledge and information about the modern Commonwealth; maintain a worldwide network of branches and societies; provide a forum for debate about Commonwealth issues. **Structure** Board of Trustees. **Languages** English. **Staff** 10.00 FTE, paid. **Finance** Grants; donations; corporate sponsorship. **Activities** Events/meetings; awards/prizes/competitions; projects/programmes. **Events** *Annual General Meeting* London (UK) 2008, *Annual General Meeting* London (UK) 2006, *Biennial international meeting* London (UK) 2006, *Annual General Meeting* London (UK) 2005, *Biennial international meeting / International Meeting* Agona Swedru (Ghana) 2004. **Publications** *Commonwealth Voices* (3 a year) – magazine; *RCS Newsletter.* Education packs; reports. Library collection at Cambridge University Library.
Members Honorary Representatives; Affiliated Societies. Branches (60) with a total indirect membership of about 15,000 in 35 countries and territories:
Australia, Bahamas, Bangladesh, Barbados, Belgium, Cameroon, Canada, Cayman Is, Cyprus, Dominican Rep, Fiji, Ghana, Gibraltar, Guernsey, Hong Kong, India, Ireland, Italy, Jamaica, Japan, Jersey, Kenya, Malaysia, Malta, Mauritius, New Zealand, Nigeria, Pakistan, Singapore, Sri Lanka, Switzerland, Trinidad-Tobago, Uganda, UK, USA.
Also members in Nordic region. Membership countries not specified.
IGO Relations Accredited to the Commonwealth by the *Commonwealth Secretariat (#04362).* Organizes: *Commonwealth Heads of Government Meeting (CHOGM, #04337).* **NGO Relations** Provides secretariat for: *Council of Commonwealth Societies (CCS, #04878).* Associate member of: *British Overseas NGO's for Development (BOND).* [2017.06.01/XF4981/**E**]

♦ Royal Commonwealth Society for the Blind / see Sightsavers International (#19270)
♦ Royal Empire Society / see Royal Commonwealth Society (#18990)
♦ Royal Family Foundation International (unconfirmed)
♦ Royal Geographical Society / see Royal Geographical Society – with the Institute of British Geographers
♦ Royal Geographical Society – with IBG / see Royal Geographical Society – with the Institute of British Geographers
♦ Royal Geographical Society – with the Institute of British Geographers (internationally oriented national body)
♦ Royal Institute of International Affairs (internationally oriented national body)
♦ Royal Institute for International Relations / see Egmont Institute

♦ Royal Institution of Chartered Surveyors (RICS) 18991
CEO RICS Head Office, 12 Great George Str, London, SW1P 3AD, UK. T. +442076868555 – +442072227000. Fax +442073343811.
Europe Office Rue Ducale 67, 1000 Brussels, Belgium. T. +3227331019. Fax +3227429748.
URL: http://www.rics.org/
History 1881, London (UK). Founded as the 'Institution of Surveyors'. Registration: Companies House, No/ID: RC000487, England; EU Transparency Register, No/ID: 12309911354-39, Start date: 12 Mar 2009. **Aims** Facilitate promotion of the *chartered surveying profession* and exchange of experience and information among professionally qualified chartered surveyors; represent members' interests to institutions; facilitate training, qualification and mutual recognition; establish worldwide standards of professional practice and codes of conduct; support and promote development of the *property* and *construction* professions for the benefit of all. **Structure** Council. Offices in Brussels (Belgium), Hong Kong, London (UK), New York NY (USA), Sydney (Australia). Brussels office – *RICS Europe (#18939)* – comprises the previous *'European Society of Chartered Surveyors'.* **Staff** 420.00 FTE, paid. **Events** *Smart Buildings Conference* Singapore (Singapore) 2020, *Future of Quantity Surveyor Seminar* Singapore (Singapore) 2019, *PropTech Innovate Summit* Singapore (Singapore) 2019, *Seminar on Primer on the SOP Act and new Amendments* Singapore (Singapore) 2019, *Seminar on Prolongation Cost* Singapore (Singapore) 2019. **Members** Individuals in 120 countries. Membership countries not specified. **Consultative Status** Consultative status granted from: *ECOSOC (#05331)* (Special). **NGO Relations** Member of (11): *Coalition for Energy Savings (#04056); Construction 2050 Alliance (#04760); European Construction Forum (ECF, #06765); European Housing Forum (EHF, #07504); European Real Estate Forum (#08331); Global Alliance for Buildings and Construction (GlobalABC, #10187); International Cost Management Standard Coalition (ICMS Coalition, #12978); International Council for Research and Innovation in Building and Construction (CIB, #13069); International Ethics Standards Coalition (IES Coalition, #13307); International Fire Safety Standards Coalition (IFSS Coalition, #13606); International Housing Coalition (IHC Global).* Partner of (1): *Global Shelter Cluster (GSC, #10594).* [2020/XG8038/y/**C**]

♦ Royal Institution of Naval Architects (internationally oriented national body)

♦ Royal Life Saving Society (RLSS) 18992

Société royale de sauvetage

Registered Office Royal Life Saving Society, Red Hill House, 227 London Road, Worcester, WR5 2JG, UK. T. +4403003230096. E-mail: commonwealth@rlss.org.uk.
URL: http://www.rlsscommonwealth.org/

History 1891, London (UK). Registration: Charity Commission, No/ID: 306094, England and Wales; Royal Charter, Start date: 1924, UK. **Aims** Facilitate drowning prevention, lifesaving and lifesaving sport activity; foster and facilitate exchanges and sharing between Member Organisations. **Structure** Board of Trustees; Council of Presidents; Committees; Working Groups. **Languages** English. **Staff** 1.00 FTE, paid. Several voluntary. **Finance** Sources: donations; grants; members' dues; sponsorship. **Activities** Awards/prizes/competitions; events/meetings; projects/programmes; training/education. **Events** *Quadrennial Conference* Alberta (Canada) 2009, *Quadrennial Conference* Edmonton, AB (Canada) 2009, *Asia Pacific conference* Singapore (Singapore) 2007, *Quinquennial Conference* Bath (UK) 2006, *Asia Pacific conference* Malaysia 2003. **Publications** *Commonwealth Newsletter* (4 a year). Annual Report. Branch magazines and publications.
Members National; Associate; Emerging; Companion. Members currently in 30 Commonwealth countries and territories:
Australia, Bangladesh, Barbados, Botswana, Brunei Darussalam, Cameroon, Canada, Cyprus, Ghana, Gibraltar, Hong Kong, India, Jamaica, Kenya, Lesotho, Malawi, Malaysia, Malta, Mauritius, New Zealand, Nigeria, Pakistan, Singapore, South Africa, Sri Lanka, St Lucia, Tanzania UR, Trinidad-Tobago, Uganda, UK.
IGO Relations Accredited by (1): *Commonwealth Secretariat (#04362).* **NGO Relations** Member of (1): *International Life Saving Federation (ILS, #14040).* [2022.05.04/XF3270/**F**]

♦ Royal Museum for Central Africa (internationally oriented national body)
♦ Royal Netherlands Institute for Sea Research (internationally oriented national body)
♦ Royal Netherlands Institute of Southeast Asian and Caribbean Studies (internationally oriented national body)
♦ Royal Netherlands International Law Association / see Royal Netherlands Society of International Law
♦ Royal Netherlands Society of International Law (internationally oriented national body)
♦ Royal Oriental Institute of Naples / see University Institute of Oriental Studies
♦ Royal Over-Seas League (internationally oriented national body)
♦ Royal Society for Asian Affairs (internationally oriented national body)
♦ Royal Society of Chemistry (internationally oriented national body)
♦ Royal Tropical Institute (internationally oriented national body)
♦ Royal United Services Institute for Defence and Security Studies (internationally oriented national body)
♦ Royal United Services Institute for Defence Studies / see Royal United Services Institute for Defence and Security Studies
♦ Royal World Peace Fund / see World Constitution Fund
♦ Royaumont Foundation for the Advancement of the Social Sciences (internationally oriented national body)
♦ Rozenkruizersgenootschap – Internationale School van het Gouden Rozenkruis (religious order)
♦ ROZRADA – International Humanitarian Centre for Rehabilitation of Survivors after Chernobyl Disaster / see International Humanitarian Centre for Rehabilitation of Survivors after Chernobyl Disaster
♦ ROZRADA – International Humanitarian Centre for Rehabilitation of Survivors after Chernobyl Disaster (internationally oriented national body)
♦ Røde Kors Nordisk United World College (internationally oriented national body)
♦ **RPA** Regional Programme of Action for the Protection of the Arctic Marine Environment from Land-based Activities (#18806)
♦ RPA – Rockefeller Philanthropy Advisors (internationally oriented national body)
♦ RPB – Sisters Adorers of the Precious Blood (religious order)
♦ **RPCA** Réseau de prévention des crises alimentaires (#18905)
♦ RPCDC / see Caribbean Child Development Centre
♦ RPC / see Piracy Reporting Centre, Kuala Lumpur (#18373)
♦ RPE / see People from Here and Elsewhere Federation (#18298)
♦ RPFI – Asian Regional Cooperative Project on Food Irradiation (inactive)
♦ RPF – Russian Peace Foundation (internationally oriented national body)
♦ **RPGA** RP Global Alliance (#18993)

♦ RP Global Alliance (RPGA) 18993

Address not obtained.
URL: https://rpglobalalliance.org/

History Jun 2015. Founded by RP Churches of Australia, Ireland, North America and Scotland. Former names and other names: *Reformed Presbyterian Global Alliance* – full title. **Aims** Work together so as to better utilize the resources already existing within the worldwide RP Church. **Structure** Advisory Committee.
Members Churches in 4 countries and territories:
Australia, Ireland, Scotland, USA. [2022/XM8417/**C**]

♦ RPGR – Recent Progress in Graphene and Two-dimensional Materials Research Conference (meeting series)
♦ RP – International Conference on Reachability Problems (meeting series)
♦ RPI – Research Policy Institute, Lund (internationally oriented national body)
♦ **RPN** Red Panda Network (#18726)
♦ RPN – Regional Powers Network (internationally oriented national body)
♦ RPPA – Global Reverse Phase Protein Array Workshop (meeting series)
♦ RPsBm / see Parliamentary Network on the World Bank and International Monetary Fund (#18219)
♦ RQ – International Conference on Rapidly Quenched and Metastable Materials (meeting series)
♦ RRB – International Conference on Renewable Resources and Biorefineries (meeting series)
♦ RRE / see Assembly of European Regions (#02316)
♦ RReFA) – Rhinology Research Forum in Asia (meeting series)
♦ **RREUSE** Re-Use and Recycling European Union Social Enterprises (#18931)
♦ **RRF** Raptor Research Foundation (#18619)
♦ RRI / see Refugee Relief International
♦ RRII – Refugee Relief International (internationally oriented national body)
♦ **RRI** Reach to Recovery International (#18625)
♦ RRI – Resource Renewal Institute (internationally oriented national body)
♦ **RRI** Rights and Resources Initiative (#18947)
♦ RRN / see Humanitarian Practice Network (#10973)
♦ RRN / see Latin American and Caribbean Research Network (#16284)
♦ **RROCM** Red Regional de Organizaciones Civiles para las Migraciones (#18728)
♦ RRRPD / see Farm Radio International (#09274)
♦ RS5C – Road Safety on Five Continents (meeting series)
♦ RSAA – Royal Society for Asian Affairs (internationally oriented national body)
♦ **RSAHC** ROPME Sea Area Hydrographic Commission (#18971)
♦ **RSAI** Regional Science Association International (#18813)
♦ RSA / see Regional Science Association International (#18813)
♦ RSA – Regional Studies Association (internationally oriented national body)
♦ RSA – Renal Society of Australasia (internationally oriented national body)
♦ RSB / see Roundtable on Sustainable Biomaterials (#18985)
♦ **RSB** Roundtable on Sustainable Biomaterials (#18985)
♦ RSCAS – Robert Schuman Centre for Advanced Studies (see: #09034)
♦ RSCM – Religiose del Sacro Cuore di Maria (religious order)
♦ RSC – Refugee Studies Centre, Oxford (internationally oriented national body)
♦ RSC – Royal Society of Chemistry (internationally oriented national body)
♦ **RSC SUN** Red de la Sociedad Civil SUN (#20035)
♦ **RSC SUN** Réseau de la société civile SUN (#20035)
♦ RSD – International Conference on Reactive Sputter Deposition (meeting series)
♦ **RSE** Rett Syndrome Europe (#18928)
♦ **RSE** Rhetoric Society of Europe (#18934)
♦ **RSF** Reporters sans frontières (#18846)
♦ **RSF** Robert Schuman Foundation for Cooperation among Christian Democrats in Europe (#18957)
♦ RSHM – Religious of the Sacred Heart of Mary (religious order)
♦ RSIF / see Federation International Football Skating (#09671)
♦ **RSI** Robert Schuman Institute for Developing Democracy in Central and Eastern Europe (#18958)
♦ RSIS Centre for Non-Traditional Security / see Centre for Non-Traditional Security Studies
♦ RSIS – S Rajaratnam School of International Studies (internationally oriented national body)
♦ RSLF – Roger Scruton Legacy Foundation (internationally oriented national body)
♦ **RSMLAC** Red de Salud de las Mujeres Latinoamericanas y del Caribe (#16288)
♦ RSM – Robert S McNamara Fellowships Program (internationally oriented national body)
♦ RSMT / see ReachAcross
♦ RSP / see Refugee Studies Centre, Oxford
♦ RSPAA – Remote Sensing and Photogrammetry Association of Australasia (inactive)
♦ RSPAS – Research School of Pacific and Asian Studies, Canberra (internationally oriented national body)
♦ **RSPC SEE** Regional Secretariat for Parliamentary Cooperation in South-East Europe (#18815)
♦ **RSPO** Roundtable on Sustainable Palm Oil (#18986)
♦ **RSSC** Radiological Society of SAARC Countries (#18602)
♦ **RSS Foundation** Robotics: Science and Systems Foundation (#18964)
♦ RSS – Rural Sociological Society (internationally oriented national body)
♦ RSTC / see World Recreational Scuba Training Council (#21747)
♦ RSV – Congregatio Religiosorum Sancti Vincentii a Paulo, Patrum et Fratrum (religious order)
♦ **RSVP** Research Society for Victorian Periodicals (#18861)
♦ RSWR – Right Sharing of World Resources (internationally oriented national body)
♦ **RTAE** Rubber Trade Association of Europe (#18995)
♦ **RTAG** Round Table Arabian Gulf (#18979)
♦ RTAL' / see Rubber Trade Association of Europe (#18995)
♦ **RTA** Red de Transparencia y Acceso a la Información (#18732)
♦ RTBI – National Association of Round Tables of Great Britain and Ireland (internationally oriented national body)
♦ RTCA / see Radio Technical Commission for Aeronautics
♦ RTCA – Radio Technical Commission for Aeronautics (internationally oriented national body)
♦ RTC – Commission pour la production et la diffusion de radio-télévision et cinéma d'expression française (inactive)
♦ RTCC – Responding to Climate Change (unconfirmed)
♦ RTCM – Radio Technical Commission for Maritime Services (internationally oriented national body)
♦ **RtDE** Right to Die Europe (#18941)
♦ **RTE** RadTech Europe (#18606)
♦ RTE – Renew the Earth (internationally oriented national body)
♦ **RTE** Right to Education Initiative (#18942)
♦ RTI International (internationally oriented national body)
♦ **RTI** Round Table International (#18982)
♦ **RTI-TN** Rural Tourism International – Training Network (#19005)
♦ RTM – Reggio Terzo Mondo (internationally oriented national body)
♦ RTO – NATO Research and Technology Organization (inactive)
♦ RTRC Asia / see SEED Institute (#19215)
♦ **RTRS** Round Table on Responsible Soy Association (#18983)
♦ **RTSA** Round Table Southern Africa (#18984)
♦ **R and TTE CA** R and TTE Compliance Association (#18994)

♦ R and TTE Compliance Association (R and TTE CA) 18994

Address not obtained.
URL: http://www.rtteca.com/

History Full title: *Radio and Telecommunications Terminal Equipment Compliance Association.* **Aims** Provide a forum for people concerned with the compliance of *radio equipment* and *telecommunications* terminal equipment with technical *standards.* **Structure** Officers: Chairman; Secretary; Treasurer. [2010/XJ2142/**D**]

♦ **RUAF Foundation** International Network of Resource Centers on Urban Agriculture and Food Security (#14319)
♦ RUAF / see International Network of Resource Centers on Urban Agriculture and Food Security (#14319)
♦ Rubber Growers' Association / see Tropical Growers' Association (#20250)

♦ Rubber Trade Association of Europe (RTAE) 18995

SG 122 Haliburton Road, Twickenham, TW1 1PH, UK. T. +442088924177 – +4420(447774249634.
URL: http://www.rtae.org/

History Founded 1992, as *Association of the International Rubber Trade (AIRT)*, deriving from the *'Rubber Trade Association of London (RTAL)'*, founded 1913. Re-organized under current title, 1 Mar 2002. Company Registered in England and Wales: 4377813. **Aims** Provide an efficient and dependable marketing service to producers, consumers and traders of rubber; promote best interests of the rubber trade. **Structure** Committee; Arbitrators (13), also available for appeal tribunals; Committees; Sub-Committees. **Languages** English. **Staff** 1.00 FTE, paid. **Finance** Members' dues. **Activities** Guidance/assistance/consulting; networking/liaising; politics/policy/regulatory; events/meetings; training/education. **Publications** Daily quotations for certain grades of rubber.
Members Members (15) in 14 countries:
Belgium, Cameroon, France, Germany, Italy, Luxembourg, Malaysia, Netherlands, Singapore, Spain, Switzerland, Thailand, UK, Vietnam.
Broker members (2) in 1 country:
UK.
Associate (6) in 4 countries:
Belgium, France, Spain, UK.
Included in the above, 1 organization listed in this Yearbook:
European Tyre and Rubber Manufacturers' Association (ETRMA, #08963).
IGO Relations Member of: Panel of Associates of *International Rubber Study Group (IRSG, #14772).* **NGO Relations** Member of: *Federation of Commodity Associations (FCA, no recent information).*
[2019.12.18/XC0043/ty/**D**]

♦ Rubber Trade Association of London / see Rubber Trade Association of Europe (#18995)
♦ Ruben and Elisabeth Rausing Trust / see Sigrid Rausing Trust
♦ **RUFORUM** Regional Universities Forum for Capacity Building in Agriculture (#18818)

♦ Rugby Africa 18996

Rugby Afrique

Gen Manager c/o SARU, PO Box 15929, Panorama 7506, Cape Town, South Africa.
URL: http://www.rugbyafrique.com/

History Jan 1986, Tunis (Tunisia), at constituent assembly, as *African Rugby Football Union – Confédération africaine de rugby (CARA)* In French previously also referred to as *Confédération africaine de rugby amateur.* **Aims** Promote rugby in Africa. **Structure** General Assembly; Steering Committee; Founding President. **Languages** Arabic, English, French. **Finance** Members' dues. **Activities** Organizes African Cup and qualifying matches for Rugby World Cup. **Events** *Meeting* Casablanca (Morocco) 1992, *Meeting* Tunis (Tunisia) 1991, *Meeting* Tunis (Tunisia) 1990.
Members Full in 20 countries:
Botswana, Burundi, Congo DR, Côte d'Ivoire, Kenya, Madagascar, Malawi, Mauritania, Mauritius, Morocco, Namibia, Nigeria, Senegal, Seychelles, South Africa, Togo, Tunisia, Uganda, Zambia, Zimbabwe.
NGO Relations Recognized by: *Association of African Sports Confederations (AASC, #02360); Rugby Europe (#18998).* Regional association of: *World Rugby (#21757).* [2018/XD4532/**D**]

♦ Rugby Afrique (#18996)

♦ Rugby Americas North (RAN) 18997

Pres PO Box 4441, Road Town, Road Town VG1110, Virgin Is UK. E-mail: info@rugbyamericasnorth.com.
URL: https://rugbyamericasnorth.com/

History Mar 2001. A regional association of *World Rugby (#21757)*. Former names and other names: *North America and West Indies Rugby Association (NAWIRA)* – former; *North America Caribbean Rugby Association (NACRA)* – former. **Aims** Grow the game of rugby in the RAN; facilitate international tournaments and implement goals and directives from World Rugby for the global game. **Structure** Board of Directors; Executive Committee. **Languages** English, French, Spanish. **Staff** 6.00 FTE, paid. **Activities** Sporting activities.
Members Full in 13 countries and territories:
Bahamas, Barbados, Bermuda, Canada, Cayman Is, Guyana, Jamaica, Mexico, St Lucia, St Vincent-Grenadines, Trinidad-Tobago, USA, Virgin Is UK.
Associate in 4 countries and territories:
Dominican Rep, Guadeloupe, Guiana Fr, Martinique.
Recognized Regional Developement Unions in 2 territories:
Curaçao, Turks-Caicos.
NGO Relations Member of (1): *Asociación de Confederaciones Deportivas Panamericanas (ACODEPA, #02119)*. [2023/XJ2082/D]

♦ Rugby Europe 18998

Secretariat 45 rue de Liège, 75008 Paris, France. E-mail: secretariat@rugbyeurope.eu.
URL: http://www.rugbyeurope.eu/

History 2 Jan 1934. Founded following meeting 4 Sep 1933, Turin (Italy), during temporary exclusion of France from the *'5 Nations Tournament'*. Commenced activities 24 Mar 1934, Hanover (Germany). 29 May 1999, Paris (France), new constitution adopted. Former names and other names: *International Amateur Rugby Federation* – former; *Fédération internationale de rugby amateur (FIRA)* – former (1999); *Federación Internacional de Aficionados de Rugby* – former (1999); *Internationale Vereinigung der Rugby Amateur* – former (1999); *FIRA – Association européenne de rugby (FIRA-AER)* – former (29 May 1999 to 2014). Registration: Start date: 10 Jun 1934, France. **Aims** Promote, develop, manage and administer the game of rugby in Europe within the European jurisdiction in accordance with bye-laws and regulations. **Structure** General Assembly (one at Congress, other in Dec, always in Paris-France). Board of Directors of at least 20 and up to 45 members and including President, General Secretary, Deputy General Secretary, General Treasurer, Deputy General Treasurer, Representative to World Rugby and 10 Vice-Presidents. Executive Committee of at least 6 and up to 14 members and including Chairman, General Secretary and General Treasurer. 2 Regional Development Managers. Committees (11): Competitions; Medical – Insurance – Anti-doping; Partnership – Communication; Women's Rugby; International relations; Referees; Legal – Administrative; Technical and Game Development; Finance; High Level; Sevens Rugby. **Languages** English, French, Russian. **Staff** 10.00 FTE, paid. **Finance** Sources: investments; members' dues; subsidies. **Activities** Events/meetings; training/education. **Events** *Annual Congress* Valletta (Malta) 2010, *Annual Congress* Moscow (Russia) 2009, *Annual Congress* Corfu (Greece) 2008, *Annual Congress* Monte Carlo (Monaco) 2007, *Annual Congress* Sorrento (Italy) 2006. **Publications** *Flash Info* (12 a year).
Members National rugby federations recognized by World Rugby in 48 countries and territories:
Andorra, Austria, Azerbaijan, Belarus, Belgium, Bosnia-Herzegovina, Bulgaria, Croatia, Cyprus, Czechia, Denmark, England, Estonia, Finland, France, Georgia, Germany, Greece, Hungary, Iceland, Ireland, Israel, Italy, Latvia, Liechtenstein, Lithuania, Luxembourg, Malta, Moldova, Monaco, Montenegro, Netherlands, Norway, Poland, Portugal, Romania, Russia, San Marino, Scotland, Serbia, Slovakia, Slovenia, Spain, Sweden, Switzerland, Türkiye, Ukraine, Wales.
NGO Relations Regional association of: *World Rugby (#21757)*. Member of: *Association of European Team Sports (ETS, #02546)*; *European Association of Sport Employers (EASE, #06218)*. [2022/XD6413/D]

♦ Rugby League European Federation / see European Rugby League (#08411)
♦ Rugmark Foundation / see GoodWeave International (#10681)
♦ RugMark International / see GoodWeave International (#10681)
♦ Rui Foundation (internationally oriented national body)
♦ RUIG – Réseau universitaire international de Genève (internationally oriented national body)
♦ RuleML+RR – International Joint Conference on Rules and Reasoning (meeting series)
♦ Rules of Arbitration and Conciliation for Settlement of International Disputes between Two Parties of Which One Only Is a State (1962 treaty)

♦ RUNDA 18999

Contact Paromlinska cesta 49, HR-10000 Zagreb, Croatia. T. +38514444310. E-mail: info@runda.online.
URL: http://runda.online/

History 15 Oct 2018. Founded by former members of and with the support of *Independent Music Companies Association (IMPALA, #11151)*. Former names and other names: *Association of Independent Discographers – Regional Association of Independent Discographers Balkans* – alias; *Music Business Balkan* – alias. **Aims** Promote the interests of record companies or individuals – professionals who make music recordings and who have the status of independent record companies. **Structure** Managing Board; Supervisory Board; Advisory Board. **Activities** Advocacy/lobbying/activism; awards/prizes/competitions; events/meetings.
Members Full (67) in 7 countries:
Bosnia-Herzegovina, Croatia, Kosovo, Montenegro, North Macedonia, Serbia, Slovenia.
NGO Relations Member of (2): *Independent Music Companies Association (IMPALA, #11151)*; *Worldwide Independent Network (WIN, #21925)*. [2021/AA2363/D]

♦ Runder Tisch für Nachhaltiges Palmöl (#18986)
♦ RUNIC / see United Nations Regional Information Centre for Western Europe (#20621)

♦ Running the European Network of Biological and retrospective Physical dosimetry (RENEB) 19000

Address not obtained.
URL: http://www.reneb.net/

History 2017. Founded within the 7th EU framework EURATOM Fission Programme. Registration: No/ID: VR 201614, Start date: 5 Jul 2017, Germany. **Aims** Advance science and research; advance fire prevention, occupational health and safety, disaster control and civil defense as well as of accident prevention. **Structure** General Assembly; Council; Board; Working Groups. **Activities** Events/meetings.
Members Organizations in 11 countries:
Belgium, Bulgaria, France, Germany, Italy, Lithuania, Norway, Portugal, Spain, Sweden, UK. [2019/AA0778/F]

♦ Rural Advancement Foundation International / see Action Group on Erosion, Technology and Concentration (#00091)
♦ Rural Advancement Fund International / see Action Group on Erosion, Technology and Concentration (#00091)
♦ Rural Development Counsellors for Christian Churches in Africa / see Rural and Urban Resources – Counselling, Outreach and Networking
♦ Rural Development Foundation Global (internationally oriented national body)
♦ Rural Development Institute / see Landesa – Rural Development Institute
♦ Rural Education and Development / see READ Global
♦ Rural Foundation for the Development of the Third World (internationally oriented national body)

♦ Ruralia 19001

Sec Arch Inst of the Hungarian Ac of Sciences, Uri utca 49, Budapest 1250, Hungary. T. +3613759011. Fax +3612253361.
URL: http://www.ruralia.cz/

History 1995. **Aims** Strengthen exchange of knowledge in, and development of, archaeologically comparable studies in *archaeology* of *mediaeval settlements* and rural life; make archaeological results available to other disciplines. **Structure** Committee; Executive Committee. **Languages** English, French, German. **Staff** None paid. **Activities** Events/meetings. **Events** *Jean-Marie Pesez Conference on Medieval Rural Archaeology* Luxembourg (Luxembourg) 2015, *Jean-Marie Pesez Conference on Medieval Rural Archaeology* Smolenice (Slovakia) 2013, *Jean-Marie Pesez Conference on Medieval Rural Archaeology* Götzis (Austria) 2011, *Jean-Marie Pesez Conference on Medieval Rural Archaeology* Lorca (Spain) 2009, *Jean-Marie Pesez Conference on Medieval Rural Archaeology* Cardiff (UK) 2007. **Publications** *Ruralia* – journal.
Members Full in 21 countries:
Austria, Belgium, Czechia, Denmark, Finland, France, Germany, Hungary, Ireland, Italy, Luxembourg, Netherlands, Norway, Portugal, Romania, Russia, Slovakia, Spain, Sweden, Switzerland, UK.
IGO Relations None. [2015.03.15/XJ8653/c/E]

♦ Ruralidad – Medio Ambiente – Desarrollo (#19003)
♦ Rural Integrated Development Program of Africa (internationally oriented national body)

♦ Rural Investment Support for Europe Foundation (RISE Foundation) 19002

Managing Dir Rue de Trèves 67, 1040 Brussels, Belgium. T. +3222343000. Fax +3222343009.
URL: http://www.risefoundation.eu/

History Set up 2006, by former *European Union (EU, #08967)* Commissioner for Agriculture, Rural Development and Fisheries, Franz Fischler and his Chief of Staff Corrado Pirzio-Biroli, with the support of *European Landowners' Organization (ELO, #07639)* and *Friends of the Countryside (FCS, #10000)*. Registration: No/ID: 0884.303.072, Start date: 16 Oct 2006, Belgium; EU Transparency Register, No/ID: 094378436020-67, Start date: 25 Sep 2019. **Aims** Support a sustainable and internationally competitive rural economy across Europe, looking for ways to preserve the European countryside, its environment and biodiversity, and its cultural heritage and traditions. See a more sustainable *agricultural* system in Europe. **Structure** Board. **Activities** Guidance/assistance/consulting.
Members Organizations in 5 countries:
Germany, Lithuania, Portugal, Sweden, UK.
Regional organizations (2):
European Landowners' Organization (ELO, #07639); *Friends of the Countryside (FCS, #10000)*.
NGO Relations Partners include: *European Water Partnership (EWP, #09083)*; *King Baudouin Foundation (KBF)*. [2020/XM6990/f/F]

♦ Ruralité – Environnement – Développement (#19003)

♦ Rurality – Environment – Development (RED) 19003

Ruralité – Environnement – Développement (RED) – Ruralidad – Medio Ambiente – Desarrollo – Ländlichkeit – Umwelt – Entwicklung

Contact Rue des Potiers 304, 6717 Attert, Belgium. T. +3263230490. Fax +3263230499. E-mail: infored@ruraleurope.org.
URL: http://www.ruraleurope.org/

History Founded Jul 1980, Arlon (Belgium). Also referred to as *Association Internationale RED*. Registered in accordance with Belgian law. **Aims** Promote a European rural development policy; facilitate contact and exchange among people involved in rural development; ascertain links between development and environmental problems and those of rural culture; seek means of participation for rural inhabitants in *European unity*; exchange and disseminate information on global rural development; stimulate and carry out research in *regional planning*, economic development, environment, methods and tools adapted to the rural world; make the European development network available to members. **Structure** General Assembly; Board of Directors. **Languages** English, French, German, Spanish. **Staff** 4.00 FTE, paid. **Finance** Members' dues. Other sources: study and research works; subsidy from Wallonia Region and Luxembourg. Annual budget: euro 240,000. **Activities** Events/meetings; projects/programmes. **Events** *International Colloquium* Brussels (Belgium) 2012, *International Colloquium* Castellón de la Plana (Spain) 2012, *International Colloquium* Montmédy (France) 2012, *International colloquium* Arlon (Belgium) 2011, *International colloquium* Grossetto (Italy) 2010. **Publications** *RED Dossier* (2 a year). Books; leaflets.
Members Individuals; Organizations. Members in 16 countries:
Belgium, Denmark, Finland, France, Germany, Hungary, Ireland, Italy, Luxembourg, Poland, Portugal, Romania, Spain, Sweden, Switzerland, UK.
Consultative Status Consultative status granted from: *Council of Europe (CE, #04881)* (Participatory Status).
IGO Relations Member of: Advisory Group on Rural Development of *European Commission (EC, #06633)*. *European Landscape Convention (2000)*. Associated with Department of Global Communications of the United Nations. **NGO Relations** Joint studies and programmes with: *Assembly of European Regions (AER, #02316)*; *Association for European Rural Universities (APURE, #02541)*; *Association internationale des mouvements familiaux de formation rurale (AIMFR, #02719)*; *Comité Européen de Droit Rural (CEDR, #04155)*; *Euromontana (#05737)*; *European Association for Rural Development Institutions (#06198)*; *European Greenways Association (EGWA, #07412)*; *European LEADER Association for Rural Development (ELARD, #07663)*; *Fédération Internationale de Tourisme Équestre (FITE, #09666)*; *Peri-Urban Regions Platform Europe (PURPLE, #18316)*. Member of: *Europa Nostra (#05767)*. [2019.12.13/XF0243/F]

♦ Rural Sociological Society (internationally oriented national body)

♦ Ruralter Platform 19004

Plate-forme ruralter – Plataforma Ruralter

Dir AVSF, 45 bis ave de la Belle Gabrielle, 94736 Nogent-sur-Marne CEDEX, France.
URL: http://www.ruralter.org/

Aims Function as a *rural development* organization in the *Andean* region. **Finance** Supported by: *European Commission (EC, #06633)*; French Government.
Members National organizations (2) in 2 countries:
Ecuador, Peru.
Regional organizations (3):
Agronomes et vétérinaires sans frontières (AVSF); *Centre international d'études pour le développement local (CIEDEL)*; *SNV Netherlands Development Organisation (SNV)*. [2014/XM1252/y/F]

♦ **RuralTour** European Federation of Rural Tourism (#07208)

♦ Rural Tourism International – Training Network (RTI-TN) 19005

Address not obtained.
URL: http://ruraltourisminternational.wordpress.com/

History 2005, to continue the work of the Hospitality in Rural Tourism project which had been funded by *LEONARDO DA VINCI (inactive)*. [2008/XM8272/F]

♦ Rural and Urban Resources – Counselling, Outreach and Networking (internationally oriented national body)

♦ Rural Water Supply Network (RWSN) 19006

Dir c/o Skat Foundation, Vadianstr 42, 9000 St Gallen, Switzerland. E-mail: ruralwater@skat.ch.
URL: http://www.rural-water-supply.net/

History Set up following a meeting held, 1992, Kenya, as *Handpump Technology Network*. Current title adopted 2004. Developed by *UNICEF (#20332)*, *Swiss Resource Centre and Consultancies for Development (SKAT)* and *Swiss Agency for Development and Cooperation (SDC)*. **Aims** Promote access for all rural people to sustainable and reliable water supplies which can be effectively managed to provide sufficient, affordable and safe water within a reasonable distance of the home. **Structure** Executive Steering Committee; Secretariat. Hosted by *SKAT Foundation*. **Languages** English, French, Portuguese, Spanish. **Finance** Supported (financial and in-kind) by: *Swiss Agency for Development and Cooperation (SDC)*; *WaterAid (#20822)*; *The World Bank Group (#21218)*; *Swiss Resource Centre and Consultancies for Development (SKAT)*; *UNICEF (#20332)*; *African Development Bank Group (ADB Group, #00284)*; *IRC (#16016)*; *Water Mission International (Water Mission)*; national organizations. **Activities** Knowledge management/information dissemination; events/meetings; networking/liaising; training/education. **Publications** *RWSN Quarterly Newsletter*. Field notes; guidance documents. **Members** Full (over 11,000) in 160 countries. Membership countries not specified. [2019.03.11/XM7243/F]

♦ Rural Youth Europe 19007

Jeunesse rurale européenne – Europäischer Landjugendverband

SG Karjalankatu 2A, FI-00520 Helsinki, Finland. T. +358452345629. E-mail: office@ruralyoutheurope.com – info@ruralyoutheurope.com.

URL: http://www.ruralyoutheurope.com/
History Feb 1957, Germany FR. Feb 1957, Rendsburg (Germany FR), on the initiative of Pieter Dijkhuis, as *European Committee for Young Farmers' Clubs Federations*. Subsequently changed title to *European Committee for Young Farmers' and 4H Clubs (ECYF4HC) – Comité européen des jeunes agriculteurs et des 4H clubs – Comité Europeo de Organizaciones de Jóvenes Agricultores y 4H Clubs – Europäisches Komitee für Jungbauern- und 4H-Clubs*. Functions widened and name changed 16 Feb 1960, Edinburgh (UK). Current title adopted, 2004. Charter revised 1965, 1974, 1990, 1997, 1998, 1999, 2004, 2016. Builds on the work of *International Four-H Youth Exchange (IFYE, inactive)*, set up 1948 to rebuild personal relations between young rural people from the USA and their counterparts in the rest of the world. **Aims** Create a platform for learning, developing and improving life for youngsters in rural areas. **Structure** General Assembly (annual); Board; Secretary-General. **Languages** English. **Staff** 1.50 FTE, paid. **Finance** Members' dues. Grants. **Activities** Events/meetings; training/education; networking/liaising; advocacy/lobbying/activism. **Events** *Annual General Assembly* Halmstad (Sweden) 2010, *Annual General Assembly* Estonia 2009, *Annual General Assembly* Jäneda (Estonia) 2009, *Annual General Assembly* Switzerland 2008, *Annual General Assembly* Germany 2007. **Publications** *Rural Voices* (annual) – magazine; *RYEurope's Monthly Newsletter*. Seminar reports.
Members Rural youth, young farmers' and 4H organizations, with total membership of 500,000 young people, in 14 countries:
Armenia, Austria, Denmark, Estonia, Finland, Germany, Hungary, Ireland, Latvia, Norway, Slovenia, Sweden, Switzerland, UK.
IGO Relations Regular relations with: *Council of Europe (CE, #04881)*; *European Commission (EC, #06633)*. Member of: *European Youth Centres (EYCs, #09138)*. **NGO Relations** Member of: *European Youth Forum (#09140)*. *European IFYE Alumni Association (#07516)* maintains contacts among ex-participants of IFYE programmes. [2019.02.12/XD0638/**E**]

♦ RURCON – Rural and Urban Resources – Counselling, Outreach and Networking (internationally oriented national body)
♦ RU – Renaissance Universal (internationally oriented national body)

♦ RURENER 19008

Office 14 av Léonard de Vinci, 63000 Clermont-Ferrand, France. E-mail: contact@rurener.eu – rurener@gmail.com.
URL: http://rurener.eu/
History Set up 2008, as of project funded by *European Commission (EC, #06633)* – Intelligent Energy Europe. Becomes independent 2017. Full title: *RURENER – Network of small RURal communities for ENERgetic-neutrality*. Current articles adopted 28 Sep 2011; revised 14 Sep 2018. Registered in accordance with French law. **Aims** Promote and support European small rural communities committed to an integrated *energy policy* at local level, aiming to reach energy neutrality. **Structure** General Assembly; Executive Committee; Secretariat. **Languages** English. **Finance** Members' dues. **Activities** Advocacy/lobbying/activism; monitoring/evaluation; networking/liaising; projects/programmes; events/meetings. **Events** *General Assembly* Rossignol (Belgium) 2019, *General Assembly* Jarnages (France) 2018.
Members Full in 7 countries:
Belgium, Cyprus, France, Greece, Hungary, Portugal, Spain.
NGO Relations *Future of Rural Energy in Europe (FREE)*; *Rurality – Environment – Development (RED, #19003)*. [2019.06.04/XM6610/**F**]

♦ RURENER – Network of small RURal communities for ENERgetic-neutrality / see RURENER (#19008)
♦ **RUSEMEG** Réseau Universitaire et Scientifique Euro-Méditerranéen sur le Genre et les Femmes (#18907)
♦ RUSI / see Royal United Services Institute for Defence and Security Studies
♦ RUSI – Royal United Services Institute for Defence and Security Studies (internationally oriented national body)
♦ Russian Association of Indigenous Peoples of the North (internationally oriented national body)
♦ Russian Association of the Peoples of the North / see Russian Association of Indigenous Peoples of the North
♦ Russian Committee of Cooperation with Latin America (internationally oriented national body)
♦ Russian and East European Centre, Oxford / see Russian and Eurasian Studies Centre, Oxford
♦ Russian and East European Institute, Bloomington IN (internationally oriented national body)
♦ Russian and East European Research Centre, Tel Aviv / see Cummings Center for Russian and East European Studies
♦ Russian and Eurasian Studies Centre, Oxford (internationally oriented national body)
♦ Russian and Euroasian Security Network (internationally oriented national body)
♦ Russian International Affairs Council (internationally oriented national body)
♦ Russian International Studies Association (internationally oriented national body)
♦ Russian Nobility Association / see Russian Nobility Union (#19009)

♦ Russian Nobility Union 19009

Union de la noblesse russe (UNR) – Sojuz Russkih Dvorjan
Pres 29 bd des Batignolles, 75008 Paris, France. E-mail: union.noblesse.russe@gmail.com.
URL: http://www.noblesse-russie.org/
History 27 Nov 1925, Paris (France). Former names and other names: *Russian Nobility Association* – former; *Association de la noblesse russe* – former. **Aims** Provide moral, legal and material assistance to people of the Russian nobility; maintain the old traditions of the nobility; raise youth in religious principles; deliver genealogical certificates to people proving member of the Russian nobility. **Structure** General Assembly; Board; Committee. **Finance** Members' dues. Annual budget: about euro 5,000. **Activities** Events/meetings; networking/liaising. **Publications** *Vestnik Sojuza Dvorjan* (4 a year).
Members Individuals in 13 countries:
Argentina, Austria, Belgium, Brazil, Finland, France, Germany, Italy, Russia, Spain, Switzerland, UK, USA.
[2020/XF0501/v/**E**]

♦ Russian Orthodox Church 19010

Contact St Daniel's Monastery 22, Danilovsky Val, Moscow MOSKVA, Russia, 115191. T. +74959556761. Fax +74956337281. E-mail: contact@sinfo-mp.ru.
URL: http://www.mospat.ru/
History 988, following the baptism of Prince Vladimir of Kiev (Old Russia). Autocephalous status since 1448. Patriarchal office established in 1589. **Aims** Carry out wide social activities, missionary work and charity. **Structure** Diocese (261) in various countries; parishes (30,675). Pastoral service carried out by 329 bishops: diocesan (240); vicar (63). Retired bishops (25). Monasteries (804): male monasteries (379); convents (400). **Languages** Arabic, English, Irish Gaelic, Russian, Ukrainian. **Staff** Administrative Department of Moscow Patriarchate. **Finance** Donations; income from enterprises. **Activities** Training/education; events/meetings. **Publications** *Tserkovnyi Vestnik – Church Messenger* (weekly); *Tserkov I Vremya – Church and Time* (12 a year); *Zhurnal Moskovskoy Patriarkhii – Journal of the Moscow Patriarchate* (12 a year). Other publications.
Members Dioceses, parishes or self-governing Orthodox churches in 57 countries and territories:
Argentina, Australia, Austria, Azerbaijan, Belarus, Belgium, Brazil, Bulgaria, Canada, Chile, Cuba, Czechia, Denmark, Egypt, Estonia, Finland, France, Germany, Greece, Hong Kong, Hungary, Iceland, Iran Islamic Rep, Ireland, Israel, Italy, Japan, Kazakhstan, Kyrgyzstan, Latvia, Lebanon, Lithuania, Mexico, Moldova, Mongolia, Montenegro, Morocco, Netherlands, Norway, Panama, Poland, Portugal, Russia, Serbia, South Africa, Spain, Sweden, Switzerland, Syrian AR, Tajikistan, Thailand, Togo, Turkmenistan, UK, Ukraine, USA, Uzbekistan.
IGO Relations *Council of Europe (CE, #04881)*; *European Court of Human Rights (#06855)*; *Organization for Security and Cooperation in Europe (OSCE, #17887)*; *UNESCO (#20322)*; *United Nations (UN, #20515)*. **NGO Relations** *European Council of Religious Leaders – Religions for Peace (ECRL, #06840)*; *World Council of Churches (WCC, #21320)*. [2014.11.13/XF5764/**F**]

♦ Russian Peace Foundation (internationally oriented national body)
♦ Russia's Institute for Strategic Studies (internationally oriented national body)
♦ Russlands Friedens Fonds (internationally oriented national body)
♦ Ruta Europea del Modernismo (#01125)
♦ **RUTA** Unidad Regional de Asistencia Técnica (#20333)

♦ Rutgers 19011

Exec Dir Arthur van Schendelstraat 696, 3511 MJ Utrecht, Netherlands. T. +31302313431. E-mail: office@rutgers.nl.
URL: http://www.rutgers.nl/
History Jul 1987, as *World Population Foundation (WPF)*. Current title adopted end 2010 when merged with Rutgers Nisso Groep (RNG). Registered in accordance with Dutch law. **Aims** Work to improve quality of life, especially sexual and reproductive health and rights, of all, in particular in the Netherlands and in low and middle income countries by: promoting *sexual* and *reproductive health* and rights (SRHR) through education and access to information and services; creating awareness of the importance of SRHR and the relationship with population growth and poverty; functioning as a centre of research and expertise, especially to women, young people and marginalized groups. **Structure** Executive Board; Supervisory Board; Divisions (7); Field Offices (2). **Languages** Dutch, English. **Staff** 70.00 FTE, paid. **Finance** Members' dues. Supported by national and international organizations, including: *European Commission (EC, #06633)*; *The William and Flora Hewlett Foundation*; *United Nations Population Fund (UNFPA, #20612)*. **Activities** Financial and/or material support; research/documentation; training/education; capacity building; knowledge management/information dissemination; projects/programmes; events/meetings. **Events** *Meeting* Amsterdam (Netherlands) 2018, *Y-SAV Conference on Acting against Youth Sexual Aggression and Victimization in Europe* Amsterdam (Netherlands) 2013, *NGO forum* The Hague (Netherlands) 1999, *The Hague international forum on international conference on population and development in Cairo* The Hague (Netherlands) 1999, *Youth forum* The Hague (Netherlands) 1999. **Publications** *Rutgers Newsletter* in Dutch, English. Annual Report in Dutch, English.
Consultative Status Consultative status granted from: *ECOSOC (#05331)* (Special). **IGO Relations** Member of: United Nations Population Fund. Involved in the *International Conference on Population and Development (ICPD)*. Works with: *Deutsche Gesellschaft für Technische Zusammenarbeit (GTZ, inactive)*; *International Bank for Reconstruction and Development (IBRD, #12317)*. **NGO Relations** Member of: *International Planned Parenthood Federation (IPPF, #14589)*; *Reproductive Health Supplies Coalition (RHSC, #18847)*. Works with: *PAI (#18025)*; numerous other organizations. [2018.03.08/XF2796/f/**F**]

♦ RVA – Returned Volunteer Action (internationally oriented national body)
♦ RVDAGE België / see Conseil des communautés africaines en Europe/Belgique
♦ RVDAGE/Vlaanderen / see Conseil des communautés africaines en Europe/Belgique
♦ RVDAGE/V – Raad van de Afrikaanse Gemeenschappen in Europe/Vlaanderen (internationally oriented national body)
♦ **RVP** Council for Research in Values and Philosophy (#04915)
♦ RwB – Rivers without Boundaries (unconfirmed)
♦ RWCHR – Raoul Wallenberg Centre for Human Rights (internationally oriented national body)
♦ **RWC** Rice-Wheat Consortium for the Indo-Gangetic Plains (#18937)
♦ RWF – Reading and Writing Foundation (internationally oriented national body)
♦ **RWG** Rail Working Group (#18610)
♦ **RWG** Refugee Working Group (#18741)
♦ RWI – Raoul Wallenberg Institutet för Mansliga Rattigheter och Humanitar Ratt (internationally oriented national body)
♦ **RWI** Reconstructing Women International (#18629)
♦ **RWISO** Roth Williams International Society of Orthodontists (#18976)
♦ **RWSN** Rural Water Supply Network (#19006)
♦ Ryan Foundation International (internationally oriented national body)
♦ RYS – Religious Youth Service
♦ RZIM – Ravi Zacharias International Ministries (internationally oriented national body)
♦ **S2B** Seattle to Brussels Network (#19190)
♦ S2R / see Shift2Rail Joint Undertaking (#19261)
♦ S4E – Sail For Ethics (internationally oriented national body)
♦ SA4D – Schweizerische Akademie für Entwicklung (internationally oriented national body)
♦ SA4D – Swiss Academy for Development (internationally oriented national body)
♦ SAAAD – South Asian Academy of Aesthetic Dentistry (unconfirmed)
♦ **SAAA** Southern African Accounting Association (#19834)
♦ SAABT – Southern African Association for Behaviour Therapy (no recent information)
♦ SAACLALS – Southern African Association for Commonwealth Literature and Language Studies (see: #02439)
♦ **SAACS** South American Academy of Cosmetic Surgery (#19700)
♦ SAAFA – Special Arab Aid Fund for Africa (inactive)
♦ SAAFSR / see Southern and Eastern African Association for Farming Systems Research-Extension (#19873)
♦ SAAIR – Southern African Association for Institutional Research (internationally oriented national body)
♦ SAALA – Southern African Applied Linguistics Association (internationally oriented national body)
♦ SAAMA – Southern African Asset Management Association (internationally oriented national body)
♦ Saamelais- ja Poronhoitoasiain Pohjoismainen Yhteistyöelin (no recent information)
♦ Saamelaisneuvosto (#19012)

♦ Saami Council 19012

Conseil Same – Consejo Same – Lappischer Rat – Samerådet – Saamelaisneuvosto – Samiraddi
SG Postboks 162, 9735 Karasjok, Norway. T. +358400725226. E-mail: saamicouncil@saamicouncil.net.
URL: http://www.saamicouncil.net/
History 1956, Karasjok (Norway), as *Nordic Saami Council – Conseil Same nordique – Consejo Nórdico Same – Lappischer Rat der Skandinavischen Länder – Nordiska Samerådet – Pohjoismaiden Saamelaisneuvosto – Davviriikkaid Samiraddi – Samiraddi Callingoddi*, at a Nordic Sami Conference. Charter: 1956, 1974, 1980; unregistered. **Aims** Consolidate affinity among the Saami people; attain recognition for the Saami as a nation; maintain cultural, political, economic and social rights of the Saami in legislation of the four states. **Structure** *Sami Conference* (every 4 years); Council; Executive Committee; National Sections; Working Groups; Committees; Secretariat. **Languages** English, Finnish, Northern Sami, Norwegian, Russian, Swedish. **Staff** 4.00 FTE, paid. **Finance** Grants. Support from: *Nordic Council of Ministers (NCM, #17260)*. **Activities** Knowledge management/information dissemination; networking/liaising. **Events** *Conference* Gällivare (Sweden) 2022, *Oktasas sapmi – a common sapmi* Trondheim (Norway) 2017, *Saami culture and increasing industrial development* Murmansk (Russia) 2013, *Conference* Rovaniemi (Finland) 2008, *Conference* Honningsvåg (Norway) 2004.
Members Saami organizations in 4 countries:
Finland, Norway, Russia, Sweden.
Consultative Status Consultative status granted from: *ECOSOC (#05331)* (Ros C); *ILO (#11123)* (Special List). **IGO Relations** A cooperation body of NMR. Permanent Participant in: *Arctic Council (#01097)*; *Emergency, Prevention, Preparedness and Response (EPPR, #05437)*; *Standing Committee of Parliamentarians of the Arctic Region (SCPAR, #19958)*. Accredited by: *United Nations Office at Vienna (UNOV, #20604)*. **NGO Relations** Permanent Participant of: *Circumpolar Biodiversity Monitoring Program (CBMP, #03941)*. Through CMPI, links with other regions: *Indian Council of South America (#11158)*. Through WCIP with: *Coordinadora de las Organizaciones Indígenas de la Cuenca Amazónica (COICA, #04811)*; *International Alliance of the Indigenous Tribal Peoples of the Tropical Forests (IAITPTF, #11629)*; *International Indian Treaty Council (IITC, #13836)*. [2018.02.10/XD0254/**D**]

♦ SAANSO – South Asia Association of National Scout Organization (unconfirmed)
♦ **SAAPD** South Asian Association of Pediatric Dentistry (#19720)
♦ **SAAPE** South Asia Alliance for Poverty Eradication (#19712)
♦ SAAPH / see General Association of Asia Pacific Sports Federations (#10106)
♦ **SAARCAA** SAARC Confederation of Anaesthesiologists (#19016)

♦ SAARC Academy of Ophthalmology (SAO) 19013

SG Dr Rajendra Prasad Ctr for Ophthalmic Sciences, AIIMS, Delhi 110029, DELHI 110029, India.
URL: http://sao.org.in/

History Also referred to as *Southasian Academy of Ophthalmology*. **Aims** Promote peace, solidarity and ocular health in the region of the SAARC countries. **Structure** Council; Officers. **Events** *Congress* Karachi (Pakistan) 2016, *Congress* Colombo (Sri Lanka) 2014.
Members Full in 8 countries:
Afghanistan, Bangladesh, Bhutan, India, Maldives, Nepal, Pakistan, Sri Lanka.
IGO Relations A *South Asian Association for Regional Cooperation (SAARC, #19721)* Recognized Body. **NGO Relations** Regional society member of: *International Council of Ophthalmology (ICO, #13057)*. [2016/XM4910/E]

♦ SAARC Agriculture Centre (see: #19721)

♦ SAARC Cardiac Society 19014

Pres PO Box 2587, Kathmandu, Nepal. T. +97714371374 – +97714371322ext123. Fax +97714371123. E-mail: csofnepal@hotmail.com.
History Recognized body of *South Asian Association for Regional Cooperation (SAARC, #19721)*. **Aims** Foster cooperation and exchange of information in the field of cardiovascular science. **Structure** Executive Committee of up to 24 members. Rotating headquarters. **Finance** Members' dues. **Events** *Biennial conference / Biennial South Asian Cardiac Conference* Kathmandu (Nepal) 2004, *Biennial conference / Biennial South Asian Cardiac Conference* Delhi (India) 2002, *Joint meeting* Colombo (Sri Lanka) 2001, *Biennial conference* Dhaka (Bangladesh) 2000. **Publications** Monographs; guidelines.
Members in 5 countries:
Bangladesh, India, Nepal, Pakistan, Sri Lanka. [2016/XE3719/E]

♦ **SAARC CCI** SAARC Chamber of Commerce and Industry (#19015)

♦ SAARC Chamber of Commerce and Industry (SAARC CCI) 19015

Contact 397 Street No 64, I-8/3, Islamabad, Pakistan. T. +92514860612 – +92514860613. Fax +92518316024. E-mail: info@saarcchamber.org.
URL: http://www.saarcchamber.org/
History Dec 1992. A recognized Regional Apex Body of *South Asian Association for Regional Cooperation (SAARC, #19721)*. Previously also known under the acronym *SCCI*. **Aims** Promote regional cooperation in the area of trade, commerce and industry; safeguard the economic and business interests of SAARC countries. **Structure** Executive Body; General Body; General Secretariat. **Languages** English. **Staff** 19.00 FTE, paid. **Finance** Financed by international donor agency of *Friedrich Naumann Foundation for Freedom*; contributions from members and all SAARC Countries National Federations of Commerce and Industry. **Activities** Events/meetings; awards/prizes/competitions; advocacy/lobbying/activism. **Events** *General Assembly* Kathmandu (Nepal) 2013, *Young Entrepreneur Summit* Kathmandu (Nepal) 2013, *China-South Asia Business Forum* Kunming (China) 2013, *General Meeting* Maldives 2006, *General Meeting* Kathmandu (Nepal) 2001. **Publications** *SAARC Biz* (12 a year) – newsletter. Sectorial Reports.
Members Federations/Chambers of 8 countries:
Afghanistan, Bangladesh, Bhutan, India, Maldives, Nepal, Pakistan, Sri Lanka.
NGO Relations Cooperates with: *South Asian Federation of Exchanges (SAFE, #19729)*; *World Chambers Network (WCN, #21270)*. Through Global Chamber Platform, links with: *Association des chambres de commerce et d'industrie européennes (EUROCHAMBRES, #02423)*. [2020/XD5721/t/D]

♦ SAARC Coastal Zone Management Centre, Maldives (see: #19721)

♦ SAARC Confederation of Anaesthesiologists (SAARCAA) 19016

Secretariat Dept of Anaesthesia, Analgesia and Intensive Care Medicine, Bangabandhu Sheikh Mujib Medical University, Shahbag, Dhaka 1000, Bangladesh. T. +92212765673. Fax +92212779718. E-mail: saarcaasecretariat@gmail.com.
URL: http://saarc-aa.com/
History 1992, Delhi (India). Founded following activities initiated in 1988 during a WFSA meeting, as *South Asian Confederation of Anaesthesiologists (SACA)*. **Aims** Promote the activities of member associations. **Structure** Executive Committee, consisting of President, Vice President, Secretary and Treasurer. **Languages** English. **Staff** Voluntary. **Finance** Self financed. **Activities** Awareness raising. **Events** *Biennial Congress* Lahore (Pakistan) 2019, *Biennial Congress* Colombo (Sri Lanka) 2017, *Biennial Congress* Kathmandu (Nepal) 2015, *Biennial Congress* Dhaka (Bangladesh) 2013, *Biennial Congress* Bangalore (India) 2011. **Publications** Congress proceedings.
Members National associations in 6 countries:
Bangladesh, India, Maldives, Nepal, Pakistan, Sri Lanka. [2019/XD3604/D]

♦ SAARC Convention on Preventing and Combating the Trafficking in Women and Children for Prostitution (2002 treaty)
♦ SAARC Convention on Regional Arrangements for the Promotion of Child Welfare in South Asia (2002 treaty)

♦ SAARC Cultural Centre, Colombo (SCC) 19017

Contact No 224 Bauddhaloka Mawatha, Colombo, 7, Sri Lanka. T. +94112584451. Fax +94112584452. E-mail: scc@saarcculture.org.
URL: http://saarcculture.org/
History Proposed Jul 1998, as a regional centre of *South Asian Association for Regional Cooperation (SAARC, #19721)*. SAARC Agenda for Culture approved Oct 2006. First Meeting, Apr 2009, Colombo (Sri Lanka). **Aims** Bring the people of South Asia together to celebrate and exchange the cultural heritage of the region and strengthen the relationship through sharing of the regional dance, music, theatre, literature, cinema and arts. **Activities** Advocacy/lobbying/activism; research/documentation; networking/liaising; awards/prizes/competitions; training/education. **Publications** *SAARC Culture Centre Newsletter*. [2019/XM0498/E*]

♦ SAARC Development Fund (SDF) 19018

CEO PO Box No 928, Norzin Lam, Thimphu, Bhutan. T. +9752321152 – +9752321153. Fax +9752321150 – +9752321203. E-mail: info@sdfsec.org – ceo@sdfsec.org.
URL: http://www.sdfsec.org/
History May 1995, Delhi (India), at 8th summit of *South Asian Association for Regional Cooperation (SAARC, #19721)*, as *South Asian Development Fund (SADF)*, when merger of *SAARC Regional Fund (SRF, inactive)*, *SAARC Fund for Regional Projects (SFRP, inactive)* and a third 'window' for social development and infrastructure building was endorsed. Establishment followed the work of *SAARC Inter-Governmental Group on South Asian Development Fund (IGG, inactive)*, set up Apr 1993, Dhaka (Bangladesh), to define size, structure, resources and operational modalities of the proposed fund. Commenced operations Jun 1996, Dhaka, at first meeting. Reconstituted under current title Nov 2005. **Aims** Promote welfare of the people of the SAARC region; improve their quality of life; accelerate economic growth, social progress and poverty alleviation in the region. **Structure** Governing Council; Board of Directors; Secretariat. **Languages** English. **Activities** Financial and/or material support. **Events** *Meeting / Meeting of the Governing Board* Maldives 2000.
Members Governments of 8 countries:
Afghanistan, Bangladesh, Bhutan, India, Maldives, Nepal, Pakistan, Sri Lanka.
IGO Relations Multinational development banks; international financial institutions. **NGO Relations** Banks; chambers of commerce and industry; trade and investment promotion agencies. [2019.06.19/XF4016/f/F*]

♦ SAARC Economic Union (unconfirmed)
♦ SAARC Energy Centre, Islamabad (see: #19721)
♦ SAARC-FAMMED – South Asian Association for Regional Cooperation in Family Medicine (no recent information)
♦ SAARC Forestry Centre, Bhutan (unconfirmed)
♦ **SAARCH** South Asian Association for Regional Cooperation of Architects (#19722)
♦ **SAARCLAW** South Asian Association for Regional Cooperation in Law (#19723)

♦ SAARC Psychiatric Federation (SPF) 19019

Contact c/o SAARC Secretariat, Tridevi Marg, PO Box 4222, Kathmandu, Nepal. T. +97714221785 – +97714226350. Fax +97714227033 – +97714223991.
History 2004, as a federation of psychiatrists in countries of *South Asian Association for Regional Cooperation (SAARC, #19721)*. **Aims** Foster collaboration between psychiatrists of SAARC member countries. **Events** *Conference* Lahore (Pakistan) 2011, *International conference / Conference* Dhaka (Bangladesh) 2008, *International conference / Conference* Kalutara (Sri Lanka) 2007, *International conference / Conference* Kathmandu (Nepal) 2006.
Members in 7 countries:
Bangladesh, Bhutan, India, Maldives, Nepal, Pakistan, Sri Lanka.
NGO Relations Affiliate member of: *World Psychiatric Association (WPA, #21741)*. [2011/XM3010/D]

♦ SAARC Regional Convention on Narcotic Drugs and Psychotropic Substances (1990 treaty)
♦ SAARC Regional Convention on Suppression of Terrorism (1987 treaty)
♦ **SAARC** South Asian Association for Regional Cooperation (#19721)

♦ SAARC Surgical Care Society (SSCS) 19020

SG Medical Fac, Univ of Peradeniya, Peradeniya, Sri Lanka. E-mail: mdyasas@yahoo.co.uk.
Founding Pres 132/7 Wariyapola Sri Sumangala Mawatha, Kandy, Sri Lanka. Fax +948389106.
History 1996, Kandy (Sri Lanka). Recognized body of *South Asian Association for Regional Cooperation (SAARC, #19721)* as of Jan 2002. **Aims** Promote understanding and cooperation among surgeons, surgical associations, colleges, societies and organizations in the SAARC countries. **Structure** Officers rotate annually. Headquarters in Sri Lanka. **Languages** English. **Staff** paid; several voluntary. **Finance** Subscriptions. **Activities** Organizes meetings. Develops database for training and exchange of expertise between countries. **Events** *Conference* Sri Lanka 2013, *Conference* Pakistan 2012, *Conference* Sri Lanka 2011, *Conference* Pakistan 2009, *Conference* Bangladesh 2007.
Members National apex surgical colleges and societies in 7 countries:
Bangladesh, Bhutan, India, Maldives, Nepal, Pakistan, Sri Lanka.
NGO Relations Associations of Surgeons; colleges; societies. [2013.08.02/XJ0480/E]

♦ SAARC Teachers' Federation (inactive)
♦ SAARC Tuberculosis and HIV/AIDS Centre (see: #19721)
♦ Saaristoyhteistyö (#17253)
♦ SAARMSE / see Southern African Association for Research in Mathematics, Science and Technology Education (#19835)
♦ **SAARMSTE** Southern African Association for Research in Mathematics, Science and Technology Education (#19835)
♦ SAAR – Society for Austro-Arab Relations (internationally oriented national body)
♦ Saarte komisjon (#16061)
♦ **SAA** Sasakawa Africa Association (#19055)
♦ **SAA** Seed Association of the Americas (#19214)
♦ **SAA** Société africaine anti-SIDA (#19518)
♦ **SAA** Society on AIDS in Africa (#19518)
♦ SAA – Society for American Archaeology (internationally oriented national body)
♦ **SAA** Society of Audiovisual Authors (#19524)
♦ **SAAS** Social Accountability Accreditation Services (#19332)
♦ SAASTEC – Southern African Association of Science and Technology Centres (internationally oriented national body)
♦ SAA – Suzuki Association of the Americas (internationally oriented national body)
♦ **SAATA** South Asian Association of Transactional Analysts (#19724)
♦ SAAWG – South Asian Association of Women Geoscientists (unconfirmed)
♦ SAAW – Sport Association of Arab Women (no recent information)
♦ SAAWS – South Asian Association for Women's Studies (inactive)
♦ **SABA** Southern African Broadcasting Association (#19837)
♦ **SABE** Society for the Advancement of Behavioral Economics (#19514)
♦ Sabin – Sabin Vaccine Institute (internationally oriented national body)
♦ Sabin Vaccine Institute (internationally oriented national body)
♦ SABISA – Southern African Bursars of Independent Schools Association (internationally oriented national body)
♦ **SABITA** Southern African Bitumen Association (#19836)
♦ **SABRAO** Society for the Advancement of Breeding Research in Asia and Oceania (#19515)
♦ **SABRN** Southern Africa Bean Research Network (#19826)
♦ SABRO – South American Brain Research Organization (inactive)
♦ SACAR / see Joint Secretariat of Agricultural Trade Associations (#16148)
♦ **SACAR** Secrétariat des Associations du Commerce Agricole Réunies (#16148)
♦ SACA / see SAARC Confederation of Anaesthesiologists (#19016)
♦ **SACAU** Southern African Confederation of Agricultural Unions (#19840)
♦ **SACBC** Southern African Catholic Bishops' Conference (#19838)
♦ SACCA – Streets Ahead Children's Centre Association (internationally oriented national body)
♦ SACCC – Southern Africa Climate Change Coalition (unconfirmed)
♦ SAC / see Communauté africaine de culture (#04373)
♦ SACCORD – Southern African Centre for the Constructive Resolution of Disputes (internationally oriented national body)
♦ **SACC** South African Council of Churches (#19699)
♦ **SACCS** South Asian Coalition on Child Servitude (#19725)
♦ SACD – Société des auteurs et compositeurs dramatiques (internationally oriented national body)
♦ **SACEP** South Asia Cooperative Environment Programme (#19714)
♦ **SACEPS** South Asia Centre for Policy Studies (#19713)
♦ Sacer et Apostolicus Ordo Canonicorum Regularium Sancti Augustini (religious order)
♦ Sacerdoti Missionari della Regalità di Cristo (religious order)
♦ Sacerdoti Operai Diocesani del Cuore di Gesù (religious order)
♦ Sacerdoti del Sacro Cuore di Gesù (religious order)
♦ Sacerdoti del Sacro Cuore di Gesù, 1950 (religious order)
♦ Sacerdoti di Santa Maria di Tinchebray (religious order)
♦ **SACE** Syndicat des agents du Conseil de l'Europe (#20079)
♦ SACGA – Southern Africa Compressed Gases Association (internationally oriented national body)
♦ **SACHES** Southern African Comparative and History of Education Society (#19839)
♦ SAC / see International Society for Advancement of Cytometry (#14900)
♦ SAC / see IOM Global Staff Association Committee (#16008)
♦ SACIS – Southern African Cultural Information System (internationally oriented national body)
♦ SACJF / see Southern African Judges Commission (#19847)
♦ SACMEQ / see Southern and Eastern Africa Consortium for Monitoring Educational Quality (#19871)
♦ **SACMEQ** Southern and Eastern Africa Consortium for Monitoring Educational Quality (#19871)
♦ SACOD – Southern Africa Communications for Development (no recent information)
♦ SACOFA – Southern Africa Community Foundation Association (internationally oriented national body)
♦ SA – Congregatio Fratrum Adunationis Tertii Regularis Ordinis Sancti Francisci (religious order)
♦ SACO – Service d'assistance canadienne aux organismes (internationally oriented national body)
♦ SACP / see Society for Asian and Comparative Philosophy
♦ **SACPN** Southern African Conflict Prevention Network (#19841)
♦ SACP – Société Africaine de Chirurgie Pédiatrique (unconfirmed)
♦ SACP – Society for Asian and Comparative Philosophy (internationally oriented national body)
♦ Sacra Congregatio pro Institutione Catholica / see Congregation for Catholic Education – for Seminaries and Educational Institutions (#04665)
♦ Sacra Congregatio de Seminariis et Studiorum Universitatibus / see Congregation for Catholic Education – for Seminaries and Educational Institutions (#04665)
♦ SACRACT – Southern African Centre for Rural and Agricultural Credit Training (meeting series)
♦ Sacramentine Sisters of Bergamo (religious order)
♦ SACRED / see Sustainable Agriculture Centre for Research, Extension and Development in Africa

- ♦ SACRED-Africa – Sustainable Agriculture Centre for Research, Extension and Development in Africa (internationally oriented national body)
- ♦ Sacred Congregation for Bishops / see Congregation for Bishops (#04664)
- ♦ Sacred Congregation for the Evangelization of Peoples / see Congregation for the Evangelization of Peoples (#04670)
- ♦ Sacred Congregation of the Holy Office / see Congregation for the Doctrine of the Faith (#04669)
- ♦ Sacred Congregation of Religious / see Congregation for Institutes of Consecrated Life and Societies of Apostolic Life (#04671)
- ♦ Sacred Congregation for the Sacraments and Divine Worship / see Congregation for Divine Worship and the Discipline of the Sacraments (#04668)
- ♦ Sacred Congregation of Seminaries and Universities / see International Federation of Catholic Universities (#13381)
- ♦ Sacred Congregation of the Universal Inquisition / see Congregation for the Doctrine of the Faith (#04669)
- ♦ Sacred Earth Network (internationally oriented national body)
- ♦ Sacred Earth Trust (internationally oriented national body)
- ♦ Sacred Heart Brothers – Institute of the Brothers of the Sacred Heart (religious order)
- ♦ Sacred Heart Congregation (religious order)
- ♦ Sacred Natural Sites Initiative (unconfirmed)
- ♦ Sacred Roman and Universal Inquisition / see Congregation for the Doctrine of the Faith (#04669)
- ♦ SACRE – Surgical Association for Clinical Research in Europe (no recent information)
- ♦ Sacrificio Quaresimale (internationally oriented national body)

♦ Sacro Occipital Technic Organization International (SOTO-I) 19021

Contact c/o SOTO-A, PO Box 2310, Burleigh QLD 4220, Australia. T. +61755762132. E-mail: hello@soto.org.au.

History 2010. **Aims** Preserve, promote, advance, and elevate the basic principles of SOT Methods and SOT Craniopathy as methods of *chiropractic* treatment.
Members Organizations (6). National organizations in 2 countries:
Brazil, Japan.
Organizations listed in this Yearbook:
Sacro Occipital Research Society International (SORSI); SOTO Australasia (SOTO-A); SOTO Europe (SOTO-E); SOTO Sudamérica (SOTO-SA). [2021/XM5792/y/**C**]

- ♦ Sacro Occipital Technique Organisation – Europe / see SOTO Europe
- ♦ SAC – SAARC Agriculture Centre (see: #19721)
- ♦ SAC – Save Africa Concerts Foundation (internationally oriented national body)
- ♦ SAC – Societas Apostolatus Catholici (religious order)
- ♦ SAC – Southern Africa Committee (internationally oriented national body)
- ♦ **SAC** Sugar Association of the Caribbean (#20033)
- ♦ SAC – Suore Missionarie dell'Apostolato Cattolico (religious order)
- ♦ SAC – Sustainable Apparel Coalition (unconfirmed)
- ♦ SACTD – South Asian Centre for Teacher Development (unconfirmed)
- ♦ **SACU** Southern African Customs Union (#19842)
- ♦ SAD / see Swiss Academy for Development
- ♦ SADA / see African Methodist Episcopal Church Service and Development Agency
- ♦ **SADAOC Foundation** Foundation for Sustainable Food Security in Central West Africa (#09975)
- ♦ Sadarbiba Mieram (#18282)
- ♦ SADC Association of Central Banks / see Committee of Central Bank Governors in SADC (#04245)
- ♦ **SADCAS** Southern African Development Community Accreditation Service (#19844)
- ♦ SADC Banco Regional de Genes / see SADC Plant Genetic Resources Centre (#19024)

♦ SADC Banking Association 19022

Manager PO Box 61674, Marshalltown, 2107, South Africa. T. +27116456718. Fax +27116456818. E-mail: secretariat@sadcbanking.org.
URL: http://www.sadcbanking.org

History 15 Jul 1998. **Aims** Provide a regional banking leadership platform for strategic direction to be given on matters pertinent to the transformation of the banking sector in the region; promote and transform the whole of SADC into a dynamic and well-integrated economic block. **Structure** Secretariat function provided by the Banking Association South Africa. **Languages** English, French, Portuguese. **Activities** Knowledge management/information dissemination; politics/policy/regulatory; training/education.
Members Open to banking associations of SADC countries. Current membership covers 13 SADC countries:
Angola, Botswana, Congo DR, Eswatini, Lesotho, Madagascar, Malawi, Mauritius, Mozambique, Namibia, South Africa, Zambia, Zimbabwe.
IGO Relations *Southern African Development Community (SADC, #19843).* **NGO Relations** Affiliate member of: *International Payments Framework Association (IPFA, #14534).* [2022.05.11/XD8046/**D**]

- ♦ SADCC Banco Regional de Genes / see SADC Plant Genetic Resources Centre (#19024)
- ♦ SADC Centre for Specialization in Public Administration and Management (see: #19843)
- ♦ SADC Committee of Stock Exchanges / see Committee of SADC Stock Exchanges (#04285)
- ♦ SADCC Regional Gene Bank / see SADC Plant Genetic Resources Centre (#19024)
- ♦ SADCC – Southern African Development Coordination Conference (inactive)
- ♦ SADC-ECF / see Electoral Commissions Forum of SADC Countries (#05414)
- ♦ SADC Election Support Network / see Southern Africa Development Community Election Support Network (#19827)
- ♦ SADC Electoral Commissions Forum / see Electoral Commissions Forum of SADC Countries (#05414)
- ♦ **SADC-ESN** Southern Africa Development Community Election Support Network (#19827)
- ♦ SADC Lawyers Association / see Southern African Development Community Lawyers Association (#19845)

♦ SADC Parliamentary Forum (SADC PF) 19023

SG SADC Forum House, Parliament Gardens, Love Street, Private Bag 13361, Windhoek, Namibia. T. +264612870000. Fax +26461254642 – +26461247569. E-mail: info@sadcpf.org.
Street Address SADC Forum House, Parliament Gardens, ERF 578 Love Street, Windhoek, Namibia.
URL: http://www.sadcpf.org/

History 1993. Founded to unite parliamentarians of countries of *Southern African Development Community (SADC, #19843).* Set up with the assistance of *Association of European Parliamentarians with Africa (AWEPA, inactive).* **Aims** Facilitate strategic partnerships within the SADC region; promote information sharing; initiate and implement projects that enhance regional integration; promote effective and professional Parliamentary practice. **Structure** Plenary Assembly, comprising Presiding Officers and 4 representatives from each member parliament. Executive Committee, comprising Presiding Officers, representatives, Secretary General, Treasurer, Chair and Vice-Chair. Standing Committees. Sub-Committees (2): Finance; Legal. Secretariat, headed by Secretary-General. **Finance** Equal subscriptions from each member parliament (US$ 30,000). Annual budget: US$ 360,000. **Activities** Standing Committees (5): Democratization, Governance and Gender Equality; Trade, Development and Integration; Inter-Parliamentary Cooperation and Capacity Building; HIV and AIDS; Regional Women's Parliamentary Caucus Committee. Programmes (6): Regional Integration; Parliamentary Leadership Training – through *SADC Parliamentary Leadership Centre (PLC)*; Elections Observations and Democratic Governance; HIV-AIDS; Engendering Parliaments; ICT for e-governance. **Events** *Plenary Assembly* Maputo (Mozambique) 2006, *Plenary Assembly* Dar es Salaam (Tanzania UR) 2002, *Regional seminar on HIV/AIDS* Gaborone (Botswana) 2001, *Plenary Assembly* Victoria Falls (Zimbabwe) 2001.
Members Parliamentarians nominated by their parliaments in the 13 SADC countries:
Angola, Botswana, Congo DR, Eswatini, Lesotho, Malawi, Mauritius, Mozambique, Namibia, South Africa, Tanzania UR, Zambia, Zimbabwe.
IGO Relations *European Union (EU, #08967); United States Agency for International Development (USAID).*
NGO Relations Member of: *Association of Secretaries General of Parliaments (ASGP, #02911).* [2021/XF3558/**F**]

- ♦ SADC Parliamentary Leadership Centre (internationally oriented national body)
- ♦ **SADC PF** SADC Parliamentary Forum (#19023)

♦ SADC Plant Genetic Resources Centre (SPGRC) 19024

Dir Private Bag CH6, Lusaka ZA-15302, Zambia. T. +26021139920010. E-mail: spgrc@zamnet.zm – registry@spgrc.org.zm.
URL: http://www.spgrc.org.zm/

History 1988, under the aegis of *Southern African Development Coordination Conference (SADCC, inactive)*, as *SADCC Regional Gene Bank – SADCC Banco Regional de Genes*, as a 20-year joint Nordic development project with *Nordic Genetic Resource Centre (NordGen, #17303).* Subsequently, name changed to *SADC Regional Gene Bank (SRGB) – SADC Banco Regional de Genes*, known also as *Regional Gene Bank for Plant Genetic Resources.* Present name adopted in Oct 1993. Second phase (1994-1997); 3rd phase (1999-2003); 4th phase (2003-2007); 5th phase (2008-2013). Now fully integrated within the Food Agriculture and Natural Resources (FANR) Directorate of *Southern African Development Community (SADC, #19843).* **Aims** Promote and coordinate a regional network for plant genetic resources management through national centres of SADC Member States; train specialists; develop national plant genetic resource management programmes; prevent erosion and loss of regional genetic resources through collection and preservation efforts. **Structure** Organized under SADC Food Agriculture and Natural Resources Directorate. Board, comprising Chairman and 15 members representing each SADC member state. Institutional building in Zambia houses Administrative and Financial Sections, 3 Technical Sections, Gene Bank, herbarium and field gene bank, and is expected to include a biotechnology laboratory. **Languages** English, French, Portuguese. **Staff** 17.00 FTE, paid. Temporary staff as required. **Finance** Contributions from SADC Member States and cooperating partners. Annual budget: US$ 1,400,000. **Activities** Networking/liaising; training/education; knowledge management/information dissemination; capacity building. **Events** *Seminar on incentive measures to enhance conservation of agrobiodiversity* Lusaka (Zambia) 2002, *Seminar on incentive measures to enhance conservation of agrobiodiversity* Lusaka (Zambia) 2001, *Plant genetic resources conference* Lusaka (Zambia) 1994. **Publications** Newsletter. Annual Report; catalogue; working group documents. **Information Services** *SPGRC Documentation and Information System (SDIS).*
Members National plant genetic resource centres in 16 countries:
Angola, Botswana, Comoros, Congo DR, Eswatini, Lesotho, Madagascar, Malawi, Mauritius, Mozambique, Namibia, Seychelles, South Africa, Tanzania UR, Zambia, Zimbabwe.
IGO Relations SADC acts as implementing agency. Formal contact with: *Bioversity International (#03262).* [2018.09.04/XF5236/**E***]

- ♦ SADC Regional Gene Bank / see SADC Plant Genetic Resources Centre (#19024)
- ♦ **SADC** Southern African Development Community (#19843)
- ♦ **SADE** Scandinavian Association for Digestive Endoscopy (#19071)
- ♦ SADEYA – Sociedad Astronómica de España y América (no recent information)
- ♦ SADF / see SAARC Development Fund (#19018)
- ♦ **SADF** South Asia Democratic Forum (#19715)
- ♦ Sa'diyah (religious order)
- ♦ SADOCC – Southern Africa Documentation and Cooperation Centre, Vienna (internationally oriented national body)
- ♦ SADP – Scandinavian Association of Directory and Database Publishers (inactive)
- ♦ SADP – South Asian Development Partnership (internationally oriented national body)
- ♦ SADRA – Southern African Development Research Association (no recent information)
- ♦ SADSEM – Southern African Defence and Security Management Network (inactive)
- ♦ SAEA – Society of Anaesthesiologists of East Africa (see: #21482)
- ♦ SAED – Scandinavian Academy of Esthetic Dentistry (internationally oriented national body)
- ♦ **SAEF** Southern Africa Editors' Forum (#19828)
- ♦ SAE International (internationally oriented national body)
- ♦ SAESCO – South American Esports Confederation (unconfirmed)
- ♦ SAE – Society for the Anthropology of Europe (internationally oriented national body)
- ♦ SAE / see World Council of Hellenes Abroad (#21329)
- ♦ **SAfAIDS** Southern Africa HIV/AIDS Information Dissemination Service (#19831)
- ♦ Safari Club International (internationally oriented national body)
- ♦ **SAfA** Society of Africanist Archaeologists (#19517)
- ♦ **SAFA** South Asian Federation of Accountants (#19727)
- ♦ SAFCEI – Southern African Faith Communities' Environment Institute (internationally oriented national body)
- ♦ **SAFE Consortium** European Association for Food Safety (#06044)

♦ SAFE Europe 19025

Sec Survial Equipment Services Ltd, Hampton Street Industrial Estate, Tetbury, GL8 8LD, UK. T. +441666505081. E-mail: info@safeeurope.co.uk.
Contact A5 Blg, Cody Technology Park, Ively Road, Farnborough, GU14 0LX, UK. T. +441252393029.
URL: http://www.safeeurope.co.uk/

History Founded 1982, as the Europe Chapter of the (US) SAFE Association, *Survival and Flight Equipment Association.* **Aims** Stimulate research and development in the fields of safety and survival; disseminate pertinent information to concerned individuals in government and industry. **Structure** Committee. **Activities** Events/meetings; awards/prizes/competitions. **Events** *Annual Symposium* Hamburg (Germany) 2021, *Annual Symposium* Hamburg (Germany) 2020, *Annual Symposium* Stockholm (Sweden) 2019. [2019/XM8321/**D**]

- ♦ SAFEFOD – Société africaine d'éducation et de formation pour le développement (internationally oriented national body)

♦ Safe Food Advocacy Europe (SAFE) 19026

SG Rue de la Science 14, 1000 Brussels, Belgium. T. +3228931058. E-mail: info@safefoodadvocacy.eu.
URL: https://www.safefoodadvocacy.eu/

History 2015, Brussels (Belgium). Registration: EU Transparency Register, No/ID: 104500414872-61, Start date: 5 Nov 2014; No/ID: 0578.909.064, Start date: 10 Jan 2015, Belgium. **Aims** Ensure that consumer's health and concerns remain at the core of EU food legislation. **Languages** English. **Staff** 4.00 FTE, paid. **Finance** Supported by: Bruxelles Environnement (BE); *European Union (EU, #08967).* **Activities** Advocacy/lobbying/activism; awareness raising; research and development; publishing activities; events/meetings; training/education.
Members Full in 10 countries:
Belgium, Bulgaria, France, Germany, Ireland, Italy, Luxembourg, Netherlands, Poland, UK.
Included in the above, 1 organization listed in this Yearbook:
European Childhood Obesity Group (ECOG, #06529).
IGO Relations Stakeholder in: *European Food Safety Authority (EFSA, #07287).* **NGO Relations** Member of: *European Public Health Alliance (EPHA, #08297).* [2021/XM7761/**D**]

♦ Safeguard for Agricultural Varieties in Europe (SAVE Foundation) . . 19027

Sauvegarde pour l'agriculture des variétés d'Europe – Sicherung der Landwirtschaftlichen Arten Vielfalt in Europa

Coordinator Gebouw De Valk, Dreijenlaan 2, 6703 HA Wageningen, Netherlands. E-mail: office@save-network.com.
Project Office Neugasse 30, 9000 St Gallen, Switzerland. T. +41712227410. Fax +41712227440.
URL: http://www.save-foundation.net/

History 1993, Netherlands. Registration: EU Transparency Register, No/ID: 1404621848-82. **Aims** Conserve and promote genetic and historically important cultural variety in agricultural *flora* and *fauna*; safeguard *agrobiodiversity* within unique human systems throughout Europe. **Structure** Council of Cooperation Partners (meets annually); Board of Directors; Network Office based in Wageningen (Netherlands); Project Office based in St Gallen (Switzerland). **Languages** English, German. **Activities** Events/meetings. **Events** *Annual Meeting* Croatia 2014, *Annual Meeting* Biezenmortel (Netherlands) 2013, *Annual Meeting* Urnäsch (Switzerland) 2012, *Annual Meeting* Schwedt-Oder (Germany) 2010, *Annual Meeting* Schwedt-Oder (Germany) 2010. **Publications** *SAVE eNews* (4 a year). **Information Services** *Arca-Net; European Agrobiodiversity Network; European Livestock Breeds Ark and Rescue Net (ELBARN); Fruit-Net: Neglected and Forgotten Fruit and Berries.*

Members Partner organizations (22 regionally and nationally active NGOs) in 15 countries:
Albania, Austria, Belgium, Bulgaria, Denmark, Germany, Greece, Hungary, Ireland, Italy, Netherlands, Poland, Serbia, Switzerland, Ukraine.
Consultative Status Consultative status granted from: *FAO (#09260)* (Specialized Consultative Status). **NGO Relations** Member of (2): *GEF CSO Network (GCN, #10087)*; *International Union for Conservation of Nature and Natural Resources (IUCN, #15766)*. Cooperates with (1): *European Regional Focal Point for Animal Genetic Resources (ERFP, #08343)* (working relationship). [2020.10.14/XM3778/f/F]

♦ Safe Injection Global Network (SIGN) 19028

Secretariat c/o WHO HSS/EHT/DCT, Ave Appia 20, 1211 Geneva 27, Switzerland. T. +41227911275. Fax +41227914836.
URL: http://www.who.int/injection_safety/
History 1999, as a voluntary coalition of stakeholders within *WHO (#20950)*. **Aims** Achieve safe and appropriate use of injections throughout the world. **Events** *Annual meeting* Dubai (United Arab Emirates) 2010, *Annual Meeting* Geneva (Switzerland) 2009, *Annual Meeting* Moscow (Russia) 2008, *Annual Meeting* Geneva (Switzerland) 2007, *Annual meeting* Mexico City (Mexico) 2006. **Publications** *SIGNpost* (weekly) – electronic newsletter. **NGO Relations** Instrumental in setting up: *Infection Control Africa Network (ICAN, #11184)*. [2013/XF6266/F]

- ♦ Safe Kids Worldwide (internationally oriented national body)
- ♦ **SAFE Network** Asia-Pacific Network for Sustainable Agriculture Food and Energy (#01976)
- ♦ Safer Africa / see Surpaz
- ♦ SaferAfrica / see Surpaz
- ♦ Safer Drug Policies – Association for Safer Drug Policies (internationally oriented national body)
- ♦ Saferworld (internationally oriented national body)
- ♦ **SAFE** Safe Food Advocacy Europe (#19026)
- ♦ Safe Seaweed Coalition (unconfirmed)
- ♦ **SAFE** South Asian Federation of Exchanges (#19729)
- ♦ SAFE – South Asian Forum for Environment (internationally oriented national body)

♦ Safe Sport International (SSI) 19029

Main Office 2 Communications Road, Greenham Business Park, Greenham, Newbury, RG19 6AB, UK. E-mail: info@safesportinternational.com.
URL: http://www.safesportinternational.com/
History Registration: Charity Commission, No/ID: 1177798, England and Wales; Companies House, No/ID: 10117650, England and Wales. **Aims** End violence and abuse against athletes. **Structure** Board. **Finance** Sources: international organizations. Supported by: *Oak Foundation*. **Activities** Events/meetings; guidance/assistance/consulting; standards/guidelines. **Events** *Conference* Nottingham (UK) 2022, *International Conference* 2021, *International Conference* Québec, QC (Canada) 2020, *International Conference* Madrid (Spain) 2018. **NGO Relations** Partners include: *International Association of Physical Education and Sport for Girls and Women (IAPESGW, #12081)*; *World Netball (WN, #21668)*; *International Paralympic Committee (IPC, #14512)*; *International Council of Sport Science and Physical Education (ICSSPE, #13077)*; *WomenSport International (WSI, #21033)*. [2022/XM7674/C]

- ♦ **SAFES** South Asian Federation of Endocrine Societies (#19728)
- ♦ **SAFE** Stroke Alliance for Europe (#20012)
- ♦ Safe and sustainable construction with plastics / see Modern Building Alliance (#16842)
- ♦ Safety and Health in Agriculture Convention (2001 treaty)
- ♦ Safety Pharmacology Society (internationally oriented national body)
- ♦ Safe-Use Pilot Project / see CropLife Asia (#04964)
- ♦ Safe Water International (internationally oriented national body)
- ♦ SafeWork – InFocus Programme on Safety and Health at Work and the Environment (see: #11123)

♦ SAFEX International 19030

SG c/o Soc Suisse des Explosifs, PO Box 636, 3900 Brig VS, Switzerland. T. +412792271111. E-mail: secretariat@safex-international.org.
URL: http://www.safex-international.org/
History 1954. Registration: Swiss Civil Code, Switzerland. **Aims** Eliminate worldwide the harmful effects of *explosives* on people, property and the planet (environment). **Structure** General Assembly; Board of Governors; Secretariat. **Activities** Events/meetings; networking/liaising; training/education. **Events** *Congress* Salzburg (Austria) 2023, *Congress* Salzburg (Austria) 2022, *Congress* Salzburg (Austria) 2021, *Congress* Helsinki (Finland) 2017, *Congress* Warsaw (Poland) 2014. **Publications** *SAFEX Newsletter*.
Members Full; Associate. Membership countries not specified. Associate members include 3 organizations listed in this Yearbook:
Association of European Manufacturers of Sporting Ammunition (#02522); *European Federation of Explosives Engineers (EFEE, #07117)*; *International Society of Explosives Engineers (ISEE)*. [2023/XM5595/y/C]

- ♦ Saffron SDGF – Saffron Social Development Global Foundation (internationally oriented national body)
- ♦ Saffron Social Development Global Foundation (internationally oriented national body)
- ♦ SAFF – South Asian Football Federation (unconfirmed)
- ♦ Safina Center (internationally oriented national body)
- ♦ **SAFIR** South Asia Forum for Infrastructure Regulation (#19716)
- ♦ **SAFMA** South Asian Free Media Association (#19731)
- ♦ SAFNGO – South Asian Federation of NGOs for the Prevention of Drug and Substance Abuse (no recent information)
- ♦ **SAFOD** Southern Africa Federation of the Disabled (#19829)
- ♦ SAFOMS – South Asian Federation of Menopause Societies (unconfirmed)
- ♦ **SAFO** Société Africaine Francophone d'Ophtalmologie (#19453)
- ♦ SAFP – Save a Family Plan (internationally oriented national body)
- ♦ SAFRG – South-Asian Fund Raising Group (internationally oriented national body)
- ♦ **SAF** South Asia Foundation (#19717)
- ♦ SAF / see South Asia Initiative to End Violence Against Children (#19719)
- ♦ **SAF** South Asian Forum on Mental Health and Psychiatry (#19730)
- ♦ SAF – South Asian Fraternity (internationally oriented national body)
- ♦ **SAFTA** South Asian Free Trade Area (#19732)
- ♦ SAG / see Société suisse d'études africaines
- ♦ SAGB / see European Association of Bioindustries (#05956)
- ♦ SAGE – Southeast Asian Gateway Evolution Meeting (meeting series)
- ♦ **SAGIM** Scandinavian Association for Neurogastroenterology and Motility (#19073)
- ♦ **SAGMA** South American Gelatin Manufacturers Association (#19703)
- ♦ **SAGO** Société africaine des Gynécologues et Obstétriciens (#19454)
- ♦ **SAGQ** South Asian Growth Quadrangle (#19733)
- ♦ SAGW – Schweizerische Akademie der Geistes- und Sozialwissenschaften (internationally oriented national body)

♦ Sahaja Yoga 19031

Address not obtained.
URL: http://www.sahajayoga.org/
History 1970, by Shri Mataji.
Members Centres in 54 countries and territories:
Algeria, Argentina, Australia, Austria, Belarus, Belgium, Bolivia, Brazil, Bulgaria, Canada, Chile, Colombia, Côte d'Ivoire, Czechia, Denmark, Finland, France, Germany, Greece, Hong Kong, Hungary, India, Ireland, Israel, Italy, Japan, Kazakhstan, Kenya, Lithuania, Malaysia, Mexico, Nepal, Netherlands, New Zealand, Peru, Poland, Portugal, Romania, Russia, Seychelles, Sierra Leone, Slovakia, South Africa, Spain, Sweden, Switzerland, Taiwan, Thailand, Tunisia, Türkiye, UK, United Arab Emirates, Uruguay, USA. [2008/XF6058/F]

♦ SaharaConservation (SC) 19032

Communications Manager 53 rue Bourdignon, B002, 94100 Saint-Maur-des-Fossés, France. T. +41218643651. E-mail: scf@saharaconservation.org – comms@saharaconservation.org.
CEO 13220 N Red Hill Rd, Marana AZ 85653, USA. T. +15206164649.
URL: http://www.saharaconservation.org/
History 2004, USA. Former names and other names: *Sahara Conservation Fund (SCF)* – former (2004 to 2022). Registration: No/ID: N00797639, Start date: 2007, USA, Missouri; No/ID: RNA W772005158, Start date: 2016, France. **Aims** Conserve the wildlife, habitats and other natural resources of the Sahara and its bordering Sahelian grasslands. **Structure** Board; Headquarters in France; Teams in Chad and Niger. **Languages** English, French. **Activities** Awareness raising; capacity building; healthcare; humanitarian/emergency aid; monitoring/evaluation; projects/programmes; training/education. **IGO Relations** Partner of (1): *Secretariat of the Convention on the Conservation of Migratory Species of Wild Animals (UNEP/CMS, #19198)*. **NGO Relations** Member of (1): *International Union for Conservation of Nature and Natural Resources (IUCN, #15766)*. [2022.10.19/XJ7740/f/F]

- ♦ Sahara Conservation Fund / see SaharaConservation (#19032)
- ♦ SAHARA for Life Trust (internationally oriented national body)
- ♦ Saharan Studies Association (internationally oriented national body)
- ♦ Sahara Resource Network (internationally oriented national body)
- ♦ Sahara and Sahel Observatory (#17636)
- ♦ SAHARA – Social Aspects of HIV/AIDS Research Alliance (internationally oriented national body)
- ♦ Sahaya / see Samaritans

♦ Sahaya International 19033

Sec/Treas 1504 Portola St, Davis CA 95616, USA. T. +15307569074. E-mail: koen@sahaya.org.
URL: http://www.sahaya.org/
History Jun 1999. Registered in the State of California (USA). **Aims** Improve the quality of life in *third world* countries. **Structure** Board of Directors; President; Secretary/Treasurer. **Languages** English. **Staff** Voluntary. **Finance** Budget (annual): about US$ 200,000. **Activities** Humanitarian/emergency aid. **Publications** Information Services: Develops educational materials on HIV/AIDS and distributes them via free online downloads. **NGO Relations** Supported by: *Gilead Foundation*. [2014.12.11/XJ2209/F]

- ♦ SAHC – International Conference on Structural Analysis of Historical Constructions (meeting series)
- ♦ Sahelian Scientific and Technological Information and Documentation Network (no recent information)
- ♦ Sahel Institute (#11357)

♦ Sahel and West Africa Club (SWAC) 19034

Club de Sahel et de l'Afrique de l'Ouest (CSAO)
Secretariat 2 rue André Pascal, 75775 Paris CEDEX 16, France. T. +33145248987. Fax +33145249031. E-mail: swac.contact@oecd.org.
URL: https://www.oecd.org/swac/
History 23 Dec 1975, Nouakchott (Mauritania), as *Amis du Sahel*, on the initiative of *OECD (#17693)* member countries and with the approval of Sahelian countries grouped within *Comité permanent inter-Etats de lutte contre la sécheresse dans le Sahel (CILSS, #04195)*. Inaugural Ministerial Session held Mar 1976, Dakar (Senegal). A semi-autonomous body of the OECD. Present name adopted, Apr 2001, when geographical coverage was expanded to 18 countries. Previously also referred to as *Club du Sahel*. **Aims** Act as a bridge between West African actors and *OECD* member countries; together with regional institutions, governments, business and civil society organizations, promote the regional dimension of *development* and support formulation and implementation of joint of intergovernmental *policies* so as to contribute to mobilizing and strengthening West African capacities. **Structure** Strategy and Policy Group (SPG – meets twice a year), consisting of representatives of funding countries/organizations and West-African partners, and headed by a President. Secretariat based at OECD in Paris (France). **Languages** English, French. **Staff** 9.00 FTE, paid. **Finance** Voluntary contributions from several development cooperation agencies from OECD member countries and regional organizations. Budget (annual): about euro 1.8 million. **Activities** Analytical work and regional workshops and fora done in partnership with West African stakeholders, such as farmers, traders, entrepreneurs, researchers, politicians, civil society and experts; up-to-date information on West Africa, events people and initiatives; access to essential data and synthesis on the "state of the debate"; information on the structural evolutions in the regional and prospective thinking on the region's future. Supports West African Regional Organizations, including: *Réseau de prévention des crises alimentaires (RPCA, #18905)*; *West African Network of Farmers' Organizations and Agricultural Producers (#20891)*. **Events** *Joint workshop on post-conflict development* Abidjan (Côte d'Ivoire) 2008, *Aid strategy* Bissau (Guinea-Bissau) 1990. **Publications** *West Africa Observer* (4 a year) – review; *SWAC Briefing Notes*. *West Africa Studies* – series. Synthesis papers; reports; cross-border diaries; CD-ROMS; promotional material.
Members No statutory membership. Funding member countries (10):
Austria, Belgium, Canada, France, Germany, Italy, Luxembourg, Netherlands, Switzerland, USA.
Geographic coverage (18 countries):
Benin, Burkina Faso, Cameroon, Cape Verde, Chad, Côte d'Ivoire, Gambia, Ghana, Guinea, Guinea-Bissau, Liberia, Mali, Mauritania, Niger, Nigeria, Senegal, Sierra Leone, Togo.
IGO Relations Close cooperation with: *Economic Community of West African States (ECOWAS, #05312)*; *Comité permanent inter-Etats de lutte contre la sécheresse dans le Sahel (CILSS, #04195)*; *Union économique et monétaire Ouest africaine (UEMOA, #20377)*. **NGO Relations** Close cooperation with: *Association of European Border Regions (AEBR, #02499)*; *Council for the Development of Social Science Research in Africa (CODESRIA, #04879)*; *Environnement et développement du Tiers-monde (enda, #05510)* – DIAPOL; *Friedrich-Ebert-Stiftung (FES)*; *Groupe de recherche et de réalisations pour le développement rural dans le Tiers-monde (GRDR)*; *West African Network of Farmers' Organizations and Agricultural Producers (#20891)*; *West African Network on Security and Democratic Governance (WANSED, #20892)*; *West and Central African Council for Agricultural Research and Development (WECARD, #20907)*. [2019/XF6027/F]

- ♦ SAHISA – Southern African Heads of Independent School Association (unconfirmed)
- ♦ **SAHRDC** South Asia Human Rights Documentation Centre (#19718)
- ♦ SAHRDN – Southern African Human Rights Defenders Network (unconfirmed)
- ♦ SAHSS – Swiss Academy of Humanities and Social Sciences (internationally oriented national body)
- ♦ SAI / see Arab Investment Company (#00996)
- ♦ SAIACS – South Asia Institute of Advanced Christian Studies (internationally oriented national body)
- ♦ SAICEM – Southern African International Conference on Environmental Management (meeting series)
- ♦ **SAICM** Strategic Approach to International Chemicals Management (#20005)
- ♦ SAIDC – Slovak Agency for International Development Cooperation (internationally oriented national body)
- ♦ **SAIEA** Southern African Institute for Environmental Assessment (#19846)
- ♦ **SAIEVAC** South Asia Initiative to End Violence Against Children (#19719)
- ♦ SAIF – Southern Africa Institute of Fundraising (internationally oriented national body)
- ♦ SAIF – Southern African Institute of Forestry (internationally oriented national body)
- ♦ SAIHC – Southern African and Islands Hydrographic Commission (see: #13825)
- ♦ SAIH – Studentenes og Akademikernes Internasjonale Hjelpefond (internationally oriented national body)
- ♦ SAIIA – South African Institute of International Affairs (internationally oriented national body)
- ♦ SAIIC – South and Meso American Indian Rights Center (inactive)
- ♦ SAIIER – Sri Aurobindo International Institute of Educational Research (internationally oriented national body)
- ♦ **SAILD** Service d'appui aux initiatives locales de développement (#19237)
- ♦ Sail For Ethics (internationally oriented national body)

♦ Sail for Europe 19035

Naviguer pour l'Europe
Address not obtained.
URL: http://www.sailforeurope.eu/

History 1976, by Patricia Colman, who launched the sail boat 'Traité de Rome', the first European boat with a European crew for around the world competition, which became the first European training school. **Aims** Promote the European idea through sailing; give a young and dynamic image to the European Union. **Activities** The first 'constitution race' started in 1987, Niewpoort (Belgium), and finished in Philadelphia PA (USA). The 2nd edition (1991) of the race started from USA and ended in Brussels (Belgium). Sail for Europe participates in races with a flag 'EUR'. **IGO Relations** *European Commission (EC, #06633).* [2010/XF1901/**F**]

- ♦ Sail of Hope – Interregional Union of Life Help for Mentally Handicapped Persons (unconfirmed)

♦ Sail Training International 19036

COO Charles House, Gosport Marina, Mumby Road, Gosport, PO12 1AH, UK. T. +442392586367. Fax +442392584661. E-mail: office@sailtraininginternational.org.
URL: http://www.sailtraininginternational.org/

History 2002. Took over activities of *International Sail Training Association (ISTA, inactive).* Registration: Charity Commission, No/ID: 1096846, England and Wales. **Staff** 5.00 FTE, paid. **Activities** Awards/prizes/competitions; events/meetings; training/education. **Events** *Annual Conference* Antwerp (Belgium) 2019, *Annual Conference* Seville (Spain) 2018, *Annual Conference* Bordeaux (France) 2017, *Annual Conference* Halmstad (Sweden) 2016, *Annual Conference* Stavanger (Norway) 2010. **Publications** *Tall Ships and Sail Training International* (2 a year).
Members National organizations in 21 countries and territories:
Australia, Belgium, Bermuda, Canada, Denmark, Finland, France, Germany, Ireland, Italy, Latvia, Netherlands, New Zealand, Norway, Poland, Portugal, Russia, Spain, Sweden, UK, USA.
NGO Relations Member of (1): *European Maritime Heritage (EMH, #07741).* [2022/XD9250/**D**]

- ♦ SAINT / see SAMARITAN INTERNATIONAL (#19046)
- ♦ Sainte Bernadette, Nevers – Soeurs de la Charité et de l'Instruction Chrétienne de Nevers (religious order)
- ♦ Sainte-Famille (religious order)
- ♦ Sainte Madeleine-Sophie Barat – Société du Sacré-Coeur de Jésus (religious order)
- ♦ Saint Francis de Sales Association (religious order)
- ♦ Saint Joseph's Hospice Association – Jospice International (internationally oriented national body)
- ♦ Saint Peter and Saint Paul's Workers' Mission (religious order)
- ♦ Saint Petersburg International Conference on Integrated Navigation Systems (meeting series)
- ♦ Saint-Saluveur-le-Vicomte – Soeurs de Sainte Marie-Madeleine Postel (religious order)
- ♦ **SAI Platform** Sustainable Agriculture Initiative (#20051)
- ♦ Sairaalahallinnon Pohjoismainen Yhteistyökomitea (inactive)
- ♦ SAI – Shark Advocates International (unconfirmed)
- ♦ **SAI** Sistema Andino de Integración (#19292)
- ♦ SAI – Social Accountability International (internationally oriented national body)
- ♦ SAIS – Paul H Nitze School of Advanced International Studies (internationally oriented national body)
- ♦ **SAI** SurfAid international (#20040)
- ♦ SAJA – Southern Africa Journalists Association (no recent information)
- ♦ **SAJC** Southern African Judges Commission (#19847)
- ♦ SAK – Sydafrika Kontakt (internationally oriented national body)
- ♦ Säkularinstitut der Schönstätter Marienschwestern (religious order)
- ♦ Säkularinstitut der Schönstatt-Patres (religious order)

♦ Sakyadhita International Association of Buddhist Women 19037

Sec 7331 Princess View Drive, San Diego CA 92120, USA. T. +18585255163. E-mail: info@sakyadhita.org.
URL: http://www.sakyadhita.org/

History 1987, Bodhgaya (India). Founded at the conclusion of the first International Conference on Buddhist Women, under the patronage of the Dalai Lama. Registration: Section 501 (c)(3), No/ID: C1414578, Start date: 12 Dec 1989, USA, State of California. **Aims** Promote world peace through the teachings of the Buddha; foster an international communications network among Buddhist women; promote harmony and understanding among the Buddhist traditions; promote the physical and spiritual welfare of the world's Buddhist women; encourage education and training projects for Buddhist women; encourage compassionate social action for the benefit of humanity. **Structure** Board of Directors; Executive Committee; National and Local Branches. **Languages** Chinese, English, French, German, Hindi, Indonesian, Japanese, Korean, Russian, Spanish, Tibetan, Vietnamese. **Staff** Voluntary. **Finance** Sources: members' dues. Annual budget: 12,000 USD. **Activities** Advocacy/lobbying/activism; awareness raising; capacity building; conflict resolution; events/meetings; guidance/assistance/consulting; knowledge management/information dissemination; networking/liaising; projects/programmes; publishing activities; religious activities; research and development; training/education. **Events** *Conference* Kuching (Malaysia) 2021, *Conference* Leura, NSW (Australia) 2019, *Conference* Hong Kong (Hong Kong) 2017, *Conference* Yogyakarta (Indonesia) 2015, *Conference* Vaishali (India) 2013. **Publications** *Sakyadhita Newsletter* (annual). *Contemporary Buddhist Women: Contemplation, Cultural Exchange, and Social ActionCompassion and Social Justice* (2017) by Karma Lekshe Tsomo; *Compassion and Social Justice* (2015) by Karma Lekshe Tsomo; *Buddhism at the Grassroots* (2012) by Karma Lekshe Tsomo; *Leading to Liberation* (2011) by Karma Lekshe Tsomo; *Buddhism in Transition: Tradition, Changes, and Challenges* (2008) by Karma Lekshe Tsomo; *Buddhist Women in a Global Multicultural Community* (2008) by Karma Lekshe Tsomo; *Out of the Shadows: Socially Engaged Buddhist Women in the Global Community* (2006) by Karma Lekshe Tsomo; *Bridging Worlds: Buddhist Women's Voices Across Generations* (2004) by Karma Lekshe Tsomo; *Sakyadhita: Daughters of the Buddha – Sakyadhita: Tochter des Buddha* (1988) by Karma Lekshe Tsomo.
Members Women in 49 countries and territories:
Argentina, Australia, Austria, Bangladesh, Belgium, Bhutan, Brazil, Cambodia, Canada, China, Costa Rica, Denmark, Estonia, Finland, France, Germany, Greece, Hong Kong, India, Indonesia, Ireland, Israel, Italy, Japan, Korea Rep, Malaysia, Mexico, Mongolia, Myanmar, Nepal, Netherlands, New Zealand, Norway, Philippines, Poland, Puerto Rico, Russia, Singapore, South Africa, Spain, Sri Lanka, Sweden, Switzerland, Taiwan, Thailand, Türkiye, UK, USA, Vietnam.
Consultative Status Consultative status granted from: *ECOSOC (#05331)* (Special).
[2022.05.11/XD5841/**D**]

- ♦ SALAHE – Southeast Asia Lutheran Association for Higher Education (inactive)
- ♦ SALALM – Seminar on the Acquisition of Latin American Library Materials (internationally oriented national body)
- ♦ Salam Institute for Peace and Justice (internationally oriented national body)
- ♦ Salamiya (religious order)
- ♦ **SALAN** Southern African Legal Assistance Network (#19849)
- ♦ SALA – Science Across Latin America
- ♦ **SALC** Scandinavian Association for Language and Cognition (#19072)
- ♦ SALC – Southern Africa Labour Commission (inactive)
- ♦ **SALC** Southern Africa Litigation Centre (#19832)
- ♦ **SALDA** Scandinavian Airline Dispatchers' Association (#19068)
- ♦ SALEM International (internationally oriented national body)
- ♦ Sales Exchange for Refugee Rehabilitation and Vocation / see SERRV International
- ♦ Salesian Cooperators (religious order)
- ♦ Salesiane di Don Bosco – Figlie di Maria Ausiliatrice (religious order)
- ♦ Salesiani – Società Salesiana di San Giovanni Bosco (religious order)
- ♦ Salesian Missionaries of Mary Immaculate (religious order)

♦ Salesian Pontifical University 19038

Università Pontificia Salesiana (UPS) – Pontificia Studiorum Universitas Salesiana

SG Piazza dell' Ateneo Salesiano 1, 00139 Rome RM, Italy. T. +3906872901. Fax +390687290318. E-mail: segreteria@unisal.it.
URL: http://www.unisal.it/

History 3 May 1940, Turin (Italy). Transfer to Rome (Italy) approved, 1965, by Pope Paul VI; new seat inaugurated on 29 Oct 1966. Became a Pontifical University with current name, 24 May 1973, by the Motu Proprio 'Magisterium Vitae' of Pope Paul VI. Originally 3 Faculties: Theology, Canon Law, Philosophy. Higher Institute of Philosophy, now Faculty of Sciences of Education, set up in the framework of the Faculty of Philosophy, 2 Jul 1956, by decree of the Holy See. *Pontificium Institutum Altioris Latinitatis*, or Faculty of Christian and Classical Letters, set up Oct 1965. Institute of Social Communication Sciences (ISCOS) set up, 17 Dec 1998, became a Faculty, 27 May 1998. Most recent statutes adopted 24 May 2020. Former names and other names: *Pontificio Ateneo Salesiano* – former; *Pontificium Athenaeum Salesianum* – former; *Pontificium Institutum Altioris Latinitatis* – former; *Istituto Superiore di Scienze Religiose – Magisterium Vitae* – former. Registration: Congregation for Catholic Education, No/ID: prot. n. 265/40, Start date: 3 May 1940, Holy See. **Aims** Promote, develop and disseminate the *theological, philosophical, canonical*, literary and social communication sciences according to the educational and pedagogical ideas of Don Bosco. **Structure** Faculties (5); 35 affiliations worldwide. **Languages** Italian. **Staff** 225.00 FTE, paid. **Finance** Salesian Congregation. **Activities** Research/documentation; training/education. **Publications** *Orientamenti Pedagogici* (6 a year); *Salesianum* (4 a year).
Members Adhering institutes (35) in 18 countries:
Argentina, Brazil, Cameroon, Chile, Congo DR, Guatemala, Holy See, India, Israel, Italy, Kenya, Mexico, Nigeria, Philippines, Senegal, Spain, Venezuela, Vietnam.
NGO Relations Member of (1): *International Federation of Catholic Universities (IFCU, #13381).* Cooperates with (1): *Society of St Francis of Sales (Salesians of Don Bosco).* [2022.10.25/XF7214/**F**]

- ♦ Salesians of Don Bosco – Society of St Francis of Sales (religious order)
- ♦ Salesian Sisters – Daughters of Mary Help of Christians (religious order)

♦ Salesian Youth Movement (SYM) 19039

Mouvement salésien des jeunes – Movimiento Juvenil Salesiano (MJS) – Movimento Giovanile Salesiano (MGS)

Contact c/o Youth Ministry Dept, Salesians of Don Bosco, Via Marsala 42, 00185 Rome RM, Italy. T. +396656121. Fax +39665612556.
Contact Youth Ministry Sector, Daughters of Mary Help of Christians, Via dell'Ateneo Salesiano 81, 00139 Rome RM, Italy. T. +396872741. Fax +39687132306.
URL: http://www.symeurope.eu/

History 1847, Turin (Italy), by St John Bosco, as groups and sodalities for young people in all Salesian schools, parishes and centres and referred to as *Associationes Juventutis Salesianae.* Officially launched as worldwide youth mouvement, 1988. **Aims** As a *Roman Catholic* youth movement, promote growth of *God's* kingdom by: fostering all round growth of young people in the setting of youth groups; enabling young leaders to serve fellow young people with generosity and responsibility, in line with the spirit and mission of St John Bosco. **Structure** Salesian Congregation provides coordination at continental and world levels. Secretariat, councils and assemblies ensure coordination among different groups, associations and federations on the provincial level. At the local level, young people from parishes, schools and centres form groups with their own leaders and animators. **Languages** English, French, German, Italian, Portuguese, Spanish. **Staff** Voluntary. **Finance** Member's due. Donations from benefactors. **Activities** Religious activities; projects/programmes; events/meetings. **Events** *EURIZON* Bratislava (Slovakia) 2006, *Meeting* Germany 2005, *EURIZON* Prague (Czech Rep) 2005, *General Assembly* Rome (Italy) 2005, *General Assembly* Rome (Italy) 2005. **Publications** *Da mihi Animas* (12 a year) in English, Italian, Spanish; *Misión Jóven* (12 a year); *Note di Pastorale Giovanile* (12 a year); *Radar ADS* (12 a year) in Italian; *Don Bosco Animacion* in Spanish; *Giovani per i Giovani* in Italian; *Juvenilia* in Italian. *Youth Pastoral Documents* in English, Italian, Spanish.
Members Associations and individuals in 120 countries and territories:
Albania, Angola, Argentina, Australia, Austria, Azerbaijan, Belarus, Belgium, Benin, Bolivia, Brazil, Bulgaria, Burkina Faso, Burundi, Cambodia, Cameroon, Canada, Cape Verde, Central African Rep, Chad, Chile, China, Colombia, Congo Brazzaville, Congo DR, Corsica, Costa Rica, Côte d'Ivoire, Croatia, Cuba, Czechia, Dominican Rep, Ecuador, Egypt, El Salvador, Eritrea, Eswatini, Ethiopia, Fiji, France, Gabon, Germany, Ghana, Guatemala, Guinea, Guinea-Bissau, Haiti, Holy See, Honduras, Hong Kong, Hungary, India, Indonesia, Iran Islamic Rep, Ireland, Israel, Italy, Japan, Kenya, Korea Rep, Lebanon, Lesotho, Liberia, Lithuania, Madagascar, Malawi, Mali, Malta, Mexico, Mongolia, Morocco, Mozambique, Myanmar, Namibia, Netherlands, Nicaragua, Nigeria, Pakistan, Panama, Papua New Guinea, Paraguay, Peru, Philippines, Poland, Portugal, Puerto Rico, Romania, Russia, Rwanda, Samoa, San Marino, Senegal, Serbia, Sierra Leone, Slovakia, Slovenia, Solomon Is, South Africa, Spain, Sri Lanka, Sudan, Sweden, Switzerland, Syrian AR, Taiwan, Tanzania UR, Thailand, Timor-Leste, Togo, Tunisia, Türkiye, Uganda, UK, Ukraine, Uruguay, USA, Venezuela, Vietnam, Zambia. [2019.07.08/XE4527/**F**]

- ♦ Salésiennes de Don Bosco – Filles de Marie-Auxiliatrice (religious order)
- ♦ Salésiennes Missionnaires de Marie Immaculée (religious order)
- ♦ Salésiens – Société Salésienne de Saint Jean Bosco (religious order)
- ♦ Sales and Marketing Executives International (internationally oriented national body)
- ♦ Sales Promotion Executives Association International / see Marketing Communications Executives International (#16586)
- ♦ La Salette Missionaries – Missionaries of Our Lady of La Salette (religious order)
- ♦ **SALF** Société d'andrologie de langue française (#19456)
- ♦ SALF – Société d'angiologie de langue française (inactive)
- ♦ SALF – South Asian Labour Forum (no recent information)
- ♦ **SALIS** Substance Abuse Librarians and Information Specialists (#20028)
- ♦ Sällskapet för Studier av Ryssland, Central-och Östeuropa samt Centralasien (internationally oriented national body)
- ♦ Sällskap för östnordisk filologi (#19223)
- ♦ **SALSA** Society for the Anthropology of Lowland South America (#19520)
- ♦ SAL – Sentient Animal Law Foundation (unconfirmed)
- ♦ SALS – Southern African Literature Society (inactive)
- ♦ **SALT Consortium** Southern African Large Telescope Consortium (#19848)
- ♦ Salt Institute (internationally oriented national body)

♦ SALTO-YOUTH 19040

Inclusion Resource Centre SALTO-JINT vzw, Gretystr 26, 1000 Brussels, Belgium. T. +3222090720. Fax +3222090749. E-mail: inclusion@salto-youth.net.
URL: http://www.salto-youth.net/

History Sep 2000, when 4 SALTO resource centres in 4 countries started cooperating. Gradually grew into a network of 8, Sep 2003. SALTO stands for: *Support, Advanced Learning and Training Opportunities.* Functions within the Youth in Action programme of *European Commission (EC, #06633).* **Aims** Provide youth work and training resources; organize training and contact-making activities to support organizations and national agencies within the framework of the Youth in Action programme and beyond. **Structure** Network of 8 Resource centres. **Languages** English. **Staff** 2-3 full-time per centre. **Finance** Financed by *European Commission (EC, #06633)* – Youth in Action programme. **Activities** Organizes training events and seminars. **Publications** Books; manuals; tools. **Information Services** *Toolbox for Training* – online bookshelf; *TOY – Trainers Online for Youth* – database.
Members Resources centres (8) in 7 countries:
Belgium (2), France, Germany, Poland, Slovenia, Sweden, UK.
IGO Relations *European Commission (EC, #06633)* – Youth Unit, DG Education and Culture; *Council of Europe (CE, #04881)* – Directorate of Youth and Sport. **NGO Relations** *European Youth Forum (#09140).*
[2013/XJ0166/**E**]

- ♦ Saltzman Institute of War and Peace Studies (internationally oriented national body)
- ♦ Salud por Derecho (internationally oriented national body)
- ♦ Salud sin Daño (#10875)
- ♦ Salute Senza Danno (#10875)
- ♦ Salutis Rete (see: #15807)

♦ Salvation Army 19041

Armée du salut – Ejército de Salvación – Heilsarmee – Leger des Heils

International Leader 101 Queen Victoria Street, London, EC4V 4EH, UK. T. +442073320101. Fax +442073328019. E-mail: websa@salvationarmy.org.
URL: http://www.salvationarmy.org/

History Founded 1865, London (UK), by General William Booth, as *The Christian Revival Association*, subsequently *The Christian Mission*. Present name adopted 1878. Became international in 1880. 1st International Congress 1886. Registered in accordance with UK law, with parallel registration in other countries. An integral part of the Christian Church although distinctive in government and practice. **Aims** Advance *Christian* religion; promote education; relieve *poverty*; carry out *charitable* activities beneficial to the community of mankind as a whole; maintain a *spiritual* and *humanitarian* ministry through Christian worship and *evangelism*; provide *social services* for the needy of all ages and groups, irrespective of race or religion. **Structure** High Council; International Headquarters, located in London (UK); Commanders in 62 territories; Commands in 126 countries; *Salvation Army International Social Justice Commission* at UN, New York NY (USA); *Salvation Army World Service Office (SAWSO, see: #19041)*. **Languages** 181. **Staff** 150000.00 FTE, paid. **Finance** Income from members, public appeals and public authorities. **Activities** Training/education; humanitarian/emergency aid; awards/prizes/competitions. **Events** *International congress* Atlanta, GA (USA) 2000, *International congress* London (UK) 1990, *International development conference / International Congress* London (UK) 1990, *European youth congress* Cologne (Germany FR) 1989, *Bicentennial congress* Sydney, NSW (Australia) 1988. **Publications** *The Officer* (6 a year); *All the World* (4 a year); *Revive* (4 a year); *Words of Life* (4 a year); *The Salvation Army Year Book*. Books; magazines.

Members Commissioned officers/ministers (26,357) and soldiers (1,150,666) – individuals subscribing to SA doctrines and giving voluntary support, adherents (169,144) and Junior Soldiers (368,749) in 126 countries and territories:

Angola, Antigua, Argentina, Australia, Austria, Bahamas, Bangladesh, Barbados, Belgium, Belize, Bermuda, Bolivia, Botswana, Brazil, Burundi, Cambodia, Canada, Chile, China, Colombia, Congo Brazzaville, Congo DR, Costa Rica, Cuba, Czechia, Denmark, Dominican Rep, Ecuador, El Salvador, Estonia, Eswatini, Faeroe Is, Fiji, Finland, France, Georgia, Germany, Ghana, Greece, Greenland, Grenada, Guam, Guatemala, Guernsey, Guiana Fr, Guyana, Haiti, Honduras, Hong Kong, Hungary, Iceland, India, Indonesia, Ireland, Isle of Man, Italy, Jamaica, Japan, Jersey, Kenya, Korea Rep, Kuwait, Latvia, Lesotho, Liberia, Lithuania, Macau, Malawi, Malaysia, Mali, Marshall Is, Mexico, Micronesia FS, Moldova, Mongolia, Mozambique, Myanmar, Namibia, Nepal, Netherlands, New Zealand, Nicaragua, Nigeria, Norway, Pakistan, Panama, Papua New Guinea, Paraguay, Peru, Philippines, Poland, Portugal, Puerto Rico, Romania, Russia, Rwanda, Sierra Leone, Singapore, Solomon Is, South Africa, Spain, Sri Lanka, St Helena, St Kitts Is, St Lucia, St Maarten, St Vincent-Grenadines, Suriname, Sweden, Switzerland, Taiwan, Tanzania UR, Togo, Tonga, Trinidad-Tobago, Turks-Caicos, Uganda, UK, Ukraine, United Arab Emirates, Uruguay, USA, Venezuela, Virgin Is UK, Zambia, Zimbabwe.

Consultative Status Consultative status granted from: *ECOSOC (#05331)* (Special); *UNICEF (#20332)*.

NGO Relations Member of:
- *Alliance of NGOs on Crime Prevention and Criminal Justice (#00709)*;
- *Committee of Religious NGOs at the United Nations (CRNGOs, #04282)*;
- *Conference of European Churches (CEC, #04593)*;
- *Conference of Non-Governmental Organizations in Consultative Relationship with the United Nations (CONGO, #04635)*;
- *Council for Education in the Commonwealth (CEC)*;
- *ECHO – International Health Services*;
- *European Anti-Poverty Network (EAPN, #05908)*;
- *Evangelical Association of the Caribbean (EAC, #09210)*;
- *International Christian Federation for the Prevention of Alcoholism and Drug Addiction (ICF-PADA, no recent information)*;
- *International Partnership on Religion and Sustainable Development (PaRD, #14524)*;
- *Joint Learning Initiative on Faith and Local Communities (JLI, #16139)*;
- *Jubilee Research (#16158)*;
- *National Council for Voluntary Organizations (NCVO)*;
- *NGO Committee on Freedom of Religion or Belief, New York NY (#17109)*;
- *NGO Committee to Stop Trafficking in Persons (NGO CSTIP)*;
- *NGO Committee on UNICEF (#17120)*;
- *Religious in Europe Networking Against Trafficking and Exploitation (RENATE, #18833)*;
- *Saskatchewan Council for International Cooperation (SCIC)*;
- *South African Council of Churches (SACC, #19699)*;
- *UK Consortium on AIDS and International Development*;
- *Vienna NGO Committee on the Status of Women (#20775)*.

Cooperates with: *Adventist Development and Relief Agency International (ADRA, #00131)*. Instrumental in setting up: *Salvation Army Guides and Guards, Brownies and Sunbeams (no recent information)*; *Salvation Army International College for Officers (ICO, see: #19041)*; *Salvation Army Medical Fellowship (SAMF, see: #19041)*; *Salvation Army Women's Ministries (#19042)*. [2019/XF3172/**F**]

- ♦ Salvation Army Home League / see Salvation Army Women's Ministries (#19042)
- ♦ Salvation Army International College for Officers (see: #19041)
- ♦ Salvation Army Medical Fellowship (see: #19041)

♦ Salvation Army Women's Ministries 19042

World Pres 101 Queen Victoria Street, London, EC4V 4EH, UK. T. +442073320101.
URL: http://www1.salvationarmy.org/

History Founded as *Salvation Army Home League*, in the framework of *Salvation Army (#19041)*. Subsequently know as *Salvation Army Women's Organizations*. **Aims** Bring women into the knowledge of Jesus Christ. **Members** Organizations in 129 countries and territories. Membership countries not specified. [2018.06.18/XF0405/**F**]

- ♦ Salvation Army Women's Organizations / see Salvation Army Women's Ministries (#19042)
- ♦ Salvation Army World Service Office (see: #19041)
- ♦ Salvatoriane – Suore del Divin Salvatore (religious order)
- ♦ Salvatoriani – Società del Divin Salvatore (religious order)
- ♦ Salvatorians – Society of the Divine Saviour (religious order)
- ♦ Salvatoriennes – Soeurs du Divin Sauveur (religious order)
- ♦ Salvatoriens – Société du Divin Sauveur (religious order)
- ♦ Salvatrucha Gang (#16570)

♦ Salzburg Congress on Urban Planning and Development (SCUPAD) . 19043

Sec c/o Groot Hertoginnelaan 51, 2517 EC The Hague, Netherlands.
Pres address not obtained.
URL: http://www.scupad.org/

History Founded 1965, by fellows of the Planning session of *Salzburg Global Seminar (#19044)*. **Aims** Promote communication among participants of urban planning and related sessions of the Salzburg Seminar; exchange research results and new concepts and *policies* in the field of urban planning and development. **Structure** General Assembly (annual), elects Committee. **Languages** English. **Staff** Voluntary. **Finance** Members' dues. Income from congresses. **Activities** Organizes: annual congress, always Salzburg (Austria); annual congress on urban planning issues. **Events** *Annual Congress* Salzburg (Austria) 2015, *Annual Congress* Salzburg (Austria) 2014, *Annual Congress* Salzburg (Austria) 2013, *Annual Congress* Salzburg (Austria) 2012, *Annual Congress* Salzburg (Austria) 2010.

Members Individuals (302) in 46 countries and territories:

Albania, Australia, Austria, Belgium, Bosnia-Herzegovina, Brazil, Bulgaria, Canada, Chile, Croatia, Czechia, Denmark, Egypt, Estonia, Ethiopia, Finland, France, Germany, Ghana, Greece, Hungary, India, Ireland, Israel, Italy, Japan, Latvia, Mali, Malta, Netherlands, Nigeria, North Macedonia, Norway, Palestine, Poland, Romania, Russia, Serbia, Slovakia, Slovenia, South Africa, Spain, Switzerland, Türkiye, UK, USA. [2013.07.30/XF5756/v/**F**]

♦ Salzburg Global Seminar 19044

Main Office Schloss Leopoldskron, Leopoldskronstr 56-58, 5020 Salzburg, Austria. T. +4366283983146. E-mail: info@salzburgglobal.org.
USA Office Eaton House, 1203 K St NW, Washington DC 20005, USA. T. +12026377683. E-mail: info@salzburgglobal.org.
URL: http://www.salzburgglobal.org/

History 1947. Founded, on the initiative of Clemens Heller (1917-2002), as a "Marshall Plan of the Mind" to bring together young intellectuals from nations recently at war to discuss topics of mutual interest. Former names and other names: *Salzburg Seminar in American Studies* – former (1947); *Salzburg Seminar* – alias. Registration: No/ID: 04-2200147, USA, Massachusetts; No/ID: FN 442195 m, Austria, Salzburg. **Aims** Challenge current and future *leaders* to shape a better world. **Structure** Board of Directors. **Languages** English. **Staff** 60.00 FTE, paid. **Finance** Institutional support; donors. **Activities** Networking/liaising; knowledge management/information dissemination. **Events** *Global Forum on Corporate Governance* Salzburg (Austria) 2018, *Conference on Students at the Margins and the Institutions that Serve Them* Salzburg (Austria) 2014, *Conference on Sustainability* Salzburg (Austria) 2014, *Global Forum for Young Cultural Innovators* Salzburg (Austria) 2014, *Meeting on Lessons from the Past, Visions for the Future* Salzburg (Austria) 2014. **Publications** President's Reports. **NGO Relations** Instrumental in setting up: *European Muslim Professionals Network (CEDAR, #07840)*; *Salzburg Congress on Urban Planning and Development (SCUPAD, #19043)*. Partner of: *International Conflict Research Institute (INCORE, see: #20642)*. [2021/XG9697/**F**]

- ♦ Salzburg Mozarteum Foundation (internationally oriented national body)
- ♦ Salzburg Seminar / see Salzburg Global Seminar (#19044)
- ♦ Salzburg Seminar in American Studies / see Salzburg Global Seminar (#19044)
- ♦ SAMA / see Southern African Asset Management Association
- ♦ **SAMAK** Samarbetsorganisationen för de Nordiska Socialdemokratiska Parterna och Fackföreningsrörelsen (#19045)
- ♦ Samarbeid mellom myndigheter og institusjoner innenfor den yrkesrettede attføring og arbeidsmarkedsoppl'ringen (1982 treaty)
- ♦ Samarbeidskomite for de Blindes Organisasjoner i de Nordiske Land (inactive)
- ♦ Samarbejde mellem myndigheder og institutioner inden for erhvervsm'ssig revalidering og arbejdsmarkedsuddannelserne (1982 treaty)
- ♦ Samarbejdsnaevnet for Nordisk Skovforskning / see Nordic Forest Research Cooperation Committee (#17296)
- ♦ Samarbete för Fred (#18282)
- ♦ Samarbete mellan myndigheter och institutioner inom den yrkesinriktade rehabiliteringen och arbetsmarknadsutbildningen (1982 treaty)
- ♦ Samarbetskommitte för de Nordiske Laendernas Vandrarhemsorg (no recent information)
- ♦ Samarbetsorganisationen for Emballagefragor i Skandinavien / see Scandinavian Packaging Association (#19095)

♦ Samarbetsorganisationen för de Nordiska Socialdemokratiska Parterna och Fackföreningsrörelsen (SAMAK) 19045

Joint Committee of the Nordic Social Democratic Labour Movement – Tervetuloa SAMAKiin – Sosiaalidemokraattien ja ay-liikkeen pohjoismaiseen

SG c/o Arbeiderpartiet, Postboks 8743, Youngstorget, 0028 Oslo, Norway.
URL: http://samak.info/

Events *Meeting* Oslo (Norway) 2017, *Annual Meeting and Baltic Sea Conference* Helsinki (Finland) 2013.
Members Social democratic parties and trade unions in 8 countries and territories:
Åland, Denmark, Faeroe Is, Finland, Greenland, Iceland, Norway, Sweden.
NGO Relations Member of: *Foundation for European Progressive Studies (FEPS, #09954)*. [2021/XJ4655/**D**]

♦ SAMARITAN INTERNATIONAL 19046

SG Sülzburgstrasse 140, 50937 Cologne, Germany. T. +4922147605338. E-mail: mail@samaritan-international.eu.
Brussels Office Rue de Pascale 4-6, 1040 Brussels, Belgium.
URL: http://www.samaritan.info/

History Aug 1994. Previously also known under the acronym *SAINT*. EU Transparency Register: 877886034945-03. **Aims** Contribute in the field of social services, rescue services, civil protection, first-aid training and humanitarian aid; coordinate activities among each other; develop new cross-border partnerships. **Structure** Advisory Committee (equivalent to General Assembly, meets every 2 years); Praesidium. **Languages** English, German. **Staff** 45000.00 FTE, paid; 140000.00 FTE, voluntary. **Finance** Members' dues. EU grants for projects. **Activities** Projects/programmes; events/meetings; awards/prizes/competitions. **Events** *Contest* Berlin (Germany) 2013, *Contest* Riga (Latvia) 2012, *Forum / Conference* Florence (Italy) 2011, *Contest* Vienna (Austria) 2010, *Help and rescue* Hainau (Germany) 2009. **Publications** *SAMARITAN news*.
Members Organizations in 19 countries:
Austria, Bosnia-Herzegovina, Croatia, Czechia, Denmark, France, Georgia, Germany, Hungary, Italy, Latvia, Lithuania, Montenegro, North Macedonia, Poland, Romania, Serbia, Slovakia, Ukraine.
NGO Relations Affiliate member of: *SOLIDAR (#19680)*. [2019.10.22/XE4226/**E**]

- ♦ Samaritans (now national)

♦ Samaritan's Purse 19047

Pres Headquarters, PO Box 3000, Boone NC 28607, USA. T. +18282621980. Fax +18282661053. E-mail: info@samaritan.org.
URL: http://www.samaritanspurse.org/

History 1970, USA, by Dr Bob Pierce. Also known as *Samaritan's Purse International Relief*. **Aims** Provide spiritual and physical aid to hurting people around the world. **Structure** International Headquarters in Boone NC (USA); Affiliate Offices (4); Field Offices. **Finance** Donations. **Activities** Humanitarian/emergency aid; religious activities. [2019.10.31/XF6121/**F**]

- ♦ Samaritan's Purse International Relief / see Samaritan's Purse (#19047)
- ♦ SAMA – South Asian Media Association (no recent information)
- ♦ SAMA – Southern African Museums Association (internationally oriented national body)
- ♦ SAMA – Strategic Account Management Association (internationally oriented national body)
- ♦ Sambandet av Europeiske Bonder / see European Coordination Via Campesina (#06795)
- ♦ Samband Islenskra Kristnibodsfélaga (internationally oriented national body)
- ♦ Samband Norraenu Felaganna (#09859)
- ♦ Samdong International (internationally oriented national body)
- ♦ Samenwerkende Rijn- en Maaswaterleidingbedrijven / see Association of River Water Companies (#02895)
- ♦ Samerådet (#19012)
- ♦ Under The Same Sun (internationally oriented national body)
- ♦ **SaM** European Search and Matching Network (#08454)
- ♦ SAMF – Salvation Army Medical Fellowship (see: #19041)
- ♦ SAMIN – Société arabe des mines de l'Inchiri (no recent information)
- ♦ Samiraddi (#19012)
- ♦ Samiraddi Callingoddi / see Saami Council (#19012)
- ♦ Sammenslutningen ag Fabrikanter af Dybfrosne Levnedsmidler i EØF (inactive)
- ♦ Sammenslutningen af Europaeiske Akvakultur Producenter / see Federation of European Aquaculture Producers (#09491)
- ♦ Sammenslutningen af Europaeiske Forlaeggere (#09536)
- ♦ Sammenslutningen af Europaeiske Journalister (#02516)
- ♦ Sammenslutningen af Europaeiske Karnevalsbyer / see Federation of European Carnival Cities (#09496)
- ♦ Sammenslutningen af Europaeiske Producenter af Optik og Finmekanik (#07193)
- ♦ Sammenslutningen af Fabrikanter af Bageri- og Konditoriartikler i EØF / see Federation of European Manufacturers of Ingredients to the Bakery, Confectionery and Patisserie Industries (#09513)
- ♦ Sammenslutningen af Faglige Organisationer for Sukkerhandelen i EF-Landene / see European Association of Sugar Traders (#06239)
- ♦ Sammenslutningen af Iskremindustrien IEF / see EUROGLACES – European Ice Cream Association (#05688)
- ♦ Sammenslutningen for TV-Oplysning om Europaeiske Anliggender (inactive)
- ♦ Sammenslutning af Europaeiske Tørrerier (#06896)
- ♦ Sammenslutninginden for Olivenolieindustrien i EØF (#09596)
- ♦ **SAMNAM** Samrådet for Nordisk Amatörmusik (#19048)
- ♦ Samningur til ad komast hj tvisköttun arfs og gjafafjar (1989 treaty)
- ♦ Samningur milli Danmerkur, Finnlands, Íslands, Noregs og Svipjódar um adgang ad aedri menntun (1996 treaty)
- ♦ Samningur milli Danmerkur, Íslands, Noregs og Svipjódar um samstarf i samkeppnismalum (2001 treaty)
- ♦ Samningur um alpjódleg einkamalaréttarakvaedi um hjúskap, aettleidingu og lögrad (1931 treaty)

- ♦ Samningur um framkv'md tiltekinna vvaeda um rikisborgararétt (2002 treaty)
- ♦ Samningur um innheimtu medlaga (1962 treaty)
- ♦ Samningur um norr'nt menntunarsamfélag a framhaldsskólastigi (2004 treaty)
- ♦ Samningur um sameiginlegan norr'nan vinnumarkad (1982 treaty)
- ♦ Samningur um samstarf stjórnvalada og stofnana a svidi starfsendurh'fingar og starfsmenntunar (1982 treaty)
- ♦ Samningur um samstarf a svidi menningarmala (1971 treaty)
- ♦ SAM / see Nordisk Företagsekonomiska Förening (#17510)
- ♦ Sam Nordisk Sknovforskning (#17296)
- ♦ SamNordisk Skogsforskning (#17296)
- ♦ Samnordiskt Organ inom Provningsområdet (#16142)
- ♦ Samorganisationen af Detailhandlere inden for Vildt- og Fjerkraesektoren i EØF-Landene / see European Poultry, Egg and Game Association (#08258)
- ♦ **SAMP** Southern African Migration Programme (#19850)

♦ Samrådet for Nordisk Amatörmusik (SAMNAM) 19048

Bureau nordique des musiciens amateurs – Nordic Board of Amateur Musicians

Contact address not obtained. T. +4586198099.

Sec Finlands- Svens sånh- och musikförbund, Handelsesplanaden 23A, FI-65100 Vaasa, Finland. Fax +35863206820.

History 1980. Former names and other names: *Nordic Amateur Music Co-operation Council* – alias. **Events** *Nordic Music Conference* Turku (Finland) 2005, *Conference* Copenhagen (Denmark) 1998.
Members Individuals belonging to national choirs and amateurs music organizations in 6 countries and territories:
Denmark, Faeroe Is, Finland, Iceland, Norway, Sweden.
NGO Relations *Nordisk Korforum (#17521)*; *Nordisk Orkestermusik Union (NOMU, #17525)*; *Nordiska Arbetarsångar- och Musikerförbundet (NASOM, #17478)*; *Organization for Nordic Children's and Youth Choirs (#17880)*. [2013.11.20/XD1876/v/**D**]

- ♦ Samrådet for Nordiske Realkredittinstitusjoner (inactive)
- ♦ **SAMRO** Southern African Music Rights Organizations (#19851)
- ♦ SAMR – Society for Ancient Mediterranean Religions (internationally oriented national body)
- ♦ **SAMSA** Southern Africa Mathematical Sciences Association (#19833)
- ♦ **SAMS International** South American Mission Society (#19705)
- ♦ SAM – Société des Auxiliaires des Missions (religious order)
- ♦ SAM – South America Mission (internationally oriented national body)
- ♦ SAMS / see Scandinavian Simulation Society (#19100)
- ♦ SAMS – Workshop on Scattering of Atoms and Molecules from Surfaces (meeting series)
- ♦ Samu Social International / see Samusocial International
- ♦ Samusocial International (internationally oriented national body)
- ♦ SAMV – Suider-Afrikaanse Museum Vereniging (internationally oriented national body)

♦ Sanabel 19049

Headquarters 34 B South Police Academy, Cairo, Egypt. T. +20226134723. Fax +20226134770.
URL: http://www.sanabelnetwork.org/

History 2002, Tunisia. Full title: *Sanabel – The Microfinance Network of Arab Countries.* Incorporated in the States of Atlanta and Georgia (USA) and also registered in accordance with the laws of Egypt. Bylaws drafted in 2002 and revised: Dec 2003, Dec 2004, Yemen 2007, Tunisia 2008, Nov 2011, Sep 2013. **Aims** Serve microfinance institutions in the Arab world. **Structure** General Assembly (annual); Board of Directors. **Activities** Research/documentation; training/education; capacity building. **Events** *Annual Conference / Conference* Dubai (United Arab Emirates) 2014, *Conference* Khartoum (Sudan) 2012, *Conference* Amman (Jordan) 2011, *Conference* Damascus (Syrian AR) 2010, *Conference* Beirut (Lebanon) 2009.
Members Full; Affiliate; Friends. Members in 17 countries and territories:
Bahrain, Egypt, France, Iraq, Jordan, Lebanon, Luxembourg, Morocco, Palestine, Qatar, Saudi Arabia, Sudan, Switzerland, Syrian AR, Tunisia, UK, Yemen.
Included in the above, 3 organizations listed in this Yearbook:
enda inter-arabe (enda-ia); *Positive Planet International (#18465)*; *Relief International.* [2015/XJ9294/y/**F**]

- ♦ Sanabel – The Microfinance Network of Arab Countries / see Sanabel (#19049)
- ♦ SANA – Scandinavian Air Navigators Association (inactive)
- ♦ SANASO – Southern African Network of AIDS Service Organizations (see: #00272)
- ♦ SANCCOB – Southern African Foundation for the Conservation of Coastal Birds (internationally oriented national body)
- ♦ SANCRA – Southern African New Crop Research Association (internationally oriented national body)
- ♦ **SANDEE** South Asian Network for Development and Environmental Economics (#19735)
- ♦ SANDRP – South Asia Network on Dams, Rivers and People (internationally oriented national body)
- ♦ **SandSI** Sport and Sustainability International (#19931)
- ♦ Saneamiento Ecológico en Latinoamérica y el Caribe (internationally oriented national body)
- ♦ SANE Education Fund / see Peace Action Education Fund
- ♦ SANE/FREEZE / see Peace Action Network
- ♦ **SANEI** South Asia Network of Economic Research Institutes (#19726)
- ♦ **SANEM** South Asian Network on Economic Modeling (#19736)
- ♦ San Francisco Arts and Athletics / see Federation of Gay Games (#09589)
- ♦ Sangharakshita / see Triratna Buddhist Community (#20243)
- ♦ **SANGIS** Southeast Asian Network for a Geological Information System (#19778)
- ♦ **SANGONeT** Southern African Non-Governmental Development Organization Network (#19854)
- ♦ SANIGMI / see Hydrometeorological Research Institute of Uzhydromet
- ♦ SANIIRI – Central Asia Research Institute for Irrigation (internationally oriented national body)
- ♦ Sanitary Convention, 1852 (1852 treaty)
- ♦ Sanitary Convention, 1903 (1903 treaty)
- ♦ Sanitary Convention, 1904 (1904 treaty)
- ♦ Sanitary Convention, 1905 (1905 treaty)

♦ The Sanitation & Hygiene Fund (SHF) 19050

Fonds pour l'Assainissement et l'Hygiène (SHF)

Exec Dir Chemin des Anémones 11, 1219 Geneva, Switzerland. T. +41792989532. E-mail: info@shfund.org.
URL: https://www.shfund.org/

History Nov 2020, Switzerland. Replaces *Water Supply and Sanitation Collaborative Council (WSSCC, inactive).* **Aims** Raise, catalyze and invest resources to accelerate delivery of sustainable sanitation, hygiene and menstrual health services for people in urban and rural settings with the highest burden and lowest ability to respond. **Languages** English. **Activities** Projects/programmes. [2021.09.27/AA2008/f/**F**]

♦ Sanitation and Water for All (SWA) 19051

Coordinator c/o UNICEF, Three UN Plaza, New York NY 10017, USA. E-mail: info@sanitationandwaterforall.org.
URL: http://www.sanitationandwaterforall.org/

History 2009. **Aims** Increase political prioritization for sanitation, *hygiene* and water; catalyze political leadership and action; improve accountability and the use of scarce resources. **Structure** High Level Meeting; Partnership Meeting; Steering Committee; Executive Chair; Secretariat. Partners divided into 6 constituencies. **Languages** English, French. **Activities** Knowledgement management/information dissemination; advocacy/lobbying/activism; capacity building; monitoring/evaluation; events/meetings. **Events** *Partnership Meeting* The Hague (Netherlands) 2015, *High Level Meeting* Washington, DC (USA) 2014, *Partnership Meeting* Geneva (Switzerland) 2013, *Partnership Meeting* South Africa 2012, *High Level Meeting* Washington, DC (USA) 2012. **Publications** *SWA Newsletter.*
Members Governments of 52 countries and territories:
Afghanistan, Angola, Bangladesh, Benin, Brazil, Burkina Faso, Burundi, Cameroon, Central African Rep, Chad, Costa Rica, Côte d'Ivoire, Egypt, Ethiopia, Gambia, Ghana, Guinea, Guinea-Bissau, Kenya, Laos, Lesotho, Liberia, Madagascar, Malawi, Maldives, Mali, Mauritania, Mexico, Mongolia, Morocco, Mozambique, Nepal, Niger, Nigeria, Pakistan, Palestine, Paraguay, Portugal, Rwanda, Senegal, Sierra Leone, South Africa, South Sudan, Sri Lanka, Sudan, Tanzania UR, Timor-Leste, Togo, Uganda, Vietnam, Zambia, Zimbabwe.
External Support Agency partners (21):
- *African Development Bank (ADB, #00283)*;
- *African Ministers' Council on Water (AMCOW, #00376)*;
- *Agence française de développement (AFD)*;
- *Australian Aid (inactive)*;
- *Austrian Development Agency (ADA)*;
- *Bill and Melinda Gates Foundation (BMGF)*;
- *Centre for Environment and Development for the Arab Region and Europe (CEDARE, #03738)*;
- *Department for International Development (DFID, inactive)*;
- Directorate General for International Cooperation of Netherlands;
- Federation Ministry for Economic Cooperation and Development of Germany;
- *International Bank for Reconstruction and Development (IBRD, #12317)* (World Bank);
- Japanese Ministry of Foreign Affairs;
- Portuguese Government;
- *Swiss Agency for Development and Cooperation (SDC)*;
- *UNDP (#20292)*;
- *UNICEF (#20332)*;
- *United Nations Human Settlements Programme (UN-Habitat, #20572)*;
- *United States Agency for International Development (USAID)*;
- *Water and Sanitation for Africa (WSA, #20836)*;
- *Water and Sanitation Programme (WSP, #20837)*;
- *Water Supply and Sanitation Collaborative Council (WSSCC, inactive).*

Civil Society Partners, including 14 organizations listed in this Yearbook:
African Civil Society Network on Water and Sanitation (ANEW, #00250); *African Water Association (AfWA, #00497)*; *Arab Water Council (AWC, #01075)*; *End Water Poverty (EWP, #05464)*; *Freshwater Action Network South Asia (FANSA, #09996)*; *Global Water Challenge (GWC)*; *Global Water Partnership (GWP, #10653)*; *International Centre for Water Management Services (cewas)*; *International Water Association (IWA, #15865)*; *PSI (#18555)*; *Red Centroamericana de Acción del Agua (#18638)*; *United Cities and Local Governments of Africa (UCLG Africa, #20500)*; *Water and Sanitation for the Urban Poor (WSUP)*; *Water for People (WFP).*
Research and Learning Partners include 9 organizations listed in this Yearbook:
International WaterCentre (IWC); *IRC (#16016)*; *SKAT Foundation*; *SNV Netherlands Development Organisation (SNV)*; *Stockholm Environment Institute (SEI, #19993)*; *Stockholm International Water Institute (SIWI)*; *United Nations University (UNU, #20642)*; *WaterAid (#20822)*; *Water, Engineering and Development Centre (WEDC).*
Private sector partners include 2 organizations listed in this Yearbook:
Global Handwashing Partnership (GHP, #10396); *International Federation of Private Water Operators (AquaFed, #13517).* [2016.11.03/XJ7130/y/**F**]

- ♦ San José Group (no recent information)
- ♦ Sankt-Peterburgskij Mezdunarodnyj Institut Menezmenta (internationally oriented national body)
- ♦ **SANNAM** Southern African Network of Nurses and Midwives (#19853)
- ♦ **SANOG** South Asian Network Operators Group (#19737)
- ♦ S-Anon International Family Groups (unconfirmed)
- ♦ **SANORD** Southern African-Nordic Centre (#19855)

♦ Sanquin Bank of Frozen Blood 19052

Chief Medical Officer Sanquin Bloodbank, Plesmanlaan 125, 1066 CX Amsterdam, Netherlands. T. +31205123010. E-mail: sbfb@sanquin.nl.
URL: http://www.sanquin.nl/

History Established 1969, Amsterdam (Netherlands), by *Council of Europe (CE, #04881).* Original title: *European Bank of Frozen Blood of Rare Groups – Banque européenne de sang congelé de groupes rares.* Present title adopted 2006. **Aims** Make available a stock of units of blood which are negative for one of the red cell antigens of very high frequency and of red cells of the 0-type of the blood group systems in which these occur, to be used for patients who have antibodies against high frequency antigen or who have a 0- genotype. **Languages** Dutch, English. **Staff** 1.00 FTE, paid. **Finance** Costs of unit, thawing and transportation paid by receiving company. **Events** *Meeting on Advances in Clinical Transfusion Science* Amsterdam (Netherlands) 2011.
Members Member states of the Council of Europe (41):
Albania, Andorra, Austria, Belgium, Bulgaria, Croatia, Cyprus, Czechia, Denmark, Estonia, Finland, France, Georgia, Germany, Greece, Hungary, Iceland, Ireland, Italy, Latvia, Liechtenstein, Lithuania, Luxembourg, Malta, Moldova, Netherlands, North Macedonia, Norway, Poland, Portugal, Romania, Russia, San Marino, Slovakia, Slovenia, Spain, Sweden, Switzerland, Türkiye, UK, Ukraine. [2017.10.26/XF0301/**F***]

- ♦ SANSAD – South Asian Network for Social and Agricultural Development (internationally oriented national body)
- ♦ SAN / see Social Agriculture Network (#19333)
- ♦ **SAN** Social Agriculture Network (#19333)
- ♦ **SAN** Société africaine de nutrition (#00400)
- ♦ SAN – South Asian Network of Self-Help Organizations of People with Disabilities (no recent information)
- ♦ SANS – Southern African Neuroscience Society (internationally oriented national body)
- ♦ **SAN** Sustainable Agriculture Network (#20052)
- ♦ Santa Maddalena Sofia Barat – Società del Sacro Cuore di Gesù (religious order)
- ♦ Santander Group – European Universities Network / see SGroup – Universities in Europe (#19254)
- ♦ Santé mentale Europe (#16715)

♦ Santé mentale et exclusion sociale – Europa (SMES Europa) 19053

Mental Health Social Exclusion – Europe

Sec Place Albert Leemans 3, 1050 Brussels, Belgium. T. +3225385887. E-mail: smeseu@smes-europa.org.
Registered Address Rue du Rempart des Moines 78, 1000 Brussels, Belgium.
URL: http://www.smes-europa.org/

History 1992, Rome (Italy). Registration: Banque Carrefour des Entreprises, No/ID: 0476.429.158, Start date: 15 Jan 2002, Belgium; EU Transparency Register, No/ID: 413244533995-30, Start date: 18 Feb 2019. **Structure** General Assembly (annual). Board, including President, Vice-President, Secretary and Treasurer. **Activities** Events/meetings. **Events** *Seminar* Lisbon (Portugal) 2017, *Seminar* Bucharest (Romania) 2011, *What has changed in mental health, access to rights, participation?* Rome (Italy) 2008, *Dignity and health – a person only exists when their voice is heard* Berlin (Germany) 2005, *Dignity and health, right and access* Prague (Czech Rep) 2004.
Members Founding members; individuals (13) in 8 countries:
Belgium, Denmark, Germany, Greece, Italy, Portugal, Spain, UK.
NGO Relations Member of (3): *EU Health Coalition*; *European Anti-Poverty Network (EAPN, #05908)*; *Mental Health Europe (MHE, #16715).* Supports: *European Alliance for the Statute of the European Association (EASEA, #05886).* [2020/XD8341/**D**]

- ♦ Santé Sud (internationally oriented national body)
- ♦ Sanúsiya (religious order)
- ♦ Sao Cambodia / see Cambodia Action
- ♦ **SAOC** South Asia Olympic Council (#19747)
- ♦ **SAON** Sustaining Arctic Observing Networks (#20071)
- ♦ **SAO** SAARC Academy of Ophthalmology (#19013)
- ♦ **SAOUG** Southern African Online User Group (#19856)
- ♦ SAPAM / see African Physical Society (#00417)
- ♦ SAPA / see Solidarity for ASEAN People's Advocacy (#19683)
- ♦ **SAPA** Solidarity for ASEAN People's Advocacy (#19683)
- ♦ SAPA – South Asia Peoples' Alliance (internationally oriented national body)
- ♦ SAPCI – Southern African Project Controls Institute (internationally oriented national body)

- **SAPES Trust** Southern African Political Economy Series Trust (#19857)
- SAPI – Save the People International (internationally oriented national body)
- **SAPI** Société africaine de pathologie infectieuse (#19455)
- **SAPNA** South Asian Perspectives Network Association (#19738)
- **SAPOA** Southern Africa Postal Operators Association (#19866)
- **SAPP** Southern African Power Pool (#19858)
- **SAP** Society for Applied Philosophy (#19521)
- **SAPS** Société Africaine de Probabilité and de Statistique (#19975)
- SAPTA – South Asian Preferential Trade Arrangement (1993 treaty)
- **SARAD** South Asian Regional Association of Dermatologists, Venereologists and Leprologists (#19739)
- Saratoga Foundation for Women Worldwide (internationally oriented national body)
- SARBICA – Southeast Asian Regional Branch of the International Council on Archives (see: #12996)
- **SARBIO** Southern African Regional Cooperation in Biochemistry, Molecular Biology and Biotechnology (#19859)
- SARCCUS – Southern African Regional Commission for the Conservation and Utilisation of the Soil (inactive)
- Sarcoidosis Europe / see European Association of Patients Organizations of Sarcoidosis and other Granulomatous Disorders (#06144)

♦ Sarcoma Patients EuroNet (SPAEN) 19054

Secretariat Am Rothenanger 1b, 85521 Riemerling, Germany. E-mail: info@sarcoma-patients.eu.
Contact Untergasse 36, 61200 Wölfersheim, Germany. E-mail: sarcomapatientseuronet@daswissenshaus.de.
URL: http://www.sarcoma-patients.eu/

History 6 Apr 2009, Bad Nauheim (Germany). Former names and other names: *European Network of Sarcoma, GIST and Desmoid Patient Advocacy Groups* – full title. Registration: Hesse District court, No/ID: VR 2609, Start date: 11 Aug 2009, Germany, Friedberg. **Aims** Support sarcoma research and improve diagnosis, treatment and care of sarcoma patients in close collaboration with clinical sarcoma experts, scientific researchers, pharmaceutical industry and other stakeholders. **Structure** Board of Directors. **Languages** English. **Staff** 1.00 FTE, paid. **Finance** Members' dues. Other sources: EU funding; industrial funding. **Activities** Knowledge management/information dissemination; advocacy/lobbying/activism; research and development. **Events** *Annual Conference* Paris (France) 2015, *Conference* Amsterdam (Netherlands) 2014, *Annual Conference / Conference* London (UK) 2013, *Annual Conference / Conference* Florence (Italy) 2012, *Conference* Berlin (Germany) 2011. **Publications** *SPAEN Newsletter*. Infographics; position papers; policy checklist; conference/project reports; abstracts.

Members Organizations (41) in 23 countries:
Australia, Austria, Bulgaria, Curaçao, Finland, France, Germany, India, Israel, Italy, Kenya, Netherlands, North Macedonia, Norway, Poland, Romania, South Africa, Spain, Sweden, Switzerland, Türkiye, UK, USA.

NGO Relations Member of (3): *European Cancer Organisation (ECO, #06432)* (Patient Advisory Committee); *Rare Cancers Europe (RCE, #18620)*; *Workgroup of European Cancer Patient Advocacy Networks (WECAN, #21054)*. Cooperates with (5): *American Society of Clinical Oncology (ASCO)*; *Connective Tissue Oncology Society (CTOS, #04682)*; *European Musculo-Skeletal Oncology Society (EMSOS, #07834)*; *European Organisation for Research and Treatment of Cancer (EORTC, #08101)*; *European Society for Medical Oncology (ESMO, #08648)*. [2018.06.01/XJ6435/**D**]

- **SARCS** Southeast Asia Regional Committee (#19793)
- SARDA – Southern African Refrigerated Distribution Association (internationally oriented national body)
- **SARDC** Southern African Research and Documentation Centre (#19861)
- SARIA – Southern Africa Regional Irrigation Association (internationally oriented national body)
- SARIMA – Southern African Research and Innovation Management Association (internationally oriented national body)
- SAR – International Convention on Maritime Search and Rescue (1979 treaty)
- **SARMAC** Society for Applied Research in Memory and Cognition (#19522)
- SAR – Multilateral Agreement on Search and Rescue (1973 treaty)
- SARN – South Asia Research Network for the Social Sciences and Humanities (internationally oriented national body)
- SARPCCO – Southern African Regional Police Chiefs Cooperation Organization (inactive)
- **SARPS** South Asian Regional Pain Society (#19740)
- **SARRA** South Asia Rural Reconstruction Association (#19748)
- **SARRNET** USAID/SADC/IITA/CIP Southern Africa Root Crops Research Network (#20734)
- SAR – Scholars at Risk (internationally oriented national body)
- **SAR** Search and Rescue (#04845)
- **SAR** Seas at Risk (#19189)
- **SAR** Society for Artistic Research (#19523)
- SARTOC – Southern Africa Regional Tourism Council (inactive)
- **SARUA** Southern African Regional Universities Association (#19860)
- Sarvodaya International Trust (internationally oriented national body)
- Sarvodaya Shramadana Movement (internationally oriented national body)
- **SARV** Suider Afrika Rekenkundige Vereniging (#19834)
- SARW – Southern African Resource Watch (unconfirmed)
- SAS Action Plan / see Action Plan for the Protection and Management of the South Asia Seas Region (#00094)

♦ Sasakawa Africa Association (SAA) 19055

Headquarters c/o Sasakawa Peace Foundation Bldg, 5th Floor, 1-15-16 Toranomon, Minato-ku, Tokyo, 105-0001 Japan. T. +81362571870. Fax +81362571874. E-mail: info@saa-safe.org.
URL: http://www.saa-safe.org/

History Headquarters established in Geneva (Switzerland), 1986; moved to Tokyo (Japan) 2017. Former names and other names: *Sasakawa Global 2000 (SG2000)* – former. Registration: Tokyo Legal Affairs Bureau, Start date: 2015, Japan; Swiss Civil Code, Start date: 1986, End date: 2015, Switzerland. **Aims** Support Africa to fulfill its aspirations in building resilient and sustainable food systems. **Structure** Board of Councillors; Board of Directors. **Languages** English, French, Japanese. **Staff** 160.00 FTE, paid. **Activities** Awareness raising; capacity building; networking/liaising; publishing activities; training/education. Strategic Plan (2021-2025): Regenerative Agriculture (RA); nutrition sensitive agriculture; market oriented agriculture. Active in: Benin, Burkina Faso, Ethiopia, Ghana, Malawi, Mali, Mozambique, Nigeria, Sierra Leone, Tanzania UR, Uganda. **Events** *Healthy Soils for Food Security in Africa: The Potential of Regenerative Agriculture* 2022. **Publications** Annual Report. [2023.02.20/XM7290/**F**]

- Sasakawa Global 2000 / see Sasakawa Africa Association (#19055)
- Sasakawa Peace Foundation (internationally oriented national body)
- Sasakawa Peace Foundation USA (internationally oriented national body)
- SASA – Society for the Advancement of Science in Africa (internationally oriented national body)
- SASA – South Asian Studies Association of Australia (internationally oriented national body)
- **SASAT** South Asian Society on Atherosclerosis and Thrombosis (#19741)
- SASCA – Southern African Spinal Cord Association (internationally oriented national body)
- SASCPB – South American Society for Comparative Physiology and Biochemistry (inactive)
- **SASCV** South Asian Society of Criminology and Victimology (#19742)
- **SASE** Society for the Advancement of Socio-Economics (#19516)
- SA – Sexaholics Anynymous (internationally oriented national body)
- SASF / see Alström Syndrome International (#00750)
- SASF – Scandinavian Association for the Study of Fertility (inactive)
- SASF / see South Asia Olympic Council (#19747)
- SASHA – Southern African Sexual Health Association (internationally oriented national body)
- SASHG – Southern African Society of Human Genetics (internationally oriented national body)
- SAS International / see Scandinavian Airlines System (#19069)
- SAS – International Small Angle Scattering Conference (meeting series)
- SAS / see International Society for the Advancement of Spine Surgery (#14903)
- Saskatchewan Council for International Cooperation (internationally oriented national body)
- SASK – Suomen Ammattiliittojen Solidaarisuuskeskus (internationally oriented national body)
- SASNET – Swedish South Asian Studies Network (internationally oriented national body)
- **SASO** South American Sports Organization (#19708)
- **SASP** Action Plan for the Protection and Management of the South Asia Seas Region (#00094)
- SASPID – Southern African Society for Paediatric Infectious Diseases (internationally oriented national body)
- SA – Sports Ambassadors (internationally oriented national body)
- **SASPP** Southern African Society for Plant Pathology (#19863)
- **SASP** Scandinavian Association for the Study of Pain (#19077)
- SASQUA – Southern African Society of Quaternary Research (internationally oriented national body)
- SA/SRDC Lusaka / see ECA Subregional Office for Southern Africa (#05276)
- SASREG – Southern African Society for Reproductive Medicine and Gynaecological Endoscopy (internationally oriented national body)
- SASRSS / see Southern African Society for Reproductive Medicine and Gynaecological Endoscopy
- **SASSCAL** Southern African Science Service Centre for Climate Change and Adaptive Land Management (#19862)
- **SAS** Scandinavian Airlines System (#19069)
- SASSDA – Southern Africa Stainless Steel Development Association (internationally oriented national body)
- **SASSM** South Asian Society for Sexual Medicine (#19743)
- SAS – Societas Arctica Scandinavica (inactive)
- **SAS** Society for Animation Studies (#19519)
- SASTA – Society for the Advancement of Science and Technology in the Arab World (internationally oriented national body)
- **SASTT** Southern African Society for Trenchless Technology (#19864)
- SASUTA / see Southern African Accounting Association (#19834)
- SASV – Soeurs de l'Assomption de la Sainte Vierge (religious order)

♦ SAT-7 19056

CEO PO Box 26760, CY-1647 Nicosia, Cyprus. T. +35722761050. Fax +35722761040. E-mail: mail@sat7.org.
URL: http://www.sat7.org/

History Nov 1995, as a division of *Middle East Media*. Became independent Jan 1996. **Aims** Serve as a *television* service for *Christians* in the *Middle East* and North Africa. **Structure** General Assembly (annual); Board of Directors; CEO. **Staff** 145.00 FTE, paid. **Finance** Members' dues. Donations. **Activities** Knowledge management/information dissemination. **Events** *Annual Meeting* Izmir (Turkey) 2015, *Annual Meeting* Izmir (Turkey) 2014, *Annual Meeting* Limassol (Cyprus) 2013, *Annual Meeting* Larnaca (Cyprus) 2012, *Annual Meeting* Limassol (Cyprus) 2012. **Publications** *Uplink* (4 a year). *Satellite Television and Social Change* (2003). Annual reports.

Members Organisations in 18 countries:
Canada, Cyprus, Denmark, Egypt, Finland, Germany, Iceland, Jordan, Kuwait, Lebanon, Netherlands, Norway, Oman, South Africa, Sweden, UK, United Arab Emirates, USA.

IGO Relations *Department for International Development Cooperation*; *Norwegian Agency for Development Cooperation (Norad)*; *Swedish International Development Cooperation Agency (Sida)*. **NGO Relations** Corporate, associates and partners (35), including the following bodies listed in this Yearbook: *Danish European Mission*; *Det Norske Misjonsselskap (NMS)*; *Finnish Evangelical Lutheran Mission (FELM)*; *IBRA Media*; *United Bible Societies (UBS, #20498)*; *World Vision International (WVI, #21904)*. Member of: *Global Connections*. [2015.05.13/XF4478/**F**]

- **SAT-AMIKARO** Union des travailleurs espérantistes des pays de langue française (#20488)
- SATA / see Southern Africa Telecommunications Association (#19867)
- **SATA** Southern Africa Telecommunications Association (#19867)
- **SAT Association** Satisfiability: Application and Theory (#19057)
- **SATA** Subsonic Aerodynamic Testing Association (#20027)
- SATCC – Southern African Transport and Communications Commission (no recent information)
- **SatCen** European Union Satellite Centre (#09015)
- SATHRI BTE-SSC / see South Asia Theological Research Institute, Bangalore
- SATHRI – South Asia Theological Research Institute, Bangalore (internationally oriented national body)
- SATIMO – Hulp van St-Andries aan de Derde Wereld (internationally oriented national body)

♦ Satisfiability: Application and Theory (SAT Association) 19057

Treas Vossberg 32a, 33100 Paderborn, Germany.
URL: http://satassociation.org/

History Registration: No/ID: VR 2589, Start date: 13 Jul 2009, Germany. **Aims** Promote science and research, in particular with regard to the Satisfiability Problem and related areas such as Formal Verification and other applications of SAT, Proof Complexity, Serial and Parallel SAT Solvers, Satisfiability Modulo Theories, Quantified Boolean Formulas, SAT Algorithms, MAX-SAT, MUS Extraction, and SAT Encodings. **Structure** General Assembly; Steering Committee; Executive Board. **Events** *International Conference on Theory and Applications of Satisfiability Testing* Paderborn (Germany) 2020, *International Conference on Theory and Applications of Satisfiability Testing* Lisbon (Portugal) 2019, *International Conference on Theory and Applications of Satisfiability Testing* Oxford (UK) 2018, *International Conference on Theory and Applications of Satisfiability Testing* Melbourne, VIC (Australia) 2017, *International Conference on Theory and Applications of Satisfiability Testing* Bordeaux (France) 2016. **Publications** *Journal on Satisfiability, Boolean Modeling, and Computation (JSAT)* – online. [2020/AA0340/**C**]

- **SATNU** Scandinavian Association of Thoracic Nurses (#19078)
- **SAT** Sennacieca Asocio Tutmonda (#16941)
- SAT – Société africaine de toxicologie (inactive)
- SAT / see SRHR Africa Trust (#19934)
- **SAT** SRHR Africa Trust (#19934)
- **SATS** Scandinavian Association for Thoracic Surgery (#19079)
- **SATUCC** Southern African Trade Union Coordination Council (#19865)
- SATW – Society of American Travel Writers (internationally oriented national body)
- Saudi Bahraini Institute for the Blind (internationally oriented national body)
- Saudi Fund for Development (internationally oriented national body)
- **SAU** Scandinavian Association of Urology (#19080)
- **SAU** South Asian University (#19744)
- Sauvegarde pour l'agriculture des variétés d'Europe (#19027)
- Pour le sauvetage des victimes de catastrophes naturelles / see Corps mondial de secours (#04845)
- Sauvons l'Europe (internationally oriented national body)
- Save Africa Concerts Foundation (internationally oriented national body)
- Save the African People CBO / see Save the People International
- Save Animals from Extinction / see EcoHealth Alliance
- Save the Children / see Save the Children International (#19058)
- Save the Children Denmark (internationally oriented national body)
- Save the Children Federation (internationally oriented national body)
- Save the Children Fund / see Save the Children UK

♦ Save the Children International 19058

CEO St Vincent House, 30 Orange Street, London, WC2H 7HH, UK. T. +442032720300. E-mail: info@savethechildren.org.
URL: http://www.savethechildren.net/

History 9 Nov 1979, Geneva (Switzerland). Founded as an international consortium of autonomous voluntary organizations, following joint response of several 'Save the Children' organizations to the 1976 earthquake in Guatemala (Guatemala). Derives historically from *Save the Children International Union (SCIU, inactive)*, set up 6 Jan 1920 but which ceased to exist in Sep 1946. Reorganized Mar 1996. Former names and other names: *International Save the Children Alliance* – former; *Alliance internationale "Save the Children"* – former; *Alianza Internacional "Save the Children"* – former; *Save the Children Union* – former; *Save the Children International* – former; *Alliance internationale d'aide à l'enfance* – former; *Alianza Internacional para el Apoyo a la Niñez* – former; *Save the Children (SC)* – alias. Registration: Charity, No/ID: 1076822, England and Wales. **Aims** As an organization fighting for children's *rights*: deliver immediate and lasting improvements to children's lives worldwide; work for a world which respects and values each child, which listens to children and learns, where all children have hope and opportunity. **Structure** Members' Meeting (annual); Board; Executive Team, headed by CEO. European Office in Brussels (Belgium). **Languages** English, French, Spanish. **Staff** 26.00 FTE, paid. **Finance** Total income of member organizations: over US$ 8,700 million. **Activities** Members work in over 115 countries worldwide, often in collaboration with other bodies. Groups of members work together on issues of common interest: global fundraising; programmes; communications; advocacy; child participation. The International Alliance Secretariat acts as focal point for mutual support, liaison and implementation of alliance strategy. Promotes implementation of *United Nations Convention on the Rights of the Child (CRC, 1989)* through programme activities, regional workshops, collaborations with other national and international NGOs and inter-governmental organizations, public information materials and children's rights advocacy work. Programme areas covered in 2005: Indian Ocean tsunami; Emergency response to conflict and disaster; Exploitation and abuse; Education; HIV/AIDS. **Events** *Ministers Responsible for Education, Gender and Humanitarian Affairs Meeting* Addis Ababa (Ethiopia) 2019, *Rights, Resources and Resilience Asia Pacific Summit* Bangkok (Thailand) 2017, *International Conference on Language and Education* Bangkok (Thailand) 2016, *Members meeting* Seoul (Korea Rep) 2008, *Members' Meeting* Sweden 2006. **Publications** Annual Report in English; online publications. Individual members publish various books and reports.

Members Autonomous national voluntary, non-profit and nongovernmental 'Save the Children' organizations in 27 countries and territories:
Australia, Canada, Denmark, Dominican Rep, Egypt, Eswatini, Fiji, Finland, Germany, Guatemala, Honduras, Iceland, Italy, Japan, Jordan, Korea Rep, Lithuania, Mexico, Netherlands, New Zealand, Norway, Romania, Spain, Sweden, Switzerland, UK, USA.
Included in the above, 5 organizations listed in this Yearbook:
Rädda Barnen – Save the Children Sweden; *Red Barnet*; *Save the Children Federation (SCF)*; *Save the Children Norway (Redd Barna)*; *Save the Children UK (SC UK)*.

Consultative Status Consultative status granted from: *ECOSOC (#05331)* (General); *ILO (#11123)* (Special List); *UNICEF (#20332)*; *UNESCO (#20322)* (Consultative Status). **IGO Relations** Global partner of: *United Nations Girls' Education Initiative (UNGEI, #20566)*. Member of: *Focusing Resources on Effective School Health (FRESH, #09809)*. Contact with: *Bioversity International (#03262)*; *Committee on the Rights of the Child (#04283)*; *European Commission (EC, #06633)*; *European Network of National Observatories on Childhood (ChildONEurope, #07951)*; *UNDP (#20292)*; *UNHCR (#20327)*; *WHO (#20950)*. Associated with Department of Global Communications of the United Nations.
NGO Relations Founder member of: *European Federation for Street Children (EFSC, inactive)*; *Steering Committee for Humanitarian Response (SCHR, #19978)*. Member of the Advisory Committee of: *Making Cents International*. Represented on the Board of: *The Sphere Project (#19918)*. Member of:
- *Alliance for Child Protection in Humanitarian Action (The Alliance, #00667)*;
- *Better Than Cash Alliance (#03220)*;
- *Child Rights Connect (#03884)*;
- *Child Rights International Network (CRIN, #03885)*;
- *CHS Alliance (#03911)*;
- *Communicating with Disaster Affected Communities Network (CDAC Network, #04379)*;
- *Confédération européenne des ong d'urgence et de développement (CONCORD, #04547)*;
- *Conference of Non-Governmental Organizations in Consultative Relationship with the United Nations (CONGO, #04635)*;
- *Cooperation Committee for Cambodia (CCC)*;
- *Global Campaign for Education (GCE, #10264)*;
- *Global Education Cluster (#10333)*;
- *End Corporal Punishment (#05457)*;
- *Global WASH Cluster (GWC, #10651)*;
- *IMPACT (#11136)*;
- *Inter-agency Network for Education in Emergencies (INEE, #11387)*;
- *International Campaign to Ban Landmines (ICBL, inactive)*;
- *International Council of Voluntary Agencies (ICVA, #13092)*;
- *Movimiento Mundial por la Infancia de Latinoamérica y El Caribe (MMI-LAC, #16873)*;
- *Neglected Tropical Diseased NGO Network (NNN, #16969)*;
- *NetHope (#16979)*;
- *NGO Working Group on the Security Council (#17128)*;
- *NGO Committee on UNICEF (#17120)*;
- *Permanent Forum of European Civil Society (#18322)*;
- *Religious in Europe Networking Against Trafficking and Exploitation (RENATE, #18833)*;
- *SDG Watch Europe (#19162)*;
- *UHC2030 (#20277)*;
- *UNITED for Intercultural Action – European Network Against Nationalism, Racism, Fascism and in Support of Migrants and Refugees (UNITED, #20511)*;
- *World Bank – Civil Society Joint Facilitation Committee (JFC, #21217)*.

German branch is member of: *Verband Entwicklungspolitik und Humanitäre Hilfe e.V. (VENRO)*. Partner of: *Global Shelter Cluster (GSC, #10594)*. Collaborates with: *Crisis Action (#04957)*; *Helen Keller International (HKI, #10902)*; *Women's Refugee Commission (WRC)*. Supports: *African Child Policy Forum (ACPF, #00246)*; *Global Call for Action Against Poverty (GCAP, #10263)*. Instrumental in setting up: *ACAPS (#00044)*.
[2019/XD4112/y/**F**]

- ♦ Save the Children International Union (inactive)
- ♦ Save the Children Norway (internationally oriented national body)
- ♦ Save the Children UK (internationally oriented national body)
- ♦ Save the Children Union / see Save the Children International (#19058)
- ♦ Save the Elephants (internationally oriented national body)
- ♦ Save a Family Plan (internationally oriented national body)
- ♦ **SAVE Foundation** Safeguard for Agricultural Varieties in Europe (#19027)
- ♦ Save a Girl – Save a Generation (internationally oriented national body)
- ♦ SAVE International (internationally oriented national body)
- ♦ SAVE International – Spoonbill Action Voluntary Echo International (internationally oriented national body)

♦ Save the Mothers (STM) 19059

Head Office 27 Legend Crt, PO Box 10126, Ancaster, Hamilton ON L9K 1P3, Canada. T. +19059287283. E-mail: info@savethemothers.org.
Exec Dir PO Box 250, Sewickley PA 15143, USA. E-mail: director@savethemothers.org.
URL: http://www.savethemothers.org/

History 2005. Registered Canadian Charity: 82876 7335 RR0001. **Aims** Promote *maternal health* in the developing world through education, public awareness and advocacy. **Structure** 3 organizations (Canada; USA; East Africa), each with their own Board of Directors. **Activities** Training/education. **NGO Relations** Member of: *PMNCH (#18410)*. [2018.01.31/XM5209/**F**]

- ♦ SaveNature.Org (internationally oriented national body)

♦ Save the Orangutan 19060

Dir Østerbrogade 146B, 1, 2100 Copenhagen Ø, Denmark. T. +4533930650. E-mail: info@savetheorangutan.org.
URL: https://savetheorangutan.org/

History Former names and other names: *Borneo Orangutan Survival International (BOS International)* – former. Registration: No/ID: CVR 36995947, Start date: 1 Apr 2015, Denmark, Copenhagen.
Members National organizations in 11 countries:
Australia, Austria, Canada, Denmark, France, Germany, Indonesia, Japan, Netherlands, Switzerland, USA.
NGO Relations Member of (1): *Roundtable on Sustainable Palm Oil (RSPO, #18986)*. [2022/XM0565/**D**]

- ♦ Save Our Seas (internationally oriented national body)
- ♦ Save our Seas Foundation (internationally oriented national body)
- ♦ Save Our Species (unconfirmed)
- ♦ Save the People International (internationally oriented national body)
- ♦ Save the Refugees Fund / see Mercy Corps International

♦ Save the Rhino International (SRI) 19061

Dir Unit 5, Coach House Mews, 217 Long Lane, London, SE1 4PR, UK. T. +442073577474. Fax +442073579666. E-mail: info@savetherhino.org.
URL: http://www.savetherhino.org/

History Founded 1992. UK Registered Charity: 1035072. **Aims** *Conserve* viable populations of rhinos in the wild by: raising funds to protect and increase rhino numbers and population distribution in African and Asian range states; facilitating exchange of technical support and information between rhino conservation stakeholders; ensuring that local communities in key rhino areas benefit from employment, capacity building, education, outreach and the sustainable use of natural resources; developing and delivering behaviour-change campaigns to reduce the demand for rhino horn in consumer countries; raising awareness throughout the world of the need for and importance of rhino conservation. **Structure** 2 Founder Patrons; 2 Founder Directors; 6 Trustees; 26 Patrons. **Languages** English. **Staff** 6.50 FTE, paid. **Finance** Sources: events; corporate fundraising; grant-making trusts and foundations; donations; legacies; membership scheme; merchandise sales; Gift Aid. **Activities** Financial and/or material support; awareness raising; knowledge capacity building. **Publications** *RhiNEWS* (12 a year) – newsletter; *Horn-E-events* (4 a year) – magazine; *The Horn* (2 a year) – magazine. Annual Report.
Members Individuals in 11 countries:
Australia, Austria, Belgium, Canada, Germany, Netherlands, New Zealand, Poland, South Africa, UK, USA.
NGO Relations Member of: *Environmental Paper Network (EPN, #05507)*. [2015.06.05/XF3834/v/**F**]

- ♦ Saveriane – Missionarie di Maria (religious order)
- ♦ Saveriani – Società di San Francesco Saverio per le Missioni Estere (religious order)
- ♦ Save the Tiger Fund (internationally oriented national body)
- ♦ Save Visions Africa (internationally oriented national body)
- ♦ Savez Alpe-Jadran (#00747)
- ♦ SAVFE – Scandinavian Association of Vacuum Field Energy (inactive)
- ♦ Savings Banks Group of the European Economic Community / see European Savings and Retail Banking Group (#08426)
- ♦ SAVS – Scandinavian Association for Vascular Surgery (no recent information)
- ♦ **SAWA** Screen Advertising World Association (#19158)
- ♦ SAWC – Southern African Wildlife College (internationally oriented national body)
- ♦ SAWC – Southern Africa Workcamps Cooperation (no recent information)
- ♦ SAWDF – South Asian Women Development Forum (internationally oriented national body)
- ♦ SAWF / see Women's Fund Asia (#21018)
- ♦ SAWG / see Advocacy Network for Africa
- ♦ SAWS / see Adventist Development and Relief Agency International (#00131)
- ♦ SAWSO – Salvation Army World Service Office (see: #19041)
- ♦ **SAWTEE** South Asia Watch on Trade, Economics and Environment (#19749)
- ♦ **SAYCC** South Asian Youth Climate Coalition (#19745)
- ♦ **SAZARC** South Asian Zoo Association for Regional Cooperation (#19746)
- ♦ **SBA** Sterile Barrier Association (#19983)
- ♦ **SBCA** Society for Benefit-Cost Analysis (#19525)
- ♦ SBCI / see Solar Cookers International (#19673)
- ♦ **SBC** Secretariat of the Basel Convention (#19196)
- ♦ SBE / see Society of Professional Economists
- ♦ **SBF** Society of Blue Friars (#19528)
- ♦ **SBH ISC** ICOMOS International Scientific Committee on Shared Built Heritage (#11081)
- ♦ **SBIC** Society of Biological Inorganic Chemistry (#19527)
- ♦ SBIF / see World Subud Association (#21836)
- ♦ SBI / see International Society on Business and Industrial Statistics (#14989)
- ♦ SBI – Société belge d'investissement international (internationally oriented national body)
- ♦ **SBI** Sozialistische Bodensee-Internationale (#16221)
- ♦ SBL – Society of Biblical Literature (internationally oriented national body)
- ♦ **SBSMP** Société Bernoulli pour la statistique mathématique et la probabilité (#03212)
- ♦ **SB** Société de biomécanique (#19458)
- ♦ **SBSP** Scandinavian-Baltic Society for Parasitology (#19081)
- ♦ **SBS** Small Business Standards (#19311)
- ♦ SBT / see Society for Immunotherapy of Cancer
- ♦ **SBU** Sociedades Biblicas Unidas (#20498)
- ♦ **SCAALA** South and Central American Assembly on Linguistic Anthropology (#19752)
- ♦ **SCA** CEV Small Countries Association (#03841)
- ♦ SCAEF – Société de cardiologie des pays d'Afrique d'expression française (inactive)
- ♦ SCAE / see Specialty Coffee Association (#19912)
- ♦ SCAHC / see Confederación de Sur y Centro America de Balonmano (#04443)
- ♦ **ScAIEM** Scandinavian Academy of Industrial Engineering and Management (#19067)
- ♦ **SCAI** Society for Complexity in Acute Illness (#19532)
- ♦ Scalabrinianas – Hermanas Misioneras de San Carlos Borromeo (religious order)
- ♦ Scalabriniane – Suore Missionarie di Santo Carlo Borromeo (religious order)
- ♦ Scalabrinian Secular Missionary Women (religious order)
- ♦ Scalabrinians – Missionary Sisters of Saint Charles Borromeo (religious order)
- ♦ Scalabriniennes – Soeurs Missionnaires de Saint Charles Borromée (religious order)

♦ Scalabrini International Migration Institute (SIMI) 19062

Dir Via Dandolo 58, 00153 Rome RM, Italy. T. +39065809764. E-mail: info@simieducation.org.
URL: https://www.simieducation.org

History 2000. Set up as an international academic institute. **Aims** Promote research and study of human mobility through interdisciplinary evaluation criteria. **Structure** Director; Vice-Director; Councillor. **Languages** English, Italian, Portuguese, Spanish. **Staff** 1.00 FTE, paid; 3.00 FTE, voluntary. **Finance** Sources: donations; private foundations; revenue from activities/projects. **Activities** Training/education. **Publications** *Quaderni SIMI*. **NGO Relations** Member of (2): *International Network on Migration and Development (INMD, #14296)*; *Refugee and Migrant Education Network (RME Network, #18740)*. Partner of (1): Refugee & Migrant Education Network. Cooperates with (1): *Scalabrini International Migration Network (SIMN, #19063)*. Affiliated with (1): *Pontificia Universitas Urbaniana (PUU, #18454)*. [2022.10.19/XQ0200/j/**F**]

♦ Scalabrini International Migration Network (SIMN) 19063

Exec Dir 307 East 60th St, New York NY 10022, USA. T. +12129130207. Fax +12122073789. E-mail: contact@simn-global.org.
URL: http://simn-global.org/

History 2005, Brussels (Belgium), within *Congregation of the Missionaries of St Charles, Scalabrinians (CS)*. New York NY (USA) office set up 2007. **Aims** Safeguard the dignity and the rights of migrants, refugees, seafarers, itinerants and people on the move worldwide. **Structure** Corporate Board; Executive Board; General Director; Executive Director; Regional Directors (5). **Languages** English, French, Italian, Portuguese, Spanish. **Staff** 8.00 FTE, paid. **Finance** Donations; grants. **Activities** Monitoring/evaluation; training/education; advocacy/lobbying/activism; capacity building. **Events** *Forum* Rome (Italy) 2017, *Forum* Berlin (Germany) 2015, *Forum* New York, NY (USA) 2013, *Forum* Mexico City (Mexico) 2011, *Forum* Bogota (Colombia) 2010. **Publications** Forum proceedings; studies.
Members Institutions (250) in 19 countries:
Argentina, Bolivia, Brazil, Chile, Colombia, Ecuador, El Salvador, Guatemala, Haiti, Italy, Mexico, Mozambique, Paraguay, Peru, Philippines, South Africa, Uruguay, USA, Venezuela.
Included in the above, 2 organizations listed in this Yearbook:

Center for Migration Studies, New York (CMS); Scalabrini Migration Centre, Manila (SMC).
Consultative Status Consultative status granted from: *ECOSOC (#05331)* (Special). **IGO Relations** Registered with: *OAS (#17629)*. Observer Status with: *International Organization for Migration (IOM, #14454)*. **NGO Relations** Member of: *International Catholic Centre of Geneva (ICCG, #12449); NGO Committee on Migration, New York (#17112).* [2018.09.05/XM1931/**E**]

♦ Scalabrini Migration Centre, Manila (internationally oriented national body)
♦ Scala Days (meeting series)

♦ Scaling Up Nutrition Movement (SUN Movement) 19064

Secretariat Dir Villa Le Bocage, Palais des Nations, 1211 Geneva, Switzerland. T. +41229177283. E-mail: info@scalingupnutrition.org.
URL: https://scalingupnutrition.org/
History 2010. Launched by the *United Nations (UN, #20515)* Secretary-General. **Aims** Unite people in a collective effort to improve nutrition. **Structure** Contains 4 SUN networks: *SUN Civil society Network (SUN CSN, #20035)*; SUN Business Network; *UN Nutrition (#20710)*; SUN Donor Network. SUN Lead Group; SUN Executive Committee; Secretariat. **Events** *Global Gathering* 2023, *Global Gathering* Kathmandu (Nepal) 2019, *Global Gathering* Abidjan (Côte d'Ivoire) 2017. **Publications** *SUN Bulletin* (12 a year).
Members Countries involved (65):
Afghanistan, Bangladesh, Benin, Botswana, Burkina Faso, Burundi, Cambodia, Cameroon, Central African Rep, Chad, Comoros, Congo Brazzaville, Congo DR, Costa Rica, Côte d'Ivoire, Djibouti, Ecuador, El Salvador, Eswatini, Ethiopia, Gabon, Gambia, Ghana, Guatemala, Guinea, Guinea-Bissau, Haiti, Honduras, Indonesia, Kenya, Kyrgyzstan, Laos, Lesotho, Liberia, Madagascar, Malawi, Mali, Mauritania, Mozambique, Myanmar, Namibia, Nepal, Niger, Nigeria, Pakistan, Papua New Guinea, Peru, Philippines, Rwanda, Sao Tomé-Principe, Senegal, Sierra Leone, Somalia, South Sudan, Sri Lanka, Sudan, Tajikistan, Tanzania UR, Timor-Leste, Togo, Uganda, Vietnam, Yemen, Zambia, Zimbabwe.
NGO Relations Partner of (1): *1,000 Days.* [2023/XJ7465/y/**F**]

♦ SCAM – Société civile des auteurs multimédia (internationally oriented national body)
♦ Scan Association (inactive)

♦ ScanBalt 19065

Gen Sec Allegade 14, 2000 Frederiksberg, Denmark. T. +4527141078. E-mail: pf@scanbalt.org.
URL: http://www.scanbalt.org/
History Aug 2004, following several projects: *ScanBalt BioRegion*, set up Jun 2002; *ScanBalt Bioregion – Network of Networks*, set up Dec 2002; *Scanbalt Agro-biotech Network*, set up Feb 2004. Registered in accordance with Danish law: 27823459. **Aims** Be the leading accelerator for inter-regional cooperation envisioning the region as a global hotspot for *health* and bio *economy*. **Structure** General Assembly; Executive Committee; Liaison Offices (4). **Languages** English. **Staff** 1-5. **Finance** Members' dues. Other sources: SME service contracts; EU project funding. **Activities** Knowledge management/information dissemination; projects/programmes; networking/liaising; publishing activities. **Events** *Forum* Tampere (Finland) 2012, *Forum* Tallinn (Estonia) 2010, *Forum* Kalmar (Sweden) 2009, *Forum* Vilnius (Lithuania) 2008, *Forum* Copenhagen (Denmark) 2007. **Publications** *ScanBalt Business Club Information* (12 a year); *ScanBalt News* (12 a year). *Macro-Regional Development and the Health Economy: Practical Experiences, Models and Concepts for Macro-Regional Collaboration between Regions and Clusters* (2016).
Members Founding; Institutional; Affiliate. Members in 10 countries:
Denmark, Estonia, Finland, Germany, Latvia, Lithuania, Netherlands, Norway, Poland, Sweden.
Co-opted Founding Members (2):
NordForsk (#17164); Nordic Innovation (#17320).
IGO Relations Partnership with: *Council of the Baltic Sea States (CBSS, #04870).* **NGO Relations** Partnership with: *Baltic Development Forum (#03111).* [2017.06.01/XJ4716/**D**]

♦ **SCANCOR** Scandinavian Consortium for Organizational Research (#19083)
♦ **SCANCOS** Scandinavian Society of Cosmetic Chemists (#19105)
♦ SCANDEM / see Nordic Microscopy Society (#17344)
♦ **SCANDEM** Nordic Microscopy Society (#17344)

♦ Scandiatransplant Association 19066

Foreningen Scandiatransplant
Medical Dir Aarhus Univ Hosp, Palle Juul-Jensens Boulevard 99, 8200 Aarhus, Denmark. T. +4578455131. E-mail: scandiatransplant.office@rm.dk.
URL: http://www.scandiatransplant.org/
History 1968. Former names and other names: *Nordiska Transplantationskommittén* – former; *Pohjoismainen Elintensiirtokomitea* – former; *Nordiska Expertkommittén för Transplantationsfrågor* – former. **Aims** Promote exchange of human organs and tissue for *transplantation* in *Scandinavia and Estonia*; maintain a transplantation database registry; facilitate in promotion of procurement of human organs and tissue for transplantation; facilitate scientific activities within field of transplantation. **Structure** Council; Board; Committees (12). **Languages** Danish, English, Norwegian, Swedish. **Staff** 8.00 FTE, paid. **Finance** Sources: members' dues. **Activities** Knowledge management/information dissemination. **Events** *Council of Representatives Meeting* Estonia 2023, *Council of Representatives Meeting* Aarhus (Denmark) 2022, *Council of Representatives Meeting* Aarhus (Denmark) 2021, *Council of Representatives Meeting* Aarhus (Denmark) 2020, *Council of Representatives Meeting* Aarhus (Denmark) 2019. **Publications** *Scandiatransplant Newsletter.* Annual report; reports from sub-groups.
Members Transplantation centres (12) in 6 countries:
Denmark, Estonia, Finland, Iceland, Norway, Sweden. [2022/XD8189/**D**]

♦ Scandinave des Associations des Travailleurs de l'Industrie du Papier (inactive)
♦ Scandinavia Against Drugs (#17157)
♦ Scandinavian Academy of Esthetic Dentistry (internationally oriented national body)

♦ Scandinavian Academy of Industrial Engineering and Management (ScAIEM) 19067

Administration Stiftelsen IMIT, SE-412 96 Gothenburg, Sweden. E-mail: info@scaiem.org.
URL: http://www.scaiem.org/
History Current statutes adopted Nov 2012, Linköping (Sweden); amended Mar 2017. **Aims** Strengthen academic education and research within the field of industrial engineering and management. **Structure** General Meeting; Board. **Activities** Advocacy/lobbying/activism; events/meetings; research and development; training/education. **Events** *ScAIEM Conference* Stockholm (Sweden) 2019. **Publications** *ScAIEM Newsletter.*
Members Departs of industrial engineering and management in 5 countries:
Denmark, Finland, Iceland, Norway, Sweden. [2021.06.08/AA0765/**D**]

♦ Scandinavian Academy of Management / see Nordisk Företagsekonomiska Förening (#17510)

♦ Scandinavian Airline Dispatchers' Association (SALDA) 19068

Pres SAS Lederne, Amager Strandvej 418, 2770 Kastrup, Denmark.
URL: http://www.salda.dk/ [2016/XD4616/**D**]

♦ Scandinavian Airlines System (SAS) 19069

Pres and CEO SAS Head Office, Frösundaviks Allé 1, SE-195 87 Stockholm, Sweden. T. +4687970000. Fax +4687972870.
Denmark Postboks 150, 2770 Kastrup, Denmark. T. +4532320000.
Norway Snarøyveien 57, LUFTHAVN, 1330 Oslo, Norway. T. +4767596050.
URL: http://www.scandinavian.net/
History 1946, as a consortium of national airlines of Denmark, Norway and Sweden. Danish DDL and Norwegian DDL each own 2/7 of SAS, while Swedish SILA owns 3/7. The three parent companies are owned fifty-fifty by private interests and the respective governments. Also referred to as *SAS International.* **Structure** President and Chief Executive Officer; Board of Directors, consisting of 9 members; Assembly of Representatives; Auditors. **NGO Relations** Instrumental in setting up: *Nordic EFQM Network (inactive).* [2013/XF2081/e/**F**]

♦ Scandinavian Air Navigators Association (inactive)
♦ Scandinavian Alliance Mission of North America / see The Evangelical Alliance Mission

♦ Scandinavian Analogue Computer Society / see Scandinavian Simulation Society (#19100)
♦ Scandinavian Association for Cerebrovascular Diseases / see Nordic Stroke Society (#17439)
♦ Scandinavian Association of Clinical Physiology / see Scandinavian Society of Clinical Physiology and Nuclear Medicine (#19104)

♦ Scandinavian Association for Dental Research 19070

Association nordique d'odontologie – Nordisk Odontologisk Forening (NOF) – Nordisk Odontologisk Förening – Nordiska Föreningen för Befrämjande af Odontologisk Undervisning och Forskning (NOF)
SG/Treas Inst of Dentistry, Univ of Turku, FI-20500 Turku, Finland.
URL: http://www.iadr-nof.com/contact-us/
History 7 Jan 1917, Gothenburg (Sweden), by a group of Scandinavian dentists, following signature, 15 Aug 1916, of a proposal for a research organization to complement *Scandinavian Dentists' Association (inactive).* Originally also referred to in English as *Nordic Association of Odontology.* Constitution amended Mar 1969, on becoming the Scandinavian Division of *International Association for Dental Research (IADR, #11838)*, included in *Continental European Division of the International Association for Dental Research (CED-IADR, #04780).* Also referred to by initials *IADR-NOF.* **Aims** Promote research and education in dental science in member countries. **Structure** General Assembly (annual); Executive Committee. **Languages** English. **Staff** 1.00 FTE, voluntary. **Finance** Members' dues. **Events** *Congress* Durham (UK) 2007, *Joint scientific meeting* Durham (UK) 2007, *Congress* Dublin (Ireland) 2006, *Congress* Amsterdam (Netherlands) 2005, *Congress* Istanbul (Turkey) 2004. **Publications** *European Journal of Oral Sciences* (6 a year).
Members Full (360), in 8 countries:
Denmark, Estonia, Finland, Iceland, Latvia, Lithuania, Norway, Sweden.
IGO Relations *WHO (#20950).* [2019.04.25/XD9150/**E**]

♦ Scandinavian Association for Digestive Endoscopy (SADE) 19071

Chair c/o CLINTEC, Alfred Nobels Allé 8, SE-141 52 Huddinge, Sweden.
URL: http://sadeendoscopy.com/
History 1982. **Activities** Annual educational course. **Events** *Annual Nordic meeting of gastroenterology* Helsinki (Finland) 2003. [2017/XD7670/**D**]

♦ Scandinavian Association of Directory and Database Publishers (inactive)
♦ Scandinavian Association for Gastrointestinal Motility / see Scandinavian Association for Neurogastroenterology and Motility (#19073)
♦ Scandinavian Association of Geneticists (no recent information)

♦ Scandinavian Association for Language and Cognition (SALC) 19072

Skandinaviska Sällskapet för Språk och Kognition (SSSK) – Det Skandinaviske Selskab for Sprog og Kognition (SSSK) – Skandinavisk Selskap for Språk og Kognisjon (SSSK) – Skandinaavinen kielen ja kognition yhdistys (SKKY)
Treas Dept of Language Studies, A Humanisthuset, korridor HE2, Umeå universitet, SE-901 87 Umeå, Sweden. T. +46907866004.
URL: http://www.salc-sssk.org/
History 11 Jun 2009, Stockholm (Sweden), during 2nd International Conference, having previously existed as the Swedish Association for Language and Cognition, set up 17 Jun 2006. **Aims** Promote study of the relationship between language and cognition. **Structure** Governing Board. **Languages** English. **Finance** Members' dues. **Events** *Conference* Turku (Finland) 2022, *Conference* Aarhus (Denmark) 2019, *Conference* Lund (Sweden) 2017, *Conference* Trondheim (Norway) 2015, *Conference* Joensuu (Finland) 2013.
Members Individuals in 4 countries:
Denmark, Finland, Norway, Sweden. [2016/XM4434/**D**]

♦ Scandinavian Association for Neurogastroenterology and Motility (SAGIM) 19073

Pres Aalborg Univ Hosp, Molleparkvej, 9000 Aalborg, Denmark. E-mail: amd@rn.dk.
URL: http://www.sagim-gastro.dk/
History 1987, Turku (Finland). Membership is compulsory for gastrointestinal motility and neurogastroenterology researchers in Scandinavia. Former names and other names: *Scandinavian Association for Gastrointestinal Motility* – former (1987 to 2012). **Aims** Promote development of research and education in gastrointestinal motility and neurogastroenterology. **Structure** Steering Committee. **Languages** English. **Staff** Voluntary. **Finance** Sources: grants; sponsorship. **Activities** Events/meetings; networking/liaising. **Events** *Annual Meeting* Copenhagen (Denmark) 2021, *Annual Meeting* Copenhagen (Denmark) 2020, *Annual Meeting* Copenhagen (Denmark) 2019, *Annual Meeting* Copenhagen (Denmark) 2018, *Annual Meeting* Copenhagen (Denmark) 2016.
Members Full in 4 countries:
Denmark, Finland, Norway, Sweden.
NGO Relations Member of (1): *European Society of Neurogastroenterology and Motility (ESNM, #08663).* [2022.05.17/XD2324/**D**]

♦ Scandinavian Association of Oral and Maxillofacial Surgeons 19074

Association scandinave des chirurgiens de la bouche – Skandinavisk Forening af Oral og Maxillofacial Kirurger (SFOMK)
Contact Flahultsringen 5, Norrahammar, SE-562 33 Jönköping, Sweden.
Contact Dept of Oral and Maxillofacial Surgery, Aalborg Univ Hosp, Hobrovej 18-22, 9000 Aalborg, Denmark. E-mail: jdj@rn.dk.
URL: http://www.sfomk.org/
History 20 Jun 1965, Copenhagen (Denmark). **Aims** Promote development in the subject area of oral and maxillofacial surgery in Scandinavia. **Structure** General Assembly; Board. **Languages** English. **Staff** 8.00 FTE, voluntary. **Finance** Members' dues. Other sources: congress; courses. **Activities** Training/education; events/meetings. **Events** *Biennial Meeting* Gothenburg (Sweden) 2024, *Biennial Meeting* Oslo (Norway) 2022, *Biennial Meeting* Reykjavik (Iceland) 2019, *Biennial Meeting* Helsinki (Finland) 2017, *Biennial Meeting* Copenhagen (Denmark) 2015.
Members Full; associate. Members in 5 countries:
Denmark, Finland, Iceland, Norway, Sweden. [2019/XD5620/**D**]

♦ Scandinavian Association of Paediatric Surgeons (no recent information)
♦ Scandinavian Association for Penal Reform (inactive)

♦ Scandinavian Association of Plastic Surgeons (SCAPLAS) 19075

Association scandinave de chirurgie plastique – Nordisk Plastikkirurgisk Forening
Sec POB 266, Helsinki Univ Hosp, FI-00029 Helsinki, Finland.
URL: http://www.scaplas.org/
History 3 Feb 1951, Stockholm (Sweden). **Aims** Safeguard the interests of recognized specialists in plastic surgery; promote professional and scientific development of plastic surgery in Nordic countries. **Structure** General Meeting (every 2 years); Council. **Languages** Danish, English, Faroese, Finnish, Icelandic, Norwegian, Swedish. **Staff** Voluntary. **Finance** Sources: members' dues. **Activities** Events/meetings; training/education. **Events** *Congress* Reykjavik (Iceland) 2022, *Biennial Congress* Reykjavik (Iceland) 2021, *Congress* Reykjavik (Iceland) 2020, *Biennial Congress* Copenhagen (Denmark) 2018, *Biennial Congress* Uppsala (Sweden) 2016. **Publications** *Journal of Hand Surgery and Plastic Surgery; Scandinavian Journal of Plastic and Reconstructive Surgery.* Congress papers.
Members National plastic surgery associations in 5 countries:
Denmark, Finland, Iceland, Norway, Sweden. [2021/XD4353/v/**D**]

♦ Scandinavian Association for Pollination Ecologists / see Scandinavian Association of Pollination Ecology (#19076)

♦ Scandinavian Association of Pollination Ecology (SCAPE) 19076

Contact Aarhus Univ, Dept of Bioscience, Ny Munkegade 116, Bldg 1540 227, 8000 Aarhus, Denmark.
URL: https://scape-pollination.org/

History Also referred to as *Scandinavian Association for Pollination Ecologists.* **Events** *Annual Meeting* Gimo (Sweden) 2022, *Annual Meeting* Checiny (Poland) 2021, *Annual Meeting* Northampton (UK) 2020, *Annual Meeting* Höör (Sweden) 2019, *Annual Meeting* Wicklow (Ireland) 2018. **Members** Membership countries not specified. [2020/XD9259/**D**]

♦ Scandinavian Association for Scolioses / see Nordic Spinal Deformities Society (#17437)
♦ Scandinavian Association for Social Medicine (inactive)
♦ Scandinavian Association for Sociology of Law (inactive)
♦ Scandinavian Association for the Study of Fertility (inactive)

♦ Scandinavian Association for the Study of Pain (SASP) 19077

Pres address not obtained. T. +4578463455. Fax +4678463455.
URL: http://www.sasp.org/

History 1977, Stockholm (Sweden). Dissolved in 2008 in order to facilitate national societies forming IASP chapters. The current version of SASP was founded in 2009. **Aims** Foster and encourage research on pain mechanisms and pain syndromes and improve the management of patients with acute and chronic pain by bringing together physicians, other health professionals and scientists with an interest in pain research and pain treatment; promote education and training in the area of pain in the Nordic countries; inform physicians, other health professionals and the general public of advances in pain research and pain therapy. **Structure** General Meeting (annual). Council, comprising one representative from each Nordic country and including President and Treasurer. **Languages** Danish, Faroese, Icelandic, Norwegian, Swedish. **Staff** Part-time, voluntary. **Finance** Members' dues. Budget (annual): Danish Kr 60,000. **Events** *Annual Meeting* Copenhagen (Denmark) 2022, *Annual Meeting* Stockholm (Sweden) 2021, *Annual Meeting* Stockholm (Sweden) 2020, *Annual Meeting* Oslo (Norway) 2019, *Annual Meeting* Tampere (Finland) 2018.
Members Physicians, scientists and other health professionals. Full in 5 countries:
Denmark, Finland, Iceland, Norway, Sweden. [2020/XD1673/**D**]

♦ Scandinavian Association of Thoracic and Cardiovascular Surgery / see Scandinavian Association for Thoracic Surgery (#19079)

♦ Scandinavian Association of Thoracic Nurses (SATNU) 19078

Contact KI-NVS-H1, Alfred Nobels Allé 23 B, SE-141 52 Huddinge, Sweden.
Sec address not obtained.
URL: http://www.satnu.org/

History 2008, Copenhagen. **Events** *Joint Scandinavian Conference in Cardiothoracic Surgery* Helsinki (Finland) 2022, *Joint Scandinavian Conference in Cardiothoracic Surgery* Bergen (Norway) 2021, *Joint Scandinavian Conference in Cardiothoracic Surgery* Bergen (Norway) 2020, *Joint Scandinavian Conference in Cardiothoracic Surgery* Stockholm (Sweden) 2019, *Joint Scandinavian Conference in Cardiothoracic Surgery* Copenhagen (Denmark) 2018. **NGO Relations** *Scandinavian Association for Thoracic Surgery (SATS, #19079); Scandinavian Society for Extracorporeal Technology (SCANSECT, #19107).* [2015/XM8232/**D**]

♦ Scandinavian Association for Thoracic Surgery (SATS) 19079

Association scandinave de chirurgie cardiothoracique – Nordisk Thoraxkirurgisk Forening (NTF)

SG address not obtained. E-mail: satsnordic@gmail.com.
URL: https://satsnordic.com/

History 17 Aug 1949, Oslo (Norway). Former names and other names: *Scandinavian Association of Thoracic and Cardiovascular Surgery* – former. **Structure** Annual Congress of members, circulating schedule; Congress President is head of the thoracic centre where meeting is held. Includes *Scandinavian Society for Research in Cardiothoracic Surgery (SSRCTS, #19117).* **Languages** English. **Finance** Membership fees: Swedish Kr 200 per annum. **Events** *Joint Scandinavian Conference in Cardiothoracic Surgery* Helsinki (Finland) 2022, *Joint Scandinavian Conference in Cardiothoracic Surgery* Bergen (Norway) 2021, *Joint Scandinavian Conference in Cardiothoracic Surgery* Bergen (Norway) 2020, *Joint Scandinavian Conference in Cardiothoracic Surgery* Stockholm (Sweden) 2019, *Joint Scandinavian Conference in Cardiothoracic Surgery* Copenhagen (Denmark) 2018. **Publications** *Scandinavian Journal of Thoracic and Cardiovascular Surgery.* Information Services: Database of members and medical companies interested in the field.
Members Individuals (307) in 5 countries:
Denmark, Finland, Iceland, Norway, Sweden.
Corresponding members (30). Membership countries not specified. [2022/XD4145/v/**D**]

♦ Scandinavian Association of Urology (SAU) 19080

Nordisk Urologisk Förening (NUF)

SG Urological Dept, Landspitali Univ Hosp, Hringbraut 101 Reykjavik, Reykjavik, Iceland. E-mail: jof0917@sak.is.
Pres Urologic Dept, Haukeland Univ Hosp of Bergen, Jonas Lies vei 65, 5021 Bergen, Norway. T. +4755972902.
URL: http://www.nuf.nu/

History Founded 1 Sep 1956, Helsinki (Finland). **Aims** Carry out studies and research and promote education in urology; provide treatment in urology. **Structure** General Assembly. **Languages** English. **Staff** 2.00 FTE, voluntary. **Finance** Members' dues. **Events** *Congress* Bergen (Norway) 2023, *Congress* Helsinki (Finland) 2022, *Biennial Congress* Helsinki (Finland) 2021, *Biennial Congress* Reykjavik (Iceland) 2019, *Biennial Congress* Odense (Denmark) 2017. **Publications** *Scandinavian Journal of Urology.*
Members Individuals (1,400) in 5 countries:
Denmark, Finland, Iceland, Norway, Sweden.
NGO Relations *International Consultation on Urological Diseases (ICUD, #12928).* [2020.02.19/XD2590/v/**D**]

♦ Scandinavian Association of Vacuum Field Energy (inactive)
♦ Scandinavian Association for Vascular Surgery (no recent information)
♦ Scandinavian Association of Women Teachers (inactive)

♦ Scandinavian-Baltic Society for Parasitology (SBSP) 19081

Pres address not obtained. E-mail: contact@sbsp.eu.
URL: http://sbsp.eu/

History 2003. Founded by fusion of *Scandinavian Society for Parasitology (SSP)*, est. 1967, Denmark, and *Baltic Society for Parasitology*, est. 1993. **Aims** Encourage research and education in parasitology in the Nordic and the Baltic countries; act as a unifying body for parasitologists and persons interested in parasitology and to represent them in the Nordic and the Baltic countries; represent Nordic and Baltic parasitologists internationally. **Languages** Danish, English, Estonian, Finnish, Icelandic, Latvian, Lithuanian, Lithuanian Sign Language, Norwegian, Swedish. **Staff** 10.00 FTE, voluntary. The board of The Scandinavian-Baltic Society for Parasitology and two webmasters. **Activities** Events/meetings; training/education. Active in: Denmark, Estonia, Finland, Iceland, Latvia, Lithuania, Norway, Sweden. **Events** *Conference* Vilnius (Lithuania) 2021, *Conference* Copenhagen (Denmark) 2019, *Conference* Riga (Latvia) 2017, *Conference* Uppsala (Sweden) 2015, *Conference* Copenhagen (Denmark) 2013. **Publications** Reports; proposals; statements. **NGO Relations** Member of (3): *European Federation of Parasitologists (EFP, #07186); International Federation for Tropical Medicine (IFTM, #13575); World Federation of Parasitologists (WFP, #21471).* [2021.06.09/XN2488/**D**]

♦ Scandinavian Baptists' Joint Committee (inactive)
♦ Scandinavian Bell Committee / see Nordisk Selskab for Campanologi og Klokkespil (#17533)
♦ Scandinavian Bishops' Conference / see Nordisk Bispekonferance (#17498)
♦ Scandinavian Clothing Council (inactive)
♦ Scandinavian Coal Importers Federation (no recent information)
♦ Scandinavian Coin Union (inactive)
♦ Scandinavian College for Brewers (internationally oriented national body)

♦ Scandinavian College of Neuropsychopharmacology (SCNP) 19082

Contact c/o Clinical Medicine Dept, Aarhus University, Universitetsbyen 13, 8000 Aarhus C, Denmark. E-mail: scnp@scnp.org.
URL: http://www.scnp.org/

History 1959. Founded following a discussion of the *subcommittee on psychopharmacology* at the 1958 Nordic Psychiatric Congress in conjunction with ideas put forth by the newly formed *Collegium Internationale Neuropsychopharmacologicum (CINP, #04115).* Former names and other names: *Scandinavian Society for Psychopharmacology (SSP)* – former (1959); *Skandinavisk Selskab for Psykofarmakologi* – former (1959). **Aims** Promote research and education in neuropsychopharmacology; advise on all aspects of neuropsychiatric drugs. **Structure** Annual Meeting; Board. **Languages** English. **Staff** 7.00 FTE, paid. **Finance** Journal; organizational activities. **Activities** Research and development; guidance/assistance/consulting; healthcare; events/meetings. **Events** *Annual Congress* Aarhus (Denmark) 2022, *Annual Congress* Aarhus (Denmark) 2021, *Annual Congress* Stockholm (Sweden) 2020, *Annual Congress* Gothenburg (Sweden) 2019, *Annual Congress* Copenhagen (Denmark) 2014. **Publications** *Acta Neuropsychiatrica* – journal.
Members Individuals psychiatrists, neurologists, pharmacologists, neurobiologists and people from the pharmaceutical industry (almost 400). 'Supportive members' pharmaceutical companies represented by 2 persons at the Annual Meeting. Members in 7 countries and territories:
Denmark, Faeroe Is, Finland, Greenland, Iceland, Norway, Sweden.
NGO Relations African College of Neuropsychopharmacology (AfCNP); *Collegium Internationale Neuropsychopharmacologicum (CINP, #04115); European College of Neuropsychopharmacology (ECNP, #06612).* [2022/XD7891/**D**]

♦ Scandinavian Committee on Materials Research and Testing (inactive)
♦ Scandinavian Committee on Production Engineering Research (inactive)
♦ Scandinavian Committee for Research in Wood Technology (inactive)
♦ Scandinavian Conference of Medical Librarians (meeting series)
♦ Scandinavian Congress for Psychiatrists (meeting series)

♦ Scandinavian Consortium for Organizational Research (SCANCOR) . 19083

Contact c/o CBS, Dept of Organization, Kilevej 14A, 2000 Frederiksberg, Denmark.
USA Office 520 Galvez Mall, CERAS 123, Stanford CA 94305-3084, USA.
URL: https://scancor.org/

History 15 Sep 1988. **Aims** Nurture the development of social scientists and their scholarship over the course of whole careers; advance research and development in the social sciences, particularly in the area of organizational studies; encourage collaboration among organizational social scientists worldwide. **Structure** Board. **Activities** Advocacy/lobbying/activism; events/meetings; networking/liaising; research and development. **Events** *Anniversary Conference* Stanford, CA (USA) 2018. [2023/AA3214/**D**]

♦ Scandinavian Contact Agency for Agricultural Research / see Nordic Joint Committee for Agricultural and Food Research (#17332)

♦ Scandinavian Copper Development Association (SCDA) 19084

Contact Tekniikantie 12, FI-02150 Espoo, Finland. T. +358405900494. E-mail: info@copperalliance.se.
Contact Murarvägen 15, SE-197 30 Bro, Sweden. T. +4621198738.
URL: http://www.copperalliance.eu/fi

Members Full in 3 countries:
Denmark, Finland, Sweden.
NGO Relations Member of: *European Copper Institute (ECI, #06796).* [2016.03.02/XD6988/**D**]

♦ Scandinavian Council of Logopedics and Phoniatrics (no recent information)
♦ Scandinavian Criminal Law Committee (inactive)
♦ Scandinavian Dentists' Association (inactive)
♦ Scandinavian Dermatological Association / see Nordic Dermatology Association (#17269)
♦ Scandinavian Development Group for Corrugated Board / see International Development Group for Corrugated Board (#13160)
♦ Scandinavian Electrophoresis Society (inactive)
♦ Scandinavian Endodontic Association / see Scandinavian Endodontic Society (#19085)

♦ Scandinavian Endodontic Society 19085

Association scandinave d'endodontie – Skandinaviska Endodontiföreningen

Contact Box 7136, SE-402 33 Gothenburg, Sweden.

History Former names and other names: *Scandinavian Endodontic Association* – alias. **Aims** Promote endodontics to specialists and general practitioners; recruit teachers. **Structure** Board, including President. **Languages** English, Norwegian. **Staff** 4.00 FTE, voluntary. **Finance** Members' dues. **Events** *SkandEndo Congress* Bergen (Norway) 2022, *SkandEndo Congress* Bergen (Norway) 2020, *SkandEndo Congress* Oslo (Norway) 2019, *ScandEndo Congress* Stockholm (Sweden) 2018, *ScandEndo Congress* Copenhagen (Denmark) 2016.
Members Specialists in endodontics; general practitioners. Members in 4 countries:
Denmark, Finland, Norway, Sweden. [2020.01.24/XD0364/**D**]

♦ Scandinavian Epilepsy Congress (meeting series)
♦ Scandinavian Episcopal Conference (#17498)
♦ Scandinavian Federation of Heating, Air Conditioning and Sanitary Engineering Associations / see Scandinavian Federation of Heating, Ventilating and Sanitary Engineering Associations (#19086)

♦ Scandinavian Federation of Heating, Ventilating and Sanitary Engineering Associations (SCANVAC) 19086

Pres c/o FINVAC, Sitratori 5, FI-00420 Helsinki, Finland. T. +35895665095.
URL: http://www.scanvac.info/

History 1956, Stockholm (Sweden). Also referred to as *Scandinavian Federation of Heating, Air Conditioning and Sanitary Engineering Associations.* **Aims** Contribute significantly to create better buildings in Scandinavia that improves the well being of people and economical sustainability of society. **Structure** Board of Directors. **Languages** English. **Finance** Members share expenses. **Activities** Events/meetings; publishing activities; research and development; awards/prizes/competitions. **Events** *Triennial International Conference on Cold Climate Heating Ventilation and Air-Conditioning* Tallinn (Estonia) 2021, *Triennial International Conference on Cold Climate Heating Ventilation and Air-Conditioning* Tallinn (Estonia) 2021, *ROOMVENT : International Conference on Air Distribution in Rooms* Turin (Italy) 2021, *ROOMVENT : International Conference on Air Distribution in Rooms* Turin (Italy) 2020, *ROOMVENT : International Conference on Air Distribution in Rooms* Espoo (Finland) 2018.
Members Full: national societies, comprising almost 20,000 individuals in 5 countries:
Denmark, Finland, Iceland, Norway, Sweden.
Associate: national societies in 3 countries:
Estonia, Latvia, Lithuania. [2018.09.21/XF1463/**F**]

♦ Scandinavian Federation for Laboratory Animal Science / see Scandinavian Society for Laboratory Animal Science (#19112)
♦ Scandinavian Fellowship for Oral Pathology and Oral Medicine (#19303)

♦ Scandinavian Folk High School in Geneva 19087

Ecole supérieure de folklore nordique à Genève – Nordiske Folkhögskolan i Genève

Rector Genevaskolan, c/o PO Box 522, SE-101 30 Stockholm, Sweden. T. +4686135045. Fax +468215276.
URL: http://www.geneveskolan.org/

History 1931, Geneva (Switzerland), primarily to make the International Labour Organization (ILO) known to young people within the Scandinavian countries. **Structure** Operated by the *Scandinavian Folk High School in Geneva (Switzerland) Association,* whose members are the workers' educational associations in Scandinavia and other national organizations which have assisted the school, and who elect the Board at a triennial meeting. **Finance** Contributions from Scandinavian countries; ILO contributes towards staff salaries.
Members Representatives of bodies in 4 countries:
Denmark, Finland, Norway, Sweden.
IGO Relations Contributing to the work of the school and receiving the triennial report: *ILO (#11123); UNESCO (#20322).* [2019.02.14/XF1820/**F**]

- ♦ Scandinavian Forum for Lipid Research and Technology / see Nordic Forum for Lipid Research and Technology (#17299)
- ♦ Scandinavian Fur Committee (inactive)
- ♦ Scandinavian Glioma Group / see Scandinavian Neuro-Oncology Society (#19092)
- ♦ Scandinavian Glioma Society / see Scandinavian Neuro-Oncology Society (#19092)
- ♦ Scandinavian Golf Union (inactive)

♦ Scandinavian Green Infrastructure Association (SGIA) 19088

Chairperson Ystadvägen 56, SE-214 42 Malmö, Sweden. T. +46723002223. E-mail: info@scandinavian-green-roof.org – helen@greenroof.se.
URL: https://green-roof.org/

History 2001. Former names and other names: *Scandinavian Green Roof Association (SGRA)* – former. **Aims** Show, tell and teach the public about the benefits of green roofs. **Structure** Board. Includes *Scandinavian Green Roof Institute (SGRI)*. **Languages** English. **Staff** 5.00 FTE, paid. **Finance** Sources: members' dues. **Activities** Advocacy/lobbying/activism; awards/prizes/competitions; events/meetings; networking/liaising. **Events** *Building Green in Cities Scandinavian Seminar* Helsinki (Finland) 2016. **Publications** *SGIA Newsletter*. **Members** Platinum; Gold; Silver. Membership countries not specified. **NGO Relations** Member of (2): *European Federation of Green Roof and Wall Associations (EFB, #07135)*; *World Green Infrastructure Network (WGIN, #21545)*. [2020/XM4312/**D**]

- ♦ Scandinavian Green Roof Association / see Scandinavian Green Infrastructure Association (#19088)
- ♦ Scandinavian Hebrew Christian Alliance (inactive)

♦ Scandinavian Herpetological Society 19089

Société nordique d'herpétologie – Nordisk Herpetologisk Forening (NHF)

Pres Smedegårds Alle 41, 8340 Malling, Denmark. T. +4525159105. E-mail: formand@nhf.dk – redaktion@nhf.dk.
URL: http://www.nhf.dk/

History 1944. **Aims** Encourage interest in and knowledge of *amphibians* and *reptiles*. **Structure** Committee of 7 Governors, elected by General Assembly. **Languages** Danish. **Staff** Voluntary work. **Finance** Members' dues. **Events** *Breeding and captive maintenance of reptiles and amphibians* Copenhagen (Denmark) 1997. **Publications** *Meddelelser fra Bestyrelsen* (6 a year) – newsletter; *Nordisk Herpetologisk Forening* (6 a year). **Members** Individuals (about 900) in 8 countries:
Denmark, Germany, Netherlands, Norway, Spain, Sweden, UK, USA. [2019/XD8796/**D**]

- ♦ Scandinavian Human Rights Lawyers (internationally oriented national body)
- ♦ Scandinavian Independent Baptist Union (inactive)
- ♦ Scandinavian Institute of African Studies / see Nordic Africa Institute (#17168)
- ♦ Scandinavian Institute of Asian Studies / see NIAS-Nordisk Institut for Asienstudier (#17132)
- ♦ Scandinavian Institute of Dental Materials / see Nordiska Institutet för Odontologisk Materialprovning (#17485)
- ♦ Scandinavian Institute of Maritime Law (#17515)
- ♦ Scandinavian International Conference on Fluid Power (meeting series)
- ♦ Scandinavian Jewish Youth Federation (no recent information)
- ♦ Scandinavian Lead Association (inactive)
- ♦ Scandinavian Lead Zinc Association (inactive)

♦ Scandinavian-Mediterranean Rail Freight Corridor (ScanMed RFC) . 19090

Registered address c/o ÖBB Infrastruktur AG, Praterstern 4, 1020 Vienna, Austria. E-mail: info@scanmedfreight.eu.
URL: http://www.scanmedfreight.eu/

History 10 Nov 2015. **Aims** Provide better railway services for freight transportation in Europe, so as to attract more goods on rail. **Structure** Executive Board; Management Board; Corridor Team. Working Groups. **Languages** English.
Members Rail infrastructure managers (7) in 6 countries:
Austria, Denmark, Germany, Italy, Norway, Sweden. [2022/XM6878/**F**]

- ♦ Scandinavian Migraine Society (inactive)
- ♦ Scandinavian Monetary Union (inactive)

♦ Scandinavian Network for the Academic Study of Western Esotericism (SNASWE) 19091

Head ToRS – Section Science of Religion, Fac Humanities – Univ of Copenhagen, Office 10-4-13, Karen Blixens Plads 8, 2300 Copenhagen 5, Denmark. T. +4593565623.

History Set up as a regional network of *European Society for the Study of Western Esotericism (ESSWE, #08749)*. [2019.12.11/XM6368/**F**]

- ♦ Scandinavian Neuro-Oncology Group / see Scandinavian Neuro-Oncology Society (#19092)

♦ Scandinavian Neuro-Oncology Society (SNOG) 19092

Pres Radiation Sciences, Oncology, University Hospital, SE-901 85 Umeå, Sweden.

History as *Scandinavian Glioma Group*. Subsequently changed title to *Scandinavian Neuro-Oncology Group (SNOG)*, 1997. Previously also referred to as *Scandinavian Glioma Society*. **Aims** Provide a basis for collaboration and exchange of experiences for all scandinavian scientists and clinicians involved in the struggle against *brain tumours*. **Languages** English. **Events** *Multidisciplinary Neuro-Oncology* Helsinki (Finland) 2022, *Meeting* Trondheim (Norway) 2018, *Meeting* Copenhagen (Denmark) 2016, *Meeting* Stockholm (Sweden) 2014, *Meeting* Helsinki (Finland) 2009.
Members Individuals in 7 countries:
Denmark, Estonia, Finland, Iceland, Latvia, Norway, Sweden. [2014/XD6098/v/**D**]

- ♦ Scandinavian Neuropaediatric Society / see Nordic Neuropediatric Society (#17367)
- ♦ Scandinavian Neuropathological Society / see Scandinavian Society of Neuropathology (#19113)

♦ Scandinavian Neurosurgical Society (SNS) 19093

Société scandinave de neurochirurgie – Nordisk Neurokirurgisk Forening

Pres c/o Dept Neurosurgery, Section 2092, Rigshospitalet, Blegdamsvej 9, 2100 Copenhagen, Denmark. T. +4535452092. Fax +4535346575.
URL: http://snsweb.org/

History 22 Sep 1945, Stockholm (Sweden). **Aims** Promote collaboration between members. **Languages** English. **Staff** 3.50 FTE, voluntary. **Finance** Members' dues. Budget (annual): SEK 200. **Events** *Scandinavian Neurosurgical Congress* Bergen (Norway) 2022, *Scandinavian Neurosurgical Congress* Bergen (Norway) 2021, *Meeting* Stockholm (Sweden) 2019, *Meeting* Copenhagen (Denmark) 2017, *Meeting* Lund (Sweden) 2015.
Members Individuals in 5 countries:
Denmark, Finland, Iceland, Norway, Sweden. [2018/XD3192/v/**D**]

- ♦ Scandinavian Optical Council / see Nordic Optical Council (#17376)
- ♦ Scandinavian Orchestra Directors Union (unconfirmed)
- ♦ Scandinavian Ornithologists Union (inactive)
- ♦ Scandinavian Orthopaedic Association / see Nordic Orthopedic Federation (#17379)

♦ Scandinavian Otolaryngological Society 19094

Société nordique d'oto-laryngologie – Nordisk Oto-Laryngologisk Forening

Pres Dept Otorhinolaryngology Head and Neck Surgery, Sahlgrenska Univ Hosp, Univ of Gothenburg, SE-413 45 Gothenburg, Sweden.
URL: http://www.nordic-ent.org/

History Also referred to as *Nordic Association of Otolaryngology*. Previously referred to in English as *Nordic Oto-Laryngological Society*. **Aims** Represent national associations of Otolaryngology in Scandinavia; support professional collaboration. **Structure** Nordic Board. **Languages** Danish, English, Finnish, Icelandic, Norwegian, Swedish. **Events** *Congress* Reykjavik (Iceland) 2023, *Congress* Reykjavik (Iceland) 2020, *Congress* Gothenburg (Sweden) 2017, *Congress* Copenhagen (Denmark) 2014, *Congress* Helsinki (Finland) 2011.
Members Full in 5 countries:
Denmark, Finland, Iceland, Norway, Sweden. [2015.07.28/XD8082/**D**]

♦ Scandinavian Packaging Association 19095

Association scandinave de l'emballage

Contact Teknologisk Inst, Emballage og Transport, Gregersensvej 5, 2630 Taastrup, Denmark. T. +4572203150. E-mail: bbi@teknologisk.dk.
URL: http://www.scanstar.org/

History 1953. Also referred to as *Nordic Packaging Association*. Previously also referred to as *Samarbetsorganisationen for Emballagefragor i Skandinavien (SES)*. **Aims** Coordinate between the national packaging organizations. **Structure** Rotating Chairmanship (every 2 years). **Languages** Danish, Norwegian, Swedish. **Staff** Voluntary. **Activities** Organizes Scanstar Packaging Competition. **Events** *EEC and its packaging directive* Norway 1993.
Members National associations, representing over 1,100 companies, in 5 countries:
Denmark, Finland, Iceland, Norway, Sweden.
IGO Relations *International Trade Centre (ITC, #15703)*. **NGO Relations** Regional federation of: *World Packaging Organisation (WPO, #21705)*. [2014/XD1160/**D**]

- ♦ Scandinavian Paint and Printing Ink Research Institute (inactive)
- ♦ Scandinavian Paper History Association / see Association of Nordic Paper Historians (#02831)
- ♦ Scandinavian Paper Industry Workers Associations Joint Committee (inactive)
- ♦ Scandinavian Patent Committee (inactive)

♦ Scandinavian Petroleum Technic Association (SPT Association) ... 19096

Contact Mailbox 2453, SE-111 75 Stockholm, Sweden. T. +46705326000. Fax +46703327477. E-mail: spt@sptass.eu.
URL: http://www.sptass.eu/

History Founded 1973, as 'Sveriges Mätare-entreprenörers Riksförbund' – 'National Organization of Fuelmeter Contractors'. Changed title to *Skandinaviska Mätarservicefirmors Förbund – Scandinavian Union of Meter Service Firms*. Current title adopted 1997. **Aims** Handle industry-specific issues and represent the industry as a whole in contact with both authorities and other organizations. **Activities** Training/education; events/meetings. **Events** *Annual Meeting and Congress* Alicante (Spain) 2019, *Conference* Stockholm (Sweden) 2018.
Members Businesses in 3 countries:
Denmark, Norway, Sweden. [2019/XM8329/**D**]

♦ Scandinavian Physiological Society (SPS) 19097

Société scandinave de physiologie – Nordisk Förening för Fysiologi

SG Dept of Veterinary Biosciences, Univ of Helsinki, Agnes Sjöberginkatu 2, FI-00014 Helsinki, Finland. T. +358505986995.
Admin Coordinator Neuroscience Center, Cultivator II Viikinkaari 4, PO Box 56, FI-00014 Helsinki, Finland.
URL: http://www.scandphys.org/

History 15 Apr 1925, Lund (Sweden). **Aims** Stimulate Scandinavian research in physiology. **Structure** General Assembly (every 2 years); Board. **Languages** English. **Staff** 1.00 FTE, paid; 1.50 FTE, voluntary. **Finance** Members' dues. Journal subscriptions. **Activities** Events/meetings. **Events** *Physiology in Focus Joint Meeting* Tallinn (Estonia) 2023, *Biennial Joint Meeting* Copenhagen (Denmark) 2022, *Ordinary Meeting* Stockholm (Sweden) 2021, *Extraordinary General Assembly* Helsinki (Finland) 2020, *General Assembly* Helsinki (Finland) 2020. **Publications** *Acta Physiologica* (12 a year).
Members Scientists (about 900) working in physiology and related fields in 5 countries:
Denmark, Finland, Iceland, Norway, Sweden.
NGO Relations Regional member of: *International Union of Physiological Sciences (IUPS, #15800)*. [2016.12.15/XD0225/v/**D**]

- ♦ Scandinavian Plant Physiology Society (#19452)
- ♦ Scandinavian Radiological Society / see Nordic Society of Medical Radiology (#17418)

♦ Scandinavian Reliability Engineers (SRE) 19098

Treas Inst for energiteknikk, PO Box 173, 1751 Halden, Norway. T. +4769212395. Fax +4769212440.

History 1980, as the Scandinavian chapter of American Society of Reliability Engineers. Independent since 1994. Statutes adopted at General Assembly of 25 May 1981; most recently amended 29 May 2001. **Aims** Serve as an interest foundation within the subject of reliability, safety and quality; develop and communicate different methods and tools within dependability and safety and promote their adaptation and development in practice; facilitate personal development through exchange of experience. **Structure** General Assembly (annual). Board, comprising President, Vice-President, Treasurer and 4 country representatives/contacts. **Languages** English. **Staff** None. **Finance** Members' dues. **Activities** Organizes joint symposia and seminars. **Events** *Annual meeting* Fredrikstad (Norway) 2005, *Annual meeting* Fredrikstad (Norway) 2005, *Annual meeting* Malmö (Sweden) 2004, *Annual meeting* Helsinki (Finland) 2003, *Annual meeting* Oslo (Norway) 2002. **Publications** *SCANNER* (1-4 a year). Annual Report.
Members Individuals (about 120) in 4 countries:
Denmark, Finland, Norway, Sweden. [2009.06.01/XD9242/v/**D**]

- ♦ Scandinavian Research Council for Criminology (#17493)
- ♦ Scandinavian Sarcoidosis Association (inactive)

♦ Scandinavian Sarcoma Group (SSG) 19099

Coordinator SSG Secretariat, Kamprad – 5th floor, Barngatan 4, SE-221 85 Lund, Sweden. T. +46768871408. E-mail: ssg@med.lu.se.
Chairman Karolinska Institute, Karolinska Vägen 37A, Solna, SE-171 76 Stockholm, Sweden.
URL: http://www.ssg-org.net/

History 3 Nov 1979, Oslo (Norway). **Aims** Uphold and improve the quality of *diagnostics*, treatment and *care* of sarcoma patients by sharing information and education, clinical studies and patient registers. **Structure** General Assembly (annual); Board; Subcommittees (8); Secretariat in Lund (Sweden). **Languages** Danish, English, Faroese, Icelandic, Norwegian, Swedish. **Finance** Sources: donations; government support. Support from national cancer foundations. Supported by: *Nordic Council (NC, #17256)*. Annual budget: 2,000,000 SEK. **Events** *Meeting* Tampere (Finland) 2022, *Meeting* Bergen (Norway) 2019, *Meeting* Aarhus (Denmark) 2017, *Meeting* Stockholm (Sweden) 2015, *Meeting* Helsinki (Finland) 2013.
Members Active in 5 countries:
Denmark, Finland, Iceland, Norway, Sweden. [2022.05.04/XJ4176/**E**]

- ♦ Scandinavian Seminar on Translational Pathology (meeting series)
- ♦ Scandinavian Shipbuilding Committee (inactive)

♦ Scandinavian Simulation Society (SIMS) 19100

Coordinator MathCore Engineering AB, Teknikringen 1F, SE-583 30 Linköping, Sweden. T. +46705281629.
Chairperson Environmental Engineering, PO Box 4300, Univ of Oulu, FI-90014 Oulu, Finland.
URL: http://www.scansims.org/

History 1958, Sweden. 1958, Västeras (Sweden), as *Scandinavian Analogue Computer Society – Skandinaviska Analoggimaskinsälskabet (SAMS)*. Activities enlarged to simulation in general and present name adopted May 1968. Formally organized with Constitution, 30 May – 1 Jun 1983, Odense (Denmark). New Bylaws adopted 19 Sep 2000. **Aims** Enhance knowledge of methods and application at numerical simulation in general; stimulate use of simulation and exchange of experience and ideas in the field. **Structure** Meeting (annual); Steering Committee (Board of Directors). **Languages** English. **Staff** 8.00 FTE, voluntary. **Finance** Members' dues. **Activities** Events/meetings; publishing activities; networking/liaising. **Events** *Annual Conference* Oulu (Finland) 2021, *Annual Conference* Oulu (Finland) 2020, *Annual Conference* Västerås (Sweden) 2019, *Annual Conference* Oslo (Norway) 2018, *Annual Conference* Reykjavik (Iceland) 2017. **Publications** Proceedings – paper and electronic; report series; handbook; pamphlets.
Members Individuals (180) and organizations in 5 countries:
Denmark, Finland, Iceland, Norway, Sweden.
NGO Relations *Society for Modeling Simulation International (SCSI, #19598)* and its: *European Council for Modelling and Simulation (ECMS, #06831)*. Member of: *Federation of European Simulation Societies (EUROSIM, #09544)*; *Integrated Spatial Potential Initiative for Renewables in Europe (INSPIRE, #11370)*. Cooperation agreement with: *International Association for Mathematics and Computers in Simulation (IMACS, #12019)*. [2016.06.01/XD3197/**D**]

♦ Scandinavian Society of Anaesthesiologists / see Scandinavian Society of Anaesthesiology and Intensive Care Medicine (#19101)

♦ Scandinavian Society of Anaesthesiology and Intensive Care Medicine (SSAI) 19101

Contact c/o HUS, PO Box 447, HUS, FI-00029 Helsinki, Finland.
URL: http://www.ssai.info/

History 25 Aug 1950, Oslo (Norway). Statutes amended: 1952, Stockholm (Sweden); 1954, Copenhagen (Denmark); 1958, Gausdal (Norway); 1966, Copenhagen; 1971, Lund (Sweden); 1977, Uppsala (Sweden); 2017, Malmö (Sweden). Former names and other names: *Scandinavian Society of Anaesthesiologists* – former (25 Aug 1950); *Société scandinave des anesthésistes* – former (25 Aug 1950); *Sociedad Escandinava de Anestesistas* – former (25 Aug 1950); *Skandinavische Gesellschaft für Anästhesiologie* – former (25 Aug 1950); *Nordisk Anästesiologisk Forening* – former (25 Aug 1950). **Aims** Work for scientific development of anaesthesiology in the Nordic countries and promote collaboration among Scandinavian anaesthesiologists. **Structure** General Assembly (every 2 years); Board; Subcommittees. **Languages** English. **Finance** Members' dues. **Activities** Events/meetings; training/education; standards/guidelines. **Events** *Congress* Oulu (Finland) 2024, *Congress* Oslo (Norway) 2022, *Congress* Oslo (Norway) 2021, *Biennial Congress* Copenhagen (Denmark) 2019, *Biennial Congress* Malmö (Sweden) 2017. **Publications** *Acta Anaesthesiologica Scandinavica* (10 a year) in English. Supplements; congress proceedings; position papers.
Members Full; Associate; Honorary. Individuals and organizations in 5 countries:
Denmark, Finland, Iceland, Norway, Sweden. [2021/XD3200/v/D]

♦ Scandinavian Society for Antimicrobial Chemotherapy / see Nordic Society for Clinical Microbiology and Infectious Diseases (#17413)

♦ Scandinavian Society for Atherosclerosis Research (SSAR) 19102

Skandinavisk Förening för Atero-sklerosforskning
Chair Dept of Clinical Biochemistry, Herlev and Gentofte Hospital, 2730 Herlev, Denmark.
URL: http://www.ssar.dk/

History 1994. **Aims** Promote atherosclerosis research with special emphasis on Scandinavian as well as international collaboration. **Structure** General Meeting (annual); Council. **Languages** English. **Staff** Voluntary. **Activities** Events/meetings. **Events** *Scandinavian Atherosclerosis Conference* Humlebaek (Denmark) 2022, *Annual Conference* Humlebaek (Denmark) 2019, *Annual Conference* Humlebaek (Denmark) 2018, *Annual Conference* Humlebaek (Denmark) 2017, *Annual Conference* Humlebaek (Denmark) 2016.
Members Atherosclerosis researchers and clinicians in 5 countries:
Denmark, Finland, Iceland, Norway, Sweden.
NGO Relations Member of (1): *International Atherosclerosis Society (IAS, #12288).* [2022/XD3832/D]

♦ Scandinavian Society for Biomaterials (ScSB) 19103

Address not obtained.
URL: http://scsb.snappages.com/

History May 2008. **Aims** Promote cross-fertilization of biomaterials research in Scandinavia, Iceland and the Baltic states. **Structure** Board. **Activities** Meeting activities; awards/prizes/competitions. **Events** *Annual Conference* Jurmala (Latvia) 2022, *Annual Conference* 2021, *Annual Conference* Jurmala (Latvia) 2020, *Annual Conference* Kirkkonummi (Finland) 2019, *Annual Conference* Fiskebäckskil (Sweden) 2018. [2017/XJ8358/D]

♦ Scandinavian Society of Cataract and Refractive Surgery (no recent information)
♦ Scandinavian Society for Cell Toxicology (inactive)
♦ Scandinavian Society for Cerebrovascular Diseases / see Nordic Stroke Society (#17439)
♦ Scandinavian Society of Clinical Chemistry / see Nordisk Förening för Klinisk Kemi (#17507)

♦ Scandinavian Society of Clinical Physiology and Nuclear Medicine (SSCPNM) 19104

Sec-Treas BFC/Clinical Physiology, Lund Univ Hospital, SE-221 85 Lund, Sweden.
Chair Clinical Physiology, Nuclear Medicine, Rigshospitalet, 2100 Copenhagen, Denmark.
URL: http://www.sscpnm.com/

History 1981, Copenhagen (Denmark). Sometimes also referred to as *Nordic Association for Clinical Physiology – Nordisk Förening för Klinisk Fysiologi* and as *Nordiska Sällskapet för Klinisk Fysiologi.* Previously referred to as *Scandinavian Association of Clinical Physiology – Skandinaviska Sällskapet för Klinisk Fysiologi.* **Aims** Promote clinical physiological methods and thinking; facilitate communications between Scandinavian countries. **Structure** Board. **Languages** English. **Activities** Coordinates clinical physiological and nuclear medicine methods in Scandinavian countries; organizes scientific meetings. **Events** *Biennial Congress* Copenhagen (Denmark) 2011, *Biennial Congress* Lillehammer (Norway) 2008, *Biennial Congress* Lund (Sweden) 2005, *Biennial Congress* Aarhus (Denmark) 2001, *Biennial Congress* Helsinki (Finland) 1998. **Publications** *Clinical Physiology and Functional Imaging* (6 a year).
Members National clinical physiological and/or nuclear medicine societies in 4 countries:
Denmark, Finland, Norway, Sweden. [2013.11.25/XD1678/D]

♦ Scandinavian Society of Cosmetic Chemists (SCANCOS) 19105

Chairman c/o Kosmolet A/S, Hvedemarken 12, 3520 Farum, Denmark. E-mail: info@scancos.com.
URL: http://www.scancos.com/

History Founded 1966. **Aims** Advance knowledge of cosmetic science and technology and associated areas; encourage dissemination of this knowledge. **Structure** Board. **Languages** English. **Staff** Voluntary. **Finance** Members' dues. **Events** *Annual Meeting* Stockholm (Sweden) 2021, *Annual Meeting* Oslo (Norway) 2019, *Annual Meeting* Stockholm (Sweden) 2018, *Annual Meeting* Copenhagen (Denmark) 2017, *Annual Meeting* Stockholm (Sweden) 2016.
Members Full in 4 countries:
Denmark, Finland, Norway, Sweden.
NGO Relations Member of: *International Federation of Societies of Cosmetic Chemists (IFSCC, #13545).* [2018.11.30/XJ8314/D]

♦ Scandinavian Society for Economic and Social History (SSESH) 19106

Société scandinave d'histoire économique et sociale
Pres address not obtained.
URL: https://sites.google.com/view/ssesh/home

History 1952. Former names and other names: *Scandinavian Society for Economic and Social History and Historical Geography* – alias. **Structure** Council, consisting of President, 3 Vice-Presidents and other Members. **Events** *Annual Conference* Gothenburg (Sweden) 2021, *Conference* Odense (Denmark) 2020. **Publications** *The Scandinavian Economic History Review* (3 a year).
Members Full in 5 countries:
Denmark, Finland, Iceland, Norway, Sweden. [2021/XD3906/D]

♦ Scandinavian Society for Economic and Social History and Historical Geography / see Scandinavian Society for Economic and Social History (#19106)
♦ Scandinavian Society for Electron Microscopy / see Nordic Microscopy Society (#17344)
♦ Scandinavian Society of Experimental Cardiothoracic Surgery / see Scandinavian Society for Research in Cardiothoracic Surgery (#19117)

♦ Scandinavian Society for Extracorporeal Technology (SCANSECT) 19107

Gen Sec Dept of Perfusion, Depy of Thorasic Anaesthesiology, Univ Hosp of Copenhagen, Rigshospitalet afd.3044, Blegdamsvej 9, 2100 Copenhagen, Denmark. T. +4528499556.
Sec address not obtained.
URL: http://www.scansect.org/

History 29 Aug 1980, Oslo (Norway). **Aims** Group Scandinavian *perfusionists.* **Structure** General Assembly (annual); Board. Committees (2): Scientific; Education. **Languages** English. **Staff** 4 voluntary (Board members). **Finance** Sources: members' dues; sponsorship. **Activities** Events/meetings; research/documentation; training/education. **Events** *Joint Scandinavian Conference in Cardiothoracic Surgery* Helsinki (Finland) 2022, *Joint Scandinavian Conference in Cardiothoracic Surgery* Bergen (Norway) 2021, *Joint Scandinavian Conference in Cardiothoracic Surgery* Bergen (Norway) 2020, *Joint Scandinavian Conference in Cardiothoracic Surgery* Stockholm (Sweden) 2019, *Joint Scandinavian Conference in Cardiothoracic Surgery* Copenhagen (Denmark) 2018. **Publications** *ScanMag* (3 a year).
Members National perfusionist organizations in 4 countries:
Denmark, Iceland, Norway, Sweden. [2021.02.24/XD4542/D]

♦ Scandinavian Society of Forensic Medicine (inactive)

♦ Scandinavian Society of Forest Economics (SSFE) 19108

Nordiska Skogsekonomers Förening
Chair Univ of Copenhagen, Rolighedsvej 25, 1958 Frederiksberg C, Denmark. T. +4535331700. E-mail: bjt@ifro.ku.dk.
URL: https://www.ssfe-network.org/

History 1958. Former names and other names: *Nordic Forest Economics Seminar* – former; *Nordisk Skogökonomisk Seminar* – former. **Aims** Promote cooperation between forest economists of Scandinavian countries and outreach to forest economists around Europe and beyond. **Structure** Board; Working Groups. **Languages** English. **Staff** None. **Finance** Each participant provides own budget. **Activities** Events/meetings; knowledge management/information dissemination; networking/liaising. **Events** *Biennial Meeting* Asikkala (Finland) 2020, *Biennial Meeting* Helsingør (Denmark) 2018, *Biennial Meeting* Drøbak (Norway) 2016, *Biennial Meeting* Uppsala (Sweden) 2014, *Biennial Meeting* Hyytiälä (Finland) 2012. **Publications** Group reports; proceedings of biennial meetings.
Members Full in 4 countries:
Denmark, Finland, Norway, Sweden. [2021.06.08/XD0277/D]

♦ Scandinavian Society for Genito-Urinary Medicine (inactive)
♦ Scandinavian Society of Glass Technology (inactive)

♦ Scandinavian Society for Head and Neck Oncology (SSHNO) 19109

Pres Dept Otorhinolaryngology – Head and Neck Surgery, Helsinki Univ Hosp, Yliopistonkatu 4, FI-00100 Helsinki, Finland. E-mail: mail@sshno.org.
URL: http://www.sshno.org/

History 1988, Stockholm (Sweden). **Aims** Encourage scientific collaboration regarding *cancer* in the head and neck region; gain knowledge about ongoing projects in the different countries both clinically and concerning research activities. **Structure** Board. **Languages** Danish, English, Faroese, Icelandic, Norwegian, Swedish. **Staff** None. **Finance** Members' dues. Exhibition fees at conferences. **Activities** Research and development; networking/liaising. **Events** *SSHNO Meeting* Aarhus (Denmark) 2022, *SSHNO Meeting* Oslo (Norway) 2021, *SSHNO Meeting* Oslo (Norway) 2020, *SSHNO Meeting* Kuopio (Finland) 2018, *SSHNO Meeting* Reykjavik (Iceland) 2016. **Publications** *Clinical Otolaryngology.* Meeting abstracts.
Members Individuals (mainly radiotherapists and otolaryngologists-head and neck surgeons, also plastic and oral surgeons and head and neck interested pathologists – about 220) in 5 countries:
Denmark, Finland, Iceland, Norway, Sweden.
NGO Relations Member of: *European Head and Neck Society (EHNS, #07452); International Federation of Head and Neck Oncologic Societies (IFHNOS, #13438).* [2021/XD2010/v/D]

♦ Scandinavian Society for the History of Medicine (no recent information)

♦ Scandinavian Society for Immunology (SSI) 19110

Association scandinave d'immunologie
Sec address not obtained.
Pres address not obtained.
URL: http://www.scandinavianimmunology.nu/

History 1970, Aarhus (Denmark). **Aims** Advance knowledge of immunology within Scandinavian countries. **Structure** Council. **Languages** English. **Staff** 3.00 FTE, paid. **Finance** Members' dues. Annual budget: euro 15,000. **Activities** Events/meetings. **Events** *Annual Meeting* Reykjavik (Iceland) 2022, *Annual Meeting* Aarhus (Denmark) 2021, *Annual Meeting* Aarhus (Denmark) 2020, *Annual Meeting* Geilo (Norway) 2019, *Annual Meeting* Stockholm (Sweden) 2017. **Publications** *Scandinavian Journal of Immunology* – 12 issues forming 2 vols per year; *The Immunologists.*
Members National Societies in 5 countries:
Denmark, Finland, Iceland, Norway, Sweden.
Individuals in 1 country:
USA.
NGO Relations Member of: *International Union of Immunological Societies (IUIS, #15781).* [2022/XD8232/D]

♦ Scandinavian Society for Jewish Studies 19111

Chairman Lund University, Room 327, PO Box 117, SE-221 00 Lund, Sweden. T. +462229041. Fax +462224426. E-mail: hanne.tk@teol.lu.se.

History 1975. **Finance** Members' dues. **Events** *Congress* Oslo (Norway) 2007, *Congress* Oslo (Norway) 2003, *Annual Meeting* Stockholm (Sweden) 1999. **Publications** *Nordisk Judaistik* (annual). [2010/XE3659/E]

♦ Scandinavian Society for Laboratory Animal Science (Scand-LAS) 19112

Société scandinave pour les animaux de laboratoires
Secretariat Karolinska Inst, Dept of Dental Medicine, Box 4064, SE-141 04 Huddinge, Sweden. E-mail: secretary@scandlas.org.
URL: http://www.scandlas.org/

History 16 Feb 1970, Gothenburg (Sweden). Constitution and bylaws adopted 1971, Uppsala (Sweden); most recently revised Apr 2018. Former names and other names: *Scandinavian Federation for Laboratory Animal Science* – former; *Fédération scandinave pour les animaux de laboratoires* – former. **Aims** Further the progress of Laboratory Animal Science (LAS) in the Scandinavian countries, where LAS is defined as the scientific, ethical and legal use of animals in biomedical research. **Structure** General Assembly (annual); Governing Board. **Languages** English. **Staff** Voluntary. **Finance** Sources: members' dues. **Activities** Events/meetings; healthcare; monitoring/evaluation; politics/policy/regulatory; training/education. **Events** *Scand-LAS Symposium* Uppsala (Sweden) 2023, *Annual Assembly* Tallinn (Estonia) 2021, *Annual Assembly* Tallinn (Estonia) 2020, *Annual Assembly* Prague (Czechia) 2019, *Annual Assembly* Kristiansand (Norway) 2018. **Publications** *Scandinavian Journal of Laboratory Animal Science* (4 a year). Annual Report; training handbooks; success stories; reports; newsletter; media contributions.
Members Individuals in 13 countries:
Austria, Denmark, Estonia, Finland, France, Germany, Greece, Iceland, Netherlands, Norway, Sweden, Switzerland, UK.
NGO Relations Member of (2): *Federation of European Laboratory Animal Science Associations (FELASA, #09509); International Council for Laboratory Animal Science (ICLAS, #13039).* [2023.02.26/XD4623/v/D]

♦ Scandinavian Society for Laser Therapy (no recent information)
♦ Scandinavian Society of Mammography (inactive)
♦ Scandinavian Society for Military Medicine (no recent information)
♦ Scandinavian Society of Nephrology / see Nordic Society of Nephrology (#17420)
♦ Scandinavian Society of Neuroanaesthesiologists (inactive)

♦ Scandinavian Society of Neuropathology 19113

Sec KI-Alzheimer Disease, Dept NVS, Novum floor 5, SE-141 86 Stockholm, Sweden.
URL: http://s-n-s.org/

History 23 Jan 1965, Copenhagen (Denmark). Also referred to as *Scandinavian Neuropathological Society (SNS).* **Aims** Promote neuropathology in the Nordic countries. **Languages** English. **Staff** Voluntary. **Finance** Members' dues. **Events** *European Congress of Neuropathology* Odense (Denmark) 2021, *European Congress of Neuropathology* Odense (Denmark) 2020, *Annual Meeting* Oslo (Norway) 2019, *Annual Meeting* Svolvaer (Norway) 2017, *Annual Meeting* Copenhagen (Denmark) 2014.
Members Individuals (60) in 5 countries:
Denmark, Finland, Iceland, Norway, Sweden.
NGO Relations Member of: *European Confederation of Neuropathological Societies (Euro-CNS, #06715).* [2013/XD5704/v/D]

♦ Scandinavian Society of Obstetricians and Gynaecologists / see Nordic Federation of Societies of Obstetrics and Gynaecology (#17286)
♦ Scandinavian Society for Oral Pathology and Oral Medicine / see Skandinavisk Förening för Oral Patologi och Oral Medicin (#19303)

♦ **Scandinavian Society of Periodontology (ScSP)** 19114
Association scandinave de parodontologie – Skandinavisk Forening for Parodontologi
Gen Sec address not obtained.
URL: https://www.scsp.info/
History 22 Apr 1972, Gothenburg (Sweden). **Aims** Promote learning and education in the understanding and treatment of periodontal health. **Structure** General Assembly. Executive Board, consisting of President, 1st Vice-President, 2nd Vice-President, Past-President, Treasurer and General Secretary. **Languages** English. **Staff** 1.00 FTE, voluntary. **Finance** Members' dues. **Events** *Congress* Thórshavn (Faeroe Is) 2022, *Congress* Longyearbyen (Norway) 2019, *Congress* Mariehamn (Finland) 2017, *Annual Meeting* Copenhagen (Denmark) 2013, *Congress* Bergen (Norway) 2011. **Publications** *Scandinavian Society of Periodontology Newsletter* (2 a year) in English.
Members Individuals in 21 countries:
Brazil, Colombia, Denmark, Finland, France, Germany, Greece, Hong Kong, Iceland, Italy, Japan, Korea Rep, Kuwait, Netherlands, Norway, Philippines, Portugal, Romania, Saudi Arabia, Sweden, USA. [2021/XD1430/D]

♦ **Scandinavian Society for Prehistoric Art (SSfPA)** 19115
Chairman c/o Underslös Rock Art Museum – Tanum, Tanums Hällristningsmuseum, Underslös, SE-457 91 Tanumshede, Sweden. T. +4523204331. E-mail: admin@rockartscandinavia.com – rockcaredenmark@mail.tele.dk.
URL: http://www.rockartscandinavia.com/
History 1952. **Aims** Focus on archeology, rock carvings, cultural heritage and digital documentation, with links to humanities, more specific digital humanities and art sciences, as well as other scientific disciplines. **Structure** Board of Directors. **Languages** Danish, English, German, Norwegian, Swedish. **Staff** 5.00 FTE, voluntary. **Finance** Sources: members' dues. **Activities** Events/meetings; networking/liaising; research and development; research/documentation; training/education. Active in all member countries. **Events** *Documenting the Past for the Future World Heritage area in Tanum* Tanumshede (Sweden) 2023, *Seminar* Tanumshede (Sweden) 2020, *Seminar* Tanumshede (Sweden) 2007. **Publications** *Adoranten* (annual) – Peer reviewed magazine; *Documentation and Registration of Rock Art in Tanum World Heritage Vol 1 – 4* in English – Gothenburg University Department of Historical Studies GOTARC, Series C. Arkeologiska Skrifter. *Prehistoric Pictures as Archaeological Source* (2004).
Members Organizations and individuals. Members in 28 countries:
Argentina, Australia, Austria, Belgium, Bolivia, Chile, China, Colombia, Czechia, Denmark, Estonia, Finland, France, Germany, Greece, Italy, Mexico, Netherlands, Norway, Poland, Portugal, Russia, Slovakia, Spain, Sweden, Switzerland, UK, USA. [2022.10.18/XD9280/D]

♦ **Scandinavian Society for Prosthetic Dentistry (SSPD)** 19116
Sec Malmö Högskola, Odontologiska Fakulteten, Carl Gustafs väg 34, SE-205 06 Malmö, Sweden. T. +4589424082.
URL: http://www.sspd.no/
History Founded 1972, by representatives from the prosthodontic departments of the dental schools in the five Nordic countries. **Aims** Promote scientific activity and advance knowledge of prosthetic dentistry within the Nordic countries. **Structure** Annual Meeting; Board; Educational Committee. **Events** *Annual Meeting* Aarhus (Denmark) 2022, *Annual Meeting* Oslo (Norway) 2021, *Annual Meeting* Gothenburg (Sweden) 2020, *Annual Meeting* Mariehamn (Finland) 2019, *Annual Meeting* Reykjavik (Iceland) 2018.
Members Full in 5 countries:
Denmark, Finland, Iceland, Norway, Sweden. [2015.01.05/XD2414/D]

♦ Scandinavian Society for Psychopharmacology / see Scandinavian College of Neuropsychopharmacology (#19082)

♦ **Scandinavian Society for Research in Cardiothoracic Surgery (SSRCTS)** 19117
Main Office Cardiothoracic Surgery, Landspitali Univ Hosp, University Hospital, 8200 Aarhus, Denmark. E-mail: ssrcts@gmail.com.
URL: https://ssrctsnordic.com/
History 1991. Founded within *Scandinavian Association for Thoracic Surgery (SATS, #19079)*. Former names and other names: *Scandinavian Society of Experimental Cardiothoracic Surgery* – former (1991 to 2001). **Aims** Exchange knowledge about ongoing cardiothoracic research in the Scandinavian countries. **Structure** Board of 3. **Languages** English. **Staff** None. **Finance** Sponsored by manufacturing companies. **Activities** Annual meeting always held at Geilo (Norway). **Events** *Annual Meeting* Geilo (Norway) 2022, *Annual Meeting* Geilo (Norway) 2017, *Annual Meeting* Geilo (Norway) 2015, *Annual Meeting* Geilo (Norway) 2013, *Annual Meeting* Geilo (Norway) 2012. **Publications** None.
Members Full in 5 countries:
Denmark, Finland, Iceland, Norway, Sweden. [2021/XJ4366/E]

♦ **Scandinavian Society for Rheumatology** 19118
Contact c/o Scandivavian Journal of Rheumatology, Lund University, 5th floor, Jan Waldenstrom gata 15, SE-20502 Malmö, Sweden. E-mail: scandjrheumatol@editorialoffice.se.
Pres Rheumatology Unit, Karolinska Hospital, Solna, SE-171 76 Stockholm, Sweden.
Journal: https://www.tandfonline.com/toc/irhe20/current
History 1946, Copenhagen (Denmark). Has been referred to as *Nordisk Reumatismekomite*. **Aims** Strengthen development of rheumatology in Scandinavia and facilitate cooperation among Scandinavian countries. **Structure** Board, comprising Chairman and Scientific Secretary of each Scandinavian country, chaired by Chairman of society organizing next congress. *Scandinavian Rheumatology Research Foundation (no recent information)* is the foundation of the society. **Languages** English. **Staff** None. **Events** *Scandinavian Congress of Rheumatology* Copenhagen (Denmark) 2023, *Scandinavian Congress of Rheumatology* Ålesund (Norway) 2021, *Scandinavian Congress of Rheumatology* Ålesund (Norway) 2020, *Scandinavian Congress of Rheumatology* Helsinki (Finland) 2018, *Scandinavian Congress of Rheumatology* Reykjavik (Iceland) 2016. **Publications** *Scandinavian Journal of Rheumatology*.
Members National organizations in 5 countries:
Denmark, Finland, Iceland, Norway, Sweden. [2022/XD2270/D]

♦ **Scandinavian Society for the Study of Diabetes (SSSD)** 19119
Société scandinave pour l'étude du diabète
Chairman NTNU Medicine-Health Sci, Public Health-Nursing, Postboks 8905, 7491 Trondheim, Norway.
URL: https://www.scandinaviandiabetes.org/
History 1965. **Aims** Promote diabetes research. **Languages** English. **Staff** 4.00 FTE, voluntary. **Finance** Members' dues. Sponsoring from companies. Budget (annual): pounds50,000. **Activities** Exchange of scientific information concerning diabetes during an annual meeting. **Events** *Annual Meeting* Reykjavik (Iceland) 2022, *Annual Meeting* 2021, *Annual Meeting* Trondheim (Norway) 2020, *Annual Meeting* Stockholm (Sweden) 2019, *Annual Meeting* Turku (Finland) 2018.
Members Active scientists involved in diabetes research. Individuals (550), mainly in the 4 Nordic countries but in a total of 10 countries:
Estonia, Finland, Germany, Iceland, Latvia, Lithuania, Norway, Russia, Sweden, UK. [2021/XD3199/v/D]

♦ **Scandinavian Society for Surgery of the Hand** 19120
Skandinavisk Handkirurgiska Föreningen
Contact address not obtained.
URL: http://sssh.site/
History 28 Jun 1951, as *Nordisk Klubb i Handkirurgi*, within the framework of *International Federation of Societies for Surgery of the Hand (IFSSH, #13551)*. 1973, present name adopted. **Structure** Meeting (every 2 years). Council, consisting of 5 members, from each Scandinavian country. Officers: Chairman, Secretary. **Finance** Members' dues: Swedish Kr 100. Also surplus from annual meetings. Budget (annual): about US$ 4,000. **Events** *Conference* Malmö (Sweden) 2021, *Biennial Conference* Tallinn (Estonia) 2019, *Biennial Conference* Levi (Finland) 2016, *Biennial Conference* Bergen (Norway) 2014, *Biennial Conference* Copenhagen (Denmark) 2012.
Members Full in 5 countries:
Denmark, Finland, Iceland, Norway, Sweden. [2021/XE0078/E]

♦ Scandinavian Society of Transport Engineering (inactive)

♦ **Scandinavian Society for Trenchless Technology (SSTT)** 19121
Contact Box 22307, SE-104 22 Stockholm, Sweden. T. +46850893800. E-mail: kontakt@sstt.se.
URL: http://www.sstt.se/
History 27 Oct 1989. **Events** *Annual Meeting* 2020, *Annual Meeting* Oslo (Norway) 2018, *Annual Meeting* Copenhagen (Denmark) 2014, *Annual meeting* Bergen (Norway) 2010, *Conference* Copenhagen (Denmark) 2002.
Members Individuals; Organizations. Members in 2 countries:
Norway, Sweden.
NGO Relations Member of: *International Society for Trenchless Technology (ISTT, #15520)*. [2019.07.01/XD4490/D]

♦ Scandinavian Society for Veterinary Pathology / see Nordic Society for Veterinary Pathology (#17432)
♦ Scandinavian Sociological Association / see Nordic Sociological Association (#17433)
♦ Scandinavian Sports Medicine Congress (meeting series)

♦ **Scandinavian Surgical Society (SSS)** 19122
Société nordique de chirurgie – Nordisk Kirurgisk Förening
Contact Finnish Society of Surgery, PL49, FI-00501 Helsinki, Finland. T. +35893930768. Fax +35893930835. E-mail: toimisto@kirurgiyhdistys.fi.
History 1893. Has also been referred to in English as *Nordic Surgical Society*. **Aims** Support the development within the field of general surgery and surgical science in all the five Nordic countries. **Structure** Board, consisting of 1 member from each country. President; Secretary General; Chairmen from 5 sections. **Languages** Danish, English, Faroese, Icelandic, Norwegian, Swedish. **Staff** Voluntary. **Activities** Annual symposium. **Events** *Breast cancer symposium / Biennial Congress* Skodsborg (Denmark) 2003, *Biennial Congress* Malmö (Sweden) 2001, *Biennial Congress* Turku (Finland) 1999, *Biennial Congress* Tromsø (Norway) 1997, *Meeting* Tromsø (Norway) 1996. **Publications** Information on congresses and courses published in 'Scandinavian Journal of Surgery'.
Members Individual surgeons (4,321) in 5 countries:
Denmark, Finland, Iceland, Norway, Sweden. [2014/XD5237/D]

♦ Scandinavian Symposium on Chemometrics (meeting series)
♦ Scandinavian Symposium on Physical Acoustics (meeting series)
♦ Scandinavian Teachers Peace Association (inactive)

♦ **Scandinavian Technical Analysts Federation (STAF)** 19123
Skandinaviens Tekniska Analytikers Förening
Sec address not obtained. E-mail: info@staf.nu.
URL: http://www.staf.nu/
History 1985. **NGO Relations** Member of: *International Federation of Technical Analysts (IFTA, #13566)*. [2015/XM1871/D]

♦ Scandinavian Telegraph and Telephone Federation (inactive)
♦ Scandinavian Textile Retailers Union (inactive)
♦ Scandinavian Theatre Laboratory (internationally oriented national body)

♦ **Scandinavian Tire and Rim Organization (STRO)** 19124
Contact Rådhusgatan 15, SE-742 42 Öregrund, Sweden. T. +4617330273 – +46173(46705284272. E-mail: info@stro.se.
URL: http://www.stronordic.com/
History Founded 1960, a Nordic organization having been set up 1960, Halmstad (Sweden). **Aims** Prepare technical norms for tyres for the Nordic countries based on national, European and international norms; provide information about tyres to authorities, media and the public. **Structure** Board; General Secretary. **Languages** Danish, English, Finnish, Norwegian, Swedish. **Staff** 1.00 FTE, paid. **Finance** Members' dues. Annual budget: about euro 200,000. **Activities** Events/meetings; networking/liaising; standards/guidelines. **Publications** *STRO Technical Data-Book* in Danish, English, Finnish, Norwegian, Swedish. International standard.
Members Full (7); Corresponding (68), in 9 countries:
Belgium, Denmark, Finland, Germany, Italy, Netherlands, Norway, Sweden, UK. [2018.03.07/XD1138/D]

♦ **Scandinavian Transplantation Society** 19125
Address not obtained.
History 1983, Aarhus (Denmark). 1983, Århus (Denmark). **Aims** Stimulate cooperative research and exchanges of ideas within the Scandinavian countries. **Structure** Informal. Biennial meeting acts as General Assembly and elects President and Councillors: 3 each from Sweden, Denmark, Finland, and Norway and 1 from Iceland. Election Committee. Secretary. **Languages** English. **Staff** Voluntary. **Finance** No membership fee. Meetings financed by President. **Events** *Congress* Aarhus (Denmark) 2024, *Congress* Reykjavik (Iceland) 2022, *Congress* Helsinki (Finland) 2020, *Congress* Oslo (Norway) 2018, *Congress* Stockholm (Sweden) 2016. **Publications** Proceedings of meetings – published by Transplantation Society.
Members Individuals in 5 countries:
Denmark, Finland, Iceland, Norway, Sweden. [2012/XD2075/v/D]

♦ Scandinavian Transport Workers Federation / see Nordiska Transportarbetarefederationen (#17496)
♦ Scandinavian Tumor Pathology Seminar (meeting series)

♦ **Scandinavian Turfgrass and Environment Research Foundation (STERF)** 19126
Dir PO Box 11016, SE-100 61 Stockholm, Sweden. T. +4686221527. E-mail: info@sterf.org.
URL: http://www.sterf.org/
History 2001. Founded by the golf federations in the Nordic countries. **Aims** Support research and development which will promote high-quality *golf* courses while guaranteeing that ecosystem protection and enhancement are fully integrated into golf facility planning, design, construction and management. **Structure** Board; Advisory Committee. **Languages** Danish, English, Finnish, Icelandic, Norwegian, Swedish. **Staff** 6.20 FTE, paid. **Finance** Funding from: participating golf associations (60%); research councils; national ministries; leading suppliers within the sector. Annual budget: Swedish KR 4,700,000. **Activities** Projects/programmes; events/meetings; standards/guidelines; publishing activities. **Events** *Law input turf grass management of golf courses* Copenhagen (Denmark) 2015, *Multifunctional golf courses* Copenhagen (Denmark) 2014, *Turf grass winter survival* Gjøvik (Norway) 2014. **Publications** *Research and Development Yearbook*; *STERF newsletter* in English, Swedish. Handbooks; fact sheets; popular scientific articles; scientific papers. Information Services: Online library.
Members Full in 5 countries:
Denmark, Finland, Iceland, Norway, Sweden.
NGO Relations Cooperates with (1): *International Turfgrass Society (ITS, #15745)*. Links with a number of Nordic and international golf organizations, as well as national organizations. [2021/XM3962/I/F]

♦ **Scandinavian UFO Information** 19127
Information scandinave sur les OVNI – Skandinavisk UFO Information (SUFOI)
Chairman Eilekiersvej 14, 4100 Ringsted, Denmark. E-mail: info@sufoi.dk.
URL: http://www.sufoi.dk/
History 17 Dec 1957, Denmark. **Aims** Promote information and carry out research regarding UFO phenomena (unidentified flying objects). **Structure** Bodies (3): Research; Report Collection; Information. **Languages** Danish. **Staff** 15.00 FTE, voluntary. **Finance** Sources: donations. **Publications** *UFO-Mail*. *Facts and Myths*. Books; reports; position statements.
Members Individuals in 1 country:
Denmark. [2021.09.01/XD8596/v/D]

♦ Scandinavian Union of Meter Service Firms / see Scandinavian Petroleum Technic Association (#19096)
♦ Scandinavian Union of Museums / see Nordic Union of Museums (#17455)
♦ Scandinavian Venous Forum (#19451)

♦ Scandinavian Visualization Society (internationally oriented national body)

♦ Scandinavian Wayfarer Association 19128

Skandinavisk Wayfarer Sammenslutning

Sec Skovgårdsvej 15, 2920 Charlottenlund, Denmark. T. +4539642007. E-mail: poul.ammentorp@wayfarer.dk.
URL: http://www.wayfarer.dk/

Members Full in 3 countries:
Denmark, Norway, Sweden.

NGO Relations *Wayfarer International Committee (WIC, #20839).* [2012/XD1943/**D**]

♦ Scandinavian Yachting Association (inactive)

♦ Scandinavian Yoga and Meditation School 19129

Skandinavisk Yoga och Meditationsskola

Secretariat International Haa Retreat Center, SE-340 13 Hamneda, Sweden. T. +4637255063. Fax +4637255036. E-mail: haa@yogameditation.com.
URL: http://www.yogameditation.com/

History Founded 1970, by Swami Janakananda Saraswati. Also referred to as *Swami Janakananda, Scandinavian Yoga and Meditation School.* **Aims** Independent of economic, political and religious interests, teach methods of yoga, *tantra* and meditation centred around the free development of the *human being.* **Languages** English. **Finance** Teaching fees; publishing activity. **Activities** Events/meetings; training/education. **Publications** *Wonderstand* by Sohan Qadri; *Yoga, Tantra and Meditation in Daily Life* by Swami Janakananda. CD; articles.

Members Associated schools in 6 countries:
Denmark, Finland, France, Germany, Norway, Sweden. [2017.06.01/XF5111/**F**]

♦ Scandinavian Zinc Association (no recent information)
♦ **Scand-LAS** Scandinavian Society for Laboratory Animal Science (#19112)
♦ SCAN – International Symposium on Scientific Computing, Computer Arithmetic and Validated Numerical Computations (meeting series)
♦ **ScanMed RFC** Scandinavian-Mediterranean Rail Freight Corridor (#19090)
♦ SCANPATH – Scandinavian Seminar on Translational Pathology (meeting series)
♦ **SCANSECT** Scandinavian Society for Extracorporeal Technology (#19107)
♦ **SCANVAC** Scandinavian Federation of Heating, Ventilating and Sanitary Engineering Associations (#19086)
♦ Scanviz – Scandinavian Visualization Society (internationally oriented national body)
♦ SCAO – Société de cardiologie de l'Afrique de l'Ouest (inactive)
♦ SCAP – Conference on Security Cooperation in the Asia Pacific (meeting series)
♦ **SCAPE** Scandinavian Association of Pollination Ecology (#19076)
♦ **SCAPLAS** Scandinavian Association of Plastic Surgeons (#19075)
♦ **SCAPR** Societies' Council for the Collective Management of Performers' Rights (#19513)
♦ ScAPS – Scandinavian Association of Paediatric Surgeons (no recent information)
♦ SCAP – Supreme Commander for the Allied Powers (inactive)
♦ S-CAR / see Jimmy and Rosalynn Carter School for Peace and Conflict Resolution
♦ Scarboro Foreign Mission Society (religious order)
♦ **SCAR** Scientific Committee on Antarctic Research (#19147)
♦ **SCA** Science Council of Asia (#19137)
♦ **SCASI** Société Civile Africaine pour la Société de l'Information (#00163)
♦ SCA – Society of the Catholic Apostolate (religious order)
♦ **SCA** Society of Core Analysts (#19537)
♦ **SCA** Softball Confederation of Asia (#19669)
♦ **SCA** Specialty Coffee Association (#19912)
♦ **SCASPEE** Society for Cultural and Scientific Progress in Central and Eastern Europe (#19539)
♦ SCAS – Society for Companion Animal Studies (internationally oriented national body)
♦ SCAT / see Association for the Prevention of Torture (#02869)
♦ SCAUL – Standing Conference of African University Libraries (no recent information)
♦ **SCBA** Smart City Business America Institute (#19318)
♦ **SCBD** Secretariat of the Convention on Biological Diversity (#19197)
♦ SCB – Shipchartering Coordinating Bureau (inactive)
♦ **SCB** Society for Conservation Biology (#19534)
♦ **SCBS** Sir Charles Bell Society (#19290)
♦ **SCCAD** Sociedad Centroamericana y del Caribe de Dermatologia (#03663)
♦ SCC-DRF / see Communication Foundation for Asia (#04380)
♦ SCCI / see SAARC Chamber of Commerce and Industry (#19015)
♦ SCCM – Society of Critical Care Medicine (internationally oriented national body)
♦ SCCN / see Stanford Center on International Conflict and Negotiation
♦ **SCC** SAARC Cultural Centre, Colombo (#19017)
♦ SCC – Scandinavian Clothing Council (inactive)
♦ SCC – Sisters of Christian Charity, Daughters of the Blessed Virgin Mary of the Immaculate Conception (religious order)
♦ **SCCS** Standing Committee of Caribbean Statisticians (#19950)
♦ SCCT – Society of Cardiovascular Computed Tomography (internationally oriented national body)
♦ **SCDA** Scandinavian Copper Development Association (#19084)
♦ SCD / see CEV Small Countries Association (#03841)
♦ SCDM – Society for Clinical Data Management (internationally oriented national body)
♦ SCD – Organisme chrétien de service volontaire international / see Service de coopération au développement (#19239)
♦ SCD – Organisme chrétien de volontariat de solidarité internationale / see Service de coopération au développement (#19239)
♦ **SCD** Service de coopération au développement (#19239)
♦ **SCEAM** Simpósio das Conferências Episcopais da Africa e Madagascar (#20077)
♦ **SCEAM** Symposium des conférences épiscopales d'Afrique et de Madagascar (#20077)
♦ SCECI – Société canadienne d'education comparée et internationale (internationally oriented national body)
♦ **SCECSAL** Standing Conference of Eastern, Central and Southern African Librarians (#19960)
♦ SCENet FB Clusters – SouthEast and Central European Network of Forest-Based Clusters (unconfirmed)
♦ SCEP / see Congregation for the Evangelization of Peoples (#04670)
♦ **SCEPSTA** Standing Conference of European Public Service Training Agencies (#19961)
♦ SCES – International Conference on Strongly Correlated Electrons systems (meeting series)
♦ SCE – Societas Caucasologica Europaea (no recent information)
♦ **SCE** Society of Computational Economics (#19533)
♦ SCEWC – Smart City Expo World Congress (meeting series)
♦ SCF / see Save the Children UK
♦ SC – Fratres a Sacratissimo Corde Iesu (religious order)
♦ SCF / see SaharaConservation (#19032)
♦ SCF – Save the Children Federation (internationally oriented national body)
♦ **SCF** Supply Chain Finance Community (#20038)
♦ SCGME – Search for Common Ground in the Middle East (internationally oriented national body)
♦ SCG – Single Cell Genomics Conference (meeting series)
♦ Scheldeverdrag, 2002 (2002 treaty)
♦ Schell Center for International Human Rights / see Orville H Schell Jr Center for International Human Rights
♦ Schengen Agreement (1985 treaty)
♦ Schengen Convention (1990 treaty)
♦ Schengen III agreement – Agreement on Cross-border Cooperation (2005 treaty)
♦ Schengen Peace Foundation (unconfirmed)
♦ Schiffsausrüster-Verband der EG-Länder / see European Ship Suppliers Organization (#08478)
♦ Schiller International University (internationally oriented national body)

♦ Schizophrenia International Research Society (SIRS) 19130

Senior Project Manager 5034-A Thoroughbred Lane, Brentwood TN 37027, USA. T. +16153242370. E-mail: info@schizophreniaresearchsociety.org.
Events Manager address not obtained.
URL: https://schizophreniaresearchsociety.org/

Aims Be a worldwide organization that aims to bring together researchers and clinicians in schizophrenia and related disorders. **Structure** Board; Advisory Committee. **Languages** English. **Activities** Awards/prizes/competitions; events/meetings; knowledge management/information dissemination. **Events** *Congress* Florence (Italy) 2026, *Congress* USA 2025, *Congress* Florence (Italy) 2024, *Congress* Toronto, ON (Canada) 2023, *Congress* Florence (Italy) 2022. **Publications** *npj: Schizophrenia* – online journal; *Schizophrenia Bulletin*; *Schizophrenia Research* – journal. [2021/XM2046/**D**]

♦ Scholarly Publishing and Academic Resources Coalition Europe / see SPARC Europe (#19902)
♦ Scholars at Risk (internationally oriented national body)
♦ Schone Kleren Campagne (#03986)
♦ Schönstatt Sisters of Mary (religious order)
♦ School of African Heritage (internationally oriented national body)
♦ School of the Americas Watch (internationally oriented national body)
♦ School of Comparative Jurisprudence and Diplomacy / see Elliott School of International Affairs
♦ School for Conflict Analysis and Resolution / see Jimmy and Rosalynn Carter School for Peace and Conflict Resolution
♦ School and Cultural Help and Equipment (internationally oriented national body)
♦ School for a Culture of Peace (internationally oriented national body)
♦ School of Development Studies (internationally oriented national body)
♦ School of Global Studies, Tempe AZ (internationally oriented national body)
♦ School of Hawaiian, Asian and Pacific Studies / see School of Pacific and Asian Studies
♦ School of Hispano-American Studies, Seville (internationally oriented national body)
♦ School of Inter-American Studies / see Center for Latin American Studies, Gainesville
♦ School of International Affairs / see School of International and Public Affairs, New York NY
♦ School of International Arbitration (internationally oriented national body)
♦ School of International and Public Affairs, New York NY (internationally oriented national body)
♦ School of International Relations, Los Angeles (internationally oriented national body)
♦ School of International Relations, Teheran (internationally oriented national body)
♦ School of International Service (internationally oriented national body)
♦ School of International Studies / see Henry M Jackson School of International Studies
♦ School of International Studies, Beijing (internationally oriented national body)
♦ School of International Studies, Delhi (internationally oriented national body)
♦ School for International Training (internationally oriented national body)
♦ School of Islamic Sufism (#16556)
♦ School for Librarians, Archivists and Documentalists (#05296)
♦ School Library Association (internationally oriented national body)
♦ School Meals Coalition (unconfirmed)

♦ School Mental Health International Leadership Exchange (SMHILE) 19131

Chair address not obtained.
URL: http://smhile.com/

History Officially launched Sep 2014, London (UK), at 8th World Congress on the Promotion of Mental Health and the Prevention of Mental and Behavioural Disorders. Builds on the work of *International Alliance for Child and Adolescent Mental Health and Schools (Intercamhs, inactive).* **Aims** Promote effective school mental health internationally by bringing together leaders from regions and countries across the world to share knowledge; co-create dissemination and leadership strategies; signal best research, policy and practice directors for the field. **Structure** Core Development Team. **Events** *World Congress on the Promotion of Mental Health and the Prevention of Mental and Behavioural Disorders* Columbia, SC (USA) 2015. [2015/XJ9273/**F**]

♦ School of Metaphysics (internationally oriented national body)

♦ School of Mining Industry and Geology 19132

Ecole des mines, de l'industrie et de la géologie (EMIG)

Dir Gen PO Box 732, Niamey, Niger. T. +22720315100. Fax +22720315797. E-mail: emig@intnet.ne.
Street Address Ecole des Mines de l'Indutrie et de la Géologie, Ministère des Mines et de l'Energie, Niamey, Niger.
URL: http://www.emig-niger.org/

History 19 Dec 1982, Yamoussoukro (Côte d'Ivoire), on signature of Constitutive Agreement, as *West African Economic Community School of Mining and Geology – Ecole des mines et de la géologie de la Communauté économique de l'Afrique de l'Ouest.* Came within the framework of *Communauté économique de l'Afrique de l'Ouest (CEAO, inactive)* and *Union économique et monétaire Ouest africaine (UEMOA, #20377).* New premises opened Jan 1990. **Aims** As an engineering school: serve the needs of engineers in the West African region for technical and engineering education in the geological, mining, mechanical, electrical, process and environmental engineering fields and informatics; provide continuing education for technicians and engineers already active in the private and public sectors. **Structure** Conference of Heads of State; Council of Ministers; Management Council; Improvement Council; Board of Directors; Education Committee. **Finance** Sources: national budget of Niger; bilateral and multilateral assistance grants and subsidies; grants and subsidies from organizations, foundations and other bodies; EMIG activities. **Activities** Provides training to engineers and technicians. **Publications** *Répertoire des prestations de service à l'EMIG*; *Répertoire des recherches à l'EMIG*; *Répertoire des élèves de l'EMIG.*

Members Governments of 7 countries:
Benin, Burkina Faso, Côte d'Ivoire, Mali, Mauritania, Niger, Senegal.

NGO Relations Member of: *Agence universitaire de La Francophonie (AUF, #00548).* [2011/XE0026/**E***]

♦ School Nurses International (unconfirmed)
♦ School of Oriental and African Studies (internationally oriented national body)
♦ School of Oriental Studies (internationally oriented national body)
♦ School of Pacific and Asian Studies (internationally oriented national body)
♦ School of Public and International Affairs / see Princeton School of Public and International Affairs
♦ School of Russian and Asian Studies, Cambridge MA (internationally oriented national body)
♦ Schools Without Borders (internationally oriented national body)
♦ School-to-School International (internationally oriented national body)
♦ Schools for Health in Europe network / see Schools for Health in Europe network foundation (#19133)

♦ Schools for Health in Europe network foundation (SHE) 19133

Manager c/o University College South Denmark, Lembckesvej 7, 6100 Haderslev, Denmark. E-mail: info@schoolsforhealth.org.
URL: http://www.schoolsforhealth.org/

History 1991. Started as a *WHO (#20950)* supported network. Since 2017, an independent legal entity. Former names and other names: *European Network of Health Promoting Schools (ENHPS)* – former; *Réseau européen des établissements scolaires attachés à la promotion de la santé* – former; *Réseau européen de la promotion de la santé dans les écoles* – former; *Schools for Health in Europe network (SHE network)* – former. **Aims** Improve the health of children and young people in Europe, including reducing health inequalities, through a specific setting focus on schools; Support members to further develop and sustain school health promotion by providing a European platform for school health promotion. **Structure** Board; Secretariat. National Coordinators; Research Group. **Languages** English. Publications translated into other languages. **Staff** 5.00 FTE, paid. . **Finance** Sources: donations. Supported by: *Council of Europe (CE, #04881)*; *European Commission*

(EC, #06633); *WHO Regional Office for Europe (#20945)*. **Activities** Advocacy/lobbying/activism; awareness raising; capacity building; events/meetings; knowledge management/information dissemination; publishing activities; research/documentation; standards/guidelines; training/education. **Events** *Assembly* Oslo (Norway) 2021, *Assembly* 2020, *Research Group Meeting* Haderslev (Denmark) 2020, *Assembly* Helsinki (Finland) 2020, *European Conference on Health Promoting Schools* Moscow (Russia) 2019. **Publications** *SHE Newsletter* (6 a year) in English – electronic; free subscription. *European Standards and Indicators* in English, Russian, Slovene; *SHE SCHOOL MANUAL 2.0 – A Methodological Guidebook to become a health promoting school* in Danish, English, Finnish, Greek, Polish, Portuguese, Russian, Slovene, Spanish. Conference resolutions; case studies; scientific publications. **Information Services** *Factsheet* in English – About topics relating to Health promoting schools; *Glossary* in English – Glossary of health promotion terminology used by SHE; *Materials for Teachers* – Available in English and other languages; *Resources during COVID-19*; *SHE Monitoring report* in English.
Members National and/or regional coordinators in 40 countries and territories:
Armenia, Austria, Azerbaijan, Belarus, Belgium, Bulgaria, Croatia, Denmark, Estonia, Finland, France, Friuli-Venezia Giulia, Germany, Greece, Hungary, Iceland, Ireland, Kazakhstan, Kosovo, Kyrgyzstan, Latvia, Lithuania, Lombardy, Luxembourg, Malta, Moldova, Netherlands, North Macedonia, Norway, Poland, Portugal, Russia, Scotland, Slovenia, Spain, Sweden, Switzerland, Tajikistan, Uzbekistan, Wales.
IGO Relations Cooperates with (3): *Council of Europe (CE, #04881)* (member of the International advisory board); *European Commission (EC, #06633)* (member of the International advisory board); *WHO Regional Office for Europe (#20945)* (member of the International advisory board). [2022/XF2808/f/**F**]

- ♦ School Sisters of Notre Dame (religious order)
- ♦ School Sisters of Saint Francis (religious order)
- ♦ School of Slavonic, Central and East European Studies, Glasgow (internationally oriented national body)
- ♦ School of Slavonic and East European Studies (internationally oriented national body)

♦ School of Spiritual Science 19134

Université libre de science spirituelle – Freie Hochschule für Geisteswissenschaft
Contact c/o Goetheanum, Rüttiweg 45, 4143 Dornach SO 1, Switzerland. T. +41617064242. Fax +41617064314. E-mail: sekretariat@goetheanum.org.
URL: http://www.goetheanum.org/
History 24 Dec 1923, Dornach (Switzerland), by Rudolf Steiner. Legally owned by *General Anthroposophical Society (#10103)*. **Aims** Research spiritual dimensions of different fields of inquiry, promote spiritual understanding of life and develop spiritual foundations for science, art and practical life; act as an organ of perception, exchange, communication and coordination for anthroposophically oriented research and initiatives; represent *Anthroposophy* to the public, providing a forum for discussions of questions, initiatives and results; offer a path of inner development and through it, the possibility of gaining a new kind of knowing that leads to creative responsible action. **Structure** Collegium. Sections (11): General Anthroposophical; Mathematics and Astronomy; Medical; Natural Science; Agriculture; Pedagogical; Visual Art; Performing Arts; Literary Arts and Humantities; Social Sciences; Youth. Includes: *International Coordination of Anthroposophic Medicine (#12957)*. **Activities** Training/education. [2015/XK2348/**E**]

- ♦ Schopenhauer-Gesellschaft (#19135)

♦ Schopenhauer Society 19135

Société Schopenhauer – Schopenhauer-Gesellschaft
Pres Schopenhauer-Forschungstelle, Univ Mainz, Colonel-Kleinmann-Weg 2, 55128 Mainz, Germany. T. +4961312920259. Fax +4961313926393.
URL: http://www.schopenhauer.de/
History 30 Oct 1911, Kiel (Germany). **Aims** Study the works of *philosopher* Schopenhauer. **Structure** Directors Board; Divisions (3). **Finance** Members' dues. Contributions. **Activities** Events/meetings; financial and/or material support; awards/prizes/competitions. **Events** *International conference* Mainz (Germany) 2006, *International seminar* Delhi (India) 2005, *International conference* Freiburg-Breisgau (Germany) 2005, *International seminar* Lecce (Italy) 2005, *International conference* Mainz (Germany) 2005. **Publications** *Schopenhauer-Jahrbuch* (annual).
Members Individuals (500) and societies, in 25 countries:
Australia, Austria, Belgium, Brazil, Bulgaria, China, Denmark, Estonia, France, Germany, India, Italy, Japan, Korea Rep, Latvia, Luxembourg, Netherlands, Poland, Russia, Spain, Sweden, Switzerland, Türkiye, UK, USA.
NGO Relations Member of: *International Federation of Philosophical Societies (FISP, #13507)*. [2016.03.01/XE0261/**E**]

- ♦ Sch P – Ordo Clericorum Regularium Pauperum Matris Dei Scholarum Piarum (religious order)
- ♦ S Chr – Societas Christi pro Emigrantibus Polonis (religious order)
- ♦ **SCHR** Steering Committee for Humanitarian Response (#19978)
- ♦ SCH – Society of Comparative Hematology (unconfirmed)
- ♦ **Schutz Circle** International Alfred Schutz Circle for Phenomenology and Interpretive Social Science (#11617)
- ♦ Schutzgemeinschaft der Fruchtsaft-Industrie / see SGF International (#19252)
- ♦ Schwab Foundation for Social Entrepreneurship (internationally oriented national body)
- ♦ The Schwarzenegger Climate Initiative (internationally oriented national body)
- ♦ Schwarzkopf Foundation for European Youth / see Schwarzkopf Foundation Young Europe (#19136)

♦ Schwarzkopf Foundation Young Europe (SF) 19136

Schwarzkopf-Stiftung Junges Europa
Hon Chairman Sophienstr 28/29, 10178 Berlin, Germany. T. +493072621950. Fax +4930726219519. E-mail: info@schwarzkopf-stiftung.de.
URL: http://www.schwarzkopf-stiftung.de/
History 1971. Originally based at *International Institute for Politics and Finance*, Hamburg (Germany); moved to NGO Europa-Union, 1991; moved to Berlin (Germany), July 2000. From Sep 2004 functions as umbrella organization for national committees comprising *European Youth Parliament (EYP, #09145)*. Former names and other names: *Heinz Schwarzkopf Foundation for European Youth* – former; *Heinz-Schwarzkopf-Stiftung Junges Europa (HSS)* – former; *Schwarzkopf Foundation for European Youth* – former. Registration: Senatskanzlei Hamburg (Stiftungsbehörde), No/ID: A 15 922.48-72, Start date: 11 May 1971, Germany, Hamburg. **Aims** Empower young people from all backgrounds to be active European citizens contributing to a pluralistic, democratic society and mutual understanding. **Structure** Board; Main Office in Berlin (Germany). **Activities** Awards/prizes/competitions; events/meetings; financial and/or material support; networking/liaising; politics/policy/regulatory; training/education. [2022.10.19/XN0708/f/**F**]

- ♦ Schwarzkopf-Stiftung Junges Europa (#19136)
- ♦ Schweizerische Afrika-Gesellschaft / see Société suisse d'études africaines
- ♦ Schweizerische Akademie für Entwicklung (internationally oriented national body)
- ♦ Schweizerische Akademie der Geistes- und Sozialwissenschaften (internationally oriented national body)
- ♦ Schweizerische Asiengesellschaft (internationally oriented national body)
- ♦ Schweizerische Flüchtlingshilfe (internationally oriented national body)
- ♦ Schweizerische Friedensbewegung (internationally oriented national body)
- ♦ Schweizerische Friedensstiftung / see Swisspeace
- ♦ Schweizerische Friedensstiftung – Institut für Konfliktlösung / see Swisspeace
- ♦ Schweizerische Friedensstiftung – Swisspeace / see Swisspeace
- ♦ Schweizerische Gesellschaft für Afrikastudien (internationally oriented national body)
- ♦ Schweizerische Gesellschaft für Asienkunde / see Swiss-Asia Society
- ♦ Schweizerische Gesellschaft für Aussenpolitik (internationally oriented national body)
- ♦ Schweizerische Gesellschaft für Skandinavische Studien (internationally oriented national body)
- ♦ Schweizerische Kommission für Forschungspartnerschaft mit Entwicklungsländern / see Commission for Research Partnerships with Developing Countries
- ♦ Schweizerische Kontaktstelle für Angepasste Technik / see Swiss Resource Centre and Consultancies for Development
- ♦ Schweizerischer Friedensrat (internationally oriented national body)
- ♦ Schweizerischer Verband für Personelle Entwicklungszusammenarbeit (internationally oriented national body)
- ♦ Schweizerisches Institut für Auslandsforschung (internationally oriented national body)
- ♦ Schweizerisches Institut für Entwicklung / see Swiss Academy for Development
- ♦ Schweizerische Stiftung für Minenräumung (internationally oriented national body)
- ♦ Schweizerisches Tropeninstitut / see Swiss Tropical and Public Health Institute
- ♦ Schweizerisches Tropen- und Public Health-Institut (internationally oriented national body)
- ♦ Schweizerische Vereinigung für Internationales Recht (internationally oriented national body)
- ♦ Schweizerische Zentralstelle für Flüchtlingshilfe / see Organisation suisse d'aide aux réfugiés
- ♦ Schwestern der Christlichen Liebe, Töchter der Allerseligsten Jungfrau Maria von der Unbefleckten Empfängnis (religious order)
- ♦ Schwestern des Erlösers (religious order)
- ♦ Schwestern Franziskanerinnen vom Heiligen Joseph (religious order)
- ♦ Schwestern der Göttlichen Heiland (religious order)
- ♦ Schwestern von der Göttlichen Vorsehung (religious order)
- ♦ Schwestern der Heiligen Maria Magdalena Postel (religious order)
- ♦ Schwestern des Schutzengels (religious order)
- ♦ Schwestern Unserer Lieben Frau (religious order)
- ♦ Schwestern vom Armen Kinde Jesus (religious order)
- ♦ Schwestern vom Göttlichen Erlöser (religious order)
- ♦ Schwestern vom Heiligen Kreuz (religious order)
- ♦ SCIAF – Scottish Catholic International Aid Fund (internationally oriented national body)
- ♦ SCICN – Stanford Center on International Conflict and Negotiation (internationally oriented national body)
- ♦ SCI – Congregatio Sacerdotum a Sacro Corde Iesu (religious order)
- ♦ SCIC – Saskatchewan Council for International Cooperation (internationally oriented national body)
- ♦ SciDev.Net (internationally oriented national body)
- ♦ SciecesPo – Centre for European Studies and Comparative Policy (internationally oriented national body)
- ♦ Science Across Latin America
- ♦ Science Based Targets Network (unconfirmed)
- ♦ Science Centre World Summit (meeting series)

♦ Science Council of Asia (SCA) 19137

SG c/o Science Council of Japan, 7-22-34 Roppongi, Minato-ku, Tokyo, 106-8555 Japan. T. +81334031949. Fax +81334031755.
Pres China Association for Science and Technology, Fuxing Rd 3, 100863 Beijing, China.
URL: http://www.scj.go.jp/en/sca/
History Founded by Science Council of Japan. Current statutes approved 14 May 2000; revised 9 May 2001, 13 May 2002, 13 May 2003, 16 Jun 2009, 4 Jul 2011, 10 Jul 2012 and 17 Jun 2014. **Aims** Provide scientists in all fields, including social as well as natural sciences and technology, a collaborative platform for promoting scientific exchange and cooperation in Asia for the improvement of human society; develop and promote a holistic vision by integrating the emerging advances in science and technology with Asian wisdom, values and heritage, focusing on sustainable development and improvement in quality of life. **Structure** General Assembly; Management Board. **Activities** Events/meetings; knowledge management/information dissemination. **Events** *Conference* Pakistan 2025, *Conference* Bangladesh 2024, *Conference* Seoul (Korea Rep) 2023, *Conference* New Delhi (India) 2022, *Conference* Guangzhou (China) 2021. **Publications** Reports.
Members Organizations (32) in 18 countries and territories:
Bangladesh, Cambodia, China, India, Indonesia, Japan, Korea Rep, Malaysia, Mongolia, Myanmar, Nepal, Pakistan, Philippines, Singapore, Sri Lanka, Taiwan, Thailand, Vietnam.
NGO Relations Observer status with (1): *InterAcademy Partnership (IAP, #11376)*. Member of (1): *International Science Council (ISC, #14796)*. Partner of (1): *Asia Oceania Geosciences Society (AOGS, #01799)*. [2021/XJ3070/**E**]

- ♦ Science Council of Japan (internationally oriented national body)
- ♦ Science for Democracy (internationally oriented national body)
- ♦ Science and Engineering Research Support Center / see Science and Engineering Research Support soCiety (#19138)

♦ Science and Engineering Research Support soCiety (SERSC) 19138

Management Office 20 Virginia Court, Sandy Bay TAS 7005, Australia. T. +61390169027. E-mail: journal@sersc.org.
URL: http://www.sersc.org/
History Founded Mar 2005, Daejeon (Korea Rep), as *Science and Engineering Research Support Center (SERSC)*. Obtained business permit to operate as an International Journal Publisher, Mar 2008. Current name adopted, Dec 2011. **Aims** Support distinguished scholars and students who are researching various areas of science and technology; provide chances for academic and industry professionals to discuss recent progress in various areas of science and technology. **Structure** Chair and Chief Executive; President; Advisory Board; Secretariat; National Parts (35). **Languages** English. **Activities** Events/meetings; financial and/or material support; guidance/assistance/consulting. **Events** *International Conference on Architecture and Civil Engineering* Cheonan (Korea Rep) 2016, *International Conference on Computer Graphics, Animation and Game* Cheonan (Korea Rep) 2016, *International Conference on Artificial Intelligence and Application* Yeosu (Korea Rep) 2016, *International Conference on Cloud-Computing and Super-Computing* Yeosu (Korea Rep) 2016, *International Conference on Web Science and Engineering* Yeosu (Korea Rep) 2016. **Publications** *International Journal of Hybrid Information Technology (IJHIT)* (12 a year); *International Journal of Advanced Science and Technology (IJAST)* (12 a year); *International Journal of u- and e- Service, Science and Technology (IJUNESST)* (12 a year); *International Journal of Software Engineering and Its Applications (IJSEIA)* (12 a year); *International Journal of Smart Home (IJSH)* (12 a year); *International Journal of Control and Automation (IJCA)* (12 a year); *International Journal of Database Theory and Application (IJDTA)* (12 a year); *International Journal of Signal Processing, Image Processing and Pattern Recognition (IJSIP)* (12 a year); *International Journal of Security and Its Applications (IJSIA)* (12 a year); *International Journal of Multimedia and Ubiquitous Engineering (IJMUE)* (12 a year); *International Journal of Future Generation Communication and Networking (IJFGCN)* (12 a year); *International Journal of Grid and Distributed Computing (IJGDC)* (12 a year); *Asia-Pacific Journal of Multimedia Services Convergent with Art, Humanities, and Sociology (AJMAHS)* (6 a year); *International Journal of Bio-Science and Bio-Technology (IJBSBT)* (6 a year); *International Journal of Energy, Information and Communications (IJEIC)* (6 a year); *Journal of Security Engineering (JSE)* (6 a year); *International Journal of Software Effectiveness and Efficiency (IJSEE)* (3 a year); *International Journal of Transportation (IJT)* (3 a year); *International Journal of Education and Learning (IJEL)* (2 a year); *International Journal of Sensor and Its Applications for Control Systems (IJSACS)* (2 a year); *International Journal of Computer Graphics (IJCG)* (2 a year); *International Journal of Artificial Intelligence and Applications for Smart Devices (IJAIASD)* (2 a year); *International Journal of Disaster Recovery and Business Continuity (IJDRBC)* (annual); *Journal of Creative Sustainable Architecture and Built Environment (CSABE)* (annual).
Members in 17 countries and territories:
Australia, Canada, China, Egypt, France, Germany, India, Japan, Korea Rep, Malaysia, Oman, Pakistan, Portugal, Spain, Taiwan, USA, Vietnam. [2016.06.01/XJ2664/s/**F**]

♦ Science Europe 19139

Contact Rue de la Science 14, 1040 Brussels, Belgium. T. +3222260300. E-mail: office@scienceeurope.org.
URL: http://www.scienceeurope.org/
History Sep 2011. Founded as an association of European Research Funding Organizations (RFO) and Research Performing Organizations (RPO). Founding General Assembly, 21 Oct 2011, Berlin (Germany), when took over functions of *European Union Research Organizations Heads of Research Councils (EUROHORCs, inactive)* and policy functions of *European Science Foundation (ESF, #08441)*. Registration: AISBL/IVZW, Belgium; EU Transparency Register, No/ID: 73131808686-11. **Aims** Define long-term perspectives for European research

and champion best-practice approaches, ensuring high quality science for the benefit of humanity and the planet. **Structure** General Assembly; Governing Board; Office; Working Groups/Task Forces/High-level Policy Networks as required. **Languages** English. **Staff** 11.00 FTE, paid. **Finance** Sources: members' dues. **Activities** Advocacy/lobbying/activism; awareness raising; events/meetings; knowledge management/information dissemination; monitoring/evaluation; networking/liaising; politics/policy/regulatory; projects/programmes; publishing activities; research and development; research/documentation; standards/guidelines; training/education. **Events** *Open Science Conference* Brussels (Belgium) 2022, *General Assembly* Luxembourg (Luxembourg) 2021, *General Assembly* Brussels (Belgium) 2019, *General Assembly* Brussels (Belgium) 2015. **Publications** Annual Report; position papers; practical guides.
Members Research Funding and Research Performing Organizations in 28 countries:
Austria, Belgium, Bulgaria, Croatia, Czechia, Denmark, Estonia, Finland, France, Germany, Hungary, Iceland, Ireland, Italy, Latvia, Lithuania, Luxembourg, Netherlands, Norway, Poland, Portugal, Romania, Slovakia, Slovenia, Spain, Sweden, Switzerland, UK.
NGO Relations Member of: *Global Research Council (GRC, #10574)* Links with; *European Network of Research Ethics and Research Integrity (ENERI); European Network of Research Integrity Offices (ENRIO, #07990); European University Association (EUA, #09027); SPARC Europe (#19902); League of European Research Universities (LERU, #16423); Conference of European Schools for Advanced Engineering Education and Research (CESAER, #04599); European Association of Research and Technology Organizations (EARTO, #06197); European Association of Research Managers and Administrators (EARMA, #06195); European Council of Doctoral Candidates and Junior Researchers (EURODOC, #06815); Marie Curie Alumni Association (MCAA, #16576); Global Young Academy (GYA, #10662); ALLEA – ALL European Academies (#00647).*
[2021.06.09/XJ4987/D]

♦ Science Journalism Association from Iberoamerica 19140

Asociación Iberoamericana de Periodismo Cientifico (AIPC)
Pres Asociación Argentina de Periodismo Cientifico, Rivadavia 3320, 9e Piso-Dto C, 1203 Buenos Aires, Argentina. Fax +541148631902.
History 1969, on the initiative of Manuel Calvo Hernando. [2008/XM0289/D]

- ♦ Science Management and Organisation Programme / see Commonwealth Partnership for Technology Management (#04356)
- ♦ Science for Peace (internationally oriented national body)
- ♦ Science Policy Research Unit / see SPRU – Science and Technology Policy Research
- ♦ Sciences Po / see Institut d'études politiques de Paris
- ♦ Les Sciences Actives / see Objectif Sciences International (#17632)
- ♦ Sciences Citoyennes (internationally oriented national body)

♦ Science of Spirituality / Sawan Kirpal Ruhani Mission (SOS) 19141

Main Office Sawan Kirpal Ruhani Mission, Kirpal Ashram, Sant Kirpal Singh Marg, Vijay Nagar, Delhi 110009, DELHI 110009, India. T. +911127117100. Fax +911127214040. E-mail: skrm@sos.org.
USA Office 4S175 Naperville Wheaton Road, Naperville IL 60563, USA. T. +16309551200. Fax +16309551205.
URL: http://www.sos.org/
History by disciples of Hazur Baba Sawan Singh Ji Maharaj (1858-1948), known as 'Sant Mat' or the 'Science of Spirituality'. **Aims** Promote personal and global *peace* through *meditation* and personal growth by sharing the teachings of Hazur Baba Sawan Singh Ji Maharaj. **Structure** 1,400 centres worldwide. **Events** *Meeting* Vienna (Austria) 2014. [2016/XF6227/F]

- ♦ SciencesPo – Centre d'études européene et de politique comparée (internationally oriented national body)

♦ Science on Stage Europe (SonSEu) 19142

Chair Am Borsigturm 15, 13507 Berlin, Germany. T. +493040006740. Fax +493040006735. E-mail: info@science-on-stage.eu.
URL: https://www.science-on-stage.eu/
History 2000. Registration: No/ID: VR 31203, Start date: 25 Jan 2012, Germany. **Aims** Improve STEM teaching by supporting educators in their professional development and growth. **Structure** Executive Board; National Steering Committees. **Activities** Awards/prizes/competitions; events/meetings; training/education. **Events** *Science on Stage* Prague (Czechia) 2022. **Publications** *Newsletter.* Teaching materials.
Members Full in 34 countries:
Albania, Austria, Belgium, Bulgaria, Canada, Cyprus, Czechia, Denmark, Finland, France, Georgia, Germany, Greece, Hungary, Iceland, Ireland, Italy, Kazakhstan, Latvia, Lithuania, Netherlands, Norway, Poland, Portugal, Romania, Serbia, Slovakia, Slovenia, Spain, Sweden, Switzerland, Türkiye, UK, Ukraine.
NGO Relations Member of (1): *EU STEM Coalition (#09201).* [2021.05.26/AA0720/F]

♦ Science and Technology Alliance for Global Sustainability (Alliance) 19143

Contact c/o Belmont Forum/IGFA, 4201 Wilson Boulevard, Ste 705, Arlington VA 22230, USA. T. +17032922250. Fax +17032829152. E-mail: belmont_secretariat@usgcrp.gov.
URL: http://www.stalliance.org/
History 2010, as an informal international partnership. **Aims** Encourage and facilitate the co-design, co-production and co-delivery of knowledge with relevant stakeholders so as to address and create solution pathways for global sustainability problems. **Structure** Co-Chairs; Secretariat. **Activities** Flagship initiative: *Future Earth (#10048).*
Members Organizations (6):
Belmont Forum (#03197); International Science Council (ISC, #14796); UNEP (#20299); UNESCO (#20322); United Nations University (UNU, #20642); World Meteorological Organization (WMO, #21649).
[2016/XM5125/y/E]

- ♦ Science, Technology, Engineering and Mathematics / see Global STEM Education Center

♦ Science and Technology Policy Asian Network (STEPAN) 19144

Contact address not obtained. T. +81482265601. Fax +81482265601.
URL: http://www.anstip.net/
History May 1988, Wollongong (Australia). Operates under the auspices of *UNESCO (#20322).* **Aims** As an official, Asia-wide network of people and institutions involved in research and training support for national science and technology *policy* and *management*: develop support programmes to assist development of science and technology management information systems; foster the linking of research with social and economic applications; promote *human resource* development. **Structure** International Coordinating Board, consisting of representatives of each member country; 'National Focal Points' – relevant national institutions formally designated by participating governments; Regional Centre responsible for overall management. **Finance** Supported by: *Asian Development Bank (ADB, #01422); Australian Aid (inactive); International Bank for Reconstruction and Development (IBRD, #12317); International Development Research Centre (IDRC, #13162); UNDP (#20292);* UNESCO; national governments. **Activities** Programme themes: Planning and integration of science and technology policy (STP) with economic development; Establishment of science and technology management information systems; Application and research and development management; Conceptual resource development and regional information exchange in STP. Major activities: establishing, developing and strengthening links; preparing resource material; formulating projects for international agencies; consultancy and limited training and research activities; conferences and workshops. **Events** *Workshop* Vietnam 1998, *Workshop* Korea Rep 1997, *International workshop on the development of S and T management learning materials for developing countries of the Southeast Asia Pacific region* Seoul (Korea Rep) 1997, *Workshop* Indonesia 1996, *Workshop* Malaysia 1996. **Publications** *STEPAN Update* (2 a year).
Members National Focal Points in 17 countries:
Australia, Bangladesh, China, India, Indonesia, Japan, Korea Rep, Laos, Malaysia, Maldives, Nepal, New Zealand, Pakistan, Philippines, Sri Lanka, Thailand, Vietnam.
Observers (2):
Brunei Darussalam, Singapore. [2010/XF1264/F]

♦ Science and Technology in Society Forum (STS forum) 19145

Secretariat Sanno Grand Bldg 419, 2-14-2 Nagatacho, Chiyoda-ku, Tokyo, 100-0014 Japan. T. +81335193351. Fax +81335193352. E-mail: press@stsforum.org – information@stsforum.org.
URL: http://www.stsforum.org/
History 2004. **Aims** Provide an informal mechanism for discussions on science and technology. **Structure** Council; Board of Directors. **Activities** Events/meetings. **Events** *Annual Meeting* Kyoto (Japan) 2022, *Annual Meeting* Tokyo (Japan) 2021, *Annual Meeting* Kyoto (Japan) 2020, *European Workshop* 2019, *Annual Meeting* Kyoto (Japan) 2019.
Members Full in 21 countries and territories:
Belgium, China, France, Germany, India, Italy, Japan, Korea Rep, Luxembourg, Malaysia, Netherlands, Oman, Qatar, Russia, Saudi Arabia, Switzerland, Taiwan, Thailand, Türkiye, UK, USA.
NGO Relations Member of: *Future Earth (#10048).* [2020/XM0573/F]

♦ Scientific Association of European Talc Industry (Eurotalc) 19146

Association scientifique de l'industrie européenne du talc
SG c/o IMA Europe, Rue des Deux Eglises 26, Box 2, 1000 Brussels, Belgium. T. +3222104422. E-mail: secretariat@ima-europe.eu.
URL: http://www.eurotalc.eu/
History 1977, Brussels (Belgium). Registered in accordance with Belgian law, 3 May 1977. **Aims** Promote research and development in the talc industry, including problems related to health, safety and environment; improve working conditions in Europe; devise and maintain standards. **Structure** General Assembly (annual, always in Brussels, Belgium); Board of Directors; Technical Committee. **Languages** English. **Staff** Managed by: *Industrial Minerals Association – Europe (IMA Europe, #11179).* **Finance** Members' dues. **Events** *Annual General Assembly* Brussels (Belgium) 1998, *Annual General Assembly* Brussels (Belgium) 1993, *Annual General Assembly* Brussels (Belgium) 1992, *Annual General Assembly* Brussels (Belgium) 1991, *Annual General Assembly* Brussels (Belgium) 1990.
Members Full (9) in 9 countries:
Austria, Belgium, Finland, France, Italy, Netherlands, Norway, Spain, Sweden.
NGO Relations Member of: *Industrial Minerals Association – Europe (IMA Europe, #11179); International Organization for Standardization (ISO, #14473).* Shares office staff with: *Calcium Carbonate Association – Europe (CCA-Europe, #03399); European Association of Feldspar Producers (EUROFEL, #06037); European Association of Industrial Silica Producers (EUROSIL, #06082); European Bentonite Producers Association (EUBA, #06328); European Borates Association (EBA, #06382); European Kaolin and Plastic Clays Association (KPC Europe, #07623); European Lime Association (EuLA, #07699); European Speciality Minerals Association (ESMA, #08811); International Diatomite Producers Association (IDPA, #13172).* [2018.09.06/XD7161/t/D]

♦ Scientific Committee on Antarctic Research (SCAR) 19147

Comité scientifique pour les recherches antarctiques
Exec Dir Scott Polar Research Inst, Lensfield Road, Cambridge, CB2 1ER, UK. T. +441223336550. Fax +441223336549. E-mail: info@scar.org.
URL: https://www.scar.org/
History Feb 1958, The Hague (Netherlands). Founded following a decision of the Executive Committee of *International Council for Science (ICSU, inactive),* Jul 1957. Currently functions within successor of ICSU: *International Science Council (ISC, #14796).* Former names and other names: *Special Committee on Antarctic Research* – former (Feb 1958). **Aims** Initiate, develop and coordinate high quality international scientific research in the Antarctic region (including the Southern Ocean), and on the role of the Antarctic region in the Earth system; provide objective and independent scientific advice to the Antarctic Treaty System and other international bodies. **Structure** Executive Committee; Permanent Science Groups (3); Standing Committees; Advisory Groups. **Languages** English. **Staff** 3.60 FTE, paid. **Finance** Sources: contributions. Annual budget: 670,000 USD. **Activities** Capacity building; events/meetings; politics/policy/regulatory; research/documentation; training/education. **Events** *Antarctic Biology Symposium* Christchurch (New Zealand) 2023, *Biennial Conference* Lisbon (Portugal) 2023, *Open Science Conference* Goa (India) 2022, *Delegates Meeting* Hyderabad (India) 2022, *Antarctic Biology Symposium* Christchurch (New Zealand) 2021. **Publications** *SCAR Bulletin* (3-4 a year) in English; *SCAR Report* (irregular). *Science in the Snow* (2nd ed 2018); *Horizon Scan* (2017). Symposium proceedings; occasional publications.
Members Full member countries (33):
Argentina, Australia, Belgium, Brazil, Bulgaria, Canada, Chile, China, Czechia, Ecuador, Finland, France, Germany, India, Italy, Japan, Korea Rep, Malaysia, Netherlands, New Zealand, Norway, Peru, Poland, Portugal, Russia, South Africa, Spain, Sweden, Switzerland, Türkiye, UK, Uruguay, USA.
Associate countries (13):
Austria, Belarus, Colombia, Denmark, Iran Islamic Rep, Luxembourg, Mexico, Monaco, Pakistan, Romania, Thailand, Ukraine, Venezuela.
Representatives of 9 international scientific unions:
International Astronomical Union (IAU, #12287); International Geographical Union (IGU, #13713); International Union for Quaternary Research (INQUA, #15811); International Union of Biological Sciences (IUBS, #15760); International Union of Geodesy and Geophysics (IUGG, #15776); International Union of Geological Sciences (IUGS, #15777); International Union of Physiological Sciences (IUPS, #15800); International Union of Pure and Applied Chemistry (IUPAC, #15809); Union radio-scientifique internationale (URSI, #20475).
IGO Relations Cooperates with (2): *Antarctic Treaty (AT, #00850); Hydrographic Commission on Antarctica (HCA, see: #13825)* (observer). **NGO Relations** Memorandum of Understanding with (2): *Asian Forum for Polar Sciences (AFoPS, #01494); ICOMOS International Polar Heritage Committee (IPHC, #11071).* Cooperates with (5): *International Antarctic Institute (#11653); International Organization for Standardization (ISO, #14473); International Union for Circumpolar Health (IUCH, #15764); Scientific Committee on Oceanic Research (SCOR, #19149); Scientific Committee on Solar-Terrestrial Physics (SCOSTEP, #19151).* Supports: Ice Sheet Mass Balance and Sea Level (ISMASS); Integrating Climate and Ecosystem Dynamics (ICED); International Partnership in Ice Core Sciences (IPICS); Southern Ocean Observing System (SOOS); Southern Ocean Regional Panel (SORP). [2023/XE3209/y/E]

♦ Scientific Committee on Frequency Allocations for Radio Astronomy and Space Science (IUCAF) 19148

Comité scientifique pour l'attribution de fréquences à la radioastronomie et à la recherche spatiale – Comité Scientifico para la Atribución de Frecuencias
Secretariat Natl Radio Astronomy Observatory, 520 Edgemont Rd, Charlottesville VA 22903-2475, USA. T. +14342276356. Fax +14342960278. E-mail: iucafchair@iucaf.org.
URL: http://www.iucaf.org/
History 1960, London (UK). Founded by *International Council for Science (ICSU, inactive),* with *Union radio-scientifique internationale (URSI, #20475), International Astronomical Union (IAU, #12287)* and *Committee on Space Research (COSPAR, #04287)* as co-equals under ICSU – currently *International Science Council (ISC, #14796).* Former names and other names: *Inter-Union Commission on Frequency Allocations for Radio Astronomy and Space Science* – former; *Comité inter-unions pour l'attribution de fréquences* – former; *Comité Interuniones para la Atribución de Frecuencias* – former. **Aims** Study requirements of scientists for frequency allocations, and for protection from *interference* of frequencies used for research in the fields of radio astronomy, space science and earth exploration; maintain contacts with International Telecommunication Union. **Structure** Committee comprises representatives each from IAU, URSI and COSPAR; additional occasional co-opted members. Representative of *ITU Radiocommunication Bureau (BR, no recent information)* is ex-officio member. **Finance** Sources: contributions; grants. Annual contributions from IAU, URSI and COSPAR. Occasional special grant from ISC. **Activities** Advocacy/lobbying/activism; events/meetings; training/education. **Events** *International Spectrum Management Seminar* Stellenbosch (South Africa) 2020, *RFI mitigation workshop* Socorro, NM (USA) 2016, *International Spectrum Management Seminar for Radio Astronomy and Space Science* Santiago (Chile) 2014, *RFI Mitigation Workshop* Groningen (Netherlands) 2010, *International Seminar in Spectrum Management for Radio Astronomy* Mitaka (Japan) 2010.
Members Individuals in 8 countries:
Australia, China, France, Japan, Korea Rep, South Africa, Sweden, USA.
Consultative Status Consultative status granted from: *ECOSOC (#05331)* (Ros C). **IGO Relations** Working relations with: *International Telecommunication Union (ITU, #15673).* [2023.02.13/XE2833/v/E]

- ♦ Scientific Committee on the Lithosphere / see International Lithosphere Program (#14059)

♦ Scientific Committee on Oceanic Research (SCOR) 19149

Comité scientifique pour les recherches océaniques

Exec Dir College of Earth/Ocean/Environment, 003 Robinson Hall, Univ of Delaware, Newark DE 19716, USA. T. +13028317011. E-mail: secretariat@scor-int.org.
URL: https://scor-int.org/

History Jul 1957. Founded by decision of the Executive Committee of *International Council for Science (ICSU, inactive)*, of which it is an interdisciplinary body. Since 2018, within *International Science Council (ISC, #14796)*. Registration: 501(c)(3), USA. **Aims** Promote international cooperation in planning and conducting oceanographic research, solve methodological and conceptual problems that hinder research, and develop capacity in ocean sciences. **Structure** Annual Meeeting; Executive Committee; Working Groups; Committees, Panels and Groups. **Languages** English. **Staff** 1.25 FTE, paid. **Finance** Sources: grants; members' dues; revenue from activities/projects. **Activities** Events/meetings; research/documentation. **Events** *Annual Meeting* Guayaquil (Ecuador) 2023, *Annual Meeting* Newark, DE (USA) 2021, *Annual Meeting* Newark, DE (USA) 2020, *Annual Meeting* Toyama City (Japan) 2019, *Meeting on Mid-Ocean Ridges and other Geological features of the Indian Ocean* Goa (India) 2018. **Publications** Reports; proceedings; newsletter; publications in scientific journals.

Members Nominated; Representative; Invited. Nominated in 33 countries and territories:
Australia, Belgium, Brazil, Canada, Chile, China, Colombia, Ecuador, Finland, France, Germany, India, Ireland, Israel, Italy, Japan, Korea Rep, Mexico, Namibia, Netherlands, New Zealand, Norway, Pakistan, Poland, Portugal, Russia, South Africa, Sweden, Switzerland, Taiwan, Türkiye, UK, USA.
Adhering scientific bodies (9):
Committee on Space Research (COSPAR, #04287); *International Association for the Physical Sciences of the Oceans (IAPSO, #12082)*; *International Association of Biological Oceanography (IABO, #11726)*; *International Association of Meteorology and Atmospheric Sciences (IAMAS, #12031)*; *International Science Council (ISC, #14796)*; *International Union of Biological Sciences (IUBS, #15760)*; *International Union of Geodesy and Geophysics (IUGG, #15776)*; *International Union of Pure and Applied Chemistry (IUPAC, #15809)*; *Scientific Committee on Antarctic Research (SCAR, #19147)*.
Affiliated organizations (3):
IAPSO; *International Association of Biological Oceanography (IABO, #11726)*; *International Association of Meteorology and Atmospheric Sciences (IAMAS, #12031)*.

NGO Relations Cooperates with (3): *Future Earth (#10048)*; *International Commission on Atmospheric Chemistry and Global Pollution (ICACGP, #12664)*; *Partnership for Observation of the Global Oceans (POGO, #18239)*. Affiliated with (2): *Global Alliance of Continuous Plankton Recorder Surveys (GACS, #10191)*; *International Ocean Colour Coordinating Group (IOCCG, #14392)*. [2022.05.04/XE3210/y/**E**]

♦ Scientific Committee on Problems of the Environment (SCOPE) ... 19150

Comité scientifique sur les problèmes de l'environnement

Pres De Bosporus 51, 1183 GE Amstelveen, Netherlands. E-mail: admin@scope-environment.org.
URL: https://scope-environment.org/

History 1969, Yerevan (Armenia). Founded by 10th Meeting of the Executive Committee of *International Council for Science (ICSU, inactive)*. Originally an ICSU interdisciplinary body. Currently an independent international organization. Current Constitution approved by 13th General Assembly, 11 Jun 2009, London (UK). Registration: France. **Aims** Advance knowledge of the influence of humans on the environment, as well as the effects of these environmental changes upon mankind, its health and welfare; serve as a source of advice for the benefit of governmental and inter-governmental organizations with respect to emerging ecological and environmental issues. **Structure** General Assembly (every 3 years). Executive Committee; Secretariat. **Languages** English, French. **Staff** 2.00 FTE, paid. **Finance** Members' dues. Other sources: specific contracts with IGOs or governmental agencies; grants from private foundations. **Activities** Networking/liaising; research and development; awards/prizes/competitions; events/meetings. **Events** *Triennial General Assembly* Prague (Czech Rep) 2014, *International symposium on urban futures and human and ecosystem wellbeing* Beijing (China) 2010, *Triennial General Assembly* London (UK) 2009, *Triennial General Assembly* Delhi (India) 2005, *Triennial General Assembly* Delhi (India) 2004. **Publications** *Environmental Development* (4 a year) – journal. *SCOPE Series* – 71 vols to date; *UNESCO-SCOPE-UNEP Policy Briefs* – series. Reports; executive summaries; articles; brochures. **Members** Governmental and inter-governmental organizations; scientific and technical research and assessment bodies; educational institutions; non-governmental and civil society organizations; industry and private sector. Membership countries not specified. **Consultative Status** Consultative status granted from: *UNEP (#20299)*; *UNESCO (#20322)* (Consultative Status). **IGO Relations** Issues examined by SCOPE reflect environmental priorities defined by: *Global Action Plan for Environment and Development in the 21st Century (Agenda 21, inactive)*. Joint projects with: *European Commission (EC, #06633)*; *Intergovernmental Oceanographic Commission (IOC, #11496)*; *NATO (#16945)*; *UNEP (#20299)*; *UNESCO (#20322)*; *WHO (#20950)*. Joint publications and projects with: *Programme on Man and the Biosphere (MAB, #18526)*. Instrumental role in: *UNEP DTIE Chemicals Branch (inactive)*. **NGO Relations** Joint projects with: *International Union of Pure and Applied Physics (IUPAP, #15810)*; IUBS; IUGS; IUPAC. Founding partner of: *DIVERSITAS – International Programme of Biodiversity Science (inactive)*. Supports: *International Nitrogen Initiative (INI, #14372)*. [2022/XE2321/y/**E**]

♦ Scientific Committee on Solar-Terrestrial Physics (SCOSTEP) 19151

Sec-Treas c/o Boston College/ISR, 885 Centre Street, Kenny Cottle Hall, Suite 205, Newton MA 02459-1148, USA. T. +16175528767. Fax +16175522818. E-mail: scostep@bc.edu.
URL: https://scostep.org

History 11 Jan 1966, Mumbai (India). Founded at 11th General Assembly of *International Council for Science (ICSU, inactive)*. Reorganized, Sep 1972, at 14th General Assembly of ICSU, and Sep 1978, at 17th General Assembly of ICSU, Athens (Greece). Constitution revised, 1988. Reorganized, 2003, at the request of ICSU. Currently functions within *International Science Council (ISC, #14796)*. Former names and other names: *Inter-Union Commission on Solar-Terrestrial Physics (IUCSTP)* – former (11 Jan 1966 to Sep 1972); *Special Committee on Solar-Terrestrial Physics* – former (Sep 1972 to Sep 1978); *Comité scientifique de la physique solaire et terrestre (CIUPST)* – former. Registration: Charitable Corporation, Start date: 2003, USA, Colorado; 501(c)(3), No/ID: 02459-0000, Start date: 2005, USA, Newton, MA. **Aims** Promote international, interdisciplinary programmes in solar-terrestrial physics. **Structure** General Meeting (every 2 years); Council; Bureau. **Languages** English. **Staff** 0.50 FTE, paid; 1.00 FTE, voluntary. **Finance** Sources: grants; members' dues. Supported by: *International Council for Science (ICSU, inactive)*. **Activities** Guidance/assistance/consulting; knowledge management/information dissemination; projects/programmes. **Events** *Quadrennial Symposium on Solar-Terrestrial Physics* Alibag (India) 2022, *Quadrennial Symposium on Solar-Terrestrial Physics* Toronto, ON (Canada) 2018, *United Nations/United States Workshop on the International Space Weather Initiative* Boston, MA (USA) 2017, *International Study of Earth-Affecting Solar Transients Workshop* Jeju (Korea Rep) 2017, *Workshop on Global Data Activities for the Study of Solar Terrestrial Variability* Koganei (Japan) 2015. **Publications** *SCOSTEP Newsletter*. Handbooks; proceedings.

Members Representatives of National Adherents in 30 countries and territories:
Australia, Austria, Bulgaria, Canada, China, Croatia, Czechia, Denmark, Egypt, Finland, France, Georgia, Germany, Hungary, India, Indonesia, Israel, Japan, Kenya, Korea Rep, New Zealand, Nigeria, Norway, Russia, Slovakia, South Africa, Switzerland, Taiwan, UK, USA.
Scientific Discipline Representatives in 23 countries and territories:
Brazil, Bulgaria, China, Czechia, Egypt, France, Germany, Greece, Hungary, India, Israel, Italy, Japan, Korea Rep, New Zealand, Nigeria, Norway, Russia, Slovakia, South Africa, Switzerland, Taiwan, USA.
Participating bodies (10):
Asociación Latinoamericana de Geofísica Espacial (ALAGE, #02226); *Committee on Space Research (COSPAR, #04287)*; *International Association of Geomagnetism and Aeronomy (IAGA, #11916)*; *International Association of Meteorology and Atmospheric Sciences (IAMAS, #12031)*; *International Astronomical Union (IAU, #12287)*; *International Science Council (ISC, #14796)*; *International Union of Geodesy and Geophysics (IUGG, #15776)*; *International Union of Pure and Applied Physics (IUPAP, #15810)*; *Scientific Committee on Antarctic Research (SCAR, #19147)*; *Union radio-scientifique internationale (URSI, #20475)*.

IGO Relations Observer status with (1): *Committee on the Peaceful Uses of Outer Space (COPUOS, #04277)*. **NGO Relations** Cooperates with (1): *ISC World Data System (ISC-WDS, #16024)*. [2021.06.08/XE2835/y/**E**]

- ♦ Scientific Council for Africa South of the Sahara (inactive)
- ♦ Scientific Foundation "Nansen International Environmental and Remote Sensing Centre / see Nansen International Environmental and Remote Sensing Centre (#16935)

♦ Scientific Information Centre of Interstate Coordination Water Commission of Central Asia (SIC ICWC) 19152

Dir B-11 Karasu 4, Tashkent, Uzbekistan, 100187. T. +998712650836. E-mail: vdukhovniy@gmail.com – info@icwc-aral.uz.
URL: http://sic.icwc-aral.uz/

History Established 1993, within the framework of *Inter-State Commission for Water Coordination of Central Asia (ICWC, #15979)*, itself a subordinate body of *International Fund for Saving the Aral Sea (IFAS, #13694)*. Part of *Central Asia Research Institute for Irrigation (SANIIRI)* transformed in SIC ICWC to act as a think-tank for the Commission. **Aims** Develop methods and approaches of prospective development; improve water management and ecological situation in the Aral Sea basin. **Structure** Divisions (5); Regional Information Centre; Branches (3). **Languages** English, Russian, Uzbek. **Staff** 36.00 FTE, paid. **Finance** Uzbekistan Ministry of Water Management; grants. **Activities** Projects/programmes; training/education; knowledge management/information dissemination; events/meetings. **Publications** Periodicals. Books. **Information Services** *CAREWIB Portal and Information System*; *Information System on Water and Land Resources*.

Members National organizations (13) based in 5 countries:
Kazakhstan, Kyrgyzstan, Tajikistan, Turkmenistan, Uzbekistan.

IGO Relations *Asian Development Bank (ADB, #01422)*; *European Commission (EC, #06633)*; *International Bank for Reconstruction and Development (IBRD, #12317)*; *International Center for Agricultural Research in the Dry Areas (ICARDA, #12466)*; *Organization for Security and Cooperation in Europe (OSCE, #17887)*; *Swiss Agency for Development and Cooperation (SDC)*; *UNDP (#20292)*; *United Nations Economic Commission for Europe (UNECE, #20555)*; *United Nations Economic and Social Commission for Asia and the Pacific (ESCAP, #20557)*; *WHO (#20950)*. [2018.08.27/XE4188/**E***]

♦ Scientific and Medical Network (SMN) 19153

Chairman 81 Larcom Street, London, SE17 1NJ, UK. T. +4402034682034. E-mail: support@scimednet.org.
Registered Office address not obtained.
Main Website: https://scientificandmedical.net/

History 1973. Statutes adopted 30 May 1987. Registration: UK. **Aims** Advance human perceptive ability and knowledge in the fields of science and medicine; extend the frameworks and assumptions of contemporary thought beyond current orthodoxy; explore the frontiers of science, *consciousness* and *spirituality*; create a climate in which science can adopt a more comprehensive and sensitive approach to human problems; acknowledge the relevance of intuitive and spiritual insights to everyday living; recognize the importance of the sense of meaning and purpose indicated by these insights; encourage dialogue and interaction between the spiritual, scientific and philosophical and the arts in open-minded enquiry. **Structure** General Meeting (annual); Board of Directors. An informal international group. **Finance** Sources: members' dues. **Activities** Events/meetings; training/education. **Events** *Mystics and Scientists Conference* East Horsley (UK) 2015, *Beyond the Brain Conference* Chesham (UK) 2013, *Annual Continental Conference* East Horsley (UK) 2013, *Annual Continental Conference* East Horsley (UK) 2012, *Annual Continental Conference* Hampshire (UK) 2011. **Publications** *Network Review Journal* (3 a year). Audios of conferences available to members online. Members' directory; books.

Members Full; Electronic. Qualified scientists, doctors, engineers, philosophers, economists and other professionals; anyone sympathetic to the aims and concerns of the Network. Members (about 2,000) in 51 countries and territories:
Argentina, Australia, Austria, Bahamas, Belgium, Brazil, Bulgaria, Canada, China, Croatia, Cyprus, Czechia, Denmark, Estonia, Finland, France, Germany, Greece, Hong Kong, Hungary, Iceland, India, Ireland, Israel, Italy, Japan, Latvia, Luxembourg, Malta, Mexico, Montenegro, Netherlands, New Zealand, Nigeria, Norway, Poland, Portugal, Romania, Russia, Serbia, Singapore, Slovakia, Slovenia, South Africa, Spain, Sweden, Switzerland, UK, Ukraine, Uruguay, USA. [2022.05.04/XF0076/v/**F**]

- ♦ Scientific and Statistical Database Management Conference (meeting series)
- ♦ Scientific Summit – Scientific Summit on Tobacco Harm Reduction: Novel products, Research & Policy (meeting series)
- ♦ Scientific Summit on Tobacco Harm Reduction: Novel products, Research & Policy (meeting series)

♦ Scientific Task Force on Avian Influenza and Wild Birds 19154

Contact UNET/CMS, Platz der Vereinten Nationen 1, 53113 Bonn, Germany. T. +492288152422. Fax +492288152449.
Contact Wildlife and Wetlands Trust, Slimbridge, GL2 7BT, UK. T. +441453891900.

History Aug 2005, by signatories to *Convention on the Conservation of Migratory Species of Wild Animals (Bonn Convention, 1979)*. **Aims** Obtain scientific advice on the conservation impact of the spread of avian influenza. **Events** *Workshop on avian influenza and wildlife* Aviemore (UK) 2007, *Seminar on avian influenza and wildlife* Nairobi (Kenya) 2006. **Members** Full; Observers. Governments of 13 countries. Membership countries not specified. **IGO Relations** *Secretariat of the Convention on the Conservation of Migratory Species of Wild Animals (UNEP/CMS, #19198)* is a member. [2016.02.22/XM1777/**F***]

- ♦ Scientific, Technical and Research Commission of the Organization of African Unity / see African Union Scientific Technical Research Commission (#00493)
- ♦ Scientific and Technological Association for the Restoration and Preservation of Monuments / see International Association for Science and Technology of Building Maintenance and Monuments Preservation (#12152)
- ♦ Les Scientifiques Amateurs / see Objectif Sciences International (#17632)
- ♦ Scientists for Global Responsibility (internationally oriented national body)
- ♦ SCIE – Self-Care Initiative Europe (internationally oriented national body)
- ♦ SCIF – Congregation of Bethlehemite Religious Women, Daughters of the Sacred Heart (religious order)
- ♦ SCI Foundation (internationally oriented national body)
- ♦ **SCIJ** Ski-club international des journalistes (#14869)
- ♦ SCI / see MindFreedom International (#16807)
- ♦ SCimPulse Foundation (unconfirmed)
- ♦ **SCIOOT** Sociedad Cientifica Interamericana de Oxigeno Ozonoterapia (#19353)
- ♦ SCIP – Society of Competitive Intelligence Professionals (internationally oriented national body)
- ♦ SCIRA – Snipe Class International Racing Association (see: #21760)
- ♦ SCI – Safari Club International (internationally oriented national body)
- ♦ SCI / see Service Civil International (#19238)
- ♦ **SCI** Service Civil International (#19238)
- ♦ SCI – Sister Cities International (internationally oriented national body)
- ♦ SCI – Society of Chemical Industry (internationally oriented national body)
- ♦ **SCI** Solar Cookers International (#19673)
- ♦ **SCI** Steel Construction Institute, The (#19977)
- ♦ SCI – Stroke Care International (internationally oriented national body)
- ♦ **SCI** Swaythling Club International (#20072)
- ♦ Scito Foundation (internationally oriented national body)
- ♦ SCIU – Save the Children International Union (inactive)
- ♦ SCJ – Congregatio Sacratissimi Cordis Jesu (religious order)
- ♦ SCJM – Soeurs de la Charité de Jésus et de Marie (religious order)
- ♦ SCJ – Science Council of Japan (internationally oriented national body)
- ♦ SCLA – Society of Construction Law for Africa (unconfirmed)
- ♦ Sclerotherapy Society of Australia / see Australasian College of Phlebology

♦ SCL International 19155

Address not obtained.
URL: https://www.sclinternational.org/

History Founded as the worldwide federation of national or regional Society of Construction Law (SCL) organizations. **Structure** Committee. **Activities** Awards/prizes/competitions; guidance/assistance/consulting; training/education.

Members Not a membership federation. Representatives from national or regional SCL organizations making up the Committee, in 10 countries and territories:

Argentina, Australia, Brazil, Hong Kong, Korea Rep, Malaysia, New Zealand, Peru, Singapore, UK.
Caribbean Society of Construction Law; *Society of Construction Law for Africa (SCLA)*; *Society of Construction Law Gulf.*
NGO Relations Sister organization: *European Society for Construction Law (ESCL, #08566).*
[2021/AA1578/y/**C**]

- SCL / see International Lithosphere Program (#14059)
- **SCL** Society for Caribbean Linguistics (#19530)
- SCMM – Sisters of Charity of Our Lady Mother of Mercy (religious order)
- **SCMR** Society for Cardiovascular Magnetic Resonance (#19529)
- SCMTM – Solidarité et coopération médicale au Tiers-monde (internationally oriented national body)
- **SCNP** Scandinavian College of Neuropsychopharmacology (#19082)
- SCN – Sisters of Charity of Nazareth (religious order)
- sCO2 – European Conference on Supercritical CO2 (meeting series)
- **SCOBA** Standing Conference of the Canonical Orthodox Bishops in the Americas (#19959)
- SCO / see BirdsCaribbean (#03267)
- **SCODC** South Caucasus Office on Drugs and Crime (#19751)
- SCOD / see Oikocredit International (#17704)
- SCOHRE – International Association on Smoking Control & Harm Reduction (unconfirmed)
- SCOLARE – Association internationale pour l'utilisation des langues régionales à l'école (no recent information)

♦ Scoliosis Research Society (SRS) 19156

Exec Dir 555 E Wells St, Suite 1100, Milwaukee WI 53202-3823, USA. T. +14142899107. Fax +14142763349. E-mail: info@srs.org.
URL: http://www.srs.org/

History 1966. **Aims** Foster optimal care for all patients with spinal deformity. **Structure** Board of Directors. **Languages** English. **Staff** 10.00 FTE, paid. **Finance** Sources: grants; meeting proceeds; members' dues. Other sources: industry advertising; exhibits; Research, Education and Outreach Endowment Fund. **Activities** Events/meetings; knowledge management/information dissemination; research/documentation; training/education. **Events** *Annual Meeting* Sydney, NSW (Australia) 2026, *Annual Meeting* Charlotte, NC (USA) 2025, *Annual Meeting* Barcelona (Spain) 2024, *IMAST : International Meeting on Advanced Spine Techniques* San Diego, CA (USA) 2024, *Annual Meeting* Seattle, WA (USA) 2023. **Publications** *Spinal Deformity* – journal. **Members** Mostly orthopaedic and neuro spine surgeons; some researchers, nurses and physician assistants and orthotists. Members in about 50 countries. Membership countries not specified.
[2021.03.18/XJ4510/v/**D**]

- SCOLMA / see SCOLMA – UK Libraries and Archives Group on Africa
- SCOLMA – UK Libraries and Archives Group on Africa (internationally oriented national body)
- Scolopi – Chierici Regolari Poveri della Madre di Dio della Scuole Pie (religious order)
- SCOM – Seminary Consultation on Mission (internationally oriented national body)
- **SCOPE** Scientific Committee on Problems of the Environment (#19150)
- **SCOPE** Skin Care in Organ Transplant Patients (#19307)
- SCOPE – Society for Conservation and Protection of Environment (internationally oriented national body)

♦ SCORAI Europe 19157

Contact address not obtained. E-mail: scoraieurope@gmail.com.
URL: https://www.scorai.eu/

History Part of *Sustainable Consumption Research and Action Initiative (SCORAI, #20053)* – International. **Aims** Support a community that contributes forward-thinking, innovative research in the area of sustainable consumption, while also fostering links between academic research, teaching, policy and practice. **Structure** Steering Committee. **Activities** Events/meetings; research/documentation; training/education. **Events** *Conference* Wageningen (Netherlands) 2023. **NGO Relations** Cooperates with (1): *European Roundtable on Sustainable Consumption and Production Society (ERSCP Society, #08408).* [2022/AA2891/**F**]

- **SCORAI** Sustainable Consumption Research and Action Initiative (#20053)
- Score More Foundation (unconfirmed)
- **SCOR** Scientific Committee on Oceanic Research (#19149)
- SC – OSCE Senior Council (inactive)
- **SCO** Shanghai Cooperation Organization (#19256)
- **SCOSS** Global Sustainability Coalition for Open Science Services (#10616)
- **SCOS** Standing Conference on Organizational Symbolism (#19962)
- **SCOSTEP** Scientific Committee on Solar-Terrestrial Physics (#19151)
- Scotland's International Development Alliance (internationally oriented national body)
- Scotland's International Development Alliance – Scotland for a fairer world / see Scotland's International Development Alliance
- Scottish Catholic International Aid Fund (internationally oriented national body)
- Scottish Education and Action for Development (internationally oriented national body)
- Scottish Refugee Council (internationally oriented national body)
- Scottish Society for Russian and East European Studies (internationally oriented national body)
- Scott Polar Research Institute (internationally oriented national body)
- Scout Esperanto League (#19309)
- Scouts marins en Europe (#08455)
- Scouts on Stamps Society International (internationally oriented national body)
- **SCPAR** Standing Committee of Parliamentarians of the Arctic Region (#19958)
- **SCP/RAC** Regional Activity Centre for Sustainable Consumption and Production (#18747)
- SCP – Service Civil pour la Paix (internationally oriented national body)
- SCP – Servicio Civil para la Paz (internationally oriented national body)
- SCRATA / see Castings Technology International (#03598)
- SCR / see Congregation for Institutes of Consecrated Life and Societies of Apostolic Life (#04671)

♦ Screen Advertising World Association (SAWA) 19158

Association mondiale de la publicité cinématographique
Secretariat 2035 Pittwater Road, Bayview, Sydney NSW 2104, Australia.
Pres Weischer Solutions GmbH, Elbberg 7, 22767 Hamburg, Germany.
URL: http://www.sawa.com/

History Jan 1963, by merger of *International Screen Publicity Association (inactive)*, set up 1955, and *International Screen Advertising Services (inactive)*, formed 1953. **Languages** English, French, Italian. **Activities** Assists the commercial organization *'International Advertising Festival Ltd'* in organizing the International Advertising Film Festival and International Advertising Press and Poster Festival, annually, always in June, Cannes (France). **Events** *Annual meeting* Cannes (France) 1986. **Members** Membership countries not specified.
[2016/XD7810/**D**]

- Screen Printing Association International / see Screenprinting and Graphic Imaging Association International (#19159)

♦ Screenprinting and Graphic Imaging Association International (SGIA) 19159

Sec Holland and Crosby Limited, 75 Superior Blvd, Mississauga ON L5T 2X9, Canada. E-mail: sgia@sgia.org.
URL: http://www.sgia.org/

History Founded 22 Oct 1948, as *Screen Process Printing Association.* Name changed, Sep 1968, to *Screen Printing Association International (SPAI).* Present name adopted Jan 1995. Also referred to as *SGIA International.* Chartered by the State of Illinois (USA). **Aims** Create a community conducive to enlightening members and stimulating growth of the specialty printing industry by: disseminating information; encouraging improvement in methods; conducting research; developing, promoting and expanding new uses and markets for the industry. **Structure** Members' Meeting (annual). Board of Directors, comprising Executive Committee of 8 members and 12 active members, 6 associate members and one representative of each affiliated national industry group. Maintains Academy of Screen Printing Technology. Standing Committees (17): Convention and Exhibition; Decal; Education; Environmental; Industrial Imaging; Ink and Chemical Manufacturers; Membership; Membrane Switch; Nominating; Safety and Health; Sign and Display Graphics; SPTF Resource Development; SPTF Research/Technical; Suppliers' Council; SPIRE; Garment Decorators Group; Travelling Squeegees. **Languages** English, Spanish. **Staff** 36.00 FTE, paid. **Finance** Members' dues (annual), based on size of member company and whether USA or international. **Activities** Events/meetings; projects/programmes. **Events** *Annual convention* Las Vegas, NV (USA) 2018, *Annual Convention* Las Vegas, NV (USA) 2014, *Annual convention / Annual Convention and Exhibition* Las Vegas, NV (USA) 2010, *Annual Convention* Las Vegas, NV (USA) 2009, *Annual Convention and Exhibition* New Orleans, LA (USA) 2009. **Publications** Bulletins; newsletters; management reports; industry surveys; technical publications.
Members Categories (6) Active; Associate; Contributory; Emeritus; Educational Institution; Honorary. Private, commercial or government firms and organizations and individuals (4,000), in 123 countries and territories:
Argentina, Aruba, Australia, Austria, Bahamas, Bahrain, Bangladesh, Barbados, Belgium, Belize, Bermuda, Bolivia, Botswana, Brazil, Brunei Darussalam, Cambodia, Cameroon, Canada, Cayman Is, Chile, China, Colombia, Costa Rica, Croatia, Cyprus, Czechia, Denmark, Dominica, Dominican Rep, Ecuador, Egypt, El Salvador, Fiji, Finland, France, Georgia, Germany, Ghana, Greece, Grenada, Guam, Guatemala, Guyana, Haiti, Honduras, Hong Kong, Hungary, Iceland, India, Indonesia, Iran Islamic Rep, Ireland, Israel, Italy, Jamaica, Japan, Jordan, Kenya, Korea Rep, Kuwait, Lebanon, Lithuania, Malaysia, Malta, Mauritius, Mexico, Monaco, Morocco, Mozambique, Nepal, Netherlands, New Caledonia, New Zealand, Nicaragua, Nigeria, Norway, Oman, Pakistan, Panama, Papua New Guinea, Paraguay, Peru, Philippines, Poland, Polynesia Fr, Portugal, Puerto Rico, Qatar, Réunion, Romania, Russia, Samoa, Samoa USA, Saudi Arabia, Serbia, Singapore, Slovakia, Slovenia, South Africa, Spain, Sri Lanka, St Kitts-Nevis, St Lucia, St Vincent-Grenadines, Sweden, Switzerland, Syrian AR, Taiwan, Tanzania UR, Thailand, Tonga, Trinidad-Tobago, Türkiye, Uganda, UK, Ukraine, United Arab Emirates, Uruguay, Venezuela, Virgin Is UK, Virgin Is USA, Zimbabwe.
[2016/XB3651/**F**]

- Screen Process Printing Association / see Screenprinting and Graphic Imaging Association International (#19159)

♦ Screenwriting Research Network (SRN) 19160

Chairperson address not obtained.
URL: http://screenwritingresearch.com/

History 2006, Leeds (UK). Established by Ian MacDonald as the 'Re-thinking the Screenplay' research group.screenwriting. Became the Screenwriting Research Network following its first annual international conference in 2008. Constitution adopted 2012; amended 2014 and 2021. **Aims** Facilitate sharing of views and information between, and collaborative working among, scholars of screenwriting studies, so as to develop research within, and in relation to, the field of screenwriting studies. **Structure** General Meeting (at Annual Conference); Executive Council. **Languages** English. **Staff** 7.00 FTE, voluntary. **Finance** Sources: in-kind support. **Activities** Awards/prizes/competitions; awareness raising; events/meetings; knowledge management/information dissemination; networking/liaising; politics/policy/regulatory; publishing activities; research and development; research/documentation; training/education. Active in all member countries. **Events** *SRN Annual International Conference* Vienna (Austria) 2022, *SRN Research Seminar* Oxford (UK) 2021, *SRN Annual International Conference* Oxford (UK) 2020, *SRN Annual International Conference* Porto (Portugal) 2019, *SRN Annual International Conference* Milan (Italy) 2018. **Publications** *Journal of Screenwriting (Intellect)* – Palgrave Macmillan Studies in Screenwriting book series.
Members Individuals (about 680) in 55 countries and territories:
Argentina, Australia, Austria, Bangladesh, Barbados, Belgium, Brazil, Canada, Chile, Colombia, Cuba, Czechia, Denmark, Egypt, England, Estonia, Finland, France, Georgia, Germany, Greece, Guatemala, India, Ireland, Italy, Japan, Korea Rep, Malta, Mexico, Netherlands, New Zealand, Nigeria, Northern Ireland, Norway, Peru, Poland, Portugal, Puerto Rico, Romania, Russia, Scotland, Serbia, Singapore, Slovakia, Slovenia, South Africa, Spain, Sweden, Switzerland, Türkiye, UK, United Arab Emirates, Uruguay, USA, Wales.
[2021.09.07/XJ9577/**F**]

- **SCRFA** Society for the Conservation of Reef Fish Aggregations (#19535)
- Scripture Gift Mission / see SGM Lifewords
- Scripture Gift Mission International / see SGM Lifewords

♦ Scripture Union International Council 19161

Ligue pour la lecture de la Bible – Conseil international – Unión Biblica – Consejo Internacional
Contact Lytchett House, 13 Freeland Park, Wareham Road, Poole, BH16 6FA, UK. E-mail: info@scriptureunion.global.
URL: http://www.scriptureunion.global/

History Registration: Charity Commission, No/ID: 1072964, UK, England and Wales. **Aims** Make God's word known to children, young people and families; help people of all ages meet God daily through the Bible and prayer; serve a world in need. **Activities** Events/meetings; publishing activities; training/education. **Events** *Global Assembly* Kuala Lumpur (Malaysia) 2017, *Conference* Kuala Lumpur (Malaysia) 2012, *Conference* Nottingham (UK) 2001, *International Conference* Nottingham (UK) 1999. **Publications** *Global News*; *Monthly Prayer News.* Annual Report; international prayer directory.
Members Involved in 111 countries and territories:
Angola, Argentina, Australia, Austria, Bangladesh, Belarus, Belgium, Benin, Bolivia, Botswana, Bulgaria, Burkina Faso, Burundi, Cambodia, Cameroon, Canada, Cape Verde, Central African Rep, Chad, Chile, Colombia, Congo Brazzaville, Congo DR, Costa Rica, Côte d'Ivoire, Croatia, Czechia, Denmark, Ecuador, Egypt, El Salvador, Eritrea, Estonia, Eswatini, Ethiopia, Fiji, Finland, France, Gabon, Gambia, Germany, Ghana, Greece, Guatemala, Guinea, Honduras, Hong Kong, Hungary, India, Indonesia, Ireland, Italy, Jamaica, Japan, Kenya, Korea Rep, Kosovo, Kyrgyzstan, Latvia, Lesotho, Liberia, Lithuania, Macau, Madagascar, Malawi, Malaysia, Mali, Mauritius, Mongolia, Myanmar, Namibia, Nepal, Netherlands, New Zealand, Niger, Nigeria, Pakistan, Papua New Guinea, Philippines, Poland, Portugal, Romania, Russia, Rwanda, Senegal, Serbia, Sierra Leone, Singapore, Slovakia, Solomon Is, South Africa, Spain, Sri Lanka, Sudan, Sweden, Switzerland, Taiwan, Tajikistan, Tanzania UR, Thailand, Togo, Tonga, Trinidad-Tobago, Uganda, UK, Ukraine, USA, Vanuatu, Venezuela, Zambia, Zimbabwe.
NGO Relations Member of (3): *Forum of Bible Agencies International (#09903)*; Global Children's Forum; *World Evangelical Alliance (WEA, #21393).*
[2021.09.21/XE2593/**E**]

- **SCR** Security Council Report (#19210)
- Scrum Alliance (unconfirmed)
- **SC** SaharaConservation (#19032)
- SCSA – Supreme Council for Sport in Africa (inactive)
- SC / see Save the Children International (#19058)
- **ScSB** Scandinavian Society for Biomaterials (#19103)
- SCSCB / see BirdsCaribbean (#03267)
- SCSC – Soeurs de Charité de la Sainte Croix (religious order)
- SC – Servants of Charity (religious order)
- SCS International / see Society for Modeling Simulation International (#19598)
- **SCSI** Society for Modeling Simulation International (#19598)
- SCSL – Sisters of Charity of St Louis (religious order)
- **SCSMI** Society for Cognitive Studies of the Moving Image (#19531)
- SC – Soeurs des Campagnes (religious order)
- **SC** Southern Connection (#19870)
- **ScSP** Scandinavian Society of Periodontology (#19114)
- SCS – Skandinaviska Celltoxikologiska Sällskapet (inactive)
- SCS – Society for Caribbean Studies (internationally oriented national body)
- SCS – Society of Combinatorial Sciences (inactive)
- SCS / see Society for Modeling Simulation International (#19598)
- **SCS** Styrenics Circular Solutions (#20022)
- SCTC – Spacecraft Charging Technology Conference (meeting series)
- SCTE / see Society for Broadband Professionals
- SCTE – International Conference on Solid Compounds of Transition Elements (meeting series)
- SCTE – Society for Broadband Professionals (internationally oriented national body)
- SCT – OAS Special Committee on Trade (no recent information)
- SCUA – Suez Canal Users' Association (inactive)
- SC UK – Save the Children UK (internationally oriented national body)
- Scuola Europea di Oncologia (#08434)
- Scuola Europea di Orgonoterapia / see International Federation of Orgonomic Colleges (#13494)
- Scuola Internazionale Ambiente Salute e Sviluppo Sostenibile (internationally oriented national body)

- ♦ Scuola Internazionale Superiore di Studi Avanzati (internationally oriented national body)
- ♦ Scuola Superiore di Musica Sacra / see Pontificio Istituto di Musica Sacra (#18455)
- ♦ **SCUPAD** Salzburg Congress on Urban Planning and Development (#19043)
- ♦ **SCUR** Society for Cutaneous Ultrastructure Research (#19540)
- ♦ SCV / see Société de Chirurgie Vasculaire et Endovasculaire de Langue Française
- ♦ SCVE – Société de Chirurgie Vasculaire et Endovasculaire de Langue Française (internationally oriented national body)
- ♦ **SCV** Sodalicio de Vida Cristiana (#19666)
- ♦ **SCWD** Society on Sarcopenia, Cachexia and Wasting Disorders (#19639)
- ♦ SCWM – Standing Commission on World Mission (internationally oriented national body)
- ♦ SCWNet – Solar Cookers World Network (inactive)
- ♦ **SDA** General Conference of Seventh-Day Adventists (#10109)
- ♦ SDBMS – Seventh Day Baptist Missionary Society (internationally oriented national body)
- ♦ SDB – Societas Sancti Francisci Salesii (religious order)
- ♦ **SDB** Societät der Bergbaukunde (#19597)
- ♦ SDB – Society for Developmental Biology (internationally oriented national body)
- ♦ SDBWF – Seventh Day Baptist World Federation (internationally oriented national body)
- ♦ SdC – Congregatio Servorum a Charitate (religious order)
- ♦ SDC – Swiss Agency for Development and Cooperation (internationally oriented national body)
- ♦ SDE – Solar Decathlon Europe (unconfirmed)
- ♦ SDEWES Centre – International Centre for Sustainable Development of Energy, Water and Environment Systems (internationally oriented national body)
- ♦ **SDF** SAARC Development Fund (#19018)
- ♦ **S and D** Group of the Progressive Alliance of Socialists and Democrats in the European Parliament (#10786)

♦ SDG Watch Europe 19162

Contact address not obtained. T. +3222741084. E-mail: sdgwatcheurope@gmail.com.
URL: http://www.sdgwatcheurope.org/

History Set up following 2015 agreement on the 2030 Agenda concerning the Sustainable Development Goals (SDGs). Functions as a European cross-sectoral civil society alliance. Registration: EU Transparency Register, No/ID: 037833727533-45, Start date: 19 Jun 2017. **Aims** Hold governments to account for the implementation of the 2030 Agenda for *Sustainable Development* (SDGs). **Structure** Steering Group. **Activities** Advocacy/lobbying/activism; monitoring/evaluation.
Members Full include 58 organizations listed in this Yearbook:
- *ACT Alliance EU (#00082)*;
- *Caritas Europa (#03579)*;
- *CEE Bankwatch Network (#03624)*;
- *CEEweb for Biodiversity (#03626)*;
- *Centre for European Volunteering (CEV, #03743)*;
- *Christian Blind Mission (CBM)*;
- *Climate Action Network Europe (CAN Europe, #04001)*;
- *Climate Alliance (#04005)*;
- *Coalition of the Flemish North South Movement – 11 11 11*;
- *COFACE Families Europe (#04084)*;
- *Conservation International (CI)* (Europe);
- *Cooperatives Europe (#04801)*;
- *Culture Action Europe (CAE, #04981)*;
- *Deutsche Stiftung Weltbevölkerung (DSW)*;
- *Don Bosco International (DBI, #05117)*;
- *Education International (EI, #05371)*;
- *Eurochild (#05657)*;
- *European Anti-Poverty Network (EAPN, #05908)*;
- *European Association for Local Democracy (ALDA, #06110)*;
- *European Association for the Education of Adults (EAEA, #06018)*;
- *European Christian Organisations in Relief and Development (EU-CORD, #06545)*;
- *European Disability Forum (EDF, #06929)*;
- *European Environmental Bureau (EEB, #06996)*;
- *European Federation for Diaconia (Eurodiaconia, #07099)*;
- *European Federation of National Organisations Working with the Homeless (#07174)*;
- *European Network for Community-Led Initiatives on Climate Change and Sustainability (ECOLISE, #07882)*;
- *European Partnership for Democracy (EPD, #08156)*;
- *European Patients' Forum (EPF, #08172)*;
- *European Public Health Alliance (EPHA, #08297)*;
- *European Women's Lobby (EWL, #09102)*;
- *European Youth Forum (#09140)*;
- *Fair Trade Advocacy Office (FTAO, #09238)*;
- *Friends of the Earth Europe (FoEE, #10001)*;
- *Global Call for Action Against Poverty (GCAP, #10263)*;
- *Global Forum for Media Development (GFMD, #10375)*;
- *Global Health Advocates (#10400)*;
- *HelpAge International (#10904)*;
- *Housing Europe – The European Federation for Public Cooperative and Social Housing (Housing Europe, #10956)*;
- *IFOAM – Organics International (IFOAM, #11105)*;
- *Inspire – the European Partnership for Sexual and Reproductive Health and Rights (Inspire, #11232)*;
- *International Council on Social Welfare (ICSW, #13076)*;
- *International Planned Parenthood Federation (IPPF, #14589)* (European Network);
- *Light for the World (#16474)*;
- *Make Mothers Matter (#16554)* (EU delegation);
- *Oxfam International (#17922)* (EU Office);
- *Plan International (#18386)* (EU Office);
- *Save the Children International (#19058)*;
- *Search for Common Ground (SFCG)*;
- *Slovenian Global Action (SLOGA)*;
- *Social Platform (#19344)*;
- *SOLIDAR (#19680)*;
- *SOS-Kinderdorf International (#19693)*;
- *Terre des Hommes International Federation (TDHIF, #20133)*;
- *Transparency International (TI, #20223)*;
- *Wetlands International (#20928)* (European Association);
- *Women Engage for a Common Future (WECF, #20992)*;
- *World Vision International (WVI, #21904)* (EU Representation Office);
- *World Wide Fund for Nature (WWF, #21922)*.

IGO Relations Member of: *European Economic and Social Committee (EESC, #06963)* Liaison Group.
[2020/XM7078/y/**F**]

- ♦ SDIA – Socialist and Democratic Interafrican (inactive)
- ♦ **SDIA** Susila Dharma International Association (#20048)
- ♦ SDIA – Sustainable Digital Infrastructure Alliance (unconfirmed)
- ♦ SDID / see Développement international Desjardins
- ♦ SDIMI – International Conference on Sustainable Development in the Minerals Industry (meeting series)
- ♦ SDI – Samdong International (internationally oriented national body)
- ♦ SDI – Secours dentaire international (inactive)
- ♦ **SDI** Shack-Slum Dwellers International (#19255)
- ♦ SDI – Social Development International (internationally oriented national body)

♦ SDL Forum 19163

Sec c/o TSE, The Laurels, Victoria Road, Windermere, LA23 2DL, UK. E-mail: admin@sdl-forum.org.
URL: https://sdl-forum.org/

History Jun 1990. Constition adopted 1996; current constitution agreed 2005. Former names and other names: *SDL Forum Society* – alias. Registration: Hessen District court, No/ID: VR 2520, Start date: 1995, Germany, Darmstadt. **Aims** Promote the *ITU Specification and Description Language (SDL)* and related languages. **Structure** Board. **Finance** Sources: members' dues. **Activities** Events/meetings. **Events** *System Analysis and Modelling (SAM) Conference* Västerås (Sweden) 2023, *System Analysis and Modelling (SAM) Conference* Montréal, QC (Canada) 2022, *System Analysis and Modelling (SAM)* Munich (Germany) 2019, *System Design Languages Forum (SDL Forum)* Budapest (Hungary) 2017, *SDL Forum* Berlin (Germany) 2015.
[2023/AA3195/**F**]

- ♦ SDL Forum Society / see SDL Forum (#19163)
- ♦ **SD-MED Association** Association for Cooperation on Sustainable Development and Sustainable Construction in the Mediterranean (#02453)
- ♦ SDNP – Sustainable Development Networking Programme – UNDP (no recent information)
- ♦ **SDN** Service Design Network (#19240)
- ♦ SDN – Société des Nations (inactive)
- ♦ SDOK / see Hulp aan de Verdrukte Kerk
- ♦ SdP – Congregatio Missionariorum Servorum Pauperum (religious order)
- ♦ SDPL – Sociedad de Dermatología Pediátrica para Latinoamérica (internationally oriented national body)
- ♦ SDP – Sisters of Divine Providence, Münster (religious order)
- ♦ **SDPS** Society for Design and Process Science (#19542)
- ♦ SDRM – Société pour l'administration du droit de reproduction mécanique des auteurs, compositeurs et éditeurs (internationally oriented national body)
- ♦ SDR – Sisters of the Divine Redeemer (religious order)
- ♦ SDSC – Strategic and Defence Studies Centre (internationally oriented national body)
- ♦ **SDSN** Sustainable Development Solutions Network (#20054)
- ♦ SDS – Sisters of the Divine Savior (religious order)
- ♦ SDS – Societas Divini Salvatoris (religious order)
- ♦ SDV – Societas Divinarum Vocationum (religious order)
- ♦ **SDWG** Working Group on Sustainable Development (#21061)
- ♦ SE4ALL / see Sustainable Energy for All (#20056)
- ♦ **SEAADE** South East Asian Association for Dental Education (#19757)
- ♦ **SEAAFSR-E** Southern and Eastern African Association for Farming Systems Research-Extension (#19873)
- ♦ SEAAGE – South East Asian Association of Graduate Employers (internationally oriented national body)
- ♦ **SEAAIR** South East Asian Association for Institutional Research (#19758)

♦ Sea Alarm Foundation 19164

General Manager Rue du Cyprès 7 -B10, 1000 Brussels, Belgium. T. +3222788744. Fax +3225027438. E-mail: secretariat@sea-alarm.org.
URL: http://www.sea-alarm.org/

History 1999, Netherlands. Registration: Start date: 1999, End date: 2007, Netherlands; Cross Bank for Enterprises, No/ID: 0894.810.152, Start date: 1 Jan 2008, Belgium. **Aims** Facilitate and motivate strategic alliances among non-governmental organizations, industry and governmental organisations, so as to respond professionally and effectively to marine wildlife incidents such as oil spills, according to international standards; be prepared for such a wildlife emergency as part of the overall incident response preparedness; work towards marine incident prevention and response capacity. **Structure** International Board of Directors. **Languages** English. **Staff** 4.00 FTE, paid. **Finance** Sources: donations; fees for services. Other sources: funding from oil and maritime industries; project funding; consultancies. Supported by: *European Commission (EC, #06633)*. **Activities** Events/meetings; guidance/assistance/consulting; humanitarian/emergency aid; networking/liaising; standards/guidelines; training/education. **Events** *International effects of oil on wildlife conference* Tallinn (Estonia) 2009, *Conference* Belgium 2007, *International workshop on oiled wildlife response planning* Brest (France) 2006, *Conference* Ireland 2004, *Conference* Netherlands 2001. **Publications** Via our website **IGO Relations** Observer status with (1): *Baltic Marine Environment Protection Commission – Helsinki Commission (HELCOM, #03126)*. Memorandum of Understanding with (1): *Regional Marine Pollution Emergency Response Centre for the Mediterranean Sea (REMPEC, #18795)*. Invited to technical meetings of: *Agreement for cooperation in dealing with pollution of the North Sea by oil and other harmful substances (Bonn Agreement, #00564)*. **NGO Relations** Member of (2): *EuroSpill Association (#09184)*; *International Spill Control Organization (ISCO, #15580)*.
[2022.10.19/XM1586/t/**F**]

- ♦ **SEAAN** Southeast Asia Astronomy Network (#19754)
- ♦ SEAASM – South East Asian Academy of Sleep Medicine (unconfirmed)
- ♦ **SEAA** Society for East Asian Archaeology (#19544)
- ♦ **SeaBRnet** Southeast Asian Biosphere Reserve Network (#19759)
- ♦ SEACAM – Secretariat for Eastern African Coastal Area Management (no recent information)
- ♦ SEACA – Secretariat for Environmental Assessment in Central Africa (inactive)
- ♦ **SEACA** South East Asian Committee for Advocacy (#19761)
- ♦ SEA-CDC / see International Copper Association Southeast Asia
- ♦ **SEACEN Centre** South East Asian Central Banks Research and Training Centre (#19760)
- ♦ SEACEN – Conference of Governors of Southeast Asian Central Banks (meeting series)
- ♦ From the Sea to the City (unconfirmed)
- ♦ The SeaCleaners (internationally oriented national body)
- ♦ SEACLEN / see International Clinical Epidemiology Network – Asia (#12599)
- ♦ SEA-CLLSD – Southeast Asian Center for Lifelong Learning for Sustainable Development (internationally oriented national body)
- ♦ **SEACONET** Southern and Eastern Africa Copyright Network (#19872)
- ♦ SEACON – Southeast Asian Council for Food Security and Fair Trade (inactive)
- ♦ **SEACSN** Southeast Asian Conflict Studies Network (#19762)
- ♦ **SEAC** Société européenne pour l'astronomie dans la culture (#19461)
- ♦ **SeaDataNet** Pan-European Infrastructure for Ocean and Marine Data Management (#18176)
- ♦ **SEADMA** South East Asia Drymix Mortar Association (#19755)
- ♦ **SEADOM** Southeast Asian Directors of Music (#19763)
- ♦ SEADPRI – Southeast Asia Disaster Prevention Research Institute (internationally oriented national body)
- ♦ SEADPRI-UKM / see Southeast Asia Disaster Prevention Research Institute
- ♦ SEAD – Scottish Education and Action for Development (internationally oriented national body)
- ♦ SEAES / see South East Asian Network of Ergonomics Societies (#19777)
- ♦ **SEA Europe** European Shipyards' and Maritime Equipment Association (#08479)
- ♦ Sea-Eye (internationally oriented national body)
- ♦ Seafarers' Identity Documents Convention (2003 treaty)
- ♦ Seafarers International Research Centre (internationally oriented national body)
- ♦ Seafarers' International Research Centre for Safety and Occupational Health / see Seafarers International Research Centre
- ♦ Seafarers' International Union of North America (internationally oriented national body)
- ♦ **SEAFCCN** Southeast Asian Federation of Critical Care Nurses (#19765)
- ♦ **SEAFDEC** Southeast Asian Fisheries Development Center (#19767)
- ♦ SEAFEA – Southeast Asian Futuristics Educators Association (no recent information)
- ♦ Sea First Foundation (internationally oriented national body)
- ♦ **SEAFOMP** Southeast Asian Federation of Organizations for Medical Physics (#19766)

♦ Seafood Choices Alliance 19165

Contact address not obtained. T. +13014959570. Fax +13014954846.
URL: http://www.seafoodchoices.com/

History 2001, USA, as a program of *SeaWeb*. **Aims** Help the seafood industry to make the seafood marketplace environmentally, economically and socially sustainable. **Events** *International Seafood Summit* St Julian's (Malta) 2016, *International seafood summit* Paris (France) 2010, *International seafood summit* San Diego, CA (USA) 2009, *International seafood summit* Barcelona (Spain) 2008, *International seafood summit* Jacksonville, FL (USA) 2007.
[2016/XM2592/**F**]

♦ Seafood Importers and Processors Alliance (SIPA) 19166

Contact Heiveldekens 4, 2550 Kontich, Belgium. T. +3234513138. Fax +3234513130. E-mail: info@seafoodalliance.org.
URL: http://www.seafoodalliance.org/

History 2002. Registration: Banque-Carrefour des Entreprises, No/ID: 0478.916.318, Start date: 5 Dec 2002, Belgium. **Aims** Facilitate scientific research into all issues relating to *food* safety and food security of fishery and aquaculture products that have been imported into the European Union. **Activities** Networking/liaising; research/documentation. **Publications** *SIPA Newsletter* (12 a year). **NGO Relations** Member of: *Federation of European and International Associations Established in Belgium (FAIB, #09508).* [2021/XJ8844/**D**]

♦ **SEAFO** South East Atlantic Fisheries Organization (#19801)
♦ **SEAF** Special Emergency Assistance Fund for Drought and Famine in Africa (#19908)
♦ **SEAGA** Southeast Asian Geography Association (#19768)
♦ **SEAGCON** Southeast Asian Gymnastics Confederation (#19770)
♦ SEAGF – South East Asia Games Federation (no recent information)

♦ Seagrass 2000 19167

Pres Univ Corse Fac Sciences, BP 52, 20250 Corte, France. E-mail: msa.seagrass2000@gmail.com.
URL: http://mediterranean.seagrassonline.org/

History Originally created to organize 'International Seagrass Biology Workshop, 2000, Corsica. Officially launched 2006, Malta. Full title: *Seagrass 2000 – a Mediterranean Seagrass Organization.* **Aims** Promote protection and *conservation* of Mediterranean seagrass species; increase awareness of seagrass issues; enhance conservation, monitoring and educational issues linked to Mediterranean seagrass systems. **Structure** Committee, comprising President, Secretary, Treasurer and 10 members. **Events** *Workshop* Oristano (Italy) 2015, *Workshop* Essaouira (Morocco) 2012, *Workshop* Hvar (Croatia) 2009, *Workshop* Malta 2006. **NGO Relations** Liaises with: *World Seagrass Association (WSA, #21775).* [2013.07.20/XJ2981/**E**]

♦ Seagrass 2000 – a Mediterranean Seagrass Organization / see Seagrass 2000 (#19167)
♦ Seagriculture – International Seaweed Conference (meeting series)
♦ **SEAGS** Southeast Asian Geotechnical Society (#19769)
♦ SEAGST / see ATESEA Theological Union (#03002)
♦ **SEAHRN** Southeast Asian Human Rights Studies Network (#19771)
♦ **SEAISI** South East Asia Iron and Steel Institute (#19756)
♦ SEALNET – Southeast Asian Laboratories Network (unconfirmed)
♦ SEALOEarth (internationally oriented national body)
♦ **SEALS** Southeast Asian Linguistics Society (#19772)
♦ Seamen's Mission – Norwegian Church Abroad (internationally oriented national body)
♦ SEAMEO BIOTROP / see Southeast Asian Regional Centre for Tropical Biology (#19782)
♦ **SEAMEO BIOTROP** Southeast Asian Regional Centre for Tropical Biology (#19782)
♦ **SEAMEO – CECCEP** SEAMEO Regional Centre for Early Childhood Care Education and Parenting (#19171)
♦ **SEAMEO CED** SEAMEO Regional Centre for Community Education Development (#19170)
♦ **SEAMEO CHAT** SEAMEO Regional Centre for History and Tradition (#19175)
♦ **SEAMEO INNOTECH** SEAMEO Regional Center for Educational Innovation and Technology (#19168)
♦ **SEAMEO QITEP in Language** SEAMEO Regional Centre for Quality Improvement of Teachers and Educational Personnel in Language (#19176)
♦ **SEAMEO QITEP in Mathematics** SEAMEO Regional Centre for Quality Improvement of Teachers and Education Personnel in Mathematics (#19177)
♦ **SEAMEO QITEP in Science** SEAMEO Regional Centre for Quality Improvement of Teachers and Education Personnel in Science (#19178)
♦ **SEAMEO RECFON** SEAMEO Regional Centre for Food and Nutrition (#19173)
♦ **SEAMEO RECSAM** SEAMEO Regional Centre for Education in Science and Mathematics (#19172)

♦ SEAMEO Regional Center for Educational Innovation and Technology (SEAMEO INNOTECH) 19168

Centre régional pour l'innovation et la technologie en matière d'éducation de la SEAMEO

Center Dir Commonwealth Avenue, UP Diliman, 1101 Quezon City, Philippines. T. +63289247684. Fax +63289210224. E-mail: info@seameo-innotech.org.
URL: https://www.seameo-innotech.org/

History 1970, Singapore (Singapore). Founded as one of the specialized Regional Centres/Networks of *Southeast Asian Ministers of Education Organization (SEAMEO, #19774).* Former names and other names: *INNOTECH* – alias. **Aims** Aid in educational development within and outside the region through its service areas: training and human resource development, research and development, knowledge management and special programmess focusing on key areas of concern in the Southeast Asian education community. **Structure** Governing Board; Center Director; Deputy Director; Office Managers (5). **Languages** English, Filipino. **Staff** 70.00 FTE, paid. **Finance** Capital and operating funds provided by the Philippine Government. Other sources: SEAMEO Secretariat; donors; programme partners. Annual budget: 155,000,000 PHP (2020). **Activities** Knowledge management/information dissemination; projects/programmes; training/education. **Events** *Regional Forum* Quezon City (Philippines) 2022, *International Conference* Quezon City (Philippines) 2015, *International INNOTECH Conference* Manila (Philippines) 2012, *International conference* Manila (Philippines) 2008, *INNOTECH international conference* Quezon City (Philippines) 2006. **Publications** *INNOTECH Monthly eNewsletter* (12 a year); *INNOTECH Quarterly Newsletter* (4 a year); *INNOTECH Journal* (irregular). Research reports; case studies; policy notes; toolkits.
Members Member countries (11):
Brunei Darussalam, Cambodia, Indonesia, Laos, Malaysia, Myanmar, Philippines, Singapore, Thailand, Timor-Leste, Vietnam.
Associate member countries (9):
Australia, Canada, France, Germany, Morocco, Netherlands, New Zealand, Spain, UK.
Affiliate members (7):
Asia-Pacific Centre of Education for International Understanding (APCEIU); British Columbia Council for International Education; *British Council* (Thailand); *China Education Association for International Exchange (CEAIE)*; *International Council for Open and Distance Education (ICDE, #13056)*; The Education University of Hong Kong; University of Tsukuba (Japan). [2022.12.14/XE6008/**E***]

♦ SEAMEO Regional Center for Graduate Study and Research in Agriculture / see Southeast Asian Regional Center for Graduate Study and Research in Agriculture (#19781)

♦ SEAMEO Regional Centre for Archaeology and Fine Arts (SEAMEO SPAFA) 19169

Contact 81/1 Si Ayutthaya Road, Thewit, Dusit, Bangkok, 10300, Thailand. T. +6622804022 – +6622804023 – +6622804029. Fax +6622804030. E-mail: spafa@seameo-spafa.org.
URL: http://www.seameo-spafa.org/

History 1985, Bangkok (Thailand). Founded as a Regional Centre of *Southeast Asian Ministers of Education Organization (SEAMEO, #19774).* The Centre is a reconstitution of the SEAMEO Project in Archaeology and Fine Arts (SPAFA), which has evolved from the initial SEAMEO Applied Research Centre for Archaeology and Fine Arts (ARCAFA). **Aims** Raise awareness of cultural and regional diversity; promote professional competence and the preservation of *cultural heritage* in the region; strive to enrich archaeological and cultural activities in Southeast Asia. **Structure** Governing Board, consisting of representatives from member countries. Director, assisted by professional and general service staff: Administrative and Financial; Academic and Professional; Library and Documentation. **Languages** English, Thai. **Staff** 20.00 FTE, paid. **Finance** Main sources: Government of Thailand for headquarters administration; SEAMEO for implementing activities. Other sources: occasional financial contributions from organizations and countries for projects of common interest and/or as part of non-regular programmes of the Centre; financial contributions from associate members and donor countries – Canada, France, Japan, New Zealand; occasional contributions from international organizations such as UNESCO or ICCROM for projects of their interest. **Activities** Events/meetings; guidance/assistance/consulting; knowledge management/information dissemination; networking/liaising; research and development; training/education. **Events** *International Conference on Southeast Asian Archaeology* Bangkok (Thailand) 2019, *Meeting* Phetchaburi (Thailand) 2018, *Meeting* Bangkok (Thailand) 2017, *International Conference on Southeast Asian Archaeology* Bangkok (Thailand) 2016, *Youth Leadership Forum* Bangkok (Thailand) 2016. **Publications** *SPAFA Journal.*
Members Governments of 11 countries:
Brunei Darussalam, Cambodia, Indonesia, Laos, Malaysia, Myanmar, Philippines, Singapore, Thailand, Timor-Leste, Vietnam.
Associate members (8):
Australia, Canada, France, Germany, Netherlands, New Zealand, Spain, UK.
NGO Relations Member of: *International Coordinating Committee on the Safeguarding and Development of the Historic Site of Angkor (ICC-Angkor, #12954).* [2020.04.15/XE1524/**E***]

♦ SEAMEO Regional Centre for Community Education Development (SEAMEO CED) 19170

Contact Ministry of Education and Sports, PO Box 67, Vientiane, Laos. T. +85621771843. Fax +85621771844. E-mail: cheanmaly@hotmail.com.

History Established by the Ministry of Education and Sport of Laos, as a regional centre of *Southeast Asian Ministers of Education Organization (SEAMEO, #19774).* Officially launched 30 Jul 2018. **Aims** Contribute to regional development. **Languages** English. **Staff** 5.00 FTE, paid. **Activities** Knowledge management/information dissemination; projects/programmes; events/meetings.
Members Governments of 11 countries:
Brunei Darussalam, Cambodia, Indonesia, Laos, Malaysia, Myanmar, Philippines, Singapore, Thailand, Timor-Leste, Vietnam.
IGO Relations *Deutsche Gesellschaft für Internationale Zusammenarbeit (GIZ)* Fit for School; *UNESCO Institute for Lifelong Learning (UIL, #20305).* **NGO Relations** *Institut für Internationale Zusammenarbeit des Deutschen Volkshochschul-Verbandes (DVV-International)*; *UNESCO International Research and Training Centre for Rural Education (INRULED).* [2019.02.27/XM6550/**E***]

♦ SEAMEO Regional Centre for Community Nutrition / see SEAMEO Regional Centre for Food and Nutrition (#19173)

♦ SEAMEO Regional Centre for Early Childhood Care Education and Parenting (SEAMEO – CECCEP) 19171

Contact Jayagiri 63, Lembang, Kabupaten, Bandung, Indonesia. E-mail: secretariat@seameo-ceccep.org.
URL: http://seameo-ceccep.org/

History Established 25 Jul 2017, as a regional centre of *Southeast Asian Ministers of Education Organization (SEAMEO, #19774).* **Aims** Enhance regional and global commitments to quality early childhood education and parenting. **Activities** Research and development; capacity building; advocacy/lobbying/activism; networking/liaising. [2018/XM6549/**E***]

♦ SEAMEO Regional Centre for Education in Science and Mathematics (SEAMEO RECSAM) 19172

Centre régional pour l'enseignement des sciences et des mathématiques de la SEAMEO

Dir Jalan Sultan Azlan Shah, Gelugor, 11700 George Town, Penang, Malaysia. T. +6046522700. Fax +6046522737.
URL: http://www.recsam.edu.my/

History May 1967, Penang (Malaysia), as one of the regional Centres/Network of *Southeast Asian Ministers of Education Organization (SEAMEO, #19774).* **Aims** Promote and enhance science and mathematics education in the SEAMEO member countries and beyond. **Structure** Governing Board (meets annually), comprising Chairman, Representatives of the respective Ministries of Education of the 11 Southeast Asian countries, SEAMEO Director or its representative (Ex-Officio), Secretariat or its representative and Director of SEAMEO RECSAM or its representative. Directorate, headed by Director, and comprising Deputy Directors of Divisions (3): Administration; Training Programme; Research and Development. **Languages** English. **Staff** 88.00 FTE, paid. **Finance** Malaysian government is primarily responsible for capital and operational costs. **Activities** Training/education; events/meetings; research and development; guidance/assistance/consulting; knowledge management/information dissemination. **Events** *International Conference on Science and Mathematics Education (COSMED)* George Town (Malaysia) 2021, *Conference on Science and Mathematics Education (COSMEd)* George Town (Malaysia) 2019, *International Conference on Education for Sustainable Development* George Town (Malaysia) 2016, *Seminar-Workshop on Developing 21st Century Skills through Science, Mathematics and Technology for Datdaruni School* George Town (Malaysia) 2016, *Workshop On Developing Technology-Enhanced Open and Distance Learning* George Town (Malaysia) 2016. **Publications** *RECSAM News* (3 a year); *Journal of Science and Mathematics Education in Southeast Asia* (2 a year); *Learning Science and Mathematics* (annual) – online journal. Annual Report; monographs; modules; assignments; catalogues; brochures; conference/workshop/symposia reports; research studies; course/project reports; academic texts.
Members Governments of 11 countries:
Brunei Darussalam, Cambodia, Indonesia, Laos, Malaysia, Myanmar, Philippines, Singapore, Thailand, Timor-Leste, Vietnam.
Associate Member countries (5):
Australia, Canada, Germany, New Zealand, Spain.
Affiliate Members (4):
Asia-Pacific Centre of Education for International Understanding (APCEIU); *British Council*; *China Education Association for International Exchange (CEAIE)*; *International Council for Open and Distance Education (ICDE, #13056).* [2021/XE9195/**E***]

♦ SEAMEO Regional Centre for Food and Nutrition (SEAMEO RECFON) 19173

Dir Jl Salemba Raya No 6, Jakarta 10430, Indonesia. T. +622131930205. Fax +62213913933. E-mail: information@seameo-recfon.org.
URL: http://www.seameo-recfon.org/

History 1970. Set as a regional centre of *SEAMEO Regional Tropical Medicine and Public Health Network (SEAMEO TROPMED, #19184)*, within the framework of *Southeast Asian Ministers of Education Organization (SEAMEO, #19774).* Restructured to become a full regional center, separate from SEMEO TROPMED Network, 26 Jan 2010, when current title was adopted. Former names and other names: *SEAMEO TROPMED Regional Centre for Community Nutrition (SEAMEO-TROPMED RCCN)* – former; *SEAMEO Regional Centre for Community Nutrition* – former; *TROPMED/Indonesia* – former. **Aims** Be the center of excellence in human resource development in the area of food and nutrition in Southeast Asia. **Structure** Program Division: Administration Division. **Languages** English, Indonesian. **Staff** 40.00 FTE, paid. **Finance** Supported by: Mlnistry of Education, Republic of Indonesia. Annual budget: 15,000,000,000 IDR (2020). **Activities** Advocacy/lobbying/activism; capacity building; knowledge management/information dissemination; networking/liaising; research and development. Active in: Brunei Darussalam, Cambodia, Indonesia, Malaysia, Myanmar, Philippines, Singapore, Thailand, Timor-Leste. **Events** *International Conference of Food and Nutrition* Jakarta (Indonesia) 2020. [2020.08.27/XK0445/**E***]

♦ SEAMEO Regional Centre for Higher Education and Development (RIHED) 19174

Centre régional pour l'enseignement supérieur et le développement de la SEAMEO (IRESD)

Dir c/o Commission on Higher Education Bldg – 5th floor, 328 Si Ayutthaya Road, Bangkok, 10400, Thailand. T. +6626449856 – +6626449863. Fax +6626445421. E-mail: rihed@rihed.seameo.org.
URL: http://www.rihed.seameo.org/

History Jul 1970, Singapore (Singapore), as *Regional Institute of Higher Education and Development – Institut régional pour l'enseignement supérieur et le développement.* On 15 Feb 1993, became a Regional Centre of *Southeast Asian Ministers of Education Organization (SEAMEO, #19774)*; commenced interim operations in this context in mid-1994. Preparation for Interim Period: 1 Jul 1993 – 30 Jun 1994; Interim Period: 1 Jul 1994 – 30 Jun 1997; Development Plan follows regular 5-year cycle of SEAMEO. Hosted by the Royal Government of Thailand. **Aims** Assist member countries of Southeast Asia in fostering efficiency and effectiveness of higher education with a focus on policy and planning processes, administrative and managing systems; serve as a regional centre and clearing house for higher education information within and outside the region; promote collaboration for the establishment of institutional linkages leading to achieve the goal of regional harmonization of higher education. **Structure** Governing Board, consisting of one representative from each member country appointed by their respective Minister of Education, ex-officio SEAMEO Secretariat Director and RIHED Director. **Languages** English, Thai. **Staff** 12.00 FTE, paid. **Finance** Main source of funds: RIHED Endowment Fund. Capital and operational costs carried by Thailand government. Specific projects additionally funded by interested partners and organizations. **Activities** Projects/programmes; training/education; research/

documentation; knowledge management/information dissemination; events/meetings; guidance/assistance/consulting; networking/liaising. **Events** *Forum for ASEAN-China Private Higher Education Development and Cooperation* Bangkok (Thailand) 2020, *Seminar on the Roles of Higher Education Internationalization in Achieving Sustainable Development Goals* Bangkok (Thailand) 2019, *Annual Meeting* Sanya (China) 2019, *Annual Meeting* Sanya (China) 2019, *Forum for ASEAN-China Private Higher Education Development and Cooperation* Sanya (China) 2019. **Publications** *RIHED Bulletin* (3 a year). Annual Report; directories; papers; seminar and conference reports. **Information Serivces** *Regional Information Network on Higher Education.*
Members Members and associate members of SEAMEO. Governments of 11 countries:
Brunei Darussalam, Cambodia, Indonesia, Laos, Malaysia, Myanmar, Philippines, Singapore, Thailand, Timor-Leste, Vietnam.
Associate members (8):
Australia, Canada, France, Germany, Netherlands, New Zealand, Norway, Spain.
IGO Relations Cooperation agreement with: *Asean Quality Assurance Network (AQAN, #01227).* Invited as observer to Governing board Meetings: *UNESCO Asia and Pacific Regional Bureau for Education (#20301).*
NGO Relations Invited as observers to Governing Board Meetings: *Association of Southeast Asian Institutions of Higher Learning (ASAIHL, #02920); Association of Universities of Asia and the Pacific (AUAP, #02968).*
[2019/XE5807/**E***]

♦ SEAMEO Regional Centre for History and Tradition (SEAMEO CHAT) 19175

Acting Dir Tha, Pyay Road, Yangon 11041, Myanmar. T. +951515180 – +951539708. Fax +951515175.
URL: http://seameochat.org

History as one of the regional Centres of *Southeast Asian Ministers of Education Organization (SEAMEO, #19774).* Inaugurated 15 Dec 2000, Yangon (Myanmar). **Aims** Promote cooperation in the study of history and tradition among member countries; develop a greater regional identity through research, human resource development, education and public awareness programmes. **Structure** Governing Board of 10 members. **Languages** English. **Staff** 27.00 FTE, paid. **Finance** Operations supported by host government; programmes supported by SEAMEO Secretariat, funding agencies and cooperating partners and by income generating activities. **Activities** Research projects; training projects; lecture series; curriculum development project; workshops; conferences; exhibitions. Projects include: 'Southeast Asian History for Southeast Asian Secondary Schools'; 'Compact Encyclopaedia of Southeast Asian History'. **Events** *International conference* Rangoon (Myanmar) 2005, *Meeting* Rangoon (Myanmar) 2004, *Meeting* Rangoon (Myanmar) 2002. **Publications** *CHAT Newsletter.* Annual Report.
Members SEAMEO member governments (11):
Brunei Darussalam, Cambodia, Indonesia, Laos, Malaysia, Myanmar, Philippines, Singapore, Thailand, Timor-Leste, Vietnam.
[2008.11.10/XE4500/**E***]

♦ SEAMEO Regional Centre for Medical Microbiology, Parasitology and Entomology / see SEAMEO TROPMED Regional Centre for Microbiology, Parasitology and Entomology (#19185)

♦ SEAMEO Regional Centre for Public Health, Hospital Administration, Occupational and Environmental Health / see SEAMEO TROPMED Regional Centre for Public Health, Hospital Administration, Environmental and Occupational Health (#19186)

♦ SEAMEO Regional Centre for Quality Improvement of Teachers and Educational Personnel in Language (SEAMEO QITEP in Language) 19176

Dir Jalan Gardu, Srengseng Sawah, Jagakarsa, Jakarta 12640, Indonesia. T. +622178884106. Fax +622178884073. E-mail: info@qiteplanguage.org – ppr@qiteplanguage.org.
URL: https://www.qiteplanguage.org/

History 13 Jul 2009. Launched as regional centre of *Southeast Asian Ministers of Education Organization (SEAMEO, #19774).* Formally set up 27 Jan 2010, Cebu (Philippines), at 45th SEAMEO Council Conference. **Aims** Provide quality programmes of professional excellence for language teachers. **Languages** Arabic, Chinese, French, German, Indonesian, Japanese. **Finance** Sources: government support. Funded by Ministry of Education, Culture, Research and Technology of the Republic of Indonesia. **Activities** Capacity building; events/meetings; knowledge management/information dissemination; research and development; training/education. **Events** *Annual International Symposium Foreign Language Learning* Jakarta (Indonesia) 2021, *Annual International Symposium Foreign Language Learning* Jakarta (Indonesia) 2020, *Annual International Symposium Foreign Language Learning* Bogor (Indonesia) 2019, *Annual International Symposium Foreign Language Learning* Serpong (Indonesia) 2018, *Annual International Symposium Foreign Language Learning* Jakarta (Indonesia) 2017. **IGO Relations** Cooperates with: *SEAMEO Regional Centre for Education in Science and Mathematics (SEAMEO RECSAM, #19172); SEAMEO Regional Center for Educational Innovation and Technology (SEAMEO INNOTECH, #19168); SEAMEO Regional Centre for Food and Nutrition (SEAMEO RECFON, #19173); SEAMEO Regional Centre for Vocational and Technical Education (VOCTECH, #19180); SEAMEO Regional Language Centre (SEAMEO RELC, #19181); SEAMEO Regional Open Learning Centre (SEAMOLEC, #19182); Southeast Asian Regional Centre for Tropical Biology (SEAMEO BIOTROP, #19782); SEAMEO Regional Centre for Early Childhood Care Education and Parenting (SEAMEO – CECCEP, #19171); SEAMEO Regional Centre for Quality Improvement of Teachers and Education Personnel in Mathematics (SEAMEO QITEP in Mathematics, #19177); SEAMEO Regional Centre for Quality Improvement of Teachers and Education Personnel in Science (SEAMEO QITEP in Science, #19178).* [2022.02.11/XJ0946/**E***]

♦ SEAMEO Regional Centre for Quality Improvement of Teachers and Education Personnel in Mathematics (SEAMEO QITEP in Mathematics) 19177

Dir Jalan Kaliurang Km 6 Sambisari, Condongcatur, Depok Sleman, Yogyakarta 55283, Indonesia. T. +62274881717. Fax +62274885752. E-mail: qitepinmath@yahoo.com – p4tkmatematika@yahoo.com.

History as a regional centre of *Southeast Asian Ministers of Education Organization (SEAMEO, #19774).* **Aims** Promote programmes and activities in improving the quality of teachers and education personnel in the areas of Mathematics. [2009/XJ0948/**E***]

♦ SEAMEO Regional Centre for Quality Improvement of Teachers and Education Personnel in Science (SEAMEO QITEP in Science) 19178

Contact Gd B Jl Dr Cipto No 9, West Java, Bandung 40171, Indonesia. T. +62224218739. Fax +62224218749. E-mail: secretariat@qitepinscience.org – info@qitepinscience.org.
Secretariat SEAQIS address not obtained. T. +6282123450630. E-mail: partnership@qitepinscience.org.
URL: https://www.qitepinscience.org/

History 13 Jul 2009. Founded simultaneously with SEAMEO QITEP in Language and SEAMEO QITEP in Mathematics. A regional centre of *Southeast Asian Ministers of Education Organization (SEAMEO, #19774).* Former names and other names: *SEAQUIS* – alias. **Aims** Provide relevant and quality programmes in professional excellence for science teachers and education personnel through capacity building activities, resource sharing, research and development and networking; improve the quality of science teachers in the region; meet the needs for more extensive networks, sharing and exchanges. **Structure** Director; Deputy Directors (2); Divisions (6). **Languages** English, Indonesian. **Staff** 38.00 FTE, paid. **Finance** Sources: government support. **Activities** Awards/prizes/competitions; events/meetings; research/documentation; training/education. **Events** *International Conference* Bandung (Indonesia) 2021, *International Conference* Jakarta (Indonesia) 2012. **Publications** Magazine; bulletin; journal; research papers; reports; proceedings; books; videos.
Members Ministries of Education of 11 countries:
Brunei Darussalam, Cambodia, Indonesia, Laos, Malaysia, Myanmar, Philippines, Singapore, Thailand, Timor-Leste, Vietnam.
[2022.10.21/XJ0950/v/**E***]

♦ SEAMEO Regional Centre for Technical Education Development (SEAMEO TED) 19179

Admin Dir c/o Ministry of Education, 80 Preah Norodom Blvd, Phnom Penh, Cambodia.
URL: https://seameoted.org/

History 2017. Established as a regional centre of *Southeast Asian Ministers of Education Organization (SEAMEO, #19774).* [2020/XM6551/**E***]

♦ SEAMEO Regional Centre for Tropical Biology / see Southeast Asian Regional Centre for Tropical Biology (#19782)

♦ SEAMEO Regional Centre for Vocational and Technical Education (VOCTECH) 19180

Centre Dir Jalan Pasar Baharu, Gadong, Brunei-Muara BE1318, Gadong BRUNEI-MUARA BE1318, Brunei Darussalam. T. +6732447992. Fax +6732447955. E-mail: info@voctech.org.
URL: http://www.voctech.org/

History 28 Aug 1990, when commenced interim operations as a Regional Centre/Project of *Southeast Asian Ministers of Education Organization (SEAMEO, #19774).* Became a full-fledged regional centre, Jul 1994. Programmes and activities fully operationalized under the first 5 year development plan (1994-1999). Also referred to as *SEAMEO VOCTECH.* **Aims** Enhance technical and vocational education and training systems of SEAMEO member countries through innovative capability building, research and development and information services. **Structure** Governing Board; Centre, managed by Centre Director; Divisions. **Languages** English, Malay. **Staff** 40.00 FTE, paid. **Finance** Grants provided by Government of Brunei Darussalam. Other sources: activities and projects. **Activities** Guidance/assistance/consulting; research and development; knowledge management/information dissemination. **Events** *Meeting* Bali (Indonesia) 2018, *Meeting* Siem Reap (Cambodia) 2017, *Meeting* Hanoi (Vietnam) 2016, *Meeting* Bandar Seri Begawan (Brunei Darussalam) 2004, *World congress of colleges and polytechnics* Québec, QC (Canada) 1999. **Publications** *The Digest* – newsletter. Annual Report; training information guide; conference proceedings; guides.
Members SEAMEO member countries (11):
Brunei Darussalam, Cambodia, Indonesia, Laos, Malaysia, Myanmar, Philippines, Singapore, Thailand, Timor-Leste, Vietnam.
Associate members countries (8):
Australia, Canada, France, Germany, Netherlands, New Zealand, Spain, UK.
Affiliate members (4) including 1 organization listed in this Yearbook:
International Council for Open and Distance Education (ICDE, #13056) (Norway).
IGO Relations Partners include: *Colombo Plan Staff College (CPSC, #04121); Deutsche Gesellschaft für Internationale Zusammenarbeit (GIZ);* German Federal Ministry for Economic Cooperation and Development (BMZ); *Japan International Cooperation Agency (JICA);* national organizations; *SEAMEO Regional Center for Educational Innovation and Technology (SEAMEO INNOTECH, #19168); SEAMEO Regional Centre for Quality Improvement of Teachers and Educational Personnel in Language (SEAMEO QITEP in Language, #19176); SEAMEO Regional Open Learning Centre (SEAMOLEC, #19182); Southeast Asian Regional Centre for Tropical Biology (SEAMEO BIOTROP, #19782); UNESCO Asia and Pacific Regional Bureau for Education (#20301); UNESCO International Centre for Technical and Vocational Education and Training (UNESCO-UNEVOC, #20307).*
NGO Relations Universities; national organizations. [2018/XE1389/**E***]

♦ SEAMEO Regional Language Centre (SEAMEO RELC) 19181

Centre régional des langues de la SEAMEO

Dir 30 Orange Grove Road, Level 3 RELC Building, Singapore 258352, Singapore. T. +6568857888. Fax +6567342753. E-mail: enquiries@relc.org.sg.
URL: http://www.relc.org.sg/

History Jul 1968, Singapore (Singapore). IS currently one of the Regional Centres of *Southeast Asian Ministers of Education Organization (SEAMEO, #19774).* Former names and other names: *Regional English Language Centre* – former (1968 to 1977); *RELC* – alias. **Aims** Assist SEAMEO member countries in language education development related to social and economic development in the multilingual context of Southeast Asia. **Structure** Governing Board. **Languages** Chinese, English. **Staff** 129.00 FTE, paid. **Finance** Self-funded. **Activities** Training/education; events/meetings; knowledge management/information dissemination; research and development. **Events** *Annual Seminar* Singapore (Singapore) 2022, *Annual Seminar* Singapore (Singapore) 2021, *Annual Seminar* Singapore (Singapore) 2020, *Annual Seminar* Singapore (Singapore) 2019, *Annual Seminar* Singapore (Singapore) 2018. **Publications** *RELC Journal: a Journal of Language Teaching and Research in Southeast Asia* (3 a year). *Anthology Series; Portfolio Series.* Annual Report. Occasional papers; library publications.
Members Governments of 11 Southeast Asian countries:
Brunei Darussalam, Cambodia, Indonesia, Laos, Malaysia, Myanmar, Philippines, Singapore, Thailand, Timor-Leste, Vietnam.
Associate members governments of 8 countries:
Australia, Canada, France, Germany, Netherlands, New Zealand, Spain, UK. [2020/XE6531/**E***]

♦ SEAMEO Regional Open Learning Centre (SEAMOLEC) 19182

Secretariat Kompleks Univ Terbuka, Jl Cabe Raya, Pondok Cabe Udik, Pamulang, Tangerang 15418, Indonesia. T. +62217423725 – +62217424154. Fax +62217422276. E-mail: secretariat@seamolec.org.
URL: http://seamolec.org/

History 27 Feb 1997. Founded as one of the Regional Centres/Network of *Southeast Asian Ministers of Education Organization (SEAMEO, #19774).* **Aims** Undertake relevant programmes that are responsive to current national and regional needs through the utilization of open and distance learning system. **Structure** Director; Deputy Directors (2); Divisions (7). **Languages** English, Indonesian. **Staff** 50.00 FTE, paid. **Finance** Sources: Government of Indonesia; SEAMEO Educational Development Fund; donors. **Activities** Events/meetings; guidance/assistance/consulting; knowledge management/information dissemination; research and development; training/education. **Events** *International seminar on open and distance learning for sustainable development* Jakarta (Indonesia) 2004, *Meeting* Jakarta (Indonesia) 2004, *Symposium* Jakarta (Indonesia) 2004, *International symposium on open distance learning* Yogyakarta (Indonesia) 2004, *Meeting* Tanjong Malim (Malaysia) 2003. **Publications** *SEAMOLEC Info* (3 a year) in English, Indonesian – Newsletter. Annual Report. **Members** Member countries of SEAMEO. **NGO Relations** Member of (2): *Asian Association of Open Universities (AAOU, #01331); International Council for Open and Distance Education (ICDE, #13056).*
[2022.11.10/XK1575/**E***]

♦ SEAMEO Regional Training Centre, Ho Chi Minh City (RETRAC) 19183

Dir 35 Le Thanh Ton St, District 1, Ho Chi Minh City HO CHI MINH, Vietnam. T. +8488245617 – +8488245618 – +8488232174. Fax +8488232175. E-mail: contact@vnseameo.org.
URL: http://www.vnseameo.org/

History Oct 1996, as one of the Regional Centres/Network of *Southeast Asian Ministers of Education Organization (SEAMEO, #19774).* **Aims** Identify and help solve common problems of *human resource development* within SEAMEO member countries, especially in *education* management. **Structure** Governing Board; Centre Director. Departments (4): Administration Office; Educational Management Department; Educational Services Department; Social Services Department. **Activities** Training/education; events/meetings. **Events** *Meeting* Bangkok (Thailand) 2004.
Members SEAMEO member countries (10):
Brunei Darussalam, Cambodia, Indonesia, Laos, Malaysia, Myanmar, Philippines, Singapore, Thailand, Vietnam.
[2017/XK1435/**E***]

♦ SEAMEO Regional Tropical Medicine and Public Health Network (SEAMEO TROPMED) 19184

SG 420/6 Ratchawithi Road, Bangkok, 10400, Thailand. T. +6623543145 – +6623549146 – +6626445135. Fax +6623549144. E-mail: secretariat@seameotropmednetwork.org.
URL: http://www.seameotropmednetwork.org/

History 1967, Bangkok (Thailand), as one of the Regional Centres/Network of *Southeast Asian Ministers of Education Organization (SEAMEO, #19774).* Previously sometimes referred to as *SEAMEO Regional Tropical Medicine and Public Health Project (TROPMED).* **Aims** Develop capacity of individuals and institutions in delivering quality healthcare in the region. **Structure** Governing Board; Council; Regional Centres: *SEAMEO TROPMED Regional Centre for Microbiology, Parasitology and Entomology (#19185),* TROPMED/Malaysia; *SEAMEO TROPMED Regional Centre for Public Health, Hospital Administration, Environmental and Occupational Health (#19186),* TROPMED/Philippines; *SEAMEO TROPMED Regional Centre for Tropical Medicine (#19187),* TROPMED/Thailand. Network Central Office, located in Bangkok (Thailand), headed by the Secretary General/Coordinator. **Languages** English. **Staff** 15.00 FTE, paid. **Finance** Financial resources through SEAMEO Secretariat – SEAMES, donor countries and international organizations. **Activities** Training/education; research and development; capacity building; advocacy/lobbying/activism; events/meetings;

knowledge management/information dissemination. **Events** *Joint international tropical medicine meeting* Bangkok (Thailand) 2009, *Seminar on food- and water-borne parasitic zoonoses* Bangkok (Thailand) 2009, *Seminar on food- and water-borne parasitic zoonoses* Bangkok (Thailand) 2006, *Meeting* Rangoon (Myanmar) 2004, *Joint international tropical medicine meeting* Nakhon Pathom (Thailand) 2002. **Publications** *Southeast Asian Journal of Tropical Medicine and Public Health* (6 a year) in English. Annual Report; technical articles; seminar and conference proceedings.
Members SEAMEO member countries (11):
Brunei Darussalam, Cambodia, Indonesia, Laos, Malaysia, Myanmar, Philippines, Singapore, Thailand, Timor-Leste, Vietnam.
Associate member countries (8):
Australia, Canada, France, Germany, Netherlands, New Zealand, Spain, UK.
Affiliate members (5):
Asia-Pacific Centre of Education for International Understanding (APCEIU); *British Council*; *China Education Association for International Exchange (CEAIE)*; *International Council for Open and Distance Education (ICDE, #13056)*; University of Tsukuba, Japan.
IGO Relations Instrumental in setting up: *SEAMEO Regional Centre for Food and Nutrition (SEAMEO RECFON, #19173).* [2019/XE8681/**E***]

- ♦ SEAMEO Regional Tropical Medicine and Public Health Project / see SEAMEO Regional Tropical Medicine and Public Health Network (#19184)
- ♦ **SEAMEO RELC** SEAMEO Regional Language Centre (#19181)
- ♦ **SEAMEO** Southeast Asian Ministers of Education Organization (#19774)
- ♦ **SEAMEO SPAFA** SEAMEO Regional Centre for Archaeology and Fine Arts (#19169)
- ♦ **SEAMEO STEM-ED** Southeast Asian Ministers of Education Organization Regional Centre for STEM Education (#19775)
- ♦ **SEAMEO TED** SEAMEO Regional Centre for Technical Education Development (#19179)
- ♦ SEAMEO-TROPMED RCCN / see SEAMEO Regional Centre for Food and Nutrition (#19173)
- ♦ SEAMEO TROPMED Regional Centre for Community Nutrition / see SEAMEO Regional Centre for Food and Nutrition (#19173)

♦ SEAMEO TROPMED Regional Centre for Microbiology, Parasitology and Entomology 19185

Dir Inst for Medical Research, Block C – Level 6, National Insts of Health Complex, No 1 Jalan Setia Murni U13/52, Setia Alam City, 40170 Shah Alam, Selangor, Malaysia. T. +60333628906. E-mail: tahir.a@moh.gov.my – seameo@moh.gov.my.
URL: https://seameotropmednetwork.org/malaysia_vision.html

History 1967. Established as a regional centre of *SEAMEO Regional Tropical Medicine and Public Health Network (SEAMEO TROPMED, #19184)*, within the framework of *Southeast Asian Ministers of Education Organization (SEAMEO, #19774)*. Former names and other names: *SEAMEO Regional Centre for Medical Microbiology, Parasitology and Entomology* – alias; *TROPMED/Malaysia* – alias. **Aims** Promote cooperation among SEAMEO member countries through various activities in the field of *tropical medicine* and *public health.* **Languages** Central Malay, English. **Finance** Operating budget funded mainly by the Malaysian Government. Other sources: research grants and training fellowships from both local and international organizations, such as: asia Pacific Malaria Elimination Network (APMEN); *Global Fund to Fight AIDS, Tuberculosis and Malaria (Global Fund, #10383)*; SEAMEO TROPMED; *WHO (#20950)*. **Activities** Guidance/assistance/consulting; research and development; training/education. Southeast Asia. **Publications** Scientific papers; technical reports; proceedings of scientific and technical meetings. [2023.02.14/XK0446/**E***]

♦ SEAMEO TROPMED Regional Centre for Public Health, Hospital Administration, Environmental and Occupational Health 19186

Dir Dean College of Public Health, Univ of the Philippines Manila, 625 Pedro Gil Street, Ermita, 1000 Manila, Philippines. T. +6325242703. Fax +6325211394. E-mail: acsantos3@up.edu.ph.
URL: http://www.seameo.org/

History as a regional centre of *SEAMEO Regional Tropical Medicine and Public Health Network (SEAMEO TROPMED, #19184)*, within the framework of *Southeast Asian Ministers of Education Organization (SEAMEO, #19774)*. Also referred to as: *SEAMEO Regional Centre for Public Health, Hospital Administration, Occupational and Environmental Health*; *TROPMED/Philippines*. The *'College of Public Health (CPH)'* of Manila (Philippines) acts as this Regional Centre. **Aims** Offer courses on *dental* public health, health promotion and *education, microbiology, parasitology, biostatistics, epidemiology, nutrition*, public health administration, hospital administration, environmental health and occupational health. [2017/XK0447/**E***]

♦ SEAMEO TROPMED Regional Centre for Tropical Medicine 19187

Dir Dean Fac of Tropical Medicine, Mahidol Univ, 420/6 Ratchawithi Road, Bangkok, 10400, Thailand. T. +6623549199 – +6626447483. Fax +6626444436 – +6623549198. E-mail: tmpsh@mahidol.ac.th – tmirunit@mahidol.ac.th.
URL: http://www.seameo.org/

History 1994, when designated as a regional centre of *SEAMEO Regional Tropical Medicine and Public Health Network (SEAMEO TROPMED, #19184)*, within the framework of *Southeast Asian Ministers of Education Organization (SEAMEO, #19774)*. Also know as *TROPMED/Thailand*. Originally, the Faculty of Tropical Medicine, Mahidol University, was appointed the TROPMED National Centre of Tropical Medicine in 1967. The activities of the Faculty of Tropical Medicine and *'TROPMED/Thailand'* are synonymous. **Aims** Offer training on endemic tropical diseases, parasitology, community and preventive medicine; conduct research on alternative control measures of diseases and the promotion of healthy lifestyles, including trials of new chemotherapeutic compounds and new vaccines; provide clinical care to patients suffering from tropical diseases. **NGO Relations** Member of: *International Federation for Tropical Medicine (IFTM, #13575).* [2011.03.05/XK0448/**E***]

- ♦ **SEAMEO TROPMED** SEAMEO Regional Tropical Medicine and Public Health Network (#19184)
- ♦ SEAMEO VOCTECH / see SEAMEO Regional Centre for Vocational and Technical Education (#19180)
- ♦ SEAMIC / see African Minerals and Geosciences Centre (#00373)
- ♦ **SEAMOLEC** SEAMEO Regional Open Learning Centre (#19182)
- ♦ **SEAMS** Southeast Asian Mathematical Society (#19773)
- ♦ **SEANAC** Southern and Eastern Africa Network of Analytical Chemists (#19874)
- ♦ **SEANAFE** Southeast Asian Network for Agroforestry Education (#19776)
- ♦ **SEANES** South East Asian Network of Ergonomics Societies (#19777)
- ♦ SEANET / see South East Asia Net (#19764)
- ♦ **SEANET** South East Asia Net (#19764)
- ♦ SEAN International (internationally oriented national body)
- ♦ SEANWFZ – Southeast Asian Nuclear Weapon-Free Zone (see: #01141)
- ♦ SEANZA – Central Banks of Southeast Asia, New Zealand and Australia (meeting series)
- ♦ **SEAOHUN** Southeast Asia One Health University Network (#19789)
- ♦ SEAPAC – South East Asia Parliamentarians Against Corruption (see: #10518)
- ♦ SEAPAL / see Asia Pacific League of Associations for Rheumatology (#01945)
- ♦ SEAPAVAA / see Southeast Asia-Pacific Audiovisual Archive Association (#19790)
- ♦ **SEAPAVAA** Southeast Asia-Pacific Audiovisual Archive Association (#19790)
- ♦ **SEAPEX** South East Asia Petroleum Exploration Society (#19791)
- ♦ SEA – Protocol on Strategic Environmental Assessment (2003 treaty)
- ♦ **SEAP** Society of European Affairs Professionals (#19553)
- ♦ SEAQUIS / see SEAMEO Regional Centre for Quality Improvement of Teachers and Education Personnel in Science (#19178)
- ♦ **SEARADO** Southeast Asia Regional Anti-Doping Organisation (#19792)
- ♦ **SEARAME** South-East Asian Regional Association for Medical Education (#19780)
- ♦ SEARCA / see Southeast Asian Regional Center for Graduate Study and Research in Agriculture (#19781)
- ♦ **SEARCA** Southeast Asian Regional Center for Graduate Study and Research in Agriculture (#19781)
- ♦ **SEARCC** South East Asia Regional Computer Confederation (#19794)
- ♦ Search for Common Ground (internationally oriented national body)
- ♦ Search for Common Ground in the Middle East (internationally oriented national body)

♦ Search and Information Industry Association (Siinda) 19188

General Manager Gotthardstr 55, 8800 Thalwil ZH, Switzerland. E-mail: info@siinda.com.
Belgium Representative Office 4th Floor South Ctr Titanium, Marcel Brother Square 8, 1060 Brussels, Belgium. T. +3228923979.
URL: http://www.siinda.com/

History 1 Jan 2014. Founded, resulting from the merger between *EIDQ Association (inactive)* and *European Association of Search and Database Publishing (EASDP, inactive)*. Registration: No/ID: CH-020.6.000.453-8, Switzerland; EU Transparency Register, No/ID: 209899418750-27, Start date: 11 Sep 2015. **Aims** Build a worldwide cooperative network of companies and associates within the Search and Information Industry. **Structure** Board of Directors. **Activities** Events/meetings. **Events** *Local Search Summit* Lisbon (Portugal) 2019, *Conference* Budapest (Hungary) 2014, *Conference* Munich (Germany) 2014.
Members Full in 41 countries and territories:
Andorra, Australia, Austria, Bahrain, Belarus, Belgium, Brazil, Bulgaria, Cyprus, Czechia, Denmark, Estonia, Finland, France, Germany, Greece, Hungary, Iceland, Ireland, Italy, Latvia, Lithuania, Macau, Malta, Mauritius, Netherlands, Norway, Palestine, Poland, Portugal, Russia, Slovakia, Slovenia, South Africa, Spain, Sri Lanka, Sweden, Switzerland, Türkiye, UK, USA.
Included in the above, 1 organization listed in this Yearbook:
Asian Local Search and Media Association (ALSMA, #01531).
NGO Relations Cooperates with various partners including: *Intergraf (#11505)*; *European Magazine Media Association (EMMA, #07723)*; *European Newspaper Publishers' Association (ENPA, #08048)*; *Federation of Business Information Services (FEBIS, #09464)*; *IAB Europe (#11002)*; *International Capital Market Association (ICMA, #12438)*; *International Federation of Library Associations and Institutions (IFLA, #13470)*; *Software and Information Industry Association (SIIA).* [2021/XJ8657/t/**C**]

- ♦ Searchlight (internationally oriented national body)
- ♦ Search and Matching research group / see European Search and Matching Network (#08454)
- ♦ Search and Rescue (#04845)
- ♦ SEARC – Southeast Asia Radiographers Conference (meeting series)
- ♦ SEARG – Southern and Eastern African Rabies Group (inactive)
- ♦ SEAR-HELLIS / see WHO South-East Asia Region Health Literature, Library and Information Services Network (#20948)
- ♦ **SEARICE** Southeast Asia Regional Initiatives for Community Empowerment (#19795)
- ♦ **SearNet** Southern and Eastern Africa Rainwater Network (#19876)
- ♦ **SEAROG** South East Asian Radiation Oncology Group (#19779)
- ♦ **SEARO** WHO Regional Office for South-East Asia (#20946)
- ♦ **SEARSOLIN** Southeast Asia Rural Social Leadership Institute (#19797)
- ♦ SEASAE – Southern and Eastern Africa Society of Agricultural Engineers (no recent information)
- ♦ SEASCO / see UNESCO Office, Jakarta – Regional Bureau for Sciences in Asia and the Pacific (#20313)
- ♦ Sea Shepherd Conservation Society / see Sea Shepherd International
- ♦ Sea Shepherd International (internationally oriented national body)
- ♦ **SEASIA** Consortium for Southeast Asian Studies in Asia (#04757)
- ♦ SEA – Single European Act (1986 treaty)
- ♦ **SEASN** South Eastern Europe Advisory Service Network (#19805)
- ♦ **SEA** Société européenne d'arachnologie (#08523)
- ♦ **SEA** Spatial Econometrics Association (#19903)
- ♦ SEASPF – Southeast Asia School Principals Forum (unconfirmed)
- ♦ SEASREP Council / see Southeast Asian Studies Regional Exchange Program Foundation (#19784)
- ♦ **SEASREP Foundation** Southeast Asian Studies Regional Exchange Program Foundation (#19784)

♦ Seas at Risk (SAR) 19189

Main Office Rue d'Edimbourg 26, 1050 Brussels, Belgium. T. +3228930965. Fax +3228930966. E-mail: secretariat@seas-at-risk.org.
URL: http://seas-at-risk.org/

History 1986. Founded by nationally based marine environmental NGOs. Previously registered in accordance with Dutch law, under the full legal title *Stichting Seas at Risk Federation.* Registration: Banque-Carrefour des Entreprises, No/ID: 0884.771.444, Start date: 6 Nov 2006. **Aims** Protect and restore the European *marine environment* of the North East Atlantic. **Structure** Assembly (annual); Board. **Languages** English. **Staff** 6.00 FTE, paid. **Finance** Grants. **Activities** Politics/policy/regulatory; advocacy/lobbying/activism. **Events** *Annual General Meeting* Lisbon (Portugal) 2015, *Annual General Meeting* Brussels (Belgium) 2014, *Conference on low impact fisheries and the reform of the CFP* Brussels (Belgium) 2010, *European conference* Copenhagen (Denmark) 1994. **Publications** *SAR Newsletter* (6 a year) – electronic.
Members National and environmental organizations in 15 countries:
Belgium, Croatia, Denmark, France, Germany, Greece, Ireland, Italy, Netherlands, Norway, Portugal, Spain, Sweden, Switzerland, UK.
Included in the above, 8 organizations listed in this Yearbook:
Environmental Investigation Agency (EIA); *European Environmental Bureau (EEB, #06996)*; *Friends of the Earth International (FoEI, #10002)*; *Marine Conservation Society (MCS)*; *North Sea Foundation*; *OceanCare*; *Project AWARE Foundation*; *World Animal Protection (#21092).*
IGO Relations Accredited observer organization within *OSPAR Commission for the Protection of the Marine Environment of the North-East Atlantic (OSPAR Commission, #17905).* Works at European Union level and within *International Maritime Organization (IMO, #14102).* **NGO Relations** Member of: *Clean Shipping Coalition (CSC, #03989)*; *Climate Action Network Europe (CAN Europe, #04001)*; *Coalition Clean Baltic (CCB, #04053)*; *Deep Sea Conservation Coalition (DSCC, #05024)*; *European Power Electronics and Drives Association (EPE, #08261)*; *Federation of European and International Associations Established in Belgium (FAIB, #09508)*; *Global Call for Climate Action (GCCA, inactive)*; *Long Distance Advisory Council (LDAC, #16511)*; *Market Advisory Council (MAC, #16584)*; *North Sea Advisory Council (NSAC, #17603)*; *North Western Waters Advisory Council (NWWAC, #17607)*; *Spring Alliance (inactive).* Instrumental in setting up: *European Seas Environmental Cooperation (ESEC, inactive).* [2021/XF4963/y/**F**]

- ♦ SEASSE / see Southeast Asian Geotechnical Society (#19769)
- ♦ **SEASTF** Southeast Asian Soft Tennis Federation (#19783)
- ♦ **SEA** Sustainable Event Alliance (#20057)
- ♦ SEATAC – Southeast Asian Agency for Regional Transport and Communications Development (inactive)
- ♦ **SEATCA** Southeast Asian Tobacco Control Alliance (#19785)
- ♦ SEATCCO – South East Asia Teachers and Counsellors Conference (meeting series)
- ♦ **SEATINI** Southern and Eastern African Trade Information and Negotiations Initiative (#19875)
- ♦ SEATO Graduate School of Engineering / see Asian Institute of Technology (#01519)
- ♦ SEATO – South-East Asia Treaty Organization (inactive)
- ♦ **SEATPA** South East Asia Theoretical Physics Association (#19799)
- ♦ **SEATTA** South East Asia Table Tennis Association (#19798)

♦ Seattle to Brussels Network (S2B) 19190

Coordinator c/o Transnational Institute, PO Box 14656, 1001 LD Amsterdam, Netherlands. T. +31206626608.
URL: http://www.s2bnetwork.org/

History 2000, Brussels (Belgium). A pan-European NGO network. The European part of the global *Our World is Not for Sale (OWINFS, #17917).* Registration: EU Transparency Register, No/ID: 059352020164-92, Start date: 4 Jan 2016. **Aims** Promote a *sustainable, democratic* and accountable system of *trade.* **Structure** Coordination Group. **Publications** *Corporate Power over EU Trade Policy: Good for Business – Bad for the World* (2006); *The EU's Corporate Trade Agenda: The Role and the Interests of Corporations and Their Lobby Groups in Trade Policy-Making in the European Union* (2005); *From Cancún to Honk Kong: Challenging Corporate Led Trade Negotiations* (2004); *Investment and Competition Negotiations in the WTO – What Is Wrong with It and What Are the Alternatives ?* (2002); *GATS and Democracy* (2001).
Members Organizations in 22 countries:
Austria, Belgium, Croatia, Czechia, Denmark, Finland, France, Germany, Hungary, Italy, Latvia, Luxembourg, Malta, Netherlands, Norway, Slovakia, Spain, Sweden, Switzerland, Türkiye, UK, Ukraine.

Included in the above, 4 organizations listed in this Yearbook:
Comhlamh; Corporate Europe Observatory (CEO, #04839); European Coordination Via Campesina (ECVC, #06795); Seattle to Brussels Network (S2B, #19190).
NGO Relations Member of (1): *Alternative Trade Mandate Alliance (ATM).* European part of: *Our World is Not for Sale (OWINFS, #17917).* Signatory to: *Alter Summit.* [2022/XG9709/y/**F**]

♦ Sea Turtle Conservancy (internationally oriented national body)
♦ Sea Turtle Restoration Project / see Turtle Island Restoration Network
♦ SEATU – Southeast Asian Taekwondo Union (no recent information)
♦ SEA / see UNESCO Associated Schools Project Network (#20302)
♦ Sea-Watch (internationally oriented national body)
♦ Sea Watch Foundation (internationally oriented national body)
♦ SeaWeb (internationally oriented national body)
♦ SeaWeb – Leading Voices for a Healthy Ocean / see SeaWeb
♦ Seaweed for Europe (unconfirmed)
♦ SEA/WP / see Asia Pacific Federation of Pharmacologists (#01903)
♦ SEA/WPFP / see Asia Pacific Federation of Pharmacologists (#01903)
♦ **SEAWUN** South East Asian Water Utilities Network (#19787)
♦ **SEAYEN** Tunza Southeast Asia Youth Environment Network (#20261)
♦ SEAZA / see Southeast Asian Zoos and Aquariums Association (#19788)
♦ **SEAZA** Southeast Asian Zoos and Aquariums Association (#19788)
♦ **SEBC** Système européen des banques centrales (#08870)
♦ SEBH – Institute for Business History (inactive)
♦ SEBI-Livestock – Centre for Supporting Evidence Based Interventions in Livestock (internationally oriented national body)
♦ SEB – Skandinaviska Enskilda Banken (internationally oriented national body)
♦ SEB – Society for Economic Botany (internationally oriented national body)
♦ SEB – Society for Experimental Biology (internationally oriented national body)
♦ SECAAR – Service chrétien d'appui à l'animation rurale (internationally oriented national body)
♦ **SECAM** Symposium of Episcopal Conferences of Africa and Madagascar (#20077)
♦ SECAP / see Association Européenne des Concessionnaires d'Autoroutes et d'Ouvrages à Péage (#02559)
♦ **SE-CEAC** Secretaria Ejecutiva del Consejo de Electrificación de América Central (#19191)
♦ **SECEC** Société européenne pour la chirurgie de l'épaule et du coude (#08752)
♦ **SECEPRO** South East and Central Europe PR Organisation (#19802)
♦ SEC / see European Society of Contraception and Reproductive Health (#08568)
♦ Sechstes protokoll zum Allgemeinen abkommen über die vorrechte und befreiungen des Europarats (1996 treaty)
♦ SECIB – Secretaria de Cooperación Iberoamericana (internationally oriented national body)
♦ SECI Center Bucharest / see Southeast European Law Enforcement Center (#19815)
♦ SECI Regional Center for Combating Trans-Border Crime / see Southeast European Law Enforcement Center (#19815)
♦ **SECI** Southeast European Cooperative Initiative (#19812)
♦ **SECIS** Service of the European Churches for International Students (#19242)
♦ **SECOF** Sociedad Europea de Cooperación Farmacéutica (#19359)
♦ Second ACP-EEC Convention (1979 treaty)
♦ Second Additional Convention Respecting the Transport of Goods by Rail (1906 treaty)
♦ Second Additional Protocol to the Convention on Cybercrime on enhanced co-operation and disclosure of electronic evidence (2022 treaty)
♦ Second Additional Protocol to the European Convention on Extradition (1978 treaty)
♦ Second Additional Protocol to the European Convention on Mutual Assistance in Criminal Matters (2001 treaty)
♦ Secondary Ion Mass Spectrometry / see International SIMS Society (#14860)
♦ Second International (inactive)
♦ Second International Tin Agreement (1960 treaty)
♦ Secondo protocollo addizionale all'Accordo generale su i privilegi e le immunità del Consiglio d'Europa (1956 treaty)
♦ Secondo protocollo addizionale alla Convenzione europea di assistenza giudiziaria in materia penale (2001 treaty)
♦ Secondo protocollo addizionale alla Convenzione europea di estradizione (1978 treaty)
♦ Secondo protocollo di modifica alla Convenzione sulla riduzione dei casi di pluralità di nazionalità e sugli obblighi militari in caso di pluralità di nazionalità (1993 treaty)
♦ Second Optional Protocol to the International Covenant on Civil and Political Rights Aiming at the Abolition of the Death Penalty (1989 treaty)
♦ Second Protocol Amending the Convention on the Canalization of the Moselle (1983 treaty)
♦ Second Protocol Amending the Convention on the Reduction of Cases of Multiple Nationality and Military Obligations in Cases of Multiple Nationality (1993 treaty)
♦ Second Protocol to the General Agreement on Privileges and Immunities of the Council of Europe (1956 treaty)
♦ Second Protocol to The Hague Convention for the Protection of Cultural Property in the Event of Armed Conflict (1999 treaty)
♦ **SECOTOX** International Society of Ecotoxicology and Environmental Safety (#15073)
♦ Secours catholique – Caritas France (internationally oriented national body)
♦ Secours dentaire international (inactive)
♦ Secours international Caritas / see International Relief Service of Caritas Catholica, Belgium
♦ Secours international d'enfants (#12551)
♦ Secours internationaux aux réfugiés (inactive)
♦ Secours aux lépreux Canada (internationally oriented national body)
♦ Secours mondial (internationally oriented national body)
♦ Secours quaker canadien (internationally oriented national body)
♦ Secrétaire régionale des architectes de la région andine (#18816)
♦ Secrétaires et assistant/e/s de direction dans la Communauté européenne / see SPACE Network (#19899)
♦ **Secretaria CITES** Secretaria de la Convención sobre el Comercio Internacional de Especies Amenazadas de Fauna y Flora Silvestres (#19199)
♦ Secretaria del Commonwealth (#04362)
♦ Secretaria de la Convención sobre el Comercio Internacional de Especies Amenazadas de Fauna y Flora Silvestres (#19199)
♦ Secretaria de la Convención de las Naciones Unidas de Lucha contra la Desertificacion (#19208)
♦ Secretaria de Cooperação Iberoamericana (internationally oriented national body)
♦ Secretaria de Cooperación Iberoamericana (internationally oriented national body)
♦ Secretariado Episcopal de América Central (#05514)
♦ Secretariado Episcopal de América Central y Panama / see Episcopal Secretariat of Central America (#05514)
♦ Secretariado Europeo de Fabricantes de Envases Metalicos Ligeros (inactive)
♦ Secretariado Europeo de las Profesiones Liberales / see European Council of Liberal Professions (#06828)
♦ Secretariado Europeu do Ambiente / see European Environmental Bureau (#06996)
♦ Secretariado Iberoamericano de Municipios (no recent information)
♦ Secretariado de Institutos Seculares en América Latina / see Confederación de Institutos Seculares en América Latina (#04451)
♦ Secretariado Internacional de Agrónomos, Economistas e Ingenieros Católicos (#19203)
♦ Secretariado Internacional del Agua (#14822)
♦ Secretariado Internacional de Artistas Cristianos / see International Society of Christian Artists (#15009)
♦ Secretariado Internacional Cristiano de Solidaridad con América Latina 'Oscar A Romero' (internationally oriented national body)
♦ Secretariado Internacional Cristiano de Solidaridad con los Pueblos de América Latina /Oscar A Romero/ / see Secretariado Internacional Cristiano de Solidaridad con América Latina 'Oscar A Romero'
♦ Secretariado Internacional del Movimiento Doce de Diciembre (internationally oriented national body)
♦ Secretariado Internacional de los Sindicatos de Artes, Medios de Communicación y Espectaculo (inactive)
♦ Secretariado Internacional de Tipógrafos (inactive)
♦ Secretariado Latinoamericano de la Compañia de Jesús (religious order)
♦ Secretariado Profesional Internacional de la Enseñanza (inactive)
♦ Secretariados Profesionales Internacionales / see Global Union Federations (#10638)
♦ Secretariado del TLCAN (#16927)
♦ Secretariado para la Unión de los Cristianos / see Pontifical Council for Promoting Christian Unity (#18446)

♦ Secretaria Ejecutiva del Consejo de Electrificación de América Central (SE-CEAC) 19191

Executive Secretariat of the Council of Electrification of Central America – Secrétariat executive du Conseil de l'électrification de l'Amérique centrale

Contact 9a Calle poniente, No 950, Entre 15 y 17 Av Norte, Centro de Gobierno, San Salvador, El Salvador. T. +50322116175 – +50322116175 – +50322116359.
URL: http://www.ceaconline.org/

History 18 Apr 1985, San José (Costa Rica), at 9th meeting of Presidents and Managers of the Electrical Enterprises of the Central American Isthmus, having been proposed at 6th meeting, 29-30 Mar 1979, Panama. Also referred to in English as *Electrification Council of Central America.* Comes within the framework of *Central American Integration System (#03671).* **Aims** Obtain the best exploitation (usage) of the resources of energy of the Member States by means of an efficient, rational and appropriate generation, transmission and distribution of electrical *energy* among Central American countries. **Structure** Joint Meeting, consisting of the highest executive authorities of member institutions. Executive Office, directed by Executive Secretary. Committees; Sub-Committees; Technical Working Groups. **Finance** Members' contributions. Other sources: donations and legacies; government loans; other contributions received from members or from third institutions or persons. **Activities** Bilateral and multilateral agreements for the electrical interconnection among Central American countries and other countries. Carries out studies and research in the field; provides scientific, technical, administrative and material assistance to integrated institutions; gives advice and information; offers personal organization and training.
Members National representative institutions appointed by 6 Member States:
Costa Rica, El Salvador, Guatemala, Honduras, Nicaragua, Panama. [2013/XE1631/**E***]

♦ Secretaria General Iberoamericana (#11024)
♦ Secretaria Geral Ibero-Americana (#11024)

♦ Secretaria de Integración Social Centroamericana (SISCA) 19192

Central American Social Integration Secretariat

Headquarters Avda Roberto F Chiari y C George W Goethal, Edificio 711, Balboa, Ancón, Panama, Panamá, Panama PANAMá, Panama. T. +15073995949. E-mail: info@sisca.int.
Sub-Headquarters Final Blv Cancilleria, Distrito el Espino, Ciudad Merliot, La Libertad, El Salvador. T. +150322488857.
URL: http://www.sica.int/sisca/

History 30 Mar 1995, El Salvador. 30 Mar 1995, Cerro Verde (El Salvador), on signature of *Tratado de Integración Social Centroamericano (1995),* by representatives of the Governments of Costa Rica, El Salvador, Guatemala (Guatemala), Honduras, Nicaragua and Panama. Functions within the framework of *Central American Integration System (#03671).* The Secretariat also functions as technical secretariat of the *Consejo de Integración Social (CIS) – Social Integration Council* created by the Treaty. The Council is composed of Heads of social cabinets in SICA signatory countries. Since Sep 2000, fully integrates *Central American Council on Housing and Human Settlements (CCVAH, inactive).* **Aims** Contribute to elaboration of social policies as well as to the design and execution of projects and programs with a social character. **Languages** English, Spanish. **Events** *CONCASIDA : Central American congress of STI/HIV/AIDS* San Salvador (El Salvador) 2005, *Central American gathering of people living with HIV/AIDS* San Salvador (El Salvador) 2005, *Latin American and Caribbean forum of HIV/AIDS/STD* San Salvador (El Salvador) 2005.
Members Member States of SICA (9):
Belize, Costa Rica, Dominican Rep, El Salvador, Guatemala, Honduras, Nicaragua, Panama.
IGO Relations Provides technical secretariat for: *Consejo de Ministros de Salud de Centroamérica (COMISCA, #04722).* [2019.02.11/XE2965/**E***]

♦ Secretaria de Integración Turistica Centroamericana (SITCA) 19193

Secretariat of Central American Tourism Integration

Exec Sec Portón principal antiguo hospital militar 1 calle al lago, 1 1/2 cuadra abajo, casa 307, Managua, Nicaragua. T. +150522663415. E-mail: contacto@sitca.info.
URL: http://sitca.info/

History 1965, as *Secretaria Técnica del Consejo Centroamericano de Turismo (ST-CCT) – Technical Secretariat of the Central American Council of Tourism – Secrétariat technique du Conseil centroaméricain du tourisme.* Comes within the framework of *Central American Integration System (#03671),* coordinated by *Secretaria Permanente del Tratado General de Integración Económica Centroamericana (SIECA, #19195).* **Aims** Lead and coordinate the general policy of Central American tourism activity at a regional level; facilitate and stimulate the development of tourism in all the region; manage and coordinate tourism promotion programmes. **Activities** Elaborates and implements policies to facilitate circulation of people who come to Central America as tourists; undertakes technical studies. [2017/XE0061/**E***]

♦ Secretaria Internacional de la Lana (inactive)
♦ Secretaria Internacional para el Servicio Voluntario (inactive)
♦ Secretaria Permanente del Acuerdo Sudamericano sobre Estupefacientes y Psicotrópicos (inactive)

♦ Secretaria Permanente del Convenio Multilateral sobre Cooperación y Asistencia Mutua entre las Direcciones Nacionales de Aduanas de América Latina, España y Portugal (COMALEP) 19194

Permanent Secretariat for the Multilateral Convention on Cooperation and Mutual Assistance among National Directions of Customs of Latin America, Spain and Portugal – Secrétariat permanent de la Convention multilatérale sur la coopération et l'assistance mutuelle entre les directions nationales des douanes de l'Amérique latine, de l'Espagne et du Portugal

Permanent Sec Aduana Mexico, Avda Hidalgo No 77 – Módulo IV – Piso 3, Col Guerrero, Deleg Cuauhtémoc, 06300 Mexico City CDMX, Mexico. T. +5258020836 – +5258020839. Fax +5258020759.

History 11 Sep 1981, Mexico City (Mexico), on signature of *Multilateral Agreement on Cooperation and Mutual Assistance between the National Customs Directors of Latin America, Spain and Portugal (1981).* The Convention came into force on 11 Dec 1981. During XX Annual Meeting, 29 Oct 1999, Agreement was modified; Protocol of the Modification came into force 17 Oct 2002. The Secretariat subsumes the functions and goals of *Sistema Latinoamericano de Capacitación e Investigación Aduaneras (inactive).* **Aims** Promote and develop cooperation and mutual assistance between international customs administration in order to standardize and simplify customs procedures meant to prevent, investigate and repress customs offences. **Structure** Plenary of National Directors of Customs of Latin America, Spain and Portugal (annual). Secretariat, located in Mexico City (Mexico). **Languages** Portuguese, Spanish. **Staff** 5.00 FTE, paid. **Finance** Funded by the 'Secretaria de Hacienda y Crédito Público' of Mexico. **Events** *Annual Meeting of National Directors of Customs* Santa Cruz (Bolivia) 2016, *Annual Meeting of National Directors of Customs* Panama 2013, *Annual Meeting of National Directors of Customs* Punta del Este (Uruguay) 2012, *Annual Meeting of National Directors of Customs* Antigua (Guatemala) 2010, *Annual meeting of national directors / Annual Meeting of National Directors of Customs* Ecuador 2009.

Members National Directions of Customs of 20 countries:
Argentina, Bolivia, Brazil, Chile, Colombia, Costa Rica, Cuba, Dominican Rep, Ecuador, El Salvador, Guatemala, Honduras, Mexico, Nicaragua, Panama, Paraguay, Peru, Portugal, Spain, Uruguay, Venezuela.
Protocol of Modification ratified by National Directions of Customs of 8 countries:
Bolivia, Colombia, Costa Rica, Cuba, Guatemala, Nicaragua, Peru, Spain.
IGO Relations Formal contacts with: *Andean Community (#00817)*; *Caribbean Customs Law Enforcement Council (CCLEC, #03487)*; *Inter-American Development Bank (IDB, #11427)*; *OAS (#17629)*; *Postal Union of the Americas, Spain and Portugal (PUASP, #18466)*; *Secretaria Permanente del Tratado General de Integración Económica Centroamericana (SIECA, #19195)*; *UNCTAD (#20285)*; *United Nations Economic Commission for Latin America and the Caribbean (ECLAC, #20556)*; *World Customs Organization (WCO, #21350)*. **NGO Relations** Formal contacts with: *Conferencia Latino Americana de Compañias Express (CLADEC, #04654)*; *International Chamber of Commerce (ICC, #12534)*; *Professional Customs Brokers Association of the Americas (#18512)*. [2019/XF0358/**E***]

♦ Secretaria Permanente del Tratado General de Integración Económica Centroamericana (SIECA) 19195

Secrétariat permanent du Traité général d'intégration économique de l'Amérique centrale – Permanent Secretariat of the General Treaty on Central American Economic Integration

Contact 4a Avenida 10-25 Z 14, Guatemala, Guatemala. T. +50223682151. E-mail: info@sieca.int.
URL: http://www.sieca.int/

History 13 Dec 1960, Managua (Nicaragua), on signature of *General Treaty on Central American Economic Integration, 1960 (1960)* by representatives of the Governments of El Salvador, Guatemala (Guatemala), Honduras and Nicaragua. Treaty came into force, Jun 1961 and by Sep 1963 was ratified by all the 5 countries. SIECA commenced activities on 12 Oct 1961. A *Central American Economic Integration Program* had been formally established, 27 Aug 1952, when Ministers of the 5 states together formed *Central American Economic Cooperation Committee (#03667)* whose first meeting was on that occasion. The General Treaty is the basic instrument of the Program, envisaging the creation of *Central American Common Market (CACM, #03666)*. The Treaty incorporates *Agreement on the System of Central American Integrated Industries (1958)*, signed 10 Jun 1958, and also takes into account and keeps in force previous agreements: *Multilateral Treaty on Free Trade and Central American Economic Integration (1958)*; *Central American Agreement on the Equalization of Import Charges (1959)*, with accompanying Protocol on Central American Preferential Tariff, adopted 1 Sep 1959. Costa Rica adhered to the Central American convention on equalization of tariff rates, 23 Jul 1962. A number of protocols to the General Treaty have been signed by member countries and ratified by some or all of them, including *Protocol to the General Treaty of Central American Economic Integration – Central American Uniform Customs Code (1963)* which contains the *Standard Central American Tariff Code (CAUCA)*. Restructuring of CACM was initiated in 1973. From Dec 1974, SIECA contributed to drawing up a Treaty establishing *Central American Economic and Social Community (inactive)* to replace CACM; and a Draft Treaty was presented to Presidents of member countries, 23 Mar 1976. In Dec 1984, *Convention on Central American Tariff and Customs Regulations (1984)* was signed by plenipotentiaries of the Governments of Costa Rica, El Salvador, Guatemala and Nicaragua and came into force in these countries on 17 Sep 1985, at first meeting of *Central American Tariff and Customs Council (no recent information)*. This adopted the Brussels (Belgium) Tariff Nomenclature (BTN) of the Customs Cooperation Council and remains open for accession to its provisions by any Central American state that is not an original signatory. *Central American Integration System (#03671)*, set up 13 Dec 1991, is the juridical and institutional framework to ensure the attainment of purposes of the Central American Integration Treaties and the follow up of regional policies and decisions adopted by summit meetings of Central American Presidents. The General Treaty of 1960 was modified in 1993 by *Protocol to the General Treaty of Central American Economic Integration, 1993 (Guatemala Protocol, 1993)*. Previous cooperation among Central American states commenced with the setting up of *Central American Federation (inactive)*, 1823. **Aims** Promote economic integration of Central America in order to obtain an equitable and sustainable economic and social development in terms of welfare of the Central American economies; coordinate economic policies of contracting states. **Structure** Original main bodies (which ceased to exist in Oct 1973): *Central American Economic Council (inactive)* and Executive Council. Current structure: *Council of Ministers Responsible for the Economic Integration and Regional Development* (the highest body), which conducts the economic integration of Central America and whose sessions are referred to as *Meeting of Ministers Responsible for the Economic Integration of Central America (ROMRIECA)*. Meeting of Presidents. Intersectoral Council of Ministers of Economic Integration. Sectoral Council. Executive Committee of Economic Integration. SIECA, headed by Secretary General, is the technical and administrative entity in charge of the economic affairs and coordinates 3 specialized Secretariats: *Central American Agricultural Council (#03657)*; *Central American Monetary Council (#03672)*; *Secretaria de Integración Turistica Centroamericana (SITCA, #19193)*. Other institutions of the economic integration of Central America: *Central American Bank for Economic Integration (CABEI, #03658)*; *Central American Institute of Public Administration (#03670)*. **Languages** Spanish. **Activities** SIECA continues in efforts to develop the Central American Common Market originally planned by ECLAC. In accordance with the current strategy for the economic integration of Central America, activities are focused on perfecting the Central American Common Market and inserting the region into the world economy. Within this framework, SIECA: supervises correct application of the legal instruments of economic integration; executes decisions of the bodies conducting economic integration; undertakes studies and other work requested by these bodies; acts as a link with these bodies and the institutions and secretariats of the integration system; exercises initiative in issues related to integration. General Directions (3): Central American Common Market; Foreign Commercial Policy; Studies of Integration and Cooperation. Was instrumental in setting up: *Asociación de Usuarios del Transporte Maritimo, Terrestre y Aéreo del Istmo Centroamericano (USUARIOS, no recent information)*; *Comisión Centroamericana de Directores de Migración (OCAM, no recent information)*; *Asociación Centroamericana de Armadores (ACAMAR, no recent information)*. Proposes setting up: *Comisión Centroamericana de Desarrollo de las Exportaciones (no recent information)*. **Events** *Seminario sobre el reglamento centraomericano del valor aduanero de las mercancias* 2005, *Joint meeting* Brussels (Belgium) 2005. **Publications** *Carta Informativa SIECA* (12 a year); *Integración en Cifras* (4 a year); *La Propriedad Intelectual en la Integración Económica Centroamericana* (4 a year); *Boletin Informativo* (2 a year); *Boletines Estadisticos. Serie: Comunidad Económica y Social Centroamericana*; *Serie: Convenies Centroamericanos de Integración Económica*; *Serie: Cuadernos de la SIECA – Colección Manuel Noriega Morales*; *Serie: Directorios y Otras Publicaciones*; *Serie: Ediciones Juridicas Centroamericanas*; *Serie: Estudios Especiales*; *Serie: Publicaciones Estadisticas*.

Members Governments of 5 countries:
Costa Rica, El Salvador, Guatemala, Honduras, Nicaragua.

IGO Relations Permanent observer status with: *World Intellectual Property Organization (WIPO, #21593)*. Observer to: *Codex Alimentarius Commission (CAC, #04081)*; *World Trade Organization (WTO, #21864)*. Special agreement with: *FAO (#09260)*; *UNIDO (#20336)*. Participates in the activities of: *UNCTAD (#20285)*. Cooperates with: *United States Agency for International Development (USAID)*; *OAS (#17629)*. Member of: *Latin American and Caribbean Research Network (#16284)*. Participates as observer in the activities of: *Codex Alimentarius Commission (CAC, #04081)*; *Sistema Económico Latinoamericano (SELA, #19294)*. **NGO Relations** Instrumental in setting up: *Federación de Colegios y Asociaciones de Profesionales de Ciencias Económicas de Centroamérica y Panama (no recent information)*. [2017/XD0996/**E***]

- ♦ Secretaria de la Regional de Arquitectos del Grupo Andino (#18816)
- ♦ Secrétariat de l'ALENA (#16927)
- ♦ Secrétariat des Associations du Commerce Agricole Réunies (#16148)

♦ Secretariat of the Basel Convention (SBC) 19196

Mailing address Av de la Paix 8-14, 1211 Geneva 10, Switzerland. T. +41229178271. Fax +41229178098. E-mail: brs@brsmeas.org.
Office 11-13 Chemin des Anémones, 1219 Châtelaine, Switzerland.
URL: http://www.basel.int/

History to administer *Basel Convention on the Control of Transboundary Movements of Hazardous Wastes and Their Disposal (UNCRTD, 1989)* – also referred to as *'Basel Convention'* – through *UNEP (#20299)*. **Aims** Protect human *health* and the environment against the adverse effects of *hazardous wastes*. **Structure** Conference of the Parties (every 2 years); "Standing" subsidiary bodies: Open-ended Working Group (OEWG); Implementation and Compliance Committee. Since 2012, joined the Secretariat of the Stockholm Convention as well as the UNEP-part of the Rotterdam Convention Secretariat to a single Secretariat with a matrix structure serving the three conventions. **Staff** Joint Secretariat: 60. **Finance** Budget operated by trust funds: general trust fund which receives contributions from country Parties; technical cooperation trust fund which received voluntary contributions for specific areas of work. **Events** *Conference of the Parties – In Person Segment* Geneva (Switzerland) 2022, *Conference of the Parties – Online Segment* Geneva (Switzerland) 2021, *Conference of the Parties* Geneva (Switzerland) 2019, *Conference of the Parties* Geneva (Switzerland) 2015, *Conference onf the Parties* Geneva (Switzerland) 2013. **Publications** Publication of the Convention; guidelines; guidance.

IGO Relations Cooperates with the following UN bodies and specialized agencies:
- *FAO (#09260)*;
- *ILO (#11123)*;
- *International Atomic Energy Agency (IAEA, #12294)*;
- *International Maritime Organization (IMO, #14102)*;
- *Pan American Health Organization (PAHO, #18108)*;
- *UNCTAD (#20285)*;
- *UNDP (#20292)*;
- UNEP;
- UNEP;
- *UNIDO (#20336)*;
- *United Nations Framework Convention on Climate Change – Secretariat (UNFCCC, #20564)*;
- *United Nations Institute for Training and Research (UNITAR, #20576)*;
- *United Nations University (UNU, #20642)*;
- *WHO (#20950)*.

Cooperates with the following UN Regional Commissions:
- *United Nations Economic Commission for Africa (ECA, #20554)*;
- *United Nations Economic Commission for Europe (UNECE, #20555)*;
- *United Nations Economic Commission for Latin America and the Caribbean (ECLAC, #20556)*;
- *United Nations Economic and Social Commission for Asia and the Pacific (ESCAP, #20557)*;
- *United Nations Economic and Social Commission for Western Asia (ESCWA, #20558)*.

Other intergovernmental bodies:
- *Caribbean Community (CARICOM, #03476)*;
- *Centro Panamericano de Ingenieria Sanitaria y Ciencias del Ambiente (CEPIS, no recent information)*;
- *Comisión Permanente del Pacifico Sur (CPPS, #04141)*;
- *Commonwealth Secretariat (#04362)*;
- *International Criminal Police Organization – INTERPOL (ICPO-INTERPOL, #13110)*;
- *NATO (#16945)*;
- *OECD (#17693)*;
- *Pacific Islands Forum (#17968)*;
- *Regional Organization for the Protection of the Marine Environment (ROPME, #18805)*;
- *Secretariat of the Pacific Regional Environment Programme (SPREP, #19205)*;
- *World Trade Organization (WTO, #21864)*.

Memorandum of Understanding signed with: *Organisation for the Prohibition of Chemical Weapons (OPCW, #17823)*; *Secretariat of the Convention on International Trade in Endangered Species of Wild Fauna and Flora (CITES Secretariat, #19199)*; *World Customs Organization (WCO, #21350)*.
NGO Relations Cooperation and collaboration with NGOs to support implementation of the Convention. [2020/XE2653/**E***]

- ♦ Secretariat of Central American Tourism Integration (#19193)
- ♦ Secrétariat central des sociétés nationales de médecins catholiques (inactive)
- ♦ **Secrétariat CITES** Secrétariat de la Convention sur le commerce international des espèces de faune et de flore sauvages menacées d'extinction (#19199)
- ♦ Secrétariat du Comité de Pilotage du Forum de la Société Civile du Partenariat Oriantal / see Eastern Partnership Civil Society Forum (#05247)
- ♦ Secretariat of the Commission for East African Cooperation / see East African Community (#05181)
- ♦ Secrétariat commun d'UNIPEDE et d'EURELECTRIC / see Union of the Electricity Industry – Eurelectric (#20379)

♦ Secretariat of the Convention on Biological Diversity (SCBD) 19197

Exec Sec World Trade Centre, 413 Saint-Jacques, Ste 800, Montréal QC H2Y 1N9, Canada. T. +15142882220. Fax +15142886588. E-mail: secretariat@cbd.int.
URL: http://www.cbd.int/

History Established in accordance with Article 24 of *Convention on Biological Diversity (Biodiversity convention, 1992)*. Convention opened for signature at the Earth Summit, 5 Jun 1992, Rio de Janeiro (Brazil); entered into force 29 Dec 1993. Secretariat administered by *UNEP (#20299)*, and also serves as the secretariat to the *Cartagena Protocol on Biosafety (2000)* and *Nagoya Protocol on Access to Genetic Resources and the Fair and Equitable Sharing of Benefits Arising from their Utilization to the Convention on Biological Diversity (Nagoya Protocol, 2010)*. **Aims** Promote the objectives of the treaty, namely: conservation of biological diversity; *sustainable* use of the components of biodiversity; fair and equitable sharing of the benefits arising from the use of *genetic resources*. Objectives of the Cartagena Protocol on *Biosafety*: contribute to ensuring an adequate level of protection in the field of the safe transfer, handling and use of living modified organisms resulting from modern biotechnology that may have adverse effects on the conservation and sustainable use of biological diversity and specifically focusing on transboundary movements. Objectives of the Nagoya Protocol: share the benefits arising from the utilization of genetic resources in a fair and equitable way, including by appropriate access to genetic resources and by appropriate transfer of relevant technologies, taking into account all rights over those resources and to technologies, and by appropriate funding, thereby contributing to the conservation of biological diversity and the sustainable use of its components. **Structure** *'Conference of the Parties (COP) to the Convention'* is the governing body, and also serves as the meeting of the Parties to the Cartagena Protocol on Biosafety. It includes a *'Bureau'*, composed of President and 10 Vice-Presidents, and is responsible for overall management of meetings of the COP and oversight of the Convention process between sessions. Bureau has overall responsibility for questions of process. Bureau members consult with their regional groups on issues of substance. It is responsible for examining the credentials of representatives of Parties attending meetings of the Conference of the Parties; it is a forum for political negotiations. In the period between sessions of the Conference of the Parties, the Bureau meets from time to time to provide advice and guidance to the Secretariat on the implementation of the agreed programmes of work, financial matters and other issues of substance. *'Secretariat'*, headed by Executive Secretary who is appointed by UN Secretary-General in consultation with the COP through its Bureau, comprises: Office of the Executive Secretary; Administration, Finance and Conference Services Division; Scientific and Policy Support Division; Mainstreaming, Cooperation and Outreach Support Division; Implementation Support Division. **Languages** Arabic, Chinese, English, French, Russian, Spanish. **Finance** Contributions made by Parties and non-Parties to the following trust funds established by the Conference of the Parties: General Trust Fund for the Convention on Biological Diversity (BY Trust Fund), funded from the assessed contributions of Parties to the CBD, based on the UN scales of assessment; Special Voluntary Trust Fund (BE Trust Fund) – provides support of approved activities; Special Voluntary Trust Fund (BZ Trust Fund) – facilitates participation of Parties in the Convention process. Voluntary Trust Fund (VB) – facilitates participation of indigenous and local communities in the Convention Process. Equivalent trust funds have been set up for the Cartagena Protocol on Biosafety. **Activities** Management of treaties and agreements: *Convention on Biological Diversity (Biodiversity convention, 1992)*; *Cartagena Protocol on Biosafety (2000)*; Nagoya Protocol on Access and Benefit-sharing. **Events** *Conference of the Parties (Second Part)* Montréal, QC (Canada) 2022, *Conference of the Parties Serving as the Meeting of the Parties to the Cartagena Protocol on Biosafety (Part II)* Montréal, QC (Canada) 2022, *Conference of the Parties Serving as the Meeting of the Parties to the Nagoya Protocol on Access and Benefit-Sharing* Pyeongchang (Korea Rep) 2022, *Catalyzing Nature-based Solutions for Biodiversity, Climate Change and Sustainable Development through Ecosystem Restoration* Tokyo (Japan) 2022, *Conference of the Parties (First Part)* Kunming (China) 2021. **Publications** *Global Biodiversity Outlook*. National reports submitted by Parties on measures taken to implement the Convention and on their effectiveness in meeting Convention objectives; COP decisions; brochures; technical series; posters; educational material used for outreach activities.

Members Parties to the Convention (196); Parties to the Cartagena Protocol (173); Parties to the Nagoya Protocol (138). Governments of 196 countries and territories:

Afghanistan, Albania, Algeria, Andorra, Angola, Antigua-Barbuda, Argentina, Armenia, Australia, Austria, Bahamas, Bahrain, Bangladesh, Barbados, Belarus, Belgium, Belize, Benin, Bhutan, Bolivia, Bosnia-Herzegovina, Botswana, Brazil, Brunei Darussalam, Bulgaria, Burkina Faso, Burundi, Cambodia, Cameroon, Canada, Cape Verde, Central African Rep, Chad, Chile, China, Colombia, Comoros, Congo Brazzaville, Congo DR, Cook Is, Costa Rica, Côte d'Ivoire, Croatia, Cuba, Cyprus, Czechia, Denmark, Djibouti, Dominica, Dominican Rep, Ecuador, Egypt, El Salvador, Equatorial Guinea, Eritrea, Estonia, Eswatini, Ethiopia, Fiji, Finland, France, Gabon, Gambia, Georgia, Germany, Ghana, Greece, Grenada, Guatemala, Guinea, Guinea-Bissau, Guyana, Haiti, Holy See, Honduras, Hungary, Iceland, India, Indonesia, Iran Islamic Rep, Iraq, Ireland, Israel, Italy, Jamaica, Japan, Jordan, Kazakhstan, Kenya, Kiribati, Korea DPR, Korea Rep, Kuwait, Kyrgyzstan, Laos, Latvia, Lebanon, Lesotho, Liberia, Libya, Liechtenstein, Lithuania, Luxembourg, Madagascar, Malawi, Malaysia, Maldives, Mali, Malta, Marshall Is, Mauritania, Mauritius, Mexico, Micronesia FS, Moldova, Monaco, Mongolia, Montenegro, Morocco, Mozambique, Myanmar, Namibia, Nauru, Nepal, Netherlands, New Zealand, Nicaragua, Niger, Nigeria, Niue, North Macedonia, Norway, Oman, Pakistan, Palau, Palestine, Panama, Papua New Guinea, Paraguay, Peru, Philippines, Poland, Portugal, Qatar, Romania, Russia, Rwanda, Samoa, San Marino, Sao Tomé-Principe, Saudi Arabia, Senegal, Serbia, Seychelles, Sierra Leone, Singapore, Slovakia, Slovenia, Solomon Is, Somalia, South Africa, South Sudan, Spain, Sri Lanka, St Kitts-Nevis, St Lucia, St Vincent-Grenadines, Sudan, Suriname, Sweden, Switzerland, Syrian AR, Tajikistan, Tanzania UR, Thailand, Timor-Leste, Togo, Tonga, Trinidad-Tobago, Tunisia, Türkiye, Turkmenistan, Tuvalu, Uganda, UK, Ukraine, United Arab Emirates, Uruguay, Uzbekistan, Vanuatu, Venezuela, Vietnam, Yemen, Zambia, Zimbabwe.

Included in the above, one regional integration EU entity, listed in this Yearbook:
European Commission (EC, #06633).

IGO Relations Partners:
- *CABI (#03393);*
- *Caribbean Environment Programme (CEP, #03497);*
- *CGIAR System Organization (CGIAR, #03843);*
- *Collaborative Partnership on Forests (CPF, #04100);*
- *Commission for Environmental Cooperation (CEC, #04211);*
- *Commission on Genetic Resources for Food and Agriculture (CGRFA, #04215);*
- *Commonwealth Secretariat (#04362);*
- Secretariat of the *Convention Concerning the Protection of the World Cultural and Natural Heritage (World Heritage Convention, 1972);*
- Secretariat of the *Convention for the Protection and Development of the Marine Environment of the Wider Caribbean Region (Cartagena Convention, 1983);*
- *European Environment Agency (EEA, #06995);*
- *FAO (#09260);*
- *Global Biodiversity Information Facility (GBIF, #10250);*
- *Global Environment Facility (GEF, #10346);*
- *Intergovernmental Oceanographic Commission (IOC, #11496);*
- *International Bank for Reconstruction and Development (IBRD, #12317);*
- *International Centre for Genetic Engineering and Biotechnology (ICGEB, #12494);*
- *International Coral Reef Initiative (ICRI, #12965);*
- *International Seabed Authority (ISBA, #14813);*
- *OECD (#17693);*
- *Organisation internationale de la Francophonie (OIF, #17809);*
- *Pan-European Ecological Network (PEEN, see: #04881);*
- *Programme on Man and the Biosphere (MAB, #18526);*
- *Regional Activity Centre for Specially Protected Areas (RAC/SPA, #18746);*
- *Secretariat of the Convention on International Trade in Endangered Species of Wild Fauna and Flora (CITES Secretariat, #19199);*
- *Secretariat of the Convention of Wetlands (#19200);*
- *Secretariat of the Pacific Regional Environment Programme (SPREP, #19205);*
- *Secretariat of the United Nations Convention to Combat Desertification (Secretariat of the UNCCD, #19208);*
- *Southern African Development Community (SADC, #19843);*
- *Standing Committee to the Bern Convention on the Conservation of European Wildlife and Natural Habitats (#19949);*
- *UN Environment Programme World Conservation Monitoring Centre (UNEP-WCMC, #20295);*
- *UNCTAD (#20285);*
- *UNDP (#20292);*
- *UNESCO (#20322);*
- *Union internationale pour la protection des obtentions végétales (UPOV, #20436);*
- United Nations Division for Ocean Affairs and the Law of the Sea(DOALOS);
- United Nations Division for Sustainable Development (UN/DSD);
- *United Nations Forum on Forests (UNFF, #20562);*
- Secretariat of the *United Nations Framework Convention on Climate Change (UNFCCC, 1992);*
- *United Nations Framework Convention on Climate Change – Secretariat (UNFCCC, #20564);*
- *United Nations Institute for Training and Research (UNITAR, #20576);*
- *United Nations University (UNU, #20642);*
- *World Intellectual Property Organization (WIPO, #21593);*
- *World Tourism Organization (UNWTO, #21861);*
- *World Water Assessment Programme (WWAP, #21907).*

Member of: *Congo Basin Forest Partnership (CBFP, #04662); UN-OCEANS (#20711); UN-Water (#20723).* Memorandum of Understanding with: *Secretariat of the Convention on the Conservation of Migratory Species of Wild Animals (UNEP/CMS, #19198).* Resolution of Cooperation with: *Conservation of Arctic Flora and Fauna (CAFF, #04728).*

NGO Relations Observers to the Convention:
- *African Centre for Technology Studies (ACTS, #00243);*
- *Biotechnology Innovation Organization (BIO);*
- *BirdLife International (#03266);*
- *Botanic Gardens Conservation International (BGCI, #03306);*
- *Catholic Youth Network for Environmental Sustainability in Africa (CYNESA, #03611)*
- *Center for International Environmental Law (CIEL);*
- *Center for International Forestry Research (CIFOR, #03646);*
- *ECNC – European Centre for Nature Conservation (#05289);*
- *European Parliament Intergroup on Climate Change, Biodiversity and Sustainable Development (Intergroup);*
- *Federation of International Civil Servants' Associations (FICSA, #09603);*
- *Greenpeace International (#10727);*
- *Indigenous Peoples' Biodiversity Network (IPBN, #11164);*
- *Inter-Agency Network for Safety in Biotechnology (IANB, inactive);*
- *International Alliance of the Indigenous Tribal Peoples of the Tropical Forests (IAITPTF, #11629);*
- *International Centre for Trade and Sustainable Development, Geneva (ICTSD, #12524);*
- *International Council for Science (ICSU, inactive);*
- *International Seed Federation (ISF, #14828);*
- *International Union of Biological Sciences (IUBS, #15760);*
- *International Union for Conservation of Nature and Natural Resources (IUCN, #15766);*
- *Inuit Circumpolar Council (ICC, #15995);*
- *Scientific Committee on Problems of the Environment (SCOPE, #19150);*
- *SYLVA-WORLD for Development and the Protection of Forests and the Environment;*
- *Wetlands International (#20928);*
- *World Business Council for Sustainable Development (WBCSD, #21254);*
- *World Resources Institute (WRI, #21753);*
- *World Wide Fund for Nature (WWF, #21922).*

Member of: *Global Gender and Climate Alliance (GGCA, no recent information); Mountain Partnership (MP, #16862).* Partner of: *Global Partnership on Forest and Landscape Restoration (GPFLR, #10535).*

[2022.10.11/XE3586/**E***]

♦ Secrétariat de la Convention sur le commerce international des espèces de faune et de flore sauvages menacées d'extinction (#19199)

♦ Secretariat of the Convention on the Conservation of Migratory Species of Wild Animals (UNEP/CMS) 19198

Exec Sec UNEP/CMS Secretariat, UN Campus, Platz der Vereinten Nationen 1, 53113 Bonn, Germany. T. +492288152401. Fax +492288152449. E-mail: cms.secretariat@cms.int.
URL: http://www.cms.int/

History under the terms of *Convention on the Conservation of Migratory Species of Wild Animals (Bonn Convention, 1979)*, concluded 23 Jun 1979, Bonn (Germany FR), which entered into force on 1 Nov 1983. Operations commenced, Nov 1984. Administered by: *UNEP (#20299).* **Aims** Provide secretariat function for the Convention on the Conservation of Migratory Species of Wild Animals; obtain information to further the objectives and implementation of the Convention and arrange for the appropriate dissemination of such information; draw the attention of the Conference of the Parties to matters pertaining to the objectives of the Convention. **Structure** Convention: Conference of the Parties; Standing Committee and Scientific Council, headed by Chairperson (any Party may appoint a qualified expert as a member of the Council, which also includes qualified experts selected and appointed by the Conference of the Parties). Secretariat headed by Executive Secretary, assisted by Deputy Executive Secretary. **Languages** English, French, Spanish. **Staff** 55.00 FTE, paid. **Finance** Secretariat financed from the Convention budget. Convention has been financed by parties to the Convention, but contributions may be accepted from other sources. Other sources: *Trust Fund for the Convention on the Conservation of Migratory Species of Wild Animals (UNEP/CMS Trust Fund, see: #20299).*

Activities Compiles, maintains and publishes a Range State list for all migratory species listed on the Appendices to the Convention; prepares reports on the work of the Secretariat and on implementation of the Convention for the Conference of the Parties; compiles reports on selected migratory species that are endangered; arranges for services for meetings of the Conference of the Parties, the Scientific Council and the Standing Committee; maintains liaison with and promotes liaison between the Parties, standing bodies set up under agreements and other international organizations concerned with migratory species; under the direction of the Conference of the Parties, promotes conclusion of agreements; maintains and makes available to the Parties a list of agreements and provides information on such agreements if required by the Conference of the Parties; maintains and publishes a list of recommendations made by the Conference of the Parties; provides information for the general public concerning the Convention and its objectives; develops annual campaigns built around migratory species or group of species.

Works on development of agreements:
- *Agreement on the Conservation of Gorillas and Their Habitats (2007)* (concluded 2007, in force 2008);
- *Agreement on the Conservation of Seals in the Wadden Sea (1990)* (concluded 1990, in force 1991);
- *Agreement on the Conservation of Populations of European Bats (EUROBATS, 1991)* (concluded 1991, in force 1994);
- *Agreement on the Conservation of Small Cetaceans of the Baltic, North East Atlantic, Irish and North Seas (ASCOBANS, 1992)* (concluded 1991, in force 1994);
- *African-Eurasian Migratory /Water Bird/ Agreement (AEWA, 1995)* (concluded 1995, in force 1999);
- *Agreement on the Conservation of Cetaceans of the Black Sea, Mediterranean Sea and contiguous Atlantic Area (ACCOBAMS, 1996)* (concluded 1996, in force 2001);
- *Agreement on the Conservation of Albatrosses and Petrels (ACAP, 2001)* (concluded 2001, in force 2004);
- *Memorandum of Understanding Concerning Conservation Measures for the Siberian Crane, 1993 (1993)* (concluded 1993, in force 1999);
- *Memorandum of Understanding Concerning Conservation Measures for the Slender-billed Curlew (1994)* (concluded 1994, in force 1994);
- *Memorandum of Understanding Concerning Conservation Measures for Marine Turtles of the Atlantic Coast of Africa (1999)* (concluded 1999, in force 1999);
- *Memorandum of Understanding on the Conservation and Management of the Middle-European Population of the Great Bustard – Otis Tarda (2000)* (concluded 2000, in force 2001);
- *Memorandum of Understanding on the Conservation and Management of Marine Turtles and Their Habitats of the Indian Ocean and South-East Asia (2001)* (concluded 2001, in force 2001);
- *Memorandum of Understanding Concerning Conservation and Restoration of the Bukhara Deer (2002)* (concluded 2002, in force 2002);
- *Memorandum of Understanding Concerning Conservation Measures for the Aquatic Warbler (2003)* (concluded 2003, in force 2003).
- *Memorandum of Understanding Concerning Conservation Measures for the West African Populations of the African Elephant – Loxodonta Africana (2005)* (concluded 2005);
- *Memorandum of Understanding Concerning Conservation, Restoration and Sustainable Use of the Saiga Antelope – Saiga Tatarica Tatarica (2005)* (concluded 2005, in force 2006);
- *Memorandum of Understanding for the Conservation of Cetaceans and Their Habitats in the Pacific Islands Region (2006)* (concluded 2006, in force 2006);
- *Memorandum of Understanding Concerning Conservation Measures for the Ruddy-headed Goose – Chloephaga Rubidiceps (2006)* (concluded 2006, in force 2006);
- *Memorandum of Understanding on the Conservation and Management of Dugongs – Dugong Dugon – and Their Habitats Throughout Their Range (UNEP/CMS Dugong MoU, 2007)* (concluded 2007, in force 2007);
- *Memorandum of Understanding on the Conservation of Southern South American Migratory Grassland Bird Species and Their Habitats (2007)* (concluded 2007, in force 2007);
- *Memorandum of Understanding on the Conservation of High Andean Flamingos and Their Habitats (2008)* (concluded 2008, in force 2008);
- *Memorandum of Understanding Concerning Conservation Measures for the Eastern Atlantic Populations of the Mediterranean Monk Seal – Monachus Monachus (2007)* (concluded 2007, in force 2007);
- *Memorandum of Understanding Concerning the Conservation of Migratory Birds of Prey in Africa and Eurasia (2008)* (concluded 2008, in force 2008);
- *Memorandum of Understanding Concerning the Conservation of the Manatee and Small Cetaceans of Western Africa and Macaronesia (2008)* (concluded 2008, in force 2008);
- *'Memorandum of understanding on the Conservation of Migratory Sharks'* (2010);
- *'Memorandum of Understanding between the Argentine Republic and the Republic of Chile concerning the Conservation of the Southern Huemul (Hippocamelus bisulcus)'* (2010).

Events *Meeting of the Signatories to the Memorandum of Understanding on the Conservation of Migratory Birds of Prey in Africa and Eurasia* Trondheim (Norway) 2015, *Meeting of the Conference of the Parties* Quito (Ecuador) 2014, *Meeting of the conference of the Parties / Conference of the Parties* Bergen (Norway) 2011, *Conference of the Parties* Rome (Italy) 2008, *Meeting of the conference of the parties* Rome (Italy) 2008. **Publications** *CMS Newsletter. CMS Technical Series* – 1-24. *Survival – Saving endangered migratory species* (2010); *A Bird's Eye View on Flyways – A brief tour by the Convention on the Conservation of Migratory Species of Wild Animals* (2009); *Convention on Migratory Species* (2008) in English, French, German, Spanish; *CMS Family Guide – The Encyclopedia on the Convention on the Conservation of Migratory Species of Wild Animals* (2007); *Migratory Species and Climate Change – Impacts of a Changing Environment on Wild Animals* (2006); *Wildlife Watching and Tourism – A study on the benefits and risks of a fast growing tourism activity and its impacts on species* (2006); *Conserving Cetaceans* (2005) in English, French, German, Spanish; *Review of Small Cetaceans: Distribution, Behaviour, Migration and Threats* (2005); *25 Years of Journeys* (2004) in English, French, Spanish; *Convention Text in Arabic* (2004) in Chinese, English, French, German, Russian, Spanish; *Conservation of Cetaceans in the Gambia and Senegal 1999-2001*; *Proceedings of Meetings of the Conference.*

Members Parties to the Convention (123) – Governments of 123 countries and one intergovernmental party:
Afghanistan, Albania, Algeria, Angola, Antigua-Barbuda, Argentina, Armenia, Australia, Austria, Bangladesh, Belarus, Belgium, Benin, Bolivia, Bosnia-Herzegovina, Brazil, Bulgaria, Burkina Faso, Burundi, Cameroon, Cape Verde, Chad, Chile, Congo Brazzaville, Cook Is, Costa Rica, Côte d'Ivoire, Croatia, Cuba, Cyprus, Czechia, Denmark, Djibouti, Dominican Rep, Ecuador, Egypt, Equatorial Guinea, Eritrea, Estonia, Eswatini, Ethiopia, Fiji, Finland, France, Gabon, Gambia, Georgia, Germany, Ghana, Greece, Guinea, Guinea-Bissau, Honduras, Hungary, India, Iran Islamic Rep, Iraq, Ireland, Israel, Italy, Jordan, Kazakhstan, Kenya, Kyrgyzstan, Latvia, Liberia, Libya, Liechtenstein, Lithuania, Luxembourg, Madagascar, Mali, Malta, Mauritania, Mauritius, Moldova, Monaco, Mongolia, Montenegro, Morocco, Mozambique, Netherlands, New Zealand, Niger, Nigeria, North Macedonia, Norway, Pakistan, Palau, Panama, Paraguay, Peru, Philippines, Poland, Portugal, Romania, Rwanda, Samoa, Sao Tomé-Principe, Saudi Arabia, Senegal, Serbia, Seychelles, Slovakia, Slovenia, Somalia, South Africa, Spain, Sri Lanka, Sweden, Switzerland, Syrian AR, Tajikistan, Tanzania UR, Togo, Tunisia, Uganda, UK, Ukraine, Uruguay, Uzbekistan, Yemen, Zimbabwe.

Intergovernmental party (1):
European Union (EU, #08967).

Signatories (2):
Central African Rep, Jamaica.

IGO Relations Member of: *Scientific Task Force on Avian Influenza and Wild Birds (#19154).* Memorandum of Understanding with: *Secretariat of the Convention on Biological Diversity (SCBD, #19197); Secretariat of the Convention on International Trade in Endangered Species of Wild Fauna and Flora (CITES Secretariat, #19199).* Memorandum of Cooperation with: *Standing Committee to the Bern Convention on the Conservation of European Wildlife and Natural Habitats (#19949).* **NGO Relations** Partners include: *Alliance of Marine Mammal Parks and Aquariums (AMMPA); BirdLife International (#03266); Union européenne des Pharmacies sociales (UEPS, #20401); Global Nature Fund (GNF, #10479); International Council for Game and Wildlife Conservation (#13024); International Crane Foundation (ICF, #13102); International Fund for Animal Welfare (IFAW, #13693); Migratory Wildlife Network (Wild Migration); SaharaConservation (SC, #19032); Whale and Dolphin Conservation (WDC); Wild for Life Campaign (Wild for Life, #20958); Wildlife Conservation Society (WCS). Wetlands International (#20928).*

[2021/XF0407/**E***]

♦ Secretariat of the Convention on Harmful Chemicals and Pesticides / see Secretariat of the Rotterdam Convention (#19206)

♦ Secretariat of the Convention on International Trade in Endangered Species of Wild Fauna and Flora (CITES Secretariat) 19199

Secrétariat de la Convention sur le commerce international des espèces de faune et de flore sauvages menacées d'extinction (Secrétariat CITES) – Secretaría de la Convención sobre el Comercio Internacional de Especies Amenazadas de Fauna y Flora Silvestres (Secretaría CITES)

SG Chemin des Anémones 11, Châtelaine, 1219 Geneva, Switzerland. T. +41229178139 – +41229178140. Fax +41227973417. E-mail: info@cites.org.

URL: http://www.cites.org/

History Article XII of *Convention on International Trade in Endangered Species of Wild Fauna and Flora (CITES, 1973)*, signed 3 Mar 1973, provides for the establishment of a Secretariat upon entry into force of Convention, 1 Jul 1975. Statutes registered in *'UNTS 1/14537'*. **Aims** Ensure that international trade in specimens of wild *animals* and *plants* does not threaten their survival. **Structure** Conference of the Parties; Standing Committee; Scientific Committees (2); Secretariat administered by *UNEP (#20299)*. **Languages** English, French, Spanish. **Staff** 26.00 FTE, paid. **Finance** Core budget contributions from Party States to Trust Fund of the Convention. Projects are externally funded by voluntary contributions from governments, intergovernmental organizations and private enterprises. Annual budget (2014): US$ 5,836,735; (2015) US$ 6,018,089; (2016) US$ 6,655,307. **Activities** Knowledge management/information dissemination; monitoring/evaluation; training/education. **Events** *Conference of the Parties* Geneva (Switzerland) 2019, *Meeting* Sochi (Russia) 2018, *Meeting* Geneva (Switzerland) 2017, *Conference of the Parties* Johannesburg (South Africa) 2016, *Meeting* Johannesburg (South Africa) 2016. **Publications** *CITES Handbook*. Checklist of CITES species; studies; reports; press releases; resolutions.

Members Contracting Parties to the Convention: governments of 182 countries:

Afghanistan, Albania, Algeria, Angola, Antigua-Barbuda, Argentina, Armenia, Australia, Austria, Azerbaijan, Bahamas, Bahrain, Bangladesh, Barbados, Belarus, Belgium, Belize, Benin, Bhutan, Bolivia, Bosnia-Herzegovina, Botswana, Brazil, Brunei Darussalam, Bulgaria, Burkina Faso, Burundi, Cambodia, Cameroon, Canada, Cape Verde, Central African Rep, Chad, Chile, China, Colombia, Comoros, Congo Brazzaville, Congo DR, Costa Rica, Côte d'Ivoire, Croatia, Cuba, Cyprus, Czechia, Denmark, Djibouti, Dominica, Dominican Rep, Ecuador, Egypt, El Salvador, Equatorial Guinea, Eritrea, Estonia, Eswatini, Ethiopia, Fiji, Finland, France, Gabon, Gambia, Georgia, Germany, Ghana, Greece, Grenada, Guatemala, Guinea, Guinea-Bissau, Guyana, Honduras, Hungary, Iceland, India, Indonesia, Iran Islamic Rep, Iraq, Ireland, Israel, Italy, Jamaica, Japan, Jordan, Kazakhstan, Kenya, Korea Rep, Kuwait, Kyrgyzstan, Laos, Latvia, Lebanon, Lesotho, Liberia, Libya, Liechtenstein, Lithuania, Luxembourg, Madagascar, Malawi, Malaysia, Maldives, Mali, Malta, Mauritania, Mauritius, Mexico, Moldova, Monaco, Mongolia, Montenegro, Morocco, Mozambique, Myanmar, Namibia, Nepal, Netherlands, New Zealand, Nicaragua, Niger, Nigeria, North Macedonia, Norway, Oman, Pakistan, Palau, Panama, Papua New Guinea, Paraguay, Peru, Philippines, Poland, Portugal, Qatar, Romania, Russia, Rwanda, Samoa, San Marino, Sao Tomé-Principe, Saudi Arabia, Senegal, Serbia, Seychelles, Sierra Leone, Singapore, Slovakia, Slovenia, Solomon Is, Somalia, South Africa, Spain, Sri Lanka, St Kitts-Nevis, St Lucia, St Vincent-Grenadines, Sudan, Suriname, Sweden, Switzerland, Syrian AR, Tajikistan, Tanzania UR, Thailand, Togo, Tonga, Trinidad-Tobago, Tunisia, Türkiye, Uganda, UK, Ukraine, United Arab Emirates, Uruguay, USA, Uzbekistan, Vanuatu, Venezuela, Vietnam, Yemen, Zambia, Zimbabwe.

Regional government:

European Union (EU, #08967).

IGO Relations Observer status at: *Standing Committee to the Bern Convention on the Conservation of European Wildlife and Natural Habitats (#19949)*. Relations with: *European Union (EU, #08967)*. Memorandum of Understanding signed with:
- Task Force for the
- *Agreement on Cooperative Enforcement Operations Directed at Illegal Trade in Wild Fauna and Flora (1994)*;
- Secretariat to the *Basel Convention on the Control of Transboundary Movements of Hazardous Wastes and Their Disposal (UNCRTD, 1989)*;
- *ECO Chamber of Commerce and Industry (ECO-CCI, #05291)*;
- *FAO (#09260)*;
- *Intergovernmental Science-Policy Platform on Biodiversity and Ecosystem Services (IPBES, #11500)*;
- *International Tropical Timber Organization (ITTO, #15737)*;
- *Secretariat of the Basel Convention (SBC, #19196)*;
- *Secretariat of the Convention on Biological Diversity (SCBD, #19197)*;
- *Secretariat of the Convention on the Conservation of Migratory Species of Wild Animals (UNEP/CMS, #19198)*;
- *Secretariat for the Vienna Convention for the Protection of the Ozone Layer and the Montreal Protocol on Substances that Deplete the Ozone Layer (Ozone Secretariat, #19209)*;
- UK Department for Environment, Food and Rural Affairs (DEFRA);
- *UN Environment Programme World Conservation Monitoring Centre (UNEP-WCMC, #20295)*;
- US Fish and Wildlife Service Office of Law Enforcement / Clark R Bavin National Fish and Wildlife Forensic Laboratory;
- *World Customs Organization (WCO, #21350)*;
- *World Trade Organization (WTO, #21864)*.

Agreement with: *International Criminal Police Organization – INTERPOL (ICPO-INTERPOL, #13110)*. Cooperates with: *Caribbean Environment Programme (CEP, #03497)*.

NGO Relations In liaison with technical committees of: *International Organization for Standardization (ISO, #14473)*. Memorandum of Understanding with: Board of Trustees of Royal Botanic Gardens, Richmond (UK); *International Union for Conservation of Nature and Natural Resources (IUCN, #15766)*; *TRAFFIC International (#20196)* (CITES Secretariat also serves as Observer); Universities of Kent (UK) and Andalucia (Spain). Founding partner of: *Wild for Life Campaign (Wild for Life, #20958)*. [2020.08.27/XE8554/E*]

♦ Secrétariat de la Convention des Nations Unies sur la Lutte contre la Désertification (#19208)

♦ Secretariat of the Convention of Wetlands 19200

Secretariat Rue Mauverney 28, 1196 Gland VD, Switzerland. T. +41229990170. Fax +41229990169. E-mail: ramsar@ramsar.org.

URL: http://www.ramsar.org/

History 1987. Established as *Ramsar Convention Bureau*, to administer *Convention on Wetlands of International Importance Especially as Waterfowl Habitat (Convention on Wetlands, 1971)*, signed, Feb 1971, Ramsar (Iran Islamic Rep). Subsequently referred to as *Secretariat of the Ramsar Convention of Wetlands. UNESCO (#20322)* is the Convention Depositary. IUCN has administrative responsibility for the Convention Secretariat. **Aims** Serve as framework for national action and international cooperation for the *conservation* and wise use of *wetland ecosystems* and *water resources*. **Structure** Convention on Wetlands Conference of the Contracting Parties; Standing Committee; Scientific and Technical Review Panel; Secretariat located in Gland (Switzerland). **Languages** English, French, Spanish. **Staff** 24.00 FTE, paid. **Finance** Contributions from Contracting Parties according to UN scale of assessments. Additional funds provided by public and private sources for project activities. Annual core budget (2019): Swiss Fr 5,080,000. **Activities** Contracting Parties designate at least one site to be included in a *'List of Wetlands of International Importance'*, according to accepted criteria, using standardized information sheet and classification of wetland types. They undertake to make wise use of all wetlands on their territories, establish and manage wetland reserves and foster international cooperation and mobilize financial assistance. The Secretariat maintains the List of Wetlands of International Importance, fosters regional activities, organizes meetings, workshops and seminars. Publishes materials to inform Member States of wetland values and Convention activities. **Events** *Conference of the Contracting Parties* Geneva (Switzerland) / Wuhan (China) 2022, *European River Symposium* Vienna (Austria) 2021, *Conference of the Contracting Parties* Dubai (United Arab Emirates) 2018, *European River Symposium* Vienna (Austria) 2016, *Conference of the Contracting Parties* Punta del Este (Uruguay) 2015. **Publications** *Ramsar Technical Reports* – series; *The Briefing Notes* – series. *Economic Evaluation of Wetlands – A Guide for Policy Makers and Planners*; *History and Development of the Convention*; *Legal Development of the Convention*; *Ramsar Handbooks for the Wise Use of Wetlands* (4th ed) – 21 vols; *Ramsar Manual* (6th ed); *Towards the Wise Use of Wetlands*; *Wetlands, Biodiversity and the Ramsar Convention*. Conference proceedings.

Members As of Mar 2017: Governments – Contracting Parties to the Convention on Wetlands – of 170 countries:

Albania, Algeria, Andorra, Antigua-Barbuda, Argentina, Armenia, Australia, Austria, Azerbaijan, Bahamas, Bahrain, Bangladesh, Barbados, Belarus, Belgium, Belize, Benin, Bhutan, Bolivia, Bosnia-Herzegovina, Botswana, Brazil, Bulgaria, Burkina Faso, Burundi, Cambodia, Cameroon, Canada, Cape Verde, Central African Rep, Chad, Chile, China, Colombia, Comoros, Congo Brazzaville, Congo DR, Costa Rica, Côte d'Ivoire, Croatia, Cuba, Cyprus, Czechia, Denmark, Djibouti, Dominican Rep, Ecuador, Egypt, El Salvador, Equatorial Guinea, Estonia, Eswatini, Fiji, Finland, France, Gabon, Gambia, Georgia, Germany, Ghana, Greece, Grenada, Guatemala, Guinea, Guinea-Bissau, Honduras, Hungary, Iceland, India, Indonesia, Iran Islamic Rep, Iraq, Ireland, Israel, Italy, Jamaica, Japan, Jordan, Kazakhstan, Kenya, Kiribati, Korea DPR, Korea Rep, Kuwait, Kyrgyzstan, Laos, Latvia, Lebanon, Lesotho, Liberia, Libya, Liechtenstein, Lithuania, Luxembourg, Madagascar, Malawi, Malaysia, Mali, Malta, Marshall Is, Mauritania, Mauritius, Mexico, Moldova, Monaco, Mongolia, Montenegro, Morocco, Mozambique, Myanmar, Namibia, Nepal, Netherlands, New Zealand, Nicaragua, Niger, Nigeria, North Macedonia, Norway, Oman, Pakistan, Palau, Panama, Papua New Guinea, Paraguay, Peru, Philippines, Poland, Portugal, Romania, Russia, Rwanda, Samoa, Sao Tomé-Principe, Senegal, Serbia, Seychelles, Sierra Leone, Slovakia, Slovenia, South Africa, South Sudan, Spain, Sri Lanka, St Lucia, Sudan, Suriname, Sweden, Switzerland, Syrian AR, Tajikistan, Tanzania UR, Thailand, Togo, Trinidad-Tobago, Tunisia, Türkiye, Turkmenistan, Uganda, UK, Ukraine, United Arab Emirates, Uruguay, USA, Uzbekistan, Venezuela, Vietnam, Yemen, Zambia, Zimbabwe.

IGO Relations Close working relations with: *European Commission (EC, #06633)*; *OECD (#17693)*; *Secretariat of the Convention on the Conservation of Migratory Species of Wild Animals (UNEP/CMS, #19198)*; *Secretariat of the Convention on International Trade in Endangered Species of Wild Fauna and Flora (CITES Secretariat, #19199)*; *UNEP (#20299)*. Accredited to the Conference of the Parties of: *Secretariat of the United Nations Convention to Combat Desertification (Secretariat of the UNCCD, #19208)*. Cooperates with: *Caribbean Environment Programme (CEP, #03497)*; *Conservation of Arctic Flora and Fauna (CAFF, #04728)*; *United Nations Institute for Training and Research (UNITAR, #20576)*. Accredited by: *United Nations Framework Convention on Climate Change – Secretariat (UNFCCC, #20564)*. Observer to: *Standing Committee to the Bern Convention on the Conservation of European Wildlife and Natural Habitats (#19949)*; *International Commission for the Protection of the Danube River (ICPDR, #12720)*. Partner of: *International Coral Reef Initiative (ICRI, #12965)*; *UN-Water (#20723)*.

Memorandum of Cooperation with:
- *Convention on Biological Diversity (Biodiversity convention, 1992)*;
- *Convention Concerning the Protection of the World Cultural and Natural Heritage (World Heritage Convention, 1972)*;
- *Convention on the Conservation of Migratory Species of Wild Animals (Bonn Convention, 1979)*;
- *Convention for the Protection and Development of the Marine Environment of the Wider Caribbean Region (Cartagena Convention, 1983)*;
- *Convention for the Protection of the Marine Environment and the Coastal Region of the Mediterranean (Barcelona Convention, 1976)*;
- *Convention on the Protection and Sustainable Development of the Carpathians (Carpathian convention, 2003)*;
- *European Environment Agency (EEA, #06995)*;
- ICPDR;
- *International Bank for Reconstruction and Development (IBRD, #12317)* (World Bank);
- *International Commission of the Congo-Ubangui-Sangha Basin (#12674)*;
- *Lake Chad Basin Commission (LCBC, #16220)*;
- *Niger Basin Authority (NBA, #17134)*;
- *OAS (#17629)*;
- *Programme on Man and the Biosphere (MAB, #18526)*;
- *Secretariat of the Pacific Regional Environment Programme (SPREP, #19205)*;
- *United Nations Convention to Combat Desertification (UNCCD, 1994)*;
- *World Tourism Organization (UNWTO, #21861)*.

NGO Relations Representatives of Convention on Wetlands Secretariat meet frequently with representatives of: *International Union for Conservation of Nature and Natural Resources (IUCN, #15766)*, to review activities and identify areas for cooperation. Member of: *East Asian – Australasian Flyway Partnership (EAAFP, #05198)*. Memorandum of Cooperation or Understanding with:
- *Albertine Rift Conservation Society (ARCOS, #00620)*;
- *ASEAN Centre for Biodiversity (ACB, #01149)*;
- *BirdLife International (#03266)*;
- *Conservation International (CI)*;
- *Ducks Unlimited (DU, #05143)*;
- *Eurosite (#09181)*;
- *International Association for Impact Assessment (IAIA, #11956)*;
- *International Lake Environment Committee Foundation (ILEC, #13998)*;
- *International Water Management Institute (IWMI, #15867)*;
- *The Nature Conservancy (TNC)*;
- *Society for Ecological Restoration International (SERI)*;
- *Society of Wetland Scientists (SWS)*;
- Stetson University College of Law (Florida, USA);
- *Université internationale de langue française au service du développement africain à Alexandrie d'Egypte (Université Senghor, #20691)*;
- *Wetlands International (#20928)*;
- *World Association of Zoos and Aquariums (WAZA, #21208)*;
- *World Wide Fund for Nature (WWF, #21922)*.

International partner organizations: Birdlife International; IUCN; IWMI; Wetlands International; *Wildfowl and Wetlands Trust (WWT)*; World Wide Fund for Nature. [2022/XE1306/E*]

♦ Secrétariat de coordination des unions nationales d'étudiants (inactive)
♦ Secretariat for Eastern African Coastal Area Management (no recent information)
♦ Secretaria Técnica del Consejo Centroamericano de Turismo / see Secretaria de Integración Turistica Centroamericana (#19193)
♦ Secretariat for Environmental Assessment in Central Africa (inactive)
♦ Secrétariat épiscopal d'Amérique centrale (#05514)
♦ Secrétariat épiscopal d'Amérique centrale et Panama / see Episcopal Secretariat of Central America (#05514)
♦ Secrétariat européen d'associations du commerce agricole réunies / see Joint Secretariat of Agricultural Trade Associations (#16148)
♦ Secrétariat européen des concessionnaires d'autoroutes à péage / see Association Européenne des Concessionnaires d'Autoroutes et d'Ouvrages à Péage (#02559)
♦ Secrétariat européen des fabricants d'emballages métalliques légers (inactive)
♦ Secretariat européen des fûts en acier / see European Association of Steel Drum Manufacturers (#06222)
♦ Secrétariat européen des professions indépendantes sociales / see Confédération internationale des travailleurs intellectuels (#04564)
♦ Secrétariat européen des professions libérales / see European Council of Liberal Professions (#06828)
♦ Secrétariat européen des professions libérales, indépendantes et sociales / see European Council of Liberal Professions (#06828)
♦ Secrétariat européen pour les publications scientifiques (internationally oriented national body)
♦ Secrétariat pour l'évaluation environnementale en Afrique centrale (inactive)
♦ Secrétariat executive du Conseil de l'électrification de l'Amérique centrale (#19191)
♦ Secrétariat du Forum / see Pacific Islands Forum Secretariat (#17970)
♦ Secrétariat du Forum du Pacifique du Sud / see Pacific Islands Forum Secretariat (#17970)
♦ Secrétariat francophone de l'Association internationale pour l'évaluation d'impacts / see Secrétariat international francophone pour l'évaluation environnementale (#19201)
♦ Secrétariat général des socialistes abstinents (inactive)
♦ Secrétariat ibéroaméricain des municipalités (no recent information)
♦ Secrétariat international des artistes chrétiens / see International Society of Christian Artists (#15009)
♦ Secrétariat international des cercles de fermières (inactive)
♦ Secrétariat international de l'eau (#14822)
♦ Secrétariat international des enseignants secondaires catholiques / see SIESC – European Federation of Christian Teachers (#19267)
♦ Secrétariat international de l'enseignement universitaire des sciences pédagogiques / see Association mondiale des sciences de l'éducation (#02811)
♦ Secrétariat international des étudiants en traduction et en interprétation (no recent information)
♦ Secrétariat international des faucons / see International Falcon Movement – Socialist Educational International (#13327)
♦ Secrétariat international des femmes socialistes (inactive)

♦ Secrétariat international francophone pour l'évaluation environnementale (SIFÉE) 19201

Dir-Gen 540 place Saint-Henri, Local A, Montréal QC H4C 2R9, Canada. T. +15142882663. Fax +15142887701.

History 1996. Founded by *International Association for Impact Assessment (IAIA, #11956)*. Former names and other names: *Secrétariat francophone de l'Association internationale pour l'évaluation d'impacts* – former (1996). **Aims** Strengthen the competence of practitioners and policy makers working in the fields of environmental assessment, public *participation* and *sustainable development* by promoting exchanges and establishing links with international bodies. **Structure** Board of Directors; Executive Committee. **Languages** French. **Staff** 3.00 FTE, paid. **Finance** Members' dues. Other sources: financial and human resources support

from governments of French-speaking countries, international organisms, NGOs, research and education institutes and public and private entities; revenue from projects and events. **Activities** Guidance / assistance / consulting; capacity building; networking / liaising; meeting activities. **Events** *Colloque international en évaluation environnementale* Canada 2020, *Colloque international en évaluation environnementale* Cotonou (Benin) 2019, *Colloque International / International Conference* Brussels (Belgium) 2014, *Colloque International / International Conference* Lomé (Togo) 2013, *Colloque International* Montréal, QC (Canada) 2012. **Publications** Symposium proceedings.
Members National associations; governmental organizations; companies; universities and research centres. Members in 10 countries:
Benin, Cameroon, Canada, Congo DR, Côte d'Ivoire, France, Madagascar, Mali, Niger, Togo. [2020/XM4640/**E**]

♦ Secrétariat international des industries de la maille (inactive)

♦ Secrétariat international des infirmières et infirmiers de l'espace francophone (SIDIIEF) 19202

Administratice 4200 Rue Molson, Montréal QC H1Y 4V4, Canada. T. +15148496060. Fax +15148497870. E-mail: info@sidiief.org.
URL: http://www.sidiief.org/

History 1 Dec 1998, Canada. Officially set up Mar 2000. Registration: Canada. **Aims** Share expertise and knowledge in *nursing* sciences throughout the francophone world; contribute to the improvement of quality care and services to the populations. **Structure** Executive Committee. **Languages** French. **Staff** 4.00 FTE, paid. **Finance** Sources: meeting proceeds; members' dues. Annual budget: 300,000 CAD. **Events** *World Congress* Ottawa, ON (Canada) 2022, *Congrès Mondial Triennal* Ottawa, ON (Canada) 2021, *Congrès Mondial Triennal* Bordeaux (France) 2018, *Congrès Mondial Triennal* Montréal, QC (Canada) 2015, *Assemblée annuelle* Paris (France) 2014. **Publications** *VIGIE Média du SIDIIEF* (weekly) – electronic bulletin; *Savoir Inf* (3 a year) – electronic bulletin; *Infolettre du SIDIIEF*. *De l'Intérêt de Parler un Même Langage Afin d'Atteindre la Reconnaissance des Soins Infirmiers dans les Programmes d'Amélioration de la Qualité des Soins* (2015); *Discipline Infirmière: Une Contribution Décisive aux Enjeux de Santé* (2015); *Indicateurs Prioritaires pour Evaluer la Contribution Infirmière à la Qualité des Soins: Revue Systématique des Ecrits* (2015); *Mémoires sur le Qualité des Soins et la Sécurityé des Patients: Une Priorité Mondiale* (2015); *La formation infirmière à l'université – Une réponse aux défis des systèmes de santé*. Reports; conference proceedings.
Members Associations (65); institutions (50); individuals (1,650); founding (2); promoter (7). Members, totalling 1,774 in 35 countries and territories:
Algeria, Belgium, Benin, Burkina Faso, Burundi, Cameroon, Canada, Chad, Congo Brazzaville, Congo DR, Côte d'Ivoire, France, Gabon, Guinea, Haiti, Italy, Lebanon, Luxembourg, Madagascar, Mali, Martinique, Mayotte, Monaco, Morocco, Netherlands, Polynesia Fr, Portugal, Romania, Senegal, Spain, Switzerland, Togo, Tunisia, Uganda, USA.
Included in the above, 1 organization listed in this Yearbook:
Association Francophone Européenne des Diagnostics Interventions Résultats Infirmiers (AFEDI, #02612). [2022/XM4641/y/**E**]

♦ Secrétariat international des ingénieurs, des agronomes et des cadres économiques catholiques (SIIAEC) 19203

International Secretariat for Catholic Engineers, Agronomists and Industry Officials – Secretariado Internacional de Agrónomos, Economistas e Ingenieros Católicos

SG Pax Romana ICMICA/MIIC, 3 rue de Varembé, 4th Floor, CP 161, 1211 Geneva, Switzerland. T. +41228230707. Fax +41228230708.

History 1951, Paris (France), as *Secrétariat international des ingénieurs catholiques (SIIC)*. A specialized secretariat of *Pax Romana, International Catholic Movement for Intellectual and Cultural Affairs (ICMICA, #18267)*. Present title adopted 1954. Also referred to as *International Secretariat of Catholic Technologists, Agriculturalists and Economists*. **Aims** Serve as a link between national associations of Catholic engineers, agriculturalists and economic managers; help in their creation and development; study and propose Christian solutions to problems raised by the practice of the members' professions, in light of the teachings of the Church. **Structure** Annual General Assembly elects International Committee, consisting of 11 members (helped by a Chaplain) for 3-year terms. **Languages** English, French, German, Spanish. **Staff** Supplied by French MCC. **Finance** National association members' dues. Other sources: grants; sale of publications. **Activities** Professional surveys and studies. **Events** *Meeting* Warsaw (Poland) 1994, *Meeting on energy and development* Bratislava (Czechoslovakia) 1992, *Annual General Assembly* Strasbourg (France) 1990, *Performante et solidaire, une Europe pour les hommes* Strasbourg (France) 1990, *Le monde face aux progrès de l'informatique – informatique: éthique et sociétés* Geneva (Switzerland) 1987. **Publications** *SIIAEC FIET INFO* in English, Spanish. *Répertoire du SIIAEC*. Congress and Assembly proceedings.
Members Associations and groups in 39 countries:
Argentina, Australia, Austria, Bolivia, Brazil, Canada, Chile, Colombia, Costa Rica, Cyprus, Ecuador, France, Germany, Ghana, Greece, Honduras, India, Ireland, Israel, Italy, Japan, Kenya, Mauritius, Mexico, Netherlands, Niger, Panama, Paraguay, Philippines, Portugal, Senegal, Singapore, Spain, Sri Lanka, Switzerland, Togo, UK, USA, Zimbabwe.
Consultative Status Consultative status granted from: *ECOSOC (#05331)* (Ros C); *ILO (#11123)* (Special List). [2015/XC2442/t/**E**]

♦ Secrétariat international des ingénieurs catholiques / see Secrétariat international des ingénieurs, des agronomes et des cadres économiques catholiques (#19203)
♦ Secrétariat international de la jeunesse catholique (inactive)
♦ Secrétariat international de la laine (inactive)
♦ Secrétariat international du mouvement 12 décembre (internationally oriented national body)
♦ Secrétariat international des ouvriers du verre (inactive)
♦ Secrétariat international des peintres et professions similaires (inactive)
♦ Secrétariat international de presse universitaire catholique (inactive)
♦ Secrétariat international des questions scientifiques (#14821)
♦ Secrétariat international des questions scientifiques de Pax Romana / see International Secretariat for Scientific Questions (#14821)
♦ Secrétariat international de recherches sur l'histoire de l'outillage agricole et alimentation (inactive)
♦ Secrétariat international du service volontaire (inactive)
♦ Secrétariat international des syndicats des arts, des mass media et du spectacle (inactive)
♦ Secrétariat international des travailleurs de la pierre (inactive)
♦ Secrétariat international de typographes (inactive)
♦ Secrétariat international pour l'unification des pharmacopées (inactive)
♦ Secrétariat Latinoaméricain de la Compagnie de Jésus (religious order)

♦ Secretariat of the Minamata Convention on Mercury 19204

Exec Sec Avenue de la Paix 8-14, 1211 Geneva 10, Switzerland. Fax +41227973460. E-mail: mea-minamatasecretariat@un.org.
URL: https://www.mercuryconvention.org/

History Secretariat to the *Minamata Convention on Mercury (2013)*. **Events** *Meeting of the Conference of the Parties* 2021, *Meeting of the Conference of the Parties* Geneva (Switzerland) 2019, *Meeting of the Conference of the Parties* Geneva (Switzerland) 2018, *Meeting of the Conference of the Parties* Geneva (Switzerland) 2017. [2021/AA2058/**E***]

♦ Secretariat for Non-Christians / see Pontifical Council for Interreligious Dialogue (#18444)
♦ Secrétariat nordique des fonctionnaires des pouvoirs locaux / see Nordisk Tjenestemannsråd (#17538)
♦ Secrétariat nordique des travailleurs de l'agriculture et de l'horticulture (inactive)
♦ Secretariato Europeo delle Concessionarie de Autostrade a Pedaggio / see Association Européenne des Concessionnaires d'Autoroutes et d'Ouvrages à Péage (#02559)

♦ Secretariat of the Pacific Regional Environment Programme (SPREP) 19205

Programme régional océanien de l'environnement (PROE)

Dir Gen PO Box 240, Apia, Samoa. T. +68521929. Fax +68520231. E-mail: sprep@sprep.org.
URL: http://www.sprep.org/

History 1982, Nouméa (New Caledonia), as *South Pacific Regional Environment Programme*, a programme/organizational unit of *Pacific Community (SPC, #17942)*. Establishment followed recommendations, 1969, of a workshop focusing on nature conservation, which led in 1973 to the inclusion in the South Pacific Commission (currently SPC) of a programme for the conservation of nature. *Convention for the Protection of the Natural Resources and Environment of the South Pacific Region (SPREP convention, 1986)* adopted 24 Nov 1986, Nouméa. Recognized, 1990, as an autonomous entity hosted by SPC. Became fully autonomous 1992, when transferred to Apia (Samoa) as an autonomous intergovernmental organization reporting to *Pacific Islands Forum (#17968)* through Director of *Pacific Islands Forum Secretariat (#17970)*, and to the South Pacific Conference (the political gathering of all states and territories of the Pacific) through SPC Secretary-General. 'Agreement Establishing SPREP' came into force 31 Aug 1995, on ratification by 10th country to do so (Niue), and provides legal basis for SPREP's existence as an autonomous regional organization. Current name adopted, 1994, dropping "South" to be more inclusive for member countries on and above the equator. Acronym SPREP stands for both the *'Pacific Regional Environment Programme'* and its Secretariat. In 2006, Vanuatu lodged its Instruments of Ratification thereby completing the ratification process of all members. **Aims** Develop regional cooperation and technical assistance on all aspects of the environment; support Pacific island member countries and territories to maintain and improve their shared environment and enhance their capacity to provide a present and future resource base to support the needs and maintain the quality of life of the people through *sustainable development*. **Structure** SPREP Meeting (annual) is governing body. Pacific Regional Environment Programme Strategic Plan (2011-2015). Secretariat, managed by Director General, assisted by Deputy Director General, a Director for each of the 4 divisions: Climate Change; Biodiversity and Ecosystem Management; Waste Management and Pollution Control; Environmental Monitoring and Governance. **Languages** English, French. **Staff** 90.00 FTE, paid. **Finance** Major donors include: Governments of Australia and France; *New Zealand Ministry of Foreign Affairs and Trade – New Zealand Aid Programme*; *United States Agency for International Development (USAID)*; *Deutsche Gesellschaft für Internationale Zusammenarbeit (GIZ)*; *Japan International Cooperation Agency (JICA)*; *European Commission (EC, #06633)*; *Global Environment Facility (GEF, #10346)*; *UNEP (#20299)*; *Commonwealth Secretariat (#04362)*; *UNDP (#20292)*; *World Meteorological Organization (WMO, #21649)*. Other funding from member government contributions. Annual Budget (2012): US$ 13,400,000. **Activities** Guidance/assistance/consulting; capacity building; training/education; monitoring/evaluation. **Events** *Pacific Islands Conference on Nature Conservation and Protected Areas* Apia (Samoa) 2020, *Intergovernmental Meeting of Officials* Apia (Samoa) 2019, *Intergovernmental Meeting of Officials* Apia (Samoa) 2017, *Intergovernmental Meeting of Officials* Alofi (Niue) 2016, *Conference on Climate Change Adaptation* Busan (Korea Rep) 2016. **Publications** *Climate Change Matters Newsletter* (12 a year); *SPREP-Tok* (12 a year). *SPREP Reports and Studies* – series. *Country Profiles Directory*. *SPREP Factsheets*. Annual Report; SPREP Meeting reports; information and educational materials. **Information Services** *Pacific Environment Information Network (PEIN)* – Virtual Environment Libraries.
Members Governments of 25 countries and territories:
Australia, Cook Is, Fiji, France, Kiribati, Marshall Is, Micronesia FS, Nauru, New Caledonia, New Zealand, Niue, Northern Mariana Is, Palau, Papua New Guinea, Polynesia Fr, Samoa, Samoa USA, Solomon Is, Tokelau, Tonga, Tuvalu, UK, USA, Vanuatu, Wallis-Futuna.
IGO Relations Part of: *Council of Regional Organisations of the Pacific (CROP, #04914)*. Works closely with: *Pacific Community (SPC, #17942)*; *Pacific Islands Forum Secretariat (#17970)*; *University of the South Pacific (USP, #20703)*. **NGO Relations** NGOs participate as active observers. [2019.06.18/XE8300/**E***]

♦ Secrétariat pour les pays du Commonwealth (#04362)
♦ Secrétariat permanent de l'Accord sud-américain sur les stupéfiants et les substances psychotropes (inactive)
♦ Secrétariat permanent du Congrès panaméricain d'éducation physique (inactive)
♦ Secrétariat permanent de la Convention multilatérale sur la coopération et l'assistance mutuelle entre les directions nationales des douanes de l'Amérique latine, de l'Espagne et du Portugal (#19194)
♦ Secrétariat permanent international des travailleurs sociaux / see International Federation of Social Workers (#13544)
♦ Secrétariat permanent du Traité général d'intégration économique de l'Amérique centrale (#19195)
♦ Secrétariat professionnel international de l'enseignement (inactive)
♦ Secretariat for Promoting Christian Unity / see Pontifical Council for Promoting Christian Unity (#18446)
♦ Secretariat of the Ramsar Convention of Wetlands / see Secretariat of the Convention of Wetlands (#19200)

♦ Secretariat of the Rotterdam Convention 19206

Joint Exec Sec c/o FAO, Plant Production and Protection Div, Viale delle Terme di Caracalla, 00100 Rome RM, Italy. T. +39657055004. Fax +39657056347. E-mail: pic@fao.org.
URL: http://www.pic.int/

History Established as *Secretariat of the Convention on Harmful Chemicals and Pesticides*, jointly administered by *FAO (#09260)* and *UNEP (#20299)*, to negotiate the *Rotterdam Convention on the Prior Informed Consent Procedure for Certain Hazardous Chemicals and Pesticides in International Trade (Rotterdam convention, 1998)*, entered into force, 24 Feb 2004. **Aims** As laid out in Article 19 of the Convention: make arrangements for the meetings of the Conference of the Parties (COP) and its subsidiary bodies and to provide them with the services they require; facilitate assistance to Parties in implementing the Convention; ensure the necessary coordination with the secretariats of other relevant international bodies; perform other secretariat functions specified in the Convention and such other functions as may be determined by the COP. **Structure** Functions performed jointly by the Executive Director of UNEP and the Director General of FAO. FAO part of Secretariat is an integral part of the FAO Plant Production and Protection Division. **Languages** Arabic, Chinese, English, French, Russian, Spanish. **Events** *Conference of the Parties* Geneva (Switzerland) 2015, *Conference of the Parties* Geneva (Switzerland) 2013, *Conference of the Parties* Geneva (Switzerland) 2011, *Simultaneous extraordinary meetings of the conferences of the parties* Nusa Dua (Indonesia) 2010, *Conference of the Parties* Rome (Italy) 2008. **Members** State Parties (153). **IGO Relations** Cooperates with: *United Nations Institute for Training and Research (UNITAR, #20576)*. Invited to meetings of: *WHO (#20950)*; *World Trade Organization (WTO, #21864)*. [2022/XE4537/**E***]

♦ Secrétariats professionnels internationaux / see Global Union Federations (#10638)
♦ Secretariat of the Steering Committee of the Eastern Partnership Civil Society Forum / see Eastern Partnership Civil Society Forum (#05247)

♦ Secretariat of the Stockholm Convention on Persistent Organic Pollutants (Secretariat of the Stockholm Convention) 19207

Contact Chemin des Anémones 11-13, Châteleine, 1219 Geneva, Switzerland. T. +41229178271. Fax +41229178098. E-mail: brs@brsmeas.org.
URL: http://www.pops.int/

History Relevant treaty: *Stockholm Convention on Persistent Organic Pollutants (POP treaty, 2001)*. **Aims** Protect human health and the environment from persistent organic pollutants. **Structure** *UNEP (#20299)* provides Secretariat. Governing Body of Convention is Conference of Parties. **Activities** Parties take action to eliminate or severely restrict production and/or use of listed persistent organic pollutants (POPs) and to reduce or eliminate releases of unintentionally produced POPs or from POPS wastes. **Events** *Conference of the Parties* Geneva (Switzerland) 2015, *Meeting* Rome (Italy) 2014, *Conference of the Parties* Geneva (Switzerland) 2013, *Meeting* Rome (Italy) 2013, *Meeting* Geneva (Switzerland) 2012. **Publications** *Guidance for Developing a National Implementation Plan for the Stockholm Convention*; *Ridding the World of POPs*. Outreach materials on the world of POPs; reports.
Members Parties in 180 countries:
Afghanistan, Albania, Algeria, Angola, Antigua-Barbuda, Argentina, Armenia, Australia, Austria, Azerbaijan, Bahamas, Bahrain, Bangladesh, Barbados, Belarus, Belgium, Belize, Benin, Bolivia, Bosnia-Herzegovina, Botswana, Brazil, Bulgaria, Burkina Faso, Burundi, Cambodia, Cameroon, Canada, Cape Verde, Chad, Chile, China, Colombia, Comoros, Congo Brazzaville, Congo DR, Cook Is, Costa Rica, Côte d'Ivoire, Croatia, Cuba, Cyprus, Czechia, Denmark, Djibouti, Dominica, Dominican Rep, Ecuador, Egypt, El Salvador, Eritrea, Estonia, Eswatini, Ethiopia, Fiji, Finland, France, Gabon, Gambia, Georgia, Germany, Ghana, Greece, Guatemala, Guinea, Guinea-Bissau, Guyana, Honduras, Hungary, Iceland, India, Indonesia, Iran Islamic Rep, Iraq, Ireland, Japan, Jordan, Kazakhstan, Kenya, Kiribati, Korea DPR, Korea Rep, Kuwait, Kyrgyzstan, Laos, Latvia, Lebanon, Lesotho, Liberia, Libya, Liechtenstein, Lithuania, Luxembourg, Madagascar, Malawi, Maldives, Mali, Malta, Marshall Is, Mauritania, Mauritius,

Mexico, Micronesia FS, Moldova, Monaco, Mongolia, Montenegro, Morocco, Mozambique, Myanmar, Namibia, Nauru, Nepal, Netherlands, New Zealand, Nicaragua, Niger, Nigeria, Niue, North Macedonia, Norway, Oman, Pakistan, Palau, Palestine, Panama, Papua New Guinea, Paraguay, Peru, Philippines, Poland, Portugal, Qatar, Romania, Russia, Rwanda, Samoa, Sao Tomé-Principe, Saudi Arabia, Senegal, Serbia, Seychelles, Sierra Leone, Singapore, Slovakia, Slovenia, Solomon Is, Somalia, South Africa, Spain, Sri Lanka, St Kitts-Nevis, St Lucia, St Vincent-Grenadines, Sudan, Suriname, Sweden, Switzerland, Syrian AR, Tajikistan, Tanzania UR, Thailand, Togo, Tonga, Trinidad-Tobago, Tunisia, Türkiye, Tuvalu, Uganda, UK, Ukraine, United Arab Emirates, Uruguay, Uzbekistan, Vanuatu, Venezuela, Vietnam, Yemen, Zambia, Zimbabwe.
Regional party:
European Union (EU, #08967).
IGO Relations Cooperates with numerous IGOs for achievement of the purposes of the Convention, such as: *FAO (#09260)*; *Global Environment Facility (GEF, #10346)*; *Inter-Organization Programme for the Sound Management of Chemicals (IOMC, #15956)*; *Secretariat of the Basel Convention (SBC, #19196)*; *Strategic Approach to International Chemicals Management (SAICM, #20005)*; *United Nations Institute for Training and Research (UNITAR, #20576)*; *World Trade Organization (WTO, #21864).* [2019.11.14/XE4513/**E***]

♦ **Secretariat of the Stockholm Convention** Secretariat of the Stockholm Convention on Persistent Organic Pollutants (#19207)
♦ Secretariat for Supporting Scientific Activities (inactive)
♦ Secrétariat technique du Conseil centroaméricain du tourisme / see Secretaria de Integración Turistica Centroamericana (#19193)
♦ **Secretariat of the UNCCD** Secretariat of the United Nations Convention to Combat Desertification (#19208)
♦ Secrétariat pour l'unité des chrétiens / see Pontifical Council for Promoting Christian Unity (#18446)

♦ Secretariat of the United Nations Convention to Combat Desertification (Secretariat of the UNCCD) 19208

Secrétariat de la Convention des Nations Unies sur la Lutte contre la Désertification – Secretaria de la Convención de las Naciones Unidas de Lucha contra la Desertificacion

Exec Sec PO Box 260129, 53153 Bonn, Germany. T. +492288152800. Fax +492288152899. E-mail: secretariat@unccd.int.
Street address Platz der Vereinten Nationen 1, 53113 Bonn, Germany.
URL: http://www.unccd.int/

History Feb 1999, Bonn (Germany). Established 1999, to service *United Nations Convention to Combat Desertification (UNCCD, 1994).* Former names and other names: *UNCCD Secretariat* – alias. **Aims** Assist the Conference of Parties by making necessary arrangements for meetings and subsidiary bodies established under the convention and provide services as required. **Structure** Headquarters in Bonn (Germany); Liaison Office in New York NY (USA); Regional Units in Bangkok (Thailand), Istanbul (Turkey), Rabat (Morocco) and Santiago (Chile). Committees (2): Review of the Implementation of the Convention (CRIC); Science and Technology (CST). **Languages** Arabic, Chinese, English, French, Russian, Spanish. **Staff** 45.00 FTE, paid. **Finance** Core budget covered by all Parties through the General Trust Fund for the Core Budget. Other trust funds (4): Special Trust Fund for Participation in the CCD Process – established to fund participation of delegates from affected developing-country Parties to sessions of COP; Trust Fund for Voluntary Financing of Activities of the UNCCD – established to support participation of NGOs from affected developing countries and other purposes appropriate to the Convention; Trust Fund for Voluntary Financing of the UNCCD Global Mechanism – established to support activities of the Global Mechanism; Trust Fund for the Supplementary Contribution to the Convention Activities by the Host Government (Bonn Fund). *Global Environment Facility (GEF, #10346)* has served as a financial mechanism to the Convention. **Activities** Events/meetings; politics/policy/regulatory. **Events** *Conference of the Parties* Delhi (India) 2019, *Session* Georgetown (Guyana) 2019, *Meeting on National Adaptation Plans* Incheon (Korea Rep) 2019, *Meeting on the Peace Forest Initiative* Seoul (Korea Rep) 2019, *Global Land Degradation Neutrality Forum* Seoul (Korea Rep) 2018. **Publications** *Policy Brief Series.* Education kits; books; booklets; thematic factsheets.

Members Parties to the Convention (197 – 196 governments and one regional entity), as of Mar 2020:
Afghanistan, Albania, Algeria, Andorra, Angola, Antigua-Barbuda, Argentina, Armenia, Australia, Austria, Azerbaijan, Bahamas, Bahrain, Bangladesh, Barbados, Belarus, Belgium, Belize, Benin, Bhutan, Bolivia, Bosnia-Herzegovina, Botswana, Brazil, Brunei Darussalam, Bulgaria, Burkina Faso, Burundi, Cambodia, Cameroon, Canada, Cape Verde, Central African Rep, Chad, Chile, China, Colombia, Comoros, Congo Brazzaville, Congo DR, Cook Is, Costa Rica, Côte d'Ivoire, Croatia, Cuba, Cyprus, Czechia, Denmark, Djibouti, Dominica, Dominican Rep, Ecuador, Egypt, El Salvador, Equatorial Guinea, Eritrea, Estonia, Eswatini, Ethiopia, Fiji, Finland, France, Gabon, Gambia, Georgia, Germany, Ghana, Greece, Grenada, Guatemala, Guinea, Guinea-Bissau, Guyana, Haiti, Honduras, Hungary, Iceland, India, Indonesia, Iran Islamic Rep, Iraq, Ireland, Israel, Italy, Jamaica, Japan, Jordan, Kazakhstan, Kenya, Kiribati, Korea DPR, Korea Rep, Kuwait, Kyrgyzstan, Laos, Latvia, Lebanon, Lesotho, Liberia, Libya, Liechtenstein, Lithuania, Luxembourg, Madagascar, Malawi, Malaysia, Maldives, Mali, Malta, Marshall Is, Mauritania, Mauritius, Mexico, Micronesia FS, Moldova, Monaco, Mongolia, Montenegro, Morocco, Mozambique, Myanmar, Namibia, Nauru, Nepal, Netherlands, New Zealand, Nicaragua, Niger, Nigeria, Niue, North Macedonia, Norway, Oman, Pakistan, Palau, Palestine, Panama, Papua New Guinea, Paraguay, Peru, Philippines, Poland, Portugal, Qatar, Romania, Russia, Rwanda, Samoa, San Marino, Sao Tomé-Principe, Saudi Arabia, Senegal, Serbia, Seychelles, Sierra Leone, Singapore, Slovakia, Slovenia, Solomon Is, Somalia, South Africa, South Sudan, Spain, Sri Lanka, St Kitts-Nevis, St Lucia, St Vincent-Grenadines, Sudan, Suriname, Sweden, Switzerland, Syrian AR, Tajikistan, Tanzania UR, Thailand, Timor-Leste, Togo, Tonga, Trinidad-Tobago, Tunisia, Türkiye, Turkmenistan, Tuvalu, Uganda, UK, Ukraine, United Arab Emirates, Uruguay, USA, Uzbekistan, Vanuatu, Venezuela, Vietnam, Yemen, Zambia, Zimbabwe.
Included in the above, 1 regional entity, listed in this Yearbook:
European Union (EU, #08967).

IGO Relations 52 Intergovernmental organizations accredited by the Conference of the Parties, include:
- *Organisation of African, Caribbean and Pacific States (OACPS, #17796)*;
- *African Development Bank (ADB, #00283)*;
- *African Organization of Cartography and Remote Sensing (AOCRS, inactive)*;
- *African Union (AU, #00488)* – previously Organization of African Unity;
- *Agence Panafricaine de la Grande Muraille Verte (APGMV, #00547)*;
- *Arab Centre for the Studies of Arid Zones and Dry Lands (ACSAD, #00918)*;
- *Arab Maghreb Union (AMU, #01004)*;
- *Arab Organization for Agricultural Development (AOAD, #01018)*;
- *Asian-African Legal Consultative Organization (AALCO, #01303)*;
- *Bioversity International (#03262)* – previously known as IPGRI;
- *CABI (#03393)*;
- *Commission des forêts d'Afrique centrale (COMIFAC, #04214)*;
- *Centre for Environment and Development for the Arab Region and Europe (CEDARE, #03738)*;
- *CGIAR System Organization (CGIAR, #03843)* / *International Crops Research Institute for the Semi-Arid Tropics (ICRISAT, #13116)*;
- *Comité permanent inter-Etats de lutte contre la sécheresse dans le Sahel (CILSS, #04195)*;
- *Common Fund for Commodities (CFC, #04293)*;
- *Commonwealth Secretariat (#04362)*;
- *Communauté économique et monétaire d'Afrique centrale (CEMAC, #04374)*;
- *Comunidade dos Paises de Lingua Portuguesa (CPLP, #04430)*;
- *Community of Sahel-Saharan States (CEN-SAD, #04406)*;
- *Council of Europe (CE, #04881)*;
- *Economic Community of Central African States (ECCAS, #05311)*;
- *Economic Community of West African States (ECOWAS, #05312)*;
- *European Space Agency (ESA, #08798)*;
- *Institut de recherche pour le développement (IRD)*;
- *Inter-American Institute for Cooperation on Agriculture (IICA, #11434)*;
- *Intergovernmental Authority on Development (IGAD, #11472)*;
- *International Center for Agricultural Research in the Dry Areas (ICARDA, #12466)*;
- *International Organization for Migration (IOM, #14454)*;
- *League of Arab States (LAS, #16420)*;
- *Observatoire du Sahara et du Sahel (OSS, #17636)*;
- *OECD (#17693)*;
- *Organisation of Islamic Cooperation (OIC, #17813)*;
- *Pacific Community (SPC, #17942)*;
- *Permanent Court of Arbitration (PCA, #18321)*;
- *Regional Environmental Centre for the Caucasus (REC Caucasus, #18781)*;
- *Regional Environmental Centre for Central and Eastern Europe (REC, #18782)*;
- *Regional Water Centre for Arid and Semi-Arid Regions of Latin America and the Caribbean (CAZALAC)*;
- *Secretariat of the Convention of Wetlands (#19200)*;
- *Secretariat of the Pacific Regional Environment Programme (SPREP, #19205)*;
- *Southern African Development Community (SADC, #19843)*;
- *Tropical Agriculture Research and Higher Education Center (#20246)*;
- *Union économique et monétaire Ouest africaine (UEMOA, #20377).*

Member of: *Collaborative Partnership on Forests (CPF, #04100)*; *UN-Water (#20723).* Partner of: *Niger Basin Authority (NBA, #17134)* (Venezuela Cooperation). Cooperates with: *United Nations Institute for Training and Research (UNITAR, #20576).*

NGO Relations 314 Civil Society Organizations (CSOs) have been accredited by the Conference of the Parties, including the following organizations listed in this Yearbook:
- *African Centre for Assistance and Protection of the Environment of the Sahel*;
- *African Forest Forum (AFF, #00318)*;
- *African Office for Development and Cooperation (OFADEC)*;
- *African Youth Movement (AYM, #00506)*;
- *Asociación Ecológica del Oriente (no recent information)*;
- *Association internationale forêts méditerranéennes (AIFM, #02699)*;
- *Association of the Network for International Research on Desertification (DesertNet International, #02823)*;
- *Both ENDS (#03307)*;
- *Caribbean Network for Integrated Rural Development (CNIRD, #03528)*;
- *Caribbean Youth Environment Network (CYEN, #03570)*;
- *Caucasus Environmental NGO Network (CENN, #03613)*;
- *Centre d'actions et de réalisations internationales (CARI)*;
- *Centre de recherche et d'information pour le développement, Paris (CRID)*;
- *Christian Aid*;
- *Commonland Foundation*;
- *Confédération des ONG d'environnement et de développement de l'Afrique centrale (CONGAC, #04572)*;
- *Conservation International (CI)*;
- *Cooperazione Internazionale Sud-Sud (CISS)*;
- *Council of European Foresters (CEF, #04889)*;
- *DESERTEC Foundation*;
- *Drylands Coordination Group (DCG, inactive)*;
- *EarthAction (EA, #05159)*;
- *Eau vive*;
- *Ecopeace Asia*;
- *EcoPeace Middle East (#05325)*;
- *Environnement et développement du Tiers-monde (enda, #05510)*;
- *Esquel Group Foundation (EGF, inactive)*;
- *Farm Radio International (#09274)*;
- *Fondation Déserts du Monde (#09816)*;
- *Forum international pour l'exploitation forestière (FIEF)*;
- *Friends of the Earth International (FoEI, #10002)*;
- *Friends World Committee for Consultation (FWCC, #10004)*;
- *Global Environmental Forum (GEF)*;
- *Global Green Environmental Network (GGEN)*;
- *Green Asia Network (GAN)*;
- *Green Cross International (GCI, #10715)*;
- *Green Earth Organization (GEO, inactive)*;
- *Hanns Seidel Foundation*;
- *Help for Children in Need (KNH)*;
- *IFOAM – Organics International (IFOAM, #11105)*;
- *Indigenous Peoples of Africa Coordinating Committee (IPACC, #11163)*;
- *Initiatives of Change International – Caux (IofC, #11213)*;
- *International Association for the Protection of the Environment in Africa (ENVIRO-PROTECT, no recent information)*;
- *International Biochar Initiative (IBI, #12342)*;
- *International Campaign for Freedom and Peace (ICFP, no recent information)*;
- *International Centre of Comparative Environmental Law (#12483)*;
- *International Centre for Environmental Education and Community Development (ICENECDEV)*;
- *International Centre for Trade and Sustainable Development, Geneva (ICTSD, #12524)*;
- *International Federation of Red Cross and Red Crescent Societies (#13526)*;
- *International Foundation for African Children (IFAC)*;
- *International Institute for Applied Systems Analysis (IIASA, #13861)*;
- *International Institute for Sustainability Analysis and Strategy (#13929)*;
- *International Trade Union Confederation (ITUC, #15708)*;
- *International Union for Conservation of Nature and Natural Resources (IUCN, #15766)*;
- *International Union of Forest Research Organizations (IUFRO, #15774)*;
- *International Union of Soil Sciences (IUSS, #15817)*;
- *International Voluntary Organisation for Women, Education and Development (IVOWED)*;
- *ISRIC – World Soil Information (#16068)*;
- *Istituto per le Relazioni tra Italia ed i Paesi dell'Africa, America Latina e Medio Oriente (IPALMO, no recent information)*;
- *Jacob Blaustein Institute for Desert Research (BIDR)*;
- *La Brique*;
- *La Route du Sel et de l'Espoir (La ROSE)*;
- *League for Pastoral Peoples and Endogenous Livestock Development (LPP)*;
- *Mediterranean Information Office for Environment, Culture and Sustainable Development (MIO-ECSDE, #16657)*;
- *Michael Succow Foundation for the Protection of Nature (Succow Foundation)*;
- *Network for Environment and Sustainable Development in Africa (NESDA, inactive)*;
- *New World Hope Organization (NWHO)*;
- *Northeast Asian Forest Forum (NEAFF)*;
- *Nubian Vault Association (#17614)*;
- *Observatorio Latinoamericano de Conflictos Ambientales, Chile (OLCA)*;
- *Ondernemers Zonder Grenzen (OZG)*;
- *Permaculture Research Institute (PRI)*;
- *Programme Solidarité eau (pS-Eau, #18529)*;
- *PROTERRA (no recent information)*;
- *Rainforest Alliance*;
- *Regional Environmental Centre for Central Asia (CAREC)*;
- *Responding to Climate Change (RTCC)*;
- *Royal Geographical Society – with the Institute of British Geographers (RGS-IBG)*;
- *Secrétariat permanent des ONG (SPONG, no recent information)*;
- *Service d'appui aux initiatives locales de développement (SAILD, #19237)*;
- *Society for Ecological Restoration International (SERI)*;
- *Solar Cookers International (SCI, #19673)*;
- *SOS SAHEL (#19695)*;
- *South African Institute of International Affairs (SAIIA)*;
- *Sovereign Military Hospitaller Order of St John of Jerusalem, of Rhodes and of Malta (SMOM)*;
- *Stockholm Environment Institute (SEI, #19993)*;
- *The Sustainability Laboratory (The Lab)*;
- *Sustainable Fibre Alliance (SFA)*;
- *Sustainable Harvest International*;
- *SYLVA-WORLD for Development and the Protection of Forests and the Environment*;
- *Tchad Agir Pour l'Environnement (TCHAPE)*;
- *Tree Aid*;
- *UNISFÉRA (#20491)*;
- *Women's Environment and Development Organization (WEDO, #21016)*;
- *World Agroforestry Centre (ICRAF, #21072)*;
- *World Business Council for Sustainable Development (WBCSD, #21254)*;
- *World Federation of UNESCO Clubs, Centres and Associations (WFUCA, #21498)*;
- *World Resources Institute (WRI, #21753)*;
- *World Vision International (WVI, #21904)*;
- *World Wide Fund for Nature (WWF, #21922)*;
- *Yves Rocher Foundation.*

Member of: *Global Gender and Climate Alliance (GGCA, no recent information)*; *Mountain Partnership (MP, #16862).* Cooperates with: *Fundación Henry Dunant América Latina (FuHD – AL, #10024).* [2020.08.31/XE3486/**E***]

♦ Secretariat of University Leaders for a Sustainable Future / see Association of University Leaders for a Sustainable Future
♦ Secretariatus ad Christianorum Unitatem Fovendam / see Pontifical Council for Promoting Christian Unity (#18446)
♦ Secretariatus pro Non Credentibus / see Pontifical Council for Culture (#18443)

♦ **Secretariat for the Vienna Convention for the Protection of the Ozone Layer and the Montreal Protocol on Substances that Deplete the Ozone Layer (Ozone Secretariat)** 19209

Exec Sec UNEP, PO Box 30552, Nairobi, 00100, Kenya. T. +254207623851 – +254207623611. E-mail: mea-ozoneinfo@un.org.
Communications Officer address not obtained.
URL: https://ozone.unep.org/

History 1989, Helsinki (Finland). Established as part of *UNEP (#20299)*, during 1st Conference of the Parties to *Vienna Convention for the Protection of the Ozone Layer (Ozone treaty, 1985)*, entered into force 22 Sep 1988, and 1st Meeting of Parties to *Montreal Protocol on Substances that Deplete the Ozone Layer (1987)*, entered into force 1 Jan 1989. Amendments to Montréal Protocol: *Amendment to the Montreal Protocol on Substances That Deplete the Ozone Layer, 1990 (London amendment, 1990)*, entered into force 1992; *Amendment to the Montreal Protocol on Substances That Deplete the Ozone Layer, 1992 (Copenhagen amendment, 1992)*, entered into force 1994; *Amendment to the Montreal Protocol on Substances That Deplete the Ozone Layer, 1997 (Montreal amendment, 1997)*, entered into force 1999, *Amendment to the Montreal Protocol on Substances That Deplete the Ozone Layer, 1999 (Beijing amendment, 1999)*, entered into force 2002; *Amendment to the Montreal Protocol on Substances that Deplete the Ozone Layer, 2016 (Kigali Amendment, 2016)*, entered into force 2019. **Aims** Facilitate and support Parties to the Vienna Convention and Montréal Protocol and other stakeholders as appropriate, in implementing the Convention and Protocol to protect and heal the ozone layer against adverse impacts resulting from its modification, thus protecting human health and the environment, including minimizing impacts on climate. **Structure** Secretariat is answerable to the Parties to the Vienna Convention and Parties to the Montréal Protocol. UN Environment is designated as Secretariat for the Convention and Protocol. UN Secretary-General appoints Executive Secretary. **Languages** Arabic, Chinese, English, French, Russian, Spanish. **Staff** 17.00 FTE, paid. **Finance** Trust Funds, contributed on an assessed basis by Parties to the Convention and Parties to the Protocol. Annual budget: 6,000,000 USD. **Activities** Events/meetings; knowledge management/information dissemination; management of treaties and agreements; politics/policy/regulatory. **Events** *Meeting of the Parties of the Montreal Protocol* 2023, *Open-Ended Working Group of the Parties to the Montreal Protocol* Brussels (Belgium) 2023, *Implementation Committee under the Non-Compliance Procedure of the Montreal Protocol Meeting* Nairobi (Kenya) 2023, *Implementation Committee under the Non-Compliance Procedure of the Montreal Protocol Meeting* 2022, *Meeting of the Parties of the Montreal Protocol* Montréal, QC (Canada) 2022. **Publications** *Handbook for the Montréal Protocol* (annual) – online; *Handbook for the Vienna Convention* (annual) – online. *Implementation Committee Primer*. Assessment panel reports; committee reports; working group publications; briefing notes; background materials.

Members Parties to the Montréal Protocol (197):
Afghanistan, Albania, Algeria, Andorra, Angola, Antigua-Barbuda, Argentina, Armenia, Australia, Austria, Azerbaijan, Bahamas, Bahrain, Bangladesh, Barbados, Belarus, Belgium, Belize, Benin, Bhutan, Bolivia, Bosnia-Herzegovina, Botswana, Brazil, Brunei Darussalam, Bulgaria, Burkina Faso, Burundi, Cambodia, Cameroon, Canada, Cape Verde, Central African Rep, Chad, Chile, China, Colombia, Comoros, Congo Brazzaville, Congo DR, Cook Is, Costa Rica, Côte d'Ivoire, Croatia, Cuba, Cyprus, Czechia, Denmark, Djibouti, Dominica, Dominican Rep, Ecuador, Egypt, El Salvador, Equatorial Guinea, Eritrea, Estonia, Eswatini, Ethiopia, Fiji, Finland, France, Gabon, Gambia, Georgia, Germany, Ghana, Greece, Grenada, Guatemala, Guinea, Guinea-Bissau, Guyana, Haiti, Holy See, Honduras, Hungary, Iceland, India, Indonesia, Iran Islamic Rep, Iraq, Ireland, Israel, Italy, Jamaica, Japan, Jordan, Kazakhstan, Kenya, Kiribati, Korea DPR, Korea Rep, Kuwait, Kyrgyzstan, Laos, Latvia, Lebanon, Lesotho, Liberia, Libya, Liechtenstein, Lithuania, Luxembourg, Madagascar, Malawi, Malaysia, Maldives, Mali, Malta, Marshall Is, Mauritania, Mauritius, Mexico, Micronesia FS, Moldova, Monaco, Mongolia, Montenegro, Morocco, Mozambique, Myanmar, Namibia, Nauru, Nepal, Netherlands, New Zealand, Nicaragua, Niger, Nigeria, Niue, North Macedonia, Norway, Oman, Pakistan, Palau, Palestine, Panama, Papua New Guinea, Paraguay, Peru, Philippines, Poland, Portugal, Qatar, Romania, Russia, Rwanda, Samoa, San Marino, Sao Tomé-Principe, Saudi Arabia, Senegal, Serbia, Seychelles, Sierra Leone, Singapore, Slovakia, Slovenia, Solomon Is, Somalia, South Africa, South Sudan, Spain, Sri Lanka, St Kitts-Nevis, St Lucia, St Vincent-Grenadines, Sudan, Suriname, Sweden, Switzerland, Syrian AR, Tajikistan, Tanzania UR, Thailand, Timor-Leste, Togo, Tonga, Trinidad-Tobago, Tunisia, Türkiye, Turkmenistan, Tuvalu, Uganda, UK, Ukraine, United Arab Emirates, Uruguay, USA, Uzbekistan, Vanuatu, Venezuela, Vietnam, Yemen, Zambia, Zimbabwe.
Included in the above, 1 regional organization:
European Union (EU, #08967). [2022.10.19/XK1276/**E***]

- ♦ Secretaries and Personal Assistants in the Community of Europe / see SPACE Network (#19899)
- ♦ **SEC** Sociedad Europea de Cultura (#08576)
- ♦ SEC – Societas Europaea Studiosorum Philologiae Classicae (no recent information)
- ♦ **SEC** Société Européenne de Cardiologie (#08536)
- ♦ SEC – Société européenne de chromatophonie (inactive)
- ♦ Secular Augustinians (religious order)
- ♦ Secular Franciscan Order (religious order)
- ♦ Secular Missionaries of the Passion (religious order)
- ♦ Secular Order of Discalced Carmelites (religious order)
- ♦ Secular Order of Servants of Mary (religious order)
- ♦ Secular Organizations for Sobriety (internationally oriented national body)
- ♦ Secular Third Order of Our Lady of Mercy (religious order)
- ♦ Secure World Foundation (internationally oriented national body)

♦ **Security Council Report (SCR)** 19210

Exec Dir 711 Third Ave, Ste 1501, New York NY 10017, USA. T. +12127599429. Fax +12127594038. E-mail: contact@securitycouncilreport.org.
URL: http://www.securitycouncilreport.org/

Aims Advance transparency and effectiveness of the UN Security Council. **Structure** Board. **Languages** English. **Staff** 14.00 FTE, paid. **Finance** Supporting Governments: Australia, Austria, Belgium, Canada, Denmark, Equatorial Guinea, Finland, Germany, Iceland, Ireland, Kuwait, Liechtenstein, Luxembourg, Netherlands, New Zealand, Norway, Peru, Poland, Korea Rep, Singapore, Spain, Sweden, Switzerland, Timor-Leste, Turkey, United Arab Emirates. Sponsoring Foundations: *Carnegie Corporation of New York*; *Humanity United*; *MacArthur Foundation*. **Activities** Knowledge management/information dissemination; events/meetings; networking/liaising; capacity building. **Publications** *What's in Blue* (daily); *Monthly Forecast*. Research reports. **NGO Relations** Member of: *NGO Working Group on the Security Council (#17128).* [2018.09.06/XM6118/**E**]

- ♦ Security and Defense Network of Latin America (#18730)
- ♦ Security Treaty (1951 treaty)
- ♦ **SEDAC** Secretariado Episcopal de América Central (#05514)
- ♦ SEDC / see smartEn (#19319)
- ♦ Sede Regional Africana da OMS (#20943)

♦ **Sedex** 19211

UK 5th Floor, 24 Southwark Bridge Rd, London, SE1 9HF, UK. T. +442079022320. E-mail: info@sedexglobal.com.
USA 26th Floor, 405 Lexington Avenue, New York NY 10174, USA.
URL: http://www.sedexglobal.com/

History 2004. **Aims** Drive improvements in responsible and ethical business practices in global *supply* chains. **Structure** Board of Directors. **Activities** Knowledge management/information dissemination; training/education. **Members** Buyer; Buyer/Supplier; Supplier. Membership countries not specified. **NGO Relations** *amfori (#00797)*; *International Trade Centre (ITC, #15703) United Nations Global Compact (#20567).* [2017/XM5561/**F**]

- ♦ SEDHU – Servicio Ecuménico para la Dignidad Humana (internationally oriented national body)
- ♦ SEDIF / see Service d'information et formation Amérique Latine – Tiers Monde
- ♦ SEDIFRALE – Sesiones Pedagógicas para Docentes e Investigatores del Francés Lengua Extranjera (meeting series)
- ♦ SEDIF – Service d'information et formation Amérique Latine – Tiers Monde (internationally oriented national body)
- ♦ **SEDI** Société européenne de droit international (#08634)
- ♦ **SEDM** South-East Europe Defense Ministerial (#19822)
- ♦ **SedNet** European Sediment Network (#08459)
- ♦ SEDOI – Société pour l'étude et le développement de l'ordre international (inactive)
- ♦ **SEDOS** Servizio di Documentazione e Studi (#19241)
- ♦ **SED** Society for Economic Dynamics (#19545)
- ♦ SED – Solidaridad, Educación y Desarrollo (internationally oriented national body)
- ♦ SEDS – Students for the Exploration and Development of Space (internationally oriented national body)
- ♦ SEEAC – Secrétariat pour l'évaluation environnementale en Afrique centrale (inactive)
- ♦ **SEEAN** South Eastern European-Adriatic Addiction Treatment Network (#19806)
- ♦ **SEEA** Société européenne d'énergie atomique (#06293)
- ♦ **SEEBRIG** South-Eastern Europe Brigade (#19808)
- ♦ SEECEL – South East European Centre for Entrepreneurial Learning (inactive)
- ♦ SEEC-Forum for Western Balkans Defense Cooperation (inactive)
- ♦ SEE Change Net Foundation (internationally oriented national body)
- ♦ **SEECOP** South-East European Consortium for Operational weather Prediction (#19810)

♦ **SEECP Parliamentary Assembly** 19212

Office 1 "Aleksandar I" Square, 1169 Sofia, Bulgaria. T. +35929878038.
URL: http://rspcsee.org/en/pages/read/seecp-parliamentary-assembly/

History 10 May 2010, Bucharest (Romania). Declaration adopted at inaugural session. Set up in accordance with the Charter on Good Neighbourly Relations, Stability, Security and Cooperation in South-Eastern Europe, signed 2000, Bucharest (Romania), the Memorandum of Understanding for Inter-Parliamentary Cooperation in SEE, signed 2008, Sofia (Bulgaria), and the Final Declarations of the Conferences of Speakers of Parliaments of the Participating States of *South East European Cooperation Process (SEECP, #19811)*. **Aims** Strengthen cooperation and coordination efforst of parliaments of all Participating States, so as to promote and further ensure peace, security, stability, solidarity and good-neighbourly cooperation in the region, in the interest of their citizens and countries, as well as of Europe in general. **Structure** Bureau; President; Standing Committee; General Committees; Ad hoc Working Groups; Secretariat. **Languages** English. **Staff** 3.00 FTE, paid. **Activities** Events/meetings. **Events** *Plenary Session* Athens (Greece) 2022, *Plenary Session* Pristina (Kosovo) 2020.

Members Parliaments of SEECP Participating States (13):
Albania, Bosnia-Herzegovina, Bulgaria, Croatia, Greece, Kosovo, Moldova, Montenegro, North Macedonia, Romania, Serbia, Slovenia, Türkiye.

IGO Relations *Parliamentary Assembly of the Organization of the Black Sea Economic Cooperation (PABSEC, #18213).* [2022/XM4185/**E***]

- ♦ **SEECP** South East European Cooperation Process (#19811)

♦ **SEED** 19213

Exec Dir DCPI-UNEP, PO Box 30552, Nairobi, 00100, Kenya.
URL: http://www.seed.uno/

History 2002, by *UNEP (#20299)*, *UNDP (#20292)* and *International Union for Conservation of Nature and Natural Resources (IUCN, #15766)*, as *SEED Initiative*. SEED stands for *Supporting Entrepreneurs for Sustainable Development*. **Aims** Contribute towards the goals in the UN's Millennium Declaration and the commitments made at the Johannesburg World Summit on Sustainable Development. **Structure** Board. **Activities** Awards/prizes/competitions; advocacy/lobbying/activism. **Publications** *SEED Newsletter*. Annual Report.

Members Partners; Supporters; Associates. Partners include 6 organizations listed in this Yearbook:
Conservation International (CI); *European Commission (EC, #06633)* (Europeaid); *Flemish International Cooperation Agency (FICA)*; *International Union for Conservation of Nature and Natural Resources (IUCN, #15766)*; *UNDP (#20292)*; *UNEP (#20299).*
Supporters include 2 organizations listed in this Yearbook:
UNIDO (#20336); *UN Women (#20724).*
Associates include 7 organizations listed in this Yearbook:
Ashoka – Innovators for the Public (#01248); *International Institute for Environment and Development (IIED, #13877)*; *Leadership for Environment and Development (LEAD International, #16416)*; *Mediterranean Marine Bird Association (MEDMARAVIS, #16661)*; *United Nations Global Compact (#20567)*; *World Business Council for Sustainable Development (WBCSD, #21254).*

NGO Relations Partner of: *Green Economy Coalition (GEC, #10717)*; *UNLEASH.* [2017/XJ0404/y/**E**]

♦ **Seed Association of the Americas (SAA)** 19214

Exec Dir 1701 Duke St, Ste 275, Alexandria VA 22314, USA. E-mail: info@saaseed.org.
URL: http://www.saaseed.org/

History 2005, USA. **Aims** Educate and support development, trade and free movement of seeds within the Americas; advocate seed industry legislation and regulation issues as to ensure plant property rights. **Structure** General Assembly; Board of Directors; Executive Director. Working Groups (4). **Languages** English, Spanish. **Staff** 5.00 FTE, paid. **Activities** Events/meetings. **Events** *Congress* Buenos Aires (Argentina) 2019, *Promoting the seed business in the Americas* Cartagena de Indias (Colombia) 2017, *Congress* Cancún (Mexico) 2015, *Congress* Punta del Este (Uruguay) 2013.

Members Full in 10 countries:
Argentina, Brazil, Canada, Chile, Colombia, Mexico, Paraguay, Peru, Uruguay, USA.
Observer in 2 countries:
Ecuador, Venezuela.
Affiliate members include:
Latin American Federation of Seed Associations (#16330).

IGO Relations Observer status with (1): *World Trade Organization (WTO, #21864).* [2023.02.14/XM2964/t/**D**]

- ♦ SeedChange (internationally oriented national body)
- ♦ SEED / see European Society of Dental Ergonomics (#08577)
- ♦ Seed Forum (unconfirmed)
- ♦ Seed Global Health (internationally oriented national body)
- ♦ SEED Initiative / see SEED (#19213)

♦ **SEED Institute** 19215

Head 73 Bras Basah Road No 07-01, NTUC Trade Union House, Singapore 189556, Singapore. T. +6563320668. Fax +6563397408. E-mail: info@seedinstitute.edu.sg.
URL: http://www.seedinstitute.edu.sg/

History Jan 1989, following an agreement of 25 Oct 1988, between *Bernard van Leer Foundation (BvLF)* and the National Trades Union Congress (NTUC) Childcare of Singapore (Singapore). Officially opened 24 Oct 1990. Original title: *Regional Training and Resource Centre in Early Childhood Care and Education for Asia (RTRC Asia)*. **Aims** Provide a solid foundation for trainers, early childhood *teachers* and *childcare* staff throughout the region. **Structure** Director leads a multi-disciplinary team of qualified trainers. **Languages** English. **Staff** Full-time trainers. **Finance** Self-financing. Occasional financial support from donors for specific projects. **Activities** Full range of training programmes, including core courses, continuing education, professional support workshops as well as customized training programmes and consultancy. Maintains *'Caterpillar's Cove Child Development and Study Centre'*. Workshops, conferences, seminars. **Events** *Regional conference on children of urban families* Singapore (Singapore) 1994. **Publications** *The Asian Network* (2 a year) – newsletter. Information Services: RTRC Resource Library; training rooms; demonstration centre. **IGO Relations** *UNICEF (#20332)*. **NGO Relations** *Save the Children Federation (SCF).* [2011/XE2138/j/**E**]

- ♦ SEED-Net – Southeast Asia Engineering Education Development Network (see: #01243)
- ♦ **SEEDNet** South East European Development Network on Plant Genetic Resources (#19813)
- ♦ Seed Programs International (internationally oriented national body)
- ♦ Seeds of Africa (internationally oriented national body)

♦ **SEEDS Asia** 19216

Contact 3-11-30-302 Okamoto, Higashi Nada-ku, Kobe HYOGO, 6580072 Japan. T. +81787669412. Fax +81787669413. E-mail: rep@seedsasia.org.
URL: http://www.seedsasia.org/

History May 2006, Kobe (Japan). SEEDS stands for: *Sustainable Environment and Ecological Development Society*. **Aims** Assist people and communities in Asia Pacific region to protect themselves from natural *disasters* or negative effects of environmental destruction, and conduct safe and sustainable livelihoods. **NGO Relations** Member of: *CHS Alliance (#03911)*. [2016.06.30/XJ9778/**D**]

- Seeds Campaign / see GRAIN (#10691)
- Seeds of Peace (internationally oriented national body)
- Seeds to Sew International (internationally oriented national body)
- SeedTree (internationally oriented national body)
- **SEEEP** Southeastern and Eastern European Parasitologists (#19803)
- SEEEPS / see Southeastern and Eastern European Parasitologists (#19803)
- SEEE / see Société internationale d'ethnographie (#19480)
- **SEEFM** South-East European Network on Formal Methods (#19816)
- **SEE Health Network** South-Eastern European Health Network (#19807)
- **SEE Heritage Network** South East European Heritage Network (#19814)
- SEEHN / see South-Eastern European Health Network (#19807)
- SEE International – Surgical Eye Expeditions International (internationally oriented national body)
- **SEEMO** South East Europe Media Organisation (#19823)
- **SEEM** Séminaire européen d'ethnomusicologie (#08463)
- SEENIR – Southeast European Network for Investigative Reporting (unconfirmed)
- **SEENPM** South East European Network for Professionalisation of the Media (#19817)
- **SEEN** SE European Bird Migration Network (#19217)
- SEEOG / see Central and East European Oncology Group (#03701)
- **SEEPAG** Southeast European Prosecutors Advisory Group (#19818)
- SEEP – International Conference on Sustainable Energy and Environmental Protection (meeting series)
- SEEP Network / see Small Enterprise Education and Promotion Network
- SEEP – Small Enterprise Education and Promotion Network (internationally oriented national body)
- SEERC – South-East European Research Centre (internationally oriented national body)
- **SEESAC** South Eastern and Eastern Europe Clearinghouse for the Control of Small Arms and Light Weapons (#19804)
- **SEE** Social Economy Europe (#19335)
- SEE – Sociedad Estudios y Expansión (inactive)
- SEE – Société d'études et d'expansion (inactive)
- SEE – Solidarité Eau Europe (internationally oriented national body)
- **SEETB** South East European Testing Board (#19820)
- **SEETO** South East Europe Transport Observatory (#19825)
- SEE Turtles (internationally oriented national body)

♦ SE European Bird Migration Network (SEEN) 19217

Contact Bird Migration Research Foundation, Przebendowo, 84-210 Choczewo, Poland. T. +48661263999. E-mail: busse@wbwp-fund.eu.
URL: http://www.seen-net.eu/

History 1995. **Aims** Enhance understanding of migratory flyways; encourage research of endangered species; promote cooperation and exchange of information relating to bird migration. **Structure** General Assembly (every 4 years); Board. **Languages** English. **Staff** 2.00 FTE, voluntary. **Finance** Sources: donations; grants. Annual budget: 500 USD. **Activities** Knowledge management/information dissemination; research/documentation. **Events** *Workshop* Riga (Latvia) 2011, *Workshop* Zwartowo (Poland) 2009, *Birds on a migration route* Krakow (Poland) 2007, *Workshop* Prague (Czech Rep) 2006, *Workshop* Przebedowo (Poland) 2005. **Publications** *The Ring* – journal. *Bird Ringing Station Manual*.
Members Institutions in 24 countries and territories:
Austria, Bangladesh, Belarus, Belgium, Bulgaria, Czechia, Egypt, Estonia, Finland, Greece, Hungary, Israel, Jordan, Kazakhstan, Latvia, Lithuania, Palestine, Poland, Romania, Russia, Slovakia, South Africa, Sweden, Türkiye, Ukraine.
NGO Relations Also links with national organizations. [2023.02.14/XF6031/**F**]

- SEEVCCC – South East European Virtual Climate Change Center (internationally oriented national body)
- SEEYC – South East European Youth Council (no recent information)
- **SEEYN** South East European Youth Network (#19821)
- SEFA / see European Association of Steel Drum Manufacturers (#06222)
- **SEFA** Syndicat européen de l'industrie des fûts en acier (#06222)
- SEFEL – Secrétariat européen des fabricants d'emballages métalliques légers (inactive)
- **SEFFI** Syndicat européen de l'industrie des fûts de fibres (#06038)
- **SEFI** Société européenne pour la formation des ingénieurs (#19462)
- **SEforALL** Sustainable Energy for All (#20056)
- **SEF** Society for Experimental Finance (#19556)
- **SEF** Sojuz Evropejskih Foniatorov (#20390)
- SEF – Stiftung Entwicklung und Frieden (internationally oriented national body)
- SE – Fundación Europea Sociedad y Educación (internationally oriented national body)
- **SEGH** Society for Environmental Geochemistry and Health (#19550)
- **SEGIB** Secretaria General Iberoamericana (#11024)
- Segretariato Europeo dei Fabbricanti di Imballaggi Metallici Leggeri (inactive)
- Segretariato Europeo delle Libere Professioni / see European Council of Liberal Professions (#06828)
- Segretariato Europeo per le Pubblicazioni Scientifiche (internationally oriented national body)
- Segretariato Internazionale degli Artisti Cristiani / see International Society of Christian Artists (#15009)
- **SEG** Sociedad Europea de las Ciencias del Grafismo (#08616)
- **SEG** Société européenne de graphologie (#08616)
- **SEG** Société Européenne de Gynécologie (#08613)
- **SEG** Society of Economic Geologists (#19546)
- SEG – Society of Exploration Geophysicists (internationally oriented national body)
- Segundo protocolo de la Convención de La Haya de 1954 para la protección de los bienes culturales en caso de conflicto armado (1999 treaty)

♦ Seguridad Humana en América Latina y el Caribe (SEHLAC) 19218

Human Security Network in Latin America and the Caribbean

Contact Acevedo 234, 8 Piso, Dpto D, CP 1414 Buenos Aires, Argentina. T. +541148561159. E-mail: redsehlac@gmail.com.
URL: http://www.sehlac.org/

History 2008. **Aims** Reduce *armed violence* and its consequences in Latin America and the Caribbean through promotion of awareness, lobbying, public policy advocacy and articulation of inclusive processes among national, regional and international actors, with respect for human rights and strengthening of democracy, thereby contributing to development and human security.
Members Full in 12 countries:
Argentina, Brazil, Chile, Colombia, Dominican Rep, El Salvador, Guatemala, Mexico, Nicaragua, Trinidad-Tobago, Uruguay, Venezuela.
NGO Relations Member of: *Campaign to Stop Killer Robots (#03405)*; *International Network on Explosive Weapons (INEW, #14266)*. Partner of: *International Campaign to Abolish Nuclear Weapons (ICAN, #12426)*. [2020/XJ8324/**F**]

- **SEHLAC** Seguridad Humana en América Latina y el Caribe (#19218)
- **SEHO** Society of Economics of the Household (#19547)
- SEHRIC – Société d'études historiques des relations internationales contemporaines (internationally oriented national body)
- **SEH** Societas Europaea Herpetologica (#07481)
- SEIAF – Sociedad de la Enciclopedia Iberoamericana de Filosofia (no recent information)
- Seibo Catechista Kai (religious order)
- SEII – Société européenne des ingénieurs et des industriels (internationally oriented national body)
- Sei Petro-Paulo Rodo Senkyokai (religious order)
- Seismological Observatory of the South West (internationally oriented national body)
- Seismological Society of the South-West Pacific (inactive)
- Seismology Section of IUGG / see International Association of Seismology and Physics of the Earth's Interior (#12157)
- SEi – Social Enterprise International (internationally oriented national body)
- SEI – Sociedad de Estudios Internacionales, Madrid (internationally oriented national body)
- SEI – Societas Ergophthalmologica Internationalis (no recent information)
- SEI – Solar Energy International (internationally oriented national body)
- **SEI** Stockholm Environment Institute (#19993)
- **SEI** Stop Ecocide International (#19998)
- SEI – Sussex European Institute (internationally oriented national body)
- SEIU – Service Employees International Union (internationally oriented national body)
- Sekai kyusei kyo (unconfirmed)
- SEKLF – Société d'études kantiennes de langue française (internationally oriented national body)
- Sekretariat für Wissenschaftliche Hilfsarbeit / Internationale Union (inactive)
- SELA / see Asian Partnership for the Development of Human Resources in Rural Asia (#01654)
- SELASI – Secretariado Latinoamericano de la Compañia de Jesús (religious order)
- **SELA** Sistema Económico Latinoamericano (#19294)
- **SELAVIP** Servicio Latinoamericano, Africano y Asiatico de Vivienda Popular (#19246)
- **SELC** Société Européenne de Littérature Comparée (#08561)
- **SELDIA** European Direct Selling Association (#06928)
- **SELEC** Southeast European Law Enforcement Center (#19815)
- SELENIUM – International Symposium on Selenium in Biology and Medicine (meeting series)

♦ Selenium-Tellurium Development Association (STDA) 19219

Pres Cavite Economic Zone Lot 6 Blk 1, Phase II Rosario, Cavite CAV, Philippines. T. +63464372526. Fax +63464372524.
URL: http://www.stda.org/

History 1938, as (US) Selenium Development Committee. Present name adopted 1963. Registered in the State of New York (USA). **Aims** Stimulate interest in selenium and tellurium; promote development and increase usage; sponsor research in connection with production, fabrication or use; develop, collect and disseminate technical and statistical information on selenium and tellurium; encourage safe industrial use and handling practices. **Structure** Board. Officers: President; Vice-President; Secretary; Assistant Secretary; Treasurer. **Languages** English. **Staff** Voluntary. **Finance** Members' dues, based on legal fees, meeting locations, project and research funding. **Activities** Promotes Selenium and Tellurium; follows and informs members of new regulations; funds projects. Organizes: regular Annual Meeting (Sep); mid-year meeting (Mar). **Events** *Symposium* Tokyo (Japan) 2012, *Symposium* Scottsdale, AZ (USA) 1998, *Symposium* Brussels (Belgium) 1994, *Symposium* Banff, AB (Canada) 1989, *Symposium* Saltsjöbaden (Sweden) 1984.
Members Companies (20) in 12 countries:
Australia, Belgium, Canada, Chile, China, Germany, India, Japan, Philippines, Russia, Sweden, USA. [2015/XN8870/**C**]

- Self-Care Initiative Europe (internationally oriented national body)
- Self Help Africa / see Self Help Africa (#19220)

♦ Self Help Africa (SHA) 19220

Chief Exec Kingsbridge House, 17-22 Parkgate Street, Dublin, 8, CO. DUBLIN, D08 NRP2, Ireland. T. +35316778880. E-mail: info@selfhelpafrica.org.
Registered Office Westgate House, Dickens Court, Hills Lane, Shrewsbury, SY1 1QU, UK. T. +441743277170.
URL: http://selfhelpafrica.org/ie/

History 2008. Founded by merger of *Harvest Help (inactive)* and *Self Help Development International (inactive)*. Merged with Gorta *Gorta – The Freedom from Hunger Council of Ireland (inactive)* organization, in 2014. Merged with *United Purpose (UP)* in 2021. Former names and other names: *Self Help Africa* – former (2008 to 2014); *Gorta – Self Help Africa* – former (2014). Registration: UK; Ireland; USA. **Aims** Provide practical support to *rural* communities to grow more food and to earn a sustainable living. **Structure** Independent Boards in each country. **Languages** English, French. **Staff** Over 60 at offices in Ireland, UK and USA; over 600 in 15 countries in sub-Saharan Africa, Bangladesh and Brazil. **Finance** Annual budget: 60,000,000 USD. **Activities** Advocacy/lobbying/activism; research and development; training/education. **NGO Relations** Member of (3): *African Smallholder Farmers Group (ASFG, inactive)*; *Farming First*; *Irish Association of Non-Governmental Development Organisations (Dóchas)*. Collaborates with over 200 local NGO and CBO partners, including: *1,000 Days*; *Irish League of Credit Unions International Development Foundation (ILCU Foundation)*. [2022.02.08/XJ1573/**F**]

- SELFHELP Crafts of the World / see Ten Thousand Villages
- Self Help Foundation / see Self-Help International
- Self-Help International (internationally oriented national body)

♦ Self Realization Fellowship (SRF) 19221

Intl Headquarters 3880 San Rafael Ave, Los Angeles CA 90065-3219, USA. T. +13232252471. Fax +13232255088. E-mail: publicaffairs@yogananda-srf.org.
URL: http://www.yogananda-srf.org/

History 1920, by Paramahansa Yogananda. **Aims** Disseminate and provide instruction on scientific methods of *meditation* taught by *Paramahansa Yogananda* for the purpose of giving the practitioner direct experience of the presence of God, and demonstrate the fundamental harmony of all true *religions*. **Structure** Annual Meeting in Los Angeles CA (USA). **Languages** English, French, German, Italian, Japanese, Portuguese, Spanish. **Staff** 1.00 FTE, paid. **Activities** Training/education; events/meetings; religious activities. **Events** *Idéologie* Paris (France) 1993. **Publications** *Self Realization* (4 a year); *Jahresheft* (annual). Books by Paramahansa Yogananda. **Members** Centres (over 600) in over 60 countries. Membership countries not specified. [2019/XF6166/**F**]

- **SELF** Société d'Ergonomie de Langue Française (#19460)
- SELF – Solar Electric Light Fund (internationally oriented national body)

♦ Self Storage Association Asia (SSAA) 19222

Exec Dir Unit 601 6/F, Tung Hip Commercial Bldg, 248 Des Voeux, Road Central, Sheung Wan, Hong Kong. T. +85229190315. E-mail: info@selfstorageasia.org.
URL: https://selfstorageasia.org/

History Founded 2014. **Aims** Provide information, education and support to facility owners/operators and industry stakeholders to develop a transparent, well-regulated, and sustainable industry through building a platform that supports the sector's development and establishes industry standards. **Structure** Board. **Languages** English. **Activities** Events/meetings. **Publications** *In Store* – magazine.
Members Operator; Supplier, Investor; Overseas. Operators in 15 countries and territories:
Brunei Darussalam, China, Hong Kong, India, Japan, Jordan, Korea Rep, Macau, Malaysia, Philippines, Singapore, Taiwan, Thailand, United Arab Emirates, Vietnam. [2020.01.16/XM8072/**D**]

- SELF – Syndicat des écrivains de langue française (internationally oriented national body)
- **SELPER** Sociedad Especialistas Latinoamericana en Percepción Remota (#19358)
- SEL – Service d'entraide et de liaison (internationally oriented national body)

♦ Selskab for østnordiskfilologi (SØF) 19223

Sällskap för östnordisk filologi (SÖF) – Gesellschaft für Ostnordische Philologie

Coordinator address not obtained.
URL: https://ostnordiskfilologi.wordpress.com/

Structure General Assembly; Board. **Activities** Events/meetings. **Events** *Conference* Stockholm (Sweden) 2021, *Conference* Cologne (Germany) 2019, *Conference* Copenhagen (Denmark) 2017, *Conference* Venice (Italy) 2015, *Conference* Uppsala (Sweden) 2013. [2021/AA0726/**D**]

- **SEL** Skolta Esperanto-Ligo (#19309)
- **SEL** Societas Europaea Lepidopterologica (#19440)

- ♦ Semaines internationales d'études pour l'enfance victime de la guerre (inactive)
- ♦ Semantics and Philosophy in Europe (meeting series)
- ♦ Semantic Technology Institute International / see STI International (#19990)

♦ Semantic Web Science Association (SWSA) 19224

Contact c/o Inst AIFB, Geb 5-20, KIT – Campus Süd, Kaiserstr 89, 76133 Karlsruhe, Germany. E-mail: swsa-feedback@lists.kit.edu.
URL: http://swsa.semanticweb.org/

Aims Promote and exchange scholarly work in semantic web and related fields worldwide. **Structure** Management Committee. **Activities** Awards/prizes/competitions; events/meetings; training/education. **Events** *International Semantic Web Conference* Hangzhou (China) 2022, *International Semantic Web Conference* Albany, NY (USA) 2021, *International Semantic Web Conference* Athens (Greece) 2020, *International Semantic Web Conference* Auckland (New Zealand) 2019, *International Semantic Web Conference* Monterey, CA (USA) 2018. [2021/XJ6655/**C**]

- ♦ SEMCO – South and East Mediterranean College of Oncology (internationally oriented national body)
- ♦ SemDial – Workshop on the Semantics and Pragmatics of Dialogue (meeting series)
- ♦ Sème l'avenir (internationally oriented national body)

♦ SEMI 19225

CEO 673 South Milpitas Blvd, Milpitas CA 95035, USA. T. +14089436900. Fax +14084289600. E-mail: semihq@semi.org.
SEMI Europe Helmholtzstrasse 2-9, House D – 3rd Floor, 10587 Berlin, Germany. T. +4930303080770. Fax +493056593055. E-mail: semieurope@semi.org.
URL: http://www.semi.org/

History 1970, USA. Founded by Bill Hugle, Fred Kulicke and John Dannelly. Former names and other names: *Semiconductor Equipment and Materials Institute* – former (1970 to 1989); *Semiconductor Equipment and Materials International (SEMI)* – full title (1989). Registration: EU Transparency Register, No/ID: 671799223-02. **Aims** Provide industry stewardship and engage members to advance the interests of the global electronics design and manufacturing supply chain. **Structure** Board of Directors. **Languages** English. **Staff** 200.00 FTE, paid. **Finance** Sources: meeting proceeds; members' dues. **Activities** Events/meetings; knowledge management/information dissemination. **Events** *Advanced Semiconductor Technology Conference* Singapore (Singapore) 2022, *SEMICON EUROPA* Munich (Germany) 2021, *Advanced Semiconductor Technology Conference* Singapore (Singapore) 2021, *Advanced Semiconductor Technology Conference* Singapore (Singapore) 2019, *FLEX Southeast Asia Meeting* Singapore (Singapore) 2019. **Publications** *Newsletters. SEMI Standards* – 11 vols a year. Membership Directory; conference proceedings; market analysts reports; technical papers; industry standards. **Information Services** *SEMICOMM Electronic Network.*
Members Corporate (over 2,000 companies) in 31 countries:
Australia, Austria, Belgium, Belize, Canada, China, Czechia, Finland, France, Germany, Hong Kong, Hungary, India, Italy, Japan, Korea Rep, Kyrgyzstan, Liechtenstein, Luxembourg, Malaysia, Netherlands, Poland, Russia, Singapore, Sweden, Switzerland, Thailand, UK, Ukraine, United Arab Emirates, USA.
NGO Relations Member of (1): *International Employee Stock Option Coalition (no recent information).* SEMI Europe is member of: *Industry4Europe (#11181).* [2020.10.13/XF0021/**F**]

♦ Semi-Arid Food Grain Research and Development (AU SAFGRAD) .. 19226

Recherche et développement des cultures vivrières dans les zones semi-arides
Coordinator 01 BP 1783, Ouagadougou 01, Burkina Faso. T. +22625311598. Fax +22625311586. E-mail: sayahe@africa-union.org.
URL: http://www.au-safgrad.org/

History Established originally within the framework of *African Union Scientific Technical Research Commission (AU STRC, #00493)*, by African Heads of State, following Resolution adopted 1976, Mauritius, by the Council of Ministers of the *Organization of African Unity (OAU, inactive)*, the current *African Union (AU, #00488).* Initial phase: 1977-1986; Phase 2: 1986-1994; Phase 3: 1994-2003. Current mandate defined in AU Assembly, 2003, and elaborated 2011. **Aims** Contribute to advancement of agricultural research, technology transfer and marketing as well as the management of natural resources by facilitating and coordinating the use of the scientific talents of National Agricultural Research Centers (NARCs), International Agricultural Research Centers (IARCs) and Scientific Research Organizations (SROs) to enhance food security, promote sustainable agriculture, develop irrigation agriculture, both in rural and peri-urban areas of the semi-arid zones of Africa. **Structure** Specialized technical office of the African Union under the Department of Agriculture, Rural Development, Blue Economy, and Sustainable Environment (ARBE). Commissioner; Director; Coordinator. **Languages** Arabic, AU languages, English, French, Portuguese. **Staff** 15.00 FTE, paid. **Finance** Development Partners. Supported by: *African Union (AU, #00488).* **Activities** Advocacy/lobbying/activism; capacity building; knowledge management/information dissemination; politics/policy/regulatory; projects/programmes; research and development.
Members Member states (55):
Algeria, Angola, Benin, Botswana, Burkina Faso, Burundi, Cameroon, Cape Verde, Central African Rep, Chad, Comoros, Congo Brazzaville, Congo DR, Côte d'Ivoire, Djibouti, Egypt, Equatorial Guinea, Eritrea, Eswatini, Ethiopia, Gabon, Gambia, Ghana, Guinea, Guinea-Bissau, Kenya, Lesotho, Liberia, Libya, Madagascar, Malawi, Mali, Mauritania, Mauritius, Morocco, Mozambique, Namibia, Niger, Nigeria, Rwanda, Sahrawi ADR, Sao Tomé-Principe, Senegal, Seychelles, Sierra Leone, Somalia, South Africa, South Sudan, Sudan, Tanzania UR, Togo, Tunisia, Uganda, Zambia, Zimbabwe.
NGO Relations Instrumental in setting up: *Association of Maize Researchers in Africa (AMRA, no recent information).* [2022.12.02/XE2407/**E***]

- ♦ Semiconductor Equipment and Materials Institute / see SEMI (#19225)
- ♦ Semiconductor Equipment and Materials International / see SEMI (#19225)
- ♦ Semiconductor Research Corporation (unconfirmed)
- ♦ **SEMIDE** Système euro-méditerranéen d'information sur les savoir-faire dans le domaine de l'eau (#05722)
- ♦ Séminaire sur l'acquisition de matériaux bibliothécaires latinoaméricains (internationally oriented national body)
- ♦ Séminaire européen d'ethnomusicologie (#08463)
- ♦ Séminaire international de la forme urbaine (#14833)
- ♦ Seminar on the Acquisition of Latin American Library Materials (internationally oriented national body)
- ♦ Seminar for Foreign and International Criminal Law / see Max Planck Institute for Foreign and International Criminal Law
- ♦ Seminario sobre la Adquisición de Materiales Latinoamericanos de Biblioteca (internationally oriented national body)
- ♦ Seminario sobre a Aquisição de Materiais Latino-americanos de Biblioteca (internationally oriented national body)
- ♦ Seminario Biblico Latinoamericano / see Universidad Biblica Latinoamericana
- ♦ Seminario Iberoamericano de Redes de Agua y Drenaje (meeting series)
- ♦ Seminario Internazionale de la Forma Urbana (#14833)
- ♦ Seminario Pedagogico Cooperazione Internazionale – Fondazione-Tovini / see Fondazione Tovini
- ♦ Seminary Consultation on Mission (internationally oriented national body)
- ♦ SEMM – European School of Molecular Medicine (internationally oriented national body)
- ♦ **Semouliers** Union of the Associations of Semolina Manufacturers of the EU (#20363)
- ♦ **SEM** Societas Europaea Mammalogica (#19441)
- ♦ SEM – Society for Ethnomusicology (internationally oriented national body)
- ♦ SEM – Society for Experimental Mechanics (internationally oriented national body)
- ♦ SEMTSI – Sociedad Española de Medicina Tropical y Salud Internacional (internationally oriented national body)
- ♦ **SENATEUROPE** Association des Sénats d'Europe (#02914)
- ♦ Send a Cow (internationally oriented national body)
- ♦ Senderos de la Paz (#18262)
- ♦ SEND International (internationally oriented national body)
- ♦ Send the Light / see OM International (#17724)
- ♦ SENDO – Southern Europe New Drug Organization (inactive)
- ♦ **SENECA** Survey in Europe on Nutrition and the Elderly (#20046)
- ♦ Senegal River Development Organization (#17815)
- ♦ **SENE** Social Epistemology Network (#19337)
- ♦ SENIA International / see Special Education Network and Inclusion Association (#19907)
- ♦ SENIA / see Special Education Network and Inclusion Association (#19907)
- ♦ **SENIA** Special Education Network and Inclusion Association (#19907)
- ♦ Senior Advisory Group on Biotechnology / see European Association of Bioindustries (#05956)

♦ Senior European Volunteers Exchange Network (SEVEN) 19227

Coordination Office Lunaria, 39 Via Buonarroti, 00185 Rome RM, Italy. E-mail: volo@lunaria.org.
URL: http://www.seven-network.eu/

History Oct 2007, following a series of projects funded by *European Commission (EC, #06633)*; first project initiated in 2001. **Aims** Promote international voluntary service in Europe as an educational and lifelong learning tool for senior citizens. **Languages** English. **Staff** 1.00 FTE, paid. **Finance** Co-funded by *European Commission (EC, #06633).* Members contribute through staff costs. **Events** *Meeting* Brussels (Belgium) 2010, *Meeting* Vienna (Austria) 2009. **Publications** Training course scheme; handbook.
Members Organizations (29) in 12 countries:
Austria, Belgium, Bulgaria, Estonia, France, Germany, Iceland, Italy, Lithuania, Spain, Türkiye, UK.
Included in the above, 2 organizations listed in this Yearbook:
Association of Voluntary Service Organisations (AVSO, no recent information); Concordia.
[2015/XJ8269/y/**E**]

♦ Senior International Health Association (SIHA) 19228

Association Internationale des Seniors pour la Santé (AISS)
Contact Rue Van Eyck 22, 1000 Brussels, Belgium. E-mail: contact@sihassociation.org.
URL: https://www.seniorinternationalhealthassociation.org/

History Registration: Banque Carrefour des Entreprises, No/ID: 0642.686.168, Start date: 5 Nov 2015, Belgium; EU Transparency Register, No/ID: 585935037174-49, Start date: 31 Jan 2020. **Aims** Promote active aging; promote full access to drugs and care for all citizens, and primarily the most vulnerable and dependent; activate a constructive dialogue between all stakeholders in the health system for the development of health systems suitable for elderly; develop a digital culture for senior population granting a better quality of life.
NGO Relations Member of (1): *EU Health Coalition.* [2020/AA1365/**D**]

♦ Seniors of the European Public Service (SEPS) 19229

Seniors de la fonction publique européenne (SFPE)
Pres c/o Council of the European Union, Rue de la Loi 175, Bureau JL 02 40 CG39, 1048 Brussels, Belgium. T. +32475472470. E-mail: info@sfpe-seps.be.
URL: http://www.sfpe-seps.be/

History 1989. Founded as *Former Officials of the European Civil Service (AFPE International) – Anciens de la fonction publique européenne (AFPE) – Ehemalige des Europäischen Öffentlichen Dienstes.* Current constitution revised 30 Sep 2008. Registration: Banque-Carrefour des Entreprises, No/ID: 0806.839.565, Start date: 3 Oct 2008. **Aims** Defend the interests of former European officials, in particular social acquired rights. **Structure** General Assembly (annual); Administration Board. **Languages** English, French, German, Italian. **Finance** Members' dues. Other sources: gifts; support from European institutions. **Activities** Events/meetings. **Publications** *Information Bulletin* (5 a year) in English, French.
Members Pensioners of European institutions in 20 countries:
Austria, Belgium, Chile, Denmark, Finland, France, Germany, Greece, Hungary, Italy, Luxembourg, Netherlands, Norway, Portugal, Spain, Sweden, Switzerland, Thailand, UK, USA. [2020/XE2072/v/**E**]

- ♦ Seniors de la fonction publique européenne (#19229)
- ♦ Senlis Council / see ICOS (#11086)
- ♦ Sennacieca Asocio Tutmonda (#16941)

♦ Senologic International Society (SIS) 19230

Société internationale de sénologie – Sociedad Internacional de Senologia
Registered Office Rue Des Grandes Arcades, 67000 Strasbourg, France. E-mail: mamcosta@yahoo.com.
Facebook: https://www.facebook.com/sisbreast/

History 10 Oct 1975, Strasbourg (France). Founded by Dr Charles-Marie Gros (1910-1984). Registration: Start date: 27 Feb 1976, France. **Aims** Foster interdisciplinary multinational cooperation in diagnosis and treatment of *breast* diseases. **Structure** Board of Directors. **Languages** English. **Finance** Sources: members' dues. **Activities** Events/meetings; training/education. **Events** *World Congress on Breast Cancer and Breast Healthcare* Rhodes Is (Greece) 2023, *Biennial Congress* Rhodes Is (Greece) 2021, *Biennial Congress* Warsaw (Poland) 2016, *European Congress on Breast Diseases* Opatija (Croatia) 2015, *Biennial Congress* Orlando, FL (USA) 2014. **Publications** *The Breast Journal.*
Members National societies in 28 countries:
Argentina, Australia, Austria, Belgium, Brazil, Bulgaria, Chile, Cuba, Czechia, Ecuador, France, Germany, Greece, Hungary, Israel, Italy, Mexico, Paraguay, Peru, Poland, Portugal, Slovakia, Spain, Switzerland, Türkiye, Uruguay, USA, Venezuela.
Scientific Centers Network includes the following organizations listed in this Yearbook (4):
Asian Breast Diseases Association (ABDA, #01365); International Breast Ultrasound School (IBUS, #12395); Latin American Federation of Mastology (#16324).
NGO Relations Joint journal with: *International Society of Breast Pathology (ISBP).* Administers: *Breast Centres Network (BCN, #03317).* [2020/XD3118/y/**C**]

- ♦ **SENP** Société européenne de neurologie pédiatrique (#19463)
- ♦ SEN – Sacred Earth Network (internationally oriented national body)
- ♦ **SENSD** Students' European Network for Sustainable Development (#20017)
- ♦ Sense International (internationally oriented national body)
- ♦ SEN – Social Employers Network (no recent information)

♦ Sensometric Society 19231

Contact address not obtained. E-mail: info@sensometric.org – secretary@sensometric.org.
URL: http://www.sensometric.org/

Aims Increase awareness of the fact that the field of sensory and consumer science needs its own special methodology and statistical methods; improve communication and cooperation between persons interested in the scientific principles, methods and applications of sensometrics; act as the interdisciplinary institution, worldwide, to disseminate scientific knowledge on the field of sensometrics. **Structure** Committee. **Activities** Events/meetings. **Events** *Sensometrics Conference* 2022, *Sensometrics Conference* Stavanger (Norway) 2020, *Sensometrics Conference* Montevideo (Uruguay) 2018, *Sensometrics Conference* Brighton (UK) 2016, *Sensometrics Conference* Chicago, IL (USA) 2014. [2021/AA1835/**C**]

- ♦ Sensorial Handicap Cooperation (internationally oriented national body)
- ♦ Senter for Europa-Rett (internationally oriented national body)
- ♦ Senter for Fredsbygging og Konflikthådtering, Oslo (internationally oriented national body)
- ♦ Senter for Fredsstudier (internationally oriented national body)
- ♦ Senter for Internasjonalisering av Høyere Utdanning (internationally oriented national body)
- ♦ Senter for Internasjonalt Universitetssamarbeid / see Norwegian Centre for International Cooperation in Higher Education
- ♦ Senter for klimaforskning (internationally oriented national body)
- ♦ Senter for Midtausten og islamske studiar (internationally oriented national body)
- ♦ Senter for Utvikling og Miljí (internationally oriented national body)
- ♦ Senter for Utviklingsstudier, Bergen / see Unifob Global
- ♦ Sentient Animal Law Foundation (unconfirmed)
- ♦ Sentiers de la paix, Les (#18262)
- ♦ Sentinelles (internationally oriented national body)
- ♦ Sentrum for Utviklingsforskning, Bergen / see Unifob Global
- ♦ SEOR / see International Federation of Orgonomic Colleges (#13494)
- ♦ SEOSP – Société européenne d'ophtalmologie de santé publique (no recent information)
- ♦ Seoul Forum for International Affairs (internationally oriented national body)

- ♦ SEPA – Société européenne de paramétrologie (inactive)
- ♦ SEPA – Société européenne de pédiatrie ambulatoire (inactive)
- ♦ **SEPCA** Southeast Europe Police Chiefs Association (#19824)
- ♦ **SE/PCF** Action Plan for the Protection of the Marine Environment and Coastal Areas in the South East Pacific (#00095)
- ♦ SEPCR – Societas Europaea Physiologiae Clinicae Respiratoriae (inactive)
- ♦ SEPERI – Société européenne pour l'étude des relations internationales (inactive)
- ♦ SEPHC – South East Pacific Hydrographic Commission (see: #13825)
- ♦ SEPIS / see Confédération internationale des travailleurs intellectuels (#04564)
- ♦ **SEPI** Society for the Exploration of Psychotherapy Integration (#19557)
- ♦ SEPLA – Sociedad latinoamericana de Economia Politica y Pensamiento Critico (unconfirmed)
- ♦ SEPLIS / see European Council of Liberal Professions (#06828)
- ♦ SEPM – Society for Sedimentary Geology (internationally oriented national body)
- ♦ **SEP** Société européenne de phlébectomie (#08701)
- ♦ SEP – Société européenne de planification à long terme (inactive)
- ♦ SEP – Société européenne de pneumologie (inactive)
- ♦ SEPS – Segretariato Europeo per le Pubblicazioni Scientifiche (internationally oriented national body)
- ♦ **SEPS** Seniors of the European Public Service (#19229)
- ♦ **SEPS** Società Europea di Psicologia della Scrittura (#08616)

♦ SEPT 19232

Chairman c/o Interlocking Concrete Pavement Inst, 14801 Murdock St, Ste 230, Chantilly VA 20151, USA.
URL: http://www.sept.org/

History SEPT stands for *Small – Element – Pavement – Technologists*. **Aims** Perpetuate the triennial International Conference on Concrete Block Paving. **Languages** English. **Staff** None. **Finance** Conference royalties. **Activities** Events/meetings. **Events** *International Conference on Concrete Block Pavement* Seoul (Korea Rep) 2018, *International Conference on Concrete Block Pavement* Dresden (Germany) 2015, *International Conference on Concrete Block Pavement* Shanghai (China) 2012, *International Conference on Concrete Block Pavement* Buenos Aires (Argentina) 2009, *International Conference on Concrete Block Pavement* San Francisco, CA (USA) 2006. **Publications** Information Services: Maintains database of conference series technical papers.
Members Full in 15 countries:
Argentina, Australia, Belgium, Brazil, Canada, China, Colombia, Germany, Israel, Italy, Netherlands, South Africa, Sweden, UK, USA. [2020.03.03/XJ6461/**C**]

- ♦ **SEQNET** European Network of Laboratories for Sequence Based Typing of Microbial Pathogens (#07936)
- ♦ Sequella Global Tuberculosis Foundation / see Aeras Global TB Vaccine Foundation
- ♦ SER / see Society for Ecological Restoration International
- ♦ SER / see Servicio Ecuménico para la Dignidad Humana
- ♦ SERAPAZ – Servicios y Asesoria para la Paz (internationally oriented national body)
- ♦ Serbest Düsünce Uluslarasi Birligi (#11906)
- ♦ SERCI – Society for Economic Research on Copyright Issues (unconfirmed)
- ♦ SEREA – Seminario Iberoamericano de Redes de Agua y Drenaje (meeting series)
- ♦ Serene Environment And Life On Earth / see SEALOEarth
- ♦ SEREN – Stowarzyszenie Ekologow na Rzecz Energii Nuklearnej (internationally oriented national body)
- ♦ SERE – Société européenne des réalisateurs de l'environnement (internationally oriented national body)
- ♦ SERFAC / see Service and Research Institute on Family and Children (#19243)
- ♦ **SERFAC** Service and Research Institute on Family and Children (#19243)
- ♦ **SERFA** Société Européenne pour la recherche en formation des adultes (#08725)
- ♦ **SERGS** Society of European Robotic Gynaecological Surgery (#19554)
- ♦ **SERG** Stowarzyseenie Europejskich Regionów Granicznych (#02499)
- ♦ Séries Formelles et Combinatoire Algébrique / see Permanent Program Committee of the Formal Power Series and Algebraic Combinatorics (#18329)
- ♦ SERI Initiative – Service Education Research and Innovation Initiative (unconfirmed)
- ♦ Serious Games Association (unconfirmed)
- ♦ SERI – Society for Ecological Restoration International (internationally oriented national body)
- ♦ **SERI** Sustainable Electronics Recycling International (#20055)
- ♦ SERI – Sustainable Europe Research Institute (internationally oriented national body)
- ♦ Serono Symposia International Foundation / see Excellence in Medical Education (#09220)
- ♦ SEROPP – Société Européenne de Recherche en Ostéopathie Périnatale and Pédiatrique (unconfirmed)
- ♦ **SERPAJ-AL** Servicio Paz y Justicia en América Latina (#19247)

♦ Serra International 19233

Contact 333 West Wacker Drive, Ste 500, Chicago IL 60606, USA. T. +13124197411. E-mail: info@serrainternational.org.
URL: http://www.serrainternational.org/

History 2 Jul 1938, by federation of 5 Serra clubs. *The Serra International Foundation* was created 25 Oct 1951, and incorporated as a non-for-profit corporation in the State of Illinois (USA). **Aims** Foster and promote *vocations* to the ministerial *priesthood* of the *Catholic* Church as a particular vocation to service and to support priests in their sacred ministry; encourage and affirm vocations to consecrated religious life in the Catholic Church; assist members to recognize and respond in their own lives to God's call to holiness in Jesus Christ and through the Holy Spirit. **Structure** Annual Convention. Officers: President; President-Elect; 4 Vice-Presidents (elected for one year at International Convention); Secretary and Treasurer (elected for 2 years). Board of Trustees, consisting of 11 trustees, 8 principal officers, Immediate Past President, together with such additional trustees, not to exceed 3, as from time to time may be determined by the Board of Trustees. Executive Director. Episcopal Adviser (3-year term). Standing Committees (8): Vocation Activities; Internal Program; Constitution and Bylaws; Membership; Finance and Budget; Communications; Long Range Planning; Audit. **Languages** English, Italian, Portuguese, Spanish. **Staff** 5.00 FTE, paid. **Finance** Worldwide budget (annual): US$ 1 million. **Events** *Convention / Annual Convention* Melbourne, VIC (Australia) 2015, *Annual Convention* Sacramento, CA (USA) 2014, *Annual Convention* Palma (Spain) 2013, *Annual Convention* Providence, RI (USA) 2012, *Annual Convention* Ottawa, ON (Canada) 2011. **Publications** *Serra Council Magazine*. District and Club newsletters.
Members Councils in 9 countries:
Australia, Brazil, Canada, Italy, Mexico, New Zealand, Spain, Thailand, UK.
Membership of 18,200 in 1,170 chartered Serra Clubs located in 46 countries on 6 continents. Membership countries not specified. [2014/XF0024/**F**]

- ♦ **SERRED** Syndicat européen des récupérateurs et rénovateurs de drums (#08333)
- ♦ SERRV International (internationally oriented national body)
- ♦ SERSC / see Science and Engineering Research Support soCiety (#19138)
- ♦ **SERSC** Science and Engineering Research Support soCiety (#19138)
- ♦ Sertoma International (internationally oriented national body)
- ♦ Servantes de l'Agneau de Dieu (religious order)
- ♦ Servantes du Coeur Immaculé de Marie (religious order)
- ♦ Servantes du Coeur de Jésus (religious order)
- ♦ Servantes de Jésus de la Charité (religious order)
- ♦ Servantes de Marie d'Anglet (religious order)
- ♦ Servantes de Marie de Madrid, Ministres des Malades (religious order)
- ♦ Servantes des Pauvres de Jeanne Delanoue (religious order)
- ♦ Servantes des Pauvres, Oblates Bénédictines (religious order)
- ♦ Servantes du Sacerdoce (religious order)
- ♦ Servantes du Sacré-Coeur (religious order)
- ♦ Servantes du Saint Esprit de l'Adoration Perpétuelle (religious order)
- ♦ Servantes du Très-Saint-Sacrement (religious order)
- ♦ Servant-Nation – Mondcivitan Republic (inactive)
- ♦ Servants to Asia's Urban Poor (internationally oriented national body)
- ♦ Servants of the Blessed Sacrament (religious order)
- ♦ Servants of Charity (religious order)
- ♦ Servants of the Holy Heart of Mary (religious order)
- ♦ Servants of the Holy Paraclete (religious order)
- ♦ Servants of the Immaculate Heart of Mary (religious order)
- ♦ Servants of Jesus of Charity (religious order)
- ♦ Servas / see SERVAS International (#19234)

♦ SERVAS International 19234

Gen Sec Beckhammer 32, 8057 Zurich ZH, Switzerland. E-mail: generalsecretary@servas.org – helpdesk@servas.org.
Pres Reimersholmsgatan 59 plan 2, SE-117 40 Stockholm, Sweden.
URL: http://www.servas.org/

History 1949, Askov (Denmark). Founded by Bob Luitweiler, following meeting in1949. Former names and other names: *Peace Builders* – former (1949 to 1952); *Servas* – former (1952 to 1972). Registration: Swiss Civil Code, Start date: 1972, Switzerland. **Aims** Seek to build world *peace*, *goodwill* and *understanding* by providing opportunities for personal contacts with people of other cultures and backgrounds; provide *educational travel* by enabling people to share *home hospitality*, discussions and exchange of ideas in homes around the world. **Structure** General Assembly (every 3 years); Executive Committee; National Organizations with a National Secretary. **Languages** English, Spanish. **Staff** Voluntary. **Finance** Sources: members' dues. **Activities** Networking/liaising. **Events** *Conference and General Assembly* Seoul (Korea Rep) 2018, *Conference and General Assembly* Matamata (New Zealand) 2015, *Conference and General Assembly / General Assembly Conference* Piaski (Poland) 2012, *Far East Asia conference* Busan (Korea Rep) 2007, *Triennial general assembly and conference / General Assembly Conference* Barcelona (Spain) 2004. **Publications** *SI News Bulletin* (4 a year).
Members Full in 77 countries and territories (Belgium and Luxembourg have single combined membership):
Argentina, Australia, Austria, Bangladesh, Belgium, Botswana, Brazil, Bulgaria, Cameroon, Canada, Chile, China, Colombia, Congo Brazzaville, Costa Rica, Croatia, Czechia, Denmark, Ecuador, Finland, France, Georgia, Germany, Greece, Guatemala, Honduras, Hong Kong, Hungary, India, Indonesia, Iran Islamic Rep, Ireland, Israel, Italy, Japan, Kazakhstan, Korea Rep, Kyrgyzstan, Lithuania, Luxembourg, Malawi, Malaysia, Mexico, Morocco, Nepal, Netherlands, New Zealand, Nigeria, Norway, Pakistan, Panama, Paraguay, Peru, Poland, Portugal, Romania, Russia, Rwanda, Sierra Leone, Singapore, Slovakia, Slovenia, South Africa, Spain, Suriname, Sweden, Switzerland, Taiwan, Thailand, Türkiye, Uganda, UK, Ukraine, Uruguay, USA, Venezuela, Vietnam, Zambia.
Consultative Status Consultative status granted from: *ECOSOC (#05331)* (Ros A). **IGO Relations** Accredited by: *United Nations Office at Geneva (UNOG, #20597)*; *United Nations Office at Vienna (UNOV, #20604)*. Associated with Department of Global Communications of the United Nations. **NGO Relations** Member of: *Abolition 2000 – Global Network to Eliminate Nuclear Weapons (Abolition 2000, #00006)*; *NGO Committee on Sustainable Development, Vienna (#17119)*; *UNITED for Intercultural Action – European Network Against Nationalism, Racism, Fascism and in Support of Migrants and Refugees (UNITED, #20511)*; *Vienna NGO Committee on the Status of Women (#20775)*. Signatory to Founding Statement of: *Alliance for Lobbying Transparency and Ethics Regulation (ALTER-EU, #00705)*. Represented on the Organizing Committee of: *Hague Appeal for Peace (HAP, #10848)*. Links with many organizations, including: *Peace 2000 Institute (#18274)*. [2020.10.12/XF3218/**F**]

♦ Serve the City International 19235

Office Place Van Meyel 15, 1040 Brussels, Belgium. T. +3227343502. E-mail: hello@servethecity.net.
URL: http://www.servethecity.net/

History 2005, Brussels (Belgium). Started as a single week of serving. Created as an umbrella organization under current title, 2017. Registration: Banque-Carrefour des Entreprises, Belgium. **Aims** Act as a global movement of volunteers showing kindness in personal and practical ways to people in *need*. **Activities** Advocacy/lobbying/activism.
Members Full in 3 countries:
Belgium, Ireland, Portugal. [2023.02.25/XM4990/**F**]

- ♦ Serve di Gesù della Carità (religious order)
- ♦ Servei Tercer Mon (internationally oriented national body)
- ♦ Serve di Maria, Ministre degli Infermi (religious order)
- ♦ Serve Secolari di Gesù Cristo Sacerdote (religious order)

♦ Servetus International Society (SIS) 19236

Chairman Gran Via de las Cortes Catalanas 421, 3o la, 08015 Barcelona, Spain. E-mail: info@servetus.org.
URL: http://www.servetus.org/

History Mar 2003, on the initiative of Juan E Naya (1968-). Named after humanist Michael Servetus (1511-1553). **Aims** Foster the spirit of humanism, tolerance of ideas and respect for the rights of the individual by promoting and preserving the *humanist philosophy* of Servetus. **Structure** General Assembly (annual). Board, comprising President, Vice-President, 4 Executive Directors, Secretary, Treasurer and Chairman. **Events** *Congress* Barcelona (Spain) 2006. **Publications** *Servetus International Society Newsletter* (4 a year). [2011/XM2835/**E**]

- ♦ Servi della Carità (religious order)
- ♦ Service d'action du citoyen européen (#06555)
- ♦ Service de l'action contre les mines des Nations Unies (#20585)

♦ Service d'appui aux initiatives locales de développement (SAILD) . 19237

Servizio d'Appoggio alle Iniziative Locali di Sviluppo

Contact 1087 rue Mengué Tsogo, Quartier Elig Essono, BP 11 955, Yaoundé, Cameroon. T. +23722224682 – +23722145654. Fax +23722225162. E-mail: secretariat@saild.org.
Main: http://www.saild.org/

History 1988. Registration: Swiss Civil Code, Switzerland. **IGO Relations** *Secretariat of the United Nations Convention to Combat Desertification (Secretariat of the UNCCD, #19208)*. [2021/XF3036/**F**]

- ♦ Service d'assistance canadienne aux organismes (internationally oriented national body)
- ♦ Servicecentralen för Utvecklingssamarbete / see Kepa – the Finnish NGO platform for global development
- ♦ Service Centre for Development Cooperation – Finnish Volunteer Service / see Kepa – the Finnish NGO platform for global development
- ♦ Service Centre for International Cultural Activities / see Dutch Centre for International Cooperation
- ♦ Service chrétien d'appui à l'animation rurale (internationally oriented national body)
- ♦ Service chrétien international pour la paix (#12564)
- ♦ Service chrétien mondial (internationally oriented national body)

♦ Service Civil International (SCI) 19238

Main Office Belgiëlei 37, 2018 Antwerp, Belgium. T. +3232265727. E-mail: info@sci.ngo – coordinator@sci.ngo.
URL: http://www.sci.ngo/

History 1920, Verdun (France). Founded by Pierre Cérésole (Swiss), as a peace and humanitarian mouvement in the aftermath of World War I. Work confined to Western Europe until 1939, except for India 1934-1937. Since 1945, developments in Africa, Asia, USA and Eastern Europe. Constitution adopted 1949, Bièvres (France); modified: 1956, 1962, 1968, 1972, 1973, 1977, 1981, 1987, 1989, 1994 and 1998. Former names and other names: *The Association of Service Civil International (SCI)* – full title; *International Voluntary Service (IVS)* – alias; *Internationaler Zivildienst (IZD)* – alias; *Internationale Freiwilligendienste* – alias; *Servizio Civile Internazionale* – alias. Registration: Banque-Carrefour des Entreprises, No/ID: 0451.967.243, Start date: 21 Jan 1994, Belgium; Start date: 1934, Switzerland; Start date: 1967, Luxembourg. **Aims**

Promote a culture of peace by organizing international volunteer projects with local and global impact. **Structure** International Committee Meeting – ICM (annual); International Executive Committee (IEC), meeting 2-3 times a year; International Insurance Committee; Financial Advisory Committee (FAC); International Secretariat, with main office in Belgium. International Working Groups, open to all SCI member branches. Administratively stable SCI groups of over 2 years duration may be granted branch status if they are officially registered with the authorities of their own country. **Languages** English. **Staff** 3.20 FTE, paid; 3.00 FTE, voluntary. **Finance** Sources: donations; grants; meeting proceeds; members' dues. **Activities** Events/meetings; projects/programmes; training/education. **Events** *International Committee Meeting* Antwerp (Belgium) 2022, *International Committee Meeting* Antwerp (Belgium) 2022, *International Committee Meeting* Antwerp (Belgium) 2021, *International Committee Meeting* Antwerp (Belgium) 2021, *International Committee Meeting* Antwerp (Belgium) 2020. **Publications** *Words about deeds* (2nd 2019) in English; *50 Years of Workcamps – a Celebration* (1981) by Harry Perry in English; *Paix, pelle et pioche* (1966) by Hélène Monastier; *Pierre Cérésole* (1962) in German; *Vivre de vérité* (1950) by Pierre Cérésole; *Pierre Cérésole – Passionate Peacemaker* by Daniel Anet – 1969 in French, 1974 in English; *SCI North-South Exchanges Guide*. Periodicals, books and reports in English, French, Spanish, German. Leaflets; slides; videos; films; photographs; posters; items from national organizations.

Members National Branches and Groups in 40 countries and territories:
Albania, Australia, Austria, Bangladesh, Belarus, Belgium, Bulgaria, Catalunya, Croatia, Finland, France, Germany, Greece, Hong Kong, Hungary, India, Indonesia, Ireland, Italy, Japan, Korea Rep, Kosovo, Malaysia, Mauritius, Moldova, Nepal, Netherlands, Nigeria, North Macedonia, Norway, Poland, Romania, Serbia, Slovenia, Spain, Sri Lanka, Sweden, Switzerland, UK, USA.
Partners in 66 countries and territories:
Algeria, Argentina, Armenia, Azerbaijan, Bangladesh, Benin, Bolivia, Bosnia-Herzegovina, Botswana, Burkina Faso, Cambodia, Chile, China, Côte d'Ivoire, Croatia, Czechia, Denmark, Ecuador, El Salvador, Estonia, Georgia, Germany, Ghana, Greenland, Iceland, Indonesia, Iran Islamic Rep, Israel, Japan, Jordan, Kenya, Kosovo, Kyrgyzstan, Lesotho, Luxembourg, Malawi, Mexico, Mongolia, Montenegro, Morocco, Mozambique, Myanmar, Netherlands, Nicaragua, Pakistan, Palestine, Peru, Philippines, Portugal, Russia, Senegal, Serbia, Slovakia, South Africa, Taiwan, Tanzania UR, Thailand, Togo, Tunisia, Türkiye, Uganda, Ukraine, USA, Vietnam, Zambia, Zimbabwe.

Consultative Status Consultative status granted from: *Council of Europe (CE, #04881)* (Participatory Status); *UNESCO (#20322)* (Consultative Status). **IGO Relations** Member of (1): *European Youth Foundation (EYF, #09141)*. **NGO Relations** Member of (6): *Coordinating Committee for International Voluntary Service (CCIVS, #04819)*; *European Youth Forum (#09140)*; *Federation of European and International Associations Established in Belgium (FAIB, #09508)*; *Fédération des employeurs ONG (FEONG)*; *NGO-UNESCO Liaison Committee (#17127)*; *UNITED for Intercultural Action – European Network Against Nationalism, Racism, Fascism and in Support of Migrants and Refugees (UNITED, #20511)*. [2022.11.29/XC2805/**B**]

♦ Service Civil pour la Paix (internationally oriented national body)
♦ Service de communication et d'information pour la promotion d'une agriculture écologique paysanne en Afrique (internationally oriented national body)
♦ Service for Cooperation to Development (#19239)

♦ Service de coopération au développement (SCD) 19239

Service for Cooperation to Development

Secretariat 18 rue de Gerland, 69007 Lyon, France. T. +33472668720. Fax +33472668729.
URL: http://www.scd.asso.fr/

History Founded 18 Oct 1979, Lyon (France), uniting *Service and Development (S and D) – Service et développement (S et D)*, set up in 1959, Lyon, by *MISSIO (#16827)* (Centre de Lyon) and *Entr'aide pour le développement intégral*, set up 1963, Rome (Italy), by *Society of the Sacred Heart of Jesus (St Madeleine-Sophie Barat)*. Subtitle: *SCD – Organisme chrétien de volontariat de solidarité internationale*. Previously also referred to as: *SCD – Organisme chrétien de service volontaire international*. **Aims** As a *Christian* international *voluntary* service organization: promote voluntary cooperation with populations in the *Third World*; assist Southern countries by sending qualified personnel on request; welcome and support development volunteers, orient them towards cooperative activities in Europe and overseas, prepare, train and assign them to suitable posts (usually in teams), support them in their mission and assist their re-integration on return, enabling them to communicate the significance of their activities to others. **Structure** General Assembly (annual); Bureau; Coordination Committee. **Languages** French. **Staff** 7.00 FTE, paid; 26.00 FTE, voluntary. **Finance** Supported by: subsidies from the French Government; *Comité Catholique contre la Faim et pour le Développement-Terre Solidaire (CCFD-Terre Solidaire)*; Coopération missionnaire – OPM; private subsidies; gifts and contributions. Budget: about euro 1,400,000. **Activities** Training/education. **Events** *Citoyenneté et mondialisation* Lyon (France) 1999. **Publications** *SCD Mag* (4 a year) in French – liaison bulletin. Activity report in French.

Members Volunteers (274, mainly from France) working in 52 countries and territories:
Afghanistan, Algeria, Angola, Argentina, Bangladesh, Benin, Bolivia, Brazil, Burkina Faso, Burundi, Cambodia, Cameroon, Central African Rep, Chad, Chile, China, Colombia, Comoros, Congo Brazzaville, Congo DR, Costa Rica, Côte d'Ivoire, Djibouti, Ecuador, El Salvador, Ethiopia, Guatemala, Guinea, Haiti, India, Indonesia, Kazakhstan, Kenya, Kosovo, Laos, Lebanon, Madagascar, Mali, Mauritania, Mongolia, Morocco, Nicaragua, Peru, Philippines, Rwanda, Senegal, Sudan, Tanzania UR, Togo, Tunisia, Ukraine, Vietnam.

IGO Relations Accredited by: French Ministry of Foreign Affairs and International Development. **NGO Relations** Member of: *Coordination SUD*; national organizations. Accredited by: L'Agence du service civique (ASC). [2015.06.01/XE2766/v/**E**]

♦ Service de coopération missionnaire au développement / see VIA Don Bosco (#20766)
♦ Service de correspondance en espéranto (#04849)
♦ Service culturel international / see International Cultural Centre

♦ Service Design Network (SDN) 19240

Office KISD Köln Intl School of Design, Ubierring 40, 50678 Cologne, Germany. T. +4922182753570. E-mail: info@service-design-network.org.
URL: http://www.service-design-network.org/

History 2011. **Aims** Promote market growth of service design; enable opportunities for members to create better and more human services worldwide. **Structure** Management Team; President. Boards (3): Event; Media; Chapter; Special Interest Groups. **Languages** English, German. **Staff** 5.00 FTE, paid. **Finance** Members' dues. Other sources: proceeds from events; sales of publications. **Events** *Conference* Copenhagen (Denmark) 2022, *Conference* Cologne (Germany) 2021, *Conference* Copenhagen (Denmark) 2020, *Conference* Toronto, ON (Canada) 2019, *Conference* Madrid (Spain) 2017. **Publications** *SDN Insider* (12 a year) – electronic newsletter; *Touchpoint* (3 year) – journal.

Members Corporate (106); Professional (448); Student (52). Chapters (18) in 15 countries:
Austria, Brazil, Chile, China, Denmark, Finland, France, Germany, Japan, Netherlands, Norway, Poland, Sweden, UK, USA.

NGO Relations Links with national organizations. [2020/XJ9018/**F**]

♦ Service and Development Agency / see African Methodist Episcopal Church Service and Development Agency

♦ Service of Documentation and Studies on Global Mission 19241

Centre de documentation et d'études – Servicio de Documentación e Investigación – Servizio di Documentazione e Studi (SEDOS)

Exec Dir Via dei Verbiti 1, 00154 Rome RM, Italy. T. +3965741350. E-mail: execdir@sedosmission.org.
URL: http://www.sedosmission.org/

History 1964, Rome (Italy). Founded by a group of 7 Superiors General of men's institutes present in the Vatican Council. Former names and other names: *Documentation and Research Centre* – former. **Aims** Provide a forum for Institutes of Consecrated Life, encouraging research and knowledge dissemination in order to deepen understanding of global mission. **Structure** General Assembly; Executive Committee; Permanent Secretariat, headed by Executive Director; ad hoc Committees. **Languages** English, French, Italian, Spanish. **Staff** 2.00 FTE, paid; 2.00 FTE, voluntary. **Finance** Sources: members' dues. **Activities** Events/meetings; knowledge management/information dissemination; religious activities; research/documentation. **Publications** *SEDOS Bulletin* (6 a year).

Members Generalates or Catholic Central Administrations of 99 international missionary-sending institutes with headquarters in 11 countries:
Belgium, Canada, France, Ireland, Italy, Mexico, Netherlands, Spain, Uganda, UK, USA.
Missionary-sending institutes (99):

- *Bethlehem Mission Society (SMB)*;
- *Brothers of the Christian Schools (Christian Brothers)*;
- *Carmelite Sisters of Charity, Vedruna (CCV)*;
- *Catholic Foreign Missionary Society of America (Maryknoll Fathers)*;
- *Comboni Missionary Sisters (CMS)*;
- *Congregatio Fratrum Christianorum (CFC)*;
- *Congregatio Missionariorum Pretiosissimi Sanguinis (CPPS)*;
- *Congregation of Jesus and Mary (CJM)*;
- *Congregation of La Retraite (RLR)*;
- *Congregation of Our Lady of Sion (NDS)*;
- *Congregation of the Blessed Sacrament (SSS)*;
- *Congregation of the Daughters of Jesus*;
- *Congregation of the Holy Spirit (Spiritans)*;
- *Congregation of the Immaculate Heart of Mary (Missionaries of Scheut)*;
- *Congregation of the Marian Clerics of the Immaculate Conception of the Most Blessed Virgin Mary (Marian Fathers)*;
- *Congregation of the Missionaries of Mariannhill (CMM)*;
- *Congregation of the Most Holy Redeemer (Redemptorists)*;
- *Congregatio Sacerdotum a Sacro Corde Iesu (SCI)*;
- *Daughters of Mary and Joseph (DMJ)*;
- *Daughters of the Heart of Mary (DHM)*;
- *Daughters of Wisdom (DW)*;
- *Dominicans of the Presentation*;
- *Filles de la Charité Canossiennes (FdCC)*;
- *Filles de Notre-Dame du Sacré-Coeur (FDNSC)*;
- *Franciscan Missionaries of Mary (FMM)*;
- *Guadalupe Missioners*;
- *Handmaids of the Sacred Heart of Jesus (ACJ)*;
- *Institut de la Bienheureuse Vierge Marie (Dames Anglaises)*;
- *Institute of Consolata Missionaries (Consolata Fathers)*;
- *Institute of the Blessed Virgin Mary, Irish Branch (Loreto)*;
- *Little Brothers of Mary (Marist Brothers)*;
- *Little Sisters of Saint Francis (LSOSF)*;
- *Little Sisters of the Assumption (LSA)*;
- *Maryknoll Sisters of Saint Dominic*;
- *Medical Missionaries of Mary (MMM)*;
- *Medical Mission Sisters*;
- *Missionalis Societas Sancti Pauli (MSSP)*;
- *Missionarie Serve dello Spirito Santo (SSpS)*;
- *Missionaries of Our Lady of La Salette (La Salette Missionaries)*;
- *Missionarii Comboniani Cordis Jesu (MCCI)*;
- *Missionarii Sacratissimi Cordis Jesu (MSC)*;
- *Missionary Franciscan Sisters of the Immaculate Conception (MFIC)*;
- *Missionary Oblates of Mary Immaculate (OMI)*;
- *Missionary Sisters of Our Lady of Africa (White Sisters)*;
- *Missionary Sisters of Our Lady of the Apostles*;
- *Missionary Sisters of Our Lady of the Holy Rosary (MSHR)*;
- *Missionary Sisters of the Immaculate Heart of Mary (ICM)*;
- *Missionary Sisters of the Precious Blood*;
- *Missionary Sisters of the Sacred Heart of Jesus (MSC)*;
- *Missionary Society of St Columban (SSCME)*;
- *Missionary Sons of the Immaculate Heart of Mary (Claretians)*;
- *Order of Brothers of the Blessed Virgin Mary of Mount Carmel (Carmelite Fathers)*;
- *Order of Friars Minor Conventual (OFM Conv)*;
- *Order of Friars Minor (OFM)*;
- *Order of Preachers (Dominicans)*;
- *Order of the Holy Cross (Crosiers)*;
- *Order of the Servants of Mary (Servites)*;
- *Ordine Ospedaliero di San Giovanni di Dio (Fatebenefratelli)*;
- *Ordo Fratrum Minorum Capuccinorum (OFM Cap)*;
- *Paris Foreign Mission Society (MEP)*;
- *Religious of the Holy Union of the Sacred Hearts (SUSC)*;
- *Religious of the Sacred Heart of Mary (RSHM)*;
- *Scarboro Foreign Mission Society (SFM)*;
- *School Sisters of Notre Dame (SSND)*;
- *Sisters Mercedarian Missionaries of Bérriz (MMB)*;
- *Sisters of Charity of Our Lady Mother of Mercy (SCMM)*;
- *Sisters of Charity of St Louis (SCSL)*;
- *Sisters of Holy Cross (CSC)*;
- *Sisters of Mercy of the Americas*;
- *Sisters of Our Lady of Charity of the Good Shepherd*;
- *Sisters of Our Lady of the Missions (RNDM)*;
- *Sisters of the Child Jesus, Puy*;
- *Sisters of the Congregation of Mary (Marist Sisters)*;
- *Sisters of the Holy Family*;
- *Società del Verbo Divino (Verbiti)*;
- *Société des Missions Etrangères de la Province de Québec (SMEPQ)*;
- *Society of African Missions (SMA)*;
- *Society of Jesus, Mary, Joseph*;
- *Society of Jesus (SJ)*;
- *Society of Mary (Marianists)*;
- *Society of Mary (Marist Fathers)*;
- *Society of Missionaries of Africa (White Fathers)*;
- *Society of St Francis Xavier for the Foreign Missions (Xaverians)*;
- *Society of the Catholic Apostolate (SCA)*;
- *Society of the Divine Saviour (Salvatorians)*;
- *Society of the Helpers of the Holy Souls (HHS)*;
- *Society of the Holy Child Jesus (SHCJ)*;
- *Society of the Sacred Heart of Jesus (St Madeleine-Sophie Barat)*;
- *Soeurs Bénédictines de Tutzing*;
- *Soeurs de Notre-Dame de Namur (SNDN)*;
- *Soeurs Missionnaires de la Consolata (MC)*;
- *Soeurs Missionnaires de la Société de Marie (SMSM)*;
- *Soeurs Servantes du Sacré-Coeur de Jésus*;
- *St Joseph's Missionary Society of Mill Hill (MHM)*;
- *St Patrick's Society for the Foreign Missions (Kiltegan Fathers)*;
- *Suore di Cristo – Unione Mysterium Christi*;
- *Tertius Ordo Regularis Sancti Francisci (TOR)*;
- *Ursulines Filles de Marie-Immaculée*;
- *Ursulines of the Roman Union*.

International organizations (2):
International Union of Superiors General (#15820); *Union of Superiors General (#20484)*. [2022.05.04/XF3930/y/**E**]

♦ Service Education Research and Innovation Initiative (unconfirmed)
♦ Service des églises européennes pour les étudiants internationaux (#19242)
♦ Service Employees International Union (internationally oriented national body)
♦ Service d'entraide et de liaison (internationally oriented national body)

♦ Service of the European Churches for International Students (SECIS) 19242

Service des églises européennes pour les étudiants internationaux – Dienst van de Europese Kerken voor Internationale Studenten

Chairwoman Calle de Añastro 1, 28033 Madrid, Spain. E-mail: universidades@conferenciaepiscopal.es.
Sec Rue de Bruxelles 61, 5000 Namur, Belgium.
URL: http://www.secis.info/

History 1996, Rome (Italy). Statutes adopted Nov 2000. Registration: Banque-Carrefour des Entreprises, No/ID: 0475.960.093, Start date: 13 Nov 2001, Belgium. **Aims** Bring together institutions that perform activities of benefit to international students. **Structure** General Assembly (annual); Executive Committee. **Languages** Dutch, English, French, German, Spanish. **Staff** 5.00 FTE, voluntary. **Finance** Sources: members' dues. **Activities** Events/meetings. **Events** *General Assembly* Namur (Belgium) 2022, *General Assembly* Namur (Belgium) 2021, *General Assembly* Namur (Belgium) 2020, *Annual Encounter & General Assembly* Namur (Belgium) 2019, *Annual Encounter & General Assembly* Madrid (Spain) 2018.
Members Full; Associate; Supporting. Members in 11 countries:
Austria, Belgium, Germany, Holy See, Ireland, Netherlands, Poland, Portugal, Spain, Switzerland, UK.
IGO Relations *Council of Europe (CE, #04881).* [2022.05.09/XF6252/**F**]

- Service européen pour l'action extérieure (#07018)
- Service d'examens des écoles internationales / see International Baccalaureate (#12306)
- Service féminin international d'information et de communication / see IO – Facilitating Space for Feminist Conversations (#16005)
- Service féminin international d'information et de communication / see Isis Women's International Cross Cultural Exchange (#16031)
- Service général autonome de la maladie du sommeil en Afrique occidentale française et au Togo / see Centre Muraz (#03773)
- Service général d'hygiène mobile et de prophylaxie / see Centre Muraz (#03773)
- Service GNSS international (#13724)
- Service GPS international / see International GNSS Service (#13724)
- Service GPS international pour la géodynamique / see International GNSS Service (#13724)
- Service d'information sur la commercialisation, la promotion, et de conseils techniques de la pêche pour les pays arabes / see Centre for Marketing Information and Advisory Services for Fishery Products in the Arab Region (#03772)
- Service d'information et formation Amérique Latine – Tiers Monde (internationally oriented national body)
- Service d'information et de formation – Tiers-monde / see Service d'information et formation Amérique Latine – Tiers Monde
- Service international d'aide aux émigrants / see International Social Service (#14886)
- Service international contre le criquet nomade (inactive)
- Service international pour les droits de l'homme (#14841)
- Service international d'échanges de maisons pour les vacances (#15989)
- Service international des indices géomagnétiques (#14840)
- Service international d'information sur l'arriération mentale / see SIIS Social Information and Research Centre (#19275)
- Service international d'information pour les étudiants (inactive)
- Service international d'information sur la paix (internationally oriented national body)
- Service international du mouvement du pôle (inactive)
- Service international de recherche d'éducation et d'action sociale (internationally oriented national body)
- Service International de Recherches / see Arolsen Archives – International Center on Nazi Persecution (#01112)
- Service international de la rotation terrestre / see International Earth Rotation and Reference Systems Service (#13216)
- Service international de la rotation de la terre et des systèmes de référence (#13216)
- Service international de la Société des amis (inactive)
- Service international des ursigrammes et jours mondiaux / see International Space Environment Service (#15572)
- Service international de vacances / see INTERVac – International Home Exchange Holiday Service (#15989)
- Service international de volontaires chrétiens (internationally oriented national body)
- Service jésuite des réfugiés (#16106)
- Service latinoaméricain, africain et asiatique des habitations sociales (#19246)
- Service latinoaméricain, asiatique et africain de logement populaire / see Servicio Latinoamericano, Africano y Asiatico de Vivienda Popular (#19246)
- Service de liaison des Nations Unies avec les organisations non gouvernementales (#20591)
- Service Management Association Ltd / see IT Service Management Forum International (#16075)
- Service for Mission and Development / see VIA Don Bosco (#20766)
- Service missionnaire évangélique (internationally oriented national body)
- Service missionnaire de l'OCIC / see SIGNIS Services Rome (#19274)
- Service missionnaire de SIGNIS / see SIGNIS Services Rome (#19274)
- Service pour un Monde Meilleur (#16869)
- Service mondial d'information sur l'énergie (#21582)
- Service oecuménique d'entraide / see CIMADE
- Service des opérations spéciales de secours (inactive)
- Service pédagogique espérantiste mondial (inactive)
- Service pédologique interafricain (inactive)
- Service permanent du niveau moyen des mers (#18333)
- Service pharmaceutique des Caraïbes orientales / see Pharmaceutical Procurement Service (#18354)
- Service de promotion et de développement des investissements en Afrique (inactive)
- Service and Research Foundation of Asia on Family and Culture / see Service and Research Institute on Family and Children (#19243)

♦ Service and Research Institute on Family and Children (SERFAC) . . 19243

Pres Post Box No 18, Tambaram West, Chennai, Tamil Nadu 600 048, Chennai TAMIL NADU 600 048, India. T. +914464625913 – +914465150118. E-mail: dirserfac@gmail.com – serfacdirfamily@gmail.com.
Street Address No 1/157, Mannimangalam Road, Varadarajapuram, Chennai, Tamil Nadu 600 048, Chennai TAMIL NADU 600 048, India.
URL: http://www.childrenserfac.org/

History Founded 1 Nov 1986, by Dr Catherine Bernard and collaborators from different parts of the world committeed to the the well being of families. Inaugurated at the First World Congress 'Family and Culture'', 1986. Original title: *Service and Research Foundation of Asia on Family and Culture (SERFAC).* Current title adopted Mar 2010. Registered in accordance with Indian law. **Aims** Revitalize the fabric of the family to exercise its transforming role in a global society; empower women, girls and family as a social unit towards working for family stability, social peace and national harmony. **Structure** Governing Board; National Advisory Board; International Advisory Board; Program Planning Committee. **Languages** English. **Staff** 8.00 FTE, paid. **Finance** Members dues'. Other sources: grants; donations; sale of products from campus; consulting fees; participant fees. **Activities** Research/documentation; networking/liaising; events/meetings; training/education; publishing activities; knowledge management/information dissemination. **Events** *Conference* Berlin (Germany) 2018, *SERFAC international conference on the family* Bangkok (Thailand) 2011, *Conference on the role of the family in building communal harmony and national integration* Chennai (India) 2010, *World congress* Delhi (India) 2009, *World congress on children and family* Delhi (India) 2008. **Publications** *Children's Voices* (12 a year) – newsletter; *Family Focus* (12 a year) – newsletter. *Nurturing Families around the World and Building a Culture of Peace* (2014); *Giving Children a Voice: The Transforming Role of the Family in a Globalised Society* (2014); *Family Heart of Humanity* (2013). Conference proceedings; monographs; pamphlets; charts; slides; video and audio cassettes; CD-ROMs.
Members Individuals and institutions in Asian and Pacific countries. Members in 25 countries and territories:
Australia, Bangladesh, Cameroon, Canada, Germany, Hong Kong, India, Indonesia, Kenya, Malaysia, Myanmar, Nepal, New Zealand, Nigeria, Pakistan, Peru, Philippines, Poland, Singapore, Sri Lanka, Tanzania UR, Thailand, Uganda, UK, USA.
Consultative Status Consultative status granted from: *ECOSOC (#05331)* (Special). **NGO Relations** Member of: *Conference of Non-Governmental Organizations in Consultative Relationship with the United Nations (CONGO, #04635); United Nations Global Compact (#20567); World Organization – Ovulation Method – Billings (WOOMB-International, #21692);* national organizations. [2019/XF2944/j/**F**]

- Services CCI pour la prévention des délits commerciaux (see: #12534)
- Services for the Health in Asian and African Regions (internationally oriented national body)
- Services internationaux de publicité cinématographique (inactive)
- Service social des étrangers / see Service international de recherche d'éducation et d'action sociale
- Service Social International (#14886)
- Service Third World (internationally oriented national body)
- Service Tiers monde (internationally oriented national body)

♦ Service- og Tjenestebranchens Union i Norden (SUN) 19244

Contact c/o Building Workers' Union, Box 70446, SE-107 25 Stockholm, Sweden. T. +46706561172.
URL: http://www.fastighets.se/om-oss/organisation/sun/

History Set up as *Nordisk Funksjonaersammenslutning (DNF).* **Aims** Promote union *solidarity* and cooperation among affiliates and members of four *industry* sectors: real estate; cleaning; insurance; security/safety.
Members Organizations (13) in 5 countries and territories:
Denmark, Faeroe Is, Finland, Norway, Sweden. [2016.06.01/XD1989/**D**]

- Service unifié pour les marins (#20661)
- Service universitaire canadien outre-mer / see SUCO

♦ Service Volontaire International (SVI) 19245

International Volunteering Service

Deputy Dir-Gen Rue Grégoire Decorte 14b, 7540 Brussels, Belgium. T. +3228886713 – +3269609065. Fax +3267857950. E-mail: info@servicevolontaire.org.
Contact Campus UC Louvain, Boucle des Métiers 21, 1348 Louvain-la-Neuve, Belgium. T. +3228886713.
Main Website: https://www.servicevolontaire.org/

History Aug 2009, Belgium. Founded as a partner organization of 'SJ Vietnam'. Former names and other names: *International Voluntary Service* – former. Registration: Moniteur Belge, No/ID: 0818.117.004, Belgium; France. **Aims** Prepare, send out and welcome volunteers who wish to take part in international projects/workcamps organised by other local, non-profit associations. **Structure** General Assembly; Administration Council. **Languages** English, French. **Staff** 5.00 FTE, paid; 900.00 FTE, voluntary. **Finance** Self-funding and state support. Annual budget: 300,000 EUR (2019). **Activities** Advocacy/lobbying/activism; humanitarian/emergency aid; projects/programmes; training/education. **Publications** *SVI Newsletter* (weekly). Guide for future volunteers (annual).
Members mainly in 5 countries:
Belgium, Canada, France, Luxembourg, Switzerland.
IGO Relations Informal contact with: *United Nations Volunteers (UNV, #20650).* **NGO Relations** Member of (4): IG Network; joint; *Network for Voluntary Development in Asia (NVDA, #17063);* relie-f. Works with several local partner organizations working mainly in the field of international youth workcamps. Regular contact with 300 voluntary nonprofit organizations worldwide which provide the projects to which the volunteers can apply. [2022.05.05/XJ4822/**E**]

- Servicio Civil para la Paz (internationally oriented national body)
- Servicio Cristiano Internacional por la Paz (#12564)
- Servicio de Documentación e Investigación (#19241)
- Servicio Ecuménico para la Dignidad Humana (internationally oriented national body)
- Servicio Ecuménico de Reintegración / see Servicio Ecuménico para la Dignidad Humana
- Servicio de Enlace No Gubernamental de las Naciones Unidas (#20591)
- Servicio Europeo de Acción Exterior (#07018)
- Servicio de Expertos Franceses / see ECTI – Professionnels Seniors Bénévoles
- Servicio Femenino Internacional de Información y de Comunicación / see Isis Women's International Cross Cultural Exchange (#16031)
- Servicio Femenino Internacional de Información y de Comunicación / see IO – Facilitating Space for Feminist Conversations (#16005)
- Servicio Internacional para los Derechos Humanos (#14841)
- Servicio Internacional GNSS (#13724)
- Servicio Internacional GPS / see International GNSS Service (#13724)
- Servicio Internacional GPS para Geodinamica / see International GNSS Service (#13724)
- Servicio Internacional de Información sobre Subnormales / see SIIS Social Information and Research Centre (#19275)
- Servicio Internacional para la Paz (internationally oriented national body)
- Servicio Jesuita a Refugiados (#16106)

♦ Servicio Latinoamericano, Africano y Asiatico de Vivienda Popular (SELAVIP) 19246

Latin American, African and Asian Social Housing Service – Service latinoaméricain, africain et asiatique des habitations sociales

Managing Dir Av de Kraainem 33, 1950 Kraainem, Belgium. T. +32475550075. E-mail: ht.selavip@gmail.com.
Santiago Chile Affiliate address not obtained. E-mail: selavip.foundation@gmail.com.
Registered Address Av Louis Jasmin 69, 1150 Brussels, Belgium.
URL: http://www.selavip.org/

History 1976. Former names and other names: *Latin American, African and Asian Low-Income Housing Service* – former; *Fédération internationale de services latino-américains et asiatiques de promotion de l'habitation populaire* – former; *Service latinoaméricain, asiatique et africain de logement populaire* – former. Registration: Banque-Carrefour des Entreprises, No/ID: 0416.969.643, Start date: 3 Dec 1976, Belgium. **Aims** Support projects that provide decent *living accommodation* for the poorest *urban families*; encourage transfer of land-title to project beneficiaries; facilitate the creation of locally-based networks and assistance to urban *poor* communities to help them obtain and/or upgrade their houses and settlements. **Structure** Headquarters in Kraainem (Belgium); Affiliate based in Santiago (Chile). **Languages** English, French, Spanish. **Staff** 2.50 FTE, paid. **Finance** Source: *'Fondation Caritative van der Rest Emsens'.* [2023.02.14/XF2556/**F**]

- Servicio Mundial de Iglesias (internationally oriented national body)
- Servicio Mundial de Información sobre la Energia (#21582)

♦ Servicio Paz y Justicia en América Latina (SERPAJ-AL) 19247

Latin American Peace and Justice Service

Coordinator Joaquin Requena 1642, CP 12000 Montevideo, Uruguay. T. +59824085301. Fax +59824085701.
Coordinator Apto 514-1002, San José, San José, San José, Costa Rica. T. +5062224857. Fax +5062224857.
URL: http://www.serpajamericalatina.org/

History Founded 1974, Medellin (Colombia), during 2nd Continental Meeting, coordinated by Adolfo Pérez Esquivel, following a consultative meeting on non-violent social change in Latin America, 1966, Montevideo (Uruguay). **Aims** Based on Christian and humanitarian principles: develop means of freeing the poor from oppression; participate in creation of a free, just and humane society; support and practice the principle of non-violence. **Structure** General Assembly (every 4 years, at Continental Meeting). Collegial Council (meets once a year), consisting of officers and national coordinators. 'Coordinación Latinoamericana (CLA)' (executive body), comprises Coordinator General and Assistant Coordinator, plus others as required by Executive Secretary. International Honorary Committee. Secretariat at location of Coordinator General. **Finance** Source: kindred organizations (not specified). Budget (annual): US$ 100,000. **Activities** Main areas of concern: education for peace and human rights; leadership training; struggle for liberation. Co-organized, 1991, *Permanent Tribunal of Communities Against Impunity in Latin America – Tribunal Permanente de los Pueblos contra la Impunidad de América Latina.* **Events** *Quadrennial continental meeting* 1998, *Quadrennial general assembly / Quadrennial Continental Meeting* San José (Costa Rica) 1994, *Quadrennial continental meeting* Rio de Janeiro (Brazil) 1990, *Meeting of women* Montevideo (Uruguay) 1989, *Meeting of women* Loja (Ecuador) 1988. **Publications** *SERPAJ-AL Informa* (12 a year); *Carta Informative SERPAJ-AL* (6 a year); *Paix et justice* (periodical). *Colección Termita* – series; *Documentos de Trabajo* – series. *No Violencia Activa: Una Estrategia Revolucionaria ? Educación para los Derechos de los Pobres*; *Principios, Objetivos y Fundamentos del SERPAJ-AL*; *Raseña Histórica del SERPAJ-AL – Vol 1.* Bibliography on non-violence and violence by topics in Portuguese. Information booklets.

Members National groups in 10 countries:
Argentina, Brazil, Chile, Costa Rica, Ecuador, Mexico, Nicaragua, Panama, Paraguay, Uruguay.
Consultative Status Consultative status granted from: *UNESCO (#20322)* (Consultative Status). **NGO Relations** Member of: *Coalition of NGOs Concerned with Impunity for Violators of Human Rights (no recent information)*; *International Network for a Culture of Nonviolence and Peace (#14247)*; *International Service for Peace (SIPAZ)*; *Consejo de Educación de Adultos de América Latina (CEAAL, #04707)*. Represented on the Organizing Committee of: *Hague Appeal for Peace (HAP, #10848)*. Cooperates with: *Permanent Peoples' Tribunal (PPT, #18328)*. [2011/XF2296/**F**]

- ♦ Servicios y Asesoria para la Paz (internationally oriented national body)
- ♦ Servicio Social Internacional (#14886)
- ♦ Servicio Tercer Mundo (internationally oriented national body)
- ♦ Servicio Unificado para Marinos (#20661)
- ♦ Servicio Universitario Mundial (#21892)
- ♦ Serviciului European de Actiune Externéa (#07018)
- ♦ Serviço para a Ação Externa (#07018)
- ♦ Serviço de Estatistica das Comunidades Européias / see Statistical Office of the European Union (#19974)
- ♦ Serviço de Estatistica da União Europeia (#19974)
- ♦ Serviço Jesuita aos Refugiados (#16106)
- ♦ Serviço de Peritos Franceses para Ultramar / see ECTI – Professionnels Seniors Bénévoles
- ♦ Serviço das Publicações da União Europeia (#18562)

♦ Serving Europe 19248

SG Ave Livingstone 13-15, 1000 Brussels, Belgium. T. +3222869484. E-mail: secretariat@servingeurope.com.
URL: https://www.servingeurope.com/en/

History 1995. Founded by major European chain restaurant operators. Former names and other names: *European Modern Restaurant Association (EMRA)* – former (1995 to 2015); *Association européenne de la restauration moderne* – former (1995 to 2015). Registration: EU Transparency Register, No/ID: 36538072001-07, Start date: 15 Jul 2009. **Aims** Promote the understanding of the chain restaurant sector through an enhanced dialogue with policy makers and opinion leaders at a European level. **IGO Relations** Partner of: *European Food Safety Authority (EFSA, #07287)*. **NGO Relations** Member of: *EU Platform for Action on Diet, Physical Activity and Health (inactive)*; *European Food Sustainable Consumption and Production Round Table (European Food SCP Roundtable, #07289)*. [2022/XM1047/**D**]

- ♦ Servi del Paraclito (religious order)
- ♦ Servi Sancti Paracliti (religious order)
- ♦ Servite Secular Institute (religious order)
- ♦ Servites de Marie (religious order)
- ♦ Servites Missionnaires de la Très Sainte Trinité (religious order)
- ♦ Servites – Order of the Servants of Mary (religious order)
- ♦ Serviteurs de la Charité de Don Guanella (religious order)
- ♦ Serviteurs de Marie-Immaculée (religious order)
- ♦ Serviteurs des Pauvres du Tiers-Monde (religious order)
- ♦ Servizi e Azione per i Cittadini Europei / see European Citizen Action Service (#06555)
- ♦ Servizi e Iniziative di Promozione E Cooperazione / see Fondazione SIPEC
- ♦ Servizio d'Appoggio alle Iniziative Locali di Sviluppo (#19237)
- ♦ Servizio Civile Internazionale / see Service Civil International (#19238)
- ♦ Servizio di Documentazione e Studi (#19241)
- ♦ Servizio Europeo per l'Azione Esterna (#07018)
- ♦ Servizio dei Gesuiti per i Rifugiati (#16106)
- ♦ Servizio Mondiale d'Informazione Energetica (#21582)
- ♦ SERWEC / see Standing International Road Weather Commission (#19965)
- ♦ SES / see Society for Standards Professionals
- ♦ SESAME – International Centre / see Synchrotron-light for Experimental Science and Applications in the Middle East (#20078)
- ♦ Sesame Network / see Réseau VERTECH CITY (#18908)
- ♦ SESAME Project / see Synchrotron-light for Experimental Science and Applications in the Middle East (#20078)
- ♦ **SESAME** Synchrotron-light for Experimental Science and Applications in the Middle East (#20078)
- ♦ Sesame Workshop (internationally oriented national body)
- ♦ **SESAM** Society in Europe for Simulation Applied to Medicine (#19555)
- ♦ SESAM – Stages européens en alternance dans les métiers (no recent information)

♦ SESAR Joint Undertaking (SJU) 19249

Exec Dir address not obtained. T. +3225078000. Fax +3225078001. E-mail: info@sesarju.eu.
URL: https://www.sesarju.eu/

History Founded as a public-private partnership, under *European Council (#06801)* Regulation (EC) 219/2007, 27 Feb 2007. Modified by Council Regulation (EC) 1361-2008 and last amended by Council Regulation (EU) 721/2014. *Single European Sky ATM Research (SESAR)* project launched 2004, as technological pillar of Single European Sky (SES). **Aims** Modernize European ATM by defining, developing and delivering new or improved technologies and procedures (SESAR Solutions). **Structure** Administrative Board; Executive Director. **Staff** 40.00 FTE, paid. **Events** *SESAR Innovation Days* 2022.
Members Founding (2):
EUROCONTROL (#05667); *European Union (EU, #08967)* (represented by European Commission EC).
IGO Relations *EUROCONTROL Maastricht Upper Area Control Centre (MUAC, #05670)*. **NGO Relations** Member of (1): *EU Agencies Network (EUAN, #05564)*. [2020/XM8722/**E**]

- ♦ SESCA – Solar Energy Society of Central Africa (internationally oriented national body)
- ♦ Sesiones Pedagógicas para Docentes e Investigatores del Francés Lengua Extranjera (meeting series)
- ♦ **SESRIC** Statistical, Economic and Social Research and Training Centre for Islamic Countries (#19971)
- ♦ SESRTCIC / see Statistical, Economic and Social Research and Training Centre for Islamic Countries (#19971)
- ♦ SESSA – Sustainable Energy Society of Southern Africa (internationally oriented national body)
- ♦ SES / see Scandinavian Packaging Association (#19095)
- ♦ Sessional Working Group of Governmental Experts on the Implementation of the International Covenant on Economic, Social and Cultural Rights / see United Nations Committee on Economic, Social and Cultural Rights (#20538)
- ♦ Sessional Working Group on the Implementation of the International Covenant on Economic, Social and Cultural Rights / see United Nations Committee on Economic, Social and Cultural Rights (#20538)
- ♦ **SES** Society for Emblem Studies (#19548)
- ♦ SES – Society for Standards Professionals (internationally oriented national body)
- ♦ SES – Studies and Expansion Society (inactive)
- ♦ Sesto protocollo addizionale all'Accordo generale su i privilegi e le immunità del Consiglio d'Europa (1996 treaty)
- ♦ Sestre Franjevke od Bezgresnog Zaceca (religious order)
- ♦ SESW – Société Européenne de Straight-Wire (unconfirmed)
- ♦ SETAC AP – SETAC Asia/Pacific (see: #19551)
- ♦ SETAC Asia/Pacific (see: #19551)
- ♦ **SETAC Europe** Society of Environmental Toxicology and Chemistry Europe (#19552)
- ♦ SETAC LA – Sociedad de Toxicologia y Quimica Ambiental en Latinoamerica (see: #19551)
- ♦ SETAC Latin America (see: #19551)
- ♦ **SETAC** Society of Environmental Toxicology and Chemistry (#19551)
- ♦ SETA – International Symposium on Econometric Theory and Applications (meeting series)
- ♦ SETE – International Symposium on Emerging Technologies for Education (meeting series)
- ♦ SETEM – Servicio Tercer Mundo (internationally oriented national body)
- ♦ **SETE** Société d'Education Thérapeutique Européenne (#19459)
- ♦ SETI League (internationally oriented national body)
- ♦ SETIS – Société européenne d'étude et d'intégration de systèmes spatiaux (inactive)
- ♦ SETM / see Solidarité étudiants du Monde
- ♦ SETM – Solidarité étudiants du Monde (internationally oriented national body)

♦ Settlements Information Network Africa (SINA) 19250

Contact c/o Mazingira Institute, PO Box 14550, Nairobi, 00800, Kenya. T. +254204409773. E-mail: sina@mazinst.org.
URL: http://sina.mazinst.org/

History Dec 1982, following a meeting of human settlements workers in Eastern and Southern Africa, Oct 1981, Lusaka (Zambia). **Aims** Advocate just governance of social and policy process for realization of human dignity and rights, gender equality and sustainable habitats in an urbanizing and globalizing world. **Structure** Operated by the Mazingira Institute of Kenya. **Finance** Funded by Shelter Sweden. **Activities** Organizes regional and national workshops, exchange visits. Links members together who are engaged in activities such as self-help construction, health, nutrition, employment projects, etc. **Events** *Regional workshop* Addis Ababa (Ethiopia) 1989, *Regional workshop* Nairobi (Kenya) 1989, *Regional NGO forum* Nairobi (Kenya) 1986. **Publications** *SINA Newsletter* (3 a year). *SINA Directory*. *NGOs and Shelter* – information package on English and Portuguese speaking Africa.
Members Organizations; Individual – community development workers, teachers, planners, health workers and other sharing a concern for improving the quality of life in human settlements. Members in 30 countries:
Algeria, Botswana, Cameroon, Congo DR, Côte d'Ivoire, Egypt, Eritrea, Eswatini, Ethiopia, Gambia, Ghana, Guinea-Bissau, Kenya, Lesotho, Malawi, Mali, Morocco, Mozambique, Namibia, Nigeria, Senegal, Sierra Leone, South Africa, Sudan, Tanzania UR, Togo, Tunisia, Uganda, Zambia, Zimbabwe.
International or internationally-oriented organizations and regional organizations or regional offices of international organizations (17), listed in this Yearbook:
Development Innovations and Networks (#05057); *Environnement et développement du Tiers-monde (enda, #05510)*; *Habitat for Humanity International (HFHI)*; *Institut Africain pour le Développement Economique et Social – Centre Africain de Formation (INADES-Formation, #11233)*; *Institut français de recherche en Afrique (IFRA)*; *International Co-operative Alliance (ICA, #12944)*; *Oxfam GB*; *Pan African Institute for Development (PAID, #18053)*; *Practical Action (#18475)*; *Rikolto*; *Sahelian Scientific and Technological Information and Documentation Network (RESADOC, no recent information)*; *Save the Children Norway (Redd Barna)*; *Save the Children UK (SC UK)*; *Southern African Catholic Development Association (no recent information)*; *Trickle Up Program (TUP, #20236)*; *World Scout Bureau (WSB, see: #21693)*; *World Vision International (WVI, #21904)*.
IGO Relations *UNICEF (#20332)*. [2008/XF1025/y/**F**]

- ♦ Settlement Study Centre / see Weitz Center for Development Studies
- ♦ **SEUD** Society of Endometriosis and Uterine Disorders (#19549)
- ♦ **SEU** Socialno-Ekologiceskij Sojuz (#19663)
- ♦ SEUS – Society of European Sonographers (inactive)
- ♦ Seva Foundation (internationally oriented national body)
- ♦ SEVC – Southern European Veterinary Conference (meeting series)
- ♦ Seven-Power Summit / see Group of Eight (#10745)
- ♦ **SEVEN** Senior European Volunteers Exchange Network (#19227)
- ♦ **Seven Sisters** Coalition of Asia Pacific Regional Networks on HIV/AIDS (#04051)
- ♦ Seventh-day Adventist Welfare Service / see Adventist Development and Relief Agency International (#00131)
- ♦ Seventh-day Adventist World Service / see Adventist Development and Relief Agency International (#00131)
- ♦ Seventh Day Baptist General Conference (internationally oriented national body)
- ♦ Seventh Day Baptist Missionary Society (internationally oriented national body)
- ♦ Seventh Day Baptist World Federation (internationally oriented national body)
- ♦ SEV / see International Society for Applied Ethology (#14930)
- ♦ SEV – Sovet Ekonomiceskoj Vzaimopomosci (inactive)
- ♦ Sewa International (internationally oriented national body)
- ♦ **SEWF** Social Enterprise World Forum (#19336)
- ♦ SEWM – Strong and ElectroWeak Matter Conference (meeting series)
- ♦ Sexaholics Anynymous (internationally oriented national body)
- ♦ Sexually Transmitted Diseases Society of Southern Africa (internationally oriented national body)

♦ Sexual Violence Research Initiative (SVRI) 19251

Contact 28 High Street, Pretoria, 0145, South Africa. E-mail: svri@svri.org.
Main Website: http://www.svri.org/

History 2003. Founded as an initiative of *Global Forum for Health Research (inactive)*. Intitially hosted by *WHO (#20950)*; moved to South Africa, 2006. Independent organization since 2019. Registration: Companies and Intellectual Property Commission, No/ID: SVRI NPC 2019/197466/08, South Africa. **Aims** Increase and strengthen action-oriented research and its uptake to improve and expand violence against women (VAW) and violence against children (VAC) prevention globally. **Structure** Leadership Council; Board; SVRI Team. **Languages** English, Spanish. **Staff** 6.00 FTE, paid. **Finance** Sources: donations. **Activities** Capacity building; events/meetings; financial and/or material support; knowledge management/information dissemination; networking/liaising; research and development; research/documentation; standards/guidelines. SVRI works in all global regions with a focus on low and middle income countries. **Events** *Forum* Cancún (Mexico) 2022, *Forum* Cape Town (South Africa) 2019, *Forum* Rio de Janeiro (Brazil) 2017, *Moving the agenda forward* Stellenbosch (South Africa) 2015, *Evidence into action* Bangkok (Thailand) 2013. **Publications** https://www.svri.org/documents/our-resources **Members** Individuals. Membeship countries not specified. [2022.10.24/XJ1527/**E**]

- ♦ Sex Workers' Rights Advocacy Network (unconfirmed)
- ♦ Seydoux Foundation for the Mediterranean World (internationally oriented national body)
- ♦ SFA – Société Francophone d'Arthroscopie (internationally oriented national body)
- ♦ **SFA** Squash Federation of Africa (#19933)
- ♦ SFA – Sustainable Fibre Alliance (internationally oriented national body)
- ♦ SFAUMB / see Société Francophone d'Echographie
- ♦ SFB – Schweizerische Friedensbewegung (internationally oriented national body)
- ♦ SFCG – Search for Common Ground (internationally oriented national body)
- ♦ **SFCG** Space Frequency Coordination Group (#19897)
- ♦ **SFCO** Société Française de Chirurgie Orale (#19464)
- ♦ **SFC** Smart Freight Centre (#19320)
- ♦ SFC – Société Francophone de Chronobiologie (internationally oriented national body)
- ♦ **SFC** Société francophone de classification (#19465)
- ♦ **SFC** Société Francophone de Contraception (#19466)
- ♦ **SfC** Society for Cryobiology (#19538)
- ♦ **SFCTCV** Société française de chirurgie thoracique et cardiovasculaire (#09993)
- ♦ **SFDP** Société francophone de primatologie (#19472)
- ♦ SFDP – Société Internationale des Docteurs en Pharmacie d'Expression Française (internationally oriented national body)
- ♦ **SFDPS** Société francophone de dermatologie psychosomatique (#19467)
- ♦ SFD – Saudi Fund for Development (internationally oriented national body)
- ♦ **SFD** Société Francophone du Diabète (#19468)
- ♦ SFDW – Steunfonds Derde Wereld (internationally oriented national body)
- ♦ SF Echo – Société Francophone d'Echographie (internationally oriented national body)
- ♦ SFE / see European Public Service Union (#08303)
- ♦ **SFERETE** Société Francophone d'Etude et de Recherche sur les Eléments Toxiques et Essentiels (#19469)
- ♦ SF – Filii Sacrae Familiae Jesu, Mariae et Ioseph (religious order)
- ♦ SFFI – Spiritual Frontiers Fellowship International (internationally oriented national body)

- ♦ SFFPC – Société française et francophone des plaies et cicatrisations (internationally oriented national body)
- ♦ SFF – Sea First Foundation (internationally oriented national body)
- ♦ SFF – Space Frontier Foundation (internationally oriented national body)
- ♦ SFG – Strategic Foresight Group (internationally oriented national body)
- ♦ SFG – Studien- und Förderungsgesellschaft (inactive)
- ♦ SFH / see Organisation suisse d'aide aux réfugiés
- ♦ SFHR – Swedish Foundation for Human Rights (internationally oriented national body)
- ♦ SFH – Schweizerische Flüchtlingshilfe (internationally oriented national body)
- ♦ **SFH** Society for Histochemistry (#19568)
- ♦ SFIA – Seoul Forum for International Affairs (internationally oriented national body)
- ♦ SFIC / see World Heart Federation (#21562)
- ♦ SFIE / see European Public Service Union (#08303)
- ♦ SFIMAR – Société Francophone pour l'informatique et le Monitorage en Anesthésie – Réanimation (unconfirmed)
- ♦ **SFIME** Stiftung für die Förderung der Inneren Medizin in Europa (#09944)
- ♦ **SFI** Société financière internationale (#13597)
- ♦ SFL – Shelter for Life (internationally oriented national body)
- ♦ SFMBCB / see Société Française de Chirurgie Orale (#19464)
- ♦ SFM – Scarboro Foreign Mission Society (religious order)
- ♦ SFM – Societas Scarborensis pro Missionibus ad Exteras Gentes (religious order)
- ♦ SFMU – Société francophone de médecine d'urgence (internationally oriented national body)
- ♦ **SFNCM** Société Francophone Nutrition Clinique et Métabolisme (#19471)
- ♦ **SFNDT** Société Francophone de Néphrologie Dialyse et Transplantation (#19470)
- ♦ SFNEP / see Société Francophone Nutrition Clinique et Métabolisme (#19471)
- ♦ SfNIRS – Society for functional Near Infrared Spectroscopy (unconfirmed)
- ♦ SFN – Société française de nutrition (internationally oriented national body)
- ♦ SfN – Society for Neuroscience (internationally oriented national body)
- ♦ **SFOMK** Skandinavisk Forening af Oral og Maxillofacial Kirurger (#19074)
- ♦ **SFOPOM** Skandinavisk Förening för Oral Patologi och Oral Medicin (#19303)
- ♦ SFO – Secular Franciscan Order (religious order)
- ♦ SFPA – Slovak Foreign Policy Association (internationally oriented national body)
- ♦ SFPA – Swiss Foreign Policy Association (internationally oriented national body)
- ♦ **SFPE** Seniors de la fonction publique européenne (#19229)
- ♦ SFPE – Society of Fire Protection Engineers (internationally oriented national body)
- ♦ SFP – Science for Peace (internationally oriented national body)
- ♦ **SFP** Smoke Free Partnership (#19329)
- ♦ SFRBM / see Society for Redox Biology and Medicine (#19628)
- ♦ **SfRBM** Society for Redox Biology and Medicine (#19628)
- ♦ **SFRR-Africa** Society for Free Radical Research Africa (#19559)
- ♦ **SFRR ASIA** Society for Free Radical Research Asia (#19560)
- ♦ SFRRA / see Society for Redox Research Australasia (#19629)
- ♦ **SFRRE** Society for Free Radical Research – Europe (#19561)
- ♦ SFRR Europe / see Society for Free Radical Research – Europe (#19561)
- ♦ SFRR / see International Society for Free Radical Research (#15131)
- ♦ SFR – Schweizerischer Friedensrat (internationally oriented national body)
- ♦ SFS / see Swisspeace
- ♦ SfSAP – Society for Sterility Assurance Professionals (unconfirmed)
- ♦ SFSA – Syngenta Foundation for Sustainable Agriculture (internationally oriented national body)
- ♦ **SF** Schwarzkopf Foundation Young Europe (#19136)
- ♦ SF – Seva Foundation (internationally oriented national body)
- ♦ SFSF – Svenska Freds- och Skiljedomsföreningen (internationally oriented national body)
- ♦ SFSR – Club Francophone des Spécialistes de la Rétine (unconfirmed)
- ♦ **SFS** Society for Financial Studies (#19558)
- ♦ SFS – Society for Freedom in Science (inactive)
- ♦ SFS – Society for Freshwater Science (internationally oriented national body)
- ♦ SF – Stakeholder Forum for a Sustainable Future (internationally oriented national body)
- ♦ SF – Strømme Foundation (internationally oriented national body)
- ♦ **SFT International** Students for a Free Tibet International (#20018)
- ♦ **SFT** Sustainable Food Trust (#20059)
- ♦ SFUM / see Société francophone de médecine d'urgence
- ♦ **SFUZO** Svitova Federacija Ukrainskih Zinocih Organizacij (#21496)
- ♦ SFV – International Convention for the Safety of Fishing Vessels (1977 treaty)
- ♦ SFV PROT 1993 – Torremolinos Protocol of 1993 Relating to the Torremolinos International Convention for the SAfety of Fishing Vessels (1993 treaty)
- ♦ SG2000 / see Sasakawa Africa Association (#19055)
- ♦ **SGAC** Space Generation Advisory Council in Support of the United Nations Programme on Space Applications (#19898)
- ♦ SGA – Schweizerische Gesellschaft für Aussenpolitik (internationally oriented national body)
- ♦ SGA – Serious Games Association (unconfirmed)
- ♦ SGA – Slavic Gospel Association (internationally oriented national body)
- ♦ SGA / see Society for Geology Applied to Mineral Deposits (#19565)
- ♦ SGAS – Schweizerische Gesellschaft für Afrikastudien (internationally oriented national body)
- ♦ **SGATAR** Study Group on Asian Tax Administration and Research (#20020)
- ♦ SGBED – Society for Global Business and Economic Development (internationally oriented national body)
- ♦ SGEPSTA / see Standing Conference of European Public Service Training Agencies (#19961)

♦ SGF International 19252

General Manager Am Hahnenbusch 14 b, 55268 Nieder-Olm, Germany. T. +4961369228140 – +49613692280. Fax +496136922810.
URL: http://www.sgf.org/

History 1972 as 'Foundation of Interessengemeinschaft Zitrussäfte (IGZ)'. Foundation of *Schutzgemeinschaft der Fruchtsaft-Industrie (SGF)* set up 1974. IGZ merges into SGF, 1976. Current title and new structure adopted 13 May 2004. Full title: *SGF International – Sure – Global – Fair.* Registered in accordance with German law. **Aims** Promote free and fair competition; contribute to improved consumer protection; control *fruit juices*, fruit nectars and other products made from fruit and vegetables. **Structure** General Assembly (annual); Executive Committee. Boards (2): International Quality Control System (IQCS); International Raw Material Assurance (IRMA). Secretariat. **Languages** English, German. **Staff** 23.00 FTE, paid. **Finance** Sources: members' dues. **Activities** Advocacy/lobbying/activism; events/meetings; research/documentation. **Events** *Annual Juice Summit* Antwerp (Belgium) 2019, *Annual Juice Summit* Antwerp (Belgium) 2018, *Annual Juice Summit* Antwerp (Belgium) 2017, *Asia Seminar* Dubai (United Arab Emirates) 2017, *Asia Seminar* Tokyo (Japan) 2017. **Publications** *SGF News* (6 a year). Business report.
Members Full in 55 countries:
Argentina, Austria, Belgium, Belize, Bolivia, Brazil, Bulgaria, China, Colombia, Costa Rica, Cuba, Czechia, Denmark, Ecuador, Egypt, Estonia, Ethiopia, Finland, France, Germany, Ghana, Greece, Guatemala, Honduras, Hungary, India, Indonesia, Israel, Italy, Kenya, Lithuania, Malawi, Mexico, Monaco, Netherlands, Pakistan, Paraguay, Peru, Philippines, Poland, Portugal, Romania, Russia, Serbia, South Africa, Spain, Sweden, Switzerland, Thailand, Türkiye, UK, Ukraine, Uruguay, USA, Vietnam.
Included in the above, 1 international member listed in this Yearbook: [2018.01.24/XM6015/y/**C**]

- ♦ SGF International – Sure – Global – Fair / see SGF International (#19252)
- ♦ SG – Fratelli dell'Istruzione Cristiana di San Gabriele (religious order)
- ♦ SGF / see SGF International (#19252)
- ♦ SGHMP / see Centre Muraz (#03773)
- ♦ SGIA International / see Screenprinting and Graphic Imaging Association International (#19159)
- ♦ **SGIA** Scandinavian Green Infrastructure Association (#19088)
- ♦ **SGIA** Screenprinting and Graphic Imaging Association International (#19159)
- ♦ **SGIDHO** Sporting Goods Industry Data Harmonization Organization (#19924)

♦ SGI Europe 19253

Gen Sec Rue des Deux Eglises 26 – Bte 5, 1000 Brussels, Belgium. T. +3222192798. Fax +3222181213. E-mail: maxime.staelens@sgieurope.org – info@sgieurope.org.
URL: http://www.sgieurope.org

History 20 Oct 1961, Brussels (Belgium). Current statutes registered Nov 1995. Former names and other names: *European Centre of Public Enterprises (ECPE)* – former (20 Oct 1961 to 1995); *Centre européen de l'entreprise publique (CEEP)* – former (20 Oct 1961 to 1995); *Europäischer Zentralverband der Öffentlichen Wirtschaft* – former (20 Oct 1961 to 1995); *Centro Europeo de la Empresa Pública* – former (20 Oct 1961 to 1995); *Centro Europeo dell'Impresa Pubblica* – former (20 Oct 1961 to 1995); *Centro Europeu da Empresa Pública* – former (20 Oct 1961 to 1995); *Europees Centrum van Gemeenschapsbedrijven* – former (20 Oct 1961 to 1995); *Evropaiko Kentro tis Dimosias Epihiriseos* – former (20 Oct 1961 to 1995); *Comhar Eorpach Eagras Poiblí* – former (20 Oct 1961 to 1995); *European Centre of Enterprises with Public Participation* – former; *Centre européen des entreprises à participation publique* – former; *Europäischer Zentralverband der Öffentlichen Wirtschaft* – former; *Centro Europeo de Empresas con Participación Pública* – former; *Centro Europeo delle Imprese a Partecipazione Pubblica* – former; *Centro Europeu das Empresas com Participação Pública* – former; *Europees Centrum van de Ondernemingen met Overheidsdeelneming* – former; *Evropaiko Kentro Epihiriseos me Simmetohi tu Dimosiu* – former; *Comhar Eorpach Eagras le Scar Stáitúil* – former; *European Centre of Enterprises with Public Participation and of Enterprises of General Economic Interest* – former (1995 to Dec 2008); *Centre européen des entreprises à participation publique et des entreprises d'intérêt économique général (CEEP)* – former (1995 to Dec 2008); *European Centre of Employers and Enterprises of Public Services (CEEP)* – former (2008 to 2013); *European Centre of Employers and Enterprises of Public Services and of Services of General Interest (CEEP)* – former (2013 to Dec 2020). Registration: Belgium; EU Transparency Register, No/ID: 59513031434-92. **Aims** Represent employers and enterprises providing services of general interest which serve the fundamental goals of the EU, supporting business, social and territorial cohesion, economic and social solidarity and a better quality of life for all citizens. **Structure** General Assembly (twice a year); Presidency; Administrative Council; Specialized Boards and Task Forces. **Languages** English, French. **Staff** 8.00 FTE, paid. **Finance** Sources: members' dues. Annual budget: 1,038,130 EUR. **Activities** Events/meetings; projects/programmes. **Events** *Public Services Summit* Brussels (Belgium) 2019, *Annual conference of local public enterprises* Brussels (Belgium) 2011, *Conference* Budapest (Hungary) 2011, *Workshop on power electronics substrates* Munich (Germany) 2010, *Workshop on advanced multilevel converter systems* Sweden 2010.
Members Full: national organizations in 18 countries:
Austria, Belgium, Bulgaria, Denmark, Finland, France, Germany, Hungary, Italy, Luxembourg, Malta, Netherlands, Norway, Portugal, Romania, Spain, Sweden, UK.
Sectoral members (3):
European Broadcasting Union (EBU, #06404); European Federation of Education Employers (EFEE, #07101); European Hospital and Healthcare Employers' Association (HOSPEEM, #07500).
IGO Relations Accredited by (1): *European Commission (EC, #06633).* Social Partner of: *European Quality Assurance in Vocational Education and Training (EQAVET, #08312).* **NGO Relations** Member of (1): *European Movement International (EMI, #07825).* Together with: *European Trade Union Confederation (ETUC, #08927)* and *BUSINESSEUROPE (#03381)*, set up: *European Centre for Industrial Relations (ECIR, inactive).*
[2021.05.31/XD0613/**E**]

- ♦ SGILWCH – Study Group on International Labor and Working Class History (internationally oriented national body)
- ♦ **SGIR** European Standing Group on International Relations (#08831)
- ♦ **SGI** Society for Gastrointestinal Intervention (#19563)
- ♦ SGI / see Society for Reproductive Investigation (#19631)
- ♦ **SGI** Soka Gakkai International (#19672)
- ♦ **SGL** Society for Germanic Linguistics (#19566)
- ♦ **SGMF** Society for Gas as a Marine Fuel (#19562)
- ♦ SGM International / see SGM Lifewords
- ♦ SGM Lifewords (internationally oriented national body)
- ♦ SGML Open / see Organization for the Advancement of Structured Information Standards
- ♦ SGPC / see Shiromani Gurdwara Parbandhak Committee (#19262)
- ♦ **SGPC** Shiromani Gurdwara Parbandhak Committee (#19262)
- ♦ SGP / see Society for Germanic Linguistics (#19566)
- ♦ SGRA / see Scandinavian Green Infrastructure Association (#19088)
- ♦ SGroup – European Universities' Network / see SGroup – Universities in Europe (#19254)

♦ SGroup – Universities in Europe 19254

Project Manager c/o University of Porto, International Relations Office, Praça de Gomes Teixeira, 4099-002 Porto, Portugal. T. +351913409416. E-mail: sgroup@sgroup-unis.eu.
Exec Sec address not obtained.
URL: https://sgroup-unis.eu/

History Dec 1988. Founded following preliminary meeting, Sep 1988, as *Santander Group – European Universities Network.* Registration: Start date: May 1992, Spain. **Aims** Strengthen institutional capacities of member universities to reinforce their international visibility, expand their collaboration opportunities in education and research, and improve the quality of their governance, teaching, research and administrative practices. **Structure** General Assembly; President; Executive Committee; Liaison Officers; Secretariat. **Languages** English. **Staff** 3.00 FTE, paid. **Finance** Sources: members' dues. Supported by: *European Union (EU, #08967).* **Activities** Advocacy/lobbying/activism; events/meetings; networking/liaising; training/education. **Events** *General Assembly* Canterbury (UK) 2019, *Liaison Officers meeting* Canterbury (UK) 2019, *General Assembly* Malmö (Sweden) 2012, *General Assembly* Le Havre (France) 2011, *Liaison Officers Meeting* Eindhoven (Netherlands) 2010. **Publications** *Santander Group News Bulletin* (10 a year). Position statements; conference proceedings; research papers; articles.
Members Full: European HEI (35) in 17 countries:
Belgium, Cyprus, Czechia, Finland, France, Germany, Greece, Italy, Malta, Netherlands, Norway, Poland, Portugal, Romania, Spain, Sweden, UK.
Associate: Non-European HEI (4) in 4 countries:
Armenia, Australia, China, Colombia.
NGO Relations Cooperates with (3): Brazilian Association for International Education – FAUBAI; *European University Association (EUA, #09027)*; Groningen Declaration Network. [2022/XF1641/v/**F**]

- ♦ SGR – Scientists for Global Responsibility (internationally oriented national body)
- ♦ SGSR / see International Society for the Systems Sciences (#15500)
- ♦ SGSS – Schweizerische Gesellschaft für Skandinavische Studien (internationally oriented national body)
- ♦ Shack Dwellers International / see Shack-Slum Dwellers International (#19255)

♦ Shack-Slum Dwellers International (SDI) 19255

Sec PO Box 13033, Mowbray, Cape Town, 7705, South Africa. T. +27214474016. Fax +27214482434. E-mail: admin@sdinet.org.
URL: http://www.sdinet.co.za/

History May 1996, South Africa. Referred to in Africa as *Shack Dwellers International* and in Asia as *Slum Dwellers International.* **Aims** Function as a worldwide network of *landless* people who empower themselves using *savings* schemes and self-build projects; create a voice of the urban poor and build inclusive and sustainable cities. **Structure** Board.
Members Organizations in 21 countries:
Argentina, Brazil, Cambodia, Colombia, Eswatini, Ghana, India, Indonesia, Kenya, Malawi, Namibia, Nepal, Philippines, South Africa, Sri Lanka, Tanzania UR, Thailand, Timor-Leste, Uganda, Zambia, Zimbabwe.
NGO Relations Supports: *Cities Alliance (#03950); Global Call for Action Against Poverty (GCAP, #10263).*
[2016.08.12/XF6147/**F**]

- ♦ **SHAC** Society for the History of Alchemy and Chemistry (#19569)
- ♦ Shadhiliya (religious order)
- ♦ SHAEF – Supreme Headquarters of the Allied Expeditionary Forces (inactive)
- ♦ **SHAFFE** Southern Hemisphere Association of Fresh Fruit Exporters (#19877)
- ♦ SHAFR – Society for Historians of American Foreign Relations (internationally oriented national body)
- ♦ Shakespeare Society of Southern Africa (internationally oriented national body)
- ♦ Shalom Achshav (internationally oriented national body)
- ♦ Shalom Incorporated / see Messianic Jewish Movement International (#16732)
- ♦ **Shamaa** Arab Educational Information Network (#00938)

♦ Shanghai Cooperation Organization (SCO) 19256

SG 7 Ritan Road, Chaoyang District, 100600 Beijing, China. T. +861065329806 – +861065329807. Fax +861065329808. E-mail: sco@sectsco.org.
URL: http://eng.sectsco.org/

History 1996, Shanghai (China). Established with the signing of the Treaty on Deepening Military Trust in Border Regions in Shanghai by the heads of states of Kazakhstan, China, Kyrgyzstan, Russia and Tajikistan. Same countries signed the Treaty on Re-education of Military Forces in Border Regions in a meeting, 1997, Moscow (Russia). Current title adopted, 15 Jun 2001, when Uzbekistan joined. Former names and other names: *Shanghai Five* – former; *Group of Shanghai* – alias. **Aims** Strengthen mutual trust and good relations among member states; promote effective cooperation in political affairs, economy and trade, scientific-technical, cultural and educational spheres as well as in energy, transportation, tourism and environment protection fields; jointly safeguard and present regional peace, security and stability; strive towards the creation of a democratic, just, rational new international political and economic order. **Structure** Council of Heads of State; Council of Heads of Government; Council of Foreign Ministers; Council of National Coordinators. Permanent bodies: Secretariat, Beijing (China); Regional Anti-Terrorism Structure (RATS), Tashkent (Uzbekistan). **Languages** Chinese, Russian. **Staff** Secretariat: 30; RCTS: 30. **Finance** Annual budget shared by member states. **Activities** Networking/liaising; events/meetings. **Events** *Annual Summit* Bishkek (Kyrgyzstan) 2019, *Annual Summit* Qingdao (China) 2018, *Annual Summit* Astana (Kazakhstan) 2017, *Annual Summit* Tashkent (Uzbekistan) 2016, *Annual Summit* Ufa (Russia) 2015.
Members Governments of 6 countries:
China, Kazakhstan, Kyrgyzstan, Russia, Tajikistan, Uzbekistan.
Observers (6):
Afghanistan, Belarus, India, Iran Islamic Rep, Mongolia, Pakistan.
Dialogue Partners (6) in 6 countries:
Armenia, Azerbaijan, Cambodia, Nepal, Sri Lanka, Türkiye. [2017.03.09/XE4275/**E***]

- ♦ Shanghai Five / see Shanghai Cooperation Organization (#19256)
- ♦ Shanghai Institute for International Studies (internationally oriented national body)
- ♦ The Shape of Enrichment (internationally oriented national body)
- ♦ Shape Modeling International (meeting series)
- ♦ SHAPE / see NATO SCHOOL Oberammergau (#16947)
- ♦ **SHAPE** Supreme Headquarters Allied Powers Europe (#20039)
- ♦ SHAPS / see School of Pacific and Asian Studies
- ♦ Share as Brothers (internationally oriented national body)
- ♦ Shared Earth (internationally oriented national body)

♦ Share International 19257

Netherlands Office PO Box 41877, 1009 DB Amsterdam, Netherlands. T. +31206946262.
UK Office PO Box 3677, London, NW5 1RU, UK. T. +442074821113. Fax +442072672881.
USA Office PO Box 971, North Hollywood CA 91603, USA. T. +18187856300.
URL: http://www.share-international.org/

History 29 Mar 1982, Amsterdam (Netherlands), following setting up of national body, Oct 1981. Incorporated in the Netherlands and USA. Took over activities of *Tara Center (inactive)*, when it merged into Share International. **Aims** Distribute publications to make known the presence of *Maitreya*, the world teacher, and to give guidance in sharing; provide a forum for the discussion and exploration of *new age* social, economic, political and cultural structures. **Staff** Voluntary. **Finance** Magazine subscriptions; donations. **Activities** Events/meetings; publishing activities. **Events** *International transmission conference* Veldhoven (Netherlands) 1991. **Publications** *Share International* (10 a year) in Dutch, English, French, German, Japanese, Spanish – magazine; *Emergence* (4 a year). Books.
Members Sister organizations in 23 countries:
Argentina, Australia, Austria, Belgium, Canada, Denmark, Finland, France, Germany, Israel, Japan, Netherlands, New Zealand, Norway, Philippines, Poland, Romania, Slovenia, Spain, Sweden, Switzerland, UK, USA.
Consultative Status Consultative status granted from: *ECOSOC (#05331)* (Special). **IGO Relations** Associated with Department of Global Communications of the United Nations. [2015.11.04/XF9599/**F**]

- ♦ Share-Net International (internationally oriented national body)
- ♦ Share-Net International – the Knowledge Platform on Sexual and Reproductive Health and Rights / see Share-Net International
- ♦ Share Our Strength (internationally oriented national body)
- ♦ SHARE – Services for the Health in Asian and African Regions (internationally oriented national body)
- ♦ **SHARE** Social sciences and Humanities in ionising radiation REsearch (#19346)
- ♦ Share the World's Resources (internationally oriented national body)
- ♦ Sharia Council / see International Shari'ah Council of the AAOIFI (#14844)
- ♦ Sharing (internationally oriented national body)
- ♦ Sharing and Building Solution Focused Practice in Organizations / see Solutions in Organisations Link-up (#19685)
- ♦ Sharing of Ministries Abroad (internationally oriented national body)
- ♦ Sharing Progress in Cancer Care (unconfirmed)
- ♦ Shark Advocates International (unconfirmed)
- ♦ Shark Alliance (inactive)

♦ Sharkhunters International 19258

Pres PO Box 1539, Hernando FL 34442, USA. T. +13526372917. Fax +13526376289. E-mail: sharkhunters@earthlink.net.
URL: http://www.sharkhunters.com/

History 1983. **Aims** Research *submarine history*, particularly of German *U-boats*. **Finance** Members' dues. **Events** *Annual Convention* Daytona Beach, FL (USA) 2000, *Annual Convention* Germany 1999, *Annual Convention* Germany 1994. **Publications** *KTB Magazine* (10 a year). **Members** Individuals (over 6,600, mostly in USA) in 70 countries. Membership countries not specified. [2017.03.09/XF3142/v/**F**]

♦ SHARKPROJECT International 19259

Contact Ottostr 13, 63150 Heusenstamm, Germany. T. +496104670984. E-mail: info@sharkproject.org.
URL: http://www.sharkproject.org/

History 2002. **Aims** Protect sharks; act in the interests of the over 500 species of *sharks* and their environment, the *marine ecosystem*. **Structure** Executive Committee. Sections (3): Germany, Austria, Switzerland. **Activities** Awareness raising. **NGO Relations** Member of: *International Union for Conservation of Nature and Natural Resources (IUCN, #15766)*. [2018/XM6798/**F**]

♦ Shark Research Institute (SRI) 19260

Exec Dir 70 Heather Lane, Princeton NJ 08540, USA. T. +16099155211. E-mail: media@sharks.org.
URL: http://www.sharks.org/

History 1991, Princeton, NJ (USA). Founded by Marie Levine. Registration: 501(c)(3) non-profit, USA. **Aims** Sponsor and conduct research on sharks; promote conservation of sharks. **Structure** Board of Trustees; Advisory Board; International Leaders. **Publications** *Member Newsletter* (4 a year); *Conservation Alerts* (irregular). **Information Services** *Global Shark Attack File*. [2020/XJ2240/j/**F**]

- ♦ Shark Trust (internationally oriented national body)
- ♦ **SHARP** Society for the History of Authorship, Reading and Publishing (#19570)
- ♦ **SHA** Self Help Africa (#19220)
- ♦ SHATiS – International Conference on Structural Health Assessment of Timber Structures (meeting series)
- ♦ SHCJ – Society of the Holy Child Jesus (religious order)
- ♦ SHC – Sensorial Handicap Cooperation (internationally oriented national body)
- ♦ **SHD Coalition** Structural Heart Disease Coalition (#20013)
- ♦ Shear Stress Symposium – International Symposium on Biomechanics in Vascular Biology and Cardiovascular Disease (meeting series)
- ♦ Sheet Metal Workers' International Alliance / see International Association of Sheet Metal, Air, Rail and Transportation Workers
- ♦ Sheet Metal Workers' International Association / see International Association of Sheet Metal, Air, Rail and Transportation Workers
- ♦ SHELA – Sociedad de Historia de la Educación Latinoamericana (unconfirmed)
- ♦ Sheldrick Wildlife Trust (internationally oriented national body)
- ♦ Shell Foundation (internationally oriented national body)
- ♦ **Shelter-Afrique** Company for Habitat and Housing in Africa (#04408)
- ♦ Shelter Asia / see Asian Network of Women's Shelters (#01562)
- ♦ ShelterBox (internationally oriented national body)
- ♦ Shelter Centre (unconfirmed)
- ♦ Shelter for Life (internationally oriented national body)
- ♦ Shelter Now International / see Shelter for Life
- ♦ SHE network / see Schools for Health in Europe network foundation (#19133)
- ♦ Shen Foundation / see Spirit Health Education Network
- ♦ SHEN – Spirit Health Education Network (internationally oriented national body)
- ♦ Sherpa (internationally oriented national body)
- ♦ **SHE** Schools for Health in Europe network foundation (#19133)
- ♦ **SHE** Solar Heat Europe (#19674)
- ♦ SHFA – Special Health Fund for Africa (no recent information)
- ♦ **SHF** Fonds pour l'Assainissement et l'Hygiène (#19050)
- ♦ **SHF** The Sanitation & Hygiene Fund (#19050)
- ♦ SHIA / see MyRight – Empower People with Disabilities

♦ Shift2Rail Joint Undertaking (Shift2Rail JU) 19261

Exec Dir White Atrium Bldg, 2nd Floor, Avenue de la Toison d'Or 56-60, 1060 Brussels, Belgium.
URL: https://shift2rail.org/

History 16 Jun 2014. Established by *Council of the European Union (#04895)* Regulation No 642/2014. Will be succeeded by *European Partnership on Rail Research and Innovation*. **Aims** Deliver, through railway research and innovation, the capabilities to bring about the most sustainable, cost-efficient, high-performing, time driven, digital and competitive customer-centred transport mode for Europe. **Structure** Governing BOard; Executive Director; States Representatives Group; Scientific Committee. **NGO Relations** Member of (1): *EU Agencies Network (EUAN, #05564)*. [2021/AA1430/**E**]

- ♦ **Shift2Rail JU** Shift2Rail Joint Undertaking (#19261)
- ♦ Shikuri Project (internationally oriented national body)
- ♦ SHILAP – Sociedad Hispano-Luso-Americana de Lepidopterologia (no recent information)
- ♦ Shiloah Centre for Middle Eastern and African Studies / see Moshe Dayan Centre for Middle Eastern and African Studies
- ♦ SHIM – Society for Humanism in Medicine (no recent information)
- ♦ Shipchartering Coordinating Bureau (inactive)
- ♦ Ship News Club / see World Ship Society (#21782)
- ♦ Ship and Ocean Foundation / see Ocean Policy Research Institute
- ♦ SHIRBRIG – Multinational Stand-by Readiness Brigade for United Nations Operations (inactive)

♦ Shiromani Gurdwara Parbandhak Committee (SGPC) 19262

Pres Teja Singh Samundri Hall, Sri Harmandar Sahib Complex, Amritsar, Punjab 143001, Amritsar PUNJAB 143001, India. T. +911832553950. E-mail: info@sgpc.net – president@sgpc.net.
Sec address not obtained.
URL: https://sgpc.net/

History 15 Nov 1920, Amritsar (India). Former names and other names: *Sikh Gurdwara Parbandhak Committee (SGPC)* – former (15 Nov 1920). Registration: The Sikh Gurdwaras Act 1925. **Aims** Administer *Sikh religious* and *cultural* institutions worldwide. **Languages** English, Hindi, Punjabi. [2022.06.21/XJ7034/**E**]

- ♦ SHJM – Sisters of the Sacred Hearts of Jesus and Mary (religious order)
- ♦ Shoah Foundation / see USC Shoah Foundation Institute for Visual History and Education
- ♦ Shoah Memorial (internationally oriented national body)
- ♦ Shooting Confederation of the Americas (#04439)
- ♦ Shop Environments Association (internationally oriented national body)
- ♦ Shop! – Shop Environments Association (internationally oriented national body)
- ♦ Shorenstein APARC – Walter H Shorenstein Asia-Pacific Research Center (internationally oriented national body)
- ♦ Shotokan Karate International Federation / see Shotokan Karate-Do International Federation (#19263)

♦ Shotokan Karate-Do International Federation (SKIF) 19263

Pres c/o Dr Philip Kwok, 7th Floor, Wing On Centre, 211 Des Voeux Road Central, Hong Kong, Central and Western, Hong Kong. T. +85228521827. Fax +85225412585. E-mail: info@skif-yudansha-kai.com – mail@rickywan.com.
URL: http://www.skif-yudansha-kai.com/

History Also referred to as *Shotokan Karate International Federation* and as *Shotokan Karate Kanazawa-Ryu International Federation (SKKIF)*. **Aims** Further and develop shotokan karate following the teachings of Kanazawa Shihan. **Activities** Organizes championships and seminars. [2008/XE4738/**E**]

- ♦ Shotokan Karate Kanazawa-Ryu International Federation / see Shotokan Karate-Do International Federation (#19263)
- ♦ **SHOT** Society for the History of Technology (#19571)
- ♦ Shrimati Pushpa Wati Loomba Memorial Trust / see The Loomba Trust – The Loomba Foundation (#16514)
- ♦ Shrine of North America / see Shriners International
- ♦ Shriners International (internationally oriented national body)
- ♦ SHRL – Scandinavian Human Rights Lawyers (internationally oriented national body)
- ♦ SHRM – Society for Human Resource Management (internationally oriented national body)
- ♦ SHR – Sisters of the Holy Redeemer (religious order)
- ♦ **SHS-AS** International Association on Self-Propagating High-Temperature Synthesis (#12158)
- ♦ SHSKI – Students Helping Street Kids International (internationally oriented national body)
- ♦ Shundahai Network (internationally oriented national body)
- ♦ SHVD – Society for Heart Valve Disease (inactive)
- ♦ SIA / see School of International and Public Affairs, New York NY
- ♦ SIA / see World Space Week Association
- ♦ SIABC – Sociedad Iberoamericana de Biologia Celular (inactive)
- ♦ **SIACE** Société Islamique pour l'Assurance des Investissements et des Crédits à l'Exportation (#16041)
- ♦ **SIACRE** Sociedad Iberoamericana y del Caribe de Restauración Ecológica (#19362)
- ♦ SIAC – Singapore International Arbitration Centre (internationally oriented national body)
- ♦ **SIAC** Sociedade Interamericana de Cardiologia (#11448)
- ♦ **SIAC** Sociedad Interamericana de Cardiologia (#11448)
- ♦ **SIAC** Société internationale des artistes chrétiens (#15009)
- ♦ **SIADEB** Sociedade Ibero-Americana para o Desenvolvimento das Biorefinarias (#19363)
- ♦ **SIADEB** Sociedad Iberoamericana para el Desarrollo de las Biorrefinarias (#19363)

- ♦ SIADTP – Sociedad Iberoamericana de Diagnóstico y Tratamiento Prenatal (no recent information)
- ♦ SIAEAC – Société internationale africaine pour la réalisation de l'Encyclopédie politique, économique, sociale et culturelle de l'Afrique contemporaine (no recent information)
- ♦ SIAEG / see Ibero-American Society of Gynecological Endoscopy and Images (#11030)
- ♦ **SIAEGI** Sociedad Iberoamericana de Endoscopia Ginecológica e Imagenes (#11030)
- ♦ **SIAEN** Sociedad Iberoamericana de Estudios Numismaticos (#19367)
- ♦ SIAE – Sociedade Interamericana de Administração da Educação (inactive)
- ♦ SIAE – Sociedad Interamericana de Administración de la Educación (inactive)
- ♦ SIAE – Société interaméricaine d'administration de l'éducation (inactive)
- ♦ **SIAF** Soroptimist International Africa Federation (#19687)
- ♦ **SIAGUA** Sistema Iberoamericano de Información sobre el Agua (#19295)
- ♦ SIAI – Sociedad Iberoamericana de Infectologia (unconfirmed)
- ♦ SIALF – Société internationale des acarologues de langue française (inactive)
- ♦ **SIAME** Sociedad Ibero-Americana de Metodologia Económica (#19374)
- ♦ SIAM – Société internationale des amis de Montaigne (internationally oriented national body)
- ♦ SIAM – Society for Industrial and Applied Mathematics (internationally oriented national body)
- ♦ SIAMU – Secretariado Iberoamericano de Municipios (no recent information)
- ♦ SIAOL – Sociedad Iberoamericana de Ortodoncia Lingual, Oclusión y Estética (no recent information)
- ♦ **SIAO** Sociedad Iberoamericana de Oculoplastica (#19376)
- ♦ SIAP – Sociedade Interamericana de Planificación (inactive)
- ♦ **SIAP** Statistical Institute for Asia and the Pacific (#19972)
- ♦ **SIAQ** Sociedad Iberoamericana de Quitina (#19378)
- ♦ SIARCT – Syndicat international des auteurs de radio, cinéma et télévision (inactive)
- ♦ SIARs – Simposio Internacional de Arte Rupestre (meeting series)

♦ SI Asia-Pacific Committee 19264

Contact c/o Socialist International, PO Box 67973, London, SW4 4DU, UK. T. +442076274449. E-mail: secretariat@socialistinternational.org.
URL: http://www.socialistinternational.org/

History Feb 1983, by the Council of *Socialist International (SI, #19340)*. Took over activities of *Asia-Pacific Socialist Organization (APSO, inactive)*.
Members Socialist member parties (21) in 18 countries:
Australia, Fiji, France, Greece, Israel (2), Italy (2), Japan (2), Malaysia, Mauritius, Mongolia, Nepal, New Zealand, Pakistan, Philippines, Spain, Sweden, Türkiye, UK. [2011/XE2945/**E**]

- ♦ SIAS / see NIAS-Nordisk Institut for Asienstudier (#17132)
- ♦ SIAS / see Nordic Africa Institute (#17168)
- ♦ SIA – Société internationale d'acupuncture, (inactive)
- ♦ **SIA** Société internationale arthurienne (#11671)
- ♦ SIA / see Soroptimist International (#19686)
- ♦ **SIA** Soroptimist International of the Americas (#19688)
- ♦ SIASS – Scuola Internazionale Ambiente Salute e Sviluppo Sostenibile (internationally oriented national body)
- ♦ Siaures Investiciju Bankas (#17327)
- ♦ **SIBAE** Sociedad Iberoamericana de Electroquimica (#19364)
- ♦ SIBAG – Sociedad Iberoamericana de Glaucoma (unconfirmed)
- ♦ **SIBC** Société internationale de bibliographie classique (#19474)
- ♦ SIBC / see World Association of Societies of Pathology and Laboratory Medicine (#21191)
- ♦ **SIBEN** Sociedad Ibero-Americana de Neonatologia (#11031)
- ♦ **SIBF** Society of International Business Fellows (#19580)
- ♦ **SIBIM** Sociedad Iberoamericana de Imagen Mamaria (#19371)
- ♦ **SIBIOS** Société internationale de biospéologie (#14975)
- ♦ **SIBI** Sociedad Internacional de Bioética (#14961)
- ♦ **SIBI** Société internationale de la bioéthique (#14961)
- ♦ **SIBMAS** Société internationale des bibliothèques et des musées des arts du spectacle (#19475)
- ♦ SIBM – Société internationale de biologie mathématique (inactive)
- ♦ **SIBOMM** Sociedad Iberoamericana de Osteologia y Metabolismo Mineral (#11032)
- ♦ **SIBR** Society of Interdisciplinary Business Research (#19578)
- ♦ **SIB** Société internationale de biométéorologie (#14969)
- ♦ SIBU – Scandinavian Independent Baptist Union (inactive)
- ♦ SICA / see Dutch Centre for International Cooperation
- ♦ **SICA** Sistema de la Integración Centroamericana (#03671)
- ♦ **SICA** Subud International Cultural Association (#20029)
- ♦ **SICCMI** Sociedad Interamericana de Cirugia de Columa Minimamente Invasiva (#19383)
- ♦ SICFP – Scandinavian International Conference on Fluid Power (meeting series)
- ♦ Sicherung der Landwirtschaftlichen Arten Vielfalt in Europa (#19027)
- ♦ **SIC ICWC** Scientific Information Centre of Interstate Coordination Water Commission of Central Asia (#19152)
- ♦ SICI / see Standing International Conference of Inspectorates (#19963)
- ♦ **SICI** Standing International Conference of Inspectorates (#19963)
- ♦ SickKids International (internationally oriented national body)
- ♦ In Sickness and In Health International Conference (meeting series)
- ♦ SICMI – Société internationale pour le check-up médical interdisciplinaire (inactive)
- ♦ **SICOFAA** Sistema de Cooperación entre las Fuerzas Aéreas Americanas (#19293)
- ♦ **SICOT** Société internationale de chirurgie orthopédique et de traumatologie (#15335)
- ♦ **SICRI Network** Small Island Cultures Research Initiative (#19313)
- ♦ SICSAL – Secretariado Internacional Cristiano de Solidaridad con América Latina 'Oscar A Romero' (internationally oriented national body)
- ♦ SICSA – Vidal Sassoon International Center for the Study of Antisemitism (internationally oriented national body)
- ♦ SICS / see International Union of Soil Sciences (#15817)
- ♦ SIC – Sociedad Interamericana de Counseling (unconfirmed)
- ♦ SIC – Société internationale de la céphalée (inactive)
- ♦ **SIC** Société internationale de chirurgie (#15496)
- ♦ **SIC** Société internationale de criminologie (#15038)
- ♦ SICTA – Sistema de Ciencia y Tecnologia Agroindustrial (no recent information)
- ♦ SICTA – Sociedade Iberoamericana de Contaminação e Toxicologia Ambiental (unconfirmed)
- ♦ SICTA – Sociedad Iberoamericana de Contaminación y Toxicologgia Ambientales (unconfirmed)
- ♦ Sida – Swedish International Development Cooperation Agency (internationally oriented national body)
- ♦ **SIDC** Solar Influences Data Analysis Centre (#19675)
- ♦ SIDEFCOOP – Sociedad Interamericana de Desarrollo de Financiamiento Cooperativo (inactive)
- ♦ SIDEME – Sociedad Iberoamericana de Derecho Médico (no recent information)

♦ Side by Side 19265

International Coordinator address not obtained.

History Founded at the instigation of *Christian Aid*, Mar 2015. Subtitle: *Faith Movement for Gender Justice*. **Aims** Shift values, beliefs, attitudes, behaviours and practices to recognize gender inequality as unacceptable and contrary to religious teaching and practice; help ensure that community level faith responses to gender injustice are more effective and sustainable, that legal systems recognize, prevent and adequately respond to gender injustice and that gender justice is an explicit aim both of religious institutions and governments; work to ensure that faith actors are no longer seen as a barrier to gender justice, but are recognized and supported to play a distinctive role in securing gender justice and the rights of both women and men, boys and girls. **Structure** Steering Group. **Publications** *Side by Side Newsletter*.
Members Regional coalitions for:
East Africa; Europe; Latin America and the Caribbean; Southern Africa; West Africa.

Sub-regional and national coalitions in 14 countries and territories:
Bolivia, Brazil, Burundi, Congo DR, Ghana, Haiti, Kenya, Malawi, Nigeria, Scotland, South Sudan, Tanzania UR, Uganda, Zimbabwe.
Organizations include 23 organizations listed in this Yearbook:
- *Anglican Alliance (#00822)*;
- *Anglican Communion (#00827)*;
- *Catholic Agency for Overseas Development (CAFOD)*;
- *CBE International*;
- *Christian Aid*;
- *Churches for Middle East Peace (CMEP)*;
- *Ecumenical Forum of European Christian Women (EFECW, #05347)*;
- *Ekklesia Foundation for Gender Education (EFOGE)*;
- *Episcopal Relief and Development*;
- *Fellowship of Christian Councils and Churches in the Great Lakes and Horn of Africa (FECCLAHA, #09723)*;
- *Finn Church Aid (FCA)*;
- *Folkekirkens Nødhjaelp (FKN)*;
- *Latin American Council of Churches (LACC, #16309)*;
- *Methodist Church of Southern Africa*;
- *Norwegian Church Aid*;
- *Pan African Christian Women Alliance (PACWA, #18043)*;
- *PMU Interlife*;
- *Restored*;
- *Sonke Gender Justice Network*;
- *We Will Speak Out (WWSO)*;
- *World Council of Churches (WCC, #21320)*;
- *World Evangelical Alliance (WEA, #21393)*;
- *World Vision International (WVI, #21904)*.

NGO Relations Member of (1): *International Partnership on Religion and Sustainable Development (PaRD, #14524)*. [2018/XM7728/y/**F**]

- ♦ **SIDF** Société Internationale de Diachronie du Français (#19476)
- ♦ **SIDG** Société Internationale de Dialectologie et Géolinguistique (#19477)
- ♦ **SIDH** Service international pour les droits de l'homme (#14841)
- ♦ **SIDH** Servicio Internacional para los Derechos Humanos (#14841)
- ♦ **SIDH** Sociedad Internacional para los Derechos Humanos (#15183)
- ♦ **SIDH** Société internationale pour les droits de l'homme (#15183)
- ♦ SIDI / see International Solidarity for Development and Investment
- ♦ **SIDIIEF** Secrétariat international des infirmières et infirmiers de l'espace francophone (#19202)
- ♦ **SIDI** Sociedad Iberoamericana de Intervencionismo (#19373)
- ♦ SIDI – Solidarité internationale pour le développement et l'investissement (internationally oriented national body)
- ♦ SIDO – Société internationale pour le développement des organisations (inactive)
- ♦ **SIDS DOCK** Small Island Developing States – Island Energy for Island Life (#19314)
- ♦ **SIDSnet** Small Island Developing States Network (#19315)
- ♦ **SID** Sociedad Internacional para el Desarrollo (#19581)
- ♦ **SID** Société internationale pour le développement (#19581)
- ♦ SID – Society for Information Display (internationally oriented national body)
- ♦ **SID** Society for International Development (#19581)
- ♦ **SIDS** Société internationale de défense sociale pour une politique criminelle humaniste (#15447)
- ♦ SIDS – Société internationale de droit social (inactive)
- ♦ **SID** Syndicat international du décolletage (#20080)
- ♦ **SIDTSS** Sociedad Internacional de Derecho del Trabajo y de la Seguridad Social (#15226)
- ♦ **SIDTSS** Société internationale de Droit du Travail et de la Sécurité Sociale (#15226)
- ♦ **SIDUO** Societas Internationalis de Diagnostica Ultrasonica in Ophthalmologia (#19443)
- ♦ **SIECA** Secretaria Permanente del Tratado General de Integración Económica Centroamericana (#19195)
- ♦ SIECD – Société internationale d'éducation continue en dentisterie (inactive)
- ♦ **SIEC** Société internationale pour l'enseignement commercial (#19479)
- ♦ **SIECV** Sociedad Iberoamericana de Enfermedad Cerebrovascular (#19365)
- ♦ **SIED** Sociedad Interamericana de Endoscopia Digestiva (#19384)
- ♦ **SIEDS** Société internationale d'étude du dix-huitième siècle (#15076)
- ♦ **SIEEC** Societas Internationalis Entomofaunistica Europae Centralis (#19444)
- ♦ SIEE – Sistema de Información Económica-Energética (see: #16313)
- ♦ **SIEFAR** Société Internationale pour l'Etude des Femmes de l'Ancien Régime (#19482)
- ♦ **SIEF** Société internationale d'ethnologie et de folklore (#19481)
- ♦ **SIEH** Sociedad Iberoamericana de Estudios Heideggerianos (#19366)
- ♦ SIEK – Sociedad Iberoamericana de Estudios Kierkegaardianos (unconfirmed)
- ♦ Siemenpuu Foundation (internationally oriented national body)
- ♦ Siemens Stiftung (internationally oriented national body)
- ♦ **SIEN** Société Internationale d'Études Néroniennes (#19484)
- ♦ **SIEPM** Société internationale pour l'étude de la philosophie médiévale (#19483)
- ♦ SIEPS – Svenska Institutet för Europapolitiska Studier (internationally oriented national body)

♦ Sierra Club International Program 19266

Contact 2101 Webster St, Ste 1300, Oakland CA 94612, USA. T. +14159775500. Fax +15102083140. E-mail: information@sierraclub.org.
URL: http://www.sierraclub.org/international/

History 1972, as the international arm of *Sierra Club (SC)*, a US body set up in 1892. **Aims** Protect the earth's *wild places*; promote responsible use of the earth's *ecosystems* and *resources*; protect and restore the quality of *natural* and human *environment*. **Languages** English. **Staff** 250.00 FTE, paid. **Finance** Members' dues. Grants; sales of publications. Budget (annual): US$ 40 million. **Activities** Advocacy/lobbying/activism. **Events** *Conservation and the environment* Ann Arbor, MI (USA) 1989. **Publications** *Sierra Magazine* (6 a year); *The Planet* (6 a year). Calendars; books.
Members Individuals, primarily North American, although over 600 individuals outside this region. Members in 73 countries. 5 or more members in each of the 27 following countries and territories:
Australia, Austria, Belgium, Brazil, Canada, Denmark, France, Germany, Hong Kong, Indonesia, Israel, Italy, Japan, Kenya, Mexico, Netherlands, New Zealand, Norway, Saudi Arabia, South Africa, Spain, Sweden, Switzerland, Thailand, UK, USA, Venezuela.
Consultative Status Consultative status granted from: *ECOSOC (#05331)* (Ros B). **IGO Relations** Observer to: *Committee of International Development Institutions on the Environment (CIDIE, no recent information)*. Associated with Department of Global Communications of the United Nations. **NGO Relations** Member of: *Antarctic and Southern Ocean Coalition (ASOC, #00849)*; *EarthAction (EA, #05159)*; *Earthcare Network (no recent information)*; *Global 100% RE (#10160)*; *Environment Liaison Centre International (ELCI, no recent information)*. Partner of: *Global Call for Climate Action (GCCA, inactive)*. [2017/XF1878/**E**]

- ♦ Sierra Club Legal Defense Fund / see Earthjustice
- ♦ Siervas del Corazón de Jesús (religious order)
- ♦ Siervas de Jesús de la Caridad (religious order)
- ♦ Siervas de Maria, Ministras de los Enfermos (religious order)
- ♦ Siervas Pobres de Jesucristo (religious order)
- ♦ Siervos Misioneros de la Santisima Trinidad (religious order)
- ♦ SIESC – Europäische Föderation Christlicher Lehrer/innen (#19267)

♦ SIESC – European Federation of Christian Teachers 19267

SIESC – Fédération européenne d'enseignants chrétiens – SIESC – Europäische Föderation Christlicher Lehrer/innen

Contact Markt 210, 2880 Kirchberg am Wechsel, Austria. E-mail: info@siesc.eu.
Registered Address 10 rue de l'Isle, 10000 Troyes, France.
URL: http://www.siesc.eu/

History 1954. Founded as a Specialized Secretariat of *Pax Romana, International Catholic Movement for Intellectual and Cultural Affairs (ICMICA, #18267).* Former names and other names: *International Secretariat of Catholic Secondary School Teachers* – former (1954); *Secrétariat international des enseignants secondaires catholiques (SIESC)* – former (1954); *Internationales Sekretariat katholischer Sekundarschullehrer* – former (1954); *European Association of Christian Teachers* – former. **Aims** Provide a European platform to promote the aims of national associations of Christian teachers; welcome colleagues of other denominations, religions or without religious denomination as guests; promote their cooperation and friendship; emphasize the close connection between professional and religious life. **Structure** Council; Executive Board. **Languages** English, French, German. **Staff** Voluntary. **Finance** Members' dues. **Activities** Events/meetings. **Events** *Annual Meeting* Gothenburg (Sweden) 2023, *Annual Meeting* Tirana (Albania) 2022, *Annual Meeting* Tainach-Tinje (Austria) 2019, *Annual Meeting* Trier (Germany) 2018, *Annual Meeting* Vichy (France) 2017. **Publications** *SIESC-Today* (2 a year) in English, French, German.
Members National associations in 10 countries:
Austria, Croatia, Czechia, France, Germany, Italy, Poland, Romania, Slovakia, Slovenia.
Individuals in 10 countries:
Belarus, Belgium, Bosnia-Herzegovina, Luxembourg, Norway, Serbia, Spain, Sweden, UK, Ukraine.
NGO Relations *Pax Romana, International Catholic Movement for Intellectual and Cultural Affairs (ICMICA, #18267); UMEC-WUCT (#20280).* [2022/XE2592/**E**]

- ♦ SIESC – Fédération européenne d'enseignants chrétiens (#19267)
- ♦ SIESC / see SIESC – European Federation of Christian Teachers (#19267)
- ♦ **SIE** Secrétariat international de l'eau (#14822)
- ♦ **SIE** Societas Iranologica Europaea (#19446)
- ♦ **SIE** Société internationale d'ethnographie (#19480)
- ♦ **SI/E** Soroptimist International of Europe (#19689)

♦ SIETAR-Europa 19268

Sec Résidences de l'Argentière – Bât E, 637 bd de la Tavernière, 06210 Mandelieu-La Napoule, France. T. +33493933659. Fax +447053492020. E-mail: communication@sietareu.org.
URL: http://www.sietareu.org/

History 1991, Haarlem (Netherlands), within *International Society for Intercultural Education, Training and Research (SIETAR-International, inactive).* Following disbanding of SIETAR-International in 1999, acts as administrative hub to coordinate activities of regional and local SIETA groups. **Aims** Encourage development and application of knowledge, values and skills which enable effective intercultural and interethnic relations at individual, group, organization and community levels. **Structure** Annual General Meeting; Board; Executive Committee; Rotating Presidency; Committees (2). **Languages** English. **Staff** 0.50 FTE, paid. **Finance** Members' dues. Other sources: donations; sponsorship. **Activities** Events/meetings. **Events** *Biennial Congress* Leuven (Belgium) 2019, *Biennial Congress* Dublin (Ireland) 2017, *Annual Congress* Valencia (Spain) 2015, *Biennial Congress* Tallinn (Estonia) 2013, *Biennial Congress* Krakow (Poland) 2011. **Publications** *Sietar Europa Journal.*
Members Full; Associate; Honorary; Sustaining. Individuals in 22 countries:
Austria, Belarus, Belgium, Bulgaria, Croatia, Czechia, Denmark, Estonia, Finland, France, Germany, Greece, Hungary, Ireland, Italy, Luxembourg, Netherlands, Norway, Poland, Spain, Türkiye, UK.
IGO Relations *Council of Europe (CE, #04881); ECOSOC (#05331); UNESCO (#20322).* [2017.10.27/XE2513/**E**]

- ♦ SIETI – Secrétariat international des étudiants en traduction et en interprétation (no recent information)
- ♦ **SIEU** Sociedad Iberoamericana de Estudios Utilitaristas (#19368)
- ♦ **SIEY** Société internationale d'études yourcenariennes (#19485)
- ♦ SIFCP – Société internationale francophone de chirurgie pelvienne (inactive)
- ♦ SIFE / see Enactus (#05451)
- ♦ **SIFÉE** Secrétariat international francophone pour l'évaluation environnementale (#19201)
- ♦ **SIFEM** Société internationale francophone d'éducation médicale (#19487)
- ♦ SIFEM – Swiss Investment Fund for Emerging Markets (internationally oriented national body)
- ♦ **SIFIV** Société Internationale pour la Fécondation In Vitro (#15545)
- ♦ **SIFoCC** Standing International Forum of Commercial Courts (#19964)
- ♦ **SIFORL** Société internationale francophone d'ORL et de chirurgie cervico-faciale (#19488)
- ♦ SIFO – Société internationale de fluorophotométrie oculaire (no recent information)
- ♦ SIF – Singapore International Foundation (internationally oriented national body)
- ♦ **SIF** Sociedad Interamericana de Filosofia (#19385)
- ♦ **SIF** Sociedad Internacional del Ferrocemento (#13587)
- ♦ **SIF** Spoqcs International Federation (#19922)
- ♦ SIF – Starr International Foundation (internationally oriented national body)
- ♦ **SIFUD-PP** Société interdisciplinaire francophone d'urodynamique et de pelvi-périnéologie (#19473)
- ♦ SIFUD / see Société interdisciplinaire francophone d'urodynamique et de pelvi-périnéologie (#19473)
- ♦ **SiFyQA** Sociedad Iberoamericana de Fisica y Quimica Ambiental (#19369)
- ♦ **SIGA** Sport Integrity Global Alliance (#19925)
- ♦ **SIGBI** Soroptimist International of Great Britain and Ireland (#19690)
- ♦ **SIGEF** Sociedad Internacional de Gestión y Economia Fuzzy (#19386)
- ♦ SightLife (internationally oriented national body)

♦ Sight and Life 19269

Mailing Address PO Box 2116, 4002 Basel BS, Switzerland. T. +41618158756. E-mail: info@sightandlife.org.
Physical office DSM Nutrional Products Ltd, Building 241 / 365, Wurmisweg 576, 4303 Kaiseraugst AG, Switzerland.
URL: http://www.sightandlife.org/

History 1986. Founded following the famine in Ethiopia (current Eritrea), by RF Hoffman-LaRoche Ltd. Transferred to DSM, a Life Sciences and Materials Sciences company, 2003. From 2011 was part of the DSM Nutrition Science and Advocacy group. An independent foundation supported by DSM since 2015. Former names and other names: *Sight and Life Foundation* – full title. Registration: Start date: 2015, Switzerland. **Aims** Innovate in *nutrition* towards eradicating *malnutrition* in *women* of childbearing age and their *children*, and so improve the lives of the world's most vulnerable populations. **Structure** Steering Committee. **Languages** English, French, German. **Staff** 6.00 FTE, paid. **Finance** Financed by DSM. **Activities** Advocacy/lobbying/activism; capacity building; networking/liaising; humanitarian/emergency aid. **Publications** *Sight and Life* (2 a year) – magazine. Guidebooks; books; manuals; CDs; DVDs. **Members** Not a membership organizations. **NGO Relations** Cooperates with (1): *Micronutrient Forum (#16748).* [2021/XJ1813/**F**]

- ♦ Sight and Life Foundation / see Sight and Life (#19269)
- ♦ Sight Savers / see Sightsavers International (#19270)

♦ Sightsavers International 19270

UK Office Bumpers Way, Bumpers Farm, Chippenham, SN14 6NG, UK. E-mail: info@sightsavers.org.
URL: http://www.sightsavers.org/

History Jan 1950, London (UK). Founded through joint action of British and Commonwealth Governments and the Royal National Institute for the Blind (RNIB). Royal Charter of Incorporation (UK) 1990. Former names and other names: *British Empire Society for the Blind* – former (1950 to 1958); *Royal Commonwealth Society for the Blind (RCSB)* – former (1958 to 1988); *Sight Savers* – former (1988 to 2005). Registration: Charity Commission, No/ID: 207544, England and Wales; Charity Commission, No/ID: SC038110, Scotland. **Aims** Prevent sight loss and avoidable blindness in some of the poorest parts of the world by treating conditions such as cataracts and fighting debilitating eye diseases; campaign for disability rights and promote equal opportunities for people with disabilities; work with governments and local communities to tackle the problems at the root of avoidable blindness and support people who need it. **Structure** Council. **Languages** English, French, Portuguese. **Staff** 560.00 FTE, paid. **Finance** Majority of income comes through voluntary fundraising; some projects are jointly financed with other NGOs and UK Government. **Activities** Guidance/assistance/consulting; training/education; advocacy/lobbying/activism. **Events** *International meeting on the prevention of childhood blindness* London (UK) 1990. **Publications** *Sightsavers News.* Annual Review; Annual Accounts and Financial Statements. Project literature; videos.
Members Located in 7 countries:
Ireland, Italy, Norway, Sweden, UK, United Arab Emirates, USA.
Regional offices, individuals and partner agencies. Partner agencies in 31 countries:
Bangladesh, Benin, Burkina Faso, Cameroon, Chad, Congo Brazzaville, Congo DR, Côte d'Ivoire, Ethiopia, Gambia, Ghana, Guinea, Guinea-Bissau, India, Kenya, Liberia, Malawi, Mali, Mozambique, Nigeria, Pakistan, Senegal, Sierra Leone, South Sudan, Sudan, Tanzania UR, Togo, Uganda, Yemen, Zambia, Zimbabwe.
Consultative Status Consultative status granted from: *African Commission on Human and Peoples' Rights (ACHPR, #00255)* (Observer); *ECOSOC (#05331)* (Ros C); *WHO (#20950)* (Official Relations). **IGO Relations** Cooperates with: *Institute for Tropical Ophthalmology in Africa (IOTA, inactive); International Bank for Reconstruction and Development (IBRD, #12317); Pan American Health Organization (PAHO, #18108).*
NGO Relations Member of:
- *Accountable Now (#00060);*
- *British Overseas NGO's for Development (BOND);*
- *ECHO – International Health Services;*
- *End Water Poverty (EWP, #05464);*
- *Gavi – The Vaccine Alliance (Gavi, #10077)* CSO Constituency;
- *Global Health Workforce Alliance (GHWA, inactive);*
- *End Corporal Punishment (#05457);*
- *Global Partnership for Disability and Development (GPDD, #10530);*
- *Grow Up Free from Poverty Coalition;*
- *ILO Global Business and Disability Network (GBDN, #11122);*
- *InsideNGO (inactive);*
- *International Coalition for Trachoma Control (ICTC, #12624);*
- *International Council for Education of People with Visual Impairment (ICEVI, #13015);*
- *International Disability and Development Consortium (IDDC, #13177);*
- *National Council for Voluntary Organizations (NCVO);*
- *Neglected Tropical Diseased NGO Network (NNN, #16969);*
- *Partnership Committee to the WHO Programme for the Prevention of Blindness (Partnership Committee, no recent information);*
- *Philanthropy Impact;*
- *Transparency, Accountability and Participation Network (TAP Network, #20222);*
- *World Blind Union (WBU, #21234).*

Cooperates with: *Caribbean Council for the Blind (CCB, #03483); Light for the World (#16474); Seva Foundation (SF); Vision Aid Overseas (VAO).* [2020/XF3167/**F**]

- ♦ **SIGI** Sisterhood Is Global Institute (#19298)

♦ SIGMA Consortium 19271

Contact address not obtained. E-mail: info@sigmaconsortium.eu.
URL: https://sigmaconsortium.eu/

History 11 Nov 2020. Founded as a contract-based alliance of research centres of *European Network of Centres for Pharmacoepidemiology and Pharmacovigilance (ENCePP, #07875).* **Aims** Provide trusted pharmacoepidemiologic and real-world evidence (PE/RWE) research through a European federated professional network of excellence. **Structure** Executive Committee.
Members Research institutions in 7 countries:
Denmark, France, Germany, Italy, Netherlands, Spain, UK.
NGO Relations Partner of (1): *Vaccine monitoring Collaboration for Europe (VAC4EU, #20740).* [2022/AA3234/**D**]

♦ SIGMA Programme 19272

Head of Programme c/o OECD, 2 rue André Pascal, 75775 Paris CEDEX 16, France. T. +33145241537. Fax +33145241305.
URL: http://www.sigmaweb.org/

History Launched 1992, as a joint initiative of *OECD (#17693)* and *European Union (EU, #08967).* **Aims** Strengthen public *governance* systems and public administration capacities through assistance in: civil service management and administrative legal framework; public finance management and external audit; public procurement; policy making and coordination; public governance strategy and reform. **Structure** Head; Central Management Unit. Expert teams: EU pre-accession countries; EU Neighbourhood South countries; EU Neighbourhood East countries; Strategy and Reform. **Languages** English, French. **Staff** 36.00 FTE, paid. **Finance** Principally financed by the EU. **Activities** Assesses: governance systems and institutions; legal frameworks; reform strategies and action plans; progress in reform implementation. Provides: methodologies and tools to support reforms; recommendations on improving laws and administrative arrangements; advice on the design and implementation of reforms; opportunities to share good practice from a wide range of countries; policy papers and multi-country studies. Active in: Albania, Algeria, Armenia, Azerbaijan, Bosnia-Herzegovina, Croatia, Egypt, Georgia, Jordan, Kosovo, Lebanon, Moldova, Montenegro, Morocco, North Macedonia, Serbia, Tunisia, Türkiye, Ukraine. **Publications** *Sigma Papers* – series. Annual assessments; policy papers; policy briefs; seminar/workshop papers and presentations. **Members** Not a membership organization. [2015.10.01/XE4197/**E***]

- ♦ Sigma Theta Tau International (internationally oriented national body)

♦ Sigmund Freud Archives 19273

Exec Dir Dept of History, Otterbein Univ, Westerville OH 43081, USA.
URL: http://www.freudarchives.org/

History 1950. **Aims** Collect, conserve and provide access to archival materials related to Sigmund Freud (1856-1939) and related persons. [2016.06.01/XN0709/**E**]

- ♦ **SIGNEA** Society of International Gastroenterological Nurses and Endoscopy Associates (#19583)
- ♦ SIGNIS Africa (see: #21264)
- ♦ SIGNIS ALC – Asociación Católica Latinoamericana y Caribeña de Comunicación (see: #21264)
- ♦ SIGNIS ALC – Catholic Association for Latin American and Caribbean Communication (see: #21264)
- ♦ SIGNIS Asia (see: #21264)
- ♦ SIGNIS Europe (see: #21264)
- ♦ SIGNIS – Missionary Service / see SIGNIS Services Rome (#19274)
- ♦ SIGNIS Pacific (see: #21264)

♦ SIGNIS Services Rome (SSR) 19274

General Manager Palazzo San Calisto, 00120 Vatican City, Vatican. T. +39669887255. Fax +39669887335. E-mail: ssr@signis.net.
SIGNIS Gen Sec ad interim Rue Royale 310, 1210 Brussels, Belgium. T. +3227349708. Fax +3227347018. E-mail: sg@signis.net.
URL: http://www.signis.net

History Founded 1953, Rome (Italy), as the missionary body of *International Catholic Organization for Cinema and Audiovisual (OCIC, inactive).* Original title: *OCIC Missionary Service – Service missionnaire de l'OCIC – OCIC Servicio Misionero.* Previously also referred to as *Missionary Service of the International Catholic Organization for Cinema and Audio-Visual (SM-OCIC).* Current title adopted, 2001, on merger of OCIC with *Unda, International Catholic Association for Radio and Television (inactive),* to become *World Catholic Association for Communication (SIGNIS, #21264).* Previously also referred to as *SIGNIS – Missionary Service – Service missionnaire de SIGNIS – SIGNIS Servicio Misionero.* **Aims** Encourage the setting-up of national, regional and diocesan centres for the production, distribution and utilization of audiovisual materials to support the work of evangelization; help local churches obtain financial support for audiovisual and other communications projects; facilitate the purchase and supply of equipment, for both the production and the utilization of audiovisual materials; provide easy access to religious and other videos suitable for use by church workers in their task of evangelization and human promotion. **Languages** English, French, Spanish. **Activities** Guidance/assistance/consulting; training/education. [2018/XF2779/**F**]

- ♦ SIGNIS Servicio Misionero / see SIGNIS Services Rome (#19274)
- ♦ **SIGNIS** World Catholic Association for Communication (#21264)
- ♦ Sign Language Linguistics Society (internationally oriented national body)
- ♦ Signpost International (internationally oriented national body)
- ♦ **SIGN** Safe Injection Global Network (#19028)
- ♦ SIgN – Singapore Immunology Network (internationally oriented national body)

♦ **SIGNUM** International Society for Mark Studies (#15247)
♦ **SIGraDI** Sociedad Iberoamericana de Grafica Digital (#19370)
♦ Sigrid Rausing Trust (internationally oriented national body)
♦ **SIGTTO** Society of International Gas Tanker and Terminal Operators (#19582)
♦ **SIGTUR** Southern Initiative on Globalisation and Trade Union Rights (#19878)
♦ Sihai – Four Seas – Association for the Exchange of Culture and Science between East and West (no recent information)
♦ Sihai – Quatre Mers – Association pour les échanges culturels et scientifiques (no recent information)
♦ Sihai – Quattro Mari – Associazione per gli Scambi Culturali e Scientifici Est-Ovest (no recent information)
♦ Sihai – Vier Meere – Gesellschaft für Kulturellen und Wissenschaftlichen Ost-West Austausch (no recent information)
♦ Sihai – Vier Zeeën – Vereniging voor Uitwisséling van Cultuur en Wetenschap tussen Oost en West (no recent information)
♦ **SIHA** Senior International Health Association (#19228)
♦ **SIHA** Strategic Initiative for Women in the Horn of Africa (#20006)
♦ SIHDA / see Société internationale Fernand De Visscher pour l'histoire des droits de l'antiquité (#19486)
♦ **SIHFLES** Société internationale pour l'histoire du français langue étrangère ou seconde (#19489)
♦ **SIHM** Societas Internationalis Historiae Medicinae (#15171)
♦ **SIHM** Société Internationale d'Histoire de la Médecine (#15171)
♦ **SIH** Société internationale d'hématologie (#15159)
♦ **SIHSPAI** Société internationale d'histoire des sciences et de la philosophie arabes et islamiques (#19490)
♦ **SIIAEC** Secrétariat international des ingénieurs, des agronomes et des cadres économiques catholiques (#19203)
♦ SIIA – Singapore Institute of International Affairs (internationally oriented national body)
♦ SIIA – Software and Information Industry Association (internationally oriented national body)
♦ SIIA – Swedish Institute of International Affairs (internationally oriented national body)
♦ SIIC / see Secrétariat international des ingénieurs, des agronomes et des cadres économiques catholiques (#19203)
♦ **SIIC** Sociedad Iberoamericana de Información Cientifica (#19372)
♦ **Siinda** Search and Information Industry Association (#19188)
♦ SIIRDT / see International Centre for Women and Child
♦ SIIS Centre de documentation et de recherche (#19275)
♦ SIIS Centro de Documentación y Estudios (#19275)
♦ **SII** Siracusa International Institute for Criminal Justice and Human Rights (#19289)
♦ SII – Social-Impact International (unconfirmed)
♦ **SII** Société interaméricaine d'investissement (#11438)
♦ SIIS – Shanghai Institute for International Studies (internationally oriented national body)
♦ SIIS / see SIIS Social Information and Research Centre (#19275)

♦ SIIS Social Information and Research Centre 19275

SIIS Centre de documentation et de recherche – SIIS Centro de Documentación y Estudios

Main Office C/ General Etxagüe 10, E-20003 San Sebastian, Santa Cruz de Tenerife, Spain. T. +34943423656. Fax +34943293007. E-mail: documentacion@siis.net.
Documentation Centre Serrano 140, 28006 Madrid, Spain. T. +34917452446. Fax +34914115502.
General: http://www.siis.net/

History Founded 1972, San Sebastian (Spain). Original title: *International Information Service on Mental Retardation – Service international d'information sur l'arriération mentale – Servicio Internacional de Información sobre Subnormales (SIIS)*. Documentation Centre set up in Madrid (Spain), 1980. **Aims** Contribute to the improvement of social wellbeing policies, organization of social services and practice of all professionals in sectors involved in social care; offer all those interested, particularly institutions, professionals and research, a document collection service specializing in social policy and social services. **Structure** Libraries (2); reading rooms (2). **Languages** Basque, English, French, Spanish. **Staff** 20.00 FTE, paid. **Finance** Public funding. Budget (annual): euro 1 million. **Activities** Knowledge management/information dissemination; research/documentation. **Publications** *Boletin del Real Patronato*; *Boletin Gizarteratuz*; *Zerbitzuan*. Electronic bulletins on various topics. **Information Services** *Center for Information and Documentation on Drug-Abuse* – created 1992; *SIIS database* – social information at local, national and international levels; *SIIS legislation database* – local, regional and national Spanish legislation on social matters. **NGO Relations** Cooperates with: *Inclusion International (#11145)*; national organizations. [2016/XF2550/**E**]

♦ SIJORI / see Indonesia-Malaysia-Thailand Growth Triangle (#11167)
♦ SIK / see Samband Islenskra Kristnibodsfélaga
♦ Sikh Gurdwara Parbandhak Committee / see Shiromani Gurdwara Parbandhak Committee (#19262)
♦ SIKR / see International Society of Refractive Surgery of the American Academy of Ophthalmology (#15416)
♦ SIK – Samband Islenskra Kristnibodsfélaga (internationally oriented national body)
♦ **SILACO** Sociedad Iberolatinoamericana de Columna (#19380)
♦ SILADEPA – Sociedad Iberolatinoamericana de Dermatopatologia (inactive)
♦ **SILAE** Società Italo-Latino Americana di Etnomedicina (#19439)

♦ Silambam Asia 19276

Founder 9, Jalan USJ 2/2B,, UEP Subang Jaya,, 47600 Petaling Jaya, Selangor, Malaysia. T. +601112347370.
URL: http://silambam.asia/

History 22 Nov 1999. Registration: Ministry of Home Affairs (JPPM), No/ID: PPM-004-10-25112016, Start date: 25 Nov 2016, Malaysia; Accounting and Corporate Regulatory Authority (ACRA), No/ID: 53269224A, Start date: 1 Aug 2014, Singapore. **Aims** Play an active role as an international organization for the development of the Indian Traditional Arts; provide expertise in Training, Research, Revive, Rejuvenate, Retention, and Restore for members and worldwide community. **Structure** General Assembly; Board Committee (Management and Executive Committee); Foreign Committee/National Representatives (Non-Voting). **Languages** English, Malay, Tamil. **Staff** 21.00 FTE, voluntary. **Finance** Sources: meeting proceeds; members' dues; revenue from activities/projects. **Activities** Awards/prizes/competitions; awareness raising; certification/accreditation; events/meetings; financial and/or material support; guidance/assistance/consulting; knowledge management/information dissemination; research/documentation; sporting activities; standards/guidelines; training/education. Active in all member countries.
Members International, Continental, National, State, Associations, Federations, Schools or Institutions, Organizations, Clubs, Students, Instructors, Teachers, Honorary and National Representatives from 12 countries:
Bangladesh, Cambodia, India, Japan, Malaysia, Maldives, Philippines, Saudi Arabia, Singapore, Sri Lanka, Thailand, United Arab Emirates.
Consultative Status Consultative status granted from: *ECOSOC (#05331)* (Consultative Status – Special). **IGO Relations** Cooperates with (3): *International Monetary Fund (IMF, #14180)*; *Internet Governance Forum (IGF, #15950)* (Civil Society/MGoS); *UNESCO (#20322)* (Intangible Cultural Heritage (ICH-UNESCO)). Cooperation agreements with: national governmental organizations and international organizations. **NGO Relations** Supports (5): *General Association of Asia Pacific Sports Federations (GAAPSF, #10106)*; *International Council of Sport Science and Physical Education (ICSSPE, #13077)*; *International Sport Network Organization (ISNO, #15592)*; Sport Academy Europe; *The Association for International Sport for All (TAFISA, #02763)*. Also links with national associations. [2022.09.21/XM5853/**D**]

♦ **SILAN** Sociedad Iberolatinoamericana de Neurorradiologia Diagnostica y Terapéutica (#19381)
♦ SILAP – Super Intense Laser-Atom Physics Conference (meeting series)
♦ **SILAT** Sociedad Iberolatinoamericana de Aterosclerosis (#19379)
♦ **SILAUHE** Sociedad Iberolatinoamericana Ulceras y Heridas (#19382)
♦ **SILBA** Société internationale Leon Battista Alberti (#19491)
♦ **SILC** Société internationale de littérature courtoise (#13100)
♦ SILC – Swedish International Liberal Centre (internationally oriented national body)
♦ SILEC – Sociedad Interamericana para la Libertad de Expresión Comercial (no recent information)
♦ **SILF** Société internationale de linguistique fonctionnelle (#19492)

♦ Silicon Europe 19277

Contact Silicon Saxony Management GmbH, Manfred-von-Ardenne-Ring 20, 01099 Dresden, Germany. T. +493518925800. E-mail: info@silicon-europe.eu.
URL: http://www.silicon-europe.eu/

History 2012. Set up within the project 'Silicon Europe – Developing a leading-edge European micro- and nanoelectronics cluster'. On termination of project, Oct 2015, *Silicon Europe Alliance* set up as a non-funded continuation of the project. **Aims** Represent, support and promote companies and organizations of regional business networks at European and global levels; act as an intermediary between relevant partners from research and academia, public authorities and industry. **Structure** Steering Committee; Chairman. A European Cluster Alliance. **Languages** English. **Staff** 25.00 FTE, voluntary. **Finance** Sources: members' dues. **Activities** Advocacy/lobbying/activism; events/meetings; guidance/assistance/consulting; knowledge management/information dissemination; networking/liaising; projects/programmes; research and development; research/documentation; training/education. Active in: Austria, Belgium, China, France, Germany, Ireland, Italy, Korea Rep, Netherlands, Spain, Sweden, Taiwan, USA.
Members Full in 9 countries:
Austria, France, Germany, Ireland, Italy, Netherlands, Spain, Sweden, UK. [2023.02.21/XM7317/**D**]

♦ Silicon Europe Alliance / see Silicon Europe (#19277)

♦ SIL International 19278

Contact 7500 W Camp Wisdom Rd, Dallas TX 75236-5629, USA. T. +19727087400. Fax +19727087350. E-mail: info_sil@sil.org.
URL: http://www.sil.org/

History 1934. Language research and development started in the Americas during late 1930s; work in Asia-Pacific commenced in Philippines, 1953, in Africa in 1962 and parts of Europe in 1974. In 2006 took over activities of *SIL UK International Programmes (inactive)*. Former names and other names: *Summer Institute of Linguistics* – former. **Aims** Advocate, build capacity and work with local communities to apply language expertise that advances meaningful development, education and engagement with Scripture. **Activities** Awareness raising; capacity building; guidance/assistance/consulting; knowledge management/information dissemination; publishing activities; research/documentation; training/education. **Events** *Celebrating 100 Years of Partnership* Antigua (Guatemala) 2019, *Inclusion, Mobility, and Multilingual Education Conference* Bangkok (Thailand) 2019, *International Language Assessment Conference* Penang (Malaysia) 2018, *International Conference on Language and Education* Bangkok (Thailand) 2016, *Conference on language development, language revitalization and multilingual education in minority communities in Asia* Bangkok (Thailand) 2003. **Publications** *Ethnologue*. Annual Update; reports. **Consultative Status** Consultative status granted from: *UNESCO (#20322)* (Consultative Status); *ECOSOC (#05331)* (Special). [2021.06.30/XG4251/**C**]

♦ SIL / see International Society of Limnology (#15232)

♦ Silkroad 19279

Exec Dir 175 North Harvard St, Boston MA 02134, USA. T. +16174968888. E-mail: hello@silkroad.org.
Deputy Dir address not obtained.
URL: http://www.silkroad.org/

History Set up 1998. Full title: *The Silk Road Project*. A US 501(c)(3) not-for-profit organization. **Aims** Create *music* that engages difference, sparking radical cultural collaboration and passion-driven learning. **Structure** Board of Directors. Includes *Silkroad Ensemble*. **Finance** Revenue from activities; grants and contributions. **Activities** Projects/programmes. [2021/XM6780/**F**]

♦ The Silk Road Project / see Silkroad (#19279)

♦ Silk Road Think Tank Network (SiLKS) 19280

Secretariat address not obtained. T. +861051780902. Fax +861065236060. E-mail: silks.secretariat@outlook.com.
URL: http://www.esilks.org/

History 16 May 2017, Beijing (China). Founded as an informal network. **Aims** Inspire the knowledge generation in an effort to jointly build the Belt and Road and promote the common development of all countries. **Structure** Steering Committee of institutional representatives, including (ex-officio) its major founders: Development Research Center of the State Council of China; *UNDP (#20292)* and *Center for International Relations and Sustainable Development (CIRSD)*. Secretariat, headed by Secretary-General. **Activities** Capacity building; knowledge management/information dissemination; research and development.
Members Members include the following organizations:
– *Asian Development Bank Institute (ADB Institute, #01423)*;
– *Asian Peace and Reconciliation Council (APRC, #01657)*;
– *Center for International Relations and Sustainable Development (CIRSD)*;
– *Centre for Strategic and International Studies, Jakarta (CSIS)*;
– *Centro Internacional de Toledo para la Paz (CITpax)*;
– *Deutsches Institut für Entwicklungspolitik (DIE)*;
– *East Asian Institute, National University of Singapore (EAI)*;
– *Finance Center for South-South Cooperation (FCSSC)*;
– *Institute for Strategic Studies, Ulaanbaatar (ISS)*;
– *Institute of Development Studies, Brighton (IDS)*;
– *Institute of Far Eastern Studies (IFES)*;
– *Institute of Strategic and International Studies, Malaysia (ISIS)*;
– *Institute of World Economics and Politics (IWEP)*;
– *Institut Mirovoj Ekonomiki i Mezdunarodnyh Otnosenij Rossijskoj Akademii Nauk (IMEMO)*;
– *International Food Policy Research Institute (IFPRI, #13622)*;
– *International Road Transport Union (IRU, #14761)*;
– *Korea Institute for International Economic Policy (KIEP)*;
– *Mekong Institute (MI, #16701)*;
– *OECD Development Centre (#17692)*;
– *Real Instituto Elcano de Estudios Internacionales y Estratégicos*;
– *Research and Information System for Developing Countries, India (RIS, India)*;
– *Royal Institute of International Affairs (RIIA)*.
IGO Relations Partner of (5): *Central European Initiative (CEI, #03708)*; *Deutsche Gesellschaft für Internationale Zusammenarbeit (GIZ)*; *European Bank for Reconstruction and Development (EBRD, #06315)*; *UNDP (#20292)*; *UNIDO (#20336)*. **NGO Relations** Partner of (1): *World Ocean Council (WOC, #21680)*. [2020/AA1151/y/**F**]

♦ Silk-road Universities Network (SUN) 19281

SG Office 909 – Main Bldg, Hankuk Univ of Foreign Studies, 107 Imun-ro Dongdaemun-gu, Seoul 02450, Korea Rep. T. +82221733581. Fax +82221733582. E-mail: sunofficial0822@gmail.com.
URL: http://www.sun-silkroadia.org/

History 2015, Seoul (Korea Rep), following symposium held Nov 2014. Registered in accordance with Korean law, Dec 2015. **Aims** Recognize and acknowledge individual differences as reason for celebration rather than segregation; pursue pace and prosperity through mutual understanding, dialogue and collective action. **Structure** General Assembly; Board. *United Presidents of the Silk-road Universities Network (UPSUN)*; *International Association for Silk-road Studies (IASS)*; *United Students of the Silk-road Universities Network (USSUN)*; *Silkroadia Philharmonic Orchestra (SPO)*. **Languages** English, Korean. **Staff** 8.00 FTE, paid; 10.00 FTE, voluntary. **Finance** Members' dues. **Activities** Awards/prizes/competitions; awareness raising; knowledge management/information dissemination; events/meetings; networking/liaising; publishing activities; research/documentation; training/education. **Events** *General Assembly* Ulaanbaatar (Mongolia) 2021, *General Assembly* Ankara (Turkey) 2020, *General Assembly* Almaty (Kazakhstan) 2019, *Annual Global Conference* Moscow (Russia) 2019, *Annual Global Conference* Gyeongju (Korea Rep) 2018.
Members Full in 28 countries and territories:
Cambodia, China, Czechia, Greece, India, Indonesia, Iran Islamic Rep, Italy, Japan, Jordan, Kazakhstan, Korea Rep, Malaysia, Mongolia, Myanmar, Oman, Poland, Portugal, Romania, Russia, Spain, Sri Lanka, Taiwan, Thailand, Türkiye, United Arab Emirates, Uzbekistan, Vietnam. [2019.03.07/XM6268/**F**]

♦ **SiLKS** Silk Road Think Tank Network (#19280)
♦ SIL LEAD (internationally oriented national body)
♦ **SIL** Societas Internationalis Limnologiae (#15232)
♦ SIL – Société internationale de linguistique (no recent information)
♦ SIL – Solidarité Internationale LGBTQI (internationally oriented national body)
♦ **Silva Network** European Forest Science Academic Network (#07300)

♦ Silver Institute (SI) 19282

Institut de l'argent

Exec Dir 1400 St NW, Ste 550, Washington DC 20005, USA. T. +12028350185. Fax +12028350155. E-mail: info@silverinstitute.org.
URL: http://www.silverinstitute.org/

History 1971, New York NY (USA). **Aims** Increase worldwide demand for silver; act as the authoritative information source for silver. **Structure** Board of Directors; Executive Committee. Officers: President; Vice-President; Executive Director/Secretary; Treasurer; Assistant Treasurer. **Activities** Organizes regular annual and interim meetings. **Events** *Annual meeting* Scottsdale, AZ (USA) 2004, *Annual meeting* San Francisco, CA (USA) 2002, *Annual meeting* Scottsdale, AZ (USA) 2001, *Annual meeting* Rancho Mirage, CA (USA) 2000, *Annual meeting* Scottsdale, AZ (USA) 1999. **Publications** *Silver News* (4 a year); *Mine Production of Silver* (annual); *World Silver Survey* (annual). Conferences; reports.
Members Companies involved in silver mining, smelting, refining, fabricating or manufacturing, in selling or distributing silver bullion, or in wholesale of silver products in 13 countries:
Argentina, Australia, Brazil, Canada, Chile, France, Germany, Japan, Mexico, Peru, Switzerland, UK, USA.
[2013/XF5357/j/**F**]

♦ SilviLaser (meeting series)
♦ SIMalliance / see Trusted Connectivity Alliance (#20254)
♦ SIMAVI (internationally oriented national body)
♦ SIMAVI – Samen Werken aan een Gezonde Ontwikkeling / see SIMAVI
♦ SIMAVI – Supporting Healthy Solutions by Local Communities / see SIMAVI
♦ SIMC – Société internationale de médecine de catastrophe (inactive)
♦ SIMC – Société internationale de médecine cybernétique (inactive)
♦ **SIMC** Société internationale pour la musique contemporaine (#15035)
♦ SIMED / see Society for Microbial Ecology and Disease (#19596)
♦ SIMEST – Società Italiana per le Imprese Miste all'Estero (internationally oriented national body)
♦ SIMFR – Solidarité internationale des maisons familiales rurales (see: #02719)
♦ SIMG – Societas Internationalis Medicinae Generalis (inactive)
♦ SIMG – Société internationale de médecine générale (inactive)
♦ **SIMHA** Société internationale de mycologie humaine et animale (#15181)
♦ SIM International (internationally oriented national body)
♦ SIM / see International Musicological Society (#14201)
♦ SIM / see International Society of Non-invasive Cardiology (#15308)
♦ **SIMI** Scalabrini International Migration Institute (#19062)
♦ **SIMN** Scalabrini International Migration Network (#19063)
♦ Simón Bolivar Andean University (#20687)

♦ Simon Bolivar Inter-American Library 19283

Bibliothèque interaméricaine Simón Bolivar – Biblioteca Interamericana Simón Bolivar

Contact Universidad de Panama, Campus Octavio Méndez Pereira, Via Transistmica 507, Panama, Panamá, Panama PANAMÁ, Panama. E-mail: sibiup@up.ac.pa.
URL: http://www.sibiup.up.ac.pa/

History Apr 1976, Panama, following Resolution AG/RES 175 (V-0/75) of 5th Regular General Assembly of the *OAS (#17629)*. **Aims** Provide an inter-American research facility specializing in *information* about the *inter-American system*, relations between Latin American countries, and *Latin America* in general. **Finance** Staff and facilities paid by the Government of Panama; inter-American activities financed by OAS. **Publications** *Boletin Bibliografico* (2 a year). [2018/XF7929/**F***]

♦ Simón Rodriguez Agreement 19284

Convention Simón Rodriguez – Convenio Simón Rodriguez (CSR)

Contact General Secretariat of the Andean Community, Paseo de la República 3895, Casilla 18-1177, San Isidro, 27, Lima, Peru. T. +51142212222. Fax +51142213329. E-mail: correspondencia@comunidadandina.org.
Contact Ministerio de Trabajo y Empleo, Asuntos Internacionales, 11vo piso, Clemente Ponce 255 y Piedrahita, Quito, Ecuador. T. +5932548900ext20601.
URL: https://www.comunidadandina.org/

History 22 Oct 1973, Caracas (Venezuela). Set up at 2nd Meeting of Ministers of Labour, as an Andean integration organ of the *Andean Subregional Integration Agreement (Cartagena Agreement, 1969)*. Functions as a *'Social Agreement'* of *Sistema Andino de Integración (SAI, #19292)* within the framework of *Andean Community (#00817)*. Full name: *Convenio de Integración Socio-Laboral Simón Rodriguez*. Currently being revitalized after a period of dormancy. **Aims** As an intergovernmental institution set up to complement integration efforts in economic and trade sectors with action the field of social and labour policy: promote and support harmonization of social and labour policies of member countries of the Cartagena Agreement; adopt plans and strategies for joint action in achieving improvements in living conditions in the Andean subregion. **Structure** Conference of Ministers of Labour; Commission of Delegates; Coordinating Secretariat. **Finance** Member contributions.
Members Governments, represented by their Ministers of Labour, of the 5 Andean countries:
Bolivia, Colombia, Ecuador, Peru, Venezuela.
IGO Relations Instrumental in setting up: *Comisión Andina de Formación Profesional (CAFP, inactive)*. **NGO Relations** Instrumental in setting up: *Instrumento Andino de Seguridad Social (IASS, inactive)*.
[2021/XF6904/**F***]

♦ Simon Wiesenthal Center (internationally oriented national body)
♦ Simon Wiesenthal Centre-Europe (internationally oriented national body)
♦ Simply Help (internationally oriented national body)
♦ Simply Help Foundation / see Simply Help

♦ Simply Neuroscience 19285

CEO 8605 Santa Monica Blvd, West Hollywood CA 90069, USA. E-mail: info@simplyneuroscience.org.
URL: https://www.simplyneuroscience.org/

History 30 May 2019. Registration: 501(c)(3) non-profit, USA. **Aims** Empower students pursuing the brain through interdisciplinary neuroscience and psychology education, outreach, and awareness. **Structure** Executive Team; Advisory Board; Board of Directors. **Staff** 300.00 FTE, voluntary. **Activities** Awareness raising; events/meetings; projects/programmes; training/education. **Events** *Simply Neurocon* West Hollywood, CA (USA) 2022, *Simply Neurocon* West Hollywood, CA (USA) 2021, *Simply Neurocon* 2020.
[2023.02.18/AA1929/v/**F**]

♦ Simposico Internacional sobre Manejo de Sedimento (meeting series)
♦ Simposi Internacional sobre Controvèrsies en Psiquiatria (meeting series)
♦ Simpósio das Conferências Episcopais da Africa e Madagascar (#20077)
♦ Simposio Internacional de Arte Rupestre (meeting series)
♦ Simposium Internacional sobre Controversias en Psiquiatría (meeting series)
♦ SIMP – Service international du mouvement du pôle (inactive)
♦ **SIMSG** Société internationale de mécanique des sols et de la géotechnique (#15452)
♦ **SIM** Sistema Inter-Americano de Metrologia (#11440)
♦ **SIM** Society for Interdisciplinary Musicology (#19579)
♦ SIM – Society for the Internet in Medicine (inactive)
♦ **SIMS** Scandinavian Simulation Society (#19100)
♦ SIM – Studie-en Informatiecentrum Mensenrechten (internationally oriented national body)
♦ Simulation Councils / see Society for Modeling Simulation International (#19598)
♦ Simvulio ton Evropaikon Kinotiton / see Council of the European Union (#04895)
♦ **SINA** Settlements Information Network Africa (#19250)
♦ Sindacato dei Funzionari Europei / see European Public Service Union (#08303)
♦ Sindacato del Personale Locale e non Locale dei Servizi Generali della FAO (#20455)
♦ Sindacato del Personale Locale e non Locale dei Servizi Generali dell'Organizzazione per l'Alimentazione e l'Agricoltura delle Nazioni Unite / see Union of Local and Non Local General Service Staff FAO/WFP (#20455)
♦ Sindesmos Demosias Evropaikis Enimerosis meso Tileoraosis (inactive)
♦ Sindesmos Viamihanion Margarinis Horon Evropaikis Kinonitas / see European Margarine Association (#07736)
♦ Sindesmos Viomihanias Eleoladu tis EOK (#09596)
♦ Sindesmos Viomihanion Sokolatopas, Biskotopas-, Friganopopas- ke Zaharodon Prionton tis EOK / see Association of the Chocolate, Biscuit and Confectionery Industries of the EU (#02427)
♦ Sindicato de los Funcionarios Europeos / see European Public Service Union (#08303)
♦ Sindicato dos Funcionarios Europeus / see European Public Service Union (#08303)
♦ Sindicato dei Funzionari Internazionali ed Europei / see European Public Service Union (#08303)
♦ Sindicato del Personal Local y no Local de los Servicios Generale de la FAO (#20455)
♦ Sindicato del Personal Local y no Local de los Servicios Generales de la Organización de las Naciones Unidas para la Agricultura y la Alimentación / see Union of Local and Non Local General Service Staff FAO/WFP (#20455)
♦ Sindicato del Personal de la Oficina Internacional del Trabajo (#19945)
♦ Sindicato del Personal de la OIT / see Staff Union of the International Labour Office (#19945)
♦ Sindicato del Personal de la OMI / see IMO Staff Association (#11135)
♦ Sindikalistiki Enosi – Evropaiki Dimosia Ipiresia / see Union Syndicale Fédérale (#20485)
♦ Sindikato Ipallilon Evropaikon Organismon / see European Public Service Union (#08303)
♦ Sinelevsi Evropaikon Ampeloinikon Periohon (#02317)
♦ Singapore Convention on Mediation – United Nations Convention on International Settlement Agreements Resulting from Mediation (2018 treaty)
♦ Singapore Immunology Network (internationally oriented national body)
♦ Singapore Institute of International Affairs (internationally oriented national body)
♦ Singapore International Arbitration Centre (internationally oriented national body)
♦ Singapore International Foundation (internationally oriented national body)
♦ Singapore International School / see United World College of South East Asia
♦ Singapore Treaty on the Law of Trademarks (2006 treaty)
♦ Singapore Treaty – Singapore Treaty on the Law of Trademarks (2006 treaty)
♦ SING – European Meeting on Game Theory (meeting series)
♦ Single Cell Genomics Conference (meeting series)
♦ Single Convention on Narcotic Drugs, 1961 (1961 treaty)
♦ Single Convention on Narcotic Drugs, 1961, as amended by the Protocol amending the Single Convention on Narcotic Drugs, 1961 (1975 treaty)
♦ Single European Act (1986 treaty)

♦ Single Global Currency Association 19286

Pres PO Box 390, Newcastle ME 04553-0390, USA. T. +12075866078.
URL: http://www.singleglobalcurrency.org/

History 2003. Registered in the State of Maine (USA). **Aims** Implement a Single Global Currency, within a Global Monetary Union and managed by a Global Central Bank by 2024. **Structure** Board of Directors; Board of Advisors; Currency Area Chapters. **Events** *Annual Conference* Boston, MA (USA) 2008, *Annual Conference* Bretton Woods, NH (USA) 2007, *Annual Conference* Bretton Woods, NH (USA) 2006, *Annual Conference* Bretton Woods, NH (USA) 2005, *Annual Conference* Bretton Woods, NH (USA) 2004. **Publications** *The Single Global Currency – Common Cents for the World* – 4 vols published to date.
Members Individuals (70) in 24 countries and territories:
Argentina, Australia, Austria, Bulgaria, Cameroon, Canada, Estonia, Fiji, Germany, Ghana, Hong Kong, India, Malaysia, Mexico, New Zealand, Peru, Spain, Sri Lanka, Sweden, Thailand, Türkiye, UK, USA, Venezuela. [2016.10.19/XJ0305/v/**F**]

♦ Single Molecule Localization Microscopy Symposium (meeting series)

♦ Single Resolution Board (SRB) 19287

Chair Treurenberg 22, 1049 Brussels, Belgium.
URL: http://srb.europa.eu/

History Established by Regulation (EU) No 806/2014 on the *Single Resolution Mechanism*. Operational as a decentralized agency of *European Union (EU, #08967)* since 1 Jan 2015. Fully operational with a complete set of resolution powers since 1 Jan 2016. **Aims** Ensure an orderly resolution of failing *banks* with minimum impact on the real economy and on public finances of participating *European Union* member states and beyond. **Structure** Board; Secretariat. **Languages** English. **Finance** Budget (2016): euro 57 million. **Events** *SRB Conference* Brussels (Belgium) 2022, *SRB Legal Conference* Brussels (Belgium) 2022, *SRB Conference* Brussels (Belgium) 2021, *SRB Conference* Brussels (Belgium) 2020, *Conference* Brussels (Belgium) 2019. **IGO Relations** Cooperates with: *Banking Union*; *European Central Bank (ECB, #06466)*; *European Commission (EC, #06633)*. **NGO Relations** Member of (2): *EU Agencies Network (EUAN, #05564)*; *Eurolib (#05703)*.
[2022/XM4610/**F***]

♦ **SINMPCC** Société internationale de nomenclature des maladies pédiatriques et congénitales du coeur (#15306)
♦ Sinn und Bedeutung (meeting series)
♦ Sinodo Europeo de Mujeres (meeting series)
♦ Sinodo dei Vescovi (#20083)
♦ Sinor Research Institute for Inner Asian Studies (internationally oriented national body)
♦ SINO – Sociedad Internacional de Neuro-Oftalmologia (inactive)
♦ Sinsinawa Dominican Congregation of the Most Holy Rosary (religious order)
♦ SINTEF (internationally oriented national body)
♦ **SINUG** Sociedad Iberoamericana de Neurourologia y Uroginecologia (#19375)
♦ Sinzleh Uhoan, Tehnikijn Medellijn Olon Ulsyn Tfb (#12514)
♦ SIODEC – Sociedad Internacional de Optometria del Desarrollo y Comportamiento (internationally oriented national body)
♦ **SIOE** Society for Institutional and Organizational Economics (#19576)
♦ **SIOG** Société internationale d'oncologie gériatrique (#19493)
♦ SIOI – Società Italiana per l'Organizzazione Internazionale (internationally oriented national body)
♦ **SIOPEN-R-NET** International Society of Paediatric Oncology European Neuroblastoma Research Network (#15340)
♦ **SIOPE** SIOP Europe (#19288)

♦ SIOP Europe (SIOPE) 19288

CEO c/o BLSI, Clos Chapelle-aux-Champs 30, Bte 1.30.30, 1200 Brussels, Belgium. T. +3228806282. E-mail: office@siope.eu.
URL: http://www.siope.eu/

History 1998. Founded as the European branch of *International Society of Paediatric Oncology (#15339)*. Statutes revised Nov 2007; 2012. Former names and other names: *European Society for Paediatric Oncology* – alias. Registration: Banque-Carrefour des Entreprises, No/ID: 0894.176.979, Start date: 13 Dec 2007, Belgium; EU Transparency Register, No/ID: 122803916413-09, Start date: 13 Mar 2015. **Aims** Represent professionals working in the field of *childhood cancers*. **Structure** General Assembly; Board of Directors; Secretariat; European Clinical Research Council for Paediatric Oncology (SIOPE CRC). **Languages** English. **Staff** 8.00 FTE, paid. **Finance** Sources: members' dues. Supported by: *European Union (EU, #08967)*. **Activities** Events/meetings; healthcare; projects/programmes; research and development. **Events** *Annual Meeting* Valencia (Spain) 2023, *Special Europe Policy Seminar* 2022, *Annual Meeting* Valencia (Spain) 2022, *Annual Meeting* 2021, *ACCELERATE Paediatric Oncology Conference* Brussels (Belgium) 2021. **Publications** *SIOPE News*. Position papers; press releases; scientific articles.

Members Members of national paediatric haemato-oncology societies (over 2,000) in 25 countries:
Austria, Belgium, Bosnia-Herzegovina, Bulgaria, Croatia, Czechia, France, Germany, Hungary, Ireland, Italy, Latvia, Luxembourg, Malta, Netherlands, North Macedonia, Poland, Portugal, Serbia, Slovakia, Slovenia, Spain, Switzerland, Türkiye, UK.
Denmark, Finland, Iceland, Lithuania, Norway and Sweden are represented by:
Nordic Society for Pediatric Hematology and Oncology (NOPHO, #17424).
NGO Relations Member of (4): *Accreditation Council for Oncology in Europe (ACOE, #00063); European Forum for Good Clinical Practice (EFGCP, #07313); EURORDIS – Rare Diseases Europe (#09175); Rare Cancers Europe (RCE, #18620).* Partner of (1): *Pan-European Network for Care of Survivors after Childhood and Adolescent Cancer (PanCare, #18178).* Cooperates with (3): *Childhood Cancer International Europe (CCI Europe, #03872); European Society of Surgical Oncology (ESSO, #08753); Innovative Therapies for Children with Cancer Consortium (ITCC, #11222).* Instrumental in setting up (2): *ACCELERATE (#00046); European Cancer Organisation (ECO, #06432).* [2022.05.04/XM1565/**E**]

- ♦ **SIOP** Société internationale d'oncologie pédiatrique (#15339)
- ♦ **SIO** Societas Internationalis Odonatologica (#19445)
- ♦ SIO – Société Internationale d'Otoneurologie (unconfirmed)
- ♦ SIPAR – Soutien à l'initiative privée pour l'aide a la reconstruction des pays du Sud-Est asiatique (internationally oriented national body)
- ♦ SIPA – School of International and Public Affairs, New York NY (internationally oriented national body)
- ♦ **SIPA** Seafood Importers and Processors Alliance (#19166)
- ♦ SIPAZ – Servicio Internacional para la Paz (internationally oriented national body)
- ♦ **SIPCC** Society for Intercultural Pastoral Care and Counselling (#19577)
- ♦ **SIPD** Sociedad Iberoamericana de Psicologia del Deporte (#19377)
- ♦ SIPED – Sociedad Iberoamericana de Psicologia del Ejercicio y el Deporte (no recent information)
- ♦ **SIPE** Sociedad Internacional de Psicologia de la Escritura (#15398)
- ♦ **SIPE** Societas Iuris Publici Europaei (#19447)
- ♦ **SIPE** Société internationale de psychologie de l'écriture (#15398)
- ♦ **SIPE** Société internationale de psychopathologie de l'expression et d'art-thérapie (#15400)
- ♦ SIPG – Société internationale de pathologie géographique (inactive)
- ♦ SIP / see International Society for Photogrammetry and Remote Sensing (#15362)
- ♦ **SIPLE** Sociedade Internacional Portugues / Lingua Estrangeira (#19356)
- ♦ **SIPP** Société Internationale de Psychanalyse et Philosophie (#15394)
- ♦ **SIPRI** Stockholm International Peace Research Institute (#19994)
- ♦ SIPRT – Sociedad Internacional de Profesionales de Radio y Televisión (inactive)
- ♦ **SIP** Sociedade Interamericana de Psicologia (#11450)
- ♦ **SIP** Sociedad Interamericana de Prensa (#11444)
- ♦ **SIP** Sociedad Interamericana de Psicologia (#11450)
- ♦ **SIP** Society for Invertebrate Pathology (#19584)
- ♦ **SIPS** Società Internazionale di Psicologia della Scrittura (#15398)
- ♦ **SIPTA** Society for Imprecise Probability: Theories and Applications (#19573)
- ♦ **SIPT** Société internationale de photogrammétrie et télédétection (#15362)
- ♦ SIPUC – Secrétariat international de presse universitaire catholique (inactive)
- ♦ **SIQS** Secrétariat international des questions scientifiques (#14821)

♦ Siracusa International Institute for Criminal Justice and Human Rights (SII) 19289

Dir Gen Via Logoteta 27, 96100 Siracusa SR, Italy. T. +39931414515 – +3993121495. Fax +3993167622. E-mail: info@siracusainstitute.org.
Pres address not obtained.
URL: http://www.siracusainstitute.org/

History Sep 1972, Siracusa (Italy). Founded by *International Association of Penal Law (IAPL, #12074).* An autonomous legal entity, under the scientific auspices of IAPL. Former names and other names: *International Institute of Higher Studies in Criminal Sciences (ISISC)* – former. Registration: Italy. **Aims** Act as a scientific institution devoted to higher education, training, studies and research in all areas of criminal sciences, including human rights: pursue a leadership role in developing United Nations norms and standards in the field of international and comparative criminal justice and human rights; work for technical assistance and justice reform projects. **Structure** Board of Directors; Executive Committee; President's Advisory Board; Regional Scientific Committee. **Languages** English, French, Italian. **Staff** 7.50 FTE, paid. **Finance** Sources: contributions; grants. Fixed contributions: Sicilian region, the city and province of Siracusa (Italy) and city of Noto (Italy). Other grants from major international sources fund some of the Institute's activities, including: Italian Ministry of Foreign Affairs; UN; *European Commission (EC, #06633).* **Activities** Events/meetings; training/education. **Events** *Europe regional conference on fighting impunity and promoting international justice* The Hague (Netherlands) 2009, *International conference on fighting impunity and promoting international justice* The Hague (Netherlands) 2009, *Workshop on typologies of money laundering and terrorist financing* Siracusa (Italy) 2008, *International conference on reining in impunity for international crimes and serious violations of human rights* Siracusa (Italy) 1997, *Seminar on international protection of human rights* Siracusa (Italy) 1988. **Publications** Books; proceedings. **Members** Not a membership organization. **Consultative Status** Consultative status granted from: *ECOSOC (#05331)* (Special). **IGO Relations** Accredited by (1): *United Nations Office at Vienna (UNOV, #20604).* Member of (1): *United Nations Crime Prevention and Criminal Justice Programme Network (#20549).* Instrumental in setting up (1): *International Criminal Court (ICC, #13108).* Works for creation of: *International Criminal Tribunal (no recent information).* Associated with Department of Global Communications of the United Nations.
NGO Relations Member of (2): *International Criminal Law Network (ICLN); World Criminal Justice Library Network (WCJLN, #21343).*
Collaborates with a number of national and international organizations, including:
- *American Refugee Committee (ARC);*
- *Amnesty International (AI, #00801);*
- *Arab Organization for Human Rights (AOHR, #01020);*
- *Basel Institute on Governance;*
- *Carnegie Endowment for International Peace (CEIP);*
- *The Carter Center;*
- *Coalition for the International Criminal Court (CICC, #04062);*
- *Defence for Children International (DCI, #05025);*
- *Global Rights;*
- *Human Rights First;*
- *Human Rights Watch (HRW, #10990);*
- *Institute of Research Against Counterfeit Medicines (IRACM);*
- *Instituto Interamericano de Derechos Humanos (IIDH, #11334);*
- *Inter-African Union of Lawyers (IAUL, inactive);*
- *International Association of Judges (IAJ, #11978);*
- *International Bar Association (IBA, #12320);*
- *International Centre for Criminal Law Reform and Criminal Justice Policy (ICCLR);*
- *International Commission of Jurists (ICJ, #12695);*
- *International Committee of the Red Cross (ICRC, #12799);*
- *International Criminal Justice and Weapons Control Center (IWCC);*
- *International Criminal Tribunal for the former Yugoslavia (ICTY, inactive);*
- *International Federation for Human Rights (#13452);*
- *International Human Rights Law Institute (IHRLI);*
- *International Law Association (ILA, #14003);*
- *International Legal Assistance Consortium (ILAC, #14025);*
- *International Penal and Penitentiary Foundation (IPPF, #14553);*
- *International Scientific and Professional Advisory Council of the United Nations Crime Prevention and Criminal Justice Programme (ISPAC, #14810);*
- *International Society of Criminology (ISC, #15038);*
- *International Society for the Reform of Criminal Law (ISRCL, #15415);*
- *International Society of Social Defence and Humane Criminal Policy (ISSD, #15447);*
- *King Faisal Centre for Research and Islamic Studies;*
- *Max Planck Institute for Foreign and International Criminal Law;*
- *Middle East Studies Center, Portland (MESC);*
- *Norwegian Centre for Human Rights (NCHR);*
- *Nuclear Age Peace Foundation;*
- *Parliamentarians for Global Action (PGA, #18208);*
- *Physicians for Human Rights, USA (PHR-USA);*
- *Special Tribunal for Lebanon (STL, #19911);*
- *Union Internationale des Avocats (UIA, #20422);*
- *United States Institute of Peace (USIP).* [2022.05.10/XF2965/j/**F**]

- ♦ Sir Alexander Robertson Centre for Tropical Veterinary Medicine / see Centre for Tropical Veterinary Medicine, Edinburgh
- ♦ Sir Arthur Lewis Institute of Social and Economic Studies (internationally oriented national body)

♦ Sir Charles Bell Society (SCBS) 19290

Sec address not obtained.
URL: http://www.sircharlesbell.org/

History 1992, Cologne (Germany), during 7th International Facial Nerve Symposium. Incorporated, 1993, in California (USA). Named after Scottish surgeon Charles Bell (1774-1842). **Aims** Increase collection, dissemination and interchange of ideas relating to facial *nerves* and their disorders. **Structure** Board of Directors. **Finance** Members' dues. **Events** *Meeting* Rome (Italy) 2009, *Meeting* Maastricht (Netherlands) 2005, *Meeting* Matsuyama City (Japan) 1997. **Publications** *SCBS Newsletter.*
Members Individuals in 30 countries and territories:
Australia, Austria, Brazil, Canada, Czechia, Denmark, Finland, France, Germany, Hungary, Ireland, Israel, Italy, Japan, Korea Rep, Mexico, Netherlands, Norway, Pakistan, Peru, Poland, Saudi Arabia, South Africa, Spain, Sweden, Switzerland, Taiwan, Türkiye, UK, USA. [2014/XM0326/**E**]

- ♦ SIRC – Seafarers International Research Centre (internationally oriented national body)
- ♦ SIREAS – Service international de recherche d'éducation et d'action sociale (internationally oriented national body)
- ♦ SIREP / see Evaluation International
- ♦ **SIRER** Société internationale de recherche et d'études sur le rachis (#19494)
- ♦ **SIRFO** Sistema Regional de Información sobre Formación Profesional (#19296)
- ♦ SIR / see International Society of the Rorschach and Projective Methods (#15430)
- ♦ SIRI / see Regional Information System (#18788)
- ♦ **SIRI** Sistema Regional de Información (#18788)
- ♦ Sirius GAO – Sirius Global Animal Organisation (internationally oriented national body)
- ♦ Sirius Global Animal Organisation (internationally oriented national body)
- ♦ SIRIUS Network / see SIRIUS – Policy Network on Migrant Education (#19291)

♦ SIRIUS – Policy Network on Migrant Education (SIRIUS) 19291

Exec Dir Rue Béliard 205, 1040 Brussels, Belgium. T. +3222305939. E-mail: sirius@migpolgroup.com.
URL: http://www.sirius-migrationeducation.org/

History 2012. Initiated by *European Commission (EC, #06633).* Restructured to become independent. Former names and other names: *European Policy Network on the Education of Children and Young People with a Migrant Background (SIRIUS)* – former (2012); *SIRIUS Network (SIRIUS)* – former. Registration: Banque Carrefour des Entreprises, No/ID: 0672.758.247, Start date: 16 Mar 2017, Belgium; EU Transparency Register, No/ID: 919723927195-44, Start date: 17 May 2017. **Aims** Research education of children and young people with migrant background. **Structure** General Assembly; Executive Board; Secretariat. **Finance** Supported by: *European Union (EU, #08967); Open Society Foundations (OSF, #17763).* **Activities** Training/education. **Publications** *SIRIUS Newsletter.*
Members Full (28); Affiliated; Observer. Full include 9 organizations listed in this Yearbook:
African and Caribbean Diversity (ACD); Don Bosco International (DBI, #05117); European Parents' Association (EPA, #08142); European Students' Union (ESU, #08848); European Trade Union Committee for Education (ETUCE, #08926); Migration Policy Group (MPG, #16801); Network of Education Policy Centers (NEPC, #17010); Organising Bureau of European School Student Unions (OBESSU, #17829).
NGO Relations Member of: *Lifelong Learning Platform – European Civil Society for Education (LLLP, #16466).* [2020/XM6569/y/**F**]

- ♦ SIRIUS / see SIRIUS – Policy Network on Migrant Education (#19291)
- ♦ **SIRIUS** SIRIUS – Policy Network on Migrant Education (#19291)
- ♦ SIRLaF – Société Internationale de Radiobiologie de Langue Française (internationally oriented national body)
- ♦ SIRMCE – Société internationale pour la recherche sur les maladies de civilisation et l'environnement (inactive)
- ♦ SIRM – International Conference on Dynamics of Rotating Machines (meeting series)
- ♦ **SIRMIP** Système d'information sur les ressources marines des îles du Pacifique (#17973)
- ♦ **SIRM** Société internationale Robert Musil (#14762)
- ♦ SIROCCO – International Colloquium on Structural Information and Communication Complexity (meeting series)
- ♦ **SIROT** Société Internationale de Recherche Orthopédique et Traumatologique (#19495)
- ♦ SIR – School of International Relations, Los Angeles (internationally oriented national body)
- ♦ SIR – School of International Relations, Teheran (internationally oriented national body)
- ♦ **SIR** Société internationale du Rorschach et des méthodes projectives (#15430)
- ♦ **SIRS** Schizophrenia International Research Society (#19130)
- ♦ SIRT – Société internationale de la radio et télévision (inactive)
- ♦ **SIRWEC** Standing International Road Weather Commission (#19965)
- ♦ SISAL / see Confederación de Institutos Seculares en América Latina (#04451)
- ♦ SIS-AP – Asia Pacific Surgical Infection Society (unconfirmed)
- ♦ SISAP – International Conference on Similarity Search and Applications (meeting series)
- ♦ SISB – Société internationale de systématique biochimique (inactive)
- ♦ **SISCA** Secretaria de Integración Social Centroamericana (#19192)
- ♦ **SISEAP** Soroptimist International South East Asia Pacific (#19691)
- ♦ SI – Sertoma International (internationally oriented national body)
- ♦ **SIS-E** Surgical Infection Society – Europe (#20043)
- ♦ **SI** Silver Institute (#19282)
- ♦ SIS / see International Society for the Interdisciplinary Study of Symmetry (#15210)
- ♦ SI – Situationist International (inactive)
- ♦ **SI** Socialist International (#19340)
- ♦ SI – Societas Jesu (religious order)
- ♦ SI – Solidaridad Internacional (internationally oriented national body)
- ♦ **SI** Soroptimist International (#19686)
- ♦ **SISR** Société internationale de sociologie des religions (#15451)
- ♦ SISSA – Scuola Internazionale Superiore di Studi Avanzati (internationally oriented national body)
- ♦ SIS – School of International Service (internationally oriented national body)
- ♦ SIS – School of International Studies, Beijing (internationally oriented national body)
- ♦ **SIS** Senologic International Society (#19230)
- ♦ **SIS** Servetus International Society (#19236)
- ♦ **SIS-Symmetry** International Society for the Interdisciplinary Study of Symmetry (#15210)

♦ Sistema Andino de Integración (SAI) 19292

Andean Integration System

Headquarters Paseo de la República 3895, esq Aramburú, San Isidro, 27, Lima, Peru. T. +51144111400. Fax +51142213329. E-mail: correspondencia@comunidadandina.org.
URL: http://www.comunidadandina.org/

History 9 Mar 1996, Trujillo (Peru). 9-10 Mar 1996, Trujillo (Peru), by the *Acta de Trujillo*, as a series of bodies and institutions within the *Andean Community (#00817)*, working in close coordination and with efforts oriented to the same objectives. The process commenced with *Andean Subregional Integration Agreement (Cartagena Agreement, 1969)* and is leading to the implementation of *Andean Common Market (ANCOM, no recent information)* and to complementary integration efforts in the fields of education, technology and culture, health and labour affairs. **Aims** Intensify Andean subregional *integration*, promote its external projection and bolster actions connected with the process.

Structure Organs:
- Highest authority – *Andean Presidential Council (see: #00817)*;
- *Andean Council of Foreign Ministers (#00818)*;
- *Commission of the Andean Community (#04203)*;
- *General Secretariat of the Andean Community – Secretaria General de la Comunidad Andina*;
- *Andean Parliament (#00820)*;
- *Court of Justice of the Andean Community (#04936)*.

Institutions:
- *Consejo Consultivo Empresarial Andino (CCEA, see: #00817)*;
- *Andean Labor Advisory Council (CCLA, see: #00817)*;
- *Development Bank of Latin America (CAF, #05055)*;
- *Latin American Reserve Fund (#16367)*;
- *Universidad Andina Simón Bolivar (UASB, #20687)*;

Social conventions -
- *Hipólito Unanue Agreement (#10921)*,
- *Convenio andino de seguridad social (CONASS, no recent information)*,
- *Simón Rodriguez Agreement (#19284)*.

IGO Relations Related treaty: *Convenio Andrés Bello de integración educativa, cientifica y cultural de América Latina y España (Convenio Andrés Bello, #04785)*. [2009/XF4919/**F***]

♦ Sistema de Ciencia y Tecnologia Agroindustrial (no recent information)

♦ Sistema de Cooperación entre las Fuerzas Aéreas Americanas (SICOFAA) 19293

System of Cooperation among the American Air Forces – Système de Coopération entre les armées de l'air des Amériques

Deputy 5385 E Madera St, Ste 316, Davis-Monthan AFB, Tucson AZ 85707, USA. T. +15202282290.
URL: http://www.sicofaa.org/

History 1961. Founded as a series of meetings with the title 'Conference of the Chiefs of the American Air Forces (CONJEFAMER)'. 2002, system charter approved. **Aims** Promote exchange of experience, knowledge and training that allows the strengthening of capacities of air forces and their equivalents; provide support for the requirements of members. **Structure** Permanent Secretariat; Committees (7). **Languages** Spanish. **Activities** Events/meetings. **Events** *CONJEFAMER Annual Meeting* Tucson, AZ (USA) 2020, *CONJEFAMER Annual Meeting* Panama (Panama) 2018, *CONJEFAMER Annual Meeting* Manaus (Brazil) 2017, *CONJEFAMER Annual Meeting* Colorado Springs, CO (USA) 2016, *CONJEFAMER Annual Meeting* Mexico City (Mexico) 2015. **Publications** *Alas del SICOFAA* – magazine. Regulations; manuals; guides; data banks.
Members National Air Force representatives in 21 countries and territories:
Argentina, Bolivia, Brazil, Canada, Chile, Colombia, Dominican Rep, Ecuador, El Salvador, Guatemala, Guyana, Honduras, Jamaica, Mexico, Nicaragua, Panama, Paraguay, Peru, Uruguay, USA, Venezuela.
Observers in 4 countries:
Belize, Costa Rica, Haiti, Trinidad-Tobago. [2020.03.03/XD7659/**D***]

♦ Sistema Econômico Latino-Americano (#19294)

♦ Sistema Económico Latinoamericano (SELA) 19294

Système économique latinoaméricain – Latin American Economic System – Sistema Econômico Latino-Americano

Permanent Sec Torre Europa – 4th Floor, Urb Campo Alegre, Av Francisco de Miranda, Caracas 1060 DF, Venezuela. T. +582129557111. Fax +582129515292. E-mail: sela@sela.org – difusion@sela.org.
Street Address Permanent Secretariat, Av Francisco de Miranda, Torre Europa – Piso 4, Urb Campo Alegre, Caracas 1060 DF, Venezuela.
URL: http://www.sela.org/

History 17 Oct 1975, Panama, through the *Panama Convention – Convenio Constitutivo de Panamá*, as successor to *Comisión Especial de Coordinación Latinoamericana (CECLA, inactive)*. Statutes registered in *'UNTS/1 21295'*. **Aims** Promote a consultation and coordination system for the consensus on joint positions and common strategies for the Latin American and Caribbean region on economic issues vis-à-vis countries, groups of countries, international fora and organizations. **Structure** *Latin American Council* (meets annually) is the principal decision-making body and comprises one representative from each Member State. Permanent Secretariat, headed by the Permanent Secretary, is located in Caracas (Venezuela) and serves as the technical administrative organ. Action Committees are flexible cooperation mechanisms set up when more than 2 Member States voice interest in promoting joint programmes and projects in specific areas; they are dissolved once their objectives are fulfilled or they may become Permanent Bodies of the System. No Action Committees at present. Permanent bodies presently functioning: *Latin American Fisheries Development Organization (#16335)*, Lima (Peru); *Red de Información Tecnológica Latinoamericana (RITLA, see: #19294)*, Rio de Janeiro (Brazil). **Languages** English, French, Portuguese, Spanish. **Staff** 42.00 FTE, paid. **Finance** Member countries' dues; contributions from international bodies.
Activities Main work areas (3):
'Extra-Regional Relations' – study of Latin American and Caribbean insertion in the world economy's globalization process and long-term development scenarios; follow-up of extra-regional economic relations, fundamentally the evolution of negotiations for the FTAA and relations between the USA and Latin America and Caribbean, implications of the EU/LA Summit on the region and progress made in the EU's expansion process and relations between Latin America/Caribbean and the Asia Pacific; analysis of specific issues on the international economic agenda, such as negotiations on agriculture and trade in services currently under way in the WTO and development financing and external debt of the region.
'Intra-Regional Relations': exchange of experiences relating to the evolution of integration processes and agreements among countries of the region, including the issue of intra-regional investments and the study of specific issues concerning articulation and convergence of regional processes; fostering of dialogue and information dissemination on national experiences relating to economic and social policies of significance for the region.
'Regional Cooperation': promotion and facilitation of activities for Technical Cooperation Among Developing Countries (TCDC) and training of human resources relating to international and regional trade negotiations, especially those involving government officials in charge of the WTO and FTAA negotiations and, in case of the CARIFORUM countries, of the preparation of post-Lomé negotiations; joint execution of programmes with the International Cooperation Agency of Spain in favor of the countries of the Caribbean and support to the Rio Group and the 1999 Iberian-American Summit; organization of meetings; coordination of actions in support of countries affected by natural disasters.
Organizes fora with the participation of government and private sector representatives and organizes meetings of experts on specific issues of the regional and global economic agenda. Develops seminars, courses and workshops on issues of economic interest for the Latin American and Caribbean region, addressing the needs of government officials, business people, workers, parliamentarians and academicians.
Events *Meeting on integration in Latin America and Caribbean and the role of higher education institutions* Caracas (Venezuela) 2006, *International culture and development congress* Havana (Cuba) 2003, *International culture and development congress* Havana (Cuba) 2001, *International culture and development congress* Havana (Cuba) 1999, *Seminar on environmental policy and market access* Bogota (Colombia) 1993. **Publications** *Bulletin on Integration* (12 a year); *Strategic Issues* (6 a year) in English, Spanish; *SELA Antenna in the United States* (4 a year); *Capitulos del SELA* (3 a year) in English, Spanish – magazine. *Economic Relations Studies* in English, Spanish – series. *Le Crisis: Es del SELA o de América Latina ?* (2002); *Agricultural Trade in the Multilateral Framework: Latin America and the Caribbean Perspectives* (1999); *El Laberinto económico: la Agenda de América Latina y el Caribe ante la Crisis Financiera Internacional* (1999) in English, Spanish; *La Economia Mundial al Fin de Siglo* (1999); *Las Industrias Culturales en la Integración Latinoamericana* (1999); *PYMES: Escenario de Oportunidades en e Sigle XXI* (1999); *Relaciones de América Latina y el Caribe con Asia-Pacifico (1997-1998)* (1999); *The Expropiation and Indemnification Process in Cuba* (1999) in English, Spanish; *Comercio y desarrollo en América Latina y el Caribe: Los Desafios del ALCA en el contexto de la globalización* by Giovanni E Reyes; *Guide to Latin American and Caribbean Integration 1999* in English, Spanish – electronic; *Keys to Latin America and the Caribbean 1999* in English, Spanish. Current situation reports; non-periodical publications; books.
Members Governments of 28 countries:
Argentina, Bahamas, Barbados, Belize, Bolivia, Brazil, Chile, Colombia, Costa Rica, Cuba, Dominican Rep, Ecuador, El Salvador, Grenada, Guatemala, Guyana, Haiti, Honduras, Jamaica, Mexico, Nicaragua, Panama, Paraguay, Peru, Suriname, Trinidad-Tobago, Uruguay, Venezuela.
IGO Relations Relationship agreement with: *FAO (#09260)*. Observer to: *ECOSOC (#05331)*; *International Fund for Agricultural Development (IFAD, #13692)*. Cooperation agreement with: *UNCTAD (#20285)*. Member of: *Intergovernmental Organizations Conference (IGO Conference, #11498)*. Special links with: *Permanent Mechanism for Consultation and Political Coordination (Rio Group, inactive)*. Participates as observer in the activities of: *Codex Alimentarius Commission (CAC, #04081)*. Invited to sessions of Intergovernmental Council of: *International Programme for the Development of Communication (IPDC, #14651)*. Instrumental in setting up: *Latin America-Caribbean Privatization Network (inactive)*.
Observers:
- *Andean Community (#00817)*;
- *Andean Parliament (#00820)*;
- *Association of Caribbean States (ACS, #02411)*;
- *Caribbean Community (CARICOM, #03476)*;
- *Central American Bank for Economic Integration (CABEI, #03658)*;
- *Central American Integration System (#03671)*;
- *Comité Intergubernamental Coordinador de los Paises de la Cuenca del Plata (CIC, #04172)*;
- *Court of Justice of the Andean Community (#04936)*;
- *Development Bank of Latin America (CAF, #05055)*;
- *European Commission (EC, #06633)*;
- *Fondo Financiero para el Desarrollo de la Cuenca del Plata (FONPLATA, #09833)*;
- *Institute for the Integration of Latin America and the Caribbean (#11271)*;
- *Inter-American Development Bank (IDB, #11427)*;
- *Inter-American Institute for Cooperation on Agriculture (IICA, #11434)*;
- *International Organization for Migration (IOM, #14454)*;
- *International Trade Centre (ITC, #15703)*;
- *Latin American Energy Organization (#16313)*;
- *Latin American Fisheries Development Organization (#16335)*;
- *Organisation of Eastern Caribbean States (OECS, #17804)*;
- *Pan American Health Organization (PAHO, #18108)*;
- *Parlamento Latinoamericano (PARLATINO, #18203)*;
- *Red de Información Tecnológica Latinoamericana (RITLA, see: #19294)*;
- *Secretaria Permanente del Tratado General de Integración Económica Centroamericana (SIECA, #19195)*;
- *UNEP (#20299)*;
- UNCTAD;
- *UNDP (#20292)*;
- *UNESCO (#20322)*;
- *UNICEF (#20332)*;
- *UNIDO (#20336)*;
- *United Nations (UN, #20515)*;
- *United Nations Economic Commission for Latin America and the Caribbean (ECLAC, #20556)*;
- *United Nations Office for Disaster Risk Reduction (UNDRR, #20595)*;
- *WHO (#20950)*;
- *World Intellectual Property Organization (WIPO, #21593)*;
- *World Trade Organization (WTO, #21864)*.

NGO Relations Observers:
- *Asociación Latinoamericana de Instituciones Financieras para el Desarrollo (ALIDE, #02233)*;
- *Banco Latinoamericano de Comercio Exterior (BLADEX, #03159)*;
- *Center for Latin American Monetary Studies (#03648)*;
- *International Society for the Study of Human Ideas on Ultimate Reality and Meaning (URAM, #15474)*. [2008/XF4530/**F***]

♦ Sistema Euromediterraneo de información sobre la Pericia en el sector del Agua (#05722)
♦ Sistema Europeo de Redes Cooperativas de Investigación Agricola (#08871)
♦ Sistema Global de Observación Terrestre (#10626)

♦ Sistema Iberoamericano de Información sobre el Agua (SIAGUA) 19295

Latin American Water Information System

Address not obtained.
URL: http://www.siagua.org/

History 12 Jul 2001, Cartagena de Indias (Colombia). **Aims** Increase information exchange and management of water resources in Latin America, Portugal and Spain. **Structure** National Focal Points. **Events** *Meeting / Conference* San José (Costa Rica) 2006, *Meeting / Conference* Cartagena de Indias (Colombia) 2005, *Taller regional iberoamericano sobre la innovacion cientifica y tecnologica para enfrentar los retos en materia de agua en la region iberoamericana* Jiutepec (Mexico) 2005, *Meeting / Conference* Santo Domingo (Dominican Rep) 2004, *Meeting / Conference* Cancún (Mexico) 2003. **Publications** *Boletin SIAGUA*.
Members in 21 countries:
Argentina, Bolivia, Brazil, Chile, Colombia, Costa Rica, Cuba, Dominican Rep, Ecuador, El Salvador, Guatemala, Honduras, Mexico, Nicaragua, Panama, Paraguay, Peru, Portugal, Spain, Uruguay, Venezuela. [2013/XM1741/**F**]

♦ Sistema de Información Económica-Energética (see: #16313)
♦ Sistema de la Integración Centroamericana (#03671)
♦ Sistema Inter-Americano de Metrologia (#11440)
♦ Sistema de Intercambio Internacional de Datos y Información Oceanograficos (#14396)
♦ Sistema Internacional de Alerta para la Seguridad y la Salud de los Trabajadores (inactive)
♦ Sistema Internacional de Información Ambiental (inactive)
♦ Sistema Internacional de Información para las Ciencias y la Tecnologia Agricolas (#13848)
♦ Sistema Latinoamericano de Capacitación e Investigación Aduaneras (inactive)
♦ Sistema Mundial de Información y Alerta sobre la Alimentación y la Agricultura (#10416)
♦ Sistema Mundial de Observación del Clima (#10289)
♦ Sistema Mundial de Observación del Nivel del Mar (see: #11496)
♦ Sistema Mundial de Observación de los Océanos (#10511)
♦ Sistema de las Naciones Unidas (#20635)
♦ Sistema Panamericano de Carreteras (#18109)
♦ Sistema de Promoción de Información Tecnológica y Comercial (#20119)
♦ Sistema Regional de Información (#18788)

♦ Sistema Regional de Información sobre Formación Profesional (SIRFO) 19296

Regional Vocational Training Information System

Contact c/o OIT/CINTERFOR, Avda Uruguay 1238, 11100 Montevideo, Uruguay. T. +59829020557 – +59829086023 – +59829029716. Fax +59829021305.
URL: http://www.oitcinterfor.org/

History 1965, and coordinated by the Information and Documentation Service (IDS) of *Centro Interamericano para el Desarrollo del Conocimiento en la Formación Profesional (OIT/Cinterfor, #03802)*. **Languages** English, Spanish. **Activities** Within SIRFO content, IDS carries out the following activities: diagnoses of information and documentation services currently existing in vocational training institutes of the region; meetings of specialists in the area of documentation to study the results obtained by the implementation of SIRFO; study of joint actions to be undertaken to ensure continuation of the pilot programme to implement SIRFO and its extension to all documentation centres of the vocational training centres belonging to the network; review and analysis of ILO Thesaurus, Facet 06 – Education/Training, in current use by IDS. **Publications** *SIRFO Bibliographical Series*. Vocational training abstracts; Catalogues of Latin American publications on vocational training; Catalogues of Latin American didactic publications on vocational training; Catalogues of Latin American audiovisual material on vocational training. Information Services: IDS produces indexes, routines, procedure manuals for organizing and standardizing the documental tasks of the documentation centres of vocational training institutions. IDS implements a database with courses and curricula that impart the vocational training institutions in the region. **Information Services** *Centros Tecnológicos de América Latina y el Caribe*; *INFOR – Información sobre Formación Profesional*. [2013/XF2607/**F***]

♦ Sistema Regional de Información en Linea para Revistas Cientificas de América Latina, el Caribe, España y Portugal (Latindex) 19297

Gen Coordinator Dep de Biblio Latinoamericana, UNAM D-G de Bibliotecas, Edificio Anexo antes CICH Cir de la Investigación Cientifica, Ciudad Universitaria, 04510 Mexico City CDMX, Mexico. E-mail: latindex@unam.mx.
URL: http://www.latindex.org/

History 1997. **Aims** Disseminate, make available and improve the quality of academic journals published in the region. **Structure** A network of institutions. **Languages** English, French, Portuguese, Spanish. **Staff** 50.00 FTE, paid. **Finance** Members' dues. Funds from national and international organizations for specific activities. **Activities** Capacity building; events/meetings; guidance/assistance/consulting; knowledge management/ information dissemination; publishing activities; research/documentation; standards/guidelines.
Members Institutions in 24 countries:
Argentina, Bolivia, Brazil, Chile, Colombia, Costa Rica, Cuba, Dominican Rep, Ecuador, El Salvador, Germany, Guatemala, Honduras, Korea Rep, Mexico, Nicaragua, Panama, Paraguay, Peru, Portugal, Puerto Rico, Spain, Uruguay, Venezuela.
IGO Relations Cooperates with: *International Nuclear Information System (INIS, #14378); ISSN International Centre (ISSNIC, #16069); UNESCO (#20322).* **NGO Relations** Cooperates with: *Bioline International (BI); International Council for Scientific and Technical Information (ICSTI, #13070); International Network for the Availability of Scientific Publications (INASP, #14233); Red Europea de Información y Documentación sobre América Latina (REDIAL, #18652).* [2020.01.21/XJ5828/**F**]

- ♦ Sistema Regional de Información del Proyecto Principal / see Regional Information System (#18788)
- ♦ Sistemas de Documentación y de Información sobre Derechos Humanos, Internacional (#10985)
- ♦ Sister Cities International (internationally oriented national body)

♦ Sisterhood Is Global Institute (SIGI) 19298

Institut pour la solidarité internationale des femmes (ISIF)
Pres 25 Central Park West, Ste 9-I, New York NY 10023, USA. E-mail: info@sigi.org.
URL: http://www.sigi.org/

History 19 Nov 1984, New York, NY (USA). Founded by contributors to *'Sisterhood Is Global: The International Women's Movement Anthology'*, and meeting arising from the book, Nov 1984, New York NY. Currently in transition, since Mar 2004. **Aims** Support and help expand multi-issue, multi-constituency women's *rights activism* at local, national, regional and global levels; alert individuals, groups, governments and international bodies to *discriminatory* or *oppressive* practices against women, generating swift, effective *protest*; conduct and publish research, distribute information and work actively to end the abuse of women, informing women of their basic rights in addition to those guaranteed them through international human rights instruments; design educational programs to help women empower themselves; develop materials for women's rights facilitators to adapt and use cross-culturally; develop partnership projects aimed at women redefining and gaining power; encourage women from all societies to work together creatively to emphasize and achieve common goals. **Structure** Executive Committee; Advisory Board; Steering Committee. Headquarters rotates periodically: from 1984-1988 based in New York NY (USA); from 1988-1993 in New Zealand; subsequently Maryland (USA); currently Montréal (Canada). **Activities** Core activities: urgent action alert program; research and communications facilities; human rights education/knowledge partnership program; ending violence against women; training human rights education facilitators. Set up: *Arab Regional Resource Center on Violence Against Women (AMAN).* **Events** *International symposium on eliminating violence against women in Muslim societies* Amman (Jordan) 1998, *International conference on women's human rights education* Washington, DC (USA) 1997, *Conference on Beijing and beyond* Washington, DC (USA) 1995, *Meeting on refugee women and children in times of conflict* Athens (Greece) 1994. **Publications** *SIGI News* (2 a year). Books, research papers; training manuals.
Members Founding members (individuals); Affiliate organizations. Members in 59 countries and territories:
Afghanistan, Argentina, Australia, Bahrain, Bangladesh, Belgium, Brazil, Canada, Chile, China, Cuba, Egypt, Ethiopia, Fiji, Finland, France, Ghana, Greece, Honduras, Hungary, India, Iran Islamic Rep, Ireland, Israel, Italy, Japan, Jordan, Lebanon, Libya, Malaysia, Mexico, Morocco, Namibia, Nepal, New Zealand, Nigeria, Norway, Pakistan, Palestine, Papua New Guinea, Peru, Philippines, Poland, Portugal, Russia, Saudi Arabia, Spain, Sri Lanka, Syrian AR, Tanzania UR, Thailand, Uganda, UK, Uruguay, USA, Uzbekistan, Venezuela, Zambia, Zimbabwe.
Consultative Status Consultative status granted from: *ECOSOC (#05331)* (Special). **IGO Relations** *United Nations Commission on Crime Prevention and Criminal Justice (CCPCJ, #20530).* **NGO Relations** Member of: *EuroMed Rights (#05733).* [2020/XF3151/**F**]

- ♦ Sisters of Adoration of the Blessed Sacrament (religious order)
- ♦ Sisters Adorers of the Precious Blood (religious order)
- ♦ Sisters of the Assumption of the Blessed Virgin (religious order)
- ♦ Sisters of the Blessed Virgin Mary of the Philippines (religious order)
- ♦ Sisters of Bon Secours of Paris (religious order)
- ♦ Sisters of the Catholic Apostolate Pallottine (religious order)
- ♦ Sisters for Change (internationally oriented national body)
- ♦ Sisters of Charity of the Blessed Virgin Mary (religious order)
- ♦ Sisters of Charity and Christian Instruction of Nevers (religious order)
- ♦ Sisters of Charity of Cincinnati (religious order)
- ♦ Sisters of Charity of Jesus and Mary (religious order)
- ♦ Sisters of Charity of Leavenworth (religious order)
- ♦ Sisters of Charity of Montreal (religious order)
- ♦ Sisters of Charity of Nazareth (religious order)
- ♦ Sisters of Charity of Ottawa (religious order)
- ♦ Sisters of Charity of Our Lady of Evron (religious order)
- ♦ Sisters of Charity of Our Lady Mother of Mercy (religious order)
- ♦ Sisters of Charity of Quebec (religious order)
- ♦ Sisters of Charity of Saint Elizabeth (religious order)
- ♦ Sisters of Charity of Saints Bartholomew Capitanio and Vincent Gerosa (religious order)
- ♦ Sisters of Charity of Seton Hill (religious order)
- ♦ Sisters of Charity – Sisters of Charity of St Vincent-de-Paul (religious order)
- ♦ Sisters of Charity of St Charles Borromeo (religious order)
- ♦ Sisters of Charity of St Hyacinthe (religious order)
- ♦ Sisters of Charity of St Jeanne-Antide Thouret (religious order)
- ♦ Sisters of Charity of St Louis (religious order)
- ♦ Sisters of Charity of St Paul the Apostle (religious order)
- ♦ Sisters of Charity of St Vincent-de-Paul (religious order)
- ♦ Sisters of Charity of St Vincent-de-Paul, Halifax (religious order)
- ♦ Sisters of the Child Jesus, Puy (religious order)
- ♦ Sisters of Christian Charity, Daughters of the Blessed Virgin Mary of the Immaculate Conception (religious order)
- ♦ Sisters of the Christian Doctrine (religious order)
- ♦ Sisters of the Congregation of Mary (religious order)
- ♦ Sisters of Congregation de Notre Dame (religious order)
- ♦ Sisters of the Cross of Chavanod (religious order)
- ♦ Sisters of the Destitute (religious order)
- ♦ Sisters of Divine Providence, Münster (religious order)
- ♦ Sisters of the Divine Redeemer (religious order)
- ♦ Sisters of the Divine Savior (religious order)
- ♦ Sister-Servants of the Holy Spirit of Perpetual Adoration (religious order)
- ♦ Sister Servants of the Most Sacred Heart of Jesus (religious order)
- ♦ Sisters of the Good Samaritan of the Order of St Benedict (religious order)
- ♦ Sisters of the Guardian Angel (religious order)
- ♦ Sisters of the Holy Angels (religious order)
- ♦ Sisters of the Holy Childhood of Jesus and Mary of St Chrétienne (religious order)
- ♦ Sisters of the Holy Cross (religious order)
- ♦ Sisters of Holy Cross (religious order)
- ♦ Sisters of the Holy Cross (religious order)
- ♦ Sisters of the Holy Cross and Passion of Our Lord Jesus Christ (religious order)
- ♦ Sisters of the Holy Family (religious order)
- ♦ Sisters of the Holy Family of Bordeaux (religious order)
- ♦ Sisters of the Holy Family of Nazareth (religious order)
- ♦ Sisters of the Holy Names of Jesus and Mary (religious order)
- ♦ Sisters of the Holy Redeemer (religious order)
- ♦ Sisters Hospitallers of the Sacred Heart of Jesus (religious order)
- ♦ Sisters of the Immaculate Conception of Saint-Méen-Le-Grand (religious order)
- ♦ Sisters of the Incarnate Word and Blessed Sacrament (religious order)
- ♦ Sister to Sister International (internationally oriented national body)
- ♦ Sisters of the Little Flower of Bethany (religious order)
- ♦ Sisters of the Love of God (religious order)
- ♦ Sisters of Marie Auxiliatrice (religious order)
- ♦ Sisters Mercedarian Missionaries of Bérriz (religious order)
- ♦ Sisters of Mercy, 1823 (religious order)
- ♦ Sisters of Mercy of the Americas (religious order)
- ♦ Sisters of Mercy of the Holy Cross (religious order)
- ♦ Sisters of the Most Precious Blood of O'Fallon, Missouri (religious order)
- ♦ Sisters of Nazareth (religious order)
- ♦ Sisters of Notre Dame (religious order)
- ♦ Sisters of Notre Dame de Namur (religious order)
- ♦ Sisters of Our Lady of Charity of the Good Shepherd (religious order)
- ♦ Sisters of Our Lady of the Missions (religious order)
- ♦ Sisters of the Poor Child Jesus (religious order)
- ♦ Sisters of the Precious Blood (religious order)
- ♦ Sisters of the Presentation of Mary (religious order)
- ♦ Sisters of Providence (religious order)
- ♦ Sisters of Providence of Ruillé-sur-Loir (religious order)
- ♦ Sisters of Providence of St Mary-of-the-Woods (religious order)
- ♦ Sisters of the Sacred Heart of Jesus (religious order)
- ♦ Sisters of the Sacred Hearts of Jesus and Mary (religious order)
- ♦ Sisters of Saint Brigid (religious order)
- ♦ Sisters of Saint Clare (religious order)
- ♦ Sisters of Saint Joseph of the Sacred Heart (religious order)
- ♦ Sisters of Saint Joseph of "Saint-Marc" (religious order)
- ♦ Sisters of Saint Joseph of the Third Order of Saint Francis (religious order)
- ♦ Sisters of Saint Martha (religious order)
- ♦ Sisters of Saints Cyril and Methodius (religious order)
- ♦ Sisters, Servants of the Immaculate Heart of Mary of Monroe (religious order)
- ♦ Sisters Servants of the Immaculate Heart of Mary of Scranton (religious order)
- ♦ Sisters Servants of Mary (religious order)
- ♦ Sisters Servants of Mary Immaculate (religious order)
- ♦ Sisters of the Society of the Divine Vocations (religious order)
- ♦ Sisters of St Anne (religious order)
- ♦ Sisters of St Francis of Dillingen (religious order)
- ♦ Sisters of St Francis of Philadelphia (religious order)
- ♦ Sisters of St Gemma Galgani (religious order)
- ♦ Sisters of St John of God (religious order)
- ♦ Sisters of St Joseph of Annecy (religious order)
- ♦ Sisters of St Joseph of the Apparition (religious order)
- ♦ Sisters of St Joseph of Cluny (religious order)
- ♦ Sisters of St Joseph of Tarbes (religious order)
- ♦ Sisters of St Louis Juilly-Monaghan (religious order)
- ♦ Sisters of St Paul of Chartres (religious order)
- ♦ Sisters of St Thomas of Villanova (religious order)
- ♦ Sisters of St Ursula of the Blessed Virgin (religious order)
- ♦ Sisters of the Third Order of St Dominic (religious order)
- ♦ SI – Survivors International (internationally oriented national body)
- ♦ SISV – Secretaria Internacional para el Servicio Voluntario (inactive)
- ♦ SISV – Secrétariat international du service volontaire (inactive)
- ♦ SI/SWP / see Soroptimist International South East Asia Pacific (#19691)

♦ SITA 19299

Shareholder Relations Ave des Olympiades 2, 1140 Brussels, Belgium. T. +3227450510. Fax +3227450517. E-mail: shareholder.relations@sita.aero.
CEO Chemin de Joinville 26, BP 31, Cointrin, 1216 Geneva, Switzerland. T. +41227476207. E-mail: info@sita.aero.
URL: http://www.sita.aero/

History 1949. Founded by 11 airlines. Former names and other names: *International Society of Aeronautical Telecommunications* – former; *Airlines Worldwide Telecommunications and Information Services* – former; *Airline Telecommunication and Information Services* – former; *Société internationale de télécommunications aéronautiques (SITA)* – former; *Sociedad Internacional de Telecomunicaciones Aeronauticas* – former. Registration: Banque-Carrefour des Entreprises, Belgium. **Aims** Bring together the airlines' existing communications facilities so that all users could take advantage of the cost efficiencies of a shared infrastructure; ensure rapid transmission of information relating to aircraft movements and flight security, passenger, cargo, flight operations and management services. **Structure** General Assembly. Board of Directors and SITA Council, comprising up to 45 members, represented on the basis of shares held in SITA. Offices in 32 countries; main office in Geneva (Switzerland). Subsidiaries: *'SITA FOR AIRCRAFT'* – specializes in Nose-to-Tail connectivity solutions for airlines; *"SITA AT AIRPORTS' – Solutions and services for airlines, airports, ground handlers operating at airport; 'SITA AT BORDERS' – Ensuring that governments can strike a balance between critical measures, and safer, easier travel; CHAMP Cargosystems'* – IT company dedicated to aviation cargo. Hosts Customer Event (annual, in Brussels). **Languages** English. **Staff** 4500.00 FTE, paid. **Activities** Provides IT business solutions and communication services to the air transport industry; manages complex communication solutions for air transport, government and GDS customers over the world's most extensive communication network, complemented by consultancy in the design, deployment and integration of communication services; provides market-leading common-use services to airports and air-to-ground communications to airlines; delivers a comprehensive portfolio of e-commerce solutions for airlines and pioneers new technologies in areas such as in-flight passenger communications and transportation security; works to simplify travel and transportation removing complexity and improving members' operational performance. **Events** *Air Transport IT Summit* Brussels (Belgium) 2017, *Annual airline IT summit and general assembly* Brussels (Belgium) 2006, *Annual airline IT summit and general assembly* Brussels (Belgium) 2005, *Annual airline IT summit and general assembly* Brussels (Belgium) 2004, *Annual airline IT summit and general assembly* Brussels (Belgium) 2003. **Publications** *Air Transport IT Review* (3 a year); *SITA Aircom Industry Report* (2 a year); *SITA Regional e-News* (2 a year); *Airline IT Trends Survey* (annual) – jointly with Airline Business; *Airport IT Trends Survey* (annual) – jointly with ACI and Airline Business; *Passenger IT Trens Survey* (annual) – jointly with ATW; *SITA Activity Reports* (annual); *SITA Baggage Report* (annual) – jointly with AATW. White papers. **Members** Airlines and air transport related companies. Total membership (over 400) in over 220 countries. Membership countries not specified. **Consultative Status** Consultative status granted from: *ECOSOC (#05331)* (Ros C); *UNCTAD (#20285)* (Special Category). **IGO Relations** Cooperates with: *International Mobile Satellite Organization (IMSO, #14174); International Telecommunication Union (ITU, #15673)* and observer member of its Radiocommunication and Telecommunication Standardization Sectors. **NGO Relations** Member of: *Airports Council International (ACI, #00611); International Air Transport Association (IATA, #11614).* In liaison with technical committees of: *International Organization for Standardization (ISO, #14473).* Australian branch is member of: *Pacific Islands Telecommunications Association (PITA, #17979).* [2021.09.01/XD7339/**F**]

- ♦ **SITA** Sociedade Internacional de Trilogia Analitica (#14917)
- ♦ **SITA** Società Internazionale Tommaso d'Aquino (#19438)
- ♦ **SITCA** Secretaria de Integración Turistica Centroamericana (#19193)
- ♦ SITC – Society for Immunotherapy of Cancer (internationally oriented national body)
- ♦ SITE / see Society for Incentive Travel Excellence (#19574)
- ♦ **SITEMSH** Société internationale de traumatologie de ski et de médecine des sports d'hiver (#15445)
- ♦ **SITE** Society for Incentive Travel Excellence (#19574)
- ♦ **SITH** Société internationale de technique hydrothermale (#19497)
- ♦ **SITIMO** Société internationale des techniques d'imagerie mentale onirique (#19498)
- ♦ SITIM / see Société internationale des techniques d'imagerie mentale onirique (#19498)
- ♦ **SITM** Société internationale pour l'étude du théâtre médiéval (#15480)
- ♦ SITP – Société internationale de thérapie psychomotrice (no recent information)
- ♦ SITRASS – Solidarité internationale sur les transports et la recherche en Afrique sub-saharienne (internationally oriented national body)
- ♦ SITREC – Stockholm International Toy Research Centre (internationally oriented national body)
- ♦ SIT – Sarvodaya International Trust (internationally oriented national body)
- ♦ SIT – School for International Training (internationally oriented national body)

♦ SITS International 19300

Exec Coordinator Karolinska Inst, CNS 5th floor, Tomtebodav[agen 18A, SE-171 77 Stockholm, Sweden. T. +46707704230. Fax +4600000000000. E-mail: info@sitsinternational.org.
Chair address not obtained.
URL: https://www.sitsinternational.org/

History 1996. **Aims** Promote safe implementation of treatments in *stroke.* **Structure** Scientific Committee; Coordination Office. **Languages** English, Swedish. **Activities** Awards/prizes/competitions; research/documentation. **Publications** Annual Reports; articles; papers. Information Services: Registries.
Members Regional networks; stroke professionals (3000) in 88 countries and territories:
Albania, Algeria, Argentina, Australia, Austria, Belarus, Belgium, Bolivia, Bosnia-Herzegovina, Brazil, Bulgaria, Chile, China, Colombia, Costa Rica, Croatia, Czechia, Denmark, Dominican Rep, Ecuador, Egypt, El Salvador, Estonia, Ethiopia, Finland, France, Georgia, Germany, Greece, Guatemala, Honduras, Hong Kong, Hungary, Iceland, India, Iran Islamic Rep, Ireland, Israel, Italy, Japan, Kazakhstan, Kenya, Korea Rep, Kuwait, Kyrgyzstan, Lebanon, Libya, Lithuania, Malta, Mexico, Moldova, Morocco, Netherlands, New Zealand, Nicaragua, Nigeria, North Macedonia, Norway, Oman, Pakistan, Panama, Paraguay, Peru, Philippines, Poland, Portugal, Qatar, Romania, Russia, Saudi Arabia, Serbia, Singapore, Slovakia, Slovenia, Spain, Sri Lanka, Sweden, Switzerland, Tanzania UR, Thailand, Tunisia, Türkiye, UK, Ukraine, United Arab Emirates, Uruguay, Venezuela, Vietnam.
[2023/XM0149/**F**]

- ♦ SITS / see International Society of Blood Transfusion (#14979)
- ♦ SIT – Society of International Treasurers (inactive)
- ♦ **SITS** Société internationale de transfusion sanguine (#14979)
- ♦ SIT – Sugar Industry Technologists (unconfirmed)
- ♦ **SIT** Systems in Transition (#20085)
- ♦ Situationist International (inactive)
- ♦ SIUNA – Seafarers' International Union of North America (internationally oriented national body)
- ♦ **SIUP** Sociedad Iberoamericana de Urologia Pediatrica (#11033)
- ♦ SIU – Schiller International University (internationally oriented national body)
- ♦ SIU – Senter for Internasjonalisering av Høyere Utdanning (internationally oriented national body)
- ♦ **SIU** Société Internationale d'Urologie (#19499)
- ♦ SIVA / see International Society for Anaesthetic Pharmacology
- ♦ Sivananda Yoga Vedanta Zentrum (#14863)
- ♦ SIW / see Foundation for International Voluntary Service
- ♦ SIW Internationale Vrijwilligersprojekten (internationally oriented national body)
- ♦ SIWI – Stockholm International Water Institute (internationally oriented national body)
- ♦ SIWO / see International Association on Social Quality (#12168)
- ♦ SIWPS – Saltzman Institute of War and Peace Studies (internationally oriented national body)
- ♦ **SIW** Socialist International Women (#19341)

♦ Six Countries Programme (6CP) 19301

Secretariat TNO, PO Box 49, 2600 AA Delft, Netherlands. T. +31888668562. E-mail: 6cp@tno.nl.
Chairman address not obtained.
URL: http://www.6cp.net/

History 1975, by France, Germany, Netherlands and UK. **Aims** Contribute to a better understanding of *innovation* processes, their impacts on the economy and society and the development of effective (public) innovation policies. **Structure** Steering Committee (meets annually). **Languages** English. **Staff** 0.50 FTE, paid. Volunteers. **Finance** Members' dues. **Activities** Organizes annual workshops. **Events** *40 years of innovation – what's next?* Vienna (Austria) 2015, *Can policy follow the dynamics of global innovation platforms?* 's Hertogenbosch (Netherlands) 2014, *Exploring the green innovation paradigm* Utrecht (Netherlands) 2010, *New economic ground for innovation policy* Bilbao (Spain) 2009, *Workshop / Annual Autumn Workshop* Karlsruhe (Germany) 2008. **Publications** *Six Countries Programme Newsletter.*
Members Governments and organizations of 11 countries:
Austria, Belgium, Canada, Finland, Germany, Hungary, Ireland, Netherlands, South Africa, Sweden, UK.
IGO Relations Contacts with: *OECD (#17693)*; *European Commission (EC, #06633).* **NGO Relations** Contacts with: *European Association of Research and Technology Organizations (EARTO, #06197)*; *European Industrial Research Management Association (EIRMA, #07531).* [2016/XM3081/**E***]

- ♦ Sixième protocole additionnel à l'Accord général sur les privilèges et immunités du Conseil de l'Europe (1996 treaty)
- ♦ Six Markets Group (no recent information)
- ♦ Six plus Two Group on Afghanistan (inactive)
- ♦ **SIX** Social Innovation Exchange (#19339)
- ♦ Sixth Protocol to the General Agreement on Privileges and Immunities of the Council of Europe (1996 treaty)
- ♦ SJC – Sisters of St Joseph of Cluny (religious order)
- ♦ SJC – Social Justice Committee (internationally oriented national body)
- ♦ **SJFA** Starptautiska Jauno Fermeru Apvieniba (#15829)
- ♦ Sjíassurandírernes Centralforening / see Nordic Association of Marine Insurers (#17198)
- ♦ **SJIA** St Joan's International Alliance (#19992)
- ♦ **SJI** Stichting Justice Initiative (#19985)
- ♦ **SJJAF** Sports Jiu-Jitsu African Federation (#19927)
- ♦ **SJJIF** Sport Jiu-Jitsu International Federation (#19926)
- ♦ SJJOF – Sport Jiu-Jitsu Oceana Federation (unconfirmed)
- ♦ SJJSAF – Sport Jiu-Jitsu South American Federation (unconfirmed)

♦ Sjögren Europe 19302

Sec Rue du Marché-Neuf 27, 2503 Biel BE, Switzerland. E-mail: contact@sjogreneurope.org.
URL: https://sjogreneurope.org/

History Feb 2019. Former names and other names: *European Federation of Sjögren's Syndrome Patient Associations (Sjögren Europe)* – former; *European Federation of Sjögren's Disease Patient Association (Sjögren Europe)* – full title. Registration: Swiss Civil Code, Switzerland. **Aims** Increase visibility, attention and solutions for Sjögren's Syndrome, by promoting the advancement of knowledge, research, information, treatment and care, by fostering patient involvement and participation in scientific research, medical, health, political institutions, pharmaceutical industry and social areas, and by increasing awareness about Sjögren's Syndrome at all levels. **Structure** General Assembly; Board. **Languages** English.
Members Organizations in 12 countries:
Belgium, Finland, France, Greece, Israel, Netherlands, Norway, Poland, Portugal, Spain, Switzerland, UK.
Associate in 1 country:
Romania. [2022.05.22/AA2345/**D**]

- ♦ Sjögren Europe / see Sjögren Europe (#19302)
- ♦ Sjømannskirken – Norsk kirke i utlandet (internationally oriented national body)
- ♦ SJ – Society of Jesus (religious order)
- ♦ SJT – Soeurs de Saint Joseph de Tarbes (religious order)
- ♦ SJUF – Skandinavisk-Judiska Ungdomsförbundet (no recent information)
- ♦ Sjundedags Adventisternas Generalkonferens (#10109)
- ♦ **SJU** SESAR Joint Undertaking (#19249)
- ♦ Skål International (#02743)
- ♦ Skandinaavinen kielen ja kognition yhdistys (#19072)
- ♦ Skandinaviens Tekniska Analytikers Förening (#19123)
- ♦ Skandinavische Gesellschaft für Anästhesiologie / see Scandinavian Society of Anaesthesiology and Intensive Care Medicine (#19101)
- ♦ Skandinavischen Textileinzelhandelsorganisationen (inactive)
- ♦ Skandinaviska Analoggimaskinsälskabet / see Scandinavian Simulation Society (#19100)
- ♦ Skandinaviska Celltoxikologiska Sällskapet (inactive)
- ♦ Skandinaviska Endodontiföreningen (#19085)
- ♦ Skandinaviska Enskilda Banken (internationally oriented national body)
- ♦ Skandinaviska Félagio um Meina-og Lyflaeknisfraedi Munns og Kjalka (#19303)
- ♦ Skandinaviska Föreningen för Elektronmikroskopi / see Nordic Microscopy Society (#17344)
- ♦ Skandinaviska Kriminalsällskapet (#04955)
- ♦ Skandinaviska Lackteknikers Förbund (#09702)
- ♦ Skandinaviska Mätarservicefirmors Förbund / see Scandinavian Petroleum Technic Association (#19096)
- ♦ Skandinaviska Sällskapet för Cerebrovaskulära Sjukdomar / see Nordic Stroke Society (#17439)
- ♦ Skandinaviska Sällskapet för Klinisk Fysiologi / see Scandinavian Society of Clinical Physiology and Nuclear Medicine (#19104)
- ♦ Skandinaviska Sällskapet för Språk och Kognition (#19072)
- ♦ Skandinaviska Samarbetskommittén för Pappersindustriarbetarförbunden (inactive)
- ♦ Skandinaviska Seglarforbund (inactive)
- ♦ Skandinaviska Tandläkareföreningen (inactive)
- ♦ Skandinaviska Transportarbetarefederationen / see Nordiska Transportarbetarefederationen (#17496)
- ♦ Skandinaviska Utvecklingsgruppen för Wellpapp / see International Development Group for Corrugated Board (#13160)
- ♦ Skandinavisk Celletoksikologisk Selskab (inactive)
- ♦ Skandinaviske Bryggerhøjskole (internationally oriented national body)
- ♦ Skandinavisk Elektroforese Forening (inactive)
- ♦ Skandinaviske Ornitologiske Union (inactive)
- ♦ Det Skandinaviske Selskab for Sprog og Kognition (#19072)
- ♦ Skandinavisk Fjørfeavls-Forbund (inactive)
- ♦ Skandinavisk Flynavigatør Forening (inactive)
- ♦ Skandinavisk Förening för Atero-sklerosforskning (#19102)
- ♦ Skandinavisk Forening af Oral og Maxillofacial Kirurger (#19074)
- ♦ Skandinavisk Forening for Oral Patologi og Oral Medicin (#19303)

♦ Skandinavisk Förening för Oral Patologi och Oral Medicin (SFOPOM) 19303

Scandinavian Fellowship for Oral Pathology and Oral Medicine – Skandinavisk Forening for Oral Patologi og Oral Medicin – Skandinavisk Forening for Oral Patologi og Oral Medisin – Pohjoismainen Suupatologian ja Suulääketieteen Yhdistys – Skandinaviska Félagio um Meina-og Lyflaeknisfraedi Munns og Kjalka

Pres Dept of Oral and Maxillofacial Diseases, Kuopio University Hospital, FI-70210 Kuopio, Finland.
URL: http://sfopom.org/

History 1971, Gothenburg (Sweden). Former names and other names: *Scandinavian Society for Oral Pathology and Oral Medicine* – former. **Aims** Promote and encourage study and practice of oral pathology and oral medicine; increase education of oral pathologists; facilitate communication between oral and general pathologists. **Structure** General Meeting (annual). Council, comprising President, Immediate Past-President and General Secretary/Treasurer. **Finance** Sources: members' dues. **Activities** Events/meetings. **Events** *Meeting* Kuopio (Finland) 2022, *Meeting* Copenhagen (Denmark) 2019, *Annual Meeting* Tromsø (Norway) 2010, *Annual Meeting* Stockholm (Sweden) 2009, *Annual Meeting* Copenhagen (Denmark) 2008.
Members Ordinary; life; honorary. Individuals in 7 countries:
Denmark, Finland, Germany, Iceland, Netherlands, Norway, Sweden. [2022/XD8058/**D**]

- ♦ Skandinavisk Forening for Oral Patologi og Oral Medisin (#19303)
- ♦ Skandinavisk Forening for Parodontologi (#19114)
- ♦ Skandinavisk Forening for Zoneterapeuter (inactive)
- ♦ Skandinavisk Forum for Lymfologi (unconfirmed)
- ♦ Skandinavisk Golf-Union (inactive)
- ♦ Skandinavisk Handkirurgiska Föreningen (#19120)
- ♦ Skandinavisk-Judiska Ungdomsförbundet (no recent information)
- ♦ Skandinavisk Kriminalselskap (#04955)
- ♦ Skandinavisk Migraeneselskab (inactive)
- ♦ Skandinavisk Museumsforbund / see Nordic Union of Museums (#17455)
- ♦ Skandinavisk Selskab for Psykofarmakologi / see Scandinavian College of Neuropsychopharmacology (#19082)
- ♦ Skandinavisk Selskap for Språk og Kognisjon (#19072)
- ♦ Skandinavisk Tandläkarförening (inactive)
- ♦ Skandinavisk Telegraf og Telefon Föderasjon (inactive)
- ♦ Skandinavisk Transportarbeiderfederasjon / see Nordiska Transportarbetarefederationen (#17496)
- ♦ Skandinavisk UFO Information (#19127)
- ♦ Skandinavisk Wayfarer Sammenslutning (#19128)
- ♦ Skandinavisk Yoga och Meditationsskola (#19129)
- ♦ Skandinawische Ausschuss für Zusammenarbeit in der Hauswirtshaftlichen Bildung (no recent information)
- ♦ Skanmek (meeting series)

♦ SKA Observatory (SKAO) 19304

Contact SKA Global Headquarters, Jodrell Bank, Lower Withington, Macclesfield, SK11 9FT, UK. E-mail: enquiries@skatelescope.org.
URL: http://www.skatelescope.org/

History Established through *Treaty for the establishment of the SKA Observatory*, which was signed 12 Mar 2019, Rome (Italy), by governments involved in *International Square Kilometre Array Project (SKA, inactive)*: Australia, China, Italy, Netherlands, Portugal, South Africa and UK. Evolved from SKA Organisation, which managed the SKA Project. Will supersede SKA Project, 2020. **Aims** Facilitate global collaboration in *radio astronomy* and build the SKA telescopes. **Events** *Congreso* Buenos Aires (Argentina) 2015.
[2022/XM8462/**E***]

- ♦ **SKAO** SKA Observatory (#19304)
- ♦ SKAT Foundation (internationally oriented national body)
- ♦ SKAT – Swiss Resource Centre and Consultancies for Development (internationally oriented national body)
- ♦ SKDA – Sportivnyj Komitet Druzeskih Armij (inactive)
- ♦ Ski-Club International der Journalisten / see International Ski Club of Journalists (#14869)
- ♦ Ski-club international des journalistes (#14869)
- ♦ **SKIF** Shotokan Karate-Do International Federation (#19263)

♦ **Skilex International** **19305**

Pres Marktplatz 16/1, 4810 Gmunden, Austria.
Sec address not obtained.
URL: https://www.skilex.eu/

History 1973, Italy. Founded by Giorgio Lazzarini, Michel Bailly and Dr Eugen Leer. Registration: Switzerland. **Structure** International Board. **Activities** Events/meetings. **Events** *International Skilex Congress* Berchtesgaden (Germany) 2023, *Conference* Zrece (Slovenia) 2020, *Conference* Val d'Isère (France) 2019, *Conference* Hradec Králové (Czechia) 2018, *Conference* Åre (Sweden) 2017. **NGO Relations** Cooperates with (1): *International Sport Lawyers Association (ISLA, #15591).* [2022/AA2976/c/**F**]

♦ Skillman.eu / see Skillman Network (#19306)

♦ **Skillman Network** **19306**

Sec Centro studi 'Cultura Sviluppo', Via Puccini 80, 51100 Pistoia PO, Italy. E-mail: secretariat@skillman.eu.
URL: https://skillman.eu/

History 1 Oct 2014. First contacts to set up network started June 2014. First project started 1 Jan 2015. Former names and other names: *Transnational platform of Centres of Vocational Excellence for the Advanced Manufacturing Sector (Skillman.eu)* – alias. Registration: EU Transparency Register, No/ID: 669084537755-08, Start date: 7 Apr 2020. **Aims** Introduce skills, competences and innovative curricula for the advanced manufacturing sector within the VET pathways. **Structure** Secretariat. **Finance** Supported by: *European Commission (EC, #06633).* **Activities** Events/meetings; projects/programmes; training/education. **Events** *Skillman International Forum* Lisbon (Portugal) 2021.

Members Regional, national and international organizations (about 630) in 93 countries. Membership countries not specified. Included in the above, 2 organizations listed in this Yearbook:
Colombo Plan Staff College (CPSC, #04121); European Photonics Industry Consortium (EPIC, #08205).
Skillman Alliance, founded 2019 and led by Skillman Network includes 4 organizations:
Assembly of European Regions (AER, #02316); European Association for Practitioner Research on Improving Learning (EAPRIL, #06161); International Vocational Education and Training Association (IVETA, #15861); The Global Association of Art and Design Education and Research (Cumulus Association, #10241). [2022/AA2626/y/**F**]

♦ SKIL – Sport Karate International (internationally oriented national body)

♦ **Skin Care in Organ Transplant Patients (SCOPE)** **19307**

Contact Hudkliniken, Karolinska Sjukhuset, SE-171 76 Stockholm, Sweden.
Sec address not obtained.
Sec address not obtained.
URL: https://www.scopenetwork.org/

History 2000. Former names and other names: *Skin Care in Organ Transplant Patients Europe* – full title. Registration: No/ID: 802418-9220, Sweden. **Aims** Meet the increasing need for qualified dermatological aftercare in this specialist group of patients. **Structure** Board of Directors. **Activities** Events/meetings. **Events** *SCOPE Network Meeting* Barcelona (Spain) 2019. [2020/AA0649/**F**]

♦ Skin Care in Organ Transplant Patients Europe / see Skin Care in Organ Transplant Patients (#19307)

♦ **Skin Inflammation and Psoriasis International Network (SPIN)** **19308**

Project Manager Fondation René Touraine, Hôpital Necker Enfants Malades Carré Necker, Cour Breteuil, 149 rue de Sèvres, 75015 Paris, France. T. +33145325417. E-mail: weboffice@spindermatology.org.
URL: http://www.spindermatology.org/

History 18 Nov 2005, Paris (France). Founding meeting comprised 20 countries willing to develop national psoriasis groups and to connect these groups into an international network, and following the European Congress on Psoriasis – PSO, 2004, Paris, when interest in developing networking activities in the field of psoriasis was shown. Initiated by FRT-Fondation René Touraine. Former names and other names: *Psoriasis International Network (PIN)* – former (2005 to 2017). **Aims** Improve the quality of health care of patients suffering from psoriasis and other chronic inflammatory skin diseases, as well as their access to quality skin care; develop national and international collaborations in the field of skin inflammation, in particular psoriasis, atopic dermatitis, vitiligo, alopecia and hidradenitis suppurativa. **Structure** Scientific Committee (around 50 members, organized in 7 functional teams); National Representatives (around 100); Executive Team. **Languages** English, French. **Staff** 1.00 FTE, paid; 1.00 FTE, voluntary. **Finance** Sources: grants; meeting proceeds; revenue from activities/projects. Supported by Fondation René Touraine. **Activities** Events/meetings; guidance/assistance/consulting; knowledge management/information dissemination; networking/liaising; research/documentation; training/education. **Events** *SPIN Congress* Paris (France) 2022, *SPIN Congress* Paris (France) 2019, *PSO Congress* Paris (France) 2016, *PSO Congress* Paris (France) 2013, *PSO Congress* Paris (France) 2010. **Publications** *SPIN Newsletter. Current Practice of Methotrexate Use for Psoriasis: Results of a worldwide survey among dermatologists* by R Gyulai et al. *International eDelphi Study to Reach Consensus on the Methotrexate Dosing Regimen in Patients With Psoriasis* (2022). Patient leaflet; social media.

Members Individuals and patient organizations in 100 countries and territories:
Algeria, Argentina, Australia, Austria, Bahrain, Bangladesh, Belarus, Belgium, Benin, Bolivia, Bosnia-Herzegovina, Brazil, Bulgaria, Burkina Faso, Cameroon, Canada, Chile, China, Colombia, Costa Rica, Côte d'Ivoire, Croatia, Cuba, Czechia, Denmark, Dominican Rep, Egypt, El Salvador, Estonia, Finland, France, Gabon, Georgia, Germany, Greece, Guinea, Honduras, Hungary, Iceland, India, Indonesia, Iran Islamic Rep, Ireland, Israel, Italy, Japan, Jordan, Kenya, Korea Rep, Kuwait, Latvia, Lebanon, Libya, Lithuania, Malaysia, Mali, Malta, Mauritania, Mexico, Moldova, Morocco, Netherlands, New Zealand, Nicaragua, Niger, Nigeria, North Macedonia, Palestine, Peru, Philippines, Poland, Portugal, Puerto Rico, Qatar, Romania, Russia, Saudi Arabia, Senegal, Serbia, Singapore, Slovakia, Slovenia, South Africa, Spain, Sri Lanka, Sweden, Switzerland, Syrian AR, Taiwan, Thailand, Togo, Tunisia, Türkiye, UK, Ukraine, United Arab Emirates, Uruguay, USA, Venezuela, Yemen. [2023.02.14/XJ2325/**F**]

♦ SKI – SickKids International (internationally oriented national body)
♦ **SKKB/CCCBR** Council of Christian Churches in the Barents Region (#04876)
♦ SKKIF / see Shotokan Karate-Do International Federation (#19263)
♦ **SKKY** Skandinaavinen kielen ja kognition yhdistys (#19072)
♦ Skoll Foundation (internationally oriented national body)
♦ Skoll Global Threats Fund (internationally oriented national body)

♦ **Skolta Esperanto-Ligo (SEL)** **19309**

Scout Esperanto League – Ligue espérantiste scoute – Liga de Exploradores Esperantistas – Esperanto-Liga der Pfadfinder – Liga dos Escoteiros Esperantistas

SG Av des Muguets 39, 1950 Kraainem, Belgium. E-mail: skoltismo@gmail.com.
URL: http://www.skolta.org/

History 1918, London (UK). **Aims** Spread the ideals of the Scout movement through Esperanto and promote the use of Esperanto by scouts and guides; create, publish and distribute scout literature in Esperanto; increase the feeling of brotherhood among the youth of all nations. **Structure** General Committee of national representatives; Executive Committee. **Languages** Esperanto. **Staff** 5.00 FTE, voluntary. **Finance** Sources: donations; members' dues. **Activities** Events/meetings. **Events** *Annual Congress* Fortaleza (Brazil) 2003, *Annual Congress* Tampere (Finland) 1995, *Annual Congress* Seoul (Korea Rep) 1994, *Annual Congress* Valencia (Spain) 1993, *Annual Congress* Vienna (Austria) 1992. **Publications** *La Skolta Mondo* (4 a year) in Esperanto. *Jamborea Lingvo* in Esperanto – direct-method textboo, with record; *Jamboree Story* in English, Esperanto; *La Patrol-sistemo* in Esperanto; *Ni Faru Grupan Planadon* in Esperanto; *Orjubileo* in Esperanto – History of SEL; *Skolta Terminaro* in Esperanto – dictionary of scout words; *Skoltismo por Knapoj* in Esperanto; *Wider Horizons* in Catalan, Dutch, English, French, German, Japanese, Norwegian, Spanish, Swedish – practical suggestions to promote international collaboration.

Members Full in 71 countries and territories:
Angola, Argentina, Australia, Austria, Belgium, Brazil, Bulgaria, Canada, Chile, China, Congo DR, Costa Rica, Côte d'Ivoire, Croatia, Czechia, Denmark, Estonia, Finland, France, Germany, Greece, Hong Kong, Hungary, Iceland, India, Indonesia, Iran Islamic Rep, Ireland, Israel, Italy, Jamaica, Japan, Korea Rep, Latvia, Lebanon, Liberia, Lithuania, Madagascar, Malaysia, Malta, Mexico, Netherlands, New Zealand, Nigeria, Norway, Pakistan, Philippines, Poland, Puerto Rico, Romania, Russia, Senegal, Serbia, Sierra Leone, Slovakia, Slovenia, South Africa, Spain, Sri Lanka, Sweden, Switzerland, Syrian AR, Tanzania UR, Thailand, UK, Ukraine, Uruguay, USA, Vanuatu, Venezuela, Zambia.

NGO Relations Member of: *Universal Esperanto Association (UEA, #20676).* SEL members are present or former members of national associations which belong to: *World Organization of the Scout Movement (WOSM, #21693).* [2020.03.03/XC3212/**C**]

♦ **SKS** Skandinaviska Kriminalsällskapet (#04955)
♦ Skupina Aliance Liberalu a Demokratu pro Evropu / see Renew Europe (#18840)
♦ Skupina Aliancie Liberalov a Demokratov za Európu / see Renew Europe (#18840)
♦ Skupina Socialdemokratov v Evropskem Parlamentu / see Group of the Progressive Alliance of Socialists and Democrats in the European Parliament (#10786)
♦ Skupina Socialnich Demokratu v Evropském Parlamentu / see Group of the Progressive Alliance of Socialists and Democrats in the European Parliament (#10786)
♦ Skupina Zaveznistva Liberalcev in Demokratov za Evropo / see Renew Europe (#18840)
♦ Skupni Raziknovalni Center (#16147)
♦ Skylark International (internationally oriented national body)
♦ SKY – Sorig Khang International (unconfirmed)
♦ SkyTruth (internationally oriented national body)
♦ SLAA / see Society for Latin American and Caribbean Anthropology
♦ **SLAAI** Sociedad Latinoamericana de Alergia, Asma e Inmunologia (#19389)
♦ **SLABO** Sociedade Latino Americana de Biomateriais, Engenharia de Tecidos e Orgãos Artificiais (#16370)
♦ SLACA – Society for Latin American and Caribbean Anthropology (internationally oriented national body)
♦ SLACIP – Sociedad Latinoamericana de Cuidados Intensives Pediatricos (unconfirmed)
♦ **SLACOM** Sociedad Latinoamericana y del Caribe de Oncologia Médica (#16286)
♦ SLAC – Sociedade Latino Americana de Coaching (internationally oriented national body)
♦ SLAC / see Sociedad Latinoamericana de Citopatologia (#19398)
♦ **SLAC** Sociedad Latinoamericana de Citopatologia (#19398)
♦ **SLADE** Sociedad Latinoamericana de Estrategia (#19404)
♦ SLADIMER – Sociedad Latinoamericana de Investigación Médica en Enfermedades Raras (no recent information)
♦ **SLADI** Sociedad Latinoamericana de Derecho Internacional (#16374)
♦ SLADP – Sociedad Latinoamericana de Dermatología Pediátrica (inactive)
♦ **SLAD** Sociedad Latinoamericana de Disfagia (#19400)
♦ **SLAGF** Sociedad Latinoamericana de Genetica Forense (#19408)
♦ **SLAGHNP** Sociedad Latinoamericana de Gastroenterologia, Hepatologia y Nutrición Pediatrica (#16382)
♦ SLAGPNH / see Latinamerican Society for Pediatric Gastroenterology, Hepatology and Nutrition (#16382)
♦ SLAGPN / see Latinamerican Society for Pediatric Gastroenterology, Hepatology and Nutrition (#16382)
♦ **SLAG** Sociedade Latino-Americana de Glaucoma (#19357)
♦ **SLAHOC** Sociedad Latino Americana de Hombro y Codo (#19409)
♦ **SLAIP** Sociedad Latinoamericana de Investigación Pediatrica (#19411)
♦ SLAI / see Sociedad Latinoamericana de Alergia, Asma e Inmunologia (#19389)
♦ SLAI / see Sociedad Latinoamericana de Medicina Sexual (#19413)
♦ SLAIS / see Sociedad Latinoamericana de Medicina Sexual (#19413)
♦ SLAM / see Latin American Federation of Mastology (#16324)
♦ SLAM – Sociedad Latinoamericana de Micotoxicologia (unconfirmed)
♦ SLAM – Solidarité Laurentides Amérique centrale (internationally oriented national body)
♦ **SLAMS** Sociedad Latinoamericana de Medicina Sexual (#19413)
♦ **SLAMTB** Sociedad Latinoamericana de Tuberculosis y Otras Micobacteriosis (#19427)
♦ **SLAMVI** Sociedad Latinoamericana de Medicina del Viajero (#19414)
♦ **SLANFE** Sociedad Latinoamericana de Neurocirugia Funcional y Esterotaxia (#16386)
♦ **SLANH** Sociedade Latinoamericana de Nefrologia e Hipertensión (#19415)
♦ **SLANH** Sociedad Latinoamericana de Nefrologia e Hipertensión (#19415)
♦ **SLAN** Sociedad Latinoamericana de Neuropsicologia (#16378)
♦ **SLAN** Sociedad Latinoamericana de Nutrición (#19417)
♦ **SLAOP** Sociedad Latinoamericana de Oncologia Pediatrica (#16383)
♦ SLAO / see Société ouest-africaine de linguistique (#19506)
♦ **SLAOTI** Sociedad Latinoamericana de Ortopedia y Traumatologia Infantil (#19419)
♦ **SLAOT** Sociedad Latinoamericana de Ortopedia y Traumatologia (#19418)
♦ SLAP / see Sociedad Latinoamericana de Primatologia (#19422)
♦ SLAPCV – Sociedad Latinoamericana de Patologia Clinica Veterinaria (unconfirmed)
♦ **SLAPPE** Sociedad Latinoamericana de Patologia Pediatrica (#19421)
♦ **SLAPrim** Sociedad Latinoamericana de Primatologia (#19422)
♦ **SLAP** Sociedad Latinoamericana de Paraplejia (#19420)
♦ **SLAP** Sociedad Latinoamericana de Patologia (#16380)
♦ SLARCF / see Sociedad Latinoamericana de Rinologia y Cirugia Plastica Facial (#19425)
♦ **SLARCF** Sociedad Latinoamericana de Rinologia y Cirugia Plastica Facial (#19425)
♦ **SLARD** Sociedad Latinoamericana de Artroscopia, Rodilla y Traumatologia Deportiva (#19390)
♦ **SLARP** Sociedad Latinoamericana de Radiologia Pediatrica (#19424)
♦ SLAR / see Sociedad Latinoamericana de Rinologia y Cirugia Plastica Facial (#19425)
♦ SLA – School Library Association (internationally oriented national body)
♦ SLAS Europe / see Society for Laboratory Automation and Screening
♦ SLA – Sociedad Latinoamericana de Acarologia (no recent information)
♦ SLA – Solar Light for Africa (internationally oriented national body)
♦ SLA – Special Libraries Association (internationally oriented national body)
♦ SLAS – Society for Laboratory Automation and Screening (internationally oriented national body)
♦ SLAS – Society for Latin American Studies (internationally oriented national body)
♦ **SLASS** Sociedad Latinoamericana de Auditoría de Servicios de Salud (#19392)
♦ **SLATME** Sociedad Latino Americana de Tumores Musculo Equeléticos (#19428)
♦ **SLAT** Sociedad Latinoamericana de Tiroides (#16390)
♦ SLAT – Sociedad Latinoamericana de Trasplantes (inactive)
♦ Slavery Convention, 1926 (1926 treaty)
♦ Slavery Convention, 1953 (1953 treaty)
♦ Slavic Gospel Association (internationally oriented national body)
♦ Slavic Studies Institute (internationally oriented national body)
♦ **SLBD** Sociedad Latino Americana de Biologica del Desarrollo (#16371)
♦ **SLB** Sociedad Latinoamericana de Briologia (#16260)
♦ SLCA / see International Association of Claim Professionals (#11777)
♦ SLCCCP – Sociedad Latina Cardiologia y Cirugia Cardiovascular Pediatrica (unconfirmed)
♦ **SLCCS** Sociedad Latinoamericana y del Caribe de Cactaceas y Otras Suculentas (#19395)
♦ SLCCT – Sociedad Latinoamericana de Cirugia Cardiovascular y Toracica (unconfirmed)
♦ SLC – Secours aux lépreux Canada (internationally oriented national body)
♦ **SLCS** Sociedad Latinoamericana de la Ciencia del Suelo (#16385)
♦ **SLDV** Sociedad Latinoamericana de Dermatologia Veterinaria (#19399)
♦ **SLEIMPN** Sociedad Latinoamericana de Errores Innatos del Metabolismo y Pesquisa Neonatal (#19401)
♦ **SLE** Linguistics Society of Europe (#19448)
♦ **SLEP** Sociedad Latinoamericana de Endocrinologia Pediatrica (#16381)
♦ **SLE** Societas Linguistica Europaea (#19448)
♦ **SLE** Société européenne de linguistique (#19448)
♦ **SLEuro** European Lupus Society (#07719)
♦ **SLF** Skandinaviska Lackteknikers Förbund (#09702)

- ♦ SLF – Sociedad Latinoamericana de Fitoquimica (inactive)
- ♦ SLF – Stichting Liliane Fonds (internationally oriented national body)
- ♦ SLHCT – Sociedad Latinoamericana de Historia de las Ciencias y la Tecnologia (no recent information)
- ♦ SLH / see Latin American Association for the Study of the Liver (#16252)
- ♦ **SLHP** Sociedad Latina de Hipertensión Pulmonar (#19388)
- ♦ **SLIMP** Sociedade Latino Americana de Interação Materno Fetal and Placenta (#16376)
- ♦ **SLIMP** Sociedad Latinoamericana de Interacción Materno-Fetal y Placenta (#16376)
- ♦ SLIP / see Asociación Latinoamericana de la Papa (#02250)
- ♦ **SLIPE** Sociedad Latinoamericana de Infectologia Pediatrica (#19410)
- ♦ **SLiR** Société de linguistique romane (#19501)
- ♦ SLLS – Sign Language Linguistics Society (internationally oriented national body)
- ♦ **SLLS** Society for Longitudinal and Life Course Studies (#19589)
- ♦ SLM – Sociedad Latinoamericana de Maiz (inactive)
- ♦ **SLNG** Service de liaison des Nations Unies avec les organisations non gouvernementales (#20591)
- ♦ **SLNG** Sociedad Latinoamericana de Neurogastroenterologia (#19416)
- ♦ SLoCaT Foundation / see Partnership on Sustainable, Low Carbon Transport Foundation (#18244)
- ♦ **SLoCaT Foundation** Partnership on Sustainable, Low Carbon Transport Foundation (#18244)
- ♦ SLOGA – Slovenian Global Action (internationally oriented national body)
- ♦ SLORL – Société latine d'oto-rhino-laryngologie (inactive)
- ♦ Slovak Agency for International Development Cooperation (internationally oriented national body)
- ♦ Slovak Foreign Policy Association (internationally oriented national body)
- ♦ Slovenian Global Action (internationally oriented national body)
- ♦ Slovenska spolocnost' pre zahranicnú politiku (internationally oriented national body)
- ♦ Slow Food International / see International Movement for the Defence of and the Right to Pleasure (#14194)
- ♦ **Slow Food** International Movement for the Defence of and the Right to Pleasure (#14194)
- ♦ SLP Conference – International Conference on Second Language Pedagogies (meeting series)
- ♦ SLS / see Society for Literature, Science and the Arts
- ♦ **SLSAeu** European Society for Literature, Science and the Arts (#08642)
- ♦ SLSA – Society for Literature, Science and the Arts (internationally oriented national body)
- ♦ **SLTBR** Society for Light Treatment and Biological Rhythms (#19588)
- ♦ **SLTB** Society for Low Temperature Biology (#19590)
- ♦ **SLTC** Sociedad Latinoamericana de Tecnologia del Caucho (#19426)
- ♦ Slum Dwellers International / see Shack-Slum Dwellers International (#19255)
- ♦ Slush (meeting series)
- ♦ SMACC – Social Media and Critical Care Conference (meeting series)
- ♦ SMACD – International Conference on Synthesis, Modeling, Analysis and Simulation Methods and Applications to Circuit Design Conference (meeting series)

♦ SMA Europe 19310

Coordinator Glebe Fold, Chipping Campden, GL55 6JP, UK.
URL: http://www.sma-europe.eu/

History Founded 1989, as *European Spinal Muscular Atrophy Task Force.* Also referred to as *European Alliance of SMA Groups (EASMA).* Formally organized, 2006, as a pan-European body of representatives. **Aims** Provide a framework to organize and drive research and clinical trial initiatives and drug approval for *spinal muscular atrophy* at European level. **Structure** Board. **Languages** English. **Staff** 0.50 FTE, paid. **Finance** Projects financed by member organizations. **Activities** Financial and/or material support; research and development. **Events** *International Scientific Congress on Spinal Muscular Atrophy* Barcelona (Spain) 2022, *International Scientific Congress on Spinal Muscular Atrophy* Evry (France) 2020, *International Scientific Congress on Spinal Muscular Atrophy* Krakow (Poland) 2018, *Meeting* UK 2001.
Members in 19 countries:
Belgium, Czechia, Denmark, Finland, France, Germany, Iceland, Italy, Netherlands, North Macedonia, Poland, Romania, Russia, Serbia, Spain, Sweden, Switzerland, UK, Ukraine.
IGO Relations *European Medicines Agency (EMA, #07767).* **NGO Relations** Member of: *EURORDIS – Rare Diseases Europe (#09175); TREAT-NMD Neuromuscular Network (TREAT-NMD, #20231).* [2020/XD5120/**D**]

- ♦ Smalkad League Treaty (1531 treaty)

♦ Small Business Standards (SBS) 19311

Gen Sec Rue Jacques de Lalaing 4, 1040 Brussels, Belgium. T. +3222850727. E-mail: info@sbs-sme.eu.
URL: https://www.sbs-sme.eu/

History Set up by *SMEunited (#19327), European Federation for Elevator Small and Medium-sized Enterprises (EFESME, #07104), European Builders Confederation (EBC, #06408), European Consortium of Anchors Producers (ECAP, #06749), European Digital SME Alliance (#06925)* and national organizations in France and Italy. Constitution adopted 25 Oct 2013. Registration: No/ID: 0546.585.694, Belgium; EU Transparency Register, No/ID: 653009713663-08. **Aims** Represent European *SMEs* in the standard making process at European and international levels. **Structure** General Assembly; Bureau; Board. **Languages** English, French, German, Spanish. **Staff** 4.00 FTE, paid. **Finance** Supported by: *EFTA (#05391); European Commission (EC, #06633).* **Activities** Projects/programmes. Europe. **Events** *Conference on SMEs Setting the Standard for Sustainable Products* Brussels (Belgium) 2022, *Forum on PPE and Textile Care* Brussels (Belgium) 2022, *ICT Forum* Brussels (Belgium) 2022, *Lift Forum* Brussels (Belgium) 2022, *Forum on Digitalisation in the Lift Sector* Brussels (Belgium) 2021. **Publications** *SBS Newsletter.* Annual Report; brochures; position papers; videos; studies.
Members Full in 4 countries:
Austria, France, Germany, Italy.
Regional organizations include 11 listed in this Yearbook:
Coiffure EU (#04088); European Association of Small and Medium sized Enterprises (SME Safety, #06207); European Builders Confederation (EBC, #06408); European Consortium of Anchors Producers (ECAP, #06749); European Digital SME Alliance (#06925); European Federation for Elevator Small and Medium-sized Enterprises (EFESME, #07104); European Metal Union (EMU, #07785); International Federation for the Roofing Trade (#13534); SMEunited (#19327); Timber Construction Europe (#20164); Union Europäischer Gerüstbaubetriebe (UEG, #20382).
NGO Relations Member of (1): *European Telecommunications Standards Institute (ETSI, #08897).* Partner of (2): *Comité européen de normalisation (CEN, #04162); European Committee for Electrotechnical Standardization (CENELEC, #06647).* Cooperates with (3): *Association européenne pour la coordination de la représentation des consommateurs pour la normalisation (ANEC, #02561); Environmental Coalition on Standards (ECOS, #05499); European Trade Union Confederation (ETUC, #08927).* [2022.05.25/XJ9358/y/**D**]

♦ Small Cell Forum 19312

CEO PO Box 23, Dursley, GL11 5WA, UK. E-mail: info@smallcellforum.org.
URL: http://www.smallcellforum.org/

Aims Make mobile cellular connectivity an accessible resource for organizations of all sizes; support digital transformation of industry, enterprise and communities. **Structure** Executive Board; CEO/CSO; Work Items. **Events** *Small Cells World Summit* London (UK) 2022. **Publications** SCF Release Program. **Members** Full; Board; Explorer. Membership countries not specified. [2022.02.09/XJ8745/**F**]

- ♦ Small Cinemas Conference (meeting series)
- ♦ Small – Element – Pavement – Technologists / see SEPT (#19232)
- ♦ Small Enterprise Education and Promotion Network (internationally oriented national body)

♦ Small Island Cultures Research Initiative (SICRI Network) 19313

Contact 417/28 College Hill, Freemans Bay, Auckland 1011, New Zealand. E-mail: kinghoodqu@gmail.com.
URL: https://www.sicri.net/

History 2004. **Aims** Research and assist maintenance and development of the language, literature, music, dance, folkloric and media cultures of small island communities. **Structure** Advisory Board; 2 co-Conveners. **Languages** English. **Staff** 1.00 FTE, paid. **Finance** No budget or funding. Registration fees and host institutions and partners fund Conference. **Activities** Events/meetings. **Events** *International Conference on Small Island Cultures* Shetland (UK) 2022, *International Small Islands Conference* Western Isles (UK) 2021, *International Small Islands Conference* Hilo, HI (USA) 2020, *International Small Islands Conference* Kingston (Jamaica) 2019, *International Small Islands Conference* Normandie (France) 2018. **Publications** *Shima: The International Journal of Research into Island Cultures* (2 a year). **Members** Over 300. Membership countries not specified. **NGO Relations** Links with universities. [2022.05.16/XJ4688/**F**]

♦ Small Island Developing States – Island Energy for Island Life (SIDS DOCK) 19314

Contact address not obtained. T. +15018221104 – +15018221094. E-mail: secretariat@sidsdock.org.
URL: http://sidsdock.org/

History Set up as an initiative among member countries of *Alliance of Small Island States (AOSIS, #00721).* **Aims** Provide Small Island Developing States (SIDS) with a collective institutional mechanism to assist them transform their national *energy* sectors into a catalyst for sustainable economic development and help generate financial resources to address adaptation to *climate change.* **Structure** Steering Committee. **IGO Relations** Instrumental in setting up: *Caribbean Centre for Renewable Energy and Energy Efficiency (CCREEE, #03470); Pacific Centre for Renewable Energy and Energy Efficiency (PCREEE, #17941).* [2017/XM6102/**E***]

♦ Small Island Developing States Network (SIDSnet) 19315

Réseau des Petits États insulaires en développement

Contact SIDS Unit, UN Div for Sustainable Development Goals, UNDESA, 405 East 42nd St, S-2610, New York NY 10017, USA. Fax +12129631267.

History as a project within *Sustainable Development Networking Programme – UNDP (SDNP, no recent information)* and with the cooperation of *Alliance of Small Island States (AOSIS, #00721)* and funds from Spain. Currently administered Small Island Developing States (SIDS) Unit of the *United Nations (UN, #20515)*'s Department of Economic and Social Affairs (DESA). **Aims** Link island nations worldwide through the Internet on issues related to *sustainable development*; build capacity development through education for sustainable development for SIDS; facilitate and coordinate partnerships; track and support international meetings and inter-governmental processes; fill in gaps in data availability through collection of data and statistical information; strengthen inter-regional exchange and SIDS-SIDS cooperation, North-South cooperation, and Triangular cooperation; enable information sharing on best practices and success stories; provide a platform to build consensus on island issues, take action and manage knowledge and information, initially on biodiversity, climate change, coastal and marine resources, energy resources, freshwater resources, land resources, natural disasters, waste management and sustainable tourism. **Events** *International Conference on Small Island Developing States* Apia (Samoa) 2014, *Meeting* Mauritius 2005, *International meeting for the 10-year review of the Barbados Programme of Action (BPoA + 10) for the sustainable development of small islands developing states* Port Louis (Mauritius) 2005, *Inter-regional preparatory meeting for the 10-year review of the Barbados Programme of Action (BPoA + 10)* Nassau (Bahamas) 2004, *Preparatory meeting for the 10-year review of the Barbados Programme of Action (BPoA + 10)* New York, NY (USA) 2004.
Members Small island nations (37):
Antigua-Barbuda, Bahamas, Barbados, Belize, Cape Verde, Comoros, Cuba, Dominica, Dominican Rep, Fiji, Grenada, Guinea-Bissau, Guyana, Haiti, Jamaica, Kiribati, Maldives, Marshall Is, Mauritius, Micronesia FS, Nauru, Palau, Papua New Guinea, Samoa, Sao Tomé-Principe, Seychelles, Singapore, Solomon Is, St Kitts-Nevis, St Lucia, St Vincent-Grenadines, Suriname, Timor-Leste, Tonga, Trinidad-Tobago, Tuvalu, Vanuatu.
Associate members of regional commissions (20):
Anguilla, Aruba, Bermuda, Cayman Is, Cook Is, Curaçao, Guadeloupe, Guam, Martinique, Montserrat, New Caledonia, Niue, Northern Mariana Is, Polynesia Fr, Puerto Rico, Samoa USA, St Maarten, Turks-Caicos, Virgin Is UK, Virgin Is USA. [2018.07.20/XK1810/**E***]

- ♦ Small Islands Initiative (internationally oriented national body)
- ♦ Small Kindness (internationally oriented national body)
- ♦ Small Medium Enterprise Fundamentals / see SMEFUNDS (#19324)

♦ Small and Medium Entrepreneurs Europe (SME Europe) 19316

Contact Rue de Pascale 22, 1040 Brussels, Belgium. T. +3225882975. E-mail: office@smeeurope.eu.
URL: http://www.smeeurope.eu/

History Constituent Meeting 16 May 2012, Brussels (Belgium). Set up as an independent political network of Christian-Democrat and Conservative political and pro-business organization. Registered in accordance with Belgian law. **Aims** Shape EU policies in a more SME friendly way. **Structure** General Assembly. Board. Working Groups.
Members Full; Observer. Full in 15 countries:
Austria, Bulgaria, Cyprus, Denmark, France, Greece, Hungary, Italy, Latvia, Luxembourg, Poland, Romania, Slovakia, Slovenia, Spain.
Observer in 1 country:
Serbia.
NGO Relations Political partner of: *European People's Party (EPP, #08185).* Cooperates with: *SME Global (#19325).* [2017/XJ8419/**E**]

- ♦ Smart Card Alliance (internationally oriented national body)

♦ Smart Cities & Sport Network 19317

Dir Escaliers du Marché 2, PO Box 6904, 1002 Lausanne VD, Switzerland. T. +41213152449. E-mail: info@smartcitiesandsport.org.
Events Manager address not obtained.
URL: https://www.smartcitiesandsport.org/

History 2014. Originates from the group of former and future Olympic Host Cities. **Aims** Empower cities to achieve their social, economic, promotional and environmental goals through sport. **Activities** Events/meetings; knowledge management/information dissemination. **Events** *Smart Cities & Sport Summit* Copenhagen (Denmark) 2021. **NGO Relations** Partner of (3): *Global Association of International Sport Federations (GAISF, inactive); International Olympic Committee (IOC, #14408); SportAccord (#19923).* [2021/AA2535/**F**]

♦ Smart City Business America Institute (SCBA) 19318

Instituto Smart City Business América – Instituto Smart City Business America

Main Office Av Paulista 726, CJ 1303 – CP 556 Bela Vista, Sao Paulo SP, 01310-910, Brazil. T. +551130422928.
URL: https://scbamerica.com/

History Apr 2013. **Aims** Accelerate the development of Smart Cities – using information and *communication technologies* to increase operational efficiency – in Latin America, through networking, qualified discussions and business generation between the public and private sectors. **Structure** Councils (4): Deliberative; Fiscal; Advisory; Technical. Executive Board. Units Brazil (Headquarters); Argentina; Bolivia; Chile; Colombia; Ecuador; Panama; USA. **Activities** Networking/liaising; events/meetings. **Events** *Smart City Business America Congress* Sao Paulo (Brazil) 2019, *Smart City Business America Congress* Medellin (Colombia) 2018, *Smart City Business America Congress* Sao Paulo (Brazil) 2018, *Smart City Business America Congress* Curitiba (Brazil) 2017, *Smart City Business America Congress* Curitiba (Brazil) 2016. [2021/XM6397/j/**D**]

- ♦ Smart City Expo World Congress (meeting series)

♦ smartEn (Smart Energy Europe) 19319

Exec Dir Rue d'Arlon 69-71, 1040 Brussels, Belgium. T. +3225117611. E-mail: info@smarten.eu.
URL: http://www.smarten.eu/

History Launched Jan 2011, following an 18-month study, as *Smart Energy Demand Coalition (SEDC)*. Current title adopted 2017. **Aims** Promote system efficiency, encourage innovation and diversity, empower energy consumers and drive the decarbonization of the energy sector. **Structure** Board; Executive Committee; Secretariat. **Languages** English. **Finance** Members' dues. **Activities** Advocacy/lobbying/activism; knowledge management/information dissemination; awareness raising; networking/liaising; events/meetings. Active in: Europe. **Events** *Annual Symposium* Brussels (Belgium) 2022, *emPOWER – The Energy Transition Summit* Brussels (Belgium) 2020, *Smart Energy Summit* Brussels (Belgium) 2019, *Annual Symposium* Brussels (Belgium) 2018, *Smart Energy Summit* Brussels (Belgium) 2018. **Publications** *smartEn Newsletter*. Reports. **Members** Executive; Regular; Associate. Membership countries not specified. **IGO Relations** *Agency for the Cooperation of Energy Regulators (ACER, #00552); European Committee of the Regions (CoR, #06665); European Commission (EC, #06633); European Council (#06801); European Parliament (EP, #08146).* **NGO Relations** *Council of European Energy Regulators (CEER, #04888)*; other NGOs, not specified. [2020.03.16/XM4227/**D**]

♦ Smart Energy Demand Coalition / see smartEn (#19319)
♦ **Smart Energy Europe** smartEn (#19319)

♦ Smart Freight Centre (SFC) 19320

Contact Keizersgracht 560, 1017 EM Amsterdam, Netherlands. T. +31646954405. E-mail: info@smartfreightcentre.org.
URL: https://www.smartfreightcentre.org/

History 2013. **Aims** Collaborate with global partners to quantify impacts, identify solutions and propagate logistics decarbonization strategies. **Structure** Board; Advisory Council. Includes *Global Logistics Emissions Council (GLEC)*. **Languages** English. **Staff** 30.00 FTE, paid. **Finance** Annual budget: 1,900,000 EUR (2021). **Activities** Advocacy/lobbying/activism; awareness raising; certification/accreditation; events/meetings; guidance/assistance/consulting; projects/programmes; publishing activities; research and development; standards/guidelines; training/education. [2022.08.02/AA2660/**F**]

♦ SMART – International Association of Sheet Metal, Air, Rail and Transportation Workers (internationally oriented national body)

♦ Smart Ticketing Alliance (STA) 19321

Manager Rue Sainte Marie 6, 1080 Brussels, Belgium. T. +3226636632. E-mail: chair@smart-ticketing.org.
URL: http://www.smart-ticketing.org/

History Founded 2015. Statutes adopted 11 May 2015, Brussels (Belgium). Registered in accordance with Belgian law. EU Transparency Register: 611701437375-68. **Aims** Promote and facilitate cooperation between national and regional Smart Ticketing schemes to establish interoperable "Smart Ticketing" in Europe and elsewhere. **Structure** General Meeting; Board. **Finance** Members' dues. **Publications** *STA Newsletter*. [2022/XM8885/**D**]

♦ Smart Water Networks Forum (SWAN) 19322

Exec Dir Elder House, St Georges Business Park, 207 Brooklands Road, Weybridge, KT13 0TS, UK. T. +442032905342. E-mail: info@swan-forum.com.
URL: http://www.swan-forum.com/

Aims Promote the use of data-driven technologies in water and wastewater networks worldwide; increase awareness about the benefits of adopting smart water and wastewater solutions. **Structure** Executive Council; Management Team. Regional Alliances (4): Americas; Europe Utility; Asia-Pacific; India. Work Groups (2): Digital Twin; Young Professional. **Activities** Events/meetings. **Events** *Conference* Glasgow (UK) 2020, *Conference* Miami, FL (USA) 2019, *Conference* Barcelona (Spain) 2018. **NGO Relations** Partners include: *Alliance to Save Energy (ASE)*. [2019/XM8351/c/**F**]

♦ SMA – Societas Missionum ad Afros (religious order)
♦ **SMBC** Sociedad Mesoamericana para la Biologia y la Conservación (#19429)
♦ **SMBE** Society for Molecular Biology and Evolution (#19599)
♦ SMBN – Sociedade Missionaria da Boa Nova (religious order)
♦ SMB – Societas Missionum Exterarum de Bethlehem in Helvetia (religious order)
♦ **SMB** Society for Mathematical Biology (#19591)
♦ SMCM – Society for Mathematics and Computation in Music (internationally oriented national body)
♦ SMC – Scalabrini Migration Centre, Manila (internationally oriented national body)
♦ **SMC** Sound and Music Computing Network (#19698)
♦ SMC – Swedish Mission Council (internationally oriented national body)
♦ SMDM – Society for Medical Decision Making (internationally oriented national body)
♦ SME (internationally oriented national body)
♦ **SME Europe** Small and Medium Entrepreneurs Europe (#19316)

♦ SME Finance Forum 19323

CEO 2121 Pennsylvania Avenue NW, Washington DC 20433, USA. E-mail: smefinanceforum@ifc.org.
URL: http://www.smefinanceforum.org/

History 2012, by *Global Partnership for Financial Inclusion (GPFI, #10534)*. **Aims** Accelerate access to finance for small and medium *business* worldwide by promoting knowledge exchange, policy change and new connections. **Structure** Managed by *International Finance Corporation (IFC, #13597)*. Advisory Board. **Activities** Events/meetings; networking/liaising. **Events** *Global SME Finance Forum* Amsterdam (Netherlands) 2019, *Global SME Finance Forum* Madrid (Spain) 2018, *Global SME Finance Forum* Berlin (Germany) 2017. **Publications** *SME Finance Forum Newsletter*.
Members Development finance institutions; Financial institutions; Industry associations. Membership countries not specified. Included in the above, 15 organizations listed in this Yearbook:
Included in the above, 15 organizations listed in this Yearbook:
Asia Securities Industry and Financial Markets Association (ASIFMA, #02094); Association of Consumer Credit Information Suppliers (ACCIS, #02451); Association of Development Financing Institutions in Asia and the Pacific (ADFIAP, #02472); Business Information Industry Association (BIIA, #03386); CapitalPlus Exchange (CapPlus); European Association of Guarantee Institutions (#06061); European Investment Bank (EIB, #07599); European Investment Fund (EIF, #07601); FCI (#09278); Global Communities; Global Private Capital Association (GPCA, #10556); Inter-American Investment Corporation (IIC, #11438); Overseas Private Investment Corporation (OPIC); The Montreal Group (TMG, #16853); World Savings Banks Institute (WSBI, #21764).
IGO Relations Partners include: *Asia-Pacific Economic Cooperation (APEC, #01887)* Business Advisory Council; *Global Partnership for Financial Inclusion (GPFI, #10534); OECD (#17693).* **NGO Relations** Partners include: *Global Alliance for Banking on Values (GABV, #10186); Global Banking Alliance for Women (GBA, #10248); Latin American Banking Association (#16254); Responsible Finance Forum (RFF).* [2019/XM5928/y/**F**]

♦ SMEFUNDS 19324

CEO The Green Place, 18B Ogundana Street, Allen Avenue, Ikeja, Lagos 101212, Nigeria. T. +2347042383761. E-mail: info@smefunds.com.
URL: http://www.smefunds.com/

History Former names and other names: *Small Medium Enterprise Fundamentals* – full title. **Aims** End *poverty* through *sustainable enterprise* development in *Africa*. **Structure** Executive Team. **Languages** English. **Staff** 54.00 FTE, paid. **IGO Relations** Partners include: *Global Environment Facility (GEF, #10346); Regions of Climate Action (R20, #18820); UNDP (#20292); UNEP (#20299); United Nations Framework Convention on Climate Change – Secretariat (UNFCCC, #20564).* **NGO Relations** Member of (1): *GEF CSO Network (GCN, #10087).* Partners include: *1% for the Planet; 350.org; CERES; Clean Cooking Alliance (#03987); The Nature Conservancy (TNC); Renewable Energy and Energy Efficiency Partnership (REEEP, #18837); United Nations Foundation (UNF, #20563); United Nations Global Compact (#20567); World Business Council for Sustainable Development (WBCSD, #21254); World Resources Institute (WRI, #21753).* [2018/XJ8800/f/**F**]

♦ SME Global 19325

Contact Rue de Pascale 22, 1040 Brussels, Belgium. T. +3222847749. Fax +3222849749.
URL: http://www.sme-global.info/

History Set up as the global counterpart of *Small and Medium Entrepreneurs Europe (SME Europe, #19316)*. **Aims** Further develop cooperation with small and medium-sized *entrepreneurs* supporting institutions all over the globe. **Structure** Board. **NGO Relations** Cooperates with: *European People's Party (EPP, #08185); Small and Medium Entrepreneurs Europe (SME Europe, #19316).* [2017.06.01/XJ8420/**E**]

♦ **SMEIC** APEC SME Innovation Center (#00873)
♦ SMEI – Sales and Marketing Executives International (internationally oriented national body)

♦ Y's Men International 19326

SG Av Sainte-Clotilde 9, 1205 Geneva, Switzerland. T. +41228091530. Fax +41228091539. E-mail: ihq@ysmen.org.
URL: http://www.ysmen.org/

History Nov 1922, Toledo, OH (USA). Founded as a Service Club to *World Alliance of Young Men's Christian Associations (YMCA, #21090)*. New International Constitution and Guidelines adopted at International Convention, 1972; ratified at International Convention, 1973; entered into force, 1 Jun 1974; most recently amended 2018. Former names and other names: *International Association of Y's Men's Clubs* – former (1922); *Y's Men International – Y Service Clubs International* – former. Registration: Start date: 26 Jan 1927, End date: 24 Jul 1964, USA, Massachusetts; Start date: 24 Jul 1964, USA, Illinois; Start date: 1995, Switzerland. **Aims** Encourage, promote and supervise the organization of Y's Men's Clubs worldwide as they assist their local *YMCA* in activities, involving community service, *youth*, YMCA membership service, world outlook and *scholarships* for prospective YMCA professionals; coordinate, standardize and direct non-local activities of member Y's Men's Clubs. **Structure** International Council; Administrative Units: 45 Regions. **Languages** English. **Staff** 4.00 FTE, paid. **Finance** Sources: members' dues. Annual budget: 1,700,000 CHF. **Events** *International Convention* Honolulu, HI (USA) 2022, *International Centenary Celebration* Taipei (Taiwan) 2022, *International Convention* Odense (Denmark) 2020, *International Convention* Yeosu (Korea Rep) 2018, *International Convention* Taipei (Taiwan) 2016. **Publications** *YMI World* (4 a year). *History of Y'sdom (1922-1953, 1953-1972 and 1972-1997)*. Leadership training material; pamphlets; brochures.
Members Local Clubs (about 1,500) for men, for women or for both, totalling about 25,000 members in 74 countries and territories:
Albania, Aruba, Australia, Bangladesh, Barbados, Bolivia, Brazil, Bulgaria, Burundi, Cambodia, Cameroon, Canada, Chile, Colombia, Costa Rica, Denmark, Ecuador, Egypt, England, Estonia, Finland, Germany, Ghana, Guatemala, Haiti, Honduras, Hong Kong, Hungary, India, Indonesia, Italy, Jamaica, Japan, Kenya, Korea Rep, Kosovo, Latvia, Lithuania, Macau, Malaysia, Malta, Moldova, Mongolia, Myanmar, Nepal, Netherlands, Nigeria, Norway, Oman, Pakistan, Palestine, Peru, Philippines, Poland, Qatar, Romania, Russia, Saudi Arabia, Sierra Leone, Singapore, Slovakia, Sri Lanka, Sweden, Taiwan, Tanzania UR, Thailand, Uganda, Ukraine, United Arab Emirates, Uruguay, USA, Vietnam, Zambia, Zimbabwe.
Consultative Status Consultative status granted from: *ECOSOC (#05331)* (Special). **NGO Relations** Member of: *Alliance for Malaria Prevention (AMP, #00706); Fédération des Institutions Internationales établies à Genève (FIIG, #09599).* [2022.05.04/XB1376/**E**]

♦ Y's Men International – Y Service Clubs International / see Y's Men International (#19326)
♦ SMEPQ – Société des Missions Etrangères de la Province de Québec (religious order)
♦ **SME Safety** European Association of Small and Medium sized Enterprises (#06207)
♦ **SME** Santé mentale Europe (#16715)
♦ SME – Service missionnaire évangélique (internationally oriented national body)
♦ **SMES Europa** Santé mentale et exclusion sociale – Europa (#19053)

♦ SMEunited 19327

SG Rue Jacques de Lalaing 4, 1040 Brussels, Belgium. T. +3222307599. Fax +3222307861. E-mail: info@smeunited.eu.
URL: https://www.smeunited.eu/

History 1980. Founded by the joint action of *International Association of Crafts and Small and Medium-Sized Enterprises (IACME, inactive)*, by: *International Federation of Small and Medium-Sized Commercial Enterprises (IFSMC, inactive); International Federation of Small and Medium-Sized Industrial Enterprises (IFSMI, inactive)*; and *Union of Craft Industries and Trades of the EEC (inactive)*, taking over the activities of UACEE which then ceased to exist. Statutes modified 1996. Former names and other names: *European Association of Craft, Small and Medium-Sized Enterprises* – former; *Union européenne de l'artisanat et des petites et moyennes entreprises (UEAPME)* – former; *Europäische Union des Handwerks und der Klein- und Mittelbetriebe* – former; *Unione Europea dell' Artigianato e delle Piccole e Medie Imprese* – former; *SMEunited – Crafts and SMEs in Europe* – full title. Registration: Banque-Carrefour des Entreprises, No/ID: 0441.251.911, Start date: 13 Aug 1990, Belgium; EU Transparency Register, No/ID: 55820581197-35, Start date: 20 Feb 2009. **Aims** Create an SME friendly climate in the EU in which SMEs can thrive; monitor EU policy and legislative process and keep members informed on all matters of relevance to crafts and SMEs; represent and promote interests of Crafts and SMEs to the EU institutions and other international organisations; support members academically, technically and legally on all areas of EU policy; support the idea of European integration and contribute to European cooperation. **Structure** General Assembly (twice a year); Board of Directors; Committees; Permanent Secretariat, located in Brussels (Belgium). **Languages** Dutch, English, French, German, Italian. **Staff** 14.00 FTE, paid. **Finance** Sources: members' dues. **Activities** Capacity building; events/meetings; networking/liaising; projects/programmes. **Events** *General Assembly* Paris (France) 2022, *General Assembly* Brussels (Belgium) 2020, *REACH 2018 Road to Successful Registration SME Workshop* Vienna (Austria) 2017, *European Forum on Co-operative Banks & SMEs* Brussels (Belgium) 2014, *Mediterranean economic leaders summit* Barcelona (Spain) 2010. **Publications** *SMEunited Weekly Newsflash*. Annual Report; position papers; online publications; press releases.
Members Full: representative national, cross-sectoral organizations representing craft activities and/or SME businesses in the different sectors of the economy within the EU. Members in 26 countries:
Austria, Belgium, Bulgaria, Croatia, Cyprus, Czechia, Denmark, Estonia, Finland, France, Germany, Greece, Hungary, Ireland, Italy, Latvia, Lithuania, Luxembourg, Malta, Netherlands, Poland, Portugal, Romania, Slovenia, Spain, Sweden.
Merger Group (exclusively formed by members from the former EUROPMI) is also a full member. Associate: national associations of craft industries and of SME businesses from European countries that are not members of the EU. Members in 4 countries:
Associate: national associations of craft industries and of SME businesses from European countries that are not members of the EU. Members in 4 countries:
Liechtenstein, Serbia, Switzerland, Türkiye.
European Sectoral organizations (22) – European and international organizations representing SMEs in a specific trade sector (Construction; Foodstuffs; Healthcare; Services; Transport):
- *BIPAR – European Federation of Insurance Intermediaries (#03263);*
- *Children's Fashion Europe (CFE, #03876);*
- *Coiffure EU (#04088);*
- *Confédération européenne des professionelles de l'esthétique cosmétique (CEPEC, #04549);*
- *Europäische Schornsteinfegermeister-Föderation (ESCHFOE, #05761);*
- *European Builders Confederation (EBC, #06408);*
- *European Cold Storage and Logistics Association (ECSLA, #06603);*
- *European Confederation of National Bakery and Confectionery Organizations (CEBP, #06714);*
- *European Digital SME Alliance (#06925);*
- *European Federation for Elevator Small and Medium-sized Enterprises (EFESME, #07104);*
- *European Federation of Accountants and Auditors for SMEs (EFAA, #07037);*
- *European Federation of Associations of Health Product Manufacturers (EHPM, #07052);*
- *European Metal Union (EMU, #07785);*
- *European Road Hauliers Association (UETR, #08393);*
- *Fédération européenne et internationale des patrons prothésistes dentaires (FEPPD, #09575);*
- *Fédération internationale des grossistes importateurs et exportateurs en fournitures automobiles (FIGIEFA, #09635);*
- *Federation of European Professional Photographers (FEP, #09533);*
- *International Federation for the Roofing Trade (#13534);*
- *Timber Construction Europe (#20164);*
- *Union Europäischer Gerüstbaubetriebe (UEG, #20382);*
- *Union internationale des entrepreneurs de peinture (UNIEP, #20425);*
- *Vereinigung Europäischer Verbände des Kachelofenbauer/Hafner-Handwerks (VEUKO, #20754).*

Other Associate and sponsoring members in 6 countries:

Belgium, France, Germany, Italy, Slovakia, UK.
Included in the above, 1 organization listed in this Yearbook:
Association of Chartered Certified Accountants (ACCA).
IGO Relations Social partner of: *European Commission (EC, #06633); European Quality Assurance in Vocational Education and Training (EQAVET, #08312).* Liaises with: *Council of the European Union (#04895); European Economic and Social Committee (EESC, #06963); European Centre for the Development of Vocational Training (Cedefop, #06474); European Parliament (EP, #08146).* **NGO Relations** Member of (3): *Eastern Partnership Civil Society Forum (EaP CSF, #05247); European Registry of Internet Domain Names (EURid, #08351); European Small Business Alliance of Small and Medium Independent Enterprises (ESBA, #08494).* Partner of (1): *Eurisy (#05625).* Together with EUROPMI, instrumental in: *European Conference on Craft and Small Enterprises.* [2022/XD7908/y/**D**]

- ♦ SMEunited – Crafts and SMEs in Europe / see SMEunited (#19327)
- ♦ SMF / see Strømme Foundation
- ♦ **SMFC** Société Méditerranéenne Francophone de Cancérologie (#19502)
- ♦ SMF – Score More Foundation (unconfirmed)
- ♦ SMG – Poor Servants of the Mother of God (religious order)
- ♦ **SMHILE** School Mental Health International Leadership Exchange (#19131)
- ♦ SMIA – Nordic Conference on the Application of Scientific Methods in Archaeology (meeting series)
- ♦ **SMIAR** Système mondiale d'information et d'alerte rapide sur l'alimentation et l'agriculture (#10416)
- ♦ **SMIA** Sistema Mundial de Información y Alerta sobre la Alimentación y la Agricultura (#10416)
- ♦ SMIER – Société médicale d'imagerie, enseignement et recherche (no recent information)
- ♦ **SMIIC** The Standards and Metrology Institute for Islamic Countries (#19947)
- ♦ Smile Africa International (internationally oriented national body)
- ♦ Smile Africa International (internationally oriented national body)

♦ Smile Train 19328

World Headquarters 633 Third Ave, 9th Floor, New York NY 10017, USA. E-mail: info@smiletrain.org.
UK Office York House, Wetherby Road, York, YO26 7NH, UK. E-mail: ukinfo@smiletrain.org.
URL: http://www.smiletrain.org.uk/

History 1999, UK. UK Registered charity: 1114748; also registered as a nonprofit in the USA: EIN 13-3661416. **Aims** Support free *cleft* surgery and comprehensive cleft care to *children* in need globally. **Structure** Board of Directors; Headquarters in New York NY (USA); Regional Offices (11). **Finance** Donations. **Activities** Training/education; financial and/or material support. Active in over 87 countries. **NGO Relations** Member of: *Face Equality International (FEI, #09232); Global Alliance for Surgical, Obstetric, Trauma and Anaesthesia Care (G4 Alliance, #10229).* Partner of: *Every Woman Every Child (EWEC, #09215).* [2019.02.13/XM7015/**F**]

- ♦ SMI – Senter for Midtausten og islamske studiar (internationally oriented national body)
- ♦ SMI – Shape Modeling International (meeting series)
- ♦ SMI – Social Marketing International Association (inactive)
- ♦ **SMI** Society for Molecular Imprinting (#19600)
- ♦ **SMI** Society for Mucosal Immunology (#19601)
- ♦ Smithsonian Institution (internationally oriented national body)
- ♦ Smithsonian Tropical Research Institute, Panama (internationally oriented national body)
- ♦ SMIT / see International Society for Medical Innovation and Technology (#15255)
- ♦ SMLMS – Single Molecule Localization Microscopy Symposium (meeting series)
- ♦ Smlouva o Ustave pro Evropu (2004 treaty)
- ♦ SMMIB – International Conference on Surface Modification of Materials by Ion Beams (meeting series)
- ♦ SMMI – Salésiennes Missionnaires de Marie Immaculée (religious order)
- ♦ SMMK – Svetski Makedonski Mladinski Kongres
- ♦ **SMML** Société méditerranéenne de médecine légale (#16677)
- ♦ SMMP – Schwestern der Heiligen Maria Magdalena Postel (religious order)
- ♦ **SMM** Service pour un Monde Meilleur (#16869)
- ♦ SMM – Societas Mariae Montfortana (religious order)
- ♦ **SMN** Scientific and Medical Network (#19153)
- ♦ SM-OCIC / see SIGNIS Services Rome (#19274)
- ♦ **SMOC** Sistema Mundial de Observación del Clima (#10289)
- ♦ **SMOC** Système mondial d'observation du climat (#10289)

♦ Smoke Free Partnership (SFP) 19329

Main Office Chaussée de Louvain 479, 1030 Brussels, Belgium. T. +32499843222. E-mail: info@smokefreepartnership.eu.
URL: http://smokefreepartnership.eu/

History Registration: EU Transparency Register, No/ID: 6403725595-50. **Aims** Promote *tobacco* control advocacy and policy research at EU and national levels; ensure effective implementation of the Framework Convention on Tobacco Control (FCTC) at EU level. **Structure** *SFP Coalition* is a network of advocacy organizations. **Languages** English, French. **Finance** Sources: contributions. **Activities** Advocacy/lobbying/activism; politics/policy/regulatory. **NGO Relations** Member of (2): *European Public Health Alliance (EPHA, #08297); Framework Convention Alliance (FCA, #09981).* Partner of (3): Action on Smoking and Health (UK); Cancer Research UK; *European Heart Network (EHN, #07467).* [2022.05.16/XJ1605/**F**]

- ♦ Smoke Prevention Association of America / see Air and Waste Management Association
- ♦ SMOM – Sovrano Militare Ordine Ospedaliero di San Giovanni di Gerusalemme, di Rodi e di Malta (religious order)
- ♦ SMO – Società Mediterranea di Ortottica (internationally oriented national body)
- ♦ SMOTJ – Sovereign Military Order of the Temple of Jerusalem (religious order)
- ♦ **SMP** Society for Mathematical Psychology (#19592)
- ♦ SMPTE – Society of Motion Picture and Television Engineers (internationally oriented national body)
- ♦ **SMRI** Solution Mining Research Institute (#19684)
- ♦ SMR – Norsk senter for menneskerettigheter (internationally oriented national body)
- ♦ SMRP – Society for Maintenance and Reliability Professionals (internationally oriented national body)
- ♦ SMR – Société des Soeurs de Marie Réparatrice (religious order)
- ♦ **SMR** Society for Melanoma Research (#19595)
- ♦ SMR – Svenska missionsrådet (internationally oriented national body)
- ♦ S de M – Siervas de Maria, Ministras de los Enfermos (religious order)
- ♦ SMSM – Soeurs Missionnaires de la Société de Marie (religious order)
- ♦ SM – Societas Mariae (religious order)
- ♦ SM – Societas Mariae (religious order)
- ♦ SM – Soeurs Maristes (religious order)
- ♦ SMSOP / see Nordic Spinal Cord Society (#17436)
- ♦ **SMS** Statistical Modelling Society (#19973)
- ♦ **SMS** Strategic Management Society (#20007)
- ♦ SMST – International Organization on Shape Memory and Superelastic Technologies (internationally oriented national body)
- ♦ SMT – International Workshop on Satisfiability Modulo Theories (meeting series)
- ♦ SMU – Scandinavian Monetary Union (inactive)
- ♦ SMWIA / see International Association of Sheet Metal, Air, Rail and Transportation Workers
- ♦ SNAME – Society of Naval Architects and Marine Engineers (internationally oriented national body)
- ♦ SNAP – Sociedad Naturalista Andino Patagónica (internationally oriented national body)
- ♦ **SNASWE** Scandinavian Network for the Academic Study of Western Esotericism (#19091)
- ♦ **SNCLF** Société de neurochirurgie de langue française (#19503)
- ♦ **SNCLF** Société de neurophysiologie clinique de langue française (#19504)
- ♦ **SNDE** Society for Nonlinear Dynamics and Econometrics (#19611)
- ♦ SND – Hermanas de Notre Dame (religious order)
- ♦ **SNDI** South North Development Initiative (#19881)
- ♦ SNDLF / see Société française de nutrition
- ♦ SNDN – Soeurs de Notre-Dame de Namur (religious order)
- ♦ SND – Sisters of Notre Dame (religious order)
- ♦ SND – Society for News Design (internationally oriented national body)
- ♦ SND/S / see Society for News Design – Scandinavia (#19609)
- ♦ **SNDS** Society for News Design – Scandinavia (#19609)
- ♦ **SNEB** Society for Nutrition Education and Behavior (#19612)
- ♦ Sneha / see Samaritans
- ♦ **SNE** Society for NeurEconomics (#19606)
- ♦ SNE / see Society for Nutrition Education and Behavior (#19612)
- ♦ **SNE** Specialised Nutrition Europe (#19909)
- ♦ **SNETP** Sustainable Nuclear Energy Technology Platform (#20063)
- ♦ **SNG** Sodruzestvo Nezavissimyh Gosudarstv (#04341)
- ♦ SNH – Symposium on Naval Hydrodynamics (meeting series)
- ♦ SNI / see Shelter for Life
- ♦ SNIA Europe / see Storage Networking Industry Association (#20000)
- ♦ **SNIA South Asia** Storage Networking Industry Association South Asia (#20001)
- ♦ **SNIA** Storage Networking Industry Association (#20000)
- ♦ SNIH – Swedish Network for International Health (internationally oriented national body)
- ♦ Snipe Class International Racing Association (see: #21760)
- ♦ SNI – School Nurses International (unconfirmed)
- ♦ **SNI** Society of Natural Immunity (#19603)
- ♦ SNJM – Sisters of the Holy Names of Jesus and Mary (religious order)
- ♦ **SNL** Society for the Neurobiology of Language (#19607)
- ♦ SNME – Society of Nuclear Medicine – Europe (inactive)
- ♦ SNMS – International Symposium on Nanomaterials and Membrane Science for Water, Energy and Environment (meeting series)
- ♦ SNOG / see Scandinavian Neuro-Oncology Society (#19092)
- ♦ **SNOG** Scandinavian Neuro-Oncology Society (#19092)

♦ SNOMED International 19330

Communications Officer 1 Kingdom Street, Paddington Central, London, W2 6BD, UK. T. +442037550974. E-mail: info@snomed.org.
Main Website: https://www.snomed.org/

History 2007. Set up by 9 countries. 31 Dec 2016, new corporate structure established in UK, with *SNOMED International* as the trading name. Former names and other names: *International Health Terminology Standards Development Organization (IHTSDO)* – legal name. Registration: Companies House, No/ID: 9915820, England and Wales. **Aims** Lead development and evolution of the world's most comprehensive clinical terminology standard for use in delivery of *health* and *social care*, as well as data analysis and health system planning. **Structure** General Assembly; Management Board; Management Team; Standing Committees; Advisory Groups; Projects Groups. **Languages** English. **Staff** 53.00 FTE, paid. **Finance** Sources: contributions of member/participating states; fees for services; members' dues. **Activities** Events/meetings; standards/guidelines. Active in: Argentina, Armenia, Australia, Austria, Belgium, Brunei Darussalam, Canada, Chile, Cyprus, Czechia, Denmark, El Salvador, Estonia, Finland, Germany, Hong Kong, Iceland, India, Ireland, Israel, Jordan, Kazakhstan, Korea Rep, Lithuania, Luxembourg, Malaysia, Malta, Netherlands, New Zealand, Norway, Portugal, Saudi Arabia, Singapore, Slovakia, Slovenia, Spain, Sweden, Switzerland, Thailand, United Arab Emirates, Uruguay, USA. **Events** *SNOMED CT Conference* Atlanta, GA (USA) 2023, *SNOMED CT Conference* Lisbon (Portugal) 2022, *Business Meeting* London (UK) 2022, *Business Meeting* London (UK) 2022, *SNOMED CT Conference* London (UK) 2021. **Publications** *SNOMED International Newsletter.* Annual Report; organizational strategy; product and services catalogue. **Members** National government agencies or other bodies endorsed by an appropriate national government authority within the country it represents (43). Membership countries not specified. [2022.10.12/XJ7770/**C***]

- ♦ **SNO** Student Network Organization (#20014)
- ♦ SNSI – Sacred Natural Sites Initiative (unconfirmed)
- ♦ **SNS** Norraenar Skógarrannsóknir (#17296)
- ♦ **SNS** Sam Nordisk Sknovforskning (#17296)
- ♦ **SNS** SamNordisk Skogsforskning (#17296)
- ♦ **SNS** Scandinavian Neurosurgical Society (#19093)
- ♦ SNS / see Scandinavian Society of Neuropathology (#19113)
- ♦ SNS – Spectroscopies in Novel Superconductors (meeting series)
- ♦ **SNSUS** Stiftelsen Nordiska Sällskapet för Upplysning om Spelberoende (#19989)
- ♦ **SNS** Yhteispohjoismainen Metsäntutkimus (#17296)
- ♦ **SNTS** Society for New Testament Studies (#19610)
- ♦ **SNTS** Studiorum Novi Testamenti Societas (#19610)
- ♦ SNV / see SNV Netherlands Development Organisation
- ♦ SNV Netherlands Development Organisation (internationally oriented national body)
- ♦ SNV – SNV Netherlands Development Organisation (internationally oriented national body)
- ♦ SNV USA / see DevWorks International
- ♦ SOAC – Système Ouest-Africain d'Accréditation (unconfirmed)
- ♦ SOAGA – Société Ouest Africaine de Gestion d'Actifs (see: #03170)
- ♦ SOAI – Société ouest africaine d'immunologie (no recent information)
- ♦ **SOAL** Société ouest-africaine de linguistique (#19506)
- ♦ **SOAM** Société Ouest africaine de malherbologie (#20899)
- ♦ SOAO / see Société Africaine Francophone d'Ophtalmologie (#19453)
- ♦ SOAP – Société ouest africaine de pharmacologie (inactive)
- ♦ **SOA** Sqay Organization of Asia (#19932)
- ♦ SOAS – School of Oriental and African Studies (internationally oriented national body)
- ♦ SOAS University of London / see School of Oriental and African Studies
- ♦ SOA – Sustainable Ocean Alliance (internationally oriented national body)
- ♦ SOA Watch – School of the Americas Watch (internationally oriented national body)
- ♦ Soberana Orden Constantiniana (religious order)
- ♦ **SoBLA** Sociedad de Biofisicos Latinoamericanos (#19351)
- ♦ SOCAP Europe / see Society for Consumer Affairs Professionals in Europe (#19536)
- ♦ SOCAP in Europe / see Society for Consumer Affairs Professionals in Europe (#19536)
- ♦ **SOCAPiE** Society for Consumer Affairs Professionals in Europe (#19536)
- ♦ SOCAP International – Society of Consumer Affairs Professionals in Business (internationally oriented national body)
- ♦ **SocBin** Society for Bioinformatics in the Nordic Countries (#19526)
- ♦ **SoCCCAD** Sociedad Centroamericana y del Caribe de Clasificación y Analisis de Datos (#19352)
- ♦ Soccer Without Borders (internationally oriented national body)
- ♦ **SocDem Asia** Social Democracy in Asia (#19334)
- ♦ **SOCECAF** Sociedad Centroamericana y del Caribe de Fisica (#03664)
- ♦ SOCECAR – Sociedad Centroamericana y Caribe de Cancerologia (no recent information)
- ♦ SOCFI / see Société internationale francophone d'ORL et de chirurgie cervico-faciale (#19488)
- ♦ **SOC** Groupe Socialistes, démocrates et verts (#19342)

♦ SOCHAIR Organization (Europe) 19331

CEO 9-10 St Andrew Square, Edinburgh, EH2 3AF, UK. T. +443003656400. Fax +443003656499. E-mail: contactcenter@sochair.org.
URL: http://sochair.org/

History Oct 2014, London (UK). European headquarters established in Edinburgh (UK), 2016. Former names and other names: *ORANG-ORANG Organization for Human* – former (2014 to 2015); *PRO Human Rights Organization CLG* – former (2015 to 2016). Registration: No/ID: SC547850, Scotland. **Aims** Provide advice and assistance in questions of *human rights* violations; support human rights *violence victims.* **Languages** Arabic, Dutch, English, German, Spanish. **Staff** 8.00 FTE, paid; 67.00 FTE, voluntary. **Finance** Sources: donations; fees for services. Annual budget: 350,000 GBP. **Activities** Awareness raising; guidance/assistance/consulting; humanitarian/emergency aid; training/education.

Members Organizations in 6 countries and territories:
Austria, Germany, Netherlands, Scotland, Switzerland, UK.
NGO Relations Participant of: *United Nations Global Compact (#20567).* [2022.05.05/XM5193/F]

♦ Sociaal-Democratische Fractie in the Europees Parlement / see Group of the Progressive Alliance of Socialists and Democrats in the European Parliament (#10786)

♦ Social Accountability Accreditation Services (SAAS) 19332

Headquarters 9 East 37th St., 10th Floor, New York NY 10016, USA. T. +12123912106. E-mail: saas@saasaccreditation.org.
URL: http://www.saasaccreditation.org/
History 1997. Set up as an accreditation department within *Centre for Refugee Studies, Moi University (no recent information).* Became an independent not-for-profit organization, 2007. **Aims** Support social responsibility and accountability by ensuring implementation of credible systems designed to protect people and their communities. **Structure** Board of Directors; Accreditation Review Panel; Advisory Committee. **Activities** Certification/accreditation. [2020.05.18/XM5560/E]

♦ Social Accountability International (internationally oriented national body)

♦ Social Agriculture Network (SAN) 19333

Exec Dir PO Box 11029-1000, San José, San José, San José, Costa Rica. T. +50622164800. Fax +50622164800.
URL: http://www.sanstandards.org/
History 1991, as *Conservation Agriculture Network.* Subsequently changed title to *Sustainable Agriculture Network (SAN) – Réseau d'agriculture durable – Red de Agricultura Sostenible.* **Aims** Improve environmental and social conditions in tropical agriculture through conservation certification.
Members Organizations in 11 countries:
Belize, Brazil, Colombia, Costa Rica, Denmark, Ecuador, El Salvador, Guatemala, Honduras, Mexico, USA.
NGO Relations *Rainforest Alliance.* Cooperates with: *Fairtrade International (FLO, #09240); IFOAM – Organics International (IFOAM, #11105); Social Accountability International (SAI).* Links indicated by *HCV Network Ltd (HCV Network, #10865).* [2013/XF6772/F]

♦ Social Aspects of HIV/AIDS Research Alliance (internationally oriented national body)
♦ Social Commission / see United Nations Commission for Social Development (#20535)
♦ Social Communication Center – Development Research Foundation / see Communication Foundation for Asia (#04380)

♦ Social Democracy in Asia (SocDem Asia) 19334

Coordinator Unit 3E Suite 122, No 122 Maginhawa Street, Teachers Village East, 1101 Diliman, Philippines. T. +6329032396. E-mail: secretariat@socdemasia.com.
URL: https://socdemasia.com/
History 2009. **Aims** Promote the values and practices of social democracy; fight for alternatives to elitist politics and neoliberal capitalist economic organization; build social democratic alternative. **Structure** Steering Committee. **Publications** *Socdem Asia Quarterly* (4 a year).
Members Parties, think tanks/institutes, labour, academics and young activists in 13 countries:
India, Indonesia, Japan, Korea Rep, Malaysia, Mongolia, Myanmar, Nepal, Pakistan, Philippines, Sri Lanka, Thailand, Timor-Leste.
NGO Relations Partner of (1): *Progressive Alliance for Freedom, Justice and Solidarity (Progressive Alliance, #18530).* [2020/AA0980/F]

♦ Socialdemokratiska Gruppen i Europaparlamentet / see Group of the Progressive Alliance of Socialists and Democrats in the European Parliament (#10786)
♦ Socialdemokratu Grupa Eiropas Parlamenta / see Group of the Progressive Alliance of Socialists and Democrats in the European Parliament (#10786)
♦ Social Development International (internationally oriented national body)
♦ Social, Economic, and Environmental / see SEE Change Net Foundation

♦ Social Economy Europe (SEE) 19335

Contact Rue Botanique 75-79, 1210 Brussels, Belgium. T. +3225150661. Fax +3225150506. E-mail: contact@socialeconomy.eu.org.
URL: http://www.socialeconomy.eu.org/
History 17 Nov 2000, as *Permanent European Conference of Cooperatives, Mutual Societies, Associations and Foundations (CEP-CMAF) – Conférence européenne permanente des coopératives, mutualités, associations et fondations (CEP-CMAF),* replacing *Consultative Committee of Cooperatives, Mutual Societies, Associations and Foundations (CMAF, inactive).* Current title adopted, 1 Jan 2008. EU Transparency Register: 739159434916-75. **Aims** Promote social economy as a sector that produces both economic and social wealth; promote the role and values of the social economy actors throughout Europe; reinforce political and legal recognition of the social economy and the CMAF at European level. **Languages** English, French. **Activities** Organizes conferences. **Events** *Social Economy Scientific Conference* Brussels (Belgium) 2020, *European Conference on Madrid, European Capital of Social Economy* Madrid (Spain) 2017, *Conference on social economy* Luxembourg (Luxembourg) 2005, *European social economy conference in the Central and Eastern Europe* Krakow (Poland) 2004. **Publications** *Creating an Inclusive Society: Mainstreaming disability based on the Social Economy example.*
Members International and European organizations (5 – '*' indicates founding):
Association internationale de la mutualité (AIM, #02721) (*); *Association of Mutual Insurers and Insurance Cooperatives in Europe (AMICE, #02816); Cooperatives Europe (#04801); European Council for Non-Profit Organizations (#06834)* (*); *European Foundation Centre (EFC, inactive)* (*).
National organizations (2) in 2 countries:
France, Spain.
Network organizations (3):
European Federation of Social Employers (#07214); European Network of Social Integration Enterprises (ENSIE, #08009); Réseau Européen des Villes and Régions de l'Économie Sociale (REVES, #18880).
IGO Relations *European Commission (EC, #06633)* – DG Employment and Social Affairs and DG Enterprise; *European Economic and Social Committee (EESC, #06963)* – Liaison Group; *European Parliament (EP, #08146)* – Social Economy Intergroup. [2020/XE4507/y/E]

♦ Social Employers Network (no recent information)
♦ Social Enterprise Europe / see Social Enterprise International
♦ Social Enterprise International (internationally oriented national body)
♦ Social Enterprise Partnership / see Social Enterprise International

♦ Social Enterprise World Forum (SEWF) 19336

Secretariat Moorpark Court, 5 Dava Street, Glasgow, G51 2JA, UK. T. +441414252926. E-mail: enquiries@sewfonline.com.
URL: https://sewfonline.com/
History 2008. Founded by Gerry Higgins. Registration: No/ID: SC425154, Scotland. **Aims** Promote social enterprise throughout the world; lead the social enterprise movement. **Structure** Board of Directors. **Languages** English. **Staff** None. **Finance** License fee paid by event hosts. **Events** *Social Enterprise World Forum* Brisbane, QLD (Australia) 2022, *Social Enterprise World Forum* Nova Scotia (Canada) 2021, *Social Enterprise World Forum – Digital* 2020, *Social Enterprise World Forum (SEWF)* Addis Ababa (Ethiopia) 2019, *Social Enterprise World Forum* Edinburgh (UK) 2018. **NGO Relations** Member of (1): *Wellbeing Economy Alliance (WEAll, #20856).* [2022/XJ7190/c/F]

♦ Social Epistemology Network (SENE) 19337

Contact address not obtained. E-mail: socialepistemologynetwork@gmail.com.
URL: http://www.socialepistemologynetwork.com/
Aims Provide a platform for cooperation and exchange among researchers from all over the world, interested in social aspects of cognition. **Structure** Steering Committee. **Activities** Events/meetings. **Events** *Meeting* New Haven, CT (USA) 2020, *Meeting* Incheon (Korea Rep) 2019, *Meeting* Oslo (Norway) 2018. [2019/XM8043/F]

♦ Social Firms Europe (CEFEC) 19338

Coordinator Oituz Street 30, 720201 Suceava, Romania. T. +40230524128. Fax +40230524128. E-mail: socialfirmseurope@gmail.com.
URL: http://socialfirmseurope.eu/
History 3 Jan 1990, Brussels (Belgium), as *Confederation of European Firms, Employment Initiatives and Cooperatives for Psychically Disabled,* at the initiative of associations in Germany, Italy and Netherlands. Subsequently changed title to *Confederation of European Social Firms, Employment Initiatives and Social Cooperatives (CEFEC).* Registered in accordance with Belgian law. **Aims** Initiate and stimulate firms, employment initiatives and cooperatives on behalf of *rehabilitation* and employment of people with *mental health* problems and other socially marginalized persons in countries of the European Union and other European states; give form and content to international cooperation in these fields. **Structure** General Assembly (at least annually); Executive Committee. **Languages** English. **Staff** 0.50 FTE, paid. **Finance** Members' dues. **Activities** Financial and/or material support; knowledge management/information dissemination; events/meetings; awards/prizes/competitions. **Events** *Conference* Dortmund (Germany) 2020, *Conference* Trieste (Italy) 2019, *Conference* Helsinki (Finland) 2018, *Conference* Gorizia (Italy) / Nova Gorica (Slovenia) 2014, *Conference* Corfu (Greece) 2013. **Publications** *The Linz Appeal.*
Members Full: Supporting; Individual. Members (48) in 22 countries:
Austria, Belgium, Bulgaria, Croatia, Czechia, Denmark, Finland, France, Germany, Greece, Italy, Japan, Moldova, North Macedonia, Poland, Portugal, Romania, Slovenia, Spain, Sweden, Switzerland, UK.
NGO Relations Member of: *European Disability Forum (EDF, #06929).* [2020.03.03/XD2303/D]

♦ Social Good Accelerator (internationally oriented national body)
♦ Social-Impact International (unconfirmed)

♦ Social Innovation Exchange (SIX) 19339

Dir 32 Cubitt Street, London, WC2R 1LA, UK.
URL: http://www.socialinnovationexchange.org/
History Launched 2008, Sydney (Australia). **Aims** Improve the methods with which societies find better solutions to challenges such as climate change, inequality and healthcare. **Structure** Global Network; Global Council; Executive Board; Nodes (4). **Activities** Events/meetings; networking/liaising; knowledge management/information dissemination; training/education. **NGO Relations** *Global Innovation Exchange (The Exchange, inactive).* [2018/XJ6903/F]

♦ Socialisme sans frontières (internationally oriented national body)
♦ Socialisme zonder Grenzen (internationally oriented national body)
♦ Socialist and Democratic Interafrican (inactive)
♦ Socialist Educational International (inactive)
♦ Socialist Group / see Socialists, Democrats and Greens Group (#19342)
♦ Socialist Group /in the Council of Europe/ / see Socialists, Democrats and Greens Group (#19342)
♦ Socialist Group in the European Parliament / see Group of the Progressive Alliance of Socialists and Democrats in the European Parliament (#10786)
♦ Socialist Group of the Parliamentary Assembly of the Council of Europe/ / see Socialists, Democrats and Greens Group (#19342)
♦ Socialisticka Skupina v Európskom Parlamente / see Group of the Progressive Alliance of Socialists and Democrats in the European Parliament (#10786)
♦ Socialisticka Telovychovna Internacionala (inactive)

♦ Socialist International (SI) 19340

Internationale Socialiste – Internacional Socialista
SG PO Box 67973, London, SW4 4DU, UK. T. +442076274449. E-mail: secretariat@socialistinternational.org.
URL: http://www.socialistinternational.org/
History 1951, Frankfurt-Main (Germany FR), following: work of *Comité international socialiste consultatif (COMISCO),* an organizational centre of several socialist parties, Dec 1947 – Jun 1951; the setting up of a temporary *International Solidarity Committee (inactive),* 1946, Clacton-on-Sea (UK); the work of *Comité international socialiste consultatif (COMISCO, inactive),* set up 1947 as a loose organization of democratic labour and socialist parties from all parts of the world. COMISCO was seen as re-establishing *Labour and Socialist International (LSI, inactive),* formed 21 May 1923, Hamburg (Germany), on merger of *Second International (inactive),* created 21 Jul 1889, Paris (France), and *International Working Union of Socialist Parties (inactive),* set up 1921. **Aims** Strengthen relations among member parties and organizations and coordinate their *political* views and activities by consent; establish contacts with progressive forces worldwide working for application of the principles of *democratic socialism* – an international movement for freedom, social justice and solidarity. **Structure** Congress (every 4 years); Council; Praesidium; Secretariat, located in London (UK) and headed by Secretary General; Statutory Committees (2); Regional Committees (9); Thematic Committees (7). **Languages** English, French, Spanish. **Finance** Members' dues. Other sources: contributions from fraternal and associated organizations; donations. Annual budget (2018): pounds1,150,000. **Activities** Events/meetings; politics/policy/regulatory. **Events** *Meeting* Geneva (Switzerland) 2018, *Meeting* Barcelona (Spain) 2017, *Meeting* Barcelona (Spain) 2017, *Meeting* New York, NY (USA) 2017, *Meeting* New York, NY (USA) 2017. **Publications** Reports of Congress, Council and other conferences.
Members Full: Member Parties (97) in 83 countries and territories:
Albania, Algeria, Andorra, Angola, Argentina, Armenia, Austria, Azerbaijan, Belarus, Belgium, Benin, Bolivia, Bosnia-Herzegovina, Brazil, Bulgaria, Burkina Faso, Cameroon, Cape Verde, Chad, Chile, Colombia, Costa Rica, Croatia, Cyprus, Czechia, Dominican Rep, Egypt, Equatorial Guinea, Finland, France, Ghana, Greece, Guatemala, Guinea, Haiti, Hungary, India, Iran Islamic Rep, Iraq, Ireland, Israel, Italy, Jamaica, Japan, Kazakhstan, Lebanon, Lithuania, Luxembourg, Mali, Mauritania, Mauritius, Mexico, Moldova, Mongolia, Montenegro, Morocco, Mozambique, Namibia, Nepal, Nicaragua, Niger, Northern Ireland, Pakistan, Palestine, Panama, Paraguay, Peru, Portugal, Puerto Rico, Romania, Russia, San Marino, Senegal, Serbia, Slovakia, South Africa, Spain, Tanzania UR, Tunisia, Türkiye, Uruguay, Venezuela, Yemen.
Consultative Parties (17) in 17 countries and territories:
Algeria, Botswana, Eswatini, Gabon, Gambia, Georgia, Guinea-Bissau, Iran Islamic Rep, Nigeria, Palestine, Sahara West, Sao Tomé-Principe, Syrian AR, Togo, Türkiye, Ukraine, Zambia.
Observer Parties (11) in 9 countries and territories:
Central African Rep, Congo DR, Eswatini, Haiti, Iran Islamic Rep, Kenya, Lesotho, Somalia, UK.
Fraternal Organizations (3), listed in this Yearbook:
International Falcon Movement – Socialist Educational International (IFM-SEI, #13327); International Union of Socialist Youth (IUSY, #15815); Socialist International Women (SIW, #19341).
Associated Organizations (11):
Arab Social Democratic Forum (ASDF); Euro-Latin American Forum of Progressive Socialist Parliamentarians; *International Federation of the Socialist and Democratic Press (IFSDP, no recent information); International League of Religious Socialists (ILRS, #14022); International Social Democratic Union for Education (ISDUE, #14881); International Workers and Amateurs in Sports Confederation (#15905);* Jewish Labour Bund (JLB); *National Democratic Institute for International Affairs (NDIIA); Parlamento Latinoamericano (PARLATINO, #18203)* (Social Democratic Group of); *Party of European Socialists (PES, #18249); World Labour Zionist Movement (WLZM, #21615).*
Consultative Status Consultative status granted from: *ECOSOC (#05331)* (General). **IGO Relations** Cooperates with: *European Commission (EC, #06633); Organization for Security and Cooperation in Europe (OSCE, #17887).* Contacts with: *FAO (#09260); ILO (#11123); International Atomic Energy Agency (IAEA, #12294); International Bank for Reconstruction and Development (IBRD, #12317); International Monetary Fund (IMF, #14180); UNESCO (#20322); United Nations Population Fund (UNFPA, #20612); World Trade Organization (WTO, #21864).* Accredited by: *United Nations (UN, #20515); United Nations Office at Geneva (UNOG, #20597); United Nations Office at Vienna (UNOV, #20604).* **NGO Relations** Instrumental in setting up: *Global Progressive Forum (GPF, #10557).* [2018.06.01/XF3220/y/F]

♦ Socialist International Women (SIW) 19341

Internationale socialiste des femmes – Internacional Socialista de Mujeres
Sec PO Box 67973, London, SW4 4DU, UK. T. +4402080582885. E-mail: socintwomen@gn.apc.org.
URL: http://www.socintwomen.org/

History 9 Jul 1955, London (UK). Founded as successor to *International Socialist Women's Secretariat (inactive)*, set up 17 Aug 1907, Stuttgart (Germany). Present name and statutes adopted, 31 Oct – 1 Nov 1978, Vancouver BC (Canada). Former names and other names: *International Council of Social Democratic Women (ICSDW)* – former (9 Jul 1955 to 1 Nov 1978); *Conseil international des femmes social-démocrates* – former (9 Jul 1955 to 1 Nov 1978); *Consejo Internacional de Mujeres Social-Demócratas* – former (9 Jul 1955 to 1 Nov 1978). **Aims** Promote gender equality, end discrimination against women and promote women's rights; strengthen relations between member organizations to coordinate political positions and activities; encourage members to ensure implementation of adopted resolutions and declarations; extend relations between members and other socialist-orientated women's groups; promote action programmes to overcome discrimination; work for development, peace and human rights in general. **Structure** Congress (every 3 years); Council; Executive Committee; Secretariat at headquarters of Socialist International. **Languages** English, French, Spanish. **Staff** 1.00 FTE, paid. **Finance** Secretariat expenses covered by Socialist International; donations. **Activities** Events/meetings; projects/programmes. **Events** *Congress* Cartagena de Indias (Colombia) 2017, *Asia Regional Meeting* Ulaanbaatar (Mongolia) 2016, *Euro-Mediterranean Regional Meeting* Marseille (France) 2015, *African Regional Meeting* Luanda (Angola) 2014, *North America Regional meeting* Mexico City (Mexico) 2013. **Members** Full; Consultative; Observer. Members in 140 countries. Membership countries not specified. **Consultative Status** Consultative status granted from: *ECOSOC (#05331)* (Special); *ILO (#11123)* (Special List). **IGO Relations** Accredited by (1): *United Nations Office at Vienna (UNOV, #20604)*. Associated with Department of Global Communications of the United Nations. **NGO Relations** Member of (7): *Committee of NGOs on Human Rights, Geneva (#04275)*; *Conference of Non-Governmental Organizations in Consultative Relationship with the United Nations (CONGO, #04635)*; *NGO Committee for Disarmament, Geneva (#17105)*; *NGO Committee on Disarmament, Peace and Security, New York NY (#17106)*; *NGO Committee on Sustainable Development, Vienna (#17119)*; *NGO Committee on the Status of Women, Geneva (#17117)*; *Vienna NGO Committee on the Status of Women (#20775)*. Affiliated with (1): *International Conference of NGOs (#12883)*. Fraternal organizations: *International Falcon Movement – Socialist Educational International (IFM-SEI, #13327)*; *International Union of Socialist Youth (IUSY, #15815)*; *Socialist International (SI, #19340)* (being represented on SI Council). Associated organizations: *Group of the Progressive Alliance of Socialists and Democrats in the European Parliament (S and D, #10786)*; *International League of Religious Socialists (ILRS, #14022)*; *International Social Democratic Union for Education (ISDUE, #14881)*; *Party of European Socialists (PES, #18249)*. [2023.02.14/XC1754/F]

♦ Socialistische Fractie Europees Parlement / see Group of the Progressive Alliance of Socialists and Democrats in the European Parliament (#10786)
♦ Socialist Labour and Sport International (inactive)

♦ Socialists, Democrats and Greens Group (SOC) 19342

Groupe Socialistes, démocrates et verts (SOC)

Pres av de l'Europe, 67000 Strasbourg, France. T. +33388412000.

History Founded 1975, Strasbourg (France), as a political group of the *Parliamentary Assembly of the Council of Europe (PACE, #18211)*. Original title: *Socialist Group of the Parliamentary Assembly of the Council of Europe/ (SOC)* and referred to in short as the *Socialist Group /in the Council of Europe/ – Groupe socialiste /au Conseil de l'Europe*. Subsequently known as: *Socialist Group – Groupe socialiste de l'Assemblée parlementaire du Conseil de l'Europe (SOC)*. **Aims** As a *political* group, represent socialist views in the Parliamentary Assembly of the Council of Europe. **Structure** Plenary Assembly. Bureau, consisting of President, Treasurer, 2 Auditors, Vice-Presidents who are members of the national delegations. Committees (16): Standing Committee; Political Affairs; Economic Affairs and Development; Social, Health and Family Affairs; Legal Affairs and Human Rights; Culture and Education; Science and Technology; Environment, Regional Planning and Local Authorities; Migration, Refugees and Demography; Rules and Procedure; Agriculture and Rural Development; Parliamentary and Public Relations; Budget and the Intergovernmental Work Programme; Equal Opportunities for Women and Men; Honouring of Obligations and Commitments by Members States of the Council of Europe (Monitoring Committee); Joint Committee. Working Groups. Secretariat. **Activities** Fights for the protection of human rights and the promotion of peace and social justice; supports independent trade-union movements and the principle of social cooperation and works for protective measures against the threatening and harmful changes occurring in the environment; invites associated members and guests to take part in its meetings. **Publications** *The Socialist Group in the Council of Europe* in English, French – brochure. Activities reports.

Members Parliamentarians (180) from 36 countries:
Albania, Andorra, Austria, Belgium, Bulgaria, Croatia, Cyprus, Czechia, Denmark, Estonia, Finland, France, Germany, Greece, Hungary, Ireland, Italy, Lithuania, Luxembourg, Malta, Moldova, Netherlands, North Macedonia, Norway, Poland, Portugal, Romania, Russia, San Marino, Slovakia, Slovenia, Spain, Sweden, Switzerland, Türkiye, UK.

NGO Relations *International Social Democratic Union for Education (ISDUE, #14881)*; *Party of European Socialists (PES, #18249)*; *Socialist International (SI, #19340)*. [2019/XF3610/v/F]

♦ Socialist Solidarity – Fund for Development Cooperation FCD (internationally oriented national body)
♦ Socialistu Frakcija Europos Parlamente / see Group of the Progressive Alliance of Socialists and Democrats in the European Parliament (#10786)
♦ Social Justice Committee (internationally oriented national body)
♦ Social Justice Committee of Montréal / see Social Justice Committee
♦ Social Justice Secretariat
♦ Social Marketing International Association (inactive)
♦ Social Media and Critical Care Conference (meeting series)
♦ Socialno-Ekologiceskij Sojuz (#19663)

♦ Social Performance Task Force (SPTF) 19343

Dir address not obtained. E-mail: info@sptfnetwork.org.
URL: http://www.sptf.info/

History Mar 2005, by *Consultative Group to Assist the Poor (CGAP, #04768)*, *Argidius Foundation* and *Ford Foundation (#09858)*. **Aims** Engage with *microfinance* stakeholders to develop, disseminate and promote standards and good practices for social performance management and reporting. **Structure** Board of Directors; Secretariat. **Languages** Arabic, English, French, Russian, Spanish. **Staff** 7.00 FTE, paid. **Finance** Grants. **Activities** Events/meetings; knowledge management/information dissemination; training/education. **Events** *Annual Meeting* Dakar (Senegal) 2014, *Annual Meeting* Panama (Panama) 2013, *Annual Meeting* Jordan 2012, *Annual Meeting* 's Hertogenbosch (Netherlands) 2011. **Publications** *The Universal Standards for Social Performance Management*. **Information Services** *Technical Assistance Providers Database*. **Members** Individual (over 1,600), representing over 1,000 organizations and over 100 countries. [2014.06.01/XJ7018/y/E]

♦ Social Platform 19344

Plate-forme sociale

Mailing Address Rue d'Egmont 11, 1000 Brussels, Belgium. E-mail: platform@socialplatform.org.
URL: http://www.socialplatform.org/

History Sep 1995. Former names and other names: *Platform of European Social NGOs (Social Platform)* – full title; *Plate-forme des ONG européennes du secteur social* – full title. **Aims** Fight for social justice and participatory democracy in Europe; organise policy and advocacy actions as well as campaigns to ensure that *EU policies* are developed in partnership with the people they affect, respecting fundamental rights, promoting solidarity and improving lives. **Structure** General Assembly (annual); Steering Group; Management Committee, including President and 5 elected members; Secretariat, headed by Secretary-General; Working Groups; Taskforces. **Finance** Sources: members' dues. Supported by: Citizens, Equality, Rights and Values Programmme (CERV); *European Commission (EC, #06633)*. **Activities** Advocacy/lobbying/activism; events/meetings. **Events** *Building Social Europe Meeting* Helsinki (Finland) 2019, *Conférence sur l'investissement dans le développement durable* Dublin (Ireland) 2004, *Meeting on forward Europe* Stockholm (Sweden) 2001, *Final conference on the inclusion of fundamental rights in the EU treaty* Brussels (Belgium) 2000, *After Amsterdam – towards a social Europe?* Luxembourg (Luxembourg) 1997. **Publications** *Social Compass* (12 a year) – newsletter. Annual Report; position papers; policy papers.

Members Full members international organizations (32), listed in this Yearbook:
– *AGE Platform Europe (#00557)*;
– *Autism-Europe (AE, #03040)*;
– *Caritas Europa (#03579)*;
– *Confédération européenne des coopératives de travail associé, des coopératives sociales et des entreprises sociales et participatives (CECOP, #04541)*;
– *ERGO Network (#05531)*;
– *EURAG – European Federation of Older Persons (#05597)*;
– *Eurochild (#05657)*;
– *European Anti-Poverty Network (EAPN, #05908)*;
– *European Association of Service Providers for Persons with Disabilities (EASPD, #06204)*;
– *European Consumer Debt Network (ECDN, #06772)*;
– *European Disability Forum (EDF, #06929)*;
– *European Federation for Diaconia (Eurodiaconia, #07099)*;
– *European Network against Racism (ENAR, #07862)*;
– *European Network of Social Integration Enterprises (ENSIE, #08009)*;
– *European Parents' Association (EPA, #08142)*;
– *European Public Health Alliance (EPHA, #08297)*;
– *European Social Action Network (ESAN, #08499)*;
– *European Women's Lobby (EWL, #09102)*;
– *European Youth Forum (#09140)*;
– *EURORDIS – Rare Diseases Europe (#09175)*;
– *Fédération européenne des femmes actives en famille (FEFAF, #09568)*;
– *Housing Europe – The European Federation for Public Cooperative and Social Housing (Housing Europe, #10956)*;
– *ILGA-Europe (#11118)*;
– *International Council on Social Welfare (ICSW, #13076)*;
– *International Federation of Social Workers (IFSW, #13544)*;
– *International Lesbian, Gay, Bisexual, Transgender, Queer and Intersex Youth and Student Organization (IGLYO, #14032)*;
– *International Union of Tenants (IUT, #15822)*;
– *Platform for International Cooperation on Undocumented Migrants (PICUM, #18401)*;
– *SOLIDAR (#19680)*;
– *SOS-Kinderdorf International (#19693)*;
– *TGEU (#20138)*;
– *Volonteurope (#20807)*.

Associate international organizations (14), listed in this Yearbook:
Association des femmes de l'Europe méridionale (AFEM, #02594); *COFACE Families Europe (#04084)*; *European Association for the Education of Adults (EAEA, #06018)*; *European Association Working for Carers (Eurocarers, #06277)*; *European Community Development Network (EuCDN, #06679)*; *European Council for Non-Profit Organizations (#06834)*; *European Forum of Muslim Women (EFOMW, #07321)*; *International Movement ATD Fourth World (#14193)*; *Make Mothers Matter (#16554)*; *Mental Health Europe (MHE, #16715)*; *Re-Use and Recycling European Union Social Enterprises (RREUSE, #18931)*; *Save the Children International (#19058)*; *Women Against Violence Europe (WAVE, #20986)*; *Youth and European Social Work (YES Forum, #22015)*.

Consultative Status Consultative status granted from: *Council of Europe (CE, #04881)* (Participatory Status). **NGO Relations** Member of (3): *Civil Society Europe*; *Observatoire social européen (OSE)*; *SDG Watch Europe (#19162)*. Founding member of: *Spring Alliance (inactive)*. [2023.02.15/XE2503/y/E]

♦ Social Progress Imperative 19345

Exec Dir 2101 L St NW, Ste 800, Washington DC 20037, USA.
URL: http://www.socialprogressimperative.org/

History 2012. Set up previously functioning as *Global Social Progress Initiative*. **Aims** Advance global human *wellbeing* by combining national social performance and capacity indicators with solutions-oriented outreach to sector leaders and grassroots champions, who together can effect large-scale change. **Structure** Board of Directors; Advisory Board. Executive Director. **Staff** 9.00 FTE, paid. **Activities** Launched *Social Progress Index*, Apr 2013. **NGO Relations** Member of (2): *European Policy Centre (EPC, #08240)*; *Wellbeing Economy Alliance (WEAll, #20856)*. [2020/XJ7617/F]

♦ Social Promotion Foundation (internationally oriented national body)
♦ Social Science Research Council (internationally oriented national body)
♦ Social Science Research Institute, Hawaii (internationally oriented national body)

♦ Social sciences and Humanities in ionising radiation REsearch (SHARE) 19346

Contact address not obtained. E-mail: share@ssh-share.eu.
URL: https://www.ssh-share.eu/

Aims Help society in its interaction with radiation risk by bringing together researchers from all relevant platforms, associations and projects related to ionising radiation. **Structure** General Assembly; Steering Committee; Stakeholder Roundtable; Working Groups. **Activities** Events/meetings; training/education. [2020/AA0779/F]

♦ SocialSec – International Symposium on Security and Privacy in Social Networks and Big Data (meeting series)

♦ Social Services Europe 19347

Policy and Project Coordinator c/o EASPD, Rue du Commerce 72, 1040 Brussels, Belgium. E-mail: info@socialserviceseurope.eu.
URL: http://www.socialserviceseurope.eu/

History 12 Dec 2011. Formalized after a phase of cooperation for some years as "Informal Network of Social Service Providers". Registration: Belgium. **Aims** Strengthen the profile and position of social services; promote the role of not-for-profit service providers in Europe. **Structure** General Assembly; Board of Directors; General Working Group; Task Forces: European Care Strategy, Social Economy Action Plan; Policy and Project Coordinator. **Languages** English, French, German. **Staff** 1.00 FTE, paid. **Finance** Sources: members' dues; revenue from activities/projects. Annual budget: 28,000 EUR (2023). **Activities** Advocacy/lobbying/activism; events/meetings; guidance/assistance/consulting; networking/liaising; politics/policy/regulatory; projects/programmes. **Publications** Reports; letters; briefings; position papers; contributions to public consultations/call for evidence of the European Commission

Members Organizations (8):
Caritas Europa (#03579); *European Ageing Network (EAN, #05841)*; *European Association of Service Providers for Persons with Disabilities (EASPD, #06204)*; *European Council for Non-Profit Organizations (#06834)*; *European Federation for Diaconia (Eurodiaconia, #07099)*; *European Federation of National Organisations Working with the Homeless (#07174)*; *European Platform for Rehabilitation (EPR, #08230)*; *Red Cross EU Office (#18643)*.

IGO Relations Cooperates with (1): *European Economic and Social Committee (EESC, #06963)*. **NGO Relations** Partner of (2): *Social Economy Europe (SEE, #19335)*; *Social Platform (#19344)*. [2023.02.16/XJ5825/y/D]

♦ Social Value International (SVI) 19348

Contact Graeme House, Derby Square, Liverpool, L2 7ZH, UK. T. +441517039229. E-mail: hello@socialvalueint.org.
URL: https://socialvalueint.org/

History Registration: Charity, No/ID: 1142874, England and Wales. **Aims** Change the way society accounts for value through principles, practice, people and power. **Structure** Board of Trustees; Social Value International Council. **Activities** Certification/accreditation; knowledge management/information dissemination; training/education. **Publications** *SVI Newsletter*.

Members Individuals in 14 countries:
Australia, Canada, Indonesia, Ireland, Malaysia, Mexico, Nigeria, Philippines, Qatar, Saudi Arabia, South Africa, Spain, Türkiye, UK.

National member networks in 5 countries:
Indonesia, Italy, Japan, Mexico, South Africa.

Associate networks in 11 countries:
Belgium, Bulgaria, France, Greece, Hungary, India, Korea Rep, Russia, Spain, Thailand, Türkiye.

NGO Relations Member of (2): *Wellbeing Economy Alliance (WEAll, #20856)*; *Worldwide Initiatives for Grantmaker Support (WINGS, #21926)*. Partners include: *Accountable Now (#00060)*; *Asian Venture Philanthropy Network (AVPN, #01778)*; *Aspen Network of Development Entrepreneurs (ANDE, #02310)*; *European Venture Philanthropy Association (EVPA, #09053)*. Subscriber to: *ISEAL (#16026)*. [2020/XM8817/C]

♦ Social Venture Network Europe (SVN Europe) 19349

Secretariat Icaruslaan 28, 1185 JM Amstelveen, Netherlands.
History Founded 1993, Amsterdam (Netherlands), with the support of the (US) Social Venture Network. **Aims** Integrate the values of a socially and environmentally *sustainable* society into day to day *business* practices. **Structure** Board of Directors. **Finance** Members' dues. **Activities** Meeting activities. **Events** *Annual Conference* Amsterdam (Netherlands) 2012, *Annual Conference* Egmond aan Zee (Netherlands) 2012, *Annual Conference* Amsterdam (Netherlands) 2011, *Annual Conference* Rotterdam (Netherlands) 2009, *Annual Conference* Rotterdam (Netherlands) 2008.
Members Full in 15 countries:
Austria, Belgium, Denmark, France, Germany, Italy, Japan, Netherlands, South Africa, Spain, Sweden, Switzerland, Thailand, UK, USA. [2013.07.18/XF5750/F]

♦ Social Watch 19350

Control Ciudadano
Coordinator 18 de Julio 2095/office 301, 11100 Montevideo, Uruguay. T. +59824031424.
URL: http://www.socialwatch.org/
History Project hosted by *Instituto del Tercer Mundo, Montevideo (ITEM)*. **Aims** Monitor and report on the implementation by governments and international organizations of the commitments undertaken at the World Summit on *Social Development*, 1995, Copenhagen (Denmark), and at the 4th World Conference on *Women*, 1995, Beijing (China). **Structure** Assembly; Coordinating Committee; Secretariat. **Events** *Civil society forum* Doha (Qatar) 2008. **Publications** *Social Watch Report* (annual) in Arabic, English, French, German, Italian, Portuguese, Spanish; *Social Watch E-Newsletter*.
Members Full in 85 countries:
Albania, Algeria, Angola, Argentina, Armenia, Azerbaijan, Bahrain, Bangladesh, Belgium, Benin, Bolivia, Brazil, Bulgaria, Cambodia, Cameroon, Canada, Central African Rep, Chile, Colombia, Congo DR, Costa Rica, Cyprus, Czechia, Ecuador, Egypt, El Salvador, Estonia, France, Germany, Ghana, Guatemala, Honduras, Hungary, India, Indonesia, Iraq, Italy, Jordan, Kenya, Korea Rep, Latvia, Lebanon, Lithuania, Malaysia, Malta, Mauritania, Mexico, Moldova, Mongolia, Mozambique, Myanmar, Nepal, Netherlands, Nicaragua, Niger, Pakistan, Palestine, Paraguay, Peru, Philippines, Poland, Portugal, Romania, Senegal, Serbia, Slovakia, Slovenia, Somalia, Spain, Sri Lanka, Sudan, Switzerland, Syrian AR, Tanzania UR, Thailand, Tunisia, Uganda, UK, Ukraine, Uruguay, USA, Venezuela, Vietnam, Yemen, Zambia.
Included in the above, 34 organizations listed in this Yearbook:
- *African Youth Growth Foundation (AYGF)*;
- *Alliance Sud, Swiss Alliance of Development Organisations Swissaid – Catholic Lenten Fund – Bread for All – Helvetas – Caritas – Interchurch Aid*;
- *American Council for Voluntary International Action (InterAction)*;
- *Arab Association for Human Rights (HRA, no recent information)*;
- *Arab NGO Network for Development (ANND, #01016)*;
- *Archive of Maori and Pacific Sound (AMPS)*;
- *Asian NGO Coalition for Agrarian Reform and Rural Development (ANGOC, #01566)*;
- *Asociación Centroamericana para la Economia, la Salud y el Ambiente (ACEPESA)*;
- *Asociación del Desarrollo para America Central (ADEPAC, no recent information)*;
- *Bread for All*;
- *Brot für die Welt*;
- *Canadian Feminist Alliance for International Action (FAFIA)*;
- *Catholic Lenten Fund*;
- *CNCD Opération 11 11 11*;
- *Coalition of the Flemish North South Movement – 11 11 11*;
- *Coordination SUD*;
- *Defence for Children International (DCI, #05025)*;
- *Europe External Programme with Africa (EEPA, #09155)*;
- *Foundation for Grassroots Initiatives in Africa (GrassRootsAfrica)*;
- *Friedrich-Ebert-Stiftung (FES)*;
- *GPF Europe (#10684)*;
- *International NGO Forum on Indonesian Development (INFID, #14366)*;
- *Latin American and Caribbean Committee for the Defense of Women's Rights (#16268)*;
- *North-South Institute (NSI)*;
- *Oikos – Cooperação e Desenvolvimento (Oikos)*;
- *Oxfam GB*;
- *Oxfam Novib*;
- *South Asia Alliance for Poverty Eradication (SAAPE, #19712)*;
- *Southern Africa Human Rights NGO Network (SAHRINGON, no recent information)*;
- *Swissaid*;
- *Third World Network-Africa (TWN Africa)*;
- *Third World Network (TWN, #20151)*;
- *UCODEP*;
- *Women in Law and Development in Africa-Afrique de l'Ouest (WiLDAF-AO, #21005)*.

NGO Relations Member of: *World Social Forum (WSF, #21797)*. Supports: *Global Call for Action Against Poverty (GCAP, #10263)*. Organizations involved include: *Arab NGO Network for Environment and Development (RAED, #01017)*; *Development Alternatives with Women for a New Era (DAWN, #05054)*; *Ford Foundation (#09858)*; *Inter-Africa Group – Centre for Dialogue on Humanitarian, Peace and Development Issues in the Horn of Africa (IAG, #11381)*; *Latin American Women's Network to Transform the Economy (#16395)*; *Women's Environment and Development Organization (WEDO, #21016)*. [2019/XF4291/y/F]

- ♦ Social Welfare and Development Centre for Asia and the Pacific (inactive)
- ♦ Sociedad Americana de Derecho Internacional (internationally oriented national body)
- ♦ Sociedad Sur Americana de Fisiologia y Bioquimica Comparadas (inactive)
- ♦ Sociedad Americana de Pesquerias (internationally oriented national body)
- ♦ Sociedad Americana de Quimioterapia de la Tuberculosis (inactive)
- ♦ Sociedad Astronómica de España y América (no recent information)

♦ Sociedad de Biofisicos Latinoamericanos (SoBLA) 19351

Society of Biophysicists of Latin America
Pres MSC 3701 NINDS PNRC, Bldg 35 Rm 3B-1016, 35 Convent Dr, Bethesda MD 20892-3701, USA. Fax +13014964268.
URL: http://sobla.weebly.com/
History at meeting of the US Biophysical Society. **Aims** Foster relations among Latin American scientists working in different countries, particularly of younger researchers with more senior scientists working abroad. **Activities** Annual business meeting at meeting of the US Biophysical Society. **Events** *Ibero-American Congress* Valparaiso (Chile) 2013, *Ibero-American Congress* Madrid (Spain) 2006, *Ibero-American Congress* Rio de Janeiro (Brazil) 2003, *Ibero-American Congress* Alicante (Spain) 2000, *Iberoamerican congress / Ibero-American Congress* Puebla (Mexico) 1993. **Publications** *Biophysics Textbook*; *Boletin de la SOBLA*. Members' directory.
Members Scientists in 19 countries:
Argentina, Bolivia, Brazil, Canada, Chile, Colombia, Costa Rica, Cuba, Ecuador, France, Mexico, Peru, Portugal, Puerto Rico, Spain, UK, Uruguay, USA, Venezuela. [2013/XD2576/v/D]

- ♦ Sociedad de Biospeologia / see International Society of Biospeleology (#14975)
- ♦ Sociedad Caribeña de Cultivos Alimenticios (#03509)
- ♦ Sociedad Centroamericana de Cardiologia (inactive)
- ♦ Sociedad Centroamericana y Caribe de Cancerologia (no recent information)

♦ Sociedad Centroamericana y del Caribe de Clasificación y Analisis de Datos (SoCCCAD) 19352

Central American and Caribbean Society of Classification and Data Analysis
Contact address not obtained. T. +50622075889. Fax +50622074918.
History Jan 2000, Costa Rica. **Aims** Promote research and exchanges on classification and multivariate data analysis and statistics in Central America and the Caribbean region. **Structure** Officers: President; Vice-President; Secretary. One Coordinator per section. **Languages** Spanish. **Staff** 1.00 FTE, paid. **Finance** Members' dues. **Activities** Organizes: biennial International Symposium on Mathematical Methods Applied to the Sciences (SIMMAC); short courses. **Events** *Biennial symposium on mathematical methods applied to the sciences* San José (Costa Rica) 2010, *Symposium* San José (Costa Rica) 2008, *Biennial international symposium on mathematical methods applied to sciences* San Pedro (Costa Rica) 2008, *International conference on applications of statistics to the social sciences* Liberia (Costa Rica) 2002, *Biennial international symposium on mathematical methods applied to the sciences / Symposium* San José (Costa Rica) 2002. **Publications** *Revista de Matematica: Teoria y Aplicaciones*. Books.
Members Sections in 9 countries:
Colombia, Costa Rica, Cuba, Guatemala, Honduras, Mexico, Nicaragua, Panama, Venezuela.
Full (57) in 10 countries and territories:
Colombia, Costa Rica, Cuba, El Salvador, Guadeloupe, Guatemala, Honduras, Mexico, Panama, Venezuela.
NGO Relations Member of: *International Federation of Classification Societies (IFCS, #13391)*. [2015/XD7951/D]

- ♦ Sociedad Centroamericana y del Caribe de Dermatologia (#03663)
- ♦ Sociedad Centroamericana y del Caribe de Fisica (#03664)
- ♦ Sociedad Centroamericana de Dermatologia / see Central American and Caribbean Dermatological Society (#03663)
- ♦ Sociedad Centroamericana de Farmacologia (inactive)
- ♦ Sociedad Centroamericana de Fisica / see Central American and Caribbean Physical Society (#03664)

♦ Sociedad Cientifica Interamericana de Oxigeno Ozonoterapia (SCIOOT) 19353

SG Centro Médico del Ozono, Avellaneda 358, Merlo, Argentina. T. +542204837234. Fax +542204837234. E-mail: draarieck@telered.com.ar.
URL: http://www.scioot.com.ar/
History 12 Sep 2008, Buenos Aires (Argentina). **Structure** Executive Committee; Scientific Committee.
Members Full in 11 countries:
Argentina, Colombia, Costa Rica, Cuba, Ecuador, Mexico, Panama, Paraguay, Peru, Uruguay, Venezuela. [2015/XJ9457/D]

♦ Sociedad Cientifica Latinoamericana de Agroecologia (SOCLA) 19354

Latin American Scientific Society of Agroecology
Pres Calle 475 No 4349, B1896 La Plata, Argentina.
URL: https://www.socla.co/
History Statutes adopted Aug 2007. **Aims** Promote study, discussion and scientific information exchange on agroecology between researchers and teachers in the region. **Structure** General Assembly; Board of Directors; Working Groups. **Languages** Spanish. **Staff** 4.00 FTE, paid. **Finance** Members' dues. **Events** *Congress* La Plata (Argentina) 2015, *Congress* Lima (Peru) 2013. **Publications** *Revista de Agroecologia*. [2019.02.19/XJ6790/D]

- ♦ Sociedad de Cirugia del Mediterraneo Latino (#20042)
- ♦ Sociedad de Cirugia Plastica Latinoamericana (inactive)
- ♦ Sociedad para la Conservación n y Estudio de las Aves Caribeñas / see BirdsCaribbean (#03267)
- ♦ Sociedad Cooperativa Internacional Agricola de Abastecimiento (inactive)
- ♦ Sociedad para la Cronobiologia (#15010)
- ♦ Sociedad de Dermatología Pediátrica para Latinoamérica (internationally oriented national body)
- ♦ Sociedad Diplomatica de St Gabriel (internationally oriented national body)
- ♦ Sociedade Africana de Ciência do Solo (#00520)
- ♦ Sociedade de Cirugia Neurológica Cono Sur (#19869)
- ♦ Sociedad para la Educación en Nutrición (#19612)
- ♦ Sociedade de Especialistas Latinoamericanos en Percepción Remota / see Sociedad Especialistas Latinoamericana en Percepción Remota (#19358)
- ♦ Sociedade Européia para a Geografia / see Association of European Geographical Societies (#02512)
- ♦ Sociedade Europeia de Urgência e Cuidados Intensivos Veterinarios (#09056)

♦ Sociedade de Filosofia da Educação de Lingua Portuguesa (SOFELP) 19355

Pres Rua da Alegria, 1714 C/42, 4200-024 Porto, Portugal. T. +351934566451. Fax +351936091610. E-mail: adcarval@gmail.com.
URL: http://sofelp.com/
Events *Congress* Porto (Portugal) 2011, *Congress* Sao Paulo (Brazil) 2009. **NGO Relations** Member of: *International Federation of Philosophical Societies (FISP, #13507)*; *Société francophone de philosophie de l'éducation (SOFPHIED)*. [2018/XJ5084/D]

- ♦ Sociedade Iberoamericana de Contaminação e Toxicologia Ambiental (unconfirmed)
- ♦ Sociedade Ibero-Americana para o Desenvolvimento das Biorefinarias (#19363)
- ♦ Sociedade Ibero-Americana de Direito Medico (no recent information)
- ♦ Sociedade Ibero-Americana de Grafica Digital (#19370)
- ♦ Sociedade Ibero-americana de Suitina (#19378)
- ♦ Sociedade Interamericana de Administração da Educação (inactive)
- ♦ Sociedade Interamericana de Cardiologia (#11448)
- ♦ Sociedade Interamericana de Endoscopia Digestiva (#19384)
- ♦ Sociedade Interamericana de Filosofia (#19385)
- ♦ Sociedade Interamericana de Hipertensão (#11449)
- ♦ Sociedade InterAmericana de Horticultura Tropical (#11451)
- ♦ Sociedade Interamericana de Imprensa (#11444)
- ♦ Sociedade Interamericana de Psicologia (#11450)
- ♦ Sociedade Internacional para a Conservação dos Fungos (#15134)
- ♦ Sociedade Internacional para o Direito de Autor (no recent information)
- ♦ Sociedade Internacional para o Estudo da Hipertensão na Gravidez (#15475)
- ♦ Sociedade Internacional de Higiene Animal (#14922)

♦ Sociedade Internacional Portugues / Lingua Estrangeira (SIPLE) .. 19356

Pres address not obtained.
URL: http://www.siple.org.br/
History Founded during 'III Congresso Brasileiro de Lingüistica Aplicada'. **Activities** Events/meetings. **Events** *Symposium* Natal (Brazil) 2018, *Symposium* Lisbon (Portugal) 2017, *Congress* Salvador (Brazil) 2016, *Symposium* Londrina (Brazil) 2014, *Congress* Macau (Macau) 2014. **NGO Relations** Member of: *International Federation of Language Teacher Associations (#13468)*. [2020.03.27/XD8038/D]

- ♦ Sociedade Internacional das Técnicas de Imagerie Mentale / see Société internationale des techniques d'imagerie mentale onirique (#19498)
- ♦ Sociedade Internacional das Técnicas de Imagerie Mentale Onirique (#19498)
- ♦ Sociedade Internacional de Trilogia Analitica (#14917)
- ♦ Sociedade Latina de Biologia e Medicina da Reprodução (#19387)
- ♦ Sociedade Latin Hipertensão Pulmonary (#19388)
- ♦ Sociedade Latinoamericana de Auditoria de Serviços de Saúde (#19392)
- ♦ Sociedade Latino Americana de Biomateriais, Engenharia de Tecidos e Orgãos Artificiais (#16370)
- ♦ Sociedade Latinoamericana de Ciencia do Solo (#16385)
- ♦ Sociedade Latino Americana de Coaching (internationally oriented national body)
- ♦ Sociedade Latinoamericana de Direito Internacional (#16374)
- ♦ Sociedade Latino-Americana de Endocrinologia Pediátrica (#16381)
- ♦ Sociedade Latino-americana de Especialistas em Mamiferos Aquaticos (#19402)
- ♦ Sociedade Latinoamericana para o Estudo da Impotência / see Sociedad Latinoamericana de Medicina Sexual (#19413)
- ♦ Sociedade Latinoamericana para o Estudo da Impotência e Sexualidade / see Sociedad Latinoamericana de Medicina Sexual (#19413)
- ♦ Sociedade Latino Americana de Estudos Imobiliarios (#16366)
- ♦ Sociedade Latino-Americana de Gastroenterologia, Hepatologia e Nutrição Pediatrica (#16382)
- ♦ Sociedade Latinoamericana de Gastroenterologia Pediatrica e Nutrição / see Latinamerican Society for Pediatric Gastroenterology, Hepatology and Nutrition (#16382)

♦ Sociedade Latino-americana de Gastroenterologia Pediatrica, Nutrição e Hepatologia / see Latinamerican Society for Pediatric Gastroenterology, Hepatology and Nutrition (#16382)

♦ Sociedade Latino-Americana de Glaucoma (SLAG) 19357

Latin American Glaucoma Society

Pres Cntr de Oftalmologia Especializada, Av São Gualter 99, Sao Paulo SP, Brazil.

Events *Meeting* Cancún (Mexico) 2000. **Publications** *Slag Revista.* **NGO Relations** Member of: *World Glaucoma Association (WGA, #21540).* [2012.08.28/XD9411/**D**]

♦ Sociedade Latino Americana de Interação Materno Fetal and Placenta (#16376)
♦ Sociedade Latinoamericana de Investigação Pediatrica (#19411)
♦ Sociedade Latinoamericana de Medicina Sexual (#19413)
♦ Sociedade Latinoamericana de Nefrologia e Hipertensión (#19415)
♦ Sociedade Latinoamericana de Neuropsicologia (#16378)
♦ Sociedade Latinoamericana de Nutrição (#19417)
♦ Sociedade Latino-Americana de Ombro e Cotovelo (#19409)
♦ Sociedade Latinoamericana de Tireóide (#16390)
♦ Sociedade Missionaria da Boa Nova (religious order)
♦ Sociedad de la Enciclopedia Iberoamericana de Filosofia (no recent information)
♦ Sociedade de Oftalmopediatria Latino Americana (#19430)
♦ Sociedade de Optometria de Europa (#08675)
♦ Sociedade Panamericana de Neurovirologia (#18130)
♦ Sociedade Panamericana de Trauma (#19436)
♦ Sociedad Ergoftalmológica Internacional (no recent information)
♦ Sociedades Biblicas Unidas (#20498)
♦ Sociedad Escandinava de Anestesistas / see Scandinavian Society of Anaesthesiology and Intensive Care Medicine (#19101)
♦ Sociedad Española de Medicina Tropical y Salud Internacional (internationally oriented national body)

♦ Sociedad Especialistas Latinoamericana en Percepción Remota (SELPER) 19358

Latin American Society of Remote Sensing and Special Systems – Société latinoaméricaine de télédétection et de systèmes spéciaux

Contact Carrero 30 No 48-51, Edificio IGAC-CIAF Of 212, Bogota, Bogota DC, Colombia. T. +5713694096. Fax +5713694096. E-mail: info@selper.org.co – info@selper.info.

SG c/o CPRSIG, Edificio Panoramico, 11 de Sept 2155, Torre A, Of 902, Santiago, Santiago Metropolitan, Chile.

URL: http://selper.info/

History Nov 1980, Quito (Ecuador). Founded at first meeting of Latin American specialists in remote sensing. Former names and other names: *Sociedade de Especialistas Latinoamericanos en Percepción Remota* – former (Nov 1980); *Sociedad Latinoamericana de Percepción Remota y Sistemas Especiales* – former alias; *Sociedad Latinoamerican de Percepción Remota y Sistemas de Información Espacial* – alias. **Aims** Promote cooperation among member countries in order to improve their already existing technical-scientific capacity; stimulate international, national and regional integration of remote sensing specialists by linking countries with similar problems. **Structure** Executive Committee, consisting of President, 3 Vice-Presidents, Secretary-General, Treasurer, Director of Institutional Relations, Director of Teaching and Investigation, Editorial Director and National Coordinators. **Languages** Portuguese, Spanish. **Staff** 35.00 FTE, voluntary. **Finance** Members' dues. Donations from research institutions, universities and private companies. **Activities** Organizes *'Latin American Symposium in Remote Sensing'* (every 2 years) and Plenary Meetings. Promotes training courses (in cooperation with other organizations). Through national chapters supports development of project research in conjunction with research institutes, universities and other interested organizations. **Events** *International Symposium* Monterrey (Mexico) 2022, *Symposium* Puerto Iguazú (Argentina) 2016, *Symposium* Medellin (Colombia) 2014, *Symposium* Cayenne (Guiana Fr) 2012, *Symposium* Guanajuato (Mexico) 2010. **Publications** *Revista Técnica* (4 a year); *Noticias SELPER* – newsletter. *SELPER Dictionary in Remote Sensing* (1989) in English, Portuguese, Spanish.

Members Individual; Institutional; Sponsored, in 22 countries:
Argentina, Bolivia, Brazil, Chile, Colombia, Costa Rica, Cuba, Dominican Rep, Ecuador, France, Germany, Guatemala, Mexico, Netherlands, Nicaragua, Panama, Paraguay, Peru, Puerto Rico, Uruguay, USA, Venezuela.

NGO Relations Member of: *International Society for Photogrammetry and Remote Sensing (ISPRS, #15362).* [2022/XD0523/**D**]

♦ Sociedad Estadounidense de Estudios de Ingenieria (#00790)
♦ Sociedad para el Estudio del Nuevo Testamento (#19610)
♦ Sociedad Estudios y Expansión (inactive)
♦ Sociedad de Estudios Internacionales, Madrid (internationally oriented national body)
♦ Sociedade Sul Americana de Cirurgia do Ombro e Cotovelo / see Sociedad Latino Americanas de Hombro y Codo (#19409)
♦ Sociedade Sul Americana de Fisiologia e Bioquimica Comparadas (inactive)
♦ Sociedade de Toxicologia e Quimica Ambiental da América Latina (see: #19551)
♦ Sociedad Europea de Artroscopia de Muñeca (#09122)
♦ Sociedad Europea de las Ciencias del Grafismo (#08616)
♦ Sociedad Europea de Conservación de Suelos (#08739)

♦ Sociedad Europea de Cooperación Farmacéutica (SECOF) 19359

European Society for Pharmaceutical Cooperation

Main Office Edif Portico, c/o Landwell – 8o plano, Concejal F Ballesteros 4, 41018 Seville, Sevilla, Spain. T. +34954981300. Fax +34954981320. E-mail: contact@secof.eu.

Admin 39 rue des Augustins, BP 2039X, 76040 Rouen CEDEX 1, France.

URL: http://www.secof.eu/

Members Pharmaceutical cooperatives in 7 countries:
Belgium, France, Greece, Italy, Portugal, Spain, Türkiye.

NGO Relations Member of: *Groupement International de la Répartition Pharmaceutique (GIRP, #10762).* [2014/XD9471/**D**]

♦ Sociedad Europea de Cultura (#08576)
♦ Sociedad Europea para la Geografia / see Association of European Geographical Societies (#02512)
♦ Sociedad Europea de Medicina de Familia (#08609)
♦ Sociedad Europea para el Medio Ambiente y el Desarrollo (inactive)
♦ Sociedad Europea de Optometria (#08675)
♦ Sociedad Europea de Radiologia de la Cabeza y del Cuello (#08617)
♦ Sociedad Europea de Semantica General (no recent information)
♦ Sociedad Europea de Sociologia Rural (#08731)
♦ Sociedad Europea Para La Sordera y La Salud Mental (#08649)
♦ Sociedad Europea de Tratamiento de Heridas / see European Wound Management Association (#09121)
♦ Sociedad Europea Veterinaria de Urgencias y Cuidados Intensivos (#09056)
♦ Sociedad europeo para investigación de la educación de adultos (#08725)
♦ Sociedad Farmacéutica del Mediterraneo Latino (#19508)
♦ Sociedad y Federación Internacional de Cardiologia / see World Heart Federation (#21562)
♦ Sociedad Hegel Internacional (#13788)
♦ Sociedad de las Hijas del Corazón de Maria (religious order)

♦ Sociedad Hispanoamericana de Hernia (SoHaH) 19360

Sec address not obtained.

URL: http://www.sohah.org/

Aims Promote the scientific progress and development of abdominal wall surgery. **Structure** Board of Directors; Scientific Committee. **Finance** Members' dues. **Events** *Congreso* Bilbao (Spain) 2020, *Congreso* Madrid (Spain) 2018. **Publications** *Revista Hispanoamericana de Hernia.* [2021/XM7632/**D**]

♦ Sociedad Hispano-Luso-Americana de Lepidopterologia (no recent information)
♦ Sociedad de Historia de la Educación Latinoamericana (unconfirmed)

♦ Sociedad Iberoamericana de Bioinformatica (SoIBio) 19361

Iberoamerican Society for Bioinformatics

Sec c/o Fundación Ciena and Vida, Computational Biology Laboratory, Avenida Zañartu 1482, ¥uñoa, Santiago, Santiago Metropolitan, Chile. T. +56223672000.

URL: http://www.soibio.org/

History 2009, Mexico, as a continuation of *Red Iberoamericana Bioinformatica (RIB, inactive)*, which was set up 2002. **Aims** Promote research and development on bioinformatics in the large international region of Iberoamerica. **Structure** Officers: President; Vice-President; Secretary. Committees (6): Admissions And Membership; Education and Training; Outreach; Scientific Collaboration; Infrastructure; Foreign Relations. Students and Young Researchers Council. **Languages** English, Portuguese, Spanish. **Staff** All voluntary. **Finance** Members' dues. **Activities** Education and training through courses, workshops and didactic material. **Events** *Meeting on Bioinformatics* Belo Horizonte (Brazil) 2014, *Congress* Rosario (Argentina) 2013.

Members Full in 11 countries:
Argentina, Brazil, Chile, Colombia, Costa Rica, Mexico, Peru, Portugal, Spain, Uruguay, Venezuela.

NGO Relations Affiliate organization of: *International Society for Computational Biology (ISCB, #15026).* Instrumental in setting up: *Global Organisation for Bioinformatics Learning, Education and Training (GOBLET, #10516).* [2015/XJ6801/**D**]

♦ Sociedad Iberoamericana de Biologia Celular (inactive)
♦ Sociedad Iberoamericana y del Caribe de Coordinadores de Trasplantes, Donación de Organos, Tejidos y Células (inactive)

♦ Sociedad Iberoamericana y del Caribe de Restauración Ecológica (SIACRE) 19362

Ibero-American and Caribbean Ecological Restoration Society

Pres Depto Ecologia y Recursos Naturales, Fac de Ciencias UNAM, Circuito Exterior, Ciudad Universitaria, 04510 Mexico City CDMX, Mexico. E-mail: siacre.org@gmail.com.

Contact Calle 118 No 70-84, Bogota, Bogota DC, Colombia. T. +5716434200. Fax +5716434200.

URL: http://www.siacre.com.co/

History Founded 2013, Bogota (Colombia), at 3rd Congress of *Red Iberoamericana y del Caribe de Restauración Ecológica (RIACRE, inactive)*, as a merger between RIACRE and *REDLAN – Latin-American Network on Ecological Restoration.* **Aims** Generate, promote, assemble, develop and spread research on ecological restoration in degraded areas in Ibero-America and the Caribbean; contribute to specialized professional training in this area of knowledge. **Structure** Directive Board. **Languages** English, Portuguese, Spanish. **Staff** Voluntary. **Finance** Members' dues. **Activities** Events/meetings. **Events** *Congress* Santa Marta (Colombia) 2021, *Congress* Santa Marta (Colombia) 2020, *Let's restore the connection with nature – hands to the ground* Lima (Peru) 2019. **Publications** *Boletin SIACRE.*

Members Full in 12 countries:
Argentina, Bolivia, Brazil, Chile, Colombia, Costa Rica, Cuba, Ecuador, Mexico, Peru, Spain, Venezuela.

NGO Relations *Society for Ecological Restoration International (SERI).* [2020.01.16/XM8461/**D**]

♦ Sociedad Iberoamericana de Contaminación y Toxicologgia Ambientales (unconfirmed)
♦ Sociedad Iberoamericana de Córnea / see Pan-American Cornea Society (#18090)
♦ Sociedad Iberoamericana de Derecho Médico (no recent information)

♦ Sociedad Iberoamericana para el Desarrollo de las Biorrefinarias (SIADEB) 19363

Sociedade Ibero-Americana para o Desenvolvimento das Biorefinarias (SIADEB) – Ibero-American Society for the Development of Biorefineries

Pres Edificio K2 – Campus do Lumiar, Estrada do Paço do Lumiar 22, 1649-038 Lisbon, Portugal. T. +351210924713. Fax +351217163636. E-mail: contact@siadeb.org.

URL: http://www.siadeb.org/

History Set up within the network of *Programa Iberoamericano de Ciencia y Tecnologia para el Desarrollo (CYTED, #18524)* (2010-2013). Registered in accordance with Portuguese law, 27 Sep 2010, Lisbon (Portugal). **Aims** Bring together experts from all relevant scientific areas, from agriculture and agro-industrial economics to process engineering, especially the key areas of *energy, biotechnology,* chemistry, *logistics* and mathematical *modelling,* for development of biorefineries and the bioeconomy. **Structure** General Assembly; Board of Directors; Secretary General. **Languages** English, Portuguese, Spanish. **Staff** None. **Finance** Members dues. Institutional support from: FundaçÆo para Ciencia e Tecnologia (Portugal); *Programa Iberoamericano de Ciencia y Tecnologia para el Desarrollo (CYTED, #18524).* **Activities** Research/documentation; awards/prizes/competitions. **Events** *Iberoamerican Congress on Biorefineries* Jaén (Spain) 2018.

Members Researchers, academics and other professionals in 19 countries:
Angola, Argentina, Brazil, Chile, Colombia, Costa Rica, Cuba, Dominican Rep, Ecuador, France, Mexico, Panama, Paraguay, Peru, Portugal, Spain, Uruguay, USA, Venezuela. [2018.09.06/XJ6788/v/**D**]

♦ Sociedad Iberoamericana de Diagnóstico y Tratamiento Prenatal (no recent information)

♦ Sociedad Iberoamericana de Electroquimica (SIBAE) 19364

Ibero-american Electrochemical Society

Pres Depto de Fisco-quimica, Inst de Quimica, Univ Estadual Paulista Júlio de Mesquita Filho, Rua Francisco Degni s/n, Araraquara SP, 14800-900, Brazil. T. +551633016653. Fax +551633227932. E-mail: mercedes@iq.unesp.br.

SG INFIQC – Depto de Fisicoquimica, Fac de Ciencias Quimicas, Univ Nac de Córdoba, Haya de la Torre y Medina Allende, Pabellón Argentina, Ala 1, Ciudad Universitaria, 5000 Córdoba, Argentina. T. +543514334169 – +543514334180. Fax +543514334188. E-mail: mlopez@mail.fcq.unc.edu.ar.

URL: http://www.sibae.org/

History Jul 1990, Santa Cruz de Tenerife (Spain). Jul 1990, Tenerife (Spain), at 9th Iberoamerican Electrochemical Congress. Name adopted at 10th Congress, Sep 1992, Córdoba (Argentina). Statutes approved at 12th Congress, 23-29 Apr 1996, Mérida (Venezuela). **Aims** Promote, in the framework of the Iberoamerican countries, the cooperation of specialists in the field of pure and applied *electrochemical* science. **Structure** General Meeting (every 2 years, at Congress). Executive Committee, consisting of President, Vice-President Secretary-General, a National Secretary for each country with members, and immediate Past-President. **Languages** Portuguese, Spanish. **Activities** Organizes the Iberoamerican Electrochemical Congress (every 2 years). **Events** *Congress* Mexico 2022, *Congress* Montevideo (Uruguay) 2020, *Biennial Congress* Madrid (Spain) 2010, *Biennial Congress* Medellin (Colombia) 2008, *Biennial Congress* La Plata (Argentina) 2006.

Members Individual Full; Correspondent; Honorary. Organizational Collaborating; Benefactor Enterprise. Individuals in 15 countries and territories:
Argentina, Brazil, Chile, Colombia, Costa Rica, Cuba, Mexico, Panama, Peru, Portugal, Puerto Rico, Spain, Uruguay, USA, Venezuela. [2021/XD5108/**D**]

♦ Sociedad Iberoamericana de Endoscopia Ginecológica / see Ibero-American Society of Gynecological Endoscopy and Images (#11030)
♦ Sociedad Iberoamericana de Endoscopia Ginecológica e Imagenes (#11030)

♦ Sociedad Iberoamericana de Enfermedad Cerebrovascular (SIECV) 19365

Ibero-American Stroke Organization (IASO)

Contact Magdalena 133, Col del Valle, Mexico City CDMX, Mexico. E-mail: iberocerebrovascular@grupodestinos.com.mx.

URL: http://siecv.cicmundiales.net/

History Oct 1998, Guayaquil (Ecuador). **Aims** Promote adequate attention and care to patients with cerebrovascular diseases in the iberoamerican countries, as well as high quality education in cerebrovascular disease; promote research in vascular neurology in iberoamerican countries; collaborate with public and private sector and the community in all matters related with the prevention of cerebrovascular disease. **Structure** General Assembly; Board. **Languages** Portuguese, Spanish. **Staff** 9.00 FTE, paid. Voluntary. **Finance** Members' dues. Other sources: industry donations; congress proceeds. **Events** *Congress* San José (Costa Rica) 2019, *Congress* Monterrey (Mexico) 2016, *Congress* Panama (Panama) 2014, *Congress* Buenos Aires (Argentina) 2013, *Congress* Brasilia (Brazil) 2012.

Members Full in 20 countries:
Argentina, Bolivia, Brazil, Chile, Colombia, Costa Rica, Cuba, Ecuador, El Salvador, Guatemala, Honduras, Mexico, Panama, Paraguay, Peru, Portugal, Spain, Uruguay, USA, Venezuela. [2020/XM0322/D]

♦ Sociedad Iberoamericana de Estudios Heideggerianos (SIEH) 19366

Contact address not obtained. E-mail: sociedadheidegger@gmail.com.
URL: http://www.sociedadheidegger.org/

History 5 Sep 2008, Buenos Aires (Argentina). **Structure** Executive Committee. **Events** *Congress* Madrid (Spain) 2019, *Congress* Puebla (Mexico) 2013, *Congress* Barranquilla (Colombia) 2009. **Publications** *Studia Heideggeriana* – series. [2019/XJ6799/D]

♦ Sociedad Iberoamericana de Estudios Kierkegaardianos (unconfirmed)

♦ Sociedad Iberoamericana de Estudios Numismaticos (SIAEN) 19367

Ibero-American Society of Numismatic Research – Société ibéroaméricaine de recherches numismatiques

Sec Calle Jorge Juan 106, 28009 Madrid, Spain. T. +34915666536. E-mail: siaen@fnmt.es.
URL: http://www.siaen.org/

History 1951, Madrid (Spain). **Structure** Directing Council, comprising President, Vice-President, Secretary, Vice-Secretary, Treasurer and 5 members. **Languages** Spanish. **Activities** Research/documentation. **Events** *Congress* Barcelona (Spain) 2018, *Congress* Madrid (Spain) 2014. **Publications** *Numisma: Revista de Estudios Numismaticos* (annual). *Museo Casa de la Moneda* – co-editor. **Members** Membership countries not specified. **NGO Relations** Member of: *International Numismatic Council (INC, #14385).* [2015.01.08/XD4553/D]

♦ Sociedad Iberoamericana de Estudios Utilitaristas (SIEU) 19368

Exec Pres Facultad de Humanidades, Campus de Esteiro, Universidad de Coruña, 15403 Ferrol, La Coruña, Spain. T. +34981337400ext3834. Fax +34981337430. E-mail: joselu@udc.es.
URL: http://sieu.es/

History 1990. **Structure** General Assembly. **Events** *Biennial Congress* London (UK) 2006, *Biennial Congress* Ferrol (Spain) 2004. **Publications** *Revista Iberoamericana de Estudios Utilitaristas.* **NGO Relations** Instrumental in setting up: *European Network of Utilitarian Scholars (E-nous).* [2020/XM3447/D]

♦ Sociedad Iberoamericana de Filosofia (no recent information)

♦ Sociedad Iberoamericana de Fisica y Quimica Ambiental (SiFyQA) . 19369

Ibero-American Society of Environmental Physics and Chemistry

Exec Sec C/C Crespo Rascón 12 5N, 37002 Salamanca, Spain. T. +34923268493. E-mail: juanf.gallardo@gmail.com.
URL: http://www.sifyqa.org.es/

History 2005. **Aims** Support Latin-American scientists and researchers dealing with environmental topics. **Structure** Headquarters in Salamanca (Spain). Maintains the Network: *'Red Iberoamericana de Fisica y Quimica Ambiental (RiFyQA)'.* **Languages** English, Portuguese, Spanish. **Staff** 15.00 FTE, voluntary. **Finance** Sources: members' dues. **Activities** Events/meetings; research/documentation. **Events** *Congress* Puebla (Mexico) 2020, *Congress* Puebla (Mexico) 2017, *Congress* Viña del Mar (Chile) 2014, *Congress* Cancún (Mexico) 2011, *Congress* Mar del Plata (Argentina) 2008. **Publications** *Materia organica de suelos* (2016); *Procesos geoquimicos superficiales en Iberoamérica* (2014); *Aguas, suelos y vegetación en cuencas iberoamericanas* (2012); *Residuos Sólidos en Iberoamérica* (2012); *Contaminación, descontaminación y restauración en Iberoamérica* (2010); *Emisiones de gases con efecto invernadero en ecosistemas iberoamericanos* (2009); *Contaminación en Iberoamérica: Xenobióticos y metales Pesados* (2008); *La Captura de C en ecosistemas terrestres iberoamericanos* (2007); *Medio Ambiente en Iberoamérica: Visión desde la Fisica y la Quimica en los albores del Siglo XXI* (2006).
Members Full in 16 countries:
Argentina, Bolivia, Brazil, Chile, Colombia, Costa Rica, Cuba, Dominican Rep, Ecuador, El Salvador, Mexico, Peru, Portugal, Spain, Uruguay, Venezuela.
IGO Relations Maintains relations with intergovernmental organizations (not specified). **NGO Relations** Maintains relations with nongovernmental organizations (not specified). [2022/XM3445/D]

♦ Sociedad Iberoamericana de Glaucoma (unconfirmed)

♦ Sociedad Iberoamericana de Grafica Digital (SIGraDI) 19370

Ibero-American Society of Digital Graphics – Sociedade Ibero-Americana de Grafica Digital

Pres Universidad Nacional del Litoral, Bv Pellegrini 2750, 3000 Santa Fé, Argentina. E-mail: info@sigradi.org.
Treas Univ of Rio de Janeiro, Rua Joaquium Nabucco 244/102, Rio de Janeiro RJ, 22080 030, Brazil.
Contact Fac de Arquitectura, Universidad de la República, Br Artigas 1031, CP11200 Montevideo, Uruguay. T. +59824001106ext147. Fax +59824006063 – +59824014142.
URL: http://www.sigradi.org/

History Founded 1997, Buenos Aires (Argentina). **Aims** Gather architects, planners, designers and artists associated with digital graphics and provide the opportunity for educators, professionals, researchers and students from Latin america and the rest of the world to meet and share their knowledge and expertise. **Structure** International Executive Committee, comprising President and 9 Full Members. Advisor Committee of 3 Full Members. **Languages** English, Portuguese, Spanish. **Staff** International Executive Committee (ad-honorem). **Finance** Members' dues (annual): US$ 30. **Activities** Organizes annual conference. Participates in CumInCAD, a cumulative index of publications about computer aided architectural design. **Events** *Annual Congress / Conference* Valparaiso (Chile) 2013, *Annual Congress / Conference* Fortaleza (Brazil) 2012, *Annual congress / Conference* Santa Fé (Argentina) 2011, *Annual congress / Conference* Bogota (Colombia) 2010, *Annual congress / Conference* Sao Paulo (Brazil) 2009. **Publications** *CumInCad: Cumulative Index of Articles about CAD.* **Members** Full; Guest. Individuals (about 1,000) in a variety of fields ranging from architecture and graphic, industrial and textile design, to urban planning, visual and performing arts, cinematography engineering, computer science and mathematics, in 30 countries. Membership countries not specified. **NGO Relations** Links with sister organizations: *Arab Society for Computer Aided Architectural Design (ASCAAD, #01044); Association for Computer Aided Design in Architecture (ACADIA); Computer Aided Architectural Design Research in Asia (CAADRIA, #04425); Education and research in Computer Aided Architectural Design in Europe (eCAADe, #05373).* [2013.04.05/XD7579/D]

♦ Sociedad Iberoamericana de Imagen Mamaria (SIBIM) 19371

Pres Head of Breast Radiology and Gynecology, UDIAT Centre Diagnostic, Parc del Tauli 1, 08208 Sabadell, Barcelona, Spain. E-mail: info@sibim.org.
URL: http://www.sibim.org/

History 20 Oct 2005. **Structure** Board of Directors, comprising President, Vice-President, Secretary and Treasurer. **Events** *Congress* Madrid (Spain) 2013, *Congress* Lima (Peru) 2012, *Congress* Puerto Vallarta (Mexico) 2011, *Congress* Cartagena de Indias (Colombia) 2010, *Congress* Buenos Aires (Argentina) 2009. [2016/XJ7200/D]

♦ Sociedad Iberoamericana de Infectologia (unconfirmed)

♦ Sociedad Iberoamericana de Información Cientifica (SIIC) 19372

Iberoamerican Society for Scientific Information

Dir Casilla de Correo 2568, C1000WAZ, Correo Central, Buenos Aires, Argentina. T. +541143424901. Fax +541143313305. E-mail: direccion@siicsalud.com.
URL: http://www.siicsalud.com/

History 1980. **Aims** Promote scientific research among the countries of the region; contribute to its diffusion through media and related scientific institutions. **Structure** Editorial and Scientific Board of Directors; Editorial Scientific Superior Committee; scientific committees (21). **Languages** English, German, Italian, Portuguese, Spanish. **Finance** Funded by users and enterprises. **Activities** Knowledge management/information dissemination; research/documentation; publishing activities. **Events** *International congress of traditional medicine* Mexico City (Mexico) 2006, *World summit on health and integral medicine* Mexico City (Mexico) 2006, *International symposium on hormonal carcinogenesis* Valencia (Spain) 2003. **Publications** *Salud Ciencia* (6 a year) – journal, electronic and paper; *Collection Trabajos Distinguidos* (4 a year) – electronic and paper. *Trabajos Distinguidos* – series. Scientific information on medicine and healthcare in English and Spanish; manuscripts.

Members Full in 63 countries and territories:
Algeria, Argentina, Armenia, Australia, Austria, Belgium, Bolivia, Bosnia-Herzegovina, Brazil, Bulgaria, Canada, Chile, China, Colombia, Croatia, Cuba, Czechia, Denmark, Ecuador, Egypt, Finland, France, Germany, Greece, Guatemala, Honduras, Hong Kong, Hungary, Iceland, India, Iraq, Ireland, Israel, Italy, Japan, Jordan, Luxembourg, Mexico, Morocco, Netherlands, New Zealand, Nicaragua, Norway, Palestine, Panama, Paraguay, Peru, Poland, Portugal, Russia, Saudi Arabia, Slovenia, South Africa, Spain, Sweden, Switzerland, Taiwan, Türkiye, UK, United Arab Emirates, Uruguay, USA, Venezuela.
NGO Relations Scientific relations with: *Asociación Latina e Ibérica Contra el Cancer (ALICC, #02173); European Federation of Neurological Societies (EFNS, inactive); European Alliance of Associations for Rheumatology (EULAR, #05862); Global Reproductive Health Forum (GRHF, no recent information); International Association for Disability and Oral Health (iADH, #11848); International Pediatric Nephrology Association (IPNA, #14543); International Society of Bioethics (ISB, #14961); International Society of Gynecological Endocrinology (ISGE, #15150); International Society of University Colon and Rectal Surgeons (ISUCRS, #15530); World Assembly on Tobacco Counters Health (WATCH); World Psychiatric Association (WPA, #21741).* [2020/XD7108/D]

♦ Sociedad Iberoamericana de Inteligencia Artificial (#11029)

♦ Sociedad Iberoamericana de Intervencionismo (SIDI) 19373

Iberoamerican Society of Interventional Radiology

Address not obtained.
URL: http://www.intervencionismosidi.org/

Structure General Assembly. Executive Committee, comprising President, Vice-President, Secretary-General, Treasurer, Scientific and Congress Secretary and 3-4 members. **Events** *Congress* Buenos Aires (Argentina) 2019, *Congress* Buenos Aires (Argentina) 2013, *Congress* Panama (Panama) 2012. **Publications** *Revista Intervencionismo.*
Members Individuals in 13 countries:
Argentina, Brazil, Chile, Colombia, Guatemala, Mexico, Nicaragua, Panama, Peru, Spain, Uruguay, USA, Venezuela.
NGO Relations Member of: *Cardiovascular and Interventional Radiological Society of Europe (CIRSE, #03427).* [2019/XJ6882/v/D]

♦ Sociedad Iberoamericana de Metodologia Económica / see Sociedad Ibero-Americana de Metodologia Económica (#19374)

♦ Sociedad Ibero-Americana de Metodologia Económica (SIAME) ... 19374

Contact Inst de Filosofia, Univ Veracruzana, Tuxpan 29, 91020 Xalapa VER, Mexico. T. +522288154285. Fax +522288154285.
URL: http://siameorg.wordpress.com/

History 2000. Previously also referred to as *Sociedad Iberoamericana de Metodologia Económica.* **Aims** Encourage study of the methodology, epistemology and philosophy of economic science. **Structure** Board of Directors. **Languages** English, Portuguese, Spanish. **Staff** 1.00 FTE, paid. **Finance** Support from Universidad Veracruzana. **Events** *Meeting* Helsinki (Finland) 2011. **Publications** *Energeia* (2 a year) – journal.
Members Full in 6 countries:
Argentina, Brazil, Mexico, Portugal, Spain, Venezuela. [2018.09.13/XJ6824/D]

♦ Sociedad Ibero-Americana de Neonatologia (#11031)
♦ Sociedad Iberoamericana de Neurouroginecologia / see Sociedad Iberoamericana de Neurourologia y Uroginecologia (#19375)

♦ Sociedad Iberoamericana de Neurourologia y Uroginecologia (SINUG) 19375

Contact c/ Teodora Lamadrid, 52 Est E Entresuelo 2o, 08022 Barcelona, Spain. T. +34934703513. E-mail: secretaria@sinug.org.
URL: http://www.sinug.org/

History 1987. Also known as *Sociedad Iberoamericana de Neurouroginecologia.* **Events** *Congress* San Sebastian (Spain) 2014, *Congress* Barcelona (Spain) 2013, *Congress* Cancún (Mexico) 2010, *Symposium* Lisbon (Portugal) 2009, *Congress* Albufeira (Portugal) 2008. **Publications** *Monograficos sobre Formación Continuada en Urologia.* [2014/XM3446/D]

♦ Sociedad Ibero Americana de Oculoplastica / see Sociedad Iberoamericana de Oculoplastica (#19376)

♦ Sociedad Iberoamericana de Oculoplastica (SIAO) 19376

Ibero American Oculoplastic Society

Pres c/o APECM, C/ Vicente Garcia Torres 46-S, Barrio San Lucas, Coyoacan, 04030 Mexico City CDMX, Mexico. E-mail: aceriotto@hotmail.com.
URL: http://www.oculoplasticaiberoamericana.com/

History Also referred to as *Sociedad Ibero Americana de Oculoplastica.* **Events** *Congress* Lima (Peru) 2019, *Congress* Mexico City (Mexico) 2018, *Congress* Novo Horizonte (Brazil) 2016, *Congress* Lisbon (Portugal) 2014, *Congress* Buenos Aires (Argentina) 2012. [2018/XM3349/D]

♦ Sociedad Iberoamericana de Ortodoncia Lingual, Oclusión y Estética (no recent information)
♦ Sociedad Iberoamericana de Osteologia y Metabolismo Mineral (#11032)

♦ Sociedad Iberoamericana de Psicologia del Deporte (SIPD) 19377

Contact Camiño dos Vilares 94, 15705 Santiago de Compostela, La Coruña, Spain. T. +34981576666. E-mail: info@mastersipd.com.
URL: https://www.mastersipd.com/

History 31 May 2005, Santiago de Compostela (Spain). 31 May 2005, Santiago de Compostella (Spain). **Languages** Spanish. **Events** *Congress* Monterrey (Mexico) 2022, *Congress* Santiago (Chile) 2018, *Congress* San José (Costa Rica) 2016, *Congress* San Juan (Puerto Rico) 2014, *Congress* Torrelavega (Spain) 2008.
Members in 27 countries:
Angola, Argentina, Bolivia, Brazil, Cape Verde, Chile, Colombia, Costa Rica, Cuba, Dominican Rep, Ecuador, El Salvador, Guatemala, Guinea-Bissau, Honduras, Mexico, Mozambique, Nicaragua, Panama, Paraguay, Peru, Portugal, Puerto Rico, Spain, Timor-Leste, Uruguay, Venezuela. [2022/XM3438/D]

♦ Sociedad Iberoamericana de Psicologia del Ejercicio y el Deporte (no recent information)

♦ Sociedad Iberoamericana de Quitina (SIAQ) 19378

Iberoamerican Chitin Society – Sociedade Ibero-americana de Suitina

Sec address not obtained. E-mail: siaq@siaq.net.
URL: http://www.siaq.net/

Aims Promote research, development and products utilizing chitin, a glucose derivative, and related compounds. **Structure** Board of Directors. **Finance** Members' dues. **Events** *Symposium* Nuevo Vallarta (Mexico) 2015, *Symposium* Natal (Brazil) 2007. **Members** Regular; Student. Membership countries not specified. [2015/XM3444/D]

♦ Sociedad Iberoamericana de Urologia Pediatrica (#11033)
♦ Sociedad Iberoamericana de Violentologia (inactive)

♦ Sociedad Iberolatinoamericana de Aterosclerosis (SILAT) 19379

Pres address not obtained. E-mail: jesus.millan.nunezcortes@madrid.org.

History 1998, by *Sociedad Latinoamericana de Aterosclerosis (SOLAT, #19391)* and 2 national organizations. **Aims** Promote knowledge exchange and progress in the understanding of the causes, natural history, prevention treatment and rehabilitation of atherosclerotic diseases. **Events** *Annual congress / Congress* Vilamoura (Portugal) 2008, *Annual Congress* Mexico City (Mexico) 2005, *Annual Congress* Montevideo (Uruguay) 1999. **NGO Relations** Member of: *International Atherosclerosis Society (IAS, #12288).* [2014/XD8986/D]

♦ Sociedad Iberolatinoamericana de Columna (SILACO) 19380

Contact WTC Torre 3, Piso 12, Av Luis Herrera 1248, 11300 Montevideo, Uruguay. Fax +5932267829. E-mail: secretaria@silaco.org – info@silaco.org.
URL: http://www.silaco.org/

History 1991, Buenos Aires (Argentina). **Aims** Strengthen relationships between spine societies in Latin America and Spain and exchange experiences and knowledge with all those interested in the field. **Structure** Officers include: President; Vice-President; General Secretary; Past-President. **Languages** Spanish. **Finance** Sources: meeting proceeds; members' dues. **Activities** Knowledge management/information dissemination. **Events** *Congress* Viña del Mar (Chile) 2023, *Biennial Congress* Barcelona (Spain) 2019, *Biennial Congress* Rio de Janeiro (Brazil) 2017, *Conference* Singapore (Singapore) 2016, *Biennial Congress* Lima (Peru) 2015.
Members National organizations in 15 countries and territories:
Argentina, Chile, Colombia, Costa Rica, Dominican Rep, Ecuador, Guatemala, Mexico, Paraguay, Peru, Portugal, Puerto Rico, Spain, Uruguay, Venezuela. [2022.03.22/XD8657/**D**]

♦ Sociedad Iberolatinoamericana de Dermatopatologia (inactive)

♦ Sociedad Iberolatinoamericana de Neurorradiologia Diagnostica y Terapéutica (SILAN) 19381

Iberian Latin American Society of Neuroradiology
Pres Beth Israel Deaconess MC, Neuroradiology Section, 330 Brookline Ave, Boston MA 02215, USA. T. +16177542009. Fax +16177542004. E-mail: carmennaba@telefonica.net.
URL: http://www.silan.org/
History 1988, Acapulco (Mexico). 22 Jun 1989, registered in accordance with Mexican law. **Aims** Develop and support standards for the training of neuroradiologists; stimulate interest in the field of diagnostic and therapeutic neuroradiology. **Structure** Executive Committee. **Languages** Portuguese, Spanish. **Staff** 1.00 FTE, paid. **Activities** Training/education. **Events** *Congress* Montevideo (Uruguay) 2022, *Congress* Porto (Portugal) 2019, *Congress* Havana (Cuba) 2018, *Congress* San Juan (Puerto Rico) 2017, *Congress* Cartagena de Indias (Colombia) 2016.
Members Active; Associate; Senior; Honorary; Correspondent; Junior; Inactive. Members (168) in 16 countries:
Argentina, Brazil, Canada, Colombia, Ecuador, France, Guatemala, Mexico, Peru, Portugal, Puerto Rico, Spain, UK, Uruguay, USA, Venezuela.
NGO Relations Member of: *World Federation of Neuroradiological Societies (WFNRS, #21463).*
[2018.03.08/XD3337/**D**]

♦ Sociedad Iberolatinoamericana Ulceras y Heridas (SILAUHE) 19382

Contact Bocemtium, Plaça gal la Placida 1, 08006 Barcelona, Spain.
URL: http://silauhe.org/
Aims Promote and defend *care* of *wounds* and *ulcers*. **Structure** General Assembly; Board of Directors. **Events** *Congress* San Miguel de Tucuman (Argentina) 2014, *Congress* Santiago (Chile) 2013.
Members Associations in 8 countries:
Argentina, Brazil, Chile, Italy, Mexico, Portugal, Spain, Uruguay. [2019.05.23/XJ7753/**D**]

♦ Sociedad Interamericana de Administración de la Educación (inactive)
♦ Sociedad Interamericana de Cardiologia (#11448)

♦ Sociedad Interamericana de Cirugia de Columa Minimamente Invasiva (SICCMI) 19383

Sec c/o Colombia Soc of Cardiology and Cardiovascular Surgery, Avenia 9 No 126-18 of 201, Bogota, Bogota DC, Colombia. E-mail: socardio@telmex.net.co.
URL: http://www.siccmi2015.com/
History 2006. Registered in accordance with the law of Chile. **Structure** Executive Council. **Events** *Congress* Asunción (Paraguay) 2015, *Congress* Guanajuato (Mexico) 2013. **NGO Relations** *World Federation of Minimally Invasive Spine Surgery (WFMISS, #21458).* [2015/XJ9721/**D**]

♦ Sociedad Interamericana de Counseling (unconfirmed)
♦ Sociedad Interamericana de Desarrollo de Financiamiento Cooperativo (inactive)

♦ Sociedad Interamericana de Endoscopia Digestiva (SIED) 19384

Interamerican Society of Digestive Endoscopy – Sociedade Interamericana de Endoscopia Digestiva
Permanent Sec c/o Hospital de Gastroenterologia Dr Carlos Bonorino Udaondo, Av Caseros 2061, C1264AAA Buenos Aires, Argentina.
URL: http://siedonline.org/
History 6 Sep 1973, Buenos Aires (Argentina). Founded 6 Sept 1973, Buenos Aires (Argentina) during XIII Congreso Panamericano de Gastroenterologia. **Structure** Council; Standing Committees (5). **Events** *International Symposium* Gramado (Brazil) 2014, *Panamerican congress of digestive endoscopy* Santiago (Chile) 2008, *Panamerican congress on digestive diseases* Santiago (Chile) 2008, *Panamerican congress of digestive endoscopy* Cancún (Mexico) 2006, *Panamerican congress on digestive diseases / Panamerican Congress of Gastroenterology* Cancún (Mexico) 2006.
Members National organizations (14) in 14 countries:
Argentina, Bolivia, Brazil, Chile, Colombia, Cuba, Dominica, Ecuador, Mexico, Paraguay, Peru, Uruguay, USA, Venezuela.
NGO Relations Member of: *World Endoscopy Organization (WEO, #21380).* [2017/XD1070/**D**]

♦ Sociedad Interamericana de Filosofia (SIF) 19385

Société interaméricaine de philosophie – Inter-American Society of Philosophy – Sociedade Interamericana de Filosofia
Headquarters Pontificia Universidad Católica del Perú, Dept de Humanidades, Av Universitaria 1801, 46112, 32, Lima, Peru.
History 15 Aug 1954, Sao Paulo (Brazil), following a series of congresses since 1947. **Aims** Collaborate in the development of philosophical studies and investigations; contribute to the interchange of ideas, doctrines, and points of view of philosophers and students of philosophy in the Americas; facilitate personal and intellectual relations of those who devote themselves to the study of philosophy in the Americas. **Structure** General Assembly (every 3 years). Executive Committee, consisting of President, Secretary-Treasurer, and 4 standing members. **Languages** English, Portuguese, Spanish. **Finance** Members' dues. **Events** *Congress* Montevideo (Uruguay) 2024, *Congress* Bogota (Colombia) 2019, *Congress* Salvador (Brazil) 2013, *Congress* Mazatlan, SIN (Mexico) 2010, *Congress* Monterrey (Mexico) 2009.
Members Collective; Individual. Members in 9 countries:
Argentina, Brazil, Chile, Colombia, Costa Rica, Mexico, Peru, USA, Venezuela. [2019/XD1141/**D**]

♦ Sociedad Interamericana de Hipertensión (#11449)
♦ Sociedad InterAmericana de Horticultura Tropical (#11451)
♦ Sociedad Interamericana para la Libertad de Expresión Comercial (no recent information)
♦ Sociedad Interamericana de Planificación (inactive)
♦ Sociedad Interamericana de Prensa (#11444)
♦ Sociedad Interamericana de Psicologia (#11450)
♦ Sociedad Interamericana de Quimioterapia (no recent information)
♦ Sociedad Internacional de Acupuntura (inactive)
♦ Sociedad Internacional del Aguacate (#12304)
♦ Sociedad Internacional de Agua Subterranea para el Desarrollo Sostenible (#15149)
♦ Sociedad Internacional de Amistad y Buena Voluntad (#15132)
♦ Sociedad Internacional de Artistas Cristianos (#15009)
♦ Sociedad Internacional de Audiologia (#14948)
♦ Sociedad Internacional para el Avance de la Investigación en Escritura (#14905)
♦ Sociedad Internacional de Bioética (#14961)
♦ Sociedad Internacional de Biometeorologia (#14969)
♦ Sociedad Internacional de Biometria (#12354)
♦ Sociedad Internacional de Biopsia Liquida (#15234)
♦ Sociedad Internacional de Biospeologia (#14975)
♦ Sociedad Internacional de la Ciencia Horticola / see International Society for Horticultural Science (#15180)
♦ Sociedad Internacional de la Ciencia del Suelo / see International Union of Soil Sciences (#15817)
♦ Sociedad Internacional de Citricultura (#15011)
♦ Sociedad Internacional para la Conservación del Bosque Tropical (#15384)
♦ Sociedad Internacional para la Conservación de los Hongos (#15134)
♦ Sociedad Internacional contra las Corridas (inactive)
♦ Sociedad Internacional de Criminologia (#15038)
♦ Sociedad Internacional de Defensa Social / see International Society of Social Defence and Humane Criminal Policy (#15447)
♦ Sociedad Internacional de Defensa Social para una Politica Criminal Humanista (#15447)
♦ Sociedad Internacional para el Derecho de Autor (no recent information)
♦ Sociedad Internacional de Derecho Militar y Derecho de la Guerra (#15270)
♦ Sociedad Internacional para los Derechos Humanos (#15183)
♦ Sociedad Internacional de Derecho del Trabajo y de la Seguridad Social (#15226)
♦ Sociedad Internacional de Dermatologia Pediatrica (#15345)
♦ Sociedad Internacional para el Desarrollo (#19581)
♦ Sociedad Internacional para el Desarrollo Comunitario (inactive)
♦ Sociedad Internacional para el Desarrollo del Transporte Combinado y del Transporte con Temperatura Dirigida (inactive)
♦ Sociedad Internacional de Ecologia Quimica (#15004)
♦ Sociedad Internacional de la Educación por el Arte (#15074)
♦ Sociedad Internacional de Educación Musical (#15287)
♦ Sociedad Internacional para la Educación a través del Arte / see International Society for Education through Art (#15074)
♦ Sociedad Internacional de Ejecutivos de Negocios de Tecnologia (#16461)
♦ Sociedad Internacional de Endocrinologia / see International Society of Endocrinology (#15086)
♦ Sociedad Internacional para la Enseñanza Comercial (#19479)
♦ Sociedad Internacional por la Equidad en Salud (#15100)
♦ Sociedad Internacional para el Estudio de la Política de Drogas (#15469)
♦ Sociedad Internacional para el Estudio de los Virus del Papiloma (#14511)
♦ Sociedad Internacional de Etnopsicologia Normal y Patológica (inactive)
♦ Sociedad Internacional de Evaluación de Tecnologias de la Salud (inactive)
♦ Sociedad Internacional del Ferrocemento (#13587)
♦ Sociedad Internacional de Fitopatologia (#15371)
♦ Sociedad Internacional de Forestales Tropicales (#15522)
♦ Sociedad Internacional de Genética Humana (no recent information)

♦ Sociedad Internacional de Gestión y Economia Fuzzy (SIGEF) 19386

International Association for Fuzzy Set Management and Economy
Sec Dep de Gestión de Empresas, Univ Rovira i Virgili, Avinguda Universitat 1, 43204 Reus, Tarragona, Spain. T. +34977759833. Fax +34977759810. E-mail: sigef@urv.cat.
URL: http://www.sigef.net/
History 1993. **Aims** Promote research, study and treatment of economic problems, in particular pertaining to management of enterprises, in the field of uncertainty, using fuzzy logic developments and application of fuzzy set theory. **Structure** General Assembly (annual); Management Board; Scientific Council. **Languages** English, French, Spanish. **Staff** 1.00 FTE, paid. **Finance** Members' dues. **Activities** Events/meetings; knowledge management/information dissemination; awards/prizes/competitions. **Events** *Annual Congress* Naples (Italy) 2019, *Annual Congress* New York, NY (USA) 2017, *Annual Congress* Girona (Spain) 2015, *Annual Congress* Reus (Spain) 2012, *Annual Congress* Reus (Spain) 2011. **Publications** *Fuzzy Economic Review* (2 a year) in English.
Members Individuals (270) in 24 countries:
Argentina, Belarus, Brazil, Bulgaria, Canada, China, Cuba, Czechia, France, Greece, Hungary, India, Italy, Japan, Mexico, Poland, Portugal, Romania, Russia, Spain, Switzerland, Türkiye, USA, Uzbekistan.
NGO Relations Member of: *International Fuzzy Systems Association (IFSA, #13697).*
[2019.10.15/XD5766/v/**D**]

♦ Sociedad Internacional de Historia de la Medicina / see International Society for the History of Medicine (#15171)
♦ Sociedad Internacional de Ingenieros Forestales Tropicales / see International Society of Tropical Foresters (#15522)
♦ Sociedad Internacional para la Investigación de las Enfermedades de la Civilización y el Medio Ambiente (inactive)
♦ Sociedad Internacional por Investigación de las Grasas (#15115)
♦ Sociedad Internacional para la Investigación de los Grupos Sanguineos Animales / see International Society for Animal Genetics (#14921)
♦ Sociedad Internacional para la Investigación y Promoción de la Música de Orquestas de Viento (#13237)
♦ Sociedad Internacional de Malacologia Médica y Aplicada (no recent information)
♦ Sociedad Internacional de Medicina Interna (#15212)
♦ Sociedad Internacional de Medicina de Rehabilitación (inactive)
♦ Sociedad Internacional de Médicos para la Terapia de Informaciones-Biofisicas (#15253)
♦ Sociedad Internacional de Mesoterapia (#15262)
♦ Sociedad Internacional de Micologia Humana y Animal (#15181)
♦ Sociedad Internacional de Muscoesquelética Laser (no recent information)
♦ Sociedad Internacional de Muscoesquelética Ultrasound (inactive)
♦ Sociedad Internacional de Música Contemporanea (#15035)
♦ Sociedad Internacional de Musicologia / see International Musicological Society (#14201)
♦ Sociedad Internacional de Nefrologia (#15294)
♦ Sociedad Internacional de Neuro-Oftalmologia (inactive)
♦ Sociedad Internacional de Oftalmologia Geografica / see International Society of Geographical and Epidemiological Ophthalmology (#15140)
♦ Sociedad Internacional de Oftalmologia Geografica y Epidemiológica (#15140)
♦ Sociedad Internacional de Oncologia Pediatrica (#15339)
♦ Sociedad Internacional de Optometria del Desarrollo y Comportamiento (internationally oriented national body)
♦ Sociedad Internacional de Ortopedagogia (inactive)
♦ Sociedad Internacional de Platonistas (#14603)
♦ Sociedad Internacional de Profesionales de Radio y Televisión (inactive)
♦ Sociedad Internacional Protectora de Animales (inactive)
♦ Sociedad Internacional de Prótesica y Ortesica (#15390)
♦ Sociedad Internacional de Prótesis y Ortosis / see International Society for Prosthetics and Orthotics (#15390)
♦ Sociedad Internacional de Psicologia Comparada (#15024)
♦ Sociedad Internacional de Psicologos de la Escritura (#15398)
♦ Sociedad Internacional de Psicólogos para el Futbol (unconfirmed)
♦ Sociedad Internacional de Psicopatologia de la Expresión (#15400)
♦ Sociedad Internacional de Quemaduras (#14986)
♦ Sociedad Internacional de Radiologia (#15412)
♦ Sociedad Internacional de Rorschach y Métodos Proyectivos (#15430)
♦ Sociedad Internacional para la Salud y Derechos Humanos (#15156)
♦ Sociedad Internacional de Senologia (#19230)
♦ Sociedad Internacional de Técnica Hidrotermal (#19497)
♦ Sociedad Internacional de Tecnólogos Azucareros (#15495)
♦ Sociedad Internacional de Telecomunicaciones Aeronauticas / see SITA (#19299)
♦ Sociedad Internacional Tomas de Aquino (#19438)
♦ Sociedad Internacional de Topografia Minera (#15272)
♦ Sociedad Internacional de Transfusión de Sangre (#14979)
♦ Sociedad Internacional sobre la Transmisión de Embriones (#13257)

♦ Sociedad Internacional de Trompas (#13810)
♦ Sociedad Internacional de Veterinarios Expertos en Cerdos (#14584)
♦ Sociedad de Inversión y de Desarrollo Internacional / see International Solidarity for Development and Investment

♦ Sociedad Latina de Biologia y Medicina de la Reproducción (SOLAMER) 19387

Latin Society of Reproductive Medicine – Société latine de biologie et médecine de la reproduction – Sociedade Latina de Biologia e Medicina da Reprodução – Società Latina di Biologia e Medicina della Riproduzione

Gen Sec c/o Clinique Pasteur, 34 rue du Moulin à Poudre, 29200 Brest, France. T. +33298313372 – +33298313319. Fax +33298313215.

History 1992, Colombia. Registration: France. **Aims** Encourage dialogue between scientists and clinicians active in the field of human reproduction; establish dialogue with other scientist societies to give an original identity to Latin research in the field. **Structure** Administrative Council, comprising President, Secretary, Treasurer and 8 members. **Languages** French, Italian, Portuguese, Spanish. **Staff** 1.00 FTE, voluntary. **Finance** Members' dues: euro 35. **Activities** Events/meetings. **Events** *Congress* Québec, QC (Canada) 2005, *Journées internationales* Québec, QC (Canada) 2005, *Congress* Salvador (Brazil) 2003, *Journées internationales* Salvador (Brazil) 2003, *Congress* Dominican Rep 2002.
Members Individuals (more than 450) in 26 countries:
Algeria, Argentina, Belgium, Bolivia, Brazil, Canada, Chile, Colombia, Dominican Rep, Ecuador, El Salvador, France, Greece, Honduras, Italy, Japan, Mexico, Morocco, Panama, Paraguay, Peru, Portugal, Romania, Spain, USA, Venezuela.
NGO Relations Associated with: *International Federation of Fertility Societies (IFFS, #13426).*
[2016/XD7541/v/**D**]

♦ Sociedad Latina Cardiologia y Cirugia Cardiovascular Pediatrica (unconfirmed)

♦ Sociedad Latina de Hipertensión Pulmonar (SLHP) 19388

Sociedade Latin Hipertensão Pulmonary

Sec address not obtained.
Pres address not obtained.
URL: https://sociedadlatinahp.org/

History 2005, Miami, FL (USA). **Structure** Board of Directors. Committees (3): Scientific; Education; Events Organizer.
Members Full in 21 countries:
Argentina, Bolivia, Brazil, Chile, Colombia, Costa Rica, Cuba, Dominican Rep, Ecuador, El Salvador, Guatemala, Honduras, Mexico, Panama, Paraguay, Peru, Puerto Rico, Spain, Uruguay, USA, Venezuela.
NGO Relations Member of (2): *Rare Diseases International (RDI, #18621); World Patients Alliance (WPA).*
[2022/XM7438/**D**]

♦ Sociedad Latinoamericana de Acarologia (no recent information)

♦ Sociedad Latinoamericana de Alergia, Asma e Inmunologia (SLAAI) 19389

Latin American Society of Allergy, Asthma and Immunology

Communications Committee – Coordinator address not obtained. E-mail: ivancev@gmail.com.
SG address not obtained.
Main: http://www.slaai.org/

History 1964. Founded as *Latin American Society of Allergology – Société latinoaméricaine d'allergologie – Sociedad Latinoamericana de Alergologia.* Later known as *Latin American Society of Allergy and Immunology – Sociedad Latinoamericana de Alergologia e Imunologia (SLAI).* **Aims** Promote and publicize the study of allergic and immunological diseases; promote and facilitate contact in the field; promote continuing education in allergy and immunology studies; promote quality and excellence in the field among members. **Languages** Portuguese, Spanish. **Activities** Events/meetings. **Events** *Congress* Asunción (Paraguay) 2019, *Congress* Cancún (Mexico) 2017, *Congress* Buenos Aires (Argentina) 2015, *Congress* Cartagena de Indias (Colombia) 2012, *South American Congress of Allergy and Asthma* Córdoba (Argentina) 2011. **Publications** *Revista Alergia.* **NGO Relations** Member of: *World Allergy Organization – IAACI (WAO, #21077).* [2020/XD2892/**D**]

♦ Sociedad Latinoamericana de Alergologia / see Sociedad Latinoamericana de Alergia, Asma e Inmunologia (#19389)
♦ Sociedad Latinoamericana de Alergologia e Imunologia / see Sociedad Latinoamericana de Alergia, Asma e Inmunologia (#19389)
♦ Sociedad Latinoamericana de Anestesia Regional (#16384)

♦ Sociedad Latinoamericana de Artroscopia, Rodilla y Traumatologia Deportiva (SLARD) 19390

Latin American Society of Arthroscopy, Knee Surgery and Orthopaedic Sports Medicine

Secretariat Av Pres Kennedy 5488, Torre Sur Of 303, Vitacura, Santiago, Santiago Metropolitan, Chile. E-mail: secretaria@slard.org.
URL: http://www.slard.org/

History 1997, Buenos Aires (Argentina). **Aims** Represent all national and regional societies in the region. **Structure** Executive Council. **Languages** English, Portuguese, Spanish. **Staff** 4.00 FTE, paid. **Events** *Congress* Cartagena de Indias (Colombia) 2022, *Encuentro Latinoamericano de Artroscopia Reconstrucción Articular y Trauma Deportivo* 2021, *Congress* Santiago (Chile) 2020, *Congress* Curitiba (Brazil) 2017, *Congress* Buenos Aires (Argentina) 2016.
Members National societies in 15 countries:
Argentina, Bolivia, Brazil, Chile, Colombia, Costa Rica, Cuba, Ecuador, Guatemala, Mexico, Panama, Paraguay, Peru, Uruguay, Venezuela. [2021/XD8629/**D**]

♦ Sociedad Latinoamericana de Aterosclerosis (SOLAT) 19391

Latin American Society of Atherosclerosis

Pres c/o Capitulo Chileno, Av. Kennedy 5757, oficina 306 Oriente, 756 0356 Santiago, Santiago Metropolitan, Chile.
URL: http://www.ateropedia.org/

Events *Congress* Buenos Aires (Argentina) 2019, *Congress* Barranquilla (Colombia) 2015, *Congress* Asunción (Paraguay) 2011, *Biennial Congress* Acapulco (Mexico) 2005, *Congress* Acapulco (Mexico) 2005. **Members** Membership countries not specified. **NGO Relations** Member of (1): *International Atherosclerosis Society (IAS, #12288).* Instrumental in setting up (1): *Sociedad Iberolatinoamericana de Aterosclerosis (SILAT, #19379).*
[2021/XD3954/**D**]

♦ Sociedad Latinoamericana de Auditoría de Servicios de Salud (SLASS) 19392

Latin American Society of Audit in Health Services – Société latinoaméricaine d'audit des services de la santé – Sociedade Latinoamericana de Auditoria de Serviços de Saúde – Latijnsamerikaanse Vereniging voor de Controle van Gezondheidsdiensten

Pres Pte Luis Saenz Peña 352, 3o Piso "B", C1110AAF Buenos Aires, Argentina. T. +541143810543. Fax +541143810543. E-mail: slass@slass.org.
URL: http://www.slass.org/

History 1999, Argentina. Registration: Argentina. **Aims** Research, train and advise in the areas of health audit and management in public and private health services and in social security. **Structure** Executive Committee, headed by President; Offices (national, regional and local), each headed by a General Coordinator. **Languages** English, French, Italian, Portuguese, Spanish. **Staff** 15.00 FTE, paid. Several researchers, advisors and teachers part-time. **Finance** Sources: revenue from activities/projects. **Activities** Events/meetings; guidance/assistance/consulting; knowledge management/information dissemination; projects/programmes; research/documentation; training/education. **Publications** Books; booklets.
Members Full in 3 countries:
Argentina, Peru, Venezuela.
NGO Relations Universities; scientific societies; professional associations. [2023.02.24/XD9387/**D**]

♦ Sociedad Latinoamericana de Biologia Matematica (#16377)
♦ Sociedad Latino Americana de Biologica del Desarrollo (#16371)
♦ Sociedad Latino Americana de Biomateriales, Ingenieria de Tejidos y Organos Artificiales (#16370)

♦ Sociedad Latinoamericana de Biotecnologia Ambiental y Algal (SOLABIAA) 19393

Latin-American Society of Environmental and Algal Biotechnology

Pres INECOL, Carretera antigua a Coatepec 351, El Haya, 91070 Xalapa VER, Mexico.
Sec address not obtained.
URL: http://www.solabiaa.org/

History 6 Oct 2008. **Structure** Executive Council, comprising President, 3 Vice-Presidents, Treasurer, Secretary and 4 members. **Finance** Members' dues. **Events** *Congress* La Paz (Bolivia) 2022, *Congress* La Paz (Bolivia) 2020, *Congress* Florianópolis (Brazil) 2015, *Congress* Chiriqui (Panama) 2013, *Congress* Cancún (Mexico) 2010. **Publications** *Revista Latinoamericana de Biotecnologia Ambiental y Algal* (periodical).
Members Founding partners in 12 countries:
Argentina, Brazil, Colombia, Costa Rica, Ecuador, Israel, Italy, Mexico, Peru, Spain, USA, Venezuela. [2020/XM4054/**D**]

♦ Sociedad Latinoamericana de Briologia (#16260)

♦ Sociedad Latinoamericana de Buiatria 19394

Associação Latinoamericana de Boiatria – Latin American Society for Buiatrics – Société latinoaméricaine de buiatrie

Address not obtained.
URL: http://www.mgar.com.br/latinbui/

History 1971, La Plata (Argentina). **Aims** Strive to improve *veterinary* profession in the field of *cattle* and other ruminants. **Structure** Commission, consisting of Honorary President, President, 1st Vice-President, 2nd Vice-President, Secretary and 9 members. **Languages** Portuguese, Spanish. **Staff** Part-time; voluntary. **Finance** Percentage of net profits from congresses organized by different affiliated associations. **Activities** Congresses and other meetings. **Events** *Congress* Lima (Peru) 2009, *Congress* Acapulco (Mexico) 2007, *Congress* Valdivia (Chile) 2005, *Congress* Salvador (Brazil) 2003, *Congress* Paysandú (Uruguay) 2002.
Members National associations, grouping about 10,000 individual members, in 12 countries:
Argentina, Brazil, Chile, Colombia, Costa Rica, Cuba, Ecuador, Mexico, Paraguay, Peru, Uruguay, Venezuela.
NGO Relations Member of: *World Association for Buiatrics (WAB, #21122).* [2017/XD7354/**D**]

♦ Sociedad Latinoamericana de Cardiologia Intervencionista (#16375)

♦ Sociedad Latinoamericana y del Caribe de Cactaceas y Otras Suculentas (SLCCS) 19395

Pres Inst Venezolano de Investigaciones Cientificas, Casa 18, Altos de Pipe, Carretera Panamericana Km 11, Caracas DF, Venezuela. T. +582125041631 – +582125041088. Fax +582125041631 – +582125041088.
URL: http://www.ibiologia.unam.mx/slccs/www/histo.htm

History 1989. **Structure** General Assembly. Board, comprising President, Honorary President, 1st and 2nd Vice-Presidents and Secretary. **Publications** *SLCCS Boletin* – electronic. [2013/XJ1125/**D**]

♦ Sociedad Latinoamericana y Caribeña de Historia Ambiental (SOLCHA) 19396

Latin American and Caribbean Society for Environmental History

Sec address not obtained.
URL: http://solcha.org/

History 2004, Havana (Cuba). Founded during 2nd Simposio de Historia Ambiental Americana. Officially launched 2006. **Structure** Board of Directors. **Events** *Symposium* Quilmes (Argentina) 2014, *Symposium* Colombia 2012, *Symposium* La Paz (Mexico) 2010, *Symposium* Belo Horizonte (Brazil) 2008, *Symposium* Carmona (Spain) 2006. **Publications** *Historia Ambiental Latinoamérica y Caribeña (HALAC).* **NGO Relations** Member of (1): *International Consortium of Environmental History Organizations (ICEHO, #12912).*
[2020/XM4053/**D**]

♦ Sociedad Latinoamericana y del Caribe de Oncologia Médica (#16286)
♦ Sociedad Latinoamericana y del Caribe de Oncologia Médica – SLACOM Asociación Civil / see Latin-American and Caribbean Society of Medical Oncology (#16286)
♦ Sociedad Latinoamericana de la Ciencia del Suelo (#16385)

♦ Sociedad Latinoamericana de Ciencia y Tecnología (SOLACYT) 19397

Latinamerica Society for Science and Technology

Contact Sierra de Pihuamo 1594, Col Las Águilas CP, 45080 Zapopan JAL, Mexico. T. +523333345654. E-mail: contacto@solacyt.org.
URL: http://solacyt.org/

History 2002, Mexico. **Aims** Promote science and technology in Latinamerica among students. **Structure** Board. **Languages** English, Portuguese, Spanish. **Staff** 4.00 FTE, paid; 80.00 FTE, voluntary. **Finance** Registration fees. **Activities** Awards/prizes/competitions; events/meetings. **Publications** *Revista ORAMA.*
Members Organizations in 12 countries:
Argentina, Bolivia, Brazil, China, Colombia, Ecuador, Guatemala, Paraguay, Peru, Romania, Spain, Tunisia.
[2022.02.15/AA0945/**D**]

♦ Sociedad Latinoamericana de Cirugia Cardiovascular y Toracica (unconfirmed)
♦ Sociedad Latinoamericana de Citologia / see Sociedad Latinoamericana de Citopatologia (#19398)
♦ Sociedad Latino Americana de Citologia Exfoliativa / see Sociedad Latinoamericana de Citopatologia (#19398)

♦ Sociedad Latinoamericana de Citopatologia (SLAC) 19398

Latin American Cytopathology Society

Secretariat Bvar Artigas 1443, Apto 513, 11200 Montevideo, Uruguay. T. +598224093945. E-mail: sec.slac@gmail.com – info@citologiala.org.
URL: http://www.citologiala.org/

History 1961, Vienna (Austria). Formally constituted under current name and structure, Buenos Aires (Argentina), 2017. Former names and other names: *Sociedad Latino Americana de Citologia Exfoliativa* – former (1961); *Latin American Society of Cytology* – former; *Sociedad Latinoamericana de Citologia (SLAC)* – former; *Latin American Cytology Society* – alias. **Events** *Congress* Bogota (Colombia) 2021, *Congress* Bogota (Colombia) 2020, *Congress* Buenos Aires (Argentina) 2017, *Cytopathology* Montevideo (Uruguay) 1993. **Members** Membership countries not specified. [2021/XD3254/**D**]

♦ Sociedad Latinoamericana de Cuidados Intensives Pediatricos (unconfirmed)
♦ Sociedad Latinoamericana de Derecho Internacional (#16374)
♦ Sociedad Latinoamericana de Dermatologia Pediátrica (inactive)

♦ Sociedad Latinoamericana de Dermatologia Veterinaria (SLDV) . . . 19399

Sec Calle 129 No 54-42, Bogota, Bogota DC, Colombia. E-mail: rodriguezblaureano@gmail.com.
Pres FC Veterinaias UNCPBA, Campus Univ, Tandil, 7000 Buenos Aires, Argentina. E-mail: sanavis@speedy.com.ar.
URL: http://sldvweb.com/

History 17 Nov 2011, Cancún (Mexico). **Aims** Bring together licensed veterinarians dedicated to veterinary dermatology in Latin America. **Structure** Committee. **Events** *Congress* Mérida (Mexico) 2018, *Congress* Buenos Aires (Argentina) 2015, *Congress* Bogota (Colombia) 2013, *Congress* Cancún (Mexico) 2011. **NGO Relations** Provisional member of: *World Association for Veterinary Dermatology (WAVD, #21203).*
[2015/XJ9410/**D**]

♦ Sociedad Latinoamericana de Disfagia (SLAD) 19400

Sec address not obtained. E-mail: info@disfagiaslad.com.
URL: https://disfagiaslad.com/

History 2019. Founded during first Congress, following a year of discussions. Former names and other names: *Latin American Dysphagia Society* – alias. **Aims** Encourage the development of multiprofessional societies in all Latin American countries; convene them to improve the level of care, teaching and research in dysphagia. **Structure** Board of Directors. **Activities** Events/meetings; training/education. **Events** *Congreso Latinoamericano de Disfagia (CLAD)* Santiago (Chile) 2023, *Congreso Latinoamericano de Disfagia (CLAD)* Brazil 2021, *Congreso Latinoamericano de Disfagia (CLAD)* Buenos Aires (Argentina) 2019.
Members National associations and institutes in 9 countries:
Argentina, Bolivia, Brazil, Chile, Colombia, Mexico, Paraguay, Peru, Venezuela. [2023/AA3090/**D**]

♦ Sociedad latinoamericana de Economia Politica y Pensamiento Critico (unconfirmed)
♦ Sociedad Latinoamericana de Endocrinología Pediatrica (#16381)

♦ Sociedad Latinoamericana de Errores Innatos del Metabolismo y Pesquisa Neonatal (SLEIMPN) 19401

Latin American Society of Inborn Errors of Metabolism and Neonatal Screening
Editor-in-Chief address not obtained.
URL: http://www.sleimpn.org/
History 13 Aug 1996, Brazil. Officially organized, Cuba, 1997. Current statutes adopted 2019, Argentina. **Structure** General Assembly; Board of Directors. **Events** *International Congress of Inborn Errors of Metabolism* Kyoto (Japan) 2025, *Congress* Punta Cana (Dominican Rep) 2022, *Congress* Punta Cana (Dominican Rep) 2020, *Congress* Buenos Aires (Argentina) 2019, *International Congress of Inborn Errors Metabolism* Rio de Janeiro (Brazil) 2017. **Publications** *Journal of Inborn Errors of Metabolism and Screening (JIEMS)*. **Members** Membership countries not specified. **NGO Relations** Member of (1): *Society for the Study of Inborn Errors of Metabolism (SSIEM, #19648)*. [2020/XD9181/**D**]

♦ Sociedad Latinoamericana de Especialistas en Mamiferos Acuaticos (SOLAMAC) 19402

Latin American Society of Aquatic Mammal Specialists – Sociedade Latino-americana de Especialistas em Mamiferos Aquaticos
Sec address not obtained. E-mail: mjose.perez@gmail.com.
URL: http://solamac.org/
History 28 Oct 1994. **Structure** Directive Committee, comprising President, President-Elect, Secretary, Treasurer and Directors. **Languages** English, Portuguese, Spanish. **Events** *Congress* Puerto Madryn (Argentina) 2012. [2017/XM4045/**D**]

♦ Sociedad Latinoamericana de Esterilización (SOLAES) 19403

Pres address not obtained. E-mail: mariaelenayperu@yahoo.es.
Events *Congress* Santa Cruz (Bolivia) 2014, *Congress* Guayaquil (Ecuador) 2012. **NGO Relations** Member of: *World Federation for Hospital Sterilisation Sciences (WFHSS, #21438)*. [2013.10.22/XJ7387/**D**]

♦ Sociedad Latino Americana de Estimulación Cardiaca / see Latin American Heart Rhythm Society (#16339)
♦ Sociedad Latinoamericana de Estimulación Cardiaca y Electrofisiologia / see Latin American Heart Rhythm Society (#16339)

♦ Sociedad Latinoamericana de Estrategia (SLADE) 19404

Pres Manuel Pagola 3126 ap 602, 11300 Montevideo, Uruguay. T. +59827096495.
URL: http://sladeinternacional.com/
History 1987, Rio de Janeiro (Brazil). **Aims** Study, develop and spread analyses related to strategy. **Structure** Assembly; Executive Committee; Board of Directors. **Languages** Spanish. **Staff** 40.00 FTE, voluntary. **Finance** Congress proceeds. **Activities** Awards/prizes/competitions; capacity building; guidance/assistance/consulting; knowledge management/information dissemination; events/meetings; research/documentation. Active in: Argentina, Brazil, Chile, Colombia, Costa Rica, Dominican Rep, Ecuador, Mexico, Paraguay, Spain, Uruguay, USA, Venezuela. **Events** *Annual Strategy Congress* Montevideo (Uruguay) 2016, *Annual Strategy Congress* Medellin (Colombia) 2015, *Annual Strategy Congress* Cochabamba (Bolivia) 2014, *Annual Strategy Congress* Buenos Aires (Argentina) 2013, *Annual Strategy Congress* San José (Costa Rica) 2012.
Members Individuals (about 350) in 12 countries:
Argentina, Bolivia, Brazil, Chile, Costa Rica, Dominican Rep, Ecuador, Mexico, Paraguay, Uruguay, USA, Venezuela.
[2015.12.04/XD2299/**D**]

♦ Sociedad Latinoamericana de Estudiantes de Psicologia (SOLEPSI) 19405

Contact address not obtained. E-mail: solepsicologia@gmail.com.
URL: http://solepsicologia.blogspot.com/
History 2005. **Events** *Congreso Latinoamericano de Estudiantes de Psicologia – COLAEPSI* Lima (Peru) 2015, *Congreso Latinoamericano de Estudiantes de Psicologia – COLAEPSI* Quito (Ecuador) 2011, *Congreso Latinoamericano de Estudiantes de Psicologia – COLAEPSI* Lima (Peru) 2007. **Publications** *Magazine SOLEPSI*.
Members Full in 6 countries:
Argentina, Brazil, Colombia, Ecuador, Peru, Venezuela. [2022/XJ9060/**D**]

♦ Sociedad Latino Americana para Estudio del Hombre Maduro (no recent information)
♦ Sociedad Latino Americana para el Estudio de la Impotencia / see Sociedad Latinoamericana de Medicina Sexual (#19413)
♦ Sociedad Latinoamericana para el Estudio de la Impotencia y Sexualidad / see Sociedad Latinoamericana de Medicina Sexual (#19413)

♦ Sociedad Latinoamericana de Estudios sobre América Latina y el Caribe (SOLAR) 19406

Latin American Society of Studies on Latin America and the Caribbean – Société latinoaméricaine d'études sur l'Amérique latine et les Caraïbes
Contact c/o CIALC, Piso 8, Torre II de Humanidades, Ciudad Universitaria, 04510 Mexico City CDMX, Mexico. E-mail: ruizg@unam.mx.
Contact Inst de Estudios Humanisticos, Univ de Talca, Juan Ignacio Molina, 2 norte 685, Talca, Maule, Chile. T. +5671200459. Fax +5671200459.
URL: http://www.cialc.unam.mx/
History Nov 1978, Mexico City (Mexico). Founded on the initiative of 1st 'Simposio para la Coordinación y Difusión de los Estudios Latinoamericanos'. Statutes approved at 2nd Symposium, 6-7 Jun 1980, Caracas (Venezuela), although the organization did not take form until 1982. *Centro de Investigaciones sobre América y el Caribe (CIALC, #03810)* and *Programa Universitario de Difusión de Estudios Latinoamericanos (PUDEL, no recent information)*, both created by the Universidad Nacional Autónoma de México (UNAM), coordinate the activities of SOLAR and *Federación Internacional de Estudios sobre América Latina y el Caribe (FIEALC, #09338)*. **Aims** Promote, coordinate and disseminate the study of the social and *cultural* reality of Latin America and the Caribbean; establish institutional links between institutions and scholars on both Latin American and world levels in view of promoting Latin American studies. **Structure** General Assembly (every 2 years); Executive Council; Consultative Council. **Languages** English, French, Portuguese, Spanish. **Staff** Paid. **Finance** Supported by the Universidad Nacional Autónoma de México (UNAM). **Activities** Training/education; knowledge management/information dissemination; events/meetings. **Events** *Congress* Bogota (Colombia) 2018, *Congress* Manta (Ecuador) 2016, *Congress* Lima (Peru) 2014, *Congress* Cartagena de Indias (Colombia) 2012, *Congress* Heredia (Costa Rica) 2010.
Members Affiliate institutions (70) in 11 countries:
Argentina, Brazil, Colombia, Cuba, Ecuador, Mexico, Nicaragua, Panama, Peru, Uruguay, Venezuela.
Of the above-mentioned affiliates, 10 bodies listed in this Yearbook:
Casa de las Américas; Centro de Documentação de América Latina, Niterói (no recent information); Centro de Estudios de la Realidad Latinoamericana (CEREL, no recent information); Centro de Estudios Latinoamericanos Rómulo Gallegos (Fundación CELARG); Centro de Estudios Latinoamericanos, São Carlos (no recent information); Centro Interdisciplinar de Estudos das Américas, Rio de Janeiro (no recent information); European-Latin American Research Center (no recent information); Instituto del Pensamiento Latinoamericano, Buenos Aires (no recent information); International Relations Institute, Rio de Janeiro (IRI); Latin American Society for the History of Sciences and Technology (LASHST, no recent information).
NGO Relations *Association of Historians of Latin America and the Caribbean (#02632)*. [2020/XD4037/**D**]

♦ Sociedad Latinoamericana de Estudios Sociales de la Ciencia y la Tecnologia (ESOCITE) 19407

Contact c/o IIS-UNAM, Circ Mario Cueva s/n, Ciudad de Humanidades, Ciudad Universitaria, Coyoacan, 04510 Mexico City CDMX, Mexico. E-mail: esocite@gmail.com.
URL: http://www.esocite.la/
History 2006. Founded following several meetings organized since 1995. **Structure** Executive Council. Chairman; Secretary. **Events** *ESOCITE-LALICS Congress* Montevideo (Uruguay) 2020, *Congress* Buenos Aires (Argentina) 2014, *Congress* Buenos Aires (Argentina) 2010. **Publications** *Revista de Estudios Sociales de la Ciencia y la Tecnologia (REDES)*. **NGO Relations** Cooperates with (1): *Latin American Network for Economics of Learning, Innovation and Competence Building Systems (LALICS, #16352)*. [2021/XJ8553/**D**]

♦ Sociedad Latinoamericana de Fenomenologia / see Circulo Latinoamericano de Fenomenologia (#03937)
♦ Sociedad Latinoamericana de Fisiologia Vegetal (no recent information)
♦ Sociedad Latinoamericana de Fitoquimica (inactive)
♦ Sociedad Latinoamericana de Gastroenterologia, Hepatologia y Nutrición Pediatrica (#16382)
♦ Sociedad Latinoamericana de Gastroenterologia Pediatrica y Nutrición / see Latinamerican Society for Pediatric Gastroenterology, Hepatology and Nutrition (#16382)
♦ Sociedad Latinoamericana de Gastroenterologia Pediatrica, Nutrición y Hepatologia / see Latinamerican Society for Pediatric Gastroenterology, Hepatology and Nutrition (#16382)

♦ Sociedad Latinoamericana de Genetica Forense (SLAGF) 19408

Latin American Society of Forensic Genetics
Registered Office SB 010-109118, 4405 NW 73 Ave, Miami FL 33166, USA.
Pres c/o Lab CIGA, San Jerónimo 167 – 2o A, 5000 Córdoba, Argentina. E-mail: argentina@slagf.org.
URL: http://www.slagf.org/
Aims Promote training for those working in forensic genetics. **Structure** Executive Committee, comprising President, Vice-President, Secretary, Treasurer, Committee representatives and President for Life.
[2018/XM4049/**D**]

♦ Sociedad Latinoamericana de Hepatologia / see Latin American Association for the Study of the Liver (#16252)
♦ Sociedad Latinoamericana de Hipertensión Arterial (#16372)
♦ Sociedad Latinoamericana de Historia de las Ciencias y la Tecnologia (no recent information)

♦ Sociedad Latino Americana de Hombro y Codo (SLAHOC) 19409

Latin American Shoulder and Elbow Society – Sociedade Latino-Americana de Ombro e Cotovelo
Contact address not obtained. E-mail: info@slahoc.net.
URL: http://slahoc.net/
History 12 Oct 1994, Salvador (Brazil), as *Sociedade Sul Americana de Cirurgia do Ombro e Cotovelo*. Statutes modified 2008. **Aims** Promote development of knowledge of, treatment of and research into shoulder and elbow diseases. **Structure** Executive Committee. **Languages** English, Portuguese, Spanish. **Staff** 4.00 FTE, paid. **Finance** None. **Activities** Events/meetings. **Events** *Congress* Quito (Ecuador) 2021, *Congress* Brazil 2020, *Congress* La Paz (Bolivia) 2018, *Congress* Lima (Peru) 2016, *Congress* Mérida (Mexico) 2015.
Members National committees in 17 countries:
Argentina, Bolivia, Brazil, Chile, Colombia, Costa Rica, Dominican Rep, Ecuador, El Salvador, Guatemala, Mexico, Nicaragua, Panama, Paraguay, Peru, Uruguay, Venezuela.
IGO Relations None. **NGO Relations** None. [2020/XM4044/**D**]

♦ Sociedad Latinoamericana de Imagenologia Mamaria (no recent information)

♦ Sociedad Latinoamericana de Infectologia Pediatrica (SLIPE) 19410

Latin American Society of Pediatric Infectious Diseases
Contact address not obtained. E-mail: contacto@slipe.org.
URL: http://www.slipe.org/
History 1984, Santiago (Chile). Legalized 16 May 1990. **Aims** Encourage development of infectology in paediatrics through study and investigation of relevant problems in the Latin American context. **Structure** Consultative Council; Advisory Council; Executive Board; Directors; Committees (12). **Languages** Spanish. **Staff** 2.00 FTE, paid. **Finance** Sources: contributions; meeting proceeds. Self financed through congresses and contributions from pharmaceutical laboratories. Annual budget: 25,000 USD. **Activities** Events/meetings; networking/liaising; projects/programmes. **Events** *Congress* Buenos Aires (Argentina) 2021, *Congress* Cartagena de Indias (Colombia) 2019, *Congress* Cancún (Mexico) 2017, *Congress* San Juan (Puerto Rico) 2015, *Congress* Sao Paulo (Brazil) 2013. **Publications** *Revista de Enfermedades Infecciosas en Pediatria* (annual) – magazine. *Vaccines in Pediatrics*.
Members Full in 18 countries:
Argentina, Bolivia, Brazil, Chile, Colombia, Costa Rica, Cuba, Ecuador, El Salvador, Guatemala, Honduras, Mexico, Panama, Peru, Portugal, Spain, Uruguay, Venezuela.
NGO Relations Member of (1): *World Society of Pediatric Infectious Diseases (WSPID, #21810)*.
[2023.02.14/XD6912/**D**]

♦ Sociedad Latinoamericana de Interacción Materno-Fetal y Placenta (#16376)
♦ Sociedad Latinoamericana de Investigaciones Biomédicas sobre el Alcoholismo (unconfirmed)
♦ Sociedad Latinoamericana de Investigación Médica en Enfermedades Raras (no recent information)

♦ Sociedad Latinoamericana de Investigación Pediatrica (SLAIP) 19411

Société latinoaméricaine de recherches pédiatriques – Latin American Society for Pediatric Research – Sociedade Latinoamericana de Investigação Pediatrica
Address not obtained.
URL: http://www.slaip.org/
History 1962. **Aims** Promote development of subjects related to paediatric research, stimulate and provide training of new elements dedicated to it, and stimulate relations among Latin American researchers; provide for discussion and analysis of current research work so that it may be improved; make health organizations and institutions aware of improvements and developments in paediatrics research. **Structure** Ordinary meeting (annual, in the country of the President); Board of Directors, consisting of President, Elected President, Secretary and representatives. **Languages** English, Portuguese, Spanish. **Staff** Voluntary. **Finance** Financed by donations. **Activities** Preparing guidelines for use of height and weight standards in evaluating growth and nutrition in children from birth to maturity; carrying out a meta-analysis of menarche in the region from (already prepared) country surveys. Individual groups also carry out their own research. **Events** *Annual Meeting* Cochabamba (Bolivia) 2015, *Annual Meeting* Paracas (Peru) 2014, *Annual Meeting* Buenos Aires (Argentina) 2012, *Annual meeting* Itapecerica da Serra (Brazil) 2010, *Annual meeting* Asunción (Paraguay) 2009. **Publications** *El Heraldo Doble Ciego*.
Members Individuals in 13 countries:
Argentina, Bolivia, Brazil, Chile, Colombia, Ecuador, Guatemala, Italy, Mexico, Paraguay, Peru, Uruguay, USA.
NGO Relations Formal contacts with: *Latin American Society for Pediatric Endocrinology (#16381)*.
[2017/XD2891/v/**D**]

♦ Sociedad Latinoamericana de Investigadores de Papa / see Asociación Latinoamericana de la Papa (#02250)
♦ Sociedad Latinoamericana de Maiz (inactive)
♦ Sociedad Latinoamericana de Mastologia / see Latin American Federation of Mastology (#16324)

♦ Sociedad Latinoamericana de Medicina Interna (SOLAMI) 19412

Latin American Society of Internal Medicine
SG c/o CMIM, Col Napoles, Insurgentes Sur No 569 piso 6, 08310 Mexico City CDMX, Mexico. E-mail: nor_mx@yahoo.com.
URL: https://solami2021.com/
History Nov 1997, Acapulco (Mexico). **Structure** General Assembly; Board. **Languages** Spanish. **Staff** Voluntary. **Events** *Congress* La Paz (Bolivia) 2021, *Congress* Dominican Rep 2015, *Congress* Punta Cana (Dominican Rep) 2015, *Congress* Asunción (Paraguay) 2013, *Congress* Guatemala (Guatemala) 2011.
[2020/XD8545/**D**]

♦ Sociedad Latinoamericana de Medicina Sexual (SLAMS) 19413

Sociedade Latinoamericana de Medicina Sexual

SG address not obtained. E-mail: info@slamsnet.orgg.
Pres address not obtained.
URL: http://www.slamsnet.org/

History Sep 1990. Latin American Chapter of *International Society for Sexual Medicine (ISSM, #15441)* since Sep 1997. Former names and other names: *Sociedad Latino Americana para el Estudio de la Impotencia (SLAI)* – former (Sep 1990); *Sociedade Latinoamericana para o Estudo da Impotência* – former (Sep 1990); *Sociedad Latinoamericana para el Estudio de la Impotencia y Sexualidad (SLAIS)* – former (Dec 2005); *Sociedade Latinoamericana para o Estudo da Impotência e Sexualidade* – former (Dec 2005). **Aims** Encourage research on sexual medicine in Latin America. **Structure** Executive Committee. **Languages** English, Portuguese, Spanish. **Events** *Congress* 2021, *Congress* Sao Paulo (Brazil) 2019, *Congress* Lima (Peru) 2017, *Symposium* Lima (Peru) 2016, *Congress* Montevideo (Uruguay) 2015. **Publications** *e-SLAMS* – electronic newsletter. Participates in publication of the ISSM Journal of Sexual Medicine and ISSM Newsbulletin.
Members must also be member of ISSM. Individuals (227) in 17 countries:
Argentina, Bolivia, Brazil, Chile, Colombia, Costa Rica, Cuba, Dominican Rep, Ecuador, Guatemala, Honduras, Mexico, Panama, Paraguay, Peru, Uruguay, Venezuela. [2021/XD6914/v/**D**]

♦ Sociedad Latinoamericana de Medicina Veterinaria de Emergencia y Cuidados Intensivos (#16392)

♦ Sociedad Latinoamericana de Medicina del Viajero (SLAMVI) 19414

Latin American Society for Travel Medicine

Secretariat Beruti 4437, piso 7 depto E, C1425BDA, Buenos Aires, Argentina.
URL: http://www.slamvi.org/

Structure Executive Board, including President, Vice-President, Secretary and Treasurer. **Events** *Congress* Miami, FL (USA) 2010, *Congress* Buenos Aires (Argentina) 2008. **NGO Relations** *International Society of Travel Medicine (ISTM, #15519)*; *International Society for Infectious Diseases (ISID, #15199).* [2017/XM4032/**D**]

♦ Sociedad Latinoamericana de Micotoxicologia (unconfirmed)

♦ Sociedad Latinoamericana de Nefrologia e Hipertensión (SLANH) . . 19415

Latin American Society of Nephrology and Hypertension – Sociedade Latinoamericana de Nefrologia e Hipertensión (SLANH)

Main Office c/o Congrex, Calle Jorge Gil, INNOVA 109, Ciudad del Saber, Panama, Panamá, Panama PANAMá, Panama. E-mail: infoslanh@congrex.com.pa – info@slanh.net.
URL: http://www.slanh.net/

History 1970, Córdoba (Argentina). Additional founding activity, Mexico 1972. **Aims** Unite nephrology societies and individuals in the field; contribute to information dissemination on nephrology and hypertension through congresses, meetings and publications; stimulate formation of study groups in cooperation with nephritic centres; promote and guide training of Latin American nephrologists and paramedical personnel in activities related to nephrology and hypertension; develop continuing education in the field. **Structure** Board of Directors. Committees. **Languages** Portuguese, Spanish. **Staff** 3.00 FTE, paid. **Finance** Members' dues. Other sources: donations; subsidies; legacies; proceeds from congresses and events. **Activities** Events/meetings; training/education. **Events** *Congreso Latinoamericano de Nefrologia e Hipertensión* 2021, *Congress* Lima (Peru) 2019, *Latin American Congress on Severe Renal Injuries* Punta Cana (Dominican Rep) 2016, *Congress* Santiago (Chile) 2014, *Congress* Cartagena de Indias (Colombia) 2012. **Publications** *SLANH* (12 a year) – electronic newsletter; *Nefrologia Latinoamericana* (3 a year) – newsletter.
Members Full in 21 countries:
Argentina, Bolivia, Brazil, Canada, Chile, Colombia, Costa Rica, Cuba, Dominican Rep, Ecuador, El Salvador, Guatemala, Honduras, Mexico, Nicaragua, Panama, Paraguay, Peru, Uruguay, USA, Venezuela.
NGO Relations Member of (1): *International Society of Nephrology (ISN, #15294).* [2021/XD4508/**D**]

♦ Sociedad Latinoamericana de Neumologia Pediatrica (no recent information)
♦ Sociedad Latinoamericana de Neurocirugia Funcional y Esterotaxia (#16386)

♦ Sociedad Latinoamericana de Neurogastroenterologia (SLNG) 19416

Technical Secretariat Permanyer, Temistocles 315 – Colonia Polanco, Delegación Miguel Hidalgo, 11560 Mexico City CDMX, Mexico. E-mail: frank.garcia@permanyer.com – permanyer@permanyer.com.
Pres Clinica Hosp San Fernando, Consultorios San Fernando, Policlinica Norte 2-14, Panama, Panamá, Panama PANAMá, Panama. T. +50766182728. Fax +5072615377.
URL: http://neurogastrolatamreviews.com/

History 13 Nov 2006, Cancún (Mexico). **Aims** Disseminate information on neurogastroenterology in Latin America; stimulate research in the field; encourage cooperation; develop training programs. **Structure** Board. **Events** *Meeting* Bangkok (Thailand) 2024, *Meeting* Panama 2012. **Publications** *NeuroGastro LATAM Reviews* (4 a year) – official journal.
Members Societies in 5 countries:
Argentina, Brazil, Chile, Mexico, Venezuela.
NGO Relations Associate member of: *Federation of Neurogastroenterology and Motility (FNM, #09696).* [2018/XM4050/**D**]

♦ Sociedad Latinoamericana de Neuropsicologia (#16378)

♦ Sociedad Latinoamericana de Nutrición (SLAN) 19417

Société latinoaméricaine de nutrition – Latin American Society of Nutrition – Sociedade Latinoamericana de Nutrição

Sec c/o ALAN, Apartado 62.778, Chacao, Caracas 1060 DF, Venezuela. E-mail: info@alanrevista.org – info@slaninternacional.org.
URL: http://www.slaninternacional.org/

History 1964, Bogota (Colombia). **Aims** Stimulate advance of nutrition sciences and allied fields in Latin America; facilitate sharing of experience among researchers. **Structure** Presidency rotates among members and names local commissions or committees. **Languages** English, Portuguese, Spanish. **Finance** Members' dues. Other supporting sources (industry, government). **Activities** Programme for technical strengthening (with support from RORIAN) addresses food and nutrition security, including food protection, food economy, nutritional deficiency, health promotion, prevention of chronic diseases related to diet and lifestyle, nutrition education, nutrition security at clinical level, clinical nutrition and nutritional epidemiology. Organizes congress at the seat of the Presidency. **Events** *Congreso Latinoamericano de Nutrición* Cuenca (Ecuador) 2023, *Congress* Asunción (Paraguay) 2021, *Congress* Guadalajara (Mexico) 2018, *Congress* Punta Cana (Dominican Rep) 2015, *Congress* Havana (Cuba) 2012. **Publications** *Archivos Latinoamericanos de Nutrición* (4 a year) – journal; *NutritionElectronic Journal* – website. Letter to members (4 a year).
Members Professionals involved solving nutrition problems (about 800) in 20 countries:
Argentina, Bolivia, Brazil, Chile, Colombia, Costa Rica, Cuba, Dominican Rep, Ecuador, El Salvador, Guatemala, Mexico, Nicaragua, Panama, Paraguay, Peru, Spain, Uruguay, USA, Venezuela.
National chapters in 6 countries:
Argentina, Chile, Cuba, Guatemala, Mexico, Venezuela.
NGO Relations Affiliate of: *International Union of Nutritional Sciences (IUNS, #15796).* [2022/XD0534/**D**]

♦ Sociedad Latinoamericana de Oftalmologia Veterinaria / see Colegio Latinoamericano de Oftalmólogos Veterinarios (#04094)
♦ Sociedad Latinoamericana de Oncologia Pediatrica (#16383)

♦ Sociedad Latinoamericana de Ortopedia y Traumatologia (SLAOT) . 19418

Latin American Society for Orthopaedics and Traumatology – Société latinoaméricaine d'orthopédie et de traumatologie

SG address not obtained. T. +552199821645. E-mail: secretario@slaot.org.
URL: http://www.slaot.org/

History 1948. **Events** *Congress* Punta Cana (Dominican Rep) 2016, *Congress* Mexico City (Mexico) 2015, *Regional congress* Willemstad (Curaçao) 2010, *World congress on external fixation* Cairo (Egypt) 2007, *SLAOT triennial congress* Mexico City (Mexico) 2007. [2014/XD2832/**D**]

♦ Sociedad Latinoamericana de Ortopedia y Traumatologia Infantil (SLAOTI) 19419

Contact Soc Brasileira de Ortopedia Pedriatrica, Al Lorena 427 – 14o Andar, Sao Paulo SP, CEP 01424-000 SP, Brazil. Fax +551121377268.
URL: http://www.slaoti.org/

History 1999, Orlando FL (USA). **Structure** Scientific Committee. Officers: President; Vice-President; Secretary. **Events** *Congress* Brazil 2010, *Congress* Sao Paulo (Brazil) 2010, *Congress* Buenos Aires (Argentina) 2002, *Congress* Colombia 2000. **NGO Relations** Member of: *International Federation of Paediatric Orthopaedic Societies (IFPOS, #13497).* [2010/XD8665/**D**]

♦ Sociedad Latinoamericana de Paraplejia (SLAP) 19420

Latin American Society of Paraplegia

Contact DOT IOT HCFMUSP, Rua Dr Ovidio Pires de Campos 333, Cerqueira Cesar, Sao Paulo SP, 05403-010, Brazil.

History 1994, Sao Paulo (Brazil). **Activities** Organizes meetings, workshops. **Events** *Meeting* Cartagena de Indias (Colombia) 2010, *Meeting* Punta del Este (Uruguay) 2008, *Meeting* Sao Paulo (Brazil) 2007, *Meeting* Belo Horizonte (Brazil) 2006, *Meeting* Miami, FL (USA) 2003. **NGO Relations** Affiliated with: *International Spinal Cord Society (ISCoS, #15581).* [2011/XD7379/**D**]

♦ Sociedad Latinoamericana de Patologia (#16380)
♦ Sociedad Latinoamericana de Patologia Clinica Veterinaria (unconfirmed)

♦ Sociedad Latinoamericana de Patologia Pediatrica (SLAPPE) 19421

Société latinoaméricaine de pathologie pédiatrique – Latin American Society for Pediatric Pathology

SG HNRG Pathology Div, Gallo 1330, 1425 Buenos Aires, Argentina.
URL: http://www.slappe.org/

History May 1985, Santiago (Chile). **Aims** Facilitate scientific exchange between paediatric pathologists in Latin America. **Structure** Scientific Committee of 7 members. Officers: President; Secretary-General. Council of Past-Presidents. Honorary Directory Committee. **Languages** Portuguese, Spanish. **Staff** 6-7 voluntary. **Finance** Members' dues. **Activities** Exchange of information through biennial conference. **Events** *Conference* Santa Cruz (Bolivia) 2015, *Conference* Oaxaca (Mexico) 2013, *Conference* Maceió (Brazil) 2011, *Conference* Guatemala 2009, *Conference* Punta del Este (Uruguay) 2007. **Publications** *Pediatric Pathology.*
Members Individuals in 17 countries:
Argentina, Bolivia, Brazil, Chile, Colombia, Costa Rica, Cuba, Ecuador, Mexico, Panama, Paraguay, Peru, Spain, UK, Uruguay, USA, Venezuela.
IGO Relations Formal contacts with: *Pan American Health Organization (PAHO, #18108).* **NGO Relations** Constituent society of: *International Paediatric Pathology Association (IPPA, #14498).* [2014/XD1328/**D**]

♦ Sociedad Latinoamericana de Percepción Remota y Sistemas Especiales / see Sociedad Especialistas Latinoamericana en Percepción Remota (#19358)

♦ Sociedad Latinoamericana de Primatologia (SLAPrim) 19422

Pres address not obtained. T. +558381214366. E-mail: contacto@slaprim.org.
URL: http://www.slaprim.org/

History Founded Nov 1986, Aguas de Lindoia (Brazil). Ceased to function, early 1990s. Revived Aug 2012, Cancún (Mexico). Previously also known under the acronym *SLAP.* Current statutes adopted August 2013. **Aims** Promote and disseminate the study, management and conservation of Neotropical Primates in Latin American countries; promote sustainable scientific development in each of the regions where they are present. **Structure** General Assembly; Board of Directors; Executive Committee. **Finance** Members' dues. **Publications** *El Aullador / O Uivador* – bulletin. [2016/XD7268/**D**]

♦ Sociedad Latinoamericana de Profesores de Terapia Fisica (inactive)

♦ Sociedad Latinoamericana de Psoriasis (SOLAPSO) 19423

Contact Avda Callao 157 piso 9 Dto "C", CABA, Buenos Aires, Argentina. T. +541143722388.
Facebook: https://www.facebook.com/solapso/

History 13 Nov 2008. **Structure** Council of Delegates. Executive Commission. **Activities** Meeting activities. **Events** *Congress* Cancún (Mexico) 2014, *Congress* Buenos Aires (Argentina) 2012. **Publications** *SOLAPSO Newsletter.*
Members Full in 18 countries:
Argentina, Bolivia, Brazil, Chile, Colombia, Costa Rica, Cuba, Dominican Rep, Ecuador, El Salvador, Guatemala, Honduras, Mexico, Nicaragua, Paraguay, Peru, Uruguay, Venezuela.
NGO Relations Cooperates with (1): *International Psoriasis Council (IPC, #14661).* [2019/XM4048/**D**]

♦ Sociedad Latinoamericana de Radiologia Pediatrica (SLARP) 19424

Latin American Society for Pediatric Radiology

Contact address not obtained. E-mail: secretaria@slarp.net.
URL: http://www.slarp.net/

History 1977, Rio de Janeiro (Brazil). Founded following the 14th International Radiology Congress. **Events** *Congress* Rio de Janeiro (Brazil) 2014, *Congress* Santiago (Chile) 2010, *Congress* Rio de Janeiro (Brazil) 2009, *Congress* Guadalajara (Mexico) 2008, *Congress* Viña del Mar (Chile) 2007. **NGO Relations** Founding member of: *World Federation of Pediatric Imaging (WFPI, #21472).* [2021/XJ4345/**D**]

♦ Sociedad Latinoamericana de Rinologia / see Sociedad Latinoamericana de Rinologia y Cirugia Plastica Facial (#19425)
♦ Sociedad Latinoamericana de Rinologia e Cirugia Facial / see Sociedad Latinoamericana de Rinologia y Cirugia Plastica Facial (#19425)

♦ Sociedad Latinoamericana de Rinologia y Cirugia Plastica Facial (SLARCF) 19425

Contact Carrera 23 No 124-87 Torre 2, Of 202, Bogota, Bogota DC, Colombia.

History 1982, Santiago (Chile), as *Sociedad Latinoamericana de Rinologia (SLAR).* Subsequently changed title to *Sociedad Latinoamericana de Rinologia e Cirugia Facial (SLARCF),* Sep 1993. **Structure** Board. **Activities** Events/meetings. **Events** *Congress* Lima (Peru) 2021, *Congress* Quito (Ecuador) 2019, *Congress* Rio de Janeiro (Brazil) 2017, *Congress* Bogota (Colombia) 2013, *Congress* Rio de Janeiro (Brazil) 1984. [2019/XJ6451/**D**]

♦ Sociedad Latinoamericana del Ritmo Cardiaco (#16339)
♦ Sociedad Latinoamericana del Sueño / see Federation of Latin American Sleep Societies (#09685)

♦ Sociedad Latinoamericana de Tecnologia del Caucho (SLTC) 19426

Latin American Society for Rubber Technology

Main Office Av Paseo Colón 275, Piso 3-B, C1063ACC Buenos Aires, Argentina. E-mail: gerencia@sltcaucho.org.
URL: http://www.sltcaucho.org/

History 1996, Medellin (Colombia). Founded during 3rd *Jornadas Latinoamericanas y Encuentros Sectoriales de la Industria del Caucho.* **Events** *Days / Meeting* Guatemala (Guatemala) 2015, *Meeting* Buenos Aires (Argentina) 2002, *Jornadas iberoamericanas* Guadalajara (Mexico) 2000, *Jornadas latinoamericanas / Meeting* Guadalajara (Mexico) 2000. **Members** Affiliates (4,000) in 31 countries. Membership countries not specified. [2021/XD7275/**D**]

♦ Sociedad Latinoamericana de Tiroides (#16390)
♦ Sociedad Latinoamericana de Trasplantes (inactive)

♦ Sociedad Latinoamericana de Tuberculosis y Otras Micobacteriosis (SLAMTB) 19427

Latin American Society of Tuberculosis and other mycobacteriosis

Contact Calle Montevideo 665, CP 1019 Buenos Aires, Argentina. E-mail: pedrefurg@gmail.com.
URL: http://www.slamtb.org/

History 24 Oct 2006. **Aims** Produce and disseminate knowledge about tuberculosis and other mycobacteriosis by promoting collaboration between researchers and institutions. **Structure** Steering Committee. Executive Council. **Languages** English. **Staff** All voluntary. **Finance** Members' dues. **Events** *Meeting* Canela (Brazil) 2014. [2016/XJ8402/**D**]

♦ **Sociedad Latino Americana de Tumores Musculo Equeléticos (SLATME)** 19428
Pres Rua Barata Ribeiro 490, 3o andar cj 33, Bela Vista, Sao Paulo SP, 01308-000, Brazil.
URL: http://www.slatme.org/
Events *Congress* Salvador (Brazil) 2014, *Congress* Antigua (Guatemala) 2012. [2013/XJ7370/**D**]

- ♦ Sociedad Latinoamerican de Percepción Remota y Sistemas de Información Espacial / see Sociedad Especialistas Latinoamericana en Percepción Remota (#19358)
- ♦ Sociedad de Legislación Comparada (#19500)
- ♦ Sociedad de Lingüistica del Caribe (#19530)
- ♦ Sociedad de Maria (religious order)
- ♦ Sociedad de Medicina Nuclear – Europa (inactive)
- ♦ Sociedad Mediterranea y Africana de Ultrasonografia (#16640)

♦ **Sociedad Mesoamericana para la Biologia y la Conservación (SMBC)** 19429
Mesoamerican Society for Biology and Conservation (MSBC)
Sec address not obtained. E-mail: melissa.rg784@gmail.com.
Pres address not obtained. E-mail: bonilla@uaem.mx.
URL: http://socmeso.org/
History 14 Jan 1996, Lago de Yojoa (Honduras). **Aims** Promote biological and cultural conservation through information exchange and research. **Structure** General Assembly; Board of Directors. **Events** *Congress* Granada (Nicaragua) 2018, *Congress* San José (Costa Rica) 2017, *Congress* Belize City (Belize) 2016, *Congress* Villahermosa (Mexico) 2015, *Entrelacing cultures and biodiversity – assets of Mesoamerica* Copan (Honduras) 2014. **Publications** *Mesoamericana* in English, Spanish – review.
Members Individuals and institutions in 9 countries:
Belize, Costa Rica, El Salvador, Guatemala, Honduras, Mexico, Nicaragua, Panama, USA.
NGO Relations Member of: *International Union for Conservation of Nature and Natural Resources (IUCN, #15766).* [2017/XD7952/**D**]

- ♦ Sociedad Mundial de Ekistica (#21801)
- ♦ Sociedad Mundial Protectora de Animales (#21092)
- ♦ Sociedad de Música Militar internacional (#14162)
- ♦ Sociedad Naturalista Andino Patagónica (internationally oriented national body)

♦ **Sociedad de Oftalmologia Pediatrica Latinoamericana (SOPLA)** ... 19430
Latin American Pediatric Ophthalmology Society – Sociedade de Oftalmopediatria Latino Americana
Pres Carrera 8A No 97-20 Ap 402, Bogota, Bogota DC, Colombia. T. +5713760285. E-mail: amfernandezd@gmail.com.
History Founded 1999. **Aims** Serve as a forum for researchers in the field of paediatric ophthalmology in Latin America.
Members Individuals in 14 countries:
Argentina, Bolivia, Brazil, Chile, Colombia, Cuba, Dominican Rep, Ecuador, Guatemala, Mexico, Paraguay, Peru, Uruguay, Venezuela.
NGO Relations Member of: *International Pediatric Ophthalmology and Strabismus Council (IPOSC, #14544); Pan-American Association of Ophthalmology (PAAO, #18081); World Society of Paediatric Ophthalmology and Strabismus (WSPOS, #21807).* [2015/XJ2747/**D**]

♦ **Sociedad de Ornitologia Neotropical (SON)** 19431
Neotropical Ornithological Society
Pres address not obtained. E-mail: info.neotropicalornithology@gmail.com.
Treas address not obtained. E-mail: nostreasurer@gmail.com.
URL: http://www.neotropicalornithology.org/
History 4 Dec 1987. **Aims** Promote scientific study of birds and their habitats in the neotropical region. **Structure** Executive Committee, including President, President-Elect, Past-President, Secretary, Treasurer and Editor. **Languages** English, Portuguese, Spanish. **Finance** Members' dues. **Events** *Ornithological Congress of the Americas* Beni (Bolivia) 2023, *Neotropical Ornithological Congress* San José (Costa Rica) 2019, *Neotropical Ornithological Congress* Manaus (Brazil) 2015, *Neotropical Ornithological Congress* Cusco (Peru) 2011, *Neotropical Ornithological Congress* Maturin (Venezuela) 2007. **Publications** *Ornitologia Neotropical* – journal. [2020/XJ6663/**D**]

- ♦ Sociedad Panamericana de Audiologia (no recent information)
- ♦ Sociedad Panamericana de Baja Visión (#18119)
- ♦ Sociedad Panamericana de Dialisis y Trasplantes (inactive)

♦ **Sociedad Panamericana de Enfermedades Inflamatorias Oculares (SPEIO)** 19432
Pan-American Society of Inflammatory Ocular Diseases
Pres Consultorios Oftalmológicos, Montevideo 1410, 1018 Buenos Aires, Argentina. T. +541148155356. Fax +541148144043.
History Original title: *Pan-American Society of Uveitis – Sociedad Panamericana de Uveitis.* **Activities** Events/meetings. **NGO Relations** Member of: *Pan-American Association of Ophthalmology (PAAO, #18081).* [2015/XD6812/**D**]

♦ **Sociedad Panamericana de Flebologia y Linfologia** 19433
Panamerican Society of Phlebology and Lymphology
SG Perú 1018, Acasusso, Buenos Aires, Argentina. T. +54114792-3243.
URL: http://www.flebologiapanam.com.ar/
History Founded 1977, Buenos Aires (Argentina), during the VI World Congress of Phlebology. **Aims** Serve as a forum of information on scientific progress in phlebology and lymphology. **Structure** Executive Committee. **Languages** English, Portuguese, Spanish. **Staff** Voluntary. **Activities** Training/education. **Events** *Biennial Congress* San Miguel de Tucuman (Argentina) 2014, *Biennial Congress* Cusco (Peru) 2012, *Biennial Congress* Lima (Peru) 2012, *Biennial Congress* Guayaquil (Ecuador) 2010, *Biennial Congress* Cancún (Mexico) 2004. **Publications** *Revista Panamericana de Flebologia y Linfologia* (4 a year).
Members National Organizations and individuals in 16 countries:
Argentina, Bolivia, Brazil, Canada, Chile, Colombia, Cuba, Dominican Rep, Ecuador, Mexico, Paraguay, Peru, Spain, Uruguay, USA, Venezuela.
Regional organization (1):
European Society of Phlebectomy (#08701).
NGO Relations Links with a large number of organizations active in the field (not specified). [2015.01.19/XD4102/**D**]

- ♦ Sociedad Panamericana de Glaucoma (#18107)
- ♦ Sociedad Panamericana de Lentes de Contacto y Refracción (inactive)
- ♦ Sociedad Panamericana de Oculoplastica (no recent information)

♦ **Sociedad Panamericana de Oncologia Oftalmológica** 19434
Panamerican Society of Opthalmic Oncology
Pres Arenales 1662, Piso 2-A, 1061 Buenos Aires, Argentina.
Activities Events/meetings. [2015/XM8110/**D**]

- ♦ Sociedad Panamericana de Patologia Ocular – Lorenz E Zimmerman (#18131)
- ♦ Sociedad Panamericana de Retina y Vitreo (#18126)

♦ **Sociedad Panamericana de Retinopatia del Prematuro (SPROP)** ... 19435
Pres 4 Norte 319 Of 101, V REGION 2520191 Viña del Mar, Valparaíso, Chile. E-mail: avazkart@gmail.com – sociedadpanamericanarop@gmail.com.
History Founded 8 Aug 2013. Also referred to as *SP-ROP.* **Aims** Improve the quality of life of premature infants and their families in the Pan American population. **Events** *Symposium* Punta del Este (Uruguay) 2014. **NGO Relations** Member of: *Pan-American Association of Ophthalmology (PAAO, #18081).* [2015/XJ8538/**D**]

♦ **Sociedad Panamericana de Trauma (SPT)** 19436
Panamerican Trauma Society – Sociedade Panamericana de Trauma
Contact Virginia Commonwealth Univ, PO Box 980454, Richmond VA 23298-0454, USA.
URL: http://www.panamtrauma.org/
History 1986, Bogota (Colombia). Officially launched 1987. Headquarters relocated from Pittsburgh PA (USA) to Richmond VA (USA), 2010. **Aims** Encourage exchange of knowledge and information between and among physicians, nurses, prehospital providers and other health care personnel involved in the care of injured patients in North, Central and South America. **Structure** Board of Directors. **Languages** English, Portuguese, Spanish. **Staff** 2.00 FTE, paid. **Activities** Advocacy/lobbying/activism; awards/prizes/competitions; awareness raising; capacity building; events/meetings; knowledge management/information dissemination; networking/liaising; publishing activities; research and development; research/documentation; standards/guidelines; training/education. South America, Central America and North America. **Events** *Trauma Symposium* 2021, *Congress* Mexico City (Mexico) 2020, *Congress* La Serena (Chile) 2019, *Congress* Cartagena de Indias (Colombia) 2018, *Congress* Mexico City (Mexico) 2017. **Publications** *Panamerican Journal of Trauma, Critical Care and Emergency Surgery* (3 a year).
Members Full in 23 countries:
Argentina, Bolivia, Brazil, Canada, Chile, Colombia, Costa Rica, Cuba, Dominican Rep, Ecuador, El Salvador, Germany, Guatemala, Honduras, Panama, Paraguay, Peru, Puerto Rico, Spain, UK, Uruguay, USA, Venezuela.
NGO Relations Cooperates with (3): *Eastern Association for the Surgery of Trauma (EAST);* The American Association for the Surgery of Trauma; *World Coalition for Trauma Care (WCTC, #21282).* [2022.06.01/XD4690/**D**]

- ♦ Sociedad Panamericana de Trauma Ocular / see Asociación Panamericana de Trauma Ocular (#02293)
- ♦ Sociedad Panamericana de Uveitis / see Sociedad Panamericana de Enfermedades Inflamatorias Oculares (#19432)
- ♦ Sociedad Papel Moneda Latinoamericana (#16359)
- ♦ Sociedad Planetaria (see: #20322)
- ♦ Sociedad para la Promoción de la Literatura de Africa, Asia y América Latina (internationally oriented national body)
- ♦ Sociedad Religiosa de los Amigos (#18834)
- ♦ Sociedad de San Vicente de Paul / see International Confederation of the Society of St Vincent-de-Paul (#12870)
- ♦ Sociedad Sri Aurobindo (internationally oriented national body)
- ♦ Sociedad Sudamericana de Cardiologia (#19707)
- ♦ Sociedad Sudamericana de Cirugia de la Mano (inactive)
- ♦ Sociedad Sudamericana de Psicologia del Deporte (no recent information)
- ♦ Sociedad Teosófica (#20141)
- ♦ Sociedad Teosófica en Europa (#20142)
- ♦ Sociedad de Toxicologia y Quimica Ambiental en Latinoamerica (see: #19551)

♦ **Sociedad de Trasplante de América Latina y el Caribe (STALYC)** ... 19437
Contact c/o Hosp Garrahan, Combate de los Pozos 1881, C 1245 AAM Buenos Aires, Argentina.
URL: http://www.stalyc.net/
History upon the merger of *Sociedad Latinoamericana de Trasplantes (SLAT, inactive)* and *Panamerican Society for Dialysis and Transplantation (PSDT, inactive).* Registered in accordance with Puerto Rican law. **Structure** Board of Directors. **Languages** Spanish. **Activities** Events/meetings. **Events** *Biennial Congress* Mérida (Mexico) 2019, *Biennial Congress* Montevideo (Uruguay) 2017, *Biennial Congress* Cancún (Mexico) 2015, *Biennial Congress* Buenos Aires (Argentina) 2013, *Biennial congress / Congress* Cartagena de Indias (Colombia) 2011.
Members Societies in 25 countries and territories:
Argentina, Barbados, Bolivia, Brazil, Chile, Colombia, Costa Rica, Cuba, Dominican Rep, Ecuador, El Salvador, Guatemala, Haiti, Honduras, Jamaica, Mexico, Nicaragua, Panama, Paraguay, Peru, Puerto Rico, Trinidad-Tobago, Uruguay, Venezuela, Virgin Is USA.
NGO Relations *European Society for Organ Transplantation (ESOT, #08676); The Transplantation Society (TTS, #20224).* [2019.07.22/XJ8123/**D**]

- ♦ Società dell'Apostolato Cattolico (religious order)
- ♦ Società di Biospeologia / see International Society of Biospeleology (#14975)
- ♦ Società di Chirurgia del Mediterraneo Latino (#20042)
- ♦ Società di Cristo per gli Emigrati della Polonia (religious order)
- ♦ Società di Cristo Signore (religious order)
- ♦ Società di Cronobiologia (#15010)
- ♦ Società Divine Vocazioni (religious order)
- ♦ Società del Divin Salvatore (religious order)
- ♦ Società Europea per l'Ambiente e lo Sviluppo (inactive)
- ♦ Società Europea di Anestesiologia Ostetrica (no recent information)
- ♦ Società Europea di Cultura (#08576)
- ♦ Società Europea di Educazione Terapeutica (#19459)
- ♦ Società Europea Ergonomia Dentale / see European Society of Dental Ergonomics (#08577)
- ♦ Società Europea per la Geografia / see Association of European Geographical Societies (#02512)
- ♦ Società Europea per l'Igiene Mentale e Sordità (#08649)
- ♦ Società Europea dell'Ipertensione (#08627)
- ♦ Società Europea di Malerbologia (#09089)
- ♦ Società Europea di Psicologia della Scrittura (#08616)
- ♦ Società Europea per la Semantica Generale (no recent information)
- ♦ Società Europea di Tossicologia (inactive)
- ♦ Società Farmaceutica del Mediterraneo Latino (#19508)
- ♦ Società delle Figlie del Cuore di Maria (religious order)
- ♦ Società delle Figlie di Santo Francesco de Sales (religious order)
- ♦ Società di Gesù, Maria e Giuseppe (religious order)
- ♦ Società Internationale de Defense Sociale pour une Politique Criminelle Humaniste (#15447)
- ♦ Società Internazionale degli Artisti Cristiani (#15009)
- ♦ Società Internazionale di Biospeologia (#14975)
- ♦ Società Internazionale del Cacao e Cioccolato in Medicina (#15008)
- ♦ Società Internazionale di Criochirurgia (#15041)
- ♦ Società Internazionale per il Diritto di Autore (no recent information)
- ♦ Società Internazionale Hegel-Marx per il Pensiero Dialettico (no recent information)
- ♦ Società Internazionale di Musica Militare (#14162)
- ♦ Società Internazionale di Musicologia / see International Musicological Society (#14201)
- ♦ Società Internazionale di Ortopedia Cranio-Mandibolare (inactive)
- ♦ Società Internazionale per la Pedagogia dell' Ingegneria (#15089)
- ♦ Società Internazionale di Psicologia della Scrittura (#15398)
- ♦ Società Internazionale di Studi Neroniani (#19484)
- ♦ Società Internazionale per lo Sviluppo de la Cultura Commerciale (#19479)
- ♦ Società Internazionale per lo Sviluppo del Trasporto Combinato e del Trasporto a Temperatura Controllata (inactive)
- ♦ Società Internazionale per le Tecniche d'Imagerie Mentale / see Société internationale des techniques d'imagerie mentale onirique (#19498)
- ♦ Società Internazionale per le Tecniche d'Imagerie Mentale Onirique (#19498)

♦ **Società Internazionale Tommaso d'Aquino (SITA)** 19438
Société internationale Thomas d'Aquin – Sociedad Internacional Tomas de Aquino
Acting Gen Dir c/o Pontificia Univ S Tommaso d'Aquino, Largo Angelicum 1, 00184 Rome RM, Italy. T. +393515411157. E-mail: segreteriasitaroma@gmail.com.
URL: http://www.sitaroma.com/

History 1974. **Aims** Study and bring up to date the work of *Thomas Aquinas*; spread his doctrine; examine contemporary fundamental problems, especially those concerning *Christian* thought, in the light of his teaching. **Structure** Assembly; Council. **Languages** English, Italian, Spanish. **Staff** 2.00 FTE, voluntary. **Finance** Sources: donations; members' dues. **Activities** Events/meetings; training/education. **Events** *Country Risk Conference* Paris (France) 2015, *L'humanisme chrétien au troisième millénaire* Rome (Italy) 2003, *Ethique et société contemporaine* Rome (Italy) 1991, *International Congress* Rome (Italy) 1991. **Publications** *Società Internazionale Tommaso d'Aquino – Notiziario.*
Members Individuals and local sections in 23 countries and territories:
Argentina, Australia, Belgium, Chile, Colombia, Czechia, Ecuador, Egypt, Holy See, Hungary, Ireland, Italy, Mexico, Peru, Poland, Puerto Rico, Senegal, Spain, Switzerland, Taiwan, UK, Uruguay, USA. [2022.03.08/XE0873/**E**]

- ♦ Società Internazionale di Traumatologia dello Sciismo e della Medicina degli Sport Invernali (#15445)
- ♦ Società Internazionale Veterinaria de Produzione Animale (inactive)
- ♦ Società Italiana per le Imprese Miste all'Estero (internationally oriented national body)
- ♦ Società Italiana per l'Organizzazione Internazionale (internationally oriented national body)

♦ Società Italo-Latino Americana di Etnomedicina (SILAE) 19439

Italo-Latin American Asian and African Ethnomedicine Society
Gen Sec Dipto Farmacia, Univ degli Studi di Salerno, Via Giovanni Paolo II, 84084 Fisciano SA, Italy. T. +3989969766. Fax +3989969602. E-mail: segreteria@silae.it.
URL: http://www.silae.it/
History 1992, Salerno (Italy). In English previously referred to as *Italo-Latin American Ethnomedicine Society*. **Aims** Promote research, development and use of *medicinal* and *food plants*. **Structure** International Organizer Committee, composed of professors from Italian and Latin American universities. **Languages** English, Italian, Portuguese, Spanish. **Staff** 3.00 FTE, voluntary. **Finance** Research programmes. **Activities** Projects/ programmes; events/meetings; networking/liaising; awards/prizes/competitions; knowledge management/ information dissemination. **Events** *Congress* Bavaro (Dominican Rep) 2015, *Congress* Punta Cana (Dominican Rep) 2015, *Congress* Marsala (Italy) 2014, *Congress* Puntarenas (Costa Rica) 2013, *Congress* Paestum (Italy) 2012. **Publications** *Pharmacologyonline (PhOL)* – journal. *SILAE Special Issues.*
Members Full (4,000) in 100 countries:
Afghanistan, Albania, Algeria, Argentina, Australia, Austria, Bangladesh, Belgium, Belize, Bolivia, Bosnia-Herzegovina, Brazil, Bulgaria, Burkina Faso, Cameroon, Canada, Chile, China, Colombia, Costa Rica, Croatia, Cuba, Czechia, Dominican Rep, Ecuador, Egypt, El Salvador, Ethiopia, Finland, France, Germany, Greece, Guatemala, Guyana, Haiti, Honduras, Hungary, India, Indonesia, Iran Islamic Rep, Iraq, Ireland, Israel, Italy, Japan, Jordan, Kazakhstan, Kenya, Korea Rep, Kuwait, Latvia, Lebanon, Libya, Madagascar, Malaysia, Mauritania, Mexico, Morocco, Nepal, Netherlands, New Zealand, Nicaragua, Niger, Nigeria, North Macedonia, Norway, Oman, Pakistan, Panama, Paraguay, Peru, Poland, Portugal, Puerto Rico, Romania, Russia, Saudi Arabia, Serbia, Slovakia, South Africa, South Sudan, Spain, Suriname, Switzerland, Syrian AR, Tajikistan, Tanzania UR, Thailand, Tunisia, Türkiye, Uganda, UK, Ukraine, United Arab Emirates, Uruguay, USA, Uzbekistan, Venezuela, Yemen, Zambia.
NGO Relations Universities; organizations. [2015.07.02/XJ0867/**D**]

- ♦ Società Latina di Biologia e Medicina della Riproduzione (#19387)
- ♦ Società di Maria (religious order)
- ♦ Società di Maria (religious order)
- ♦ Società Mediterranea e Africana di Ultrasonografia (#16640)
- ♦ Società Mediterranea di Educazione Comparata (inactive)
- ♦ Società Mediterranea di Medicina dello Stile di Vita (internationally oriented national body)
- ♦ Società Mediterranea di Oftalmologia (#16679)
- ♦ Società Mediterranea di Ortottica (internationally oriented national body)
- ♦ Società Mediterranea di Talassologia e Talassoterapia (no recent information)
- ♦ Società dei Missionari d'Africa (religious order)
- ♦ Società Missionaria di San Giuseppe di Mill Hill (religious order)
- ♦ Società Missionaria di San Paolo (religious order)
- ♦ Società delle Missioni Africane (religious order)
- ♦ Società delle Missioni Estere di Betlemme in Svizzera (religious order)
- ♦ Società per le Missioni Estere di Parigi (religious order)
- ♦ Società per le Missioni Estere della Provincia di Québec (religious order)
- ♦ Società per le Missioni Estere di Scarboro (religious order)
- ♦ Società per le Missioni Estere degli Stati Uniti d'America (religious order)
- ♦ Società d'Optometria d'Europa (#08675)
- ♦ Società Organizzatrice di Conferenze Internazionali in Esperanto (internationally oriented national body)
- ♦ Società dei Sacerdoti Missionari di San Paolo Apostolo (religious order)
- ♦ Società dei Sacerdoti di San Giuseppe Benedetto Cottolengo (religious order)
- ♦ Società del Sacro Cuore di Gesù (religious order)
- ♦ Societas Ad Studia De Hominis Condicione Colenda (#13238)
- ♦ Società Salesiana di San Giovanni Bosco (religious order)
- ♦ Societas Anatomica Africae Australis (internationally oriented national body)
- ♦ Societas Ancillarum Sanctissimi Sacramenti (religious order)
- ♦ Società di San Colombano per le Missioni Estere (religious order)
- ♦ Società di San Edmondo (religious order)
- ♦ Società di San Francesco Saverio per le Missioni Estere (religious order)
- ♦ Società di San Giuseppe del Sacro Cuore (religious order)
- ♦ Società San Paolo (religious order)
- ♦ Società di San Patrizio per le Missioni Estere (religious order)
- ♦ Società del Santo Bambino Gesù (religious order)
- ♦ Societas Apostolatus Catholici (religious order)
- ♦ Societas Arctica Scandinavica (inactive)
- ♦ Societas Caucasologica Europaea (no recent information)
- ♦ Societas Christi pro Emigrantibus Polonis (religious order)
- ♦ Societas Divinarum Vocationum (religious order)
- ♦ Societas Divini Salvatoris (religious order)
- ♦ Societas Ergophthalmologica Internationalis (no recent information)
- ♦ **Societas Ethica** European Society for Research in Ethics (#08726)
- ♦ Societas Europaea Anatomorum Veterinariorum (#06268)
- ♦ Societas Europaea Herpetologica (#07481)
- ♦ Societas Europaea Ichthyologorum / see European Ichthyological Society (#07513)

♦ Societas Europaea Lepidopterologica (SEL) 19440

SG Naturalis Biodiversity Center, PO Box 9517, 2300 RA Leiden, Netherlands. E-mail: jadranka.rota@ gmail.com.
URL: http://www.soceurlep.eu/
History 1976. **Aims** Further closer cooperation among *lepidopterists* of Europe, Western Asia and North Africa. **Structure** Council. **Languages** English, French, German. **Staff** 3.00 FTE, voluntary. **Finance** Subscriptions. **Activities** Events/meetings. **Events** *European Congress of Lepidopterology* Laulasmaa (Estonia) 2022, *European Congress of Lepidopterology* Campobasso (Italy) 2019, *European Congress of Lepidopterology* Pogdora (Croatia) 2017, *European Congress of Lepidopterology* Radebeul (Germany) 2015, *European Congress of Lepidopterology* Blagoevgrad (Bulgaria) 2013. **Publications** *News-Nouvelles-Nachrichten* – newsletter; *Nota Lepidopterologia* – journal.
Members Corporate (16) in 8 countries:
Denmark, Finland, France, Germany, Netherlands, Spain, Switzerland, UK.
Individuals in 41 countries and territories:
Argentina, Australia, Austria, Belgium, Brazil, Bulgaria, Canada, Chile, China, Croatia, Czechia, Denmark, Estonia, Finland, France, Germany, Greece, Hungary, Iran Islamic Rep, Ireland, Italy, Japan, Korea Rep, Latvia, Lithuania, Netherlands, Norway, Poland, Portugal, Romania, Russia, Slovakia, Slovenia, Spain, Sweden, Switzerland, Taiwan, Türkiye, UK, Ukraine, USA.
IGO Relations *UNESCO (#20322).* [2015/XD2198/**D**]

♦ Societas Europaea Mammalogica (SEM) 19441

Contact c/o PTES, 15 Cloisters House, 8 Battersea Park Road, London, SW8 4BG, UK.
URL: http://www.european-mammals.org/
History Founded 1988, Paris (France). **Aims** Promote links between European mammalogists; encourage the study and conservation of European mammals; publish an atlas of European mammals. **Activities** Research/ documentation; financial and/or material support. **Events** *European Congress of Mammology* Warsaw (Poland) 2019, *European Congress of Mammology* Stockholm (Sweden) 2015, *European congress of mammalogy* Paris (France) 2011, *European congress of mammalogy* Siena (Italy) 2007. [2017.11.06/XM3213/**D**]

- ♦ Societas Europaea Physiologiae Clinicae Respiratoriae (inactive)
- ♦ Societas Europaea Pneumologica (inactive)
- ♦ Societas Europaea Studiosorum Philologiae Classicae (no recent information)
- ♦ Societas Europensis Ophthalmologiae Traditionalis (no recent information)

♦ Societas Heraldica Scandinavica 19442

Société héraldique du nord – Heraldisk Selskab – Heraldiska Sällskapet – Heraldisk Selskap
Contact Örja Byväg 11 A, SE-261 51 Landskrona, Sweden. E-mail: sekretariat@heraldik.org.
URL: https://heraldik.org/
History 27 May 1959. **Aims** Promote knowledge of heraldry in the nordic countries. **Structure** Board; Editorial Committee. **Languages** Danish, Norwegian, Swedish. **Staff** None; Board members and members of Editorial Committee voluntary. **Finance** Sources: grants; members' dues. **Activities** Events/meetings. Active in: Denmark, Finland, Iceland, Norway, Sweden. **Events** *Nordic Heraldry Conference* Røskilde (Denmark) 2023, *Nordic Heraldry Conference* Turku (Finland) 2022, *Nordic Heraldry Conference* Turku (Finland) 2021, *Nordic Heraldry Conference* Oslo (Norway) 2019, *Nordic Heraldry Conference* Lund (Sweden) 2017. **Publications** *Heraldisk Tidsskrift* (2 a year) – abstracts in English. *Heraldiske Studier*, *Skandinavisk Vapenrulla.*
Members Individuals in 20 countries:
Australia, Austria, Belgium, Canada, Denmark, Finland, France, Germany, Iceland, Italy, Japan, Monaco, Netherlands, New Zealand, Norway, Spain, Sweden, Switzerland, UK, USA. [2022.10.18/XD9176/v/**D**]

- ♦ Societas Internationalis pro Aerosolibus in Medicina (#14907)
- ♦ Societas Internationalis Dermatologiae Tropicae / see International Society of Dermatology (#15048)

♦ Societas Internationalis de Diagnostica Ultrasonica in Ophthalmologia (SIDUO) 19443

International Society on Ultrasonic Diagnostics in Ophthalmology (ISUDO)
Pres 13 bd de Montchalamet, Royat, 63130 Clermont-Ferrand, France.
Sec address not obtained.
URL: http://www.siduo.org/
History 1964, Berlin (Germany). Former names and other names: *International Society for Ophthalmic Ultrasound (ISOU)* – former. **Aims** Promote scientific work in the physical principles, technical developments, modes of examination and measurement, and diagnostic and therapeutic capabilities of *ultrasound* in ophthalmology; develop and spread clinical applications of ophthalmic ultrasound; facilitate communication and cooperation on an international level between those engaged in research and/or clinical applications of ophthalmic ultrasound. **Structure** General Assembly; Executive Board. **Languages** English. **Staff** None. **Finance** Sources: donations; gifts, legacies; grants; members' dues. **Events** *Biennial Congress* Paris (France) 2022, *Biennial Congress* Paris (France) 2020, *Biennial Congress* Puerto Varas (Chile) 2018, *Biennial Congress* Naples (Italy) 2016, *Biennial Congress* Berlin (Germany) 2014. **Publications** *SIDUO Newsletter* (annual). Congress proceedings.
Members Regular, Honorary, Associate/Physician, Associate/Physicist, Associate/Technician, Affiliate. Members in 51 countries:
Argentina, Australia, Austria, Belgium, Brazil, Bulgaria, Canada, Chile, China, Colombia, Costa Rica, Croatia, Czechia, Denmark, Ecuador, Egypt, Finland, France, Germany, Greece, Guatemala, Hungary, India, Indonesia, Israel, Italy, Japan, Jordan, Lebanon, Malta, Mexico, Montenegro, Netherlands, Paraguay, Peru, Philippines, Poland, Portugal, Romania, Russia, Serbia, Slovakia, Slovenia, Spain, Sweden, Switzerland, Türkiye, UK, United Arab Emirates, USA, Venezuela. [2023.02.15/XC6420/v/**C**]

♦ Societas Internationalis Entomofaunistica Europae Centralis (SIEEC) 19444

Pres Postfach 202731, 01193 Dresden, Germany.
History Set up during Symposium Internationale Entomofaunisticum Europae Centralis, 1964, Opava (Czechoslovakia). Former names and other names: *Permanent International Committee of SIEEC* – alias. **Structure** Executive Committee. **Activities** Awards Prize during Symposium. **Events** *Symposium internationale entomofaunisticum Europae centralis* Bratislava (Slovakia) 2015, *Symposium internationale entomofaunisticum Europae centralis* Bolzano (Italy) 2013, *Symposium internationale entomofaunisticum Europae centralis* Varazdin (Croatia) 2011, *Symposium* Ceské Budejovice (Czech Rep) 2009, *Symposium* Cluj-Napoca (Romania) 2007.
Members in 14 countries:
Austria, Belarus, Croatia, Czechia, Germany, Hungary, Netherlands, Poland, Romania, Russia, Slovakia, Slovenia, Switzerland, Ukraine. [2014/XJ1873/**F**]

- ♦ Societas Internationalis Historiae Medicinae (#15171)
- ♦ Societas Internationalis Lenti Conformatae Indagandae (#15033)
- ♦ Societas Internationalis Limnologiae (#15232)
- ♦ Societas Internationalis Limnologiae Theoreticae et Applicatae / see International Society of Limnology (#15232)
- ♦ Societas Internationalis Medicinae Generalis (inactive)
- ♦ Societas Internationalis Mycologiae Humanae et Animalis (#15181)

♦ Societas Internationalis Odonatologica (SIO) 19445

International Odonatological Foundation
Exec Dir Osmylus Scientific Publishers, Odonatologica Editorial Office, Postfach 1212, 85283 Wolnzach, Germany. E-mail: odonatologica@osmylus.com.
URL: http://www.odonatologica.com/
Structure Includes *International Odonata Research Institute (IORI)*. **Languages** English, German. **Staff** 0.50 FTE, voluntary. **Finance** Subscriptions; sales. **Publications** *Notulae odonatologicae* (2 a year); *Odonatologica* (2 a year).
Members Individuals in 4 countries:
Canada, Mexico, Puerto Rico, USA.
NGO Relations *International Odonata Research Institute (IORI)*; national organizations. [2022/XD8231/f/**D**]

- ♦ Societas Internationalis Studiis Neolatinis Provehendis (#12048)
- ♦ Societas Internationalis Universitaria Chirurgorum Colonis et Recti (#15530)

♦ Societas Iranologica Europaea (SIE) 19446

Pres Univ of Bologna, Via Zamboni 33, 40126 Bologna BO, Italy.
Sec Inst of Iranian Studies, Apostelgasse 23, 1030 Vienna, Austria.
URL: http://www.societasiranologicaeu.org/
Aims Enforce, develop and support Ancient, Middle and Modern Iranian Studies in all subject areas – philology, linguistics, literature, history and history of religions, arts, archaeology, philosophy, ethnology, geography, human sciences, jurisprudence. **Structure** Board, comprising President, Vice-President, Secretary, Treasurer and 5 members. **Activities** Awards/prizes/competitions. **Events** *Quadrennial Conference* Berlin (Germany) 2019, *Quadrennial Conference* St Petersburg (Russia) 2015, *International Colloquium* Paris (France) 2013, *Quadrennial Conference / European Conference* Krakow (Poland) 2011, *European Conference* Bamberg (Germany) 2009.
Members Full in 20 countries:
Belgium, Canada, Czechia, Denmark, France, Georgia, Germany, Hungary, Iran Islamic Rep, Israel, Italy, Japan, Netherlands, Poland, Russia, Spain, Sweden, Switzerland, UK, USA.
NGO Relations *International Union for Oriental and Asian Studies (IUOAS, inactive).* [2016/XE1788/**E**]

♦ Societas Iuris Publici Europaei (SIPE) 19447

SG Eberhard-Karls-Uni Tübingen, Juristische Fak, Geschister-Scholl-Platz, 72071 Tübingen, Germany. T. +4970712972560 – +4970712978101. Fax +497071295847.
Pres Andreou Metaxa 2, 106 81 Athens, Greece. T. +302103826083. Fax +302103805413. E-mail: juliostr@ law.uoa.gr.
URL: http://www.sipe-online.eu/

History Apr 2003, Frankfurt-Main (Germany). Statutes adopted 5 Apr 2003. Registered in accordance with German law. **Aims** Discuss and clarify questions of public *law*, especially in Europe, including their impact on the legal system as a whole. **Structure** General Meeting. Executive Committee, including President and Secretary General. **Languages** English, French, German. **Finance** Members' dues. **Events** *Congress* Berlin (Germany) 2015, *Congress / Conference* Athens (Greece) 2014, *Conference* Krakow (Poland) 2013, *Congress / Conference* Lisbon (Portugal) 2011, *International Congress* Lisbon (Portugal) 2011. **Publications** *Societas Iuris Publici Europaei (SIPE)* – series.
Members Full in 21 countries:
Austria, Belgium, Czechia, Estonia, Finland, France, Germany, Greece, Hungary, Italy, Luxembourg, Norway, Poland, Portugal, Romania, Slovakia, Spain, Sweden, Switzerland, Türkiye, UK. [2015.03.11/XJ5514/**D**]

♦ Societas Jesu (religious order)

♦ Societas Linguistica Europaea (SLE) 19448

Société européenne de linguistique (SLE) – Linguistics Society of Europe (SLE)
Sec Andreas Schelfhoutstraat 31 H, 1058 HR Amsterdam, Netherlands. E-mail: treasurersle@ gmail.com.
URL: http://www.societaslinguistica.eu/

History 27 Feb 1966, Kiel (Germany). Registration: Chamber of Commerce, No/ID: 34276576, Start date: 2018, Netherlands. **Aims** Advance, in European countries and elsewhere, the scientific study of language in all its aspects. **Structure** Annual Meeting; Executive Committee; Scientific Committee; Nominating Committee. **Languages** English. **Finance** Sources: members' dues. **Activities** Events/meetings; publishing activities; research and development. **Events** *Annual Meeting* Athens (Greece) 2023, *Annual Meeting* Bucharest (Romania) 2022, *Annual Meeting* 2021, *Annual meeting* 2020, *Annual Meeting* Leipzig (Germany) 2019. **Publications** *Folia Linguistica*; *Folia Linguistica Historica*.
Members Regular; Associate. Members in 76 countries and territories:
Albania, Algeria, Argentina, Australia, Austria, Azerbaijan, Belarus, Belgium, Benin, Bosnia-Herzegovina, Brazil, Bulgaria, Canada, Chile, China, Costa Rica, Croatia, Czechia, Denmark, Ecuador, Egypt, Estonia, Finland, France, Georgia, Germany, Ghana, Greece, Hong Kong, Hungary, Iceland, Iran Islamic Rep, Ireland, Israel, Italy, Japan, Jordan, Kazakhstan, Kenya, Korea Rep, Kuwait, Latvia, Lithuania, Luxembourg, Malaysia, Malta, Mexico, Montenegro, Nepal, Netherlands, New Zealand, Nigeria, North Macedonia, Norway, Pakistan, Peru, Philippines, Poland, Portugal, Puerto Rico, Romania, Russia, Serbia, Slovakia, Slovenia, South Africa, Spain, Sweden, Switzerland, Taiwan, Thailand, Tunisia, Türkiye, UK, Ukraine, USA.
NGO Relations Member of (1): *Comité international permanent des linguistes (CIPL, #04182).* [2022.05.10/XD3222/**D**]

♦ Societas Liturgica – International Society for Liturgical Study and Renewal 19449

Société liturgique internationale
Co-Sec 11 Princess St, Toronto ON M5C 4A8, Canada. T. +14162036671.
URL: http://www.societas-liturgica.org/

History Founded 29 Jun 1967, Driebergen (Netherlands), when statutes were adopted, on the initiative of Wiebe Vos, a pastor of the Dutch Reformed Church, after he called a conference of 25 liturgists from Europe and North America, 1965, Neuchâtel (Switzerland), when it was resolved to found the Society. **Aims** Encourage research in the field of *worship* and allied subjects, with the pastoral implications of such research; facilitate exchange of results in this research; seek to deepen the mutual understanding of the various liturgical traditions and ways to make clear the relevance of liturgy in the contemporary world. **Structure** General Meeting (every 2 years, at Congress); Council; Specific Committees. **Languages** English, French, German. **Finance** Sources: members' dues. **Events** *Biennial Congress* Durham (UK) 2019, *Biennial Congress* Leuven (Belgium) 2017, *Biennial Congress* Québec, QC (Canada) 2015, *Biennial Congress* Würzburg (Germany) 2013, *Biennial congress* Reims (France) 2011. **Publications** *Studia Liturgica* (2 a year); *Societas Liturgica Newsletter* (periodical) in English.
Members Open to those: teaching or doing research in liturgical related studies; who are actively engaged in official liturgical commissions; who are making significant contributions to the liturgical life of the churches; such other persons as the Society may wish to invite; and to those in church responsible for promotion or revision of liturgy. Individuals (about 400) in 51 countries and territories:
Argentina, Australia, Austria, Belgium, Brazil, Canada, Congo DR, Costa Rica, Cuba, Cyprus, Czechia, Denmark, Estonia, Fiji, Finland, France, Germany, Hungary, Iceland, India, Iraq, Ireland, Italy, Jamaica, Japan, Kenya, Korea Rep, Latvia, Malta, Netherlands, New Zealand, Nigeria, Norway, Philippines, Poland, Qatar, Romania, Russia, Serbia, Sierra Leone, South Africa, Spain, Sweden, Switzerland, Taiwan, Tanzania UR, Tonga, UK, Uruguay, USA, Venezuela. [2018.09.05/XC3223/**C**]

♦ Societas Mariae (religious order)
♦ Societas Mariae (religious order)
♦ Societas Mariae pro Educatione Surdorum et Mutorum (religious order)
♦ Societas Mariae Montfortana (religious order)
♦ Societas de Maryknoll pro Missionibus Exteris (religious order)
♦ Societas Missionariorum Africae (religious order)
♦ Societas Missionariorum Domesticorum Americae (religious order)
♦ Societas Missionariorum a Sancti Joseph (religious order)
♦ Societas Missionariorum Sancti Joseph de Mill Hill (religious order)
♦ Societas pro Missionibus Exteris Provinciae Quebecensis (religious order)
♦ Societas Missionum ad Afros (religious order)
♦ Societas Missionum Exterarum de Bethlehem in Helvetia (religious order)
♦ Societas Mundi Medica / see World Medical Association (#21646)
♦ Societas Oecumenica – Europäische Gesellschaft für Oekumenische Forschung (#19450)

♦ Societas Oecumenica – European Society for Ecumenical Research 19450

Societas Oecumenica – Société européenne de recherche oecuménique – Societas Oecumenica – Europäische Gesellschaft für Oekumenische Forschung
Sec Evangelische Theologische Fac – Leuven, Sint-Jansbergsesteenweg 95-97, 3001 Leuven, Belgium.

History 1978, Driebergen (Netherlands), on the occasion of 3rd *Conférence des instituts oecuméniques d'Europe*. **Aims** Coordinate research in ecumenical *theology* to further communication between institutes and individuals engaged in ecumenical theology. **Structure** General Assembly (every 2 years at Consultation); Standing Committee. **Languages** English, French, German. **Staff** Voluntary. **Finance** Members' dues. Other sources: consultation fee; grants. **Activities** Events/meetings. **Events** *Biennial Scientific Consultation* Helsinki (Finland) 2016, *Biennial Scientific Consultation* Budapest (Hungary) 2014, *Biennial Scientific Consultation* Belfast (UK) 2012, *Biennial Scientific Consultation* Belgrade (Serbia) 2010, *Biennial Scientific Consultation* Leuven (Belgium) 2008. **Publications** *Signalia* – newsletter. Consultation proceedings.
Members Institutes (about 50); Individuals (140) concerned with research and teaching ecumenical theology, in 33 countries and territories:
Austria, Belarus, Belgium, Botswana, Croatia, Czechia, Denmark, Estonia, Finland, France, Germany, Greece, Holy See, Hungary, Iceland, India, Ireland, Israel, Italy, Malta, Netherlands, Norway, Poland, Portugal, Romania, Russia, Serbia, Spain, Sweden, Switzerland, UK, Ukraine, USA. [2017.10.16/XD0104/**D**]

♦ Societas Oecumenica – Société européenne de recherche oecuménique (#19450)
♦ Societas Ophthalmologica Europaea (#08674)
♦ Societas Oto-Rhino-Laryngologica (inactive)
♦ Societas Oto-Rhino-Laryngologica Latina (inactive)
♦ Societas Parisiensis Missionum ad Exteras Gentes (religious order)
♦ Societas Pathologorum Europae (#08689)
♦ Societas Patrum Sancti Edmundi (religious order)

♦ Societas Phlebologica Scandinavica (SVS) 19451

Scandinavian Venous Forum
Chairman address not obtained.
URL: http://www.venforum.org/

History Sep 1963, Snekkersten (Denmark). **Structure** General Assembly; Board. **Languages** Danish, Finnish, Icelandic, Norwegian, Swedish. **Staff** Voluntary. **Activities** Research and development; events/ meetings. **Events** *General Assembly / Congress* Stockholm (Sweden) 2014, *Scandinavian Venous Forum* Lübeck (Germany) 2012, *Congress* Copenhagen (Denmark) 2011, *Scandinavian Venous Forum* Copenhagen (Denmark) 2010, *Scandinavian venous forum* Trondheim (Norway) 2008.
Members Surgeons, clinical physiologists, dermatologists and radiologists in 5 countries:
Denmark, Finland, Iceland, Norway, Sweden.
NGO Relations Member of: *International Union of Phlebology (#15797).* [2019/XD8580/v/**D**]

♦ Societas Physiologiae Plantarum Scandinavica / see Societas Physiologiae Plantarum Scandinavica (#19452)

♦ Societas Physiologiae Plantarum Scandinavica (SPPS) 19452

Scandinavian Plant Physiology Society
Sec c/o Plant Physiology, Umeå Univ, SE-907 36 Umeå, Sweden.
SG Dept of Biology, Fac of Natural Sciences, NTNU, Realfagbygget DU1-119, HØgskoleringen 5, 7491 Trondheim, Norway. T. +4773596096.
URL: http://www.spps.se/

History 27 Oct 1947, Copenhagen (Denmark). Former names and other names: *Societas Physiologiae Plantarum Scandinavica (SPPS)* – former; *Nordisk Förening för Fysiologisk Botanik* – alias. Registration: Sweden. **Aims** Promote all aspects of experimental plant biology, from molecular cell biology and biochemistry to ecophysiology; serve as a forum for contact and communication among plant biologists. **Structure** Ordinary General Meeting (every 2 years, at Congress); Council; Committees (2); Secretarial Office, headed by Secretary-General and Office Secretary. **Languages** English, Swedish. **Staff** 0.60 FTE, paid. **Finance** Members' dues. Income from journal. **Activities** Financial and/or material support; research/documentation; publishing activities. **Events** *Congress* Longyearbyen (Norway) 2022, *Congress* Longyearbyen (Norway) 2021, *Biennial PhD Student Conference* Turku (Finland) 2020, *Biennial Congress* Umeå (Sweden) 2019, *Biennial PhD Student Conference* Copenhagen (Denmark) 2018. **Publications** *Physiologia Plantarum* (12 a year) – journal. **Members** Individuals (about 300); Organizations (about 10) in 30 countries. Membership countries not specified. **NGO Relations** Member of: *Global Plant Council (#10550)*. Affiliated with: *Federation of European Societies of Plant Biology (FESPB, #09548)*. Memorandum of Understanding with: *European Plant Science Organization (EPSO, #08211).* [2022/XD3198/v/**D**]

♦ Societas Presbyterorum Sacratissimi Cordis Jesu de Bétharram (religious order)
♦ Societas Presbyterorum Sancti Iosephi Benedicti Cottolengo (religious order)
♦ Societas Presbyterorum a Sancto Sulpitio (religious order)
♦ Societas Sacerdotum Missionariorum a Sancto Paulo Apostolo (religious order)
♦ Societas Sancti Columbani pro Missionibus ad Exteros (religious order)
♦ Societas Sancti Francisci Salesii (religious order)
♦ Societas Sancti Francisci Xaverii pro Exteris Missionibus (religious order)
♦ Societas Sancti Patritii pro Missionibus ad Exteros (religious order)
♦ Societas Sancti Pauli (religious order)
♦ Societas a Sancto Paulo Apostolo (religious order)
♦ Societas Scarborensis pro Missionibus ad Exteras Gentes (religious order)
♦ Societas Sodalium Sancti Joseph a Sacro Corde (religious order)
♦ Societas pro Studio Rhythmi Biologici / see International Society for Chronobiology (#15010)
♦ Società di Suore di Maria Riparatrice (religious order)
♦ Societas Verbi Divini (religious order)
♦ Societät der Bergbaukunde (#19597)
♦ Societatea Europeana de Urgente si Terapie Intensiva Veterinara (#09056)
♦ Società del Verbo Divino (religious order)
♦ Société des académies européennes (internationally oriented national body)
♦ Société pour l'administration du droit de reproduction mécanique des auteurs, compositeurs et éditeurs (internationally oriented national body)
♦ Société africaine anti-SIDA (#19518)
♦ Société Africaine de Chirurgie Pédiatrique (unconfirmed)
♦ Société africaine de culture / see Communauté africaine de culture (#04373)
♦ Société africaine de droit international et comparé (no recent information)
♦ Société africaine d'éducation et de formation pour le développement (internationally oriented national body)

♦ Société Africaine Francophone d'Ophtalmologie (SAFO) 19453

SG 08 BP 674, Abidjan 08, Côte d'Ivoire. T. +22520218411. Fax +22520226101. E-mail: info@safo-info.org.
URL: https://safo-info.org/

History 1992, Abidjan (Côte d'Ivoire). Former names and other names: *Société Ouest Africaine d'Ophtalmologie (SOAO)* – former; *West African Society of Ophthalmology* – former. **Structure** Executive Council. **Events** *Congrès* Niamey (Niger) 2015, *Congrès* Yamoussoukro (Côte d'Ivoire) 2013. **Publications** *Revue SOAO*.
Members Societies in 10 countries:
Benin, Burkina Faso, Cameroon, Côte d'Ivoire, Gabon, Guinea, Mali, Niger, Senegal, Togo.
NGO Relations Member of (1): *Middle East African Council of Ophthalmology (MEACO, #16752)*. Regional society member of: *International Council of Ophthalmology (ICO, #13057).* [2021/XJ8818/**D**]

♦ Société africaine de la gérontologie (inactive)
♦ Société africaine de gynécologie – obstétrique / see Société africaine des Gynécologues et Obstétriciens (#19454)

♦ Société africaine des Gynécologues et Obstétriciens (SAGO) 19454

African Society of Gynaecologists and Obstetricians
Secretariat address not obtained.
Dep Gen Sec address not obtained.
Pres address not obtained. E-mail: alguma@yahoo.fr.
URL: http://sago.sante.gov.ml/

History Mar 1988, Cotonou (Benin). Previously also referred to as *Société africaine de gynécologie – obstétrique*. **Structure** General Assembly. Executive Board, comprising President, General Secretary, Deputy General Secretary, General Treasurer and Deputy General Treasurer. **Events** *Congress* Ouagadougou (Burkina Faso) 2016, *Congress* Brazzaville (Congo Brazzaville) 2014, *Congress* Niamey (Niger) 2013, *Congress* Libreville (Gabon) 2010, *Congress* Bamako (Mali) 2003. **Publications** *Journal de la SAGO*.
Members in 10 countries:
Benin, Burkina Faso, Cameroon, Congo DR, Côte d'Ivoire, Guinea, Mali, Senegal, Togo, Tunisia.
NGO Relations Cooperates with: *Fédération Internationale de Gynécologie et d'Obstétrique (FIGO, #09638); New European Surgical Academy (NESA, #17084).* [2015/XJ0850/**D**]

♦ Société Africaine de Medicine Sexuelle (#00470)
♦ Société africaine de nutrition (#00400)

♦ Société africaine de pathologie infectieuse (SAPI) 19455

Pres FANN Teaching Hospital, Dakar, Senegal.

History 1993, Abidjan (Côte d'Ivoire). **Aims** Offer specialist and expertise services to organizations involved in healthcare management of populations; set up recommendations and guidelines for management of infectious and tropical diseases in Africa; facilitate multi-centre research of infectious diseases and tropical medicine in Africa; participate in training of residents and students. **Structure** Executive Office, comprising President, Vice-President, Secretary-General, Treasurer, Assistant Treasurer, Secretary, Accounts Manager. **Languages** French. **Staff** 2.00 FTE, paid. Voluntary. **Finance** Members' dues. Other sources: registration fees; donations; sponsorship. **Activities** Organizes scientific events related to infectious diseases and tropical medicine. **Events** *Congrès* Grand-Bassam (Côte d'Ivoire) 2020, *Congrès* Dakar (Senegal) 2017, *Les infections associées aux soins* Brazzaville (Congo Brazzaville) 2013, *Les infections associées aux soins* Bamako (Mali) 2011, *Infections et système nerveux* Dakar (Senegal) 2009.

Members Organizations; individuals in 13 countries:
Benin, Burkina Faso, Cameroon, Chad, Congo Brazzaville, Congo DR, Côte d'Ivoire, Gabon, Gambia, Guinea, Mali, Mauritania, Niger, Rwanda, Senegal.
IGO Relations *WHO (#20950).* **NGO Relations** *FHI 360.* [2013/XD6414/D]

- Société africaine de physiciens et de mathématiciens / see African Physical Society (#00417)
- Société Africaine de Probabilité and de Statistique (#19975)
- Société africaine de réassurance (#00438)
- Société africaine de toxicologie (inactive)
- Société des africanistes (internationally oriented national body)
- Société agricole européenne et Comité consultatif des organisateurs d'expositions (#07043)
- Société allemande de politique étrangère (internationally oriented national body)
- Société américaine de chimiothérapie de la tuberculose (inactive)
- Société américaine de droit international (internationally oriented national body)
- Société américaine pour la formation des ingénieurs (#00790)
- Société américaine des pêches (internationally oriented national body)
- Société américaine pour la qualité (internationally oriented national body)
- Société d'Amérique de malherbologie (internationally oriented national body)
- Société des Amici Thomae Mori / see Amici Thomae Mori (#00799)
- Société des amis du français universel / see Biennale de la langue française (#03231)
- Société des amis de Tyr (internationally oriented national body)
- Société des anches doubles internationale (#13194)
- Société andine de développement / see Development Bank of Latin America (#05055)

♦ Société d'andrologie de langue française (SALF) 19456

French-Speaking Andrology Society

Secretariat CHU de Grenoble, Labo Aide à la procréation CECOS, BP 217, 38043 Grenoble CEDEX, France. E-mail: secretariatsalf@yahoo.fr – contact@salf.fr.
URL: http://www.salf.fr/

History 1982, Paris (France), taking over the activities of a *'Club d'andrologie'*. **Aims** Propagate and increase knowledge of andrology in French-speaking countries or those belonging to the French-speaking community. **Structure** Executive Council. **Languages** French. **Staff** 15.00 FTE, paid. **Finance** members' dues. **Events** *Congrès Annuel* Caen (France) 2021, *Congrès Annuel* Nancy (France) 2020, *Congrès Annuel* Paris (France) 2019, *Congrès Annuel* Lille (France) 2018, *Scientific Meeting on Male Contraception* Paris (France) 2018. **Publications** *Andrologie* (4 a year). *Progrès en andrologie* – collection.
Members Full in 20 countries:
Algeria, Belgium, Canada, Congo Brazzaville, Côte d'Ivoire, Egypt, Gabon, Germany, Greece, Iran Islamic Rep, Israel, Italy, Jordan, Lebanon, Morocco, Portugal, Senegal, Slovenia, Switzerland, Tunisia. [2022/XF2370/F]

♦ Société de l'Anesthésie Réanimation d'Afrique Francophone 19457

Pres 32 rue Henri de Gastines, 53160 Vimarcé, France. E-mail: ramur-secretariat@web-saraf.net.
URL: https://web-saraf.net/

History 15 Dec 1984, Cotonou (Benin). **Aims** In the framework of creation of a 'French-speaking African Society': unite medical anaesthetists and reanimators, medical doctors who either work in Africa South of the Sahara or are native of that geographical region; promote exchange of experience among them; ensure continuing education in the specialty; train specialist nurses and technicians in the field; provide authorities with expertise in order to develop the specialty and define its norms and standards; promote international cooperation in the field. **Structure** General Assembly; Bureau. **Languages** French. **Staff** 7.00 FTE, voluntary. **Finance** Members' dues. Benefactors. **Activities** Events/meetings. Working to create *Société panafricaine d'anesthésiologie (no recent information).* **Events** *Annual Congress* Cotonou (Benin) 2022, *Congrès Annuel* Bamako (Mali) 2019, *Congrès Annuel* Abidjan (Côte d'Ivoire) 2018, *Congrès Annuel* Libreville (Gabon) 2017, *Congrès Annuel* Yaoundé (Cameroon) 2016. **Publications** *Revue Africaine d'Anesthésiologie et de Médecine d'Urgence* (3 a year) in French.
Members Full medical doctors in the field of anaesthesia from or practising in Africa South of the Sahara; Associate other interested persons. Members in 15 countries:
Benin, Burkina Faso, Cameroon, Central African Rep, Chad, Congo Brazzaville, Congo DR, Côte d'Ivoire, Gabon, Guinea, Madagascar, Mauritania, Niger, Senegal, Togo.
NGO Relations Participates in conferences of: *World Federation of Societies of Anaesthesiologists (WFSA, #21482).* Member of WFSA African Regional Section, set up Apr 1997, Harare (Zimbabwe). [2022/XD1449/v/D]

- Société d'angiologie de langue française (inactive)
- Société anthroposophique universelle (#10103)
- Société anti-esclavagiste pour la protection des droits de l'homme / see Anti-Slavery International (#00860)
- Société de l'Apostolat Catholique (religious order)
- Société arabe de construction et de reparation navales (see: #17854)
- Société arabe de développement des richesses animales / see Arab Company for Livestock Development (#00927)
- Société arabe d'imprimerie / see Arab Federation for Paper, Printing and Packaging Industries (#00950)
- Société arabe des industries des produits pharmaceutiques et instruments médicaux (#00926)
- Société arabe et internationale de transport terrestre / see Arab Union of Land Transport (#01069)
- Société arabe d'investissement (#00996)
- Société arabe d'investissements pétroliers (#01026)
- Société arabe des mines de l'Inchiri (no recent information)
- Société arabe de navigation maritime (inactive)
- Société arabe de nephrologie et de transplantation rénale (#01047)
- Société arabe d'orthodontie (#01022)
- Société arabe des pêches (#00959)
- Société arabe de services pétroliers (see: #17854)
- Société des archéologues de la céramique romaine (#18827)
- Société des arts électroniques / see ISEA International (#16025)
- Société asiatique de réassurance (#01685)
- Société pour l'Asie et du Pacifique de malherbologie (#01646)
- Société des associations des matières plastiques en Europe (inactive)
- Société d'assurance mutuelle du personnel contre la maladie (#20629)
- Société des Auteurs Audiovisuels / see Society of Audiovisual Authors (#19524)
- Société des auteurs et compositeurs dramatiques (internationally oriented national body)
- Société autrichienne de science politique (internationally oriented national body)
- Société des Auxiliaires des Missions (religious order)
- Société basimétrique internationale (inactive)
- Société belge d'investissement international (internationally oriented national body)
- Société belge de médecine tropicale (internationally oriented national body)
- Société bénéluxienne de phlébologie (#03204)
- Société Bernoulli pour la statistique mathématique et la probabilité (#03212)
- Société de bibliographie classique / see Société internationale de bibliographie classique (#19474)
- Société de bioélectrochimie (#03244)

♦ Société de biomécanique (SB) 19458

Pres Lab de Biomécanique, ENSAM Paris Tech, 151 bd de l'Hôpital, 75013 Paris, France.
URL: http://www.biomecanique.org/

History 1975. Registered in accordance with French law. **Aims** Encourage and promote research in *biomechanics.* **Structure** Officers: President; Vice-President; Secretary-General; Treasurer. **Languages** French. **Staff** 4.00 FTE, paid. **Activities** Organizes annual congress and thematic workshops. Grants: Senior researcher award; Society of biomechanics award (for students). **Events** *Congrès Annuel / Annual Congress* Marseille (France) 2013, *Congrès Annuel / Annual Congress* Toulouse (France) 2012, *Annual Congress* Besançon (France) 2011, *Congrès annuel* Besançon (France) 2011, *Symposium on sport modelling and simulation* Poitiers (France) 2011. **Publications** Congress abstracts.
Members Active (about 200); Honorary (21). Members mainly in 4 countries and territories:
Belgium, France, Québec, Switzerland. [2013.06.01/XM2038/D]

- Société de biospéologie / see International Society of Biospeleology (#14975)
- Société de broncho-oesophagologie et de gastroscopie de langue française (inactive)
- Société canadienne d'éducation comparative et internationale / see Comparative and International Education Society of Canada
- Société canadienne d'éducation comparée et internationale (internationally oriented national body)
- Société canadienne pour la médecine tropicale et la santé internationale / see Canadian Association Global Health
- Société Caraïbe des plantes alimentaires (#03509)
- Société de cardiologie de l'Afrique de l'Ouest (inactive)
- Société de cardiologie d'Amérique centrale (inactive)
- Société de cardiologie des pays d'Afrique d'expression française (inactive)
- Société cardiologique Asie-Pacifique (#01631)
- Société catholique écossaise de secours international (internationally oriented national body)
- Société centroaméricaine de pharmacologie (inactive)
- Société de Chirurgie de la Méditerranée Latine (#20042)
- Société chirurgie orthopédique et traumatologique de la Méditerranée et du Moyen-Orient (inactive)
- Société de chirurgie plastique de l'Amérique latine (inactive)
- Société de chirurgie thoracique et cardio-vasculaire de langue française / see French Society for Thoracic and Cardiovascular Surgery (#09993)
- Société de Chirurgie Vasculaire et Endovasculaire de Langue Française (internationally oriented national body)
- Société de chirurgie vasculaire de langue française / see Société de Chirurgie Vasculaire et Endovasculaire de Langue Française
- Société chrétienne évangélique d'Asie (inactive)
- Société du Christ Seigneur (religious order)
- Société Civile Africaine pour la Société de l'Information (#00163)
- Société civile des auteurs multimédia (internationally oriented national body)
- Société du Commonwealth pour les sourds (inactive)
- Société de communication par satellite pour radio-amateurs (#18601)
- Société pour une confédération au Moyen-Orient (inactive)
- Société pur la conservation et l'etude des oiseaux de la Caraïbe / see BirdsCaribbean (#03267)
- Société de Conservation du Rift Albertine (#00620)
- Société de coopération pour le développement international (internationally oriented national body)
- Société coopérative internationale agricole d'achat et de vente (inactive)
- Société coopérative internationale de gros (inactive)
- Société coopérative oecuménique pour le développement / see Oikocredit International (#17704)
- Société de correspondance internationale des allergologistes (no recent information)
- Société Cousteau / see Cousteau Society
- Société danoise d'études européennes (internationally oriented national body)
- Société dentaire américaine de l'Europe (#00779)
- Société de Dermatologie et Vénéréologie (#00460)
- Société dermatologique de l'Amérique centrale / see Central American and Caribbean Dermatological Society (#03663)
- Société d'études rousseauistes / see Rousseau Association
- Société de développement international Desjardins / see Développement international Desjardins
- Société diplomatique de St Gabriel (internationally oriented national body)
- Société du Divin Sauveur (religious order)
- Société de droit international John Bassett Moore (internationally oriented national body)
- Société d'échange international des enfants et des jeunes gens (inactive)
- Société écologique d'Asie (inactive)
- Société d'économétrie (#05310)
- Société d'éditeurs de journaux de la région du Pacifique (inactive)
- Société d'éducation comparée en Asie (#04409)
- Société d'éducation comparée de langue néerlandaise (internationally oriented national body)
- Société pour l'éducation en nutrition (#19612)

♦ Société d'Education Thérapeutique Européenne (SETE) 19459

European Society for Therapeutic Education – Società Europea di Educazione Terapeutica

Contact 32 Boulevard Carnot, 47000 Agen, France. E-mail: contact@socsete.org.
URL: http://www.socsete.org/

History 2002, Paris (France). **Aims** Develop and diffuse interdisciplinary research on therapeutic education and follow up strategies in acute and chronic diseases. **Structure** General Assembly; Board of Directors. **Finance** Members' dues. **Activities** Events/meetings. **Events** *Congress* Montpellier (France) 2022, *Congress* Montpellier (France) 2021, *Congrès* Toulouse (France) 2019, *Santé, créativité* Geneva (Switzerland) 2016, *Congrès* Paris (France) 2014. **Publications** *Education thérapeutique du patient – Therapeutic patient education* – journal. [2020/XJ7180/D]

- Société d'électro-encéphalographie de langue française / see Société de neurochirurgie de langue française (#19503)

♦ Société d'Ergonomie de Langue Française (SELF) 19460

Francophone Ergonomics Society

Sec 13 rue Planty, 78200 Mantes-la-Jolie, France. T. +33634664750.
URL: http://www.ergonomie-self.org/

History 1963. International since 1972. Statutes amended, 1998. **Aims** Promote research, action and training in ergonomics in order to improve living and working environments and to ensure individual health, wellbeing, safety and development; represent ergonomic principles before national and international authorities. **Structure** General Assembly (annual); Administrative Council; Bureau. **Languages** French. **Staff** 3.50 FTE, voluntary. **Finance** Sources: members' dues. **Activities** Events/meetings; training/education; awards/prizes/competitions. **Events** *Annual Congress* Geneva (Switzerland) 2022, *Annual Congress* Paris (France) 2021, *Annual Congress* Paris (France) 2020, *Annual Congress* Tours (France) 2019, *Annual Congress* Bordeaux (France) 2018. **Publications** *Bulletin de liaison de la SELF* (3 a year).
Members Active (about 700); Honorary (20). Individuals in 25 countries:
Algeria, Belgium, Bulgaria, Canada, Colombia, Côte d'Ivoire, Czechia, Denmark, Finland, France, Germany, Greece, Italy, Luxembourg, Mexico, Morocco, Netherlands, Norway, Poland, Portugal, Romania, Spain, Switzerland, Tunisia, USA. [2020/XD0982/v/D]

- Société Espagnole pour le Droit International des Droits Humains (internationally oriented national body)
- Société d'éthologie vétérinaire / see International Society for Applied Ethology (#14930)
- Société pour l'étude des croisades et de l'Orient latin (#19644)
- Société pour l'étude et le développement de l'ordre international (inactive)
- Société d'étude de l'histoire de l'Eglise en Afrique (inactive)
- Société pour l'étude du Nouveau Testament (#19610)
- Société d'études et de correspondance internationales, Internationalis Concordia (inactive)
- Société d'études et d'expansion (inactive)
- Société d'études historiques des relations internationales contemporaines (internationally oriented national body)
- Société d'études kantiennes de langue française (internationally oriented national body)
- Société d'études religieuses (inactive)
- Société EURODIF (#05676)
- Société européenne d'agronomie (#08515)
- Société européenne d'alimentation parentérale et entérale / see European Society for Clinical Nutrition and Metabolism (#08550)

- ♦ Société européenne d'anesthésie régionale / see European Society of Regional Anaesthesia and Pain Therapy (#08722)
- ♦ Société européenne d'aquaculture (#05909)
- ♦ Société européenne d'arachnologie (#08523)
- ♦ Société européenne d'astronomie (#06288)

♦ Société européenne pour l'astronomie dans la culture (SEAC) 19461

European Society for Astronomy in Culture

Pres Incipit – CSIC, Avda de Vigo s/n, 15705 Santiago de Compostela, La Coruña, Spain. E-mail: info@incipit.csic.es.
Sec address not obtained.
URL: http://www.archeoastronomy.org/

History 1992, Strasbourg (France). **Aims** Promote interdisciplinary study of astronomical practise in its cultural context as a topic of considerable importance within the general study of human societies and their relationship to their environment; promote research seeking to develop our understanding of the cultural significance of astronomical knowledge through the integration of techniques and methods within the humanities, natural sciences, social sciences and other disciplines. **Structure** Executive Committee. **Languages** English, French, German, Russian, Spanish. **Staff** No fixed staff. **Finance** Members' dues. **Activities** Events/meetings; awards/prizes/competitions; publishing activities. **Events** *Annual Conference* Bern (Switzerland) 2019, *Annual Conference* Graz (Austria) 2018, *Annual Conference* Santiago de Compostela (Spain) 2017, *Annual conference* Bath (UK) 2016, *Annual Conference* Rome (Italy) 2015. **Publications** *Proceeding Book of Annual Meetings*. **Members** Individuals (about 90) in 18 countries. Membership countries not specified. **NGO Relations** *International Society for Archaeoastronomy and Astronomy in Culture (ISAAC, #14937)*; Sociedad Interamericana de Astronomia en la Cultura (SIAC). [2019.10.17/XM1404/**D**]

- ♦ Société européenne d'athérosclérose (#06289)
- ♦ Société européenne de biomécanique / see European Society of Biomechanics (#08531)
- ♦ Société européenne de bio-médecine sous-marine / see European Underwater and Baromedical Society (#08965)
- ♦ Société européenne des blessures / see European Wound Management Association (#09121)
- ♦ Société Européenne de Cardiologie (#08536)
- ♦ Société européenne de la cataracte et chirurgie réfractive (#08539)
- ♦ Société européenne du cerveau et du comportement (#06390)
- ♦ Société Européenne de Chimie (#06524)
- ♦ Société européenne de chirurgie cardiovasculaire / see European Society for Cardiovascular and Endovascular Surgery (#08537)
- ♦ Société européenne de chirurgie cardiovasculaire et endovasculaire (#08537)
- ♦ Société européenne de chirurgie cranio-maxillo-faciale (#05995)
- ♦ Société européenne pour la chirurgie de l'épaule et du coude (#08752)
- ♦ Société européenne de chirurgie gériatrique (no recent information)
- ♦ Société européenne de chirurgie maxillo-faciale / see European Association for Cranio-Maxillo-Facial Surgery (#05995)
- ♦ Société européenne de chirurgie orthopédique de la polyarthrite chronique évolutive (#08387)
- ♦ Société européenne de chirurgie reconstructive de la tête et du cou (inactive)
- ♦ Société européenne de chromatophonie (inactive)
- ♦ Société européenne de chronobiologie (no recent information)
- ♦ Société européenne de la contraception / see European Society of Contraception and Reproductive Health (#08568)
- ♦ Société européenne contre les maladies à virus (inactive)
- ♦ Société Européenne de Cryochirurgie (inactive)
- ♦ Société européenne de culture (#08576)
- ♦ Société européenne de culture de tissus (inactive)
- ♦ Société européenne des déformations rachidiennes (inactive)
- ♦ Société européenne des déformations du rachis (inactive)
- ♦ Société européenne de dermatologie pédiatrique (#08691)
- ♦ Société européenne sur les dermatoses de contact (#08567)
- ♦ Société européenne des dirigeants d'associations / see European Society of Association Executives (#08526)
- ♦ Société européenne de droit international (#08634)
- ♦ Société européenne d'économie écologique (#08587)
- ♦ Société européenne d'endocrinologie comparée (#08558)
- ♦ Société européenne d'énergie atomique (#06293)
- ♦ Société européenne de l'énergie nucléaire (#08059)
- ♦ Société européenne pour l'environnement et le développement (inactive)
- ♦ Société européenne d'ergonomie dentaire / see European Society of Dental Ergonomics (#08577)
- ♦ Société européenne d'ethnomusicologie (#08598)
- ♦ Société européenne d'étude et d'intégration de systèmes spatiaux (inactive)
- ♦ Société européenne pour l'étude de la motilité gastro-intestinale / see European Society of Neurogastroenterology and Motility (#08663)
- ♦ Société européenne pour l'étude et la prévention de la mort subite des enfants (inactive)
- ♦ Société européenne pour l'étude des relations internationales (inactive)
- ♦ Société européenne d'études de monstres / see European Teratology Society (#08900)
- ♦ Société européenne d'études du strabisme / see European Strabismological Association (#08840)
- ♦ Société européenne du film (inactive)

♦ Société européenne pour la formation des ingénieurs (SEFI) 19462

European Society for Engineering Education – Europäische Gesellschaft für Ingenieurausbildung – Europese Genootschap voor Ingenieursopleiding

Exec Dir Rue des Deux Eglises 39, 1000 Brussels, Belgium. T. +3225023609. Fax +3225029611.
URL: http://www.sefi.be/

History 19 Jan 1973, Louvain-la-Neuve (Belgium). Founded at a meeting of official representatives of engineering education institutions and technical universities from 10 European countries. New statutes adopted 30 Apr 1979; modified 11 Sep 1996, 4 Sep 1998 and 24 Mar 2006. Registration: AISBL/IVZW, Start date: 4 May 1973, Belgium. **Aims** Develop and improve engineering training and the professional status of engineers; promote information on engineering education; improve communication and exchanges between teachers, researchers and students in Europe; develop cooperation between educational engineering institutions; contribute to the development and improvement of engineering education in the economic, social and cultural framework of Europe; promote cooperation between engineering educators and industry. **Structure** General Assembly (annual). Administrative Council of up to 21 members. Bureau. Head Office. **Languages** English, French, German. **Staff** 5.00 FTE, paid. **Finance** Sources: members' dues; revenue from activities/projects. **Activities** Awards/prizes/competitions; events/meetings. **Events** *Annual Conference* Lausanne (Switzerland) 2024, *Annual Conference* Dublin (Ireland) 2023, *European Convention of Engineering Deans* Enschede (Netherlands) 2023, *Annual Conference* Barcelona (Spain) 2022, *International Conference on Physics Teaching in Engineering Education* Tampere (Finland) 2022. **Publications** *News'at'sefi* (12 a year); *European Journal of Engineering Education* (6 a year). *SEFI-Guide on Eastern-Central European Countries* (1993); *SEFI-Guide on Engineering Education in Europe* (1990). Annual reports. Working group reports; documents; cahiers; conference proceedings; position papers.
Members Institutional; Individual; Industrial and related organizations; Associate. Members (412) in 47 countries. Institutional in 28 countries:
Australia, Belgium, Croatia, Czechia, Denmark, Estonia, Finland, France, Germany, Greece, Hungary, Ireland, Italy, Kazakhstan, Latvia, Lithuania, Netherlands, Norway, Poland, Portugal, Romania, Russia, Slovakia, Spain, Sweden, Switzerland, Türkiye, UK.
Associate in 19 countries:
Australia, Belgium, Croatia, Denmark, Finland, France, Germany, Ghana, Greece, Hungary, Ireland, Italy, Netherlands, North Macedonia, Norway, Portugal, Russia, Spain, UK.
Included in the above, 2 organizations listed in this Yearbook:
European Higher Engineering and Technical Professionals Association (EurEta, #07484); *Fédération Européenne d'Associations Nationales d'Ingénieurs (FEANI, #09558)*.
Consultative Status Consultative status granted from: *UNESCO (#20322)* (Consultative Status). **NGO Relations** Member of (2): *EDEN Digital Learning Europe (EDEN, #05356)*; *International Federation of Engineering Education Societies (IFEES, #13412)*. Instrumental in setting up (2): *European Technology Management Initiative (ETMI, no recent information)*; *International Institute for Developing Engineering Academics (IIDEA, #13873)*. Founding member of: *International Association for Continuing Engineering Education (IACEE, #11817)*. Associate member of: *European Network for Accreditation of Engineering Education (ENAEE, #07859)*. [2022/XD4224/y/**D**]

- ♦ Société Européenne pour la gastro-entérologie, d'hépatologie et de nutrition pédiatriques (#08680)
- ♦ Société européenne pour la géographie / see Association of European Geographical Societies (#02512)
- ♦ Société européenne de graphologie (#08616)
- ♦ Société Européenne de Gynécologie (#08613)
- ♦ Société européenne d'hématologie (inactive)
- ♦ Société européenne d'hématologie et d'immunologie pédiatriques (#08681)
- ♦ Société européenne d'herpétologie (#07481)
- ♦ Société européenne d'histotechnologie (inactive)
- ♦ Société européenne d'ichthyologie (#07513)
- ♦ Société européenne d'imagerie thoracique (#08759)
- ♦ Société européenne d'infection en chirurgie (#20043)
- ♦ Société européenne des ingénieurs et des industriels (internationally oriented national body)
- ♦ Société européenne de kinésithérapie respiratoire et cardio-vasculaire (inactive)
- ♦ Société européenne de laryngologie (#07653)
- ♦ Société européenne de linguistique (#19448)
- ♦ Société Européenne de Littérature Comparée (#08561)
- ♦ Société européenne des maladies infectieuses pédiatriques (#08682)
- ♦ Société européenne de malherbologie (#09089)
- ♦ Société Européenne pour les Mathématiques et les Arts (internationally oriented national body)
- ♦ Société européenne de médecine interne cancérologique / see European Society for Medical Oncology (#08648)
- ♦ Société européenne de médecine naturelle classique (no recent information)
- ♦ Société européenne de médecine nucléaire (inactive)
- ♦ Société Européenne pour la Médecine d'Urgence (#08590)
- ♦ Société européenne des méthodes nucléaires en agriculture (inactive)
- ♦ Société européenne de microbiologie clinique et des maladies infectieuses (#08548)
- ♦ Société européenne de microcirculation (#08651)
- ♦ Société européenne de néphrologie pédiatrique (#08684)
- ♦ Société européenne de neurochimie (#08662)
- ♦ Société européenne de neurochirurgie pédiatrique (#08685)
- ♦ Société européenne de neurochirurgie stéréotaxique et fonctionnelle (#08742)
- ♦ Société européenne de neurologie (inactive)

♦ Société européenne de neurologie pédiatrique (SENP) 19463

Secretariat 154 av de Lodève, 34000 Montpellier, France. T. +33467109223. E-mail: senp-secretariat@ant-congres.com.
URL: https://www.senp-neuropediatrie.eu/

History 1971, Paris (France). **Aims** Promote scientific and clinical research in all domains related to diseases of the *nervous system* in *childhood*. **Structure** Board. **Languages** English, French. **Staff** 7.00 FTE, voluntary. **Finance** Subscriptions; contributions; congress proceeds. **Activities** Events/meetings. **Events** *Annual Meeting* Lausanne (Switzerland) 2021, *Annual Meeting* Paris (France) 2019, *Annual Meeting* Barcelona (Spain) 2018, *Annual Meeting* Turin (Italy) 2017, *Annual Meeting* Lugano (Switzerland) 2016.
Members Active French-speaking child neurologists in 7 countries:
Belgium, France, Italy, Luxembourg, Portugal, Spain, Switzerland.
Associate in 22 countries:
Algeria, Argentina, Belgium, Brazil, Chile, Colombia, France, Germany, Greece, Israel, Italy, Japan, Luxembourg, Netherlands, Poland, Portugal, Spain, Switzerland, Tunisia, UK, USA, Venezuela.
NGO Relations National neuropediatrician societies. [2020/XD3434/**D**]

- ♦ Société européenne de neuroradiologie (#08664)
- ♦ Société européenne d'oncologie chirurgicale (#08753)
- ♦ Société européenne d'ophtalmologie (#08674)
- ♦ Société européenne d'ophtalmologie de santé publique (no recent information)
- ♦ Société européenne des ophtalmologistes contactologues (#06775)
- ♦ Société européenne pour les organes artificiels (#08525)
- ♦ Société européenne d'ostéoarthrologie (inactive)
- ♦ Société européenne de paléontologie (inactive)
- ♦ Société européenne de paramétrologie (inactive)
- ♦ Société européenne de pathologie (#08689)
- ♦ Société européenne de pathologie cellulaire analytique (inactive)
- ♦ Société européenne de pathologie unguéale (#07850)
- ♦ Société européenne de pathologie vétérinaire (#08785)
- ♦ Société européenne de pédiatrie ambulatoire (inactive)
- ♦ Société Européenne de Pharmacogénomique et Théranostique / see European Society of Pharmacogenomics and Personalised Therapy (#08696)
- ♦ Société Européenne de Pharmacogénomique et Thérapie Personalisée (#08696)
- ♦ Société européenne de pharmacologie biochimique (inactive)
- ♦ Société européenne pour la philosophie de la médecine et de la santé (#08698)
- ♦ Société européenne de phlébectomie (#08701)
- ♦ Société européenne de phraséologie (#08705)
- ♦ Société européenne de physiologie et de biochimie comparées (#08562)
- ♦ Société européenne de physiopathologie clinique respiratoire (inactive)
- ♦ Société européenne de physique (#08207)
- ♦ Société européenne de planification à long terme (inactive)
- ♦ Société européenne de pneumologie (inactive)
- ♦ Société européenne de psychiatrie de l'enfant et de l'adolescent (#08543)
- ♦ Société européenne de radiobiologie / see European Radiation Research Society (#08319)
- ♦ Société européenne de radiologie cardio-vasculaire et de radiologie d'intervention (inactive)
- ♦ Société européenne de radiologie pédiatrique (#08686)
- ♦ Société européenne de radiologie de la tête et du cou (#08617)
- ♦ Société européenne des réalisateurs de l'environnement (internationally oriented national body)
- ♦ Société européenne de recherche en dermatologie (#08578)
- ♦ Société européenne de recherche en éthique (#08726)
- ♦ Société Européenne pour la recherche en formation des adultes (#08725)
- ♦ Société européenne pour la recherche sur les groupes sanguins des animaux / see International Society for Animal Genetics (#14921)
- ♦ Société Européenne de Recherche sur le Handicap (#00751)
- ♦ Société européenne de recherche sur les matériaux (#07753)
- ♦ Société Européenne de Recherche en Ostéopathie Périnatale and Pédiatrique (unconfirmed)
- ♦ Société européenne de recherche en pédiatrie (#08687)
- ♦ Société européenne de recherches biomédicales sur l'alcoolisme (#08532)
- ♦ Société européenne de recherches chirurgicales (#08754)
- ♦ Société Européenne pour les Recherches en Education Mathématique (#08728)
- ♦ Société européenne de recherche sur le sommeil (#08493)
- ♦ Société européenne de reproduction humaine et d'embryologie (#08625)

♦ Société européenne réticuloendothéliale (inactive)
♦ Société européenne de santé mentale et surdité (#08649)
♦ Société européenne de science fiction (#08440)
♦ Société européenne de sémantique générale (no recent information)
♦ Société européenne de sociologie rurale (#08731)
♦ Société européenne de soins intensifs et de médecine d'urgence (#09056)
♦ Société européenne de soins intensifs pédiatriques / see European Society of Paediatric and Neonatal Intensive Care (#08683)
♦ Société européenne de soins intensifs pédiatriques et neonataux (#08683)
♦ Société Européenne de Straight-Wire (unconfirmed)
♦ Société européenne de technologie cellulaire animale (#08520)
♦ Société européenne de télémédecine (internationally oriented national body)
♦ Société européenne de tératologie (#08900)
♦ Société Européenne de Tête et Cou (#07452)
♦ Société européenne de la tête et du cou (inactive)
♦ Société européenne de toxicologie (inactive)
♦ Société européenne pour le traitement chimique des combustibles irradiés (inactive)
♦ Société européenne d'urologie de l'enfant (#08688)
♦ Société européenne de la vermiculite (no recent information)
♦ Société et fédération internationale de cardiologie / see World Heart Federation (#21562)
♦ Société des Filles du Coeur de Marie (religious order)
♦ Société des Filles de Saint François de Sales (religious order)
♦ Société financière de l'ANASE (#01186)
♦ Société financière pour le développement international d'ententes économiques, intellectuelles et sociales (inactive)
♦ Société financière européenne (inactive)
♦ Société financière internationale (#13597)

♦ Société Française de Chirurgie Orale (SFCO) 19464

Pres Fac d'Odontologie, 545 av Pr JL Viala, 34193 Montpellier CEDEX, France. E-mail: presidence@sfco.online.
SG Fac d'Odontologie, 27 bd Jean Moulin, 13385 Marseille, France. E-mail: secretariat@sfco.online.
URL: http://www.societechirorale.com/

History 1970. Current statutes adopted 18 May 2019. Former names and other names: *Société francophone de chirurgie buccale* – former; *Société francophone de médecine buccale et chirurgie buccale (SFMBCB)* – former. **Aims** Promote study, continuing education, research and progress in *oral medicine* and *oral surgery*. **Structure** General Assembly (annual); Council; Committees (3). **Languages** French. **Staff** 8.00 FTE, voluntary. **Finance** Sources: donations; meeting proceeds; members' dues. Annual budget: 70,000 EUR. **Activities** Awards/prizes/competitions; events/meetings; financial and/or material support; knowledge management/information dissemination; publishing activities; training/education. **Events** *Congrès* Aix-les-Bains (France) 2022, *Congrès* Bordeaux (France) 2021, *Congrès* Aix-en-Provence (France) 2019, *Congrès* Paris (France) 2018, *Congrès* Rouen (France) 2017. **Publications** *Journal of Oral Medicine and Oral Surgery (JOMOS).*
Members Full; Associate. Members in 11 countries:
Algeria, Canada, Côte d'Ivoire, France, Germany, Madagascar, Morocco, Senegal, Spain, Switzerland, Tunisia.
NGO Relations Also links with national organizations. [2022.05.10/XD7021/**D**]

♦ Société française de chirurgie thoracique et cardiovasculaire (#09993)
♦ Société française et francophone des plaies et cicatrisations (internationally oriented national body)
♦ Société française de nutrition (internationally oriented national body)
♦ Société franco-panafricaine des sciences vasculaires (unconfirmed)
♦ Société Francophone d'Analyse du Mouvement chez l'Enfant et l'Adulte (internationally oriented national body)
♦ Société francophone pour l'application des ultrasons à la médecine et la biologie / see Société Francophone d'Echographie
♦ Société Francophone d'Arthroscopie (internationally oriented national body)
♦ Société francophone de chirurgie buccale / see Société Française de Chirurgie Orale (#19464)
♦ Société Francophone de Chronobiologie (internationally oriented national body)

♦ Société francophone de classification (SFC) 19465

French-speaking Classification Society
Sec Inst Galilée, Univ Paris Nord, 99 ave Jean-Baptiste Clément, 93430 Villetaneuse, France. T. +33149403590. Fax +33148260712.
URL: http://www.sfc-classification.net/

History 1977. **Aims** Group *French-speaking* conceptors and users of clustering and classification methods. **Structure** Council. Officers: President; 2 Vice-Presidents; Secretary; Treasurer; Newsletter Editor. **Languages** French. **Staff** Voluntary. **Finance** Members' dues. **Activities** Awards 'Prix Simon Regnier' for an original contribution to classification published in French. Organizes annual congress. **Events** *Congrès* Lyon (France) 2022, *Congrès* Nancy (France) 2019, *Congrès* Paris (France) 2018, *Congrès* Lyon (France) 2017, *Congrès* Rabat (Morocco) 2014. **Publications** *Bulletin de la SFC* (annual).
Members Individuals in 6 countries:
Belgium, Burundi, France, Germany, Italy, Switzerland.
NGO Relations Founder member of: *International Federation of Classification Societies (IFCS, #13391).* [2017/XD1484/v/**D**]

♦ Société Francophone de Contraception (SFC) 19466

Contact 9 rue de Villersexel, 75007 Paris, France. T. +33490810042. Fax +33413334627. E-mail: contact@societe-francophone-contraception.com.
URL: http://www.societe-francophone-contraception.com/

History Founded 28 Apr 2000, Paris (France). Registered in accordance with French law. **Aims** Promote contraception in all its aspects in French-speaking countries; initiate and encourage contraceptive research. **Structure** Bureau; Scientific Committee. **Activities** Events/meetings; networking/liaising. **Publications** *Journal de Contraception de la SFC.*
Members Full in 18 countries:
Algeria, Belgium, Burkina Faso, Cameroon, Canada, Côte d'Ivoire, France, Gabon, Guinea, Lebanon, Mali, Malta, Mauritania, Morocco, Senegal, Switzerland, Tunisia, Vietnam.
NGO Relations *International Consortium for Male Contraception (ICMC, #12919).* [2020.03.13/XM8447/**C**]

♦ Société francophone de dermatologie psychosomatique (SFDPS) .. 19467

Francophone Society of Psychosomatic Dermatology
Pres 186 rue de la Convention, 75015 Paris, France. T. +33145312020.

History Founded 1992. **Aims** Gather francophone members of the medical and para-medical professions to study psychosomatic problems in dermatology. **Members** Membership countries not specified. **NGO Relations** *European Society for Dermatology and Psychiatry (ESDaP, #08579).* [2017.12.20/XD8939/**D**]

♦ Société Francophone du Diabète (SFD) 19468

Secretariat 60 rue Saint-Lazare, 75009 Paris, France. T. +33140098907. Fax +33140092914. E-mail: secretariat@sfdiabete.org.
URL: http://www.sfdiabete.org/

History 23 Mar 1974. Replaced *Association des diabétologues de langue française* founded 29 Mar 1954. Reorganized in May 1984. Former names and other names: *Association de langue française pour l'étude du diabète et des maladies métaboliques (ALFEDIAM)* – former; *French-Language Association for Research on Diabetes and Metabolic Diseases* – former. Registration: RNA, No/ID: W751030940, France. **Aims** Contribute to improving knowledge on diabetes and metabolic diseases and developing links among all specialists concerned. **Structure** General Assembly (annual); Administrative Board; Bureau; Scientific Committee; Permanent Secretariat in Paris (France). **Languages** French. **Staff** 1.00 FTE, paid. **Finance** Members's dues. **Activities** Events/meetings; training/education. **Events** *Paris NASH Meeting* Paris (France) 2022, *Paris NASH Meeting* Paris (France) 2021, *Annual Congress* Strasbourg (France) 2021, *Annual Congress* Paris (France) 2020, *Paris NASH Meeting* Paris (France) 2020. **Publications** *Diabetes and Metabolism* (6 a year) in English, French – official journal; *Lettre des paramédicaux* – internal liaison publication.
Members Individuals (about 1,200) mainly in France but in a total of 34 countries:
Albania, Algeria, Belgium, Benin, Canada, Chad, China, Congo Brazzaville, Czechia, Egypt, France, Germany, Greece, Israel, Italy, Lebanon, Luxembourg, Madagascar, Mali, Morocco, New Zealand, Norway, Poland, Saudi Arabia, Senegal, Slovakia, Spain, Switzerland, Syrian AR, Togo, Tunisia, Türkiye, UK, United Arab Emirates, USA, Vietnam.
NGO Relations Member of (1): *European Foundation for the Study of Diabetes (EFSD, #07351).* [2021/XD0137/v/**D**]

♦ Société Francophone de Dialyse / see Société Francophone de Néphrologie Dialyse et Transplantation (#19470)
♦ Société Francophone d'Echographie (internationally oriented national body)

♦ Société Francophone d'Etude et de Recherche sur les Eléments Toxiques et Essentiels (SFERETE) 19469

Pres ENS de Lyon, 15 parvis René Descartes – BP 7000, 69342 Lyon CEDEX 07, France.
Sec Inst de Biologie et Pathologie, CHUCGA CS 10217, 38043 Grenoble CEDEX 9, France.
URL: http://www.sferete.fr/

History 1986 as *Société francophone d'étude et de recherche sur les éléments trace essentiels.* Registered in accordance with French law. **Aims** Promote knowledge in the field of *trace elements* by pluridisciplinary exchanges among researchers, clinicians and biologists. **Structure** Bureau. **Languages** French. **Staff** None. **Finance** Members' dues. **Activities** Events/meetings; publishing activities; awards/prizes/competitions; research/documentation; training/education. **Events** *International symposium on trace elements in man and animals* Évian (France) 1999, *International congress on trace elements in medicine and biology* Chamonix (France) 1993.
Members in 6 countries:
Algeria, Belgium, France, Morocco, Switzerland, Tunisia.
NGO Relations *Federation of European Societies on Trace Elements and Minerals (FESTEM, #09550).* [2017.11.21/XD7426/**D**]

♦ Société francophone d'étude et de recherche sur les éléments trace essentiels / see Société Francophone d'Etude et de Recherche sur les Eléments Toxiques et Essentiels (#19469)
♦ Société francophone d'histoire de l'ophtalmologie (internationally oriented national body)
♦ Société Francophone pour l'informatique et le Monitorage en Anesthésie – Réanimation (unconfirmed)
♦ Société francophone de médecine buccale et chirurgie buccale / see Société Française de Chirurgie Orale (#19464)
♦ Société francophone de médecine d'urgence (internationally oriented national body)

♦ Société Francophone de Néphrologie Dialyse et Transplantation (SFNDT) 19470

Admin Dir 24 Montée des Roches, Saint-Sorlin, 69440 Chabanière, France. T. +33637560927. E-mail: secretariat.sfndt@gmail.com – communication.sfndt@gmail.com.
URL: https://www.sfndt.org/

History 29 Jan 2003. Current title adopted on merger with Société de Néphrologie, 2016. Former names and other names: *Société Francophone de Dialyse* – former. Registration: RNA, No/ID: W623002835, Start date: 2015, France. **Aims** Study and evaluate techniques of treatment of *kidney diseases*, chronic *renal* insufficiency by dialysis and transplantation. **Structure** General Assembly (annual); Board. **Languages** French. **Staff** 1.00 FTE, paid; 7.00 FTE, voluntary. **Finance** Members' dues. Other sources: income from congress; industry grants. **Activities** Events/meetings; research/documentation; knowledge management/information dissemination; training/education. **Events** *Congrès* Liège (Belgium) 2023, *Congrès* Rennes (France) 2022, *Congrès* Toulouse (France) 2021, *Congrès* Wimereux (France) 2020, *Congrès* Nancy (France) 2019. **Publications** *Néphrologie et Thérapeutique* – journal.
Members Active; Associate; Honorary. Members in 13 countries:
Algeria, Belgium, Cameroon, Canada, Côte d'Ivoire, France, Mali, Morocco, Niger, Senegal, Switzerland, Tunisia, USA.
IGO Relations Agence de biomdicine; HAS; French Ministry of Health. **NGO Relations** Member of (1): *European Kidney Health Alliance (EKHA, #07626)* (Affiliate). American Society of Nephrology; *European Renal Association – European Dialysis and Transplant Association (ERA-EDTA, #08353); International Society of Nephrology (ISN, #15294).* [2022/XM2019/**D**]

♦ Société francophone nutrition clinique et métabolisme / see Société Francophone Nutrition Clinique et Métabolisme (#19471)

♦ Société Francophone Nutrition Clinique et Métabolisme (SFNCM) .. 19471

Secretariat 37 rue des Mathurins, 75008 Paris, France. E-mail: contact@sfncm.org.
Registered Office Tour CIT, 3 rue de l'Arrivée, BP05, 75749 Paris Cedex 15, France.
URL: https://www.sfncm.org/

History 1982. Former names and other names: *Société francophone de nutrition entérale et parentérale (SFNEP)* – former (1982 to 2006); *Société francophone nutrition clinique et métabolisme (SFNEP)* – former (2006). Registration: France. **Aims** Contribute to development of clinical and fundamental research in nutrition; disseminate, promote and teach diagnosis and management of malnutrition. **Structure** Administrative Council; Scientific Council. Committees (3). **Languages** French. **Staff** 1.00 FTE, paid. **Finance** Members' dues. Budget (annual): about euro 200,000. **Activities** Research/documentation; training/education; events/meetings. **Events** *Journées Francophones de Nutrition / Annual Conference* Brussels (Belgium) 2014, *Journées Francophones de Nutrition* Bordeaux (France) 2013, *Annual Conference* Lyon (France) 2012, *Annual Conference* Reims (France) 2011, *Annual Conference* Lille (France) 2010. **Publications** *Nutrition Clinique et Métabolisme (NCM)* (6 a year) – journal. Text books; educational tools. **Members** Full (about 470) in 8 countries. Membership countries not specified. **IGO Relations** with national organizations. [2021/XD8621/**D**]

♦ Société francophone de nutrition entérale et parentérale / see Société Francophone Nutrition Clinique et Métabolisme (#19471)
♦ Société francophone de philosophie de l'éducation (internationally oriented national body)

♦ Société francophone de primatologie (SFDP) 19472

French-speaking Primatological Society
Treas Fort Foch, 67207 Niederhausbergen, France. T. +33388567855. Fax +33388137879. E-mail: info@sfdp-primatologie.fr.
URL: http://sfdp-primatologie.fr/

History 25 May 1987, Paris (France), at Constituent Assembly. First General Assembly 17 Dec 1987, Paris. Registered in accordance with French law. **Aims** Further multidisciplinary research in primatology; unite French-speaking scientists interested in breeding, conservation and study of primates; confront ethical issues for protection of endangered species used in exhibitions and laboratories. **Structure** General Assembly (annual); Council (meets twice a year); Bureau. **Languages** English, French. **Staff** Voluntary. **Finance** Members' dues. **Activities** Events/meetings; financial and/or material support. **Events** *Colloque* Le Guerno (France) 2019, *Colloque* Paris (France) 2018, *Colloque* Strasbourg (France) 2017, *Colloque* Rennes (France) 2016, *Quand les primates communiquent* Strasbourg (France) 2015. **Publications** *Folia Primatologica* (annual) – abstracts of colloquia; *Revue de Primatologie* – journal.
Members Individuals in 14 countries:
Barbados, Belgium, Brazil, Canada, Congo DR, France, Germany, Italy, Saudi Arabia, Senegal, Spain, Switzerland, UK, USA.
NGO Relations An affiliate of: *International Primatological Society (IPS, #14642).* [2021/XD1700/v/**D**]

♦ Société francophone des urgences médicale / see Société francophone de médecine d'urgence
♦ Société de gastroentérologie pédiatrique pour l'Asie et le Pacifique (inactive)
♦ Société de géologie appliquée aux gîtes minéraux / see Society for Geology Applied to Mineral Deposits (#19565)
♦ Société Géologique de l'Afrique (#10135)
♦ Société germanophone de la chirurgie de la main (#05048)
♦ Société Gutenberg – Association internationale pour l'histoire et le développement contemporain de l'imprimerie et du livre / see International Gutenberg Society (#13766)
♦ Société pour l'habitat et le logement territorial en Afrique (#04408)
♦ Société d'hématologie de l'Asie et du Pacifique (inactive)

- ♦ Société héraldique du nord (#19442)
- ♦ Société d'histoire de l'alchimie et de la chimie (#19569)
- ♦ Société ibéroaméricaine de biologie cellulaire (inactive)
- ♦ Société ibéroaméricaine de endoscopie et imagénologie gynécologique (#11030)
- ♦ Société ibéroaméricaine de philosophie (no recent information)
- ♦ Société ibéroaméricaine de recherches numismatiques (#19367)
- ♦ Société des indexeurs (#19575)
- ♦ Société de l'information maritime (internationally oriented national body)
- ♦ Société des ingénieurs de l'automobile internationale / see SAE International
- ♦ Société interaméricaine d'administration de l'éducation (inactive)
- ♦ Société interaméricaine d'anthropologie et de géographie (inactive)
- ♦ Société interaméricaine de cardiologie (#11448)
- ♦ Société interaméricaine de chimiothérapie (no recent information)
- ♦ Société interaméricaine de développement du financement coopératif (inactive)
- ♦ Société interaméricaine d'investissement (#11438)
- ♦ Société interaméricaine de philosophie (#19385)
- ♦ Société interaméricaine de psychologie (#11450)
- ♦ Société interaméricaine d'urbanisme (inactive)

♦ Société interdisciplinaire francophone d'urodynamique et de pelvi-périnéologie (SIFUD-PP) 19473

Secretariat 10 rue du Docteur Baillat, 66100 Perpignan, France. E-mail: info@sifud-pp.org.
URL: http://www.sifud-pp.org/

History 30 Apr 1977, Lyon (France). Statutes adopted during 1st Extraordinary General Assembly, 13 Oct 1977, Paris (France). Former names and other names: *Société internationale francophone d'uro-dynamique (SIFUD)* – former (1977). **Aims** Study the methods of diagnosis and treatment of excremental disfunctions of the urinary tract. **Structure** Managing Board; Coordinating Committees. **Languages** French. **Staff** Voluntary. **Finance** Members' dues. **Activities** Organizes CONAMES Congress (annual); symposia; satellite conferences. **Events** *Annual Congress* Saint-Malo (France) 2022, *Annual Congress* Perpignan (France) 2021, *Annual Congress* La Rochelle (France) 2019, *Congrès Annuel* Arcachon (France) 2014, *Congrès Annuel* Nice (France) 2013. **Publications** *Pelvi Périnéologie* – official magazine. CD-Roms.
Members Urologists, gynaecologists, geriatricians, paediatricians, general practitioners, surgeons, neurologists and paramedics (nurses, physiotherapists, midwives) in 19 countries:
Algeria, Belgium, Benin, Brazil, Burundi, Canada, France, Gabon, Germany, Italy, Madagascar, Monaco, Morocco, Netherlands, Portugal, Romania, Spain, Switzerland, Tunisia. [2022/XD8942/v/**D**]

- ♦ Société intergouvernementale de télévision et radio (no recent information)
- ♦ Société internationale des acarologues de langue française (inactive)
- ♦ Société internationale pour l'action réciproque entre la mécanique et les mathématiques (#15208)
- ♦ Société internationale d'acupuncture, (inactive)
- ♦ Société internationale des administrateurs des arts et du spectacle / see International Society for the Performing Arts Foundation (#15350)
- ♦ Société internationale pour les aérosols en médecine (#14907)
- ♦ Société internationale africaine pour la réalisation de l'Encyclopédie politique, économique, sociale et culturelle de l'Afrique contemporaine (no recent information)
- ♦ Société internationale de l'alto / see International Viola Society (#15855)
- ♦ Société internationale pour l'amélioration des cuirs et des peaux bruts (inactive)
- ♦ Société internationale des amis de Montaigne (internationally oriented national body)
- ♦ Société internationale d'amitié et de bonne volonté (#15132)
- ♦ Société internationale des analystes d'image automatique (inactive)
- ♦ Société internationale d'annotation (#14959)
- ♦ Société internationale d'anthroscopie, de la chirurgie du genou et de la médecine orthopédique sportive (#14941)
- ♦ Société internationale des apocryphes (inactive)
- ♦ Société internationale arthurienne (#11671)
- ♦ Société internationale des artistes chrétiens (#15009)
- ♦ Société internationale des arts graphiques (inactive)
- ♦ Société internationale d'assistance aux enfants estropiés / see RI Global (#18948)
- ♦ Société internationale d'athérosclérose (#12288)
- ♦ Société internationale d'audiologie (#14948)

♦ Société internationale de bibliographie classique (SIBC) 19474

International Society of Classical Bibliography

Gen Sec Univ Paris-Sorbonne (Paris IV), UFR de Latin, 1 rue Victor Cousin, 75230 Paris CEDEX 05, France.
Registered Seat 12 allée Georges Brassens, 92220 Châtenay-Malabry, France.
URL: http://www.bibliographie-classique.org/

History 1923, Paris (France), as *Society of Classical Bibliography – Société de bibliographie classique*. Reconstructed under present name in 1948. Current Statutes adopted 24 May 2014. **Aims** Alert the academic world to publications on *ancient Greece* and *Rome* in the widest sense. **Structure** General Assembly (annual); Executive Committee. **Languages** English, French, German, Italian, Spanish. **Staff** Voluntary. **Finance** Subsidies; sales of publications. **Activities** Publishing activities; knowledge management/information dissemination; events/meetings. **Events** *Meeting* Bordeaux (France) 2014, *Meeting* Berlin (Germany) 2009, *Meeting* Ouro Preto (Brazil) 2004, *Meeting* Kavala (Greece) 1999, *Meeting* Québec, QC (Canada) 1994. **Publications** *L'Année philologique* (annual). Retrospective bibliographies.
Members Individuals in 12 countries:
Brazil, Denmark, Finland, France, Germany, Greece, Italy, Japan, Spain, Switzerland, UK, USA.
NGO Relations Member of: *Fédération internationale des associations d'études classiques (FIEC, #09607).* [2018.09.07/XD2477/v/**D**]

♦ Société internationale des bibliothèques et des musées des arts du spectacle (SIBMAS) 19475

International Association of Libraries and Museums of the Performing Arts

Main Office c/o Bibliothèque Nationale, Département des arts du spectacle, 58 rue de Richelieu, 75002 Paris, France. E-mail: info@sibmas.org.
URL: https://www.sibmas.org/

History Sep 1954, Zagreb (Croatia). Founded as the International Section for Performing Arts Libraries and Museums of *International Federation of Library Associations and Institutions (IFLA, #13470).* Became autonomous and present name adopted during 10th International Congress of Performing Arts Libraries and Museums, Oct 1972, Brussels (Belgium). **Aims** Promote practical and theoretical research in documentation on the performing arts; develop cooperation among libraries, museums, documentation centres and public and private organizations specializing in documentation concerning *theatre*, dance, opera, circus, cinema, marionettes, mime, festival, son et lumière, radio and television. **Structure** Congress (every 2 years); Committee; Working Committees; International Directory of Performing Arts Collections. **Languages** English, French. **Staff** Voluntary. **Finance** Sources: members' dues. **Activities** Events/meetings. **Events** *Conference* Hong Kong (Hong Kong) 2024, *Conference* Warsaw (Poland) 2022, *Conference* Warsaw (Poland) 2020, *Conference* Paris (France) 2018, *Conference* Copenhagen (Denmark) 2016. **Publications** *International Bibliography of Theatre (IBT)* (annual) – jointly with Theatre Research Data Center, New York NY. *International Directory of Performing Arts Collections* (1996); *Performing Arts Libraries and Museums of the World* (3rd ed 1992) in English, French; *World Encyclopedia of Contemporary Theatre* (1992) – together with UNESCO, IFTR and AICT. Congress proceedings.
Members National Centres; Full and Associate (individuals). Members in 38 countries:
Australia, Austria, Belgium, Canada, Congo DR, Czechia, Denmark, Estonia, Finland, France, Germany, Ghana, Greece, Hungary, India, Ireland, Israel, Italy, Korea Rep, Malta, Netherlands, Nigeria, Norway, Poland, Portugal, Romania, Russia, Serbia, Slovakia, Slovenia, South Africa, Spain, Sweden, Switzerland, Türkiye, UK, Ukraine, USA.
IGO Relations *UNESCO (#20322).* **NGO Relations** Member of (3): *International Council of Museums (ICOM, #13051)* (as Affiliated member of); *International Federation for Theatre Research (IFTR, #13570)* (as Associate member); *International Theatre Institute (ITI, #15683)* (as Associate member). [2022.06.28/XC2451/**C**]

- ♦ Société internationale pour les billets de banque (#12316)
- ♦ Société Internationale de Bioacoustique (#12341)
- ♦ Société internationale de bioclimatologie et de biométéorologie / see International Society of Biometeorology (#14969)
- ♦ Société internationale de la bioéthique (#14961)
- ♦ Société internationale de biologie cellulaire (inactive)
- ♦ Société internationale de biologie clinique / see World Association of Societies of Pathology and Laboratory Medicine (#21191)
- ♦ Société internationale de biologie mathématique (inactive)
- ♦ Société internationale des biologistes du développement (#15052)
- ♦ Société internationale de biométéorologie (#14969)
- ♦ Société internationale de biométrie (#12354)
- ♦ Société internationale de biorhéologie (#14972)
- ♦ Société internationale de biospéologie (#14975)
- ♦ Société Internationale de Brecht / see International Brecht Society (#12397)
- ♦ Société internationale de broncho-oesophagologie (#12401)
- ♦ Société internationale des brûlures (#14986)
- ♦ Société internationale des cadres en transfert des technologies (#16461)
- ♦ Société internationale du camelia (#12425)
- ♦ Société internationale de cardiologie non-invasive (#15308)
- ♦ Société internationale de la carte à jouer (#14605)
- ♦ Société internationale de la céphalée (inactive)
- ♦ Société internationale pour le check-up médical interdisciplinaire (inactive)
- ♦ Société internationale du chien de berger (#14845)
- ♦ Société internationale de chimiothérapie / see International Society of Antimicrobial Chemotherapy (#14925)
- ♦ Société internationale de chimiothérapie et d'immunothérapie (inactive)
- ♦ Société internationale de chirurgie (#15496)
- ♦ Société internationale de chirurgie dermatologique (#15047)
- ♦ Société internationale de chirurgie esthétique plastique (#14908)
- ♦ Société internationale de chirurgie orthopédique / see International Society of Orthopaedic Surgery and Traumatology (#15335)
- ♦ Société Internationale de Chirurgie Orthopédique de la Méditerranée (unconfirmed)
- ♦ Société internationale de chirurgie orthopédique et de traumatologie (#15335)
- ♦ Société internationale de chirurgie réfractive / see International Society of Refractive Surgery of the American Academy of Ophthalmology (#15416)
- ♦ Société internationale de chronobiologie (#15010)
- ♦ Société internationale de collectionneurs de tirelires (inactive)
- ♦ Société internationale pour les computers mini et micro (inactive)
- ♦ Société Internationale pour la Conservation Fongique (#15134)
- ♦ Société internationale de construction par méthode sandwich agglutinante (inactive)
- ♦ Société internationale contre les corridas (inactive)
- ♦ Société internationale des cornistes (#13810)
- ♦ Société internationale de criminologie (#15038)
- ♦ Société internationale de cryochirurgie (#15041)
- ♦ Société internationale de cryptozoologie (inactive)
- ♦ Société internationale pour les cultures sans sol (inactive)
- ♦ Société internationale de cytologie expérimentale (inactive)
- ♦ Société internationale de défense sociale / see International Society of Social Defence and Humane Criminal Policy (#15447)
- ♦ Société internationale de défense sociale pour une politique criminelle humaniste (#15447)
- ♦ Société internationale de dermatologie (#15048)
- ♦ Société internationale de dermatopathologie (#15049)
- ♦ Société internationale pour le développement (#19581)
- ♦ Société internationale du développement des communautés (inactive)
- ♦ Société internationale pour le développement de l'enseignement commercial (inactive)
- ♦ Société internationale pour le développement des organisations (inactive)
- ♦ Société internationale pour le développement du transport combiné et du transport sous température dirigée (inactive)

♦ Société Internationale de Diachronie du Français (SIDF) 19476

Sec address not obtained.
URL: https://diachronie.org/

History 2010, France. **Aims** Establish links between researchers all over the world interested in the diachrony of French; create international networks; organize study days on methodological and theoretical issues; disseminate information on research, events, corpora concerning the diachrony of French. **Structure** General Assembly; Bureau. **Finance** Sources: members' dues. **Activities** Awards/prizes/competitions; events/meetings; knowledge management/information dissemination; networking/liaising. **Events** *Colloque* Berlin (Germany) 2021, *Colloque* Neuchâtel (Switzerland) 2018. [2020.06.23/XM8437/**D**]

♦ Société Internationale de Dialectologie et Géolinguistique (SIDG) . . 19477

International Society for Dialectology and Geolinguistics – Internationale Gesellschaft für Dialektologie und Geolinguistik

Pres Filologia Catalana – Lingüística, Univ de Barcelona, Gran Via Corts Catalanes 585, 08007 Barcelona, Spain. E-mail: president@geo-linguistics.org – secretary@geo-linguistics.org.
URL: http://www.geo-linguistics.org/

History Founded 1989. **Aims** Promote dialectology and geolinguistics at the international level; increase collaboration and the exchange of knowledge in the field; preserve, in whatever form, data, dialects, jargons and slangs, terminologies of traditional trades and any other linguistic forms associated with disappearing ways of life. **Structure** Assembly (every 3 years); Executive Committee; Committees (2). **Languages** English, French, German. **Finance** Members' dues (annual): Ordinary and Institutional – euro 50; Student – euro 25. **Activities** Events/meetings; knowledge management/information dissemination. **Events** *Congress* Vilnius (Lithuania) 2018, *Congress* Famagusta (Cyprus) 2015, *Congress* Vienna (Austria) 2012, *Congress* Maribor (Slovenia) 2009, *Congress* Braga (Portugal) 2006. **Publications** *Dialectologia et Geolinguistica* (annual) – journal; *SIDGBulletin.*
Members Organizations in 9 countries:
Austria, Canada, Denmark, Estonia, Finland, Germany, Lithuania, Spain, Sweden.
Individuals in 37 countries:
Albania, Australia, Austria, Belarus, Belgium, Brazil, Canada, Croatia, Cyprus, Czechia, Denmark, Estonia, Finland, France, Germany, Hungary, Ireland, Italy, Japan, Korea Rep, Latvia, Lithuania, Netherlands, Nigeria, Norway, Poland, Portugal, Romania, Russia, Serbia, Slovenia, Spain, Sweden, Switzerland, UK, USA, Venezuela.
NGO Relations *Comité international permanent des linguistes (CIPL, #04182).* [2017/XD7786/**D**]

- ♦ Société internationale de dialectologie romane (inactive)
- ♦ Société internationale pour la didactique de l'histoire (#15167)
- ♦ Société internationale de différenciation (#15059)
- ♦ Société internationale de diffusion (inactive)
- ♦ Société Internationale des Docteurs en Pharmacie d'Expression Française (internationally oriented national body)
- ♦ Société internationale pour le droit d'auteur (no recent information)

♦ Société internationale de droit canonique et de législations religieuses comparées 19478

Secretariat 21 rue d'Assas, 75006 Paris, France. T. +33144345282. E-mail: droit.canonique@icp.fr.
URL: http://www.droitcanonique.fr/

History 1956, Paris (France). Registered in accordance with French law. **Aims** Unite persons interested in study and practice of canon law and the different religious legislations; provide members with practical means to carry out their research and activities. **Structure** Secretariat in Paris (France). **Languages** French. **Staff** Voluntary. **Finance** Sources: members' dues. **Activities** Promotes: meetings; conferences; exchange of information. **Events** *Biennial Colloquium* 2000, *Biennial colloquium* Paris (France) 1998. **Publications** *L'année canonique* (annual).
Members Full (individuals); Associate (university establishments, libraries and congregations). Members in 33 countries:
Angola, Argentina, Australia, Belgium, Brazil, Burkina Faso, Cameroon, Canada, Colombia, Congo Brazzaville, Congo DR, Côte d'Ivoire, Dominican Rep, Germany, Haiti, Holy See, Hungary, Ireland, Italy, Lebanon, Luxembourg, Mali, Montenegro, Poland, Portugal, Rwanda, Serbia, Spain, Switzerland, Türkiye, Uganda, UK, USA. [2018.12.19/XD4126/**C**]

♦ Société internationale de droit militaire et de droit de la guerre (#15270)
♦ Société internationale pour les droits de l'homme (#15183)
♦ Société internationale de droit social (inactive)
♦ Société internationale de Droit du Travail et de la Sécurité Sociale (#15226)
♦ Société internationale pour l'écologie de l'enfant (inactive)
♦ Société internationale d'écologie tropicale (#15521)
♦ Société internationale d'écotoxicologie et de protection de l'environnement (#15073)
♦ Société internationale des écrivains de l'aviation (inactive)
♦ Société Internationale pour l'Education à travers l'Art (#15074)
♦ Société internationale pour l'éducation artistique / see International Society for Education through Art (#15074)
♦ Société internationale d'éducation continue en dentisterie (inactive)
♦ Société internationale pour l'éducation musicale (#15287)
♦ Société internationale des électriciens (inactive)
♦ Société internationale d'électromyographie (inactive)
♦ Société internationale d'électrophysiologie clinique de la vue (#15016)
♦ Société internationale d'électrorétinographie clinique / see International Society for Clinical Electrophysiology of Vision (#15016)
♦ Société internationale d'électro-stimulation (inactive)
♦ Société internationale d'endocrinologie / see International Society of Endocrinology (#15086)
♦ Société internationale d'endoscopie urologique (inactive)
♦ Société internationale d'énergie solaire (#15564)
♦ Société internationale des enseignants, chercheurs et créateurs en danse à l'université (inactive)

♦ Société internationale pour l'enseignement commercial (SIEC) 19479

International Society for Business Education – Sociedad Internacional para la Enseñanza Comercial – Internationale Gesellschaft für Kaufmännisches Bildungswesen – Società Internazionale per lo Sviluppo de la Cultura Commerciale
Gen Sec Campus Box 5500, Illinois State Univ – College of Business, Peoria IL 61790, USA.
URL: http://www.siec-isbe.org/
History 1901, Zurich (Switzerland). Reorganized: 25 Sep 1926, Zurich; 1948. Former names and other names: *Internationale Gesellschaft für Wirtschaftliche Bildung* – alias. **Aims** Organize international courses and congresses on *economic development* and business education; stimulate discussion of general questions related to the field. **Structure** Assembly of Delegates; Presidency; Permanent Office; Regional Vice Presidents; Professional Development Committee. **Languages** English. **Staff** 1.00 FTE, paid. **Finance** Sources: members' dues. **Activities** Events/meetings. **Events** *Conference* Vienna (Austria) 2023, *Conference* Vienna (Austria) 2022, *Conference* Trieste (Italy) 2021, *Annual Conference* Trieste (Italy) 2020, *Annual Conference* Argostolion (Greece) 2019. **Publications** *International Journal for Business Education (IJBE)*.
Members National groups in 15 countries and territories:
Australia, Austria, Bahamas, Denmark, Faeroe Is, Finland, Germany, Iceland, Korea Rep, Malta, Poland, Puerto Rico, Sweden, Switzerland, USA.
Also individual members. Membership countries not specified. [2023.02.15/XC2475/**C**]

♦ Société internationale pour l'épidémiologie et l'économie vétérinaires (#15540)
♦ Société internationale Erard (internationally oriented national body)
♦ Société internationale d'ergophtalmologie (no recent information)
♦ Société internationale Ernst Cassirer (#13295)
♦ Société internationale espérantiste d'architectes et urbanistes (inactive)
♦ Société internationale d'éthique, d'économie et de gestion (#14988)

♦ Société internationale d'ethnographie (SIE) 19480

Pres 7 Le Feuil, 35580 Saint-Senoux, France.
URL: http://riethno.org/
History 1999, Lecce (Italy), as *Européenne d'Ethnographie de l'Education (SEEE)*. Present title adopted 2011, when restructured into current form. **Aims** Encourage development of ethnography research, in a critical perspective, and its use in advancement of education; promote cooperation and exchange between those engaged in relevant research; promote international teams of searches. **Structure** General Assembly; Board. **Languages** Arabic, English, French, Italian, Portuguese, Spanish. **Finance** Sources: grants; members' dues; sale of publications. **Activities** Events/meetings; research/documentation. **Events** *Annual International Meeting* Lecce (Italy) 2015. **Publications** *Revue Internationale d'Ethnographie*.
Members Full in 11 countries and territories:
Argentina, Australia, Belgium, France, Italy, Lebanon, Macau, Mexico, Morocco, Portugal, Spain. [2016.06.18/XM4366/**C**]

♦ Société internationale d'ethnologie et de folklore (SIEF) 19481

International Society for Ethnology and Folklore – Internationale Gesellschaft für Ethnologie und Volkskunde
Exec Vice-Pres c/o Meertens Inst, PO Box 10855, 1001 EW Amsterdam, Netherlands. T. +31204628500. E-mail: sief@meertens.knaw.nl.
URL: http://www.siefhome.org/
History 1928, Prague (Czechia). Founded at International Congress, held under the auspices of *International Institute of Intellectual Cooperation (IICI, inactive)*. New statutes and present name adopted 8 Sep 1964, Athens (Greece). Latest statutes adopted 28 Mar 2017, Göttingen (Germany). Former names and other names: *International Commission on Folk Arts and Folklore* – former (1928 to 1964); *Commission internationale des arts et traditions populaires (CIAP)* – former (1928 to 1964). **Aims** Facilitate cooperation among scholars working within European Ethnology, Anthropology, Folklore Studies and adjoining fields; develop scholarly work in the field; promote publication in the field; stimulate cooperation among scholars and scientific organizations; contribute to advancement of knowledge. **Structure** General Assembly (at International Congress); Executive Board; Sections; Scholarly Commissions; Working Groups (14); Secretariat. **Languages** English, French, German. **Finance** Sources: members' dues. **Activities** Events/meetings. **Events** *International Ethnological Food Research Conference* Antwerp (Belgium) 2022, *Congress* Helsinki (Finland) 2021, *International Ethnological Food Research Conference* Antwerp (Belgium) 2020, *Congress* Santiago de Compostela (Spain) 2019, *Working Group on the Ritual Work Conference* Bucharest (Romania) 2018. **Publications** *Cultural Analysis: An Interdisciplinary Forum on Folklore and Popular Culture* (2 a year) – open access journal; *Ethnologia Europaea* (2 a year) – open access journal; *SIEF Newsletter* (2 a year). **Members** Individual scholars and students. Membership countries not specified. **NGO Relations** Member of (1): *World Council of Anthropological Associations (WCAA, #21317)*. [2021.06.08/XD1082/**D**]

♦ Société internationale d'ethnopsychologie normale et pathologique (inactive)
♦ Société internationale pour l'étude des algues nuisibles (#15473)
♦ Société internationale pour l'étude de l'Altra Medicina (inactive)
♦ Société internationale d'étude de la colonne vertébrale lombaire (#15479)
♦ Société internationale pour l'étude comparée des civilisations (internationally oriented national body)
♦ Société internationale pour l'étude du développement du comportement (#15465)
♦ Société internationale d'étude du dix-huitième siècle (#15076)
♦ Société internationale pour l'étude des écosystèmes de la mangrove (#15245)

♦ Société Internationale pour l'Etude des Femmes de l'Ancien Régime (SIEFAR) 19482

Registered Office 4 rue de Chevreuse, 75006 Paris, France. E-mail: contact@siefar.org.
URL: http://www.siefar.org/
History 10 Oct 2000, Paris (France). Registered in accordance with French law. **Structure** Board of Directors. **Languages** English, French. [2017.10.25/XJ9532/**E**]

♦ Société internationale pour l'étude de l'hypertension de la grossesse (#15475)
♦ Société internationale pour l'étude des idées européennes (#15470)
♦ Société internationale d'étude des interactions (inactive)
♦ Société internationale pour l'étude des maladies du côlon et du rectum (inactive)
♦ Société internationale pour l'étude des maladies infectieuses et parasitaires (inactive)
♦ Société internationale d'étude des maladies de l'oesophage (#15064)
♦ Société internationale pour l'étude des maladies du trophoblaste (#15489)
♦ Société internationale pour l'étude des maladies vulvaires / see International Society for the Study of Vulvovaginal Disease (#15491)
♦ Société internationale pour l'étude de l'origine de la vie (#15481)

♦ Société internationale pour l'étude de la philosophie médiévale (SIEPM) 19483

International Society for the Study of Medieval Philosophy
SG Inst of Philosophy, Kardinaal Mercierplein 2 – box 3200, 3000 Leuven, Belgium. E-mail: siepm@kuleuven.be.
URL: https://hiw.kuleuven.be/siepm/
History 2 Sep 1958, Leuven (Belgium). Latest statutes adopted 2002. Registered in accordance with Belgian law. **Aims** Promote the study of medieval thought. **Structure** General Assembly; (every 5 years); Board; Secretariat. Commissions (6): Electronic Tools; Critical Editions; Latin Philosophy; Islamic Philosophy; Jewish Philosophy; Byzantine Philosophy. **Languages** English, French. **Finance** Sources: members' dues. **Activities** Research/documentation. **Events** *Quinquennial Congress* Paris (France) 2022, *Annual Colloquium* Porto (Portugal) 2021, *Annual Colloquium* Porto (Portugal) 2020, *Annual Colloquium* Varna (Bulgaria) 2019, *Annual Colloquium* Leuven (Belgium) 2018. **Publications** *Bulletin de philosophie médiévale* (annual). *Rencontres de Philosophie Médiévales*.
Members Individuals in 39 countries:
Argentina, Austria, Belgium, Brazil, Bulgaria, Canada, Chile, Colombia, Cyprus, Czechia, Denmark, Finland, France, Georgia, Germany, Greece, Hungary, Iran Islamic Rep, Ireland, Israel, Italy, Japan, Lebanon, Morocco, Netherlands, New Zealand, Peru, Poland, Portugal, Russia, South Africa, Spain, Sweden, Switzerland, Türkiye, UK, Ukraine, USA, Venezuela.
NGO Relations Member society of: *International Federation of Philosophical Societies (FISP, #13507)*. [2019.12.12/XC2521/v/**C**]

♦ Société internationale pour l'étude des primates / see International Primatological Society (#14642)
♦ Société internationale pour l'étude des questions d'assistance (inactive)
♦ Société internationale d'études pour l'exploration des régions arctiques par dirigeable (inactive)
♦ Société internationale d'études gémellaires (#15526)

♦ Société Internationale d'Études Néroniennes (SIEN) 19484

International Society for Neronian Studies – Internationale Gesellschaft für Neronischen Studien – Società Internazionale di Studi Neroniani
Sec Maître de conférences en histoire ancienne, Univ Jean Monnet – Fac SHS, 35 rue du 11 novembre, 42023 Saint-Étienne CEDEXS 2, France.
Sec Univ Michel de Montaigne, Bordeaux III, Domaine Universitarire, 33607 Pessac CEDEX, France.
URL: http://www.sien-neron.fr/
History 1976, Clermont-Ferrand (France). **Aims** Encourage and promote research concerning the Neronian age (from Claudius to Titus) and the Roman Empire in the first century AD; act as a forum for exchanges and debates. **Structure** Governing Council; Officers. **Events** *Neronia Conference* Come (Italy) 2012, *Neronia Conference* Paris (France) 2008, *Neronia Conference* Athens (Greece) 2004, *Neronia Conference* Rome (Italy) 1999, *Neronia Conference* Clermont-Ferrand (France) 1994. **Publications** *Neronia electronica* – review.
Members Individuals in 19 countries:
Belgium, Canada, Cyprus, Estonia, France, Germany, Greece, Hungary, Italy, Netherlands, Poland, Portugal, Romania, South Africa, Spain, Switzerland, Tunisia, UK, USA. [2015/XN1908/**D**]

♦ Société internationale d'études orientales (no recent information)
♦ Société internationale pour l'étude du squelette (#14867)
♦ Société internationale d'études socialistes (inactive)

♦ Société internationale d'études yourcenariennes (SIEY) 19485

Pres 2 rue Abbé Girard, 63000 Clermont-Ferrand, France. T. +33473908027.
URL: https://www.yourcenariana.org/
History 1987, Tours (France). Registration: France. **Aims** Gather people interested in the work of *Marguerite Yourcenar*. **Structure** General Assembly; Bureau; Administrative Council. **Languages** French. **Staff** 12.00 FTE, voluntary. **Finance** Sources: members' dues. **Activities** Events/meetings; research/documentation. **Events** *Marguerite Yourcenar et le souci du monde* Torun (Poland) 2022, *Marguerite Yourcenar et les Passions de l'Ame* Naples (Italy) 2021, *Marguerite Yourcenar et les Passions de l'Ame* Naples (Italy) 2020, *Marguerite Yourcenar et les Amériques* Bogota (Colombia) 2019, *Marguerite Yourcenar et le monde des lettres* Clermont-Ferrand (France) 2017. **Publications** *Bulletin de la SIEY*. Books on the works of Marguerite Yourcenar; proceedings.
Members Individuals in 31 countries:
Argentina, Australia, Austria, Belgium, Brazil, Canada, China, Colombia, Cyprus, Egypt, France, Germany, Greece, Ireland, Italy, Japan, Korea Rep, Luxembourg, Netherlands, North Macedonia, Poland, Portugal, Romania, South Africa, Spain, Sweden, Switzerland, Thailand, Tunisia, UK, USA. [2022.05.04/XE3636/v/**E**]

♦ Société internationale pour l'étude du théâtre médiéval (#15480)
♦ Société internationale d'étude des tourbes /du moor/ (inactive)
♦ Société internationale pour l'évaluation de la technologie (inactive)
♦ Société internationale d'évaluation de la technologie en soins de santé (inactive)
♦ Société internationale pour l'exploration des régions arctiques par aéroned (inactive)
♦ Société internationale de facteurs d'orgues (#15329)
♦ Société Internationale pour la Fécondation In Vitro (#15545)

♦ Société internationale Fernand De Visscher pour l'histoire des droits de l'antiquité 19486

Contact Univ de Liège, Place des Orateurs 1, 4000 Liège, Belgium.
History Founded by Fernand de Visscher (14 Oct 1885 – 15 Dec 1964). Met for the first time during the academic year 1941-1942, as *Société d'histoire des droits de l'antiquité (SHDA)* as a meeting of Belgian specialists only. First international meeting organized Dec 1945. Former names and other names: *Société internationale pour l'histoire des droits de l'antiquité (SIHDA)* – former. **Aims** Contribute to research into legal systems of *antiquity*, in particular Roman law. **Structure** Informal group without finance or membership. **Languages** English, French, German, Italian, Spanish. **Staff** None paid. **Finance** Sources: contributions of participants to annual congress; subsidies. **Activities** Events/meetings. **Events** *Session* Helsinki (Finland) 2023, *Session* Brussels (Belgium) / Ghent (Belgium) 2022, *Session* Santiago (Chile) 2022, *Session* Santiago (Chile) 2021, *Session* Edinburgh (UK) 2019. **Publications** *Revue internationale des droits de l'antiquité (RIDA)* (annual). Articles.
Members No formal membership. Individual legal historians invited to Annual Congress in 50 countries:
Argentina, Austria, Belgium, Bosnia-Herzegovina, Brazil, Bulgaria, Canada, Chile, China, Colombia, Croatia, Czechia, Denmark, Ecuador, Egypt, Estonia, Finland, France, Germany, Greece, Holy See, Hungary, Ireland, Israel, Italy, Japan, Korea Rep, Lithuania, Mexico, Montenegro, Netherlands, North Macedonia, Peru, Poland, Portugal, Romania, Russia, Serbia, Slovakia, South Africa, Spain, Sweden, Switzerland, Türkiye, UK, USA. [2017.10.25/XF3753/v/**F**]

♦ Société internationale des filarioses (inactive)
♦ Société internationale de fluorophotométrie oculaire (no recent information)
♦ Société internationale des forestiers tropicaux (#15522)

♦ Société internationale francophone de chirurgie pelvienne (inactive)

♦ Société internationale francophone d'éducation médicale (SIFEM) . 19487

SG CFR-PS, 4 rue Kirschleger, 67085 Strasbourg CEDEX, France. E-mail: pelaccia@unistra.fr – info.sifem@gmail.com.
URL: http://www.sifem.net/

History 24 Apr 2004. Replaces *Association francophone pour le développement de l'éducation médicale (AFDEM, inactive)*. **Activities** Working Groups (3): Communication; Research; Health-Society. **Events** *Congrès international francophone en pédagogie en science de la santé* Strasbourg (France) 2021, *Congrès* Marseille (France) 2017, *Congrès* Brussels (Belgium) 2015, *Congrès* Lyon (France) 2012, *Compétences et finalités de l'éducation des professionnels de la santé. Comment faire évoluer les institutions, les programmes et les pratiques pédagogiques* Grenoble (France) 2009. **Publications** *Pédagogie Médicale: Revue Internationale Francophone d'Education Médicale.* **Members** Individuals (267) in 24 countries. Membership countries not specified. [2020/XJ3017/D]

♦ Société internationale francophone d'ORL et de chirurgie cervico-faciale (SIFORL) 19488

Main Office 26 rue Lalo, 75116 Paris, France. E-mail: contact@siforl.org.
URL: http://siforl.org/

History 1988. Previously also referred to as: *Société ORL des pays francophones*; *Société d'oto-rhino-laryngologie et de chirurgie cervico-faciale des pays francophones (SOCFI)*; *Société internationale d'otorhinolaryngologie et de chirurgie cervico-faciale des pays francophones.* **Aims** Promote the development of French expression and literature in *otorhinolaryngologic medicine* and *surgery* of the *head* and *neck*; facilitate exchanges of students and teachers in these fields between countries of French expression. **Structure** Officers: President; Treasurer; Vice-Presidents. **Events** *Congress* Réunion 2021, *Congress* Réunion 2020, *Congress* Algiers (Algeria) 2018, *Congrès* Lille (France) 2016, *Congrès* Montréal, QC (Canada) 2014. **Members** Individuals. Membership countries not specified. [2020/XE1342/v/E]

♦ Société internationale francophone d'uro-dynamique / see Société interdisciplinaire francophone d'urodynamique et de pelvi-périnéologie (#19473)
♦ Société internationale des gazons (#15745)
♦ Société internationale de génétique animale (#14921)
♦ Société internationale du genou (inactive)
♦ Société internationale Gottfried-Wilhelm-Leibniz (#10683)
♦ Société internationale Gustav Mahler (#13765)
♦ Société internationale de Gutenberg (#13766)
♦ Société internationale Hegel-Marx pour la pensée dialectique (no recent information)
♦ Société internationale Heinrich Schütz (#13248)
♦ Société internationale d'hématologie (#15159)
♦ Société internationale de l'hibernation (inactive)
♦ Société internationale pour l'histoire des droits de l'antiquité / see Société internationale Fernand De Visscher pour l'histoire des droits de l'antiquité (#19486)
♦ Société internationale d'histoire de l'éducation physique et du sport (#15175)

♦ Société internationale pour l'histoire du français langue étrangère ou seconde (SIHFLES) 19489

SG Univ de Tours, 3 rue des Tanneurs, 37041 Tours CEDEX 1, France. E-mail: dprovata@frl.uoa.gr.
Office FIPF, 9 rue Jean de Beauvais, 75005 Paris, France.
URL: :

History Founded 5 Dec 1987, Paris (France), at Constituent Assembly. Registered in accordance with French law. **Aims** Promote the history of French as a foreign or second language both within and outside of France, and linguistic education in general. **Structure** General Assembly (annual); Council; Bureau. **Languages** French. **Staff** 8.00 FTE, voluntary. **Finance** Members' dues. Other sources: universities' punctual subsidies; sales of publications. **Activities** Events/meetings; training/education; research/documentation. **Events** *Colloque* Mons (Belgium) 2018, *Colloque* Athens (Greece) 2017, *Innovations pédagogiques dans l'enseignement des langues étrangères – perspective historique* Faro (Portugal) 2016, *The linguistic and cultural foreign policies of European countries* Leiden (Netherlands) 2015, *Colloque* Nottingham (UK) 2014. **Publications** *Documents pour l'histoire du français langue étrangère ou seconde* (2 a year) – online; *La lettre de la SIHFLES* (2 a year).
Members Honorary; Supporting; Active. Individuals in 29 countries:
Belgium, Bulgaria, Canada, Chile, China, Cyprus, Czechia, Finland, France, Germany, Greece, Iceland, Ireland, Israel, Italy, Japan, Malaysia, Malta, Netherlands, Norway, Poland, Portugal, Romania, Spain, Sweden, Switzerland, Türkiye, UK, USA.
NGO Relations *Association de didactique du français langue étrangère (ASDIFLE)*; *Association internationale de linguistique appliquée (AILA, #02713)*; *Fédération internationale des professeurs de français (FIPF, #09652)*; *International Centre for Educational Research, Sèvres (CIEP)*; national organizations. [2019/XC0065/v/E]

♦ Société internationale d'histoire des idées (inactive)
♦ Société Internationale d'Histoire de la Médecine (#15171)
♦ Société internationale d'histoire de la pharmacie (#15173)

♦ Société internationale d'histoire des sciences et de la philosophie arabes et islamiques (SIHSPAI) 19490

International Society for the History of Arabic and Islamic Science and Philosophy

Permanent Sec Univ de Paris Diderot/CNRS, UMR 7219, 5 rue Thomas Mann, Case 7093, 75205 Paris CEDEX 13, France.
Pres address not obtained.
URL: https://www.sihspai.org

History 25 Nov 1989, Paris (France). Founded during International Colloquium on the History of Arabic Science and Philosophy. Registration: France. **Aims** Increase cooperation and information exchange between specialists of Arabic and Islamic science and philosophy. **Structure** General Assembly (every 4 years); Council; Board. **Languages** Arabic, English, French. **Staff** 5.00 FTE, paid. **Finance** Sources: members' dues. **Activities** Events/meetings; research and development. **Events** *Meeting* Naples (Italy) 2019, *Meeting* Paris (France) 2014, *Meeting* London (UK) 2010, *Meeting* Florence (Italy) 2006, *Meeting* Namur (Belgium) / Brussels (Belgium) 2003. **Publications** *Arabic Sciences and Philosophy: A Historical Journal (CUP).* Conference proceedings.
Members Individuals in 24 countries:
Algeria, Australia, Belgium, Brazil, Canada, Egypt, France, Germany, Iran Islamic Rep, Israel, Italy, Japan, Lebanon, Mexico, Morocco, Pakistan, Portugal, Spain, Switzerland, Tunisia, Türkiye, UK, United Arab Emirates, USA. [2023.02.14/XM2708/D]

♦ Société internationale pour l'histoire de la science, de la technologie et de la médecine en asie orientale (#15168)
♦ Société internationale des hydroglisseurs (inactive)
♦ Société internationale d'hydrologie et de climatologie médicale (#15254)
♦ Société internationale d'hydrologie médicale / see International Society of Medical Hydrology and Climatology (#15254)
♦ Société internationale pour l'hygiene animale (#14922)
♦ Société internationale pour l'hygiène de la race (inactive)
♦ Société internationale d'hypertension (#15189)
♦ Société internationale d'hypnose (#15190)
♦ Société internationale d'hypnose clinique et expérimentale (inactive)
♦ Société internationale d'hypnose médicale et psychologique (#15257)
♦ Société internationale d'ichtyologie et d'hydrobiologie (inactive)
♦ Société internationale pour l'immunologie de la reproduction (#15193)
♦ Société internationale d'immunopharmacologie (inactive)
♦ Société internationale des ingénieurs forestiers tropicaux / see International Society of Tropical Foresters (#15522)
♦ Société internationale d'ingénieurs pédagogues / see International Society for Engineering Pedagogy (#15089)
♦ Société internationale des intellectuels (inactive)
♦ Société internationale de kératoplastie réfractive / see International Society of Refractive Surgery of the American Academy of Ophthalmology (#15416)
♦ Société internationale de kinésiologie électromyographique / see International Society of Electrophysiology and Kinesiology (#15081)
♦ Société internationale de kinésiologie électrophysiologique (#15081)
♦ Société internationale Kodaly (#13990)
♦ Société internationale du laser en ophtalmologie (inactive)

♦ Société internationale Leon Battista Alberti (SILBA) 19491

Pres c/o Fondation Maison des Sciences de l'Homme, Bur 108-109, 54 bd Raspail, 75270 Paris CEDEX 06, France. Fax +33149542133. E-mail: lbasoc@msh-paris.fr.
SG address not obtained.
URL: http://www.silba.msh-paris.fr/

History Founded 15 Apr 1995, Paris (France). Statutes adopted Oct 1996. Registered in accordance with French law. **Aims** Promote and facilitate the study of the works, life and times of the Italian *Renaissance humanist* and *architect* Leon Battista Alberti (1404-1472). **Structure** General Assembly (annual); Council of 4 members; Scientific Council. Housed at: *Fondation de la maison des sciences de l'homme (MSH).* **Languages** English, French, German, Italian, Portuguese, Spanish. **Staff** 5-6 FTE. **Activities** Events/meetings. **Events** *Congrès international sur l'humanisme de Pétrarque à Alberti et Valla* Tours (France) 2004, *Congrès international sur Pétrarque* Paris (France) / Tours (France) 2003, *Représentations du mouvement* Metz (France) 2002, *Congrès international sur les sciences et les arts* Paris (France) / Tours (France) 2002, *Séminaire* Tours (France) 2002. **Publications** *Albertiana* (annual). *L B Alberti Opera Omnia*; *Nova Humanistica.* Studies.
Members Individuals and organizations in 25 countries:
Andorra, Argentina, Australia, Austria, Belgium, Brazil, Canada, Chile, Denmark, France, Germany, Greece, Holy See, Italy, Japan, Netherlands, New Zealand, Poland, Portugal, Russia, Spain, Sweden, Switzerland, UK, USA. [2015.11.10/XE3758/E]

♦ Société internationale des libres-penseurs espérantistes (inactive)
♦ Société internationale de limnologie / see International Society of Limnology (#15232)
♦ Société internationale de linguistique (no recent information)

♦ Société internationale de linguistique fonctionnelle (SILF) 19492

International Society of Functional Linguistics

Pres 26 rue de Clichy, 75009 Paris, France. T. +33148747982. Fax +33145960611.
Registered Office c/o Ecole pratique des hautes études, 4e section, 45 rue des Ecoles, 75005 Paris, France.
URL: http://www.silf-la-linguistique.org/

History Founded 11 Oct 1978, Paris (France), the journal *'La Linguistique'* having been published since 1965 and the society having functioned as a French national association since Oct 1976. Registered in accordance with French law. **Aims** Promote and coordinate research in functional linguistics and disseminate the results obtained by functionalists from all the countries and of all tendencies. **Structure** General Meeting; Executive Committee. **Languages** English, French, Italian, Spanish. **Staff** 2.50 FTE, voluntary. **Finance** Sources: meeting proceeds; members' dues; sale of publications. **Activities** Events/meetings; research/documentation. **Events** *Annual Colloquium* Paris (France) 2020, *Annual Colloquium* Florina (Greece) 2019, *Annual Colloquium* Cadiz (Spain) 2018, *Annual Colloquium* Brno (Czech Rep) 2013, *Annual Colloquium* Oaxaca (Mexico) 2012. **Publications** *La Linguistique* (2 a year) – journal. Conference and study reports; colloquium proceedings.
Members Individuals in 35 countries:
Algeria, Argentina, Australia, Belarus, Belgium, Brazil, Canada, Chile, China, Colombia, Cyprus, Czechia, France, Germany, Greece, Italy, Japan, Jordan, Mexico, Morocco, Netherlands, Norway, Peru, Poland, Portugal, Romania, Russia, Serbia, Spain, Sweden, Switzerland, Tunisia, Türkiye, UK, USA.
NGO Relations Cooperates with: *Linguistic Association of Canada and the United States (LACUS).* [2020.03.03/XD7162/v/C]

♦ Société internationale de linguistique historique (#15166)
♦ Société internationale de littérature courtoise (#13100)
♦ Société Internationale pour les Littératures Orales d'Afrique (#15327)
♦ Société internationale pour la lutte contre le cancer du sein (inactive)
♦ Société internationale de lymphologie (#15238)
♦ Société internationale des maladies métaboliques de l'oeil (#15263)
♦ Société internationale pour les maladies du sang et les tumeurs (inactive)
♦ Société internationale de malherbologie sur le désherbage (#15875)
♦ Société internationale des matières grasses (#15115)
♦ Société internationale de mécanique des sols et de la géotechnique (#15452)
♦ Société internationale de mécanique des sols et de travaux de fondations / see International Society for Soil Mechanics and Geotechnical Engineering (#15452)
♦ Société internationale de mécanocardiographie / see International Society of Non-invasive Cardiology (#15308)
♦ Société internationale de médecine de catastrophe (inactive)
♦ Société internationale de médecine cybernétique (inactive)
♦ Société internationale de médecine générale (inactive)
♦ Société internationale de médecine interne (#15212)
♦ Société internationale de médecine physique (inactive)
♦ Société internationale de médecine prophylactique et d'hygiène sociale (inactive)
♦ Société internationale de médecine tropicale (inactive)
♦ Société internationale de médecine vétérinaire porcine (#14584)
♦ Société internationale de la médecine des voyages (#15519)
♦ Société internationale des médecins pour la thérapie de l'information biophysique (#15253)
♦ Société Internationale des Médiévistes, Paris (#14142)
♦ Société internationale de mésothérapie (#15262)
♦ Société internationale de métaphysique (#15265)
♦ Société internationale de microbiologie / see International Union of Microbiological Societies (#15794)
♦ Société internationale de microchirurgie (inactive)
♦ Société internationale de micro-électronique hybride (inactive)
♦ Société internationale de micropatrologie (inactive)
♦ Société internationale missionnaire / see SIM International
♦ Société internationale pour le modèle écologique (#15070)
♦ Société internationale des modèles radio-commandés (inactive)
♦ Société internationale des monarchistes (inactive)
♦ Société internationale des morphologistes de la vie végétale (#15370)
♦ Société internationale de morphomédecine (no recent information)
♦ Société internationale de la Moselle (#13263)
♦ Société internationale de musicologie / see International Musicological Society (#14201)
♦ Société internationale de musique (inactive)
♦ Société internationale de musique Arthur Rubinstein (#01120)
♦ Société internationale pour la musique contemporaine (#15035)
♦ Société internationale de mycologie humaine et animale (#15181)
♦ Société internationale de néphrologie (#15294)
♦ Société internationale de neurochimie (#15295)
♦ Société internationale de neuropathologie (#15300)
♦ Société internationale de la neuroscience du développement (#15054)
♦ Société internationale de nomenclature des maladies pédiatriques et congénitales du coeur (#15306)
♦ Société internationale de nutrition parentérale (inactive)
♦ Société internationale d'obstétrique et de gynécologie psychosomatiques (#15402)

♦ Société internationale d'odonto-stomatologie légale / see International Organization for Forensic Odonto-Stomatology (#14448)

♦ Société internationale d'oncologie gériatrique (SIOG) 19493

International Society of Geriatric Oncology

Contact c/o International Environment House 2, 7-9 Chemin de Balexert, 1219 Châtelaine, Switzerland. T. +41225523305. E-mail: info@siog.org.

Main Website: https://www.siog.org

History 2000, New York, NY (USA). Registration: Swiss Civil Code, Start date: 2012, Switzerland. **Aims** Foster development of health professionals in the field of geriatric oncology in order to optimize treatment of older adults with *cancer*. **Structure** Executive Committee; Board of Directors; Permanent Committees (5); ad-hoc Committees (5); Interest Groups (2); Task Forces; Working Groups. **Languages** English. **Staff** 3.00 FTE, paid; 10.00 FTE, voluntary. **Finance** Sources: grants; members' dues; sponsorship. **Activities** Events/meetings; research and development; training/education. **Events** *Annual Conference* Geneva (Switzerland) 2022, *Annual Conference* Châtelaine (Switzerland) 2021, *Annual Conference* Châtelaine (Switzerland) 2020, *Annual Conference* Geneva (Switzerland) 2019, *Annual Conference* Amsterdam (Netherlands) 2018. **Publications** *Journal of Geriatric Oncology*. **Members** Individuals and societies in over 80 countries and territories. Membership countries not specified. **NGO Relations** Member of (1): *Union for International Cancer Control (UICC, #20415)*. Also links with national societies. [2022.05.12/XD8542/v/**D**]

♦ Société internationale d'oncologie pédiatrique (#15339)
♦ Société internationale d'oncologie préventive (no recent information)
♦ Société internationale d'ophtalmologie géographique / see International Society of Geographical and Epidemiological Ophthalmology (#15140)
♦ Société internationale d'ophtalmologie géographique et épidémiologique (#15140)
♦ Société internationale d'ophtalmologie pédiatrique (no recent information)
♦ Société internationale de l'orbite oculaire (no recent information)
♦ Société internationale des organes artificiels / see International Federation for Artificial Organs (#13357)
♦ Société internationale pour l'organisation des congrès mondiaux de psychiatrie (inactive)
♦ Société internationale pour l'organisation des connaissances (#15224)
♦ Société internationale d'orthopédagogie (inactive)
♦ Société internationale d'orthopédie cranio-mandibulaire (inactive)
♦ Société Internationale d'Otoneurologie (unconfirmed)
♦ Société internationale d'otorhinolaryngologie et de chirurgie cervico-faciale des pays francophones / see Société internationale francophone d'ORL et de chirurgie cervico-faciale (#19488)
♦ Société internationale pour la papyrologie arabe (#14934)
♦ Société internationale de pathologie géographique (inactive)
♦ Société internationale des pathologistes en gynécologie (#15151)
♦ Société internationale de pathophysiologie (#15343)
♦ Société internationale de pharmacologie clinique (inactive)
♦ Société internationale de phénoménologie (inactive)
♦ Société internationale de phénoménologie et littérature (see: #21725)
♦ Société internationale de photogrammétrie / see International Society for Photogrammetry and Remote Sensing (#15362)
♦ Société internationale de photogrammétrie et télédétection (#15362)
♦ Société internationale de phycologie (#14576)
♦ Société internationale de phytopathologie (#15371)
♦ Société internationale pour la prévention des complications iatrogéniques (inactive)
♦ Société internationale pour la prévention des mauvais traitements et négligences envers les enfants / see International Society for Prevention of Child Abuse and Neglect (#15385)
♦ Société internationale de primatologie (#14642)
♦ Société internationale des professeurs en maladies du côlon et du rectum (#15530)
♦ Société internationale pour le progrès des théories économiques dans leurs relations avec les statistiques et les mathématiques (inactive)
♦ Société internationale pour la promotion des études hégéliennes (#13788)
♦ Société internationale pour la promotion des recherches sur l'écriture (#14905)
♦ Société internationale des propagateurs de plantes (#14594)
♦ Société internationale de prophylaxie criminelle (inactive)
♦ Société internationale pour la protection des animaux (inactive)
♦ Société internationale pour la protection de l'environnement (#15097)
♦ Société internationale pour la protection des invalides / see RI Global (#18948)
♦ Société internationale pour la protection des pêcheurs d'éponge (inactive)
♦ Société internationale pour la protection et la reproduction de l'aurochs (inactive)
♦ Société internationale de prothèse et orthèse / see International Society for Prosthetics and Orthotics (#15390)
♦ Société Internationale de Psychanalyse et Philosophie (#15394)
♦ Société internationale de psychiatrie de l'adolescence / see International Society for Adolescent Psychiatry and Psychology (#14897)
♦ Société internationale de psychiatrie infantile (inactive)
♦ Société internationale de psychologie comparée (#15024)
♦ Société internationale de psychologie de l'écriture (#15398)
♦ Société internationale de psychologie politique (#15374)
♦ Société internationale psychologique religieuse (inactive)
♦ Société internationale de psychoneuroendocrinologie (#15399)
♦ Société internationale de psychopathologie de l'expression et d'art-thérapie (#15400)
♦ Société internationale de psycho-prophylaxie obstétricale (inactive)
♦ Société internationale de psychothérapie non verbale (inactive)
♦ Société internationale de radiobiologie (inactive)
♦ Société Internationale de Radiobiologie de Langue Française (internationally oriented national body)
♦ Société internationale de radiologie (#15412)
♦ Société internationale de la radio et télévision (inactive)
♦ Société internationale de radiothérapie (inactive)

♦ Société internationale de recherche et d'études sur le rachis (SIRER) 19494

Pres Clinique du Parc, 155 bd Stalingrad, 69006 Lyon, France. T. +33472448728. Fax +33478949698. E-mail: sirer@wanadoo.fr.

URL: http://www.sirer.net/

History 11 Jun 1964, Florence (Italy). **Aims** Promote research in the area of treatment of spinal diseases; disseminate information on spinal deformations and their treatment to specialists in this field. **Structure** Bureau. Includes: *Centre européen de la colonne vertébrale (CECV)*. **Languages** English, French, Italian, Spanish. **Staff** Part-time, voluntary. **Finance** Members' dues: euro 130. Sponsorship. **Events** *Congrès annuel* Bari (Italy) 2010, *Congrès annuel* Lyon (France) 2009, *SOSORT international conference on conservative management of spinal deformities* Lyon (France) 2009, *Congrès annuel* Palermo (Italy) 2008, *Congrès annuel* Marseille (France) 2007. **Publications** *Résonances Européenne du Rachis* (4 a year). Congress proceedings. **Members** Full in 9 countries:
Belarus, Belgium, Brazil, Canada, France, Italy, North Macedonia, Poland, Spain. [2015.01.12/XD7251/**D**]

♦ Société internationale de recherche sur le folklore oral (#15124)
♦ Société internationale de recherche en littérature d'enfance et de jeunesse (#14742)
♦ Société internationale pour la recherche sur les maladies de civilisation et l'environnement (inactive)
♦ Société internationale pour la recherche sur les maladies de civilisation et les substances vitales (inactive)

♦ Société Internationale de Recherche Orthopédique et Traumatologique (SIROT) 19495

International Research Society of Orthopaedics and Traumatology

Pres Rue de la Loi 26, Boîte 13, 1040 Brussels, Belgium. T. +3226486823. Fax +3226498601.

SG address not obtained.

URL: http://www.sicot.org/

History 1978, Kyoto (Japan), as the research branch of *International Society of Orthopaedic Surgery and Traumatology (#15335)*. **Aims** Encourage research related to orthopaedic *surgery*; provide a forum for exchange of technical, scientific and practical information related to the science and practice of orthopaedic surgery and for presentation of recent advances in the field; encourage young orthopaedic researchers to acquire and develop new research skills, and give them the opportunity to present their work to an international forum, to discuss their work with colleagues from around the world and to meet individuals at the 'sharp end' of orthopaedic research. **Structure** General Meeting (every 3 years, at congress); Executive Committee. **Languages** English. **Staff** None. **Finance** Members' dues for 3 years: US$ 45. Other sources: Profit from scientific meetings; donations. **Activities** Events/meetings; training/education; awards/prizes/competitions. **Events** *SICOT Orthopaedic World Congress* Muscat (Oman) 2019, *Annual International Conference* Pattaya (Thailand) 2009, *Triennial World Congress* Hong Kong (Hong Kong) 2008, *AIC : annual international conference* Marrakech (Morocco) 2007, *AIC : annual international conference* Buenos Aires (Argentina) 2006. **Publications** *SIROT Newsletter*. Abstracts of scientific meetings.

Members Professionals in fields related to orthopaedics and traumatology in 36 countries and territories:
Australia, Austria, Bangladesh, Belgium, Bosnia-Herzegovina, Brazil, Canada, China, Finland, France, Germany, Greece, Hong Kong, Hungary, India, Israel, Italy, Japan, Korea Rep, Kyrgyzstan, Mexico, Netherlands, Pakistan, Poland, Portugal, Romania, Russia, Saudi Arabia, Slovenia, Spain, Sweden, Switzerland, Taiwan, Türkiye, UK, USA.

NGO Relations Affiliated to SICOT. [2013/XC0061/v/**E**]

♦ Société internationale de recherche sur la posture et la marche (#15378)
♦ Société internationale de recherches en anesthésiologie (internationally oriented national body)
♦ Société internationale des recherches astrologiques (#14945)
♦ Société internationale de recherches biomédicales sur l'alcoolisme (#14968)
♦ Société internationale de recherches cardiaques (#15158)
♦ Société internationale de recherches aux frontières de la médecine (inactive)
♦ Société internationale de recherches sur les Ordres (inactive)
♦ Société internationale de recherches psychiques (inactive)
♦ Société internationale pour les recherches sur le système réticuloendothélial (inactive)
♦ Société internationale de recherche en stéréoencéphalotomie / see World Society for Stereotactic and Functional Neurosurgery (#21812)
♦ Société internationale renardienne (#14750)

♦ Société internationale rencesvals 19496

Sec ULG, Section Langues et littératures romanes, Pl Cockerill 3 – Bât A2, 4000 Liège, Belgium. T. +3243665451. Fax +3243665816.

URL: http://rencesvals.net/

History 1955, as *Société rencesvals internationale*. Also referred to as *Société rencesvals pour l'étude des épopées romanes*. Refounded in 2008. **Aims** Study epic *poetry* of *mediaeval* Europe. **Structure** International Bureau, comprising Honorary Presidents, President, 2 Vice-Presidents and Founding members. Board of Directors. **Languages** French, Italian, Spanish. **Finance** Members' dues. **Events** *Triennial Congress* Rome (Italy) 2015, *Triennial Congress* Rome (Italy) 2015, *Triennial Congress* Oxford (UK) 2012, *Triennial Congress* Coppet (Switzerland) 2009, *Triennial Congress* Geneva (Switzerland) 2009. **Publications** *Bulletin bibliographique* (annual).

Members National branches (11) in 11 countries:
Belgium, Canada, France, Germany, Italy, Japan, Netherlands, Spain, Switzerland, UK, USA.
Also a Scandinavian branch.
Individuals in 26 countries:
Belgium, Canada, Denmark, Finland, France, Germany, Greece, Iceland, Ireland, Israel, Italy, Jamaica, Japan, Korea Rep, Netherlands, Norway, Poland, Portugal, Romania, Russia, Serbia, Spain, Switzerland, Tunisia, UK, USA. [2013.07.12/XD6422/**D**]

♦ Société internationale pour le renouveau de la musique sacrée catholique (inactive)
♦ Société internationale de rhinologie / see International Rhinologic Society (#14753)
♦ Société internationale rhinologique (#14753)
♦ Société internationale Robert Musil (#14762)
♦ Société internationale du Rorschach et des méthodes projectives (#15430)
♦ Société internationale de la science horticole / see International Society for Horticultural Science (#15180)
♦ Société internationale de science sociale (inactive)
♦ Société internationale des sciences phonétiques (#15361)
♦ Société internationale de la science des systèmes dans le domaine de la santé (no recent information)
♦ Société internationale scientifique des champignons comestibles (#15286)
♦ Société internationale pour la sécurité en ski (#15443)
♦ Société internationale de sémantique générale (inactive)
♦ Société internationale de sénologie (#19230)
♦ Société internationale pour la sociologie des connaissances (inactive)
♦ Société internationale de sociologie des religions (#15451)
♦ Société internationale pour les soins palliatifs (inactive)
♦ Société internationale de sophrologie (inactive)
♦ Société internationale de spécialistes de verres de contact (#15034)
♦ Société internationale pour la suppression des machines pour le traitement automatique des données (inactive)
♦ Société internationale de systématique biochimique (inactive)
♦ Société Internationale Szondi (#15648)
♦ Société internationale des techniciens de la canne à sucre (#15495)

♦ Société internationale de technique hydrothermale (SITH) 19497

Sociedad Internacional de Técnica Hidrotermal – International Society for Hydrothermal Techniques

Chief Sec Rúa do Balneario 5, 36670 Cuntis, La Coruña, Spain. T. +34986532535. Fax +34986532151. E-mail: termas@termasdecuntis.com.

URL: http://www.sithomth.com/

History 1969, Italy. **Aims** Improve balneology and hydrothermal technics. **Structure** General Assembly; Presidency, consisting of Presidents (3), Vice-Presidents (3), Secretary General and Treasurer; Executive Committee; International Committee. **Languages** English, French. **Staff** 5.00 FTE, voluntary. **Finance** Members' dues. **Events** *Annual Congress / International Congress* Cuntis (Spain) 2014, *Annual congress / International Congress* Cuntis (Spain) 2008, *Future perspectives of thermalism and its legislation in Europe and in different geographical areas* Trento (Italy) 2005, *International Congress* Trento (Italy) 2005, *Congress / International Congress* Beppu (Japan) 2003. **Publications** *SITH-News-Actualités* (4 a year).

Members Individuals in 39 countries:
Albania, Algeria, Argentina, Austria, Belgium, Benin, Bolivia, Brazil, Bulgaria, Chile, Colombia, Cuba, Czechia, Ecuador, Egypt, France, Germany, Greece, Hungary, Iran Islamic Rep, Israel, Italy, Japan, Luxembourg, Malaysia, Mongolia, Morocco, Peru, Poland, Romania, Saudi Arabia, Serbia, Spain, Switzerland, Tunisia, Türkiye, UK, USA, Venezuela.
Members also in the former USSR; countries not specified.

NGO Relations Instrumental in setting up: *Organisation mondiale du thermalisme (OMTh, #17820)*, with which it has close links. [2019/XD0001/v/**D**]

♦ Société internationale des techniques d'imagerie mentale / see Société internationale des techniques d'imagerie mentale onirique (#19498)

♦ Société internationale des techniques d'imagerie mentale onirique (SITIMO) 19498

International Society for Oneiric Mental Imagery Techniques – Sociedade Internacional das Técnicas de Imagerie Mentale Onirique – Società Internazionale per le Tecniche d'Imagerie Mentale Onirique

Contact 56 rue Sedaine, 75011 Paris, France.

History 12 Apr 1968, Paris (France). Founded by by a small group of practitioners of psychotherapeutic health imagery techniques, on the initiative of André Virel (1920-2000). Statutes modified 24 Oct 1998. Former names and other names: *Association internationale d'onirothérapie* – former (12 Apr 1968 to 21 Jun 1968); *International Society for Mental Imagery Techniques* – former (21 Jun 1968); *Société internationale des techniques d'imagerie mentale (SITIM)* – former (21 Jun 1968); *Sociedade Internacional das Técnicas de Imagerie Mentale* – former (21 Jun 1968); *Società Internazionale per le Tecniche d'Imagerie Mentale* – former (21 Jun 1968). Registration: Répertoire National des Associations, No/ID: W751011036, France. **Aims** Facilitate links between *research* workers, *psychotherapists* and *therapists* for exchange of information and joint research efforts. **Structure** General Assembly (annual). Executive Council (meets at least annually) of up to 15 members. Bureau, consisting of Founder-President, one or more Vice-Presidents, Secretary-General and Treasurer. Committee of Honour; Scientific Committee; Committee on Professional Training. **Languages** French. **Staff** 5.00 FTE, voluntary. **Finance** Members' dues. **Activities** Teaching seminars; congresses; scientific meetings. **Events** *Images de l'homme, images du monde* Paris (France) 1991, *Congress / International Meeting* Paris (France) 1988, *International meeting* Turin (Italy) 1987, *International Meeting* Paris (France) 1976, *International Meeting* Porto (Portugal) 1972. **Publications** *Le modèle fonctionnel du corps* (2008); *Les univers de l'imaginaire* (2000); *L'imagerie mentale* (1968); *Histoire de notre image* (1965).

Members Full; Corresponding. Research workers, psychotherapists and other individuals in 3 countries:
France, Italy, Portugal. [2020/XD5285/v/**D**]

- ♦ Société internationale de technique de soudage (#10144)
- ♦ Société internationale de télécommunications aéronautiques / see SITA (#19299)
- ♦ Société internationale du test de Rorschach et autres méthodes projectives / see International Society of the Rorschach and Projective Methods (#15430)
- ♦ Société internationale de thérapeutique en rhumatologie (no recent information)
- ♦ Société internationale de thérapie psychomotrice (no recent information)
- ♦ Société internationale Thomas d'Aquin (#19438)
- ♦ Société internationale de thrombose et d'hémostase (#15511)
- ♦ Société internationale de la topographie électromagnétique du cerveau (#14984)
- ♦ Société internationale de topographie minière (#15272)
- ♦ Société internationale de la tourbe / see International Peatland Society (#14538)
- ♦ Société Internationale de Toxinologie (#15512)
- ♦ Société internationale de transfusion sanguine (#14979)
- ♦ Société internationale de traumatologie de ski et de médecine des sports d'hiver (#15445)
- ♦ Société internationale des travailleurs de l'agrumiculture (#15011)
- ♦ Société internationale de trilogie analytique (#14917)
- ♦ Société internationale pour les ultrasons en obstétrique et gynécologie (#15527)

♦ Société Internationale d'Urologie (SIU) 19499

Exec Dir 1155 Robert-Bourassa Blvd, Suite 1012, Montréal QC H3B 3A7, Canada. T. +15148755665. Fax +15148750205. E-mail: communications@siu-urology.org.
URL: http://www.siu-urology.org/

History 1907, Paris (France). Founded by Dr Jean Casimir Félix-Guyon. Permanent headquarters established in Montréal (Canada), 1999. Former names and other names: *Association internationale d'urologie* – former. **Aims** Enable urologists in all nations, through international cooperation in education and research, to apply the highest standards of *urological* care to their patients. **Structure** General Assembly (annual, during Congress); Board of Directors. Foundation (FSIU). **Languages** English. **Staff** 12.50 FTE, paid. **Finance** Sources: meeting proceeds; members' dues; sponsorship. **Activities** Certification/accreditation; events/meetings; financial and/or material support; networking/liaising; training/education. **Events** *Congress* Istanbul (Türkiye) 2023, *SIU Regional Meeting in Urological Care* Istanbul (Türkiye) 2022, *Congress* Montréal, QC (Canada) 2022, *Congress* Dubai (United Arab Emirates) 2021, *GU Cancer Triad Meeting* Montréal, QC (Canada) 2020. **Publications** *The Société Internationale d'Urologie Journal (SIUJ)* (6 a year) in English. **Information Services** *SIU Academy* – eLearning resource.

Members Active; Senior; Associate; Affiliate; Trainee; Honorary: individuals (over 9,000) in over 130 countries and territories. Membership countries not specified.
Affiliated societies (3):
Caribbean Urological Association (CURA, #03563); Society of Genitourinary Reconstructive Surgeons (GURS, #19564); World Uro Oncology Federation (WUOF, #21895). [2022/XB2574/y/**B**]

- ♦ Société internationale du vin et de l'alimentation (#15890)
- ♦ Société international pour la garde des animaux de ferme (#15236)
- ♦ Société international du SIDA (#11601)
- ♦ Société d'investissement et de développement international / see International Solidarity for Development and Investment
- ♦ Société d'investissements des Caraïbes (inactive)
- ♦ Société Islamique pour le Développement du Secteur Privé (see: #16044)
- ♦ Société Islamique pour l'Assurance des Investissements et des Crédits à l'Exportation (#16041)
- ♦ Société italienne pour l'organisation internationale (internationally oriented national body)
- ♦ Societeit van Jesus-Maria-Josef (religious order)
- ♦ Société de Jésus-Christ (religious order)
- ♦ Société de Jésus, Marie et Joseph (religious order)
- ♦ Société des juristes francophones du Commonwealth (no recent information)
- ♦ Société latine de biologie et médecine de la reproduction (#19387)
- ♦ Société latine d'oto-rhino-laryngologie (inactive)
- ♦ Société latinoaméricaine d'allergologie / see Sociedad Latinoamericana de Alergia, Asma e Inmunologia (#19389)
- ♦ Société latinoaméricaine d'audit des services de la santé (#19392)
- ♦ Société latinoaméricaine de buiatrie (#19394)
- ♦ Société latino-américaine de droit international (#16374)
- ♦ Société latinoaméricaine d'études sur l'Amérique latine et les Caraïbes (#19406)
- ♦ Société latinoaméricaine d'histoire des sciences et de la technologie (no recent information)
- ♦ Société latinoaméricaine du maïs (inactive)
- ♦ Société latinoaméricaine de malherbologie (#16394)
- ♦ Société latino-américaine de neuropsychologie (#16378)
- ♦ Société latinoaméricaine de nutrition (#19417)
- ♦ Société latinoaméricaine d'orthopédie et de traumatologie (#19418)
- ♦ Société latinoaméricaine de pathologie (#16380)
- ♦ Société latinoaméricaine de pathologie pédiatrique (#19421)
- ♦ Société latinoaméricaine de physiologie végétale (no recent information)
- ♦ Société latinoaméricaine des professeurs de thérapie physique (inactive)
- ♦ Société latinoaméricaine de recherches pédiatriques (#19411)
- ♦ Société latinoaméricaine de télédétection et de systèmes spéciaux (#19358)
- ♦ Société latinoaméricaine de la thyroïde (#16390)
- ♦ Société latino-ibéroaméricaine de recherche opérationnelle (#16398)

♦ Société de législation comparée 19500

Society of Comparative Legislation – Sociedad de Legislación Comparada

Headquarters 28 rue Saint-Guillaume, 75007 Paris, France. T. +33144398623. Fax +33144398628. E-mail: emmanuelle.bouvier@legiscompare.com – slc@legiscompare.com.
Representative at UN c/o Columbia Univ of Law, 435 West 116th St, New York NY 10027, USA.
URL: http://www.legiscompare.com/

History 1869, Paris (France). Recognized by French Ministerial Decree, 4 Dec 1873. **Aims** Study and compare the statutes and *laws* of different countries and search for practical means of improving the different branches of the law. **Structure** General Assembly; Executive Council. **Languages** English, French, Spanish. **Staff** 1.50 FTE, paid. **Finance** Members' dues. Other sources: grants from CNRS (France); French Ministry of Justice; private companies. **Activities** Events/meetings. **Events** *Journées juridiques franco-latino-américaines* Rio de Janeiro (Brazil) 2001, *Journées juridiques* Tokyo (Japan) / Sapporo (Japan) 2001, *Journées juridiques* Helsinki (Finland) 2000, *Journées juridiques* Trier (Germany) 2000, *French-Nordic juridical days* Toulouse (France) 1997. **Publications** *Revue internationale de droit comparé* (4 a year). Books.

Members Individual or collective in 42 countries and territories:
Argentina, Australia, Belgium, Brazil, Canada, Chile, China, Colombia, Croatia, Czechia, Finland, France, Germany, Greece, Hungary, India, Ireland, Italy, Japan, Lebanon, Luxembourg, Mexico, Monaco, Morocco, Netherlands, Panama, Peru, Poland, Portugal, Romania, Russia, Senegal, Serbia, Spain, Sweden, Switzerland, Taiwan, Tunisia, Türkiye, UK, USA, Venezuela.

Consultative Status Consultative status granted from: *ILO (#11123)* (Special List). **IGO Relations** Associated with Department of Global Communications of the United Nations. [2017.03.21/XF0250/**F**]

- ♦ Société Letterstedt (#16447)
- ♦ Société pour la liberté de la science (inactive)
- ♦ Société linguistique de l'Afrique occidentale / see Société ouest-africaine de linguistique (#19506)
- ♦ Société de linguistique des Caraïbes (#19530)

♦ Société de linguistique romane (SLiR) 19501

Society of Romance Linguistics

Sec-Treas Univ Heidelberg, Romanisches Seminar, Seminarstr 3, 69117 Heidelberg, Germany. E-mail: info@slir.org.
Sec Admin Romanisches Seminar, Zürichbergstr 8, Postfach, 8044 Zurich ZH, Switzerland.
URL: http://www.slir.org/

History 30 May 1924, Dijon (France). Founded on the initiative of Adolphe Terracher and Oscar Bloch. Reorganized 11 Apr 1953, Barcelona (Spain). Registration: France. **Aims** Study both the linguistic and philological aspects of the Romance languages and literatures. **Structure** Congress (every 3 years); Bureau; Administrative Council. **Languages** Catalan, French, Friulian, Italian, Ladin, Latin, Occitan, Portuguese, Romance languages, Romanian, Romansh, Spanish. **Staff** 1.50 FTE, voluntary. **Finance** Sources: members' dues. Annual budget: 50,000 EUR. **Activities** Awards/prizes/competitions; events/meetings. **Events** *Congrès International de Linguistique et de Philologie Romanes* La Laguna (Spain) 2022, *Triennial Congress* Copenhagen (Denmark) 2019, *Triennial Congress* Rome (Italy) 2016, *Triennial Congress* Nancy (France) 2013, *Triennial congress* Valencia (Spain) 2010. **Publications** *Revue de linguistique romane* (2 a year). *Bibliothèque de Linguistique Romane*; *Editions de Linguistique et de Philologie*.

Members Societies; Individuals. Members in 49 countries:
Algeria, Australia, Austria, Belgium, Brazil, Bulgaria, Cameroon, Canada, Chile, Croatia, Czechia, Denmark, Estonia, Finland, France, Germany, Greece, Hungary, Israel, Italy, Japan, Korea Rep, Latvia, Luxembourg, Mexico, Moldova, Montenegro, Morocco, Netherlands, New Zealand, North Macedonia, Norway, Peru, Poland, Portugal, Romania, Russia, Senegal, Serbia, Slovenia, South Africa, Spain, Sweden, Switzerland, Trinidad-Tobago, Tunisia, UK, Ukraine, USA. [2022.06.17/XC3854/**C**]

- ♦ Société liturgique internationale (#19449)
- ♦ Société de lutte contre les rongeurs pour l'Asie et le Pacifique (inactive)
- ♦ Société de lutte contre le SIDA pour l'Asie et le Pacifique (#00592)
- ♦ Société de malherbologie de l'Afrique de l'Est (inactive)
- ♦ Société de Marie (religious order)
- ♦ Société de Marie (religious order)
- ♦ Société de mathématiques d'Asie du Sud-Est (#19773)
- ♦ Société de médecine gériatrique de l'Union européenne (#07392)
- ♦ Société de médecine sous-marine du Pacifique Sud (#19890)
- ♦ Société de médecine nucléaire – Europe (inactive)
- ♦ Société des médecins d'hôpitaux de langue française (inactive)
- ♦ Société médicale d'Afrique Noire de langue française (inactive)
- ♦ Société médicale d'imagerie, enseignement et recherche (no recent information)
- ♦ Société médicale mycologique des Amériques (#16625)
- ♦ Société méditerranéenne et africaine d'ultrasonographie (#16640)
- ♦ Société méditerranéenne de chimiothérapie / see Mediterranean Society of Chemotherapy and Infection (#16675)
- ♦ Société méditerranéenne de coloproctologie (#16676)

♦ Société Méditerranéenne Francophone de Cancérologie (SMFC) . . . 19502

Contact Ctr Hospitalier Universitaire Saint-Louis, 1 avenue Claude Vellefaux, 75010 Paris, France.
URL: http://www.smfc-cancer.com/

History 2008. Registered in accordance with French law. **Structure** General Assembly. Board of Directors, comprising Board (President, 2 Vice-Presidents, Secretary, Deputy Secretary, Treasurer, Deputy Treasurer) and 5 members. **Activities** Organizes congress at 'Eurocancer', always in Paris (France). **Events** *Eurocancer Congress* Paris (France) 2013. [2013/XJ7231/**D**]

- ♦ Société méditerranéenne de médecine légale (#16677)
- ♦ Société méditerranéenne d'ophtalmologie (#16679)
- ♦ Société méditerranéenne d'otologie et d'audiologie (#16680)
- ♦ Société méditerranéenne de thérapeutique (inactive)
- ♦ Société métallographique internationale (#14151)
- ♦ Société météorologique européenne (#07786)
- ♦ Société missionnaire allemande (internationally oriented national body)
- ♦ Société des Missionnaires d'Afrique (religious order)
- ♦ Société Missionnaire de Saint Paul (religious order)
- ♦ Société des Missions Africaines (religious order)
- ♦ Société pour les Missions Etrangères des Etats-Unis d'Amérique (religious order)
- ♦ Société des Missions Etrangères de la Province de Québec (religious order)
- ♦ Société des missions norvégiennes (internationally oriented national body)
- ♦ Société des Mohicans des Nations Unies (inactive)
- ♦ Société du monde futur (#21534)
- ♦ Société mondiale d'agriculture (inactive)
- ♦ Société mondiale de buiatrie (#21122)
- ♦ Société mondiale d'ékistique (#21801)
- ♦ Société mondiale d'endoscopie, d'endobiopsie et de cytologie (inactive)
- ♦ Société mondiale d'histoire méthodiste (#21651)
- ♦ Société mondiale de mariculture (#21099)
- ♦ Société mondiale de neurochirurgie stéréotatique et fonctionnelle (#21812)
- ♦ Société mondiale pour la protection des animaux (#21092)
- ♦ Société mondiale de résonance magnétique (#15240)
- ♦ Société mondiale de sexologie / see World Association for Sexual Health (#21187)
- ♦ Société mondiale de victimologie (#21815)
- ♦ Société du Mont-Pèlerin (#16852)
- ♦ Société de la musique militaire internationale (#14162)
- ♦ Société de mycologie de langue allemande (#05051)
- ♦ Société napoléonnienne internationale (#14211)
- ♦ Société des Nations (inactive)

♦ Société de neurochirurgie de langue française (SNCLF) 19503

French-Speaking Society of Neurosurgery

Gen Sec Service de Neurochirurgie, CHU Ibn Rochd, 1 Rue des Hôpitaux, 20360 Casablanca, Morocco.
Exec Sec Service de Neurochirurgie, Hôpital d'Enfants, 4 rue du Morvan, 54500 Vandoeuvre-les-Nancy, France.
Registered Office Service de neurochirurgie, Hôpital Sainte Anne, 1 rue Cabanis, 75674 Paris CEDEX 14, France.
URL: http://www.snclf.fr/

History Founded 1948, Paris (France), as *Société d'électro-encéphalographie de langue française.* **Aims** Promote *electroencephalography* and functional exploration of the *nervous system.* **Structure** Managing and Scientific Committee, comprising President, Secretary-General, Treasurer and 12 members. Delegate to Candidates, the person responsible for relations with SFNC and 7 representatives (Canada, Belgium, Sub-Saharan Africa, Middle East, USA, Latin America and Switzerland). Committees (5): Executive; Membership; Finance; Scientific Programme; Review. **Languages** French. **Staff** 4.00 FTE, voluntary. **Finance** Sources: members' dues. Annual budget: 53,355 EUR. **Activities** Organizes: winter congress in Paris (France); summer congress, alternately in France and in another country; joint educational and scientific meetings. **Events** *Réunion Annuelle de Paris* Paris (France) 2021, *Réunion Annuelle de Paris* Paris (France) 2020, *Réunion Annuelle de Paris* Paris (France) 2019, *Annual Summer Congress* Grenoble (France) 2018, *Réunion Annuelle de Paris* Paris (France) 2018. **Publications** *Neurochirurgie* (6 a year). Monographs.
Members Regular: individuals (709) in 57 countries and territories:
Algeria, Argentina, Australia, Austria, Bahamas, Belgium, Bolivia, Bosnia-Herzegovina, Brazil, Bulgaria, Cambodia, Canada, Chile, Colombia, Costa Rica, Côte d'Ivoire, Denmark, Dominican Rep, Egypt, El Salvador, France, Gabon, Germany, Greece, Haiti, Hungary, Israel, Italy, Lebanon, Luxembourg, Martinique, Mexico, Morocco, Myanmar, Netherlands, North Macedonia, Norway, Panama, Peru, Polynesia Fr, Portugal, Réunion, Romania, Saudi Arabia, Senegal, Spain, Switzerland, Syrian AR, Tunisia, Türkiye, UK, Ukraine, United Arab Emirates, USA, Venezuela, Vietnam, Zimbabwe.
Corresponding members (81) in 21 countries and territories:
Algeria, Argentina, Belgium, Brazil, Canada, Chile, France, Greece, Israel, Italy, Lebanon, Mexico, Morocco, Peru, Réunion, Spain, Switzerland, Syrian AR, Tunisia, Ukraine, USA.
NGO Relations Member of: *International Federation of Clinical Neurophysiology (IFCN, #13393).* [2019/XC5997/v/**C**]

- Société de neurochirurgie du Moyen-Orient (no recent information)

♦ Société de neurophysiologie clinique de langue française (SNCLF) . 19504

Secretariat ANT Congrès, 154 av de Lodéve, 34070 Montpellier, France. T. +33467109223.
SG Service de Physiologie – Explorations Fonctionnelles, Hôp Henri Mondor, 51 av du Maréchal de Lattre de Tassigny, 94010 Créteil CEDEX, France. T. +33149812694.
URL: http://www.sncIf.net/

Aims Facilitate exchange of scientific information, encourage research, and promote contact between researchers in the field of Clinical and Experimental Neurophysiology. **Structure** General Assembly. Executive Board, comprising President, Vice-President, Past President, Secretary General, Treasurer and 5 members. Administrative Council of 21 members. Scientific Council of 24 members. **Events** *Congrès* Brussels (Belgium) 2009, *Réunion d'hiver* Paris (France) 2009, *Réunion d'hiver* Paris (France) 2008. [2013/XJ0514/**C**]

♦ Société de neuropsychologie de langue française 19505

French-Speaking Neuropsychological Society
SG Inserm U897, Univ Victor Segalen Bordeaux 2, 146 rue Léo Saignat, 33076 Bordeaux CEDEX, France. T. +33557571510. Fax +33557571486.
Pres Unité de Neuropsychologie, Fac de Psychologie et Sciences de l'Education, Univ de Liège, Bd du Rectorat 3 (B33), 4000 Liège, Belgium. T. +3243662274. Fax +3243662808.
URL: http://www.snlf.net/

History 14 Apr 1977, Paris (France). **Aims** Develop, study and observe behaviour in relation to: cerebral processes; clinical and experimental analysis; therapeutic and socio-professional implications of these processes. **Structure** General Assembly (annual). Board, consisting of at least 6 and up to 10 members. Officers: President; Secretary General; Treasurer. **Languages** French. **Staff** 3.00 FTE, voluntary. **Finance** Members' dues. **Activities** Twice yearly scientific meetings; annual thematic forum. **Events** *Spring Meeting* Liège (Belgium) 2016, *Joint Meeting* London (UK) 2016, *Spring Meeting* Angers (France) 2015, *Spring Meeting* Fribourg (Switzerland) 2014, *Spring Meeting* Caen (France) 2013. **Publications** *Revue de neuropsychologie* (4 a year).
Members Individuals (500) in 12 countries:
Algeria, Argentina, Belgium, Brazil, Canada, France, Greece, Italy, Morocco, Spain, Switzerland, USA. [2016/XD6129/v/**D**]

- Société des neuroscientifiques d'Afrique (#19608)
- Société nord-américaine pour la littérature française du dix-septième siècle (internationally oriented national body)
- Société nordique d'allergologie (inactive)
- Société nordique de chimie clinique (#17507)
- Société nordique de chirurgie (#19122)
- Société nordique de chirurgie infantile (no recent information)
- Société nordique d'ergonomie (#17480)
- Société nordique d'études latino-américaines (inactive)
- Société nordique d'étude des techniques de transport (inactive)
- Société nordique du film 16mm (inactive)
- Société nordique d'herpétologie (#19089)
- Société nordique d'histoire de la médecine (no recent information)
- Société nordique d'hydrologie (#17194)
- Société nordique d'illustration biologique et médicale (inactive)
- Société nordique de neuroradiologie (#17421)
- Société nordique d'odontologie pour les handicapés / see Nordic Association for Disability and Oral Health (#17190)
- Société nordique d'orthodontie (#17378)
- Société nordique d'oto-laryngologie (#19094)
- Société nordique de pharmacologie (no recent information)
- Société nordique de philatélie specialisée (inactive)
- Société nordique de la radiologie médicale (#17418)
- Société nordique de réadaptation (inactive)
- Société de numismatique orientale (#17893)
- Société de nutrition et de diététique de langue française / see Société française de nutrition
- Société des Océanistes (internationally oriented national body)
- Société oncologique centro américaine et des caraïbes (no recent information)
- Société d'ophtalmologie latine (inactive)
- Société pour l' optimisation mathématique (#16601)
- Société d'optométrie d'Europe (#08675)
- Société d'organisation de colloques internationaux en Espéranto (internationally oriented national body)
- Société ORL des pays francophones / see Société internationale francophone d'ORL et de chirurgie cervico-faciale (#19488)
- Société d'orthopédie pédiatrique européenne (#08128)
- Société d'oto-rhino-laryngologie (inactive)
- Société d'oto-rhino-laryngologie et de chirurgie cervico-faciale des pays francophones / see Société internationale francophone d'ORL et de chirurgie cervico-faciale (#19488)
- Société d'oto-rhino-laryngologique du Maghreb arabe (inactive)
- Société Ouest Africaine de Gestion d'Actifs (see: #03170)
- Société ouest africaine d'immunologie (no recent information)

♦ Société ouest-africaine de linguistique (SOAL) 19506

West African Linguistics Society (WALS)
Sec-Treas 06-BP 829, Abidjan 06, Côte d'Ivoire. T. +225478015. Fax +225440299.
URL: http://www.journalofwestafricanlanguages.org/

History 1965, Accra (Ghana). Also referred to in French as *Société linguistique de l'Afrique occidentale (SLAO).* **Aims** Encourage research and publication in the *languages* of West Africa. **Structure** Council of English-speaking and French-speaking members. **Activities** Undertakes research on the development of languages. Acts as sub-regional network of *Network of Educational Innovation for Development in Africa (NEIDA, no recent information).* Organizes Congresses (every 2 years). **Events** *Biennial Congress* Abidjan (Côte d'Ivoire) 2019, *Biennial Congress* Winneba (Ghana) 2017, *Biennial Congress* Ibadan (Nigeria) 2013, *Biennial Congress* Abidjan (Côte d'Ivoire) 2011, *Biennial Congress* Ibadan (Nigeria) 2004. **Publications** *Journal of West African Languages* (2 a year).
Members Academics, research workers, field workers and teachers in 20 countries:
Benin, Burkina Faso, Cameroon, Canada, Chad, Côte d'Ivoire, France, Ghana, Kenya, Liberia, Mali, Netherlands, Niger, Nigeria, Senegal, Sierra Leone, Spain, Togo, UK, USA. [2019/XD2170/**D**]

- Société Ouest africaine de malherbologie (#20899)
- Société Ouest Africaine d'Ophtalmologie / see Société Africaine Francophone d'Ophtalmologie (#19453)
- Société ouest africaine de pharmacologie (inactive)

♦ Société Palmophile Francophone (SPF) 19507

SG U Giardinu di l'Isuli, Costa-Baca, 20144 Sainte Lucie de Porto-Vecchio, France.
URL: http://www.societepalmophilefrancophone.org/

History 2014. Registered in accordance with French law. **Aims** Promote – in a scientific framework and by means of the French language – the study of the *Arecaceae,* their spreading, culture and conservation. **Structure** Bureau; Executive Committee. **Finance** Sources: members' dues. **Publications** *PRINCEPS* – journal; *SPF Newsletter.* **NGO Relations** Affiliate of: *International Palm Society (IPS).* [2018/XJ9061/**C**]

- Société panafricaine de cardiologie (#18066)
- Société Pan Africaine de Statistiques / see Statistics and Probability African Society (#19975)
- Société panaméricaine colombienne (inactive)
- Société panaméricaine de cytologie du cancer (inactive)
- Société de Pathologie Exotique (#09225)
- Société de pathologie infectieuse de langue française (internationally oriented national body)
- Société des pêches de l'Afrique (no recent information)
- Société des pédiatres d'Amérique centrale (inactive)
- Société de pédiatrie de langue française / see Association des pédiatres de langue française (#02855)

♦ Société de pharmacie de la Méditerranée latine 19508

Sociedad Farmacéutica del Mediterraneo Latino – Società Farmaceutica del Mediterraneo Latino – Latin Mediterranean Society of Pharmacy – Romanorum juxta mare pharmacopolum collegium
Contact Facultad de Farmacia, Universidad de Granada, Campus Universitario de Cartuja, 18071 Granada, Spain.
URL: http://farmacia.ugr.es/sfml/

History 1 May 1953, Palma (Spain). Former names and other names: *Association des sociétés de pharmacie de la Méditerranée latine* – alias; *Asociación de Sociedades Farmacéuticas del Mediterraneo Latino* – alias; *Associazione delle Società Farmaceutiche del Mediterraneo Latino* – alias. **Aims** Establish scientific, professional and cultural links between member pharmacists. **Structure** International Congress and General Assembly (every 2 years, in France, Spain or Italy); Local Assemblies. Administrative Committee. **Languages** French, Italian, Spanish. **Staff** 21.00 FTE, paid. **Finance** Members' dues. Donations; legacies. **Events** *Congress* Valencia (Spain) 2022, *Congress* Naples (Italy) 2018, *Congress* Seville (Spain) 2016, *Congress* Montpellier (France) 2014, *Biennial Congress* Rome (Italy) 2012.
Members Individuals (Founder, Full, Associate, Honorary, Emeritus) in 3 countries:
France, Italy, Spain. [2019/XD2899/v/**D**]

♦ Société de Physiologie 19509

Secretariat 5 allée des Fauvettes, 44116 Vieillevigne, France. T. +33650127863.
URL: http://www.societedephysiologie.org/

History Founded 1927, Paris (France), as *Association des physiologistes de langue française.* Registered in accordance with French law. Subsequently referred to as *Physiological Association – Association des physiologistes.* Present title adopted 1994. **Aims** Promote research and discussion of all branches of physiology from gene to being. **Structure** General Assembly (annual). Council (meets at least annually) consisting of 20 members, including Board, President of the Scientific Committee and 9 representatives of different branches of physiology (sectoral groups). External Relations Committee. **Languages** English, French. **Staff** 3.50 FTE, voluntary. **Finance** Members' dues. Annual budget: about euro 25,000. **Activities** Events/meetings; knowledge management/information dissemination. **Events** *Joint Congress* Paris (France) 2016, *Annual Meeting* Strasbourg (France) 2015, *Annual Meeting* Poitiers (France) 2014, *Annual Meeting* Angers (France) 2013, *Annual Meeting* Dijon (France) 2012. **Publications** *Physiome-info* (24 a year) – electronic newsletter. Abstracts; position papers.
Members Full and corresponding, individuals in 38 countries and territories:
Algeria, Australia, Belgium, Bosnia-Herzegovina, Brazil, Bulgaria, Cameroon, Canada, Congo Brazzaville, Côte d'Ivoire, Croatia, Czechia, Denmark, Finland, France, Germany, Hungary, Iran Islamic Rep, Italy, Japan, Luxembourg, Morocco, Netherlands, New Zealand, Poland, Romania, Russia, Senegal, Serbia, Slovakia, Slovenia, Spain, Switzerland, Tahiti Is, Togo, Tunisia, USA, Vietnam. [2015.11.24/XD4640/v/**D**]

- Société Phytochimique d'Europe (#18370)
- Société planétaire (internationally oriented national body)
- Société planétaire (see: #20322)
- Société planétaire pour l'assainissement de l'énergie (#18381)
- Société Platonicienne Internationale (#14603)

♦ Société de pneumologie de langue française (SPLF) 19510

French-Language Society of Pneumology
Sec Maison de la Pneumologie, 66 boulevard St Michel, 75006 Paris, France. T. +33146340387. Fax +33146345827.
URL: https://splf.fr/

History 1903. Registration: France. **Aims** Study respiratory diseases in all their aspects. **Structure** General Assembly; Board; Administrative Council; Scientific Council. Working Group: *Groupe d'Endoscopie de Langue Française (GELF).* **Finance** Members' dues. **Events** *Congrès de Pneumologie de Langue Française (CPLF)* Marseille (France) 2023, *Journées de Recherche Respiratoire* Brussels (Belgium) 2019, *BPCO, granulomatoses* Marseille (France) 2019, *Oncologie thoracique, le poumon et son environnement* Lyon (France) 2018, *Congrès* Paris (France) 2018. **Members** Membership countries not specified. **NGO Relations** Member of: *Global Alliance Against Chronic Respiratory Diseases (GARD, #10182).* [2022/XE3226/**D**]

- Société de politique étrangère (internationally oriented national body)
- Société des professionnels en affaires européennes (#19553)
- Société pour la Promotion de l'Evolution Artificielle en Europe et Alentours (#19625)
- Société de promotion des littératures d'Afrique, d'Asie et d'Amérique latine (internationally oriented national body)
- Société de promotion et de participations pour la coopération économique, Paris (internationally oriented national body)
- Société de promotion des recherches sur l'élevage en Asie et en Océanie (#19515)
- Société protectrice des animaux en Afrique du Nord / see Society for the Protection of Animals Abroad
- Société protectrice des animaux outre mer (internationally oriented national body)
- Société de psychogériatrie de langue française (internationally oriented national body)
- Société de psychologie médicale et de psychiatrie de liaison de langue française (no recent information)

♦ Société de Radiologie d'Afrique Noire Francophone (SRANF) 19511

Pres Service de Radiologie et Imagerie Médicale, HGOPY, BP 13 765, Yaoundé, Cameroon. T. +23777704784. E-mail: jgonsu@gmail.com.
SG Service de radiologie et Imagerie Médicale, Hôp Central, Yaoundé, Cameroon.

Aims Promote the development of radiology in all countries of francophone Africa; promote research in radiology and medical imaging; promote medical education through scientific meetings and training. **Structure** Bureau, comprising President, Past-President, Vice-President, Secretary-General, Deputy Secretary-General, Treasurer-General, Deputy Treasurer-General and 5 members. **Events** *Ingénierie médicale au coeur du développement sanitaire en Afrique noire francophone* Lomé (Togo) 2011, *Congress* Lomé (Togo) 2010, *Congress* Yaoundé (Cameroon) 2008, *Congress* Ouagadougou (Burkina Faso) 2006, *Congress* Cotonou (Benin) 2002. **Publications** *Journal Officiel de la Société de Radiologie d'Afrique Noire Francophone (JAIM).*

Members Active; Honorary; Associate; Junior. Members in 19 countries:
Benin, Burkina Faso, Burundi, Cameroon, Central African Rep, Chad, Comoros, Congo Brazzaville, Congo DR, Côte d'Ivoire, Gabon, Guinea, Madagascar, Mali, Mauritania, Niger, Rwanda, Senegal, Togo.
NGO Relations *International Society of Radiology (ISR, #15412).* [2010/XJ1972/**D**]

♦ Société de réanimation de langue française (SRLF) 19512

French Intensive Care Society (FITC)
Contact 48 av Claude Vellefaux, 75010 Paris, France. T. +33145867400.
URL: http://www.srlf.org/
History 1971, Paris (France). **Aims** Promote research, education and training in critical care medicine. **Structure** General Assembly (during annual congress); President; Executive Council; Bureau; Task Forces (12). **Languages** French. **Staff** 5.00 FTE, paid. **Finance** Members' dues. Congress activities. **Activities** Events/meetings; training/education; publishing activities. **Events** *Congrès* Paris (France) 2023, *Congrès* Paris (France) 2022, *Congrès* Paris (France) 2021, *Congrès* Paris (France) 2020, *Congrès* Paris (France) 2019. **Publications** *Médicine Intensive Réanimation* (6 a year) – journal; *Annals of Intensive Care* – journal.
Members Full (by election of General Assembly); Associate. Specialists (1,441) in 26 countries:
Argentina, Belgium, Brazil, Burkina Faso, Canada, Egypt, Gabon, Germany, Greece, Israel, Italy, Lebanon, Libya, Luxembourg, Netherlands, Norway, Portugal, Senegal, Spain, Switzerland, Syrian AR, Togo, Tunisia, UK, Uruguay, Venezuela.
Included in the above, 1 organization listed in this Yearbook:
Groupe francophone de réanimation et urgences pédiatriques (GFRUP). [2019.06.25/XD5223/v/**F**]

- ♦ Société de recherche des plantes médicinales / see GA – Society for Medicinal Plant and Natural Product Research (#10075)
- ♦ Société de recherches sur les périodiques de l'époque victorienne (#18861)
- ♦ Société de recherches psychothérapiques de langue française (no recent information)
- ♦ Société religieuse des amis (#18834)
- ♦ Société rencesvals pour l'étude des épopées romanes / see Société internationale rencesvals (#19496)
- ♦ Société rencesvals internationale / see Société internationale rencesvals (#19496)
- ♦ Société Richelieu / see Richelieu International (#18938)
- ♦ Société Rorschach internationale / see International Society of the Rorschach and Projective Methods (#15430)
- ♦ Société royale de l'agriculture du Commonwealth (#18987)
- ♦ Société royale de sauvetage (#18992)
- ♦ Société Sacerdotale de Saint Joseph-Benoît Cottolengo (religious order)
- ♦ Société du Sacré-Coeur de Jésus (religious order)
- ♦ Société de Saint Colomban pour les Missions Etrangères (religious order)
- ♦ Société de Saint François Xavier pour les Missions Etrangères (religious order)
- ♦ Société de Saint Joseph du Sacré-Coeur (religious order)
- ♦ Société de Saint Paul (religious order)
- ♦ Société de Saint Vincent-de-Paul / see International Confederation of the Society of St Vincent-de-Paul (#12870)
- ♦ Société Salésienne de Saint Jean Bosco (religious order)
- ♦ Société scandinave des anesthésistes / see Scandinavian Society of Anaesthesiology and Intensive Care Medicine (#19101)
- ♦ Société scandinave pour les animaux de laboratoires (#19112)
- ♦ Société scandinave pour l'étude du diabète (#19119)
- ♦ Société scandinave d'étude de la migraine (inactive)
- ♦ Société scandinave d'histoire économique et sociale (#19106)
- ♦ Société scandinave de médecine légale (inactive)
- ♦ Société scandinave de médecine militaire (no recent information)
- ♦ Société scandinave de neurochirurgie (#19093)
- ♦ Société scandinave de physiologie (#19097)
- ♦ Sociétés chimiques des pays nordiques (inactive)
- ♦ Société Schopenhauer (#19135)
- ♦ Société pour la science des animaux de laboratoire (#19585)
- ♦ Société pour la science de la paix – internationale (internationally oriented national body)
- ♦ Société des sciences criminologiques / see International Society of Criminology (#15038)
- ♦ Société séismologique du Pacifique du Sud-Ouest (inactive)
- ♦ Société de sociologie rurale (internationally oriented national body)
- ♦ Société des Soeurs de Marie Réparatrice (religious order)
- ♦ Société des Soeurs du Prado (religious order)
- ♦ Société Sri Aurobindo (internationally oriented national body)
- ♦ Société sud-américaine de la chirurgie de la main (inactive)
- ♦ Société Suisse-Asie (internationally oriented national body)
- ♦ Société suisse de droit international (internationally oriented national body)
- ♦ Société suisse d'études africaines (internationally oriented national body)
- ♦ Société suisse d'études asiatiques / see Swiss-Asia Society
- ♦ Société suisse d'études scandinaves (internationally oriented national body)
- ♦ Société pour la théorie de la gestalt et ses applications (internationally oriented national body)
- ♦ Société théosophique (#20141)
- ♦ Société théosophique en Europe (#20142)
- ♦ Société de transplantation (#20224)
- ♦ Société des transports aériens de l'Afrique orientale (inactive)
- ♦ Société unitive (inactive)
- ♦ Société universelle d'ophtalmologie (inactive)
- ♦ Société universelle du théâtre (inactive)
- ♦ Société universitaire européenne de recherches financières (#20032)
- ♦ Société d'urologie de la Méditerranée latine (inactive)
- ♦ Société du Verbe Divin Steyler Missionare (religious order)
- ♦ Société vexillologique nordique (#17294)
- ♦ Société de vie évangélique du Coeur de Jésus (religious order)
- ♦ Société des Vocations Divines (religious order)

♦ Societies' Council for the Collective Management of Performers' Rights (SCAPR) 19513

Secretariat Av de Cortenbergh 116, 1000 Brussels, Belgium. T. +3227325984. E-mail: secretariat@scapr.org.
URL: http://www.scapr.org/
History 27 Sep 2001, Oslo (Norway), following a series of informal meetings since 1986. **Aims** Serve as a platform for cooperation among performers' collective management organizations in order to improve exchange of data and payment of performers' rights internationally. **Structure** General Assembly (annual); Board. **Languages** English. **Events** *General Assembly* Paris (France) 2018, *General Assembly* Amsterdam (Netherlands) 2014, *Asian regional conference* Kuala Lumpur (Malaysia) 2005, *General Assembly* Vienna (Austria) 2005. **Members** Full (61) in 43 countries. Membership countries not specified. [2019.09.30/XJ3906/**E**]

♦ Society for the Advancement of Behavioral Economics (SABE) 19514

Pres c/o ICEF, Miasnitsky Proezd 4/3, Moscow MOSKVA, Russia, 107078. E-mail: info@sabeconomics.org.
Sec Paderborn University, Warburger Str 100, 33098 Paderborn, Germany.
URL: https://sabeconomics.org/
History 1982. Following a dormant period, revived in 1992. **Aims** Develop behavioral economic analysis. **Structure** Board; Executive Committee. **Events** *Joint Conference on Economic Psychology and Behavioural Economics* Nice (France) 2023, *Conference* Stateline, NV (USA) 2022, *Joint Conference on Economic Psychology and Behavioural Economics* 2021, *Joint Conference on Economic Psychology and Behavioural Economics* Kristiansand (Norway) 2020, *Joint Conference on Economic Psychology and Behavioural Economics* Dublin (Ireland) 2019. **Publications** *Journal of Behavioral Economics for Policy (JBEP)*; *SABE Newsletter.*
Members Individuals in 44 countries and territories:
Argentina, Australia, Austria, Canada, Chile, China, Colombia, Costa Rica, Czechia, Denmark, Ecuador, Egypt, Finland, France, Germany, Ghana, Greece, Guatemala, Hungary, Ireland, Israel, Italy, Japan, Malta, Mauritius, Mexico, Morocco, Netherlands, New Zealand, Peru, Poland, Portugal, Romania, Russia, South Africa, Spain, Sweden, Switzerland, Taiwan, Tunisia, Türkiye, UK, Uruguay, USA.
NGO Relations With *International Association for Research in Economic Psychology (IAREP, #12132)* instrumental in setting up: *International Confederation for the Advancement of Behavioral Economics and Economic Psychology (ICABEEP, #12842).* Occasional joint conferences with IAREP or *Western Economic Association International (WEA International).* [2023/XW1412/v/**C**]

♦ Society for the Advancement of Breeding Research in Asia and Oceania (SABRAO) 19515

Société de promotion des recherches sur l'élevage en Asie et en Océanie
Coordinator 99 Daehak-ro, Yuseong-gu, Chungnam National University, Daejeon 34134, Korea Rep.
SG address not obtained.
Journal: https://sabraojournal.org/
History 1968, Japan. Former names and other names: *Society for the Advancement of Breeding Researches in Asia and Oceania* – former (1968). **Aims** Foster communication among scientists working in plant breeding and *genetics*; promote scientific and technical cooperation primarily in Asia and Oceania, in order to contribute towards progress in agricultural production and food ssecurity within the region. **Structure** Congress (every 4 years); Executive Board; Regional Secretaries; Editorial Board. **Languages** English. **Staff** Voluntary. **Finance** Members' dues. Publication fees. **Activities** Knowledge management/information dissemination; events/meetings; networking/liaising. **Events** *Quadrennial Congress* Gwangju (Korea Rep) 2019, *Quadrennial Congress* Bogor (Indonesia) 2015, *Quadrennial Congress* Chiang Mai (Thailand) 2012, *Quadrennial Congress* Cairns, QLD (Australia) 2009, *Quadrennial congress* Tsukuba (Japan) 2005. **Publications** *SABRAO Journal of Breeding and Genetics* (4 a year) – plus special issues.
Members Individuals (about 500); Corporate (40). Members in 17 countries and territories:
Australia, Bangladesh, Canada, China, India, Indonesia, Japan, Korea Rep, Malaysia, Nepal, New Zealand, Pakistan, Philippines, Sri Lanka, Taiwan, Thailand, USA.
IGO Relations *International Rice Research Institute (IRRI, #14754).* **NGO Relations** Member of: *International Genetics Federation (IGF, #13711).* [2022/XD5336/**D**]

- ♦ Society for the Advancement of Breeding Researches in Asia and Oceania / see Society for the Advancement of Breeding Research in Asia and Oceania (#19515)
- ♦ Society for the Advancement of General Systems Theory / see International Society for the Systems Sciences (#15500)
- ♦ Society for the Advancement of Science in Africa (internationally oriented national body)
- ♦ Society for the Advancement of Science and Technology in the Arab World (internationally oriented national body)

♦ Society for the Advancement of Socio-Economics (SASE) 19516

Exec Dir Paulstr 3, 50676 Cologne, Germany. T. +4922153006683. E-mail: saseexecutive@sase.org.
URL: http://www.sase.org/
History 1989. Bylaws amended: 8 July 1999; 27 Sep 2019. Former names and other names: *Association pour le développement de la socio-économie (ADSE)* – former. Registration: Section 501(c)(3), USA, Washington DC. **Aims** Advance understanding of economic behaviour across a broad range of academic disciplines; support intellectual exploration of economic behaviour and its policy implications within the context of societal, institutional, historical, philosophical, psychological and ethical factors; balance inductive and deductive approaches to the study of economic behaviour at both micro and macro levels of analysis. **Structure** Executive Council; Executive Committee; Executive Director; Committees. **Activities** Awards/prizes/competitions; events/meetings. **Events** *Annual Conference* Limerick (Ireland) 2024, *Annual Meeting* Rio de Janeiro (Brazil) 2023, *Annual Meeting* Amsterdam (Netherlands) 2022, *Annual Meeting* 2021, *Annual Meeting* 2020. **Publications** *SASE Blog*; *Socio-Economic Review* – journal. **Members** Individuals in 50 countries. Membership countries not specified. [2023.02.15/XN5614/**C**]

- ♦ Society for Afghan Studies / see Society for South Asian Studies
- ♦ Society for African Church History (inactive)
- ♦ Society of African Culture / see Communauté africaine de culture (#04373)

♦ Society of Africanist Archaeologists (SAfA) 19517

Main Office PO Box 1892, Houston TX 77251-1892, USA. E-mail: safa@rice.edu.
Pres Dept of Anthropology, Stony Brook Univ, 100 Nicolls Rd, Stony Brook NY 11794, USA.
URL: http://safa.rice.edu/
History Founded Apr 1971, Urbana IL (USA), at first meeting of Africanist Archaeologists. **Aims** Promote archaeological research in Africa and on African-related topics and the management and protection of Africa's cultural heritage. **Structure** Executive Committee. **Languages** English, French. **Staff** None. **Finance** Members' dues. Donations. **Events** *Biennial Conference* Houston, TX (USA) 2023, *Biennial Conference* Oxford (UK) 2021, *Biennial Conference* Oxford (UK) 2020, *Biennial Conference* Toronto, ON (Canada) 2018, *Biennial Conference* Toulouse (France) 2016. **Publications** *Nyame Akuma* (2 a year) – online. **Members** Individuals worldwide. Membership countries not specified. **NGO Relations** Cooperates with: *British Institute in Eastern Africa (BIEA)*; *Pan-African Archaeological Association (PAA, #18035)*; *World Archaeological Congress (WAC, #21103).* Affiliate society of: *African Studies Association (ASA)*; Society for American Archaeology (SAA). [2020/XD0478/v/**D**]

- ♦ Society of African Missions (religious order)
- ♦ Society of African Physicists and Mathematicians / see African Physical Society (#00417)

♦ Society on AIDS in Africa (SAA) 19518

Société africaine anti-SIDA (SAA)
Secretariat PO Box AF2072, Accra, Ghana. T. +233302913739. Fax +233302913694. E-mail: info@saafrica.org.
URL: http://www.saafrica.org/
History 1990, during 5th conference. **Aims** Decrease the spread and mitigate the impact of *HIV/AIDS*, *STIs*, *tuberculosis* and *malaria* on the *African* continent. **Structure** Board of Trustees; Secretariat. **Languages** English, French. **Staff** 10.00 FTE, paid. **Finance** UN System; conference proceeds. **Activities** Events/meetings. **Events** *ICASA : International Conference on HIV/AIDS and Sexually Transmitted Infections in Africa* Durban (South Africa) 2021, *ICASA : International Conference on HIV/AIDS and Sexually Transmitted Infections in Africa* Kigali (Rwanda) 2019, *International Workshop on HIV Pediatrics* Mexico City (Mexico) 2019, *ICASA : International Conference on HIV/AIDS and Sexually Transmitted Infections in Africa* Abidjan (Côte d'Ivoire) 2017, *International Workshop on HIV Pediatrics* Paris (France) 2017.
Members Individuals and organizations engaged in reproductive health and HIV/AIDS-related activities in 26 countries:
Belgium, Benin, Botswana, Burkina Faso, Burundi, Cameroon, Canada, Comoros, Congo DR, Côte d'Ivoire, Egypt, Ethiopia, Gabon, Ghana, India, Kenya, Mali, Morocco, Netherlands, Nigeria, Rwanda, Senegal, South Africa, Sudan, Tanzania UR, UK.
IGO Relations Governments of: Burkina Faso; Cameroon; Ethiopia; Ghana; Kenya; Kinshasa; Morocco; Nigeria; Senegal; South Africa; Uganda; Zimbabwe. **NGO Relations** Member of: *Network of AIDS Researchers of Eastern and Southern Africa (NARESA, #16990).* [2019/XD2781/**F**]

- ♦ Society of Air Safety Investigators / see International Society of Air Safety Investigators (#14914)
- ♦ Society for American Archaeology (internationally oriented national body)
- ♦ Society of American Travel Writers (internationally oriented national body)
- ♦ Society of Anaesthesiologists of East Africa (see: #21482)
- ♦ Society of Anaesthesiologists of West Africa – Anglophone (inactive)
- ♦ Society of Analytical Cytology / see International Society for Advancement of Cytometry (#14900)
- ♦ Society for Ancient Mediterranean Religions (internationally oriented national body)

♦ Society for Animation Studies (SAS) **19519**
Sec address not obtained.
URL: http://www.animationstudies.org/
History 1987. Founded by Harvey Deneroff. Registration: 501(c)3, USA, California. **Aims** Promote the study of animation history, theory and practice. **Structure** Board. **Activities** Awards/prizes/competitions; events/meetings. **Events** *Conference* Glassboro, NJ (USA) 2023, *Conference* Teesside (UK) 2022, *Conference* 2021, *Conference* New Orleans, LA (USA) 2020, *Conference* Lisbon (Portugal) 2019. [2022/XM7911/**C**]

♦ Society for the Anthropology of Europe (internationally oriented national body)

♦ Society for the Anthropology of Lowland South America (SALSA) .. **19520**
Sec-Treas address not obtained. E-mail: salsasectreas@gmail.com – salsatipiti.webmaster@gmail.com.
URL: https://www.salsa-tipiti.org/
History 2001. Bylaws last amended Sep 2019. Registration: Section 501(c)(3) organization, No/ID: EIN: 72-1517376, Start date: 2013, USA. **Aims** Bring together specialists who live in Latin America, Europe, North America, and elsewhere and facilitate connections and develop exchanges of information among them, disseminate original scholarship of high quality, and encourage students to learn about and carry out research in this region. **Structure** Board of Directors. **Languages** English, Portuguese, Spanish. **Finance** Sources: members' dues. **Events** *Conference* Charlottesville, VA (USA) 2021, *Conference* Vienna (Austria) 2019, *Conference* Lima (Peru) 2017. [2023/AA0594/**C**]

♦ Society for Applied Philosophy (SAP) **19521**
Administrator LLMVC – Taylor Bldg, Univ of Aberdeen, Aberdeen, AB24 3UB, UK. E-mail: admin@appliedphil.org.
URL: http://www.appliedphil.org/
History Founded 1982. A UK Registered Charity: 287331. **Aims** Promote philosophical work that has a direct bearing on areas of practical concern. **Structure** Executive Committee. **Activities** Events/meetings. **Events** *Annual Conference* Cardiff (UK) 2019, *Annual Conference* Utrecht (Netherlands) 2018. **Publications** *Journal of Applied Philosophy.* [2019/XM7807/**D**]

♦ Society for Applied Research in Memory and Cognition (SARMAC) . **19522**
Exec Dir Room H128, Dept of Psychology, Univ of Warwick, University Road, Coventry, CV4 7AL, UK. T. +442476523096.
URL: http://www.sarmac.org/
History 1994, Baltimore, MD (USA). Founded at the 3rd *International Conference on Practical Aspects of Memory (PAM).* **Aims** Enhance collaboration and cooperation between basic and applied researchers in memory and cognition. **Structure** Governing Board; Executive Officers; Publications Committee; Membership Committee; Student Caucus. **Languages** English. **Finance** Sources: members' dues. **Activities** Awards/prizes/competitions; events/meetings. **Events** *Biennial Meeting* Nagoya (Japan) 2023, *Regional Meeting* Portsmouth (UK) 2022, *Biennial Meeting* Nagoya (Japan) 2021, *Biennial Meeting* Brewster, MA (USA) 2019, *Biennial Meeting* Sydney, NSW (Australia) 2017. **Publications** *Journal of Applied Research in Memory and Cognition.* **Members** Full (about 500). Membership countries not specified. [2022/XJ2280/**C**]

♦ Society of Arab Neuroscientists (unconfirmed)
♦ Society for Arthroscopy and Joint-Surgery (#10141)

♦ Society for Artistic Research (SAR) **19523**
Contact Oranje Nassaulaan 1, PO Box 53028, 1007 RA Amsterdam, Netherlands. E-mail: info@societyforartisticresearch.org – backoffice@societyforartisticresearch.org.
URL: http://www.societyforartisticresearch.org/
History 2010, Bern (Switzerland). **Aims** Nurture, connect and disseminate artistic research as specific practices of creating knowledge and insight. **Structure** Executive Board. **Finance** Sources: members' dues. **Activities** Events/meetings; knowledge management/information dissemination. **Events** *International Conference on Artistic Research* Vienna (Austria) 2021, *SAR International Conference on Artistic Research* Bergen (Norway) 2020, *Conference* The Hague (Netherlands) 2016, *Members' Meeting* London (UK) 2015, *Members' Meeting* Stockholm (Sweden) 2014. **Publications** *Journal for Artistic Research (JAR).* Research catalogue.
Members Individual; Institutional. Institutions in 11 countries:
Austria, Belgium, Estonia, Finland, Germany, Netherlands, Norway, Spain, Sweden, Switzerland, UK. [2018/XM4284/**D**]

♦ The Society of ASEAN Rhinologists / see ASEAN Rhinology Society (#01231)
♦ Society for Asian and Comparative Philosophy (internationally oriented national body)
♦ Society for Asian and Comparative Philosophy, Oneonta / see Society for Asian and Comparative Philosophy
♦ Society for Asian Political and Economic Studies, Tokyo / see Japan Association for Asian Studies
♦ Society of Asian Rotomoulders (internationally oriented national body)

♦ Society of Audiovisual Authors (SAA) **19524**
Communications Manager Rue du Prince Royal, 87B, 1050 Brussels, Belgium. T. +3228949330. E-mail: info@saa-authors.eu.
URL: http://www.saa-authors.eu/
History 2010, Belgium. Founded by *Société des auteurs et compositeurs dramatiques (SACD)* and 2 German companies. Former names and other names: *Société des Auteurs Audiovisuels* – former. Registration: EU Transparency Register:, No/ID: 99336382936-11. **Aims** Support and strengthen the economic and moral rights of audiovisual authors (screenwriters and directors); secure fair and proportional remuneration for audiovisual authors for every use of their works; develop, promote and advance the collective management of rights by member organisations to provide a cost effective, transparent and efficient system to facilitate dissemination of audiovisual works and distribution of royalties to authors. **Structure** General Assembly; Board of Directors. **Languages** English, French. **Staff** 4.00 FTE, paid. **Activities** Advocacy/lobbying/activism. **Events** *Young Creators Have Rights, Right?* 2022, *Collective management: A safety net for authors and performers* 2021, *Lights and Action on Authors' Royalties* 2021, *Seminar on the Copyright Directive, Article 18* 2021, *The New Copyright Legislation – Making the Most for Next Generation Authors* 2020. **Publications** White Papers.
Members Institutions (33) in 25 countries:
Albania, Austria, Belgium, Bulgaria, Croatia, Czechia, Estonia, Finland, France, Germany, Greece, Hungary, Italy, Lithuania, Netherlands, Norway, Poland, Portugal, Romania, Slovakia, Slovenia, Spain, Sweden, Switzerland, UK. [2022.05.10/XG7832/**D**]

♦ Society of Australasian Neurological Surgeons / see Neurosurgical Society of Australasia
♦ Society for Austro-Arab Relations (internationally oriented national body)
♦ Society of Automotive Engineers International / see SAE International

♦ Society for Benefit-Cost Analysis (SBCA) **19525**
Contact 222 S Westmonte Dr, Ste 111, Altamonte Springs FL 32714, USA. T. +14077880. E-mail: info@benefitcostanalysis.org.
URL: https://www.benefitcostanalysis.org/
History 2007, USA. Founded by the Benefit-Cost Analysis Center at the Evans School of Public Affairs, University of Washington, with the support of *MacArthur Foundation.* **Aims** Improve the theory and practice of benefit-cost analysis; support evidence-based policy decisions. **Structure** Board of Directors. **Activities** Awards/prizes/competitions; events/meetings. **Events** *Annual Conference* 2022, *European Conference* Stockholm (Sweden) 2021, *European Conference* 2020, *European Conference* Toulouse (France) 2019. **Publications** *Journal of Benefit Cost Analysis (JBCA).* **Members** Individuals. Organizational affiliates. Membership countries not specified. [2022/AA2459/**C**]

♦ Society of Biblical Literature (internationally oriented national body)

♦ Society for Bioinformatics in the Nordic Countries (SocBin) **19526**
Pres Science for Life Laboratory, Box 1031, SE-171 21 Solna, Sweden. T. +46855378568. Fax +46855378214.
URL: http://www.socbin.org/
Events *Annual Conference* Moscow (Russia) 2016, *Annual Conference* Oslo (Norway) 2014, *Annual Conference* Torun (Poland) 2013, *Annual Conference* Stockholm (Sweden) 2012, *FORTE : International Conference on Formal Techniques for Networked and Distributed Systems* Stockholm (Sweden) 2012. **NGO Relations** Affiliated regional group of: *International Society for Computational Biology (ISCB, #15026).* [2018/XD8984/**D**]

♦ Society of Biological Inorganic Chemistry (SBIC) **19527**
Main Office 7918 Jones Branch Dr, Ste 300, McLean VA 22102, USA. E-mail: info@sbichem.org.
URL: http://www.sbichem.org/
History 1995. **Structure** Council. **Activities** Awards/prizes/competitions; events/meetings. Sponsors several conferences, including *International Conference on Biological Inorganic Chemistry (ICBIC); European Biological Inorganic Chemistry Conference (EuroBIC); Asian Biological Inorganic Chemistry Conference (AsBIC); Latin American Meeting on Biological Inorganic Chemistry (LABIC).* **Events** *International Conference on Biological Inorganic Chemistry (IBIC22)* UK 2027, *International Conference on Biological Inorganic Chemistry (IBIC21)* Irvine, CA (USA) 2025, *EuroBIC – European Biologic Inorganic Chemistry Conference* Münster (Germany) 2024, *International Conference on Biological Inorganic Chemistry (IBIC20)* Adelaide, SA (Australia) 2023, *AsBIC – Asian Biological Inorganic Chemistry Conference* Kobe (Japan) 2022. **Publications** *Journal of Biological Inorganic Chemistry.*
Members Individuals (648) in 41 countries and territories:
Argentina, Australia, Austria, Belgium, Brazil, Bulgaria, Canada, China, Croatia, Czechia, Denmark, Finland, France, Germany, Greece, Hungary, India, Ireland, Israel, Italy, Japan, Korea Rep, Mexico, Netherlands, New Zealand, Norway, Philippines, Poland, Portugal, Puerto Rico, Russia, Slovenia, South Africa, Spain, Sweden, Switzerland, Taiwan, UK, Uruguay, USA, Venezuela. [2022/XM2140/**D**]

♦ Society for Biological Therapy / see Society for Immunotherapy of Cancer
♦ Society of Biophysicists of Latin America (#19351)

♦ Society of Blue Friars (SBF) **19528**
Contact Grand Abbott, 1733 16th St NW, Washington DC 20009-3103, USA.
SG address not obtained.
URL: http://www.societyofbluefriars.org/
History 1932. Comes within the *Masonic Movement (#16593).* **Aims** Recognize *Masonic* authors. **Structure** Officers: President; Secretary-General; Deputy Grand Abbot. **Activities** Organizes annual meeting.
Members Individuals (21) in 4 countries:
Canada, Israel, UK, USA. [2019/XM0799/**F**]

♦ Society for Broadband Professionals (internationally oriented national body)
♦ Society of Business Economists / see Society of Professional Economists
♦ Society for Cable Television Engineers / see Society for Broadband Professionals
♦ Society of Cardiology of African French-Speaking Countries (inactive)
♦ Society of Cardiovascular Computed Tomography (internationally oriented national body)

♦ Society for Cardiovascular Magnetic Resonance (SCMR) **19529**
CEO 19 Mantua Rd, Mount Royal NJ 08061, USA. T. +18564238955. Fax +18564233420. E-mail: hq@scmr.org.
Events Manager address not obtained. E-mail: meetings@scmr.org.
URL: http://smcr.org/
Aims Improve cardiovascular health by advancing the field of CMR. **Structure** Executive Committee; Board of Trustees. Committees (13): Annual Scientific Session; Clinical Practice; Clinical Trials; Education; Global CMR Registry; International Outreach Program; Membership; Nominating; Publications; Public Relations; Science; Technologist; Web. **Activities** Certification/accreditation; events/meetings; standards/guidelines; training/education. **Events** *Annual Scientific Session* San Diego, CA (USA) 2021, *Annual Scientific Session* Orlando, FL (USA) 2020, *Annual Scientific Session* Bellevue, WA (USA) 2019, *Joint Meeting* Barcelona (Spain) 2018, *Annual Scientific Session* Washington, DC (USA) 2017. **Publications** *Journal of Cardiovascular Magnetic Resonance (JCMR); SCMR Bulletin* – electronic. [2016/XM5243/**C**]

♦ Society for Caribbean Linguistics (SCL) **19530**
Société de linguistique des Caraïbes – Sociedad de Lingüística del Caribe – Vereniging voor Taalkunde van het Caraibisch Gebied – Sosaiyiti fi Kyaribiyan Linggwistiks – Organisashon di Lingwistika Karibense – Sosyété pou lengwistik kawayib-la
Treas Dept Modern Languages and Linguistics, Fac of Humanities and Education, Univ of the West Indies, St Augustine, Trinidad-Tobago. T. +18686622002ext2035. Fax +18686635059. E-mail: treasurer@scl-online.net.
Sec Dept Languages/Literatures/Linguistics, 140 Founder's College, York Univ, 4700 Keele Street, Toronto ON M3J 1P3, Canada. E-mail: secretary@scl-online.net.
URL: http://www.scl-online.net/
History 1972, St Augustine (Trinidad), at 1st biennial Conference. **Aims** Advance scientific study of language and language-related problems in the Caribbean area; promote study of language with special reference to the Caribbean; involve interested persons from all parts of the world. **Structure** General Meeting (every 2 years); Executive Committee; Special Committees. **Languages** Dutch, English, French, French-based creoles and pidgins, Spanish. **Staff** 0.00 FTE, paid. **Finance** Members' dues. Income (annual): about US$ 2,500. Expenditure (annual): non-conference year US$ 1,000; conference year: US$ 8,000. **Events** *Biennial Conference* St Augustine (Trinidad-Tobago) 2022, *Biennial Conference* St Augustine (Trinidad-Tobago) 2020, *Biennial Conference* Heredia (Costa Rica) / Limón (Costa Rica) 2018, *Biennial Conference* Mona (Jamaica) 2016, *Biennial Conference* Oranjestad (Aruba) 2014. **Publications** *SCL Occasional Papers. SCL Popular Series. Ivory Towers: The Memoirs of a Pidgin Fancier* by Robert B LePage; *Studies in Caribbean Language; Studies in Caribbean Language II; Vini Chanté an Patwa: Come Sing in Patois – Patois Songs of Trinidad and Tobago.* Conference proceedings.
Members Regular; Student; Honorary, in 31 countries and territories:
Aruba, Australia, Bahamas, Barbados, Belize, Bonaire Is, Canada, Colombia, Costa Rica, Curaçao, Dominica, France, Germany, Grenada, Guadeloupe, Guyana, Haiti, Italy, Jamaica, Kenya, Martinique, Netherlands, Portugal, Puerto Rico, Spain, St Lucia, St Vincent-Grenadines, Suriname, Trinidad-Tobago, USA, Virgin Is USA. [2022/XD0161/**v/D**]

♦ Society of Caribbean Ornithology / see BirdsCaribbean (#03267)
♦ Society for Caribbean Studies (internationally oriented national body)
♦ Society of the Catholic Apostolate (religious order)
♦ Society of Chemical Industry (internationally oriented national body)
♦ Society of Christ for Polish Emigrants (religious order)
♦ Society of Classical Bibliography / see Société internationale de bibliographie classique (#19474)
♦ Society for Clinical Data Management (internationally oriented national body)
♦ Society for Clinical and Experimental Oral Oncology / see International Society for Oral Oncology (#15328)
♦ Society for Coaching Psychology / see International Society for Coaching Psychology (#15019)

♦ Society for Cognitive Studies of the Moving Image (SCSMI) **19531**
Sec UWI-M Communication Arts, 821 University Ave, Madison WI 53706, USA. T. +16082633132.
Pres School of Performing Arts, Virginia Tech, 251B Henderson Hall, 195 Alumni Mall, Blacksburg VA 24061, USA. T. +15402316014.
URL: http://scsmi-online.org/
History 1997, at University of Kansas, Lawrence KS (USA), as *'Center for Cognitive Studies of the Moving Image'.* Current title adopted 2006. Migrated to Georgia State University, Atlanta GA (USA) and then to University of Central Arkansas, Conway AR (USA). **Aims** Investigate the contribution of cognitive science to our understanding of moving images as well as the contribution of scholarship on moving image form, style, aesthetics and history to our understanding of psychology and the cognition of art. **Structure** Board of Directors. **Languages** English. **Staff** Voluntary. **Finance** Sources: members' dues. **Events** *Conference* Gandia (Spain) 2022, *Conference* Madison, WI (USA) 2021, *Conference* Madison, WI (USA) 2020, *Conference* Hamburg (Germany) 2019, *Conference* Bozeman, MT (USA) 2018. **Publications** *Projections: The Journal for Movies and Mind.*
Members Individuals in 25 countries and territories:
Australia, Austria, Belgium, Brazil, Canada, China, Croatia, Denmark, Finland, France, Germany, Hong Kong, Ireland, Italy, Jordan, Korea Rep, Mexico, Netherlands, Portugal, Spain, Sweden, Switzerland, Türkiye, UK, USA. [2022/XJ8659/**C**]

- ♦ Society of Combinatorial Sciences (inactive)
- ♦ Society for Companion Animal Studies (internationally oriented national body)
- ♦ Society of Comparative Hematology (unconfirmed)
- ♦ Society of Comparative Legislation (#19500)
- ♦ Society of Competitive Intelligence Professionals (internationally oriented national body)

♦ Society for Complexity in Acute Illness (SCAI) 19532

Pres c/o Denver Health, 777 Bannock St, Denver CO 80204, USA.
URL: http://scai.iccai.org/

Structure Board of Directors, comprising President, Vice-President, Secretary and Treasurer. **Activities** *International Conference on Complexity in Acute Illness (ICCAI)*. **Events** *Conference* Denver, CO (USA) 2019, *Conference* Budapest (Hungary) 2013, *Conference* Ottawa, ON (Canada) 2012, *International conference / Conference* Bonn (Germany) 2011, *International conference / Conference* Atlanta, GA (USA) 2010. **NGO Relations** Cooperates with: *European Shock Society, The (ESS, #08480)*. [2015/XM4076/D]

♦ Society of Computational Economics (SCE) 19533

Sec-Treas Dept of Economics, Penn State Univ, 304 Kern Bldg, University Park PA 16801, USA. T. +13153123444.
URL: http://comp-econ.org/

History Founded 1984. **Aims** Promote computational methods in economics and finance. **Structure** Officers: President, Secretary-Treasurer; Advisory Council. **Staff** None. **Events** *International Conference on Computing in Economics and Finance (CEF)* Tokyo (Japan) 2021, *International Conference on Computing in Economics and Finance* Warsaw (Poland) 2020, *International Conference on Computing in Economics and Finance* Ottawa, ON (Canada) 2019, *International Conference on Computing in Economics and Finance* Milan (Italy) 2018, *International Conference on Computing in Economics and Finance* New York, NY (USA) 2017. **Publications** *Computational Economics*; *Journal of Economic Dynamics and Control*.
Members Individuals (357) in 19 countries and territories:
Australia, Austria, Canada, Chile, Denmark, France, Germany, Italy, Japan, Netherlands, New Zealand, Norway, Russia, Spain, Sweden, Switzerland, Taiwan, UK, USA. [2020/XF4690/F]

- ♦ Society for Computer Simulation / see Society for Modeling Simulation International (#19598)
- ♦ Society for Computers and Law (internationally oriented national body)

♦ Society for Conservation Biology (SCB) 19534

Exec Dir 1017 O St NW, Washington DC 20001-4229, USA. T. +12022344133. Fax +17039954633. E-mail: information@conbio.org.
URL: http://www.conservationbiology.org/

History 1985. Registered in accordance with USA law. **Aims** Develop the scientific and technical means for the *protection*, maintenance and restoration of life on Earth (species, ecosystems and the processes that sustain them); promote scientific study of the phenomena that affect maintenance, loss and restoration of *biodiversity*. **Structure** Annual Meeting. Board of Governors, comprising President, President Elect, Secretary, Chief Financial Officer, 3 Past Presidents, 16 voting members and 12 ex-officio members. Sections (7): Africa; Asia; Austral and Neotropical America; Australasia; Europe; Marine; North America. Committees (8). **Staff** 11.00 FTE, paid. **Finance** Members' dues. Donations from foundations, international and national organizations and governmental agencies, including the following listed in this Yearbook: *Conservation International (CI)*; *MacArthur Foundation*; *World Wide Fund for Nature (WWF, #21922)*. **Activities** Organizes meetings and workshops; offers awards. Committees (8): Awards; Conference; Education; Membership; Nominations; Planning and Development; Policy; Student Affairs. **Events** *International Congress for Conservation Biology* Kuala Lumpur (Malaysia) 2019, *International Marine Conservation Congress* Kuching (Malaysia) 2018, *Congress* St Augustine (Trinidad-Tobago) 2018, *Conservation in a changing world* Wellington (New Zealand) 2018, *International Congress for Conservation Biology* Cartagena de Indias (Colombia) 2017. **Publications** *Conservation Biology* (6 a year) – journal; *NeoCons* (6 a year) – online newsletter; *Conservation in Practice* (4 a year) – magazine; *Society for Conservation Biology Newsletter* (4 a year); *Pacific Conservation Biology* – journal. Annual Report. **Members** Individuals (8,000); Institutions (3,000), in 120 countries. Membership countries not specified. **IGO Relations** *UNESCO (#20322)*. **NGO Relations** Member of: *International Union for Conservation of Nature and Natural Resources (IUCN, #15766)*. Collaborates with: *American Association for the Advancement of Science (AAAS)*. [2012/XF2305/F]

- ♦ Society for the Conservation of Endangered Carnivores and their International Ecological Study (unconfirmed)
- ♦ Society for Conservation and Protection of Environment (internationally oriented national body)

♦ Society for the Conservation of Reef Fish Aggregations (SCRFA) ... 19535

Dir 3/F Kadoorie BioSci Bldg, Univ of Hong Kong, Pok Fu Lam, Hong Kong, Central and Western, Hong Kong. Fax +85225176082. E-mail: scrfa.org@gmail.com.
URL: http://www.scrfa.org/

Aims Raise awareness about the vulnerability of reef fish spawning aggregations and work towards their better protection and management. **Structure** Board of 8. **Publications** *SCRFA Update*. **Members** Individuals (about 300). Membership countries not specified. **NGO Relations** Member of: *Global Coral Reef Monitoring Network (GCRMN, #10306)*. [2010/XM3982/D]

- ♦ Society for the Conservation and Study of Caribbean Birds / see BirdsCaribbean (#03267)
- ♦ Society of Construction Law for Africa (unconfirmed)
- ♦ Society of Construction Law Gulf (internationally oriented national body)
- ♦ Society of Construction Law – UAE / see Society of Construction Law Gulf
- ♦ Society of Consumer Affairs Professionals / see Society of Consumer Affairs Professionals in Business
- ♦ Society of Consumer Affairs Professionals in Business (internationally oriented national body)

♦ Society for Consumer Affairs Professionals in Europe (SOCAPiE) .. 19536

Registered Office Wexford Lodge, Symington, KA1 5QN, UK.
URL: http://www.socapie.eu/

History as *SOCAP Europe*. Registered in accordance with Belgian law. Present name adopted 2003 when merged with SOCAP UK. Previously also known as *SOCAP in Europe*. **Structure** Officers: President, Vice-President, Secretary and Treasurer. **Events** *Social Capital Markets Conference* Amsterdam (Netherlands) 2011, *Annual Conference* London (UK) 2005. **Members** Membership countries not specified. **NGO Relations** *Society of Consumer Affairs Professionals in Business (SOCAP International)*. [2013/XD4693/t/D]

♦ Society of Core Analysts (SCA) 19537

Exec Dir 139 Whittaker Road, Rusagonis NB E3B 7X3, Canada. E-mail: office@scaweb.org.
Pres TOTAL, av Larribau, 64000 Pau, France. T. +33663153983.
URL: http://www.scaweb.org/

History Founded 1986. A chapter of *Society of Petrophysicists and Well Log Analysts (SPWLA, #19617)*. Current by-laws revised 2013. **Aims** Serve the interests of all persons who use or obtain *reservoir* evaluation information from *rock* and core samples. **Structure** Board of 8 officers. **Languages** English. **Staff** 1.00 FTE, paid. **Activities** Events/meetings. Annual International Symposium. **Events** *Symposium* Austin, TX (USA) 2021, *Symposium* Austin, TX (USA) 2020, *Symposium* Pau (France) 2019, *Symposium* Trondheim (Norway) 2018, *Maximizing the value from your core* Vienna (Austria) 2017. **Publications** *SCANews*. [2019/XJ6449/C]

- ♦ Society of Cotton Products Analysts / see American Oil Chemists' Society
- ♦ Society of Criminological Sciences / see International Society of Criminology (#15038)
- ♦ Society of Critical Care Medicine (internationally oriented national body)

♦ Society for Cryobiology (SfC) 19538

Exec Dir 245 W Chase St, Baltimore MD 21201, USA. E-mail: admin@societyforcryobiology.org.
Sec Univ of Saskatchewan, College Arts and Science, Saskatoon SK S7N 5A2, Canada. T. +13069664404.
URL: http://www.societyforcryobiology.org/

History 1964. Former names and other names: *Society for Cryobiology – International Society for Low-Temperature Biology and Medicine* – full title; *Society for Cryobiology – Scientific Society for Low-Temperature Biology and Medicine* – former. **Aims** Promote scientific research in low temperature biology; improve scientific understanding in this field; disseminate and apply this knowledge to the benefit of mankind. **Structure** Board of Governors; Executive Committee. **Languages** English. **Staff** 1.60 FTE, paid. **Finance** Sources: donations; meeting proceeds; members' dues; sale of publications. **Activities** Events/meetings; publishing activities. **Events** *Virtual Annual Meeting* Chicago, IL (USA) 2022, *Virtual Annual Meeting* Baltimore, MD (USA) 2021, *Virtual Annual Meeting* Baltimore, MD (USA) 2020, *Annual Meeting* San Diego, CA (USA) 2019, *Annual Meeting* Madrid (Spain) 2018. **Publications** *Cryobiology* – journal; *SfC Newsletter*.
Members Full in 30 countries and territories:
Argentina, Australia, Brazil, Canada, China, Czechia, Denmark, France, Germany, Greece, Hungary, India, Iran Islamic Rep, Israel, Italy, Japan, Korea Rep, Netherlands, New Zealand, Nigeria, Russia, Slovakia, Spain, Sweden, Switzerland, Taiwan, Türkiye, UK, Ukraine, USA. [2023.02.14/XJ6488/C]

- ♦ Society for Cryobiology – International Society for Low-Temperature Biology and Medicine / see Society for Cryobiology (#19538)
- ♦ Society for Cryobiology – Scientific Society for Low-Temperature Biology and Medicine / see Society for Cryobiology (#19538)

♦ Society for Cultural and Scientific Progress in Central and Eastern Europe (SCASPEE) 19539

Headquarters Kőrakas 47, floor 2 – door 6, Budapest 1157, Hungary.
Main: http://scaspee.com/

History Founded Aug 2012, Budapest (Hungary). **Aims** Promote and facilitate cooperation among scientists; encourage and support scientific education and science outreach for progress and development in the region; enhance and support scientific activities among students; sharpen students' talents for scientific research and creativity; strengthen ties between students and researchers; improve scientific collaboration between scientists of the region. **Structure** Board of Governors. **Languages** English, Hungarian, Russian, Ukrainian. **Staff** 6.00 FTE, voluntary. **Activities** Events/meetings. **Events** *Advances in the natural sciences and engineering* Budapest (Hungary) 2015, *Humanities and social sciences in the era of globalization* Budapest (Hungary) 2015, *Pedagogy and psychology in an era of increasing flow of information* Budapest (Hungary) 2015, *Philology and linguistics in the digital age* Budapest (Hungary) 2015, *Urgent problems of pedagogy and psychology* Budapest (Hungary) 2015. **Publications** *Science and Education – a New Dimension* – journal.
Members Full (112) in 12 countries:
Armenia, Belarus, Bulgaria, Hungary, Poland, Romania, Russia, Serbia, Slovakia, UK, Ukraine, Uzbekistan. [2019.12.12/XJ6601/D]

♦ Society for Cutaneous Ultrastructure Research (SCUR) 19540

Sec Univ Milano, Biomedical Sciences Dept, Via Mangiagalli 31, 20133 Milan MI, Italy. E-mail: volker.huck@scur.org – contact@scur.org.
URL: http://www.scur.org/

History Founded 1978. **Aims** Promote research in electron microscopy and other combined visualization techniques applied to cutaneous biology and pathology; advance understanding of human skin ultrastructure in health and disease. **Structure** Board. **Languages** English. **Finance** Members' dues. Other sources: conference proceeds; sustaining members. Annual budget: about euro 3,500. **Activities** Awards/prizes/competitions; financial and/or material support. **Events** *Annual Meeting* Milan (Italy) 2019, *Annual Meeting* Lyon (France) 2016, *Annual Meeting* Mannheim (Germany) 2015, *Meeting* Mannheim (Germany) 2015, *Annual Meeting / Meeting* Rome (Italy) / Frascati (Italy) 2014. **Publications** Meeting abstracts. **Members** Individuals (about 80) in 19 countries. Membership countries not specified. **NGO Relations** Affiliate member of: *International League of Dermatological Societies (ILDS, #14018)*. [2019.01.29/XD6491/D]

- ♦ Society of Daughters of St Francis de Sales (religious order)

♦ Society of Deontic Logic and Normative Systems (DEON) 19541

Contact Maison du Nombre – 3rd floor, Belval, L-4002 Esch-sur-Alzette, Luxembourg.
URL: http://deonticlogic.org/

History Conference series organized since 1991. **Aims** Foster research and communication on deontic logic and normative systems by building build bridges between disciplines like ethics, law, linguistics, philosophy, computer science, game theory, the social sciences, artificial intelligence, and mathematics. **Structure** Steering Committee. **Activities** Events/meetings. **Events** *Conference* Munich (Germany) 2021, *Conference* Munich (Germany) 2020, *Conference* Utrecht (Netherlands) 2018, *Conference* Bayreuth (Germany) 2016, *Conference* Ghent (Belgium) 2014. [2020.01.16/XM7809/C]

♦ Society for Design and Process Science (SDPS) 19542

Main Office 3824 Cedar Springs Rd, Ste 368, Dallas TX 75219, USA. T. +12142539025. Fax +12145200227. E-mail: admin@sdpsnet.org.
URL: http://www.sdpsnet.org/

History 1995. Incorporated by the State of Texas (USA). **Aims** Encourage and foster research and development to advance the discipline of process science. **Structure** Board of Directors; Officers: President, Vice-President, Secretary and Treasurer. **Languages** English. **Staff** Voluntary. **Finance** Conferences; publications; sponsorship donations. **Activities** Events/meetings; awards/prizes/competitions; publishing activities. **Events** *International Conference on Emerging Trends and Technologies in Designing Healthcare Systems* Orlando, FL (USA) 2016, *International Conference on Emerging Trends and Technologies in Designing Healthcare Systems* Fort Worth, TX (USA) 2015, *International Conference on Emerging Trends and Technologies in Designing Healthcare Systems* Kuching (Malaysia) 2014, *International Conference on Emerging Trends and Technologies in Designing Healthcare Systems* Sao Paulo (Brazil) 2013, *International Conference on Emerging Trends and Technologies in Designing Healthcare Systems* Berlin (Germany) 2012. **Publications** *Journal of Design and Process Science*. Book series.
Members Full in 25 countries and territories:
Australia, Austria, Brazil, Canada, China, Finland, France, Germany, India, Ireland, Italy, Japan, Korea Rep, Malaysia, Netherlands, Norway, Poland, Romania, Saudi Arabia, South Africa, Taiwan, Türkiye, UK, United Arab Emirates, USA. [2016.06.01/XM0330/D]

- ♦ Society for Developmental Biology (internationally oriented national body)
- ♦ Society for Development Alternatives (internationally oriented national body)

♦ Society of Dialysis Access Specialists (SoDAS) 19543

Contact 10 Anson Road #27-15 International Plaza, Singapore 079903, Singapore. T. +6563221209.
URL: https://www.sodas.live/

Aims Induce synergy among healthcare professionals to improve the holistic care for dialysis access. **Structure** Executive Committee. **Finance** Sources: members' dues. **Activities** Events/meetings; training/education. **Events** *DASy – Dialysis Access Synergy Annual Conference* Singapore (Singapore) 2019. [2020/AA0176/v/D]

- ♦ Society of the Divine Saviour (religious order)
- ♦ Society of Divine Vocations (religious order)
- ♦ Society of the Divine Word (religious order)

♦ Society for East Asian Archaeology (SEAA) 19544

Pres Dept Archaeology, Chungnam Natl Univ, Daejeon 305-764, Korea Rep. T. +82428216384. Fax +82428229880.
URL: http://www.seaa-web.org/

History Apr 1990, Chicago, IL (USA). Founded during annual meeting of *Association for Asian Studies, Ann Arbor (AAS)*. Reorganized under current title, Jun 1996, Honolulu HI (USA). Former names and other names: *East Asian Archaeology Network (EAAN)* – former (Apr 1990 to Jun 1996); *EAANetwork* – alias. **Aims** Promote interest and research in the field of East Asian archaeology. **Structure** Council; Executive Board. **Languages** English. **Staff** None. **Finance** Members' dues. Other sources: conference fees; institutional subscription fees; bequests; endowments; special project funding. **Activities** Events/meetings; research/documentation. **Events** *Worldwide Conference* Daegu (Korea Rep) 2022, *Worldwide Conference* Daejeon (Korea Rep) 2021, *Worldwide Conference* Nanjing (China) 2018, *Worldwide Conference* Ulaanbaatar (Mongolia) 2014, *Worldwide*

Conference Fukuoka (Japan) 2012. **Publications** *Bulletin of the Society for East Asian Archaeology* – vol 1-3 (2007-2009); *Journal of East Asian Archaeology* – vol 1-5 (1999-2006). *EAANnouncements* (1990-1998); *Bibliographic Reviews of Far Eastern Archaeology* (1990); *Western Language Bibliography for East Asian Archaeology* – online.
Members Scholars (over 370) in 24 countries and territories:
Australia, Canada, China, Denmark, France, Germany, Guam, Hong Kong, Israel, Japan, Korea Rep, Malaysia, Mexico, Mongolia, Netherlands, New Zealand, Philippines, Russia, Sweden, Switzerland, Taiwan, UK, USA, Vietnam.
NGO Relations Member of: Association for Asian Studies, Ann Arbor (AAS); *European Association for Japanese Studies (EAJS, #06096).* [2015.06.16/XF3199/v/**F**]

- Society for Ecological Restoration / see Society for Ecological Restoration International
- Society for Ecological Restoration International (internationally oriented national body)
- Society for Economic Botany (internationally oriented national body)

♦ Society for Economic Dynamics (SED) 19545

Sec c/o Stony Brook – Econ Dept, 100 Nicolls Rd, Stony Brook NY 11794-4384, USA.
URL: http://www.economicdynamics.org/
Structure Officers: President; Treasurer; Secretary; Editor. **Staff** None. **Events** *Annual Meeting* Madison, WI (USA) 2022, *Annual Meeting* Barcelona (Spain) 2021, *Annual Meeting* Minneapolis, MN (USA) 2021, *Annual Meeting* Barcelona (Spain) 2020, *Annual Meeting* St Louis, MO (USA) 2019. **Publications** *Review of Economic Dynamics* (4 a year); *Economic Dynamics Newsletter* (2 a year). [2020/XM0595/**F**]

♦ Society of Economic Geologists (SEG) 19546

Exec Dir 7811 Shaffer Pkwy, Littleton CO 80127-3732, USA. T. +17209817882. Fax +17209817874. E-mail: seg@segweb.org.
URL: http://www.segweb.org/
History 28 Dec 1920. Founded at constituting meeting of 60 distinguished professionals. Originated from a gathering, 1919, of a group of *'Geological Society of America (GSA)'* members who were especially interested in economic geology. **Aims** Advance the science of geology through scientific investigation of mineral deposits and mineral resources and the application thereof to exploration, mineral resource appraisal, mining and mineral extraction; disseminate basic and applied scientific information arising from investigations of mineral deposits and mineral resources; advance the status of the profession of economic geology, and maintain a high professional and ethical standard among members. **Structure** Council (meets twice a year); Executive Committee; Regions (8). **Languages** English. **Staff** 12.00 FTE, paid. **Finance** Sources: contributions; donations; grants; investments; members' dues. **Activities** Awards/prizes/competitions; events/meetings; publishing activities; research and development; training/education. **Events** *Conference* London (UK) 2023, *Conference* Denver, CO (USA) 2022, *Conference* Whistler, BC (Canada) 2021, *Conference* Whistler, BC (Canada) 2020, *South American metallogney – Sierra to craton* Santiago (Chile) 2019. **Publications** *SEG Newsletter* (4 a year); *Economic Geology Journal* (8 a year). *Compilation CD/DVD* – series; *Fieldtrip Guidebook* – series; *Reviews in Economic Geology* – series; *Special Publications* – series. **Members** Fellow; Member; Student. Members (7,000) in 100 countries. Membership countries not specified. **NGO Relations** Member of (5): American Geosciences Institute (AGI); Association for Mineral Exploration British Columbia (AMEBC); *Geological Society of America (GSA)*; Prospectors and Developers Association of Canada (PDAC); *Society for Geology Applied to Mineral Deposits (#19565).* Together with *American Association of Petroleum Geologists (AAPG), European Association of Geoscientists and Engineers (EAGE, #06055)* and *Society of Petroleum Engineers (SPE, #19616)*, sponsors *International Petroleum Technology Conference (IPTC).* [2021.05.24/XD0446/v/**F**]

- Society of Economic Geophysicists / see Society of Exploration Geophysicists
- Society of Economic Paleontology and Mineralogy / see Society for Sedimentary Geology
- Society for Economic Research on Copyright Issues (unconfirmed)

♦ Society of Economics of the Household (SEHO) 19547

Pres Paris School of Economics, Campus Jourdan, 48 Boulevard Jourdan, 75014 Paris, France.
History Founded 2017, by Dr Shoshana Grossbard. **Aims** Promote economic research about households. **Structure** Executive Committee. **Languages** English. **Staff** None paid. **Finance** Conferences mostly paid by participants. **Activities** Events/meetings; knowledge management/information dissemination. **Events** *Economics of the household* Venice (Italy) 2020, *Conference* Lisbon (Portugal) 2019, *Conference* Paris (France) 2018, *Conference* San Diego, CA (USA) 2017. **Publications** *Review of Economics of the Household (REHO).* [2020.03.12/XM8364/**C**]

♦ Society for Emblem Studies (SES) 19548

Chair address not obtained.
Treas address not obtained.
URL: https://www.emblemstudies.org/
History 1987. **Aims** Foster the study of emblem books and related materials in literature and the visual arts, their origins and influence on other cultural forms, in all periods, countries and languages. **Structure** Executive Board; Advisory Board. **Finance** Sources: members' dues. **Activities** Events/meetings; research/documentation. **Events** *International Conference* Coimbra (Portugal) 2021, *International Conference* Coimbra (Portugal) 2020, *International Conference* Nancy (France) 2017, *International Conference* Kiel (Germany) 2014, *International Conference* Glasgow (UK) 2011. **Publications** *SES Newsletter* (2 a year). [2020/AA0286/**C**]

- Society of Emissaries / see Emissaries of Divine Light (#05442)

♦ Society of Endometriosis and Uterine Disorders (SEUD) 19549

Secretariat 15 Bd Grawitz, 13016 Marseille, France. E-mail: secretariat@seud.org.
URL: http://seud.org/
History 2015. **Aims** Provide an international scientific platform supporting better management of benign *gynaecological* diseases and related uterine dysfunctions. **Structure** Board; Secretariat. **Languages** English. **Staff** None paid. **Activities** Awareness raising; events/meetings. **Events** *Update on Endometriosis and Uterine Disorders – Dispelling Myths, Removing Stigma* Stockholm (Sweden) 2021, *Congress* Marseille (France) 2020, *Congress* Stockholm (Sweden) 2020, *Abnormal uterine bleeding and fibroids – from bench to bedside* Montréal, QC (Canada) 2019, *Congress* Florence (Italy) 2018. **Publications** *Journal of Endometriosis and Pelvic Pain Disorders (JEPPD).* [2019.09.25/XM4701/**B**]

♦ Society for Environmental Geochemistry and Health (SEGH) 19550

Sec address not obtained.
Pres address not obtained.
URL: http://www.segh.net/
History 1971. **Aims** Provide a forum for scientists to work together in understanding the interaction between the geochemical environment and the health of plants, animals and humans; recognizing the importance of interdisciplinary research, represent, through members, expertise in a diverse range of scientific fields, such as biology, engineering, geology, hydrology, epidemiology, chemistry, medicine, nutrition and toxicology. **Structure** Main Board comprises President; Secretary; Membership Secretary/Treasurer; Webmaster and 4 sections: African chairs; Americas chairs; Asia/Middle East chairs; European chairs. **Languages** English. **Staff** Voluntary. **Finance** Sources: members' dues. **Activities** Events/meetings; research/documentation. **Events** *International Conference on Geochemistry and Health* Eldoret (Kenya) 2022, *International Conference on Geochemistry and Health* Eldoret (Kenya) 2021, *International Conference on Geochemistry and Health* Eldoret (Kenya) 2020, *International Conference on Geochemistry and Health* Manchester (UK) 2019, *International Conference on Geochemistry and Health* Livingstone (Zambia) 2018. **Publications** *Environmental Geochemistry & Health* (6 a year) in English. **Members** Scientists and students in environmental science, medicine, agricultural science, earth science, veterinary science and life science worldwide. Membership countries not specified. [2022.10.25/XD1607/v/**D**]

♦ Society of Environmental Toxicology and Chemistry (SETAC) 19551

EMEA Office Av des Arts 53, 1000 Brussels, Belgium. T. +3227727281. Fax +3227705386. E-mail: setaceu@setac.org.
North America Office 229 S Baylen St, 2nd Floor, Pensacola FL 32502, USA. T. +18504691500. Fax +18504699778. E-mail: setac@setac.org.
Asia Pacific Office 27/2 Masthead Drive, Cleveland QLD 4163, Australia. E-mail: ap@setac.org.
URL: http://www.setac.org/
History 1979. **Aims** Provide a forum for individuals and institutions engaged in: study of environmental issues; management and *conservation* of *natural resources*; environmental education; environmental research and development. Balance interests of academia, business and government. **Structure** SETAC World Council (SWC), comprising President, Immediate Past President, Vice President and Secretary-Treasurer of each geographical unit. Executive Director and a number of representatives Geographic Units (4), each with its own administration: *SETAC Asia/Pacific (SETAC AP, see: #19551)*; *Society of Environmental Toxicology and Chemistry Europe (SETAC Europe, #19552)*; *SETAC Latin America (SETAC LA, see: #19551)*; *SETAC North America.* Committees (14): Awards and Fellowship; Education; Elections/Nominations; Finance; Government Affairs; International Affairs; Long-Range Planning; Meetings; Membership; Publications; Publications Advisory Council; Regional Chapters; Short Course; Technical. **Activities** Events/meetings. **Events** *Conference* Fitzroy, VIC (Australia) 2022, *Annual North America Meeting* Pittsburgh, PA (USA) 2022, *World Congress* Singapore (Singapore) 2022, *Annual North America Meeting* Portland, OR (USA) 2021, *Biennial Meeting* Valdivia (Chile) 2021. **Publications** *Environmental Toxicology and Chemistry* (12 a year); *Integrated Environmental Assessment and Management* (4 a year). Books.
Members Individuals (about 5,000) in 61 countries and territories:
Albania, Argentina, Australia, Austria, Bahrain, Belgium, Bermuda, Brazil, Bulgaria, Canada, Chile, China, Costa Rica, Croatia, Cuba, Czechia, Denmark, Egypt, Estonia, Finland, France, Germany, Greece, Haiti, Hong Kong, Hungary, India, Indonesia, Ireland, Israel, Italy, Japan, Korea DPR, Korea Rep, Lithuania, Luxembourg, Malawi, Malaysia, Mexico, Monaco, Netherlands, Nicaragua, Nigeria, Norway, Peru, Poland, Portugal, Serbia, Slovenia, South Africa, Spain, Sweden, Switzerland, Taiwan, Trinidad-Tobago, Türkiye, UK, Uruguay, USA, Vietnam, Zimbabwe.
NGO Relations In liaison with technical committees of: *International Organization for Standardization (ISO, #14473).* [2020/XF6912/v/**F**]

♦ Society of Environmental Toxicology and Chemistry Europe (SETAC Europe) 19552

Exec Dir Av des Arts 53, 1000 Brussels, Belgium. T. +3227727281. Fax +3227705386. E-mail: setaceu@setac.org.
URL: http://www.setac.org/
History 1989. Set up as sister organization to, and now regional chapter geographic unit of, *Society of Environmental Toxicology and Chemistry (SETAC, #19551).* Registration: Banque-Carrefour des Entreprises, No/ID: 0998.493.056, Start date: 31 Dec 1994, Belgium; EU Transparency Register, No/ID: 940910825833-38, Start date: 9 Feb 2017. **Aims** Support development of principles and practices for protection, enhancement and management of sustainable environmental quality and ecosystem integrity. **Structure** General Assembly; Council; Executive Committee. **Languages** English. **Staff** 7.00 FTE, paid. **Finance** Members' dues. **Activities** Events/meetings; awards/prizes/competitions; financial and/or material support. **Events** *Annual Meeting* Seville (Spain) 2024, *Annual Meeting* Dublin (Ireland) 2023, *LCA Case Studies Symposium* Brussels (Belgium) 2022, *Annual Meeting* Copenhagen (Denmark) 2022, *Annual Meeting* Brussels (Belgium) 2021. **Publications** *Environmental Toxicology and Chemistry* (12 a year) – journal; *Integrated Environmental Assessment and Management* (6 a year) – journal; *SETAC Globe* (6 a year). Books; reports; membership directory.
Members Member; Student; Sustaining. Individuals (over 1,020) in 42 countries:
Argentina, Australia, Austria, Belgium, Brazil, Bulgaria, Canada, China, Cyprus, Czechia, Denmark, Finland, France, Germany, Greece, Hungary, India, Indonesia, Ireland, Italy, Japan, Latvia, Luxembourg, Malaysia, Netherlands, Norway, Poland, Portugal, Romania, Russia, Serbia-Montenegro, Slovenia, South Africa, Spain, Sweden, Switzerland, Tanzania UR, Türkiye, UK, Ukraine, USA, Vietnam.
IGO Relations Cooperates with: *UNEP (#20299)*; UNEP-SETAC Life Cycle Initiative. **NGO Relations** Member of: *Federation of European and International Associations Established in Belgium (FAIB, #09508).* [2021/XE3521/**E**]

- Society for Ethnomusicology (internationally oriented national body)
- Society of European Academies (internationally oriented national body)

♦ Society of European Affairs Professionals (SEAP) 19553

Société des professionnels en affaires européennes
Secretariat Rue du Trône 60, 1050 Brussels, Belgium.
URL: http://www.seap.be/
History 1997, as *European Federation of Lobbying and Public Affairs – Fédération européenne du lobbying et public affairs (FELPA).* Current name adopted 7 Apr 2000, when current statutes were adopted. Registered in accordance with Belgian law. **Aims** Advance the European affairs profession so that it will contribute to ever better policy outcomes. **Structure** General Assembly; Board Committees (2); Secretary-General. **Languages** English. **Staff** 0.50 FTE, paid. **Finance** Members' dues. **Activities** Events/meetings. **Events** *Annual General Meeting* Brussels (Belgium) 2021, *Annual General Meeting* Brussels (Belgium) 2020, *Annual General Meeting* Brussels (Belgium) 2018. **Publications** *SEAP Newsletter.* Position papers; press releases. **Members** Individuals. Membership countries not specified. **IGO Relations** *European Commission (EC, #06633)*; *European Parliament (EP, #08146)*; *OECD (#17693).* **NGO Relations** Cooperates with (2): *European Centre for Public Affairs (ECPA, #06498)*; *European Public Affairs Consultancies' Association (EPACA, #08294).* [2019/XD8609/tv/**D**]

♦ Society of European Robotic Gynaecological Surgery (SERGS) 19554

Secretariat c/o CoWorking Prague, Karlovo namesti 7, 120 00 Prague 2, Czechia. T. +420777100429. E-mail: info@sergsmail.org.
URL: http://www.sergs.org/
History 2009. **Aims** Develop knowledge in robotic surgery in Europe. **Structure** Council. Committees (2): Education; By-Laws. **Activities** Training/education; events/meetings; research and development; knowledge management/information dissemination. **Events** *Annual Meeting* Lille (France) 2017, *Annual Meeting* Barcelona (Spain) 2016. [2018/XM5307/**D**]

- Society of European Sonographers (inactive)

♦ Society in Europe for Simulation Applied to Medicine (SESAM) 19555

Pres Fac de Médecine Paris Descartes, 15 rue de l'école de médecine, 75006 Paris, France. E-mail: president@sesam-web.org – contact@sesam-web.org.
URL: http://www.sesam-web.org/
History Aug 1994, Copenhagen (Denmark). Current constitution adopted 18 Apr 1998, Leiden (Netherlands); amended 31 Mar 2001, Stirling (UK) and 19 May 2005, Bristol (UK). Registered in accordance with German law. **Aims** Encourage and support the use of simulation in *health care* for the purpose of training and research. **Structure** General Assembly; Executive Committee. **Languages** English. **Finance** Members' dues. **Events** *Asia Collaborative Simulation Conference* Singapore (Singapore) 2019, *Annual Meeting* Paris (France) 2017, *Asia Collaborative Simulation Conference* Singapore (Singapore) 2017, *Middle East and North Africa Regional Conference* Dubai (United Arab Emirates) 2016, *Annual Meeting* Lisbon (Portugal) 2016. **Publications** *SESAM Newsletter.* [2019/XJ2515/**D**]

- Society for Experimental Biology (internationally oriented national body)

♦ Society for Experimental Finance (SEF) 19556

Contact c/o Dept of Banking and Finance, Univ of Innsbruck, Universitätsstr 15/4, 6020 Innsbruck, Austria. E-mail: office@experimentalfinance.org.
URL: https://www.experimentalfinance.org/
History 2011, Innsbruck (Austria). Registration: No/ID: ZVR 291045388, Start date: Oct 2013, Austria. **Aims** Advance scientific research in the area of experimental finance. **Structure** Managing Board; Scientific leadership. **Activities** Awards/prizes/competitions; events/meetings; training/education. **Events** *Experimental Finance Conference* Bonn (Germany) 2022, *Experimental Finance Conference* Innsbruck (Austria) 2021, *Experimental Finance Conference* Innsbruck (Austria) 2020, *North American Regional Conference* USA 2020, *Asia Pacific Regional Conference* Singapore (Singapore) 2019. **Publications** *Journal of Behavioral and Experimental Finance.* [2022/AA2552/**D**]

- Society for Experimental Mechanics (internationally oriented national body)
- The Society for Experimental Stress Analysis / see Society for Experimental Mechanics

♦ Society of Exploration Geophysicists (internationally oriented national body)

♦ Society for the Exploration of Psychotherapy Integration (SEPI) . . . 19557
Contact 801 Key Hwy, No 412, Baltimore MD 21230, USA. E-mail: sepimembership@gmail.com.
URL: http://sepiweb.com/
History Founded 1983. **Aims** Promote exploration and development of psychotherapies that integrate theoretical orientation, clinical practice, and diverse methods of inquiry; seek to bring clinicians and researchers together to an unprecedented degree and facilitate collaboration between clinician and researcher, helping both learn from each other; promote dialogue between therapists of differing theoretical orientations; advance understanding of the sources of therapeutic change; meet the needs of the growing ranks of integrative therapists. **Structure** Elected Executive Committee of 6. **Languages** English. **Staff** 1.00 FTE, paid. **Finance** Members' dues. Annual scientific conference. Annual gross income about US$ 100,000. **Events** *Annual Meeting* Lisbon (Portugal) 2019, *Annual Meeting* Dublin (Ireland) 2016, *Annual Meeting* Baltimore, MD (USA) 2015, *Annual Meeting* Montréal, QC (Canada) 2014, *Annual Meeting* Barcelona (Spain) 2013. **Publications** *Journal of Psychotherapy Integration* (4 a year). **Members** Full (about 500); two-thirds in North America. Membership countries not specified. [2015.06.24/XM0813/**D**]

♦ Society for Financial Studies (SFS) 19558
Managing Dir PO Box 28494, Raleigh NC 17611, USA.
URL: http://www.sfs.org/
History Incorporated in the State of California (USA), 1987. Current bylaws adopted Jun 2012. **Structure** Council. **Activities** Events/meetings. **Publications** *Review of Asset Pricing Studies*; *Review of Corporate Finance Studies*; *Review of Financial Studies.* [2019/XM7865/**C**]

♦ Society of Fire Protection Engineers (internationally oriented national body)
♦ Society of Forensic Haemogenetics / see International Society for Forensic Genetics (#15128)
♦ Society for Freedom in Science (inactive)
♦ Society for Free Radical Biology and Medicine / see Society for Redox Biology and Medicine (#19628)

♦ Society for Free Radical Research Africa (SFRR-Africa) 19559
Exec Sec address not obtained.
Pres address not obtained.
History A regional society under *International Society for Free Radical Research (ISFRR, #15131).* **Events** *International Conference* Stellenbosch (South Africa) 2021, *International Conference* Ebene (Mauritius) 2015, *International Conference* South Africa 2011, *International Conference* Mauritius 2006, *International Conference* Tetouan (Morocco) 2005. **Publications** *Archives of Medical and Biomedical Research.* [2021/AA2091/**D**]

♦ Society for Free Radical Research Asia (SFRR ASIA) 19560
SG c/o Dept of Molecular Gastroenterology and Hepatology, Grad School of Med Science, Kyoto Prefect Univ of Medicine, Kamigyo-ku, Kyoto, 602-8566 Japan. Fax +81752515650. E-mail: sfrrasia@koto.kpu-m.ac.jp.
URL: http://sfrrj.umin.jp/asia
History 1995. An autonomous regional group of *International Society for Free Radical Research (ISFRR, #15131).* **Aims** Advance knowledge of free radicals and the processes in which they participate with particular reference to those processes of industrial and medical importance, such knowledge being for the benefit of the public. **Structure** Committee. **Events** *Biennial Meeting* Seoul (Korea Rep) 2022, *Biennial Meeting* Daegu (Korea Rep) 2021, *Biennial Meeting* Kyoto (Japan) 2019, *Biennial Meeting* Xian (China) 2017, *Biennial Meeting* Chiang Mai (Thailand) 2015. **Publications** *Free Radical Research.*
Members Full in 7 countries and territories:
China, India, Japan, Korea Rep, Malaysia, Taiwan, Thailand. [2020/AA0168/**D**]

♦ Society for Free Radical Research Australasia / see Society for Redox Research Australasia (#19629)

♦ Society for Free Radical Research – Europe (SFRRE) 19561
Gen Sec Dept of Physiology, School of Pharmacy, Univ of Valencia, Avda Vicente Andrés Estellés s/n, 46100 Burjassot, Valencia, Spain. Fax +34963543395. E-mail: info@sfrr-europe.org.
URL: https://www.sfrr-europe.org/
History 1988. An automous regional group of *International Society for Free Radical Research (ISFRR, #15131).* Former names and other names: *SFRR Europe* – alias. **Structure** Council; Executive Committee. **Activities** Awards/prizes/competitions; events/meetings; training/education. **Events** *Annual Meeting* Belgrade (Serbia) 2021, *Annual Meeting* Berlin (Germany) 2017, *Annual Meeting* Paris (France) 2014, *Annual Meeting* Oslo (Norway) 2010, *Annual Meeting* Rome (Italy) 2009. **Publications** *Free Radical Biology and Medicine (FRBM)* (12 a year); *Redox Biology.* **Members** Full (over 300). Membership countries not specified. [2022/AA0169/**D**]

♦ Society for Free Radical Research International / see International Society for Free Radical Research (#15131)
♦ Society of French-Speaking Hospital Physicians (inactive)
♦ Society for Freshwater Science (internationally oriented national body)
♦ Society of Friends / see Religious Society of Friends (#18834)
♦ Society for functional Near Infrared Spectroscopy (unconfirmed)

♦ Society for Gas as a Marine Fuel (SGMF) 19562
General Manager 50 Liverpool Str, London, EC2M 7PY, UK. T. +442036371455. E-mail: office@sgmf.info.
URL: http://www.sgmf.info/
History Launched 3 Sep 2014, Singapore (Singapore). Registration: Bermuda; No/ID: FC 031569, UK, Isle of Man. **Aims** Promote safety and industry best practice in the use of gas as a marine fuel. **Structure** General Meeting (annual); Board of Directors. **Finance** Sources: members' dues. [2023.02.15/XJ9614/**C**]

♦ Society for Gastrointestinal Intervention (SGI) 19563
Contact 12 Hakdong-ro 31, Gangnam-gu, Seoul 06052, Korea Rep. T. +8224730089. Fax +825052730089. E-mail: sgisci@sgiw.org.
URL: http://www.sgiw.org/
History 2007, Seoul (Korea Rep). **Aims** Improve public health through disease management and minimally invasive, image-guided gastrointestinal interventions. **Structure** Steering Committee; Executive Committee. Committees. Secretariat. **Languages** English, Korean. **Staff** 1.00 FTE, paid. **Finance** Members' dues. **Activities** Events/meetings. **Events** *Annual Meeting* Incheon (Korea Rep) 2021, *Annual Meeting* Hyderabad (India) 2020, *Annual Meeting* Incheon (Korea Rep) 2019, *Meeting* Nanjing (China) 2018, *Serum phosphate as a prognostic factor in post-endoscopic retrograde cholangiopancreatography pancreatitis* Incheon (Korea Rep) 2017. **Publications** *International Journal of Gastrointestinal Intervention (IJGII)* (4 a year).
Members Individuals in 8 countries:
Argentina, China, Egypt, Japan, Spain, Taiwan, UK, USA.
NGO Relations *European Society of Gastrointestinal Endoscopy (ESGE, #08606).* [2020/XJ0229/**D**]

♦ Society for General Systems Research / see International Society for the Systems Sciences (#15500)

♦ Society of Genitourinary Reconstructive Surgeons (GURS) 19564
Sec/Treas Dept of Urologic Reconstruction, Univ of Minnesota School of Medicine, 420 Delaware St SE, MMC 394, Minneapolis MN 55455, USA. T. +16126257486. Fax +16126260428. E-mail: info@societygurs.org.
Street address c/o Urology Management Services, 1000 Corporate Blvd, Linthicum MD 21090, USA. T. +14106893950. Fax +14106893824.
URL: http://www.societygurs.org/
History 1986, Virginia Beach VA (USA). **Aims** Encourage the study of, promote research in, improve the practice of, elevate the standards of, and otherwise advance genitourinary reconstructive surgery. **Structure** Board of Directors. **Languages** English. **Finance** Sources: grants; members' dues. **Activities** Events/meetings; events/meetings; networking/liaising. **Events** *Academic Congress* Montréal, QC (Canada) 2022, *Annual Meeting* Las Vegas, NV (USA) 2021, *Annual Meeting* San Diego, CA (USA) 2016, *Annual Meeting* New Orleans, LA (USA) 2015, *Session / Scientific Session* Glasgow (UK) 2014. **Members** Full in 26 countries. Membership countries not specified. **NGO Relations** Affiliate of: American Urological Association; *Société Internationale d'Urologie (SIU, #19499).* [2016/XJ6876/**C**]

♦ Society for Geology Applied to Mineral Deposits 19565
Exec Sec Czech Geological Survey, Geologicka 6, 152 00 Prague 5, Czechia. T. +420251085506. E-mail: info@e-sga.org.
Registered address 13 rue des Maraîchers, 1205 Geneva, Switzerland.
URL: http://e-sga.org/
History 1965, Heidelberg (Germany). Founded following decision of an international group of economic geologists. Former names and other names: *Société de géologie appliquée aux gîtes minéraux (SGA)* – former; *Gesellschaft für Lagerstättenforschung* – former. **Aims** Advance application of scientific knowledge in the study and development of mineral resources and their environment; promote the profession of geology in science and industry; cultivate contacts for mutually beneficial relationships; protect and improve professional and ethical standards among members. **Structure** Council; Executive Committee. **Languages** English, French, German. **Staff** 38.00 FTE, voluntary. **Finance** Sources: members' dues. **Activities** Events/meetings; financial and/or material support; training/education. **Events** *Biennial Meeting* Zurich (Switzerland) 2023, *Biennial Meeting* Rotorua (New Zealand) 2022, *Biennial Meeting* Rotorua (New Zealand) 2021, *Biennial Meeting* Glasgow (UK) 2019, *Biennial Meeting* Québec, QC (Canada) 2017. **Publications** *SGA News* (2 a year); *Mineralium Deposita* (8 a year). Meeting proceedings; special publications.
Members Honorary; Senior; Regular; Student; Corporate. Professional geologists and companies specifically concerned with mineral deposits, in 76 countries and territories:
Algeria, Argentina, Australia, Austria, Belgium, Benin, Bolivia, Brazil, Bulgaria, Burkina Faso, Cameroon, Canada, Chad, Chile, China, Colombia, Côte d'Ivoire, Cyprus, Czechia, Denmark, Ecuador, Estonia, Ethiopia, Finland, France, Gabon, Georgia, Germany, Ghana, Greece, Greenland, Guiana Fr, Hong Kong, India, Indonesia, Iran Islamic Rep, Ireland, Italy, Japan, Mexico, Mongolia, Morocco, Myanmar, Netherlands, New Zealand, Niger, Nigeria, North Macedonia, Norway, Peru, Philippines, Poland, Portugal, Romania, Russia, Senegal, Serbia, Slovakia, South Africa, Spain, Sudan, Suriname, Sweden, Switzerland, Taiwan, Tanzania UR, Thailand, Tunisia, Türkiye, UK, Ukraine, United Arab Emirates, Uruguay, USA, Uzbekistan, Zambia.
NGO Relations Affiliated with (1): *International Union of Geological Sciences (IUGS, #15777).* [2022.10.12/XC4642/**C**]

♦ Society for Germanic Linguistics (SGL) 19566
Pres Dept of Linguistics, College of Arts and Sciences, University at Buffalo, North Campus, 609 Baldy Hall, Buffalo NY 14260-6420, USA.
URL: http://societyforgermaniclinguistics.org/
History 1968. Former names and other names: *Society for Germanic Philology (SGP)* – former. **Aims** Foster research into Germanic *languages.* **Structure** Executive Committee, comprising President, Vice-President, Secretary-Treasurer and 6 members. **Languages** English, German. **Staff** Voluntary. **Finance** Sources: members' dues. **Activities** Events/meetings. **Events** *Annual Conference* Banff, AB (Canada) 2023, *Annual Conference* Athens, GA (USA) 2022, *Annual Conference* Iowa City, IA (USA) 2021, *Annual Conference* Athens, GA (USA) 2020, *Annual Conference* Iowa City, IA (USA) 2019. **Publications** *Journal of Germanic Linguistics*; *SGL Newsletter.*
Members in 18 countries:
Australia, Austria, Belgium, Canada, Denmark, France, Germany, Ireland, Israel, Italy, Japan, Netherlands, Norway, Poland, Russia, Sweden, Switzerland, USA. [2022/XD6755/**D**]

♦ Society for Germanic Philology / see Society for Germanic Linguistics (#19566)
♦ Society of German-Speaking Anatomists / see Anatomische Gesellschaft (#00813)
♦ Society of German-Speaking Lymphologists (internationally oriented national body)
♦ Society for Gestalt Theory and its Applications (internationally oriented national body)
♦ Society for Global Business and Economic Development (internationally oriented national body)
♦ Society of the Golden Keys / see Union Internationale des Concierges d'Hôtels "Les Clefs d'Or" (#20424)
♦ Society for Gynecologic Investigation / see Society for Reproductive Investigation (#19631)

♦ Society of Hair Testing (SoHT) 19567
Sec Cooper Gold Forensic Consultancy Ltd, 40 Main Road, East Wemyss, KY1 4RA, UK.
Treas Bayerisches Landeskriminalamt, Maillingerstr 15, 80636 Munich, Germany. Fax +498912123223.
URL: http://www.soht.org/
History Dec 1995. Registered in accordance with French law. **Aims** Promote research in hair testing technologies in *forensic*, clinical and occupational sciences; develop international proficiency tests; encourage scientific cooperation and exchanges among members. **Structure** Board. **Finance** Members' dues. **Events** *IALM Intersocietal Symposium* Venice (Italy) 2016, *Annual Meeting / Meeting* Sao Paulo (Brazil) 2015, *Scientific Meeting* Strasbourg (France) 2015, *Annual Meeting / Meeting* Bordeaux (France) 2014, *Annual Meeting / Meeting* Geneva (Switzerland) 2013. [2015/XJ9943/**D**]

♦ Society for Heart Valve Disease (inactive)
♦ Society of the Helpers of the Holy Souls (religious order)

♦ Society for Histochemistry (SFH) 19568
Gesellschaft für Histochemie
Pres Ctr for Anatomy and Cell Biology, Medical Univ of Vienna, Schwarzspanierstr 17, 1090 Vienna, Austria. E-mail: info@histochemistry.eu.
URL: http://histochemistry.eu/
History 1952. Current by-laws adopted Aug 2015. Registration: Baden-Württemberg District court, No/ID: VR 380392, Start date: 23 Aug 1973, Germany, Stuttgart. **Aims** Advance histochemical methodology and new developments in the field; stimulate contacts between the novice and the more experienced young scientists on the one hand and the celebrities on the other; create a platform where young scientists can present their data and expose themselves to top players in the field; stimulate the development of new approaches in histochemistry. **Structure** General Assembly; Board. **Languages** English. **Staff** 3.00 FTE, paid. **Finance** Members' dues. **Activities** Events/meetings; awards/prizes/competitions. **Events** *International Congress of Histochemistry and Cytochemistry* Prague (Czechia) 2022, *International Congress of Histochemistry and Cytochemistry* Prague (Czechia) 2021, *Symposium* Prague (Czechia) 2018. **Publications** *Histochemistry and Cell Biology* – journal. **Members** Full (145) in 30 countries. Membership countries not specified. **NGO Relations** Member of: *International Federation of Societies for Histochemistry and Cytochemistry (IFSHC, #13548).* [2022/XM7826/**D**]

♦ Society for Historians of American Foreign Relations (internationally oriented national body)

♦ Society for the History of Alchemy and Chemistry (SHAC) 19569
Société d'histoire de l'alchimie et de la chimie
Honorary Sec Hawthorn House, Checkendon, Reading, RG8 0SU, UK. E-mail: society@ambix.org.
URL: https://www.ambix.org/
History 1935, London (UK). Former names and other names: *Society for the Study of Alchemy and Early Chemistry* – former. **Aims** Promote study of, and interest in, the history of alchemy and chemistry. **Structure** Council. **Languages** English. **Staff** Voluntary. **Finance** Sources: members' dues; sale of publications. Annual budget: 25,000 GBP. **Activities** Awards/prizes/competitions; events/meetings. **Events** *Spring Meeting* Durham (UK) 2019, *Spring Meeting* London (UK) 2018, *Autumn Meeting* Louvain-la-Neuve (Belgium) 2018, *New chemical biography* London (UK) 1999, *Meeting* London (UK) 1992. **Publications** *Ambix* – journal; *Chemical Intelligence* – newsletter.
Members Individuals. Members in 15 countries:
Australia, Austria, Belgium, Brazil, Canada, France, Germany, Italy, Japan, Netherlands, Norway, Spain, Sweden, UK, USA. [2021.03.19/XD4678/v/**D**]

♦ Society for the History of Asian Casting Technology (unconfirmed)

♦ Society for the History of Authorship, Reading and Publishing (SHARP) 19570
Pres English and Linguistics, Univ of Otago, PO Box 56, Dunedin 9054, New Zealand. T. +6434798892. E-mail: president@sharpweb.org.
URL: http://www.sharpweb.org/

History 1991. **Aims** Promote teaching, research and publication in the field of book history. **Structure** Executive Council. **Languages** English, French, German, Spanish. **Staff** None. **Finance** Sources: members' dues. Annual budget: 42,000 USD. **Activities** Events/meetings; research/documentation; training/education. **Events** *Annual Conference* Amsterdam (Netherlands) 2022, *Annual Conference* Münster (Germany) 2021, *Annual Conference* Amherst, MA (USA) 2019, *Annual Conference* Sydney, NSW (Australia) 2018, *Annual Conference* Victoria, BC (Canada) 2017. **Publications** *Book History* (annual); *SHARP News*. **Information Services** *SHARP-L* – electronic bulletin board linking hundreds of book historians worldwide.
Members Academic and non-academic members – literary scholars, historians, bibliophiles, sociologists, journalists, publishing professionals, art historians, editors, linguists, reading instructors, librarians, booksellers and printers – (mostly in USA and UK) in 43 countries and territories:
Argentina, Australia, Austria, Belgium, Brazil, Bulgaria, Canada, Croatia, Cyprus, Czechia, Denmark, Egypt, Estonia, Finland, France, Germany, Hong Kong, Iceland, India, Ireland, Israel, Italy, Japan, Korea Rep, Lithuania, Mexico, Netherlands, New Zealand, Norway, Peru, Philippines, Poland, Portugal, Romania, Russia, Singapore, South Africa, Spain, Sweden, Switzerland, Taiwan, UK, USA.
NGO Relations Member of (1): *American Literature Association (ALA, #00786)*. Links with American Council of Learned Societies and national societies. [2022.05.06/XF3802/v/**F**]

♦ Society for the History of Technology (SHOT) 19571

Sec c/o Eindhoven Univ of Technology, Atlas Bldg 8-8401, PO Box 513, 5600 MB Eindhoven, Netherlands. T. +31402474641. E-mail: shot.secretariaat@tue.nl.
URL: http://www.historyoftechnology.org/

History 1958. **Aims** Encourage study of the development of technology and its relations with society and culture. **Structure** Executive Council; Committees (7). **Events** *Annual Meeting* Long Beach, CA (USA) 2023, *Annual Meeting* New Orleans, LA (USA) 2022, *Annual Meeting* New Orleans, LA (USA) 2021, *Annual Meeting* Eindhoven (Netherlands) 2020, *Annual Meeting* Milan (Italy) 2019. **Publications** *SHOT Newsletter* (4 a year); *Technology and Culture* (4 a year) – journal. *Historical Perspectives on Technology, Society, and Culture*.
Members Individuals in 48 countries. Membership countries not specified. [2021.02.24/XW0511/**C**]

- ♦ Society of the Holy Child Jesus (religious order)
- ♦ Society of the Holy Name (religious order)
- ♦ Society for Human Ecology (internationally oriented national body)
- ♦ Society for Humanism in Medicine (no recent information)
- ♦ Society for Human Resource Management (internationally oriented national body)
- ♦ Society for Human Rights / see International Society for Human Rights (#15183)

♦ Society for Imaging Science and Technology (IS&T) 19572

Exec Dir 7003 Kilworth Lane, Springfield VA 22151, USA. T. +17036429090. Fax +17036429094. E-mail: info@imaging.org.
URL: http://www.imaging.org/

History 1947. **Aims** Advance understanding and application of all fields related to imaging science and technology through conferences and publications that promote exchange of ideas among colleagues. **Languages** English. **Staff** 6.50 FTE, paid. **Finance** Sources: meeting proceeds; members' dues; sale of publications. **Activities** Events/meetings; knowledge management/information dissemination; publishing activities. **Events** *Electronic Imaging* San Francisco, CA (USA) 2023, *Annual Color and Imaging Conference* Scottsdale, AZ (USA) 2022, *Printing for Fabrication Annual Conference* Chiba (Japan) 2021, *Annual Color Imaging Conference* Springfield, VA (USA) 2020, *Printing for Fabrication Annual Conference* Springfield, VA (USA) 2020. **Publications** *Journal of Electronic Imaging* (6 a year); *Journal of Imaging Science and Technology* (6 a year); *Journal of Perceptual Imaging* (2 a year). Books; conference proceedings.
Members Chapters (3) in 43 countries and territories:
Australia, Austria, Belgium, Brazil, Canada, China, Croatia, Czechia, Denmark, Ecuador, Egypt, Finland, France, Germany, Greece, Hong Kong, Hungary, India, Indonesia, Ireland, Israel, Italy, Japan, Korea Rep, Lithuania, Malaysia, Mexico, Netherlands, New Zealand, Norway, Poland, Portugal, Russia, Singapore, Slovakia, Spain, Sweden, Switzerland, Taiwan, Thailand, Türkiye, UK, Vietnam.
NGO Relations Many national and international organizations serve as cooperating societies on conferences. [2022.10.18/XD6758/**D**]

- ♦ Society for Immunotherapy of Cancer (internationally oriented national body)

♦ Society for Imprecise Probability: Theories and Applications (SIPTA) 19573

Address not obtained.
URL: http://www.sipta.org/

History Feb 2002. Registration: Swiss Civil Code, Switzerland. **Activities** Events/meetings; knowledge management/information dissemination; research/documentation. **Events** *Biennial Symposium* Ghent (Belgium) 2019, *Biennial Symposium* Lugano (Switzerland) 2017, *Biennial Symposium* Pescara (Italy) 2015, *Biennial Symposium* Compiègne (France) 2013, *Biennial Symposium* Innsbruck (Austria) 2011. [2020/AA0271/v/**D**]

♦ Society for Incentive Travel Excellence (SITE) 19574

CEO 330 North Wabash Ave, Chicago IL 60611, USA. T. +13126735876. E-mail: site@siteglobal.com – events@siteglobal.com.
Events Manager address not obtained.
URL: http://www.site-intl.org/

History 1973, New York NY (USA), as *Society of Incentive and Travel Executives (SITE)*. Previously also referred to as *Society of International Travel Executives*. Later known only by acronym *SITE*. Present name adopted, 2014. **Aims** As an association devoted exclusively to the pursuit of excellence in incentive travel: link *professional* incentive travel executives dedicated to recognition and development of travel as the key to motivational and performance improvement strategies; recognize the global cultural differences and practices in developing these strategies; serve as a networking and educational opportunity for members. **Structure** Board of Directors, consisting of President, President-Elect, Immediate Past President, Executive Vice President/CEO, 3 further Vice-Presidents – for Education, Finance and Marketing – and 17 board members. Includes *SITE Belgium/Luxembourg* as well as 33 other chapters. **Languages** English. **Finance** Members' dues. Other sources: conference proceeds; education fees. **Activities** Provides educational seminars and information services to those who design, develop, promote, sell, administer and operate travel programs as an incentive to increase productivity in business. **Events** *Global Conference* New York, NY (USA) 2023, *Global Conference* Vancouver, BC (Canada) 2020, *Global Conference* Bangkok (Thailand) 2019, *Global Conference* Rome (Italy) 2018, *Global Forum* Rome (Italy) 2018. **Publications** *SITE Resource Directory* (annual); *In-SITE Magazine*.
Members Individuals (about 2,000) representing airlines, cruise lines, ground transportation companies, hotels and resorts, incentive houses, destination management companies, official tourist organizations, trade publications, travel agencies and supporting organizations such as restaurants and visitor attractions. Mainly in North America but in a total of 82 countries and territories:
Argentina, Aruba, Australia, Austria, Bahamas, Barbados, Belgium, Bermuda, Brazil, Canada, Chile, China, Costa Rica, Croatia, Curaçao, Cyprus, Czechia, Denmark, Dominican Rep, Ecuador, Egypt, England, Fiji, Finland, France, Germany, Greece, Guatemala, Hong Kong, Iceland, India, Indonesia, Ireland, Israel, Italy, Jamaica, Japan, Jordan, Kenya, Korea Rep, Lebanon, Luxembourg, Malaysia, Malta, Mexico, Monaco, Morocco, Nepal, Netherlands, New Zealand, Norway, Oman, Panama, Peru, Poland, Portugal, Puerto Rico, Russia, Scotland, Singapore, South Africa, Spain, St Lucia, St Maarten, St Martin, St Thomas Is, Sweden, Switzerland, Syrian AR, Tanzania UR, Thailand, Trinidad-Tobago, Tunisia, Türkiye, Uganda, United Arab Emirates, Uruguay, USA, Venezuela, Vietnam, Wales, Zimbabwe.
NGO Relations Member of (2): *Events Industry Council (EIC, #09212)*; *Joint Meetings Industry Council (JMIC, #16140)*. Partner of (1): *International Institute for Peace through Tourism (IIPT)*. [2023/XF2292/v/**F**]

- ♦ Society of Incentive and Travel Executives / see Society for Incentive Travel Excellence (#19574)

♦ Society of Indexers 19575

Société des indexeurs

Office Manager Woodbourn Business Centre, 10 Jessell Street, Sheffield, S9 3HY, UK. E-mail: admin@indexers.org.uk.
URL: http://www.indexers.org.uk/

History 30 Mar 1957, London (UK). **Aims** Safeguard and improve indexing standards; promote professional interests of indexers. **Structure** General Meeting (annual); Executive Board. **Languages** English. **Staff** 1.00 FTE, paid. **Finance** Sources: members' dues. **Activities** Events/meetings; publishing activities. **Events** *Conference* London (UK) 2019, *Conference* Lancaster (UK) 2018, *Conference* Oxford (UK) 2017, *Conference* Birmingham (UK) 2016, *Conference* York (UK) 2015.
Members Individuals in 17 countries and territories:
Australia, Canada, France, Germany, Iceland, India, Ireland, Italy, Japan, Korea Rep, Netherlands, South Africa, Spain, Switzerland, Taiwan, UK, USA.
NGO Relations Member of (1): *Association of Learned and Professional Society Publishers (ALPSP, #02786)*. [2021.08.31/XC3241/**F**]

- ♦ Society for Industrial and Applied Mathematics (internationally oriented national body)
- ♦ Society for Industrial and Technological Research at NTH / see SINTEF
- ♦ Society for Information Display (internationally oriented national body)

♦ Society for Institutional and Organizational Economics (SIOE) 19576

Sec c/o Olin Business School, 1 Brookings Dr, CB 1133, St Louis MO 63130, USA.
URL: http://sioe.org/

History 21 Sep 1997, St Louis, MO (USA). Former names and other names: *International Society for New Institutional Economics (ISNIE)* – former (1997 to 2015). **Aims** Stimulate and disseminate interdisciplinary research on economic, political and social institutions and their effects on economic activity; encourage rigorous theoretical and empirical investigation using approaches drawn from economics, organization theory, law, political science and other social sciences; encourage participation from scholars worldwide, with special commitment to young scholars and those from developing countries and transitional economies. **Finance** Members' dues (2010): US$ 40-60. **Activities** Organizes: Annual Conference; *European School on New Institutional Economics*, a combination of spring schools and autumn workshops; joint sessions with other societies. Topics of interest include: organization and boundaries of the firm; structure and performance of contractual arrangements; determinants and impacts of property rights and transactions costs on resource allocation and governance institutions; causes and effects of government regulatory and competition policies; structure and effects of legal, social and political institutions on economic performance; role and response of organizations to innovation and technological change; nature of economic development and transition economies. **Events** *Annual Conference* 2021, *Annual Conference* Cambridge, MA (USA) 2020, *Annual Conference* Stockholm (Sweden) 2019, *Annual Conference* Montréal, QC (Canada) 2018, *Annual Conference* New York, NY (USA) 2017. **Publications** *ISNIE Newsletter*.
Members Individuals, mainly in the USA but in a total of 31 countries:
Argentina, Australia, Austria, Belarus, Brazil, Canada, Colombia, Croatia, Denmark, Finland, France, Germany, Greece, India, Israel, Italy, Japan, Korea Rep, Mexico, Netherlands, New Zealand, Norway, Poland, Russia, Slovakia, Spain, Sweden, Switzerland, Türkiye, UK, USA.
NGO Relations Joint sessions with: *American Political Science Association (APSA)*; *European Association of Law and Economics (EALE, #06104)*; *European Association for Research in Industrial Economics (EARIE, #06193)*; *International Economic History Association (IEHA, #13224)*. [2020/XC0084/v/**C**]

- ♦ Society of Integral Psychoanalysis / see International Society of Analytical Trilogy (#14917)

♦ Society for Intercultural Pastoral Care and Counselling (SIPCC) . . . 19577

Gesellschaft für Interkulturelle Seelsorge und Beratung

Chairman Friederike-Fliedner-Weg 72, 40489 Düsseldorf, Germany. T. +492114790525. Fax +492114790526.
URL: https://www.sipcc.org/

History 1995. Registration: North Rhine-Westphalia District court, No/ID: VR 8102, Start date: 27 Mar 1996, Germany, Düsseldorf. **Aims** Promote international exchange and mutual learning in pastoral care and counselling. **Structure** General Assembly; Executive Committee; Coordinating Committee. **Finance** Sources: members' dues. **Activities** Events/meetings; training/education. **Members** Full (289) in 38 countries. Membership countries not specified. **NGO Relations** Member of (1): *International Council on Pastoral Care and Counselling (ICPCC, #13059)*. [2021/AA1229/**C**]

♦ Society of Interdisciplinary Business Research (SIBR) 19578

Secretariat address not obtained. E-mail: secretary@sibresearch.org.
URL: https://sibresearch.org/

History 2008. **Aims** Extend researchers' knowledge and understanding of the real business world from interdisciplinary perspectives. **Structure** Committee. **Activities** Events/meetings; research/documentation. **Events** *Conference on Interdisciplinary Business and Economics Research* Tokyo (Japan) 2023, *Conference on Interdisciplinary Business and Economics Research* Seoul (Korea Rep) 2022, *Conference on Interdisciplinary Business and Economics Research* Osaka (Japan) 2021, *Conference on Interdisciplinary Business and Economics Research* Seoul (Korea Rep) 2021, *Conference* Tokyo (Japan) 2021. **Publications** *Review of Integrative Business and Economics Research*. [2021/AA1733/**C**]

♦ Society for Interdisciplinary Musicology (SIM) 19579

Contact Merangasse 70, 8010 Graz, Austria. T. +433163808161.
URL: http://www.idmusicology.com/

History Jan 2012. Proposed at 2008 *Conference on Interdisciplinary Musicology*, of which it is now its sole organizer. **Aims** Promote collaboration between humanities and sciences in musicology. **Structure** General Meeting. **Activities** Events/meetings. **Events** *Conference on Interdisciplinary Musicology* Edinburgh (UK) 2022, *Conference on Interdisciplinary Musicology (CIM)* Graz (Austria) 2019, *Conference on Interdisciplinary Musicology (CIM)* Poznań (Poland) 2018, *Conference on Interdisciplinary Musicology (CIM)* Shanghai (China) 2015, *Conference on Interdisciplinary Musicology* Berlin (Germany) 2014. **Publications** *Journal of Interdisciplinary Music Studies (JIMS)*.
Members Individuals in 26 countries:
Australia, Austria, Azerbaijan, Belgium, Canada, Estonia, Finland, France, Georgia, Germany, Greece, Iran Islamic Rep, Ireland, Israel, Lithuania, Mexico, Norway, Poland, Russia, Serbia, South Africa, Spain, Switzerland, Türkiye, UK, USA. [2022/AA2510/cv/**E**]

♦ Society of International Business Fellows (SIBF) 19580

Main Office 715 Peachtree St NE, Ste 200, Atlanta GA 30308, USA. T. +14703781156. E-mail: info@sibf.org.
URL: http://www.sibf.org/

History 1981. **Aims** Educate and connect leaders throughout the world to further their professional and personal success. **Activities** Events/meetings; networking/liaising; training/education. **Events** *Annual Summit* Atlanta, GA (USA) 2020, *Annual Summit* Park City, UT (USA) 2012, *Annual Summit* San Francisco, CA (USA) 2011, *Meeting* Hong Kong (Hong Kong) 1997. **Members** Individuals (1,100) in over 60 countries. Membership countries not specified. [2020/XN8163/**C**]

♦ Society for International Development (SID) 19581

Société internationale pour le développement (SID) – Sociedad Internacional para el Desarrollo (SID)

Managing Dir Via degli Etruschi 7, 00185 Rome RM, Italy. T. +39064872172. Fax +39064872170. E-mail: sidsec.rom@sidint.org.
URL: http://www.sidint.net/

History 19 Oct 1957, Washington, DC (USA). Constitution adopted 22 Jan 1958; amended: Nov 1960; Mar 1964; May 1971; Dec 1976; July 2011. Registration: USA; Italy; Kenya. **Aims** Promote social justice; foster democratic participation in the development process. **Structure** General Assembly (every 4 years, at World Conference); Governing Council; Executive Committee; International Secretariat; Local Chapters (15). **Languages** English, French, Italian, Spanish. **Staff** 15.00 FTE, paid. **Finance** Sources: contributions; government support; international organizations; members' dues; private foundations. Supported by: *Deutsche Gesellschaft für Internationale Zusammenarbeit (GIZ)*; *Ford Foundation (#09858)*; *Heinrich Böll Foundation*; *Norwegian Agency for Development Cooperation (Norad)*; *Open Society Foundations (OSF, #17763)*; *Swedish International Development Cooperation Agency (Sida)*; Wellspring Foundation. **Activities** Awareness raising; knowledge management/information dissemination; monitoring/evaluation; networking/liaising; politics/policy/regulatory; research and development; research/documentation. Active in all member

countries. **Events** *World Conference* Tanzania UR 2016, *World conference* Washington, DC (USA) 2011, *World conference* The Hague (Netherlands) 2007, *Conference on Europe and the South* The Hague (Netherlands) 2004, *World conference* Dar es Salaam (Tanzania UR) 2002. **Publications** *Development* (4 a year) – journal. **Members** Institutional (55); Individuals (3,000), including Sustaining and Life categories. Membership countries not specified. Chapters in 14 countries:
Chapters in 14 countries:
Argentina, Austria, Bangladesh, Bolivia, Burundi, Germany, Haiti, India, Israel, Mauritius, Netherlands, Sri Lanka, Türkiye, USA.
Included in the above, 13 organizations listed in this Yearbook:
AIESEC Alumni International (AAI, #00594); Asian Research Centre for Migration (ARCM); Association for Women's Rights in Development (AWID, #02980); Centre for International Studies, Managua (CEI); Development Alternatives with Women for a New Era (DAWN, #05054); Development Training International (DTI); European Association of Development Research and Training Institutes (EADI, #06012); European Centre for Development Policy Management (ECDPM, #06473); Food Basket Foundation International (FBFI); International Drug Awareness Research Foundation; Red Latinoamericana de Comercialización Comunitaria (RELACC, #18707); Société africaine d'éducation et de formation pour le développement (SAFEFOD); Women's Environment and Development Organization (WEDO, #21016).
Consultative Status Consultative status granted from: *ECOSOC (#05331)* (General); *UNESCO (#20322)* (Consultative Status); *FAO (#09260)* (Liaison Status); *ILO (#11123)* (Special List); *UNCTAD (#20285)* (General Category); *UNEP (#20299)*; *UNICEF (#20332)*; *UNIDO (#20336)*; *United Nations Population Fund (UNFPA, #20612)*. **IGO Relations** Accredited by (1): *United Nations Office at Vienna (UNOV, #20604)*. Cooperates with (2): *International Fund for Agricultural Development (IFAD, #13692)*; *United Nations University (UNU, #20642)*. Associated with Department of Global Communications of the United Nations. **NGO Relations** Member of (5): *Geneva Global Health Hub (G2H2, #10122)*; *GLOBAL RESPONSIBILITY – Austrian Platform for Development and Humanitarian Aid*; *NGO Committee on Sustainable Development, Vienna (#17119)*; *NGO Committee on UNICEF (#17120)*; *Verband Entwicklungspolitik und Humanitäre Hilfe e.V. (VENRO)*. Partner of (2): *Centro di Studi di Politica Internazionale (CeSPI)*; *FIAN International (#09743)*. Represented on the Organizing Committee of: *Hague Appeal for Peace (HAP, #10848)*. [2023.02.20/XB3228/y/**B**]

♦ Society for the International Exchange of Children and Young People (inactive)

♦ Society of International Gas Tanker and Terminal Operators (SIGTTO) 19582

Gen Manager 42 New Broad Street, London, EC2M 1JD, UK. T. +442076281124. Fax +442076283163. E-mail: reception@sigtto.org – manager@sigtto.org.
Registered Office PO Box 1022, Clarendon House, Church Street West, Hamilton 5-31, Bermuda.
URL: http://www.sigtto.org/

History Oct 1979, Bermuda. Incorporated under the laws of Bermuda. **Aims** Define and promote international best practice in operation of liquefied gas tankers and liquefied gas loading and receiving terminals. **Structure** General meeting (annual). Board of Directors; Chairman; General Purposes Committee (GPC). Specialist working groups from membership. **Languages** English. **Staff** 5.00 FTE, paid. **Finance** Sources: members' dues. **Activities** Events/meetings. **Events** *Autumn Board Meeting and Annual General Meeting* Athens (Greece) 2020, *Asian Tanker Conference* Singapore (Singapore) 2019, *Asian Tanker Conference* Singapore (Singapore) 2018, *LNG Ship/Shore Interface Asia Conference* Singapore (Singapore) 2018, *LNG Ship/Shore Interface Conference* Singapore (Singapore) 2018. **Publications** *SIGTTO Newsletter* (2 a year). Annual Report; reviews; records; consultative documents; recommendations; guidelines; guides, jointly with ICS and OCIMF; films.
Members Individuals in 39 countries and territories:
Algeria, Argentina, Australia, Bahrain, Belgium, Brunei Darussalam, China, Costa Rica, Denmark, Dominican Rep, France, Germany, Greece, India, Indonesia, Iran Islamic Rep, Italy, Korea Rep, Kuwait, Libya, Malaysia, Mexico, Monaco, Netherlands, Nigeria, Norway, Oman, Portugal, Puerto Rico, Qatar, Saudi Arabia, Singapore, Spain, Sweden, Taiwan, Trinidad-Tobago, Türkiye, UK, United Arab Emirates.
Consultative Status Consultative status granted from: *ECOSOC (#05331)* (Ros C); *International Maritime Organization (IMO, #14102)*. **NGO Relations** Member of: *Maritime Piracy Humanitarian Response Programme (MPHRP, #16583)*. [2021/XD1147/v/**C**]

♦ Society of International Gastroenterological Nurses and Endoscopy Associates (SIGNEA) 19583

Contact address not obtained. T. +18472975088. Fax +18477450800.
URL: http://www.signea.org/

History Initial organizational meeting for an international group of gastroenterological nurses, 1982, New Orleans LA (USA). **Aims** Facilitate communication and collaboration between gastroenterology nurses and associates throughout the world; establish international standards to ensure quality patient care; develop education and training opportunities for nurses and associates worldwide; support related research and disseminate information in the field. **Structure** Executive Committee, comprising President, Treasurer, Executive Director, Newsletter Editor and 5 members-at-large. **Events** *ESGENA annual conference* Barcelona (Spain) 2010, *ESGENA annual conference / Educational Meeting / Annual Conference* London (UK) 2009, *Educational Meeting* Montréal, QC (Canada) 2005, *International educational meeting / Educational Meeting* Bangkok (Thailand) 2002, *International educational meeting / Educational Meeting* Vienna (Austria) 1998. **Publications** *SIGNEA Newsletter* (3 a year). [2013/XD6942/**D**]

♦ Society for International Studies, Madrid (internationally oriented national body)
♦ Society of International Travel Executives / see Society for Incentive Travel Excellence (#19574)
♦ Society of International Treasurers (inactive)
♦ Society for the Internet in Medicine (inactive)
♦ Society for Intestinal Microbial Ecology and Disease / see Society for Microbial Ecology and Disease (#19596)
♦ Society for Intravenous Anesthesia / see International Society for Anaesthetic Pharmacology

♦ Society for Invertebrate Pathology (SIP) 19584

Pres Wuhan Institute of Virology, Chinese Academy of Sciences, Xiao Hong Shan 44, Wuhan, 430071 Hubei, China. T. +862787197180.
Sec Wageningen Univ, Laboratory of Virology, Droevendaalsesteeg 1, 6708 PB Wageningen, Netherlands. T. +31317485082.
URL: http://www.sipweb.org/

History Founded 9 May 1967, Seattle WA (USA), during a meeting of the Organizing Committee comprising 7 members. **Aims** Promote scientific knowledge of pathology of invertebrate animals and of related subjects through discussions, reports, and publications; stimulate scientific investigations and the application of the research data; plan, organize and administer projects for advancement of scientific knowledge in invertebrate pathology; improve education and professional qualifications in the field; promote international cooperation. **Structure** General Meeting; Governing Council; Divisions (7); Committees (11); Executive Secretary (1). **Languages** English. **Staff** 0.50 FTE, paid. Voluntary. **Finance** Members' dues. **Activities** Research/documentation; training/education; publishing activities; awards/prizes/competitions. **Events** *Annual Meeting* Port Elizabeth (South Africa) 2022, *Annual Meeting* Port Elizabeth (South Africa) 2021, *Annual Meeting* Mérida (Mexico) 2020, *Annual Meeting* Valencia (Spain) 2019, *Congress on Invertebrate Pathology and Microbial Control* Valencia (Spain) 2019. **Publications** *SIP Newsletter* (3 a year); *Membership Directory* (every 2 years); *The Journal of Invertebrate Pathology* – refereed.
Members Full (303); Student (59); Emeritus (49); Honorary (9); Endowed (14). Members in 52 countries and territories:
Argentina, Australia, Austria, Belgium, Benin, Brazil, Bulgaria, Canada, China, Colombia, Cuba, Czechia, Denmark, Dominican Rep, Egypt, Finland, France, Georgia, Germany, Greece, Honduras, India, Iran Islamic Rep, Ireland, Israel, Italy, Japan, Jordan, Kenya, Korea Rep, Latvia, Mexico, Moldova, Netherlands, New Zealand, Norway, Peru, Philippines, Poland, Portugal, Romania, Russia, South Africa, Spain, Sri Lanka, Sweden, Switzerland, Taiwan, Thailand, Türkiye, UK, USA. [2018.09.17/XE5988/v/**D**]

♦ Society for Iranian Studies / see Association for Iranian Studies
♦ Society of Jesus (religious order)
♦ Society of Jesus, Mary, Joseph (religious order)
♦ Society of King Charles the Martyr (internationally oriented national body)

♦ Society for Laboratory Animal Science (GV-SOLAS) 19585

Société pour la science des animaux de laboratoire – Gesellschaft für Versuchstierkunde (GV-SOLAS)

Hon Sec Universitätsklinikum Freiburg, CEMT-FR, Stefan-Meier-Straße 8, 79104 Freiburg, Germany. T. +497612037759. E-mail: sekretariat@gv-solas.de.
URL: http://www.gv-solas.de/

History 30 Apr 1964, Wiesbaden (Germany). Registration: Germany. **Aims** Promote science in the area of laboratory animal science as a basic for biomedical research. **Structure** General Assembly (annual); Executive Board; Duties; Advisory Council; Working Committees (8). **Languages** English, German. **Staff** Voluntary. **Finance** Sources: members' dues. **Activities** Awards/prizes/competitions; events/meetings; publishing activities; research/documentation. **Events** *Annual Congress* Würzburg (Germany) 2020, *Annual Congress* Brussels (Belgium) 2016, *Annual Congress* Hannover (Germany) 2015, *Annual Congress* Frankfurt-Main (Germany) 2014, *Annual Congress* Barcelona (Spain) 2013. **Publications** *Laboratory Animals* (6 a year).
Members Ordinary; Extraordinary; Promotive; Honorary; Corresponding; Free. Members in 22 countries:
Australia, Austria, Belgium, Canada, Denmark, Estonia, Finland, France, Germany, India, Israel, Italy, Japan, Luxembourg, Netherlands, Spain, Sweden, Switzerland, Taiwan, Türkiye, UK, USA. [2020.05.12/XC3229/**F**]

♦ Society for Laboratory Automation and Screening (internationally oriented national body)

♦ Society of Lateral Access Surgery (SOLAS) 19586

US Office 10755 Scripps Poway Pkwy #502, San Diego CA 92131, USA. T. +16195509591.
Netherlands Office Barbara Strozzilaan 201, 1083 HN Amsterdam, Netherlands.
Twitter: https://twitter.com/lateralaccess

History 2006. Former names and other names: *Stichting Society of Lateral Access Surgery* – full title. Registration: RSIN, No/ID: 855611911, Netherlands. **Aims** Shape the future of lateral access spine surgery. **Structure** Board of Directors; Executive Committee; Board of Trustees. **Activities** Events/meetings; knowledge management/information dissemination; research/documentation; training/education. **Events** *Asia Pacific and Japan Combined Meeting* Tokyo (Japan) 2019. **Publications** *SOLAS Newsletter* (12 a year). [2020/AA0148/**C**]

♦ Society for Latin American Anthropology / see Society for Latin American and Caribbean Anthropology
♦ Society for Latin American and Caribbean Anthropology (internationally oriented national body)
♦ Society for Latin American Studies (internationally oriented national body)
♦ Society for Latin Ophthalmologists (inactive)

♦ Society for Learning Analytics Research (SoLAR) 19587

Exec Manager address not obtained. E-mail: info@solaresearch.org.
URL: https://solaresearch.org/

History Current constitution and by-laws adopted 2013. Registered in accordance with Canadian law. Registration: Canada, Alberta. **Aims** Foster the highest standards of academic research into learning analytics; promote development of open educational resources in learning analytics; raise awareness of learning analytics amongst policy and decision-makers in educational institutions and governments. **Structure** Annual General Meeting; Executive Committee. **Finance** Sources: members' dues. **Activities** Awareness raising; events/meetings; training/education. *Learning Analytics Summer Institute (LASI)*. **Events** *International Conference on Learning Analytics and Knowledge (LAK)* Arlington, TX (USA) 2023, *International Conference on Learning Analytics and Knowledge (LAK)* Newport Beach, CA (USA) 2022, *International Conference on Learning Analytics and Knowledge (LAK)* Irvine, CA (USA) 2021, *Nordic Learning Analytics Summer Institute (LASI-Nordic)* Stockholm (Sweden) 2021, *International Conference on Learning Analytics and Knowledge* Frankfurt-Main (Germany) 2020. **Publications** *Journal of Learning Analytics*.
Members Institutions in 9 countries:
Australia, Canada, Germany, Japan, Netherlands, New Zealand, Singapore, UK, USA. [2021/XM8009/**C**]

♦ Society for Light Treatment and Biological Rhythms (SLTBR) 19588

Main Office c/o GroupAdvance Consulting GmbH, Gubelstrasse, 12, 6300 Zug, Switzerland. E-mail: info@groupadvance.com.
Pres Fac of Science and Engineering, Univ of Groningen, GELIFES, Nijenborgh 7, 9747 AG Groningen, Netherlands.
URL: https://sltbr.org/

History 1988. **Structure** Executive, comprising President, Past-Presidents, Board of Directors and Executive Director. **Events** *Annual Meeting* Manchester (UK) 2022, *Annual Meeting* Vienna (Austria) 2021, *Annual Meeting* Manchester (UK) 2020, *Annual Meeting* Chicago, IL (USA) 2019, *Annual Meeting* Groningen (Netherlands) 2018. [2021/XM8192/**D**]

♦ Society for Literature and Science / see Society for Literature, Science and the Arts
♦ Society for Literature, Science and the Arts (internationally oriented national body)
♦ Society of Logistics Engineers / see SOLE – The International Society of Logistics (#19679)

♦ Society for Longitudinal and Life Course Studies (SLLS) 19589

Sec 6 New Exeter Street, Chudleigh, Newton Abbot, TQ13 0DB, UK. T. +441626683101. E-mail: info@slls.org.uk.
Registered Office 20 Bedford Way, London, WC1H 0AL, UK.
URL: https://www.slls.org.uk/

History Sep 2010, Cambridge (UK). UK Registered Charity: 1144426. **Aims** Promote interdisciplinary and inter-study understanding and collaboration in longitudinal and life course research; provide a forum for discussion and publication of new ideas about all aspects of this topic. **Structure** Executive Committee. **Events** *Conference* Cleveland, OH (USA) 2022, *Conference* Newton Abbot (UK) 2021, *Conference* Potsdam (Germany) 2019, *Conference* Milan (Italy) 2018, *Education and the life course – determinants and consequences of unequal educational opportunities* Bamberg (Germany) 2016. **Publications** *Longitudinal and Life Course Studies* – journal. [2022/XJ7527/**C**]

♦ Society for Low Temperature Biology (SLTB) 19590

Communications Officer address not obtained. E-mail: arics@us.es.
Communications Officer address not obtained.
URL: http://www.sltb.info/

History 1964. **Aims** Carry out and promote studies and research in low temperature biology and the application of *cryobiology* in various fields. **Structure** Committee. **Languages** English. **Staff** Voluntary. **Finance** Members' dues. **Activities** Events/meetings. **Events** *Annual General Meeting* Seville (Spain) 2019, *Annual General Meeting* Prague (Czechia) 2018, *Symposium* Copenhagen (Denmark) 2008, *Annual General Meeting* Derby (UK) 2007, *Annual General Meeting* Hamburg (Germany) 2006.
Members Individuals in 25 countries:
Argentina, Australia, Belgium, Brazil, Canada, Czechia, Denmark, France, Germany, India, Italy, Japan, Korea Rep, Malaysia, Netherlands, Nigeria, Russia, Serbia, Singapore, South Africa, Spain, Switzerland, Türkiye, UK, USA. [2019/XD8200/v/**D**]

♦ Society of Magnetic Resonance / see International Society for Magnetic Resonance in Medicine (#15241)
♦ Society for Maintenance and Reliability Professionals (internationally oriented national body)
♦ Society of Manufacturing Engineers / see SME
♦ Society of Mary (religious order)
♦ Society of Mary (religious order)

♦ Society for Mathematical Biology (SMB) 19591

Membership Committee address not obtained. E-mail: membership@smb.org.
URL: http://www.smb.org/

History 1972. **Aims** Promote and foster interactions between mathematical and biological sciences communities through membership, journal publications, travel support and conferences. **Structure** Officers: President; President-Elect; Secretary; Treasurer. Committees (9). **Finance** Sources: members' dues. **Activities** Awards/prizes/competitions; events/meetings; training/education. **Events** *Annual Meeting* Riverside, CA (USA) 2021, *Annual Meeting* Guttenberg, NJ (USA) 2020, *Annual Meeting* Montréal, QC (Canada) 2019, *Annual Meeting* Sydney, NSW (Australia) 2018, *Annual Meeting* Salt Lake City, UT (USA) 2017. **Publications** *SMB Newsletter* (3 a year); *Bulletin of Mathematical Biology*. **Members** Individuals (791). Membership countries not specified. [2022.02.02/XW0071/**C**]

♦ **Society for Mathematical Psychology (SMP)** **19592**
Sec Dept of Psychology, Carnegie Mellon Univ,, 5000 Forbes Ave, Baker Hall 345C, Pittsburgh PA 15213, USA. E-mail: treasurer@mathpsych.org.
URL: http://mathpsych.org/
History 1977, USA. Originally registered in the State of Illinois (USA), 1977. Reincorporation in the state of Utah (USA), 1985. Registration: USA. **Aims** Promote the advancement and communication of research in mathematical psychology and related disciplines. **Structure** Executive Committee. **Activities** Awards/prizes/competitions; events/meetings; research/documentation; training/education. **Events** *Annual Meeting* Montréal, QC (Canada) 2019. **Publications** *SMP Newsletter* (annual); *Computational Brain & Behavior*, *Journal of Mathematical Psychology*. [2020/AA0411/**C**]

♦ Society for Mathematics and Computation in Music (internationally oriented national body)
♦ Society for Medical Decision Making (internationally oriented national body)
♦ Society for Medical Innovation and Technology / see International Society for Medical Innovation and Technology (#15255)
♦ Society of Medical Technologists, West Indies / see Caribbean Association of Medical Technologists (#03453)
♦ Society for Medicinal Plant Research / see GA – Society for Medicinal Plant and Natural Product Research (#10075)

♦ **Society for Medieval Canon Law** **19593**
Iuris Canonici Medii Aevi Consociatio (ICMAC)
Pres Dept of History, School of Humanities, Keele Univ, Keele, ST5 5BG, UK. Fax +441782583195.
Treas Univ Zurich, Rechtswissenschaftliches Inst, Rämistr 74, 8001 Zurich ZH, Switzerland. Fax +41446343034.
URL: http://icmac.rch.uky.edu/
History Founded 1988, San Diego CA (USA). **Aims** Support research, publications and instruction in medieval canon law. **Structure** General Assembly; Board; Advisory Board. **Languages** English, French, German, Italian. **Staff** 4.00 FTE, voluntary. **Finance** Members' dues. **Activities** Research/documentation; events/meetings. **Events** *International Congress* St Louis, MI (USA) 2022, *International Congress* St Louis, MI (USA) 2020, *International Congress* Paris (France) 2016, *Congress* Toronto, ON (Canada) 2012, *International congress* Toronto, ON (Canada) 2012. **Publications** *Bulletin of the Stephan Kuttner Institute of Medieval Canon Law* (annual).
Members Individuals in 22 countries:
Australia, Austria, Belgium, Canada, Czechia, Finland, France, Germany, Holy See, Hungary, Ireland, Israel, Italy, Japan, Netherlands, Poland, Portugal, Russia, Spain, Switzerland, UK, USA. [2020.01.20/XD7827/v/**D**]

♦ **Society for the Medieval Mediterranean** **19594**
Sec address not obtained.
Pres address not obtained.
URL: https://www.societymedievalmediterranean.com/
History 1997. **Aims** Foster cross-cultural and inter-disciplinary investigation, create a forum of ideas, and encourage debate on crosspollination within the Medieval Mediterranean. **Structure** Committee. **Finance** Sources: members' dues. **Activities** Awards/prizes/competitions; events/meetings. **Events** *Biennial Conference* Rethimno (Greece) 2022, *Biennial Conference* Rethimno (Greece) 2021, *Biennial Conference* Barcelona (Spain) 2019, *Biennial Conference* Ghent (Belgium) 2017, *Biennial Conference* Lincoln (UK) 2015. **Publications** *Al-Masāq: Journal of the Medieval Mediterranean*. [2020/AA0644/**D**]

♦ Society of Mediterranean Ecologists / see International Society of Mediterranean Ecology (#15259)

♦ **Society for Melanoma Research (SMR)** **19595**
Association Manager c/o Site Solutions Worldwide, PO Box 113, Clifton Park NY 12065, USA. T. +18663746338. E-mail: info@societymelanomaresearch.org.
URL: http://www.societymelanomaresearch.org/
History 2003, Philadelphia, PA (USA). **Aims** Bring together members who vary widely in their professions – from basic researchers to translational researchers to clinicians – but share an abiding devotion to improving the lives of those suffering from melanoma through research. **Structure** Steering Committee. Officers: President; Vice-President; Secretary/Treasurer; Past President. **Finance** Sources: donations; members' dues. **Events** *International Congress* Edinburgh (UK) 2022, *International Congress* Salt Lake City, UT (USA) 2019, *International Congress* Manchester (UK) 2018, *International Congress* Brisbane, QLD (Australia) 2017, *International Congress* Boston, MA (USA) 2016. **Publications** *Pigment Cell and Melanoma Research* – offical journal. [2022/XM3999/**C**]

♦ **Society for Microbial Ecology and Disease (SOMED)** **19596**
Pres Uzhhorod National Univ, 46 Pidgirna St, Uzhhorod, Zakarpattia, 88000, Ukraine.
Sec address not obtained.
URL: http://www.somed.nu/
History 1978. Former names and other names: *Society for Intestinal Microbial Ecology and Disease (SIMED)* – former (1978 to 1988). **Aims** Promote scientific knowledge and encourage research and technology in the field of microbial ecology and its relation to diseases; disseminate information relative to this field; unify the efforts of those in the field; cooperate with national and international organizations in the field; hold and sponsor scientific meetings. **Structure** Executive Council, comprising including President-elect, President, Immediate Past-President, Secretary, Treasurer and 6 Councillors. **Languages** English. **Staff** 1.00 FTE, paid; 5.50 FTE, voluntary. **Finance** Members' dues. Budget (annual): about US$ 5,000. **Events** *Congress* Alexandroupoli (Greece) 2022, *Congress* Budapest (Hungary) 2018, *Congress* Tokyo (Japan) 2017, *Congress* Verona (Italy) 2015, *Congress* Chicago, IL (USA) 2014. **Publications** *SOMED News* (4 a year).
Members Full in 21 countries:
Australia, Austria, Brazil, Canada, Czechia, Estonia, Finland, France, Germany, Greece, Hungary, Italy, Japan, Netherlands, Norway, Romania, Russia, Spain, Sweden, UK, USA.
NGO Relations Joint meeting with: *International Association for Gnotobiology (IAG, #11921)*. [2021/XM8285/**D**]

♦ Society for Middle East Confederation (inactive)
♦ Society for Minimally Invasive Therapy / see International Society for Medical Innovation and Technology (#15255)

♦ **Society of Mining Professors (SOMP)** **19597**
Societät der Bergbaukunde (SDB)
SG School of Mining Eng, Univ of New South Wales, Sydney NSW 2052, Australia. T. +61293855160. Fax +61293137269. E-mail: info@mineprofs.org.
Deputy SG and Treas PO Box 5048, 2600 GA Delft, Netherlands. T. +31152785001.
URL: http://www.mineprofs.org/
History Founded 1990, Leoben (Austria). Successor to *Societät der Bergbaukunde*, founded in the early 18th century. **Aims** Promote responsible practice of mining engineering as an engineering discipline; facilitate information exchange, research and teaching collaboration and other collaborative activities among members. **Structure** Annual General Meeting; Council. **Languages** English. **Staff** Voluntary. **Finance** Members' dues. **Events** *Annual Meeting* Medellin (Colombia) 2021, *Annual Meeting* Bochum (Germany) 2019, *Annual Meeting* Beijing (China) 2018, *Annual Meeting* Turin (Italy) 2017, *Annual Meeting* Washington, DC (USA) 2016. **Publications** *SOMP Newsletter*.
Members Professors and academic staff involved in mining engineering education (over 250) in 39 countries:
Albania, Australia, Austria, Belgium, Brazil, Bulgaria, Canada, Chile, China, Colombia, Croatia, Czechia, Estonia, Finland, France, Germany, Greece, Hungary, India, Italy, Japan, Namibia, Netherlands, Norway, Peru, Poland, Portugal, Romania, Russia, Serbia, Slovakia, Slovenia, South Africa, Spain, Sweden, Türkiye, UK, Ukraine, USA. [2016.06.01/XD6604/v/**D**]

♦ Society of Missionaries of Africa (religious order)
♦ Society for Missions to Africa and the East / see Church Mission Society

♦ **Society for Modeling Simulation International (SCSI)** **19598**
Dir 2598 Fortune Way, Ste I, Vista CA 92081, USA. T. +18582773888. Fax +18582773930. E-mail: scs@scs.org.
URL: http://www.scs.org/
History Founded 1952, as *Simulation Councils*, originally in the aerospace context. Also referred to as *SCS International*. Part of *Society for Computer Simulation (SCS)*. **Aims** Advance the use of modelling and simulation to solve real-world problems; advocate simulation and allied computer arts in all fields across all industries; facilitate communication and further education among professionals in the field of simulation. **Structure** Board of Directors; Executive Committee; Regional Councils. **Finance** Members' dues. Other sources: conference registrations; sales of publications. Budget (annual): US$ 1.2 million. **Activities** Events/meetings. **Events** *Summer International Simulation Multiconference* Berlin (Germany) 2019, *Power Plant Simulation International Conference* Tampa, FL (USA) 2019, *Annual Spring Simulation Conference* Tucson, AZ (USA) 2019, *Annual Spring Simulation Conference* Baltimore, MD (USA) 2018, *Summer International Simulation Multiconference* Bordeaux (France) 2018. **Publications** *Simulation* (12 a year) – journal; *Transactions* (4 a year) – journal; *Modeling and Simulation Magazine*. Books. Conference proceedings.
Members Full individuals involved or appropriately qualified in the subject; Student; Corporate governments, non-profit organizations and businesses; Academic educational institutions. Associations in 7 countries:
Belgium, France, Germany, Italy, Japan, Netherlands, USA.
Individuals mainly in North America but in total in 50 countries and territories:
Argentina, Australia, Austria, Belgium, Brazil, Bulgaria, Canada, China, Colombia, Cyprus, Czechia, Denmark, Egypt, Finland, France, Germany, Greece, Honduras, Hong Kong, Iceland, India, Iran Islamic Rep, Iraq, Ireland, Israel, Italy, Japan, Jordan, Korea Rep, Kuwait, Mexico, Netherlands, New Zealand, Norway, Pakistan, Philippines, Portugal, Saudi Arabia, Serbia, Singapore, South Africa, Spain, Sweden, Switzerland, Taiwan, Thailand, UK, United Arab Emirates, USA, Venezuela.
Autonomous member:
European Council for Modelling and Simulation (ECMS, #06831).
NGO Relations Member of: *International Centre for Earth Simulation (ICES Foundation)*. [2015.06.01/XF1389/y/**F**]

♦ **Society for Molecular Biology and Evolution (SMBE)** **19599**
Sec Nat'l Univ of Ireland, Maynooth, CO. KILDARE, Ireland.
URL: http://www.smbe.org/
History 1992, University Park PA (USA). Became operational 1 Jan 1993. **Aims** Provide facilities for association and conference among molecular evolutionists so as to further the goals of molecular evolutionary biology and its practitioners. **Structure** Council, comprising President, Past President, President-Elect, Secretary, Treasurer and 3 Councillors. **Languages** English. **Staff** None. **Finance** Member' dues. **Activities** Awards/prizes/competitions; events/meetings. **Events** *Annual Conference* Maynooth (Ireland) 2021, *Annual Conference* Québec, QC (Canada) 2020, *Annual Conference* Manchester (UK) 2019, *Annual Conference* Yokohama (Japan) 2018, *Annual Conference* Austin, TX (USA) 2017. **Publications** *Genome Biology and Evolution* – journal; *Molecular Biology and Evolution* – journal.
Members Full in 39 countries and territories:
Australia, Austria, Belgium, Brazil, Canada, Chile, China, Czechia, Denmark, Estonia, Finland, France, Germany, Greece, Hong Kong, Hungary, India, Ireland, Israel, Italy, Japan, Korea Rep, Mexico, Netherlands, New Zealand, Norway, Portugal, Russia, Singapore, Slovenia, South Africa, Spain, Sweden, Switzerland, Taiwan, Thailand, UK, Uruguay, USA. [2020/XM0342/**D**]

♦ **Society for Molecular Imprinting (SMI)** **19600**
Secretariat Dept Pure/Applied Biochemistry, Ctr for Chemistry and Chemical Engineering, Lund Univ, PO Box 124, SE-221 00 Lund, Sweden. E-mail: lei.ye@tbiokem.lth.se.
Pres address not obtained. E-mail: mike@mipdatabase.com.
URL: http://mipsoc.org/SMI/index.php/
History 17 Sep 1997. **Aims** Pursue excellence in and advance the science and technology of molecular imprinting. **Structure** General Assembly; Administrative Council; Board. **Events** *International Conference on Molecular Imprinting – MIP* Hiroshima (Japan) 2021, *International Conference on Molecular Imprinting – MIP* ZhenJiang (China) 2014, *International Conference on Molecular Imprinting – MIP* Paris (France) 2012, *International Conference on Molecular Imprinting – MIP* New Orleans, LA (USA) 2010, *International Conference on Molecular Imprinting – MIP* Kobe (Japan) 2008.
Members Individuals in 55 countries and territories:
Argentina, Australia, Austria, Belgium, Brazil, Canada, China, Croatia, Czechia, Denmark, Egypt, Estonia, Finland, France, Germany, Greece, Hong Kong, Hungary, India, Iran Islamic Rep, Iraq, Ireland, Israel, Italy, Japan, Jordan, Kazakhstan, Korea Rep, Malaysia, Mexico, Netherlands, New Zealand, Nigeria, Oman, Pakistan, Philippines, Poland, Portugal, Romania, Russia, Singapore, Slovenia, South Africa, Spain, Sri Lanka, Sweden, Switzerland, Taiwan, Tanzania UR, Thailand, Tunisia, Türkiye, UK, Ukraine, USA. [2020/XJ7403/v/**C**]

♦ Society of Motion Picture Engineers / see Society of Motion Picture and Television Engineers
♦ Society of Motion Picture and Television Engineers (internationally oriented national body)

♦ **Society for Mucosal Immunology (SMI)** **19601**
Exec Dir N83 W13410 Leon Rd, Menomonee Falls WI 53051, USA. T. +14143591650ext1104. Fax +14143591671. E-mail: info@socmucimm.org.
URL: http://www.socmucimm.org/
History 1987, Niagara Falls (Canada), following 4th Congress. **Aims** Advance the research, literacy and educational aspects of the scientific field of mucosal immunology. **Structure** Officers: President; President-elect; Secretary/Treasurer; Councillors; Committees. **Languages** English. **Staff** 1.50 FTE, paid. **Activities** National and international research congresses, seminars and workshops. **Events** *Biennial Congress* Brisbane, QLD (Australia) 2019, *Biennial Congress* Washington, DC (USA) 2017, *Biennial Congress* Berlin (Germany) 2015, *Biennial Congress* Vancouver, BC (Canada) 2013, *Biennial Congress* Paris (France) 2011. **Publications** *Journal of Mucosal Immunology*. **Members** Individual immunologists, physicians, dentists, veterinarians, biochemists or other scientists doing research or with active interest in mucosal immunology (400), in 25 countries. Membership countries not specified. **NGO Relations** International affiliate of: *International Union of Immunological Societies (IUIS, #15781)*. Instrumental in setting up: *European Mucosal Immunology Group (EMIG, #07826)*. [2016/XD2820/v/**C**]

♦ **Society for Multi-Ethnic Studies: Europe and Americas (MESEA)** ... **19602**
Sec address not obtained.
URL: http://www.mesea.org/
History 1998. Registered in accordance with German law. **Aims** Promote the study of ethnic cultures of Europe and the Americas; support scholarly and cultural exchanges; act as a forum for cooperation between universities, political institutions and ethnic communities to further multi-ethnic understanding. **Structure** Membership Meeting (every 2 years). Executive Board, comprising President, Vice-President, Treasurer, Secretary and Programme Chair. Advisory Board. **Finance** Members 'dues. **Events** *Biennial Conference* Larnaca (Cyprus) 2022, *Biennial Conference* Larnaca (Cyprus) 2020, *Biennial Conference* Graz (Austria) 2018, *Biennial Conference* Warsaw (Poland) 2016, *Biennial Conference* Saarbrücken (Germany) 2014. **Publications** *Atlantic Studies* (2 a year); *MESEA NEWS* (2 a year).
Members Individuals (250) and organizations in 31 countries and territories:
Australia, Austria, Belgium, Bulgaria, Canada, Croatia, Finland, France, Germany, Greece, Hong Kong, Hungary, Israel, Italy, Japan, Korea Rep, Netherlands, New Zealand, Nigeria, Poland, Portugal, Romania, Russia, Slovakia, South Africa, Spain, Switzerland, Tunisia, UK, United Arab Emirates, USA.
NGO Relations *Collegium for African American Research (CAAR)*; national organizations. [2014/XM1872/**D**]

♦ **Society of Natural Immunity (SNI)** **19603**
Pres Howard Hughes Medical Inst, 400 Jones Bridge Rd, Chevy Chase MD 20815-6789, USA. T. +13012158500. Fax +1301215-8937.
URL: http://www.upci.upmc.edu/sni/
History Set up 1991. **Aims** Provide a framework to support meetings and symposia. **Finance** Members' dues: Regular: US $50; Postdoctoral/Student: US $20. **Events** *International Meeting / Biennial Meeting* Heidelberg (Germany) 2013, *International Meeting / Biennial Meeting* Asilomar, CA (USA) 2012, *International Meeting / Biennial Meeting* Dubrovnik (Croatia) 2010, *International Meeting / Biennial Meeting* Perth, WA (Australia) 2009, *International Meeting / Biennial Meeting* Cambridge (UK) 2007. **Members** Membership countries not specified. [2014/XJ6660/c/**F**]

♦ Society of Naval Architects and Marine Engineers (internationally oriented national body)
♦ Society for Near Eastern Studies (internationally oriented national body)
♦ Society for Near Eastern Studies in Japan (internationally oriented national body)

♦ Society of Nematologists (SON) 19604

Business Office SON Business Office, PO Box 190, Mesilla NM 88047, USA. T. +15756393327. E-mail: societyofnematologists@gmail.com.
URL: http://www.nematologists.org/

History Dec 1961. Founded under the aegis of *Society of Nematologists (SON, #19604)*. **Aims** Advance the science of nematology, in both its fundamental and economic aspects. **Structure** Executive Board; Standing Committees (15). **Languages** English. **Staff** 0.50 FTE, paid. **Finance** Sources: gifts, legacies; investments; members' dues; sale of publications. **Activities** Events/meetings; knowledge management/ information dissemination. **Events** *Annual Meeting* Anchorage, AK (USA) 2022, *Annual Meeting* Gulf Shores, AL (USA) 2021, *Annual Meeting* Mesilla, NM (USA) 2020, *Annual Meeting* Raleigh, NC (USA) 2019, *Annual Meeting* Albuquerque, NM (USA) 2018. **Publications** *Journal of Nematology*; *Nematology Newsletter*.
Members Individuals in 53 countries and territories:
Argentina, Australia, Austria, Belgium, Bolivia, Brazil, Canada, Chile, China, Costa Rica, Ecuador, Egypt, France, Germany, Greece, Hungary, India, Indonesia, Iran Islamic Rep, Ireland, Israel, Italy, Jamaica, Japan, Jordan, Korea DPR, Korea Rep, Lesotho, Malaysia, Martinique, Mexico, Morocco, Netherlands, New Zealand, Norway, Pakistan, Paraguay, Peru, Poland, Portugal, Russia, Saudi Arabia, Serbia, South Africa, Spain, Sweden, Taiwan, Thailand, Türkiye, Uganda, UK, USA.
NGO Relations Member of (1): *International Federation of Nematology Societies (IFNS, #13488)*. Affiliated with (2): American Institute of Biological Science; National Science Collections Alliance.
[2022.06.03/XE0048/v/E]

♦ Society for the Neural Control of Movement (NCM) 19605

Administrator 2661 Queenswood Drive, Victoria BC V8N 1X6, Canada. E-mail: management@ncm-society.org.
URL: http://ncm-society.org/

History 1990. Inaugural conference Apr 1991, Marco Island FL (USA). **Aims** Bring together scientists seeking to understand neural mechanisms that guide meaningful activities of daily life, primarily through the brain's control of the eyes, head, trunk, and limbs. **Structure** Board of Directors; Executive Committee. **Languages** English. **Activities** Events/meetings. **Events** *Annual Meeting* Victoria, BC (Canada) 2023, *Annual Meeting* Dublin (Ireland) 2022, *Annual Meeting* 2021, *Annual Meeting* Dubrovnik (Croatia) 2020, *Annual Meeting* Toyama City (Japan) 2019. **Members** Principal Investigators and Students in over 30 countries. Membership countries not specified. [2021.06.15/XJ6493/C]

♦ Society for NeurEconomics (SNE) 19606

Secretariat Podium Conference Specialists, 2661 Queenswood Drive, Victoria BC V8N 1X6, Canada. T. +12504727644.
URL: https://neuroeconomics.org/

Aims Foster research on the foundations of economic behavior by promoting collaboration and discussion among scholars from the psychological, economic, and neural sciences; ensure the continued advancement of the field of neuroeconomics by supporting young researchers. **Structure** Board of Directors. **Finance** Sources: members' dues. **Activities** Awards/prizes/competitions; events/meetings. **Events** *Annual Meeting* 2021, *Annual Meeting* 2020, *Annual Meeting* Dublin (Ireland) 2019, *Annual Meeting* Philadelphia, PA (USA) 2018, *Annual Meeting* Toronto, ON (Canada) 2017. [2021/AA1652/v/C]

♦ Society for the Neurobiology of Language (SNL) 19607

Address not obtained.
URL: https://www.neurolang.org/

History Nov 2010, USA. **Aims** Foster progress in understanding the neurobiological basis for language via the interdisciplinary exchange of ideas. **Structure** Board of Directors. **Activities** Awards/prizes/competitions; events/meetings. **Events** *Annual Meeting* Brisbane, QLD (Australia) 2024, *Annual Meeting* Marseille (France) 2023, *Annual Meeting* Philadelphia, PA (USA) 2022, *Annual Meeting* 2021, *Annual Meeting* 2020. **Publications** *Neurobiology of Languagge* – online. [2020/AA0526/C]

- ♦ Society for Neuronal Regulation / see International Society for Neurofeedback and Research
- ♦ Society for Neuroscience (internationally oriented national body)

♦ Society of Neuroscientists of Africa (SONA) 19608

Société des neuroscientifiques d'Afrique

Secretariat The Conference Company, 13 Claribel Rd, Morningside, Durban, 4001, South Africa. T. +27313039852. E-mail: sona@confco.co.za.
SG School of Anatomical Sciences, Fac of Health Sciences, Univ of the Witwatersrand, 7 York Rd, Parktown, Johannesburg, 2193, South Africa.
Assistant SG address not obtained.
URL: https://sonafrica.org/

History 1993. Founded as a regional chapter of *International Brain Research Organization (IBRO, #12392)*. **Aims** Promote research and teaching in neuroscience in Africa. **Events** *Biennial Congress* Johannesburg (South Africa) 2023, *Biennial Congress* Accra (Ghana) 2021, *Biennial Congress* Lagos (Nigeria) 2019, *Biennial Congress* Entebbe (Uganda) 2017, *Biennial Congress* Durban (South Africa) 2015. **Publications** *SONA Newsletter* (2 a year).
Members Neuroscientists in 62 countries:
Algeria, Angola, Australia, Benin, Botswana, Burkina Faso, Burundi, Cameroon, Canada, Cape Verde, Central African Rep, Chad, Comoros, Congo Brazzaville, Congo DR, Côte d'Ivoire, Djibouti, Egypt, Equatorial Guinea, Eritrea, Eswatini, Ethiopia, France, Gabon, Gambia, Ghana, Guinea, Guinea-Bissau, Italy, Kenya, Lesotho, Liberia, Libya, Madagascar, Malawi, Mali, Mauritania, Mauritius, Morocco, Mozambique, Namibia, Niger, Nigeria, Rwanda, Sao Tomé-Principe, Senegal, Seychelles, Sierra Leone, Somalia, South Africa, Spain, Sudan, Sweden, Switzerland, Tanzania UR, Togo, Tunisia, Uganda, UK, USA, Zambia, Zimbabwe.
[2022.05.11/XD2067/v/D]

- ♦ Society for News Design (internationally oriented national body)

♦ Society for News Design – Scandinavia (SNDS) 19609

Secretariat address not obtained.
URL: http://www.snds.org/

History 1985. Founded within *Society for News Design (SND)*. Former names and other names: *Society of Newspaper Design/Scandinavia (SND/S)* – former. **Structure** Board, comprising Presidents, 2 Vice-Presidents, Secretary and Treasurer. **Events** *Design Matters Conference* Copenhagen (Denmark) 2019, *Design Matters Conference* Copenhagen (Denmark) 2018, *Conference* Copenhagen (Denmark) 2017, *Seminar* Copenhagen (Denmark) 2015, *Seminar* Copenhagen (Denmark) 2014. **Publications** *SNDS Magazine* (4 a year).
Members in 4 countries:
Denmark, Finland, Norway, Sweden. [2020/XD3457/v/D]

- ♦ Society of Newspaper Design / see Society for News Design
- ♦ Society of Newspaper Design/Scandinavia / see Society for News Design – Scandinavia (#19609)

♦ Society for New Testament Studies (SNTS) 19610

Société pour l'étude du Nouveau Testament – Sociedad para el Estudio del Nuevo Testamento – Gesellschaft für das Studium des Neuen Testaments – Studiorum Novi Testamenti Societas (SNTS)

Sec Lethenty Byre, Inverurie, AB51 0HQ, UK. T. +441467624131. E-mail: secretary@snts.international.
Assistant Sec George W Truett Theological Seminary, One Bear Place, Box 97126, Waco TX 76798, USA.
URL: http://snts.international/

History Sep 1938, Birmingham (UK). Founded on the initiative of an International Group of scholars formed at the Faith and Order Conference 1937, Edinburgh (UK). **Aims** Stimulate research into the New Testament across the globe. **Structure** General Meeting (annual); Committee; Officers. Observers admitted to the General Meeting. **Languages** English, French, German. **Staff** Voluntary. **Events** *Annual General Meeting* Marburg (Germany) 2019, *Annual General Meeting* Athens (Greece) 2018, *Annual General Meeting* Pretoria (South Africa) 2017, *Annual General Meeting* Montréal, QC (Canada) 2016, *Annual General Meeting* Amsterdam (Netherlands) 2015. **Publications** *New Testament Studies* – journal (1953-); *SNTS Bulletin* – 1950/1952-. *SNTS Monograph Series*.
Members Elected by General Meeting on recommendation of Committee and on presentation by 2 members (candidates must have a background equivalent to that necessary for a university lecturing post). Individuals (about 940) in 50 countries:
Argentina, Australia, Austria, Barbados, Belgium, Brazil, Bulgaria, Canada, Chile, Congo DR, Costa Rica, Croatia, Czechia, Denmark, Finland, France, Germany, Ghana, Greece, Holy See, Hong Kong, Hungary, Iceland, India, Ireland, Israel, Italy, Jamaica, Japan, Kenya, Korea Rep, Netherlands, New Zealand, Nigeria, Norway, Peru, Poland, Romania, Russia, Samoa, Serbia, Slovakia, South Africa, Spain, Sweden, Switzerland, Türkiye, UK, Uruguay, USA. [2019.02.13/XC3236/v/C]

♦ Society for Nonlinear Dynamics and Econometrics (SNDE) 19611

Pres address not obtained.
URL: https://sndeecon.org/

History Current bylawss approved Mar 2015. **Aims** Promote the use of nonlinear methods in economics and finance from both a theoretical and empirical perspective. **Structure** Executive Committee. **Activities** Events/ meetings. **Publications** *Studies in Nonlinear Dynamics and Econometrics (SNDE)* (4 a year). **NGO Relations** Supports (1): *International Workshop in Financial Markets and Nonlinear Dynamics (FMND)*.
[2020/AA0874/C]

- ♦ Society of Nuclear Medicine – Europe (inactive)
- ♦ Society for Nutrition Education / see Society for Nutrition Education and Behavior (#19612)

♦ Society for Nutrition Education and Behavior (SNEB) 19612

Société pour l'éducation en nutrition – Sociedad para la Educación en Nutrición

Main Office 3502 Woodview Trace, Suite 300, Indianapolis IN 46268, USA. T. +13173284627. Fax +13172808527. E-mail: info@sneb.org.
Main: http://www.sneb.org/

History 1967. Former names and other names: *Society for Nutrition Education (SNE)* – former. **Aims** Represent the professional interests of nutrition educators; promote effective nutrition education and healthy behaviour through research, policy and practice. **Structure** Board of Directors; Special Interest Divisions. **Events** *Annual Conference* Washington, DC (USA) 2023, *Annual Conference* Atlanta, GA (USA) 2022, *Annual Conference* Indianapolis, IN (USA) 2021, *Annual Conference* Indianapolis, IN (USA) 2020, *Annual Conference* Orlando, FL (USA) 2019. **Publications** *Journal of Nutrition Education and Behavior* (10 a year); *SNEB eCommunicator*. **Members** Full in over 27 countries. Membership countries not specified. **Consultative Status** Consultative status granted from: *ECOSOC (#05331)* (Special). **IGO Relations** United States Department of Agriculture (USDA). [2020.06.22/XD5651/D]

- ♦ Society of Open Innovation: Technology, Market, and Complexity (internationally oriented national body)
- ♦ Society for Ophthalmo-Immunoinfectiology in Europe (unconfirmed)
- ♦ Society for Oral Oncology / see International Society for Oral Oncology (#15328)
- ♦ Society for Organic Petrology (internationally oriented national body)

♦ Society for Organizational Learning (SOL) 19613

Pres/CEO PO Box 131, North Andover MA 01845, USA. E-mail: info@solonline.org.
Chair address not obtained.
URL: http://www.solonline.org/

History Apr 1997. Founded on the initiative of Dr Peter Senge. **Aims** Discover, integrate and implement theories and practices for the interdependent development of people and their institutions. **Structure** Includes: SOL Europe. **Activities** North America. **Events** *SoL European Learning Plaza* Budapest (Hungary) 2019, *Global forum* Vienna (Austria) 2005, *Global forum* Espoo (Finland) 2003, *Leading towards sustainable organisations* Helsinki (Finland) 2002, *Conference* Jyväskylä (Finland) 2001. **Publications** *SOL Journal*.
Members Communities in 31 countries:
Australia, Austria, Brazil, Chile, China, Colombia, Denmark, Egypt, Finland, France, Germany, Hungary, India, Iran Islamic Rep, Israel, Japan, Malaysia, Mexico, Netherlands, Norway, Palestine, Peru, Poland, Singapore, Spain, Sweden, Thailand, Türkiye, UK, USA, Venezuela. [2021/XD9314/D]

♦ Society for Orthopaedic Traumatologic Sports Medicine 19614

Gesellschaft für Orthopädisch-Traumatologische Sportmedizin (GOTS)

Secretariat Bachstrasse 18, 07743 Jena, Germany. T. +4936414724158. Fax +4936414721921. E-mail: info@gots.org – office@gots.org.
URL: http://www.gots.org/

History 1986. Statutes adopted 22 Jun 2007. Registered in accordance with German law. **Aims** Unite interests of the different specialities orthopaedic surgery, trauma surgery, biomechanics, physiotherapy, physical therapy and sports sciences. **Structure** Board. **Languages** German. **Activities** Events/meetings. **Events** *Annual Meeting* Salzburg (Austria) 2019, *Annual Meeting* Basel (Switzerland) 2015, *Annual Congress* Munich (Germany) 2015, *Annual Congress / Annual Meeting* Munich (Germany) 2014, *Annual Congress / Annual Meeting* Mannheim (Germany) 2013. **Publications** *Sports Orthopaedic and Traumatology (SOT)* – journal. **Members** Individuals (about 1,500). Membership countries not specified. [2020.03.11/XJ8315/D]

- ♦ Society of Orthopaedic and Traumatologic Surgery of the Mediterranean and Middle East Countries (inactive)
- ♦ Society of Otorhinolaryngology (inactive)
- ♦ Society of Our Lady of the Way (religious order)
- ♦ Society for Participatory Research in Asia (internationally oriented national body)
- ♦ Society for Pediatric Pathology (internationally oriented national body)

♦ Society for Persuasion and Technology (SPT) 19615

Sec address not obtained.
URL: http://persuasivetech.org/

History Created formally to give a more formalized structure for the organization of the International Conference on Persuasive Technology. **Aims** Provide an open forum for all those interested in the education, science and applications of Persuasive Technology. **Structure** Steering Committee. **Events** *International Conference on Persuasive Technology* Doha (Qatar) 2022, *International Conference on Persuasive Technology* Bournemouth (UK) 2021, *International Conference on Persuasive Technology* Aalborg (Denmark) 2020, *International Conference on Persuasive Technology* Limassol (Cyprus) 2019, *International Conference on Persuasive Technology (ICPT)* Waterloo, ON (Canada) 2018. [2022/AA2632/C]

♦ Society of Petroleum Engineers (SPE) 19616

Mailing Address PO Box 833836, Richardson TX 75083-3836, USA. T. +19729529393. Fax +19729529435. E-mail: spedal@spe.org.
URL: http://www.spe.org/

History 1985. **Aims** Collect, disseminate and exchange technical knowledge concerning exploration, development and production of oil and gas resources and related technologies for the public benefit; provide opportunities for professionals to enhance their technical and professional competence. **Structure** Board of Directors; Board Committees. Offices (7) in 6 countries: Canada; Dubai; Malaysia; Moscow; UK; USA. **Staff** 300.00 FTE, paid. **Activities** Knowledge management/information dissemination; events/meetings; awards/prizes/competitions. **Events** *Symposium on the Decarbonisation Initiative* Abu Dhabi (United Arab Emirates) 2022, *Workshop on Advances in Technology and Solutions for Well Integrity* Abu Dhabi (United Arab Emirates) 2022, *SPE Asia Pacific Oil and Gas Conference* Adelaide, SA (Australia) 2022, *Asia Pacific Drilling Technology Conference* Bangkok (Thailand) 2022, *SPE Annual Technical Conference and Exhibition (ATCE)* Houston, TX (USA) 2022. **Publications** *Journal of Petroleum Technology*; *Oil and Gas Facilities*; *SPE Drilling and Completion*; *SPE Economics and Management*; *SPE Journal*; *SPE Production and Operations*; *SPE Reservoir Evaluation and Engineering*; *The Way Ahead*. *Monograph Series*. Handbooks; reports; training courses; technical papers; standards; surveys; videos. **Information Services** *OnePetro* – library of technical literature. **Members** Professional; Student. Over 168,000 members in 144 countries. Membership countries not specified. **NGO Relations** Member of (1): *ABET*. Together with *American Association of Petroleum Geologists (AAPG)*, *European Association of Geoscientists and Engineers (EAGE, #06055)* and *Society of Economic Geologists (SEG, #19546)*, sponsors *International Petroleum Technology Conference (IPTC)*.
[2020/XF0838/v/F]

- ♦ Society of Petroleum Geophysicists / see Society of Exploration Geophysicists

♦ Society of Petrophysicists and Well Log Analysts (SPWLA) **19617**

Secretariat 8866 Gulf Freeway, Ste 320, Houston TX 77017, USA. T. +17139478727. Fax +17139477181. E-mail: foundation@spwla.org.
URL: http://www.spwla.org/

History 1959, USA. **Aims** Promote: advancement of the science of petrophysics and formation evaluation through well logging and other formation evaluation techniques; application of these techniques to the exploitation of *petroleum gas*, *oil* and other *minerals*. **Structure** Board of Directors. Chapter at Large: *Society of Core Analysts (SCA, #19537)*. **Languages** English. **Staff** 2.00 FTE, paid. **Finance** Members' dues. Proceeds from Annual Symposium. Budget (annual): less than US$ 1,000 million. **Events** *Annual Symposium* Boston, MA (USA) 2021, *Annual Symposium* The Woodlands, TX (USA) 2019, *Abu Dhabi Topical Conference* Abu Dhabi (United Arab Emirates) 2018, *Annual Symposium* London (UK) 2018, *Joint Meeting* Bangkok (Thailand) 2017. **Publications** *Petrophysics* (6 a year) – journal.
Members Chapters in 21 countries:
Angola, Argentina, Australia, Brazil, China, France, Hungary, India, Indonesia, Japan, Malaysia, Mexico, Netherlands, Nigeria, Norway, Russia, Saudi Arabia, UK, United Arab Emirates, USA, Venezuela. [2022/XF2879/**F**]

♦ Society for Phenomenology and Media (SPM) **19618**

Acting Sec address not obtained. E-mail: socphenmedia@yahoo.com.
URL: https://www.societyforphenomenologyandmedia.org/

History 1998. **Aims** Encourage *philosophical* diversity. **Structure** Board. **Languages** English. **Staff** 4.00 FTE, voluntary. **Finance** Sources: members' dues. **Events** *International Conference* Shanghai (China) / Puebla (Mexico) 2023, *International Conference* Tallinn (Estonia) 2020, *International Conference* Puebla (Mexico) 2019, *International Conference* Akureyri (Iceland) 2018, *International Conference* Brussels (Belgium) 2017. **Publications** *Glimpse* – journal; *Outis*. Proceedings.
Members Participants in 32 countries:
Argentina, Australia, Austria, Belgium, Canada, China, Czechia, Denmark, Estonia, Ethiopia, Finland, France, Germany, Greece, Hungary, Iceland, India, Italy, Japan, Lithuania, Mexico, New Zealand, Nigeria, North Macedonia, Norway, Poland, Slovenia, Spain, Sweden, Türkiye, UK, USA.
NGO Relations Founding member of: *Organization of Phenomenological Organizations (OPO, #17883)*. [2019/XJ6863/**C**]

♦ Society for Philosophy of Science in Practice (SPSP) **19619**

Contact address not obtained.
URL: http://www.philosophy-science-practice.org/

History 2007. **Aims** Build meaningful bridges between the philosophy of science and the newer fields of philosophy of technology and philosophy of medicine. **Structure** Organizing Committee; Advisory Board. **Activities** Events/meetings. **Events** *Biennial Conferece* Ghent (Belgium) 2022, *Biennial Conference* East Lansing, MI (USA) 2021, *Biennial Conference* East Lansing, MI (USA) 2020, *Biennial Conference* Ghent (Belgium) 2018, *Biennial Conference* Glassboro, NJ (USA) 2016. **Publications** *SPSP Newsletter*. [2022/XM7887/c/**C**]

♦ Society for Philosophy and Technology (SPT) **19620**

Sec Philosophy Dept, texas A&M University, 418 YMCA Bldg, MS 4237, College Station TX 77843-4237, USA.
URL: http://www.spt.org/

History 1976. **Aims** Facilitate, support and encourage literary and educational projects aiming to advance philosophical understanding of technology. **Structure** Board of Directors. **Languages** English. **Finance** Sources: members' dues. **Activities** Events/meetings. **Events** *Biennial Conference* Rohnert Park, CA (USA) 2021, *Biennial Conference* College Station, TX (USA) 2019, *Biennial Conference* Darmstadt (Germany) 2017, *Biennial Conference* Shenyang (China) 2015, *Biennial Conference* Lisbon (Portugal) 2013. **Publications** *Techné* (3 a year) – scientific journal; *SPT Newsletter*. **Members** Individuals. Membership countries not specified. [2022/XJ8475/v/**D**]

- ♦ Society of Photographic Instrumentation Engineers / see SPIE (#19919)
- ♦ Society for Photo-Optical Instrumentation Engineers / see SPIE (#19919)
- ♦ Society of Photo-Technologists (internationally oriented national body)

♦ Society for Pidgin and Creole Linguistics (SPCL) **19621**

Exec Sec address not obtained. E-mail: spclsociety@gmail.com.
URL: https://sites.google.com/site/societypidgncreolelinguistics/

History Jan 1989, Washington, DC (USA). Constitution most recently approved June 2017, Tampere (Finland). **Aims** Study and document pidgin and Creole languages worldwide, together with other languages or dialects of other languages influencing them or influenced by them. **Structure** Annual Business Meeting; Executive Council. **Finance** Sources: members' dues. **Events** *Winter Meeting* New York, NY (USA) 2024, *Winter Meeting* Denver, CO (USA) 2023, *Winter Meeting* 2022, *Summer Meeting* Paris (France) 2021, *Winter Meeting* San Francisco, CA (USA) 2021. **Members** Regular; Student. Membership countries not specified. [2020/AA0344/v/**C**]

- ♦ Society of Plastics Associations in Europe (inactive)
- ♦ Society of Plastics Engineers (internationally oriented national body)
- ♦ Society of Police Futurists International (internationally oriented national body)

♦ Society of Porphyrins and Phthalocyanines (SPP) **19622**

Main Office UBFC – ICMUB – SPP, 9 ave Alain Savary, 21000 Dijon, France. E-mail: spp@spp-jpp.org.
URL: https://www.spp-jpp.org/

History Jun 2000, Dijon (France). Founded during the First International Conference on Porphyrins and Phthalocyanines (ICPP-1). **Aims** Serve the interests of scientists working in any area of porphyrins, phthalocyanine, and related macrocycles, independent of their scientific discipline, be it chemistry, physics, biology, biochemistry, or material science. **Structure** Committee. **Activities** Awards/prizes/competitions; events/meetings. **Events** *ICPP: International Conference on Porphyrins & Phthalocyanines* Kyoto (Japan) 2026, *ICPP: International Conference on Porphyrins & Phthalocyanines* Niagara Falls, NY (USA) / Buffalo, NY (USA) 2024, *International Conference on Porphyrins and Phthalocyanines (ICPP-12)* Madrid (Spain) 2022, *International Conference on Porphyrins and Phthalocyanines (ICPP-11)* Buffalo, NY (USA) 2021, *International Conference on Porphyrins and Phthalocyanines (ICPP-10)* Munich (Germany) 2018. **Publications** *Journal of Porphyrins and Phthalocyanines (JPP)* (12 a year). [2023/AA2892/c/**E**]

- ♦ Society of Prayer for World Peace / see World Peace Prayer Society
- ♦ Society of the Precious Blood (religious order)
- ♦ Society for the Preservation of the Fairy Tales of the European Peoples / see Europäische Märchengesellschaft (#05755)
- ♦ Society for the Preservation of the Fauna of the Empire / see Fauna & Flora International (#09277)
- ♦ Society for the Preservation of the Natural History Collections (internationally oriented national body)
- ♦ Society for the Preservation of the Wild Fauna of the Empire / see Fauna & Flora International (#09277)
- ♦ Society of the Priests of St Sulpice (religious order)
- ♦ Society of Professional Economists (internationally oriented national body)

♦ Society for Progress and Innovation in the Near East (SPINE) **19623**

Contact address not obtained. E-mail: tannoury@bu.edu – raja@chaftari.com – hassan.serhan@neareastspine.org.
URL: http://www.neareastspine.org/

History 2008. **Aims** Serve people with *pain* from *spine disorders* and other causes through education, information, advocacy and support; improve the quality of life of people. **Structure** Faculty. **Events** *Annual Meeting* Beirut (Lebanon) 2014, *Annual Meeting* Beirut (Lebanon) 2013, *Annual Meeting* Beirut (Lebanon) 2012, *Annual meeting* Beirut (Lebanon) 2010, *Annual meeting* Beirut (Lebanon) 2009. [2013/XJ1629/**D**]

♦ Society for Promoting Christian Knowledge (SPCK) **19624**

Gen Sec 36 Causton Street, London, SW1P 4ST, UK. T. +442075923900. Fax +442075923939. E-mail: spck@spck.org.uk.
URL: http://www.spck.org.uk/

History 8 Mar 1698, London (UK). UK Registered Charity: 231144. **Aims** Promote Christian knowledge by: communicating the Christian faith in its rich diversity; helping people to understand it and to develop their personal faith; equipping Christians for *mission* and *ministry*. **Structure** Annual General Meeting. Governing Body, comprising elected, unpaid members acting as trustees. Executive staff: General Secretary; Publishing Director; Executive Administrator. Patron – Her Majesty the Queen; President; 5 Vice-Patrons; 14 Elected Vice-Presidents; Ex-Officio Vice-Presidents – Archbishops and Bishops of the Anglican Communion who are members of the Society; 3 Honorary Life Members. Operating arms (3): Diffusion; Publishing; Worldwide. Committees (3). **Staff** 30.00 FTE, paid. **Finance** Donations; legacies; funds. **Activities** Publishes books; assists churches throughout the world in development of their own literature and communications ministries; provides support for theological colleges and students training for ministry; awards grants. Grantmaking support classified in the following categories: Education for Development; Training and Communications for Development; Publishing for Development; Theological Education. Committees (3): Standing; Governing Body Membership; Audit. **Publications** *Theology* (6 a year) – journal. Annual Report. Books; booklets; stationery; biographies.
Members Full (110) as of 30 Apr 2013; sister societies in 4 countries:
Australia, India, Ireland, USA.
NGO Relations Member of: *Partnership for World Mission (PWM)*. [2013.08.27/XF4983/**F**]

- ♦ Society for the Promotion of Adult Literacy in Africa (inactive)
- ♦ Society for the Promotion of African, Asian and Latin American Literature (internationally oriented national body)
- ♦ Society for the Promotion of EC In Europe and Surroundings / see Society for the Promotion of Evolutionary Computation in Europe and its Surroundings (#19625)
- ♦ Society for Promotion of Engineering Education / see American Society for Engineering Education (#00790)

♦ Society for the Promotion of Evolutionary Computation in Europe and its Surroundings (SPECIES) **19625**

Société pour la Promotion de l'Evolution Artificielle en Europe et Alentours (SPEA2)
Contact address not obtained. E-mail: info@species-society.org.
URL: http://species-society.org/

History 16 Jul 2014, Vancouver, BC (Canada). Former names and other names: *Society for the Promotion of EC In Europe and Surroundings* – alias. Registration: RNA, No/ID: W943004050, Start date: Mar 2015, France. **Aims** Promote evolutionary algorithmic thinking within Europe and wider; promote inspiration of parallel algorithms derived from natural processes. **Structure** Executive Board. **Activities** Awards/prizes/competitions; events/meetings. **Events** *Evostar Conference* Seville (Spain) 2021. [2021/AA2064/**C**]

- ♦ Society for the Propagation of the Gospel in Foreign Parts / see USPG (#20736)
- ♦ Society for the Protection of Animals Abroad (internationally oriented national body)
- ♦ Society for the Protection of Animals in North Africa / see Society for the Protection of Animals Abroad
- ♦ Society for the Protection of Human and Environmental Rights International (unconfirmed)
- ♦ Society for the Protection of Unborn Children (internationally oriented national body)
- ♦ Society for Protective Coatings (internationally oriented national body)
- ♦ Society of Protozoologists / see International Society of Protozoologists
- ♦ Society of Protozoologists / see International Society of Protistologists (#15392)
- ♦ Society for Psychological Study of Social Issues (internationally oriented national body)
- ♦ Society for Psychophysiological Research (internationally oriented national body)

♦ Society for Psychotherapy Research (SPR) **19626**

Exec Officer 4320 Glenarm Rd, Crestwood KY 40014, USA. E-mail: sprexecutive@gmail.com.
URL: http://www.psychotherapyresearch.org/

History 1969. **Aims** Support development of knowledge in psychotherapy by fostering communication among investigators. **Structure** Officers: President; Vice-President; President-Elect; General Vice-President; Executive Officer. **Finance** Sources: meeting proceeds; members' dues. **Activities** Events/meetings. **Events** *Annual Conference* Krakow (Poland) 2025, *Annual Conference* Ottawa, ON (Canada) 2024, *Annual Conference* Dublin (Ireland) 2023, *Annual Conference* Denver, CO (USA) 2022, *Annual Conference* Heidelberg (Germany) 2021. **Publications** *Psychotherapy Research* (6 a year). **Members** Individuals (about 1,000) in 35 countries. Membership countries not specified. [2022.10.18/XD8614/**D**]

- ♦ Society of Publishers in Asia (internationally oriented national body)

♦ Society of Radiopharmaceutical Sciences (SRS) **19627**

Exec Dir 223 Green Oaks Loop, Fredericksburg TX 78624-4576, USA. T. +18303706554.
URL: http://www.srsweb.org/

History Jun 2001, Interlaken (Switzerland), as *International Society for Radiopharmaceutical Chemistry and Biology (ISRCB)*, during 14th International Symposium on Radiopharmaceutical Chemistry (ISRC) and 12th International Symposium on Radiopharmacology, organized by *International Association of Radiopharmacology (IAR, #12121)*. Incorporated in the State of Missouri. **Aims** Advance excellence in education and research in radiopharmaceutical chemistry and in the study and use of radiopharmaceuticals. **Structure** General Assembly; Board of Directors; Executive Committee. **Finance** Members' dues. **Activities** Financial and/or material support; knowledge management/information dissemination; standards/guidelines. **Events** *China-Japan-Korea Symposium on Radiopharmaceutical Sciences* Seoul (Korea Rep) 2021, *Symposium* Beijing (China) 2019, *Symposium* Dresden (Germany) 2017, *Symposium* Columbia, MO (USA) 2015, *International Symposium on Radiopharmaceutical Chemistry / Symposium* Jeju (Korea Rep) 2013. **Publications** *Nuclear Medicine and Biology* – journal. [2018/XJ3364/**D**]

♦ Society for Redox Biology and Medicine (SfRBM) **19628**

Exec Dir 8365 Keystone Xing, Ste 107, Indianapolis IN 46240, USA. T. +13172059482. Fax +13172059481. E-mail: info@sfrbm.org.
URL: http://www.sfrbm.org/

History 1987, as *Oxygen Society*. Subsequently changed title to *Society for Free Radical Biology and Medicine (SFRBM)*. A regional group of *International Society for Free Radical Research (ISFRR, #15131)*. **Aims** Be the premier scientific organization for discovery and exchange of knowledge in the field of redox biology, a unifying theme in the pathophysiology of human diseases. **Activities** Events/meetings; networking/liaising; training/education; awards/prizes/competitions. **Events** *Annual Conference* Punta del Este (Uruguay) 2023, *Annual Conference* Orlando, FL (USA) 2022, *Annual Conference* Savannah, GA (USA) 2021, *Annual Meeting* Orlando, FL (USA) 2020, *Annual Meeting* Las Vegas, NV (USA) 2019. **Publications** *DOT* – newsletter; *FRBM* – journal; *Redox Biology* – journal. *Critical Methods* – series. Articles. **Members** Individuals (over 1,500) in over 60 countries. Membership countries not specified. [2019.12.16/XE4627/**E**]

♦ Society for Redox Research Australasia **19629**

Pres address not obtained. E-mail: sfrrasecretariat@gmail.com.
URL: https://www.sfrr-australasia.org/

History 1988. Former names and other names: *Society for Free Radical Research Australasia (SFRRA)* – former. **Aims** Support research conducted in the field of free radical biology and medicine. **Structure** President; President-Elect; Treasurer; Secretary. **Languages** English. **Staff** No full-time staff. **Finance** Members' dues. **Activities** Events/meetings; networking/liaising; research/documentation. **Events** *SFRR Australasia & Japan Conference* Christchurch (New Zealand) 2022, *Joint Meeting* Tokyo (Japan) 2017, *Scientific Meeting* Gold Coast, QLD (Australia) 2016, *Scientific Meeting* Melbourne, VIC (Australia) 2014, *Scientific Meeting* Sydney, NSW (Australia) 2013. **Members** About 100 active members. Membership countries not specified. **NGO Relations** Regional member of: *International Society for Free Radical Research (ISFRR, #15131)*. Links with national societies. [2022/XM0879/**D**]

♦ Society of Regional Anaesthesia / see European Society of Regional Anaesthesia and Pain Therapy (#08722)
♦ Society of Relay Engineers / see Society for Broadband Professionals
♦ Society for Religious Studies (inactive)

♦ Society for Reproductive and Infant Psychology (SRIP) 19630

Sec School of Health & Social Sciences, University of West London, St Mary's Rd, London, W5 5RF, UK. E-mail: admin@srip.org.
URL: https://srip.org/

History 1980. Registration: Charity, No/ID: 1013235, England and Wales. **Aims** Promote the scientific study, both pure and applied, of all psychological and behavioural matters related to human reproduction. **Structure** Committee. **Finance** Sources: members' dues. **Activities** Awards/prizes/competitions; events/meetings. **Events** *Annual Conference* 2022, *Annual Conference* 2021, *Annual Conference* Chester (UK) 2020, *Annual Conference* London (UK) 2019. **Publications** *SRIP Journal*. Journal of Reproductive and Infant Psychology [2022.07.14/AA0314/**D**]

♦ Society for Reproductive Investigation (SRI) 19631

Exec Dir 555 East Wells St, Ste 1100, Milwaukee WI 53202-3823, USA. T. +14149189888. Fax +14142763349. E-mail: info@sri-online.org.
Meetings Manager address not obtained.
URL: http://www.sri-online.org/

History 1953, New York, NY (USA). Former names and other names: *Society of University Gynecologists* – former (1953); *Society for Gynecologic Investigation (SGI)* – former. **Aims** Inspire creative investigation of global problems in women's reproductive health through: discovering, reviewing, reporting and transferring new knowledge; training scholars of the future; working with practitioners and stakeholders. **Structure** Executive Council. **Languages** English. **Staff** 3.00 FTE, paid. **Events** *Annual Scientific Meeting* Brisbane, QLD (Australia) 2023, *Annual Scientific Meeting* Denver, CO (USA) 2022, *Annual Scientific Meeting* Boston, MA (USA) 2021, *Annual Scientific Meeting* Vancouver, BC (Canada) 2021, *Annual Scientific Meeting* Vancouver, BC (Canada) 2020. **Publications** *Reproductive Sciences Journal* (12 a year). **Members** Individuals (about 1,000) in 30 countries and territories. Membership countries not specified. [2021/XM8234/**D**]

♦ Society of Research Administrators International (internationally oriented national body)

♦ Society for Research in Asiatic Music 19632

Toyo Ongaku Gakkai

Contact 307 Miharu Bldg, 3-6-3 Ueno, Taitô-Ku, Tokyo, 110-0005 Japan. T. +81338325152. Fax +81338325152. E-mail: len03210@nifty.com.
URL: http://tog.a.la9.jp/

History 1936. **Aims** Promote research in Japanese and other Asian music and ethnomusicology. **Events** *Meeting* Tokyo (Japan) 2015. **Publications** *Toyo Ongaku Kenkyu* (annual) – journal.
Members Individuals in 16 countries and territories:
Australia, Austria, Canada, China, France, Germany, Indonesia, Israel, Japan, Korea Rep, New Zealand, Philippines, Sweden, Taiwan, UK, USA. [2012/XD4545/v/**D**]

♦ Society for Research on Biological Rhythms (SRBR) 19633

Pres 5034-A Thoroughbred Lane, Brentwood TN 37027, USA. T. +16156493087. E-mail: info@srbr.org.
URL: https://srbr.org/

History 1986. **Aims** Advance rigorous, peer-reviewed science and evidence-based policies related to sleep and circadian biology. **Structure** Board of Directors; Executive Committee. **Activities** Advocacy/lobbying/activism; events/meetings; research/documentation. **Events** *Biennial Meeting* Amelia Island, FL (USA) 2022, *Biennial Meeting* Brentwood, TN (USA) 2020, *Biennial Meeting* Amelia Island, FL (USA) 2018, *Biennial Meeting* Palm Harbor, FL (USA) 2016, *Biennial Meeting* Big Sky, MT (USA) 2014. **Publications** *SRBR Newsletter* (4 a year); *Journal of Biological Rhythms*. [2022/AA1986/**D**]

♦ Society for Research in Child Development (internationally oriented national body)
♦ Society for Research into Higher Education (internationally oriented national body)

♦ Society for Research into Hydrocephalus and Spina Bifida (SRHSB) 19634

Registered Address The Dan Young Building, 6 Craighalbert Way, Dullatur, G68 0LS, UK.
URL: http://www.srhsb.com/

History 1957. Registration: Charity Commission, No/ID: 256115, England and Wales. **Aims** Advance education and promote research into hydrocephalus and spina bifida; bring together workers in different medical, scientific and sociological fields to aid their joint endeavour to identify causation of and prevent, cure or alleviate these conditions. **Structure** Executive Committee, comprising President, Honorary Secretary, President Elect, Honorary Treasurer, 2 Honorary Publications Secretaries, North American Corresponding Member, Folic Acid Spokesperson, Webmaster and 2 members. **Languages** English. **Staff** Voluntary. **Finance** Sources: donations; members' dues; sponsorship. **Activities** Organizes scientific meetings. **Events** *Annual Conference* Doha (Qatar) 2020, *Annual Conference* La Laguna (Spain) 2019, *Annual Conference* Bristol (UK) 2018, *Annual Conference* St Louis, MO (USA) 2017, *Annual Conference* Stirling (UK) 2016. **Publications** *A Short History of Spina Bifida* by J D van Gool and A B van Gool. Conference proceedings.
Members Individuals (188) Honorary (16), Senior (18), Ordinary (154), residing in 30 countries:
Australia, Austria, Belgium, Canada, Chile, Estonia, Germany, India, Ireland, Italy, Japan, Montenegro, Netherlands, Nigeria, Norway, Poland, Portugal, Romania, Russia, Saudi Arabia, Serbia, Singapore, Slovakia, Spain, Sudan, Sweden, Switzerland, Tanzania UR, UK, USA. [2020/XD6160/v/**C**]

♦ Society for Research on Identity Formation / see International Society for Research on Identity (#15422)
♦ Society for Research and Initiatives for Sustainable Technologies and Institutions (internationally oriented national body)
♦ Society for Research on the Nature of Human Individual (internationally oriented national body)
♦ Society for Research on Nicotine and Tobacco (internationally oriented national body)

♦ Society for Research Synthesis Methods (SRSM) 19635

Contact address not obtained. E-mail: srsm.asst@gmail.com.
URL: http://www.srsm.org/

Aims Develop and promote innovative and robust methods of research synthesis. **Structure** Officers. **Activities** Events/meetings; advocacy/lobbying/activism; awards/prizes/competitions. **Events** *Annual Meeting* Portland, OR (USA) 2022, *Annual Meeting* Bern (Switzerland) 2021, *Annual Meeting* Bern (Switzerland) 2020, *Annual Meeting* Chicago, IL (USA) 2019, *Annual Meeting* Bristol (UK) 2018. **Publications** *Research Synthesis Methods* – journal. [2017/XM6262/**D**]

♦ Society for Ricoeur Studies (SRS) 19636

Pres Philosohy, School of European Culture and Languages, Univ of Kent, Canterbury, CT2 7NF, UK.
Treas/Sec address not obtained.
URL: http://www.ricoeursociety.org/

History Founded 2007, as an interdisciplinary organization for scholars of the work of French philosopher Paul Ricoeur (1913-2005). Registered in the State of Pennsylvania (USA). **Aims** Preserve and build upon the legacy of Ricoeur's work through collective study, critique and interpretation. **Structure** Annual Meeting; Board of Directors. **Languages** English, French, Spanish. **Finance** Members' dues. **Activities** Events/meetings; awards/prizes/competitions. **Events** *Conference* Montréal, QC (Canada) 2019, *Conference* Stellenbosch (South Africa) 2018, *Conference* Boston, MA (USA) 2017, *Conference* Chicago, IL (USA) 2016, *Conference on Paul Ricoeur in Asia* Manila (Philippines) / Quezon City (Philippines) 2015. **Publications** *Etudes Ricoeuriennes/Ricoeur Studies (ERRS)* – journal.
Members Individuals (230) in 23 countries and territories:
Argentina, Australia, Belgium, Brazil, Canada, Finland, Germany, Greece, Hungary, Ireland, Italy, Lithuania, Mexico, Netherlands, Philippines, Portugal, Russia, South Africa, Spain, Taiwan, Türkiye, UK, USA. [2017.10.12/XM3918/**F**]

♦ Society for Risk Analysis – Asia (unconfirmed)

♦ Society for Risk Analysis – Europe (SRA-Europe) 19637

Pres Avenue Louise 240, box 14, 1050 Brussels, Belgium. T. +3223464624. E-mail: sraeurope.mail@gmail.com.
URL: http://www.sraeurope.eu-vri.eu/

History Set up within *Society for Risk Analysis International (SRA International)*. Registration: EU Transparency Register, No/ID: 172772547768-46, Start date: 28 Sep 2022. **Aims** Bring together individuals and organizations interested in risk assessment, risk management and risk communication in Europe. **Structure** Board; Secretariat. **Staff** 1.00 FTE, paid. **Finance** Sources: members' dues. **Activities** Events/meetings. **Events** *Annual Conference* Lund (Sweden) 2023, *Conference* Novi Sad (Serbia) 2022, *Annual Conference* Espoo (Finland) 2021, *Annual Conference* Espoo (Finland) 2020, *Nordic Conference* Copenhagen (Denmark) 2019. **Publications** *Journal of Risk Research* (4 a year). [2022/XE2506/**E**]

♦ Society for Risk Analysis International (internationally oriented national body)
♦ Society of Robotic Surgery / see Minimally Invasive Robotic Association (#16811)
♦ Society of Robotic Surgery (unconfirmed)
♦ Society of Romance Linguistics (#19501)
♦ Society for Rousseau Studies / see Rousseau Association
♦ Society of the Sacred Heart of Jesus (religious order)
♦ Society of the Sacred Hearts of Jesus and Mary (religious order)

♦ Society of Saint John Chrysostom 19638

Contact PO Box 146, Fairfax VA 22038, USA. T. +17036918862. Fax +17036910513.
URL: http://orientale-lumen.blogspot.com/

History 1926, UK. Named after St John Chrysostom (347-407). **Aims** Promote Eastern *Christianity* and *ecumenical* dialogue between the Eastern and Western Churches. **Events** *Annual Conference* Melbourne, VIC (Australia) 2000, *Annual Conference* Washington, DC (USA) 1997. **Publications** *Chrysostom* (4 a year). [2020/XM0795/**F**]

♦ Society on Sarcopenia, Cachexia and Wasting Disorders (SCWD) 19639

Main Office c/o Intercomptas, Vers-chez-les-Blanc, Route du Jorat 67, 1000 Lausanne VD 26, Switzerland. E-mail: scwd@mededgs.com.
URL: https://society-scwd.org/

History 2008. **Aims** Further research on cachexia and sarcopenia and wasting disorders; bring practical solutions to health-care teams worldwide grappling with treatment. **Structure** Board. **Finance** Sources: members' dues. **Activities** Events/meetings. **Events** *International Conference of the Society on Cachexia, Sarcopenia & Muscle Wasting* Stockholm (Sweden) 2023, *International Conference of the Society on Cachexia, Sarcopenia & Muscle Wasting* Lisbon (Portugal) 2022, *International Meeting* Berlin (Germany) 2019, *International Meeting* Maastricht (Netherlands) 2018, *International Meeting* Maastricht (Netherlands) 2018. **Publications** *SCWD newsletter* (12 a year) – electronic; *Journal of Cachexia, Sarcopenia and Muscle*. **Members** Full Adherent; Associate Adherent; Adherent Corporate; Fellow. Membership countries not specified. [2022/XM7816/**C**]

♦ Society for Satellite Professionals International (internationally oriented national body)
♦ Society for Scandinavian Seamen's Homes in Foreign Ports (inactive)
♦ Society for the Science and Technology of Handwriting and Other Graphic Skills / see International Graphonomics Society (#13734)
♦ Society for Scientific Exploration (internationally oriented national body)
♦ Society for the Scientific Investigation of Para-Science (internationally oriented national body)

♦ Society for the Scientific Study of Reading (SSSR) 19640

Contact PO Box 5999, Irvine CA 92616-5999, USA. E-mail: sdaysssr@gmail.com.
URL: http://www.triplesr.org/

History 1993. Bylaws adopted 10 Aug 1993; updated Jul 2006. **Aims** Promote the scientific study of reading; disseminate information about reading and related areas such as *language* and *literacy*. **Structure** Board. Committees (3): Publications; Membership; Award. **Finance** Sources: members' dues. **Activities** Awards/prizes/competitions; events/meetings. **Events** *Annual Meeting* Newport Beach, CA (USA) 2020, *Annual Meeting* Toronto, ON (Canada) 2019, *Annual Meeting* Brighton (UK) 2018, *Annual Meeting* Halifax, NS (Canada) 2017, *Annual Meeting* Porto (Portugal) 2016. **Publications** *SSSR Journal*. [2020/XJ6735/**C**]

♦ Society for Sedimentary Geology (internationally oriented national body)
♦ Society of Sisters of Mary Reparatrix (religious order)

♦ Society for Social Choice and Welfare 19641

Contact Institut SCW, MRSH, Univ de Caen, 14032 Caen CEDEX, France. T. +33231566248. Fax +33231565513.
URL: http://www.unicaen.fr/mrsh/scw/

History 1992, Caen (France). **Structure** Council, including President, President-Elect and Secretary-Treasurer. **Languages** English. **Finance** Members' dues. **Activities** Awards 'Social Choice and Welfare Prize', to honour young scholars of excellent accomplishment in the area of social choice theory and welfare economics. **Events** *Meeting* Caen (France) 2020, *Meeting* Mexico City (Mexico) 2020, *Meeting* Seoul (Korea Rep) 2018, *Meeting* Lund (Sweden) 2016, *Meeting* Boston, MA (USA) 2014. **Publications** *Social Choice and Welfare* (8 a year).
Members in 26 countries and territories:
Austria, Belgium, Brazil, Cameroon, Canada, France, Germany, Greece, Hong Kong, India, Israel, Italy, Japan, Korea Rep, Mexico, Netherlands, Northern Ireland, Norway, Poland, Portugal, Russia, Spain, Switzerland, Türkiye, UK, USA. [2019/XM1164/**D**]

♦ Society for Social Studies of Science (4S) 19642

Sec Dep Sociology, Univ Southern Indiana, Evansville IN 47712, USA. T. +18124641981.
Pres Dept of Sociology, Univ of Wisconsin-Madison, Madison WI 53706-1393, USA. T. +16082652724.
URL: http://www.4sonline.org/

History 1975. **Aims** Facilitate communication among those interested in understanding science, technology and medicine, including the way they develop and interact with their social contexts. **Structure** Council; Officers (4); Standing and ad hoc Committees. **Languages** English. **Staff** 3.50 FTE, paid. **Finance** Sources: meeting proceeds; members' dues. **Activities** Events/meetings; publishing activities. **Events** *Annual Meeting* Seattle, WA (USA) 2025, *Annual Meeting* Honolulu, HI (USA) 2023, *Annual Meeting* Cholula (Mexico) 2022, *Annual Meeting* Toronto, ON (Canada) 2021, *Annual Meeting* Prague (Czechia) 2020. **Publications** *Backchannels*; *Engaging Science, Technology, and Society* – journal; *Science, Technology, and Human Values* – journal. Book series. **Information Services** *Technoscience*. **Members** Individuals (about 2,000). Membership countries not specified. **NGO Relations** Member of (1): *International Science Council (ISC, #14796)*. [2021.06.08/XD8537/**D**]

♦ Society of Soft Drink Technologists / see International Society of Beverage Technologists
♦ Society for South Asian Studies / see British Association for South Asian Studies
♦ Society for South Asian Studies (internationally oriented national body)
♦ Society for Standards Professionals (internationally oriented national body)
♦ Society of St Edmund (religious order)
♦ Society for Sterility Assurance Professionals (unconfirmed)
♦ Society of St Francis of Sales (religious order)
♦ Society of St Francis Xavier for the Foreign Missions (religious order)
♦ Society of St John the Evangelist (religious order)
♦ Society of St Paul (religious order)
♦ Society of St Peter the Apostle for Native Clergy (religious order)
♦ Society of St Teresa of Jesus (religious order)
♦ Society for the Study of Alchemy and Early Chemistry / see Society for the History of Alchemy and Chemistry (#19569)

♦ Society for the Study of Behavioural Phenotypes (SSBP) 19643

Admin Dir 32 Willows Road, Bourne End, SL8 5HG, UK.
URL: https://ssbp.org.uk/

History 1987. Registration: Charity Commission, No/ID: 1013849, England and Wales. **Aims** Study the development, learning and behaviours of individuals with genetic disorders and ways of helping to improve lives. **Structure** Executive Committee. **Activities** Events/meetings; knowledge management/information dissemination. **Events** *International Research Symposium* Oslo (Norway) 2022, *International Research Symposium* 2021, *International Research Symposium* Oslo (Norway) 2020, *International Research Symposium* Birmingham (UK) 2019, *International Research Symposium* Melbourne, VIC (Australia) 2018. [2021/AA1817/**C**]

♦ Society for the Study of Biological Rhythm / see International Society for Chronobiology (#15010)

♦ Society for the Study of the Crusades and the Latin East (SSCLE) . . 19644

Société pour l'étude des croisades et de l'Orient latin

Pres Dept Archaeology, Univ of Haifa, Mount Carmel, 31905 Haifa, Israel.
SG Dépt d'Histoire et d'Archéologie, Univ François-Rabelais, 3 rue des Tanneurs, 37000 Tours, France.
URL: https://societyforthestudyofthecrusadesandthelatineast.wildapricot.org/

History 1980, London (UK). Affiliated as an internal commission of *International Committee of Historical Sciences (ICHS, #12777)* in 1987; became a fully-fledged affiliated organization of ICHS in 2000. **Aims** Serve as a liaison body and disseminate information among *historians* of the Crusades and the Latin East, including the Spanish Reconquest, crusades along the Baltic shores and crusades against heretics and political enemies of the papacy and allied topics in *Byzantine*, *Islamic* and *Mongol* history. **Structure** Committee. **Languages** English, French, German, Italian, Spanish. **Finance** Members' dues. **Events** *Congress* London (UK) 2022, *Quadrennial Congress* London (UK) 2020, *Quadrennial Congress* Odense (Denmark) 2016, *Quadrennial Congress* Caceres (Spain) 2012, *Quadrennial Congress* Avignon (France) 2008. **Publications** *Bulletin* (annual); *Crusades* – journal.

Members Individuals in 31 countries:
Australia, Austria, Belgium, Brazil, Bulgaria, Canada, Cyprus, Czechia, Denmark, Egypt, France, Germany, Greece, Hungary, Ireland, Israel, Italy, Japan, Lebanon, Luxembourg, Malta, Netherlands, New Zealand, Russia, Saudi Arabia, South Africa, Spain, Switzerland, Türkiye, UK, USA.

NGO Relations Member of: ICHS. [2020/XE0559/v/**E**]

♦ Society for the Study and the Development of International Order (inactive)

♦ Society for the Study of Economic Inequality (ECINEQ) 19645

Secretariat Dipto di Scienze Economiche, Univ di Verona, Via dell'Artigliere 19, 37129 Verona BL, Italy. E-mail: secretariat.ecineq@ateneo.univr.it.
URL: http://www.ecineq.org/

History Jul 2005, Palma (Spain). Registered in accordance with Italian law. **Aims** Support the study of economic inequality and related fields. **Structure** General Assembly; Council; Executive Committee. **Finance** Sources: members' dues. **Activities** Events/meetings; training/education. **Events** *Conference* Paris (France) 2019, *Conference* Bari (Italy) 2013, *Conference* Catania (Italy) 2011, *Conference* Buenos Aires (Argentina) 2009, *Conference* Berlin (Germany) 2007. **Publications** *Journal of Economic Inequality. ECINEQ Working Paper Series.* [2014/XJ8701/**C**]

♦ Society for the Study of Emerging Markets (SSEM) 19646

Dir address not obtained.
URL: http://www.emergingecons.org/

Aims Promote research and publication about emerging market economies; provide a way for academics, policy makers, and members of the business community to exchange views and share information and research about emerging markets. **Structure** Board of Directors. **Languages** English. **Activities** Events/meetings. **Events** *World Congress of Comparative Economics* St Petersburg (Russia) 2017, *World Congress of Comparative Economics* Rome (Italy) 2015. **Publications** *Emerging Markets Finance and Trade (EMFT)* – journal. [2019.02.12/XM5319/**C**]

♦ Society for the Study of Fetal Physiology / see Fetal and Neonatal Physiological Society (#09740)

♦ Society for the Study of the History of Analytical Philosophy (SSHAP) 19647

Founder/Pres Dept of Philosophy, McMaster Univ, University Hall 310A, 1280 Main Street West, Hamilton ON L8S 4K1, Canada.
URL: http://sshap.org/

History 1 Sep 2009, USA. **Aims** Promote discussion in all areas of scholarship concerning the development of philosophical logic, philosophy of language, the philosophy of mind, metaphysics, the philosophy of science and epistemology. **Structure** General Assembly; Board; Steering Committee. **Finance** Sources: members' dues. **Activities** Events/meetings. **Events** *Annual Conference* Taiyuan (China) 2022, *Annual Conference* Vienna (Austria) 2021, *Annual Conference* Vienna (Austria) 2020, *Annual Conference* Boston, MA (USA) 2019, *Annual Conference* Hamilton, ON (Canada) 2018. **Publications** *Journal for the History of Analytical Philosophy.* [2022/AA2441/**C**]

♦ Society for the Study of Human Biology (internationally oriented national body)

♦ Society for the Study of Inborn Errors of Metabolism (SSIEM) 19648

Mailing Address PO Box 3375, Croydon, CR2 1PN, UK.
Registered Office c/o Stone King LLP, Boundary House, 91 Charterhouse Street, London, EC1M 6HR, UK.
URL: http://www.ssiem.org/

History 1963, UK. Registration: Charity Commission, No/ID: 1010639, England and Wales; Companies House, No/ID: 2567711, England and Wales. **Aims** Promote exchange of ideas between professional workers in different disciplines who are interested in inherited metabolic *disease*. **Structure** General Meeting (annual); Executive Council; Advisory Council. **Languages** English. **Staff** None. **Finance** Sources: members' dues. **Activities** Awards/prizes/competitions; events/meetings; training/education. **Events** *International Congress of Inborn Errors of Metabolism* Kyoto (Japan) 2025, *Annual Symposium* Porto (Portugal) 2024, *Annual Symposium* Jerusalem (Israel) 2023, *Annual Symposium* Freiburg-Breisgau (Germany) 2022, *International Congress of Inborn Errors of Metabolism (ICIEM)* Sydney, NSW (Australia) 2021. **Publications** *Journal of Inherited Metabolic Diseases (JIMD)* (4 a year). Symposium proceedings (annual). Monographs.

Members National societies in 32 countries and territories:
Australia, Belgium, Canada, Croatia, Denmark, Finland, France, Germany, Greece, Hong Kong, Hungary, India, Iran Islamic Rep, Ireland, Israel, Italy, Japan, Morocco, Netherlands, New Zealand, Norway, Pakistan, Poland, Portugal, Russia, Spain, Sweden, Switzerland, Tunisia, Türkiye, UK, USA.

Regional member:
Sociedad Latinoamericana de Errores Innatos del Metabolismo y Pesquisa Neonatal (SLEIMPN, #19401).
Also member in the Baltic.

NGO Relations Cooperates with (1): *Galactosemia Network (GalNet, #10063).* [2021/XD5080/**C**]

♦ Society for the Study of the Indigenous Languages of the Americas (internationally oriented national body)

♦ Society for the Study of Labour History 19649

Sec/Pres Univ of Huddersfield, Queensgate, Huddersfield, HD1 3DH, UK.
Vice Pres 1 Chelea Road Brincliffe, Sheffield, S11 9BP, UK. T. +441142582541.
URL: http://www.sslh.org.uk/

History 1960. UK Registered Charity: 288599. **Aims** Increase public knowledge and awareness of labour history; ensure the preservation of labour movement *archives*; promote study, teaching and research into the past of the labour movement; promote international collaboration and exchange in the field of labour history. **Structure** Annual General Meeting; Executive Committee; Labour Archives Liaison. **Finance** Members' dues. **Activities** Knowledge management/information dissemination; events/meetings. **Events** *Labour and nationalism* Huddersfield (UK) 2018, *The labours of Asa Briggs* Leeds (UK) 2017. **Publications** *Labour History Review* (3 a year) – journal. *Aids to Research* – series. Guides; reports.

Members Organizations and Individuals () in 10 countries:
Austria, Belgium, Denmark, France, Germany (*), Israel, Italy, Netherlands (*), Sweden, Switzerland.
[2017.06.01/XF5489/**F**]

♦ Society for the Study of Neuronal Regulation / see International Society for Neurofeedback and Research

♦ Society for the Study of Pathophysiology of Pregnancy / see Organization Gestosis (#17869)

♦ Society for the Study of the Short Story in English (SSSS) 19650

Exec Dir Dept of English – Office 414, Boston Univ, 236 Bay STate Road, Boston MA 02215, USA.

History Chartered 1992, following a conference organized 1998. **Structure** Board. **Finance** Members' dues. **Activities** Events/meetings. **Events** *International Conference* Singapore (Singapore) 2022, *International Conference* Rende (Italy) 2021, *International Conference* Lisbon (Portugal) 2018, *International Conference* Shanghai (China) 2016, *International Conference* Vienna (Austria) 2014. **Publications** *SSSS Newsletter.* [2018/XM7958/c/**E**]

♦ Society for the Study of Social Problems (internationally oriented national body)

♦ Society for the Study of Symbolic Interaction (SSSI) 19651

Contact address not obtained. E-mail: sssinteraction@gmail.com.
URL: http://www.symbolicinteraction.org/

Aims Current constitution and bylaws adopted, 2014. **Structure** Annual Meeting; Executive Council; Publications Committee. Includes: *European Society for the Study of Symbolic Interaction (EU SSSI).* **Activities** Awards/prizes/competitions; events/meetings. **Events** *Annual Meeting* New York, NY (USA) 2019, *Annual Meeting* Lancaster (UK) 2018, *Annual Meeting* Seattle, WA (USA) 2016, *International conference on postmodern culture, global capitalism and democratic action* College Park, MD (USA) 1997. **Publications** *SSSI Notes* – newsletter; *Symbolic Interaction* – journal. [2019.12.12/XW0241/**C**]

♦ Society of St Vincent-de-Paul / see International Confederation of the Society of St Vincent-de-Paul (#12870)

♦ Society for Symbiosis and Cell Research / see International Society of Endocytobiology (#15087)

♦ Society for Telecommunication Engineers / see Society for Broadband Professionals

♦ Society for Tennis Medicine and Science (STMS) 19652

Admin attn: S Higgins, 434 Homestead Rd, Ste 3, La Grange Park IL 60526, USA. E-mail: info@tennismedicine.org.
URL: https://www.tennismedicine.org/

History 1991, USA. Founded following earlier initiatives. **Structure** Board, including President, Past-President, Vice-President, Treasurer and Secretary. Regional committees (3): Europe; North America; South America. Scientific Committee. **Events** *World Congress* Tokyo (Japan) 2021, *World Congress* Stockholm (Sweden) 2019, *World Congress* Rome (Italy) 2015, *World Congress* Buenos Aires (Argentina) 2013, *World Congress* Paris (France) 2011. **Publications** *Medicine and Science in Tennis* (3 a year). **NGO Relations** *International Tennis Federation (ITF, #15676).* [2021/XD8884/**D**]

♦ Society for Terrorism Research (STR) 19653

Pres PO Box 590094, Newton MA 02459, USA. E-mail: sfortr@gmail.com.
Sec address not obtained.
URL: http://www.societyforterrorismresearch.org/

History Founded Jun 2006, in reaction to the absence of any then-existing integrated and multidisciplinary organization dedicated to the area of terrorism and political violence research, and conceived by Dr Samuel Justin Sinclair, with the assistance of Dr Alice LoCicero, Dr Michael Commons, and Dr Sarah Ross. **Aims** Enhance knowledge and understanding of terrorism and political violence; encourage research that includes and integrates theoretical frameworks and findings from multiple disciplines, thus informing more effective policies worldwide by giving the ability to reflect diverse models of complex causation; provide a forum to support efforts to coherently communicate substantive additions to knowledge of terrorism and political violence. **Structure** Governing Board; Advisory Board. **Finance** Members' dues. **Activities** Research/documentation; networking/liaising; events/meetings. **Events** *International Conference* London (UK) 2020, *Annual International Conference* Oslo (Norway) 2019, *Postgraduate Conference on Emerging Developments in the Study of Terrorism and Counter-Terrorism* Nottingham (UK) 2016, *Annual International Conference* The Hague (Netherlands) 2016, *Annual International Conference* Birmingham (UK) 2015. **Publications** *Behavioral Sciences of Terrorism and Political Aggression* (3 a year) – journal; *STR Newsletter* (2 a year). *Radicalization, Terrorism, and Conflict – vol 2* (2013). **Members** Researchers and thought leaders from a wide range of social science disciplines that include, but are not limited to, political science, psychology, sociology, criminology, anthropology, economics, journalism and law. Membership countries not specified. **NGO Relations** Joint conference organized with *International Colloquium on Conflict and Aggression (#12653).* [2020/XM3889/**D**]

♦ Society for Test Anxiety Research / see Stress, Trauma, Anxiety, and Resilience Society (#20011)

♦ Society for Theatre Research (internationally oriented national body)

♦ Society for Threatened Peoples International (STP International) . . 19654

Association pour les peuples menacés international (APM International) – Gesellschaft für Bedrohte Völker International (GfbV International) – Asociación para la Defensa de los Pueblos Amenazados Internacional – Associazione per i Popoli Minacciati Internazionale (APM Internazionale)

Mailing Address Post Box 2024, 37010 Göttingen, Germany. E-mail: info@gfbv.de.
URL: http://www.gfbv.de/

History Jun 1968, Hamburg (Germany). Founded by Tilman Zülch and Klaus Guerke, as *Aktion Biafra-Hilfe* (Help Biafra), a Federal German national organization. Scope widened and current title adopted in 1970. Transferred to Göttingen (Germany FR) in 1979. **Aims** Campaign against genocide and discrimination of threatened ethnic and religious minorities or nationalities worldwide. **Structure** General Assembly (annual). Management Board. Executive Committee, comprising President and 6 members. Arbitration Commission. Advisory Council. Central Office in Göttingen (Germany). International Chapters (6) in: Bolzano (Italy); Paris (France); Bern (Switzerland); Sarajevo (Bosnia-Herzegovina); Vienna (Austria); New York NY (USA); Temuco (Chile); Arbil/Kurdistan-Iraq. Regional groups; voluntary coordinators. **Languages** English, French, German, Italian, Spanish. **Finance** Members' dues. Grants; donations (over 30,000 donors). **Activities** Advocacy/lobbying/activism; events/meetings; training/education. **Events** *Joint meeting* Bratislava (Czechoslovakia) 1992. **Publications** *Progrom* (6 a year) in German. Electronic newsletter. Work records; reports; press releases; short portraits. Information Services: Documentation centre, including large archives on: Europe; Sinti and Romanies; Near East; Africa; Asia; the Pacific; the Americas; Asylum; general information on minorities and indigenous peoples. On-line service.

Members in 43 countries:
Albania, Australia, Austria, Belgium, Bosnia-Herzegovina, Brazil, Burundi, Canada, Chile, Colombia, Croatia, Denmark, France, Germany, Greece, India, Ireland, Israel, Italy, Liechtenstein, Luxembourg, Malaysia, Mauritania, Mexico, Micronesia FS, Netherlands, New Zealand, Nigeria, North Macedonia, Papua New Guinea, Poland, Portugal, Samoa, Slovenia, Sudan, Sweden, Switzerland, Tajikistan, Timor-Leste, Türkiye, Turkmenistan, UK, USA.

Consultative Status Consultative status granted from: *ECOSOC (#05331)* (Special); *Council of Europe (CE, #04881)* (Participatory Status). **IGO Relations** Accredited by (2): *United Nations Framework Convention on Climate Change – Secretariat (UNFCCC, #20564); United Nations Office at Vienna (UNOV, #20604).* **NGO Relations** Member of (3): *UNITED for Intercultural Action – European Network Against Nationalism, Racism, Fascism and in Support of Migrants and Refugees (UNITED, #20511); World Heritage Watch (WHW); World Uyghur Congress (WUC, #21896).* [2019/XD0038/**D**]

♦ Society for Thrombosis and haemostasis Research (#10146)

♦ Society for Traumatic Stress Studies / see International Society for Traumatic Stress Studies (#15518)

♦ Society of Tribologists and Lubrication Engineers (STLE) 19655

Exec Dir 840 Busse Highway, Park Ridge IL 60068-2302, USA. T. +18478255536. Fax +18478251456. E-mail: information@stle.org.
URL: http://www.stle.org/

History 1944, USA, as American Society of Lubrication Engineers (ASLE). Present name adopted 1987. **Structure** Board of Directors. Administrative Committees. **Activities** Awards/prizes/competitions; certification/accreditation; events/meetings; training/education. **Events** *Annual Meeting* Long Beach, CA (USA) 2022, *Annual Meeting* Park Ridge, IL (USA) 2021, *Annual Meeting* Chicago, IL (USA) 2020, *Annual Meeting* Nashville, TN (USA) 2019, *Annual Meeting* Minneapolis, MN (USA) 2018. **Publications** *Tribology and Lubrication Technology* (12 a year) – magazine; *Tribology Letters*; *Tribology Transactions.*

Members Individuals (13,000) and companies (200) in 5 countries:
Australia, Belgium, Canada, Indonesia, USA.
NGO Relations Cooperates with: *American Society of Mechanical Engineers (ASME).* [2016/XJ4046/**C**]

♦ Society for Tropical Ecology (internationally oriented national body)

♦ Society for Tropical Veterinary Medicine (STVM) 19656

Sec-Treas 250 McElroy Hall, Oklahoma State Univ, Stillwater OK 74078-2008, USA. T. +14057446726. Fax +14057445275.
Sec-Treas address not obtained. T. +14057447271.
URL: http://www.soctropvetmed.org/

History 1978. Former names and other names: *American Society for Tropical Veterinary Medicine* – former (1978 to 1993). **Aims** Promote international advancement of tropical veterinary medicine, hygiene and related disciplines. **Structure** Officers: President; President-Elect; Past-President; 2 Secretary/Treasurers. Councillors (8). **Languages** English. **Staff** 5.00 FTE, voluntary. **Finance** Members' dues. Grants and non-monetary contributions from international organizations, biologics producers, universities, *European Commission (EC, #06633)* and USDA agencies. **Activities** Events/meetings; awards/prizes/competitions. **Events** *Joint Conference on Tropical Animal Diseases and Veterinary Public Health* Buenos Aires (Argentina) 2018, *Joint Conference on Tropical Animal Diseases and Veterinary Public Health* Berlin (Germany) 2016, *Biennial Meeting* Orvieto (Italy) 2012, *Regional Conference* Phuket (Thailand) 2012, *Biennial Meeting* Lübeck (Germany) 2009. **Publications** *STVM Newsletter.* Conference proceedings.
Members in 47 countries and territories:
Argentina, Australia, Austria, Barbados, Belgium, Belize, Botswana, Brazil, Burkina Faso, Cameroon, Canada, China, Colombia, Congo Brazzaville, Congo DR, Costa Rica, Cuba, Czechia, Dominica, France, Germany, Ghana, Israel, Italy, Kenya, Mauritania, Mexico, Morocco, Netherlands, Nigeria, Panama, Portugal, South Africa, Spain, Sri Lanka, St Kitts Is, Sudan, Sweden, Switzerland, Taiwan, Thailand, Trinidad-Tobago, UK, USA, Venezuela, Vietnam, Zimbabwe.
NGO Relations *Association of Institutions of Tropical Veterinary Medicine (AITVM, #02648).* [2019.04.30/XD6534/**D**]

♦ Society of Typographic Designers / see International Society of Typographic Designers
♦ Society of Ultrasound in Medical Education (internationally oriented national body)
♦ Society for Ultrastructural Pathology (internationally oriented national body)

♦ Society for Underwater Technology (SUT) 19657

Exec Dir 2 John St, London, WC1N 2ES, UK. E-mail: info@sut.org.
Events Manager address not obtained.
URL: http://www.sut.org/

History 1966, London (UK). 1992, absorbed the *Underwater Association*, founded in 1966. Took over activities of *Engineering Committee on Oceanic Resources (ECOR, inactive)*, 2013. Registration: Companies House, No/ID: 00932590, Start date: 1968, England and Wales. **Aims** Promote further understanding of the underwater environment. Encourage: cross-fertilization and dissemination of ideas, experience and information amongst workers in academic and applied research and technology, industry and government; development of techniques and tools to explore, study and exploit the oceans; proper economic and sociological use of resources in and beneath the oceans; further education of scientists and technologists to maintain high standards in *marine* science and technology. **Structure** Council; Committees (13). **Languages** English. **Staff** 5.50 FTE, paid. **Finance** Sources: donations; meeting proceeds; members' dues. Annual budget: 1,148,000 GBP. **Activities** Research/documentation; standards/guidelines; training/education; awards/prizes/competitions; events/meetings. **Events** *Meeting* Singapore (Singapore) 2019, *All-Energy Conference* Glasgow (UK) 2017, *Annual Optoelectronic Technologies for the Oil and Gas Industry Technical Meeting* Bergen (Norway) 2011, *Conference on coasts, marine structures and breakwaters* Edinburgh (UK) 2009, *Subsea controls and data acquisition* 2002. **Publications** *UT2 Magazine* (6 a year); *Underwater Technology* (3 a year); *UT3* – electronic magazine. *Underwater Technology, Ocean Science and Offshore Engineering* – in 33 vols. Members' yearbook; conference proceedings.
Members Individual (including Fellow, Associate and Student) and Corporate (company). Members, mostly in the UK, but in a total of Corporate; Fellow; Individual; Associate; Student. Members (mostly in UK) in 40 countries and territories:
Australia, Austria, Azerbaijan, Belgium, Brazil, Canada, China, Denmark, Egypt, France, Germany, Greece, Hong Kong, India, Indonesia, Ireland, Italy, Japan, Korea Rep, Malaysia, Malta, Mexico, Netherlands, New Zealand, Nigeria, Norway, Panama, Qatar, Russia, Saudi Arabia, Singapore, South Africa, Spain, Switzerland, Thailand, Trinidad-Tobago, Türkiye, United Arab Emirates, USA, Venezuela.
NGO Relations Member of (1): *Association of Learned and Professional Society Publishers (ALPSP, #02786).* [2020/XC0365/**F**]

♦ Society of University Gynecologists / see Society for Reproductive Investigation (#19631)
♦ Society of University Patent Administrators / see Association of University Technology Managers

♦ Society for Urban Development in East Africa (SUDEA) 19658

Dir PO Box 31673, Addis Ababa, Ethiopia. T. +2519200514. E-mail: sudea@ethionet.et. [2008/XM0981/**D**]

♦ Society for Urban Ecology (SURE) 19659

Pres Urban and Landscape Ecology, Paris Londron Univ Salzburg, Dept of Geogrpahy and Geology, Hellbrunnerstr 34, 5020 Salzburg, Austria.
URL: http://www.society-urban-ecology.org/

History 2009. Registered in accordance with Austrian law. **Aims** Foster and develop knowledge and implementation of urban ecology worldwide. **Structure** General Assembly (every 4 years); Executive Committee; Working Groups (2); Chapters (5). **Languages** English. **Finance** Sources: meeting proceeds; members' dues. **Activities** Events/meetings; training/education. **Events** *World Conference* Poznań (Poland) 2021, *World Conference* Poznań (Poland) 2020, *World Conference* Shanghai (China) 2016, *World Conference* Berlin (Germany) 2013. **Publications** Conference outcomes; books; special issues. **Members** Institutional; Regular; Low income/developing countries; Student. Membership countries not specified. [2021/XJ8676/**C**]

♦ Society for Veterinary Ethology / see International Society for Applied Ethology (#14930)
♦ Society of Virology (internationally oriented national body)
♦ Society for West African Internal Audit Practitioners (unconfirmed)
♦ Society of Wetland Scientists (internationally oriented national body)
♦ Society of Women Engineers (internationally oriented national body)

♦ Society of World Deaf Magicians 19660

SG 212 W Hidden Trail, Elkhorn WI 53121, USA.

History Founded 1990. **Aims** Unite all deaf young and adult magicians – amateur, part-time professional and professional – to participate in international festivals for camaraderie, exchange of ideas and improvement in their performance skills; solve technical problems; participate in competitions; attend magic lectures with interpreters provided to learn new tricks or improve their skills; learn where to purchase magic apparatus or props; promote their magic shows available to other national deaf clubs and associations in different countries. **Structure** Board of 3 officers. **Languages** English, International Sign Language. **Staff** Voluntary. **Finance** Members' dues. Festival financed by organizing festival host country and admission charges. **Activities** Events/meetings. **Events** *Festival* Chicago, IL (USA) 2014, *Festival* Helsinki (Finland) 2012, *Festival* Cattolica (Italy) 2010, *Festival* Riverside, CA (USA) 2008, *Festival* St Petersburg (Russia) 2006. **Publications** *Magic Hands* (3-4 a year) – electronic newsletter.
Members Full in 21 countries:
Canada, Cuba, Cyprus, France, Germany, Hungary, India, Italy, Japan, Lithuania, Malaysia, Mexico, Poland, Portugal, Russia, Spain, Sri Lanka, UK, Ukraine, USA, Uzbekistan.
NGO Relations Recognized by: *International Brotherhood of Magicians (IBM, #12402).* [2015.11.20/XF6907/**F**]

♦ Society for Worldwide Interbank Financial Telecommunication (SWIFT) 19661

CEO Avenue Adèle 1, 1310 La Hulpe, Belgium. T. +3226553111. Fax +3226553226.
URL: http://www.swift.com/

History May 1973, Brussels (Belgium). Founded as a member-owned cooperative society. Operational system launched Sep 1977. Registration: Belgium. **Aims** Provide the communications platform, products and services to connect banking organizations, securities institutions and corporate customers; enable users to exchange automated, standardized financial information securely and reliably, thereby lowering costs, reducing operational risk and eliminating operational inefficiencies; bring the financial community together to work collaboratively to shape market practice, define standards and debate issues of mutual interest. **Structure** Board of Directors; Executive Committee. **Languages** English. **Staff** 2000.00 FTE, paid. **Activities** Guidance/assistance/consulting. **Events** *Sibos Annual Conference* Toronto, ON (Canada) 2023, *Sibos Annual Conference* Amsterdam (Netherlands) 2022, *Operations Forum Europe* 2021, *SWIFT African Regional Conference* 2021, *Sibos Annual Conference* 2021. **Publications** *Market Infrastructure Forum Magazine*; *SWIFT Annual Review.* Newsletters. **Members** Financial institutions (over 10,500) connected to SWIFT in 215 countries and territories. Membership countries not specified. [2022/XF6413/e/**F**]

♦ Society for Worldwide Medical Exchange (SWME) 19662

Exec Dir 1688 Meridian Ave, Ste 900, Miami Beach FL 33139, USA. T. +13054079222. Fax +13054337128. E-mail: info@worldwidemedicalexchange.org.
URL: http://www.worldwidemedicalexchange.org/

History 2009. A US 501(c)3 non-profit. **Aims** Advance global *health* through medical education. **Structure** Advisory Board. **Activities** Events/meetings; financial and/or material support; training/education. [2018/XJ5769/**C**]

♦ Socio-Ecological Union 19663

Socialno-Ekologiceskij Sojuz (SEU)

Contact address not obtained. T. +74951247178. Fax +74951247178.
URL: http://www.seu.ru/

History 24 Dec 1988, Moscow (USSR). **Aims** Promote cooperation for the preservation of the environment, wildlife, human health and rights. **Structure** Council. Centre for Coordination and Information (CCI). **Languages** English, Russian. **Staff** 15.00 FTE, paid. **Finance** Grants; donations; programmes. **Activities** CCI is the working body: networks and programmes (6): (1) Environmental Education; (2) Ecological Settlements for 21st century; (3); Chemical Safety for Peoples and Nature; (4) Nuclear and Radioactive Safety; (5) Environment and Children Health; (6) Local initiatives – Alternatives for Humanity. The Union, through its publications, networks and programmes: promotes environmental awareness; carries out human rights activities in the environmental field; cooperates in developing national and international legislation and in carrying out environmental impact assessments in this respect; promotes the development of environmentally friendly technologies; carries out the prevention of damage to ecosystems and human settlements from industrial projects of different kinds. **Events** *Conference* Kiev (Ukraine) 2000, *International conference / Biennial Meeting* Moscow (Russia) 2000, *Conference* Temirtau (Kazakhstan) 1997. **Publications** *Bereginya* (12 a year) – newsletter; *SEU Times* (12 a year) – bulletin; *Vestnik of Association of Environmental Education* (4 a year) – magazine. Newspapers; journals; bulletins.
Members Organizations (over 290) in 17 countries:
Armenia, Azerbaijan, Belarus, Finland, Georgia, Kazakhstan, Kyrgyzstan, Moldova, Norway, Russia, Spain, Tajikistan, Turkmenistan, UK, Ukraine, USA, Uzbekistan.
International organization (2):
Initiative for Social Action and Renewal in Eurasia (ISAR, no recent information); Sacred Earth Network (SEN).
IGO Relations Collaborates with: *Global Environment Facility (GEF, #10346)*, in particular with respect to *United Nations Human Settlements Programme (UN-Habitat, #20572); United States Agency for International Development (USAID); UNESCO (#20322).* **NGO Relations** Member of: *Taiga Rescue Network (TRN, inactive).* Collaborates with: *Friends of the Earth International (FoEI, #10002); Living Economies Forum (LEF); International NGO Network on Desertification (inactive).* Also links with a large number of national organizations active in the field. [2012/XD4286/**D**]

♦ Socio-Economic Life in Asia / see Asian Partnership for the Development of Human Resources in Rural Asia (#01654)

♦ Socio-Gerontechnology Network 19664

Sec address not obtained. E-mail: info@socio-gerontechnology.net.
Chair address not obtained.
URL: https://www.socio-gerontechnology.net/

History Emerged from loosely organised conference sessions since 2010, and formalised during inaugural meeting in Vienna, 2017. **Aims** Strengthen critical and reflexive thinking and research by emphasising the complex and co-constitutive relationship between ageing, technology and society. **Activities** Events/meetings. **Events** *International Workshop on Socio-Gerontechnology* Bristol (UK) 2022, *International Workshop on Socio-Gerontechnology* Stockholm (Sweden) 2019, *International Workshop on Socio-Gerontechnology* Barcelona (Spain) 2018, *International Workshop on Socio-Gerontechnology* Vienna (Austria) 2017. [2022.02.16/AA0773/**F**]

♦ Sociologists without Borders 19665

Sociólogos sin Fronteras

Treas VT Dept of Sociology, 654 McBryde Hall, PC 0137, Blacksburg VA 24061-0002, USA.
Pres – SSF USA Univ of Connecticut, Dept of Sociology – Unit 1068, 344 Mansfield Rd, Storrs CT 06269, USA.
URL: http://sociologistswithoutborders.org/

History Founded 2001, Spain. Registered in accordance with USA law 2002. **Aims** Develop a globally inclusive sociological curricula; advance human rights by working through communities, societies, the workplace and other social institutions. **Structure** Executive Council. **Languages** English. **Finance** Members' dues. **Activities** Advocacy/lobbying/activism. **Publications** *Societies without Borders: Human Rights and the Social Sciences* – journal.
Members Chapters in 7 countries:
Brazil, Canada, Chile, Iran Islamic Rep, Italy, Spain, USA. [2014.06.01/XJ1817/**F**]

♦ Sociólogos sin Fronteras (#19665)
♦ Sociology of Development Research Centre, Bielefeld / see Transnationalisation and Development Research Centre, Bielefeld
♦ **SOCLA** Sociedad Cientifica Latinoamericana de Agroecologia (#19354)
♦ **SOCODEVI** – Société de coopération pour le développement international (internationally oriented national body)
♦ **SOC** / see Socialists, Democrats and Greens Group (#19342)
♦ **SOC** Socialists, Democrats and Greens Group (#19342)
♦ SoDA – The Digital Society (unconfirmed)

♦ Sodalicio de Vida Cristiana (SCV) 19666

Sodalitium christianae Vitae

Superior Genera Calle Dos 553, Monterrico Norte, San Borja, 41, Lima, Peru. T. +5114188333. E-mail: prensa@sodalitium.org.
URL: http://sodalicio.org/

History Founded 1971, Lima. Approved as a Society of Pontifical Right by Pope John Paul II, 1997. **Aims** Be of apostolic service in Christian solidarity to the poor, the needy and the young. **Structure** General Assembly; Council Superior; Superior General. **Languages** English, Italian, Portuguese, Spanish. **Staff** 7.00 FTE, paid.
Members Individuals (152) in 9 countries:
Argentina, Brazil, Chile, Colombia, Costa Rica, Ecuador, Italy, Peru, USA. [2020.03.13/XM6381/**E**]

♦ Sodalitium christianae Vitae (#19666)
♦ Sodality of Christian Mothers (religious order)
♦ Sodality of St Rita and St Claire (religious order)
♦ SoDA – SoDA – The Digital Society (unconfirmed)
♦ **SoDAS** Society of Dialysis Access Specialists (#19543)
♦ SODEIT / see Social Development International
♦ SODEPAU – Solidaridat per al Desenvolupament i la Pau (internationally oriented national body)
♦ SODEPAX – Committee on Society, Development and Peace of the World Council of Churches and the Pontifical Commission Justice and Peace (inactive)

♦ SODEPAZ – Solidaridad para el Desarrollo y la Paz (internationally oriented national body)
♦ SODI – Solidaritätsdienst International (internationally oriented national body)
♦ Sodisse Europskih Skupnosti / see Court of Justice of the European Union (#04938)
♦ Sodisse Evropske Unije (#04938)

♦ Sodium Sulphate Producers Association (SSPA) 19667

Manager CEFIC, Rue Belliard 40, Box 15, 1040 Brussels, Belgium. T. +32475941003. E-mail: ppa@cefic.be – caj@cefic.be.
URL: http://specialty-chemicals.eu/
History as a sector group of *Conseil européen de l'industrie chimique (CEFIC, #04687).* **Aims** Promote and encourage safety and best environmental practices in production, transport and use of sodium sulphate.
Members Full in 5 countries:
Austria, Germany, Spain, Sweden, Türkiye.
IGO Relations Cooperates with (1): *European Commission (EC, #06633).* [2022/XK1876/**E**]

♦ Sodruzestvo Nezavissimyh Gosudarstv (#04341)
♦ SOEC / see Statistical Office of the European Union (#19974)
♦ **SOE** European Society of Ophthalmology (#08674)
♦ **SOE** Societas Ophthalmologica Europaea (#08674)
♦ **SOE** Société d'optométrie d'Europe (#08675)
♦ Soeurs de l'Adoration Réparatrice (religious order)
♦ Soeurs de l'Adoration du Sacré-Coeur de Jésus (religious order)
♦ Soeurs de l'Adoration du Saint Sacrement (religious order)
♦ Soeurs de l'Adoration du Très Précieux Sang (religious order)
♦ Soeurs de l'Amour de Dieu (religious order)
♦ Sœurs de l'Ange Gardien (religious order)
♦ Soeurs de l'Apostolat Catholique Pallottines (religious order)
♦ Soeurs de l'Assomption de la Sainte Vierge (religious order)
♦ Soeurs Augustines (religious order)
♦ Soeurs Augustines – Hospitalières de l'Immaculée Conception (religious order)
♦ Soeurs Augustines Missionnaires (religious order)
♦ Soeurs Bénédictines (religious order)
♦ Soeurs Bénédictines de la Congrégation de Saint Benoît (religious order)
♦ Soeurs Bénédictines de la Fédération de Sainte Gertrude (religious order)
♦ Soeurs Bénédictines de la Fédération de Sainte Scolastique (religious order)
♦ Soeurs Bénédictines de Tutzing (religious order)
♦ Soeurs de Béthanie du Sacré-Coeur (religious order)
♦ Soeurs Blanches – Soeurs Missionnaires de Notre-Dame d'Afrique (religious order)
♦ Soeurs Bleues de Castres – Soeurs de Notre-Dame de l'Immaculée-Conception (religious order)
♦ Soeurs du Bon Pasteur de Québec – Servantes du Coeur Immaculé de Marie (religious order)
♦ Soeurs du Bon Sauveur (religious order)
♦ Soeurs du Bon Secours de Paris (religious order)
♦ Soeurs camilliennes (religious order)
♦ Soeurs des Campagnes (religious order)
♦ Soeurs Capucines de la Sainte Famille (religious order)
♦ Soeurs Carmélites de la Charité, Vedruna (religious order)
♦ Soeurs du Carmel Saint Joseph (religious order)
♦ Soeurs du Carmel Saint-Joseph (religious order)
♦ Soeurs de la Charité de Besançon (religious order)
♦ Soeurs de Charité de la Bienheureuse Vierge Marie (religious order)
♦ Soeurs de la Charité Chrétienne, Filles de la Bienheureuse Vierge Marie de l'Immaculée Conception (religious order)
♦ Soeurs de Charité de Cincinnati (religious order)
♦ Soeurs de la Charité, Dominicaines de la Présentation de la Sainte Vierge (religious order)
♦ Soeurs de la Charité et de l'Instruction Chrétienne de Nevers (religious order)
♦ Soeurs de la Charité de Jésus et de Marie (religious order)
♦ Soeurs de la Charité Maternelle (religious order)
♦ Soeurs de la Charité de Montréal (religious order)
♦ Soeurs de la Charité de Namur (religious order)
♦ Soeurs de Charité de Nazareth (religious order)
♦ Soeurs de la Charité de Notre-Dame du Bon et Perpétuel Secours (religious order)
♦ Soeurs de la Charité de Notre-Dame d'Evron (religious order)
♦ Soeurs de Charité de Notre-Dame de la Merci (religious order)
♦ Soeurs de Charité de Notre-Dame Mère de Miséricorde (religious order)
♦ Soeurs de la Charité d'Ottawa (religious order)
♦ Soeurs de la Charité de Québec (religious order)
♦ Soeurs de Charité de Saint Charles Borromée (religious order)
♦ Soeurs de la Charité de Saint-Charles de Nancy (religious order)
♦ Soeurs de Charité de la Sainte Croix (religious order)
♦ Soeurs de Charité de Sainte Elizabeth (religious order)
♦ Soeurs de la Charité de Sainte Jeanne-Antide Thouret (religious order)
♦ Soeurs de la Charité de Sainte-Marie-d'Angers (religious order)
♦ Soeurs de la Charité de Sainte-Marie-la-Forêt (religious order)
♦ Soeurs de Charité des Saintes Bartolomea Capitanio et Vincenza Gerosa de Marie Enfant (religious order)
♦ Soeurs de la Charité de Saint-Hyacinthe (religious order)
♦ Soeurs de la Charité de Saint Vincent-de-Paul (religious order)
♦ Soeurs de la Charité de St Louis (religious order)
♦ Soeurs de la Charité de Strasbourg (religious order)
♦ Soeurs du Christ Rédempteur de Fougères (religious order)
♦ Soeurs Clarisses Franciscaines (religious order)
♦ Soeurs du Coeur Immaculée de Marie de Blon (religious order)
♦ Soeurs de la Congrégation de Notre-Dame (religious order)
♦ Soeurs de la Croix de Chavanod (religious order)
♦ Soeurs de la Croix de Strasbourg (religious order)
♦ Soeurs de la Divine Providence, Münster (religious order)
♦ Soeurs de la Divine Providence de Ribeauvillé (religious order)
♦ Soeurs de la Divine Providence de Saint-Jean-de-Bassel (religious order)
♦ Soeurs du Divin Rédempteur (religious order)
♦ Soeurs du Divin Sauveur (religious order)
♦ Soeurs de la Doctrine Chrétienne de Nancy (religious order)
♦ Soeurs Dominicaines (religious order)
♦ Soeurs Dominicaines de la Congrégation du Très Saint Rosaire (religious order)
♦ Soeurs Dominicaines de Maryknoll (religious order)
♦ Soeurs dominicaines de Sainte-Catherine de Sienne (religious order)
♦ Soeurs de l'Education Chrétienne (religious order)
♦ Soeurs de l'Enfance de Jésus et Marie de Sainte Chrétienne (religious order)
♦ Soeurs de l'Enfant-Jésus (religious order)
♦ Soeurs de l'Enfant-Jésus de Chauffailles (religious order)
♦ Soeurs de l'Enfant Jésus – Nicolas Barré (religious order)
♦ Soeurs de l'Enfant-Jésus, Puy (religious order)
♦ Soeurs Enseignantes de Notre-Dame (religious order)
♦ Soeurs Féliciennes – Congrégation des Soeurs de Saint Félix de Cantalice (religious order)
♦ Soeurs Franciscaines (religious order)
♦ Soeurs Franciscaines de Dillingen (religious order)
♦ Soeurs Franciscaines Elisabethines (religious order)
♦ Soeurs Franciscaines, Filles des Sacrés Coeurs de Jésus et de Marie (religious order)
♦ Soeurs Franciscaines Hospitalières de l'Immaculée Conception (religious order)
♦ Soeurs Franciscaines Missionnaires du Coeur Immaculé de Marie d'Egypte (religious order)
♦ Soeurs franciscaines des pauvres (religious order)
♦ Soeurs Franciscaines de Philadelphie (religious order)
♦ Soeurs Franciscaines de Saint Georges Martyr (religious order)
♦ Soeurs Grises – Soeurs de la Charité de Montréal (religious order)
♦ Soeurs Grises – Soeurs de la Charité d'Ottawa (religious order)
♦ Soeurs Grises – Soeurs de la Charité de Québec (religious order)
♦ Soeurs Grises – Soeurs de la Charité de Saint-Hyacinthe (religious order)
♦ Soeurs Hospitalières du Sacré-Coeur de Jésus (religious order)
♦ Soeurs de l'Immaculée-Conception de Notre-Dame de Lourdes (religious order)
♦ Soeurs de l'Immaculée-Conception de Saint-Méen-Le-Grand (religious order)
♦ Soeurs de Jeanne Delanoue – Servantes des Pauvres de Jeanne Delanoue (religious order)
♦ Soeurs de Jésus Rédempteur (religious order)
♦ Soeurs de Jésus au Temple (religious order)
♦ Soeurs Maîtresses de Sainte Dorothée, 1838 (religious order)
♦ Soeurs des Malades de Saint François (religious order)
♦ Soeurs de Marie-Joseph et de la Miséricorde (religious order)
♦ Soeurs de Marie Réconciliatrice (religious order)
♦ Soeurs de Marie de Schönstatt (religious order)
♦ Soeurs Maristes (religious order)
♦ Soeurs Mercédaires Missionnaires de Bérriz (religious order)
♦ Soeurs de la Mère du Carmel (religious order)
♦ Soeurs Minimes du Saint-Coeur de Marie (religious order)
♦ Soeurs ministres des infirmes (religious order)
♦ Soeurs de la Miséricorde, 1823 (religious order)
♦ Soeurs de la Miséricorde des Amériques (religious order)
♦ Soeurs de la Miséricorde de Billom (religious order)
♦ Soeurs de la Miséricorde de Moissac (religious order)
♦ Soeurs Missionnaires de l'Apostolat Catholique (religious order)
♦ Soeurs Missionnaires du Coeur Immaculé de Marie (religious order)
♦ Soeurs Missionnaires de la Consolata (religious order)
♦ Soeurs Missionnaires de l'Immaculée Conception (religious order)
♦ Soeurs Missionnaires de l'Immaculée-Conception (religious order)
♦ Soeurs Missionnaires de Jésus Crucifié (religious order)
♦ Soeurs Missionnaires de Notre-Dame d'Afrique (religious order)
♦ Soeurs Missionnaires de Notre-Dame des Anges (religious order)
♦ Soeurs Missionnaires de Notre-Dame des Apôtres (religious order)
♦ Soeurs Missionnaires de Notre-Dame du Saint Rosaire (religious order)
♦ Soeurs Missionnaires du Précieux Sang (religious order)
♦ Soeurs Missionnaires du Sacré-Coeur de Jésus (religious order)
♦ Soeurs missionnaires du Sacré-Coeur de Jésus (religious order)
♦ Soeurs Missionnaires de Saint Charles Borromée (religious order)
♦ Soeurs Missionnaires de Saint Columban (religious order)
♦ Soeurs Missionnaires du Saint-Esprit (religious order)
♦ Soeurs Missionnaires de Saint Pierre Claver (religious order)
♦ Soeurs Missionnaires de la Société de Marie (religious order)
♦ Soeurs des Missions Etrangères (religious order)
♦ Soeurs du Monde Rural (religious order)
♦ Soeurs de Nazareth (religious order)
♦ Soeurs de Niederbronn (religious order)
♦ Soeurs de Notre-Dame (religious order)
♦ Soeurs de Notre-Dame de Bon Secours de Troyes (religious order)
♦ Soeurs de Notre-Dame du Calvaire (religious order)
♦ Soeurs de Notre-Dame de Charité du Bon Pasteur (religious order)
♦ Soeurs de Notre-Dame de la Compassion (religious order)
♦ Soeurs de Notre-Dame de l'Immaculée-Conception (religious order)
♦ Soeurs de Notre-Dame-du-Mont-Carmel (religious order)
♦ Soeurs de Notre-Dame de Namur (religious order)
♦ Soeurs de Notre-Dame de la Retraite au Cénacle (religious order)
♦ Soeurs de Notre-Dame de la Visitation (religious order)
♦ Soeurs Oblates du Très Saint Rédempteur (religious order)
♦ Soeurs de l'Oeuvre de Saint Paul (religious order)
♦ Soeurs Ouvrières de la Sainte-Maison de Nazareth (religious order)
♦ Soeurs du Pauvre Enfant Jésus (religious order)
♦ Soeurs des Pauvres de Saint François (religious order)
♦ Soeurs des Petites Filles Pauvres de l'Institut Palazzolo (religious order)
♦ Soeurs de Picpus (religious order)
♦ Soeurs du Précieux Sang (religious order)
♦ Soeurs de la Présentation de Marie (religious order)
♦ Soeurs de la Providence (religious order)
♦ Soeurs de la Providence de Gap (religious order)
♦ Soeurs de la Providence et de l'Immaculée Conception (religious order)
♦ Soeurs de la Providence de La Pommeraye (religious order)
♦ Soeurs de la Providence de Portieux (religious order)
♦ Soeurs de la Providence de Rouen (religious order)
♦ Soeurs de la Providence de Ruillé-sur-Loir (religious order)
♦ Soeurs de la Providence de Saint André (religious order)
♦ Soeurs de la Providence de Saint Gaetan de Thiene (religious order)
♦ Soeurs de la Providence de Sees (religious order)
♦ Soeurs du Rédempteur (religious order)
♦ Soeurs de la Retraite Chrétienne (religious order)
♦ Soeurs Sacramentines de Bergame (religious order)
♦ Soeurs du Sacré-Coeur d'Ernemont (religious order)
♦ Soeurs du Sacré-Coeur de Jésus (religious order)
♦ Soeurs des Sacrés Coeurs de Jésus et de Marie (religious order)
♦ Soeurs de Saint Charles d'Angers (religious order)
♦ Soeurs de Saint-Charles-de-Lyon (religious order)
♦ Soeurs des Saint-Coeurs de Jésus et de Marie (religious order)
♦ Soeurs de Sainte Agnès (religious order)
♦ Soeurs de Sainte Anne (religious order)
♦ Soeurs de la Sainte Croix (religious order)
♦ Soeurs de Sainte-Croix (religious order)
♦ Soeurs de Sainte Elisabeth (religious order)
♦ Soeurs de la Sainte-Famille (religious order)
♦ Soeurs de la Sainte Famille de Bordeaux (religious order)
♦ Soeurs de la Sainte-Famille de la Délivrande (religious order)
♦ Soeurs de la Sainte Famille de Nazareth (religious order)
♦ Soeurs de la Sainte-Famille du Sacré-Coeur (religious order)
♦ Soeurs de la Sainte-Famille de Villefranche-de-Rouergue (religious order)
♦ Soeurs de Sainte Marie-Madeleine Postel (religious order)
♦ Soeurs de Sainte-Marthe (religious order)

- ♦ Soeurs du Saint-Enfant Jésus de Reims (religious order)
- ♦ Soeurs de Saint François d'Assise (religious order)
- ♦ Soeurs de Saint-François-d'Assise (religious order)
- ♦ Soeurs de Saint François de Sales (religious order)
- ♦ Soeurs de Saint Jean de Dieu (religious order)
- ♦ Soeurs de Saint Joseph d'Annecy (religious order)
- ♦ Soeurs de Saint Joseph de l'Apparition (religious order)
- ♦ Soeurs de Saint Joseph de Bourg (inactive)
- ♦ Soeurs de Saint-Joseph de Chambéry (religious order)
- ♦ Soeurs de Saint-Joseph de Champagnole (religious order)
- ♦ Soeurs de Saint-Joseph de Clermont-Ferrand (religious order)
- ♦ Soeurs de Saint-Joseph de Cluny (religious order)
- ♦ Soeurs de Saint Joseph de Lyon (religious order)
- ♦ Soeurs de Saint-Joseph du Puy (religious order)
- ♦ Soeurs de Saint-Joseph de Rodez (religious order)
- ♦ Soeurs de Saint Joseph du Sacré-Coeur (religious order)
- ♦ Soeurs de Saint-Joseph, Saint-Etienne (religious order)
- ♦ Soeurs de Saint Joseph de "Saint-Marc" (religious order)
- ♦ Soeurs de Saint Joseph de Saint-Vallier (religious order)
- ♦ Soeurs de Saint Joseph de Tarbes (religious order)
- ♦ Soeurs de Saint-Joseph de Viviers (religious order)
- ♦ Soeurs de Saint-Louis (religious order)
- ♦ Soeurs du Saint Nom de Jésus et de Marie (religious order)
- ♦ Soeurs de Saint Paul de Chartres (religious order)
- ♦ Soeurs de Saint-Roch (religious order)
- ♦ Soeurs de Saint Thomas de Villeneuve (religious order)
- ♦ Soeurs du Sauveur et de la Sainte Vierge (religious order)
- ♦ Soeurs, Servantes du Coeur Immaculé de Marie de Monroe (religious order)
- ♦ Soeurs Servantes du Coeur Immaculé de Marie de Scranton (religious order)
- ♦ Soeurs Servantes de Marie Immaculée (religious order)
- ♦ Soeurs Servantes du Sacré-Coeur de Jésus (religious order)
- ♦ Soeurs Servantes du Saint-Coeur de Marie (religious order)
- ♦ Soeurs du Très-Saint-Sacrement (religious order)
- ♦ Soeurs Trinitaires de Valence (religious order)
- ♦ Soeurs Ursulines du Sacré-Coeur de Jésus Agonisant (religious order)
- ♦ Soeurs Ursulines de Somasca (religious order)
- ♦ SOF / see Ocean Policy Research Institute
- ♦ SOFAMEA – Société Francophone d'Analyse du Mouvement chez l'Enfant et l'Adulte (internationally oriented national body)
- ♦ **SOFELP** Sociedade de Filosofia da Educação de Lingua Portuguesa (#19355)

♦ SOFICATRA – European Group for the Development of Participative Enterprises 19668

Contact Av Jules César 2, bte 7, 1150 Brussels, Belgium. T. +3227701562. Fax +3222307541.
URL: http://www.soficatra.org/

History 6 Jul 1993. Founded with the initial support of the DG XXIII of the *European Commission (EC, #06633)*. A limited company in accordance with Belgian law, comprising the centre of a European financing mechanism. **Aims** Act as a financing mechanism to provide funding (in the form of equity and quasi equity) for enterprises associated with cooperative, mutual and associative economy and to participating entreprises, with the participation of personnel in company management and equity. **Structure** A European network of partners; each partner is a direct actor in its sector and has connections with the rest of the national economy. **Finance** Source: private capital invested by the partners. **Activities** Financial and/or material support.
Members Partners in 6 countries:
Belgium, France, Italy, Netherlands, Portugal, Spain.
NGO Relations Member of: *Confédération européenne des coopératives de travail associé, des coopératives sociales et des entreprises sociales et participatives (CECOP, #04541).* [2021/XF2872/ef/**F**]

- ♦ SOFPHIED – Société francophone de philosophie de l'éducation (internationally oriented national body)
- ♦ **SÖF** Sällskap för östnordisk filologi (#19223)

♦ Softball Confederation of Asia (SCA) 19669

Pres 53 Jalan Maarof, Bangsar, 59000 Kuala Lumpur, Malaysia. T. +60322820820. Fax +60322827026.
SG 46 Jalan Cenderai 1, Lucky Garden, Bangsar, 59100 Kuala Lumpur, Malaysia. T. +60320941292. Fax +60320941275. E-mail: bclow@bclowco.com.

Languages English. **Activities** Sporting activities; events/meetings.
Members Full in 16 countries and territories/:
Brunei Darussalam, China, Hong Kong, India, Indonesia, Iran Islamic Rep, Iraq, Japan, Korea DPR, Korea Rep, Malaysia, Pakistan, Philippines, Singapore, Taiwan, Thailand.
NGO Relations Regional federation of: *World Baseball Softball Confederation (WBSC, #21222).* [2013.09.27/XM4063/**D**]

- ♦ Software and Information Industry Association (internationally oriented national body)
- ♦ Software Technologies: Applications and Foundations (meeting series)
- ♦ SOGA – Social Good Accelerator (internationally oriented national body)
- ♦ SOGH – Swedish Organization for Global Health (internationally oriented national body)
- ♦ SOG – Südosteuropa-Gesellschaft (internationally oriented national body)
- ♦ **SoHaH** Sociedad Hispanoamericana de Hernia (#19360)
- ♦ **SoHI** Star of Hope International (#19967)
- ♦ **SoHT** Society of Hair Testing (#19567)
- ♦ **SOIA** Synthetic Organic Ion Exchangers and Adsorbents (#20084)
- ♦ **SolBio** Sociedad Iberoamericana de Bioinformatica (#19361)

♦ Soi Dog Foundation 19670

Contact 167/9 Moo 4, Soi Mai Khao 10, Tambon Mai Khao, Amphur Thalang, Phuket, 83110, Thailand. T. +6676681029. E-mail: info@soidog.org.
Registered Address c/o Dryden Associates SA, 7th floor, 47 Avenue Blanc, 1202 Geneva, Switzerland.
URL: https://www.soidog.org/

History 2003, Phuket (Thailand). Former names and other names: *Soi Dog Foundation International* – alias. Registration: No/ID: 39/2548, Thailand; No/ID: CHE-393.768.679, Switzerland; 501(c)(3) nonprofit, USA; No/ID: 58982568831, Australia; Handelsregister, No/ID: KVK 37120202, Netherlands; Charity Commission, No/ID: 1176305, England and Wales; No/ID: 981179-6, Canada. **Aims** Improve the welfare of dogs and cats in Asia, resulting in better lives for both the animal and human communities; create a society without homeless animals; ultimately end animal cruelty. **Structure** Board. **Languages** English, German, Thai. **Staff** 320.00 FTE, paid. **Finance** Annual budget: 20,000,000 USD (2022). **Activities** Active in: Cambodia, Korea DPR, Thailand, Vietnam. **NGO Relations** Member of (1): *Action for Animal Health (A4AH, #00088).* [2022.05.04/AA2387/f/**F**]

- ♦ Soi Dog Foundation International / see Soi Dog Foundation (#19670)
- ♦ SOIE – Society for Ophthalmo-Immunoinfectiology in Europe (unconfirmed)
- ♦ Soil Association (internationally oriented national body)

♦ Soil Science Society of East Africa (SSSEA) 19671

Chairperson c/o KALRO, PO Box 57811, City Square, Nairobi, 00200, Kenya.

History 1975. **Structure** Annual General Meeting elects: Chairman; 2 Regional Vice Chairmen (from countries other than that of Chairman); Secretary General; Treasurer General; 2 Regional Treasurers (from countries other than that of Treasurer General); 6 members. **Languages** English. **Staff** None. **Finance** Members' dues. Registration fees; grants. **Activities** Holds meetings for presentation of professional papers and for discussion; stimulates and promotes publishing of papers; liaises with other organizations in disseminating information. **Events** *Conference* Naivasha (Kenya) 2019, *Conference* Morogoro (Tanzania UR) 2015, *Annual Conference* Moshi (Tanzania UR) 2009, *Annual general meeting / Annual Conference* Arusha (Tanzania UR) 2004, *Annual general meeting / Annual Conference* Eldoret (Kenya) 2003. **Publications** Congress proceedings; summaries and bibliographies on soil science research; advisory notes.
Members Currently effective in 3 countries:
Kenya, Tanzania UR, Uganda.
NGO Relations *African Academy of Sciences (AAS, #00193); International Union of Soil Sciences (IUSS, #15817).* [2019/XD1511/**D**]

- ♦ Soil Security and Planetary Health Conference (meeting series)
- ♦ Soil and Water Conservation Society (internationally oriented national body)
- ♦ SOIR / see Swedish Development Partner
- ♦ SOI – Society of Open Innovation: Technology, Market, and Complexity (internationally oriented national body)
- ♦ **SOI** Special Olympics International (#19910)
- ♦ Sojuz Evropejskih Foniatorov (#20390)
- ♦ Sojuz Russkih Dvorjan (#19009)
- ♦ Sojuz Sovetskih Socialisticeskih Respublik (inactive)

♦ Soka Gakkai International (SGI) 19672

Office of Peace and Global Issues 15-3 Samon-cho, Shinjuku-ku, Tokyo, 160-0017 Japan. T. +81353609831. Fax +81333534368.
URL: http://www.sgi.org/

History 1975. **Aims** As a Nichiren *Buddhist* association, foster a network of empowered global citizens contributing to the promotion of peace, education and culture, based on respect for the *sanctity* of life. **Structure** Committee of Standing Directors; Board of Directors; Executive Office (administrative body). **Languages** English, Japanese. **Finance** Donations. **Activities** Events/meetings; advocacy/lobbying/activism; training/education. **Events** *General Assembly* France 1991, *General Assembly* Japan 1990. **Publications** *SGI Quarterly* (4 a year) – magazine. Booklets. **Members** 12 million members in 192 countries and territories, of which 94 have local organizations, affiliated to SGI. Membership countries not specified. **Consultative Status** Consultative status granted from: *ECOSOC (#05331)* (Ros A).
NGO Relations Member of:
- *Committee of NGOs on Human Rights, Geneva (#04275);*
- *Committee of Religious NGOs at the United Nations (CRNGOs, #04282);*
- *Conference of Non-Governmental Organizations in Consultative Relationship with the United Nations (CONGO, #04635);*
- *Global Movement for the Culture of Peace (GMCOP);*
- *Human Rights Education Associates (HREA);*
- *International Campaign to Abolish Nuclear Weapons (ICAN, #12426);*
- *Joint Learning Initiative on Faith and Local Communities (JLI, #16139);*
- *NGO Committee for Disarmament, Geneva (#17105);*
- *NGO Committee on Disarmament, Peace and Security, New York NY (#17106);*
- *NGO Committee on Freedom of Religion or Belief, Geneva (see: #04275);*
- *NGO Committee on Freedom of Religion or Belief, New York NY (#17109);*
- *NGO Committee on Sustainable Development, Vienna (#17119);*
- *Vienna NGO Committee on the Status of Women (#20775).*

Associate member of: *World Federation of United Nations Associations (WFUNA, #21499).* [2015.12.22/XF0086/**F**]

- ♦ SOL / see Solutions in Organisations Link-up (#19685)
- ♦ **SOLABIAA** Sociedad Latinoamericana de Biotecnologia Ambiental y Algal (#19393)
- ♦ SoLaBiMa – Asociación Latinoamericana de Biomatematica (inactive)
- ♦ **SOLABIMA** Sociedad Latinoamericana de Biologia Matematica (#16377)
- ♦ **SOLACI** Sociedad Latinoamericana de Cardiologia Intervencionista (#16375)
- ♦ **SOLACYT** Sociedad Latinoamericana de Ciencia y Tecnología (#19397)
- ♦ SOLADIM – Sociedad Latinoamericana de Imagenologia Mamaria (no recent information)
- ♦ SOLAECE / see Latin American Heart Rhythm Society (#16339)
- ♦ SOLAEC / see Latin American Heart Rhythm Society (#16339)
- ♦ **SOLAES** Sociedad Latinoamericana de Esterilización (#19403)
- ♦ SOLAGRAL – Solidarités agricoles et alimentaires (internationally oriented national body)
- ♦ **SOLA International** International Society for Oral Laser Applications (#15326)
- ♦ **SOLAMAC** Sociedad Latinoamericana de Especialistas en Mamiferos Acuaticos (#19402)
- ♦ **SOLAMER** Sociedad Latina de Biologia y Medicina de la Reproducción (#19387)
- ♦ **SOLAMI** Sociedad Latinoamericana de Medicina Interna (#19412)
- ♦ Solanaceae Conference (meeting series)
- ♦ SOLANEP – Sociedad Latinoamericana de Neumologia Pediatrica (no recent information)
- ♦ **SOLAPSO** Sociedad Latinoamericana de Psoriasis (#19423)
- ♦ SolarAid (internationally oriented national body)
- ♦ Solar Box Cookers International / see Solar Cookers International (#19673)

♦ Solar Cookers International (SCI) 19673

Executive Director 2400 22nd St, Ste 210, Sacramento CA 95818, USA. T. +19164554499. E-mail: info@solarcookers.org.
URL: http://www.solarcookers.org/

History 1987. Former names and other names: *Solar Box Cookers International (SBCI)* – former (1987 to 1993). Registration: Section 501(c)(3), No/ID: 68-0153141, USA. **Aims** Improve human and environmental health by supporting the expansion of effective carbon-free solar cooking in world regions of greatest need. **Structure** Board of Directors; Executive Director; Global Advisory Council; Solar Cookers International Association. **Languages** English, French, Hindi, Spanish, Thai. **Staff** 8.00 FTE, paid. Several voluntary. **Finance** Sources: donations; grants; sale of products. **Activities** Advocacy/lobbying/activism; events/meetings; humanitarian/emergency aid; knowledge management/information dissemination; research and development; training/education. **Events** *Solar cooking – A transformative approach for the SDGs* Hastings-on-Hudson, NY (USA) 2020, *World Conference on Solar Cookers* India 2017, *Solar Cooking Convention* Sacramento, CA (USA) 2014, *International solar cookers conference and food processing* Granada (Spain) 2006, *International information exchange meeting* Harare (Zimbabwe) 2000. **Publications** *Solar Cookers International Newsletter. SCI Blog.* Annual Report; conference papers; field guides; training manuals; statements; submissions to external publications; press. **Members** Individuals and organizations in over 145 countries. **Consultative Status** Consultative status granted from: *ECOSOC (#05331)* (Special). **IGO Relations** Associated with Department of Global Communications of the United Nations. **NGO Relations** Member of (2): *American Council for Voluntary International Action (InterAction);* American Solar Energy Society. [2022.02.08/XF3039/**F**]

- ♦ Solar Cookers World Network (inactive)
- ♦ Solar Decathlon Europe (unconfirmed)
- ♦ Solar Electric Light Fund (internationally oriented national body)
- ♦ Solar Energy International (internationally oriented national body)
- ♦ Solar Energy Society / see International Solar Energy Society (#15564)
- ♦ Solar Energy Society of Central Africa (internationally oriented national body)

♦ Solar Heat Europe (SHE) 19674

ESTIF

SG Place du Champ de Mars 2, 1050 Brussels, Belgium. T. +3223184060. E-mail: info@solarheateurope.eu.
URL: http://solarheateurope.eu/

History 1992. 2002, name changed on merger with *Active Solar Thermal Industry Group (ASTIG)*. Former names and other names: *European Solar Industry Federation (ESIF)* – former (1992 to 2002); *Association européenne de l'industrie solaire* – former (1992 to 2002); *European Solar Thermal Industry Federation (ESTIF)* – former (2002 to 2017); *Association européenne de l'industrie solaire thermique* – former (2002 to 2017). Registration: Banque-Carrefour des Entreprises, No/ID: 0478.331.744, Start date: 17 Sep 2002, Belgium; EU Transparency Register, No/ID: 10790718699-18, Start date: 2 May 2012. **Aims** Promote the growth of solar heat solutions in Europe through different actions, such as advocating for better regulation or encouraging the EU policy makers to shape a fair context for heating and cooling solutions; represent directly or indirectly the industry. **Languages** English, French, Italian, Portuguese, Spanish. **Activities** Certification/accreditation; events/meetings; guidance/assistance/consulting; politics/policy/regulatory; projects/programmes; research and development; standards/guidelines. **Events** *Joint Session* Brussels (Belgium) 2022, *Youth fight against climate change – from knowledge to action* 2021, *International Conference on Solar Heating and Cooling for Buildings and Industry* Santiago (Chile) 2019, *International Conference on Solar Heating and Cooling for Buildings and Industry* Abu Dhabi (United Arab Emirates) 2017, *International Conference on Solar Heating and Cooling for Buildings and Industry* Istanbul (Turkey) 2015. **Members** National industrial associations; manufacturers and service providers. Membership countries not specified. **NGO Relations** Member of (2): *Federation of European and International Associations Established in Belgium (FAIB, #09508)*; *Industry4Europe (#11181)*. [2022.05.10/XD7481/t/**D**]

♦ Solar Influences Data Analysis Centre (SIDC) 19675

Address not obtained.
URL: http://sidc.oma.be/

History 1 Jan 1981, Brussels (Belgium), at Royal Observatory of Belgium, in cooperation with Locarno Specola Solare Ticinese (Switzerland) and Institute of Astronomy and Astrophysics, Free University of Brussels, taking over previous activities of Zurich (Switzerland) Federal Observatory. Original title: *Sunspot Index Data Centre – World Data Centre – Centre mondial de données pour les indices d'activité solaire*. Previously also referred to as *WDC-C for Sunspot Index*. Previously an analysis service of *Federation of Astronomical and Geophysical Data Analysis Services (FAGS, inactive)*. Part of the *ISC World Data System (ISC-WDS, #16024)*. Since 1 Jan 2000, also a Regional Warning Centre (RWC) of *International Space Environment Service (ISES, #15572)*. Other interested unions: *International Union of Geodesy and Geophysics (IUGG, #15776)*; *International Astronomical Union (IAU, #12287)*; *Union radio-scientifique internationale (URSI, #20475)*. Since 2003 one of the Service Development Activities (SDAs) of the ESA Space Weather Pilot Project, incorporated into *Space Weather European Network (SWENET, #19900)*. **Aims** Collect, analyse and provide data on solar activity and its consequences for the *environment* of the earth in space and on the earth itself by setting up a monitoring, alerting and forecasting service for *space weather*. **Structure** Includes all service activities of the Solar Physics Department of the Royal Observatory of Belgium. Several permanent scientists work in the team, one of which takes the role of main responsible and carries the title of SIDC Director. Administrative and technical staff assist in carrying out duties. **Languages** Dutch, English, French. **Finance** Bulletin fees; Belgian government; FAGS; IUGG; IAU; URSI; activities also supported by research projects. **Activities** Deduces daily, monthly, yearly and smoothed monthly Sunspot Numbers from local Wolf numbers observed by network, including from 40 stations (provisional Sunspot Number) to 110 stations (definitive Sunspot Number), with Locarno (Switzerland) as reference station. Since 1992, also provides daily provisional hemispheric sunspot numbers and their monthly means. Since 1 Jan 2000, distributes daily ursigrams with space weather data and forecasts, and fast alert warnings when required. Organizes *'European Space Weather Week'* (in Nov). **Events** *Annual European Space Weather Week* Liège (Belgium) 2014, *Annual European Space Weather Week* Antwerp (Belgium) 2013, *Annual European Space Weather Week* Bruges (Belgium) 2010, *European space weather week* Bruges (Belgium) 2009, *European space weather week* Brussels (Belgium) 2008. **Publications** *Sunspot Bulletin* (12 a year); *SIDC News* (4 a year) – daily, monthly, annual Sunspot Numbers, daily and monthly hemispheric Sunspot Numbers; *Quarterly Bulletin for Solar Activity* – International Sunspot Numbers, central zone Sunspot Numbers and estimates of the spotted area. Annual report to FAGS; reports to IAU commission 10; publications related to solar physics – statistical and spectral analysis of the sunspot time series, helioseismology, coronal structure, instruments. Sunspot data from 1812 (1 a day), 1750 (12 a year), 1700 (1 a year) and 1992 – hemispheric – online, e-mail and ftp files. **Members** Institutions; individuals. Membership countries not specified. [2019/XF0604/**E**]

♦ Solar Light for Africa (internationally oriented national body)

♦ SolarPower Europe 19676

CEO Rond-Point Robert Schuman 3, 1040 Brussels, Belgium. T. +3227095520. Fax +3227253284. E-mail: info@solarpowereurope.org.
Pres address not obtained.
URL: http://www.solarpowereurope.org/

History Mar 1985, London (UK). Former names and other names: *European Photovoltaic Industry Association (EPIA)* – former (1985). Registration: Banque-Carrefour des Entreprises, No/ID: 0427.557.687, Start date: 15 Apr 1985, Belgium; EU Transparency Register, No/ID: 2680046412-48, Start date: 22 Sep 2008. **Aims** Shape the regulatory environment and enhance business opportunities for *solar* power in Europe; promote solar-based energy solutions at European and national levels to policymakers and the energy sector; ensure financing and funding of solar-based energy solutions throughout Europe; communicate the benefits of *solar* power through all relevant communication channels. **Structure** General Meeting (annual); Board of Directors; Strategy Committee. **Languages** English. **Staff** 14 – 19. **Finance** Members' dues. **Activities** Events/meetings; research/documentation; advocacy/lobbying/activism; knowledge management/information dissemination. **Events** *Summit* Brussels (Belgium) 2022, *Summit* Brussels (Belgium) 2021, *Summit* Brussels (Belgium) 2020, *Digital Solar and Storage Conference* Brussels (Belgium) 2019, *Summit* Brussels (Belgium) 2019. **Publications** *Ahead of the Pack: Solar, the new Gateway to the decentralised Energy System*; *Designing EU Policy to Encourage New Solar Business Models*; *Digitalisation and Solar Report*; *EU-wide solar PV business models*; *Global Market Outlook for Solar Power 2018-2021*; *Operations and Maintenance Best Practices Guidelines Version 2.0*; *Solar PV Jobs and Value Added in Europe*; *Tenders for the Solar Projects*.
Members Upstream and downstream organisations (200) from the entire solar value chain: national PV associations, material and components, silicon, wafer and cells, module production, BOS (balance of system), systel and power sales. Company headquarters in 36 countries:
Austria, Belgium, Bulgaria, Canada, Chile, China, Croatia, Czechia, Denmark, Finland, France, Germany, Greece, Hungary, Ireland, Italy, Japan, Korea Rep, Latvia, Lithuania, Luxembourg, Netherlands, Norway, Poland, Portugal, Saudi Arabia, Slovakia, Slovenia, Spain, Sweden, Switzerland, Tunisia, Türkiye, UK, United Arab Emirates, USA.
IGO Relations Accredited by: *United Nations Framework Convention on Climate Change – Secretariat (UNFCCC, #20564)*. **NGO Relations** Member of (4): *Federation of European and International Associations Established in Belgium (FAIB, #09508)*; *Global Solar Council (GSC, #10609)*; *RE-Source Platform (RE-Source, #18916)* (Founding); *World Alliance for Efficient Solutions*. Technical Liaison Partner with: *European Committee for Electrotechnical Standardization (CENELEC, #06647)*. Sponsoring Supportive member of: *European Forum for Renewable Energy Sources (EUFORES, #07329)*. Instrumental in setting up: *Alliance for Rural Electrification (ARE, #00719)*. [2021/XD5421/**D**]

♦ **SOLAR** Sociedad Latinoamericana de Estudios sobre América Latina y el Caribe (#19406)
♦ **SoLAR** Society for Learning Analytics Research (#19587)
♦ Solar Solidarity International (unconfirmed)

♦ SOLARUNITED 19677

German Office Bruchköbeler Landstr 37, 63452 Hainau, Germany. T. +4961819828020. E-mail: ekus@ipvea.com.
Exec Dir PO Box 771507, Orlando FL 32877, USA. T. +14078569100.
URL: http://www.ipvea.org/

History Set up as *International Photovoltaic Equipment Association (IPVEA)*. Previously Also referred to as *International PV Equipment Association*. **Aims** Promote a path of cooperation and mutual support in achieving proactive solutions between all sectors within the Upstream *Photovoltaic* (PV) *Power* Generation and Battery Storage Technology value chain. **Structure** Board. **Finance** Sources: members' dues. **Events** *European Photovoltaic Solar Energy Conference* Hamburg (Germany) 2015, *European Photovoltaic Solar Energy Conference* Amsterdam (Netherlands) 2014, *European Photovoltaic Solar Energy Conference* Kyoto (Japan) 2014, *World Conference on Photovoltaic Energy Conversion* Kyoto (Japan) 2014, *International Photovoltaic Power Generation Conference* Shanghai (China) 2014. **Publications** *IPVEA Newsletter*. **NGO Relations** Founding member of: *International Battery and Energy Storage Alliance (IBESA)*. Member of: *European Technology and Innovation Platform Photovoltaics (ETIP PV, #08884)*. [2018/XJ5392/**C**]

♦ Solar Wind Conference (meeting series)
♦ SOLAS AGR 1996 – Agreement Concerning Specific Stability Requirements for Ro-ro Passenger Ships Undertaking Regular Scheduled International Voyages Between, to or from Designated Ports in North West Europe and the Baltic Sea (1996 treaty)
♦ SOLAS – International Convention for the Safety of Life at Sea, 1960 (1960 treaty)
♦ SOLAS – International Convention for the Safety of Life at Sea, 1974 (1974 treaty)
♦ SOLAS PROT 1988 – Protocol of 1988 Relating to the International Convention for the Safety of Life at Sea (1988 treaty)
♦ **SOLAS** Society of Lateral Access Surgery (#19586)
♦ **SOLAT** Sociedad Latinoamericana de Aterosclerosis (#19391)
♦ **SOLCHA** Sociedad Latinoamericana y Caribeña de Historia Ambiental (#19396)
♦ Soldiers for Peace / see Soldiers of Peace International Association (#19678)

♦ Soldiers of Peace International Association (SPIA) 19678

Association internationale des soldats de la paix (AISP)
Pres 178 rue Garibaldi, 69003 Lyon, France. T. +33478954503. Fax +33478603298. E-mail: direction@aisp.fr.
URL: http://www.aisp.fr/

History 1988, Lyon (France). Originally referred to as *Soldiers for Peace (SP)*. Currently also referred to in English as *International Association of Soldiers for Peace*. Registered in accordance with French law. **Aims** Inform civil population of the ONU mission; serve the principals of the Charter of the *United Nations*; assist people who have suffered casualties, widows and orphans; coordinate and contribute to *humanitarian* and peace actions; reinforce the bonds of friendship between people. **Structure** General Assembly (annual); Administrative Council. Officers: President; 4 Vice-Presidents. **Activities** Participates in conferences and debates on peace-keeping operations; intervenes with international organizations in order to contribute to the improvement of the statute of the blue helmets in the world and to peace. **Events** *Dynamisme et doctrine du maintien de la paix face à la diversité des intervenants – UE, OTAN, OSCE, ONU* Strasbourg (France) 2003, *Peacekeeping operations and their development* Paris (France) 1999. **Publications** *Bulletin d' Adhésion* (4 a year) – magazine; *Blue Helmet News* – journal.
Members National associations in 8 countries:
Denmark, Finland, France, Ireland, Norway, Russia, Sweden, Ukraine.
Individuals in 7 countries:
Fiji, Germany, Ghana, Kenya, Pakistan, UK, USA.
Consultative Status Consultative status granted from: *ECOSOC (#05331)* (General). **IGO Relations** *UNHCR (#20327)*. **NGO Relations** Member of (1): *International Campaign to Ban Landmines – Cluster Munition Coalition (ICBL-CMC, #12427)*. [2020/XE0096/**E**]

♦ SOLE – The International Society of Logistics 19679

Exec Dir DML, 14625 Baltimore Avenue, Ste 303, Laurel MD 20707-4902, USA. T. +13014598446. Fax +13014591522.
URL: http://www.sole.org/

History 1966, as *Society of Logistics Engineers*. Current title adopted, 1996. **Aims** Engage in scientific, educational and literary endeavours to enhance the art of logistics *technology*, education and management. **Languages** English. **Staff** 4.00 FTE, paid. **Finance** Budget (annual): US$ 1.5 million. **Activities** Events/metings; financial and/or material support; training/education; projects/programmes; networking/liaising. **Events** *Annual Conference* Jacksonville, FL (USA) 2012, *Annual Conference* Dallas, TX (USA) 2011, *Annual Conference* Dallas, TX (USA) 2010, *Annual Conference* Dallas, TX (USA) 2009, *Annual Conference* Orlando, FL (USA) 2008. **Publications** Technical papers.
Members Individuals and companies, mainly in USA but in a total of 55 countries and territories:
Argentina, Australia, Austria, Belgium, Brazil, Bulgaria, Canada, China, Cyprus, Czechia, Denmark, Dominican Rep, Finland, France, Germany, Greece, Guyana, Hong Kong, India, Indonesia, Iran Islamic Rep, Ireland, Israel, Italy, Jamaica, Japan, Kenya, Korea Rep, Luxembourg, Malaysia, Mexico, Montenegro, Netherlands, New Zealand, Nigeria, Norway, Philippines, Portugal, Romania, Russia, Saudi Arabia, Serbia, Singapore, South Africa, Spain, Sri Lanka, Sweden, Switzerland, Taiwan, Thailand, Türkiye, UK, United Arab Emirates, USA, Venezuela. [2016.01.04/XC0042/**F**]

♦ **SOLEPSI** Sociedad Latinoamericana de Estudiantes de Psicologia (#19405)
♦ SOLE – Student Organisation of Linguistics in Europe (unconfirmed)
♦ Solidaarisuus (internationally oriented national body)
♦ Solidagro (internationally oriented national body)

♦ SOLIDAR 19680

SG Avenue des Arts 50, Bte 5, 2ème étage, 1000 Brussels, Belgium. E-mail: communications@solidar.org.
Communications Officer address not obtained.
URL: http://www.solidar.org/

History 1948. Took over activities of the Matteotti Funds created, 1933, by the 2nd Socialist International, and on the initiative of *COMISCO*, a precursor of the reconstituted *Socialist International (SI, #19340)*. Moved to Brussels (Belgium), 1995. Former names and other names: *International Workers' Aid (IWA)* – former; *Entraide ouvrière internationale (EOI)* – former; *Internationales Arbeiter-Hilfswerk (IAM)* – former; *Ayuda Obrera Internacional (AOI)* – former; *COMISCO* – former. Registration: Banque-Carrefour des Entreprises, No/ID: 0458.458.721, Start date: 8 Aug 1996, Belgium; EU Transparency Register, No/ID: 31087615802-06, Start date: 9 May 2011. **Aims** Advance *social justice* through a Just Transition in Europe and worldwide. **Structure** General Assembly (annual); Board of Directors; Secretariat in Brussels (Belgium), headed by Secretary-General. Includes SOLIDAR Foundation. **Languages** Dutch, English, French, German, Italian, Spanish. **Staff** 13.00 FTE, paid. **Finance** Sources: members' dues. Erasmus+ supports SOLIDAR Foundation. Supported by: *European Commission (EC, #06633)*. **Activities** Advocacy/lobbying/activism; awards/prizes/competitions; events/meetings. **Events** *Annual General Assembly* Brussels (Belgium) 2003, *Annual General Assembly* Brussels (Belgium) 1998. **Publications** *Social Rights Monitor* – countries in EU and worldwide; *SOLIDAR NEWS Round Up*. Annual Report; briefings on thematic issues.
Members NGOs (60) in 27 countries. Membership countries not specified.
Included in the above, 12 organizations listed in this Yearbook:
Asamblea de Cooperación por la Paz (ACPP); *Fonds voor Ontwikkelingssamenwerking – Socialistische Solidariteit (FOS)*; *Foundation for European Progressive Studies (FEPS, #09954)*; *Foundation Max van der Stoel (FMS)*; *Instituto Sindical de Cooperación al Desarrollo, Madrid (ISCOD)*; *International Federation of Training Centres for the Promotion of Progressive Education (#13572)*; *International Federation of Workers' Education Associations (IFWEA, #13580)*; *International Solidarity Foundation (ISF)*; *Movement for Peace, Disarmament and Freedom (MPDL)*; *Olof Palme International Center, Stockholm*; *Solidarité laïque*; *Volunteering Matters*.
Affiliated members (17) in 14 countries:
Australia, Austria, Belgium, Bulgaria, Estonia, Germany, Italy, Latvia, Lithuania, North Macedonia, Portugal, Serbia, Slovakia, Spain.
Included in the above, 3 organizations listed in this Yearbook:
Foundation for European Progressive Studies (FEPS, #09954); *SAMARITAN INTERNATIONAL (#19046)*; *Union Aid Abroad-APHEDA*.
Consultative Status Consultative status granted from: *ILO (#11123)* (Special List). **IGO Relations** Observer status with (1): *International Organization for Migration (IOM, #14454)*. **NGO Relations** Member of (7): *Civil Society Europe*; *Confédération européenne des ong d'urgence et de développement (CONCORD, #04547)*; *European NGO Platform Asylum and Migration (EPAM, #08051)*; *Foundation for European Progressive Studies (FEPS, #09954)*; *Lifelong Learning Platform – European Civil Society for Education (LLLP, #16466)*; *SDG Watch Europe (#19162)*; *Social Platform (#19344)*. Cooperates with (2): *Group of the Progressive Alliance of Socialists and Democrats in the European Parliament (S and D, #10786)*; *Party of European Socialists (PES, #18249)*. [2023.02.16/XD5552/y/**F**]

♦ Solidaridad para el Desarrollo y la Paz (internationally oriented national body)
♦ Solidaridad, Educación y Desarrollo (internationally oriented national body)

- ♦ Solidaridad Foundation / see SOLIDARIDAD Network (#19681)
- ♦ Solidaridad Internacional (internationally oriented national body)
- ♦ Solidaridad Internacional Antifascista (inactive)
- ♦ Solidaridad Internacional para el Desarrollo y la Inversión (internationally oriented national body)
- ♦ Solidaridad entre Mujeres (internationally oriented national body)
- ♦ Solidaridad con Mujeres en Apuro (internationally oriented national body)

♦ SOLIDARIDAD Network 19681

Exec Dir 't Goylaan 15, 3525 AA Utrecht, Netherlands. T. +31302759450. E-mail: info@solidaridadnetwork.org.
URL: http://www.solidaridadnetwork.org/

History 1969. Founded by Catholic bishops as an Advent campaign to provide development aid to Latin America. Founded as a Dutch ecumenical organization, 15 June 1976. From 2010 became independent from the churches which gave way to the development of an international network organization composed of 8 legally bound Solidaridad organizations worldwide. Former names and other names: *Interkerkelijke Aktie voor Latijns Amerika (Solidaridad)* – former (1969 to 2010); *Interchurch Action for Latin America* – former (1969 to 2010); *Solidaridad Foundation* – former (2010 to Dec 2010); *Stichting Solidaridad* – former (2010 to Dec 2010). **Aims** Enable farmers and workers to earn a living income, shape their own future, and produce in balance with nature by working throughout the whole supply chain to make sustainability the norm. **Structure** International Supervisory Board; Continental Supervisory Boards (5); Executive Board of Directors; Regional Expertise Centres (8). **Languages** All local languages where Solidaridad works. **Staff** 985.00 FTE, paid. **Finance** Sources: fundraising; gifts, legacies; government support; grants; private foundations. Public and private funding from private persons and organizations; corporate funding. Annual budget: 56,306,000 EUR (2022). **Activities** Advocacy/lobbying/activism; awareness raising; capacity building; knowledge management/information dissemination; networking/liaising; politics/policy/regulatory; training/education. **NGO Relations** Member of (6): *Better Cotton Initiative (BCI, #03218); European Partnership for Responsible Minerals (EPRM, #08159); Global Coffee Platform (GCP, #10298); Global Roundtable for Sustainable Beef (GRSB, #10583); Sustainable Apparel Coalition (SAC); World Benchmarking Alliance (WBA, #21228).* Partner of (2): *Mastercard Foundation; Tropical Forest Alliance (TFA, #20249).* Instrumental in setting up (2): *Impunity Watch (#11138); Max Havelaar Foundation.* Subscriber to: *ISEAL (#16026).*
[2023.02.14/XN1437/**F**]

- ♦ Solidaridad Olimpica (#17721)
- ♦ Solidaridad / see SOLIDARIDAD Network (#19681)
- ♦ Solidaritat per al Desenvolupament i la Pau (internationally oriented national body)
- ♦ **SOLIDARIOS** Consejo de Fundaciones Americanas de Desarrollo (#04712)
- ♦ SOLIDARIOS, Council of American Development Foundations (#04712)
- ♦ Solidarität mit Frauen in Not (internationally oriented national body)
- ♦ Solidaritätsdienst International (internationally oriented national body)
- ♦ Solidaritätsfonds für Soziale Befreiungskämpfe in der Dritten Welt (internationally oriented national body)
- ♦ Solidarité (internationally oriented national body)
- ♦ Pour la Solidarité (internationally oriented national body)
- ♦ Solidarité chrétienne internationale (#03909)
- ♦ Solidarité et coopération médicale au Tiers-monde (internationally oriented national body)
- ♦ Solidarité eau / see Programme Solidarité eau (#18529)
- ♦ Solidarité Eau Europe (internationally oriented national body)
- ♦ Solidarité et Entraide / see Solidarité protestante
- ♦ Solidarité étudiants du Monde (internationally oriented national body)
- ♦ Solidarité Etudiants Tiers-Monde / see Solidarité étudiants du Monde

♦ Solidarité européenne, Luxembourg 19682

Contact address not obtained. E-mail: osp-se@ec.europa.eu.
URL: http://www.solidarite-euro.org/

History to unite personnel of *European Commission (EC, #06633)* based in Luxembourg. **NGO Relations** Member of: *Confédération syndicale européenne (CSE, no recent information).* Together with: *Confédération syndicale des fonctionnaires du Parlement européen (inactive), Syndicat autonome du personnel de la Cour des comptes européenne (inactive)* and SFE (Brussels), co-founder of *European Public Service Union (#08303).*
[2014/XE2535/**E**]

- ♦ Solidarité européenne pour une participation égale des peuples / see Europe External Programme with Africa (#09155)
- ♦ Solidarité européenne pour une participation égalitaire entre les peuples / see Europe External Programme with Africa (#09155)
- ♦ Solidarité avec des femmes en détresse (internationally oriented national body)
- ♦ Solidarité internationale (unconfirmed)
- ♦ Solidarité internationale antifasciste (inactive)
- ♦ Solidarité internationale pour le développement et l'investissement (internationally oriented national body)
- ♦ Solidarité Internationale LGBTQI (internationally oriented national body)
- ♦ Solidarité internationale des maisons familiales rurales (see: #02719)
- ♦ Solidarité internationale sur les transports et la recherche en Afrique sub-saharienne (internationally oriented national body)
- ♦ Solidarité laïque (internationally oriented national body)
- ♦ Solidarité Laurentides Amérique centrale (internationally oriented national body)
- ♦ Solidarité Mondiale / see WSM
- ♦ Solidarité olympique (#17721)
- ♦ Solidarité et partenariat Nord-Sud (internationally oriented national body)
- ♦ Solidarité protestante (internationally oriented national body)
- ♦ Solidarités / see Solidarités International
- ♦ Solidarités agricoles et alimentaires (internationally oriented national body)
- ♦ Solidarités agroalimentaires / see Solidarités agricoles et alimentaires
- ♦ Solidarités – Aide humanitaire d'urgence / see Solidarités International
- ♦ Solidarite para sa Mga Babaeng Nasa Mahirap ang Katayuan (internationally oriented national body)
- ♦ Solidarité sans frontières, Berne (internationally oriented national body)
- ♦ Solidarités International (internationally oriented national body)
- ♦ Solidarités internationales / see Solidarités International
- ♦ Solidarité socialiste – Fonds de coopération au développement (internationally oriented national body)
- ♦ Solidaritetsaksjon for utvikling (internationally oriented national body)
- ♦ Solidarité union coopération / see SUCO

♦ Solidarity for ASEAN People's Advocacy (SAPA) 19683

Contact c/o Forum-Asia, SPD Building 3rd Floor, 79/2 Krungthonburi Road, Khlong Ton Sai, Khlong San, Bangkok, 10600, Thailand. E-mail: info@forum-asia.org.

History 3 Feb 2006, Bangkok (Thailand). 3-4 Feb 2006, Bangkok (Thailand). Former names and other names: *Solidarity for Asian People's Advocacy (SAPA)* – former. **Structure** General Forum (meets annually). Regional Steering Group. Working Groups and Committee (3): WG-ASEAN; Human Right Council (WG-HRC); Migration and Labour (WG-ML). **Events** *General forum* Kathmandu (Nepal) 2010, *General forum* Bangkok (Thailand) 2008, *General forum* Bangkok (Thailand) 2007. **NGO Relations** Organizations involved: *Asian Forum for Human Rights and Development (FORUM-ASIA, #01491); Asian Partnership for the Development of Human Resources in Rural Asia (AsiaDHRRA, #01654); Focus on the Global South (Focus, #09807); Migrant Forum in Asia (MFA, #16798); South East Asian Committee for Advocacy (SEACA, #19761); Third World Network (TWN, #20151).*
[2019/XJ0385/**F**]

- ♦ Solidarity for Asian People's Advocacy / see Solidarity for ASEAN People's Advocacy (#19683)
- ♦ Solidarity Center (internationally oriented national body)
- ♦ Solidarity Among Children in Africa and the World (internationally oriented national body)
- ♦ Solidarity for Development and Peace (internationally oriented national body)
- ♦ Solidarity with East Timor (internationally oriented national body)
- ♦ Solidarity, Education and Development (internationally oriented national body)
- ♦ Solidarity Fund for the Social Struggles for Liberation in the Third World (internationally oriented national body)
- ♦ Solidarity Humanity International Aid / see MyRight – Empower People with Disabilities
- ♦ Solidarity Human Rights Inclusion Accessibility / see MyRight – Empower People with Disabilities
- ♦ Solidarity International (internationally oriented national body)
- ♦ Solidarity in Literacy (internationally oriented national body)
- ♦ Solidarity Tourism for Development (internationally oriented national body)
- ♦ Solidarity Water Europe (internationally oriented national body)
- ♦ Solidarity among Women – Development Initiatives for Women in the Third World (internationally oriented national body)
- ♦ Solidarity With Women in Distress (internationally oriented national body)
- ♦ SolidarMed (internationally oriented national body)
- ♦ SolidarMed – Schweizer Organisation für Gesundheit in Afrika / see SolidarMed
- ♦ Solid Handle – Arabo-African Union of Ageing, Pensioners and of Intergenerational Alliance (no recent information)
- ♦ SOLIFONDS – Solidaritätsfonds für Soziale Befreiungskämpfe in der Dritten Welt (internationally oriented national body)
- ♦ SOLOVE / see Colegio Latinoamericano de Oftalmólogos Veterinarios (#04094)
- ♦ Sol sem Fronteiras (internationally oriented national body)
- ♦ **SOL** Society for Organizational Learning (#19613)
- ♦ SOL – Solanaceae Conference (meeting series)

♦ Solution Mining Research Institute (SMRI) 19684

Address not obtained.
URL: http://www.solutionmining.org/

History 1959, as Brine Cavity Research Group (BCRG). Present name adopted 1965. **Aims** Sponsor and engage in research related to solution mining, cavern storage and utilization and *environmental* effects thereof. **Finance** Members' dues. **Events** *Fall Conference* Berlin (Germany) 2019, *Spring Conference* New York, NY (USA) 2015, *Fall Conference* Santander (Spain) 2015, *Fall Conference* Groningen (Netherlands) 2014, *Spring Conference* San Antonio, TX (USA) 2014.
Members Full companies. Honorary individuals. Members in 19 countries:
Australia, Austria, Belgium, Canada, China, Denmark, France, Germany, Mexico, Netherlands, Norway, Poland, Portugal, Russia, Switzerland, Thailand, Türkiye, UK, USA.
[2012/XM3115/j/**E**]

♦ Solutions in Organisations Link-up (SOLWorld) 19685

Contact 26 Christchurch Road, Cheltenham, GL50 2PL, UK. T. +441242511441. Fax +441242510941.
URL: http://www.solworld.org/

History 2002. Former names and other names: *Sharing and Building Solution Focused Practice in Organizations* – alias; *SOL* – former. **Aims** Promote the use of Solutions Focused ideas at work, in consulting, managing, training, HR practice, strategic planning, performance management, team building and *organizational development.* **Structure** Steering Group. **Languages** English. **Finance** Sources: meeting proceeds. **Activities** Events/meetings; training/education. **Events** *International Conference* Stockholm (Sweden) 2014, *International Conference* Bad Pyrmont (Germany) 2013, *International Conference* Oxford (UK) 2012, *International Conference* Balatonfüred (Hungary) 2011, *International Conference* Bucharest (Romania) 2010. **Publications** *Positive Approaches to Change: Applications of Solutions Focus and Appreciative Inquiry at Work* (2005).
Members Individuals (over 1,500). Membership countries not specified.
[2018/XJ3082/**F**]

- ♦ SOLWODI – Solidarity With Women in Distress (internationally oriented national body)
- ♦ **SOLWorld** Solutions in Organisations Link-up (#19685)
- ♦ Somali Studies International Association (internationally oriented national body)
- ♦ Somascan Fathers – Clerics Regular of Somasca (religious order)
- ♦ SOMA – Sharing of Ministries Abroad (internationally oriented national body)
- ♦ SOMA – Société d'oto-rhino-laryngologique du Maghreb arabe (inactive)
- ♦ **SoMeCoP** Société méditerranéenne de coloproctologie (#16676)
- ♦ **SOMED** Society for Microbial Ecology and Disease (#19596)
- ♦ SOMET – International Conference on Intelligent Software Methodologies, Tools, and Techniques (meeting series)
- ♦ Sommet euro-asiatique / see Asia-Europe Meeting (#01272)
- ♦ Sommet européen (meeting series)
- ♦ Sommet franco-africain (meeting series)
- ♦ Sommet de la Francophonie / see Conférence au sommet des chefs d'Etat et de gouvernement des pays ayant le français en partage (#04648)
- ♦ **Sommet de la Francophonie** Conférence au sommet des chefs d'Etat et de gouvernement des pays ayant le français en partage (#04648)
- ♦ Sommet de la grande région (meeting series)
- ♦ Sommet des huit pays les plus industrialisés / see Group of Eight (#10745)
- ♦ Sommet mondial de la nordicité (meeting series)
- ♦ Sommet des pays les plus industrialisés / see Group of Eight (#10745)
- ♦ Sommet des sept / see Group of Eight (#10745)
- ♦ Sommet des sept pays les plus industrialisés / see Group of Eight (#10745)
- ♦ Sommets des parlements d'Europe (meeting series)
- ♦ SOMO – Stichting Onderzoek Multinationale Ondernemingen (internationally oriented national body)
- ♦ **SOMP** Society of Mining Professors (#19597)
- ♦ SOM – School of Metaphysics (internationally oriented national body)
- ♦ **SONA** Society of Neuroscientists of Africa (#19608)
- ♦ SONGE / see Soutien aux ONG à l'Est et au Sud
- ♦ SONGES – Soutien aux ONG à l'Est et au Sud (internationally oriented national body)
- ♦ Sonke Gender Justice Network (internationally oriented national body)
- ♦ Sons of Charity – Canossians (religious order)
- ♦ **SonSEu** Science on Stage Europe (#19142)
- ♦ Sons of the Holy Family (religious order)
- ♦ Sons of the Immaculate Conception (religious order)
- ♦ Sons of Mary Immaculate, Fathers of Chavagnes (religious order)
- ♦ Sons of Mary Immaculate – Pavonians (religious order)
- ♦ **SON** Sociedad de Ornitologia Neotropical (#19431)
- ♦ **SON** Society of Nematologists (#19604)
- ♦ SOPAC – Pacific Islands Applied Geoscience Commission (inactive)
- ♦ **SOPAC** Société panafricaine de cardiologie (#18066)
- ♦ SOPANOC – Sociedad Panamericana de Oculoplastica (no recent information)
- ♦ SOPAR-Bala Vikasa (internationally oriented national body)
- ♦ SOPA – Society of Publishers in Asia (internationally oriented national body)
- ♦ Sopimus elatusavun perimisestä pakkotoimin (1962 treaty)
- ♦ Sopimus Euroopan Perustuslaista (2004 treaty)
- ♦ Sopimus kulttuuriyhteistyöstä (1971 treaty)
- ♦ Sopimus Pohjoismaiden yhteisistä työmarkkinoista (1982 treaty)
- ♦ Sopimus Suomen, Islannin, Norjan, Ruotsin ja Tanskan viranomaisten ja laitosten välisestä yhteistyöstä ammatillisen kuntoutuksen ja työllisyyskoulutuksen alalla (1982 treaty)
- ♦ Sopimus Tanskan, Suomen, Islannin, Norjan ja Ruotsin välillä eräiden kansalaisuutta koskevien määräysten voimaansaattamisesta (2002 treaty)
- ♦ Sopimus Tanskan, Suomen, Islannin, Norjan ja Ruotsin välillä pääsystä korkeampaan koulutukseen (1996 treaty)
- ♦ Sopimus Tanskan, Suomen, Islannin, Norjan ja Ruotsin välillä perintö- ja lahjaveroja koskevan kaksinkertaisen verotuksen välttämiseksi (1989 treaty)

- ♦ **SOPLA** Sociedad de Oftalmologia Pediatrica Latinoamericana (#19430)
- ♦ Sorelle della Carità di San Vincenzo de Paoli (religious order)
- ♦ Sorelle Mariane di Schönstatt (religious order)
- ♦ Sorelle della Misericordia (religious order)
- ♦ Sorghum ID – Sorghum – International Development (unconfirmed)
- ♦ Sorghum – International Development (unconfirmed)
- ♦ Sorig Khang International (unconfirmed)
- ♦ SORLL – Societas Oto-Rhino-Laryngologica Latina (inactive)
- ♦ Soroptimist Federation of the Americas / see Soroptimist International of the Americas (#19688)

♦ Soroptimist International (SI) 19686

Pres 8A Romsey Terrace, Cambridge, CB1 3NH, UK. T. +441223311833. E-mail: hq@soroptimistinternational.org – admin@soroptimistinternational.org.
URL: http://www.soroptimistinternational.org/

History 1928, Washington, DC (USA). Founded uniting the American Federation – the first Soroptimist Club having been established in 1921, Oakland CA (USA) – with the European Federation, which had developed from the first Soroptimist club in Europe, the Greater London (UK) Club, set up 1923; each Federation was self-governed and self-supporting. In 1934, the Federation of Soroptimist Clubs of Great Britain and Ireland was formed as a third Federation, separate from the European. The Association functioned through a Liaison Secretary until 1952 when International Officers and a Governing body were elected. In 1978, the SI/South West Pacific was formed as a fourth Federation. Soroptimist International Africa Federation (SIAF) was inaugurated 30 June 2020. Former names and other names: *Soroptimist International Association (SIA)* – former; *Association soroptimiste internationale* – former; *Asociación Internacional Soroptimista* – former. **Aims** Create a world where women and girls together achieve their individual and collective potential, realize aspirations and have an equal voice in creating strong, peaceful communities worldwide; inspire action and create opportunities to transform the lives of *women* and girls through a global network of members and international partnerships. **Structure** International Board; Officers; Standing Committees. **Languages** English. **Staff** 4.00 FTE, paid. **Finance** Sources: members' dues. **Events** *Convention* Dublin (Ireland) 2023, *100 Year Anniversary Meeting* Cambridge (UK) 2021, *Nordic Soroptimist Meeting* Oslo (Norway) 2020, *Convention* Kuala Lumpur (Malaysia) 2019, *Convention* Istanbul (Turkey) 2015. **Publications** *Global Voice* (12 a year) – newsletter. Periodicals issued by Regional Federations.

Members In all, comprises about 72,000 club members in 126 countries and territories:
Albania, Anguilla, Antigua-Barbuda, Argentina, Australia, Austria, Bangladesh, Barbados, Belgium, Benin, Bolivia, Bosnia-Herzegovina, Brazil, Bulgaria, Burkina Faso, Cameroon, Canada, Chile, China, Colombia, Côte d'Ivoire, Croatia, Cyprus, Czechia, Denmark, Ecuador, Egypt, Estonia, Ethiopia, Fiji, Finland, France, Gambia, Georgia, Germany, Ghana, Greece, Grenada, Guadeloupe, Guam, Guernsey, Guiana Fr, Guinea, Haiti, Hungary, Iceland, India, Indonesia, Ireland, Isle of Man, Israel, Italy, Jamaica, Japan, Jersey, Kenya, Korea Rep, Kosovo, Kuwait, Latvia, Liechtenstein, Lithuania, Luxembourg, Madagascar, Malawi, Malaysia, Mali, Malta, Martinique, Mauritius, Mexico, Moldova, Monaco, Mongolia, Morocco, Netherlands, New Caledonia, New Zealand, Niger, Nigeria, Norway, Pakistan, Panama, Papua New Guinea, Paraguay, Peru, Philippines, Poland, Portugal, Puerto Rico, Réunion, Romania, Russia, Rwanda, Samoa, San Marino, Senegal, Seychelles, Sierra Leone, Singapore, Slovakia, Slovenia, Solomon Is, South Africa, Spain, Sri Lanka, St Vincent-Grenadines, Sudan, Suriname, Sweden, Switzerland, Tahiti Is, Taiwan, Thailand, Togo, Trinidad-Tobago, Tunisia, Türkiye, Turks-Caicos, Uganda, UK, Ukraine, United Arab Emirates, USA, Venezuela, Zimbabwe.

Member Federations (5):
Soroptimist International Africa Federation (SIAF, #19687); Soroptimist International of Europe (SI/E, #19689); Soroptimist International of Great Britain and Ireland (SIGBI, #19690); Soroptimist International of the Americas (SIA, #19688); Soroptimist International South East Asia Pacific (SISEAP, #19691).

Consultative Status Consultative status granted from: *ECOSOC (#05331)* (General); *UNESCO (#20322)* (Consultative Status); *FAO (#09260)* (Liaison Status); *ILO (#11123)* (Special List); *UNICEF (#20332)*; *UNIDO (#20336)*; *UNEP (#20299)*. **IGO Relations** Associated with Department of Global Communications of the United Nations. **NGO Relations** Member of (14): *Alliance of NGOs on Crime Prevention and Criminal Justice (#00709); Committee of NGOs on Human Rights, Geneva (#04275); Conference of Non-Governmental Organizations in Consultative Relationship with the United Nations (CONGO, #04635); NGO Committee on Financing for Development, New York (#17108)* (Full member); *NGO Committee on Mental Health, New York NY (#17111); NGO Committee on Sustainable Development, Vienna (#17119); NGO Committee on the Status of Women, Geneva (#17117); NGO Committee on the Status of Women, New York NY (see: #04635); NGO Committee on UNICEF (#17120); NGO Forum on Environment (FOE, #17125); NGO-UNESCO Liaison Committee (#17127); Ockenden International; Vienna NGO Committee on Drugs (VNGOC, #20773); Vienna NGO Committee on the Status of Women (#20775).* [2021.09.02/XB3245/y/**B**]

♦ Soroptimist International Africa Federation (SIAF) 19687

Address not obtained.
URL: https://siafrica.org/

History A member federation of *Soroptimist International (SI, #19686)*. Former names and other names: *Soroptimist International – Future African Federation* – alias. **Aims** Enhance human rights and the status of women and girls so they can achieve their individual and collective potential, realize aspirations and have an equal voice in creating strong, peaceful communities worldwide. **Structure** General Assembly; African Federation Board. **Events** *General Assembly* Abidjan (Côte d'Ivoire) 2021.

Members Full in 26 countries:
Benin, Burkina Faso, Cameroon, Côte d'Ivoire, Egypt, Gambia, Ghana, Guinea, Kenya, Madagascar, Malawi, Mali, Mauritius, Morocco, Niger, Nigeria, Rwanda, Senegal, Seychelles, Sierra Leone, South Africa, Tanzania UR, Togo, Tunisia, Uganda, Zimbabwe. [2021/AA2099/**D**]

♦ Soroptimist International of the Americas (SIA) 19688

Soroptimist international des Amériques

Dir 1709 Spruce St, Philadelphia PA 19103-6103, USA. T. +12158939000. Fax +12158935200. E-mail: siahq@soroptimist.org.
URL: http://www.soroptimist.org/

History 1921, Oakland, CA (USA). Founded as a federation of *Soroptimist International (SI, #19686)*. Former names and other names: *American Federation of Soroptimist Clubs* – former (1921); *Soroptimist Federation of the Americas* – former. **Aims** Maintain high *ethical* standards in *business, professions*, and other aspects of life; strive for *human rights* and, in particular, advance the status of *women*; develop the spirit of *friendship* and unity among Soroptimists of all countries; quicken the spirit of service and human *understanding*; contribute to international understanding and universal friendship. **Structure** Comprises clubs set up within the area assigned by SI, each club being assigned to a region in that area (some regions divided into districts). Board of Directors, consisting of President, President-Elect, Secretary-Treasurer and 10 other members. Regional Officers: Governor, Secretary, Treasurer and/or Board members according to regional standing procedures. **Languages** English. **Staff** 20.00 FTE, paid. **Finance** Sources: members' dues. **Activities** Awards/prizes/competitions; events/meetings; projects/programmes. **Events** *Biennial Convention* Bellevue, WA (USA) 2024, *Biennial Convention* 2022, *Biennial Convention* Bellevue, WA (USA) 2020, *Japan Chuo Region Conference* Kyoto (Japan) 2019, *Board of Directors Meeting* Montréal, QC (Canada) 2019. **Publications** *The Soroptimist of the Americas.*

Members Comprises 1,466 clubs with a total membership of over 45,000 women in 19 countries and territories:
Argentina, Bolivia, Brazil, Canada, Chile, Costa Rica, Ecuador, Guam, Japan, Korea Rep, Mexico, Panama, Paraguay, Peru, Philippines, Puerto Rico, Taiwan, USA, Venezuela.

IGO Relations Associated with Department of Global Communications of the United Nations. [2022/XE9319/**E**]

- ♦ Soroptimist international des Amériques (#19688)
- ♦ Soroptimist International Association / see Soroptimist International (#19686)

♦ Soroptimist International of Europe (SI/E) 19689

Soroptimist International d'Europe

Exec Dir Route de Florissant 72, 1206 Geneva, Switzerland. T. +41223460880. E-mail: siehq@soroptimisteurope.org.
URL: http://www.soroptimisteurope.org/

History 1928, Paris (France). First Club: 1924, France; first Union: 1927, Netherlands; first Associated Club: 1972, Madagascar; first Single Club: 1978, Monaco. Current Constitution and By-Laws approved at Governors' Meeting, Mar 1979, Noordwijk (Netherlands) and most recently amended by Governors' Meeting in 2021 (online). One of 5 Federations of *Soroptimist International (SI, #19686)*. **Aims** Maintain high *ethical* standards in *business, profession* and other aspects of life; strive for *human rights* for all people; in particular, advance the status of *women*; develop a spirit of friendship and unity among Soroptimists of all countries; quicken the spirit of service and human understanding; contribute to international understanding and universal friendship. **Structure** Committee of Governors (convenes annually); Board; Technical Committees; Programme Coordinators. **Languages** English, French. **Staff** 5.00 FTE, paid. **Finance** Sources: members' dues. **Activities** Financial and/or material support; projects/programmes; training/education. **Events** *Governors Meeting* Kortrijk (Belgium) 2022, *Governors meeting* Geneva (Switzerland) 2021, *Governors Meeting* Zagreb (Croatia) 2019, *Governors meeting* Lucerne (Switzerland) 2018, *European Quadrennial Congress* Florence (Italy) 2017. **Publications** *The Link Newsletter* (12 a year). *Le Trait d'union.*

Members Unions of Soroptimist Clubs and Single Clubs in 43 countries:
Armenia, Austria, Belgium, Benin, Bosnia-Herzegovina, Bulgaria, Croatia, Cyprus, Czechia, Denmark, Estonia, Finland, France, Georgia, Germany, Greece, Haiti, Hungary, Iceland, Israel, Italy, Kosovo, Kuwait, Latvia, Liechtenstein, Lithuania, Luxembourg, Moldova, Monaco, Netherlands, Norway, Poland, Portugal, Romania, Russia, San Marino, Slovakia, Slovenia, Spain, Sweden, Switzerland, Türkiye, Ukraine.

Consultative Status Consultative status granted from: *Council of Europe (CE, #04881)* (Participatory Status); *ECOSOC (#05331)* (Special). **NGO Relations** Member of (2): *European Women's Lobby (EWL, #09102); Women for Water Partnership (WfWP, #21041).* [2022.05.04/XD8740/**E**]

- ♦ Soroptimist International d'Europe (#19689)
- ♦ Soroptimist International – Future African Federation / see Soroptimist International Africa Federation (#19687)
- ♦ Soroptimist international de Grande-Bretagne et d'Irlande (#19690)

♦ Soroptimist International of Great Britain and Ireland (SIGBI) 19690

Soroptimist international de Grande-Bretagne et d'Irlande

Sec 2nd Floor, Beckwith House, 1-3 Wellington Road North, Stockport, SK4 1AF, UK. T. +441614807686. Fax +441614776152. E-mail: hq@sigbi.org.
Membership/Website Officer address not obtained.
URL: http://www.sigbi.org/

History Set up as one of 4 federations of *Soroptimist International (SI, #19686)*. Registered as a charity in England and Wales: 1179433. **Aims** Commit to a world where *women* and *girls* together achieve their individual and collective potential, realize aspirations and have an equal voice in creating strong, peaceful communities worldwide. **Structure** Board of Directors. **Languages** English. **Staff** 3.00 FTE, paid. **Finance** Members' dues. **Activities** Advocacy/lobbying/activism; awareness raising; conflict resolution; events/meetings; financial and/or material support; healthcare; knowledge management/information dissemination; monitoring/evaluation; projects/programmes. **Events** *Annual Conference* Manchester (UK) 2018, *Annual Conference* Cardiff (UK) 2017, *Annual Conference* St Julian's (Malta) 2016, *Annual Conference / Conference* Glasgow (UK) 2015, *Annual Conference / Conference* Harrogate (UK) 2014. **Publications** *Soroptimist News* – online publication and App.

Members Soroptimist clubs (320) with 8,000 individual members in 28 countries and territories:
Anguilla, Bangladesh, Barbados, Cameroon, Gambia, Grenada, Guernsey, India, Ireland, Jamaica, Jersey, Malawi, Malta, Mauritius, Nepal, Nigeria, Pakistan, Seychelles, Sierra Leone, South Africa, Sri Lanka, St Vincent-Grenadines, Tanzania UR, Trinidad-Tobago, Turks-Caicos, Uganda, UK, Zimbabwe.

Consultative Status Consultative status granted from: *ECOSOC (#05331)* (Special). **NGO Relations** Member of: *International Campaign to Ban Landmines – Cluster Munition Coalition (ICBL-CMC, #12427).* [2019.04.24/XE4018/**E**]

- ♦ Soroptimist international du Pacifique Sud-Ouest / see Soroptimist International South East Asia Pacific (#19691)

♦ Soroptimist International South East Asia Pacific (SISEAP) 19691

Admin Dir PO Box 1400, Strawberry Hills NSW 2012, Australia. T. +61280966072. Fax +61296902261. E-mail: hq@siswp.org.
www.siseap.org: https://siseap.org/

History 1978, as one of 4 federations of *Soroptimist International (SI, #19686)*. Former names and other names: *Soroptimist International of the South West Pacific (SI/SWP)* – former (6 Jun 2022); *Soroptimist international du Pacifique Sud-Ouest* – former (6 Jun 2022). **Aims** Transform the lives and status of women and girls through education, empowerment and enabling opportunities. **Structure** A network of Clubs. **Activities** Events/meetings. **Events** *Convention* Sydney, NSW (Australia) 2016, *Biennial Conference / Convention* Kuching (Malaysia) 2014, *Biennial Conference / Convention* Greymouth (New Zealand) 2012, *Biennial Conference / Convention* Gold Coast, QLD (Australia) 2010, *Biennial conference / Convention* Chiang Rai (Thailand) 2008.

Members Clubs (131) with about 2,500 individual members in 13 countries and territories:
Australia, Cambodia, Fiji, Hong Kong, Indonesia, Malaysia, Mongolia, Myanmar, New Zealand, Papua New Guinea, Samoa, Singapore, Thailand.

Consultative Status Consultative status granted from: *ECOSOC (#05331)* (Special). **IGO Relations** Operational relations with: *UNESCO (#20322).* [2023.02.14/XE9626/**E**]

- ♦ Soroptimist International of the South West Pacific / see Soroptimist International South East Asia Pacific (#19691)
- ♦ Sorores Divini Salvatoris (religious order)
- ♦ Sosaiyiti fi Kyaribiyan Linggwistiks (#19530)
- ♦ SOS Amazonia Association (internationally oriented national body)
- ♦ SOS Bambini Senza Frontiere (internationally oriented national body)
- ♦ SOS boîtes de lait (internationally oriented national body)

♦ SOS Catastrophes – European Disaster Victims Network (SOS Catastrophes) 19692

Contact Place des Barricades 1, 1000 Brussels, Belgium. T. +32465726287.
Facebook: https://www.facebook.com/pages/category/Non-Governmental-Organization – NGO-/SOS-Catastrophes-European-network-of-victims-595987493829427/

History 2013. Registration: Belgium. **Aims** Facilitate mutual assistance between disaster victims; promote solidarity within the community in response to such tragedies. **Structure** Board of Directors; Committees. **Members** Full; Support; Associate. Membership countries not specified. [2015/XJ8845/**F**]

- ♦ **SOS Catastrophes** SOS Catastrophes – European Disaster Victims Network (#19692)
- ♦ SOS Children's Villages International (#19693)
- ♦ SOS Chrétiens d'Orient (internationally oriented national body)
- ♦ SOS Christians of the Middle East (internationally oriented national body)
- ♦ SOS Cristiani d'Oriente (internationally oriented national body)
- ♦ SOS-enfants sans frontières (internationally oriented national body)
- ♦ SOS Faim – Action pour le développement – SOS Faim (internationally oriented national body)
- ♦ SOSF – Save our Seas Foundation (internationally oriented national body)
- ♦ SOSF – Solidarité sans frontières, Berne (internationally oriented national body)
- ♦ SOS Hunger – Aktion für die Entwicklung (internationally oriented national body)
- ♦ Sosiaalidemokraattien ja ay-liikkeen pohjoismaiseen (#19045)
- ♦ SOSJ – Sisters of Saint Joseph of the Sacred Heart (religious order)

♦ SOS-Kinderdorf International 19693

SOS Children's Villages International – SOS Villages d'Enfants International – Aldeas Infantiles-SOS Internacional

COO Hermann-Gmeiner-Str 51, 6020 Innsbruck, Austria. Fax +4351233105085. E-mail: info@sos-childrensvillages.org.
URL: http://www.sos-kinderdorfinternational.org/

History 1949, Imst (Austria), by Hermann Gmeiner, when first SOS Children's Village was set up. International organization set up 1960, as the umbrella organization for all national SOS children's associations. Statutes revised and adopted 1993, Innsbruck (Austria). Current statutes adopted by 18th ordinary General Assembly, 2008, Innsbruck (Austria). **Aims** Provide direct services in areas of care, education and health for children and young people at risk of losing parental care, and those who have lost parental care; build capacity of children's caregivers, their families and communities to provide adequate care. **Structure** General Assembly (every 4 years); International Senate; Management Council; General Secretariat, consisting of international office and regional offices. **Languages** English, French, German, Spanish. **Staff** 35000.00 FTE, paid. General Secretariat (2010): 386. **Finance** Main source: private and corporate donations. Activities often coordinated by government departments or existing agencies; services funded through domestic governmental subsidies. SOS Promoting and Supporting Agencies raise 84% of total financial revenue. **Activities** Humanitarian/emergency aid; projects/programmes; training/education. **Events** *General Assembly* Innsbruck (Austria) 2016, *Meeting* Innsbruck (Austria) 2013, *General Assembly* Innsbruck (Austria) 2012, *General Assembly* Innsbruck (Austria) 2008, *General Assembly* Innsbruck (Austria) 2003. **Publications** *Care for Me*; *I Matter*. Annual Report; reports; studies.
Members National associations; promoting and supporting associations. Members in 134 countries and territories:
Albania, Algeria, Angola, Argentina, Armenia, Australia, Austria, Azerbaijan, Bangladesh, Belarus, Belgium, Benin, Bolivia, Bosnia-Herzegovina, Botswana, Brazil, Bulgaria, Burkina Faso, Burundi, Cambodia, Cameroon, Canada, Cape Verde, Central African Rep, Chad, Chile, China, Colombia, Congo DR, Costa Rica, Côte d'Ivoire, Croatia, Cyprus, Czechia, Denmark, Djibouti, Dominican Rep, Ecuador, Egypt, El Salvador, Equatorial Guinea, Estonia, Eswatini, Ethiopia, Finland, France, Gambia, Georgia, Germany, Ghana, Greece, Guatemala, Guinea, Guinea-Bissau, Haiti, Honduras, Hungary, Iceland, India, Indonesia, Iraq, Israel, Italy, Jamaica, Japan, Jordan, Kazakhstan, Kenya, Korea Rep, Kosovo, Kyrgyzstan, Laos, Latvia, Lebanon, Lesotho, Liberia, Lithuania, Luxembourg, Madagascar, Malawi, Mali, Mauritius, Mexico, Mongolia, Morocco, Mozambique, Namibia, Nepal, Netherlands, Nicaragua, Niger, Nigeria, North Macedonia, Norway, Pakistan, Palestine, Panama, Paraguay, Peru, Philippines, Poland, Polynesia Fr, Portugal, Romania, Russia, Rwanda, Senegal, Serbia, Sierra Leone, Somalia, South Africa, South Sudan, Spain, Sri Lanka, Sudan, Sweden, Switzerland, Syrian AR, Taiwan, Tanzania UR, Thailand, Togo, Tunisia, Uganda, UK, Ukraine, Uruguay, USA, Uzbekistan, Venezuela, Vietnam, Zambia, Zimbabwe.
Consultative Status Consultative status granted from: *ECOSOC (#05331)* (Special); *Council of Europe (CE, #04881)* (Participatory Status); *African Committee of Experts on the Rights and Welfare of the Child (ACERWC, #00257)* (Observer Status). **IGO Relations** Associated with Department of Global Communications of the United Nations. **NGO Relations** Accredited by (1): *International Child and Youth Care Network (CYC-Net)*. Member of (10): *Eurochild (#05657)*; *Girls not Brides (#10154)*; *Global Coalition to End Child Poverty (#10292)*; *Global Partnership to End Violence Against Children (End Violence Against Children, #10533)*; *International Foster Care Organization (IFCO, #13663)*; *Keeping Children Safe*; *NetHope (#16979)*; *NGO Committee on UNICEF (#17120)*; *SDG Watch Europe (#19162)*; *Transparency, Accountability and Participation Network (TAP Network, #20222)*. Supports (1): *End Corporal Punishment (#05457)*. Shareholder in: *International Civil Society Centre (#12589)*. [2018.10.23/XB3246/**B**]

♦ SOS Layettes (internationally oriented national body)
♦ SOS Layettes Solidarité et Développement / see SOS Layettes

♦ SOS MEDITERRANEE 19694

Communications Manager Postbox 44 03 52, 12003 Berlin, Germany. T. +493023525682. E-mail: contact@sosmediterranee.org.
Main Website: https://en.sosmediterranee.org/

History May 2015. **Aims** Rescue and advocate on behalf of all people in distress at sea. **Structure** A network with teams in France, Germany, Italy and Switzerland jointly financing and operating a rescue ship. **Languages** English, French, German, Italian. **Activities** Advocacy/lobbying/activism; humanitarian/emergency aid. **NGO Relations** Member of (1): *United4Rescue*. [2022.10.19/AA1022/**F**]

♦ **SO** Solidarité olympique (#17721)
♦ **SOSORT** International Society on Scoliosis Orthopaedic and Rehabilitation Treatment (#15437)
♦ SOS racisme international (internationally oriented national body)

♦ SOS SAHEL 19695

CEO 2 avenue Jeanne, 72604 Asnières-sur-Seine CEDEX, France. T. +33146889370. E-mail: contact@sossahel.org.
URL: http://www.sossahel.org/

History 1976, Dakar (Senegal), by Sahelians and Europeans concerned by the consequences of the desertification. Original full title: *Association SOS-Sahel International*. Previously also referred to as *SOS-SAHEL International*. Registered in accordance with the Senegalese law. Registered in accordance with French law. **Aims** Assist villagers of Sahel to manage their own rural development and to strive to achieve alimentary self-sufficiency; hinder rural emigration and alleviate the work of women. **Structure** General Assembly; Board of Directors; Permanent Team. **Languages** English, French. **Finance** Grants; subsidies. Budget (annual) about euro 5,335,715. **Activities** Advocacy/lobbying/activism. **Events** *Annual general assembly* Paris (France) 1996, *Annual General Assembly* Nouakchott (Mauritania) 1993, *Annual General Assembly* Dakar (Senegal) 1986. **Publications** *La lettre du Sahel* (4 a year). Annual activity report.
Members SOS-Sahel International associations in 9 countries:
Burkina Faso, France, Luxembourg, Mali, Mauritania, Niger, Senegal, Sudan, UK.
IGO Relations Accredited to the Conference of the Parties of: *Secretariat of the United Nations Convention to Combat Desertification (Secretariat of the UNCCD, #19208)*. **NGO Relations** Full member of: *British Overseas NGO's for Development (BOND)*. Member of: *Consortium of Christian Relief and Development Association (CCRDA)*; *Council of Non-Governmental Organizations for Development Support (#04911)*; *Groupe de Travail Désertification (GTD)*. [2015/XD7603/**F**]

♦ SOS-SAHEL International / see SOS SAHEL (#19695)
♦ SOS – Save Our Seas (internationally oriented national body)
♦ SOS – Save Our Species (unconfirmed)
♦ **SOS** Science of Spirituality / Sawan Kirpal Ruhani Mission (#19141)
♦ SOS – Secular Organizations for Sobriety (internationally oriented national body)
♦ SOS – Share Our Strength (internationally oriented national body)
♦ SOSSI – Scouts on Stamps Society International (internationally oriented national body)
♦ Sostrene af det dyrebare blod (religious order)
♦ SOSUPE – Sociedad Sudamericana de Psicologia del Deporte (no recent information)
♦ SOS Villages d'Enfants International (#19693)
♦ SOS Wereldhandel / see Fair Trade Original
♦ Sosyété pou lengwistik kawayib-la (#19530)
♦ SOTA – Stichting Onderzoek Turkestan (internationally oriented national body)

♦ Soteria International 19696

Main office Avdeoerevej 35, 2980 Kokkedal, Denmark. T. +4530953679.
URL: http://soteriainternational.org/

History Jul 2007. **Aims** Establish a constructive dialogue between state and social actors together with *spiritual* practitioners in order to decrease the gap of misunderstanding and stop abuse of human rights that result from it. **Structure** International centre; national offices. **Languages** English. **Finance** Members' dues. Donations. **Activities** Events/meetings; networking/liaising. **Events** *International conference on peace for the 21st century / Conference* Berlin (Germany) 2009, *International conference on spiritual human rights / Conference* Copenhagen (Denmark) 2009. **Members** Individuals and organizations. Membership countries not specified. **IGO Relations** *European Parliament (EP, #08146)*. **NGO Relations** Member of: *European Federation for Freedom of Belief (FOB)*. [2017.12.16/XJ8146/**E**]

♦ SOTO-A – SOTO Australasia (internationally oriented national body)
♦ SOTO Australasia (internationally oriented national body)
♦ SOTO-E – SOTO Europe (internationally oriented national body)
♦ SOTO Europe (internationally oriented national body)
♦ **SOTO-I** Sacro Occipital Technic Organization International (#19021)
♦ SOTO-SA – SOTO Sudamérica (unconfirmed)
♦ SOTO Sudamérica (unconfirmed)

♦ Soudni dvur Evropskych Spolecentstvi / see Court of Justice of the European Union (#04938)
♦ Soudniho dvora Evropské Unie (#04938)
♦ SOUFFLE – Groupement professionnel des organismes d'enseignement du français langue étrangère (internationally oriented national body)
♦ The Soul of Europe (#00772)

♦ A Soul for Europe (ASF) 19697

Contact c/o European House for Culture, Sainctelettesquare 17, 1000 Brussels, Belgium. T. +3226444800. E-mail: asfe@houseforculture.eu.
Germany office c/o Stiftung Zukunft Berlin, Klingelhoferstr 7, 10785 Berlin, Germany. T. +493026392290. Fax +4930263922922. E-mail: mail@asoulforeurope.eu.
URL: https://asoulforeurope.eu/

History Emerged from 1st Berlin Conference, 2004. A grouping of the type *European Economic Interest Grouping (EEIG, #06960)*. Registration: Banque-Carrefour des Entreprises, No/ID: 0809.751.347, Start date: 11 Feb 2009, Belgium. **Aims** Connect and mobilize citizens and democratic institutions across Europe, fostering a sense of *responsibility* for the future of Europe and *democracy* through *culture*; connect communities so as to build a commont European public space and a culture of proactive citizenship. **Structure** Advisory Board; Strategy Group, subdivided into Topic Groups and City Clusters. EEIG Board. Offices (4): Amsterdam (Netherlands); Berlin (Germany); Brussels (Belgium); Porto (Portugal). Associated partner offices in: Belgrade (Serbia); Tbilisi (Georgia). **Languages** English. **Staff** 4.00 FTE, voluntary. **Finance** Financed by members of the EEIG. **Activities** Events/meetings; projects/programmes; knowledge management/information dissemination; advocacy/lobbying/activism. **Events** *A Soul for Europe Conference* Berlin (Germany) 2019, *Conference* Berlin (Germany) 2015. **Publications** No regular publications.
Members Partners in 20 countries:
Albania, Armenia, Austria, Belgium, Croatia, France, Georgia, Germany, Hungary, Italy, Moldova, Montenegro, Netherlands, Portugal, Romania, Serbia, Slovenia, Sweden, Türkiye, UK.
Included in the above, 31 organizations listed in this Yearbook:
– *Analytical Centre on Globalization and Regional Cooperation (ACGRC)*;
– *British Council*;
– *Calouste Gulbenkian Foundation*;
– *Deutscher Akademischer Austauschdienst (DAAD)*;
– *EUROCITIES (#05662)*;
– *Europa Nostra (#05767)*;
– *European Alternatives (EA, #05891)*;
– *European Cities and Regions for Culture (LIKE, #06554)*;
– *European Committee of the Regions (CoR, #06665)*;
– *European Cultural Foundation (ECF, #06868)*;
– *European Cultural Parliament (ECP, #06870)*;
– *European Economic and Social Committee (EESC, #06963)*;
– *European Festivals Association (EFA, #07242)*;
– *European Forum Alpbach (#07304)*;
– *European League of Institutes of the Arts (ELIA, #07670)*;
– *European Stability Initiative (ESI, #08828)*;
– *European University Institute (EUI, #09034)*;
– *European Youth Forum (#09140)*;
– *EUSTORY (#09202)*;
– *IETM – International Network for Contemporary Performing Arts (#11098)*;
– *Institut für Auslandsbeziehungen, Stuttgart (ifa)*;
– *Institut Jacques Delors (IJD)*;
– *International Network for Educational Exchange (INEX)*;
– *King Baudouin Foundation (KBF)*;
– *Konrad Adenauer Foundation (KAF)*;
– *Network for Reporting on Eastern Europe (n-ost)*;
– *Network of European Foundations (NEF, #17019)*;
– *Robert Bosch Foundation*;
– *Southeast European Cooperative Initiative (SECI, #19812)*;
– *Trans Europe Halles – A Network of Independent Cultural Centres (TEH, #20211)*;
– *Verein für Sprach- und Kulturaustausch in Mittel-, Ost- und Südosteuropa (MitOst)*.
IGO Relations *European Commission (EC, #06633)*; *European Parliament (EP, #08146)*. **NGO Relations** Member of (1): *Citizens for Europe (CFEU, #03956)*. [2022/XJ9591/**E**]

♦ Sound and Music Computing Network (SMC) 19698

Pres AC Meyers Vaenge 15, 2450 Copenhagen, Denmark.
URL: http://www.smcnetwork.org/

Structure Board; Steering Committee. **Activities** Events/meetings. **Events** *Sound and Music Computing Conference* Malaga (Spain) 2019. [2020/AA0784/**F**]

♦ Sound Seekers – Commonwealth Society for the Deaf (inactive)
♦ Sounds of Lusofonia Association (#02335)
♦ Source européenne de rayonnement synchrotron / see European Synchrotron Radiation Facility (#08868)
♦ Sources d'Europe – Centre d'information sur l'Europe / see Toute l'Europe
♦ SOU – Scandinavian Ornithologists Union (inactive)
♦ SOU – Skandinaviske Ornitologiske Union (inactive)

♦ South African Council of Churches (SACC) 19699

Gen Sec Khotso House, 62 Marshall Street, Johannesburg, 2001, South Africa. T. +27112417800. Fax +27114921448. E-mail: support@sacc.org.za.
URL: http://www.sacc.org.za/

History 1968. **Aims** Give expression to the Lordship of Christ over every aspect and area of human life by promoting the spiritual, social, intellectual and physical welfare of all people; foster that unity which is both God's will for creation and God's gift to the Church. **Structure** National Conference (every 3 years). Central Committee (meets at least once a year). Executive Committee, including President, Vice-President and General Secretary. **Finance** Members' fees. **Events** *Triennial Conference* Kempton Park (South Africa) 2014.
Members Full; observer; associate; affiliate. Churches (26), including 14 Churches listed in this Yearbook: *African Methodist Episcopal Church (AME)*; *Anglican Church of Southern Africa (ACSA, #00826)*; *Council of African Instituted Churches (no recent information)*; *International Federation of Christian Churches (IFCC, #13389)*; *Methodist Church of Southern Africa*; *Presbyterian Church of Africa (PCA, #18485)*; *Religious Society of Friends (Quakers, #18834)*; *Salvation Army (#19041)*; *Southern African Catholic Bishops' Conference (SACBC, #19838)*; *United Congregational Church of Southern Africa (UCCSA, #20503)*; *United Evangelical Lutheran Church in Southern Africa (UELCSA)*; *Uniting Presbyterian Church in Southern Africa (UPCSA, #20668)*; *Uniting Reformed Church in Southern Africa (URCSA)*; *Volkskerk van Afrika*. [2016/XM2238/y/**D**]

♦ South African Institute of International Affairs (internationally oriented national body)
♦ South African Society for Plant Pathology / see Southern African Society for Plant Pathology (#19863)
♦ South African Society of University Teachers in Accounting / see Southern African Accounting Association (#19834)
♦ South America Indian Mission / see South America Mission
♦ South America Mission (internationally oriented national body)

♦ South American Academy of Cosmetic Surgery (SAACS) 19700

Pres Santiago del Estero 102, Martinez, 1640 Buenos Aires, Argentina. T. +541147922061 – +541147938240. Fax +541147938240.

History 1998. **Aims** Promote teaching and research in the field of cosmetic surgery; promote and diffuse information through congresses, courses and publication of papers. **Languages** English, Spanish. **Activities** Organizes International Congress of Medicine and Cosmetic Surgery (always in Buenos Aires, Argentina). **Events** *International congress of medicine and cosmetic surgery* Buenos Aires (Argentina) 2008, *International symposium of applied aesthetics* Buenos Aires (Argentina) 2008, *International symposium* Buenos Aires (Argentina) 2008, *International Congress of Medicine and Cosmetic Surgery* Buenos Aires (Argentina) 2006, *International Symposium of Applied Aesthetics* Buenos Aires (Argentina) 2006. **NGO Relations** Division of: *International Academy of Cosmetic Surgery (IACS, #11543)*. [2015/XE4294/**E**]

♦ South American Agreement on Narcotic Drugs and Psychotropic Substances (1973 treaty)
♦ South American Armwrestling Confederation (inactive)
♦ South American Association of the Chlor-Alkali and Derivatives Industry / see Latin American Chlor-Alkali and Derivatives Industry Association (#16295)
♦ South American Association of Geopolitical and International Studies, Montevideo (no recent information)
♦ South American Association of Master Athletes (#02299)
♦ South American Association of Theological Institutions / see Association of Seminaries and Theological Institutions (#02912)
♦ South American Atherosclerosis Group (inactive)

♦ South American Athletic Confederation 19701

Confédération sudaméricaine d'athlétisme – Confederación Sudamericana de Atletismo (CONSUDATLE)

Contact Av Pedro Teixeira 400 – Bloco 3, Dom Pedro I Vila Olimpica de Manaus, Manaus AM, 69040-000, Brazil. E-mail: south-america@aa.iaaf.org.
URL: http://www.consudatle.org/

History 24 May 1918, Buenos Aires (Argentina), by delegates from Argentina, Chile and Uruguay, during a ceremony commemorating Argentinian independence. Registered in accordance with Brazilian laws, 20 Sep 1993. **Aims** Unite South American associations, federations and confederations which promote and govern athletics in their respective countries; issue regulations and adopt measures, in accordance with constitution and regulations of IAAF; homologate South American records from affiliated organs, providing they have been set according to IAAF norms; organize South American Championships and other events in the area, establishing rules and regulations for their execution; promote ethical values and combat all kinds of doping and of racial, political, religious or any other kind of discrimination within sport; promote development of athletics in South America and diffusion of technical knowledge within member federations; grant titles of honorary member, awards and other distinctions to persons or organizations which have distinguished themselves in developing and promoting athletics. **Structure** Congress of member federations (annual, in connection with the South American Championships). Council (meets at least twice a year), comprising President, Vice-President and 3 other Directors elected by each member body. Secretariat in the country of the President's residence. **Languages** Spanish. **Staff** Employees, paid; directors, voluntary. **Finance** Members' dues. Other sources: grants from IAAF; sponsorship programme. **Activities** Organizes every year: Marathon, Race Walking, Cross Country and Junior Championships; Grand Prix, Half Marathon and Road Race Circuits; Road Mile; South American 10 Miles Championships. Even-numbered years – Youth Championships; odd-numbered years – Senior Championships. **Events** *Annual Congress* Manaus (Brazil) 2001, *Annual Congress* São Leopoldo (Brazil) 2000, *Annual Congress* Bogota (Colombia) 1999, *Annual Congress* Bogota (Colombia) 1999, *Annual Congress* Manaus (Brazil) 1998. **Publications** *Atletismo Sudamericano Magazine* (3 a year); *El Atletismo Sudamericano* (annual). *Libro de Oro del Atletismo Sudamericano* (1999); *Historia del Atletismo 1867-1958* by Luis Galvez Chipoco; *Historia del Atletismo 1968-1991* by Pedro Galvez Velarde.
Members National Athletic Confederations, Federations and Associations in 13 countries:
Argentina, Bolivia, Brazil, Chile, Colombia, Ecuador, Guyana, Panama, Paraguay, Peru, Suriname, Uruguay, Venezuela.
NGO Relations Continental association of: *World Athletics (#21209)*. Member of: *Asociación de Confederaciones Deportivas Sudamericanas (ACODESU, no recent information)*. [2017/XD3932/**D**]

♦ South American Athletics Officials Association (inactive)
♦ South American Badminton Confederation (#04481)
♦ South American Billiards Confederation (inactive)
♦ South American Bowling Confederation (#04483)
♦ South American Brain Research Organization (inactive)
♦ South American Commission for the Control of Foot-and-Mouth Disease (#04143)
♦ South American Community of Nations / see Union of South American Nations (#20481)
♦ South American Confederation of Pediatric Societies / see Latin American Pediatric Association (#16360)

♦ South American Confederation of Squash 19702

Confederación Sudamericana de Squash Racket (CSSR)

Pres 360 Street 1121, Ranelagh, 1876 Buenos Aires, Argentina. T. +541142588923. Fax +541142588923. E-mail: presidenciasudamericasquash@hotmail.com.

History 1982. Also referred to as *South American Squash Federation*. **Aims** Promote, organize and develop the *game* of squash in South America. **Structure** Annual General Meeting. General Committee, consisting of President, Honorary Secretary and Presidents of affiliated national associations. Executive Committee, comprising President, Honorary Secretary and other members. **Finance** Members' dues. Other sources: income from activities; sponsorship. **Activities** Approves, auspices and organizes or delegates the organization of all major international squash events in South America and between member countries; organizes the South American squash players ranking order; encourages the formation of referees and trainers of squash and similar activities.
Members National associations in 9 countries:
Argentina, Brazil, Chile, Colombia, Ecuador, Paraguay, Peru, Uruguay, Venezuela.
NGO Relations Member of: *Asociación de Confederaciones Deportivas Sudamericanas (ACODESU, no recent information)*; *Federación Panamericana de Squash (FPS, #09384)*. [2010/XE4094/**E**]

♦ South American Confederation of Subaquatic Activities (no recent information)
♦ South American Cycling Confederation (inactive)
♦ South American Esports Confederation (unconfirmed)
♦ South American Federation of YMCAs / see Latin American and Caribbean Alliance of YMCAs (#16264)
♦ South American Fencing Confederation (#04486)

♦ South American Gelatin Manufacturers Association (SAGMA) 19703

Asociación de Fabricantes de Gelatina de América del Sur – Associação dos Fabricantes de Gelatina da América do Sul

Secretariat Rua Salvador Correa 364, Aclimaçao, Sao Paulo SP, 04109-070, Brazil. E-mail: sagmasec@arnet.com.ar.
URL: http://www.sagma-gelatina.com/

NGO Relations Cooperates with: *Gelatin Manufacturers Association of Asia Pacific (GMAP, #10089)*; *Gelatin Manufacturers Association of Europe (GME, #10090)*. [2014/XD6507/**D**]

♦ South American Golf Confederation (no recent information)
♦ South American Gymnastics Confederation (#04488)
♦ South American Handball Confederation (no recent information)

♦ South American Judo Confederation 19704

Confederación Sudamericana de Judo (CSJ)

Pres c/o CAJ, 9 de Julio 2015, Dpto 9, 5003 Córdoba, Argentina.
URL: http://mmunoz950.wixsite.com/sudamericanajudo/

NGO Relations Affiliated with: *Pan American Judo Union (PJU, #18115)*; *South American Sports Organization (SASO, #19708)*. [2017/XJ4317/**D**]

♦ South American Karate Confederation (#04489)
♦ South American Maritime Pilots Federation (no recent information)
♦ South American Missionary Society / see South American Mission Society (#19705)
♦ South American Mission Prayer League / see World Mission Prayer League

♦ South American Mission Society (SAMS International) 19705

UK Office c/o Church Mission Society, Watlington Road, Oxford, OX4 6BZ, UK. T. +441865787400. E-mail: info@churchmissionsociety.org.
URL: http://www.samsinternational.org/

History 1844, UK. Founded to carry on missionary work within *The Anglican Church of South America (#00825)*. SAMS Great Britain integrated into *Church Mission Society (CMS)*, Feb 2010. Former names and other names: *South American Missionary Society* – former (1864 to 1995); *Patagonia Missionary Society* – former (1844 to 1864). Registration: Companies House, No/ID: 00065048, Start date: 15 Feb 1900, England; Charity Commission, No/ID: 221328, Start date: 16 Jul 1963, England and Wales. **Aims** Enable and encourage Latin Americans and Iberians to train their own church leadership within the framework of the *Anglican* and Episcopalian churches and continue as an evangelistic and missionary church in their own right. **Languages** English, Portuguese, Spanish. **Staff** 41.00 FTE, paid. **Finance** Donations; voluntary contributions. **Events** *International conference* Swanwick (UK) 1995.
Members Chapters and individuals. Members in 20 countries:
Angola, Argentina, Australia, Bolivia, Brazil, Canada, Chile, Ecuador, Guatemala, Honduras, Ireland, Mozambique, New Zealand, Paraguay, Peru, Portugal, Spain, UK, Uruguay, USA.
NGO Relations Member of: *Global Connections*; *Jubilee Research (#16158)*; *Partnership for World Mission (PWM)*. [2020/XD0434/**D**]

♦ South American Modern Pentathlon Confederation (#04492)
♦ South American Museums Association (inactive)
♦ South American Ostomy Association (inactive)
♦ South American Panathlon Confederation (inactive)
♦ South American Pelota Confederation (inactive)
♦ South American Petroleum Institute (inactive)
♦ South American Postal Convention (1911 treaty)
♦ South American Postal Order Convention (1911 treaty)
♦ South American Regional Agreement on Radiocommunications, 1935 (1935 treaty)
♦ South American Regional Agreement on Radiocommunications, 1937 (1937 treaty)
♦ South American Regional Agreement on Radiocommunications, 1940 (1940 treaty)
♦ South American Rugby Confederation / see Sudamérica Rugby (#20030)

♦ South American Sailing Confederation 19706

Confederación Sudamericana de Vela

Pres c/o Chilean Sailing Federation, Ramon Cruz No 1176 – of 401, Santiago, Santiago Metropolitan, Chile. T. +5626358323. Fax +56226358323. E-mail: presidente@fedevela.cl.
URL: http://www.csudamvela.org/

NGO Relations Affiliate member of: *World Sailing (#21760)*. Affiliated with: *South American Sports Organization (SASO, #19708)*. [2016/XJ4315/**D**]

♦ South American Society of Cardiology 19707

Sociedad Sudamericana de Cardiologia (SSC)

Contact Av Garibaldi 2593, 11600 Montevideo, Uruguay. T. +59824806567. Fax +59824872565. E-mail: presidencia@sscardio.org.
URL: http://www.sscardio.org/

History 4 Dec 1962, as *Union of Cardiology Societies of South America – Union de Sociedades de Cardiologia de América del Sur (USCAS)*. Present name adopted, 2006. **Events** *Biennial Congress* Santiago (Chile) 2021, *Biennial Congress* Santiago (Chile) 2020, *Biennial Congress* Peru 2018, *Biennial Congress* Pereira (Colombia) 2016, *Biennial Congress* Quito (Ecuador) 2014.
Members Full in 10 countries:
Argentina, Bolivia, Brazil, Chile, Colombia, Ecuador, Paraguay, Peru, Uruguay, Venezuela. [2014/XD6164/**D**]

♦ South American Society for Comparative Physiology and Biochemistry (inactive)
♦ South American Society for Surgery of the Hand (inactive)
♦ South American Softball Confederation (no recent information)
♦ South American Sport Psychology Society (no recent information)

♦ South American Sports Organization (SASO) 19708

Organisation sportive sudaméricaine – Organización Deportiva Sudamericana (ODESUR)

Office Autopista Nu Guasu, Parque Olimpico, Gran Asunción, Luque, Central, Paraguay. T. +59521649650. E-mail: info@odesur.org.
URL: http://www.odesur.org/

History 27 Mar 1976, La Paz (Bolivia). Former names and other names: *Organización Deportiva Suramericana* – alias. **Structure** Congress; Executive Committee, comprising President, 2 Vice-Presidents, Treasurer, General Secretary, Executive Secretary. **Languages** Spanish. **Staff** 1.50 FTE, voluntary. **Finance** Members' dues. Other sources: South American Games. Budget (annual): US$ 500. **Activities** Sporting activities. **Events** *Academic congress* Asunción (Paraguay) 1998, *Academic congress* Córdoba (Argentina) 1997, *Academic congress* Medellin (Colombia) 1997, *Academic congress* Montevideo (Uruguay) 1996.
Members National Olympic Committees in 15 countries and territories:
Argentina, Aruba, Bolivia, Brazil, Chile, Colombia, Ecuador, Guyana, Neth Antilles, Panama, Paraguay, Peru, Suriname, Uruguay, Venezuela.
NGO Relations Partner of (1): *Global ESports Federation (GEF, #10348)*.
Recognized by: *International Olympic Committee (IOC, #14408)*. Affiliated organizations:
– *Confederación Panamericana de Bochas (CPB, #04470)*;
– *Confederación Panamericana de Taekwondo (no recent information)*;
– *Confederación Sudamericana de Bowling (#04483)*;
– *Confederación Sudamericana de Esgrima (#04486)*;
– *Confederación Sudamericana de Gimnasia (#04488)*;
– *Confederación Sudamericana de Handball (no recent information)*;
– *Confederación Sudamericana de Karate (CSK, #04489)*;
– *Confederación Sudamericana de Lucha (#04490)*;
– *Confederación Sudamericana de Natación (CONSANAT, #04491)*;
– *Confederación Sudamericana de Softbol (no recent information)*;
– *Pan American Hockey Federation (PAHF, #18110)*;
– *South American Judo Confederation (#19704)*;
– *South American Sailing Confederation (#19706)*;
– *South American Triathlon Confederation (#19710)*. [2018/XD1703/**D**]

♦ South American Squash Federation / see South American Confederation of Squash (#19702)
♦ South American Structural Engineering Association (#02336)
♦ South American Sumo Union (no recent information)
♦ South American Swimming Confederation (#04491)
♦ South American Table Tennis Confederation (#04493)
♦ South American Taekwondo Confederation (no recent information)

♦ South American Tennis Confederation 19709

Confederación Sudamericana de Tenis (COSAT)

Technical Coordinator Avenida Santisimo Sacramento 3100, Asunción, Paraguay. E-mail: cosat@cosat.org.
URL: https://cosat.org/

History 20 Oct 1947. **Languages** English, Spanish. **Events** *Congress* Brasilia (Brazil) 2006. **Publications** *Boletin Noticosat* (6 a year).
Members National federations in 10 countries:
Argentina, Bolivia, Brazil, Chile, Colombia, Ecuador, Paraguay, Peru, Uruguay, Venezuela.
NGO Relations Member of (2): *Asociación de Confederaciones Deportivas Panamericanas (ACODEPA, #02119)*; *Asociación de Confederaciones Deportivas Sudamericanas (ACODESU, no recent information)*. Affiliated regional association of: *International Tennis Federation (ITF, #15676)*. [2018/XD6640/**D**]

♦ South American Thoroughbred Breeding Organization (#17850)

♦ South American Triathlon Confederation 19710

Confederación Sudamericana de Triatlón (COSUTRI)

Vice-Pres Ramsay 2496, 6e Piso, C1428 BAN Buenos Aires, Argentina. T. +541147884433 – +5411(5491162109685.

Structure Officers: President, Vice-President, Secretary-General. **Languages** Portuguese, Spanish. **Staff** 3.00 FTE, paid. **NGO Relations** Affiliated with: *South American Sports Organization (SASO, #19708)*. [2015.02.05/XJ4316/**D**]

♦ South American Union of Engineers' Associations (inactive)

♦ South American University Sports Confederation 19711

Confederación Sudamericana Universitaria de Deportes (COSUD) – Confederação Sulamericana de Esportes

Pres address not obtained.
Sec FEDUP, Estadio Nacional Puerta 13, 2do Piso, 01, Lima, Peru. T. +5113323783. Fax +5114316530.

History Founded 1985. **Structure** General Assembly. **Events** *South American University Games* Brazil 2008, *South American University Games* Curitiba (Brazil) 2006.
Members in 10 countries:
Argentina, Bolivia, Brazil, Chile, Colombia, Ecuador, Paraguay, Peru, Uruguay, Venezuela.
IGO Relations Agreement signed with: *Consejo Sudamericano de Deportes (CONSUDE, #04726).*
[2016/XM1300/D]

♦ South American Volleyball Confederation (#04495)
♦ South American Weightlifting Confederation (inactive)
♦ South American Wrestling Confederation (#04490)
♦ South America Powerlifting Federation (#09393)

♦ South Asia Alliance for Poverty Eradication (SAAPE) 19712

Coordinator GPO Box 8130, 288 Gairidhara Marg, Gairidhara, Kathmandu, Nepal. T. +97714004976 – +97714004813 – +97714004985. Fax +97714004508. E-mail: saape@saape.org – praman@saape.org.
URL: http://www.saape.org/

History Founded Dec 2001, Kathmandu (Nepal), following a consultation, 2000, Manesar (India). **Aims** Fight against poverty and injustice in South Asia. **Structure** General Assembly; Annual General Meeting; Core Committee; Campaign Focal Organisations; Secretariat. **Languages** English. **Staff** 4.00 FTE, paid. **Finance** Support from funding agencies. **Activities** Policy research; advocacy; lobbying; campaigns; meeting activities. **Publications** *South Asia Poverty Report* (every 3 years); *SAAPE Newsletter*. *Regional Status Papers of Thematic Areas.* Proceedings.
Members Country focal organizations in 7 countries:
Afghanistan, Bangladesh, India, Maldives, Nepal, Pakistan, Sri Lanka.
IGO Relations *European Union (EU, #08967); South Asian Association for Regional Cooperation (SAARC, #19721).* **NGO Relations** *European Network on Debt and Development (EURODAD, #07891); Europe External Programme with Africa (EEPA, #09155); Financial Transparency Coalition (FTC, #09772); Humanistisch Instituut voor Ontwikkelingssamenwerking (Hivos); Jubilee South – Asian Peoples' Movement on Debt and Development (JSAPMDD, #16160); LDC Watch (#16412); Oxfam Novib; Oxfam International (#17922); Social Watch (#19350).* [2020/XF6662/F]

♦ South Asia Association of National Scout Organization (unconfirmed)

♦ South Asia Centre for Policy Studies (SACEPS) 19713

Contact c/o RIS, Core 4B, Fourth Floor, India Habitat Centre Lodhi Road, Delhi 110003, DELHI 110003, India. E-mail: dgoffice@ris.org.in.
URL: http://saceps.org.in/

History 1998. First housed at Centre for Policy Research, Delhi (India), 1999. Jul 2000 moved to Centre for Policy Dialogue, Dhaka (Bangladesh). Moved permanently to Kathmandu (Nepal) following Board Meeting decision, Aug 2005. MOU signed with Ministry of Foreign Affairs of the Government of Nepal, 3 Jan 2009. Founding institutions include: Centre for Policy Dialogue, Bangladesh; *Research and Information System for Developing Countries, India (RIS, India)*; Centre for Policy Research, India; *Institute for Integrated Development Studies (IIDS)*; Lahore University of Management Science, Pakistan; Institute for Policy Studies, Sri Lanka; *Marga Institute.* **Aims** Serve as an independent think tank for regional cooperation and integration; promote policy dialogue, research and interaction between policy makers, business community and civil society by drawing a wider constituency of people committed to promoting regional cooperation in South Asia; strengthen and influence national as well as regional policy making processes. **Structure** Board of 26 members – representing Bangladesh, Bhutan, India, Maldives, Nepal, Pakistan and Sri Lanka – including 2 Co-Chairs. Executive Committee; International Advisors; Executive Director. Secretariat located in Kathmandu (Nepal). **Languages** English. **Staff** 5.00 FTE, paid. 4 interns. **Finance** Core institutional support (3 year period, effective Oct 2007) from *Ford Foundation (#09858).* Funds also from *'Supporting Network of Research Institutes and Think Tanks in South Asia Phase II (RETA 6417)'.* **Activities** Overarching research area includes both national and regional policy issues. Project, together with International IDEA, to develop the South Asia Democratic Charter. Works as implementing agency for RETA 6417. Provides set of recommendations to the SAARC Summit for consideration as part of the final Declaration to enhance the process of regional integration in South Asia. Organizes regional conferences and seminars. **Publications** *SACEPS Newsletter. Economic and Political Empowerment of the Poor* (2009) – monograph series; *Structural Dimensions of the Poverty in Nepal* (2009) – monograph series; *Poverty Reduction Strategies in South Asia: A Comparative Study* (2007) – monograph series; *Poverty Reduction Strategies of the International Development Community: The Scope for Structural Change* (2007) – monograph series. Policy papers; books; maps. [2015/XJ0986/E]

♦ South Asia Cooperative Environment Programme (SACEP) 19714

Programme coopératif sur l'environnement pour l'Asie du Sud

Dir Gen 69/4 Maya Avenue, Colombo, 06, Sri Lanka. T. +94112596443. Fax +94112589369. E-mail: info@sacep.org.
URL: http://www.sacep.org/

History 1982, upon adoption of the Colombo (Sri Lanka) Declaration and the Articles of Association of SACEP at the meeting of South Asian Environment Ministers, Feb 1981, Colombo. Secretariat in Colombo, under a host country agreement with Government of Sri Lanka. **Aims** Promote regional cooperation in South Asia in the field of environment, both natural and human, in the context of *sustainable development* and on issues of economic and social development, which also impinge on the environment and vice versa; support *conservation* and management of *natural resources* of the region; work closely with all national, regional and international institutions, governmental and non-governmental, as well, as experts and groups engaged in such cooperation and conservation efforts. **Structure** Governing Council (meets periodically), represented at the ministerial level. Consultative Committee, comprising representatives of Diplomatic Missions of member countries. Secretaries of Ministries of the Environment serve as National Focal Points. Secretariat. **Languages** English. **Staff** At Secretariat: Director General; professional, administrative and support staff. **Finance** Members' contributions. Other sources: hosting facilities provided by government of Sri Lanka; project based funds from various bilateral and multilateral donor agencies. **Activities** Advocacy/lobbying/activism. Serves as secretariat for: *Action Plan for the Protection and Management of the South Asia Seas Region (SASP, #00094); South Asia Environment and Natural Resources Information Centre (SENRIC).* **Events** *Meeting* Islamabad (Pakistan) 2013, *Meeting* Colombo (Sri Lanka) 2010, *Intergovernmental Ministerial Meeting* Jaipur (India) 2008, *Meeting* Jaipur (India) 2008, *Regional environmentally sustainable transport forum in Asia* Singapore (Singapore) 2008. **Publications** *SACEP Newsletter. Alternative Livelihoods through Income Diversification: An Option for Sustainable Coral Reef and Associated Ecysystem Management in Sri Lanka* (2004) – SACEP and CORDIO; *South Asia Environmental Education and Training Action Plan 2003-2007 – Learning to Live in Harmony with Nature and Environment* (2003); *Children of the Monsoon: South Asia: State of the Environment 2002 – Youth Version.*
Members Governments of 8 countries;:
Afghanistan, Bangladesh, Bhutan, India, Maldives, Nepal, Pakistan, Sri Lanka.
IGO Relations Memorandum of Understanding with: *Global Programme of Action for the Protection of the Marine Environment from Land-Based Activities (GPA, see: #20299); International Coral Reef Initiative (ICRI, #12965); International Maritime Organization (IMO, #14102); South Asian Association for Regional Cooperation (SAARC, #19721); UNEP (#20299); UNESCO (#20322); World Meteorological Organization (WMO, #21649).* Cooperates with: *Colombo Plan for Cooperative Economic and Social Development in Asia and the Pacific (CPS, #04120); International Coral Reef Action Network (ICRAN, #12964).* Also collaborates with: *Swedish International Development Cooperation Agency (Sida).* **NGO Relations** Memorandum of Understanding with: *International Union for Conservation of Nature and Natural Resources (IUCN, #15766); RECOFTC – The Center for People and Forests (RECOFTC, #18628); TRAFFIC International (#20196).* Member of: *International Network for Environmental Compliance and Enforcement (INECE, #14261).* Cooperates with: *Global Coral Reef Monitoring Network (GCRMN, #10306); Stockholm Environment Institute (SEI, #19993).*
[2015/XF0820/F*]

♦ South Asia Democratic Forum (SADF) 19715

Contact Av des Arts 19, 1210 Brussels, Belgium. T. +3228084208. E-mail: info@sadf.eu.
URL: https://www.sadf.eu/

History 3 Feb 2011. Registration: Banque-Carrefour des Entreprises, No/ID: 0833.606.320, Start date: 9 Feb 2011, Belgium; EU Transparency Register, No/ID: 92070807286-46. **Aims** Bring together people and private and public institutions that can contribute to Europe-South Asia related cooperation and understanding. **Structure** General Assembly; Board of Directors; Executive Director. **Languages** English. **Staff** 4.00 FTE, paid; 2.00 FTE, voluntary. **Finance** Annual budget: 175,000 EUR (2020). **Activities** Events/meetings; guidance/assistance/consulting; knowledge management/information dissemination; networking/liaising; research/documentation. **Publications** Research reports; working papers; policy briefs; focus; comments; and books.
[2021.05.20/XJ2888/F]

♦ South Asia Forum for Ending Violence Against Children / see South Asia Initiative to End Violence Against Children (#19719)

♦ South Asia Forum for Infrastructure Regulation (SAFIR) 19716

Secretariat c/o CERC, 4th floor – Chanderlok Bldg, 36 Janpath, Delhi 110001, DELHI 110001, India. T. +911123353503 ext 100. Fax +911123753920. E-mail: asecy.safir@gmail.com.
URL: http://www.safirasia.org/

History May 1999. Founded with support from the *The World Bank Group (#21218).* **Aims** Provide high quality capacity building and training on infrastructure regulation and related topics, in South Asia; stimulate research on the subject by building a network of regional and international institutions and individuals active in the field; facilitate effective and efficient regulation of utility and infrastructure industries; initiate beneficial exchange of knowledge and expertise; set the trend of rapid implementation of global best practices. **Structure** General Meeting (at annual conference); Steering Committee; Executive Committee. **Finance** Sources: members' dues. **Events** *World Forum on Energy Regulation (WFER)* Istanbul (Turkey) 2015.
Members Representatives of regulatory bodies in 5 countries:
Bangladesh, Bhutan, India, Pakistan, Sri Lanka.
NGO Relations Member of (1): *International Confederation of Energy Regulators (ICER, #12859).*
[2021.06.15/XJ4640/F]

♦ South Asia Foundation (SAF) 19717

Sec SAF-India, A-33 Vasant Marg, Vasant Vihar, Delhi 110 057, DELHI 110 057, India. T. +911126153721 – +911126153724. Fax +911126155871. E-mail: nihar@safmail.org.
URL: http://www.southasiafoundation.org/

History Founded 2000, India, by Madanjeet Singh. **Aims** Promote *cooperation* among South Asian communities through education, cultural interaction and sustainable economic development; eventually establish a common *currency* in SAARC countries. **Structure** Governing Council. **Languages** English. **Finance** Private sources. Flexible budget. **Activities** Capacity building; financial and/or material support; networking/liaising; events/meetings. **Publications** *Kashmiriyat.*
Members Autonomous chapters in 8 countries:
Afghanistan, Bangladesh, Bhutan, India, Maldives, Nepal, Pakistan, Sri Lanka.
Consultative Status Consultative status granted from: *UNESCO (#20322)* (Foundations). **IGO Relations** Apex Body of: *South Asian Association for Regional Cooperation (SAARC, #19721).* [2019.02.15/XJ0031/f/F]

♦ South Asia Human Rights Documentation Centre (SAHRDC) 19718

Exec Dir 22 Northend Complex, Ramakrishna Ashram Marg, Delhi 110001, DELHI 110001, India. T. +911123361120 – +911123342717.
URL: http://www.hrdc.net/sahrdc/

History Oct 1990, Delhi (India). Registered in accordance with Indian law. **Aims** Protect and promote human rights and *fundamental rights* in South Asia, based on the Universal Declaration of Human Rights and other international human rights instruments. **Structure** Board. Executive Director. **Languages** English, Hindi. **Staff** 2.00 FTE, paid. **Finance** Members' dues. Other sources: donations, subscriptions and fees for research services. **Activities** Research/documentation; knowledge management/information dissemination; training/education; guidance/assistance/consulting. **Events** *Asia Pacific human rights NGO congress* Nepal 2002, *APHRN consultation on national human rights institutions* Colombo (Sri Lanka) 2001, *Asia Pacific NGO congress on human rights* Delhi (India) 1996. **Publications** *Human Rights Features Service* (12 a year) – electronic. *Handbook of Human Rights and Criminal Justice in India* (2008). Reports; studies; analysis of human rights issues in South Asian countries; human rights news and documentation services.
Members Individuals in 16 countries:
Australia, Bangladesh, Bhutan, Canada, Germany, India, Indonesia, Italy, Nepal, Netherlands, Pakistan, Sri Lanka, Switzerland, Thailand, UK, USA.
IGO Relations Cooperates with: *Office of the United Nations High Commissioner for Human Rights (OHCHR, #17697).* **NGO Relations** Member of: *International League for Human Rights (ILHR, inactive); Minority Rights Group International (MRG, #16820); World Organisation Against Torture (OMCT, #21685).* Serves as secretariat for *Asia Pacific Human Rights Network (APHRN, no recent information).* Cooperates with: *Amnesty International (AI, #00801); Committee to Protect Journalists (CPJ, #04280); Human Rights Watch (HRW, #10990),* Asia Division; *IFEX (#11100); International PEN (#14552); International Service for Human Rights (ISHR, #14841).* [2017.06.01/XF1424/v/E]

♦ South Asia Initiative to End Violence Against Children (SAIEVAC) . . 19719

Dir Gen GPO 5850, House No 122, Sujan Marg, Lazimpat 2, Kathmandu, Nepal. T. +97714001601 – +97714001685. Fax +97714001602. E-mail: info@saievac.org.
URL: http://www.saievac.org/

History Set up 2005, as *South Asia Forum for Ending Violence Against Children (SAF).* Transformed into a new institutional structure under current title, 2010. **Aims** Prevent and respond to all forms of neglect, abuse, exploitation and violence against children through a comprehensive child protection system at regional and national levels where governments, civil society and children are empowered to share experience, formalize linkages and reinforce cooperation to end violence against children. **Structure** Governing Board, including Member State representatives, Chairperson of *South Asia Coordinating Group on Action Against Violence Against Women and Children (SACG),* child representatives and Civil Society representatives. Regional Secretariat; National Mechanism. **Activities** Knowledge management/information dissemination; standards/guidelines; training/education; awareness raising. **Publications** *SAIEVAC Newsletter.*
Members Governments of SAARC countries (8):
Afghanistan, Bangladesh, Bhutan, India, Maldives, Nepal, Pakistan, Sri Lanka.
IGO Relations An apex body of: *South Asian Association for Regional Cooperation (SAARC, #19721).* **NGO Relations** Member of: *Global Partnership to End Violence Against Children (End Violence Against Children, #10533).* [2019/XM4489/E*]

♦ South Asia Institute of Advanced Christian Studies (internationally oriented national body)
♦ South Asia Institute, Austin TX (internationally oriented national body)
♦ South Asia Institute, Heidelberg (internationally oriented national body)
♦ South Asian Academy of Aesthetic Dentistry (unconfirmed)
♦ Southasian Academy of Ophthalmology / see SAARC Academy of Ophthalmology (#19013)

♦ South Asian Association of Pediatric Dentistry (SAAPD) 19720

SG Room No 516, Dept of Pediatric Dentistry, Maulana Azad Inst of Dental Sciences, New Delhi, Delhi 110002, New Delhi DELHI 110002, India.
URL: http://www.saapd.asia/

Aims Build a disease-free and healthy community of children for holistic development of the South Asian countries. **Structure** Working Body; Committees. **Finance** Sources: members' dues. **Activities** Events/meetings. **Events** *Congress* Kathmandu (Nepal) 2019, *Conference* New Delhi (India) 2018. **Publications** *Journal of South Asian Association of Pediatric Dentistry* – online.
Members Individuals in 6 countries:
Bangladesh, Bhutan, India, Maldives, Nepal, Sri Lanka. [2021/AA2251/v/D]

♦ South Asian Association for Regional Cooperation (SAARC) 19721

Association sud-asiatique de coopération régionale (ASACR)

SG PO Box 4222, Tridevi Marg, Kathmandu, Nepal. T. +97714221792 – +97714221785 – +97714226350. Fax +97714227033 – +97714223991. E-mail: saarc@saarc-sec.org.
URL: http://www.saarc-sec.org/

History 8 Dec 1985, Dhaka (Bangladesh), on adoption of the SAARC Charter at the 1st Meeting of Heads of State or Government of 7 founder-member countries (Bangladesh, Bhutan, India, Maldives, Nepal, Pakistan and Sri Lanka) following: official proposal, 2 May 1980, by the President of Bangladesh; informal meeting of Foreign Ministers, Feb 1981, Delhi (India); official meeting of Foreign Secretaries, Apr 1981, Colombo (Sri Lanka); identification, later in 1981, of 5 broad areas for regional cooperation by a Committee of the Whole; and 1st Official Meeting of Foreign Ministers, Aug 1983, Delhi, when *Declaration on South Asian Regional Cooperation (SARC)* – or *Delhi Declaration* – was adopted and *Integrated Programme of Action for South Asian Regional Cooperation* launched in 9 selected areas. Afghanistan admitted as member of SAARC at the 14th SAARC Summit, 3 Apr 2007, Delhi. **Aims** Accelerate the process of economic and social development in member states through collective action in agreed areas of cooperation, including: Agriculture and Rural Development; Human Resource Development; Environment; Meteorology and Forestry; Science and Technology; Transport and Communications; Energy; Social Development; Poverty Alleviation.
Structure Summit Meeting of Heads of State or Government (annual) is the highest authority. Council of Ministers (meets twice a year), comprises Foreign Ministers of Member States and is responsible for formulating policies and considering new projects. Standing Committee (meets twice a year), comprises Foreign Secretaries of Member States and monitors and coordinates cooperative programmes. Programming Committee, consisting of senior officials of Member States. Technical Committees (6) and Working Groups (4) are responsible for individual areas of the Association's activities. Secretariat, established 16 Jan 1987, Kathmandu (Nepal), headed Secretary-General, monitors, facilitates and promotes activities and services meetings, and serves as a channel of communication between the Association, Member States and other regional and inter-governmental institutions. Secretariat Divisions (8): Media and Integration of Afghanistan (MIA); Agriculture and Rural Development (ARD); Environment, Bio-technology and Observers (EBO); Economic, Trade and Finance (ETF); Social Affairs (SA); ICT and Poverty Alleviation (IPA); Energy, Tourism and Science (ETS); Human Resource Development, Security Aspects and Culture (HTS).
Regional Centres:
- *SAARC Agriculture Centre (SAC, see: #19721)*, Dhaka (Bangladesh);
- *SAARC Meteorological Research Centre (SMRC, no recent information)*, Dhaka;
- *SAARC Tuberculosis and HIV/AIDS Centre (STAC, see: #19721)*, Kathmandu (Nepal);
- *SAARC Coastal Zone Management Centre, Maldives (see: #19721)*;
- *SAARC Energy Centre, Islamabad (see: #19721)*;
- *SAARC Disaster Management Centre, Delhi*;
- *SAARC Forestry Centre, Bhutan*;
- *SAARC Cultural Centre, Colombo (SCC, #19017)*.

Languages English. **Staff** Secretary-General (on deputation for 3 years), Directors (8 – on deputation for 3 years), General Services Staff – regionally recruited (13), locally recruited (39). **Finance** Activities of Secretariat and Regional Centres funded through assessed contributions of Member States.
Activities Areas of cooperation:
- *'Poverty Alleviation'* – A two-tier mechanism (Ministers and Secretaries dealing with Poverty Alleviation) meets regularly to review progress in this area, including progress in the realization of the 22 SAARC Development Goals (SDGs) and the implementation of the SAARC Action Plan on Poverty Alleviation. Regional Poverty Profile on designated themes – provides analysis of regional situation (published every 2 years).
- *'Agriculture and Rural Development'* – Cooperation pursued based on SAARC Agriculture Perspectives/Vision 2020 (2008), Regional Food Security Strategy (2008). A major regional project with FAO on Control of Trans-boundary Animal Diseases, underway since Jun 2010. Food Security project with AusAID also under implementation. A set of regional food security projects is being developed with assistance of ADB. Cooperation in this area is being steered by the meetings of the SAARC Agriculture Ministers and the Technical Committee on Agriculture and Rural Development. SAARC Food Bank established and operational since 2008. Establishment of Regional Seed Bank under consideration.
- *'Biotechnology'* – Plan of Action for Cooperation in Biotechnology covers: Plant Tissue Culture; Medicinal and Aromatic Plants; Plant Biotechnology including Therapeutic and Edible Vaccines; Vaccines and Diagnostics for Human Health; Aquaculture; Human Resource Development.
- *'Communications, Information and Media'* – stresses the importance of developing infrastructure and adequate communications networks among member countries to reinforce the process of economic cooperation; highlights the need for simplification of complex documentation procedures and transactional software to facilitate economic interaction across the region.
- *'Economic' – South Asian Preferential Trade Arrangement (SAPTA, 1993)* entered into force Dec 1995. Subsequently, *South Asian Free Trade Area (SAFTA, #19732)* Agreement entered into force with effect from 1 Jan 2006. *Agreement on trade in services under SAFTA* signed Apr 2010; ratification by Members States under process. Agreement on *South Asian Regional Standards Organization (SARSO)*, signed Aug 2008; ratification by Member States under process. *'SAARC Arbitration Council'* established 2010. Three trade facilitation agreements signed in 2005: Customs Cooperation; Avoidance of Double Taxation; Arbitration Council. *'Agreement on protection and promotion of investments'* under consideration. Cooperation in economic and financial sector pursued by, inter alia, SAFTA Ministerial Council, SAFTA Committee of Experts, Committee on Economic Cooperation, SAARCFINANCE (Central Bank Governors of Member States), Inter-governmental Expert Group on Financial Issues.
- *'Transport Connectivity'* – Decade of Intra-regional Connectivity in SAARC (2010-2020). SAARC Regional Multimodal Transport Study (2006) provides for measures/corridors to be developed. *'Regional Motor Vehicle Agreement'*, *'Regional Railways Agreement'* and *'Comprehensive Regional Transit Agreement'* under consideration. Meetings of Transport Ministers, Inter-governmental Group on Transport and Technical Committee on Transport guide cooperation in this area.
- *'Energy'* – Concept of Energy Ring developed Jan 2009. Working Group on Energy has prepared a Plan of Action, Jun 2004, under implementation. Experts Groups work on Oil and Gas, Electricity, Renewable Energy and Technology/Knowledge Sharing. Task Force has finalized a common template on technical and commercial aspects of electricity grid interconnection amongst SAARC Member States. Road Map on Energy Efficiency and Energy Conservation for implementation by Member States has been developed. SAARC Energy Trade Study (SRETS) completed with assistance of ADB, identifying 4 trade options.
- *'Environment'* – Plan of Action on Environment (1997); Plan of Action on Climate Change (2008); Thimphu Statement on Climate Change (2010); SAARC Convention on Cooperation on Environment (2010 – ratification by Member State under process). Four regional initiatives on mountain, marine, monsoon and climate-related disasters being commissioned. Common SAARC position on climate change presented at COP15 and COP16. SAARC Natural Disaster Rapid Response Mechanism under consideration. SAARC Environment Ministers and Technical Committee on Environment and Forestry guide cooperation in this area.
- *'Human Resources Development'* – covers education and culture and establishment of a network of centers of higher learning and training and Skill Development Institutes across South Asia.
- *'Human Resources Development'* – Work underway on harmonization of professional/academic degrees in the region. SAARC Chairs, Fellowship and Scholarship Programme facilitates students/scholars from the region to pursue higher studies. South Asian University, Delhi (India), established 2010.
- *'Security'* – Legal instruments concluded in this area: *SAARC Regional Convention on Suppression of Terrorism (1987)* and its Additional Protocol; *SAARC Regional Convention on Narcotic Drugs and Psychotropic Substances (1990)*; *SAARC Convention on Mutual Assistance in Criminal Matters.* Mechanisms that address cooperation in this area: Meetings of Interior/Home Ministers and Secretaries; Conference on Cooperation in Police Matters; SAARC Terrorist Offences Monitoring Desk (STOMD); SAARC Drug Offences Monitoring Desk (SDOMD); Coordination Group on Drug Law Enforcement Agencies. High Level Group of Eminent Experts to strengthen SAARC Anti-Terrorism Mechanism.
- *'Science, Technology and Meteorology'* – SAARC Plan of Action on Science and Technology (2008-2013). SAARC Initiative for Industrial Research and Development underway. Meetings of Ministers of Science and Technology and Technical Committee on Science and Technology guide cooperation in this area.
- *'Social'* – Major initiatives include: SAARC Social Charter; SAARC Gender Info Base; Goodwill Ambassador for HIV/AIDS; Regional Strategy for HIV/AIDS; SAARC Award; SAARC Youth Award; Telemedicine Network; Regional Strategy on Communicable Diseases; *SAARC Convention on Preventing and Combating the Trafficking in Women and Children for Prostitution (2002)*; *SAARC Convention on Regional Arrangements for the Promotion of Child Welfare in South Asia (2002).* Ministerial Meetings and Technical Committee on Women, Children and Youth, and Technical Committee on Health and Population guide cooperation in this area.
- *'Tourism'* – Plan of Action on Tourism (2006). Meetings of SAARC Tourism Ministers and Working Group on Tourism guide cooperation in this area.

SAARC Apex Bodies: *South Asia Initiative to End Violence Against Children (SAIEVAC, #19719)*; *Foundation of SAARC Writers and Literature (FOSWAL, #09972)*; *SAARC Chamber of Commerce and Industry (SAARC CCI, #19015)*; *South Asian Association for Regional Cooperation in Law (SAARCLAW, #19723)*; *South Asian Federation of Accountants (SAFA, #19727)*; *South Asia Foundation (SAF, #17917)*.
SAARC Recognized Bodies:
1. *Association of Management Development Institutions in South Asia (AMDISA, #02792)*;
2. *South Asian Association for Regional Cooperation of Architects (SAARCH, #19722)*;
3. *Federation of State Insurance Organizations of SAARC Countries (FSIO, inactive)*;
4. *'SAARC Diploma Engineers Forum (SDEF)'*;
5. *Radiological Society of SAARC Countries (RSSC, #18602)*;
6. *SAARC Teachers' Federation (STF, inactive)*;
7. *SAARC Surgical Care Society (SSCS, #19020)*;
8. *South Asian Free Media Association (SAFMA, #19731)*;
9. *'SAARC Women's Association in Sri Lanka (SWA)'*;
10. *'Hindukush Himalayan Grassroots Women's Natural Resources Management (HIMAWANTI)'*;
11. *Federation of Associations of Pediatric Surgeons of SAARC Countries (FAPSS)*;
12. *South Asian Federation of Exchanges (SAFE, #19729)*;
13. *SAARC Federation of Oncologists (SFO)*;
14. *South Asia Association of National Scout Organization (SAANSO)*;
15. *South Asia Network of Economic Research Institutes (SANEI, #19726)*;
16. *SAARC Academy of Ophthalmology (SAO, #19013)*;
17. *South Asian Women Development Forum (SAWDF)*;
18. Self Employed Women Association (SEWA).

SAARC Development Fund (SDF, #19018), as funding mechanism for regional/sub-regional projects with 3 windows: social; economic; infrastructure. Initial paid up capital of US$ 300 million.
Cooperation Agreements / Memoranda of Understanding not mentioned above:
- Agreement establishing SAARC-Japan Special Fund, signed 27 Sep 1993 by SAARC and the Ambassador of Japan in Kathmandu;
- Memorandum of Understanding between SAARC and PTB, signed 25 Nov 2003 by SAARC and the President of PTB;
- Revised Memorandum Guidelines for the SAARC-Japan Special Fund, signed 6 Feb 2006 by SAARC and the Ambassador of Japan to Nepal.

Designated SAARC Years – since 1989, designated SAARC Years to focus on specific themes of common concern to Member States:
- 1989 – SAARC Year of Combating Drug Abuse and Drug Trafficking;
- 1990 – SAARC Year of Girl Child;
- 1991 – SAARC Year of Shelter;
- 1992 – SAARC Year of Environment;
- 1993 – SAARC Year of Disabled Persons;
- 1994 – SAARC Year of the Youth;
- 1995 – SAARC Year of Poverty Eradication;
- 1996 – SAARC Year of Literacy;
- 1997 – SAARC Year of Participatory Governance;
- 1999 – SAARC Year of Biodiversity;
- 2002-2003 – SAARC Years of Contribution of Youth to Environment;
- 2004 – SAARC Awareness Year for TB and HIV/AIDS;
- 2005 – South Asia Tourism Year;
- 2006 – South Asia Tourism Year;
- 2007 – Green South Asia Year.

Designated SAARC Decades:
- 1991-2000 – SAARC Decade of the Girl Child;
- 2001-2010 – SAARC Decade of the Rights of the Child;
- 2006-2015 – SAARC Decade of Poverty Alleviation.

Instrumental in setting up *Independent South Asian Commission on Poverty Alleviation (ISACPA, see: #19721)*.
Events *Korea-SAARC Partnership Seminar* Seoul (Korea Rep) 2019, *Regional Workshop for the Utilization of Space-Based and Geospatial Information for Achieving the Targets of the Sendai Framework for Disaster Risk Reduction* Ahmedabad (India) 2018, *Special Session on Antimicrobial Resistance* Bangkok (Thailand) 2016, *Korea-South Asia Culture Ministers Meeting* Seoul (Korea Rep) 2016, *Korea-SAARC Partnership Seminar* Seoul (Korea Rep) 2014. **Publications** *SAARC in Brief* (periodical); *SAARC and Women in Development*; *SAARC – A Profile*. *Declarations of SAARC Summits* – series; *SAARC Documents* – series; *SAARC Reports* – series; *Statements of the SAARC Heads of State or Government* – series. Agreements; conventions; ministerial declarations/statements; press releases.
Members Governments of 8 countries:
Afghanistan, Bangladesh, Bhutan, India, Maldives, Nepal, Pakistan, Sri Lanka.
Observers in 8 countries:
Australia, China, Iran Islamic Rep, Japan, Korea Rep, Mauritius, Myanmar, USA.
Observer organization:
European Commission (EC, #06633).
IGO Relations Observer status with (1): *United Nations (UN, #20515)* (General Assembly).
Cooperation Agreements / Memoranda of Understanding with:
- *Asia-Pacific Telecommunity (APT, #02064)*;
- *Asian Development Bank (ADB, #01422)*;
- *Canadian International Development Agency (CIDA, inactive)*;
- *Centre on Integrated Rural Development for Asia and the Pacific (CIRDAP, #03750)*;
- *European Commission (EC, #06633)*;
- *FAO (#09260)*;
- *International Bank for Reconstruction and Development (IBRD, #12317)* (World Bank);
- *International Telecommunication Union (ITU, #15673)*;
- *Joint United Nations Programme on HIV/AIDS (UNAIDS, #16149)*;
- *South Asia Cooperative Environment Programme (SACEP, #19714)*;
- *UNEP (#20299)*;
- *UN Women (#20724)*;
- *UNCTAD (#20285)*;
- *UNDP (#20292)*;
- *UNESCO (#20322)*;
- *UNICEF (#20332)*;
- *United Nations Economic and Social Commission for Asia and the Pacific (ESCAP, #20557)*;
- *United Nations Office for Disaster Risk Reduction (UNDRR, #20595)*;
- *United Nations Population Fund (UNFPA, #20612)*;
- *WHO (#20950)*.

Participates as observer in the activities of: *Codex Alimentarius Commission (CAC, #04081)*. Also cooperates with: *ASEAN (#01141)*; *Deutsche Gesellschaft für Internationale Zusammenarbeit (GIZ)*.
NGO Relations Memorandum of Understanding with: *Asian Disaster Preparedness Center (ADPC, #01426)*.
[2017.07.20/XD5720/**D***]

♦ South Asian Association for Regional Cooperation of Architects (SAARCH) 19722

Association sud-asiatique pour la coopération régionale des architectes

Chair c/o Bhutan Inst of Architects, PO Box 233, Thimphu, Bhutan. T. +97517946075. Fax +9752321285. E-mail: bhutanarchitects@gmail.com.
URL: http://saarch.org/

History 1991, Colombo (Sri Lanka). Recognized body of *South Asian Association for Regional Cooperation (SAARC, #19721)*. **Aims** Discuss and develop professional affairs among architects of the SAARC region; develop architectural education and institutional affairs in the region; coordinate architectural activities. **Structure** Assembly of Presidents of members; Council. **Languages** English. **Staff** Shares Secretariat staff with Institute of Architects, Sri Lanka. **Finance** Members' dues. Sponsorship. **Activities** Prepares construction of SAARC Millennium Centre; arranges cross border exchanges of architects and students of architecture. **Events** *Conference* Thimphu (Bhutan) 2012, *Conference* Colombo (Sri Lanka) 2009, *Conference* Delhi (India) 2008, *Conference* Dhaka (Bangladesh) 2006, *Conference* Karachi (Pakistan) 2004. **Publications** *SAARCH* – newsletter.
Members in 7 countries:
Bangladesh, Bhutan, India, Maldives, Nepal, Pakistan, Sri Lanka. [2012/XD6999/**D**]

♦ South Asian Association for Regional Cooperation in Family Medicine (no recent information)

♦ South Asian Association for Regional Cooperation in Law (SAARCLAW) 19723

Vice-Pres c/o Goeman Bind HTO, Prehem House, A 57/2, DLF City Phase 1 – Behind PVR Cinemas Mega Mall, National Capital Region, Delhi 122002, DELHI 122002, India. T. +919818266278 – +91981(911244309481. Fax +911244040194. E-mail: info@saarclaw.org.
URL: http://www.saarclaw.org/

History 24 Oct 1991, Colombo (Sri Lanka). A Recognized Regional Apex Body of *South Asian Association for Regional Cooperation (SAARC, #19721)*. Former names and other names: *Association of Persons of the Legal Communities of the SAARC Countries* – former. **Aims** Bring together the legal communities within the region for closer cooperation, developing understanding, promoting exchange of ideas and information dissemination; use and develop law as a source and instrument towards social change for development as well as for building cooperation among the peoples of the region. **Structure** Executive Council. **Languages** English. **Staff** 35.00 FTE, paid. **Finance** Sources: subscriptions. **Activities** Events/meetings; knowledge management/information dissemination; publishing activities. **Events** *Chief justices conference* Paro (Bhutan) 2005, *Conference* Paro (Bhutan) 2005, *Chief justices conference* Karachi (Pakistan) 2004, *Conference* Karachi (Pakistan) 2004, *Good governance for development – a challenge of the new millennium* Kathmandu (Nepal) 2000. **Publications** *SAARCLAW Newsletter*. Papers; recommendations; observations.
Members Full in 8 countries:
Afghanistan, Bangladesh, Bhutan, India, Maldives, Nepal, Pakistan, Sri Lanka. [2020.06.24/XD5718/**D**]

♦ South Asian Association of Transactional Analysts (SAATA) 19724

Contact c/o Asha, 91 Krishna Colony, Trichy Road, Singanallur, Coimbatore, Tamil Nadu 641005, Coimbatore TAMIL NADU 641005, India.
URL: http://saata.org/
Aims Promote global standards in Transactional Analysis practice, training and certification; network and develop professional competencies in transactional analysis. **Structure** Board of Trustees. **Activities** Events/meetings; training/education; certification/accreditation; networking/liaising. **Events** *Joint Conference* Raleigh, NC (USA) 2019, *Joint Conference* Kochi (India) 2018, *South Asian Transactional Analysis Conference* Coimbatore (India) 2016, *Joint Conference* Chennai (India) 2012. **Publications** *SAATA Journal*.
Members Full in 3 countries:
Bangladesh, India, Iran Islamic Rep.
NGO Relations *International Transactional Analysis Association (ITAA, #15719)*. [2018.02.08/XM4888/**D**]

- ♦ South Asian Association of Women Geoscientists (unconfirmed)
- ♦ South Asian Association for Women's Studies (inactive)
- ♦ South Asian Centre for Teacher Development (unconfirmed)

♦ South Asian Coalition on Child Servitude (SACCS) 19725

Coalition de l'Asie du Sud contre la servitude enfantine
Sec 74 Aravali Apartment, D D A Kalkaji, Delhi 110019, DELHI 110019, India. T. +911126210807. Fax +911126224899.
History 1989, Delhi (India). **Aims** Create a child labour free society, where all children attend school; identify, liberate, rehabilitate and educate children in servitude through direct intervention, coalition building and mass mobilization. **Structure** Headquarters in Delhi (India). National Offices (4), headed by a Coordinator. Committee of representatives from partner NGOs, headed by Chairperson. **Finance** Financed by funding agencies and contributions. **Activities** Direct action includes: rescue operation; Rehabilitation measures. Indirect action includes: Marches/rallies; campaigns. Runs 'Bal Mitra Gram' (Child Friendly Village). Fora and Committees; Workshops and seminars; Training and orientation programmes; Networking and coordination; Primary education centres. **Events** *Meeting on psychology in the context of public health* Tampere (Finland) 1997. **Publications** *Freedom Now. Break the Chains – Save the Childhood* (1995). Book on RUGMARK labelling system. Research and Documentation Centre.
Members NGOs (about 350) in 5 countries:
Bangladesh, India, Nepal, Pakistan, Sri Lanka.
IGO Relations *United Nations Commission on Human Rights (inactive)*. [2009/XF5445/**F**]

- ♦ South Asian Concern / see South Asian Development Partnership
- ♦ South Asian Concern (internationally oriented national body)
- ♦ South Asian Confederation of Anaesthesiologists / see SAARC Confederation of Anaesthesiologists (#19016)
- ♦ South Asian Development Fund / see SAARC Development Fund (#19018)
- ♦ South Asian Development Partnership (internationally oriented national body)
- ♦ South Asia Network on Dams, Rivers and People (internationally oriented national body)

♦ South Asia Network of Economic Research Institutes (SANEI) 19726

Address not obtained.
URL: http://www.saneinetwork.net/
History Set up 1998. **Aims** Foster networking amongst economic research institutions in the South Asia region for establishing strong research interlinkages pertaining to broader concerns of regional cooperation, understanding and development. **Structure** Steering Committee. **Activities** Training/education; events/meetings.
Members Institutes in 5 countries:
Bangladesh, India, Nepal, Pakistan, Sri Lanka.
IGO Relations A *South Asian Association for Regional Cooperation (SAARC, #19721)* Recognized body. [2016/XM6863/**F**]

♦ South Asian Federation of Accountants (SAFA) 19727

Main Office c/o ICAI Bhawan, PO Box No 7100, Indraprastha Marg, Delhi 110002, DELHI 110002, India. E-mail: safa@icai.org – safa@icai.in.
URL: http://www.esafa.org/
History 1984, as a sub-regional organization of *Confederation of Asian and Pacific Accountants (CAPA, #04511)*. A Recognized Regional Apex Body of *South Asian Association for Regional Cooperation (SAARC, #19721)*. **Aims** Serve the accountancy profession in the South Asian Region. **Activities** Training/education; standards/guidelines; networking/liaising; research/documentation. **Events** *Transformation of accounting profession* Karachi (Pakistan) 2005, *Corporate governance – challenges in implementation* Colombo (Sri Lanka) 2004, *Integrated financial sector in the SAARC region* Delhi (India) 2004, *Conference* Colombo (Sri Lanka) 2000, *The global village – opportunities and challenges* Bhurban (Pakistan) 1996. **Publications** Studies; Guidelines.
Members Individual (over 180,000) of national chartered accountancy and cost and management accountancy institutions in 5 countries:
Bangladesh, India, Nepal, Pakistan, Sri Lanka.
Observer bodies in 6 countries:
Afghanistan, Bhutan, China, Japan, Korea Rep, Maldives.
NGO Relations Affiliated to: *International Federation of Accountants (IFAC, #13335)*. [2019/XE1525/v/**E**]

♦ South Asian Federation of Endocrine Societies (SAFES) 19728

Secretariat Room 1320 – 13th floor, BIRDEM General Hosp, 122 Kazi Nazrul Islam Eve, Shahbag, Dhaka 1000, Bangladesh. E-mail: fariasafes@gmail.com.
URL: http://2ndsafessummit2015.com/
Events *Summit* Dhaka (Bangladesh) 2015, *Summit* Hyderabad (India) 2013.
Members Full in 5 countries:
Bangladesh, India, Nepal, Pakistan, Sri Lanka. [2015/XM4115/**D**]

♦ South Asian Federation of Exchanges (SAFE) 19729

Contact address not obtained. T. +92512826763 – +92512274163. Fax +92512804215. E-mail: usman@safe-asia.com – info@safe-asia.com.
URL: http://www.safe-asia.com/
History 2000, under the initiative of Chittagong Stock Exchange, Bangladesh. **Aims** Provide a platform to share, exchange and promote technologies, experiences for rapid growth and development of capital market and work towards regional as well as global integration. **Structure** Executive Board. Secretariat. **Languages** English. **Staff** 5.00 FTE, paid. **Finance** Members' dues. **Activities** Acts as a forum for promoting mutual cooperation, regulatory alignment, exchange of information and technological linkage to facilitate the process of integration and harmonization of the region's capital market and to accelerate the common economic growth of South Asia; promotes the investment potential of the region by attracting foreign institutional and portfolio investments into the region's markets by regularly conducting seminars, events, conferences and roundtables; engages, both independently and in association with other domestic, regional and international entities, in capacity building programmes to develop skills and expertise of human capital for effective management of the region's markets; works for adoption of consumer/investor protection standards in the region; provides advisory and consulting services regarding financial and capital market issues, matters and projects, both within and outside the region. **Publications** *Capital Markets* (12 a year) – e-newsletter; *Trading Places* (4 a year) – newsletter. *SAFE Almanac 2010*; *SAFE Handbook*. **Information Services** *News-wire* – (daily) – market data from regional member exchanges and capital market entities, released on the website.
Members Stock exchanges in 10 countries:
Bangladesh, Bhutan, India, Kazakhstan, Maldives, Mauritius, Nepal, Pakistan, Sri Lanka, United Arab Emirates.
IGO Relations Recognized by: *South Asian Association for Regional Cooperation (SAARC, #19721)*. **NGO Relations** Memorandum of Understanding with: *Association of Futures Markets (AFM, #02621)*; *Federation of Euro-Asian Stock Exchanges (FEAS, #09486)*. Affiliate Member of: *African Securities Exchanges Association (ASEA, #00452)*; *World Federation of Exchanges (WFE, #21434)*. Cooperates with: *SAARC Chamber of Commerce and Industry (SAARC CCI, #19015)*; national organizations. [2013.09.27/XD8988/**D**]

- ♦ South Asian Federation of Menopause Societies (unconfirmed)
- ♦ South Asian Federation of NGOs for the Prevention of Drug and Substance Abuse (no recent information)
- ♦ South Asian Football Federation (unconfirmed)
- ♦ South Asian Forum for Environment (internationally oriented national body)

♦ South Asian Forum on Mental Health and Psychiatry (SAF) 19730

SG Sri Lanka Psychiatric Assn, SLMA House, Wijevama Mawatha, Colombo, 7, Sri Lanka.
Events *International conference* Dhaka (Bangladesh) 2010, *IRBD Asia Pacific conference* Kochi (India) 2009, *Conference* Bangkok (Thailand) 2008, *World congress of Asian psychiatry* Goa (India) 2007.
Members Chapters in 10 countries:
Australia, Bangladesh, Canada, India, Malaysia, Pakistan, Sri Lanka, Thailand, UK, USA. [2013/XM2086/**F**]

- ♦ South Asian Fraternity (internationally oriented national body)

♦ South Asian Free Media Association (SAFMA) 19731

General Secretariat c/o South Asian Media Centre, 177-A Shadman II, Lahore, Pakistan. T. +924237555621-8. Fax +924237555629.
SG 9 Lower Ground, Edent Heights, Jail Road, Lahore, Pakistan. T. +9242587251 – +92425879253. Fax +92425879254. E-mail: safma@hotmail.com.
URL: http://www.mediawitty.com/test/
Aims Promote networking among the media in the region; improve professional standards; facilitate exchanges between journalists. **IGO Relations** Affiliate member of: *Asia-Pacific Institute for Broadcasting Development (AIBD, #01934)*. Recognized body of: *South Asian Association for Regional Cooperation (SAARC, #19721)*. [2011/XM1950/**D**]

♦ South Asian Free Trade Area (SAFTA) 19732

Contact SAARC, PO Box 4222, Kathmandu, Nepal. T. +9771221794 – +9771221785. Fax +9771227033 – +9771223991. E-mail: saarc@saarc-sec.org.
History 6 Nov 2001, Bandar Seri Begawan (Brunei Darussalam), following a proposal 1997, Male (Maldives), during the 9th Summit of *South Asian Association for Regional Cooperation (SAARC, #19721)*. Agreement reached at the 12th SAARC summit, Islamabad (Pakistan), Jan 2004, and entered into force, 1 Jan 2006. Follows the signing, 11 Apr 1993, Dhaka (Bangladesh), of the *South Asian Preferential Trade Arrangement (SAPTA, 1993)*, which came into force, 7 Dec 1995. Group of Experts, comprising officials from SAARC member states, is mandated to make concrete and detailed recommendations towards realization of SAFTA. **Aims** Create a framework for the creation of a free trade zone covering Afghanistan, India, Pakistan, Nepal, Sri Lanka, Bangladesh, Bhutan and the Maldives. [2009/XF6460/t/**F***]

- ♦ South-Asian Fund Raising Group (internationally oriented national body)

♦ South Asian Growth Quadrangle (SAGQ) 19733

Address not obtained.
History 1997.
Members Participating countries (4):
Bangladesh, Bhutan, India, Nepal. [2008/XJ0461/**F***]

- ♦ South Asian Humanist Network (see: #10972)

♦ South Asian Initiative on Disaster Migration (Duryog Nivaran) 19734

Secretariat c/o Practical Action, No 5 Lionel Edirisinghe Mawatha, Kirulapone, Colombo, 5, Sri Lanka. T. +94112829142. Fax +94112856188.
URL: http://www.duryognivaran.org/
History 1995. **Events** *Round table meeting* Bangkok (Thailand) 1999, *Policy forum / Forum* Delhi (India) 1999.
Members Organizations in 6 countries:
Bangladesh, India, Nepal, Pakistan, Sri Lanka, Thailand.
Included in the above, 1 international organization listed in this Yearbook:
Asian Disaster Preparedness Center (ADPC, #01426). [2015/XG6528/**F**]

- ♦ South Asian Labour Forum (no recent information)
- ♦ South Asian Media Association (no recent information)

♦ South Asian Network for Development and Environmental Economics (SANDEE) 19735

Contact PO Box 8975, EPC 1056, Kathmandu, Nepal. T. +97715003222. Fax +97715003299. E-mail: info@sandeeonline.org.
URL: http://www.sandeeonline.org/
History Nov 1999. **Aims** Strengthen capacity in South Asia to undertake research on the inter-linkages among economic development, poverty and environmental change. **Structure** Located at: *International Union for Conservation of Nature and Natural Resources (IUCN, #15766)* (Kathmandu Office). **Publications** *SANDEE Newsletter*. **IGO Relations** *International Centre for Integrated Mountain Development (ICIMOD, #12500)*. **NGO Relations** Cooperates with: *Economy and Environment Programme for Southeast Asia (EEPSEA, #05324)*. [2020/XF6621/**F**]

- ♦ South Asian Network of Economic Institutes (internationally oriented national body)

♦ South Asian Network on Economic Modeling (SANEM) 19736

Secretariat Flat Number K-5, House Number 1/B, Road 35, Gulshan 2, Dhaka 1212, Bangladesh. T. +8828813075. Fax +8829883445. E-mail: sanemnet@yahoo.com.
URL: http://www.sanemnet.org/
History 1 Jan 2007, by *Partnership for Economic Policy (PEP, #18233)* and *Global Trade Analysis Project (GTAP, #10631)*. **Aims** Promote production, exchange and dissemination of basic research knowledge in the areas of regional integration, multilateral and domestic trade liberalization, environment and poverty. **Structure** Coordinating Committee.
Members Institutions in 8 countries:
Bangladesh, Belgium, Canada, India, Nepal, Sri Lanka, UK, USA.
Included in the above, 8 organizations listed in this Yearbook:
Bangladesh Institute of Development Studies (BIDS); *Consumer Unity and Trust Society (CUTS)*; *Global Trade Analysis Project (GTAP, #10631)*; *Indian Council for Research on International Economic Relations (ICRIER)*; *Pakistan Institute of Development Economics (PIDE)*; *Partnership for Economic Policy (PEP, #18233)*; *Research and Information System for Developing Countries, India (RIS, India)*; *South Asia Watch on Trade, Economics and Environment (SAWTEE, #19749)*.
NGO Relations Member of: *Asia-Pacific Research and Training Network on Trade (ARTNeT, #02014)*. [2016/XJ5312/y/**F**]

♦ South Asian Network Operators Group (SANOG) 19737

Secretariat GPO Box 13655, Kathmandu, Nepal. Fax +97714362480 – +97715012546. E-mail: info@sanog.org.
Street address c/o Nepal Research and Education Network, Gusingal, Kupandole, Lalitpur, Nepal.
URL: http://www.sanog.org/

Aims Provide a regional forum to discuss operational issues and technologies of interest to data operators in the South Asian Region. **Structure** Core Committee; Programme Committee; Fellowship Committee; Advisory Committee. **Languages** English. **Activities** Events/meetings. **Events** *Meeting* Pakistan 2024, *Meeting* Bhutan / Bangladesh 2023, *Meeting* Pakistan 2023, *Meeting* Kathmandu (Nepal) 2022, *Meeting* Padukka (Sri Lanka) 2021. **NGO Relations** Cooperates with (1): *Asia Pacific Network Operators Group (APNOG, #01972)*. Memorandum of Understanding with: *Asia and Pacific Internet Association (APIA, #01936)*; *Asian-Pacific Network Information Centre (APNIC)*. Member ofl *DotAsia Organisation (DotAsia, #05124)*.
[2021/XM2135/**F**]

♦ South Asian Network of Self-Help Organizations of People with Disabilities (no recent information)
♦ South Asian Network for Social and Agricultural Development (internationally oriented national body)

♦ South Asian Perspectives Network Association (SAPNA) 19738

Chairman 75 Kynsey Road, Colombo, 8, Sri Lanka. T. +94112695625. Fax +94112688676.
URL: http://www.propoor.org/

History Mid 1970s. **Aims** Work on decentralization, participatory development and social mobilization/capacity building for *poverty* eradication and *peace building*, including analysing and monitoring of the process. **Structure** Regional Network. Consultative Committee. Chairman; Associate Coordinator/Advisor; Director Administration. **Languages** English, Sinhala, Tamil. **Staff** 2.00 FTE, paid. Voluntary. **Events** *Conférence sur la Passion de la Mission* Paris (France) 2020, *Seminar on poverty in Asia* Colombo (Sri Lanka) 2002. **Publications** *Economic Democracy Through Pro-Poor Growth* (2009); *Pro Poor Growth and Governance in South Asia: Decentralisation and participatory development* (2004) by Ponna Wignaraja and Susil Sirivardana; *Readings on Pro-Poor Planning through Social Mobilisation in South Asia: The strategic option for poverty eradication* (1998) by Ponna Wignaraja and Susil Sirivardana; *New Social Movements in the South* (1993) by Ponna Wignaraja; *Participatory Development: Learning from South Asia* (1991) by Ponna Wignaraja et al; *Women, Poverty and Resources* (1990) by Ponna Wignaraja; *The Challenge in South Asia: Development, democracy and regional cooperation* (2nd ed 1989) by Ponna Wignaraja and Akmal Hussain; *Towards a Theory of Rural Development* (1988) by G V S De Silva et al. Progress reports.
[2009.06.01/XF6889/**F**]

♦ South Asian Preferential Trade Arrangement (1993 treaty)

♦ South Asian Regional Association of Dermatologists, Venereologists and Leprologists (SARAD) 19739

Gen Sec Dept of Dermatology, BPKIHS, PO Box 7053, Kathmandu, Nepal. E-mail: saradvd2019@gmail.com.
URL: http://www.sarcd2019.com/

History 2 Oct 1999, Kathmandu (Nepal), during 1st South Asian Regional Conference of Dermatology. **Aims** Establish and promote close personal and professional relations among dermatologists, venereologists and leprologists in the SAARC region; encourage common strategies towards advancement of education, care and prevention of skin diseases, leprosy and sexually transmitted diseases in the region; promote research and mutual exchange of knowledge and data for the benefit and care of SAARC countries communities. **Structure** Executive Committee, consisting of President, Vice-President, Secretary-General, Joint Secretary, Treasurer and members. **Languages** English. **Staff** None. **Finance** Members' dues. **Activities** Organizes 'South Asian Regional Conference of Dermatology (SARCD)'. **Events** *Conference* Pokhara (Nepal) 2019, *Conference* Lahore (Pakistan) 2017, *Conference* Mysore (India) 2015, *Conference* Colombo (Sri Lanka) 2013, *Conference* Dhaka (Bangladesh) 2011.
Members Full in 6 countries:
Bangladesh, India, Maldives, Nepal, Pakistan, Sri Lanka.
NGO Relations Member of: *International League of Dermatological Societies (ILDS, #14018)*.
[2019.11.22/XM1949/**D**]

♦ South Asian Regional Pain Society (SARPS) 19740

Contact Bangladesh Society of Anaesthesiologists, Dept of Anaesthesia, Analgesia and Intensive Care Medicine, Bangabandhu Sheikh Mujib Medical Univ, Shahbag, Dhaka 1000, Bangladesh. T. +88028619115. Fax +88029669444.

Events *Pain – reduce, relieve, remove* Ahmedabad (India) 2014, *Congress* Karachi (Pakistan) 2012, *Congress* Dhaka (Bangladesh) 2008, *Congress* Dhaka (Bangladesh) 2006, *Congress* Colombo (Sri Lanka) 2005.
[2014/XD9001/**D**]

♦ South Asian Seas Action Plan / see Action Plan for the Protection and Management of the South Asia Seas Region (#00094)

♦ South Asian Society on Atherosclerosis and Thrombosis (SASAT) .. 19741

Contact 12500 Park Potomac Ave, Unit 306N, Potomac MD 20854, USA.
URL: http://www.sasat.org/

History 1993. **Aims** Promote better heart health for South Asians. **Structure** Executive Board. **Finance** Members' dues. **Activities** Events/meetings. **NGO Relations** Member of: *Paediatric Radiation Oncology Society (PROS, #18019)*.
[2020.01.16/XM7021/**D**]

♦ South Asian Society of Criminology and Victimology (SASCV) 19742

Sec 55 Saibaba Colony, 4th Street, Thiyagaraja Nagar, Tirunelveli, Rajapalayam, Tamil Nadu, Rajapalayam TAMIL NADU, India. E-mail: southasiancsv@gmail.com.
URL: http://www.sascv.org/

History Registration: No/ID: 83/2009, India. **Aims** Nurture criminology and victimology in the South Asian region. **Structure** Executive Board. **Languages** English. **Events** *International Conference* Goa (India) 2016, *International Conference* Kanyakumari (India) 2013, *International Conference* Jaipur (India) 2011. **Publications** *International Journal of Criminal Justice Sciences*. Conference proceedings.
Members Individuals in 8 South Asian countries:
Afghanistan, Bangladesh, Bhutan, India, Maldives, Nepal, Pakistan, Sri Lanka.
Also members outside South Asian region. Membership countries not specified. [2019/XM4090/**D**]

♦ South Asian Society for Sexual Medicine (SASSM) 19743

Exec Sec B 701 Renaissance Temple Bells, Yeshwanthpur Industrial Suburb, Mahalakshmi Layout opp Iskon Temple, Bengaluru, Bangalore, Karnataka 560022, Bangalore KARNATAKA 560022, India. T. +917899852991. E-mail: info.sassm@gmail.com.
URL: http://sassm.in/

History Aug 2012, by a group of Indian specialists. **Aims** Encourage the highest standards of practice, education and research in the field of human sexuality and andrology; develop scientific methods for the diagnosis, prevention and treatment of conditions affecting human sexual – reproductive function; promote the publication of medical and scientific literature in the field of sexual – reproductive function. **Structure** Steering Committee; Executive Committee; Board of Directors. **Languages** English. **Staff** 1.00 FTE, paid. **Finance** No budget. **Activities** Research/documentation. **Events** *Meeting* Dhaka (Bangladesh) 2015. **Publications** None.
Members Full in 13 countries:
Afghanistan, Bangladesh, Bhutan, India, Kazakhstan, Kyrgyzstan, Maldives, Nepal, Pakistan, Sri Lanka, Tajikistan, Turkmenistan, Uzbekistan.
IGO Relations None. **NGO Relations** Regional society of: *International Society for Sexual Medicine (ISSM, #15441)*.
[2018.09.09/XJ9392/**D**]

♦ South Asian Studies Association of Australia (internationally oriented national body)

♦ South Asian University (SAU) 19744

Contact Akbar Bhawan, Satya Marg, Chanakyapure, New Delhi, Delhi 110021, DELHI 110021, India. T. +9111241122512 – +911124122514. Fax +911124122511.
URL: http://www.sau.int/

History Proposed 2005, Dhaka (Bangladesh). Agreement for Establishment of South Asian University signed 4 Apr 2007, by all *South Asian Association for Regional Cooperation (SAARC, #19721)* countries. **Aims** Create an institution of learning bringing together students from South Asia; build a South Asian community of learning where students can develop their intellectual potential; create a South Asian community by strengthening regional consciousness; impart education towards capacity building; contribute to promotion of regional peace and security; foster sound civic sense and train students to become useful citizens of democratic societies. **Structure** Governing Board; Executive Council; Finance Committee; Academic Council; President. **Activities** Training/education; research/documentation. **Events** *Convocation* Delhi (India) 2018, *Convocation* Delhi (India) 2017.
Members SAARC Governments (8):
Afghanistan, Bangladesh, Bhutan, India, Maldives, Nepal, Pakistan, Sri Lanka. [2019.08.31/XM6730/**F***]

♦ South Asian Women Development Forum (internationally oriented national body)

♦ South Asian Youth Climate Coalition (SAYCC) 19745

Contact c/o OSVSWA, B-14 – 15, Phase-1 Krishna Garden, Jagamara, Bhubaneswar, Sundargarh, Odisha, Sundargarh ODISHA, India. T. +916742350384.
URL: http://southasianyouthclimatecoalition.yolasite.com/

Aims Involve, educate and promote a new generation of youth volunteers to respond to the challenges communities must face and help them address the humanitarian consequences of climate change. **Structure** Advisory Board; Steering Committee. **Activities** Networking/liaising; research/documentation; advocacy/lobbying/activism.
Members Full in 8 countries:
China, India, Indonesia, Malaysia, Myanmar, Nepal, Sri Lanka, Thailand.
NGO Relations Partner of: *Global Call for Climate Action (GCCA, inactive)*. [2015/XM4336/**D**]

♦ South Asian Zoo Association for Regional Cooperation (SAZARC) .. 19746

Dir c/o Zoo Outreach Organisation, No 12 Thiruvannamalai Nagar, Saravanampatti, Coimbatore, Rajapalayam, Tamil Nadu 641 035, Rajapalayam TAMIL NADU 641 035, India. T. +914222665298. Fax +914222665472.
URL: http://www.zooreach.org/

History 2000. **Aims** Unite and inform zoos of the South Asian region; introduce modern zoo philosophy and best practice in conservation, education, research and animal care; lobby for zoo legislation including optimum standards of welfare and focus on conservation; lobby for change of administrative rules. **Structure** Informal structure. President elected by annual conference attendees from the country which has agreed to host next annual conference. Secretariat provided by Zoo Outreach Organisation. Director is also the Director of Zoo Outreach Organisation. **Languages** English. **Staff** 17.00 FTE, paid. **Finance** Sources: grants and donations from a variety of western zoos, welfare NGOs and governments. Fees not collected from zoos as their governments do not permit them to pay. **Activities** Events/meetings; training/education; knowledge management/information dissemination. **Events** *Annual Meeting* Chitwan (Nepal) 2010, *Annual Meeting* Dehiwela (Sri Lanka) 2009, *Annual meeting* Ahmedabad (India) 2008, *Annual meeting* Ho Chi Minh City (Vietnam) 2006, *Annual meeting* Coimbatore (India) 2005. **Publications** *SAZARC Newsletter*. **Members** Zoos and their personnel in South Asia. Membership countries not specified. **NGO Relations** Member of: *World Association of Zoos and Aquariums (WAZA, #21208)*. [2016.11.23/XJ3561/**D**]

♦ South Asia Olympic Council (SAOC) 19747

Contact address not obtained. T. +911124366950. Fax +911124365953.

History 1981, Delhi (India), as *South Asia Sports Federation (SASF)*. **Aims** Help develop in the youth in the region those physical and moral qualities that come from fair competition in amateur sports and promote international respect and goodwill among them. **Structure** President, Secretary-General, Treasurer; Executive Committee of 7 members. **Languages** English. **Activities** Games; conferences; meetings.
Members Sports federations from 8 countries:
Afghanistan, Bangladesh, Bhutan, India, Maldives, Nepal, Pakistan, Sri Lanka.
NGO Relations *Olympic Council of Asia (OCA, #17718)*. [2010/XD0997/**D**]

♦ South Asia Peoples' Alliance (internationally oriented national body)
♦ South Asia Research Network for the Social Sciences and Humanities (internationally oriented national body)

♦ South Asia Rural Reconstruction Association (SARRA) 19748

Association pour la reconstruction rurale de l'Asie du Sud

Contact Lumbini, St 30, 2nd Cross, 1st Main, Veerabadranagar, Marathahalli Post, Bangalore, Karnataka 560 037, Bangalore KARNATAKA 560 037, India. T. +91805232227. E-mail: sarraindia@gmail.com – grassit2001@yahoo.com.

History May 1984, by 70 NGOs inspired by *International Institute of Rural Reconstruction (IIRR, #13921)* and its founder. Registered according to Indian law. **Aims** Enhance capabilities of NGO network partners in South Asia for promoting participatory and integrated development of rural communities through utilization of current knowledge on rural reconstruction; design strategies for participatory planning, implementation, monitoring, feedback and evaluation; learn from experiential wisdom of grassroots development agencies in the region; promote training programs in South Asia in order to enhance awareness, knowledge and skills related to sustainable agriculture and family level food security. **Structure** General Body of 13. Executive Committee of 7. Regional Council. Advisory Committee. **Languages** English. **Staff** 20.00 FTE, paid. **Finance** Financed through international donor agencies. Annual budget: US$ 50,000. **Activities** Training/education; research and development; events/meetings. **Events** *Workshop on reproductive health* Bangalore (India) 1995. **Publications** Books.
Members Founder NGOs (70) in 20 countries:
Bangladesh, Bhutan, Egypt, Germany, India, Indonesia, Kenya, Korea Rep, Lebanon, Malaysia, Maldives, Nepal, Netherlands, Pakistan, Philippines, Sri Lanka, Sudan, Switzerland, Thailand, Zimbabwe.
NGO Relations Member of: *International Land Coalition (ILC, #13999)*. Working partnership with alumni associations, institutions, agencies and individuals world-wide. [2018.07.07/XD1426/**D**]

♦ South Asia Science Cooperation Office / see UNESCO Asia-Pacific Regional Bureau for Communication and Information (#20300)
♦ South Asia Sports Federation / see South Asia Olympic Council (#19747)
♦ South Asia Table Tennis Federation (no recent information)
♦ South Asia Theological Research Institute, Bangalore (internationally oriented national body)
♦ South Asia Theological Research Institute of the Board of Theological Education of Senate of Serampore College / see South Asia Theological Research Institute, Bangalore

♦ South Asia Watch on Trade, Economics and Environment (SAWTEE) 19749

Contact PO Box 19366, Tukucha Marg, Baluwatar, Kathmandu, Nepal. T. +97714424360 – +97714444438. Fax +97714444570. E-mail: sawtee@sawtee.org.
URL: http://www.sawtee.org/

History Dec 1994. Registered in accordance with Nepalese law, 1999. **Aims** Enable stakeholders, particularly the poor and marginalized, to derive net benefits from changing political economy and environmental landscapes. **Structure** Advisory Board; Executive Committee. **Languages** English, Nepali. **Staff** 22.00 FTE, paid. **Finance** Support from: *Oxfam Novib*. **Activities** Events/meetings; research/documentation; training/education. **Publications** *Trade Insight* (4 a year). Briefing papers; issue papers; policy briefs; discussion papers.
Members Organizations (11) in 5 countries:
Bangladesh, India, Nepal, Pakistan, Sri Lanka. [2014.06.02/XF0844/t/**F**]

♦ South Asia Women's Fund / see Women's Fund Asia (#21018)
♦ South Association for Cooperation and Development (internationally oriented national body)

♦ South Atlantic Maritime Area 19750

Area Maritima del Atlantico Sur (AMAS)

Contact Estado Mayor General de la Armada Argentina, Comodoro Py 2055, piso 11 oficina 130 C1104, Ciudad Autónoma, Buenos Aires, Argentina. T. +541143172000. Fax +541143172509. E-mail: colcoar@ara.mil.ar.

URL: http://www.coamas.org/
History 1966. Established by the Governments of Argentina, Brazil, Paraguay and Uruguay. Former names and other names: *South Atlantic Maritime Area Coordination* – alias; *Coordinador del Area Maritima del Atlantico Sur (CAMAS)* – alias. **Aims** Control maritime traffic in the South Atlantic. **Structure** Operations Officer; Advisors. **Languages** English, Portuguese, Spanish. **Staff** 9.00 FTE, paid. [2023.02.15/XF6097/**F***]

♦ South Atlantic Maritime Area Coordination / see South Atlantic Maritime Area (#19750)

♦ South Caucasus Office on Drugs and Crime (SCODC) 19751

Dir 20 Panaskerteli St, 0160 Tbilisi, Georgia. T. +995322363675 – +995322362093.
History Feb 2010. Registration: Georgia. **Aims** Conduct monitoring of implementation of relevant UN Conventions and other international treaties and prepare reports in the areas of drugs and crime. **Structure** Board (meets at least twice a year). **Languages** English, Georgian, Russian. **Staff** 6.00 FTE, voluntary. **Finance** Donor resources; private donations. Annual budget: 5,000 USD. **Activities** Advocacy/lobbying/activism; events/meetings; knowledge management/information dissemination; projects/programmes; research/documentation; training/education. **Consultative Status** Consultative status granted from: *ECOSOC (#05331)* (Special). **IGO Relations** PADOR; *United Nations Office on Drugs and Crime (UNODC, #20596).* [2021.06.08/XM7269/**D**]

♦ South and Central America Handball Confederation / see Confederación de Sur y Centro America de Balonmano (#04443)

♦ South and Central American Assembly on Linguistic Anthropology (SCAALA) 19752

Address not obtained.
Aims Redefine the way South and Central American and Caribbean language and society are viewed. **Languages** English. **Activities** Advocacy/lobbying/activism; awards/prizes/competitions; awareness raising; capacity building; events/meetings; financial and/or material support; guidance/assistance/consulting; knowledge management/information dissemination; networking/liaising; publishing activities; research/documentation; training/education. **NGO Relations** Constitutes *Global Network in Linguistic Anthropology*, together with *Global Council for Anthropological Linguistics (GLOCAL, #10310), Conference on Mediterranean and European Linguistic Anthropology (COMELA, #04628), Conference on Oceanian Linguistic Anthropology (COOLA, #04636), Middle Eastern Association of Linguistic Anthropology (MEALA, #16760)* and *African Assembly of Linguistic Anthropology (AFALA, #00204).* [2020.05.02/XM8715/c/**F**]

♦ South Centre 19753

Centre Sud – Centro del Sur
Exec Dir Chemin de Balexert 7-9, PO Box 228, 1211 Geneva 19, Switzerland. T. +41227918050. E-mail: south@southcentre.int.
URL: http://www.southcentre.int/
History 1 Nov 1990. Established as a temporary mechanism to follow up work of *South Commission (inactive)*, set up Aug 1987, Geneva (Switzerland), following *Conference of Heads of State or Government of Non-Aligned Countries*, 1986, Harare (Zimbabwe). Work of the South Commission terminated at final meeting, Oct 1990, Arusha (Tanzania UR). South Centre established on a new basis as an intergovernmental organization of developing countries by the 1994 intergovernmental *'Agreement to Establish the South Centre'*, which came into force 31 Jul 1995. **Aims** Help *developing countries* combine their efforts and expertise to promote their common interests in the international arena; pursue objectives as listed in the intergovernmental agreement; work towards South unity in diversity and South progress through *cooperation.* **Structure** Council of Representatives; Board; Secretariat located in Geneva (Switzerland). **Languages** English, French, Spanish. **Staff** 16.00 FTE, paid. *Administrative Tribunal of the International Labour Organization (ILO Tribunal, #00118)* is competent to settle disputes. **Finance** Sources: contributions of member/participating states. **Activities** Capacity building; guidance/assistance/consulting; politics/policy/regulatory; research/documentation. **Events** *International conference on challenges to the South in the nineties with special reference to the Asian region* 1993, *Regional seminar / Annual Conference of Ministers Responsible for Economic and Social Development and Planning* Addis Ababa (Ethiopia) 1993, *Regional seminar* Delhi (India) 1993. **Publications** *SouthNews and SouthViews.* Research papers; policy briefs; reprints; books.
Members As at March 2021 countries (54):
Algeria, Angola, Argentina, Barbados, Benin, Bolivia, Brazil, Burundi, Cambodia, Cape Verde, China, Côte d'Ivoire, Cuba, Dominican Rep, Ecuador, Egypt, Gabon, Ghana, Guyana, Honduras, India, Indonesia, Iran Islamic Rep, Iraq, Jamaica, Jordan, Korea DPR, Liberia, Libya, Malawi, Malaysia, Mali, Mauritius, Micronesia FS, Morocco, Mozambique, Namibia, Nicaragua, Nigeria, Pakistan, Palestine, Panama, Philippines, Seychelles, Sierra Leone, South Africa, Sri Lanka, Sudan, Suriname, Tanzania UR, Uganda, Venezuela, Vietnam, Zimbabwe.
IGO Relations Observer status with:
- *Convention on Biological Diversity (Biodiversity convention, 1992);*
- *Basel Convention on the Control of Transboundary Movements of Hazardous Wastes and Their Disposal (UNCRTD, 1989);*
- *ECOSOC (#05331);*
- *Framework Convention on Tobacco Control (FCTC, 2003);*
- *Green Climate Fund (GCF, #10714);*
- *Intergovernmental Group of Twenty-Four on International Monetary Affairs (Group of Twenty-Four, #11495);*
- *Intergovernmental Panel on Climate Change (IPCC, #11499);*
- *International Criminal Court (ICC, #13108);*
- *Rotterdam Convention on the Prior Informed Consent Procedure for Certain Hazardous Chemicals and Pesticides in International Trade (Rotterdam convention, 1998);*
- *Stockholm Convention on Persistent Organic Pollutants (POP treaty, 2001);*
- *UNCTAD (#20285);*
- *Union internationale pour la protection des obtentions végétales (UPOV, #20436);*
- *United Nations (UN, #20515)* General Assembly;
- *United Nations Framework Convention on Climate Change – Secretariat (UNFCCC, #20564);*
- *WHO (#20950);*
- *World Intellectual Property Organization (WIPO, #21593);*
- *World Trade Organization (WTO, #21864)* Committee on Trade and Development. [2021.03.05/XE1177/**E***]

♦ South China Growth Triangle (no recent information)
♦ South Continent Boxing Federation (unconfirmed)
♦ South and East African Society of Agricultural Engineering (unconfirmed)
♦ South East Asia Amateur Radio Network / see South East Asia Net (#19764)
♦ South East Asia Association for the Promotion of Christian Church Music (inactive)
♦ South East Asia Association for the Promotion of Church Music / see World Association for Chinese Church Music (#21125)

♦ Southeast Asia Astronomy Network (SEAAN) 19754

Address not obtained.
History 2007, Thailand. **Activities** Events/meetings. **Events** *Meeting* Singapore (Singapore) 2019, *Meeting* Lampung (Indonesia) 2018, *Meeting* Mandalay (Myanmar) 2017, *Meeting* Hanoi (Vietnam) 2016, *Meeting* Chiang Mai (Thailand) 2011. [2019/AA0207/c/**F**]

♦ South East Asia Clinical Epidemiology Network / see International Clinical Epidemiology Network – Asia (#12599)
♦ Southeast Asia Disaster Prevention Research Initiative / see Southeast Asia Disaster Prevention Research Institute
♦ Southeast Asia Disaster Prevention Research Institute (internationally oriented national body)

♦ South East Asia Drymix Mortar Association (SEADMA) 19755

Pres Tegernseer Landstr 26, 81541 Munich, Germany. T. +498962000232. Fax +498962009911. E-mail: info@seadma.org.
Registered Office 80 South Bridge Road, No 03-01, Singapore 058710, Singapore.
URL: http://www.seadma.org/
History 2006, when charter was adopted. Registered in accordance with Singapore law: ROS 2089/2006. **Aims** Promote an integrative, quality minded approach to drymix (factory made) mortars to the South East Asia. **Structure** Board (Executive Committee). Executive Secretary. National Chapters; Technical Committee. **Languages** English. **Staff** 3.00 FTE, voluntary. **Finance** Members' dues. Other sources: sponsoring; meeting and publication proceeds. **Activities** Events/meetings; training/education; knowledge management/information dissemination; certification/accreditation; publishing activities. **Events** *Annual Conference / Annual SEADMA Conference* Bangkok (Thailand) 2015, *Annual Conference / Annual SEADMA Conference* Singapore (Singapore) 2014, *Annual SEADMA Conference* Kuala Lumpur (Malaysia) 2013, *Annual SEADMA Conference* Jakarta (Indonesia) 2012, *Annual SEADMA Conference* Jakarta (Indonesia) 2009. **Publications** *SEADMA Newsletter*; *SEADMA Technical Bulletin.*
Members Full in 5 countries:
Indonesia, Malaysia, Philippines, Singapore, Thailand. [2015.01.14/XJ9051/**D**]

♦ Southeast Asia Engineering Education Development Network (see: #01243)
♦ South East Asia Games Federation (no recent information)
♦ South East Asia Graduate School of Theology / see ATESEA Theological Union (#03002)
♦ South East Asia Institute for Community Education / see Southeast Asia Regional Initiatives for Community Empowerment (#19795)

♦ South East Asia Iron and Steel Institute (SEAISI) 19756

Institut de la sidérurgie du Sud-Est asiatique
Manager – Admin and IT PO Box 7094, 40702 Shah Alam, Selangor, Malaysia. T. +60355191102. Fax +60355191159. E-mail: seaisi@seaisi.org.
Street Address 2E – 5th Floor – Block 2, Worldwide Business Park, Jalan Tinju 13/50, 40675 Shah Alam, Selangor, Malaysia.
URL: http://www.seaisi.org/
History 1971, under the auspices of United Nations Economic Commission for Asia and the Far East (ECAFE), now *United Nations Economic and Social Commission for Asia and the Pacific (ESCAP, #20557).* Registered as a limited company in Singapore. **Aims** Further the development of iron and steel industries; encourage regional cooperation between governments, industries and organizations and supporting member countries; provide a forum for exchange of knowledge and discussion; provide advisory services and promote the scientific, technological and economic aspects of iron and steel industry development in member countries; encourage establishment and extension of training programmes; promote standardization and utilization of steel products; collect, collate and publish appropriate statistics; disseminate the results of its activities by publication and other means. **Structure** Board of Directors (governing body), comprising 10 country members, one from each regular member country and supporting member country. Regular Member Countries: Indonesia; Malaysia; Philippines; Thailand; Singapore; Vietnam. Supporting Member Countries: Australia; Japan; Korea Rep; Taiwan. Each Regular Member Country and Supporting Member Country represented by a National Committee. Independent Committees (4): National; Technical; Environmental and Safety; Statistical. Technical Committee advises Board on technical matters. Secretariat located in Malaysia since 1992. **Languages** English. **Staff** 8.00 FTE, paid. **Finance** Members' dues. **Activities** Organizes international conference (annually), travelling seminars and lectures; collects and publishes appropriate statistical data; provides training programmes for industry personnel; provides advisory services; promotes standardization and utilization of steel products. **Events** *Sustainable development of ASEAN steel value chain* Bangkok (Thailand) 2019, *Forum* Ho Chi Minh City (Vietnam) 2018, *ASEAN steel industry – next leap of transformation* Jakarta (Indonesia) 2018, *Forum* Manila (Philippines) 2017, *Conference* Singapore (Singapore) 2017. **Publications** *SEAISI Directory* (2 a year); *Country Reports* (annual); *Steel Statistical Yearbook* (annual); *SEAISI Monthly Newsletter*; *SEAISI Quarterly Journal.* Technical Papers presented at Conferences; Bibliographies. Information Services: Information Centre including contract research services.
Members Companies Regular; Associate; Affiliated. Individuals. Members (829 worldwide of which 537 in South East Asia) in 40 countries and territories:
Argentina, Australia, Austria, Bahrain, Belgium, Brunei Darussalam, Canada, China, France, Germany, Greece, Hong Kong, India, Indonesia, Italy, Japan, Korea Rep, Malaysia, Mauritius, Mexico, Myanmar, Netherlands, New Zealand, Norway, Philippines, Portugal, Qatar, Singapore, South Africa, Spain, Sri Lanka, Sweden, Switzerland, Taiwan, Thailand, Türkiye, UK, Ukraine, USA, Vietnam.
Included in the above, 1 regional organization:
International Iron Metallics Association (IIMA, #13953).
IGO Relations Participates in the work of: *United Nations Economic Commission for Europe (UNECE, #20555).* Regular relations with: *UNDP (#20292).* **NGO Relations** In liaison with technical committees of: *International Organization for Standardization (ISO, #14473).* [2019/XD3977/j/**D**]

♦ Southeast Asia Lutheran Association for Higher Education (inactive)
♦ South East Asian Academy of Sleep Medicine (unconfirmed)
♦ Southeast Asian Agency for Regional Transport and Communications Development (inactive)

♦ South East Asian Association for Dental Education (SEAADE) 19757

Secretariat Faculty of Dentistry, Univ Teknologi MARA, 40540 Shah Alam, Selangor, Malaysia.
Pres address not obtained. E-mail: mibrahim@salam.uitm.edu.my.
URL: http://www.seaade.org/
History 1990, Singapore (Singapore). **Aims** Promote advancement of dental education, research and service in all institutions; encourage and facilitate cooperative effort and achievement by dental educators in the region. **Structure** General Meeting (annual). Council, consisting of President, President-elect, Secretary, Treasurer and 4 councillors. **Languages** English. **Staff** Voluntary. **Finance** No dues. Expenses absorbed by faculties and dental schools in the region, essential expenditure from donations. **Events** *Annual General Meeting* Bali (Indonesia) 2015, *Annual General Meeting* Kuching (Malaysia) 2014, *Annual General Meeting* Bangkok (Thailand) 2013, *Annual General Meeting* Hong Kong (Hong Kong) 2012, *Annual General Meeting* Hong Kong (Hong Kong) 2012. **Publications** Membership directory.
Members Dental schools and other dental educational institutions (31); individuals. Members in 11 countries:
China, Hong Kong, India, Malaysia, Myanmar, Philippines, Singapore, Sri Lanka, Taiwan, Thailand, Vietnam.
NGO Relations Member of: *International Federation of Dental Educators and Associations (IFDEA, #13404).* [2015/XD3401/**D**]

♦ South East Asian Association of Graduate Employers (internationally oriented national body)

♦ South East Asian Association for Institutional Research (SEAAIR) . . 19758

Sec c/o International Studies Inst, 2086 7th floor RU Printing Press Bldg, Ramkhamhaeng Road, Bangkok, 10240, Thailand.
URL: http://www.seaairweb.info/
History Sep 2000, Kuala Lumpur (Malaysia). **Aims** Advance research leading to improved understanding, planning and operation of institutions of post-secondary education; disseminate information and interchange of ideas on problems of common interest in the field of institutional research. **Structure** Executive Committee. **Events** *Annual Conference* Seoul (Korea Rep) 2022, *Diversity in Education* 2021, *Conference* Taipei (Taiwan) 2019, *Conference* Jakarta (Indonesia) 2018, *Annual Conference* Singapore (Singapore) 2017. [2020/XM1830/**D**]

♦ Southeast Asian Biosphere Reserve Network (SeaBRnet) 19759

Contact UNESCO Office Jakarta, Jl Galuh II No 5, Kebayoran Baru, Jakarta, Indonesia. T. +62217399818. Fax +622172796489. E-mail: jakarta@unesco.org.
URL: http://www.unesco.org/new/en/jakarta/about-this-office/regional-networks/
History Oct 1998, Ho Chi Minh City (Vietnam), within the framework of *Programme on Man and the Biosphere (MAB, #18526)* and with the support of *UNESCO Office, Jakarta – Regional Bureau for Sciences in Asia and the Pacific (#20313).* **Aims** Foster cooperation of scientific, ecosystem and biosphere reserve management related issues such as communication and visibility, ecotourism, partnership, green economy and climate change. **Events** *Meeting* Chiang Mai (Thailand) 2018, *Meeting* Bali (Indonesia) 2017, *Meeting* Malang (Indonesia) 2015, *Meeting* Siem Reap (Cambodia) 2014, *Meeting* Puerto Princesa (Philippines) 2013.
Members Full in 9 countries:
Cambodia, Indonesia, Laos, Malaysia, Myanmar, Philippines, Thailand, Timor-Leste, Vietnam. [2017.04.04/XF6554/**F**]

♦ Southeast Asian Center for Lifelong Learning for Sustainable Development (internationally oriented national body)

♦ South East Asian Central Banks Research and Training Centre (SEACEN Centre) 19760

Contact Level 5 – Sasana Kijang, Bank Negara Malaysia, 2 Jalan Dato'Onn, 50480 Kuala Lumpur, Malaysia. T. +60391951888. E-mail: enquiries@seacen.org.
URL: http://www.seacen.org/

History Idea conceived 1967, Baguio (Philippines), at 2nd *Conference of Governors of Southeast Asian Central Banks (SEACEN)*, with feasibility discussed at subsequent annual conferences. Single centre for both research and training agreed at 7th meeting, 1972, Kuala Lumpur (Malaysia). Officially opened 15 Jan 1977. Became a legal entity when formal agreement was signed at 17th Conference, 3 Feb 1982, Bangkok (Thailand). **Aims** Promote a better understanding of the financial, monetary, banking and economic development matters which are of interest to the central banks and monetary authorities of the countries in South East Asia or of interest to the region as a whole; stimulate and facilitate cooperation among central banks and monetary authorities in the area of research and training. **Structure** Board of Governors (meeting annually in conjunction with SEACEN Governors' Conference), comprises Governors and Managing Directors of central banks and monetary authorities. Executive Committee, comprising Deputy Governors; Board of Directors (meets annual), comprising Governor and Deputy Governor of Bank Negara Malaysia, plus Executive Director. Departments (3): Learning Design and Development; Research and Learning Contents; Performance and Support Services. *SEACEN Trust Fund*, set up by 23rd SEACEN Conference, Jan 1988, Singapore. **Languages** English. **Staff** 26.00 FTE, paid. **Finance** Contributions from member central banks and monetary authorities. Annual budget (2014): US$ 2,568,000. **Activities** Events/meetings; research/documentation; training/education. **Events** *Annual Governors Conference* Colombo (Sri Lanka) 2018, *Seminar on Mitigating Misconduct Risk in the Financial Sector* Singapore (Singapore) 2018, *Annual Governors Conference* Bangkok (Thailand) 2017, *Seminar on Financial Cycles and Crises* Daegu (Korea Rep) 2017, *Annual Governors Conference* Port Moresby (Papua New Guinea) 2014. **Publications** *SEACEN Financial Stability Journal* (2 a year); *SEACEN Profile* (annual); *SEACEN Program* (annual). Research studies series; working papers series; conference proceedings; research monographs; seminar papers; training brochures; database.
Members Central banks and monetary authorities of 19 economies:
Brunei Darussalam, Cambodia, China, Hong Kong, India, Indonesia, Korea Rep, Laos, Malaysia, Mongolia, Myanmar, Nepal, Papua New Guinea, Philippines, Singapore, Sri Lanka, Taiwan, Thailand, Vietnam.
Associate members in 8 countries and territories:
Australia, Bangladesh, Bhutan, Fiji, Macau, Pakistan, Tonga, Vanuatu.
Observer in 8 countries and territories:
Afghanistan, Iran Islamic Rep, Japan, Maldives, New Zealand, Samoa, Solomon Is, Timor-Leste.
IGO Relations Cooperates with: APEC Training Initiative; *ASEAN (#01141)*; *Asia-Pacific Economic Cooperation (APEC, #01887)* Business Advisory Council (ABAC); *Asian Development Bank (ADB, #01422)*; *Asian Development Bank Institute (ADB Institute, #01423)*; *Bank for International Settlements (BIS, #03165)*; *Financial Stability Institute (FSI, #09771)*; *IMF Institute (see: #14180)*; *International Bank for Reconstruction and Development (IBRD, #12317)* (World Bank); *International Monetary Fund (IMF, #14180)*; *Irving Fisher Committee on Central Bank Statistics (IFC, #16020)*; *Islamic Development Bank (IsDB, #16044)*; national banks; *World Bank Institute (WBI, #21220)*. **NGO Relations** Cooperates with: *Center for Latin American Monetary Studies (#03648)*; *The Iclif Leadership and Governance Centre (Iclif)*; *International Association of Deposit Insurers (IADI, #11843)*.
[2020/XD6488/**E***]

♦ South East Asian Committee for Advocacy (SEACA) 19761

Secretariat 29 D Mayaman St, UP Village, Diliman, Quezon City, Philippines. T. +6329206228.
URL: http://www.seaca.net/

Aims Focus on advocacy capacity building of *civil society* organizations (CSOs) in Southeast Asia.
Members Organizations in 8 countries and territories:
Cambodia, Indonesia, Malaysia, Myanmar, Philippines, Thailand, Timor-Leste, Vietnam.
Included in the above, 4 organizations listed in this Yearbook:
Asian Centre for Women's Human Rights (ASCENT, no recent information); *Asian Cultural Forum on Development Foundation (ACFOD, no recent information)*; *Asian Partnership for the Development of Human Resources in Rural Asia (AsiaDHRRA, #01654)*; *Southeast Asia Consortium (SEACON, no recent information)*.
NGO Relations Involved in: *Solidarity for ASEAN People's Advocacy (SAPA, #19683)*. [2014/XE4413/y/**E**]

♦ Southeast Asian Conflict Studies Network (SEACSN) 19762

Contact Research and Education for Peace Unit, School of Social Sciences, Universiti Sains Malaysia, 11800 Minden, Malaysia. T. +6046532123. Fax +6046577070.
Facebook: https://www.facebook.com/pages/category/Education/Southeast-Asian-Conflict-Studies-Network-SEACSN-992602784112541/

Aims Promote cooperation and collaboration among researchers working in the area of peace and conflict research in Southeast Asia. **Activities** Organizes Consolidation for Peace in the regions of Aceh (Indonesia), Southern Thailand and Mindanao (since 2006). **Events** *Issues and challenges for peace and conflict resolution in Southeast Asia* Penang (Malaysia) 2004, *Regional workshop* Chiang Mai (Thailand) 2003, *Regional workshop* Phnom Penh (Cambodia) 2003, *Regional workshop* Sanur (Indonesia) 2003. **Members** Membership countries not specified. **NGO Relations** Member of: *Global Partnership for the Prevention of Armed Conflict (GPPAC, #10538)*; *Mediation Support Network (MSN, #16622)*; *Southeast Asian Human Rights Studies Network (SEAHRN, #19771)*. [2010.09.20/XF7065/**F**]

♦ South East Asian Copper Development Centre / see International Copper Association Southeast Asia
♦ Southeast Asian Council for Food Security and Fair Trade (inactive)

♦ Southeast Asian Directors of Music (SEADOM) 19763

CEO College of Music, Mahidol Univ 25/25, Phuttamonthon Sai 4, Salaya Nakhon Pathom, Bangkok, 73170, Thailand. T. +662800252534 ext 3202. Fax +6628002530. E-mail: contact@seadom.org – ir_music@mahidol.ac.th.
URL: http://www.seadom.org/

History Founded 2008. **Aims** Advance Southeast Asia music education with a particular focus on professional training for musician as they engage with music, the arts and culture in contemporary society and for future generations. **Structure** Executive Council. **Activities** Events/meetings. **Events** *Congress* Yogyakarta (Indonesia) 2019, *Congress* Nakhon Pathom (Thailand) 2018, *Congress* Yangon (Myanmar) 2017, *Congress* Vientiane (Laos) 2016, *Congress* Quezon City (Philippines) 2015.
Members Active in 4 countries:
Indonesia, Malaysia, Singapore, Thailand.
Associate in 10 countries:
Australia, China, Estonia, Hong Kong, Korea Rep, Malaysia, Norway, Singapore, Sweden, UK.
Consultative Status Consultative status granted from: *ASEAN (#01141)*. [2022/XM8411/**D**]

♦ South-East Asian Ergonomics Society / see South East Asian Network of Ergonomics Societies (#19777)

♦ South East Asia Net (SEANET) 19764

Contact c/o RAST, GPO Box 2008, Bangkok, 10501, Thailand.
URL: http://seanet.asia

History 29 Nov 1963. Former names and other names: *South East Asia Amateur Radio Network (SEANET)* – alias. **Aims** Bring together *amateur radio* operators (HAMs). **Activities** Organizes a convention. **Events** *Convention* 2021, *Convention* Thailand 2020, *Convention* Johor Bahru (Malaysia) 2019, *Convention* Yogyakarta (Indonesia) 2018, *Convention* Siem Reap (Cambodia) 2017. [2020/XJ6960/**F**]

♦ Southeast Asian Federation of Critical Care Nurses (SEAFCCN) 19765

Contact address not obtained. E-mail: seafccn.info@gmail.com.
URL: http://seafccn.com/

History 2018. **Aims** Link critical care nursing associations and nurses throughout the Southeast Asian region and the world; strengthen the influence and contribution of critical care nurses to health care in the Southeast Asian region; be a collective voice and advocate for critical care nurses and patients at an international level. **Structure** Council. **Events** *Congress* Makati (Philippines) 2022, *Congress* Kuching (Malaysia) 2019.
Members Full in 6 countries:
Brunei Darussalam, Cambodia, Indonesia, Malaysia, Myanmar, Philippines. [2019/AA2392/**D**]

♦ Southeast Asian Federation of Organizations for Medical Physics (SEAFOMP) 19766

Contact BHDT, Dept of Health, San Lazaro Compound, Tayuman, Sta Cruz, 1003 Manila, Philippines. T. +6327116061. Fax +6327116061.
URL: http://seafomp.fisika.ui.ac.id/

History 2000, following informal discussions initiated in 1996. **Aims** Promote cooperation and communication between medical physics organizations in the ASEAN region; promote advancement in status and standard of practice of the medical physics profession. **Structure** Council, including President, Vice-President, Secretary-General and Treasurer. **Events** *International Conference on Medical Physics (ICMP)* Mumbai (India) 2023, *Congress* Kuala Lumpur (Malaysia) 2018, *Congress* Singapore (Singapore) 2013, *Congress* Bandung (Indonesia) 2010, *Congress* Vietnam 2008.
Members in 7 countries:
Brunei Darussalam, Indonesia, Malaysia, Philippines, Singapore, Thailand, Vietnam.
NGO Relations Regional chapter of: *International Organization for Medical Physics (IOMP, #14453)*.
[2010/XJ1589/**D**]

♦ Southeast Asian Fisheries Development Center (SEAFDEC) 19767

Centre de développement des pêches de l'Asie du Sud-Est
SG PO Box 1046, Kasetsart Post Office, Chatuchak, Bangkok, 10903, Thailand. T. +6629406326. Fax +6629406336. E-mail: sg@seafdec.org – saowanee@seafdec.org – secretariat@seafdec.org.
URL: http://www.seafdec.org/

History 28 Dec 1967, Bangkok (Thailand), following recommendation of the Ministerial Conference on Economic Development of Southeast Asia, 1966, Tokyo (Japan). Protocol amending agreement signed 13 Jan 1968, Bangkok. **Aims** Promote fisheries and *aquaculture* development in Southeast Asia; provide training, research and information. **Structure** Council of Directors. Secretariat in Thailand, headed by Secretary-General. Departments (4): Training (TD) in Thailand; Marine Fisheries Research (MFRD) in Singapore; Aquaculture (AQD) in Philippines; Marine Fishery Resources Development and Management (MFRDMD) in Malaysia. **Languages** English. **Staff** 500.00 FTE, paid. **Finance** Contributions from Member countries and other donor organizations. **Activities** Promotes sustainable development of fisheries in the Southeast Asian region through research, training, technology transfer and information dissemination. Works through its departments: *'Training Department'* – Fishery resources surveys and explorations; development of fishing gear technologies; promotion of responsible fishing gear and practices; promotion of sustainable fisheries management. *'Marine Fisheries Research Department (MFRD)'* – Development and promotion of appropriate fishery post-harvest technologies and practices; improving quality and safety of fish and fishery products. *'Aquaculture Department'* – Development of aquaculture technologies for economically important species and species under international concern. *'Marine Fishery Resources Development and Management Department (MFRDMD)'* – Conduct of research and development on marine fishery resources; inland fisheries management. **Events** *Meeting* Bangkok (Thailand) 2020, *Meeting* Siem Reap (Cambodia) 2018, *Meeting* Bandar Seri Begawan (Brunei Darussalam) 2017, *Oceans and Fisheries Partnership Regional Gender and Ecosystem Approach to Fisheries Management Workshop* Bangkok (Thailand) 2017, *Meeting* Nha Trang (Vietnam) 2016. **Publications** *SEAFDEC Newsletter* (4 a year); *Fish for the People* (3 a year); *Fishery Statistical Bulletin of Southeast Asia* (annual).
Members Governments of 11 countries:
Brunei Darussalam, Cambodia, Indonesia, Japan, Laos, Malaysia, Myanmar, Philippines, Singapore, Thailand, Vietnam.
NGO Relations Associate member of: *International Network on Genetics in Aquaculture (INGA, see: #21507)*. Partner of: *WorldFish (#21507)*. [2020/XE4956/**E***]

♦ Southeast Asian Futuristics Educators Association (no recent information)
♦ Southeast Asian Gateway Evolution Meeting (meeting series)

♦ Southeast Asian Geography Association (SEAGA) 19768

Contact c/o HSSE, 1 Nanyang Walk, Singapore 637616, Singapore. E-mail: seaga@nie.edu.sg.
URL: http://www.seaga.info/

History 1990. Registered in accordance with the law of Singapore, Feb 2006. **Events** *Biennial Conference* Siem Reap (Cambodia) 2014, *Biennial Conference* Singapore (Singapore) 2012, *Biennial Conference* Hanoi (Vietnam) 2010, *Seminar on teaching and learning geography that matters* Singapore (Singapore) 2010, *Biennial Conference* Vietnam 2010. **Publications** *SEAGA focus* (2 a year) – electronic newsletter.
[2015.01.08/XD6535/**D**]

♦ Southeast Asian Geotechnical Society (SEAGS) 19769

SG c/o Asian Inst of Technology, 58 Moo 9, Km 42 Paholyothin Highway, Klong Luang, Pathumthani, Bangkok, 12120, Thailand. T. +6625245864. E-mail: seags@ait.ac.th.
URL: http://www.seags.ait.ac.th/

History 29 Apr 1967, at 1st Southeast Asian Conference on Soil Engineering, as *South East Asian Society of Soil Engineering (SEASSE)*. **Aims** Promote cooperation among engineers and scientists for the advancement of knowledge in the field of soil *engineering* – geotechnical engineering, rock mechanics and mining engineering. **Structure** General Committee. **Languages** English. **Finance** Members' dues. Sponsorship by: *Asian Institute of Technology (AIT, #01519)*. **Events** *Southeast Asian Geotechnical Conference* Jakarta (Indonesia) 2018, *Symposium* Pathum Thani (Thailand) 2017, *Southeast Asian Geotechnical Conference* Subang Jaya (Malaysia) 2016, *Southeast Asian Geotechnical Conference* Singapore (Singapore) 2013, *International symposium on sustainable geosynthetisis and green technology for climate change* Bangkok (Thailand) 2011. **Publications** *Geotechnical Engineering Journal* (4 a year). Newsletters (2 a year); conference, symposium and specialty session proceedings (annual).
Members Individuals interested or engaged in geotechnical engineering, engineering geology, rock mechanics or mining engineering in 29 countries and territories:
Australia, Bangladesh, Brunei Darussalam, Canada, China, Egypt, Hong Kong, India, Indonesia, Iraq, Israel, Italy, Japan, Korea DPR, Korea Rep, Malaysia, Myanmar, New Zealand, Norway, Papua New Guinea, Philippines, Saudi Arabia, Singapore, Switzerland, Taiwan, Thailand, UK, USA, Vietnam.
NGO Relations Instrumental in setting up with *Association of Geotechnical Societies in Southeast Asia (AGSSEA, #02625)*, with which it is now allied. Constituent member of: *International Society for Soil Mechanics and Geotechnical Engineering (ISSMGE, #15452)*. Member of *International Association of Engineering Geology and the Environment (IAEG, #11872)*; *International Society for Rock Mechanics and Rock Engineering (ISRM, #15428)*. SEAGS members automatically become members of ISSMGE and of IAEG and/or ISRM.
[2020.03.06/XD3258/v/**D**]

♦ Southeast Asian Gymnastics Confederation (SEAGCON) 19770

Pres c/o Malaysian Gymnastics Federation – MGF, 2 Jalan Langat II, Taman Sri Langat, 43000 Kajang, Selangor, Malaysia. T. +60391323029. Fax +60391323029. [2011/XD7921/**D**]

♦ Southeast Asian Human Rights Studies Network (SEAHRN) 19771

Convenor CHRSD, Mahidol Univ, Salaya Campus, Phuttamonthon, Nakhon Pathom, 73170, Thailand. E-mail: seahrn@gmail.com – seahrn.secretariat@gmail.com.
URL: http://www.seahrn.org/

History 2009, as a consortium of academic institutions. **Aims** Strengthen higher education devoted to the study of human rights in Southeast Asia through faculty and course development; develop deeper understanding and enhancement of human rights knowledge through collaborative research; achieve excellent regional academic and civil society cooperation in realizing human rights in Southeast Asia; conduct public advocacy through critical engagement with civil society actors, including inter-governmental bodies, in Southeast Asia. **Events** *International Conference on Human Rights and Peace and Conflict in Southeast Asia* Bangkok (Thailand) 2016, *International Conference on Human Rights and Peace and Conflict in Southeast Asia* Kuala Lumpur (Malaysia) 2014, *Conference* Bangkok (Thailand) 2010, *Conference* Bangkok (Thailand) 2009.
Members Network; Individual. Members in 6 countries:
Indonesia, Laos, Malaysia, Philippines, Thailand, Vietnam.
Included in the above, 2 organizations listed in this Yearbook:
Centre for Southeast Asian Social Studies (CESASS); *Southeast Asian Conflict Studies Network (SEACSN, #19762)*. [2020/XJ2202/y/**D**]

♦ Southeast Asian Laboratories Network (unconfirmed)

♦ Southeast Asian Linguistics Society (SEALS) 19772

Pres c/o Language Intelligence, 14 Malindi Place, Giralang ACT 2617, Australia.
Journal: http://jseals.org/

History 1991. First meeting took place at Wayne State University, Detroit MI (USA). **Aims** Facilitate and promote contact and communication among scholars and students of Southeast Asian Linguistics; disseminate their scholarly works. **Structure** Operates as a spontaneous voluntary collective. **Events** *Meeting* Manoa, HI (USA) 2020, *Meeting* Tokyo (Japan) 2019, *Annual Meeting* Chiang Mai (Thailand) 2015, *Annual meeting* Bangkok (Thailand) 2011, *Annual meeting* Kuala Lumpur (Malaysia) 1998. **Publications** *Journal of the Southeast Asian Linguistics Society (JSEALS).* Conference proceedings. [2021.09.01/XN8501/**D**]

♦ Southeast Asian Mathematical Society (SEAMS) 19773

Société de mathématiques d'Asie du Sud-Est

Sec address not obtained.
Pres address not obtained.
URL: http://www.seams-math.org/

History 1972. Regional network of *UNESCO Office, Jakarta – Regional Bureau for Sciences in Asia and the Pacific (#20313).* **Aims** Promote the advancement of mathematical science in Southeast Asia; facilitate information exchange about current research work and teaching methods between mathematicians in Southeast Asia; encourage and foster friendly collaboration with the members of other recognized mathematical and scientific institutions. **Structure** Council. **Languages** English. **Staff** Voluntary. **Finance** Sources: grants; members' dues. **Activities** Events/meetings; training/education. **Events** *Asian Mathematical Conference* Vietnam 2020, *Asian Mathematical Conference* Bali (Indonesia) 2016, *Asian Mathematical Conference* Busan (Korea Rep) 2013, *Asian Mathematical Conference* Kuala Lumpur (Malaysia) 2009, *AMC Asian mathematical conference / Asian Mathematical Conference* Singapore (Singapore) 2005. **Publications** *SEAMS Newsletter*; *Southeast Asian Bulletin of Mathematics.*

Members Societies in 9 countries and territories:
Cambodia, Hong Kong, Indonesia, Malaysia, Myanmar, Philippines, Singapore, Thailand, Vietnam.

NGO Relations Member of (1): *International Mathematical Union (IMU, #14121).* Represented on International Scientific Council of: *Centre international de mathématiques pures et appliquées (CIMPA, #03758).* [2022/XD1257/**D**]

♦ Southeast Asian Ministers of Education Organization (SEAMEO) ... 19774

Organisation des ministres d'éducation de l'Asie du Sud-Est (OMEASE)

Dir Mom Luang Pin Malakul Centenary Bldg, 920 Sukhumvit Road, Klongtoey, Bangkok, 10110, Thailand. T. +6623910144. Fax +6623812587. E-mail: secretariat@seameo.org.
URL: http://www.seameo.org/

History 30 Nov 1965, Bangkok (Thailand). Established at 1st Ministerial Conference, as an intergovernmental organization. Charter signed 7 Feb 1968, Singapore (Singapore), and ratified by all 7 founding member countries by Jan 1969. **Aims** Enhance regional understanding, cooperation and unity of purpose among Member Countries for a better quality of life through the establishment of networks and partnerships, the provision of fora among policy makers and experts, and the promotion of sustainable human resource development.

Structure SEAMEO Council, comprising Ministers of Education of all member countries, is the policy-making body; SEAMEO Secretariat. Directorship rotates every 4 years among member states.

Regional Centres (26):
- *Southeast Asian Ministers of Education Organization Regional Centre for STEM Education (SEAMEO STEM-ED, #19775),* Bangkok (Thailand);
- *Southeast Asian Regional Centre for Tropical Biology (SEAMEO BIOTROP, #19782),* Bogor (Indonesia);
- *SEAMEO Regional Centre for Early Childhood Care Education and Parenting (SEAMEO – CECCEP, #19171);*
- *SEAMEO Regional Centre for Community Education Development (SEAMEO CED, #19170);*
- *SEAMEO Regional Centre for Technical Education Development (SEAMEO TED, #19179);*
- *SEAMEO Regional Centre for History and Tradition (SEAMEO CHAT, #19175),* Yangon (Myanmar);
- *SEAMEO Regional Centre for Lifelong Learning (SEAMEO CELLL),* Ho Chi Minh City (Vietnam);
- *SEAMEO Regional Centre for Special Education (SEN),* Melaka (Malaysia);
- *SEAMEO Regional Open Learning Centre (SEAMOLEC, #19182),* Ciputat (Indonesia);
- *SEAMEO Regional Centre for Archaeology and Fine Arts (SEAMEO SPAFA, #19169),* Bangkok (Thailand);
- *SEAMEO Regional Centre for Education in Science and Mathematics (SEAMEO RECSAM, #19172),* Penang (Malaysia);
- *SEAMEO Regional Center for Educational Innovation and Technology (SEAMEO INNOTECH, #19168),* Manila (Philippines);
- *SEAMEO Regional Centre for Higher Education and Development (RIHED, #19174),* Bangkok;
- *Southeast Asian Regional Center for Graduate Study and Research in Agriculture (SEARCA, #19781),* Laguna (Philippines);
- *SEAMEO Regional Centre for Vocational and Technical Education (VOCTECH, #19180),* Bandar Seri Begawan (Brunei Darussalam);
- *SEAMEO Regional Language Centre (SEAMEO RELC, #19181),* Singapore (Singapore);
- *SEAMEO Regional Tropical Medicine and Public Health Network (SEAMEO TROPMED, #19184),* Bangkok;
- *SEAMEO Regional Training Centre, Ho Chi Minh City (RETRAC, #19183),* Ho Chi Minh City (Vietnam);
- *SEAMEO Regional Centre for Quality Improvement of Teachers and Educational Personnel in Language (SEAMEO QITEP in Language, #19176),* Jakarta (Indonesia);
- *SEAMEO Regional Centre for Quality Improvement of Teachers and Education Personnel in Mathematics (SEAMEO QITEP in Mathematics, #19177),* Yogyakarta (Indonesia);
- *SEAMEO Regional Centre for Quality Improvement of Teachers and Education Personnel in Science (SEAMEO QITEP in Science, #19178),* Bandung (Indonesia).

SEAMEO TROPMED Regional Centres in the region:
- *SEAMEO Regional Centre for Food and Nutrition (SEAMEO RECFON, #19173),* Jakarta (Indonesia);
- *SEAMEO TROPMED Regional Centre for Tropical Medicine (#19187),* Bangkok;
- *SEAMEO TROPMED Regional Centre for Microbiology, Parasitology and Entomology (#19185),* Kuala Lumpur (Malaysia);
- *SEAMEO TROPMED Regional Centre for Public Health, Hospital Administration, Environmental and Occupational Health (#19186),* Manila.

Languages English. **Staff** Professional staff of the Secretariat and the Centres are recruited from member countries; foreign experts are seconded under technical assistance. **Finance** SEAMEO Secretariat operating costs are underwritten by member countries. Capital and annually recurring operational costs of projects are the responsibility of the member country hosting a project or centre. Implementation of programmes of regional centres and projects are covered by SEAMEO Educational Development Fund (SEDF), with contributions from member and associate member governments and from other donor governments and agencies. **Activities** Training/education; events/meetings; research and development; projects/programmes; networking/liaising; financial and/or material support. **Events** *Ministerial Conference* 2021, *Congress* Bangkok (Thailand) 2021, *Southeast Asia Global Citizenship Education Policy Meeting* Seoul (Korea Rep) 2021, *Congress* Bangkok (Thailand) 2020, *High Officials Meeting* Bangkok (Thailand) 2019. **Publications** *SEAMEO Calendar of Activities*; *SEAMEO Education Agenda* – magazine. Technical publications; report status; brochures.

Members Governments of 11 countries:
Brunei Darussalam, Cambodia, Indonesia, Laos, Malaysia, Myanmar, Philippines, Singapore, Thailand, Timor-Leste, Vietnam.

Associate members (8):
Australia, Canada, France, Germany, Netherlands, New Zealand, Spain, UK.

Affiliate members (5):
Asia-Pacific Centre of Education for International Understanding (APCEIU); *British Council*; China Education Association for International Exchange (CEAIE); *International Council for Open and Distance Education (ICDE, #13056)*; University of Tsukuba (Japan).

IGO Relations Formal agreement with: *UNESCO (#20322).* Agreement with: *United Nations University (UNU, #20642).* Invited to sessions of Intergovernmental Council of: *International Programme for the Development of Communication (IPDC, #14651).* Cooperation agreement with: *Islamic World Educational, Scientific and Cultural Organization (ICESCO, #16058).* **NGO Relations** Affiliate member of: *International Council for Open and Distance Education (ICDE, #13056).* [2022/XD3257/y/**D***]

♦ Southeast Asian Ministers of Education Organization Regional Centre for STEM Education (SEAMEO STEM-ED) 19775

Program Dir 920 Sukhumvit Rd, Phra Khanong, Khlong Toei, Bangkok, 10110, Thailand. E-mail: secretariat@seameo-stemed.org.
URL: http://www.seameo-stemed.org/

History Established Nov 2019, Bangkok (Thailand), as a regional centre of *Southeast Asian Ministers of Education Organization (SEAMEO, #19774).* **Aims** Develop, maintain and continuously build capacities in STEM Education; serve as regional knowledge repository and creator through high-quality research in STEM education in Southeast Asia in a way that builds evidences of good practices, experiments and demonstrates pragmatic solutions, and guides effective policy formulation and capacity building of policymakers, professionals, and practitioners. **Structure** Governing Board. **Languages** English, Thai. **Staff** 8.00 FTE, paid. **Finance** Operating budgets from Thai government; programmatic budgets from fundraising with corporate sector. Starting annual budget: about US$ 15,000,000. **Activities** Advocacy/lobbying/activism; awareness raising; capacity building; knowledge management/information dissemination; research/documentation; training/education. **Publications** *Southeast Asian Journal of STEM Education.*

Members Governments (11):
Brunei Darussalam, Cambodia, Indonesia, Laos, Malaysia, Myanmar, Philippines, Singapore, Thailand, Timor-Leste, Vietnam.
[2020.02.17/XM8887/**E***]

♦ Southeast Asian Network for Agroforestry Education (SEANAFE) ... 19776

Contact 2/F Florencio-Tamesis Hall, College of Forestry and Natural Resources, University of the Philippines Los Banos, 4031 Santa Cruz LAG, Philippines. T. +63495363809.
URL: http://www.seanafe.org/

History Apr 1999. **Aims** Help improve agroforestry education, training, research and extension; contribute to socioeconomic development, empowerment of farming communities and sustainable natural resources and environmental management in the Southeast Asian region. **Structure** General Meeting (every 2 years). Board of 5 members. **Finance** Grant from: *Swedish International Development Cooperation Agency (Sida).* **Activities** Main activity areas: agroforestry curriculum development; teaching material support; theses research grants; research and field links; training of teachers. Organizes courses and workshops. **Publications** *SEANAFE Enews* – online E-J journal; *SEANAFE Trunk Line* – newsletter. *A Guide to Learning Agroforestry: A Framework for Developing Agroforestry Curricula in Southeast Asia* (2001) by Per G Rudebjer et al.

Members National networks (5) in 5 countries:
Indonesia, Laos, Philippines, Thailand, Vietnam.

IGO Relations Partners: *FAO Regional Office for Asia and the Pacific (RAP, #09266)*; *Southeast Asian Regional Center for Graduate Study and Research in Agriculture (SEARCA, #19781).* **NGO Relations** Partners: *African Network for Agriculture, Agroforestry and Natural Resources Education (ANAFE, #00380)*; *World Agroforestry Centre (ICRAF, #21072)*; *International Institute of Rural Reconstruction (IIRR, #13921)*; *RECOFTC – The Center for People and Forests (RECOFTC, #18628).* [2013/XF6674/**F**]

♦ South East Asian Network of Ergonomics Societies (SEANES) 19777

Pres De La Salle Univ, GCOE, Br Andrew Gonzales Hall, 2401 Taft Ave, 1004 Manila, Philippines.
URL: http://www.acedseanes2020.com/

History 1984, Indonesia, as *South-East Asian Ergonomics Society (SEAES).* **Aims** Promote learning and advance education in countries of South-East Asia concerning the relationship between man and his occupation, equipment and environment. **Structure** Officers: President, Vice-Presidents (2), Honorary Secretary-Treasurer and 5 members. **Languages** English. **Finance** Members' dues. **Events** *SEANES and ACED Joint Conference* Bohol (Philippines) 2020, *International Conference* Bangkok (Thailand) 2018, *International Conference* Bandung (Indonesia) 2016, *International Conference* Singapore (Singapore) 2014, *Conference* Langkawi (Malaysia) 2012.

Members Individuals in 13 countries:
Australia, Brunei Darussalam, China, Hong Kong, India, Indonesia, Japan, Malaysia, Philippines, Singapore, Sweden, Thailand, USA.

NGO Relations Cooperates with (1): *Asian Council on Ergonomics and Design (ACED).* Federated society of: *International Ergonomics Association (IEA, #13294).* [2020/XD1352/v/**F**]

♦ Southeast Asian Network for a Geological Information System (SANGIS) 19778

Réseau sud-est asiatique pour un système d'information géologique

Contact address not obtained. T. +33238643884. Fax +33238643472.
URL: http://sangis.brgm.fr/

History 1996, by *Centre international pour la formation et les échanges en géosciences (CIFEG, #03754)*; *IUGS Commission on Management and Application of Geoscience Information (CGI, #16081)*; *UNESCO (#20322)* (Division of Earth Sciences). **Aims** Optimize earth sciences information management in South-East Asian Geological Surveys; maximize the value of geosciences data on a regional scale; exchange geodata. **Languages** English. **Finance** Supported by the French Government and the following international organizations: UNESCO. **Activities** Organizes workshops and training. **Events** *Regional technical workshop* Bangkok (Thailand) 1999.

Members Full (Geological Surveys); Associate (Regional and international organizations). Full in 11 countries:
Cambodia, China, Indonesia, Japan, Korea Rep, Laos, Malaysia, Papua New Guinea, Philippines, Thailand, Vietnam.

Organizations (5):
CIFEG; *Coordinating Committee for Geoscience Programmes in East and Southeast Asia (CCOP, #04816)*; UIGS/COGEOINFO; UNESCO/Earth Sciences Division; *United Nations Economic and Social Commission for Asia and the Pacific (ESCAP, #20557).* [2008.06.01/XF5803/**F**]

♦ Southeast Asian Nuclear Weapon-Free Zone (see: #01141)
♦ Southeast Asian Outreach / see Cambodia Action

♦ South East Asian Radiation Oncology Group (SEAROG) 19779

Contact c/o PORI, Jl Diponegoro 71, Jakarta DKI 10430 ID, Indonesia.
URL: http://www.searog.org/

History Inaugurated 12 May 2007. **Aims** Improve the quality of radiation oncology practice in the South East Asian Region by means of enhancing cooperation in education, research and Quality Assurance initiatives. **Activities** Advocacy/lobbying/activism; training/education; events/meetings.

Members Societies in 6 countries:
Brunei Darussalam, Indonesia, Malaysia, Philippines, Singapore, Thailand.

Individuals in 3 countries:
Cambodia, Myanmar, Vietnam. [2018/XM8343/**D**]

♦ South-East Asian Regional Association for Medical Education (SEARAME) 19780

Asociación Regional de Educación Médica para el Sureste Asiatico

SG Dept Medical Education, PSG Inst of Medical Sciences and Research, Coimbatore, Tamil Nadu 641004, Coimbatore TAMIL NADU 641004, India. T. +914222570247 – +914224345803. Fax +914222594400. E-mail: searame@gmail.com.
Main: http://www.searame.org/

History A regional association of *World Federation for Medical Education (WFME, #21454).* Previously referred to as *Association for Medical Education in South-East Asia.* **Aims** Improve the quality and relevance of medical education at all levels – undergraduate, postgraduate and continuing professional development in line with WFME Global Standards. **Structure** General Assembly (annual); Executive Committee. **Languages** English. **Staff** 10.50 FTE, voluntary. **Finance** Members' dues. **Activities** Standards/guidelines; training/education; networking/liaising; knowledge management/information dissemination; events/meetings. **Events** *International Conference* Dhaka (Bangladesh) 2021, *International Conference* Yogyakarta (Indonesia) 2018, *International Conference* Yangon (Myanmar) 2016, *International Conference* Colombo (Sri Lanka) 2014, *International conference* Coimbatore (India) 2012. **Publications** *South-East Asian Journal of Medical Education (SEAJME)* (2 a year) – printed and online. Newsletter; bulletin; booklet.

Members Full in 12 countries:
Bangladesh, Bhutan, Denmark, India, Indonesia, Korea DPR, Maldives, Myanmar, Nepal, Sri Lanka, Thailand, Timor-Leste.

NGO Relations Member of: *World Federation for Medical Education (WFME, #21454).*
[2015.09.04/XD0780/**D**]

♦ Southeast Asian Regional Branch of the International Council on Archives (see: #12996)

♦ **Southeast Asian Regional Center for Graduate Study and Research in Agriculture (SEARCA)** **19781**

Dir c/o SEARCA, College, 4031 Los Baños LAG, Philippines. T. +63495549330 – +63495362290 – +63286571300. Fax +63495367097. E-mail: post@searca.org.
URL: http://www.searca.org/

History 27 Nov 1966. Established as the 1st of 26 specialist institutions set up by *Southeast Asian Ministers of Education Organization (SEAMEO, #19774)*. First operated on an interim basis from 1 Jul 1967 to 30 Jun 1969. Former names and other names: *SEAMEO Regional Center for Graduate Study and Research in Agriculture (SEARCA)* – alias. **Aims** Strengthen institutional capacities in agricultural and rural development in Southeast Asia by providing nationals of SEAMEO member countries with high-quality graduate education and training in agriculture and related fields; promote, undertake and coordinate research programs related to the needs and problems of the region; disseminate findings of agricultural research and experimentation. **Structure** Governing Board; Project Development and Management Department. **Languages** English. **Staff** 71.00 FTE, paid. **Finance** Sources: donations; government support; revenue from activities/projects. Other sources: Philippine government; SEAMEO Secretariat; donor agencies; government and non-government organizations and institution; interest earning. **Activities** Events/meetings; guidance/assistance/consulting; knowledge management/information dissemination; projects/programmes; research and development; training/education. **Events** *International Conference on Asian Highland Natural Resources Management* Chiang Mai (Thailand) 2015, *International Conference on Agricultural and Rural Development in Southeast Asia / International Conference* Manila (Philippines) 2014, *Conference on Regional Integration of Myanmar's Agricultural Trade* Nay Pyi Taw (Myanmar) 2013, *ICAFS : international conference on Asian food security* Singapore (Singapore) 2011, *International conference on developing tomorrow's leaders in agriculture and rural development* Los Baños (Philippines) 2008. **Publications** *SEARCA Diary* (4 a year); *Asian Journal of Agriculture and Development* (2 a year). *Southeast Asian Agriculture and Development Primer Series.* Discussion paper series. Conference proceedings; books; monographs; policy briefs.
Members Governments of SEAMEO member states (11):
Brunei Darussalam, Cambodia, Indonesia, Laos, Malaysia, Myanmar, Philippines, Singapore, Thailand, Timor-Leste, Vietnam.
Associate members in 9 countries:
Australia, Canada, France, Germany, Morocco, Netherlands, New Zealand, Spain, UK.
Affiliate members:
Asia-Pacific Centre of Education for International Understanding (APCEIU); British Columbia Council for International Education (BCCIE); *British Council*; *China Education Association for International Exchange (CEAIE)*; *International Council for Open and Distance Education (ICDE, #13056)*; University of Tsukuba, Japan.
NGO Relations Cooperates with (1): *Southeast Asian University Consortium for Graduate Education in Agriculture and Natural Resources (UC, #19786).* [2021.10.27/XE7377/y/**E***]

♦ Southeast Asian Regional Centre for Tropical Biology / see Southeast Asian Regional Centre for Tropical Biology (#19782)

♦ **Southeast Asian Regional Centre for Tropical Biology (SEAMEO BIOTROP)** **19782**

Centre régional de biologie tropicale de la SEAMEO

Contact Jl Raya Tajur Km 6, Bogor 16134, Indonesia. T. +622518323848. Fax +622518326851. E-mail: gau@biotrop.org.
URL: http://www.biotrop.org/

History 6 Feb 1968, under the name *Regional Centre for Training Research and Post-Graduate Study in Tropical Biology*, as one of the Regional Centres/Project of *Southeast Asian Ministers of Education Organization (SEAMEO, #19774)*. Name changed, 10 Jan 1969, to *SEAMEO Regional Centre for Tropical Biology (BIOTROP) – Centre régional de biologie tropicale de la SEAMEO* and subsequently to *Southeast Asian Regional Centre for Tropical Biology (SEAMEO BIOTROP) – Centre régional de biologie tropicale de l'Asie du Sud-Est*, 1 Jul 1982. Current name readopted as previously changed, 10 Jan 1969. **Aims** Increase capability in *biological research* and *training* relevant to regional and economic needs; assist the member states to identify biological problems. **Structure** Governing Board; Director; Deputy Director for Programme and Marketing, including Marketing Coordinator and Academic Staff/Scientist; Deputy Director Resource Management and Communication; Laboratory Coordinator and Units (8): Human Resources Management; General Administration; Finance; Facility; Information Resource; MIT Coordinator; Information Technology; Community Development. **Languages** English, Indonesian. **Staff** 115.00 FTE, paid. **Finance** Government of Indonesia; SEAMEO organization; donor countries. Budget (annual): US$ 1,086,957. **Activities** Research; consultancy; training; meeting activities. **Events** *Meeting* Malaysia 2004, *Symposium on forest diversity* Bogor (Indonesia) 1998, *Symposium on brackishwater aquaculture management* Bogor (Indonesia) 1997, *Symposium on the use of remote sensing and GIS for monitoring natural resource development and management* Bogor (Indonesia) 1997, *Seminar on grains postharvest technology* Manila (Philippines) 1997. **Publications** *Information Technology for Natural Resources Management* (2 a year) – journal; *Biotropia* (2 a year) – journal; *BIOTROP Courier* – newsletter. Proceedings. Information Services: Library with 13,120 copies of books and 740 titles of serial journals.
Members Southeast Asian States (11):
Brunei Darussalam, Cambodia, Indonesia, Laos, Malaysia, Myanmar, Philippines, Singapore, Thailand, Timor-Leste, Vietnam.
Associate Governments of 6 countries:
Australia, Canada, France, Germany, Netherlands, New Zealand.
IGO Relations Partner of: *UNESCO Office, Jakarta – Regional Bureau for Sciences in Asia and the Pacific (#20313).* **NGO Relations** Member of: *International Association for Ecology (INTECOL, #11856).* Together with: *Global Change System for Analysis, Research and Training (START, #10278)* and *Global Change and Terrestrial Ecosystems Project (GCTE, inactive)*, set up: *Global Change Impacts Centre for Southeast Asia (IC-SEA, no recent information).* [2014.01.16/XE7078/**E***]

♦ South East Asian Social Science Association (inactive)
♦ South East Asian Society of Soil Engineering / see Southeast Asian Geotechnical Society (#19769)

♦ **Southeast Asian Soft Tennis Federation (SEASTF)** **19783**

Pres Univ of Perpetual Help, Dalta Medical Ctr, Alabang Zapote Rd, Pamplona, Las Piñas, Philippines. E-mail: softtennispilipinas@gmail.com.
URL: http://softtennispilipinas.weebly.com/seastf.html

Structure General Assembly. Officers: 2 Honorary Chairmen; President; 4 Vice-Presidents; Secretary General/Treasurer. **Activities** Championships. **Events** *General Assembly* Chiayi City (Taiwan) 2013.
Members Full in 6 countries:
Cambodia, Indonesia, Laos, Malaysia, Philippines, Thailand. [2014/XJ3707/**D**]

♦ **Southeast Asian Studies Regional Exchange Program Foundation (SEASREP Foundation)** **19784**

Exec Dir Unit 612/613, Residencia de Regina, 94 Xavierville Ave, Brgy. Loyola Heights, 1108 Quezon City, Philippines. T. +63287090854. Fax +63287090891. E-mail: seasrep@pldtdsl.net – seasrepfoundation@gmail.com.
Tokyo Joint Secretariat c/o Toyota Foundation, Shinjuku Mitsui Bldg 37F, 2-1-1 Nishi-Shinjuko, Shinjuku-ku, Tokyo, 163-0437 Japan. T. +81333441701 – +8139262897. Fax +81333426911.
URL: http://www.seasrepfoundation.org/

History May 1994, Kuala Lumpur (Malaysia). Former names and other names: *Southeast Asian Studies Regional Exchange Programme Council (SEASREP Council)* – former. **Aims** Expand the pool of Southeast Asian scholars engaged in studies of the region, contribute meaningfully to the body of work published in the region, and strengthen SEASREP's network with Southeast Asianists in the region and in the larger community of Asia and the world. **Languages** English. **Finance** Supported by: *Japan Foundation*; *Toyota Foundation.* **Activities** Awards/prizes/competitions; financial and/or material support; knowledge management/information dissemination; training/education. **Events** *Conference* Yogyakarta (Indonesia) 2015, *Conference* Chiang Mai (Thailand) 2005. **Publications** *Southeast Asian Studies E-Bulletin* (2 a year). Annual Report.
Members Scholars from 10 countries:
Brunei Darussalam, Cambodia, Indonesia, Laos, Malaysia, Myanmar, Philippines, Singapore, Thailand, Vietnam.
Consultative Status Consultative status granted from: *ASEAN (#01141).* [2022.02.14/XD7291/t/**F**]

♦ Southeast Asian Studies Regional Exchange Programme Council / see Southeast Asian Studies Regional Exchange Program Foundation (#19784)
♦ Southeast Asian Taekwondo Union (no recent information)

♦ **Southeast Asian Tobacco Control Alliance (SEATCA)** **19785**

Contact Apartment 4D, Thakolsuk Place, 115 Thoddamri Road, Dusit, Bangkok, 10300, Thailand. T. +6626683650. E-mail: info@seatca.org.
URL: http://www.seatca.org/

History 2001. **Aims** Work together to achieve the tobacco endgame by demonalizing the tobacco industry and advancing effective tobacco control policies and their enforcement. **Finance** Supported by: *Bill and Melinda Gates Foundation (BMGF)*; Thai Health Promotion Foundation. **Activities** Capacity building; events/meetings; projects/programmes; research/documentation. **Events** *Asia Pacific Smoke-Free Meeting* Baguio (Philippines) 2022, *Regional tobacco industry surveillance workshop* Bangkok (Thailand) 2009, *Regional lawyer's fellowship programme workshop* Manila (Philippines) 2009. **Publications** Regional Summaries; country report cards; video; research reports.
Members in 10 countries:
Brunei Darussalam, Cambodia, Indonesia, Laos, Malaysia, Myanmar, Philippines, Singapore, Thailand, Vietnam.
NGO Relations Member of (1): *Framework Convention Alliance (FCA, #09981).* Partner of (1): *Global Smokefree Partnership (GSP, #10602).* [2023.02.14/XF6319/**F**]

♦ **Southeast Asian University Consortium for Graduate Education in Agriculture and Natural Resources (UC)** **19786**

Secretariat SEAMEO SEARCA, College, 4031 Los Baños LAG, Philippines. T. +63495362290. E-mail: mcnc@searca.org – geidd@searca.org.
URL: http://www.uc.searca.org/

History Initiated 1989 by *Southeast Asian Regional Center for Graduate Study and Research in Agriculture (SEARCA, #19781).* Former names and other names: *University Consortium* – former. **Aims** Provide highly trained personnel in agriculture, environment and natural resources for development of the Southeast Asian region; promote cooperation among members by optimizing utilization of scarce resources and expertise; develop strong links among members through collaborative research projects and faculty and student exchange programmes. **Structure** Executive Board; Coordinators; Secretariat, provided by *Southeast Asian Regional Center for Graduate Study and Research in Agriculture (SEARCA, #19781).* **Languages** English. **Staff** 1.50 FTE, paid. **Finance** Sources: members' dues; revenue from activities/projects. **Activities** Events/meetings; financial and/or material support; networking/liaising; projects/programmes; training/education. **Publications** *UC Newsletter.*
Members Founding universities (5) in 4 countries:
Indonesia, Malaysia, Philippines, Thailand.
Associate country:
Japan. [2020.05.07/XJ7919/**E**]

♦ **South East Asian Water Utilities Network (SEAWUN)** **19787**

Exec Dir 71 Nguyen Chi Than Building, Room 1305 – 13th Floor, Dong Da District, Hanoi, Vietnam. T. +84462752677. Fax +84462752679.
URL: http://www.seawun.org/

History Aug 2002, Hanoi (Vietnam). Became operational Aug 2003. **Aims** Improve services of member organizations. **Structure** Board. Executive Committee, including President and Executive Director.
Members Organizations and companies (57) in 7 countries:
Australia, Indonesia, Laos, Malaysia, Philippines, Thailand, Vietnam.
IGO Relations *Asian Development Bank (ADB, #01422).* **NGO Relations** Member of: *Global Water Operators' Partnerships Alliance (GWOPA, #10652).* [2016/XM2725/**F**]

♦ South East Asian/Western Pacific Federation of Pharmacologists / see Asia Pacific Federation of Pharmacologists (#01903)
♦ South East Asian/Western Pacific Regional Federation of Pharmacologists / see Asia Pacific Federation of Pharmacologists (#01903)
♦ South-East Asian Zoological Parks Association / see Southeast Asian Zoos and Aquariums Association (#19788)

♦ **Southeast Asian Zoos and Aquariums Association (SEAZA)** **19788**

Secretariat c/o Avilon Wildlife Conservation Foundation, 9003 GP Sitio Gulod, San Isidro, 1860 Rodriguez RIZ, Philippines. T. +639776913178. E-mail: info@seaza.asia – seaza.secretariat@gmail.com.
URL: https://www.seaza.asia/

History 1990, Bogor (Indonesia). Former names and other names: *South East Asian Zoos Association (SEAZA)* – former; *South East Asia Zoological Gardens' Association* – alias; *South-East Asian Zoological Parks Association* – alias. **Events** *Zoos Moving Forward with Nature: Nurturing the Wild, Saving Our Future* Manila (Philippines) 2021, *Annual Conference* Yangon (Myanmar) 2020, *Annual Conference* Phú Quôc (Vietnam) 2019, *Annual Conference* Chiang Mai (Thailand) 2018, *Annual Conference* Manila (Philippines) 2017. **NGO Relations** Member of (1): *World Association of Zoos and Aquariums (WAZA, #21208).* [2021.11.30/XD3615/**D**]

♦ South East Asian Zoos Association / see Southeast Asian Zoos and Aquariums Association (#19788)

♦ **Southeast Asia One Health University Network (SEAOHUN)** **19789**

Exec Dir 119/85 Moo 5, Suthep, Muang, Chiang Mai, 50200, Thailand. T. +6652010069. E-mail: secretariat@seaohun.org.
Main Website: http://www.seaohun.org/

History 2011. Founded with support from *United States Agency for International Development (USAID).* **Aims** Develop a resilient and competent One Health workforce to effectively prevent, detect and respond to infectious disease threats by leveraging education, research, and training excellence provided by member Universities. **Structure** Executive Board; Foundation Board; One Health University Networks (Country Networks); Secretariat. **Languages** English. **Staff** 11.00 FTE, paid. **Finance** Supported by: Chevron; *United States Agency for International Development (USAID)* (One Health Workforce – Next Generation (OHW-NG)). **Activities** Events/meetings; training/education. **Events** *International Conference* Nonthaburi (Thailand) 2022, *International Conference* Hanoi (Vietnam) 2018. **Publications** Annual Report.
Members Universities (99) in 8 countries:
Cambodia, Indonesia, Laos, Malaysia, Myanmar, Philippines, Thailand, Vietnam.
IGO Relations *ASEAN (#01141)* Secretariat; *Asian Development Bank (ADB, #01422)*; *Centre de coopération internationale en recherche agronomique pour le développement (CIRAD, #03733)*; *FAO (#09260)*; *International Bank for Reconstruction and Development (IBRD, #12317)* (World Bank); *International Livestock Research Institute (ILRI, #14062)*; *Korea International Cooperation Agency (KOICA)*; *OIE – World Organisation for Animal Health (#17703)*; *SEAMEO Regional Centre for Higher Education and Development (RIHED, #19174)*; *United States Agency for International Development (USAID)*; *WHO (#20950).* **NGO Relations** *Wildlife Conservation Society (WCS).* [2022.11.03/XM7475/**F**]

♦ South East Asia-Pacific Audio Visual Archive Association / see Southeast Asia-Pacific Audiovisual Archive Association (#19790)

♦ **Southeast Asia-Pacific Audiovisual Archive Association (SEAPAVAA)** **19790**

Administrative Coordinator 1 Scotts Road, #24-10 Shaw Centre, Singapore 228208, Singapore. E-mail: secretariat@seapavaa.net – secretarygeneral@seapavaa.net.
MANILA OFFICE c/o UP School of Library and Information Studies, UP School of Library and Information Studies, Quirino Avenue, Diliman, 1101 Quezon City, Philippines.
Corporate Website: http://seapavaa.net/

History Feb 1996, Manila (Philippines). Legally constituted and launched at First General Assembly, where Constitution was ratified and officers elected. Initiated at Conference Workshop on ASEAN Audio/Video and Film Retrieval, Restoration and Archiving, Manila (Philippines), 1993, where a framework for a comprehensive program for film/video archiving in the region and a recommendation to form an ASEAN confederation of film

archivists was drew up. Idea of a regional association pursued at ASEAN Training Seminar on Film and Video Archive Management, a project of the ASEAN Committee on Culture and Information, Canberra (Australia), May 1995. Former names and other names: *South East Asia-Pacific Audio Visual Archive Association (SEAPAVAA)* – former. Registration: Registry of Societies, Singapore, Start date: 2014, Singapore. **Aims** Provide a regional forum for addressing common issues and concerns related to the collection and preservation of, and provision of access to, the audiovisual heritage of member countries; promote development of audiovisual archiving at the national, regional and international levels; strengthen national capabilities in audiovisual acquisition, management, preservation and provision of access to collections through research, training and technology transfer, among other methods; establish regionwide standards, methods and procedures; advance the professional development and recognition of audiovisual archivists; cooperate with relevant international bodies toward achieving international recognition and support of AV archiving in the region. **Structure** General Assembly; Executive Council. **Languages** English. **Staff** 1.00 FTE, paid. **Finance** Sources: meeting proceeds; members' dues. **Activities** Awareness raising; capacity building; events/meetings; knowledge management/information dissemination; standards/guidelines; training/education. **Events** *Annual Conference* Hanoi (Vietnam) 2021, *Annual Conference* Nouméa (New Caledonia) 2019, *Annual Conference* Bangkok (Thailand) 2018, *Annual Conference* Manila (Philippines) 2017, *Annual Conference* Guam 2016. **Publications** *SEAPAVAA Bulletin* – 2011; *Southeast Asia-Pacific AV Archives Bulletin* – 1996- 2009. *Lost Films of Asia* (2006); *Film in Southeast Asia: Views from the Region* (1st ed 2001); *Film Preservation Handbook*. **Information Services** *ASEAN Database of Film and Television Productions*; *Audiovisual (AV) Archive Checklist*.
Members Full Institutional (32); Associate Institutional (25); Associate Individual (33). Archive institutions and professional archivists in 24 countries and territories:
Australia, Cambodia, Canada, China, France, Hong Kong, India, Indonesia, Italy, Japan, Kiribati, Korea Rep, Laos, Malaysia, Netherlands, New Caledonia, New Zealand, Philippines, Singapore, Switzerland, Taiwan, Thailand, USA, Vietnam.
Consultative Status Consultative status granted from: *UNESCO (#20322)* (Consultative Status). **NGO Relations** Member of (1): *Co-ordinating Council of Audiovisual Archives Associations (CCAAA, #04820)*.
[2022.03.07/XD5572/**D**]

- ♦ South East Asia and Pacific League Against Rheumatism / see Asia Pacific League of Associations for Rheumatology (#01945)
- ♦ South-East Asia and Pacific Region Islamic Dawah Council / see Regional Islamic Da'wah Council of Southeast Asia and the Pacific (#18792)
- ♦ South East Asia Parliamentarians Against Corruption (see: #10518)

♦ South East Asia Petroleum Exploration Society (SEAPEX) 19791

Secretariat Tanglin PO Box 423, Singapore 912415, Singapore. T. +6566225358. Fax +6566225999. E-mail: seapex@seapex.org.
URL: http://www.seapex.org/

History 31 Jul 1973, Singapore (Singapore), as a technically orientated regional petroleum exploration association. **Aims** Advance the understanding of geology and related earth sciences, particularly with reference to petroleum and natural gas in Southeast Asia; foster the spirit of scientific research, throughout the membership; disseminate information relating to geosciences and the associated technology of petroleum and natural gas; inspire a high standard of professional conduct on the part of members. **Structure** Council, comprising President, 1st Vice-President Programs, 2nd Vice-President Membership, Treasurer, Secretary and 4 Councillors. **Languages** English. **Finance** Members' dues: Life members, US$ 200; Active members, US$ 40 per year; Associated members, US$ 40 per year. **Events** *Asia Pacfic Scout Check Meeting* Singapore (Singapore) 2020, *Exploration Conference* Singapore (Singapore) 2019, *Farm Out Forum* Singapore (Singapore) 2019, *Asia Pacfic Scout Check Meeting* Singapore (Singapore) 2018, *Asia-Pacific Assembly* Singapore (Singapore) 2018. **Publications** *SEAPEX Membership Directory*. SEAPEX Proceedings. Offshore Southeast Asia Conference Papers. **Members** Honorary; Life; Active; Associated, in Southeast Asian region. Membership countries not specified. [2020/XF2850/**F**]

- ♦ Southeast Asia Radiographers Conference (meeting series)

♦ Southeast Asia Regional Anti-Doping Organisation (SEARADO) 19792

Dir Gen Singapore Sports Council, 3 Stadium Drive, Singapore 397630, Singapore.
URL: https://www.searado.com/

History 30 Nov 2006, Doha (Qatar). Founded by National Olympic Committees and governmental representatives from the region, with the assistance of *World Anti-Doping Agency (WADA, #21096)*. **Aims** Promote, coordinate and enhance anti-doping programmes in Southeast Asia. **Structure** Board. Committees. **Activities** Advocacy/lobbying/activism; capacity building; monitoring/evaluation.
Members National committees in 11 countries:
Brunei Darussalam, Cambodia, Indonesia, Laos, Malaysia, Myanmar, Philippines, Singapore, Thailand, Timor-Leste, Vietnam.
[2022/AA2502/**D**]

♦ Southeast Asia Regional Committee (SARCS) 19793

Secretariat Natl Central Univ, 300 Jhongda Rd, Chung Li 320, Taiwan. T. +88634227151ext34030 – +886333400. E-mail: ncusts@gmail.com.
URL: http://www.sarcs.org/

History 1993. **Aims** Address critical *environmental* change issues: adaptation to *global change*; the monsoon system; food and water security; coastal and forest degradation; air quality; sustainable development; biodiversity; climate variability. **Structure** Regional Council; Regional Scientific Committee; Secretariat. **Finance** Sponsored by National Science Council of Taiwan. **Activities** Organizes conferences and workshops; facilitates water and carbon research projects. **Publications** *SARCS Environmental Newsletter* (12 a year). **Members** Membership countries not specified. [2015/XE4595/**E**]

♦ South East Asia Regional Computer Confederation (SEARCC) 19794

Executive Officer Level 27, Tower One, 100 Barangaroo Avenue, Sydney NSW 2000, Australia. T. +61414672161.
URL: http://www.searcc.org/

History 1978. Founded under the auspices of *International Federation for Information Processing (IFIP, #13458)*. **Aims** Promote cooperation among national computer societies in the Asia Pacific region for the express or implicit purpose of advancing knowledge and application of information processing in the region. **Languages** English. **Finance** Annual budget: US$ 100,000. **Activities** Projects/programmes; events/meetings; networking/liaising; awards/prizes/competitions. **Events** *Conference* 2021, *Conference* Colombo (Sri Lanka) 2019, *Conference* Melbourne, VIC (Australia) 2018, *Annual Conference* Colombo (Sri Lanka) 2017, *Annual Conference* Sydney, NSW (Australia) 2016. **Publications** Policies; standards; better practice guides; research papers; conference papers.
Members Member Economies in 7 countries:
Australia, China, Fiji, India, Malaysia, Papua New Guinea, Sri Lanka.
NGO Relations *International Federation for Information Processing (IFIP, #13458)*. [2021/XD9148/**D**]

♦ Southeast Asia Regional Initiatives for Community Empowerment (SEARICE) 19795

Contact No 14D Maalalahanin Str, Teachers Village, Diliman, 1101 Quezon City, Philippines. T. +63289226710. Fax +6329226710. E-mail: searice@searice.org.ph.
URL: http://www.searice.org.ph/

History 1977. Started as a "circle of friends" among activists from Thailand, Malaysia, Indonesia and the Philippines. These activists initially shared experiences and supported each other in helping empower grassroots communities at a time when dictatorship and authoritarian regimes ruled the region. Evolved into an action-oriented, policy advocacy-driven, and research-based organization focused on agricultural biodiversity and the protection of farmers' rights, following a model of convergence of ideas and efforts among the grassroots, government institutions, and private entities. Former names and other names: *Southeast Asia Rural Institute for Community Education* – former; *South East Asia Institute for Community Education* – former; *Southeast Asia Regional Institute for Community Education* – former; *Southeast Asia Regional Institute for Community Empowerment* – former. Registration: Start date: 1981, Philippines. **Aims** Empower farming communities through agricultural research and development by strengthening their control over agricultural resources, particularly plant genetic resources; work towards policy and structural reforms to ensure agricultural biodiversity. **Structure** Board of Trustees (BT); Office based in Quezon City (Philippines). **Finance** Financial support received from funding partners based in Sweden, Netherlands and Switzerland **Activities** Advocacy/lobbying/activism; capacity building; politics/policy/regulatory; research and development. **Publications** *SEARICE Notes* (4 a year); *SEARICE Review* (2 a year); *Farmers' Rights Monitor*. *Field Manual on Agroecology – Manwal ng Agroekolohiya* (2021) in English. Brochures; proceedings. **Consultative Status** Consultative status granted from: *ASEAN (#01141)*. **NGO Relations** Member of (2): *Association for Plant Breeding for the Benefit of Society (APBREBES, #02861)*; *NGO Forum on ADB (#17123)*.
[2023.02.15/XE0645/**E**]

- ♦ Southeast Asia Regional Institute for Community Education / see Southeast Asia Regional Initiatives for Community Empowerment (#19795)
- ♦ Southeast Asia Regional Institute for Community Empowerment / see Southeast Asia Regional Initiatives for Community Empowerment (#19795)

♦ South East Asia Regional Network for Capacity Building in IWRM (AguaJaring) 19796

Coordinator c/o IHE Indonesia – Consultant Office, Balai Diklat VI Jakiarta, Ground Floor, Jl Sapta Taruna Raya, Pasar Jumat, Jakarta 12310, Indonesia. T. +62217597110. E-mail: web.aguajaring@gmail.com.

Aims Enhance capacity in *integrated water resources management* (IWRM) in the region through support for training, education, research and development, and outreach, by sharing complementary expertise and resources. **Structure** Steering Committee; Advisory Board; Secretariat. **Languages** English.
Members Full in 8 countries:
Cambodia, Indonesia, Laos, Malaysia, Myanmar, Philippines, Thailand, Vietnam.
NGO Relations Member of: *Network for Capacity Building in Integrated Water Resources Management (CAP-Net, #17000)*. [2015.01.13/XJ2386/**F**]

- ♦ Southeast Asia Rural Institute for Community Education / see Southeast Asia Regional Initiatives for Community Empowerment (#19795)

♦ Southeast Asia Rural Social Leadership Institute (SEARSOLIN) 19797

Main Office Fr WF Masterson Ave, 9000 Cagayan de Oro MSR, Philippines. T. +63888588062. Fax +63888588062. E-mail: searsolin@xu.edu.ph.
URL: https://www.xu.edu.ph/searsolin

History Mar 1964, Philippines. Founded by Fr William F Masterson. **Aims** Train rural social leaders and sharpen their skills in assisting rural peoples to achieve more rewarding and responsible human existence. **Structure** Director; Associate Director; Assistant Director. **Languages** English. **Staff** 10.00 FTE, paid. **Finance** Some financial assistance with sending sponsor. **Activities** Gives modular courses on rural social leadership development. 6-month rural leadership training and 1 month credit union/cooperative short courses. Conducts seminars/workshops on community development, cooperatives, micro-enterprise development and marketing, micro-finance for the poor, participatory approaches to working with communities. Monitors and evaluates development projects relating to sustainable agriculture. **Publications** *SEARSOLINE Newsletter* (3 a year). Brochures.
Members Alumni in 39 countries and territories:
Bangladesh, Bhutan, Cambodia, China, Fiji, Ghana, Hong Kong, India, Indonesia, Japan, Kenya, Korea Rep, Laos, Liberia, Malaysia, Mozambique, Myanmar, Nepal, Nigeria, Northern Mariana Is, Pakistan, Papua New Guinea, Philippines, Rwanda, Samoa, Sierra Leone, Solomon Is, Sri Lanka, Sudan, Sweden, Taiwan, Tanzania UR, Thailand, Timor-Leste, Tonga, Uganda, Vietnam, Zambia, Zimbabwe.
IGO Relations *Colombo Plan for Cooperative Economic and Social Development in Asia and the Pacific (CPS, #04120)*; *FAO (#09260)*; *International Development Research Centre (IDRC, #13162)*; *United Nations Volunteers (UNV, #20650)*. **NGO Relations** Member regional organization of: *Asian NGO Coalition for Agrarian Reform and Rural Development (ANGOC, #01566)*. Member of: *Asia Caucus (no recent information)*. Partner of: *Development Innovations and Networks (#05057)*. [2014/XE0310/j/**E**]

- ♦ Southeast Asia School Principals Forum (unconfirmed)
- ♦ South-East Asia Shariah Association (inactive)

♦ South East Asia Table Tennis Association (SEATTA) 19798

Hon SG c/o Table Tennis Assoc of Malaysia, 1st Floor, No 11-23-1 Jalan Jalil Perkas 15, Bukit Jalil, 55700 Kuala Lumpur, Malaysia. T. +60389961497. Fax +60389991491.
History Founded Sep 1995. **NGO Relations** Recognized by: *International Table Tennis Federation (ITTF, #15650)*. [2017.07.04/XD7134/**D**]

- ♦ South East Asia Teachers and Counsellors Conference (meeting series)

♦ South East Asia Theoretical Physics Association (SEATPA) 19799

Association de physique théorique de l'Asie du Sud-Est

Pres NTU Institute of Advanced Studies, Nanyang Exec Ctre 02-18, 60 Nanyang View, Singapore 639673, Singapore. T. +6567906491. Fax +6567944941.
Events *Workshop on future directions on research education in physics* Singapore (Singapore) 1999, *Rencontres du Vietnam* Ho Chi Minh City (Vietnam) 1995, *International Conference on High Energy Physics* Singapore (Singapore) 1990. **NGO Relations** Member of: *Association of Asia Pacific Physical Societies (AAPPS, #02388)*. [2011/XD5680/**D**]

- ♦ South-East Asia Treaty Organization (inactive)

♦ Southeast Asia Women's Caucus on ASEAN (WC) 19800

Secretariat c/o APWLD, 189/3 Changklan Road, A Muang, Chiang Mai, 50100, Thailand. T. +6653284527. Fax +6653280847. E-mail: apwld@apwld.org.
URL: http://womenscaucusonasean.wordpress.com/

History Co-convened by *Asia Pacific Forum on Women, Law and Development (APWLD, #01912)* and *International Women's Rights Action Watch Asia Pacific (IWRAW Asia Pacific, #15902)*. Also referred to as *Women's Caucus*. **Aims** Engage the Association of Southeast Asian Nations (ASEAN) to advance women's human rights. **Structure** Coordinating Group. **Languages** English. **Activities** Advocacy/lobbying/activism; capacity building; knowledge management/information dissemination.
Members Organizations in 11 countries:
Brunei Darussalam, Cambodia, Indonesia, Laos, Malaysia, Myanmar, Philippines, Singapore, Thailand, Timor-Leste, Vietnam.
[2014.06.01/XJ6523/**E**]

- ♦ South East Asia Zoological Gardens' Association / see Southeast Asian Zoos and Aquariums Association (#19788)

♦ South East Atlantic Fisheries Organization (SEAFO) 19801

Exec Sec Strand Street 1, Box 4862, Vineta, Swakopmund, Namibia. T. +26464406885. Fax +26464406884. E-mail: info@seafo.org.
URL: http://www.seafo.org/

History 1997, Windhoek (Namibia). Established under *Convention on the Conservation and Management of Fishery Resources in the South-East Atlantic Ocean (2001)*, following initiatives starting in 1995, Namibia, with negotiations for the convention taking place between 1997-2001. Convention signed, Apr 2003. Permanent Secretariat established, Mar 2005. **Aims** Ensure long-term conservation and sustainable use of living marine resources in the South East Atlantic. **Structure** Commission; Scientific Committee; Compliance Committee; Standing Committee on Administration and Finance; Secretariat. **Languages** English, Portuguese. **Staff** 2.00 FTE, paid. **Finance** Sources: contributions of member/participating states. Annual budget: 3,800,000 NAD (2021). **Activities** Capacity building; events/meetings; guidance/assistance/consulting; knowledge management/information dissemination; management of treaties and agreements; monitoring/evaluation; networking/liaising; politics/policy/regulatory; research and development; research/documentation. **Events** *Annual Commission Meeting* Swakopmund (Namibia) 2022, *Annual Commission Meeting* Swakopmund (Namibia) 2021, *Annual Commission Meeting* Swakopmund (Namibia) 2020, *Annual Commission Meeting* Swakopmund (Namibia) 2019, *Annual Commission Meeting* Swakopmund (Namibia) 2018.
Members Governments of 5 countries:

Angola, Japan, Korea Rep, Namibia, South Africa.
Regional organization:
European Union (EU, #08967).
IGO Relations Memorandum of Understanding with (2): *Agreement on the Conservation of Albatrosses and Petrels (ACAP, 2001); Commission for the Conservation of Antarctic Marine Living Resources (CCAMLR, #04206).* [2023.02.14/XM1750/**D***]

♦ SouthEast and Central European Network of Forest-Based Clusters (unconfirmed)

♦ South East and Central Europe PR Organisation (SECEPRO) 19802

Contact address not obtained. E-mail: info@secepro.org.
URL: http://secepro.org/
History Founding meeting May 2011, Ljubljana (Slovenia) in cooperation with *South East Europe Media Organisation (SEEMO, #19823).* **Aims** Provide a platform for exchange and collaboration among *public relations* agencies and *media* experts in the SEE region; facilitate cross-border and regional cooperation; represent the industry on PR issues; enhance the image of publication relations in South, East and Central Europe; attract the best PR talent in the region. **Finance** Members' dues. **Activities** Training/education; events/meetings. **Events** *Conference* Ljubljana (Slovenia) 2011. **Publications** *Media Handbook.* **Members** Full in 35 countries. Membership countries not specified. [2017.03.07/XJ6826/**D**]

♦ Southeastern and Eastern European Parasitological Society / see Southeastern and Eastern European Parasitologists (#19803)

♦ Southeastern and Eastern European Parasitologists (SEEEP) 19803

Address not obtained.
History Also referred to as *Southeastern and Eastern European Parasitological Society (SEEEPS).* **Structure** General Assembly. **Events** *Conference* Zagreb (Croatia) 2011. **NGO Relations** Member of: *European Federation of Parasitologists (EFP, #07186); World Federation of Parasitologists (WFP, #21471).* [2011/XJ3723/**D**]

♦ South Eastern and Eastern Europe Clearinghouse for the Control of Small Arms and Light Weapons (SEESAC) 19804

Coordinator Bulevar Zorana Dindica 64, Belgrade, PAK 11000, Serbia. Fax +3814155499. E-mail: seesac@undp.org.
URL: http://www.seesac.org/
History 8 May 2002, Belgrade (Serbia). Launched under the auspices of the *Stability Pact for South Eastern Europe (inactive)* (later succeeded by *Regional Cooperation Council (RCC, #18773)*) and *UNDP (#20292)* to function as an executive arm of the *Regional Implementation Plan on Combating the Proliferation of Small Arms and Light Weapons (SALW)* and a focal point for SALW-related activities in South East Europe. The *Regional Implementation Plan* was formulated and adopted Nov 2001; revised in 2006 and 2014. **Aims** Work to strengthen capacities of national and regional stakeholders to control and reduce proliferation and misuse of small arms and light weapons, advance gender equality, facilitate regional cooperation and thus contribute to enhanced stability, security and development in South Eastern and Eastern Europe. **Structure** Regional Steering Group (RSG) for Small Arms and Light Weapons (meets annually) provides political and strategic guidance and indigenous support, and is composed of representatives of the governments of the states concerned, *Regional Cooperation Council (RCC, #18773)*, UNDP and observers from institutions such as *European Union (EU, #08967), NATO (#16945), Organization for Security and Cooperation in Europe (OSCE, #17887)* and civil society. **Languages** Albanian, Bosnian, Croatian, English, Macedonian, Montenegrin, Romanian, Russian, Serbian, Slovene. **Staff** 29.00 FTE, paid. **Finance** Support from: European Union (EU), Germany, France, USA, Norway, Slovakia, the UK, Sweden and the Netherlands. **Activities** Awareness raising; capacity building; events/meetings; guidance/assistance/consulting; knowledge management/information dissemination; management of treaties and agreements; monitoring/evaluation; networking/liaising; politics/policy/regulatory; projects/programmes; research and development; research/documentation; standards/guidelines; training/education. **Events** *Regional Meeting of the South-East Europe Firearms Expert Network* Belgrade (Serbia) 2021, *Regional Workshop for Border Officials of Western Balkans* Belgrade (Serbia) 2021, *Regional meeting of the Firearm Focal Points* Belgrade (Serbia) 2021, *Regional workshop of Criminal Police Representatives* Belgrade (Serbia) 2021, *A Way Forward on Gender Equality in the Defence Sector in the Western Balkans* Budva (Montenegro) 2021.
Members Active in 9 countries:
Albania, Belarus, Bosnia-Herzegovina, Kosovo (*), Moldova, Montenegro, North Macedonia, Serbia, Ukraine.
*References to Kosovo shall be understood to be in the context of Security Council resolution 1244 (1999).
NGO Relations Partner of: *Bonn International Center for Conversion (BICC, #03300); International Action Network on Small Arms (IANSA, #11585); ITF Enhancing Human Security (ITF); Norwegian People's Aid (NPA); Peace Research Institute Oslo (PRIO); Saferworld; Stockholm International Peace Research Institute (SIPRI, #19994).* Cooperates with: Flemish Peach Institute; *International Association of Women Police (IAWP, #12270); Nordic Centre for Gender in Military Operations (NCGM); Parliamentary Forum on Small Arms and Light Weapons (Parliamentary Forum on SALW, #18218);* Small Arms Survey. [2022.03.17/XM0265/**F***]

♦ South Eastern Europe Advisory Service Network (SEASN) 19805

Pres Savska cesta 41, HR-10000 Zagreb, Croatia. T. +38514882714.
Sec address not obtained.
URL: https://www.seasn.com.hr/en/
History 22 Oct 2015, Sofia (Bulgaria). Initiative board meeting held Apr 2014, Belgrade (Serbia). **Aims** Increase the efficiency of agricultural advisory services so as to develop agriculture and rural areas in the region. **Structure** General Assembly; Executive Board; Officers. **Activities** Events/meetings; networking/liaising; training/education. **NGO Relations** Cooperates with (2): *European Forum for Agricultural and Rural Advisory Services (EUFRAS, #07303); Internationale Akademie land- und hauswirtschaftlicher Beraterinnen und Berater (IALB, #13212).* [2020/AA2293/**F**]

♦ South Eastern European Addiction Treatment Network / see South Eastern European-Adriatic Addiction Treatment Network (#19806)

♦ South Eastern European-Adriatic Addiction Treatment Network (SEEAN) 19806

Pres Sound of Reflection Foundation, Zaloska 29, 1000 Ljubljana, Slovenia. T. +38615443516. Fax +38615443518. E-mail: seea.net@gmail.com.
URL: http://www.seea.net/
History Sarajevo (Bosnia-Herzegovina). Also referred to as *South Eastern European Addiction Treatment Network.* **Structure** Board. **Events** *Adriatic Drug Addiction Treatment Conference* Thessaloniki (Greece) 2019, *Adriatic Drug Addiction Treatment Conference* Budva (Montenegro) 2017, *Adriatic Drug Addiction Treatment Conference* Ljubljana (Slovenia) 2015, *Adriatic Drug Addiction Treatment Conference* Tirana (Albania) 2012, *Adriatic Drug Addiction Treatment Conference* Ohrid (Macedonia) 2010. **Publications** *SEEA Addiction* – magazine.
Members in 8 countries:
Albania, Bosnia-Herzegovina, Bulgaria, Croatia, Italy, North Macedonia, Serbia, Slovenia. [2017/XM0393/**F**]

♦ South-Eastern European Health Network (SEE Health Network) 19807

Action pour le développement sanitaire en Europe du sud-est – Aktion Gesundheitsentwicklung für Südosteuropa
Secretariat Dir SEEHN, 50ta Divizija 6, 1000 Skopje, North Macedonia. T. +38923125235. E-mail: secretariat@seehn.org.
URL: http://seehn.org
History 2001, by *Council of Europe (CE, #04881)* and *WHO Regional Office for Europe (#20945)*, as a health component to *Stability Pact for South Eastern Europe (inactive).* Also known under the acronym *SEEHN.* **Aims** Improve health and well-being, and promote peace and reconciliation in the countries of South-Eastern Europe. **Structure** Presidency; Executive Committee; Secretariat. Since 1 Jan 2010, took over ownership of the regional cooperation for health and development under the auspices of *Regional Cooperation Council (RCC, #18773).* **Languages** English. **Staff** 3.00 FTE, paid. **Finance** Member States' contributions. **Activities** Healthcare; capacity building; networking/liaising; training/education; research and development. **Events** *Meeting* Sofia (Bulgaria) 2011, *Meeting* Belgrade (Serbia) 2009, *Meeting* Brussels (Belgium) 2008, *Meeting* Chisinau (Moldova) 2008, *Meeting* Zagreb (Croatia) 2008. **Publications** *Boosting the Implementation of Health 2020 and the Sustainable Development Goals in South-Eastern Europe.*
Members Governments (9):
Albania, Bosnia-Herzegovina, Bulgaria, Israel, Moldova, Montenegro, North Macedonia, Romania, Serbia.
Partner governments (2):
Croatia, Slovenia. [2019.02.20/XJ3094/y/**E***]

♦ South-Eastern Europe Brigade (SEEBRIG) 19808

Contact Camp "Boro Menkov", 1300 Kumanovo, North Macedonia. T. +38931387909. Fax +38931387976. E-mail: seebrig@sedmprocess.org.
URL: http://www.seebrig.org/
History 1998, Macedonia. *Agreement on the Multinational Peace Force South-Eastern Europe (MPFSEE)* signed 26 Sep 1998, Skopje (Macedonia). SEEBRIG established and activated 31 Aug 1999, Plovdiv (Bulgaria), by 7 participating nations. **Aims** Be available for possible employment in peace support operations mandated by UN or OSCE and led by NATO or EU. **Structure** Brigade-sized force. **Languages** English. **Staff** Permanent HQ Nucleus Staff 42 military personnel, to increase to 105 upon activation for exercises or deployments. **Finance** Common budget approved annually by Defense Ministers of participating nations. Annual budget: 250,000 EUR. **Activities** Events/meetings; humanitarian/emergency aid; knowledge management/information dissemination; management of treaties and agreements; projects/programmes; training/education. **Publications** *STARS INFORMER* (annual) – magazine.
Members Nations (6):
Albania, Bulgaria, Greece, North Macedonia, Romania, Türkiye.
IGO Relations Cooperates with (5): *Centre for Security Cooperation (RACVIAC, #03785); European Union (EU, #08967); NATO (#16945); Organization for Security and Cooperation in Europe (OSCE, #17887); United Nations (UN, #20515).* Operational body of: *South-East Europe Defense Ministerial (SEDM, #19822).* **NGO Relations** Open to cooperation with NGOs for preparation and conduct of Peace Support Operations under a Comprehensive/Integrated Approach. [2022.12.14/XM5718/**F***]

♦ South Eastern Europe Regional Rural Development Standing Working Group (SWG RRD) 19809

SG Goce Delcev 18, Macedonian TV Bldg, Floor 12, PO Box 659, 1000 Skopje, North Macedonia. T. +38923217708. Fax +38923217244. E-mail: swgsecretariat@swg-seerural.org.
URL: http://seerural.org/
History Set up Jun 2005, Macedonia and Serbia, during Agricultural Policy Forum 2005. **Aims** Empower and promote sustainable principles on rural development, through networking and permanent cooperation between all stakeholders of rural development in SEE region. **Structure** Assembly; Secretariat.
Members Ministries. Full member countries (6):
Albania, Bosnia-Herzegovina, Kosovo, Montenegro, North Macedonia, Serbia.
Observers countries (8):
Austria, Bulgaria, Croatia, Germany, Hungary, Italy, Serbia, Slovenia.
IGO Relations Partners include: *Central European Initiative (CEI, #03708); Deutsche Gesellschaft für Internationale Zusammenarbeit (GIZ); European Commission (EC, #06633); FAO (#09260); CIHEAM – International Centre for Advanced Mediterranean Agronomic Studies (CIHEAM, #03927); Regional Cooperation Council (RCC, #18773).* **NGO Relations** Member of: *TP Organics – European Technology Platform (TP Organics, #20180). SWG RRD Newsletter.* [2018/XM6464/**E***]

♦ South-East European Association of Neurologists and Psychiatrists / see South East European Society for Neurology and Psychiatry (#19819)
♦ South East European Centre for Entrepreneurial Learning (inactive)

♦ South-East European Consortium for Operational weather Prediction (SEECOP) 19810

Address not obtained.
URL: http://seecop.meteo.co.me/
History Established Mar 2015. Consortium Agreement approved, Oct 2015. **Aims** Provide Members with a state-of-the-art NWP system based on the application of the Non-hydrostatic Multiscale Model on the B grid (NMMB model) developed by NCEP, both for research and development activities and for operational usage in meteorological and hydrological forecasting, other applications driven by the atmosphere, and corresponding warning services. **Structure** Consortium Council; Coordination Experts Team; Working Groups.
Members Governments of 5 countries:
Albania, Bosnia-Herzegovina, Montenegro, North Macedonia, Serbia. [2018/XM7822/**D***]

♦ South East European Cooperation Process (SEECP) 19811

Contact Hellenic Ministry of Foreign Affairs, A3 Directorate for Southeastern Europe Countries, 1 Akadimias Street, 106 71 Athens, Greece. E-mail: athenscioseecp@mfa.gr.
Office 1 "Aleksandar I" Square, 1169 Sofia, Bulgaria. T. +35929878038.
URL: https://www.seecp.info/
History Jul 1996. Established at the ministerial meeting in Sofia (Bulgaria). **Aims** Strengthen security and political cooperation; intensify economic relations and cooperation in human resources, democracy and justice; combat organized crime. **Structure** Rotating chairmanship. Coordinated by *Regional Secretariat for Parliamentary Cooperation in South-East Europe (RSPC SEE, #18815).* **Languages** English. **Staff** 3.00 FTE, paid. **Activities** Events/meetings. **Events** *Meeting* Zagreb (Croatia) 2007, *Regional conference for South Eastern Europe* Bucharest (Romania) 2001, *Conference of the presidents of the parliaments from Southeastern Europe* Skopje (Macedonia) 2001, *Summit of the heads of state and government* Skopje (Macedonia) 2001, *Meeting* Ohrid (Macedonia) 2000.
Members Governments of 13 countries:
Albania, Bosnia-Herzegovina, Bulgaria, Croatia, Greece, Kosovo, Moldova, Montenegro, North Macedonia, Romania, Serbia, Slovenia, Türkiye.
IGO Relations *Regional Cooperation Council (RCC, #18773)* and *Migration, Asylum, Refugees Regional Initiative (MARRI, #16800)* function under SEECP's umbrella. [2022/XF6480/**F***]

♦ Southeast European Cooperative Initiative (SECI) 19812

Contact c/o OSCE, Hofburg Congress Centre, Hofburg, Heldenplatz 1, 1010 Vienna, Austria. T. +431514366422. E-mail: office@seci.org.
URL: http://www.seci.org/
History 6 Dec 1996, Geneva (Switzerland). **Aims** Facilitate cooperation among participating states; monitor and evaluate cooperation progress and trends; support the integration of countries into Euro-atlantic structures; focus on economic development, policy-making, policy facilitation and international cooperation. **Structure** Head office based in Vienna (Austria); Special Coordinator and Executive Chairman; Network of National Coordinators, regional coordination bodies and secretariats. Affiliated Offices: Business Advisory Council for SEE, based in Thessaloniki (Greece); Regional Center *Southeast European Law Enforcement Center (SELEC, #19815)*, based in Bucharest (Romania). **Languages** English. **Staff** 2.00 FTE, paid. **Finance** Voluntary contributions from supporting and participating states: Austria; Czech Rep; North Macedonia; Romania; Switzerland; USA. **Activities** Research and development; politics/policy/regulatory; networking/liaising; knowledge management/information dissemination. **Events** *Meeting of the Partnerships for Improvement of Danube Infrastructure and Navigation* Vienna (Austria) 2011, *Meeting* Istanbul (Turkey) 1998. **Publications** *The Danube Region: Transformation and Emergence* (2010) by E Busek and A Gjoreska; *10 Years Southeast European Cooperative Initiative: From Dayton to Brussels* (2006). Policy paper.
Members Participating States (13):
Albania, Bosnia-Herzegovina, Bulgaria, Croatia, Greece, Hungary, Moldova, Montenegro, North Macedonia, Romania, Serbia, Slovenia, Türkiye.
IGO Relations Cooperation with: *Regional Cooperation Council (RCC, #18773).* Observer to: *Central Asian Regional Information and Coordination Centre for Combating Illicit Trafficking of Narcotic Drugs, Psychotropic Substances and Their Precursors (CARICC, #03683); International Organization for Migration (IOM, #14454).* Close cooperation with: *European Bank for Reconstruction and Development (EBRD, #06315); European Commission (EC, #06633); International Bank for Reconstruction and Development (IBRD, #12317).* Located

at: *Organization for Security and Cooperation in Europe (OSCE, #17887).* Regional initiatives with: *Central European Initiative (CEI, #03708); Commission du Danube (CD, #04210); International Commission for the Protection of the Danube River (ICPDR, #12720); International Sava River Basin Commission (#14783); Organization of Black Sea Economic Cooperation (BSEC, #17857); Working Community of the Danube Regions (#21056).* Project implementation in cooperation with: *International Development Law Organization (IDLO, #13161); OECD (#17693); UNDP (#20292); UNEP (#20299); World Customs Organization (WCO, #21350).* **NGO Relations** Regional initiatives with: *Danube Tourist Commission (#05005).* Project implementation in cooperation with: *European Forum Alpbach (#07304); Institut für den Donauraum und Mitteleuropa (IDM); Vienna Economic Forum (VEF, #20770).* [2019/XF4396/F*]

♦ South East European Development Network on Plant Genetic Resources (SEEDNet) 19813

Contact address not obtained. T. +4640415587. Fax +4640415576.
History 2004. **Aims** Promote long-term conservation and sustainable utilization of the diversity of Plant Genetic Resources (PGR) within the region. **Structure** Regional Steering Committee. Regional Working Groups. **Finance** Supported by: *Swedish International Development Cooperation Agency (Sida).* **Activities** Working Groups (7): Cereals and Maize; Medicinal and Aromatic Plants; Vegetables; Fruit Crops and Vitis; Fodder Crops; Industrial Crops; Documentation and Information.
Members Institutions (13) in 12 countries:
Albania, Bosnia-Herzegovina, Bulgaria, Croatia, Hungary, Kosovo, Moldova, Montenegro, North Macedonia, Romania, Serbia, Slovenia. [2011/XJ2331/D]

♦ South East European Heritage Network (SEE Heritage Network) 19814

Sec PO Box 85, 85330 Kotor, Montenegro. T. +381641989577. Fax +38232302521. E-mail: secretary@seeheritage.net.
URL: http://www.seeheritage.net/
History 2006. **Aims** Protect and promote the common cultural heritage so as to encourage sustainable development of the region. **Languages** English, Macedonian, Serbo-Croatian.
Members NGOs in 10 countries:
Albania, Bosnia-Herzegovina, Bulgaria, Croatia, Greece, Kosovo, Montenegro, North Macedonia, Romania, Serbia.
NGO Relations Member of (1): *European Heritage Alliance 3.3 (#07477).* [2022/AA0961/F]

♦ Southeast European Law Enforcement Center (SELEC) 19815

Contact No 1-5 – Calea 13 Septembrie, Sector 5, Palace of the Parliament – 10th floor, 050711 Bucharest, Romania. T. +40213036009. Fax +40213036077. E-mail: secretariat@selec.org.
URL: http://www.selec.org/
History Set up by *Southeast European Cooperative Initiative (SECI, #19812)*, when *'Agreement on Cooperation to Prevent and Combat Trans-border Crime (SECI Agreement)'* entered into force, after being signed by 12 Southeast European countries on 26 May 1999. Transformed into SELEC, 7 Oct 2011, when Convention of the Southeast European Law Enforcement Center entered into force, the SELEC Convention being ratified by all Member States. Former names and other names: *SECI Regional Center for Combating Trans-Border Crime (SECI Center Bucharest)* – former. **Aims** Provide support for Member States in exchanging information and coordinating joint investigations and regional operations; enhance coordination in preventing and combating *crime*, including serious and organized crime, where such crime involves or appears to involve an element of trans-border activity. **Structure** SELEC Council, composed of high level representatives of Member States; Management. Police and Customs Authorities' Liaison Officers posted at SELEC headquarters. Under SELEC umbrella: *Southeast European Prosecutors Advisory Group (SEEPAG, #19818).* **Languages** English. **Staff** 15.00 FTE, paid. **Finance** Sources: contributions; contributions of member/participating states; revenue from activities/projects. **Activities** Networking/liaising. **Publications** *Organised Crime Threat Assessment for Southeast Europe (OCTA-SEE).* Annual Activity Report; controlled delivery manual; operational reports; press releases; leaflets; manuals; booklets.
Members Participating States (11):
Albania, Bosnia-Herzegovina, Bulgaria, Greece, Hungary, Moldova, Montenegro, North Macedonia, Romania, Serbia, Türkiye.
Operational Partners:
Italy, Saudi Arabia, UK, USA.
International organization:
International Criminal Police Organization – INTERPOL (ICPO-INTERPOL, #13110).
International observers (6):
European Union Border Assistance Mission to Moldova and Ukraine (EUBAM); *Gulf Cooperation Council (GCC, #10826); International Organization for Migration (IOM, #14454); UN Interim Administration Mission in Kosovo (UNMIK, #20343); United Nations Office on Drugs and Crime (UNODC, #20596); World Customs Organization (WCO, #21350).*
IGO Relations Memorandum of Understanding with (2): *United Nations Office on Drugs and Crime (UNODC, #20596); World Customs Organization (WCO, #21350).* Cooperates with (1): *International Criminal Police Organization – INTERPOL (ICPO-INTERPOL, #13110).* [2022.12.12/XE4515/y/E*]

♦ South-East European Network on Formal Methods (SEEFM) 19816

Chair International Faculty, City College, 3 Leontos Sofou Street, 546 26 Thessaloniki, Greece. T. +302310536544 – +302310528450. Fax +302310282384.
URL: http://www.seefm.info/
Aims Bring together researchers of South-Eastern European countries who are interested in formal methods. **Structure** Steering Committee of 9 members, headed by Chair. **Events** *Workshop* Thessaloniki (Greece) 2009, *Workshop* Thessaloniki (Greece) 2007, *Workshop* Ohrid (Macedonia) 2005, *Workshop* Thessaloniki (Greece) 2003. [2011/XJ2697/F]

♦ Southeast European Network for Investigative Reporting (unconfirmed)

♦ South East European Network for Professionalisation of the Media (SEENPM) 19817

Exec Dir address not obtained. E-mail: office@seenpm.org.
Communication Officer address not obtained.
URL: http://www.seenpm.org/
History 1999. **Aims** Increase professional standards of the media in South East Europe; work towards democratization of the media; increase regional cooperation and contacts between media professionals in the region. **Structure** General Assembly; Network Coordination Committee; Network Coordinators; Secretariat. **Finance** Financed through donors' programmes. Main donors: Danish government; Open Society Institute, Budapest (Hungary); Swiss government through *Swiss Agency for Development and Cooperation (SDC).* Other donors: *Council of Europe (CE, #04881);* German government; Guardian Foundation; *International Federation of Journalists (IFJ, #13462);* US State Department. Annual budget: euro 600,000. **Activities** Events/meetings; training/education. **Events** *General Assembly* Belgrade (Serbia) 2017. **Publications** Manuals; media studies; surveys.
Members Media centres (18) in 10 countries:
Albania, Bosnia-Herzegovina, Bulgaria, Croatia, Hungary, Moldova, North Macedonia, Romania, Serbia, Slovenia.
NGO Relations Member of (3): *Ethical Journalism Network (EJN, #05554); Global Forum for Media Development (GFMD, #10375); IFEX (#11100).* [2021/XF6205/t/F]

♦ South and East European Oncology Group / see Central and East European Oncology Group (#03701)

♦ Southeast European Prosecutors Advisory Group (SEEPAG) 19818

Secretariat c/o SELEC, No 1-5 – Calea 13 Septembrie, Sector 5, Palace of Parliament 10th Floor, 050711 Bucharest, Romania. T. +40213036083. Fax +40213036075. E-mail: seepag@selec.org.
URL: https://www.selec.org/about-seepag/
History Dec 2003. **Aims** Increase *judicial* cooperation in Southeast Europe; assist SELEC in operational matters and facilitate rapid exchange of information and evidence in transborder investigations; provide guidance, assistance and feedback to lawmakers in the region on justice and law enforcement issues. **Structure** Contact Points (1 from each member state); Chairmanship rotates annually; Secretariat provided by *Southeast European Law Enforcement Center (SELEC, #19815)*, based in Bucharest (Romania). **Languages** English. **Activities** Events/meetings. **Events** *Conference* Istanbul (Turkey) 2019, *Conference* Belgrade (Serbia) 2018, *Conference* Podgorica (Montenegro) 2016, *Conference* Chisinau (Moldova) 2015, *Conference* Budapest (Hungary) 2014.
Members National representatives in 11 countries:
Albania, Bosnia-Herzegovina, Bulgaria, Greece, Hungary, Moldova, Montenegro, North Macedonia, Romania, Serbia, Türkiye.
IGO Relations Cooperates with (4): *Eurojust (#05698); European Judicial Network (EJN, #07615); Regional Cooperation Council (RCC, #18773); United Nations Office on Drugs and Crime (UNODC, #20596).* Supports (1): *Southeast European Law Enforcement Center (SELEC, #19815).* [2021.09.07/XM2649/E*]

♦ South-East European Research Centre (internationally oriented national body)
♦ South-East European Research Institute on Geo Sciences (internationally oriented national body)

♦ South East European Society for Neurology and Psychiatry 19819

Contact address not obtained. E-mail: inpc2010@gmail.com.
History 1972, Thessaloniki (Greece). Previously also referred to as *South-East European Association of Neurologists and Psychiatrists.* **Aims** Cooperate research within Europe and the neighbourhood. **Structure** Executive Board. Chairmen (2); General Secretary. **Languages** English. **Staff** 3.00 FTE, paid. **Finance** Members' dues. Congress fees. **Activities** Presents academic lectures for an overview of the present knowledge; organizes post-graduate courses. **Events** *International Neuropsychiatric Pula Congress* Pula (Croatia) 2019, *International Neuropsychiatric Pula Congress* Pula (Croatia) 2018, *International Neuropsychiatric Pula Congress* Pula (Croatia) 2017, *International Neuropsychiatric Pula Congress* Pula (Croatia) 2016, *International Neuropsychiatric Pula Congress* Pula (Croatia) 2013. **Publications** *Neurologia et Psychiatria* (4 a year).
Members Full in 13 countries:
Austria, Bulgaria, Croatia, Czechia, Egypt, Germany, Hungary, Israel, Italy, Poland, Romania, Slovenia, Switzerland. [2010/XD2543/D]

♦ South East European Testing Board (SEETB) 19820

Main Office Ivan Vazov District, 1 Balsha St, Fl 3, 1408 Sofia, Bulgaria. E-mail: info@seetb.org.
URL: http://www.seetb.org/
History 2005. **Aims** Support the ISTQB qualification scheme aimed at software and system testing professionals in South East Europe. **Languages** English. **Activities** Certification/accreditation; events/meetings. **Events** *South East European Software Testing Confeence SEETEST* Sofia (Bulgaria) 2022, *Software Testing Conference* Belgrade (Serbia) 2021, *South East European Software Testing Conference* Bucharest (Romania) 2016, *South East European Software Testing Conference* Sofia (Bulgaria) 2015, *South East European Software Testing Conference* Bucharest (Romania) 2014. **Publications** *Quality Matters* – magazine. **NGO Relations** Member of: *International Software Testing Qualifications Board (ISTQB, #15559).* [2022/XM3093/E]

♦ South East European Virtual Climate Change Center (internationally oriented national body)
♦ South East European Youth Council (no recent information)

♦ South East European Youth Network (SEEYN) 19821

Exec Dir Skenderija 15, 1st Floor, 71000 Sarajevo, Bosnia-Herzegovina.
URL: http://www.seeyn.org/
History Dec 1999. **Aims** Empower civil society organizations (CSOs) and young people in the region to engage in peace and reconciliation, community development, economic empowerment and solidarity programmes. **Structure** General Assembly; Steering Board; Advisory Board; Executive Director. **Languages** English. **Staff** 49.00 FTE, paid. Voluntary trainers. **Finance** Supported by: Danish Ministry for Foreign Affairs; *Erasmus Student Network (ESN, #05529);* EuropeAid; *European Instrument for Democracy and for Human Rights (EIDHR, #07576);* PeaceNexus Foundation. **Activities** Advocacy/lobbying/activism; capacity building; networking/liaising; projects/programmes; research and development. **Publications** Handbooks; research papers; policy papers.
Members Organizations in 12 countries:
Albania, Bosnia-Herzegovina, Bulgaria, Croatia, Greece, Hungary, Kosovo, Montenegro, North Macedonia, Serbia, Slovenia, Türkiye.
NGO Relations Member of (2): Anna Lindh Foundation Bosnia-Herzegovina; *Centre for European Volunteering (CEV, #03743).* [2019.02.11/XJ3140/F]

♦ Southeast Europe Association (internationally oriented national body)

♦ South-East Europe Defense Ministerial (SEDM) 19822

Secretariat Devlet Mah Inönü Bulv, Merasim Sok Kor M Sirri Seyrek Kislasi, MSB Ek Hizmet Binasi Kat 4 No 412, Bakanliklar, Ankara/Ankara, Türkiye. T. +903124194387. Fax +903124193445. E-mail: sedm_pmsc@msb.gov.tr.
URL: http://www.sedmprocess.org/
History SEDM Process started Mar 1996, Tirana (Albania). **Aims** Strengthen understanding and politico-military cooperation in the region in order to enhance the stability and security in South-East Europe. **Structure** Coordination Committee (SEDM-CC); Political Military Steering Committee (PMSC). **Activities** Politics/policy/regulator; events/meetings. **Events** *SEESIM (South-Eastern Europe SIMulation) Command Post/Computer Assisted Exercise Meeting* Bucharest (Romania) 2016, *Meeting* Nevsehir (Turkey) 2016, *Meeting* Nevsehir (Turkey) 2016, *Ministerial Meeting* Rome (Italy) 2016.
Members National Ministries of Defence (14):
Albania, Bosnia-Herzegovina, Bulgaria, Croatia, Georgia, Greece, Italy, Montenegro, North Macedonia, Serbia, Slovenia, Türkiye, Ukraine, USA.
Observer nation:
Moldova.
IGO Relations *Centre for Security Cooperation (RACVIAC, #03785); South-Eastern Europe Brigade (SEEBRIG, #19808).* [2017/XM5717/F*]

♦ South East Europe Media Organisation (SEEMO) 19823

SG Spiegelgasse 2-29, 1010 Vienna, Austria. T. +4315133940. Fax +4315129015. E-mail: info@seemo.org.
URL: http://www.seemo.org/
History 15 Oct 2000, Zagreb (Croatia). **Aims** Promote and safeguard freedom of the press in the South East European region; improve the standards and practices of journalism; promote cooperation, understanding and the free exchange of news; ensure safety of journalists. **Structure** Board. **Languages** English. **Staff** 4.00 FTE, paid. **Activities** Awards/prizes/competitions; events/meetings; projects/programmes. **Events** *South East Europe Media Forum (SEEMF)* 2021, *Conference* Vienna (Austria) 2010, *Congress* Sofia (Bulgaria) 2008, *Congress* Zagreb (Croatia) 2007, *Congress* Belgrade (Serbia) 2006. **Publications** *DeScripto* (4 a year) – magazine; *SEEMO Media Handbook for South East and Central Europe* (annual) – in 2 vols. *Investigative Reporting Handbook* (2008); *Media and Minorities* (2006).
Members Editors; media executives; journalists and media organizations in 20 countries:
Albania, Belarus, Bosnia-Herzegovina, Bulgaria, Croatia, Cyprus, Czechia, Greece, Hungary, Kosovo, Moldova, Montenegro, North Macedonia, Poland, Romania, Serbia, Slovakia, Slovenia, Türkiye, Ukraine.
IGO Relations Close cooperation with: *Southeast European Cooperative Initiative (SECI, #19812).* **NGO Relations** Member of (1): *Ethical Journalism Network (EJN, #05554).* Close cooperation with: *Balkan Point; European Academy of Sciences and Arts (EASA, #05814); European Institute for the Media (EIM, no recent information);* International Center for Education of Journalists; *International Press Institute (IPI, #14636); South East European Network for Professionalisation of the Media (SEENPM, #19817).* [2021/XD8339/D]

♦ Southeast Europe Police Chiefs Association (SEPCA) 19824

Address not obtained.
URL: http://www.sepca-see.eu/
History Jan 2002, Pula (Croatia), with the help of the Canadian government, *Canadian International Development Agency (CIDA, inactive)* and Royal Canadian Mounted Police. Statutes adopted Oct 2002, Bucharest (Romania). New statutes signed 2007. As per Memorandum of Understanding, signed 2014, transformed in a voluntary network without legal status. **Aims** Improve police cooperation between members and other existing law-enforcement formats in identifying current threats and countering all types of crime. **Structure** General Assembly; Rotating Presidency; National Coordinators. **Activities** Capacity building. **Events** *Annual General Assembly* Ohrid (Macedonia) 2010, *Annual General Assembly* Belgrade (Serbia-Montenegro) 2003.
Members Countries and territories (8):
Albania, Bosnia-Herzegovina, Bulgaria, Montenegro, North Macedonia, Romania, Serbia, Srpska.

IGO Relations Partners include: BK Austria; *European Police Office (Europol, #08239)*; *Geneva Centre for Security Sector Governance (DCAF, #10121)*; *Migration, Asylum, Refugees Regional Initiative (MARRI, #16800)*; *Regional Cooperation Council (RCC, #18773)*; *Southeast European Law Enforcement Center (SELEC, #19815)*. [2016.09.28/XJ2471/**F***]

♦ South East Europe Transport Observatory (SEETO) 19825

General Manager SIV III, Omlandinskih Brigada 1, 5th Floor Office 555, P FAh (PO Box) 14, Belgrade, PAK 11198, Serbia. T. +381113131799 – +381113131805. Fax +381113131800. E-mail: office@seetoint.org.
URL: http://www.seetoint.org/

History Established by Memorandum of Understanding, signed 11 Jun 2004, by governments of Albania, Bosnia-Herzegovina, Croatia, Macedonia, Montenegro, Serbia, Kosovo and *European Commission (EC, #06633)*. **Aims** Promote cooperation on the development of the main and ancillary infrastructure on the multimodal SEETO Comprehensive Network; promote and enhance local capacity for the implementation of investment programmes, management and data collection and analysis on the SEETO Comprehensive Network. **Structure** Meeting of Ministers (annual, in December); Steering Committee; National Coordinators (one for each Regional Participant); Secretariat, based in Belgrade (Serbia). Working Groups (2): Railway and Intermodality; Road Safety. **Languages** English. **Staff** Region-wide. **Finance** Regional Participants' contributions. **Activities** Knowledge management/information dissemination; meeting activities. **Publications** Multi Annual Plans; transport-related reports.
Members Countries (7):
Albania, Bosnia-Herzegovina, Croatia, Kosovo, Montenegro, North Macedonia, Serbia. [2013.11.25/XJ2474/**F***]

- ♦ South and East Mediterranean College of Oncology (internationally oriented national body)
- ♦ South East Pacific Action Plan / see Action Plan for the Protection of the Marine Environment and Coastal Areas in the South East Pacific (#00095)
- ♦ South East Pacific Hydrographic Commission (see: #13825)
- ♦ Southern Africa AIDS Information Dissemination Service / see Southern Africa HIV/AIDS Information Dissemination Service (#19831)

♦ Southern Africa Bean Research Network (SABRN) 19826

Coordinator PO Box 158, Lilongwe, Malawi. T. +265999962851. Fax +2651707146.
URL: http://www.pabra-africa.org/

History 1987, as a regional organization of *Pan-African Bean Research Alliance (PABRA, #18040)*. **Aims** Ensure wider availability and increased utilization of demand driven bean-based technologies that increase agricultural sustainability and productivity, add value to bean commodity and are utilized for improving nutrition and food security and incomes of rural and urban poor in Southern Africa. **Finance** Main donors: *Canadian International Development Agency (CIDA, inactive)*; *Swiss Agency for Development and Cooperation (SDC)*. Also support from: *Department for International Development (DFID, inactive)*.
Members National Agricultural Research Systems (NARS) and their partners in 12 countries:
Angola, Botswana, Congo DR, Eswatini, Lesotho, Malawi, Mauritius, Mozambique, South Africa, Tanzania UR, Zambia, Zimbabwe.
IGO Relations *Southern African Development Community (SADC, #19843)*. [2018.09.06/XM3907/**E**]

- ♦ Southern Africa Climate Change Coalition (unconfirmed)
- ♦ Southern Africa Committee (internationally oriented national body)
- ♦ Southern Africa Communications for Development (no recent information)
- ♦ Southern Africa Community Foundation Association (internationally oriented national body)
- ♦ Southern Africa Compressed Gases Association (internationally oriented national body)
- ♦ Southern Africa Consortium for Monitoring Educational Quality / see Southern and Eastern Africa Consortium for Monitoring Educational Quality (#19871)
- ♦ Southern Africa Contact (internationally oriented national body)
- ♦ Southern Africa Cooperative Network (inactive)

♦ Southern Africa Development Community Election Support Network (SADC-ESN) 19827

Host Dir 10 Rochester Crescent Belravia, Harare, HARARE, Zimbabwe.
Coordinator address not obtained. E-mail: sadcesn@gmail.com.
URL: http://www.sadc-esn.org/

History 2010. Also referred to as *SADC Election Support Network*. **Aims** Promote democratic elections in the SADC region through networking of domestic observer groups. **Structure** General Assembly. Board. Secretariat. **Languages** English. **Staff** Seconded staff from member organization in Zimbabwe. **Finance** Donor funding. **Activities** Election Observation; Capacity Building Projects; Electoral Observatory Seminar.
Members Organizations in 15 countries:
Angola, Botswana, Congo DR, Eswatini, Lesotho, Madagascar, Malawi, Mauritius, Mozambique, Namibia, Seychelles, South Africa, Tanzania UR, Zambia, Zimbabwe.
IGO Relations *Southern African Development Community (SADC, #19843)*. [2013.11.20/XJ7528/**E**]

- ♦ Southern Africa Documentation and Cooperation Centre, Vienna (internationally oriented national body)

♦ Southern Africa Editors' Forum (SAEF) 19828

SG 19 Pine Valley Road, East Dalriach, PO Box 1793, Mbabane, H100, Eswatini.

History Nov 2003, South Africa. **Aims** Promote press freedom, professionalism and ethics among senior editorial executives in the print, broadcast and electronic news media. **Structure** General Meeting (2 a year). Regional Council consisting of Chairperson of national Editors Forum of SADC countries. Management Committee, comprising Chair, Deputy Chair, Secretary-General and Treasurer. Administrator. **Languages** English. **Staff** 1.00 FTE, paid. **Finance** Members' dues: US$ 1,000. **Activities** Standing Committees on: Press Freedom; Professionalism and Self-Regulation; Legal Defence and Constitutionalism; Membership development; Education and life-long learning.
Members Full in 14 countries:
Angola, Botswana, Congo DR, Eswatini, Lesotho, Madagascar, Malawi, Mauritius, Mozambique, Namibia, South Africa, Tanzania UR, Zambia, Zimbabwe.
NGO Relations Affiliated with: *African Editors' Forum (TAEF, #00293)*. [2008.06.01/XM1958/**F**]

♦ Southern Africa Federation of the Disabled (SAFOD) 19829

Federação de Deficientes da Africa Austral

Dir Gen Malawi Office – Blantyre, PO Box 1693, Blantyre, Malawi. T. +265111585119. E-mail: programs@safod.net – info@safod.net.
URL: http://www.safod.net/

History 1986. **Aims** Promote cross-disability interventions throughout Southern Africa. **Events** *General Assembly* Manzini (Swaziland) 1997, *Equileg regional meeting* Malawi 1995, *Seminar* Lusaka (Zambia) 1994, *Equal opportunities legislation for disabled people* Maseru (Lesotho) 1992.
Members Organizations in 10 countries:
Angola, Botswana, Eswatini, Lesotho, Malawi, Mozambique, Namibia, South Africa, Zambia, Zimbabwe.
NGO Relations Affiliated with: *Disabled Peoples' International (DPI, #05097)*; *Pan African Federation of the Disabled (PAFOD, no recent information)*. Cooperates with: *Africa Disability Alliance (ADA)*. [2016.06.01/XD2630/**D**]

♦ Southern Africa Gender Protocol Alliance 19830

CEO 9 Derrick Avenue, Cyrildene, Johannesburg, 2198, South Africa. T. +27116222877. Fax +27116224732.
URL: http://www.genderlinks.org.za/page/sadc-and-gender-protocol/

History 2005. **Aims** Work for the implementation of the SADC Protocol on Gender and Development. **Structure** Coordinated by *Gender Links (GL, #10098)*.
Members Full in 15 countries:
Angola, Botswana, Congo DR, Eswatini, Lesotho, Madagascar, Malawi, Mauritius, Mozambique, Namibia, Seychelles, South Africa, Tanzania UR, Zambia, Zimbabwe.
IGO Relations *Southern African Development Community (SADC, #19843)*. [2013/XJ7288/**E**]

♦ Southern Africa HIV/AIDS Information Dissemination Service (SAfAIDS) 19831

Exec Dir 17 Beveridge Road, PO Box A509, Avondale, Harare, HARARE, Zimbabwe. T. +2634336193. Fax +2634335005. E-mail: reg@safaids.net.
URL: http://www.safaids.net/

History 1994, Harare (Zimbabwe), as *Southern Africa AIDS Information Dissemination Service*. **Aims** Help strengthen capacity in the subregion to understand and effectively address the socio-economic impact of AIDS and promote HIV *prevention*. **Structure** Board of Trustees, comprising Chairperson, Vice-Chairperson, Treasurer, 4 members and 1 ex-officio member. **Finance** Supporters include: Dutch Government; *Humanistisch Instituut voor Ontwikkelingssamenwerking (Hivos)*; *Irish Aid*; *Swedish International Development Cooperation Agency (Sida)*. **Activities** Knowledge management/information dissemination; research/documentation. **Events** *Regional conference for Southern and Eastern Africa on AIDS and agriculture* Harare (Zimbabwe) 1998. **Publications** *SAfAIDS News* (4 a year); *Sexual Health Exchange* (4 a year); *Southern Africa Aids Action* (4 a year). Media materials, including occasional papers, books, posters and pamphlets. **Members** Not a membership organization. **IGO Relations** *Joint United Nations Programme on HIV/AIDS (UNAIDS, #16149)*. **NGO Relations** Partnerships and cooperation with several international, national and regional organizations. Member of: *Africa Capacity Alliance (ACA, #00160)*; *AIDS and Rights Alliance for Southern Africa (ARASA)*; *Regional Inter-Agency Task Team on Children and AIDS in Eastern and Southern Africa (RIATT-ESA, #18791)*. [2012/XF4536/**F**]

- ♦ Southern Africa Institute of Fundraising (internationally oriented national body)
- ♦ Southern Africa Journalists Association (no recent information)
- ♦ Southern Africa Labour Commission (inactive)

♦ Southern Africa Litigation Centre (SALC) 19832

Litigation Dir PO Box 52250, Saxonwold, 2132, South Africa. T. +27105968538. E-mail: enquiries@salc.org.za.
Street Address President Place, 1 Hood Avenue/ 148 Jan Smuts Avenue, Rosebank, Johannesburg, 2196, South Africa.
URL: http://www.southernafricalitigationcentre.org/

History Officially launched 20 Jun 2005, by *International Bar Association (IBA, #12320)* and Open Society Initiative for Southern Africa (OSISA). **Aims** Promote and advance human rights and the rule of law in southern Africa, primarily through strategic litigation support and capacity building. **Structure** Trustees. **Staff** 9.00 FTE, paid. **Activities** Advocacy/lobbying/activism; training/education; events/meetings. Active in: Angola, Botswana, Congo DR, Eswatini, Lesotho, Malawi, Mozambique, Namibia, Zambia, Zimbabwe. **Consultative Status** Consultative status granted from: *African Commission on Human and Peoples' Rights (ACHPR, #00255)* (Observer). **NGO Relations** Member of: *Coalition for an Effective African Court on Human and Peoples' Rights (African Court Coalition, #04055)*. [2020/XJ6557/**D**]

♦ Southern Africa Mathematical Sciences Association (SAMSA) 19833

Pres Stellenbosch Univ, Dept of Mathematical Sciences, P Bag X1, Matieland, South Africa.
Sec Univ of Malawi, Mathematics and Statistics Dept, P/Bag 303, Chichiri, Blantyre, Malawi.
URL: http://samsa-math.org/

History 1981. **Aims** Promote cooperation and exchange of ideas in mathematical sciences research and teaching of mathematical sciences; stimulate communication between mathematical scientists in the region. **Structure** Annual General Meeting; Executive Committee. **Languages** English. **Staff** 6.00 FTE, voluntary. **Finance** Members' dues. **Activities** Capacity building; projects/programmes; training/education; knowledge management/information dissemination; publishing activity; awards/prizes/competitions. **Events** *Conference* Blantyre (Malawi) 2019, *Mathematical sciences – a catalyst in driving a knowledge based economy* Palapye (Botswana) 2018, *Conference* Arusha (Tanzania UR) 2017, *Through the deserts of Namibia, discover the oasis of the mathematical knowledge* Windhoek (Namibia) 2015, *Conference* Victoria Falls (Zimbabwe) 2014. **Publications** *SAMSA Newsletter* (4 a year); *Southern Africa Journal of Pure and Applicable Mathematics (SAJPAM)* (2 a year). *SAMSA Expositions in Mathematical Sciences*. Conference proceedings.
Members Full in 11 countries:
Angola, Botswana, Eswatini, Kenya, Lesotho, Madagascar, Malawi, Mozambique, Namibia, South Africa, Tanzania UR, Uganda, Zambia, Zimbabwe. [2015.09.06/XD1409/**D**]

♦ Southern African Accounting Association (SAAA) 19834

Suider Afrika Rekenkundige Vereniging (SARV)

Pres Univ of the Witwatersrand, Richard Ward, 1 Jan Smuts Ave, Braamfontein, Johannesburg, 2000, South Africa. T. +271171718186.
URL: http://www.saaa.org.za/

History Founded Jul 1974, as *South African Society of University Teachers in Accounting (SASUTA)*. **Aims** Promote teaching of and *education* in accounting on the tertiary level in Southern Africa, including *auditing*, internal auditing, financial management, taxation and information systems. **Structure** General Meeting (every 2 years at International Conference); Executive Committee; Subject Interest Groups (SIG) (5). Regions (6): Western Cape; Eastern Cape; KwaZulu-Natal; Gauteng-North; Johannesburg (South Africa); Central. **Languages** Afrikaans, English. **Staff** None. **Finance** Members dues. **Activities** Events/meetings; research/documentation; standards/guidelines; awareness raising; knowledge management/information dissemination. **Events** *Biennial Conference* Johannesburg (South Africa) 2019, *Biennial Conference* Central Drakensberg (South Africa) 2017, *Biennial Conference* East London (South Africa) 2015, *Biennial Conference* Cape Town (South Africa) 2013, *Biennial Conference* George (South Africa) 2011. **Publications** *SAAA Accounting Education Forum* (2 a year) – newsletter; *South African Journal of Accounting Research SAJAR* (2 a year).
Members Lecturers at the tertiary level, chartered accountants, commercial and financial accountants, certified management accountants. Individuals (500), mainly in South Africa but in a total of 6 countries:
Botswana, Eswatini, Lesotho, Namibia, South Africa, Zimbabwe. [2016.10.19/XD4280/**D**]

- ♦ Southern African AIDS Training Programme / see SRHR Africa Trust (#19934)
- ♦ Southern African AIDS Trust / see SRHR Africa Trust (#19934)
- ♦ Southern African Applied Linguistics Association (internationally oriented national body)
- ♦ Southern African Asset Management Association (internationally oriented national body)
- ♦ Southern African Association for Behaviour Therapy (no recent information)
- ♦ Southern African Association for Commonwealth Literature and Language Studies (see: #02439)
- ♦ Southern African Association for Farming Systems Research / see Southern and Eastern African Association for Farming Systems Research-Extension (#19873)
- ♦ Southern African Association for Institutional Research (internationally oriented national body)
- ♦ Southern African Association for Research in Mathematics and Science Education / see Southern African Association for Research in Mathematics, Science and Technology Education (#19835)

♦ Southern African Association for Research in Mathematics, Science and Technology Education (SAARMSTE) 19835

Secretariat address not obtained. E-mail: saarmste@gmail.com.
URL: http://www.saarmste.org/

History 1992, South Africa. Former names and other names: *Southern African Association for Research in Mathematics and Science Education (SAARMSE)* – former. Registration: No/ID: 229-825 NPO, Start date: 12 Jun 2019, South Africa. **Aims** Advance research in mathematics, science and technology education in Southern Africa. **Structure** Executive Committee. **Languages** English. **Staff** 0.50 FTE, paid. **Finance** Sources: meeting proceeds; members' dues. **Activities** Events/meetings; training/education. **Events** *Annual Conference* 2022, *Annual Conference* Roma (Lesotho) 2021, *Annual Conference* Port Elizabeth (South Africa) 2020, *Annual Conference* Durban (South Africa) 2019, *Annual Conference* Gaborone (Botswana) 2018. **Publications** *AJRMSTE Journal*. Conference proceedings.
Members Full in 21 countries:
Australia, Botswana, Brazil, China, Eswatini, Ethiopia, Finland, Germany, Hungary, Japan, Lesotho, Malawi, Mozambique, Namibia, New Zealand, Norway, South Africa, UK, USA, Zambia, Zimbabwe. [2022.03.28/XN9131/**D**]

- ♦ Southern African Association of Science and Technology Centres (internationally oriented national body)

♦ Southern African Bitumen Association (SABITA) **19836**

CEO Postnet Ste 56, Private Bag X21, Howard Place, 7450, South Africa. T. +27215312718. Fax +27215312606. E-mail: info@sabita.co.za.
Street address No 5 Lonsdale Bldg, Lonsdale Way, Pinelands, 7405, South Africa.
URL: http://www.sabita.co.za/

History 1979, Cape Town (South Africa). **Aims** Advance best practice in Southern Africa in: use and application of bituminous materials; worker safety and environmental conservation; education and training; contact with government on the value of *road* provision and preservation. **Structure** Board of Trustees; Council; Working Group Committees. **Languages** Afrikaans, English. **Staff** 4.00 FTE, paid. **Finance** Members' dues. Other sources: investment growth; training. **Activities** Research and development; training/education; knowledge management/information dissemination; events/meetings. **Events** *Conference on Asphalt Pavements for Southern Africa* Sun City (South Africa) 2019, *Conference on Asphalt Pavements for Southern Africa* Sun City (South Africa) 2015, *Conference on Asphalt Pavements for Southern Africa* Victoria Falls (Zimbabwe) 1999. **Publications** *asphaltNEWS* (3 a year); *Roads Review* (annual). Manuals; technical guidelines; DVDs.
Members Full (95) in 6 countries:
Eswatini, Korea Rep, Namibia, South Africa, Zambia, Zimbabwe. [2020.03.05/XD7391/**D**]

♦ Southern African Broadcasting Association (SABA) **19837**

SG Radio Park Henley Road, Private Bag X1, Room 2323, Auckland Park, Johannesburg, 2006, South Africa. T. +27117144918. Fax +27117144869.
URL: http://saba-digital.org/

History Nov 1993. Current statutes revised 9 Aug 1997, Johannesburg (South Africa), and ratified 19 Oct 1997, Cologne. **Aims** Enhance professionalism and credibility of public broadcasting in the region. Through SABANEWS news exchange system: broaden the knowledge of radio listeners in the region on events in neighbouring countries and, where relevant to the region, further afield; contribute to enhancing a sense of regionalism in southern Africa, improving south-south flow of information and making newsroom operations more professional; uphold the principles of free speech and expression and free access to communication. **Structure** General Assembly (annual). Board of 6 (meets twice a year), comprising Directors General or Chief Executives of 5 member broadcasting corporations, including President and Secretary General (Chief Executive) who heads the Secretariat in Lusaka (Zambia). **Languages** English. **Staff** 2.00 FTE, paid. **Finance** Budget (annual): US$ 250,000. **Activities** *SABANEWS* news exchange service, launched 1 Mar 1995, Johannesburg (South Africa). **Events** *Annual General Assembly* Maputo (Mozambique) 2006, *Annual general assembly* Cape Town (South Africa) 1999, *Annual general assembly* Port Louis (Mauritius) 1998, *Annual General Assembly* Livingstone (Zambia) 1997, *Annual General Assembly* Maputo (Mozambique) 1996.
Members Full: public service broadcasting corporations of Southern Africa. Associate: similar corporations in other countries and other organizations in Southern Africa. Full members in 14 countries:
Angola, Botswana, Congo DR, Eswatini, Lesotho, Malawi, Mauritius, Mozambique, Namibia, Seychelles, South Africa, Tanzania UR, Zambia, Zimbabwe.
Associate members in 4 countries:
Germany, South Africa, UK, Zambia.
Included in the above, 1 organization listed in this Yearbook:
European Telecommunications Satellite Organization (EUTELSAT IGO, #08896).
IGO Relations *United States Agency for International Development (USAID).* [2016/XD5354/**D**]

♦ Southern African Bursars of Independent Schools Association (internationally oriented national body)

♦ Southern African Catholic Bishops' Conference (SACBC) **19838**

Conférence des évêques catholiques de l'Afrique méridionale – Suider-Afrikaanse Katolieke Biskopperaad

Contact SACBC, 399 Paul Kruger Street, PO Box 941, Pretoria, 0001, South Africa. T. +27123236458. Fax +27123266218. E-mail: communication@sacbc.org.za.
URL: http://www.sacbc.org.za/

History 1947. **Aims** Provide members of Conference with a platform for joint consultation, planning and policy making; promote united action in matters of common concern to the membership of the Church and in certain instances to fellow citizens as a whole; coordinate the work of 29 dioceses or ecclesiastical territories; act as a suitable link between the Church in Southern Africa, the Apostolic Delegation and the Holy See. **Structure** Plenary Session Meeting (2 a year); Administrative Board. Departments (6); Office (10); Associate Bodies (12); Forums (2). **Languages** Afrikaans, English, French, German, Italian, Portuguese. **Staff** 62.00 FTE, paid. **Finance** Financed by annual contributions made by dioceses. Budget (annual): South African Rand 3.5 million. **Activities** Departments (6): Pastoral Planning; Christian Education and Liturgy; Ecumenism and Inter-Religious Dialogue; Finance; Justice and Peace; Seminaries. Evangelization, AIDS Office; Human Trafficking Desk. **Events** *Plenary Session* Mariannhill (South Africa) 1996, *Annual plenary session* Pretoria (South Africa) 1989, *Annual plenary session* Harare (Zimbabwe) 1988. **Publications** *UmAfrika* (weekly) in Zulu; *Southern Cross* (weekly); *Catholic Directory of Southern Africa* (every 2 years). *Pastoral Action Series.* Lumko Institutes publications; other publications produced by SACBC's different Departments, Offices and Associate bodies.
Members Bishops in 3 countries:
Botswana, Eswatini, South Africa.
NGO Relations Member of: *Global Network of Domestic Election Monitors (GNDEM, #10487); International Catholic Migration Commission (ICMC, #12459); Oikocredit International (Oikocredit, #17704); South African Council of Churches (SACC, #19699).* Contacts with Vatican City and with all Bishops' Conferences, especially in African territories, Europe, Canada and the United States of America. Set up: *Catholic Theological Society of Southern Africa (CTSSA).* [2014/XD8787/v/**D**]

♦ Southern African Centre for the Constructive Resolution of Disputes (internationally oriented national body)
♦ Southern African Centre for Rural and Agricultural Credit Training (meeting series)
♦ Southern African Chief Justices Forum / see Southern African Judges Commission (#19847)

♦ Southern African Comparative and History of Education Society (SACHES) **19839**

Contact PO Box 13455, Hatfield, 0028, South Africa. T. +27849290170. E-mail: info@saches.co.za.
URL: http://www.saches.co.za/

History 1991. **Structure** General Meeting (annual); Core Executive Committee. **Languages** English. **Staff** Voluntary. **Finance** Members' dues. Other sources: income from annual conference; sales of journal. **Activities** Training/education; research/documentation; awards/prizes/competitions. **Events** *Annual Conference* Windhoek (Namibia) 2019, *Annual Conference* Skukuza (South Africa) 2018, *Annual Conference* Livingstone (Zambia) 2017, *Annual Conference* Bloemfontein (South Africa) 2015, *Annual Conference* Port Elizabeth (South Africa) 2012. **Publications** *SACHES eNEWS; SARE with EWP* – journal.
Members Organizations, not specified but including:
Working Group of Indigenous Minorities in Southern Africa (WIMSA, no recent information).
NGO Relations Member of: *World Council of Comparative Education Societies (WCCES, #21322).* [2017/XD4651/y/**D**]

♦ Southern African Confederation of Agricultural Unions (SACAU) ... **19840**

CEO PO Box 10480, Centurion, 0046, South Africa. T. +27126440808. Fax +27126671335. E-mail: info@sacau.org.
URL: http://www.sacau.org/

Aims Stimulate an environment that allows southern African farmers to realize their productive potential by influencing regional, continental and global policies and programmes related to agriculture. **Structure** Board of Directors. **Events** *Annual General Meeting* Victoria Falls (Zimbabwe) 2018, *Annual General Meeting* Cape Town (South Africa) 2017. **Publications** *SACAU Magazine.* Annual Report.
Members Full (17) in 12 countries:
Botswana, Eswatini, Lesotho, Madagascar, Malawi, Mozambique, Namibia, Seychelles, South Africa, Tanzania UR, Zambia, Zimbabwe.
NGO Relations Cooperates with: *Eastern African Farmers Federation (EAFF, #05223); West African Network of Farmers' Organizations and Agricultural Producers (#20891); Union Magrébine et Nord Africaine des Agriculteurs (UMNAGRI).* Member of: *PanAfrican Farmers' Organization (PAFO, #18049).* [2018/XJ8877/**D**]

♦ Southern African Conflict Prevention Network (SACPN) **19841**

Acting Coordinator c/o SACCORD, 5 Beit Road, Rhodespark, Box 37660, Lusaka, Zambia. T. +2601250027. Fax +2601250027.
Members in 10 countries:
Angola, Botswana, Eswatini, Lesotho, Malawi, Mozambique, Namibia, South Africa, Zambia, Zimbabwe. [2007.09.10/XJ2024/**F**]

♦ Southern African Cultural Information System (internationally oriented national body)

♦ Southern African Customs Union (SACU) **19842**

Union douanière d'Afrique australe (UDAA)

Exec Sec Private Bag 13285, Windhoek, Namibia. T. +264612958000. Fax +26461245611. E-mail: lindiwe.dlamini@sacu.int – info@sacu.int.
URL: http://www.sacu.int/

History 11 Dec 1969, on signature of the Customs Union Agreement (CUA) between Botswana, Lesotho, Swaziland and South Africa which entered into force 1 Mar 1970; replaced *Customs Union Agreement between the Governments of South Africa, Botswana, Lesotho and Swaziland (1910)* of 1910. Agreement amended, 1990, to make provisions for accession of additional contracting parties, Namibia becoming a de jure member from 10 Jul 1990 having been accepted de facto since 21 Mar 1990. New agreement signed 2002. **Aims** Maintain free interchange of goods between parties and apply the same tariffs and trade regulations to goods imported from outside on a basis designed to ensure continued economic development of the customs area as a whole; ensure in particular that arrangements encourage development of less advanced members of the customs union and diversification of their economies and afford all parties equitable benefits arising from trade among themselves and with other countries. **Structure** Customs Union Commission (meeting annually); Liaison Committees (3); Ad-hoc Committee on Agriculture. **Languages** English. **Staff** Provided by Namibian Customs and Excise Directorate: 374. **Finance** Government funding. **Activities** Networking/liaising; monitoring/evaluation. **Events** *Annual meeting* Swaziland 1990.
Members Governments of 5 countries:
Botswana, Eswatini, Lesotho, Namibia, South Africa.
IGO Relations Participates in the activities of: *UNCTAD (#20285).* Special agreement with: *EFTA (#05391).* Close working relations with: *Agency for International Trade Information and Cooperation (AITIC, #00553).* [2014.10.27/XD4612/**D***]

♦ Southern African Defence and Security Management Network (inactive)

♦ Southern African Development Community (SADC) **19843**

Communauté de développement de l'Afrique australe (CDAA) – Comunidade de Desenvolvimento da Africa Austral

Exec Sec SADC House, Plot No 54385 – Central Business District, Private Bag 0095, Gaborone, Botswana. T. +2673951863. Fax +2673972848. E-mail: registry@sadc.int.
Chairperson address not obtained.
URL: http://www.sadc.int/

History 17 Aug 1992, Windhoek (Namibia). Established on signature of Declaration and Treaty by Heads of State of member nations, to replace *Southern African Development Coordination Conference (SADCC, inactive)*, created 1 Apr 1980, Lusaka (Zambia), a meeting of Council of Ministers of SADCC, Jan 1992, Maputo (Mozambique), having endorsed a plan to transform the Conference into an economic community with common policies in areas such as trade and exchange rates, and with a majority-ruled South Africa as a full member. Restructured 2001. **Aims** Achieve development and *economic* growth, alleviate poverty, enhance living standards and quality of life of the peoples of Southern Africa and support the socially disadvantaged through regional integration; evolve common political values, systems and institutions; promote and defend peace and security; promote self-sustaining development on the basis of collective self reliance and the interdependence of member states; achieve complementarity between national and regional strategies and programmes; promote and maximize productive *employment* and utilization of the region's resources; achieve sustainable utilization of natural resources and effective protection of the environment; strengthen and consolidate historical, social and cultural affinities and links among the peoples of the region. **Structure** Institutional framework: Summit of Heads of State or Government (annual); Summit Troika of the Organ/SADC Organ on Politics Defence and Security; SADC Tribunal; SADC Council of Ministers. Sectoral and Cluster Ministerial Committees: Trade, Industry, Finance and Investment; Infrastructure and Services; Food, Agriculture, Natural Resources and Environment; Social and Human Development and Special Programmes; Politics, Defence and Security; Legal Affairs and Judicial Matters. Standing Committee of Senior Officials. SADC Secretariat, comprising Executive Secretary, 2 Deputies Executive Secretary (Regional Integration; Finance and Administration). SADC National Committees, including SADC Committee of Ambassadors and High Commissioners. SADC Parliamentary Forum. **Languages** English, French, Portuguese. **Staff** 92.00 FTE, paid. **Finance** Operating costs of Secretariat borne by member states in proportions agreed by Council (at least 5% and maximum 20%). Member states also fund and staff their respective Sector Coordinating Units and meet the expenses of their delegations at meetings. Donors include: *African Development Bank (ADB, #00283); European Union (EU, #08967);* governments of Italy and USA.
Activities Research/documentation; politics/policy/regulatory. Manages and sets up SADC Protocols (currently 26):
– Against Corruption (2001);
– Combating Illicit Drugs Trafficking (1996);
– Control of Firearms Ammunition and other Related Materials (2001);
– Culture, Information and Sport (2001);
– Education and Training (1997);
– Energy (1996);
– Extradition (2002);
– Facilitation and Movement of Persons (2005);
– Finance and Investment (2006);
– Fisheries (2001);
– Forestry (2002);
– Gender and Development (2008);
– Health (1999);
– Treaty Establishing SADC on Immunities and Privileges (1992);
– Legal Affairs (2002);
– Mutual Legal Assistance in Criminal Matters (2002);
– Mining (1997);
– Politics, Defence and Security Cooperation (2001);
– Science, Technology and Innovation (2008);
– Shared Watercourses (2000);
– Development of Tourism (1998);
– Trade (1996);
– Trade in Services (2012);
– Transport, Communications and Meteorology (1996);
– Tribunal and Rules Thereof (2000);
– Wildlife Conservation and Law Enforcement (1999);
– Shared Watercourses – revised (2000).

Other SADC legal instruments currently operational: Charter of *Regional Tourism Organisation of Southern Africa (RETOSA, #18817).* Memoranda of Understanding on: *'Macroeconomic Convergence', 'Cooperation in Taxation and Related Matters'* and *Standardization, Quality Assurance, Accreditation and Meteorology (SQUAM).* Summit has also signed: *'Declaration on Gender and Development'; 'Declaration on Productivity'; 'Declaration on Information and Communications Technology'; 'HIV and AIDS Declaration'*; Charter on Fundamental Social Rights; Mutual Defence Pact.
Committee of SADC Stock Exchanges (CoSSE, #04285) and *Committee of Central Bank Governors in SADC (CCBG, #04245)* coordinate regional developments in the financial markets. Other SADC organizations include:
– *Southern African Development Community Accreditation Service (SADCAS, #19844);*
– *Association of SADC Chambers of Commerce and Industry (ASCCI, #02901);*
– *Committee of Central Bank Governors in the Southern African Development Community (#04246);*
– *Development Training International (DTI);*
– *SADC Cooperation in Measurement Traceability (SADCMET);*
– *SADC Cooperation in Accreditation (SADCA);*
– *SADC Cooperation on Standardization (SADCSTAN);*

– *SADC Cooperation in Legal Metrology (SADCMEL)*;
– *SADC Council of NGOs (CNGO)*;
– *Electoral Commissions Forum of SADC Countries (ECF-SADC, #05414)*;
– *SADC Plant Genetic Resources Centre (SPGRC, #19024)*;
– *SADC Regional and National Early Warning System (no recent information)*, which monitors crop and food situation in the subregion and alerts on impending food crises;
– *Southern African Development Community Logistical Advisory Centre (no recent information)*;
– *Southern African Development Research Association (SADRA, no recent information)*;
– *Southern African Transport and Communications Commission (SATCC, no recent information)*;
– *USAID/SADC/IITA/CIP Southern Africa Root Crops Research Network (SARRNET, #20734)*;
– *Southern African Regional Police Chiefs Cooperation Organization (SARPCCO)*, set up on signature of Southern African regional police chiefs cooperation organization agreement (SARPCCO agreement).

From 1996, *'Employment and Labour Sector (ELS)'*, comprising 3 social partners – government, employers and workers – replaced *Southern Africa Labour Commission (SALC, inactive)*, which existed as an independent commission from Jan 1980. Instrumental in setting up: *SADC Centre for Specialization in Public Administration and Management (CESPAM, see: #19843)*. Established through a Memorandum of Understanding: *Southern African Power Pool (SAPP, #19858)*. Together with *East African Community (EAC, #05181)* and *Common Market for Eastern and Southern Africa (COMESA, #04296)*, announced setting up of *African Continental Free Trade Area (AfCFTA, #00267)*, Oct 2008.
Events *Summit of Heads of State and Government* Windhoek (Namibia) 2018, *SFSA : Science Forum South Africa* Pretoria (South Africa) 2017, *Summit of Heads of State and Government* Pretoria (South Africa) 2017, *Summit of Heads of State and Government* Mbabane (Swaziland) 2016, *SFSA : Science Forum South Africa* Pretoria (South Africa) 2016. **Publications** *SADC Facts and Figures*; *SADC Gender Monitor*; *SADC Official Trade and Investment Review*. Annual Report. Progress reports; proceedings; reports; pamphlets. **Information Services** *SADC-Information Centre* – database covers all SADC activity.
Members Governments of 15 countries:
Angola, Botswana, Congo DR, Eswatini, Lesotho, Madagascar, Malawi, Mauritius, Mozambique, Namibia, Seychelles, South Africa, Tanzania UR, Zambia, Zimbabwe.
Cooperating Governments (18):
Australia, Austria, Belgium, Brazil, Canada, China, Cuba, Egypt, Germany, Greece, Ireland, Italy, Netherlands, Nigeria, Portugal, Switzerland, UK, USA.
IGO Relations *Revised Protocol on Shared Watercourses (2000)*; *World Trade Organization (WTO, #21864)* (Observer Status). Memorandum of Understanding signed with: *Commonwealth Secretariat (#04362)*; *UNESCO (#20322)*. Relationship agreement with: *FAO (#09260)*. Permanent observer status with: *ECOSOC (#05331)*; *World Intellectual Property Organization (WIPO, #21593)*. Participates as observer in the activities of: *Codex Alimentarius Commission (CAC, #04081)*. Regional Economic Community of: *African Union (AU, #00488)*. Member of: *Africa Partnership Forum (APF, #00510)*. Observer to General Assembly of: *United Nations (UN, #20515)*. Accredited to the Conference of the Parties of: *Secretariat of the United Nations Convention to Combat Desertification (Secretariat of the UNCCD, #19208)*. Accredited by: *United Nations Framework Convention on Climate Change – Secretariat (UNFCCC, #20564)*. Agreement with: *Disaster Management Training Programme (DMTP, inactive)*. Close cooperation with: *International Civil Aviation Organization (ICAO, #12581)*; *United Nations Institute for Training and Research (UNITAR, #20576)*. Discussions on cooperation/possible merger, initiated by: *Preferential Trade Area for Eastern and Southern African States (PTA, inactive)*, are currently continuing with its successor, *Common Market for Eastern and Southern Africa (COMESA, #04296)*. Cooperates with: *New Partnership for Africa's Development (NEPAD, #17091)*, especially through *SADC Regional Indicative Strategic Development Plan (RISDP)*. Member of: *Eastern and Southern African Anti-Money Laundering Group (ESAAMLG, #05252)*. Close cooperation with: *International Crops Research Institute for the Semi-Arid Tropics (ICRISAT, #13116)*. Instrumental in setting up: *African Economic Community (AEC, #00290)*. **NGO Relations** Cooperates with: *International Fertilizer Development Center (IFDC, #13590)*; *International Institute of Tropical Agriculture (IITA, #13933)*; *Southern African Research and Documentation Centre (SARDC, #19861)*. Formal relations with: *Association of Power Utilities in Africa (APUA, #02867)*. Supports: *Academy for Educational Development (AED, inactive)*; *Southern African Network of AIDS Service Organizations (SANASO, see: #00272)*. Member of: *International Accreditation Forum (IAF, #11584)*; *Forus (#09934)*. Participates in: *Global Island Partnership (GLISPA, #10436)*. Partner of: *WorldFish (#21507)*. Instrumental in setting up: *Communications Regulators' Association of Southern Africa (CRASA, #04384)*; *Food, Agriculture and Natural Resources Policy Analysis Network (FANRPAN, #09839)*; *Regional Electricity Regulators Association of Southern Africa (RERA, #18779)*; *Southern Africa Bean Research Network (SABRN, #19826)*; *Southern Africa Telecommunications Association (SATA, #19867)*. [2020/XF2522/F*]

♦ Southern African Development Community Accreditation Service (SADCAS) 19844

CEO Plot 50669, Unit 2A, Tholo Office Park, Fairgrounds, Private Bag 00320, Gaborone, Botswana. T. +2673132909 – +2673132910. Fax +2673132922. E-mail: info@sadcas.org.
URL: http://www.sadcas.org/
History A subsidiary body of *Southern African Development Community (SADC, #19843)*. Incorporated in Botswana as a non-profit limited company. **Aims** Provide credible, cost effective, accreditation services for SADC Member States aimed at supporting trade, enhance protection of consumers and the environment, and improve competitiveness of SADC products and services in both voluntary and regulatory areas. **Structure** General Assembly; Board. Units (3): Technical; Administration; Financial Administration. **Activities** Certification/accreditation; training/education. **Publications** *SADCAS Newsletter*. Annual Report.
Members National Accreditation Focal Points (NAFPS) in 13 countries:
Angola, Botswana, Congo DR, Eswatini, Lesotho, Madagascar, Malawi, Mozambique, Namibia, Seychelles, Tanzania UR, Zambia, Zimbabwe.
NGO Relations Arrangement member of: *African Accreditation Cooperation (AFRAC, #00196)*.
[2018/XM5876/E]

♦ Southern African Development Community Lawyers Association .. 19845

Contact c/o Law Society of Botswana, PO Box 50889, Gaborone, Botswana.
History also referred to as *SADC Lawyers Association*. **Consultative Status** Consultative status granted from: *African Commission on Human and Peoples' Rights (ACHPR, #00255)* (Observer). **NGO Relations** Cooperates with: *East Africa Law Society (EALS, #05173)*. [2010/XM8121/D]

♦ Southern African Development Coordination Conference (inactive)
♦ Southern African Development Research Association (no recent information)
♦ Southern African Faith Communities' Environment Institute (internationally oriented national body)
♦ Southern African Foundation for the Conservation of Coastal Birds (internationally oriented national body)
♦ Southern African Heads of Independent School Association (unconfirmed)
♦ Southern African Human Rights Defenders Network (unconfirmed)
♦ Southern African Hypertension Society (internationally oriented national body)

♦ Southern African Institute for Environmental Assessment (SAIEA) . 19846

Exec Dir PO Box 6322, Windhoek, Namibia. T. +26461220579. Fax +26461259183. E-mail: bwa@saiea.co.za.
URL: http://www.saiea.com/
Aims Support *sustainable development* in Southern Africa through promoting the effective and efficient use of Environmental Assessment as a planning tool. **Structure** Board of Directors, comprising Chair, Vice-Chair and 7 members. Offices in: Windhoek (Namibia); Cape Town (South Africa). **Activities** Provides strategic support to SADC, governments, local authorities, development agencies, NGO's and private sector clients who are increasingly aware of the need to incorporate Environmental Assessment (EA) as an integral part of their planning. Services: guiding, monitoring and reviewing EA studies; monitoring the implementation of EA's and the impact of mitigation measures; basic and advanced training in EA; strategic research (eg EA effectiveness studies, sustainable development planning, Strategic Environmental Assessments, etc); needs-based information and networking. Projects: Cleaner Production; CBBIA; Capacity Building; Calabash. **Publications** *Environmental Assessment Legislation in the SADC Region*; *Environmental Impact Assessment in Southern Africa* – handbook. Trainin materials; workshop proceedings. **IGO Relations** Provides strategic support to: *Southern African Development Community (SADC, #19843)*. **NGO Relations** Member of: *Capacity Development and Linkages for Environmental Assessment in Africa (CLEAA, no recent information)*. Operates under the guidance of: *International Association for Impact Assessment (IAIA, #11956)*.
[2011.06.01/XJ0189/j/D]

♦ Southern African Institute of Forestry (internationally oriented national body)
♦ Southern African International Conference on Environmental Management (meeting series)
♦ Southern African and Islands Hydrographic Commission (see: #13825)

♦ Southern African Judges Commission (SAJC) 19847

Contact Constitutional Court of South Africa, Constitution Hill, c/o Sam Hancock and Queens Streets / Private Bag X1, Braamfontein, 2017, South Africa. T. +27113597537. Fax +27114038743.
History 7 Dec 2003, Johannesburg (South Africa). Sometimes also referred to as *Southern African Chief Justices Forum (SACJF)*. **Aims** Promote: cooperation among courts in the Southern African region; the rule of law, democracy and the independence of the courts in the region; the welfare and dignity of judges in the member countries. **Structure** Management Committee, comprising Chairperson, Deputy Chairperson and Immediate Past Chairperson. **Activities** Organizes meetings.
Members Chief justices and senior judges in 13 countries:
Angola, Botswana, Eswatini, Lesotho, Malawi, Mozambique, Namibia, Seychelles, South Africa, Tanzania UR, Uganda, Zambia, Zimbabwe.
IGO Relations *European Commission for Democracy through Law (Venice Commission, #06636)*.
[2014/XJ3560/E]

♦ Southern African Large Telescope Consortium (SALT Consortium) . 19848

Chairman American Museum of Natural History, Central Park West at 79th St, New York NY 10024-5192, USA. T. +12127695488. Fax +12127695007. E-mail: salt@salt.ac.za.
URL: http://www.salt.ac.za/
Aims Build a 10 metre class telescope near Sutherland (South Africa).
Members Partners (8) in 6 countries:
Germany, New Zealand, Poland, South Africa, UK, USA. [2014.11.26/XF5949/F]

♦ Southern African Legal Assistance Network (SALAN) 19849

Secretariat Legal and Human Rights Ctr, Justice Lugakingira House, Kijitomyama Area, PO Box 75254, Dar es Salaam, Tanzania UR. T. +255222773038 – +255222773048. Fax +255222773037. E-mail: salan@humanrights.or.tz.
URL: http://www.salan.org/
History 1994. **Aims** Encourage dialogue and information sharing on human rights in Southern Africa. **Events** *Annual General Meeting* Johannesburg (South Africa) 2014. **Publications** *SALAN Newsletter*.
Members National centres (15) in 9 countries:
Botswana, Lesotho, Malawi, Mozambique, Namibia, South Africa, Tanzania UR, Zambia, Zimbabwe. [2014/XM2064/F]

♦ Southern African Literature Society (inactive)
♦ Southern African Maintenance Association / see Southern African Asset Management Association

♦ Southern African Migration Programme (SAMP) 19850

Project Dir International Migration Research Centre, Balsillie School of International Affairs, 67 Erb St West, Waterloo ON N2L 6C2, Canada. T. +16133296289.
Southern African Office 6 Spin Street, CHurch Square, Cape Town, South Africa.
URL: http://www.queensu.ca/samp/
History Founded 1996. **Aims** Promote awareness of linkages between migration and *development* in the Southern African Development Community (SADC). **Structure** International network of organizations. **Activities** Conducts applied research on migration and development issues; provides policy advice and expertise; offers training in migration policy and management; conducts public education campaigns on migration-related issues. **Publications** *SAMP Migration Policy Briefs*. *SAMP Migration Policy Series*.
Members in 10 countries:
Botswana, Canada, Eswatini, Lesotho, Malawi, Mozambique, Namibia, South Africa, Zambia, Zimbabwe.
[2013.06.12/XJ0531/F]

♦ Southern African Museums Association (internationally oriented national body)

♦ Southern African Music Rights Organizations (SAMRO) 19851

CEO PO Box 31609, Braamfontein, Johannesburg, 2017, South Africa. T. +27117128000. Fax +27866744391. E-mail: customerservices@samro.org.za.
Street Adress 20 De Korte Street, Braamfontein, 2001, South Africa.
URL: http://www.samro.org.za/
History 1961. **Aims** Protect the intellectual property of composers and authors, as well as ensure that composers and authors talents are adequately credited both locally and internationally for music usage. **Structure** Board of Directors. SAMRO Foundation. **Members** Composers and authors (over 7,000) from all nationalities in Southern Africa. Membership countries not specified. **NGO Relations** Affiliated to: *Confédération internationale des sociétés d'auteurs et compositeurs (CISAC, #04563)*. [2019/XM1357/D]

♦ Southern African Natural Products Trade Association (PhytoTrade Africa) 19852

Europe Office 16 Benson House, Ligonier Street, London, E2 7HH, UK. T. +447813791497.
URL: http://phytotrade.com/
History 2001. **Aims** Develop a *fair trade* and environmentally sustainable natural products industry in Southern Africa. **Structure** Board. **Languages** English. **Finance** Members' dues. Other sources: donations; service fees. **Activities** *Natural Products Information Service (NPIS)*.
Members Companies and individuals 8 countries:
Botswana, Eswatini, Malawi, Mozambique, Namibia, South Africa, Zambia, Zimbabwe.
NGO Relations Member of: *International Union for Conservation of Nature and Natural Resources (IUCN, #15766)*; *World Fair Trade Organization (WFTO, #21396)*. [2019.10.30/XM3277/t/D]

♦ Southern African Network of AIDS Service Organizations (see: #00272)
♦ Southern African Network on Equity in Health / see Network for Equity in Health in East and Southern Africa (#17011)

♦ Southern African Network of Nurses and Midwives (SANNAM) 19853

Exec Dir PO Box 1280, Pretoria, 0001, South Africa. T. +27123446135. Fax +27123446135. E-mail: sannamco@denosa.org.za.
History Jul 2000, Durban (South Africa). Officially launched, 23 may 2001. **Aims** Improve the quality of health care services through a comprehensive response to HIV/AIDS and other critical health care challenges in the region within the context of the Millennium Development Goals. **Structure** Executive Committee, comprising Chairperson, Vice-Chairperson, Treasurer and 2 members. Secretariat. **Events** *Conference & AGM* Gaborone (Botswana) 2011.
Members Associations in 15 countries:
Angola, Botswana, Congo DR, Eswatini, Lesotho, Madagascar, Malawi, Mauritius, Mozambique, Namibia, Seychelles, South Africa, Tanzania UR, Zambia, Zimbabwe.
NGO Relations Member of: *Global Health Workforce Alliance (GHWA, inactive)*. [2014/XJ1583/E]

♦ Southern African Neuroscience Group / see Southern African Neuroscience Society
♦ Southern African Neuroscience Society (internationally oriented national body)
♦ Southern African New Crop Research Association (internationally oriented national body)

♦ Southern African Non-Governmental Development Organization Network (SANGONeT) 19854

Exec Dir PO Box 31392, Braamfontein, 2017, South Africa. T. +27114034935. Fax +27114030130. E-mail: info@sangonet.org.za.
Street Address Maths Centre Bldg, 28 Juta Street, Braamfontein, South Africa.
URL: http://www.sangonet.org.za/

History Founded 1987, Johannesburg (South Africa). **Aims** Support effective use of ICTs in Southern African civil society organizations by providing quality services and initiatives. **Structure** General Meeting (annual); Board. Includes: *MIET Africa*. **Languages** English. **Staff** 3.00 FTE, voluntary. 23-26 FTE, paid. **Finance** Internet services; training and fundraising projects. **Activities** Guidance/assistance/consulting; training/education; knowledge management/information dissemination; advocacy/lobbying/activism; events/meetings. **Events** *Annual ICTs for civil society conference* Cape Town (South Africa) / Johannesburg (South Africa) 2009, *Annual ICTs for civil society conference* Johannesburg (South Africa) 2008, *Annual ICTs for civil society conference* Johannesburg (South Africa) 2006, *Annual General Meeting* Braamfontein (South Africa) 2005, *Annual ICTs for civil society conference* Johannesburg (South Africa) 2005. **Publications** *NGP Pulse* – newsletter. Annual Report. **Members** Not a membership organizations. **NGO Relations** Member of: *Association for Progressive Communications (APC, #02873)*; *CIVICUS: World Alliance for Citizen Participation (#03962)*. [2016.06.01/XF2742/**F**]

♦ Southern African-Nordic Centre (SANORD) 19855

Admin University of the Western Cape, Private Bag X17, Bellville, Cape Town, 7535, South Africa. T. +27219593802 – +27219593811.
URL: http://sanord.uwc.ac.za/

History 2007. **Aims** Promote multilateral research cooperation on matters of importance to the *development* of both regions. **Structure** Council; Board. **Languages** English. **Staff** 2.00 FTE, paid. **Finance** Members' dues. **Activities** Training/education; financial and/or material support; events/meetings; networking/liaising. **Events** *Annual Conference* Bergen (Norway) 2021, *Annual Conference* Bergen (Norway) 2020, *Annual Conference* Gaborone (Botswana) 2019, *Annual Conference* Jyväskylä (Finland) 2018, *Annual Conference* Uppsala (Sweden) 2016. **Publications** *SANORD Newsletter*. *Knowledge for justice – Critical perspectives from southern African-Nordic research partnerships* (2017); *Knowledge for a sustainable world – A southern African-Nordic contribution* (2015); *One world, many knowledges – Regional experiences and cross-regional links in Higher Education* (2009). *Strengthening the Roles of Universities as Hubs of Development* (2012) – e-publication. **Information Services** *SANORD Portal*.
Members Higher Education institutions (48) in 11 countries:
Botswana, Denmark, Finland, Iceland, Malawi, Namibia, Norway, South Africa, Sweden, Zambia, Zimbabwe.
NGO Relations *Nordic Africa Institute (NAI, #17168)*. [2020/XJ5129/E]

♦ Southern African Online User Group (SAOUG) 19856

Chair PostNet Ste 104, Private Bag X1, Menlo Park, Pretoria, 0102, South Africa. T. +27124203791. E-mail: saoug.chair@gmail.com – events.saoug@gmail.com.
URL: http://www.saoug.org.za/

Aims Promote development and use of online and other *computerized information retrieval* systems. **Structure** Executive Committee. **Finance** Sources: grants; members' dues. **Activities** Events/meetings. **Events** *Biennial Southern African Online Information Meeting* 2018, *Biennial Southern African Online Information Meeting* Pretoria (South Africa) 2016, *Biennial Meeting* Pretoria (South Africa) 2014, *Biennial Southern African Online Information Meeting* Johannesburg (South Africa) 2012, *Biennial Southern African Online Information Meeting* Pretoria (South Africa) 2010. **Publications** *Southern African Online User Group Blog*. [2022.02.02/XE2398/**E**]

♦ Southern African Political Economy Series Trust (SAPES Trust) 19857

Main Office PO Box MP 111, Mount Pleasant, Harare, HARARE, Zimbabwe. T. +2634252962 – +2634252963 – +2634252965. Fax +2634252963. E-mail: admin@sapes.org.zw.
URL: http://sapes.org.zw/

History Oct 1987, by *African Association of Political Science (AAPS)*. **Structure** Includes *Southern Africa Regional Institute for Policy Studies (SARIPS, no recent information)*. **Events** *Annual Colloquium* 1999. [2020/XF3561/**F**]

♦ Southern African Power Pool (SAPP) 19858

Exec Dir PO EH 52, Emerald Hill, Harare, HARARE, Zimbabwe. T. +2634335468 – +2634335558 – +2634335517. Fax +2634307063. E-mail: info@sapp.co.zw.
Street Address 24 Golden Stairs, Emerald Hill, Harare, HARARE, Zimbabwe.
URL: http://www.sapp.co.zw/

History 28 Aug 1995. Established by *Southern African Development Community (SADC, #19843)*, on signature of an Intergovernmental Memorandum of Understanding (IGMOU). Revised IGMOU signed, 23 Feb 2006, Gaborone (Botswana). **Aims** Coordinate provision of a reliable and economical electricity supply, facilitate electricity trading, and promote regional cooperation in power projects, both generation and transmission, while increasing access to electricity among SAPP member utilities in the SADC region. **Structure** General Meeting (twice a year); SADC Directorate of Infrastructure and Services; Executive Committee; Management Committee; Coordination Centre Board; Coordination Centre. Sub-Committees (4): Planning; Operating; Markets; Environmental. **Languages** English, French, Portuguese. **Staff** 16.00 FTE, paid. **Finance** Sources: government support; international organizations; members' dues. Members meet all other expenses. Supported by: *Development Bank of Southern Africa (DBSA)*; Government of Norway; *International Bank for Reconstruction and Development (IBRD, #12317)*; *Swedish International Development Cooperation Agency (Sida)*; *United States Agency for International Development (USAID)*. Annual budget: 1,000,000 USD. **Activities** Projects/programmes. Current projects: Implementation of the SAPP Telecommunications Study; SAPP Generation and Transmission Priority Projects; Competitive Electricity Market; Transmission Pricing Policy and Ancillary Services Markets; Environmental Management Guidelines. **Events** *General Meeting* Walvis Bay (Namibia) 2013, *Annual Meeting* Livingstone (Zambia) 2012, *General Meeting* Mangochi (Malawi) 2012, *General Meeting* Johannesburg (South Africa) 2011, *General Meeting* Victoria Falls (Zimbabwe) 2011. **Publications** *Sustainable Development Bulletin* (12 a year); *Operations Report* (12 a year); *Monthly Report*. Annual Report.
Members Operating and non-operating (indicated by ") utility companies in 12 countries:
Angola (*), Botswana, Congo DR, Eswatini, Lesotho, Malawi (*), Mozambique, Namibia, South Africa, Tanzania UR (*), Zambia, Zimbabwe. [2023.02.16/XF6484/**F***]

- ♦ Southern African Project Controls Institute (internationally oriented national body)
- ♦ Southern African Refrigerated Distribution Association (internationally oriented national body)
- ♦ Southern African Regional Commission for the Conservation and Utilisation of the Soil (inactive)

♦ Southern African Regional Cooperation in Biochemistry, Molecular Biology and Biotechnology (SARBIO) 19859

Coordinator NUST Envir Science / Health, PO Box AC 939, Ascot, Bulawayo, BULAWAYO, Zimbabwe.
History 1995, on the initiative of Prof Julia A Hasler. **Members** in 6 countries. Membership countries not specified. **NGO Relations** Member of: *AFASSA (no recent information)*. [2009/XF6965/**F**]

- ♦ Southern African Regional Police Chiefs Cooperation Organization (inactive)

♦ Southern African Regional Universities Association (SARUA) 19860

CEO Gnd Fl Chardonnay House, Vineyards Office Estate, 99 Jip de Jager Drive, Bellville, 7530, South Africa. E-mail: info@sarua.org.
URL: http://www.sarua.org/

History 2005. **Aims** Strengthen *higher education* leadership and institutions in Southern Africa, thus consolidating a Southern African agenda for higher education leading to a significant contribution by higher education to national and regional development. **Activities** Events series: Vice Chancellor Dialogue Exchange; Executive Focus. **Publications** *SARUA Handbook – Guide to Public Universities*. Leadership Dialogue Series. **Members** Public universities in the SADC region. Membership countries not specified. **NGO Relations** Member of: *International Association of Universities (IAU, #12246)*. [2018/XJ0520/**D**]

♦ Southern African Research and Documentation Centre (SARDC) ... 19861

Main Office JK Nyerere House, 15 Downie Avenue, Harare, HARARE, Zimbabwe. T. +2634791141. E-mail: sardc@sardc.net.
Chairperson c/o Parliament of Namibia, Private Bag 13323, Windhoek, Namibia.
URL: http://www.sardc.net/

History 1985. Established 1987 in Harare (Zimbabwe) and Maputo (Mozambique) in response to an expressed need within southern Africa for greater access to cross-border and regional information. **Aims** Strengthen regional integration and community building in partnership with the Southern African Development Community (SADC) adn others by tracking progress and raising awareness of regional development issues, achievements and challenges. **Structure** Board; Institutes (5); Service Departments (5); sub-office in Maputo (Mozambique). **Languages** English, French, Portuguese. **Staff** 35.00 FTE, paid. **Finance** Financed through consultancies and subscriptions, and by development agencies and other donors, including: Governments of Netherlands, Zimbabwe, China, Norway; *Austrian Development Agency (ADA)*; *Deutsche Gesellschaft für Internationale Zusammenarbeit (GIZ)*; Trust Africa; Zambezi Watercourse Commission (ZAMCOM); *Global Environment Facility (GEF, #10346)*; Open Society Initiative of Southern Africa (OSISA); *Swedish International Development Cooperation Agency (Sida)*; *UNEP (#20299)*; *Norwegian Agency for Development Cooperation (Norad)*; *United States Agency for International Development (USAID)*; *African Development Bank (ADB, #00283)*. **Activities** Politics/policy/regulatory; research/documentation; knowledge management/information dissemination; training/education; publishing activities. **Publications** *SADC Today* (6 a year) – newsletter; *The Zambezi* (2 a year) – newsletter; *Southern African News Features (SANF)* (24 a year). Books; special reports; directories; guides; country profiles; fact sheets.
Members Full in 1 country:
Netherlands.
Consultative Status Consultative status granted from: *African Commission on Human and Peoples' Rights (ACHPR, #00255)* (Observer). **IGO Relations** Cooperates with: *Southern African Development Community (SADC, #19843)*. Associated with Department of Global Communications of the United Nations. **NGO Relations** Ms member of: *International Federation of Library Associations and Institutions (IFLA, #13470)*. Cooperates with: *International Federation of Red Cross and Red Crescent Societies (#13526)*; *International Union for Conservation of Nature and Natural Resources (IUCN, #15766)*. [2021/XF2957/**E**]

- ♦ Southern African Research and Innovation Management Association (internationally oriented national body)
- ♦ Southern African Resource Watch (unconfirmed)

♦ Southern African Science Service Centre for Climate Change and Adaptive Land Management (SASSCAL) 19862

Exec Dir address not obtained.
Aims Conduct problem-oriented research in the area of adaptation to climate and change and sustainable land management; provide evidence-based advice for all decision-makers and stakeholders to improve the *livelihoods* of people in the region; contribute to the creation of an African knowledge-based society. **Structure** Governing Board. **Finance** Sponsored by German Federal Ministry of Education and Research. **Publications** *SASSCAL Newsletter*.
Members Governments (6):
Angola, Botswana, Germany, Namibia, South Africa, Zambia. [2014/XJ7858/**D***]

- ♦ Southern African Sexual Health Association (internationally oriented national body)
- ♦ Southern African Society of Human Genetics (internationally oriented national body)
- ♦ Southern African Society for Paediatric Infectious Diseases (internationally oriented national body)

♦ Southern African Society for Plant Pathology (SASPP) 19863

Contact Univ of the Free State, PO Box 339, Bloemfontein, 9300, South Africa. T. +27514012378. E-mail: contact@saspp.co.za.
URL: https://saspp.co.za/

History 1962, Stellenbosch (South Africa). Former names and other names: *South African Society for Plant Pathology* – former; *Suid-Afrikaanse Vereniging vir Plantpatologie* – former. **Aims** Promote plant pathology in Southern Africa by acting as official mouthpiece of plant pathologists in the region. **Structure** General Meeting (biennial, at Congress); Council. **Languages** English. **Staff** Voluntary. **Finance** Sources: donations; members' dues. **Activities** Events/meetings; knowledge management/information dissemination; networking/liaising. **Events** *Biennial Congress* Pretoria (South Africa) 2022, *Conference* Pretoria (South Africa) 2021, *Biennial Congress* Langebaan (South Africa) 2019, *Biennial Congress* Winterton (South Africa) 2017, *Biennial Congress* Bloemfontein (South Africa) 2015. **Publications** Conference abstracts printed in SA Journal of Science.
Members Full in 9 countries:
Botswana, France, Ghana, Netherlands, South Africa, Tanzania UR, UK, USA, Zimbabwe.
NGO Relations Member of (1): *International Association of Botanical and Mycological Societies (IABMS, #11730)*. [2022.05.13/XD4378/**D**]

- ♦ Southern African Society of Quaternary Research (internationally oriented national body)
- ♦ Southern African Society of Reproductive Biology / see Southern African Society for Reproductive Medicine and Gynaecological Endoscopy
- ♦ Southern African Society for Reproductive Medicine and Gynaecological Endoscopy (internationally oriented national body)
- ♦ Southern African Society of Reproductive Science and Surgery / see Southern African Society for Reproductive Medicine and Gynaecological Endoscopy

♦ Southern African Society for Trenchless Technology (SASTT) 19864

Pres c/o Trenchless Technologies cc, 11Villa Pala 220, Belami Drive, Sonstraalhoogte, 7550, Durbanville. T. +27825517458. E-mail: director@sastt.org.za.
Vice-Pres address not obtained.
URL: http://www.sastt.org.za/

History 26 Feb 1992, Pretoria (South Africa). **Aims** From an ethical and neutral base, promote the use of trenchless technology for providing and maintaining *underground* services with a minimum of surface and environmental disruption. **Structure** Board. **Languages** English. **Staff** 0.50 FTE, paid. **Finance** Sources: members' dues. **Activities** Financial and/or material support; guidance/assistance/consulting. **Publications** *SASTT News* (irregular). *SASTT Construction Standards for Trenchless Technology*. **Members** in Southern Africa. Membership countries not specified. **NGO Relations** Affiliated with (1): *International Society for Trenchless Technology (ISTT, #15520)*. [2022.05.13/XD4766/**D**]

- ♦ Southern African Spinal Cord Association (internationally oriented national body)

♦ Southern African Trade Union Coordination Council (SATUCC) 19865

Conseil de coordination des syndicats d'Afrique australe – Conselho de Coordenação dos Sindicatos da Africa Austral

Exec Sec Plot 5071 Kabelo Way, Extension 10, PO Box 601557, Gaborone, Botswana. T. +2673901449 – +2673160401. Fax +2673184453. E-mail: info@satucc.org.
URL: http://www.satucc.org/

History Mar 1983, Gaborone (Botswana). Set up as a regional trade union organization representing all major trade union federations in *Southern African Development Community (SADC, #19843)*. **Aims** Unite working people and the poor and voiceless in the struggle to free southern Africa from exploitation, injustice and oppression through providing a dynamic, inclusive and sustainable platform to influence regional policy in favour of the working populations and the poor. **Structure** Delegates Congress (every 4 years); Executive Council (at least annual); Central Executive Committee; Committees (2); Secretariat, headed by Executive Secretary. **Languages** English, French, Portuguese. **Staff** 4.00 FTE, paid. **Finance** Sources: donations; government support; grants; international organizations; members' dues. **Activities** Advocacy/lobbying/activism; capacity building; events/meetings; projects/programmes; research and development; training/education. **Publications** Booklets; research papers; reports.
Members Trade Union Centres (23) in 15 SADC countries:
Angola, Botswana, Comoros, Congo DR, Eswatini, Lesotho, Madagascar, Malawi, Mauritius, Mozambique, Namibia, South Africa, Tanzania UR, Zambia, Zimbabwe.
IGO Relations Consultative Status with: *African Union (AU, #00488)*; *Southern African Development Community (SADC, #19843)*. **NGO Relations** Collaborative relations with: *Fellowship of Christian Councils in Southern Africa (FOCCISA)*; *International Trade Union Confederation (ITUC, #15708)*; *International Trade Union Confederation – African Regional Organization (#15709)*; *Organisation of African Trade Union Unity (OATUU, #17798)*. [2023.02.14/XE6122/t/**E**]

♦ Southern African Transport and Communications Commission (no recent information)
♦ Southern African Wildlife College (internationally oriented national body)

♦ Southern Africa Postal Operators Association (SAPOA) 19866

Secretary address not obtained.
URL: http://www.upu.int/

History 2001. A Restricted Union of *Universal Postal Union (UPU, #20682)*. **Aims** Promote development, establishment and operation of efficient, affordable and accessible postal service that meet the diverse needs of customers while being economically and commercially sustainable. **Structure** General Meeting (annual). Management Board. Secretariat headed by Executive Director. Task Forces (5). **Finance** Members' dues.
Members Public postal operators in 14 countries:
Angola, Botswana, Congo DR, Eswatini, Lesotho, Malawi, Mauritius, Mozambique, Namibia, Seychelles, South Africa, Tanzania UR, Zambia, Zimbabwe. [2014/XD8681/**D***]

♦ Southern Africa Regional Irrigation Association (internationally oriented national body)
♦ Southern Africa Regional Tourism Council (inactive)
♦ Southern Africa Stainless Steel Development Association (internationally oriented national body)
♦ Southern Africa Telecommunications Administrations / see Southern Africa Telecommunications Association (#19867)

♦ Southern Africa Telecommunications Association (SATA) 19867

Exec Sec Ave Martires de Inhaminga 170-2 Andar, PO Box 2677, Maputo, Cidade de Maputo, Mozambique. T. +2581302194. Fax +2581431288. E-mail: sata@sata-sec.net.
URL: http://www.sata-sec.net/

History 1980, as *Southern Africa Telecommunications Administrations (SATA)*, within: *Southern African Development Community (SADC, #19843)*. Present name adopted, 1999. **Aims** Establish efficient telecommunications networks and services in the region. **Events** *Conference* Kasane (Botswana) 2016, *Conference* Namibia 2014, *Annual Conference* Livingstone (Zambia) 2013, *Conference* Livingstone (Zambia) 2005, *Conference* Windhoek (Namibia) 2003. **IGO Relations** Support from: *Commonwealth Telecommunications Organisation (CTO, #04365)*. [2015/XM2239/**D**]

♦ Southern Africa Trust (internationally oriented national body)
♦ Southern Africa Workcamps Cooperation (no recent information)
♦ Southern Africa Working Group / see Advocacy Network for Africa
♦ Southern Asian Institute, New York (internationally oriented national body)

♦ Southern Common Market 19868

Marché commun du Sud – Mercado Común del Sur (MERCOSUR) – Mercado Comum do Sul (MERCOSUL)

Contact c/o MERCOSUR, Dr Luis Piera 1992, 1er Piso, Edificio MERCOSUR, CP 11200 Montevideo, Uruguay. T. +59824129024. Fax +59824180557.
URL: http://www.mercosur.int/

History Dec 1994 following the signing of *Ouro Preto Protocol* by Brazil, Argentina, Paraguay and Uruguay. Integration process involving the four countries was established by the *Treaty of Asunción*, signed 26 Mar 1991. Agreements for a Free Trade Area signed by Chile, Bolivia and Peru (since Dec 2003). Also referred to in English as *Common Market of the South*. Expected to merge with *Andean Community (#00817)*; complete integration expected by Summit, Colombia, Dec 2007. **Aims** Promote free movement of goods, services and factors of production between States Parties; establish a common external tariff and adopt a common trade policy in relation to third States; coordinate macroeconomic and sectoral policies between States Parties; harmonize legislation in relevant areas in order to strengthen the integration process. **Structure** *Consejo del Mercado Común – Conselho do Mercado Comum* – Common Market Council (governing body), consisting of Ministers of Finance and Foreign Relations; *Grupo Mercado Común del MERCOSUR (GMC, see: #19868)*; *Comisión de Comercio del MERCOSUR (no recent information)*; *Parlamento del MERCOSUR (#18205)*; Permanent Court of Revision; *Foro Económico y Social del MERCOSUR (no recent information)*; Secretariat. **Languages** Guarani, Portuguese, Spanish. **Events** *Extraordinary Health Ministers Meeting* Montevideo (Uruguay) 2016, *Presidential Summit* Asunción (Paraguay) 2015, *Presidential Summit* Brasilia (Brazil) 2015, *MERCOSUR Meeting of Networks of Employers and Trade Unions against Child Labour* Buenos Aires (Argentina) 2015, *Regional Conference* Buenos Aires (Argentina) 2015.
Members State Parties (5):
Argentina, Brazil, Paraguay, Uruguay, Venezuela.
Associate States (6):
Chile, Colombia, Ecuador, Guyana, Peru, Suriname. [2016.02.03/XF9180/**F***]

♦ Southern Cone Regional Phytosanitary Committee (#04197)

♦ Southern Cone Society of Neurological Surgeons 19869

Sociedade de Cirugia Neurológica Cono Sur

Pres Dept of Neurosurgery, Fac of Medicine, Valparaiso Univ, Av Libertad 1405-Of 301, CP 254-1194 Viña del Mar, Valparaíso, Chile. T. +56322683860. Fax +56322683861. E-mail: leonquin@gmail.com – rene@corvalan.cl.
URL: http://www.wfns.org/

Activities Events/meetings. **Events** *Congress* Santiago (Chile) 2013, *Congress* Armação de Búzios (Brazil) 2011, *Congress* Rosario (Argentina) 2011, *Congress* Salta (Argentina) 2009, *Congress* Bariloche (Argentina) 2005.
Members in 6 countries:
Argentina, Bolivia, Brazil, Chile, Paraguay, Uruguay.
NGO Relations Member of: *Latin American Federation of Neurosurgical Societies (#16325)*. [2017.02.01/XJ4038/**D**]

♦ Southern Cone Trade Union Coordinating Body (#04805)

♦ Southern Connection (SC) 19870

Contact Dept of Environmental Management, NRE 183, PO Box 85084, Lincoln Univ, Christchurch 7647, New Zealand. T. +6434230442.

History 1992, Hawaii (USA). **Aims** Promote *research* of southern *temperate ecosystems*. **Structure** Council, including President and Vice-President. **Languages** English. **Staff** 9.00 FTE, voluntary. **Finance** Income from conferences. **Events** *Conference* Chile 2016, *Conference* Dunedin (New Zealand) 2013, *Conference* Bariloche (Argentina) 2010, *Conference* Adelaide, SA (Australia) 2007, *Conference* Cape Town (South Africa) 2004. **Publications** Books; articles; conference proceedings.
Members Individuals in 23 countries:
Argentina, Australia, Brazil, Canada, Chile, China, Costa Rica, Denmark, Finland, Germany, Indonesia, Japan, Korea Rep, Mexico, Netherlands, New Zealand, Papua New Guinea, South Africa, Sweden, Switzerland, UK, Uruguay, USA. [2014.11.27/XF6334/v/**F**]

♦ Southern and Eastern Africa Consortium for Monitoring Educational Quality (SACMEQ) 19871

Consortium d'Afrique australe pour le pilotage de la qualité de l'éducation

Dir Plot 4775 Notwane Road, Gaborone, Botswana. T. +2673552055. Fax +2673184535. E-mail: info@sacmeq.org.
Technical Manager address not obtained.
URL: http://www.sacmeq.org/

History 1995. Previously known in English as *Southern Africa Consortium for Monitoring Educational Quality (SACMEQ)*. **Aims** Undertake integrated research and training activities to: expand opportunities for educational *planners* to gain necessary technical skills to monitor and evaluate quality of basic education; generate information for use by decision makers when planning and improving quality of education. **Structure** Assembly of Ministers (every 2 years, always in Paris-France). Managing Committee. *SACMEQ Coordinating Centre (SCC)*, Harare (Zimbabwe), managed by Director under guidance of Managing Committee. National Research Coordinators (one per country). **Activities** Conducts activities for *International Institute for Educational Planning (IIEP, #13874)* in association with Ministries of Education in the Southern Africa sub-region. Policy research projects cover high-priority concerns defined in consultation with Ministries of Education, assessing conditions of schooling and quality of education provided by primary education systems. Cooperative initiatives coordinated and facilitated by SCC, which also works with partners to obtain funding for sub-regional research and training programmes. **Publications** National educational policy reports.
Members Ministries of Education of 15 countries and territories:
Botswana, Eswatini, Kenya, Lesotho, Malawi, Mauritius, Mozambique, Namibia, Seychelles, South Africa, Tanzania UR, Uganda, Zambia, Zimbabwe.
IGO Relations *UNESCO (#20322)*. [2006.10.18/XF6449/**F***]

♦ Southern and Eastern Africa Copyright Network (SEACONET) 19872

Secretariat Copyright Society of Malawi, Johnstone Rd, PO Box 30784, Lilongwe, Malawi. T. +2631751148. Fax +2631753018.

History Jul 2008. **Aims** Strengthen regional collaboration and cooperation in the field of creative industries, copyright and related rights. **Structure** Executive Council. President. Secretariat.
Members Full in 17 countries:
Angola, Botswana, Eswatini, Kenya, Lesotho, Madagascar, Malawi, Mauritius, Morocco, Namibia, Seychelles, South Africa, Sudan, Tanzania UR, Uganda, Zambia, Zimbabwe.
Consultative Status Consultative status granted from: *World Intellectual Property Organization (WIPO, #21593)* (Permanent Observer Status). [2010/XJ0942/**D**]

♦ Southern and Eastern African Association for Farming Systems Research-Extension (SEAAFSR-E) 19873

Contact address not obtained. E-mail: anandaponniah@gmail.com.
URL: http://www.ruralinnovationsystems.za.org/

History 1993, Swaziland, as *Southern African Association for Farming Systems Research (SAAFSR)*. Present name adopted 1998. **Aims** Promote farmer-extension-research participation in the development, adaptation and adoption of farming systems approaches. **Structure** Council, comprising President, President-elect, Secretary and 4 to 5 Councillors, supported by Country Coordinators. **Languages** English. **Staff** None. **Finance** Members' dues. Donations. **Activities** Organizes annual conferences and workshops. **Events** *Conference* South Africa 2012, *Conference* Malawi 2005, *Conference* Kampala (Uganda) 2003, *Conference* Nakuru (Kenya) 2001, *Workshop* Njoro (Kenya) 2001. **Publications** *SEAAFSR-E Newsletter* (4 a year). *The Institutionalisation of the Farming Systems Approach in Eastern and Southern Africa* (1998).
Members Full in 14 countries:
Botswana, Eswatini, Ethiopia, Kenya, Lesotho, Madagascar, Malawi, Mozambique, Namibia, South Africa, Tanzania UR, Uganda, Zambia, Zimbabwe. [2012/XD7638/**D**]

♦ Southern and Eastern Africa Network of Analytical Chemists (SEANAC) 19874

SG Dept of Chemistry, Univ of Botswana, Private Bag UB 00704, Gaborone, Botswana. T. +2673552502. Fax +267355283. E-mail: secretarygeneral@seanac.org.
Chief Programme Officer address not obtained. T. +26735552488. Fax +2673552836.
URL: http://www.seanac.org/

History 10 Jul 2003, Gaborone (Botswana). **Aims** Promote analytical chemistry in the region through collaboration, research, training, and information sharing; facilitate inventory, access, operation, maintenance and repairs of analytical equipment. **Structure** Board of 11 members. Executive Committee, including Secretary General, Treasurer and 4 Programme Officers. **Events** *Conference* Gaborone (Botswana) 2019, *Conference* Kasane (Botswana) 2016, *Conference* Mombasa (Kenya) 2014, *Analytical chemistry for the environment health and water* Maputo (Mozambique) 2012, *Conference* Ezulwini (Swaziland) 2009.
Members Universities in 17 countries:
Botswana, Egypt, Eritrea, Eswatini, Ethiopia, Ghana, Kenya, Lesotho, Malawi, Morocco, Mozambique, Nigeria, South Africa, Tanzania UR, Uganda, Zambia, Zimbabwe. [2016/XF6987/**F**]

♦ Southern and Eastern African Mineral Centre / see African Minerals and Geosciences Centre (#00373)
♦ Southern and Eastern African Rabies Group (inactive)

♦ Southern and Eastern African Trade Information and Negotiations Initiative (SEATINI) 19875

Exec Dir SEATINI Uganda, Plot 806 Block 213, Bukoto-Kisaasi Road, PO Box 3138, Kampala, Uganda. T. +256414540856. E-mail: seatini@infocom.co.ug.
URL: http://www.seatiniuganda.org/

History 1996, under the auspices of *International South Group Network (ISGN, no recent information)*. SEATINI Uganda established 2001. **Aims** Strengthen Africa's capacity to take a more effective part in the emerging global trading system and to better manage the process of globalization. **Structure** Board of Trustees; Director. Regional Coordinating Offices in Harare (Zimbabwe); Kampala (Uganda); Nairobi (Kenya). **Languages** English. **Finance** Donor funds. Project funding from: *Department for International Development Cooperation*; *Norwegian Agency for Development Cooperation (Norad)*; *Rockefeller Brothers Fund (RBF)*; *The Rockefeller Foundation (#18966)*; *Swedish International Development Cooperation Agency (Sida)*; *UNDP (#20292)*; *World Trade Organization (WTO, #21864)*. Annual budget: about US$ 200,000. **Activities** Events/meetings; research/documentation. **Publications** Bulletin; briefing papers. **Members** Full in Africa. Membership countries not specified. **NGO Relations** Member of: *Our World is Not for Sale (OWINFS, #17917)*; *Tax Justice Network-Africa (TJN-A, #20101)*. [2019.01.18/XF6432/t/**F**]

♦ Southern and Eastern Africa Rainwater Network (SearNet) 19876

Address not obtained.
URL: http://www.searnet.net

History Jan 2003, Nairobi (Kenya), following workshops and conferences dating back to 1998. **Aims** Promote rainwater harvesting and utilization in the region. **Structure** Umbrella organization comprised of legally registered National Rainwater Associations. Regional organization of *International Rainwater Catchment Systems Association (IRCSA, #14694)*. **Languages** English. **Staff** 3.00 FTE, paid. **Events** *Annual Conference* Nairobi (Kenya) / Naivasha (Kenya) 2012, *International Conference* Naivasha (Kenya) 2012. **Publications** *SearNet Newsletter* (12 a year) – online. Annual Report; abstracts; studies; brochure.
Members National Rainwater Associations in 10 countries:
Botswana, Ethiopia, Kenya, Malawi, Rwanda, Somalia, Tanzania UR, Uganda, Zambia, Zimbabwe.
IGO Relations Partner of: *UNEP (#20299)*; *United Nations (UN, #20515)* Millennium Development Goals. **NGO Relations** Secretariat provided by: *World Agroforestry Centre (ICRAF, #21072)*. Partner of: *Green Belt Movement (#10713)*; *Rainwater Harvesting Implementation Network (RAIN)*; *Rainwater Partnership (no recent information)*; *Stockholm Environment Institute (SEI, #19993)*; *William J Clinton Foundation*; *World Agroforestry Centre (ICRAF, #21072)*; national organizations. [2015/XM0980/**F**]

♦ Southern and Eastern Africa Society of Agricultural Engineers (no recent information)
♦ Southern European Veterinary Conference (meeting series)
♦ Southern Europe New Drug Organization (inactive)

♦ Southern Hemisphere Association of Fresh Fruit Exporters (SHAFFE) 19877

Gen Delegate Rue de Trèves 49-51, 1040 Brussels, Belgium. T. +3227771580. Fax +3227771581. E-mail: shaffe@shaffe.net.
URL: http://www.shaffe.net/

Aims Improve conditions for exporting fruit to the Northern Hemisphere; promote free trade and improve global market access.
Members Full in 8 countries:
Argentina, Australia, Brazil, Chile, New Zealand, Peru, South Africa, Uruguay. [2012.06.01/XM3885/**D**]

♦ Southern Initiative on Globalisation and Trade Union Rights (SIGTUR) 19878

Contact address not obtained. E-mail: sigtur.solidarity@gmail.com.
URL: http://www.sigtur.com/

History Launched May 1991, Australia, at a meeting of democratic unions from the Global South. **Aims** Share a common southern experience; develop an alternative vision to that of neo-liberal globalization. [2019/XM8379/**F**]

♦ Southern Refugee Legal Aid Network (SRLAN) **19879**
Contact Box 282 266 Banbury Road, Summertown, Oxford, OX2 7DL, UK. E-mail: kravin24@gmail.com.
URL: https://srlanetwork.wordpress.com/
History Started 2007, Nairobi (Kenya), on conclusion of the Nairobi Code. **Aims** Formalize cooperation, so as to channel disparate refugee rights organizations into a movement for refugee rights in the global South. **Structure** Steering Committee. Secretariat at UK address of *International Refugee Rights Initiative (IRRI, #14708).*
Members Organizations in 22 countries and territories:
Australia, Burundi, Congo DR, Egypt, Hong Kong, Indonesia, Israel, Italy, Japan, Jordan, Kenya, Korea Rep, Lebanon, Pakistan, Poland, Senegal, South Africa, Türkiye, Uganda, UK, USA, Zambia.
Included in the above, 6 organizations listed in this Yearbook:
AMERA International; *Arab Renaissance for Democracy and Development (ARDD)*; *Asylum Access*; *HIAS*; *International Refugee Rights Initiative (IRRI, #14708)*; *Jesuit Refugee Service (JRS, #16106).*
[2018/XM6951/y/**F**]

♦ Southern Voice on Post-MDG International Development Goals (Southern Voice) **19880**
Secretariat House no 6/2, Block F, Kazi Nazrul Islam Road, Lalmatia Housing Estate, Dhaka 1207, Bangladesh. T. +88029141734. Fax +88028130951. E-mail: info@southernvoice.org – info@cpd.org.bd.
URL: http://southernvoice.org/
History Proposed Jun 2012, Cape Town (South Africa). Activity plan endorsed Jan 2013, Dhaka (Bangladesh). **Aims** Provide a platform as well as strengthen participation of southern researchers in the SDG debate by improving their analytical contributions and strategic engagements. **Structure** Steering Committee; Regional Coordinators; Secretariat. **Languages** English. **Staff** 5.00 FTE, paid; 50.00 FTE, voluntary. **Finance** Project grants from international development partners, including *The William and Flora Hewlett Foundation.* Additional support from *International Development Research Centre (IDRC, #13162).* Annual budget: about US$ 315,000. **Activities** Research/documentation; events/meetings. **Publications** *Southern Voice Occasional Papers (SV OPs)* – series. *Southern Perspectives on the Post-2015 International Development Agenda* (2016).
Members Think tanks (49) in 22 countries:
Bangladesh, Benin, Bolivia, Burkina Faso, Ecuador, El Salvador, Ethiopia, Ghana, Guatemala, Honduras, India, Kenya, Nepal, Nigeria, Pakistan, Paraguay, Peru, Rwanda, Senegal, Sri Lanka, Tanzania UR, Uganda.
NGO Relations Member of: *Global Partnership for Sustainable Development Data (Data4SDGS, #10542).*
[2017/XM4977/**F**]

♦ **Southern Voice** Southern Voice on Post-MDG International Development Goals (#19880)
♦ South and Meso American Indian Rights Center (inactive)

♦ South North Development Initiative (SNDI) **19881**
Sur Norte Inversión y Desarrollo
Address not obtained.
URL: http://www.surnorte.org.ar/
History by a coalition of Southern and Northern organizations, including: *Esquel Group Foundation (EGF, inactive)*; *Partners (no recent information)*; *Synergos (#20082).* Incorporated in the State of New York (USA). Argentinian organization founded in 1999; most operations transferred to Argentina office circa 2005. **Aims** Develop sustainable, market-driven systems for *funding* local economic and social development with positive social impact in Southern countries. **Structure** Board of Directors (international); Venture Capital Advisory Committee. **Activities** Advocacy/lobbying/activism. **IGO Relations** Registered with: *United States Agency for International Development (USAID).* **NGO Relations** Technical cooperation with: *International Cooperative University (ICU, #12952).*
[2009/XF5115/**F**]

♦ South-North Solidarity and Culture (internationally oriented national body)
♦ South-North Trust / see Patronat Sud-Nord Solidaritat i Cultura
♦ South Pacific Airlines Darts Association (unconfirmed)
♦ South Pacific Air Transport Council (inactive)
♦ South Pacific Arts Festival Council / see Pacific Cultural Council (#17944)
♦ South Pacific Asbestos Association (inactive)
♦ South Pacific Association for Commonwealth Literature and Language Studies (see: #02439)
♦ South Pacific Association of Supreme Audit Institutions / see Pacific Association of Supreme Audit Institutions (#17935)
♦ South Pacific Association of Teacher Education (inactive)

♦ South Pacific Association of Theological Schools (SPATS) **19882**
SG PO Box 2426, Govt Bldg, Suva, Fiji. T. +6793303924 – +6793301942. Fax +6793307005. E-mail: info@spats.org.fj.
URL: https://spats.org.fj/
History 1969. **Aims** Strengthen theological education among Churches in the Pacific region. **Structure** Council (meet every 2 years); Executive Committee; *Weavers Committee (#20843)* (Women in Theological Education); Accreditation Committee; Editorial Board; Secretariat. **Languages** English. **Staff** 3.50 FTE, paid. **Finance** Members' dues. Other sources: registration fees for seminars and workshops; donations; subscription income. Funds from: *Association of Protestant Churches and Missions in Germany (EMW)*; *Global Ministries of The United Methodist Church (GM-UMC)*; *Methodist Church Britain – World Church Office*; *MISSIO (#16827)*; *World Council of Churches (WCC, #21320).* **Activities** Networking/liaising; knowledge management/information dissemination; guidance/assistance/consulting; events/meetings. **Publications** *Pacific Journal of Theology* (2 a year). Educational curricula; handbooks; manuals.
Members Full in 13 countries and territories:
Australia, Cook Is, Fiji, Kiribati, Marshall Is, New Caledonia, New Zealand, Samoa, Samoa USA, Solomon Is, Tahiti Is, Tonga, Vanuatu.
NGO Relations Member of: *World Association for Christian Communication (WACC, #21126)*; *World Conference of Associations of Theological Institutions (WOCATI, #21296).*
[2016/XD3144/**D**]

♦ South Pacific Bars' Secretariat / see South Pacific Lawyers' Association (#19887)
♦ South Pacific Board for Educational Assessment (inactive)

♦ South Pacific Bodybuilding Federation (SPBBF) **19883**
Pres BP 11441, 98802 CEDEX Nouméa, New Caledonia. E-mail: spbbf@outlook.com.
Secretariat 35 Tannery Road, Tannery Block 04-01, Ruby Industrial Complex, Singapore 347740, Singapore.
Aims Steward, modernise and develop the sporting disciplines of bodybuilding in conjunction with member federations, national Olympic committees, and international, regional and other stakeholders in accordance with Olympic values; secure participation for bodybuilding at Pacific *Games* events; achieve full IOC recognition. **Structure** Executive Council. **Languages** English, French.
Members National federations of 15 countries and territories:
Cook Is, Fiji, Guam, New Caledonia, Niue, Norfolk Is, Northern Mariana Is, Palau, Papua New Guinea, Polynesia Fr, Samoa, Solomon Is, Tonga, Vanuatu, Wallis-Futuna.
NGO Relations Affiliated to: *World Bodybuilding and Physique Sports Federation (WBPF, #21237).*
[2020.03.03/XM7404/**D**]

♦ South Pacific Bridge Federation (SPBF) **19884**
Sec PO Box 5242, Palmerston North 4441, New Zealand. T. +6463583449. Fax +6463583440.
Pres address not obtained.
URL: http://www.southpacbridge.org/
History 1990. A zone of *World Bridge Federation (WBF, #21246).* **Structure** Management Committee.
Members Organizations in 4 countries and territories:
Australia, New Caledonia, New Zealand, Polynesia Fr.
[2020/AA0989/**D**]

♦ South Pacific Bureau for Economic Co-operation / see Pacific Islands Forum Secretariat (#17970)
♦ South Pacific Chiefs of Police Conference / see Pacific Islands Chiefs of Police (#17964)
♦ South Pacific Commission / see Pacific Community (#17942)
♦ South Pacific Electoral Administrators Conference / see Pacific Islands, Australia and New Zealand Electoral Administrators Network (#17962)
♦ South Pacific Electoral Administrators Network / see Pacific Islands, Australia and New Zealand Electoral Administrators Network (#17962)

♦ South Pacific Environmental Radioactivity Association (SPERA) ... **19885**
Sec c/o ANSTO, New Illawarra Road, Lucas Heights NSW 2234, Australia.
URL: http://www.spera.org.au/
History 1991, Tahiti (Polynesia Fr). 1991, Tahiti. Registered in accordance with Australian law. **Aims** Encourage and facilitate communication among scientists studying occurrence, behaviour and impact of radioactive species present in the environment due either to natural processes or resulting from human activities. **Structure** Executive Committee. **Languages** English. **Staff** None. **Finance** Members' dues. **Events** *Connecting People, Developing Solutions for a Changing Environment* Christchurch (New Zealand) 2022, *Connecting People, Developing Solutions for a Changing Environment* Christchurch (New Zealand) 2021, *Biennial Conference* Christchurch (New Zealand) 2020, *Biennial Conference* Perth, WA (Australia) 2018, *Biennial Conference* Bali (Indonesia) 2016.
Members Individuals (98) in 10 countries and territories:
Australia, Austria, Chile, China, France, New Zealand, Oman, Portugal, Spain, Sweden.
[2020/XD4010/**D**]

♦ South Pacific Evangelical Alliance (SPEA) **19886**
Chairman PO Box 112287, Penrose, Auckland 1642, New Zealand. T. +6494199699. E-mail: admin@nzchristiannetwork.org.nz.
URL: http://www.worldevangelicals.org/
History Founded 1989, Suva (Fiji), as *Evangelical Fellowship of the South Pacific (EFSP).* Replaced *Evangelical Alliance of the South Pacific Islands (inactive)*, which became the national Papua New Guinea organization. **Aims** Strengthen, equip and mobilize National Evangelical Alliances/Fellowships (EF), local *churches* and other evangelical movements and agencies to extend the kingdom of God; promote revival in churches; assist in equipping Church leaders in the South Pacific; establish cooperative networks of evangelicals in South Pacific nations; mobilize a united missionary movement to take the Gospel from the 'uttermost parts of the earth' to the least evangelized people of the world and promote a prayer movement. **Structure** Annual Conference; Council; Executive Secretariat; Task Forces. **Languages** English. **Staff** 1.00 FTE, voluntary. **Finance** Organizational members' dues. Other sources: donations; events; offerings. Budget (annual): Australian $ 10,000. **Activities** Events/meetings; training/education; religious activities. **Events** *Annual South Pacific Prayer Assembly* Port Moresby (Papua New Guinea) 1999, *Annual conference / Annual South Pacific Prayer Assembly* Nuku'alofa (Tonga) 1998, *Annual South Pacific Prayer Assembly* Apia (Samoa) 1997, *General assembly / Annual South Pacific Prayer Assembly* Suva (Fiji) 1996, *General Assembly* Suva (Fiji) 1995. **Publications** *The Uttermost.*
Members Full in 5 countries:
Fiji, Papua New Guinea, Samoa, Solomon Is, Tonga.
Associate members listed in this Yearbook (2):
Compassion International (CI, #04413) (Australian branch); *South Sea Evangelical Church (no recent information).*
NGO Relations Member of: *World Evangelical Alliance (WEA, #21393).*
[2015.11.09/XD3011/y/**D**]

♦ South Pacific Fisheries Treaty (1987 treaty)
♦ South Pacific Forum / see Pacific Islands Forum (#17968)
♦ South Pacific Forum Fisheries Agency / see Pacific Islands Forum Fisheries Agency (#17969)
♦ South Pacific Forum Secretariat / see Pacific Islands Forum Secretariat (#17970)
♦ South Pacific Games Council / see Pacific Games Council (#17951)
♦ South Pacific Humpback Whale Consortium / see South Pacific Whale Research Consortium (#19891)

♦ South Pacific Lawyers' Association (SPLA) **19887**
Contact Law Council of Australia Secretariat, GPO Box 1989, Canberra ACT 2601, Australia. T. +61262463788. Fax +61262480639. E-mail: info@southpacificlawyers.org.
URL: http://www.southpacificlawyers.org/
History Set up 2007, by Pacific bar leaders, with support from *International Bar Association (IBA, #12320).* Original title: *South Pacific Bars' Secretariat.* Constitutions adopted Jul 2011; amended Nov 2013. Officially launched Jul 2011. **Aims** Advocate the administration of justice and the development and improvement of law throughout the South Pacific region. **Structure** General Meeting (annual). **Languages** English. **Staff** 1.00 FTE, paid. **Finance** Support from Law Council of Australia. **Activities** Knowledge management/information dissemination. **Events** *LAWASIA Alternative Dispute Resolution Conference* Denarau (Fiji) 2022, *Conference* Brisbane, QLD (Australia) 2015, *Conference* Port Vila (Vanuatu) 2013. **Publications** *newSPLAsh.*
Members Full in 16 countries and territories:
Australia, Cook Is, Fiji, Kiribati, Nauru, New Zealand, Niue, Norfolk Is, Papua New Guinea, Samoa, Samoa USA, Solomon Is, Timor-Leste, Tonga, Tuvalu, Vanuatu.
NGO Relations *Global Science and Technology Forum (GSTF).*
[2017/XJ1257/**E**]

♦ South Pacific Nuclear Free Zone Treaty (1985 treaty)

♦ South Pacific Nurses Forum (SPNF) **19888**
Secretariat Australian Nursing and Midewifery Federation, Level 1, 365 Queen Street, Melbourne VIC 3000, Australia. T. +61396028500. Fax +61396028567.
URL: http://www.spnf.org.au/
History 1982, Fiji. **Aims** Promote and improve health services and nursing in the South Pacific region. **Structure** Governing Board. **Languages** English. **Finance** Members' dues. **Activities** Events/meetings. **Events** *Biennial Forum / Biennial Conference* Melbourne, VIC (Australia) 2012, *Biennial forum / Biennial Conference* Auckland (New Zealand) 2010, *Biennial forum / Biennial Conference* Suva (Fiji) 2008, *Biennial forum* Apia (Samoa) 2006, *South Pacific chief nursing officers meeting* Apia (Samoa) 2006. **Publications** *SPNF Newsletter.*
Members National organizations (16) in 16 countries and territories:
Australia, Cook Is, Fiji, Kiribati, Nauru, New Zealand, Niue, Papua New Guinea, Samoa, Samoa USA, Solomon Is, Timor-Leste, Tokelau, Tonga, Tuvalu, Vanuatu.
International organizations (2):
Commonwealth Nurses and Midwives Federation (CNMF, #04353); *International Council of Nurses (ICN, #13054).*
[2019.07.16/XG1310/c/**F**]

♦ South Pacific Oceania Council of Trade Unions (unconfirmed)
♦ South Pacific Organizations Coordinating Committee / see Council of Regional Organisations of the Pacific (#04914)
♦ South Pacific Peoples Foundation of Canada / see Pacific Peoples' Partnership
♦ South Pacific Ports Association / see Pacific Maritime Transport Alliance (#17982)
♦ South Pacific Regional Association (inactive)
♦ South Pacific Regional Environment Programme / see Secretariat of the Pacific Regional Environment Programme (#19205)

♦ South Pacific Regional Fisheries Management Organisation (SPRFMO) **19889**
Exec Sec PO Box 3797, Wellington 6140, New Zealand. T. +6444999893. Fax +6444739579. E-mail: secretariat@sprfmo.int.
Communications Officer Level 26 Plimmer Towers, 2-6 Gilmer Terrace, Wellington, New Zealand.
URL: http://www.sprfmo.int/
History Process of consultations initiated by Australia, Chile and New Zealand, 2006, resulting in *Convention on the Conservation and Management of High Seas Fishery Resources in the South Pacific Ocean (2009)*, 14 Nov 2009. Entered into force 24 Aug 2012, with first Commission meeting held 28 Jan-1 Feb 2013, Auckland (New Zealand). **Aims** Through application of precautionary approach and an ecosystem approach to fisheries management, ensure long-term conservation and sustainable use of fishery resources and, in doing so, safeguard the *marine ecosystems* in which these resources occur. **Structure** Commission (meets annually); Committees (3); Secretariat. **Languages** English. **Staff** 5.00 FTE, paid. **Finance** Sources:

members' dues. Varying annual budget. **Activities** Guidance/assistance/consulting; standards/guidelines. **Events** *Commission Meeting* Port Vila (Vanuatu) 2020, *Commission Meeting* The Hague (Netherlands) 2019, *Commission Meeting* Lima (Peru) 2018, *Commission Meeting* Adelaide, SA (Australia) 2017, *Commission Meeting* Valdivia (Chile) 2016. **Publications** *Convention, Conservation and Management Measures (CMMs)*. Reports; rules of procedure; regulations.
Members Contracting Parties to the Convention (14):
Australia, Chile, China, Cook Is, Cuba, Denmark (Faeroe Is), Ecuador, Korea Rep, New Zealand, Peru, Russia, Taiwan, USA, Vanuatu.
Regional entity:
European Union (EU, #08967).
Cooperating non-Contracting Parties (CNCPs – 3):
Curaçao, Liberia, Panama.
Observer States (4):
Japan, Polynesia Fr, Tonga, Wallis-Futuna.
IGO Relations Observer status with (5): *Advisory Centre on WTO Law (ACWL, #00138)*; *FAO (#09260)*; *Inter-American Tropical Tuna Commission (IATTC, #11454)*; *Pacific Islands Forum Fisheries Agency (FFA, #17969)*; *World Meteorological Organization (WMO, #21649)*. Memorandum of Understanding with (3): *Agreement on the Conservation of Albatrosses and Petrels (ACAP, 2001)*; *Comisión Permanente del Pacífico Sur (CPPS, #04141)*; *Commission for the Conservation of Antarctic Marine Living Resources (CCAMLR, #04206)*. **NGO Relations** Observer status with (9): *BirdLife International (#03266)*; *Centro Desarrollo y Pesca Sustenable (CeDePesca, #03796)*; *Deep Sea Conservation Coalition (DSCC, #05024)*; *Greenpeace International (#10727)*; *International Coalition of Fisheries Associations (ICFA, #12614)*; *Marine Stewardship Council (MSC, #16580)*; *Oceana*; *Pew Charitable Trusts*; *World Wide Fund for Nature (WWF, #21922)*. Also links with national organizations. [2020.10.15/XM4321/**D***]

- ♦ South Pacific Regional Trade and Economic Cooperation Agreement (1980 treaty)
- ♦ South Pacific Regional Trade and Economic Cooperation Agreement, 1980 (1980 treaty)
- ♦ South Pacific Shooting Region / see Oceania Shooting Federation (#17674)
- ♦ South Pacific Social Sciences Association (inactive)
- ♦ South Pacific Society of Lifestyle Medicine (internationally oriented national body)
- ♦ South Pacific Tourism Organisation / see Pacific Tourism Organization (#18008)
- ♦ South Pacific Trade Commission / see Pacific Islands Trade and Invest (#17980)

♦ South Pacific Underwater Medicine Society (SPUMS) 19890

Société de médecine sous-marine du Pacifique Sud
Sec c/o Australian and New Zealand College of Anaesthetists, 630 St Kilda Road, Melbourne VIC 3004, Australia. E-mail: secretary@spums.org.au.
URL: http://www.spums.org.au/
History Founded 3 May 1971, Sydney (Australia). Incorporated in Victoria (Australia), 1990. **Aims** Promote and facilitate information and research on all aspects of underwater and *hyperbaric* medicine; provide information on underwater medicine to all interested groups, including diving organizations, industry, the military and the individual diver; promote exchange of information between members on all aspects of underwater medicine and related subjects. **Structure** Executive Committee, composed of President, Past President, Secretary, Treasurer, Editor, Public Officer, Education Officer, Webmaster and 3 members. **Languages** English. **Staff** 9.00 FTE, voluntary. 3 appointed. **Finance** Members' dues (in Australian Dollars): Full – AU$ 175 if paid online before 31 Jan, and AU$ 200 if paid after 31 Jan; Associate, Retired or Student – AU$ 130; Corporate – AU$ 440. Paper renewals incur extra AU$ 10 fee. **Activities** Issues Diploma of Diving and Hyperbaric Medicine on completion of approved basic and advanced examined diving and hyperbaric medicine courses, submission of a suitable thesis and completion of six months full time employment in an approved hyperbaric unit. Candidates must be medically qualified and be a current financial member of the Society. **Events** *Annual Scientific Meeting* 2022, *Annual Scientific Meeting* Labuan Bajo (Indonesia) 2021, *Annual Scientific Meeting* Tutukaka (New Zealand) 2020, *Tri-Continental Annual Scientific Meeting* Durban (South Africa) 2018, *Annual Scientific Meeting* Fiji 2016. **Publications** *Diving and Hyperbaric Medicine* (4 a year) – journal, jointly with European Underwater and Baromedical Society.
Members Individuals from diving and medical communities in 29 countries and territories:
Australia, Canada, China, Denmark, Fiji, France, Germany, Hong Kong, India, Indonesia, Ireland, Israel, Japan, Malaysia, Netherlands, New Zealand, Norway, Oman, Palau, Papua New Guinea, Saudi Arabia, Singapore, Solomon Is, South Africa, Sweden, Thailand, UK, USA, Vanuatu. [2012.06.11/XD2625/v/**D**]

♦ South Pacific Whale Research Consortium (SPWRC) 19891

Chair CCRC, PO Box 3069, Avarua, Avarua, Rarotonga, Avarua RAROTONGA, Cook Is. E-mail: nan@whaleresearch.org – info@whaleresearch.org.
URL: http://www.whaleresearch.org/spwrc.htm
History 2000, as *South Pacific Humpback Whale Consortium*. **Aims** Coordinate and facilitate research on large whales in the South Pacific region. **Structure** Executive Committee of 5. Executive Officers (4). **Activities** Field work and analysis; Conservation initiatives. **Events** *Annual Meeting* Apia (Samoa) 2011, *Annual Meeting* Auckland (New Zealand) 2010, *Annual Meeting* Auckland (New Zealand) 2009, *Annual Meeting* Auckland (New Zealand) 2008, *Annual meeting* Auckland (New Zealand) 2007. **IGO Relations** Signatory to: *Memorandum of Understanding for the Conservation of Cetaceans and Their Habitats in the Pacific Islands Region (2006)*. [2013.06.01/XM3137/**D**]

- ♦ South Pole Neutrino Observatory (unconfirmed)
- ♦ South Research (internationally oriented national body)

♦ South and Southeast Asian Association for the Study of Culture and Religion (SSEASR) 19892

SG Research Inst for Languages and Cultures of Asia, Mahidol Univ, Nakhon Pathom, 73170, Thailand. E-mail: sseasr@gmail.com.
URL: http://www.sseasr.org/
History 30 Jan 2005, Delhi (India), as *South and Southeast Asian Association for the Study of Religion (SSEASR)*. Current name adopted, 2006. **Aims** Bring out the genius of local regional scholarship; create a network of scholars by cooperating with related agencies in the region of South and Southeast Asia to develop healthy academic atmospheres; offer native scholars, writers and artists a platform to share with the international academic fraternity. **Structure** General Assembly; Executive Committee. **Languages** English. **Staff** 0.50 FTE, paid; 5.00 FTE, voluntary. **Finance** Membership; accrued interest; contributions; journal subscriptions; occasional funding from *International Association for the History of Religions (IAHR, #11936)* at the time of the announcement of the bi-annual conference. Annual budget: about US$ 5,100. **Activities** Events/meetings; publishing activities; knowledge management/information dissemination; networking/liaising; research/documentation. **Events** *Conference* Yangon (Myanmar) 2021, *Rivers and religion – connecting cultures in South and Southeast Asia* Dhaka (Bangladesh) 2019, *ASEAN region's culture and religion by the end of 21st Century – a dialogue of past with present?* Ho Chi Minh City (Vietnam) 2017, *Conference* Colombo (Sri Lanka) 2015, *Healing, belief systems, cultures and religions of South and Southeast Asia* Manila (Philippines) 2013. **Publications** *SSEASR Journal on Culture and Religion of South and Southeast Asia* (annual).
Members in 16 countries:
Bangladesh, Bhutan, Brunei Darussalam, Cambodia, Germany, India, Indonesia, Laos, Malaysia, Myanmar, Nepal, Philippines, Sri Lanka, Switzerland, Thailand, Vietnam.
NGO Relations A regional association of: *International Association for the History of Religions (IAHR, #11936)*. Contact with: *International Council for Philosophy and Human Sciences (CIPSH, #13061)*. [2019/XM0029/**D**]

- ♦ South and Southeast Asian Association for the Study of Religion / see South and Southeast Asian Association for the Study of Culture and Religion (#19892)

♦ SouthSouthNorth (SSN) 19893

Dir PO Box 12842, Mill Street, Gardens, Cape Town, 8010, South Africa. T. +27214612881. Fax +27214613507. E-mail: info@southsouthnorth.org.
Street Address 55 Salt River Road, Salt River, Cape Town, 7925, South Africa.
URL: http://www.southsouthnorth.org/
History 1999, Bonn (Germany), during climate change negotiations under *United Nations Framework Convention on Climate Change (UNFCCC, 1992)*. Registered in accordance with South African law, 1996. **Aims** Support the transition towards *climate* compatible economies and societies in *developing countries*. **Consultative Status** Consultative status granted from: *UNEP (#20299)*. **NGO Relations** Member of: *Climate and Development Knowledge Network (CDKN, #04012)*. [2015.05.26/XJ7059/**F**]

- ♦ South and West Asian Regional Branch of the International Council on Archives (see: #12996)
- ♦ South and West Asia Postal Union (inactive)
- ♦ South-West Atlantic Action Plan (no recent information)
- ♦ South West Atlantic Hydrographic Commission (see: #13825)
- ♦ South Western Waters Regional Advisory Council / see South West Waters Advisory Council (#19896)

♦ South West Indian Ocean Fisheries Commission (SWIOFC) 19894

Commission des pêches pour le sud-ouest de l'océan indien (CPSOOI)
Secretariat c/o FAO-SFS, Rua Consiglieri Pedroso 347, 4th Fl, Maputo, Cidade de Maputo, Mozambique. E-mail: swiofc-secretariat@fao.org.
URL: http://www.fao.org/fishery/rfb/swiofc/en
History Nov 2004, by *FAO (#09260)*. **Aims** Promote sustainable utilization of the living marine resources of the South West Indian Ocean. **Events** *Session* Maputo (Mozambique) 2015, *Session* Flic en Flac (Mauritius) 2012, *Session* Malé (Maldives) 2011, *Session* Mombasa (Kenya) 2010, *Session* Mahe Is (Seychelles) 2007.
Members States (12):
Comoros, France, Kenya, Madagascar, Maldives, Mauritius, Mozambique, Seychelles, Somalia, South Africa, Tanzania UR, Yemen. [2019/XM0772/**E***]

- ♦ Southwest Medical Teams / see International Relief Teams

♦ South-West Pacific Dialogue (SWPD) 19895

Address not obtained.
History 5 Oct 2002, Yogyakarta (Indonesia). Also referred to as *West Pacific Forum* and as *West Pacific Dialogue*. **Events** *Ministerial Meeting* Cambodia 2012, *Ministerial Meeting* Bali (Indonesia) 2011, *Ministerial Meeting* Hanoi (Vietnam) 2010, *Ministerial Meeting* Phuket (Thailand) 2009, *Ministerial Meeting* Singapore (Singapore) 2008.
Members Participating countries (6):
Australia, Indonesia, New Zealand, Papua New Guinea, Philippines, Timor-Leste. [2012/XJ3783/c/**F***]

- ♦ South West Pacific Hydrographic Commission (see: #13825)

♦ South West Waters Advisory Council (SWWAC) 19896

Conseil Consultatif des Eaux Occidentales Australes (CC SUD) – Consejo Consultivo para las Aguas Occidentales Australes (CC SUR) – Conselho Consultivo para as Águas Ocidentais Austrais (CC SUL)
Contact 6 rue Alphonse Rio, 56100 Lorient, France. T. +33297831169. Fax +33297839184. E-mail: adrillet@cc-sud.eu – info@cc-sud.eu.
URL: http://www.cc-sud.eu/
History Apr 2007, in respect of *European Commission (EC, #06633)* Council Decision 2004/585/EC. Original title: *South Western Waters Regional Advisory Council (CCR-S)*. Current functioning by EU 2015/242. EU Transparency Register: 94788066865-39. **Aims** Contribute to achieve the goals of a sustainable exploitation like it is fixed by the Common *Fisheries* Policy. **Structure** General Assembly; Executive Committee; Working Groups (4). **Languages** French, Portuguese, Spanish. **Staff** 3.00 FTE, paid. **Finance** Sources: DG Mare; Members States; Atlantic regions; members' dues. Budget (annual): euro 350,000. **Activities** Programmes/projects. **Publications** None.
Members Stakeholders in 5 countries:
Belgium, France, Netherlands, Portugal, Spain.
NGO Relations *Baltic Sea Advisory Council (BSAC, #03139)*; *Long Distance Advisory Council (LDAC, #16511)*; *Mediterranean Advisory Council (MEDAC, #16639)*; *North Sea Advisory Council (NSAC, #17603)*; *North Western Waters Advisory Council (NWWAC, #17607)*; *Pelagic Advisory Council (Pelagic AC, #18289)*. [2017/XJ9741/**E**]

- ♦ Soutien à l'initiative privée pour l'aide a la reconstruction des pays du Sud-Est asiatique (internationally oriented national body)
- ♦ Soutien à l'initiative privée pour l'aide aux réfugiés des pays du Sud-Est asiatique / see Soutien à l'initiative privée pour l'aide a la reconstruction des pays du Sud-Est asiatique
- ♦ Soutien aux ONG à l'Est / see Soutien aux ONG à l'Est et au Sud
- ♦ Soutien aux ONG à l'Est et au Sud (internationally oriented national body)
- ♦ Souveräner Konstantinorden (religious order)
- ♦ Sovereign Constantinian Order (religious order)
- ♦ Sovereign Military Hospitaller Order of St John of Jerusalem, of Rhodes and of Malta (religious order)
- ♦ Sovereign Military Order of the Temple of Jerusalem (religious order)
- ♦ Sovereign Order of World Guards (see: #21543)
- ♦ Sovereignty International (internationally oriented national body)
- ♦ Sovereign Wealth Fund Institute (internationally oriented national body)
- ♦ Sovereign World Trust (internationally oriented national body)
- ♦ Sovet Ekonomiceskoj Vzaimopomosci (inactive)
- ♦ Soviet Institute of World Economy and International Relations / see Institut Mirovoj Ekonomiki i Mezdunarodnyh Otnosenij Rossijskoj Akademii Nauk
- ♦ Sovrano Militare Ordine Ospedaliero di San Giovanni di Gerusalemme, di Rodi e di Malta (religious order)
- ♦ SOWG – Sovereign Order of World Guards (see: #21543)
- ♦ Sozialdemokratische Fraktion im Europäischen Parlament / see Group of the Progressive Alliance of Socialists and Democrats in the European Parliament (#10786)
- ♦ Sozialdemokratische Partei Europas (#18249)
- ♦ Sozialistische Arbeiter-Sportinternationale (inactive)
- ♦ Sozialistische Bodensee-Internationale (#16221)
- ♦ Sozialistische Fraktion Europäisches Parlament / see Group of the Progressive Alliance of Socialists and Democrats in the European Parliament (#10786)
- ♦ Sozialistische Jugendinternationale (inactive)
- ♦ Sozopol Foundation (internationally oriented national body)
- ♦ **SØF** Selskab for østnordiskfilologi (#19223)
- ♦ SPAA – South Pacific Asbestos Association (inactive)
- ♦ Spa Association Africa / see Spa & Wellness Association of Africa (#19904)
- ♦ Spacecraft Charging Technology Conference (meeting series)
- ♦ SPACE – European Network for Languages and Business Studies / see SPACE Network (#19899)
- ♦ SPACE – European Network for Languages, Business Studies and Hotel and Tourism Management / see SPACE Network (#19899)
- ♦ SPACE – European Network for Languages, Business Studies and Tourism / see SPACE Network (#19899)
- ♦ Space-Eye (internationally oriented national body)
- ♦ Space-Eye e.V. / see Space-Eye
- ♦ Space Foundation (internationally oriented national body)

♦ Space Frequency Coordination Group (SFCG) 19897

Exec Sec c/o ESOC/OPS-SF, Robert-Bosch-Str 5, 64293 Darmstadt, Germany.
URL: http://www.sfcgonline.org/
Aims Provide a less formal and more flexible environment for the solution of frequency management problems encountered by member space agencies. **Events** *Annual Meeting (SFCG-42)* Toulouse (France) 2023, *Annual Meeting* Palm Cove, QLD (Australia) 2022, *Annual Meeting* Berlin (Germany) 2019, *Annual Meeting* Montréal, QC (Canada) 2017, *Annual Meeting* Mainz (Germany) 2016.
Members National and international governmental space agencies, represented by individuals. Full in 24 countries and territories:

Argentina, Australia, Austria, Brazil, Canada, China, France, Germany, India, Italy, Japan, Korea Rep, Malaysia, Netherlands, Nigeria, Russia, South Africa, Spain, Sweden, Taiwan, UK, Ukraine, United Arab Emirates, USA.
Regional entities (2):
European Organisation for the Exploitation of Meteorological Satellites (EUMETSAT, #08096); European Space Agency (ESA, #08798). [2022/XJ7447/E]

♦ Space Frontier Foundation (internationally oriented national body)

♦ Space Generation Advisory Council in Support of the United Nations Programme on Space Applications (SGAC) 19898

Space Generation Beirates des Programmes für Weltraumanwendungen der Vereinten Nationen
Exec Dir c/o ESPI, Schwarzenbergplatz 6, 1030 Vienna, Austria. E-mail: info@spacegeneration.org.
Chair address not obtained.
URL: http://www.spacegeneration.org/
History Conceived at 3rd United Nations Conference on the Exploration and Peaceful Uses of Space (UNISPACE-III), 1999, Vienna (Austria). Registration: 501(c)3, USA. **Aims** Represent students and young space professionals to the United Nations, industry, agencies and academia. **Structure** General Assembly (annual); Executive Committee; Secretariat; Honorary Board; Advisory Board; Election Oversight Committee. **Languages** English. **Staff** 1.00 FTE, paid; 100.00 FTE, voluntary. **Activities** Advocacy/lobbying/activism; events/meetings; training/education. **Events** *Space Generation Congress* Paris (France) 2022, *Space Generation Congress* Dubai (United Arab Emirates) 2021, *Annual SGx Conference* 2019, *Workshop* Paris (France) 2019, *Annual Space Generation Congress* Washington, DC (USA) 2019. **Publications** *SGAC Newsletter* (12 a year). Annual Report with summary; congress and forum reports.
Members Full (about 10,000) in over 110 countries. Members represented by National Points of Contact (NPoC). NPoCs in 80 countries and territories:
Afghanistan, Albania, Argentina, Australia, Austria, Bangladesh, Belarus, Belgium, Bolivia, Brazil, Bulgaria, Cameroon, Canada, Chile, China, Colombia, Costa Rica, Czechia, Ecuador, Egypt, Ethiopia, France, Georgia, Germany, Ghana, Greece, Guatemala, Hungary, India, Indonesia, Iran Islamic Rep, Ireland, Israel, Italy, Jamaica, Japan, Kazakhstan, Kenya, Korea Rep, Kuwait, Lebanon, Lesotho, Lithuania, Malaysia, Mauritius, Mexico, Montenegro, Nepal, Netherlands, New Zealand, Nicaragua, Nigeria, Norway, Pakistan, Palestine, Peru, Philippines, Poland, Portugal, Romania, Russia, Saudi Arabia, Serbia, Slovenia, South Africa, Spain, Sri Lanka, Sudan, Sweden, Switzerland, Thailand, Türkiye, UK, Ukraine, Uruguay, USA, Venezuela, Vietnam, Zambia, Zimbabwe.
Consultative Status Consultative status granted from: *ECOSOC (#05331)* (Ros A). **IGO Relations** Observer status with: *Committee on the Peaceful Uses of Outer Space (COPUOS, #04277).* **NGO Relations** Member of: *Asia-Pacific Regional Space Agency Forum (APRSAF, #02010); International Astronautical Federation (IAF, #12286).* Links with national, regional and international organizations, including: *European Space Policy Institute (ESPI, #08801); International Association for the Advancement of Space Safety (IAASS, #11689); International Space Safety Foundation (ISSF); International Space University (ISU, #15575);* national organizations; *Planetary Society (PS); Secure World Foundation (SWF); Society for Satellite Professionals International (SSPI); Space Foundation; Space Frontier Foundation (SFF); Women in Aerospace Europe (WIA Europe, #20984).* [2022/XJ4218/E]

♦ Space Generation Beirates des Programmes für Weltraumanwendungen der Vereinten Nationen (#19898)
♦ Space for Giants (internationally oriented national body)

♦ SPACE Network 19899

Head Office Premises VLHORA/EURASHE, Ravensteingalerij 27/3, 1000 Brussels, Belgium. E-mail: julie.verstraeten@space-network.org.
URL: http://www.space-network.org/
History 1989, as *Secretaries and Personal Assistants in the Community of Europe (SPACE).* Previous constitution and byelaws approved 13-15 Mar 1997, Ålborg (Denmark). Current constitution and byelaws approved Apr 2009, Tallinn (Estonia). Subsequently changed title to *Studies for Personal Assistants in the Countries of Europe (SPACE) – Secrétaires et assistant/e/s de direction dans la Communauté européenne,* when constitution was adapted, Sep 2001, Lyngby (Denmark). Adopted new title, *SPACE – European Network for Languages, Business Studies and Hotel and Tourism Management,* published in the 'Moniteur belge' of 27 Jun 2003. Also known as *SPACE – European Network for Languages, Business Studies and Tourism.* Adopted new title, 24 Jan 2011: *SPACE – European Network for Languages and Business Studies.* Registered in accordance with Belgian law, 31 Mar 1998. **Aims** Develop educational programmes; enhance entrepreneurship in education; develop a spirit for quality in teaching and a sense for research; make education more accessible to all; facilitate the bridging of the gap between higher education institutions and the business community and key stakeholders. **Structure** General Conference (annual); Council; Professional Sections (committees – 8). **Languages** Dutch, English. **Staff** 2.00 FTE, paid. **Finance** Members' dues. **Activities** Training/education; projects/programmes; events/meetings. **Events** *Annual General Meeting and Conference* Guarda (Portugal) 2021, *Annual General Meeting and Conference* Guarda (Portugal) 2020, *Annual General Meeting and Conference* Kavala (Greece) 2019, *Annual General Meeting and Conference* Kolding (Denmark) 2018, *Annual General Meeting and Conference* Porto (Portugal) 2017. **Publications** *Journal of Advances in Higher Education* (annual). Conference proceedings.
Members Institutional (HEI); Affiliated; Associate; Honorary. Full in 22 countries:
Austria, Belgium, Croatia, Cyprus, Denmark, Estonia, Finland, France, Germany, Greece, Hungary, Kosovo, Latvia, Lithuania, Norway, Poland, Portugal, Romania, Slovakia, Spain, Switzerland, UK.
Associate in 2 countries:
Kenya, USA.
Affiliated members (7):
EDEN Digital Learning Europe (EDEN, #05356); Educational Innovation in Economics and Business Network (EDiNEB Network, #05367); EFMD – The Management Development Network (#05387); European Access Network (EAN, #05819); European Council on Hotel, Restaurant and Institutional Education (EuroCHRIE, #06823); Network of International Business Schools (NIBS, #17041); Ulixes European Union Training and Research EEIG (ULIXES, #20279).
NGO Relations Member of: *Federation of European and International Associations Established in Belgium (FAIB, #09508).* [2019/XD6821/y/D]

♦ **SpaceOps** International Committee on Technical Interchange for Space Mission Operations (#12808)
♦ SpaceOps Organization / see International Committee on Technical Interchange for Space Mission Operations (#12808)
♦ SPACE / see SPACE Network (#19899)

♦ Space Weather European Network (SWENET) 19900

Contact c/o ESA Headquarters, Space Environments and Effects Section, 8-10 rue Mario Nikis, 75738 Paris CEDEX 15, France. T. +33153697654. Fax +33153697560. E-mail: contactesa@esa.int.
URL: http://esa-spaceweather.net/swenet/index.html
History 2005, within *European Space Agency (ESA, #08798).* **Aims** Serve as a central resource centre for space weather activities, providing interested users access to space weather data and services. [2011/XM3396/F*]

♦ Spaceweek International Association / see World Space Week Association
♦ SPACLALS – South Pacific Association for Commonwealth Literature and Language Studies (see: #02439)
♦ SPADA – South Pacific Airlines Darts Association (unconfirmed)
♦ **SPAEN** Sarcoma Patients EuroNet (#19054)
♦ **SPAG** Sociedad Panamericana de Glaucoma (#18107)
♦ SPAI / see Regional Anti-Corruption Initiative (#18750)
♦ SPAI / see Screenprinting and Graphic Imaging Association International (#19159)
♦ SPANA – Society for the Protection of Animals Abroad (internationally oriented national body)
♦ Spanish Agency of International Cooperation / see Agencia Española de Cooperación Internacional para el Desarrollo
♦ Spanish Agency of International Cooperation for Development (internationally oriented national body)
♦ Spanish Centre for International Relations (internationally oriented national body)
♦ Spanish Commission for Refugee Assistance (internationally oriented national body)
♦ Spanish Development Finance Company (internationally oriented national body)
♦ Spanish Society of Americanists (internationally oriented national body)
♦ Spanish Society for International Human Rights Law (internationally oriented national body)
♦ Spanish Society of Tropical Medicine and International Health (internationally oriented national body)
♦ Spanish World Gospel Mission / see Spanish World Ministries (#19901)

♦ Spanish World Ministries (SWM) 19901

El Camino de la Vida
Exec Dir PO Box 542, Winona Lake IN 46590, USA. T. +15742678821. Fax +15742673524. E-mail: info@spanishworld.org.
URL: http://www.spanishworld.org/
History 1959, as *Spanish World Gospel Mission (SWGM).* Registered in the State of Indiana (USA). **Aims** Assist local *churches* in the Spanish speaking world to carry out the ministry of communicating the *Gospel* of *Christ* and to edify those who believe. **Structure** Board of Directors. **Languages** Spanish. **Staff** 3.50 FTE, paid. **Finance** Church and individual contributions. Annual budget: US$ 500,000. **Activities** Events/meetings; knowledge management/information dissemination; guidance/assistance/consulting. **Events** *Conference* Lima (Peru) 2012, *Conference* Buenos Aires (Argentina) 2005, *Conference* Mendoza (Argentina) 2003, *Conference* Miami, FL (USA) 2000, *Conference* Miami, FL (USA) 1995.
Members Nationals from 16 countries:
Argentina, Bolivia, Chile, Colombia, Cuba, Dominican Rep, Ecuador, Guatemala, Honduras, Mexico, Paraguay, Peru, Spain, Uruguay, USA, Venezuela. [2018.07.30/XF1190/F]

♦ SPARC Europe 19902

Dir Watermanstraat 98, 7324 AK Apeldoorn, Netherlands. E-mail: info@sparceurope.org.
URL: https://www.sparceurope.org/
History 2004. Founded by *Association of European Research Libraries (#02540).* Statutes revised 2017; 2020. Former names and other names: *Stichting SPARC Europe* – legal name; *Scholarly Publishing and Academic Resources Coalition Europe* – full title. Registration: No/ID: KVK 30193812, Netherlands; RSIN, No/ID: 815 414 213, Netherlands; EU Transparency Register, No/ID: 126724615363-50, Start date: 22 Dec 2014. **Aims** Advocate change in scholarly communications for the benefit of researchers and society. **Structure** Board of Directors. **Languages** Dutch, English, German, Irish Gaelic, Italian, Polish. **Staff** 3.00 FTE, paid. Several consultants. **Finance** Sources: grants; members' dues; revenue from activities/projects. Annual budget: 231,835 EUR (2020). **Activities** Advocacy/lobbying/activism; networking/liaising; research/documentation; training/education. **Events** *Munin Conference on Scholarly Publishing* Tromsø (Norway) 2021, *OpenCon Conference* Toronto, ON (Canada) 2018, *Munin Conference on Scholarly Publishing* Tromsø (Norway) 2018, *OpenCon Conference* Berlin (Germany) 2017, *Munin Conference on Scholarly Publishing* Tromsø (Norway) 2017.
Members Libraries in 24 countries:
Austria, Belgium, Croatia, Cyprus, Czechia, Denmark, Finland, France, Germany, Greece, Hungary, Ireland, Italy, Latvia, Luxembourg, Netherlands, Norway, Poland, Slovakia, Spain, Sweden, Switzerland, Türkiye, UK.
IGO Relations Cooperates with (1): *UNESCO (#20322).* **NGO Relations** Member of (1): *Global Sustainability Coalition for Open Science Services (SCOSS, #10616).* Cooperates with (8): *Association of European Research Libraries (#02540); Confederation of Open Access Repositories (COAR, #04573);* Digital Curation Centre (DCC); *European Bureau of Library, Information and Documentation Associations (EBLIDA, #06413); European University Association (EUA, #09027); International Federation of Library Associations and Institutions (IFLA, #13470); Open Access Scholarly Publishers Association (OASPA, #17747); Science Europe (#19139).* Official relations with: *Electronic Information for Libraries (EIFL, #05425).* [2021.05.18/XF6809/F]

♦ Spark M Matsunaga Institute for Peace and Conflict Resolution (internationally oriented national body)
♦ SPARTECA – South Pacific Regional Trade and Economic Cooperation Agreement (1980 treaty)
♦ SPASAI / see Pacific Association of Supreme Audit Institutions (#17935)
♦ SPAS – School of Pacific and Asian Studies (internationally oriented national body)
♦ SPAS / see Statistics and Probability African Society (#19975)
♦ **SPAS** Statistics and Probability African Society (#19975)
♦ SPAS – Swedish Peace and Arbitration Society (internationally oriented national body)
♦ SPATC – South Pacific Air Transport Council (inactive)
♦ SPATE – South Pacific Association of Teacher Education (inactive)

♦ Spatial Econometrics Association (SEA) 19903

Sec address not obtained. E-mail: secretary@spatialeconometricsassociation.org.
URL: http://www.spatialeconometricsassociation.org/
Structure Board of Directors. **Activities** Events/meetings; training/education. **Events** *Annual Conference* Warsaw (Poland) 2022, *Inrternational Workshop on Spatial Econometrics and Statistics* Nantes (France) 2021, *Annual Conference* Tokyo (Japan) 2021, *Annual Conference* Jönköping (Sweden) 2020, *Annual Conference* Jönköping (Sweden) 2020. **Publications** *Journal of Spatial Econometrics.* [2019/XM7990/C]

♦ **SPATS** South Pacific Association of Theological Schools (#19882)

♦ Spa & Wellness Association of Africa (SWAA) 19904

Pres C/O Executive Services, 2nd floor – Les Jamalacs Bldg, Vieux Conseil Street, Port Louis, Mauritius. T. +2302083013.
URL: https://swaafrica.org/
History 2010. Former names and other names: *Spa Association Africa* – former. Registration: Republic of Mauritius, No/ID: C112822, Start date: 17 Oct 2012, Mauritius. **Aims** Make wellness accessible to all in Africa; support Africa's wellness industry in leading standards, education and productivity for future generations. **Staff** 1.00 FTE, paid; 50.00 FTE, voluntary. **Activities** Advocacy/lobbying/activism; awards/prizes/competitions; certification/accreditation; events/meetings. **Publications** *Insight.*
Members Chapters in 6 countries:
Ethiopia, Kenya, Mauritius, Morocco, Nigeria, South Africa.
NGO Relations Partner of (1): *World Wellness Weekend (WWW).* [2020.07.08/AA0947/D]

♦ **SPBBF** South Pacific Bodybuilding Federation (#19883)
♦ SPBEA – South Pacific Board for Educational Assessment (inactive)
♦ **SPBF** South Pacific Bridge Federation (#19884)
♦ SPCA International (internationally oriented national body)
♦ SPCC – Sharing Progress in Cancer Care (unconfirmed)
♦ SPCI – International Symposium on the Science and Processing of Cast Iron (meeting series)
♦ **SPCK** Society for Promoting Christian Knowledge (#19624)
♦ **SPCL** Society for Pidgin and Creole Linguistics (#19621)
♦ SPCO / see Pharmaceutical Procurement Service (#18354)
♦ **SPC** Pacific Community (#17942)
♦ SPCPC / see Pacific Islands Chiefs of Police (#17964)
♦ SPCU / see Pontifical Council for Promoting Christian Unity (#18446)
♦ SPDT – Sociedad Panamericana de Dialisis y Trasplantes (inactive)
♦ **SPEA2** Société pour la Promotion de l'Evolution Artificielle en Europe et Alentours (#19625)
♦ Speakers Research Committee for the United Nations / see Communications Coordination Committee for the United Nations
♦ SPEA / see Marketing Communications Executives International (#16586)
♦ Spearhead Group / see Melanesian Spearhead Group (#16704)
♦ **SPEA** South Pacific Evangelical Alliance (#19886)
♦ **SPECA** UN Special Programme for the Economies of Central Asia (#20715)
♦ Special Agreement Concerning Telegraphic Relations (1921 treaty)
♦ Special Arab Aid Fund for Africa (inactive)
♦ Special Central American Agreement on the Equalization of Import Duties on Textiles Manufactured from Rayon or from other Artificial or Synthetic Fibres (1965 treaty)
♦ Special Committee of 24 on Decolonization / see Special Committee on Decolonization (#19906)
♦ Special Committee on Antarctic Research / see Scientific Committee on Antarctic Research (#19147)

♦ Special Committee on the Charter of the United Nations and on the Strengthening of the Role of the Organization 19905

Comité spécial de la Charte des Nations Unies et du raffermissement du rôle de l'Organisation

Contact c/o United Nations, 405 E 42nd St, Room M-13065, New York NY 10017, USA. T. +12129635375. Fax +12129631963.

URL: https://legal.un.org/committees/charter/

History 1975. Established under resolution 3499 (XXX) of the General Assembly of the *United Nations (UN, #20515)*, having existed as an ad hoc committee to review the UN Charter since 1974. **Aims** Consider all proposals concerning the question of the maintenance of international peace and security in all its aspects in order to strengthen the role of the United Nations. **Events** *Substantive session* New York, NY (USA) 2010, *Substantive session* New York, NY (USA) 2007, *Substantive session* New York, NY (USA) 2005, *Substantive session* New York, NY (USA) 2004, *Substantive session* New York, NY (USA) 2003. **Members** Pursuant to General Assembly resolution 50/52, 11 Dec 1995, open to all UN member states. [2020/XE1134/**E***]

♦ Special Committee on Decolonization (C-24) 19906

Comité spécial de la décolonisation – Comité Especial de Descolonización (C-24)

Chair United Nations, Room S-2977D, New York NY 10017, USA. T. +12129635305. Fax +12129635305. E-mail: c24@un.org.

URL: https://www.un.org/dppa/decolonization/en/c24/about

History 27 Nov 1961, New York, NY (USA). Established by resolution 1654 (XVI) of the General Assembly of *United Nations (UN, #20515)*, following adoption by the General Assembly, 14 Dec 1960, in resolution 1514 (XV), of the *Declaration on the Granting of Independence to Colonial Countries and Peoples*, in response to growing concern over the slowness of progress towards independence of many peoples and lands outside the Trusteeship system and still under colonial rule. Came within the remit of *United Nations Trusteeship Council (#20639)*. Currently functions within Department of Political and Peacebuilding Affairs – Decolonization Unit. Former names and other names: *Special Committee of 24 on Decolonization* – alias; *Comité spécial des Vingt-Quatre* – alias; *United Nations Special Committee on the Situation with Regard to the Implementation of the Declaration on the Granting of Independence to Colonial Countries and Peoples (Special Committee of Twenty Four)* – full title. **Aims** As the main body in the United Nations dealing with the progress of peoples in dependent territories towards self-determination and independence, monitor the Declaration on Decolonization which states that: "Immediate steps shall be taken, in Trust and Non-Self-Governing Territories or all other Territories which have not yet attained independence, to transfer all powers to the peoples of those Territories, without any conditions or reservations, in accordance with their freely expressed will and desire, without any distinction as to race, creed or colour, in order to enable them to enjoy complete independence and freedom". **Structure** Special Committee meets annually from mid-February to late Jun and includes Chairman and other officers. Representatives of non-self-governing territories may attend. A government which is not member of the Committee may, if it wishes, and with the Committee's consent, be invited to speak before the Committee on any agenda item. Bureau. **Staff** 2.00 FTE, paid. **Activities** Events/meetings; politics/policy/regulatory. **Events** *Meeting* New York, NY (USA) 2010, *Meeting* New York, NY (USA) 2010, *Meeting* New York, NY (USA) 2007, *Pacific regional seminar* Dili (Timor-Leste) 2006, *Meeting* New York, NY (USA) 2006. **Publications** *Annual Working Papers on the Non-Self-Governing Territories*. Reports to the General Assembly; other special reports.

Members The Committee originally consisted of 18 Member States; it was expanded to 24 in 1962 and has since fluctuated. Current membership comprises governments of 29 countries:
Antigua-Barbuda, Bolivia, Chile, China, Congo Brazzaville, Côte d'Ivoire, Cuba, Dominica, Ecuador, Ethiopia, Fiji, Grenada, India, Indonesia, Iran Islamic Rep, Iraq, Mali, Nicaragua, Papua New Guinea, Russia, Sierra Leone, St Kitts-Nevis, St Lucia, St Vincent-Grenadines, Syrian AR, Tanzania UR, Timor-Leste, Tunisia, Venezuela.

IGO Relations Close working relationships with: *Caribbean Community (CARICOM, #03476)*; *Pacific Islands Forum (#17968)*. [2022/XE0586/**E***]

- ♦ Special Committee of International NGOs on Human Rights / see Committee of NGOs on Human Rights, Geneva (#04275)
- ♦ Special Committee on Solar-Terrestrial Physics / see Scientific Committee on Solar-Terrestrial Physics (#19151)
- ♦ Special Committee of Twenty Four / see Special Committee on Decolonization (#19906)
- ♦ Special Convention Relative to Economic Matters (1918 treaty)
- ♦ Special Education Network in Asia / see Special Education Network and Inclusion Association (#19907)

♦ Special Education Network and Inclusion Association (SENIA) 19907

Contact address not obtained. E-mail: seniaboard@seniainternational.org.

URL: https://seniainternational.org/

History 2002, China. Former names and other names: *SENIA International* – alias; *Special Education Network in Asia (SENIA)* – former. **Aims** Advocate for and provide resources and support for differently-abled individuals. **Structure** Board. **Languages** English. **Activities** Advocacy/lobbying/activism; awards/prizes/competitions; awareness raising; certification/accreditation; events/meetings; networking/liaising; projects/programmes; training/education. **Events** *Annual Conference* 2021, *Annual Conference* 2020, *Annual Conference* Hong Kong (Hong Kong) 2019, *Annual Conference* Bangkok (Thailand) 2018, *Annual Conference* Yokohama (Japan) 2017. [2022.06.15/XJ9597/**F**]

♦ Special Emergency Assistance Fund for Drought and Famine in Africa (SEAF) 19908

Fonds spécial d'assistance d'urgence pour la lutte contre la sécheresse et la famine en Afrique

Contact ADB Headquarters, Rue Joseph Anoma, 01 BP 1387, Abidjan 01, Côte d'Ivoire. T. +22520204444. Fax +22520204959. E-mail: afdb@afdb.org.

History 12 Nov 1984, Addis Ababa (Ethiopia). 12-15 Nov 1984, Addis Ababa (Ethiopia), at 20th Ordinary Session of the Assembly of Heads of State and Government of *Organization of African Unity (OAU, inactive)*. Statute adopted at 21st Ordinary Session of the Assembly of Heads of State and Government of OAU, 18-20 Jul 1985, Addis Ababa. The Fund is also referred to as *Special Relief Fund* and is operated by *African Development Bank Group (ADB Group, #00284)*. Currently administered by *African Development Bank (ADB, #00283)*. **Aims** Provide emergency assistance to African countries affected by drought and/or famine; provide immediate financial and material assistance in support of national activities and programmes designed to reduce the impact of drought and/or famine in Africa. **Structure** Policy Committee (meets annually in ordinary session), consisting of 13 Member States. Secretariat lies with OAU Secretariat. **Finance** Sources: voluntary financial contributions from Member States; contributions from OAU; contributions from other countries, organizations, associations and individuals.

Members Governments of 53 countries:
Algeria, Angola, Benin, Botswana, Burkina Faso, Burundi, Cameroon, Cape Verde, Central African Rep, Chad, Comoros, Congo Brazzaville, Congo DR, Côte d'Ivoire, Djibouti, Egypt, Equatorial Guinea, Eritrea, Eswatini, Ethiopia, Gabon, Gambia, Ghana, Guinea, Guinea-Bissau, Kenya, Lesotho, Liberia, Libya, Madagascar, Malawi, Mali, Mauritania, Mauritius, Mozambique, Namibia, Niger, Nigeria, Rwanda, Sahara West, Sao Tomé-Principe, Senegal, Seychelles, Sierra Leone, Somalia, South Africa, Sudan, Tanzania UR, Togo, Tunisia, Uganda, Zambia, Zimbabwe.

IGO Relations *UNDP (#20292)*; *United Nations Economic Commission for Africa (ECA, #20554)*. **NGO Relations** Member of: *Aspen Network of Development Entrepreneurs (ANDE, #02310)*. [2010/XF1058/f/**F***]

- ♦ Special Fund for the Social Transformation of Central America (see: #03658)
- ♦ Special Health Fund for Africa (no recent information)
- ♦ Special Initiative for Africa / see TrustAfrica (#20251)
- ♦ Special Interest Group on MCDM / see International Society on Multiple Criteria Decision Making (#15283)

♦ Specialised Nutrition Europe (SNE) 19909

Secretariat Ave des Nerviens 9-31, 1040 Brussels, Belgium. T. +3225081070. Fax +3225081025. E-mail: secretariat@specialisednutritioneurope.eu.

URL: http://www.specialisednutritioneurope.eu/

History 23 Sep 1959, as *Association of Dietetic Foods Industries of the EEC – Association des industries des aliments diététiques de la CEE – Verband der Diätetischen Lebensmittelindustrie der EWG*. Later known as *Association des industries des aliments diététiques de l'Union européenne (IDACE) – Association of the Food Industries for Particular Nutritional Uses of the European Union – Verband der Diätetischen Lebensmittelindustrie der EU*, and previously also referred to as *Association of Dietetic Foods Industries of the EU*. Current title adopted Oct 2013. Registered in accordance with Belgian law. EU Transparency Register: 33498019160-40. **Aims** Increase awareness and understanding of foods for populations with very specific nutritional needs and the way in which they meet the needs of European consumers with particular dietary requirements. **Structure** Operational Board. **Languages** English. **Activities** Knowledge management/information dissemination; awareness raising; standards/guidelines. **Events** *General Assembly* London (UK) 2001, *General Assembly* Copenhagen (Denmark) 1996, *General Assembly* Madrid (Spain) 1991, *General Assembly* France 1987, *General Assembly* Sorrento (Italy) 1986.

Members National trade associations in 16 countries:
Austria, Denmark, France, Germany, Greece, Hungary, Ireland, Italy, Netherlands, Poland, Portugal, Romania, Spain, Sweden, Switzerland, UK.

IGO Relations Recognized by: *European Commission (EC, #06633)*. Participates as observer in the activities of: *Codex Alimentarius Commission (CAC, #04081)*. **NGO Relations** Affiliated member of: *FoodDrinkEurope (#09841)*. [2017.06.19/XE0124/**D**]

- ♦ Spécialistes baltes de biologie marine (#03125)
- ♦ Speciality Coffee Association of Europe / see Specialty Coffee Association (#19912)
- ♦ Specialized Committee on Fertilizers and Pesticides of Agricultural Cooperatives in the EEC Countries / see General Confederation of Agricultural Cooperatives in the European Union (#10107)
- ♦ Special Libraries Association (internationally oriented national body)
- ♦ Special Olympics / see Special Olympics International (#19910)

♦ Special Olympics International (SOI) 19910

Contact 1133 19th St NW, Washington DC 20036, USA. T. +12026283630. Fax +12028240200. E-mail: info@specialolympics.org.

URL: http://www.specialolympics.org/

History Dec 1968, as *Special Olympics*, when established under the laws of the District of Columbia (USA). Officially recognized and endorsed, 15 Feb 1988, by *International Olympic Committee (IOC, #14408)*. Current name adopted 1990. **Aims** Provide year-round sports training and athletic competition in a variety of Olympic-type sports for children and adults with intellectual *disabilities*. **Structure** Board of Directors; Global Leadership Team; Regional Branches (7). **Languages** Arabic, Chinese, English, French, Russian, Spanish. **Staff** 250.00 FTE, paid. **Finance** Private funding from individual donations; corporate partnerships; special fundraising projects. **Activities** Events/meetings; training/education; sporting activities; awards/prizes/competitions. **Events** *Delegation Medical Staff Meeting* Abu Dhabi (United Arab Emirates) 2019, *Global Youth Leadership Summit* Abu Dhabi (United Arab Emirates) 2019, *Head of Delegations Meeting* Abu Dhabi (United Arab Emirates) 2019, *Heads of Delegations Meeting* Abu Dhabi (United Arab Emirates) 2018, *Seminar on the Role of Sport in Public Diplomacy* Singapore (Singapore) 2011. **Publications** Annual Report; Reach Report.

Members Special Olympics National Programs in 174 countries and territories:
Afghanistan, Albania, Algeria, Andorra, Argentina, Armenia, Aruba, Australia, Austria, Azerbaijan, Bahamas, Bahrain, Bangladesh, Barbados, Belarus, Belgium, Belize, Benin, Bermuda, Bhutan, Bolivia, Bonaire Is, Bosnia-Herzegovina, Botswana, Brazil, Brunei Darussalam, Bulgaria, Burkina Faso, Cambodia, Canada, Cayman Is, Chile, China, Colombia, Congo DR, Costa Rica, Côte d'Ivoire, Croatia, Cuba, Curaçao, Cyprus, Czechia, Denmark, Dominica, Dominican Rep, Ecuador, Egypt, El Salvador, Estonia, Eswatini, Faeroe Is, Fiji, Finland, France, Gambia, Georgia, Germany, Ghana, Gibraltar, Great Britain, Greece, Guam, Guatemala, Guyana, Haiti, Honduras, Hong Kong, Hungary, Iceland, India, Indonesia, Iran Islamic Rep, Iraq, Ireland, Isle of Man, Israel, Italy, Jamaica, Japan, Jordan, Kazakhstan, Kenya, Kiribati, Korea Rep, Kosovo, Kyrgyzstan, Laos, Latvia, Lebanon, Libya, Liechtenstein, Lithuania, Luxembourg, Macau, Malawi, Malaysia, Mali, Malta, Mauritania, Mauritius, Mexico, Moldova, Monaco, Mongolia, Montenegro, Morocco, Myanmar, Namibia, Nepal, Netherlands, New Zealand, Nicaragua, Nigeria, North Macedonia, Norway, Oman, Pakistan, Palestine, Panama, Papua New Guinea, Paraguay, Peru, Philippines, Poland, Portugal, Qatar, Romania, Russia, Rwanda, Samoa, Samoa USA, San Marino, Saudi Arabia, Senegal, Serbia, Seychelles, Singapore, Slovakia, Slovenia, South Africa, Spain, Sri Lanka, St Kitts-Nevis, St Lucia, St Maarten, St Vincent-Grenadines, Sudan, Suriname, Sweden, Switzerland, Syrian AR, Taiwan, Tajikistan, Tanzania UR, Thailand, Timor-Leste, Togo, Tonga, Trinidad-Tobago, Tunisia, Türkiye, Turkmenistan, Uganda, Ukraine, United Arab Emirates, Uruguay, USA, Uzbekistan, Vanuatu, Venezuela, Vietnam, Virgin Is USA, Zambia, Zimbabwe.

Consultative Status Consultative status granted from: *ECOSOC (#05331)* (Special); *ILO (#11123)* (Special List); *Council of Europe (CE, #04881)* (Participatory Status). **IGO Relations** Accredited by: *United Nations Office at Vienna (UNOV, #20604)*. Associated with Department of Global Communications of the United Nations. **NGO Relations** Member of (4): *International Council for Coaching Excellence (ICCE, #13008)*; *International Council of Sport Science and Physical Education (ICSSPE, #13077)*; *Olympic Movement (#17719)*; *Sport Integrity Global Alliance (SIGA, #19925)* (Founding). Participates in: *Global Partnership on Children with Disabilities (GPcwd, #10529)*. [2020/XF0277/**F**]

- ♦ Special Operations in Rescue Team (internationally oriented national body)
- ♦ Special Protocol on Basic Grains (1965 treaty)
- ♦ Special Protocol Concerning Statelessness (1930 treaty)
- ♦ Special Relief Fund / see Special Emergency Assistance Fund for Drought and Famine in Africa (#19908)
- ♦ Special Relief Operations Service (inactive)
- ♦ Special Standing Committee for the International Police Conference (inactive)
- ♦ Special Trade Passenger Ships Agreement, 1971 (1971 treaty)

♦ Special Tribunal for Lebanon (STL) 19911

Tribunal spécial pour le Liban (TSL)

Public Information and Communications Dokter van der Stamstraat 1, 2265 BC Leidschendam, Netherlands. E-mail: stl-pressoffice@un.org.

URL: http://www.stl-tsl.org/

History Set up following request by the Government of Lebanon to the UN, 13 Dec 2005. Pursuant to *United Nations Security Council (UNSC, #20625)* resolution 1664 (2006), *United Nations (UN, #20515)* and Lebanese Republic negotiated agreement on the establishment of the Special Tribunal. Established under Chapter VII of the UN Charter by UN Security Council Resolution 1757 (2007), implementing the Agreement between the UN and the Lebanese Republic on the establishment of a Special Tribunal for Lebanon, 30 May 2007. Began functioning 1 Mar 2009. Main trial began 16 Jan 2014. **Aims** Hold trials for individuals responsible for the attack of 14 Feb 2005, resulting in the death of 22 people, including former prime minister, Rafiq Hariri, and injuring 226 others; investigate and try other connected attacks that occurred in Lebanon between 1 Oct 2004 and 12 Dec 2005, or any later date decided by Lebanon and the United Nations with the consent of the UN Security Council, determined to be connected to the 2005 attack. **Structure** Organs (4): Chambers; Office of the Prosecutor; Defence Office; Registry. **Languages** Arabic, English, French. **Staff** 401.00 FTE, paid. **Finance** Sources: Lebanese Government (49%); voluntary contributions by states (51%). Annual budget (2019): euro 55,100,000. **Activities** Networking/liaising; events/meetings; training/education; projects/programmes; publishing activities. **Publications** *STL Bulletin* (12 a year). *Judicial Briefs*. Annual Report; casebooks; press releases; case information sheets. **IGO Relations** Full member of: *United Nations Joint Staff Pension Fund (UNJSPF, #20581)*. [2019.02.12/XJ6563/**F***]

♦ Specialty Coffee Association (SCA) 19912

CEO 117 West 4th St, Ste 300, Santa Ana CA 92701, USA. T. +15626244100. E-mail: executivedirector@sca.coffee – hello@sca.coffee.

UK Office Oak Lodge Farm, Leighams Road, Bicknacre, Chelmsford, CM3 4HF, UK. T. +441245426060. E-mail: membership@sca.coffee.

URL: http://sca.coffee/

History 5 Jun 1998, London (UK). Current title adopted on merger of SCAE with its USA counterpart, the *Specialty Coffee Association of America*, set up 1982. Former names and other names: *Speciality Coffee Association of Europe (SCAE)* – former (1998 to 2017). Registration: 501(c)(6), USA, California. **Aims** Develop a forum for exchanging information and promotion through education for the coffee industry. **Structure** Board of Directors; Presidents Council. **Staff** 13.00 FTE, paid. **Activities** Awards/prizes/competitions; events/meetings; training/education. **Events** *World of Coffee Event* Athens (Greece) 2023, *World of Coffee Event* Warsaw (Poland) 2022, *World of Coffee Event* Athens (Greece) 2021, *World of Coffee Event* Warsaw (Poland) 2020, *World of coffee meeting* Maastricht (Netherlands) 2011.

Members National chapters in 25 countries:
Austria, Belgium, Bulgaria, Croatia, Czechia, Denmark, Estonia, France, Germany, Greece, Iceland, Israel, Italy, Netherlands, Norway, Poland, Portugal, Russia, Serbia, Slovenia, Spain, Sweden, Switzerland, UK, USA. [2021/XD8886/**D**]

♦ Special Union for the International Classification of Goods and Services for the Purposes of the Registration of Marks (Nice Union) 19913

Union particulière pour la classification internationale des produits et des services aux fins de l'enregistrement des marques (Union de Nice)

Contact c/o WIPO, Chemin des Colombettes 34, Case Postale 18, 1211 Geneva 20, Switzerland. T. +41223389111. Fax +41227335428. E-mail: nivilo@wipo.int.
URL: http://www.wipo.int/classifications/nice/en/

History 18 Mar 1970. Established on the entry into force of *Nice Agreement Concerning the International Classification of Goods and Services for the Purposes of the Registration of Marks (1957)*, signed 15 Jun 1957, Nice, revised 14 Jul 1967, Stockholm (Sweden); 13 May 1977, Geneva (Switzerland). Amended 1979. Some parties objected to an instrument deposited which by one interpretation brought the agreement into force on 12 Nov 1969; countries to which this agreement applies constitute a special union. A union administered by *World Intellectual Property Organization (WIPO, #21593)*. **Aims** Establish and maintain a classification of goods and services for the purposes of registering marks. **Structure** Assembly (meets in ordinary session every 2 years); Committee of Experts (meets every year); International Bureau. **Languages** English, French. **Staff** WIPO Secretariat. **Finance** WIPO unitary contribution system. **Activities** Knowledge management/information dissemination; management of treaties and agreements. Manages the following treaties/agreements: *Nice Agreement Concerning the International Classification of Goods and Services for the Purposes of the Registration of Marks (1957)*. **Publications** *Nice Classification* (annual).

Members Open to States Party to the Nice Agreement. States party to the Agreement, as of 18 Oct 2022 (92):
Albania, Algeria, Antigua-Barbuda, Argentina, Armenia, Australia, Austria, Azerbaijan, Bahrain, Barbados, Belarus, Belgium, Benin, Bosnia-Herzegovina, Bulgaria, Canada, China, Croatia, Cuba, Czechia, Denmark, Dominica, Egypt, Estonia, Finland, France, Georgia, Germany, Greece, Guinea, Hungary, Iceland, India, Iran Islamic Rep, Ireland, Israel, Italy, Jamaica, Japan, Jordan, Kazakhstan, Korea DPR, Korea Rep, Kyrgyzstan, Latvia, Lebanon, Liechtenstein, Lithuania, Luxembourg, Malawi, Malaysia, Mexico, Moldova, Monaco, Mongolia, Montenegro, Morocco, Mozambique, Netherlands, New Zealand, North Macedonia, Norway, Paraguay, Peru, Poland, Portugal, Romania, Russia, Saudi Arabia, Serbia, Singapore, Slovakia, Slovenia, Spain, St Kitts-Nevis, St Lucia, Suriname, Sweden, Switzerland, Syrian AR, Tajikistan, Tanzania UR, Trinidad-Tobago, Tunisia, Türkiye, Turkmenistan, UK, Ukraine, United Arab Emirates, Uruguay, USA, Uzbekistan. [2022.10.11/XF4431/**F***]

♦ Species 2000 19914

Exec Sec/Chair c/o Naturalis, PO Box 9517, 2300 RA Leiden, Netherlands. T. +31717519362. E-mail: sp2000@sp2000.org.
Street Address Darwinweg 2, 2333 CR Leiden, Netherlands.
URL: http://www.sp2000.org/

History 10 Mar 1996, Manila (Philippines). 10-13 Mar 1996, Manila (Philippines), at workshop sponsored by *UNEP (#20299)*, the Species 2000 Programme having been established by *International Union of Biological Sciences (IUBS, #15760)* in cooperation with *Committee on Data for Science and Technology (CODATA, #04247)* and *International Union of Microbiological Societies (IUMS, #15794)*. UK Registered Company: 3479405. Registration: Companies House, No/ID: 3479405, England. **Aims** As a federation of existing *taxonomic databases*, stimulate establishment of global species databases by accelerating completion of existing databases and developing new ones, so as to eventually provide a uniform and validated quality *index* of names of all known species of *plants, animals, fungi* and *micro-organisms*, to be used as a neutral scientific baseline in relation to world species *biodiversity*; develop procedures to maintain the databases and update taxonomy; cooperate with international authorities in stabilizing *nomenclature*. **Structure** General Assembly (annual). Project Team, comprising 11 individuals including Chair and Vice-Chair. 5 Directors. **Finance** Contributions from national and international bodies, including CODATA and IUBS. Project funding from: *European Commission (EC, #06633)*. Additional funding from: GBIF. **Activities** Technical Groups (2): Software; Taxonomic. Organizes meetings and workshops. Together with Integrated Taxonomic Information System (ITIS) of North America formed the *'Catalogue of Life (CoL)'* programme, collating a uniform and validated index to the world's known species, for use as a practical tool in inventorying and monitoring biodiversity worldwide. **Events** *Millennium symposium* Wellington (New Zealand) 2000, *Species 2000 international workshop* Tsukuba (Japan) 1999. **Publications** Other information services: Information Services: Operates a dynamic Common Access System on the Internet through which users can locate a species by name across an array of online databases. **Information Services** *Species 2000 and ITIS CoL Annual Checklist* – Internet and CD-ROM (updated annually).

Members Individuals and institutions in 11 countries:
Australia, Belgium, Brazil, France, Germany, Ireland, Italy, Japan, Netherlands, UK, USA.

IGO Relations Member of: *Global Biodiversity Information Facility (GBIF, #10250)*. **NGO Relations** Supports: *WorldFish (#21507)*. [2020/XE3769/**E**]

♦ Species360 19915

Main Office 7900 International Dr, Ste 1040, Bloomington MN 55425, USA. T. +19522238030.
URL: http://www.species360.org/

History 1973, as *International Species Inventory System (ISIS)*. 1989, incorporated as an nonprofit organization with the name *International Species Information System (ISIS)*. 2016, present name adopted. **Aims** Contribute to the preservation of biotic diversity by providing global specimen, species catalogues and auxiliary information services; support long-term collective species conservation and preservation programmes. **Structure** Board of Trustees. Computer-based information system on specimens in over 800 zoos. **Staff** 17 full-time plus additional part-time, paid. **Finance** Members' dues. Grants and other financial support, especially from USA agencies and foundations. **Activities** Knowledge management/information dissemination. **Publications** DVDs. **Information Services** *Animal Record Keeping System (ARKS)*; *Central Specimen Database* – registering 2 million individuals of 10,000 species, including pedigree details and population demographics; *Medical Animal Records Keeping System (MedARKS)*; *Single Population Analysis and Records Keeping System (SPARKS)*; *Zoological Information Management System (ZIMS)*.

Members Zoos and aquariums in 72 countries and territories:
Argentina, Australia, Austria, Bahamas, Belarus, Belgium, Brazil, Bulgaria, Canada, Chile, China, Colombia, Costa Rica, Croatia, Czechia, Denmark, Dominican Rep, Ecuador, Egypt, Estonia, Finland, France, Georgia, Germany, Greece, Guatemala, Hungary, India, Ireland, Israel, Italy, Jamaica, Japan, Kazakhstan, Latvia, Lithuania, Luxembourg, Malaysia, Mexico, Moldova, Namibia, Nepal, Netherlands, New Zealand, Norway, Peru, Poland, Portugal, Qatar, Romania, Russia, Saudi Arabia, Singapore, Slovakia, Slovenia, South Africa, Spain, Sri Lanka, Sweden, Switzerland, Taiwan, Thailand, Trinidad-Tobago, Tunisia, Türkiye, Uganda, UK, Ukraine, United Arab Emirates, USA, Zambia, Zimbabwe.

NGO Relations Member of: *International Union for Conservation of Nature and Natural Resources (IUCN, #15766)*; *World Association of Zoos and Aquariums (WAZA, #21208)*. [2017/XF2803/**F**]

- ♦ SPECIES – Society for the Conservation of Endangered Carnivores and their International Ecological Study (unconfirmed)
- ♦ **SPECIES** Society for the Promotion of Evolutionary Computation in Europe and its Surroundings (#19625)

♦ Species Survival Network (SSN) 19916

Chair 2100 L St NW, Washington DC 20037, USA. T. +13015487769. Fax +12023180891. E-mail: info@ssn.org.
URL: http://www.ssn.org/

History 1992. **Aims** Promote, enhance and enforce the Convention on international trade in endangered species of wild fauna and flora (CITES). **Structure** Board. Regional offices (6): Africa; Asia; Central and South America and the Caribbean; Europe; North America; Oceania. Working Groups. **Activities** Advocacy/lobbying/activism; networking/liaising; research/documentation; training/education.

Members Nongovernmental organizations (over 80) in 34 countries and territories:
Argentina, Australia, Austria, Belgium, Brazil, Canada, China, Croatia, Czechia, France, Gambia, Germany, Guatemala, Hong Kong, India, Indonesia, Japan, Kenya, Malawi, Malta, Mexico, Nepal, Netherlands, Poland, Romania, Singapore, South Africa, Switzerland, Taiwan, Thailand, UK, USA, Vietnam, Zimbabwe.

- *ACTAsia (#00084)*;
- *Animal Defenders International (ADI)*;
- *Animals Asia Foundation (AAF, #00842)*;
- *Born Free Foundation*;
- *Cetacean Society International (CSI)*;
- *David Shepherd Wildlife Foundation*;
- *Earthtrust*;
- *Eastern Caribbean Coalition for Environmental Awareness (ECCEA, #05233)*;
- *Eurogroup for Animals (#05690)*;
- *Franz Weber Foundation*;
- *Future for Elephants*;
- *Global Federation of Animal Sanctuaries (GFAS)*;
- *Greenpeace International (#10727)*;
- *International Primate Protection League (IPPL, #14641)*;
- *International Ranger Federation (IRF, #14697)*;
- *OceanCare*;
- *Orangutan Foundation International (OFI, #17784)*;
- *Pan African Conservation Network, Kenya*;
- *Pan African Sanctuary Alliance (PASA, #18064)*;
- *Rainforest Concern*;
- *Save the Elephants (STE)*;
- *Whale and Dolphin Conservation (WDC)*;
- *WildAid*;
- *World Animal Protection (#21092)*.

IGO Relations *Convention on International Trade in Endangered Species of Wild Fauna and Flora (CITES, 1973)*. **NGO Relations** Member of (1): *International Tiger Coalition (ITC)*. [2022/XM1281/y/**F**]

- ♦ SPECOM – International Conference on Speech and Computer (meeting series)
- ♦ SPEC / see Pacific Islands Forum Secretariat (#17970)
- ♦ Spectroscopies in Novel Superconductors (meeting series)
- ♦ SPEE / see American Society for Engineering Education (#00790)
- ♦ Speech in Noise Workshop (meeting series)
- ♦ **SPEED** Student Platform for Engineering Education Development (#20016)
- ♦ **SPEIO** Sociedad Panamericana de Enfermedades Inflamatorias Oculares (#19432)
- ♦ Speleological Federation of the European Community / see Fédération Spéléologique Européenne (#09705)
- ♦ Speleological Federation of the European Union / see Fédération Spéléologique Européenne (#09705)

♦ Speleological Federation of Latin America and the Caribbean 19917

Federación Espeleológica de América Latina y el Caribe (FEALC)

SG address not obtained. E-mail: secretariogeneral@fealc.org.
Pres HC-02 Box 7429, Camuy PR 00627, USA. T. +17873839252.
URL: http://www.fealc.org/

History Founded 1981, Bowling Green KY (USA), during 8th International Speleological Congress of *International Union of Speleology (#15818)*. Registered in accordance with the laws of the USA and Puerto Rico. **Aims** Exchange experience, techniques and publications among members; promote the conservation of caves and karst regions. **Structure** General Assembly. Executive Committee. Board, consisting of President, Vice-President, Secretary-General and 4 Assistant Regional Secretaries. **Languages** English, Portuguese, Spanish. **Staff** 2.50 FTE, voluntary. **Finance** Each Officer or his supporting society pays his expenses. **Events** *Congress* Colombia 2018, *Congress* Catacamas (Honduras) 2014, *General Assembly and Scientific Meeting* Mérida (Mexico) 2013, *Congress / General Assembly and Scientific Meeting* Matanzas (Cuba) 2010, *General Assembly* Malargüe (Argentina) 2008. **Publications** *FEALC Newsletter* (periodical) in Spanish; *FEALC Geoespeleological Bulletin*. Proceedings of meetings in the periodicals of sponsoring country.

Members in 14 countries and territories:
Argentina, Bolivia, Brazil, Colombia, Costa Rica, Cuba, Dominican Rep, Honduras, Mexico, Paraguay, Peru, Puerto Rico, Uruguay, Venezuela. [2013/XD9562/**D**]

- ♦ SpellAfrica Initiative (internationally oriented national body)
- ♦ **SPERA** South Pacific Environmental Radioactivity Association (#19885)
- ♦ SPE – Semantics and Philosophy in Europe (meeting series)
- ♦ **SPE** Société de Pathologie Exotique (#09225)
- ♦ **SPE** Society of Petroleum Engineers (#19616)
- ♦ SPE – Society of Plastics Engineers (internationally oriented national body)
- ♦ SPE – Society of Professional Economists (internationally oriented national body)
- ♦ SPF / see Swisspeace
- ♦ SPFII / see United Nations Permanent Forum on Indigenous Issues (#20609)
- ♦ SPFI – Society of Police Futurists International (internationally oriented national body)
- ♦ **SPF** SAARC Psychiatric Federation (#19019)
- ♦ SPF – Sasakawa Peace Foundation (internationally oriented national body)
- ♦ **SPF** Société Palmophile Francophone (#19507)
- ♦ SPFS / see Pacific Islands Forum Secretariat (#17970)
- ♦ SPF-USA – Sasakawa Peace Foundation USA (internationally oriented national body)
- ♦ SPG / see Society of Exploration Geophysicists
- ♦ **SPGRC** SADC Plant Genetic Resources Centre (#19024)
- ♦ SPG / see USPG (#20736)

♦ The Sphere Project 19918

Contact c/o ICVA, Av Giuseppe Motta 26-28, 1202 Geneva, Switzerland. T. +41229509691. Fax +41229509609. E-mail: info@sphereproject.org.
URL: http://www.sphereproject.org/

History Founded Jul 1997. Originally due to end in 2004; restructured Apr 2005 with transition from Management Committee to Board, to continue until end 2009; Board developed new strategy during 2008, extending Project until end 2015. **Aims** Improve the quality of *humanitarian* assistance and *accountability* of humanitarian actors to their constituents, donors and affected populations by developing a set of universal minimum *standards* in life-saving areas of humanitarian response. **Structure** Governing Board, including representatives from: *ACT Alliance (#00081)*; Aktion Deutschland Hilft; *African Office for Development and Cooperation (OFADEC)*; *American Council for Voluntary International Action (InterAction)*; *CARE International (CI, #03429)*; *Caritas Internationalis (CI, #03580)*; Humanitarian Response Network of Canada; *International Council of Voluntary Agencies (ICVA, #13092)*; *International Federation of Red Cross and Red Crescent Societies (#13526)* (IFRC); *International Medical Corps (IMC)*; *The Lutheran World Federation (LWF, #16532)*; *Oxfam International (#17922)*; *Plan International (#18386)*; *RedR International (#18729)*; *Salvation Army (#19041)*; *Save the Children International (#19058)*; Sphere India; *World Vision International (WVI, #21904)*. Project office hosted by ICVA. **Languages** Arabic, English, French, Spanish. **Staff** 4.50 FTE, paid. **Finance** Core costs supported by contributions from Board organizations; programme activities covered by international donors / funding partners. **Activities** Humanitarian/emergency aid; publishing activities. **Publications** *Newsletter* (11 a year) in English, French, Spanish – electronic. *Sphere Unpacked* – series. *Humanitarian Charter and Minimum Standards in Humanitarian Response* (2011) in Arabic, English, French, Russian, Spanish. **Members** Not a membership organization. **IGO Relations** Cooperates with: *FAO (#09260)*; *Office of the United Nations High Commissioner for Human Rights (OHCHR, #17697)*; *UNDP (#20292)*; *UNEP (#20299)*; *UNHCR (#20327)*; *UNICEF (#20332)*; *United Nations Human Settlements Programme (UN-Habitat, #20572)*; *United Nations Office for the Coordination of Humanitarian Affairs (OCHA, #20593)*; *WHO (#20950)*; *World Food Programme (WFP, #21510)*. **NGO Relations** Cooperates with: *Active Learning Network for Accountability and Performance in Humanitarian Action (ALNAP, #00101)*; *Coordination SUD*; *Groupe urgence, réhabilitation et développement (Groupe URD)* Observer status with: *Global Health Cluster (GHC, #10401)*. [2015.06.01/XE4209/**E**]

- ♦ **SPHERIC** International Smoothed Particle Hydrodynamics European Research Interest Community (#14878)
- ♦ SPHER International – Society for the Protection of Human and Environmental Rights International (unconfirmed)
- ♦ **SPIA** Soldiers of Peace International Association (#19678)
- ♦ SPICA – International Symposium on Preparative Chromatography and Allied techniques (meeting series)
- ♦ SPIDH – International Permanent Secretariat Human Rights and Local Governments (internationally oriented national body)

♦ **SPIE** **19919**

Manager Marketing Dept PO Box 10, Bellingham WA 98227-0010, USA. T. +13606763290. Fax +13606471445. E-mail: spie@spie.org – customerservice@spie.org.
SPIE Europe 2 Alexandra Gate, Ffordd Pengam, Cardiff, CF24 2SA, UK. T. +442920894747. Fax +442920894750. E-mail: info@spieeurope.org.
URL: http://spie.org/

History 1955, Studio City CA (USA), as *Society of Photographic Instrumentation Engineers*. Subsequently changed title to *Society for Photo-Optical Instrumentation Engineers*. Changed title to *SPIE – The International Society for Optical Engineering*, 1981. Since 2007, only known under acronym, with full title *SPIE – international society for optics and photonics*. **Aims** Advance exchange, collection and dissemination of knowledge in optics, *photonics* and *imaging*. **Structure** Headquarters in Bellingham WA (USA); SPIE Europe in Cardiff (UK). **Languages** English. **Staff** 160.00 FTE, paid. **Finance** Members' dues. Other sources: revenue from conferences, exhibitions, publications and education. **Activities** Events/meetings; training/education; knowledge management/information dissemination; awards/prizes/competitions; advocacy/lobbying/activism. **Events** *Congress* Yokohama (Japan) 2023, *Astronomical Telescopes and Instrumentation Conference* Montréal, QC (Canada) 2022, *International Symposium on Photomask and Next Generation Lithography Mask Technology* Tokyo (Japan) 2022, *Congress* Yokohama (Japan) 2022, *Congress* Yokohama (Japan) 2021. **Publications** *SPIE Professional* (4 a year) – magazine. Research papers; e-books; articles; proceedings; monographs; tutorial texts; field guides; reference books; articles. **Information Services** *SPIE Digital Library*.
Members Student Chapters in 54 countries and territories:
Argentina, Armenia, Australia, Belgium, Bolivia, Brazil, Cameroon, Canada, Chile, China, Colombia, Czechia, Denmark, Ecuador, Egypt, Estonia, Finland, France, Germany, India, Indonesia, Ireland, Israel, Italy, Japan, Korea Rep, Latvia, Lithuania, Malaysia, Mexico, Netherlands, New Zealand, Pakistan, Peru, Poland, Portugal, Romania, Russia, Saudi Arabia, Senegal, Singapore, Slovakia, South Africa, Spain, Sweden, Switzerland, Taiwan, Thailand, Tunisia, Türkiye, UK, Ukraine, USA, Venezuela.
IGO Relations Cooperates with: *UNESCO Office, Jakarta – Regional Bureau for Sciences in Asia and the Pacific (#20313)*. **NGO Relations** Member of (1): *ABET*. Cooperates with (1): *International Society for Photogrammetry and Remote Sensing (ISPRS, #15362)*. Joint meetings with: *European Optical Society (EOS, #08091)*; *Institute of Electrical and Electronics Engineers (IEEE, #11259)*; *Institution of Engineering and Technology (IET, #11320)*; *International Commission for Optics (ICO, #12710)*. [2020/XD0175/**F**]

- ♦ SPIEF – St Petersburg International Economic Forum (meeting series)
- ♦ SPIE – The International Society for Optical Engineering / see SPIE (#19919)
- ♦ SPIE – international society for optics and photonics / see SPIE (#19919)
- ♦ SPIE – Secretariado Profesional Internacional de la Enseñanza (inactive)
- ♦ SPIE – Secrétariat professionnel international de l'enseignement (inactive)
- ♦ SPI / see Global Union Federations (#10638)
- ♦ SPILF – Société de pathologie infectieuse de langue française (internationally oriented national body)
- ♦ Spine Arthroplasty Society / see International Society for the Advancement of Spine Surgery (#14903)

♦ **The Spinelli Group** **19920**

Secretariat Square de Meeûs 25, 1000 Brussels, Belgium. T. +3225083030.
URL: http://www.spinelligroup.eu/

History Launched Sep 2010, by members of *European Parliament (EP, #08146)*. **Aims** Create a network of citizens, politicians, academics and writers who oppose the current trend of moving towards a looser *European Union*; promote a closer, post-national Europe. **Structure** Steering Group; MEP Spinelli Group; Spinelli Network Group. **Events** *Forum* Brussels (Belgium) 2013. **Publications** *Spinelli Newsletter*. **IGO Relations** *European Parliament (EP, #08146)*. **NGO Relations** Partners: *Bertelsmann Foundation*; *King Baudouin Foundation (KBF)*. [2018.05.18/XJ5112/v/**E**]

- ♦ **SPINE** Society for Progress and Innovation in the Near East (#19623)
- ♦ **SPIN** Skin Inflammation and Psoriasis International Network (#19308)
- ♦ SpiN – Speech in Noise Workshop (meeting series)
- ♦ SPIN – Stichting Promotie Internationale Neerlandistiek (see: #11854)
- ♦ SPIN – Study Platform on Interlocking Nationalisms (unconfirmed)
- ♦ S.PIO V – Istituto di Studi Politici (internationally oriented national body)
- ♦ Spiritaines – Soeurs Missionnaires du Saint-Esprit (religious order)
- ♦ Spiritains – Congrégation du Saint-Esprit (religious order)
- ♦ Spiritains – Fraternité du Saint-Esprit (religious order)
- ♦ Spiritans – Congregation of the Holy Spirit (religious order)
- ♦ Spirit of Enterprise Group (internationally oriented national body)
- ♦ Spirit Health Education Network (internationally oriented national body)

♦ **spiritsEUROPE** **19921**

Dir General Rue Belliard 12 – bte 5, 1040 Brussels, Belgium. T. +3227792423. E-mail: info@spirits.eu.
URL: https://www.spirits.eu/

History Sep 1993, Brussels (Belgium). Together with *European Union of Ethanol Producers (UEPA, inactive)*, jointly took over activities of *European Alcohol, Brandy and Spirits Union (UEAES, inactive)*. Merged with *European Forum for Responsible Drinking (EFRD, inactive)*, 27 Nov 2012. Former names and other names: *Confédération européenne des producteurs de spiritueux (CEPS)* – former; *European Spirits Organization* – former; *European Confederation of Spirits Producers* – former. Registration: No/ID: 0451.407.613, Start date: 17 Feb 1994, Belgium; EU Transparency Register, No/ID: 64926487056-58, Start date: 2 Nov 2011. **Aims** Encourage development of an environment in which producers and *distributors* can meet expectations of individual customers and society at large, while competing effectively for sustained growth. **Structure** General Assembly; Board; Standing Committees (4). **Languages** English. **Staff** 6.00 FTE, paid. **Finance** Sources: members' dues. **Events** *Spirits Summit* Brussels (Belgium) 2022, *Annual Summit* Brussels (Belgium) 2020, *Annual Summit* Brussels (Belgium) 2019, *Annual Summit* Brussels (Belgium) 2018, *Annual Summit* Brussels (Belgium) 2016. **Publications** *spiritsEUROPE Newsletter*.
Members Full (28) in 22 countries:
Austria, Belgium, Bulgaria, Cyprus, Czechia, Finland, France, Germany, Greece, Hungary, Ireland, Italy, Latvia, Malta, Netherlands, Poland, Portugal, Romania, Slovakia, Spain, Sweden, UK.
Observer (3) in 2 countries:
Norway, Switzerland.
Consultative Status Consultative status granted from: *World Intellectual Property Organization (WIPO, #21593)* (Observer Status). **NGO Relations** Member of (2): *European Tourism Manifesto (#08921)*; *FoodDrinkEurope (#09841)*. Partner of (1): *Transnational Alliance to Combat Illicit Trade (TRACIT)*. Associate Expert Group of *Business and Industry Advisory Committee to the OECD (BIAC, #03385)*. Liaison Organization of: *Comité européen de normalisation (CEN, #04162)*. [2022/XD3819/t/**D**]

- ♦ Spiritual Frontiers Fellowship / see Spiritual Frontiers Fellowship International
- ♦ Spiritual Frontiers Fellowship International (internationally oriented national body)
- ♦ Spiritual Unity of Nations (inactive)
- ♦ SPI – Seed Programs International (internationally oriented national body)
- ♦ SPI – Service pédologique interafricain (inactive)
- ♦ **SPI** Sports Philatelists International (#19928)
- ♦ Spitzen-Verband der Handelskammern des Commonwealths (inactive)
- ♦ SPJc – Siervas Pobres de Jesucristo (religious order)
- ♦ Splash International (unconfirmed)
- ♦ Splash – Splash International (unconfirmed)
- ♦ **SPLA** South Pacific Lawyers' Association (#19887)
- ♦ SPLC – International Software Product Line Conference (meeting series)
- ♦ **SPLF** Société de pneumologie de langue française (#19510)
- ♦ SPLF – Société de psychogériatrie de langue française (internationally oriented national body)
- ♦ SPLSLM – South Pacific Society of Lifestyle Medicine (internationally oriented national body)
- ♦ **SPM** Society for Phenomenology and Media (#19618)
- ♦ **SPM** Sustainable Project Management- Public-Private Partnerships for the Urban Environment (#20064)
- ♦ SPMUDA International Organization for Peace and Development (internationally oriented national body)
- ♦ SPMUDA International – SPMUDA International Organization for Peace and Development (internationally oriented national body)
- ♦ **SPNF** South Pacific Nurses Forum (#19888)
- ♦ SPNHC – Society for the Preservation of the Natural History Collections (internationally oriented national body)
- ♦ SPNS – Solidarité et partenariat Nord-Sud (internationally oriented national body)
- ♦ SPOCC / see Council of Regional Organisations of the Pacific (#04914)
- ♦ Spojené Vyskumné Centrum (#16147)
- ♦ Spojeny Ustav Jadernych Vyzjumú / see Joint Institute for Nuclear Research (#16134)
- ♦ Spolecné Vyzkumné Centrum (#16147)
- ♦ Spoonbill Action Voluntary Echo International (internationally oriented national body)
- ♦ SPOON Foundation (internationally oriented national body)

♦ **Spoqcs International Federation (SIF)** **19922**

Coordination Headquarters address not obtained. E-mail: info@spoqcs.org – spoqcs@gmail.com.
SG address not obtained. E-mail: hjj@spoqcs.org.
URL: http://spoqcs.org/

History 5 May 2011, Iran Islamic Rep. **Aims** Develop spoqcs as a major world media and entertainment sport through world-class planning and organization of competitions, marketing and development activities. **Structure** Executive Committee. **Activities** Sporting activities. **NGO Relations** Member of (1): *The Association for International Sport for All (TAFISA, #02763)*. [2021/XM7397/**C**]

♦ **SportAccord** **19923**

Acting Managing Dir Maison du Sport International, Avenue de Rhodania 54, 1007 Lausanne VD, Switzerland. T. +41216123070. E-mail: info@sportaccord.sport.
Events Manager address not obtained.
URL: https://www.sportaccord.sport/

History 2003. Created by *Global Association of International Sport Federations (GAISF, inactive)*, *Association of Summer Olympic International Federations (ASOIF, #02943)* and *Association of the International Olympic Winter Sports Federations (AIOWF, #02757)*. Former names and other names: *SportAccord – World Sport & Business Summit* – full title. **Aims** Drive positive change internationally; engage and connect international sport federations, right holders, organizing committees, cities, press and media, businesses and other organizations involved in the development and business of sport. **Structure** Executive Committee; Steering Committee. **Activities** Events/meetings. **Events** *World Sport and Business Summit* Ekaterinburg (Russia) 2022, *World Sport and Business Summit* Ekaterinburg (Russia) 2021, *World Sport and Business Summit* Lausanne (Switzerland) 2020, *World Sport and Business Summit* Gold Coast, QLD (Australia) 2019, *World Sport and Business Summit* Bangkok (Thailand) 2018.
Members Stakeholders (4), bringing together over 125 international sport federations:
Alliance of Independent recognised Members of Sport (AIMS, #00690); *Association of Summer Olympic International Federations (ASOIF, #02943)*; *Association of the International Olympic Winter Sports Federations (AIOWF, #02757)*; *Association of the IOC Recognized International Sports Federations (ARISF, #02767)*.
NGO Relations Full support of: *International Olympic Committee (IOC, #14408)*. [2022/AA1448/cy/**E**]

- ♦ SportAccord Asia-Pacific Headquarters / see General Association of Asia Pacific Sports Federations (#10106)
- ♦ SportAccord – World Sport & Business Summit / see SportAccord (#19923)
- ♦ Sport Association of Arab Women (no recent information)
- ♦ Sport and Citizenship (internationally oriented national body)
- ♦ Sport et Citoyenneté (internationally oriented national body)
- ♦ Sportcom – Asociación Iberoamericana de Información Deportiva (no recent information)
- ♦ Sport and Cooperation Network (internationally oriented national body)
- ♦ Sport and Development International Platform / see International Platform on Sport and Development
- ♦ Sport and Discrimination Conference (meeting series)
- ♦ **Sport&EU** Association for the Study of Sport and the European Union (#02941)

♦ **Sporting Goods Industry Data Harmonization Organization (SGIDHO)** **19924**

Contact Wölflistr 2, 3006 Bern, Switzerland. E-mail: info@sgidho.com.
URL: https://www.sgidho.com/

History 1997. Current statutes adopted Sep 2016. Former names and other names: *Federation of European Sporting Goods Retail Associations (FEDAS)* – former (2016); *Fédération européenne des associations de détaillants en articles de sport* – former (2016); *Europäische Vereinigung der Sporthändlerverbände* – former (2016). Registration: Switzerland. **Aims** Promote, develop, manage and distribute SGIDHO product data standards for sporting goods. **Structure** General Assembly; Board of Directors. **Finance** Sources: members' dues. **Events** *Annual conference / Conference* Bordeaux (France) 2009, *Annual conference / Conference* Dresden (Germany) 2008, *Annual conference / Conference* Naples (Italy) 2006, *Annual conference / Conference* Crans-Montana (Switzerland) 2005, *Annual conference / Conference* Marseille (France) 2004.
Members Active; national organizations (6) in 6 countries:
Austria, Czechia, France, Germany, Italy, Switzerland.
Partner; regional organization (1):
World Federation of the Sporting Goods Industry (WFSGI, #21487). [2020/XD8764/**D**]

♦ **Sport Integrity Global Alliance (SIGA)** **19925**

CEO House of Sport, Avenue des Arts 43, 1040 Brussels, Belgium. E-mail: info@siga-sport.com.
URL: https://siga-sport.com/

History Founded Nov 2015, by 20 organizations. EU Transparency Register: 355616337528-60. **Aims** Provide global leadership, promote good governance and safeguard the integrity of sport through a set of universal standards operated by an independent, neutral and global body. **Structure** General Assembly; Council. Standing Committees. **Finance** Sources: members' dues. **Activities** Events/meetings. **Events** *Sport Integrity Forum* New York, NY (USA) 2020, *World Congress on Global Leadership and Anti-Corruption in Sport* Rome (Italy) 2020, *Sport Integrity Forum* New York, NY (USA) 2019. **Publications** *SIGA Newsletter*.
Members Founding members include 8 organizations listed in this Yearbook:
Basel Institute on Governance; *Caribbean Association of National Olympic Committees (CANOC, #03454)*; *International Centre for Sport Security (ICSS, #12518)*; *International Mixed Martial Arts Federation (IMMAF, #14173)*; *Ligue européenne de natation (LEN, #16477)*; *McCain Institute for International Leadership*; *Special Olympics International (SOI, #19910)*; *Union Internationale des Avocats (UIA, #20422)*.
Regular members include 5 organizations listed in this Yearbook:
Alliance of European Football Coaches' Associations (AEFCA, #00674); *Association Internationale des Avocats du Football (AIAF, #02672)*; *Association of Certified Anti-Money Laundering Specialists (ACAMS)*; *IBLF Global*; *Parkour Earth (#18200)*.
NGO Relations Cooperation agreement with: *Union of European Football Associations (UEFA, #20386)*. [2020/XM8976/y/**C**]

- ♦ Sportivnyj Komitet Druzeskih Armij (inactive)

♦ **Sport Jiu-Jitsu International Federation (SJJIF)** **19926**

Contact address not obtained. E-mail: staff@sjjif.com.
URL: https://sjjif.com/

History Founded Jun 2012. Current statutes adopted 2015. **Aims** Acquire International Olympic Committee sport recognition and admittance into the Olympic program. **Structure** General Assembly; Board of Directors; Secretariat. **Languages** English.
Members Continental Federations (6):
Asian Sport Jiu-Jitsu Federation (ASJJF); *European Sport Jiu Jitsu Federation (ESJJF)*; North American Brazilian Jiu-jitsu Federation; *Sport Jiu-Jitsu Oceana Federation (SJJOF)*; *Sport Jiu-Jitsu South American Federation (SJJSAF)*; *Sports Jiu-Jitsu African Federation (SJJAF, #19927)*.
National federations in 44 countries and territories:

Algeria, Angola, Argentina, Australia, Belize, Brazil, Cameroon, Canada, Chile, Colombia, Ecuador, Egypt, El Salvador, Guatemala, Honduras, Hong Kong, India, Japan, Korea Rep, Malaysia, Mauritania, Mauritius, Mexico, Moldova, Mongolia, Morocco, New Caledonia, New Zealand, Nigeria, Pakistan, Panama, Peru, Philippines, Polynesia Fr, Portugal, Seychelles, Singapore, South Africa, Taiwan, Tunisia, UK, Ukraine, Uruguay, USA.
NGO Relations Member of: *International Council of Sport Science and Physical Education (ICSSPE, #13077); The Association for International Sport for All (TAFISA, #02763); World Martial Arts Games Committee (WMAGC, #21637).* [2019/XM8623/y/**C**]

- Sport Jiu-Jitsu Oceana Federation (unconfirmed)
- Sport Jiu-Jitsu South American Federation (unconfirmed)
- Sport Karate International (internationally oriented national body)
- Sport and Recreation Council of the Central American Isthmus (#04716)
- Sports Ambassadors (internationally oriented national body)
- Sport sans frontières / see PLAY International
- Sports Without Borders / see PLAY International
- Sports Committee of Friendly Armies (inactive)
- Sports Federation of Islamic Solidarity Games / see Islamic Solidarity Sports Federation (#16052)

♦ Sports Jiu-Jitsu African Federation (SJJAF) 19927

Contact Shop ub4g Suninghill village, Sunninghill, Johannesburg, South Africa. T. +27782254502. E-mail: admin@sabjjf.org.
URL: http://sjjaf.org/
Aims Help support and bring quality services and tools to individual practitioners, competitors, academy owners, independent promoters and instructors. **Activities** Sporting activities.
Members Federations in 10 countries:
Algeria, Angola, Cameroon, Mauritania, Mauritius, Morocco, Nigeria, Seychelles, South Africa, Tunisia.
NGO Relations Continental federation of: *Sport Jiu-Jitsu International Federation (SJJIF, #19926).* Associate member of: *International Martial Art Games Committee (IMGC, #14107).* [2018/XM8627/**D**]

♦ Sports Philatelists International (SPI) 19928

Pres 9936 Kika Ct. #3623, San Diego CA 92129, USA.
URL: http://www.sportstamps.org/
History 1962, USA. Former names and other names: *Sports on Stamps Unit of American Topical Association* – former. **Aims** Serve *collectors* of *Olympic* and sports *stamps* and related material throughout the world. **Languages** English. **Staff** Voluntary. **Finance** Sources: members' dues. **Activities** Knowledge management/information dissemination. **Publications** *Journal of Sports Philately (JSP)* (4 a year); *Journal Index 1953-2012. Postal History and Vignettes of the 1932 Olympic Games.* Handbooks; monographs.
Members Individuals (mostly in USA) in 32 countries and territories:
Australia, Austria, Belgium, Brazil, Canada, Czechia, Denmark, Finland, France, Germany, Greece, Hong Kong, Hungary, Iceland, Israel, Italy, Japan, Mexico, Netherlands, New Zealand, Portugal, Russia, Slovenia, South Africa, Spain, Sweden, Switzerland, Thailand, Türkiye, UK, Ukraine, USA.
NGO Relations American Philatelic Society (APS); *Association Internationale des Collectionneurs Olympiques (AICO, #02677); International Olympic Committee (IOC, #14408).* [2020.04.29/XF2945/v/**F**]

♦ Sports Rights Owners Coalition (SROC) 19929

Contact c/o FOTA, 49 Welbeck Street, London, W1G 9XN, UK.
URL: http://www.sroc.info/
History as an informal group of representatives. **Aims** Enable discussion of sharing of best practice on key legal, political and regulatory issues; raise awareness of new developments and innovation in sports rights; enable sports to take joint action to protect and promote their rights. **Publications** Position papers.
Members National and regional sports organizations in 7 countries and territories:
Australia, England, France, Germany, India, Scotland, Wales.
Regional organizations included in this Yearbook (13):
ATP World Tour (#03011); European Leagues (#07672); Fédération Équestre Internationale (FEI, #09484); International Cricket Council (ICC, #13105); International Federation of Association Football (#13360); International Federation of Horseracing Authorities (IFHA, #13449); International Tennis Federation (ITF, #15676); Ligue européenne de natation (LEN, #16477); Union of European Football Associations (UEFA, #20386); World Athletics (#21209); World Professional Billiards and Snooker Association (WPBSA, #21740); World Rugby (#21757).
IGO Relations Member of Consultative Committee of: *Enlarged Partial Agreement on Sport (EPAS, #05487).* [2012/XJ5299/y/**F**]

- Sports on Stamps Unit of American Topical Association / see Sports Philatelists International (#19928)
- Sports Tourism International Council (no recent information)

♦ Sports Union for athletes with Down Syndrome (SU-DS) 19930

Contact address not obtained. E-mail: president@su-ds.org.
URL: http://www.SU-DS.org/
History Proposed 16 May 2012, Portugal. **Aims** Promote sport worldwide for athletes with Down Syndrome to the highest levels of sporting excellence. **Languages** English. **Finance** Self-funded through voluntary contributions. **Activities** Sporting events.
Members Organizations (9) in 53 countries:
Basketball for Down Syndrome (IB21); *Down Syndrome International Gymnastic Organization (DSIGO); Down Syndrome International Swimming Organisation (DSISO, #05129); Football International Federation for Players with Down syndrome (FIFDS);* Handball for players with Down Syndrome (HANDOWN); *International Athletic Association for Persons with Down Syndrome (IAADS, #12289);* International Table Tennis Association for Down Syndrome (ITTADS); Judo for Down Syndrome (JUDOWN); Skiing International for Down Syndrome (SKiDS). [2019.12.12/XJ6949/y/**D**]

♦ Sport and Sustainability International (SandSI) 19931

SG Maison du Sport, Ave de Rhodanie 54, 1007 Lausanne VD, Switzerland. E-mail: info@sportsustainability.org.
URL: http://www.sandsi.org/
History 16 Nov 2016. Registration: Switzerland. **Aims** Promote healthy, sustainable and just communities, aligning itself on the United Nations Sustainable Development Goals. **Structure** General Assembly; Board of Directors; Administration Committee; Secretariat. Committees. **Activities** Awareness raising; guidance/assistance/consulting; knowledge management/information dissemination; projects/programmes; sporting activities; training/education. **Members** Organizations; Individuals. Membership countries not specified. [2022.03.12/XM6632/**F**]

- SPPF / see Pacific Peoples' Partnership
- SPP – International Conference on Surface Plasmon Photonics (meeting series)
- SPP – Society for Pediatric Pathology (internationally oriented national body)
- **SPP** Society of Porphyrins and Phthalocyanines (#19622)
- SPPS / see Societas Physiologiae Plantarum Scandinavica (#19452)
- **SPPS** Societas Physiologiae Plantarum Scandinavica (#19452)
- SPR / see Just Detention International
- Språkkonvensjonen (1981 treaty)
- Språkkoventionen (1981 treaty)
- SPREP convention – Convention for the Protection of the Natural Resources and Environment of the South Pacific Region (1986 treaty)
- **SPREP** Secretariat of the Pacific Regional Environment Programme (#19205)
- **SPRFMO** South Pacific Regional Fisheries Management Organisation (#19889)
- SPRI – Scott Polar Research Institute (internationally oriented national body)
- Sprogkonventionen (1981 treaty)
- SP-ROP / see Sociedad Panamericana de Retinopatia del Prematuro (#19435)
- **SPROP** Sociedad Panamericana de Retinopatia del Prematuro (#19435)
- SPR – Society for Psychophysiological Research (internationally oriented national body)
- **SPR** Society for Psychotherapy Research (#19626)
- SPRU – Science and Technology Policy Research (internationally oriented national body)
- **SPRV** Sociedad Panamericana de Retina y Vitreo (#18126)
- SPRYWA – South Pacific Regional Association (inactive)
- SPS agreement – WTO Agreement on the Application of Sanitary and Phytosanitary Measures (1993 treaty)
- SP – Servi Sancti Paracliti (religious order)
- SP – Sisters of Providence (religious order)
- SP / see Soldiers of Peace International Association (#19678)
- **SPSP** Society for Philosophy of Science in Practice (#19619)
- SPS – Safety Pharmacology Society (internationally oriented national body)
- SPSSA – South Pacific Social Sciences Association (inactive)
- **SPS** Scandinavian Physiological Society (#19097)
- SPSSI – Society for Psychological Study of Social Issues (internationally oriented national body)
- SPS – Societas Sancti Patritii pro Missionibus ad Exteros (religious order)
- SPS – Sustainable Phosphorus Summit (meeting series)
- **SPT Association** Scandinavian Petroleum Technic Association (#19096)
- SPTC / see Pacific Islands Trade and Invest (#17980)
- **SPTF** Social Performance Task Force (#19343)
- SPTO / see Pacific Tourism Organization (#18008)
- **SPTO** Pacific Tourism Organization (#18008)
- **SPT** Sociedad Panamericana de Trauma (#19436)
- **SPT** Society for Persuasion and Technology (#19615)
- **SPT** Society for Philosophy and Technology (#19620)
- SPT – Society of Photo-Technologists (internationally oriented national body)
- **SPT** Subcommittee on Prevention of Torture and other Cruel, Inhuman or Degrading Treatment or Punishment (#20023)
- SPUC / see Pontifical Council for Promoting Christian Unity (#18446)
- SPUC – Society for the Protection of Unborn Children (internationally oriented national body)
- SPUDM / see European Association for Decision Making (#06006)
- **SPUMS** South Pacific Underwater Medicine Society (#19890)
- SPW / see Restless Development
- **SPWLA** Society of Petrophysicists and Well Log Analysts (#19617)
- SPWP / see World Peace Prayer Society
- **SPWRC** South Pacific Whale Research Consortium (#19891)
- SQAY Asia / see Sqay Organization of Asia (#19932)

♦ Sqay Organization of Asia (SOA) 19932

Sec Drangbal, Pampore, 192121, Pampore 192121, India. T. +917006190566. E-mail: sqayasia@gmail.com.
URL: https://www.sqayasia.tk/
History 2000, India. A continental federation of *International Council of Sqay (ICS).* Former names and other names: *SQAY Asia* – alias. **Aims** Promote the indigenous martial art of Kashmir throughout Asia. **Structure** Annual General Meeting; Executive Committee. Commissions. **Languages** English, Kashmiri, Urdu. **Activities** Awards/prizes/competitions; sporting activities.
Members Federations in 19 countries and territories:
Bangladesh, Bhutan, China, Hong Kong, India, Indonesia, Iran Islamic Rep, Iraq, Jordan, Korea Rep, Malaysia, Nepal, Pakistan, Philippines, Sri Lanka, Syrian AR, Thailand, United Arab Emirates, Uzbekistan.
NGO Relations Member of (2): *General Association of Asia Pacific Sports Federations (GAAPSF, #10106); International Sport Network Organization (ISNO, #15592).* [2022.11.12/AA1104/**D**]

- SQM – International Conference on Strangeness in Quark Matter (meeting series)

♦ Squash Federation of Africa (SFA) 19933

SG PO Box 613, Northlands, 2116, South Africa. T. +27114428056. Fax +27114428036.
Chief Exec address not obtained.
URL: http://squashafrica.org/
History Founded 1988, as *African Squash Rackets Federation.* Subsequently name changed to *African Squash Federation.* Present name adopted 1992. Regional federation of: *World Squash Federation (WSF, #21826).* **Aims** Promote the growth and development of squash in Africa. **Activities** Sporting activities.
Members Full in 19 countries:
Algeria, Botswana, Congo DR, Egypt, Ghana, Kenya, Lesotho, Malawi, Mauritius, Morocco, Namibia, Nigeria, Somalia, South Africa, Sudan, Tanzania UR, Uganda, Zambia, Zimbabwe. [2016/XD2372/**D**]

- SRA-Asia – Society for Risk Analysis – Asia (unconfirmed)
- **SRA-Europe** Society for Risk Analysis – Europe (#19637)
- SRA International – Society for Risk Analysis International (internationally oriented national body)
- SRAM / see Association of Catholic Education for Africa and Madagascar (#02415)
- **SRANF** Société de Radiologie d'Afrique Noire Francophone (#19511)
- SRA – Society of Research Administrators International (internationally oriented national body)
- SRAS – School of Russian and Asian Studies, Cambridge MA (internationally oriented national body)
- **SRBR** Society for Research on Biological Rhythms (#19633)
- **SRB** Single Resolution Board (#19287)
- SRCD – Society for Research in Child Development (internationally oriented national body)
- SRC – Scottish Refugee Council (internationally oriented national body)
- SRC – Semiconductor Research Corporation (unconfirmed)
- SREN – European Cooperative Research Network on Sustainable Rural Environmental and Energy (see: #08871)
- **SRE** Scandinavian Reliability Engineers (#19098)
- SREU – Ständiger Rat der Europäischen Übersetzer (inactive)
- **SRFC** Sub-Regional Fisheries Commission (#20026)
- SRF – International Conference of RF Superconductivity (meeting series)
- **SRF** Self Realization Fellowship (#19221)
- SRGB / see SADC Plant Genetic Resources Centre (#19024)
- SRHE – Society for Research into Higher Education (internationally oriented national body)
- SRHR / see Share-Net International

♦ SRHR Africa Trust (SAT) 19934

Regional Office PO Box 411919, Craighall Park, Johannesburg, 2024, South Africa. T. +27114788300.
Street address 1st Floor, South Tower 1 Sixty Jan Smuts, c/o Jan Smuts Ave and 7th Ave, Rosebank, Johannesburg, 2196, South Africa.
URL: http://www.satregional.org/
History 1990, as *Southern African AIDS Training Programme,* as a project of *Canadian International Development Agency (CIDA, inactive).* Subsequent name *Southern African AIDS Trust (SAT)* adopted 2003, when SAT became an independent organization. **Aims** Shift and transform society to meet the needs of Africa's youthful population, pressing adolescent healthcare needs, particularly Sexual and Reproductive Health and Rights (SRHR); root out systemic issues which are responsible for gender inequality. **Structure** Board. **Languages** English. **Staff** 43.00 FTE, paid. **Finance** Joint funding arrangement, including from: *Canadian International Development Agency (CIDA, inactive); Swedish International Development Cooperation Agency (Sida); Swiss Agency for Development and Cooperation (SDC).* **Activities** Advocacy/lobbying/activism; projects/programmes; knowledge management/information dissemination; monitoring/evaluation. **Publications** Information Services: Data exchange platform.
Members Offices in 4 countries:
Malawi, South Africa, Zambia, Zimbabwe.
NGO Relations Member of: *Africa Capacity Alliance (ACA, #00160); PMNCH (#18410); Regional Inter-Agency Task Team on Children and AIDS in Eastern and Southern Africa (RIATT-ESA, #18791).* Cooperates with: *ICASO (#11040).* [2018.11.02/XM1893/**F**]

- ♦ **SRHSB** Society for Research into Hydrocephalus and Spina Bifida (#19634)
- ♦ Sri Agathiar Sanmaarga Charitable Trust (internationally oriented national body)
- ♦ Sri Aurobindo Center of Los Angeles / see East-West Cultural Center
- ♦ Sri Aurobindo International Institute of Educational Research (internationally oriented national body)
- ♦ Sri Aurobindo Society (internationally oriented national body)
- ♦ SRIFIAS – Sinor Research Institute for Inner Asian Studies (internationally oriented national body)
- ♦ SRIF / see International Society for Research on Identity (#15422)
- ♦ SRI International (internationally oriented national body)
- ♦ SRI – International Conference on Synchrotron Radiation Instrumentation (meeting series)
- ♦ Sri Lanka Center for Development Studies / see Marga Institute
- ♦ **SRIP** Society for Reproductive and Infant Psychology (#19630)
- ♦ **SRI** Save the Rhino International (#19061)
- ♦ **SRI** Shark Research Institute (#19260)
- ♦ **SRI** Society for Reproductive Investigation (#19631)
- ♦ SRISTI – Society for Research and Initiatives for Sustainable Technologies and Institutions (internationally oriented national body)
- ♦ SRI – swissinfo – Swiss Radio International (internationally oriented national body)
- ♦ **SRLAN** Southern Refugee Legal Aid Network (#19879)
- ♦ **SRLF** Société de réanimation de langue française (#19512)
- ♦ **SRN** Screenwriting Research Network (#19160)

♦ SRNT Europe 19935

Member Delegate Univ of Helsinki, Dept of Public Health, PO Box 41, FI-00014 Helsinki, Finland. T. +358504151268.
URL: http://www.srnteurope.org/

History within *Society for Research on Nicotine and Tobacco (SRNT)*. **Events** *Annual Conference* Oslo (Norway) 2019, *Annual Conference* Maastricht (Netherlands) 2015, *Annual Conference* Santiago de Compostela (Spain) 2014, *Annual Conference* Boston, MA (USA) 2013, *Annual European Conference / Annual Conference* Helsinki (Finland) 2012. **Publications** *Nicotine and Tobacco Research* – journal. **NGO Relations** Member of: *Federation of European Neuroscience Societies (FENS, #09522).* [2016/XD9404/E]

- ♦ SRNT – Society for Research on Nicotine and Tobacco (internationally oriented national body)
- ♦ **SROC** Sports Rights Owners Coalition (#19929)
- ♦ **SRO-EA Kigali** ECA Sub-Regional Office for Eastern Africa (#05275)
- ♦ **SRO-SA Lusaka** ECA Subregional Office for Southern Africa (#05276)
- ♦ **SRO-WA** ECA Sub-Regional Office for West Africa (#05277)
- ♦ **SRP** Sustainable Rice Platform (#20065)
- ♦ **SRSM** Society for Research Synthesis Methods (#19635)
- ♦ **SRS** Scoliosis Research Society (#19156)
- ♦ **SRS** Society of Radiopharmaceutical Sciences (#19627)
- ♦ **SRS** Society for Ricoeur Studies (#19636)
- ♦ SRS – Society of Robotic Surgery (unconfirmed)
- ♦ SRTY – Suomen Rauhantutkimusyhdistys Ry (internationally oriented national body)
- ♦ **SSAA** Self Storage Association Asia (#19222)
- ♦ SSAC / see Nordic Society for Clinical Microbiology and Infectious Diseases (#17413)

♦ SSAFE 19936

Contact address not obtained. E-mail: info@ssafe-food.org.
URL: http://www.ssafe-food.org/

History Founded 2004. **Aims** Foster continuous improvement and global acceptance of internationally recognized *food* protection systems and *standards* through public-private partnerships. **Languages** English. **Finance** Members' dues. **IGO Relations** Observer to: *Codex Alimentarius Commission (CAC, #04081).* **NGO Relations** *Global Food Safety Initiative (GFSI, #10366)*; *Health for Animals (#10870)*; *International Organization for Standardization (ISO, #14473)*; national organizations. [2019.02.04/XM7045/F]

- ♦ **SSAI** Scandinavian Society of Anaesthesiology and Intensive Care Medicine (#19101)
- ♦ SSANAAS / see African Forum for Agricultural Advisory Services (#00320)
- ♦ **SSAR** Scandinavian Society for Atherosclerosis Research (#19102)
- ♦ SSA – Saharan Studies Association (internationally oriented national body)
- ♦ SSA – Sisters of St Anne (religious order)
- ♦ SSAS – Stockholm School of Asian Studies (internationally oriented national body)
- ♦ SSA – Stroke Society of Australasia (internationally oriented national body)
- ♦ **SSATP** Africa Transport Policy Program (#00527)
- ♦ **SSBP** Society for the Study of Behavioural Phenotypes (#19643)
- ♦ SSC / see Weitz Center for Development Studies
- ♦ SSC / see We Effect
- ♦ SSCC – Congregatio Sacrorum Cordium Jesu et Mariae necnon Adorationis Perpetuae Sacratissimi Sacramenti Altaris (religious order)
- ♦ SSCJ – Sisters of the Sacred Heart of Jesus (religious order)
- ♦ **SSCLE** Society for the Study of the Crusades and the Latin East (#19644)
- ♦ SSCME – Societas Sancti Columbani pro Missionibus ad Exteros (religious order)
- ♦ SSC – Missionary Sisters of St Columban (religious order)
- ♦ SSCM – Soeurs Servantes du Saint-Coeur de Marie (religious order)
- ♦ **SSCPNM** Scandinavian Society of Clinical Physiology and Nuclear Medicine (#19104)
- ♦ SSCRS – Scandinavian Society of Cataract and Refractive Surgery (no recent information)
- ♦ SSCS / see Sea Shepherd International
- ♦ SSC – Scandinavian Symposium on Chemometrics (meeting series)
- ♦ **SSC** Sociedad Sudamericana de Cardiologia (#19707)
- ♦ SSC – Societas Presbyterorum Sancti Iosephi Benedicti Cottolengo (religious order)
- ♦ **SSCS** SAARC Surgical Care Society (#19020)
- ♦ SSCT – Scandinavian Society for Cell Toxicology (inactive)
- ♦ SSDBM – Scientific and Statistical Database Management Conference (meeting series)
- ♦ SSD – Congregazione delle Suore di Santa Dorotea della Frassinetti (religious order)
- ♦ SSDI – Société suisse de droit international (internationally oriented national body)
- ♦ SSDT / see International Society of Beverage Technologists
- ♦ SSEA – Société suisse d'études africaines (internationally oriented national body)
- ♦ SSEASR / see South and Southeast Asian Association for the Study of Culture and Religion (#19892)
- ♦ **SSEASR** South and Southeast Asian Association for the Study of Culture and Religion (#19892)
- ♦ SSEES – School of Slavonic and East European Studies (internationally oriented national body)
- ♦ SSEFI / see SSE International Forum (#19937)
- ♦ SSE Forum International – Réseau International D'Économie Sociale et Solidaire / see SSE International Forum (#19937)

♦ SSE International Forum 19937

ESS Forum International

General Delegate 34 bis rue Vignon, 75009 Paris, France. E-mail: contact@essfi.coop.
URL: https://www.essforuminternational.com/

History 2004. Founded following the activities of *Mont-Blanc Meetings (MBM, #16850)*. Former names and other names: *SSE International Forum – International Network of Social and Solidarity Economy (SSEFI)* – full title; *SSE Forum International – Réseau International D'Économie Sociale et Solidaire (ESSFI)* – full title; *ESS Forum International – Red Internacional de Economia Social y Solidaria (ESSFI)* – full title. **Aims** Promote *social* and *solidarity economy* within a *pluralistic* economy and on all continents. **Structure** Board of Directors; Executive Committee; Scientific Committee; Co-Presidency. **Languages** English, French, Spanish. **Staff** 2.00 FTE, paid. **Finance** Members' dues. **Activities** Events/meetings. **Events** *Mont Blanc Meeting* Cartagena de Indias (Colombia) 2022. **Publications** Books.
Members Benefactor members in 2 countries:
Canada, France.
Active members in 10 countries:
Belgium, Cameroon, Comoros, Costa Rica, Dominican Rep, France, Guinea, Madagascar, Mali, Togo.
Included in the above, 1 organization listed in this Yearbook:
Global Social Economy Forum (GSEF, #10603).
IGO Relations *European Commission (EC, #06633)*; *ECOSOC (#05331)*. **NGO Relations** Partners include: *Centre international de recherches et d'information sur l'économie publique, sociale et coopérative (CIRIEC, #03764)*; *FMDV (#09804)*; *International Association of Investors in the Social Economy (INAISE, #11971)*; *Institut de coopération sociale internationale (ICOSI, #11237).* [2022/XM7499/c/F]

- ♦ SSE International Forum – International Network of Social and Solidarity Economy / see SSE International Forum (#19937)
- ♦ **SSEM** Society for the Study of Emerging Markets (#19646)
- ♦ **SSESH** Scandinavian Society for Economic and Social History (#19106)
- ♦ SSE – Societas Patrum Sancti Edmundi (religious order)
- ♦ SSF / see PLAY International
- ♦ **SSFE** Scandinavian Society of Forest Economics (#19108)
- ♦ SSF-IIIHS Centre for Psychospiritual Studies (internationally oriented national body)
- ♦ SSFM – Scandinavian Society of Forensic Medicine (inactive)
- ♦ **SSfPA** Scandinavian Society for Prehistoric Art (#19115)
- ♦ SSF – Socialisme sans frontières (internationally oriented national body)
- ♦ SSGM – Scandinavian Society for Genito-Urinary Medicine (inactive)
- ♦ **SSG** Scandinavian Sarcoma Group (#19099)
- ♦ **SSHAP** Society for the Study of the History of Analytical Philosophy (#19647)
- ♦ SSH / see Net4Society (#16976)
- ♦ **SSHNO** Scandinavian Society for Head and Neck Oncology (#19109)
- ♦ SSIA – Somali Studies International Association (internationally oriented national body)
- ♦ **SSIEM** Society for the Study of Inborn Errors of Metabolism (#19648)
- ♦ SSIF / see Excellence in Medical Education (#09220)
- ♦ SSIHRL – Spanish Society for International Human Rights Law (internationally oriented national body)
- ♦ SSILA – Society for the Study of the Indigenous Languages of the Americas (internationally oriented national body)
- ♦ SSIS / see ISC-Foundation
- ♦ **SSI** Safe Sport International (#19029)
- ♦ SSI – Samusocial International (internationally oriented national body)
- ♦ **SSI** Scandinavian Society for Immunology (#19110)
- ♦ **SSI** Service Social International (#14886)
- ♦ **SSI** Servicio Social Internacional (#14886)
- ♦ SSI – Sustainable Sciences Institute (internationally oriented national body)
- ♦ **SSI** Sustainable Shipping Initiative (#20067)
- ♦ SSJE – Society of St John the Evangelist (religious order)
- ♦ SSJG – Sisters of St John of God (religious order)
- ♦ SSJ – Societas Sodalium Sancti Joseph a Sacro Corde (religious order)
- ♦ SSMI – Sisters Servants of Mary Immaculate (religious order)
- ♦ SSMI – Soeurs Servantes de Marie Immaculée (religious order)
- ♦ SSML – Typology of Small-Scale Multilingualism (meeting series)
- ♦ SSM – Sarvodaya Shramadana Movement (internationally oriented national body)
- ♦ SSND – School Sisters of Notre Dame (religious order)
- ♦ **SSN** SouthSouthNorth (#19893)
- ♦ **SSN** Species Survival Network (#19916)
- ♦ **SSN** Surveillance Studies Network (#20045)
- ♦ **SSN** Sykepleiernes Samarbeid i Norden (#17371)
- ♦ SSOSA – Shakespeare Society of Southern Africa (internationally oriented national body)
- ♦ SSPA – Scandinavian Symposium on Physical Acoustics (meeting series)
- ♦ **SSPA** Sodium Sulphate Producers Association (#19667)
- ♦ SSPC / see Society for Protective Coatings
- ♦ SSPC – Missionary Sisters of St Peter Claver (religious order)
- ♦ SSPC – Society for Protective Coatings (internationally oriented national body)
- ♦ **SSPD** Scandinavian Society for Prosthetic Dentistry (#19116)
- ♦ SSPI – Society for Satellite Professionals International (internationally oriented national body)
- ♦ SSpSAP – Sister-Servants of the Holy Spirit of Perpetual Adoration (religious order)
- ♦ SSP / see Scandinavian College of Neuropsychopharmacology (#19082)
- ♦ SSpS – Missionarie Serve dello Spirito Santo (religious order)
- ♦ SSP – Societas a Sancto Paulo Apostolo (religious order)
- ♦ **SSPX** Priestly Society of Saint Pius X (#18494)
- ♦ SSRC – Social Science Research Council (internationally oriented national body)
- ♦ **SSRCTS** Scandinavian Society for Research in Cardiothoracic Surgery (#19117)
- ♦ SSREES – Scottish Society for Russian and East European Studies (internationally oriented national body)
- ♦ SSRI – Social Science Research Institute, Hawaii (internationally oriented national body)
- ♦ **SSR** SIGNIS Services Rome (#19274)
- ♦ SSS – Congregazione del Santissimo Sacramento (religious order)
- ♦ **SSSD** Scandinavian Society for the Study of Diabetes (#19119)
- ♦ **SSSEA** Soil Science Society of East Africa (#19671)
- ♦ SSSF – School Sisters of Saint Francis (religious order)
- ♦ SSS – International Space Syntax Symposium (meeting series)
- ♦ **SSSI** Society for the Study of Symbolic Interaction (#19651)
- ♦ **SSSK** Skandinaviska Sällskapet för Språk och Kognition (#19072)
- ♦ **SSSK** Det Skandinaviske Selskab for Sprog og Kognition (#19072)
- ♦ **SSSK** Skandinavisk Selskap for Språk og Kognisjon (#19072)
- ♦ SSSP – Society for the Study of Social Problems (internationally oriented national body)
- ♦ **SSSR** Society for the Scientific Study of Reading (#19640)
- ♦ SSSR – Sojuz Sovetskih Socialisticeskih Respublik (inactive)
- ♦ **SSS** Scandinavian Surgical Society (#19122)
- ♦ SSS – Societas Ancillarum Sanctissimi Sacramenti (religious order)
- ♦ **SSSS** Society for the Study of the Short Story in English (#19650)
- ♦ SSSWP – Seismological Society of the South-West Pacific (inactive)
- ♦ SSTD – International Symposium on Spatial and Temporal Databases (meeting series)
- ♦ **SSTT** Scandinavian Society for Trenchless Technology (#19121)
- ♦ STAA – Student Travel Association of Asia (inactive)
- ♦ Stability Pact Anti-corruption Initiative / see Regional Anti-Corruption Initiative (#18750)
- ♦ STAB – International Conference on the Stability of Ships and Ocean Vehicles (meeting series)
- ♦ STAC – SAARC Tuberculosis and HIV/AIDS Centre (see: #19721)
- ♦ Städteverband für Recycling / see Association of Cities and Regions for Sustainable Resource Management (#02433)
- ♦ Stående Udvalg for Laegerne i EF / see Standing Committee of European Doctors (#19955)
- ♦ Staff Association of the African Development Bank / see Staff Council of the African Development Bank (#19943)
- ♦ Staff Association of the European Region of the World Health Organization / see Staff Association of the WHO Regional Office for Europe (#19941)

♦ Staff Association of the International Atomic Energy Agency 19938

Contact c/o Staff Council IAEA, Room A0423, Wagramer Strasse 5, 1400 Vienna, Austria. E-mail: presidentstaffcouncil@iaea.org.

History Jul 1957, Vienna (Austria), as integral party of *International Atomic Energy Agency (IAEA, #12294)*. Revised version of Statutes adopted: Nov 1968; Mar 1971; Jul 1979; Nov 1980; Dec 1982. Also referred to as *IAEA Staff Association*. **Aims** Safeguard the rights and represent the interests of IAEA staff in a fair and unbiased manner. **Structure** Referendum; Staff Assembly; Staff Council and its Officers. **Languages** Arabic, Chinese, English, French, Russian, Spanish. **Finance** Voluntary contributions. Anual budget: Austrian Sch 380,000. **Members** Any IAEA staff member, as defined in AM.II/1, Regulation 14.02, holding an appointment in the Secretariat for a period of at least three months or with at least four months of continuous service shall be considered a member of the Staff Association. **NGO Relations** *Federation of International Civil Servants' Associations (FICSA, #09603)*. [2016.07.21/XE2014/v/E]

♦ Staff Association of the International Civil Aviation Organization (ICAO Staff Association) 19939

Association du personnel de l'Organisation de l'aviation civile internationale – Asociación del Personal de la Organización de Aviación Civil Internacional

Contact 999 Robert-Bourassa Blvd, Ste 8/30, Montréal QC H3C 5H7, Canada. T. +15149548219 ext8380. Fax +15149546379. E-mail: staficao@icao.int.
URL: http://www.icao.int/

History 16 Dec 1948, Montréal (Canada), to represent staff members of *International Civil Aviation Organization (ICAO, #12581)*. **Members** Staff members of the International Civil Aviation Organization. [2018.06.19/XE2129/v/E]

♦ Staff Association of the OECD 19940

Association du personnel de l'OCDE

Exec Sec c/o OCDE, 2 rue André Pascal, 75775 Paris CEDEX 16, France. T. +33145248809. Fax +33145247578.

History to represent staff members of *OECD (#17693)*. **Aims** Protect professional interests, including financial and non-material, of staff as a whole and of the different categories thereof; improve material living conditions of staff and strengthen links between members of staff of different nationalities; strengthen links between the Organization and staff as a whole. **Structure** Executive Committee; Staff Representatives (45). **Languages** English, French. **Staff** 10.00 FTE, paid. **Finance** Members' dues. Other sources: investment returns; OECD's facilities (secondments, etc). **Activities** Events/meetings; networking/liaising; guidance/assistance/consulting. **Publications** Annual activity report; fact files. **Members** as of Jul 2019: about 2,833. Membership countries not specified. [2019.08.16/XE0207/v/E]

♦ Staff Association of the Organization of American States / see OAS Staff Association (#17631)

♦ Staff Association of the WHO Regional Office for Europe (EURSA) 19941

Secretariat c/o WHO/EURO, Marmorvej 51, 2100 Copenhagen Ø, Denmark. T. +4545336777. E-mail: eursa@who.int.

History Established to represent staff members of *WHO (#20950)* European Region. Statutes adopted 10 May 1984; amended: 13 May 1986, 8 Dec 1988, 8 May 1990, 24 Nov 1994, 23 Nov 1995, 4 May 1999; 27 Jan 2004. Former names and other names: *Staff Association of the European Region of the World Health Organization* – former; *Association du personnel de la Région européenne de l'Organisation mondiale de la santé* – former; *WHO/EUR Staff Association, Copenhagen* – alias. **Aims** Promote the welfare, interests and career development of all staff, both collectively and individually, to safeguard their rights and to foster conditions in which staff of the region can work harmoniously and effectively, while helping the Organization in attaining the aims set out in its constitution; ensure that the terms and conditions of service of all staff accord with the principles established in the constitution of WHO and in the staff regulations and rules and other provisions applicable to staff, providing always that such principles and provisions are not deemed to conflict with the rights, interests and welfare of staff. **Structure** General Assembly (annual); Executive Committee. **Members** in Member States of the WHO European Region (53). Membership countries not specified. **NGO Relations** Member of (1): *Federation of International Civil Servants' Associations (FICSA, #09603)*. [2021.08.31/XE2273/v/E]

♦ Staff Association of the World Intellectual Property Organization (WIPO Staff Association) 19942

Association du personnel de l'Organisation mondiale de la propriété intellectuelle (Association du personnel de L'OMPI)

Contact Office of the Secretariat, NC 0 102, 1211 Geneva 20, Switzerland. T. +41223389532. Fax +41223388865.

History Founded 3 Dec 1958, Geneva (Switzerland), following removal from Bern (Switzerland) to Geneva of the then *'United International Bureaux for the Protection of Intellectual Property – Bureaux internationaux réunis pour la protection de la propriété intellectuelle (BIRPI)'*, currently *World Intellectual Property Organization (WIPO, #21593)*, when it was intended to integrate the organization into the United Nations "common system". Current statutes adopted, 23 May 2006. **Aims** Safeguard collective and individual rights and interests of all staff, whether in service or retired; maintain and enhance unity within the staff as a body of international civil servants; ensure staff working conditions are satisfactory and remain in conformity with the principles set forth in Staff Regulations and Staff Rules of WIPO and any other applicable provisions; improve the professional condition of members and afford assistance to those in difficulty; organize cultural, recreational and sporting activities for the staff. **Structure** General Assembly (annual); Staff Council; Executive Committee; subsidiary bodies. **Languages** English, French. **Staff** 643.00 FTE, paid. **Finance** Members' contributions; gifts; WIPO Staff Association Emergency Fund. **Members** Staff of WIPO and UPOV (710). **NGO Relations** *Federation of International Civil Servants' Associations (FICSA, #09603)*. [2015.12.30/XE0445/v/E]

♦ Staff Council of the African Development Bank 19943

Conseil du Personnel de la Banque africaine de développement

Contact c/o AfDB, Avenue Joseph Anoma, 01 BP 1387, Abidjan 01, Côte d'Ivoire. T. +22520263900. E-mail: staffcouncil@afdb.org.
Contact c/o AfDB, Immeuble CCIA Abidjan Plateau, Ave Jean-Paul II, 01 BP 1387, Abidjan 01, Côte d'Ivoire. T. +22520262126.
URL: http://www.afdb.org/

History 1989, Abidjan (Côte d'Ivoire). Founded to represent staff members of *African Development Bank (ADB, #00283)*. Former names and other names: *Staff Association of the African Development Bank* – former. **Aims** Safeguard the rights, promote and defend the legitimate interests and aspirations of all staff; improve cooperation and morale within the Bank; promote healthy relations between Staff and Management. **Structure** General Assembly; Staff Council Bureau; Country Offices. **Languages** English, French. **Staff** 2046.00 FTE, paid. **Finance** Staff contributions; administrative budget. **Activities** Conflict resolution; events/meetings; guidance/assistance/consulting. **Publications** Staff Communique, Internal Staff Council Website. **Members** All staff members of the African Development Bank Group are eligible. **NGO Relations** Cooperates with (5): *Asian Development Bank Staff Association and Staff Council (#01424)*; Caribbean Development Bank Staff Association; European Bank for Reconstruction and Development staff council; European Investment Bank Staff Association; International Monetary Fund Staff Association. [2020.06.24/XE1627/v/E]

♦ **Staff Council** UNDP/UNFPA/UNOPS/UN Women Staff Association (#20291)
♦ **Staff Union-ESCWA** Staff Union of the United Nations Economic and Social Commission for Western Asia (#19946)

♦ Staff Union of the European Patent Office (SUEPO) 19944

Union syndicale de l'Office européen des brevets (USOEB) – Internationale Gewerkschaft im Europäischen Patentamt (IGEPA)

Administrator Veraartlaan 8, 2288 GM Rijswijk, Netherlands. T. +31704129391. Fax +491636937474. E-mail: central@suepo.org – hague@suepo.org – munich@suepo.org.
URL: https://suepo.org/

History 1979. Founded as the staff union within *European Patent Office (EPO, #08166)*; the successor body to *Syndicat du personnel de l'Institut international des brevets (SPIIB)*, which represented staff of *International Patent Institute (IIB, inactive)*. **Aims** Represent the interests of EPO staff in general and those of members in particular. **Structure** Local Unions (4) in: Berlin (Germany), Munich (Germany), The Hague (Netherlands) and Vienna (Austria). Central Chairmanship rotates among the 4 towns. Central Committee, consisting of Chairman (*Rotating presidency/Rotierende Präsidentschaft/Présidence rotative*), 3 Deputy Chairmen, Treasurer, Secretary and Deputy Members. Executive Committees (4), located in the 4 above-mentioned towns, each composed of President, Vice-President, Treasurer, Secretary and members. **Languages** English, French, German. **Finance** Self-financing. **Publications** *Bulletin IGEPA – SUEPO – USOEB*; *Tribune*.
Members Staff members recruited in 38 States:
Albania, Austria, Belgium, Bulgaria, Croatia, Cyprus, Czechia, Denmark, Estonia, Finland, France, Germany, Greece, Hungary, Iceland, Ireland, Italy, Latvia, Liechtenstein, Lithuania, Luxembourg, Malta, Monaco, Netherlands, North Macedonia, Norway, Poland, Portugal, Romania, San Marino, Serbia, Slovakia, Slovenia, Spain, Sweden, Switzerland, Türkiye, UK.
NGO Relations Consultative status with: *European Federation of Public Service Unions (EPSU, #07202)*; *Federation of International Civil Servants' Associations (FICSA, #09603)*; *Union Syndicale Fédérale (USF, #20485)*. [2022.05.04/XE0209/v/E]

♦ Staff Union of the International Labour Office 19945

Syndicat du personnel de l'Organisation internationale du travail – Sindicato del Personal de la Oficina Internacional del Trabajo

Address not obtained.
URL: http://www.ilostaffunion.org/

History to represent staff members of *ILO (#11123)*. Also referred to as *ILO Staff Union – Syndicat du personnel de l'OIT – Sindicato del Personal de la OIT*. **Publications** *Union* (4 a year); *Staff Union Bulletin* (irregular).
Members Persons employed by the International Labour Office (ILO), based in Geneva (Switzerland) and field offices. Members in 47 countries:
Algeria, Argentina, Bangladesh, Belgium, Brazil, Cambodia, Cameroon, Chile, China, Congo Brazzaville, Congo DR, Costa Rica, Côte d'Ivoire, Egypt, Ethiopia, Fiji, France, Germany, Hungary, India, Indonesia, Italy, Japan, Kuwait, Lebanon, Madagascar, Mexico, Myanmar, Nepal, Nigeria, Pakistan, Peru, Philippines, Russia, Senegal, South Africa, Sri Lanka, Tanzania UR, Thailand, Trinidad-Tobago, Türkiye, UK, Uruguay, USA, Vietnam, Zambia, Zimbabwe.
NGO Relations Member of: *Coordinating Committee for International Staff Unions and Associations of the United Nations System (CCISUA, #04818)*. [2019/XE1946/v/E]

♦ Staff Union of the International Training Centre of the ILO (internationally oriented national body)

♦ Staff Union of the United Nations Economic and Social Commission for Western Asia (Staff Union-ESCWA) 19946

Chairperson c/o ESCWA, PO Box 11-8575, Riad El-Solh 1107 2812, Beirut, Lebanon. T. +9611978554 – +9611978000. Fax +9611981517. E-mail: council1@un.org.
URL: http://www.ccisua.org/

History Founded 1975, when 1st Staff Council was elected. Set up by: *United Nations Economic and Social Commission for Western Asia (ESCWA, #20558)*. **Aims** Represent staff members of ESCWA. **Structure** General Meeting (annual); Referendum. Staff Council of 6 members. **Finance** Members' dues. **Activities** Guidance/assistance/consulting. **Members** Staff members of ESCWA. **NGO Relations** Member of: *Coordinating Committee for International Staff Unions and Associations of the United Nations System (CCISUA, #04818)*. Cooperates with: *ECLAC Staff Association (#05285)*; *ESCAP Staff Council (no recent information)*; *UNECA Staff Union (#20293)*. [2015.08.17/XE0227/v/E]

♦ Staff Union of the UN Office at Vienna / see United Nations Staff Union, Vienna (#20631)
♦ **STAF** Scandinavian Technical Analysts Federation (#19123)
♦ STAF – Software Technologies: Applications and Foundations (meeting series)
♦ Stages européens en alternance dans les métiers (no recent information)
♦ STAI – Supersonic Tunnel Association, International (internationally oriented national body)
♦ Stakeholder Forum for Our Common Future / see Stakeholder Forum for a Sustainable Future
♦ Stakeholder Forum for a Sustainable Future (internationally oriented national body)
♦ **STALYC** Sociedad de Trasplante de América Latina y el Caribe (#19437)
♦ STAMDA – International Society for the Theory and Application of Multi-Objective Decision Analysis (inactive)
♦ Stamford International University (internationally oriented national body)
♦ Stamp Out Poverty (internationally oriented national body)
♦ Stamps for Evangelism (internationally oriented national body)
♦ Standardization and Metrology Organization for Gulf Cooperation Council Countries (no recent information)
♦ Standardized Electronic Commerce Forum for Companies with Interests in Computing, Electronics and Telecommunication / see Global Network for B2B Integration in High Tech Industries (#10481)
♦ Standards Engineering Society / see Society for Standards Professionals

♦ The Standards and Metrology Institute for Islamic Countries (SMIIC) 19947

Contact Istanbul Dünya Ticaret Merkezi A1, Blok No 437-438 K-14 Yesilköy, Bakirköy, 34149 Istanbul/Istanbul, Türkiye. T. +902124656507 – +902124656508. Fax +902124656509. E-mail: secretariat@smiic.org – info@smiic.org.
URL: http://www.smiic.org/

History Proposed 1984, at first Meeting of *Standing Committee for Economic and Commercial Cooperation (COMCEC, #19952)* of *Organisation of Islamic Cooperation (OIC, #17813)*. Standardization Experts Group for Islamic States (SEG) et up 1985. SMIIC Statutes approved at 14th COMCEC Meeting, 1998. Statutes submitted for signature, Jul 1999, Istanbul (Turkey), at 15th COMCEC Meeting. Statutes entered into force May 2010. Institute established Aug 2010, as an affiliate organ of OIC. **Aims** Develop harmonized standards and other relevant specific standards through voluntary standardization process to expedite exchange of goods and services among member bodies/states. **Structure** General Assembly; Board of Directors; General Secretariat. Councils (3): Standardization Management; Metrology; Accreditation. **Languages** Arabic, English, French. **Activities** Events/meetings; standards/guidelines; training/education. **Events** *General Assembly* Medina (Saudi Arabia) 2020, *General Assembly* Makkah (Saudi Arabia) 2019, *General Assembly* Makkah (Saudi Arabia) 2018.
Members States (35):
Afghanistan, Algeria, Azerbaijan, Benin, Burkina Faso, Cameroon, Côte d'Ivoire, Djibouti, Egypt, Gabon, Gambia, Guinea, Iran Islamic Rep, Iraq, Jordan, Kyrgyzstan, Lebanon, Libya, Malaysia, Mali, Mauritania, Morocco, Niger, Pakistan, Palestine, Qatar, Saudi Arabia, Senegal, Somalia, Sudan, Suriname, Tunisia, Türkiye, Uganda, United Arab Emirates.
Observers (3):
Bosnia-Herzegovina, Northern Cyprus, Thailand.
IGO Relations Partner of (5): *African Organisation for Standardisation (ARSO, #00404)*; *Arab Industrial Development, Standardization and Mining Organization (AIDSMO, #00981)*; *GCC Standardization Organization (GSO, #10084)*; *International Islamic Fiqh Academy (IIFA, #13960)*; *International Trade Centre (ITC, #15703)*. [2021.04.16/XM6810/E*]

♦ Standards and Trade Development Facility (STDF) 19948

Fonds pour l'application des normes et le développement du commerce – Fondo para la Aplicación de Normas y el Fomento del Comercio

Secretariat World Trade Org, Ctr William Rappard, Rue de Lausanne 154, 1211 Geneva, Switzerland. T. +41227395295. Fax +41227395760. E-mail: stdfsecretariat@wto.org.
URL: http://www.standardsfacility.org/

History Aug 2002, by *FAO (#09260)*, *OIE – World Organisation for Animal Health (#17703)*, *International Bank for Reconstruction and Development (IBRD, #12317)*, *WHO (#20950)* and *World Trade Organization (WTO, #21864)*. First Business Plan adopted Sep 2004. **Aims** Support developing countries in building their capacity to implement international sanitary and phytosanitary (SPS) standards, guidelines and recommendations as a means to improve their human, animal and plant health status and ability to gain or maintain access to markets. **Structure** Policy Committee, consisting of high-level representatives. Working Group, consisting of technical-level representatives. Secretariat. **Finance** Voluntary contributions to Trust Fund.

Members Partners (5):
FAO (#09260); International Bank for Reconstruction and Development (IBRD, #12317) (World Bank); *OIE – World Organisation for Animal Health (#17703); WHO (#20950); World Trade Organization (WTO, #21864).*
Observers (3):
International Trade Centre (ITC, #15703); UNCTAD (#20285); UNIDO (#20336).
IGO Relations *Interafrican Bureau for Animal Resources (AU-IBAR, #11382).* [2020/XJ6591/ty/**E***]

- ♦ Stand Up for Europe (internationally oriented national body)
- ♦ Ständige Europäische Konferenz für Straffälligen- und Bewährungshilfe / see Confederation of European Probation (#04530)
- ♦ Ständige Konferenz der Europäischen Emaillewarenindustrie (inactive)
- ♦ Ständige Konferenz der Industrie- und Handelskammern der EWG / see Association des chambres de commerce et d'industrie européennes (#02423)
- ♦ Ständiger Arbeitsausschuss für die Tagungen der Nobelpreisträger in Lindau / see Council for the Lindau Nobel Laureate Meetings (#04909)
- ♦ Ständiger Ausschuss der Ärzte der EWG / see Standing Committee of European Doctors (#19955)
- ♦ Ständiger Ausschuss der Glas-Industrien in Europa / see Glass Alliance Europe (#10156)
- ♦ Ständiger Ausschuss der Glas-Industrien in der EWG / see Glass Alliance Europe (#10156)
- ♦ Ständiger Ausschuss der Internationalen Konferenz für Soziale Arbeit / see International Council on Social Welfare (#13076)
- ♦ Ständiger Ausschuss der Internationalen Tierärztlichen Kongresse (inactive)
- ♦ Ständiger Ausschuss der Krankenhäuser der Europäischen Union / see European Hospital and Healthcare Federation (#07501)
- ♦ Ständiger Internationaler Ausschuss für Acetylen, Autogen-Schweisstechnick und Verwandte Industriezweige / see European Industrial Gases Association (#07525)
- ♦ Ständiger Rat der Europäischen Übersetzer (inactive)
- ♦ Ständiges Forum der Zivilgesellschaft (#18322)
- ♦ Standing Commission for Afro-Arab Cooperation (no recent information)
- ♦ Standing Commission for International Congresses on the History of Religions (inactive)
- ♦ Standing Commission on World Mission (internationally oriented national body)

♦ Standing Committee to the Bern Convention on the Conservation of European Wildlife and Natural Habitats 19949

Comité permanent de la Convention de Berne relative à la conservation de la vie sauvage et du milieu naturel de l'Europe

Contact Biodiversity Unit, DG Democracy, Council of Europe, 67075 Strasbourg CEDEX, France. E-mail: bern.convention@coe.int.
URL: http://www.coe.int/bernconvention/

History Established 1 Jun 1982, Strasbourg (France), under the auspices of *Council of Europe (CE, #04881)*, on coming into force of *Convention on the Conservation of European Wildlife and Natural Habitats (Bern convention, 1979)*, which had been adopted 19 Sep 1979. Previously also referred to as *Standing Committee to the Bern Convention on the Conservation of European Wildlife and Natural Habitats.* **Aims** Act as a responsible body for the convention, which aims to: conserve *wild flora* and *fauna* and their *natural habitats*, especially those species and habitats whose conservation requires cooperation of several states; promote such cooperation; give particular emphasis to *endangered* and *vulnerable species*, including endangered and vulnerable *migratory* species. **Structure** Standing Committee (meets annually, usually in November or December, at Council of Europe's Headquarters in Strasbourg (France)) is governing body of Bern Convention; Bureau (meets twice a year, generally in the first and third quarters of each year) of 5 members; Groups of Experts; Secretariat. **Languages** English, French. **Staff** 4.00 FTE, paid. **Finance** Council of Europe Ordinary Budget and voluntary contributions from Contracting Parties. **Events** *Meeting* Berlin (Germany) 2007, *Meeting* Reykjavik (Iceland) 2007, *Meeting* Strasbourg (France) 2007, *Meeting* Strasbourg (France) 2006, *Meeting* Strasbourg (France) 2005. **Publications** *Environmental Encounters* – series; *Nature and Environment* – series; *Questions and Answers* – series. Brochures; conference proceedings; information documents. All publications in English/French.
Members Contracting States (51):
Albania, Andorra, Armenia, Austria, Azerbaijan, Belarus, Belgium, Bosnia-Herzegovina, Bulgaria, Burkina Faso, Croatia, Cyprus, Czechia, Denmark, Estonia, Finland, France, Georgia, Germany, Greece, Hungary, Iceland, Ireland, Italy, Latvia, Liechtenstein, Lithuania, Luxembourg, Malta, Moldova, Monaco, Montenegro, Morocco, Netherlands, North Macedonia, Norway, Poland, Portugal, Romania, Senegal, Serbia, Slovakia, Slovenia, Spain, Sweden, Switzerland, Tunisia, Türkiye, UK, Ukraine.
Included in the above, one regional organization:
European Union (EU, #08967).
Observer states (5):
Algeria, Holy See, Jordan, Russia, San Marino.
National and international organization observers including the following 51 organizations listed in this Yearbook:
- *Agreement on the Conservation of Cetaceans of the Black Sea, Mediterranean Sea and contiguous Atlantic Area (ACCOBAMS, 1996)* (Secretariat of);
- *Agreement on the Conservation of Populations of European Bats (EUROBATS, 1991)* (Secretariat of);
- *Agreement on the Conservation of Small Cetaceans of the Baltic, North East Atlantic, Irish and North Seas (ASCOBANS, 1992)* (Secretariat of);
- *Arab League Educational, Cultural and Scientific Organization (ALECSO, #01003);*
- *BirdLife International (#03266);*
- *CEEweb for Biodiversity (#03626);*
- *Committee Against Bird Slaughter (CABS);*
- *Conservation International (CI)* (Europe);
- *Convention for the Protection of the Marine Environment and the Coastal Region of the Mediterranean (Barcelona Convention, 1976)* (Secretariat of);
- *Convention on Biological Diversity (Biodiversity convention, 1992)* (Secretariat of);
- *Convention on Environmental Impact Assessment in a Transboundary Context (Espoo Convention, 1991)* (Secretariat of);
- *Convention on the Protection of the Black Sea Against Pollution (Bucharest convention, 1992)* (Secretariat of);
- *ECNC – European Centre for Nature Conservation (#05289);*
- *Eurogroup for Animals (#05690);*
- *EUROPARC Federation (#05768);*
- *European and Mediterranean Plant Protection Organization (EPPO, #07773);*
- *European Anglers Alliance (EAA, #05900);*
- *European Association of Zoos and Aquaria (EAZA, #06283);*
- *European Council for the Conservation of Fungi (ECCF, #06811);*
- *European Environment Agency (EEA, #06995);*
- *European Foundation Il Nibbio (FEIN);*
- *European Habitats Forum (EHF, #07443);*
- *European Herpetological Society (#07481);*
- *European Science Foundation (ESF, #08441);*
- *European Squirrel Initiative (ESI);*
- *Federation of Associations for Hunting and Conservation of the EU (#09459);*
- *Humane Society International (HSI, #10966);*
- *Infrastructure Ecology Network Europe (IENE, #11207);*
- *International Association for Falconry and Conservation of Birds of Prey (IAF, #11888);*
- *International Council for Game and Wildlife Conservation (#13024);*
- *International Fund for Animal Welfare (IFAW, #13693);*
- *International Plant Protection Convention, 1951 (IPPC, 1951)* (Secretariat of);
- *International Union for Conservation of Nature and Natural Resources (IUCN, #15766);*
- *Large Carnivore Initiative for Europe (LCIE, #16232);*
- *Mediterranean Association to Save the Sea Turtles (MEDASSET, #16647);*
- *Mediterranean NGO Network for Ecology and Sustainable Development (MED Forum, no recent information);*
- *Oceana;*
- *OECD (#17693);*
- *Oiseaux migrateurs du paléarctique occidental (OMPO, #17712);*
- *Permanent Secretariat to the Agreement on the Conservation of African-Eurasian Migratory Waterbirds (#18330);*
- *Plantlife International;*
- *Protocol Concerning Mediterranean Specially Protected Areas (1982)* (Secretariat of);
- *Sea Shepherd International;*
- *Secretariat of the Convention of Wetlands (#19200);*
- *Secretariat of the Convention on International Trade in Endangered Species of Wild Fauna and Flora (CITES Secretariat, #19199);*
- *Secretariat of the Convention on the Conservation of Migratory Species of Wild Animals (UNEP/CMS, #19198);*
- *UN Environment Programme World Conservation Monitoring Centre (UNEP-WCMC, #20295);*
- *UNEP (#20299);*
- *UNESCO (#20322);*
- *United Nations Economic Commission for Europe (UNECE, #20555);*
- *World Wide Fund for Nature (WWF, #21922).*

IGO Relations Memorandum of Understanding with: European Environment Agency; *Secretariat of the Convention on Biological Diversity (SCBD, #19197); Secretariat of the Convention on the Conservation of Migratory Species of Wild Animals (UNEP/CMS, #19198).* Set up: *Emerald Network (see: #19949).* **NGO Relations** Memorandum of Understanding with: *International Union for Conservation of Nature and Natural Resources (IUCN, #15766).* [2020.03.04/XE3253/y/**E***]

- ♦ Standing Committee for the Bibliographic Directory of Mathematical Sciences (inactive)
- ♦ Standing Committee of the British Commonwealth Scientific Official Conference / see Commonwealth Science Council (#04361)

♦ Standing Committee of Caribbean Statisticians (SCCS) 19950

Comité permanent des statisticiens des Caraïbes

Contact CARICOM, PO Box 10827, Georgetown, Guyana. T. +592222000175. Fax +5922220098. E-mail: stats1@caricom.org.
URL: http://www.caricomstats.org/

History Established 1974, in accordance with Resolution No 54/74/4 of 4th Meeting of Council of Ministers of *Caribbean Community (CARICOM, #03476).* **Aims** Foster increased recognition of the importance of adequate statistical services to the countries of the region; widen scope and coverage of statistical data collection; improve the quality, comparability and timeliness of statistics produced. **Activities** Meetings held annually. **Events** *Meeting* Barbados 2015, *Meeting* Providence (Guyana) 2014, *Meeting* Frigate Bay (St Kitts-Nevis) 2013, *Meeting* St George's (Grenada) 2012, *Meeting* Belize City (Belize) 2011.
Members Governments of the 13 CARICOM countries and territories:
Antigua-Barbuda, Bahamas, Barbados, Belize, Dominica, Grenada, Guyana, Jamaica, Montserrat, St Kitts-Nevis, St Lucia, St Vincent-Grenadines, Trinidad-Tobago.
Associate members (4):
Bermuda, Cayman Is, Turks-Caicos, Virgin Is UK.
Observer status (1):
Neth Antilles. [2016/XD3271/**E***]

♦ Standing Committee on Commonwealth Forestry 19951

Secretariat Commonwealth Forestry Association, The Crib, Dinchope, Craven Arms, SY7 9JJ, UK. T. +441588672868. E-mail: cfa@cfa-international.org.
URL: http://www.cfa-international.org/sccf.php

History 1923, Canada. Established at 2nd *Empire Forestry Conference*, now *Commonwealth Forestry Conference*, following the setting up, 1920, London (UK), at 1st Conference, of a standing committee to coordinate activities between conferences. **Aims** Take appropriate follow-up action on Commonwealth Forestry Conference recommendations; provide continuity between Conferences; provide a forum for discussion on forestry matters of common interest to member Governments, which may be brought to Committee's notice by any member country or organization. **Structure** Director General of Forestry Commission of Great Britain (Chairman); one representative from *Commonwealth Secretariat (#04362)* and from each independent Commonwealth Government; one representative each from *Commonwealth Forestry Association (CFA, #04329)*, the Department for International Development; plus the Conference Organizers. **Finance** Money raised for Conference from donors. **Events** *Commonwealth Forestry Conference* Vancouver, BC (Canada) 2022, *Commonwealth Forestry Conference* 2021, *Commonwealth Forestry Conference* Dehradun (India) 2017, *Commonwealth forestry conference* Edinburgh (UK) 2010, *Commonwealth forestry conference* Colombo (Sri Lanka) 2005.
Members All 53 Commonwealth countries:
Antigua-Barbuda, Australia, Bahamas, Bangladesh, Barbados, Belize, Botswana, Brunei Darussalam, Cameroon, Canada, Cyprus, Dominica, Eswatini, Fiji, Ghana, Grenada, Guyana, India, Jamaica, Kenya, Kiribati, Lesotho, Malawi, Malaysia, Maldives, Malta, Mauritius, Mozambique, Namibia, Nauru, New Zealand, Nigeria, Pakistan, Papua New Guinea, Samoa, Seychelles, Sierra Leone, Singapore, Solomon Is, South Africa, Sri Lanka, St Kitts-Nevis, St Lucia, St Vincent-Grenadines, Tanzania UR, Tonga, Trinidad-Tobago, Tuvalu, Uganda, UK, Vanuatu, Zambia, Zimbabwe. [2022.10.11/XF3286/**E***]

- ♦ Standing Committee of Congresses on Low-Cost Housing (inactive)
- ♦ Standing Committee for Cooperation with National Social Science Councils and Analogous Bodies / see International Federation of Social Science Organizations (#13543)
- ♦ Standing Committee of EC Doctors / see Standing Committee of European Doctors (#19955)

♦ Standing Committee for Economic and Commercial Cooperation (COMCEC) 19952

Comité permanent pour la coopération économique et commerciale entre les Etats membres de l'OCI

Cooordination Office Necatibey Cad 108, Ankara/Ankara, Türkiye. T. +903122945718. Fax +903122945777. E-mail: comcec@comcec.org.
Contact c/o OIC, PO Box 178, Jeddah 21411, Saudi Arabia.
URL: http://www.comcec.org/

History Jan 1981, Makkah, as a specialized committee of *Organisation of Islamic Cooperation (OIC, #17813)*, in accordance with the resolution adopted by 3rd *Islamic Summit of Kings and Heads of States and Governments (#16053).* Commenced operations, Jan 1984, following 4th Summit. Full title: *Standing Committee for Economic and Commercial Cooperation of the Organization of the Islamic Conference – Comité permanent pour la coopération économique et commerciale de l'Organisation de la conférence islamique.* **Aims** Follow up implementation of resolutions adopted by OIC in the economic and commercial fields; examine means of strengthening cooperation among *Islamic* States; put forward programmes and proposals likely to improve the capabilities of Islamic States in those sectors. **Activities** Organizes Annual Session, always in Istanbul (Turkey). **Events** *Annual session* Istanbul (Turkey) 2019, *Annual session* Istanbul (Turkey) 2011, *Annual Session* Istanbul (Turkey) 2010, *Annual Session* Izmir (Turkey) 2009, *Annual Session* Antalya (Turkey) 2008. **Members** Representatives of all OIC Member States. **IGO Relations** Links with all subsidiary, specialized and affiliated bodies of OIC. [2021/XE1033/**E***]

- ♦ Standing Committee for Economic and Commercial Cooperation of the Organization of the Islamic Conference / see Standing Committee for Economic and Commercial Cooperation (#19952)

♦ Standing Committee of the EFTA States 19953

Comité permanent de l'AELE

Contact EFTA Brussels Secretariat, Rue Joseph II 12-16, 1000 Brussels, Belgium. T. +3222861711. Fax +3222861750. E-mail: mail.bxl@efta.int.
URL: http://secretariat.efta.int/

History 1994, by *EFTA (#05391)* in the context of the *European Economic Area (EEA, #06957).* **Aims** Manage the EFTA side of the EEA Agreement; act as a forum for coordinating the positions of EFTA/EEA States on all EEA-related matters. **Structure** Normally meets in Brussels (Belgium) and comprises government representatives of EFTA countries (one vote per country) who also represent their countries within the *EEA Joint Committee (#05381).* May also meet at ministerial level. Switzerland has observer status, which also can be issued to the *EFTA Surveillance Authority (ESA, #05392).* Consultative bodies: the *Committee of Members of Parliament of the EFTA States Party to the EEA (EFTA MPS, #04270)*; EFTA Consultative Committee (CC). Subcommittees (5); Working Groups. Secretariat provided by EFTA Secretariat in Brussels. **Activities** Main task is to ensure the good functioning of the EEA Agreement. Prepares elaboration of decisions taken by EEA Council and EEA Joint Committee. Transmits information between EFTA States and the European Commission and vice versa. Subcommittees: I. Free Movement of Goods; II. Free Movement of Capital and Services and Company Law; III. Free Movement of Persons; IV. Flanking and Horizontal Policies; V. Legal and Institutional Matters. Current concerns include possible implications for EEA and EFTA of the *Treaty of Amsterdam (1997).*
IGO Relations *European Commission (EC, #06633).* [2015.09.24/XE3022/**E***]

♦ Standing Committee for Esperanto Congresses (inactive)

♦ Standing Committee Euro-Mediterranean Partnership of the Local and Regional Authorities 19954

Comité permanent pour le partenariat euroméditerranéen des pouvoirs locaux et régionaux – Comitato Permanente per il Partenariato Euromediterraneo dei Poteri Locali e Regionali (COPPEM)

Gen Sec Via Emerico Amari 162, 90139 Palermo PA, Italy. T. +39916622238. Fax +39916622304. E-mail: i.puccio@coppem.org – coppem@coppem.org.
Press Office address not obtained.
URL: http://www.coppem.org/

History 27 Nov 2000, Palermo (Italy). Founded upon initiative of *Council of European Municipalities and Regions (CEMR, #04891)* and *Arab Towns Organization (ATO, #01059)*, following the initial setting up of a regulation agreed upon, Jul 2000, at Gaza (West Bank-Gaza), by representatives of Local Administrations. Formally set up, Dec 2002, during 3rd Plenary Assembly. **Aims** Promote both dialogue and cooperation for local development between towns, municipalities, local authorities, and regions of the member countries, and their active and concrete participation in achieving the objectives established within the Barcelona Declaration in 1995. **Structure** General Assembly, composed of 120 members, of which: 117 are Accredited Members (each with an alternate) appointed in their personal capacity by their national associations (for the EU they are CERM sections); 3 Full Members, including COPPEM Secretary General, a representative of CEMR, and a representative of ATO. Distribution of both Accredited and Alternate members representing global and regional authorities from the 27 signatory states of the Barcelona Declaration of 1995, and regional and local authorities from countries members of the Union for the Mediterranean. General Assembly Elective Members must hold an elective term of office at local, provincial or regional level, or they shall have responsibility in the framework of local or regional authorities, or they must be members of an association of local or regional authorities. Presidency Council (2-year terms, renewable); Standing Commissions; Working Commissions (5) on: institutional cooperation; migration; economic development; cultural and environment cooperation; cooperation for fostering human rights and gender equality. **Languages** English, French, Italian, Spanish. **Staff** 13.00 FTE, paid. **Finance** Mainly funded by Sicilian Region. Other funds can be provided by the European Commission and/or other donors for implementation of specific projects submitted in the framework of thematic calls for proposals. Annual budget: 500,000 EUR. **Activities** Networking/liaising; projects/programmes; research and development. **Events** *International Conference on Immigration and Cooperation* Palermo (Italy) 2015, *General Assembly* Palermo (Italy) 2014, *General Assembly* Palermo (Italy) 2013, *General Assembly* Palermo (Italy) 2012, *General Assembly* Palermo (Italy) 2011. **Publications** *COPPEM News*.

Members Full (117); Alternate (117). Representatives of local authorities in European and Mediterranean countries. Delegations of regional and local authorities from countries members of the Union for the Mediterranean in 43 countries (number of seats):
Albania (2), Algeria (5), Austria (2), Belgium (2), Bosnia-Herzegovina (2), Bulgaria (2), Croatia (3), Cyprus (1), Czechia (2), Denmark (2), Egypt (6), Estonia (1), Finland (2), France (5), Germany (6), Greece (2), Hungary (2), Ireland (2), Israel (2), Italy (6), Jordan (2), Latvia (1), Lebanon (2), Lithuania (1), Luxembourg (1), Malta (1), Mauritania (2), Monaco (1), Montenegro (1), Morocco (5), Netherlands (2), Palestine (2), Poland (5), Portugal (2), Romania (2), Slovakia (2), Slovenia (1), Spain (5), Sweden (2), Syrian AR (4), Tunisia (2), Türkiye (6), UK (6).

IGO Relations Observer status with (1): *Congress of Local and Regional Authorities of the Council of Europe (#04677)*. **NGO Relations** Member of (1): *Association for the Documentation, Preservation and Enhancement of the Euro-Mediterranean Cultural Heritage (HERIMED, no recent information)*. [2021/XM2970/D]

♦ Standing Committee of European Doctors 19955

Comité permanent des médecins européens (CPME)

SG Rue Guimard 15, 1040 Brussels, Belgium. T. +3227327202. Fax +3227327344. E-mail: secretariat@cpme.eu.
URL: http://www.cpme.eu/

History 1959, Amsterdam (Netherlands). Founded by the original 6 National Medical Associations (NMAs) of the member states of the European Economic Community, namely France, Germany, Italy, Luxembourg, Netherlands and Belgium, and which were also members of the World Medical Association. Original title: *Standing Committee of EC Doctors – Comité permanent des médecins de la CE – Comité Permanente de Médicos de la CE – Ständiger Ausschuss der Ärzte der EWG – Comité Permanente dos Médicos da CE – Comitato Permanente dei Medici della CE – Permanent Comité der Artsen in de EG – Stående Udvalg for Laegerne i EF – Monimis Epitropi Iatron tis EK*. Present name adopted 1994. Registration: Banque-Carrefour des Entreprises, No/ID: 0462.509.658, Start date: 12 Feb 1998, Belgium; EU Transparency Register, No/ID: 9276943405-41, Start date: 18 Sep 2008. **Aims** Represent national medical associations across Europe; contribute the medical profession's point of view to EU institutions and European policy-making through pro-active cooperation on a wide range of health and healthcare related issues. **Structure** General Assembly; Board; Executive Committee; Secretariat. **Languages** English. **Staff** 7.00 FTE, paid. **Finance** Members' dues. EU funding projects. **Activities** Politics/policy/regulatory; projects/programmes; events/meetings. **Events** *General Assembly* Brussels (Belgium) 2021, *Joint Conference* Berlin (Germany) 2020, *Meeting* Budapest (Hungary) 2014, *General Assembly* Cyprus 2012, *Meeting* Cyprus 2012. **Publications** *CPME Newsletter*. *Summary Policy Statement 1959-2000* (3rd ed). Policies; position papers; press releases.

Members National medical associations in 29 countries:
Austria, Belgium, Bulgaria, Croatia, Cyprus, Czechia, Denmark, Estonia, Finland, France, Germany, Greece, Hungary, Iceland, Ireland, Latvia, Lithuania, Luxembourg, Malta, Netherlands, Norway, Poland, Portugal, Romania, Slovakia, Slovenia, Sweden, Switzerland, UK.
Associated Members (2) in 2 countries:
Andorra, Türkiye.
Observer in 4 countries:
Albania, Georgia, Israel, Serbia.
International associated organizations (11):
Association européenne des médecins des hôpitaux (AEMH, #02577); *EANA – European Working Group of Physicians in Private Practice (#05154)*; *European Council of Medical Orders (ECMO, #06830)*; *European Federation of Salaried Doctors (#07209)*; *European Junior Doctors Association (EJD, #07620)*; *European Medical Students' Association (EMSA, #07764)*; *European Union of General Practitioners / Family Physicians (#08993)*; *European Union of Insurance and Social Security Medicine (EUMASS, #08995)*; *European Union of Medical Specialists (UEMS, #09001)*; *International Federation of Medical Students' Associations (IFMSA, #13478)*; *World Medical Association (WMA, #21646)*.

Consultative Status Consultative status granted from: *Council of Europe (CE, #04881)* (Participatory Status). **IGO Relations** Recognized by: *European Commission (EC, #06633)*. Member of: *European Economic and Social Committee (EESC, #06963)* Liaison Group. **NGO Relations** Member of: *Centre for European Policy Studies (CEPS, #03741)*; *EU Platform for Action on Diet, Physical Activity and Health (inactive)*; *International Society of Mediterranean Ecology (ISOMED, #15259)*. Supports: *European Alliance for the Statute of the European Association (EASEA, #05886)*. Stakeholder in: *European Network for Health Technology Assessment (EUnetHTA, #07921)*. [2020/XE3280/y/E]

♦ Standing Committee of European Glass Industries / see Glass Alliance Europe (#10156)
♦ Standing Committee of European Local Authority Chief Executives / see Union of Local Authority Chief Executives of Europe (#20454)

♦ Standing Committee on the Food Chain and Animal Health 19956

Comité permanent de la chaîne alimentaire et de la santé publique

Address not obtained.
URL: http://ec.europa.eu/food/food/biosafety/index_en.htm

History Founded as *Standing Veterinary Committee of the European Union – Comité vétérinaire permanent de l'Union européenne*, within *European Commission (EC, #06633)*.

Members Senior government veterinarians in 25 countries:
Austria, Belgium, Cyprus, Czechia, Denmark, Estonia, Finland, France, Germany, Greece, Hungary, Ireland, Italy, Latvia, Lithuania, Luxembourg, Malta, Netherlands, Poland, Portugal, Slovakia, Slovenia, Spain, Sweden, UK. [2014/XE2713/E]

♦ Standing Committee of Glass Industries of the EEC / see Glass Alliance Europe (#10156)
♦ Standing Committee of the Hospitals of the European Union / see European Hospital and Healthcare Federation (#07501)
♦ Standing Committee of the ICIAM / see International Council for Industrial and Applied Mathematics (#13032)
♦ Standing Committee for Information and Cultural Affairs (see: #17813)
♦ Standing Committee for International Congresses on Apiculture (inactive)
♦ Standing Committee on the International Congresses of Chambers of Commerce and Industrial Associations (inactive)
♦ Standing Committee of International Congresses of Gynaecology and Obstetrics (inactive)
♦ Standing Committee of the International Congresses for Improving the Welfare of the Deaf and Dumb (inactive)
♦ Standing Committee for International Congresses of Medical Electrology and Radiology (inactive)
♦ Standing Committee for International Congresses of Military Medicine and Pharmacy / see International Committee of Military Medicine (#12785)
♦ Standing Committee for International Congresses of Physiotherapy (inactive)
♦ Standing Committee for the International Embryological Conference (inactive)
♦ Standing Committee for Latin American Zoological Congresses (inactive)
♦ Standing Committee of NGOs / see NGO-UNESCO Liaison Committee (#17127)
♦ Standing Committee for Nobel Prize Winners' Congresses in Lindau / see Council for the Lindau Nobel Laureate Meetings (#04909)
♦ Standing Committee of Nordic Ironmongers (inactive)
♦ Standing Committee of Nurses of the EC / see European Federation of Nurses Associations (#07180)
♦ Standing Committee of Nurses of the EU / see European Federation of Nurses Associations (#07180)

♦ Standing Committee of the Pacific Islands Conference of Leaders 19957

Contact East-West Center, 1601 East-West Rd, Honolulu HI 96848-1601, USA. T. +18089447724. Fax +18089447670. E-mail: ewcinfo@eastwestcenter.org.
URL: http://www.eastwestcenter.org/pacific-islands-development-program/

History 1980, to follow up *Pacific Islands Conference (PIC)*, Heads of Government meeting originally every 5, now every 3 years, involving leaders from throughout the Pacific Islands region. PIC is also referred to as *Pacific Islands Conference of Leaders (PICL)* and the Standing Committee as *Standing Committee of the Pacific Islands Conference of Leaders*. **Aims** Ensure follow-up on development problems discussed at each Pacific Islands Conference. **Structure** Standing Committee; Programme Planning Committee; Pacific Islands Development Programme. Officers: PIDP officers; Chairman of the Conference; Chairman and Vice-Chairman of Standing Committee; Observers: *Pacific Islands Development Program (PIDP, see: #05263)* *East-West Center (EWC, #05263)*, which serves as Secretariat for PIC and for the Standing Committee; *Pacific Community (SPC, #17942)*; *Pacific Islands Forum Fisheries Agency (FFA, #17969)*; *Pacific Islands Forum Secretariat (#17970)*; *Secretariat of the Pacific Regional Environment Programme (SPREP, #19205)*; *Pacific Tourism Organization (SPTO, #18008)*; *University of the South Pacific (USP, #20703)*. **Events** *Pacific Island Conference* Honolulu, HI (USA) 2007, *Pacific Island Conference* Honolulu, HI (USA) 2005, *Pacific Island Conference* Honolulu, HI (USA) 2002, *Pacific Island Conference* Honolulu, HI (USA) 2000, *Pacific Island Conference* Honolulu, HI (USA) 1997.

Members Leaders of 21 Pacific Islands countries and territories:
Cook Is, Fiji, Guam, Hawaii, Kiribati, Marshall Is, Micronesia FS, Nauru, New Caledonia, Niue, Northern Mariana Is, Palau, Papua New Guinea, Polynesia Fr, Samoa, Samoa USA, Solomon Is, Tokelau, Tonga, Tuvalu, Vanuatu. [2017/XE1107/E*]

♦ Standing Committee of Parliamentarians of the Arctic Region (SCPAR) 19958

Chair Christiansborg, Parliament of Denmark, 1240 Copenhagen, Denmark. T. +4561623007.
SG address not obtained.
URL: http://www.arcticparl.org/

History Sep 1994. Established following a decision taken at 1st Parliamentary Conference concerning Arctic cooperation, 1993, Reykjavik (Iceland). **Aims** Promote the work of the Arctic Council; monitor how the 8 States members of the Arctic Council implement the Conference statement; initiate further Arctic cooperation. **Structure** Standing Committee. **Languages** English, Russian. **Activities** Events/meetings. **Events** *Arctic Parliamentarian Summit* Nuuk (Greenland) 2022, *Conference of Arctic Parliamentarians* Oslo (Norway) 2021, *Conference of Parliamentarians of the Arctic Region* Oslo (Norway) 2020, *Meeting* Kiruna (Sweden) 2019, *Meeting* Murmansk (Russia) 2019.

Members Organizations in 8 countries:
Canada, Denmark, Finland, Iceland, Norway, Russia, Sweden, USA.
Regional organization (1):
European Parliament (EP, #08146).

IGO Relations Observer status with (5): *Arctic Council (#01097)*; *Baltic Sea Parliamentary Conference (BSPC, #03146)*; *Barents Euro-Arctic Council (BEAC, #03177)*; *Conservation of Arctic Flora and Fauna (CAFF, #04728)*; *Nordic Council (NC, #17256)*. [2022.10.11/XE3288/y/E*]

♦ Standing Committee on Statistics in Business and Industry / see International Society on Business and Industrial Statistics (#14989)
♦ Standing Committee on Statistics in Industry / see International Society on Business and Industrial Statistics (#14989)
♦ Standing Committee of Trade Unions of the Graphic Industry (inactive)
♦ Standing Conference of African Library Archives and Information Studies Schools (inactive)
♦ Standing Conference of African University Libraries (no recent information)

♦ Standing Conference of the Canonical Orthodox Bishops in the Americas (SCOBA) 19959

SG 10 East 79th St, New York NY 10075, USA. T. +12127740526. Fax +12127740202.
URL: http://www.scoba.us/

History 1960, New York NY (USA). **Aims** Coordinate Orthodox Church activities in the Western hemisphere; promote Orthodox cooperative activities aimed at eventual organic unity of the various Orthodox Churches. **Structure** Officers: Chairman; Vice-Chair; General Secretary; Treasurer; Canonical Advisor. **Activities** Agencies and Commissions (10): Study and Planning Commission; Orthodox Christian Education Commission; International Orthodox Christian Charities; Orthodox Christian Mission Center; Scouting Commission; Ecumenical Commission; Military Chaplaincy Commission; Orthodox Campus Fellowship; Social and Moral Issues Commission; Orthodox Christian Network. **Events** *Semi-annual meeting* 1987, *Semi-annual meeting* 1987. **Publications** *Upbeat* (10 a year); *Young Life* (10 a year); *Concern* (4 a year); *American Orthodox Directory* (annual).

Members Presiding hierarchs of 10 Eastern Orthodox ecclesiastical jurisdictions in America, covering 15 countries and territories:
Argentina, Bahamas, Bermuda, Bolivia, Brazil, Canada, Chile, Colombia, Cuba, Mexico, Panama, Peru, Uruguay, USA, Venezuela.

NGO Relations Supervises: *Orthodox Christian Mission Center (OCMC)*. [2010/XD7606/v/D]

♦ Standing Conference of Delegates of the National Basketball Federations of Europe / see FIBA-Europe (#09747)
♦ Standing Conference of Directors of South Pacific Departments for French Studies (inactive)

♦ Standing Conference of Eastern, Central and Southern African Librarians (SCECSAL) 19960

Secretariat address not obtained. E-mail: constantinebu@yahoo.com.
URL: http://www.scecsal.org/

History as a result of a proposal made at the biennial conference of *East African Library Association (EALA, inactive)*, 1972. SCECSAL subsequently took over the activities of EALA. Regulations revised 1976, Lusaka (Zambia), and adopted 2 Sep 1978, Nairobi (Kenya). **Aims** Organize biennial conferences. 'Objectives': Promote and support development of libraries, i e: libraries, information services and documentation services; forge, maintain and strengthen professional links between librarians in member countries; discuss matters of mutual benefit and interest. **Structure** General Meeting (meets once every 2 years during the Conference). Acting Executive Committee, provided by the Library Association to host the last conference. **Languages** English. **Finance** Hosting Library Association is responsible for financing the conference. **Events** *Biennial Conference* Windhoek (Namibia) 2021, *Biennial Conference* Windhoek (Namibia) 2020, *Biennial Conference* Entebbe (Uganda) 2018, *Biennial Conference* Ezulwini (Swaziland) 2016, *Biennial Conference* Lilongwe (Malawi) 2014. **Publications** Conference proceedings.

Members Library Associations in 23 countries:
Angola, Botswana, Burundi, Central African Rep, Congo DR, Djibouti, Eswatini, Ethiopia, Kenya, Lesotho, Madagascar, Malawi, Mauritius, Mozambique, Namibia, Rwanda, Seychelles, Somalia, Sudan, Tanzania UR, Uganda, Zambia, Zimbabwe.
IGO Relations *Deutsche Stiftung für Internationale Entwicklung (DSE, inactive).* [2010.07.19/XF1408/c/**F**]

- Standing Conference of European Ethics Committees / see European Conference of National Ethics Committees (#06734)
- Standing Conference of European Jewish Community Services / see European Council of Jewish Communities (#06825)

♦ Standing Conference of European Public Service Training Agencies (SCEPSTA) 19961

Chair Verwaltungsakademie, Rotensterngasse 9-11, 1020 Vienna, Austria. T. +431400082273. Fax +43140009982273.
URL: http://www.scepsta.eu/

History 1973. Previously referred to as *Study Group of European Public Service Training Agencies (SGEPSTA).* **Aims** Provide a forum for exchange of experiences, ideas and new information on everything related to training and development of public services in Europe. **Structure** General Assembly (meets at Annual Conference); Executive Committee. **Languages** English. **Staff** None. **Finance** Conference fees. **Activities** Events/meetings; publishing activities; networking/liaising. **Events** *Annual Conference* St Julian's (Malta) 2018, *Annual Conference* Dublin (Ireland) 2017, *Annual Conference* Prague (Czechia) 2016, *Annual Conference* Berlin (Germany) 2015, *Annual Conference* Stockholm (Sweden) 2014. **Publications** *SCEPSTA Newsletter. SCEPSTA Directory.*
Members Institutions (26) in 13 countries:
Austria, Belgium, Czechia, Denmark, Finland, Germany, Latvia, Lithuania, Malta, Poland, Portugal, Sweden, UK.
[2016.10.19/XD7007/**F**]

- Standing Conference on Library Materials on Africa / see SCOLMA – UK Libraries and Archives Group on Africa
- Standing Conference of Local and Regional Authorities of Europe / see Congress of Local and Regional Authorities of the Council of Europe (#04677)
- Standing Conference of National Basketball Federations of Europe / see FIBA-Europe (#09747)

♦ Standing Conference on Organizational Symbolism (SCOS) 19962

Chairperson c/o School for Business and Society, Church Lane Building, Univ of York, Leicester, YO10 5ZF, UK. E-mail: scos@gmail.com.
Sec address not obtained.
URL: http://www.scos.org/

History Mar 1981, Glasgow (UK). Founded as an autonomous working group of *European Group for Organizational Studies (EGOS, #07428).* Currently an independent academic venture. Former names and other names: *Organizational Symbolism* – former. **Aims** Provide an international forum for organizational studies research dealing with symbolism, *culture* and change, articulated in the broadest possible sense and informed by a commitment to *inter-disciplinary* and transdisciplinary understandings of organization and management. **Structure** Executive Board. **Languages** English. **Staff** 12.50 FTE, voluntary. **Finance** Sources: meeting proceeds. **Activities** Events/meetings. **Events** *Annual Conference* Paris (France) 2023, *Annual Conference* Krakow (Poland) 2022, *Symposium* Leicester (UK) 2022, *Annual Conference* Copenhagen (Denmark) 2021, *Annual Conference* Copenhagen (Denmark) 2020. **Publications** *Culture and Organization* (6 a year) – official journal; *Notework* (2 a year) – newsletter. Conference proceedings. **Members** Academic and non-academic scholars (over 900) in over 40 countries. Membership countries not specified. [2022.10.24/XF1091/v/**E**]

- Standing European Road Weather Commission / see Standing International Road Weather Commission (#19965)
- Standing International Committee for Congresses of Archivists and Librarians (inactive)
- Standing International Committee of International Congresses on Administrative Sciences (inactive)
- Standing International Committee for International Congresses of Hygiene and Demography (inactive)
- Standing International Committee on Physical Education (inactive)
- Standing International Committee for the Reproduction of Manuscripts, Medals and Seals (inactive)
- Standing International Conference of Building Centres / see International Union of Building Centres (#15761)
- Standing International Conference of Central and General Inspectorates of Education / see Standing International Conference of Inspectorates (#19963)

♦ Standing International Conference of Inspectorates (SICI) 19963

Conférence internationale permanente des inspections de l'éducation

SG SICI Secretariat, Henrik Consciencegebouw 2B15, Koning Albert II-laan 15, 1210 Brussels, Belgium. T. +3225538802.
URL: http://www.sici-inspectorates.eu/

History Founded 17 Oct 1995, as *Standing International Conference of Central and General Inspectorates of Education (SICI) – Conférence internationale permanente des inspections centrales et générales de l'éducation.* **Aims** Serve as a forum for members for: exchange of experiences; gaining information regarding developments within, or integral development of, education systems; discussion of ways and means to improve inspection; promotion of partnership and cooperation between inspectorates of education. **Structure** Executive Committee. **Languages** English. **Staff** 1.50 FTE, paid. **Finance** Members' dues (annual): euro 3,000. **Activities** Guidance/assistance/consulting; events/meetings; networking/liaising. **Events** *Annual General Assembly* Dresden (Germany) 2014, *Annual General Assembly* Edinburgh (UK) 2013, *Annual General Assembly* Glasgow (UK) 2013, *Annual General Assembly* Prague (Czech Rep) 2012, *Workshop* Stockholm (Sweden) 2011. **Publications** *SICI Review* (annual).
Members Full in 22 countries:
Albania, Austria, Belgium, Bulgaria, Czechia, Denmark, Estonia, France, Germany, Ireland, Lithuania, Malta, Montenegro, Netherlands, Norway, Portugal, Romania, Serbia, Slovakia, Sweden, Türkiye, UK.
IGO Relations Cooperates with: *European Commission (EC, #06633); European Schoolnet (EUN, #08433); OECD (#17693).* **NGO Relations** Cooperates with: *Consortium of Institutions for Development and Research in Education in Europe (CIDREE, #04749).* [2014.06.01/XF7085/**F**]

- Standing International Delegation on Sanitation and Hygiene in Communes (inactive)

♦ Standing International Forum of Commercial Courts (SIFoCC) 19964

Contact 4th Floor, Rolls Bldg, Fetter Lane, London, EC4A 1NL, UK. T. +442071730318.
URL: https://sifocc.org/

History 4 May 2017. **Aims** Promote best practice in commercial dispute resolution and further the Rule of Law. **Structure** Steering Group; Secretariat. **Events** *Meeting* Sydney, NSW (Australia) 2022, *Meeting* Singapore (Singapore) 2021, *Meeting* New York, NY (USA) 2018, *Meeting* London (UK) 2017.
Members Courts in 35 countries and territories:
Abu Dhabi, Australia, Bahrain, Bermuda, Brazil, Canada, Cayman Is, China, Dubai, England and Wales, France, Gambia, Germany, Ghana, Hong Kong, Ireland, Jamaica, Japan, Kazakhstan, Kenya, Korea Rep, Malaysia, Netherlands, New Zealand, Nigeria, Northern Ireland, Philippines, Qatar, Rwanda, Scotland, Sierra Leone, Singapore, Sri Lanka, Uganda, USA.
Eastern Caribbean Supreme Court (ECSC, #05236). [2022.05.04/AA1507/**F**]

♦ Standing International Road Weather Commission (SIRWEC) 19965

Sec Canadian Meteor Center, 2121 Trans-Canada Highway, North Service Road, Dorval QC H9P 1J3, Canada. T. +15144214729.
URL: http://www.sirwec.org/

History Mar 1985, Copenhagen (Denmark). March 1985, Copenhagen (Denmark), during 2nd International Road Weather Conference, as *Standing European Road Weather Commission (SERWEC).* Present name adopted in 1992. **Aims** Encourage *meteorologists,* weather *forecasters,* highway engineers, road masters and others who are interested in road weather problems to exchange ideas to make our roads *safer* to drive on in all weather conditions. **Structure** Executive Committee (meets annually), comprising President, Vice-President, Secretary and up to 2 members from each interested country. **Languages** English. **Staff** 3.00 FTE, voluntary. **Finance** No budget; conference costs covered by participants. **Activities** Operates as a forum for exchange of information relevant to the field of highway meteorology, including management, maintenance, road safety, meteorology and environmental protection; seeks to identify those areas where increased and/or new research and development may yield improvements in practices, techniques, systems and methodology, to the general benefits of the art; encourages the undertaking of trials, studies and research; organizes international congress (every 2 years). **Events** *Biennial Conference* La Massana (Andorra) 2014, *Biennial Conference* Helsinki (Finland) 2012, *Biennial Conference* Québec, QC (Canada) 2010, *Biennial Conference* Prague (Czech Rep) 2008, *Biennial Conference* Turin (Italy) / Sestriere (Italy) 2006. **Publications** Conference proceedings.
Members Individuals in 19 countries:
Austria, Belgium, Canada, Czechia, Denmark, Estonia, Finland, France, Germany, Iceland, Italy, Japan, Korea Rep, Norway, Slovenia, Sweden, Switzerland, UK, USA.
NGO Relations *World Road Association (PIARC, #21754).* [2010/XE2991/v/**E**]

- Standing Liaison Committee of Speech and Language Therapists /Logopedists of the European Union / see European Speech and Language Therapy Association (#08812)
- Standing Nordic Committee on Food / see Committee of Senior Officials of the Nordic Countries, Estonia, Latvia and Lithuania in the Field of Food Issues (#04286)
- Standing Veterinary Committee of the European Union / see Standing Committee on the Food Chain and Animal Health (#19956)
- Standing Voice (internationally oriented national body)
- STAND International (internationally oriented national body)
- Stanford Center on Conflict and Negotiation / see Stanford Center on International Conflict and Negotiation
- Stanford Center on International Conflict and Negotiation (internationally oriented national body)
- Stanford IIS / see Freeman Spogli Institute for International Studies
- Stanford Institute for International Studies / see Freeman Spogli Institute for International Studies
- Stanley Center for Peace and Security (internationally oriented national body)
- Stanley Foundation / see Stanley Center for Peace and Security
- St Anthony Messenger Press / see Franciscan Media
- St Anthony Messenger Press and Franciscan Communications / see Franciscan Media
- STAR Andina Paint / see Asociación de Técnicos Andinos en Recubrimientos (#02302)
- STAR / see ASEAN Rhinology Society (#01231)
- **STAR** Asociación de Técnicos Andinos en Recubrimientos (#02302)

♦ Starch Europe 19966

Managing Dir Ave des Arts 43, 1040 Brussels, Belgium. T. +3222896760. Fax +3225135592. E-mail: info@starch.eu.
URL: http://www.starch.eu/

History 17 Mar 1963, Brussels (Belgium), as *Association of the Maize Starch Industries of the EEC – Association des amidonneries de maïs de la CEE (AAM).* Name changed to *Association of the Cereal Starch Industries of the EU – Association des amidonneries de céréales de l'UE (AAC)* 1 Oct 1988, on merger with *EEC Wheat Starch Manufacturers' Association (EWSA, inactive).* Subsequently known as *Association des amidonniers et féculiers (AAF) – European Starch Industry Association.* Present name adopted, 2014. EU Transparency Register: 57787966531-03. Registration: EU Transparency Register, No/ID: 57787966531-03. **Aims** Promote and protect the interests of EU starch producers to EU and international institutions and stakeholders, in order to assure a reliable and sustainable supply of safe starch based ingredients in a fair competitive environment. **Structure** General Assembly; Executive Committee; Secretariat. **Languages** English. **Finance** Members' dues. **Activities** Politics/policy/regulatory; advocacy/lobbying/activism.
Members Individual firms (24) in 21 countries:
Austria, Belgium, Bulgaria, Czechia, Denmark, Finland, France, Germany, Greece, Hungary, Italy, Latvia, Lithuania, Netherlands, Poland, Portugal, Romania, Slovakia, Spain, Sweden, UK.
IGO Relations Recognized by: *European Commission (EC, #06633).* **NGO Relations** Member of: *European Bioeconomy Alliance (EUBA, #06334); FoodDrinkEurope (#09841); European Feed Ingredients Platform (EFIP, #07237); European Feed and Food Ingredients Safety Certification (EFISC-GTP, #07236); European Policy Centre (EPC, #08240); Primary Food Processors (PFP, #18496).* In liaison with technical committees of: *Comité européen de normalisation (CEN, #04162); International Organization for Standardization (ISO, #14473).*
[2020/XE2942/**E**]

♦ Star of Hope International (SoHI) 19967

Hoppets Stjärna Stiftelsen

CEO Kärrsjö, SE-890 54 Trehörningsjö, Sweden. T. +4666246100. E-mail: info@starofhope.org.
USA Office PO Box 427, Ellinwood KS 67526, USA. T. +16205643355. Fax +16205643355.
URL: http://www.starofhope.org/

History 1970. **Aims** Provide *children* with a stable foundation and tools needed to change their lives and communities, through education, health care and nutritional food. **Structure** Headquarters located in Kärrsjö (Sweden). Network branch offices located in Norway and USA. **Finance** Financed through gifts and contributions from private, corporate and individual organizations. **Activities** Training/education; projects/programmes. Active in: Argentina, Belarus, Brazil, Ghana, Haiti, Kenya, Latvia, Moldova, Philippines, Romania, Russia, Trinidad-Tobago. **Events** *Annual international relief aid and mission conference* Sweden 1997, *Annual international relief aid and mission conference* Sweden 1996. **Publications** *Star of Hope Magazine* (annual). **IGO Relations** Regularly cooperates with: *UNICEF (#20332).* **NGO Relations** Regularly cooperates with: *Caritas Internationalis (CI, #03580); International Federation of Red Cross and Red Crescent Societies (#13526).* [2018.06.01/XF2929/f/**F**]

- Starlight Foundation (internationally oriented national body)
- Starptautiska Jauno Fermeru Apvieniba (#15829)
- Starr International Foundation (internationally oriented national body)

♦ STARS International 19968

UK PO Box 175, Stratford-upon-Avon, CV37 8YD, UK. T. +441789450564.
URL: http://www.stars-international.org/

History STARS stands for *Syncope Trust And Reflex anoxic Seizures.* An umbrella organization for national organizations.
Members Organizations in 12 countries:
Denmark, France, Ireland, Italy, Japan, Netherlands, Norway, Poland, Spain, Sweden, UK, USA.
NGO Relations *AFA International; European Society of Cardiology (ESC, #08536).* [2014/XJ7958/**F**]

- StAR – Society of Asian Rotomoulders (internationally oriented national body)
- Star Spirit International (internationally oriented national body)
- **StAR** Stolen Asset Recovery Initiative (#19996)
- **STAR** Stress, Trauma, Anxiety, and Resilience Society (#20011)
- START / see Global Change System for Analysis, Research and Training (#10278)
- **START** Global Change System for Analysis, Research and Training (#10278)

♦ Start Network 19969

Dir Wework Aviation House, 125 Kingsway, London, WC2B 6NH, UK. E-mail: info@startnetwork.org.
URL: http://startnetwork.org/

History 2010, as *Consortium of British Humanitarian Agencies (CBHA).* Current title adopted 2012. Registration: Company, No/ID: 09286835, England and Wales; Charity, No/ID: 1159483, England and Wales. **Aims** Deliver effective *aid,* harnessing the power and knowledge of the Network to make faster and better decisions to help people affected by *crises.* **Structure** General Assembly; Board of Trustees. **Finance** Financing from *Department for International Development (DFID, inactive).* Other donors include: Dutch Aid; *European Union (EU, #08967);* governments of Belgium and Estonia; *Irish Aid.* **Activities** Financial and/or material support; advocacy/lobbying/activism. Programmes include: *Start Fund.*
Members Organizations, including national federations of international organizations, and including 31 organizations listed in this Yearbook:
– *Action Against Hunger (#00086);*
– *ActionAid (#00087);*
– *African Development Solutions (Adeso, #00287);*
– *Agency for Technical Cooperation and Development (ACTED);*

- *ALIMA (#00636)*;
- *Arab Renaissance for Democracy and Development (ARDD)*;
- *Catholic Agency for Overseas Development (CAFOD)*;
- *Catholic Organization for Relief and Development (Cordaid)*;
- *Catholic Relief Services (CRS, #03608)*;
- *Christian Aid*;
- *Community World Service Asia (#04407)*;
- *Concern Worldwide*;
- *Dorcas (#05123)*;
- *GOAL*;
- *HelpAge International (#10904)*;
- *International Medical Corps (IMC)*;
- *International Rescue Committee (IRC, #14717)*;
- *Islamic Relief Worldwide (IRWW, #16048)*;
- *Mercy Corps International (MCI)*;
- *Mines Advisory Group (MAG)*;
- *Muslim Aid*;
- *Norwegian Refugee Council (NRC)*;
- *Oxfam GB*;
- *Plan International (#18386)*;
- *Relief International*;
- *Save the Children UK (SC UK)*;
- *Solidarités International*;
- *Tearfund, UK*;
- *Trocaire – Catholic Agency for World Development*;
- *Welthungerhilfe*;
- *World Jewish Relief (WJR, #21600)*.

NGO Relations Partners include: *Communicating with Disaster Affected Communities Network (CDAC Network, #04379)*. [2020/XM6948/y/**F**]

♦ START treaty – Strategic Arms Reduction Treaty (1991 treaty)
♦ **STA** Smart Ticketing Alliance (#19321)
♦ Statens investeringsfond for næringsvirksomhet i utviklingsland (internationally oriented national body)
♦ Statewatch (internationally oriented national body)
♦ Station scientifique du Jungfraujoch, fondation internationale / see International Foundation of the High Altitude Research Stations Jungfraujoch and Gornergrat (#13671)
♦ Station spatiale internationale (#15574)

♦ Statistical Center for the Cooperation Council for the Arab Countries of the Gulf (GCC Stat) 19970

Executive Secretariat PO Box 840, 133, Muscat, Oman. T. +96824346499. E-mail: info@gccstat.org.
Registered Address Al Maardih St 677, 2nd Floor, Murtafa'at Al Matar, Al Seeb, 113, Muscat, Oman.
URL: http://gccstat.org/

History Jun 2011. Approved by *Gulf Cooperation Council (GCC, #10826)* Ministerial Council, Sep 2011. Charter officially endorsed Dec 2012 by GCC Supreme Council. Former names and other names: *GCC-STAT* – alias. **Aims** Serve as a common official pool of statistics and data for GCC member states. **Structure** Board. **Activities** Events/meetings; training/education. **Events** *Meeting of Board Directors* Muscat (Oman) 2014, *Meeting of Board Directors* Muscat (Oman) 2014, *Meeting of Board Directors* Muscat (Oman) 2014, *Meeting of Board Directors* Muscat (Oman) 2014.
Members Governments (6):
Bahrain, Kuwait, Oman, Qatar, Saudi Arabia, United Arab Emirates. [2023/XJ8403/**E***]

♦ Statistical, Economic and Social Research and Training Centre for Islamic Countries (SESRIC) 19971

Centre de recherches statistiques, économiques et sociales et de formation pour les pays islamiques

Secretariat Kudüs Cad No 9, Diplomatik Site, ORAN, 06450 Ankara/Ankara, Türkiye. T. +903124686172. Fax +903124685726. E-mail: library@sesric.org – oicankara@sesric.org.
URL: http://www.sesric.org/

History Set up as a subsidiary organ of *Organisation of Islamic Cooperation (OIC, #17813)*, following resolution 2/8-E, adopted by 8th Islamic Conference of *Council of Foreign Ministers (CFM, see: #17813)*, May 1977, Tripoli (Libyan AJ). Activities started 1 Jun 1978. Also known as *Ankara Centre – Centre d'Ankara*. Previously known under the acronym *SESRTCIC* and *CRSESFPI*. **Aims** Support the process of cooperation and development among member states by activities in statistics, research, training and technical cooperation, and publish results; compile and disseminate economic and social statistics relating to OIC members; undertake research work based on such data; study economic structures in member states; prepare technical reports and background documents for presentation to related OIC fora; act as computerized source of information; function as focal point for technical cooperation; organize and conduct training courses. **Structure** General Assembly (annual), consisting of one representative of each OIC member state, as *Islamic Commission for Economic, Cultural and Social Affairs (ICECSA, #16038)*, elects 9 members of Board of Directors (meets annually) which also includes Director General of the Centre and OIC Secretary-General as ex-officio members. **Languages** Arabic, English, French. **Staff** 70.00 FTE, paid. **Finance** Mandatory and voluntary contributions of member states; revenues from services rendered. Budget (annual): US$ 2.25 million. **Activities** Implemented through project-oriented annual work programmes. Participates in and contributes to many OIC economic fora. **Events** *International Halal congress* Ankara (Turkey) 2011, *International conference on Islamic economics and finance* Doha (Qatar) 2011, *Islamic Countries Conference on Statistical Sciences* Shah Alam (Malaysia) 2007, *Meeting of heads of OIC statistical organizations* Lahore (Pakistan) 2003, *Meeting of heads of OIC statistical organizations* Cairo (Egypt) 2001. **Publications** *Journal of Economic Cooperation and Development* (4 a year) in English; *SESRIC Information Report* (4 a year) in Arabic, English, French; *Economic Cooperation and Development Review* (2 a year) in English; *Basic Facts and Figures on OIC Member Countries* (annual); *Statistical Yearbook of the OIC Countries* (annual) in English; *Annual Economic Report on the OIC Countries* in Arabic, English, French. Reports; annals; directories; reference material; books; monographs – in the fields of economics and finance, information and statistics, legislation, etc. Information Services: Collects, collates and keeps available exhaustive data and information on selected subjects. /Library and Documentation Unit/ – includes about 17,000 books, over 145 periodicals, over 7,100 documents and reports and over 500 SESRTCIC reports. Library is a Depository Library of *International Bank for Reconstruction and Development (IBRD, #12317)* (World Bank) and *International Monetary Fund (IMF, #14180)*. /Computerized Information Systems/ – installed in 2004 and maintains online databases, designed at the Centre's computer facilities, which provide different sets and types of information extracted from various sources: *'Documentation System'*; *'Article Abstracts'*; *'Technical Cooperation'*; *BASEIND Statistical Database*. /Research/ Centre produces reports and/or technical background documents for OIC meetings, staff papers and articles to be published in the Centre's journal. /Training/ Short to medium term courses are organized in collaboration with national and regional training institutions. Participants selected from the member states are placed into training programmes in the member states themselves. **Information Services** *Article Abstracts* – abstracts and bibliographic information on articles in learned journals; *BASEIND Statistical Database* – basic socio-economic indicators on member states; *Documentation System* – bibliographic database of books, documents and statistical publications; *Technical Cooperation* – information on research, training, consultancy, mass-media and higher learning institutions within OIC community, collected through periodic questionnaires.
Members All OIC member states (57):
Afghanistan, Albania, Algeria, Azerbaijan, Bahrain, Bangladesh, Benin, Brunei Darussalam, Burkina Faso, Cameroon, Chad, Comoros, Côte d'Ivoire, Djibouti, Egypt, Gabon, Gambia, Guinea, Guinea-Bissau, Guyana, Indonesia, Iran Islamic Rep, Iraq, Jordan, Kazakhstan, Kuwait, Kyrgyzstan, Lebanon, Libya, Malaysia, Maldives, Mali, Mauritania, Morocco, Mozambique, Niger, Nigeria, Oman, Pakistan, Palestine, Qatar, Saudi Arabia, Senegal, Sierra Leone, Somalia, Sudan, Suriname, Syrian AR, Tajikistan, Togo, Tunisia, Türkiye, Turkmenistan, Uganda, United Arab Emirates, Uzbekistan, Yemen.
NGO Relations Formal contacts with: *Arab Institute for Training and Research in Statistics (AITRS, #00987)*; *Association of National Development Finance Institutions in Member Countries of the Islamic Development Bank (ADFIMI, #02817)*; *Federation of Consultants from Islamic Countries (FCIC, #09476)*; *Islamic Chamber of Commerce, Industry and Agriculture (ICCIA, #16036)*; national statistical offices in OIC member countries; *Organization of the Islamic Shipowners' Association (OISA, #17876)*. [2018.06.28/XE8148/**E***]

♦ Statistical Institute for Asia and the Pacific (SIAP) 19972

Institut de statistique pour l'Asie et le Pacifique (ISAP)

Main Office JETRO-IDE, 2-2 Wakaba 3-chome, Mihama-ku, Chiba-shi, Chiba, 261-8787 Japan. E-mail: escap-siap@un.org.
URL: http://www.unsiap.or.jp/

History 1970, Tokyo (Japan). Founded with support from the *UNDP (#20292)*, as a regional training institute operating under the aegis of *United Nations Economic and Social Commission for Asia and the Pacific (ESCAP, #20557)*. Subsidiary body of ESCAP since 1995. Former names and other names: *Asian Statistical Institute (ASI)* – former. **Aims** Strengthen, through practically oriented training of official statisticians, capability of countries in the Asia-Pacific region to collect, process, analyse and disseminate statistics; produce timely and high-quality statistics; assist in establishing or strengthening their statistical training capability and other related activities. **Structure** Governing Council, consisting of a representative nominated by the host country, Japan, and 8 representatives, nominated by other members and associate members of ESCAP and elected by ESCAP. Executive Secretary and chiefs of concerned divisions of ESCAP attend meetings of the Council in non-voting capacities. The Director of SIAP serves as Secretary of the Council. **Finance** Sources: annual contributions from member countries; Government of Japan. **Activities** Training; networking; partnerships; courses; meeting activities. **Events** *Session* Chiba (Japan) 2019, *Session* Incheon (Korea Rep) 2018, *Session* Bangkok (Thailand) 2016, *Management Seminar for the Heads of National Statistical Offices* Tokyo (Japan) 2015, *Regional Workshop on Production and Use of Vital Statistics* Daejeon (Korea Rep) 2014.
Members Governments of the ESCAP region (53):
Afghanistan, Armenia, Australia, Azerbaijan, Bangladesh, Bhutan, Brunei Darussalam, Cambodia, China, Fiji, France, Georgia, India, Indonesia, Iran Islamic Rep, Japan, Kazakhstan, Kiribati, Korea DPR, Korea Rep, Kyrgyzstan, Laos, Malaysia, Maldives, Marshall Is, Micronesia FS, Mongolia, Myanmar, Nauru, Nepal, Netherlands, New Zealand, Pakistan, Palau, Papua New Guinea, Philippines, Russia, Samoa, Singapore, Solomon Is, Sri Lanka, Tajikistan, Thailand, Timor-Leste, Tonga, Türkiye, Turkmenistan, Tuvalu, UK, USA, Uzbekistan, Vanuatu, Vietnam.
Associate Members in 9 countries and territories:
Cook Is, Guam, Hong Kong, Macau, New Caledonia, Niue, Northern Mariana Is, Polynesia Fr, Samoa USA.
NGO Relations Member of: *Asia-Pacific Regional Space Agency Forum (APRSAF, #02010)*.
[2020/XE0295/j/**E***]

♦ Statistical Modelling Society (SMS) 19973

Sec address not obtained. E-mail: secretary@statmod.org.
Chair address not obtained. E-mail: chair@statmod.org.
URL: http://www.statmod.org/

History Jun 2003. Registered in accordance with Dutch law. **Aims** Promote statistical modelling as the general framework for the application of statistical ideas; promote important developments, extensions, and applications; bring together statisticians working on statistical modelling from various disciplines. **Structure** General Meeting (annual, at Workshop). Executive Committee, including Chair, Secretary and Treasurer. **Languages** English. **Finance** Sources: members' dues. **Activities** Events/meetings; training/education. **Events** *International Workshop on Statistical Modelling* Natal (Brazil) 2023, *International Workshop on Statistical Modelling* Trieste (Italy) 2022, *International Workshop on Statistical Modelling* Bilbao (Spain) 2021, *International Workshop on Statistical Modelling* Bilbao (Spain) 2020, *International Workshop on Statistical Modelling* Guimarães (Portugal) 2019. **Publications** *Statistical Modelling: An International Journal*. **Members** Individuals. Membership countries not specified. [2014/XJ6919/v/**C**]

♦ Statistical Office of the European Communities / see Statistical Office of the European Union (#19974)

♦ Statistical Office of the European Union (Eurostat) 19974

Office statistique de l'Union européenne – Oficina Estadística de la Unión Europea – Statistischen Amt der Europäischen Union – Serviço de Estatística da União Europeia – Istituto Statistico dell'Unione Europea – Bureau voor de Statistiek van de Europese Unie – Europeiska Unionens Statistikkontor – Europ'iske Unions Statistiske Kontor

Dir Gen Bâtiment Bech, Rue Alphonse Weicker 5, L-2920 Luxembourg, Luxembourg. T. +35243011.
URL: http://ec.europa.eu/eurostat/

History Established 1953 to meet requirements of *European Coal and Steel Community (ECSC, inactive)*. When *European Community (inactive)* was established 1958, became a Directorate-General of *European Commission (EC, #06633)*, with the title *Statistical Office of the European Communities (Eurostat) – Office statistique des Communautés européennes – Oficina Estadística de las Comunidades Europeas – Statistisches Amt der Europäischen Gemeinschaften – Serviço de Estatística das Comunidades Europeias – Istituto Statistico delle Comunità Europee – Bureau voor de Statistiek van de Europese Gemeenschappen – Europeiska Gemenskapernas Statistik Kontor – Europaeiske Faellesskabers Statistiske Kontor – Statistiko Grafio ton Evropaikon Kinotiton*. Originally also referred to by English initials *SOEC* and French initials *OSCE*. Currently based in Luxembourg with a department in Brussels. Legal basis: Regulation (EC) No 223/2009 of *European Parliament (EP, #08146)* and *Council of the European Union (#04895)*, 11 Mar 2009 on European statistics. **Aims** Provide high-quality statistics for Europe; collect, harmonize and disseminate statistical information on the *European Union* (EU) and the main countries with which EU maintains relations; together with national statistical institutes, harmonize statistics in order to obtain comparable data for EU member states. **Structure** Directorates: A – Resources; B – Methodology, Dissemination, Cooperation in the European Statistical System; C – Macro-economic Statistics; D – Government Finance Statistics (GFS); E – Sectoral and Regional Statistics; F – Social Statistics; G – Business and Trade Statistics. **Languages** Bulgarian, Croatian, Czech, Danish, Dutch, English, Estonian, Finnish, French, German, Hungarian, Irish Gaelic, Italian, Latvian, Lithuanian, Maltese, Polish, Portuguese, Romanian, Slovakian, Slovene, Spanish, Swedish. **Staff** 800.00 FTE, paid. **Finance** EU budget. Operational budget (2018): euro 58,500,000; subdelegated credits (2017): euro 31,500,000. **Activities** Research/documentation; knowledge management/information dissemination. **Events** *European Conference on Quality in Official Statistics* Vilnius (Lithuania) 2022, *European Conference on Quality in Official Statistics* Budapest (Hungary) 2020, *Meeting* Brussels (Belgium) 2018, *European Conference on Quality in Official Statistics* Krakow (Poland) 2018, *Meeting* Lisbon (Portugal) 2017. **Publications** *Regional Yearbook*. Digital publications; statistical books; manuals and guidelines; working papers and reports; leaflets; brochures; news releases. **Information Services** *Statistics Explained*.
Members Member States of the European Union (27):
Austria, Belgium, Bulgaria, Croatia, Cyprus, Czechia, Denmark, Estonia, Finland, France, Germany, Greece, Hungary, Ireland, Italy, Latvia, Lithuania, Luxembourg, Malta, Netherlands, Poland, Portugal, Romania, Slovakia, Slovenia, Spain, Sweden.
EFTA countries (3):
Iceland, Liechtenstein, Norway.
IGO Relations Close cooperation with: *European Central Bank (ECB, #06466)*. **NGO Relations** In liaison with technical committees of: *International Organization for Standardization (ISO, #14473)*. Member of: *International Association for Research in Income and Wealth (IARIW, #12134)*; *International Maritime Statistics Forum (IMSF, #14105)*. Observer to: *European Umbrella Organization for Geographical Information (EUROGI, #08964)*. [2019.07.10/XE7358/**E***]

♦ Statistical Pan African Society / see Statistics and Probability African Society (#19975)

♦ Statistics and Probability African Society (SPAS) 19975

Société Africaine de Probabilité and de Statistique (SAPS)

Coordinator UFR SAT, Univ Gaston Berger, Route de Ngallèle, BP 234, Saint Louis, Senegal.
URL: http://www.statpas.net/

History May 2008. Also referred to as *Société Pan Africaine de Statistiques (SPAS) – Statistical Pan African Society*. **Aims** Promote and sustain development of Probability Theory and Statistics within Africa, and in the world. **Structure** Continental Committee; Executive Committee; General Coordinator; Technical Committees. **Languages** English, French. **Events** *General Assembly* Saint Louis (Senegal) 2011, *General Assembly* Saint Louis (Senegal) 2011. **Publications** *Afrika Statistika*. **Members** Individuals. Membership countries not specified. [2020.03.03/XM3931/**D**]

♦ Statistiko Grafio ton Evropaikon Kinotiton / see Statistical Office of the European Union (#19974)
♦ Statistischen Amt der Europäischen Union (#19974)
♦ Statistisches Amt der Europäischen Gemeinschaften / see Statistical Office of the European Union (#19974)
♦ STA / see UNESCO Staff Union (#20321)

♦ Stay Behind Network / see Allied Coordination Committee (#00733)

♦ **STAY GROUNDED** 19976
Coordinator Periskop, c/o GLOBAL 2000, Neustiftgasse 36, 1070 Vienna, Austria. E-mail: office@kollektiv-periskop.org.
URL: https://stay-grounded.org/
History Oct 2016. **Aims** Foster mutual support and exchange of experiences; campaign for a reduction of aviation and its negative impacts, as well as against problematic climate strategies like offsetting emissions and biofuels. **Activities** Advocacy/lobbying/activism; events/meetings; networking/liaising; research/documentation; training/education. **Events** *International Conference On Degrowth Of Aviation* Barcelona (Spain) 2019. **Members** Full (over 150). Membership countries not specified. [2021.09.08/AA0645/**F**]

♦ Staying Alive Foundation (internationally oriented national body)
♦ St Bernadette, Nevers – Sisters of Charity and Christian Instruction of Nevers (religious order)
♦ **STCAA** Sustainable Tourism Certification Alliance Africa (#20068)
♦ ST-CCT / see Secretaria de Integración Turistica Centroamericana (#19193)
♦ STCI – Synthetic Turf Council International (unconfirmed)
♦ **STCNA** Sustainable Tourism Certification Network of the Americas (#20069)
♦ STC – Sea Turtle Conservancy (internationally oriented national body)
♦ STC – Synthetic Turf Council (internationally oriented national body)
♦ STCW-F – International Convention on Standards of Training, Certification and Watchkeeping for Fishing Vessel Personnel (1995 treaty)
♦ STCW – International Convention on Standards of Training, Certification and Watchkeeping for Seafarers (1978 treaty)
♦ St Cyril and St Methodius International Foundation (internationally oriented national body)
♦ **STDA** Selenium-Tellurium Development Association (#19219)
♦ STD Forum – Third World Science Technology and Development Forum (internationally oriented national body)
♦ **STDF** Standards and Trade Development Facility (#19948)
♦ STDSSA – Sexually Transmitted Diseases Society of Southern Africa (internationally oriented national body)

♦ **Steel Construction Institute, The (SCI)** 19977
Main Office Silwood Park, Ascot, SL5 7QN, UK. T. +441344636525. Fax +441344636570. E-mail: reception@steel-sci.com.
URL: http://www.steel-sci.com/
History 1986. **Aims** Design and produce technical content that sits behind and drives the sources of steel construction information used by engineers globally; develop and promote proper and effective use of steel in construction. **Structure** General Meeting (annual); Advisory Council; Board. **Languages** English, French, Portuguese, Spanish. **Staff** 30.00 FTE, paid. **Finance** Subscriptions; funding from UK and other government sponsors. **Activities** Training/education; awards/prizes/competitions; guidance/assistance/consulting. **Events** *Conference on blast and fire engineering for topside structures* London (UK) 1998, *Symposium / Annual Symposium* Birmingham (UK) 1994. **Publications** *Connect* (12 a year) – newsletter; *New Steel Construction* (10 a year). Technical publications; design guides. **Information Services** *Steelbiz online*.
Members Corporate members in 37 countries:
Australia, Belgium, Brazil, Canada, Chile, Croatia, Egypt, Finland, France, Germany, Greece, Hong Kong, India, Ireland, Italy, Kenya, Korea Rep, Liechtenstein, Lithuania, Malaysia, Malta, Netherlands, New Zealand, Norway, Pakistan, Philippines, Portugal, Qatar, Romania, Singapore, Slovenia, South Africa, Spain, Sweden, Türkiye, United Arab Emirates, USA.
[2022/XE3405/j/**E**]

♦ Steel Structures Painting Council / see Society for Protective Coatings
♦ The Steel Treaters Club / see ASM International
♦ Steel Treating Research Society / see ASM International
♦ Steering Committee for Equality between Women and Men (inactive)

♦ **Steering Committee for Humanitarian Response (SCHR)** 19978
Exec Sec Chemin des Crêtes 17, 1209 Geneva, Switzerland. T. +41797083255. E-mail: schr@ifrc.org.
URL: http://www.schr.info/
History 1972, Geneva (Switzerland). Former names and other names: *Licross/Volags Steering Committee for Disasters* – former. **Aims** Promote actively a world in which local communities, civil society, governments and regional institutions can respond effectively to humanitarian emergencies, based on universally accepted humanitarian principles and with disaster-affected people at the centre of these responses; save lives, reduce human suffering and preserve human dignity. **Structure** SCHR Principals (meet at least once a year); Working Group; Secretariat managed by Executive Secretary, based in Geneva (Switzerland). **Languages** English. **Staff** 1.00 FTE, paid. **Finance** Sources: members' dues. Annual budget: 250,000 CHF (2022). **Activities** Advocacy/lobbying/activism; events/meetings; knowledge management/information dissemination. **Events** *Principals Conference* Geneva (Switzerland) 2023, *Conference* Geneva (Switzerland) 1986.
Members Representatives of 9 international humanitarian organizations:
ACT Alliance (#00081); CARE International (CI, #03429); Caritas Internationalis (CI, #03580); International Committee of the Red Cross (ICRC, #12799); International Federation of Red Cross and Red Crescent Societies (#13526); Oxfam International (#17922); Save the Children International (#19058); The Lutheran World Federation (LWF, #16532); World Vision International (WVI, #21904).
IGO Relations Standing invitee of: *Inter-Agency Standing Committee (IASC, #11393)*. **NGO Relations** Member of (1): *Active Learning Network for Accountability and Performance in Humanitarian Action (ALNAP, #00101)*. Cooperates with (2): *CHS Alliance (#03911); Humanitarian Quality Assurance Initiative (HQAI, #10974)*. Instrumental in setting up (1): *The Sphere Project (#19918)*. [2022.10.19/XE5231/y/**E**]

♦ Steering Committee for Nordic Cooperation on Adult and General Education / see Nordisk Folkeoplysnings- og Voksenundervisningssamarbejde (#17504)

♦ **Steering Committee on Trade Capacity and Standards (CTCS)** 19979
Comité directeur des capacités et des normes commerciales
Contact Div on Economic Cooperation and Trade, UNECE, Palais des Nations, 8-14 Avenue de la Paix, 1211 Geneva 10, Switzerland. T. +41229172745 – +41229172895. Fax +41229170037. E-mail: ceci@unece.org.
URL: http://www.unece.org/tradewelcome/home.html
History Established in Geneva (Switzerland) as a Principal Subsidiary Body of *United Nations Economic Commission for Europe (UNECE, #20555)*. Original title: *Committee on Trade (CT) – Comité du commerce*. Reports to *ECOSOC (#05331)*. First session Dec 1997; first session of current Committee, Jun 2006; 6th session, Feb 2014. Also has a title in Russian. **Aims** Support: development of trade in the UNECE region; better integration of all member states into the regional and global *economy*. Facilitate trade by introducing trade facilitation measures and electronic commerce; eliminate technical barriers to trade; promote international *standardization* and *regulatory* cooperation among member states; develop agricultural *quality* standards used in trade and reflected in the legislation of many countries as well as in EU directives; carry out studies on regulatory and procedural barriers to trade in selected countries; support the Aid for Trade Initiative in the ECE region. **Structure** Annual Plenary Sessions in Geneva (Switzerland); Bureau. **Languages** English, French, Russian. **Finance** Regular UN budget. **Activities** Capacity building; politics/policy/regulatory; standards/guidelines; research/documentation; events/meetings. Support for trade facilitation globally and the general expansion and diversification of trade in the UNECE region with special reference to the further integration of the countries in transition. **Events** *Annual plenary session* Geneva (Switzerland) 2003, *Seminar on analysis, methodology of treatment and remediation of soils and groundwater* Geneva (Switzerland) 2003, *Seminar on barriers to industrial restructuring resulting from overmanning in steel companies* Krakow (Poland) 2002, *Annual plenary session* Geneva (Switzerland) 2001, *Seminar on analysis, methodology of treatment and remediation of contaminated soils and groundwaters* Paris (France) 2001. **Publications** *Code for Ports and Other Locations (UN/LOCODE); Trade Facilitation Recommendations and Conventions; UNECE Agricultural Quality Standards; United Nations Directories for Electronic Data Interchange for Administration, Commerce and Transport (UN/EDIFACT); United Nations Trade Data Elements Directory (UNTDED). Core Components Specifications and Core Components Library for e-Business; Norms, Standards and Practices for Trade Faciliation and International Business.* Trade guides and briefings; studies on regulatory and procedural barriers to trade. **Information Services** *Trade Facilitation Implementation Guide* – online knowledge platform. **Members** All 56 member States of UNECE can participate in CTCS activities, as well as any other UN member State. Regional integration EU entity, listed in this Yearbook:
Regional integration EU entity, listed in this Yearbook:
European Union (EU, #08967). [2017/XE3245/t/**E***]

♦ Steering Group for Adult Education / see Nordisk Folkeoplysnings- og Voksenundervisningssamarbejde (#17504)
♦ Steering Group of the Catholic Family Organizations in Europe / see Federation of Catholic Family Associations in Europe (#09468)
♦ Steering group for Folkeoplysning and Adult Education / see Nordisk Folkeoplysnings- og Voksenundervisningssamarbejde (#17504)

♦ **Steering Group on Influenza Vaccination** 19980
Secretariat address not obtained. T. +32499887116. E-mail: sginfluenzavacc@hanovercomms.com.
URL: http://eufightingflu.com/
History Set up, 2017, with support of *Vaccines Europe (VE, #20741)*. **Aims** Disseminate the Manifesto on Influenza Vaccination. **Structure** 2 Co-Chairs. **Events** *Meeting* Brussels (Belgium) 2018. **NGO Relations** Supported by: *Vaccines Europe (VE, #20741)*. Endorsed by: *Association of European Cancer Leagues (ECL, #02500); European Academy of Paediatrics (EAP, #05811); European Association of Hospital Pharmacists (EAHP, #06074); European Brain Council (EBC, #06391); European Federation of Allergy and Airways Diseases Patients' Associations (EFA, #07045); European Forum for Primary Care (EFPC, #07326); European Patients' Forum (EPF, #08172); European Pharmaceutical Students' Association (EPSA, #08197); European Scientific Working Group on Influenza (ESWI, #08450); European Specialist Nurses Organisation (ESNO, #08808); International Primary Care Respiratory Group (IPCRG, #14640); Pharmaceutical Group of the European Union (PGEU, #18352); World Medical Association (WMA, #21646).* [2019/XM7751/**E**]

♦ Steering Group for Nordic School Cooperation (inactive)

♦ **Stefan Banach International Mathematical Center at the Institute of Mathematics of the Polish Academy of Sciences** 19981
Centre international mathématique pour le relèvement de la qualification des cadres scientifiques 'Stefan Banach'
Contact Sniadeckich 8, 00-656 Warsaw, Poland. T. +48225228232. Fax +48226225750. E-mail: banach@impan.gov.pl.
URL: http://www.impan.pl/
History 13 Jan 1972, Warsaw (Poland), on signature of an agreement by representatives of Academies of Science in the then 7 European socialist countries. Cooperation with *European Mathematical Society (EMS, #07755)* since 1993. Also known as *Banach Centre*. **Aims** Create opportunities for prolonged personal contacts between mathematicians with similar scientific interest; exchange information and ideas; stimulate research and international cooperation. **Structure** Scientific Director; Scientific Council. **Languages** English. **Staff** Supplied by Institute of Mathematics of Polish Academy of Sciences. **Finance** Polish Academy of Sciences. **Activities** Training/education; research/documentation; events/meetings. **Events** *Conference on PDEs, submanifolds and affine differential geometry* Bedlewo (Poland) 2003, *Conference on conformal geometry, discrete groups and surfaces* Bedlewo (Poland) 2003, *Conference on nonlocal elliptic and parabolic problems* Bedlewo (Poland) 2003, *Conference on statistical inference in linear models* Bedlewo (Poland) 2003, *Workshop on mathematics of gravitation* Warsaw (Poland) 2003. **Publications** *Banach Centre Publications* (1976-) – in 115 vols. Reprints of research papers. **NGO Relations** Member of: *European Research Centres of Mathematics (ERCOM, #08360).* [2018.07.25/XE0656/**E**]

♦ Stefanus-Lahetys Ry (#20804)
♦ **STELA-World** World Solar Thermal Electricity Association (#21817)
♦ STELO – Studenta Tutmonda Esperanto-Ligo (inactive)
♦ STEM – Stichting voor Europees Milieubeleid (see: #11261)

♦ **STEP** 19982
Chief Exec Artillery House, 11-19 Artillery Row, London, SW1P 1RT, UK. T. +442037523700. E-mail: step@step.org.
URL: http://www.step.org/
History Jul 1991, London (UK). Acronym derives from: *Society of Trust and Estate Practitioners*. Former names and other names: *STEP – Advising Families Across Generations* – full title. Registration: Companies House, No/ID: 2632423, England and Wales; EU Transparency Register, No/ID: 64339983762-18. **Aims** Improve public understanding of the issues families face in relation to *inheritance* and succession planning; promote education and high professional standards among members. **Structure** Board of Directors; Council; Committees; Panels; Special Interest Groups; Regional Committees; Branches and Chapters. **Activities** Training/education; standards/guidelines; knowledge management/information dissemination. **Events** *Arabia Conference* Abu Dhabi (United Arab Emirates) 2022, *International Conference* Channel Is (UK) 2022, *Europe Conference* Luxembourg (Luxembourg) 2022, *Latin America Conference* Panama (Panama) 2022, *Asia Conference* Singapore (Singapore) 2022. **Publications** *STEP Journal*; *Trust Quarterly Review*. **Members** Full (21,500) in 96 countries. Membership countries not specified. [2020/XM5224/**F**]

♦ STEP – Advising Families Across Generations / see STEP (#19982)
♦ **STEPAN** Science and Technology Policy Asian Network (#19144)
♦ STEPS Centre (internationally oriented national body)
♦ Stereopsia – World Immersion Forum (meeting series)
♦ **STERF** Scandinavian Turfgrass and Environment Research Foundation (#19126)

♦ **Sterile Barrier Association (SBA)** 19983
Dir Gen 4 King Square, Bridgwater, TA6 3YF, UK. E-mail: director.general@sterilebarrier.org.
URL: http://www.sterilebarrier.org/
History 1992, as *European Sterilization Packaging Association (ESPA)*. **Aims** Represent manufacturers of sophisticated barrier materials, sterilization systems and processing equipment for the medical industry allowing single use medical devices and products to be sterilized and then to maintain that sterility up to the point of use. **Structure** Board of 7 members, including Chairman. **Languages** English. **Staff** 1.00 FTE, paid. **Finance** Members' dues. **Activities** Organizes biannual conference. **Events** *Software and process validation for medical devices* Amsterdam (Netherlands) 1997, *Conference* London (UK) 1997, *Medical device packaging issues* Vienna (Austria) 1996. **Publications** *What's New* (2 a year) – online.
Members Companies (21) in 12 countries:
Finland, France, Germany, Ireland, Italy, Luxembourg, Netherlands, Sweden, Switzerland, Türkiye, UK, USA.
NGO Relations Member of: *MedTech Europe (#16692).* [2022/XD5041/**D**]

♦ STE – Save the Elephants (internationally oriented national body)
♦ STETE / see Finnish Committee for European Security
♦ STETE – Finnish Committee for European Security (internationally oriented national body)
♦ Steunfonds Derde Wereld (internationally oriented national body)
♦ Steun Ontwikkelings Streken / see Fair Trade Original
♦ Steyler Missionsschwestern (religious order)
♦ STF / see Nordiska Transportarbetarefederationen (#17496)
♦ STF – SAARC Teachers' Federation (inactive)
♦ STF – Save the Tiger Fund (internationally oriented national body)
♦ StfTE – Studienkreis für Tourismus und Entwicklung (internationally oriented national body)
♦ St Gabriel's Union / see World Union Saint Gabriel (#21885)
♦ St Gallen Foundation for International Studies / see ISC-Foundation
♦ St Galler Stiftung für Internationale Studien / see ISC-Foundation
♦ STI2 / see STI International (#19990)
♦ Stichting 100 Million campaign / see 100 Million (#22042)

- ♦ Stichting Advocaten voor Advocaten (internationally oriented national body)
- ♦ Stichting AIESEC International / see AIESEC (#00593)
- ♦ Stichting Amazon Fund (unconfirmed)
- ♦ Stichting Arab West Foundation (internationally oriented national body)
- ♦ Stichting Archives Portal Europe Foundation / see Archives Portal Europe Foundation (#01090)
- ♦ Stichting BankTrack / see BankTrack (#03166)
- ♦ Stichting van de Belgische Rotary Clubs voor Ontwikkelingssamenwerking / see Association des Rotary clubs belges pour la coopération au développement
- ♦ Stichting van de Belgisch-Luxemburgse Rotary Clubs voor Hulp aan de Derde Wereld / see Association des Rotary clubs belges pour la coopération au développement
- ♦ Stichting Berenbos Rhenen / see Bears in Mind
- ♦ Stichting Bernard van Leer Foundation (internationally oriented national body)
- ♦ Stichting Bos / see Vereniging Tropische Bossen
- ♦ Stichting Caraïbisch Marien Biologisch Instituut / see Caribbean Research and Management of Biodiversity
- ♦ Stichting Care4BrittleBones (#09943)
- ♦ Stichting CEFLEX / see Circular Economy for Flexible Packaging (#03935)
- ♦ Stichting Centre for Safety and Development / see Centre for Safety and Development

♦ Stichting Changing Markets 19984

Changing Markets Foundation

Contact Newtonlaan 115, 3584 BH Utrecht, Netherlands. E-mail: contact@changingmarkets.org.
URL: https://changingmarkets.org/

History Registration: Handelsregister, No/ID: 68014635, Netherlands; Section 501(c)(3), USA, State of New York; EU Transparency Register, No/ID: 482789528099-85. **Aims** Accelerate and scale up solutions to *sustainability* challenges by leveraging the power of markets. **Structure** Board. **NGO Relations** Member of (1): *European Environmental Bureau (EEB, #06996).* [2021.08.31/XM8665/f/**F**]

- ♦ Stichting CMC / see Mensen met een Missie
- ♦ Stichting CMC – Mensen met een Missie (internationally oriented national body)
- ♦ Stichting Concawe / see Oil Companies' European Association for Environment, Health and Safety in Refining and Distribution (#17708)
- ♦ Stichting DOEN (internationally oriented national body)
- ♦ Stichting Drinkable Rivers / see Drinkable Rivers
- ♦ Stichting EMDA / see Network for European Monitoring and Development Assistance
- ♦ Stichting ETC Consultants for Development Programmes / see ETC
- ♦ Stichting EuroBSDcon (#05650)
- ♦ Stichting EUROCAM / see EUROCAM (#05653)
- ♦ Stichting EUROGI / see European Umbrella Organization for Geographical Information (#08964)
- ♦ Stichting Europalia International (internationally oriented national body)
- ♦ Stichting Europeana (#05839)
- ♦ Stichting European Climate Foundation / see European Climate Foundation (#06574)
- ♦ Stichting European Football for Development Network / see European Football for Development Network (#07291)
- ♦ Stichting European Grid Initiative / see EGI Foundation (#05395)
- ♦ Stichting Europees Centrum voor Conflictpreventie / see Global Partnership for the Prevention of Armed Conflict Foundation
- ♦ Stichting voor Europees Milieubeleid (see: #11261)
- ♦ Stichting van de Europese Carnavalssteden / see Federation of European Carnival Cities (#09496)
- ♦ Stichting Europese Mime Federatie (inactive)
- ♦ Stichting Europese Ontwikkelingssamenwerking / see Network for European Monitoring and Development Assistance
- ♦ Stichting Feedback EU / see Feedback EU
- ♦ Stichting Fonds Schrijvers in Nood (internationally oriented national body)
- ♦ Stichting Gered Gereedschap (internationally oriented national body)
- ♦ Stichting Greenpeace Council / see Greenpeace International (#10727)
- ♦ Stichting Iatrogenic Europe Unite-Alliance / see Iatrogenic Europe Unite – Alliance (#11010)
- ♦ Stichting Iconic Houses / see ICONIC HOUSES
- ♦ Stichting IDA / see IDA Foundation (#11091)
- ♦ Stichting IEA Secretariaat Nederland / see International Association for the Evaluation of Educational Achievement (#11882)
- ♦ Stichting IEU-Alliance / see Iatrogenic Europe Unite – Alliance (#11010)
- ♦ Stichting Internationaal Belasting Documentatie Bureau / see International Bureau of Fiscal Documentation (#12415)
- ♦ Stichting voor the Internationaal Decennium voor een Cultuur van Vrede en Geweldloosheid voor de Kinderen in de Wereld (internationally oriented national body)
- ♦ Stichting Internationale Culturele Activiteiten / see Dutch Centre for International Cooperation
- ♦ Stichting Internationale Werkkampen / see Foundation for International Voluntary Service
- ♦ Stichting International Institute for Environment and Development Europe / see International Institute for Environment and Development – Europe (#13878)
- ♦ Stichting International Kidney Cancer Coalition / see International Kidney Cancer Coalition (#13983)
- ♦ Stichting International Parents Alliance / see Parents International (#18198)
- ♦ Stichting International Pole and Line (#14610)
- ♦ Stichting International SOS / see International SOS Foundation (#15570)
- ♦ Stichting The International Well Control Forum / see International Well Control Forum (#15877)
- ♦ Stichting IPA / see Parents International (#18198)
- ♦ Stichting JourNetwork / see Journalism in the Eastern Mediterranean – Strategy, Training, Organization (#16154)
- ♦ Stichting Justdiggit Foundation / see Justdiggit

♦ Stichting Justice Initiative (SJI) 19985

Contact PO Box 19318, 3501 DH Utrecht, Netherlands. E-mail: srji.org@gmail.com.
URL: https://www.srji.org/

History 2001. Registration: Handelsregister, No/ID: KVK 30176053, Netherlands. **Aims** Legally protect victims of human rights violations connected to armed conflict and counter-terrorism operations, torture and gender-based violence in the post-Soviet region. **Structure** Governing Board; Committee of Recommendation; Advisory Committee. **Consultative Status** Consultative status granted from: *Council of Europe (CE, #04881)* (Participatory Status). **NGO Relations** Member of (2): *Conference of INGOs of the Council of Europe (#04607); European Implementation Network (EIN, #07521).* [2021/AA2430/f/**F**]

- ♦ Stichting Justitia et Pax Nederland / see Justice and Peace Netherlands
- ♦ Stichting voor de Kunsten te Brussel (internationally oriented national body)
- ♦ Stichting Liliane Fonds (internationally oriented national body)

♦ Stichting Lupus Academy Foundation (Lupus Academy) 19986

Secretariat Maasdijk 409, 4264 AS Veen, Netherlands. T. +31416693925. E-mail: secretariat@lupus-academy.org.
URL: https://lupus-academy.org/

History 2012, Netherlands. Registration: Handelsregister, No/ID: KVK 54535891, Netherlands. **Aims** Improve patient outcomes in systemic lupus erythematosus and allied diseases. **Structure** Lupus Academy Consortium; Steering Committee. **Activities** Research and development; research/documentation; training/education. **Events** *Annual Meeting* Barcelona (Spain) 2023, *Annual Meeting* 2022, *Annual Meeting* 2021, *Annual Meeting* 2020, *Annual Meeting* Warsaw (Poland) 2019. [2023/AA3251/v/**C**]

- ♦ Stichting Max Havelaar (internationally oriented national body)
- ♦ Stichting voor Milieueducatie (#09949)
- ♦ Stichting voor Milieueducatie in Europa / see Foundation for Environmental Education (#09949)
- ♦ Stichting voor Nederlandse Bosbouw-Ontwikkelingssamenwerking / see Vereniging Tropische Bossen
- ♦ Stichting Nederlandse Raad voor Juridische Samenwerking met Indonesië / see Center for International Legal Cooperation
- ♦ Stichting der Nederlandse Universiteiten en Hogescholen voor Internationale Samenwerking / see Netherlands Organization for International Cooperation in Higher Education
- ♦ Stichting Nederlandse Vrijwilligers / see SNV Netherlands Development Organisation
- ♦ Stichting De Noordzee (internationally oriented national body)
- ♦ Stichting De Ondergrondse Kerk / see Hulp aan de Verdrukte Kerk
- ♦ Stichting Onderzoek Multinationale Ondernemingen (internationally oriented national body)
- ♦ Stichting Onderzoek Turkestan (internationally oriented national body)
- ♦ Stichting Orfeus / see Observatories and Research Facilities for European Seismology (#17639)
- ♦ Stichting Partnership of a European Group of Aeronautics and Space Universities Foundation / see Partnership of a European Group of Aeronautics and Space UniversitieS (#18236)
- ♦ Stichting Partnership on Sustainable, Low Carbon Transport / see Partnership on Sustainable, Low Carbon Transport Foundation (#18244)
- ♦ Stichting Permits (#18334)
- ♦ Stichting Prins Claus Fonds voor Cultuur en Ontwikkeling (internationally oriented national body)
- ♦ Stichting Promotie Internationale Neerlandistiek (see: #11854)
- ♦ Stichting Re-course International / see Recourse (#18630)
- ♦ Stichting reNature / see reNature Foundation
- ♦ Stichting Respect International West-East Bridges Foundation / see West-East Bridges Foundation (#20909)
- ♦ Stichting Seas at Risk Federation / see Seas at Risk (#19189)
- ♦ Stichting Society of Lateral Access Surgery / see Society of Lateral Access Surgery (#19586)
- ♦ Stichting Solidaridad / see SOLIDARIDAD Network (#19681)
- ♦ Stichting SOS / see Fair Trade Original
- ♦ Stichting SPARC Europe / see SPARC Europe (#19902)
- ♦ Stichting Stem van Afrika (internationally oriented national body)
- ♦ Stichting Steun voor Onderontwikkelde Streken / see Fair Trade Original
- ♦ Stichting TEAR Fund Nederland / see Tear
- ♦ Stichting tot Internationale Natuurbescherming / see Van Tienhoven Foundation for International Nature Protection
- ♦ Stichting Tribunaal voor de Vrede (internationally oriented national body)
- ♦ Stichting Tropenbos International / see Tropenbos International
- ♦ Stichting voor Vermiste en Seksueel Uitgebuite Kinderen / see European Centre for Missing and Sexually Exploited Children
- ♦ Stichting Vluchteling (internationally oriented national body)
- ♦ Stichting Vredeseducatie (internationally oriented national body)
- ♦ Stichting tegen Vrouwenhandel / see Coördinatiecentrum Mensenhandel
- ♦ Stichting Wereld Verbond van Wereld Federalisten / see World Federalist Movement – Movement for a Just World Order through a Strengthened United Nations (#21404)
- ♦ Stichting Wereldverbond van Wereld Federalisten (#21404)
- ♦ Stichting Werkgroep Internationaal Wad- en Watervogelonderzoek (#09976)
- ♦ Stichting Werkgroep Noordzee / see North Sea Foundation
- ♦ Stichting voor Wetenschappelijk Onderzoek van de Tropen / see WOTRO Science for Global Development

♦ Stichting ZDHC Foundation (ZDHC Foundation) 19987

Exec Dir Oudezijds Voorburgwal 316-B, 1012 GM Amsterdam, Netherlands. E-mail: media@zdhc.org.
URL: https://www.roadmaptozero.com/

History 2015. Initiated in 2011. ZDHC stands for: Zero Discharge of Hazardous Chemicals. Registration: No/ID: 62332252, Netherlands. **Aims** Enable brands and retailers in the textile, apparel, and footwear industries to implement sustainable chemical management best practice across the value chain. **Structure** Board; Management Team. **Activities** Advocacy/lobbying/activism; standards/guidelines. **Publications** *News.* Annual Reports. **NGO Relations** Cooperates with (1): *Asia Dyestuff Industry Federation (ADIF).* [2022.05.10/AA0639/f/**F**]

- ♦ Stiftelsen för Acta Odontologica Scandinavica / see Acta Odontologica Scandinavica Society (#00083)
- ♦ Stiftelsen Barn og Krig Children and War / see Children and War Foundation
- ♦ Stiftelsen för ett Levande Östersjön (internationally oriented national body)
- ♦ Stiftelsen Flyktningerådet (internationally oriented national body)
- ♦ Stiftelsen Globträdet (internationally oriented national body)

♦ Stiftelsen IMTEC 19988

IMTEC Foundation

Dir Grínland 58, 3045 Drammen, Norway. T. +4723203900. E-mail: imtec@imtec.org.
URL: http://www.imtec.org/

History 1972, as a 4-year OECD project on the management of educational change. Became independent in 1977, as *International Learning Cooperative.* Subsequently changed title to *IMTEC – International Movements Towards Educational Change.* Registered in accordance with Norwegian law. **Aims** Study the way that educational change works. **Structure** Governing Board, headed by Chairman. Director. *IMTEC Foundation.* **Activities** Research and development; research/documentation; monitoring/evaluation; networking/liaising; events/meetings; training/education. **Events** *International Seminar* Mölndal (Sweden) 2000, *International Seminar* Beitostølen (Norway) 1997, *School year 2020 conference / International Seminar* Berlin (Germany) 1993, *International Seminar* Oxford (UK) 1990, *International Seminar* Snowmass, CO (USA) 1989. **Publications** File of 300 international case studies. **Members** Individuals and institutions worldwide. Membership countries not specified. [2020/XD2518/**F**]

- ♦ Stiftelsen for industriell og teknisk forskning / see SINTEF
- ♦ Stiftelsen Kidlink / see Kidlink Association (#16189)
- ♦ Stiftelsen Kulturarv utan gränser / see Cultural Heritage without Borders

♦ Stiftelsen Nordiska Sällskapet för Upplysning om Spelberoende (SNSUS) 19989

Nordic Society Foundation for Information about Problem Gambling

Contact c/o Sustainable Interaction AB, Winstrupsgatan 1, SE-222 22 Lund, Sweden. T. +46703330570.
URL: http://www.snsus.org/

History 1999. **Aims** Disseminate knowledge and information about problem gambling. **Structure** Board, comprising 5 regular members and 1 honorary member. **Languages** English. **Staff** 5.00 FTE, paid. **Finance** Donations. **Events** *Conference* Tampere (Finland) 2019, *Conference* Stockholm (Sweden) 2015, *Conference* Hamar (Norway) 2013, *Treatment, prevention and responsible gaming* Reykjavik (Iceland) 2011, *Problem gambling, treatment and prevention* Helsinki (Finland) 2009.
Members Full in 5 countries:
Denmark, Finland, Iceland, Norway, Sweden. [2017/XJ0369/f/**D**]

- ♦ Stiftelsen ReGeneration 2030 sr / see ReGeneration 2030 (#18742)
- ♦ Stiftelsen för Utbildning och Forskning Avseende Inflammatoriska Tarmsjukdom / see International Organization for the Study of Inflammatory Bowel Disease (#14475)
- ♦ Stiftelsen Utbildning Nordkalotten – Utbildning Nord (#01102)
- ♦ Stiftung Deutsches Übersee-Institut / see GIGA – German Institute of Global and Area Studies
- ♦ Stiftung DIAKONIA Weltbund von Verbänden und Gemeinschaften der Diakonie / see World Federation of Diaconal Associations and Diaconal Communities (#21429)
- ♦ Stiftung DIAKONIA / see World Federation of Diaconal Associations and Diaconal Communities (#21429)
- ♦ Stiftung für die Förderung der Inneren Medizin in Europa (#09944)

- ♦ Stiftung Die Schwelle (internationally oriented national body)
- ♦ Stiftung Drittes Millennium (internationally oriented national body)
- ♦ Stiftung ECARF – Europäische Stiftung für Allergieforschung (internationally oriented national body)
- ♦ Stiftung Entwicklung und Frieden (internationally oriented national body)
- ♦ Stiftung Europa und Gesellschaft / see Association Europe and Society (#02586)
- ♦ Stiftung der Europäischen Karnevalsstädte / see Federation of European Carnival Cities (#09496)
- ♦ Stiftung des Europäischen Verdienstordens (internationally oriented national body)
- ♦ Stiftung Europäisches Naturerbe / see EuroNatur – European Nature Heritage Fund (#05738)
- ♦ Stiftung für Europäische Sprach- und Bildungszentren / see Foundation for Language and Educational Centres (#09964)
- ♦ Stiftung für Europäische Umweltpolitik (see: #11261)
- ♦ Stiftung Europa-Kolleg Hamburg (internationally oriented national body)
- ♦ Stiftung zur Förderung der Gesundheit – IHCF (#11109)
- ♦ Stiftung für den Fortschritt des Menschen / see Fondation Charles Léopold Mayer pour le progrès de l'homme (#09815)
- ♦ Stiftung für Gesundheit, Religiosität und Spiritualität (internationally oriented national body)
- ♦ Stiftung Global Werte Allianz (internationally oriented national body)
- ♦ Stiftung GRS – Stiftung für Gesundheit, Religiosität und Spiritualität (internationally oriented national body)
- ♦ Stiftung Internationales Centrum für Begabungsforschung (internationally oriented national body)
- ♦ Stiftung für Internationales Kulturschaffen in Gebirge (#09813)
- ♦ Stiftung für Internationale Verständigung / see Folmer Wisti Foundation for International Understanding
- ♦ Stiftung Kinderdorf Pestalozzi (internationally oriented national body)
- ♦ Stiftung Lebende Ostsee (internationally oriented national body)
- ♦ Stiftung Leukämiepatientvertreter (unconfirmed)
- ♦ Stiftung Menschen gegen Minen (internationally oriented national body)
- ♦ Stiftung Mercator (internationally oriented national body)
- ♦ Stiftung Mozarteum Salzburg (internationally oriented national body)
- ♦ Stiftung für nachhaltige Entwicklung und interkulturellen Austausch (internationally oriented national body)
- ♦ Stiftung Neues Europa-Kolleg Hamburg / see Stiftung Europa-Kolleg Hamburg
- ♦ Stiftung der Niederländischen Hochschuler für Internationale Zusammenarbeit / see Netherlands Organization for International Cooperation in Higher Education
- ♦ Stiftung Nord-Süd-Brücken (internationally oriented national body)
- ♦ Stiftung für Ökologische Entwicklung (internationally oriented national body)
- ♦ Stiftung 'Populorum Progressio' (#09969)
- ♦ Stiftung für Sprach- und Bildungszentren (#09964)
- ♦ Stiftung Tinnitus Research Initiative / see Tinnitus Research Initiative (#20166)
- ♦ Stiftung für Umwelterziehung (#09949)
- ♦ Stiftung für Umwelterziehung in Europa / see Foundation for Environmental Education (#09949)
- ♦ Stiftung UNESCO – Bildung für Kinder in Not / see YOU Stiftung – Bildung für Kinder in Not
- ♦ Stiftung für Vermisste und Sexuell Ausgebeuteter Kinder / see European Centre for Missing and Sexually Exploited Children
- ♦ Stiftung Volkswagenwerk / see Volkswagen Foundation
- ♦ Stiftung Weltethos (internationally oriented national body)
- ♦ Stiftung Welt ohne Minen (internationally oriented national body)
- ♦ Stiftung Weltvertrag (internationally oriented national body)
- ♦ Stiftung Wissenschaft und Politik (internationally oriented national body)
- ♦ Stiftung Wissenschaft und Politik – Deutsches Institut für Internationale Politik und Sicherheit / see Stiftung Wissenschaft und Politik
- ♦ Stigmatines – Pauvres Filles des Sacrés Stigmates de Saint François d'Assise (religious order)

♦ STI International 19990

Treas Augasse 5-7/25, 1090 Vienna, Austria. T. +436643964684.
Contact Univ of Innsbruck, Technikerst 21a, 6020 Innsbruck, Austria. T. +4351250753710.
URL: http://www.sti2.org/

History Founded as *Semantic Technology Institute International (STI2)*. Registered in accordance with Austrian law. **Aims** Establish semantics as a main pillar of modern *computer* engineering; exploit semantic technologies to address the various challenges associated with communication and collaboration at large scales. **Structure** General Assembly (annual); Board; Executive Board. Fellows; Auditor; Board of Arbitrators. **Finance** Sources: members' dues. **Activities** Awards/prizes/competitions; events/meetings; training/education. **Events** *General Assembly* Heraklion (Greece) 2016, *General Assembly* Heraklion (Greece) 2015, *General Assembly* Portoroz (Slovenia) 2015, *General Assembly* Crete (Greece) 2014, *Extraordinary General Assembly* Bonn (Germany) 2013.
Members Ordinary; Extraordinary. Members in 8 countries:
Austria, Belgium, Germany, Korea Rep, Netherlands, Russia, Spain, UK. [2020/XJ8820/j/**C**]

- ♦ Stimmatini – Congregazione delle Sacre Stimmate di Nostro Signore Gesù Cristo (religious order)

♦ Stirling International Association 19991

Contact Via Sandro Totti 3, 60131 Ancona AN, Italy. E-mail: info@stirlinginternational.org.
URL: http://www.stirlinginternational.org/

History Registered in accordance with Italian law, 3 Apr 2012. **Aims** Foster initiatives aimed to promote cultural relations between members and the international scientific community; contribute to activities and development of research in the sector of *Stirling-cycle* machines; collect, circulate and promote information about members and their activities; encourage young people, students and enthusiasts to study the Stirling-cycle machine and explore its *thermal fluid-dynamic* aspect. **Structure** General Meeting (at ISEC); International Stirling Engine Council; Executive Committee; Scientific and Organizing Committees; President. **Languages** English. **Staff** 1.00 FTE, voluntary. **Finance** Members' dues. Other sources: sponsorship; participant fees. **Activities** Events/meetings; knowledge management/information dissemination. **Events** *Conference* Tainan (Taiwan) 2018, *Conference* Newcastle upon Tyne (UK) 2016, *Conference* Bilbao (Spain) 2014, *Conference* Dubrovnik (Croatia) 2012, *Conference* Groningen (Netherlands) 2009. **Publications** Conference proceedings. **Members** Worldwide membership. Membership countries not specified. **NGO Relations** Links with universities. [2016.12.22/XJ6651/**E**]

- ♦ STI – Sustainable Travel International (internationally oriented national body)
- ♦ STISWB – International Conference on Science, Technology and Innovation for Sustainable Well-Being (meeting series)
- ♦ STIU – Stamford International University (internationally oriented national body)

♦ St Joan's International Alliance (SJIA) 19992

L'Alliance terre des femmes – Alleanza Internazionale Giovanna d'Arco (AIGA)

Contact 1360 University Avenue West, Ste 463, Minneapolis MN 55104, USA.
URL: http://www.stjoansinternationalalliance.org/

History 1931, Paris (France), as an international body, developing from 'Catholic Women's Suffrage Society', set up 1911, London (UK), the only association of Catholics then working for woman's suffrage. Name changed, 1923, to *St Joan's Social and Political Alliance*. Current English title adopted following formation of sections, the French title being *Alliance Internationale Sainte Jeanne d'Arc*. Constitution amended: 1947, Brussels (Belgium); 1953, Paris; 1961, London; 1985; 10-11 Aug 2001, Brussels, when current French title adopted. **Aims** Secure equal *rights* and opportunities for *women* and men in state, society, and *Church*. **Structure** General Assembly (every 2 years) of 2 delegates per national section, elects President, Vice-Presidents, Treasurer, Secretary (who, with the departing President, comprise the Executive Committee which meets annually), representatives at the United Nations and other intergovernmental and non-governmental bodies, and Editor (2-year terms). **Languages** English, French. **Staff** Voluntary. **Finance** Members' annual dues. Subscriptions to periodical; donations. **Activities** Resaerch/documentation. **Events** *Biennial international council meeting and general assembly / Biennial International Council Meeting* Brussels (Belgium) 2001, *Biennial International Council Meeting* Ravenna (Italy) 1999, *Biennial international council meeting and general assembly / Biennial International Council Meeting* Leuven (Belgium) 1997, *Biennial International Council Meeting* Leuven (Belgium) 1995, *Biennial International Council Meeting* Ravenna (Italy) 1993. **Publications** *Terre des femmes* (4 a year) in French; *The Catholic Citizen* (2 a year) in English. **Members** National sections; independent members in countries where there is no national section. Membership countries not specified. **Consultative Status** Consultative status granted from: *ECOSOC (#05331)* (Special). **IGO Relations** Accredited by: *United Nations Office at Vienna (UNOV, #20604)*. Associated with Department of Global Communications of the United Nations. **NGO Relations** Member of: *Women's Ordination Worldwide (WOW, #21032)*. [2019/XF3169/**F**]

- ♦ St Joan's Social and Political Alliance / see St Joan's International Alliance (#19992)
- ♦ St Joseph's Missionary Society of Mill Hill (religious order)
- ♦ St Joseph's Society of the Sacred Heart (religious order)
- ♦ STJ – Society of St Teresa of Jesus (religious order)
- ♦ **STLE** Society of Tribologists and Lubrication Engineers (#19655)
- ♦ **STL** Special Tribunal for Lebanon (#19911)
- ♦ St Madeleine-Sophie Barat – Society of the Sacred Heart of Jesus (religious order)
- ♦ STM Group / see International Association of Scientific, Technical and Medical Publishers (#12154)
- ♦ **STM** International Association of Scientific, Technical and Medical Publishers (#12154)
- ♦ ST – Missionari Servi della Santissima Trinità (religious order)
- ♦ **STM** Save the Mothers (#19059)
- ♦ **STMS** Society for Tennis Medicine and Science (#19652)
- ♦ STNSA / see Sustainable Tourism Certification Alliance Africa (#20068)
- ♦ Stockholm Club / see European Confederation of International Trading Houses Associations (#06708)
- ♦ Stockholm Convention on Persistent Organic Pollutants (2001 treaty)

♦ Stockholm Environment Institute (SEI) 19993

Exec Dir Box 24218, SE-104 51 Stockholm, Sweden. E-mail: info-hq@sei.org – executive.director@sei.org.
Street Address Linnégatan 87D, SE-115 23 Stockholm, Sweden. T. +468308044.
URL: http://www.sei.org

History 1989, Stockholm (Sweden). Founded on the initiative of the Swedish government. **Aims** Support decision-making and induce change towards sustainable development around the world by providing integrative knowledge that bridges science and policy in the field of environment and development. **Structure** International Board; Offices/Centres (7): Africa; America (USA); Asia; Europe (Oxford, Tallinn, York); Latin America. **Finance** Sources: government support; international organizations. Supported by: *African Development Bank (ADB, #00283)*; *Asian Development Bank (ADB, #01422)*; *European Commission (EC, #06633)*; *Every Home for Christ International (EHCI, #09214)*; *German Marshall Fund of the United States (GMF)*; *Nordic Council of Ministers (NCM, #17260)*; *OECD (#17693)*; *Swedish International Development Cooperation Agency (Sida)*; *The Rockefeller Foundation (#18966)*; *UNDP (#20292)*; *UNEP (#20299)*; *United Nations Economic Commission for Europe (UNECE, #20555)*; *World Meteorological Organization (WMO, #21649)*. **Activities** Events/meetings; knowledge management/information dissemination; research and development. **Events** *Sustainable Development Forum* Tallinn (Estonia) 2018, *Climate Adaptation Governance Workshop* Stockholm (Sweden) 2017, *International Workshop on the Politics of Fossil Fuel Subsidies* Stockholm (Sweden) 2016, *Low-Carbon Development in Africa Workshop* Nairobi (Kenya) 2015, *Research Forum* Stockholm (Sweden) 2012. **Publications** *Renewable Energy for Development* – newsletter. *Atmospheric Environment in Developing Countries Series*; *Energy, Environment and Development Series (EED Series)*; *PoleStar Series*. Books; articles.
Members Previous and current (*) Board members in 20 countries:
Canada (*), China, Costa Rica (*), Egypt, Estonia (*), Ghana, Guyana (*), India, Indonesia, Italy (*), Japan (*), Kuwait, Mexico, Poland, Russia (*), Sudan (*), Sweden (*), Switzerland (*), UK (*), USA (*).
Consultative Status Consultative status granted from: *ECOSOC (#05331)* (Ros A); *UNEP (#20299)*. **IGO Relations** Accredited by (2): *Green Climate Fund (GCF, #10714)*; *United Nations Framework Convention on Climate Change – Secretariat (UNFCCC, #20564)*. Cooperates with (3): *Inter-American Institute for Cooperation on Agriculture (IICA, #11434)*; *Intergovernmental Panel on Climate Change (IPCC, #11499)*; *South Asia Cooperative Environment Programme (SACEP, #19714)*. Accredited to the Conference of the Parties of: *Secretariat of the United Nations Convention to Combat Desertification (Secretariat of the UNCCD, #19208)*. **NGO Relations** Member of (10): *Asian Energy Institute (AEI, #01436)*; *Climate and Clean Air Coalition (CCAC, #04010)*; *Climate Knowledge Brokers (CKB, #04016)*; *European Forum on Integrated Environmental Assessment (EFIEA, no recent information)*; *Global Alliance of Disaster Research Institutes (GADRI, #10194)*; *Institute for European Environmental Policy (IEEP, #11261)*; *LEDS Global Partnership (LEDS GP, #16435)*; *Nordic Network on Climate Change Governance (NordClimGov, inactive)*; *Resilience Alliance (RA, #18911)*; *Sustainable Sanitation Alliance (SuSanA, #20066)*. Partner of (4): *Many Strong Voices (MSV, #16568)*; *Partnership on Sustainable, Low Carbon Transport Foundation (SLoCaT Foundation, #18244)*; *Sanitation and Water for All (SWA, #19051)*; *Southern and Eastern Africa Rainwater Network (SearNet, #19876)*. Supports (1): *International Centre for Tropical Agriculture (#12527)*. Instrumental in setting up (1): *Beijer Institute – International Institute of Ecological Economics*. Main collaborating institutions listed in this Yearbook: *African Academy of Sciences (AAS, #00193)*; *African Centre for Technology Studies (ACTS, #00243)*; *AFREPREN/FWD (#00153)*; *Environnement et développement du Tiers-monde (enda, #05510)*; *Institute for International Urban Development (I2UD)*; *International Institute for Environment and Development (IIED, #13877)*; *International Institute of Tropical Agriculture (IITA, #13933)*; *World Business Council for Sustainable Development (WBCSD, #21254)*; *World Resources Institute (WRI, #21753)*; *World Wide Fund for Nature (WWF, #21922)*. [2022.10.19/XE3018/j/**E**]

♦ Stockholm International Peace Research Institute (SIPRI) 19994

Institut international de recherche sur la paix de Stockholm – Stockholms Internationella Fredsforskningsinstitut

Dir Signalistgatan 9, SE-169 72 Solna, Sweden. T. +4686559700. E-mail: director@sipri.org.
URL: http://www.sipri.org/

History 1 Jul 1966, Stockholm (Sweden). Current Statutes adopted by the Swedish Government in 1994, amended in 1995, entered into force 1997. Former names and other names: *International Institute for Peace and Conflict Research* – former. **Aims** As an institute for scientific research, further understanding on conditions for peaceful solutions to international *conflicts* and for a stable peace; offer a unique platform for researchers from different countries to work in close cooperation. **Structure** Governing Board; Advisory Committee; Director; Deputy Director; Research Staff Collegium. **Languages** English. **Staff** 100.00 FTE, paid. **Finance** Financed by Swedish Parliament and a range of public and private sources. **Activities** Events/meetings; guidance/assistance/consulting; research/documentation. **Events** *Stockholm Forum on Peace and Development* Stockholm (Sweden) 2022, *Stockholm Forum on Peace and Development* Stockholm (Sweden) 2021, *Stockholm Security Conference* Stockholm (Sweden) 2021, *Stockholm Forum on Peace and Development* Stockholm (Sweden) 2020, *Stockholm Security Conference* Stockholm (Sweden) 2020. **Publications** *SIPRI Yearbook* – in several languages. Research reports; series; books; monographs; fact sheets; policy papers; press releases. **Members** Not a membership organization. **IGO Relations** Partner of (1): *South Eastern and Eastern Europe Clearinghouse for the Control of Small Arms and Light Weapons (SEESAC, #19804)*. Cooperates with (3): *Organisation for the Prohibition of Chemical Weapons (OPCW, #17823)* (Preparatory Commission); *Organization for Security and Cooperation in Europe (OSCE, #17887)*; *United Nations (UN, #20515)*. **NGO Relations** Member of (4): *Euro-Mediterranean Study Commission (EuroMeSCo, #05727)* (Observer); *European Information Network on International Relations and Area Studies (EINIRAS, #07534)*; *Global Partnership for the Prevention of Armed Conflict (GPPAC, #10538)*; *International Peace Research Association (IPRA, #14537)*. Partner of (1): *European Leadership Network (ELN, #07666)*. Joint project with: *Pugwash Conferences on Science and World Affairs (#18574)*. Jointly manages: *European Network of Independent Non-Proliferation Think Tanks (EU Non-Proliferation Network, #07930)*. [2022.05.05/XE4571/j/**E**]

- ♦ Stockholm International Toy Research Centre (internationally oriented national body)
- ♦ Stockholm International Water Institute (internationally oriented national body)

♦ **Stockholm Resilience Centre** **19995**
Dir Stockholm Univ, Albanovägen 28, SE-106 91 Stockholm, Sweden. T. +4686747070. E-mail: info@stockholmresilience.su.se.
URL: http://www.stockholmresilience.org/

History Jan 2007. Launched as a joint initiative between Stockholm University and *Beijer Institute – International Institute of Ecological Economics*. Registration: No/ID: 202100-3062, Sweden. **Aims** Advance research for governance and management of social-ecological systems to secure *ecosystem* services for human wellbeing and resilience for long-term *sustainability*. **Structure** Independent international Board. **Languages** English. **Staff** 100.00 FTE, paid. **Finance** Funded by Foundation for Strategic Environmental Research (Mistra). **Activities** Events/meetings; research/documentation; training/education. **Publications** *Stockholm Resilience Centre Newsletter* (12 a year) – electronic. [2023.02.20/XM4493/**E**]

♦ Stockholm School of Asian Studies (internationally oriented national body)
♦ Stockholms Internationella Fredsforskningsinstitut (#19994)

♦ **Stolen Asset Recovery Initiative (StAR)** **19996**
Contact 1818 H St NW, Washington DC 20433, USA. E-mail: starinitiative@worldbank.org.
URL: http://www1.worldbank.org/finance/star_site/

History 2007, as a partnership between *The World Bank Group (#21218)* and *United Nations Office on Drugs and Crime (UNODC, #20596)*. **Aims** Support international efforts to end safe havens for corrupt funds; cooperate with developing countries and financial centers to prevent the laundering of the proceeds of corruption and facilitate more systematic and timely return of stolen assets. **Finance** Financed by World Bank Group and UNODC. Contributions from governments of Australia, France, Luxembourg, Norway, Sweden and Switzerland. **Activities** Training/education; guidance/assistance/consulting; networking/liaising. **Events** *Arab Forum on Asset Recovery* Marrakech (Morocco) 2013. **Publications** *StAR News*. Policy notes; handbooks. [2012/XJ5635/**E***]

♦ STO – NATO Science and Technology Organization (unconfirmed)
♦ Stone Center for Latin American Studies, New Orleans (internationally oriented national body)
♦ STOP AIDS NOW ! (internationally oriented national body)

♦ **STOP the Destruction of the World** **19997**
Association STOP à la destruction du monde
Main Office Avenida Rebouças 3819, Sao Paulo SP, 05401-450, Brazil. T. +551130323616. E-mail: stop@stop.org.br.
URL: http://www.stop.org.br/english/

History 28 Jun 1992. Registered in accordance with French law. **Aims** Make the public aware of the *problems* the *planet* is facing; gather people willing to work towards solutions. **Languages** English, Finnish, French, German, Italian, Portuguese, Spanish. **Staff** 11.00 FTE, paid; 50.00 FTE, voluntary. **Finance** Funded by: donations; activities; sale of products. Budget (annual): about US$ 150,000. **Events** *Meeting* Cambuquira (Brazil) 2006, *Meeting* Cambuquira (Brazil) 2005, *Meeting* Sao Paulo (Brazil) 2004, *Meeting* Sao Paulo (Brazil) 2003, *Meeting* Sao Paulo (Brazil) 2002. **Publications** *The Integral Psychoanalysis*.
Members National committees in 7 countries:
Brazil, Finland, France, Portugal, Russia, Sweden, UK.
Individuals in 14 countries:
Austria, Côte d'Ivoire, Denmark, Germany, Greece, Italy, Japan, Nigeria, Panama, Poland, Saudi Arabia, Somalia, Spain, USA.
NGO Relations *International Society of Analytical Trilogy (ISAT, #14917)*. [2008/XF3223/**F**]

♦ **Stop Ecocide International (SEI)** **19998**
Exec Dir Willow Court, Beeches Green, Stroud, GL5 4BJ, UK. E-mail: team@stopecocide.earth – press@stopecocide.earth.
Registered Address Nieuwe Herengracht 18, 1018 DP Amsterdam, Netherlands.
URL: https://www.stopecocide.earth/

History 2017. Founded by barrister Polly Higgins (1968-2019) and Jojo Mehta. Managed from UK by Stop Ecocide International Ltd. Charitable entity Stop Ecocide Foundation created Nov 2019, Netherlands. Registration: Companies House, No/ID: 10830859, Start date: 22 Jun 2017, England and Wales; Handelsregister, No/ID: KVK 76532054, Netherlands. **Aims** Make ecocide an international crime. **Structure** Board; Advisory Board. **Finance** Stop Ecocide Foundation acts as main fundraising and commissioning vehicle. **Activities** Advocacy/lobbying/activism; networking/liaising. **Publications** *Stop Ecocide Newsletter*.
Members National branches in 25 countries:
Australia, Belgium, Canada, Chile, Croatia, Cyprus, Denmark, Finland, Germany, Italy, Kenya, Korea Rep, Mauritius, Netherlands, New Zealand, Norway, Peru, Portugal, Serbia, Spain, Sweden, Switzerland, Tunisia, USA, Zambia.
IGO Relations Cooperates with (1): *United Nations Commission on Crime Prevention and Criminal Justice (CCPCJ, #20530)*. **NGO Relations** Partner of (7): *1% for the Planet*; *Climate Counsel (#04011)*; *Earth Law Center*; *Fridays For Future (FFF, #09997)*; *Global Witness (GW)*; *International Council on Environmental Economics and Development (ICEED, #13017)*; *International Parliamentary Alliance for the Recognition of Ecocide (Ecocide Alliance, #14517)*. [2022/AA2672/**C**]

♦ Stop Hunger Now / see Rise Against Hunger
♦ Stop LFAS Worldwide (internationally oriented national body)
♦ Stop Prisoner Rape / see Just Detention International

♦ **Stop TB Partnership** **19999**
Exec Sec Chemin de Blandonnet 2, 1214 Vernier GE, Switzerland. T. +41227912967. Fax +41227914886. E-mail: communications@stoptb.org.
Contact address not obtained. T. +41225522818 – +4122(41794755534.
URL: http://www.stoptb.org/

History 2000, with the original title: *Global Partnership to Stop TB*. **Aims** Ensure that every TB patient has access to effective diagnosis, treatment and cure; stop transmission of TB; reduce the inequitable social and economic toll of TB; develop and implement new preventive, diagnostic and therapeutic tools and strategies to stop TB. **Structure** Partners' Forum (meets every 3 years); Coordinating Board; Working Groups (7); Secretariat in Geneva (Switzerland). **Languages** English, French, Spanish. **Staff** 45.00 FTE, paid. **Finance** Donations. **Activities** Advocacy/lobbying/activism. **Events** *Coordinating Board Meeting* Kuala Lumpur (Malaysia) 2012, *International Tuberculosis Symposium* Takatsuki (Japan) 2011, *Forum* Rio de Janeiro (Brazil) 2008, *Forum* Delhi (India) 2003, *World congress on tuberculosis* Washington, DC (USA) 2002. **Publications** *Stop TB News*. *Global Plan to Stop TB 2016-2020*. Progress reports.
Members Partners (over 1,600). Board members (34) in 19 countries:
Brazil, Bulgaria, Canada, China, Eswatini, France, India, Japan, Kenya, Lesotho, Myanmar, Netherlands, Pakistan, South Africa, Switzerland, Syrian AR, UK, USA, Zambia.
Included in the above, 8 organizations listed in this Yearbook:
Bill and Melinda Gates Foundation (BMGF); *Canadian International Development Agency (CIDA, inactive)*; *Global Fund to Fight AIDS, Tuberculosis and Malaria (Global Fund, #10383)*; *International Union Against Tuberculosis and Lung Disease (The Union, #15752)*; *Joint United Nations Programme on HIV/AIDS (UNAIDS, #16149)*; *TB Alliance (#20103)*; *United States Agency for International Development (USAID)*; *WHO (#20950)*.
IGO Relations Secretariat provided by: WHO. Partners include: *Canadian International Development Agency (CIDA, inactive)*; *Department for International Development (DFID, inactive)*; *Global Fund to Fight AIDS, Tuberculosis and Malaria (Global Fund, #10383)*; *International Bank for Reconstruction and Development (IBRD, #12317)* (World Bank); *Joint United Nations Programme on HIV/AIDS (UNAIDS, #16149)*; *UNDP (#20292)*.
NGO Relations Partners include:
- *Amref Health Africa (#00806)*;
- *Bill and Melinda Gates Foundation (BMGF)*;
- *Damien Foundation – Voluntary Organization for Leprosy and TB Control (AF)*;
- *Every Woman Every Child (EWEC, #09215)*;
- *Global Health Council (GHC, #10402)*;
- *Icons of Europe*;
- *International Council of Nurses (ICN, #13054)*;
- *International Federation of Medical Students' Associations (IFMSA, #13478)*;
- *International Federation of Red Cross and Red Crescent Societies (#13526)*;
- *International Union Against Tuberculosis and Lung Disease (The Union, #15752)*;
- *PATH (#18260)*;
- *The Rockefeller Foundation (#18966)*;
- *Social Development International (SDI)*;
- *TB Alliance (#20103)*;
- *World Economic Forum (WEF, #21367)*;
- *World Vision International (WVI, #21904)*.

Member of: *Global Health Workforce Alliance (GHWA, inactive)*. [2017.06.01/XF6853/y/**F**]

♦ **Storage Networking Industry Association (SNIA)** **20000**
Headquarters 5201 Great America Parkway, Suite 320, Santa Clara CA 95054, USA. T. +17196941380. Fax +17196941385. E-mail: info@snia.org.
URL: http://www.snia.org/

History 1 Dec 1997. Former names and other names: *Storage Networking Industry Association Europe (SNIA Europe)* – former. **Aims** Promote high-level knowledge exchange, thought-leadership and the acceptance of storage networks as open, trusted and valued solutions across the IT community. **Structure** Board of Directors. Secretariat. **Staff** 5.00 FTE, paid. **Activities** Events/meetings. **Events** *SDC : Storage Developer Conference* Fremont, CA (USA) 2022, *SDC : Storage Developer Conference* Santa Clara, CA (USA) 2018, *Conference* Santa Clara, CA (USA) 2016, *Conference* Santa Clara, CA (USA) 2015, *Storage Developer Conference* Santa Clara, CA (USA) 2014. **Members** Membership countries not specified. [2023.02.14/XD9261/t/**D**]

♦ Storage Networking Industry Association Europe / see Storage Networking Industry Association (#20000)

♦ **Storage Networking Industry Association South Asia (SNIA South Asia)** **20001**
Exec Dir 111 North Bridge Road, No 27-01/02 Peninsula Plaza, Singapore 179098, Singapore. T. +61424665024. E-mail: admin@snia-sa.org.
URL: https://www.snia.org/south-asia/

History Set up as the regional affiliate of the US Storage Networking Industry Association (SNIA). **Aims** Lead the storage industry worldwide in developing and promoting standards, technologies, and educational services to empower organizations in the management of information. **Structure** Board. **Finance** Sources: members' dues. [2021/XJ7775/t/**D**]

♦ Storbyens Hjerte Og Smerte – Nordisk Storbykonference (meeting series)
♦ Stowarzyseenie Europejskich Regionów Granicznych (#02499)
♦ Stowarzyszenie Ekologow na Rzecz Energii Nuklearnej (internationally oriented national body)
♦ Stowarzyszenie Koalicja Karat (#16179)
♦ Støtteordningen for Nordisk Ungdomssamarbejde (inactive)
♦ STP and A – International Conference of Social Theory, Politics and the Arts (meeting series)
♦ St Patrick's Society for the Foreign Missions (religious order)
♦ St Petersburg International Economic Forum (meeting series)
♦ **STP International** Society for Threatened Peoples International (#19654)
♦ STP – Special Trade Passenger Ships Agreement, 1971 (1971 treaty)

♦ **La Strada International (LSI)** **20002**
Mailing Address Postbus 15865, 1001 NJ Amsterdam, Netherlands. T. +31206881414. E-mail: info@lastradainternational.org.
URL: http://www.lastradainternational.org/

History First project started Sep 1995 between organizations in Czech Rep, Netherlands and Poland. Became operational 1 Jan 2005. 2019, network and platform merged. Former names and other names: *La Strade International – European Network Against Trafficking in Human Beings* – full title; *International La Strada Association* – former. Registration: EU Transparency Register, No/ID: 552173642688-57, Start date: 10 May 2021. **Aims** Raise awareness of human *trafficking* as a violation of human rights; inform *women* and girls about the risks of trafficking and how to protect themselves; protect short- and long-term assistance to women and girls who have become victims of trafficking; defend and advocate their rights; build up strong and independent NGOs in Central and Eastern Europe, working in this area. **Structure** General Assembly (2 a year); Board; Advisory Board; International Secretariat in Amsterdam (Netherlands). **Languages** English. **Staff** 135.00 FTE, paid. **Finance** Initial funding from Dutch Ministry of Justice and *Phare Programme (inactive)*. Currently main funding from Dutch donors, *King Baudouin Foundation (KBF)*, *Sigrid Rausing Trust* and *European Commission (EC, #06633)*. Donors vary per year, per country and per project. European Commission. Budget (annual): about euro 400,000. **Activities** Advocacy/lobbying/activism; awareness raising. **Events** *Annual meeting* Skopje (Macedonia) 2007. **Publications** *La Strada Newsletter* (4 a year). *Violation of Women's Rights: A Cause and Consequence of Trafficking in Women* (2008); *La Strada Facts and Figures* (2005). Prevention material; manuals; guidelines.
Members Organizations (8) in 8 countries:
Belarus, Bulgaria, Czechia, Moldova, Netherlands, North Macedonia, Poland, Ukraine.
Consultative Status Consultative status granted from: *Council of Europe (CE, #04881)* (Participatory Status); *ECOSOC (#05331)* (Special). **IGO Relations** *European Union Agency for Fundamental Rights (FRA, #08969)*; *International Organization for Migration (IOM, #14454)*; *Organization for Security and Cooperation in Europe (OSCE, #17887)*; *United Nations (UN, #20515)*. **NGO Relations** *Amnesty International (AI, #00801)*; *Association for Women's Rights in Development (AWID, #02980)*; *Coördinatiecentrum Mensenhandel (CoMensha)*; *Global Alliance Against Traffic in Women (GAATW, #10184)*; *Global Fund for Women (GFW, #10384)*; *Human Rights and Democracy Network (HRDN, #10980)*; *Human Rights Watch (HRW, #10990)*; *Oxfam Novib*; *Platform for International Cooperation on Undocumented Migrants (PICUM, #18401)*; *UNCAC Coalition (#20283)*. [2021/XM1643/**D**]

♦ La Strade International – European Network Against Trafficking in Human Beings / see La Strada International (#20002)
♦ **STRADEMED** Association internationale des pays du pourtour de la Méditerranée et de l'Union européenne (#02726)
♦ Straits Commission (inactive)
♦ Strana Aliance Liberalu a Demokratu pro Evropu (#00703)
♦ Strana Aliancie liberalov Demokratov za Európu (#00703)
♦ Stranka Evropskih liberalcev, demokratov in reformistov / see Alliance of Liberals and Democrats for Europe Party (#00703)
♦ Stranka Zaveznistva Liberalcev in Demokratov za Evropo (#00703)
♦ St Raphael's Society (religious order)
♦ Strasbourg Agreement Concerning the International Patent Classification (1971 treaty)

♦ **Strasbourg Astronomical Data Centre** **20003**
Centre de données astronomiques de Strasbourg (CDS)
Dir Observatoire Astronomique, Univ de Strasbourg, 11 rue de l'Université, 67000 Strasbourg, France. T. +33368852487. E-mail: cds-question@unistra.fr.
URL: http://cds.unistra.fr/

History 1972, with the title *Centre of Stellar Data – Centre de données stellaires*, originally as a permanent service of *Federation of Astronomical and Geophysical Data Analysis Services (FAGS, inactive)*. Current responsible union: *International Astronomical Union (IAU, #12287)*. Since 2008: Infrastructure de Recherche, France. **Aims** Collect information on astronomical objects outside the *solar system*; improve them through critical evaluation and comparison; develop value-added information services for worldwide usage by professional astronomers; participate in definition of international exchange standards in astronomy and in International Virtual Observatory. **Languages** English, French. **Staff** 30.00 FTE, paid. **Finance** Annual budget: about euro 3,000,000. **Activities** Knowledge management/information dissemination; research and development. **Events** *Conference on astronomy from large databases* Haguenau (France) 1992, *Errors, uncertainties and bias in astronomy* Strasbourg (France) 1989. **Information Services** *ALADIN* – interactive sky atlas; *SIMBAD (Set of Identification, Bibliography, for Astronomical Data)* – database; *VIZIER* – catalogues. **NGO Relations** Member of: *ISC World Data System (ISC-WDS, #16024)*. Certified by: Data Seal of Approval. [2019.12.11/XE0314/**E**]

♦ Stratagem Strategic Research / see RAND Europe

♦ Strategic Account Management Association (internationally oriented national body)
♦ Strategic Alliance for Asian Studies / see European Alliance for Asian Studies (#05861)

♦ Strategic Alliance of the National Convention Bureaux of Europe .. 20004

Co-Chair GCB German Convention Bureau e. V., Kaiserstr. 53, 60329 Frankfurt-Main, Germany. T. +49692429300. E-mail: info@gcb.de.
Co-Chair address not obtained.
URL: https://convention-europe.com/

History 2014. **Aims** Unite individual and unique offerings of members, to simplify and strengthen the approach towards key markets, such as USA and China. **Activities** Research/documentation; events/meetings. **Events** *Meeting* Lisbon (Portugal) 2022, *Meeting* Reykjavik (Iceland) 2018, *Meeting* Munich (Germany) 2016, *Meeting* Warsaw (Poland) 2015.
Members National Convention Bureaux in 23 countries:
Austria, Czechia, Denmark, Estonia, Finland, France, Germany, Hungary, Iceland, Ireland, Italy, Latvia, Montenegro, Netherlands, Norway, Poland, Portugal, Serbia, Slovakia, Slovenia, Spain, Sweden, Switzerland. [2022/XM4233/D]

♦ Strategic Approach to International Chemicals Management (SAICM) 20005

Secretariat UN Environment, Chemin des Anémones 11-13, Chatelaine, 1219 Geneva, Switzerland. T. +41229178532. Fax +41227973460. E-mail: saicm.chemicals@unep.ch.
URL: http://www.saicm.org/

History 6 Feb 2006, Dubai (United Arab Emirates), at International Conference on Chemicals Management (ICCM), after being proposed at World Summit on Sustainable Development, 2002, Johannesburg (South Africa). **Aims** Promote chemical safety around the world; achieve sound management of chemicals throughout their life cycle so that, by 2020, chemicals are produced and used in ways that minimize significant adverse impacts on human health and the environment. **Structure** Secretariat at: *UNEP DTIE Chemicals Branch (inactive)*. **Finance** Donor governments: Australia, Austria, Canada, Denmark, Finland, Germany, Kenya, Netherlands, Nigeria, Norway, Senegal, Slovenia, Sweden, Switzerland, Thailand, United Arab Emirates, UK and Uruguay. Donor Organizations: *European Commission (EC, #06633)*; *International Bank for Reconstruction and Development (IBRD, #12317)* (World Bank); *OECD (#17693)*; *UNDP (#20292)*; *UNEP (#20299)*; *UNIDO (#20336)*; *WHO (#20950)*; Zayed International Prize for the Environment. **Activities** Awareness raising. **Events** *African regional meeting* Nairobi (Kenya) 2011, *Latin American and Caribbean regional meeting* Panama (Panama) 2011, *Seminar* Tokyo (Japan) 2011, *African regional meeting* Abidjan (Côte d'Ivoire) 2010, *Latin American and Caribbean regional meeting* Kingston (Jamaica) 2010. **IGO Relations** Cooperates with: *Inter-Organization Programme for the Sound Management of Chemicals (IOMC, #15956)*. [2017.10.27/XM3845/E*]

♦ Strategic Arms Reduction Treaty (1991 treaty)
♦ Strategic and Corporate Europlanners Society (inactive)
♦ Strategic and Defence Studies Centre (internationally oriented national body)
♦ Strategic Foresight Group (internationally oriented national body)

♦ Strategic Initiative for Women in the Horn of Africa (SIHA) 20006

Secretariat Plot 2A Lugogo Lane, Naguru, PO Box 2793, Kampala, Uganda. T. +256414286263. E-mail: sihahornofafrica@gmail.com.
Sudan Office PO Box 1805, Omdurman, Ahmed Khair Str, 3, Khartoum, Sudan. T. +249183571789.
URL: http://www.sihanet.org/

History 1995. **Aims** Strengthen women's capacities and build regional solidarity for advocacy; share lessons in relation to women's rights in the Horn of Africa region. **Structure** Board of Directors; Secretariat. **Languages** English. **Finance** Funding through various embassies and international donors. **Activities** Projects/programmes. **Publications** *Women in Islam* (annual) – journal. Country publications.
Members Full in 7 countries:
Djibouti, Eritrea, Ethiopia, Somalia, South Sudan, Sudan, Uganda.
Consultative Status Consultative status granted from: *African Commission on Human and Peoples' Rights (ACHPR, #00255)* (Observer). **IGO Relations** *African Commission on Human and Peoples' Rights (ACHPR, #00255)*. [2022/XJ9985/F]

♦ Strategic Management Society (SMS) 20007

Exec Office 134 N LaSalle St, Suite 1005, Chicago IL 60607-3567, USA. T. +13124926224. Fax +13124926223. E-mail: sms@strategicmanagement.net.
URL: http://www.strategicmanagement.net/

History 1981, London (UK). Founding group of officers elected 1982, Montréal (Canada), served as Founding Board. Registration: Start date: 1983, USA. **Aims** Develop and disseminate insight into the strategic management process; foster contacts and interchange among academics, business practitioners and consultants worldwide. **Structure** Board. **Languages** English. **Staff** 5.00 FTE, paid. **Finance** Sources: members' dues. **Activities** Events/meetings. **Events** *Conference* London (UK) 2022, *Special Conference* Milan (Italy) 2022, *Conference* Toronto, ON (Canada) 2021, *Conference* Chicago, IL (USA) 2020, *Annual Conference* London (UK) 2020. **Publications** *Strategic Management Journal* (12 a year); *Global Strategy Journal* (4 a year); *Strategic Entrepreneurship Journal* (4 a year). **Members** Regular, student and emeritus, individual academics, business practitioners and consultants (over 3,000) in over 80 countries and territories. Membership countries not specified. [2022.02.02/XC0064/v/C]

♦ Strategie der EU für den Alpenraum (#09203)
♦ Stratégies et Développement en Méditerranée / see Association internationale des pays du pourtour de la Méditerranée et de l'Union européenne (#02726)

♦ Strategies for Peace 20008

Administrator 61 Sedlescombe Road, London, SW6 1RE, UK. T. +442073856738.

History Founded 1981, with the title *Generals for Peace and Disarmament (GPD)*, as a small group of retired senior officers from NATO countries who questioned the wisdom of NATO defence strategy depending on the nuclear deterrent. In 1989, the retired generals and admirals of NATO and Warsaw Treaty Organization merged into a single group. Adopted new title *Worldwide Consultative Association of Retired Generals and Admirals (WCARGA)* in 1990, on expanding constituency to include non-European countries and constitution of a new modus operandi based on a global consultancy association. Has in the past also been referred to as *Retired Generals and Admirals for Peace and Disarmament*, as *Worldwide Association of Retired Generals and Admirals* and as *International Consultative Association of Retired Generals and Admirals*. **Aims** Use the skills and experience of senior retired *military* personnel to strengthen initiatives for *conflict* prevention, conflict resolution and peace building; disseminate information on these initiatives as widely as possible. **Structure** A forum acting as a pressure group directing recommendations to decision-makers. **Languages** English. **Staff** 1.00 FTE, voluntary. **Finance** Funding derives from: individual donations; sale of literature. Annual budget: pounds10,000. **Activities** Conflict resolution; knowledge management/information dissemination. **Events** *Biennial Conference* 2005, *Biennial Conference* Amman (Jordan) 2002, *Biennial conference / Biennial Meeting* Colombo (Sri Lanka) 2000, *Biennial Meeting* Arusha (Tanzania UR) 1998, *Biennial Meeting* London (UK) 1995. **Publications** Booklets; occasional papers; memoranda. **Members** Individuals. Membership countries not specified. [2018.06.01/XF1349/v/F]

♦ Stratégie de l'Union européenne pour la région Alpine (#09203)
♦ Stredisko Mezinarodnich Studii Jana Masaryka (internationally oriented national body)

♦ streetfootballworld 20009

Contact Waldenserstr 2, 10551 Berlin, Germany. T. +493078006240. E-mail: contact@streetfootballworld.org.
URL: http://www.streetfootballworld.org/

History 2002. **Aims** Contribute to social change on a global scale through the power of football; promote partnerships for development, using *football* to unite grassroots organizations, corporations and public bodies in the pursuit of positive social development. **Structure** Board. Headquarters in Berlin (Germany); Regional Offices in: Cape Town (South Africa); New York NY (USA); Rio de Janeiro (Brazil). **Activities** Projects/programmes; guidance/assistance/consulting; events/meetings.
Members Community organizations (over 100) in 50 countries:
Argentina, Australia, Bosnia-Herzegovina, Botswana, Brazil, Burkina Faso, Burundi, Cambodia, Cameroon, Cape Verde, Chile, Colombia, Costa Rica, Cuba, Denmark, Ecuador, France, Germany, Ghana, Haiti, Hungary, India, Indonesia, Iraq, Ireland, Israel, Kenya, Lesotho, Liberia, Mali, Mozambique, Netherlands, Nigeria, Peru, Portugal, Rwanda, Sierra Leone, South Africa, Spain, St Lucia, Sudan, Switzerland, Tanzania UR, Uganda, UK, Uruguay, USA, Vietnam, Zambia, Zimbabwe.
Included in the above, 6 organizations listed in this Yearbook:
Coaches Across Continents (CAC); *Peres Center for Peace, The*; *PLAY SOCCER Nonprofit International (PSNI)*; *Soccer Without Borders (SWB)*; *WASH United*; *Women Win (#21042)*.
Consultative Status Consultative status granted from: *ECOSOC (#05331)* (Special). **IGO Relations** *European Commission (EC, #06633)*. **NGO Relations** Partners include: *Ashoka – Innovators for the Public (#01248)*; *Confédération africaine de football (CAF, #04500)*; *International Federation of Association Football (#13360)*; *Union of European Football Associations (UEFA, #20386)*. [2016.10.07/XM1227/F]

♦ StreetNet International 20010

Coordinator PO Box 61139, Bishopsgate, Durban, 4008, South Africa. T. +27313074038. Fax +27313067490. E-mail: sharonpillay847@gmail.com – coordinator@streetnet.org.za.
URL: http://www.streetnet.org.za/

Aims Promote the exchange of information and ideas on critical issues facing street vendors and market *vendors* and hawkers (mobile vendors) and on practical organizing and advocacy strategies. **Structure** International Council, comprising officers and 12 members. Executive Committee, comprising President, Vice-President, Secretary and Treasurer. **Events** *Congress* Cotonou (Benin) 2010, *Congress* Atibaia (Brazil) 2007, *Congress* Seoul (Korea Rep) 2004, *Congress* Durban (South Africa) 2002.
Members Affiliates in 30 countries:
Argentina, Bangladesh, Benin, Brazil, Congo Brazzaville, Congo DR, Ghana, Guinea, Honduras, India, Kenya, Korea Rep, Lesotho, Malawi, Mexico, Mozambique, Namibia, Nepal, Nicaragua, Niger, Peru, Senegal, South Africa, Tanzania UR, Togo, Uganda, USA, Venezuela, Zambia, Zimbabwe.
NGO Relations Member of: *Women in Informal Employment: Globalizing and Organizing (WIEGO, #21003)*. [2014/XJ2018/C]

♦ Streets Ahead Children's Centre Association (internationally oriented national body)
♦ Streit Council – Streit Council for a Union of Democracies (internationally oriented national body)
♦ Streit Council for a Union of Democracies (internationally oriented national body)
♦ Stress and Anxiety Research Society / see Stress, Trauma, Anxiety, and Resilience Society (#20011)

♦ Stress, Trauma, Anxiety, and Resilience Society (STAR) 20011

Pres Berlin School of Economics and Law, Campus Lichtenberg, Alt-Friedrichsfelde 60, 10315 Berlin, Germany. E-mail: contact@star-society.org.
Sec address not obtained.
Treas address not obtained.
Main Website: http://star-society.org/

History 1980, Antwerp (Belgium). Former names and other names: *Stress and Anxiety Research Society* – former; *Society for Test Anxiety Research* – former. Registration: Berlin District Court, No/ID: VR 38633, Start date: 7 Jan 2021, Germany, Charlottenburg. **Aims** Foster research and understanding in stress, anxiety, and related phenomena in a multi-disciplinary fashion. **Structure** General Assembly, Board; Officers; Committees. **Languages** English. **Staff** Voluntary. **Finance** Sources: members' dues. **Activities** Events/meetings. **Events** *Annual Conference* Palma (Spain) 2019, *Annual Conference* Lublin (Poland) 2018, *Annual Conference* Hong Kong (Hong Kong) 2017, *Annual Conference* Cluj-Napoca (Romania) 2014, *Annual Conference* Faro (Portugal) 2013. **Publications** *STAR Newsletter* (4 a year); *Journal of Stress, Trauma, Anxiety, and Resilience (J-STAR)* (2 a year) – official journal. *Stress and Anxiety – Application to Life Span Development and Health Promotion* (2008); *Stress and Psychosocial Resources – Coping with life changes, occupational demands, educational challenges, and threats to physical and emotional well being* (2008); *Stress and Anxiety – Application to Health, Community, Work Place and Education* (2006); *Advances in Test Anxiety Research* – in 7 vols. Research reports; proceedings; theoretical papers; reviews; analyses.
Members National representatives in 38 countries and territories:
Argentina, Australia, Belgium, Brazil, Canada, Costa Rica, Croatia, Czechia, Dominican Rep, Egypt, Estonia, Finland, France, Germany, Greece, Hungary, India, Ireland, Israel, Italy, Japan, Malaysia, Mexico, Netherlands, New Zealand, Norway, Pakistan, Poland, Portugal, Puerto Rico, Romania, Russia, Slovakia, Spain, Switzerland, Türkiye, UK, USA.
Individuals in 40 countries and territories:
Argentina, Australia, Austria, Belgium, Brazil, China, Czechia, Denmark, Egypt, Estonia, Finland, France, Germany, Greece, Hungary, India, Iran Islamic Rep, Ireland, Israel, Italy, Japan, Malaysia, Mexico, Netherlands, New Zealand, Norway, Poland, Portugal, Romania, Russia, Serbia, Slovakia, Slovenia, Spain, Sweden, Switzerland, Taiwan, Türkiye, UK, USA. [2022.02.10/XD0986/F]

♦ Strings (meeting series)
♦ Strings and Geometry Conference (meeting series)
♦ STRI – Smithsonian Tropical Research Institute, Panama (internationally oriented national body)
♦ **STRN** Sustainability Transitions Research Network (#20050)

♦ Stroke Alliance for Europe (SAFE) 20012

Secretariat Rue Washington 40, 1050 Brussels, Belgium. T. +447866758813. E-mail: info@safestroke.eu.
URL: http://www.safestroke.eu/

History Oct 2004. Registration: Banque-Carrefour des Entreprises, No/ID: 0661.651.450, Start date: 23 Aug 2016, Belgium. **Aims** Raise awareness and understanding of stroke and stroke prevention with policymakers at pan-European and national levels. **Structure** General Assembly (annual); Board. **Languages** English. **Staff** 3.00 FTE, paid. **Finance** Sources: grants; members' dues; revenue from activities/projects; sponsorship. **Activities** Events/meetings. **Events** *European Life After Stroke Forum* Barcelona (Spain) 2023, *European Life After Stroke Seminar* 2022, *European Life After Stroke Forum Seminar* 2021, *European Life After Stroke Forum Seminar* 2021, *European Life after Stroke Forum Seminar* 2021. **Publications** *Economic Impact of Stroke in Europe* (2019); *Stroke Action Plan for Europe 2018-2030* (2018); *Burden of Stroke in Europe* (2017).
Members National organizations (31) in 30 countries:
Belgium, Bulgaria, Croatia, Cyprus, Czechia, Denmark, Finland, Georgia, Germany, Greece, Hungary, Iceland, Ireland, Israel, Italy, Luxembourg, Netherlands, North Macedonia, Norway, Poland, Portugal, Romania, Serbia, Slovakia, Slovenia, Spain, Sweden, Türkiye, UK, Ukraine.
NGO Relations Member of (2): *European Alliance for Cardiovascular Health (EACH, #05863)*; *European Federation of Neurological Associations (EFNA, #07177)*. Cooperates with (5): *European Alliance for Access to Safe Medicines (EAASM, #05859)*; *European Patients' Forum (EPF, #08172)*; *European Stroke Organisation (ESO, #08843)*; *Federation of European and International Associations Established in Belgium (FAIB, #09508)*; *World Stroke Organization (WSO, #21831)*. [2022.10.19/XM1937/y/F]

♦ Stroke Care International (internationally oriented national body)
♦ Stroke Society of Australasia (internationally oriented national body)
♦ Strong and ElectroWeak Matter Conference (meeting series)
♦ **STRO** Scandinavian Tire and Rim Organization (#19124)
♦ Strømme Foundation (internationally oriented national body)
♦ Strømme Memorial Foundation / see Strømme Foundation
♦ Strømmestiftelsen (internationally oriented national body)
♦ **STR** Society for Terrorism Research (#19653)
♦ STR – Society for Theatre Research (internationally oriented national body)
♦ Structural Funds of the European Community (inactive)

♦ Structural Heart Disease Coalition (SHD Coalition) 20013

Contact c/o RPP Group Brussels, Rue Guimard 10, 1040 Brussels, Belgium. E-mail: secretariat@structuralheartdiseasecoalition.eu.
URL: https://structuralheartdiseasecoalition.eu/

History Former names and other names: *EU Structural Heart Disease Coalition (EU SHD Coalition)* – alias. Registration: EU Transparency Register, No/ID: 625204542275-25, Start date: 13 Apr 2021. **Aims** Work towards a European Joint Action on Structural Heart Disease with an emphasis on early diagnosis and treatment. **Structure** Steering Committee. **Activities** Advocacy/lobbying/activism. [2021/AA1595/D]

♦ **STS forum** Science and Technology in Society Forum (#19145)

- ♦ STSI – Sister to Sister International (internationally oriented national body)
- ♦ **ST** Sociedad Teosófica (#20141)
- ♦ **ST** Société théosophique (#20141)
- ♦ STS – School-to-School International (internationally oriented national body)
- ♦ STTC – European Sustainable Tropical Timber Coalition (unconfirmed)
- ♦ Studenta Tutmonda Esperanto-Ligo (inactive)
- ♦ Studentenes og Akademikernes Internasjonale Hjelpefond (internationally oriented national body)
- ♦ Student Movement for African Unity (inactive)
- ♦ Student Movement of the Afro-Malagasy Common Organization (inactive)

♦ Student Network Organization (SNO) 20014

Address not obtained.
URL: http://www.the-networktufh.org/sno

History 1993, Malaysia, as the student chapter of *The Network: Towards Unity for Health (The Network: TUFH, #17060).* **Aims** Promote interaction among TUFH student members and facilitate their participation in network activities. **Structure** Executive Committee. **Languages** English. **Activities** Events/metings. **Events** *Meeting* Mexico City (Mexico) 1997, *Meeting* Durban (South Africa) 1996, *International medical student workshop on the future of medical education* Maastricht (Netherlands) 1994. **NGO Relations** *International Federation of Medical Students' Associations (IFMSA, #13478).* [2019/XE2868/**E**]

- ♦ Student Organisation of Linguistics in Europe (unconfirmed)

♦ Student Planning Network (PlaNet) 20015

Contact address not obtained. E-mail: planningnetwork@gmail.com.

History Sep 1998, Berlin (Germany). Name derives from: Planning Network. **Aims** Provide a platform for students in the urban and regional planning disciplines. **Activities** Organizes congress. **Events** *Congress* Wroclaw (Poland) 2004, *International planet congress / Congress* Copenhagen (Denmark) 2002, *International student congress* Berlin (Germany) 1998.
Members Local groups (13) in 10 countries:
Austria, Canada, Denmark, France, Germany, Greece, Italy, Netherlands, Portugal, USA.
NGO Relations *Association of European Schools of Planning (AESOP, #02542); International Society of City and Regional Planners (ISOCARP, #15012).* [2008/XF4674/**F**]

♦ Student Platform for Engineering Education Development (SPEED) . 20016

Pres address not obtained. E-mail: info@worldspeed.org.
URL: http://www.worldspeed.org/

History 2006. Founded following *American Society for Engineering Education (ASEE, #00790)* 5th Global Colloquium on Engineering Education (GCEE). **Aims** Advance engineering education (EE) by providing a platform for global communication about EE among students as well as between students and other stakeholders. **Structure** General Assembly; Executive Committee; Board of Advisors. Working Groups. **Activities** Events/meetings; training/education. **Events** *World Engineering Education Forum* Kuala Lumpur (Malaysia) 2017, *African Student Forum for Engineering Education* Bloemfontein (South Africa) 2016, *Global Student Forum* Seoul (Korea Rep) 2016, *Global Student Forum* Florence (Italy) 2015, *World Engineering Education Forum* Florence (Italy) 2015. **Publications** *SPEED Newsletter.* **NGO Relations** Member of (1): *International Federation of Engineering Education Societies (IFEES, #13412).* [2020/XM5298/**F**]

♦ Students' European Network for Sustainable Development (SENSD) 20017

Registered Office 13 impasse Monvoisin Autard, 84000 Avignon, France.
URL: https://www.facebook.com/sensd/

History Aug 2010, France. **Aims** Gather European students together to promote sustainable development, by exchanging knowledge and information. **Structure** Board, comprising President, Secretary and Treasurer. [2015/XJ5371/**F**]

- ♦ Students for the Exploration and Development of Space (internationally oriented national body)
- ♦ Students in Free Enterprise / see Enactus (#05451)

♦ Students for a Free Tibet International (SFT International) 20018

Headquarters 602 East 14th St, 2nd Floor, New York NY 10009, USA. T. +12123580071. Fax +12123581771. E-mail: info@studentsforafreetibet.org.
URL: http://www.studentsforafreetibet.org/

History 1994, New York NY (USA). **Aims** Help Tibetan people regain their freedom. **Structure** Board of Directors.
Members Chapters (over 650) in 15 countries and territories:
Australia, Austria, Bangladesh, Canada, Denmark, France, Germany, India, Italy, Japan, Mexico, Poland, Taiwan, UK, USA. [2022/XJ8959/**E**]

- ♦ Students Helping Street Kids International (internationally oriented national body)
- ♦ Students International Union / see Institute of World Affairs
- ♦ Students Partnership Worldwide / see Restless Development
- ♦ Student Travel Association of Asia (inactive)
- ♦ Student University Network for Social and International Health (internationally oriented national body)

♦ Student World Assembly (SWA) 20019

Asamblea Mundial de Estudiantes

Contact 2 W 64th St, Ste 408, New York NY 10023, USA.

History 22 Sep 2003, USA. **Aims** Promote global democracy by engaging students in the democratic process throughout the world. **Structure** Board of Directors; Advisory Board; Executive Directs. Teams (5): Management; Program Development and Growth; Information Technology; Global Initiative and Outreach; Advocacy. **Languages** English. **Staff** 1.00 FTE, paid; 10.00 FTE, voluntary. **Finance** Donations by private foundations and individuals. Budget (annual): about US$ 130,000. **Events** *Annual international convention / Annual Convention* Peshawar (Pakistan) 2008, *Annual international convention / Annual Convention* Accra (Ghana) 2007, *Annual international convention / Annual Convention* Montréal, QC (Canada) 2006, *Annual international convention* Montréal, QC (Canada) 2005, *Annual international convention / Annual Convention* San Luis Obispo, CA (USA) 2004. **Publications** Annual Report. Monthly Updates; Membership Manual; Toolkits.
Members Students (about 18,000) in 149 countries and territories:
Albania, Algeria, Andorra, Antigua-Barbuda, Argentina, Australia, Austria, Azerbaijan, Bahrain, Bangladesh, Barbados, Belarus, Belgium, Belize, Benin, Bhutan, Bolivia, Bosnia-Herzegovina, Botswana, Brazil, Bulgaria, Burundi, Cambodia, Cameroon, Canada, Cape Verde, Central African Rep, Chile, China, Colombia, Congo Brazzaville, Congo DR, Costa Rica, Côte d'Ivoire, Croatia, Cuba, Cyprus, Czechia, Denmark, Dominican Rep, Ecuador, Egypt, El Salvador, Equatorial Guinea, Eritrea, Estonia, Ethiopia, Finland, France, Gabon, Gambia, Georgia, Germany, Ghana, Gibraltar, Greece, Guinea, Guyana, Haiti, Honduras, Hong Kong, Hungary, India, Indonesia, Iran Islamic Rep, Iraq, Ireland, Israel, Italy, Jamaica, Japan, Jordan, Kenya, Korea Rep, Kyrgyzstan, Latvia, Lebanon, Liberia, Lithuania, Madagascar, Malawi, Malaysia, Mauritania, Mauritius, Mexico, Moldova, Mongolia, Morocco, Mozambique, Myanmar, Nepal, Netherlands, New Zealand, Nicaragua, Niger, Nigeria, North Macedonia, Norway, Pakistan, Palestine, Papua New Guinea, Peru, Philippines, Poland, Polynesia Fr, Portugal, Puerto Rico, Qatar, Romania, Russia, Rwanda, Samoa USA, Saudi Arabia, Senegal, Serbia, Seychelles, Sierra Leone, Singapore, Slovakia, Slovenia, Somalia, South Africa, Spain, Sri Lanka, Sudan, Sweden, Switzerland, Syrian AR, Tajikistan, Tanzania UR, Thailand, Togo, Trinidad-Tobago, Tunisia, Türkiye, Uganda, UK, Ukraine, United Arab Emirates, Uruguay, USA, Uzbekistan, Venezuela, Vietnam, Virgin Is UK, Virgin Is USA, Yemen, Zambia, Zimbabwe. [2009.07.29/XM1672/**F**]

- ♦ Studie-Comité van de Westeuropese Steenkolenproducenten / see European Association for Coal and Lignite (#05978)
- ♦ Studie-en Informatiecentrum Mensenrechten (internationally oriented national body)
- ♦ Studie- en Informatiecentrum voor Vredes- en Ontwikkelingsproblematie (internationally oriented national body)
- ♦ Studienausschuss des Westeuropäischen Kohlenbergbaus / see European Association for Coal and Lignite (#05978)
- ♦ Studien- und Förderungsgesellschaft (inactive)
- ♦ Studiengruppe Europäischer Ernährungswissenschaftler / see Accademia Europea di Scienza della Nutrizione (#00045)
- ♦ Studienkreis für Tourismus und Entwicklung (internationally oriented national body)
- ♦ Studies Without Borders International (#05561)
- ♦ Studies and Expansion Society (inactive)
- ♦ Studies for Personal Assistants in the Countries of Europe / see SPACE Network (#19899)
- ♦ Studie Zentrum für Auswanderung Fragen (internationally oriented national body)
- ♦ Studio Globo (internationally oriented national body)
- ♦ Studiorum Novi Testamenti Societas (#19610)
- ♦ Study Center for the Historical Demography of Latin America (internationally oriented national body)
- ♦ Study Centre for the Third World (internationally oriented national body)
- ♦ Study Committee of the Hospital Organizations in the Common Market / see European Hospital and Healthcare Federation (#07501)
- ♦ Study Committee on the Legal Status of International Non-Governmental Organizations (inactive)

♦ Study Group on Asian Tax Administration and Research (SGATAR) . 20020

Contact Intl Tax Affairs and Relations Branch, Inland Revenue Authority of Singapore, 55 Newton Road, Singapore 307987, Singapore. T. +6563513251. Fax +6563513250.

History May 1970, during Fifth Southeast Asian Ministerial Conference for Economic Development (SEAMCED). **Aims** Provide a forum to discuss issues related to *taxation*; share best practices and experiences related to tax administration. **Structure** Has no formal organization, structure, charter or constitution, permanent secretariat or governing board. **Activities** Annual Meetings. Three topics are selected for deliberation each year. **Events** *Annual Meeting* Japan 2021, *Annual Meeting* Singapore (Singapore) 2015, *Annual Meeting* Sydney, NSW (Australia) 2014, *Annual Meeting* Jeju (Korea Rep) 2013, *Annual meeting* Fukuoka (Japan) 2010. **Publications** Reports.
Members Tax administrations in 13 countries and territories:
Australia, China, Hong Kong, Indonesia, Japan, Korea Rep, Malaysia, New Zealand, Philippines, Singapore, Taiwan, Thailand, Vietnam. [2013.09.13/XE0605/**F**]

- ♦ Study Group on Bone and Joint Infection / see European Bone and Joint Infection Society (#06380)
- ♦ Study Group on European Labor and Working-Class History / see Study Group on International Labor and Working Class History
- ♦ Study Group of European Public Service Training Agencies / see Standing Conference of European Public Service Training Agencies (#19961)
- ♦ Study Group on Historical Peace Research / see Arbeitskreis Historische Friedens- und Konfliktforschung
- ♦ Study Group on International Labor and Working Class History (internationally oriented national body)
- ♦ Study Group on Meat / see Intergovernmental Group on Meat and Dairy Products (#11491)
- ♦ Study Group on Rice / see Intergovernmental Group on Rice (#11493)
- ♦ Study Group for Saxon Research / see Internationales Sachsensymposion – Arbeitsgemeinschaft zur Archäologie der Sachsen und ihrer Nachbarvölker in Nordwesteuropa (#13305)
- ♦ Study Group of Tanners and Dressers in the EEC / see Confédération des associations nationales de tanneurs et mégissiers de la Communauté européenne (#04515)
- ♦ Study Platform on Interlocking Nationalisms (unconfirmed)

♦ Study and Research Group on Democracy, Economic and Social Development in Africa (GERDDES-Africa) 20021

Groupe d'étude et de recherche sur la démocratie et le développement économique et social en Afrique (GERDDES-Afrique)

Exec Sec 01 BP 1258, Cotonou, Benin. T. +229309268. Fax +229309273. E-mail: contact@gerddes.org.
Seat BP 16 Akpro-Missérété, Porto-Novo, Benin.
URL: http://www.gerddes.org/

History 1990, Cotonou (Benin). **Aims** Promote the democracy for favouring the economic and social development of African countries. **Structure** General Assembly; Bureau; Board of Directors; *Centre international de recherche sur la démocratie et le développement (CIRD) – International Research Centre on Democracy and Development (IRCD)*; Secretariat. **Finance** Subventions for seminars; assistance from international partners. **Activities** Research/documentation; events/meetings. **Events** *The role of the military in the democratic process* Ouagadougou (Burkina Faso) 1997, *Regional seminar* Cotonou (Benin) 1996, *Meeting on the struggle against impunity in Africa / Ordinary Session* Ouagadougou (Burkina Faso) 1996, *Regional seminar* Ouagadougou (Burkina Faso) 1996. **Publications** *African Democracy and Development* (4 a year) in English, French; *Development and Democracy* (4 a year) in English, French – newsletter; *Conflic Prevention in Africa* in English, French; *Role of the African Armed Forces in Democratic Process in Africa* in English, French.
Members National chapters in 31 countries:
Benin, Botswana, Burkina Faso, Cameroon, Canada, Central African Rep, Chad, Congo Brazzaville, Congo DR, Côte d'Ivoire, Equatorial Guinea, France, Gabon, Gambia, Ghana, Guinea, Guinea-Bissau, Kenya, Madagascar, Mali, Mauritania, Namibia, Niger, Nigeria, Rwanda, Senegal, Seychelles, South Africa, Togo, Tunisia, USA.
Consultative Status Consultative status granted from: *African Commission on Human and Peoples' Rights (ACHPR, #00255)* (Observer). **NGO Relations** Member of: *Inter-African Union of Human Rights (IUHR, inactive).* [2020/XF3037/**F**]

- ♦ STUF United Fund (internationally oriented national body)
- ♦ **STU** UNESCO Staff Union (#20321)
- ♦ STV / see Coördinatiecentrum Mensenhandel
- ♦ St Vincent Declaration Primary Care Diabetes Group / see Primary Care Diabetes Europe (#18495)
- ♦ **STVM** Society for Tropical Veterinary Medicine (#19656)
- ♦ STV – Sisters of St Thomas of Villanova (religious order)
- ♦ STWR – Share the World's Resources (internationally oriented national body)
- ♦ Styrelsen för internationellt utvecklingssamarbete (internationally oriented national body)
- ♦ Styrelsen för Nordiska Biståndsprojekt (inactive)

♦ Styrenics Circular Solutions (SCS) 20022

Contact Avenue des Arts 6-9, 1210 Brussels, Belgium. E-mail: info@styrenics-circular-solutions.com.
URL: http://styrenics-circular-solutions.com/

History Dec 2018. Registration: Banque-Carrefour des Entreprises, No/ID: 0720.728.311, Start date: 14 Feb 2019, Belgium; EU Transparency Register, No/ID: 198696432927-14, Start date: 20 Oct 2018. **Aims** Transform the styrenics industry by un-leashing polystyrene's value as a fully and infinitely recyclable material. **Structure** General Assembly.
Members Manufacturers. Membership countries not specified.
European Extruded Polystyrene Insulation Board Association (EXIBA, #07019); European Manufacturers of Expanded Polystyrene (EUMEPS, #07732); European Plastics Converters (EuPC, #08216); Plastics Recyclers Europe (PRE, #18394).
NGO Relations Member of (1): *Circular Plastics Alliance (#03936).* Partner of (1): *European Coalition for Chemical Recycling.* [2022.10.12/AA2026/ty/**D**]

- ♦ SUA 2005 – Protocol of 2005 to the Convention for the Suppression of Unlawful Acts against the Safety of Maritime Navigation (2005 treaty)
- ♦ SUA – Convention for the Suppression of Unlawful Acts Against the Safety of Maritime Navigation (1988 treaty)
- ♦ SUA PROT 2005 – Protocol of 2005 to the Protocol for the Suppression of Unlawful Acts against the Safety of Fixed Platforms Located on the Continental Shelf (2005 treaty)
- ♦ SUA PROT – Protocol for the Suppression of Unlawful Acts Against the Safety of Fixed Platforms Located on the Continental Shelf (1988 treaty)
- ♦ SUA / see World Council of Arameans – Syriacs (#21318)
- ♦ Subcomisión de la COI para el Caribe y Regiones Adyacentes (#16003)
- ♦ Subcommittee on Prevention of Torture / see Subcommittee on Prevention of Torture and other Cruel, Inhuman or Degrading Treatment or Punishment (#20023)

♦ Subcommittee on Prevention of Torture and other Cruel, Inhuman or Degrading Treatment or Punishment (SPT) — 20023

Address not obtained.
URL: https://www.ohchr.org/EN/HRBodies/OPCAT/Pages/OPCATIndex.aspx

History Feb 2007. Established pursuant to the provisions of *Optional Protocol to the UN Convention Against Torture and other Cruel, Inhuman or Degrading Treatment or Punishment (OPCAT, 2002).* A treaty body of *Office of the United Nations High Commissioner for Human Rights (OHCHR, #17697).* Former names and other names: *Subcommittee on Prevention of Torture* – alias. **Structure** Committee of 25 independent and impartial experts. **Activities** Advocacy/lobbying/activism; guidance/assistance/consulting.
Members Experts from 25 countries (term of expiry is last day of indicated year):
Argentina (2020), Chile (2022), Croatia (2022), Cyprus (2020), France (2022), Georgia (2022), Germany (2020), Greece (2022), Lebanon (2022), Mauritania (2020), Mauritius (2020), Moldova (2020), Montenegro (2020), Morocco (2020), Norway (2022), Panama (2022), Peru (2022), Philippines (2020), Senegal (2022), Serbia (2020), Spain (2022), Switzerland (2020), Togo (2022), UK (2020), Uruguay (2022).
States Parties to OPCAT, as at Aug 2020 (90):
Afghanistan, Albania, Argentina, Armenia, Australia, Austria, Azerbaijan, Belize, Benin, Bolivia, Bosnia-Herzegovina, Brazil, Bulgaria, Burkina Faso, Burundi, Cambodia, Cape Verde, Central African Rep, Chile, Congo DR, Costa Rica, Croatia, Cyprus, Czechia, Denmark, Ecuador, Estonia, Finland, France, Gabon, Georgia, Germany, Ghana, Greece, Guatemala, Honduras, Hungary, Iceland, Italy, Kazakhstan, Kyrgyzstan, Lebanon, Liberia, Liechtenstein, Lithuania, Luxembourg, Madagascar, Maldives, Mali, Malta, Mauritania, Mauritius, Mexico, Moldova, Mongolia, Montenegro, Morocco, Mozambique, Nauru, Netherlands, New Zealand, Nicaragua, Niger, Nigeria, North Macedonia, Norway, Palestine, Panama, Paraguay, Peru, Philippines, Poland, Portugal, Romania, Rwanda, Senegal, Serbia, Slovenia, South Africa, South Sudan, Spain, Sri Lanka, Sweden, Switzerland, Togo, Tunisia, Türkiye, UK, Ukraine, Uruguay.
IGO Relations *United Nations (UN, #20515).* [2020/AA1010/**E***]

- ♦ Sub-Committee on the Status of Women, Geneva / see NGO Committee on the Status of Women, Geneva (#17117)
- ♦ Subgrupo Intergubernamental sobre los Cueros y Pieles (#11502)
- ♦ Subilee Sur (#16159)
- ♦ Subjective Probability, Utility and Decision Making / see European Association for Decision Making (#06006)

♦ SUBMARINER Network for Blue Growth EEIG (SUBMARINER Network) — 20024

Managing Dir Kärntener Str 20, 10827 Berlin, Germany. T. +4930832141740. E-mail: asz@submariner-network.eu.
URL: http://www.submariner-network.eu/

History 2014, Berlin (Germany). An organization of the type *European Economic Interest Grouping (EEIG, #06960).* Registration: Amtsgericht Charlottenburg, No/ID: HRA 49838 B, Germany, Berlin. **Aims** Promote innovative approaches to the *sustainable* use of *marine resources*; offer a cooperation platform to related actors and initiatives in the *Baltic* Sea Region. **Structure** Executive Board; Secretariat. **Languages** English, German. **Activities** Advocacy/lobbying/activism; events/meetings; projects/programmes. **Publications** *SUBMARINER Newsletter.*
Members Full; Associate. Full in 6 countries:
Denmark, Finland, Germany, Lithuania, Poland, Sweden.
Associate in 8 countries:
Estonia, Finland, Germany, Latvia, Lithuania, Norway, Poland, Sweden.
NGO Relations Member of (1): *European Centre for Information on Marine Science and Technology (EurOcean).* [2020.11.18/XM6660/**F**]

- ♦ **SUBMARINER Network** SUBMARINER Network for Blue Growth EEIG (#20024)

♦ SubOptic — 20025

Sec address not obtained. E-mail: info@suboptic.org.
URL: http://www.suboptic.org/

History 1986. Former names and other names: *SubOptic Association* – current – now national. **Aims** Promote the interests of organizations and individuals involved in the submarine telecommunications industry, including with respect to the planning, deployment and operation of submarine cable systems, the technology used in such systems and the regulation of all related activity. **Structure** Executive Committee; Working Groups. **Staff** 1.00 FTE, paid. **Activities** Events/meetings; networking/liaising. **Events** *Conference* New Orleans, LA (USA) 2019, *Conference* Dubai (United Arab Emirates) 2016, *From ocean to cloud* Paris (France) 2013, *Conference* Yokohama (Japan) 2010, *Conference* Baltimore, MD (USA) 2007. [2022.02.08/XJ4811/**F**]

- ♦ SubOptic Association / see SubOptic (#20025)

♦ Sub-Regional Fisheries Commission (SRFC) — 20026

Commission sous-régionale des pêches (CSRP) – Comissão Sub-Regional das Pescas
Permanent Secretariat 116 Allées Khalifa Ababacar SY, BP 25485, Dakar, Senegal. T. +221338640475. Fax +221338640477. E-mail: spcsrp@spcsrp.org – spcsrp@gmail.com.
URL: http://www.spcsrp.org/

History 29 Mar 1985, Dakar (Senegal). Established through a Convention amended 14 July 1993, Praia (Cape Verde). **Aims** Ensure harmonization of national policies of Member States on preservation, conservation and exploitation of fisheries resources; strengthen cooperation for the well-being of the populations (Article 2 of the SRFC Convention of 1985). **Structure** Conference of Ministers (every 2 years); Coordinating Committee (meets annually); Permanent Secretariat. **Languages** English, French, Portuguese. **Staff** 37.00 FTE, paid. **Finance** Sources: contributions of member/participating states; grants; revenue from activities/projects. **Activities** Knowledge management/information dissemination; monitoring/evaluation; politics/policy/regulatory; research/documentation. **Events** *Ordinary session of the conference of ministers* Guinea 1998, *Round table donors conference* Praia (Cape Verde) 1997, *Ordinary session of the conference of ministers* Banjul (Gambia) 1996, *Séminaire sur les problèmes de délimitation de frontières maritimes* Rabat (Morocco) 1990. **Publications** *Flash info* – newsletter. Guides; documents; books; reports.
Members Member States (7):
Cape Verde, Gambia, Guinea, Guinea-Bissau, Mauritania, Senegal, Sierra Leone.
IGO Relations Cooperates with (1): *International Maritime Organization (IMO, #14102).* [2023.02.13/XE1355/**E***]

- ♦ Sub-Saharan African Network on Agricultural Advisory Services / see African Forum for Agricultural Advisory Services (#00320)
- ♦ Sub-Saharan Africa Transport Policy Program / see Africa Transport Policy Program (#00527)
- ♦ Sub-Saharan Africa Transport Program / see Africa Transport Policy Program (#00527)
- ♦ Subscriptions to Newspapers and Periodicals Agreement (1984 treaty)
- ♦ SuB – Sinn und Bedeutung (meeting series)

♦ Subsonic Aerodynamic Testing Association (SATA) — 20027

Sec address not obtained.
URL: http://www.sata.aero/

History Mar 1965. **Activities** Events/meetings. **Events** *Conference (SATA 2023)* Kyoto (Japan) 2024, *Conference* Kyoto (Japan) 2020, *Conference* Toronto, ON (Canada) 2019. [2020/AA0279/**C**]

♦ Substance Abuse Librarians and Information Specialists (SALIS) — 20028

Exec Dir PO Box 9513, Berkeley CA 94709-0513, USA. T. +15108656225. E-mail: salis@salis.org.
URL: https://salis.org/

History 1978, Houston, TX (USA). The Canadian ' Librarians and Information Specialists in Addictions (LISA)' merged with SALIS, 1986. *European Association of Libraries and Information Services on Addictions (ELISAD, inactive)* merged into SALIS, 2013-2014. Registration: Incorporated, Start date: 1988, USA, CA; 501(c)(3) organization, No/ID: EIN: 02-0408988, Start date: 1993, USA, CA. **Aims** Promote dissemination of knowledge and objective, accurate information about the use and consequences of alcohol, tobacco, and other *drugs*; provide a communications network for those working in the ATOD field; encourage cooperation and linkages among members and libraries/information centers; serve as an advocate for members on matters of common interest; support professional development through training programs. **Structure** Executive Board. Special Interest Groups; Committees. **Finance** Sources: donations; fundraising; meeting proceeds; members' dues; sponsorship. Annual budget: 25,000 USD (2021). **Activities** Events/meetings; knowledge management/information dissemination; networking/liaising; projects/programmes; training/education. **Events** *Annual Conference* New York, NY (USA) 2022, *Annual Conference* Berkeley, CA (USA) 2021, *Annual Conference* Washington, DC (USA) 2020, *Annual Conference* Boston, MA (USA) 2019, *Annual Conference* Berkeley, CA (USA) 2018. **Publications** *SALIS News* (4 a year) – newsletter; *SALIS Journal* (annual) – conference proceedings.
Members Full in 6 countries:
Australia, Canada, France, Portugal, UK, USA.
NGO Relations Affiliate member of: *International Council on Alcohol and Addictions (ICAA, #12989).* Member of: *International Confederation of Alcohol, Tobacco and other Drug Research Associations (ICARA, #12843).* [2022.10.12/XM4725/**C**]

- ♦ Subud Brotherhood International Foundation / see World Subud Association (#21836)

♦ Subud International Cultural Association (SICA) — 20029

Chair 9509 Ketona Cove, Austin TX 78759-6260, USA. E-mail: sica@subud-sica.org.
URL: https://sica-usa.org/

History 1992, as the independent cultural affiliate of *World Subud Association (WSA, #21836).* Registered in the State of Virginia (USA). **Aims** Encourage peace, harmony and understanding among people regardless of age, gender, ethnic origin, or religion; facilitate creative learning and education opportunities for the development of the full potential of human beings; advance and celebrate activities that emerge from the awakening, development and expression of one's inner gifts and talents; nurture and promote cultural and artistic activities and values than enliven and enrich the human spirit. **Structure** General Assembly. **Languages** English, French, German, Indonesian, Italian, Russian, Spanish. **Staff** Voluntary. **Finance** Grants and contributions. **Activities** Programs: Triennial SICA Prize; Interculture and Interfaith; Development of Human Societies; Education and Creativity Training; Human Values and Development; Creative Arts; Humanities, Science and Technology across all genres and disciplines. Provides technical assistance, advocacy and support services for individuals and organizations. Stages international and national exhibitions, festival and cultural events. Organizes seminars and workshops. **Events** *General Assembly* Christchurch (New Zealand) 2010, *General Assembly* New York, NY (USA) 2004, *General Assembly* Indonesia 2001, *General Assembly* Palangkaraya (Indonesia) 2001, *General Assembly* Argentina 2000. **Publications** *SICA Update* (12 a year) – electronic bulletin; *Celebrate* (2 a year) – online magazine. Annual Report.
Members National organizations and national contacts in 47 countries:
Argentina, Australia, Austria, Brazil, Canada, Chile, Colombia, Congo Brazzaville, Cuba, Denmark, Ecuador, Finland, France, Germany, Greece, India, Indonesia, Ireland, Israel, Italy, Jamaica, Japan, Kenya, Malaysia, Mexico, Moldova, Netherlands, New Zealand, Nigeria, Norway, Peru, Philippines, Portugal, Russia, Singapore, South Africa, Spain, Sri Lanka, Suriname, Sweden, Switzerland, UK, Ukraine, USA, Venezuela, Vietnam, Zambia.
NGO Relations Cooperates with: *Puppeteers Without Borders*; *Susila Dharma International Association (SDIA, #20048).* [2018/XK0079/**E**]

- ♦ Succow Foundation – Michael Succow Foundation for the Protection of Nature (internationally oriented national body)
- ♦ SUCO (internationally oriented national body)

♦ Sudamérica Rugby — 20030

Pres address not obtained.
Communications Officer address not obtained.
URL: https://www.sudamerica.rugby/

History 1988. Regional association of: *World Rugby (#21757).* Former names and other names: *South American Rugby Confederation (CONSUR)* – former; *Confederación Sud Americana de Rugby (CONSUR)* – former. **Structure** Board.
Members Full in 9 countries:
Argentina, Brazil, Chile, Colombia, Costa Rica, Paraguay, Peru, Uruguay, Venezuela.
NGO Relations Member of (1): *Asociación de Confederaciones Deportivas Panamericanas (ACODEPA, #02119).* [2023/XD9461/**D**]

♦ Sudan Consortium — 20031

Contact PO Box 603, Kampala, Uganda. E-mail: info@sudanconsortium.org.
URL: http://sudanconsortium.org/

History Sep 2004. Former names and other names: *Darfur Consortium* – former. **Aims** Promote a just, *peaceful* and sustainable end to the ongoing humanitarian and human rights crisis in Darfur.
Members National and international organizations (over 50) including the following 24 organizations listed in this Yearbook:

- *African Centre for Democracy and Human Rights Studies (ACDHRS, #00239);*
- *African Women's Development and Communication Network (FEMNET, #00503);*
- *Alliances for Africa (AfA);*
- *Anti-Slavery International (#00860);*
- *Arab Programme for Human Rights Activists (APHRA);*
- *Association africaine de défense des droits de l'homme (ASADHO);*
- *Cairo Institute for Human Rights Studies (CIHRS, #03397);*
- *Citizens for Global Solutions;*
- *East Africa Law Society (EALS, #05173);*
- *Femmes Africa solidarité (FAS, #09732);*
- *Human Rights First;*
- *Institute for Human Rights and Development in Africa (IHRDA);*
- *Inter-African Union of Human Rights (IUHR, inactive);*
- *International Commission of Jurists (ICJ, #12695);*
- *International Federation for Human Rights (#13452);*
- *International Refugee Rights Initiative (IRRI, #14708);*
- *Justice Africa;*
- *Media Foundation for West Africa (MFWA, #16617);*
- *Minority Rights Group International (MRG, #16820);*
- *Never Again International;*
- *Pan African Movement (PAM);*
- *Rencontre africaine pour la défense des droits de l'homme (RADDHO);*
- *Unitarian Universalist Service Committee (UUSC);*
- *Universal Human Rights Network.* [2020/XM2403/y/**F**]

- ♦ Sudan United Mission / see Pioneers UK
- ♦ Südasien Institut, Heidelberg (internationally oriented national body)
- ♦ **SUDEA** Society for Urban Development in East Africa (#19658)
- ♦ Súdneho dvora Európskej Unie (#04938)
- ♦ Súdney dvor Európskych Spolocenstiev / see Court of Justice of the European Union (#04938)
- ♦ Südosteuropa-Gesellschaft (internationally oriented national body)
- ♦ Sud-ouest sans frontières (internationally oriented national body)
- ♦ **SU-DS** Sports Union for athletes with Down Syndrome (#19930)
- ♦ SÜDWIND – Verein für Entwicklungspolitische Bildungs- und Öffentlichkeitsarbeit (internationally oriented national body)
- ♦ **SUEPO** Staff Union of the European Patent Office (#19944)
- ♦ **SUERA** Stratégie de l'Union européenne pour la région Alpine (#09203)

♦ SUERF – The European Money and Finance Forum — 20032

Société universitaire européenne de recherches financières
Secretariat c/o OeNB, Otto Wagner-Platz 3, 1090 Vienna, Austria. T. +431404207216 – +431404207206. E-mail: suerf@oenb.at.
URL: http://www.suerf.org/

History Founded 25 Nov 1963, Louveciennes (France). Constitution amended: 13 Oct 2006, Lisbon (Portugal); 3 Sep 2009, Utrecht (Netherlands); 10 Dec 2010, Barcelona (Spain); 15 Sep 2018, Helsinki (Finland). Registered in accordance with French law. **Aims** Provide a forum for information, research, networking and debate on financial and monetary issues, financial regulation, and supervision and monetary policy.

Structure General Assembly; Council of Management; Secretariat. **Languages** English, French. **Staff** 1.75 FTE, paid. **Finance** Members' dues. Contributions from most European national central banks, *Bank for International Settlements (BIS, #03165)* and *European Central Bank (ECB, #06466)*. **Activities** Events/meetings; networking/liaising; publishing activities. **Events** *The Euro area in an uncertain world* Paris (France) 2019, *Conference on Financial Disintermediation and the Future of the Banking Sector* Madrid (Spain) 2018, *Colloquium* Helsinki (Finland) 2017, *Colloquium* Frankfurt-Main (Germany) 2016, *Conference on Liquidity and Market Efficiency* Helsinki (Finland) 2015. **Publications** *SUERF Policy Notes*. Studies; conference proceedings and reports; book reviews.
Members Personal: academics, researchers, economists, consultants and members from the financial community in 30 countries and territories:
Australia, Austria, Belgium, Bulgaria, Canada, China, Denmark, Estonia, Finland, France, Germany, Greece, Hungary, Ireland, Italy, Japan, Luxembourg, Malta, Netherlands, New Zealand, Poland, Romania, Russia, Singapore, South Africa, Spain, Sweden, Switzerland, UK, USA.
Academic Institutions: universities, business schools and research institutions in 13 countries and territories:
Austria, Belgium, Bulgaria, Czechia, France, Germany, Hungary, Ireland, Italy, Poland, Switzerland, Taiwan, UK.
Corporate: banks, financial institutions, banking associations and public sector agencies in 15 countries:
Austria, Belgium, Denmark, Finland, France, Germany, Italy, Luxembourg, Netherlands, Portugal, Spain, Sweden, Switzerland, UK, USA.
Included in the above, one organization listed in this Yearbook:
European Investment Bank (EIB, #07599).
Central Banks, supervisors and international organizations in 21 countries:
Albania, Austria, Belgium, Croatia, Denmark, Finland, France, Germany, Hungary, Iceland, Ireland, Italy, Latvia, Luxembourg, Netherlands, Poland, Portugal, Slovakia, South Africa, Spain, Switzerland. [2020.03.03/XD4564/**D**]

- ♦ Suez Canal Users' Association (inactive)
- ♦ SUFIT / see International Organization for the Study of Inflammatory Bowel Disease (#14475)
- ♦ **SUFOI** Skandinavisk UFO Information (#19127)

♦ Sugar Association of the Caribbean (SAC) 20033

Mailing Address c/o Caroni, Brechin Castle, Couva, Trinidad-Tobago. T. +18686362449.
Chairman c/o Jamaica Cane Products Sales, 5 Trevennion Park Rd, Kingston, Jamaica. T. +8769293650.
History Founded 26 Jan 1942, as *British West Indies Sugar Association*. Name changed, 13 Dec 1966, to *West Indies Sugar Association*. Present title adopted 1 Dec 1975. Incorporated under the Companies Act of Trinidad and Tobago, 26 Jan 1942. **Aims** Promote and protect sugar *industry* in the Caribbean region; promote research and other scientific work in connection with the sugar industry; publish material in regard to the sugar industry. **Structure** Annual General Meeting; Board of Directors. Committees (3): Research and Cane Breeding; Sugar Technologists; Accountants. **Languages** English. **Staff** 1.00 FTE, paid. **Finance** Members' dues (annual), based on respective tonnages of sugar production. **Activities** Finances and administers *West Indies Central Sugar Cane Breeding Station (CBS, #20922)*. Exchanges and disseminates information amongst members and with others. Organizes periodic meetings of Caribbean sugar technologists. **Events** *Technologists conference / Conference* Port-of-Spain (Trinidad-Tobago) 2001, *Technologists conference* Georgetown (Guyana) 1997, *Meeting* Jamaica 1989. **Publications** Annual Report.
Members National associations in 4 countries:
Barbados, Belize, Guyana, Jamaica.
IGO Relations *Caribbean Community (CARICOM, #03476)*. **NGO Relations** *West Indies Sugarcane Breeding and Evaluation Network (WISBEN, see: #20922).* [2013.12.01/XD4153/**D**]

- ♦ Sugar Convention, 1864 (1864 treaty)
- ♦ Sugar Convention, 1866 (1866 treaty)
- ♦ Sugar Industry Technologists (unconfirmed)
- ♦ Sugar Union (inactive)
- ♦ Suhrawardiya (religious order)
- ♦ Suicide Prevention / see Samaritans
- ♦ Suid-Afrikaanse Instituut van Internasionale Aangeleenthede (internationally oriented national body)
- ♦ Suid-Afrikaanse Vereniging vir Plantpatologie / see Southern African Society for Plant Pathology (#19863)
- ♦ Suider-Afrikaanse Katolieke Biskopperraad (#19838)
- ♦ Suider-Afrikaanse Museum Vereniging (internationally oriented national body)
- ♦ Suider Afrikaanse Vereniging vir Kwarternavorsing (internationally oriented national body)
- ♦ Suider-Afrikaanse Vereniging vir Toegepaste Linguistiek (internationally oriented national body)
- ♦ Suider Afrika Rekenkundige Vereniging (#19834)
- ♦ Sulabh International Institute for Rural Development and Training / see International Centre for Women and Child
- ♦ Sulabh International Social Service Organization (internationally oriented national body)
- ♦ SUL – Associação para a Cooperação e Desenvolvimento (internationally oriented national body)

♦ Sulphur Institute, The (TSI) 20034

Institut international du soufre – Instituto del Azufre
CEO Don Messick, 1020 19th St NW, Ste 520, Washington DC 20036, USA. T. +12023319640. Fax +12022932940. E-mail: dmessick@sulphurinstitute.org – kkurowski@sulphurinstitute.org.
URL: http://www.sulphurinstitute.org/
History 1960. **Aims** Be the global advocate for sulphur, representing all stakeholders engaged in producing, buying, selling, handling, transporting or adding value to sulphur. **Structure** Board of Directors; Executive Committee. **Languages** Chinese, Dutch, English, Portuguese, Spanish. **Staff** 7.00 FTE, paid. **Finance** Contributions from producers of sulphur and affiliated industries, traders and brokers and consumers, and service providers for sulphur. **Events** *World Symposium* Barcelona (Spain) 2015, *World Symposium* Long Beach, CA (USA) 2014, *World Symposium / Sulphur World Symposium* Beijing (China) 2013, *World symposium / Sulphur World Symposium* New York, NY (USA) 2011, *World symposium / Sulphur World Symposium* Doha (Qatar) 2010. **Publications** Newsletter (weekly) – online; quarterly reports.
Members Full in 11 countries:
Canada, China, Germany, Japan, Korea Rep, Kuwait, Netherlands, Qatar, South Africa, Switzerland, USA.
Consultative Status Consultative status granted from: *ECOSOC (#05331)* (Ros C); *FAO (#09260)* (Liaison Status). **NGO Relations** Cooperates with: *International Fertilizer Development Center (IFDC, #13590).* [2017/XE2607/j/**E**]

- ♦ Sulpicians – Society of the Priests of St Sulpice (religious order)
- ♦ Sulpiciens – Compagnie des Prêtres de Saint-Sulpice (religious order)
- ♦ Sulpiziani – Compagnia dei Sacerdoti di Santo Sulpizio (religious order)
- ♦ SUM / see Pioneers UK
- ♦ Suma Ching Hai International Association / see Supreme Master Ching Hai International Association
- ♦ Sumaitri / see Samaritans
- ♦ **SUMERNET** Sustainable Mekong Research Network (#20062)
- ♦ Sumithrayo / see Samaritans
- ♦ Summer Institute of Linguistics / see SIL International (#19278)
- ♦ Summit of the Americas (meeting series)
- ♦ Summit of the Eight Most Industrialized Countries / see Group of Eight (#10745)
- ♦ Summit Level Group of Developing Countries / see Group of Fifteen (#10778)
- ♦ Summit of the Most Industrialized Countries / see Group of Eight (#10745)
- ♦ Summit of the Seven Most Industrialized Countries / see Group of Eight (#10745)
- ♦ SumOfUs (internationally oriented national body)
- ♦ SUM – Senter for Utvikling og Miljі (internationally oriented national body)
- ♦ **SUM** Servicio Universitario Mundial (#21892)
- ♦ **SUNAMCO** International Commission on Symbols, Units, Nomenclature, Atomic Masses and Fundamental Constants (#12733)

♦ SUN Civil society Network (SUN CSN) 20035

Réseau de la société civile SUN (RSC SUN) – Red de la Sociedad Civil SUN (RSC SUN)
Head Secretariat c/o Save the Children UK, 1 St John's Lane, London, EC1M 4AR, UK. E-mail: sun.csnetwork@savethechildren.org.uk.
URL: https://www.suncivilsociety.com/
History Part of *Scaling Up Nutrition Movement (SUN Movement, #19064)*. **Aims** Raise the voices of those who are affected by malnutrition. **Structure** Steering Group; Secretariat. **Activities** Advocacy/lobbying/activism; knowledge management/information dissemination; training/education.
Members Local and international organizations (over 4,000). Membership countries not specified. International members include 19 organizations listed in this Yearbook:
1,000 Days; *ACTION (#00085)*; *Action Against Hunger (#00086)*; *African Nutrition Society (ANS, #00400)*; *Agency for Technical Cooperation and Development (ACTED)*; *ALIMA (#00636)*; *Concern Worldwide*; *CUAMM – Medici con l'Africa*; *Helen Keller International (HKI, #10902)*; *Hunger Project (#10994)*; *International Federation of Red Cross and Red Crescent Societies (#13526)*; *Nutrition International (#17627)*; *Results for Development (R4D, #18923)*; *Save the Children International (#19058)*; *SNV Netherlands Development Organisation (SNV)*; *Society for Conservation and Protection of Environment (SCOPE)*; *Terre des Hommes International Federation (TDHIF, #20133)*; *WaterAid (#20822)*; *World Vision International (WVI, #21904).*
NGO Relations Member of (1): *International Coalition for Advocacy on Nutrition (ICAN).* [2023/AA3156/y/**F**]

- ♦ **SUN CSN** SUN Civil society Network (#20035)
- ♦ Sundance Institute (internationally oriented national body)
- ♦ **SUN Movement** Scaling Up Nutrition Movement (#19064)
- ♦ **SUN** Service- og Tjenestebranchens Union i Norden (#19244)
- ♦ Sunshine without Borders (internationally oriented national body)
- ♦ SUNSIH – Student University Network for Social and International Health (internationally oriented national body)
- ♦ **SUN** Silk-road Universities Network (#19281)
- ♦ SUN – Spiritual Unity of Nations (inactive)
- ♦ Sunspot Index Data Centre – World Data Centre / see Solar Influences Data Analysis Centre (#19675)
- ♦ Sun-Do World Federation (inactive)
- ♦ Suomalaiset Kehitysjärjestöt (internationally oriented national body)
- ♦ Suomalais-Ugrilaisten Kirjallisuuksien Liitto (unconfirmed)
- ♦ Suoma Rafibealusteaddjit (internationally oriented national body)
- ♦ Suomen Ammattiliittojen Solidaarisuuskeskus (internationally oriented national body)
- ♦ Suomen Lähetysseuran (internationally oriented national body)
- ♦ Suomen Pakolaisapu (internationally oriented national body)
- ♦ Suomen Rauhanliitto (internationally oriented national body)
- ♦ Suomen Rauhanpuolustajat ry (internationally oriented national body)
- ♦ Suomen Rauhantutkimusyhdistys Ry (internationally oriented national body)
- ♦ Suomen Toimikunta Euroopan Turvallisuuden Edistamiseksi / see Finnish Committee for European Security
- ♦ Suomen Vapaa Ulkolähetys / see Fida International
- ♦ Suore degli Abbandonati (religious order)
- ♦ Suore Adoratrici del Preziosissimo Sangue di Nostro Signore Gesù Cristo dell'Unione de Saint-Hyacinthe (religious order)
- ♦ Suore Adoratrici del Santissimo Sacramento (religious order)
- ♦ Suore dell'Adorazione del Preziosissimo Sangue (religious order)
- ♦ Suore dell'Adorazione del Santissimo Sacramento (religious order)
- ♦ Suore Agostiniane (religious order)
- ♦ Suore Agostiniane Missionarie (religious order)
- ♦ Suore dell'Amor di Dio (religious order)
- ♦ Suore Ancelle di Beata Vergine Maria Immacolata (religious order)
- ♦ Suore Ancelle del Cuore Immacolato di Maria (religious order)
- ♦ Suore Ancelle del Sacro Cuore di Maria (religious order)
- ♦ Suore degli Angeli (religious order)
- ♦ Suore dell'Angelo Custode (religious order)
- ♦ Suore dell'Apostolato Cattolico Pallottine (religious order)
- ♦ Suore dell'Assunzione della Santa Vergine (religious order)
- ♦ Suore del Bambin Gesù, Puy (religious order)
- ♦ Suore del Bambino Gesù (religious order)
- ♦ Suore del Bambino Gesù, Chauffailles (religious order)
- ♦ Suore della Beata Vergine Maria delle Filippine (religious order)
- ♦ Suore Benedettine (religious order)
- ♦ Suore Benedettine della Congregazione di San Benedetto (religious order)
- ♦ Suore Benedettine della Federazione di Santa Scholastica (religious order)
- ♦ Suore Betlemite (religious order)
- ♦ Suore Bianche – Suore Missionarie di Nostra Signora d'Africa (religious order)
- ♦ Suore del Buon Pastore – Suore Ancelle del Cuore Immacolato di Maria (religious order)
- ♦ Suore del Buon Samaritano (religious order)
- ♦ Suore Cappuccine della Sacra Famiglia (religious order)
- ♦ Suore di Carità della Beata Vergine Maria (religious order)
- ♦ Suore di Carità di Cincinnati (religious order)
- ♦ Suore della Carità Cristiana, Figlie della Beata Vergine Maria dell'Immacolata Concezione (religious order)
- ♦ Suore della Carità e dell'Istruzione Cristiana (religious order)
- ♦ Suore della Carità Leavenworth (religious order)
- ♦ Suore di Carità di Nazareth (religious order)
- ♦ Suore della Carità di Nostra Signora (religious order)
- ♦ Suore di Carità di Nostra Signora del Buono e Perpetuo Soccorso (religious order)
- ♦ Suore di Carità di Nostra Signora Madre della Misericordia (religious order)
- ♦ Suore della Carità dell'Ospedale Generale (religious order)
- ♦ Suore della Carità di Ottawa (religious order)
- ♦ Suore della Carità di Québec (religious order)
- ♦ Suore della Carità di San Luigi (religious order)
- ♦ Suore di Carità di San Paolo Apostolo (religious order)
- ♦ Suore di Carità di Santa Anna (religious order)
- ♦ Suore di Carità della Santa Croce (religious order)
- ♦ Suore di Carità di Santa Elisabetta (religious order)
- ♦ Suore della Carità di Santa Giovanna Antida Thouret (religious order)
- ♦ Suore di Carità delle Sante Bartolomea Capitanio e Vincenza Gerosa, dette di Maria Bambina (religious order)
- ♦ Suore di Carità di Santo Carlo Borromeo (religious order)
- ♦ Suore della Carità Seton Hill (religious order)
- ♦ Suore Carmelitane della Carità, Vedruna (religious order)
- ♦ Suore Carmelitane del Divin Cuore di Gesù (religious order)
- ♦ Suore Carmelitane di San Giuseppe (religious order)
- ♦ Suore Carmelitane di Santa Teresa (religious order)
- ♦ Suore Carmelitane – Suore della Beata Vergine Maria del Monte Carmelo (religious order)
- ♦ Suore Carmelitane Teresiane Verapoly (religious order)
- ♦ Suore Clarisse Francescane (religious order)
- ♦ Suore Clarisse Francescane Missionarie del Santissimo Sacramento – Bertinoro (religious order)
- ♦ Suore della Congregazione di Maria (religious order)
- ♦ Suore della Congregazione di Nostra Signora (religious order)
- ♦ Suore di Cristo – Unione Mysterium Christi (religious order)

- Suore della Divina Provvidenza, Ribeauvillé (religious order)
- Suore della Divina Provvidenza, Saint-Jean-de-Bassel (religious order)
- Suore del Divin Redentore (religious order)
- Suore del Divin Salvatore (religious order)
- Suore Domenicane della Congregazione di Santa Caterina da Siena (religious order)
- Suore Domenicane di Maryknoll (religious order)
- Suore Dominicane della Congregazione di Nostra Signora del Santissimo Rosario (religious order)
- Suore della Dottrina Cristiana (religious order)
- Suore Feliciane – Congregazione delle Suore di San Felice da Cantalice (religious order)
- Suore Francescane del Cuore Immacolato di Maria (religious order)
- Suore Francescane Elisabettine (religious order)
- Suore Francescane dell'Immacolata Concezione (religious order)
- Suore Francescane Insegnanti (religious order)
- Suore Francescane Missionarie del Cuore Immacolato di Maria dette d'Egitto (religious order)
- Suore Francescane Missionarie di Gesù Bambino (religious order)
- Suore Francescane Missionarie del Sacro Cuore (religious order)
- Suore Francescane Ospedaliere dell' Immacolata Concezione (religious order)
- Suore Francescane della Penitenza e della Carità Cristiana (religious order)
- Suore Francescane dei Poveri (religious order)
- Suore Francescane di San Giuseppe (religious order)
- Suore di Francesco d'Assisi (religious order)
- Suore Franciscane, Filie dei Sacri Cuori di Gesù e Maria (religious order)
- Suore di Gesù Redentore (religious order)
- Suore Grigie del Sacro Cuore (religious order)
- Suore Grigie – Suore della Carità dell'Ospedale Generale (religious order)
- Suore dell'Immacolata Concezione (religious order)
- Suore dell'Immacolata Concezione di Nostra Signora di Lourdes (religious order)
- Suore della Madre del Carmelo (religious order)
- Suore Maestre di Santa Dorotea, 1838 (religious order)
- Suore Maestre di Santa Dorotea, Figlie dei Sacri Cuori (religious order)
- Suore Mercedarie Missionarie di Bérriz (religious order)
- Suore della Misericordia, 1823 (religious order)
- Suore Missionarie dell'Apostolato Cattolico (religious order)
- Suore Missionarie Comboniane, Pie Madri della Nigrizia (religious order)
- Suore Missionarie della Consolata (religious order)
- Suore Missionarie del Cuore Immacolato di Maria (religious order)
- Suore Missionarie Francescane dell' Immacolata Concezione di Maria (religious order)
- Suore Missionarie di Gesù Crocifisso (religious order)
- Suore Missionarie dell'Immacolata Concezione (religious order)
- Suore Missionarie di Maria Aiuto dei Cristiani (religious order)
- Suore Missionarie di Nostra Signora d'Africa (religious order)
- Suore Missionarie di Nostra Signora degli Apostoli (religious order)
- Suore Missionarie di Nostra Signora del Santo Rosario (religious order)
- Suore Missionarie del Preziosissimo Sangue (religious order)
- Suore Missionarie del Sacro Cuore di Gesù di Hiltrup (religious order)
- Suore Missionarie di San Pietro Claver (religious order)
- Suore Missionarie di Santo Carlo Borromeo (religious order)
- Suore Missionarie di Santo Colombano (religious order)
- Suore Missionarie della Società di Maria (religious order)
- Suore Missionarie dello Spirito Santo (religious order)
- Suore di Nazareth (religious order)
- Suore di Nostra Signora (religious order)
- Suore di Nostra Signora del Buon Soccorso (religious order)
- Suore di Nostra Signora della Carità del Buon Pastore (religious order)
- Suore di Nostra Signora della Compassione (religious order)
- Suore di Nostra Signora dell'Immacolata Concezione (religious order)
- Suore di Nostra Signora della Mercede (religious order)
- Suore di Nostra Signora delle Missioni (religious order)
- Suore di Nostra Signora di Namur (religious order)
- Suore di Nostra Signora del Ritiro al Cenacolo (religious order)
- Suore Oblate del Santo Redentore (religious order)
- Suore Orsoline (religious order)
- Suore Orsoline del Sacro Cuore di Gesù Agonizzante (religious order)
- Suore Orsoline di Tildonk (religious order)
- Suore Ospedaliere del Sacro Cuore di Gesù (religious order)
- Suore Passioniste di Santo Paolo della Croce (religious order)
- Suore del Piccolo Fiore di Betania (religious order)
- Suore dei Picpus (religious order)
- Suore delle Poverelle dell'Istituto Palazzolo (religious order)
- Suore dei Poveri di Santo Francesco (religious order)
- Suore del Povero Bambino Gesù (religious order)
- Suore della Presentazione di Maria (religious order)
- Suore del Preziosissimo Sangue (religious order)
- Suore della Provvidenza (religious order)
- Suore della Provvidenza e dell'Immacolata Concezione (religious order)
- Suore della Provvidenza, Ruillé-sur-Loir (religious order)
- Suore della Provvidenza di San Gaetano da Thiene (religious order)
- Suore della Provvidenza di Sant'Andrea (religious order)
- Suore del Redentore (religious order)
- Suore della Sacra Famiglia (religious order)
- Suore della Sacra Famiglia di Nazareth (religious order)
- Suore Sacramentine di Bergamo (religious order)
- Suore dei Sacri Cuori di Gesù et di Maria (religious order)
- Suore del Salvatore e della Santa Vergine (religious order)
- Suore di San Giuseppe (religious order)
- Suore di San Giuseppe dell'Apparizione (religious order)
- Suore di San Giuseppe del Sacro Cuore di Gesù (religious order)
- Suore di San Giuseppe di Tarbes (religious order)
- Suore di San Paolo di Chartres (religious order)
- Suore di Santa Agnese (religious order)
- Suore di Santa Anna (religious order)
- Suore di Santa Brigida (religious order)
- Suore di Santa Clotilda (religious order)
- Suore della Santa Croce (religious order)
- Suore della Santa Croce (religious order)
- Suore della Santa Croce e Passione di Nostro Signore Gesù Cristo (religious order)
- Suore di Santa Elisabetta (religious order)
- Suore della Santa Famiglia di Bordeaux (religious order)
- Suore di Santa Marcellina (religious order)
- Suore di Santa Maria, Francescane (religious order)
- Suore di Santa Maria Maddalena di Postel (religious order)
- Suore di Santa Marta (religious order)
- Suore della Santa Unione dei Sacri Cuori (religious order)
- Suore dei Santi Cirillo e Metodio (religious order)
- Suore dei Santi Nomi di Gesù e di Maria (religious order)
- Suore del Santissimo Sacramento (religious order)
- Suore di Santo Francesco di Sales (religious order)
- Suore di Santo Giovanni di Dio (religious order)
- Suore di Santo Luigi (religious order)
- Suore di Santo Tommaso da Villanova (religious order)
- Suore Scolastiche di Nostra Signora (religious order)
- Suore Scolastiche di San Francesco (religious order)
- Suore del Verbo Incarnato e del Santo Sacramento (religious order)
- SUPA / see Association of University Technology Managers
- Super Intense Laser-Atom Physics Conference (meeting series)
- Superior Royal Oriental Institute of Naples / see University Institute of Oriental Studies
- Supersonic Tunnel Association / see Supersonic Tunnel Association, International
- Supersonic Tunnel Association, International (internationally oriented national body)

♦ Supervised Visitation Network (SVN) 20036

Exec Dir 3955 Riverside Ave, Jacksonville FL 32205, USA. T. +19044197861. Fax +19042395888.
URL: http://svnworldwide.org/

History 1991. **Aims** Establish standards, promote education and advance professionalism in the field of supervised visitation. **Structure** Board of Directors of 15 members, with a minimum of 2 members per geographical region. **Activities** Collects and disseminates information; organizes annual conference; maintains a library of training and program materials. [2011/XJ2861/**F**]

♦ Superyacht Builders Association (SYBAss) 20037

Secretariat Diemerzeedijk 27-B, 1095 KK Amsterdam, Netherlands. T. +3122900061. E-mail: info@sybass.org.
Registered Office 34 Quai Jean-Charles Rey, 98000 Monte Carlo, Monaco. T. +377793304800.
URL: http://www.sybass.org/

History Feb 2007. Consultative status granted at *International Maritime Organization (IMO, #14102)*, 2011. Involved in the development of the Red Ensign Group Yacht Code, launched in 2017. The creation of the SYBAss Sustainability Committee in 2017 organically resulted in a new non-profit, Water Revolution Foundation, established in 2018 to drive sustainability in the superyacht industry. Registration: Monaco. **Aims** Ensure that the unique needs of the world's leading superyacht builders are addressed on the international stage; enhance the professionalism of the sector; assure central positions for its members. **Structure** General Assembly; Board; Committees; Working Groups; Secretariat. **Languages** Czech, Dutch, English, French, German, Indonesian, Italian, Spanish, Turkish. **Staff** 4.00 FTE, paid. **Finance** Sources: contributions. **Activities** Guidance/assistance/consulting; knowledge management/information dissemination; networking/liaising; politics/policy/regulatory. **Publications** *SYBAss Economic Impact Study*. Economic Report; Statistics Report.

Members Individuals in 9 countries and territories:
Australia, Finland, Germany, Italy, Netherlands, Taiwan, Türkiye, United Arab Emirates, USA.

Consultative Status Consultative status granted from: *International Maritime Organization (IMO, #14102)*. [2022.06.20/XJ6629/**C**]

- Supplementary Agreement to the Application of the European Convention on Social Security (1972 treaty)
- Supplementary Arrangement Respecting the Measurement of the Tonnage of Vessels in Inland Navigation (1908 treaty)
- Supplementary Arrangements for the Regulation of Antarctic Pelagic Whaling (1962 treaty)
- Supplementary Convention on the Abolition of Slavery, the Slave Trade, and Institutions and Practices Similar to Slavery (1956 treaty)
- Supplementary Convention Amending the Convention Concerning the Tenure and Disposal of Real and Personal Property (1936 treaty)
- Supplementary Monetary Convention (1908 treaty)
- Supplementary Protocol to the Convention on the Recognition and Enforcement of Foreign Judgments in Civil and Commercial Matters (1971 treaty)

♦ Supply Chain Finance Community (SCF) 20038

Contact Campus 2-6, 8017 CA Zwolle, Netherlands. E-mail: admin@scfcommunity.org.
URL: http://www.scfcommunity.org/

History 2013. Registration: Netherlands. **Aims** Promote and accelerate understanding, development and implementation of supply chain finance models. **Structure** Board. **Activities** Awards/prizes/competitions; events/meetings. **Events** *Seminar on Distributor Financing* Singapore (Singapore) 2020, *Forum Europe* Amsterdam (Netherlands) 2019, *Forum Europe* Amsterdam (Netherlands) 2018. **Publications** *SCF Briefing* – newsletter. [2020/XM8015/**D**]

- Support, Advanced Learning and Training Opportunities / see SALTO-YOUTH (#19040)
- Support Coalition International / see MindFreedom International (#16807)
- Support Group for African Peacekeeping Capabilities (no recent information)
- Supporting Entrepreneurs for Sustainable Development / see SEED (#19213)
- Support for NGOs in the East / see Soutien aux ONG à l'Est et au Sud
- Support for NGOs in the East and in the South (internationally oriented national body)
- Supreme Allied Command Transformation / see Allied Command Transformation (#00732)
- Supreme Commander for the Allied Powers (inactive)
- Supreme Council for Sport in Africa (inactive)
- Supreme Headquarters of the Allied Expeditionary Forces (inactive)

♦ Supreme Headquarters Allied Powers Europe (SHAPE) 20039

Grand quartier général des puissances alliées en Europe

Headquarters SHAPE, 7010 Shape, Belgium. T. +3265447111. E-mail: media@shape.nato.int.
URL: http://www.shape.nato.int/

History Established 2 Apr 1951, Paris (France), as the headquarters of *Allied Command Operations (ACO, #00731)*, one of two Supreme Allied Commands of *NATO (#16945)*, following the appointment, 19 Dec 1950, of a *Supreme Allied Commander Europe (SACEUR)*. Permanent headquarters set up, 23 Jul 1951, Rocquencourt (France); moved to current site, Mar 1967, at SHAPE (Belgium), on withdrawal of French military forces from the allied military structure of NATO. Also referred to in French as *Commandement suprême des forces alliées en Europe*. **Aims** Function as headquarters of SACEUR, whose task is to coordinate *defence* of Allied Command Europe, the area from the North Cape to the Mediterranean and from the Atlantic to the eastern border of Turkey, excluding Portugal. In peace-time: develop requirements, plans and procedures for the *military forces* assigned to ACE to perform their missions in peace, crises and war. In crises: recommend and conduct military measures to reinforce political actions and thereby contribute to crisis management. In wartime: assist SACEUR in commanding the forces committed to ACE for collective defence of NATO territory. **Structure** SHAPE is organized on normal military lines. Staff divisions (6): Operations and Logistics; Policy and Requirements; Resources; Intelligence; Communications and Information Systems; Budget and Finance. International Headquarters and Support Command. National military representatives (NMRs) accredited to SACEUR have particular responsibilities at SHAPE. Includes: *NATO Programming Centre (NPC, inactive)*; *NATO SCHOOL Oberammergau (NSO, #16947)*. Maintenance and supply through *NATO Maintenance and Supply Agency (NAMSA)*. Exercises and other operational functions for ACE are planned and conducted at SHAPE by SACEUR and his international allied staff. *Allied Rapid Reaction Corps (ARRC, #00736)* is under SACEUR operational command in peacetime. *NATO Response Force (NRF)*, launched 15 Oct 2003, is also based at SHAPE. **Languages** English, French. **Staff** The International SHAPE Staff is composed of approximately 2,500 personnel – officers, other ranks and civilians. In addition, there are 1,300 persons who are part of NMR echelon and support elements at SHAPE. With the addition of locally employed civilians and some 3,800 dependents, SHAPE community consists of over 10,000 people. The approximate breakdown by nations of the international staff is: USA – 26%, UK – 14%, Germany – 16%, Belgium 6%, Netherlands – 6%, Italy – 7%, and the other nations combined – 20%. The average length of tour at SHAPE for military personnel is 3-4 years. **Events** *Meteorological and oceanographical meeting* Madrid (Spain) 2003.

Members NATO member countries (27 – Iceland, having no military forces, is not represented):
Albania, Belgium, Bulgaria, Canada, Croatia, Czechia, Denmark, Estonia, France, Germany, Greece, Hungary, Italy, Latvia, Lithuania, Luxembourg, Netherlands, Norway, Poland, Portugal, Romania, Slovakia, Slovenia, Spain, Türkiye, UK, USA.
[2016.02.12/XE5515/**E***]

- ♦ Supreme Master Ching Hai International Association (internationally oriented national body)
- ♦ SUP – Society for Ultrastructural Pathology (internationally oriented national body)
- ♦ SU – Religieuses de la Compagnie de Sainte-Ursule (religious order)
- ♦ **SURE** Society for Urban Ecology (#19659)

♦ SurfAid international (SAI) 20040

Contact PO Box 603, Avalon NSW 2107, Australia. T. +61299657325. E-mail: aus@surfaid.org.
URL: http://www.surfaid.org/

History Jan 2000, by surf enthusiast Dave Jenkins. **Aims** Run health, disaster preparedness, and water and sanitation programmes in the Mentawai and Nias islands; improve health, wellbeing and self-reliance of people living in isolated regions connected through surfing. **Structure** Board of Directors, headed by Chairman/Secretary.
Members Organizations in 4 countries:
Australia, Indonesia, New Zealand, USA.
NGO Relations Member of: *PMNCH (#18410).* [2018.08.01/XM0433/**F**]

♦ Surfrider Foundation Europe 20041

Main Office 33 allée du Moura, 64200 Biarritz, France. T. +33559235499. E-mail: contact@surfrider.eu.
URL: http://www.surfrider.eu/

History 1990, Biarritz (France). Registration: EU Transparency Register, No/ID: 58969291154-50, Start date: 17 Feb 2009. **Aims** Protect and enhance lakes, rivers, oceans, waves and the coastline. **Structure** Board of Directors. **Languages** English, French. **Consultative Status** Consultative status granted from: *ECOSOC (#05331)* (Special); *UNEP (#20299)*; *UNESCO (#20322)* (Consultative Status). [2022/XJ5199/f/**F**]

♦ Surgery Society of the Latin Mediterranean 20042

Société de Chirurgie de la Méditerranée Latine – Sociedad de Cirugia del Mediterraneo Latino – Societa di Chirurgia del Mediterraneo Latino

SG Hosp Univ Sagrat Cor, Viladomat 288, 08029 Barcelona, Spain. E-mail: bibhsc@hscor.com.

History 1951, Turin (Italy). Former names and other names: *Latin Mediterranean Medical Union* – former (1951); *Union médicale de la Méditerranée latine (UMML)* – former (1951); *Unione Medica Mediterranea Latina* – former (1951). **Aims** Facilitate friendly meetings between doctors united by common Latin cultures and the spirit of Greco-Latin humanism to discuss problems in their specialized fields: general surgery, general medicine, experimental medicine. **Structure** General Presidential Committee; National Sections (3); Surgical Section (meets every 2 years). **Languages** French, Italian, Spanish. **Staff** 7.00 FTE, voluntary. **Finance** Members' dues. **Events** *Biennial Congress* Barcelona (Spain) 2013, *Biennial Congress* Italy 2011, *Biennial Congress* Montpellier (France) 2009, *Biennial Congress* Alicante (Spain) 2007, *Biennial Congress* Naples (Italy) 2005.
Members Individuals adhering to independent Societies forming National Sections (3) in 3 countries:
France, Italy, Spain.
Individuals in 20 countries:
Algeria, Andorra, Argentina, Belgium, Brazil, Bulgaria, Egypt, Greece, Iraq, Luxembourg, Malta, Monaco, Morocco, Portugal, Romania, Senegal, Serbia, Switzerland, Syrian AR, Tunisia. [2015.02.02/XD2898/**D**]

- ♦ Surgical Association for Clinical Research in Europe (no recent information)
- ♦ Surgical Eye Expeditions International (internationally oriented national body)

♦ Surgical Infection Society – Europe (SIS-E) 20043

Société européenne d'infection en chirurgie

Secretary SIS-E Secretariat, c/o Conference Partners, 11-13 The Hyde Building – The Park, Carrickmines, Dublin, D18 YX22, CO. DUBLIN, Ireland. T. +35312968688. E-mail: sis-e@conferencepartners.ie.
Pres address not obtained.
URL: http://www.sis-e.org/

History May 1987, Hamburg (Germany). Founded by the European members of the Surgical Infection Society North America. **Aims** Promote and encourage education and research in the nature, prevention, diagnosis and treatment of surgical infections. **Structure** Council; Education Committee. **Languages** English. **Finance** Sources: grants; members' dues. Annual budget: 100,000 CHF. **Activities** Events/meetings; standards/guidelines; training/education. **Events** *Annual Congress* Dublin (Ireland) 2021, *Annual Congress* Madrid (Spain) 2020, *Annual Congress* Dublin (Ireland) 2019, *Annual Congress* Athens (Greece) 2018, *Annual Congress* Hamburg (Germany) 2017. **Publications** *Surgical Infection Journal.*
Members Full in 35 countries:
Austria, Belgium, Canada, Croatia, Cyprus, Czechia, Denmark, Egypt, Finland, France, Germany, Greece, Hungary, Indonesia, Israel, Italy, Jordan, Kuwait, Netherlands, Norway, Poland, Portugal, Romania, Saudi Arabia, Serbia, Slovenia, South Africa, Spain, Sweden, Switzerland, Thailand, Türkiye, UK, United Arab Emirates, USA. [2020/XE3189/**E**]

- ♦ Surpaz (internationally oriented national body)
- ♦ Surtseyjarfelagid (#20044)

♦ Surtsey Research Society 20044

Surtseyjarfelagid

Sec PO Box 352, 121 Reykjavik, Iceland. E-mail: surtsey@ni.is.
URL: http://www.surtsey.is/

History 1965. **Aims** Coordinate scientific research on the *geological* and *biological* phenomena of the Isle of Surtsey formed in 1963-1967 by *volcanic* activity. **Publications** *Surtsey Research* (every 5 years). **Members** Scientists in 5 countries. Membership countries not specified. [2016/XE1754/**E**]

- ♦ Surveillance de l'Environnement en Afrique pour un Développement Durable (inactive)

♦ Surveillance Studies Network (SSN) 20045

Contact School of Law Politics and Sociology, Univ of Sussex – Freeman Ctr, Southern Ring Road, Falmer, Brighton, BN1 9QE, UK.
URL: https://www.surveillance-studies.net/

History Registration: Charity Commission, No/ID: 1117449, England and Wales. **Aims** Study surveillance in all its forms. **Structure** Executive Board. **Activities** Awards/prizes/competitions; events/meetings; knowledge management/information dissemination; research/documentation. **Events** *Conference* 2024, *Conference* Rotterdam (Netherlands) 2022, *Conference* Rotterdam (Netherlands) 2020, *Conference* Aarhus (Denmark) 2018, *Conference* Barcelona (Spain) 2016. **Publications** *Surveillance and Society.* [2022/AA1712/j/**F**]

♦ Survey in Europe on Nutrition and the Elderly (SENECA) 20046

Contact Dept of Human Nutrition, Wageningen Agricultural Univ, PO Box 8129, 6700 EV Wageningen, Netherlands. T. +31317482589 – +31317484214. Fax +31317483342.

History 1987, within the framework of *Concerted Action on Nutrition and Health in the European Community (EURONUT, inactive)*, a programme of *European Commission (EC, #06633)*. Currently, since 1991, a concerted action independent of the European Commission. **Aims** Examine nutrition and *health* of elderly people across Europe. **Structure** Network of universities, research institutes and industry. **Finance** Participants' contributions. **Activities** Carries out research, particularly coordination, data analysis and standardized blood chemistry. **Events** *European Congress* Warsaw (Poland) 2008, *European congress on nutrition and health in the elderly / European Congress* Warsaw (Poland) 2006, *European congress on nutrition and health in the elderly / European Congress* Toulouse (France) 2004, *European congress on nutrition and health in the elderly / European Congress* Madrid (Spain) 2000, *European congress on nutrition and health in the elderly / European Congress* Helsingør (Denmark) 1996. **Publications** Monographs.
Members Participating centres in 15 countries:
Belgium, Denmark, France, Greece, Hungary, Ireland, Italy, Netherlands, Norway, Poland, Portugal, Spain, Switzerland, UK, USA. [2009.07.02/XF3400/**F**]

- ♦ Survival and Flight Equipment Association / see SAFE Europe (#19025)

♦ Survival International 20047

Dir Gen 6 Charterhouse Bldgs, Goswell Road, London, EC1M 7ET, UK. T. +442076878700. E-mail: info@survivalinternational.org.
URL: http://www.survivalinternational.org/

History 1969, London (UK). **Aims** Support tribal and Indigenous peoples in defending their lives, protecting their lands and determining their own futures. **Structure** International Secretariat based in London (UK); Offices in: France, Germany, Italy, Spain, UK, USA. **Languages** English, French, German, Italian, Portuguese, Spanish. **Finance** Sources: donations; gifts, legacies; private foundations. **Activities** Advocacy/lobbying/activism; awareness raising; financial and/or material support; research/documentation; training/education. **Publications** Annual Report in English, French, German, Italian, Spanish; press releases; e-news; films. **Members** Associated individuals in 121 countries and territories. Membership countries not specified. **Consultative Status** Consultative status granted from: *African Commission on Human and Peoples' Rights (ACHPR, #00255)* (Observer); *ECOSOC (#05331)* (Ros A); *ILO (#11123)* (Special List).
[2022.02.14/XF0007/v/**F**]

- ♦ SURVIVE-MIVA (internationally oriented national body)
- ♦ Survivors International (internationally oriented national body)
- ♦ Survivors of the Shoah Visual History Foundation / see USC Shoah Foundation Institute for Visual History and Education
- ♦ **SuSanA** Sustainable Sanitation Alliance (#20066)
- ♦ **SusChem** European Technology Platform for Sustainable Chemistry (#08893)
- ♦ SUSC – Suore della Santa Unione dei Sacri Cuori (religious order)
- ♦ Susila Budhi Dharma / see World Subud Association (#21836)

♦ Susila Dharma International Association (SDIA) 20048

Exec Dir 572 Empire St, Greenfield Park, Québec QC J4V 1W2, Canada. T. +14507610592. E-mail: virginia@susiladharma.org – info@susiladharma.org.
URL: http://www.susiladharma.org/

History Founded 1983, Windsor (UK), to coordinate social and humanitarian activities of *World Subud Association (WSA, #21836)* as its charitable arm. Activities started in 1968, prior to official founding. Registration: No/ID: 98-0156249, Start date: 1994, USA. **Aims** Work globally for just and sustainable development through empowering individuals and communities to engage in positive human, social and economic change and creating partnerships to achieve grassroots, participatory initiatives. **Structure** General Assembly (annual); International Board of Directors. Network comprises: Susila Dharma National Organizations; Susila Dharma Projects. Head office in Montréal QC (Canada). **Languages** English, French, Spanish. **Staff** 2.00 FTE, paid. **Finance** Donations from members, individuals, enterprises, foundations, trust and NGOs. **Activities** Capacity building; networking/liaising; financial and/or material support; awareness raising; events/meetings; publishing activities. **Events** *General Assembly* Assisi (Italy) 2020, *General Assembly* Salobreña (Spain) 2019, *General Assembly* Freiburg (Germany) 2018, *General Assembly* Montréal, QC (Canada) 2017, *General Assembly* Olsztynek (Poland) 2016. **Publications** *SDIA eNews* (6 a year); *SDIA Magazine* (every 4 years). Annual Report.
Members Organizations in 24 countries:
Australia, Canada, Colombia, Congo DR, Cuba, Ecuador, France, Germany, India, Indonesia, Japan, Mexico, Netherlands, New Zealand, Norway, Paraguay, Portugal, South Africa, Spain, Sweden, UK, Uruguay, USA, Vietnam.
Included in the above, 1 organizations listed in this Yearbook:
International Child Development Programme (ICDP, #12548).
Consultative Status Consultative status granted from: *ECOSOC (#05331)* (Special); *UNICEF (#20332)*. **IGO Relations** Associated with Department of Global Communications of the United Nations. **NGO Relations** Member of: *Conference of Non-Governmental Organizations in Consultative Relationship with the United Nations (CONGO, #04635)*; *NGO Committee on UNICEF (#17120).* [2020.01.20/XF0613/y/**E**]

- ♦ SUSME – Society of Ultrasound in Medical Education (internationally oriented national body)
- ♦ Sussex European Institute (internationally oriented national body)
- ♦ SUSTAIN (internationally oriented national body)

♦ The Sustainability Consortium (TSC) 20049

COO 777 East University Dr, 3rd Floor, Tempe AZ 85281, USA.
Managing Dir – Europe PO Box 29703, 2502 LS The Hague, Netherlands. T. +31703358235.
URL: http://www.sustainabilityconsortium.org/

History 2009. **Aims** Design and implement credible, transparent and scalable science-based measurement and reporting systems accessible for all producers, retailers, and users of consumer products. **Structure** Board of Directors of 10. Managing Board. CEO. Advisory Councils (3): Corporate; Civil Society; Academic. Working Groups.
Members Corporate; Civil Society and Government. Including in the above, 2 organizations listed in this Yearbook:
The Nature Conservancy (TNC); World Wide Fund for Nature (WWF, #21922).
NGO Relations Member of (2): *GLOBALG.A.P (#10386)* (Associate); *Natural Capital Coalition (NCC, #16952).* Partner of (2): *Cool Farm Alliance (CFA)*; *Livestock Environmental Assessment and Performance Partnership (LEAP, #16500).* [2022/XJ7334/y/**F**]

- ♦ The Sustainability Laboratory (internationally oriented national body)

♦ Sustainability Transitions Research Network (STRN) 20050

Chair address not obtained. E-mail: sustainabilitytransitions@gmail.com.
URL: https://transitionsnetwork.org/

Aims Deepen the scientific understanding of sustainability transitions. **Structure** Steering Committee; Board. **Activities** Events/meetings; networking/liaising; research/documentation; training/education. **Events** *International Sustainability Transition Conference* Vienna (Austria) 2020, *International Sustainability Transition Conference* Ottawa, ON (Canada) 2019, *International Sustainability Transition Conference* Manchester (UK) 2018, *International Sustainability Transition Conference* Gothenburg (Sweden) 2017, *International Sustainability Transition Conference* Wuppertal (Germany) 2016. **Publications** *Environmental Innovation and Societal Transitions*; *STRN Newsletter.* [2021/AA1467/**F**]

- ♦ Sustainable Agriculture Centre for Research and Development in Africa / see Sustainable Agriculture Centre for Research, Extension and Development in Africa
- ♦ Sustainable Agriculture Centre for Research, Extension and Development in Africa (internationally oriented national body)

♦ Sustainable Agriculture Initiative (SAI Platform) 20051

Dir Gen Av des Nerviens 9-31, 1040 Brussels, Belgium. T. +3225008757. Fax +3225081025. E-mail: info@saiplatform.org.
Registered Address Av Jules Crosnier 6, 1206 Geneva, Switzerland. T. +41223090600.
URL: http://www.saiplatform.org/

History 2002, by Nestlé, Unilever and Danone. **Aims** Grow a sustainable, thriving and resilient agricultural sector that safeguards farm viability and protects and preserves the earth's resources, human rights and animal welfare while supporting members and adding value across the food and drink industry. **Structure** Executive Committee; Advisory Council; Secretariat headed by General Manager. **Languages** English. **Staff** 11.00 FTE, paid. **Finance** Members' dues. External funding grants. **Activities** Projects/programmes; events/meetings; training/education. **Events** *Annual Event* Parma (Italy) 2021, *General Assembly* Parma (Italy) 2020, *Annual Event and General Assembly* Chicago, IL (USA) 2019, *Annual Event and General Assembly* Aarhus (Denmark) 2018, *Reporting session* Parma (Italy) 2011. **Publications** Annual Report; guidelines; presentations; practical tools. [2020/XM3780/**F**]

- ♦ Sustainable Agriculture Network / see Social Agriculture Network (#19333)

♦ Sustainable Agriculture Network (SAN) 20052

Red de Agricultura Sostenible (RAS)

Exec Dir Gracias Cowork Escalante, San José, San José, San José, 10101, Costa Rica. T. +50622729312. E-mail: info@san.eco.
URL: https://www.sustainableagriculture.eco

History 1 Jun 2010, Mexico City (Mexico). **Aims** Transform agriculture to secure a sustainable future for food, nature and rural communities. **Structure** General Assembly; Board of Directors; Secretariat. **Languages** English, German, Spanish. **Activities** Advocacy/lobbying/activism; capacity building; guidance/assistance/consulting; monitoring/evaluation; networking/liaising; projects/programmes; training/education. Active in all member countries.
Members Member-led organizations combining global and local reach. Membership countries not specified. Included in the above, 6 organizations listed in the Yearbook:
CABI (#03393); Fundación Global Nature; Inter-American Foundation for Tropical Research, Guatemala (FIIT); Participatory Ecological Land Use Management (PELUM Association, #18225); Preferred by Nature (#18477); Rainforest Alliance.
IGO Relations Partner of (2): *Bioversity International (#03262); Inter-American Institute for Cooperation on Agriculture (IICA, #11434).* **NGO Relations** Member of (3): *European Fruit Juice Association (AIJN, #07362); Global Landscapes Forum (GLF, #10451)* (Charter member); *ISEAL (#16026).* Partner of (2): *International Centre for Tropical Agriculture (#12527); Tropical Forest Alliance (TFA, #20249).* [2022.11.18/XM8963/y/**F**]

♦ Sustainable Apparel Coalition (unconfirmed)
♦ Sustainable Cities Foundation / see International Centre for Sustainable Cities, Vancouver

♦ Sustainable Consumption Research and Action Initiative (SCORAI) . 20053

Contact address not obtained. E-mail: orgscorai@gmail.com.
URL: https://scorai.net/
Aims Provide a forum for scholars and practitioners striving to understand the drivers of the consumerist economy in affluent technological societies; formulate and analyse options for post-consumerist lifestyles, social institutions, and economic systems; provide the knowledge for emergent grassroots innovations, social movements, and public policies. **Structure** Executive Board; Advisory Board. Regional networks (5): China; North America; *SCORAI Europe (#19157)*; Israel; Brazil. **Activities** Events/meetings; knowledge management/information dissemination; research/documentation. **Events** *Conference* Wageningen (Netherlands) 2023, *SCORAI : Sustainable Consumption Research and Action Initiative* Boston, MA (USA) 2020, *International Conference* Copenhagen (Denmark) 2018, *Workshop* Budapest (Hungary) 2016, *Conference* Orono, ME (USA) 2016. **Publications** *SCORAI Newsletter* (12 a year). *SCORAI Studies in Sustainable Consumption* – series. **NGO Relations** Member of (1): *Wellbeing Economy Alliance (WEAll, #20856).* Cooperates with (1): *European Roundtable on Sustainable Consumption and Production Society (ERSCP Society, #08408). Global Research Forum on Sustainable Production and Consumption (GRF, #10575); International Sustainable Development Research Society (ISDRS, #15636)*; Tellus Institute. [2022/XM7549/**F**]

♦ Sustainable Development Foundation (internationally oriented national body)
♦ Sustainable Development Networking Programme – UNDP (no recent information)

♦ Sustainable Development Solutions Network (SDSN) 20054

Réseau des solutions pour le développement durable des Nations-unies
Exec Dir 4 Rue de Chevreuse, 75006 Paris, France. T. +33144102449. E-mail: info@unsdsn.org.
URL: http://unsdsn.org/
History 9 Aug 2012, by *United Nations (UN, #20515)* Secretary-General. Also referred to as *United Nations Sustainable Development Solutions Network.* **Aims** Mobilize scientific and technical expertise from academia, civil society, and the private sector in support of sustainable-development problem solving at local, national, and global scales. **Structure** Leadership Council, headed by 2 Co-Chairs; Executive Committee; Secretariat. Includes *SDSN Youth.* **Languages** Arabic, English, French, German, Spanish. **Staff** 25.00 FTE, paid. **Activities** Knowledge management/information dissemination. **Events** *2030 Sustainable Development and Korea's Response Meeting* Seoul (Korea Rep) 2017, *Meeting on Global Companies and the 2030 Agenda* Tokyo (Japan) 2017, *Meeting* Sydney, NSW (Australia) 2016, *Green Korea Meeting* Incheon (Korea Rep) 2014. **Publications** *SDSN Newsletter.* **Members** Over 900 members in over 100 countries. Membership countries not specified. **NGO Relations** Member of: *Future Earth (#10048); Global Partnership for Sustainable Development Data (Data4SDGS, #10542); United Nations Global Compact (#20567); World Benchmarking Alliance (WBA, #21228).* Core partner of: *Food and Land Use Coalition (FOLU).* [2019.02.15/XJ7855/y/**F**]

♦ Sustainable Digital Infrastructure Alliance (unconfirmed)

♦ Sustainable Electronics Recycling International (SERI) 20055

Exec Dir PO Box 721, Hastings MN 55033, USA. T. +16514383608. E-mail: info@sustainableelectronics.org.
URL: https://sustainableelectronics.org/
Aims Advance safe and sustainable reuse and recycling of used electronics through consensus-driven standards. **Structure** Board of Directors. **Activities** Training/education; standards/guidelines. **NGO Relations** Subscriber to: *ISEAL (#16026).* [2020/XM8967/**F**]

♦ Sustainable Energy for All (SEforALL) 20056

CEO Andromeda Tower 15th floor, Donau City Strasse 6, 1220 Vienna, Austria. T. +43676846727200. E-mail: info@seforall.org.
URL: http://www.seforall.org/
History Sep 2011. Founded by UN Secretary-General Ban Ki-Moon. Former names and other names: *SE4ALL* – former. Registration: Austria; EU Transparency Register, No/ID: 365585639064-33, Start date: 29 Jul 2020. **Aims** Ensure universal access to modern energy services; double the global rate of improvement in energy efficiency; double the share of renewable energy in the global energy mix. **Structure** Administrative Board; Funders' Council; CEO. **Finance** Sources: government support. Governments: Austria; Iceland; Denmark; Korea Rep; UK; Germany; Sweden. Supported by: *Charles Stewart Mott Foundation; ClimateWorks Foundation (#04024); Shell Foundation; Swiss Agency for Development and Cooperation (SDC); The Rockefeller Foundation (#18966); United Nations Foundation (UNF, #20563); Wallace Global Fund.* **Events** *Annual Sustainable Energy for All Forum* Kigali (Rwanda) 2021, *Annual Sustainable Energy for All Forum* Kigali (Rwanda) 2020, *Annual Sustainable Energy for All Forum* Lisbon (Portugal) 2018, *VEF : Vienna Energy Forum Special Session* Vienna (Austria) 2018, *VEF : Biennial Vienna Energy Forum* Vienna (Austria) 2017. **Publications** *SE4ALL Newsletter.* **IGO Relations** Partners include: *African Development Bank (ADB, #00283); Asian Development Bank (ADB, #01422); Inter-American Development Bank (IDB, #11427); International Bank for Reconstruction and Development (IBRD, #12317)* (World Bank); *International Renewable Energy Agency (IRENA, #14715); Norwegian Agency for Development Cooperation (Norad); OPEC Fund for International Development (OFID, #17745); UNEP (#20299); UNDP (#20292); UNIDO (#20336).* Supporters include: *Global Bioenergy Partnership (GBEP, #10251); UNHCR (#20327).*
NGO Relations Partners include:
- *Alliance for Rural Electrification (ARE, #00719);*
- *Global Alliance for Energy Productivity (#10196);*
- *International Electrotechnical Commission (IEC, #13255);*
- *International Institute for Applied Systems Analysis (IIASA, #13861);*
- *SNV Netherlands Development Organisation (SNV);*
- *Practical Action (#18475);*
- *Renewable Energy and Energy Efficiency Partnership (REEEP, #18837);*
- *REN21 (#18836);*
- *United Nations Foundation (UNF, #20563);*
- *United Nations Global Compact (#20567).*

Maintains: *Global LPG Partnership (GLPGP, #10461).* Member of: *Global Alliance for Buildings and Construction (GlobalABC, #10187).* Supporters include: *AHEAD Energy; Associação Lusófona de Energias Renovaveis (ALER); Clean Cooking Alliance (#03987); Energy 4 Impact (#05465).* [2020/XJ9277/**E**]

♦ Sustainable Energy Society of Southern Africa (internationally oriented national body)
♦ Sustainable Environment and Ecological Development Society / see SEEDS Asia (#19216)
♦ Sustainable Europe Research Institute (internationally oriented national body)

♦ Sustainable Event Alliance (SEA) 20057

Contact address not obtained. E-mail: info@sustainable-event-alliance.org.
URL: http://sustainable-event-alliance.org/
History Registered in accordance with Australian law: INC9893674. **Aims** Provide a knowledge bank for *event practitioners*; offer a portal for networking and discussion around sustainable event management; communicate and create a commonality of best practice in sustainable event management across all industry sectors and the supply chain; spread the desire to reduce impacts; open up opportunities for development of sustainable production solutions within the industry. **Structure** General Meeting. Board of Directors, comprising President, Secretary and members. Management Sub-Committee; Country Coordinators; Advisory Group. [2013.03.22/XJ2678/**F**]

♦ Sustainable Fibre Alliance (internationally oriented national body)

♦ Sustainable Fisheries Partnership 20058

CEO 4348 Waialae Avenue No 692, Honolulu HI 96816, USA.
URL: http://www.sustainablefish.org/
History Founded 2006, as a program of the Trust for Conservation Innovation. Granted nonprofit status in US, 2010. **Aims** Engage and catalyze global seafood supply chains in rebuilding depleted fish stocks and reducing the environmental impacts of fishing and fish farming. **Structure** Board of Directors, comprising Chairman, President/CEO, Secretary/Vice Chair and 2 members. **Publications** *SFP Update* – newsletter. **IGO Relations** Observer to meeting of: *International Commission for the Conservation of Atlantic Tunas (ICCAT, #12675).* **NGO Relations** Participates in: *Global Partnership for Oceans (GPO, #10537). Centro Desarrollo y Pesca Sustenable (CeDePesca, #03796).* [2012.07.19/XJ2497/**E**]

♦ Sustainable Food Trust (SFT) 20059

Contact 38 Richmond Street, Totterdown, Bristol, BS3 4TQ, UK. E-mail: info@sustainablefoodtrust.org.
URL: http://www.sustainablefoodtrust.org/
History 2011, Bristol (UK). **Aims** Accelerate the transition to more sustainable food systems. **Structure** Board. **Activities** Events/meetings. **Events** *The future of UK farming* Lower Swell (UK) 2018, *Harmony in food and farming* Llandovery (UK) 2017, *The true cost of American food* San Francisco, CA (USA) 2016. [2017.03.09/XJ2732/**F**]

♦ Sustainable Fuels 20060

SG c/o CEFIC, Rue Belliard 40, Box 15, 1040 Brussels, Belgium. T. +3224369482. E-mail: info@sustainablefuels.eu.
URL: http://www.sustainablefuels.eu/
History Nov 1985. Founded as a sector group of *Conseil européen de l'industrie chimique (CEFIC, #04687).* Former names and other names: *European Fuel Oxygenates Association (EFOA)* – former. **Aims** Supports and disseminate state-of-the art scientific research on the benefits and impact of fuel ethers on vehicle performance, health and the environment; advocate for science-based policy making through active cooperation with all stakeholders: regulators, legislators, industry, NGOs and the academic community. **Structure** General Assembly; Steering Committee; Technical Committee; Advocacy Committee; Safety and Health Environment Committee; Communication Committee; Working Groups. **Languages** English. **Activities** Networking/liaising; politics/policy/regulatory. **Publications** Technical documents; communication documents.
Members Full; Associate. Companies (8) in 7 countries:
Bulgaria, France, Germany, Italy, Netherlands, Spain, UK. [2020.05.27/XE5992/**E**]

♦ Sustainable Harvest International (internationally oriented national body)

♦ Sustainable Hospitality Alliance 20061

CEO 137 Shepherdess Walk, London, N1 7RQ, UK. T. +442075668711. E-mail: info@sustainablehospitalityalliance.org.
URL: https://sustainablehospitalityalliance.org/
History 1992. Founded as a programme of *The Prince of Wales International Business Leaders Forum (PWIBLF, inactive)*, following signature by a number of international hotel chains of a *'Charter for Environmental Action in the International Hotel and Catering Industry'.* Became a programme of *'Business in the Community'*, Oct 2013. Became an independent charity, 1 Oct 2020. Former names and other names: *International Hotels Environment Initiative (IHEI)* – former (1992 to 2004); *International Tourism Partnership (ITP)* – former (2004). Registration: Charity, No/ID: 1188731, Start date: 2020, England and Wales; Company limited by guarantee, No/ID: 12373950, Start date: 2020, England. **Aims** Bring together engaged hospitality companies; use the collective power of the industry to deliver impact locally and on a global scale. **Structure** Board of Trustees; Senior Advisory Council; Executive Committee. Working Groups; Expert Panel. **Languages** English. **Staff** 12.00 FTE, paid. **Finance** Sources: donations; grants; members' dues. **Activities** Networking/liaising. **Events** *World green tourism conference* Abu Dhabi (United Arab Emirates) 2011, *World green tourism conference* Abu Dhabi (United Arab Emirates) 2010, *HICAP : annual Asia Pacific hotel investment conference* Hong Kong (Hong Kong) 2009. **Publications** *Greenhotelier* – magazine. **Members** Companies. Membership countries not specified. **IGO Relations** Partner of (3): *ILO (#11123); International Finance Corporation (IFC, #13597); International Organization for Migration (IOM, #14454).* **NGO Relations** Partner of (3): *Global Fund to End Slavery; Humanity United; Sightsavers International (#19270).* Cooperates with: *World Travel and Tourism Council (WTTC, #21871).* [2020/XF2842/**F**]

♦ Sustainable, Innovative and United Agriculture and Food Network (internationally oriented national body)

♦ Sustainable Mekong Research Network (SUMERNET) 20062

Contact c/o Stockholm Environment Inst (SEI), 10th Floor, Kasem Uttayanin Bldg, 254 Chulalongkorn Univ, Henri Dunant Rd, Pathumwan, Bangkok, 10330, Thailand. T. +6620730040. Fax +6620730045. E-mail: secretariat@sumernet.org.
URL: http://www.sumernet.org/
History SUMERNET Phase 1 covered 2005–2009; Phase 2, 2010–2013; Phase 3, 2014–Apr 2018; and the present phase 2019–2028. **Aims** Inform and influence sustainable development in the Mekong Region by supporting credible, collaborative research, stimulating independent discussions on key regional issues and engaging with decisionmakers and stakeholders to foster more effective and sustainable policies and programmes. **Structure** Steering Committee; Network Members; Secretariat. **Languages** Burmese, Central Khmer, Chinese, English, Laotian, Thai, Vietnamese. **Finance** Supported by: *Climate and Development Knowledge Network (CDKN, #04012); Swedish International Development Cooperation Agency (Sida).* **Activities** Networking/liaising; projects/programmes; publishing activities; research and development; training/education. Active in all member countries. **Publications** *Climate Risks, Regional Integration and Sustainability in the Mekong Region* (2014); *Meeting Regional and Global Demands for Rubber: A Key to Poverty Alleviation in Lao PDR* (2008); *Challenges to Sustainable Development in the Mekong Delta* (2007). Studies; guides; policy papers.
Members Organizations in 7 countries:
Cambodia, China, Laos, Myanmar, Philippines, Thailand, Vietnam.
NGO Relations Partner of (4): *Asian Institute of Technology (AIT, #01519); International Centre for Tropical Agriculture (#12527); International Water Management Institute (IWMI, #15867); Stockholm Environment Institute (SEI, #19993)* (Asia Centre). [2021.05.19/XM4175/**F**]

♦ Sustainable Nuclear Energy Technology Platform (SNETP) 20063

Secretariat 13 rue Marivaux, 75002 Paris, France. T. +3223188477. E-mail: secretariat@snetp.eu.
URL: http://www.snetp.eu/
History 21 Sep 2007. **Aims** Promote research, development and demonstration of nuclear fission technologies. **Structure** General Assembly; Governing Board; Executive Committee; Secretariat. **Languages** English. **Staff** 2.00 FTE, paid. **Finance** Members' dues. Budget (annual): euro 50,000 – 100,000. **Events** *General Assembly* Brussels (Belgium) 2019, *General Assembly* Brussels (Belgium) 2018, *General Assembly* Brussels (Belgium) 2015, *General Assembly* Vilnius (Lithuania) 2013, *General Assembly* Warsaw (Poland) 2011. **Publications** *SNETP Newsletter.* Factsheets; position papers; strategic documents.
Members Stakeholders from industry, research, academia, technical safety organizations, NGOs and national representatives. Members in 20 countries:
Belgium, Bulgaria, Czechia, Finland, France, Germany, Greece, Hungary, Italy, Latvia, Lithuania, Netherlands, Poland, Romania, Slovakia, Slovenia, Spain, Sweden, Switzerland, UK.
European organizations (7) included in the above:

Confrontations for a European Participative Democracy (Confrontations Europe); European Commission (EC, #06633) (DGs ENER and RTD); *European Committee for Electrotechnical Standardization (CENELEC, #06647); European Nuclear Education Network (ENEN, #08057); European Nuclear Society (ENS, #08059); Joint Research Centre (JRC, #16147); nucleareurope (#17616).* [2020/XJ4823/y/F]

♦ Sustainable Ocean Alliance (internationally oriented national body)
♦ Sustainable Phosphorus Summit (meeting series)

♦ Sustainable Project Management- Public-Private Partnerships for the Urban Environment (SPM) 20064

Chairman Chalet Fleurs de Savigny, 1659 Rougemont VD, Switzerland. T. +41269258000. Fax +41269259500.

History 1994. Founded by *Sustainable Project Management – Innovative Partnerships for Sustainable Development (SPM, inactive)* and *UNDP (#20292)*. Operational 1995. Formerly known as *Public-Private Partnerships for the Urban Environment*. **Aims** Promote the concept and culture of sustainable development, eco-efficiency and public participation through collaborative project identification, development and implementation; identify development problems for which public-private partnerships can provide cost-effective business solutions; engage private sector investors in partnership with the public sector to promote sustainable development through eco-efficient business projects in the developing world and transition economies; ensure long-term viability and poverty alleviation by integrating capacity building and human resource development; stimulate both preventive and remedial pragmatic and replicable solutions to widespread environmental problems affecting urban dwellers and small island developing states; establish new forms of public-private cooperation to finance sustainable development business projects; accelerate technological advance and 'leapfrogging' to meet urban environmental needs; act in a catalytic and supportive role in establishing replicable models of public-private cooperation and shared responsibility to address environmental problems in major urban areas; turn urban environmental problems into viable business opportunities and sustainable, economically sound and socially conscious investments providing reliable, affordable, eco-efficient services related to water treatment, waste management and energy conservation. **Structure** An international collaboration involving governments donors, businesses, nongovernmental organizations and the scientific and academic community. **Finance** Pilot phase funded by UNDP: US$ 1 million. Further funding provided by: *New Zealand Ministry of Foreign Affairs and Trade – New Zealand Aid Programme* for work in the Asia/Pacific region; US$ 250,000 grant from *Asian Development Bank (ADB, #01422)* for project. **Activities** Projects bring together private investors and public sector authorities to address: water and air pollution; inadequate water supply provision; insufficient sanitation infrastructure; excessive waste of natural resources in industrial production processes; inadequate or non-existent waste management procedures; environmentally unfriendly technology; lack of environmental education; lack of environmental consideration in industrial and urban development initiatives; ineffective and wasteful energy sources and technology, including public transport and industrialization.

Members in 7 countries:
Australia, Indonesia, New Zealand, Philippines, Samoa, Switzerland, USA. [2021/XF3676/F]

♦ Sustainable Rice Platform (SRP) 20065

Exec Dir UN Environment Asia and the Pacific Office, UN Bldg, Rajdamnern Nok Ave, Bangkok, 10200, Thailand. T. +6622881801. E-mail: secretariat@sustainablerice.org.
URL: http://www.sustainablerice.org/

History Founded Dec 2011. Co-convened by *UNEP (#20299)* and *International Rice Research Institute (IRRI, #14754)*. **Aims** Promote resource efficiency and sustainability in the global rice sector through an alliance that links research, production, policy making, trade and consumption. **Structure** Executive Board. Technical Committees; Task Forces; Secretariat. **IGO Relations** *Deutsche Gesellschaft für Internationale Zusammenarbeit (GIZ); International Rice Research Institute (IRRI, #14754); UNEP (#20299).* **NGO Relations** Subscriber to: *ISEAL (#16026).* [2020/XM8969/F]

♦ Sustainable Sanitation Alliance (SuSanA) 20066

Secretariat c/o GIZ, Friedrich-Ebert-Allee 36 + 40, 53113 Bonn, Germany. T. +4922844600. Fax +4922844601766. E-mail: info@susana.org.
URL: http://www.susana.org/

History 2007. Registration: Amtsgericht, No/ID: HRB 18384, Germany, Bonn; Amtsgericht, No/ID: HRB 12394, Germany, Frankfurt am Main. **Aims** Ensure access to sustainable sanitation, without distinction of any kind as to race, colour, sex, gender, language, religion, political or other opinion, national or social origin, property, birth, disability or other status. **Structure** Core Group; Secretariat. Working Groups. Loose network of organizations and individuals. **Languages** English. Website translation tool. **Activities** Awareness raising; events/meetings; healthcare; knowledge management/information dissemination; networking/liaising; projects/programmes; publishing activities; research and development; research/documentation; standards/guidelines; training/education. **Events** *Meeting* Kampala (Uganda) 2020, *International Faecal Sludge Management Conference* Abidjan (Côte d'Ivoire) 2019. **Information Services** *Online Library.*

Members Partner organizations (over 380) in 37 countries and territories:
Australia, Austria, Bangladesh, Bolivia, Brazil, Burkina Faso, Cameroon, China, Colombia, Costa Rica, Denmark, Ethiopia, Finland, France, Germany, India, Italy, Japan, Kenya, Malawi, Mali, Mexico, Nepal, Netherlands, Norway, Pakistan, Peru, Philippines, Singapore, South Africa, Sri Lanka, Sweden, Switzerland, UK, USA, Zambia, Zimbabwe.

Included in the above, the following organizations listed in this Yearbook (34):
- *Akvo Foundation;*
- *Asociación Centroamericana para la Economia, la Salud y el Ambiente (ACEPESA);*
- *Bremen Overseas Research and Development Association (BORDA);*
- *Climate Foundation;*
- *Deutsche Gesellschaft für Internationale Zusammenarbeit (GIZ);*
- *FAO (#09260)* (Land and Water Division of);
- *Fondation ensemble;*
- *Gender and Water Alliance (GWA, #10102);*
- *Global Dry Toilet Association of Finland;*
- *IHE Delft Institute for Water Education (#11110);*
- *International Code Council (ICC);*
- *International Ecological Engineering Society (IEES, #13220);*
- *International Rainwater Harvesting Alliance (IRHA, #14695);*
- *International Water Association (IWA, #15865);*
- *International Water Management Institute (IWMI, #15867);*
- *IRC (#16016);*
- *Kreditanstalt für Wiederaufbau (KfW);*
- *Local Governments for Sustainability (ICLEI, #16507);*
- *Oxfam GB;*
- *Plan International (#18386);*
- *Saneamiento Ecológico en Latinoamérica y el Caribe (ECOSANLAC);*
- *SNV Netherlands Development Organisation (SNV);*
- *Stockholm Environment Institute (SEI, #19993);*
- *Sulabh International Social Service Organization;*
- *Swedish International Development Cooperation Agency (Sida);*
- *Toilets for All;*
- *UNICEF (#20332);*
- *United Nations Human Settlements Programme (UN-Habitat, #20572);*
- *WASTE;*
- *Water and Sanitation for Africa (WSA, #20836);*
- *Water and Sanitation Programme (WSP, #20837);*
- *Wherever the Need (WTN);*
- *Women Engage for a Common Future (WECF, #20992);*
- *World Toilet Organization (WTO, #21854).* [2022.02.23/XJ8220/y/F]

♦ Sustainable Sciences Institute (internationally oriented national body)

♦ Sustainable Shipping Initiative (SSI) 20067

Registered Office 19 Eastbourne Terrace, Paddington, London, W2 6LG, UK. T. +447415091372. E-mail: info@sustainableshipping.org.
Main Website: https://www.ssi2040.org/

History 2010. Founded by *Forum for the Future*. Developed into an independent charity. Registration: Charity Commission, No/ID: 1157491, England and Wales. **Aims** Bring together like-minded and leading organizations with shared goals and equal determination in improving sustainability of the shipping industry in terms of social, environmental and economic impacts. **Structure** Board of Trustees; Secretariat. **Languages** English. **Staff** 4.00 FTE, paid. **Activities** Awareness raising; networking/liaising; projects/programmes. **Events** *Annual Round Table on Sustainable Ship Recycling* Singapore (Singapore) 2017. **Publications** *SSI Impact* – Newsletter. Annual Progress Report; case studies; slide decks; videos; podcasts; reports; white papers; press releases. **Members** Individuals; organizations. Membership countries not specified. **IGO Relations** None. [2022.05.18/XJ9798/F]

♦ Sustainable Tourism Certification Alliance Africa (STCAA) 20068

Address not obtained.

History Previous title: *Sustainable Tourism Network Southern Africa (STNSA).* **Aims** Serve as a platform for generating and sharing knowledge, skills, capacity, networks and other resources to create a more enabling environment for sustainable tourism standards and certification in Africa. **Structure** Executive Committee; Rotating Secretariat. **Activities** Knowledge management/information dissemination; advocacy/lobbying/activism. **Events** *Annual Conference* Durban (South Africa) 2013, *Annual Conference* Durban (South Africa) 2012.

Members Registered members in 23 countries:
Angola, Botswana, Congo DR, Egypt, Eswatini, Germany, Ghana, Kenya, Lesotho, Malawi, Mauritius, Mozambique, Namibia, Netherlands, Nigeria, Seychelles, South Africa, Switzerland, Tanzania UR, UK, USA, Zambia, Zimbabwe.

Included in the above, 9 organizations listed in this Yearbook:
African Safari Lodge Foundation (ASL Foundation, #00448); Deutsche Gesellschaft für Internationale Zusammenarbeit (GIZ); Fair Trade Tourism; Global Sustainable Tourism Council (GSTC, #10619); International Trade Centre (ITC, #15703); Open Africa; Rainforest Alliance; Regional Tourism Organisation of Southern Africa (RETOSA, #18817); Sustainable Travel International (STI).

NGO Relations Secretariat provided by: *Better Tourism Africa.* [2015/XJ7299/y/F]

♦ Sustainable Tourism Certification Network of the Americas (STCNA) 20069

Red de Certificación en Turismo Sostenible de las Américas

Secretariat 665 Broadway, Ste 500, New York NY 10012, USA. E-mail: sustainabletourism@ra.org.
URL: http://www.certificationnetwork.org/

History Jan 2003, after a study of *Sustainable Tourism Stewardship Council*, which serves as its accreditation body. Launched Sep 2003, Bahia (Brazil), with the support of *Inter-American Development Bank (IDB, #11427).* **Aims** Promote sustainable tourism in the region. **Structure** Secretariat, organized by *Rainforest Alliance.*

Members Full (over 130) in 21 countries.
Argentina, Belize, Bolivia, Brazil, Chile, Colombia, Costa Rica, Dominican Rep, Ecuador, El Salvador, Guatemala, Honduras, Jamaica, Mexico, Nicaragua, Panama, Paraguay, Peru, Trinidad-Tobago, Uruguay, USA.

Regional institutions include the following listed in this Yearbook (4):
Asociación Centroamericana para la Economia, la Salud y el Ambiente (ACEPESA); Caribbean Alliance for Sustainable Tourism (CAST, #03439); Federación de Camaras de Turismo de Centroamérica (FEDECATUR, #09295); Mesoamerican Ecotourism Alliance (MEA, #16731). [2011/XJ1871/y/F]

♦ Sustainable Tourism Network Southern Africa / see Sustainable Tourism Certification Alliance Africa (#20068)

♦ The Sustainable Trade Initiative (IDH) 20070

CEO PO Box 1241, 3500 BE Utrecht, Netherlands. T. +31302305660. E-mail: office@idhtrade.org.
Street Address Arthur van Schendelstraat 500, 3511 MH Utrecht, Netherlands.
URL: https://www.idhsustainabletrade.com/

History 2008. Former names and other names: *Initiatief Duurzame Handel (IDH)* – former. Registration: EU Transparency Register, No/ID: 022874548279-90, Start date: 8 Dec 2022. **Aims** Convene companies, civil society organizations (CSOs), governments and others in public-private partnerships, so as to drive the joint design, co-funding and prototyping of new economically viable approaches to realize green abd inclusive growth at scale in commodity sectors and sourcing areas. **Structure** Supervisory Board; Executive Board; Global Management Team; Impact Committee. **Staff** 0.50 FTE, paid. **Finance** Sources: government support; grants. Supported by multiple European governments, including Netherlands, Switzerland, Denmark – *DANIDA*, and Norway. Annual budget: 52,865,000 EUR (2021). **NGO Relations** Member of (2): *Better Cotton Initiative (BCI, #03218); World Benchmarking Alliance (WBA, #21228).* Partner of (1): *Tropical Forest Alliance (TFA, #20249).* [2022/XM8559/f/F]

♦ Sustainable Transport Africa (internationally oriented national body)
♦ Sustainable Travel International (internationally oriented national body)

♦ Sustaining Arctic Observing Networks (SAON) 20071

Secretariat AMAP, The Fram Ctr, PO Box 6606 Langnes, 9296 Tromsø, Norway. T. +4523618177.
URL: http://www.arcticobserving.org/

History Mandate given to *Arctic Monitoring and Assessment Programme (AMAP, #01100)* in Salekhard Declaration of *Arctic Council (#01097)*, Nov 2006. *World Meteorological Organization (WMO, #21649)* endorsed development of network, May 2007. SAON established through Arctic council Nuuk Declaration, 2011, as a joint initiative with *International Arctic Science Committee (IASC, #11668).* **Aims** Facilitate, coordinate and advocate for coordinated international pan-Arctic observations; mobilize the supported needed to sustain them. **Structure** Board; Executive Committee; Committees (2); Secretariat. **Languages** English. **Finance** National contributions to Secretariat. **Activities** Research/documentation; knowledge management/information dissemination; events/meetings. **Events** *Biennial Arctic Observing Summit* Tromsø (Norway) 2022, *Biennial Arctic Observing Summit* Akureyri (Iceland) 2020, *Biennial Arctic Observing Summit* Davos (Switzerland) 2018, *Annual Arctic Science Summit* Fairbanks, AK (USA) 2016, *Biennial Arctic Observing Summit* Fairbanks, AK (USA) 2016. **Publications** *The International Arctic Observations Assessment Framework.*

Members Full in 16 countries:
Canada, Denmark, Finland, France, Germany, Iceland, Italy, Japan, Korea Rep, Norway, Poland, Russia, Spain, Sweden, UK, USA.

IGO Relations Partner of: *Group on Earth Observations (GEO, #10735).* **NGO Relations** *International Arctic Science Committee (IASC, #11668).* [2019.12.11/XM6847/F]

♦ Suster-Suster Santa Bunda Maria (religious order)
♦ SUSY – International Conference on Supersymmetry and Unification of Fundamental Interactions (meeting series)
♦ **SUT** Society for Underwater Technology (#19657)
♦ SUW / see International Development Group for Corrugated Board (#13160)
♦ **SUW** International Development Group for Corrugated Board (#13160)
♦ Suzuki Association of the Americas (internationally oriented national body)
♦ SVA – Save Visions Africa (internationally oriented national body)
♦ SVD – Societas Verbi Divini (religious order)
♦ SVECJ – Société de vie évangélique du Coeur de Jésus (religious order)
♦ SVE / see International Society for Applied Ethology (#14930)
♦ Svenska Freds- och Skiljedomsföreningen (internationally oriented national body)
♦ Svenska Handikapporganisationeres Internationella Biståndsförening / see MyRight – Empower People with Disabilities
♦ Svenska Institutet för Europapolitiska Studier (internationally oriented national body)
♦ Svenska missionsrådet (internationally oriented national body)
♦ Svenskt Internationellt Liberalt Centrum (internationally oriented national body)
♦ Svet Evropske Unije (#04895)
♦ Svetovna Organizacija Mladih Proti Klimatski Spremembi (inactive)
♦ Svetski Makedonski Mladinski Kongres
♦ Sviluppo Sostenibile e Lotta alla Povertà nel Mediterraneo e nel Mal Nero (#13562)
♦ Svinesund Committee (internationally oriented national body)
♦ SvinesundKommittén (internationally oriented national body)

- ♦ SVIR – Schweizerische Vereinigung für Internationales Recht (internationally oriented national body)
- ♦ **SVI** Service Volontaire International (#19245)
- ♦ **SVI** Social Value International (#19348)
- ♦ Svitova Federacija Ukrainskih Zinocih Organizacij (#21496)
- ♦ Svjetska Federacija Lijecnika i Drugih Zdravstvenih Radnika Koji Postuju Ljudski Zivot (#21432)
- ♦ **SVN Europe** Social Venture Network Europe (#19349)
- ♦ **SVN** Supervised Visitation Network (#20036)
- ♦ **SVRI** Sexual Violence Research Initiative (#19251)
- ♦ **SVS** Societas Phlebologica Scandinavica (#19451)
- ♦ **SWAA** Spa & Wellness Association of Africa (#19904)
- ♦ SWAC / see Commission for Controlling the Desert Locust in South-West Asia (#04209)
- ♦ **SWAC** Commission for Controlling the Desert Locust in South-West Asia (#04209)
- ♦ **SWAC** Sahel and West Africa Club (#19034)
- ♦ SWAIAP – Society for West African Internal Audit Practitioners (unconfirmed)
- ♦ Swakopmund Protocol on the protection of traditional knowledge and expressions of folklore (2010 treaty)
- ♦ Swami Janakananda, Scandinavian Yoga and Meditation School / see Scandinavian Yoga and Meditation School (#19129)
- ♦ Swaminathan Research Foundation – Centre for Research on Sustainable Agriculture and Rural Development (internationally oriented national body)
- ♦ SWAN – Sex Workers' Rights Advocacy Network (unconfirmed)
- ♦ **SWAN** Smart Water Networks Forum (#19322)
- ♦ SWAPU – South and West Asia Postal Union (inactive)
- ♦ SWARBICA – South and West Asian Regional Branch of the International Council on Archives (see: #12996)
- ♦ **SWA** Sanitation and Water for All (#19051)
- ♦ **SWA** Student World Assembly (#20019)
- ♦ SWAtHC – South West Atlantic Hydrographic Commission (see: #13825)

♦ Swaythling Club International (SCI) 20072

Sec address not obtained.
Pres address not obtained. E-mail: e.d.schoeler@unitybox.de.
URL: https://www.ittf.com/committees/swaythling-club/sc-info/

History 20 Apr 1967, Stockholm (Sweden), at 29th World Table Tennis Championships, by Victor Barna. **Aims** Make it possible for older players, many of whom may be in bad health or without the means, to meet once again at *table tennis* World Championships; develop the game; foster international friendship; encourage younger players; help the younger generation understand the importance of *sportsmanship*. **Structure** Executive Committee, consisting of President, Deputy President, Secretary, Treasurer and Rules Expert. Sub Committees (5): Press and Publicity; National and International Relations; Sponsoring and Advertising; Public Relations; World Veteran Championships (WVC). **Languages** English. **Staff** 25.00 FTE, voluntary. **Finance** Members' dues (annual): Swiss Fr 20. **Activities** Grants "Best Player" Award at World Team Championships (at annual General Meeting). Also organizes: biennial World Veteran Championships. **Events** *Annual Meeting / Annual General Meeting* Tokyo (Japan) 2014, *Annual Meeting / Annual General Meeting* Paris (France) 2013, *Annual Meeting / Annual General Meeting* Dortmund (Germany) 2012, *Annual Meeting / Annual General Meeting* Rotterdam (Netherlands) 2011, *Annual Meeting / Annual General Meeting* Moscow (Russia) 2010. **Publications** *SCI News* (2 a year); *SCI Booklet* (every 2-4 years).
Members Individuals (540) in 56 countries and territories:
Armenia, Australia, Austria, Azerbaijan, Belarus, Belgium, Brazil, Bulgaria, Canada, Croatia, Curaçao, Cyprus, Czechia, Denmark, Egypt, England, Estonia, Finland, France, Germany, Greece, Hungary, India, Iran Islamic Rep, Ireland, Israel, Italy, Japan, Jersey, Jordan, Kazakhstan, Kenya, Lebanon, Luxembourg, Malaysia, Mexico, Netherlands, New Zealand, Norway, Portugal, Romania, Russia, Scotland, Serbia, Slovakia, Slovenia, South Africa, Spain, Sri Lanka, Sweden, Switzerland, Türkiye, Ukraine, Uruguay, USA, Wales.
NGO Relations Recognized by: *International Table Tennis Federation (ITTF, #15650).* [2018/XF0679/v/**F**]

- ♦ SWB – Schools Without Borders (internationally oriented national body)
- ♦ SWB – Soccer Without Borders (internationally oriented national body)
- ♦ SWC – Simon Wiesenthal Center (internationally oriented national body)
- ♦ SWCS – Soil and Water Conservation Society (internationally oriented national body)
- ♦ SWDCAP – Social Welfare and Development Centre for Asia and the Pacific (inactive)
- ♦ SWEA International / see Swedish Women's Educational Association International (#20075)
- ♦ **SWEA** Swedish Women's Educational Association International (#20075)

♦ Swedenborg Foundation 20073

Address not obtained.
URL: http://www.swedenborg.com/

History 1849, New York, NY (USA). Incorporated 1850. Administrative offices moved, from New York NY to West Chester PA (USA) in 1993. **Aims** Preserve the *literary* heritage of Emanuel Swedenborg; promote his *spiritual* insights worldwide; foster an affirmative and increasingly broad engagement with his *theological* thought among persons desiring to apply spiritual principles to life. **Structure** Meeting (annual); Board of Directors. **Languages** English. **Staff** 9.00 FTE, paid. **Finance** Sources: members' dues. **Activities** Events/meetings; projects/programmes. **Events** *International conference on altered states of consciousness* Albuquerque, NM (USA) 2002. **Publications** *Logos* (2 a year) – newsletter. Annual report; biographies and translations of Swedenborg; spiritual transformation materials; spiritual trade books; videos. **Members** in 45 countries (not specified). [2020.05.14/XF2906/f/**F**]

- ♦ Swedenborgian – General Conference of the New Church (inactive)

♦ Swedenborg Society 20074

Administrator 20-21 Bloomsbury Way, London, WC1A 2TH, UK. T. +442074057986. Fax +442078315848. E-mail: admin@swedenborg.org.uk.
URL: http://www.swedenborg.org.uk/

History 1810, London (UK). A charity registered in accordance with British law. **Aims** Publish and distribute the works of Emanuel Swedenborg, *theologian* and *philosopher*. **Structure** Council; Advisory and Revision Board. **Languages** English, Latin. **Staff** 6.00 FTE, paid. **Finance** Members' dues. Other sources: investment income; office rents; room hire; sale of publications. **Activities** Publishing activities; events/meetings. **Publications** *Journal of the Swedenborg Society*; *Things Heard and Seen* – newsletter. Annual Report; books.
Members Individuals in 31 countries and territories:
Argentina, Australia, Barbados, Canada, Canaries, Denmark, Finland, France, Germany, Ghana, Iceland, India, Italy, Jamaica, Japan, Korea Rep, Liberia, Mauritania, Mexico, Monaco, Netherlands, New Zealand, Nigeria, Norway, South Africa, Spain, Sweden, Switzerland, UK, USA, Zimbabwe. [2015/XF5107/v/**E**]

- ♦ SWEDESD – Swedish International Centre of Education for Sustainable Development (internationally oriented national body)
- ♦ Swedfund – International (internationally oriented national body)
- ♦ Swedish Cooperative Centre / see We Effect
- ♦ Swedish Development Aid Organization (internationally oriented national body)
- ♦ Swedish Development Partner (internationally oriented national body)
- ♦ Swedish Foundation for Human Rights (internationally oriented national body)
- ♦ Swedish Free Church Aid / see Diakonia
- ♦ Swedish Fund for Industrial Cooperation with Developing Countries / see Swedfund – International
- ♦ Swedish Helsinki Committee for Human Rights / see Civil Rights Defenders
- ♦ Swedish Institute for European Policy Studies (internationally oriented national body)
- ♦ Swedish Institute of International Affairs (internationally oriented national body)
- ♦ Swedish International Centre of Education for Sustainable Development (internationally oriented national body)
- ♦ Swedish International Centre for Local Democracy (internationally oriented national body)
- ♦ Swedish International Development Cooperation Agency (internationally oriented national body)
- ♦ Swedish International Liberal Centre (internationally oriented national body)
- ♦ Swedish Medical Mission Foundation / see Läkarmissionen
- ♦ Swedish Mission Council (internationally oriented national body)
- ♦ Swedish Network for International Health (internationally oriented national body)
- ♦ Swedish NGO Centre for Development Cooperation (internationally oriented national body)
- ♦ Swedish NGO Foundation for Human Rights / see Swedish Foundation for Human Rights
- ♦ Swedish Organization of Disabled Persons International Aid Association / see MyRight – Empower People with Disabilities
- ♦ Swedish Organization for Global Health (internationally oriented national body)
- ♦ Swedish Organization of the Handicapped – International Aid Foundation / see MyRight – Empower People with Disabilities
- ♦ Swedish Organization for Individual Relief / see Swedish Development Partner
- ♦ Swedish Peace and Arbitration Society (internationally oriented national body)
- ♦ Swedish Pentecostal Mission Relief and Development Cooperation Agency / see PMU Interlife
- ♦ Swedish Society for the Study of Russia, Central and Eastern Europe and Central Asia (internationally oriented national body)
- ♦ Swedish South Asian Studies Network (internationally oriented national body)

♦ Swedish Women's Educational Association International (SWEA) .. 20075

Mailing Address PO Box 4128, Fort Lauderdale FL 33338, USA. E-mail: office@swea.org.
URL: http://www.swea.org/

History 1979, Los Angeles, CA (USA). Founded by Swedish and Swedish speaking women. Former names and other names: *SWEA International* – alias. **Aims** Safeguard the Swedish language; support and convey information regarding Swedish culture and traditions; encourage contacts between Swedish women worldwide. **Activities** Awards 2 scholarships (annual); selects 'Swedish Woman of the Year'; organizes Spring meeting (annual) and Autumn meeting (annual). **Events** *International board meeting* Brussels (Belgium) 2001, *Congress* Madrid (Spain) 1995. **Publications** *SWEA Forum* (2 a year).
Members Chapters in 33 countries:
Argentina, Austria, Belgium, Canada, China, France, Germany, Greece, Hong Kong, Hungary, Ireland, Israel, Italy, Japan, Korea Rep, Latvia, Lithuania, Netherlands, Norway, Poland, Portugal, Saudi Arabia, Singapore, South Africa, Spain, Sweden, Switzerland, Thailand, Tunisia, Türkiye, UK, United Arab Emirates, USA. [2020/XD8607/**D**]

- ♦ SWEDO – Swedish Development Aid Organization (internationally oriented national body)
- ♦ Sweets Global Network (internationally oriented national body)
- ♦ SWEHR / see Swedish Foundation for Human Rights
- ♦ SWEMP – International Symposium on Environmental Issues and Waste Management in Energy and Minerals Production (meeting series)
- ♦ **SWENET** Space Weather European Network (#19900)
- ♦ SWE – Society of Women Engineers (internationally oriented national body)
- ♦ SWE – Solidarity Water Europe (internationally oriented national body)
- ♦ SWFI – Sovereign Wealth Fund Institute (internationally oriented national body)
- ♦ SWF – Secure World Foundation (internationally oriented national body)
- ♦ SWGEN – Conference on Stochastic Weather Generators (meeting series)
- ♦ SWGM / see Spanish World Ministries (#19901)
- ♦ **SWG RRD** South Eastern Europe Regional Rural Development Standing Working Group (#19809)
- ♦ Swiatowej Federacji Zwiezkow Swiety Gabriel (#21885)
- ♦ Swiatowy Kongres Górniczy (#21654)
- ♦ **SWIFT** Society for Worldwide Interbank Financial Telecommunication (#19661)
- ♦ **SWIOFC** South West Indian Ocean Fisheries Commission (#19894)
- ♦ SWI – Safe Water International (internationally oriented national body)
- ♦ SwiSca – Symposium on Swearing in the Nordic Countries (meeting series)
- ♦ Swiss Academy for Development (internationally oriented national body)
- ♦ Swiss Academy of Humanities and Social Sciences (internationally oriented national body)
- ♦ Swiss Agency for Development and Cooperation (internationally oriented national body)
- ♦ Swissaid (internationally oriented national body)
- ♦ Swiss Aid Agencies Coalition / see Alliance Sud, Swiss Alliance of Development Organisations Swissaid – Catholic Lenten Fund – Bread for All – Helvetas – Caritas – Interchurch Aid
- ♦ Swiss-Asia Society (internationally oriented national body)
- ♦ Swiss Association for the Exchange of Personnel in Development Cooperation (internationally oriented national body)
- ♦ Swiss Association for Responsible Development / see Public Eye
- ♦ Swiss Catholic Lenten Fund / see Catholic Lenten Fund
- ♦ Swiss Centre of Competence for International Cooperation / see Centre for Information, Counseling and Training Professions Relating to International Cooperation and Humanitarian Aid
- ♦ Swiss Centre for Development Cooperation in Technology and Management / see Swiss Resource Centre and Consultancies for Development
- ♦ Swiss Coalition of Development Organizations Swissaid – Catholic Lenten Fund – Bread for All – Helvetas – Caritas / see Alliance Sud, Swiss Alliance of Development Organisations Swissaid – Catholic Lenten Fund – Bread for All – Helvetas – Caritas – Interchurch Aid
- ♦ Swiss Commission for Research Partnerships with Developing Countries / see Commission for Research Partnerships with Developing Countries
- ♦ Swiss Committee Against Torture / see Association for the Prevention of Torture (#02869)
- ♦ Swisscontact – Fondation suisse de coopération au développement technique (internationally oriented national body)
- ♦ Swisscontact – Fundación Suiza para la Cooperación para el Desarrollo Técnica (internationally oriented national body)
- ♦ Swisscontact – Schweizerische Stiftung für Technische Entwicklungszusammenarbeit (internationally oriented national body)
- ♦ Swisscontact – Swiss Foundation for Technical Cooperation (internationally oriented national body)
- ♦ Swiss Foreign Policy Association (internationally oriented national body)
- ♦ Swiss Foundation for Mine Action (internationally oriented national body)
- ♦ swissinfo – Swiss Radio International (internationally oriented national body)
- ♦ Swiss Institute of International Studies (internationally oriented national body)
- ♦ Swiss Interchurch Aid (internationally oriented national body)
- ♦ Swiss Investment Fund for Emerging Markets (internationally oriented national body)
- ♦ Swisspeace (internationally oriented national body)
- ♦ Swiss Peace Council (internationally oriented national body)
- ♦ Swiss Peace Foundation / see Swisspeace
- ♦ Swiss Peace Foundation – Institute for Conflict Resolution / see Swisspeace
- ♦ Swiss Peace Movement (internationally oriented national body)
- ♦ Swiss Radio International / see swissinfo – Swiss Radio International
- ♦ Swiss Refugee Council (internationally oriented national body)
- ♦ Swiss Resource Centre and Consultancies for Development (internationally oriented national body)
- ♦ Swiss Society for African Studies (internationally oriented national body)
- ♦ Swiss Society of International law (internationally oriented national body)
- ♦ Swiss TPH – Swiss Tropical and Public Health Institute (internationally oriented national body)
- ♦ Swiss Tropical Institute / see Swiss Tropical and Public Health Institute
- ♦ Swiss Tropical and Public Health Institute (internationally oriented national body)
- ♦ Swiss Volunteer Service Cooperating for Development (internationally oriented national body)
- ♦ **SWME** Society for Worldwide Medical Exchange (#19662)
- ♦ **SWM** Spanish World Ministries (#19901)
- ♦ SWP / see Stiftung Wissenschaft und Politik
- ♦ **SWPD** South-West Pacific Dialogue (#19895)
- ♦ SWPHC – South West Pacific Hydrographic Commission (see: #13825)
- ♦ SWP – Stiftung Wissenschaft und Politik (internationally oriented national body)
- ♦ **SWSA** Semantic Web Science Association (#19224)

- ♦ SWS – Society of Wetland Scientists (internationally oriented national body)
- ♦ SWT – Sheldrick Wildlife Trust (internationally oriented national body)
- ♦ **SWWAC** South West Waters Advisory Council (#19896)
- ♦ SX – Societas Sancti Francisci Xaverii pro Exteris Missionibus (religious order)
- ♦ **SYBAss** Superyacht Builders Association (#20037)
- ♦ Sydafrika Kontakt (internationally oriented national body)
- ♦ SYDEPI – Synergie Développement et Partenariat International (internationally oriented national body)

♦ SYFIA International 20076

Secretariat 58 bis avenue Maurice de Sauret, 34000 Montpellier, France. T. +33685734602. E-mail: magnes.leplaideur@gmail.com.
URL: http://www.syfia.com/

History as *Système francophone d'information*, as an independent press agency under the management of *Agence intergouvernementale de La Francophonie (inactive)*. **Aims** Provide *information* on *agriculture, economics* and *environment* for *African* countries. **Activities** Active in: Algeria, Benin, Burkina Faso, Burundi, Cameroon, Central African Rep, Chad, Comoros, Congo Brazzaville, Congo DR, Côte d'Ivoire, Gabon, Gambia, Ghana, Guinea, Guinea-Bissau, Madagascar, Mali, Mauritania, Mauritius, Morocco, Niger, Nigeria, Rwanda, Senegal, South Africa, Togo, Tunisia, Uganda. **Publications** *SYFIA* (12 a year) – bulletin. **NGO Relations** Member of: *Coordination SUD*. [2014/XF0869/**F**]

- ♦ SYFODIP – Synergy for Development and International Partnership (internationally oriented national body)
- ♦ Sykepleiernes Samarbeid i Norden (#17371)
- ♦ Sykes-Picot agreement (inactive)
- ♦ Sylva-Monde pour le Développement et la Protection des Forêts et de l'Environnement (internationally oriented national body)
- ♦ SYLVA-WORLD for Development and the Protection of Forests and the Environment (internationally oriented national body)
- ♦ SymBioSE (meeting series)
- ♦ Symposium on Algorithmic Approaches for Transportation Modeling, Optimization, and Systems (meeting series)
- ♦ Symposium on Bacterial Genetics and Ecology (meeting series)
- ♦ Symposium of Biotechnology Applied to Lignocelluloses (meeting series)
- ♦ Symposium of the Central and Eastern European Chambers of Physicians (meeting series)
- ♦ Symposium des conférences épiscopales d'Afrique et de Madagascar (#20077)
- ♦ Symposium on Conformal and Probabilistic Prediction with Applications (meeting series)

♦ Symposium of Episcopal Conferences of Africa and Madagascar (SECAM) 20077

Symposium des conférences épiscopales d'Afrique et de Madagascar (SCEAM) – Simpósio das Conferências Episcopais da Africa e Madagascar (SCEAM)

SG 4 Senchi Street, PO Box 9156, Airport Residential Area, Accra, Ghana. T. +233302778867 – +233302778868. Fax +233302772548. E-mail: secamsec@yahoo.com.
URL: http://www.secam-sceam.org/

History Jul 1969, Kampala (Uganda), following a meeting of 6 African bishops, Apr 1968, Rome (Italy), and superseding the functions and objectives of *Pan African Episcopal Conference (inactive)*, dissolved after Vatican II. Constitution approved 1970, Abidjan (Côte d'Ivoire). Statutes revised 2003. **Aims** Promote the Symposium's role as a sign and instrument of salvation; build the Church as a Family of God in Africa; preserve and foster communion, collaboration and joint action among all the Episcopal Conferences of Africa and the Islands; promote propagation of Faith, human development, ecumenism, communications, formation and consultation. **Structure** Plenary Assembly of representatives (every 3 years). Standing Committee, consisting of President, 2 Vice-Presidents (belonging to language groups different from the President's – English, French or Portuguese) and 8 members from each of the 8 episcopal regions. Each of the Regional Episcopal Conferences represented in membership of the Standing Committee. Presidential Council, comprising President and 2 Vice-Presidents. Departments and offices: *'Department of Evangelisation'*, including *Catholic Biblical Centre for Africa and Madagascar (BICAM, #03599)*, Theological Committee (COMITHEOL) and *Equipe panafricaine de coordination des laïcs (EPACL, #05523)*; *'Department of Justice, Peace, Development and Good Governance'*, including Office of Justice, Peace and Development, Office of Good Governance, *Association of Catholic Education for Africa and Madagascar (#02415)*, Office of HIV/AIDS. Other offices: Communications; Administrative; Accounts. **Languages** English, French, Portuguese. **Staff** 4 priests; 1 lay man; 12 support staff. **Finance** Mainly funded through contributions of member Episcopal Conferences with levies paid by each diocese. Subsidies from: *Congregation for the Evangelization of Peoples (CEP, #04670)*; Vatican City; various religious organizations and partner agencies, mainly in Europe and USA. **Activities** carried out through internal commissions: CEPACS; CETAP; *Theological Committee – Comité théologique (COMITHEOL)*; *Committee for the Biblical Apostolate – Comité pour l'apostolat biblique (COMIBIBLE)*, which set up BICAM. General Assemblies each cover a specific theme. **Events** *Congrès continental de justice et paix* Kinshasa (Congo DR) 2008, *Triennial plenary assembly* Abidjan (Côte d'Ivoire) 2006, *Symposium of African and European bishops* Rome (Italy) 2004, *Triennial plenary assembly* Dakar (Senegal) 2003, *Triennial plenary assembly* Rome (Italy) 2000. **Publications** *As Family* (6 a year) in English, French, Portuguese; *Symposium* – bulletin. *SECAM at 40*; *What is SECAM*. Meeting reports; pastoral letters; documents.

Members (a) National Episcopal Conferences – or Inter-Territorial Conference – (35), covering 51 countries:
Algeria, Angola, Benin, Botswana, Burkina Faso, Burundi, Cameroon, Cape Verde, Central African Rep, Chad, Comoros, Congo Brazzaville, Congo DR, Côte d'Ivoire, Equatorial Guinea, Eritrea, Ethiopia, Gabon, Gambia, Ghana, Guinea, Guinea-Bissau, Kenya, Lesotho, Liberia, Libya, Madagascar, Malawi, Mali, Mauritania, Mauritius, Morocco, Mozambique, Namibia, Niger, Nigeria, Rwanda, Sao Tomé-Principe, Senegal, Seychelles, Sierra Leone, Somalia, South Africa, South Sudan, Sudan, Tanzania UR, Togo, Tunisia, Uganda, Zambia, Zimbabwe.
(b) All Cardinals of Africa.
(c) Members of the Council of 24 of the Congregation for the Evangelization of Peoples belonging to the African Episcopate:
(d) Members of the Standing Committee of SECAM.
(e) Regional Episcopal Conferences (10), including the following 7 organizations listed in this Yearbook:
Association des conférences épiscopales de l'Afrique centrale (ACEAC, #02448); *Association of Member Episcopal Conferences in Eastern Africa (AMECEA, #02805)*; *Association of the Episcopal Conferences of the Central African Region (#02491)*; *Conférence des évêques de la région du Nord de l'Afrique (CERNA, #04605)*; *Conférence épiscopale de l'Océan Indien (CEDOI, #04592)*; *Inter-Regional Meeting of Bishops of Southern Africa (IMBISA, #15971)*; *Regional Episcopal Conference of West Africa (RECOWA, #18783)*.
NGO Relations Partner of: *World Catholic Association for Communication (SIGNIS, #21264)*. Member of: *African Council of Religious Leaders – Religions for Peace (ACRL-RfP, #00276)*. [2012.09.24/XD3948/y/**D**]

- ♦ Symposium of European Bishops (meeting series)
- ♦ Symposium européen du génie électrochimique (meeting series)
- ♦ Symposium des évêques d'Europe (meeting series)
- ♦ Symposium on Flavonoids in Biology and Medicine (meeting series)
- ♦ Symposium international pour l'étiquetage d'entretien des textiles / see Groupement International de l'Etiquetage pour l'Entretien des Textiles (#10761)
- ♦ Symposium international sur l'impédance cérébrale (meeting series)
- ♦ Symposium international sur les jets moléculaires (meeting series)
- ♦ Symposium international de morphologie (meeting series)
- ♦ Symposium international sur le nerf facial (meeting series)
- ♦ Symposium international de phytopharmacie et phytiatrie (meeting series)
- ♦ Symposium international de télévision (meeting series)
- ♦ Symposium International Théorie Quantique et Symétries (meeting series)
- ♦ Symposium on Mathematical Theory of Networks and Systems (meeting series)
- ♦ Symposium on Naval Hydrodynamics (meeting series)
- ♦ Symposium on Prospects in the Physics of Discrete Symmetries (meeting series)
- ♦ Symposium on Swearing in the Nordic Countries (meeting series)
- ♦ Symposium on Trends in Functional Programming (meeting series)
- ♦ Symposium on UltraSonic Electronics (meeting series)
- ♦ Symposium on World Trends in Science Education / see International Organization for Science and Technology Education (#14469)
- ♦ **SYM** Salesian Youth Movement (#19039)
- ♦ Synchronicity Earth (internationally oriented national body)
- ♦ Synchrotron-light for Experimental Science and Applications in the Middle East / see Synchrotron-light for Experimental Science and Applications in the Middle East (#20078)

♦ Synchrotron-light for Experimental Science and Applications in the Middle East (SESAME) 20078

Centre international de rayonnement synchrotron pour les sciences expérimentales et appliquées au Moyen-Orient

Admin Assistant PO Box 7, Allan 19252, Jordan. T. +9625351134 – +96253511361ext228. Fax +96253511423.
Admin Dir address not obtained.
URL: http://www.sesame.org.jo/

History First proposed in 1997. Interim council set up in 1999. Establishment under auspices of *UNESCO (#20322)* approved by UNESCO Executive Board, May 2002; ceremony, 6 Jan 2003. Soft inauguration, 3 Nov 2008. Also referred to as *SESAME Project* and *Synchrotron-light for Experimental Science and Applications in the Middle East (SESAME) – International Centre*. Facility officially opened 16 May 2017. **Aims** Establish a scientific center of excellence in which scientists from all countries of the Middle East and the rest of the world work together to enhance peace and prosperity. **Structure** Users' Meeting (annual, in Dec); Council; Directors (4); Committees (4). **Languages** English. **Staff** 52.00 FTE, paid. **Finance** Members' dues. Donation from other countries and scientific centres around the world. Annual budget: US$ 3,500,000. **Activities** Research and development; events/meetings; training/education; capacity building; networking/liaising. **Events** *SESAME Users Meeting* Allan (Jordan) 2019, *SESAME Users Meeting* Allan (Jordan) 2018, *SESAME Users Meeting* Amman (Jordan) 2017, *SESAME Users Meeting* Amman (Jordan) 2016, *SESAME users meeting* Amman (Jordan) 2015. **Publications** Scientific and technical papers by staff and visitors.

Members Governments of 9 countries and territories:
Bahrain, Cyprus, Egypt, Iran Islamic Rep, Israel, Jordan, Pakistan, Palestine, Türkiye. [2018.09.05/XE4575/**E***]

- ♦ Syndesmos Viomichanion Pagotou tis EOK / see EUROGLACES – European Ice Cream Association (#05688)
- ♦ **Syndesmos** World Fellowship of Orthodox Youth (#21504)

♦ Syndicat des agents du Conseil de l'Europe (SACE) 20079

Council of Europe Staff Trade Union

Main Office Bureau D110, Conseil de l'Europe, 67075 Strasbourg, France. E-mail: sace@coe.int.
URL: https://unionsyndicale.eu/en/organisations-membres-usf/sace-syndicat-agents-conseil-europe/

History 1966. Founded to represent staff members of *Council of Europe (CE, #04881)*. **NGO Relations** Founding member of: *Union Syndicale Fédérale (USF, #20485)*. [2022/XE1847/v/**E**]

- ♦ Syndicat des écrivains de langue française (internationally oriented national body)
- ♦ Syndicat européen des fûts en acier / see European Association of Steel Drum Manufacturers (#06222)
- ♦ Syndicat européen de l'industrie des fûts en acier (#06222)
- ♦ Syndicat européen de l'industrie des fûts de fibres (#06038)
- ♦ Syndicat européen des récupérateurs et rénovateurs de drums (#08333)
- ♦ Syndicat des fonctionnaires européens / see European Public Service Union (#08303)
- ♦ Syndicat des fonctionnaires internationaux et européens / see European Public Service Union (#08303)
- ♦ Syndicat de la fonction publique européenne (#08303)
- ♦ Syndicat international des auteurs de radio, cinéma et télévision (inactive)

♦ Syndicat international du décolletage (SID) 20080

Contact SNDEC, 780 av de Colomby, BP 20200, 74304 Cluses CEDEX, France. T. +33450980768. Fax +33450961498.
Contact PMPA, 6700 W Snowville Rd, Brecksville OH 44141, USA. T. +14405260300. Fax +14405265803.
URL: https://sidgroup.org/

History 1963. **Aims** Promote friendly contact among producers of precision machine *tools* – screw machine products and turned parts – in Europe and North America. **Structure** Steering Committee, comprising 2 representatives of each member association and 3 Officers. **Activities** Events/meetings. **Events** *Congress* Switzerland 2030, *Congress* France 2028, *Congress* UK 2026, *Congress* USA 2024, *Congress* Barcelona (Spain) 2022.

Members National associations (7) in 7 countries:
France, Germany, Ireland, Spain, Sweden, Switzerland, USA. [2021/XF3772/**D**]

- ♦ Syndicat du personnel du Centre OIT à Turin / see Staff Union of the International Training Centre of the ILO
- ♦ Syndicat du personnel local et non local des services généraux de la FAO (#20455)
- ♦ Syndicat du personnel local et non local des services généraux de l'Organisation des Nations Unies pour l'alimentation et l'agriculture / see Union of Local and Non Local General Service Staff FAO/WFP (#20455)
- ♦ Syndicat du personnel des Nations Unies (#20630)
- ♦ Syndicat du personnel de l'OIT / see Staff Union of the International Labour Office (#19945)
- ♦ Syndicat du personnel de l'OMI / see IMO Staff Association (#11135)
- ♦ Syndicat du personnel de l'ONUDI (#20335)
- ♦ Syndicat du personnel de l'Organisation internationale du travail (#19945)
- ♦ Syndicat du personnel de l'Organisation des Nations Unies (#20561)
- ♦ Syndicat du personnel de l'UNESCO (#20321)
- ♦ Synergie Développement et Partenariat International (internationally oriented national body)

♦ Synergies Africaines contre le SIDA et les Souffrances (Synergies Africaines) 20081

Contact Boîte Postale 3526, Yaoundé, Cameroon. T. +23722230915. Fax +23722231163. E-mail: contact@synergiesafricaines.org.
URL: http://www.synergiesafricaines.org/

History Founded 15 Nov 2002, Yaoundé (Cameroon). **Aims** Eliminate transmission of *HIV* from mother to child; reduce maternal and *infant* mortality; alleviate suffering of the African child; fight against non-transmissible diseases. **Structure** Conference des Premières Dames; Comité de Suivi; Executive Secretariat. **Languages** Arabic, English, French, Portuguese, Spanish. **Staff** 25.00 FTE, paid. **Finance** Members' dues. Other sources: donations; subsidies. Annual budget: US$ 300,000. **Activities** Advocacy/lobbying/activism; capacity building; awards/prizes/competitions; healthcare; financial and/or material support; events/meetings.

Members First and former First Ladies in 28 countries:
Angola, Benin, Burkina Faso, Burundi, Cameroon, Cape Verde, Central African Rep, Chad, Comoros, Egypt, Equatorial Guinea, Eswatini, Eswatini, Gabon, Guinea, Kenya, Mali, Mauritius, Morocco, Mozambique, Namibia, Niger, Nigeria, Senegal, Sierra Leone, Sudan, Togo, Uganda.

IGO Relations *FAO (#09260)*; *International Criminal Police Organization – INTERPOL (ICPO-INTERPOL, #13110)*; *Joint United Nations Programme on HIV/AIDS (UNAIDS, #16149)*; *UNDP (#20292)*; *UNESCO (#20322)*; *UNICEF (#20332)*; *United Nations Population Fund (UNFPA, #20612)*; *WHO (#20950)*. **NGO Relations** Member of: *PMNCH (#18410)*; *Smile Train (#19328)*; *Union for International Cancer Control (UICC, #20415)*. [2018.10.24/XM6998/v/**F**]

- ♦ **Synergies Africaines** Synergies Africaines contre le SIDA et les Souffrances (#20081)

♦ **Synergos** **20082**

Contact 3 East 54th St, 14th Floor, New York NY 10022, USA. T. +16469632100. Fax +16462015220. E-mail: synergos@synergos.org.
URL: https://www.synergos.org/

History 1986, New York NY (USA). Former names and other names: *Synergos Institute* – former. **Aims** Mobilize resources and bridge social and economic divides to reduce *poverty* and increase equity around the world. **Structure** Board of Directors; International Advisory Council. Standing Committees (6): Finance; Nominating; Governance; Development; Program and Planning; Executive and Management. **Staff** 37.00 FTE, paid. **Finance** Sources: grants and contributions from foundations, corporations, international organizations and individuals. **Activities** Works through partnerships, networks and knowledge sharing. Worked in over 30 countries and regions worldwide. Currently runs 2 global networks: Senior Fellows; Global Philanthropists Circle. Organizes annual 'University for a Night'. Instrumental in setting up *South North Development Initiative (SNDI, #19881)*. **Events** *Conference* 1997, *Regional workshop* Maputo (Mozambique) 1996, *Meeting on strengthening sustainable community initiatives in Southern Mexico* Oaxaca (Mexico) 1996. **Publications** *Global Giving Matters* (5 a year); *The Commons* (4 a year) – newsletter. Papers and presentations by Synergos staff.

Members Individuals in 20 countries and territories:
Argentina, Brazil, Canada, Ecuador, Egypt, Ghana, India, Indonesia, Japan, Jordan, Lebanon, Mexico, Morocco, Mozambique, Namibia, Palestine, Philippines, South Africa, USA, Zimbabwe.

NGO Relations Member of (2): *Humentum (#10993)*; *Worldwide Initiatives for Grantmaker Support (WINGS, #21926)*. [2022/XF1477/jv/**F**]

- ♦ Synergos Institute / see Synergos (#20082)
- ♦ SYNERGY (no recent information)
- ♦ Synergy for Development and International Partnership (internationally oriented national body)
- ♦ Syngenta Foundation for Sustainable Agriculture (internationally oriented national body)
- ♦ Syngenta Stiftung für Nachhaltige Landwirtschaft (internationally oriented national body)

♦ **Synod of Bishops** **20083**

Synode des evêques – Sinodo dei Vescovi – Synodus Episcoporum

SG Via della Conciliazione 34, 00120 Vatican City, Vatican. T. +39669884821 – +39669884324. Fax +39669883392. E-mail: synodus@synod.va.
URL: http://www.synod.va/

History 15 Sep 1965, Vatican City, when instituted by Pope Paul VI. **Aims** Encourage close union and valued assistance between the Sovereign Pontiff and the bishops of the entire world; ensure that direct and real information is provided on questions and situations touching upon the internal action of the Church and its necessary activity in the world of today; facilitate better understanding of essential points of doctrine and promote pastoral initiatives in the life of the Church. **Structure** Ordinary General Assembly; Ordinary Council; Special Councils; General Secretary. **Languages** English, French, Italian, Spanish. **Staff** 11.00 FTE, paid. **Activities** Knowledge management/information dissemination; advice/assistance/consulting. **Events** *Ordinary General Assembly* Vatican City (Vatican) 2015, *Extraordinary General Assembly* Vatican City (Vatican) 2014, *Ordinary General Assembly* Vatican City (Vatican) 2012, *Special assembly for the Middle East* Vatican City (Vatican) 2010, *Special assembly for Africa* Vatican City (Vatican) 2009. **NGO Relations** Comes within the: *Administrative Hierarchy of the Roman Catholic Church (#00117)*. [2019.02.19/XF9238/**F**]

- ♦ Synode européen des femmes (meeting series)
- ♦ Synode des evêques (#20083)
- ♦ Synodus Episcoporum (#20083)
- ♦ Synowie Matki Bozej Bolesnej (religious order)
- ♦ Synskadades Nordiska Samarbetskomitté (inactive)

♦ **Synthetic Organic Ion Exchangers and Adsorbents (SOIA)** **20084**

Contact c/o CEFIC, Rue Belliard 40, Box 15, 1040 Brussels, Belgium. E-mail: ywu@cefic.be.
URL: http://soia.cefic.org/

History 28 Feb 1990. Founded as a sector group of *Conseil européen de l'industrie chimique (CEFIC, #04687)*. **Structure** General Assembly.

Members Companies (5) in 5 countries:
Belgium, Finland, Germany, Italy, UK.

IGO Relations Recognized by: *European Commission (EC, #06633)*. [2021.09.01/XK0236/**E**]

- ♦ Synthetic Turf Council (internationally oriented national body)
- ♦ Synthetic Turf Council International (unconfirmed)
- ♦ Syriac Universal Alliance / see World Council of Arameans – Syriacs (#21318)
- ♦ Syrian Orthodox Patriarchate of Antioch and All the East / see Greek Orthodox Patriarchate of Antioch and All the East (#10710)
- ♦ SysMus – International Conference of Students of Systematic Musicology (meeting series)
- ♦ System of Cooperation among the American Air Forces (#19293)
- ♦ Système d'accès aux données et informations sur le milieu marin (no recent information)
- ♦ Système CEI d'assurance de la qualité des composants électroniques (#11095)
- ♦ Système CEI d'essais de conformité et de certification des équipements électriques / see IEC System of Conformity Assessment Schemes for Electrotechnical Equipment and Components (#11096)
- ♦ Système CEI d'essais de conformité aux normes de sécurité de l'équipement électrique / see IEC System of Conformity Assessment Schemes for Electrotechnical Equipment and Components (#11096)
- ♦ Système de Coopération entre les armées de l'air des Amériques (#19293)
- ♦ Système d'échanges d'énergie électrique ouest africain (#20894)
- ♦ Système des écoles associées appliquant un programme d'éducation pour la coopération internationale et la paix / see UNESCO Associated Schools Project Network (#20302)
- ♦ Système des écoles associées de l'UNESCO / see UNESCO Associated Schools Project Network (#20302)
- ♦ Système des écoles associées de l'UNESCO pour la promotion de l'éducation en faveur de la paix, des droits de l'homme, de la démocratie et de la compréhension internationale / see UNESCO Associated Schools Project Network (#20302)
- ♦ Système économique latinoaméricain (#19294)
- ♦ Système euro-méditerranéen d'information sur les savoir-faire dans le domaine de l'eau (#05722)
- ♦ Système européen des banques centrales (#08870)
- ♦ Système européen de réseaux coopératifs de recherche en agriculture (#08871)
- ♦ Système francophone d'information / see SYFIA International (#20076)
- ♦ Système global d'observation terrestre (#10626)
- ♦ Système d'information sur les ressources marines des îles du Pacifique (#17973)
- ♦ Système international d'alerte pour la sécurité et la santé des travailleurs (inactive)
- ♦ Système international d'information sur l'aide alimentaire (inactive)
- ♦ Système international de l'information environnementale (inactive)
- ♦ Système international d'information nucléaire (#14378)
- ♦ Système international d'information pour les sciences et la technologie agricoles (#13848)
- ♦ Système international de satellites pour les recherches et le sauvetage / see International Cospas-Sarsat Programme (#12975)
- ♦ Système Intra-Africain de Métrologie (#15992)
- ♦ Système latinoaméricain de formation et de recherches douanières (inactive)
- ♦ Système mondial d'information et d'alerte rapide sur l'alimentation et l'agriculture (#10416)
- ♦ Système mondial d'observation du climat (#10289)
- ♦ Système mondial d'observation du cycle de l'eau (#21573)
- ♦ Système mondial d'observation du niveau de la mer de la COI (see: #11496)
- ♦ Système mondial d'observation de l'océan (#10511)
- ♦ Système des Nations Unies (#20635)
- ♦ Système Ouest-Africain d'Accréditation (unconfirmed)
- ♦ Système panaméricain des routes (#18109)
- ♦ Systèmes d'information et de documentation sur les droits de l'homme, international (#10985)
- ♦ System of the South Pacific / see Comisión Permanente del Pacifico Sur (#04141)
- ♦ Systems Science European Union / see Union Européenne de Systémique (#20403)

♦ **Systems in Transition (SIT)** **20085**

Contact c/o Scharwiess, Damaschkestr 36, 10711 Berlin, Germany. E-mail: epasit@chello.at – sit@systems-in-transition.com.
URL: https://www.systems-in-transition.com/

History 1992, by mental health professionals and social scientists. Registered in accordance with German law. **Aims** Bring together *mental health* professionals to study psychological effects of transition and change; identify common values integrating individual and cultural diversity. **Structure** Plenary Meeting (annual). Board. **Languages** English. **Staff** None. **Finance** Members' dues. Grants. Annual budget: less than US$ 10,000. **Activities** Organizes: international meetings; lectures; courses. **Events** *Annual Working Meeting* Prizren (Kosovo) 2013, *Annual Working Meeting* Szczecin (Poland) 2012, *Annual Working Meeting* Brno (Czech Rep) 2011, *Annual Working Meeting* Lviv (Ukraine) 2010, *Annual Working Meeting* Mikulov (Czech Rep) 2009. **Publications** *Systems in Transition Newsletter* (3-4 a year). *A Decade of Dialogue: Psychological Dimensions of Transition in Central Europe since 1989*.

Members Individuals in 19 countries:
Austria, Azerbaijan, Bosnia-Herzegovina, Bulgaria, Croatia, Czechia, Denmark, Germany, Hungary, North Macedonia, Norway, Poland, Portugal, Romania, Russia, Serbia, Slovakia, Slovenia, UK. [2019/XD7058/**D**]

- ♦ Szabadelvü Vallasok Nemzetközi Szövetsege (#12130)
- ♦ SZA – Scandinavian Zinc Association (no recent information)
- ♦ T1International (internationally oriented national body)
- ♦ **T21RS** Trisomy 21 Research Society (#20244)
- ♦ **T2M Association** International Association for the History of Transport, Traffic and Mobility (#11937)
- ♦ **TAALS** American Association of Language Specialists (#00774)
- ♦ Taani Kultuuri Instituut (internationally oriented national body)
- ♦ TAA – Tropical Agriculture Association (internationally oriented national body)
- ♦ **TABC** Trans-Atlantic Business Council (#20201)
- ♦ Table ronde sur le développement durable à l'OCDE (see: #17693)
- ♦ Table Ronde des Hommes d'Affaires d'Afrique (#00232)
- ♦ Table ronde internationale (#18982)
- ♦ Table ronde internationale pour le développement de l'orientation / see International Association for Counselling (#11821)
- ♦ Table ronde internationale pour l'orientation scolaire et la guidance professionnelle / see International Association for Counselling (#11821)
- ♦ Table rond huile de palme durable (#18986)
- ♦ Table Tennis Federation of Asia (inactive)
- ♦ TABS International (internationally oriented national body)
- ♦ **TAB** Type Association Benelux (#20272)
- ♦ Tabulae Orbis Terrarum Civium / see Registre des Citoyens du Monde (#18822)
- ♦ **TACD** Transatlantic Consumer Dialogue (#20203)
- ♦ **TACEUSS** Trans-Atlantic Consortium for European Union Studies and Simulations (#20202)
- ♦ TACKERS – Transplant Adventure Camps for Kids (unconfirmed)
- ♦ TackleAfrica (internationally oriented national body)
- ♦ TACSS – Turkish Asian Centre for Strategic Studies (internationally oriented national body)
- ♦ Tactical Tech (unconfirmed)

♦ **Tactical Technology Collective** **20086**

Exec Dir Brunnenstrasse 9, 10119 Berlin, Germany. T. +493041715333. E-mail: ttc@tacticaltech.org.
Registered Office Kingsfordweg 151, 1043 GR Amsterdam, Netherlands.
URL: http://www.tacticaltech.org/

History 2003. Registered in accordance with Dutch law. **Aims** Educate, advocate and create practical solutions that contribute to the wider socio-political debate around digital security, privacy and the ethics of data. **Structure** Governing Board. **Activities** Training/education; guidance/assistance/consulting; knowledge management/information dissemination. [2019.05.09/XJ1599/**F**]

- ♦ TAC / see Traditional Anglican Church (#20193)
- ♦ **TAC** Traditional Anglican Church (#20193)
- ♦ TAC – Treaty of Amity and Cooperation in Southeast Asia (1976 treaty)
- ♦ **TAdEN** Tutmonda Agado de Esperantistaj Nefumantoj (#20265)
- ♦ **TAEF** African Editors' Forum (#00293)
- ♦ Taekwondo Europe / see European Taekwondo Union (#08874)
- ♦ **TAE** Taxpayers Association of Europe (#20102)
- ♦ Tafelrondes Suidelike Afrika (#18984)
- ♦ **TAFISA** The Association for International Sport for All (#02763)

♦ **TAFISA Europe** **20087**

Contact Hostatostrasse 2, 65929 Höchst, Germany. T. +49699739359920. Fax +49699739359925. E-mail: info@tafisa.org.
URL: http://www.tafisa.net/europe/

History Founded 11 Nov 2006, Bordeaux (France), as *European Sport for All Network (ESFAN)*. Restructured Nov 2011 as a regional body of *The Association for International Sport for All (TAFISA, #02763)*. Registered in accordance with French law, Jun 2007. **Aims** Promote Sport for All and physical activity in Europe; provide a network to promote and support systematic transfer and exchange of experience, best practice examples, know how, etc, in this field. **Structure** Steering Group, consisting of Chairman, Deputy Chairperson and 3 members. **Languages** English. **Events** *Conference* Ljubljana (Slovenia) 2016, *Conference* Bordeaux (France) 2009.

Members Full: European members of TAFISA in 36 countries and territories:
Albania, Austria, Belarus, Belgium, Bosnia-Herzegovina, Bulgaria, Croatia, Cyprus, Denmark, Estonia, Faeroe Is, Finland, France, Germany, Greece, Hungary, Iceland, Italy, Latvia, Liechtenstein, Lithuania, Netherlands, North Macedonia, Poland, Portugal, Romania, Russia, Serbia, Slovakia, Slovenia, Spain, Sweden, Switzerland, Türkiye, UK, Ukraine.

IGO Relations Observer status with: *Enlarged Partial Agreement on Sport (EPAS, #05487)*. [2019/XJ0917/**D**]

- ♦ TAFTA – Trans-Atlantic free trade agreement (unconfirmed)
- ♦ TAFTIE – European Network of Innovation Agencies / see Taftie – The European Network of leading national innovation agencies (#20088)

♦ **Taftie – The European Network of leading national innovation agencies (TAFTIE)** **20088**

Assistant Secretary address not obtained.
URL: http://www.taftie.eu

History Former names and other names: *TAFTIE – European Network of Innovation Agencies* – alias; *Association for Technology Implementation in Europe (TAFTIE)* – former. Registration: Start date: 1992, France. **Aims** Play an important role in the sharing of information and best practice to enable its Members to better implement R&D and innovation programmes within their countries and internationally. **Structure** Board; Executive Working Group; Task Forces and Working Groups. Annual rotating Presidency: Innovate UK (2022); HAMAG-BICRO (2023); Innosuisse (2024). **Activities** Events/meetings. **Events** *Annual Conference* Paris (France) 2016, *Annual Conference* Berlin (Germany) 2015, *Annual Conference* Warsaw (Poland) 2014, *General Meeting / Annual General Meeting* Antwerp (Belgium) 2013, *Executive Working Group Meeting* Vienna (Austria) 2013.

Members Innovation agencies (34) in 28 countries:
Austria, Belgium, Croatia, Czechia, Denmark, Estonia, Finland, France, Germany, Hungary, Iceland, Ireland, Israel, Italy, Lithuania, Luxembourg, Netherlands, Norway, Poland, Portugal, Serbia, Slovakia, Slovenia, Spain, Sweden, Switzerland, Türkiye, UK. [2022.10.18/XD8135/**D**]

- ♦ TAFTIE / see Taftie – The European Network of leading national innovation agencies (#20088)

- ♦ **TAFTIE** Taftie – The European Network of leading national innovation agencies (#20088)
- ♦ TAG Alliances (internationally oriented national body)
- ♦ Tagar Zionist Student Activist Movement (see: #03217)

♦ Tag International Development (Tag) 20089

Chief Exec address not obtained. T. +442077540341. E-mail: info@tagdevelopment.org.
URL: http://www.tagdevelopment.org/

History 1 Dec 2009, London (UK). Registration: Companies House, No/ID: 07219378, Start date: 22 Jul 2010, UK; USA; Charity Commission, No/ID: 1137017, England and Wales. **Aims** Deploy unique *humanitarian* expertise and proven social models to create *sustainable* solutions for *developing countries*. **Activities** Capacity building; knowledge management/information dissemination. **IGO Relations** *MASHAV – Centre for International Cooperation*; *UNDP (#20292)*; *United States Agency for International Development (USAID)*. **NGO Relations** *Asian Disaster Preparedness Center (ADPC, #01426)*; *Weitz Center for Development Studies*; *Golda Meir Mount Carmel International Training Centre (MCTC)*; *International Blue Crescent (IBC)*; national partners. [2020.05.13/XM4188/**F**]

- ♦ **Tag** Tag International Development (#20089)
- ♦ TAHA – Lagos-Mombasa Trans-African Highway Authority (inactive)
- ♦ **TAHMO** Trans-African HydroMeteorological Observatory (#20199)
- ♦ T/AI / see Transparency and Accountability Initiative (#20221)
- ♦ **TAI** The Access Initiative (#00050)
- ♦ TAI – AJC Transatlantic Institute (internationally oriented national body)
- ♦ **TAIC** Arab Investment Company (#00996)
- ♦ TAIM / see Association of Industrial Ceiling Manufacturers (#02641)
- ♦ **TAIM** Association of Industrial Ceiling Manufacturers (#02641)
- ♦ T/A Initiative / see Transparency and Accountability Initiative (#20221)
- ♦ Taipei Overseas Peace Service (internationally oriented national body)
- ♦ **TAI** Transparency and Accountability Initiative (#20221)
- ♦ Taiwan AID – Taiwan Alliance in International Development (internationally oriented national body)
- ♦ Taiwan Alliance in International Development (internationally oriented national body)
- ♦ Taiwan Foundation for Democracy (internationally oriented national body)
- ♦ TAI / see World Taxpayers Associations (#21847)
- ♦ Taizé Community (religious order)
- ♦ Takeonejetsu Martial Arts World Federation (unconfirmed)
- ♦ **TAKE** Tutmonda Asocio de Konstruistoj Esperantistaj (#20266)
- ♦ Takfir Wa al-Hjira (#18829)
- ♦ Taking IT Global (internationally oriented national body)
- ♦ TAKIS – Tutmonda Asocio pri Kibernetiko, Informadiko, kaj Sistemiko (inactive)
- ♦ Talaa' al-Fateh / see Al-Jihad (#00637)
- ♦ TALC / see Health Books International
- ♦ TAL – International Symposium on Tonal Aspects of Languages (meeting series)

♦ Talitha Kum – International Network against Trafficking in Persons (Talitha Kum) 20090

Coordinator Piazza di Ponte Sant'Angelo 28, 00186 Rome RM, Italy. T. +3966840020. E-mail: coordinator@talithakum.info.
URL: https://www.talithakum.info/

History Founded 2009, as a project of *International Union of Superiors General (#15820)* and *Union of Superiors General (#20484)*. **Aims** Promote networking between consecrated persons, social organizations, religious and political leaders at national and international level; strengthen existing activities and initiatives, optimizing resources of consecrated life, to promote preventative actions, awareness raising, protection and assistance of victims as well as official reporting of trafficking. **Structure** General Assembly. **Activities** Training/education; awareness raising; advocacy/lobbying/activism; guidance/assistance/consulting; knowledge management/information dissemination; politics/policy/regulatory.
Members National networks in 43 countries:
Albania, Argentina, Australia, Brazil, Burkina Faso, Cameroon, Canada, Colombia, Costa Rica, Dominican Rep, El Salvador, Germany, Ghana, Guatemala, Honduras, India, Indonesia, Ireland, Italy, Japan, Kenya, Korea Rep, Mexico, Myanmar, New Zealand, Nicaragua, Nigeria, Pakistan, Paraguay, Peru, Philippines, Poland, Romania, South Africa, Sri Lanka, Taiwan, Thailand, Timor-Leste, Tunisia, Uganda, Uruguay, USA, Zimbabwe.
NGO Relations Member of: *Religious in Europe Networking Against Trafficking and Exploitation (RENATE, #18833)*. [2022/XM8893/**F**]

- ♦ **Talitha Kum** Talitha Kum – International Network against Trafficking in Persons (#20090)
- ♦ Talking Bibles International (internationally oriented national body)
- ♦ Tall Clubs International Europe / see European Federation of Tall People (#07223)
- ♦ El Taller / see El Taller International (#20091)
- ♦ Talleres de Santa Rita (religious order)

♦ El Taller International 20091

Contact address not obtained. T. +21671753738. E-mail: eltaller.international@gmail.com.
URL: http://www.eltaller.in/

History 20 Nov 1991, Santiago (Chile), as a world network of non-governmental organizations of development, environment, gender and human rights groups/movements from diverse cultures and communities. Originally referred to as *El Taller*. Since Mar 1992, headquarters located in Tunis (Tunisia), where an official 'Accord de Siège' with the government of Tunisia was signed. **Aims** Participate in a worldwide movement of *NGOs* and social movements working towards building a strong *civil society*; offer a space for analysis and action learning on critical issues, networking and innovation around issues of justice and peace, challenging dominant discourses on human rights, development and peace and working towards alternative concepts/praxis of justice, democracy, subjugated knowledge, etc. **Structure** International Board, comprising 15 members from 6 regions of the world (Africa, Asia, Central and Latin America, Arab, Europe and USA). International Secretariat based in Tunis (Tunisia). **Languages** Arabic, English, French, Spanish. **Staff** Paid and voluntary. **Finance** Funds from: bilateral and multilateral organizations and foundations; NGOs. **Activities** Training/education; events/meetings; networking/liaising; research/documentation. **Events** *Assises méditerranéennes / Mediterranean Meeting* Tunis (Tunisia) 2001, *Annual Mediterranean youth exchange* Cairo (Egypt) 1997, *General Assembly* Manila (Philippines) 1997, *International meeting on women and violence* Ethiopia 1996, *Conference on the Arab world* Tunisia 1995. **Publications** *Daring to claim the Sky* (2007); *Singing in the Dark Time* (2003); *Asking, We Walk: South as New Political Imaginary* – 4 vols by 2012. Reports; research discussion papers. **Members** NGOs worldwide. Membership countries not specified. **Consultative Status** Consultative status granted from: *UNEP (#20299)*. **IGO Relations** *UNDP (#20292)* in Asia. [2012.07.31/XF5424/**F**]

- ♦ Tallinna Acelikooli Balti Filmi-ja Meediakooli / see Tallinna Ülikool – Balti filmi, meedia, kunstide ja kommunikatsiooni instituut (#20092)

♦ Tallinna Ülikool – Balti filmi, meedia, kunstide ja kommunikatsiooni instituut 20092

Tallinn University – Baltic Film, Media, Arts and Communication School

Contact Narva Rd 27, 10120 Tallinn, Estonia. T. +3726199900. Fax +3726199901. E-mail: tlu@tlu.ee.
URL: http://www.bfm.ee/

History 2005, Tallinn (Estonia). Founded within Tallinn University, on the instigation of *Nordic-Baltic Film Fund (no recent information)*. Former names and other names: *Tallinna Acelikooli Balti Filmi-ja Meediakooli (BFM)* – former (2005); *Tallinn University Baltic Film and Media School* – former (2005). **Aims** Train *students* for international careers in the world's rapidly growing *audiovisual* and media industry. **Languages** English, Estonian. **Activities** Training/education. **Members** Students (about 430) from 25 countries. Membership countries not specified. **NGO Relations** Universities. [2017.11.24/XM2798/**D**]

- ♦ Tallinn University – Baltic Film, Media, Arts and Communication School (#20092)
- ♦ Tallinn University Baltic Film and Media School / see Tallinna Ülikool – Balti filmi, meedia, kunstide ja kommunikatsiooni instituut (#20092)
- ♦ Tall Oil Association / see Pine Chemicals Association

♦ Talloires Network 20093

Secretariat 23 Bellevue St, Medford MA 02155, USA. T. +17818749731. E-mail: talloiresnetwork@tufts.edu.
URL: http://talloiresnetwork.tufts.edu/

History Sep 2005, at Talloires Conference, which led to *'Talloires Declaration on the Civic Roles and Social Responsibilities of Higher Education'*. **Aims** Strengthen the *civic* roles and social *responsibilities* of *higher education*. **Structure** Steering Committee, comprising Chair and 9 members. Secretariat shared between Tisch College of Citizenship and Public Service, Tufts University, and Innovations in Civic Participation, Washington DC (USA). **Activities** Organizes annual MacJannet Prize for Global Citizenship. Also awards 8 cash prizes to outstanding student civic engagement initiatives. **Events** *Leaders Conference* Madrid (Spain) 2011.
Members Institutions and universities (over 185) in 57 countries and territories:
Argentina, Australia, Brazil, Canada, Chile, Colombia, Costa Rica, Croatia, Egypt, Germany, Ghana, Hong Kong, India, Indonesia, Ireland, Israel, Italy, Kazakhstan, Kenya, Korea Rep, Kuwait, Latvia, Lebanon, Lesotho, Liberia, Lithuania, Malaysia, Mexico, Netherlands, Nigeria, Pakistan, Palestine, Peru, Philippines, Puerto Rico, Russia, Rwanda, Samoa, Saudi Arabia, Senegal, Serbia, South Africa, Spain, Sri Lanka, Sudan, Sweden, Switzerland, Taiwan, Tanzania UR, Türkiye, UK, Ukraine, United Arab Emirates, USA, Venezuela, Vietnam, Zimbabwe.
Included in the above, one university listed in this Yearbook:
University of the West Indies (UWI, #20705).
NGO Relations Formal partnerships with: *Latin American Center for Service Learning (#16291)*; national universities and organizations. [2014/XJ1814/**F**]

- ♦ Talous-ja Sosiaalikomitea / see European Economic and Social Committee (#06963)
- ♦ TAMC – Annual Conference on Theory and Applications of Models of Computation (meeting series)
- ♦ Tami Steinmetz Centre for Peace Research, Tel Aviv (internationally oriented national body)
- ♦ **TAMPEP** European Network for the Promotion of Rights and Health among Migrant Sex Workers (#07976)
- ♦ TAMPEP International Foundation / see European Network for the Promotion of Rights and Health among Migrant Sex Workers (#07976)
- ♦ Tampere Convention on the Provision of Telecommunication Resources for Disaster Mitigation and Relief Operations (1998 treaty)
- ♦ Tampere Peace Research Institute (internationally oriented national body)
- ♦ TAM – Teresian Apostolic Movement (religious order)
- ♦ TAN – The African Network (internationally oriented national body)

♦ Tangent Club International (TCI) 20094

Pres address not obtained. E-mail: president@tangentclubinternational.org – secretary@tangentclubinternational.org – tcinewseditor@gmail.com.
URL: http://www.tangentclubinternational.org/

History Inaugurated 26 Oct 2013, with Charter signed 3 May 2014. **Aims** Promote and strengthen international friendships established through *Ladies* Circle International; promote, encourage and support new international friendships between Tangent Clubs worldwide. **Structure** General Meeting (annual); Council; Board. **Events** *Annual General Meeting* Landshut (Germany) 2016, *Half-Yearly Meeting* Birmingham (UK) 2015, *Annual General Meeting* Limassol (Cyprus) 2015.
Members Full in 5 countries:
Cyprus, Denmark, Norway, Sweden, UK.
Associate in 6 countries and territories:
Belgium, France, Gibraltar, Lithuania, Netherlands, Spain.
NGO Relations *41 International (#22047)*; *Ladies Circle International (LCI, #16217)*; *Round Table International (RTI, #18982)*. [2023/XJ9191/**E**]

- ♦ Tangiers-Cairo Trans-African Highway Coordinating Committee (inactive)
- ♦ Tangiers-Lagos Trans-African Highway Coordinating Committee (inactive)
- ♦ Tanker owners voluntary agreement concerning liability for oil pollution (inactive)

♦ Tantalum-Niobium International Study Center (T.I.C.) 20095

Centre international d'étude de tantale et niobium

SG Chaussée de Louvain 490, 1380 Lasne, Belgium. T. +3226495158. E-mail: info@tanb.org.
URL: https://www.tanb.org/

History 27 Mar 1974, Brussels (Belgium). Statutes modified 17 Oct 2016; 30 June 2020. Former names and other names: *Tantalum Producers International Study Center* – former; *Centre international d'étude des producteurs de tantale* – former. Registration: Banque-Carrefour des Entreprises, No/ID: 0414.408.447, Start date: 6 Aug 1974, Belgium. **Aims** Increase awareness and promote the properties of tantalum and niobium. **Structure** General Assembly; Executive Committee. **Languages** English. **Staff** 1.80 FTE, paid. **Finance** Sources: meeting proceeds; members' dues. **Activities** Awards/prizes/competitions; events/meetings; knowledge management/information dissemination; publishing activities; research/documentation. **Events** *General Assembly* Geneva (Switzerland) 2021, *General Assembly* Brussels (Belgium) 2020, *General Assembly* Hong Kong (Hong Kong) 2019, *General Assembly* Kigali (Rwanda) 2018, *General Assembly* Vancouver, BC (Canada) 2017. **Publications** *T.I.C. Quarterly Bulletin* (4 a year) in English; *T.I.C. Bulletin Review* (annual) in Chinese, French, Japanese, Portuguese. Symposium proceedings.
Members Companies and organizations active in the field of tantalum and/or niobium, in 27 countries and territories:
Australia, Austria, Bolivia, Brazil, Burundi, Canada, China, Congo DR, Estonia, France, Germany, Hong Kong, India, Israel, Japan, Kazakhstan, Luxembourg, Malaysia, Netherlands, Russia, Rwanda, Singapore, South Africa, Thailand, UK, United Arab Emirates, USA.
Included in the above, 1 organization listed in this Yearbook:
International Conference on the Great Lakes Region (ICGLR, #12880).
NGO Relations Member of (5): *Critical Raw Materials Alliance (CRM Alliance, #04959)*; *European Partnership for Responsible Minerals (EPRM, #08159)*; *Federation of European and International Associations Established in Belgium (FAIB, #09508)*; *Minor Metals Trade Association (MMTA, #16821)*; *Responsible Minerals Initiative (RMI)*. [2021.05.03/XC4571/**C**]

- ♦ Tantalum Producers International Study Center / see Tantalum-Niobium International Study Center (#20095)
- ♦ Tantur / see Tantur Ecumenical Institute (#20096)

♦ Tantur Ecumenical Institute 20096

Institut oecuménique de recherches théologiques

Rector PO Box 11381, 9111301 Jerusalem, Israel. T. +97225422900. Fax +97226760914. E-mail: tantur@tantur.org.
URL: http://www.tantur.org/

History 1971, Israel. Founded following proposals, 1967, by non-Catholic observers at Vatican Council II, including *International Federation of Catholic Universities (IFCU, #13381)*. Former names and other names: *Ecumenical Institute for Theological Research* – former; *Tantur Ecumenical Institute for Theological Studies* – alias; *Tantur* – alias. **Aims** Advance ecumenical scholarship and understanding by continuing the ecumenical work of Vatican II; offer opportunities for residential research and multilateral ecumenical encounter between *Catholic*, *Orthodox* and *Protestant Churches* at international and national levels. **Structure** International Advisory Board; Executive Administrative Committee. **Activities** Projects/programmes; religious activities; training/education. Projects/programmes; training/education; religious activities. **Events** *Symposium on teaching about Islam, Christianity and Judaism in Israeli and Palestinian education* Jerusalem (Israel) 1997. [2022.05.04/XF8379/jv/**F**]

- ♦ Tantur Ecumenical Institute for Theological Studies / see Tantur Ecumenical Institute (#20096)
- ♦ **TAOIT** Tribunal administratif de l'Organisation internationale du travail (#00118)
- ♦ tAontas Eorpach (#08967)
- ♦ TAP / see Cohesive Communities Development Initiative

- ♦ **TAPA Asia** Transported Asset Protection Association Asia (#20226)
- ♦ **TAPA-EMEA** Transported Asset Protection Association Europe (#20227)
- ♦ TAP / see Ending Clergy Abuse (#05460)
- ♦ TAPHOS – International Conference on Taphonomy and Fossilisation (meeting series)
- ♦ **TAP Network** Transparency, Accountability and Participation Network (#20222)
- ♦ TAPPC – True Animal Protein Price Coalition (internationally oriented national body)
- ♦ TaPP – International Workshop on Theory and Practice of Provenance (meeting series)
- ♦ **TAPPI** Technical Association of the Pulp and Paper Industry (#20114)
- ♦ TAPRI – Tampere Peace Research Institute (internationally oriented national body)
- ♦ TAP – Trans Africa Pipeline (internationally oriented national body)

♦ Tarab Institute International 20097

Contact St Sohoj, Horsholm Kongevej 40, 2970 Hørsholm, Denmark.
URL: http://www.tarab-institute.org/

Aims Promote teaching, training and research in unity in *duality*, inner science of mind and reality, personal development, art-of-relating as well as psychotherapeutic and *spiritual* application, based on universalities from Ancient *Eastern* Inner Science extracted by Lharampa Geshe Dr Phil Tarab Tulku Rinpoche. **Languages** English, French, German, Slovakian. **Activities** Organizes: 4-year training programmes; conferences; courses. **Events** *International meeting* Copenhagen (Denmark) 2004. **Publications** *Unity in Duality* – newsletter.
Members Institutes in 9 countries:
Denmark, Finland, France, Germany, India, Netherlands, Slovakia, Sweden, UK. [2013.07.24/XE4475/j/**E**]

- ♦ TARA – Technology and Action for Rural Advancement (internationally oriented national body)
- ♦ TARA – Trust for African Rock Art (internationally oriented national body)
- ♦ TAREA – Regional Assistance Treaty on Food Emergencies (treaty)
- ♦ Tariff Union of Balkan and Near East Countries (no recent information)
- ♦ Tarifunion Balkan Naher Osten (inactive)
- ♦ Tarptautine Jaunuju Ukininku Sajunga (#15829)
- ♦ Tarptautinio santykio ir politikos mokslo institutas (internationally oriented national body)
- ♦ Tarptautinis Politikos Mokslu Institutas (internationally oriented national body)
- ♦ **TAR** Trans-Asian Railway Network (#20200)
- ♦ TASAM – Türk Asya Stratejik Arastirmalar Merkezi (internationally oriented national body)
- ♦ Task Force for Child Survival / see Task Force for Global Health (#20098)
- ♦ Task Force for Child Survival and Development / see Task Force for Global Health (#20098)
- ♦ Task force des commissaires de police européens (no recent information)
- ♦ Task Force on Cultural and Spiritual Values of Protected Areas / see IUCN WCPA Specialist Group on Cultural and Spiritual Values of Protected Areas (#16080)
- ♦ Task Force der Europäischen Polizeichefs (no recent information)
- ♦ Task Force on Financial Integrity and Economic Development / see Financial Transparency Coalition (#09772)

♦ Task Force for Global Health (TFGH) 20098

President 330 W Ponce de Leon Ave, Decatur GA 30030, USA. T. +14046875635 – +14046875611. Fax +14043711087. E-mail: info@taskforce.org.
URL: http://www.taskforce.org

History Founded Mar 1984, Bellagio (Italy), during Bellagio Conference, as *Task Force for Child Survival*, as a collaborative effort among *WHO (#20950), UNICEF (#20332), UNDP (#20292), International Bank for Reconstruction and Development (IBRD, #12317)* (World Bank) and *The Rockefeller Foundation (#18966)*, to achieve the goal of raising child immunization to 80%, which was reached by 1990. *United Nations Population Fund (UNFPA, #20612)* joined as 6th sponsor in 1994, as well as other organizations. Following UN World Summit for Children, changed title to *Task Force for Child Survival and Development (TFCSD)*, 1990. Current name adopted, 1 Mar 2009. Registered under the laws of the State of Georgia (USA), 5 May 1986. **Aims** Solve large-scale health problems affecting vulnerable populations around the world; focus on controlling and eliminating debilitating diseases; build sustainable health systems that protect and promote health. **Structure** Board of Directors. Includes: *Children Without Worms (CWW, #03881); International Trachoma Initiative (ITI, #15701); Training Programs in Epidemiology and Public Health Interventions NETwork (TEPHINET, #20198)*. **Languages** English, French, Spanish. **Staff** 150.00 FTE, paid. **Finance** Funded by a broad range of donors including foundations, corporations and governmental entities. **Activities** Guidance/assistance/consulting; financial and/or material support; projects/programmes; healthcare. **Events** *Bellagio conference / International Conference* Delhi (India) 1994, *International conference* Delhi (India) 1994, *Bellagio conference* Bangkok (Thailand) 1990, *International conference* Bangkok (Thailand) 1990, *International conference* Talloires (France) 1988. **Consultative Status** Consultative status granted from: *ECOSOC (#05331)* (Special). **IGO Relations** *International Bank for Reconstruction and Development (IBRD, #12317)* (World Bank); *United Nations (UN, #20515); WHO (#20950)*. **NGO Relations** Member of (4): *Gavi – The Vaccine Alliance (Gavi, #10077)* (CSO Constituency); *Global Coalition Against Child Pneumonia (#10290); Global Partnership for Zero Leprosy (#10543); InsideNGO (inactive)*. Cooperates with: *African Field Epidemiology Network (AFENET, #00315); CARE International (CI, #03429); The Carter Center, PMNCH (#18410); RTI International; Sightsavers International (#19270)*. Houses: *Coalition for Operational Research on Neglected Tropical Diseases (COR-NTD)*. [2020/XF1555/**F**]

- ♦ Task Force for International Cooperation on Holocaust Education, Remembrance and Research / see International Holocaust Remembrance Alliance (#13803)
- ♦ Task Force on Money Laundering in Central Africa (unconfirmed)
- ♦ Task Force on Non Material Values of Protected Areas / see IUCN WCPA Specialist Group on Cultural and Spiritual Values of Protected Areas (#16080)

♦ Task Force on Organized Crime in the Baltic Sea Region 20099

Secretariat Central Criminal Police, Tööstuse 52, 10414 Tallinn, Estonia. T. +3726123648. Fax +3726123812.

History Following a decision of the Heads of Government during the Baltic Sea States Summit, May 1996, Visby (Sweden). Mandate extended, Dec 1998 until Dec 2000; extended again, Apr 2000, at Baltic Sea States Summit, until Dec 2004; further extended, Jun 2004, at Baltic Sea States Summit, until 31 Dec 2008; most recently extended, 2 Jun 2010, Vilnius (Lithuania), at 8th Baltic Sea States Summit, until 31 Dec 2016. **Aims** Strengthen ability to prevent and combat organized crime in the Baltic Sea Region; deepen and reinforce *law enforcement* cooperation; improve *border* arrangements. **Structure** Composed of representatives of the Heads of Government or Ministers responsible for police cooperation (Task Force) of member states of *Council of the Baltic Sea States (CBSS, #04870)* and the Presidency of the European Union and *European Commission (EC, #06633)*. Reports directly to the Heads of Government. Operative Committee (OPC); expert groups. **Languages** English. **Activities** Fields: improved and increased exchange of information; joint concrete and operative measures/actions; judicial cooperation; special surveys, training and other cooperation. Expert groups (5): Drugs; Money Laundering; Environmental Crime; Trafficking in Persons; Trafficking in Goods. **Events** *Meeting* Helsinki (Finland) 2006, *Biennial meeting of ministers responsible for police cooperation in the Baltic sea region* Koli (Finland) 2006, *Meeting* Vantaa (Finland) 2006, *Meeting* Vilnius (Lithuania) 2006, *Meeting* Visby (Sweden) 2006. **Publications** *Report on Organized Crime in the Baltic Sea Region* (1st ed 2001-2002, 2nd ed 2002-2003); *Task-Force Contact Manual*.
Members Participating countries (11):
Denmark, Estonia, Finland, Germany, Iceland, Latvia, Lithuania, Norway, Poland, Russia, Sweden.
Observers in 7 countries:
France, Italy, Netherlands, Slovakia, UK, Ukraine, USA.
Regional organization (1), listed in this Yearbook:
European Commission.
IGO Relations *European Police Office (Europol, #08239)*. [2010/XF5741/**F***]

- ♦ Task Force on Permanent Access / see Alliance for Permanent Access (#00712)
- ♦ Task Force on World Hunger / see Presbyterian Hunger Program
- ♦ TASSC International (internationally oriented national body)
- ♦ **TAS** Tribunal Arbitral del Deporte (#04933)
- ♦ **TAS** Tribunal arbitral du sport (#04933)
- ♦ Tata Energy and Resources Institute / see Energy and Resources Institute
- ♦ **TA** Traité sur l'Antarctique (#00850)
- ♦ **TA** Tratado Antártico (#00850)
- ♦ TAUESG – Tuber aestivum / uncinatum European Scientific Group (meeting series)
- ♦ TAUS – Balkanska Asocijacija za Transakcionu Analizu (unconfirmed)
- ♦ **TAUS Data Association** Translation Automation User Society Data Association (#20215)
- ♦ **TAUS** Translation Automation User Society (#20214)
- ♦ Tavola della Pace (internationally oriented national body)
- ♦ TAWS – World Association for Transport Animal Welfare and Studies (internationally oriented national body)
- ♦ Tax Executives Institute (internationally oriented national body)
- ♦ Tax Free World Association (internationally oriented national body)

♦ Tax Justice Network (TJN) 20100

Chief Exec C/O Godfrey Wilson Ltd, 5th Floor Mariner House, 62 Prince Street, Bristol, BS1 4QD, UK. E-mail: info@taxjustice.net.
URL: http://www.taxjustice.net/

History Mar 2003, UK. Launched at British Houses of Parliament, London (UK). Registration: England and Wales. **Aims** Promote high-level research, analysis and advocacy in the area of international tax and financial regulation. **Structure** Directors (10). **Finance** Supported by: *Adessium Foundation; Campaign for Tobacco-Free Kids; European Commission (EC, #06633); Financial Transparency Coalition (FTC, #09772); Ford Foundation (#09858); Norwegian Agency for Development Cooperation (Norad); Wallace Global Fund.* **Activities** Advocacy/lobbying/activism; research/documentation. **Publications** *Tax Justice Focus* (2-4 a year) – newsletter; *Tax Justice Research Bulletin*. Reports; briefing papers. **NGO Relations** Signatory to: *Alter Summit*. [2023.02.14/XJ6047/**F**]

♦ Tax Justice Network-Africa (TJN-A) 20101

Exec Dir George Padmore Ridge, 2nd Fl Wing 'B', George Padmore Lane, Kilimani, PO Box 25112-00100, Nairobi, Kenya. T. +254202473373. E-mail: info@taxjusticeafrica.net.
URL: http://www.taxjusticeafrica.net/

History Launched Jan 2007, Nairobi (Kenya), during World Social Forum. **Aims** Spearhead tax justice in Africa's development by enabling citizens and institutions to promote equitable tax systems through research, capacity-building and policy-influencing. **Structure** Board; Secretariat. **Publications** *TJN-A Newsletter*.
Members Organizations in 16 countries:
Benin, Cameroon, Congo DR, Côte d'Ivoire, Egypt, Ghana, Kenya, Malawi, Nigeria, Sierra Leone, South Africa, Tanzania UR, Togo, Uganda, Zambia, Zimbabwe.
Included in the above, 4 organizations listed in this Yearbook:
African Forum and Network on Debt and Development (AFRODAD, #00321); African Network of Centres for Investigative Reporting (ANCIR); Economic Justice Network for Churches in Eastern and Southern Africa (EJN, #05317); Southern and Eastern African Trade Information and Negotiations Initiative (SEATINI, #19875).
Consultative Status Consultative status granted from: *UNCTAD (#20285)* (General). **NGO Relations** Coordinating Committee partner of: *Financial Transparency Coalition (FTC, #09772).* [2017.08.23/XM4470/y/**F**]

♦ Taxpayers Association of Europe (TAE) 20102

Association européenne des contribuables

SG Nymphenburgerstrasse 118, 80636 Munich, Germany. T. +498912600820. Fax +498912600847. E-mail: info@taxpayers-europe.org.
Dir – Brussels Office Rue de Pascale 22, 1040 Brussels, Belgium. T. +3225881520. E-mail: info@taxpayers-europe.org.
URL: http://www.taxpayers-europe.org/

History 12 May 1969, Luxembourg. Former names and other names: *European Taxpayers Association (ETA)* – former. Registration: Luxembourg; Banque-Carrefour des Entreprises, No/ID: 0682.805.665, Start date: 11 Oct 2017, End date: 2017, Belgium; Eu Transparency Register, No/ID: 5903604107-54, Start date: 30 Jun 2008. **Aims** Increase contact among European taxpayer unions by reciprocal exchange of experience and information, reciprocal granting of aid, common consultation and conferences on fiscal policy and law; foster inter-organizational contacts with non-member and extra-European organizations. **Structure** Board; Offices in Brussels (Belgium) and Munich (Germany). **Languages** English, German. **Staff** 2.00 FTE, paid; 12.00 FTE, voluntary. **Finance** Members' and others' voluntary allowances. Board members bear own expenses. **Activities** Knowledge management/information dissemination; guidance/assistance/consulting; networking/liaising; events/meetings; awards/prizes/competitions. **Events** *Congress* Batumi (Georgia) 2014, *Congress* Brussels (Belgium) 2014, *Congress* Kiev (Ukraine) 2014, *Congress* Brussels (Belgium) 2013, *Congress* Brussels (Belgium) 2012. **Publications** *Taxpayers' Glasshouse* – newsletter. *Expenditure of the European Communities (Exposé and Critique)* in English, French, German.
Members National taxpayer organizations and institutions in 31 countries:
Austria, Belarus, Belgium, Bulgaria, Croatia, Czechia, Denmark, Estonia, Finland, France, Georgia, Germany, Greece, Hungary, Italy, Latvia, Lithuania, Luxembourg, Netherlands, Norway, Poland, Portugal, Romania, Russia, Serbia, Slovakia, Spain, Sweden, Switzerland, UK, Ukraine. [2022/XD3892/**D**]

- ♦ Taxpayers Associations International / see World Taxpayers Associations (#21847)

♦ TB Alliance 20103

Contact 40 Wall St, 24th Fl, New York NY 10005, USA. T. +12122277540.
Pretoria Office Boardwalk Office Park, Block 1 – Suite 5, 107 Haymeadow St, Pretoria, 0043, South Africa. T. +27129916328.
URL: http://www.tballiance.org/

History Feb 2000, Cape Town (South Africa). Former names and other names: *Global Alliance for Tuberculosis Drug Development* – full title; *Global Alliance for TB Drug Development (GATB)* – former (Feb 2000). Registration: EU Transparency Register, No/ID: 636752920377-18, Start date: 20 Jan 2016. **Aims** Accelerate the discovery, development and delivery of better, faster-acting and affordable tuberculosis drugs that are available to those who need them. **Structure** Board of Directors; Advisory Boards (4). **Staff** 0.80 FTE, paid. **Finance** Sources: grants. Supported by: Australia's Department of Foreign Affairs; *Bill and Melinda Gates Foundation (BMGF)*; Cystic Fibrosis Foundation; *Department for International Development (DFID, inactive); European and Developing Countries Clinical Trials Partnership (EDCTP, #06912)*; Germany's Federal Ministry of Education and Research through *Kreditanstalt für Wiederaufbau (KfW)*; Global Health Innovative Technology Fund; Indonesia Health Fund; *Irish Aid*; Medical Research Council UK; National Institute of Allergy and Infectious Disease; Netherlands Ministry of Foreign Affairs; *United States Agency for International Development (USAID)*. Annual budget: 70,000,000 EUR (2020). **Activities** Research and development; networking/liaising. **Publications** Annual Report; reports; statements; research papers. **Consultative Status** Consultative status granted from: *ECOSOC (#05331)* (Special). **NGO Relations** Member of (3): *Global Health Council (GHC, #10402); Global Health Technologies Coalition (GHTC); InsideNGO (inactive)*. Partner of (1): *Stop TB Partnership (#19999)*. [2022/XF6224/**E**]

- ♦ **TBA** Tropical Biology Association (#20247)
- ♦ **TBC** Toilet Board Coalition (#20171)
- ♦ **TBEC** TB Europe Coalition (#20104)
- ♦ TBE / see Tiles and Bricks Europe (#20163)
- ♦ **TBE** Tiles and Bricks Europe (#20163)

♦ TB Europe Coalition (TBEC) 20104

Contact address not obtained. E-mail: coordinator@tbcoalition.eu.
URL: https://www.tbcoalition.eu/

History Registration: EU Transparency Register, No/ID: 115064941687-78, Start date: 25 Mar 2021. **Aims** Raise awareness of tuberculosis (TB); increase the political will required to effectively control the disease throughout the WHO Europe Region and worldwide. **Structure** Steering Committee.
Members Organizations in 11 countries:
Bulgaria, France, Germany, Latvia, Lithuania, Moldova, Netherlands, Romania, Spain, UK, Ukraine.
Included in the above, 10 organizations listed in this Yearbook:

ACTION (#00085); *Aeras Global TB Vaccine Foundation* (Europe); *European AIDS Treatment Group (EATG, #05850)*; *Frontline AIDS (#10007)*; *Global Health Advocates (#10400)*; *International AIDS Vaccine Initiative (IAVI, #11602)*; *International Federation of Red Cross and Red Crescent Societies (#13526)*; *PATH (#18260)*; *Stop TB Partnership (#19999)*; *TuBerculosis Vaccine Initiative (TBVI, #20257)*. [2022/XJ8390/y/**D**]

♦ TBI / see KeraLink International
♦ TBI – Tropenbos International (internationally oriented national body)
♦ TBMSG / see Triratna Buddhist Community (#20243)

♦ TBnet 20105

Sec Research Ctr Borstel, Medical Clinic, Parkallee 35, 23845 Borstel, Germany. T. +4945371883678.
Registered Office Armenberg 6, 23843 Bad Oldesloe, Germany.
URL: https://www.tbnet.eu/

History Nov 2006, Borstel (Germany). Registration: Schleswig-Holstein District court, No/ID: VR 3140 HL, Start date: 1 Jul 2009, Germany, Lübeck. **Aims** Promote clinically oriented *research* in the field of *tuberculosis* in *Europe* by sharing and developing ideas and research protocols. **Structure** Steering Committee. **Activities** Events/meetings; research/documentation; training/education. *European Advanced Course on Clinical Tuberculosis (EACCTB)*. **Events** *Meeting* Borstel (Germany) 2020, *Meeting* Paris (France) 2018, *Biennial Meeting* Milan (Italy) 2017. **Publications** *TBnet Newsletter*.
Members Full (nearly 700) in 44 countries and territories:
Argentina, Australia, Austria, Belarus, Belgium, Brazil, Bulgaria, Colombia, Croatia, Czechia, Denmark, Egypt, Finland, France, Germany, Greece, Hungary, India, Iran Islamic Rep, Italy, Kenya, Korea Rep, Kuwait, Mexico, Moldova, Namibia, Netherlands, Norway, Pakistan, Poland, Portugal, Romania, Russia, Serbia, Slovakia, Spain, Sweden, Switzerland, Taiwan, Tanzania UR, Türkiye, UK, Ukraine, USA. [2022/XM6473/**F**]

♦ **TBVI** TuBerculosis Vaccine Initiative (#20257)
♦ **TCA** The Cyclists' Alliance (#04990)
♦ **TCA** Thyroid Cancer Alliance (#20157)
♦ **TCA** Trusted Connectivity Alliance (#20254)

♦ TCCA 20106

CEO 14 Blandford Square, Newcastle upon Tyne, NE1 4HZ, UK. T. +441912314328. Fax +441912453802.
URL: http://tcca.info/

History Founded Dec 1994, as *TETRA Memorandum of Understanding Association (TETRA MoU Association)*. Current title adopted 2011. Full title: *TETRA and Critical Communications Association (TCCA)*. Registered in accordance with UK law. **Aims** Promote and support the development of current and evolving mobile *digital radio* standards for critical communications. **Structure** Annual General Meeting; Executive Board. Groups, including *International Critical Control Rooms Alliance (ICCRA, #13112)*. **Languages** English. **Staff** 2.00 FTE, paid. **Finance** Members' dues. Annual budget: pounds1,000,000. **Activities** Events/meetings; standards/guidelines. **Events** *Critical Communications World Congress* Berlin (Germany) 2018, *Critical Communications MENA Congress* Dubai (United Arab Emirates) 2018, *Critical Communications MENA Congress* Dubai (United Arab Emirates) 2017, *International Critical Control Rooms Congress* Geneva (Switzerland) 2017, *Critical Communications World Congress* Hong Kong (Hong Kong) 2017. **Publications** *TETRA Today*.
Members Full in 35 countries and territories:
Australia, Austria, Belgium, Canada, China, Denmark, Estonia, Finland, France, Germany, Greece, Hong Kong, Hungary, India, Ireland, Italy, Korea Rep, Luxembourg, Malaysia, Mexico, Netherlands, Norway, Poland, Qatar, Romania, Saudi Arabia, Serbia, Singapore, South Africa, Spain, Sweden, Switzerland, UK, United Arab Emirates, USA. [2018/XJ6509/**E**]

♦ TCC – Transatlantic Christian Council (internationally oriented national body)
♦ TCC – World Tai Chi Chuan Federation (unconfirmed)
♦ **TCEN** The Commonwealth Equality Network (#04327)
♦ **TC** ESCAP/WMO Typhoon Committee (#05534)
♦ TCE – Trail Club of Europe (internationally oriented national body)
♦ **TCEurope** Technical Communication in Europe (#20116)
♦ TCF / see The Century Foundation
♦ TCF – Christensen Fund (internationally oriented national body)
♦ TC – Fratres Tertii Ordinis Sancti Francisci Capulatorum a Beata Virgine Perdolente (religious order)
♦ **TCF** Turtle Conservation Fund (#20263)
♦ Tchad Agir Pour l'Environnement (internationally oriented national body)
♦ TCHAPE – Tchad Agir Pour l'Environnement (internationally oriented national body)
♦ **TCIA** Twin Cities International Association (#20271)

♦ TCI Network (TCI) 20107

CEO Passeig de Gracia 129, 80008 Barcelona, Spain. T. +34933094834. E-mail: info@tci-network.org.
URL: http://www.tci-network.org/

History Founded Nov 1998. Full title: *TCI Network – The Competitiveness Institute (TCI)*. Registered in accordance with Spanish law: 21602. **Aims** Promote the cluster concept, improve methodologies and raise professional standards in the field so as so improve *living standards* and *local* competitiveness of regions worldwide. **Structure** General Assembly (annual); Board of Directors. Chapters (3): Latin America; Oceania; Asia. **Languages** English, Spanish. **Staff** 3.00 FTE, paid. **Finance** Members' dues. **Activities** Events/meetings; networking/liaising. **Events** *Global Conference* Durban (South Africa) 2022, *Annual Conference* Antwerp (Belgium) 2019, *Asia Chapter Meeting* Daegu (Korea Rep) 2018, *Annual Conference* Toronto, ON (Canada) 2018, *Annual Conference* Bogota (Colombia) 2017. **Publications** *TCI Newsletter* – online.
Members Organizational non-profit organizations, regional development agencies, multilateral organizations, academic institutions and companies; Individual. Organizational members in 37 countries and territories:
Argentina, Australia, Austria, Belgium, Brazil, Canada, Chile, Colombia, Denmark, Egypt, Estonia, France, Germany, India, Italy, Korea Rep, Mexico, Morocco, Netherlands, New Zealand, Nigeria, Norway, Peru, Poland, Portugal, Russia, Senegal, Serbia, Slovenia, Spain, Sweden, Switzerland, Taiwan, Türkiye, Uganda, UK, USA. [2017/XM1216/y/**E**]

♦ TCI Network – The Competitiveness Institute / see TCI Network (#20107)
♦ **TCI** Tangent Club International (#20094)
♦ TCI / see TCI Network (#20107)
♦ **TCI** TCI Network (#20107)
♦ TCIU – Transportation Communications International Union (internationally oriented national body)
♦ TCOR – Special Relief Operations Service (inactive)
♦ TCPEC / see Peace Education Center, Columbia University
♦ TCPI – The Children's Project International (internationally oriented national body)
♦ TCPM – Tracking the Creative Process in Music – International Conference (meeting series)
♦ **TCS** The Crustacean Society (#04974)
♦ TCSP / see Pacific Tourism Organization (#18008)
♦ **TCS** Trilateral Cooperation Secretariat (#20239)
♦ **TC** Trilateral Commission (#20237)
♦ TC – Turtle Conservancy (internationally oriented national body)
♦ TC / see UNECE Committee on Forests and the Forest Industry (#20294)
♦ **tDA Asia** the Design Alliance Asia (#05043)
♦ **TDB** Trade and Development Bank (#20181)
♦ **T and D EUROPE** European Association of the Electricity Transmission and Distribution Equipment and Services Industry (#06023)
♦ **TDHFI** Terre des Hommes Fédération Internationale (#20133)
♦ **Tdh Foundation** Terre des hommes Foundation (#20132)
♦ **TDHIF** Terre des Hommes International Federation (#20133)
♦ TDH / see Terre des hommes Foundation (#20132)
♦ **TDI** Democracy International (#05033)
♦ TDL – Thinking, Doing, Learning (meeting series)
♦ **TDL** Trust in Digital Life (#20253)
♦ **TDMA** Titanium Dioxide Manufacturers' Association (#20168)
♦ TDRC – Transnationalisation and Development Research Centre, Bielefeld (internationally oriented national body)
♦ TDRC – Tropical Diseases Research Centre (internationally oriented national body)
♦ TDR / see UNICEF/UNDP/World Bank/WHO Special Programme for Research and Training in Tropical Diseases (#20331)
♦ **TDR** UNICEF/UNDP/World Bank/WHO Special Programme for Research and Training in Tropical Diseases (#20331)
♦ TDS – Tourisme et développement solidaires (internationally oriented national body)
♦ **TDWG** Biodiversity Information Standards (#03243)

♦ Teach For All 20108

CEO address not obtained. E-mail: media@teachforall.org – generalinquiry@teachforall.org.
URL: http://teachforall.org/

Aims Develop collective leadership to ensure all children have the opportunity to fulfill their potential. **Structure** Board; Global Advisory Council. **Activities** Awareness raising; networking/liaising.
Members Partners in 40 countries:
Argentina, Armenia, Australia, Austria, Bangladesh, Belgium, Brazil, Bulgaria, Chile, China, Colombia, Denmark, Ecuador, Estonia, France, Germany, Ghana, Haiti, India, Israel, Japan, Latvia, Lebanon, Lithuania, Malaysia, Mexico, Nepal, New Zealand, Panama, Peru, Philippines, Qatar, Romania, Slovakia, Spain, Sweden, Thailand, UK, Uruguay, USA.
NGO Relations Member of: *InsideNGO (inactive)*. [2022/XM5430/**F**]

♦ TeachBeyond (internationally oriented national body)

♦ Teacher Education Policy in Europe (TEPE) 20109

Coordinator Hogeschool van Amsterdam, Postbus 36180, 1020 MD Amsterdam, Netherlands.
URL: http://tepe.au.dk

History 2006, Umeå (Sweden). **Aims** Bring together stakeholders around teacher education, focusing on improving the quality of teacher education in Europe. **Structure** Board. **Activities** Events/meetings. **Events** *Annual Conference* Ljubljana (Slovenia) 2021, *Annual Conference* Helsinki (Finland) 2020, *Annual Conference* Krakow (Poland) 2019, *Annual Conference* Braga (Portugal) 2018, *Annual Conference* Limerick (Ireland) 2017. [2021/AA1689/**F**]

♦ Teacher Education in Sub Saharan Africa (internationally oriented national body)

♦ Teacher Network of Latin America and the Caribbean (KIPUS) 20110

Red Docente de América Latina y El Caribe (KIPUS)

Exec Sec UNIPE, Paraguay 1583, CABA, Buenos Aires, Argentina. T. +5491148114107.
Tech Sec address not obtained.
URL: http://www.redkipus.org/

History 2003, following the signing of the 'Carta de Santiago'. **Aims** Provide a platform for exchange between institutions and individuals dealing with teacher issues. **Languages** Spanish. **Activities** Research/documentation; projects/programmes. **Events** *Meeting* Buenos Aires (Argentina) 2016, *Meeting* Mexico City (Mexico) 2010, *Meeting* Lima (Peru) 2008. [2016.02.04/XM2806/**F**]

♦ Teachers Without Borders (internationally oriented national body)
♦ Teachers College Peace Education Program / see Peace Education Center, Columbia University
♦ Teachers College Peacemaking in Education Program / see Peace Education Center, Columbia University
♦ Teachers of English to Speakers of Other Languages / see TESOL International Association
♦ Teaching Aids at Low Cost / see Health Books International
♦ Teaching English for Specific Purposes (meeting series)
♦ Teach A Man To Fish (internationally oriented national body)
♦ Teadusuuringute Ühiskeskus (#16147)
♦ TEAHA – Cairo-Gaborone Trans East African Highway Authority (inactive)

♦ Tea and Herbal Infusions Europe (THIE) 20111

SG Sonninstr 28, 20097 Hamburg, Germany. T. +494023601621. Fax +494023601610 – +494023601611. E-mail: thie@wga-hh.de.
URL: http://www.thie-online.eu/

History 22 Jan 2015. Founded as successor to *European Tea Committee (ETC, inactive)* and *European Herbal Infusions Association (EHIA, inactive)*. **Aims** Establish a common European policy with regard to tea and herbal infusions; make contact with EU-officials and representatives of other organizations and collaborate constructively with them in any matter related to the tea and herbal infusions trade and industry. **Structure** Executive Board. **Languages** English.
Members National associations in 10 countries:
Austria, Denmark, France, Germany, Ireland, Italy, Netherlands, Spain, Switzerland, UK.
Companies in 3 countries:
Croatia, Romania, Slovakia.
Observer in 1 country:
Türkiye.
IGO Relations Observer status with (1): *Codex Alimentarius Commission (CAC, #04081)*. **NGO Relations** Member of (1): *FoodDrinkEurope (#09841)*. [2019.12.20/XM5986/**D**]

♦ TEAK-NET / see International Teak Information Network (#15665)
♦ **TEAKNET** International Teak Information Network (#15665)
♦ Team Drivers International Union (TDIU) / see International Brotherhood of Teamsters
♦ **TEAM** European Alliance of EU-critical Movements (#05870)
♦ TEAM – The Evangelical Alliance Mission (internationally oriented national body)
♦ **TEAM-NB** European Association Medical Devices of Notified Bodies (#06117)
♦ Team-PRRC – European Association of Persons Responsible for Regulatory Compliance of Medical Devices (unconfirmed)

♦ Teams of Our Lady 20112

Equipes Notre-Dame (END) – Equipos de Nuestra Señora – Ehegruppen END – Equipas de Nossa Senhora

Int Secretariat 49 rue de la Glacière, 7ème Etage, 75013 Paris, France. T. +33143319621. E-mail: contact@equipes-notre-dame.com.
URL: http://www.equipes-notre-dame.com/

History 1939, Paris (France). Charter promulgated in 1947. Also referred to as *Equipes Notre-Dame "International"*. **Aims** Foster *Catholic* married people spiritual training within the framework of conjugal and family life. **Finance** Members' dues. **Events** *International Gathering* Brasilia (Brazil) 2012, *International Gathering* Lourdes (France) 2006, *International Gathering* Santiago de Compostela (Spain) 2000, *International gathering* Fatima (Portugal) 1994, *International gathering* Lourdes (France) 1988. **Members** 125,519 (including 7,820 priests) – in 70 countries. Membership countries not specified. [2019/XD4407/**F**]

♦ TEAM STAINLESS 20113

Contact c/o ISSF, Av de Tervuren 270, 1150 Brussels, Belgium. T. +3227028915. Fax +3227028912.
URL: http://www.teamstainless.org/

Aims Promote the benefits of stainless *steel* to a *sustainable* society. **Structure** An informal cooperation between associations. **Languages** English. **Publications** *TEAM STAINLESS News* (12 a year); *Achievements*.
Members Organizations (6):
European Steel Association (EUROFER, #08835); *International Chromium Development Association (ICDA, #12567)*; *International Molybdenum Association (IMOA, #14178)*; *International Nickel Study Group (INSG, #14370)*; *Nickel Institute (#17133)*; *world stainless association (worldstainless, #21828)*. [2019.12.12/XJ6009/y/**F**]

♦ Teamsters / see International Brotherhood of Teamsters
♦ Teamsters – Fédération internationale des routiers, chauffeurs, magasiniers et aides d'Amérique (internationally oriented national body)
♦ TEAR / see Tearfund, UK

♦ Tear (internationally oriented national body)
♦ TEAR Australia (internationally oriented national body)
♦ TEAR Fund / see Tear
♦ Tear Fund / see Tearfund, UK
♦ TEAR Fund (internationally oriented national body)
♦ Tearfund, Belgium (internationally oriented national body)
♦ Tearfund Canada (internationally oriented national body)
♦ Tearfund, Ireland (internationally oriented national body)
♦ TearFund, Schweiz (internationally oriented national body)
♦ TearFund, Switzerland (internationally oriented national body)
♦ Tearfund, UK (internationally oriented national body)
♦ Tebtebba Foundation – Indigenous Peoples' International Centre for Policy Research and Education (internationally oriented national body)
♦ **TECAC** TEsticular CAncer Consortium (#20134)
♦ TECH-FAB Europe – European Association of Technical Fabrics producers (unconfirmed)
♦ TECHNART (meeting series)
♦ Technical Association of the European Lubricant Industry (#02950)
♦ Technical Association of Industrial Metal Ceilings / see Association of Industrial Ceiling Manufacturers (#02641)
♦ Technical Association of Latin American Newspapers (#02301)

♦ Technical Association of the Pulp and Paper Industry (TAPPI) 20114

Secretariat 15 Technology Pkwy South, Ste 115, Peachtree Corners GA 30092, USA. T. +17704461400. Fax +17704466947. E-mail: memberconnection@tappi.org.
URL: http://www.tappi.org/

History 1915, USA. Founded as a new technical arm of the *'American Paper and Pulp Association (APPA)'*. **Aims** Provide an open forum for communication and an environment to cultivate relationships in the paper and packaging industry, with a focus on emerging technologies and driving innovation. **Structure** Headquarters located just outside Atlanta GA (USA). **Activities** Knowledge management/information dissemination; networking/liaising; events/meetings; training/education; standards/guidelines. **Events** *International Conference on Nanotechnology for Renewable Materials* Helsinki (Finland) 2022, *International Conference on Nanotechnology for Renewable Materials* 2021, *Advanced Coating Fundamentals Symposium* Zurich (Switzerland) 2020, *International Conference on Nanotechnology for Renewable Materials* Chiba (Japan) 2019, *International Conference on Nanotechnology for Renewable Materials* Madison, WI (USA) 2018. **Publications** *TAPPI Journal* (12 a year); *Paper360 Magazine*; *Tissue 360 Magazine*. Books; industry specific newsletters; videos; CD-Roms. **Information Services** *Member Connection*.
Members Organizations in 27 countries:
Argentina, Austria, Brazil, Canada, Chile, China, Colombia, Czechia, Finland, France, Germany, India, Japan, Korea Rep, Mexico, Norway, Philippines, Poland, Russia, Slovakia, South Africa, Spain, Sweden, Thailand, UK, USA, Venezuela.
Engineers, managers, scientists, academics, suppliers and others in the paper industry (about 34,000) in 75 countries and territories:
Argentina, Austria, Bahamas, Belgium, Belize, Bolivia, Brazil, Canada, Chile, China, Colombia, Costa Rica, Cuba, Cyprus, Czechia, Denmark, Dominican Rep, Ecuador, Egypt, El Salvador, Finland, France, Georgia, Germany, Greece, Hong Kong, India, Indonesia, Ireland, Israel, Italy, Japan, Jordan, Kenya, Korea Rep, Latvia, Lebanon, Liechtenstein, Luxembourg, Madagascar, Malaysia, Mauritius, Mexico, Morocco, Netherlands, Norway, Pakistan, Palestine, Panama, Paraguay, Peru, Philippines, Poland, Portugal, Puerto Rico, Romania, Russia, Saudi Arabia, Singapore, Slovakia, South Africa, Spain, Sri Lanka, Sweden, Switzerland, Taiwan, Thailand, Tunisia, Türkiye, UK, Uruguay, USA, Venezuela, Vietnam, Zimbabwe.
IGO Relations Member of: *International Organization for Standardization (ISO, #14473)*. **NGO Relations** Member of: *Inter-Society Color Council (ISSC)*; TC6. [2021/XF3431/t/**F**]

♦ Technical Centre for Agricultural and Rural Cooperation (inactive)
♦ Technical Commission for Telecommunications in Central America / see Comisión Técnica Regional de Telecomunicaciones (#04144)

♦ Technical Committee of Petroleum Additive Manufacturers in Europe (ATC) 20115

Main Office Ave de Tervueren 188A, Bte 4, 1140 Brussels, Belgium.
Contact European Registration Centre, 6555 Penn Ave, Pittsburgh PA 15206, USA. T. +14123651032. Fax +14123651027. E-mail: jac@atc-erc.org.
URL: http://www.atc-europe.org/

History 1974. Originally a sectoral group of *Conseil européen de l'industrie chimique (CEFIC, #04687)*. Now an autonomous affiliated organization. Registration: AISBL/IVZW, Belgium.
Members Companies (17) in 6 countries:
Belgium, France, Germany, Netherlands, Switzerland, UK.
NGO Relations Member of: *Coordinating European Council for the Development of Performance Tests for Transportation Fuels, Lubricants and Other Fluids (CEC, #04822)*. [2020/XE1466/**E**]

♦ Technical Committee for Technology Transfer between Latin America and the Caribbean (inactive)

♦ Technical Communication in Europe (TCEurope) 20116

Communication Technique en Europe (CTeurope)
Main Office Ave Chazal 125, 1030 Brussels, Belgium.
Twitter: https://mobile.twitter.com/tceuropeorg

History 25 Mar 2002, Brussels (Belgium). **Aims** Promote the quality of technical documentation in Europe. **Structure** General Assembly (annual); Board. **Languages** English. **Finance** Members' dues. **Activities** Events/meetings; training/education. **Events** *Annual Colloquium* Brussels (Belgium) 2013, *Annual Colloquium* Aveiro (Portugal) 2012, *Annual Colloquium* Brussels (Belgium) 2011, *Annual colloquium for user-friendly product information / Annual Colloquium* Paris (France) 2010, *Annual colloquium for user-friendly product information / Annual Colloquium* Stockholm (Sweden) 2009. **Publications** Working group reports.
Members Organizations (4) in 4 countries:
Finland, France, Portugal, Sweden. [2019.03.14/XF6661/**F**]

♦ Technical Cooperation Network on Citrus Production, Improvement and Trade Development in Latin America and the Caribbean / see Inter-American Citrus Network (#11407)

♦ Technical Cooperation Network on National Parks, Other Protected Areas and Wildlife in Latin America and the Caribbean 20117

Red Latinoamericana de Cooperación Técnica en Parques Nacionales, otras Areas Protegidas, Flora y Fauna Silvestres (REDPARQUES)
Contact FAO-RLC, Avenida Dag Hammarskjöld 3241, Vitacura, PO Box 10095, Santiago, Santiago Metropolitan, Chile. T. +56229232100. E-mail: fao-rlc@fao.org.
Regional Coordinator address not obtained. E-mail: coordinacionredparques@gmail.com.
URL: http://redparques.com/

History Jun 1983, Santiago (Chile). Set up at a roundtable organized by *FAO Regional Office for Latin America and the Caribbean (FAO/RLC, #09268)*. **Aims** Ensure *conservation* of an adequate sample of *biological diversity* through effective management of *protected areas*; improve training level of personnel involved in managing protected areas and wildlife; cooperate in improving contribution of these areas to local and regional *socio-economic development*. **Structure** Regional Coordination; National Coordinators (19). Sub-networks: *Subred de Areas Protegidas del Amazonas (SURAPA, no recent information)*; *Subred de Fauna del Cono Sur (no recent information)*. **Activities** Training/education; events/meetings; guidance/assistance/consulting. **Events** *Latin American congress on national parks and other protected areas* Santa Marta (Colombia) 1997. **Publications** Information Services: Textbooks; bulletins; technical documents; directory institutions and professionals. Computerized directory of professionals and institutions.
Members National institutions (approx 800) in 19 countries:
Argentina, Bolivia, Brazil, Chile, Colombia, Costa Rica, Cuba, Dominican Rep, Ecuador, El Salvador, Guatemala, Honduras, Mexico, Nicaragua, Panama, Paraguay, Peru, Uruguay, Venezuela.
IGO Relations *UNEP (#20299)*. [2022/XF0693/**E***]

♦ Technical Cooperation Network among Veterinary Research and Diagnostic Laboratories in Latin America and the Caribbean (see: #09268)

♦ Technical Image Press Association (TIPA) 20118

Office Calle Valderribas 10, 6oB dcha, 28007 Madrid, Spain. T. +34699375390. Fax +34911820166. E-mail: office@tipa.com.
Contact Rosa de Luxemburgo s/n, CC Rosa de Luxemburgo, local 19, 28023 Madrid, Spain.
URL: http://www.tipa.com/

History 16 Apr 1991, Paris (France). Registration: Spain. **Structure** General Assembly. **Languages** English. **Staff** 1.00 FTE, paid. **Finance** Sources: members' dues; revenue from activities/projects. **Activities** Awards/prizes/competitions; events/meetings. Active in all member countries.
Members Photo and video publications in 13 countries:
Australia, China, France, Germany, Greece, Hungary, India, Italy, Netherlands, Spain, Türkiye, UK, USA.
Camera Journal Press Club in 1 country:
Japan.
Individual in 1 country:
Japan. [2023.02.14/XD9498/**D**]

♦ Technical Office for International Studies and Cooperation (internationally oriented national body)
♦ Technical Secretariat of the Central American Council of Tourism / see Secretaria de Integración Turistica Centroamericana (#19193)
♦ Technical University of Central America (internationally oriented national body)
♦ Technical University of Latin America, San Salvador (internationally oriented national body)
♦ Technische Organisation der Europäischen Reifen- und Felgenhersteller (#08962)
♦ Technological Information Pilot System / see Technological Trade and Information Promotion System (#20119)

♦ Technological Trade and Information Promotion System (TIPS) 20119

Sistema de Promoción de Información Tecnológica y Comercial
Address not obtained.
URL: http://www.tips.co.za/

History Oct 1986, as *Technological Information Pilot System (TIPS)*, an inter-regional project of *UNDP (#20292)* within the framework of South-South cooperation. Fully operational since 1987. Currently implemented by *DEVNET International (#05059)*. Also referred to as *TIPS Network*. **Aims** Expand technology and trade transaction of *developing countries* through information. **Structure** Intergovernmental Steering Committee (policy). International Operations Centre (management) in Rome (Italy). Regional Centres (coordination): Regional Centre for Asia (Manila); Regional Centre for Latin America (Caracas); Sub-Regional Centre for Central America (San José, Costa Rica). National Bureaux (sourcing, processing, distribution). **Languages** English, Spanish. **Finance** Donors: *European Community (inactive)*; Austria, Italy, Netherlands. **Events** *Regional coordination meeting for Asia* Seoul (Korea Rep) 1994. **Publications** *Daily Bulletin – Agro-Industry*; *Daily Bulletin – Business Opportunities*; *Daily Bulletin – Electronics*; *Daily Bulletin – Energy*; *Daily Bulletin – Food Processing*; *Daily Bulletin – Machinery*; *Daily Bulletin – Pharmaceuticals*; *Weekly Bulletin – Biotechnology*; *Weekly Bulletin – Building Materials*; *Weekly Bulletin – Chemicals*; *Weekly Bulletin – Fisheries*; *Weekly Bulletin – Mining*; *Weekly Bulletin – Packaging*; *Weekly Bulletin – Textiles*. Information Services: Database of offers and requests.
Members National Bureaux in 17 countries:
Argentina, Brazil, Chile, China, Colombia, Costa Rica, Cuba, Egypt, India, Mexico, Pakistan, Peru, Philippines, Saudi Arabia, Uruguay, Venezuela, Zimbabwe.
IGO Relations *Andean Community (#00817)*; *European Commission (EC, #06633)*; *International Trade Centre (ITC, #15703)*; *Sistema Económico Latinoamericano (SELA, #19294)*; *Southern Common Market (#19868)*; *UNCTAD (#20285)*; *UNESCO (#20322)*; *UNIDO (#20336)*; *World Intellectual Property Organization (WIPO, #21593)*. **NGO Relations** *Asociación Latinoamericana de Instituciones Financieras para el Desarrollo (ALIDE, #02233)*; *Latin American Confederation of the Graphics Industry (#16303)*. [2014/XF0659/t/**F**]

♦ Technologies for Interactive Digital Storytelling (meeting series)
♦ Technology and Action for Rural Advancement (internationally oriented national body)
♦ Techno-Ocean Network (internationally oriented national body)
♦ Technoscan / see African Centre for Technology Studies (#00243)

♦ TechnoServe 20120

Pres and CEO 1777 N Kent Stree, Suite 1100, Arlington VA 22209, USA. T. +12027854515. Fax +12027854544. E-mail: info@technoserve.org – online@technoserve.org.
URL: http://www.technoserve.org/

History 14 Feb 1969, USA. Registration: Section 501(c)(3), No/ID: 13-2626135, USA. **Aims** Help *entrepreneurial* men and women in *poor rural* areas of the *developing world* to build *business* that create income, opportunity and economic growth for their families, their communities and their countries. **Structure** Board of Directors; Council; Committees of the Board of Directors (7); Worldwide Offices (9). **Languages** English, French, Portuguese, Spanish. **Staff** 1433.00 FTE, paid. **Finance** Sources: foundations; corporations; religious organizations; individuals; host-country institutions; international private voluntary organizations; various multilateral organizations. **Activities** Training/education. Active in: Benin, Bolivia, Brazil, Burkina Faso, Chile, Colombia, Côte d'Ivoire, Ecuador, El Salvador, Eswatini, Ethiopia, Ghana, Guatemala, Haiti, Honduras, India, Kenya, Malawi, Mexico, Mozambique, Nicaragua, Nigeria, Peru, Rwanda, South Africa, Tanzania UR, Uganda, Venezuela, Zambia, Zimbabwe. **Events** *Meeting on cost effectiveness in the nonprofit sector* Palo Alto, CA (USA) 1991. **Publications** *Working Newsletter* (3 a year). Annual Report; findings; field studies; sector studies; case histories; reprints; other papers.
Members Individuals in 14 countries:
Austria, Belgium, Costa Rica, El Salvador, Germany, Ghana, Nicaragua, Nigeria, Panama, Peru, Poland, Switzerland, UK, USA.
NGO Relations Member of: *Global Coffee Platform (GCP, #10298)*; *Global Impact*; *InsideNGO (inactive)*. Supports: *Farming First*. Partner of: *International Centre for Tropical Agriculture (#12527)*; *Mastercard Foundation*. [2021/XF1341/v/**F**]

♦ TECHO 20121

Communications Officer Departamental Avenue 440, San Joaquin, Santiago, Santiago Metropolitan, Chile. T. +56228387300. E-mail: info@techo.org.
USA 2050 SW 22nd St, Suite 306, Miami FL 33145, USA. T. +13058604090. E-mail: info.usa@techo.org.
URL: http://www.techo.org/

History 1997. Former names and other names: *TECHO Internacional* – former. Registration: Chile. **Aims** Build a fair, integrated and *poverty*-free society, where everyone has the opportunities needed to develop their capacities and fully exercise their rights. **Structure** Board of Directors. **Languages** English, Portuguese, Spanish. Haitian Creole. **Activities** Advocacy/lobbying/activism; projects/programmes. **Members** Full in 19 countries. Membership countries not specified. [2022/XM4962/**F**]

♦ TECHO Internacional / see TECHO (#20121)

♦ TechSoup Global 20122

Main Office 435 Brannan St, San Francisco CA 94107-1780, USA.
URL: http://www.techsoupglobal.org/

History 1987, USA, as *CompuMentor*. Present name adopted 2010. Registered in accordance with USA law. **Aims** Increase the programme impact of *nonprofit* organizations through technology assistance; increase the *philanthropic* impact of corporations and foundations. **Structure** Board. European office: *Fundacja TechSoup (#10038)*. **NGO Relations** Member of: *Worldwide Initiatives for Grantmaker Support (WINGS, #21926)*. [2016/XM3873/**F**]

♦ TECLAC – Comité Técnico para la Transferencia de Tecnologia Agricola entre América Latina y el Caribe (inactive)
♦ Tecnalia Research and Innovation Foundation (internationally oriented national body)
♦ Tecnalia – Tecnalia Research and Innovation Foundation (internationally oriented national body)
♦ TED – International Association for Training, Education and Development (inactive)
♦ TEEB For Business Coalition / see Natural Capital Coalition (#16952)
♦ Teen Challenge International / see Global Teen Challenge
♦ **TEEN** Tripartite Environmental Education Network (#20241)
♦ **T and E** European Federation for Transport and Environment (#07230)

- ♦ **T and E** Fédération européenne pour le transport et l'environnement (#07230)
- ♦ **TEFI** Tourism Education Futures Initiative (#20177)
- ♦ TEFMA – Tertiary Education Facilities Management Association (internationally oriented national body)
- ♦ TEF – Tony Elumelu Foundation (unconfirmed)
- ♦ **TEGOVA** European Group of Valuers' Associations (#07439)
- ♦ Tehran Convention – Framework Convention for the Protection of the Marine Environment of the Caspian Sea (2003 treaty)
- ♦ **Tehran ICH Centre** Regional Research Centre for Safeguarding Intangible Cultural Heritage in West and Central Asia (#18808)
- ♦ TEH / see Trans Europe Halles – A Network of Independent Cultural Centres (#20211)
- ♦ **TEH** Trans Europe Halles – A Network of Independent Cultural Centres (#20211)
- ♦ **TEI Consortium** Consortium for the Maintenance of the Text Encoding Initiative (#04753)
- ♦ TEI – International Conference on Tangible, Embedded and Embodied Interaction (meeting series)
- ♦ TEIMUN – The European International Model United Nations (internationally oriented national body)
- ♦ TE – Internationale Konferenz für die Technische Einheit im Eisenbahnwesen (inactive)
- ♦ TEI – Tax Executives Institute (internationally oriented national body)
- ♦ **TEJA** Tutmonda Esperantista Jurnalista Asocio (#21138)
- ♦ **TEJO** Tutmonda Esperantista Junulara Organizo (#20268)
- ♦ Teknis-Luonnontieteellisen Tutkimuksen Pohjoismainen Yhteistyöelin (inactive)
- ♦ **tekom Europe** European Association for Technical Communication (#06251)
- ♦ Telecentre-Europe / see ALL DIGITAL (#00646)
- ♦ Télécommunauté Asie-Pacifique (#02064)
- ♦ Telecommunication Development Bureau (#03358)
- ♦ Telecommunications Industry Association (internationally oriented national body)
- ♦ Telecommunications Regulators' Association of Southern Africa / see Communications Regulators' Association of Southern Africa (#04384)
- ♦ Telecommunication Standardization Bureau (see: #15673)
- ♦ Telecommunications Treaty (1966 treaty)
- ♦ Télécoms sans frontières (internationally oriented national body)
- ♦ TELECOM – World Telecommunication Forum (meeting series)
- ♦ Telefone da Amizade / see Samaritans
- ♦ Telefon Zaufania / see Samaritans
- ♦ **Teleforum** Forum for Telecom Operators of Small States (#09929)
- ♦ Telegraph Convention (1912 treaty)
- ♦ Telegraph Convention, 1858 (1858 treaty)
- ♦ Telegraph Convention, 1871 (1871 treaty)
- ♦ Telegraph Regulations, Telephone Regulations (1973 treaty)

♦ TeleManagement Forum (TM Forum) 20123

CEO 240 Headquarters Plaza, East Tower – 10th Fl, Morristown NJ 07960-6628, USA. T. +19739445100. Fax +19739445110. E-mail: info@tmforum.org.
European Office 47 Lower Brook Street, Ipswich, IP4 1AQ, UK. T. +442077486615.
URL: http://www.tmforum.org/

History 1988. Founded as a non-profit consortium. Since May 2007, includes *Global Billing Association (GBA, inactive)*. Former names and other names: *OSI / Network Management Forum (NMF)* – former. **Aims** Assist member *telecommunications* service providers, suppliers and users. **Structure** Board of Trustees. Committees (4): Approval; Finance and Business Development; Membership and Governance; Technical. **Finance** Sources: members' dues. **Activities** Events/meetings. **Events** *DTW Asia Forum* Bangkok (Thailand) 2023, *Digital Transformation World Forum* Copenhagen (Denmark) 2022, *Digital Transformation World Forum* Copenhagen (Denmark) 2021, *Digital Transformation World Forum* Morristown, NJ (USA) 2020, *Management World Asia Forum* Singapore (Singapore) 2017. **Members** About 850 in 65 countries. Membership countries not specified. [2022.10.21/XG5808/**F**]

- ♦ Telemedicine Development Center of Asia (unconfirmed)
- ♦ Televisión Educativa Iberoamericana / see Asociación de Televisión Educativa Iberoamericana (#02303)
- ♦ Televisión Educativa Latinoamericana / see Asociación de Televisión Educativa Iberoamericana (#02303)
- ♦ Television Trust for the Environment / see TVE International
- ♦ TELFA / see Trans European Law Firms Alliance (#20207)
- ♦ **TELFA** Trans European Law Firms Alliance (#20207)
- ♦ TeLL-Net – International Transfer Live Lessons Network (unconfirmed)
- ♦ Tellus Institute (internationally oriented national body)
- ♦ **TEL** Tutmonda Ekumena Ligo (#20267)
- ♦ TEMDEC – Telemedicine Development Center of Asia (unconfirmed)
- ♦ TEMM – Tripartite Environment Ministers Meeting (meeting series)
- ♦ Témoignage mondial, Eglise presbytérienne réformée-associée (internationally oriented national body)
- ♦ Témoins de Jéhovah (#16096)
- ♦ Temple de la compréhension (#20124)

♦ Temple of Understanding (ToU) 20124

Temple de la compréhension

Chairman/Exec Dir 777 United Nations Plaza, Office 3E, New York NY 10017, USA. T. +19146105146. E-mail: alison@templeofunderstanding.org – info@templeofunderstanding.org.
URL: http://www.templeofunderstanding.org/

History 1960, by Judith Hollister, as a global interfaith association. Registered in USA. **Aims** Promote interfaith dialogue and education worldwide; achieve understanding and harmony among the different *religions* and beyond; recognize the oneness of the human family; maintain a strong commitment to the integrity of each religion or faith tradition in the belief that each can better remain true to itself by honouring truths inherent in all traditions; work together to meet the challenges of today and build a harmonious future for the world's people. **Structure** Board of Directors; Council of Trustees; International Council. Officers: Founder, President, Chairman, Secretary, Treasurer. **Finance** Members' dues. Other sources: Board and Council donations; foundation grants. Budget (annual): US$ 165,000. **Activities** Annual Pilgrimage to places of current religious interest and unrest, visiting holy sites and meeting with political and religious leaders. Organizes roundtables and retreats. Collaborative sacred arts project. Spring and Fall Lecture Series. **Events** *Consultation on interfaith education for a global society* Barcelona (Spain) 2004, *Consultation on interfaith education for a global society* New York, NY (USA) 2004, *Consultation on interfaith education for a global society* New York, NY (USA) 2003, *Consultation on interfaith education for a global society* New York, NY (USA) 2003, *Conference on education* Delhi (India) 2002. **Publications** *Temple of Understanding Newsletter* (3 a year).
Members Individuals and organizations in 47 countries:
Algeria, Argentina, Australia, Austria, Bahamas, Bangladesh, Belgium, Bolivia, Brazil, Canada, China, Colombia, Costa Rica, Cyprus, Denmark, Dominican Rep, Egypt, France, Germany, Ghana, Greece, Hong Kong, India, Ireland, Israel, Italy, Japan, Jordan, Kenya, Korea Rep, Lebanon, Liberia, Malaysia, Netherlands, Nigeria, Pakistan, Peru, Philippines, Russia, Singapore, South Africa, Spain, Sri Lanka, Switzerland, Syrian AR, Thailand, UK.
Consultative Status Consultative status granted from: *ECOSOC (#05331)* (Special). **IGO Relations** Associated with Department of Global Communications of the United Nations. **NGO Relations** Founding member of: *NGO Forum on Environment (FOE, #17125)*. Member of: *Committee of Religious NGOs at the United Nations (CRNGOs, #04282)*; *Conference of Non-Governmental Organizations in Consultative Relationship with the United Nations (CONGO, #04635)*; *Faith and Ethics Network for the International Criminal Court*; *International Interfaith Organizations Network (IION, #13945)*; *Mining Working Group at the UN (MWG, #16813)*. Instrumental in setting up: *Global Forum of Spiritual and Parliamentary Leaders on Human Survival (inactive)*. [2015/XF5057/**F**]

- ♦ TEMPMEKO – International Symposium on Temperature and Thermal Measurements in Industry and Science (meeting series)
- ♦ Temporary Agreement Concerning the Registration and Disbanding of Sailors at Memel and Danzig (1922 treaty)
- ♦ Temporary Agreement for the Regulation of the Fisheries in Waters Contiguous to the Northern Coasts of the Territory of the Union of Soviet Socialist Republics (1930 treaty)
- ♦ Temporary International Council for Educational Reconstruction (inactive)
- ♦ Temporary International Presence in Hebron (inactive)
- ♦ TEMPUS IV (inactive)
- ♦ **TEM** Trans-European North-South Motorway Project (#20208)
- ♦ Tennis Europe / see European Tennis Federation (#08898)
- ♦ TENOR – International Conference on Technologies for Music Notation and Representation (meeting series)

♦ TensiNet Association 20125

Contact Lombeekweg 26, 1740 Ternat, Belgium. E-mail: info@tensinet.com.
URL: http://www.tensinet.com/

History Founded to fulfil the initial objectives of the *European Commission (EC, #06633)* thematic network TensiNet (2001-2004). Became an international non-profit association, 2020. **Aims** As a platform for all parties interested in *tensioned membrane* construction, offer the opportunity to exchange and share multidisciplinary knowledge about *tensile* structures in order to increase the quality of tensile *architecture*; interact with all parties involved in membrane construction; enhance the positive image of tensile structures. **Structure** General Assembly; Board of Directors. **Languages** English. **Staff** 0.50 FTE, paid. Several voluntary. **Finance** Sources: members' dues. **Activities** Awards/prizes/competitions; events/meetings; knowledge management/information dissemination; training/education. **Events** *Membrane Architecture – The Seventh Established Building Material – Designing Reliable and Sustainable Structures for the Urban Environment* Nantes (France) 2023, *Softening the habitats – sustainable innovations in minimal mass structures and lightweight architectures* Milan (Italy) 2019, *Symposium* Newcastle upon Tyne (UK) 2016, *Symposium* Istanbul (Turkey) 2013, *Symposium* Sofia (Bulgaria) 2010. **Publications** *TensiNews* (2 a year). Design guides and recommendations; symposium proceedings. **Information Services** *Projects Database*.
Members Full in 59 countries and territories:
Armenia, Australia, Austria, Bahrain, Belgium, Brazil, Bulgaria, Canada, Chile, China, Colombia, Croatia, Czechia, Denmark, Finland, France, Germany, Greece, Guatemala, Hong Kong, Hungary, India, Indonesia, Iran Islamic Rep, Israel, Italy, Japan, Korea Rep, Kuwait, Lithuania, Malaysia, Mexico, Morocco, Netherlands, Nicaragua, Norway, Pakistan, Peru, Philippines, Poland, Portugal, Qatar, Romania, Russia, Saudi Arabia, Singapore, South Africa, Spain, Sweden, Switzerland, Taiwan, Thailand, Türkiye, UK, Ukraine, United Arab Emirates, Uruguay, USA, Vietnam.
IGO Relations *Comité européen de normalisation (CEN, #04162)* CEN/TC 250 Structural Eurocodes. [2022.10.19/XM2073/**D**]

- ♦ TENT – The European Nature Trust (internationally oriented national body)
- ♦ **TEN** Third World Tourism European Ecumenical Network (#20153)
- ♦ Ten Thousand Villages (internationally oriented national body)
- ♦ Tent Schools International (internationally oriented national body)
- ♦ TEN-T – Trans-European Transport Network (inactive)
- ♦ Teollisen Yhteistyön Rahasto (internationally oriented national body)
- ♦ **TEPAL** Organización de Asociaciones y Empresas de Telecomunicaciones para América Latina (#17832)
- ♦ **TEPE** Teacher Education Policy in Europe (#20109)
- ♦ **TEPHINET** Training Programs in Epidemiology and Public Health Interventions NETwork (#20198)
- ♦ Te Pokapu Take Rautaki Aotearoa (internationally oriented national body)
- ♦ **TEPPFA** The European Plastic Pipes and Fittings Association (#08215)
- ♦ **TEPSA** Trans European Policy Studies Association (#20209)
- ♦ TEPS – Tutmonda Esperantista Pedagogia Servo (inactive)
- ♦ TERATEC (internationally oriented national body)
- ♦ Tercera Orden Carmelitana (religious order)
- ♦ Terciarios Capuchinos de Nuestra Señora de los Dolores (religious order)
- ♦ Teresa Lozano Long Institute of Latin American Studies, Austin (internationally oriented national body)
- ♦ Teresian Apostolic Movement (religious order)
- ♦ Teresian Association (religious order)
- ♦ Teresian Carmelites of Verapoly (religious order)
- ♦ Teresianischer Karmel-Gemeinschaft (religious order)
- ♦ TERI / see Energy and Resources Institute
- ♦ TERI – Energy and Resources Institute (internationally oriented national body)
- ♦ TERMIA – International Association of Terminology (inactive)
- ♦ **TERMIS** Tissue Engineering and Regenerative Medicine International Society (#20167)
- ♦ **TermNet** International Network for Terminology (#14332)

♦ ternYpe International Roma Youth Network (ternYpe) 20126

Contact Rue de Flandre 86, 1070 Brussels, Belgium. E-mail: ternype@romayouth.com.
URL: http://www.ternype.eu/

History Jan 2010. **Aims** Create space for young people to become active citizens through empowerment, mobilization, self-organization and participation; promote respect between Roma and non-Roma youth. **Structure** General Assembly; Board; Managing Director; Working Groups. **Languages** English. **Publications** *Education for Remembrance of the Roma Genocide: Scholarship, Commemoration and the Role of Youth* (2015).
Members Full in 10 countries:
Albania, Bulgaria, Germany, Hungary, Italy, North Macedonia, Poland, Romania, Slovakia, Spain. [2016.06.01/XJ8830/**F**]

- ♦ **ternYpe** ternYpe International Roma Youth Network (#20126)
- ♦ Terra Atlantica (no recent information)

♦ TerrAfrica 20127

Secretariat African Union Development Agency – NEPAD, 230 15th Road, Randjiespark, Midrand, 1685, South Africa. T. +27112563600. Fax +27112063762.
URL: http://www.terrafrica.org/

History 2005. **Aims** Serve as a partnership among sub-Saharan *African* countries, donor countries and agencies, civil society and the research community in order to scale up harmonized support for effective and efficient country-driven *sustainable land management*. **Structure** Two-tier decision-making structure – at country level and at regional platform level, including Consultative Forum (CF), Executive Committee and Secretariat. Special Advisory Groups. **Languages** English, French. **Staff** 1.00 FTE, paid. **Publications** Annual Report; briefs/modules; resource publications. **IGO Relations** Partner of: *International Center for Agricultural Research in the Dry Areas (ICARDA, #12466)*. **NGO Relations** *Forum for Agricultural Research in Africa (FARA, #09897)*. Supports: *Confédération des ONG d'environnement et de développement de l'Afrique centrale (CONGAC, #04572)*. [2019.07.24/XJ1703/**F**]

- ♦ Terra do Futuro (internationally oriented national body)
- ♦ TerraGraphics International Foundation (internationally oriented national body)

♦ TerraLex 20128

Chief Business Officer 8350 NW 52nd Ter, Ste 410, Miami FL 33166, USA. T. +13055390001 – +13055390010.
URL: http://www.terralex.org/

Aims Help member firms serve their clients' *legal* needs and business interests through a worldwide network of quality *law* firms that meet high *professional* standards. **Structure** Board of Directors. **Events** *Global Meeting* Miami, FL (USA) 2022, *Global Meeting* Oslo (Norway) 2022, *Global Meeting* Oslo (Norway) 2021, *Global Meeting* Miami, FL (USA) 2020, *Global Meeting* Phoenix, AZ (USA) 2019. **Members** Firms; professionals. Membership countries not specified. [2020.08.18/XM8348/**C**]

- ♦ Terralingua – Associação para a Defesa da Diversidade Linguistica e Biológica / see Terralingua – Unity in Biocultural Diversity (#20129)
- ♦ Terralingua – Association pour la diversité linguistique et biologique / see Terralingua – Unity in Biocultural Diversity (#20129)

♦ Terralingua – Cooperazione per la Diversità Linguistica e Biologica / see Terralingua – Unity in Biocultural Diversity (#20129)
♦ Terralingua – Partnerships for Linguistic and Biological Diversity / see Terralingua – Unity in Biocultural Diversity (#20129)
♦ Terralingua – Partnerskap för Lingvistisk och Biologisk Mångfald / see Terralingua – Unity in Biocultural Diversity (#20129)
♦ **Terralingua** Terralingua – Unity in Biocultural Diversity (#20129)

♦ Terralingua – Unity in Biocultural Diversity (Terralingua) 20129

Dir 217 Baker Road, Salt Spring Island BC V8K 2N6, Canada. T. +12505380939. Fax +12505380940. E-mail: admin@terralingua.org.
URL: http://www.terralingua.org/

History 1996. Former names and other names: *Terralingua – Partnerships for Linguistic and Biological Diversity (TL)* – former (1996); *Terralingua – Association pour la diversité linguistique et biologique* – former (1996); *Terralingua – Associação para a Defesa da Diversidade Linguistica e Biológica* – former (1996); *Terralingua – Cooperazione per la Diversità Linguistica e Biologica* – former (1996); *Terralingua – Partnerskap för Lingvistisk och Biologisk Mångfald* – former (1996). Registration: 501(c)3, Start date: 1996, USA; Charity Commission, Start date: 2012, Canada. **Aims** Sustain the biocultural diversity of life – the world's invaluable heritage of biological, cultural and linguistic diversity – through research, education, policy-relevant work and on-the-ground action. **Structure** Board of Governors; Advisory Panel; Working Committees. **Languages** English, French, Italian, Spanish. **Staff** 1.50 FTE, paid; 1.00 FTE, voluntary. **Finance** Members' dues. Other sources: programme grants; donations. Operating expenses (annual): about US$ 120,000. Annual budget varies. **Activities** Training/education; research/documentation. **Events** *Conference* Berkeley, CA (USA) 1996. **Publications** *Langscape* (2 a year) – magazine. Books. **Members** Individuals (1,400) from over 50 countries. Membership countries not specified. **NGO Relations** Cooperates with: *Biodiversity Indicators Partnership (BIP, #03242); Society for the Study of the Indigenous Languages of the Americas (SSILA).* [2022/XN8683/**F**]

♦ Terra Madre Foundation 20130

Fondazione Terra Madre

Headquarters Via Mendicità Istruita 14, 12042 Bra CN, Italy. T. +39172419611. Fax +39172419725. E-mail: terramadre@slowfood.it.
Registered Office Piazza Palazzo di Città 1, 10122 Turin TO, Italy.
URL: http://www.terramadre.info/

History On the initiative of *International Movement for the Defence of and the Right to Pleasure (Slow Food, #14194).* **Aims** Support rural and small food producers in relation to the pressures of *globalization* and intensive commercial *agriculture.* **Activities** Biennial meeting in Turin (Italy); workshops; regional meetings. **Events** *Nordic Meeting* Copenhagen (Denmark) 2018, *Biennial meeting* Turin (Italy) 2018, *Biennial Meeting* Turin (Italy) 2008, *Biennial Meeting* Turin (Italy) 2006, *Biennial Meeting* Turin (Italy) 2004. [2008/XM8142/f/**F**]

♦ Terra Nuova (internationally oriented national body)
♦ Terra Nuova – Centro per la Solidarietà e la Cooperazione tra i Popoli ONLUS / see Terra Nuova
♦ Terra Renaissance (internationally oriented national body)
♦ Pro Terra Sancta Association (internationally oriented national body)
♦ TerraWatt Initiative (internationally oriented national body)
♦ Terre / see Autre Terre (#03044)

♦ TERRE DES FEMMES 20131

Gen Sec Brunnenstr 128, 13355 Berlin, Germany. T. +493040504699-0. Fax +493040504699-99. E-mail: info@frauenrechte.de – geschaeftsfuehrung@frauenrechte.de.
URL: http://www.frauenrechte.de/

History 1 Jul 1981. Registration: Germany. **Aims** Ensure that *human rights* become *women's rights,* and that women all over the world can live in dignity, freedom and fair partnership with men. **Structure** General Assembly (annual); Committee Board; Main Office. **Languages** English, German. **Staff** 41.00 FTE, paid. **Finance** Sources: donations; grants; members' dues. **Activities** Guidance/assistance/consulting; networking/liaising. **Publications** Books; book calendar; flyer. **Members** (about 2,500). Membership countries not specified. **NGO Relations** Member of: *End FGM European Network (#05458); European Women's Lobby (EWL, #09102); Girls not Brides (#10154).* [2022.02.10/XF5299/**F**]

♦ Terre des hommes / see Terre des hommes Foundation (#20132)
♦ Terre des Hommes Fédération Internationale (#20133)

♦ Terre des hommes Foundation (Tdh Foundation) 20132

Dir-Gen Av de Montchoisi 15, 1006 Lausanne VD, Switzerland. T. +41586110666. Fax +41586110677.
URL: http://www.tdh.ch/

History 1960, Switzerland. Founded by Edmond Kaiser (1914-2000). Former names and other names: *Terre des hommes (TDH)* – former (1960 to 1988). Registration: Switzerland. **Aims** Increase chances of survival and *wellbeing* of the most *vulnerable children;* pay attention to children's distress wherever they are, to the limit of available human, technical and financial resources; combat processes endangering children's physical and moral integrity; help *rehabilitate* the poorest children, where possible associating their families or communities of origin; make society aware of children's distress. **Structure** Governing Council; Executive Departments (8); Secretary General/CEO; Support Groups. **Languages** English, French, German, Italian. **Staff** 141.00 FTE, paid. **Finance** Annual budget: 104,000,000 CHF (2017). **Activities** Awareness raising; events/meetings; humanitarian/emergency aid. **Events** *Conference* Lausanne (Switzerland) 2021, *Latin American Regional Conference* Buenos Aires (Argentina) 2019, *American Regional Conference* Mérida (Mexico) 2019, *World Congress on Justice for Children* Paris (France) 2018, *World Congress on Justice for Children* Geneva (Switzerland) 2015. **Publications** *Magazine Terre des Hommes – Courage* (4 a year) in French, German, Italian. Annual Report; research reports.
Members Swiss-based organization with activities in 36 countries and territories:
Afghanistan, Albania, Bangladesh, Benin, Brazil, Burkina Faso, Burundi, Colombia, Ecuador, Egypt, Greece, Guinea, Haiti, Hungary, India, Jordan, Kenya, Kosovo, Lebanon, Mali, Mauritania, Moldova, Morocco, Myanmar, Nepal, Nicaragua, Pakistan, Palestine, Panama, Peru, Philippines, Romania, Senegal, South Sudan, Syrian AR, Togo.
IGO Relations Member of: *Interagency Panel on Juvenile Justice (IPJJ, #11390).* **NGO Relations** Member of: *Centre de recherche et d'information pour le développement, Paris (CRID); Consortium of Christian Relief and Development Association (CCRDA); Federation of European and International Associations Established in Belgium (FAIB, #09508); Global WASH Cluster (GWC, #10651); Maison des Tiers monde et de la solidarité internationale (MTM SI); NGO Committee on UNICEF (#17120); Terre des Hommes International Federation (TDHIF, #20133).* Partner of: *CartONG (#03591).* Supports: *Global Call for Action Against Poverty (GCAP, #10263).* [2021/XF5082/f/**F**]

♦ Terre des Hommes International Federation (TDHIF) 20133

Terre des Hommes Fédération Internationale (TDHFI)

Headquarters Chemin du Pré-Picot 3, Cologny, 1223 Geneva, Switzerland. T. +41227363372. E-mail: info@terredeshommes.org.
European Office Rue de la Pépinière 10, 1000 Brussels, Belgium.
URL: http://www.terredeshommes.org/

History 1966. Founded when several TDH groups joined together. Former names and other names: *International Federation Terre des Hommes (IFTDH)* – former; *Fédération internationale Terre des hommes (FITDH)* – former. Registration: Swiss Civil Code, Switzerland; EU Transparency Register, No/ID: 030107317058-64, Start date: 22 Apr 2015. **Aims** Promote equitable *development* through work for the *rights* of the *child,* without racial, religious, political, cultural or gender-based discrimination. **Structure** General Assembly (annual); International Board; Presidency; International Secretariat, based in Geneva (Switzerland) with a liaison office in Brussels (Belgium); Working Groups. **Languages** English, French. **Staff** 354.00 FTE, paid; 7150.00 FTE, voluntary. **Finance** Sources: donations; members' dues; private foundations. Members' dues (for the International Secretariat). Annual budget: 211,691,247 EUR (2019). **Activities** Advocacy/lobbying/activism; humanitarian/emergency aid; networking/liaising; projects/programmes. **Events** *Psychosocial Support Forum (PSS Forum)* Windhoek (Namibia) 2019, *Annual General Assembly* Berlin (Germany) 2014, *Annual General Assembly* The Hague (Netherlands) 2013, *Annual General Assembly* The Hague (Netherlands) 2013, *Annual General Assembly* Luxembourg (Luxembourg) 2012. **Publications** Annual Report; research papers; position papers; handbooks; press releases.
Members National branches 9 in 8 countries:
Denmark, France, Germany, Italy, Luxembourg, Netherlands, Spain, Switzerland (2).
Consultative Status Consultative status granted from: *ECOSOC (#05331)* (Special); *ILO (#11123)* (Special List); *UNICEF (#20332); Council of Europe (CE, #04881)* (Participatory Status). **IGO Relations** Partner of (1): *Interagency Panel on Juvenile Justice (IPJJ, #11390).* Cooperates with (1): *European Union Agency for Fundamental Rights (FRA, #08969).* **NGO Relations** Partner of (9): *Child Rights Connect (#03884); Conference of Non-Governmental Organizations in Consultative Relationship with the United Nations (CONGO, #04635); Confédération européenne des ong d'urgence et de développement (CONCORD, #04547); Destination Unknown (#05047); Global Partnership to End Violence Against Children (End Violence Against Children, #10533); Human Rights and Democracy Network (HRDN, #10980); Keeping Children Safe; NGO Committee on UNICEF (#17120); Save the Children International (#19058).* [2021.05.26/XF1872/**F**]

♦ Terre et Humanisme (internationally oriented national body)
♦ Terre Nouvelle / see Solidagro
♦ Terre sans frontières (internationally oriented national body)
♦ Terres et vie (internationally oriented national body)
♦ Terre Tiers-monde et information / see Autre Terre (#03044)
♦ Tertiaires Carmélites du Sacré-Coeur de Jésus (religious order)
♦ Tertiary Education Facilities Management Association (internationally oriented national body)
♦ Tertius Ordo Minimorum (religious order)
♦ Tertius Ordo Regularis Sancti Francisci (religious order)
♦ Tertius Ordo Sancti Francisci (religious order)
♦ **TER** Trans-European Railway Project (#20210)
♦ Tervetuloa SAMAKiin (#19045)
♦ Terziari Cappuccini di Nostra Signora Addolorata (religious order)
♦ Terzo protocollo addizionale all'Accordo generale su i privilegi e le immunità del Consiglio d'Europa (1959 treaty)
♦ Terzo protocollo addizionale al Protocollo all'Accordo europeo per la protezione delle emissioni televisive (1989 treaty)
♦ Terz'Ordine dei Minimi (religious order)
♦ Terz'Ordine Regolare di Santo Francesco (religious order)
♦ TESEC – European Centre of Technological Safety (internationally oriented national body)
♦ TES / see The International Ecotourism Society (#13225)
♦ TESOL / see TESOL International Association
♦ TESOL International Association (internationally oriented national body)
♦ TESOL International Research Foundation / see The International Research Foundation for English Language Education (#14725)
♦ TESSA – Teacher Education in Sub Saharan Africa (internationally oriented national body)
♦ Testausalan Yhteispohjoismainen Elin (#16142)

♦ TEsticular CAncer Consortium (TECAC) 20134

Address not obtained.
URL: http://www.tecac.org/

Aims Pool together resources of all genome-wide association studies (GWAS) to identify new genetic markers of risk, further characterize the existing genomic regions with risk markers, examine potential maternal or parent-of-origin effects though case-parent triads and dyads and finally create a consortium that formalizes the existing research alliances. **Activities** Research/documentation. **Events** *Workshop* Copenhagen (Denmark) 2018.
Members Individuals in 11 countries:
Canada, Denmark, Germany, Iceland, Italy, Netherlands, Norway, Spain, Sweden, UK, USA.
Associate members in 4 countries:
Denmark, Italy, Netherlands, USA. [2017/XM7502/v/**C**]

♦ TETHYS / see Tethys Research Institute
♦ Tethys Research Institute (internationally oriented national body)
♦ TETRA and Critical Communications Association / see TCCA (#20106)
♦ Tetrahedron Symposium (meeting series)
♦ TETRA Memorandum of Understanding Association / see TCCA (#20106)
♦ TETRA MoU Association / see TCCA (#20106)
♦ TETRA – Transdisciplinary European Training and Research in Anthropology (internationally oriented national body)
♦ Te Tuao Tawahi (internationally oriented national body)
♦ Teutonic Order (religious order)
♦ **TEVA** Tutmonda Esperantista Vegetarana Asocio (#21389)
♦ TeV Particle Astrophysics (meeting series)
♦ TeVPA – TeV Particle Astrophysics (meeting series)
♦ Texans for Educational Excellence / see Intercultural Development Research Association
♦ Texas International Education Consortium (internationally oriented national body)
♦ Texas A and M International University (internationally oriented national body)
♦ Texas Symposium on Relativistic Astrophysics (meeting series)
♦ TEXERE – Textile Education and Research in Europe (see: #08903)
♦ TEXTIL CREDIT – Organisation européenne de la protection du crédit textile (inactive)
♦ Textile and Clothing Information Center (internationally oriented national body)
♦ Textile and Clothing Workers Trade Unions International (inactive)
♦ Textile Education and Research in Europe (see: #08903)

♦ Textile Exchange 20135

Contact 511 South 1st St, Lamesa TX 79331, USA. T. +18064283411. Fax +18064283475.
URL: http://textileexchange.org/

History 2002. Former names and other names: *Organic Exchange* – former (2002 to 2010). **Aims** Create leaders in the sustainable *fiber* and materials industry by providing learning opportunities, tools, standards, measurements and benchmarking. Promote a responsible expansion of textile sustainability across the global textile value chain. **Structure** Board of Directors; Executive Committee. **Languages** English, French, German, Japanese, Mandarin Chinese, Spanish, Swedish. **Staff** 30.00 FTE, paid. **Activities** Events/meetings; standards/guidelines; training/education. **Events** *Textile Exchange Conference* Colorado Springs, CO (USA) 2022. [2022/XM4128/**C**]

♦ Textile Industry Federation of Africa and Madagascar (inactive)

♦ The Textile Institute (TI) 20136

Main Office 8th Fl, St James's Bldgs, 79 Oxford Street, Manchester, M1 6FQ, UK. T. +441612371188. Fax +441612361991. E-mail: tiihq@textileinst.org.uk.
URL: http://www.textileinstitute.org/

History Apr 1910, Manchester (UK). Founded following decision 20 Jul 1909, based on original idea conceived May 1907, Brussels (Belgium). Incorporated in UK by Royal Charter 1925. Supplemental Charter: 1965; 1975. Recognized as a non-profit association under the laws of many countries. Registration: Charity Commission, No/ID: 222478, England and Wales. **Aims** Promote professionalism in all areas associated with textile industries worldwide. **Structure** Council; Standing Committees; Sections; Special Interest Groups. **Languages** English. **Staff** 5.00 FTE, paid. **Finance** Sources: fees for services; meeting proceeds; members' dues; sale of publications. **Activities** Certification/accreditation; events/meetings; knowledge management/information dissemination; training/education. **Events** *Annual World Conference* Huddersfield (UK) 2023, *Annual World Conference* Leeds (UK) 2018, *Annual World Conference* Poznań (Poland) 2016, *Annual World Conference* Wuhan (China) 2014, *Annual World Conference* Shah Alam (Malaysia) 2012. **Publications** *International Textile Calendar* (daily); *Journal of the Textile Institute* (12 a year); *Textile Progress* (4 a year); *Textiles* (3 a year) – magazine; *Textile Terms and Definitions.* Textbooks; monographs; catalogues of textile processes and analytical methods for identifying textile fibres. **Members** Licentiates; Associates; Fellows. A total of over 4,000 members in 80 countries (not specified). **NGO Relations** In liaison with technical committees of: *International Organization for Standardization (ISO, #14473).* [2022.11.30/XC4439/j/**B**]

♦ Textile Technology Transfer Network / see TEXTRANET (#20137)
♦ Textile Transfer Network / see TEXTRANET (#20137)

♦ TEXTRANET **20137**

Head Office 14 rue des Reculettes, 75013 Paris, France. E-mail: pcadeia@textranet.net.
Contact address not obtained. T. +351252300300. Fax +351252300300. E-mail: bz@textranet.net.
URL: http://www.textranet.net/

History 1989. Former names and other names: *Textile Technology Transfer Network (TEXTRANET)* – former; *Textile Transfer Network* – full title; *European Network for Textile Research Organizations* – alias. **Aims** Provide technical and commercial benefit by participation for all members; promote exchange of information between members; facilitate establishment of transnational project, with particular emphasis on those receiving European funding; develop and maintain cooperative links with professional and textile associations, particularly those having pan-European activity; provide a forum for promotion of technical progress within the European textile *industry*. **Structure** Executive Council (Bureau), composed of up to 6 members drawn from Full Member organizations, including President, Vice-President, Treasurer, Secretary and 2 additional members. **Languages** English. **Staff** 1.00 FTE, paid.

Members Full (25) textile research and technology organizations deriving the majority of their income from commercial operations, registered within the European Union or EFTA. Associate textile research and technology organizations deriving the majority of their income from commercial operations, registered outside the EU or EFTA. Transitional organizations which have served a minimum of 2 years as an Associate Member and whose countries are in the active process of becoming a member of the EU or EFTA. Supporting EU or EFTA registered associations or companies. Members in 18 countries:
Austria, Belgium, Czechia, Denmark, Finland, France, Germany, Greece, Hungary, Italy, Netherlands, Poland, Portugal, Spain, Sweden, Switzerland, Tunisia, UK.

IGO Relations *European Commission (EC, #06633)*. **NGO Relations** Joint meeting with: *European Group for the Development of Textile Research (GEDRT)*. [2023.02.13/XF4872/**F**]

♦ TFA / see Food and Trees for Africa
♦ TFA – Family Africa (internationally oriented national body)
♦ **TFAF** Trade Facilitation Agreement Facility (#20182)
♦ TFA – Trade Facilitation Agreement (2014 treaty)
♦ **TFA** Tropical Forest Alliance (#20249)
♦ TFCSD / see Task Force for Global Health (#20098)
♦ TFD – Taiwan Foundation for Democracy (internationally oriented national body)
♦ TFEU – Treaty on the Functioning of the European Union (1957 treaty)
♦ **TFF** Thought For Food (#20155)
♦ **TFF** Transnational Foundation for Peace and Future Research (#20217)
♦ TFF – Tropical Forest Foundation (internationally oriented national body)
♦ **TFGH** Task Force for Global Health (#20098)
♦ TFGI – Future Group International, The (unconfirmed)
♦ **TFI** The Family International (#09253)
♦ TFI – The Forgotten International (internationally oriented national body)
♦ **TFI** Thyroid Federation International (#20158)
♦ **TFI** WHO Tobacco Free Initiative (#20949)
♦ **TFNet** International Tropical Fruits Network (#15736)
♦ TFP – Symposium on Trends in Functional Programming (meeting series)
♦ TFSR / see Tools for Self Reliance
♦ **TfS** Together for Sustainability (#20170)
♦ TFTF – Trees for the Future (internationally oriented national body)
♦ TF – Tolstoy Foundation (internationally oriented national body)
♦ TFWA – Tax Free World Association (internationally oriented national body)
♦ **TGA** Touristische Gemeinschaft der Alpenländer (#00745)
♦ **TGA** Tropical Growers' Association (#20250)
♦ **TGE** Transnational Giving Europe (#20218)

♦ TGEU **20138**

Exec Dir Heidelberger Str 63/64, 12435 Berlin, Germany. E-mail: tgeu@tgeu.org.
URL: http://tgeu.org

History 2 Feb 2005, Vienna (Austria). Founded at 1st Council. Current constitution adopted, Dec 2006. Former names and other names: *European Transgender – Network and Council (TGEU)* – former; *Transgender Europe eV* – legal name. Registration: Amtsgericht Berlin (Charlottenburg), No/ID: VR 32583 B, Germany, Berlin; EU Transparency Register, No/ID: 384028912403-82, Start date: 9 Dec 2013. **Aims** Strengthen the rights and wellbeing of trans people in Europe and Central Asia. **Structure** General Assembly (every 2 years); Board; Working Groups. **Languages** English, Russian. **Staff** 10.00 FTE, paid. **Finance** Funding and support from: *European Commission (EC, #06633)*; *Heinrich Böll Foundation*; Open Society Foundations; governmental departments of Netherlands and USA. **Activities** Advocacy/lobbying/activism; awareness raising; capacity building; events/meetings; monitoring/evaluation; networking/liaising; research/documentation; training/education. **Events** *European Transgender Council Meeting* Antwerp (Belgium) 2018, *European Transgender Council Meeting* Bologna (Italy) 2016, *European Transgender Council Meeting* Budapest (Hungary) 2014, *European Transgender Council Meeting* Dublin (Ireland) 2012, *European Transgender Council Meeting* Malmö (Sweden) 2010. **Publications** *Trans Murder Monitoring update* in English, Spanish; *Trans Rights Map* in English, Russian. Catalogue; reports; guides; toolkits; recommendations.

Members Organisations (183) in 46 countries:
Albania, Armenia, Austria, Belarus, Belgium, Bosnia-Herzegovina, Bulgaria, Croatia, Cyprus, Czechia, Denmark, Estonia, Finland, France, Georgia, Germany, Greece, Hungary, Iceland, Ireland, Italy, Kazakhstan, Kosovo, Kyrgyzstan, Lithuania, Luxembourg, Malta, Montenegro, Netherlands, North Macedonia, Norway, Poland, Portugal, Romania, Russia, Serbia, Slovakia, Slovenia, Spain, Sweden, Switzerland, Tajikistan, Türkiye, UK, Ukraine, Uzbekistan.
International Lesbian, Gay, Bisexual, Transgender, Queer and Intersex Youth and Student Organization (IGLYO, #14032); *Network of European LGBTIQ Families Associations (NELFA, #17021)*; Post-Soviet Trans Coalition; Trans* Network Balkan.

Consultative Status Consultative status granted from: *Council of Europe (CE, #04881)* (Participatory Status). **IGO Relations** Participant in Fundamental Rights Platform of: *European Union Agency for Fundamental Rights (FRA, #08969)*. **NGO Relations** Member of (3): *ILGA-Europe (#11118)*; *ILGA World (International Lesbian, Gay, Bisexual, Trans and Intersex Association, #11120)*; *Social Platform (#19344)*. [2022.02.09/XM1742/**F**]

♦ TGH – Triangle génération humanitaire (internationally oriented national body)
♦ **TG** Theosophische Gesellschaft (#20141)
♦ THAF – Tropical Health Alliance Foundation (internationally oriented national body)
♦ Thailand International Development Cooperation Agency (internationally oriented national body)

♦ Thalassaemia International Federation **20139**

Exec Dir PO Box 28807, CY-2083 Nicosia, Cyprus. T. +35722319129. Fax +35722314552. E-mail: thalassaemia@cytanet.com.cy.
Street Address Ifigeneias Street 31, Strovolos, CY-2007 Nicosia, Cyprus.
URL: http://www.thalassaemia.org.cy/

History 1987. **Aims** Promote and implement national control programmes for prevention and treatment of thalassaemia and other *haemoglobin* disorders in every affected country. **Structure** Board of Directors. **Languages** English, Irish Gaelic. **Staff** 7.00 FTE, paid. **Finance** Members' dues. Other sources: grants; donations. **Activities** Events/meetings. **Events** *Pan-Middle East (MEGMA) Conference on Haemoglobinopathies* Amman (Jordan) 2016, *Pan-Asian Conference on Haemoglobinopathies* Hanoi (Vietnam) 2015, *Pan-European Conference on Haemoglobinopathies and Rare Anaemias* Athens (Greece) 2014, *International Conference for Parents and Patients* Abu Dhabi (United Arab Emirates) 2013, *International Conference on Thalassaemia and Haemoglobinopathies* Abu Dhabi (United Arab Emirates) 2013. **Publications** *TIF Magazine* (4 a year). *Prevention of Thalassaemias and other Haemoglobinopathies* – 2 vols. Annual Report. Books; educational booklets; manuals; guidelines; DVD; booklets.

Members Voting; General; Associate (100). Voting in 35 countries and territories:
Albania, Australia, Azerbaijan, Bahrain, Bangladesh, Brazil, Bulgaria, Canada, China, Cyprus, Egypt, Greece, India, Indonesia, Iraq, Israel, Italy, Jordan, Lebanon, Malaysia, Maldives, Morocco, Nepal, Pakistan, Palestine, Romania, South Africa, Sri Lanka, Syrian AR, Thailand, Tunisia, Türkiye, UK, United Arab Emirates, USA.
General in 29 countries:
Argentina, Australia, Bangladesh, Belgium, Bulgaria, Cambodia, Canada, China, France, Germany, Greece, India, Iran Islamic Rep, Iraq, Italy, Luxembourg, Malaysia, Malta, Netherlands, Pakistan, Philippines, Portugal, Singapore, Spain, Taiwan, Trinidad-Tobago, Türkiye, UK, United Arab Emirates.
Individual/Associate in 37 countries and territories:
Argentina, Australia, Azerbaijan, Bangladesh, Belgium, Brazil, Bulgaria, Canada, China, Cyprus, Denmark, Egypt, Finland, Germany, Greece, India, Iraq, Israel, Kuwait, Malaysia, Nepal, Netherlands, New Zealand, Nigeria, Norway, Oman, Pakistan, Palestine, Saudi Arabia, South Africa, Sri Lanka, Switzerland, Syrian AR, UK, United Arab Emirates, USA, Vietnam.

Consultative Status Consultative status granted from: *WHO (#20950)* (Official Relations); *ECOSOC (#05331)* (Special); *Council of Europe (CE, #04881)* (Participatory Status). **NGO Relations** Member of: *DigitalHealthEurope (DHE, #05078)*; *EURORDIS – Rare Diseases Europe (#09175)*; *International Alliance of Patients' Organizations (IAPO, #11633)*; *Rare Diseases International (RDI, #18621)*. Cooperates with: *European Hematology Association (EHA, #07473)*. [2018.06.01/XD2836/**D**]

♦ **THA** Triple Helix Association (#20242)
♦ Théatins – Clercs Réguliers Théatins (religious order)
♦ Theatre Without Borders (internationally oriented national body)
♦ Theatre of Nations / see International Association of Theatre Critics (#12226)
♦ Théâtre des Nations / see International Association of Theatre Critics (#12226)
♦ Théâtre sans frontières (internationally oriented national body)
♦ THE FUNDS / see Danish International Investment Funds
♦ **THE-ICE** International Centre of Excellence in Tourism and Hospitality Education (#12491)
♦ THE INTERLEX Group – International Law Firm Network / see Interlex Group (#11518)
♦ THEnet – Training for Health Equity Network (unconfirmed)
♦ TheoBio – International Theoretical Biophysics Symposium (meeting series)
♦ Theological Libraries of Latin America / see Red Latinoamericana de Información Teologica (#18713)
♦ **TheoPhilos** ICOMOS International Committee on Theory and Philosophy of Conservation and Restoration (#11067)

♦ Théophraste Network **20140**

Réseau Théophraste

Pres c/o Ecole supérieure de journalisme de Lille, 50 rue Gauthier-de-Châtillon, 59046 Lille CEDEX, France. T. +33320304400. Fax +33320304494. E-mail: theophraste@theophraste.org.
URL: http://www.theophraste.org/

History 11 Mar 1994, Lille (France). An institutional network member of *Agence universitaire de La Francophonie (AUF, #00548)* and its *Université des réseaux d'expression française (UREF, inactive)*. Full title in French is *Réseau des centres francophones de formation au journalisme*. **Aims** Create *French language* schools of *journalism* where none exist; provide training for trainers; reinforce members' documentation and information centres; make students aware of *media* management and professional training; make students of journalism aware of cultural differences through foreign exchanges. **Activities** Networking/liaising; training/education; knowledge management/information dissemination. **Events** *Annual General Assembly* Lille (France) 2004, *Annual General Assembly* Québec, QC (Canada) 2003, *Annual General Assembly* Houston, TX (USA) 2000, *Annual General Assembly* Tunis (Tunisia) 2000, *Annual General Assembly* Moncton, NB (Canada) 1999.

Members Schools of journalism (19) in 13 countries:
Belgium, Bosnia-Herzegovina, Bulgaria, Cameroon, Canada, France, Madagascar, Moldova, Morocco, Romania, Senegal, Switzerland, Tunisia.

NGO Relations Member of: *World Journalism Education Council (WJEC, #21602)*. [2019.10.17/XF3283/**F**]

♦ Theory of Inventive Problem Solving / see European TRIZ Association (#08949)
♦ Theosophical Order of Service (see: #20141)
♦ Theosophical Society (internationally oriented national body)

♦ Theosophical Society (TS) **20141**

Société théosophique (ST) – Sociedad Teosófica (ST) – Theosophische Gesellschaft (TG)

Pres Adyar, Chennai, Tamil Nadu 600 020, Chennai TAMIL NADU 600 020, India. T. +914424912474. E-mail: president.hq@ts-adyar.org – intl.hq@ts-adyar.org.
URL: http://www.ts-adyar.org/

History Founded 17 Nov 1875, New York NY (USA), by Helena P Blavatsky, Henry S Olcott, William Q Judge and others. Headquarters transferred, 1882, to Adyar, Chennai (India). In the years following the death of Helena Blavatsky in 1891, the Theosophical Movement divided into several separate organizations. *Theosophical Society* remained in New York NY, with William Q Judge, subsequently transferring to Pasadena CA (USA), while the Adyar Society, following H S Olcott and Annie Besant, retained its international headquarters in Chennai and was registered in accordance with Indian law on 3 Apr 1905. The *'Theosophical Society'* is currently established internationally. **Aims** Form a nucleus of the universal *brotherhood* of humanity, without distinction of race, creed, sex, caste or colour; encourage the study of *comparative religion, philosophy* and science; investigate unexplained laws of *nature* and the powers latent in man. **Structure** General Council (annual), consisting of Officers, General Secretaries of national societies and 5 to 12 additional members, elects Executive Committee. Membership open to all over the age of 10. Conferences and conventions partly open to the public. Through *Theosophical Order of Service (TOS, see: #20141)*, members and non-members collaborate with other organizations in social service, protection of animals, prison reform and other community service activities. In Adyar (India): School of the Wisdom – for students (annually Oct-Mar); Olcott Memorial Secondary High School for underprivileged (with 550 students); Social Welfare Centre providing day-care, free meals and medical care to 90-150 poor children; Vocational Training Centre gives one year sewing training for young women. **Languages** English. **Finance** Members' dues. Other sources: donations; interest on investments and endowment funds. **Activities** Events/meetings; knowledge management/information dissemination. **Events** *Annual Convention* Varanasi (India) 2019, *Annual Convention* Chennai (India) 2018, *World congress* Singapore (Singapore) 2018, *Annual Convention* Chennai (India) 2017, *Annual Convention* Chennai (India) 2016. **Publications** *The Theosophist* (12 a year); *Adyar Newsletter* (4 a year); *Wake Up India* (4 a year); *Adyar Library Bulletin* (annual). Books on spiritual, metaphysical, philosophical, scientific and religious subjects. Information Services: *Peace Library and Research Centre*, Quezon City (Philippines), set up by Philippine branch.

Members Lodges and study centres (1,097), totalling over 28,000 individual members; national societies, sections, regional associations and presidential agencies and lodges. Individuals in 56 countries and territories:
Argentina, Australia, Austria, Bangladesh, Belgium, Bolivia, Brazil, Canada, Chile, Colombia, Costa Rica, Côte d'Ivoire, Croatia, Cuba, Denmark, Dominican Rep, Estonia, Finland, Germany, Ghana, Greece, Hungary, Iceland, India, Indonesia, Ireland, Israel, Italy, Japan, Kenya, Liberia, Malaysia, Mexico, Netherlands, New Zealand, Norway, Paraguay, Peru, Philippines, Portugal, Puerto Rico, Russia, Singapore, Slovenia, South Africa, Spain, Sri Lanka, Sweden, Switzerland, Tanzania UR, Togo, Uganda, UK, Ukraine, Uruguay, USA.
Regional organizations (4):
Indo-Pacific Theosophical Federation (IPTF, #11172); *Inter-American Theosophical Federation (IATF, #11453)*; *Pan African Theosophical Federation (PATF, #18069)*; *Theosophical Society in Europe (#20142)*.

NGO Relations Instrumental in setting up: *Theosophical World Trust for Education and Research (TWTER, no recent information)*; *Theosophy Science Centre (TSC, no recent information)*. [2022/XB3316/y/**F**]

♦ Theosophical Society in Europe **20142**

Société théosophique en Europe – Sociedad Teosófica en Europa – Theosophische Gesellschaft in Europa

Chairman 67 rue des Pommiers, 45000 Orléans, France. T. +33171504869. E-mail: info@ts-efts.eu.
URL: http://www.ts-efts.eu/

History 23 Jul 1903, London (UK). Operated since 1928 under the name *Federation of Theosophical Societies in Europe – Fédération des sociétés théosophiques d'Europe*. Also referred to as *European Federation of National Theosophical Societies*. Constitution adopted Jun 1904, Amsterdam (Netherlands); most recently amended Nov 1987. All affiliated societies are chartered by *Theosophical Society (TS, #20141)* in Adyar (India).

Aims Encourage and extend the work of the Society throughout Europe; strengthen bonds between European national societies and encourage cooperation among them. **Structure** *Council of the European Federation of National Societies*; Executive Committee. **Languages** English. **Staff** Voluntary. **Finance** Members' dues. Other sources: legacies; donations; sale of publications. **Activities** Training/education; events/meetings; networking/liaising. **Events** *Triennial European Congress* York (UK) 2021, *Triennial European Congress* York (UK) 2020, *Triennial European Congress* Barcelona (Spain) 2017, *Triennial European Congress* Paris (France) 2014, *Triennial European congress* Rome (Italy) 2010. **Publications** *Circles* in English; *Gangleri* in Icelandic; *Ilosos* in Greek; *Insight* in English; *Le lotus bleu* in French; *Osiris* in Portuguese – magazine; *Rivista Italiana di Teosofia* in Italian; *Sophia* in Spanish; *Teosofi* in Finnish; *Teosofi i Tiden* in Norwegian; *Teozofska Misel* in Slovene; *Theosofia* in Dutch; *Theosophie Adyar* in German; *Tidlös Visdom* in Swedish; *Tidzens Teosofi* in Danish.

Members National societies, regional associations of lodges and presidential agencies in 40 countries:
Argentina, Australia, Austria, Belgium, Brazil, Canada, Central African Rep, Chile, Colombia, Costa Rica, Cuba, Dominican Rep, Finland, France, Germany, Greece, Iceland, India, Indonesia, Ireland, Israel, Italy, Kenya, Mexico, Netherlands, New Zealand, Norway, Peru, Poland, Portugal, Singapore, Slovenia, South Africa, Spain, Sri Lanka, Sweden, Switzerland, UK, Uruguay, USA.
Individuals in 21 countries:
Bangladesh, Belarus, Bosnia-Herzegovina, Bulgaria, Congo Brazzaville, Congo DR, Côte d'Ivoire, Croatia, Denmark, Estonia, Hungary, Japan, Lithuania, Malaysia, Pakistan, Philippines, Poland, Russia, Togo, Ukraine, Vietnam.
NGO Relations Instrumental in setting up: *European School of Theosophy*. [2016.11.28/XD3317/**D**]

- ♦ Theosophische Gesellschaft (#20141)
- ♦ Theosophische Gesellschaft in Europa (#20142)
- ♦ Theranostics World Congress (meeting series)
- ♦ THERMEC – International Conference on Processing and Manufacturing of Advanced Materials (meeting series)
- ♦ THERMINIC – International Workshop on Thermal Investigations of ICs and Systems (meeting series)
- ♦ Thermophiles – International Thermophiles Conference (meeting series)
- ♦ Thesaurus Islamicus Foundation (internationally oriented national body)
- ♦ Thesaurus Linguae Graecae (internationally oriented national body)
- ♦ Thesaurus Linguae Latinae (internationally oriented national body)
- ♦ THET – Tropical Health and Education Trust (internationally oriented national body)
- ♦ **THIE** Tea and Herbal Infusions Europe (#20111)
- ♦ THIMUN – The Hague International Model United Nations (internationally oriented national body)
- ♦ Thin Green Line Foundation (internationally oriented national body)
- ♦ Think Global – Development Education Association (internationally oriented national body)
- ♦ Thinking, Doing, Learning (meeting series)

♦ Think Pink Europe 20143

Acting Managing Dir Researchdreef 12, 1070 Anderlecht, Belgium. E-mail: office@thinkpinkeurope.org.
URL: https://www.thinkpinkeurope.org/

History Mar 2018. Founded by 5 organizations in Belgium, Bosnia-Herzegovina, Greece, Italy and Romania. Registration: Banque-Carrefour des Entreprises, No/ID: 0693.907.514, Start date: 4 Apr 2018, Belgium; EU Transparency Register, No/ID: 929009941953-43, Start date: 24 Mar 2021. **Aims** Improve and accelerate the exchange of information and best practices on health care and research.
Members Members in 31 countries:
Albania, Belgium, Bosnia-Herzegovina, Bulgaria, Croatia, Cyprus, Czechia, Estonia, France, Georgia, Greece, Hungary, Ireland, Italy, Kosovo, Luxembourg, Malta, Moldova, Netherlands, North Macedonia, Poland, Portugal, Romania, Russia, Serbia, Slovenia, Spain, Sweden, Switzerland, UK, Ukraine. [2021/AA1506/**F**]

- ♦ ThinkWell (internationally oriented national body)

♦ ThinkYoung 20144

Brussels Place Luxembourg 6, 1050 Brussels, Belgium. T. +3226088210. E-mail: info@thinkyoung.eu.
URL: http://www.thinkyoung.eu/

History 2009, Brussels (Belgium). Registration: No/ID: 0822.537.531, Start date: 22 Jan 2010, Belgium. **Aims** Make the world a better place for young people, by involving them in decision making processes and by providing decision makers with high quality researchers on youth's conditions. **Activities** Research/documentation; training/education; advocacy/lobbying/activism. **Publications** Research reports; videos. **NGO Relations** Member of (1): *EU STEM Coalition (#09201)*. Partners include: *AIESEC (#00593)*; *Association des états généraux des étudiants de l'Europe (AEGEE-Europe, #02495)*; *Erasmus Student Network (ESN, #05529)*; *ERSTE Foundation*; *European Association of Aerospace Students (EUROAVIA, #05930)*; *European Geography Association for Students and Young Geographers (EGEA, #07388)*; *Friedrich-Ebert-Stiftung (FES)*; *International Association of Students in Agricultural and Related Sciences (IAAS, #12191)*; *Junior Enterprises Europe (JE Europe, #16169)*; *Students' European Network for Sustainable Development (SENSD, #20017)*; *Vodafone Group Foundation*; *Wilfried Martens Centre for European Studies (Martens Centre, #20962)*. [2019.06.15/XM4162/**F**]

- ♦ Third ACP-EEC Convention (1984 treaty)
- ♦ Third Additional Protocol to the European Convention on Extradition (2010 treaty)
- ♦ Third Additional Protocol to the Protocol to the European Agreement on the Protection of Television Broadcasts (1989 treaty)

♦ Third Generation Partnership Project (3GPP) 20145

Contact 3GPP Mobile Competence Ctr, c/o ETSI, 650 route des Lucioles, 06921 Sophia Antipolis CEDEX, France. E-mail: 3gppcontact@3gpp.org – info@3gpp.org.
URL: http://www.3gpp.org/

History Dec 1998. **Aims** Produce technical specifications and technical reports for a 3G *mobile telephone* system based on evolved GSM core networks and the radio access technologies that they support; maintain and develop the Global System for Mobile *Communication* technical specifications and technical reports. **Structure** Coordination Group. **Activities** Events/meetings. **Events** *Third Generation Partnership Project Ran Access Network Plenary Meeting* Budapest (Hungary) 2022, *Third Generation Partnership Project Ran Access Network Plenary Meeting* Jeju (Korea Rep) 2020, *Meeting* Barcelona (Spain) 2019, *A4-EVS Adhoc on IVAS Codex Meeting* Busan (Korea Rep) 2019, *Meeting* Busan (Korea Rep) 2019.
Members Individual members are members of organizational partners. Individual members (362) in 37 countries and territories:
Austria, Belgium, Brazil, Canada, China, Croatia, Cyprus, Czechia, Denmark, Finland, France, Germany, Greece, India, Ireland, Israel, Italy, Japan, Korea Rep, Luxembourg, Netherlands, Norway, Portugal, Romania, Russia, Serbia, Singapore, Slovenia, South Africa, Spain, Sweden, Switzerland, Taiwan, Türkiye, UK, United Arab Emirates, USA.
NGO Relations Partner of (1): *European Telecommunications Standards Institute (ETSI, #08897)*. [2020.11.19/XJ0285/**E**]

♦ Third Generation Partnership Project 2 (3GGP2) 20146

Dir 1320 North Courthouse Rd, Ste 200, Arlington VA 22201, USA. T. +17039077779. Fax +17039077728.
URL: http://www.3gpp2.org/

Activities Events/meetings. **Events** *Super Meeting* Seoul (Korea Rep) 2011, *Meeting* Osaka (Japan) 2008.
Members Standard Development Organizations (5) in 4 countries:
China, Japan, Korea Rep, USA. [2017.06.27/XJ0284/**E**]

- ♦ Third International Tin Agreement (1965 treaty)

♦ Third Millennium Foundation (3MF) 20147

Exec Dir Palazzo Baldeschi, Via Sensini 4, 06060 Paciano PG, Italy. T. +3975730540.
Sec/Treas 119 E Young Avenue, Henderson NC 27536, USA. T. +12524382588. Fax +12524913455.
URL: http://3mf.org/

History 1987, by David McTaggart, former Chairman of *Greenpeace International (#10727)*. Also referred to as *3rd Millennium Foundation*. **Aims** Support global peace, ecological balance and international cooperation; encourage forward-thinking efforts to foster greater awareness and understanding of the planet and the issues and challenges it faces, with special focus on the *oceans* and on *conservation* and *protection* of *marine life*. **Structure** Executive Director; Secretary/Treasurer. Includes *International Whales Network (IWN, see: #20147)*. [2019/XJ6764/t/**F**]

- ♦ Third Order Capuchin of Our Lady of Sorrows (religious order)
- ♦ Third Order Conventual Dominican (religious order)
- ♦ Third Order of Mary (religious order)
- ♦ Third Order Regular of St Francis (religious order)
- ♦ Third Order Secular of Minims (religious order)
- ♦ Third Order Secular of the Most Holy Trinity (religious order)
- ♦ Third Order Secular of St Dominic (religious order)
- ♦ Third Order of the Society of St Pius X (religious order)
- ♦ Third Order of St Norbert (religious order)
- ♦ Third Protocol Amending the Convention on the Canalization of the Moselle (1987 treaty)
- ♦ Third Protocol to the Central American Agreement on Fiscal Incentives to Industrial Development (1977 treaty)
- ♦ Third Protocol to the General Agreement on Privileges and Immunities of the Council of Europe (1959 treaty)
- ♦ Third Protocol to the General Treaty of Central American Economic Integration to Guarantee Free Trade in Paper and Glass Containers (1966 treaty)

♦ Third Sector European Policy Network (TSEP) 20148

Contact SSPSSR, Cornwallis Bldg, Univ of Kent, Canterbury, CT2 7NF, UK.
URL: http://www.kent.ac.uk/tsep/

History 2002, as a collaborative research project. **Publications** *Handbook on European Third Sector Policy: Multi-level Processes and Organised Civil Society* (2010). Workshop reports; working papers.
Members Participants from 10 countries:
Czechia, France, Germany, Italy, Netherlands, Spain, Sweden, Switzerland, UK. [2009/XJ8232/**F**]

- ♦ Third World Academy of Sciences / see TWAS (#20270)
- ♦ Third World Action (internationally oriented national body)
- ♦ Third World Center for Water Management (internationally oriented national body)
- ♦ Third World Centre, Nijmegen / see Centre for International Development Issues, Nijmegen
- ♦ Third World Conference Foundation (internationally oriented national body)
- ♦ Third World Development Forum / see Third World Science Technology and Development Forum
- ♦ Third World First / see People and Planet

♦ Third World Forum (TWF) 20149

Forum du Tiers-monde (FTM) – Foro del Tercer Mundo

African Office Dir BP 3501, Dakar, Senegal. T. +221338211144. Fax +221338211144.

History Apr 1973, Santiago (Chile). Inaugural meeting: 1975, Karachi (Pakistan). **Aims** As a network of social scientists and other scientists and intellectuals from the *developing countries*, contribute to the creation of a more just and equitable world, in which the basic needs of every human being are adequately satisfied in the context of a self-reliant, needs-oriented, endogenous *development*. **Structure** General Assembly; Council; Executive Committee (meets annually); Director. **Languages** Arabic, English, French, Spanish. **Finance** Sources: grants; members' dues. **Activities** Events/meetings; knowledge management/information dissemination; research and development. **Events** *Assemblée générale* Cochabamba (Bolivia) 2012, *Conférence monde Arabe – Asia* Delhi (India) 2011, *Symposium* Cairo (Egypt) 1988. **Publications** Papers; books. **Members** Individuals (around 3,000) in 85 countries. Membership countries not specified. **IGO Relations** *UNESCO (#20322)*; *University of the West Indies (UWI, #20705)*. **NGO Relations** Founding member of: *World Forum for Alternatives (WFA, #21513)*. Instrumental in setting up: *Communications for Development (CODEV, inactive)*. [2018.07.03/XC0048/v/**C**]

- ♦ Third World Foundation / see Third World Foundation for Social and Economic Studies (#20150)

♦ Third World Foundation for Social and Economic Studies (TWF) . . . 20150

Fondation du Tiers-monde

Contact 25 Upper Shirley Road, Croydon, CR0 5EB, UK. T. +442086554211. E-mail: ma-hmood.hasan80@yahoo.com.

History 1978, London (UK). Also referred to as *Third World Foundation*. UK Registered Charity: 275515. **Aims** Relieve poverty and sickness and advance education among inhabitants of Third World countries through the establishment of programmes of research and investigation, the results of which will be disseminated to the general public and to organizations; directly concerned with improving the conditions of life in the Third World. **Events** *International conference on the changing international realities and their likely impact on the future world order* Havana (Cuba) 1990. **Consultative Status** Consultative status granted from: *ECOSOC (#05331)* (Ros C); *UNCTAD (#20285)* (General Category); *UNIDO (#20336)*. **IGO Relations** *OPEC Fund for International Development (OFID, #17745)*. Associated with Department of Global Communications of the United Nations. [2019/XF1914/f/**F**]

- ♦ Third World Health Aid / see Viva Salud
- ♦ Third World House, Bielefeld / see World House, Bielefeld
- ♦ Third World Information Network (internationally oriented national body)
- ♦ Third World Institute, Montevideo (internationally oriented national body)
- ♦ Third World Journalists (inactive)
- ♦ Third World Medical Collaboration Solidarity (internationally oriented national body)
- ♦ Third World Missions Advance / see Third World Missions Association
- ♦ Third World Missions Association (internationally oriented national body)

♦ Third World Network (TWN) 20151

Dir Programmes 131 Jalan Macalister, 10400 Penang, Malaysia. T. +6042266159. Fax +6042264505. E-mail: twn@twnetwork.org.
URL: http://www.twn.my/

History 14 Nov 1984, Penang (Malaysia). **Aims** Bring about a greater articulation of the needs and rights of peoples in the South, a fair distribution of world resources, and forms of development which are ecologically sustainable and fulfill human needs. **Structure** International Secretariat, located in Penang (Malaysia). Offices (2): Kuala Lumpur (Malaysia); Geneva (Switzerland). Regional Secretariats (2): Montevideo (Uruguay); *Third World Network-Africa (TWN Africa)*. **Languages** English. **Activities** Publishing activities; events/meetings. **Events** *Civil society forum* Doha (Qatar) 2008, *People's health assembly* Dhaka (Bangladesh) 2000. **Publications** *South-North Development Monitor (SUNS)* (daily) – bulletin; *Third World Economics* (bi-weekly) in English, Spanish; *Third World Resurgence* (12 a year) in English, Spanish; *Africa Agenda*; *Third World Network Features*. **Members** Organizations and individuals involved in greater articulation of needs and rights of peoples in the Third World. Membership countries not specified. **Consultative Status** Consultative status granted from: *ECOSOC (#05331)* (Ros C); *UNCTAD (#20285)* (General Category); *World Intellectual Property Organization (WIPO, #21593)* (Permanent Observer Status); *UNEP (#20299)*. **IGO Relations** Accredited to: *Green Climate Fund (GCF, #10714)*; *United Nations Framework Convention on Climate Change – Secretariat (UNFCCC, #20564)*; Conference of the Parties of: *Convention on Biological Diversity (Biodiversity convention, 1992)*; *Intergovernmental Panel on Climate Change (IPCC, #11499)*; *UNEP (#20299)* Governing Council/Global Ministerial Environment Forum (GC/GMEF).
NGO Relations Member of: *Association for Plant Breeding for the Benefit of Society (APBREBES, #02861)*; *Climate Justice Now ! (CJN!, inactive)*; *Just Net Coalition (JNC, #16173)*; *People's Health Movement (PHM, #18305)*; *Social Watch (#19350)*; *World Social Forum (WSF, #21797)*. Collaborates with:
- *African Centre for Biodiversity (ACB)*;
- *Arab NGO Network for Development (ANND, #01016)*;
- *Bureau international des Médecins sans frontières (MSF International, #03366)*;
- *Center for Development Studies and Promotion (DESCO)*;
- *EarthRights International (ERI)*;
- European Group for Ecological Action;
- *Friends of the Earth International (FoEI, #10002)*;
- *HAI – Asia-Pacific (HAIAP, #10852)*;
- *Institute for Global Justice (IGJ)*;
- national organizations;
- *Our World is Not for Sale (OWINFS, #17917)*;
- *Oxfam Novib*;
- *Oxfam GB*;
- *Red por una América Latina Libre de Transgénicos (RALLT, #18733)*;
- *World Rainforest Movement (WRM, #21745)*. [2022/XF1170/**F**]

- ♦ Third World Network-Africa (internationally oriented national body)
- ♦ Third World Organization for Women in Science / see Organization for Women in Science for the Developing World (#17890)
- ♦ Third World Relief Fund (internationally oriented national body)
- ♦ Third World Science Technology and Development Forum (internationally oriented national body)
- ♦ Third World Scientific and Technological Development Forum / see Third World Science Technology and Development Forum
- ♦ Third World Sociological Association (inactive)
- ♦ Third World Solidarity Action (internationally oriented national body)

♦ Third World Studies Center (TWSC) 20152

Dir Lower Ground Floor, Palma Hall, PO Box 210, Manuel A Roxas St, Univ of the Philippines – Diliman, 1101 Quezon City, Philippines. Fax +63289205428. E-mail: twsc.updiliman@up.edu.ph.
URL: http://twsc.upd.edu.ph/

History 5 Feb 1977. Founded as a program affiliated to the Office of the Dean of the College of Arts and Sciences of the University of Philippines Diliman. Became a unit of the College of Arts and Sciences, 29 Mar 1979. Formally recognized as a Center in the College of Social Sciences and Philosophy, University of the Philippines Diliman by the Board of Regents, University of the Philippines, 30 Mar 2000. **Aims** As a *social science* research center, develop critical, alternative paradigms to promote progressive scholarship and action for change by: undertaking pioneering research on issues of national and international concern; creating spaces for discussion and dialogue; publishing original, empirically-grounded, and innovative studies; building a community of activist-scholars and public intellectuals. **Structure** Director; Deputy Director; University Researcher; University Research Associates; administrative staff. **Languages** English, Filipino. **Staff** 9.00 FTE, paid. **Finance** Sources: donations; grants. Funding from the University of the Philippines. **Activities** Events/meetings; networking/liaising; publishing activities; research/documentation. **Publications** *Kasarinlan: Philippine Journal of Third World Studies* (2 a year). Books; mimeographs. **Members** Not a membership organization. **IGO Relations** *UNDP (#20292)*; *United Nations Economic and Social Commission for Asia and the Pacific (ESCAP, #20557)*; *United Nations Research Institute for Social Development (UNRISD, #20623)*; *United Nations University (UNU, #20642)*. **NGO Relations** Links with non-governmental organizations including: *Asian Regional Exchange for New Alternatives (ARENA, #01684)*; *Focus on the Global South (Focus, #09807)*; *Friedrich Naumann Foundation for Freedom*; *Oxfam Novib*; *Southeast Asian Studies Regional Exchange Program Foundation (SEASREP Foundation, #19784)*. [2020.05.06/XE3966/**E**]

- ♦ Third World Tourism Ecumenical European Network / see Third World Tourism European Ecumenical Network (#20153)

♦ Third World Tourism European Ecumenical Network (TEN) 20153

Contact address not obtained. T. +4922881012302. Fax +492288101150. E-mail: tourism-watch@eed.de.
URL: http://www.ten-tourism.org/

History 1984. Also known as *Third World Tourism Ecumenical European Network*. **Aims** Link European groups working on Third World tourism issues. **Activities** Exchanges information on Third World tourism developments; coordinates joint projects; organizes annual meeting for members. **Events** *Annual meeting* UK 2010, *Annual Meeting* Italy 2004, *Annual meeting* Italy 1995, *Annual Meeeting* Bernried (Germany) 1994.
Members Organizations (12) in 8 countries:
Austria, Belgium, France, Germany, Italy, Netherlands, Switzerland, UK.
Included in the above, 4 organizations listed in this Yearbook:
RETOUR Foundation (no recent information); *Studienkreis für Tourismus und Entwicklung (StfTE)*; *Tourism Watch*; *Working Group on Tourism and Development (akte)*.
NGO Relations Located at: Tourism Watch. [2010/XF0494/y/**F**]

- ♦ THIRUVANANTHAPURAM / see Peace and Disarmament Society of Kerala
- ♦ ThIL – Thesaurus Linguae Latinae (internationally oriented national body)

♦ Thomas More Institute 20154

Institut Thomas More (TMI)
CEO 8 rue Monsigny, 75002 Paris, France. T. +33149490330. Fax +33149490333.
Contact Av Walkiers 45, 1160 Brussels, Belgium. T. +3223742313. E-mail: info@institut-thomas-more.org.
URL: http://www.institut-thomas-more.org/

History 2004, as an independent European think tank. **Aims** Influence *European decision-making* bodies, at both community and national levels. **Structure** Board of Trustees; Advisory Board. **Languages** English, French. **Staff** 3.00 FTE, paid. 16 Fellows, paid and voluntary. **Finance** Donations; contracts. Annual budget: euro 350,000. **Activities** Advocacy/lobbying/activism; monitoring/evaluation; politics/policy/regulatory; research and development. **Events** *Meeting on Magreb and the UE* Brussels (Belgium) 2010. **Publications** *TMI Newsletter* (25 a year). *L'utopie du tout renoubelable* (2017) by Jean-Pierre Schaeken Willemaers; *L'enfant Oublié – Propositions pour la famille de demain* (2016). News notes; reports.
Members Individuals mainly in 2 countries:
Belgium, France. [2017.11.17/XJ2467/j/**E**]

- ♦ Thomson Foundation (internationally oriented national body)
- ♦ Thomson Media Foundation / see Thomson Foundation
- ♦ Thomson Reuters Foundation (internationally oriented national body)
- ♦ The THOR Network / see Trauma Hemostasis & Oxygenation Research (#20229)
- ♦ THOR / see Trauma Hemostasis & Oxygenation Research (#20229)
- ♦ **THOR** Trauma Hemostasis & Oxygenation Research (#20229)

♦ Thought For Food (TFF) 20155

Contact address not obtained. E-mail: info@thoughtforfood.org.
URL: https://thoughtforfood.org/

History 2011. **Aims** Empower the next generation of leaders to develop bold, out-of-the-box *innovations* that help to build new solutions transforming world's food system. **Languages** English. **Finance** Sources: sponsorship. **Activities** Advocacy/lobbying/activism; events/meetings. **Events** *Global Summit* New York, NY (USA) 2022, *Global Summit* Zurich (Switzerland) 2016, *Global Summit* Lisbon (Portugal) 2015, *Global Summit* Berlin (Germany) 2013. **Publications** *TFF Newsletter* (12 a year). **Members** Students, ambassadors and mentors (over 1000) from about 100 countries worldwide. Membership countries not specified. [2022/XJ8954/**F**]

- ♦ The Thousand / see International Society for Philosophical Enquiry (#15358)
- ♦ Thredbo – International Conference Series on Competition and Ownership in Land Passenger Transport (meeting series)
- ♦ Three Kings Action (internationally oriented national body)
- ♦ Threshold Foundation / see Stiftung Die Schwelle
- ♦ Threshold Test Ban Treaty, 1974 (treaty)
- ♦ Thrive Networks (internationally oriented national body)

♦ Thrombosis and Hemostasis Societies of North America (THSNA) .. 20156

Contact 2111 Chestnut Avenue Ste 145, Glenview IL 60025, USA. T. +18479782001. E-mail: info@thsna.org.
URL: https://www.thsna.org/

History 2013. **Aims** Advance the prevention, early diagnosis, management, and cure of bleeding and clotting disorders. **Structure** Board of Directors. **Activities** Advocacy/lobbying/activism; awards/prizes/competitions; events/meetings; training/education. **Events** *Thrombosis & Hemostasis Summit of North America* Chicago, IL (USA) 2022, *Thrombosis & Hemostasis Summit of North America* 2020, *Thrombosis & Hemostasis Summit of North America* Chicago, IL (USA) 2016.
Members Organizations in 3 countries:
Canada, Mexico, USA. [2021/AA1806/c/**D**]

- ♦ THS / see International Federation of Hydrographic Societies (#13453)
- ♦ **THSNA** Thrombosis and Hemostasis Societies of North America (#20156)
- ♦ T and H – Terre et Humanisme (internationally oriented national body)
- ♦ Thunderbird / see Thunderbird – The Garvin School of International Management
- ♦ Thunderbird – The American Graduate School of International Management / see Thunderbird – The Garvin School of International Management
- ♦ Thunderbird – The Garvin School of International Management (internationally oriented national body)
- ♦ Thunderbird Graduate School of International Management / see Thunderbird – The Garvin School of International Management

♦ Thyroid Cancer Alliance (TCA) 20157

Contact Burgemeester Bosstraat 46, 3043 GD Rotterdam, Netherlands. E-mail: info@thyroidcanceralliance.org.
URL: https://thyroidcanceralliance.org/

Aims Work together towards providing support, information and encouragement to those affected by thyroid cancer throughout the world. **Structure** Board; Medical Advisory Panel.
Members Organizations in 9 countries:
Argentina, Bulgaria, Colombia, France, Mexico, Netherlands, Peru, Spain, UK.
NGO Relations Member of (4): *European Cancer Organisation (ECO, #06432)* (Patient Advisory Committee); *European Cancer Patient Coalition (ECPC, #06433)*; *EURORDIS – Rare Diseases Europe (#09175)*; *Workgroup of European Cancer Patient Advocacy Networks (WECAN, #21054)*. [2016/AA0349/**C**]

♦ Thyroid Federation International (TFI) 20158

Admin Coordinator PO Box 471, Bath ON K0H 1G0, Canada. E-mail: tfi@thyroid-fed.org.
URL: http://www.thyroid-fed.org/

History Sep 1995, Toronto ON (Canada). Registered in accordance with Swedish law. **Aims** Work for the benefit of those affected by thyroid *disorders* throughout the world. **Structure** Annual General Meeting; Board of Directors; Executive Committee. **Languages** English. **Staff** 0.50 FTE, paid. **Finance** Corporate donations. Annual budget: 10,000 EUR. **Activities** Events/meetings. **Events** *Annual Conference* Leiden (Netherlands) 2013, *Annual Conference* Pisa (Italy) 2012, *Annual Conference* Krakow (Poland) 2011, *Annual Conference* Paris (France) 2010, *Annual Conference* Lisbon (Portugal) 2009. **Publications** *ThyroWorld*.
Members Organizations in 24 countries:
Australia, Belgium, Brazil, Bulgaria, Canada, Croatia, Denmark, Finland, France, Georgia, Germany, India, Italy, Japan, Nepal, Netherlands, Nigeria, Norway, Philippines, Portugal, Russia, Spain, Sweden, USA.
NGO Relations Associate member of: *EURORDIS – Rare Diseases Europe (#09175)*. Cooperates with: American Thyroid Association; *Asia and Oceania Thyroid Association (AOTA, #01810)*; *European Thyroid Association (ETA, #08913)*; *Latin American Thyroid Society (LATS, #16390)*. [2018/XE3698/**C**]

- ♦ TIA / see US Travel Association
- ♦ **TIACA** The International Air Cargo Association (#11608)
- ♦ **TIAFT** International Association of Forensic Toxicologists (#11902)
- ♦ TIA / see The International Alliance for Women (#11640)
- ♦ **TIAMSA** The International Art Market Studies Association (#11674)
- ♦ **TIAS** Integrated Assessment Society, The (#11367)
- ♦ TIA – Telecommunications Industry Association (internationally oriented national body)
- ♦ TIA – Tire Industry Association (internationally oriented national body)
- ♦ TIA – Transportation Intermediaries Association (internationally oriented national body)
- ♦ **TIAW** The International Alliance for Women (#11640)

♦ Tibet Justice Center 20159

Treas 440 Grand Avenue, Suite 425, Oakland CA 94610, USA. E-mail: tjc@tibetjustice.org.
URL: http://www.tibetjustice.org/

History 1989. Founded as an independent body at the request of the Tibetan Government-in-Exile, which recognized the importance of having an international legal organization devoted exclusively to Tibetan issues. Former names and other names: *International Committee of Lawyers for Tibet (ICLT)* – former. **Aims** As an independent volunteer committee of lawyers and other experts: advocate human rights and self-determination for the Tibetan people; promote human rights, environmental governance, refugee protection and self-governance; promote *self-determination* through legal research, analysis and education; advocate *human rights*, *environmental* governance and *peaceful resolution* of the situation in Tibet. **Structure** Board of Directors. **Staff** 1.00 FTE, paid. **Finance** Sources: donations; fundraising; grants; private foundations. **Activities** Advocacy/lobbying/activism; awareness raising; capacity building; events/meetings; research/documentation; training/education. **Publications** UN human rights treaty bodies submissions; reports on situation for Tibetans in Nepal and India; reports on Tibet's environment and development; reports on Tibet's history, sovereignty and right to self-determination. **NGO Relations** Accredited by (9): *Amnesty International (AI, #00801)*; *International Campaign for Tibet (ICT, #12429)*; *International Tibet Network (#15690)*; *International Union for Conservation of Nature and Natural Resources (IUCN, #15766)*; *Students for a Free Tibet International (SFT International, #20018)*; Tibet Advocacy Coalition; Tibetan Legal Association; Tibet Society; *Unrepresented Nations and Peoples Organization (UNPO, #20714)*. [2023.02.28/XE3188/v/**E**]

- ♦ **TICAD** Tokyo International Conference on African Development (#20172)
- ♦ TICA – The International Cat Association (internationally oriented national body)
- ♦ TICA – Thailand International Development Cooperation Agency (internationally oriented national body)
- ♦ **TICCIH** International Committee for the Conservation of the Industrial Heritage (#12754)

♦ TIC Council 20160

Gen Dir Rue du Commerce 20-22, 1000 Brussels, Belgium. T. +322802137. E-mail: secretariat@tic-council.org.
URL: http://www.tic-council.org/

History Dec 2018. Founded on merger of *International Federation of Inspection Agencies (IFIA, inactive)* and *CEOC International – International Confederation of Inspection and Certification Organisations (inactive)*. Registration: Banque-Carrefour des Entreprises, No/ID: 0724.881.295, Start date: 12 Apr 2019, Belgium. **Aims** Be the voice of the global independent testing, inspection and certification industry; engage governments and key stakeholders to advocate for effective solutions that protect the public, support innovation and facilitate trade; be a valuable resource to policy-makers around the world on how the use of TIC services brings value to society; support development of international standards and regulations that protect consumers without hindering innovation or adding unnecessary burden on industry. **Structure** General Assembly; Global Board; Senior Advisory Committee. Committees; Working Groups. **Languages** English. **Finance** Members' dues. **Activities** Events/meetings; certification/accreditation. **Events** *General Assembly* Brussels (Belgium) 2019, *Asia Meeting* Singapore (Singapore) 2019. **Publications** Position papers; bulletins; reports; codes and guidelines.
Members Full (88); Associate (8); Observer (3). Membership countries not specified. Associate members include 1 organization listed in this Yearbook:
Associate members include 1 organization listed in this Yearbook:
European Federation of National Associations of Measurement, Testing and Analytical Laboratories (EUROLAB, #07168).
NGO Relations Member of: *International Accreditation Forum (IAF, #11584)*. [2021/XM8482/**D**]

- ♦ TICER – Temporary International Council for Educational Reconstruction (inactive)
- ♦ TICH – Tropical Institute of Community Health and Development in Africa (internationally oriented national body)

♦ Tics and Tourette Across the Globe (TTAG) 20161

Contact address not obtained. E-mail: ttagcontact@gmail.com.
URL: https://ticsandtourette.org

History 2022, Germany. Proposed 2020. **Aims** Promote TS awareness and information on a global level, promoting evidence-based treatment and supporting member efforts throughout the world, combating ignorance, stigma and intolerance with regard to TS; promote equality, participation, and opportunities for people with TS through collaboration between advocates, clinicians, and scientists around the world, to benefit those affected by Tourette Syndrome or tic disorders. **Structure** Board. **Languages** English, French, German, Portuguese, Spanish. **Staff** 5.00 FTE, voluntary. **Activities** Advocacy/lobbying/activism; guidance/assistance/consulting; knowledge management/information dissemination; networking/liaising. Active in all member countries. **Members** Groups worldwide. Membership countries not specified. **NGO Relations** Member of (1): *European Federation of Neurological Associations (EFNA, #07177)* (provisional). [2022.02.19/AA2339/**C**]

♦ **T.I.C.** Tantalum-Niobium International Study Center (#20095)
♦ Tides (internationally oriented national body)
♦ Tides Foundation / see Tides
♦ Tidjaniya (religious order)
♦ TIDSE – Technologies for Interactive Digital Storytelling (meeting series)
♦ TIEC – Texas International Education Consortium (internationally oriented national body)
♦ **TIEMS** International Emergency Management Society (#13261)
♦ van Tienhoven Foundation / see Van Tienhoven Foundation for International Nature Protection
♦ van Tienhoven Stichting / see Van Tienhoven Foundation for International Nature Protection
♦ Tierärztlicher-Weltverein der Kleintier-Spezialisten (#21795)
♦ Tierra del Futuro (internationally oriented national body)
♦ **TIER** Red Internacional de Escritores por la Tierra (#18698)
♦ Tiers-Ordre Capucin de Notre-Dame des Douleurs (religious order)
♦ Tiers-Ordre Carmélitain (religious order)
♦ Tiers-Ordre Conventuel Dominicain (religious order)
♦ Tiers ordre franciscain (religious order)
♦ Tiers-Ordre Régulier de Saint François (religious order)
♦ Tiers Ordre Seculier Dominicain (religious order)
♦ Tiers-Ordre Seculier de Marie (religious order)
♦ Tiers-Ordre Seculier des Minimes (religious order)
♦ Tiers-Ordre Seculier de Notre-Dame de la Miséricorde (religious order)
♦ Tiers-Ordre Séculier de la Très-Sainte-Trinité (religious order)
♦ **TIES** The International Ecotourism Society (#13225)
♦ **TIES** International Environmetrics Society (#13284)
♦ Tieteellisen Informaation Pohjoismainen Yhteistyöelin (inactive)
♦ Tietoa Meistä (#17348)
♦ **TIE** Toy Industries of Europe (#20179)
♦ TIE – Transnationals Information Exchange (internationally oriented national body)
♦ TIFO – TerraGraphics International Foundation (internationally oriented national body)
♦ **TIF** Tilapia International Foundation (#20162)
♦ TIG – Taking IT Global (internationally oriented national body)
♦ Tihookeanskaja Naucnaja Associacija / see Pacific Science Association (#18003)
♦ **TII** European Association for the Transfer of Technologies, Innovation and Industrial Information (#06259)
♦ Tijani Sufi tariqa (religious order)
♦ **Tikal Protocol** Association of Electoral Organizations of Central America and the Caribbean (#02484)

♦ Tilapia International Foundation (TIF) 20162

Main Office PO Box 2375, 3500 GJ Utrecht, Netherlands. T. +31302948700. Fax +31302936810. E-mail: info@tilapiastichting.nl.
URL: http://www.tilapiastichting.nl/

History 1952, by Mgr Jan D F Heijne (1914-2000). Registered in accordance with Netherlands law. **Aims** Fight against *hunger* by spreading the Foundation's activities throughout the world. **Structure** Board, consisting of President, Vice-President, Secretary/Treasurer and 3 members; Recommendation Committee; Advisors. **Activities** Projects in various countries of Africa, Asia and Latin America. Informs the general public by participating in conferences, projections of films, producing brochures for the promotion of the 'Tilapia' idea. **Members** Active in the majority of countries where there is shortage of animal protein. Currently present in 24 countries:
Benin, Brazil, Cameroon, Central African Rep, Chad, Congo DR, Egypt, Ethiopia, Ghana, Haiti, Honduras, India, Indonesia, Kenya, Libya, Malawi, Mali, Nicaragua, Nigeria, Sri Lanka, Tanzania UR, Togo, Uganda, Venezuela.
Advisors, cooperators and contributors in 7 countries:
Belgium, France, Germany, Italy, Netherlands, Taiwan, USA.
NGO Relations *Tilapia Food Aid Organization (TFAO, inactive).* [2015/XF2044/f/**F**]

♦ Tilburg Group / see European Group on Tort Law (#07437)

♦ Tiles and Bricks Europe (TBE) 20163

SG Rue Belliard 12, 1040 Brussels, Belgium. T. +3228083880. Fax +3225115174.
URL: http://www.tiles-bricks.eu/

History 16 May 1952, Paris (France). Former names and other names: *European Federation of Tile and Brick Manufacturers* – former (1952); *European Association of Roofing Tile and Brick Manufacturers (TBE)* – full title; *Fédération européenne des fabricants de tuiles et de briques* – full title; *Verband der Europäischen Dachziegel- und Mauerziegelfabrikanten* – full title; *Federatie van Baksteen en Dakpannen Fabrikanten* – full title. Registration: Start date: 2008, Belgium. **Aims** Ensure the basis of the brick and roofing tile industry; maintain its ability to compete by representing and implementing joint interests at a European level, mainly regarding standardization (CEN and ISO), and by combating additional levies and taxation in the context of environmental protection and social legislation. **Structure** General Assembly (annual, at conference); Executive Committee; Technical Product Groups (4); Office in Brussels (Belgium). **Languages** English. **Staff** 1.00 FTE, paid. **Finance** Members' dues. Annual budget: euro 220,000. **Activities** Events/meetings; advocacy/lobbying/activism. **Events** *Congress* 2021, *Congress* 2020, *Congress* Copenhagen (Denmark) 2019, *Congress* Lucerne (Switzerland) 2016, *Congress* Leuven (Belgium) 2015.
Members National organizations in 22 countries and territories:
Austria, Belgium, Croatia, Cyprus, Czechia, Denmark, Estonia, Finland, France, Germany, Greece, Hungary, Italy, Netherlands, Norway, Poland, Portugal, Serbia, Spain, Sweden, Switzerland, UK.
IGO Relations Recognized by: *European Commission (EC, #06633)*; *European Parliament (EP, #08146).*
NGO Relations Member of: *Industry4Europe (#11181).* Associate member of: *European Ceramic Industry Association (CERAME-UNIE, #06506).* In liaison with technical committees of: *International Organization for Standardization (ISO, #14473).* [2018.06.01/XD0759/**D**]

♦ Timber Committee / see UNECE Committee on Forests and the Forest Industry (#20294)

♦ Timber Construction Europe 20164

Europäische Vereinigung des Holzbaus (EVH)
Secretariat Kronenstr 55-58, 10117 Berlin, Germany. T. +493020314533. Fax +493020314566. E-mail: info@timber-construction.eu.
URL: http://www.timber-construction.eu/

History Previously also referred to as *European Federation of Timber Construction (EFCT) – Fédération européenne de la construction en bois.* **Aims** Represent political interests in timber construction relevant areas; work towards a practical design of the European standard; coordinate and cooperate in practice-relevant research and education projects; stimulate cross-border information and experience exchange. **Structure** General Assembly; Praesidium; General Secretariat. **Events** *Congress* Leipzig (Germany) 1999.
Members Full in 5 countries:
Austria, France, Germany, Luxembourg, Switzerland.
NGO Relations Member of: *Small Business Standards (SBS, #19311)*; *SMEunited (#19327).* [2018/XD7452/**D**]

♦ TIME Association 20165

SG c/o CentraleSupélec, Bât Eiffel, Dir Relations Internationales, 8-10 rue Joliot-Curie, 91190 Gif-sur-Yvette, France.
URL: http://timeassociation.org/

History 1989, Paris (France). Founded by 16 members. Former names and other names: *Top Industrial Managers for Engineering* – former; *Top International Managers in Engineering* – full title. Registration: Start date: 15 May 1997, France. **Aims** Facilitate exchange of *students* for Double Master Degrees in *engineering.* **Structure** General Assembly (annual); Advisory Committee; Management Committee. **Staff** 1.00 FTE, paid. **Finance** Sources: members' dues. **Activities** Training/education. **Events** *Annual General Assembly* Wroclaw (Poland) 2023, *Annual General Assembly* Brisbane, QLD (Australia) 2022, *Annual General Assembly* 2021, *Annual General Assembly* 2020, *Annual General Assembly* Paris (France) 2019.
Members Institutions in 25 countries:
Argentina, Austria, Belgium, Brazil, Canada, Czechia, Denmark, Finland, France, Germany, Greece, Hungary, Italy, Japan, Latvia, Norway, Poland, Portugal, Romania, Russia, Spain, Sweden, Switzerland, Türkiye, UK. [2020.10.13/XM2978/**F**]

♦ **Time Perspective Network** International Research Network on Time Perspective (#14737)
♦ Time Series Analysis and Forecasting Society (inactive)
♦ The Timeshare Council / see Resort Development Organisation (#18913)
♦ Timor Aid (internationally oriented national body)
♦ TIMS / see Institute for Operations Research and the Management Sciences (#11286)
♦ **TIMS** The International Molinological Society (#14177)
♦ TIMSS and PIRLS International Study Center (internationally oriented national body)
♦ **TINC** The International NanoScience Community (#14209)
♦ Tinerii Europeni Federalisti (#21984)
♦ Tinker Foundation (internationally oriented national body)
♦ Tinker Institute on International Law and Organizations (internationally oriented national body)

♦ Tinnitus Research Initiative (TRI) 20166

Chair Bezirksklinikum Regensburg, Universitätsstr 84, 93053 Regensburg, Germany. T. +499419412096. E-mail: info@tinnitusresearch.org.
URL: https://tinnitusresearch.net/

History Jan 2006. Former names and other names: *Tinnitus Research Initiative Foundation* – legal name; *Stiftung Tinnitus Research Initiative* – legal name. Registration: Germany, Regensburg. **Aims** Develop effective treatments for all types of tinnitus so that relief can be obtained by everyone who suffers from it; improve quality of life for *patients* who suffer from tinnitus and tinnitus-related disorders. **Structure** Board of Directors; Executive Committee; Scientific Committee; Research Coordinator. **Activities** Events/meetings; research/documentation. **Events** *Conference* Dublin (Ireland) 2023, *Conference* Vancouver, BC (Canada) 2020, *Conference* Taipei (Taiwan) 2019, *Conference* Auckland (New Zealand) 2014. [2023/XM5166/**F**]

♦ Tinnitus Research Initiative Foundation / see Tinnitus Research Initiative (#20166)
♦ Tin Research Institute / see International Tin Association (#15692)
♦ Tin, Sheet Iron, and Cornice Workers' International Association / see International Association of Sheet Metal, Air, Rail and Transportation Workers
♦ TIOF – The International Osprey Foundation (internationally oriented national body)
♦ **TIPA** Technical Image Press Association (#20118)
♦ TIPH – Temporary International Presence in Hebron (inactive)
♦ TIPS Network / see Technological Trade and Information Promotion System (#20119)
♦ TIPS / see Technological Trade and Information Promotion System (#20119)
♦ **TIPS** Technological Trade and Information Promotion System (#20119)
♦ TIR Convention – Customs Convention on the International Transport of Goods under Cover of TIR Carnets, 1959 (1959 treaty)
♦ TIR convention – Customs Convention on the International Transport of Goods under Cover of TIR Carnets, 1975 (1975 treaty)
♦ Tire Industry Association (internationally oriented national body)
♦ **TIRF** The International Research Foundation for English Language Education (#14725)
♦ TIRI – The governance – Access – Learning Network / see Integrity Action
♦ TIRI – Making Integrity Work / see Integrity Action
♦ TIRN – Turtle Island Restoration Network (internationally oriented national body)
♦ TIS – International Conference on Tethers in Space (meeting series)
♦ TISPOL – European Traffic Police Organisation (inactive)
♦ Tissue Banks International / see KeraLink International

♦ Tissue Engineering and Regenerative Medicine International Society (TERMIS) 20167

Administrator 2563 Shadow Mountain Dr, San Ramon CA 94583, USA.
URL: http://www.termis.org/

History 2005. *European Tissue Engineering Society (ETES, inactive)* and *Tissue Engineering Society International (TESI, inactive)* became European chapter. **Aims** Advance science and technology of tissue engineering and regenerative medicine. **Structure** Board. Executive Committee, comprising President, President-Elect, Immediate Past President, Continental Chairmen, Secretary and Treasurer. Nominating Committee; Meeting Committee. Chapters (3): Asia-Pacific; Europe; North America. **Languages** English. **Staff** 1.00 FTE, paid. **Finance** Sources: members' dues. **Events** *Americas Conference* Boston, MA (USA) 2023, *European Chapter Meeting* Manchester (UK) 2023, *Asia-Pacific Conference TERMIS-AP* Shatin (Hong Kong) 2023, *Asia-Pacific Conference TERMIS-AP* Jeju (Korea Rep) 2022, *Americas Conference* Toronto, ON (Canada) 2022. **Publications** *Tissue Engineering* – official journal. **NGO Relations** Memorandum of Understanding with (1): *International Society for Biofabrication (ISBF, #14962).* European chapter has links with: *European Society for Biomaterials (ESB, #08530).* [2021/XM2316/**C**]

♦ Titanium Dioxide Manufacturers' Association (TDMA) 20168

Manager CEFIC, Rue Belliard 40, Box 15, 1040 Brussels, Belgium. T. +3224369300. E-mail: bpi@cefic.be – tdma@cefic.be.
URL: http://www.tdma.info/

History Founded 1974, as a sector group of *Conseil européen de l'industrie chimique (CEFIC, #04687).* **Aims** Ensure that robust scientific information on product *safety* is made available to members, customers and authorities; demonstrate that TiO2, in its intended uses, is safe to use in all applications. **Structure** General Committee, Committees (3); Working Parties.
Members Titanium dioxide producers (10) in 12 countries:
Belgium, Czechia, Finland, France, Germany, Italy, Netherlands, Norway, Poland, Slovenia, Spain, UK. [2020/XK1195/**E**]

♦ **TI** The Textile Institute (#20136)
♦ **TI** Toastmasters International (#20169)
♦ TI – Toothfriendly International (internationally oriented national body)
♦ **TI** Transfrigoroute International (#20213)
♦ **TI** Transparency International (#20223)
♦ Tiyatien Health / see Last Mile Health
♦ TIYE International – International Platform for Black, Migrant and Refugee Women's Organizations (internationally oriented national body)
♦ **TIY** European Research Network on Transitions in Youth (#08377)
♦ Tjenesten for EU's Optraeden Udadtil (#07018)
♦ **TJN-A** Tax Justice Network-Africa (#20101)
♦ **TJN** Tax Justice Network (#20100)
♦ TJSGA – Jus Semper Global Alliance (internationally oriented national body)
♦ **TJUS** Tarptautine Jaunuju Ukininku Sajunga (#15829)
♦ TLI-AP – Logistics Institute – Asia Pacific (internationally oriented national body)
♦ **TLMI** Leprosy Mission International (#16446)
♦ TLM / see Leprosy Mission International (#16446)
♦ TL / see Terralingua – Unity in Biocultural Diversity (#20129)
♦ TLT – International Workshop on Treebanks and Linguistic Theory (meeting series)
♦ TLT – Trademark Law Treaty (1994 treaty)
♦ TLWNSI / see Jus Semper Global Alliance
♦ **TMA Europe** Turnaround Management Association – Europe (#20262)
♦ TMA Global – Turnaround Management Association – Global (internationally oriented national body)
♦ T M C Asser Institute / see TMC Asser Institute – Centre for International and European Law
♦ TMC Asser Institute – Centre for International and European Law (internationally oriented national body)
♦ T M C Asser Instituut / see TMC Asser Institute – Centre for International and European Law
♦ **TMEA** TradeMark East Africa (#20183)
♦ **TM Forum** TeleManagement Forum (#20123)
♦ **TMG** The Montreal Group (#16853)
♦ **TMI** Institut Thomas More (#20154)
♦ TMI – Mountain Institute, The (internationally oriented national body)

- ♦ **TMS** Micropalaeontology Society, The (#16749)
- ♦ TMS – Minerals, Metals and Materials Society (internationally oriented national body)
- ♦ TNC – The Nature Conservancy (internationally oriented national body)
- ♦ TNFIS – The Nordic Frugal Innovation Society (unconfirmed)
- ♦ TNF – The Network Forum (unconfirmed)
- ♦ **TNI** Transnational Institute (#20219)
- ♦ **TNS** The Natural Step (#16958)
- ♦ TO'AI World Federation (unconfirmed)

♦ Toastmasters International (TI) 20169

Headquarters 9127 S Jamaica St, Ste 400, Englewood CO 80112, USA. T. +17204395050. Fax +13037997753. E-mail: membership@toastmasters.org – pr@toastmasters.org.
URL: http://www.toastmasters.org/

History Oct 1924, Santa Ana, CA (USA). **Aims** Empower individuals to become more effective communicators and leaders through public speaking and leadership skills teaching. **Structure** Board of Directors; Executive Committee; Strategic Planning Committee; Finance Committee. Worldwide network of clubs. **Activities** Events/meetings. **Events** *Annual International Convention* Nashville, TN (USA) 2022, *Annual International Convention* 2021, *Annual International Convention* Mission Viejo, CA (USA) 2020, *District Council Meeting* Singapore (Singapore) 2020, *Executive Council Meeting* Singapore (Singapore) 2020. **Publications** *Toastmaster* (12 a year) – Magazine for communicator and leaders. **Members** About 345,000 members in over 15,900 clubs in 142 countries. Membership countries not specified. [2020/XN0594/**C**]

- ♦ TOBS – Tourism Organization of the Baltic States (no recent information)
- ♦ Töchter der Göttlichen Liebe (religious order)
- ♦ Toda Institute / see Toda Institute for Global Peace and Policy Research
- ♦ Toda Institute for Global Peace and Policy Research (internationally oriented national body)
- ♦ TOF – The Ocean Foundation (internationally oriented national body)
- ♦ TOF – Tertius Ordo Sancti Francisci (religious order)
- ♦ TOF – Tiers ordre franciscain (religious order)
- ♦ Together, Achieving, Believing, Sustaining / see TABS International
- ♦ Together Against the Death Penalty / see ECPM
- ♦ Together for Girls (unconfirmed)

♦ Together for Sustainability (TfS) 20170

Communications Manager Rue Belliard 40, bus 20, 1040 Brussels, Belgium. T. +3224369620. E-mail: info@tfs-initiative.com.
URL: https://tfs-initiative.com/

History 2011. Registration: Banque-Carrefour des Entreprises, No/ID: 0589.936.479, Start date: 13 Jan 2015, Belgium. **Aims** Drive and foster resilience, efficiency, and sustainability of global supply chains in the chemical industry. **Structure** General Assembly; Steering Committee. **Activities** Capacity building; guidance/assistance/consulting; standards/guidelines. **Events** *TfS 10th Anniversary celebration Meeting* Brussels (Belgium) 2021, *TogetherForSustainability Meeting* Antwerp (Belgium) 2020. **Members** Chemical companies (33). Membership countries not specified. [2022.02.09/AA1418/**F**]

- ♦ Together Women Rise (internationally oriented national body)
- ♦ Toho Gakkai (internationally oriented national body)

♦ Toilet Board Coalition (TBC) 20171

Exec Dir/CEO Rue Fendt 1, 1201 Geneva, Switzerland. E-mail: secretariat@toiletboard.org.
URL: http://www.toiletboard.org/

History 2015, Geneva (Switzerland). **Aims** Catalyze a robust *business* sector delivering universal access to sanitation; accelerate business solutions that deliver *sanitation* at scale by innovating at the social, economic and organizational levels. **Structure** Steering Committee; Board of Directors; Partnership Council; Secretariat. **Languages** English, French, Portuguese, Spanish. **Staff** 12.00 FTE, paid. **Activities** Advocacy/lobbying/activism; awareness raising; networking/liaising; projects/programmes; standards/guidelines. **NGO Relations** Member of (1): *World Alliance for Efficient Solutions*. Partner of (8): *Aspen Network of Development Entrepreneurs (ANDE, #02310)*; *Global Citizen (#10281)*; *Global Handwashing Partnership (GHP, #10396)*; *GSM Association (GSMA, #10813)*; *International Centre for Water Management Services (cewas)*; *Sustainable Sanitation Alliance (SuSanA, #20066)*; *Waterforeveryone*; *Waterpreneurs (#20833)*. [2022.02.02/XM6747/**C**]

- ♦ Toilets for All (unconfirmed)
- ♦ Tokyo Club Foundation for Global Studies (internationally oriented national body)
- ♦ Tokyo convention – Convention on Offences and Certain other Acts Committed on Board Aircraft (1963 treaty)

♦ Tokyo International Conference on African Development (TICAD) .. 20172

Coordinator c/o TICAD/UNDP Africa Bureau, One United Nations Plaza DC1-24, New York NY 10017, USA. T. +12129065926.
URL: http://www.mofa.go.jp/region/africa/ticad/

History 1993, as a joint effort of the Government of Japan and *United Nations (UN, #20515)* and its then *United Nations Office of the Special Coordinator for Africa and the Least Developed Countries (OSCAL, inactive)*. *International Bank for Reconstruction and Development (IBRD, #12317)* joined 2000. UN entities currently responsible: *UNDP (#20292)* and Office of the Secretary General's Special Adviser on Africa (OSSA). **Aims** Promote high-level policy dialogue between African leaders and development partners; mobilize support for African-owned development initiatives. **Events** *Conference* Tunisia 2022, *Conference* Yokohama (Japan) 2019, *Meeting on the African Clean Cities Platform* Tokyo (Japan) 2018, *Ministerial Meeting* Tokyo (Japan) 2018, *Conference* Nairobi (Kenya) 2016. **IGO Relations** Partners: *African Union (AU, #00488)*; *UNIDO (#20336)*; *UNCTAD (#20285)*; *United Nations Volunteers (UNV, #20650)*; *Africa Rice Center (AfricaRice, #00518)*. [2013/XJ1763/**E***]

- ♦ **Tokyo MOU** Memorandum of Understanding on Port State Control in the Asia-Pacific Region (#16709)
- ♦ Toledo International Centre for Peace (internationally oriented national body)
- ♦ Tolstoy Foundation (internationally oriented national body)
- ♦ **TomatoEurope** European Organisation of Tomato Industries (#08104)
- ♦ Tomorrow People Organization (internationally oriented national body)
- ♦ TOM – Tertius Ordo Minimorum (religious order)
- ♦ TONNAGE – International Convention on Tonnage Measurement of Ships (1969 treaty)
- ♦ TON – Techno-Ocean Network (internationally oriented national body)
- ♦ Tony Elumelu Foundation (unconfirmed)
- ♦ Tools for Self Reliance (internationally oriented national body)
- ♦ Toonan Ajia Gakkai (internationally oriented national body)
- ♦ Toonan Ajia Shigakkai / see Japan Society for Southeast Asian Studies

♦ Toothfriendly Foundation 20173

Contact Bundesstrasse 29, 4054 Basel BS, Switzerland. T. +41612737707. Fax +41612737703. E-mail: contact@toothfriendly.ch.
URL: http://www.toothfriendly-foundation.org/

History 2004. **Aims** Improve oral *health* in less developed countries, mainly focusing on *caries* prevention among underprivileged children. **Structure** Board of 3. **Languages** English, German. **Staff** 1.00 FTE, paid; 25.00 FTE, voluntary. **Finance** Members' dues of *Toothfriendly International (TI)*. Budget (annual): about euro 22,000. **NGO Relations** Partner of: *Toothfriendly International (TI)*. Supporting member of: *FDI – World Dental Federation (#09281)*. [2016.06.01/XM3640/f/**F**]

- ♦ Toothfriendly International (internationally oriented national body)
- ♦ Toothfriendly Sweets International / see Toothfriendly International

♦ Top E – European Consulting Engineering Network 20174

Address not obtained.

History Sep 1990. Founded as a grouping of the type *European Economic Interest Grouping (EEIG, #06960)*. Registered in accordance with Belgian law. **Structure** General Meeting (annual); Board. **Languages** English. **Finance** Capital: euro 50,000. Annual turnover of members: euro 100 million. **Activities** Events/meetings. **Events** *International annual seminar* Munich (Germany) 1992. **Publications** *Top E Communiqué* – journal.
Members Consulting engineers' practices (one per country) in 12 countries of the European Union:
Austria, Belgium, France, Germany, Greece, Ireland, Italy, Luxembourg, Netherlands, Norway, Spain, UK.
Affiliate (1) in 1 country:
USA. [2009/XF5099/**F**]

- ♦ Topeka Center for Peace and Justice (internationally oriented national body)
- ♦ Topeka Peace Resource Center / see Topeka Center for Peace and Justice
- ♦ Top Industrial Managers for Engineering / see TIME Association (#20165)
- ♦ Top International Managers in Engineering / see TIME Association (#20165)
- ♦ TOPLAP (unconfirmed)
- ♦ **TOPRA** The Organization for Professionals in Regulatory Affairs (#17885)
- ♦ TOPS – Taipei Overseas Peace Service (internationally oriented national body)
- ♦ Toques d'Or International / see Euro-Toques International (#09190)
- ♦ Torch Trust for the Blind (internationally oriented national body)
- ♦ TORMED – Mediterranean Confederation of Centres for Chelonian Conservation (inactive)
- ♦ Torremolinos charter – European Regional/spatial Planning Charter (1983 treaty)
- ♦ Torremolinos Protocol of 1993 Relating to the Torremolinos International Convention for the SAfety of Fishing Vessels (1993 treaty)
- ♦ Törtèneti Varosok ès Falvak Nemzetközi Bizottsaga / see ICOMOS International Committee on Historic Cities, Towns and Villages (#11063)
- ♦ TOR – Tertius Ordo Regularis Sancti Francisci (religious order)

♦ Tortoise Trust 20175

Contact BM Tortoise, London, WC1N 3XX, UK. T. +441267211578. Fax +441267211578.
URL: http://www.tortoisetrust.org/

History 1986. **Aims** Promote *protection* of tortoises worldwide. **Finance** Members' dues. **Activities** Runs fieldwork projects in Egypt, Greece, Morocco, Tunisia and Turkey; specializes in veterinary care and nursing of sick tortoises and turtles. **Publications** *Tortoise Trust Newsletter*. Books; videos.
Members Individuals in 25 countries and territories:
Belgium, Canada, Cyprus, Denmark, Egypt, Finland, France, Germany, Ireland, Italy, Japan, Malta, Netherlands, Norway, Portugal, Saudi Arabia, Singapore, South Africa, Spain, Sweden, Switzerland, Taiwan, Türkiye, UK, USA.
NGO Relations Cooperates with: *International Union for Conservation of Nature and Natural Resources (IUCN, #15766)*. [2009/XF4944/**F**]

- ♦ Torture Abolition Support Coalition International / see TASSC International
- ♦ Torture Abolition and Survivors Support Coalition International / see TASSC International
- ♦ TOSC@ – Transnational Opera Studies Conference (meeting series)
- ♦ TOSD – Third Order Secular of St Dominic (religious order)
- ♦ Toshiba International Foundation (internationally oriented national body)
- ♦ **TOS** Oceanography Society (#17684)

♦ Tostan 20176

Headquarters 5 Cité Aelmas, Ouest Foire VDN, en face CICES, BP 29371, Dakar, Senegal. T. +221338205589. E-mail: info@tostan.org.
US Address 1199 North Fairfax Street, Suite 300, Alexandria VA 22314, USA. T. +12025053925.
URL: http://www.tostan.org/

History 1991. Former names and other names: *Tostan International* – former. Registration: 501(c)(3) non-profit, No/ID: EIN 98-0118676, USA. **Aims** Empower communities to develop and achieve their vision for the future and inspire large-scale movements leading to dignity for all. **Structure** Board of Directors; Leadership Team. **Languages** English, French, Portuguese. **Finance** Sources: donations; fundraising; gifts, legacies; government support; grants; private foundations. Supported by: *Bill and Melinda Gates Foundation (BMGF)*; *Conrad N Hilton Foundation (CNHF)*; *European Union (EU, #08967)*; *Just World International (JWI)*; *Mastercard Foundation*; *Norwegian Agency for Development Cooperation (Norad)*; *Orchid Project*; *Skoll Foundation*; *Swedish International Development Cooperation Agency (Sida)*; *The Carter Center*; *UNICEF (#20332)*; *United Nations Population Fund (UNFPA, #20612)*; *United States Agency for International Development (USAID)*. **Activities** Awareness raising; capacity building; conflict resolution; financial and/or material support; monitoring/evaluation; projects/programmes; research/documentation; training/education. Active in: Gambia, Guinea, Guinea-Bissau, Mali, Senegal. **Publications** Annual Report; research reports. **NGO Relations** Member of (1): *Humentum (#10993)*. *Every Woman Every Child (EWEC, #09215)* *Girls not Brides (#10154)* Catalyst 2030. [2021.09.01/XJ1728/**F**]

- ♦ Tostan International / see Tostan (#20176)
- ♦ TOS – Theosophical Order of Service (see: #20141)
- ♦ Tourism Council of the South Pacific / see Pacific Tourism Organization (#18008)
- ♦ Tourisme et développement solidaires (internationally oriented national body)

♦ Tourism Education Futures Initiative (TEFI) 20177

Chair Inst for Kultur og Global Studier, AC Meyers Vaenge 15, Bldg A – Room B3, Aalborg Univ, 2450 Copenhagen SV, Denmark.
URL: http://tourismeducationfutures.org/

History 2006. **Aims** Progress an alternative type of tourism that is sustainable and just, that delivers blended social, economic and environmental value, and that promotes vibrant flourishing communities. **Structure** Executive Committee; Advisory Board. **Activities** Events/meetings; training/education; advocacy/lobbying/activism. **Events** *Biennial Conference* York (UK) 2020, *Biennial Conference* Finland 2018, *European Conference* Copenhagen (Denmark) 2017, *Biennial Conference* Kamloops, BC (Canada) 2016, *Biennial Conference* Guelph, ON (Canada) 2014. [2017/XM6276/**F**]

- ♦ Tourism Organization of the Baltic States (no recent information)

♦ Tourism Promotion Organization for Asia Pacific Cities (TPO) 20178

SG 4F, No 357 Geumgok-daero, Buk-gu, Busan 46523, Korea Rep. T. +82515022984. Fax +82515021968. E-mail: secretariat@aptpo.org.
Gen Dir address not obtained.
URL: http://www.aptpo.org/

History Aug 2002, Fukuoka (Japan). Proposed 2000, Busan (Korea Rep). Secretariat opened, Nov 2002. **Aims** Serve as a centre of marketing, information and communication. **Structure** General Assembly (every 2 years); Executive Committee; Secretariat. **Languages** Chinese, English, Japanese, Korean. **Staff** 8.00 FTE, paid. **Finance** Sources: members' dues. Annual budget: 1,600,000 USD. **Activities** Events/meetings; knowledge management/information dissemination; advocacy/lobbying/activism; training/education; networking/liaising. **Events** *Seminar for Global Tourism Policy* Busan (Korea Rep) 2021, *TPO Introduction Meeting for Indonesian Cities* Busan (Korea Rep) 2021, *General Assembly* Busan (Korea Rep) 2019, *Regional Meeting* Busan (Korea Rep) 2019, *Forum* Ho Chi Minh City (Vietnam) 2018. **Publications** *TPO News* (12 a year). *Tourism Scope*.
Members City members (129) in 16 countries and territories:
China, Indonesia, Japan, Korea Rep, Laos, Malaysia, Mongolia, Nepal, Philippines, Russia, Taiwan, Thailand, Timor-Leste, Uzbekistan, Vanuatu, Vietnam.
Private members in 9 countries:
China, India, Japan, Korea Rep, Malaysia, Mongolia, Russia, USA, Vietnam. [2021/XJ6706/**D**]

- ♦ Tourism Watch (internationally oriented national body)
- ♦ Tourism Watch – Zusammenarbeit – Entwicklung – Bildung / see Tourism Watch
- ♦ Tourist Alliance of the Indian Ocean (inactive)
- ♦ Touristische Gemeinschaft der Alpenländer (#00745)
- ♦ Toute l'Europe (internationally oriented national body)

♦ **ToU** Temple of Understanding (#20124)
♦ TOVALOP – Tanker owners voluntary agreement concerning liability for oil pollution (inactive)
♦ Towarzystwo Chrystusowe dla Polonii Zagranicznej (religious order)
♦ Town Affiliation Association of the United States / see Sister Cities International

♦ Toy Industries of Europe (TIE) 20179

Dir Gen Bd de Waterloo 36, 1000 Brussels, Belgium. T. +3222134190. Fax +3222134199. E-mail: info@toyindustries.eu.
URL: http://www.toyindustries.eu/

History 12 Mar 1997. Founded on merger of *Fédération européenne des industries du jouet – jeux, jouets, puériculture (FEJ, inactive)* and *Toy Manufacturers of Europe (TME, inactive)*. Registration: Banque-Carrefour des Entreprises, No/ID: 0444.581.979, Start date: 29 Nov 1990, Belgium. **Aims** Promote the value of toys and play in psychological, physical and social development of *children*; raise awareness of the positive role that toys play in society. **Structure** General Assembly (annual); Board of Directors; Technical Committee; Secretariat. **Languages** English. **Staff** 4.00 FTE, paid. **Finance** Self-financed.
Members Corporate (13); national associations (9); affiliate (6). Members in 9 countries:
Bulgaria, Denmark, France, Germany, Italy, Netherlands, Spain, Sweden, UK.
IGO Relations *European Commission (EC, #06633)*; *European Council (#06801)*; *European Parliament (EP, #08146)*. **NGO Relations** Member of (2): *Alliance for Internet of Things Innovation (AIOTI, #00697)*; *Federation of European and International Associations Established in Belgium (FAIB, #09508)*. In liaison with technical committees of: *Comité européen de normalisation (CEN, #04162)*; *European Committee for Electrotechnical Standardization (CENELEC, #06647)*; *International Organization for Standardization (ISO, #14473)*. [2021/XD6229/t/**D**]

♦ TOY – International Union of Allied, Novelty and Production Workers (internationally oriented national body)
♦ Toyo Ongaku Gakkai (#19632)
♦ Toyota Foundation (internationally oriented national body)
♦ Toy Traders of Europe (no recent information)
♦ TPA / see Tube and Pipe Association International
♦ TPAA – Transatlantic Partners Against AIDS (internationally oriented national body)
♦ **TPDL** International Conference on Theory and Practice of Digital Libraries (#12887)
♦ **TPE** Trade Promotion Europe (#20184)
♦ TPIR – Tribunal pénal international pour le Rwanda (inactive)
♦ TPIY – Tribunal pénal international pour l'ex-Yougoslavie (inactive)
♦ **TPN** Transatlantic Policy Network (#20204)
♦ TPNW – Treaty on the Prohibition of Nuclear Weapons (2017 treaty)

♦ TP Organics – European Technology Platform (TP Organics) 20180

Secretariat c/o IFOAM EU, Rue du Commerce 124, 1000 Brussels, Belgium. T. +3224162761. Fax +3227357381.
URL: http://tporganics.eu/

History Set up as a European Technology Platform (ETP), officially recognized by *European Commission (EC, #06633)*. Registration: EU Transparency Register, No/ID: 321531633059-83. **Aims** Strengthen research and innovation for organics and other *agroecological* approaches that contribute to *sustainable food* and *farming* systems. **Structure** Steering Committee; Secretariat. **Activities** Networking/liaising; research/documentation; knowledge management/information dissemination. **Events** *Organic Innovation Days* Brussels (Belgium) 2022, *Organic Innovation Days* Brussels (Belgium) 2021, *Organic Innovation Days* Brussels (Belgium) 2020, *Organic Innovation Days* Brussels (Belgium) 2019.
Members Umbrella organizations and international networks; Enterprise members; National platforms and members. Umbrella organizations and international networks (29):
– *ACT Alliance EU (#00082)*;
– *AgroBioMediterraneao (ABM, #00579)*;
– *BERAS International Foundation (#03210)*;
– *BirdLife International (#03266)* (Europe);
– *Conseil européen des jeunes agriculteurs (CEJA, #04689)*;
– *COPA – european farmers (COPA, #04829)*;
– *Donau Soja (#05116)*;
– *Ecologica International Association (#05299)*;
– *Eurogroup for Animals (#05690)*;
– *Euromontana (#05737)*;
– *European Agroforestry Federation (EURAF, #05848)*;
– *European Community of Consumer Cooperatives (EURO COOP, #06678)*;
– *European Consortium for Organic Plant Breeding (ECO-PB, #06761)*;
– *European Coordination Via Campesina (ECVC, #06795)*;
– *European Draught Horse Federation (#06944)*;
– *European Environmental Bureau (EEB, #06996)*;
– *European Federation of Food, Agriculture and Tourism Trade Unions (EFFAT, #07125)*;
– *European Landowners' Organization (ELO, #07639)*;
– *European Organic Certifiers Council (EOCC, #08094)*;
– *Friends of the Earth Europe (FoEE, #10001)*;
– *General Confederation of Agricultural Cooperatives in the European Union (#10107)*;
– *Greenpeace International (#10727)* (EU Unit);
– *IFOAM Organics Europe (#11104)*;
– *Innovation for Development and South-South cooperation (IDEASS)*;
– *International Research Association for Organic Food Quality and Health (FQH, #14719)*;
– *International Society of Organic Farming Research (ISOFAR, #15331)*;
– *Pesticide Action Network Europe (#18338)*;
– *Sciences Citoyennes*;
– *South Eastern Europe Regional Rural Development Standing Working Group (SWG RRD, #19809)*.
National technology platforms and national members in 17 countries:
Austria, Belgium, Bulgaria, Czechia, Denmark, Finland, France, Germany, Hungary, Italy, Netherlands, Norway, Portugal, Spain, Switzerland, Türkiye, UK. [2018/XM6454/y/**F**]

♦ **TP Organics** TP Organics – European Technology Platform (#20180)
♦ **TPO** Tourism Promotion Organization for Asia Pacific Cities (#20178)
♦ TPP – Trans-Pacific Partnership Agreement (2016 treaty)
♦ **TPP** Tribunale Permanente dei Popoli (#18328)
♦ **TPP** Tribunal Permanente de los Pueblos (#18328)
♦ **TPP** Tribunal Permanent des Peuples (#18328)
♦ **TPSEP** Trans-Pacific Strategic Economic Partnership (#20220)
♦ **TPW** Philanthropy Workshop (#18359)
♦ TQC – Conference on the Theory of Quantum Computation, Communication and Cryptography (meeting series)
♦ Trabajar Juntos por los Derechos Humanos (internationally oriented national body)
♦ TRAC / see CorpWatch
♦ TraCCC – Transnational Crime and Corruption Center (internationally oriented national body)
♦ TRACECA / see Transport Corridor from Europe-Caucasus-Asia (#20225)
♦ **TRACECA** Transport Corridor from Europe-Caucasus-Asia (#20225)
♦ Trace Element – Institute for UNESCO (internationally oriented national body)
♦ Tracé élément – institut pour l'UNESCO (internationally oriented national body)
♦ TRACE International (unconfirmed)
♦ TRACE – TRACE International (unconfirmed)
♦ TRACIT – Transnational Alliance to Combat Illicit Trade (unconfirmed)
♦ Tracking the Creative Process in Music – International Conference (meeting series)
♦ Trade Bureau / see Pacific Islands Forum Secretariat (#17970)

♦ Trade and Development Bank (TDB) 20181

Chief Exec Africa Fl Place, Lot No 13, Wall Street, PO Box 43, Cybercity, Ebene 72201, Mauritius. T. +2304601500. E-mail: info@tdbgroup.org.
Bujumbura Principal Office Chaussée Prince Louis, Rwagasore, PO Box 1750, Bujumbura, Burundi. T. +25722224966 – +25722224975.
URL: http://www.tdbgroup.org/

History Dec 1983, Bujumbura (Burundi). Established as financial arm of *Preferential Trade Area for Eastern and Southern African States (PTA, inactive)*. Since 8 Dec 1994, comes within *Common Market for Eastern and Southern Africa (COMESA, #04296)*. Operational from 1985. Currently located in Nairobi (Kenya). Former names and other names: *Eastern and Southern African Trade and Development Bank (PTA Bank)* – former (Dec 1983 to 2017); *Banque de commerce et de développement pour l'Afrique de l'Est et du Sud (Banque de la Zep)* – former (Dec 1983 to 2017). **Aims** Finance and foster trade, socio-economic development and regional economic integration through trade and development finance, funds management as well as advisory and agency services. **Structure** Board of Governors; Board of Directors. Principal offices in Mauritius and Burundi. Regional Offices in Kenya, Ethiopia and Zimbabwe. **Staff** 8.00 FTE, paid. **Finance** Total liabilities and equity (2020): over 6,000,000,000. **Activities** Financial and/or material support. **Events** *Conference on oil marketing, risk management and finance in Sub- Saharan Africa* Harare (Zimbabwe) 1996. **Publications** Annual Report and Accounts.
Members Governments. Regional members (22):
Burundi, Comoros, Congo DR, Djibouti, Egypt, Eritrea, Eswatini, Ethiopia, Kenya, Madagascar, Malawi, Mauritius, Mozambique, Rwanda, Seychelles, Somalia, South Sudan, Sudan, Tanzania UR, Uganda, Zambia, Zimbabwe.
Non-Regional members (2):
Belarus, China.
Institutional members (14).
Denmark, Mauritius, Mozambique, Rwanda, Seychelles, Uganda.
African Development Bank (ADB, #00283); *African Economic Research Consortium (AERC, #00292)*; *African Reinsurance Corporation (AFRICA RE, #00438)*; *Arab Bank for Economic Development in Africa (#00904)*; *Investeringsfonden for Udviklingslande (IFU)*; *OPEC Fund for International Development (OFID, #17745)*; *PTA Reinsurance Company (ZEP-RE, #18561)*.
IGO Relations Member of (3): *African Trade Insurance Agency (ATI, #00485)*; *Eastern and Southern African Anti-Money Laundering Group (ESAAMLG, #05252)*; *Intergovernmental Organizations Conference (IGO Conference, #11498)*. **NGO Relations** Member of (3): *Association of African Development Finance Institutions (AADFI, #02353)*; *Global Network of Export-Import Banks and Development Finance Institutions (G-NEXID, #10489)*; *International Development Finance Club (IDFC, #13159)*. [2020/XF0203/t/**F***]

♦ Trade Expansion and Economic Cooperation Agreement between India, Egypt and Yugoslavia (1967 treaty)
♦ Trade Facilitation Agreement (2014 treaty)

♦ Trade Facilitation Agreement Facility (TFAF) 20182

Mécanisme pour l'Accord sur la facilitation des échanges – Mecanismo para el Acuerdo sobre Facilitación del Comercio

Contact c/o WTO, Ctr William Rappard, Rue de Lausanne 154, 1211 Geneva 21, Switzerland. T. +41227395111. E-mail: tfaf@wto.org.
URL: https://www.tfafacility.org/

History Launched 22 Jul 2014, by *World Trade Organization (WTO, #21864)* Director-General Roberto Azevêdo; operational 27 Nov 2014 when Members adopted the Protocol of Amendment to insert *Trade Facilitation Agreement (TFA, 2014)* into Annex 1A of the WTO Agreement. **Aims** Support Developing and Least-Developed Country Members to assess their specific needs and to identify possible development partners to help them meet those needs. **Finance** Contributions from governments of Australia, Austria, China, Finland, France, New Zealand, Norway, UK and of *European Union (EU, #08967)*. [2019/XM8533/t/**F***]

♦ TradeMark East Africa (TMEA) 20183

CEO 2nd Floor, Fidelity Insurance, Centre Waiyaki Way, Westlands, Nairobi, 00800, Kenya. T. +254204235000. E-mail: info@trademarkea.com.
URL: http://www.trademarkea.com/

Aims Promote rapid advances in East Africa's integration, *trade* and global *competitiveness* for all East Africans. **Structure** Council; Board. **Finance** Support from governments of Belgium, Netherlands and Denmark, and through the following governmental agencies: *Swedish International Development Cooperation Agency (Sida)*; *Department for International Development (DFID, inactive)*. **Publications** *The Update*. **IGO Relations** Memorandum of Understanding with: *World Customs Organization (WCO, #21350)*. Cooperates with: *East African Community (EAC, #05181)*; *East African Legislative Assembly (EALA, #05185)*. **NGO Relations** Partners include: *East Africa Philanthropy Network (EAPN, #05192)*; *East African Business Council (EABC, #05177)*; *Eastern African Farmers Federation (EAFF, #05223)*; *The Eastern African Sub-Regional Support Initiative for the Advancement of Women (EASSI, #05225)*. [2020/XJ3016/t/**D**]

♦ Trademark Law Treaty (1994 treaty)
♦ Trademark Registration Treaty (1973 treaty)

♦ Trade Promotion Europe (TPE) 20184

SG Boulevard du Roi Albert II 37, Zenith Bldg, 8th floor, 1030 Brussels, Belgium. E-mail: secretariat@tradepromotioneurope.eu.
URL: https://tradepromotioneurope.eu/

History 31 Oct 2018. Former names and other names: *European Trade Promotion Organizations Association (ETPOA)* – former (2022). Registration: Banque-Carrefour des Entreprieses, No/ID: 0722.594.669, Start date: 11 Mar 2019, Belgium. **Aims** Promote the interests of European trade promotion organisations (TPOs) in dialogue and collaboration with European institutions and other competent authorities. **Structure** Board of Directors.
Members Full in 19 countries:
Austria, Belgium, Bulgaria, Cyprus, Estonia, France, Germany, Greece, Hungary, Ireland, Italy, Lithuania, Malta, Netherlands, Portugal, Slovenia, Spain, Switzerland, UK.
NGO Relations Member of (1): *Federation of European and International Associations Established in Belgium (FAIB, #09508)*. [2022/AA3228/**D**]

♦ Trades Union International of Workers in the Building, Wood, Building Materials and Allied Industries (UITBB) 20185

Union internationale des syndicats des travailleurs du bâtiment, du bois et des matériaux de construction (UITBB) – Unión Internacional de Sindicatos de Trabajadores de la Construcción – Internationale Vereinigung der Arbeiter der Bau-, Holz- und Baumaterialienindustrie – Mezdunarodnoe Obedinenie Trudjascihsja Profsojuzov Stroitelstva, Derevoobrabatyvajuscej Promyslennosti i Promyslennosti Stroitelnyh Materialov

Gen Sec 1514, 31-35 Archermos St, CY-1514 Nicosia, Cyprus. T. +35722866411. E-mail: uitbb@peo.org.cy.
URL: http://www.uitbb.org/

History 14 Jul 1949, Milan (Italy). Statutes approved by 5th International Conference, 26 May 1967, Berlin (German DR). New Constitution adopted by 9th International Conference, 16 Oct 1983, Sofia (Bulgaria). Present Constitution adopted by 11th International Conference, Oct 1993, Helsinki (Finland). **Aims** Promote trade unions in building, wood and building materials industries. **Structure** International Conference (every 4 years); Executive Committee (meeting annually); Commissions and Working Groups; Secretariat. **Languages** English, French, Spanish. **Finance** Sources: members' dues. **Activities** Advocacy/lobbying/activism; networking/liaising. **Events** *Conference* Athens (Greece) 2020, *Conference* Montevideo (Uruguay) 2015, *Conference* Salvador (Brazil) 2010, *Conference* Athens (Greece) 2006, *Conference* Cyprus 2002. **Members** National trade unions (50), totalling 10 million unionized workers, in 50 countries. Membership countries not specified.
NGO Relations Autonomous organization working within the framework of: *World Federation of Trade Unions (WFTU, #21493)*. Affiliated organization: *Latin American Federation of Building, Wood and Building Materials Unions (#16318)*. [2022.02.02/XB3328/ty/**B**]

♦ Trade Union Advisory Committee to the OECD (TUAC) 20186

Commission syndicale consultative auprès de l'OCDE (CSC)

SG 15 rue Lapérouse, 75016 Paris, France. T. +33155373737. Fax +33147549828. E-mail: tuac@tuac.org.

URL: http://www.tuac.org/
History Dec 1948, Paris (France), as a trade union advisory committee in connection with the European recovery programme (Marshall Plan). On creation of *OECD (#17693)*, 1962, became its advisory committee. Full title: *Trade Union Advisory Committee to the Organisation for Economic Cooperation and Development (TUAC-OECD) – Commission syndicale consultative auprès de l'Organisation de coopération et de développement économiques (CSC-OCDE).* **Aims** Appraise OECD Secretariat, Committees and Member governments of the views of the trade union movement on the issues on the OECD agenda. **Structure** Plenary Session (twice a year), consisting of all affiliates and representatives of the international organizations. Administrative Committee, consisting of President, Vice-Presidents, General Secretary and representatives of central organizations of trade unions from Germany, Austria, Belgium, Canada, Denmark, France, Italy, Japan, Sweden, USA and UK. Working Groups. **Languages** English, French. **Staff** 9.00 FTE, paid. **Finance** Members' dues. **Activities** Working Groups on: Economic Policy; Global Trade and Investment; Education, Training and Employment Policy. Regular consultations with various OECD bodies on: economic policies; structural adjustment and labour market policies; impact of globalization on employment; education and training; multinational enterprises; OECD relations with non-member countries; environment; science and technology policy. Labour/Management Programme. Regular meetings and conferences. **Events** *Plenary Session* Paris (France) 2013, *Plenary Session* Paris (France) 2009, *Plenary Session* Paris (France) 2006, *Seminar on the OECD guidelines for multinational enterprises* Montevideo (Uruguay) 2004, *Plenary Session* Paris (France) 2004. **Publications** *Exiting from the Crisis: Towards a Model of More Equitable and Sustainable Growth* (2011); *Users' Guide for Trade Unionists to the OECD Guidelines to Multinational Enterprises* (2003) – reissued; *Korea and the OECD: The Social Dimension of Economic Integration* (1996) in English; *Adaptability versus Flexibility* (1995) in English, French. Symposium proceedings; statements; declarations.
Members Central organizations of trade unions (59), representing 61.5 million individual members, in 31 countries:
Australia, Austria, Belgium, Canada, Czechia, Denmark, Finland, France, Germany, Greece, Hungary, Iceland, Ireland, Israel, Italy, Japan, Korea Rep, Luxembourg, Mexico, Netherlands, New Zealand, Norway, Poland, Portugal, Slovakia, Spain, Sweden, Switzerland, Türkiye, UK, USA.
Consultative Status Consultative status granted from: *OECD (#17693).* **IGO Relations** Represented in Steering Group of: *Anti-Corruption Network for Eastern Europe and Central Asia (ACN, #00853).* **NGO Relations** Member of (2): *Global Labour University (GLU, #10448); Global Union Federations (GUF, #10638).* Instrumental in setting up (1): *Global Unions Committee on Workers' Capital (CWC, #10639).*
[2013/XE3320/t/E]

- ♦ Trade Union Advisory Committee to the Organisation for Economic Cooperation and Development / see Trade Union Advisory Committee to the OECD (#20186)
- ♦ Trade Union Confederation of the Americas (#04480)
- ♦ Trade Union Confederation of Latin American Workers (inactive)
- ♦ Trade Union Council of Andean Workers (inactive)

♦ Trade Union Eurocontrol Maastricht (TUEM) 20187
Union syndicale Eurocontrol Maastricht
Sec Horsterweg 11, 6199 AC Maastricht, Netherlands. T. +31433661110. E-mail: info@tuem.org – office@tuem.org.
URL: https://tuem.org/
History Founded within the framework of *EUROCONTROL (#05667)*, to represent staff of *EUROCONTROL Maastricht Upper Area Control Centre (MUAC, #05670).* **Structure** Executive Board. **Finance** Sources: members' dues. [2022/XK0756/v/E]

♦ Trade Union International of Chemical, Energy, Metal, Oil and Allied Industries (TUI CHEMISTRY-ENERGY) 20188
Gen Sec address not obtained. E-mail: info@wftucentral.org.
URL: http://www.wftucentral.org/trade-union-internationals/
History Founded at constituent conference, on merger of: *Trade Unions International of Chemical, Oil and Allied Workers (ICPS, inactive); Trade Unions International of Workers in Energy (TUIWE, inactive); Trade Unions International of Workers in the Metal Industry (inactive).* Finalization of draft constitution by Working Group of the Initiative Committee, 28 Feb 1996, Prague (Czech Rep). One of the Trade Union Internationals (TUIs) of *World Federation of Trade Unions (WFTU, #21493).* Former names and other names: *Trade Unions International of Workers in the Chemical, Energy, Oil, Metal and Allied Industries (TUI WCEOM)* – former; *Trade Union International of Workers of the Energy, Metal, Chemistry, Petroleum and Compatible Industries (TUI WEMCORI)* – former; *Trade Union International of Workers of Energy, Metal, Chemical, Oil and Allied Industries (TUI EMCOAI)* – former (1998); *Union internationale de syndicats de travailleurs de l'énergie, du métal, de la chimie, du pétrole et des industries analogues (UIS TEMCPIA)* – former (1998); *Unión Internacional de Sindicatos de Trabajadores de la Energia, el Metal, La Quimica, el Petróleo e Industrias Afines (UIS TEMQPIA)* – former (1998); *Trade Union International of Energy (TUI ENERGY)* – former (Sep 2007); *TUI ENERGY* – former. **Structure** Conference (every 5 years); Executive Committee. Secretariat. **Finance** Sources: members' dues. **Events** *International trade unions congress of energy workers* Mexico City (Mexico) 2007.
Members Trade unions in 33 countries:
Algeria, Chile, Colombia, Cuba, Cyprus, Czechia, Dominican Rep, Ecuador, El Salvador, Ethiopia, France, Haiti, India, Iraq, Korea Rep, Kuwait, Libya, Mali, Mauritania, Mauritius, Mexico, Nicaragua, Pakistan, Peru, Philippines, Poland, Portugal, Senegal, Spain, Sri Lanka, Sudan, Syrian AR, Vietnam. [2020/XB0005/ty/B]

- ♦ Trade Union International of Energy / see Trade Union International of Chemical, Energy, Metal, Oil and Allied Industries (#20188)
- ♦ Trade Union International of Mining, Metallurgy and Metal (unconfirmed)
- ♦ Trade Union International of Workers in Defence and Specialized Enterprises (no recent information)
- ♦ Trade Union International of Workers of Energy, Metal, Chemical, Oil and Allied Industries / see Trade Union International of Chemical, Energy, Metal, Oil and Allied Industries (#20188)
- ♦ Trade Union International of Workers of the Energy, Metal, Chemistry, Petroleum and Compatible Industries / see Trade Union International of Chemical, Energy, Metal, Oil and Allied Industries (#20188)

♦ Trade Union International of Workers in Geology, Geodesy and Cartography 20189
Pres 42 Leninsky Prospekt, Moscow MOSKVA, Russia, 119119. T. +74959388147. Fax +74952370476.
Members Trade unions in the CIS region (membership countries not specified). **NGO Relations** Affiliated with: *General Confederation of Trade Unions (GCTU, #10108).* [2014/XM2458/t/D]

- ♦ Trade Union International of Workers in Innovation Enterprises and Small Businesses (no recent information)
- ♦ Trade Union International of Workers in Shipbuilding (no recent information)
- ♦ Trade Unions of Christian Workers in the Pacific (inactive)
- ♦ Trade Unions International of Agricultural, Forestry and Plantation Workers (inactive)

♦ Trade Unions International of Agriculture, Food, Commerce, Textile and Allied Industries 20190
Union internationale syndicale des travailleurs de l'agriculture, alimentation, commerce, textiles et industries similaires (UISTAACT)
SG UIS TAACT – c/o FNAF-CGT, Case 428, 263 rue de Paris, 93514 Montreuil CEDEX, France. T. +33155828445. Fax +33148515749. E-mail: uis@fnaf.cgt.fr.
URL: http://www.wftucentral.org/
History 1996. Founded on amalgamation of *Trade Unions International of Agricultural, Forestry and Plantation Workers (TUIAFPW, inactive), Trade Unions International of Food, Tobacco, Hotel and Allied Industries' Workers (inactive), Union internationale des syndicats des travailleurs du commerce (UISTC, inactive)* and *Trade Unions International of Workers in Textile, Clothing, Leather, Shoe and Allied Industries (inactive).* One of the Trade Union Internationals (TUIs) of *World Federation of Trade Unions (WFTU, #21493).* Former names and other names: *Trade Unions International of Agriculture, Food, Commerce and Textile Workers* – former. **Languages** French. **Publications** *Bulletin UIS* (3 a year). **Consultative Status** Consultative status granted from: *ECOSOC (#05331)* (Ros C). [2023.02.28/XB0006/t/B]

- ♦ Trade Unions International of Agriculture, Food, Commerce and Textile Workers / see Trade Unions International of Agriculture, Food, Commerce, Textile and Allied Industries (#20190)
- ♦ Trade Unions International of Chemical, Oil and Allied Workers (inactive)
- ♦ Trade Unions International of Food, Tobacco, Hotel and Allied Industries' Workers (inactive)
- ♦ Trade Unions International of Land and Air Transport Workers (inactive)
- ♦ Trade Unions International of Postal, Telegraph, Telephone and Radio Workers / see Trade Unions International of Public and Allied Employees (#20191)

♦ Trade Unions International of Public and Allied Employees 20191
Union internationale des syndicats des travailleurs de la fonction publique et assimilés – Unión Internacional de Sindicatos de Trabajadores de Servicios Públicos y Similares – Internationale Vereinigung der Gewerkschaften der Werktätigen des Öffentlichen Dienstes und Verwandter Berufe – Mezdunarodnoe Obedinenie Profsojuzov Trudjascihsja Obscestvennogo Obsluzivanija
Contact address not obtained. E-mail: congresstuips@gmail.com.
URL: http://www.tui-ps.org/
History 27 Oct 1949, Berlin (Germany). Present name adopted Vienna (Austria). Current Statute adopted by 8th International Trades Congress of Public and Allied Employees, Mar 1988, Sofia (Bulgaria); last amended at 10th Congress, Mar 2006, Johannesburg (South Africa). Headquarters moved to Delhi, Jun 1996, and to Kolkata (India), 1998. Former names and other names: *Trade Unions International of Postal, Telegraph, Telephone and Radio Workers* – former (27 Oct 1949 to 12 Apr 1995); *Union internationale des syndicats des travailleurs des postes, télégraphes, téléphones et radio* – former (27 Oct 1949 to 12 Apr 1995). **Aims** Unite *trade unions* of officials, workers, employees, engineers, cadres and technicians employed in state, municipal, postal, telecommunication and health services, banks, finance and insurance institutions; help implement improvements in their *working conditions*; activate for security of employment; contribute to protective social legislation; promote international trade union unity; support the struggle for improvement of the social, economic and professional situation of public employees and for the fulfillment of their demands; defend democratic and trade union rights and liberties; activate workers' common struggle against the penetration of monopolies and transnational corporations into the public services, against discrimination and against detrimental effects of the introduction and application of new technology; strengthen the role and importance of trade unions in every social order and safeguard their rights to fully participate in negotiations and develop their work at all levels; guard interests of workers, safeguard rights already gained, work for success of their trade union demands and struggle for international understanding, lasting peace and peaceful coexistence on the basis of mutual respect, independence, sovereignty and non-interference in the affairs of other peoples, against war and aggression, for the final liquidation of colonialism and neo-colonialism, for international détente and for the achievement of general and complete disarmament. **Structure** International Trades Congress (every 5 years), composed of delegates elected by member unions in accordance with specific norms. Directive Committee regulates activity in the period between Trades Congresses. Directive Committee, consisting of President, 2 Vice-Presidents, General Secretary and 14 members. Secretariat, composed of General Secretary and 3 Secretaries. Branch Commissions (5): State Service; Municipal Service; Health Service; Postal and Telecommunication Services; Banks, Finance and Insurance Institutions. Financial Control Commission, elected by Congress from among representatives of organizations which have affiliated member status and are not members of the Directive Committees. **Languages** English, French, Russian, Spanish. **Staff** 30.00 FTE, paid. **Finance** Subscriptions of affiliated and associate organizations. **Activities** Main areas: strengthening relations among member unions; organizing consultative meetings and congresses, sessions, colloquia and exchanges of experience; encouraging national and international trade union cooperation in the public services; studying and publishing trade union and related news and experience. **Events** *Congress* Johannesburg (South Africa) 2006, *World Congress / Congress* Kolkata (India) 1998, *Congress* Berlin (Germany) 1992, *Meeting* Berlin (Germany FR) 1989, *Congress* Sofia (Bulgaria) 1988. **Publications** *Public Service* (4 a year) in English.
Members Trade unions (198), totalling 20 million members, in 33 countries:
Austria, Bangladesh, Benin, Congo Brazzaville, Costa Rica, Cuba, Cyprus, Czechia, Ethiopia, Fiji, Ghana, India, Indonesia, Japan, Korea DPR, Lesotho, Mauritius, Mongolia, Nepal, Nicaragua, Nigeria, Pakistan, Panama, Philippines, South Africa, Sri Lanka, Sudan, Syrian AR, Trinidad-Tobago, Turkmenistan, Vietnam, Yemen, Zimbabwe.
Trade unions (15) whose activities are suppressed and therefore their links with TUI are interrupted, in 4 countries:
Chile, Iraq, Sudan, Türkiye.
NGO Relations Member of: *World Federation of Trade Unions (WFTU, #21493).* [2015/XB3324/t/B]

- ♦ Trade Unions International of Seamen, Inland Waterways Workers, Fishermen and Port Workers (inactive)

♦ Trade Unions International of Transport, Fisheries and Communication (TUI Transport) 20192
Address not obtained.
History 12 Mar 1953, Prague (Czechia). 12-18 Mar 1953, Prague (Czech Rep), by merger of *Trade Unions International of Seamen, Inland Waterways Workers, Fishermen and Port Workers (inactive)*, set up Jul 1949, Marseille (France), and *Trade Unions International of Land and Air Transport Workers (inactive)*, formed Dec 1949, Bucharest (Romania). Original title: *Trade Unions International of Transport Workers – Union internationale des syndicats des travailleurs des transports – Unión Internacional de Sindicatos de Trabajadores de los Transportes – Mezdunarodnoe Obedinenie Profsojuzov Trudjascihsja Transporta.* **Aims** Coordinate trade union action; organize meetings and seminars on professional issues. **Structure** International Trade Conference (every 4 years). General Council (annually). **Languages** English, Spanish. **Staff** 1.00 FTE, paid. **Finance** Sources: members' dues. **Activities** Events/meetings. **Events** *Quadrennial Conference* Santiago (Chile) 2014, *Quadrennial Conference* Belo Horizonte (Brazil) 2007, *Quadrennial Conference* Damascus (Syrian AR) 2002, *Quadrennial Conference* Damascus (Syrian AR) 1998, *Quadrennial Conference* Kuwait 1996. **Publications** *TUI Reporter* (6 a year).
Members Affiliated organizations, totalling 15 million individual members, in 36 countries and territories:
Bangladesh, Brazil, Burkina Faso, China, Cuba, Cyprus, Eritrea, Fiji, Georgia, Greece, Grenada, Honduras, India, Iran Islamic Rep, Iraq, Japan, Jordan, Korea DPR, Kuwait, Laos, Lebanon, Liberia, Libya, Nicaragua, Pakistan, Palestine, Peru, Philippines, Russia, Slovakia, Sudan, Syrian AR, Trinidad-Tobago, Uruguay, Vietnam, Yemen.
IGO Relations *ILO (#11123).* **NGO Relations** Affiliated to: *World Federation of Trade Unions (WFTU, #21493).* [2005.11.02/XD3325/t/B]

- ♦ Trade Unions International of Transport Workers / see Trade Unions International of Transport, Fisheries and Communication (#20192)
- ♦ Trade Unions International of Workers in the Chemical, Energy, Oil, Metal and Allied Industries / see Trade Union International of Chemical, Energy, Metal, Oil and Allied Industries (#20188)
- ♦ Trade Unions International of Workers in Commerce (inactive)
- ♦ Trade Unions International of Workers in Energy (inactive)
- ♦ Trade Unions International of Workers in the Metal Industry (inactive)
- ♦ Trade Unions International of Workers in Textile, Clothing, Leather, Shoe and Allied Industries (inactive)
- ♦ Trade Union Solidarity Centre of Finland (internationally oriented national body)
- ♦ Trade Unions' Portuguese Speaking Countries Community (#04431)

♦ Traditional Anglican Church (TAC) 20193
Office of the Primate 980 Falmouth Road, Victoria BC V8X 3A3, Canada. E-mail: ccsje@shaw.ca.
URL: http://traditionalanglicanchurch.com/
History 29 Sep 1990, Victoria, BC (Canada). Established on completion of final draft of agreement – *'Concordat'* – following several organizational meetings and provisional formation 29 Sep 1989, Orlando FL (USA). Concordat amended 13-14 May 1995, at meeting of College of Bishops. Former names and other names: *Traditional Anglican Communion (TAC)* – former (29 Sep 1990 to 2019). **Aims** Continue in the Catholic Faith, Apostolic Order, Orthodox Worship and Evangelical Witness of the historic Anglican Church, with its traditional liturgy, music and patrimony. **Structure** College of Bishops of all Provinces having ratified the Constitution (meeting at least every 5 years). Assistance ministry through worldwide charity arm: *International Anglican Fellowship (IAF, see: #20193).* **Languages** English, Spanish. **Finance** No fixed budget; funds provided as needed by Provinces.

Members Provinces in 12 countries:
Australia, Canada, El Salvador, Guatemala, India, Ireland, South Africa, UK, USA, Venezuela, Zambia, Zimbabwe.
[2020.04.29/XF4848/**F**]

♦ Traditional Anglican Communion / see Traditional Anglican Church (#20193)
♦ Traditional Healers Organization for Africa (inactive)

♦ Traditional Textile Arts Society of South East Asia (TTASSEA) 20194

SG Museum Tekstil Jakarta, JL KS Tubun 2-4, Jakarta, Indonesia. E-mail: waworuntusidik@gmail.com – ttasseaindonesia@gmail.com.
History 2009. Founded as *ASEAN Traditional Textile Arts Community (ASEAN TTAC)*, at 2nd ASEAN Traditional Textile Symposium, the first having been organized 2005. Current title adopted 2016. Registration: Foundation, No/ID: AHU 0027929.AH, Indonesia. **Aims** Save traditional textiles through science, preservation and conservation activities, education; inspire people to value *cultural heritage*. **Languages** English, Indonesian. **Finance** Members' dues. Donations. **Activities** Guidance/assistance/consulting; training/education; knowledge management/information dissemination; research/documentation; events/meetings. **Events** *ASEAN Traditional Textiles Symposium* Singapore (Singapore) 2023, *ASEAN Traditional Textiles Symposium* Putrajaya (Malaysia) 2022, *ASEAN Traditional Textiles Symposium* Putrajaya (Malaysia) 2021, *ASEAN Traditional Textiles Symposium* Yogyakarta (Indonesia) 2019, *ASEAN Traditional Textiles Symposium* Bandar Seri Begawan (Brunei Darussalam) 2017. **Publications** Books; symposium proceedings.
Members Members in 10 countries:
Brunei Darussalam, Cambodia, Indonesia, Laos, Malaysia, Myanmar, Philippines, Singapore, Thailand, Vietnam.
Consultative Status Consultative status granted from: *ASEAN (#01141)*. **IGO Relations** *UNESCO (#20322)*. **NGO Relations** National universities and institutes. [2022/XM8412/**D**]

♦ Traditions pour Demain (#20195)

♦ Traditions for Tomorrow 20195

Traditions pour Demain
Contact Promenade John Berney 10A, 1180 Rolle VD, Switzerland. T. +41218252331. Fax +41218252362. E-mail: tradi@tradi.info.
Contact BP 134, 01216 Ferney-Voltaire CEDEX, France. T. +33147051624. Fax +33145560551.
URL: http://www.tradi.info/
History 1986. Registration: Start date: 14 Jul 1986, Switzerland, Geneva; Start date: 2015, France. **Aims** Restore the sense of confidence, dignity and self-esteem amongst *indigenous* peoples and afro-descendant communities in Latin America through *cultural*, educational and communication initiatives designed and carried out by the beneficiaries themselves, and in post conflict situations. **Structure** General Assembly; Board of Directors; Advisory Board. **Languages** English, French, German, Spanish. **Staff** 2.00 FTE, paid. Voluntary. **Finance** Members' dues. Other sources: private donations; public subsidies; private foundation support; corporate sponsorship; co-financing of projects with cooperation and development organizations. Annual budget: about US$ 300,000. **Activities** Financial and/or material support; advocacy/lobbying/activism; projects/programmes. **Publications** *Le patrimoine culturel matériel et immatériel: quelle protection en cas de conflit armé?* (2013) by Christiane Johannot-Gradis; *Madre Tierra ! Por el renacimiento indigena* (2004); *Madre Tierra: Pour une renaissance Amérindienne* (2002) by Daniel Wermus in French, Spanish; *Amérindiens: des traditions pour demain* (1996) by Geneviève Herold. **Members** Individuals (about 500) in 10 countries, mainly in Europe. Membership countries not specified. **Consultative Status** Consultative status granted from: *ECOSOC (#05331)* (Special); *UNESCO (#20322)* (Associate Status); *World Intellectual Property Organization (WIPO, #21593)* (Observer). **NGO Relations** Board member of: *Centre de recherche et d'information pour le développement, Paris (CRID)*. [2019.03.12/XF3510/**F**]

♦ Traducteurs sans Frontières (#20216)

♦ TRAFFIC International 20196

Exec Dir David Attenborough Bldg, Pembroke Street, Cambridge, CB2 3QZ, UK. T. +441223277427. Fax +441223277237. E-mail: traffic@traffic.org.
URL: http://www.traffic.org/
History 1976, by *International Union for Conservation of Nature and Natural Resources (IUCN, #15766)* – Species Survival Commission (SSC). From 1 Jul 1991, functions as a joint conservation programme of *World Wide Fund for Nature (WWF, #21922)* and IUCN. Registered UK Charity: 1076722. **Aims** Ensure that trade in *wild plants* and *animals* is not a threat to the conservation of nature; contribute to wildlife trade-related priorities of these partners; find solutions for a sustainable future. **Structure** TRAFFIC Committee (governing body), composed of members of *World Wide Fund for Nature (WWF, #21922)* and *International Union for Conservation of Nature and Natural Resources (IUCN, #15766)*. TRAFFIC Network Offices (14); Regional Organizations (6); Secretariat based in Cambridge (UK). **Languages** English, French, Spanish. **Staff** 126.00 FTE, paid. **Finance** Funding from: *International Union for Conservation of Nature and Natural Resources (IUCN, #15766)*; *World Wide Fund for Nature (WWF, #21922)*. Projects funds from NGOs, international development agencies, private corporations, foundations and national governments. **Activities** Projects/programmes; awareness raising; management of treaties and agreements: *Convention on Biological Diversity (Biodiversity convention, 1992)*; *Convention on International Trade in Endangered Species of Wild Fauna and Flora (CITES, 1973)*. **Publications** *e-Dispatches* (weekly); *TRAFFIC Bulletin* (2 a year). Annual Report – electronic; regional reports. **Consultative Status** Consultative status granted from: *UNEP (#20299)*. **IGO Relations** Memorandum of Understanding with: *Secretariat of the Convention on International Trade in Endangered Species of Wild Fauna and Flora (CITES Secretariat, #19199)*; *South Asia Cooperative Environment Programme (SACEP, #19714)*; *World Customs Organization (WCO, #21350)*. Observer at: *Commission for the Conservation of Southern Bluefin Tuna (CCSBT, #04207)*. Member of: *Congo Basin Forest Partnership (CBFP, #04662)*; *Global Tiger Forum (GTF, #10628)*. **NGO Relations** Partner organizations: *International Union for Conservation of Nature and Natural Resources (IUCN, #15766)*; *Wild for Life Campaign (Wild for Life, #20958)*; *World Wide Fund for Nature (WWF, #21922)*. [2016.11.08/XF5436/**F**]

♦ Trägertechnologie-Kontrollregime (#16826)
♦ Traidcraft Exchange (internationally oriented national body)
♦ Traidlinks (internationally oriented national body)
♦ Traidmission (internationally oriented national body)
♦ Trail Club of Europe (internationally oriented national body)
♦ Trailokya Bauddha Mahasangha Sahayak Gana / see Triratna Buddhist Community (#20243)
♦ Train4Dev / see learn4dev (#16427)
♦ Training Center for Tropical Resources and Ecosystems Sustainability (internationally oriented national body)

♦ Training Centre for Regional Integration 20197

Centro de Formación para la Integración Regional (CEFIR)
Contact Avda Joaquin Suarez 3568, CP-11700, Montevideo, Uruguay. T. +59823365232. Fax +59823363695. E-mail: info@cefir.org.uy.
European Contact EIPA Headquarters, Onze Lieve Vrouweplein 22, PO Box 1229, 6201 BE Maastricht, Netherlands. T. +31433296222. Fax +31433296296. E-mail: info@eipa.eu.
URL: http://www.cefir.org.uy/
History Mar 1993, Montevideo (Uruguay), on the joint initiative of member countries of *Permanent Mechanism for Consultation and Political Coordination (Rio Group, inactive)* and *European Union (EU, #08967)*, to implement, manage and coordinate a *'Regional Integration Training Programme'*, agreed at 2nd *EU-Rio Group Institutionalized Ministerial Meeting (CE-RIO, inactive)*, 28-29 May 1992, Santiago (Chile). At 4th ministerial meeting, 22-23 Apr 1994, Sao Paulo (Brazil), became part of the *EU/Rio Group Human Resources Training Programme (FOR CE-RIO)*; Programme reaffirmed at 7th meeting, 7-8 Apr 1997, Noordwijk (Netherlands). **Aims** Promote exchange of knowledge and experience between *Europe* and *Latin America* in matters related to *development*, *management* and implementation of *public policies* aimed at regional integration; create a permanent forum for exchange of ideas and experience and promote added value in this exchange; work jointly with the authorities in addressing issues related to integration, attempting to generate a "chain reaction" for the benefit of agencies and participants involved; to this effect, implement, manage and coordinate throughout Latin America, a joint programme to promote *Latin American – European Union* cooperation in training *personnel* in the field of regional integration; strengthen and develop the capacity of Latin American countries to implement and manage integration programmes; target high-level public and private officials involved in formulation, management and implementation of public policies on integration, within the context of MERCOSUR, the Andean Pact, the Group of Three and other regional *free trade* agreements. **Structure** Permanent team of 7 in Latin America, including Director. Permanent staff of 2 at EIPA (Europe), including Director. The 2 Directors function as Co-Directors of the Training Programme. Permanent headquarters in Montevideo (Uruguay). **Languages** English, Spanish. **Staff** 3.00 FTE, paid. **Finance** Budget resources from the Economic Cooperation Programme of the European Union, under Financing Agreement signed by the EU and the Rio Group; supplementary contributions from Rio Group member countries; infrastructure support from Government of Uruguay. **Activities** Training/education; awards/prizes/competitions; projects/programmes. **Events** *Seminar on integration and its impact over the regions* Buenos Aires (Argentina) 1999. **Publications** *CEFIR Book Series*. Information Services: Specialized European Documentation Centre – on-line access to the database of the European Union; Specialized Library in Integration Management. **Information Services** *CEFIR Network* – internet access to training and documentation on integration in Europe, Latin America and other regions.
Members Member countries of the European Union and the Rio Group, 27 countries in all:
Argentina, Austria, Belgium, Bolivia, Brazil, Chile, Colombia, Denmark, Ecuador, Finland, France, Germany, Greece, Ireland, Italy, Luxembourg, Mexico, Netherlands, Panama, Paraguay, Peru, Portugal, Spain, Sweden, UK, Uruguay, Venezuela.
IGO Relations *Andean Community (#00817)*; *European Commission (EC, #06633)*; *Group of Three (G-3, #10791)*; *Southern Common Market (#19868)*. [2016.06.22/XE2618/**E***]

♦ Training for Health Equity Network (unconfirmed)

♦ Training Programs in Epidemiology and Public Health Interventions NETwork (TEPHINET) 20198

Main Office 325 Swanton Way, Decatur GA 30030, USA. T. +14045921447 – +14045921412. Fax +14043710415. E-mail: secretariat@tephinet.org.
URL: https://www.tephinet.org/
History 1997. Since Oct 2008, an independent part of *Task Force for Global Health (TFGH, #20098)*. Registration: Start date: 1999, USA, Georgia. **Aims** Empower and mobilize a competent field epidemiology workforce to serve all people. **Structure** Advisory Board; Secretariat. **Languages** English, French, Portuguese, Spanish. **Staff** 22.00 FTE, paid. **Finance** Support from Centers for Disease Control and Prevention; Tulane University; US Department of State. **Activities** Training/education; monitoring/evaluation; knowledge management/information dissemination; networking/liaising; events/meetings; financial and/or material support. **Events** *Global Scientific Conference* Panama (Panama) 2022, *Regional Scientific Conference of the Americas* 2021, *Southeast Asia and Western Pacific Bi-regional TEPHINET Scientific Conference* Taipei (Taiwan) 2021, *Global Scientific Conference* Atlanta, GA (USA) 2019, *Global Scientific Conference* Chiang Mai (Thailand) 2017. **Publications** *TEPHINET Newsletter*. **Members** Training programmes working across over 100 countries. Membership countries not specified. **NGO Relations** Partners include: *African Field Epidemiology Network (AFENET, #00315)*; *Eastern Mediterranean Public Health Network (EMPHNET, #05245)*. [2022/XM0041/**E**]

♦ Training Through Research Programme / see Floating University (#09796)
♦ Traité d'alliance (1942 treaty)
♦ Traité d'alliance de coopération politique et d'assistance mutuelle (1954 treaty)
♦ Traité américain de règlement pacifique (1948 treaty)
♦ Traité d'amitié et de collaboration (1953 treaty)
♦ Traité d'amitié et de coopération (1976 treaty)
♦ Traité d'amitié et de coopération dans l'Asie du Sud-Est (1976 treaty)
♦ Traité d'amitié, de coopération et d'assistance mutuelle (1955 treaty)
♦ Traité d'Amsterdam (1997 treaty)
♦ Traité sur l'Antarctique (#00850)
♦ Traité sur l'asile et les réfugiés politiques (1939 treaty)
♦ Traité d'assistance mutuelle, 1683 (1683 treaty)
♦ Traité d'assistance mutuelle, 1939 (1939 treaty)
♦ Traité d'association économique (1960 treaty)
♦ Traité de l'Atlantique nord (1949 treaty)
♦ Traité ayant pour but de prévenir les différends internationaux (1936 treaty)
♦ Traité Benelux sur l'exécution des décisions judiciaires rendues en matière pénale (1968 treaty)
♦ Traité Benelux d'extradition et d'entraide judiciaire en matière pénale (1962 treaty)
♦ Traité sur brevets d'invention, modèles et dessins industriels et marques de fabrique ou de commerce (1902 treaty)
♦ Traité de Bruxelles – Traité de collaboration en matières économique, sociale et culturelle, et leur légitime défense collective (1948 treaty)
♦ Traité de Budapest sur la reconnaissance internationale du dépôt des micro-organismes aux fins de la procédure en matière de brevets (1977 treaty)
♦ Traité sur la charte de l'énergie (1994 treaty)
♦ Traité ciel ouvert (1992 treaty)
♦ Traité de collaboration en matières économique, sociale et culturelle, et leur légitime défense collective (1948 treaty)
♦ Traité de commerce (1701 treaty)
♦ Traité sur le Commerce des Armes (2013 treaty)
♦ Traité de commerce et de navigation, 1925 (1925 treaty)
♦ Traité concernant l'enregistrement international des découvertes scientifiques (1978 treaty)
♦ Traité concernant l'enregistrement des marques (1973 treaty)
♦ Traité concernant l' exploitation et la conservation des ressources marines du Pacifique Sud (1952 treaty)
♦ Traité concernant la renonciation aux droits d'exterritorialité en Chine (1943 treaty)
♦ Traité concernant le Spitsberg (1920 treaty)
♦ Traité de coopération amazonienne (1978 treaty)
♦ Traité de coopération en matière de brevets (1970 treaty)
♦ Traité de dénucléarisation de l'Asie du sud-est (1995 treaty)
♦ Traité sur le droit des brevets (2000 treaty)
♦ Traité sur le droit civil international, 1940 (1940 treaty)
♦ Traité sur le droit des marques (1994 treaty)
♦ Traité sur le droit pénal international, 1940 (1940 treaty)
♦ Traité sur l'enregistrement international des oeuvres audiovisuelles (1989 treaty)
♦ Traité établissant une Constitution pour l'Europe (2004 treaty)
♦ Traité d'extradition des criminels et de protection contre l'anarchie (1902 treaty)
♦ Traité sur les forces armées conventionnelles en Europe (1990 treaty)
♦ Traité de garantie mutuelle (1925 treaty)
♦ Traité général d'arbitrage interaméricain (1929 treaty)
♦ Traité général d'intégration économique de l'Amérique centrale, 1960 (1960 treaty)
♦ Traité général d'intégration économique de l'Amérique centrale, 1968 (1968 treaty)
♦ Traité général de renonciation à la guerre comme instrument de politique nationale (1928 treaty)
♦ Traité Gondra – Traité pour le règlement pacifique des conflits entre les Etats américains (1923 treaty)
♦ Traité instituant la Communauté économique africaine (1991 treaty)
♦ Traité instituant la Communauté européenne du charbon et de l'acier (1951 treaty)
♦ Traité interaméricain d'assistance mutuelle (1947 treaty)
♦ Traité interaméricain sur les bons offices et la médiation (1936 treaty)
♦ Traité sur l'interdiction des armes nucléaires (2017 treaty)
♦ Traité d'interdiction complète des essais nucléaires (1996 treaty)
♦ Traité interdisant les essais d'armes nucléaires dans l'atmosphère, dans l'espace extra-atmosphérique et sous l'eau (1963 treaty)
♦ Traité interdisant de placer des armes nucléaires et d'autres armes de destruction massive sur le fond des mers et des océans, ainsi que dans leur sous-sol (1971 treaty)

♦ Traité international pour la limitation et la réduction des armements navals (1930 treaty)
♦ Traité de la Ligue d'Augsburg (1686 treaty)
♦ Traité de la ligue de Cambrai (1508 treaty)
♦ Traité pour la limitation des armements navals, 1936 (1936 treaty)
♦ Traité de Locarno – Traité de garantie mutuelle (1925 treaty)
♦ Traité de Maastricht – Traité sur l'Union européenne (1992 treaty)
♦ Traité pour le maintien de la paix en Amérique centrale (1903 treaty)
♦ Traité multilatéral de libre-échange et d'intégration économique de l'Amérique centrale (1958 treaty)
♦ Traité de Nairobi concernant la protection du Symbole olympique (1981 treaty)
♦ Traité de Nice (2001 treaty)
♦ Traité de non-agression (1937 treaty)
♦ Traité sur la non-prolifération des armes nucléaires (1968 treaty)
♦ Traité de l'OMPI sur le droit d'auteur (1996 treaty)
♦ Traité de l'OMPI sur les interprétations ou exécutions et les phonogrammes (1996 treaty)
♦ Traité pacifique de non-agression et de conciliation (1933 treaty)
♦ Traité de paix avec l'Italie (1947 treaty)
♦ Traité de Paris – Traité instituant la Communauté européenne du charbon et de l'acier (1951 treaty)
♦ Traité sur les pêcheries du Pacifique Sud (1987 treaty)
♦ Traité de la petite entente (1921 treaty)
♦ Traité sur les principes régissant les activités des Etats en matière d'exploration et d'utilisation de l'espace extra-atmosphérique, y compris la lune et les autres corps célestes (1967 treaty)
♦ Traité sur la propriété intellectuelle (1939 treaty)
♦ Traité sur la protection des biens meubles de valeur historique (1935 treaty)
♦ Traité pour la protection de l'Escaut, 1994 (1994 treaty)
♦ Traité pour la protection d'institutions artistiques et scientifiques et de monuments historiques (1935 treaty)
♦ Traité sur la protection de la propriété intellectuelle en matière de circuits intégrés (1989 treaty)
♦ Traité de la quadruple alliance, 1745 (1745 treaty)
♦ Traité de la quadruple – alliance, 1834 (1834 treaty)
♦ Traité de la quadruple alliance, 1840 (1840 treaty)
♦ Traité pour le règlement par décision arbitrale des réclamations de dommages pécuniaires (1902 treaty)
♦ Traité pour le règlement pacifique des conflits entre les Etats américains (1923 treaty)
♦ Traité relatif au droit civil (1901 treaty)
♦ Traité relatif au droit international (1901 treaty)
♦ Traité relatif au droit pénal et à l'extradition (1901 treaty)
♦ Traité relatif au droit procédural (1901 treaty)
♦ Traité relatif à la limitation des armements navals, 1922 (1922 treaty)
♦ Traité relatif à leurs possessions et dominions insulaires dans l'Océan Pacifique (1921 treaty)
♦ Traité relatif à la propriété littéraire artistique et industrielle (1901 treaty)
♦ Traité relatif à la réglementation de la pêche au saumon dans le bassin du Rhin (1995 treaty)
♦ Traité relatif aux télécommunications (1966 treaty)
♦ Traité de Rio – Traité interaméricain d'assistance mutuelle (1947 treaty)
♦ Traité de Rome (1957 treaty)
♦ Traité de la Sainte alliance, 1495 (1495 treaty)
♦ Traité de la Sainte alliance, 1526 (1526 treaty)
♦ Traité de la Sainte-alliance, 1684 (1684 treaty)
♦ Traité de la Sainte alliance, 1815 (1815 treaty)
♦ Traité de la Sainte ligue, 1511 (1511 treaty)
♦ Traité de sécurité (1951 treaty)
♦ Traité de Sécurité Collective de la CEI (1992 treaty)
♦ Traité de Singapore sur le droit des marques (2006 treaty)
♦ Traité START (1991 treaty)
♦ Traité de Tachkent – Traité de Sécurité Collective de la CEI (1992 treaty)
♦ Traité de travail (1956 treaty)
♦ Traité de la triple-alliance, 1668 (1668 treaty)
♦ Traité de la triple-alliance, 1699 (1699 treaty)
♦ Traité de la triple alliance, 1717 (1717 treaty)
♦ Traité de la triple alliance, 1882 (1882 treaty)
♦ Traité de la triple alliance, 1902 (1902 treaty)
♦ Traité de la triple entente, 1907 (1907 treaty)
♦ Traité sur l'Union européenne (1992 treaty)
♦ Traité de Versailles (1919 treaty)
♦ Traité visant l'interdiction des armes nucléaires en Amérique latine et les Caraïbes (1967 treaty)
♦ Traktat om den Europaeiske Union (1992 treaty)
♦ Traktat om en Forfatning for Europa (2004 treaty)
♦ Traktat for det Nord-Atlantiske område (1949 treaty)
♦ Traktat om oprettelse af det Europaeiske Kul- og Stålfaellesskab (1951 treaty)
♦ Traktat ustanawiajacy Konstytucje dla Europy (2004 treaty)
♦ Trans*Coalition (unconfirmed)
♦ Trans Africa Forum (internationally oriented national body)
♦ Trans-African Highway Bureau (no recent information)

♦ Trans-African HydroMeteorological Observatory (TAHMO) 20199

CEO address not obtained. E-mail: info@tahmo.org.
Co-Dir address not obtained.
Co-Dir address not obtained.
URL: http://tahmo.org/

History 25 Apr 2014, Delft (Netherlands). The Trans-African Hydro-Meteorological Observatory (TAHMO) aims to develop a vast network of weather stations across Africa. Current and historic weather data is important for agricultural, climate monitoring, and many hydro-meteorological applications. Registration: Netherlands Chamber of Commerce, No/ID: 60544481, Start date: 25 Apr 2014, Netherlands, Zuid-Holland; Ministry of Devolution and Planning, No/ID: OP.218/051/14-0255/9673, Start date: 6 Nov 2014, Kenya, Nairobi. **Aims** Develop a network of self-sustaining *weather* stations across Africa. **Languages** English. **Staff** 20.00 FTE, paid; 10.00 FTE, voluntary. **Finance** Sources: investments; revenue from activities/projects. **Activities** Capacity building; knowledge management/information dissemination; monitoring/evaluation; research and development. Active in: Benin, Burkina Faso, Cameroon, Chad, Congo DR, Côte d'Ivoire, Ethiopia, Ghana, Kenya, Lesotho, Malawi, Mali, Mozambique, Netherlands, Nigeria, Rwanda, Senegal, South Africa, Tanzania UR, Togo, Uganda, USA, Zambia, Zimbabwe. **Publications** *TAHMO Newsletter.* [2022.10.25/XJ9464/F]

♦ Trans Africa Pipeline (internationally oriented national body)
♦ Transaid (internationally oriented national body)
♦ Trans-ASEAN Energy Network (unconfirmed)

♦ Trans-Asian Railway Network (TAR) 20200

Contact UNESCAP, United Nations Building, Rajadamnern Nok Avenue, Bangkok, 10200, Thailand.
URL: http://www.unescap.org/ttdw/common/TIS/TAR/TARintergovagreement.asp

History 30 Nov 2005, Bangkok (Thailand), by intergovernmental agreement. Project originally initiated in the 1960s by *United Nations Economic and Social Commission for Asia and the Pacific (ESCAP, #20557).* **Aims** Promote and develop international rail transport in Asia and with neighbouring regions. **Events** *International Convention* Busan (Korea Rep) 2011.
Members Railways in 28 countries:
Armenia, Azerbaijan, Bangladesh, Cambodia, China, Georgia, India, Indonesia, Iran Islamic Rep, Kazakhstan, Korea DPR, Korea Rep, Kyrgyzstan, Laos, Malaysia, Mongolia, Myanmar, Nepal, Pakistan, Russia, Singapore, Sri Lanka, Tajikistan, Thailand, Türkiye, Turkmenistan, Uzbekistan, Vietnam. [2012/XU7262/F*]

♦ Transatlantic Academy (internationally oriented national body)

♦ Trans-Atlantic Business Council (TABC) 20201

Contact 919 18th St NW, Ste 220, Washington DC 20006, USA. T. +12028289104. Fax +12028288106.
Brussels Office Av de Cortenbergh 168, 1000 Brussels, Belgium. T. +3225140501.
URL: http://www.transatlanticbusiness.org/

History 1 Jan 2013, on merger of *Trans Atlantic Business Dialogue (TABD, inactive)* and *European-American Business Council, Washington DC (EABC, inactive).* EU Transparency Register: 89092554724-82. **Aims** Serve as the main business interlocutor to both the US government and the EU institutions on issues impacting transatlantic *economy.* **Structure** Board of Directors. [2017/XM5491/E]

♦ Transatlantic Christian Council (internationally oriented national body)

♦ Trans-Atlantic Consortium for European Union Studies and Simulations (TACEUSS) 20202

Address not obtained.
URL: http://www.eusimulations.org/

History Also known under its main activity: *EuroSim,* organized since 1988. **Aims** Bring together students and faculty from colleges and universities in the USA and Europe. **Finance** Members' dues. **Activities** Events/meetings. [2018/XM7795/c/F]

♦ Transatlantic Consumer Dialogue (TACD) 20203

Dialogue transatlantique des consommateurs

Coordinator c/o Consumers Int'l, 24 Highbury Crescent, London, N5 1RX, UK. T. +442072266663. Fax +442073540607. E-mail: tacd@consint.org.
URL: http://www.tacd.org/

History Founded Sep 1998, Washington DC (USA). Secretariat provided by: *Consumers International (CI, #04773).* **Aims** Serve as a formal mechanism for American and European Union consumers' representatives to provide input in transatlantic trade-policy decision-making; explore ways of strengthening the consumer's view at EU and US. **Structure** Annual Meeting, alternately in Brussels (Belgium) and Washington DC (USA); Steering Committee; Working Groups (5): Food; Information Society; Intellectual Property; Financial Services; Nanotechnology; Secretariat. **Languages** English. **Staff** 1.00 FTE, paid. **Finance** Grants from *European Commission (EC, #06633)* and US charitable foundations. **Activities** Politics/policy/regulatory. **Events** *Joint Conference on the Financial Crisis Ten Years Later* Brussels (Belgium) 2018, *Annual Meeting* Brussels (Belgium) 2013, *Annual meeting* Brussels (Belgium) 2011, *Annual meeting* Washington, DC (USA) 2010, *Annual meeting* Brussels (Belgium) 2009. **Publications** Resolutions; position papers; open letters; surveys.
Members Leading organizations (75) representing consumer interest, in 21 countries:
Austria, Belgium, Bulgaria, Czechia, Denmark, Finland, France, Germany, Greece, Hungary, Ireland, Italy, Netherlands, Norway, Portugal, Romania, Slovenia, Spain, Sweden, UK, USA.
Included in the above, 6 organizations listed in this Yearbook:
Association européenne pour la coordination de la représentation des consommateurs pour la normalisation (ANEC, #02561); Bureau Européen des Unions de Consommateurs (BEUC, #03360); European Community of Consumer Cooperatives (EURO COOP, #06678); European Digital Rights (EDRi, #06924); European Public Health Alliance (EPHA, #08297); Health Action International (HAI, #10868).
IGO Relations Cooperates with: *European Commission (EC, #06633);* US Government. [2014.12.15/XF5985/y/F]

♦ Trans-Atlantic free trade agreement (unconfirmed)
♦ Transatlantic Partners Against AIDS (internationally oriented national body)

♦ Transatlantic Policy Network (TPN) 20204

Contact Rue Froissart 115, 1st Floor, 1040 Brussels, Belgium. T. +3222306149. Fax +3222305896. E-mail: tpnoffice@tpnonline.org.
Washington Office 1800 K St NW, Sixth Floor, Washington DC 20006, USA. T. +12027753165. Fax +12022896582.
URL: http://www.tpnonline.org/

History as an informal network of businessmen and politicians in Europe and North America. EU Transparency Register: 923710115785-95. **Aims** Facilitate informal dialogue at a strategic level by helping the transatlantic partners identify common interests and adjust to new challenges and opportunities. **Structure** Management Committee; Chairman; Secretariat in Brussels (Belgium) and Washington DC (USA). **Members** No formal membership. **NGO Relations** Member of: *European Policy Centre (EPC, #08240).* [2020/XF2781/F]

♦ Transatlantic Studies Association (TSA) 20205

Vice Chairperson address not obtained.
URL: https://www.transatlanticstudies.com/

History 11 Jul 2002. Registration: Charity Commission, England and Wales. **Aims** Promote the study of transatlantic relations. **Structure** Management Committee. **Activities** Awards/prizes/competitions; events/meetings. **Events** *Annual Conference* Plymouth (UK) 2023, *Annual Conference* Canterbury (UK) 2022, *Annual Conference* Lisbon (Portugal) 2021, *Annual Conference* Lisbon (Portugal) 2020, *Annual Conference* Lancaster (UK) 2019. **Publications** *Journal of Transatlantic Studies.* [2020/AA0377/D]

♦ TRANSCEND-A Peace Development Environment Network 20206

Contact address not obtained. E-mail: info@transcend.org.
Co-Founder address not obtained.
URL: http://www.transcend.org/

History 19 Jun 1993, Honolulu, HI (USA). Former names and other names: *TRANSCEND International* – alias; *Transcend: A Peace and Development Network* – former. **Aims** Bring about a more peaceful world and transform conflict nonviolently, with empathy and creativity, for acceptable and sustainable outcomes. **Structure** Board; Executive Committee. **Languages** English. **Staff** Voluntary. **Finance** Sources: donations; private foundations. No budget. **Activities** Knowledge management/information dissemination; projects/programmes; research/documentation; training/education. **Events** *General Meeting* Vienna (Austria) 2007, *General Meeting* Cluj-Napoca (Romania) 2004, *General Meeting* London (UK) 1999. **Publications** Books; manuals. **Information Services** *TRANSCEND Media Service.*
Members Individuals (over 350) in 29 countries:
Armenia, Australia, Austria, Azerbaijan, Canada, China, Costa Rica, Croatia, Denmark, France, Georgia, Germany, India, Italy, Japan, Korea Rep, Malaysia, Nicaragua, North Macedonia, Norway, Romania, Russia, Serbia, Spain, Sweden, Switzerland, Thailand, UK, USA.
NGO Relations Member of: *EarthAction (EA, #05159).* Instrumental in setting up: *Nytt Institutt for Fredsforskning (NIFF, no recent information).* [2020.05.28/XF4857/F]

♦ TRANSCEND International / see TRANSCEND-A Peace Development Environment Network (#20206)
♦ Transcend: A Peace and Development Network / see TRANSCEND-A Peace Development Environment Network (#20206)
♦ TRANSCRIME – Joint Research Centre on Transnational Crime (internationally oriented national body)
♦ Transcultural Relations Group (internationally oriented national body)
♦ Transdisciplinary European Training and Research in Anthropology (internationally oriented national body)
♦ TRANSED – International Conference on Mobility and Transport for Elderly and Disabled Persons (meeting series)
♦ **Transeo** European Association for SME Transfer (#06208)

♦ Trans European Law Firms Alliance (TELFA) 20207

Pres PO Box 3045, 6802 DA Arnhem, Netherlands. E-mail: info@telfa.law.
Registered Address Av Louise 208, 1050 Brussels, Belgium.
URL: https://www.telfa.law/

History 1989. Former names and other names: *Trans European Law Firms Association (TELFA)* – former (1989 to 1999). Registration: Banque-Carrefour des Entreprises, No/ID: 0455.489.432, Start date: 13 Jul 1995, Belgium, Brussels; UK. **Aims** Build a network of independent, similar minded law firms. **Structure** Board of Directors of 11. **Events** *General Meeting* Brussels (Belgium) 2023, *Conference on New Mobilities* Athens (Greece) 2022, *General Meeting* 2021, *General Meeting* Brussels (Belgium) 2020, *General Meeting* Warsaw (Poland) 2019. **Members** Lawyers and firms (over 700). Membership countries not specified. [2023/XN7175/D]

♦ Trans European Law Firms Association / see Trans European Law Firms Alliance (#20207)

♦ Trans-European North-South Motorway Project (TEM) 20208

Autoroute transeuropéenne Nord-Sud

Strategy Coordinator Project Central Office, Wronia 53, 00-874 Warsaw, Poland. T. +48223758633.
Executing Agency c/o UNO/ECE, Palais des Nations, 1211 Geneva 10, Switzerland. T. +41229173298. Fax +41229170039. E-mail: nenad.nikolic@unece.org.
URL: http://www.unece.org/

History 1 Sep 1977, Geneva (Switzerland), the *United Nations Economic Commission for Europe (UNECE, #20555)* being the executive agency responsible for technical and administrative support of the project. Financed and managed through a 'Cooperation Trust Fund'. **Aims** Work to promote sustainable transport which is safe, clean and competitive through development of freight and personal mobility by inland transport modes, by improving traffic safety, environmental performance, energy efficiency, inland transport security and efficient service provision in the transport sector. **Structure** Steering Committee (meets twice a year); Working Groups; Project Central Office. **Languages** English. **Finance** Centralized management and administration funded by member countries. In addition, each country is responsible for financing the construction of motorway sections on its own territory and also contributes in-kind to planning, design, coordination and training activities. **Activities** TEM Project 2017-2021 within 3 main fields: (I) Network and funding. (II) Operational proficiency, with 5 strategic areas: Environmental protection; Organization and financing of roads and motorways; Information systems for management of road infrastructure; Innovations in infrastructure management; Road safety. (III) Designing strategies for upcoming trends in transportation. **Events** *International conference on ITS in Central and Eastern European countries* Brno (Czech Rep) 2001, *Conference on strategic environmental impact assessment of sustainable multimodal transport networks* Gdansk (Poland) 1998, *Seminar on highway electronic engineering* Prague (Czech Rep) 1993, *East-West conference* Warsaw (Poland) 1993, *Seminar on road project evaluation techniques* Prague (Czechoslovakia) 1989. **Publications** Reports, studies and standards related to motorway planning, construction and operation.
Members Governments of 14 countries:
Armenia, Bosnia-Herzegovina, Bulgaria, Croatia, Czechia, Georgia, Hungary, Italy, Lithuania, Poland, Romania, Slovakia, Slovenia, Türkiye.
Associate members (1):
Austria.
Observer members (4):
Montenegro, Serbia, Sweden, Ukraine. [2018.07.26/XF8317/**F***]

♦ Trans-European North-South Railway Project / see Trans-European Railway Project (#20210)

♦ Trans European Policy Studies Association (TEPSA) 20209

Exec Dir Rue d'Egmont 11, 1000 Brussels, Belgium. T. +3225113470. Fax +3225116770.
URL: http://www.tepsa.eu/

History 1974. Founded on the initiative of a number of European research institutes. Former names and other names: *Association transeuropéenne d'études politiques* – former. Registration: Banque-Carrefour des Entreprises, No/ID: 0459.192.456, Start date: 5 Jul 1995, Belgium. **Aims** Provide and strengthen high quality international research on European integration in order to stimulate discussion on policies and political options for Europe. **Structure** General Assembly; Board. **Languages** English, French. **Staff** 2-5. **Finance** Sources: members' dues. Other sources: European Union grants and participation in EU funded projects; occasional grants from other organizations. **Activities** Events/meetings; politics/policy/regulatory; research/documentation. **Events** *Conference on Researching and Teaching EU-Turkey Relations* Brussels (Belgium) 2020, *Conference on the German presidency of the European Union* Bonn (Germany) 1998, *Conference on common foreign and security policy* Brussels (Belgium) 1998, *Conference on new transatlantic agenda* Brussels (Belgium) 1998, *Conference on monitoring the EU enlargement process* Lódz (Poland) 1998. **Publications** Results of trans-European research and studies; books; conference reports.
Members Research institutes and associations (33):
- *Center for Comparative and International Studies (CIS)* (Switzerland);
- *Centre of International Relations, Ljubljana (CIR)* (Slovenia);
- *Danish Institute for International Studies (DIIS)* (Denmark);
- *Eesti Välispoliitika Instituut (EVI)* (Estonia);
- EGE Network (Belgium);
- *Federal Trust for Education and Research* (UK);
- *Finnish Institute of International Affairs (FIIA)* (Finland);
- *Foundation for European Studies – European Institute, Lodz* (Poland);
- *Greek Centre of European Studies and Research (EKEME)* (Greece);
- Institute for Advanced Studies (Austria);
- *Institute for Development and International Relations (IRMO)* (Croatia);
- *Institute for European Studies, Malta* (Malta);
- *Institute for World Economics of the Hungarian Academy of Sciences (IWE)* (Hungary);
- *Institute of International European Affairs, Dublin (IIEA)* (Ireland);
- *Institute of International Relations and Political Sciences, Vilnius (IIRPS)* (Lithuania);
- *Institute of International Relations, Prague (IIR)* (Czech Rep);
- *Institut für Europäische Politik, Berlin (IEP)* (Germany);
- *Instituto Português de Relações Internacionais (IPRI)* (Portugal);
- *Istituto Affari Internazionali, Roma (IAI)* (Italy);
- Iustinianus Primus Faculty of Law (North Macedonia);
- *Latvian Institute of International Affairs (LIIA)* (Latvia);
- Liechtenstein Institute;
- *Middle East Technical University (METU)*;
- *Netherlands Institute of International Relations – Clingendael* (Netherlands);
- New Bulgarian University (Bulgaria);
- *Norwegian Institute of International Affairs (NUPI)*;
- Razumkov Centre (Ukraine);
- *Real Instituto Elcano de Estudios Internacionales y Estratégicos* (Spain);
- Robert Schuman Institute – Institute of Political Science – University of Luxembourg (Luxembourg);
- *Romanian Center for European Policies (CRPE)* (Romania);
- *SciencesPo – Centre d'études europénne et de politique comparée* (France);
- Slovakia: Institute of European Studies and International Relations (IESIR);
- *Swedish Institute of International Affairs (SIIA)* (Sweden).

Associate member institutes (9):
Austrian Society for European Politics; *Centre for International Information and Documentation, Barcelona (CIDOB Foundation)*; *Centre international de formation européenne (CIFE, #03755)* (EU); *College of Europe (#04105)* (EU: Bruges – Belgium, and Natolin – Poland); Economics Faculty – Univ of Montenegro; *European Institute of Public Administration (EIPA, #07569)* (EU); Institute of European Studies, Krakow; Istanbul Policy Center; *Robert Schuman Centre for Advanced Studies (RSCAS, see: #09034)*.
NGO Relations Member of (1): *Euro-Mediterranean Study Commission (EuroMeSCo, #05727)* (Observer). [2021/XD8747/y/**D**]

♦ Trans-European Railway Project (TER) 20210

Project Central Office Namestie Slobody 6, PO Box 100, 810 05 Bratislava, Slovakia. T. +421259494728. Fax +421252442005.
Executing Agency c/o UNECE, Palais des Nations, 1211 Geneva 10, Switzerland. T. +41229171128. Fax +41229170039.
URL: http://www.unece.org/trans/main/ter/ter.html

History 17 Dec 1992. Founded when *TER Cooperation Trust Fund Agreement* opened for signature. Former names and other names: *Trans-European North-South Railway Project* – former. **Aims** Improve the quality and efficiency of international rail and combined transport, passenger and freight on the main international lines in accordance with AGC and AGTC agreements and implementation of TER technical standards and operational parameters on TER lines. **Structure** Steering Committee (meets annually). Working Parties on (2): Infrastructure Matters (WP1); Economic, Financial and Management Matters (WP2). Ad-hoc Working Groups. Project Central Office based in Budapest (Hungary). *United Nations Economic Commission for Europe (UNECE, #20555)* is Executive Agency. **Languages** English. **Finance** Centralized management and administration financed by member countries. Overall activities through voluntary contributions. Countries are responsible for financing and implementing TER decisions. **Activities** Total length of TER lines is 28,577 km railway lines of which 3/4 are electrified lines and over half are double track lines. Main activities are to: ensure coordinated upgrading of existing railway infrastructure up to the level of AGC and AGTC standards; contribute to the modernization of rolling stock; help participating countries in improving rail efficiency and adoption of the railway organization to market orientated management; develop a database on the railway and combined transport system in the region; coordinate improvement of operation parameters and facilitation of border crossings to the view of eliminating bottlenecks; develop cooperation in preparation of studies; promote development of combined transport; organize training activities for experts. **Events** *Seminar on the consequences of the European directives in Central and Eastern European countries* Paris (France) 2002, *Séminaire sur la transposition dans les pays d'Europe Centrale et Orientale des directives européennes sur la libéralisation du transport ferroviaire* Paris (France) 1999, *Round table on TER investments* Gardony (Hungary) 1993. **Publications** Reports; studies; brochure.
Members Governments of 16 countries:
Austria, Bosnia-Herzegovina, Bulgaria, Croatia, Czechia, Georgia, Greece, Hungary, Italy, Lithuania, Poland, Romania, Russia, Slovakia, Slovenia, Türkiye.
Observer countries (6):
Belarus, Latvia, Moldova, North Macedonia, Serbia, Ukraine. [2022/XF5465/**F***]

♦ Trans-European Transport Network (inactive)
♦ TransEuropeHalles: Association of Independent Cultural Centres / see Trans Europe Halles – A Network of Independent Cultural Centres (#20211)

♦ Trans Europe Halles – A Network of Independent Cultural Centres (TEH) 20211

Managing Dir c/o Mejeriet, Stora Södergatan 64, SE-222 23 Lund, Sweden. T. +46762901450. Fax +46762901450.
Contact address not obtained.
URL: http://www.teh.net/

History Mar 1983, Brussels (Belgium). Former names and other names: *TransEuropeHalles: Association of Independent Cultural Centres (TEH)* – former. Registration: Sweden; EU Transparency Register, No/ID: 213259743057-23, Start date: 8 Jun 2021. **Aims** Repurpose abandoned buildings for arts, culture and activism. **Structure** General Meeting (twice a year); Executive Committee. **Languages** English. **Staff** 9.00 FTE, paid. **Finance** Sources: members' dues. Other sources: Swedish Art Council; Region Skane; City of Lund. Supported by: *European Commission (EC, #06633)*; *Nordic Council of Ministers (NCM, #17260)*. **Activities** Capacity building; events/meetings; guidance/assistance/consulting; networking/liaising; projects/programmes; training/education. **Events** *TEH Camp Meeting* Fengersfors (Sweden) 2022, *TEH Camp Meeting* Prague (Czechia) 2022, *TEH Camp Meeting* Bratislava (Slovakia) 2021, *Cultural Impact Now! European Conference of Cultural and Creative Spaces* Ebeltoft (Denmark) 2021, *TEH Camp Meeting* Nicosia (Cyprus) 2020. **Publications** *TEH Newsletter* (12 a year). *The Lift Handbook* (2009); *TEH Factories of the Imagination* (2000).
Members Cultural centres (129) in 39 countries:
Armenia, Austria, Azerbaijan, Belarus, Belgium, Bulgaria, Congo DR, Croatia, Cyprus, Czechia, Denmark, Estonia, Finland, France, Georgia, Germany, Greece, Hungary, Ireland, Italy, Kosovo, Latvia, Lithuania, Luxembourg, Malta, Netherlands, North Macedonia, Norway, Poland, Romania, Russia, Serbia, Slovakia, Slovenia, Spain, Sweden, Switzerland, UK, Ukraine.
IGO Relations *Asia-Europe Foundation (ASEF, #01270)*. **NGO Relations** Member of (3): *A Soul for Europe (ASF, #19697)*; *European Alliance for Culture and the Arts (#05866)*; *European Heritage Alliance 3.3 (#07477)*. Founding member of: *Culture Action Europe (CAE, #04981)*. Contacts with other cultural networks; including: *Artfactories – International Resource Platform for Independent Art Spaces*; *freeDimensional (fD)*; *IETM – International Network for Contemporary Performing Arts (#11098)*; *Intercult*; *On the Move (OTM, #16868)*; *Worldwide Network of Artists Residencies (Res Artis, #21928)*. [2022.05.19/XD0292/**D**]

♦ transform! europe (transform) 20212

Contact Gusshausstr 14/3, 1040 Vienna, Austria. T. +4315046686. Fax +43125330332683. E-mail: office@transform-network.net.
URL: http://www.transform-network.net/

History Full title: *transform! european network for alternative thinking and political dialogue*. **Aims** Utilize work of independent non-profit organizations, institutes, foundations and people to contribute to peaceful relations among people and to *transform* the present world. **Structure** Members' Assembly; Board. Offices in: Vienna (Austria); Paris (France); Athens (Greece); Rome (Italy); Brussels (Belgium). **Languages** Czech, English, French, German, Irish Gaelic, Spanish. **Activities** Events/meetings; projects/programmes; publishing activities; research/documentation; training/education. **Events** *Cities for Future Communal Forum* Vienna (Austria) 2021, *Finding a New Path International Conference* Brussels (Belgium) 2017, *Just Transition Conference* Brussels (Belgium) 2016, *Analysing European Social Democracy Workshop* Helsinki (Finland) 2016. **Publications** *transform! europe Newsletter*. Yearbook; papers.
Members European organizations (29). Full in 12 countries:
Austria, Czechia, Denmark, Finland, France, Germany, Greece, Italy, Luxembourg, Portugal, Spain, Sweden.
Included in the above, 2 organizations listed in this Yearbook:
Fundación por la Europa de los Ciudadanos (FEC); *Rosa Luxemburg Stiftung (RLS)*.
Observer organizations in 10 countries:
Cyprus, France, Hungary, Italy, Moldova, Norway, Poland, Romania, Slovenia, Türkiye.
NGO Relations Recognized corresponding political foundation of: *European Left (EL, #07676)*. [2017.03.02/XM5394/y/**E**]

♦ **TRANSFORM** European Alliance for Transformative Therapies (#05889)
♦ transform! european network for alternative thinking and political dialogue / see transform! europe (#20212)
♦ Transforming Education Through Information Technologies (internationally oriented national body)
♦ **transform** transform! europe (#20212)
♦ Transfrigoroute Europe / see Transfrigoroute International (#20213)

♦ Transfrigoroute International (TI) 20213

Address not obtained.
URL: http://www.transfrigoroute.eu/

History 28 Mar 1955, Basel (Switzerland), as *Transfrigoroute Europe*, under the auspices of the *International Road Transport Union (IRU, #14761)*, and at the request of the Inland Transport Committee of *United Nations Economic Commission for Europe (UNECE, #20555)*. Present title adopted 26 Oct 1984. Previously also known as *International Umbrella Organization for Road Transport of Goods under Controlled Temperatures – Organisation faîtière du transport routier international à température dirigée – Dachverband des internationalen Strassentransports temperaturgeführter Güter*. Currently also known as *Inter-professional Organization Serving Temperature-Controlled Transport and Logistics – Organisation interprofessionalle au service du transport et de la logistique à température dirigée – Interprofessionelle Organisation im Dienste des Transports und der Logistik Temperaturgeführter Güter*. Statutes adopted 1979. Third revised version of statutes approved by Assembly of Delegates 17 Sep 1994, entered into force 1 Jan 1995. Current version incorporates changed made up to 31 Dec 2004. Registered in accordance with Swiss Civil Code. EU Transparency Register: 49864752280-23. **Aims** Take all suitable measures to develop international road transport of refrigerated, frozen or deep-frozen products; study problems relating to development of transport of temperature-controlled foodstuffs and goods in solid or liquid form; contribute to preserving wholesomeness and other characteristics of such perishable goods; improve the logistics of the cold chain, from production to distribution; encourage technical progress; participate in improving security of transportation by road; minimize pollution caused by transport; promote coordination and exchange of experience among national member groups and enterprises; maintain and develop professionalism and increase profitability, productivity and quality of benefits and services.
Structure General Assembly of Delegates (annual). Executive Committee, comprising President, Vice-President/President FCI Board, Vice-President/CCT President, Vice-President/Treasurer, 2 Vice-Presidents and 3 Honorary Presidents. Technical Advisory Committee (CCT) of body-builders and constructors, meets in Plenary Sessions and includes CCT Management Committee and CCT Committee of Experts. *Frigoclub International (FCI, see: #20213)* is the official arm representing operators of temperature-controlled vehicles. General Secretariat, based in Brussels (Belgium).

Membership categories: Active (MA) – National Groups bearing the name "TRANSFRIGOROUTE" set up and constituted in any country under valid legislation by specialized transport firms and managed by a road transport professional or a professional actively involved in road transport; Advisory (CCT) – manufacturers of vehicles, accessories and equipment, of materials for construction of special vehicles and also technical test stations responsible for ATP vehicle. Members of Frigoclub International (FCI) – individual firms actively involved in international road transport of temperature-controlled goods, with consent of their National Group member; Extraordinary (ME) – members admitted by National Groups, such as registered manufacturers of packaging, cold storage plants and providers of services in the fields of technical assistance, insurance and damage appraisal, who do not wish to become direct members; Correspondent (MC) – interested parties from outside Europe who fulfil requirements.
Languages English, French, German. **Finance** Members' dues. Other sources: fees and other income from publicity measures; donations; revenues from assets.
Activities *'Technical field'*: prepares, updates and disseminates technical provisions for the manufacture and operation of temperature-controlled equipment; encourages dialogue and exchange of experience among body-builders and manufacturers of refrigerating units, measuring instruments and other appliances. *'Economic and financial field'*: encourages cooperation between haulier (freight exchange) and takes action against unfair competition. *'Regulatory field'*: advises and exerts influence on international, European Union and national authorities in their political decision-making. *'Legal field'*: ensures immediate distribution of information relating to the *Agreement on the International Carriage of Perishable Foodstuffs and on the Special Equipment to be Used for Such Carriage (ATP, 1970)*, to international, European and national regulations and standards, to the highway code, to working practices and to customs requirements, weights and dimensions. *'Operational field'*: develops multinational cooperation within the sector and training for drivers. *'Social field'*: acts as privileged meeting point for all professionals in the temperature-controlled transport industry and takes action on working conditions and personnel training. *'Public field'*: disseminates information to the public at large via the press, radio and television.
'Means of action' – Organizes: triennial congress; annual meeting; annual forum, in which national and international politicians, administrators and technical experts are invited to participate; seminars; conferences. Adopts resolutions for the attention of inter-governmental organizations. Promotes the profession through press conferences, interviews and articles in the press; provides hauliers with the services of a network of lawyers; disseminates technical documents (technical provisions, brochures, driver manuals, etc); assists in establishing Transfrigoroute national groups being established in member countries (currently 25) and carries out surveys through them. Frigoclub International promotes commercial cooperation among ATP transporters. **Events** *Annual General Meeting* Naples (Italy) 2019, *Annual General Meeting* Paris (France) 2018, *Annual General Meeting* Madrid (Spain) 2017, *Annual General Meeting* London (UK) 2016, *Annual General Meeting* Amsterdam (Netherlands) 2015. **Publications** *Frigoriscope* in English, French, German – official newsletter; *TI Yearbook* in English, French, German – at annual meeting and at congress. *Technical Provisions CCT* in English, French, German – series (16 to date). Annual Report; annual reports of national groups; meeting proceedings.
Members total about 1,700. Active members in 23 countries:
Belgium, Bulgaria, Croatia, Cyprus, Czechia, Denmark, France, Germany, Greece, Hungary, Italy, Luxembourg, Morocco, Netherlands, Norway, Portugal, Romania, Serbia, Slovakia, Slovenia, Spain, Switzerland, UK.
Extraordinary members of national groups in 7 countries:
France, Germany, Hungary, Italy, Netherlands, Switzerland, UK.
Consultative Status Consultative status granted from: *ECOSOC (#05331)* (Ros A); *UNIDO (#20336)*. **IGO Relations** Member of: *International Institute of Refrigeration (IIR, #13918)*. Cooperates with: *European Commission (EC, #06633)*; *International Transport Forum (ITF, #15725)*; *FAO (#09260)*; *OECD (#17693)*; *United Nations Economic Commission for Europe (UNECE, #20555)* (makes representations to Inland Transport Committee and Working Group for Transportation of Perishable Goods). **NGO Relations** Associate member of: *International Road Transport Union (IRU, #14761)*. Partner in: *Global Cold Chain Alliance (GCCA, #10299)*. Cooperates with: *European Cold Storage and Logistics Association (ECSLA, #06603)*; *International Association of Refrigerated Warehouses (IARW, #12125)*. [2018/XD3330/**D**]

- ♦ Transgender Europe eV / see TGEU (#20138)
- ♦ TransitData – International Symposium Use of Public Transit Automated Data for Planning and Operations (meeting series)
- ♦ Transition Network (internationally oriented national body)
- ♦ Transitions Without Borders (internationally oriented national body)
- ♦ Transit Transport Coordination Authority of the Northern Corridor / see Northern Corridor Transit and Transport Coordination Authority (#17582)
- ♦ Translational Research In Oncology (internationally oriented national body)

♦ Translation Automation User Society (TAUS) 20214

Office Address Danzigerkade 65A, 1013 AP Amsterdam, Netherlands. E-mail: memberservices@taus.net.
Registered Address Oosteinde 9, 1483 AB De Rijp, Netherlands.
URL: https://www.taus.net/
History 2005. **Events** *Round Table* Vienna (Austria) 2017. **NGO Relations** Instrumental in setting up: *Translation Automation User Society Data Association (TAUS Data Association, #20215)*. Member of: *Cracking the Language Barrier (#04942)*. [2021/XM8129/**F**]

♦ Translation Automation User Society Data Association (TAUS Data Association) 20215

Dir Oosteinde 9, 1483 AB De Rijp, Netherlands. T. +31207734172. E-mail: memberservices@taus.net.
Office Address Molenpad 7, 1016 GL Amsterdam, Netherlands.
URL: https://www.taus.net/
History 30 Jun 2008, on the initiative of *Translation Automation User Society (TAUS, #20214)*. [2008/XM8128/**E**]

- ♦ Translation Centre for the Bodies of the European Union (#03790)

♦ Translators without Borders 20216

Traducteurs sans Frontières (TSF)
Contact Ste 500, 30 Main St, Danbury CT 06810, USA. E-mail: info@translatorswithoutborders.org.
URL: http://translatorswithoutborders.com/
History 1993. **Aims** Provide aid in humanitarian crisis response through translation and interpretation; provide translation and simplification services that are culturally appropriate, accessible and open-source; building language translation capacity at local level; raise awareness of language barriers. **Structure** Board of Directors; Advisory Board. Management Team. **Activities** Humanitarian/emergency aid; capacity building; awareness raising. **Publications** *Translators without Borders Newsletter*. *Words of Relief Impact Study*. **NGO Relations** Member of: *Communicating with Disaster Affected Communities Network (CDAC Network, #04379)*; Digital Humanitarian Network (DHN); *International Council of Voluntary Agencies (ICVA, #13092)*; *Multilingual Europe Technology Alliance (META, #16892)*. Supports: *Women Enabled International (WEI, #20991)*. Partner of: *North Star Alliance (#17605)*. [2016.06.01/XJ8595/**F**]

- ♦ Trans-Mediterranean Renewable Energy Cooperation (internationally oriented national body)
- ♦ Transnational AIDS/STD Prevention Among Migrant Prostitutes in Europe Project / see European Network for the Promotion of Rights and Health among Migrant Sex Workers (#07976)
- ♦ Transnational Alliance to Combat Illicit Trade (unconfirmed)
- ♦ Transnational Centre for Peace and Nonviolent Action / see Anuvrat Global Organization
- ♦ Transnational Civic Service Trust (#02959)
- ♦ Transnational Commercial Law Teachers Meeting (meeting series)
- ♦ Trans-national Committee of African Geotechnical Engineers (#04199)
- ♦ Transnational Crime and Corruption Center (internationally oriented national body)

♦ Transnational Foundation for Peace and Future Research (TFF) . . . 20217

Transnationella Stiftelsen för Freds-och Framtidsforskning
Dir Vegagatan 25, SE-224 57 Lund, Sweden. T. +46738525200. E-mail: tff@transnational.org.
URL: https://transnational.live/
History 1986, Lund (Sweden). Registration: Lansstyrelsen 1985, No/ID: 845001-4637, Sweden, Skåne. **Aims** Inspire a passion for the principle of peace by peaceful means from the grassroots to the corridors of power; focus on former Yugoslavia, the Middle East in general, Iraq, Burundi, Iran, Somaliland, Syria and Swedish immigration. **Structure** Board; Founders; Director; Associates. **Languages** Danish, English, Swedish. **Staff** 2.00 FTE, voluntary. about 60 TFF Associates contributing analyses. **Finance** Sources: contributions; grants; international organizations; members' dues. No government nor corporate funding. **Activities** Advocacy/lobbying/activism; conflict resolution; knowledge management/information dissemination; projects/programmes; research/documentation; training/education. **Publications** *TFF Pressinfo*; *Transnational Affairs*. Books; reports. **Members** Not a membership organization. **IGO Relations** Also links with various UN peacekeeping missions. **NGO Relations** Member of (1): *International Peace Research Association (IPRA, #14537)*. Also links with national organizations. [2023.02.28/XF1548/f/**F**]

♦ Transnational Giving Europe (TGE) 20218

Contact c/o King Baudouin Foundation, Rue Brederode 21, 1000 Brussels, Belgium. T. +3225490231. E-mail: info@transnationalgiving.eu.
URL: http://www.transnationalgiving.eu/
History 1998. Founded by a consortium of 4 foundations: *Fondation de France*; *King Baudouin Foundation (KBF)*; *Juliana Welzijn Fonds (inactive)*; *Charities Aid Foundation (CAF)*. **Aims** Facilitate cross-border philanthropy in Europe by providing a secure and efficient solution to enable individual and corporate donors to give tax-efficiently; promote cross-border *philanthropy* through the exchange of information and best practices; improve and extend the TGE network to new countries as a trusted and practical service for a tax-effective philanthropy across Europe. **Languages** English. **Staff** 2.00 FTE, paid. **Activities** Advocacy/lobbying/activism; guidance/assistance/consulting; knowledge management/information dissemination; networking/liaising. Active in Europe. **Publications** *TGE Newsletter*. Reports.
Members Partners (19) in 19 countries:
Belgium, Bulgaria, Croatia, Estonia, France, Germany, Greece, Hungary, Ireland, Italy, Luxembourg, Netherlands, Poland, Portugal, Slovakia, Slovenia, Spain, Switzerland, UK.
Partners include the following 10 organizations:
Academy for the Development of Philanthropy in Poland (Poland); *Charities Aid Foundation (CAF)* (UK); Empresa y Sociedad Fundaçion; *Europska zaklada za filantropiju i drusveni razvoj* (Croatia); *Fondation de France* (France); Fondazione Donor Italia; *Fundação Oriente, Lisboa* (Portugal); *King Baudouin Foundation (KBF)* (Netherlands); *Maecenata International (MINT, inactive)*; Open Estonia Foundation. [2022.10.24/XM8613/y/**F**]

- ♦ Transnational Immigration and Refugee Group / see Universal Human Rights Network

♦ Transnational Institute (TNI) 20219

Dir De Wittenstraat 25, 1052 AK Amsterdam, Netherlands. T. +31206626608. E-mail: tni@tni.org.
URL: http://www.tni.org/
History 1974. Founded as the international programme of *Institute for Policy Studies, Washington DC (IPS)*. An independent institution since 1992. Registration: Netherlands. **Aims** Strengthen international *social* movements with rigorous research, reliable information, sound analysis and constructive proposals that advance progressive, *democratic policy change* and common solutions to global problems; act as a unique nexus between social movements, engaged scholars and policy makers. **Structure** Board of Directors (international); Management Team (local). **Languages** English, Spanish. **Staff** 23.13 FTE, paid; 0.40 FTE, voluntary. 18 consultants. **Finance** Fees; grants; subsidies. Donors include: *Deutsche Gesellschaft für Internationale Zusammenarbeit (GIZ)*; Dutch Ministry of Foreign Affairs; *European Union (EU, #08967)*; Funders for Fair Trade; *International Development Research Centre (IDRC, #13162)*; NWO-Dfid; *Open Society Foundations (OSF, #17763)*; Referendum Committee Netherlands; *Rockefeller Brothers Fund (RBF)*; *Swedish International Development Cooperation Agency (Sida)*; *Swiss Agency for Development and Cooperation (SDC)*. Annual budget: euro 4,865,757. **Activities** Research/documentation; events/meetings; capacity building; advocacy/lobbying/activism. **Events** *Inter-generational dialogue for the 21st century* Amsterdam (Netherlands) 1999, *International seminar on global competition versus global cooperation* Amsterdam (Netherlands) 1998, *International seminar on media and conflict* Cairo (Egypt) 1998, *Asia-Europe people's forum* London (UK) 1998, *Interregional conference on democratisation* Manila (Philippines) 1998. **Publications** *TNI News* (18 a year). *TNI Briefing Series* in English, Spanish. Annual Report; working papers; reports; books; monographs; studies; policy papers; infographics; videos.
Members Individuals: Fellows (8); Associates (116). Members in 16 countries:
Australia, Brazil, Colombia, France, Germany, India, Netherlands, Norway, Philippines, Russia, South Africa, Switzerland, UK, Uruguay, USA, Venezuela.
Consultative Status Consultative status granted from: *UNCTAD (#20285)* (General Category). **IGO Relations** Observer status with: *ECOSOC (#05331)*. **NGO Relations** Member of (15): *Alternative Trade Mandate Alliance (ATM)*; *Asia-Europe People's Forum (AEPF, #01274)*; *Climate Justice Now ! (CJN!, inactive)*; *ETO Consortium (ETOs, #05560)*; *EU-LAT Network (#05585)*; *European Association of Development Research and Training Institutes (EADI, #06012)*; *Financial Transparency Coalition (FTC, #09772)*; *Global Water Operators' Partnerships Alliance (GWOPA, #10652)*; *International Drug Policy Consortium (IDPC, #13205)*; *International Science Council (ISC, #14796)*; *Observatori Internacional de la Democràcia Participativa (OIDP, #17640)*; *Seattle to Brussels Network (S2B, #19190)*; *transform! europe (transform, #20212)*; *Vienna NGO Committee on Drugs (VNGOC, #20773)*; *World Social Forum (WSF, #21797)*. Cooperates with (13): *ActionAid (#00087)* (Netherlands); *Both ENDS (#03307)*; *Clean Clothes Campaign (CCC, #03986)*; *Coalition of the Flemish North South Movement – 11 11 11*; *Economy for the Common Good (ECG, #05323)*; *FIAN International (#09743)* (and national sections in Austria, Germany and Netherlands); *Focus on the Global South (Focus, #09807)*; *Friends of the Earth International (FoEI, #10002)* (and affiliates in Europe, Netherlands, Nigeria, Uruguay and Colombia); *Institute of Global Responsibility (IGO)*; *La Via Campesina (#20765)*; *Stichting Onderzoek Multinationale Ondernemingen (SOMO)*; *Traidcraft Exchange*; *World Forum of Fisher Peoples (WFFP, #21517)*. Supports: *European Citizens' Initiative Campaign (ECI Campaign, #06558)*. [2019.02.13/XF0065/j/**F**]

- ♦ Transnationalisation and Development Research Centre, Bielefeld (internationally oriented national body)
- ♦ Transnational Network for Young European Women (see: #10689)
- ♦ Transnational Opera Studies Conference (meeting series)
- ♦ Transnational platform of Centres of Vocational Excellence for the Advanced Manufacturing Sector / see Skillman Network (#19306)
- ♦ Transnational Radical Party / see Nonviolent Radical Party, Transnational and Transparty (#17154)
- ♦ Transnational Resource and Action Center / see CorpWatch
- ♦ Transnationals Information Exchange (internationally oriented national body)
- ♦ Transnational Transparty Radical Party / see Nonviolent Radical Party, Transnational and Transparty (#17154)
- ♦ Transnational Working Group for the Study of Gender and Sport (unconfirmed)
- ♦ Transnationella Stiftelsen för Freds-och Framtidsforskning (#20217)
- ♦ Trans-Pacific Partnership Agreement (2016 treaty)

♦ Trans-Pacific Strategic Economic Partnership (TPSEP) 20220

Address not obtained.
History Established following agreement, signed 3 Jun 2005 by governments of Brunei Darussalam, Chile, New Zealand and Singapore, entered into force 28 May 2006. Former names and other names: *P4 Agreement* – alias. **Aims** Encourage expansion and diversification of *trade* among each party's territory; eliminate barriers to trade in, and facilitate cross-border movement of, goods and services among parties' territories; promote conditions of fair competition in the *free trade* area; substantially increase investment opportunities; provide adequate and effective protection and enforcement of intellectual property rights; create an effective mechanism to prevent and resolve trade disputes. **Structure** CPTPP Commission.
Members Full parties to the agreement (4):
Brunei Darussalam, Chile, New Zealand, Singapore. [2022/XJ4926/**F***]

♦ Transparency and Accountability Initiative (TAI) 20221

Contact address not obtained. E-mail: contact@transparency-initiative.org.
URL: http://www.transparency-initiative.org/

History Set up as a donor collaborative. Former names and other names: *T/A Initiative* – former; *T/AI* – former. **Aims** Expand the impact and scale of transparency, accountability and participation interventions. **Languages** English. **Staff** 5.00 FTE, paid. **Publications** *TAI Weekly*. Briefs; reports; thinkpieces.
Members Funders (6):
Ford Foundation (#09858); Luminate; *MacArthur Foundation*; *Open Society Foundations (OSF, #17763)*; *The William and Flora Hewlett Foundation*.
NGO Relations Member of (2): *Transparency, Accountability and Participation Network (TAP Network, #20222)*; *Worldwide Initiatives for Grantmaker Support (WINGS, #21926)*. [2023.02.28/XM4982/y/F]

♦ Transparency, Accountability and Participation Network (TAP Network) 20222

Secretariat 205 E 42nd St, New York NY 10017, USA. E-mail: secretariat@tapnetwork2030.org.
URL: http://tapnetwork2030.org/

Aims Ensure that open, inclusive, accountable and effective governance is at the heart of the UN's Post-2015 Development Agenda, and that civil society is recognized and mobilized as indispensable partners in the design, implementation and accountability of sustainable development policies, at all levels. **Structure** Steering Committee. Secretariat hosted by *World Federation of United Nations Associations (WFUNA, #21499)*. **Finance** Funded by grants. **Activities** Advocacy/lobbying/activism; monitoring/evaluation; events/meetings. **Events** *Asian Civil Society Forum on Sustainable Development Goals* Bangkok (Thailand) 2016. **Publications** *TAP Newsletter*. Position papers.
Members Organizations in 50 countries:
Australia, Austria, Bangladesh, Belgium, Brazil, Cambodia, Cameroon, Canada, China, Colombia, Côte d'Ivoire, Fiji, France, Gambia, Germany, Ghana, Guinea, Hungary, Iceland, India, Indonesia, Ireland, Israel, Japan, Jordan, Kenya, Korea Rep, Liberia, Malawi, Malaysia, Mexico, Nepal, Netherlands, Nigeria, Pakistan, Peru, Philippines, Rwanda, Senegal, South Africa, Spain, Sri Lanka, Sweden, Tanzania UR, Togo, Tunisia, Uganda, UK, USA, Zambia.
Included in the above, 51 organizations listed in this Yearbook:
- *Access Info Europe*;
- *ADD International*;
- *African Law Foundation (AFRILAW)*;
- *AfroLeadership*;
- *AIESEC (#00593)*;
- *Amnesty International (AI, #00801)*;
- *ARTICLE 19 (#01121)*;
- *Asia Democracy Network (ADN, #01265)*;
- *Avocats Sans Frontières (ASF, #03050)*;
- *CARE International (CI, #03429)*;
- *Caritas Internationalis (CI, #03580)*;
- *Catholic Agency for Overseas Development (CAFOD)*;
- *Centre on Integrated Rural Development for Asia and the Pacific (CIRDAP, #03750)*;
- *CIVICUS: World Alliance for Citizen Participation (#03962)*;
- *Confédération européenne des ong d'urgence et de développement (CONCORD, #04547)*;
- *Consumer Unity and Trust Society (CUTS)*;
- *Echoes of Women in Africa (ECOWA)*;
- *Environnement et développement du Tiers-monde (enda, #05510)*;
- *European Network on Debt and Development (EURODAD, #07891)*;
- *German NGO Forum on Environment and Development*;
- *Global Forum for Media Development (GFMD, #10375)*;
- *Global Network of Civil Society Organizations for Disaster Reduction (GNDR, #10485)*;
- *Global Organization of Parliamentarians Against Corruption (GOPAC, #10518)*;
- *Global Witness (GW)*;
- *Institut für Internationale Zusammenarbeit des Deutschen Volkshochschul-Verbandes (DVV-International)*;
- *International Alert (#11615)*;
- *International Budget Partnership (IBP, #12406)*;
- *International Catholic Migration Commission – Europe (ICMC – Europe, #12460)*;
- *International Centre of Comparative Environmental Law (#12483)*;
- *International Federation of Library Associations and Institutions (IFLA, #13470)*;
- *International Institute of Social Studies, The Hague (ISS)*;
- *International NGO Forum on Indonesian Development (INFID, #14366)*;
- *Korea Civil Society Forum on International Development Cooperation (KoFID)*;
- *ONE (#17728)*;
- *Oxfam GB*;
- *Oxfam International (#17922)*;
- *Pacific Disability Forum (PDF, #17945)*;
- *Plan International (#18386)*;
- *Publish What You Fund*;
- *Restless Development*;
- *Saferworld*;
- *Save the Children UK (SC UK)*;
- *Sightsavers International (#19270)*;
- *SOS-Kinderdorf International (#19693)*;
- *Stakeholder Forum for a Sustainable Future (SF)*;
- *Stiftung Wissenschaft und Politik (SWP)*;
- *Transparency and Accountability Initiative (TAI, #20221)*;
- *Transparency International (TI, #20223)*;
- *Trocaire – Catholic Agency for World Development*;
- *WaterAid (#20822)*;
- *West Africa Civil Society Institute (WACSI)*.

NGO Relations Member of: *Global Partnership for Sustainable Development Data (Data4SDGS, #10542)*. [2020/XM4979/y/F]

♦ Transparency International (TI) 20223

Headquarters Alt-Moabit 96, 10559 Berlin, Germany. T. +49303438200. Fax +493034703912. E-mail: ti@transparency.org.
URL: http://www.transparency.org/

History Founded May 1993, Berlin (Germany). Registered in accordance with German law. **Aims** Work towards a world in which government, politics, business, civil society and the daily lives of people are free of *corruption*; focus on combating international and national corruption, increasing government accountability and raising public awareness of the need to curb corruption, through international and national coalitions encouraging governments to establish and implement effective laws, policies and anti-corruption programmes; strengthen public support and understanding for anti-corruption programmes and enhance public transparency and accountability in international business transactions and in the administration of public procurement; encourage all parties to international business transactions to operate at the highest levels of integrity, guided in particular by TI Standards of Conduct. **Structure** General Meeting (annual). Board of Directors, consisting of Chairman, 2 Vice-Chairmen and 10 members. Advisory Council, including Chairman. **Staff** 150.00 FTE, paid. **Finance** Contributions and pledges by the governments of Austria, Canada, Denmark, Finland, France, Netherlands, Norway, Sweden, UK, corporations and various organizations, including:
- *Australian Aid (inactive)*;
- *Bill and Melinda Gates Foundation (BMGF)*;
- *Canadian International Development Agency (CIDA, inactive)*;
- *Chr Michelsen Institute – Development Studies and Human Rights (CMI)*;
- *DANIDA*;
- *Department for International Development (DFID, inactive)*;
- *Deutsche Gesellschaft für Technische Zusammenarbeit (GTZ, inactive)*;
- *European Commission (EC, #06633)*;
- *The William and Flora Hewlett Foundation*;
- *Inter-American Development Bank (IDB, #11427)*;
- *Irish Aid*;
- *Norwegian Agency for Development Cooperation (Norad)*;
- *Stockholm International Water Institute (SIWI)*;
- *Swedish International Development Cooperation Agency (Sida)*;
- *Swiss Agency for Development and Cooperation (SDC)*;
- *United States Agency for International Development (USAID)*.

Activities Works through the National Chapters, which fight corruption on national level through: bringing together relevant players from government, civil society, business and the media to promote transparency in elections, public administration, procurement and business; advocacy campaigns to lobby governments to implement anti-corruption reforms. *'Global Corruption Barometer'* – survey assessing general public attitudes towards and experience of corruption. *'National Integrity System'* – country studies. *'Promoting Revenue Transparency Project'* – raise awareness in both government and private sector of steps required for revenue transparency to be achieved, sustained and mainstreamed. *'Integrity Pact (IP)'* – aims to prevent corruption in public contracting. *'Business Principles for Countering Bribery'* – provide a framework for companies to develop comprehensive anti-bribery programmes. Annual TI Integrity Awards. **Events** *Biennial International Anticorruption Conference* 2020, *Biennial International Anticorruption Conference* Copenhagen (Denmark) 2018, *Financial Transparency Conference* Jakarta (Indonesia) 2015, *Conference on Managing Risk for Result and Financial Corruption* Oslo (Norway) 2013, *Biennial International Anticorruption Conference* Brasilia (Brazil) 2012. **Publications** *Corruption Perceptions Index (CPI)* (annual); *Global Corruption Report* (annual); *Bribe Payers Index (BPI)* (every 2 years); *Global Corruption Barometer* (every 2 years); *Bribe Payers Index* (every 3 years). *National Integrity System Studies Policy* – working papers. Annual Report; OECD Anti-Bribery Convention Progress Report.
Members Organizations and individuals worldwide. National Chapters accredited in 84 countries and territories:
Albania, Argentina, Armenia, Australia, Austria, Azerbaijan, Bangladesh, Belgium, Bosnia-Herzegovina, Bulgaria, Cameroon, Canada, Chile, China, Colombia, Croatia, Czechia, Denmark, Dominican Rep, Estonia, Fiji, Finland, France, Georgia, Germany, Ghana, Greece, Guatemala, Haiti, Hungary, India, Indonesia, Ireland, Israel, Italy, Japan, Kazakhstan, Kenya, Korea Rep, Kyrgyzstan, Latvia, Lithuania, Madagascar, Malaysia, Mauritius, Mexico, Moldova, Mongolia, Nepal, Netherlands, New Zealand, Nicaragua, Niger, North Macedonia, Norway, Pakistan, Panama, Papua New Guinea, Peru, Philippines, Romania, Russia, Rwanda, Senegal, Serbia, Sierra Leone, Slovakia, Solomon Is, Spain, Sri Lanka, Sweden, Switzerland, Taiwan, Thailand, Trinidad-Tobago, Türkiye, Uganda, UK, Uruguay, USA, Vanuatu, Venezuela, Zambia, Zimbabwe.
National Chapters in formation in 12 countries and territories:
Bahrain, Burundi, El Salvador, Ethiopia, Kuwait, Lebanon, Liberia, Luxembourg, Morocco, Mozambique, Palestine, Slovenia.
National Contacts in 14 countries:
Belarus, Bolivia, Brazil, Cambodia, Cyprus, Guyana, Honduras, Jamaica, Kosovo, Maldives, Portugal, Ukraine, Vietnam, Yemen.
Consultative Status Consultative status granted from: *ECOSOC (#05331)* (Special); *Council of Europe (CE, #04881)* (Participatory Status); *UNESCO (#20322)* (Consultative Status). **IGO Relations** Consultative Status with: *OECD (#17693)*. Associated with Department of Global Communications of the United Nations. Partner of: *Anti-Corruption Initiative for Asia and the Pacific (#00852)*. Member of Steering Group of: *Anti-Corruption Network for Eastern Europe and Central Asia (ACN, #00853)*.
NGO Relations Provides secretariat for: *International Anti-Corruption Conference Council (IACC Council, #11655)*; *Water Integrity Network (WIN, #20830)*. Provides Help Desk for: *U4 Anti-Corruption Resource Centre (#20273)*. Member of:
- *CHS Alliance (#03911)*;
- *CIVICUS: World Alliance for Citizen Participation (#03962)*;
- *Climate Action Network Europe (CAN Europe, #04001)*;
- *European Association of Communication Directors (EACD, #05982)*;
- *GEF CSO Network (GCN, #10087)*;
- *Gavi – The Vaccine Alliance (Gavi, #10077)* CSO Constituency;
- *Global Call for Climate Action (GCCA, inactive)*;
- *Global Partnership for Sustainable Development Data (Data4SDGS, #10542)*;
- *SDG Watch Europe (#19162)*;
- *Transparency, Accountability and Participation Network (TAP Network, #20222)*.

Steering Committee member of: *International Aid Transparency Initiative (IATI, #11604)*. Instrumental in setting up: *Publish What You Pay Coalition (PWYP, #18573)*. Supports: *Global Call for Action Against Poverty (GCAP, #10263)*. Partner of: *Basel Institute on Governance*. Links with professional, national and international organizations worldwide, including:
- *Amnesty International (AI, #00801)*;
- *ESMT Berlin*;
- *European Business Ethics Network (EBEN, #06418)*;
- *Extractive Industries Transparency Initiative (EITI, #09229)*;
- *Foundation for Environmental Education (FEE, #09949)*;
- *Global Organization of Parliamentarians Against Corruption (GOPAC, #10518)*;
- *Global Transparency Initiative (GTI, #10634)*;
- *Global Witness (GW)*;
- *International Chamber of Commerce (ICC, #12534)*;
- *International Federation of Journalists (IFJ, #13462)*;
- *International Federation of Red Cross and Red Crescent Societies (#13526)*;
- *Jeunesses Musicales International (JMI, #16110)*;
- *ONE (#17728)*;
- *Partnership for Transparency Fund (PTF, #18245)*;
- *Publish What You Fund*;
- *United Nations Global Compact (#20567)*;
- *World Vision International (WVI, #21904)*. [2019/XF2663/F]

♦ Transplant Adventure Camps for Kids (unconfirmed)

♦ The Transplantation Society (TTS) 20224

Société de transplantation

Address not obtained.
URL: http://www.tts.org/

History Feb 1966, New York, NY (USA). Founded at 7th International Transplantation Conference. International Headquarters established 1999, Montréal QC (Canada). Current by-laws approved 2013. Registration: USA, Delaware. **Aims** Provide focus for global leadership in transplantation; promote: development of the science and clinical practice; scientific communication; continuing education; guidance on ethical practice. **Structure** Council (Board of Directors), consisting of 8 Officers and 12 Councillors-at-Large, representing 6 regions (North America, Latin America, Europe, Asia, Africa/Middle East, Oceania). Committees. Sections (9): *Cell Transplant and Regenerative Medicine Society (CTRMS, #03630)*; *International Society of Vascularized Composite Allotransplantation (ISVCA, #15536)*; *International Pancreas and Islet Transplant Association (IPITA, #14504)*; *International Pediatric Transplant Association (IPTA, #14549)*; *International Society for Organ Donation and Procurement (ISODP, #15330)*; *Intestinal Rehabilitation and Transplant Association (IRTA, #15990)*; *International Xenotransplantation Association (IXA, #15919)*; *Society of Pediatric Liver Transplantation (SPLIT)*; *Transplant Infectious Disease (TID)*. **Languages** English, French. **Finance** Sources: members' dues; sponsorship. **Activities** Awards/prizes/competitions; events/meetings; training/education. **Events** *International Congress* Buenos Aires (Argentina) 2022, *Asian Regional Meeting of the Transplantation Science Symposium* Kyoto (Japan) 2022, *International Congress* Montréal, QC (Canada) 2020, *International Transplant Infectious Disease Conference* Dubai (United Arab Emirates) 2019, *Biennial Congress* Madrid (Spain) 2018. **Publications** *Transplantation* (12 a year) – journal; *Tribune* (4 a year) – newsletter. **Members** Full; Trainee; Emeritus; Associate; Honorary. Members (over 6,500) in over 100 countries. Membership countries not specified. **Consultative Status** Consultative status granted from: *WHO (#20950)* (Official Relations). **NGO Relations** Affiliated societies: *International Transplant Nurses Society (ITNS)*. Associate organizations: *Asian Society of Transplantation (AST, #01745)*; *European Donation and Transplant Coordination Organisation (EDTCO, #06939)*; *European Society for Organ Transplantation (ESOT, #08676)*; *Federation of Clinical Immunology Societies (FOCIS, #09472)*; *International Pediatric Transplant Association (IPTA, #14549)*; *Middle East Society for Organ Transplantation (MESOT, #16790)*; *Scandinavian Transplantation Society (#19125)*; *Sociedad de Trasplante de América Latina y el Caribe (STALYC, #19437)*. [2020/XC3331/B]

♦ Transportation Communications International Union (internationally oriented national body)
♦ Transportation Intermediaries Association (internationally oriented national body)

♦ Transport Corridor from Europe-Caucasus-Asia (TRACECA) 20225

SG 8/2 General Aliyarbekov Street, AZ 1005 Baku, Azerbaijan. T. +994125982718 – +994124989234 – +994124987247. Fax +994124986426. E-mail: office@ps.traceca-org.org.
URL: http://www.traceca-org.org/

History May 1993, within the framework of *Tacis Programme (inactive)* as a programme of External Relations Directorate-General of the *European Commission (EC, #06633)*, with the full title *Transport Corridor from Europe through the Caucasus and Central Asia (TRACECA)*. Founding conference organized by *European Union (EU, #08967)*. Since 2007 supported by *European Neighbourhood and Partnership Instrument (ENPI)*. Basic Multilateral Agreement on International Transport for Development of the Transport Corridor Europe-the Caucasus – Asia (MLA) signed by 12 countries, 1998, Baku (Azerbaijan). Office inaugurated, 2000. **Aims** Gradually develop trends of trade and economic development in the regions of the Black Sea basin, South Caucasus and Central Asia. **Structure** Intergovernmental Commission (IGC TRACECA) – meets annually; Permanent Secretariat, located in Baku (Azerbaijan); National Secretariats. **Languages** English, Russian. **Staff** 10.00 FTE, paid. **Finance** Country contributions. **Activities** Advocacy/lobbying/activism; financial and/or material support; guidance/assistance/consulting; knowledge management/information dissemination; research/documentation. **Events** *IGC Annual Conference* Issyk-Kul Lake (Kyrgyzstan) 2009, *IGC Annual Conference* Astana (Kazakhstan) 2007, *IGC Annual Conference* Sofia (Bulgaria) 2006, *IGC Annual Conference* Baku (Azerbaijan) 2005, *IGC Annual Conference* Yerevan (Armenia) 2003. **Publications** *TRACECA Today Magazine*.

Members Members countries (13):
Armenia, Azerbaijan, Bulgaria, Georgia, Iran Islamic Rep, Kazakhstan, Kyrgyzstan, Moldova, Romania, Tajikistan, Türkiye, Ukraine, Uzbekistan.

IGO Relations Memorandum of Understanding with: *Economic Cooperation Organization (ECO, #05313)*. *European Civil Aviation Conference (ECAC, #06564)*; *Organization of Black Sea Economic Cooperation (BSEC, #17857)*; *United Nations Economic and Social Commission for Asia and the Pacific (ESCAP, #20557)*. [2018.09.24/XK0978/**E***]

- ♦ Transport Corridor from Europe through the Caucasus and Central Asia / see Transport Corridor from Europe-Caucasus-Asia (#20225)

♦ Transported Asset Protection Association Asia (TAPA Asia) 20226

Exec Dir Secretariat Office, c/o Global E2C Pte Ltd, 1 Gateway Drive, Westgate Tower 07-01, Singapore 608531, Singapore. T. +6565149648. E-mail: info@tapa-apac.org.
General Manager address not obtained.
URL: https://www.tapa-apac.org/

Aims Establish and maintain best asset protection for the technology industry. **Structure** Management Committee, comprising Chairperson, Vice-Chairperson, Secretary, Treasurer and 8 members. **Events** *Supply Chain Security Conference* Singapore (Singapore) 2012. **NGO Relations** *Transported Asset Protection Association Europe (TAPA-EMEA, #20227)*. [2018/XJ1401/**E**]

♦ Transported Asset Protection Association Europe (TAPA-EMEA) . . . 20227

Exec Dir 1st Floor – Cordes House, Factory Road, Newport, NP20 5FA, UK. T. +441633251325.
URL: https://tapa-global.org/

History Full title: *Transported Asset Protection Association, Europe Middle East and Africa*. Registered in accordance with Dutch law. **Aims** Work towards the reduction of losses in the manufacture, transportation and distribution of high value and theft attractive products. **Structure** Board of Directors, comprising Chairman, Vice Chairman, Treasurer and 10 members. **Events** *Conference* Berlin (Germany) 2019, *Conference* Paris (France) 2016, *Conference* Madrid (Spain) 2015, *Meeting* Copenhagen (Denmark) 2013, *Meeting* Vienna (Austria) 2009. **Publications** *vigilant* (12 a year) – newsletter. [2020/XJ1400/**E**]

- ♦ Transported Asset Protection Association, Europe Middle East and Africa / see Transported Asset Protection Association Europe (#20227)
- ♦ Transport and Environment / see European Federation for Transport and Environment (#07230)
- ♦ Transport Research Arena (meeting series)
- ♦ Transport Study Center for the Western Mediterranean (internationally oriented national body)
- ♦ Trans Rescue (unconfirmed)

♦ TRANSROMANICA 20228

Contact Danzstr 1, 39104 Magdeburg, Germany. T. +493917384350. Fax +493917384352. E-mail: info@transromanica.com.
URL: http://www.transromanica.com/

History Nov 2007, Magdeburg (Germany), previously existing as a project. **Aims** Represent the common *Romanesque heritage* of eight countries in *Europe* between the Baltic and the Mediterranean Sea.
Members Full in 7 countries:
Austria, France, Germany, Italy, Portugal, Serbia, Spain.
IGO Relations *Council of Europe (CE, #04881)*; *European Commission (EC, #06633)*. **NGO Relations** *European Institute of Cultural Routes (EICR)*. [2019/XJ5964/**E**]

- ♦ Trans United Europe (unconfirmed)
- ♦ TransWorld Development Initiatives (internationally oriented national body)
- ♦ Trans World Radio (internationally oriented national body)
- ♦ Trappistes – Ordre Cistercien de la Stricte Observance (religious order)
- ♦ Trappisti – Cistercensi della Stretta Osservanza (religious order)
- ♦ Trappists – Cistercian Order of the Strict Observance (religious order)
- ♦ Traprock Peace Center (internationally oriented national body)
- ♦ TRASA / see Communications Regulators' Association of Southern Africa (#04384)
- ♦ Tratado americano des soluciones pacificas (1948 treaty)
- ♦ Tratado Antártico (#00850)
- ♦ Tratado antibélico de não-agressão e conciliação (1933 treaty)
- ♦ Tratado antibélico de no agresión y conciliación (1933 treaty)
- ♦ Tratado sobre asilo y refugio politicos (1939 treaty)
- ♦ Tratado del Atlantico Norte (1949 treaty)
- ♦ Tratado do Atlântico Norte (1949 treaty)
- ♦ Tratado del Canal de Panama (1977 treaty)
- ♦ Tratado sobre el Comercio de Armas (2013 treaty)
- ♦ Tratado constitutivo de la Comunidad Europea del Carbon y del Acero (1951 treaty)
- ♦ Tratado de Cooperação Amazônica (1978 treaty)
- ♦ Tratado de Cooperación Amazónica (1978 treaty)
- ♦ Tratado de cooperación en materia de patentes (1970 treaty)
- ♦ Tratado de derecho civil internacional, 1889 (1889 treaty)
- ♦ Tratado de derecho civil internacional, 1940 (1940 treaty)
- ♦ Tratado de derecho comercial internacional de Montevideo, 1889 (1889 treaty)
- ♦ Tratado de derecho comercial terrestre internacional (1940 treaty)
- ♦ Tratado de derecho penal internacional, 1889 (1889 treaty)
- ♦ Tratado de derecho penal internacional, 1940 (1940 treaty)
- ♦ Tratado de derecho penal internacional, 1940 (1940 treaty)
- ♦ Tratado de derecho procesal internacional (1940 treaty)
- ♦ Tratado de derecho procesal internacional, 1889 (1889 treaty)
- ♦ Tratado para evitar o prevenir conflictos entre los Estados Americanos (1923 treaty)
- ♦ Tratado para evitar ou prevenir conflitos entre os Estados Americanos (1923 treaty)
- ♦ Tratado de extradição contra o anarquismo (1902 treaty)
- ♦ Tratado de extradición y protección contra el anarquismo (1902 treaty)
- ♦ Tratado general de arbitraje Interamericano (1929 treaty)
- ♦ Tratado general de arbitramento Interamericano (1929 treaty)
- ♦ Tratado general de integración económica centroamericana, 1960 (1960 treaty)
- ♦ Tratado general de integración económica centroamericana, 1968 (1968 treaty)
- ♦ Tratado de Ginebra relativo al registro internacional de descubrimientos cientificos (1978 treaty)
- ♦ Tratado de Integración Social Centroamericano (1995 treaty)
- ♦ Tratado interamericano de asistencia reciproca (1947 treaty)
- ♦ Tratado interamericano sobre bons oficios e mediação (1936 treaty)
- ♦ Tratado interamericano sobre buenos oficios y mediación (1936 treaty)
- ♦ Tratado sobre marcas de comercio y de fabricas (1889 treaty)
- ♦ Tratado de Montevideo (1960 treaty)
- ♦ Tratado de Montevideo 1980 (1980 treaty)
- ♦ Tratado de Montevidéu (1960 treaty)
- ♦ Tratado de Montevidéu 1980 (1980 treaty)
- ♦ Tratado de Nice (2001 treaty)
- ♦ Tratado de Niza (2001 treaty)
- ♦ Tratado de no proliferación de armas nucleares (1968 treaty)
- ♦ Tratado sobre patentes de invenção, desenhos e modelos industriais, e marcas de comércio et de fabrica (1902 treaty)
- ♦ Tratado sobre patentes de invención (1889 treaty)
- ♦ Tratado sobre patentes de invención, dibujos y modelos industriales, y marcas de comercio y de fabrica (1902 treaty)
- ♦ Tratado sobre la Prohibición de las Armas Nucleares (2017 treaty)
- ♦ Tratado sobre propiedad artistica y literaria (1889 treaty)
- ♦ Tratado sobre propiedad intelectual (1939 treaty)
- ♦ Tratado para a proscrição de armas nucleares na América Latina e nas Caraibas (1967 treaty)
- ♦ Tratado para la proscripción de las armas nucleares en la América Latina y el Caribe (1967 treaty)
- ♦ Tratado para a proteção das instituções artisticas, cientificas e monumentos históricos (1935 treaty)
- ♦ Tratado sobre a proteção de móveis de valor histórico (1935 treaty)
- ♦ Tratado para la protección de instituciones artisticas y cientificas y monumentos históricos (1935 treaty)
- ♦ Tratado sobre la protección de muebles de valor histórico (1935 treaty)
- ♦ Tratado sobre la protección de la propiedad intelectual respecto de los circuitos integrados (1989 treaty)
- ♦ Tratado que estabelece uma Constituição pare a Europa (2004 treaty)
- ♦ Tratado que institui a Comunidade Europeia do Carvão e do Aço (1951 treaty)
- ♦ Tratado per el que se establece una Constitución para Europa (2004 treaty)
- ♦ Tratado sobre reclamaciones por daños y perjuicios pecuniarios (1902 treaty)
- ♦ Tratado sobre reclamações pecuniarias (1902 treaty)
- ♦ Tratado sobre el reconocimiento en matiera de patentes (1977 treaty)
- ♦ Tratado sobre la registración internacional de las obras audiovisuales (1989 treaty)
- ♦ Tratado relativo à prevenção de controvérsias (1936 treaty)
- ♦ Tratado relativo a la prevención de controversias (1936 treaty)
- ♦ Tratado relativo al registro de marcas (1973 treaty)
- ♦ Tratado de Rio – Tratado interamericano de asistencia reciproca (1947 treaty)
- ♦ Tratado de Tlatelolco – Tratado para la proscripción de las armas nucleares en la América Latina y el Caribe (1967 treaty)
- ♦ Tratado da União Européia (1992 treaty)
- ♦ Tratado de la Unión Europea (1992 treaty)
- ♦ Tratodo Gondra – Tratado para evitar o prevenir conflictos entre los Estados Americanos (1923 treaty)
- ♦ Tratodo Gondra – Tratado para evitar ou prevenir conflitos entre os Estados Americanos (1923 treaty)
- ♦ TRA – Transport Research Arena (meeting series)
- ♦ Trattat li jistabbilixxi Kostituzzjoni ghall-Ewropa (2004 treaty)
- ♦ Trattato che adotta una Costituzione per l'Europa (2004 treaty)
- ♦ Trattato che istituisce la Comunità Europea del Carbone e dell'Acciaio (1951 treaty)
- ♦ Trattato di Nizza (2001 treaty)
- ♦ Trattato Nord Atlantico (1949 treaty)
- ♦ Trattato sull'Unione Europea (1992 treaty)

♦ Trauma Hemostasis & Oxygenation Research (THOR) 20229

C-Chair Center for Military Medicine Research, Univ of Pittsburgh, Bridgeside Point II, 450 Technology Drive, Pittston PA 15219, USA.
URL: https://rdcr.org/

History Former names and other names: *The THOR Network* – alias; *The Hemostasis and Oxygenation Research Network (THOR)* – former. **Aims** Develop and implement best practices for prehospital care through to the completion of the acute phase of hemorrhagic shock resuscitation. **Structure** Steering Committee. **Activities** Events/meetings; research/documentation; training/education; advocacy/lobbying/activism. **Events** *Symposium* Bergen (Norway) 2019, *Symposium* Bergen (Norway) 2018. **Publications** *The Journal of Trauma and Acute Care Surgery*. **Members** Full (nearly 300) in 22 countries. Membership countries not specified. [2021/XM8055/**F**]

- ♦ Travailleurs industrialles du Monde (internationally oriented national body)
- ♦ Travel Industry Association of America / see US Travel Association
- ♦ Travel Program for Foreign Diplomats / see Executive Council on Diplomacy
- ♦ Travel and Tourism Research Association (internationally oriented national body)
- ♦ TREAT Asia (unconfirmed)

♦ Treat Me Nice Fan Club 20230

Club Treat Me Nice
Pres 306 rue de Belleville, 75020 Paris, France. T. +33143642364. Fax +33143642364. E-mail: amiselvis@wanadoo.fr.
URL: http://treatmenice.org/

History Mar 1965. As of 1979, also referred to in French as *Les Amis d'Elvis*. **Aims** Promote the name and image of Elvis Presley in France and in the world. **Staff** 1.00 FTE, paid. Voluntary. **Finance** Members' dues. **Activities** Events/meeting; publishing activities. **Events** *Meeting* Paris (France) 2000, *Meeting* Memphis, TN (USA) 1994, *International meeting / Meeting* Paris (France) 1993, *International meeting / Meeting* Memphis, TN (USA) 1992.
Members Individuals (7,030) in 26 countries and territories:
Algeria, Argentina, Belgium, Brazil, Canada, Denmark, England, France, Germany, Iran Islamic Rep, Israel, Italy, Luxembourg, Madagascar, Mauritius, Mexico, Netherlands, Norway, Peru, Poland, Scotland, Spain, Sweden, Switzerland, Thailand, USA. [2016.06.20/XE4150/v/**F**]

♦ TREAT-NMD Neuromuscular Network (TREAT-NMD) 20231

Main Office The Catalyst, 3 Science Square, Intl Centre for Life, Newcastle upon Tyne, NE4 5TG, UK. E-mail: info@treat-nmd.org – info@treat-nmd.com.
URL: http://www.treat-nmd.org/

History 2007. Charter adopted Jan 2012; amended Jan 2016. **Aims** Provide the neuromuscular field with the infrastructure needed to ensure that the most promising new *therapies* reach *patients* as quickly as possible. **Structure** Executive Committee; Global Database Oversight Committee; Education Committee; Project Ethics Council; Secretariat. **Languages** English. **Activities** Events/meetings; training/education. **Events** *Conference* Leiden (Netherlands) 2019, *Conference* Freiburg (Germany) 2017, *Conference* Washington, DC (USA) 2015, *Conference* Newcastle upon Tyne (UK) 2013, *Conference* Geneva (Switzerland) 2011. **Publications** *TGDOC Newsletter*, *TREAT-NMD Newsletter*.
Members Individual; Organization. Individuals in 65 countries and territories:
Argentina, Australia, Austria, Belgium, Brazil, Bulgaria, Canada, Chile, China, Colombia, Croatia, Czechia, Denmark, Egypt, Finland, France, Germany, Greece, Hong Kong, Hungary, India, Indonesia, Iran Islamic Rep, Ireland, Israel, Italy, Japan, Kazakhstan, Korea Rep, Latvia, Lebanon, Malaysia, Mexico, Moldova, Montenegro, Netherlands, New Zealand, North Macedonia, Norway, Pakistan, Peru, Philippines, Poland, Portugal, Qatar, Romania, Russia, Saudi Arabia, Serbia, Slovenia, South Africa, Spain, Sudan, Sweden, Switzerland, Syrian AR, Taiwan, Thailand, Türkiye, Turkmenistan, UK, Ukraine, United Arab Emirates, USA, Venezuela.
Organizations in 54 countries:
Algeria, Argentina, Australia, Austria, Belgium, Brazil, Bulgaria, Canada, Chile, China, Colombia, Croatia, Cyprus, Czechia, Denmark, Egypt, Finland, France, Germany, Greece, Hungary, Iceland, India, Ireland, Israel, Italy, Japan, Kuwait, Lebanon, Lithuania, Malaysia, Mexico, Moldova, Nepal, Netherlands, New Zealand, Norway, Pakistan, Poland, Portugal, Romania, Russia, Saudi Arabia, Serbia, Slovakia, Slovenia, Spain, Sweden, Switzerland, Türkiye, UK, Ukraine, USA, Vietnam.
Included in the above, 6 organizations listed in this Yearbook:
Australasian Neuromuscular Network (ANN); *Cooperative International Neuromuscular Research Group (CINRG)*; *European Alliance of Neuromuscular Disorders Associations (EAMDA, #05876)*; *European Neuromuscular Centre (ENMC, #08042)*; *FSHD Europe (#10011)*; *SMA Europe (#19310)*. [2022.10.19/XM7628/y/**F**]

♦ **TREAT-NMD** TREAT-NMD Neuromuscular Network (#20231)
♦ Treaty on Abolition of African Slave Trade, 1815 (1815 treaty)
♦ Treaty on Abolition of Slave Trade, 1822 (1822 treaty)
♦ Treaty of Alliance (1942 treaty)
♦ Treaty of Alliance, Political Cooperation and Mutual Assistance (1954 treaty)
♦ Treaty for Amazonian Cooperation (1978 treaty)
♦ Treaty of Amity and Cooperation in Southeast Asia (1976 treaty)
♦ Treaty of Amsterdam (1997 treaty)
♦ Treaty of Arbitration for Pecuniary Claims (1902 treaty)
♦ Treaty on Asylum and Political Refugees (1939 treaty)
♦ Treaty to Avoid or Prevent Conflicts between the American States (1923 treaty)
♦ Treaty Banning Nuclear Weapon Tests in the Atmosphere, in Outer Space and under Water (1963 treaty)
♦ Treaty of Central American Fraternity (1934 treaty)
♦ Treaty on Central American social integration (1995 treaty)
♦ Treaty of Chaguaramas (1973 treaty)
♦ Treaty of Chaguaramas – Revised (2001 treaty)
♦ Treaty for the Civil Law (1901 treaty)
♦ Treaty for Collaboration in Economic, Social and Cultural Matters and for Collective Self-defence (1948 treaty)
♦ Treaty of Commerce (1701 treaty)
♦ Treaty of Commerce and Navigation, 1691 (1691 treaty)
♦ Treaty of Commerce and Navigation, 1925 (1925 treaty)
♦ Treaty on Compulsory Arbitration (1902 treaty)
♦ Treaty Concerning Cooperation in the Field of Transport and Communications (1972 treaty)
♦ Treaty Concerning the Permanent Neutrality and Operation of the Panama Canal (1977 treaty)
♦ Treaty Concerning the Regulation of Salmon Fishery in the Rhine River Basin (1995 treaty)
♦ Treaty on Conventional Armed Forces in Europe (1990 treaty)
♦ Treaty of Cooperation between Denmark, Finland, Iceland, Norway and Sweden (1962 treaty)
♦ Treaty on Cooperation among States Members of the Commonwealth of Independent States in Combating Terrorism (1999 treaty)
♦ Treaty of Economic Association (1960 treaty)
♦ Treaty Establishing the African Economic Community (1991 treaty)
♦ Treaty Establishing a Constitution for Europe (2004 treaty)
♦ Treaty Establishing the European Atomic Energy Community (1957 treaty)
♦ Treaty Establishing the European Coal and Steel Community (1951 treaty)
♦ Treaty on European Union (1992 treaty)
♦ Treaty for the Extradition of Criminals and for Protection Against Anarchism (1902 treaty)
♦ Treaty of Friendship and Collaboration (1953 treaty)
♦ Treaty of Friendship and Cooperation (1976 treaty)
♦ Treaty of Friendship, Cooperation and Mutual Assistance (1955 treaty)
♦ Treaty on the Functioning of the European Union (1957 treaty)
♦ Treaty for Integrated International Telecommunications Services and Networks (1988 treaty)
♦ Treaty on Intellectual Property (1939 treaty)
♦ Treaty on International Civil Law, 1889 (1889 treaty)
♦ Treaty on International Civil Law, 1940 (1940 treaty)
♦ Treaty on International Commercial Law, 1889 (1889 treaty)
♦ Treaty on International Commercial Terrestrial Law (1940 treaty)
♦ Treaty on International Penal Law, 1889 (1889 treaty)
♦ Treaty on International Penal Law, 1940 (1940 treaty)
♦ Treaty on International Procedural Law, 1889 (1889 treaty)
♦ Treaty on International Procedural Law, 1940 (1940 treaty)
♦ Treaty on the International Registration of Audiovisual Works (1989 treaty)
♦ Treaty on International Service of Railroads, 1848 (1848 treaty)
♦ Treaty on International Transport by Rail, 1852 (1852 treaty)
♦ Treaty of Joint Defence and Economic Cooperation between the Arab League States (1950 treaty)
♦ Treaty of Lausanne – Treaty of Peace between the Allied Powers and Turkey (1923 treaty)
♦ Treaty on the Law of International Commercial Navigation (1940 treaty)
♦ Treaty for the Limitation of Naval Armament, 1922 (1922 treaty)
♦ Treaty for the Limitation of Naval Armament, 1936 (1936 treaty)
♦ Treaty of Lisbon (2007 treaty)
♦ Treaty on Literary and Artistic Property (1889 treaty)
♦ Treaty for the Maintenance of Peace in Central America (1903 treaty)
♦ Treaty of Mutual Assistance, 1939 (1939 treaty)
♦ Treaty of Mutual Guarantee (1925 treaty)
♦ Treaty of Non-aggression (1937 treaty)
♦ Treaty on the Non-proliferation of Nuclear Weapons (1968 treaty)
♦ Treaty on a Nuclear-Weapon-Free Zone in Central Asia (2006 treaty)
♦ Treaty on Open Skies (1992 treaty)
♦ Treaty of Paris, 1856 (1856 treaty)
♦ Treaty of Paris – Treaty Establishing the European Coal and Steel Community (1951 treaty)
♦ Treaty on Patents of Invention (1889 treaty)
♦ Treaty on Patents of Invention, Industrial Drawings and Models and Trademarks (1902 treaty)
♦ Treaty of Peace between the Allied and Associated Powers and Germany (1919 treaty)
♦ Treaty of Peace between the Allied Powers and Turkey (1920 treaty)
♦ Treaty of Peace between the Allied Powers and Turkey (1923 treaty)
♦ Treaty of Peace with Italy (1947 treaty)
♦ Treaty on the Prevention of Controversies (1936 treaty)
♦ Treaty on Principles Governing the Activities of States in the Exploration and Use of Outer Space, Including the Moon and other Celestial Bodies (1967 treaty)
♦ Treaty on the Prohibition of the Emplacement of Nuclear Weapons and other Weapons of Mass Destruction on the Sea-bed and the Ocean Floor and in the Subsoil Thereof (1971 treaty)
♦ Treaty on the Prohibition of Nuclear Weapons (2017 treaty)
♦ Treaty for the Prohibition of Nuclear Weapons in Latin America and the Caribbean (1967 treaty)
♦ Treaty on the Protection of Artistic and Scientific Institutions and Historic Monuments (1935 treaty)
♦ Treaty on the Protection of Intellectual Property in Respect of Integrated Circuits (1989 treaty)
♦ Treaty on the Protection of Movable Property of Historic Value (1935 treaty)
♦ Treaty of Rarotonga – South Pacific Nuclear Free Zone Treaty (1985 treaty)
♦ Treaty Regulating the Status of Spitsbergen and Conferring the Sovereignty on Norway (1920 treaty)
♦ Treaty Relating to Their Insular Possessions and Insular Dominions in the Pacific Ocean (1921 treaty)
♦ Treaty for the Relinquishment of Extra-territorial Rights in China (1943 treaty)
♦ Treaty Respecting Civil Law (1901 treaty)
♦ Treaty Respecting Criminal Law and Extradition (1901 treaty)
♦ Treaty Respecting International Law (1901 treaty)
♦ Treaty Respecting Literary, Artistic and Industrial Property (1901 treaty)
♦ Treaty Respecting Procedural Law (1901 treaty)
♦ Treaty of Rome – Treaty Establishing the European Atomic Energy Community (1957 treaty)
♦ Treaty of Sèvres – Treaty of Peace between the Allied Powers and Turkey (1920 treaty)
♦ Treaty on the Southeast Asia Nuclear Weapon-free Zone (1995 treaty)
♦ Treaty on Stability, Coordination and Governance in the Economic and Monetary Union (2012 treaty)
♦ Treaty of Tlatelolco – Amendment to the Treaty for the Prohibition of Nuclear Weapons in Latin America, 1992 (1992 treaty)
♦ Treaty of Tlatelolco – Treaty for the Prohibition of Nuclear Weapons in Latin America and the Caribbean (1967 treaty)
♦ Treaty on Trademarks (1889 treaty)
♦ Treaty of the Triple Alliance, 1902 (1902 treaty)
♦ Treaty for the Union, League and Perpetual Confederation of Latin American (1826 treaty)
♦ Treaty of Versailles – Treaty of Peace between the Allied and Associated Powers and Germany (1919 treaty)
♦ TREC – Trans-Mediterranean Renewable Energy Cooperation (internationally oriented national body)
♦ Tree Aid (internationally oriented national body)
♦ Tree of Life International (internationally oriented national body)
♦ Tree of Peace Society (internationally oriented national body)

♦ Tree-Ring Society 20232

Contact 3021 Zodiac Ct, Loveland CO 80537, USA. T. +15206618590.
URL: http://www.treeringsociety.org/

History 1935, Santa Fe, NM (USA). Bylaws revised: 5 Apr 2015; Feb 2023. Registration: 501(c)3 non-profit, USA. **Aims** Promote and encourage research in *dendrochronology* throughout the world. **Structure** Executive Council. **Languages** English. **Staff** 0.50 FTE, paid. **Finance** Sources: members' dues. **Activities** Awards/prizes/competitions; events/meetings; knowledge management/information dissemination; networking/liaising; research/documentation. **Events** *AmeriDendro Meeting* Montréal, QC (Canada) 2022, *WorldDendro : International Conference on Dendrochronology* Thimphu (Bhutan) 2018, *WorldDendro: International Conference on Dendrochronology* Melbourne, VIC (Australia) 2014, *WorldDendro: International Conference on Dendrochronology* Rovaniemi (Finland) 2010, *WorldDendro: International Conference on Dendrochronology* Beijing (China) 2006. **Publications** *Tree-Ring Research* – digital only; formerly Tree-Ring Bulletin; *Tree-Ring Society Newsletter.* **Members** Members in over 30 countries. Membership countries not specified. [2023.02.16/XJ3684/**C**]

♦ Trees for Africa / see Food and Trees for Africa
♦ Trees for Climate Justice / see Plant-for-the-Planet Foundation (#18390)
♦ Trees FTF / see Trees for the Future
♦ Trees for the Future (internationally oriented national body)
♦ Trees for Life / see Trees for Life International
♦ Trees for Life International (internationally oriented national body)
♦ TREES – Training Center for Tropical Resources and Ecosystems Sustainability (internationally oriented national body)
♦ Trends in Brewing – International Malting and Brewing Symposium (meeting series)
♦ Trends in Brewing – Trends in Brewing – International Malting and Brewing Symposium (meeting series)

♦ Tres Dias 20233

Head Office 3512 Springwheat, Rockford IL 61114-5649, USA. T. +18156360840. E-mail: tresdias@tresdias.org.
URL: http://www.tresdias.org/

History Founded Jul 1980, when statutes ratified. Statutes most recently revised in 2012. **Aims** Function as an *ecumenical Christian renewal* ministry. **Structure** General Assembly (annual); Secretariat. **Events** *Assembly* Poughkeepsie, NY (USA) 2016, *Assembly* Rockford, IL (USA) 2015, *Unity in the spirit* Atlanta, GA (USA) 2014, *Assembly* Birmingham, AL (USA) 2013, *Assembly* Seoul (Korea Rep) 2012.
Members Communities (100) in 13 countries and territories:
Canada, Denmark, Ecuador, Germany, Ireland, Japan, Korea Rep, Peru, Russia, Taiwan, UK, Ukraine, USA.
[2015.09.07/XF5946/**F**]

♦ Trevi Group (inactive)
♦ **TRF** Rosicrucian Fellowship, The (#18972)
♦ TRF – Thomson Reuters Foundation (internationally oriented national body)
♦ TRF – Tropical Rainforest Foundation (internationally oriented national body)

♦ Triads 20234

Address not obtained.

History 1674, when first recorded as secret societies aiming to overthrow the Chinese Manchurians and restore the Ming Dynasty to power. Subsequently evolved from a patriotic movement to a network of ethnic Chinese crime syndicates centred around Hong Kong but active in a number of countries. **Aims** Among others, *money launder* the proceeds of legal and *illegal* activities – *narcotics trafficking*, gambling, prostitution – to fund legitimate business. **Structure** Currently 15-20 triads are thought to be actively involved in criminal activity in Hong Kong, with membership varying from about 50 individuals to over 30,000. **Activities** Gangs are involved in gambling, prostitution, arms sales, drug smuggling but also legitimate enterprises such as real estate, public transportation and film-making. Also active in China, Macau and Chinatowns in Australia, Europe, New Zealand, North America and South Africa. [2010/XF6535/s/**F**]

♦ TRIAL International (internationally oriented national body)
♦ Trialog – Research Association for Planning and Building in Developing Countries (internationally oriented national body)
♦ TRIAL – track impunity always / see TRIAL International
♦ Triangle génération humanitaire (internationally oriented national body)
♦ TRIAS (internationally oriented national body)
♦ TRIAS Make the South your Business / see TRIAS
♦ **Tri-Association** Association of American Schools of Central America, Colombia, Caribbean and Mexico (#02367)
♦ Tribal Link Foundation (internationally oriented national body)
♦ Tribunal administratif de la Banque mondiale (#21216)
♦ Tribunal administratif des Nations Unies (inactive)
♦ Tribunal administratif de l'Organisation de coopération et de développement économiques (#00119)
♦ Tribunal administratif de l'Organisation des Etats américains (see: #17629)
♦ Tribunal administratif de l'Organisation internationale du travail (#00118)
♦ Tribunal administratif de la Société des Nations (inactive)
♦ Tribunal administratif d'UNIDROIT (see: #13934)
♦ Tribunal Administrativo de la Organización de los Estados Americanos (see: #17629)
♦ Tribunal Andino de Justicia / see Court of Justice of the Andean Community (#04936)
♦ Tribunal de Arbitraje Deportivo / see Court of Arbitration for Sport (#04933)
♦ Tribunal Arbitral del Deporte (#04933)
♦ Tribunal arbitral du sport (#04933)
♦ Tribunal de la Banque internationale pour la reconstruction et le développement, de l'Association internationale de développement et de la Société financière internationale / see World Bank Administrative Tribunal (#21216)
♦ Tribunal Centroamericano / see Corte Centroamericana de Justicia (#04850)
♦ Tribunal des Communautés européennes (inactive)
♦ Tribunal de las Comunidades Europeas (inactive)
♦ Tribunal das Comunidades Européias (inactive)
♦ Tribunal de Contas Europeu (#06854)
♦ Tribunal de Cuentas Europeo (#06854)
♦ Tribunale delle Comunità Europee (inactive)
♦ Tribunale Internazionale dell'Ambiente (see: #13097)
♦ Tribunale Permanente dei Popoli (#18328)
♦ Tribunal Internacional del Derecho del Mar (#15731)
♦ Tribunal international centroaméricain (inactive)
♦ Tribunal international du droit de la mer (#15731)
♦ Tribunal international pour l'environnement (see: #13097)
♦ Tribunal de Justiça das Comunidades Europeias / see Court of Justice of the European Union (#04938)
♦ Tribunal de Justica da União Europeia (#04938)

♦ Tribunal de Justicia del Acuerdo de Cartagena / see Court of Justice of the Andean Community (#04936)
♦ Tribunal de Justicia de la Comunidad Andina (#04936)
♦ Tribunal de Justicia de las Comunidades Europeas / see Court of Justice of the European Union (#04938)
♦ Tribunal de Justicia de la Unión Europea (#04938)
♦ Tribunal pour la paix (internationally oriented national body)
♦ Tribunal pénal international pour l'ex-Yougoslavie (inactive)
♦ Tribunal pénal international pour le Rwanda (inactive)
♦ Tribunal Permanente de los Pueblos (#18328)
♦ Tribunal Permanent des Peuples (#18328)
♦ Tribunal spécial pour le Liban (#19911)

♦ TRICALS 20235

Registered Address Jansdam 2A, 3512 HB Utrecht, Netherlands. E-mail: info@tricals.org.
URL: https://www.tricals.org/

History Registration: Netherlands. **Aims** Find effective treatments for ALS. **Structure** Executive Board. **Activities** Events/meetings; training/education. **Events** *Meeting* Utrecht (Netherlands) 2019.
Members Centres in 14 countries:
Belgium, Croatia, Denmark, France, Ireland, Italy, Netherlands, Norway, Poland, Slovenia, Spain, Sweden, Switzerland, UK.
[AA0495/**D**]

♦ The Trickledown Trust / see Prospero World

♦ Trickle Up Program (TUP) 20236

Address not obtained.
URL: http://www.trickleup.org/

History 1979, USA. 1979, Weston CT (USA). **Aims** Create new opportunities for *self employment* and economic and social *well-being* among low income populations of the world; encourage the poorest of the *poor* to invest their time, skills and resources in productive, sustainable, profit-making enterprises they plan themselves, which can lead them to economic independence; increase productivity; reduce *unemployment* and underemployment; stimulate development with equity and greater opportunities for women; encourage *development* agencies, governmental, non-governmental and intergovernmental, to incorporate the Trickle Up process into their development strategies. **Structure** Founder/Chair of the Board; Board President; President; Board of Directors of 24 members; Trickle Up Advisory Council of 16 members. **Languages** English, French, Spanish. **Staff** 17.00 FTE, paid. **Finance** Contributions from individuals, corporations, foundations, governments and organizations, including the following bodies listed in this Yearbook: *Stanley Center for Peace and Security*; *UNDP (#20292)*. Budget (annual): US$ 5 million. **Activities** Financial and/or material support; training/education. **Events** *Annual meeting* New York, NY (USA) 2000, *Annual women's studies conference* New Haven, CT (USA) 1999. **Publications** *Trickle Update* (12 a year) – e-mail newsletter; *Trickle Up Program Newsletter* (3 a year). Annual Report.
Members Not a membership programme, but enterprises have been started or expanded by the Trickle Up process, through volunteer local and international non-governmental and intergovernmental organizations, which has assigned grants in 8 countries:
Burkina Faso, Ethiopia, Guatemala, India, Mali, Nepal, Nicaragua, Uganda.
IGO Relations Associated with Department of Global Communications of the United Nations. Cooperation with: UNDP; *United Nations Volunteers (UNV, #20650)*. **NGO Relations** Member of: *American Council for Voluntary International Action (InterAction)*; *InsideNGO (inactive)*. Coordinating Agencies, 2 of which are listed in this Yearbook: *CARE International (CI, #03429)*; *Habitat for Humanity International (HFHI)*. [2020/XF1836/**F**]

♦ Tricontinental Centre (internationally oriented national body)
♦ TRIDO / see International Association for Counselling (#11821)
♦ Triennial Nordic Shoulder and Elbow Conference (meeting series)
♦ Trier – Franziskanerbrüder vom Heiligen Kreuz (religious order)
♦ Trieste International Foundation (internationally oriented national body)
♦ Trifinio plan – Agreement Concluded between the Governments of El Salvador, Honduras and Guatemala, the Inter-American Institute for Cooperation on Agriculture and the OAS General Secretariat Relative to an Extension for the Technical Cooperation for Execution of the Integral Development Plan for the Border Region Shared by the Three Countries (1994 treaty)

♦ Trilateral Commission (TC) 20237

Commission trilatérale – Comisión Trilateral

Dir – European Group 5 rue de Téhéran, 75008 Paris, France. T. +33145614180. Fax +33145614287. E-mail: trilateral.europe@wanadoo.fr – european.office@trilateral.fr.
Dir – North American Group 1156 Fifteenth St NW, Washington DC 20005, USA. T. +12024675410. Fax +12024675415. E-mail: contactus@trilateral.org.
Dir – Pacific Asia Group Japan Centre Int Exchange, 4-9-17 Minami-Azabu, Minato-ku, Tokyo, 106-0047 Japan. T. +81334467781. Fax +81334437580. E-mail: admin@jcie.or.jp.
URL: http://www.trilateral.org/

History Jul 1973, New York NY (USA), by individuals in Western Europe, Japan and North America. Originally set up for 3 years, but continues to be renewed every 3 years. Current triennium to be completed in 2015. **Aims** Encourage closer *cooperation* among democratic *industrialized* regions of Western Europe, Pacific Asia and North America on matters of common concern; analyse major issues facing these regions; improve public understanding of such problems; develop and support proposals for handling them jointly; nurture habits and practices of working together. **Structure** Executive Committee. Groups (3) each with own Chairman, Deputy Chairman and Directors: Pacific Asia; North America; Europe. Task forces. **Finance** Grants from foundations and corporations. **Activities** Events/meetings. **Events** *Asia Pacific Regional Meeting* Tokyo (Japan) 2022, *Annual Meeting* Paris (France) 2019, *European Regional Meeting* Stockholm (Sweden) 2019, *Annual Meeting* Singapore (Singapore) 2018, *Asia Pacific Regional Meeting* Tokyo (Japan) 2017. **Publications** *Task Force Reports*.
Members Membership is restricted. Individuals in 40 countries:
Australia, Austria, Belgium, Bulgaria, Canada, Cyprus, Czechia, Denmark, Estonia, Finland, France, Germany, Greece, Hungary, Indonesia, Ireland, Italy, Japan, Korea Rep, Latvia, Lithuania, Luxembourg, Malaysia, Malta, Mexico, Netherlands, New Zealand, Norway, Philippines, Poland, Portugal, Romania, Singapore, Slovakia, Slovenia, Spain, Sweden, Thailand, UK, USA.
Consultative Status Consultative status granted from: *ECOSOC (#05331)* (Ros B). **IGO Relations** Accredited by: *United Nations Office at Vienna (UNOV, #20604)*. Associated with Department of Global Communications of the United Nations. [2018/XF5306/v/**F**]

♦ Trilateral Committee for Wildlife and Ecosystem Conservation and Management 20238

Comité trilatéral de conservation et de gestion des espèces sauvages et des écosystèmes – Comité Trilateral de Conservación y Manejo de Vida Silvestre y Ecosistemas

Coordinator c/o USFWS, 5275 Leesburg Pike, Falls Church VA 22014, USA.
URL: http://www.trilat.org/

History 1996. **Aims** Facilitate and enhance cooperation and coordination among the members in projects and programmes for the conservation and management of wildlife, plants, biological diversity and ecosystems of mutual interest. **Events** *Annual Meeting* Gatineau, QC (Canada) 2022, *Annual Meeting* Falls Church, VA (USA) 2021, *Annual Meeting* Mérida (Mexico) 2020, *Annual Meeting* Victoria, BC (Canada) 2019, *Annual Meeting* Shepherdstown, WV (USA) 2018.
Members Governmental agencies (3) in 3 countries:
Canada, Mexico, USA.
IGO Relations Partner: *Commission for Environmental Cooperation (CEC, #04211)*. **NGO Relations** Partners: *International Association of Fish and Wildlife Agencies (IAFWA, inactive)*; national organizations. [2021/XE4335/**E***]

♦ Trilateral Cooperation Secretariat (TCS) 20239

Secretariat S-Tower 20th Fl, 82 Saemunan-ro, Jongno-gu, Seoul 03185, Korea Rep. T. +8227334700. Fax +8227332525. E-mail: tcs@tcs-asia.org.
URL: http://www.tcs-asia.org/

History Officially inaugurated, Sep 2011, Seoul (Korea Rep), upon signing and ratification of agreement. **Aims** Promote peace and comon prosperity among the People's Republic of China, Japan and the Republic of Korea. **Structure** Consultative Board. Departments (4): Political Affairs; Economic Affairs; Socio-cultural Affairs; Management and Coordination. **Finance** Operation budget shared equally by participating governments. **Activities** Events/meetings. **Events** *International Forum for Trilateral Cooperation* Seoul (Korea Rep) 2021, *Trilateral Entrepreneurs Forum* Seoul (Korea Rep) 2021, *Summit* Chengdu (China) 2019, *Tourism Ministers Meeting* Incheon (Korea Rep) 2019, *ROK-Japan-China Trilateral Heads of Government Agency Meeting on Disaster Management* Seoul (Korea Rep) 2019.
Members Governments (3):
China, Japan, Korea Rep. [2021/XM7771/**F***]

♦ Trilateral Forum on North Pacific Security (meeting series)
♦ Trim and Fitness International Sport for All Association / see The Association for International Sport for All (#02763)

♦ Tri-nation Alliance 20240

Address not obtained.

History 2010. A formal collaboration between medical colleges in Australia, New Zealand and Canada. **Activities** Events/meetings. **Events** *Tri-nation Alliance International Medical Symposium* Sydney, NSW (Australia) 2020, *International Medical Symposium* Auckland (New Zealand) 2019, *International Medical Symposium* Sydney, NSW (Australia) 2018.
Members Colleges in 3 countries:
Australia, Canada, New Zealand. [2018/XM8010/c/**E**]

♦ Trinitarian Sisters of Valence (religious order)
♦ Trinitarians – Order of the Most Holy Trinity for the Redemption of Captives (religious order)
♦ Trinitari – Ordine della Santissima Trinità (religious order)
♦ TRIO – Translational Research In Oncology (internationally oriented national body)
♦ Tripartite Agreement on Road Transport (1998 treaty)
♦ Tripartite Agreement – Trade Expansion and Economic Cooperation Agreement between India, Egypt and Yugoslavia (1967 treaty)
♦ Tripartite Commission for the Development of the River Basin of Rio Pilcomayo (#04145)
♦ Tripartite Commission for the Restitution of Monetary Gold (inactive)
♦ Tripartite Declaration of Principles Concerning Multinational Enterprises and Social Policy (1977 treaty)

♦ Tripartite Environmental Education Network (TEEN) 20241

Contact Ministry of the Environment – Govt of Japan, Godochosha No 5, Kasumigaseki 1-2-2, Chivoda-ku, Tokyo, 100-8975 Japan. T. +81335813351.
URL: http://www.temm.org/

History following 1st *Tripartite Environment Ministers Meeting (TEMM)*, Jan 1999, Seoul (Korea Rep). **Aims** Conduct projects promoting environmental awareness. **Activities** Runs 'Database Creation Project on Environmental Education'. Organizes workshops. **Events** *Symposium* Hangzhou (China) 2019, *Symposium* Kitakyushu (Japan) 2018, *Symposium* Suwon (Korea Rep) 2017, *Symposium* Shenzhen (China) 2016, *Workshop* Japan 2006.
Members Institutes (3) in 3 countries:
China, Japan, Korea Rep. [2010/XM3121/**F**]

♦ Tripartite Environment Ministers Meeting (meeting series)
♦ Tripartite Inland Waterways Agreement (1998 treaty)
♦ Tripartite Pact (1940 treaty)
♦ Tripartite Shippers' Group / see Global Shippers' Forum (#10596)
♦ Triple Alliance (inactive)
♦ Triple Alliance (inactive)
♦ Triple Alliance Treaty, 1668 (1668 treaty)
♦ Triple Alliance Treaty, 1699 (1699 treaty)
♦ Triple Alliance Treaty, 1717 (1717 treaty)
♦ Triple Alliance Treaty, 1882 (1882 treaty)
♦ Triple Entente Treaty, 1907 (1907 treaty)

♦ Triple Helix Association (THA) 20242

Exec Dir address not obtained.
URL: http://www.triplehelixassociation.org/

History 2009, Turin (Italy), following a series of conferences organized since 1996. Registered in accordance with Italian law. **Aims** Advance scientific knowledge and operational capacity to ignite and manage academy/industry/government interactions (Triple Helix) to foster research, innovation, entrepreneurship and regional sustainable developments. **Structure** General Assembly; Executive Committee; Operational Committees. **Activities** Awards/prizes/competitions; events/meetings; publishing activities; research/documentation; training/education. **Events** *International Conference* Florence (Italy) 2022, *International Conference* Tampere (Finland) 2020, *International Conference* Cape Town (South Africa) 2019, *International Summit* Dubai (United Arab Emirates) 2018, *International Conference* Manchester (UK) 2018. **Publications** *THA Newsletter* (12 a year); *Hélice* (4 a year) – magazine; *Spiral*; *Triple Helix Journal*. **Members** Individuals (120). Membership countries not specified. **NGO Relations** Member of: *EFMD – The Management Development Network (#05387)*. [2019.02.13/XM4874/**C**]

♦ Tripoli-Windhoek Highway Coordinating Committee (inactive)
♦ TRIPS – WTO Agreement on Trade Related Aspects of Intellectual Property Rights (1994 treaty)
♦ Triratna Bauddha Mahasangha (#20243)

♦ Triratna Buddhist Community 20243

Buddhistische Gemeinschaft Triratna – Buddhistiska Gemenskapen Triratna – Buddhalainen Yhteiso Triratna – Triratna Bauddha Mahasangha

Contact Adhisthana, Coddington Court, Coddington, Ledbury, HR8 1JL, UK. E-mail: munisha@triratnadevelopment.org.
URL: http://www.thebuddhistcentre.com/text/what-triratna-buddhist-community/

History 6 Apr 1967, London (UK). Founded by an English Buddhist teacher, Venerable Urgyen *Sangharakshita*. Former names and other names: *Friends of the Western Buddhist Order (FWBO)* – former; *Amigos del Orden Budista Occidental (AOBO)* – former; *Freunde des Westlichen Buddhistischen Orden* – former; *Västerländska Buddhistordens Vänner* – former; *Länsimaisen Buddhalaisen Veljeskunnan Ystävät* – former; *Trailokya Bauddha Mahasangha Sahayak Gana (TBMSG)* – former; *Sangharakshita* – former; *Western Buddhist Order (WBO)* – former (1968); *Orden Budista Triratna* – former. **Aims** Teach Buddhism as presented by Sangharakshita; enable people to follow the Buddhist path in the context of the modern world. **Structure** Network of legally independent centres, communities and right livelihood business, administered by members of *Triratna Buddhist Order*. **Finance** All centres are independent charities and are responsible for their own financial support. This may come from course fees, right livelihood businesses, donations. **Activities** Awareness raising; knowledge management/information dissemination; networking/liaising; publishing activities; religious activities; standards/guidelines; training/education. **Members** Buddhist centres, retreat centres and other enterprises in 28 countries. Membership countries not specified. **NGO Relations** Member of national Buddhist umbrella groups. [2023.02.14/XF1863/**F**]

♦ Triratna Buddhist Order (religious order)
♦ TRI – Remanufacturing Institute (internationally oriented national body)
♦ TRI – Rensselaerville Institute (internationally oriented national body)

♦ Trisomy 21 Research Society (T21RS) 20244

Groningen Office Dept of Neurology, Univ Medical Ctr Groningen, Hanzeplein 1, 9713 GZ Groningen, Netherlands. T. +31503611485. E-mail: info@t21rs.org.
Paris Office Brain and Spine Inst, 47 boulevard de l'Hôpital, 75013 Paris, France.
URL: http://www.t21rs.org/

History 17 Apr 2014, Groningen (Netherlands). Registered in accordance with Dutch law. **Aims** Promote basic and applied research on Down *syndrome*; stimulate translational research; apply new scientific knowledge to develop improved treatments and cures. **Structure** Executive Board; Advisory Board; Committees. **Finance** Sources: members' dues. **Activities** Events/meetings; research/documentation; training/education. **Events** *International Conference* Barcelona (Spain) 2019, *International Conference* Chicago, IL (USA) 2017, *International Conference* Paris (France) 2015. [2020.03.03/XM4706/**C**]

- ♦ **TRI** Tinnitus Research Initiative (#20166)
- ♦ TRI – Tropical Resources Institute (internationally oriented national body)
- ♦ tRNA Conference (meeting series)
- ♦ Trocaire – Catholic Agency for World Development (internationally oriented national body)
- ♦ **TroCCAP** Tropical Council for Companion Animal Parasites (#20248)
- ♦ Trois cultures méditerranéennes (internationally oriented national body)
- ♦ Troisième accord international sur l'étain (1965 treaty)
- ♦ Troisième convention ACP-CEE (1984 treaty)
- ♦ Troisième protocole additionnel à l'Accord général sur les privilèges et immunités du Conseil de l'Europe (1959 treaty)
- ♦ Troisième Protocole additionnel à la Convention européenne d'extradition (2010 treaty)
- ♦ Troisième protocole additionnel au Protocole à l'Arrangement européen pour la protection des émissions de télévision (1989 treaty)
- ♦ Troisième protocole portant amendement à la Convention au sujet de la canalisation de la Moselle (1987 treaty)
- ♦ TROMEFO – Tropisch Medisch Fonds (internationally oriented national body)

♦ TropEd 20245

Exec Sec Teaching & Training Unit, Div of Infectious Diseases and Tropical Medicine – LMU, Leopoldstr 5, 80802 Munich, Germany. E-mail: tropedsecretariat@gmail.com.
URL: http://www.troped.org/

History Former names and other names: *European Network for Education in International Health (tropEd)* – former; *Network for Education in International Health (TropEd)* – alias. Registration: Berlin District court, No/ID: VR 23235, Start date: 4 Mar 2004, Germany, Charlottenburg. **Aims** Improve management of health services for disadvantaged populations. **Structure** General Assembly; Executive Committee. **Languages** English. **Activities** Training/education.
Members Institutional Full; Collaborating institutions; Individual. Institutions (27) in 18 countries:
Belgium, China, Germany, Indonesia, Italy, Mali, Mexico, Morocco, Netherlands, Norway, Portugal, Spain, Sweden, Switzerland, Tanzania UR, Thailand, UK, Vietnam.
Barcelona Institute for Global Health (ISGlobal); Bernhard Nocht Institut für Tropenmedizin (BNITM); Centre for International Health, Bergen (CIH); Heidelberg Institute of Global Health (HIGH); Institute de Higiene e Medicina Tropical, Universidade Nova e Lisboa; Institute for Global Health and Development, Edinburgh (IGHD); Institute of Tropical Medicine Antwerp (IMT); Institut für Tropenmedizin und Internationale Gesundheit; Royal Tropical Institute (KIT); Swiss Tropical and Public Health Institute (Swiss TPH); UCL Institute for Global Health (IGH).
NGO Relations Member of (1): *World Federation of Academic Institutions for Global Health (WFAIGH, inactive).* [2016.10.18/XM3226/y/**F**]

- ♦ tropEd / see TropEd (#20245)
- ♦ Tropenbos Foundation / see Tropenbos International
- ♦ Tropenbos International (internationally oriented national body)
- ♦ Tropical Agriculture Association (internationally oriented national body)

♦ Tropical Agriculture Research and Higher Education Center 20246

Centre agronomique tropical de recherche et d'enseignement – Centro Agronómico Tropical de Investigación y Enseñanza (CATIE)

Dir Gen 7170 Cartago, Cartago, Turrialba, Turrialba, 30501, Costa Rica. T. +50625582000. E-mail: comunica@catie.ac.cr – catie@catie.ac.cr.
URL: http://www.catie.ac.cr/

History 12 Jan 1973, Turrialba (Costa Rica), as *Tropical Agriculture Research and Training Center*, by a contract between the then *'Inter-American Institute of Agricultural Sciences (IAIAS)'*, currently *Inter-American Institute for Cooperation on Agriculture (IICA, #11434)*, and the Government of Costa Rica, taking over the activities of *IAIAS Training and Research Center* which had operated at the same site since 17 Oct 1942. Activities commenced officially on 1 Jul 1973. Contract revised 1982 and ratified May 1983, when *Inter-American Board of Agriculture (IABA, see: #11434)* met as the Constituent Assembly of the Center. **Aims** Improve well-being by applying scientific research and higher education to *development*, *conservation* and *sustainable* use of *natural resources*; make a substantive, measurable impact on economic growth and social development in the *American Tropics* and on *conservation* of its natural resources and *environment*; develop educational and training activities at postgraduate level and specialization so as to qualify professionals to solve *agrosilvopastural* development problems of member countries and of *Latin America* and the *Caribbean* in general. **Structure** *'Inter-American Board of Agriculture (JIA)'*, comprising Ministers of Agriculture of all countries of the American continent, acts as General Assembly. Governing Council, consisting of member countries' Ministers of Agriculture and/or Natural Resources. Board of Directors, composed of 5 eminent scientists from the international community, 4 distinguished businessmen from member countries, one representative of IICA and one of IABA, both acting in their personal capacity; Director General acts as ex-officio Secretary. Directorate of Administration and Finances; Directorate of Strategic Planning. National Technical Offices in: Colombia; Costa Rica; Dominican Rep; El Salvador; Guatemala (Guatemala); Honduras; Mexico; Nicaragua; Panama; Venezuela. **Languages** English, Spanish. **Staff** 150.00 FTE, paid. **Finance** Major sources: annual fees from member countries and IICA (8% of budget); donors and development agencies (36% – for project funding); contributions from Denmark, Sweden and Switzerland (15% – for central budget); resources generated by activities (15%); support foundations – *FUNDATROPICOS* (2%); administered funds (24%). Other sources: American Cacao Research Institute; *European Commission (EC, #06633); International Bank for Reconstruction and Development (IBRD, #12317); Inter-American Development Bank (IDB, #11427).* Budget (annual): US$ 19 million. **Activities** Research/documentation; knowledge management/information dissemination; training/education. **Events** *Latin American congress on agroforestry for sustainable animal production* Havana (Cuba) 2006, *Congress on agroforestry and livestock production in Latin America* San José (Costa Rica) 2001, *International symposium on silvopastoral systems* San José (Costa Rica) 2001, *Conference on criteria and indicators for sustainable forest management at the forest management unit level* Nancy (France) 2000, *Latin American symposium* Santo Domingo (Dominican Rep) 1999. **Publications** *Integrated Pest Management Journal* (4 a year); *Agroforestry in the Americas Review*; *Central American Forestry Review.* Annual Report.
Members Full governments of 12 countries:
Belize, Bolivia, Colombia, Costa Rica, Dominican Rep, El Salvador, Guatemala, Honduras, Mexico, Nicaragua, Panama, Venezuela.
Full regional member:
IICA.
Associate governments of countries that are not IICA members, intergovernmental and nongovernmental organizations, international centers and private organizations (not specified).
IGO Relations Accredited to the Conference of the Parties of: *Secretariat of the United Nations Convention to Combat Desertification (Secretariat of the UNCCD, #19208).* Accredited by: *United Nations Framework Convention on Climate Change – Secretariat (UNFCCC, #20564).* Involved in development and participation of: *Caribbean Action Plan (CAR, #03432).* Supports: *Bioversity International (#03262).* Observer to: *International Fund for Agricultural Development (IFAD, #13692).* **NGO Relations** Working relations with universities worldwide and with national research and training institutions in member countries. Member of: *Asociación Universitaria Iberoamericana de Postgrado (AUIP, #02307); Association of International Research and Development Centers for Agriculture (AIRCA, #02760); Global Alliance for Climate-Smart Agriculture (GACSA, #10189); International Foundation for Science (IFS, #13677); International Union for Conservation of Nature and Natural Resources (IUCN, #15766); LEDS Global Partnership (LEDS GP, #16435); Mountain Partnership (MP, #16862).* Supports: *Red Iberoamericana de Bosques Modelo (RLABM, #18659).* Partner of: *Climate Technology Centre and Network (CTCN, #04023).* [2017/XF4511/**E***]

- ♦ Tropical Agriculture Research and Training Center / see Tropical Agriculture Research and Higher Education Center (#20246)

♦ Tropical Biology Association (TBA) 20247

European Office Attenborough Bldg, Pembroke St, Cambridge, CB2 3QZ, UK. T. +441223336619. E-mail: tba@tropical-biology.org.
African Office PO Box 44486, Nairobi, 00100, Kenya. T. +254203537568. E-mail: tba-africa@tropical-biology.org.
URL: http://www.tropical-biology.org/

History 1990. UK Registered Charity: 1116111. Incorporated 24 May 2006. **Aims** Meet the challenge of biodiversity conservation through building expertise, creating regional and international collaboration and providing resources and support to African *conservationists*. **Languages** English. **Finance** Members' dues. Grants. **Activities** Training/education; networking/liaising. **Events** *Annual Conference* Brussels (Belgium) 2013. **Publications** *TBA Skill Series.* Annual Report.
Members Universities and institutes (29) in 11 countries:
Australia, Austria, Germany, Ireland, Malaysia, Netherlands, Poland, Sweden, Switzerland, UK, USA.
Included in the above, 1 institute listed in this Yearbook:
Swiss Tropical and Public Health Institute (Swiss TPH). [2020.03.03/XD3861/**D**]

- ♦ Tropical Botanic Garden and Research Institute (internationally oriented national body)
- ♦ Tropical Conservancy / see Biodiversity Conservancy International

♦ Tropical Council for Companion Animal Parasites (TroCCAP) 20248

Exec Sec address not obtained.
URL: https://www.troccap.com/

History Registration: Australian Public Company, No/ID: 27 607 698 439, Start date: 22 Oct 2015, Australia. **Aims** Independently inform, guide and make best-practice recommendations to veterinarians and allied health professionals for the diagnosis, treatment and control of companion animal parasites in the tropics and sub-tropics, with the aim of protecting animal and human health. **Structure** Council. [2019/AA0201/**C**]

- ♦ Tropical Disease Research Centre / see Community Information, Empowerment and Transparency
- ♦ Tropical Diseases Research Centre (internationally oriented national body)

♦ Tropical Forest Alliance (TFA) 20249

Secretariat c/o WEF, Route de la Capite 91-93, 1223 Cologny GE, Switzerland. E-mail: tfa@weforum.org.
URL: https://www.tropicalforestalliance.org/

History Founded 2012, Rio de Janeiro (Brazil), at 3rd UN Conference on Sustainable Development. EU Transparency Register: 089099737489-51. **Aims** Catalyze the power of collective action and responsibility for a forest positive future. **Structure** Steering Committee. Secretariat based at *World Economic Forum (WEF, #21367).* **Finance** Funders include: governments of Netherlands, Norway, Germany and UK; Gordon and Betty Moore Foundation. **Events** *Annual Meeting* Bogota (Colombia) 2019. **Publications** Annual Report. Studies; discussion papers. **IGO Relations** *Global Environment Facility (GEF, #10346); Global Green Growth Institute (GGGI, #10392); Inter-American Development Bank (IDB, #11427); UNEP (#20299); UNDP (#20292).*
NGO Relations Partners include:
- *CDP (#03621);*
- *Center for International Forestry Research (CIFOR, #03646);*
- *Climate Policy Initiative (CPI, #04020);*
- *CERES;*
- *Code REDD;*
- *Conservation International (CI);*
- *The Consumer Goods Forum (CGF, #04772);*
- *Earth Innovation Institute (#05165);*
- *Earthworm Foundation (#05172);*
- *EcoAgriculture Partners (#05290);*
- *Environmental Defense Fund (EDF);*
- *Fauna & Flora International (FFI, #09277);*
- *Finance Alliance for Sustainable Trade (FAST, #09763);*
- *Forest Peoples Programme (FPP, #09865);*
- *Forest Stewardship Council (FSC, #09869);*
- *Forest Trends (#09870);*
- *Global Canopy (#10271);*
- *HCV Network Ltd (HCV Network, #10865);*
- *The Sustainable Trade Initiative (IDH, #20070);*
- *Instituto de Pesquisa Ambiental da Amazônia (IPAM);*
- *International Bank for Reconstruction and Development (IBRD, #12317)* (World Bank);
- *International Centre for Tropical Agriculture (#12527);*
- *International Sustainability and Carbon Certification (ISCC);*
- *International Union for Conservation of Nature and Natural Resources (IUCN, #15766);*
- *Lutheran World Relief (LWR);*
- *The Nature Conservancy (TNC);*
- *SNV Netherlands Development Organisation (SNV);*
- *Preferred by Nature (#18477);*
- *Rainforest Alliance;*
- *Sustainable Agriculture Network (SAN, #20052);*
- *SOLIDARIDAD Network (#19681);*
- *Tropenbos International (TBI);*
- *WeForest (#20852);*
- *Wildlife Conservation Society (WCS);*
- *Winrock International;*
- *World Agroforestry Centre (ICRAF, #21072);*
- *World Cocoa Foundation (WCF);*
- *World Resources Institute (WRI, #21753);*
- *World Wide Fund for Nature (WWF, #21922).* [2020/XM8962/**C**]

- ♦ Tropical Forest Foundation (internationally oriented national body)
- ♦ Tropical Forest Trust / see Earthworm Foundation (#05172)

♦ Tropical Growers' Association (TGA) 20250

Sec Langley, Bures, CO8 5EA, UK. T. +441787227002.
Contact 3 Clanricarde Gardens, Tunbridge Wells, TN1 1HQ, UK.

History 1907. Incorporated 1912. Constitution revised: 1970; 1975; 1982. Former names and other names: *Rubber Growers' Association (RGA)* – former; *Association des planteurs d'hévéas* – former; *International Association of Growers of Rubber Oil Palms and other Tropical Crops* – former; *International Association of Growers of Tropical Crops* – alias. Registration: UK. **Aims** Represent growers of tropical agricultural crops. **Structure** General meeting (annual); Council; Secretariat. **Languages** English. **Staff** 1.00 FTE, paid. **Finance** Sources: members' dues. **Activities** Events/meetings. **Events** *Biennial seminar* Oxford (UK) 1997. **Members** Corporate (plantations), Tropical Commodity Associations and Individuals. Membership countries not specified. **Consultative Status** Consultative status granted from: *ECOSOC (#05331)* (Ros C); *FAO (#09260)* (Liaison Status). [2023.02.23/XC4141/**C**]

- ♦ Tropical Health Alliance Foundation (internationally oriented national body)
- ♦ Tropical Health and Education Trust (internationally oriented national body)
- ♦ Tropical Institute of Community Health and Development in Africa (internationally oriented national body)
- ♦ Tropical Rainforest Foundation (internationally oriented national body)
- ♦ Tropical Resources Institute (internationally oriented national body)
- ♦ Tropical Science Center, Costa Rica (internationally oriented national body)
- ♦ Tropical Science Research Institute (internationally oriented national body)
- ♦ TROPICA VERDE (internationally oriented national body)

- ♦ Tropisch Medisch Fonds (internationally oriented national body)
- ♦ TROPMEDEUROP – Council of Directors of Institutes of Tropical Medicine in Europe (inactive)
- ♦ TROPMED/Indonesia / see SEAMEO TROPMED Regional Centre for Food and Nutrition (#19173)
- ♦ TROPMED/Malaysia / see SEAMEO TROPMED Regional Centre for Microbiology, Parasitology and Entomology (#19185)
- ♦ TROPMED/Philippines / see SEAMEO TROPMED Regional Centre for Public Health, Hospital Administration, Environmental and Occupational Health (#19186)
- ♦ TROPMED / see SEAMEO Regional Tropical Medicine and Public Health Network (#19184)
- ♦ TROPMED/Thailand / see SEAMEO TROPMED Regional Centre for Tropical Medicine (#19187)
- ♦ TRP / see Nonviolent Radical Party, Transnational and Transparty (#17154)
- ♦ TRP – Rainforest Project Foundation (internationally oriented national body)
- ♦ TRRF / see World Food Logistics Organization
- ♦ **TRSA** Tafelrondes Suidelike Afrika (#18984)
- ♦ **TRTF** The Round Table Foundation (#18981)
- ♦ TRT Union – Union for the International Registration of Trademarks (inactive)
- ♦ True Animal Protein Price Coalition (internationally oriented national body)

♦ TrustAfrica 20251

Exec Dir Lot 4, Almadies Ngor, BP 45435, Fann-Dakar, Senegal. T. +221338694686. Fax +221338241567. E-mail: info@trustafrica.org.
URL: http://www.trustafrica.org/

History 2001, as *Special Initiative for Africa*, under the aegis of *Ford Foundation (#09858)*. Present name adopted 2006. **Aims** Strengthen African initiatives that address the most difficult challenges confronting the continent. **Structure** Board of Trustees. **Languages** English, French. **Staff** 18.00 FTE, paid. **Finance** Supported mainly by *Ford Foundation (#09858)*. Other sources: *Bill and Melinda Gates Foundation (BMGF)*; *Carnegie Corporation of New York*; David and Lucile Packard Foundation; *Humanity United*; *MacArthur Foundation*; Netherlands Ministry of Foreign Affairs (MDG3 Dutch Fund); *Oak Foundation*; Open Society Institute; *UniversalGiving*. **Activities** Networking/liaising; knowledge management/information dissemination. **Events** *Looking back, looking ahead – African philanthropy for political, economic and social justice in the 21st century* Addis Ababa (Ethiopia) 2016, *Joint workshop* Istanbul (Turkey) 2010. **Publications** *TrustAfrica Now* – newsletter. *Social Justice and Philanthropy in Africa: Transforming Power Relations and the Balance of Stories* (2010) by Akwasi Aidoo. Annual Report; brochure. **Information Services** *TrustAfrica Blog*. **Consultative Status** Consultative status granted from: *ECOSOC (#05331)* (Special). **IGO Relations** Works with: *African Union (AU, #00488)*; *ECOSOC (#05331)*; *Pan-African Parliament (PAP, #18058)*; *United Nations Economic Commission for Africa (ECA, #20554)*. Global partner of: *Global Partnership for Social Accountability (GPSA, #10541)*. **NGO Relations** Member of (2): *Africa Philanthropy Network (APN, #00512)*; *Philanthropy Europe Association (Philea, #18358)*. Supports: *Eastern and Southern Africa small scale Farmers' Forum (ESAFF, #05256)*; *Global Fund for Community Foundations (GFCF, #10382)*. [2018/XM2634/F]

- ♦ Trust for African Rock Art (internationally oriented national body)

♦ The Trust for the Americas 20252

Fundación para las Américas

SG 1801 Constitution Ave, Washington DC 20006, USA. T. +12024586978. Fax +12024586892. E-mail: info@trust-oea.org – lbersano@trust-oea.org.
URL: http://trustfortheamericas.org/

History Nov 1997, as a private sector arm in support of *Inter-American Council for Integral Development (#11423)* within the framework of *OAS (#17629)*. Registration: Section 501 (c)(3), USA. **Aims** Promote social and economic inclusion for vulnerable communities in the Americas through partnerships with the public, private and non-profit sector. **Structure** Board of Directors, comprising President, Secretary, Treasurer, Chief of Staff to the OAS Secretary General and 9 Executives from the Private Sector. OAS Secretary General is Ex-officio member. **Languages** English, French, Portuguese, Spanish. **Finance** Public Sector partners include governments of: Argentina; Canada; Costa Rica; Colombia; Ecuador; Guatemala; Honduras; Mexico; Paraguay; Panama; Peru; El Salvador; St Lucia; US Department of State through *United States Agency for International Development (USAID)*. Private Sector partners; various civil society organizations and local partners. **Activities** Initiatives include: Partnership in Opportunities for Employment through Technology in the Americas (POETA) – teaching ICT and job skills training. Initiatives organize workshops, strategic planning sessions, training and conferences. Organizes annual 'Gala for the Americas'.

Members Full in 14 countries:
Argentina, Brazil, Colombia, Costa Rica, Dominican Rep, Ecuador, El Salvador, Guatemala, Honduras, Mexico, Nicaragua, Panama, Peru, Venezuela.

NGO Relations Member of: *Freedom of Information Advocates Network (FOIAnet, #09985)*. [2021/XK1805/f/F]

- ♦ Trust for Civil Society in Central and Eastern Europe (internationally oriented national body)

♦ Trust in Digital Life (TDL) 20253

Office Maurice Dekeyserlaan 11, 1090 Brussels, Belgium. T. +441738583533. E-mail: office@trustindigitallife.eu.
URL: https://trustindigitallife.eu/

Aims Create a trusted ecosystem based on innovative and trustworthy ICT products and solutions that protects the data and assets of European citizens and enterprises. **Structure** Board of Directors. **NGO Relations** *European Association for e-Identity and Security (EEMA, #06077)*. [2019/XM8530/F]

♦ Trusted Connectivity Alliance (TCA) 20254

General Secretary c/o Alliances Management, 544 Hillside Road, Redwood City CA 94062, USA. T. +16502602387.
URL: https://trustedconnectivityalliance.org/

History 2000. Registered in the UK. Former names and other names: *SIMalliance* – former (Feb 2020). **Aims** Facilitate the sustained growth of connected objects through trusted connectivity which offers protection for service provider assets, application and device data, and end user privacy. **Structure** Board, comprising Chair, General Secretary and 4 directors. **Languages** English. **Activities** Organizes: annual 'SIMposium'; annual SIMposium Asia; annual SIMposium USA; annual 'SIMagine – competition. **Events** *SIMposium* Berlin (Germany) 2013, *SIMposium* Berlin (Germany) 2012, *SIMposium Asia* Singapore (Singapore) 2012, *SIMposium* Berlin (Germany) 2011, *SIMposium Asia* Kuala Lumpur (Malaysia) 2011. **Publications** *SIMalliance Newsletter* (4 a year). Specifications; recommendations; white papers. [2020/XJ1328/F]

- ♦ Trust Fund for the Convention on the Conservation of Migratory Species of Wild Animals (see: #20299)
- ♦ Trust Fund for the International Year of Disabled Persons / see United Nations Voluntary Fund on Disability (#20648)
- ♦ Trust Fund for Population Activities / see United Nations Population Fund (#20612)
- ♦ Trust Fund for the Protection of the Mediterranean Sea Against Pollution / see Mediterranean Trust Fund (#16686)
- ♦ Trust for Mutual Understanding (internationally oriented national body)
- ♦ Trust Territory of the Pacific Islands (inactive)
- ♦ Trybunal Sprawiedliwosci Wspólnot Europejskich / see Court of Justice of the European Union (#04938)
- ♦ Trybunau Sprawiedliwos'ci Unii Europejskiej (#04938)
- ♦ TSA / see Ottoman and Turkish Studies Association
- ♦ TSA Europe – Tuberous Sclerosis Association Europe (inactive)
- ♦ **TSA** Transatlantic Studies Association (#20205)
- ♦ **TSA** Turtle Survival Alliance (#20264)
- ♦ TSB – Telecommunication Standardization Bureau (see: #15673)
- ♦ TSCG – Treaty on Stability, Coordination and Governance in the Economic and Monetary Union (2012 treaty)
- ♦ **TSCI** International Association of Technical Survey and Classification Institutions (#12223)
- ♦ **TSCi** Tuberous Sclerosis Complex International (#20258)
- ♦ **TSC** The Sustainability Consortium (#20049)
- ♦ tSeirbhis Eorpach Gniomhaiochta Eachtrai (#07018)
- ♦ **TSEP** Third Sector European Policy Network (#20148)
- ♦ TSFP – International Symposium on Turbulence and Shear Flow Phenomena (meeting series)
- ♦ TSF – Télécoms sans frontières (internationally oriented national body)
- ♦ TSF – Terre sans frontières (internationally oriented national body)
- ♦ **TSF** Traducteurs sans Frontières (#20216)
- ♦ TSGA – Turner Syndrome Global Alliance (internationally oriented national body)
- ♦ TSG / see Global Shippers' Forum (#10596)
- ♦ TSI / see Toothfriendly International
- ♦ **TSI** Sulphur Institute, The (#20034)
- ♦ **TSL** Tribunal spécial pour le Liban (#19911)
- ♦ TSOP – Society for Organic Petrology (internationally oriented national body)
- ♦ TSPMI – Tarptautinio santykio ir politikos mokslo institutas (internationally oriented national body)
- ♦ **TSRU** Tuberculosis Surveillance Research Unit (#20256)
- ♦ **TS** Theosophical Society (#20141)
- ♦ **TS** Tsunami Society International (#20255)

♦ Tsunami Society International (TS) 20255

Contact 1741 Ala Moana Blvd No 70, Honolulu HI 96815, USA. E-mail: postmaster@tsunamisociety.org.
URL: http://www.tsunamisociety.org/

History 1982, Honolulu HI (USA). Also referred to as *International Tsunami Society*. **Aims** Promote theoretical and applied tsunami research; support efforts in increasing and disseminating knowledge about tsunamis; devise methodology for effective risk assessments; development of early warning systems and management of programs for preparedness. **Structure** Officers: President; Vice-President; Secretary/Treasurer. **Languages** English. **Staff** 9.00 FTE, voluntary. **Finance** Members' dues. Nominal publication fees. Annual budget: less than US$ 10,000. **Activities** Guidance/assistance/consulting; events/meetings; knowledge management/information dissemination. **Events** *Symposium* Nicoya (Costa Rica) 2014, *Symposium* Ispra (Italy) 2012, *Symposium* Toronto, ON (Canada) 2010, *Symposium* Honolulu, HI (USA) 2006, *Symposium* Honolulu, HI (USA) 2002. **Publications** *Science of Tsunami Hazards* – electronic journal. **Members** Full; Associate, in 55 countries. Membership countries not specified. **IGO Relations** Many international organizations, including: *Intergovernmental Oceanographic Commission (IOC, #11496)*; *Joint Research Centre (JRC, #16147)*. **NGO Relations** Universities and academic institutions that carry relevant research in earthquakes, tsunamis, volcanoes, etc. [2016.10.19/XJ4976/D]

- ♦ **TTAG** Tics and Tourette Across the Globe (#20161)
- ♦ **TTASSEA** Traditional Textile Arts Society of South East Asia (#20194)
- ♦ TTCA / see Northern Corridor Transit and Transport Coordination Authority (#17582)
- ♦ TTE – Toy Traders of Europe (no recent information)
- ♦ TTFA – Table Tennis Federation of Asia (inactive)
- ♦ TTMI / see Autre Terre (#03044)
- ♦ TTP / see World Without War Council
- ♦ TTRA – Travel and Tourism Research Association (internationally oriented national body)
- ♦ TTR / see Floating University (#09796)
- ♦ TTSGI – Twinless Twins Support Group International (internationally oriented national body)
- ♦ **TTS** The Transplantation Society (#20224)
- ♦ TUAC-OECD / see Trade Union Advisory Committee to the OECD (#20186)
- ♦ **TUAC** Trade Union Advisory Committee to the OECD (#20186)
- ♦ TUBEHYDRO – International Conference on Tube Hydroforming (meeting series)
- ♦ Tube and Pipe Association International (internationally oriented national body)
- ♦ Tube and Pipe Fabricators Association International / see Tube and Pipe Association International
- ♦ Tuber aestivum / uncinatum European Scientific Group (meeting series)

♦ Tuberculosis Surveillance Research Unit (TSRU) 20256

Unité de recherche sur la surveillance de la tuberculose

Contact c/o KNCV Tuberculosis Foundation, Postbus 146, 2501 CC The Hague, Netherlands. T. +31704167222. Fax +31703584004.
Street Address Van Bylandt Huis, Benoordenhoutseweg 46, 2596 BC The Hague, Netherlands.
URL: http://www.kncvtbc.org/

History Originally coordinated by *International Union Against Tuberculosis and Lung Disease (The Union, #15752)*, *WHO (#20950)* and KNCV Tuberculosis Foundation. Has been referred to in French as *Groupe de travail international sur la surveillance de la résistance aux anti-tuberculeux*. **Aims** Host a forum to discuss tuberculosis epidemiology relevant to TB control and surveillance. **Languages** English. **Finance** Members' dues. **Activities** Events/meetings. **Events** *Meeting* Paris (France) 1992. **Publications** Annual Report.

Members Full in 9 countries:
Finland, Germany, Japan, Korea Rep, Malawi, Netherlands, Switzerland, Tanzania UR, Vietnam.
International organizational members (2):
International Union Against Tuberculosis and Lung Disease (The Union, #15752); *WHO (#20950)*. [2018.07.25/XE7724/y/F]

♦ TuBerculosis Vaccine Initiative (TBVI) 20257

Contact Runderweg 6, 8219 PK Lelystad, Netherlands. T. +31320277550. E-mail: info@tbvi.eu.
URL: http://www.tbvi.eu/

History Founded 2008, on suggestion of *European Commission (EC, #06633)*. **Aims** Support, integrate, translate and prioritize research and development efforts to discover and develop new tuberculosis vaccines that are accessible and affordable for all people. **Structure** Governing Board; Advisory Committee; Operational Office; Product and Clinical Development Team. **Languages** English. **Staff** 7.00 FTE, paid. **Finance** Donations and sponsorship, including from: *Bill and Melinda Gates Foundation (BMGF)*; *European Commission (EC, #06633)* – 7th Framework Programme; *Norwegian Agency for Development Cooperation (Norad)*; companies. **Activities** Networking/liaising; events/meetings. **Events** *Symposium* Les Diablerets (Switzerland) 2016, *Symposium* Berlin (Germany) 2015, *Symposium* Ijmuiden (Netherlands) 2015, *Global Forum / Global Forum on TB Vaccines* Shanghai (China) 2015, *Symposium on TB Vaccines* Madrid (Spain) 2014. **Publications** *TBVI Newsletter*.

Members Partners in 17 countries:
Australia, Belgium, Denmark, France, Gambia, Germany, Ireland, Italy, Korea Rep, Netherlands, Norway, Senegal, South Africa, Spain, Switzerland, UK, USA.

IGO Relations Cooperates with: *WHO (#20950)*. **NGO Relations** Member of: *Developing Countries Vaccine Manufacturers Network (DCVMN, #05052)*; *TB Europe Coalition (TBEC, #20104)*. Cooperates with: *Aeras Global TB Vaccine Foundation*; *Amis du Fonds mondial Europe (AFM Europe)*; *Bureau international des Médecins sans frontières (MSF International, #03366)*; *European Foundation Centre (EFC, inactive)*; *European-Latin-American-Caribbean-Tuberculosis Consortium (EurolacTB, #07655)*; *European Vaccine Initiative (EVI, #09043)*; Fundacion Ramon Areces; *Global Health Advocates (#10400)*; KNCV Tuberculosis Foundation; *Mérieux Foundation*; Sclavo Vaccines Association; *Stop TB Partnership (#19999)*. [2020/XJ8383/F]

- ♦ Tuberous Sclerosis Association Europe (inactive)

♦ Tuberous Sclerosis Complex International (TSCi) 20258

Sec 801 Roder Rd, Ste 750, Silver Spring MD 20708, USA. T. +13015629890.
URL: http://www.tscinternational.org/

History Founded 1986, as *Tuberous Sclerosis International*. **Aims** Increase knowledge of tuberous sclerosis complex (TSC) throughout the world; establish internationally recognized diagnostic criteria, surveillance and treatment guidelines; stimulate, coordinate and originate research; interest statutory international organizations in the welfare of those with tuberous sclerosis complex and their families; support national tuberous sclerosis complex associations and organizations in their work; initiate the realization of new tuberous sclerosis complex associations in additional countries; exchange information of mutual interest between tuberous sclerosis complex associations. **Languages** English. **Staff** None. **Events** *Research Conference* Toronto, ON (Canada) 2019, *Research Conference* Tokyo (Japan) 2018, *Research Conference* Lisbon (Portugal) 2016, *TSC international research conference* Berlin (Germany) 2006, *TSC international research conference* Cambridge (UK) 2004.

Members National tuberous sclerosis associations in 30 countries:
Australia, Austria, Belgium, Brazil, Canada, China, Colombia, Denmark, France, Germany, Greece, Israel, Italy, Japan, Mexico, Netherlands, New Zealand, North Macedonia, Norway, Poland, Portugal, Russia, Slovakia, South Africa, Spain, Sweden, Switzerland, Taiwan, UK, USA.
Included in the above, 1 organizations listed in this Yearbook:
Australasian Tuberous Sclerosis Society (ATSS). [2020/XF3471/y/**C**]

- Tuberous Sclerosis International / see Tuberous Sclerosis Complex International (#20258)
- **TUCA** Trade Union Confederation of the Americas (#04480)
- **TUEM** Trade Union Eurocontrol Maastricht (#20187)

♦ Tug of War International Federation (TWIF) 20259

Association internationale de la traction à la corde

SG Lytse Dyk 2, 9026 BD Jellum, Netherlands. T. +31623271158. E-mail: 10cc@hetnet.nl.
Pres PO BOx 163, Paarl, 7620, South Africa. T. +27218702900.
URL: http://www.tugofwar-twif.org/

History 1960. Constitution amended; 14 May 1983, Engelberg (Switzerland); 11 Apr 1992, Drogheda (Ireland); 24 Apr 1993, London (UK); 18 Apr 1998, Rochester MN (USA); 21 Apr 2004, Cento (Italy); 7 May 2005, Cape Town (South Africa); 6 May 2006, Minehead (UK); 12 May 2007, Stenungsund (Sweden); 26 Apr 2008, Amsterdam (Netherlands); 2 May 2009, Pretoria (South Africa); 30 Apr 2016, Belfast (UK); 28 Apr 2018, Cork (Ireland). **Aims** Provide the structure and good governance necessary for the well-being and development of the sport of tug of war throughout the world; attain a sufficiently high level of excellence and universality to expedite acceptance by the International Olympic Committee as a sport within the programme of the Olympic Games, a status held in the early years of the 20th century. **Structure** Congress (annual); Executive Committee; Commissions (5). **Languages** English. **Staff** Voluntary. **Finance** Licence fees; IOC grants. **Activities** Events/meetings; sporting activities; training/education. **Events** *Annual Congress* Lucerne (Switzerland) 2022, *Annual Congress* Malmö (Sweden) 2015, *Annual Congress* Belfast (UK) 2014, *Annual Congress* Madison, WI (USA) 2013, *Annual Congress* Volendam (Netherlands) 2012. **Publications** *TWIF Magazine* (3 a year). Manuals; brochure.
Members Affiliated associations in 74 countries and territories:
Australia, Basque Country, Belgium, Brazil, Brunei Darussalam, Cambodia, Cameroon, Canada, Channel Is, China, Colombia, Congo DR, Czechia, Denmark, Dominican Rep, England, Estonia, Finland, France, Gambia, Georgia, Germany, Ghana, Greece, Haiti, Hong Kong, Hungary, India, Iran Islamic Rep, Ireland, Israel, Italy, Japan, Kenya, Korea Rep, Kyrgyzstan, Laos, Latvia, Lithuania, Macau, Malaysia, Malta, Mauritius, Mongolia, Morocco, Myanmar, Namibia, Nepal, Netherlands, Nigeria, Northern Ireland, Pakistan, Philippines, Poland, Romania, Russia, Scotland, Serbia, Sierra Leone, Singapore, Slovakia, South Africa, Sri Lanka, Sweden, Switzerland, Taiwan, Thailand, Türkiye, Ukraine, USA, Vietnam, Wales, Zambia, Zimbabwe.
NGO Relations Member of (3): *Association of the IOC Recognized International Sports Federations (ARISF, #02767); International World Games Association (IWGA, #15914); Olympic Movement (#17719).* Cooperates with (1): *International Testing Agency (ITA, #15678).* Recognized by: *International Olympic Committee (IOC, #14408).* [2022.02.06/XD3647/**C**]

- Tuhamiyyan (religious order)
- TUIAFPW – Trade Unions International of Agricultural, Forestry and Plantation Workers (inactive)
- **TUI CHEMISTRY-ENERGY** Trade Union International of Chemical, Energy, Metal, Oil and Allied Industries (#20188)
- TUI EMCOAI / see Trade Union International of Chemical, Energy, Metal, Oil and Allied Industries (#20188)
- TUI ENERGY / see Trade Union International of Chemical, Energy, Metal, Oil and Allied Industries (#20188)
- TUI Metal – Trade Union International of Mining, Metallurgy and Metal (unconfirmed)
- **TUI Transport** Trade Unions International of Transport, Fisheries and Communication (#20192)
- TUI WCEOM / see Trade Union International of Chemical, Energy, Metal, Oil and Allied Industries (#20188)
- TUI WEMCORI / see Trade Union International of Chemical, Energy, Metal, Oil and Allied Industries (#20188)
- TUIWE – Trade Unions International of Workers in Energy (inactive)
- Tulane University School of Public Health and Tropical Medicine (internationally oriented national body)

♦ Tularemia International Society (TULISOC) 20260

Office Manager address not obtained.
URL: https://tularemia.org/

History 1 Jan 2009, Berlin (Germany). Founded during 6th International Conference on Tularemia. **Aims** Facilitate and encourage assembly, acquaintance and association of scientists from all geographical regions engaged in tularaemia research; foster and encourage discussion and dissemination of results of research and related matters of interest in this field; provide a means to convene appropriate specialists that will serve as a ready resource in case of specific needs and emergencies; promote awareness of the field and of implications of research findings; promote education and training in the field. **Structure** General Business Meeting (at triennial conference); Executive Council; Standing Committees (5). **Languages** English. **Finance** Sources: members' dues. **Activities** Events/meetings; financial and/or material support; knowledge management/information dissemination. **Events** *International Conference on Tularemia* Grenoble (France) 2023, *International Conference on Tularemia* Montréal, QC (Canada) 2018, *International Conference on Tularemia* Opatija (Croatia) 2015, *International Conference on Tularemia* Breckenridge, CO (USA) 2012, *International Conference on Tularemia* Berlin (Germany) 2009. [2023.02.14/XJ1653/**E**]

- Tulenarkoja ja Räjähdysaineita Valvovien Viranomaisten Pohjoismainen Yhteistyö (#17247)
- Tulevaisuuden Tutkimuskeskus (internationally oriented national body)
- **TULISOC** Tularemia International Society (#20260)
- Tulun Rai Timor (internationally oriented national body)
- Tuna Commission / see Western and Central Pacific Fisheries Commission (#20912)
- Tungumalasattmalinn (1981 treaty)
- Tunis International Centre for Environmental Technologies (internationally oriented national body)

♦ Tunza Southeast Asia Youth Environment Network (SEAYEN) 20261

Secretariat Natl Youth Achievement Award Council, 151 Lorong Chuan, 06-01B, New Tech Park (Lobby A), Singapore 556741, Singapore. T. +6567336753. Fax +6567336754. E-mail: nyaac@singnet.com.sg.
URL: http://www.seayen.org/

History Set up jointly by *UNEP (#20299)* – Regional Office for Asia and the Pacific, Bayer and National Youth Achievement Award (NYAA) Council, Singapore. **Aims** Unite youth in activities to share experience, stimulate cross-cultural and international activity and participate in regional decision-making by providing the youth with a voice in consultation on ASEAN environment for *sustainable development* issues. **Events** *Regional Meeting* Singapore (Singapore) 2016. **Publications** Reports.
Members Full in 10 countries:
Brunei Darussalam, Cambodia, Indonesia, Laos, Malaysia, Myanmar, Philippines, Singapore, Thailand, Vietnam.
[2022/XJ7829/**F**]

- **TUP** Trickle Up Program (#20236)
- Turin Centre / see International Training Centre of the ILO (#15717)
- Turismforskningsinstitutet (internationally oriented national body)
- Türk Asya Stratejik Arastirmalar Merkezi (internationally oriented national body)
- Türk Dili Konusan Ülkeler Isbirligi Koseyi (#04793)
- **Türk Donseyi – TDIK** Türk Dili Konusan Ülkeler Isbirligi Koseyi (#04793)
- **Turkic Council** Cooperation Council of Turkic Speaking States (#04793)
- Turkish Asian Center for Strategic Studies (internationally oriented national body)
- Turkish Asian Centre for Strategic Studies (internationally oriented national body)
- Turkish Foreign Policy Institute / see Foreign Policy Institute, Ankara
- Turkish Missions Aid Society / see Embrace the Middle East
- Turkish Studies Association / see Ottoman and Turkish Studies Association
- Türk Kültür ve Sanatlari Ortak Yönetimi / see International Organization of Turkic Culture (#14482)
- **TURKPA** Parliamentary Assembly of Turkic Speaking Countries (#18215)
- TÜRKSOY / see International Organization of Turkic Culture (#14482)
- **TURKSOY** International Organization of Turkic Culture (#14482)

♦ Turnaround Management Association – Europe (TMA Europe) 20262

General Manager 122 Havelock Road, London, SW19 8HB, UK. T. +442082863025.
URL: http://www.tma-europe.org/

History Set up, 2001, as the umbrella organization for the European chapters of *Turnaround Management Association – Global (TMA Global).* **Aims** Serve as a forum for the interchange of ideas and as a networking opportunity for developing relationships across the continent. **Structure** Board. **Activities** Events/meetings. **Events** *Annual Conference* Hamburg (Germany) 2023, *Annual Conference* London (UK) 2020, *East European Conference* Prague (Czechia) 2020, *Annual Conference* Vienna (Austria) 2019, *East European Conference* Zagreb (Croatia) / Czechia 2019. **Publications** *TMA Europe Newsletter.*
Members Chapters in 12 countries:
Austria, Czechia, Finland, France, Germany, Ireland, Italy, Netherlands, Romania, Spain, Sweden, UK.
NGO Relations *European Association of Certified Turnaround Professionals (EACTP, #05969).*
[2023/XM4221/**E**]

- Turnaround Management Association – Global (internationally oriented national body)
- Turner Syndrome Global Alliance (internationally oriented national body)
- Turn Toward Peace / see World Without War Council
- Turtle Conservancy (internationally oriented national body)

♦ Turtle Conservation Fund (TCF) 20263

Contact address not obtained.
URL: http://www.turtleconservationfund.org/

History Founded 2002, as a partnership initiative of *Conservation International (CI), International Union for Conservation of Nature and Natural Resources (IUCN, #15766)* Tortoise and Freshwater Turtle Specialist Group and *Turtle Survival Alliance (TSA, #20264).* **Aims** Ensure the long-term survival of tortoises and freshwater turtles. **Structure** Executive Board. **Activities** Advocacy/lobbying/activism; awards/prizes/competitions.
Members Coalition members (9):
Andrew Sabin Family Foundation; Chelonian Research Institute; *Humane Society International (HSI, #10966)* (Australia); *International Union for Conservation of Nature and Natural Resources (IUCN, #15766)* (Tortoise and Freshwater Turtle Specialist Group); *Latin American Association of Capital Goods Manufacturers (ALABIC, no recent information)* (Shellshock Campaign); *Re:wild; Turtle Conservancy (TC); Turtle Survival Alliance (TSA, #20264).* [2018/XM7361/f/**F**]

- Turtle Island Restoration Network (internationally oriented national body)

♦ Turtle Survival Alliance (TSA) 20264

Main Office 1989 Colonial Pkwy, Fort Worth TX 76110, USA. T. +18438681872. E-mail: cclark@turtlesurvival.org.
URL: http://www.turtlesurvival.org/

History Jan 2001, Fort Worth, TX (USA). Jan 2001, Forth Worth TX (USA), by *International Union for Conservation of Nature and Natural Resources (IUCN, #15766)* – SSC Tortoise and Freshwater Turtle Specialist Group (TFTSG) as part of TCF Global Action Plan for Conservation of Tortoises and Freshwater Turtles. **Aims** Transform passion for turtles into effective conservation through global networks of living collections and range country actions. **Structure** Board of Directors. Divisions: Austral-Asia; Europe; USA. **Activities** *Symposium on the Conservation and Biology of Tortoises and Freshwater Turtles.* **Events** *Joint Symposium on the Conservation and Biology of Tortoises and Freshwater Turtles* New Orleans, LA (USA) 2016, *Symposium* Tucson, AZ (USA) 2015, *Annual Conference* Atlanta, GA (USA) 2007, *Meeting* Atlanta, GA (USA) 2007, *Annual Conference* St Louis, MO (USA) 2006. **Publications** *TSA Newsletter.* **Members** Individuals, organizations and institutions (over 300). Membership countries not specified. **NGO Relations** Instrumental in setting up: *Turtle Conservation Fund (TCF, #20263).* Member of: *Alliance for Zero Extinction (AZE, #00730); International Union for Conservation of Nature and Natural Resources (IUCN, #15766).* [2017/XM2855/**F**]

- TUSK (internationally oriented national body)
- Tusk Trust / see TUSK

♦ Tutmonda Agado de Esperantistaj Nefumantoj (TAdEN) 20265

Contact Zwaansmeerstraat 48, 1946 AE Beverwijk, Netherlands.

History 1995. **Aims** Serve the interests of *non-smoking* esperantists. **Structure** General Assembly (annual). **Languages** Esperanto. **Staff** 1.00 FTE, voluntary. **Finance** Members' dues: euro 4,50. Budget (annual): about euro 450. **Activities** Annual Assembly at Universal Esperanto Congress. **Events** *Annual Assembly* Reykjavik (Iceland) 2013, *Annual assembly* Hanoi (Vietnam) 2012, *Annual assembly* Copenhagen (Denmark) 2011, *Annual assembly* Havana (Cuba) 2010, *Annual assembly* Bialystok (Poland) 2009. **Publications** *Puraj Pulmoj* (3-4 a year).
Members Individuals in 36 countries:
Austria, Belgium, Benin, Brazil, Bulgaria, Canada, China, Croatia, Cuba, Czechia, Denmark, Estonia, Finland, France, Germany, Hungary, Iran Islamic Rep, Italy, Japan, Korea Rep, Lithuania, Nepal, Netherlands, Poland, Portugal, Romania, Russia, Serbia, Slovakia, Spain, Sweden, Switzerland, Togo, UK, Ukraine, Uruguay, USA.
NGO Relations Associated with: *Universal Esperanto Association (UEA, #20676).* [2012.04.30/XD5535/v/**D**]

- Tutmonda Asocio de Geinstruistoj Esperantistaj (inactive)

♦ Tutmonda Asocio de Konstruistoj Esperantistaj (TAKE) 20266

Association mondiale des esperantophones professionnels du bâtiment et des travaux publics

Contact RN 83 rue de Tiefenbach, 68920 Wintzenheim, France. T. +33389793227. Fax +33389794073. E-mail: verdapigo@gmail.com.
URL: http://take.esperanto.free.fr/

History 4 May 1993, Colmar (France). Registered in accordance with French law. **Aims** Unite Esperanto-speaking professional *builders*; promote *Esperanto* in the economic world; provide information for members at every level and for their clients. **Structure** President; Secretary-General; 4 Vice-Presidents; Treasurer; Editor. **Finance** Members' dues. Bulletin subscriptions. **Activities** Ecological reforestation projects in Brazil, Benin and Burundi. **Publications** *La Domo* (4 a year). **Information Services** *Database on Building Terminology* in English, Esperanto, French, German, Russian.
Members Individuals in 45 countries:
Albania, Australia, Austria, Belarus, Belgium, Benin, Brazil, Burundi, Canada, Chile, China, Congo DR, Croatia, Cuba, Czechia, Denmark, Finland, France, Germany, Greece, Hungary, Israel, Italy, Japan, Korea Rep, Lithuania, Luxembourg, Madagascar, Netherlands, New Zealand, Norway, Poland, Portugal, Romania, Russia, Slovakia, Spain, Sweden, Switzerland, Togo, Türkiye, UK, Ukraine, USA, Vietnam.
NGO Relations Associated with: *Universal Esperanto Association (UEA, #20676).* [2019/XF3265/v/**F**]

- Tutmonda Asocio pri Kibernetiko, Informadiko, kaj Sistemiko (inactive)

♦ Tutmonda Ekumena Ligo (TEL) 20267

Address not obtained.

History 1985. **Aims** Provide contacts and *ecumenical* collaboration with all the *religions* worldwide. **Structure** Board; Secretary. **Languages** Esperanto. **Finance** Members' dues. Budget (annual): Italian Lire 10 million. **Events** *Meeting* Jerusalem (Israel) 1996, *Meeting* Annan (UK) 1989. **Publications** *Ekumenismo* (4 a year).
Members Full in 80 countries and territories:
Albania, Angola, Argentina, Armenia, Australia, Austria, Belgium, Bolivia, Bosnia-Herzegovina, Brazil, Bulgaria, Burundi, Cameroon, Canada, Central African Rep, Chile, China, Colombia, Congo Brazzaville, Costa Rica, Côte d'Ivoire, Croatia, Cuba, Czechia, Denmark, Dominican Rep, El Salvador, Estonia, Ethiopia, Finland, France, Germany, Greece, Holy See, Hong Kong, Hungary, India, Indonesia, Ireland, Israel, Italy, Japan, Jordan, Kazakhstan, Korea DPR, Korea Rep, Lebanon, Libya, Lithuania, Madagascar, Malta, Mexico, Netherlands, New Zealand, Norway, Pakistan, Panama, Paraguay, Peru, Philippines, Poland, Portugal, Romania, Russia, San Marino, Serbia, Slovakia, Slovenia, South Africa, Spain, Sri Lanka, Sweden, Switzerland, Taiwan, Türkiye, UK, Ukraine, Uruguay, USA, Venezuela.
IGO Relations *UNESCO (#20322).* **NGO Relations** Associated with: *Universal Esperanto Association (UEA, #20676).* [2012/XF0632/**F**]

♦ Tutmonda Esperantista Junulara Organizo (TEJO) 20268

Organisation Mondiale de la Jeunesse Espérantophone – Organización Mundial de la Juventud Esperantista – Welt-Esperanto-Jugend – World Esperanto Youth Organization

Gen Sec Nieuwe Binnenweg 176, 3015 BJ Rotterdam, Netherlands. T. +31104361044. Fax +31104361751. E-mail: oficejo@tejo.org.
URL: http://www.tejo.org/

History 2 Aug 1938, Groet (Netherlands). New statute approved 1985, Eringerfeld (Germany FR). Former names and other names: *Tutmonda Junular-Organizo* – former (1938 to 1954); *Organisation mondiale de la jeunesse espérantiste* – former (1938 to 1954); *Weltbund Junger Esperantisten* – former (1938 to 1954). Registration: EU Transparency Register, No/ID: 099332335142-02, Start date: 1 Jul 2019. **Aims** Spread the use of the international language Esperanto; work to raise the level of consciousness among young people concerning world language problems; facilitate international communication and take action to solve language problems in international relations; facilitate all kinds of human relationship, spiritual and material, irrespective of differences with regard to nationality, race, sex, religion, politics or language; foster a strong sense of solidarity among members by developing their understanding and respect for other people. **Structure** Council (meets twice a year); Executive Committee. **Languages** Esperanto. **Staff** 3.50 FTE, paid; 3.00 FTE, voluntary. **Finance** Sources: donations; grants; meeting proceeds; members' dues; sale of products. Arranged with Universal Esperanto Association (UEA). **Activities** Events/meetings; networking/liaising; projects/programmes. **Events** *Annual Congress* Westelbeers (Netherlands) 2022, *Annual Congress* Rotterdam (Netherlands) 2020, *Annual Congress* Liptovsky Hradok (Slovakia) 2019, *Annual Congress* Badajoz (Spain) 2018, *Annual Congress* Aného (Togo) 2017. **Publications** *Kontakto* (6 a year); *TEJO-Tutmonde* (6 a year); *Pasporta Servo* (annual) – address-list of TEJO accommodation service for travellers; *EJO Aktuale.* Congress and seminar reports.

Members Individuals in 44 countries:
Argentina, Austria, Benin, Brazil, Bulgaria, Burundi, Canada, China, Colombia, Congo DR, Croatia, Cuba, Czechia, Denmark, Finland, France, Germany, Greece, Haiti, Hungary, Iran Islamic Rep, Israel, Italy, Japan, Korea Rep, Lithuania, Madagascar, Mexico, Nepal, Netherlands, Norway, Poland, Portugal, Romania, Russia, Serbia, Slovakia, Spain, Sweden, Switzerland, UK, Ukraine, USA, Vietnam.
National organizations in 48 countries and territories. Membership countries not specified.

IGO Relations *European Youth Foundation (EYF, #09141).* Relations with United Nations and other bodies through UEA. **NGO Relations** Associated with: *Universal Esperanto Association (UEA, #20676).* Member of: *Council for International Cooperation of Nongovernmental Youth Organizations (EUROPOLIS, no recent information); European Youth Forum (#09140).* [2022.07.03/XC3566/**C**]

- ♦ Tutmonda Esperantista Jurnalista Asocio (#21138)
- ♦ Tutmonda Esperantista Kuracista Asocio / see Universala Medicina Esperanto-Asocio (#20672)
- ♦ Tutmonda Esperantista Pedagogia Servo (inactive)
- ♦ Tutmonda Esperantista Vegetarana Asocio (#21389)
- ♦ Tutmonda Junulara Organizo Kontraux Sxangxo de Klimato (inactive)
- ♦ Tutmonda Junular-Organizo / see Tutmonda Esperantista Junulara Organizo (#20268)

♦ TV5Monde (TV5) 20269

Managing Dir 131 avenue de Wagram, 75017 Paris, France. T. +33144185555. Fax +33144185510. E-mail: contact@tv5.org.
URL: http://www.tv5monde.com/

History 2 Jan 1984, by French language stations in Belgium (RTBF), France (TFI, Antenne 2 and FR3, grouped together under the banner of Satellimages) and Switzerland (SSR). Since formalization of *Organisation internationale de la Francophonie (OIF, #17809)*, 14-16 Nov 1997, Hanoi (Vietnam), an operating institution of 'La Francophonie'. **Aims** Promote *French language*, culture and society in diverse forms, through offering the best possible selection of *television* programmes already shown in the producing countries. **Structure** Chairman of the Board; Managing Director; 13 Directors; 7 Network Directors. **Languages** French. **Staff** 240.00 FTE, paid. **Finance** Funded through the French Ministry of Culture and Communications; contributions of French Authorities, French Community of Belgium, Canada, Québec, Switzerland, and African governments. Budget: euro 106 million. **Activities** Present in over 215 million homes in 200 countries 24 hours a day and 7 days a week. Comprises 9 television channels: *TV5MONDE France-Belgium-Switzerland*; *TV5MONDE Europe (see: #20269)*, the name taken in 1988 by the original European stations after a Canadian (Québec-Canada) consortium (CTQC) joined TV5 in 1986; *TV5MONDE Afrique (see: #20269)* launched Jun 1992; *TV5MONDE Middle East*; *TV5 Québec-Canada*; *TV5MONDE Asie*; *TV5MONDE Etats-Unis*; *TV5MONDE Latin America (see: #20269)* launched Oct 1992; *TV5MONDE Pacifique*, launched Sep 2009. Provides subtitles for a proportion of its programmes in: French; English; Spanish; Arabic; Portuguese; Dutch; German; Japanese; Korean; Romanian; Russian.

Members French-language television stations in 4 countries:
Belgium, Canada, France, Switzerland.

IGO Relations Direct operator of: *Conférence au sommet des chefs d'Etat et de gouvernement des pays ayant le français en partage (Sommet de la Francophonie, #04648).* Member of: *Asia-Pacific Institute for Broadcasting Development (AIBD, #01934).* **NGO Relations** Member of (2): *Conference of International Broadcasters' Audience Research Services (CIBAR, #04611); European Broadcasting Union (EBU, #06404).* Cooperates with (1): *Fondation des Alliances Françaises (AF, #09814).* [2011/XF0037/**F***]

- ♦ TV5MONDE Afrique (see: #20269)
- ♦ TV5MONDE Europe (see: #20269)
- ♦ TV5MONDE Latin America (see: #20269)
- ♦ **TV5** TV5Monde (#20269)
- ♦ **TVA** Vermiculite Association (#20755)
- ♦ TVE / see TVE International
- ♦ TVE International (internationally oriented national body)
- ♦ TVET – International Chair-Network UNESCO/ICES on "Technical and Vocational Education and Training" (see: #12487)
- ♦ **TVNI** The Vetiver Network International (#20763)
- ♦ TVN / see The Vetiver Network International (#20763)

♦ TWAS 20270

Exec Dir ICTP Enrico Fermi Bldg – Room 108, Strada Costiera 11, Enrico Fermi Bldg – 1st floor, 34151 Trieste TS, Italy. T. +39402240327. Fax +3940224559. E-mail: edoffice@twas.org – info@twas.org.
URL: https://www.twas.org/

History 10 Nov 1983, Trieste (Italy). Founded at foundation meeting sponsored by *Fondazione Internazionale Trieste per il Progresso e la Libertà delle Scienze (FIT).* Officially launched by United Nations Secretary General, 5 Jul 1985. Currently located in the premises of *Abdus Salam International Centre for Theoretical Physics (ICTP, #00005).* Former names and other names: *Third World Academy of Sciences (TWAS)* – former; *TWAS, the Academy of Sciences for the Developing World* – former alias; *The World Academy of Sciences for the advancement of science in developing countries (TWAS)* – full title. **Aims** Recognize, support and promote excellence in *scientific research* in the *developing world*; respond to the needs of young scientists in countries that are lagging in science and technology; promote South-South and South-North cooperation in science, technology and innovation; encourage scientific research and sharing of experiences in solving major problems facing developing countries. **Structure** General Meeting; Council of 7 members; Secretariat. Regions (5): Africa; Arab Region; Central and South Asia; East and Southeast Asia; Latin American and Caribbean. **Languages** English. **Finance** Sources: Ministry of Foreign Affairs, Italy; *Swedish International Development Cooperation Agency (Sida)*; Chinese Academy of Sciences; *OIC Ministerial Standing Committee on Scientific and Technological Cooperation (COMSTECH, #17702)*; Kuwait Foundation for the Advancement of Sciences; Elsevier Foundation, USA; *European Commission (EC, #06633)* Seventh Framework Programme; *UNESCO (#20322).* Governments and scientific organizations in developing countries cover local expenses for visits to their countries under fellowship and exchange programmes. **Activities** Awards/prizes/competitions; events/meetings. **Events** *General Conference* Changzhou (China) 2022, *Annual General Meeting* Trieste (Italy) 2018, *General Conference* Trieste (Italy) 2018, *Annual General Meeting* Kigali (Rwanda) 2016, *Annual General Conference* Vienna (Austria) 2015. **Publications** *TWAS Plus* (6 a year) – bulletin; *TWAS Newsletter. Excellence in Science* – series. Annual Report; Research Reports.

Members Fellows (1,262, including Founding Fellows): scientists of developing countries having made outstanding contributions in their respective fields of science, in 98 countries and territories:
Algeria, Argentina, Australia, Austria, Azerbaijan, Bahrain, Bangladesh, Barbados, Belgium, Benin, Bolivia, Botswana, Brazil, Cameroon, Canada, Chile, China, Colombia, Congo Brazzaville, Congo DR, Côte d'Ivoire, Cuba, Denmark, Ecuador, Egypt, Eswatini, Ethiopia, Finland, France, Germany, Ghana, Guatemala, Hungary, India, Iran Islamic Rep, Iraq, Italy, Jamaica, Japan, Jordan, Kazakhstan, Kenya, Korea DPR, Korea Rep, Kuwait, Laos, Lebanon, Libya, Madagascar, Malawi, Malaysia, Mali, Mauritius, Mexico, Mongolia, Morocco, Nepal, Netherlands, Nicaragua, Nigeria, Norway, Oman, Pakistan, Palestine, Panama, Peru, Philippines, Russia, Saudi Arabia, Senegal, Sierra Leone, Singapore, Slovenia, South Africa, Spain, Sri Lanka, Sudan, Sweden, Switzerland, Syrian AR, Taiwan, Tajikistan, Tanzania UR, Thailand, Togo, Trinidad-Tobago, Tunisia, Türkiye, Uganda, UK, United Arab Emirates, Uruguay, USA, Uzbekistan, Venezuela, Vietnam, Zambia, Zimbabwe.

Consultative Status Consultative status granted from: *ECOSOC (#05331)* (Ros B). **IGO Relations** Cooperates with: *Abdus Salam International Centre for Theoretical Physics (ICTP, #00005); International Science, Technology and Innovation Centre for South-South Cooperation under the auspices of UNESCO (ISTIC, #14799).* **NGO Relations** Cooperates with: *Fondazione Internazionale Trieste per il Progresso e la Libertà delle Scienze (FIT); Gender in science, innovation, technology and engineering (GenderInSITE, #10100); Global Research Council (GRC, #10574); Global Young Academy (GYA, #10662); InterAcademy Partnership (IAP, #11376); International Science Council (ISC, #14796); Organization for Women in Science for the Developing World (OWSD, #17890)*; national organizations. [2023/XF0440/v/**F**]

- ♦ TWAS, the Academy of Sciences for the Developing World / see TWAS (#20270)
- ♦ TWAS / see TWAS (#20270)
- ♦ TWB – Teachers Without Borders (internationally oriented national body)
- ♦ **TWCA** The World Calendar Association – International (#21255)
- ♦ TWCF – Third World Conference Foundation (internationally oriented national body)
- ♦ TWC – Theranostics World Congress (meeting series)
- ♦ TWDI – TransWorld Development Initiatives (internationally oriented national body)
- ♦ Twelve Gates Foundation (internationally oriented national body)
- ♦ Twentieth Century Fund / see The Century Foundation
- ♦ **TWF** Third World Forum (#20149)
- ♦ **TWF** Third World Foundation for Social and Economic Studies (#20150)
- ♦ TWF – TO'AI World Federation (unconfirmed)
- ♦ **TWFTW International** Word for the World, The (#21048)
- ♦ TWHA / see Viva Salud
- ♦ **TWIF** Tug of War International Federation (#20259)

♦ Twin Cities International Association (TCIA) 20271

Mezdunarodnaja Associacija 'Porodnennye Goroda' (MAPG)

Contact address not obtained. T. +74957081101 – +74957081075 – +74957081076. Fax +74957081101 – +74957081075.

History Dec 1991, USSR. Dec 1991, Tver (USSR), under present title and new charter, having previously existed since 1964 as *Association for Relations between Soviet and Foreign Cities.* **Aims** Bring together sister cities and local governments operating in the territories of the Commonwealth of Independent States – CIS; develop the *twinning* movement in Russia and other sovereign states within the regions of the former *Soviet Union*; promote participation of city populations in civic affairs. **Structure** General Conference (every 4 years); Board of Directors; Officers. **Languages** English, French, German, Russian. **Staff** 10.00 FTE, paid. **Finance** Members' dues. Budget (annual): about US$ 170,000. **Activities** Networking/liaising; events/meetings. **Events** *Ukraine-Russia cities conference* Kharkiv (Ukraine) 2001, *Russia-Bulgaria cities conference* Krasnogorsk (Russia) 2001, *Russia-Great Britain twinned cities congress* Volgograd (Russia) 2001, *General Assembly* Moscow (Russia) 2000, *Russia and Belarus twinned cities congress* Mytishchy (Belarus) 2000. **Publications** *Sister Cities* – magazine; *TCIA Bulletin.*

Members Twinned cities and regions and their associations, under new charter, public and commercial organizations and individuals with professional interest in twinning, local government and public administration and personnel training. Members in all 12 countries of the CIS:
Armenia, Azerbaijan, Belarus, Georgia, Kazakhstan, Kyrgyzstan, Moldova, Russia, Tajikistan, Turkmenistan, Ukraine, Uzbekistan. [2015/XD3976/**D**]

- ♦ Twinless Twins Support Group International (internationally oriented national body)
- ♦ TWIN – Third World Information Network (internationally oriented national body)
- ♦ TWI – TerraWatt Initiative (internationally oriented national body)
- ♦ TWMA – Third World Missions Association (internationally oriented national body)
- ♦ TWN Africa – Third World Network-Africa (internationally oriented national body)
- ♦ **TWN** Third World Network (#20151)
- ♦ TWOWEEKS International Volunteer Network (unconfirmed)
- ♦ TWOWEEKS – TWOWEEKS International Volunteer Network (unconfirmed)
- ♦ TWOWS / see Organization for Women in Science for the Developing World (#17890)
- ♦ TWR – Trans World Radio (internationally oriented national body)
- ♦ **TWSC** Third World Studies Center (#20152)
- ♦ TWTH INT – The Way to Happiness Foundation International (internationally oriented national body)
- ♦ Tyndall Centre for Climate Change Research (internationally oriented national body)

♦ Type Association Benelux (TAB) 20272

Association typologique Benelux

Contact Meerstraat 3, 2880 Bornem, Belgium. T. +3252376854. Fax +3252376855. E-mail: info@type-association.org.
Netherlands Dalmatië 2, 3831 EG Leusden, Netherlands. T. +31334321434. Fax +31334321434.
URL: http://www.type-association.org/

History 2003. **Finance** Members' dues. **NGO Relations** Member of: *European Association for Psychological Type (EAPT, #06173).* [2013/XJ6506/**D**]

- ♦ TYPES – International Conference on Types for Proofs (meeting series)
- ♦ Typhoon Committee / see ESCAP/WMO Typhoon Committee (#05534)
- ♦ Typology of Small-Scale Multilingualism (meeting series)
- ♦ Tzu Chi Foundation / see Buddhist Tzu Chi Foundation (#03347)
- ♦ Tzu Chi Merits Society / see Buddhist Tzu Chi Foundation (#03347)

♦ U4 Anti-Corruption Resource Centre 20273

Dir c/o CMI, PO Box 6033, 5892 Bergen, Norway. E-mail: u4@u4.no – u4@cmi.no.
URL: http://www.u4.no/

History 2002. A permanent centre at *Chr Michelsen Institute – Development Studies and Human Rights (CMI).* "U4" derives from the "*Utstein-partnership*" which developed following aid-harmonization and anti-corruption discussions in 1999 among ministers from Germany, Netherlands, Norway and the UK. **Aims** Assist *donor* practitioners in more effectively addressing corruption challenges through their development support. **Activities** Training/education; publishing activities. **Events** *Interdisciplinary Corruption Research Forum* Bergen (Norway) 2020. **IGO Relations** Cooperates with: Australian Department of Foreign Affairs and Trade; *DANIDA*; *Department for International Development (DFID, inactive)*; *Deutsche Gesellschaft für Internationale Zusammenarbeit (GIZ)*; Finnish Ministry of Foreign Affairs; German Federal Ministry of Economic Cooperation and Development (BMZ); *Norwegian Agency for Development Cooperation (Norad)*; *Swedish International Development Cooperation Agency (Sida)*; *Swiss Agency for Development and Cooperation (SDC).* **NGO Relations** Help Desk provided by: *Transparency International (TI, #20223). Chr Michelsen Institute – Development Studies and Human Rights (CMI)* provides secretariat. [2021/XJ0300/**F**]

- ♦ **UAAA** Union of Asian Alpine Associations (#20359)
- ♦ **UAA** Union des Architectes d'Afrique (#00529)
- ♦ **UAA** Union des avocats arabes (#01002)
- ♦ **UAA** Urban Affairs Association (#20728)
- ♦ **UAA** Urological Association of Asia (#20733)
- ♦ UAB / see Arab Federation of Exchanges (#00944)
- ♦ **UA-BIRA** Bureau interafricain des ressources animales (#11382)
- ♦ **UAB** Union of Arab Banks (#20349)

♦ **UACCC** Union of Arab Constitutional Courts and Councils (#20351)
♦ **UACES** University Association for Contemporary European Studies (#20697)
♦ UACF – Union arabe des chemins de fer (inactive)
♦ **UACI** Confederazione Internazionale Unione Apostolica del Clero (#12844)
♦ **UA/CIEFFA** Centre international pour l'éducation des filles et des femmes en Afrique de l'Union Africaine (#03752)
♦ UAC / see International Confederation Apostolic Union of Clergy (#12844)
♦ **UACMC** Union arabe du ciment et des matériaux de construction (#01065)
♦ UACSJ – Union arabe des clubs scientifiques pour jeunes (no recent information)
♦ **UAC** Union africaine des chemins de fer (#20347)
♦ **UAC** Union of Arab Chambers (#20350)
♦ UAC – Union of Arab Chemists (no recent information)
♦ UACVAO – Union des associations de chantiers de volontaires de l'Afrique de l'Ouest (inactive)
♦ **UADC** Université africaine de développement coopératif (#00494)
♦ UADE / see African Water Association (#00497)
♦ UADW – Universal Alliance of Diamond Workers (inactive)
♦ **UAECNE** Union of Armenian Evangelical Churches in the Near East (#20358)
♦ UAEE – Union des associations européennes d'étudiants (inactive)
♦ **UAEIF** Union des associations européennes des ingénieurs ferroviaires (#20362)
♦ **UAEM** Universities Allied for Essential Medicines (#20692)
♦ UAEPS – Union Arabe de l'éducation physique et du sport (inactive)
♦ **UAE** Union arabe d'électricité (#01066)
♦ **UAE** Union des avocats européens (#20365)
♦ **UAFA** Union arabe du fer et de l'acier (#00998)
♦ **UAFA** Union arabe de football associations (#20353)
♦ **UAFA** Union of Arab Football Associations (#20353)
♦ UAFE / see Intergovernmental Collaborative Action Fund for Excellence
♦ UAF – Urgent Action Fund for Women's Human Rights (internationally oriented national body)
♦ **UAG** Union africaine de gymnastique (#00334)
♦ UAH – Union of Arab Historians (no recent information)
♦ UAH – United Against Hunger (internationally oriented national body)
♦ **UAIA** Unión de Asóciaciones Ibéricas e Iberoamericanas del Benelux (#20361)
♦ **UAI** Union académique internationale (#20345)
♦ **UAI** Union des associations internationales (#20414)
♦ **UAI** Union astronomique internationale (#12287)
♦ UAI – Universidad Abierta Interamericana (internationally oriented national body)
♦ **UAJ** Union africaine de judo (#00350)
♦ **UAJ** Union of Arab Jurists (#20354)
♦ UAM / see Arab Maghreb Union (#01004)
♦ UAMBD – Union africaine des banques pour le développement (inactive)
♦ UAMD – Union africaine et malgache de défense (inactive)
♦ UAM / see FIM Asia (#09759)
♦ UAMI / see European Union Intellectual Property Office (#08996)
♦ UAMPI – Union africaine et malgache pour la propriété industrielle (inactive)
♦ UAMS – Union africaine de médecine du sport (no recent information)
♦ UANA / see PanAm Aquatics (#18077)
♦ **UAN** United Animal Nations (#20497)
♦ UAOD – United Ancient Order of Druids (religious order)
♦ UAP / see African Parliamentary Union (#00412)
♦ UAPA – Union of African Performing Artists (no recent information)
♦ UAPCU – Universal Association of Professional Colleges and Universities (internationally oriented national body)
♦ UAPDD – Union of African Parties for Democracy and Development (inactive)
♦ **UAPNA** Union des administrations portuaires du Nord de l'Afrique (#17556)
♦ UAPP / see Arab Federation of Fish Producers (#00945)
♦ **UAPS** Union for African Population Studies (#20346)
♦ **UAPS** Union of Arab Paediatric Societies (#20355)
♦ UAPTDE / see Arab Union of Electricity (#01066)
♦ UAPT – Union africaine des postes et télécommunications (inactive)
♦ UAP – Union africaine de physique (inactive)
♦ **UAP** Union of Arab Pharmacists (#20356)
♦ **UArctic** University of the Arctic (#20696)
♦ **UAR** Union Africaine de Radiodiffusion (#00490)
♦ **UAR** Union of African Railways (#20347)

♦ UAS4EUROPE 20274

Contact address not obtained. E-mail: info@uas4europe.eu.
URL: http://uas4europe.eu/

History Set up as a joint initiative of *European Association of Institutions of Higher Education (EURASHE, #06086)*, *Universities of Applied Sciences Network (UASNET, #20693)*, and national institutions in Switzerland, Germany and Austria. **Aims** Promote the voice of *universities* of applied *sciences* (UAS) in Europe for applied research and innovation. **Structure** Organisation Committee; Board. **Activities** Events/meetings; research/documentation. **Events** *Conference* Brussels (Belgium) 2019, *Universities of applied sciences – maximising success in horizon 2020 and beyond – Learn! Network! Lobby!* Brussels (Belgium) 2017.
Members Partners (5). National institutions in 3 countries:
Austria, Germany, Switzerland.
Regional institions (2):
European Association of Institutions of Higher Education (EURASHE, #06086); *Universities of Applied Sciences Network (UASNET, #20693).* [2017/XM5550/y/**F**]

♦ **UASA** Union of Arab Securities Authorities (#20357)
♦ UASA – Union des artistes de spectacle africains (no recent information)
♦ **UASB** Universidad Andina Simón Bolívar (#20687)
♦ **UASC** Union of African Shippers' Councils (#20348)
♦ UASC – United Arab Shipping Company (no recent information)
♦ UASE / see Arab Federation of Exchanges (#00944)
♦ UASG / see Asian Gymnastics Union (#01499)
♦ UASNET / see Universities of Applied Sciences Network (#20693)
♦ **UASNET** Universities of Applied Sciences Network (#20693)
♦ **UATCM** Union des associations de techniciens de culture méditerranéenne (#20364)
♦ UATI / see Union internationale des associations et organismes scientifiques et techniques (#20421)
♦ **UATI** Union internationale des associations et organismes scientifiques et techniques (#20421)
♦ UAT – Union africaine des télécommunications (inactive)
♦ **UAT** Union africaine des télécommunications (#00482)
♦ UAT – Union of African Towns (inactive)
♦ **UA** Union africaine (#00488)
♦ **UA** Universal Alliance (#20671)
♦ UAV DACH – Unmanned Aviation Association (internationally oriented national body)
♦ UAW – International Union, United Automobile, Aerospace and Agricultural Implement Workers of America (internationally oriented national body)
♦ UAWS / see African Water Association (#00497)
♦ UBAC / see Commercial Bank Centrafrique
♦ **UBAF** Union de Banques Arabes et Françaises (#20367)
♦ UBCCE / see Union of Black Sea and Caspian Business (#20369)
♦ UBCHEA – United Board for Christian Higher Education in Asia (internationally oriented national body)
♦ **UBC** Union of the Baltic Cities (#20366)
♦ UBE – European Basketball Players' Union (internationally oriented national body)
♦ Übereinkommen des Europarats zur verhütung des terrorismus (2005 treaty)
♦ Übereinkommen zum schutz des menschen bei der automatischen verarbeitung personenbezogener daten (1981 treaty)
♦ Übereinkommen über computerkriminalität (2001 treaty)
♦ Übereinkommen über die anerkennung von qualifikationen im hochschulbereich in der europäischen region (1997 treaty)
♦ Übereinkommen über die ausarbeitung eines europäischen arzneibuches (1964 treaty)
♦ Übereinkommen über die beteiligung von ausländern am kommunalen öffentlichen leben (1992 treaty)
♦ Übereinkommen über die gegenseitige amtshilfe in steuersachen (1988 treaty)
♦ Übereinkommen über die haftung der gastwirte für die von ihren gästen eingebrachten sachen (1962 treaty)
♦ Übereinkommen über die information und verfahrenshilfe bezüglich der "dienstleistungsgesellschaften von informationen" (2001 treaty)
♦ Übereinkommen über die leichenbeförderung (1973 treaty)
♦ Übereinkommen über die regelung von wasserentnahmen aus dem Bodensee (1966 treaty)
♦ Übereinkommen über die schaffung eines systems zur registrierung von testamenten (1972 treaty)
♦ Übereinkommen über die schiffahrt auf dem Bodensee (1973 treaty)
♦ Übereinkommen über die überstellung verurteilter personen (1983 treaty)
♦ Übereinkommen über die verringerung der mehrstaatigkeit und über die wehrpflicht von mehrstaatern (1963 treaty)
♦ Übereinkommen über die vorübergehende zollfreie einfuhr von medizinischem, chirurgischem und laboratoriumsmaterial zur leihweisen verwendung für diagnose- und behandlungszwecke in krankenhäusern und anderen einrichtungen des gesundheitswesens (1960 treaty)
♦ Übereinkommen über geldwäsche sowie ermittlung, beschlagnahme und einziehung von erträgen aus straftaten (1990 treaty)
♦ Übereinkommen über insidergeschäfte (1989 treaty)
♦ Übereinkommen über den Internationalen Eisenbahnverkehr, 1980 (1980 treaty)
♦ Übereinkommen über den Internationalen Eisenbahnverkehr, 1999 (1999 treaty)
♦ Übereinkommen über den schutz des lachsbestandes in der Ostsee (1962 treaty)
♦ Übereinkommen über den umgang von und mit kindern (2003 treaty)
♦ Übereinkommen über den unerlaubten verkehr auf see zur durchführung des artikels 17 des übereinkommens der Vereinten Nationen gegen den unerlaubten verkehr mit suchtstoffen und psychotropen stoffen (1995 treaty)
♦ Übereinkommen über den widerspruch bei international gehandelten inhaberpapieren (1970 treaty)
♦ Übereinkommen zur vereinheitlichung gewisser begriffe des materiellen rechts der erfindungspatente (1963 treaty)
♦ Übereinkommen zwischen den mitgliedstaaten des Europarats über die ausgabe eines internationalen gutscheinhefts für die instandsetzung von prothesen und orthopädischen hilfsmitteln an militärische und zivile kriegsbeschädigte (1962 treaty)
♦ **UBE** Union bouddhiste d'Europe (#06407)
♦ Ubhaliso Lwabantu Belizwe Jukelele / see Registre des Citoyens du Monde (#18822)
♦ UBIFRANCE / see Agence française pour le développement international des entreprises
♦ **UBLA** Union of Baptists in Latin America (#20368)
♦ **UBLA** Unión Bautista Latino-Americana (#20368)
♦ UBL – Universidad Biblica Latinoamericana (internationally oriented national body)
♦ UBM – Union balkanique mathématique (inactive)
♦ UB – Observatory of Globalization (internationally oriented national body)
♦ **UBO** Universal Boxing Organization (#20673)
♦ **UBS** United Bible Societies (#20498)
♦ UBUNTU Liberation Movement (unconfirmed)

♦ UbuntuNet Alliance for Research and Education Networking 20275

CEO PO Box 2550, Lilongwe, Malawi. T. +2651754535. Fax +2651754535.
Street Address Onions Office Complex, Lilongwe, Malawi.
URL: http://www.ubuntunet.net/

History Founded in the latter half of 2005, by 5 established and emerging National Research and Education Networks (NRENs) in Eastern and Southern Africa, namely MAREN (Malawi), MoRENet (Mozambique), KENET (Kenya), RwEdNet (Rwanda) and TENET (South Africa). Originally registered in accordance with Dutch law in 2006; registered in accordance with Malawi law, 2014. **Aims** Build and operate UbuntuNet, the regional high-speed backbone network interconnecting NRENs and connecting them to other regional RENs in the world and the Internet in general; develop and provide high speed and affordable interconnectivity among NRENs and with the rest of the world; develop and share the knowledge and skills of ICT practitioners in NRENs; provide related auxiliary services to NRENs; lead and participate in research aimed at improving networking infrastructure. **Structure** Annual General Meeting. Board of Trustees, composed of 7 elected Trustees and 2 ex officio Trustees, Chairperson and CEO. Trustees are nominated by NREN members, and are elected at the Annual General Meeting for a 2-year term. **Languages** English, French. **Staff** 7.00 FTE, paid. **Activities** Events/meetings. **Events** *Annual Conference* Entebbe (Uganda) 2016, *Annual Conference* Maputo (Mozambique) 2015, *Annual Conference* Lusaka (Zambia) 2014, *Annual Conference* Kigali (Rwanda) 2013, *Annual Conference* Dar es Salaam (Tanzania UR) 2012. **Publications** *NUANCE* (12 a year).
Members NRENs in 15 countries:
Burundi, Congo DR, Ethiopia, Kenya, Madagascar, Malawi, Mozambique, Namibia, Rwanda, Somalia, South Africa, Sudan, Tanzania UR, Uganda, Zambia.
IGO Relations Cooperates with: *European Commission (EC, #06633)*; *International Development Research Centre (IDRC, #13162)*. **NGO Relations** Development partners include: *Association of African Universities (AAU, #02361)*; *Southern African Regional Universities Association (SARUA, #19860)*; *Trans-European Research and Education Networking Association (TERENA, inactive).* [2021/XJ7071/**D**]

♦ UCAC – Université catholique d'Afrique centrale (unconfirmed)
♦ UCADIA – Unión Centroamericana de Asociaciones de Ingenieros y Arquitectos (inactive)
♦ UCAL – Unión de Cinematecas de América Latina (no recent information)
♦ UCA News / see Union of Catholic Asian News (#20371)
♦ **UCAN** Union of Catholic Asian News (#20371)
♦ UCAO – Union des chercheurs d'Afrique de l'ouest (no recent information)
♦ **UCAPE** Union pour la culture et l'avenir professionnel en Europe (#20373)
♦ UCA – União das Cidades Africanas (inactive)
♦ UCA – Union coopérative arabe (inactive)
♦ UCA – Universidad Centroamericana José Simeón Cañas (internationally oriented national body)
♦ UCA – Universidad Centroamericana, Managua (internationally oriented national body)
♦ **UCA** University of Central Asia (#20698)
♦ UC Berkeley Center of Evaluation for Global Action (internationally oriented national body)
♦ UCBR – Union pour le commerce des bois résineux dans l'UE (inactive)
♦ UCB – United Christian Broadcasters (internationally oriented national body)
♦ UCBWM / see Common Global Ministries Board
♦ **UCCA** União dos Conselhos dos Carregadores Africanos (#20348)
♦ **UCCA** Union des conseils des chargeurs africains (#20348)
♦ UCCEE / see UNEP Copenhagen Climate Centre (#20296)
♦ UCCIFE / see Chambres de Commerce et d'Industrie Françaises à l'International (#03849)
♦ UCCIOI / see Cap Business Océan Indien (#03419)
♦ **UCCI** União de Cidades Capitais Ibero-Americanas (#20412)

♦ **UCCI** Unión de Ciudades Capitales Iberoamericanas (#20412)
♦ **UCCLA** União das Cidades Capitais Luso-Afro-Américo-Asiaticas (#20328)
♦ UCCRN – Urban Climate Change Research Network (internationally oriented national body)
♦ **UCCSA** United Congregational Church of Southern Africa (#20503)
♦ UCDEC – Union chrétienne démocrate d'Europe centrale (inactive)
♦ UCEA – University Council for Educational Administration (internationally oriented national body)
♦ UCEE – Unione Camere Esperti Europei (unconfirmed)
♦ UCEM – Union de Centros de Estudios del Mediterraneo (internationally oriented national body)
♦ UCENS – Union of Central Eurasian Neonatal Societies (inactive)
♦ UCEP / see Ecotechnie (#05333)
♦ UCESA – Union of Economic and Social Councils of Africa (no recent information)
♦ UCESIF – Union des Conseils Economiques et Sociaux et Institutions Similaires Francophones (unconfirmed)
♦ **UCESM** Unio Conferentiarum Europae Superiorum Maiorum (#20344)
♦ UCF / see Union culturelle et technique de langue française (#20374)
♦ **UCGIA** United Church of God – International Association (#20499)
♦ UCG / see United Church of God – International Association (#20499)
♦ UCILS – Utrecht Centre for International Legal Studies (internationally oriented national body)
♦ UCIP / see International Christian Organisation of the Media (#12563)
♦ UCISS / see Centre for International Security and Strategic Studies, Kiev
♦ UCISS – Ukrainian Centre for International Security Studies (internationally oriented national body)
♦ UCISS – Union catholique internationale de service social (inactive)
♦ UCISS – Unión Católica Internacional de Servicio Social (inactive)
♦ UCIS – University Center for International Studies, Pittsburgh (internationally oriented national body)
♦ **UCI** Union canine internationale (#20370)
♦ **UCI** Union Cycliste Internationale (#20375)
♦ **UCI** Universidad Cooperativa Internacional (#12952)
♦ **UCI** Université coopérative internationale (#12952)
♦ **UCJG** Alliance universelle des unions chrétiennes de jeunes gens (#21090)
♦ **UCKG** Universal Church of the Kingdom of God (#20674)
♦ UCLA Center for international Relations / see Burkle Center for International Relations
♦ UCLA Center for Middel East Development / see Center for Middle East Development
♦ UCLA Globalization Research Centre of Africa (internationally oriented national body)
♦ UCLAS – Unisa Centre for Latin American Studies (internationally oriented national body)
♦ UCL Centre for European Studies (internationally oriented national body)
♦ UCL CES – UCL Centre for European Studies (internationally oriented national body)
♦ UCLGA / see United Cities and Local Governments of Africa (#20500)
♦ **UCLG Africa** United Cities and Local Governments of Africa (#20500)
♦ **UCLG ASPAC** United Cities and Local Governments Asia Pacific (#20501)
♦ **UCLG-MEWA** United Cities and Local Governments Middle East and West Asia (#20502)
♦ **UCLG** World Organization of United Cities and Local Governments (#21695)
♦ UCL Institute for Global Health (internationally oriented national body)
♦ UCMS – United Christian Missionary Society (internationally oriented national body)
♦ UCNC – International Conference on Unconventional Computation and Natural Computation (meeting series)
♦ UCODEP (internationally oriented national body)
♦ UCODEP – per un' mondo a dimensione umana / see UCODEP
♦ UCOS – Universitair Centrum voor Ontwikkelingssamenwerking, Brussel (internationally oriented national body)
♦ UCO / see UNESCO Office, Cairo – Regional Bureau for Sciences in the Arab States (#20312)
♦ UCPBL – Aalborg Centre for Problem Based Learning in Engineering Science and Sustainability (internationally oriented national body)
♦ UCPCCRS / see Center for Peace, Conversion and Foreign Policy of Ukraine
♦ UCRIF / see Ethic étapes
♦ Ucrif étapes jeunes / see Ethic étapes
♦ **UCSA** Union des confédérations sportives africaines (#02360)
♦ **UCSEEC** Union of Central and South-Eastern European Capitals (#20372)
♦ UCSJ – Union of Councils for Jews in the Former Soviet Union (internationally oriented national body)
♦ **UC** Southeast Asian University Consortium for Graduate Education in Agriculture and Natural Resources (#19786)
♦ UCS – Union of Concerned Scientists (internationally oriented national body)
♦ UCTE – Union for the Coordination of Transmission of Electricity (inactive)
♦ **UCTF** Union culturelle et technique de langue française (#20374)
♦ UCUE – Union des capitales de l'Union européenne (inactive)
♦ UC – United Cultures Foundation (internationally oriented national body)
♦ UCWM / see UnitingWorld
♦ **UDAA** Union douanière d'Afrique australe (#19842)
♦ UDAO – Union douanière de l'Afrique de l'Ouest (inactive)
♦ **UDC Consortium** Universal Decimal Classification Consortium (#20675)
♦ UDCEC – Unión Democratica Cristiana de Europa Central (inactive)
♦ **UDC** Unity-and-Diversity World Council (#20670)
♦ UDEAC – Union douanière et économique de l'Afrique centrale (inactive)
♦ **UDEFAL** Unión de Escuelas y Facultades de Arquitectura Latinoamericanas (#20380)
♦ Det Udenrigspolitiske Selskab (internationally oriented national body)
♦ UDE – Union démocratique européenne (inactive)
♦ UDHR – Universal Declaration of Human Rights (1948 treaty)
♦ UD – International Conference on Universal Design (meeting series)
♦ **UDITE** Union des dirigeants territoriaux de l'Europe (#20454)
♦ **UDI** Union démocratique internationale (#13147)
♦ UDLA – Universidad de las Américas (internationally oriented national body)
♦ **UDMS** Urban Data Management Society (#20730)
♦ **UDNI** Undiagnosed Diseases Network International (#20288)
♦ **UDOFAO** Union des ordres fiscaux de l'Afrique de l'ouest (#20898)
♦ Udruzenje Evropskih Karnevalskih Grazdova / see Federation of European Carnival Cities (#09496)
♦ UdS / see Union Syndicale Fédérale (#20485)
♦ **UDUAL** Unión de Universidades de América Latina y el Caribe (#02970)
♦ Udvalget for det EØFs Fabrikanter af Gaer til Brødfremstilling / see Confédération des Fabricants de Levure de l'Union Européenne (#04551)
♦ **UEAC** Union économique de l'Afrique centrale (#20376)
♦ UEAC – Union des Etats de l'Afrique centrale (inactive)
♦ UEADM – Union européenne des associations de délégués médicaux (inactive)
♦ UEAES – Union européenne des alcools, eaux-de-vie et spiritueux (inactive)
♦ **UEAI** Union européenne des arabisants et islamisants (#08976)
♦ UEAPME / see SMEunited (#19327)
♦ **UEAtc** Union européenne pour l'agrément technique dans la construction (#20393)
♦ **UEA** Union des entrepreneurs arabes (#09419)
♦ **UEA** Union européenne de l'ameublement (#07370)
♦ **UEA** Union Européenne des Aveugles (#06350)
♦ **UEA** Universal Esperanto Association (#20676)
♦ **UEA** Urban Economics Association (#20731)
♦ **UEA** Urban Environmental Accords (#20732)
♦ UEB / see Badminton Europe (#03058)
♦ **UEBL** Union économique belgo-luxembourgeoise (#03195)
♦ **UEBT** Union for Ethical BioTrade (#20381)
♦ UEB – Union Europäischer Bankpersonalverbände (no recent information)
♦ UECA – Union européenne du commerce ambulant (no recent information)
♦ **UECB** Union européenne des consommateurs de bière (#06325)
♦ **UECBV** Union européenne du commerce du bétail et de la viande (#20394)
♦ UECCA – CEFACEF / see European Committee for the Advancement of Thermal Sciences and Heat Transfer (#06640)
♦ UECCA – Union européenne des constructeurs de chaudières en acier (inactive)
♦ UECC / see Union of European Chambers of Commerce for Transport (#20384)
♦ **UECC** Union of European Chambers of Commerce for Transport (#20384)
♦ UECGPT / see European Potato Trade Association (#08257)
♦ UECL / see Build Europe (#03350)
♦ **UECNA** Union Européenne Contre les Nuisances des Avions (#20395)
♦ UE – Comité de liaison des praticiens de l'art dentaire / see Council of European Dentists (#04886)
♦ UECP – Union européenne des coupeurs de poil pour chapellerie et filature (inactive)
♦ **UECT** Union européenne de cyclotourisme (#20396)
♦ UEC – Union européenne de la carrosserie (inactive)
♦ UEC – Union européenne de chaudières (inactive)
♦ **UEC** Union européenne de cyclisme (#06876)
♦ UEC – Union européenne des experts comptables économiques et financiers (inactive)
♦ UEDA – Utility Economic Development Association (internationally oriented national body)
♦ UEDC – Union européenne démocrate chrétienne (inactive)
♦ UEDE – Union économique et douanière européenne (inactive)
♦ UEE / see Institut Européen d'Ecriture
♦ **UEEIV** Union Europäischer Eisenbahn-Ingenieur-Verbände (#20362)
♦ **UEEJ** Union Européenne des Etudiants Juifs (#08997)
♦ UEEP – Vereinigung Nationaler Stuck-Putz-Trockenbauverbände in Europa (inactive)
♦ UEF / see Alliance of European Football Coaches' Associations (#00674)
♦ **UEFA** Union of European Football Associations (#20386)
♦ UEFCO – Union of European Federation of Corporate Football (unconfirmed)
♦ UEFDC / see EPP Women (#05516)
♦ UEF / see Learning for Well-being Foundation (#16431)
♦ UEFM – Union européenne des femmes de militaires (no recent information)
♦ UEFPC – Union européenne des fédérations du personnel communal (inactive)
♦ **UEFS** Unione Europea delle Farmacie Sociali (#20401)
♦ **UEFS** Union Europea de Futsal (#07371)
♦ **UEF** Union of European Federalists, The (#20385)
♦ **UEF** Union of European Foresters (#20387)
♦ **UEF** Union européenne féminine (#09022)
♦ **UEG** / see European Gymnastics (#07442)
♦ UEGF / see United European Gastroenterology (#20506)
♦ **UEG** Union Europäischer Gerüstbaubetriebe (#20382)
♦ **UEG** United European Gastroenterology (#20506)
♦ UEHHA / see European Historic Houses Association (#07491)
♦ **UEHMSU** Union européenne d'hygiène et de médecine scolaires et universitaires (#09016)
♦ **UEHP** Union européenne de l'hospitalisation privée (#20397)
♦ UEIL / see Union Européenne de l'Industrie des Lubrifiants (#20398)
♦ **UEIL** Union Européenne de l'Industrie des Lubrifiants (#20398)
♦ UEITP / see EUPPA – European Potato Processors' Association (#05592)
♦ **UEJ** Union européenne de judo (#20399)
♦ UELCSA – United Evangelical Lutheran Church in Southern Africa (internationally oriented national body)
♦ **UELDC** Unione Europea dei Lavoratori Democratici Cristiani (#08981)
♦ UEL / see European Association of Violin and Bow Makers (#06273)
♦ UELF – Union des éditeurs de langue française (no recent information)
♦ **UEL** Group of the Unified European Left (#10794)
♦ **UELRSE** Union des élus locaux et régionaux socialistes d'Europe (#20479)
♦ **UEMASS** Union européenne de médecine d'assurance et de sécurité sociale (#08995)
♦ UEM – Communion of Churches in Three Continents / see United Evangelical Mission (#20507)
♦ **UEMC** Union européenne des magistrats statuant en matière commerciale (#08998)
♦ UEMDC / see EPP Women (#05516)
♦ UEMD – Unione Europea dei Medici Dentisti (inactive)
♦ UEME – Union européenne des mandataires, des entreprises et professions libérales (no recent information)
♦ UEM / see FIM Europe (#09760)
♦ UEMOA Court of Justice (#04932)
♦ **UEMOA** Union économique et monétaire Ouest africaine (#20377)
♦ UEMO / see European Union of General Practitioners / Family Physicians (#08993)
♦ **UEMO** Union européenne des médecins omnipraticiens / médecins de famille (#08993)
♦ **UEMS** European Union of Medical Specialists (#09001)
♦ UEMS – Unione Europea di Medicina Sociale (no recent information)
♦ **UEMS** Union Européenne des Médecins Spécialistes (#09001)
♦ UEMTA – Union européenne contre l'emploi abusif des animaux (inactive)
♦ **UEM** Union économique et monétaire (#06961)
♦ UEM – Union européenne des musiciens (inactive)
♦ **UEM** United Evangelical Mission (#20507)
♦ **UEMV** Union européenne des miroitiers vitriers (#07394)
♦ UEM / see World Evangelical Alliance (#21393)
♦ UENCPB – Union européenne des négociants en cuirs et peaux bruts (no recent information)
♦ **UENF** Union européenne de la navigation fluviale (#06318)
♦ **UENFW** Union of European national football teams of winemakers (#20388)
♦ **UENPS** Union of European Neonatal and Perinatal Societies (#20389)
♦ **UEN** Union européenne des non-fumeurs (#09006)
♦ UEO – Union de l'Europe occidentale (inactive)
♦ UEPAC – Union des éditeurs de presse d'Afrique centrale (no recent information)
♦ UEPA – European Union of Ethanol Producers (inactive)
♦ **UEPA** Union pour l'étude de la population africaine (#20346)
♦ UEPC / see Build Europe (#03350)
♦ UEP / see European Society of Child and Adolescent Psychiatry (#08543)
♦ **UEPG** Aggregates Europe (#00558)
♦ **UEPG** Union européenne des producteurs de granulats (#00558)
♦ **UEPS** Unione Europea delle Pharmacies sociales (#20401)
♦ **UEPS** Union européenne de la presse sportive (#08822)
♦ **UEPS** United Elvis Presley Society (#20504)
♦ **UEP** Union der Europäischen Phoniater (#20390)
♦ **UEP** Union of European Phoniatricians (#20390)
♦ **UEP** Union européenne des parachutistes (#09008)
♦ UERP / see European Union of Public Relations (#09011)
♦ **UERP** Unione Europea di Relazioni Pubbliche (#09011)
♦ **UER** Union européenne de radio-télévision (#06404)
♦ UESC – Union européenne du spectacle cinématographique (inactive)
♦ **UESpT** European Sport for All Federation (#08819)
♦ **UESpT** Union Européenne Sport pour Tous (#08819)
♦ **UES** Union Européenne de Systémique (#20403)
♦ UES – United Economic Space (unconfirmed)

- UETA – Union européenne des travailleurs aveugles (inactive)
- UETA – United European Tattoo Artists (internationally oriented national body)
- **UETDC** Union européenne des travailleurs démocrates-chrétiens (#08981)
- UETR / see European Road Hauliers Association (#08393)
- **UETR** European Road Hauliers Association (#08393)
- **UET** Union européenne du trot (#08952)
- **UE** União Europeia (#08967)
- **UE** Unione Europea (#08967)
- **UE** Unión Europea (#08967)
- **UE** Union européenne (#08967)
- UEVA – Union européenne des vétérinaires d'abattoirs (inactive)
- **UEVF** Union européenne des vétérinaires fonctionnaires (#06221)
- **UEVH** Union of European Veterinary Hygienists (#20404)
- **UEVH** Union européenne des vétérinaires hygiénistes (#20404)
- UEVH / see Union internationale des vélodromes (#20440)
- **UEVP** Union européenne des vétérinaires praticiens (#20405)
- UEV – Université européenne du volontariat (see: #02978)
- UEYBDA – Union européenne de yoseikan budo et disciplines assimilées (inactive)
- **UEY** Unione Europea di Yoga (#09131)
- UFAI – Union féminine artistique internationale (inactive)
- **UFAI** Union francophone de l'audit interne (#20409)
- UFAK – Union des fédérations africaines de karaté (see: #21608)
- **UFA** Union Francophone des Aveugles (#20410)
- UFAW / see Universities Federation for Animal Welfare
- UFAW – The International Animal Welfare Science Society / see Universities Federation for Animal Welfare
- UFAW – Universities Federation for Animal Welfare (internationally oriented national body)
- **UFBAL** Union Femenil Bautista de America Latina (#16255)
- UFCE / see Federal Union of European Nationalities (#09396)
- UFCWIU / see United Food and Commercial Workers Union
- UFCW – United Food and Commercial Workers Union (internationally oriented national body)
- **UFDWR** United for Foreign Domestic Workers' Rights (#20510)
- **UFEMAT** Union européenne des fédérations nationales des négociants en matériaux de construction (#06128)
- UFER / see Unis pour l'Equite et la Fin du Racisme (#20490)
- **UFER** Unis pour l'Equite et la Fin du Racisme (#20490)
- **UFER** United for Equity and Ending Racism (#20490)
- UFE / see Union des féculeries de pommes de terre de l'Union européenne (#20406)
- **UFE** Union des féculeries de pommes de terre de l'Union européenne (#20406)
- **UFE** Union des Finanzpersonals in Europa (#20407)
- **UFE** Union foraine européenne (#08483)
- Ufficio per l'Armonizzazione nel Mercato Interno – Marchi, Disegni e Modelli / see European Union Intellectual Property Office (#08996)
- Ufficio Centrale Svizzero per l'Aiuto ai Rifugiati / see Organisation suisse d'aide aux réfugiés
- Ufficio Comunitario delle Varietà Vegetali (#04404)
- Ufficio Europeo dell' Ambiente / see European Environmental Bureau (#06996)
- Ufficio Europeo per la Lotta Antifrode (#05906)
- Ufficio Internazionale delle Associazioni di Fabbricanti, Grossisti e Dettaglianti di Gioielleria, Oreficeria e Argenteria / see CIBJO – The World Jewellery Confederation (#03923)
- Ufficio Internazionale per la Standardizzazione del Raion e delle Fibre Artificiali e Sintetiche / see Bureau international pour la standardisation de la rayonne et des fibres synthétiques (#03369)
- Ufficio delle Pubblicazioni dell'Unione Europea (#18562)
- Ufficio dell'Unione Europea per la Proprietà Intellettuale (#08996)
- UFGC – Urban Future global conference (meeting series)

♦ UFI – The Global Association of the Exhibition Industry 20276

Managing Dir – CEO UFI Headquarters, 17 rue Louise Michel, 92300 Levallois-Perret, France. T. +33146397500. Fax +33146397501. E-mail: info@ufi.org – media@ufi.org.
Events Manager address not obtained.
URL: http://www.ufi.org/

History 15 Apr 1925, Milan (Italy). Statutes modified: 1955, Paris (France); 1960, Casablanca (Morocco); 1969, Leipzig (German DR); 1970, London (UK); 1973, Cologne (Germany FR) (when UFI was first composed of member-organizers); 1981, Québec (Canada); 1982, Tokyo (Japan); 1983, Funchal (Portugal); 1985, Düsseldorf (Germany FR); 1986, Budapest (Hungary); 1988, Jakarta (Indonesia); 1992, Valencia (Spain); 1994, Singapore (Singapore); 1995, London (UK); 1999, Bilbao (Spain); 2001, Cologne (Germany); 2004, Bangkok (Thailand); 2006, Beijing (China); 2009, Zagreb (Croatia). Former names and other names: *Union of International Fairs* – former; *Union des foires internationales (UFI)* – former; *Verband internationaler Messen* – former. Registration: France. **Aims** Globally represent, promote and support the business interests of members and the exhibition industry. **Structure** General Assembly; Board of Directors; Executive Committee; The Trio (President and 2 Executive Vice-Presidents); Regional Chapters (4). **Languages** English. **Finance** Sources: members' dues. **Activities** Events/meetings; networking/liaising. **Events** *UFI Global Congress* Las Vegas, NV (USA) 2023, *Global CEO Summit* Lisbon (Portugal) 2023, *European Conference* Maastricht (Netherlands) 2023, *Latin American Conference* San José (Costa Rica) 2023, *UFI Global Congress* Muscat (Oman) 2022. **Publications** *M+A-UFI Exhibition Newsletter* (weekly); *UFI Info* (10 a year) – e-bulletin; *Exhibition World* (4 a year) – magazine.
Members Organizations (800) in 86 countries and territories:
Albania, Algeria, Argentina, Australia, Austria, Azerbaijan, Bahrain, Belgium, Bolivia, Brazil, Bulgaria, Canada, Chile, China, Colombia, Croatia, Cuba, Czechia, Egypt, El Salvador, Finland, France, Georgia, Germany, Greece, Guatemala, Hong Kong, Hungary, India, Indonesia, Iraq, Italy, Japan, Jordan, Kazakhstan, Kenya, Korea Rep, Kosovo, Kuwait, Lebanon, Libya, Lithuania, Luxembourg, Macau, Malaysia, Mexico, Moldova, Montenegro, Morocco, Mozambique, Netherlands, Nigeria, North Macedonia, Oman, Pakistan, Peru, Philippines, Poland, Portugal, Qatar, Romania, Russia, Rwanda, Saudi Arabia, Serbia, Singapore, Slovakia, Slovenia, South Africa, Spain, Sudan, Sweden, Switzerland, Taiwan, Tanzania UR, Thailand, Tunisia, Türkiye, UK, Ukraine, United Arab Emirates, Uruguay, USA, Uzbekistan, Vietnam, Zimbabwe.
Included in the above, 1 organization listed in this Yearbook:
International Association of Exhibitions in Latin America (#11886).
Consultative Status Consultative status granted from: *ECOSOC (#05331)* (Ros A); *UNCTAD (#20285)* (General Category); *UNIDO (#20336)*. **IGO Relations** Cooperates with (6): *Bureau International des Expositions (BIE, #03365)*; *ILO (#11123)*; *International Trade Centre (ITC, #15703)*; *OECD (#17693)*; *United Nations Office at Vienna (UNOV, #20604)*; *World Trade Organization (WTO, #21864)*. Associated with Department of Global Communications of the United Nations. **NGO Relations** Cooperates with (1): *International Organization for Standardization (ISO, #14473)*. Links with a large number of national and international associations of the exhibition industry, including: *European Exhibition Industry Alliance (EEIA, #07012)*; *European Major Exhibition Centres Association (EMECA, #07726)*; *International Association of Convention Centres (AIPC, #11818)*; *International Chamber of Commerce (ICC, #12534)*; *International Congress and Convention Association (ICCA, #12892)*; *International Exhibition Logistics Association (IELA, #13322)*; *International Federation of Exhibition and Event Services (IFES, #13420)*; *Joint Meetings Industry Council (JMIC, #16140)*.
[2022.10.11/XB3354/ty/**B**]

- UFIPTE – Union franco-ibérique pour la coordination de la production et du transport d'électricité (inactive)
- UFI / see UFI – The Global Association of the Exhibition Industry (#20276)
- UFI – Union fédéraliste inter-universitaire (inactive)
- **UFI** United Families International (#20508)
- UFK – Umweltschützer für die Kernenergie (internationally oriented national body)
- **UFLC** Union internationale des femmes libérales chrétiennes (#11999)
- UFM International / see Crossworld
- UFMUCM / see World Fellowship of Methodist and Uniting Church Men (#21503)
- **UfM** Union for the Mediterranean (#20457)
- UFROAT – Union des femmes rurales ouest-africaines et du Tchad (internationally oriented national body)
- UFSI / see Institute of World Affairs
- **UFTAA** United Federation of Travel Agents' Associations (#20509)
- UFWH – Universities Fighting World Hunger (unconfirmed)
- **UGAA** Union générale arabe d'assurance (#10104)
- UGAL / see Independent Retail Europe (#11154)
- **UGB** Universal Great Brotherhood (#20677)
- UGEAO – Union générale des étudiants de l'Afrique de l'Ouest (inactive)
- UGEL / see Independent Retail Europe (#11154)
- **UGGI** Union géodésique et géophysique internationale (#15776)
- **UGI** Union géographique internationale (#13713)
- UGPA – Union générale des paysans et des coopératives arabes (no recent information)
- UGPFE / see AFILIATYS (#00151)
- UGSA – UroGynaecological Society of Australasia (internationally oriented national body)
- UGSS / see Union of Local and Non Local General Service Staff FAO/WFP (#20455)
- UGTAN – Union générale des travailleurs d'Afrique noire (inactive)
- UHAI EASHRI – East African Sexual Health and Rights Initiative (unconfirmed)
- UHAI – UHAI EASHRI – East African Sexual Health and Rights Initiative (unconfirmed)

♦ UHC2030 20277

Geneva Office c/o WHO, Dept of Health Systems Governance and Financing, Av Appia 20, 1211 Geneva 27, Switzerland. T. +41227915574. E-mail: info@internationalhealthpartnership.net.
Washington DC Office c/o World Bank, 1818 H Str NW, Washington DC 20433, USA. T. +12024580447.
URL: http://www.uhc2030.org/

History 2007, as a group of partners, including developing country governments, international development partners, Civil Society Organizations (CSOs) and other non-state actors, who all signed the Global Compact. Original title: *International Health Partnership (IHP+)*. Transformed under current title, 2016. Full title: *International Health Partnership for UHC 2030 (UHC2030)*. **Aims** Create a movement for accelerating equitable and sustainable progress towards universal *health* coverage (UHC). **Structure** Steering Committee; Reference Group; Core Team; Technical Working Groups. Civil Society Engagement Mechanism (CSEM) acts as civil society arm. **Languages** English, French. **Staff** 2.00 FTE, paid. **Activities** Financial and/or material support; networking/liaising; politics/policy/regulatory; advocacy/lobbying/activism; knowledge management/information dissemination. **Events** *Country Health Teams Meeting* Siem Reap (Cambodia) 2014, *Country Health Teams Meeting* Nairobi (Kenya) 2012, *Country Health Teams Meeting* Brussels (Belgium) 2010, *Country Health Teams Meeting* Bamako (Mali) 2009, *Country Health Teams Meeting* Lusaka (Zambia) 2008. **Publications** *UHC2030 Newsletter* (6 a year).
Members Signatories include 80 Partner countries:
Afghanistan, Australia, Bahrain, Belgium, Benin, Burkina Faso, Burundi, Cambodia, Cameroon, Canada, Cape Verde, Chad, Chile, Comoros, Congo Brazzaville, Congo DR, Côte d'Ivoire, Denmark, Djibouti, Egypt, El Salvador, Ethiopia, Finland, France, Gambia, Georgia, Germany, Ghana, Guinea, Guinea-Bissau, Haiti, Indonesia, Iran Islamic Rep, Iraq, Italy, Japan, Jordan, Kenya, Kuwait, Kyrgyzstan, Lebanon, Liberia, Libya, Luxembourg, Madagascar, Mali, Mauritania, Morocco, Mozambique, Myanmar, Nepal, Netherlands, Niger, Nigeria, Norway, Oman, Pakistan, Palestine, Portugal, Qatar, Rwanda, Senegal, Sierra Leone, Somalia, South Africa, Spain, Sudan, Sweden, Switzerland, Syrian AR, Thailand, Togo, Tunisia, Uganda, UK, United Arab Emirates, USA, Vietnam, Yemen, Zambia.
Regional entity:
European Union (EU, #08967).
Development partners includes 16 countries:
Australia, Belgium, Canada, Denmark, Finland, France, Germany, Italy, Japan, Luxembourg, Netherlands, Norway, Poland, Spain, Sweden, UK.
Multilateral organizations and global health initiatives (12):
African Development Bank (ADB, #00283); *Gavi – The Vaccine Alliance (Gavi, #10077)*; *Global Financing Facility (GFF, #10360)*; *Global Fund to Fight AIDS, Tuberculosis and Malaria (Global Fund, #10383)*; *ILO (#11123)*; *International Bank for Reconstruction and Development (IBRD, #12317)* (World Bank); *Joint United Nations Programme on HIV/AIDS (UNAIDS, #16149)*; *OECD (#17693)*; *UNDP (#20292)*; *UNICEF (#20332)*; *United Nations Population Fund (UNFPA, #20612)*; *WHO (#20950)*.
Philanthropic Organizations (3):
Bill and Melinda Gates Foundation (BMGF); *The Rockefeller Foundation (#18966)*; *United Nations University (UNU, #20642)*.
Civil society organizations having signed the UHC2030 Global Compact include 11 organizations listed in this Yearbook:
African Health Economics and Policy Association (AfHEA, #00335); *Amref Health Africa (#00806)*; *CORE Group*; *Global Alliance for Surgical, Obstetric, Trauma and Anaesthesia Care (G4 Alliance, #10229)*; *International Federation of Medical Students' Associations (IFMSA, #13478)*; *International Federation of Red Cross and Red Crescent Societies (#13526)*; *International Pharmaceutical Students' Federation (IPSF, #14568)*; *Management Sciences for Health (MSH)*; *Medicus Mundi International – Network Health for All (MMI, #16636)*; *Save the Children International (#19058)*; *Worldwide Hospice Palliative Care Alliance (WHPCA, #21924)*.
[2019/XJ6640/**E**]

- UHEA – Union hydroélectrique africaine (inactive)
- Ühenduse Sordiamet (#04404)
- **UHMS** Undersea and Hyperbaric Medical Society (#20286)
- UHR – United for Human Rights (internationally oriented national body)
- **UIAA** Union internationale des associations d'alpinisme (#20420)
- **UIAA** Union internationale des assureurs aéronautiques (#15750)
- UIAA / see World Federation of Advertisers (#21407)
- UIACM – Union internationale des automobile-clubs médicaux (no recent information)
- **UIADM** Union internationale des associations de délégués médicaux (#15791)
- UIAE / see Union internationale des alsaciens (#20418)
- UIAFR – Union internationale des agriculteurs français pour le renouveau (internationally oriented national body)
- **UIAGM** Union internationale des associations de guides de montagne (#15756)
- **UIA** Internationaler Architekten Union (#20419)
- **UIA** International Union of Architects (#20419)
- UIA / see International Union of Food, Agricultural, Hotel, Restaurant, Catering, Tobacco and Allied Workers Associations (#15772)
- **UIA** Keren Hayesod – United Israel Appeal (#16183)
- UIAMS – Union internationale d'action morale et sociale (inactive)
- UIAPME – Union internationale de l'artisanat et des petites et moyennes entreprises (inactive)
- **UIAPPA** Union internationale des associations pour la prévention de la pollution de l'air et la protection de l'environnement (#15753)
- UIASM – Union internationale d'aide à la santé mentale (no recent information)
- **UIA** Uniao Internacional dos Arquitetos (#20419)
- **UIA** Unión Internacional de los Arquitectos (#20419)
- **UIA** Union of International Associations (#20414)
- **UIA** Union internationale des alsaciens (#20418)
- **UIA** Union internationale des architectes (#20419)
- **UIA** Union Internationale des Avocats (#20422)
- UIA – Universidad Iberoamericana, México (internationally oriented national body)
- **UIBA** União-Ibero-americana dos Colégios e Ordens dos Advogados (#20411)
- **UIBA** Unión Iberoamericana de Colegios y Agrupaciones de Abogados (#20411)
- **UIBC** International Union of Bakers and Confectioners (#15757)
- UIBEB – Union internationale des bègues éliminant leur bégaiement (no recent information)
- UIBE – University of International Business and Economics (internationally oriented national body)

- ♦ **UIBG** Union internationale des biologistes du gibier (#15775)
- ♦ UIB / see International Union of Bakers and Confectioners (#15757)
- ♦ **UICB** Union internationale des centres du bâtiment (#15761)
- ♦ UICC / see Union for International Cancer Control (#20415)
- ♦ **UICC** Union for International Cancer Control (#20415)
- ♦ **UICC** Union internationale contre le cancer (#20415)
- ♦ UIC / see Fédération Internationale de Tir aux Armes Sportives de Chasse (#09665)
- ♦ **UICG** Unión Internacional de Ciencias Geológicas (#15777)
- ♦ **UICH** Union Internationale des Concierges d'Hôtels "Les Clefs d'Or" (#20424)
- ♦ UICM – Union internationale catholique des classes moyennes (inactive)
- ♦ **UICN** Unión Internacional para la Conservación de la Naturaleza y de los Recursos Naturales (#15766)
- ♦ **UICPA** Union internationale de chimie pure et appliquée (#15809)
- ♦ UICP – Union internationale de la couverture et plomberie (inactive)
- ♦ **UICR** Union internationale des chauffeurs routiers (#15802)
- ♦ UICTER / see International Union Against Tuberculosis and Lung Disease (#15752)
- ♦ UICT / see International Union Against Tuberculosis and Lung Disease (#15752)
- ♦ UICTMR / see International Union Against Tuberculosis and Lung Disease (#15752)
- ♦ **UIC** Union internationale des chemins de fer (#15813)
- ♦ UIDA – Union internationale des arts (inactive)
- ♦ UIDA – Union internationale des organisations de détaillants de la branche alimentaire (inactive)
- ♦ UIDD – Université internationale du développement durable (internationally oriented national body)
- ♦ UIDH – Union interafricaine des droits de l'homme (inactive)
- ♦ **UIDIP** Union Internationale des Ingénieurs Professionnels (#15803)
- ♦ UIDP – Union internationale de droit pénal (inactive)
- ♦ UIEA – Union internationale des étudiants en architecture (inactive)
- ♦ UIEA – Universala Islama Esperanto-Asocio (internationally oriented national body)
- ♦ UIEC / see International Union of Cinemas (#15763)
- ♦ **UIECP** Unión Internacional para el Estudio Científico de la Población (#15814)
- ♦ UIECS / see European Public Service Union (#08303)
- ♦ **UIEIS** Union internationale pour l'étude des insectes sociaux (#15819)
- ♦ UIEOA – Union internationale des études orientales et asiatiques (inactive)
- ♦ UIEO / see Union internationale des associations et organismes scientifiques et techniques (#20421)
- ♦ UIES / see International Union for Health Promotion and Education (#15778)
- ♦ **UIESP** Union internationale pour l'étude scientifique de la population (#15814)
- ♦ UIES – Union internationale des employés de services (internationally oriented national body)
- ♦ UIES – Union internationale d'études sociales (inactive)
- ♦ UIE / see UNESCO Institute for Lifelong Learning (#20305)
- ♦ **UIE** Unión Internacional de Editores (#14675)
- ♦ **UIE** Union internationale pour les applications de l'électricité (#15770)
- ♦ **UIE** Union internationale des éditeurs (#14675)
- ♦ **UIE** Université international de l'espace (#15575)
- ♦ UIFAB / see World Billiards Union (#21230)
- ♦ **UIFA** Union internationale des femmes architectes (#15828)
- ♦ UIFL – Union internationale des fédérations de détaillants en produits laitiers (inactive)
- ♦ UIFTCA – Union internationale pour la formation technique et culturelle des adultes (inactive)
- ♦ UIGDC – Unione Internazionale dei Giovani Democratici Cristiani (inactive)
- ♦ **UIGSE-FSE** Union Internationale des Guides et Scouts d'Europe – Fédération du Scoutisme Européen (#20426)
- ♦ **UIG** Union Internationale du Gaz (#13700)
- ♦ **UIHJ** Union internationale des huissiers de justice et officiers judiciaires (#15785)
- ♦ UIHP – Union internationale de l'hospitalisation privée (no recent information)
- ♦ UIH – Union internationale des hôteliers (inactive)
- ♦ UIIDE – Union internationale des infirmières diplômées d'Etat (inactive)
- ♦ UIIG / see International Gas Union (#13700)
- ♦ **UIIN** University Industry Innovation Network (#20699)
- ♦ **UIJA** Union internationale des journalistes africains (#20428)
- ♦ UIJDC – Unión Internacional de Jóvenes Demócrata Cristianos (inactive)
- ♦ UIJDC – Union internationale des jeunes démocrates-chrétiens (inactive)
- ♦ UIJPLF / see Union internationale de la presse francophone (#20435)
- ♦ UILE – Union internationale pour la liberté d'enseignement (inactive)
- ♦ UILFC / see World Union of Catholic Women's Organisations (#21876)
- ♦ **UILI** Union internationale des laboratoires indépendants (#20429)
- ♦ UILP – Union internationale des associations scoutes-guides pluralistes-laïques (no recent information)
- ♦ **UIL** UNESCO Institute for Lifelong Learning (#20305)
- ♦ **UIMC** Union internationale des services médicaux des chemins de fer (#20437)
- ♦ **UIME** Union internationale de médecine esthétique (#15771)
- ♦ UIMH – Union internationale des maîtres d'hôtel (inactive)
- ♦ **UIMLA** Union of International Mountain Leader Associations (#20442)
- ♦ **UIM** Unión Iberoamericana de Municipalistas (#11034)
- ♦ **UIM** Union internationale des magistrats (#11978)
- ♦ UIM – Union internationale des métis (inactive)
- ♦ UIM – Union internationale monarchiste (no recent information)
- ♦ **UIM** Union internationale Motonautique (#20431)
- ♦ UIMV / see European Glaziers Association (#07394)
- ♦ UIMVT / see International Union against Sexually Transmitted Infections (#15751)
- ♦ UINF – Union internationale de la navigation fluviale (inactive)
- ♦ UINL / see International Union of Notaries (#15795)
- ♦ **UINL** Union internationale du Notariat (#15795)
- ♦ **UIOE** Union internationale des oenologues (#20432)
- ♦ UIOF / see World Family Organization (#21399)
- ♦ UIOG – Union internationale des orphelins de guerre (inactive)
- ♦ UIOPE – Union inter-africaine des organisations professionnelles d'éleveurs (no recent information)
- ♦ UIO – União Internacional de Orações (religious order)
- ♦ UIO – Unión Internacional de Oraciones (religious order)
- ♦ UIP / see Asociación Universitaria Iberoamericana de Postgrado (#02307)
- ♦ **UIPA** Union interparlementaire arabe (#00995)
- ♦ UIPCG – Union internationale de la pâtisserie, confiserie et glacerie (inactive)
- ♦ UIPC / see International Christian Organisation of the Media (#12563)
- ♦ UIPD / see International Federation of Eurhythmics Teachers (#13418)
- ♦ **UIPES** Union internationale de promotion de la santé et d'éducation pour la santé (#15778)
- ♦ UIPE – Union internationale de protection de l'enfance (inactive)
- ♦ UIPFB / see International Union of Property Owners (#15804)
- ♦ UIPGH / see Union Internationale des Concierges d'Hôtels "Les Clefs d'Or" (#20424)
- ♦ UIP / see International Union of Wagon Keepers (#15827)
- ♦ UIPI – Unión Internacional de Protección a la Infancia (inactive)
- ♦ **UIPI** Union internationale de la propriété immobilière (#15804)
- ♦ UIPMB / see World Penthathlon (#21720)
- ♦ UIPM – Union internationale de la presse médicale (no recent information)
- ♦ UIPM / see World Penthathlon (#21720)
- ♦ **UIPM** World Penthathlon (#21720)
- ♦ UIPN / see International Union for Conservation of Nature and Natural Resources (#15766)
- ♦ **UIPPA** Union internationale de physique pure et appliquée (#15810)
- ♦ **UIPRE** Union internationale de la presse électronique (#20433)
- ♦ UIPS – Union internationale de logique, méthodologie et philosophie des sciences (inactive)
- ♦ UIP / see UNESCO Institute for Lifelong Learning (#20305)
- ♦ UIP – Unione Internazionale di Preghiere (religious order)
- ♦ **UIP** Union Internationale de Phlébologie (#15797)
- ♦ UIP – Union Internationale de Prières de Banneux Notre-Dame (religious order)
- ♦ UIP – Union internationale des professeurs et maîtres de conférences des universités techniques et scientifiques et des instituts post-universitaires de perfectionnement technique et scientifique (inactive)
- ♦ UIP – Union internationale des publicitaires (inactive)
- ♦ **UIP** Union interparlementaire (#15961)
- ♦ UIRD – Union internationale de la résistance et de la déportation (no recent information)
- ♦ UIR / see International Union of Radioecology (#15812)
- ♦ **UIRR** Internationale Vereinigung der Gesellschaften für den Kombinierten Verkehr Schiene-Strasse (#15765)
- ♦ **UIRR** International Union for Combined Road – Rail Transport (#15765)
- ♦ **UIRR** Union internationale des sociétés de transport combiné rail – route (#15765)
- ♦ **UIR** Union internationale de radioécologie (#15812)
- ♦ **UISAE** Union Internationale des Sciences Anthropologiques et Ethnologiques (#15755)
- ♦ UISA – Union internationale des sciences agricoles (inactive)
- ♦ **UISB** Union internationale des sciences biologiques (#15760)
- ♦ UISE – Union internationale de secours aux enfants (inactive)
- ♦ UISF / see Federación Iberoamericana de Sociedades de Fisica (#09321)
- ♦ **UISF** Union internationale des ingénieurs et des scientifiques utilisant la langue française (#20427)
- ♦ **UISG** Union internationale des sciences géologiques (#15777)
- ♦ **UISG** Union internationale des supérieures générales (#15820)
- ♦ UISIF – Union internationale des sociétés d'ingénieurs forestiers (no recent information)
- ♦ **UISL** Union internationale des sociétés de lipoplastie (#20438)
- ♦ **UISM** Union internationale des sociétés de microbiologie (#15794)
- ♦ UISN / see International Waterski and Wakeboard Federation (#15872)
- ♦ **UISN** Union internationale des sciences de la nutrition (#15796)
- ♦ **UISPP** Union internationale des sciences préhistoriques et protohistoriques (#15801)
- ♦ UISPTT – Union internationale sportive des PTT (inactive)
- ♦ UISP – Union internationale des sanatoriums privés (inactive)
- ♦ UISP – Union internationale des sociétés de la paix (inactive)
- ♦ UISP – Union internationale des syndicats de police (inactive)
- ♦ **UISS** Union internationale de la science du sol (#15817)
- ♦ **UISTAACT** Union internationale syndicale des travailleurs de l'agriculture, alimentation, commerce, textiles et industries similaires (#20190)
- ♦ UISTABP – Unión Internacional de Sindicatos de Trabajadores de la Agricultura, de los Bosques y de las Plantaciones (inactive)
- ♦ UISTAFP – Union internationale des syndicats des travailleurs de l'agriculture, des forêts et des plantations (inactive)
- ♦ **UISTAV** Union internationale pour la science, la technique et les applications du vide (#15826)
- ♦ UISTC – Union internationale des syndicats des travailleurs du commerce (inactive)
- ♦ UIS TEMCPIA / see Trade Union International of Chemical, Energy, Metal, Oil and Allied Industries (#20188)
- ♦ UIS TEMQPIA / see Trade Union International of Chemical, Energy, Metal, Oil and Allied Industries (#20188)
- ♦ UISTE – Union internationale des syndicats des travailleurs de l'énergie (inactive)
- ♦ UIS-TIMMM – Unión Internacional del Sindicatos de Trabajadores de la Mineria, la Metalurgia y el Metal (unconfirmed)
- ♦ **UIS** UNESCO Institute for Statistics (#20306)
- ♦ UIS – Union internationale de secours (inactive)
- ♦ **UIS** Union internationale de spéléologie (#15818)
- ♦ UITA / see International Union of Food, Agricultural, Hotel, Restaurant, Catering, Tobacco and Allied Workers Associations (#15772)
- ♦ **UITA** Unión Internacional de Trabajadores de la Alimentación, Agricolas, Hoteles, Restaurantes, Tabaco y Afines (#15772)
- ♦ **UITA** Union internationale des travailleurs de l'alimentation, de l'agriculture, de l'hôtellerie-restauration, du tabac et des branches connexes (#15772)
- ♦ **UITBB** Trades Union International of Workers in the Building, Wood, Building Materials and Allied Industries (#20185)
- ♦ **UITBB** Union internationale des syndicats des travailleurs du bâtiment, du bois et des matériaux de construction (#20185)
- ♦ UITCA – Union internationale de tourisme coopératif et associatif (inactive)
- ♦ UITF / see Union internationale des ingénieurs et des scientifiques utilisant la langue française (#20427)
- ♦ Uitgeversvereniging voor Europese Juridische en Economische Literatuur (inactive)
- ♦ **UITIC** Union internationale des techniciens de l'industrie de la chaussure (#20439)
- ♦ UIT / see International Shooting Sport Federation (#14852)
- ♦ **UITP** Union internationale des transports publics (#12118)
- ♦ **UIT** Unión Internacional de Telecomunicaciones (#15673)
- ♦ **UIT** Union internationale des télécommunications (#15673)
- ♦ UITU – Union internationale des théâtres universitaires (inactive)
- ♦ UI – Utrikespolitiska Institutet, Stockholm (internationally oriented national body)
- ♦ **UIV** Union internationale des vélodromes (#20440)
- ♦ UIV – Union internationale des villes et pouvoirs locaux (inactive)
- ♦ UI / see World Nuclear Association (#21674)
- ♦ UIYA / see Union internationale Motonautique (#20431)
- ♦ **UJAO** Union des journalistes de l'Afrique de l'Ouest (#20885)
- ♦ UJA / see Union internationale des journalistes africains (#20428)
- ♦ **UJCL** Union of Jewish Congregations in Latin America and the Caribbean (#20446)
- ♦ UJDH – Unión de Juventudes Democraticas Hispanoamericanas (no recent information)
- ♦ UJE – Union de la jeunesse européenne (inactive)
- ♦ UJOA – Union de la jeunesse Ouest-Africaine (inactive)
- ♦ UJSA – Union des journalistes sportifs africains (inactive)
- ♦ UJ – Ursulines de Jésus (religious order)
- ♦ UKCISA – UK Council for International Student Affairs (internationally oriented national body)
- ♦ UK Consortium on AIDS and International Development (internationally oriented national body)
- ♦ UKCOSA / see UK Council for International Student Affairs
- ♦ UK Council for International Student Affairs (internationally oriented national body)
- ♦ UKFIET – United Kingdom Forum for International Education and Training (internationally oriented national body)
- ♦ UKFSP / see Just World Partners
- ♦ UK-Latin America Political Philosophy Research Network (unconfirmed)
- ♦ UKNA – Urban Knowledge Network Asia (unconfirmed)
- ♦ UKOWLA – United Kingdom One World Linking Association (internationally oriented national body)
- ♦ UK Race and Europe Network (internationally oriented national body)
- ♦ Ukrainian Center for Peace, Conversion and Conflict Resolution Studies / see Center for Peace, Conversion and Foreign Policy of Ukraine
- ♦ Ukrainian Centre for International Security Studies / see Centre for International Security and Strategic Studies, Kiev
- ♦ Ukrainian Centre for International Security Studies (internationally oriented national body)

- ♦ Ukrainian World Congress / see World Congress of Free Ukrainians (#21305)
- ♦ UKREN – UK Race and Europe Network (internationally oriented national body)
- ♦ UKUSA agreement – United Kingdom United States Agreement (1947 treaty)
- ♦ ULACIT – Universidad Latinoamericana de Ciencia y Tecnologia (internationally oriented national body)
- ♦ **ULAC** Unión Latinoamericana de Ciegos (#16256)
- ♦ **ULADE** Unión Latinoamericana del Embalaje (#16358)
- ♦ **ULAERGO** Unión Latinoamericana de Ergonomía (#20450)
- ♦ ULAJE – Unión Latinoamericana de Juventudes Ecuménicas (no recent information)
- ♦ U-landsorganisationen Ibis (internationally oriented national body)
- ♦ **ULAPSI** Unión Latinoamericana de Entidades de Psicologia (#20449)
- ♦ ULAST – Unión Latinoamericana de Sociedades de Tisiologia (inactive)
- ♦ ULAU / see Association of Universities of Latin America and the Caribbean (#02970)
- ♦ ULA – Universidad de los Andes (internationally oriented national body)
- ♦ ULAViM – Union Latinoamericana de Visitadores Médicos (no recent information)
- ♦ **ULBA** Universal Love and Brotherhood Association (#20678)
- ♦ **ULCM** União Libanese Cultural Mundial (#21622)
- ♦ ULCRA – Unión Latinoamericana y del Caribe de Radiodifusión (inactive)

♦ ULD CARE 20278

Contact 4 Place Ville Marie, Suite 600, Montréal QC H3B 2E7, Canada. E-mail: admin@uldcare.com.
URL: https://www.uldcare.com/

History Founded 1971, as ULD Control and Procedures Committee (UCPC) by *International Air Transport Association (IATA, #11614)*. Became *Interline ULD User Group (IULDUG)*, an IATA Interest Group. Became an independent legal entity, 2011. Current title adopted 2012. A non-profit corporation registered in accordance with Canadian law: 1166467002. **Aims** Use the collective resources, skills and grass roots experience of members to provide direction and deliver appropriate change in ULD operations throughout the global *air* cargo operating environment. **Structure** Board. **Activities** Knowledge management/information dissemination. **Events** *Annual Conference* Montréal, QC (Canada) 2019. **Members** Airlines; non-airlines. Membership countries not specified. [2019/XM8763/**E**]

- ♦ Ulemaailmne Eesti Kesknoukogu (#05550)
- ♦ **ULEPICC** Unión Latina de Economia Politica de la Información, la Comunicación ya la Cultura (#20447)
- ♦ **ULE** Unión Latinoamericana de Espeleologia (#20451)
- ♦ ULFIS – Convention Relating to a Uniform Law on the Formation of Contracts for the International Sale of Goods (1964 treaty)
- ♦ ULIM – Universitatea Libera Internationala din Moldova (internationally oriented national body)
- ♦ ULIS – Convention Relating to a Uniform Law on the International Sale of Goods (1964 treaty)
- ♦ ULI – Université libre internationale de Bruxelles (internationally oriented national body)
- ♦ ULI – Urban Land Institute (internationally oriented national body)

♦ Ulixes European Union Training and Research EEIG (ULIXES) 20279

Sec Via G Giglioli Valle 11, 42124 Reggio Emilia RE, Italy. T. +39522329243 – +39522329273. Fax +39522284708. E-mail: secretariat@ulixesnet.eu – headoffice@ulixesnet.eu.
URL: http://www.ulixesnet.eu/

History Founded 1994. An organization of the type *European Economic Interest Grouping (EEIG, #06960)*. **Aims** Pool information, expertise, knowledge and resources in order to increase performance of members; support local, national, European and international development in the fields of human resources and economic growth; initiate and promote Ulixes EEIG image and ensure representation on all levels. **Structure** Executive Committee. **Activities** Develops programmes designed to facilitate mutual exchanges at all levels. **Members** Full in 9 countries:
Austria, Belgium, Denmark, France, Italy, Lithuania, Portugal, Spain, UK.
NGO Relations Affiliate member of: *SPACE Network (#19899)*. [2018.01.26/XJ6078/**F**]

- ♦ **ULIXES** Ulixes European Union Training and Research EEIG (#20279)
- ♦ Ulkopoliittinen Instituutti (internationally oriented national body)
- ♦ **ULLA** European University Consortium for Pharmaceutical Research (#09029)
- ♦ ULLO – Union of Liberal Labour Organizations (no recent information)
- ♦ ULM / see FIM Latin America (#09762)
- ♦ ULOR – Unión Latinoamericana de Organismos de Rescate (inactive)
- ♦ ULPGL – Université libre des pays des Grands Lacs (internationally oriented national body)
- ♦ ULSF – Association of University Leaders for a Sustainable Future (internationally oriented national body)
- ♦ **ULTM** Unión Latinoamericana de Tenis de Mesa (#20453)
- ♦ UltraTeslan International (internationally oriented national body)
- ♦ **ULT** United Lodge of Theosophists (#20512)
- ♦ UL – Underwriters Laboratories (internationally oriented national body)
- ♦ UL – Union latine (inactive)
- ♦ UL – Universala Ligo (inactive)
- ♦ Uluslararasi Mavi Hilal (internationally oriented national body)
- ♦ Uluslar arasi Mavi Hilal Insani Yardim ve Kalkinma Vakfi / see International Blue Crescent
- ♦ Uluslararasi Sert Meyveler Komitesi / see International Nut and Dried Fruit Council Foundation (#14387)
- ♦ Uluslararasy Türk Kültürü Tetkilaty (#14482)
- ♦ **ULY** União Latino Americana de Yoga (#20329)
- ♦ **UMAC** ICOM International Committee for University Museums and Collections (#11058)
- ♦ **UMAC** Union monétaire de l'Afrique centrale (#20463)
- ♦ UMAEL / see Union mondiale des anciens élèves Lasalliens (#20462)
- ♦ **UMAEL** Union mondiale des anciens élèves Lasalliens (#20462)
- ♦ **UMALCA** Unión Matematica de América Latina y el Caribe (#20456)
- ♦ UMAPF – Union mondiale des associations d'anciens parlementaires francophones (inactive)
- ♦ **UMAP** University Mobility in Asia and the Pacific (#20700)
- ♦ **UMAR** Union méditerranéenne des architectes (#20459)
- ♦ **UMA** Union du Maghreb arabe (#01004)
- ♦ **UMA** Union mathématique africaine (#00370)
- ♦ **UMA** Union des médecins arabes (#01007)
- ♦ **UMA** Union mondiale des aveugles (#21234)
- ♦ UMA – Unión de Mujeres Americanas (inactive)
- ♦ UMA – Universal Medical Assistance International Centre (inactive)
- ♦ UMAV – Union maghrébine des associations de volontariat (no recent information)
- ♦ **UMB** Union médicale balkanique (#03078)
- ♦ **UMB** Union mondiale de billard (#21230)
- ♦ Umbutho Wasemazantsi E-Afrika Wezingokusetyenziswa Kolwimi (internationally oriented national body)
- ♦ UMCOR – United Methodist Committee on Relief (internationally oriented national body)
- ♦ **UMC** Unión Mundial de Ciegos (#21234)
- ♦ **UMC** The United Methodist Church (#20514)
- ♦ UMDC / see Centrist Democrat International (#03792)
- ♦ UMDD / see International University on Sustainable Development
- ♦ **UMEA** Universala Medicina Esperanto-Asocio (#20672)
- ♦ UMEC / see UMEC-WUCT (#20280)

♦ UMEC-WUCT 20280

SG Clivo Monte del Gallo 48, 00165 Rome RM, Italy. T. +396634651 – +396(393286298436. E-mail: umec.wuct@gmail.com – umec@org.va.
Pres address not obtained. T. +32475582419.
URL: http://wuct-umec.blogspot.com

History Founded 1910, Bochum (Germany), as *World Union of Catholic Educators – Weltverband Katholischer Pädagogen*, the activities of which ceased with World War II. Re-established on a world-wide basis at 1st World Congress of Catholic Teachers, 1951, Rome (Italy). Full name: *World Union of Catholic Teachers (WUCT) – Union mondiale des enseignants catholiques (UMEC) – Unión Mundial de Educadores Católicos – Weltunion Katholischer Lehrer – Unione Mondiale Insegnanti Cattolici – Wereldverbond van Katholieke Onderwijsgevenden.* **Aims** Study, assert and promote Catholic *doctrine* in connection with education and the school; compile and exchange news regarding economic and social status of teachers in various countries and study possibilities for improving them; further and support establishment of Catholic teachers' associations in countries where they do not yet exist; exchange information concerning initiatives and experience in the field of religious, moral and professional training of teachers and of apostolic action in the teaching sphere; defend and respect the rights, liberties and interests of the teacher, as far as he/she is a Catholic, notably within the Church's framework. **Structure** General Assembly (every 4 years); Council; Executive Committee; Chaplain. Meetings closed. **Languages** English, French, German, Italian, Spanish. **Staff** 4.00 FTE, paid. **Finance** Sources: members' dues. Other sources: symbolic or solidarity contributions from non-member countries. **Activities** Events/meetings; networking/liaising. **Events** *Quadrennial Congress* Rome (Italy) 2012, *Quadrennial International Congress* Rome (Italy) 2008, *Quadrennial Congress* Bangkok (Thailand) 2003, *European Seminar* Malta 2000, *Quadrennial congress* Hoeven (Netherlands) 1999. **Publications** *UMEC-WUCT NEWS.*

Members National: national or regional organizations of Catholic teachers of all types of duly recognized educational organizations. Correspondent: all Catholic teachers who, between one General Assembly and the next, intend to establish an organization of Catholic teachers where one does not exist; Honorary: persons who have distinguished themselves in UMEC-WUCT. National associations in 35 countries and territories:
Antigua-Barbuda, Argentina, Barbados, Belgium, Burundi, Cameroon, Canada, Chile, Colombia, Congo Brazzaville, Congo DR, Curaçao, Czechia, Denmark, France, Germany, Grenada, Haiti, Hungary, Italy, Jamaica, Malta, Mauritius, Mexico, Netherlands, Philippines, Portugal, Romania, Slovakia, Spain, St Lucia, Thailand, Trinidad-Tobago, UK, USA.
Consultative Status Consultative status granted from: *UNESCO (#20322)* (Consultative Status). **NGO Relations** Member of: *Forum of Catholic Inspired NGOs (#09905)*. [2020.03.03/XC3593/**C**]

- ♦ **UMEJ** Union Mondiale des Etudiants Juifs (#21878)
- ♦ **UMEJ** Unión Mundial de Estudiantes Judios (#21878)
- ♦ **UMEMPS** Union of Middle Eastern and Mediterranean Paediatric Societies (#20461)
- ♦ UMEM – Union mondiale des écrivains-médecins (inactive)
- ♦ UMFIA – Union médicale latine (inactive)
- ♦ **UMFR** Union mondiale des femmes rurales (#02338)
- ♦ **UMG** Union Méditerranéenne des Géomètres (#20460)
- ♦ UMHP – Union mondiale des sociétés d'histoire pharmaceutique (inactive)
- ♦ UMIOR – University Mobility in the Indian Ocean Region (internationally oriented national body)
- ♦ **UMI** Union mathématique internationale (#14121)
- ♦ **UMI** Union Mundial pro Interlingua (#20464)
- ♦ UMLP – Union mondiale des libres penseurs (inactive)
- ♦ UMML / see Surgery Society of the Latin Mediterranean (#20042)
- ♦ **UMMM** Unión Mundial de Mercados Mayoristas (#21889)
- ♦ UMMM / see World Union of Wholesale Markets (#21889)
- ♦ UMM – Union médicale méditerranéenne (inactive)
- ♦ **UMM** Unión Mundial Macabi (#16537)
- ♦ **UMM** Universidad Maritima Mundial (#21633)
- ♦ **UMM** Université maritime mondiale (#21633)
- ♦ UMNAGRI – Union Magrébine et Nord Africaine des Agriculteurs (unconfirmed)
- ♦ **UMNS** Union mondiale des nationaux socialistes (#21880)
- ♦ UMN – United Mission to Nepal (internationally oriented national body)
- ♦ UMOA – Union monétaire Ouest africaine (inactive)
- ♦ **UMOFC** Union mondiale des organisations féminines catholiques (#21876)
- ♦ **UMOFC** Unión Mundial de las Organizaciones Femeninas Católicas (#21876)
- ♦ Umoja na Wanawake Wenye Shida (internationally oriented national body)
- ♦ UMOSEA – Union mondiale pour la sauvegarde de l'enfance et de l'adolescence (inactive)
- ♦ **UMPL** Union mondiale des professions libérales (#21882)
- ♦ UMR – United Mission for Relief & Development (internationally oriented national body)
- ♦ **UMSB** Union mondiale des clubs de Saint Bernard (#21887)
- ♦ UMSN / see International Waterski and Wakeboard Federation (#15872)
- ♦ **UMSR** Universal Movement for Scientific Responsibility (#20679)
- ♦ UMTAPO Centre – Peace Education Centre (internationally oriented national body)
- ♦ UMU Foundation – European Muslim Union (unconfirmed)
- ♦ Umut Foundation (internationally oriented national body)
- ♦ UMVF – Union mondiale des voix françaises (inactive)
- ♦ UMVIM – United Methodist Volunteers in Mission (internationally oriented national body)
- ♦ **UMV** Union méditerranéenne de voile (#16673)
- ♦ UMV – Ustav Mezinarodnich Vztahu, Praha (internationally oriented national body)
- ♦ Umweltberatung Europa – Europäischer Verband der UmweltberaterInnen (inactive)
- ♦ Umweltschützer für die Kernenergie (internationally oriented national body)
- ♦ UMYS – Union of Maghreb Youth and Students (inactive)
- ♦ UN+ / see UN Plus (#20713)
- ♦ UN2020 Initiative – Coalition for the UN We Need (unconfirmed)
- ♦ UNA-AUSTRIA – Foreign Policy and United Nations Association of Austria (internationally oriented national body)
- ♦ UNAccc – Unity of Nations Action for Climate Change Council (internationally oriented national body)
- ♦ **UN-ACT** United Nations Action for Cooperation against Trafficking in Persons (#20517)
- ♦ **UNAEC-Europe** Union européenne des anciens et anciennes élèves de l'enseignement catholique (#08992)
- ♦ **UNAFEI** United Nations Asia and Far East Institute for the Prevention of Crime and the Treatment of Offenders (#20521)
- ♦ **UNAFPA** Union des associations de fabricants de pâtes alimentaires de l'UE (#20468)
- ♦ **UNAFRI** United Nations African Institute for the Prevention of Crime and the Treatment of Offenders (#20519)
- ♦ **Una** Global Learning Initiative on Children and Ethnic Diversity (#10455)
- ♦ **UNAIDS** Joint United Nations Programme on HIV/AIDS (#16149)
- ♦ UNAIDS Secretariat Staff Association (see: #16149)
- ♦ **UNAI** United Nations Academic Impact (#20516)
- ♦ **UNAL** UNESCO Network of Associated Libraries (#20311)
- ♦ UNAMA – United Nations African Mothers' Association (internationally oriented national body)
- ♦ **UNAMA** United Nations Assistance Mission in Afghanistan (#20522)
- ♦ **UNAMAZ** Association of Amazonian Universities (#02366)
- ♦ UNAMET – United Nations Mission in East Timor (inactive)
- ♦ UNAMID – African Union/United Nations Hybrid Operation in Darfur (inactive)

♦ UNANIMA International 20281

Exec Dir 777 UN Plaza, 6th floor – Suite 6-F, New York NY 10017, USA. T. +19292592105. E-mail: director@unanima-international.org – info@unanima-international.org.
URL: http://www.unanima-international.org/

History 2002. Founded by seven congregations of religious women. **Aims** Advocate on behalf of women and children, homeless and displaced, migrants and refugees, and the environment; educate and influence policy makers at the global level and work for systemic change to achieve a more just world. **Structure** Board of Directors. **Languages** English, French, Portuguese, Spanish. **Staff** 2.50 FTE, paid. **Finance** Voluntary contributions of member congregations. **Activities** Advocacy/lobbying/activism; events/meetings; research and development. **Publications** *UNANIMA International Newsletter* (5 a year) in English, French, Portuguese,

Spanish. *Family Homelessness Through the Lens of the 2030 Agenda* – in 2 vols; *Hidden Faces of Homelessness: International Research on Families* – in 2 vols. *The Intersections of Family Homelessness and Human Trafficking.*
Members Congregations (23):
- *Carmelite Sisters of Charity, Vedruna (CCV)*;
- Congregation of Mary (Marists) (SM);
- *Congregation of Our Lady of Sion (NDS)*;
- *Congregation of Sisters of St Agnes (CSA)*;
- *Daughters of Wisdom (DW)*;
- *Handmaids of the Sacred Heart of Jesus (ACJ)*;
- *Missionary Sisters of the Sacred Heart of Jesus (MSC)* (Stella Maris Province);
- Religious of Jesus and Mary;
- *Religious of the Holy Union of the Sacred Hearts (SUSC)*;
- Religious Sisters of Charity (RSC);
- *Sisters of Bon Secours of Paris (CBS)*;
- Sisters of Notre Dame de Sion (NDS);
- Sisters of Notre Dame (SND);
- *Sisters of Providence (SP)*;
- *Sisters of Saint Brigid (CSB)*;
- *Sisters of St Anne (SSA)*;
- *Sisters of the Assumption of the Blessed Virgin (SASV)*;
- *Sisters of the Divine Savior (SDS)*;
- *Sisters of the Holy Names of Jesus and Mary (SNJM)*;
- *Society of the Holy Child Jesus (SHCJ)*;
- *Soeurs de la Congrégation de Notre-Dame (CND)*;
- Ursuline Charism Group;
- *Ursuline Sisters of Mount St Joseph (OSU)*.

Individuals (23,000) in 91 countries and territories:
Albania, Algeria, Argentina, Australia, Austria, Belgium, Benin, Bolivia, Brazil, Cambodia, Cameroon, Canada, Chad, Chile, China, Colombia, Comoros, Congo DR, Costa Rica, Cuba, Denmark, Dominican Rep, Ecuador, Egypt, El Salvador, England, Equatorial Guinea, Eswatini, Fiji, France, Gabon, Gambia, Germany, Ghana, Guatemala, Haiti, Honduras, Hungary, India, Indonesia, Ireland, Israel, Italy, Japan, Jordan, Kenya, Korea Rep, Lebanon, Lesotho, Libya, Madagascar, Malaysia, Mexico, Morocco, Mozambique, Netherlands, New Zealand, Nicaragua, Nigeria, Northern Ireland, Norway, Pakistan, Panama, Papua New Guinea, Paraguay, Peru, Philippines, Poland, Portugal, Puerto Rico, Romania, Scotland, Senegal, South Africa, Spain, Sri Lanka, Syrian AR, Taiwan, Tanzania UR, Timor-Leste, Togo, Tunisia, Türkiye, Uganda, Ukraine, Uruguay, USA, Venezuela, Vietnam, Wales, Zambia.
Consultative Status Consultative status granted from: *ECOSOC (#05331)* (Special); *United Nations Framework Convention on Climate Change (UNFCCC, 1992)* (Observer Status). **IGO Relations** Associated with Department of Global Communications of the United Nations. **NGO Relations** Member of (2): *Laudato Si' Movement (#16403)*; *Religious in Europe Networking Against Trafficking and Exploitation (RENATE, #18833)*.
[2022.05.03/XM0846/y/**F**]

♦ UNAN – Union Americana de Numismática (unconfirmed)
♦ **UNAOC** United Nations Alliance of Civilizations (#20520)
♦ **UNAPSA** Union of National African Paediatric Societies and Associations (#20465)

♦ UNASMA – Fundación Internacional de Asma y Alergias 20282

UNASMA – International Foundation for Asthma and Allergies

Pres E Finochietto 894, C1272AAB Buenos Aires, Argentina. T. +541143074050. Fax +541142932083. E-mail: email@haama.org.
Hon Pres address not obtained. T. +541143074050. Fax +541143004756.
URL: http://www.unasma.org.ar/

History 1996, New Orleans LA (USA), as *Pan American Union of Asthma and Allergy Foundations – Union Panamericana de Fundaciones de Asma y Alergia (UNASMA)*. Oct 2003, re-founded in Argentina under current title. **Aims** Promote, coordinate and develop *athletic* events for *asthmatic* patients and educational activities for patients and their families; promote the study and exchange of investigations in this field. **Structure** Permanent Council, comprising President, Honorary President, Secretary, Treasurer 2 Vice-Presidents and 6 Members at large. 7 Associate Members; 7 Honorary Committee Members. **Languages** English, Spanish. **Staff** Part-time, voluntary. **Finance** Members' dues. Voluntary collaborations. **Activities** Educational activities; national and regional meetings; *'International Sports Asthmatic Games'*. **Events** *International Olympic Games for Children with Asthma* Salzburg (Austria) 2012, *International Olympic Games for Children with Asthma* Madrid (Spain) 2010, *International Olympic Games for Children with Asthma* Mexico City (Mexico) 2008, *International Olympic Games for Children with Asthma* Los Angeles, CA (USA) 2006, *International Olympic Games for Children with Asthma* Maldonado (Uruguay) 2004. **Publications** *FUNDALER y la Salud*; *Guia en Asma para el Docente*; *Orientacion para el Alérgico y Asmatico*. Booklets.
Members Full; Individual. Full in 12 countries:
Argentina, Brazil, Colombia, Ecuador, Mexico, Panama, Paraguay, Peru, Spain, Uruguay, USA, Venezuela.
Individual in 1 country:
Egypt.
NGO Relations Member of: *Global Allergy and Airways Patient Platform (GAAPP, #10178)*.
[2012.09.28/XD7601/f/**F**]

♦ UNASMA – International Foundation for Asthma and Allergies (#20282)
♦ UNASMA / see UNASMA – Fundación Internacional de Asma y Alergias (#20282)
♦ **UNASUL** União das Nações Sul-Americanas (#20481)
♦ **UNASUR** Unión de Naciones Suramericanas (#20481)
♦ UNATAC – Union d'assistance technique pour l'automobile et la circulation routière (no recent information)
♦ **UNATECH** Union européenne pour la promotion des formations techniques dans les métiers de l'hôtellerie (#20402)
♦ Una Terra Mondo di Tutti (internationally oriented national body)
♦ UNA – Una Terra Mondo di Tutti (internationally oriented national body)
♦ **UNA** Union of OIC News AGencies (#20467)
♦ Unbound (internationally oriented national body)

♦ UNCAC Coalition 20283

Secretariat Widerhofergasse 8/2/4, 1090 Vienna, Austria. E-mail: info@uncaccoalition.org.
URL: http://www.uncaccoalition.org/

History Aug 2006. Founded as a global network in support of *United Nations Convention Against Corruption (UNCAC, 2003)*. **Aims** Promote the ratification, implementation and monitoring of the UN Convention against *Corruption* (UNCAC). **Structure** Coordination Committee of 12 Seats (Americas; East Asia, Central Asia and Pacific; 2 Europe; Middle East and North Africa; South Asia; 2 Sub-Saharan Africa; 2 International Member; Individual Affiliate). Secretariat located in Vienna (Austria).
Members Civil society networks (380). Included in the above, 31 organizations listed in this Yearbook:
- *Africa Centre for Open Governance (AfriCOG)*;
- *African Network for Environment and Economic Justice (ANEEJ)*;
- *Africa Youth for Peace and Development (AYPAD)*;
- *Anti-Slavery International (#00860)*;
- *Arab Organization for International Cooperation (AICO)*;
- *Arab Thought Forum (ATF, #01055)*;
- *ARTICLE 19 (#01121)*;
- *Bread for All*;
- *Catholic Agency for Overseas Development (CAFOD)*;
- *Chamber of Computer Logistics People Worldwide (CCLP Worldwide, #03847)*;
- *Christian Aid*;
- *CIVICUS: World Alliance for Citizen Participation (#03962)*;
- *Commonwealth Human Rights Initiative (CHRI, #04340)*;
- *Fondation humanus – Humanus International*;
- *Free World Foundation (FWF)*;
- *Global Alliance Against Traffic in Women (GAATW, #10184)*;
- *Global Network for Good Governance (GNGG, #10490)*;
- *Global Witness (GW)*;
- *Governance Institutes Network International (GINI)*;
- *Human Rights and Development Trust of Southern Africa (Huridetsa, #10981)*;
- *International Alliance of Women (IAW, #11639)*;
- *International Trade Union Confederation (ITUC, #15708)*;
- *Islamic Relief Worldwide (IRWW, #16048)*;
- *La Strada International (LSI, #20002)*;
- *Public Services International (PSI, #18572)*;
- *Rainbow Warriors International (RWI, no recent information)*;
- *Raoul Wallenberg Institute of Human Rights and Humanitarian Law (RWI)*;
- *Sherpa*;
- *South Asian Network for Social and Agricultural Development (SANSAD)*;
- *Tearfund, UK*;
- *Voluntary Service Overseas (VSO)*.

[2020.05.08/XJ5746/y/**E**]

♦ UNCAC – United Nations Convention Against Corruption (2003 treaty)
♦ UNCA – United Nations Correspondents Association (internationally oriented national body)
♦ UNCCD Secretariat / see Secretariat of the United Nations Convention to Combat Desertification (#19208)
♦ UNCCD – United Nations Convention to Combat Desertification (1994 treaty)
♦ **UN CC:Learn** One UN Climate Change Learning Partnership (#17735)
♦ UNCCP – United Nations Conciliation Commission for Palestine (no recent information)
♦ **UNCC** United Nations Compensation Commission (#20548)
♦ **UNCDF** United Nations Capital Development Fund (#20524)
♦ UNCED – United Nations Conference on Environment and Development (meeting series)
♦ **UN/CEFACT** United Nations Centre for Trade Facilitation and Electronic Business (#20527)
♦ UNCG – United Nations Communications Group (inactive)
♦ UNCITRAL Arbitration Rules (1976 treaty)
♦ UNCITRAL Conciliation Rules (1980 treaty)
♦ UNCITRAL Model Law on Cross-border Insolvency (1997 treaty)
♦ UNCITRAL Model Law on Electronic Commerce (1996 treaty)
♦ UNCITRAL Model Law on Electronic Signatures (2001 treaty)
♦ UNCITRAL Model Law on International Commercial Arbitration (1985 treaty)
♦ UNCITRAL Model Law on International Commercial Conciliation (2002 treaty)
♦ UNCITRAL Model Law on International Credit Transfers (1992 treaty)
♦ UNCITRAL Model Law on Procurement of Goods and Construction (1993 treaty)
♦ UNCITRAL Model Law on Procurement of Goods, Construction and Services (1994 treaty)
♦ **UNCITRAL** United Nations Commission on International Trade Law (#20531)
♦ UNCIVPOL / see United Nations Police (#20611)
♦ Uncle Erik's Children and Relief Support / see Erikshjälpen

♦ UN Climate Resilience Initiative (A2R) 20284

Contact address not obtained. E-mail: info@a2rinitiative.org.
URL: http://www.a2rinitiative.org/

History Launched Dec 2015, Paris (France), by former Secretary General Ban Ki-moon. Full title: *UN Climate Resilience Initiative – Anticipate, Absorb, Reshape (A2R)*. **Aims** Strengthen climate resilience for vulnerable countries and people. **Structure** Leadership Group; Support Team, comprising Executive Office of the UN Secretary-General, *FAO (#09260)* and *UNEP (#20299)*. **Activities** Awareness raising; research/documentation; advocacy/lobbying/activism.
Members Participating organizations include:
Africa Adaptation Initiative (AAI); *BRAC (#03310)*; *Earth Institute at Columbia University*; Executive Office of the UN Secretary General; *FAO (#09260)*; *Global Resilience Partnership (GRP, #10577)*; *Red Cross Red Crescent Climate Centre (Climate Centre)*; *The World Bank Group (#21218)*; *UNEP (#20299)*; *United Nations Framework Convention on Climate Change (UNFCCC, 1992)* (Representatives of the Presidents of); *United Nations Office for Disaster Risk Reduction (UNDRR, #20595)*.
NGO Relations Participates in: *Global Center on Adaptation (GCA)*.
[2018/XM7164/y/**E**]

♦ UN Climate Resilience Initiative – Anticipate, Absorb, Reshape / see UN Climate Resilience Initiative (#20284)
♦ UNCLOS – United Nations Conference on the Law of the Sea (inactive)
♦ UNCLOS – United Nations Convention on the Law of the Sea (1982 treaty)
♦ **UNCMAC** United Nations Command Military Armistice Commission (#20529)
♦ UNCOPUOS / see Committee on the Peaceful Uses of Outer Space (#04277)
♦ **UNCRD** United Nations Centre for Regional Development (#20526)
♦ UNCRTD – Basel Convention on the Control of Transboundary Movements of Hazardous Wastes and Their Disposal (1989 treaty)
♦ UNCSGN / see United Nations Group of Experts on Geographical Names (#20569)
♦ UNCSTD – United Nations Centre for Science and Technology for Development (inactive)
♦ **UNCTAD** Conferencia de las Naciones Unidas sobre Comercio y Desarrollo (#20285)

♦ UNCTAD – United Nations Conference on Trade and Development . . 20285

Conférence des Nations Unies sur le commerce et le développement (CNUCED) – Conferencia de las Naciones Unidas sobre Comercio y Desarrollo (UNCTAD)

SG Palais des Nations, Avenue de la Paix 8-14, 1211 Geneva 10, Switzerland. T. +41229175806. Fax +41229170051. E-mail: sgo@unctad.org – unctadinfo@unctad.org.
New York Office DC2-1120, United Nations, New York NY 10017, USA. E-mail: unctadny2@unctad.org.
URL: http://www.unctad.org/

History 30 Dec 1964, Geneva (Switzerland). Established under General Assembly resolution 1995 (XIX), as a permanent organ of the *United Nations (UN, #20515)*, following 1st Session, 23 Mar-16 Jun 1964; linked to *ECOSOC (#05331)* within *United Nations System (#20635)*. Based at *United Nations Office at Geneva (UNOG, #20597)*. **Aims** Provide a forum for discussion to consider development *strategies* and *policies* in a globalized world *economy*; give special attention to analysing, exchanging and drawing lessons from successful developmental experience. In analytical and deliberative work, focus on: *globalization* and development; international trade in goods and services; commodity issues; *investment*, *enterprise* development and technology; service *infrastructure* for development and trade efficiency. **Structure** *'Conference'*, the highest policymaking body comprising all member states, meets every 4 years at ministerial level to formulate policy guidelines and set work priorities. *'Trade and Development Board'*, the governing (executive) body, meeting annually in regular session and up to 3 times a year in 1-day executive sessions. Divisions (5): Africa, least developed countries and special programmes; Globalization and development strategies; Investment and enterprise; International trade and commodities; Technology and logistics. Since Jul 1993, UNCTAD Secretariat has been servicing *United Nations Commission on Science and Technology for Development (CSTD, #20534)*. Also provides secretariat for: *Intergovernmental Working Group of Experts on International Standards of Accounting and Reporting (ISAR, #11503)*. **Languages** Arabic, Chinese, English, French, Russian, Spanish. **Staff** 456.00 FTE, paid. **Finance** Annual operational budget drawn from the UN regular budget. Annual budget: 68,000,000 USD (2020).
Activities Financial and/or material support; guidance/assistance/consulting; projects/programmes. *'Evolution of UNCTAD'*:
UNCTAD has helped to forge new perceptions, concepts, approaches and action on issues of international economic cooperation. Its early years were marked by high rates of trade and economic growth, particularly in developed countries, worsening terms of trade for developing country commodity exports and an increasing income gap between them and the developed countries. Recognition of these factors led to consensus on needs to increase financial flows to developing countries, strengthen and stabilize commodity markets and support developing countries' participation in world trade. The specific actions agreed at UNCTAD I in 1964, at UNCTAD II in 1968 and at UNCTAD III in 1972 reflected this consensus.
Negotiations under UNCTAD auspices in the 1970s led to significant decisions to deal with the adverse consequences for the trade and economic development of developing countries resulting from erosion of the multilateral trading system and slowdown in world economic growth. These included: *Integrated Programme for Commodities (IPC)* to stabilize the commodity market; Generalized System of Preferences (GSP), giving preferential treatment for the exports of developing countries. UNCTAD VII, 1987, focused on revitalization of development, growth and international trade in response to difficult world economic situation in particular

for developing countries, with tension between demand for a *New International Economic Order (NIEO)* and requirements of states using UNCTAD as a forum for negotiations. The Conference dealt with the issues facing the world economy and with policies and measures required to address them, leading to new prospects for action on multilateral cooperation for development. UNCTAD VIII, 1992, faced the huge political and economic changes since the previous Conference and the need for further action to support the international trade and economic development of developing countries. The concept of development evolved from a narrow focus on economic growth and capital accumulation to a multidimensional, people-centred process in which the aim of economic and social policy is to improve conditions for individuals. Recognizing the urgency of making the international trading and financial systems more responsive to the needs of economic growth and development, with emphasis on economic interdependence and shared responsibility for supportive action by of all countries, UNCTAD VIII adopted the Cartagena Commitment, pledging a New Partnership for Development, giving priority to development as a means of securing economic, social and human security and affirming UNCTAD as the focal point for facilitating and implementing the new development consensus. Greater recognition was given to the need for improved policy coordination, the importance of links between the external environment and domestic policies and the contribution of public and private sectors. UNCTAD VIII also undertook far-reaching reforms of UNCTAD's intergovernmental machinery and methods of work. UNCTAD IX, 1996, reaffirmed UNCTAD's role as focal point within the United Nations for integrated treatment of development and interrelated issues in trade, finance, technology, investment and sustainable development. Member states agreed that UNCTAD should continue to facilitate the integration of developing countries and countries in transition into the international trading system, complementing the work of the WTO, and to promote development through trade and investment in cooperation and coordination with *International Trade Centre (ITC, #15703)* and with relevant institutions of the United Nations system and other international organizations.

UNCTAD X, 2000, included participation of civil society and keynote speakers from major international organizations for the first time, in a series of interactive debates. It made a number of recommendations for all countries to benefit from globalization, including increased policy coherence at national and international level and more effective cooperation and coordination among multilateral institutions, and for furthering UNCTAD's capacity-building activities tailored to needs of developing countries. UNCTAD was confirmed as a knowledge-based institution and forum for discussion and consensus building.

In its Decision 529 (LXIII) of December 2016, the Trade and Development Board "*reiterates the relevance of the technical cooperation pillar of UNCTAD, as reaffirmed in the Nairobi Maafikiano, in contributing to inclusive development in the context of the 2030 Agenda for Sustainable Development and in achieving the Sustainable Development Goals*".

'Main Achievements':

– A number of international commodity agreements, or commodity study groups involving producing and consuming countries.

– Adoption of the generalized system of preferences (GSP), involving tariff concessions granted by the developed countries to the developing ones (1971).

– A resolution on retroactive adjustment of terms of the official development assistance debt of low-income developing countries (1978).

– Guidelines for international action in the area of debt rescheduling (1980).

– Set of principles and rules for the control of restrictive business practices (1980), (the Set is the only universally applicable international instrument on competition policy).

– Establishment of the Common Fund for Commodities to facilitate the financing of commodity agreements and support research and development activities for individual commodities (1989).

– *Agreement on a Global System of Trade Preferences among Developing Countries (GSTP, 1988)*, in force 19 Apr 1989.

– Conventions in the area of maritime transport: *Convention on a Code of Conduct for Liner Conferences (1974)*; *United Nations Convention on International Multimodal Transport of Goods (1980)*; *United Nations Convention on Conditions for Registration of Ships (1986)*; *International Convention on Maritime Liens and Mortgages (1993)*.

– Global Trade Point Network (GTPN) launched in 1994 as a result of the United Nations International Symposium on Trade Efficiency.

– Action in favour of the least developed countries, including organization of 3 United Nations Conferences on the Least Developed Countries: 1981, Paris (France), which adopted the Substantial New Programme of Action for the 1980s for the Least Developed Countries (SNPA), defining the measures to be taken by these countries to promote their own development together with international support; 1990, Paris, which reviewed the implementation of the SNPA and adopted a strengthened Programme of Action, which the LDCs and their developed partners undertook to implement through the 1990s; 2001, Brussels (Belgium), adopted a programme of action for the next decade that addresses development assistance, debt cancellation, and private investment in the 49 LDCs.

In addition to those mentioned above, UNCTAD is associated with the following treaties:

- *Food Aid Convention, 1995 (1994)*;
- *General Agreement on Tariffs and Trade, 1994 (GATT 1994, 1994)*;
- *Grains Trade Convention (GTC, 1994)*;
- *International Agreement on Jute and Jute Products, 1989 (1989)*;
- *International Sugar Agreement, 1992 (1992)*;
- *International Tropical Timber Agreement, 1983 (ITTA, 1983)*;
- *Protocol Relating to Trade Negotiations among Developing Countries (GATT Protocol, 1971)*;
- *Trade Expansion and Economic Cooperation Agreement between India, Egypt and Yugoslavia (Tripartite Agreement, 1967)*.

Events *Annual Session* Geneva (Switzerland) 2023, *World Summit on the Information Society (WSIS) Forum* Geneva (Switzerland) 2022, *E-Commerce Week for Asia* Abu Dhabi (United Arab Emirates) 2021, *World Investment Forum* Abu Dhabi (United Arab Emirates) 2021, *World Conference on Creative Economy* Dubai (United Arab Emirates) 2021. **Publications** *Transnational Corporations* (3 a year) – journal. *Current Studies on Science, Technology and Innovation* – series. Information Services: Databases on foreign direct investment include statistics on inward and outward stocks and flows, by origin and sectoral distribution, on transnational corporations from developed and developing countries and their foreign activities, and on small and medium-sized transnational corporations. Computerized HS-based databank covers: tariff and para-tariff measures; quantity control measures; automatic licensing measures; finance measures; price control measures; monopolistic measures; technical measures. **Information Services** *Advance Cargo Information System (ACIS)*; *Automated System for Customs Data (ASYCUDA)*; *Debt Management and Financial Analysis System (DMFAS)*; *'IMPORTES Database' of the International Trade Centre UNCTAD/WTO*; *Software for Market Access and Restrictions to Trade (SMART)*; *Trade Analysis and Information System (TRAINS)* – services include searching external databases, compilation of reference lists, information analysis and document delivery.

Members Member countries (195):

Afghanistan, Albania, Algeria, Andorra, Angola, Antigua-Barbuda, Argentina, Armenia, Australia, Austria, Azerbaijan, Bahamas, Bahrain, Bangladesh, Barbados, Belarus, Belgium, Belize, Benin, Bhutan, Bolivia, Bosnia-Herzegovina, Botswana, Brazil, Brunei Darussalam, Bulgaria, Burkina Faso, Burundi, Cambodia, Cameroon, Canada, Cape Verde, Central African Rep, Chad, Chile, China, Colombia, Comoros, Congo Brazzaville, Congo DR, Costa Rica, Côte d'Ivoire, Croatia, Cuba, Cyprus, Czechia, Denmark, Djibouti, Dominica, Dominican Rep, Ecuador, Egypt, El Salvador, Equatorial Guinea, Eritrea, Estonia, Eswatini, Ethiopia, Fiji, Finland, France, Gabon, Gambia, Georgia, Germany, Ghana, Greece, Grenada, Guatemala, Guinea, Guinea-Bissau, Guyana, Haiti, Holy See, Honduras, Hungary, Iceland, India, Indonesia, Iran Islamic Rep, Iraq, Ireland, Israel, Italy, Jamaica, Japan, Jordan, Kazakhstan, Kenya, Kiribati, Korea DPR, Korea Rep, Kuwait, Kyrgyzstan, Laos, Latvia, Lebanon, Lesotho, Liberia, Libya, Liechtenstein, Lithuania, Luxembourg, Madagascar, Malawi, Malaysia, Maldives, Mali, Malta, Marshall Is, Mauritania, Mauritius, Mexico, Micronesia FS, Moldova, Monaco, Mongolia, Montenegro, Morocco, Mozambique, Myanmar, Namibia, Nauru, Nepal, Netherlands, New Zealand, Nicaragua, Niger, Nigeria, North Macedonia, Norway, Oman, Pakistan, Palau, Palestine, Panama, Papua New Guinea, Paraguay, Peru, Philippines, Poland, Portugal, Qatar, Romania, Russia, Rwanda, Samoa, San Marino, Sao Tomé-Principe, Saudi Arabia, Senegal, Serbia, Seychelles, Sierra Leone, Singapore, Slovakia, Slovenia, Solomon Is, Somalia, South Africa, South Sudan, Spain, Sri Lanka, St Kitts-Nevis, St Lucia, St Vincent-Grenadines, Sudan, Suriname, Sweden, Switzerland, Syrian AR, Tajikistan, Tanzania UR, Thailand, Timor-Leste, Togo, Tonga, Trinidad-Tobago, Tunisia, Türkiye, Turkmenistan, Tuvalu, Uganda, UK, Ukraine, United Arab Emirates, Uruguay, USA, Uzbekistan, Vanuatu, Venezuela, Vietnam, Yemen, Zambia, Zimbabwe.

Consultative Status External actors such as the private sector, the business community, trade unions, the academic community and nongovernmental organizations and other international bodies are closely associated with UNCTAD's work. Rule 77 of the rules of procedure of the Trade and Development Board provides for participation of NGOs in UNCTAD's activities. In accordance with Board decision 43 (VII), a distinction is made between international NGOs which exercice functions, and have a basic interest, in most of the activities of the Board and of all of its Committees, and those which have a special competence in, and are concerned with, specific matters falling within the terms of reference of one or two Committees or of the Board itself. The former are placed in the General Category and the latter in the Special Category. National NGOs of recognized standing which are deemed to have a significant contribution to make to the work of UNCTAD may be entered by UNCTAD Secretary-General in a Register established for that purpose. As of Feb 2021, 242 NGOs, of which 149 in the general category and 93 in the special category. Organizations listed in this Yearbook are included below.

Organizations granted consultative status:

General Category (127):

- *ACT Alliance EU (#00082)*;
- *ActionAid (#00087)*;
- *African Business Roundtable (ABR, #00232)*;
- *African Centre for Monetary Studies (ACMS, inactive)*;
- *African Insurance Organization (AIO, #00343)*;
- *African Office for Development and Cooperation (OFADEC)*;
- *Afro-Asian Peoples' Solidarity Organization (AAPSO, #00537)*;
- *Arab Federation for Engineering Industries (AFEI, #00943)*;
- *Arab NGO Network for Development (ANND, #01016)*;
- *Arab-Swiss Chamber of Commerce and Industry (CASCI, #01053)*;
- *Asociación Latinoamericana de Industrias Farmacéuticas (ALIFAR, #02232)*;
- *Asociación Latinoamericana de Instituciones Financieras para el Desarrollo (ALIDE, #02233)*;
- *Asociación Latinoamericana del Acero (Alacero, #02176)*;
- *Association Africa 21 (Africa 21)*;
- *Association des chambres de commerce et d'industrie européennes (EUROCHAMBRES, #02423)*;
- *Association of Economists of Latin America and the Caribbean (AELAC, #02480)*;
- *Bread for All*;
- *BUSINESSEUROPE (#03381)*;
- *Catholic Agency for Overseas Development (CAFOD)*;
- *Center for Economic and Policy Research (CEPR)*;
- *Center for Latin American Monetary Studies (#03648)*;
- *Centrist Democrat International (CDI, #03792)*;
- *CIDSE (CIDSE, #03926)*;
- *Computer and Communications Industry Association (CCIA)*;
- *Conference of Iberoamerican Authorities on Informatics (#04606)*;
- *Confédération européenne des ong d'urgence et de développement (CONCORD, #04547)*;
- *Conseil européen de l'industrie chimique (CEFIC, #04687)*;
- *Consumers International (CI, #04773)*;
- *Consumer Unity and Trust Society (CUTS)*;
- *Coordination SUD*;
- *Development Innovations and Networks (#05057)*;
- *Environnement et développement du Tiers-monde (enda, #05510)*;
- *"Eurasian Economic Club of Scientists" Association (EECSA, no recent information)*;
- *European Business Council for Africa (EBCAM, #06416)*;
- *European Confederation of International Trading Houses Associations (CITHA, #06708)*;
- *European Network on Debt and Development (EURODAD, #07891)*;
- *European Shipyards' and Maritime Equipment Association (SEA Europe, #08479)*;
- *Europe – Third World Centre (CETIM)*;
- *Exchange and Cooperation Centre for Latin America (ECCLA)*;
- *Fair Trade Advocacy Office (FTAO, #09238)*;
- *Focus on the Global South (Focus, #09807)*;
- *Friends World Committee for Consultation (FWCC, #10004)*;
- *Fundación Global Democracia y Desarrollo (FUNGLODE)*;
- *Fédération Mondiale des Zones Franches (FEMOZA, #09693)*;
- *Global Express Association (GEA, #10351)*;
- *Global Foundation for Democracy and Development (GFDD)*;
- *Global Traders Conference (GTC, #10632)*;
- *Ibero-American Association of Chambers of Commerce (IACC, #11014)*;
- *Ingénieurs du monde (IdM)*;
- *Institute for Agriculture and Trade Policy (IATP)*;
- *Inter-American Council of Commerce and Production (IACCP, no recent information)*;
- *Intercontinental Network for the Promotion of the Social Solidarity Economy (INPSSE, #11463)*;
- *International Actuarial Association (IAA, #11586)*;
- *International Agency for Rural Industrialization (INARI, no recent information)*;
- *International Alliance of Women (IAW, #11639)*;
- *International Association of Agricultural Economists (IAAE, #11695)*;
- *International Association of Crafts and Small and Medium-Sized Enterprises (IACME, inactive)*;
- *International Association of Trading Organizations for a Developing World (ASTRO, inactive)*;
- *International Bar Association (IBA, #12320)*;
- *International Centre for Trade and Sustainable Development, Geneva (ICTSD, #12524)*;
- *International Chamber of Commerce (ICC, #12534)*;
- *International Chamber of the Transport Industry (#12536)*;
- *International Christian Union of Business Executives (#12566)*;
- *International Co-operative Alliance (ICA, #12944)*;
- *International Council of Environmental Law (ICEL, #13018)*;
- *International Council of Women (ICW, #13093)*;
- *International Council on Social Welfare (ICSW, #13076)*;
- *International Federation of Business and Professional Women (BPW International, #13376)*;
- *International Federation of Operational Research Societies (IFORS, #13493)*;
- *International Federation of Pharmaceutical Manufacturers and Associations (IFPMA, #13505)*;
- *International Federation of Purchasing and Supply Management (IFPSM, #13525)*;
- *International Fertilizer Association (IFA, #13589)*;
- *International Hotel and Restaurant Association (IH&RA, #13813)*;
- *International Institute for Sustainable Development (IISD, #13930)*;
- *International Law Association (ILA, #14003)*;
- *International Network for Standardization of Higher Education Degrees (INSHED, #14329)*;
- *International Organisation of Employers (IOE, #14428)*;
- *International Organization for Standardization (ISO, #14473)*;
- *International Peace Research Association (IPRA, #14537)*;
- *International Pole and Line Foundation (IPNLF, #14610)*;
- *International Road Transport Union (IRU, #14761)*;
- *International South Group Network (ISGN, no recent information)*;
- *International Textile Manufacturers Federation (ITMF, #15679)*;
- *International Trademark Association (INTA, #15706)*;
- *International Trade Union Confederation (ITUC, #15708)*;
- *International Union of Marine Insurance (IUMI, #15789)*;
- *IQsensato (#16015)*;
- *Islamic Chamber Research and Information Center (ICRIC, #16037)*;
- *Junior Chamber International (JCI, #16168)*;
- *Latin American Federation of International Transport Users' Councils (FELACUTI, no recent information)*;
- *Latin American Industrialists Association (#16341)*;
- *LDC Watch (#16412)*;
- *Mandat International*;
- *Organisation camerounaise de promotion de la coopération économique internationale (OCAPROCE internationale)*;
- *Organisation of African Trade Union Unity (OATUU, #17798)*;
- *Oxfam International (#17922)*;
- *Pan African Organization for Sustainable Development (POSDEV, #18057)*;
- *Public Services International (PSI, #18572)*;
- *Resource Africa*;
- *Rockefeller Brothers Fund (RBF)*;
- *Society for International Development (SID, #19581)*;
- *Tax Justice Network-Africa (TJN-A, #20101)*;
- *TerraWatt Initiative (TWI)*;
- *The Lutheran World Federation (LWF, #16532)*;
- *The World Veterans Federation (WVF, #21900)*;
- *Third World Foundation for Social and Economic Studies (TWF, #20150)*;
- *Third World Network (TWN, #20151)*;
- *Traidcraft Exchange*;
- *Transnational Institute (TNI, #20219)*;
- *UFI – The Global Association of the Exhibition Industry (#20276)*;

- *Union of Arab Banks (UAB, #20349);*
- *Women's International League for Peace and Freedom (WILPF, #21024);*
- *World Assembly of Youth (WAY, #21113);*
- *World Association for Small and Medium Enterprises (WASME, #21189);*
- *World Association of Former United Nations Internes and Fellows (WAFUNIF, #21141);*
- *World Council of Churches (WCC, #21320)* (Commission of the Churches on International Affairs);
- *World Economic Processing Zones Association (WEPZA, #21368);*
- *World Federation of Trade Unions (WFTU, #21493);*
- *World Federation of United Nations Associations (WFUNA, #21499);*
- *World Free Zones Organization (World FZO, #21530);*
- *World Peace Council (WPC, #21717);*
- *World Savings Banks Institute (WSBI, #21764);*
- *World Trade Centers Association (WTCA, #21862);*
- *World Vision International (WVI, #21904);*
- *World Wide Fund for Nature (WWF, #21922);*
- *Youth for Development and Cooperation (YDC, inactive);*
- *Zentrum für Wissenschaftliche Kommunikation mit Ibero-America (CCC).*

Special Category (84):
- *Action Group on Erosion, Technology and Concentration (ETC Group, #00091);*
- *Advanced Networked Cities and Regions Association (ANCARA, no recent information);*
- *Arab Federation for the Protection of Intellectual Property Rights (AFPIPR, #00951);*
- *Asia Pacific Forum on Women, Law and Development (APWLD, #01912);*
- *Asociación Centroamericana de Armadores (ACAMAR, no recent information);*
- *Association internationale villes et ports – réseau mondial des villes portuaires (AIVP, #02751);*
- *Association mondiale de dispacheurs (AMD, #02809);*
- *Association of Export Credit Insurers and of Export Promotion Organizations (Dakar Union, inactive);*
- *Association of the Chocolate, Biscuit and Confectionery Industries of the EU (CAOBISCO, #02427);*
- *BIMCO (#03236);*
- *BIPAR – European Federation of Insurance Intermediaries (#03263);*
- *Bureau international des containers et du transport intermodal (BIC, #03364);*
- *Bureau of International Recycling (BIR, #03368);*
- *Caribbean Shipping Association (CSA, #03554);*
- *Center for Democracy and Technology (CDT);*
- *Center for International Environmental Law (CIEL);*
- *CIRFS – European Man-made Fibres Association (#03944);*
- *Comité européen des fabricants de sucre (CEFS, #04159);*
- *Comité maritime international (CMI, #04192);*
- *Committee for International Cooperation between Cotton Associations (CICCA, #04265);*
- *EURATEX – The European Apparel and Textile Confederation (EURATEX, #05616);*
- *EURO-CHINA (#05658);*
- *European Association for the Trade in Jute and Related Products (Eurojute, #06256);*
- *European Sea Ports Organisation (ESPO, #08453);*
- *European Shippers' Council (ESC, #08477);*
- *European Tyre and Rubber Manufacturers' Association (ETRMA, #08963);*
- *Federación Interamericana de Empresas de Seguros (FIDES, #09331);*
- *Federation of African National Insurance Companies (#09408);*
- *Federation of Afro-Asian Insurers and Reinsurers (FAIR, #09413);*
- *Federation of Commodity Associations (FCA, no recent information);*
- *Federation of National Associations of Shipbrokers and Agents (FONASBA, #09694);*
- *Fundación Futuro Latinoamericano (FFLA, #10022);*
- *Fédération européenne des industries de corderie ficellerie et de filets (EUROCORD, #09573);*
- *Fédération internationale des associations de transitaires et assimilés (FIATA, #09610);*
- *Fédération Internationale des Conseils en Propriété Intellectuelle (FICPI, #09624);*
- *Fédération internationale des experts-comptables francophones (FIDEF, #09630);*
- *General Arab Insurance Federation (GAIF, #10104);*
- *Global Reporting Initiative (GRI, #10567);*
- *Grain and Feed Trade Association (GAFTA, #10692);*
- *IFOAM – Organics International (IFOAM, #11105);*
- *Institute of Chartered Shipbrokers (#11247);*
- *Institute of International Container Lessors (IICL, #11273);*
- *Instituto Iberoamericano de Derecho Marítimo (IIDM);*
- *Insurance Europe (#11362);*
- *International Air Transport Association (IATA, #11614);*
- *International Aluminium Institute (IAI, #11643);*
- *International Association for the Protection of Intellectual Property (#12112);*
- *International Association of Classification Societies (IACS, #11778);*
- *International Association of Dry Cargo Shipowners (INTERCARGO, #11853);*
- *International Association of Independent Tanker Owners (INTERTANKO, #11959);*
- *International Association of Islamic Banks (IAIB, no recent information);*
- *International Association of Ports and Harbors (IAPH, #12096);*
- *International Chamber of Shipping (ICS, #12535);*
- *International Chromium Development Association (ICDA, #12567);*
- *International Confederation of European Beet Growers (CIBE, #12860);*
- *International Council of Nurses (ICN, #13054);*
- *International Council on Mining and Metals (ICMM, #13048);*
- *International Environmental Law Research Centre (IELRC);*
- *International Federation of Beekeepers' Associations (APIMONDIA, #13370);*
- *International Federation of Inventors' Associations (IFIA, #13461);*
- *International Federation of Multimedia Associations (IFMA, #13483);*
- *International Food Policy Research Institute (IFPRI, #13622);*
- *International Group of P and I Clubs (#13751);*
- *International Ocean Institute (IOI, #14394);*
- *International Ship Suppliers and Services Association (ISSA, #14850);*
- *International Tungsten Industry Association (ITIA, #15743);*
- *International Union for Conservation of Nature and Natural Resources (IUCN, #15766);*
- *International Union of Railways (#15813);*
- *International Wrought Copper Council (IWCC, #15917);*
- *Joint Secretariat of Agricultural Trade Associations (#16148);*
- *Jubilee Research (#16158);*
- *Latin American and Caribbean Federation of National Associations of Cargo (#16276);*
- *Latin American Association of Navigational Law and Law of the Sea (ALDENAVE, no recent information);*
- *Latin American Shipowners Association (LASA, #16369);*
- *Licensing Executives Society International (LESI, #16461);*
- *Multiport Ship Agencies Network (MSAN, #16900);*
- *Organization of the Islamic Shipowners' Association (OISA, #17876);*
- *PIANC (#18371);*
- *Professional Association of Natural Rubber in Africa (ANRA, no recent information);*
- *SITA (#19299);*
- *The International Air Cargo Association (TIACA, #11608);*
- *World Association of Industrial and Technological Research Organizations (WAITRO, #21145);*
- *World Association of Investment Promotion Agencies (WAIPA, #21149);*
- *World Bureau of Metal Statistics (WBMS, #21250).*

IGO Relations *World Trade Organization (WTO, #21864)* (Observer Status). Member of: *Global Bioenergy Partnership (GBEP, #10251); UN-Water (#20723).* Cooperates with other United Nations agencies, including:
- *FAO (#09260);*
- *International Atomic Energy Agency (IAEA, #12294);*
- *International Civil Aviation Organization (ICAO, #12581);*
- *International Fund for Agricultural Development (IFAD, #13692);*
- *International Telecommunication Union (ITU, #15673);*
- *UNEP (#20299);*
- *UNDP (#20292);*
- *UNESCO Office, Jakarta – Regional Bureau for Sciences in Asia and the Pacific (#20313);*
- *UNIDO (#20336);*
- *United Nations Economic Commission for Latin America and the Caribbean (ECLAC, #20556);*
- *United Nations Group on the Information Society (UNGIS, #20570);*
- *Universal Postal Union (UPU, #20682);*
- *WHO (#20950).*

Governmental organization with Consultative Status: *Parlamento Latinoamericano (PARLATINO, #18203)* (General Category). Governmental organization listed on the register: *Research and Information System for Developing Countries, India (RIS, India).* Represented on: *United Nations System Chief Executives Board for Coordination (CEB, #20636).* Has been represented in meetings of: *Round Table on Sustainable Development at the OECD (see: #17693).*

Representatives of inter-governmental organizations, designated for this purpose by the Conference or the Trade and Development Board, may participate without the right to vote in deliberations of UNCTAD on questions within the scope of their activities. UNCTAD has official cooperation agreements with:
- *Agencia Española de Cooperación Internacional para el Desarrollo (AECID);*
- *Andean Community (#00817);*
- Latin American Parliament (PARLATINO);
- *Organisation of Islamic Cooperation (OIC, #17813).*

The following inter-governmental organizations also currently participate in the work of the Conference, in accordance with the rules of procedure:
- *ACP-EU Joint Parliamentary Assembly (#00077);*
- *African-Asian Rural Development Organization (AARDO, #00203);*
- *Organisation of African, Caribbean and Pacific States (OACPS, #17796);*
- *African Development Bank (ADB, #00283);*
- *African Export-Import Bank (Afreximbank, #00305);*
- *African Groundnut Council (AGC, #00332);*
- *African Reinsurance Corporation (AFRICA RE, #00438);*
- *African Union (AU, #00488);*
- *Agency for International Trade Information and Cooperation (AITIC, #00553);*
- *Alliance of Cocoa Producing Countries (COPAL, no recent information);*
- *Andean Presidential Council (see: #00817);*
- *Arab Administrative Development Organization (ARADO, #00893);*
- *Arab Authority for Agricultural Investment and Development (AAAID, #00902);*
- *Arab Bank for Economic Development in Africa (#00904);*
- *Arab Federation of Fish Producers (AFFP, #00945);*
- *Arab Federation of Shipping (AFS, #00953);*
- *Arab Fund for Economic and Social Development (AFESD, #00965);*
- *Arab Fund for Technical Assistance to African Countries (AFTAAC, #00966);*
- *Arab Industrial Development, Standardization and Mining Organization (AIDSMO, #00981);*
- *Arab Labour Organization (ALO, #01001);*
- *Arab League Educational, Cultural and Scientific Organization (ALECSO, #01003);*
- *Arab Maghreb Union (AMU, #01004);*
- *Arab Monetary Fund (AMF, #01009);*
- *Arab Organization for Agricultural Development (AOAD, #01018);*
- *Arab Tourism Organization (ATO, #01057);*
- *Asia-Pacific Telecommunity (APT, #02064);*
- *Asian-African Legal Consultative Organization (AALCO, #01303);*
- *Asian Clearing Union (ACU, #01380);*
- *Asian Reinsurance Corporation (Asian Re, #01685);*
- *Association of African Trade Promotion Organizations (AATPO, no recent information);*
- *Association of Iron Ore Exporting Countries (APEF, inactive);*
- *Association of Natural Rubber Producing Countries (ANRPC, #02822);*
- *Association of Tin Producing Countries (ATPC, inactive);*
- *Banque centrale des Etats de l'Afrique de l'Ouest (BCEAO, #03167);*
- *Caribbean Community (CARICOM, #03476);*
- *Caribbean Development Bank (CDB, #03492);*
- *Central American Integration System (#03671);*
- *Comisión Centroamericana de Transporte Marítimo (COCATRAM, #04131);*
- *Common Fund for Commodities (CFC, #04293);*
- *Common Market for Eastern and Southern Africa (COMESA, #04296);*
- *Commonwealth of Independent States (CIS, #04341);*
- *Commonwealth Secretariat (#04362);*
- *Communauté économique et monétaire d'Afrique centrale (CEMAC, #04374);*
- *Communauté économique des pays des Grands Lacs (CEPGL, #04375);*
- *Comunidade dos Países de Língua Portuguesa (CPLP, #04430);*
- *Consejo Centroamericano de Superintendentes de Bancos, de Seguros y de Otras Instituciones Financieras (CCSBSO, #04704);*
- *Council of Arab Economic Unity (CAEU, #04859);*
- *Development Bank of Latin America (CAF, #05055);*
- *Economic Community of West African States (ECOWAS, #05312);*
- *Economic Cooperation Organization (ECO, #05313);*
- *EFTA (#05391);*
- *Entente Council (#05491);*
- *Eurasian Development Bank (EDB, #05605);*
- *European Union (EU, #08967);*
- *Grupo de Países Latinoamericanos y del Caribe Exportadores de Azúcar (GEPLACEA, inactive);*
- *Gulf Cooperation Council (GCC, #10826);*
- *The Hague Conference on Private International Law (HCCH, #10850);*
- *Inter-African Coffee Organization (IACO, #11383);*
- *Inter-African Conference on Insurance Markets (#11385);*
- *Inter-American Development Bank (IDB, #11427);*
- *Intergovernmental Council of Copper Exporting Countries (CIPEC, inactive);*
- *Organisation intergouvernementale pour les transports internationaux ferroviaires (OTIF, #17807);*
- *Inter-Governmental Standing Committee on Shipping (ISCOS, #11501);*
- *International Bank for Economic Co-operation (IBEC, #12310);*
- *International Centre for Promotion of Enterprises (ICPE, #12509);*
- *International Cocoa Organization (ICCO, #12627);*
- *International Coffee Organization (ICO, #12630);*
- *International Copper Study Group (ICSG, #12963);*
- *International Cotton Advisory Committee (ICAC, #12979);*
- *International Criminal Police Organization – INTERPOL (ICPO-INTERPOL, #13110);*
- *International Customs Tariffs Bureau (#13124);*
- *International Grains Council (IGC, #13731);*
- *International Institute for the Unification of Private Law (UNIDROIT, #13934);*
- *International Investment Bank (IIB, #13951);*
- *International Jute Study Group (IJSG, no recent information);*
- *International Lead and Zinc Study Group (ILZSG, #14012);*
- *International Natural Rubber Organization (INRO, inactive);*
- *International Olive Council (IOC, #14405);*
- *International Organization of Legal Metrology (#14451);*
- *International Organization for Migration (IOM, #14454);*
- *International Rubber Study Group (IRSG, #14772);*
- *International Sugar Organization (ISO, #15623);*
- *International Tea Promotion Association (ITPA, inactive);*
- *International Textiles and Clothing Bureau (ITCB, #15680);*
- *International Tropical Timber Organization (ITTO, #15737);*
- *International Wool Study Group (IWSG, inactive);*
- *Islamic Development Bank (IsDB, #16044);*
- *Italian-Latin American Institute (ILAI, #16071);*
- *Latin American Energy Organization (#16313);*
- *League of Arab States (LAS, #16420);*
- *Mano River Union (MRU, #16566);*
- *Maritime Organization of West and Central Africa (MOWCA, #16582);*
- *OAS (#17629);*
- *OECD (#17693);*
- *OPEC Fund for International Development (OFID, #17745);*
- *Organisation of Eastern Caribbean States (OECS, #17804);*
- *Organisation internationale de la Francophonie (OIF, #17809);*
- *Organisation of Islamic Cooperation (OIC, #17813);*
- *Organization of Arab Petroleum Exporting Countries (OAPEC, #17854);*
- *Organization of the Petroleum Exporting Countries (OPEC, #17881);*
- *Pacific Islands Forum Secretariat (#17970);*
- *Permanent Consultative Committee of the Maghreb (PCCM, inactive);*
- *Red de Información Tecnológica Latinoamericana (RITLA, see: #19294);*
- *Secretaría Permanente del Tratado General de Integración Económica Centroamericana (SIECA, #19195);*
- *Sistema Económico Latinoamericano (SELA, #19294);*
- *South Centre (#19753);*

- *Southern African Customs Union (SACU, #19842)*;
- *Union of African Shippers' Councils (UASC, #20348)*;
- *Union économique et monétaire Ouest africaine (UEMOA, #20377)*;
- *Union monétaire de l'Afrique centrale (UMAC, #20463)*;
- *Unión de Países Exportadores de Banano (UPEB, inactive)*;
- *West African Monetary Agency (WAMA, #20887)*.

The following bodies have links:
- *African Regional Centre of Technology (ARCT, #00432)*;
- *African Regional Intellectual Property Organization (ARIPO, #00434)*;
- *Arab Investment and Export Credit Guarantee Corporation (DHAMAN, #00997)*;
- *ASEAN (#01141)*;
- *Asian Development Bank (ADB, #01422)*;
- *Asian and Pacific Centre for Transfer of Technology (APCTT, #01603)*;
- *Asian and Pacific Skill Development Programme (APSDEP, no recent information)*;
- *Central American Common Market (CACM, #03666)*;
- *Conference of Ministers of African Least Developed Countries (no recent information)*;
- *Coordination Committee on Multilateral Payments Arrangements and Monetary Cooperation among Developing Countries (no recent information)*;
- *Court of Justice of the Andean Community (#04936)*;
- *Economic Community of Central African States (ECCAS, #05311)*;
- *European Commission (EC, #06633)*;
- *Federation of Arab Scientific Research Councils (FASRC, no recent information)*;
- *Group of 77 (G-77, #10732)*;
- *Indian Ocean Marine Affairs Cooperation (IOMAC, no recent information)*;
- *Intergovernmental Group on Oilseeds, Oils and Fats (#11492)*;
- *Intergovernmental Group on Rice (#11493)*;
- *Intergovernmental Negotiating Committee for a Framework Convention on Climate Change (INC/FCCC, inactive)*;
- *International Bank for Reconstruction and Development (IBRD, #12317)* (World Bank);
- *International Maritime Organization (IMO, #14102)*;
- *International Nickel Study Group (INSG, #14370)*;
- *International Pepper Community (IPC, #14557)*;
- *Islamic Centre for Development of Trade (ICDT, #16035)*;
- *Joint Ministerial Committee of the Boards of Governors of the Bank and the Fund on the Transfer of Real Resources to Developing Countries (Development Committee, #16141)*;
- *Port Management Association of Eastern and Southern Africa (PMAESA, #18462)*;
- *Port Management Association of West and Central Africa (PMAWCA, #18463)*;
- *Secretariat of the Convention on Biological Diversity (SCBD, #19197)*;
- *South Asian Association for Regional Cooperation (SAARC, #19721)*;
- *Southern African Development Community (SADC, #19843)*;
- *Southern Common Market (#19868)*;
- *Statistical, Economic and Social Research and Training Centre for Islamic Countries (SESRIC, #19971)*;
- *Transmar Project (no recent information)*;
- *United Nations Economic Commission for Africa (ECA, #20554)*;
- *United Nations Economic Commission for Europe (UNECE, #20555)*;
- *United Nations Framework Convention on Climate Change – Secretariat (UNFCCC, #20564)*;
- *United Nations Human Settlements Programme (UN-Habitat, #20572)*;
- *United Nations Non-Governmental Liaison Service (NGLS, #20591)*;
- *United Nations University (UNU, #20642)*;
- *WHO Tobacco Free Initiative (TFI, #20949)*.

NGO Relations Official cooperation agreements with: *Centre for International Cooperation and Development (CICD)*; *World Federation of Development Financing Institutions (WFDFI, #21428)*. [2021/XE3381/**E***]

♦ UNCTC – United Nations Centre on Transnational Corporations (inactive)
♦ **UN-CTSU** United Nations Criminal Tribunals Staff Union (#20550)
♦ **UNC** United Nations Unified Command in Korea (#20641)
♦ Unda, Asociación Católica Internacional para la Radio y la Televisión (inactive)
♦ Unda, Association catholique internationale pour la radio et la télévision (inactive)
♦ Unda, International Catholic Association for Radio and Television (inactive)
♦ UNDCP – United Nations International Drug Control Programme (inactive)
♦ Undeb Celtaidd (#03633)
♦ **UNDEF** United Nations Democracy Fund (#20551)

♦ Undersea and Hyperbaric Medical Society (UHMS) 20286

Exec Dir 631 US Highway 1, Ste 307, North Palm Beach FL 33408, USA. T. +15612713276. Fax +15616225220. E-mail: uhms@uhms.org.
URL: http://www.uhms.org/

History 1967. Former names and other names: *Undersea Medical Society* – former (1967 to 1986). **Aims** Provide scientific information to protect the health of sport, military and commercial *divers*; improve scientific basis of hyperbaric oxygen therapy; promote sound treatment protocols and standards of practice and provide CME accreditation and pressure chamber accreditation. **Structure** Board of Directors. **Languages** English. **Staff** 6.50 FTE, paid. **Finance** Sources: fees for services; meeting proceeds; members' dues; sale of publications. Annual budget: 1,000,000 USD. **Activities** Awards/prizes/competitions; certification/accreditation; events/meetings; publishing activities. **Events** *Annual Scientific Meeting* New Orleans, LA (USA) 2024, *Annual Scientific Meeting* San Diego, CA (USA) 2023, *Annual Scientific Meeting* Reno, NV (USA) 2022, *Annual Scientific Meeting* North Palm Beach, FL (USA) 2021, *Annual Scientific Meeting* Río Grande (Puerto Rico) 2019. **Publications** *Pressure* (4 a year) – mpembership newsletter; *Undersea and Hyperbaric Medicine* (4 a year) – journal. *Hyperbaric Oxygen Therapy Indications* (14th ed); *UHMS Guidelines for Hyperbaric Facility Operation* (3rd ed). **Members** Individuals (2,000) in over 50 countries. Membership countries not specified. [2022.02.08/XF7211/**F**]

♦ Undersea Medical Society / see Undersea and Hyperbaric Medical Society (#20286)

♦ Understanding Risk Network (UR Network) 20287

Contact c/o GFDRR, World Bank, 1818 H Str NW, Washington DC 20433, USA.
URL: http://www.understandrisk.org/

History 2010. **Events** *UR Asia Forum* Singapore (Singapore) 2021, *Understanding Risk Global Forum* 2020, *UR Asia Forum* Singapore (Singapore) 2020, *Understanding Risk Global Forum* Mexico City (Mexico) 2018, *Understanding Risk Global Forum* Venice (Italy) 2016. **Members** Individuals. Membership countries not specified. **IGO Relations** *Global Facility for Disaster Reduction and Recovery (GFDRR, #10352)*. [2022/XJ9508/v/**F**]

♦ Underwriters Laboratories (internationally oriented national body)
♦ UNDG / see United Nations Sustainable Development Group (#20634)

♦ Undiagnosed Diseases Network International (UDNI) 20288

Contact address not obtained. Fax +39649904370. E-mail: udni@iss.it.
URL: http://www.udninternational.org/

History Set up 2014. **Aims** Improve the rate of definite diagnosis for persons living with undiagnosed conditions. **Structure** Board of Directors. **Activities** Research/documentation; knowledge management/information dissemination; events/meetings. **Events** *Conference* Stockholm (Sweden) 2017. **Publications** *UDNI Newsletter.*
Members Clinical investigators in 18 countries:
Australia, Austria, Belgium, Canada, France, Germany, Hungary, India, Israel, Italy, Japan, Korea Rep, Netherlands, Spain, Sri Lanka, Sweden, Thailand, USA. [2018/XM6499/v/**F**]

♦ **UNDL Foundation** Universal Networking Digital Language Foundation (#20680)
♦ **UNDOF** United Nations Disengagement Observer Force (#20553)
♦ UNDP Drylands Development Centre (inactive)

♦ UNDP International Policy Centre for Inclusive Growth (IPC-IG) 20289

Acting Dir Sector Bancario Sul Quadra 1, Bloco J, Ed BNDES, 13o andar, UNDP/IPC-IG, Brasilia DF, 70076-900, Brazil. T. +556121055000. Fax +556121055001. E-mail: ipc@ipc-undp.org.
URL: http://www.ipc-undp.org/

History 2002, as *UNDP International Poverty Centre (IPC)*, within *UNDP (#20292)*, as a partnership between UNDP's Poverty Group, Bureau for Development Policy (BDP) and Government of Brazil with the support of Institute for Applied Economic Research (IPEA). Current title adopted 2009. **Aims** As a global forum for South-South dialogue on innovative development policies, promote production and dissemination of studies and policy recommendations, exchange of best practices in development initiatives, and expansion of South-South learning. **Structure** Subordinated to UNDP (New York NY – USA) and Government of Brazil's Institute of Applied Economic Research (Brasilia, Brazil). **Languages** English. **Staff** 25.00 FTE, paid. Additional visiting fellows and researchers. **Finance** Funding from: UNDP headquarters and country offices; UN agencies; bilateral organizations; Brazilian Government. **Activities** Research and development; networking/liaising; publishing activities; advocacy/lobbying/activism; knowledge management/information dissemination; capacity building; training/education; events/meetings. **Events** *International conference on the many dimensions of poverty* Brasilia (Brazil) 2005. **Publications** *One Pager*; *Policy Research Brief*; *Poverty In Focus* – magazine. *Country Study.* Working papers; technical papers; evaluation notes; conference papers. **IGO Relations** Partners include: *African Development Bank (ADB, #00283)*; Australian Government Department of Foreign Affairs and Trade (DFAT); Brazilian Ministry of Social Development and Fight against Hunger (MDS); *Department for International Development (DFID, inactive)*; *Deutsche Gesellschaft für Internationale Zusammenarbeit (GIZ)*; *FAO (#09260)*; *International Bank for Reconstruction and Development (IBRD, #12317)* (World Bank); *UN Women (#20724)*; *UNDP (#20292)* Independent Evaluation Office (IEO); *UNICEF (#20332)*; *United Nations Economic Commission for Latin America and the Caribbean (ECLAC, #20556)*; *United Nations Economic and Social Commission for Asia and the Pacific (ESCAP, #20557)*; *World Food Programme (WFP, #21510)*. [2014.12.09/XM0562/**E***]

♦ UNDP International Poverty Centre / see UNDP International Policy Centre for Inclusive Growth (#20289)

♦ UNDP Oslo Governance Centre (OGC) 20290

Main Office Kongens Gate 12, 0153 Oslo, Norway. T. +4722121600. E-mail: oslo.governance.centre@undp.org.
URL: http://www.undp.org/content/undp/en/home/ourwork/global-policy-centres/

History 2002. Founded within *UNDP (#20292)*. Registration: Brønnøysund Register Centre, No/ID: 894 665 432, Norway. **Aims** Help position UNDP as a champion of democratic governance. **Languages** English. **Staff** 10.00 FTE, paid. **Finance** Financed through a cost-share agreement between UNDP and the Government of Norway. Annual budget: 2,500,000 USD. **Activities** Knowledge management/information dissemination; networking/liaising; politics/policy/regulatory; research/documentation. **Publications** Guides; reports; discussion papers; notes; manuals. [2020.11.17/XM0563/**E**]

♦ UNDP Staff Association / see UNDP/UNFPA/UNOPS/UN Women Staff Association (#20291)
♦ UNDP / UNFPA Staff Association / see UNDP/UNFPA/UNOPS/UN Women Staff Association (#20291)

♦ UNDP/UNFPA/UNOPS/UN Women Staff Association (Staff Council) . 20291

Contact One UN Plaza – 44th Street, CD1-24 floor, Room DC1-2488, New York NY 10017, USA. T. +12129066633. Fax +12122974905. E-mail: registry.staff-council@undp.org.
URL: http://www.staffcouncil.org/

History 1973. Initially founded to represent staff members of *UNDP (#20292)*. Expanded to represent staff of *United Nations Population Fund (UNFPA, #20612)*; *United Nations Office for Project Services (UNOPS, #20602)*; and *UN Women (#20724)*. Mandate from Chapter VIII of the UN Staff Rules and Regulations (ST/SGB/2017/1). Constitution updated: 2013. Former names and other names: *UNDP Staff Association* – former; *UNDP / UNFPA Staff Association* – former. **Aims** Promote and safeguard the rights, interests and welfare of UNDP/UNFPA staff; serve as channel of communication with the Administration; foster cooperation with other UN common system staff associations on matters concerning conditions of service of the United Nations. **Structure** Staff Council, consisting of 11 members. **Events** *Regional Meeting* Harare (Zimbabwe) 1993. **Members** Individuals worldwide. **NGO Relations** Member of (1): *United Nations International Civil Servants Federation (UNISERV, #20579)*. [2021/XE0282/v/**E**]

♦ UNDP – United Nations Development Programme 20292

Programme des Nations Unies pour le développement (PNUD) – Programa de las Naciones Unidas para el Desarrollo (PNUD) – Entwicklungsprogramm der Vereinten Nationen

Administrator One United Nations Plaza, New York NY 10017, USA. T. +12129065000. Fax +12129065364.
European Office Palais des Nations, 1211 Geneva 10, Switzerland. T. +41229178542. Fax +41229178001.
URL: http://www.undp.org/

History Nov 1965. Established pursuant to resolution 1020 (XXXVII) of *ECOSOC (#05331)*, approved by the General Assembly in resolution 2029 (XX). Set up by merger of *United Nations Expanded Programme of Technical Assistance (EPTA) – Programme élargi d'assistance technique des Nations Unies – Programa Ampliado de Asistencia Técnica de las Naciones Unidas* and of *United Nations Special Fund (inactive)* – note that this is not the same as the later *United Nations Special Fund, 1974 (UNSF, no recent information)*. The Governing Council, originally consisting of 37 members, was increased to 48 members by General Assembly resolution 2813 (XXVI) of 14 Dec 1971 and replaced by a 36-member Executive Board in 1994. UNDP is an organ of *United Nations (UN, #20515)* within the framework of *United Nations System (#20635)*, linked to the General Assembly and to ECOSOC. **Aims** Work to eradicate poverty while protecting the planet; help countries develop strong policies, skills, partnerships and institutions so they can sustain their progress.
Structure Executive Board, consisting of representatives of 36 nations (on a rotating basis) representing African States, Asian and Pacific States, Latin America and Caribbean States, Eastern European and other States and Western European and other States, and includes President and 4 Vice-Presidents. The Executive Board, is responsible for providing inter-governmental support to, and supervision of, the activities of UNDP and for ensuring that it is responsive to the needs of programme countries. Executive Board secretariat is headed by Director/Secretary and includes Senior Editor, Editor, Documents/Editorial Associate and Administrative Associate. UNDP Headquarters in New York NY (USA) headed by an Administrator, supported by an Associate Administrator. Reporting to the Administrator:
- Executive Office;
- Development Operations Coordination Office;
- Human Development Report Office;
- Evaluation Office;
- Office of Audit and Investigation;
- Communications Office;
- Partnerships Bureau;
- Bureau for Development Policy;
- Bureau of Management;
- Bureau for Crisis Prevention and Recovery.

Reporting to the Associate Administrator:
- Operations Support Group;
- Regional Bureaux (5): UNDP Africa, UNDP Asia and the Pacific, UNDP Latin America and the Caribbean, UNDP Arab States and UNDP Europe and the CIS;
- Special Unit for South-South Cooperation (SU/SCC);
- *United Nations Volunteers (UNV, #20650)*;
- *United Nations Capital Development Fund (UNCDF, #20524)*.

Resident Representatives oversee work in over 130 Country Offices in developing countries and normally serve as Resident Coordinators of development activities of the UN system and, in crisis situations, as humanitarian coordinators. They report to the UN Secretary-General through UNDP Administrator.
Languages English, French, Spanish. **Staff** 6500.00 FTE, paid. 21% at Headquarters and 79% in country offices. Personnel negotiations through *UNDP/UNFPA/UNOPS/UN Women Staff Association (Staff Council, #20291)*. **Finance** Core (voluntary contributions) and non-core (targeted) resources amount to over US$ 5,000,000,000 annually. Core funds, averaging US$ 700,000,000 annually, comprise voluntary contributions of member countries of the United Nations or its agencies.
Activities On the ground in about 170 countries and territories to help them find their own solutions to global and national development challenges. As they develop local capacity, they draw on the people of UNDP and UNDP's partners. Focuses on helping countries build and share solutions to the challenges of: Democratic Governance; Poverty Reduction; Crisis Prevention and Recovery; Energy and Environment; Information and Communications Technology; HIV/AIDS. In these 6 practices, UNDP seeks out and shares ways to promote: gender equality as an essential dimension of ensuring political participation and accountability; economic

empowerment and effective development planning; crisis prevention and conflict resolution; access to clean water, sanitation and energy services; the best use of technologies for development purposes; society-wide mobilization against HIV/AIDS. Helps developing countries attract and use aid effectively; engages in extensive advocacy work; sponsors workshops.

'Human Development Report' contains substantive data on most development indicators, ranking every country each year in such areas as per capita income, literacy, life expectancy and respect for women's rights. The goal of the report is to put people back at the centre of the development process. An independent team of experts, drawn from a worldwide network of leaders from academia, government and civil society, write the report. Developing countries and their international partners use the report to gauge results and shape new policies. UNDP has also helped more than 120 developing countries produce their own national human development reports which provide a basis for informed local debate about priorities and policies and help donor governments measure the impact of their aid dollars and to communicate the way in which aid is making a positive difference both to direct beneficiaries and to electorates at home.

'Millennium Development Goals (MDGs)' adopted at United Nations Millennium Summit, Sep 2000, set clear targets for reducing poverty, hunger, disease, illiteracy, environmental degradation and discrimination against women by 2015. UNDP uses its global network to help the UN system and its partners raise awareness and track progress, while connecting countries to the knowledge and resources needed to achieve these goals. *UNDP International Policy Centre for Inclusive Growth (IPC-IG, #20289)* and *UNDP Oslo Governance Centre (OGC, #20290)* were set up to advance UNDP's objective of assisting countries to achieve these goals. The MDGs are:

- 1. Eradicate extreme poverty and hunger – Target: halve the proportion of people living on less than a dollar a day and those who suffer from hunger.
- 2. Achieve universal primary education – Target: ensure that all boys and girls complete primary school.
- 3. Promote gender equality and empower women – Target (for 2005 and 2015): eliminate gender disparities in primary and secondary education preferably by 2005, and at all levels by 2015.
- 4. Reduce child mortality – Target: reduce by two-thirds the mortality rate among children under five.
- 5. Improve maternal health – Target: reduce by three-quarters the ratio of women dying in childbirth.
- 6. Combat HIV/AIDS, malaria and other disease – Target: halt and begin to reverse the spread of HIV/AIDS and the incidence of malaria and other major diseases.
- 7. Ensure environmental sustainability – Targets: integrate the principles of sustainable development into country policies and programmes and reverse the loss of environmental resources; by 2015, reduce by half the proportion of people without access to safe drinking water; by 2020, achieve significant improvement in the lives of at least 100 million slum dwellers.
- 8. Develop a global partnership for development Targets: develop further an open trading and financial system that includes a commitment to good governance, development and poverty reduction, nationally and internationally; address the least developed countries' special needs and the special needs of landlocked and small island developing States; deal comprehensively with developing countries' debt problems; develop decent and productive work for youth; in cooperation with pharmaceutical companies, provide access to affordable essential drugs in developing countries; in cooperation with the private sector, make available the benefits of new technologies, especially information and communications technologies.

/Funds and Funding Projects Associated with UNDP/

United Nations Capital Development Fund (UNCDF): provides capital grants and concessional loans for povertyreduction programmes in the leastdeveloped countries; supports government efforts to decentralize administrative control of social services and local government capacity to take on that responsibility; implements local development projects and promotes mechanisms to provide credit to for the poor so as to encourage use of sustainable natural resources.

World Solidarity Fund (#21818): contributes to the eradication of poverty and promotes social and human development in the poorest regions of the world.

– United Nations Development Fund for Women (UNIFEM): promotes women's empowerment and gender equality through support for participation of women at all levels of development planning and practice; acts as a catalyst in the UN system linking needs and concerns of women to critical social and economic issues on national, regional and global agendas.

– United Nations Volunteers: provides programme countries with technically qualified volunteer specialists and field workers (currently 3,500 from 140 countries) who work alongside their host country peers in: technical cooperation; community-based initiatives for self-reliance; humanitarian relief and rehabilitation; support for electoral and peace-building processes.

– Special Unit for South-South Cooperation (SU/SSC): promotes South-South cooperation in support of development directives and as a means of helping developing countries to participate more effectively in the global economy.

– *Energy and Environment Group (see: #20292)*, comprising UNDP units executing: *Global Environment Facility (GEF, #10346)*; *Network for Capacity Building in Integrated Water Resources Management (CAP-Net, #17000)*; activities concerning *Montreal Protocol on Substances that Deplete the Ozone Layer (1987)*; Energy Unit; and other core areas. GEF provides grants and concessional funding to help countries translate global concerns into national action to combat ozone depletion, global warming, loss of biodiversity and pollution of international waters. UNDP is an implementing agency, together with the World Bank and UNEP.

– *Joint United Nations Programme on HIV/AIDS (UNAIDS, #16149)* – UNDP is one of 6 UN sponsors of this Programme.

/Other Activities/

– *'CAPACITY 21'*: helps developing countries implement *Global Action Plan for Environment and Development in the 21st Century (Agenda 21, inactive)* by funding efforts to marshall the necessary skills and financial resources for evolving sustainable development strategies in key environmental areas and establishing policies to protect essential stocks of ecological capital on which future economic development depends.

– *Multilateral Fund for the Implementation of the Montreal Protocol (#16885)*: assists developing countries in the planning, preparation and implementation of country programmes, projects and sectoral activities to replace and phase out chlorofluorocarbons, halons and other substances that destroy the earth's protective ozone layer.

– *UNDP Energy Account (no recent information)*: acts as channel for specific contributions towards energy projects for developing countries using existing trust-fund arrangements.

– *Local Initiative Facility for the Environment (LIFE, inactive)*: demonstrates local solutions for urban environmental problems and works at community, country, regional and interregional levels to promote local dialogue and action by NGOs and local authorities to improve living conditions in low-income urban communities.

Events *World Summit on the Information Society (WSIS) Forum* Geneva (Switzerland) 2022, *Asia-Pacific Conference on the Promotion of Gender-Responsive Judicial Systems* Tokyo (Japan) 2022, *Solidarity of Women Entrepreneurs in Africa and Japan* Tokyo (Japan) 2022, *Youth Co:Lab: Social Innovation Challenge Japan 2022* Tokyo (Japan) 2022, *AEC : African Economic Conference* Cape Verde 2021. **Publications** *Millennium Development Goals Report* (annual); *Human Development Report* (annual) – also CD-ROM; *Creating Value for All: Strategies for Doing Business with the Poor* – report; *UNDP Illustrated Annual Report*; *UNDP Online News Bulletin*. *A Handbook on Working with Political Parties* (2006); *ERRA – UN Early Recovery Plan* (2006); *Getting to the CORE: A Global Survey on the Cost of Registration and Elections* (2006); *Mainstreaming HIV and AIDS in Sectors and Programmes* (2006); *Niger Delta Human Development Report* (2006); *The New Public Finance* (2006); *The United Nations Development Programme: A Better Way ?* (2006); *Asia-Pacific Human Development Report 2006*; *Democratic Dialogue – A Handbook for Practitioners*; *Governance for the Future: Democracy and Development in the Least Developed Countries*; *Water Rights and Wrongs: A Young People's Summary of the United Nations Development Report 2006*; *Youth and Violent Conflict*. *Making the Law Work for Everyone* – report; *MDG Gap Task Force Report*. Information Services: INRES became *SSC WIDE (no recent information)* – a computerized service since 1985. **Information Services** *UNDP Information Referral System for Technical Cooperation among Developing Countries (INRES)* – set up May 1977.

Members Open to all members and observers of the United Nations, of the Specialized Agencies and of the International Atomic Energy Agency (IAEA). The following 200 countries and territories participate in UNDP:
Afghanistan, Albania, Algeria, Andorra, Angola, Anguilla, Antigua-Barbuda, Argentina, Armenia, Australia, Austria, Azerbaijan, Bahamas, Bahrain, Bangladesh, Barbados, Belarus, Belgium, Belize, Benin, Bermuda, Bhutan, Bolivia, Bosnia-Herzegovina, Botswana, Brazil, Brunei Darussalam, Bulgaria, Burkina Faso, Burundi, Cambodia, Cameroon, Canada, Cape Verde, Cayman Is, Central African Rep, Chad, Chile, China, Colombia, Comoros, Congo Brazzaville, Congo DR, Cook Is, Costa Rica, Côte d'Ivoire, Croatia, Cuba, Cyprus, Czechia, Denmark, Djibouti, Dominica, Dominican Rep, Ecuador, Egypt, El Salvador, Equatorial Guinea, Eritrea, Estonia, Eswatini, Ethiopia, Fiji, Finland, France, Gabon, Gambia, Georgia, Germany, Ghana, Greece, Grenada, Guatemala, Guinea, Guinea-Bissau, Guyana, Haiti, Holy See, Honduras, Hungary, Iceland, India, Indonesia, Iran Islamic Rep, Iraq, Ireland, Israel, Italy, Jamaica, Japan, Jordan, Kazakhstan, Kenya, Kiribati, Korea DPR, Korea Rep, Kuwait, Kyrgyzstan, Laos, Latvia, Lebanon, Lesotho, Liberia, Libya, Liechtenstein, Lithuania, Luxembourg, Madagascar, Malawi, Malaysia, Maldives, Mali, Malta, Marshall Is, Mauritania, Mauritius, Mexico, Micronesia FS, Moldova, Monaco, Mongolia, Montserrat, Morocco, Mozambique, Myanmar, Namibia, Nauru, Nepal, Netherlands, New Zealand, Nicaragua, Niger, Nigeria, Niue, North Macedonia, Norway, Pakistan, Palau, Panama, Papua New Guinea, Paraguay, Peru, Philippines, Poland, Portugal, Qatar, Romania, Russia, Rwanda, Samoa, San Marino, Sao Tomé-Principe, Saudi Arabia, Senegal, Serbia, Seychelles, Sierra Leone, Singapore, Slovakia, Slovenia, Solomon Is, Somalia, South Africa, Spain, Sri Lanka, St Kitts-Nevis, St Lucia, St Vincent-Grenadines, Sudan, Suriname, Sweden, Switzerland, Syrian AR, Tajikistan, Tanzania UR, Thailand, Togo, Tokelau, Tonga, Trinidad-Tobago, Tunisia, Türkiye, Turkmenistan, Turks-Caicos, Tuvalu, Uganda, UK, Ukraine, United Arab Emirates, Uruguay, USA, Uzbekistan, Vanuatu, Venezuela, Vietnam, Virgin Is UK, Yemen, Zambia, Zimbabwe.

Members of the Executive Board (expery date in brackets):
Algeria (2023), Bangladesh (2023), Bulgaria (2022), Cameroon (2024), Chad (2024), China (2022), Colombia (2022), Costa Rica (2024), Côte d'Ivoire (2024), Cuba (2023), Czechia (2022), Finland (2023), Germany (2024), Greece (2024), Guatemala, Iran Islamic Rep (2023), Japan (2022), Kazakhstan (2024), Kenya (2024), Kuwait (2022), Lesotho (2024), Myanmar (2024), Netherlands (2024), New Zealand (2023), Nigeria (2023), Norway (2022), Peru (2022), Qatar (2024), Russia (2023), Somalia (2022), Spain (2023), Sweden (2024), Switzerland (2022), UK (2023), Ukraine (2024), USA (2022).

IGO Relations *World Trade Organization (WTO, #21864)* (Observer Status). Cooperation agreement with: *Organisation internationale de la Francophonie (OIF, #17809)*. Partner of: *United Nations Forum on Forests (UNFF, #20562)*. Projects are or have been carried out with the assistance of United Nations regional commissions: *United Nations Economic Commission for Africa (ECA, #20554)*; *United Nations Economic Commission for Europe (UNECE, #20555)*; *United Nations Economic Commission for Latin America and the Caribbean (ECLAC, #20556)*; *United Nations Economic and Social Commission for Asia and the Pacific (ESCAP, #20557)*; *United Nations Economic and Social Commission for Western Asia (ESCWA, #20558)*, and with the following executing and associated agencies:

- *African Development Bank (ADB, #00283)*;
- *Arab Fund for Economic and Social Development (AFESD, #00965)*;
- *Asian Development Bank (ADB, #01422)*;
- *Caribbean Development Bank (CDB, #03492)*;
- *FAO (#09260)*;
- *ILO (#11123)*;
- *Inter-American Development Bank (IDB, #11427)*;
- *International Atomic Energy Agency (IAEA, #12294)*;
- *International Bank for Reconstruction and Development (IBRD, #12317)* (World Bank);
- *International Civil Aviation Organization (ICAO, #12581)*;
- *International Development Association (IDA, #13155)*;
- *International Finance Corporation (IFC, #13597)*;
- *International Fund for Agricultural Development (IFAD, #13692)*;
- *International Maritime Organization (IMO, #14102)*;
- *International Monetary Fund (IMF, #14180)*;
- *International Telecommunication Union (ITU, #15673)*;
- *International Trade Centre (ITC, #15703)*;
- *Islamic Development Bank (IsDB, #16044)*;
- United Nations Environment Programme – *UNEP (#20299)*;
- United Nations Conference on Trade and Development – *UNCTAD (#20285)*;
- United Nations Educational, Scientific and Cultural Organization – *UNESCO (#20322)*;
- Office of the United Nations High Commissioner for Refugees – *UNHCR (#20327)*;
- United Nations Children's Fund – *UNICEF (#20332)*;
- *United Nations Centre on Transnational Corporations (UNCTC, inactive)*;
- *United Nations Group on the Information Society (UNGIS, #20570)*;
- *United Nations Human Settlements Programme (UN-Habitat, #20572)*;
- *United Nations Population Fund (UNFPA, #20612)*;
- *United Nations University (UNU, #20642)*;
- *Universal Postal Union (UPU, #20682)*;
- World Health Organization – *WHO (#20950)*;
- *World Food Programme (WFP, #21510)*;
- *World Intellectual Property Organization (WIPO, #21593)*;
- *World Meteorological Organization (WMO, #21649)*;
- *World Tourism Organization (UNWTO, #21861)*.

Panel member of: *Interagency Panel on Juvenile Justice (IPJJ, #11390)*. Represented on: *United Nations System Chief Executives Board for Coordination (CEB, #20636)*. Has been represented in meetings of: *Round Table on Sustainable Development at the OECD (see: #17693)*. Close cooperation with: *United Nations Institute for Training and Research (UNITAR, #20576)*. On Board of: *International Training Centre of the ILO (ITC, #15717)*. Member of Steering Committee of: *Caspian Environment Programme (CEP, #03596)*. Member of: *Committee of International Development Institutions on the Environment (CIDIE, no recent information)*; *Inter-Agency Standing Committee (IASC, #11393)*; *UN-Water (#20723)*. Partner of: *World Water Assessment Programme (WWAP, #21907)*. Supports: *CIS-7 Initiative (no recent information)*. Observer to: *United Nations Framework Convention on Climate Change – Secretariat (UNFCCC, #20564)*; *International Organization for Migration (IOM, #14454)*; *UNESCO Office, Jakarta – Regional Bureau for Sciences in Asia and the Pacific (#20313)* (under Asia Pacific Gender Programme). Previously responsible for day-to-day management of: *United Nations Border Relief Operations (UNBRO, inactive)*. Cooperation agreement with: *Islamic World Educational, Scientific and Cultural Organization (ICESCO, #16058)*.

Instrumental in setting up and/or assists in the administering of:

- *Africa Project Development Facility (APDF, inactive)*;
- *Arab Planning Institute (API, #01027)*;
- *Arab Trade Financing Programme (ATFP, #01060)*;
- *Asian and Pacific Skill Development Programme (APSDEP, no recent information)*;
- *Caribbean Institute for Meteorology and Hydrology (CIMH, #03520)*;
- *Caribbean Regional Technical Assistance Centre (CARTAC, #03550)*;
- *Consultative Group to Assist the Poor (CGAP, #04768)*;
- *Digital Opportunity Task Force (DOT Force, no recent information)*;
- *INFOPESCA (#11192)*;
- *Liptako-Gourma Integrated Development Authority (LGA, no recent information)*;
- *Operational Net of Regional Cooperation of Central American Maritime Authorities (ROCRAM-CA, no recent information)*;
- *Organization for the Management and Development of the Kagera River Basin (KBO, no recent information)*;
- *Pacific Sustainable Development Networking Programme (PSDNP, inactive)*;
- *Programme on Credit for Income Generating Activities of the Poor in Asia and the Pacific (CIGAP, inactive)*;
- *Special Measures Fund for Least-Developed Countries (inactive)*;
- *Statistical Institute for Asia and the Pacific (SIAP, #19972)*;
- *UNICEF/UNDP/World Bank/WHO Special Programme for Research and Training in Tropical Diseases (TDR, #20331)*;
- *United Nations Fund for Science and Technology for Development (UNFSTD, inactive)*;
- *United Nations Office for Project Services (UNOPS, #20602)*;
- *United Nations Trust Fund for Sudano-Sahelian Activities (no recent information)*.

NGO Relations Cooperates through programmes that: support participatory, community-based development; promote dialogue and collaboration among NGOs, governments and multilateral agencies; encourage and support NGO involvement in sustainable development activities; strengthen the capacity, impact and sustainability of NGOs and other grass-roots groups. Instrumental in setting up and/or assists in the administering of: *World Alliance of Cities Against Poverty (WACAP, #21080)*; *ABA-UNDP International Legal Resource Centre (ILRC)*. Observer to: *International Committee of the Red Cross (ICRC, #12799)*; *International Federation of Red Cross and Red Crescent Societies (#13526)*; *International Red Cross and Red Crescent Movement (#14707)*. Partner of: *WorldFish (#21507)*. [2022/XE3382/**E***]

♦ UNDP-World Bank Water and Sanitation Programme / see Water and Sanitation Programme (#20837)
♦ UNDP/World Bank/WHO Special Programme for Research and Training in Tropical Diseases / see UNICEF/UNDP/World Bank/WHO Special Programme for Research and Training in Tropical Diseases (#20331)
♦ UNDRO – Office of the United Nations Disaster Relief Coordinator (inactive)
♦ **UNDRR** United Nations Office for Disaster Risk Reduction (#20595)
♦ Undugu Group (meeting series)
♦ UnEAS – Union of European Accountancy Students (inactive)
♦ UNEBIF – Union européenne des fabricants de bijouterie fantaisie (inactive)
♦ UNECA / see United Nations Economic Commission for Africa (#20554)
♦ UNECA/MULPOC / see ECA Office for North Africa (#05273)
♦ UNECA/SDRC-CA / see ECA Sub-Regional Office for Central Africa (#05274)
♦ UNECA/SDRC-EA / see ECA Sub-Regional Office for Eastern Africa (#05275)
♦ UNECA/SDRC-NA / see ECA Office for North Africa (#05273)

- ♦ UNECA/SDRC-SA / see ECA Subregional Office for Southern Africa (#05276)
- ♦ UNECA/SDRC-WA / see ECA Sub-Regional Office for West Africa (#05277)

♦ UNECA Staff Union 20293

Pres c/o ECA, PO Box 3001, Addis Ababa, Ethiopia. T. +25115550174 – +25115517200ext34634. Fax +25115515309.
URL: http://www.uneca.org/staff-union/

History to represent staff members of *United Nations Economic Commission for Africa (ECA, #20554)*. **Aims** Promote, defend and safeguard the *rights, privileges*, interests and welfare of all staff members of ECA, especially with regard to their terms and conditions of *employment*; ensure that staff-management relations are in conformity with the principles laid down in the UN Charter, the Universal Declaration of Human Rights, international *labour* norms and the UN Staff Rules and Regulations; contribute to promotion and achievement of the objectives of the UN Charter and development goals of the Organization and its member states; maintain working relations and cooperation with other staff unions or associations of the United Nations System with a view to promoting collective interest; promote a healthy and conducive work environment so as to enhance staff performance; promote good work practices and ethics among Union members to contribute to the achievement of the objectives of ECA. **Structure** General Meeting; Council; Executive Committee. **Languages** English. **Staff** 980.00 FTE, paid. Comprises staff in Ethiopia, Zambia, Morocco, Cameroon, Niger, Senegal and Rwanda. **Finance** Budget (annual): US$ 100,000. **Activities** Advocacy/lobbying/activism; events/meetings; research/documentation. **Members** All ECA staff with international staff worldwide. **IGO Relations** Member of: Staff-Management Coordination Committee (SMCC) of *United Nations (UN, #20515)*, which includes all presidents of UN staff unions and their management counterparts of UN offices around the world.
[2016/XE1764/v/**E**]

- ♦ UNECE / see United Nations Economic Commission for Europe (#20555)
- ♦ UNECE Committee on Environmental Policy / see Committee on Environmental Policy (#04253)

♦ UNECE Committee on Forests and the Forest Industry (COFFI) 20294

Contact Forestry and Timber Section, Forests-Land-Housing Div, Palais des Nations, 1211 Geneva 10, Switzerland. T. +41229171379. Fax +41229170041. E-mail: info.ece-faoforests@unece.org.
URL: http://www.unece.org/forests/

History Established 1947, Geneva (Switzerland), as a Sub-Committee of *United Nations Economic Commission for Europe (UNECE, #20555)*. Original title: *UNECE Timber Committee (TC)*. Also referred to as *Timber Committee*. **Aims** Strengthen the *forest* sector and its contribution to *sustainable development* throughout the UNECE region, through monitoring, analysis, capacity building and the provision of a forum for discussion, taking into account the changing policy environment, notably as regards to climate change and bioenergy. **Structure** *Joint FAO/ECE Working Party on Forest Economics and Statistics*; *Joint UNECE/FAO/ILO Expert Network on Implementing Sustainable Forest Management*. **Languages** English, French, Russian. **Staff** Serviced by joint UNECE/FAO Secretariat, based at UNECE Forests, Land and Housing Division: 7 FTE (UNECE) and 3.5 FTE (FAO). **Finance** Financed through UN regular budget: Economic Development for Europe – subprogramme 7 on timber and forestry. **Activities** Knowledge management/information dissemination; research/documentation; politics/policy/regulatory; guidance/assistance/consulting; networking/liaising; capacity building. **Events** *Session* San Marino (San Marino) 2023, *Session* Geneva (Switzerland) 2022, *Session* Rome (Italy) 2021, *Joint ECE/FAO Working Party on Forest Statistics, Economics and Management Session* Geneva (Switzerland) 2019, *European Forest Pedagogics Congress* Riga (Latvia) 2019. **Publications** *Geneva Timber and Forest Discussion Papers*; *Geneva Timber and Forest Study Papers*.
Members UNECE member countries (56).
Albania, Andorra, Armenia, Austria, Azerbaijan, Belarus, Belgium, Bosnia-Herzegovina, Bulgaria, Canada, Croatia, Cyprus, Czechia, Denmark, Estonia, Finland, France, Georgia, Germany, Greece, Hungary, Iceland, Ireland, Israel, Italy, Kazakhstan, Kyrgyzstan, Latvia, Liechtenstein, Lithuania, Luxembourg, Malta, Moldova, Monaco, Montenegro, Netherlands, North Macedonia, Norway, Poland, Portugal, Romania, Russia, San Marino, Serbia, Slovakia, Slovenia, Spain, Sweden, Switzerland, Tajikistan, Türkiye, Turkmenistan, UK, Ukraine, USA, Uzbekistan.
IGO Relations *European Forest Institute (EFI, #07297)* has Observer status. [2016.06.01/XE3248/t/**E***]

- ♦ UNECE Committee on Human Settlements / see Committee on Housing and Land Management (#04259)
- ♦ UNECE Committee on Sustainable Energy / see Committee on Sustainable Energy (#04288)
- ♦ UNECE Inland Transport Committee / see Committee on Inland Transport (#04262)
- ♦ UNECE Timber Committee / see UNECE Committee on Forests and the Forest Industry (#20294)
- ♦ **UNECE** United Nations Economic Commission for Europe (#20555)
- ♦ UNECOLAIT – Union européenne du commerce laitier (inactive)
- ♦ UnECS – Union européenne des experts-comptables stagiaires (inactive)
- ♦ UNECTES – Union européenne des conseillers techniques et scientifiques (inactive)
- ♦ **UNEDBAS** UNESCO Regional Office for Education in the Arab States (#20320)
- ♦ UNED-UK / see Stakeholder Forum for a Sustainable Future
- ♦ **UNeECC** University Network of the European Capitals of Culture (#20701)
- ♦ UNEFA – Union de Escuelas Familiares Agrarias (internationally oriented national body)
- ♦ UNEF – United Nations Emergency Force (inactive)
- ♦ UNEGA – Union européenne des fondeurs et fabricants de corps gras animaux (inactive)
- ♦ **UNEG** United Nations Evaluation Group (#20560)
- ♦ UN Environment / see UNEP (#20299)

♦ UN Environment Programme World Conservation Monitoring Centre (UNEP-WCMC) 20295

Centre de surveillance de la conservation mondiale de la nature

Address not obtained.
URL: https://www.unep-wcmc.org/

History 1 Jul 2000. Established through cooperation of *UNEP (#20299)*, *International Union for Conservation of Nature and Natural Resources (IUCN, #15766)* and the UK government. Originally founded by IUCN in 1979. Subsequently became an independent organization with a joint Board of IUCN, UNEP and *World Wide Fund for Nature (WWF, #21922)*. Former names and other names: *IUCN Conservation Monitoring Unit* – former (1979 to 1988); *World Conservation Monitoring Centre (WCMC)* – former (1988 to 2000); *Centre mondial de surveillance continue de la conservation* – former (1988 to 2000); *Centre for World Biodiversity Information and Assessment* – former (2000); *UN Environment WCMC* – former. **Aims** Provide authoritative information about biodiversity and ecosystem services in a way that is useful to decision makers who are driving change in environment and development policy. **Structure** Director; Deputy Director; CEO. **Languages** English, French, German, Italian, Persian, Portuguese, Russian, Spanish. **Staff** About 200 experts. **Finance** Support from *UNEP (#20299)*. Other resources through services. Projects supported by organizations and sponsorship. **Activities** Guidance/assistance/consulting; knowledge management/information dissemination. **Events** *International workshop on the 2010 biodiversity indicators and post-2010 indicator development* Reading (UK) 2009, *COHAB : international conference on health and biodiversity* Galway (Ireland) 2008, *Global diversity forum* Curitiba (Brazil) 2006, *COHAB : international conference on the importance of biodiversity to human health* Galway (Ireland) 2005, *2010 – the global biodiversity challenge* London (UK) 2003. **Publications** *Mountain Watch*; *WCMC Biodiversity Bulletin*. *WCMC Biodiversity Series*. *United Nations List of Protected Areas* – with IUCN; *World Atlas of Biodiversity*; *World Atlas of Coral Reefs*. Annual Report; project reports; atlases of ecosystems; books; papers; CD-ROMs. Information Services: /Services to International Agreements/: information service to over 20 international agreements (not specified). Data management service to *Convention on International Trade in Endangered Species of Wild Fauna and Flora (CITES, 1973)* and *Programme on Man and the Biosphere (MAB, #18526)* and *Convention Concerning the Protection of the World Cultural and Natural Heritage (World Heritage Convention, 1972)*; background reporting and assessment; analysis of achievements, gaps and priorities; information systems planning for Bonn Convention and CITES; assistance in developing clearinghouse mechanisms for *Convention on Biological Diversity (Biodiversity convention, 1992)*. Databases on: threatened species; wildlife trade; protected areas; arctic waterfowl. **Information Services** *Geographic Information System – GIS – Database on Critical Sites and Habitat* – particularly tropical forest wetlands, coral reefs and mangroves; *Multimedia Information Service* – includes access to databases, expert advice, map library, interactive mapping and downloading service via the Internet and customer service facility for WCMC users. **Members** Not a membership body. **IGO Relations** Observer status at: *Standing Committee to the Bern Convention on the Conservation of European Wildlife and Natural Habitats (#19949)*. Memorandum of Understanding or formal links with: *African-Eurasian Migratory /Water Bird/ Agreement (AEWA, 1995)*; *Convention on the Conservation of Migratory Species of Wild Animals (Bonn Convention, 1979)*; *Convention on Wetlands of International Importance Especially as Waterfowl Habitat (Convention on Wetlands, 1971)*; *Department for International Development (DFID, inactive)*; *International Bank for Reconstruction and Development (IBRD, #12317)*; *Bioversity International (#03262)*; *Permanent Secretariat to the Agreement on the Conservation of African-Eurasian Migratory Waterbirds (#18330)*. Participates in development and implementation of: *Action Plan for the Protection and Management of the South Asia Seas Region (SASP, #00094)*. Instrumental in setting up: *Pan-European Ecological Network (PEEN, see: #04881)*.
Project partners include:
- *Convention on the Conservation of European Wildlife and Natural Habitats (Bern convention, 1979)*;
- *European Commission (EC, #06633)*;
- *European Environment Agency (EEA, #06995)*;
- *FAO (#09260)*;
- *Global Environment Facility (GEF, #10346)*;
- *Plan Bleu pour l'environnement et le développement en Méditerranée (Plan Bleu, #18379)*;
- *Secretariat of the Convention on Biological Diversity (SCBD, #19197)*;
- *Secretariat of the Convention on International Trade in Endangered Species of Wild Fauna and Flora (CITES Secretariat, #19199)*;
- *Secretariat of the Convention of Wetlands (#19200)*;
- *UNESCO (#20322)*;
- *World Heritage Committee (#21567)*.

NGO Relations IUCN Publications Service; part of IUCN Species Survival Commission. Member of: *Biodiversity Indicators Partnership (BIP, #03242)*. Participates in: *Global Island Partnership (GLISPA, #10436)*; *Science Based Targets Network*. Instrumental in setting up: *Biodiversity and Economics for Conservation (BIOECON, #03240)*.
Memorandum of Understanding or formal links with:
- *Arctic Offshore Research Centre (no recent information)*; *Center for International Earth Science Information Network (CIESIN)*; *Conservation International (CI)*; *ECNC – European Centre for Nature Conservation (#05289)*; *EUROPARC Federation (#05768)*; *International Centre for Conservation Education (ICCE, inactive)*; *International Society for Mangrove Ecosystems (ISME, #15245)*; *WorldFish (#21507)*.

As of 1999, project partners include:
- *BirdLife International (#03266)*; *British Council*; *Center for International Forestry Research (CIFOR, #03646)*; *College of African Wildlife Management, Mweka (CAWM)*; *The Conservation Foundation, UK*; *Fauna & Flora International (FFI, #09277)*; *International Centre for Integrated Mountain Development (ICIMOD, #12500)*; *International Institute for Environment and Development (IIED, #13877)*; *International Union of Forest Research Organizations (IUFRO, #15774)*; *IUCN Species Survival Commission (SSC)*; *Raleigh International*; *United Nations Foundation (UNF, #20563)*; *Wetlands International (#20928)*; *World Commission on Protected Areas (WCPA / CMAP)*; *World Resources Institute (WRI, #21753)*. [2023/XE8372/**E***]

- ♦ UN Environment WCMC / see UN Environment Programme World Conservation Monitoring Centre (#20295)
- ♦ UNEPA / see Union of European Practitioners in Intellectual Property (#20392)
- ♦ UNEP Caribbean Environment Programme / see Caribbean Action Plan (#03432)
- ♦ UNEP/CMS Dugong MoU – Memorandum of Understanding on the Conservation and Management of Dugongs – Dugong Dugon – and Their Habitats Throughout Their Range (2007 treaty)
- ♦ **UNEP/CMS** Secretariat of the Convention on the Conservation of Migratory Species of Wild Animals (#19198)
- ♦ UNEP/CMS Trust Fund – Trust Fund for the Convention on the Conservation of Migratory Species of Wild Animals (see: #20299)
- ♦ UNEP Collaborating Centre on Energy and Environment / see UNEP Copenhagen Climate Centre (#20296)

♦ UNEP Copenhagen Climate Centre 20296

Dir Marmorvej 51, 2100 Copenhagen Ø, Denmark. T. +4545335250.
Communications Officer address not obtained.
URL: http://www.unepdtu.org/

History 1 Oct 1990, Røskilde (Denmark). Founded based on an agreement between *UNEP (#20299)*, Technical University of Denmark and Danish Ministry of Foreign Affairs. Former names and other names: *UNEP Collaborating Centre on Energy and Environment (UCCEE)* – former; *UNEP Risø Centre on Energy, Climate and Sustainable Development (URC)* – former; *UNEP DTU Partnership* – former. **Aims** Facilitate a shift towards cleaner and more efficient *energy* systems; support more climate resilient *sustainable* development, mainly in *developing countries*, by providing internationally leading research, policy analysis and *capacity building*. **Structure** Management and Policy Committee; Scientific Advisory Committee. Centres (2): Centre on Energy, Climate and Sustainable Development; Copenhagen Centre on Energy Efficiency. **Languages** English. **Staff** 48.00 FTE, paid. **Finance** Funded jointly by: UNEP; *DANIDA*; Technical University of Denmark. **Activities** Research/documentation; capacity building; awareness raising; training/education. **Events** *Latin American carbon forum* Quito (Ecuador) 2006, *European photovoltaic solar energy conference* Paris (France) 2004, *Towards sustainable product design international conference* Brussels (Belgium) 1999, *African regional workshop on ozone depletion and management of ODS phase-out in small and medium enterprises* Pretoria (South Africa) 1997, *Regional symposium on energy and environment* Manila (Philippines) 1992. **Publications** *E+ Energy, Climate and Sustainable Development* – newsletter. Project newsletters; guidebooks; reports; summaries; working papers; academic publications. **Members** Not a membership body. **IGO Relations** Collaborates with: *United Nations Framework Convention on Climate Change – Secretariat (UNFCCC, #20564)*; *Global Environment Facility (GEF, #10346)*; *International Bank for Reconstruction and Development (IBRD, #12317)*; *Latin American Energy Organization (#16313)*; *UNCTAD (#20285)*; *UNDP (#20292)*; *United Nations Institute for Training and Research (UNITAR, #20576)*. **NGO Relations** Collaborates with a large number of organizations worldwide, including: *AFREPREN/FWD (#00153)*; *Asian Institute of Technology (AIT, #01519)*; *International Research Centre on Environment and Development (CIRED)*. Represented in: *Bariloche Foundation (FB)*; *Environnement et développement du Tiers-monde (enda, #05510)*; *Energy and Resources Institute (TERI)*. Member of: *United Nations Foundation (UNF, #20563)*. Participates in: *Global Center on Adaptation (GCA)*. [2022/XE0678/**E**]

- ♦ UNEP DTIE Chemicals Branch (inactive)
- ♦ UNEP DTU Partnership / see UNEP Copenhagen Climate Centre (#20296)
- ♦ UNEP Environment Fund (see: #20299)

♦ UNEP/EUROBATS Secretariat 20297

Secretariat United Nations Campus, Platz der Vereinten Nationen 1, 53113 Bonn, Germany. T. +492288152420. Fax +492288152445. E-mail: eurobats@eurobats.org.
URL: http://www.eurobats.org/

History Agreement on the Conservation of Populations of European Bats came into force in 1994. Secretariat was established1995 by the First Session of the Meeting of Parties of *Agreement on the Conservation of Populations of European Bats (EUROBATS, 1991)*. Became operational in 1996, Bonn (Germany). **Aims** Act as a point for information exchange and coordinate international research and monitoring initiatives; arrange Meetings of the Parties and meetings of the Standing Committee and the Advisory Committee; stimulate proposals for improving effectiveness of the Agreement and attract more countries to participate in and join the Agreement; stimulate public awareness of the threats to *bat* populations in Europe, northern Africa and the Middle East; support activities at all levels to prevent their numbers dwindling further. **Structure** Meeting of the Parties (every 4 years); Standing Committee; Advisory Committee; Secretariat. **Languages** English. **Staff** 2.50 FTE, paid. **Finance** Financed by a Trust Fund, consisting of annual contributions of the Parties to EUROBATS, as well as voluntary contributions. Annual budget: 500,251 EUR (2022). **Activities** Events/meetings. Active in: Europe; Northern Africa; Middle East. **Events** *Meeting of the Parties* Brioni (Croatia) 2022, *Meeting of the Parties* Monte Carlo (Monaco) 2018, *Meeting of the Parties* Brussels (Belgium) 2014, *Meeting of the Parties* Prague (Czech Rep) 2010, *Meeting of the Parties* Ljubljana (Slovenia) 2006. **Publications** *EUROBATS Implementation Guide*. Publication series; leaflets.
Members Parties to the EUROBATS Agreement (38):
Albania, Belgium, Bosnia-Herzegovina, Bulgaria, Croatia, Cyprus, Czechia, Denmark, Estonia, Finland, France, Georgia, Germany, Hungary, Ireland, Israel, Italy, Latvia, Lithuania, Luxembourg, Malta, Moldova, Monaco, Montenegro, Netherlands, North Macedonia, Norway, Poland, Portugal, Romania, San Marino, Serbia, Slovakia, Slovenia, Sweden, Switzerland, UK, Ukraine. [2022.10.19/XE3687/**E***]

♦ **UNEP FI** United Nations Environment Programme Finance Initiative (#20559)
♦ UNEP/GRID / see Global Resource Information Database (#10578)
♦ **UNEP-IEMP** UNEP-International Ecosystem Management Partnership (#20298)
♦ UNEP/IETC / see International Environmental Technology Centre (#13282)

♦ UNEP-International Ecosystem Management Partnership (UNEP-IEMP) 20298

Dir c/o Inst of Geographic Sciences and Natural Resources Research, No 11A Datun Road, 10010 Beijing, China.
URL: http://unep-iemp.org/

History 2011. **Aims** Provide science, policy, and capacity support to developing countries to integrate ecosystem management approaches into national policies and development plans to enhance the delivery of ecosystem services for human well-being. **Structure** Steering Committee; Science Advisory Group; Director; Programme Coordination Group; Senior Advisors. **Languages** Chinese, English. **Staff** 11.00 FTE, paid. **Finance** Mainly financed through projects and programmes. Annual budget: Chinese Renminbi over 3,000,000. **Activities** Capacity building; research/documentation; events/meetings. **Publications** *UNEP-IEMP Quarterly Bulletin*. Annual Report. **IGO Relations** Partner of: *UNEP (#20299)*. [2018.06.20/XM6657/**E**]

♦ UN/EPOC – UNESCAP Pacific Operations Centre (see: #20557)
♦ UNEP Regional Seas Programme / see Regional Seas Programme (#18814)
♦ UNEP Risø Centre on Energy, Climate and Sustainable Development / see UNEP Copenhagen Climate Centre (#20296)
♦ UNEPSA / see European Paediatric Association (#08124)
♦ UNEP-UK / see Stakeholder Forum for a Sustainable Future

♦ UNEP – United Nations Environment Programme 20299

Programme des Nations Unies pour l'environnement (PNUE) – Programa de las Naciones Unidas para el Medio Ambiente (PNUMA)

Exec Dir United Nations Avenue, Gigiri, PO Box 30552, Nairobi, 00100, Kenya. E-mail: executiveoffice@unep.org – unenvironment-executiveoffice@un.org.
URL: https://www.unep.org/

History 15 Dec 1972. Established by General Assembly resolution 2997 (XXVII), in response to the report of the Secretary-General on the United Nations Conference on the Human Environment, 5-16 Jun 1972, Stockholm (Sweden). In operation by Jan 1973, working out of temporary headquarters first in Geneva (Switzerland) and then in Nairobi (Kenya). Restructured following approval by special session of Governing Council, May 1998. An organ of *United Nations (UN, #20515)* within the *United Nations System (#20635)*. Former names and other names: *UN Environment* – alias. **Aims** Provide *leadership* and encourage *partnership* in caring for the environment by inspiring, informing and enabling nations and peoples to improve their quality of life without compromising that of future generations.

Structure United Nations Environment Assembly (UNEA), meets every 2 years, and reports to UN General Assembly through *ECOSOC (#05331)*, and comprising all 193 UN Member States. Committee of Permanent Representatives (CPR), serves as subsidiary inter-sessional body, consisting of accredited Permanent Representatives. UNEA is led by President and a Bureau.

Executive Office, based at *United Nations Office at Nairobi (UNON, #20600)*, set up May 1998, comprising Executive Director, Deputy Executive Director and Chief of Staff. Also reporting to Executive Office: New York Office/Secretariat of the Environment Management Group; Governance Affairs Office/Secretariat of Governing Bodies; Chief Scientist; Evaluation Office; Regional Presence; Divisions (7). Also hosts several convention secretariats.

Divisions (7): Communication; Corporate Services; Economy; Ecosystems; Governance Affairs Office; Law; Policy and Programme; Science.

Regional Presence: Africa Office in Nairobi (Kenya), includes West Africa Sub-regional Office, South Africa Country Office and Addis Ababa Liaison Office; Asia and the Pacific Office in Bangkok (Thailand), includes Pacific Sub-regional Office, China Country Office and India Office; Europe Office in Geneva (Switzerland), includes Central Asia Sub-regional Office, Russian Federation Country Office, Brussels Liaison Office and Vienna Programme Office; Latin America and the Caribbean Office in Panama (Panama), includes Caribbean Sub-regional Office, Southern Cone Sub-regional Office, Brazil Country Office and Mexico Country Office; West Asia Office in Manama (Bahrain).

Partners:
– *Basel Agency for Sustainable Energy (BASE)*;
– BCA Centre for Sustainable Buildings (CSB);
– *Environmental Management Group (EMG, #05506)*;
– Frankfurt School of Finance and Management;
– Global Efficient Lighting Centre (GELC);
– *Global Reporting Initiative (GRI, #10567)*;
– *Global Resource Information Database (GRID, #10578)*;
– *Global Environment Facility (GEF, #10346)*;
– UN Environment Collaborating Centre on Water and Environment (UCC-Water);
– *UNEP Copenhagen Climate Centre (#20296)*;
– *UN Environment Programme World Conservation Monitoring Centre (UNEP-WCMC, #20295)*;
– *UNEP-International Ecosystem Management Partnership (UNEP-IEMP, #20298)*;
– *United Nations Scientific Committee on the Effects of Atomic Radiation (UNSCEAR, #20624)*.

Languages Arabic, Chinese, English, French, Russian, Spanish. **Staff** 1144.00 FTE, paid. Personnel negotiations through *UNEP Staff Association (no recent information)*. **Finance** Sources: Regular budget of the United Nations; *UNEP Environment Fund (see: #20299)*, also referred to as *'Environment Fund'*; trust funds; earmarked contributions; Global Environment Fund.

Activities Advocacy/lobbying/activism; awards/prizes/competitions; knowledge management/information dissemination; monitoring/evaluation; networking/liaising; politics/policy/regulatory; research/documentation; training/education. Hosts secretariats of multilateral environment agreements and research bodies:
– *Secretariat for the Vienna Convention for the Protection of the Ozone Layer and the Montreal Protocol on Substances that Deplete the Ozone Layer (Ozone Secretariat, #19209)*;
– Secretariat for the *Convention on the Ban of the Import of Hazardous Wastes into Africa and on the Control of Their Transboundary Movements within Africa (Bamako Convention, 1991)*;
– *Secretariat of the Basel Convention (SBC, #19196)*;
– Interim Secretariat of *Convention on the Protection and Sustainable Development of the Carpathians (Carpathian convention, 2003)*;
– *Secretariat of the Convention on Biological Diversity (SCBD, #19197)*;
– *Secretariat of the Convention on International Trade in Endangered Species of Wild Fauna and Flora (CITES Secretariat, #19199)*;
– *Secretariat of the Convention on the Conservation of Migratory Species of Wild Animals (UNEP/CMS, #19198)*;
– Secretariat of the *Minamata Convention on Mercury (2013)*;
– *Multilateral Fund for the Implementation of the Montreal Protocol (#16885)*;
– *Secretariat of the Rotterdam Convention (#19206)*;
– *Secretariat of the Stockholm Convention on Persistent Organic Pollutants (Secretariat of the Stockholm Convention, #19207)*;
– Secretariat of *Framework Convention for the Protection of the Marine Environment of the Caspian Sea (Tehran Convention, 2003)*;
– Caribbean Regional Coordinating Unit / *Convention for the Protection and Development of the Marine Environment of the Wider Caribbean Region (Cartagena Convention, 1983)*;
– *Coordinating Body on the Seas of East Asia (COBSEA, #04814)* Secretariat;
– Eastern African Regional Coordinating Unit / *Convention for the Protection, Management and Development of the Marine and Coastal Environment of the Eastern African Region (Nairobi Convention, 1985)*;
– *Mediterranean Action Plan (MAP, #16638) / Convention for the Protection of the Marine Environment and the Coastal Region of the Mediterranean (Barcelona Convention, 1976)*.
– *Action Plan for Protection, Development and Management of the Marine Environment of the Northwest Pacific Region (NOWPAP, #00092)* / Regional Coordinating Unit;
– *West and Central African Action Plan (WACAF, no recent information) / Convention for Cooperation in the Protection and Development of the Marine and Coastal Environment of the West and Central African Region (Abidjan convention, 1981)*.

Work is categorized into thematic areas (7): Climate change; Disasters and conflicts; Ecosystem management; Environmental governance; Chemicals and waste; Resource efficiency; Environment under review. Subdivided into 20 topics through which programmes and projects are organized:
– *'Air'*, includes *Climate and Clean Air Coalition (CCAC, #04010)*;
– *'Biosafety'*, includes *Cartagena Protocol on Biosafety (2000)*;
– *'Chemicals and waste'*, include *Strategic Approach to International Chemicals Management (SAICM, #20005)*;
– *'Climate change'*, includes CCAC and *Climate Technology Centre and Network (CTCN, #04023)*;
– *'Disasters and conflicts'*;
– *'Ecosystems'*;
– *'Education and training'*;
– *'Energy'*, includes *Sustainable Energy for All (SEforALL, #20056)* and *Global Alliance for Buildings and Construction (GlobalABC, #10187)*;
– *'Environment under review'*;
– *'Environmental governance'*;
– *'Extractives'*;
– *'Forests'*, include *United Nations Collaborative Programme on Reducing Emissions from Deforestation and Forest Degradation in Developing Countries (UN-REDD Programme, #20528)* and *Global Peatlands Initiative*;
– *'Gender'*;
– *'Green Economy'*, includes *Green Growth Knowledge Platform (GGKP, #10719)*;
– *'Oceans and seas'*, include Global Programme of Action and *Regional Seas Programme (#18814)*.

Of the 18 Regional Seas programmes, 7 are administered by UN Environment: *Caribbean Action Plan (CAR, #03432)*; *Action Plan for the Protection and Development of the Marine Environment and Coastal Areas of the East Asian Region (EAS, #00093)*; *Eastern African Action Plan (EAF, no recent information)*; Mediterranean Action Plan; North-West Pacific Region; Western Africa Region; *Caspian Environment Programme (CEP, #03596)*. Non-UN Environment administered (7): *Black Sea Action Plan (BSAP, no recent information)*; *Plan of Action for Cooperation in the Protection and Sustainable Development of the Marine and Coastal Environment of the Northeast Pacific (no recent information)*; *Regional Organization for the Conservation of the Environment of the Red Sea and Gulf of Aden (PERSGA, #18804)*; *Kuwait Action Plan (KAP, no recent information)* / ROPME Sea Area; *Action Plan for the Protection and Management of the South Asia Seas Region (SASP, #00094)*; *Action Plan for the Protection of the Marine Environment and Coastal Areas in the South East Pacific (SE/PCF, #00095)*. Independent programmes (4): Arctic Region; Antarctic Region; Baltic Sea; North-East Atlantic Region.
– *'Resource efficiency'*, includes *Life Cycle Initiative (LCI, #16464)*;
– *'Sustainable Development Goals'*;
– *'Technology'*, includes Climate Technology Centre and Network, Climate and Clean Air Coalition, *International Environmental Technology Centre (IETC, #13282)* and Global Alliance for Buildings and Construction;
– *'Transport'*, includes *Partnership for Clean Fuels and Vehicles (PCFV, #18231)* and *Global Fuel Economy Initiative (GFEI, #10381)*;
– *'Water'*, includes *Global Programme of Action for the Protection of the Marine Environment from Land-Based Activities (GPA, see: #20299)* and *GEMS/Water (see: #20299)*.

Agreements concluded under UN Environment auspices and not mentioned above:
– *Phyto-sanitary Convention for Africa (1967)*;
– *Convention on Wetlands of International Importance Especially as Waterfowl Habitat (Convention on Wetlands, 1971)*;
– *Convention Concerning the Protection of the World Cultural and Natural Heritage (World Heritage Convention, 1972)*;
– *Convention on International Trade in Endangered Species of Wild Fauna and Flora (CITES, 1973)*;
– *Protocol Concerning Cooperation in Combating Pollution of the Mediterranean Sea by Oil and other Harmful Substances in Cases of Emergency (1976)*;
– *Protocol for the Prevention of Pollution of the Mediterranean Sea by Dumping from Ships and Aircraft (Dumping Protocol, 1976)*;
– *Convention on the Conservation of Migratory Species of Wild Animals (Bonn Convention, 1979)*;
– *Convention on the Conservation of Antarctic Marine Living Resources (CCAMLR, 1980)*;
– *International Tropical Timber Agreement, 1983 (ITTA, 1983)*;
– *Protocol Amending the International Convention for the Conservation of Atlantic Tunas, 1984 (1984)*;
– *Vienna Convention for the Protection of the Ozone Layer (Ozone treaty, 1985)*;
– *Montreal Protocol on Substances that Deplete the Ozone Layer (1987)*;
– *Basel Convention on the Control of Transboundary Movements of Hazardous Wastes and Their Disposal (UNCRTD, 1989)*;
– *Convention for the Prohibition of Fishing with Long Driftnets in the South Pacific (1989)*;
– *Protocol Amending the Convention for the Prevention of Marine Pollution by Dumping from Ships and Aircraft (1983)*;
– *Amendment to the Montreal Protocol on Substances That Deplete the Ozone Layer, 1990 (London amendment, 1990)*;
– *Protocol I to the Convention for the Prohibition of Fishing with Long Driftnets in the South Pacific (1990)*;
– *Protocol II to the Convention for the Prohibition of Fishing with Long Driftnets in the South Pacific (1990)*;
– *Agreement on the Conservation of Small Cetaceans of the Baltic, North East Atlantic, Irish and North Seas (ASCOBANS, 1992)*;
– *Convention on the Ban of the Import of Hazardous Wastes into Africa and on the Control of Their Transboundary Movements within Africa (Bamako Convention, 1991)*;
– *Convention for the Protection of the Alps (Alpine convention, 1991)*;
– *Amendment to the Montreal Protocol on Substances That Deplete the Ozone Layer, 1992 (Copenhagen amendment, 1992)*;
– *Convention on Biological Diversity (Biodiversity convention, 1992)*;
– *Convention for the Conservation of the Biodiversity and the Protection of Wilderness Areas in Central America (1992)*;
– *Convention on the Protection of the Marine Environment of the Baltic Sea Area, 1992 (Helsinki Convention, 1992, 1992)*;
– *Convention for the Protection on the Marine Environment for the North-East Atlantic (OSPAR Convention, 1992)*;
– *Protocol Amending the International Convention for the Conservation of Atlantic Tunas, 1992 (1992)*;
– *Protocol to the International Convention on Civil Liability for Oil Pollution Damage, 1992 (1992)*;
– *Agreement to Promote Compliance with the International Conservation and Management Measures by Fishing Vessels on the High Seas (1993)*;
– *Convention on Civil Liability for Damage Resulting from Activities Dangerous to the Environment (1993)*;
– *Convention for the Conservation of Southern Bluefin Tuna (1993)*;
– *Convention on the Prevention of Major Industrial Accidents (1993)*;
– *Torremolinos Protocol of 1993 Relating to the Torremolinos International Convention for the SAfety of Fishing Vessels (SFV PROT 1993, 1993)*;
– *Agreement on Cooperative Enforcement Operations Directed at Illegal Trade in Wild Fauna and Flora (1994)*;
– *Convention on Nuclear Safety (1994)*;
– *Protocol for the Protection of the Mediterranean Sea Against Pollution Resulting from Exploration and Exploitation of the Continental Shelf and the Seabed and its Subsoil (1994)*;
– *United Nations Convention to Combat Desertification (UNCCD, 1994)*;
– *African-Eurasian Migratory /Water Bird/ Agreement (AEWA, 1995)*;
– *Amendments to the Convention for the Protection of the Mediterranean Sea Against Pollution (1995)*;
– *Amendments to the Protocol for the Prevention of Pollution of the Mediterranean Sea by Dumping from Ships and Aircraft (1995)*;
– *Protocol Concerning Specially Protected Areas and Biological Diversity in the Mediterranean (Barcelona protocol, 1995)*;
– *Agreement on the Conservation of Cetaceans of the Black Sea, Mediterranean Sea and contiguous Atlantic Area (ACCOBAMS, 1996)*;
– *Protocol on the Prevention of Pollution of the Mediterranean Sea by Transboundary Movements of Hazardous Wastes and Their Disposal (1996)*;
– *Amendments to the Protocol for the Protection of the Mediterranean Sea Against Pollution from Land-based Sources and Activities (1996)*;
– *Rotterdam Convention on the Prior Informed Consent Procedure for Certain Hazardous Chemicals and Pesticides in International Trade (Rotterdam convention, 1998)*;
– *Convention on the Protection of the Marine Environment of the Baltic Sea Area, 1999 (Helsinki Convention, 1999, 1999)*;
– *Protocol on the Prevention, Reduction and Control of Land-based Sources and Activities (1999)*;
– *Stockholm Convention on Persistent Organic Pollutants (POP treaty, 2001)*;
– *Framework Convention for the Protection of the Marine Environment of the Caspian Sea (Tehran Convention, 2003)*.

Events *IMDC: International Marine Debris Conference* Busan (Korea Rep) 2022, *Stockholm+50* Stockholm (Sweden) 2022, *Asia Pacific Clean Air Partnership Joint Forum* Suwon (Korea Rep) 2022, *International Conference on Environmental Peacebuilding* Switzerland 2022, *Forum of Ministers and Environment Authorities of Asia and the Paicfic* Suwon (Korea Rep) 2021. **Publications** *Our Planet* – flagship magazine. *Emissions Gap Report 2018*; *Global Environment Outlook*. Annual Report; books; guides; guidelines; atlases; reports; procededings. Information Services: Maintains *Information Unit for Conventions /Environmental/ (IUC, inactive)*. **Information Services** *Environment Live*; *Industry and Environment Database*; *Knowledge Repository*; *Open Data Portal*; *UNEPNet Information System*. **Members** All 193 UN Member States.

IGO Relations Links with other UN agencies and related programmes through: *United Nations System Chief Executives Board for Coordination (CEB, #20636)*. Observer to: *International Council for the Exploration of the Sea (ICES, #13021)*; *Sistema Económico Latinoamericano (SELA, #19294)*; *Standing Committee to the Bern Convention on the Conservation of European Wildlife and Natural Habitats (#19949)*; *World Trade Organization (WTO, #21864)*. Participates in: *Inter-Organization Programme for the Sound Management of Chemicals (IOMC, #15956)*. Member of: *Baltic 21 (inactive)*; *Collaborative Partnership on Forests (CPF, #04100)*; *United Nations Sustainable Development Group (UNSDG, #20634)*; *UN-OCEANS (#20711)*; *UN-Water (#20723)*. Programme partners: *Protection of the Arctic Marine Environment (PAME, #18547)* and its *Regional Programme of Action for the Protection of the Arctic Marine Environment from Land-based Activities (RPA, #18806)*; *Baltic Marine Environment Protection Commission – Helsinki Commission (HELCOM, #03126)*; *Commission for the Conservation of Antarctic Marine Living Resources (CCAMLR, #04206)*; *OSPAR Commission for the Protection of the Marine Environment of the North-East Atlantic (OSPAR Commission,*

#17905). Accredited organizations: *Centre for Science and Technology of the Non-Aligned and Other Developing Countries (NAM S and T Centre, #03784); Global Biodiversity Information Facility (GBIF, #10250); Regional Environmental Centre for the Caucasus (REC Caucasus, #18781); Pacific Islands Forum Secretariat (#17970); Regions of Climate Action (R20, #18820).*
Close cooperation with: *International Agency for Research on Cancer (IARC, #11598); Programme on Man and the Biosphere (MAB, #18526); United Nations Human Settlements Programme (UN-Habitat, #20572); United Nations Office for the Coordination of Humanitarian Affairs (OCHA, #20593).* Has been represented in meetings of: *Round Table on Sustainable Development at the OECD (see: #17693).* Special links with: *Global Action Plan for Environment and Development in the 21st Century (Agenda 21, inactive).* Provides Secretariat for: *African Ministerial Conference on the Environment (AMCEN, #00374).* Administers: *Regional Trust Fund for the Implementation of the Action Plan for the Caribbean Environment Programme (see: #20299); Trust Fund for the Convention on the Conservation of Migratory Species of Wild Animals (UNEP/CMS Trust Fund, see: #20299).* Cooperation agreement with: *Global Learning and Observations to Benefit the Environment (GLOBE); Islamic World Educational, Scientific and Cultural Organization (ICESCO, #16058).* Close links with: *Caribbean Environment Programme (CEP, #03497).* Instrumental in setting up: *Regional Organization for the Protection of the Marine Environment (ROPME, #18805); United Nations Habitat and Human Settlements Foundation (UNHHSF, inactive)*, currently incorporated into HABITAT.
NGO Relations Representatives of Major Groups and Stakeholders, having an interest in the environment are invited to lend their full support and collaboration with a view to achieving the largest possible degree of cooperation. Un Environment's rules of procedure allow Major Groups and Stakeholders to designate representatives to sit as observers at public meetings of the UNEA and CPR, and, by invitation, to make oral statements; and it draws on their expertise in planning and implementing programmes and projects and maintains links with NGOs worldwide through nongovernmental networks. Accredited NGOs (609) include the following organizations listed in this Yearbook:
- *Academic Council on the United Nations System (ACUNS, #00020);*
- *ACT Alliance (#00081);*
- *Action Group on Erosion, Technology and Concentration (ETC Group, #00091);*
- *ActionAid (#00087);*
- *Association des états généraux des étudiants de l'Europe (AEGEE-Europe, #02495);*
- *Africa Network for Animal Welfare (ANAW, #00301);*
- *Réseau pour la Qualité de l'Environnement en Afrique Sub-Saharienne (AFRICACLEAN);*
- *African Biodiversity Network (ABN, #00222);*
- *African Centre for Technology Studies (ACTS, #00243);*
- *African Council for Communication Education (ACCE, #00273);*
- *African Council of Religious Leaders – Religions for Peace (ACRL-RfP, #00276);*
- *African Forest Forum (AFF, #00318);*
- *FARMAPU-INTER and CECOTRAP-RCOGL;*
- *African Network of Young Leaders for Peace and Sustainable Development (ANYL4PSD, #00399);*
- *African Population and Health Research Center (APHRC, #00420);*
- *Institut africain de gestion urbaine (IAGU);*
- *African Wildlife Foundation (AWF, #00498);*
- *ACORD – Agency for Cooperation and Research in Development (#00073);*
- *All Africa Conference of Churches (AACC, #00640);*
- *Amnesty International (AI, #00801);*
- *Anglican Consultative Council (ACC, #00828);*
- *Arab Forum for Environment and Development (AFED, #00960);*
- *Arab Group for the Protection of Nature (APN, #00970);*
- *Arab Office for Youth and Environment (AOYE);*
- *Asia Indigenous Peoples Pact (AIPP, #01282);*
- *Asian Environmental Society (AES, #01438);*
- *Association Africa 21 (Africa 21);*
- *Association of African Women for Research and Development (AAWORD, #02362);*
- *Atlantic States Legal Foundation (ASLF);*
- *Baha'i International Community (#03062);*
- *Bellona Europa;*
- *Biosphere Expeditions (#03260);*
- *Stiftung für Ökologische Entwicklung (Biovision);*
- *BirdLife International (#03266);*
- *Brahma Kumaris World Spiritual University (BKWSU, #03311);*
- *Brighter Green;*
- *Buddhist Tzu Chi Foundation (#03347);*
- *Caribbean Natural Resources Institute (CANARI, #03525);*
- *Caribbean Network for Integrated Rural Development (CNIRD, #03528);*
- *Caribbean Policy Development Centre (CPDC, #03540);*
- *Carmelite NGO (#03583);*
- *Carnegie Council for Ethics in International Affairs (CCEIA);*
- *Catholic Youth Network for Environmental Sustainability in Africa (CYNESA, #03611);*
- *Caucasus Environmental NGO Network (CENN, #03613);*
- *CDP (#03621);*
- *Center for International Environmental Law (CIEL);*
- *Center for Oceanic Awareness, Research and Education (COARE);*
- *CEEweb for Biodiversity (#03626);*
- *Central European University (CEU, #03717);*
- *Centre for International Governance Innovation (CIGI);*
- *International Centre of Comparative Environmental Law (#12483);*
- *Children and Youth International (CYI, #03882);*
- *Clean Air Asia (#03983);*
- *Clean Up the World (CUW, #03992);*
- *Climate Action Network (CAN, #03999);*
- *Climate Alliance (#04005);*
- *Common Seas;*
- *Compassion in World Farming (CIWF, #04414);*
- *Conservation International (CI);*
- *Conserve Africa Foundation;*
- *Consumer Unity and Trust Society (CUTS);*
- *Consumers International (CI, #04773);*
- *Coordinadora de las Organizaciones Indígenas de la Cuenca Amazónica (COICA, #04811);*
- *Coordinating Board of Jewish Organizations (CBJO, #04813);*
- *CropLife International (#04966);*
- *Cruelty Free International;*
- *Defensores do Planeta;*
- *Dominicans for Justice and Peace (OP, #05113);*
- *Earth Charter International (ECI, #05161);*
- *Earth Council Alliance (ECA, inactive);*
- *Earth Day Network (EDN, #05164);*
- *Earth Island Institute (EII);*
- *EARTH University (#05170);*
- *EarthAction (EA, #05159);*
- *EarthCare Africa (ECAF);*
- *Earthcorps;*
- *Eastern Africa Environmental Network (EAEN, #05221);*
- *Global Society for Ecology and Sound Economy (ECO2TERRA International);*
- *El Taller International (#20091);*
- *Ellen MacArthur Foundation;*
- *Embajada Mundial de Activistas por la Paz (EMAP);*
- *Foundation for Woodstove Dissemination (FWD, inactive);*
- *Environment Liaison Centre International (ELCI, no recent information);*
- *Environmental Ambassadors for Sustainable Development (Environmental Ambassadors);*
- *Environmental Defense Fund (EDF);*
- *Environmental Investigation Agency (EIA);*
- *Environmental Law Institute (ELI);*
- *European Citizen Science Association (ECSA, #06557);*
- *European Environmental Bureau (EEB, #06996);*
- *The European Law Students' Association (ELSA, #07660);*
- *WindEurope (#20965);*
- *Ev-K2-CNR Committee (#16175);*
- *Fauna & Flora International (FFI, #09277);*
- *Fight Against Desert Encroachment (FADE);*
- *Food Industry Asia (FIA);*
- *Forest Peoples Programme (FPP, #09865);*
- *Forest Stewardship Council (FSC, #09869);*
- *Foundation for Environmental Education (FEE, #09949);*
- *Friedrich-Ebert-Stiftung (FES);*
- *Friends of the Earth International (FoEI, #10002);*
- *Future Earth (#10048);*
- *Future Forest;*
- *Gallifrey Foundation;*
- *Gender and Water Alliance (GWA, #10102);*
- *Global Alliance for Incinerator Alternatives (GAIA, #10203);*
- *Global Dairy Platform (GDP, #10314);*
- *Global Ecovillage Network (GEN, #10331);*
- *Global Energy Interconnection Development and Cooperation Organization (GEIDCO, #10342);*
- *Global Environment Centre (GEC);*
- *Global Farmer Network (GFN, #10354);*
- *Global Footprint Network (#10367);*
- *Global Forest Coalition (GFC, #10368);*
- *Global Foundation for Democracy and Development (GFDD);*
- *Global Organization of Parliamentarians Against Corruption (GOPAC, #10518);*
- *Global Voices;*
- *Global Wind Energy Council (GWEC, #10656);*
- *Global One;*
- *Globetree Foundation;*
- *Green Africa Foundation;*
- *Greenpeace International (#10727);*
- *GRID-Arendal;*
- *GERES;*
- *Gulf Research Centre;*
- *Hanns Seidel Foundation;*
- *Hazardous Waste Europe (HWE);*
- *Health and Environment Alliance (HEAL, #10879);*
- *Health of Mother Earth Foundation (HOMEF);*
- *HEART International (no recent information);*
- *Heifer International;*
- *Heinrich Böll Foundation;*
- *Horn of Africa Voluntary Youth Committee (HAVOYOCO);*
- *IBON International (#11037);*
- *Indigenous Peoples of Africa Coordinating Committee (IPACC, #11163);*
- *Information Africa;*
- *Institute for European Environmental Policy (IEEP, #11261);*
- *Institute for Governance and Sustainable Development (IGSD);*
- *Institute of Development Studies, Brighton (IDS);*
- *Institute for Global Environmental Strategies (IGES, #11266);*
- *Institute for Planetary Synthesis (IPS, #11287);*
- *International Academy of Oral Medicine and Toxicology (IAOMT);*
- *International Alliance of the Indigenous Tribal Peoples of the Tropical Forests (IAITPTF, #11629);*
- *International Association of Ports and Harbors (IAPH, #12096);*
- *International Association of Public Transport (#12118);*
- *International Association of Students in Agricultural and Related Sciences (IAAS, #12191);*
- *International Centre for Environmental Social and Policy Studies (ICESPS);*
- *World Agroforestry Centre (ICRAF, #21072);*
- *International Centre for Trade and Sustainable Development, Geneva (ICTSD, #12524);*
- *International Centre for Environmental Education and Community Development (ICENECDEV);*
- *International Chamber of Commerce (ICC, #12534);*
- *International Christian Embassy Jerusalem (ICEJ, #12560);*
- *International Committee of the Red Cross (ICRC, #12799);*
- *The ICCF Group (#11045);*
- *Local Governments for Sustainability (ICLEI, #16507);*
- *International Council of Chemical Associations (ICCA, #13003);*
- *International Council of Environmental Law (ICEL, #13018);*
- *International Council of Voluntary Agencies (ICVA, #13092);*
- *International Council of Women (ICW, #13093);*
- *International Council on Mining and Metals (ICMM, #13048);*
- *International Dairy Federation (IDF, #13128);*
- *International Dialogue for Environmental Action (IDEA);*
- *International Environmental Law Research Centre (IELRC);*
- *International Eurasia-Press Fund (IEPF, #13309);*
- *International Federation for Housing and Planning (IFHP, #13450);*
- *Fédération internationale des associations de transitaires et assimilés (FIATA, #09610);*
- *IFOAM – Organics International (IFOAM, #11105);*
- *International Federation of Red Cross and Red Crescent Societies (#13526);*
- *International Federation of Surveyors (FIG, #13561);*
- *International Federation of Women Lawyers (FIDA, #13578);*
- *International Fertilizer Association (IFA, #13589);*
- *International Forestry Students' Association (IFSA, #13628);*
- *International Fund for Animal Welfare (IFAW, #13693);*
- *International Association 'Znanie';*
- *International Hydropower Association (IHA, #13828);*
- *International Institute for Applied Systems Analysis (IIASA, #13861);*
- *International Institute for Environment and Development (IIED, #13877);*
- *Instituto Internacional de Derecho y Medio Ambiente (IIDMA);*
- *International Institute for Sustainable Development (IISD, #13930);*
- *International Lake Environment Committee Foundation (ILEC, #13998);*
- *International Law Association (ILA, #14003);*
- *International Law Institute, Washington DC (ILI);*
- *International Movement for Advancement of Education Culture Social and Economic Development (IMAECSED);*
- *International Nuclear Societies Council (INSC, #14382);*
- *Organisation internationale pour la protection des animaux (OIPA, #17810);*
- *International Organisation of Employers (IOE, #14428);*
- *International Petroleum Industry Environmental Conservation Association (IPIECA, #14562);*
- *International Planned Parenthood Federation (IPPF, #14589);*
- *International Plant Nutrition Institute (IPNI, inactive);*
- *International Pollutants Elimination Network (IPEN, #14616);*
- *International Public Relations Association (IPRA, #14671);*
- *International Risk Governance Council (IRGC, #14756);*
- *International Seed Federation (ISF, #14828);*
- *International Solid Waste Association (ISWA, #15567);*
- *International Trade Union Confederation (ITUC, #15708);*
- *International Union of Forest Research Organizations (IUFRO, #15774);*
- *Inuit Circumpolar Council (ICC, #15995);*
- *Islamic Foundation for Ecology and Environmental Sciences (IFEES);*
- *Islamic Relief Worldwide (IRWW, #16048);*
- *Jesuit Justice and Ecology Network Africa (JENA, #16105);*
- *Leadership for Environment and Development (LEAD International, #16416);*
- *MADRE;*
- *MarViva Foundation (#16591);*
- *Maryknoll Sisters of Saint Dominic;*
- *MEDITERRANEAN SOS Network (MEDSOS);*
- *Mercy Corps International (MCI);*
- *Minority Rights Group International (MRG, #16820);*
- *New World Hope Organization (NWHO);*
- *Nuffield International – Nuffield Farming Scholarships Trust (#17624);*
- *Ocean Conservancy;*
- *Ocean Recovery Alliance (ORA, #17686);*
- *OceanCare;*
- *International Office for Water (IOW, #14399);*
- *Panafrican Climate Justice Alliance (PACJA, #18046);*

- *Foundation for Sustainable Development Intercultural Exchange (PanEco)*;
- *Parliament of the World's Religions (PoWR, #18222)*;
- *Parliamentarians for Global Action (PGA, #18208)*;
- *PAX*;
- *Pax Romana, International Catholic Movement for Intellectual and Cultural Affairs (ICMICA, #18267)*;
- *Peace Child International (PCI, #18278)*;
- *Plastic Change*;
- *Plastic Soup Foundation (PSF)*;
- *Population Institute (PI)*;
- *Practical Action (#18475)*;
- *PROTERRA (no recent information)*;
- *ProVeg International (#18554)*;
- *Pure Earth (#18578)*;
- *Quaker Earthcare Witness (QEW)*;
- *Race for Water Foundation*;
- *Rare*;
- *Regional Environmental Centre for Central Asia (CAREC)*;
- *Regions4 Sustainable Development (Regions4, #18819)*;
- *REN21 (#18836)*;
- *Rotary International (RI, #18975)*;
- *Russian Association of Indigenous Peoples of the North (RAIPON)*;
- *Scientific Committee on Problems of the Environment (SCOPE, #19150)*;
- *Society for Conservation and Protection of Environment (SCOPE)*;
- *Society for Ecological Restoration International (SERI)*;
- *Society for International Development (SID, #19581)*;
- *Soroptimist International (SI, #19686)*;
- *South Asian Forum for Environment (SAFE)*;
- *SouthSouthNorth (SSN, #19893)*;
- *Stakeholder Forum for a Sustainable Future (SF)*;
- *Global Change System for Analysis, Research and Training (START, #10278)*;
- *Stiftung Wissenschaft und Politik (SWP)*;
- *Stockholm Environment Institute (SEI, #19993)*;
- *Surfrider Foundation Europe (#20041)*;
- *Taking IT Global (TIG)*;
- *Tearfund, UK*;
- *Indigenous Peoples' International Centre for Policy Research and Education (Tebtebba Foundation)*;
- *TerraGraphics International Foundation (TIFO)*;
- *African Roundtable for Sustainable Consumption and Production (ARSCP, #00444)*;
- *Donkey Sanctuary, The (#05120)*;
- *Conseil européen de l'industrie chimique (CEFIC, #04687)*;
- *GenderCC – Women for Climate Justice (GenderCC, #10095)*;
- *Grain and Feed Trade Association (GAFTA, #10692)*;
- *Green Belt Movement (#10713)*;
- *Lions Clubs International (LCI, #16485)*;
- *International Council for Adult Education (ICAE, #12983)*;
- *The Lutheran World Federation (LWF, #16532)*;
- *Millennium Institute*;
- *The Nature Conservancy (TNC)*;
- *Northern Forum, The (#17592)*;
- *The Ocean Cleanup*;
- *Pew Charitable Trusts*;
- *The SeaCleaners*;
- *World Federation of Public Health Associations (WFPHA, #21476)*;
- *Third World Network (TWN, #20151)*;
- *TRAFFIC International (#20196)*;
- *UNISFÉRA (#20491)*;
- *World Organization of United Cities and Local Governments (UCLG, #21695)*;
- *United Nations Foundation (UNF, #20563)*;
- *Institute for Development, Environment and Peace (Vitae Civilis)*;
- *Water Environment Federation (WEF)*;
- *Western Indian Ocean Marine Science Association (WIOMSA, #20916)*;
- *Wetlands International (#20928)*;
- *Wildlife Justice Commission (WJC, #20960)*;
- *Women Engage for a Common Future (WECF, #20992)*;
- *Women Organizing for Change in Agriculture and Natural Resource Management (WOCAN)*;
- *Women's Environment and Development Organization (WEDO, #21016)*;
- *Women's International League for Peace and Freedom (WILPF, #21024)*;
- *World Animal Protection (#21092)*;
- *World Association of Girl Guides and Girl Scouts (WAGGGS, #21142)*;
- *World Business Council for Sustainable Development (WBCSD, #21254)*;
- *World Coatings Council (#21283)*;
- *World Council of Churches (WCC, #21320)*;
- *World Environment Center (WEC, #21386)*;
- *World Evangelical Alliance (WEA, #21393)*;
- *World Farmers' Organisation (WFO, #21401)*;
- *World Federalist Movement – Movement for a Just World Order through a Strengthened United Nations (WFM, #21404)*;
- *World Federation of Engineering Organizations (WFEO, #21433)*;
- *World Future Council Foundation (WFC, #21533)*;
- *World Muslim Congress (WMC, #21664)*;
- *World Organization of the Scout Movement (WOSM, #21693)*;
- *World Phosphate Institute (#21728)*;
- *World Plastics Council (WPC, #21730)*;
- *World Resources Institute (WRI, #21753)*;
- *World Sustainability Fund (WSF)*;
- *World Toilet Organization (WTO, #21854)*;
- *World Wide Fund for Nature (WWF, #21922)*;
- *World Youth Foundation (WYF)*;
- *Youth and Environment Europe (YEE, #22012)*;
- *Zero Waste Europe (#22035)*;
- *Zoï Environment Network*.

Co-hosts: *Great Apes Survival Project (GRASP, #10699)*. Supports: *Action Plan for the Environment in Latin America and the Caribbean (no recent information)*; *Climate Institute*. Contact with: *SYLVA-WORLD for Development and the Protection of Forests and the Environment*. Instrumental in setting up: *Environnement et développement du Tiers-monde (enda, #05510)*; *Global Information Network on Chemicals (GINC, no recent information)*; *UNESCO World Network of Microbiological Resources Centres MIRCEN (no recent information)*; *UNU Institute for Natural Resources in Africa (UNU-INRA, #20718)*. Close relationship with: *World Federation of Advertisers (WFA, #21407)*. Cooperates with: *International Hotel and Restaurant Association (IH&RA, #13813)*. Partner of: *WorldFish (#21507)*. Agreement with: *International Olympic Committee (IOC, #14408)*. The Interim Secretariat of the Carpathian Convention has Memorandum of Understanding with: *Carpathian Ecoregion Initiative (CERI, #03587)*. [2022/XE4161/**E***]

- ♦ **UNEP-WCMC** UN Environment Programme World Conservation Monitoring Centre (#20295)
- ♦ UNESCAP / see United Nations Economic and Social Commission for Asia and the Pacific (#20557)
- ♦ UNESCAP Pacific Operations Centre (see: #20557)
- ♦ UNESCO Apia Office / see UNESCO Office for the Pacific States (#20315)
- ♦ UNESCO-APNIEVE / see Asia-Pacific Network for International Education and Values Education (#01970)

♦ UNESCO Asia-Pacific Regional Bureau for Communication and Information 20300

Contact c/o UNESCO House, 1 San Martin Marg, Chanakyapuri, Delhi 110 021, DELHI 110 021, India. T. +911126111867 – +911126111869. Fax +911126111861. E-mail: h.dlamini@unesco.org – newdelhi@unesco.org.

URL: http://www.unesco.org/new/en/newdelhi/home

History 1948, Delhi (India), as *South Asia Science Cooperation Office*, as the first decentralized office in Asia, within the framework of *UNESCO (#20322)*, to deal with science and technology programmes in 11 South and Central Asian countries and later expanded to include communication, education and culture programmes. Subsequent name changes: *Field Science Office for South Asia*, 1968; *UNESCO Regional Office for Science and Technology for South and Central Asia (UNESCO/ROSTSCA) – Bureau régional de l'UNESCO de science et technologie pour l'Asie du Sud et l'Asie centrale*, 1974, during 18th Session of UNESCO General Conference; *UNESCO Regional Bureau for Communication and Information for South and Central Asia*. Previously also referred to by the initials *ROSTSCA*. From 1995, functions as *UNESCO Delhi Office – Bureau de l'UNESCO à Delhi*, also referred to as: *UNESCO Office in Delhi*; *Office of the United Nations Educational, Scientific and Cultural Organization in Delhi*. As part of UNESCO's new decentralization policy, UNESCO Delhi was designated as a Cluster Office for 6 countries in South Asia (Bangladesh, Bhutan, India, Maldives, Nepal and Sri Lanka) and assumed its current title, 2001. **Aims** Contribute to peace and security by *collaboration* among the nations through education, science and culture in order to further universal respect for justice, for the rule of law, for human rights and fundamental freedoms, which are affirmed for the peoples of the world, without distinction of race, sex, language or religion, by the Charter of the United Nations; promote the use of information and *communication technologies* (ICTs) to support *peace* and *development* in the region. **Structure** Office comprises 5 sectors: Education; Natural Sciences; Social and Human Science; Culture; Communication and Information. Administrative Unit. **Languages** English, French. **Staff** 18.00 FTE, paid. **Finance** Regular Programme Budget as approved by the UNESCO General Conference, is decentralized by UNESCO Headquarters, Paris (France). Extrabudgetary funding received from UNDP and other bilateral and multilateral donors. **Activities** Implements UNESCO's activities in all its fields of competence, namely, Education, Science, Culture, Communication and Information; acts as an advisory body to the Asia Pacific Member States; plans and implements regional programme activities in cooperation with other UNESCO Clusters/National Offices and with partners in the region. **Events** *Regional seminar on the role of women in utilising results of technological innovation* Colombo (Sri Lanka) 1990, *International workshop on physics of materials* Delhi (India) 1987, *Regional seminar on ecology of tropical mountain slopes* Kathmandu (Nepal) 1987, *Regional workshop on integrated water management in urban areas* Mumbai (India) 1987, *Regional workshop on application of informatics in medical services* Teheran (Iran Islamic Rep) 1987. **Publications** *UNESCO Delhi Office Newsletter* (4 a year). *Different Approaches to Achieving – Indian Experience* (2004); *Fish and Shellfish Health Management* (2004); *Water Users' Association for Sustainable Water Management* (2004); *Communication, Education and Media Needs in India* (2002) by B P Sanjay in English, Hindi; *Public Service Broadcasting: A Comparative Legal Survey* (2000) by Toby Mendel in English, Russian; *Teacher Training Manual on HIV/AIDS and Life Skills Education*. *EFA in South Asia Analytical Study on Dakar Goals* – series of booklets. Annual Report; reports; studies; case studies; papers; self learning materials on HIV/AIDS; books; CD-Roms; videos; films; posters. Publishes/sponsors publication of reports/proceedings of seminars, workshops and training courses. **Information Services** *Library, Documentation and Information Services (LDIS)* – set up 1948, Delhi (India): provides information and documentation support to regional and country programmes for sharing and exchange of information materials; provides bibliographic information for researchers and books on interlibrary loan; retrieves information from CD-ROM and UNESCO database internet searches; promotes the sale and distribution of books; participates in book fairs; *Periodicals Received in UNESCO Office Library (PERIOD)* – database; *ROSTCADOC* – bibliographic database. **Members** Countries covered (45). Membership countries not specified. **IGO Relations** Cooperates with: *Abdus Salam International Centre for Theoretical Physics (ICTP, #00005)*; *Australian Aid (inactive)*; *DANIDA*; *Department for International Development (DFID, inactive)*; *Intergovernmental Oceanographic Commission (IOC, #11496)*; *International Hydrological Programme (IHP, #13826)*; *Swedish International Development Cooperation Agency (Sida)*; *UNDP (#20292)*; *UNICEF (#20332)*; *United Nations Economic and Social Commission for Asia and the Pacific (ESCAP, #20557)*; *United States Agency for International Development (USAID)*. Involved in: *Asian Physics Education Network (ASPEN, #01664)*. **NGO Relations** Set up: *International Institute for Special Education (IISE)*. Involved in: *Asian Network of Analytical Chemistry (ANAC, #01546)*; *Asian Network for Biological Sciences (ANBS, no recent information)*. [2020/XE9703/**E***]

♦ UNESCO Asia and Pacific Regional Bureau for Education 20301

Contact Mom Luang Pin Malakul Centenary Building 920 Sukhumvit Road, Prakanong, Klongtoey, Bangkok, 10110, Thailand. T. +6623910577. Fax +6623910866. E-mail: bangkok@unesco.org.

URL: https://bangkok.unesco.org/

History 1961, Bangkok (Thailand). Established following a Resolution at 11th Session of General Conference, 1960, of *UNESCO (#20322)*. Set up as regional office for education in 1961 and expanded to cover culture in 1976, social and human sciences in 1977, and information programmes and services in 1987. From 1995, functions as *UNESCO Bangkok Office – Bureau de l'UNESCO à Bangkok – Oficina de la UNESCO en Bangkok*. Former names and other names: *UNESCO Regional Office for Education in Asia and the Pacific (ROEAP)* – former; *Bureau régional de l'UNESCO pour l'éducation en Asie et dans le Pacifique* – former; *Oficina Regional de la UNESCO de Educación para Asia y el Pacifico* – former; *UNESCO Principal Regional Office for Asia and the Pacific (PROAP)* – former (1986); *Bureau régional principal de l'UNESCO en Asie et dans le Pacifique* – former (1986); *Oficina Principal Regional de la UNESCO para Asia y el Pacifico* – former (1986); *UNESCO/PROAP* – former; *UNESCO Regional Bureau for Education in Asia and the Pacific* – alias; *UNESCO Bangkok* – alias. **Aims** Promote and organize activities in the fields of education, social and human sciences, culture, communication, information and informatics, including: development and reform of education at all levels from early childhood education to *higher education*; *social sciences*, *human sciences* and UNESCO's programme in the region related to women, human rights, peace and youth; preservation of *cultural heritage*, *traditions* and cultural identity; regional projects to facilitate access to exchange and use of *information* and *data*, including action to strengthen and develop libraries, archives and information systems. **Structure** Office of the Director; Executive Office; Administration and Finance; Communication and Information Unit; Culture Unit; Section for Educational Innovation and Skills Development; Section for Inclusive Quality Education; Natural Sciences Unit; IOC Sub-Commission for the Western Pacific; Social and Human Sciences Unit; Assessment, Information System, Monitoring and Statistics Unit. **Staff** 69.00 FTE, paid. **Finance** Sources: UNESCO Regular Programme; *Asian Development Bank (ADB, #01422)*; *UNDP (#20292)*; *United Nations Population Fund (UNFPA, #20612)*; Funds-in Trust; voluntary contributions.

Activities Acts as permanent secretariat to 'Conference of Ministers of Education and Those Responsible for Economic Planning in Asia and the Pacific' and to 'Advisory Committee on Regional Cooperation in Education in Asia and the Pacific'; implements UNESCO regular and extra-budgetary programmes in the region. Works through inter-country cooperative projects and networks and exchange of experience in: universalization of primary education; continuing education; secondary education; adult education; teacher education; educational planning and management; educational facilities; vocational and technical education; science and technology education; population education/aids education; higher education; environmental education. Coordinates the following networks and information services:

- *Asia-Pacific Programme of Educational Innovation for Development (APEID, #02001)*;
- *Asia-Pacific Programme of Education for All (APPEAL, #02002)*, whose projects include *Community Learning Centres (CLC, see: #02002)*;
- *Asian-Pacific Information Network on Medicinal and Aromatic Plants (APINMAP, no recent information)*;
- *Educational Policy-Making, Planning, Management and Statistics Network (EMPS, no recent information)*;
- Consortia in Higher Education (3) relating to innovations, policy planning and management and special research studies.

Work of APEID and APPEAL monitored by *Intergovernmental Regional Committee on Education in Asia and the Pacific (EDCOM, no recent information)*.

Events *Conference in Digital Citizenship Education in Asia-Pacific* Bangkok (Thailand) 2017, *International Symposium on Girls Education in STEM* Bangkok (Thailand) 2017, *Asia Pacific Meeting on Education 2030* Bangkok (Thailand) 2015, *Regional Meeting on Assessing Gender Issues in Pre-Service and In-Service Teacher Training in Asia* Bangkok (Thailand) 2015, *Regional Policy Forum on the Promotion of ASEAN Regional Integration through Open and Distance Higher Education* Bangkok (Thailand) 2015. **Publications** *UNESCO Bangkok Newsletter* (4 a year); *Adolescent Education Newsletter*. **Information Services** *LIB Database*; *Population and Adolescent Reproductive Health (POP)* – bibliographic database; *PROAP Database* – education, social science, culture in Asia and the Pacific; *UNE Database*.

Members Member states of UNESCO in Asia and the Pacific region (46):

Afghanistan, Australia, Bangladesh, Bhutan, Brunei Darussalam, Cambodia, China, Cook Is, Fiji, India, Indonesia, Iran Islamic Rep, Japan, Kazakhstan, Kiribati, Korea DPR, Korea Rep, Kyrgyzstan, Laos, Malaysia, Maldives, Marshall Is, Micronesia FS, Mongolia, Myanmar, Nauru, Nepal, New Zealand, Niue, Pakistan, Palau, Papua New Guinea, Philippines, Samoa, Singapore, Solomon Is, Sri Lanka, Tajikistan, Thailand, Timor-Leste, Tonga, Turkmenistan, Tuvalu, Uzbekistan, Vanuatu, Vietnam.

NGO Relations Instrumental in setting up (1): *Asia-Pacific Performing Arts Network (APPAN, #01994)*. [2021.02.25/XE9576/**E***]

♦ UNESCO Associated Schools Project / see UNESCO Associated Schools Project Network (#20302)

♦ UNESCO Associated Schools Project Network (ASPnet) 20302

Address not obtained.
URL: https://aspnet.unesco.org/

History Nov 1953, Paris (France), by *UNESCO (#20322)*, following a preparatory meeting. Also referred to as *Associated Schools Project in Education for International Cooperation and Peace – Système des écoles associées appliquant un programme d'éducation pour la coopération internationale et la paix – Plan de Escuelas Asociadas en la Educación para la Cooperación Internacional y la Paz* and as *UNESCO Associated Schools Project – Système des écoles associées de l'UNESCO – Plan de Escuelas Asociadas de la UNESCO*; *UNESCO Associated Schools Project for Promoting Education for Peace, Human Rights, Democracy and International Understanding (ASP) – Système des écoles associées de l'UNESCO pour la promotion de l'éducation en faveur de la paix, des droits de l'homme, de la démocratie et de la compréhension internationale (SEA) – Plan de Escuelas Asociadas de la UNESCO para el Fomento de la Educación por la Paz, los Derechos Humanos, la Democracia y la Comprensión Internacional.* **Aims** Promote the ideals of UNESCO by conducting pilot projects in favour of better preparing children and young people to meet effectively the challenges of an increasingly complex and interdependent world. **Structure** *Associated Schools Project Network (ASP Network)* of pre-schools, primary schools, secondary schools and teacher training institutions, coordinated through national coordinators and *ASPnet Coordination Unit.* **Languages** English, French, Spanish. **Staff** 3.00 FTE, paid. **Finance** UNESCO Regular programme funds; extrabudgetary funds or public-private partnerships for specific projects. **Activities** Projects, including: *Baltic Sea Project (BSP, #03147).* **Events** *International Forum on Cultural Diversity* Seoul (Korea Rep) 2019, *SDG4 Education 2030 Forum* Seoul (Korea Rep) 2019, *International Seminar on Getting Climate-Ready* Paris (France) 2015, *International Forum* Okayama (Japan) 2014, *International Forum* Suwon (Korea Rep) 2013. **Publications** *ASPnet News Infos* (2 a year) in English, French, Spanish.

Members Participating institutions (over 9,700) in 180 countries and territories:
Albania, Algeria, Andorra, Angola, Argentina, Armenia, Australia, Austria, Azerbaijan, Bahrain, Bangladesh, Barbados, Belarus, Belgium, Belize, Benin, Bhutan, Bolivia, Bosnia-Herzegovina, Botswana, Brazil, Bulgaria, Burkina Faso, Cambodia, Cameroon, Canada, Cape Verde, Central African Rep, Chad, Chile, China, Colombia, Comoros, Congo Brazzaville, Congo DR, Cook Is, Costa Rica, Côte d'Ivoire, Croatia, Cuba, Curaçao, Cyprus, Czechia, Denmark, Dominica, Dominican Rep, Ecuador, Egypt, El Salvador, Equatorial Guinea, Estonia, Eswatini, Ethiopia, Fiji, Finland, France, Gabon, Gambia, Georgia, Germany, Ghana, Greece, Grenada, Guatemala, Guinea, Guyana, Haiti, Honduras, Hungary, Iceland, India, Indonesia, Iran Islamic Rep, Iraq, Ireland, Israel, Italy, Jamaica, Japan, Jordan, Kazakhstan, Kenya, Kiribati, Korea Rep, Kuwait, Kyrgyzstan, Laos, Latvia, Lebanon, Lesotho, Liberia, Libya, Lithuania, Luxembourg, Madagascar, Malawi, Malaysia, Mali, Malta, Marshall Is, Mauritania, Mauritius, Mexico, Micronesia FS, Moldova, Mongolia, Montenegro, Morocco, Mozambique, Myanmar, Namibia, Nauru, Nepal, Netherlands, New Zealand, Nicaragua, Niger, Nigeria, Niue, North Macedonia, Norway, Oman, Pakistan, Palau, Palestine, Panama, Papua New Guinea, Paraguay, Peru, Philippines, Poland, Portugal, Qatar, Romania, Russia, Rwanda, Samoa, Sao Tomé-Principe, Saudi Arabia, Senegal, Serbia, Seychelles, Sierra Leone, Slovakia, Slovenia, Solomon Is, South Africa, Spain, Sri Lanka, St Lucia, St Vincent-Grenadines, Sudan, Sweden, Switzerland, Syrian AR, Tajikistan, Tanzania UR, Thailand, Togo, Tokelau, Tonga, Trinidad-Tobago, Tunisia, Türkiye, Turkmenistan, Tuvalu, Uganda, UK, Ukraine, United Arab Emirates, Uruguay, USA, Uzbekistan, Vanuatu, Venezuela, Vietnam, Virgin Is UK, Yemen, Zambia, Zimbabwe.

IGO Relations Links with all UNESCO sectors, field offices and UN agencies. [2019/XF8270/**F***]

♦ UNESCO Associated Schools Project for Promoting Education for Peace, Human Rights, Democracy and International Understanding / see UNESCO Associated Schools Project Network (#20302)
♦ UNESCO Bangkok / see UNESCO Asia and Pacific Regional Bureau for Education (#20301)
♦ UNESCO Beirut Office / see UNESCO Regional Office for Education in the Arab States (#20320)
♦ Unesco: Bureau international d'éducation / see International Bureau of Education (#12413)
♦ UNESCO Cairo Office / see UNESCO Office, Cairo – Regional Bureau for Sciences in the Arab States (#20312)
♦ UNESCO Caracas Office / see UNESCO International Institute for Higher Education in Latin America and the Caribbean (#20309)
♦ UNESCOCAT – Centre UNESCO de Catalunya (internationally oriented national body)
♦ UNESCO Centre Basque Country / see Centro UNESCO del Pais Vasco
♦ UNESCO Centre of Catalonia (internationally oriented national body)
♦ UNESCO Centre européen pour l'enseignement supérieur (inactive)
♦ UNESCO Centre for Membrane Science and Technology (unconfirmed)
♦ UNESCO Centre for Water Law, Policy and Science (internationally oriented national body)

♦ UNESCO Centre for Women and Peace in the Balkan Countries 20303

Centre UNESCO pour les femmes et la paix dans les Balkans

Pres 30 Ploutonos, G Papandreou Str, 546 55 Thessaloniki, Greece. T. +302310422270 – +302310423152. Fax +302310422271. E-mail: unescenter@gmail.com.
URL: http://www.unescocenter.gr/

History Proposed by *Association of Interbalkan Women's Cooperation Societies, Thessaloniki (AIWCS, #02653)*, with resolution adopted by 27th General Conference and Memorandum of Understanding concluded between *UNESCO (#20322)* and AIWCS. Officially declared open 18 May 1994. Originally within the framework of *UNESCO Mediterranean Programme (inactive)* as a component of *Network of Mediterranean Women for Cooperation and Parity (no recent information).* **Aims** Establish links of friendship and good understanding among women in countries of the regional through cooperation in common programmes and activities; promote respect of human rights and elimination of all forms of discrimination against women; encourage women's advancement in all sectors, their empowerment and their ever increasing participation in development; support the implementation of the UNESCO strategy aimed at building a culture of peace. **Structure** General Assembly; Directing Board; Committees (7). **Languages** English. **Staff** 2.00 FTE, voluntary. **Finance** Support from: *European Commission (EC, #06633)*; UNESCO participation programme; private-sector donors in Thessaloniki. **Activities** Projects/programmes; guidance/assistance/consulting; events/meetings; training/education. **Publications** *Directory of Women's Associations in the Balkans.* Annual Report; newsletters; brochures; leaflets; booklets; reports. Information Services: Documentation centre on the status of women in Balkan countries.

Members Organizations, institutions and individuals in 7 countries:
Albania, Bulgaria, Cyprus, Greece, Romania, Serbia, Türkiye. [2021/XK1512/**E***]

♦ UNESCO-CEPES – UNESCO Centre européen pour l'enseignement supérieur (inactive)
♦ UNESCO Cluster Office for the Pacific States / see UNESCO Office for the Pacific States (#20315)
♦ UNESCO-Cousteau Ecotechnie Programme / see Ecotechnie (#05333)
♦ UNESCO CSI Programme – UNESCO Environment and Development in Coastal Regions and Small Islands (see: #20322)
♦ UNESCO Delhi Office / see UNESCO Asia-Pacific Regional Bureau for Communication and Information (#20300)
♦ UNESCO Environment and Development in Coastal Regions and Small Islands (see: #20322)
♦ UNESCO-EOLSS Joint Committee (internationally oriented national body)
♦ UNESCO Etxea – Centro UNESCO del Pais Vasco (internationally oriented national body)
♦ UNESCO – European Centre for Higher Education (inactive)
♦ UNESCO Fellowships Programme (see: #20322)
♦ UNESCO Field Office for South East Asian Science Cooperation / see UNESCO Office, Jakarta – Regional Bureau for Sciences in Asia and the Pacific (#20313)
♦ UNESCO Havana Office / see UNESCO Regional Bureau for Culture for Latin America and the Caribbean (#20317)
♦ UNESCO-Hebrew University of Jerusalem International School for Molecular Biology and Microbiology and Science for Peace (internationally oriented national body)
♦ UNESCO-HUJ ISMBM – UNESCO-Hebrew University of Jerusalem International School for Molecular Biology and Microbiology and Science for Peace (internationally oriented national body)
♦ UNESCO-ICOM Museum Information Centre (see: #13051)
♦ **UNESCO-IESALC** Instituto Internacional de la UNESCO para la Educación Superior en América Latina y el Caribe (#20309)
♦ UNESCO – IHE Institute for Water Education / see IHE Delft Institute for Water Education (#11110)
♦ UNESCO Infoyouth Network / see INFOYOUTH – Worldwide Information Network on Youth Related Issues (#11204)
♦ UNESCO INRULED / see UNESCO International Research and Training Centre for Rural Education
♦ UNESCO Institute for Education / see UNESCO Institute for Lifelong Learning (#20305)

♦ UNESCO Institute for Information Technologies in Education (IITE) . 20304

Institut UNESCO pour l'application des technologies de l'information à l'éducation

Dir 8 Kedrova St, Bldg 3, Moscow MOSKVA, Russia, 117292. T. +74991292990. Fax +74991291225. E-mail: liste.info.iite@unesco.org.
URL: https://iite.unesco.org/

History Nov 1997. Founded on adoption of resolution 6 of the 29th General Conference of *UNESCO (#20322)* and signature of an agreement between UNESCO and the Government of Russia. **Aims** Contribute to the design and implementation of UNESCO programmes in regard to application of information and communication technologies in education. **Structure** Governing Board of 11 members, appointed by UNESCO Director-General on a geographical distribution basis. **Languages** English, Russian. **Staff** 20.00 FTE, paid. **Activities** Events/meetings; guidance/assistance/consulting; knowledge management/information dissemination; networking/liaising; projects/programmes; training/education. **Publications** Policy briefs; analytical surveys; training, methodological and information materials. Information Services: Information System on Information Technologies in Education (ISITE). **Information Services** *Information System on Information Technologies in Education (ISITE).* **IGO Relations** Cooperates with (5): *International Bureau of Education (IBE, #12413)*; *International Institute for Educational Planning (IIEP, #13874)*; *International Telecommunication Union (ITU, #15673)*; *UNESCO Institute for Lifelong Learning (UIL, #20305)*; *UNESCO Institute for Statistics (UIS, #20306).* [2022.12.02/XE4170/j/**E***]

♦ UNESCO Institute for Lifelong Learning (UIL) 20305

Institut de l'UNESCO pour l'apprentissage tout au long de la vie – UNESCO-Institut für Lebenslanges Lernen

Dir Feldbrunnenstrasse 58, 20148 Hamburg, Germany. T. +4940448041-0. Fax +49404107723. E-mail: uil@unesco.org.
Public Relations Specialist address not obtained. E-mail: uil-pr@unesco.org.
URL: http://uil.unesco.org/

History 1952, Hamburg (Germany). Founded within the framework of *UNESCO (#20322).* Former names and other names: *UNESCO Institute for Education (UIE)* – former; *Institut de l'UNESCO pour l'éducation (IUE)* – former; *Instituto de la UNESCO para la Educación (IUE)* – former; *UNESCO-Institut für Pädagogik (UIP)* – former; *IUAV* – former. **Aims** Strengthen the capacities of Member States to build effective and inclusive lifelong learning policies and systems, in line with Sustainable Development Goal 4; develop learning ecosystems that work across life, in every setting and benefit everyone through building capacity at local and national levels, strengthening partnerships, and offering data and knowledge. **Structure** Governing Board, comprising Chair, Vice-Chair, 12 members and 12 alternates. **Languages** English, French, Spanish. **Staff** 50.00 FTE, paid. **Finance** Sources: revenue from activities/projects; sponsorship. Major sponsors: UNESCO; Germany; Norway; Sweden; City of Hamburg (Germany). Allocation from the general budget of UNESCO; contribution and premises from German national and Hamburg city governments. Project funding from various partners. **Activities** Advocacy/lobbying/activism; capacity building; guidance/assistance/consulting; publishing activities; research/documentation; training/education. **Events** *CONFINTEA : International Conference on Adult Education* Marrakech (Morocco) 2022, *Arab Regional Consultation for the Seventh International Conference on Adult Education* Beirut (Lebanon) 2021, *Arab Regional Consultation for the Seventh International Conference on Adult Education* Beirut (Lebanon) 2021, *International Conference on Learning Cities* Incheon (Korea Rep) 2021, *International Conference on Learning Cities* Medellin (Colombia) 2019. **Publications** *UIL Bulletin* (12 a year) in English, French, Spanish; *International Review of Education – Journal of lifelong learning* (6 a year). *UIL Virtual Annual Report 2020* (2021) in English, French. *Curriculum globALE: competency framework for adult educators* (2021) in English; *Guidelines on open and distance learning for youth and adult literacy* (2021) in English; *Inclusive lifelong learning in cities: Policies and practices for vulnerable groups* (2021) in English; *Integrated approaches to literacy and skills development* (2021) in English; *Snapshots of learning cities' responses to COVID-19* (2021) in English; *Embracing a culture of lifelong learning – Adopter une culture de l'apprentissage tout au long de la vie* (1st ed 2020) in English, French; *4th global report on adult learning and education: leave no one behind: participation, equity and inclusion – 4ème rapport mondial sur l'apprentissage et l'éducation des adultes: ne laisser personne pour compte: participation, équité et inclusion – 4° informe mundial sobre el aprendizaje y la educación de adultos: no dejar a nadie atrás: participación, equidad e inclusión* (1st ed 2019) in Arabic, Chinese, English, French, Portuguese, Russian, Spanish. Annual Report; various general or programmes-related brochure and publications. Information Services: Maintains library with about 50,000 books, documents and audio-visual items. **Information Services** *Adult Learning Documentation and Information Network (ALADIN)* – connecting about 100 document centres worldwide.

Members Not a membership organization. [2022.02.10/XE5646/j/**E***]

♦ UNESCO Institute for Statistics (UIS) 20306

Institut de statistique de l'UNESCO

Dir CP 6128, Succursale Centre-Ville, Montréal QC H3C 3J7, Canada. T. +15143436880. Fax +15143435740. E-mail: uis.director@unesco.org.
Street address 5255 avenue Decelles, 7th floor, Montréal QC H3T 2B1, Canada.
URL: http://www.uis.unesco.org/

History Established 1999, by *UNESCO (#20322)*, developing from its Statistics Division. Initially based in UNESCO headquarters in Paris (France), the institute moved to its permanent location in Montréal (Canada), Sep 2001. **Aims** Serve as the UN depository for global statistics in the fields of education, science and technology, culture and communication; develop and disseminate the timely, accurate and policy-relevant data needed for effective policy-making at national and international levels; develop methodologies, standards and indicators needed to achieve SDG 4-Education 2030 and key targets in science and innovation, culture and communication. **Structure** Governing Board, consisting of 12 experts representing different regions and international organizations. Director reports to the Governing Board and UNESCO Director-General. **Languages** Arabic, Chinese, English, French, Russian, Spanish. **Staff** 55.00 FTE, paid. **Finance** Annual budget (2019): US$ 11,000,000. **Activities** Knowledge management/information dissemination; standards/guidelines; training/education. Data production and analysis; indicator development; methodological development. **Events** *Technical Cooperation Group Meeting* Dubai (United Arab Emirates) 2018, *Meeting of the Technical Advisory Group on Culture Satellite Accounts* Tokyo (Japan) 2018, *Technical Cooperation Group Meeting* Montréal, QC (Canada) 2017, *Global meeting on measuring the information society* Geneva (Switzerland) 2008, *Congress on library statistics for the 21st century world* Montréal, QC (Canada) 2008. **Publications** Data; guides; visualizations; e-Atlases; technical papers; analytical reports; manuals.

Members Full in 195 countries and territories:
Afghanistan, Albania, Algeria, Andorra, Angola, Antigua-Barbuda, Argentina, Armenia, Australia, Austria, Azerbaijan, Bahamas, Bahrain, Bangladesh, Barbados, Belarus, Belgium, Belize, Benin, Bhutan, Bolivia, Bosnia-Herzegovina, Botswana, Brazil, Brunei Darussalam, Bulgaria, Burkina Faso, Burundi, Cambodia, Cameroon, Canada, Cape Verde, Central African Rep, Chad, Chile, China, Colombia, Comoros, Congo Brazzaville, Congo DR, Cook Is, Costa Rica, Côte d'Ivoire, Croatia, Cuba, Cyprus, Czechia, Denmark, Djibouti, Dominica, Dominican Rep, Ecuador, Egypt, El Salvador, Equatorial Guinea, Eritrea, Estonia, Eswatini, Ethiopia, Fiji, Finland, France, Gabon, Gambia, Georgia, Germany, Ghana, Greece, Grenada, Guatemala, Guinea, Guinea-Bissau, Guyana, Haiti, Honduras, Hungary, Iceland, India, Indonesia, Iran Islamic Rep, Iraq, Ireland, Israel, Italy, Jamaica, Japan, Jordan, Kazakhstan, Kenya, Kiribati, Korea DPR, Korea Rep, Kuwait, Kyrgyzstan, Laos, Latvia, Lebanon, Lesotho, Liberia, Libya, Lithuania, Luxembourg, Madagascar, Malawi, Malaysia, Maldives, Mali, Malta, Marshall Is, Mauritania, Mauritius, Mexico, Micronesia FS, Moldova, Monaco, Mongolia, Montenegro, Morocco, Mozambique, Myanmar, Namibia, Nauru, Nepal, Netherlands, New Zealand, Nicaragua, Niger, Nigeria, Niue, North Macedonia, Norway, Oman, Pakistan, Palau, Palestine, Panama, Papua New Guinea, Paraguay, Peru, Philippines, Poland, Portugal, Qatar, Romania, Russia, Rwanda, Samoa, San Marino, Sao Tomé-Principe, Saudi Arabia, Senegal, Serbia, Seychelles, Sierra Leone, Singapore, Slovakia, Slovenia, Solomon Is, Somalia, South Africa, South Sudan, Spain, Sri Lanka, St Kitts-Nevis, St Lucia, St Vincent-Grenadines, Sudan, Suriname, Sweden, Switzerland, Syrian AR, Tajikistan, Tanzania UR, Thailand, Timor-Leste, Togo, Tonga, Trinidad-Tobago, Tunisia, Türkiye, Turkmenistan, Tuvalu, Uganda, UK, Ukraine, United Arab Emirates, Uruguay, USA, Uzbekistan, Vanuatu, Venezuela, Vietnam, Yemen, Zambia, Zimbabwe.

Associate in 9 countries and territories:
Anguilla, Aruba, Cayman Is, Curaçao, Faeroe Is, Macau, St Maarten, Tokelau, Virgin Is UK.

NGO Relations Member of: *Global Partnership for Sustainable Development Data (Data4SDGS, #10542).* [2022/XE3686/j/**E***]

♦ UNESCO-Institut für Lebenslanges Lernen (#20305)

♦ UNESCO-Institut für Pädagogik / see UNESCO Institute for Lifelong Learning (#20305)
♦ UNESCO: International Bureau of Education / see International Bureau of Education (#12413)

♦ UNESCO International Centre for Technical and Vocational Education and Training (UNESCO-UNEVOC) 20307

Centre international de l'UNESCO pour l'enseignement et la formation techniques et professionnels

Head of Office UN Campus, Platz der Vereinten Nationen 1, 53113 Bonn, Germany. T. +492288150100. Fax +492288150199. E-mail: unevoc@unesco.org.
URL: http://www.unevoc.unesco.org/

History 2000. Established within *UNESCO (#20322)*. Inaugurated in Apr 2002. **Aims** Act as a part of the United Nations mandate to promote peace, justice, equity, poverty alleviation and great social cohesion; assist member states in development of policies and practices concerning education for the world of work and skills development for employability and citizenship to achieve access for all, high quality, relevant and effective programmes, and learning opportunities throughout life; contribute to increased opportunities for productive work, sustainable livelihoods, personal empowerment and socio-economic development, especially for youth, girls, women and the disadvantaged, with emphasis on developing countries, countries in transition and those in a post-conflict situation. **Languages** English, French. **Staff** 20.00 FTE, paid. **Finance** *UNESCO (#20322)*; German government; other international donors. **Activities** Advocacy/lobbying/activism; events/meetings; knowledge management/information dissemination; networking/liaising; training/education. **Events** *Mapping Current Trends in TVET for Sustainable and Digital Transformation* Helsinki (Finland) 2022, *International Congress on Technical and Vocational Education and Training* Paris (France) 2012, *International seminar on vocational content in mass higher education* Bonn (Germany) 2005. **Publications** *UNEVOC Quarterly – Revue Trimestrielle UNEVOC* (4 a year) in English, French. *UNEVOC TVET Forum* in English – The UNESCO-UNEVOC TVET Forum is an online discussion board where TVET experts from around the world can share information and knowledge about different aspects of TVET.. Promising practices; case studies; conference, seminar and workshop proceedings. **Information Services** *TVET Country Profiles* in English – The UNESCO-UNEVOC TVET Country Profiles aim to provide concise, reliable and up-to-date information on TVET systems worldwide. Dynamic education system diagrams illustrate education systems at a glance, with a focus on TVET.; *TVETipedia Glossary* in English – The TVETipedia glossary is a collection of terms that are commonly used in the area of Technical and Vocational Education and Training..

Members Centres (254) in 167 countries:
Afghanistan, Albania, Algeria, Antigua-Barbuda, Argentina, Armenia, Australia, Austria, Bahamas, Bahrain, Bangladesh, Barbados, Belarus, Belize, Benin, Bhutan, Botswana, Brazil, Brunei Darussalam, Burkina Faso, Burundi, Cambodia, Cameroon, Canada, Cape Verde, Central African Rep, Chad, Chile, China, Colombia, Comoros, Congo Brazzaville, Congo DR, Cook Is, Costa Rica, Côte d'Ivoire, Croatia, Cuba, Cyprus, Czechia, Denmark, Dominica, Ecuador, Egypt, Eritrea, Estonia, Eswatini, Ethiopia, Fiji, Finland, France, Gabon, Gambia, Georgia, Germany, Ghana, Grenada, Guatemala, Guinea, Guinea-Bissau, Guyana, Haiti, Hungary, India, Indonesia, Iran Islamic Rep, Iraq, Ireland, Israel, Italy, Jamaica, Japan, Jordan, Kazakhstan, Kenya, Kiribati, Korea Rep, Kuwait, Kyrgyzstan, Laos, Latvia, Lebanon, Lesotho, Liberia, Libya, Lithuania, Luxembourg, Madagascar, Malawi, Malaysia, Maldives, Mali, Malta, Marshall Is, Mauritania, Mauritius, Mexico, Moldova, Mongolia, Morocco, Mozambique, Myanmar, Namibia, Nauru, Nepal, Netherlands, New Zealand, Nicaragua, Niger, Nigeria, Niue, North Macedonia, Norway, Oman, Pakistan, Palau, Palestine, Papua New Guinea, Paraguay, Peru, Philippines, Poland, Qatar, Romania, Russia, Rwanda, Samoa, Saudi Arabia, Senegal, Serbia, Seychelles, Sierra Leone, Singapore, Slovakia, Solomon Is, South Africa, Spain, Sri Lanka, St Kitts-Nevis, St Lucia, St Vincent-Grenadines, Sudan, Suriname, Sweden, Switzerland, Syrian AR, Tanzania UR, Thailand, Togo, Tonga, Trinidad-Tobago, Tunisia, Türkiye, Tuvalu, Uganda, UK, Ukraine, United Arab Emirates, Uruguay, USA, Uzbekistan, Vanuatu, Venezuela, Vietnam, Yemen, Zambia, Zimbabwe.

IGO Relations Cooperates with (1): *Colombo Plan Staff College (CPSC, #04121)*. Close cooperation with: *UNESCO Regional Office for Education in the Arab States (UNEDBAS, #20320)*; *UNESCO Asia and Pacific Regional Bureau for Education (#20301)*; *UNESCO Regional Bureau for Education in Latin America and the Caribbean (#20318)*. [2022.11.29/XK1984/**E***]

♦ UNESCO International Centre for Water Security and Sustainable Management (internationally oriented national body)
♦ UNESCO International Clearinghouse on Children and Violence on the Screen / see International Clearinghouse on Children, Youth and Media
♦ UNESCO International Committee of Bioethics / see International Bioethics Committee of UNESCO (#12348)

♦ UNESCO – International Institute for Capacity Building in Africa (IICBA) 20308

Institut international de l'UNESCO pour le renforcement des capacités en Afrique (IIRCA)

Contact IICBA Secretariat, PO Box 2305, Addis Ababa, Ethiopia. T. +251115515184 – +251115445685. Fax +251115514936. E-mail: info@unesco-iicba.org – info.iicba@unesco.org.
URL: http://www.iicba.unesco.org/

History 20 Oct 1997, when an agreement was signed between *UNESCO (#20322)* and the Government of the Federal Democratic Republic of Ethiopia, in which the two parties agreed to establish the institute in order to meet the demand for human resource development and capacity-building in African Member States in particular, and the developing world in general. The Director of the Institute was appointed as of 1 Dec 1998. The Director-General of UNESCO appointed an Interim Board which held its first meeting 10-11 Feb 1999, Paris (France). The Institute's temporary offices, provided free of charge by the Ministry of Education in Addis Ababa (Ethiopia), were officially opened May 1999 by the Assistant Director-General for Africa (ADG/Africa). One of 6 UNESCO Institutes and Centres under the direction of the UNESCO Secretariat. **Aims** Strengthen the capacities of *teacher education* institutions in member States; introduce information and *communication* technologies (ICTs) for education; establish networks of partner institutions to foster the sharing of experiences; undertake research and development on teacher education institutions in Africa; utilize distance education for improving the capacities of teacher education institutions; link educational development to economic development through collaboration with the African Union, subregional and regional educational institutions; promote international cooperation for the development of education through the New Partnership for Africa's Development. **Structure** Governing Board, consisting of 12 full members chosen for their eminence in fields relevant to education and the aims of the Institute and sitting in a personal capacity, plus an alternate member to each full member representing the same field of competence. Members, together with their alternates, appointed by the Director-General of UNESCO as follows: (1) Nine members and their alternates appointed for a period of 4 years having regard for equitable geographical, linguistic and gender distribution; one of the members and his/her alternate must be a national of the host country; (2) Two members and their alternates from regional organizations in Africa designated, for a period of 3 years, in rotation – *African Union (AU, #00488)*, *United Nations Economic Commission for Africa (ECA, #20554)*, *African Development Bank (ADB, #00283)* and *Association for the Development of Education in Africa (ADEA, #02471)*; (3) One member and his/her alternate appointed for a period of 3 years to represent the bilateral donor community, including foundations. **Languages** English, French, Portuguese. **Staff** 19.00 FTE, paid. **Finance** Regular budget of UNESCO; voluntary contributions of UNESCO member states. **Activities** Programme areas (3): Teacher Development Policy (including education, training, career development, welfare, etc); ICTs in Education; Research and Advocacy. Areas of activities geared towards implementation of TTISSA, a UNESCO action framework for teacher development in SSA. Support to member States through 4 main modalities and services: capacity building and training; ODL; research and development; partnership and networking. Strategic priorities (2005-2010): building capacity for education policy and leadership; applying distance education to address problems of teacher shortages in Africa; incorporating ICTs into teacher training; exploring innovative approaches to address challenges faced by African teachers including HIV/AIDS; networking and nurturing strategic partnerships. **Publications** *IICBA Newsletter* (2 a year) in English, French, Portuguese. Training series – CD-ROM; research monographs. **Information Services** *IICBA Electronic Library* – electronic and paper; *IICBA Teacher Education Network* – online discussion forum, DVDs, official website, resoure materials on ICT in Education and HIV/AIDS. **IGO Relations** Representatives of the following may be invited to Board meetings without the right to vote: *International Bureau of Education (IBE, #12413)*; *International Institute for Educational Planning (IIEP, #13874)*; *UNESCO Institute for Lifelong Learning (UIL, #20305)*. **NGO Relations** Partners: international and bilateral donor agencies (not specified). Founding Member of: *Federation of African Societies of Chemistry (FASC, #09411)*. [2021/XE4185/j/**E***]

♦ UNESCO International Institute for Higher Education in Latin America and the Caribbean 20309

Institut International de l'UNESCO pour l'enseignement supérieur en Amérique latine et dans les Caraïbes – Instituto Internacional de la UNESCO para la Educación Superior en América Latina y el Caribe (UNESCO-IESALC)

Dir Edificio Asovincar, Av Los Chorros con Calle Acueducto, Altos de Sebucan, Caracas DF, Venezuela. T. +582122860555 – +582122861020. Fax +582122860527.
URL: http://www.iesalc.unesco.org.ve/

History 14 Feb 1978, Caracas (Venezuela), within the framework of *UNESCO (#20322)*. Original title *UNESCO Regional Centre for Higher Education in Latin America and the Caribbean – Centre régional de l'UNESCO pour l'enseignement supérieur en Amérique latine et dans les Caraïbes – Centro Regional de la UNESCO para la Educación Superior en América Latina y el Caribe (CRESALC)*. From 1995, functions as *UNESCO Caracas Office*. Transformed into an institute under current title during a transition period 1998-1999, following decision of 29th General Conference of UNESCO. Also referred to as *International Institute for Higher Education in Latin America and the Caribbean – Institut International pour l'enseignement supérieur en Amérique latine et dans les Caraïbes – Instituto Internacional para la Educación Superior en América Latina y el Caribe*. **Aims** Strengthen cooperation among member states in the field of higher education; contribute to renewal of higher education in the region and to improvement in reciprocal knowledge of *tertiary education* systems; assist member states' efforts to develop or improve their systems and institutions of learning and research; lay the basis for *sustainable human development* founded on justice, equity, freedom, solidarity and peace by emphasizing *human resource* development, capacity building and cooperation agreements targeting a "new social pact"; achieve better utilization of human and educational resources by promoting greater mobility of professionals in higher education systems; act as a clearing house and reference centre supporting member states and institutions in improving higher education; facilitate exchange of information and experience among institutions in the region and elsewhere.

Main thrusts:
- Promotion of research on higher education, evaluation and accreditation of academic programmes and institutions, development of a regional system of information and documentation and improving technological capacity in higher education;
- Fostering lifelong education for all and promoting links between higher education and society;
- Stimulating development of new models of institutional management and training of public policy-makers in higher education;
- Putting in place new forms of inter-institutional cooperation focused on further developing *postgraduate* studies of excellence.

Structure Administrative Council of 13, including President and Vice-President. Includes: *Regional Unit for Social and Human Sciences in Latin America and the Caribbean (URSHLAC, no recent information)*; *Regional Unit for Information and Informatics in Latin America and the Caribbean (CII/LAC, no recent information)*. **Languages** English, French, Portuguese, Spanish. **Staff** 7.00 FTE, paid. **Finance** Main source: allocation under regular programme of UNESCO. Other sources: voluntary contributions of UNESCO member states and international organizations, foundations and other donors (not specified); fees for training and research projects. **Activities** Research/documentation; events/meetings. Management of treaties and agreements: *Regional Convention on the Recognition of Titles, Studies and Diplomas (1911)*. **Events** *Conference* Córdoba (Argentina) 2018, *International Conference on Diversity, Quality and Improvement* Santiago (Chile) 2018, *Conference* Cartagena de Indias (Colombia) 2008, *Meeting on integration in Latin America and Caribbean and the role of higher education institutions* Caracas (Venezuela) 2006, *Meeting* San José (Costa Rica) 2006. **Publications** *Bibliografia Selectiva de Educación Superior en América Latina y el Caribe* (2 a year); *Educación Superior / Resúmenes Analíticos – Higher Education / Analytical Abstracts – Enseignement supérieur / Résumés analytiques* (2 a year); *Revista Educación Superior – Higher Education Review – Enseignement supérieur revue* (2 a year). Monograph series by country on higher education in Latin America and the Caribbean. Series of working documents; books. Information Services: Information and Documentation Service (SID) – gathers and distributes documentation and information related to higher education, in collaboration with existing national, sub-regional and regional services. **Information Services** *Banco de Datos de Información Cualitativa sobre Educación Superior (BANIC)*; *Diccionario de Descriptores (ITEM)*; *LOGO* – bibliographic database on education, social sciences; *POB* – bibliographic database on population education, sexuality, family, demography; *SID* – bibliographic database on higher education; *Sistema de Información Referencial – Proyectos (GENTE)* – database; *STADT* – database of statistical information.

Members Countries covered (34):
Antigua-Barbuda, Argentina, Bahamas, Barbados, Belize, Bolivia, Brazil, Chile, Colombia, Costa Rica, Cuba, Dominica, Dominican Rep, Ecuador, El Salvador, Grenada, Guatemala, Guyana, Haiti, Honduras, Jamaica, Mexico, Neth Antilles, Nicaragua, Panama, Paraguay, Peru, St Kitts-Nevis, St Lucia, St Vincent-Grenadines, Suriname, Trinidad-Tobago, Uruguay, Venezuela.

NGO Relations Through SID is a member of: *Information Network on Education for Latin America (no recent information)*. Member of: *Red Iberoamericana para el Aseguramiento de la Calidad en la Educación Superior (RIACES, #18657)*. Cooperates in: *UNITWIN/UNESCO Chairs Programme (#20669)*. Instrumental in setting up: *Network of Macrouniversities of Latin America and the Caribbean (#17047)*. Cooperates with: *International Association of Universities (IAU, #12246)*. Through UNITWIN, links with: *Network of UNESCO Chairs and Training Centres in Cultural Policy and Management (NETCULT, no recent information)*. [2017/XE8660/j/**E***]

♦ UNESCO International Network of Textbook Research Institutes / see UNESCO International Research Network on Educational Resources
♦ UNESCO International Research Network on Educational Resources (internationally oriented national body)
♦ UNESCO International Research and Training Centre for Rural Education (internationally oriented national body)
♦ UNESCO Jakarta Office / see UNESCO Office, Jakarta – Regional Bureau for Sciences in Asia and the Pacific (#20313)
♦ UNESCO Jakarta Regional Office for Science and Technology for Southeast Asia / see UNESCO Office, Jakarta – Regional Bureau for Sciences in Asia and the Pacific (#20313)

♦ UNESCO Mahatma Gandhi Institute of Education for Peace and Sustainable Development (UNESCO MGIEP) 20310

Dir ICSSR Bldg – 1st Floor, 35 Ferozshan Road, Delhi 11001, DELHI 11001, India. T. +911123072356 – +911123072357 – +911123072360. E-mail: mgiep@unesco.org.
URL: https://mgiep.unesco.org/

History Proposed 2009, by *UNESCO (#20322)* General Conference. Launched 2012. A UNESCO category 1 Research Institute. **Aims** Achieve Sustainable Development Goad 4-7 towards education to foster peaceful and sustainable societies. **Structure** Governing Board; Office of the Director. **Finance** Support from Indian government. **Activities** Projects/programmes; capacity building. **Publications** *The Blue Dot*. Working Paper Series. [2019/XM9006/**E**]

♦ UNESCO Mediterranean Programme (inactive)
♦ **UNESCO MGIEP** UNESCO Mahatma Gandhi Institute of Education for Peace and Sustainable Development (#20310)
♦ UNESCO Montevideo Office / see UNESCO Office, Montevideo – Regional Bureau for Sciences in Latin America and the Caribbean (#20314)

♦ UNESCO Network of Associated Libraries (UNAL) 20311

Réseau UNESCO de bibliothèques associées – Red UNESCO de Bibliotecas Asociadas

Main Office CI/INF UNESCO, 1 rue Miollis, 75732 Paris CEDEX 15, France. T. +33145684497. Fax +33145685583.
URL: http://www.unesco.org/

History 1990, Paris (France), as a project of the General Information Programme of *UNESCO (#20322)*. **Aims** Bring together and support a group of libraries, working in association with UNESCO and cooperating organizations, to: foster international understanding; promote dialogue between cultures; encourage multicultural initiatives; spread knowledge of minority cultures; increase awareness of international issues and pursue some of UNESCO's main goals – promotion of peace and human rights, work for literacy, protection of environment, cultural development. **Finance** Limited budget. Project financing usually met by member libraries. **Activities** Events/meetings; knowledge management/information dissemination; awards/prizes/competitions. **Events** *International Conference* Florence (Italy) 1998, *Asia regional seminar* 1996, *Latin America regional seminar* Cuba 1996, *International Conference* Florence (Italy) 1994, *Workshop on libraries without boundaries / International Conference* Moscow (Russia) 1994. **Publications** *UNAL-Info* (occasional) – bulletin. Monographs; meeting reports.

Members Libraries open to the public (450) in 88 countries and territories:
Algeria, Argentina, Bangladesh, Belgium, Benin, Bolivia, Brazil, Bulgaria, Burkina Faso, Burundi, Cameroon, Chad, Chile, Colombia, Congo Brazzaville, Congo DR, Costa Rica, Côte d'Ivoire, Croatia, Cuba, Dominica, Dominican Rep, Ecuador, Egypt, El Salvador, Eritrea, Estonia, Fiji, Finland, France, Gambia, Germany, Greece, Guinea, Haiti, Honduras, Hong Kong, Hungary, India, Iran Islamic Rep, Ireland, Israel, Italy, Jamaica, Jordan, Kenya, Laos, Latvia, Lebanon, Malawi, Maldives, Mali, Malta, Mexico, Moldova, Morocco, New Zealand, Niger, Nigeria, North Macedonia, Pakistan, Papua New Guinea, Peru, Philippines, Poland, Portugal, Puerto Rico, Russia, Senegal, Slovakia, Slovenia, Solomon Is, Spain, Sri Lanka, St Kitts-Nevis, St Vincent-Grenadines, Sweden, Tanzania UR, Thailand, Togo, Uganda, UK, USA, Venezuela, Virgin Is UK, Zambia, Zimbabwe.

Of the above mentioned libraries, 4 listed in this Yearbook:
African Heritage Research Library and Cultural Center (AHRLC, #00337); Institute for Black Peoples (IBP, no recent information); International Maize and Wheat Improvement Center (#14077); International Youth Library (IYL, #15936).

IGO Relations UNESCO. **NGO Relations** *International Association of Universities (IAU, #12246); World Federation of UNESCO Clubs, Centres and Associations (WFUCA, #21498); World Library Partnership (WLP, no recent information).* [2008/XF1763/y/**F**]

♦ UNESCO Office, Cairo – Regional Bureau for Sciences in the Arab States (ROSTAS) 20312

Bureau régional de l'UNESCO de science et de technologie pour les Etats arabes

Dir 8 Abdel-Rahman Fahmy Street, Garden City, Cairo, 11541, Egypt. T. +2027950424 – +2027945599. Fax +2027945296. E-mail: cairo@unesco.org.
URL: https://en.unesco.org/news/unesco-regional-bureau-sciences-arab-states-arab-republic-egypt-cairo

History 1947, Cairo (Egypt), within the framework of *UNESCO (#20322)*. Agreement between UNESCO and host country: 25 Apr 1952. Sometimes referred to as *UNESCO Regional Bureau for Science in the Arab States – Bureau régional de l'UNESCO de science pour les Etats arabes*. From 1995, also functions as *UNESCO Cairo Office (UCO) – Bureau de l'UNESCO au Caire.* **Aims** Contribute to the scientific development of Arab member states of UNESCO through planning and implementation of UNESCO's decentralized science and *informatics* programme for the region; support the national host country in implementing education and culture programmes. **Structure** General Conference (every 2 years); Executive Board; Secretariat. **Activities** Provides training and advisory services; carries out research; holds regional and subregional training workshops, seminars and symposia. Set up *Science and Technology Management Arab Regional Network (STEMARN, no recent information).* **Events** *International conference on wadi hydrology* Sanaa (Yemen) 2005, *Regional workshop on the utilization of agricultural residues in the Near East region* Damascus (Syrian AR) 1994, *Regional seminar* Doha (Qatar) 1988, *International conference in Africa on computer methods and their application to water resources* Rabat (Morocco) 1988, *Regional seminar on the major regional project on the rational use and conservation of water resources in rural areas in the Arab States* Tunis (Tunisia) 1987. **Publications** *UNESCO Cairo Office Newsletter* (2 a year). Annual report – online. **Information Services** *GRIDOC* – multidisciplinary database.

Members Countries and territories served by UNESCO Cairo Office (21):
Algeria, Bahrain, Djibouti, Egypt, Iraq, Jordan, Kuwait, Lebanon, Libya, Mauritania, Morocco, Oman, Palestine, Qatar, Saudi Arabia, Somalia, Sudan, Syrian AR, Tunisia, United Arab Emirates, Yemen.

NGO Relations Represented on Steering Committee of: *Arab Biosciences Network (AraBN, no recent information).* [2008/XE9588/**E***]

♦ UNESCO Office in Delhi / see UNESCO Asia-Pacific Regional Bureau for Communication and Information (#20300)

♦ UNESCO Office for Education in the Arab States / see UNESCO Regional Office for Education in the Arab States (#20320)

♦ UNESCO Office, Jakarta – Regional Bureau for Sciences in Asia and the Pacific 20313

Dir UNESCO House, Jalan Galuh (II) No 5, Kebayoran Baru, Jakarta 12110, Indonesia. T. +62217399818. Fax +622172796489. E-mail: jakarta@unesco.org.
Office for Science and Technology in China UNESCO Beijing Office, Jianwaigongyu 5-15-3, 100600 Beijing, China. T. +86165321725 – +86165322828 – +86165326469. Fax +86165324854. E-mail: beijing@unesco.org.
URL: http://www.unesco.org/jakarta/

History 1951, Jakarta (Indonesia), within the framework of *UNESCO (#20322)*, as *UNESCO Field Office for South East Asian Science Cooperation (SEASCO)*. Originally hosted by Indonesia, temporarily transferred to Bangkok (Thailand) in 1965, but returned to Jakarta in 1967 as *UNESCO Regional Office for Science and Technology for Southeast Asia (ROSTSEA) – Bureau régional de l'UNESCO de science et de technologie pour l'Asie du Sud-Est* or *UNESCO Jakarta Regional Office for Science and Technology for Southeast Asia – Bureau régional de l'UNESCO de Jakarta de science et de technologie pour l'Asie du Sud-Est*, and also referred to by the initials *UNESCO/ROSTSEA*. Subsequent name changes: *UNESCO Jakarta Office – Bureau de l'UNESCO à Jakarta*, 1993; *UNESCO Office, Jakarta – Regional Science Bureau for Asia and the Pacific*, 2001, and also started functioning as the *Office for the UNESCO Representative to Indonesia, Malaysia and the Philippines*. Since 2003, also functions as the *Office for the UNESCO Representative to Indonesia, Malaysia, the Philippines and Timor-Leste*, following signing of the instrument of Acceptance of Membership by Timor-Leste in 2002. Since 2005, also functions as the *Office for the UNESCO Representative to Brunei Darussalam, Indonesia, Malaysia, the Philippines and Timor-Leste*, when Brunei Darussalam became 191st member of UNESCO. **Aims** Contribute to peace and human development in a era of globalization through *education, sciences, culture* and *communication*; reduce poverty through education for all, applying scientific knowledge to the benefit of the poor and removing social, cultural and communications barriers to equity; humanize globalization through building cultural and communication bridges, assurance of cultural heritage and empowerment of the marginalized to participate; bridge the digital divide through socio-technical innovation; redress marginalization of women and young people; assist in combating the threat of HIV/AIDS through providing essential knowledge and changing negative attitudes and behaviours through education and advocacy; empower indigenous cultures confronting the modern world; create a sustainable world for present and future generations through linking science and ecological knowledge with an understanding of community and social processes; promote freedom of expression, free flow of information and press freedom; promote peace by addressing the challenges of globalization. **Languages** English.

Activities Organizes training courses, workshops, seminars and symposia in cooperation with the relevant government ministries or departments, universities, institutions, professional bodies, scientific councils and academics, intergovernmental and non-governmental bodies. Training programmes: (i) Long-term international training courses (6 months – 2 years) for post-graduate students from developing countries; (ii) Short-term training courses (1 week – 3 months), mostly on a regional or sub-regional basis; (iii) Individual fellowships for senior scientists, technologists and engineers to attend a non-UNESCO training activity in another country; (iv) Awards within regional network programmes supported by UNESCO, for exchange of scientists, technologists and engineers within the region (normally among the developing countries); (v) Study awards and travel awards, mainly for young scientists, technologists and engineers; (vi) visiting lecturers and professors.

Field of activities: Education; Science, including Water, Environmental, Earth, Engineering Sciences and Technology, Basic, and Coastal Regional and Small Islands; Social and Human Science; Culture; Communication; Intersectoral; Special Focus.

Regional Networks:
'Education':
– *Asia/Pacific Cultural Centre for UNESCO (ACCU, #01879)*;
– *SEAMEO Regional Center for Educational Innovation and Technology (SEAMEO INNOTECH, #19168)*;
– *UNESCO International Research and Training Centre for Rural Education (INRULED)*;
– *Asia-Pacific Network for International Education and Values Education (APNIEVE, #01970)*;
– *Asia-Pacific Programme of Educational Innovation for Development (APEID, #02001).*
'Sciences':
– *Science and Technology Policy Asian Network (STEPAN, #19144)*;
– *Asian Physics Education Network (ASPEN, #01664)*;
– *UNESCO Regional Network for Microbiology and Microbial Biotechnology in Southeast Asia (#20319)*;
– *ASEAN Institute of Physics (ASEANIP, #01199)*;
– *Association of Asia Pacific Physical Societies (AAPPS, #02388)*;
– *Federation of Engineering Institutions of Asia and the Pacific (FEIAP, #09480)*;
– *Association for Engineering Education in Southeast Asia and the Pacific (AEESEAP, #02487)*;
– Regional Steering Committee of the *International Hydrological Programme (IHP, #13826)* Southeast Asia and the Pacific (RSC);
– *Asian Pacific FRIEND (FRIEND/APF, no recent information)*;
– *UNESCO Environment and Development in Coastal Regions and Small Islands (UNESCO CSI Programme, see: #20322)*;
– *East Asian Biosphere Reserve Network (EABRN, #05199)*;
– *Southeast Asian Biosphere Reserve Network (SeaBRnet, #19759).*
'Communication':
– *Asia Pacific Information Network (APIN, #01931).*

Instrumental in setting up: *Regional Network for Community Technology for Southeast Asia and the Pacific (RNTCD, inactive); Regional Secretariat for Gender, Science and Technology in Southeast Asia and the Pacific (RESGEST, see: #20313).*

Events *Workshop on integrated ecosystem management* Pakse (Laos) 2005, *Regional workshop on agriwastes* Beijing (China) 1992, *Regional seminar on waste treatment and recovery technology* Bogor (Indonesia) 1992, *Regional seminar on world heritage convention* Jakarta (Indonesia) 1992, *Conference on function and analysis and global analysis* Manila (Philippines) 1992. **Publications** Annual Report; specialized activity reports; research papers; wall chart series; meeting proceedings; brochures; leaflets. Information Services: Library. **Information Services** *Coral Reef Database; Library; UNESCO ROSTSEA Holdings* – database.

Members Covers 30 countries and territories:
Australia, Cambodia, China, Cook Is, Fiji, Hong Kong, Indonesia, Japan, Kiribati, Korea Rep, Macau, Malaysia, Marshall Is, Micronesia FS, Mongolia, Nauru, New Zealand, Niue, Palau, Papua New Guinea, Philippines, Samoa, Solomon Is, Thailand, Timor-Leste, Tokelau, Tonga, Tuvalu, Vanuatu, Vietnam.

IGO Relations Carries out initiatives in close cooperation with National Commissions for UNESCO, UNESCO Headquarters and relevant field offices. Cooperating organizations:
– *Abdus Salam International Centre for Theoretical Physics (ICTP, #00005)*;
– *ASEAN (#01141)*;
– *Asia-Pacific Institute for Broadcasting Development (AIBD, #01934)*;
– *Asian Development Bank (ADB, #01422)*;
– *Australian Aid (inactive)*;
– *Centre de coopération internationale en recherche agronomique pour le développement (CIRAD, #03733)*;
– *International Bank for Reconstruction and Development (IBRD, #12317)* (World Bank);
– *International Tropical Timber Organization (ITTO, #15737)*;
– *Japan International Cooperation Agency (JICA)*;
– *Programme on Man and the Biosphere (MAB, #18526)*;
– *Regional Humid Tropics Hydrology and Water Resources Centre for South East Asia and the Pacific (HTC, #18787)*;
– *Southeast Asian Regional Centre for Tropical Biology (SEAMEO BIOTROP, #19782)*;
– *UNEP (#20299)*;
– *UNDP (#20292)* (Asia Pacific Gender Programme – APGEN);
– *UNICEF (#20332)*;
– *United Nations Commission on Science and Technology for Development (CSTD, #20534)*;
– *United Nations Economic and Social Commission for Asia and the Pacific (ESCAP, #20557)*;
– *United Nations Mission of Support in East Timor (UNMISET, inactive)*;
– *United Nations University (UNU, #20642)*;
– *United Nations Volunteers (UNV, #20650).*

Cooperates in *'World Solar Programme'* managed by: *World Solar Commission (no recent information).*

NGO Relations Cooperating organizations:
– *Asia-Pacific Centre for Theoretical Physics (APCTP)*;
– *Asian Alliance of Appropriate Technology Practitioners (APPROTECH ASIA, #01306)*;
– *Asian Coordinating Group for Chemistry (ACGC, no recent information)*;
– *Asian Institute of Technology (AIT, #01519)*;
– *Asian Symposium on Medicinal Plants, Spices and Other Natural Products (ASOMPS)*;
– *Association of Universities of Asia and the Pacific (AUAP, #02968)*;
– *Centre for International Cooperation and Computerization (CICC)*;
– *Center for International Forestry Research (CIFOR, #03646)*;
– *Centre for Research on Sustainable Agriculture and Rural Development (Swaminathan Research Foundation)*;
– *Conservation International (CI)* Indonesia Programme;
– *Greater Mekong Subregion Academic and Research Network (GMSARN, no recent information)*;
– *Hearing International (#10895)* (Japan);
– *International Centre for Biotechnology, Osaka University (no recent information)*;
– *International Society for Mangrove Ecosystems (ISME, #15245)*;
– *The Nature Conservancy (TNC)*;
– *Oxfam GB*;
– *Pacific Foundation for the Advancement of Women (PACFAW, #17950)*;
– *SPIE (#19919)*;
– *World Council for Renewable Energy (WCRE, #21340)*;
– *World Vision International (WVI, #21904).* [2018.03.08/XE9604/**E***]

♦ UNESCO Office, Jakarta – Regional Science Bureau for Asia and the Pacific / see UNESCO Office, Jakarta – Regional Bureau for Sciences in Asia and the Pacific (#20313)

♦ UNESCO Office, Montevideo – Regional Bureau for Sciences in Latin America and the Caribbean 20314

Bureau régional de science de l'UNESCO pour l'Amérique latine et les Caraïbes – Oficina Regional de Ciencia de la UNESCO para América Latina y el Caribe (ORCYT)

Contact Edificio MERCOSUR, Calle Dr Luis Piera 1992, 2do piso, 11200 Montevideo, Uruguay. T. +58924132075. E-mail: montevideo@unesco.org.
URL: http://www.unesco.org.montevideo/

History Jan 1949, Montevideo (Uruguay), as *Centre for Scientific Cooperation of UNESCO for Latin America*, within the framework of *UNESCO (#20322)*. In 1975, adopted the title *UNESCO Regional Office for Science and Technology for Latin America and the Caribbean (ROSTLAC) – Bureau régional de science et de technologie de l'UNESCO pour l'Amérique latine et les Caraïbes – Oficina Regional de Ciencia y Tecnologia de la UNESCO para América Latina y el Caribe (ORCYT)*, also known by initials *UNESCO/ROSTLAC*. Agreement signed between UNESCO and the Government of Uruguay, Oct 1987. From 1995, functions as *UNESCO Montevideo Office – Bureau de l'UNESCO à Montevideo – Oficina de UNESCO en Montevideo*, also referred to as *UNESCO Oficina de Montevideo*. 1995, incorporation of the Education Sector, followed by Social Sciences Programme and Communication and Information Sector, 1999. In 2000, Culture Sector joins the Office. **Aims** Work to strengthen scientific, technological and innovation policies and ensure international cooperation in various environmental sciences, basic sciences, engineering and science policy. **Structure** Director; International Programme Specialists (7); National Programme Officers (2); Secretariat Assistants; Administration Unit. **Languages** English, Spanish. **Staff** 17 permanent; 16 temporary. **Finance** UNESCO's regular budget; extra budgetary funds from donors. **Activities** Research and development; knowledge management/information dissemination; capacity building; networking/liaising. Management of treaties and agreements: *Convention for the Protection of Cultural Property in the Event of Armed Conflict (The Hague Convention, 1954, 1954); Convention on the Protection and Promotion of the Diversity of Cultural Expressions (2005).* **Events** *International symposium on hydrology in the humid tropics environment* Kingston (Jamaica) 1996. **Publications** *SE¥AL Newsletter.* Online books and documents; kits; posters.

Members Countries covered (33):
Antigua-Barbuda, Argentina, Bahamas, Barbados, Belize, Bolivia, Brazil, Chile, Colombia, Costa Rica, Cuba, Dominica, Dominican Rep, Ecuador, El Salvador, Grenada, Guatemala, Guyana, Haiti, Honduras, Jamaica, Mexico, Nicaragua, Panama, Paraguay, Peru, St Kitts-Nevis, St Lucia, St Vincent-Grenadines, Suriname, Trinidad-Tobago, Uruguay, Venezuela.

Associate Members of UNESCO covered by ROSTLAC (2):
Neth Antilles, Virgin Is UK.

IGO Relations Through programmes, links with:
– *Andean Community (#00817)*;
– *Association of Caribbean States (ACS, #02411)*;
– *Caribbean Community (CARICOM, #03476)*;
– *Central American Integration System (#03671)*;
– *Centre for the Sustainable Management of Water Resources in the Caribbean Island States (CEHICA)*;

- *Centro Latino-Americano de Fisica (CLAF, #03815)*;
- *Centro Regional sobre la Gestión del Agua en Zonas Urbanas para América Latina y el Caribe*;
- *Centro Regional de Sismologia para América del Sur (CERESIS, #03818)*;
- *Coalition of Latin American and Caribbean Cities for the Fight against Racism, Discrimination and Xenophobia*;
- *Comité Intergubernamental Coordinador de los Paises de la Cuenca del Plata (CIC, #04172)*;
- *Comité Regional de Recursos Hidraulicos del Istmo Centroamericano (CRRH, #04196)*;
- *FAO (#09260)*;
- *Fundação Centro Internacional de Educação, Capacitação e Pesquisa Aplicada em Aguas (HidroEx)*;
- *Global Environment Facility (GEF, #10346)*;
- *Global Water Partnership – South America and Central America*;
- *Ibero-American General Secretariat (#11024)*;
- *Information Society Program for Latin America and the Caribbean (INFOLAC, inactive)*;
- *'Intergovernmental Committee (UNESCO/IGC)'*;
- *Intergovernmental Oceanographic Commission (IOC, #11496)*;
- *International Centre on Hydroinformatics (CIH)*;
- *International Centre for Water Hazard and Risk Management (ICHARM)*;
- *International Geoscience Programme (IGCP, #13715)*;
- *International Hydrological Programme (IHP, #13826)*;
- *IOC Sub-Commission for the Caribbean and Adjacent Regions (IOCARIBE, #16003)*;
- *Latin American Faculty of Social Sciences (#16316)*;
- *OAS (#17629)*;
- *Programa Iberoamericano de Ciencia y Tecnologia para el Desarrollo (CYTED, #18524)*;
- *Regional Water Centre for Arid and Semi-Arid Regions of Latin America and the Caribbean (CAZALAC)*;
- *Simon Bolivar Inter-American Library (#19283)*;
- *Sistema Económico Latinoamericano (SELA, #19294)*;
- *Southern Common Market (#19868)*;
- all specialized UN agencies, programmes and funds in the region and sub-region;
- *UNEP (#20299)*;
- *Union of South American Nations (#20481)*;
- *United Nations Human Settlements Programme (UN-Habitat, #20572)*;
- *World Meteorological Organization (WMO, #21649)*.

NGO Relations Through programmes, links with:
- *Academia de Ciencias de América Latina (ACAL, #00010)*;
- *Asia Centre*;
- *Centro de Coordinación para la Prevención de los Desastres Naturales en América Central (CEPREDENAC, #03795)*;
- *Centro Internacional de Ecologia Tropical (CIET, #03805)*;
- *Consejo Latinoamericano de Ciencias Sociales (CLACSO, #04718)*;
- *IHE Delft Institute for Water Education (#11110)*;
- *International Association of Seismology and Physics of the Earth's Interior (IASPEI, #12157)*;
- *International Brain Research Organization (IBRO, #12392)*;
- *International Cell Research Organization (ICRO, #12463)*;
- *International Council for Science (ICSU, inactive)*;
- *International Union for Conservation of Nature and Natural Resources (IUCN, #15766)*;
- *Red Latinoamericana de Ciencias Biológicas (RELAB, #18706)*;
- *Latin American Programme for the Human Genome (no recent information)*;
- *Network for Science and Technology Popularization in Latin America and the Caribbean (#17057)*;
- *Red de Programas de Postgrado en Planificación y Gestión de Ciencia y Tecnologia en América Latina (Red POST, no recent information)*;
- *Regional Project for Research and Training on Coastal Systems of Latin America and the Caribbean and their relations with the Continental Shelf (COSALC, no recent information)*;
- *UNESCO World Network of Microbiological Resources Centres MIRCEN (no recent information)*;
- *Unión Panamericana de Asociaciones de Ingenieros (UPADI, #20469)*;
- *UNU Programme for Biotechnology in Latin America and the Caribbean (UNU/BIOLAC, see: #20642)*.

Instrumental in setting up: *Red de Redes Cientificas de América Latina y el Caribe (CCRCLA, no recent information)*. Provides secretariat for: *Red Latinoamericana y del Caribe de Bioética (REDBIOETICA, #18702)*. [2011.01.15/XE9595/E*]

♦ UNESCO Office, Nairobi – Regional Bureau for Sciences in Africa (inactive)

♦ UNESCO Office for the Pacific States 20315

Bureau de l'UNESCO pour les Etats du Pacifique

Sec PO Box 615, Matautu Uta, Apia, Samoa. T. +68524276. Fax +68526593. E-mail: apia@unesco.org.
Dir address not obtained.
URL: https://en.unesco.org/fieldoffice/apia/about/

History 17 Sep 1984, Apia (Samoa). Set up within the framework of *UNESCO (#20322)*. Functions as *UNESCO Apia Office – Bureau de l'UNESCO à Apia*; also referred to as *UNESCO Cluster Office for the Pacific States*. **Aims** Develop and provide technical assistance in *cultural development* policies; promotes *traditional* and *natural heritage*. **Finance** UNESCO Regular Programme and extra-budgetary resources for electronic and print-media projects and promotion of science and culture. Principal funding agencies: NZODA; *UNDP (#20292)*; *International Programme for the Development of Communication (IPDC, #14651)*. **Activities** Projects include: Secondary in-school teacher training; Associated Schools Project; Pacific schools management (training of inspectors and school principals); Pacific secondary vocational curriculum development (industrial arts, commercial studies and home economics); Educational planning (Vanuatu); Pacific educational publishing; Science and technology education, with emphasis on teacher education; Promotion of literacy; Water resources field research projects; Project on traditional knowledge of marine resources. **Events** *Consultation for Pacific UNESCO National Members States* Tonga 1997, *High-Level Consultation of Pacific Educators* Honiara (Solomon Is) 1996, *Biennial high-level consultation of Pacific educators* Honiara (Solomon Is) 1995, *Biennial consultation for Pacific UNESCO national member states / Consultation for Pacific UNESCO National Members States* Port Moresby (Papua New Guinea) 1995, *High-level consultation of Pacific directors of culture* Apia (Samoa) 1994. **Publications** *Commercial Studies Manual*; *Multiclass Teaching in Primary Schools*; *Pacific Islands Literacy Levels Study*; *Practical Innovations for Clinical Supervision in Education*; *Standardized Appraisal Manual* – field guide for headteachers; *The Samoan Fale*; *Words of Accounting, Small Business, Bookkeeping, Economics and Commerce* in English, Samoan – lexicon. **Information Services** *Apia Library Database*; *Educational Management Information System* – micro-computer based system adapted to upper level management in small states.

Members Covers 15 countries and territories:
Australia, Cook Is, Fiji, Kiribati, Marshall Is, Micronesia FS, Nauru, New Zealand, Niue, Papua New Guinea, Samoa, Solomon Is, Tonga, Tuvalu, Vanuatu.

NGO Relations Coordinates: *Regional Information and Informatics Network for South Pacific Island Nations (RIINPIN, no recent information)*. [2022/XE8323/E*]

♦ UNESCO Office in Venice – UNESCO Regional Bureau for Science and Culture in Europe (BRESCE) 20316

Dir Palazzo Zorzi, Castello 4930, 30122 Venice VE, Italy. T. +39412601511. Fax +39415289995. E-mail: veniceoffice@unesco.org.
URL: http://www.unesco.org/venice/

History Established 1971, as *Regional Bureau for European Scientific Cooperation*, by *UNESCO (#20322)*, and located at UNESCO Headquarters. Transferred to Venice (Italy) and name changed, 1988, to *UNESCO Regional Office for Science and Technology for Europe (ROSTE) – Bureau régional de science et de technologie pour de l'UNESCO pour l'Europe*. Name changed, 1999, *UNESCO Regional Bureau for Science in Europe (ROSTE)*. Previously also referred to as *UNESCO Venice Office – Regional Office for Science and Technology for Europe (UVO-ROSTE)*. Present name adopted in 2006. **Aims** Enhance UNESCO's role in scientific and cultural cooperation within the South East European region; foster East-West cooperation in Europe; increase scientific and cultural exchanges among countries of the *Mediterranean*. **Finance** On regular budget of UNESCO. Other sources include subsidy for offices and operating expenses from Government of Italy. **Activities** Administers all UNESCO activities and liaison functions in Venice (Italy). Collaborates with national and international academies, universities and other scientific and cultural institutions by: promoting research; organizing training activities; improving information exchange through new means of communication, promoting mobility of experts and researchers and sponsoring their participation at scientific meetings and workshops; organizing high-level colloquia and stimulating debates; disseminating information. Fields of competence: basic sciences; engineering and applied research; environment; transformation of scientific communities in Europe; cultural initiatives. Major programmes include: The sciences in the service of development; Cultural development – heritage and creativity. Instrumental in setting up: *International Radioecology Laboratory (IRL)*; *European Network Man Against Virus (no recent information)*; *International Centre for a Water Civilization (CICA)*; *UNESCO-Hebrew University of Jerusalem International School for Molecular Biology and Microbiology and Science for Peace (UNESCO-HUJ ISMBM)*; *UNESCO International School of Science for Peace (no recent information)*. **Events** *International symposium on sharing heritages* Valencia (Spain) 2008, *Why invest in science in South Eastern Europe international conference* Ljubljana (Slovenia) 2006, *Joint international workshop on MAB biosphere reserves and transboundary cooperation in the SEE region* Belgrade (Serbia-Montenegro) 2004, *European Symposium on Polymer Blends* Capri (Italy) 1993, *Italian-East consultation on biomedical research* Siena (Italy) 1993. **Publications** *UNESCO Venice Office E-Newsletter*. *Science for Peace* – series; *UVO Technical Reports* – series. Annual Report; newsletters.

Members Covers 45 countries:
Albania, Armenia, Austria, Azerbaijan, Belarus, Belgium, Bosnia-Herzegovina, Bulgaria, Canada, Croatia, Cyprus, Czechia, Denmark, Estonia, Finland, France, Georgia, Germany, Greece, Hungary, Iceland, Ireland, Israel, Italy, Latvia, Lithuania, Luxembourg, Malta, Moldova, Monaco, Netherlands, North Macedonia, Norway, Poland, Portugal, Romania, Russia, San Marino, Slovakia, Slovenia, Spain, Sweden, Switzerland, Türkiye, Ukraine.

IGO Relations Operates in close consultation with: *Abdus Salam International Centre for Theoretical Physics (ICTP, #00005)*; *International Centre for Science and High Technology (ICS, inactive)*. **NGO Relations** Member of: *Dinaric Arc Initiative (DAI, no recent information)*. [2016/XE0963/E*]

♦ UNESCO Oficina de Montevideo / see UNESCO Office, Montevideo – Regional Bureau for Sciences in Latin America and the Caribbean (#20314)
♦ UNESCO – OREALC / see UNESCO Regional Bureau for Education in Latin America and the Caribbean (#20318)
♦ UNESCO-PIPS – UNESCO PROAP Information Programmes and Services (no recent information)
♦ UNESCO-PNUE Programme international d'éducation relative à l'environnement (inactive)
♦ UNESCO Principal Regional Office for Asia and the Pacific / see UNESCO Asia and Pacific Regional Bureau for Education (#20301)
♦ UNESCO/PROAP / see UNESCO Asia and Pacific Regional Bureau for Education (#20301)
♦ UNESCO PROAP Information Programmes and Services (no recent information)
♦ UNESCO Regional Bureau for Communication and Information for Latin America (no recent information)
♦ UNESCO Regional Bureau for Communication and Information for South and Central Asia / see UNESCO Asia-Pacific Regional Bureau for Communication and Information (#20300)

♦ UNESCO Regional Bureau for Culture for Latin America and the Caribbean 20317

Bureau régional de l'UNESCO pour la culture en Amérique latine et dans les Caraïbes – Oficina Regional de Cultura de la UNESCO para América Latina y el Caribe (ORCALC)

Dir Calzada 551 – Esq a D, El Vedado, Código Postal 10400, Código Postal 10400 Havana, Cuba. T. +5378333438. Fax +5378333144. E-mail: habana@unesco.org.
URL: http://www.unesco.org/havana/

History 24 Feb 1950, as 'Regional Office – Western Hemisphere'. Adopted the current title in 1972, by an agreement between *UNESCO (#20322)* and the Government of Cuba. Also referred to in English as *UNESCO Regional Office for Culture in Latin America and the Caribbean*. Since 1995, functions as *UNESCO Havana Office – Bureau de l'UNESCO à la Havane – Oficina de la UNESCO en la Havana*. After UNESCO reform 2002-2003, Office in Havana was ratified as Regional Office for Office for Culture and UNESCO Representation to the government of Cuba. **Aims** Represent UNESCO in Latin America and the Caribbean in the fields of culture, cultural heritage, studies on culture, research on cultures, cultural development and cultural policies. **Structure** Director; Administration Service. **Languages** English, French, Spanish. **Staff** 40.00 FTE, paid. **Finance** Supported by: UNESCO. **Activities** Programs of cultural development; Safeguard of Cultural Heritage; Promotion of Pluralism and Intercultural Dialogue; Reinforcement of links between Culture and Development and of other activities on culture. **Events** *Reading 2007 congress* Havana (Cuba) 2007, *Reading 2005 congress* Havana (Cuba) 2005, *International congress on cultural heritage* Havana (Cuba) 2003, *Reading 2003 congress* Havana (Cuba) 2003, *International meeting* Mexico 1999. **Publications** *Oralidad* (annual). Digital publications and books. Information Services: Maintains 'Jaime Torres Bodet' Documentation Centre, including Public Library. CD-ROM with UNESCO Databases. **Information Services** *ICOMOS Database*; *Información Cultural Database (IC)*; *REU Database*. **NGO Relations** Coordinates: *Teacher Network of Latin America and the Caribbean (KIPUS, #20110)*. [2015/XE6224/E*]

♦ UNESCO Regional Bureau for Education in Africa (inactive)
♦ UNESCO Regional Bureau for Education in Asia and the Pacific / see UNESCO Asia and Pacific Regional Bureau for Education (#20301)

♦ UNESCO Regional Bureau for Education in Latin America and the Caribbean 20318

Bureau régional de l'UNESCO d'éducation pour l'Amérique latine et la région des Caraïbes – Oficina Regional de Educación de la UNESCO para América Latina y el Caribe (OREALC/UNESCO Santiago)

Dir Calle Enrique Delpiano 2058, Providencia, Casilla 127, 7511019 Santiago, Santiago Metropolitan, Chile. T. +56224724600 – +56224724632. E-mail: santiago@unesco.org.
URL: http://www.unesco.org/santiago/

History Established 1967, within the framework of *UNESCO (#20322)*. Also referred to as *Regional Office for Education in Latin America and the Caribbean – UNESCO* and by the acronym *UNESCO – OREALC*. Since May 2009, also acts as UNESCO Office for Chile: *UNESCO Santiago Office – Bureau de l'UNESCO à Santiago – Oficina de la UNESCO en Santiago*. **Aims** Assist Member States in defining strategies and programmes to implement the 2030 Sustainable Development Agenda and its 17 sustainable development goals (SDGs), notably SDG-4: "Ensure inclusive and equitable quality education and promote lifelong learning opportunities for all". **Structure** Includes *Latin American Laboratory for Assessment of Quality in Education (#16346)*. **Languages** English, French, Portuguese, Spanish. **Staff** 37.00 FTE, paid. **Finance** Partially by UNESCO regular resources to support *IGU Commission on Geographical Monitoring and Forecasting (inactive)*; *ECHO (inactive)*; *Joint United Nations Programme on HIV/AIDS (UNAIDS, #16149)*; projects funded by private sector, Chilean Government and Spanish cooperation through *Agencia Española de Cooperación Internacional para el Desarrollo (AECID)*. **Activities** Knowledge management/information dissemination; standards/guidelines; research/documentation; guidance/assistance/consulting; politics/policy/regulatory; events/meetings. **Events** *Latin America and the Caribbean Regional GCED Network Meeting* Seoul (Korea Rep) 2021, *Latin America and Caribbean regional preparatory conference to CONFINTEA VI* Mexico City (Mexico) 2008, *Regional conference on policies and strategies for high education reform in Latin America and Caribbean* Havana (Cuba) 1996, *Regional conference of ministers of education of Latin America and the Caribbean* Kingston (Jamaica) 1996, *Orientation workshop on the adaptation of early childhood education training materials* Santiago (Chile) 1987. **Publications** Electronic newsletter. Annual Report; books; studies; press releases; conventions and recommendations; multimedia. **Information Services** *Centro de Documentación UNESCO-Santiago* – documentation centre and library; *LLECE Database* – surveys, reports, teaching guidelines and publications; *PERIO* – bibliographic database to OREALC library.

Members Governments of 39 countries and territories:
Anguilla, Antigua-Barbuda, Argentina, Aruba, Bahamas, Barbados, Belize, Bolivia, Brazil, Cayman Is, Chile, Colombia, Costa Rica, Cuba, Curaçao, Dominica, Dominican Rep, Ecuador, El Salvador, Grenada, Guatemala, Guyana, Haiti, Honduras, Jamaica, Mexico, Nicaragua, Panama, Paraguay, Peru, St Kitts-Nevis, St Lucia, St Maarten, St Vincent-Grenadines, Suriname, Trinidad-Tobago, Uruguay, Venezuela, Virgin Is UK.

IGO Relations UN Co-convenors in the Education 2030 Agenda: *ILO (#11123)*; *International Bank for Reconstruction and Development (IBRD, #12317)* (World Bank); *UN Women (#20724)*; *UNDP (#20292)*; *UNHCR (#20327)*; *UNICEF (#20332)*; *United Nations Population Fund (UNFPA, #20612)*. Additional partners: *Global Partnership for Education (GPE, #10531)*; *OECD (#17693)*. **NGO Relations** Instrumental in setting up: *Latin American and Caribbean Education Innovation Network (INNOVEMOS, #16275)*. [2017.10.10/XE9580/E*]

♦ UNESCO Regional Bureau for Science in the Arab States / see UNESCO Office, Cairo – Regional Bureau for Sciences in the Arab States (#20312)

♦ UNESCO Regional Bureau for Science in Europe / see UNESCO Office in Venice – UNESCO Regional Bureau for Science and Culture in Europe (#20316)
♦ UNESCO Regional Centre for Higher Education in Latin America and the Caribbean / see UNESCO International Institute for Higher Education in Latin America and the Caribbean (#20309)

♦ UNESCO Regional Network for Microbiology and Microbial Biotechnology in Southeast Asia 20319

Exec Sec Nat'l Ctre for Genetic Engineering and Biotechnology, 113 Paholyothin Road, Klong 1, Klong Luang, Pathum Thani, 12120, Thailand. T. +6625646700. Fax +6625646705.
Public Information Assistant UNESCO Office Jakarta, Jl Galuh II No 5, Kebayoran Baru, Jakarta 12110, Indonesia. T. +62217399818ext851. Fax +622172796489. E-mail: jakarta@unesco.org.
URL: http://.unesco.org/

History Established 1974, under the auspices of *UNESCO Office, Jakarta – Regional Bureau for Sciences in Asia and the Pacific (#20313)*, at the initiative of *UNESCO (#20322)*. Previously referred to a *Regional Network for Microbiology in Southeast Asia – Réseau de l'Asie du Sud-Est sur la microbiologie.* **Aims** Strengthen research and training capabilities of national faculties and institutions through regional programmes; promote regional cooperation in the advancement of science. **Structure** Coordinating Board (meets annually); National Points of Contact. **Languages** English. **Finance** Financed from UNESCO's regular budget and other resources. **Activities** Participates in cooperative research; arranges exchange of scientists' scheme which provides to young scientists the opportunity to study at institutions in other countries of the regional network; organizes training courses and regional workshops; offers travel grants provided to scientists to attend scientific conferences. **Events** *Annual Coordinating Board Meeting* Bangkok (Thailand) 2005, *Annual Coordinating Board Meeting* Bangkok (Thailand) 2004, *Annual Coordinating Board Meeting* Bangkok (Thailand) 2003, *Annual Coordinating Board Meeting* Hong Kong (Hong Kong) 2001, *Annual Coordinating Board Meeting* Auckland (New Zealand) 1999.
Members Covers 11 countries and territories:
Australia, China, Hong Kong, Indonesia, Japan, Korea Rep, Malaysia, New Zealand, Philippines, Thailand, Vietnam.
[2013.10.09/XF1277/**F***]

♦ UNESCO Regional Office for Culture in Latin America and the Caribbean / see UNESCO Regional Bureau for Culture for Latin America and the Caribbean (#20317)

♦ UNESCO Regional Office for Education in the Arab States (UNEDBAS) 20320

Bureau régional de 'Unesco de l'éducation pour les Etats arabes
Main Office PO Box 11-5244, Beirut, Lebanon. T. +9611850013 – +9611850015. Fax +9611824854. E-mail: beirut@unesco.org.
Street Address c/o UNESCO Office Beirut, Cité Sportive Avenue, Beirut, Lebanon.
URL: http://www.unesco.org/new/en/beirut/home

History 1961, Beirut (Lebanon), by *UNESCO (#20322)*, as *Arab Centre for Administration and Training of Education Personnel (ASCATEP)*. Present name adopted 1972. Also referred to as *UNESCO Office for Education in the Arab States – Bureau de l'UNESCO de l'éducation pour les Etats arabes* and as *UNESCO/UNEDBAS*. From 1995, functions as *UNESCO Beirut Office – Bureau de l'UNESCO à Beirut.* **Aims** Enhance national efforts directed to the development of educational systems in the Arab region. **Structure** Office of the Director. Divisions (4): Educational Planning, Administration, Economics and Facilities; Primary Education, Literacy, Adult Education and Education for Rural Development, Technical and Vocational Education; Higher Education, Training of Educational Personnel; Population Education, HIV/AIDS. Editorial Committees; Administrative Unit; Translation and Dissemination Section; Supporting Services. **Languages** Arabic, English, French. **Staff** 0.50 FTE, paid; 1.00 FTE, voluntary. 11 temporary, paid; 17 regular contracts. **Finance** Sources: UNESCO budget; voluntary contributions. **Activities** Provides training and advisory services; carries out studies and research; disseminates information; organizes or sponsors national, subregional and regional conferences and seminars; coordinates UNESCO activities for the region. Includes *Regional Programme for the Universalization and Renewal of Primary Education and the Eradication of Illiteracy in the Arab States by the Year 2000 (ARABUPEAL, no recent information).* **Events** *Arab states regional preparatory conference to CONFINTEA VI* Tunis (Tunisia) 2009, *Session* Cairo (Egypt) 1997, *Scientific conference on the future of science and mathematics teaching and the needs of Arab society / Scientific Conference* Tunis (Tunisia) 1996. **Publications** *Education Today* – translated into Arabic.
Members Countries served by UNESCO/UNEDBAS (20):
Algeria, Bahrain, Djibouti, Egypt, Iraq, Jordan, Kuwait, Lebanon, Libya, Mauritania, Morocco, Oman, Qatar, Saudi Arabia, Somalia, Sudan, Syrian AR, Tunisia, United Arab Emirates, Yemen.
IGO Relations Special links with:
- *FAO (#09260)*;
- *ILO (#11123)*;
- *UNEP (#20299)*;
- *UNDP (#20292)*;
- *UNESCO Institute for Lifelong Learning (UIL, #20305)*;
- *UNESCO Office, Cairo – Regional Bureau for Sciences in the Arab States (ROSTAS, #20312)*;
- *UNICEF (#20332)*;
- *United Nations Economic and Social Commission for Western Asia (ESCWA, #20558)*;
- *United Nations Population Fund (UNFPA, #20612)*;
- *United Nations Relief and Works Agency for Palestine Refugees in the Near East (UNRWA, #20622)*;
- *WHO (#20950)*;
- *World Food Programme (WFP, #21510)*.

Close relations with:
- *Arab Bureau of Education for the Gulf States (ABEGS, #00910)*;
- *Arab Federation for Technical Education (AFTE, no recent information)*;
- *Arab Gulf Programme for United Nations Development Organizations (AGFUND, #00971)*;
- *Arab League Educational, Cultural and Scientific Organization (ALECSO, #01003)*;
- *Gulf Arab States Educational Research Centre (GASERC, #10822)*;
- *International Bureau of Education (IBE, #12413)*;
- *International Institute for Educational Planning (IIEP, #13874)*;
- *Islamic World Educational, Scientific and Cultural Organization (ICESCO, #16058)*;
- *Regional Centre for Adult Education (ASFEC, no recent information)*;
- *UNESCO International Centre for Technical and Vocational Education and Training (UNESCO-UNEVOC, #20307)*.

[2017/XE9760/**E***]

♦ UNESCO Regional Office for Education in Asia and the Pacific / see UNESCO Asia and Pacific Regional Bureau for Education (#20301)
♦ UNESCO Regional Office for Science and Technology for Europe / see UNESCO Office in Venice – UNESCO Regional Bureau for Science and Culture in Europe (#20316)
♦ UNESCO Regional Office for Science and Technology for Latin America and the Caribbean / see UNESCO Office, Montevideo – Regional Bureau for Sciences in Latin America and the Caribbean (#20314)
♦ UNESCO Regional Office for Science and Technology for South and Central Asia / see UNESCO Asia-Pacific Regional Bureau for Communication and Information (#20300)
♦ UNESCO Regional Office for Science and Technology for Southeast Asia / see UNESCO Office, Jakarta – Regional Bureau for Sciences in Asia and the Pacific (#20313)
♦ UNESCO/ROSTLAC / see UNESCO Office, Montevideo – Regional Bureau for Sciences in Latin America and the Caribbean (#20314)
♦ UNESCO/ROSTSCA / see UNESCO Asia-Pacific Regional Bureau for Communication and Information (#20300)
♦ UNESCO/ROSTSEA / see UNESCO Office, Jakarta – Regional Bureau for Sciences in Asia and the Pacific (#20313)
♦ UNESCO Santiago Office / see UNESCO Regional Bureau for Education in Latin America and the Caribbean (#20318)
♦ UNESCO Staff Association / see UNESCO Staff Union (#20321)

♦ UNESCO Staff Union (STU) 20321

Syndicat du personnel de l'UNESCO
Pres c/o UNESCO, 7 place de Fontenoy, 75007 Paris, France. T. +33145685585. E-mail: un-esco.stu@unesco.org – president.stu@unesco.org.
URL: http://www.unesco-stu.org/

History 1947. Founded to represent staff members of *UNESCO (#20322)*. Former names and other names: *UNESCO Staff Association (STA)* – former (1947); *Association du personnel de l'UNESCO* – former (1947). **Aims** Safeguard the collective and individual rights and interests of international *civil servants* in UNESCO; strengthen unity and improve *working conditions*. **Structure** Assembly; Council; Executive Bureau. **Languages** Arabic, English, French. **Staff** 1.50 FTE, paid. **Finance** Sources: members' dues. Supported by: *UNESCO (#20322)* (annual subvention). **Activities** Guidance/assistance/consulting. **Publications** *STU Flash* – newsletter. **Members** Full (international civil servants of UNESCO); Associated (retired staff). Membership countries not specified. **NGO Relations** Member of (1): *Federation of International Civil Servants' Associations (FICSA, #09603)*.
[2022.05.10/XE3250/v/**E**]

♦ UNESCO Statistical Data Bank System (inactive)
♦ UNESCO/UNEDBAS / see UNESCO Regional Office for Education in the Arab States (#20320)
♦ UNESCO/UNEP International Environmental Education Programme (inactive)
♦ **UNESCO-UNEVOC** UNESCO International Centre for Technical and Vocational Education and Training (#20307)

♦ UNESCO – United Nations Educational, Scientific and Cultural Organization 20322

Organisation des Nations Unies pour l'éducation, la science et la culture – Organización de las Naciones Unidas para la Educación, la Ciencia y la Cultura
Dir Gen UNESCO Headquarters, 7 place de Fontenoy, 75352 Paris 07SP, France. T. +33145681000. Fax +33145685555.
Contact 1 rue Miollis, 75732 Paris CEDEX 15, France.
URL: https://www.unesco.org/

History Established on adoption of Constitution signed by 37 countries, at conclusion of *United Nations Conference for Establishment of an Educational and Cultural Organization (ECO/CONF)*, 1-16 Nov 1945, London, comprising representatives of 44 governments. Establishment followed proposal of *Conference of Allied Ministers of Education (CAME, inactive)*, commenced Nov 1942, London, continuing until 5 Dec 1945, at which 18 governments were represented. Preparatory Commission was established on signature of UNESCO Constitution, 16 Nov 1945; first session of the General Conference took place 19 Nov-10 Dec 1946, Paris, with participation of representatives from 30 governments entitled to vote. Constitution came into force 4 Nov 1946, on 20th ratification, on which date agreement between the United Nations and UNESCO was approved by General Assembly of the United Nations at its Oct-Dec 1946 Session, New York NY (USA).
Main predecessors: *Commission internationale de la coopération intellectuelle (CICI, inactive)*, Geneva (Switzerland) 1922-1946; *International Institute of Intellectual Cooperation (IICI, inactive)*, Paris (France) 1925-1946; *International Bureau of Education (IBE, #12413)*, Geneva 1925-1968; from 1969 the latter has been part of the Charter of UNESCO Secretariat under its own statutes. CICI and IICI together comprised *International Organization for Intellectual Cooperation (IOIC, inactive)*, whose official establishment was prevented by World War II but which would have performed a similar function to that of UNESCO. UNESCO is a specialized agency of *United Nations (UN, #20515)* within *United Nations System (#20635)*.
Aims Contribute to lasting peace and security by promoting cooperation among nations through education, science, culture and communication in order to further universal respect for justice, for the rule of law and for human rights and fundamental freedoms which are affirmed for the peoples of the world, without distinction of race, sex, language or religion, by the Charter of the United Nations; give fresh impulse to education for all throughout a person's lifetime and to the spread of culture through fostering ever wider access to and sharing of knowledge, and through building of endogenous capabilities encourage cooperation among nations in all branches of intellectual activity; initiate methods of international cooperation aimed at giving the people of all countries access to printed, published and electronically transmitted materials produced by any of them.
/Strategic Objectives/
- *'Education'*: promote education as a fundamental right in accordance with the Universal Declaration of Human Rights; improve the quality of education through diversification of contents and methods and promotion of universally shared values; promote experimentation, innovation and the diffusion and sharing of information and best practices and policy dialogue in education.
- *'Natural Sciences'*: promote principles and ethical norms to guide scientific and technological development and social transformation; improve human security by better management of the environment and social change; enhance scientific, technical and human capacities to participate in the emerging knowledge societies.
- *'Social and Human Sciences'*: promote principles and ethical norms to guide scientific and technological development and social transformation; improve human security by better management of the environment and social change; enhance scientific, technical and human capacities to participate in the emerging knowledge society.
- *'Culture'*: promote the drafting and implementation of standard-setting instruments in the cultural field; safeguard cultural diversity and encourage dialogue among cultures and civilizations; enhance links between culture and development through capacity-building and sharing of knowledge.
- *'Communication and Information'*: promote free flow of ideas and universal access to information; promote expression of pluralism and cultural diversity in the media and world information networks; promote access for all to information and communication technology, especially in the public domain.

Structure General Conference of representatives of member states (currently 193, plus 11 associate members) meets at Paris HQ every 2 years, elects Executive Board of 58 members. Board meets twice a year at Paris HQ and also after General Conference. Secretariat in Paris. National Commissions in most member states act as liaison bodies and advise their governments on UNESCO affairs; they comprise representatives of principal interested national bodies and civil society.
/Secretariat – Headquarters/:
- *'Director-General (DG)'*;
- *'Deputy Director-General (DDG)'*;
- *'Executive Office of the Director General (CAB)'*;
- *'Secretariat of the Governing Bodies (GBS)'*;
- *'Office of International Standards and Legal Affairs (LA)'*;
- *'Office of Internatioanl Oversight (IOS)'*;
- *'Ethics Office (ETH)'*;
- *'Bureau of Strategic Planning (BSP)'*;
- *'Division for Gender Equality (CAB/GE)'*;
- *'Division of Public Information (CAB/DPI)'*.
- Education Sector (ED);
- Natural Sciences Sector (SC);
- Social and Human Sciences Sector (SHS);
- Culture Sector (CLT);
- Communication and Information Sector (CI);
- Priority Africa and External Relations Sector (PAX);
- Sector for Administration and Management (ADM);
- *Intergovernmental Oceanographic Commission (IOC, #11496)*.

/UNESCO Offices/ -
- *'Africa'*:
- /Cluster Offices and Regional Bureaux/:
- UNESCO Office – Abuja;
- UNESCO Office – Addis Ababa;
- UNESCO Office – Dakar;
- UNESCO Office – Harare;
- UNESCO Office – Nairobi;
- UNESCO Office – Yaoundé.
- /National Offices/:
- UNESCO Office – Abidjan;
- UNESCO Office – Accra;
- UNESCO Office – Bamako;
- UNESCO Office – Brazzaville;
- UNESCO Office – Bujumbura;
- UNESCO Office – Dar es Salaam;
- UNESCO Office – Juba;
- UNESCO Office – Kinshasa;

- UNESCO Office – Libreville;
- UNESCO Office – Maputo;
- UNESCO Office – Windhoek.
- *'Arab States'*:
- /Cluster Offices and Regional Bureaux/:
- UNESCO Office – Beirut, including *UNESCO Regional Office for Education in the Arab States (UNEDBAS, #20320)* (Cluster Office and Regional Bureau);
- UNESCO Office – Cairo, including *UNESCO Office, Cairo – Regional Bureau for Sciences in the Arab States (ROSTAS, #20312)* (Cluster Office and Regional Bureau);
- UNESCO Office – Doha;
- UNESCO Office – Rabat.
- /National Offices/:
- UNESCO Office – Amman;
- UNESCO Office for Iraq;
- UNESCO Office – Khartoum;
- UNESCO Office – Ramallah.
- *'Asia and the Pacific'*:
- /Cluster Offices and Regional Bureaux/:
- UNESCO Office – Almaty;
- UNESCO Office – Apia;
- UNESCO Office – Bangkok, including *UNESCO Asia and Pacific Regional Bureau for Education (#20301)* (Cluster Office and Regional Bureau);
- UNESCO Office – Beijing;
- UNESCO Office – Jakarta, including *UNESCO Office, Jakarta – Regional Bureau for Sciences in Asia and the Pacific (#20313)* (Cluster Office and Regional Bureau);
- UNESCO Office – New Delhi, including *UNESCO Asia-Pacific Regional Bureau for Communication and Information (#20300)*;
- UNESCO Office – Teheran.
- /National Offices/:
- UNESCO Office – Dhaka;
- UNESCO Office – Hanoi;
- UNESCO Office – Islamabad;
- UNESCO Office – Kabul;
- UNESCO Office – Kathmandu;
- UNESCO Office – Phnom Penh;
- UNESCO Office – Tashkent.
- *'Europe'*:
- /Cluster Offices and Regional Bureaux/:
- UNESCO Office – Moscow;
- UNESCO Office – Venice (Regional Bureau).
- *'Latin America and the Caribbean'*:
- /Cluster Offices and Regional Bureaux/:
- UNESCO Office – Havana, including *UNESCO Regional Bureau for Culture for Latin America and the Caribbean (#20317)* (Cluster Office and Regional Bureau);
- UNESCO Office – Kingston;
- UNESCO Office – Montevideo, including *UNESCO Office, Montevideo – Regional Bureau for Sciences in Latin America and the Caribbean (#20314)* (Cluster Office and Regional Bureau);
- UNESCO Office – Quito, including *UNESCO Regional Bureau for Communication and Information for Latin America (ORCILAC, no recent information)*;
- UNESCO Office – San José;
- UNESCO Office – Santiago (Chile), including *UNESCO Regional Bureau for Education in Latin America and the Caribbean (#20318)* (Regional Bureau).
- /National Offices/:
- UNESCO Office – Brasilia;
- UNESCO Office – Guatemala;
- UNESCO Office – Port-au-Prince;
- UNESCO Office – Lima;
- UNESCO Office – Mexico City;
- /Liaison Offices/ -
- Liaison Office – Brussels;
- Liaison Office to the United Nations – Geneva;
- Liaison Office to the United Nations – New York.

/Institutes and Centres/ -
- *Abdus Salam International Centre for Theoretical Physics (ICTP, #00005)*;
- UNESCO International Bureau of Education (IBE);
- UNESCO *International Institute for Educational Planning (IIEP, #13874)*;
- *UNESCO Institute for Lifelong Learning (UIL, #20305)*;
- *UNESCO Institute for Information Technologies in Education (IITE, #20304)*;
- *UNESCO International Centre for Technical and Vocational Education and Training (UNESCO-UNEVOC, #20307)*;
- *UNESCO – International Institute for Capacity Building in Africa (IICBA, #20308)*;
- *UNESCO International Institute for Higher Education in Latin America and the Caribbean (#20309)*;
- *UNESCO Institute for Statistics (UIS, #20306)*;
- *IHE Delft Institute for Water Education (#11110)*;
- *World Heritage Centre (WHC, #21566)*;
- *UNESCO Mahatma Gandhi Institute of Education for Peace and Sustainable Development (UNESCO MGIEP, #20310)*.

Designated International and Regional Institutes and Centres as Category 2.

Languages Arabic, Chinese, English, French, Russian, Spanish. **Staff** 2022: about 2,200. Personnel represented through *International Staff Association of UNESCO (ISAU, #15597)*, *UNESCO Staff Union (STU, #20321)* and *Association of Former UNESCO Staff Members (AFUS Paris, #02601)*. The *Administrative Tribunal of the International Labour Organization (ILO Tribunal, #00118)* is competent to settle disputes. **Finance** Integrated budget framework 2020-2021 adopted Nov 2019: regular programme budget amounting to US$ 534,647,000, consisting of assessment on Member States (based on the scale of assessments adopted by UN General Assembly), and additional appropriation funded from unspent balance of budget framework 2016-2017; extrabudgetary funds amounting to US$ 794,468,300, consisting of funds from Special Account for Management Costs, revenue-generating funds and voluntary contributions, on the understanding that the amounts for these extrabudgetary funds are provisional and are to be funded by resource mobilization.

Activities Activities are defined by the Programme, approved every 2 years by General Conference and, since 1977, by Medium-Term Plans or Strategies.

/Major Programmes/ (5):

'Major Programme I – Education' – Includes *Education for All (EFA)*. Education Institutes (6):
- *International Bureau of Education (IBE, #12413)*;
- *International Institute for Educational Planning (IIEP, #13874)*;
- *UNESCO Institute for Lifelong Learning (UIL, #20305)*;
- *UNESCO Institute for Information Technologies in Education (IITE, #20304)*;
- *UNESCO – International Institute for Capacity Building in Africa (IICBA, #20308)*;
- *UNESCO International Institute for Higher Education in Latin America and the Caribbean (#20309)*.

Education communities/networks supported and/or coordinated by UNESCO include:
- *African Network of Scientific and Technological Institutions (ANSTI, #00395)*;
- *Asia-Pacific Programme of Education for All (APPEAL, #02002)*;
- *Asia-Pacific Programme of Educational Innovation for Development (APEID, #02001)*;
- *UNESCO Associated Schools Project Network (ASPnet, #20302)*;
- *Child Rights International Network (CRIN, #03885)*;
- *Community of Practice in Curriculum Development*;
- *E-Network on Educational Planning and Management (EMPA)*;
- *Educational Leadership Network*;
- *UNESCO International Centre for Technical and Vocational Education and Training (UNESCO-UNEVOC, #20307)*;
- *Latin American Laboratory for Assessment of Quality in Education (#16346)*;
- *Mediterranean Education Initiative for Environment and Sustainability (MEdIES)*;
- *Palestinian European Academic Cooperation in Education (PEACE)*;
- *Regional Information System (#18788)* for Latin America and the Caribbean;
- *Southern and Eastern Africa Consortium for Monitoring Educational Quality (SACMEQ, #19871)*;
- *Teacher Network of Latin America and the Caribbean (KIPUS, #20110)*;
- *Inter-agency Network for Education in Emergencies (INEE, #11387)*;
- *Latin American and Caribbean Education Innovation Network (INNOVEMOS, #16275)*;
- *United Nations Girls' Education Initiative (UNGEI, #20566)*;
- *UNITWIN/UNESCO Chairs Programme (#20669)*;
- *UNESCO/NGO Collective Consultation on Higher Education*.

'Major Programme II – Natural Sciences' – Communities/networks involved:
- *IHE Delft Institute for Water Education (#11110)*;
- *CONOSUR – Network of Ecumenical Lay Centres – OIKOSNET Latin America (no recent information)*;
- *UNESCO Institute for Statistics (UIS, #20306)*;
- *International Hydrological Programme (IHP, #13826)*;
- *Intergovernmental Oceanographic Commission (IOC, #11496)*;
- *Programme on Man and the Biosphere (MAB, #18526)*;
- *International Geoscience Programme (IGCP, #13715)*.

'Major Programme III – Social and Human Sciences' – Includes the programme *Management of Social Transformations (MOST, #16562)*.

'Major Programme IV – Culture' – includes *Intergovernmental Committee for the Safeguarding of the Intangible Cultural Heritage (#11477)*.

'Major Programme V – Communication and Information' – Includes *Memory of the World Programme (Memoria Mundi, see: #20322)*. Programmes (2):
- *International Programme for the Development of Communication (IPDC, #14651)*;
- *Information for All Programme (IFAP, see: #20322)*.

Portals include: *UNESCO Network of Associated Libraries (UNAL, #20311)*.

'Instrumental in setting up':
- *African Network of Scientific and Technological Institutions (ANSTI, #00395)*;
- *African Training Centre for Literacy and Adult Education (inactive)*;
- *Arab Network on Staff Development in Higher Education (ANSD, no recent information)*;
- *Asia/Pacific Cultural Centre for UNESCO (ACCU, #01879)*;
- *Asia Pacific Information Network (APIN, #01931)*;
- *Asia Pacific Network for Tolerance (APNT, inactive)*;
- *Asia-Pacific Programme of Educational Innovation for Development (APEID, #02001)*;
- *Asian Network of Analytical Chemistry (ANAC, #01546)*;
- *Asian-Pacific Information Network on Medicinal and Aromatic Plants (APINMAP, no recent information)*;
- *Caribbean Coastal Marine Productivity (CARICOMP, no recent information)*;
- *Central and Eastern European Media Centre Foundation (EMF-FCP, #03694)*;
- *Centre d'information sur le patrimoine mondial de Luang Prabang (no recent information)*;
- *Centre international pour le dialogue des cultures, St Pétersbourg (inactive)*;
- *Centro de Cooperación Regional para la Educación de Adultos en América Latina y el Caribe (CREFAL, #03794)*;
- *Centro Internacional de Ciencias Biológicas (CICB)*;
- *COMARNORTH (no recent information)*;
- *COSTED-IBN (inactive)*;
- *Culturelink – the Network of Networks for Research and Cooperation in Cultural Development (#04982)*;
- *European Network on Staff Development in Higher Education (ENSDHE, inactive)*;
- *European Regional Centre for Ecohydrology of the Polish Academy of Sciences, Lodz (ERCE PAS, #08341)*;
- *Focusing Resources on Effective School Health (FRESH, #09809)*;
- *Global Alliance on Cultural Diversity (inactive)*;
- *Global Geoparks Network (GGN, #10389)*;
- *Global Movement for a Culture of Peace and Non-Violence (see: #20322)*;
- *Information Society Program for Latin America and the Caribbean (INFOLAC, inactive)*;
- *INFOYOUTH – Worldwide Information Network on Youth Related Issues (INFOYOUTH, #11204)*;
- *Institut Africain pour le Développement Economique et Social – Centre Africain de Formation (INADES-Formation, #11233)*;
- *Institute for Black Peoples (IBP, no recent information)*;
- *Intergovernmental Committee for Physical Education and Sport (#11475)*;
- *Intergovernmental Regional Committee on Education in Asia and the Pacific (EDCOM, no recent information)*;
- *International Centre for Chemical Studies (ICCS, no recent information)*;
- *International Centre for Integrated Mountain Development (ICIMOD, #12500)*;
- *International Centre for Physical Land Resources (ICPLR, #12507)*;
- *International Centre for Water Hazard and Risk Management (ICHARM)*;
- *International Clearinghouse on Children, Youth and Media*;
- *International Fund for the Promotion of Culture (IFPC, inactive)*;
- *International Information Centre for Terminology (INFOTERM, #13846)*;
- *International Institute for Central Asian Studies (IICAS, #13868)*;
- *International Network for the Availability of Scientific Publications (INASP, #14233)*;
- *International Network of Centres for Computer Applications (INCCA, #14239)*;
- *International Research and Training Centre on Erosion and Sedimentation (IRTCES, #14745)*;
- *International Scientific Committee for the Drafting of a General History of the Caribbean (inactive)*;
- *International Scientific Committee for the Drafting of a General History of Latin America (inactive)*;
- *International Scientific Committee for the Drafting of a History of Civilizations of Central Asia (no recent information)*;
- *International Scientific Committee for the Drafting of a Work on the Various Aspects of Islamic Culture (no recent information)*;
- *International Scientific Committee for the 'Iron Routes in Africa' (inactive)*;
- *International Statistical Education Centre (ISEC, #15602)*;
- *International Youth Library (IYL, #15936)*;
- *Latin American Network for Tolerance and Solidarity (inactive)*;
- *Mediterranean and Black Sea Regional Network against Intolerance, Discrimination and Violence (no recent information)*;
- *Molecular and Cell Biology Network (MCBN, inactive)*;
- *Observatory on the Information Society (inactive)*;
- *ORBICOM – International Network of UNESCO Chairs in Communication (#17785)*;
- *Panel international sur la construction de la démocratie (no recent information)*;
- *Planet Society (PS, see: #20322)*;
- *Regional Centre for Biotechnology Training and Education, India (RCB)*;
- *Regional Centre for Training and Water Studies of Arid and Semiarid Zones, Cairo (RCTWS)*;
- *Regional Centre on Urban Water Management*;
- *Regional Centre on Urban Water Management, Teheran (RCUWM, #18761)*;
- *Regional Network for the Chemistry of Natural Products in Southeast Asia (inactive)*;
- *Regional Programme for the Universalization and Renewal of Primary Education and the Eradication of Illiteracy in the Arab States by the Year 2000 (ARABUPEAL, no recent information)*;
- *Regional Project for Research and Training on Coastal Ecosystems in Africa (COMARAF, inactive)*;
- *Regional Project for Research and Training on Coastal Systems of Latin America and the Caribbean and their relations with the Continental Shelf (COSALC, no recent information)*;
- *Regional Water Centre for Arid and Semi-Arid Regions of Latin America and the Caribbean (CAZALAC)*;
- *Réseau coopératif inter-universitaire de formation et de perfectionnement du personnel d'enseignement supérieur (no recent information)*;
- *South-Eastern Mediterranean Programme (SEMEP, inactive)*;
- *UNESCO Co-Action Programme (Co-Action, inactive)*;
- *UNESCO Early Childhood Cooperating Centre, Mali (no recent information)*;
- *UNESCO Environment and Development in Coastal Regions and Small Islands (UNESCO CSI Programme, see: #20322)*;
- *UNESCO Fellowships Programme (see: #20322)*;
- *UNESCO-ICOM Museum Information Centre (see: #13051)*;
- *UNESCO International Research Network on Educational Resources*;
- *UNESCO/UNEP International Environmental Education Programme (IEEP, inactive)*;
- *UNESCO World Network of Microbiological Resources Centres MIRCEN (no recent information)*;
- *Water and Development Information for Arid Lands Global Network (G-WADI, #20826)*;
- *World Heritage Fund (#21568)*.

Agreements concluded under UNESCO auspices:
- *Agreement for Facilitating the International Circulation of Visual and Auditory Materials of an Educational, Scientific and Cultural Character (Beirut Agreement, 1948)*;
- *Agreement on the Importation of Educational, Scientific and Cultural Materials (1950)*;
- *International Convention to Facilitate the Importation of Commercial Samples and Advertising Material (1952)*;
- *Protocol 1 Annexed to the Universal Copyright Convention Concerning the Application of That Convention to the Works of Stateless Persons and Refugees, 1952 (1952)*;
- *Protocol 2 Annexed to the Universal Copyright Convention, Concerning the Application of That Convention to the Works of Certain International Organizations, 1952 (1952)*;
- *Protocol 3 Annexed to the Universal Copyright Convention (1952)*;
- *Universal Copyright Convention, 1952 (1952)*;
- *Convention for the Protection of Cultural Property in the Event of Armed Conflict (The Hague Convention, 1954, 1954)*;
- *Protocol for the Protection of Cultural Property in the Event of Armed Conflict (1954)*;
- *Convention Concerning the Exchange of Official Publications and Government Documents between States (1958)*;
- *Convention Concerning the International Exchange of Publications (1958)*;
- *Convention Against Discrimination in Education (1960)*;
- *Customs Convention Concerning Facilities for the Importation of Goods for Display or Use at Exhibitions, Fairs, Meetings or Similar Events (1961)*;
- *International Convention for the Protection of Performers, Producers of Phonograms and Broadcasting Organizations (Rome Convention, 1961)*;
- *Protocol Instituting a Conciliation and Good Offices Commission to be Responsible for Seeking the Settlement of Any Disputes Which May Arise between States Parties to the Convention Against Discrimination in Education (1962)*;
- *Déclaration des Principes de la Coopération Culturelle Internationale (1966)*;

- *Convention on the Means of Prohibiting and Preventing the Illicit Import, Export and Transfer of Ownership of Cultural Property (Paris, 1970, 1970)*;
- *Convention for the Protection of Producers of Phonograms Against Unauthorized Duplication of Their Phonograms (Geneva Convention, 1971)*;
- *Convention on Wetlands of International Importance Especially as Waterfowl Habitat (Convention on Wetlands, 1971)*;
- *Protocol 1 Annexed to the Universal Copyright Convention Concerning the Application of That Convention to Works of Stateless Persons and Refugees, 1971 (1971)*;
- *Protocol 2 Annexed to the Universal Copyright Convention Concerning the Application of That Convention to the Works of Certain International Organizations, 1971 (1971)*;
- *Universal Copyright Convention, 1971 (1971)*;
- *Convention Concerning the Protection of the World Cultural and Natural Heritage (World Heritage Convention, 1972)*;
- *Declaration of Guiding Principles on the Use of Satellite Broadcasting for the Free Flow of Information, the Spread of Education and Greater Cultural Exchange (1972)*;
- *Déclaration des Principes Directeurs de L'utilisation de la Radiodiffusion par Satellites pour la Libre Circulation de L'information, L'extension de L'éducation et le Développement des échanges Culturels (1972)*;
- *Declaration on Race and Racial Prejudice (1978)*;
- *Convention Relating to the Distribution of Programme-carrying Signals Transmitted by Satellite (Brussels Convention, 1974)*;
- *Regional Convention on the Recognition of Studies, Diplomas and Degrees in Higher Education in Latin America and the Caribbean (1974)*;
- *International Convention on the Recognition of Studies, Diplomas and Degrees in Higher Education in the Arab States and European States Bordering on the Mediterranean (1976)*;
- *Protocol to the Agreement on the Importation of Educational, Scientific and Cultural Materials (1976)*;
- *Convention on the Recognition of Studies, Diplomas and Degrees in Higher Education in the Arab States (1978)*;
- *Declaration on Fundamental Principles Concerning the Contribution of the Mass Media to Strengthening Peace and International Understanding, to the Promotion of Human Rights and to Countering Racialism, Apartheid and Incitement to War (1978)*;
- *Déclaration sur les Principes Fondamentaux Concernant la Contribution des Organes D'information au Renforcement de la Paix et de la Compréhension Internationale, à la Promotion des Droits de L'homme et à la Lutte Contre le Racisme et L'apartheid et L'incitation à la Guerre (1978)*;
- *Déclaration sur la Race et les Préjugés Raciaux (1978)*;
- *International Charter of Physical Education and Sport (1978)*;
- *Convention on the Recognition of Studies, Diplomas and Degrees in Higher Education in the States Belonging to the Europe Region (1979)*;
- *Multilateral Convention for the Avoidance of Double Taxation of Copyright Royalties and Additional Protocol (Madrid Multilateral Convention, 1979)*;
- *Regional Convention on the Recognition of Studies, Certificates, Diplomas, Degrees and other Academic Qualifications in Higher Education in the African States (1981)*;
- *Protocol to Amend the Convention on Wetlands of International Importance Especially as Waterfowl Habitat (1982)*;
- *Regional Convention on the Recognition of Studies, Diplomas and Degrees in Higher Education in Asia and the Pacific (1983)*;
- *Convention on Technical and Vocational Education (1989)*;
- *Convention on Stolen or Illegally Exported Cultural Objects (1995)*;
- *Convention on the Recognition of Qualifications Concerning Higher Education in the European Region (1997)*;
- *Declaration on the Responsibilities of Present Generations Towards Future Generations (1997)*;
- *Universal Declaration on the Human Genome and Human Rights (1997)*;
- *Convention on the Protection of the Underwater Cultural Heritage (2001)*;
- *Convention for the Safeguarding of Intangible Cultural Heritage (2003)*;
- *International Declaration on Human Genetic Data (2003)*;
- *Convention on the Protection and Promotion of the Diversity of Cultural Expressions (2005)*;
- *Universal Declaration on Bioethics and Human Rights (2005)*.

Events *European Biomass Conference* Bologna (Italy) 2023, *World Human Rights Cities Forum* Gwangju (Korea Rep) 2022, *UNESCO World Conference on Cultural Policies and Sustainable Development – MONDIACULT* Mexico City (Mexico) 2022, *World Conference on Early Childhood Care and Education* Tashkent (Uzbekistan) 2022, *Memory of the World Global Policy Forum* Tokyo (Japan) 2022. **Publications** *UNESCO Sources* (12 a year); *UNESCO Courier* (12 a year) – magazine in 35 languages; *Copyright Bulletin* (4 a year) in English, French, Russian, Spanish; *Impact: Science on Society* (4 a year) in Arabic, Chinese, English, French, Korean, Russian, Spanish; *International Social Science Journal* (4 a year) in Chinese, English, French, Spanish; *Museum* (4 a year) in English, French, Spanish; *Nature and Resources* (4 a year) in Chinese, English, French, Russian, Spanish; *Prospects* (4 a year) in English, French, Spanish – review of education; *UNESCO Publishing* – catalogue of publications, also on the Internet and Minitel; *UNESCO Statistical Digest*; *UNESCO Statistical Yearbook*. *Challenges*; *Culture of Peace*. *World Culture Report* (1998); *World Education Report* (3rd ed 1998); *World Information Report* (1998); *World Science Report* (3rd ed 1998); *World Social Science Report* (1998); *Historia General de América Latina* – in 9 vols; *UNESCO List of Documents and Publications* – from UNESCO Bibliographic Database; *World History of the Caribbean* – in 6 vols. Multi-media CD-ROM on UNESCO's history (1995) – on its 50th anniversary. Books and periodicals on education, science and technology, social sciences, culture, communication, librarianship and documentation maps atlases. Subject categories: /Reference Books/ – statistical yearbooks glossaries guide to scholarships bibliographies. /Education/ – educational policy, planning and administration literacy adult education lifelong education technical and vocational education training of educational personnel. /Science/ – ecology hydrology earth sciences oceanography biotechnology engineering education science and technology policies science and technology research and higher education. /Social Sciences/ – socio-economic analysis socio-cultural studies human rights and peace studies on population, development, youth, women's issues /Culture/ – cultural heritage history museology and conservation cultural development cultural policy. /Communication/ – communication policy information networks communication planning book promotion copyright. /Documentation, Libraries, Archives/ – development organization management. /Official Publications/ – reports on UNESCO activities records of UNESCO conferences. Information Services: Library: archives include those of the previous International Institute of Intellectual Cooperation and Conference of Allied Ministers of Education (CAME). **Information Services** *African Development Networks (AFRODEVNET)*; *UNESCO International Comparative Study on the Organization, Productivity and Effectiveness of Research Teams and their Institutions 1973-1990 (ICSOPRU)*; *PEDDRO* – the previous Prévention – Education – Drogues (PEDDRO); *Speeches by the Director General of UNESCO (DGDATA) Database*; *SPGEN Database* – national central policy-making organizations for planning, organization and coordination of scientific and technological activities; *SPINES Thesaurus (SPINES) Database*; *Study Abroad Database*; *TRUSP Database* – specialists, projects and periodicals dealing with policy related issues in science and technology; *UHSINFO (UHS) Database* – UNESCO Regional Offices' Information Services; *UNDAYS* – database of international years, decades and days observed by the UN; *UNESCDOC* – database of UNESCO resolutions and decisions; *UNESCO Bibliographic Data Base (UNESBIB) – Base de données UNESBIB – Base de Datos UNESBIB* – established 1972 as UNESCO Computerized Documentation System (CDS) – Système de documentation informatisée de l'UNESCO – Sistema de Documentación Automatica de la UNESCO; *UNESCO Databases CD-ROM* – details of bibliographic, reference and factual databases (about 90) produced by UNESCO; *UNESCO Libraries Portal* – access to library resources; *Journalism and Other Media Schools Database*; *UNESCO List of Documents and Publications* – from UNESCO Bibliographic Database; *UNESCO Radio Programme (RADIO) Database*; *UNESCO Statistical Data Bank*; *UNESCOTERM* – terminology database; *UNESCO Thesaurus (UNESTHES)*; *UNESDATA* – UNESCO databases; *UNESIS* – UNESCO information services; *World Decade for Cultural Development (DECADE) Database*; *World Heritage Portal*; *World Poetry Directory* – database; *Young Child and the Family Environment International (YCFE International)* – database; *Man and the Biosphere (MAB) Database*; *ISISDIF Database* – national distributors of Micro CDS-ISIS software; *AIDS / SIDA Database*; *GRIDOC Database* – grey literature in education; *Archives Portal* – information gateway; *Broadcasting Laws Database*; *Catalogue of Documents* – database; *CI Publications* – Communications and Information Society Sector publications; *Culture and Development Bibliography*; *Culture and Development Reference Texts*; *DARE Database* – social sciences; *East-West Media Professionals Training Programme Database*; *Education Facilities (EDFAC) Database*; *ENERGY Database*; *European Development Networks (EURODEVNET) Database*; *HEDBIB Database* – literature on higher education; *International Network for Information in Science and Technology Education (INISTE)* – database; *Human Rights Research and Training Institutes Database*; *IAUDOC Database* – higher education, jointly with IAU; *IBEDOCS Database* – education, jointly with IBE; *IBETHES Database* – jointly with IBE; *ICOMMOS Database* – jointly with ICOMOS; *ICONFLEX Database* – resolutions of UNESCO General Conference and related documents; *IIPNET Database* – research and training institutions specialized in informatics; *Index Translationum (XTRANS) Database* – citations of translated books; *International Directory of Experts Specializing in Informatics (IDESI)* – database; *International Directory of Institutions Specializing in Informatics (IIPNET)* – database; *Internationally Developed Data Analysis and Management Software Package (IDAMS)*; *Youth Database*.

Members All United Nations member states are eligible. Countries which are not UN members may become members of UNESCO by two-thirds vote of General Conference. Territories or groups of territories not responsible for the conduct of their external relations may be admitted as associate members, at the request of the member state or governing authority assuming responsibility for the conduct of the external relations of the territory in question. Member states (193):

Afghanistan, Albania, Algeria, Andorra, Angola, Antigua-Barbuda, Argentina, Armenia, Australia, Austria, Azerbaijan, Bahamas, Bahrain, Bangladesh, Barbados, Belarus, Belgium, Belize, Benin, Bhutan, Bolivia, Bosnia-Herzegovina, Botswana, Brazil, Brunei Darussalam, Bulgaria, Burkina Faso, Burundi, Cambodia, Cameroon, Canada, Cape Verde, Central African Rep, Chad, Chile, China, Colombia, Comoros, Congo Brazzaville, Congo DR, Cook Is, Costa Rica, Côte d'Ivoire, Croatia, Cuba, Cyprus, Czechia, Denmark, Djibouti, Dominica, Dominican Rep, Ecuador, Egypt, El Salvador, Equatorial Guinea, Eritrea, Estonia, Eswatini, Ethiopia, Fiji, Finland, France, Gabon, Gambia, Georgia, Germany, Ghana, Greece, Grenada, Guatemala, Guinea, Guinea-Bissau, Guyana, Haiti, Honduras, Hungary, Iceland, India, Indonesia, Iran Islamic Rep, Iraq, Ireland, Italy, Jamaica, Japan, Jordan, Kazakhstan, Kenya, Kiribati, Korea DPR, Korea Rep, Kuwait, Kyrgyzstan, Laos, Latvia, Lebanon, Lesotho, Liberia, Libya, Lithuania, Luxembourg, Madagascar, Malawi, Malaysia, Maldives, Mali, Malta, Marshall Is, Mauritania, Mauritius, Mexico, Micronesia FS, Moldova, Monaco, Mongolia, Montenegro, Morocco, Mozambique, Myanmar, Namibia, Nauru, Nepal, Netherlands, New Zealand, Nicaragua, Niger, Nigeria, Niue, North Macedonia, Norway, Oman, Pakistan, Palau, Palestine, Panama, Papua New Guinea, Paraguay, Peru, Philippines, Poland, Portugal, Qatar, Romania, Russia, Rwanda, Samoa, San Marino, Sao Tomé-Principe, Saudi Arabia, Senegal, Serbia, Seychelles, Sierra Leone, Singapore, Slovakia, Slovenia, Solomon Is, Somalia, South Africa, South Sudan, Spain, Sri Lanka, St Kitts-Nevis, St Lucia, St Vincent-Grenadines, Sudan, Suriname, Sweden, Switzerland, Syrian AR, Tajikistan, Tanzania UR, Thailand, Timor-Leste, Togo, Tonga, Trinidad-Tobago, Tunisia, Türkiye, Turkmenistan, Tuvalu, Uganda, UK, Ukraine, United Arab Emirates, Uruguay, Uzbekistan, Vanuatu, Venezuela, Vietnam, Yemen, Zambia, Zimbabwe.

Associate member states (12):

Åland, Anguilla, Aruba, Cayman Is, Curaçao, Faeroe Is, Macau, Montserrat, New Caledonia, St Maarten, Tokelau, Virgin Is UK.

Consultative Status Directives concerning partnership with Non-Governmental Organizations approved by General Conference. As at Oct 2020, official partnership with 401 NGOs and 33 foundations.

Organizations granted consultative status:

Associate Status (68):

- *Academic Council on the United Nations System (ACUNS, #00020)*;
- *Africa Network Campaign on Education for All (ANCEFA, #00302)*;
- *Agence universitaire de La Francophonie (AUF, #00548)*;
- *Amnesty International (AI, #00801)*;
- *Arab Institute for Human Rights (AIHR, #00983)*;
- *Asia-Pacific Broadcasting Union (ABU, #01863)*;
- *Asia South Pacific Association for Basic and Adult Education (ASPBAE, #02098)*;
- *Association Internationale des Amis des Musées d'Egypte (AME, no recent information)*;
- *Association mondiale des radiodiffuseurs communautaires (AMARC, #02810)*;
- *Association of African Universities (AAU, #02361)*;
- *Association of Arab Universities (AARU, #02374)*;
- *Association of Commonwealth Universities, The (ACU, #02440)*;
- *Association of Universities of Latin America and the Caribbean (#02970)*;
- *B'nai B'rith International (BBI, #03290)*;
- *Caritas Internationalis (CI, #03580)*;
- *Club of Rome (COR, #04038)*;
- *Committee to Protect Journalists (CPJ, #04280)*;
- *Consejo Latinoamericano de Ciencias Sociales (CLACSO, #04718)*;
- *Coordinating Committee for International Voluntary Service (CCIVS, #04819)*;
- *Council for International Organizations of Medical Sciences (CIOMS, #04905)*;
- *Education International (EI, #05371)*;
- *ENCATC (#05452)*;
- *European Broadcasting Union (EBU, #06404)*;
- *European University Association (EUA, #09027)*;
- *Forum for African Women Educationalists (FAWE, #09896)*;
- *Fédération africaine des associations nationales de parents d'élèves et étudiants (FAPE, #09398)*;
- *Human Variome Project (HVP, #10992)* (Global Variome);
- *Inter American Press Association (IAPA, #11444)*;
- *International Association of Broadcasting (IAB, #11738)*;
- *International Association of Universities (IAU, #12246)*;
- *International Council for Adult Education (ICAE, #12983)*;
- *International Council for Film, Television and Audiovisual Communication (IFTC, #13022)*;
- *International Council for Philosophy and Human Sciences (CIPSH, #13061)*;
- *International Council of Museums (ICOM, #13051)*;
- *International Council of Organizations for Folklore Festivals and Folk Art (#13058)*;
- *International Council of Sport Science and Physical Education (ICSSPE, #13077)*;
- *International Council on Archives (ICA, #12996)*;
- *International Council on Monuments and Sites (ICOMOS, #13049)*;
- *International Federation of Journalists (IFJ, #13462)*;
- *International Federation of Library Associations and Institutions (IFLA, #13470)*;
- *International Movement ATD Fourth World (#14193)*;
- *International Music Council (IMC, #14199)*;
- *International PEN (#14552)*;
- *International Press Institute (IPI, #14636)*;
- *International Radio and Television Union (#14689)*;
- *International Science Council (ISC, #14796)*;
- *International Scientific Council for Island Development (INSULA, no recent information)*;
- *International Theatre Institute (ITI, #15683)*;
- *International Union for Conservation of Nature and Natural Resources (IUCN, #15766)*;
- *Junior Chamber International (JCI, #16168)*;
- *Observatory of Cultural Policies in Africa (OCPA, #17644)*;
- *Pax Romana, International Catholic Movement for Intellectual and Cultural Affairs (ICMICA, #18267)*;
- *Pax Romana, International Movement of Catholic Students (IMCS, #18268)*;
- *Rotary International (RI, #18975)*;
- *Shoah Memorial*;
- *Simon Wiesenthal Center (SWC)*;
- *Traditions for Tomorrow (#20195)*;
- *Union internationale des architectes (UIA, #20419)*;
- *Union internationale des associations et organismes scientifiques et techniques (UATI, #20421)*;
- *Union of International Associations (UIA, #20414)*;
- *World Assembly of Youth (WAY, #21113)*;
- *World Association of Newspapers and News Publishers (WAN-IFRA, #21166)*;
- *World Federation of Engineering Organizations (WFEO, #21433)*;
- *World Federation of UNESCO Clubs, Centres and Associations (WFUCA, #21498)*;
- *World Federation of United Nations Associations (WFUNA, #21499)*;
- *World Jewish Congress (WJC, #21599)*;
- *World Organization of the Scout Movement (WOSM, #21693)*;
- *World Water Council (WWC, #21908)*.

Consultative Status (313):

- *Academia Europaea (#00011)*;
- *ActionAid (#00087)*;
- *African Union of Broadcasting (AUB, #00490)*;
- *Afro-Asian Peoples' Solidarity Organization (AAPSO, #00537)*;
- *AFS Intercultural Programs (AFS, #00541)*;
- *AIESEC (#00593)*;
- *All-Africa Students Union (AASU, #00644)*;
- *Alliance de Villes Euro-méditerranéennes de Culture (AVEC, #00726)*;
- *Arab Council for Childhood and Development (ACCD, #00929)*;
- *Arab Educational Information Network (Shamaa, #00938)*;
- *Arabic Language International Council (#00978)*;
- *Arab Lawyers' Union (ALU, #01002)*;
- *Arab Organization for Human Rights (AOHR, #01020)*;
- *Art Education for the Blind (AEB)*;
- *ARTerial Network (#01118)*;
- *Asian Media Information and Communication Centre (AMIC, #01536)*;
- *Asia-Pacific Regional Network for Early Childhood (ARNEC, #02009)*;
- *Asociación Latinoamericana de Educación y Comunicación Popular (ALER, #02207)*;
- *Assistance a l'intégration des enfants démobilisés (AIED, no recent information)*;
- *Associated Country Women of the World (ACWW, #02338)*;
- *Association Catholique Internationale de Services pour la Jeunesse Féminine (ACISJF/In Via, #02417)*;

- *Association des états généraux des étudiants de l'Europe (AEGEE-Europe, #02495);*
- *Association for the Promotion of the International Circulation of the Press (DISTRIPRESS, #02876);*
- *Association francophone d'amitié et de liaison (AFAL, #02605);*
- *Association Internationale des Charités (AIC, #02675);*
- *Association internationale des critiques d'art (AICA, #02680);*
- *Association Montessori Internationale (AMI, #02812);*
- *Association nationale cultures du monde (ANCT);*
- *Association of Asian Social Science Research Councils (AASSREC, #02382);*
- *Association of European Journalists (AEJ, #02516);*
- *Association of Interbalkan Women's Cooperation Societies, Thessaloniki (AIWCS, #02653);*
- *Association of International Private Committees for the Safeguarding of Venice (#02758);*
- *Association of Moving Image Archivists (AMIA);*
- *Association of National Olympic Committees (ANOC, #02819);*
- *Association of Southeast Asian Institutions of Higher Learning (ASAIHL, #02920);*
- *Campaña Latinoamericana por el Derecho a la Educación (CLADE, #03407);*
- *Canadian Centre for International Studies and Cooperation (CECI);*
- *Catholic International Education Office (#03604);*
- *Central Africa Protected Areas Network (#03656);*
- *Centre d'étude et de prospective stratégique (CEPS, #03739);*
- *Centre international de phonétique appliquée (CIPA);*
- *Childhood Education International (CE International);*
- *China Education Association for International Exchange (CEAIE);*
- *China Folklore Photographic Association (CFPA);*
- *CISV International (#03949);*
- *Clowns Without Borders International (CWBI, #04029);*
- *COJEP International – Conseil pour la Justice, l'Egalité et la Paix (COJEP International, #04090);*
- *Communauté africaine de culture (#04373);*
- *Community of Mediterranean Universities (CMU, #04403);*
- *Confederación Mundial de Educación (COMED, #04464);*
- *Confédération internationale des sociétés d'auteurs et compositeurs (CISAC, #04563);*
- *Conseil international des radios-télévisions d'expression française (CIRTEF, #04694);*
- *Consejo Europeo de Investigaciones Sociales de América Latina (CEISAL, #04710);*
- *Consultative Council of Jewish Organizations (CCJO, no recent information);*
- *Defence for Children International (DCI, #05025);*
- *Development Innovations and Networks (#05057);*
- *Dhaka Ahsania Mission (DAM);*
- *DIANOVA International (#05068);*
- *Disabled Peoples' International (DPI, #05097);*
- *Documentation and Conservation of the Modern Movement (DOCOMOMO International, #05110);*
- *Dyslexia and Literacy International (inactive);*
- *Electronic Information for Libraries (EIFL, #05425);*
- *Europa Nostra (#05767);*
- *European Academy of Arts, Sciences and Humanities (EAASH, #05781);*
- *European and International Booksellers Federation (EIBF, #07584);*
- *European Association for the Education of Adults (EAEA, #06018);*
- *European Association of History Educators (EUROCLIO, #06069);*
- *European Athletics (#06291);*
- *European Capitals and Cities of Sport Federation (ACES Europe, #06440);*
- *European Cultural Network for Development Cooperation (#06869);*
- *European Dyslexia Association – International Organisation for Specific Learning Disabilities (EDA, #06951);*
- *European Students' Union (ESU, #08848);*
- *European Youth Forum (#09140);*
- *Federación Latinoamericana de Facultades de Comunicación Social (FELAFACS, #09353);*
- *Federation for EDucation in Europe (FEDE, #09479);*
- *Femmes Africa solidarité (FAS, #09732);*
- *FIPP (#09776);*
- *First Multipurpose Women Cooperative in Gassim (Herfah);*
- *Fondazione Idis-Città della Scienza;*
- *Forest Peoples Programme (FPP, #09865);*
- *Foundation for Environmental Education (FEE, #09949);*
- *Friendship Ambassadors Foundation (FAF);*
- *Fédération internationale des associations de personnes âgées (FIAPA, #09609);*
- *Fédération internationale des professeurs de français (FIPF, #09652);*
- *Fédération internationale des véhicules anciens (FIVA, #09669);*
- *Fédération internationale syndicale de l'enseignement (FISE, #09662);*
- *General Arab Women Federation (GAWF, no recent information);*
- *Global Alliance of Lesbian, Gay, Bisexual and Transgender Education (GALE);*
- *Global Campaign for Education (GCE, #10264);*
- *Graduate Women International (GWI, #10688);*
- *HOPE '87 – Hundreds of Original Projects for Employment;*
- *Hostelling International (#10950);*
- *Humanists International (#10972);*
- *Human Rights Information and Documentation Systems, International (HURIDOCS, #10985);*
- *Inclusion International (#11145);*
- *Indigenous Peoples of Africa Coordinating Committee (IPACC, #11163);*
- *Institut Afrique Monde (IAM);*
- *Institut de la Culture Afro-européenne à Paris (ICAEP);*
- *Institut Destrée;*
- *Institute of Cultural Affairs International (ICAI, #11251);*
- *Institut international d'études administratives de Montréal;*
- *Inter-American Organization for Higher Education (IOHE, #11442);*
- *International Academy of Ceramics (IAC, #11540);*
- *International Advertising Association (IAA, #11590);*
- *International Alliance of Women (IAW, #11639);*
- *International Amateur Theatre Association (AITA/IATA, #11647);*
- *International Association for Continuing Engineering Education (IACEE, #11817);*
- *International Association for Counselling (IAC, #11821);*
- *International Association for Educational and Vocational Guidance (IAEVG, #11862);*
- *International Association for Educational Assessment (IAEA, #11861);*
- *International Association for Media and Communication Research (IAMCR, #12022);*
- *International Association for Mongol Studies (IAMS, #12035);*
- *International Association for Political Science Students (IAPSS, #12095);*
- *International Association for the Evaluation of Educational Achievement (IEA, #11882);*
- *International Association for the Exchange of Students for Technical Experience (IAESTE, #11885);*
- *International Association of Academies of Sciences (IAAS, #11679);*
- *International Association of Art (IAA, #11710);*
- *International Association of Cinema, Audiovisual and Media Schools (#11771);*
- *International Association of Conference Interpreters (#11807);*
- *International Association of Democratic Lawyers (IADL, #11837);*
- *International Association of Educators for Peace (IAEP);*
- *International Association of Hydrogeologists (IAH, #11953);*
- *International Association of Sound and Audiovisual Archives (IASA, #12172);*
- *International Association of Students in Agricultural and Related Sciences (IAAS, #12191);*
- *International Association of University Presidents (IAUP, #12248);*
- *International Association of University Professors and Lecturers (IAUPL, #12250);*
- *International Association to Save Tyre (IAST, #12144);*
- *International Astronautical Federation (IAF, #12286);*
- *International Astronomical Union (IAU, #12287);*
- *International Baccalaureate (IB, #12306);*
- *International Cartographic Association (ICA, #12446);*
- *International Catholic Child Bureau (#12450);*
- *International Catholic Cooperation Centre for UNESCO (CCIC, #12454);*
- *International Christian Organisation of the Media (ICOM, #12563);*
- *International Commission of Jurists (ICJ, #12695);*
- *International Communications Volunteers (ICVolunteers, #12817);*
- *International Consortium on Landslides (ICL, #12917);*
- *International Coordination Council of Educational Institutions Alumni (INCORVUZ-XXI, #12959);*
- *International Council for Education of People with Visual Impairment (ICEVI, #13015);*
- *International Council for Health, Physical Education, Recreation, Sport and Dance (ICHPER-SD, #13028);*
- *International Council for Open and Distance Education (ICDE, #13056);*
- *International Council for Traditional Music (ICTM, #13087);*
- *International Council of Associations for Science Education (ICASE, #12997);*
- *International Council of Jewish Women (ICJW, #13036);*
- *International Council of Women (ICW, #13093);*
- *International Council on Education for Teaching (ICET, #13016);*
- *International Council on Social Welfare (ICSW, #13076);*
- *International Cultural Youth Exchange (ICYE Federation, #13122);*
- *International Dance Council (#13130);*
- *International Eurasian Academy of Sciences (IEAS, no recent information);*
- *International Federation for Home Economics (IFHE, #13447);*
- *International Federation for Housing and Planning (IFHP, #13450);*
- *International Federation for Human Rights (#13452);*
- *International Federation for Information Processing (IFIP, #13458);*
- *International Federation for Parent Education (IFPE, #13499);*
- *International Federation "Musique Espérance" (#13487);*
- *International Federation of Actors (#13337);*
- *International Federation of Arts Councils and Culture Agencies (IFACCA, #13358);*
- *International Federation of Business and Professional Women (BPW International, #13376);*
- *International Federation of Catholic Universities (IFCU, #13381);*
- *International Federation of Coalitions for Cultural Diversity (IFCCD, #13394);*
- *International Federation of East-Central European Institutes (no recent information);*
- *International Federation of Film Archives (#13427);*
- *International Federation of Landscape Architects (IFLA, #13467);*
- *International Federation of Language Teacher Associations (#13468);*
- *International Federation of Medical Students' Associations (IFMSA, #13478);*
- *International Federation of Musicians (#13486);*
- *International Federation of Photographic Art (#13509);*
- *International Federation of Red Cross and Red Crescent Societies (#13526);*
- *International Federation of Reproduction Rights Organizations (IFRRO, #13527);*
- *International Federation of Rural Adult Catholic Movements (#13535);*
- *International Federation of Television Archives (IFTA, #13568);*
- *International Federation of Training Centres for the Promotion of Progressive Education (#13572);*
- *International Federation of Translators (#13574);*
- *International Federation of Women in Legal Careers (IFWLC, #13579);*
- *International Federation of Women Lawyers (FIDA, #13578);*
- *International Federation of Workers' Education Associations (IFWEA, #13580);*
- *International Fellowship of Reconciliation (IFOR, #13586);*
- *International House of Poetry (no recent information);*
- *International Information Centre for Terminology (INFOTERM, #13846);*
- *International Institute for Peace (IIP, #13907);*
- *International Institute of Humanitarian Law (IIHL, #13885);*
- *International Jacques Maritain Institute (#13967);*
- *International Juvenile Justice Observatory (IJJO);*
- *International Lesbian, Gay, Bisexual, Transgender, Queer and Intersex Youth and Student Organization (IGLYO, #14032);*
- *International Literacy Association (ILA, #14057);*
- *International Literacy Institute (ILI);*
- *International Mediterranean Women's Forum (IMWF, #14143);*
- *International Network of Quality Assurance Agencies in Higher Education (INQAAHE, #14312);*
- *International Network of Women Engineers and Scientists (INWES, #14345);*
- *International Ocean Institute (IOI, #14394);*
- *International Organization for Chemical Sciences in Development (IOCD, #14440);*
- *International Organization for Standardization (ISO, #14473);*
- *International Organization for the Right to Education and Freedom of Education (#14468);*
- *International Organization of Folk Art (IOV World, #14447);*
- *International Pharmaceutical Students' Federation (IPSF, #14568);*
- *International Planned Parenthood Federation (IPPF, #14589);*
- *International Police Association (IPA, #14612);*
- *International Public Television (INPUT, #14674);*
- *International Publishers Association (IPA, #14675);*
- *International School Psychology Association (ISPA, #14788);*
- *International Seismological Centre (ISC, #14830);*
- *International Social Tourism Organisation (ISTO, #14889);*
- *International Society for Chinese Language Teaching;*
- *International Society for Education through Art (INSEA, #15074);*
- *International Society of City and Regional Planners (ISOCARP, #15012);*
- *International Solar Energy Society (ISES, #15564);*
- *International Statistical Institute (ISI, #15603);*
- *International Trade Union Confederation (ITUC, #15708);*
- *International Union for Health Promotion and Education (IUHPE, #15778);*
- *International Union for Vacuum Science, Technique and Applications (IUVSTA, #15826);*
- *International Union of Notaries (#15795);*
- *International Work Group for Indigenous Affairs (IWGIA, #15907);*
- *International Young Catholic Students (IYCS, #15926);*
- *International Young Christian Workers (IYCW, #15927);*
- *Internet Society (ISOC, #15952);*
- *Internews International (inactive);*
- *ISIC Association (#16029);*
- *Jeunesses Musicales International (JMI, #16110);*
- *Kuwait Society for the Advancement of Arab Children;*
- *Latin American and Caribbean Committee for the Defense of Women's Rights (#16268);*
- *Latin American Association for Human Rights (#16243);*
- *Leonard Cheshire Disability (#16443);*
- *Lifelong Learning Platform – European Civil Society for Education (LLLP, #16466);*
- *Linguapax International (#16482);*
- *Lions Clubs International (LCI, #16485);*
- *Maison de sagesse (MdS);*
- *Make Mothers Matter (#16554);*
- *Mediterranean Information Office for Environment, Culture and Sustainable Development (MIO-ECSDE, #16657);*
- *Mother Child Education Foundation (ACEV);*
- *Mouvement international de la jeunesse agricole et rurale catholique (MIJARC, #16865);*
- *New Humanity (#17088);*
- *North American Broadcasters Association (NABA, #17561);*
- *Organisation mondiale des anciens élèves de l'enseignement catholique (OMAEC, #17816);*
- *Organización Continental Latinoamericana y Caribeña de Estudiantes (OCLAE, #17834);*
- *Organización de Telecomunicaciones de Iberoamérica (OTI, #17851);*
- *Pacific Islands News Association (PINA, #17975);*
- *Pan African Women's Organization (PAWO, #18074);*
- *Pan American Association of Student Loan Institutions (#18084);*
- *Pan Pacific and South East Asia Women's Association (PPSEAWA, #18186);*
- *Patrimoine sans frontières (PSF);*
- *Pax Christi – International Catholic Peace Movement (#18266);*
- *Peace and Sport;*
- *Plan International (#18386);*
- *Project Aladdin (#18531);*
- *Religions for Peace (RfP, #18831);*
- *Reporters sans frontières (RSF, #18846);*
- *Russian Peace Foundation (RPF);*
- *Save the Children International (#19058);*
- *Scholars at Risk (SAR);*
- *Scientific Committee on Problems of the Environment (SCOPE, #19150);*
- *Service Civil International (SCI, #19238);*
- *Servicio Paz y Justicia en América Latina (SERPAJ-AL, #19247);*
- *SIL International (#19278);*
- *Society for International Development (SID, #19581);*
- *Société européenne pour la formation des ingénieurs (SEFI, #19462);*
- *Solidarity in Literacy (ALFASOL);*
- *Soroptimist International (SI, #19686);*
- *Southeast Asia-Pacific Audiovisual Archive Association (SEAPAVAA, #19790);*
- *Sozopol Foundation;*
- *Surfrider Foundation Europe (#20041);*

- *The Association for International Sport for All (TAFISA, #02763)*;
- *The European Law Students' Association (ELSA, #07660)*;
- *The Global Association of Art and Design Education and Research (Cumulus Association, #10241)*;
- *Trace Element – Institute for UNESCO*;
- *Transparency International (TI, #20223)*;
- *UMEC-WUCT (#20280)*;
- *Union internationale de la marionnette (UNIMA, #20430)*;
- *Union internationale de la presse francophone (UPF, #20435)*;
- *United Bible Societies (UBS, #20498)*;
- *Universal Esperanto Association (UEA, #20676)*;
- *University of the Arctic (UArctic, #20696)*;
- *Water Security Management, Assessment, Research & Technology (W-SMART)*;
- *West India Committee (WIC, #20920)*;
- *Wildlife Conservation Society (WCS)*;
- *Women for Water Partnership (WfWP, #21041)*;
- *Women's International League for Peace and Freedom (WILPF, #21024)*;
- *Women without Borders (WwB)*;
- *World Academy of Art and Science (WAAS, #21065)*;
- *World Alliance of Young Men's Christian Associations (YMCA, #21090)*;
- *World Association for Small and Medium Enterprises (WASME, #21189)*;
- *World Association for the School as an Instrument of Peace (#21184)*;
- *World Association of Girl Guides and Girl Scouts (WAGGGS, #21142)*;
- *World Association of Industrial and Technological Research Organizations (WAITRO, #21145)*;
- *World Catholic Association for Communication (SIGNIS, #21264)*;
- *World Committee for Lifelong Learning (WCLLL)*;
- *World Council of Comparative Education Societies (WCCES, #21322)*;
- *World Crafts Council AISBL (WCC International, #21342)*;
- *Worlddidac Association (#21361)*;
- *World Energy Council (WEC, #21381)*;
- *World Family Organization (WFO, #21399)*;
- *World Federation of Scientific Workers (WFSW, #21480)*;
- *World Federation of the Deaf (WFD, #21425)*;
- *World Federation of Tourist Guide Associations (WFTGA, #21492)*;
- *World Federation of Trade Unions (WFTU, #21493)*;
- *World Fellowship of Buddhists (WFB, #21501)*;
- *World Futures Studies Federation (WFSF, #21535)*;
- *World Islamic Call Society (WICS, inactive)*;
- *World Martial Arts Masterships Committee (WMC)*;
- *World Martial Arts Union (WoMAU, #21638)*;
- *World Mountain People Association (WMPA, #21658)*;
- *World Organization for Early Childhood Education (OMEP, #21689)*;
- *World ORT (WO, #21698)*;
- *World Peace Council (WPC, #21717)*;
- *World Technopolis Association (WTA, #21850)*;
- *World Underwater Federation (#21873)*;
- *World Union of Catholic Women's Organisations (WUCWO, #21876)*;
- *World Union of Jewish Students (WUJS, #21878)*;
- *World University Service (WUS, #21892)*;
- *World Young Women's Christian Association (World YWCA, #21947)*;
- *World Youth Student and Educational Travel Confederation (WYSE Travel Confederation, #21959)*;
- *Yachay Wasi (#21970)*;
- *Zonta International (#22038)*.

Foundations (21):
- *AMAR International Charitable Foundation (AICF)*;
- *Arab Thought Foundation (ATF, #01056)*;
- *Association Mondiale des Amis de l'Enfance (AMADE, #02808)*;
- *Bariloche Foundation (FB)*;
- *Centre for International Heritage Activities (CIE)*;
- *Centro UNESCO del Pais Vasco (UNESCO Etxea)*;
- *Education Above All (EAA)*;
- *Fondation Léopold Sédar Senghor*;
- *Fondation Paul Gérin-Lajoie*;
- *Freunde der Erziehungskunst Rudolf Steiners*;
- *Fundación Global Democracia y Desarrollo (FUNGLODE)*;
- *Goi Peace Foundation*;
- *Green Cross International (GCI, #10715)*;
- *Marangopoulos Foundation for Human Rights (MFHR)*;
- *Patronat Sud-Nord Solidaritat i Cultura*;
- *South Asia Foundation (SAF, #19717)*;
- *World Anti-Doping Agency (WADA, #21096)*;
- *World Foundation for AIDS Research and Prevention (#21525)*;
- *World Monuments Fund (WMF, #21657)*;
- *World Wide Fund for Nature (WWF, #21922)*;
- *YOU Stiftung – Bildung für Kinder in Not (YOU Stiftung)*.

IGO Relations As a Specialized Agency of the United Nations, UNESCO has established Agreements with:
- *FAO (#09260)*;
- *ILO (#11123)*;
- *International Atomic Energy Agency (IAEA, #12294)*;
- *International Bank for Reconstruction and Development (IBRD, #12317)*;
- *International Telecommunication Union (ITU, #15673)*;
- *Office of the United Nations High Commissioner for Human Rights (OHCHR, #17697)*;
- *Secretariat of the United Nations Convention to Combat Desertification (Secretariat of the UNCCD, #19208)*;
- *UNEP (#20299)*;
- *UN Women (#20724)*;
- *UNDP (#20292)*;
- *UNHCR (#20327)*;
- *UNICEF (#20332)*;
- *UNIDO (#20336)*;
- *United Nations (UN, #20515)*;
- *United Nations Economic Commission for Latin America and the Caribbean (ECLAC, #20556)*;
- *United Nations Human Settlements Programme (UN-Habitat, #20572)*;
- *United Nations Institute for Training and Research (UNITAR, #20576)*;
- *United Nations Population Fund (UNFPA, #20612)*;
- *United Nations Relief and Works Agency for Palestine Refugees in the Near East (UNRWA, #20622)*;
- *United Nations Volunteers (UNV, #20650)*;
- *WHO (#20950)*;
- *World Food Programme (WFP, #21510)*;
- *World Meteorological Organization (WMO, #21649)*;
- *World Tourism Organization (UNWTO, #21861)*.

Member of: *United Nations Sustainable Development Group (UNSDG, #20634)*. Cooperates closely with: *ECOSOC (#05331)* and the other Specialized Agencies. Agreements with and permanent observer to: *World Intellectual Property Organization (WIPO, #21593)*. On board of: *International Training Centre of the ILO (ITC, #15717)*. Observer to: *Committee for the Development of the Pan-European Ecological Network (STRA-REP, inactive)*; *Standing Committee to the Bern Convention on the Conservation of European Wildlife and Natural Habitats (#19949)*. Represented on: *United Nations System Chief Executives Board for Coordination (CEB, #20636)*. Cooperates with: *Bibliotheca Alexandrina Council of Patrons (#03227)*. Shares in the running costs of: Administrative Tribunal of the International Labour Organization (ILO Tribunal); *Joint Inspection Unit of the United Nations (JIU, #16133)*; *United Nations Committee for Programme and Coordination (CPC, #20546)*.

As of Feb 2006, formal agreements with the following interregional intergovernmental organizations not belonging to the United Nations system:
- *Organisation of African, Caribbean and Pacific States (OACPS, #17796)*;
- *CABI (#03393)*;
- *CIHEAM – International Centre for Advanced Mediterranean Agronomic Studies (CIHEAM, #03927)*;
- *Commonwealth of Learning (COL, #04346)*;
- *Commonwealth Secretariat (#04362)*;
- *Comunidade dos Países de Língua Portuguesa (CPLP, #04430)*;
- *Conférence des ministres de l'éducation des Etats et gouvernements de la Francophonie (CONFEMEN, #04632)*;
- *Conférence des ministres de la jeunesse et des sports de la Francophonie (CONFEJES, #04634)*;
- *International Centre for Genetic Engineering and Biotechnology (ICGEB, #12494)*;
- *International Centre for Promotion of Enterprises (ICPE, #12509)*;
- *International Criminal Police Organization – INTERPOL (ICPO-INTERPOL, #13110)*;
- *International Institute for the Unification of Private Law (UNIDROIT, #13934)*;
- *International Organization of Legal Metrology (#14451)*;
- *Islamic Broadcasting Union (IBU, #16033)*;
- *Islamic Development Bank (IsDB, #16044)*;
- *Islamic World Educational, Scientific and Cultural Organization (ICESCO, #16058)*;
- *Observatoire du Sahara et du Sahel (OSS, #17636)*;
- *Organisation internationale de la Francophonie (OIF, #17809)*, replacing *Agence intergouvernementale de La Francophonie (inactive)*;
- *Organisation of Islamic Cooperation (OIC, #17813)*;
- *Research Centre for Islamic History, Art and Culture (IRCICA, #18852)*;
- *University for Peace (UPEACE, #20702)*;
- *World Customs Organization (WCO, #21350)*.

As of Feb 2006, formal agreements with the following regional intergovernmental bodies:
- *African Centre for Applied Research and Training in Social Development (ACARTSOD, #00237)*;
- *African Development Bank (ADB, #00283)*;
- *African Intellectual Property Organization (#00344)*;
- *African Union (AU, #00488)*;
- *Amazonian Parliament (#00767)*;
- *Andean Parliament (#00820)*;
- *Arab Bank for Economic Development in Africa (#00904)*;
- *Arab Bureau of Education for the Gulf States (ABEGS, #00910)*;
- *Arab Centre for the Studies of Arid Zones and Dry Lands (ACSAD, #00918)*;
- *Arab Federation for Technical Education (AFTE, no recent information)*;
- *Arab Gulf Programme for United Nations Development Organizations (AGFUND, #00971)*;
- *Arab Gulf States Folklore Centre (no recent information)*;
- *Arab Gulf States Information Documentation Centre (AGSIDC, inactive)*;
- *Arab League Educational, Cultural and Scientific Organization (ALECSO, #01003)*;
- *Arab Organization for Agricultural Development (AOAD, #01018)*;
- *Arab States Broadcasting Union (ASBU, #01050)*;
- *ASEAN (#01141)*;
- *Caribbean Community (CARICOM, #03476)*;
- *Central American Bank for Economic Integration (CABEI, #03658)*;
- *Central American Integration System (#03671)*;
- *Parlamento Centroamericano (PARLACEN, #18201)*;
- *Centro Latino-Americano de Física (CLAF, #03815)*;
- *Comité permanent inter-Etats de lutte contre la sécheresse dans le Sahel (CILSS, #04195)*;
- *Communauté économique et monétaire d'Afrique centrale (CEMAC, #04374)* (replacing *Union douanière et économique de l'Afrique centrale (UDEAC, inactive)*);
- *Community of Sahel-Saharan States (CEN-SAD, #04406)*;
- *Convenio Andrés Bello de integración educativa, científica y cultural de América Latina y España (Convenio Andrés Bello, #04785)*;
- *Coordinación Educativa y Cultural Centroamericana (CECC, #04803)*;
- *Council of Europe (CE, #04881)*;
- *Economic Community of West African States (ECOWAS, #05312)*;
- *Economic Cooperation Organization (ECO, #05313)*;
- *European Commission (EC, #06633)*;
- *European Organization for Nuclear Research (CERN, #08108)*;
- *Federation of Arab Scientific Research Councils (FASRC, no recent information)*;
- *Gulf Organization for Industrial Consulting (GOIC, #10837)*;
- *Inter-American Development Bank (IDB, #11427)*;
- *Intergovernmental TV and Radio Corporation (ITRC MIR, no recent information)*;
- *International Organization of Turkic Culture (TURKSOY, #14482)*;
- *Italian-Latin American Institute (ILAI, #16071)*;
- *Joint Institute for Nuclear Research (JINR, #16134)*;
- *Latin American Faculty of Social Sciences (#16316)*;
- *League of Arab States (LAS, #16420)*;
- *OAS (#17629)*;
- *OECD (#17693)*;
- *Organisation of Eastern Caribbean States (OECS, #17804)*;
- *Organization of Ibero-American States for Education, Science and Culture (#17871)*;
- *Pacific Community (SPC, #17942)*;
- *Parlamento Indígena de América (PIA, #18202)*;
- *Parlamento Latinoamericano (PARLATINO, #18203)*;
- *Regional Council for Adult Education and Literacy in Africa (CREAA, no recent information)*;
- *Sistema Económico Latinoamericano (SELA, #19294)*;
- *Southeast Asian Ministers of Education Organization (SEAMEO, #19774)*;
- *Southern African Development Community (SADC, #19843)*;
- *Supreme Council for Sport in Africa (SCSA, inactive)*.

NGO Relations *International Conference of NGOs (#12883)* meets every 2 years to review the state of cooperation with UNESCO, conduct collective cooperation between organizations having common interests. The NGO-UNESCO Liaison Committee, made up of 10 NGO partners elected by the Conference, represents the interests of all the NGO partners with regard to UNESCO. [2020.02.28/XB3383/**B***]

♦ UNESCO Venice Office – Regional Office for Science and Technology for Europe / see UNESCO Office in Venice – UNESCO Regional Bureau for Science and Culture in Europe (#20316)

♦ UNESCO-WHC / see World Heritage Centre (#21566)

♦ UNESCO World Commission on the Ethics of Scientific Knowledge and Technology (#04235)

♦ UNESCO World Heritage Centre / see World Heritage Centre (#21566)

♦ UNESDA Soft Drinks Europe (UNESDA) 20323

Dir Gen Rue du Trône 14-16, 1000 Brussels, Belgium. T. +3227370130. E-mail: mail@unesda.eu.
Office and Events Manager address not obtained.
URL: http://www.unesda.eu/

History 20 Feb 1959, Brussels (Belgium). Took over the activities of *Confederation of International Beverages Associations (CISDA, inactive)*. Former names and other names: *Union of Aerated Drinks Associations of EEC Countries* – former; *Union des associations de boissons gazeuses des pays membres de la CEE* – former; *Union of EC Soft Drinks Associations* – former; *Union des associations de boissons rafraîchissantes des pays membres de la CE* – former; *Vereinigung der Kohlesaürehaltigen Getränke in den EG-Ländern* – former; *Union of EU Soft Drinks Associations (UNESDA)* – former; *Union des associations de boissons rafraîchissantes des pays membres de l'UE* – former; *Vereinigung der Erfrischungsgetränke in den EU-Ländern* – former; *Vereinigung der Kohlesaürehaltigen Getränke in den EU-Ländern* – former; *Union des associations de boissons non-alcoolisées* – former; *Union of European Beverages Associations (UNESDA)* – former. Registration: Banque-Carrefour des Entreprises, No/ID: 0450.702.679, Start date: 29 Jun 1993, Belgium; EU Transparency Register, No/ID: 25492952296-56, Start date: 21 Sep 2009. **Aims** Represent, protect and promote members' interests on a European Union-wide basis; support acceptance, growth and development of the soft drinks *industry*; monitor and ensure fairness of proposed and actual European legislation. **Structure** General Assembly (annual); Board of Directors; Executive Committee; Secretariat; Working Committees (4). **Languages** Dutch, English, French. **Staff** 4.00 FTE, paid. **Finance** Sources: members' dues. **Activities** Standards/guidelines; networking/liaising. **Events** *Annual General Assembly* Berlin (Germany) 2015, *Annual General Assembly* Warsaw (Poland) 2014, *Annual General Assembly* Budapest (Hungary) 2013, *Annual General Assembly* Lisbon (Portugal) 2013, *Annual General Assembly* Oslo (Norway) 2012.

Members National federations of industries of soft drinks in 23 countries:
Austria, Belgium, Bulgaria, Denmark, Estonia, Finland, France, Germany, Greece, Ireland, Italy, Luxembourg, Netherlands, Norway, Poland, Portugal, Romania, Slovakia, Slovenia, Spain, Sweden, Switzerland, UK.

IGO Relations Recognized by: *European Commission (EC, #06633)*. **NGO Relations** Member of (7): *Business and Industry Advisory Committee to the OECD (BIAC, #03385)* (Affiliate); *Centre for European Policy Studies (CEPS, #03741)* (Institutional); *Circular Plastics Alliance (#03936)*; *CIUS – European Sugar Users (#03961)*; *European Policy Centre (EPC, #08240)*; *Federation of European and International Associations Established in Belgium (FAIB, #09508)*; *FoodDrinkEurope (#09841)* (Affiliate). [2020/XE3243/**E**]

♦ UNESDA / see UNESDA Soft Drinks Europe (#20323)

♦ **UNESDA** UNESDA Soft Drinks Europe (#20323)

- ♦ UNet – International Symposium on Ubiquitous Networking (meeting series)
- ♦ UNETPSA – United Nations Educational and Training Programme for Southern Africa (inactive)
- ♦ Unevangelized Fields Mission – International / see Crossworld
- ♦ UNF3S – Université Numérique Francophone des Sciences de la Santé et du Sport (internationally oriented national body)
- ♦ UNFCCC Climate Change Secretariat / see United Nations Framework Convention on Climate Change – Secretariat (#20564)
- ♦ UNFCCC – United Nations Framework Convention on Climate Change (1992 treaty)
- ♦ **UNFCCC** United Nations Framework Convention on Climate Change – Secretariat (#20564)
- ♦ **UNFF** United Nations Forum on Forests (#20562)
- ♦ **UNFICYP** United Nations Peace-keeping Force in Cyprus (#20608)
- ♦ **UNFIP** United Nations Fund for International Partnerships (#20565)
- ♦ UNFM – Université Numérique Francophone Mondiale (internationally oriented national body)
- ♦ **UNFPA** United Nations Population Fund (#20612)
- ♦ UNFR / see United Nations Friends in Rotary
- ♦ UNFR – United Nations Friends in Rotary (internationally oriented national body)
- ♦ UNFSTD – United Nations Fund for Science and Technology for Development (inactive)
- ♦ UNFSU / see United Nations Field Staff Union (#20561)
- ♦ **UNFSU** United Nations Field Staff Union (#20561)
- ♦ **UNF** United Nations Foundation (#20563)
- ♦ Unga Europeiska Federalister (#21984)
- ♦ Ungdomens Nordiska Råd (#17474)
- ♦ Ungdommens Nordiske Råd (#17474)
- ♦ Unge Europeiske Föderalister (#21984)
- ♦ **UNGEGN** United Nations Group of Experts on Geographical Names (#20569)
- ♦ **UNGEI** United Nations Girls' Education Initiative (#20566)
- ♦ **UN-GGIM Americas** Regional Committee of the UN on Global Geospatial Information Management for the Americas (#18765)
- ♦ **UN-GGIM-AP** Regional Committee of United Nations Global Geospatial Information Management for Asia and the Pacific (#18766)
- ♦ **UN-GGIM GS** UN-GGO: Geospatial Societies (#20324)
- ♦ **UN-GGIM** United Nations Committee of Experts on Global Geospatial Information Management (#20540)

♦ UN-GGO: Geospatial Societies (UN-GGIM GS) 20324

Chair c/o FIG, Kalvebod Brygge 31-33, 1780 Copenhagen, Denmark. T. +4593910810.
URL: http://www.fig.net/unggimgs/

History 1999. A thematic network of *United Nations Committee of Experts on Global Geospatial Information Management (UN-GGIM, #20540)*. Former names and other names: *Joint Board of the Geospatial Information Societies (JB GIS)* – former. **Aims** Serve as a coalition of leading international geospatial societies which can speak on behalf of the geospatial profession at international level, especially to the United Nations and other global stakeholders; coordinate activities within the geospatial society and organizations. **Structure** No formal structure. **Languages** English. **Staff** None. Office services provide by FIG. **Finance** No fixed budget.
Members International organizations (9):
Institute of Electrical and Electronics Engineers (IEEE, #11259) (Geosciences and Remote Sensing Society IEEE GRSS); *International Association of Geodesy (IAG, #11914)*; *International Cartographic Association (ICA, #12446)*; *International Federation of Surveyors (FIG, #13561)*; *International Geographical Union (IGU, #13713)*; *International Map Industry Association (IMIA, #14085)*; *International Society for Digital Earth (ISDE, #15061)*; *International Society for Photogrammetry and Remote Sensing (ISPRS, #15362)*; *International Union of Geodesy and Geophysics (IUGG, #15776)*.
Observing members (2):
International Hydrographic Organization (IHO, #13825); *Urban and Regional Information Systems Association (URISA)*.
IGO Relations Partner of: *Group on Earth Observations (GEO, #10735)*; *United Nations Committee of Experts on Global Geospatial Information Management (UN-GGIM, #20540)*. [2019/XJ3664/y/E]

- ♦ UN-GIFT – Global Initiative to Fight Human Trafficking (inactive)
- ♦ **UNGIS** United Nations Group on the Information Society (#20570)
- ♦ UNGIWG – United Nations Geographic Information Working Group (unconfirmed)

♦ UN Global Impact 20325

Main Office 2 UN Plaza, UN DC2-612, New York NY 10017, USA. T. +12129071301. E-mail: wynhoven@un.org – ungc4@unglobalcompact.org.
URL: http://www.unglobalcompact.org/

History 26 Jul 2000. **Aims** Align business operations and strategies everywhere with universally accepted *principles* in the areas of human rights, labour, environment and anti-corruption. **Structure** Leaders Summit (every 3 years). Board. **Events** *Forum* Seoul (Korea Rep) 2011. **Members** Participants (over 7,700) in 130 countries. Membership countries not specified. **IGO Relations** Special partner of: *UN-Water (#20723)*. [2018/XJ1953/E]

- ♦ Ung Nordisk Musik (inactive)
- ♦ UNGSII Foundation (unconfirmed)
- ♦ UN-HABITAT / see United Nations Human Settlements Programme (#20572)
- ♦ **UN-Habitat** United Nations Human Settlements Programme (#20572)

♦ UNHCR Global Staff Council 20326

Chairperson c/o UNHCR Headquarters, 94 rue de Montbrillant, 1202 Geneva, Switzerland. T. +41227398591. E-mail: hqsr00@unhcr.org.

History Founded to represent staff members of *UNHCR (#20327)*. Former names and other names: *UNHCR Staff Council* – former; *UNHCR Staff Association* – former. **Aims** Safeguard *rights* of UNHCR staff members and defend their interests as regards conditions of *employment*, *work* and general *welfare*. **Members** Elected representatives (15). **NGO Relations** Member of (1): *Coordinating Committee for International Staff Unions and Associations of the United Nations System (CCISUA, #04818)*. [2022.10.19/XE2051/E]

- ♦ UNHCR Staff Association / see UNHCR Global Staff Council (#20326)
- ♦ UNHCR Staff Council / see UNHCR Global Staff Council (#20326)

♦ UNHCR – United Nations High Commissioner for Refugees 20327

Haut commissariat des Nations Unies pour les réfugiés (HCR) – Oficina del Alto Comisionado de las Naciones Unidas para los Refugiados (ACNUR)

High Commissioner Case Postale 2500, 1211 Geneva 2 Dépôt, Switzerland. T. +41227398111. Fax +41227397377.
UNHCR New York Office – UN Affairs 220 East 42nd St, New York NY 10017, USA. T. +12129630032. Fax +12129630074.
URL: http://www.unhcr.org/

History 1 Jan 1951. Established initially for a 3-year period, by General Assembly Resolutions: 319 (IV) of 3 Dec 1949; 428 (V) of 14 Dec 1950. Subsequently, the mandate of the High Commissioner's Office was renewed at 5-year intervals until 2003 when the time limitation was removed and the mandate extended until the refugee problem is solved, by General Assembly Resolution 58/153 of 22 Dec 2003. Previous organizations from which UNHCR developed were: *League of Nations High Commission for Refugees (inactive)*, set up in 1921, within the framework of *League of Nations (SDN, inactive)*; *Nansen International Office for Refugees (inactive)*, set up 30 Sep 1930, Geneva (Switzerland), replacing the High Commission as an autonomous body under the authority of the League; *'High Commission for Refugees coming from Germany'*, set up in 1933; *Office of the High Commissioner for Refugees under the Protection of the League (inactive)*, established 1 Jan 1939, London (UK), superseding these two latter bodies. UNHCR is not a specialized agency but a programme within the *United Nations System (#20635)*, forming an integral part of *United Nations (UN, #20515)* linked to the General Assembly and to *ECOSOC (#05331)*. Based in Geneva (Switzerland). **Aims** Provide international protection to refugees and seek durable solutions to their plight; extend assistance to other groups, notably returnees, internally displaced, stateless persons and others in need of international protection. **Structure** High Commissioner, elected by UN General Assembly on nomination of the UN Secretary-General, reports directly to the General Assembly, and to ECOSOC on coordination aspects. Present High Commissioner is Filippo Grandi (Italy); his term in office began 1 Jan 2016 and currently extends to 2020. Executive Committee of the High Commissioner's Programme (ExCom), meets annually in October in Geneva (Switzerland) and currently comprises 102 members. ExCom was established in 1958 under the terms of General Assembly Resolution 1166 (XII) and ECOSOC Resolution 672 (XXV). It authorizes the Office's annual programme of material assistance and provides advice to the High Commissioner, at his/her request, in the exercise of his/her mandated functions. **Languages** English, French. **Staff** Dec 2020: 17,878 staff in about 130 countries. Personnel negotiations dealt with by *UNHCR Global Staff Council (#20326)*. **Finance** Main source: voluntary contributions mainly from governments, as well as some funding from the private sector. Other sources: UN budget (about 2% of annual funding needs). Biennial programme budget approved annually by ExCom. Annual budget: 9,150,000,000 USD (2021).
Activities The basis of refugee protection activities is the 1951 *Convention Relating to the Status of Refugees (1951)*, which was drawn up in parallel with the creation of UNHCR. This legally binding treaty defines the term *'refugee'* as: *'a person who, owing to well-founded fear of being persecuted for reasons of race, religion, nationality, membership of a particular social group or political opinion, is outside the country of his nationality and is unable to or, owing to such fears is unwilling to avail himself of the protection of that country'*. The convention enunciates the principle of *'non-refoulement'*, under which no person may be returned against his/her will to a territory where he or she may be exposed to persecution; and sets standards for the treatment of refugees, including their legal status, employment and welfare. The Convention originally concerned only people who had become refugees as a result of events that took place before 1 Jan 1951; and signatory States had the option of limiting its geographical application to Europe. *Protocol Relating to the Status of Refugees (1967)* abolished the 1951 dateline, making the Convention truly universal. By Dec 2008, 147 States were party to one or both of these instruments. UNHCR promotes accession to the Convention and its 1967 Protocol.
Other relevant legal instruments include:
- *Convention Relating to the Status of Stateless Persons (1954)*;
- *Convention on the Reduction of the Number of Cases of Statelessness (1973)*;
- *Agreement Relating to Refugee Seamen (1957)*;
- *Protocol Relating to Refugee Seamen (1973)*;
- *European Agreement on the Abolition of Visas for Refugees (1959)*;
- *OAU Convention Governing the Specific Aspects of Refugee Problems in Africa (1969)*;
- African Union Convention for the Protection and Assistance of Internally Displaced Persons in Africa.

Other important texts related to refugee protection activities are:
- *Inter-American Convention on Human Rights (Pact of San José de Costa Rica, 1969)*, adopted by the Inter-American Specialized Conference on Human Rights;
- Cartagena Declaration of 1984.

Measures in favour of refugees have also been adopted in the legislation of a number of countries.
/Internally displaced persons/ Since 2005, working in close collaboration with other concerned organizations to establish an effective inter-agency framework for action in response to the challenges of protecting and finding solutions for IDPs due to conflict and human rights abuses. Has leadership role for the protection, emergency shelter and camp coordination and camp management clusters in situations of conflict-induced internal displacement.
/Material assistance/ is provided when shelter, food supplies, medical aid or other forms of relief are required on a large scale, from the outset of an emergency until such time as the beneficiaries have found a solution to their plight. Particular attention is paid to the needs of refugee women, children, adolescents and the elderly.
/Durable solutions/ The solution benefiting most refugees is voluntary repatriation, whereby refugees return to their homes and resume their lives in a sustainable manner. When repatriation is impossible, UNHCR tries to help refugees settle locally in the country of asylum. When neither of these solutions is possible, resettlement in third countries is explored for people who meet specific criteria. Resettlement remains an important instrument of international protection.
/Preventing refugee crises/ Increasingly involved in development initiatives from the outset of refugee crises. Such efforts frequently take place in the broader context of humanitarian-development cooperation.
/Population of concern to UNHCR/ In 2017, the number of persons 'of concern' stood at 65.6 million. This reflects various increases in numbers among the different groups assisted, including refugees, returnees, IDPs, asylum-seekers and stateless persons.
/Cooperation with other organizations/ In 2017, disbursed US$ 1,500,000,000 to over 1,000 partners.
Also maintains strong ties with partners in the UN system and remains engaged in the work of the Inter-Agency Standing Committee.
Instrumental in setting up: *Inter-Governmental Consultations on Migration, Asylum and Refugees (IGC, #11479)*.
Events *AidEx : Europe's Leading Humanitarian and Development Aid Conference* Brussels (Belgium) 2019, *International Solidarity Conference on the Venezuelan Refugee and Migrant Crisis* Brussels (Belgium) 2019, *Session* Geneva (Switzerland) 2019, *Regional Conference on Enhanced Collaboration within Western Balkans in Providing International Protection and Respecting the Human Rights of Refugees* Ohrid (North Macedonia) 2019, *Seminar on Private Sector Partnership in UNHCR* Tokyo (Japan) 2018. **Publications** *Global Appeal* (annual); *Global Report* (annual); *Statistical Yearbook*. Various guidelines and documents on protection and assistance (updated as necessary).
Members Member States of the Executive Committee of the High Commissioner's Programme (102):
Afghanistan, Algeria, Argentina, Armenia, Australia, Austria, Azerbaijan, Bangladesh, Belarus, Belgium, Benin, Brazil, Bulgaria, Cameroon, Canada, Chad, Chile, China, Colombia, Congo Brazzaville, Congo DR, Costa Rica, Côte d'Ivoire, Croatia, Cyprus, Czechia, Denmark, Djibouti, Ecuador, Egypt, Estonia, Ethiopia, Fiji, Finland, France, Georgia, Germany, Ghana, Greece, Guinea, Holy See, Hungary, India, Iran Islamic Rep, Ireland, Israel, Italy, Japan, Jordan, Kenya, Korea Rep, Latvia, Lebanon, Lesotho, Lithuania, Luxembourg, Madagascar, Mexico, Moldova, Montenegro, Morocco, Mozambique, Namibia, Netherlands, New Zealand, Nicaragua, Nigeria, North Macedonia, Norway, Pakistan, Paraguay, Peru, Philippines, Poland, Portugal, Romania, Russia, Rwanda, Senegal, Serbia, Slovakia, Slovenia, Somalia, South Africa, Spain, Sudan, Sweden, Switzerland, Tanzania UR, Thailand, Togo, Tunisia, Türkiye, Turkmenistan, Uganda, UK, Uruguay, USA, Venezuela, Yemen, Zambia, Zimbabwe.
IGO Relations Contributes actively to: *United Nations System Chief Executives Board for Coordination (CEB, #20636)* and its subsidiary bodies. Maintains strong ties with partners in the UN system. **NGO Relations** Long history of working with NGOs in implementation of programmes and in promotion of refugee rights. Committed to reach target of providing 25% of programme expenditure to local and national responses which deliver assistance and protection to persons of concern by 2020. Annual consultations with NGOs held at Headquarters, bringing together over 500 participants. In the context of Comprehensive Refugee Response Framework, created reference group together with *International Federation of Red Cross and Red Crescent Societies (#13526)* and *International Council of Voluntary Agencies (ICVA, #13092)*. [2022/XE3016/E*]

- ♦ UNHHSF – United Nations Habitat and Human Settlements Foundation (inactive)
- ♦ UNIA / see Universal Negro Improvement Association and African Communities League of the World
- ♦ UNIA-ACLW – Universal Negro Improvement Association and African Communities League of the World (internationally oriented national body)
- ♦ **UniAdrion** Virtual University of the Adriatic-Ionic Basin (#20792)
- ♦ Unia Europejska (#08967)
- ♦ UNI-Africa / see UNI Global Union – Africa Region (#20339)
- ♦ **UNI-Africa** UNI Global Union – Africa Region (#20339)
- ♦ UNI-Americas / see UNI Global Union – Americas Regional Office (#20340)
- ♦ **UNI-Americas** UNI Global Union – Americas Regional Office (#20340)
- ♦ União dos Advogados Europeus (#20365)
- ♦ União Africana Postal e de Telecomunicações (inactive)
- ♦ União Americana de Numismática (unconfirmed)
- ♦ União das Associações de Distribuidores de Agua dos Paises Membros das Comunidades Européias / see European Federation of National Associations of Water and Waste Water Services (#07170)
- ♦ União das Cidades Africanas (inactive)
- ♦ União de Cidades Capitais Ibero-Americanas (#20412)
- ♦ União das Cidades Capitais de Lingua Portuguesa / see União das Cidades Capitais Luso-Afro-Américo-Asiaticas (#20328)

♦ União das Cidades Capitais Luso-Afro-Américo-Asiaticas (UCCLA) . 20328
Union of Luso-Afro-America-Asiatic Capital Cities – Union des villes-capitales luso-afro-américano-asiatiques – Unión de Ciudades Capitales Luso-Afro-Américo-Asiaticas
SG Avda da India no 110, Belém, 1300-300 Lisbon, Portugal. T. +351218171617. E-mail: uccla@uccla.pt.
URL: http://www.uccla.pt/
History 28 Jun 1985, Lisbon (Portugal), as *União das Cidades Capitais de Lingua Portuguesa – Union of Portuguese-Speaking Capital Cities – Union des villes capitales de langue portugaise – Unión de Ciudades Capitales de Lengua Portuguesa.* Constitution signed 26 Jun 1987. **Aims** Promote North / South cooperation and decentralization; stimulate understanding and cooperation between Portuguese-speaking people through town twinning schemes and close exchange between capital city autarchies; study problems concerning their lives and activities with a view to their harmonious and balanced development; promote rights of good neighbourliness and citizen participation in public affairs; provide meetings where knowledge and experience in economic, cultural, touristic and professional training may be exchanged. **Structure** General Meeting (annual); Executive Committee; Audit Committee/Revenue Council; Head Office in Lisbon (Portugal), headed by Secretary-General. **Languages** Portuguese. **Staff** 22.00 FTE, paid. Staff seconded from Lisbon (Portugal) City Council. **Finance** Members' dues. Other sources: support from Lisbon (Portugal) City Council; subsidies. **Activities** Training/education; financial and/or material support; events/meetings; networking/liaising. **Events** *Annual General Meeting* Salvador (Brazil) 2005, *Annual General Meeting* Salvador (Brazil) 2005, *Annual General Meeting* Luanda (Angola) 2004, *Annual General Meeting* Lisbon (Portugal) 2003, *Annual General Meeting* Praia (Cape Verde) 2002. **Publications** *Revista Cidades UCCLA.* Book.
Members Full (17); Associated (5); Supporter (51). Cities (22) and companies and institutions (over 50) within those cities in 9 Portuguese-speaking countries and territories:
Angola, Brazil, Cape Verde, Guinea-Bissau, Macau, Mozambique, Portugal, Sao Tomé-Principe, Timor-Leste.
IGO Relations Accredited by: *United Nations Office at Vienna (UNOV, #20604).* Cooperates with: Portuguese Speaking Countries Cooperation Office within *UNESCO (#20322)*; North/South Working Group within *Congress of Local and Regional Authorities of the Council of Europe (#04677).* **NGO Relations** Member of: *Union of Ibero-American Capital Cities (#20412).* Set up: *United Cities and Local Governments of Africa (UCLG Africa, #20500).* [2017.11.30/XD2072/**D**]

- ♦ União dos Conselhos dos Carregadores Africanos (#20348)
- ♦ União para a Cultura e o Futuro Profissional na Europa (#20373)
- ♦ União Européia (#08967)
- ♦ União Européia das Associações Nacionais dos Distribuidores de Agua / see European Federation of National Associations of Water and Waste Water Services (#07170)
- ♦ União Européia de Clinicos Gerais / see European Union of General Practitioners / Family Physicians (#08993)
- ♦ União Européia do Comércio por Grosso em Papel, Cartão e Embalagens / see European Paper Merchants Association (#08138)
- ♦ União Europeia das Farmacias Sociais (#20401)
- ♦ União Européia dos Médicos Especialistas / see European Union of Medical Specialists (#09001)
- ♦ União Européia das Pequenhas e Médias Empresas (no recent information)
- ♦ União Européia dos Trabalhadores da Administração Local (inactive)
- ♦ União Franco-Ibérica para a Coordenação de Produção e do Transporte da Eletricidade (inactive)
- ♦ União-Ibero-americana dos Colégios e Ordens dos Advogados (#20411)
- ♦ União Interamericana para a Habitação (#11433)
- ♦ Uniao Internacional dos Arquitetos (#20419)
- ♦ União Internacional das Ciências Pré-Históricas e Proto-Históricas (#15801)
- ♦ União Internacional das Entidades de Crédito Imobiliario e Poupança / see International Union for Housing Finance (#15780)
- ♦ União Internacional de Orações (religious order)
- ♦ União Internacional de Organismos Turisticos e Culturais dos Correios e Telecomunicações (inactive)
- ♦ União International Socialista para Educação (#14881)
- ♦ União Latina (inactive)

♦ União Latino Americana de Yoga (ULY) 20329
Unión Latinoamericana de Yoga – Latin American Yoga Union
Main Office Calle Piedras 3364 esq, Rivera, Fray Bentos, Río Negro, Uruguay. T. +5985623340. E-mail: info@unionlatinoamericanadeyoga.org.
URL: http://www.unionlatinoamericanadeyoga.org/
History 1985. **Events** *Congress / Meeting* Punta del Este (Uruguay) 2011, *Congress / Meeting* Medellin (Colombia) 2010, *Congress / Meeting* Cancún (Mexico) 2009, *Congress / Meeting* Cancún (Mexico) 2008, *Congress / Meeting* Mexico City (Mexico) 2007.
Members National federations or institutions in 18 countries:
Argentina, Bolivia, Brazil, Canada, Chile, Costa Rica, Cuba, France, Italy, Mexico, Panama, Paraguay, Peru, Portugal, Spain, Uruguay, USA, Venezuela.
NGO Relations Full member of: *International Yoga Federation (IYF, #15923).* Member of: *World Yoga Union (no recent information).* [2011/XD5985/**D**]

- ♦ União Libanese Cultural Mundial (#21622)
- ♦ União das Nações Sul-Americanas (#20481)
- ♦ União Panamericana de Associações de Engenheiros (#20469)
- ♦ União Panamericana de Judo (#18115)
- ♦ União Sindical – Serviço Público Europeu / see Union Syndicale Fédérale (#20485)
- ♦ União das Universidades de América Latina e das Caraïbes (#02970)
- ♦ UNIAPAC / see International Christian Union of Business Executives (#12566)
- ♦ **UNIAPAC** Union internationale chrétienne des dirigeants d'entreprise (#12566)
- ♦ **UNIAPA** Unión Iberoamericana de Padres de Familia y Padres de Alumnos (#11035)
- ♦ **UNIAPRAVI** Unión Interamericana para la Vivienda (#11433)
- ♦ UNI-Apro / see UNI Global Union – Asia and Pacific Regional Office (#20341)
- ♦ UNIAP – United Nations Inter-Agency Project on Human Trafficking (inactive)
- ♦ UNI-Asia and Pacific / see UNI Global Union – Asia and Pacific Regional Office (#20341)
- ♦ **UNI-Asia and Pacific** UNI Global Union – Asia and Pacific Regional Office (#20341)
- ♦ UNIATEC – Union internationale des associations techniques cinématographiques (inactive)
- ♦ **UNICAE** Unión Internacional de Ciencias Antropológicas y Etnológicas (#15755)
- ♦ **UNICA** Network of Universities from the Capitals of Europe (#17061)
- ♦ **UNICA** Unione Intercontinentale Casalinghe (#20378)
- ♦ **UNICA** Union internationale du cinéma (#20423)
- ♦ UNICA / see Universities Caribbean (#20694)
- ♦ UNICC / see International Computing Centre (#12839)
- ♦ UNICE / see BUSINESSEUROPE (#03381)

♦ UNICEF Global Staff Association (GSA) 20330
Contact 3 UN Plaza, Room 22-34, New York NY 10017, USA. T. +12128246137.
URL: http://www.xunicef.org/
History to represent staff members of *UNICEF (#20332).* **Structure** General Meeting (annual). Officers: Chairperson; 1st and 2nd Vice-Chairpersons; Treasurer. **Finance** Sources: contributions. Other sources: management. Annual budget: 76,500 USD. **Publications** *UNICEF Global Staff Association E-bulletin.* **Members** Worldwide. Membership countries not specified. **NGO Relations** Member of (1): *Coordinating Committee for International Staff Unions and Associations of the United Nations System (CCISUA, #04818).* [2022/XE2049/**E**]

- ♦ UNICEF/PNUD/Banco Mundial/OMS Programa Especial de Investigaciones y Enseñanzas sobre Enfermedades Tropicales (#20331)
- ♦ UNICEF/PNUD/Banque mondiale/OMS Programme spécial de recherche et de formation concernant les maladies tropicales (#20331)
- ♦ UNICEF-UNAC Advisory Committee of Non-Governmental Organizations / see NGO Committee on UNICEF (#17120)

♦ UNICEF/UNDP/World Bank/WHO Special Programme for Research and Training in Tropical Diseases (TDR) 20331
UNICEF/PNUD/Banque mondiale/OMS Programme spécial de recherche et de formation concernant les maladies tropicales – UNICEF/PNUD/Banco Mundial/OMS Programa Especial de Investigaciones y Enseñanzas sobre Enfermedades Tropicales
Contact TDR/WHO, Avenue Appia 20, 1211 Geneva 27, Switzerland. T. +41227911538. Fax +41227914854. E-mail: suderi@who.int.
URL: http://www.who.int/tdr/
History Established mid-1970s, as *UNDP/World Bank/WHO Special Programme for Research and Training in Tropical Diseases (TDR) – PNUD/Banque mondiale/OMS Programme spécial de recherche et de formation concernant les maladies tropicales – PNUD/Banco Mundial/OMS Programa Especial de Investigaciones y Enseñanzas sobre Enfermedades Tropicales.* **Aims** Support research to improve control of infectious diseases of poverty; strengthen the capability of disease affected countries to perform essential health research. **Structure** Joint Coordinating Board – JCB (meets annually), comprising: 12 governments selected by TDR funding partners; 6 governments selected by WHO regional committees; 6 cooperating parties selected by JCB; 4 co-sponsors. Standing Committee; Scientific and Technical Advisory Committee (STAC). **Languages** English, French. **Staff** 30.00 FTE, paid. **Finance** Sponsors: *UNICEF (#20332); UNDP (#20292); International Bank for Reconstruction and Development (IBRD, #12317)* (World Bank); *WHO (#20950).* Contributions from governments, foundations, private corporations, public-private partnerships and academic institutions. Budget (2014-2015): US$ 50,000,000. **Activities** Advocacy/lobbying/activism; events/meetings. **Events** *Session* Accra (Ghana) 2006, *Meeting on Chagas disease in Andean countries* Bogota (Colombia) 1997, *Annual Session* Geneva (Switzerland) 1991, *Colloquium on diagnostic approaches to schistosomiasis* Beijing (China) 1990, *Annual Session* Geneva (Switzerland) 1990. **Publications** *TDR e-news* (12 a year); *TDR Annual Programme Report.* Various technical reports and monographs; guidelines, manuals. Information Services: TDR Communications Unit supplies basic information and images on the diseases and TDR Programme and offers advice to others preparing such information in book, e-news or video form.
Members WHO member states involved in collaborative projects. Joint Coordinating Board comprises representatives of UNICEF, World Bank, UNDP and WHO, one NGO and governments (including constituencies) of 29 countries:
Afghanistan, Armenia, Belgium, Burkina Faso, China, Comoros, Cuba, Fiji, Germany, Ghana, India, Japan, Luxembourg, Malaysia, Maldives, Moldova, Nigeria, Norway, Panama, Peru, Spain, Suriname, Sweden, Switzerland, Thailand, Türkiye, UK, USA, Zambia.
IGO Relations Hosted at: *WHO (#20950).* **NGO Relations** Member of (1): *ORCID (#17790).* Supports (1): *Council on Health Research for Development (COHRED, no recent information).* Supported setting up of: *Regional Network for Research, Surveillance and Control of Asian Schistosomiasis (RNSA, #18801).* [2018/XF7414/**F***]

- ♦ UNICEF / see UNICEF (#20332)

♦ UNICEF – United Nations Children's Fund 20332
Fonds des Nations Unies pour l'enfance – Fondo de las Naciones Unidas para la Infancia
Exec Dir UNICEF House, Three United Nations Plaza, New York NY 10017, USA. T. +12123267000 – +12128246000. Fax +12128887465 – +12128887454.
URL: http://www.unicef.org/
History 11 Dec 1946. Established by resolution 57 (I) of the UN General Assembly, to provide relief for children in Europe and China in the aftermath of World War II. By resolution 417 (V) of 1 Dec 1950, the UN General Assembly extended the life of the Fund, expanded its scope to give greater emphasis to developing countries and decided to consider its future again at the end of 3 years, with the object of continuing it on a permanent basis. By resolution 802 (VIII) of 6 Oct 1953, the General Assembly voted unanimously to continue the Fund for an indefinite period and shortened its name to United Nations Children's Fund, although the well-known acronym was retained. Within *United Nations System (#20635),* it is an integral part of the *United Nations (UN, #20515)* reporting to the General Assembly through *ECOSOC (#05331).* Former names and other names: *United Nations International Children's Emergency Fund (UNICEF)* – former (11 Dec 1946 to 6 Oct 1953); *Fonds international des Nations Unies pour le secours à l'enfance (FISE)* – former (11 Dec 1946 to 6 Oct 1953). **Aims** Guided by the Convention on the Rights of the Child, the Convention on the Elimination of All Forms of Discrimination against Women and the Convention on the Rights of Persons with Disabilities, and other human rights instruments, focus on equity for universal realization of children's rights. In particular: work for the well-being of children and women and advocate the protection of their rights worldwide; establish children's rights as enduring ethical principles and international standards of behaviour towards children. Ensure that: children get the best possible start in life in their early years; all boys and girls, no matter how disadvantaged, complete a quality basic education; adolescents have every opportunity to develop their capabilities and participate meaningfully in society. **Structure** Executive Board (meeting in 1 annual and 2 regular sessions a year), consists of representatives of 36 governments: 8 seats for Africa; 7 for Asia; 4 for Eastern Europe; 5 for Latin America and the Caribbean; and 12 for Western Europe and other states. These are elected by ECOSOC for a 3-year term, with about one-third of the seats expiring annually, and are presided over by a President and 4 Vice-Presidents. Secretariat, with headquarters in New York NY (USA), headed by Executive Director appointed by UN Secretary-General in consultation with the Board. Offices in Geneva (Switzerland), Brussels (Belgium) and Tokyo (Japan); Supply Division in Copenhagen (Denmark); Office of Research in Florence (Italy); Regional Offices (8) – in Geneva (2, for Europe and for Central and Eastern Europe, CIS and Baltic States), Dakar (Senegal), Amman (Jordan), Bangkok (Thailand), Kathmandu (Nepal), Nairobi (Kenya) and Panama (Panama). Country and Zone Offices (125) each headed by a country or area representative. National Committees for UNICEF (37) – private organizations working with UNICEF in advocacy and fund-rising activities. Affiliate organization: Office of Research, previously referred to as *UNICEF Innocenti Research Centre.* **Languages** Arabic, Chinese, English, French, Russian, Spanish. **Staff** As of Jan 2013, over 10,200 personnel of about 90% serve in regional and country offices. Personnel negotiations through *UNICEF Global Staff Association (GSA, #20330).* Relevant staff associations include: *Coordinating Committee for International Staff Unions and Associations of the United Nations System (CCISUA, #04818).* **Finance** Voluntary contributions from: governments/intergovernmental organizations (about 69% of total income in 2011); nongovernmental/private sector; National Committees; other contributors. Main private source: support from National Committees in advocacy and fund-raising.
Activities Supports community-based programmes in over 150 countries and territories, through an extensive field network and in partnership with governments, local communities, non-governmental organizations, other UN agencies and the private sector.
/Child Survival/ – aiming to end preventable child death to support effective and life-saving actions. Globally the number of children under 5 who died dropped to 6.9 million in 2011, compared to over 12 million in 1990. Works closely with *Gavi – The Vaccine Alliance (Gavi, #10077)* on vaccine supply to developing countries. Partners WHO, UNDP and the World Bank in the 'Roll Back Malaria' campaign to improve prevention and treatment of malaria in affected countries, particularly in Sub-Saharan Africa.
With other partners: contributes to national efforts to prevent mother-to-child transmission of HIV; providees paediatric treatment and care; prevents infection among adolescents and young people; protects and cares for children affected by HIV/AIDS. In 2011, 57% of pregnant women with HIV received effective combination antiretrovirals, compared to 11% in 2005, with new infections among children standing at 330,000 compared to 560,000 in 2003.
As part of *PMNCH (#18410),* works with *WHO (#20950),United Nations Population Fund (UNFPA, #20612)* and others in countries with high maternal mortality to improve maternal health and prevent maternal mortality. Works with governments and policy makers to ensure that emergency obstetric care is a priority in national health plans.
/Safe drinking water supply and basic sanitation/ Despite the Millennium Development Goal target on drinking water being met in 2010, 783 million people still lack access to improved drinking water and 2,500 million people not having access to improved sanitation. Promotes sustainable safe drinking water supply and basic sanitation and hygiene in developing countries and supports national efforts to invest in a safe, supportive environment for children. Works with key partners towards making schools healthier and more attractive to

children, especially girls, through school-based water, sanitation and hygiene programmes. Takes the lead in the provision of water and sanitation services in emergencies and crises around the world. WHO/UNICEF Joint Monitoring Programme for Water Supply and Sanitation reports on progress towards achieving MDG's goal on sustainable access to safe drinking water and basic sanitation.
/Undernutrition/ Supports national efforts to reduce undernutrition, fortifying some staple foods with such micronutrients as iron and iodine, widening women's access to education, improving household food security and basic health services and promoting sound child care and feeding practices, including breast feeding. Active participant in *Scaling Up Nutrition (SUN)*.
/Poverty Reduction/ Works with governments and partners to achieve United Nations Millennium Development Goals to break the cycle of poverty and bring about sustainable development. Supports developing social protection policies and programmes in over 90 countries.
/Basic Education and Gender/ Works in close cooperation with UNESCO, UNDP and the World Bank to achieve universal access to basic education for all, focusing on girls' education – reducing the number of girls out of school, improving quality, and ensuring primary school completion. Acts as lead agency and Secretariat for *United Nations Girls' Education Initiative (UNGEI, #20566)*.
/Child Protection/ Works for the wellbeing and improved protection of children from violence, abuse and exploitation. Advocates adoption of strong protection laws and policies and helps countries implement them. Helps children obtain education and life skills to prevent abuse and exploitation. Promotes full implementation of the *Optional Protocol to the Convention on the Rights of the Child on the Involvement of Children in Armed Conflict (CRC-OP-AC, 2000)* and the *Optional Protocol to the Convention on the Rights of the Child on the Sale of Children, Child Prostitution and Child Pornography (CRC-OP-SC, 2000)*.
/Emergency/ Between 2006-2012, responded to some 250 humanitarian situations a year, guided by its Core Commitments for Children in Humanitarian Action (CCCs). In partnership with national governments, civil society partners and other UN agencies, works worldwide to protect and support millions of children and women affected by natural disasters or complex emergencies. Provides emergency relief assistance, supports education, health, mine-awareness and psychosocial activities and helps demobilize and rehabilitate child soldiers in areas affected by armed conflict.
/Nobel Peace Prize/ In 1965, received Nobel Peace Prize for achievements in promoting development, peace and children's wellbeing. In 2001, as part of the United Nations family, shared the honour of the UN and its Secretary-General receiving the Nobel Peace Prize for working for a better organized and more peaceful world.
Events *Joint Review Meeting* Jakarta (Indonesia) 2019, *Workshop on Country Profiles on Children's Health and Environment in East-Asia and Pacific Region* Seoul (Korea Rep) 2019, *Child Friendly City Conference* Gunsan (Korea Rep) 2018, *Regional Symposium on Sustainable Food Systems for Healthy Diets in Europe and Central Asia* Budapest (Hungary) 2017, *Joint IAEA-WHO-UNICEF Technical Meeting on Analysis of Biological Pathways to Better Understand the Double Burden of Malnutrition* Vienna (Austria) 2017. **Publications** *The State of the World's Children* (annual) in English, French, Spanish – also in at least 30 other national languages; *Progress for Children* in English, French, Spanish; *UNICEF Annual Report* in English, French, Japanese, Spanish. *UNICEF at a Glance* in English, French, Spanish. Reports. Headquarters, Office of Research and country and regional offices publish analyses of the situation of women and children in individual developing countries and a variety of books, reports and serials on: women and children; health; nutrition; HIV/AIDS; education; children's rights; child protection; children in wars and disasters, working children; water, sanitation and the environment; partnerships; economic, social and development policies.
Members No membership, but governments of 36 countries are represented on the Executive Board (expiry date between brackets):
Algeria (2024), Argentina (2023), Australia (2024), Bangladesh (2024), Belgium (2023), Chad (2024), China (2022), Comoros (2024), Costa Rica (2023), Côte d'Ivoire (2024), Cuba (2022), Denmark (2022), Estonia (2022), Ethiopia (2023), France (2024), Germany (2024), Grenada (2024), Italy (2022), Kazakhstan (2023), Korea Rep (2023), Lebanon (2024), Liberia (2023), Monaco (2024), Netherlands (2023), Norway (2022), Paraguay (2022), Poland (2024), Russia (2022), Rwanda (2024), Slovakia (2023), Sweden (2023), UK (2022), United Arab Emirates (2024), USA (2023), Yemen (2022), Zimbabwe (2022).
IGO Relations *'Inter-Agency Relations'*
Represented on: *United Nations System Chief Executives Board for Coordination (CEB, #20636)*. Member of: *United Nations Group on the Information Society (UNGIS, #20570)*; UN Interagency Framework Team for Coordinating Early Warning and Preventive Action; *'UN Interagency Framework Team for Coordinating Early Warning and Preventive Action (Framework Team)'*; *Inter-Agency Standing Committee (IASC, #11393)*. Panel member of: *Interagency Panel on Juvenile Justice (IPJJ, #11390)*. Member of: *UN-Water (#20723)*. Main partners for inter-agency cooperation:
- *Asian Development Bank (ADB, #01422)*;
- *Economic Community of Central African States (ECCAS, #05311)*;
- *Economic Community of West African States (ECOWAS, #05312)*;
- *FAO (#09260)*;
- *ILO (#11123)*;
- *International Bank for Reconstruction and Development (IBRD, #12317)* (World Bank);
- *International Fund for Agricultural Development (IFAD, #13692)*;
- *International Monetary Fund (IMF, #14180)*;
- *Joint United Nations Programme on HIV/AIDS (UNAIDS, #16149)*;
- *Office of the United Nations High Commissioner for Human Rights (OHCHR, #17697)*;
- *Pan American Health Organization (PAHO, #18108)*;
- *UNEP (#20299)*;
- *UNDP (#20292)*;
- *UNESCO (#20322)*;
- *UNHCR (#20327)*;
- *United Nations (UN, #20515)*;
- *United Nations Economic Commission for Africa (ECA, #20554)*;
- *United Nations Economic Commission for Europe (UNECE, #20555)*;
- *United Nations Economic Commission for Latin America and the Caribbean (ECLAC, #20556)*;
- *United Nations Economic and Social Commission for Asia and the Pacific (ESCAP, #20557)*;
- *United Nations Economic and Social Commission for Western Asia (ESCWA, #20558)*;
- *United Nations Human Settlements Programme (UN-Habitat, #20572)*;
- *United Nations Office for the Coordination of Humanitarian Affairs (OCHA, #20593)*;
- *United Nations Office on Drugs and Crime (UNODC, #20596)*;
- *United Nations Population Fund (UNFPA, #20612)*;
- *United Nations University (UNU, #20642)*;
- *United Nations Volunteers (UNV, #20650)*;
- *WHO (#20950)*;
- *World Food Programme (WFP, #21510)*.

Cooperation agreement with: *Islamic World Educational, Scientific and Cultural Organization (ICESCO, #16058)*; *Organisation internationale de la Francophonie (OIF, #17809)*.
'Other Intergovernmental Relations':
- *African Union (AU, #00488)*;
- *Andean Community (#00817)*;
- *Arab Maghreb Union (AMU, #01004)*;
- *ASEAN (#01141)*;
- *Asia-Pacific Economic Cooperation (APEC, #01887)*;
- *Caribbean Community (CARICOM, #03476)*;
- *Commonwealth Secretariat (#04362)*;
- *East African Community (EAC, #05181)*;
- *Economic Cooperation Organization (ECO, #05313)*;
- *European Commission (EC, #06633)*;
- *Group of 77 (G-77, #10732)* and China;
- *Group of Fifteen (G-15, #10778)*;
- *Group of Latin American and Caribbean States (#10784)*;
- *Gulf Cooperation Council (GCC, #10826)*;
- *Inter-American Development Bank (IDB, #11427)*;
- *League of Arab States (LAS, #16420)*;
- *Non-Aligned Movement (NAM, #17146)*;
- *OAS (#17629)*;
- *Organisation of Islamic Cooperation (OIC, #17813)*;
- *Pacific Islands Forum (#17968)*;
- *Permanent Mechanism for Consultation and Political Coordination (Rio Group, inactive)*;
- *South Asian Association for Regional Cooperation (SAARC, #19721)*;
- *Southern African Development Community (SADC, #19843)*.

NGO Relations Cooperation with NGOs is fostered through the Civil Society Partnerships Section in the Programme Division New York NY (USA) and other HQ Sections, and includes advocacy for specific action on behalf of children and planning and implementation of joint programmes. NGOs already holding consultative status with ECOSOC are welcome to observe and make interventions during meetings of UNICEF Executive Board. Consultative status is granted to NGOs already holding consultative status with ECOSOC based on Article 71 of the UN Charter and wishing to formalize their relationship with UNICEF. NGOs may also choose to become members of *NGO Committee on UNICEF (#17120)*, which serves to facilitate their work with the organization. The following organizations are listed as having consultative status with UNICEF:
- *African Association of Education for Development (ASAFED, no recent information)*;
- *Agudath Israel World Organization (AIWO, #00584)*;
- *All India Women's Conference (AIWC, #00737)*;
- *All Pakistan Women's Association (APWA)*;
- *Amref Health Africa (#00806)*;
- *Anglican Consultative Council (ACC, #00828)*;
- *Anti-Slavery International (#00860)*;
- *Asian Cultural Forum on Development Foundation (ACFOD, no recent information)*;
- *Associated Country Women of the World (ACWW, #02338)*;
- *Childhood Education International (CE International)*;
- *Association Mondiale des Amis de l'Enfance (AMADE, #02808)*;
- *Association for World Education (AWE, #02983)*;
- *Baha'i International Community (#03062)*;
- *Baptist World Alliance (BWA, #03176)*;
- *Brahma Kumaris World Spiritual University (BKWSU, #03311)*;
- *CARE International (CI, #03429)*;
- *Caritas Internationalis (CI, #03580)*;
- *Catholic International Education Office (#03604)*;
- *Catholic Relief Services (CRS, #03608)*;
- *ChildFund International (#03869)*;
- Children's Defense Fund (USA);
- *Christian Life Community (CLC, #03905)*;
- *Church World Service (CWS)*;
- *Commonwealth Medical Association (CMA, #04351)*;
- *Consultative Council of Jewish Organizations (CCJO, no recent information)*;
- *Consumers International (CI, #04773)*;
- *Coordinating Board of Jewish Organizations (CBJO, #04813)*;
- *Council of International Programs USA (CIPUSA)*;
- *Covenant House*;
- *Dayemi Complex Bangladesh (DCB)*;
- *Defence for Children International (DCI, #05025)*;
- *Education International (EI, #05371)*;
- *EngenderHealth*;
- *Environnement et développement du Tiers-monde (enda, #05510)*;
- *International Federation of Fe y Alegria (FIFyA, #13425)*;
- *Fédération internationale des communautés éducatives (FICE-International, #09622)*;
- *Fraternité Notre Dame (FND)*;
- *Friends World Committee for Consultation (FWCC, #10004)*;
- *Graduate Women International (GWI, #10688)*;
- *Greek Orthodox Archdiocesan Council of America (GOAC, #10708)*;
- *Helen Keller International (HKI, #10902)*;
- *Human Rights Internet (HRI, #10986)*;
- *Human Rights Watch (HRW, #10990)*, Children's Rights Division;
- *Inclusion International (#11145)*;
- *Institute of Cultural Affairs International (ICAI, #11251)*;
- *International Academy of Architecture (IAA, #11535)*;
- *International African Institute (IAI, #11596)*;
- *International Agency for the Prevention of Blindness (IAPB, #11597)*;
- *International Alliance of Women (IAW, #11639)*;
- *International Association for Community Development (IACD, #11793)*;
- *International Association for Counselling (IAC, #11821)*;
- *International Association of Democratic Lawyers (IADL, #11837)*;
- *International Association of Educators for World Peace (IAEWP)*;
- *International Association of Logopedics and Phoniatrics (IALP, #12005)*;
- *International Association for Religious Freedom (IARF, #12130)*;
- *International Association of Schools of Social Work (IASSW, #12149)*;
- *International Board on Books for Young People (IBBY, #12366)*;
- *International Catholic Child Bureau (#12450)*;
- *International Catholic Committee of Nurses and Medico-social Assistants (#12451)*;
- *International Catholic Migration Commission (ICMC, #12459)*;
- *International Centre of Films for Children and Young People (#12493)*;
- *International College of Surgeons (ICS, #12650)*;
- *International Confederation of Midwives (ICM, #12863)*;
- *International Co-operative Alliance (ICA, #12944)*;
- *International Council for Adult Education (ICAE, #12983)*;
- *International Council for Education of People with Visual Impairment (ICEVI, #13015)*;
- *International Council on Jewish Social and Welfare Services (INTERCO, #13035)*;
- *International Council of Jewish Women (ICJW, #13036)*;
- *International Council on the Management of Population Programs (ICOMP, #13043)*;
- *International Council of Nurses (ICN, #13054)*;
- *International Council of Psychologists (ICP, #13065)*;
- *International Council on Social Welfare (ICSW, #13076)*;
- *International Council of Voluntary Agencies (ICVA, #13092)*;
- *International Dairy Federation (IDF, #13128)*;
- *International Educational Development – Humanitarian Law Project*;
- *International Falcon Movement – Socialist Educational International (IFM-SEI, #13327)*;
- *International Federation of Business and Professional Women (BPW International, #13376)*;
- *International Federation for Home Economics (IFHE, #13447)*;
- *International Federation for Parent Education (IFPE, #13499)*;
- *International Federation of Pedestrians (IFP, #13502)*;
- *International Federation of Pharmaceutical Manufacturers and Associations (IFPMA, #13505)*;
- *International Federation of Red Cross and Red Crescent Societies (#13526)*;
- *International Federation of Settlements and Neighbourhood Centres (IFS, #13538)*;
- *International Federation of Social Workers (IFSW, #13544)*;
- *International Federation of Women in Legal Careers (IFWLC, #13579)*;
- *Humanists International (#10972)*;
- *International Institute of Rural Reconstruction (IIRR, #13921)*;
- *International Lactation Consultant Association (ILCA)*;
- *International League of Associations for Rheumatology (ILAR, #14016)*;
- *International Movement of Apostolate of Children (IMAC, #14192)*;
- *International Movement ATD Fourth World (#14193)*;
- *International Pediatric Association (IPA, #14541)*;
- *International Planned Parenthood Federation (IPPF, #14589)*;
- *International Play Association (IPA, #14604)*;
- *International Public Relations Association (IPRA, #14671)*;
- *International Romani Union (IRU, #14765)*;
- *International Social Service (ISS, #14886)*;
- *International Society for Prevention of Child Abuse and Neglect (ISPCAN, #15385)*;
- *International Society for Traumatic Stress Studies (ISTSS, #15518)*;
- *International Union Against Tuberculosis and Lung Disease (The Union, #15752)*;
- *International Union for Health Promotion and Education (IUHPE, #15778)*;
- *International Union of Nutritional Sciences (IUNS, #15796)*;
- *International Union of Socialist Youth (IUSY, #15815)*;
- *Italian Centre of Solidarity (CeIS)*;
- *Junior Chamber International (JCI, #16168)*;
- *Kiwanis International (#16195)*;
- *La Leche League International (LLLI, #16433)*;
- *Lions Clubs International (LCI, #16485)*;
- *Unis pour l'Equite et la Fin du Racisme (UFER, #20490)*;
- *Muslim World League (MWL, #16917)*;
- *Organisation mondiale des anciens élèves de l'enseignement catholique (OMAEC, #17816)*;

- *Organization for Child and Youth Welfare of the World (no recent information);*
- *Organization of Islamic Capitals and Cities (OICC, #17875);*
- *Pan African Institute for Development (PAID, #18053);*
- *Pan American Development Foundation (PADF, #18094);*
- *Pan Pacific and South East Asia Women's Association (PPSEAWA, #18186);*
- *PATH (#18260);*
- *Pathways To Peace (PTP, #18262);*
- *Pax Christi – International Catholic Peace Movement (#18266);*
- *Peaceways – Young General Assembly;*
- *Pearl S Buck International (PSBI);*
- *Perhaps Kids Meeting Kids can make a Difference (KMK);*
- *Plan International (#18386);*
- *PAI (#18025);*
- *Population Council (#18458);*
- *Rädda Barnen – Save the Children Sweden;*
- *Religions for Peace (RfP, #18831);*
- *RI Global (#18948);*
- *Rissho Kosei-Kai (RKK);*
- *Rotary International (RI, #18975);*
- *Salvation Army (#19041);*
- *Save the Children Federation (SCF);*
- *Save the Children International (#19058);*
- *Save the Children UK (SC UK);*
- *Society for International Development (SID, #19581);*
- *Society for Psychological Study of Social Issues (SPSSI);*
- *Soroptimist International (SI, #19686);*
- *SOS-Kinderdorf International (#19693);*
- *Susila Dharma International Association (SDIA, #20048);*
- *Terre des Hommes International Federation (TDHIF, #20133);*
- *Union internationale des architectes (UIA, #20419);*
- *United Schools International (USI, #20660);*
- *United Way Worldwide (#20663);*
- *Universal Esperanto Association (UEA, #20676);*
- *Women's International Democratic Federation (WIDF, #21022);*
- *Women's International League for Peace and Freedom (WILPF, #21024);*
- *Women's International Zionist Organization (WIZO, #21030);*
- *World Alliance for Breastfeeding Action (WABA, #21079);*
- *World Alliance of Young Men's Christian Associations (YMCA, #21090);*
- *World Assembly of Youth (WAY, #21113);*
- *World Association of Girl Guides and Girl Scouts (WAGGGS, #21142);*
- *World Blind Union (WBU, #21234);*
- *World Confederation for Physical Therapy (WCPT, #21293);*
- *World Council of Churches (WCC, #21320);*
- *World Crafts Council AISBL (WCC International, #21342);*
- *World Education (WE);*
- *World Family Organization (WFO, #21399);*
- *World Federation of Democratic Youth (WFDY, #21427);*
- *World Federation for Mental Health (WFMH, #21455);*
- *World Federation of Methodist and Uniting Church Women (WFM and UCW, #21457);*
- *World Federation of Trade Unions (WFTU, #21493);*
- *World Federation of Ukrainian Women's Organizations (WFUWO, #21496);*
- *World Federation of United Nations Associations (WFUNA, #21499);*
- *World Jewish Congress (WJC, #21599);*
- *World Leisure Organization (WLO, #21624);*
- *World Muslim Congress (WMC, #21664);*
- *World Organization for Early Childhood Education (OMEP, #21689);*
- *World Organization of Family Doctors (WONCA, #21690);*
- *World Organization of the Scout Movement (WOSM, #21693);*
- *World Union of Catholic Women's Organisations (WUCWO, #21876);*
- *World Union for Progressive Judaism (WUPJ, #21883);*
- *The World Veterans Federation (WVF, #21900);*
- *World Vision International (WVI, #21904);*
- *World Young Women's Christian Association (World YWCA, #21947);*
- *Youth for Development and Cooperation (YDC, inactive);*
- *Zonta International (#22038).* [2022/XF3380/f/**F***]

♦ UNICEF USA – United States Fund for UNICEF (internationally oriented national body)
♦ UNICELPE – Association européenne des producteurs de protéines unicellulaires (inactive)
♦ UNICEO – United Networks of International Corporate Events Organizers (unconfirmed)
♦ UNICHAL / see Euroheat and Power (#05694)
♦ UNICOCYM – Union internationale du commerce et de la réparation du cycle et du motocycle (inactive)
♦ Unicode Consortium (internationally oriented national body)
♦ UNICON – International University Consortium for Executive Education (internationally oriented national body)
♦ **UNICRI** United Nations Interregional Crime and Justice Research Institute (#20580)
♦ **UNICs** United Nations Information Centres (#20574)
♦ **UNIC** Union internationale des cinémas (#15763)
♦ **UNIDA** African Association for a Unified System of Business Laws (#00218)

♦ Unidad Regional de Asistencia Técnica (RUTA) 20333

Regional Unit of Technical Assistance
Address not obtained.
URL: http://www.ruta.org/

Members in 7 countries:
Belize, Costa Rica, El Salvador, Guatemala, Honduras, Nicaragua, Panama.
IGO Relations Cooperates with: *Department for International Development (DFID, inactive); FAO (#09260); Inter-American Development Bank (IDB, #11427); Inter-American Institute for Cooperation on Agriculture (IICA, #11434); International Bank for Reconstruction and Development (IBRD, #12317); UNDP (#20292).* [2009/XE4530/**E**]

♦ Unidea – Fondazione UniCredito Italiano (internationally oriented national body)
♦ Unidea – UniCredit Foundation (internationally oriented national body)
♦ UNIDF / see Industrial Development Fund (#11173)
♦ **UNIDIR** United Nations Institute for Disarmament Research (#20575)

♦ UNIDO International Solar Energy Centre for Technology Promotion and Transfer (ISEC) 20334

Contact 20 People Road, Lanzhou, Gansu, China. T. +869318386009 – +869318386010. Fax +869318386011.
URL: http://www.unido-isec.org/

History 2006, by *UNIDO (#20336)*, following the work of the *Gansu Natural Energy Research Institute (GNERI)*. **Aims** Facilitate promotion and transfer of solar and other renewable energy technologies. **NGO Relations** Member of: *Green Industry Platform (GIP, #10722).* [2014/XM2863/**E***]

♦ UNIDO Staff Union 20335

Syndicat du personnel de l'ONUDI
Address not obtained.

History 1967, Vienna (Austria), to represent staff members of *UNIDO (#20336)*. **Structure** General Assembly (annual). Staff Council, consisting of President, elected by the staff at large, 13 representatives elected by their respective electoral units, and a Correspondent for Outposted Staff, elected by the Council. The Council elects First and Second Vice-Presidents, Executive Secretary and Treasurer who, together with President, constitute the Executive Committee. **Finance** Members' dues. **NGO Relations** Member of: *Coordinating Committee for International Staff Unions and Associations of the United Nations System (CCISUA, #04818).* [2012/XE0389/v/**E**]

♦ UNIDO – United Nations Industrial Development Organization 20336

Organisation des Nations Unies pour le développement industriel (ONUDI) – Organización de las Naciones Unidas para el Desarrollo Industrial (ONUDI)
Dir-Gen Vienna Intl Centre, PO Box 300, 1400 Vienna, Austria. T. +431260260. Fax +4312692669. E-mail: unido@unido.org.
Advocacy/Media Relations address not obtained.
URL: http://www.unido.org/

History 1 Jan 1967. Established by General Assembly resolution 2152 (XXI) of 17 Nov 1966. New constitution adopted 8 Apr 1979, Vienna (Austria), and entered into force 21 June 1985. Became, 17 Dec 1985, the 16th specialized agency of the *United Nations (UN, #20515)*, with mandate to act as the central coordinating body for industrial activities within the *United Nations System (#20635)* and to promote industrial development and cooperation at global, regional, national and sectoral levels. Cooperates with *ECOSOC (#05331)* on matters of inter-agency concern within UNIDO competence. **Aims** Promote and accelerate inclusive and sustainable industrial development (ISID) in developing countries and economies in transition. **Structure** Policy-making organs: General Conference (every 2 years), comprising all member states; Industrial Development Board, (meets once in Conference years and twice in other), comprising 53 members states; Programme and Budget Committee (meets annually), comprising 27 member states. Secretariat based in Vienna (Austria). Offices (3): Brussels (Belgium); Geneva (Switzerland); New York NY (USA). Also comprises: Office of the Director-General (ODG); Programme Development and Technical Cooperation Division (PTC); External Relations and Policy Research (ERP); Corporate Management and Operations (CMO); Offices of evaluation and internal oversight, legal affairs, strategic planning, coordination and quality assurance; Departments of Agri-business, Energy, Environment, Trade, Investment and Innovation; Programme Partnerships and Field Integration; Field Offices (47); External Relations; Policy, Research and Statistics; Liaison Offices (3); Human Resource Management; Finance; Operational Support Services. **Languages** UN languages. **Staff** Vienna (Austria) Headquarters, field offices and projects staff. Personnel negotiations through *UNIDO Staff Union (#20335)*. The *Administrative Tribunal of the International Labour Organization (ILO Tribunal, #00118)* is competent to settle disputes. **Finance** Biennial budget comprises 2 components: 'Regular Budget' – funded primarily from assessed contributions of member states, with marginal proportion provided by interest income, sales publications and government contributions to field offices. 'Operational Budget' – mainly financed from support cost income (5-13%) through implementation of technical cooperation activities, which are mostly financed by external donor (voluntary contributions). Annual budget: 258,557,201 EUR. **Activities** Events/meetings; projects/programmes. Thematic priorities: Creating Shared Prosperity; Advancing Economic Competitiveness; Safeguarding the Environment; Strengthening Knowledge and Institutions. **Events** *Seminar on Business and Investment in Senegal* Tokyo (Japan) 2022, *Seminar on Tech Transfer from Japan during COVID-19 pandemic* Tokyo (Japan) 2022, *General Conference Session* Vienna (Austria) 2021, *Session* Vienna (Austria) 2021, *Session* Vienna (Austria) 2021. **Publications** *Making It* (4 a year) – magazine; *International Yearbook of Industrial Statistics (INDSTAT)* (annual). *Industrial Development Report (IDR). Demand for Manufacturing: Driving Inclusive and Sustainable Industrial Development* (2018); *Delivering the Sustainable Development – seizing the opportunity in global manufacturing.*. Annual Report; Industrial Development Abstracts; studies; reports; CD-ROMS; videos. **Information Services** *Open Data Platform* – publications database.

Members Governments of 171 countries:
Afghanistan, Albania, Algeria, Angola, Antigua-Barbuda, Argentina, Armenia, Austria, Azerbaijan, Bahamas, Bahrain, Bangladesh, Barbados, Belarus, Belize, Benin, Bhutan, Bolivia, Bosnia-Herzegovina, Botswana, Brazil, Bulgaria, Burkina Faso, Burundi, Cambodia, Cameroon, Cape Verde, Central African Rep, Chad, Chile, China, Colombia, Comoros, Congo Brazzaville, Congo DR, Costa Rica, Côte d'Ivoire, Croatia, Cuba, Cyprus, Czechia, Djibouti, Dominica, Dominican Rep, Ecuador, Egypt, El Salvador, Equatorial Guinea, Eritrea, Eswatini, Ethiopia, Fiji, Finland, Gabon, Gambia, Georgia, Germany, Ghana, Grenada, Guatemala, Guinea, Guinea-Bissau, Guyana, Haiti, Honduras, Hungary, India, Indonesia, Iran Islamic Rep, Iraq, Ireland, Israel, Italy, Jamaica, Japan, Jordan, Kazakhstan, Kenya, Kiribati, Korea DPR, Korea Rep, Kuwait, Kyrgyzstan, Laos, Lebanon, Lesotho, Liberia, Libya, Luxembourg, Madagascar, Malawi, Malaysia, Maldives, Mali, Malta, Marshall Is, Mauritania, Mauritius, Mexico, Micronesia FS, Moldova, Monaco, Mongolia, Montenegro, Morocco, Mozambique, Myanmar, Namibia, Nepal, Netherlands, Nicaragua, Niger, Nigeria, North Macedonia, Norway, Oman, Pakistan, Palau, Palestine, Panama, Papua New Guinea, Paraguay, Peru, Philippines, Poland, Qatar, Romania, Russia, Rwanda, Samoa, Sao Tomé-Principe, Saudi Arabia, Senegal, Serbia, Seychelles, Sierra Leone, Slovenia, Somalia, South Africa, Spain, Sri Lanka, St Kitts-Nevis, St Lucia, St Vincent-Grenadines, Sudan, Suriname, Sweden, Switzerland, Syrian AR, Tajikistan, Tanzania UR, Thailand, Timor-Leste, Togo, Tonga, Trinidad-Tobago, Tunisia, Türkiye, Turkmenistan, Tuvalu, Uganda, Ukraine, United Arab Emirates, Uruguay, Uzbekistan, Vanuatu, Venezuela, Vietnam, Yemen, Zambia, Zimbabwe.

IGO Relations Member of (1): *Global Bioenergy Partnership (GBEP, #10251).* Cooperates with (1): *World Trade Organization (WTO, #21864).*
Represented on: *United Nations System Chief Executives Board for Coordination (CEB, #20636)* and its committees, including High-level Committee on Programmes (HLCP), High-level Committee on Management (HLCM) and *United Nations Sustainable Development Group (UNSDG, #20634).* Participates in: UN-Energy; *UN-Water (#20723);* UN management-related coordination groups. Collaboration agreement with: *FAO (#09260); ILO (#11123); International Fund for Agricultural Development (IFAD, #13692); International Trade Centre (ITC, #15703); UNDP (#20292); UNESCO (#20322); United Nations Office on Drugs and Crime (UNODC, #20596); The World Bank Group (#21218); World Intellectual Property Organization (WIPO, #21593).*
Executing agency under: *Global Environment Facility (GEF, #10346).* Implementing agency for: *Montreal Protocol on Substances that Deplete the Ozone Layer (1987); Stockholm Convention on Persistent Organic Pollutants (POP treaty, 2001); United Nations Framework Convention on Climate Change (UNFCCC, 1992).*
In accordance with Article 19.1 (b) of the Constitution, the following organization enjoys consultative status: *Cairo Regional Centre for International Commercial Arbitration (CRCICA, #03398).*
NGO Relations In accordance with Article 19.1 (b) of the Constitution, the following organizations enjoy consultative status:
- *Afro-Asian Peoples' Solidarity Organization (AAPSO, #00537);*
- *Agri-Energy Roundtable (AER);*
- *AIESEC (#00593);*
- *All-Russia Market Research Institute (VNIKI);*
- *Arab Federation for Food Industries (AFFI, #00946);*
- *Arab Fertilizer Association (AFA, #00958);*
- *Arab Iron and Steel Union (AISU, #00998);*
- *Asociación Latinoamericana del Acero (Alacero, #02176);*
- *Asociación Latinoamericana de Industrias Farmacéuticas (ALIFAR, #02232);*
- *Asociación Latinoamericana de Instituciones Financieras para el Desarrollo (ALIDE, #02233);*
- *Asociación Regional de Empresas del Sector Petróleo, Gas y Biocombustibles en Latinoamérica y el Caribe (ARPEL, #02296);*
- *Association of African Development Finance Institutions (AADFI, #02353);*
- *Association of Former United Nations Industry and Development Experts (AFIDE, #02602);*
- *Association of Power Utilities in Africa (APUA, #02867);*
- *Austrian Senior Experts Pool (ASEP);*
- *Austrian Society for Environment and Technology (ÖGUT);*
- *Austro-Arab Chamber of Commerce;*
- *Austro-Egyptian Chamber of Commerce;*
- *AVSI Foundation;*
- *BUSINESSEUROPE (#03381);*
- *Centre international de formation de la profession bancaire (CIFPB, inactive);*
- *Collaborative International Pesticides Analytical Council (CIPAC, #04099);*
- *Comité International des Plastiques en Agriculture (CIPA, #04185);*
- *Compagnia delle Opere (CDO);*
- *Consumers International (CI, #04773);*
- *Environnement et développement du Tiers-monde (enda, #05510);*
- *European Federation of Management Consultancies Associations (#07159);*
- *European Federation of National Maintenance Societies (EFNMS, #07173);*
- *European Organization for Quality (EOQ, #08112);*
- *European Union of Public Relations (EUPR, #09011);*
- *Federation of African Consultants (FEAC, inactive);*
- *Fédération Européenne d'Associations Nationales d'Ingénieurs (FEANI, #09558);*
- *Fédération Mondiale des Zones Franches (FEMOZA, #09693);*
- *Fertilizers Europe (#09738);*
- *Forum francophone des affaires (FFA, #09916);*
- *DEULA-Nienburg;*
- *Global Alliance of SMEs (GASME, #10228);*
- *Institut Supérieur de Gestion (ISG);*
- *ICC – International Association for Cereal Science and Technology (#11048);*

- *International Academy of Architecture (IAA, #11535);*
- *International Academy of Engineering (IAE, inactive);*
- *International Academy of Technological Sciences (IATS, no recent information);*
- *International Alliance of Women (IAW, #11639);*
- *International Association for Continuing Engineering Education (IACEE, #11817);*
- *International Association of Crafts and Small and Medium-Sized Enterprises (IACME, inactive);*
- *International Association for the Exchange of Students for Technical Experience (IAESTE, #11885);*
- *International Association for Hydro-Environment Engineering and Research (IAHR, #11950);*
- *International Association of Islamic Banks (IAIB, no recent information);*
- *International Association for the Protection of Intellectual Property (#12112);*
- *International Association of Trading Organizations for a Developing World (ASTRO, inactive);*
- *International Association 'Znanie';*
- *International Centre for Earth Construction (#12485);*
- *International Centre on Small Hydro-Power (IC-SHP);*
- *International Centre for Trade and Sustainable Development, Geneva (ICTSD, #12524);*
- *International Chamber of Commerce (ICC, #12534);*
- *International Congress of Industrialists and Entrepreneurs (ICIE, #12895);*
- *International Co-operative Alliance (ICA, #12944);*
- *International Council of Design (ICoD, #13013);*
- *International Council for Research and Innovation in Building and Construction (CIB, #13069);*
- *International Council of Women (ICW, #13093);*
- *International Electrotechnical Commission (IEC, #13255);*
- *International Energy Foundation (IEF, #13273);*
- *International Federation of Automatic Control (IFAC, #13367);*
- *International Federation of Business and Professional Women (BPW International, #13376);*
- *International Federation of Consulting Engineers (#13399);*
- *International Federation for Heat Treatment and Surface Engineering (IFHTSE, #13443);*
- *International Federation for Information Processing (IFIP, #13458);*
- *International Federation for Medical and Biological Engineering (IFMBE, #13477);*
- *International Federation of Pharmaceutical Manufacturers and Associations (IFPMA, #13505);*
- *International Fertilizer Association (IFA, #13589);*
- *International Forum (IF);*
- *International Foundation for the Promotion of Privatization and Foreign Investments (FPI, inactive);*
- *International Institute of Applied Technologies (IIAT, inactive);*
- *International Institute of Welding (IIW, #13935);*
- *International Measurement Confederation (IMEKO, #14124);*
- *International Multiracial Shared Cultural Organization (IMSCO);*
- *International Network for Environmental Management (INEM, #14263);*
- *International Network for Small and Medium Sized Enterprises (INSME, #14325);*
- *International Network of Subcontracting, Industrial Cooperation and Partnership Organizations (inactive);*
- *International Organisation of Employers (IOE, #14428);*
- *International Organization for Standardization (ISO, #14473);*
- *International Professors' Association (IPA, inactive);*
- *International Society for Engineering Pedagogy (#15089);*
- *International Statistical Institute (ISI, #15603);*
- *International Trade Union Confederation (ITUC, #15708);*
- *International Union of Food Science and Technology (IUFoST, #15773);*
- *International Union of Leather Technologists and Chemists Societies (IULTCS, #15788);*
- *ISEKI-Food Association (#16027);*
- *Islamic Chamber of Commerce, Industry and Agriculture (ICCIA, #16036);*
- *Latin American Industrialists Association (#16341);*
- *Licensing Executives Society International (LESI, #16461);*
- *Moscow International Energy Club (MIEC, inactive);*
- Nimtech;
- *Oasis Open City Foundation, Brazil;*
- *Organisation internationale des experts (ORDINEX, #17808);*
- *Organization for International Economic Relations (OiER, #17873);*
- *Organization of Islamic Capitals and Cities (OICC, #17875);*
- *Pan American Standards Commission (#18133);*
- *Pio Manzù International Research Centre on the Environment (inactive);*
- *Society of Chemical Industry (SCI);*
- *Society for International Development (SID, #19581);*
- *Soroptimist International (SI, #19686);*
- *Third World Foundation for Social and Economic Studies (TWF, #20150);*
- *Transfrigoroute International (TI, #20213);*
- *UFI – The Global Association of the Exhibition Industry (#20276);*
- *Union internationale des architectes (UIA, #20419);*
- *Union internationale des associations et organismes scientifiques et techniques (UATI, #20421);*
- *Union internationale pour la coopération au développement (UNICOS, inactive);*
- *Women's International Democratic Federation (WIDF, #21022);*
- *World Association of Industrial and Technological Research Organizations (WAITRO, #21145);*
- *World Association for Small and Medium Enterprises (WASME, #21189);*
- *World Coal Association (WCA, #21280);*
- *World Design Organization (WDO, #21358);*
- *World Economic Processing Zones Association (WEPZA, #21368);*
- *World Federation of Development Financing Institutions (WFDFI, #21428);*
- *World Federation of Engineering Organizations (WFEO, #21433);*
- *World Federation of Trade Unions (WFTU, #21493);*
- *World LPG Association (WLPGA, #21629);*
- *World Organization of Building Officials (WOBO, #21687);*
- *World Packaging Organisation (WPO, #21705);*
- *World Savings Banks Institute (WSBI, #21764);*
- *World Vision International (WVI, #21904).*

Core agency of: *United Nations Global Compact (#20567).* Set up: *International Centre for Materials Technology Promotion (ICM, see: #20336).* Project: *International Centre for Advancement of Manufacturing Technology, Bangalore (ICAMT, see: #20336).* Maintains direct collaboration agreements with civil society organizations, academia, para-statal institutions and transnational corporations. [2023/XE3386/**B***]

- ♦ UNIDROIT Convention on International Interests in Mobile Equipment (2001 treaty)
- ♦ UNIDROIT Convention on Substantive Rules for Intermediated Securities (2009 treaty)
- ♦ **UNIDROIT** International Institute for the Unification of Private Law (#13934)
- ♦ Unie van Aardappelzetmeelindustrieen binnen de Europese Unie (#20406)
- ♦ Unie van Beroepsgroeperingen van de Aardappelmeelindustrie in de EEG / see Union des féculeries de pommes de terre de l'Union européenne (#20406)
- ♦ Unie voor Cultuur en de Toekomst van het Beroep in Europa (#20373)
- ♦ Unie der Europese Federalisten / see Union of European Federalists, The (#20385)
- ♦ Unie van Europese Kamers van Koophandel en Fabrieken – Rijn, Rhône, Donau, Alpen / see Union of European Chambers of Commerce for Transport (#20384)
- ♦ Unie van Europese Kamers van Koophandel en Fabrieken voor Vervoersvraagstukken / see Union of European Chambers of Commerce for Transport (#20384)
- ♦ Unie van Europese Kamers van Koophandel voor Vervoersvraagstukken (#20384)
- ♦ Unie van het Financiënpersoneel in Europa (#20407)
- ♦ Unie van de Internationale Verenigingen (#20414)
- ♦ Unie van de Kamers van Koophandel van het Rijngebied / see Union of European Chambers of Commerce for Transport (#20384)
- ♦ UNIENPOR – Union internationale pour l'enseignement des populations rurales par des projections lumineuses scientifiques (inactive)
- ♦ **UNIEP** Union internationale des entrepreneurs de peinture (#20425)
- ♦ **UN-IESCO** International Ecological Safety Collaborative Organization (#13221)
- ♦ Unie van Thaise Sanghas in Europa (unconfirmed)
- ♦ UNI Europa / see UNI Global Union – Europa (#20342)
- ♦ **UNI Europa** UNI Global Union – Europa (#20342)
- ♦ Unie van Verenigingen van Fabrikanten van Deegwaren in de EEG / see Union of Organizations of manufacturers of Pasta Products of the EU (#20468)
- ♦ Unie der Verenigingen van Waterleidingbedrijven uit de Landen van de Europese Gemeenschap / see European Federation of National Associations of Water and Waste Water Services (#07170)
- ♦ Unie van de Westeuropese Kamers van Koophandel en Fabrieken van het Rijn-, Rhône- en Donaugebied / see Union of European Chambers of Commerce for Transport (#20384)
- ♦ **UNIFE** Association of the European Rail Supply Industry (#02536)
- ♦ **UNIFE** Union des industries ferroviaires européennes (#02536)
- ♦ UNIFIB – Unión de Ferias Iberoamericanas (meeting series)
- ♦ Unification of the Central American Consular Services at Geneva, Bremen, Vigo, Le Havre and Liverpool (1913 treaty)
- ♦ Unified Family (religious order)
- ♦ Unified Theory of Information Research Group / see Institute for a Global Sustainable Information Society (The)
- ♦ **UNIFIL** United Nations Interim Force in Lebanon (#20577)
- ♦ Unifob Global (internationally oriented national body)
- ♦ Uniform Rules on Contract Clauses for an Agreed Sum Due Upon Failure of Performance (1983 treaty)

♦ UNIGIS Network 20337

Main Office GeoInformatics Dept, Schillerstr 30, 5020 Salzburg, Austria. E-mail: office.uia@unigis.net.
URL: http://www.unigis.net/

History 1990. **Aims** As a worldwide network of universities, cooperate in the design and delivery of *distance learning* in *Geographical Information* Systems and Science. **Languages** English. **Activities** Training/education. **Events** *Annual Conference* Amsterdam (Netherlands) 2007, *Annual Conference* San Diego, CA (USA) 2006, *GIS PLANET : conference on geographic information* Estoril (Portugal) 2005, *Annual Conference* George (South Africa) 2001.
Members Universities (14) in 13 countries:
Austria, Canada, Czechia, Ecuador, Hungary, Italy, Netherlands, Portugal, Russia, South Africa, Spain, UK, USA.
[2021/XF6552/**F**]

♦ UNI Global Union 20338

Gen Sec Av Reverdil 8-10, 1260 Nyon VD, Switzerland. T. +41223652100. Fax +41223652121. E-mail: communications@uniglobalunion.org.
URL: http://www.uniglobalunion.org/

History 1 Jan 2000. Founded on merger of *Communications International (CI, inactive), Fédération internationale des employés, techniciens et cadres (FIET, inactive), International Graphical Federation (IGF, inactive)* and *Media and Entertainment International (MEI, inactive).* Former names and other names: *Union Network International (UNI)* – former (1 Jan 2000). **Aims** Build power for working people in service sectors worldwide through growth of unions and expansion of collective bargaining; improve working and living conditions for workers; support decent jobs for all and sustainable economic growth. **Structure** World Congress (every 4 years); World Executive Committee; Management Committee. Regional organizations (4) each with a substantial degree of autonomy: *UNI Global Union – Africa Region (UNI-Africa, #20339); UNI Global Union – Asia and Pacific Regional Office (UNI-Asia and Pacific, #20341); UNI Global Union – Europa (UNI Europa, #20342); UNI Global Union – Americas Regional Office (UNI-Americas, #20340).* Major workers' groups organized in 11 Sectors and 4 Cross-sector groups. **Languages** English, French, German, Italian, Japanese, Portuguese, Spanish, Swedish. **Finance** Annual affiliation fees. **Events** *World Congress* Liverpool (UK) 2018, *Commerce Global Conference* Berlin (Germany) 2017, *General Assembly* Lisbon (Portugal) 2015, *ICTS World Conference* Stockholm (Sweden) 2015, *World Congress* Cape Town (South Africa) 2014. **Members** Unions, totalling over 20 million workers in 150 countries and territories. Membership countries not specified. **Consultative Status** Consultative status granted from: *World Intellectual Property Organization (WIPO, #21593)* (Permanent Observer Status). **IGO Relations** *European Economic and Social Committee (EESC, #06963).* **NGO Relations** Member of (4): *Fédération des Institutions Internationales établies à Genève (FIIG, #09599); Global Labour University (GLU, #10448); Global Union Federations (GUF, #10638); International Peace Bureau (IPB, #14535).* Trade Secretariat in cooperation with: *International Trade Union Confederation (ITUC, #15708)* (replacing *International Confederation of Free Trade Unions (ICFTU, inactive)*). Media and Entertainment section is member of: *International Arts and Entertainment Alliance (IAEA, #11676).* Partner of: *International Campaign to Abolish Nuclear Weapons (ICAN, #12426).* In liaison with technical committees of: *International Organization for Standardization (ISO, #14473).* Supports: *Global Call for Action Against Poverty (GCAP, #10263).* [2022/XB0009/**B**]

♦ UNI Global Union – Africa Region (UNI-Africa) 20339

Regional Sec Résidence Latrille, Appt 169 Bat O, Blvd Latrille, 01 BP 6811, Abidjan 01, Côte d'Ivoire. T. +22522526700. Fax +22522425087. E-mail: uni-africa@uniglobalunion.org.
URL: http://www.uni-africa.org/

History as *African Regional Organization of the International Federation of Commercial, Clerical, Professional and Technical Employees (Afro-FIET) – Organisation régionale africaine de la Fédération internationale des employés techniciens et cadres.* Name changed to *Union Network International – Africa Region (UNI-Africa),* 1 Jan 2000. Also previously referred to as *Union Network International Africa Regional Office.* Regional organization of *UNI Global Union (#20338).* **Aims** Build union power and influence in the workplace to ensure that all service employees are organized into strong unions and protected by collective agreements. **Structure** Executive Committee (meets annually); Geographical/linguistic areas (6); Subregional offices in Johannesburg (South Africa) and Tunis (Tunisia). **Languages** Arabic, English, French, Portuguese. **Staff** 11.00 FTE, paid. **Finance** Members' dues. Other sources: funding. Budget (annual): Swiss Fr 1 million. **Activities** Capacity building. **Events** *Regional Conference* Nairobi (Kenya) 2013, *Regional Conference* Hammamet (Tunisia) 2009, *Africa graphical regional conference* South Africa 2004, *Africa regional women's conference / Regional Conference* Johannesburg (South Africa) 2003, *Regional conference* Johannesburg (South Africa) 2003. **Members** About 1 million individual members, in 177 unions, in 43 African countries. Membership countries not specified. [2014.07.02/XE9996/**E**]

♦ UNI Global Union – Americas Regional Office (UNI-Americas) 20340

Federación Internacional de Empleados, Técnicos y Profesionales

Regional Sec Colonia 993, Office 101, Plaza PO Box 11100, Montevideo, Uruguay. T. +59829030500 – +59829006474. Fax +59829030083.
URL: http://www.uni-americas.org/

History Sep 1970, Caracas (Venezuela), as *Inter-American Regional Organization of the International Federation of Commercial, Clerical, Professional and Technical Employees (IRO-FIET) – Organisation régionale interaméricaine de la Fédération internationale des employés, techniciens et cadres – Organización Regional Interamericana de la Federación Internacional de Empleados, Técnicos y Profesionales.* Regional union of *UNI Global Union (#20338).* Changed name to *Union Network International Americas Regional Office (UNI-Americas)* 1 Jan 2000. **Aims** Build power for working people in service sectors through growth of unions and expansion of collective bargaining; improve working and living conditions for workers; support decent jobs for all and sustainable economic growth. **Structure** Congress (every 4 years); Executive Committee; Sectors (17); Regional Office in Montevideo (Uruguay). **Languages** English, Spanish. **Staff** 13.00 FTE, paid. **Finance** Members' dues. **Activities** Training/education; knowledge management/information dissemination. **Events** *Meeting* Buenos Aires (Argentina) 2015, *Americas youth conference* Panama 2006, *Americas regional conference* Rio de Janeiro (Brazil) 2002, *Youth conference* Mexico 1997, *Meeting* Sao Paulo (Brazil) 1997.
Members Affiliated unions in 29 countries:
Antigua-Barbuda, Argentina, Bahamas, Barbados, Bolivia, Brazil, Canada, Chile, Colombia, Costa Rica, Dominica, Dominican Rep, El Salvador, Grenada, Guatemala, Guyana, Honduras, Jamaica, Mexico, Nicaragua, Panama, Paraguay, Peru, St Lucia, St Vincent-Grenadines, Suriname, Trinidad-Tobago, Uruguay, USA. [2016.06.01/XE6277/**E**]

♦ UNI Global Union – Asia and Pacific Regional Office (UNI-Asia and Pacific) 20341

Regional Sec 170 Upper Bukit Timah Rd, 14-03 Bukit Timah Shopping Centre, Singapore 588179, Singapore. T. +654677888. Fax +654681410.
URL: http://www.uniglobalunion.org/Apps/iportal.nsf/pages/reg_20081016_gc9rEn/

History May 1973, Singapore (Singapore), as *Asia-FIET*, at the Founding Conference. Regional union of *UNI Global Union (#20338)*. Name changes, at 5th Ordinary Conference, Oct 1986, Bangkok (Thailand), from Asia-FIET to *Asian and Pacific Regional Organization of the International Federation of Commercial, Clerical, Professional and Technical Employees (APRO-FIET) – Organisation régionale pour l'Asie et le Pacifique de la Fédération internationale des employés, techniciens et cadres (ORAP-FIET)* to reflect the geographical representation of FIET in the region. Changed name to *Union Network International Asia and Pacific Regional Office (UNI-Asia and Pacific)* 1 Jan 2000. Also referred to as *UNI-Apro*. **Aims** Secure new members for UNI and coordinate the activities of UNI affiliates in the region directed at dealing with the problems of commercial, clerical, professional and technical *employees*. **Structure** Regional Conference (every 4 years). Regional Executive Committee (meets annually), consisting of President, Vice President, Regional Secretary and 6 members elected from among the affiliates in 4 areas, namely: East Asia, South East Asia, South Asia and the Pacific; Coordinator for APRO UNI Women Activities is a member of the Regional Executive Committee; UNI General Secretary is ex-officio member of the Regional Executive Committee. Regional Secretary is the chief executive of APRO UNI. Secretariat Office situated in Singapore (Singapore). **Finance** Members' dues. Additional sources: donations from affiliates for the implementation of extensive educational activities. Budget (annual): about US$ 500,000. **Activities** Organizes Conferences and seminars. Organizes (annually) 5 regional training courses in specialized areas such as leadership training for young unionists and women unionists. Organizes trade union education and industrial advocacy and research. **Events** *Meeting* Singapore (Singapore) 2010, *Meeting* Singapore (Singapore) 2009, *Asia-Pacific film production workers conference* Manila (Philippines) 2006, *Asia Pacific regional youth conference* Kuala Lumpur (Malaysia) 2005, *Asia-Pacific freelance film production and creators conference* Bangkok (Thailand) 2004. **Publications** Reports; surveys. **Members** Trade Unions, representing some 1.7 million members, grouped in 80 unions, in 17 countries:
Australia, Bangladesh, Fiji, India, Indonesia, Japan, Korea Rep, Malaysia, Nepal, New Zealand, Pakistan, Papua New Guinea, Philippines, Samoa, Singapore, Sri Lanka, Thailand. [2010/XE0092/**E**]

♦ UNI Global Union – Europa (UNI Europa) 20342

Regional Sec Rue Joseph II 40, 1000 Brussels, Belgium. T. +3222345656. Fax +3222350870. E-mail: uni-europa@uniglobalunion.org.
SG Av Reverdil 8-10, 1260 Nyon VD, Switzerland. T. +41223652100. Fax +41223652121.
URL: http://www.uni-europa.org/

History 1 Jan 2000, Copenhagen (Denmark), as European regional branch of *UNI Global Union (#20338)*, on merger of *European Regional Organization of the International Federation of Commercial, Clerical, Professional and Technical Employees (inactive)*, *European Committee of International Communications (inactive)*, *European Federation of Media and Entertainment International (EURO-MEI, inactive)* and *European Graphical Federation (EGF, inactive)*. Previously referred to as: *Union Network International Europa Regional Office*. Subsequently changed name to *Union Network International Europa (UNI Europa)*. EU Transparency Register: 43785827982-59. **Aims** Build a social and *democratic* Europe; promote social and economic development; promote social dialogue and collective bargaining; support *trade union* development and educational programmes and projects aiming to improve the educational, cultural, economic and social welfare of affiliates' members in the region; encourage solidarity among affiliates. **Structure** Regional Conference (every 4 years); Regional Executive Committee; Regional Management Committee; Regional Trade Sections. **Languages** English, French, German, Swedish. **Finance** Funded by regional affiliation fees and voluntary contributions from affiliates. **Activities** Politics/policy; advocacy/lobbying/activism; knowledge management/information dissemination. **Events** *Regional Conference* Brussels (Belgium) 2021, *Meeting* Brussels (Belgium) 2019, *Symposium on the Unchecked Power of Amazon in Today's Economy and Society* Brussels (Belgium) 2019, *Graphical Conference* Budapest (Hungary) 2012, *Regional conference* Toulouse (France) 2011. **Members** National organizations affiliated to UNI in Europe. Membership countries not specified. **NGO Relations** Member of (5): *European Responsible Investment Network (ERIN)*; *European Sunday Alliance (#08856)*; *European Tourism Manifesto (#08921)*; *European Trade Union Confederation (ETUC, #08927)*; *Finance Watch (#09764)*. Instrumental in setting up (1): *European Trade Union Liaison Committee on Tourism (ETLC, #08929)*. Links with relevant sectoral employers' organizations. [2021/XE3878/**E**]

- ♦ **UNI-IIGH** UNU International Institute for Global Health (#20719)
- ♦ UNIJEAPAJ – Union internationale des jeunes écrivains et artistes pour la paix, l'amour et la justice (internationally oriented national body)
- ♦ UNIMATTER – Universalis Matter (internationally oriented national body)
- ♦ UNIMA – Union internationale de grands magasins (inactive)
- ♦ **UNIMA** Union internationale de la marionnette (#20430)
- ♦ **UNIMED** Mediterranean Universities Union (#16687)

♦ UN Interim Administration Mission in Kosovo (UNMIK) 20343

Mission d'administration intérimaire des Nations unies au Kosovo – Misión de Administración Provisional de las Naciones Unidas en Kosovo

Address not obtained.
URL: https://unmik.unmissions.org/

History 10 Jun 1999, New York, NY (USA). Established by resolution 1244 (1999) of *United Nations Security Council (UNSC, #20625)*, within *United Nations System (#20635)*, in the framework of *United Nations (UN, #20515)*. **Aims** Implement a recovery plan to assist the process of *building peace*, democracy, stability and *self-government* in Kosovo; perform basic civilian *administration* functions; promote establishment of substantial autonomy and self-government; facilitate a political process to determine future status; coordinate *humanitarian* and *disaster relief* activities of all international agencies; support reconstruction of key *infrastructure*; promote *human rights*; ensure safe and unimpeded return of all *refugees* and *displaced persons*; maintain law and order in conjunction with the Kosovo Police Force. **Structure** Comprises political, humanitarian, civil affairs, legal, police, military, public information, administrative and logistic personnel and consultants, headed by the Special Representative of the UN Secretary-General for Kosovo (SRSG). Regional Administrators (5); Municipal Administrators (30). Municipal Boards, headed by Chief Executive Officers, act as executive bodies at local level and are responsible for day-to-day running of services. **Staff** 18.00 FTE, paid. Deployed personnel (2021): 355 of which 312 civilians. **Finance** Annual budget: 44,192,100 USD (2022). **Activities** Recovery plan: emergency and humanitarian support; creation of a joint political mechanism to administer the territory; holding of municipal elections; reconstruction of physical and institutional infrastructure. Under this plan, tasks have included: tackling the emergency situation; re-establishing normal life; stabilizing and sharing administration; organizing civil registration and holding elections; managing the reconstruction and recovery process. Currently putting into practice: *'Joint Interim Administrative Structure (JIAS)'*, set up 15 Dec 1999, which is headed by Office of the SRSG and includes 20 Administrative Departments, headed by 2 Co-Heads, one Kosovar and one member of UNMIK international staff; *'Interim Administrative Council (IAC)'* for democratic procedures and tolerance building; *'IAC Advisory Council'*. **Publications** *UNMIK Chronicle*. **IGO Relations** Member of: *Southeast European Law Enforcement Center (SELEC, #19815)*. Close collaboration with: *KFOR (#16187)*; *NATO (#16945)*. **NGO Relations** Member of: *International Council on Archives (ICA, #12996)*. Cooperative agreement with: *European Centre for Peace and Development (ECPD, #06496)*. [2022/XE3802/**E***]

♦ Unio Conferentiarum Europae Superiorum Maiorum (UCESM) 20344

Union des Conférences Européennes des Supérieur/e/s Majeur/e/s – Unione delle Conferenze Europee dei Superiori Maggiori – Union of European Conferences of Major Superiors

Gen Sec Rue du Progrès 333/2, 1030 Brussels, Belgium. T. +3222650156. E-mail: ucesm@ucesm.net.
URL: http://www.ucesm.net/

History 1981. Approbation of the first canonical statutes in 1982. Statutory General Assembly, 25 Dec 1983, Rome (Italy). Registration: Banque-Carrefour des Entreprises, Start date: 17 Jun 1999, Belgium. **Aims** Support *religious* life in Europe. **Structure** General Assembly (at least every 2 years); Executive Committee; General Secretariat. **Languages** English, French, German, Italian. **Staff** 1.00 FTE, paid; 1.00 FTE, voluntary. **Finance** Sources: members' dues. **Activities** Training/education. **Events** *General Assembly* Roggenburg (Germany) 2020, *General Assembly* Snagov (Romania) 2018, *General Assembly* Rome (Italy) 2016, *General Assembly* Tirana (Albania) 2015, *General Assembly* Kiev (Ukraine) 2014.
Members Unions or Conferences of Major Superiors (39) in 28 countries:
Albania, Austria, Belgium, Bosnia-Herzegovina, Bulgaria, Croatia, Czechia, France, Germany, Greece, Hungary, Ireland, Italy, Latvia, Lithuania, Luxembourg, Malta, Netherlands, Poland, Portugal, Romania, Russia, Slovakia, Slovenia, Spain, Switzerland, UK, Ukraine.
NGO Relations Member of (1): *Religious in Europe Networking Against Trafficking and Exploitation (RENATE, #18833)*. [2022.05.19/XD7363/**D**]

- ♦ Unio Filiarum Dei (religious order)
- ♦ Unio Internationalis Contra Cancrum / see Union for International Cancer Control (#20415)
- ♦ Unio Internationalis Laicorum in Servitio Ecclesiae (inactive)
- ♦ Unió Llatina (inactive)
- ♦ Unio Mundialis Sancti Gabrielis Archangeli (#21885)
- ♦ Unión de Abogados Europeos (#20365)
- ♦ Union académique des affaires étrangères – Autriche / see United Nations Youth and Student Association of Austria – Academic Forum for Foreign Affairs

♦ Union académique internationale (UAI) 20345

International Union of Academies

Deputy Gen Sec Palais des Académies, Rue Ducale 1, 1000 Brussels, Belgium. T. +3225502200. Fax +3225502205.
Gen Sec address not obtained.
URL: http://www.unionacademique.org/

History 18 Oct 1919, Paris (France). Founded on the initiative of the 'Académie des inscriptions et belles-lettres', Paris, when statutes and by-laws were adopted. Statutes adopted in 1920, Brussels (Belgium); revised 14 Jun 1955, Brussels; 28 May 2005, Ankara (Turkey); 2019. Assigned the functions previously carried out by *International Association of Academies (inactive)*, set up 1889, Wiesbaden (Germany). Former names and other names: *International Academic Union* – former. Registration: Start date: 14 Jul 1955, Belgium. **Aims** Promote international cooperation between affiliated academies and bodies of similar scientific standing in the fields of *philology*, *archaeology*, *history*, *art* history, *moral*, political and social sciences, through appropriate coordination of activities and projects. **Structure** General Assembly (annual); Bureau; Managerial Committee; Committee of Finance and Accounts; Sections (6); Administrative Secretariat. **Languages** English, French. **Staff** 1.00 FTE, paid. **Finance** Sources: donations; members' dues; sale of publications. Other sources: subventions. **Activities** Projects/programmes. **Events** *Biennial General Assembly* 2021, *Biennial General Assembly* Paris (France) 2019, *Biennial General Assembly* Tokyo (Japan) 2017, *Biennial General Assembly* Brussels (Belgium) 2015, *Biennial General Assembly* Mainz (Germany) 2013. **Publications** *Atlas du monde grec et romain*; *Lexique de codicologie*; *Encyclopaedia Iranica*; *Encyclopaedia of Indian Poetics*; *Epistolae Pontificum Romanorum*; *Etudes islamiques*; *Fontes Historiae Africanae*; *Forma Orbis Romani*; *Greek-Old Church Slavonic Lexicon*; *Histoire comparée des Litératures de langues européennes*; *Hobogirin*; *Index de l'art juif*; *Inventaire critique du Ramayana*; *Language Atlas of the Pacific Area*; *Langues de communication interculturelle dans le Pacifique*; *Lexique iconographique de la mythologie classique*; *Ecole de Médecine de Salerne*; *Monde scytho-sarmate et civilisation gréco-romaine*; *Monumenta Musicae Byzantinae*; *Monumenta Palaeographica Medii Aevi*; *Moravia Magna*; *Norse-Icelandic Skaldic Poetry of the Scandinavian Middle Ages*; *Oeuvres complètes de Voltaire*; *Oeuvres de Grotius*; *Oeuvres d'Erasme*; *Papyrus Archives – Editions and Studies*; *Sources narratives pour l'histoire du Rio de la Plata*; *Sources pour l'histoire du théâtre en Espagne*; *Suppléments au Corpus des inscriptions grecques et latines*; *Sylloge Nummorum Graecorum*; *Tabula Imperii Romani*; *Edition of Iusti Lipsi Epistolae*; *Documents historiques inédits concernant le Japon*; *Catalogue des manuscrits orientaux*; *Corpus Epistolarum Ioannis Dantisci*; *Catalogus Translationum et Commentariorum*; *Chartae Latinae*; *China and the Mediterranean World*; *Civilisations de l'Asie centrale*; *Clavis Monumentorum Litterarum Bohemiae*; *Compendium Auctorum Latinorum Medii Aevi*; *Corpus Christianorum Series Apocryphorum*; *Corpus de la peinture monumentale byzantine and Corpus de la peinture murale mexicaine en Amérique*; *Corpus des antiquités phéniciennes et puniques*; *Corpus des antiquités précolombiennes*; *Corpus des astronomes byzantins*; *Corpus des manuscrits littéraires coptes*; *Corpus des papyrus philosophiques grecs et latins*; *Corpus des troubadours*; *Corpus Fontium Manichaeorum*; *Dictionnaires sumérien et assyrien*; *Corpus Inscriptionum Iranicarum*; *Corpus International des timbres amphoriques*; *Corpus Iuris Islamici*; *Corpus Iuris Sanscriticum*; *Corpus Philosophorum Medii Aevi*; *Corpus Praefationum Hamanisticarum*; *Corpus Rubenianum Ludwig Burchard*; *Corpus Vasorum Antiquorum*; *Corpus Vitrearum*; *Dictionnaire du latin médiéval*; *Dictionnaire du Moyen Perse*; *Dictionnaire du sanscrit des textes bouddhiques de la collection Turfan et de la littérature canonique du Sarvastivada*; *Dictionnaire espagnol et international des termes littéraires*; *Dictionnaire pâli*; *Textes alchimiques*. Summary of the first 75 years' work; assembly proceedings.
Members National academies or similar scientific bodies in 69 countries:
Albania, Argentina, Australia, Austria, Belgium, Bosnia-Herzegovina, Brazil, Bulgaria, Burkina Faso, Canada, Chile, China, Costa Rica, Côte d'Ivoire, Croatia, Czechia, Denmark, Egypt, Estonia, Ethiopia, Finland, France, Georgia, Germany, Ghana, Greece, Holy See, Hungary, India, Iran Islamic Rep, Ireland, Israel, Italy, Japan, Korea Rep, Kosovo, Latvia, Luxembourg, Madagascar, Mexico, Moldova, Montenegro, Morocco, Netherlands, New Zealand, North Macedonia, Norway, Paraguay, Peru, Poland, Portugal, Romania, Russia, Senegal, Serbia, Slovakia, Slovenia, South Africa, Spain, Sweden, Switzerland, Thailand, Tunisia, Türkiye, UK, Ukraine, Uruguay, USA, Vietnam.
International associate members (3), listed in this Yearbook:
African Academy of Languages (ACALAN, #00192); *International Academy of History of Science (#11550)*; *Islamic World Academy of Sciences (IAS, #16057)*.
IGO Relations *UNESCO (#20322)*. **NGO Relations** Founder member of: *International Council for Philosophy and Human Sciences (CIPSH, #13061)*. Member of: *International Science Council (ISC, #14796)*. Cooperates in related fields of interests with: *European Science Foundation (ESF, #08441)*. Instrumental in setting up: *International Council for the Publication of the Opera Omnia of Erasmus (#13066)*. [2023/XC2679/y/**C**]

- ♦ Union des administrations portuaires du Nord de l'Afrique (#17556)
- ♦ Union des Adoratrices du Très Saint-Sacrement (religious order)
- ♦ Unión Aduanera y Económica de Africa Central (inactive)
- ♦ Union of Aerated Drinks Associations of EEC Countries / see UNESDA Soft Drinks Europe (#20323)
- ♦ Union africaine (#00488)
- ♦ Union africaine des arts et des lettres (inactive)
- ♦ Union Africaine des Aveugles (#00489)
- ♦ Union africaine des banques pour le développement (inactive)
- ♦ Union Africaine de Boxe (#00229)
- ♦ Union africaine des chemins de fer (#20347)
- ♦ Union africaine de cultivateurs agricoles (inactive)
- ♦ Union africaine des distributeurs d'eau / see African Water Association (#00497)
- ♦ Union africaine de gymnastique (#00334)
- ♦ Union africaine de judo (#00350)
- ♦ Union africaine et malgache (inactive)
- ♦ Union africaine et malgache de défense (inactive)
- ♦ Union africaine et malgache pour la propriété industrielle (inactive)
- ♦ Union africaine de médecine du sport (no recent information)
- ♦ Union africaine de physique (inactive)
- ♦ Union africaine des postes et des télécommunications (inactive)
- ♦ Union africaine des postes et télécommunications (inactive)
- ♦ Union Africaine de Radiodiffusion (#00490)
- ♦ Union africaine Sport pour tous (inactive)
- ♦ Union africaine des télécommunications (#00482)
- ♦ Union africaine des télécommunications (inactive)
- ♦ Unión Africana de Judo (#00350)
- ♦ Union of African Architects / see Africa Union of Architects (#00529)
- ♦ Union of African Journalists / see Union internationale des journalistes africains (#20428)
- ♦ Union of African Karatedo Federations (see: #21608)
- ♦ Union of African Parliaments / see African Parliamentary Union (#00412)
- ♦ Union of African Parties for Democracy and Development (inactive)
- ♦ Union of African Performing Artists (no recent information)

♦ Union for African Population Studies (UAPS) 20346

Union pour l'étude de la population africaine (UEPA)

Secretariat Regional Inst for Population Studies, Univ of Ghana, Legon, PMB CT 224 Cantonments, Accra, Ghana. T. +233302500274. Fax +233302500273. E-mail: uaps@uaps-uepa.org.
URL: http://www.uaps-uepa.org/

History Mar 1984, Addis Ababa (Ethiopia), by *United Nations Economic Commission for Africa (ECA, #20554) – Conference of African Planners, Statisticians and Population and Information Specialists (PSD, inactive)*. Registered, Jan 1987, in Senegal. **Aims** Further the scientific study of population in Africa. **Structure** General Assembly (every 4 years); Council; Executive Secretariat, headed by Executive Director. **Languages** English, French. **Staff** 5.00 FTE, paid. **Finance** Members' dues. Donations. Funds from: *African Development Bank (ADB, #00283)*; *Canadian International Development Agency (CIDA, inactive)*; *Centre Population et développement (Ceped)*; *The William and Flora Hewlett Foundation*; *Swedish International Development Cooperation Agency (Sida)*; UNFPA; the Netherlands Government; national organizations. **Activities** Knowledge management/information dissemination; training/education; research/documentation; guidance/assistance/consulting; events/meetings. **Events** *African Population Conference* Kampala (Uganda) 2019, *African Population Conference* Pretoria (South Africa) 2015, *African population conference / General Conference* Ouagadougou (Burkina Faso) 2011, *African population conference / General Conference* Arusha (Tanzania UR) 2007, *General Conference* Johannesburg (South Africa) 2004. **Publications** *African Population Studies* (2 a year) in English, French – journal; *UAPS Newsletter* (2 a year) in English, French. Occasional Papers Series. Conference and seminar reports; research reports. **Members** Scholars and other professionals working in the field of population and development in Africa (over 1,500). Membership countries not specified. **Consultative Status** Consultative status granted from: *United Nations Population Fund (UNFPA, #20612)*. **NGO Relations** Member of: *African Books Collective (ABC, #00226)*. [2017.03.08/XD1895/v/**D**]

♦ Union of African Railways (UAR) 20347

Union africaine des chemins de fer (UAC)

Contact address not obtained. T. +251911683271. E-mail: kajange@africa-union.org.

History 23 Sep 1972, Addis Ababa (Ethiopia), as a specialized agency of *Organization of African Unity (OAU, inactive)*, currently *African Union (AU, #00488)*. **Aims** Study means of unifying African railways; improve existing railway services; connect existing railways; normalize and standardize railway equipment; coordinate with other modes of transport. **Structure** General Assembly. Executive Board, consisting of Chairman, 5 Vice-Chairmen and Secretary General. **Languages** English, French. **Staff** 10.00 FTE, paid. **Finance** Members' contributions. **Activities** Technical committees, seminars, studies, information distribution. **Events** *General Assembly* Tripoli (Libyan AJ) 2010, *General Assembly* Libreville (Gabon) 2006, *General Assembly* Nairobi (Kenya) 2005, *Réunion sur le transport ferroviaire et les chemins de fer dans les pays membres de la CEN-SAD* Tripoli (Libyan AJ) 2005, *General Assembly* Luanda (Angola) 2004.

Members Railway administrations in 29 African countries:
Algeria, Angola, Benin, Burkina Faso, Cameroon, Congo Brazzaville, Congo DR, Côte d'Ivoire, Djibouti, Egypt, Eswatini, Ethiopia, Gabon, Ghana, Guinea, Kenya, Libya, Malawi, Mali, Mauritania, Morocco, Mozambique, Niger, Nigeria, Sudan, Tanzania UR, Togo, Tunisia, Zambia.

IGO Relations Relationship agreement with: *UNIDO (#20336)*. Represented at Founding Conference of: *African Organisation for Standardisation (ARSO, #00404)*. [2016/XD4386/**D***]

♦ Union of African Shippers' Councils (UASC) 20348

Union des conseils des chargeurs africains (UCCA) – União dos Conselhos dos Carregadores Africanos (UCCA)

SG BP 12969, Centre des Affaires Maritimes, Bonajo, Douala, Cameroon. T. +237233437045. Fax +237233437075. E-mail: infos.ucca.sg@gmail.com.
URL: http://www.ucca-sg.org/

History Feb 1977, Accra (Ghana), as a specialized organ of *Maritime Organization of West and Central Africa (MOWCA, #16582)*. **Aims** Strengthen the *consultative* and negotiating mechanisms with *maritime* conferences and ship owners; reduce the incidence of transport cost on the economies of West and Central African countries; promote any cooperation policy protecting the interests of member states vis-à-vis carriage of goods; simplify administrative formalities in international maritime traffic; promote sub-regional trade; contribute to sub-regional economic integration policies. **Structure** General Assembly (every 2 years); Steering Committee; Lobby, composed of Board Chairmen and General Managers; Bureau, comprising Chairman and Vice-Chairman (2-year terms), Secretary General (4-year term), Treasurer and Auditors (from 2 countries, 2-year terms); General Secretariat in Douala (Cameroon); Standing Committees (2): Trade and Transport, Cooperation and Regulation. **Languages** English, French, Portuguese. **Finance** Members' contributions. Other sources: donations; subventions. **Activities** Projects/programmes; capacity building; events/meetings; networking/liaising. **Events** *General Assembly* Congo DR 2006, *General Assembly* Abidjan (Côte d'Ivoire) 2004. **Publications** *The African Shippers' News*. *UASC Yearbook* (1st ed 1998).

Members Shippers' Councils and similar organizations in 19 countries:
Angola, Benin, Burkina Faso, Cameroon, Central African Rep, Congo Brazzaville, Congo DR, Côte d'Ivoire, Equatorial Guinea, Gabon, Ghana, Guinea, Guinea-Bissau, Mali, Mauritania, Niger, Nigeria, Senegal, Togo.

IGO Relations Participates in the activities of: *African Union (AU, #00488)*; *Communauté économique et monétaire d'Afrique centrale (CEMAC, #04374)*; *Economic Community of West African States (ECOWAS, #05312)*; *European Commission (EC, #06633)*; *European Union (EU, #08967)*; *International Maritime Organization (IMO, #14102)*; *Maritime Organization of West and Central Africa (MOWCA, #16582)*; MOWCA; *Port Management Association of West and Central Africa (PMAWCA, #18463)*; *UNCTAD (#20285)*; *Union économique et monétaire Ouest africaine (UEMOA, #20377)*; *United Nations Commission on International Trade Law (UNCITRAL, #20531)*; *United Nations Economic Commission for Africa (ECA, #20554)*; *World Customs Organization (WCO, #21350)*; *World Trade Organization (WTO, #21864)*. [2020.01.21/XE0791/**E***]

♦ Union of African States (inactive)
♦ Union of African Towns (inactive)
♦ Union of African Water Suppliers / see African Water Association (#00497)
♦ Union des agences de presse de l'OCI (#20467)
♦ Union des agences de voyages nordiques (inactive)
♦ Union des agents en brevets européens / see Union of European Practitioners in Intellectual Property (#20392)
♦ Union Aid Abroad-APHEDA (internationally oriented national body)
♦ Unión Amateur de Natación de las Américas / see PanAm Aquatics (#18077)
♦ Unión Americana de Natación / see PanAm Aquatics (#18077)
♦ Union Americana de Numismática (unconfirmed)
♦ Union of American Republics / see OAS (#17629)
♦ Union pour l'amitié mondiale (inactive)
♦ Union APARE-CME / see OPUS (#17780)
♦ Union apostolique du clergé / see International Confederation Apostolic Union of Clergy (#12844)

♦ Union of Arab Banks (UAB) 20349

Union des banques arabes – Ittihad Al Massaref Al Arabiya

Head Office PO Box 11-2416, Riad el-Solh 1107 2210, Beirut, Lebanon. T. +9611377800 – +9611364881 – +9611364885. Fax +9611364927 – +9611364952. E-mail: uab@uabonline.org – sg@uabonline.org.
URL: http://www.uabonline.org/

History 22 Nov 1972, Beirut (Lebanon), at 1st Arab Conference on Bank Management. Established 13 Mar 1973 in accordance with first General Assembly. Statutes approved by Constituent Assembly, 12 Mar 1974, Beirut. **Aims** Be the leading financial and banking organization in the Arab world; progress the Arab banking and financial industry to an advanced level of professionalism. **Structure** General Assembly (annual); Board of Directors; General Secretariat, headed by Secretary-General. **Languages** Arabic, English, French. **Finance** Members' dues. Other sources: Revenues from consultation; training; publications; lessons; subsidies and donations. **Activities** Research and development; standards/guidelines; training/education; capacity building; events/meetings. **Events** *International Arab Banking Summit* Frankfurt-Main (Germany) 2020, *International Arab Banking Summit* Rome (Italy) 2019, *International Arab Banking Summit* Paris (France) 2018, *International Arab Banking Summit* London (UK) 2017, *International Arab Banking Summit* Paris (France) 2014. **Publications** *The Arab Banking Review* (4 a year); *Ittihad Al Masaref Al Arabiya* – magazine. Books. **Information Services** *Data and Information Center (DIC)*. **Members** Arab banks, central banks, banking associations and unions (over 340) in 21 countries. Membership countries not specified. **Consultative Status** Consultative status granted from: *UNCTAD (#20285)* (General Category). **IGO Relations** Specialized agency of: *League of Arab States (LAS, #16420)*. Member of: *Gulf International Bank (GIB, #10832)*. **NGO Relations** Instrumental in setting up: *Arab Academy of Banking and Financial Sciences (AABFS)*. [2019.02.28/XD4543/**D**]

♦ Union of Arab Chambers (UAC) 20350

Union des Chambres Arabes

Pres PO Box 11-2837, Adnan Kassar Edifice for Arab Economy, Sports City Avenue, Beirut, Lebanon. T. +9611826020 – +9611826027 – +9611826030. Fax +9611826021. E-mail: admin@uac.org.lb.
URL: http://www.uac-org.org/

History 16 Dec 1951, Beirut (Lebanon). Established by resolution of Conference of Arab Chambers. Statutes revised: Jun 1981; May 1992; Apr 2001. Former names and other names: *General Union of Chambers of Commerce, Industry and Agriculture for Arab Countries (GUCCIAAC)* – former; *Union générale des chambres de commerce, d'industrie et d'agriculture des pays arabes* – former. **Aims** Achieve Arab economic integration; represent all economic sectors from the perspective of Arab businessmen; enhance the role of member chambers and their federations; increase efficiency and effectiveness of programmes, plans and development efforts; strive to establish and develop integrated developing partnership among Arab countries. **Structure** Council; Executive Committee; General Secretariat. **Languages** Arabic, English, French. **Staff** 24.00 FTE, paid. **Finance** Sources: members' dues; revenue from activities/projects. **Activities** Events/meetings; research/documentation; publishing activities; knowledge management/information dissemination. **Events** *Arab Private Sector Forum* Riyadh (Saudi Arabia) 2013, *German-Arab Energy Forum* Berlin (Germany) 2012, *German-Arab Energy Forum* Berlin (Germany) 2011, *German-Arab energy forum* Berlin (Germany) 2010, *Conference / Arab Businessmen and Investors Conference* Abu Dhabi (United Arab Emirates) 2007. **Publications** *Al-Omran Al-Arabi* (12 a year) – magazine; *Arab Economic Bulletin*. *Arab Economic Report* in Arabic, English. Books; studies.

Members Arab Chambers and Federations in 22 countries and territories:
Algeria, Bahrain, Comoros, Djibouti, Egypt, Iraq, Jordan, Kuwait, Lebanon, Libya, Mauritania, Morocco, Oman, Palestine, Qatar, Saudi Arabia, Somalia, Sudan, Syrian AR, Tunisia, United Arab Emirates, Yemen.

Arab-Foreign Joint Chambers in 17 non-Arab countries:
Argentina, Australia, Austria, Belgium, Brazil, France, Germany, Greece, Ireland, Italy, Kenya, Luxembourg, Malta, Portugal, Switzerland, UK, USA.

Consultative Status Consultative status granted from: *ECOSOC (#05331)* (Roster); *ILO (#11123)* (Regional). **IGO Relations** Special links with: *League of Arab States (LAS, #16420)*. **NGO Relations** Instrumental in setting up: *Arab Industrial Development Organization (AIDO, inactive)* and *Arab Organization for Standardization and Metrology (ASMO, inactive)* – both currently superseded by *Arab Industrial Development, Standardization and Mining Organization (AIDSMO, #00981)*; *Arab Monetary Fund (AMF, #01009)*; *Arab Investment and Export Credit Guarantee Corporation (DHAMAN, #00997)*. [2023/XD5575/**D**]

♦ Union of Arab Chemists (no recent information)
♦ Union of Arab Community-Based Associations (internationally oriented national body)

♦ Union of Arab Constitutional Courts and Councils (UACCC) 20351

Union des cours et des conseils constitutionnels arabes

Presidency Supreme Constituioual Court, Kournish El-Nile, Maadi, Cairo, Egypt. Fax +2027958048. E-mail: info@sccourt.gov.eg.
SG address not obtained. E-mail: rana_elnaggar@hotmail.com.
URL: http://www.uaccc.org/

History Feb 1997, Cairo (Egypt). **Structure** General Assembly; Council; Secretariat General. **Events** *Symposium on the economic and political rights from a constitutional point of view* Tripoli (Libyan AJ) 2010, *Conference on the relations between the constitutional court and parliament / Colloquium* Algiers (Algeria) 2009.

Members Constitutional councils and courts in 11 countries and territories:
Algeria, Egypt, Kuwait, Lebanon, Libya, Mauritania, Morocco, Palestine, Sudan, Tunisia, Yemen.

IGO Relations *European Commission for Democracy through Law (Venice Commission, #06636)*; *World Conference on Constitutional Justice (WCCJ, #21298)*. [2010/XJ8258/**D**]

♦ Union of Arab Doctors in Europe 20352

Union Arabischer Mediziner in Europa (ARABMED)

Contact Weberstr 4, 71691 Freiberg, Germany. T. +497141708013. Fax +497141708027.
URL: http://www.arabmed.de/

History 1985, Ludwigsburg (Germany). Former names and other names: *Arab Medical Union in Europe* – alias. **Aims** Promote scientific, social and cultural relationships between Arab doctors in Europe and European doctors and medical organizations. **Structure** Executive Council, comprising President, Vice-President and General Secretary. **Languages** Arabic, English, German. **Staff** 6.00 FTE, voluntary. **Finance** Members' dues. **Activities** Involved in disaster relief work in Arab and third world countries. Organizes regional conferences and meetings. **Events** *Annual Conference* Vienna (Austria) 2016, *Annual Conference* Fujairah (United Arab Emirates) 2015, *Annual Conference* Rome (Italy) 2014, *Annual Conference* Berlin (Germany) 2013, *Annual Conference* Paris (France) 2012. **Publications** *ARABMED Journal* (3 a year).

Members Individuals and organizations in 16 countries:
Austria, Bosnia-Herzegovina, Egypt, France, Germany, Iraq, Ireland, Italy, Jordan, Palestine, Saudi Arabia, Sierra Leone, Syrian AR, Türkiye, UK, United Arab Emirates.

Consultative Status Consultative status granted from: *ECOSOC (#05331)* (Special). **NGO Relations** Member of: *Conference of Non-Governmental Organizations in Consultative Relationship with the United Nations (CONGO, #04635)*. [2014/XD6087/**D**]

♦ Union arabe (inactive)
♦ Union arabe des agronomes (no recent information)
♦ Union arabe des bibliothèques et de l'information (#00947)
♦ Union arabe des bourses de valeur / see Arab Federation of Exchanges (#00944)
♦ Union arabe des chemins de fer (inactive)
♦ Union arabe des chirurgiens vétérinaires (inactive)
♦ Union arabe du ciment et des matériaux de construction (#01065)
♦ Union arabe des clubs scientifiques pour jeunes (no recent information)
♦ Union Arabe de l'éducation physique et du sport (inactive)
♦ Union arabe d'électricité (#01066)
♦ Union arabe du fer et de l'acier (#00998)
♦ Union arabe de football associations (#20353)
♦ Union arabe de l'industrie du cuir (inactive)
♦ Union arabe des industries papetières et de l'imprimerie (#00950)
♦ Union arabe des ouvriers de banques, des assurances et des finances (inactive)
♦ Union arabe de papeterie et des imprimeurs / see Arab Federation for Paper, Printing and Packaging Industries (#00950)
♦ Union arabe des producteurs, transporteurs et distributeurs d'électricité / see Arab Union of Electricity (#01066)
♦ Union arabe des produits de la pêche / see Arab Federation of Fish Producers (#00945)
♦ Union arabe des télécommunications (inactive)
♦ Unión Arabe de Telecomunicaciones (inactive)
♦ Union arabe de tourisme / see Arab Tourism Organization (#01057)
♦ Union arabe des transporteurs maritime / see Arab Federation of Shipping (#00953)
♦ Union arabe des transports routiers (#01069)
♦ Union arabe des travailleurs des postes, télégrammes et téléphones (inactive)

♦ Union of Arab Football Associations (UAFA) 20353

Union arabe de football associations (UAFA)

Gen Sec PO Box 62997, Riyadh 11595, Saudi Arabia.
URL: http://www.uafaonline.com/

History 1974. **Aims** Support activities of, and develop relations between, member federations; establish technical programs, operations and plans to ensure development of the *game* of *soccer*, foster uniform attitudes among members. **Structure** General Assembly. Executive Committee, consisting of President, 3 Vice-Presidents and 6 members, in addition to honorary members and Arab members in the international, Asian and African football federations. 'Urgent Matters Commission', chaired by President or the 1st Vice President, members the 2nd and 3rd Vice President and the Secretary General Treasures. Standing Sub-Committees (8): Tournament and Competition; Technical; Referees; Medical; Coordination and International Relations; Marketing; TV Media; Commentators. General Secretariat, headed by Secretary-General. **Languages** Arabic, English, French. **Staff** 42.00 FTE, voluntary. **Finance** Members' dues. Other sources: annual subsidy from Saudi Arabian General Presidency of Youth Welfare; share in proceeds of matches within competitions and tournaments; revenue from advertisements and promotions in the stadia; donations; grants. Budget (annual): Riyals 5 million. **Activities** Supervises and organizes: tournaments; competitions; meetings; congresses; informational, technical, training and scientific courses and seminars. **Events** *General Assembly* Riyadh (Saudi Arabia) 2014, *General Assembly* Riyadh (Saudi Arabia) 2003, *General Assembly* Kuwait 2002, *General Assembly* Jeddah (Saudi Arabia) 2001, *General Assembly* Jeddah (Saudi Arabia) 1998. **Publications** *UAFA Magazine* (6 a year); *Sports Medicine Book and Football Encyclopedia*; *UAFA Directory*.
Members Federations in 21 countries and territories:
Algeria, Bahrain, Djibouti, Egypt, Iraq, Jordan, Kuwait, Lebanon, Libya, Mauritania, Morocco, Oman, Palestine, Qatar, Saudi Arabia, Somalia, Sudan, Syrian AR, Tunisia, United Arab Emirates, Yemen. [2014/XD8110/**D**]

- Union of Arab and French Banks / see Union de Banques Arabes et Françaises (#20367)
- Union of Arab Historians (no recent information)
- Union Arabischer Mediziner in Europa (#20352)

♦ Union of Arab Jurists (UAJ) 20354

Union des juristes arabes
Address not obtained.
History 15 Jan 1975, Baghdad (Iraq). Also known as *Arab Jurists Union*. **Aims** Accomplish political and economic liberation of Arab homeland; work for its unity; care for Arab *legal* heritage; develop Arab laws and work for their unification and unity of their terms; formulate constitutional and legal frameworks for progressive political and social principles in the Arab homeland; work for defence of human rights, with particular reference to international humanitarian law. **Structure** General Conference; Permanent Bureau; Secretariat General. **Languages** Arabic, English. **Staff** 12.00 FTE, paid. 12. **Finance** Contributions from Unions, members and others. **Activities** Arranges seminars and meetings at national and international levels. **Publications** *Al-Huqoqi Al-Arabi* (2 a year).
Members National jurists associations in 12 countries:
Bahrain, Egypt, Iraq, Jordan, Lebanon, Libya, Mauritania, Morocco, Sudan, Tunisia, United Arab Emirates, Yemen.
Consultative Status Consultative status granted from: *ECOSOC (#05331)* (Special). **IGO Relations** Accredited by: *United Nations Office at Vienna (UNOV, #20604)*. **NGO Relations** Member of: *NGO Committee on Disarmament, Peace and Security, New York NY (#17106)*. [2015/XD6090/**D**]

- Union of the Arab Maghreb / see Arab Maghreb Union (#01004)
- Union of Arab Maghreb Workers' Trade Unions (no recent information)

♦ Union of Arab Paediatric Societies (UAPS) 20355

Union des sociétés arabes de pédiatrie (USAP)
Pres c/o St George Hospital, PO Box 166378, Beirut, Lebanon.
History 1968, Cairo (Egypt). **Aims** Ensure progress and development of paediatrics in Arab countries; carry out collaborative studies in the field. **Structure** Executive Committee, consisting of President, Vice President, Secretary General, Treasurer and 4 Councillors. Administration moves to the country where next Paediatric Day will take place. **Languages** Arabic. **Staff** All voluntary. **Finance** Contribution of each member society. Donations. **Activities** Organizes 'Paediatric Days' in various Arab countries. Studies and research. **Events** *Pediatric Middle East Allergy and Respiratory Conference 2021 (MEARC)* Dubai (United Arab Emirates) 2021, *Joint Meeting* Beirut (Lebanon) 2019, *Meeting* Beirut (Lebanon) 2005, *Meeting* Bahrain 2003, *Meeting* Amman (Jordan) 1995. **Publications** *Journal of Arab Child* in English.
Members Pediatric Societies in 17 Arab countries:
Algeria, Bahrain, Egypt, Iraq, Jordan, Kuwait, Lebanon, Libya, Morocco, Oman, Qatar, Saudi Arabia, Sudan, Syrian AR, Tunisia, United Arab Emirates, Yemen.
NGO Relations Affiliate Society of: *International Pediatric Association (IPA, #14541)*. Close contacts with: *Union of Middle Eastern and Mediterranean Paediatric Societies (UMEMPS, #20461)*. [2021/XD7000/**D**]

♦ Union of Arab Pharmacists (UAP) 20356

Headquarters 2 Street Alawi, Kasr El-Nil, Cairo, Egypt. T. +20223917896. E-mail: apharmu2020@gmail.com.
Contact 4 Street Sheikh Mahmoud Abu Eyes, off Hijaz Street, Cairo, Egypt. T. +20226357032 – +20226447122. Fax +20226357032.
URL: http://www.apharmu.com/
History 1945, Cairo (Egypt). Former names and other names: *Arab Pharmacists Union* – alias. **Aims** Promote pharmaceutical research in Arab countries; encourage Arab pharmacists to establish national organizations of pharmacy in their countries; enable Arab pharmacists to contribute to the development of their countries through industrial pharmacy and transfer of technology between drug manufacturers; support faculties of pharmacy and develop pharmaceutical education; facilitate transfer of Arab drugs between Arab pharmaceutical production companies and pharmacists. **Structure** Supreme Council; Executive Bureau; Scientific Board, consisting of Scientific Sections. **Finance** Sources: members' dues. Annual budget: 150,000 USD. **Events** *Scientific Congress on Appropriate Use of Medication* Beirut (Lebanon) 2015, *Scientific conference / Congress of Arab Pharmaceutical Sciences* Amman (Jordan) 2008, *Congress of Arab pharmaceutical sciences* Damascus (Syrian AR) 1995, *Meeting / Supreme Council Meeting* Tunis (Tunisia) 1994. **Publications** *Arab Pharmacists Magazine*.
Members Pharmaceutical syndicates and societies, pharmacists (represented through Scientific Sections). Members in 17 countries:
Algeria, Bahrain, Egypt, Iraq, Jordan, Kuwait, Lebanon, Libya, Morocco, Oman, Qatar, Saudi Arabia, Sudan, Syrian AR, Tunisia, United Arab Emirates, Yemen.
NGO Relations *Arab Academy of Pharmacy (AAP, no recent information)*; *Arab Union of Manufacturers of Pharmaceuticals and Medical Appliances (AUPAM, #01070)*. [2020/XD1411/**D**]

- Union of Arab Physicists and Mathematicians (inactive)

♦ Union of Arab Securities Authorities (UASA) 20357

SG PO Box 117555, Dubai, United Arab Emirates. T. +97142900000 – +97142900055. Fax +97142900059. E-mail: info@uasa.ae.
URL: http://www.uasa.ae/
History 2007. **Aims** Enhance development of Arab securities exchanges and capital markets regulators. **Structure** Board; Secretary General; Permanent Committees. **Activities** Events/meetings; training/education. **Publications** *UNION NEWS*. Annual Report.
Members Active in 15 countries:
Algeria, Egypt, Iraq, Jordan, Kuwait, Lebanon, Libya, Morocco, Oman, Palestine, Qatar, Saudi Arabia, Syrian AR, Tunisia, United Arab Emirates.
Associate (2):
Arab Federation of Exchanges (AFE, #00944); Dubai Financial Services Authority. [2023.02.14/XJ9437/**D**]

- Union of Arab Stock Exchanges / see Arab Federation of Exchanges (#00944)
- Union of Arab Stock Exchanges and Securities Commissions / see Arab Federation of Exchanges (#00944)
- Union des Architectes d'Afrique (#00529)

♦ Union of Armenian Evangelical Churches in the Near East (UAECNE) 20358

Pres PO Box 11-377, Beirut, Lebanon. T. +9611565628 – +9611443547. Fax +9611565629. E-mail: office.director@uaecne.org.
URL: http://www.uaecne.org/
History in the 19th century, within the Armenian Orthodox Church. Became independent 1846, Istanbul (Turkey).
Members Congregations (24) in 8 countries:
Australia, Cyprus, Egypt, Greece, Iran Islamic Rep, Lebanon, Syrian AR, Türkiye.
NGO Relations Member of: *Oikocredit International (Oikocredit, #17704)*; *World Communion of Reformed Churches (WCRC, #21289)*; *World Council of Churches (WCC, #21320)*. [2011.06.01/XF5463/**F**]

- Union des artistes de spectacle africains (no recent information)

♦ Union of Asian Alpine Associations (UAAA) 20359

Contact 6F Kingkong bldg, 86 Chungdamdong, Gangnamgu, Seoul, Korea Rep. T. +8225583331. Fax +8225018848. E-mail: info@uaaa.org.
URL: http://www.theuaaa.org/
History Founded 1932. **Aims** Promote cultural exchange and strengthening friendship among alpinists and mountaineers; disseminate climbing skills, encourage safe climbing, establish a mountain rescue body, protect the environment and introduce competitive climbing. **Structure** General Assembly; Council. **Languages** English. **Activities** Events/meetings; training/education. **Events** *General Assembly* Kathmandu (Nepal) 2023, *General Assembly* New Delhi (India) 2022, *General Assembly* Bishkek (Kyrgyzstan) 2019, *General Assembly* Shiraz (Iran Islamic Rep) 2017, *General Assembly* Kathmandu (Nepal) 2016. **Publications** *UAAA Handbook*.
Members National federations in 14 countries and territories:
Bangladesh, China, Hong Kong, India, Iran Islamic Rep, Japan, Kazakhstan, Korea Rep, Kyrgyzstan, Mongolia, Nepal, Pakistan, Russia, Taiwan.
NGO Relations Continental federation of *Union internationale des associations d'alpinisme (UIAA, #20420)*. [2023/XD8555/**D**]

♦ Union of Asian Philosophers 20360

Pres Philsophy Dept NTU, No 1 Sec 4, Roosevelt Rd, Taipei 106, Taiwan. E-mail: tran@ntu.edu.tw. [2010/XJ1938/**D**]

- Unión Asiatica de Judo (#16162)
- Union asiatique des aveugles (#01360)
- Union asiatique de gymnastique (#01499)
- Union asiatique de judo (#16162)
- Unión de las Asociaciones de Distribuidores de Agua de los Paises Miembros de las Comunidades Europeas / see European Federation of National Associations of Water and Waste Water Services (#07170)
- Unión de las Asociaciones Europeas de los Estudiantes (inactive)
- Unión de Asociaciones de Fabricantes de Harinas de Pescado de la Comunidad Económica Europea / see European Fismeal and Fish Oil Producers (#07268)

♦ Unión de Asociaciones Ibéricas e Iberoamericanas del Benelux (UAIA) 20361

Pres Stadhouderslaan 68, 2517 JA The Hague, Netherlands. E-mail: bergans12@kpnmail.nl – secretaria@asoha.nl.
URL: http://www.uaia.nl/
History Founded May 1974. **Structure** Council. **Publications** *Jornada Hispanica* (annual).
Members Organizations (14) in 3 countries:
Belgium, Luxembourg, Netherlands.
Included in the above, 1 organization listed in this Yearbook:
Asociación Belgo-Ibero-Americana (ABIA, no recent information). [2019/XD7767/**D**]

- Unión de Asociaciones Internacionales (#20414)
- Unión de Asociaciones Técnicas Internacionales / see Union internationale des associations et organismes scientifiques et techniques (#20421)
- Union d'assistance technique pour l'automobile et la circulation routière (no recent information)
- Union Association pour la Participation et l'Action Régionale – Centre Méditerranéen de l'Environnement / see OPUS (#17780)
- Union des associations de boissons gazeuses des pays membres de la CEE / see UNESDA Soft Drinks Europe (#20323)
- Union des associations de boissons non-alcoolisées / see UNESDA Soft Drinks Europe (#20323)
- Union des associations de boissons rafraîchissantes des pays membres de la CE / see UNESDA Soft Drinks Europe (#20323)
- Union des associations de boissons rafraîchissantes des pays membres de l'UE / see UNESDA Soft Drinks Europe (#20323)
- Union des associations de chantiers de volontaires de l'Afrique de l'Ouest (inactive)
- Union des associations des distributeurs d'eau de pays membres des Communautés européennes / see European Federation of National Associations of Water and Waste Water Services (#07170)
- Union of the Association of Semolina Manufacturers of the EEC / see Union of the Associations of Semolina Manufacturers of the EU (#20363)
- Union d'associations européennes de demeures historiques / see European Historic Houses Association (#07491)
- Union des associations européennes d'étudiants (inactive)
- Union des associations européennes de football (#20386)

♦ Union des associations européennes des ingénieurs ferroviaires (UAEIF) 20362

Union of European Railway Engineer Associations – Union Europäischer Eisenbahn-Ingenieur-Verbände (UEEIV)
SG Kaiserstr 61, 60329 Frankfurt-Main, Germany. T. +4969259329. Fax +4969259220.
URL: http://www.ueeiv.eu/
History Also referred to as *Union of European Railroad Engineers*. **Events** *Conference on System Engineering* Vienna (Austria) 2016, *Do railways need engineers?* Vienna (Austria) 2014, *International conference* Athens (Greece) 2008, *Conference on the development of the Croatian railway* Sibenik (Croatia) 2008, *Technical and economical conditions of railroad-transport development between Europe and Asia with the second Pan-European corridor* Warsaw (Poland) 2008. [2019/XD3728/**D**]

- Union des associations européennes de seniors golfeurs / see European Senior Golf Association (#08464)
- Union des Associations Européennes de Seniors Golfeurs Amateurs / see European Senior Golf Association (#08464)
- Union des associations des fabricants de farine de poisson de la Communauté économique européenne / see European Fismeal and Fish Oil Producers (#07268)
- Union des associations de fabricants de pâtes alimentaires de la CE / see Union of Organizations of manufacturers of Pasta Products of the EU (#20468)
- Union des associations de fabricants de pâtes alimentaires de la CEE Vereinigung der Verbände der Teigwarenindustrie in der EWG / see Union of Organizations of manufacturers of Pasta Products of the EU (#20468)
- Union des associations de fabricants de pâtes alimentaires de l'UE (#20468)
- Union of Associations of Fish Meal Manufacturers in the EEC / see European Fismeal and Fish Oil Producers (#07268)
- Union of Associations of Fishmeal Manufacturers in the European Economic Community / see European Fismeal and Fish Oil Producers (#07268)
- Union des associations des ingénieurs et des architectes de l'Amérique centrale (inactive)
- Union des associations internationales (#20414)
- Union of Associations of Pasta Manufacturers of the EEC / see Union of Organizations of manufacturers of Pasta Products of the EU (#20468)

♦ Union of the Associations of Semolina Manufacturers of the EU (Semouliers) 20363

Union des associations des semouliers de l'UE

Contact Via Loviano 6, 00198 Rome RM, Italy. E-mail: semouliers@semouliers.org.
URL: http://www.semouliers.org/

History 29 Mar 1961, Rome (Italy), as *Union of the Association of Semolina Manufacturers of the EEC – Union des associations des semouliers de la CEE.* Present name adopted in 1994. EU Transparency Register: 31076147941-02. **Events** *General Assembly* Cologne (Germany) 1994.
Members National organizations in 8 countries:
Belgium, France, Germany, Italy, Luxembourg, Portugal, Spain, UK.
IGO Relations Recognized by: *European Commission (EC, #06633).* **NGO Relations** Supporting member of: *International Pasta Organisation (IPO, #14528).* [2019/XE3369/E]

- ♦ Union des associations des semouliers de la CEE / see Union of the Associations of Semolina Manufacturers of the EU (#20363)
- ♦ Union des associations des semouliers de l'UE (#20363)

♦ Union des associations de techniciens de culture méditerranéenne (UATCM) 20364

Main Office c/o AFTPVA, 5 rue Etex, 75018 Paris, France. T. +33142634591. Fax +33142633150.
URL: http://www.aftpva.org/

History Founded 21 May 1992, Sète (France), on signature of an agreement by the 3 founding associations. First EUROCOAT Congress, 1993, Nice. Registered in accordance with French law. **Aims** Promote exchanges among member associations so as to balance their common Mediterranean culture against the over-pervasive influence of the industrialized countries of Northern Europe; also promote exchange of technology and ideas among members in their fields of paint, varnish, printing ink, glues and adhesives, and of their source materials; promote product and process improvement while developing respect for the environment. **Structure** General Assembly; Board; Executive Bureau. **Languages** English, French. **Staff** 0.50 FTE, paid. Officers voluntary. **Finance** Members' dues. **Events** *EUROCOAT Annual Congress* Paris (France) 2016, *EUROCOAT Annual Congress / Annual EUROCOAT Congress* Paris (France) 2014, *Annual EUROCOAT Congress* Italy 2013, *EUROCOAT Annual Congress* Piacenza (Italy) 2013, *EUROCOAT Annual Congress / Annual EUROCOAT Congress* Barcelona (Spain) 2012.
Members National organizations in 5 countries:
France, Italy, Portugal, Romania, Spain. [2019.06.26/XD2816/D]

- ♦ Union des associations techniques internationales / see Union internationale des associations et organismes scientifiques et techniques (#20421)
- ♦ Union d'assureurs pour le contrôle des crédits internationaux / see International Union of Credit and Investment Insurers (#15767)
- ♦ Union d'assureurs des crédits internationaux / see International Union of Credit and Investment Insurers (#15767)
- ♦ Union d'assureurs des crédits et des investissements internationaux (#15767)
- ♦ Union astronomique internationale (#12287)
- ♦ Union des avocats d'Afrique centrale (inactive)
- ♦ Union des avocats arabes (#01002)

♦ Union des avocats européens (UAE) 20365

European Lawyers Union – Unión de Abogados Europeos – Europäischer Anwaltsverein – União dos Advogados Europeus – Unione degli Avvocati Europei – Europese Advocaten Unie – Foreningen af Europaeiske Advokater – Euroopan Asianajajaliitto

Contact 9A Cité Mont-Rose, L-8445 Steinfort, Luxembourg.
Pres c/o Morais Leitão, Galvão Teles, Soares da Silva, Rua Castilho 165, 1070-050 Lisbon, Portugal. T. +351210091730. Fax +351213817411.
URL: http://www.uae.lu/

History 21 Nov 1986, Luxembourg. Registration: Mémorial C, No/ID: F0004458, Start date: 21 Nov 1986, Luxembourg. **Aims** Unite lawyers who are members of a European Union bar so as to promote: professional practice within the Community; teaching and continuing education; right of establishment and the free movement of services; harmonization of legal statute, professional and deontological practices; practice of EC law as derived from the European Convention for the Protection of Human Rights and Fundamental Freedoms. **Structure** General Assembly (annual). Executive Committee. Bureau, consisting of President, 2 Vice-Presidents, Secretary-General, Deputy Secretary-General and Treasurer. **Languages** Danish, Dutch, English, Finnish, French, German, Irish Gaelic, Italian, Polish, Portuguese, Spanish, Swedish, Turkish. **Staff** Voluntary. **Finance** Members' dues. Grants from *European Community (inactive).* **Activities** Organizes: Scientific Congress (held annually in May/June); colloquia and seminars; study days. Relevant treaty: *Convention for the Protection of Human Rights and Fundamental Freedoms (1950).* **Events** *Annual Congress* Porto (Portugal) 2022, *General Assembly* Luxembourg (Luxembourg) 2019, *Annual Congress* Naples (Italy) 2019, *Annual Congress* The Hague (Netherlands) 2018, *Annual Congress* Barcelona (Spain) 2012. **Publications** *UAE Journal* (10 a year). Members Directory (annual). Books.
Members Full individuals in 19 countries:
Austria, Belgium, Bulgaria, Cyprus, Denmark, France, Germany, Greece, Hungary, Ireland, Italy, Luxembourg, Malta, Netherlands, Poland, Portugal, Romania, Spain, UK.
Associate in 4 countries:
Monaco, Russia, Switzerland, Türkiye.
Consultative Status Consultative status granted from: *Council of Europe (CE, #04881)* (Participatory Status). **IGO Relations** Close cooperation with: *Court of Justice of the European Union (CJEU, #04938); European Commission (EC, #06633); European Parliament (EP, #08146).* [2021/XD2492/D]

- ♦ Union balkanique mathématique (inactive)

♦ Union of the Baltic Cities (UBC) 20366

SG UBC Secretariat, Waly Jagiellonskie 1, 80-853 Gdansk, Poland. T. +48583010917 – +48583019123. Fax +48583017637. E-mail: info@ubc.net.
Pres Kaunas Miesto Savivaldybė, Laisves Al 96, LT-44251 Kaunas, Lithuania. T. +37062703246.
URL: http://www.ubc.net/

History 20 Sep 1991, Gdansk (Poland). Created at founding conference, on signature of declaration of creation by 32 cities, when Statutes were adopted. Former names and other names: *Baltic Club* – former. Registration: EU Transparency Register, No/ID: 5216035819-77. **Aims** Develop cooperation and exchange among member cities; contribute to positive democratic, social, economic and environmentally friendly development of the Baltic Sea region for the benefit of the people living in Baltic cities; promote municipal cooperation in such domains as environmental protection, education, business youth contacts, communications and social affairs. **Structure** General Conference (every 2 years); Executive Board; Working Commissions (7); Secretariat in Gdansk, headed by Secretary-General. **Languages** English. **Staff** 4.00 FTE, paid. **Finance** Sources: contributions of member/participating states; donations; gifts, legacies; members' dues; revenue from activities/projects. **Activities** Events/meetings. **Events** *General Conference* Kaunas (Lithuania) 2019, *General Conference* Växjö (Sweden) 2017, *Meeting* Gdansk (Poland) 2015, *General Conference* Gdynia (Poland) 2015, *Youth Conference* Gdynia (Poland) 2015. **Publications** *Baltic Cities Environmental Bulletin* (4 a year); *Baltic Cities Bulletin* (2 a year); *UBC Newsletter.*
Members Towns and cities (67) in 10 countries:
Denmark, Estonia, Finland, Germany, Latvia, Lithuania, Norway, Poland, Russia, Sweden.
IGO Relations *Baltic Marine Environment Protection Commission – Helsinki Commission (HELCOM, #03126); Baltic Sea Parliamentary Conference (BSPC, #03146); European Committee of the Regions (CoR, #06665); Congress of Local and Regional Authorities of the Council of Europe (#04677); Council of the Baltic Sea States (CBSS, #04870). Parliamentary Conference on Cooperation in the Baltic Sea Area. Baltic Sea States Subregional Cooperation (BSSSC, #03150) Nordic Council (NC, #17256); Nordic Council of Ministers (NCM, #17260); Northern Dimension Partnership in Public Health and Social Well-being (NDPHS, #17587); Swedish International Development Cooperation Agency (Sida);.* **NGO Relations** Member of: *Energy Cities (#05467).* Cooperation agreement with: *EUROCITIES (#05662).* Partner of: *Conference of European Cross-border and Interregional Cities Network (CECICN, #04595).* [2020.07.03/XD4173/D]

- ♦ Union of Banana Exporting Countries (inactive)
- ♦ Union bancaire en Afrique centrale / see Commercial Bank Centrafrique
- ♦ Union des banques arabes (#20349)

♦ Union de Banques Arabes et Françaises (UBAF) 20367

Main Office Tour EQHO, 2 av Gambetta, 92400 Courbevoie, France. T. +33146406101. Fax +33147381388.
URL: http://www.ubaf.fr/

History 1970, France. Former names and other names: *Union of Arab and French Banks* – former. **Aims** Promote and finance international *trade* with countries in the Arab world. **Structure** Board of Directors; General Management; Representative Offices (4); Branches (4); Subsidiary in Hong Kong. **Languages** Arabic, English, French. **Staff** 284.00 FTE, paid. **Finance** Shareholders: France – 47.01%; Arab World – 52.99%. Capital: euro 250,727,220. **Activities** Knowledge management/information dissemination. **Events** *Séminaire sur le Financement du Commerce International* Abidjan (Côte d'Ivoire) 2017. **Publications** Annual Report.
Members Main shareholders in 6 countries:
Algeria, Egypt, France, Libya, Morocco, Saudi Arabia. [2020/XF3698/e/F]

- ♦ Union baptiste indépendante scandinave (inactive)

♦ Union of Baptists in Latin America (UBLA) 20368

Unión Bautista Latino-Americana (UBLA)

Regional Sec Calle 8 No 4285-1923 Berisso, Buenos Aires, Argentina. T. +542214642384.
URL: http://ubla.net/

History as a regional office of *Baptist World Alliance (BWA, #03176).* **Events** *Congress* Lima (Peru) 2009, *Congress* Cochabamba (Bolivia) 2001, *Congress* Guatemala (Guatemala) 1998.
Members Full in 18 countries:
Argentina, Bolivia, Brazil, Chile, Colombia, Costa Rica, Cuba, Ecuador, El Salvador, Guatemala, Honduras, Mexico, Nicaragua, Panama, Paraguay, Peru, Uruguay, Venezuela. [2012/XE2960/E]

- ♦ Unión Bautista Latino-Americana (#20368)
- ♦ Union Benelux (#03207)
- ♦ **Unión de Berna** Unión Internacional para la Protección de las Obras Literarias y Artisticas (#15806)
- ♦ **Unión de Berna** Unión de Seguros y de Créditos Internacionales (#15767)
- ♦ **Union de Berne** Union d'assureurs des crédits et des investissements internationaux (#15767)
- ♦ **Union de Berne** Union internationale pour la protection des oeuvres littéraires et artistiques (#15806)
- ♦ Unión Biblica – Consejo Internacional (#19161)
- ♦ Union biologique africaine (inactive)

♦ Union of Black Sea and Caspian Business (BCB) 20369

SG Mesrutiyet cad No 46, Tepebasi, 34420 Istanbul/Istanbul, Türkiye. T. +902122491929. Fax +902122925375.
URL: http://www.bcbusiness.org/

History Set up 2006, as *Union of Black Sea and Caspian Confederation of Enterprises (UBCCE).* Registered in accordance with Turkish law. **Aims** Establish institutionalized cooperation and facilitate communication among business organizations of member countries; assist economic and social development of the region through fostering trade and investment activities and entrepreneurial spirit; promote social and economic interests of companies represented by member organizations; contribute to the functioning of free market economies in member countries. **Structure** General Assembly. Executive Committee. International Secretariat, headed by Secretary General. **Languages** English. **Events** *General Assembly* Istanbul (Turkey) 2013. **Publications** *BCB Quarterly Bulletin.*
Members Organizations (15) in 13 countries:
Albania, Armenia, Austria, Azerbaijan, Bulgaria, Georgia, Germany, Greece, Iran Islamic Rep, Kazakhstan, Romania, Türkiye, Ukraine.
IGO Relations Close contacts with: *Organization of Black Sea Economic Cooperation (BSEC, #17857)* and related bodies. Cooperates with: *OECD (#17693)* Eurasia Competitiveness Programme; *UNDP (#20292)* Black Sea Trade and Development Programme. **NGO Relations** Memorandum of Understanding with: Confederation of Employers and Industries of Spain (CEOE); *International Congress of Industrialists and Entrepreneurs (ICIE, #12895); Union of Mediterranean Confederations of Enterprises (BUSINESSMED, #20458); Vienna Economic Forum (VEF, #20770).* Member of: *International Federation for Sustainable Development and Fight to Poverty in the Mediterranean-Black Sea (FISPMED, #13562).* Close cooperation with national organizations. [2014/XJ2415/D]

- ♦ Union of Black Sea and Caspian Confederation of Enterprises / see Union of Black Sea and Caspian Business (#20369)
- ♦ Union of Black Sea Region NGOs (unconfirmed)
- ♦ Union bouddhiste d'Europe (#06407)
- ♦ Union de Budapest pour la reconnaissance internationale du dépôt des microorganismes aux fins de la procédure en matière de brevets (#03345)

♦ Union canine internationale (UCI) 20370

Internationale Hunde-Union (IHU)

Contact Mittelmühle 2, 31863 Coppenbrügge, Germany. T. +495156785014. E-mail: collievision@aol.com.
URL: http://www.uci-ihu.de/

History 2 Apr 1932, Paris (France). Subtitle: *Groupement international des fédérations cynologiques.* Registered in accordance with Belgian law. **Members** Kennel federations. Membership countries not specified. [2015/XF2484/D]

- ♦ Union des capitales ibéroaméricaines (#20412)
- ♦ Union des capitales de l'Union européenne (inactive)
- ♦ Union of the Capitals of the European Union (inactive)
- ♦ Union of Cardiology Societies of South America / see South American Society of Cardiology (#19707)
- ♦ Union of Caribbean Towns (inactive)

♦ Union of Catholic Asian News (UCAN) 20371

Admin Office PO Box 69626, Kwun Tong, Hong Kong. T. +85223496179. Fax +85227727656. E-mail: ucanews@ucanews.com.
URL: http://www.ucanews.com/

History 1979, Hong Kong. Also referred to as *UCA News.* **Aims** Provide news in English, Chinese, Indonesian and Vietnamese about and of interest to the Catholic Church in Asia. **Languages** Chinese, English, Indonesian, Vietnamese. **Staff** In 13 offices: 30 FTE; over 50 reporters throughout Asia. **Finance** Sources: funding agencies; self generated income. **Publications** *UCAN Daily Service; UCAN Language Services* in Chinese, Indonesian, Vietnamese. *Diocesan Profiles Series.*
Members Subscribers (160) in more than 25 countries and territories. Covers 23 countries and territories:
Bangladesh, Bhutan, Brunei Darussalam, Cambodia, China, Hong Kong, India, Indonesia, Japan, Korea Rep, Laos, Macau, Malaysia, Myanmar, Nepal, Pakistan, Philippines, Singapore, Sri Lanka, Taiwan, Thailand, Timor-Leste, Vietnam. [2017.06.30/XD8346/D]

- ♦ Union catholique des études internationales (inactive)
- ♦ Union catholique internationale de la presse / see International Christian Organisation of the Media (#12563)
- ♦ Union catholique internationale de service social (inactive)
- ♦ Unión Católica Internacional de la Prensa / see International Christian Organisation of the Media (#12563)
- ♦ Unión Católica Internacional de Servicio Social (inactive)
- ♦ Union of Central African Lawyers (inactive)
- ♦ Union of Central African States (inactive)
- ♦ Union of Central Eurasian Neonatal Societies (inactive)

♦ Union of Central and South-Eastern European Capitals (UCSEEC) .. 20372

Acting Exec Sec c/o Athens City Council International Affairs, 63 Athinas Str, 105 52 Athens, Greece. T. +302103722056. Fax +302103722333.
Contact c/o Department of International Cooperation, Athens City Hall, 63 Athinas Str, 105 52 Athens, Greece. T. +302103722053. Fax +302103722345.
URL: http://www.cseecunion.org/

History 1995, as *Permanent Conference of Mayors of Capitals of Southeastern Europe*. Transformed under current title, Sep 2002, Ljubljana (Slovenia). **Aims** Maintain permanent ties between the municipalities of the member cities and encourage exchanges between their citizens in every field, so as to develop a keen sense of European fraternity based on mutual understanding. **Structure** General Assembly (annual). Standing Committee. Rotating chairmanship. **Languages** English. **Events** *Annual Conference* Athens (Greece) 2013, *Annual conference / Conference* Zagreb (Croatia) 2010, *Annual Conference* Vienna (Austria) 2009, *Annual Conference* Tirana (Albania) 2008, *Annual Conference* Skopje (Macedonia) 2007.
Members Capital cities of 15 countries:
Albania, Austria, Bulgaria, Croatia, Cyprus, Greece, Hungary, Kosovo, Montenegro, North Macedonia, Romania, Serbia, Slovakia, Slovenia, Ukraine. [2013/XJ1381/**E**]

- ♦ Union des centres de rencontres internationales de France / see Ethic étapes
- ♦ Union centroaméricaine (unconfirmed)
- ♦ Unión Centroamericana de Asociaciones de Ingenieros y Arquitectos (inactive)
- ♦ Union de Centros de Estudios del Mediterraneo (internationally oriented national body)
- ♦ Union of Cereal Storage Firms in the EEC / see Unistock Europe (#20492)
- ♦ Union of Chambers of Commerce, Industry, and Agriculture of the Arab Gulf States / see Federation of GCC Chambers (#09590)
- ♦ Union des Chambres Arabes (#20350)
- ♦ Union des chambres de commerce et d'industrie françaises à l'étranger / see Chambres de Commerce et d'Industrie Françaises à l'International (#03849)
- ♦ Union des chambres de commerce et de l'industrie de l'Océan Indien / see Cap Business Océan Indien (#03419)
- ♦ Union des chambres de commerce rhénanes / see Union of European Chambers of Commerce for Transport (#20384)
- ♦ Union des chercheurs d'Afrique de l'ouest (no recent information)
- ♦ Union chrétienne démocrate d'Europe centrale (inactive)
- ♦ Union-Chrétienne de Saint-Chaumond (religious order)
- ♦ Unión de Cinematecas de América Latina (no recent information)
- ♦ Unión de Ciudades Capitales Iberoamericanas (#20412)
- ♦ Unión de Ciudades Capitales de Lengua Portuguesa / see União das Cidades Capitais Luso-Afro-Américo-Asiaticas (#20328)
- ♦ Unión de Ciudades Capitales Luso-Afro-Américo-Asiaticas (#20328)
- ♦ Unión de Ciudades del Caribe (inactive)
- ♦ Union pour la classification internationale des brevets (#20443)
- ♦ Union pour la classification internationale pour les dessins et modèles industriels (#20416)
- ♦ Union pour le commerce des bois résineux dans l'UE (inactive)
- ♦ Union communiste internationaliste (#13965)
- ♦ Unión Comunista Internacionalista (#13965)
- ♦ Union of Concerned Scientists (internationally oriented national body)
- ♦ Union des confédérations de l'industrie et des employeurs d'Europe / see BUSINESSEUROPE (#03381)
- ♦ Union des confédérations sportives africaines (#02360)
- ♦ Union des Conférences Européennes des Supérieur/e/s Majeur/e/s (#20344)
- ♦ Union des conseils des chargeurs africains (#20348)
- ♦ Union des Conseils Economiques et Sociaux et Institutions Similaires Francophones (unconfirmed)
- ♦ Union des conseils européens en brevets et autres mandataires agréés auprès de l'Office européen des brevets / see Union of European Practitioners in Intellectual Property (#20392)
- ♦ Union des conseils en relations publiques d'Europe (inactive)
- ♦ Union continentale de la publicité (inactive)
- ♦ Union coopérative arabe (inactive)
- ♦ Union for the Coordination of Transmission of Electricity (inactive)
- ♦ Union Corps Saint Lazarus International / see Lazarus Union (#16411)
- ♦ Unión de los Correos Sudamericanos / see Postal Union of the Americas, Spain and Portugal (#18466)
- ♦ Union of Councils / see UCSJ – Union of Councils for Jews in the Former Soviet Union
- ♦ Union of Councils for Soviet Jews / see UCSJ – Union of Councils for Jews in the Former Soviet Union
- ♦ Union des cours et des conseils constitutionnels arabes (#20351)

♦ Union for the Cultural and Professional Future in Europe 20373

Union pour la culture et l'avenir professionnel en Europe (UCAPE) – Unión para la Cultura y el Porvenir Profesional en Europa – Vereinigung für die Kultur und die Berufliche Zukunft in Europe – União para a Cultura e o Futuro Profissional na Europa – Unione per la Cultura e l'Avvenire Professionale in Europa – Unie voor Cultuur en de Toekomst van het Beroep in Europa

Pres Chaussée de Namur 124 – Bte E02, 5030 Gembloux, Belgium. T. +3271215685. Fax +3271215685.
SG address not obtained. T. +33241480580.
URL: http://www.ucape.eu/

History 10 Mar 1993, Brussels (Belgium). Statutes adopted 25 Mar 1994; amended 18 Oct 2000. Registration: Banque-Carrefour des Entreprises, No/ID: 0452.103.043, Start date: 15 Feb 1994, Belgium. **Aims** By means of education and training exchange programmes, unite teachers, students, researchers, practising experts and business people so as to become part of the professional fabric of Europe; design European cultural models for use in all educational programmes from a very early age so as to give the perspective of a citizen of Europe; assist the citizens of Europe to develop a humanistic approach, not simply through learning foreign languages but also through a deep understanding of the environment, history and habits of each European region; assure recognition of specific attainments through award of professionally established qualifications with the aim of harmonization and complementarity; encourage European educational initiatives. **Structure** General Assembly. Board of Directors, consisting of President, 2 Vice-Presidents, Secretary General, Treasurer and President of Ethical Committee. National Representatives (12). Head Office in Brussels (Belgium). **Finance** Members' dues: euro 75 to euro 100. **Activities** Awards various *'Diplômes européens de compétence (DEC)'*, administered by *'"Collèges" d'enseignements et de professionnels européens (CEE – CPE)'*, currently in: scholastic education; human sciences; hospitality and tourism. Current training programmes and examinations: general and technical education (secondary and post-baccalaureate); social psychology; hostesses; linguistic competence; European culture. Organizes or participates in congresses, symposia and other meetings. **Events** *International teachers colloquium* Luxembourg (Luxembourg) 2000, *Youth professional training in Europe* Strasbourg (France) 1999, *Expériences pédagogiques européennes* Charleroi (Belgium) 1997, *Colloque* Brussels (Belgium) 1996, *Assises culturelles* France 1996. **Publications** *Point-Info – UCAPE* (4 a year); *Bulletin UCAPE scolaire (BUS)* (3 a year) – only for members. **Information Services** *UCAPE Database on European Culture*.
Members Individuals and organizations in 12 countries and territories:
Belgium, Canada, Czechia, France, Germany, Netherlands, Poland, Portugal, Scotland, Spain, UK, Ukraine.
National Representatives in 10 countries and territories:
Belgium, Canada, Czechia, France, Poland, Portugal, Scotland, Spain, UK, Ukraine.
Consultative Status Consultative status granted from: *Council of Europe (CE, #04881)* (Participatory Status). **NGO Relations** Member of: *Federation of European and International Associations Established in Belgium (FAIB, #09508)*. Instrumental in setting up: *Centre de développement, information et recherche sur l'Europe (CEDIRE, no recent information)*; *Centre européen de documentation sur l'éducation, Charleroi (no recent information)*. [2020/XF3028/t/**F**]

- ♦ Unión para la Cultura y el Porvenir Profesional en Europa (#20373)
- ♦ Union pour la culture et l'avenir professionnel en Europe (#20373)
- ♦ Union culturelle française / see Union culturelle et technique de langue française (#20374)

♦ Union culturelle et technique de langue française (UCTF) 20374

French-Language Cultural and Technical Union

Pres c/o AFAL, 48 Quai Alphonse Le Gallo, 92100 Boulogne-Billancourt, France. T. +33147701083. Fax +3310957940931. E-mail: afalassociation@gmail.com.
URL: http://www.afalassociation.com/

History 1954, Montréal QC (Canada), as *French Cultural Union – Union culturelle française (UCF)*. Subsequently became *International Group of Associations for French Language and Culture – Groupement international d'associations de langue et de culture françaises*. Present title adopted 1969. Registered in accordance with Swiss Civil Code and in accordance with French law. **Aims** Facilitate contacts among peoples and national groups of French thought, language and culture; link these groups by a common action of reciprocal understanding; bring tangible cultural aid to French *minorities*; promote the spread of French language and culture; aid development of economic relations among countries and groups within the French language and cultural sphere. **Structure** General Assembly; International Council. **Languages** French. **Staff** 3.00 FTE, paid. **Finance** Sources: members' dues. **Activities** Awards/prizes/competitions; events/meetings; knowledge management/information dissemination; research/documentation; training/education. **Events** *Annual General Assembly* Paris (France) 2012, *Annual General Assembly* Paris (France) 2011, *Annual General Assembly* Paris (France) 2010, *Annual General Assembly* Paris (France) 2009, *Annual General Assembly* Paris (France) 2008. **Publications** Catalogue. **Members** National and regional Committees; Associations; Individuals. Membership countries not specified. **IGO Relations** *Organisation internationale de la Francophonie (OIF, #17809)*; *UNESCO (#20322)*. **NGO Relations** Member of: *Association francophone d'amitié et de liaison (AFAL, #02605)*. [2020.03.03/XC0975/**C**]

- ♦ Union culturiste internationale (inactive)

♦ Union Cycliste Internationale (UCI) 20375

Pres Allée Ferdi Kübler 12, 1860 Aigle VD, Switzerland. T. +41244685811. E-mail: admin@uci.ch.
URL: http://www.uci.org/

History 14 Apr 1900. Included *Permanent Bureau of International Sporting Federations (inactive)*, 31 May 1921 to 1936. Constitution modified 3 Sep 1965, San Sebastian (Spain), when the *'Fédération internationale amateur de cyclisme (FIAC)'* and *'Fédération internationale du cyclisme professionnel (FICP)'* were set up as constituent federations. From Jan 1993, these two federations were united in UCI, FIAC as *Conseil du cyclisme amateur de l'UCI (CCA, inactive)* and FICP as *Conseil du cyclisme professionnel de l'UCI (inactive)*. The two Councils were disbanded in Oct 1997. Former names and other names: *International Cycling Union* – former. **Aims** Develop and promote all aspects of cycling without discrimination of any kind, in close cooperation with national federations and major associates; develop, regulate and control cycling; strengthen friendship between sportsmen in all countries without racial, political and religious or other discrimination. **Structure** Congress (annual); Management Committee (meets 3 times a year); Executive Office. Also includes: *World Cycling Centre (WCC)*. **Languages** English, French. **Finance** Sources: members' dues. Other sources: championship fees; sponsoring fees; TV rights; *International Olympic Committee (IOC, #14408)*. **Activities** Events/meetings. **Events** *Annual congress* Aigle (Switzerland) 2020, *Annual congress* Harrogate (UK) 2019, *Annual congress* Innsbruck (Austria) 2018, *Annual congress* Bergen (Norway) 2017, *Annual congress* Doha (Qatar) 2016. **Publications** Annual Report; Financial Report; Yearbook.
Members National Federations in 196 countries and territories. Membership countries not specified.
Continental confederations (5):
Continental confederations (5):
Asian Cycling Confederation (ACC, #01417); *Confédération africaine de cyclisme (CAC, #04499)*; *European Cycling Union (#06876)*; *Oceania Cycling Federation (#17659)*; *Pan American Cycling Confederation (#18092)*.
NGO Relations Member of (7): *Association of Paralympic Sports Organisations (APSO, #02850)*; *Association of Summer Olympic International Federations (ASOIF, #02943)*; *International Committee for Fair Play (#12769)*; *International Council for Coaching Excellence (ICCE, #13008)*; *International Masters Games Association (IMGA, #14117)*; *International Paralympic Committee (IPC, #14512)*; *Olympic Movement (#17719)*. Cooperates with (1): *International Testing Agency (ITA, #15678)*. Recognized by: *International Olympic Committee (IOC, #14408)*. [2020.02.06/XB1779/y/**B**]

- ♦ Union of Cypriots (internationally oriented national body)
- ♦ Union de Dakar – Association des organismes d'assurance-crédit à l'exportation et de promotion du commerce extérieur (inactive)
- ♦ Union of the Daughters of God (religious order)
- ♦ Union pour la défense de la personne humaine par la collaboration internationale sociale et économique (inactive)
- ♦ Unión Democratica Cristiana de Europa Central (inactive)
- ♦ Union démocratique Asie Pacifique (#01881)
- ♦ Union démocratique européenne (inactive)
- ♦ Union démocratique internationale (#13147)
- ♦ Union démocratique Pacifique / see Asia Pacific Democrat Union (#01881)
- ♦ Union pour le dépôt international des dessins ou modèles industriels (#20417)
- ♦ Union des dirigeants territoriaux de l'Europe (#20454)
- ♦ Union des distributeurs arabes (inactive)
- ♦ Union douanière d'Afrique australe (#19842)
- ♦ Union douanière de l'Afrique de l'Ouest (inactive)
- ♦ Union douanière belgo-néerlando-luxembourgeoise (inactive)
- ♦ Union douanière et économique de l'Afrique centrale (inactive)
- ♦ Union douanière nordique (inactive)
- ♦ Unione Apostolica del Clero / see International Confederation Apostolic Union of Clergy (#12844)
- ♦ Unione Apostolica dei Presbiteri Diocesani / see International Confederation Apostolic Union of Clergy (#12844)
- ♦ Unione Apostolica dei Presbiteri Secolari / see International Confederation Apostolic Union of Clergy (#12844)
- ♦ Unione delle Associazioni delle Aziende Distributrici d'Acqua dei Paesi Membri delle Comunità Europee / see European Federation of National Associations of Water and Waste Water Services (#07170)
- ♦ Unione delle Associazioni Europee Studentesche (inactive)
- ♦ Unione delle Associazioni degli Industriali Pastificatori della CEE / see Union of Organizations of manufacturers of Pasta Products of the EU (#20468)
- ♦ Union EA – Union européenne des artistes (inactive)
- ♦ Unione degli Avvocati Europei (#20365)
- ♦ Unione Camere Esperti Europei (unconfirmed)
- ♦ Union des écoles familiales agraires (internationally oriented national body)
- ♦ Unione Comunista Internazionalista (#13965)
- ♦ Unione delle Conferenze Europee dei Superiori Maggiori (#20344)
- ♦ Union of Economic and Social Councils of Africa (no recent information)

♦ Union économique de l'Afrique centrale (UEAC) 20376

Central African Economic Union

Contact c/o BEAC, BP 1917, Yaoundé, Cameroon. T. +2372234030 – +2372234060. Fax +2372233329 – +2372233350.

History as an institution of *Communauté économique et monétaire d'Afrique centrale (CEMAC, #04374)*, gradually taking over the functions which came within the framework of the previous *Union douanière et économique de l'Afrique centrale (UDEAC, inactive)*. Set up under a convention which also includes the composition, function and field of competence of the 2 chambers comprising *Cour de justice communautaire de la CEMAC (CJ-CEMAC, #04931)*. The transition was formalized in a agreement signed by CEMAC Council of Ministers, 5 Feb 1997, Libreville (Gabon), effective 1 Jan 1998. Based at *Banque des Etats de l'Afrique centrale (BEAC, #03169)*. **Structure** Council of Ministers, comprising 3 ministers of each member state, is a principal organ of CEMAC.

Members CEMAC member states (6):
Cameroon, Central African Rep, Chad, Congo Brazzaville, Equatorial Guinea, Gabon.
IGO Relations Instrumental in setting up: *Union monétaire de l'Afrique centrale (UMAC, #20463).*
[2009/XE3882/**E***]

♦ Union économique belgo-luxembourgeoise (#03195)
♦ Union économique Benelux / see Benelux Union (#03207)
♦ Union économique et douanière européenne (inactive)
♦ Union économique et monétaire (#06961)

♦ Union économique et monétaire Ouest africaine (UEMOA) 20377

West Africa Economic and Monetary Union

Executive Organ Commission de l'UEMOA, 380 rue du Pr Joseph Kl-Zerbo, 01 BP 543, Ouagadougou 01, Burkina Faso. T. +22650318873 – +22650318874 – +22650318876. Fax +22650318872. E-mail: commission@uemoa.int.
URL: http://www.uemoa.int/

History 1 Aug 1994, on coming into effect of a Treaty, signed 10 Jan 1994, Dakar (Senegal), by Heads of State and Government of 7 countries of the subregion: Benin; Burkina Faso; Côte d'Ivoire; Mali; Niger; Senegal; Togo. Guinea-Bissau became the 8th member state on 2 May 1997. Commenced activities, Jan 1995. Set up in response to devaluation of the CFA Franc, 11 Jan 1994. By signing the UEMOA Treaty, the 7 first member states indicated their intention to complete the *Union monétaire Ouest africaine (UMOA, inactive)*, which had existed between them since 12 May 1962, into an economic and monetary Union. In this regard, UEMOA complements and rounds off work of UMOA and replaces 'Union douanière économique des Etats de l'Afrique de l'Ouest (UDEAO)', set up 9 Jun 1959 and reorganized as *Communauté économique de l'Afrique de l'Ouest (CEAO, inactive)* on coming into force of the 'Treaty of Abidjan', 1 Jan 1974. Common monetary zone launched Jan 2000. Member states are also members of *Pays africains de la Zone franc (PAZF, #18270)*. Following convergence process, merger would be negotiated between the first monetary zone UEMOA and *West African Monetary Zone (WAMZ, #20889)* to create ECOWAS single monetary zone. **Aims** Strengthen competition in the context of an open, competitive market and a streamlined, harmonized legal framework; ensure the convergence of economic performance and policies by instituting a multilateral surveillance procedure; create a common market among member states, based on the free flow of persons, goods, services and capital; work towards an common external tariff and a common trade policy; establish the coordination of national sectoral policies; harmonize member states' laws to the extent necessary for proper functioning of the common market.
Structure I. *'Management Organs'*: (i) Conference of Heads of State and Government, the supreme authority, usually meets at least once a year and defines major trends of Union policy and general trends. (ii) Council of Ministers (meeting at least twice a year), ensures implementation of the general trends defined by the Conference by means of regulations, directives and decisions. It is a common organ of UMOA and UEMOA, drawing up monetary and credit policy and following UEMOA Commission activities; (iii) *Commission de l'UEMOA (see: #20377)*, the executive organ, proposes regulations, directives and decisions to the Council, formulates recommendations and advice and ensures follow-up.
II. *'Monitoring Organs'*: (i) *Cour de justice de l'UEMOA (#04932)*, based at Ouagadougou, comprises 8 members and ensures adherence to the law relating interpretation and application of the founding Treaty. (ii) *Cour des comptes de l'UEMOA (see: #20377)*, based at Ouagadougou, comprises 3 members and keeps overall control of the Union's accounts.
III. *'Comité Interparlementaire'* (interparliamentary committee) anticipates a future *Parlement de l'Union* (Parliament of the Union), comprises 40 members (5 per country) and is based at Bamako (Mali). Draft treaty on creation of a regional parliament was adopted by UEMOA Council of Ministers, 18 Nov 2002, Ouagadougou and by Head of State, 28 Jan 2003, Dakar (Senegal). The treaty is ratified by 7 of the 8 Member States.
IV. *'Consultative Organ'*: *Chambre consulaire régionale* (Regional Consular Chamber) is a federation of the consular chambers of member countries and is based at Lomé (Togo) (56 members).
V. *'Specialized Autonomous Financial Institutions'*: (i) *Banque centrale des Etats de l'Afrique de l'Ouest (BCEAO, #03167)*; (ii) *Banque ouest africaine de développement (BOAD, #03170)*.
Languages French. **Finance** The monetary unit is the CFA franc, the franc of the *Communauté financière africaine (CFA, #04377)*, which is linked to the euro within the *Zone franc (#22037)* and is legal tender throughout the territory of the Union. **Activities** Maintains and develops a network of cooperation with similar integration organizations in Africa.*Economic and Statistical Observatory for Sub-Saharan Africa (AFRISTAT, #05321)* assists in harmonizing consumer price indexes in member countries. Instrumental in setting up: *Centre africain d'études supérieures en gestion (CESAG, #03724)*; *School of Mining Industry and Geology (#19132)*. **Events** *Conférence Régionale sur les Enjeux Transfrontaliers* Dakar (Senegal) 2013, *Session of the Conference of Heads of State and Government* Dakar (Senegal) 2013, *Session of the Conference of Heads of State and Government* Lomé (Togo) 2012, *Session of the conference of heads of state and government* Bamako (Mali) 2011, *Extraordinary session of the conference of heads of state and government* Lomé (Togo) 2011. **Publications** *Bulletin Hebdomadaires de l'UEMOA* (12 a year); *Rapport Semestriel d'Exécution de la Surveillance Multilatérale* (2 a year); *Indice Harmonisé des prix à la Consommation* (annual). *Etude sur l'Enseignement Supérieur dans les Pays de l'UEMOA*; *Le Traité de l'UEMOA*: Activity reports; extracts of official UEMOA bulletins; reports; brochure.
Members Governments of 8 countries:
Benin, Burkina Faso, Côte d'Ivoire, Guinea-Bissau, Mali, Niger, Senegal, Togo.
Consultative Status Consultative status granted from: *World Intellectual Property Organization (WIPO, #21593)* (Observer Status).
IGO Relations Accredited to the Conference of the Parties of: *Secretariat of the United Nations Convention to Combat Desertification (Secretariat of the UNCCD, #19208)*. Cooperative Agreement with: *International Fund for Agricultural Development (IFAD, #13692)*; *World Trade Organization (WTO, #21864)* (Observer Status). Participates in the activities of: *UNCTAD (#20285)*. *Union of African Shippers' Councils (UASC, #20348)* participates in activities. Partner of: *Niger Basin Authority (NBA, #17134)*. Cooperates with: *ECOSOC (#05331)*; *West African Science Service Center on Climate Change and Adapted Land Use (WASCAL, #20897)*. Observer to: *Codex Alimentarius Commission (CAC, #04081)*. Supports: *Africa Rice Center (AfricaRice, #00518)*; *Institut International d'Ingénierie de l'Eau et de l'Environnement (2iE, #11313)*. Links with the following organizations listed in this Yearbook:
- *African Civil Aviation Commission (AFCAC, #00248)*;
- *Centre technique de coopération agricole et rurale (CTA, inactive)*;
- *Comité permanent inter-Etats de lutte contre la sécheresse dans le Sahel (CILSS, #04195)*;
- *Conference of Ministers of Agriculture of West and Central Africa (CMA/WCA, #04631)*;
- *Conférence des ministres des finances des pays de la Zone franc (#04633)*;
- *Economic Community of West African States (ECOWAS, #05312)*;
- *European Union (EU, #08967)*;
- *Higher School of Fishing Sciences and Techniques (no recent information)*;
- *Institut du Sahel (INSAH, #11357)*;
- *International Bank for Reconstruction and Development (IBRD, #12317)*;
- *International Monetary Fund (IMF, #14180)*;
- *Maritime Organization of West and Central Africa (MOWCA, #16582)*;
- *Société Ouest Africaine de Gestion d'Actifs (SOAGA, see: #03170)*;
- *West African Investment Fund (FOAI, see: #03170)*;
- *World Customs Organization (WCO, #21350)*.

NGO Relations Through UMOA, member of: *International Organization of Securities Commissions (IOSCO, #14470)*. Member of: *Assemblée parlementaire de la Francophonie (APF, #02312)*; *Association des hautes juridictions de cassation des pays ayant en partage l'usage du Français (AHJUCAF, #02629)*; *Association of National Numbering Agencies (ANNA, #02818)*; *Association of Secretaries General of Parliaments (ASGP, #02911)*; *Réseau de prévention des crises alimentaires (RPCA, #18905)*. Inter-Parliamentary Committee is member of: *Inter-Parliamentary Union (IPU, #15961)*. Partner of: *Conférence interafricaine de la prévoyance sociale (CIPRES, #04610)*. Supports: *Water and Sanitation for Africa (WSA, #20836)*. Cooperates with: *International Fertilizer Development Center (IFDC, #13590)*. [2009.11.16/XF3713/**F***]

♦ Union des économistes arabes (no recent information)
♦ Union des écrivains et artistes latins (inactive)
♦ Union of EC Soft Drinks Associations / see UNESDA Soft Drinks Europe (#20323)
♦ Unione per la Cultura e l'Avvenire Professionale in Europa (#20373)
♦ Union des éditeurs de langue française (no recent information)
♦ Union des éditeurs de presse d'Afrique centrale (no recent information)
♦ Unión de Educación Superior Privada (#09009)
♦ Unione Europea (#08967)
♦ Unione Europea degli Alcoli, Acquaviti e Liquori (inactive)
♦ Unione Europea dell' Artigianato e delle Piccole e Medie Imprese / see SMEunited (#19327)
♦ Unione Europea delle Associazioni dei Grossisti in Vetro e Ceramica (inactive)
♦ Unione Europea delle Associazioni degli Informatori Scientifici (inactive)
♦ Unione Europea delle Associazioni Nazionali dei Distributori d'Acqua / see European Federation of National Associations of Water and Waste Water Services (#07170)
♦ Unione Europea dei Commercianti Ambulanti (no recent information)
♦ Unione Europea dei Commercianti dei Prodotti Lattiero Caseari (#06003)
♦ Unione Europea del Commercio all'Ingrosso delle Uova, dei Prodotti d'Uova, del Pollame e della Selvaggina (#09021)
♦ Unione Europea del Commercio del Bestiame e della Carne (#20394)
♦ Unione Europea del Commercio di Latte (inactive)
♦ Unione Europea Democratica-Cristiana (inactive)
♦ Unione Europea Dipendenti Enti Locali (inactive)
♦ Unione Europea dei Fabbricanti di Letti, Oggetti Letterecci e Affini (inactive)
♦ Unione Europea delle Farmacie Sociali (#20401)
♦ Unione Europea delle Farmacie Sociali, Mutualiste e Cooperativiste / see Union européenne des Pharmacies sociales (#20401)
♦ Unione Europea dei Federalisti / see Union of European Federalists, The (#20385)
♦ Unione Europea dei Fonditori di Sego (inactive)
♦ Unione Europea dei Grossisti in Carte, Cartoni e Imbalaggi / see European Paper Merchants Association (#08138)
♦ Unione Europea degli Impreditori di Applicatori di Gesso, Staff, Stucco et Altre Attività Annesse (inactive)
♦ Unione Europea degli Indipendenti Lubricanti / see Union Européenne de l'Industrie des Lubrifiants (#20398)
♦ Unione Europea delle Industrie Trasformatrici di Patate / see EUPPA – European Potato Processors' Association (#05592)
♦ Unione Europea dei Lavoratori Democratici Cristiani (#08981)
♦ Unione Europea dei Medici Dentisti (inactive)
♦ Unione Europea dei Medici Generali / see European Union of General Practitioners / Family Physicians (#08993)
♦ Unione Europea di Medicina Sociale (no recent information)
♦ Unione Europea dei Medici Specialisti / see European Union of Medical Specialists (#09001)
♦ Unione Europea delle Mogli dei Militari (no recent information)
♦ Unione Europea dell'Ospedalità Privata (#20397)
♦ Unione Europea delle Piccole e Medie Imprese (no recent information)
♦ Unione Europea di Relazioni Pubbliche (#09011)
♦ Unione Europea di Relazioni Pubbliche – Organizzazione Internazionale di Servizi / see European Union of Public Relations (#09011)
♦ Unione Europea dello Spettacolo Cinematografico (inactive)
♦ Unione Europea di Yoga (#09131)
♦ Unione Fitopatologica Mediterranea (#16672)

♦ Unione Intercontinentale Casalinghe (UNICA) 20378

Intercontinental Union of Women Working in the Home – Unión Intercontinental de Amas de Casa

Founder/Pres c/o MOICA, Via B Castelli 4, Mompiano, 25133 Brescia BS, Italy. T. +39302006951. Fax +39302099323. E-mail: moicanazionale@moica.it.
SG/Treas address not obtained.
URL: https://www.moica.it/presentazione/moica_international/unica.html

History 26 May 1994, Bologna (Italy). **Aims** Represent housewives before world institutions; promote, favour and support women who work at home; promote laws for their protection; promote the rights of the family and its participation in institutional decision making. **Structure** Board. **Languages** English, French, Italian, Spanish. **Staff** Voluntary. **Finance** Members' subscriptions; public and private sponsorship. **Events** *Biennial World Congress / World Congress* Brescia (Italy) 2012, *Biennial World Congress / World Congress* Asunción (Paraguay) 2011, *Biennial World Congress / World Congress* Salvador (Brazil) 2010, *Biennial World Congress / World Congress* Asunción (Paraguay) 2008, *Biennial World Congress / World Congress* Brescia (Italy) 2007.
Members Regional/national organizations and individuals in 9 countries:
Argentina, Brazil, Chile, Congo DR, Dominican Rep, Italy, Peru, Spain, Uruguay. [2022/XC0108/y/**D**]

♦ Unione Internazionale Assicurazioni Trasporti (#15789)
♦ Unione Internazionale delle Associazione di Guide di Montagna (#15756)
♦ Unione Internazionale delle Associazioni Alpinistiche (#20420)
♦ Unione Internazionale delle Associazioni Tecniche Cinematografiche (inactive)
♦ Unione Internazionale degli Avvocati / see Union Internationale des Avocats (#20422)
♦ Unione Internazionale d'Azione Morale e Sociale (inactive)
♦ Unione Internazionale dei Cinema (#15763)
♦ Unione Internazionale del Commercio all'Ingrosso dei Fiori / see UNION FLEURS (#20408)
♦ Unione Internazionale contro il Cancro (#20415)
♦ Unione Internazionale dei Giovani Democratici Cristiani (inactive)
♦ Unione Internazionale degli Istituti di Archeologia, Storia e Storia dell'Arte in Roma (#15782)
♦ Unione Internazionale dei Maestri Liutai e Archettai d'Arte (#15542)
♦ Unione Internazionale dei Magistrati (#11978)
♦ Unione Internazionale del Notariato (#15795)
♦ Unione Internazionale del Notariato Latino / see International Union of Notaries (#15795)
♦ Unione Internazionale degli Organismi Familiari / see World Family Organization (#21399)
♦ Unione Internazionale di Preghiere (religious order)
♦ Unione Internazionale de la Proprietà Immobiliaria (#15804)
♦ Unione Internazionale della Resistenza e della Deportazione (no recent information)
♦ Unione Internazionale delle Società per il Trasporto Combinato Strada – Rotaia / see International Union for Combined Road – Rail Transport (#15765)
♦ Unione Internazionale della Spedalità Privata (no recent information)
♦ Unione Internazionale Superiore Generali (#15820)
♦ Unione Latina (inactive)

♦ Union of the Electricity Industry – Eurelectric 20379

SG Bvd de l'Impératrice 66, boite 2, 1000 Brussels, Belgium. T. +3225151001 – +3225151002. E-mail: aerkens@eurelectric.org – alizin@eurelectric.org.
Head of Finance , Administration & Payroll address not obtained.
URL: https://www.eurelectric.org/

History 7 Dec 1999. Founded by merger of *European Grouping of the Electricity Supply Industry (EURELECTRIC, inactive)*, set up Nov 1989, Brussels (Belgium), and *UNIPEDE – International Union of Producers and Distributors of Electrical Energy (inactive)*, set up 1925, Paris (France). Commenced operations under listed title, 1 Jan 2000. The Secretariat of UNIPEDE (the association of the European electricity supply industry) moved to Brussels in Mar 1998, to link up with the existing structure of EURELECTRIC (the association of the European Union electricity supply industry); but the two organizations maintained distinct identities until their full merger. Former names and other names: *Joint Secretariat of UNIPEDE and EURELECTRIC* – former; *Secrétariat commun d'UNIPEDE et d'EURELECTRIC* – former. Registration: Banque-Carrefour des Entreprises, No/ID: 0462.679.112, Start date: 29 Sep 1997, Belgium; EU Transparency Register, No/ID: 4271427696-87, Start date: 1 Dec 2008. **Aims** Contribute to competitiveness of the electricity industry; provide effective representation for the industry in public affairs; promote the role of electricity in the advancement of

society. **Structure** General Assembly (annual); Board of Directors. **Languages** English. **Staff** 35.00 FTE, paid. **Activities** Events/meetings; knowledge management/information dissemination. **Events** *EVision 2022 – Power Sector Accelerating e-mobility* Brussels (Belgium) 2022, *Global DSO Event* Brussels (Belgium) 2022, *Power Summit* Brussels (Belgium) 2022, *Power Summit* Brussels (Belgium) 2021, *Conference on E-Invest* Brussels (Belgium) 2019. **Publications** Reports; position papers; responses to consultations.
Members Full; Affiliate. Full in 32 countries:
Austria, Belgium, Bulgaria, Croatia, Cyprus, Czechia, Denmark, Estonia, Finland, France, Germany, Greece, Hungary, Iceland, Ireland, Italy, Latvia, Lithuania, Luxembourg, Netherlands, North Macedonia, Norway, Poland, Portugal, Romania, Slovakia, Slovenia, Spain, Sweden, Switzerland, Türkiye, UK.
Affiliate in 8 countries and territories:
Algeria, Bosnia-Herzegovina, Egypt, Japan, Jersey, Kazakhstan, Serbia, Ukraine.
NGO Relations Member of: *Alliance for a Competitive European Industry (ACEI, #00670); European Association for Electromobility (AVERE, #06024); European Association for the Streamlining of Energy Exchange-gas (EASEE-gas, #06224); European Energy Forum (EEF, #06986); Federation of European and International Associations Established in Belgium (FAIB, #09508); MEDELEC (#16614).* Cooperates with: *European Committee for Electrotechnical Standardization (CENELEC, #06647).* [2022.05.23/XE3484/t/**D**]

♦ Union des élus locaux et régionaux socialistes d'Europe (#20479)
♦ Unione Medica Mediterranea Latina / see Surgery Society of the Latin Mediterranean (#20042)
♦ Unione Mediterranea delle Confederazioni d'Impresa (#20458)
♦ Unione Mondiale Democratica Cristiana / see Centrist Democrat International (#03792)
♦ Unione Mondiale di S Gabriele (#21885)
♦ Unione Mondiale Insegnanti Cattolici / see UMEC-WUCT (#20280)
♦ Unione Mondiale dei Mercati all'Ingrosso (#21889)
♦ Unione Mondiale dei Mercati all'Ingrosso in seno all'IULA / see World Union of Wholesale Markets (#21889)
♦ Unione Mondiale per la Pace ed i Diritti Fondamentali dell'Uomo e dei Popoli (internationally oriented national body)
♦ Unionen af Finanstjenestemaend i Europa (#20407)
♦ Union of Engineers and Technicians Utilizing the French Language / see Union internationale des ingénieurs et des scientifiques utilisant la langue française (#20427)
♦ Union pour l'enregistrement international des marques (#20445)
♦ Union pour l'enregistrement international des oeuvres audiovisuelles (#20444)
♦ Union des enseignants des Caraïbes (#03562)
♦ Union des entrepreneurs arabes (#09419)
♦ Unionen af Vandforsyningsforeninger i de Europaeiske Faellesskabers Medlemslande / see European Federation of National Associations of Water and Waste Water Services (#07170)
♦ Unione Paneuropea / see International Paneuropean Union (#14509)
♦ Unione del Personale Finanziero in Europa (#20407)
♦ Unione Professionale dei Depositari di Cereali nella CEE / see Unistock Europe (#20492)
♦ Unione Radiofónica e Televisiva Internacional / see International Radio and Television Union (#14689)
♦ Unión Escandinava del Personal de Banco (inactive)

♦ Unión de Escuelas y Facultades de Arquitectura Latinoamericanas (UDEFAL) 20380

Union of Latin American Schools and Faculties of Architecture
SG Facultad de Arquitectura, Construcción y Diseño, Av Collao 1202, Universidad del Bio-Bio, Concepción, Bio Bio, Chile. T. +56412731401. Fax +56412731016.
URL: http://udefal.blogspot.com/
History 23 Sep 1994, Mendoza (Argentina). **Structure** Executive Council, comprising President, Secretary-General, 4 Vice-Presidents. **Events** *Conference* Buenos Aires (Argentina) 2013, *Latin American conference of schools and faculties of architecture of Latin America / Conference* Buenos Aires (Argentina) 2009, *Latin American conference of schools and faculties of architecture of Latin America* La Paz (Bolivia) 2008, *Latin American conference of schools and faculties of architecture of Latin America / Conference* Antigua (Guatemala) 2007, *Latin American conference of schools and faculties of architecture of Latin America* Loja (Ecuador) 2005. **NGO Relations** *Conferencia Latinoamericana de Escuelas y Facultades de Arquitectura (CLEFA).* [2012/XD5877/**D**]

♦ Union de Escuelas Familiares Agrarias (internationally oriented national body)
♦ Unione Sindacale – Servizio Pubblico Europeo / see Union Syndicale Fédérale (#20485)
♦ Union espérantiste européenne (#07006)
♦ Unione delle Suore della Presentazione della Beata Vergine Maria (religious order)
♦ Unione Superiori Generali (#20484)
♦ Union des établissements religieux de l'Europe (no recent information)
♦ Union des Etats africains (inactive)
♦ Union des Etats de l'Afrique centrale (inactive)

♦ Union for Ethical BioTrade (UEBT) 20381

Exec Dir De Ruiterkade 6, 1013 AA Amsterdam, Netherlands. T. +31202234567. E-mail: info@ethicalbiotrade.org.
Financial Admin c/o CR Gestion et Fiduciaire SA, Rue de la Vallée 3, 1204 Geneva, Switzerland. T. +41225661585.
URL: http://www.ethicalbiotrade.org/
History Founded Oct 2007. EU Transparency Register: 20071577456-10. **Aims** Promote, support and verify companies' commitments to innovation and sourcing that contribute to a world in which people and biodiversity thrive; support and validate best practices of companies committed to ethical sourcing and innovation of natural ingredients for the benefit of people and biodiversity. **Structure** General Assembly (annual); Board; Committees (2); Secretariat. **Languages** English. **Staff** 6.00 FTE, paid. **Finance** Sources: members' dues; revenue from activities/projects. Annual budget: 800,000 EUR. **Activities** Awareness raising; capacity building; certification/accreditation; events/meetings; guidance/assistance/consulting; monitoring/evaluation; standards/guidelines; training/education. **Events** *Beauty of Sourcing with Respect Conference* Paris (France) 2019, *Beauty of Sourcing with Respect Conference* Paris (France) 2015. **Publications** *UEBT Newsletter. UEBT Biodiversity Barometer.* Annual Report.
Members Trading (43). Members in 23 countries:
Brazil, Burkina Faso, Chile, Colombia, Croatia, Czechia, France, Germany, India, Italy, Madagascar, Mexico, Nigeria, Peru, South Africa, Spain, Switzerland, Tanzania UR, Türkiye, UK, USA, Vietnam, Zimbabwe. [2019.02.13/XJ6089/ty/**C**]

♦ Union pour l'étude de la population africaine (#20346)
♦ Unione delle Università del Mediterraneo (#16687)
♦ Union der Europäischen Fussball-Verbände (#20386)
♦ Union der Europäischen Phoniater (#20390)
♦ Union der Europäischen Rundfunkorganisationen / see European Broadcasting Union (#06404)
♦ Union Europäischer Bankpersonalverbände (no recent information)
♦ Union Europäischer Berater für Geistiges Eigentum (#20392)
♦ Union Europäischer Berater für den Gewerblichen Rechtsschutz / see Union of European Practitioners in Intellectual Property (#20392)
♦ Union Europäischer Chiropraktoren (#06538)
♦ Union Europäischer Eisenbahn-Ingenieur-Verbände (#20362)
♦ Union Europäischer Elektro-Grosshändler (#08987)
♦ Union Europäischer Föderalisten / see Union of European Federalists, The (#20385)
♦ Union Europäischer Forstberufsverbände (#20387)

♦ Union Europäischer Gerüstbaubetriebe (UEG) 20382

Union of European Scaffolding Contractors
SG Rösrather Str 645, 51107 Cologne, Germany. T. +492218706020. Fax +49221870605520. E-mail: generalsecretariat@ueg-eu.org.
URL: http://www.ueg-eu.org/
History 25 Oct 2008. Legally registered as *Association of European Scaffolding Companies.* Registered in accordance with German law. **Aims** Collate, represent and promote common technical, human, commercial, social and cultural interests of members at European level; develop comparable and general standards in scaffolding; evaluate European legislative processes in respect of their effect on scaffolding; provide expert representation to European bodies; facilitate permanent links and exchanges between members. **Structure** General Assembly; Chair; General Secretariat. Working Groups. **Languages** English, German. **Staff** 1.00 FTE, paid. **Finance** Members' dues.
Members Organizations in 11 countries:
Czechia, Denmark, Finland, Germany, Luxembourg, Netherlands, Norway, Poland, Sweden, Switzerland, UK.
NGO Relations Member of: *SMEunited (#19327); Small Business Standards (SBS, #19311).* [2019/XJ7885/**D**]

♦ Union Europäischer Handelskammern für Verkehrsfragen (#20384)
♦ Union Europäischer Industrie- und Handelskammern – Rhein, Rhône, Donau, Alpen / see Union of European Chambers of Commerce for Transport (#20384)
♦ Union Europäischer Industrie- und Handelskammern für Verkehrsfragen / see Union of European Chambers of Commerce for Transport (#20384)
♦ Union Europäischer Kinderpsychiater / see European Society of Child and Adolescent Psychiatry (#08543)
♦ Union Europäischer Patentanwälte / see Union of European Practitioners in Intellectual Property (#20392)
♦ Union Europäischer Pianomacher-Fachverbände (#20391)
♦ Unión Europea (#08967)
♦ Unión Europea de Almácenistas de Papel, Cartón y Embalajes / see European Paper Merchants Association (#08138)
♦ Unión Europea de Antiguos Alumnos y Antiguas Alumnas de la Enseñanza Católica (#08992)

♦ Unión Europea de Asociaciones de Entrenadores de Baloncesto (EUABC) 20383

European Union of Basketball Coaches' Associations
Pres c/o AEEB, Calle de Fernan Gonzalez 18, 28009 Madrid, Spain. T. +34915753565. Fax +34915775073. E-mail: aeeb@aeeb.es.
History Founded 8 Sep 2007, Madrid (Spain).
Members in 6 countries:
France, Greece, Italy, Russia, Serbia, Spain. [2015/XM3302/**D**]

♦ Unión Europea de Asociaciones Nacionales de Distribuidores de Agua / see European Federation of National Associations of Water and Waste Water Services (#07170)
♦ Unión Europea de Asociaciones del Personal de la Banca (no recent information)
♦ Unión Europea del Comercio de Patatas / see European Potato Trade Association (#08257)
♦ Unión Europea de Comercios de Semillas, Semillas Oleaginosas, Alimentos del Ganado y Derivados / see Committee of the Trade in Cereals, Oilseeds, Pulses, Olive Oil, Oils and Fats, Animal Feed and Agrosupply of the EU (#04289)
♦ Unión Europea de Concursos de Música para Jóvenes (#09003)
♦ Unión Europea de los Concursos de Música por la Juventud / see European Union of Music Competitions for Youth (#09003)
♦ Unión Europea de los Concursos Nacionales de Música por la Juventud / see European Union of Music Competitions for Youth (#09003)
♦ Unión Europea de Contadores Públicos (inactive)
♦ Unión Europea de Federaciones de Personal Comunal (inactive)
♦ Unión Europea de Futsal (#07371)
♦ Unión Europea de Independientes en Lubricantes / see Union Européenne de l'Industrie des Lubrifiants (#20398)
♦ Unión Europea de Judo (#20399)
♦ Unión Europea de Medicina Social (no recent information)
♦ Unión Europea de Médicos Especialistas / see European Union of Medical Specialists (#09001)
♦ Unión Europea de Médicos Generalistas / see European Union of General Practitioners / Family Physicians (#08993)
♦ Unión Europea – Mercosur (inactive)
♦ Union Europea de Mujeres Demócrata Cristianas / see EPP Women (#05516)
♦ Union of European Accountancy Students (inactive)
♦ Union of European Associations of Bank Employees (no recent information)
♦ Union of European Association of Stove-Fitters Trade (#20754)
♦ Union of European Beverages Associations / see UNESDA Soft Drinks Europe (#20323)
♦ Union of European Chambers of Commerce and Industry – Rhine, Rhône, Danube, Alps / see Union of European Chambers of Commerce for Transport (#20384)
♦ Union of European Chambers of Commerce and Industry for Transport / see Union of European Chambers of Commerce for Transport (#20384)

♦ Union of European Chambers of Commerce for Transport (UECC) 20384

Union européenne des chambres de commerce pour la politique des transports – Union Europäischer Handelskammern für Verkehrsfragen – Unie van Europese Kamers van Koophandel voor Vervoersvraagstukken
SG St Jakobs Str 25, 4010 Basel BS, Switzerland. T. +41612706010. Fax +41612706005. E-mail: contact@uecc-chambers.eu.
Public Relations address not obtained.
URL: http://www.uecc.org/
History 9 Sep 1949, Rotterdam (Netherlands). Permanent secretariat since 1966. Current statutes adopted 18 Apr 2011. Former names and other names: *Union ouest-européenne des chambres de commerce et d'industrie des régions rhénane, rhodanienne et danubienne* – former; *Union Westeuropäischer Industrie- und Handelskammern des Rhein-, Rhône- und Donaugebietes* – former; *Unie van de Westeuropese Kamers van Koophandel en Fabrieken van het Rijn-, Rhône- en Donaugebied* – former; *Union of European Chambers of Commerce and Industry – Rhine, Rhône, Danube, Alps* – former; *Union européenne des chambres de commerce et d'industrie – Rhin, Rhône, Danube, Alpes* – former; *Union Europäischer Industrie- und Handelskammern – Rhein, Rhône, Donau, Alpen* – former; *Unie van Europese Kamers van Koophandel en Fabrieken – Rijn, Rhône, Donau, Alpen* – former; *Union of European Chambers of Commerce and Industry for Transport (UECC)* – former; *Union européenne des chambres de commerce et d'industrie pour la politique des transports* – former; *Union Europäischer Industrie- und Handelskammern für Verkehrsfragen* – former; *Unie van Europese Kamers van Koophandel en Fabrieken voor Vervoersvraagstukken* – former; *Rhine Union of Chambers of Commerce* – former; *Union des chambres de commerce rhénanes* – former; *Union der Handelskammern des Rheingebietes* – former; *Unie van de Kamers van Koophandel van het Rijngebied* – former. Registration: EU Transparency Register, No/ID: 66355731387-11. **Aims** Facilitate economic development in Europe. **Structure** General Assembly (annual); Executive Committee; Working Group; General Secretariat. **Languages** English, French, German. **Staff** 2.00 FTE, paid. **Finance** Sources: members' dues. Annual budget: 90,000 EUR. **Events** *Annual General Assembly* Zurich (Switzerland) 2020, *Annual General Assembly* Luxembourg (Luxembourg) 2019, *Annual General Assembly* Mannheim (Germany) 2018, *Annual General Assembly* Vienna (Austria) 2017, *Annual General Assembly* Bonn (Germany) 2016. **Publications** *UECC Newsletter.* Annual Report.
Members Chambers of Commerce (51) in 6 countries:
Austria, France, Germany, Luxembourg, Netherlands, Switzerland. [2022/XD4390/**D**]

♦ Union of European Choral Federations (inactive)
♦ Union of European Civil Servants / see European Public Service Union (#08303)
♦ Union of European Conferences of Major Superiors (#20344)
♦ Union of European Experts Chambers (unconfirmed)
♦ Union of European Fashion Jewellery Manufacturers (inactive)

♦ Union of European Federalists, The (UEF) 20385

Dir Rue d'Arlon 53, 1040 Brussels, Belgium. T. +3225083030. E-mail: secretariat@federalists.eu.
SG address not obtained.
URL: http://www.federalists.eu/

History 15 Dec 1946, Paris (France). In 1956, divided into two separate movements: *European Centre for Federalist Action (AEF, inactive)* and *Movement of European Federalists (MFE, inactive)*. Agreement to form present Union, 7-9 Apr 1972, Nancy (France); set up Apr 1973. Statutes adopted 13 Apr 1973, Brussels (Belgium). Statutes modified: at 10th Congress, 16 Mar 1980, Strasbourg (France); at 15th Congress, 16 May 1992, Milan (Italy); at 17th Congress, 18 Apr 1997; at 22nd Congress, 11 Oct 2008. Former names and other names: *Union des fédéralistes européens* – former; *Unión de Federalistas Europeos* – former; *Union Europäischer Föderalisten* – former; *Unione Europea dei Federalisti* – former; *Unie der Europese Federalisten* – former. Registration: Netherlands. **Aims** Promote the constitution of a European Federation to overcome the divisions of the past and ensure a future of peace and economic prosperity. **Structure** Congress (General Assembly); Federal Committee; Bureau; Arbitration Board. An autonomous political movement without any political party affiliation. **Languages** English, French, German. **Staff** 2.00 FTE, paid. **Finance** Sources: gifts, legacies; grants; members' dues. **Activities** Advocacy/lobbying/activism; awards/prizes/competitions; awareness raising. **Events** *Biennial Congress* Valencia (Spain) 2021, *Biennial Congress* Vienna (Austria) 2018, *Biennial Congress* Berlin (Germany) 2013, *Biennial Congress* Brussels (Belgium) 2011, *Biennial Congress* Paris (France) 2008. **Publications** *UEF Update* (4 a year); *Federalist Debate* (3 a year) – journal.
Members Individual members organized at local, regional and national level, in 23 countries:
Austria, Belgium, Bulgaria, Cyprus, Czechia, Finland, France, Germany, Greece, Hungary, Italy, Lithuania, Luxembourg, Montenegro, Poland, Portugal, Romania, Serbia, Slovakia, Slovenia, Spain, Sweden, Switzerland.
Also a UEF European Union Group. [2021.02.22/XD0713/D]

♦ Union of European Federation of Corporate Football (unconfirmed)

♦ Union of European Football Associations (UEFA) 20386

Union des associations européennes de football – Union der Europäischen Fussball-Verbände – Unión de Federaciones Europeas de Fútbol

Gen Sec Route de Genève 46, Case postale, 1260 Nyon VD 2, Switzerland. T. +41848002727. Fax +41848012727.
URL: http://www.uefa.com/

History Founded 15 Jun 1954, Switzerland, at World Cup Finals. Statutes most recently amended: 2014. Also referred to as *European Football Union*. Registered Office located in Switzerland. EU Transparency Register: 39217046408-27. **Aims** Consider matters relating to European football; promote development of friendly sporting relations between member associations in the spirit of peace and mutual understanding and the safeguard of their interests; assist in promoting the game of Association football in Europe in any way the members shall think proper, without racial, religious or political discrimination; reconcile the various points of view of member associations concerning problems of football, agree on common policy, if possible, and resolve any disputes which may arise between member associations. **Structure** Congress (annual); Executive Committee; Professional Football Strategy Council; Committees and Panels. **Languages** English, French, German. **Staff** 574.00 FTE, paid. **Activities** Events/meetings; awards/prizes/competitions; standards/guidelines. **Events** *Safety and Security Meeting* Amsterdam (Netherlands) 2019, *Annual Congress* Rome (Italy) 2019, *Annual Congress* Bratislava (Slovakia) 2018, *Annual Congress* Helsinki (Finland) 2017, *Workshop* Vienna (Austria) 2017. **Publications** *UEFADIRECT* (12 a year). Other publications.
Members Affiliated national associations in 55 countries and territories:
Albania, Andorra, Armenia, Austria, Azerbaijan, Belarus, Belgium, Bosnia-Herzegovina, Bulgaria, Croatia, Cyprus, Czechia, Denmark, England, Estonia, Faeroe Is, Finland, France, Georgia, Germany, Gibraltar, Greece, Hungary, Iceland, Ireland, Israel, Italy, Kazakhstan, Kosovo, Latvia, Liechtenstein, Lithuania, Luxembourg, Malta, Moldova, Montenegro, Netherlands, North Macedonia, Northern Ireland, Norway, Poland, Portugal, Romania, Russia, San Marino, Scotland, Serbia, Slovakia, Slovenia, Spain, Sweden, Switzerland, Türkiye, Ukraine, Wales. [2018/XD3347/D]

♦ Union of European Foresters (UEF) 20387

Union européenne des forestiers – Union Europäischer Forstberufsverbände

Pres c/o Bund Deutcher Forstleute, Reiterweg 12, 56290 Uhler, Germany. T. +496762408511. E-mail: h.nr@wanadoo.fr.
URL: http://www.european-foresters.eu/

History 1958, Paris (France). Founded Sep 1967, Paris (France), when first official Presidency elected and statutes were adopted. Foundations laid when foresters from Belgium, Netherlands, Luxembourg, Germany, Switzerland, Spain and France met in their first annual meeting, 1958, Brussels (Belgium), during the World Exhibition "Expo 58". The meeting was a follow-up to collaboration and close contacts between foresters from Netherlands, Belgium, Denmark and Germany since the 1850's. Subsequent meeting, 1962, Silkeborg (Denmark). Final step towards founding of the Union made by "Bund Deutscher Forstmänner, May 1965, Essen (Germany FR), during general meeting when statutes temporarily approved. EU Transparency Register: 28640971351-85. **Aims** Help reveal the essential role of forests in the balance of *nature* and protection of the *environment* and also the importance of their economic and social role; within the European framework, defend and promote the professional, ethical and material interests of associations and their members; improve the position of professional foresters within Europe. **Structure** Congress (every 4 years); Governing Council; Presidency. **Languages** English. **Staff** 7.00 FTE, voluntary. **Finance** Members' dues. **Activities** Advocacy/lobbying/activism; training/education; politics/policy/regulatory; networking/liaising; knowledge management/information dissemination. **Events** *Meeting* Cosenza (Italy) 2018, *Presidency Meeting* Brussels (Belgium) 2017, *Meeting* Nødebo (Denmark) 2016, *Meeting* Ustron (Poland) 2015, *International Workshop on Forest Pedagogy* Yundola (Bulgaria) 2015. **Publications** *Presidency Newsletter* (4 a year); *Presidency Flash Info. Union of European Foresters, 55 Years of History and Stories.*
Members Associations (25) in 21 countries:
Albania, Austria, Belgium, Bulgaria, Croatia, Cyprus, Czechia, Denmark, Finland, France, Germany, Ireland, Italy, Liechtenstein, Luxembourg, Moldova, Poland, Spain, Sweden, Switzerland, Türkiye.
IGO Relations *European Commission (EC, #06633)* – civilian dialogue and advisory groups; *European State Forest Association (EUSTAFOR, #08832)*; *FAO (#09260)*; *Intergovernmental Negotiating Committee for a Legally Binding Agreement on Forests in Europe (INC-Forests, inactive)*; *Ministerial Conference on the Protection of Forests in Europe (FOREST EUROPE, #16817)*. **NGO Relations** *Confederation of European Forest Owners (CEPF, #04525)*; *European Federation of Local Forest Communities (#07157)*; *PEFC Council (#18288)*. [2019.02.13/XD4655/v/D]

♦ Union of European Glass and Pottery Wholesalers Associations (inactive)
♦ Union of European Historic Houses Associations / see European Historic Houses Association (#07491)
♦ Union of European and International Public Services Unions / see Union Syndicale Fédérale (#20485)
♦ Union of the European Lubricants Industry (#20398)
♦ Union of European Manufacturers of Gas Meters / see Association of European Manufacturers of Gas Meters, Gas Pressure Regulators, Safety Devices and Stations (#02521)

♦ Union of European national football teams of winemakers (UENFW) 20388

Verband der europäischen Fußballnationalmannschaften der Winzer

Gen Sec c/o Hochschule Geisenheim Univ, Von-Lade-Lstr 1, 65366 Geisenheim, Germany. T. +496722502788. E-mail: generalsecretary@uenfw.com.
Pres address not obtained. T. +4915116751835. E-mail: president@uenfw.com.
URL: http://www.uenfw.com/

History 1 Jul 2018, Apace (Slovenia). Statutes adopted on foundation. Registration: Hesse District court, No/ID: VR 7216, Start date: 18 Sep 2018, Germany, Wiesbaden; EU Transparency Register, No/ID: 938672534075-19, Start date: 23 Feb 2019. **Aims** Bring together all national football teams in Europe, winegrowers and association promoted of the arts, culture and sport; raise awareness of the cultural assets of wine and football. **Structure** General Assembly; Executive Committee; Presidium. **Languages** English, German. **Staff** Voluntary. **Finance** Sources: members' dues. Annual budget: 8,000 EUR. **Activities** Events/meetings; sporting activities; training/education.
Members Full in 8 countries:
Austria, Czechia, Germany, Hungary, Italy, Portugal, Slovenia, Switzerland.
NGO Relations *International Organisation of Vine and Wine (OIV, #14435)*. [2022/XM7463/D]

♦ Union of European Neonatal and Perinatal Societies (UENPS) 20389

Secretariat Via Bonaventura Zumbini 29, 20143 Milan MI, Italy. T. +390234934404. Fax +390234934397. E-mail: secretariat@uenps.eu.
URL: https://www.uenps.eu/

History 1 Jul 2006, Vienna (Austria). Registration: No/ID: 51972, Start date: 17 Apr 2008, Italy. **Aims** Improve healthcare quality in perinatal and neonatal medicine in the European countries by integrating, coordinating and adding national and scientific society's efforts. **Structure** Executive Board; Scientific Board. **Events** *Congress* Krakow (Poland) 2022, *JENS : Congress of Joint European Neonatal Societies* 2021, *Congress* Rome (Italy) 2020, *JENS : Congress of Joint European Neonatal Societies* Maastricht (Netherlands) 2019, *Congress* Bucharest (Romania) 2018.
Members National organizations in 27 countries:
Bosnia-Herzegovina, Bulgaria, Croatia, Czechia, Estonia, Finland, France, Georgia, Greece, Hungary, Ireland, Israel, Italy, Latvia, Lithuania, Netherlands, North Macedonia, Poland, Portugal, Romania, Russia, Serbia, Slovakia, Slovenia, Spain, Türkiye, Ukraine.
NGO Relations Partner of (4): *European Board of Neonatology (EBN, #06363)*; *European Foundation for the Care of Newborn Infants (EFCNI, #07344)*; *European Milk Bank Association (EMBA, #07804)*; *Federation of Asia-Oceania Perinatal Societies (FAOPS, #09452)*. [2022/XJ1787/D]

♦ Union of European Officials / see European Public Service Union (#08303)
♦ Union of European Paedopsychiatrists / see European Society of Child and Adolescent Psychiatry (#08543)
♦ Union of European Patent Agents / see Union of European Practitioners in Intellectual Property (#20392)
♦ Union of European Patent Attorneys and other Representatives before the European Patent Office / see Union of European Practitioners in Intellectual Property (#20392)
♦ Union of European Petroleum Independents / see UPEI – The voice of Europe's independent fuel suppliers (#20726)
♦ Union of European Phoniaters / see Union of European Phoniatricians (#20390)

♦ Union of European Phoniatricians (UEP) 20390

Union des phoniatres européens (UPE) – Union der Europäischen Phoniater (UEP) – Sojuz Evropejskih Foniatorov (SEF)

Address not obtained.
URL: https://www.uep.phoniatrics.eu/

History 17 Oct 1971, Belgrade (Serbia). 17-21 Oct 1971, Belgrade (Yugoslavia). By-laws adopted 1977. Registered in accordance with Swiss law. Also referred to as *Union of European Phoniaters*. **Aims** Promote the speciality of phoniatrics, professional conditions of phoniatricians and scientific relations among members; encourage use of phoniatrics by doctors working in public health service and in private practice, for the benefit of medical care; consolidate solidarity among these medical doctors; study professional, social and ethical problems and seek their solution, in the interest of the phoniatricians and their patients; improve living and working conditions of members. **Structure** General Assembly (annual). Board, consisting of 12 members, including President, 2 Vice-Presidents, General Secretary, Vice-Secretary, General Treasurer and Vice-Treasurer. Advisory Board, composed of the initiators of the Union and all previous Presidents. **Languages** English, French, German, Russian. **Finance** Members' dues. **Events** *Congress* Prague (Czechia) 2025, *Congress* Antalya (Türkiye) 2023, *Congress* Turkey 2021, *Congress* Helsinki (Finland) 2018, *Congress* Bilbao (Spain) 2016.
Members National organizations; individual members; national liaison officers. Members in 28 countries:
Albania, Austria, Bahrain, Belarus, Belgium, China, Czechia, Denmark, Egypt, Finland, France, Germany, Italy, Lithuania, Mexico, Poland, Portugal, Romania, Russia, Saudi Arabia, Slovenia, Spain, Sweden, Switzerland, Türkiye, UK, United Arab Emirates, Uzbekistan.
IGO Relations *WHO (#20950)*. **NGO Relations** Member of: *Confederation of European Otorhinolaryngology – Head and Neck Surgery (Confederation of European ORL-HNS, #04528)*. [2016/XD7642/D]

♦ Union of European Piano Builders' Associations (Europiano) 20391

Union européenne des associations des facteurs de pianos – Union Europäischer Pianomacher-Fachverbände – Pianobygger-Fagforbundenes Europeiske Union

Sec Nonnenweg 18, 4055 Basel BS, Switzerland.
Treas Habsburgstrasse 17, 8037 Zurich ZH, Switzerland.
URL: http://www.europiano.org/

History 1966. In English also referred to as *European Association of Pianomaker Unions* and *European Union of Piano Makers Associations*. In German also referred to as *Europäische Union der Pianofachverbände*. **Aims** Provide consulting services for members; promote their professional expertise. **Events** *Piano Congress* Warsaw (Poland) 2022, *Congress* Cavalese (Italy) 2018, *Congress* Moscow (Russia) 2015, *Congress* Leusden (Netherlands) 2012, *Congress* Prague (Czech Rep) / Hradec Kralové (Czech Rep) 2009. **Publications** *Euro-Piano Magazine*.
Members National associations in 15 countries:
Austria, Czechia, Denmark, Estonia, Finland, France, Germany, Italy, Netherlands, Norway, Russia, Spain, Sweden, Switzerland, UK. [2016/XD9494/D]

♦ Union of European Practitioners in Industrial Property / see Union of European Practitioners in Intellectual Property (#20392)

♦ Union of European Practitioners in Intellectual Property (UNION) .. 20392

Union des praticiens européens en propriété intellectuelle – Union Europäischer Berater für Geistiges Eigentum

SG UNION-IP c/o CABINET BEDE, Bd Général Wahis 15, 1030 Brussels, Belgium. E-mail: mail@bede.be.
URL: https://www.union-ip.org/

History 9 Dec 1961, Brussels (Belgium). Set up on signature of an Act of Constitution by patent agents from 9 countries. Former names and other names: *Union of European Patent Agents* – former (1961 to 1975); *Union des agents en brevets européens* – former (1961 to 1975); *Union Europäischer Patentanwälte* – former (1961 to 1975); *Union of European Professional Patent Representatives* – former; *Union of European Patent Attorneys and other Representatives before the European Patent Office (UNEPA)* – former (1975 to 1979); *Union des conseils européens en brevets et autres mandataires agréés auprès de l'Office européen des brevets* – former (1975 to 1979); *Union of European Practitioners in Industrial Property* – former (1979 to 2005); *Union des praticiens européens en propriété industrielle* – former (1979 to 2005); *Union Europäischer Berater für den Gewerblichen Rechtsschutz* – former (1979 to 2005). Registration: No/ID: 0548.830.057, Start date: 24 Mar 2014, Belgium; EU Transparency Register, No/ID: 041311320851-72, Start date: 29 Feb 2016. **Aims** Study problems relating to the protection of industrial property and to the profession of members in Europe; come to conclusions on these problems and convey these conclusions to the authorities and other interested parties as recommendations or opinions or as drafts. **Structure** General Assembly (at least every 3 years); Executive Committee; Bureau; Working Commissions (10). **Languages** English, French, German. **Staff** None. **Finance** Sources: members' dues. **Activities** Events/meetings. **Events** *Congress* Berlin (Germany) 2014, *Congress* Brussels (Belgium) 2011, *Congress* Porto (Portugal) 2008, *Autumn meeting* Edinburgh (UK) 2006, *Spring meeting* Tampere (Finland) 2006. **Publications** *UNION Newsletter*.
Members National groups in 27 countries:
Austria, Belgium, Bulgaria, Czechia, Denmark, Finland, France, Germany, Greece, Hungary, Iceland, Ireland, Italy, Latvia, Liechtenstein, Luxembourg, Netherlands, Norway, Poland, Portugal, Serbia, Slovakia, Spain, Sweden, Switzerland, UK, Ukraine.
Consultative Status Consultative status granted from: *World Intellectual Property Organization (WIPO, #21593)* (Permanent Observer Status). **IGO Relations** Recognized by: *European Commission (EC, #06633)*. Observer to: *Union internationale pour la protection des obtentions végétales (UPOV, #20436)*. Cooperates with: *European Union Intellectual Property Office (EUIPO, #08996)*. [2022/XD4527/D]

♦ Union of European Professional Patent Representatives / see Union of European Practitioners in Intellectual Property (#20392)
♦ Union of European Railroad Engineers / see Union des associations européennes des ingénieurs ferroviaires (#20362)
♦ Union of European Railway Engineer Associations (#20362)

- ♦ Union of European Railways Road Services (inactive)
- ♦ Union of European Scaffolding Contractors (#20382)
- ♦ Union of European Senior Amateur Golf Associations / see European Senior Golf Association (#08464)
- ♦ Union of European Seniors Golf Associations / see European Senior Golf Association (#08464)
- ♦ Union of European Student Associations (inactive)
- ♦ Union of European Trans-Siberian Operators and Forwarders / see Gemeinschaft der Europäischen Transsibirien Operateure (#10091)
- ♦ Union of European Veterinary Hygienists (#20404)
- ♦ Unión Europea de Pequeñas y Medianas Empresas (no recent information)
- ♦ Unión Europea de Radiodifusión / see European Broadcasting Union (#06404)
- ♦ Unión Europea de Relaciones Públicas (#09011)
- ♦ Unión Europea de Relaciones Públicas – Organización Internacional de Servicios / see European Union of Public Relations (#09011)
- ♦ Unión Europea de Veterinarios Practicos (#20405)
- ♦ Union européen des entrepreneurs de plâterie, stuc et activités annexes (inactive)
- ♦ Union Européen Naturiste (inactive)
- ♦ Union européenne (#08967)
- ♦ Union européenne (inactive)

♦ Union européenne pour l'agrément technique dans la construction (UEAtc) 20393

European Union of Agrément – Europäische Union für das Agrément im Bauwesen

Secretariat c/o UBAtc, Lombardstraat 42, 1000 Brussels, Belgium.
Registered Address Lozenberg 7, 1932 Sint-Stevens-Woluwe, Belgium.
URL: http://www.ueatc.eu/

History First Statutes adopted 10 Oct 1960, Madrid (Spain). Present Statutes adopted 5 Mar 1998, London (UK). Registration: Banque-Carrefour des Entreprises, No/ID: 0849.554.407, Start date: 1 Oct 2012, Belgium. **Aims** Bring together officially recognized national institutes and organizations in Europe engaged in the issue of 'National Approvals' for construction products; ensure that, in the various countries of Europe, the equivalence of the 'National Approvals' issued by members can be established, whilst striving to facilitate export of construction products between countries. **Structure** Coordination Commission (convened by the President at least once a year); Coordination Council; General Secretariat. **Languages** English, French, German. **Staff** Voluntary. **Finance** No budget; financial sources supplied by the members institutes. **Events** *Meeting* Madrid (Spain) 2008, *Meeting* Berlin (Germany) 2007, *Meeting* Dublin (Ireland) 2007, *Meeting* Warsaw (Poland) 2006, *Meeting* Rome (Italy) 2005.

Members Institutes in 18 countries:
Belgium, Czechia, Denmark, Finland, France, Germany, Hungary, Ireland, Italy, Netherlands, Norway, Poland, Portugal, Romania, Slovakia, Spain, Sweden, UK.

NGO Relations Member of (1): *European Council for Construction Research, Development and Innovation (ECCREDI, #06813).* [2017/XD7309/**D**]

- ♦ Union européenne des alcools, eaux-de-vie et spiritueux (inactive)
- ♦ Union européenne de l'ameublement (#07370)
- ♦ Union européenne des anciens et anciennes élèves de l'enseignement catholique (#08992)
- ♦ Union européenne des arabisants et islamisants (#08976)
- ♦ Union européenne de l'artisanat et des petites et moyennes entreprises / see SMEunited (#19327)
- ♦ Union européenne des artistes (inactive)
- ♦ Union européenne des associations de délégués médicaux (inactive)
- ♦ Union européenne des associations des facteurs de pianos (#20391)
- ♦ Union européenne des associations de grossistes en céramique et verrerie (inactive)
- ♦ Union européenne des associations de journalistes scientifiques (#09017)
- ♦ Union européenne des associations nationales des distributeurs d'eau / see European Federation of National Associations of Water and Waste Water Services (#07170)
- ♦ Union européenne des associations nationales des distributeurs d'eau et de services d'assainissement / see European Federation of National Associations of Water and Waste Water Services (#07170)
- ♦ Union européenne des associations du personnel de la banque (no recent information)
- ♦ Union européenne des associations philatéliques (inactive)
- ♦ Union Européenne des Aveugles (#06350)
- ♦ Union européenne de badminton / see Badminton Europe (#03058)
- ♦ Union européenne des cadres du tourisme (inactive)
- ♦ Union européenne de la carrosserie (inactive)
- ♦ Union européenne des centrales de production et de gros des sociétés coopératives de consommation (inactive)
- ♦ Union européenne des céréales (inactive)
- ♦ Union européenne des chambres de commerce et d'industrie pour la politique des transports / see Union of European Chambers of Commerce for Transport (#20384)
- ♦ Union européenne des chambres de commerce et d'industrie – Rhin, Rhône, Danube, Alpes / see Union of European Chambers of Commerce for Transport (#20384)
- ♦ Union européenne des chambres de commerce pour la politique des transports (#20384)
- ♦ Union européenne de chaudières (inactive)
- ♦ Union européenne du commerce ambulant (no recent information)
- ♦ Union européenne du commerce du bétail et des métiers de la viande / see Union européenne du commerce du bétail et de la viande (#20394)

♦ Union européenne du commerce du bétail et de la viande (UECBV) . 20394

European Livestock and Meat Trading Union – Vieh- und Fleischhandelsunion – Unione Europea del Commercio del Bestiame e della Carne – Europese Unie van de Handel in Vee en Vlees – Europaeiske Union for Handelen med Kvaeg og Kod

SG Rue de la Loi 81-A, Bte 9, 1040 Brussels, Belgium. T. +3222304603. Fax +3222309400. E-mail: info@uecbv.eu.
Pres c/o Viangro SA, Rue de la Bienvenue 10, 1070 Brussels, Belgium. T. +3225583211. Fax +3225583200. E-mail: phb@viangro.be.
Registered Office Bourse de Commerce, 67000 Strasbourg, France.
URL: http://www.uecbv.eu/

History 1951, Strasbourg (France). Former names and other names: *European Livestock and Meat Trades Union* – alias; *Union européenne du commerce du bétail et des métiers de la viande* – alias. Registration: Start date: 2 Jul 1975, France; Banque-Carrefour des Entreprises, No/ID: 0420.669.402, Start date: 10 Jul 1980, Belgium; EU Transparency Register, No/ID: 4422649896-52, Start date: 30 Dec 2008. **Aims** Represent livestock and meat traders of European countries; facilitate and increase trade in animals on the hoof and meat; examine and study problems arising for the livestock and meat trade and propose solutions; inform traders of regulations and decisions made by European and international authorities which affect livestock and meat trading; safeguard equality of conditions for competition and defend the commercial firm. **Structure** General Assembly (annual); Board; Legal and Working Commissions. Includes *Young European Meat Committee (YEMCo).* **Languages** English, French, German. **Staff** 8.00 FTE, paid. **Finance** Members' dues. **Activities** Research/documentation. **Events** *Annual General Assembly* Dublin (Ireland) 2022, *Annual General Assembly* Poznań (Poland) 2021, *Annual General Assembly* Rotterdam (Netherlands) 2016, *Annual General Assembly* Düsseldorf (Germany) 2015, *Annual General Assembly* Barcelona (Spain) 2014. **Publications** Informative circulars (about 100 a year).

Members Federations in 28 countries:
Austria, Belgium, Bulgaria, Croatia, Cyprus, Czechia, Denmark, Finland, France, Germany, Greece, Hungary, Ireland, Italy, Japan, Luxembourg, Netherlands, Norway, Poland, Portugal, Romania, Russia, Slovenia, Spain, Sweden, Switzerland, UK, Ukraine.

International member associations (3), listed in this Yearbook:
European Association of Livestock Markets (#06109); European Natural Sausage Casings Association (ENSCA, #07854); European Ship Suppliers Organization (OCEAN, #08478).

IGO Relations Recognized by: *European Commission (EC, #06633).* **NGO Relations** Member of: *European Liaison Committee for Agricultural and Agri-Food Trades (#07687); Federation of European and International Associations Established in Belgium (FAIB, #09508); Industry4Europe (#11181).* In liaison with technical committees of: *Comité européen de normalisation (CEN, #04162).* [2020/XD0604/y/**D**]

- ♦ Union européenne du commerce de gros, d'expédition, d'importation et d'exportation en fruits et légumes (inactive)
- ♦ Union européenne du commerce de gros des oeufs, produits d'oeufs, volaille et gibier (#09021)
- ♦ Union européenne du commerce de gros des pommes de terre / see European Potato Trade Association (#08257)
- ♦ Union européenne du commerce des houblons (inactive)
- ♦ Union européenne du commerce laitier (inactive)
- ♦ Union européenne du commerce des pommes de terre / see European Potato Trade Association (#08257)
- ♦ Union européenne du commerce des produits laitiers et dérivés / see European Association of Dairy Trade (#06003)
- ♦ Union européenne des commerces des grains, graines oléagineuses, aliments du bétail et dérivés / see Committee of the Trade in Cereals, Oilseeds, Pulses, Olive Oil, Oils and Fats, Animal Feed and Agrosupply of the EU (#04289)
- ♦ Union européenne des commerces de gros en papiers, cartons et emballages / see European Paper Merchants Association (#08138)
- ♦ Union européenne des communautés israélites orthodoxes (inactive)
- ♦ Union européenne des concours de musique pour la jeunesse (#09003)
- ♦ Union européenne des concours nationaux de musique pour la jeunesse / see European Union of Music Competitions for Youth (#09003)
- ♦ Union européenne des conseillers techniques et scientifiques (inactive)
- ♦ Union européenne des consommateurs de bière (#06325)
- ♦ Union européenne des constructeurs de chaudières en acier (inactive)
- ♦ Union européenne des constructeurs de logements /Secteur privé/ / see Build Europe (#03350)
- ♦ Union européenne contre l'emploi abusif des animaux (inactive)

♦ Union Européenne Contre les Nuisances des Avions (UECNA) 20395

European Union Against Aircraft Nuisance – Europäische Vereinigung gegen die Schädlichen Auswirkungen des Luftverkehrs – Europese Vereniging tegen Geluidshinder door Vliegtuigen

Pres BP 8, 60112 Milly-sur-Thérain, France.
Registered Address Rue d'Edimbourg 26, 1050 Brussels, Belgium.
URL: https://www.uecna.eu/

History 13 Oct 1968, Mörfelden-Walldorf (Germany). Registration: Start date: 31 Mar 2012, Belgium. **Aims** Promote *noise* abatement and traffic regulation. **Structure** Board, comprising President, Secretary, Treasurer, Vice-President and 4 members. **Languages** English, French, German. **Finance** Sources: members' dues. **Events** *Meeting* Brussels (Belgium) 2009, *Meeting* Brussels (Belgium) 2008, *Meeting* Brussels (Belgium) 2007, *Meeting* Paris (France) 2006, *Meeting* Brussels (Belgium) 2005.

Members Members in 10 countries:
Austria, Belgium, France, Germany, Greece, Netherlands, Spain, Sweden, Switzerland, UK.

NGO Relations Member of (1): *European Environmental Bureau (EEB, #06996).* [2020/XD1247/**D**]

- ♦ Union européenne des coupeurs de poil pour chapellerie et filature (inactive)
- ♦ Union européenne de cyclisme (#06876)

♦ Union européenne de cyclotourisme (UECT) 20396

European Union of Cycle Tourism

Pres 12 rue Louis Bertrand, 94207 Ivry-sur-Seine, France. T. +33681111137. E-mail: info@uect.org.
URL: https://uect.org/en/

History 9 Nov 2002. Statutes adopted 27 Feb 2003. Registration: France. **Aims** Organize, develop and promote all forms of cycling tourism in Europe, and in doing so contribute to protection of landscapes, tourist sites, nature and environment; form a space for meeting, exchange and collaboration between European cycling federations and associations. **Structure** General Assembly; Board of Directors. **Languages** English, French. **Finance** Sources: members' dues. **Activities** Events/meetings.

Members Adhering organizations in 7 countries:
Belgium, Bosnia-Herzegovina, France, Netherlands, Poland, Portugal, Spain. [2022.02.17/XJ9499/**D**]

- ♦ Union européenne de défense des animaux en danger (no recent information)
- ♦ Union européenne démocrate chrétienne (inactive)
- ♦ Union européenne des écoles de musique (#05756)
- ♦ Union Européenne de l'enseignement supérieure privé (#09009)
- ♦ Union européenne des entrepreneurs du paysage (#07642)
- ♦ Union européenne des entreprises du paysage / see European Landscape Contractors Association (#07642)
- ♦ Union européenne des étudiants démocrates-chrétiens et conservateurs / see European Democrat Students (#06901)
- ♦ Union Européenne des Etudiants Juifs (#08997)
- ♦ Union européenne des experts comptables économiques et financiers (inactive)
- ♦ Union européenne des experts-comptables stagiaires (inactive)
- ♦ Union européenne des fabricants de bijouterie fantaisie (inactive)
- ♦ Union européenne des fédérations des entreprises de carrelage (#05762)
- ♦ Union européenne des fédérations nationales des négociants en matériaux de construction (#06128)
- ♦ Union européenne des fédérations du personnel communal (inactive)
- ♦ Union européenne féminine (#09022)
- ♦ Union européenne des femmes baptistes / see European Baptist Women United (#06317)
- ♦ Union européenne des femmes démocrates-chrétiennes / see EPP Women (#05516)
- ♦ Union européenne des femmes de militaires (no recent information)
- ♦ Union européenne des feuillets en polyolefin (inactive)
- ♦ Union européenne des fondeurs et fabricants de corps gras animaux (inactive)
- ♦ Union européenne des forestiers (#20387)
- ♦ Union européenne de forestiers aux conceptions de gestion proche de la nature / see PRO SILVA (#18543)
- ♦ Union européenne des géosciences (inactive)
- ♦ Union européenne des greffiers de justice / see European Union of Rechtspfleger (#09012)
- ♦ Union européenne des grossistes en matériel électrique (#08987)
- ♦ Union européenne des grossistes en produits de tabac / see European Tobacco Wholesalers Association (#08919)
- ♦ Union européenne des groupements des grossistes spécialistes en papeterie (inactive)
- ♦ Union européenne de gymnastique / see European Gymnastics (#07442)
- ♦ Union européenne de gynécologie holistique (inactive)

♦ Union européenne de l'hospitalisation privée (UEHP) 20397

European Union of Private Hospitals – Europäische Union der Privatkliniken – Unione Europea dell'Ospedalità Privata

SG Av de la Joyeuse Entrée 1, Boîte 11, 1040 Brussels, Belgium. T. +3222861237. E-mail: secretarygeneral@uehp.eu.
URL: https://www.uehp.eu/

History Set up by *European Committee for Private Hospitals (inactive),* within the framework of *International Union of Private Hospitals (UIHP, no recent information),* to extend representation from European Community countries to all the countries of Europe. Replaced CEHP, set up 13 Jul 1971, Rome (Italy). Declaration of Principles/Charter adopted 18 Jun 1993, Rome. New bylaws adopted 2004. Former names and other names: *European Union of Independent Hospitals* – former. Registration: Banque Carrefour des Entreprises, No/ID: 0875.026.211, Start date: 1 Jan 2005, Belgium; EU Transparency Register, No/ID: 281433223148-81, Start

date: 26 Aug 2016. **Aims** Defend and represent independent hospitals in Europe; generate political and economic conditions favouring independent initiative in the health field; study and create better conditions for operation and management of independent hospitals. **Structure** General Assembly; Council; Board of Directors. **Languages** English, French, German, Italian. **Staff** 1.50 FTE, paid. **Finance** Sources: members' dues. **Activities** Advocacy/lobbying/activism; events/meetings. **Events** *General Assembly* Frankfurt-Main (Germany) 2023, *General Assembly* Zurich (Switzerland) 2020, *General Assembly* Brussels (Belgium) 2018, *Healthcare Workforce Planning Summit* Berlin (Germany) 2017, *eHealth Week Session* St Julian's (Malta) 2017. **Publications** Books; conference proceedings.
Members Federations in 12 countries:
Austria, France, Germany, Greece, Hungary, Italy, Monaco, Poland, Portugal, Romania, Spain, Switzerland.
NGO Relations Member of (2): *EU Health Coalition*; *Health First Europe (HFE, #10881)*. Associate Expert Group of *Business and Industry Advisory Committee to the OECD (BIAC, #03385)*. [2023/XD2172/t/D]

♦ Union européenne d'hygiène et de médecine scolaires et universitaires (#09016)
♦ Union européenne des indépendants en lubrifiants / see Union Européenne de l'Industrie des Lubrifiants (#20398)
♦ Union européenne de l'industrie du gaz naturel / see Eurogas (#05682)

♦ Union Européenne de l'Industrie des Lubrifiants (UEIL) 20398

Union of the European Lubricants Industry
Main Office Ave des Arts 46, 1000 Brussels, Belgium. T. +3225049003. E-mail: secretariat@ueil.org.
URL: http://www.ueil.org/
History 6 Jun 1963, Paris (France). Until 2005, based in Paris (France); currently based in Brussels (Belgium). Former names and other names: *European Union of Independent Lubricant Companies* – former; *Union européenne des indépendants en lubrifiants (UEIL)* – former; *Unión Europea de Independientes en Lubricantes* – former; *Europäische Union der Unabhängigen Schmierstoffverbände* – former; *Unione Europea degli Indipendenti Lubricanti* – former; *Europese Unie van de Onafhankelijken in Smeerstoffen* – former; *Union indépendante de l'industrie européenne des lubrifiants* – former; *Independent Union of the European Lubricant Industry* – former. **Aims** Represent the interests of companies involved in the lubricants industry; facilitate resolution of EU regulatory, investment, political and competitiveness issues that impact members and play a role in creating better understanding of EU matters with members. **Structure** General Assembly; Board of Directors; Secretariat. Committees (3). Also includes: *GEIR (#10088)*. **Languages** English, French, Italian, Spanish. **Staff** 6.00 FTE, paid. **Finance** Members' dues. **Activities** Monitoring/evaluation; politics/policy/regulatory. **Events** *Congress* Athens (Greece) 2020, *Congress* Cannes (France) 2019, *Congress* Budapest (Hungary) 2018, *Congress* Bologna (Italy) 2017, *Congress* Berlin (Germany) 2016. **Publications** *LUBE Magazine*; *UEIL Quarterly* – online. Position papers.
Members National organizations in 16 countries:
Belgium, Bulgaria, Finland, France, Germany, Greece, Ireland, Italy, Netherlands, Poland, Portugal, Spain, Sweden, Switzerland, Türkiye, UK.
IGO Relations Recognized by: *European Commission (EC, #06633)*. [2021/XD0893/t/D]

♦ Union européenne des industries de transformation de la pomme de terre / see EUPPA – European Potato Processors' Association (#05592)

♦ Union européenne de judo (UEJ) 20399

European Judo Union (EJU) – Unión Europea de Judo – Europäische Judo-Union
Gen Sec Wehlistrasse 29/1/111, 1200 Vienna, Austria.
Presidential Offie Kolokolnikov per 7, bloc 1, Moscow MOSKVA, Russia, 107045. T. +74957373236. Fax +74957373213. E-mail: president@eju.net.
URL: http://www.eju.net/
History 29 Oct 1949, Bloemendaal (Netherlands). Has been referred to as *European Judo Federation*. **Aims** Unite all the European Judoka and promote cordial and friendly relations between Member National Federations and supervise judo activity throughout Europe. **Structure** Congress; Directing Committee; Executive Committee. **Languages** English, French, German, Russian. **Staff** 6.00 FTE, paid. **Finance** Members' dues. Other sources: sponsors; entry fees. **Activities** Sporting activities. **Events** *Congress* Rio de Janeiro (Brazil) 2013, *Congress* Budapest (Hungary) 2012, *Congress* Paris (France) 2011, *Congress* Bucharest (Romania) 2006, *Congress* Moscow (Russia) 2005.
Members National federations in 51 countries and territories:
Albania, Andorra, Armenia, Austria, Azerbaijan, Belarus, Belgium, Bosnia-Herzegovina, Bulgaria, Croatia, Cyprus, Czechia, Denmark, Estonia, Faeroe Is, Finland, France, Georgia, Germany, Greece, Hungary, Iceland, Ireland, Israel, Italy, Kosovo, Latvia, Liechtenstein, Lithuania, Luxembourg, Malta, Moldova, Monaco, Montenegro, Netherlands, North Macedonia, Norway, Poland, Portugal, Romania, Russia, San Marino, Serbia, Slovakia, Slovenia, Spain, Sweden, Switzerland, Türkiye, UK, Ukraine.
NGO Relations Continental Union of: *International Judo Federation (IJF, #13975)*. [2020/XD5424/D]

♦ Union européenne de la literie (inactive)
♦ Union européenne des magistrats statuant en matière commerciale (#08998)
♦ Union européenne des mandataires, des entreprises et professions libérales (no recent information)
♦ Union européenne des marchands en combustibles (inactive)
♦ Union européenne de médecine d'assurance et de sécurité sociale (#08995)
♦ Union européenne de médecine sociale (no recent information)
♦ Union européenne des médecins dentaires (inactive)
♦ Union européenne des médecins omnipraticiens / see European Union of General Practitioners / Family Physicians (#08993)
♦ Union européenne des médecins omnipraticiens / médecins de famille (#08993)
♦ Union Européenne des Médecins Spécialistes (#09001)
♦ Union Européenne – Mercosur (inactive)
♦ Union européenne du métal (#07785)
♦ Union européenne des miroitiers vitriers (#07394)

♦ Union européenne des modélistes ferroviaires et des amis des chemins de fer 20400

European Union of Railway Modellers and Friends of the Railway – Verband der Modelleisenbahner und Eisenbahnfreunde Europas (MOROP)
Pres Akazienstr 14, 86899 Landsberg am Lech, Germany. E-mail: presi-praesi@morop.eu.
URL: http://www.morop.eu/
History 1954, Genoa (Italy). Registration: Swiss Civil Code, Switzerland. **Aims** Create technical standards for model *trains*; promote railway in general. **Structure** Executive Committee; Head office in Bern (Switzerland). **Languages** English, French, German. **Staff** Voluntary. **Finance** Sources: members' dues. **Events** *Congress* Budapest (Hungary) 2022, *Congress* Budapest (Hungary) 2021, *Congress* Koblenz (Germany) 2020, *Congress* Biel (Switzerland) 2019, *Electric traction on three gauges* Vienna (Austria) 2018. **Publications** *MOROP-Inform* in French, German – electronic, only as necessary.
Members Associations (22), totalling some 1,000 clubs with some 53,000 individual members, in 16 countries:
Austria, Belgium, Czechia, Denmark, France, Germany, Hungary, Italy, Luxembourg, Netherlands, Norway, Poland, Portugal, Slovakia, Spain, Switzerland.
NGO Relations Also links with national associations. [2022.05.11/XD2638/D]

♦ Union européenne de motocyclisme / see FIM Europe (#09760)
♦ Union européenne des musiciens (inactive)
♦ Union européenne de la navigation fluviale (#06318)
♦ Union européenne des négociants en cuirs et peaux bruts (no recent information)
♦ Union européenne des non-fumeurs (#09006)
♦ Union européenne des ophthalmologues (inactive)
♦ Union européenne des organisateurs de musique nouvelle (#06736)
♦ Union européenne de paiements (inactive)
♦ Union européenne des parachutistes (#09008)
♦ Union européenne de pédopsychiatres / see European Society of Child and Adolescent Psychiatry (#08543)
♦ Union européenne des petites et moyennes entreprises (no recent information)

♦ Union européenne des Pharmacies sociales (UEPS) 20401

European Union of the Social Pharmacies (EUSP) – Verband der Europäischen Sozialen Apoteken (VESA) – Unione Europea delle Farmacie Sociali (UEFS) – União Europeia das Farmacias Sociais – Europese Unie van de Sociale Apoteken (EUSA)
SG Square Marie Curie 30, 1070 Brussels, Belgium. T. +3225299241. Fax +3225299376. E-mail: ophaco@ophaco.org.
URL: http://www.eurosocialpharma.org/
History 7 Nov 1961, Brussels (Belgium). Former names and other names: *European Union of Social, Mutual and Cooperative Pharmacies* – former; *Union européenne des pharmacies sociales, mutuellistes et coopératives* – former; *Verband der Europäischen Sozialen und Genossenschaftlichen Apoteken* – former; *Unione Europea delle Farmacie Sociali, Mutualiste e Cooperativiste* – former; *EUSMCP* – alias. **Aims** Promote development of cooperative and social pharmacies in EU countries where these exist and their creation where they do not yet exist; defend interests of affiliates against corporatism both in pharmacy – dispensing and distribution – and prostheses – optics, audiometry, surgical dressings; establish links with organizations involved in sickness and disablement insurance; promote health education; establish and promote exchange of information among members; promote quality, efficiency, safety, accessibility of medicines for patients. **Structure** General Meeting; Management Committee. **Languages** Dutch, English, French, German, Italian, Portuguese. **Staff** 5.00 FTE, paid. **Finance** Sources: members' dues. Annual budget: 81,500 EUR. **Activities** European Sanitary Campaign. **Events** *Annual General Assembly* Nice (France) 2011, *Annual General Assembly* Geneva (Switzerland) 2010, *Annual General Assembly* Ghent (Belgium) 2009, *Annual General Assembly* Verona (Italy) 2007, *Annual General Assembly* Porto (Portugal) 2006.
Members Organizations in 4 countries:
Belgium, France, Italy, Switzerland.
IGO Relations *European Economic and Social Committee (EESC, #06963)*. Recognized by: *European Commission (EC, #06633)*. **NGO Relations** Links, through Belgian national organization, with: *International Co-operative Alliance (ICA, #12944)*. Member of: *Cooperatives Europe (#04801)*. [2020/XD0901/D]

♦ Union européenne des pharmacies sociales, mutuellistes et coopératives / see Union européenne des Pharmacies sociales (#20401)
♦ Union européenne des photos de presse (inactive)
♦ Union européenne des pompes funèbres (inactive)
♦ Union européenne de la presse sportive (#08822)
♦ Union européenne des producteurs de granulats (#00558)
♦ Union européenne des promoteurs-constructeurs / see Build Europe (#03350)

♦ Union européenne pour la promotion des formations techniques dans les métiers de l'hôtellerie (UNATECH) 20402

Treas 33 rue Paul Armandot, 89000 Auxerre, France. E-mail: contact@promatel.info.
Pres address not obtained.
URL: http://www.unatech.eu/
History 25 Feb 1978. Initially founded as a French national organization. Registration: France. **Aims** Promote training and bring together alumni of educational institutions in the *hotel* trade; award a plaque to inform consumers of the professionalism of the welcome which is extended as a result of such training. **Languages** French. **Staff** Voluntary. **Finance** Members' dues. **Activities** Awards *'EUROPROMOTEL'* plaque to graduates of schools in the culinary tradition; provides employment exchange. Instrumental in setting up *Groupement pour l'emploi des diplômés de l'enseignement hôtelier (GEDEH, inactive)*. **Events** *Annual meeting* Paris (France) 1996, *Annual meeting* Paris (France) 1995, *Annual meeting* Paris (France) 1994, *Annual meeting* Paris (France) 1992. **Publications** Guide to training and specialized education in the countries of the European Community and the European Free Trade Area.
Members Individuals in 21 countries:
Australia, Austria, Belgium, Brazil, Canada, Denmark, Finland, France, Germany, Greece, Italy, Luxembourg, Mexico, Monaco, Morocco, Portugal, Spain, Sweden, Switzerland, Tunisia, USA. [2021/XD2167/v/D]

♦ Union européenne pour la protection des animaux (inactive)
♦ Union européenne de radiodiffusion / see European Broadcasting Union (#06404)
♦ Union européenne de radio-télévision (#06404)
♦ Union européenne des rechtspfleger (#09012)
♦ Union européenne de relations publiques (#09011)
♦ Union européenne de relations publiques – Organisation internationale de services / see European Union of Public Relations (#09011)
♦ Union européenne des seniors (#08466)
♦ Union européenne du spectacle cinématographique (inactive)
♦ Union Européenne Sport pour Tous (#08819)

♦ Union Européenne de Systémique (UES) 20403

European Union for Systemics (EUS)
Gen Sec Rue Wafelaerts 47/51, 1060 Brussels, Belgium.
Pres address not obtained.
URL: https://www.ues-eus.org
History 1988. Former names and other names: *Systems Science European Union* – former. **Aims** Provide an environment to progress in theoretical foundations, methodology and applications of systems science, thus favouring cross-fertilization in transdisciplinary fields; enable scientists, engineers, managers, teachers, public administrators, therapists and decision-makers to adapt to change and handle creative processes more effectively. **Structure** Board. **Languages** English, French. **Staff** Voluntary. **Finance** Support from associative partners. **Activities** Events/meetings; publishing activities; training/education. **Events** *Triennial Congress* Athens (Greece) 2021, *Triennial Congress* Brussels (Belgium) 2018, *Triennial Congress* Valencia (Spain) 2014, *European Systemic Seminar* Charleroi (Belgium) 2013, *Triennial Congress* Brussels (Belgium) 2011. **Publications** *Acta Systemica Europeana* (annual) in English, French. Congress papers; books.
Members National societies in 6 countries and territories:
Belgium, England, France, Greece, Italy, Spain.
IGO Relations Activities sponsored by: *European Commission (EC, #06633)*; *UNESCO (#20322)*. [2022.02.15/XD3348/D]

♦ Union européenne des techniciens du film et de la télévision (inactive)
♦ Union européenne pour la technopédie, l'orthopédie et la réadaptation (inactive)
♦ Union européenne de tennis de table (#08873)
♦ Union européenne des transporteurs routiers / see European Road Hauliers Association (#08393)
♦ Union européenne des travailleurs aveugles (inactive)
♦ Union européenne des travailleurs démocrates-chrétiens (#08981)
♦ Union européenne des travailleurs du film et de la télévision (inactive)
♦ Union européenne de triathlon (#08948)
♦ Union européenne du trot (#08952)
♦ Union européenne des végétariens (#09048)
♦ Union européenne des vélodromes d'hiver / see Union internationale des vélodromes (#20440)
♦ Union européenne des vétérinaires d'abattoirs (inactive)
♦ Union européenne des vétérinaires fonctionnaires (#06221)

♦ Union européenne des vétérinaires hygiénistes (UEVH) 20404

Union of European Veterinary Hygienists (UEVH)
Contact c/o Federation of Veterinarians of Europe, Avenue de Tervueren 12, 1040 Brussels, Belgium. T. +3225337024. E-mail: info@fve.org.
SG address not obtained.
URL: https://uevh.fve.org/
History Oct 1966, Paris (France). Constituted definitively 1 Jul 1967, Geneva (Switzerland). Modification of name and Statutes, 1976, so as to be qualified to adhere to *Federation of Veterinarians of Europe (#09713)*, of which it is currently a Section. Current Statutes adopted 21 Oct 1977, Verona (Italy); amended: 13 Nov 1991, Brussels (Belgium); 5 Apr 1995, Seville (Spain). Former names and other names: *Association européenne des directeurs d'abattoirs publics* – former (1 Jul 1967 to 1976); *European Union of Veterinary Hygienists* – former.

Aims Study and recommend any measures permitting the improvement of the quality and safety of foodstuffs so as to protect veterinary public health and improvement of conditions for humans, by using veterinary science; promote the role of the veterinarian in the whole of the food chains, from stable to table. **Structure** General Assembly (2 a year). Board, comprising President, Vice-President, Secretary General, Treasurer and Senior President. **Languages** English. **Finance** Sources: members' dues. Annual budget: 17,000 EUR. **Activities** Events/meetings; healthcare; monitoring/evaluation; training/education. Current concerns include, among others: implementation and review of the "Hygiene Package"; veterinary education in food hygiene and public health; meat inspection. **Events** *Meeting* Brussels (Belgium) 2006, *Meeting* Malaga (Spain) 2006, *Meeting* Berlin (Germany) 2000, *Meeting* Brussels (Belgium) 2000, *Joint meeting* Brussels (Belgium) 1999.
Members Organizations in 20 countries:
Austria, Belgium, Czechia, Denmark, Finland, France, Germany, Greece, Ireland, Italy, Latvia, Luxembourg, Netherlands, Norway, Poland, Portugal, Spain, Sweden, Switzerland, UK.
Observers in 1 country:
Argentina.
Observer organization:
World Association of Veterinary Food Hygienists (WAVFH, #21204).
NGO Relations Instrumental in setting up (1): *European College for Veterinary Public Health (ECVPH, #06629).* [2022/XD9231/**D**]

♦ Union européenne des vétérinaires praticiens (UEVP) 20405

European Union of Veterinary Practitioners – Unión Europea de Veterinarios Practicos – Europäische Union Praktischer Tierärzte

Office Manager c/o FVE, Rue Victor Oudart 7, 1030 Brussels, Belgium. T. +3225337020.
URL: http://uevp.fve.org/

History 2 Oct 1970, Garmisch-Partenkirchen (Germany). Founded at 1st European Congress of Practising Veterinarians, on adoption of Constitution drawn up by Provisional Committee, set up 1968, St Malo (France). Former names and other names: *European Union of Practising Veterinary Surgeons* – alias. Registration: Banque-Carrefour des Entreprises, Belgium; EU Transparency Register, No/ID: 37687314978-15. **Aims** Represent veterinary practitioners at international level; coordinate the work of European veterinary practitioners in the fields of practice, public health, animal welfare, relations with farmers, consumers and the European courts. **Structure** General Assembly (twice a year); Administrative Council; Board; Working Groups. **Languages** English, French, German. **Staff** 1.00 FTE, paid. **Finance** Sources: members' dues. **Activities** Advocacy/lobbying/activism. **Events** *General Assembly* London (UK) 2022, *General Assembly* Brussels (Belgium) 2021, *General Assembly* Brussels (Belgium) 2021, *General Assembly* Brussels (Belgium) 2020, *General Assembly* Brussels (Belgium) 2020. **Publications** *UEVP Newsletter* (12 a year).
Members Veterinary associations in 26 countries:
Austria, Belgium, Croatia, Cyprus, Czechia, Denmark, Estonia, Finland, France, Germany, Greece, Hungary, Ireland, Italy, Latvia, Luxembourg, Netherlands, Norway, Poland, Romania, Serbia, Slovakia, Slovenia, Spain, Switzerland, UK.
Observers in 4 countries:
Albania, North Macedonia, Portugal, Sweden.
Included in the above, 4 organizations listed in this Yearbook:
European Association of Porcine Health Management (EAPHM, #06159); European Association of Zoo and Wildlife Veterinarians (EAZWV, #06284); Federation of European Companion Animal Veterinary Associations (FECAVA, #09497); Federation of European Equine Veterinary Associations (FEEVA, #09503).
IGO Relations Recognized by: *European Commission (EC, #06633).* **NGO Relations** Member of: *Federation of Veterinarians of Europe (#09713).* In liaison with technical committees of: *International Organization for Standardization (ISO, #14473).* [2022.05.10/XD0897/**D**]

- ♦ Union européenne de yoga (#09131)
- ♦ Union européenne de yoseikan budo et disciplines assimilées (inactive)
- ♦ Union de l'Europe occidentale (inactive)
- ♦ Union of EU Soft Drinks Associations / see UNESDA Soft Drinks Europe (#20323)
- ♦ Union évangélique mondiale / see World Evangelical Alliance (#21393)
- ♦ Unione Vegetariana Internazionale (#15842)
- ♦ Unione Volontariato Internazionale per lo Sviluppo e La Pace (internationally oriented national body)
- ♦ Unión de Fabricantes de Harinas y Aceites de Pescado de la Comunidad Europea / see European Fismeal and Fish Oil Producers (#07268)
- ♦ Union des fabricants européens de compteurs de gaz / see Association of European Manufacturers of Gas Meters, Gas Pressure Regulators, Safety Devices and Stations (#02521)
- ♦ Union des fabricants de farine et huile de poisson de la Communauté européenne / see European Fismeal and Fish Oil Producers (#07268)

♦ Union des féculeries de pommes de terre de l'Union européenne (UFE) 20406

Union of Potato Starch Factories of the European Union – Union der Kartoffelstärkefabriken der Europäischen Union – Unie van Aardappelzetmeelindustrieen binnen de Europese Unie

Address not obtained.

History 14 Jan 1960, Brussels (Belgium), as *Union of Professional Groups of the Potato-Starch Industry of the EEC – Union des groupements professionnels de l'industrie de la féculerie de pommes de terre de la CEE (UFE) – Zentralverband der Berufsverbände der Kartoffelstärkeindustrie der EWG – Unie van Beroepsgroeperingen van de Aardappelmeelindustrie in de EEG.*
Members Producing companies in 10 countries:
Austria, Czechia, Denmark, Finland, France, Germany, Latvia, Netherlands, Poland, Sweden.
IGO Relations Recognized by *European Commission (EC, #06633).* **NGO Relations** In liaison with technical committees of: *International Organization for Standardization (ISO, #14473).* [2010/XE3362/t/**E**]

- ♦ Union de Federaciones de las Asociaciones de Agencias de Viajes (#20509)
- ♦ Unión de Federaciones Europeas de Fútbol (#20386)
- ♦ Unión de Federalistas Europeos / see Union of European Federalists, The (#20385)
- ♦ Union fédéraliste des communautés ethniques européennes (#09396)
- ♦ Union fédéraliste des communautés et régions européennes / see Federal Union of European Nationalities (#09396)
- ♦ Union fédéraliste inter-universitaire (inactive)
- ♦ Union des fédéralistes européens / see Union of European Federalists, The (#20385)
- ♦ Union des fédérations africaines de karaté (see: #21608)
- ♦ Union des fédérations des associations d'agences de voyages (#20509)
- ♦ Union des fédérations chorales européennes (inactive)
- ♦ Union des fédérations d'étudiants d'universités catholiques latinoaméricaines (inactive)
- ♦ Union of Federations of Latin American Catholic University Students (inactive)
- ♦ Union des fédérations nationales du cinéma non professionnel / see Union internationale du cinéma (#20423)
- ♦ Union des fédérations nationales des négociants en matériaux de construction de la CEE / see European Association of National Builders' Merchants Associations (#06128)
- ♦ Union Femenil Bautista de America Latina (#16255)
- ♦ Union féminine artistique internationale (inactive)
- ♦ Union des femmes des Amériques (inactive)
- ♦ Union des femmes baptistes d'Afrique (#03174)
- ♦ Union des femmes baptistes d'Amérique latine (#16255)
- ♦ Union des femmes rurales ouest-africaines et du Tchad (internationally oriented national body)
- ♦ Unión de Ferias Iberoamericanas (meeting series)
- ♦ Union des Filles de Dieu (religious order)

♦ Union of Finance Personnel in Europe 20407

Union du personnel des finances en Europe – Union des Finanzpersonals in Europa (UFE) – Unione del Personale Finanziero in Europa – Unie van het Financiënpersoneel in Europa – Unionen af Finanstjenestemaend i Europa

Gen Sec Friedrichstrasse 169/170, 10117 Berlin, Germany. T. +4930206256600. Fax +4930206256601. E-mail: post@ufe-online.eu.
Pres 80-82 rue de Montreuil, Boite 29, 75011 Paris, France. T. +33144646407. Fax +33143489616.
URL: http://www.finanzpersonal-europa.de/

History 22 May 1963. Statutes adopted 12 Nov 1963, Luxembourg; amended 26 Sep 1976, Luxembourg. **Aims** Unite finance *trade unions* in Europe; join their national societies in full acknowledgement of their legal and economic independence; make their work fruitful through permanent exchange of opinions and experience and through mutual support; represent joint interests of all European finance administration personnel, in particular with the cosmopolitical European institutions, with governments and parliaments of each state and with top trade union organizations. **Structure** Committee of Presidents of member societies (meets biennially); Praesidium, comprising President and 5 Vice-Presidents (of whom 2 come from tax and 2 from customs administrations). **Languages** English, French, German, Italian. **Staff** 6.00 FTE, paid. **Finance** Members' dues. **Events** *Session* Brussels (Belgium) 2007, *Session* Luxembourg (Luxembourg) 2007, *Meeting* Helsinki (Finland) 1999, *Meeting* Slagharen (Netherlands) 1989.
Members National finance trade unions (whose members become indirect individual members of UFE), national societies gathering public tax officers and/or public customs officers, in 20 countries:
Austria, Belgium, Czechia, Denmark, Finland, France, Germany, Greece, Hungary, Iceland, Ireland, Italy, Luxembourg, Netherlands, Norway, Portugal, Spain, Sweden, Switzerland, UK.
IGO Relations Recognized by: *European Commission (EC, #06633).* [2021/XD1274/**D**]

- ♦ Union des Finanzpersonals in Europa (#20407)
- ♦ Union of Fishmeal and Fishoil Manufacturers in the European Community / see European Fismeal and Fish Oil Producers (#07268)

♦ UNION FLEURS 20408

SG Av Arnaud Fraiteur 15-23, Box A91, 1050 Brussels, Belgium. T. +32498595938. E-mail: secgen@unionfleurs.org – info@unionfleurs.org.
URL: http://www.unionfleurs.org/

History 19 Sep 1959, Brussels (Belgium), as *Union internationale du commerce de gros en fleurs (Union fleurs) – International Union of Flower Wholesale Trade – Internationaler Verband des Blumengrosshandels – Unione Internazionale del Commercio all'Ingrosso dei Fiori – Internationaal Verbond van de Groothandel in Bloemkwekerijprodukten – Internationale Union for Engros-Handelen med Blomster.* Also known as *International Flower Trade Association.* EU Transparency Register: 14864192565-82. Registration: Banque-Carrefour des Entreprises, No/ID: 835.017.273, Start date: 2011, Belgium. **Aims** Represent and promote the interests of traders, wholesalers and distributors of cut flowers, cut foliage and pot plants. **Structure** General Assembly; Board of Directors; Committees; ad hoc Working Groups. **Languages** English. **Staff** 1.00 FTE, paid. **Finance** Sources: members' dues. **Activities** Advocacy/lobbying/activism; events/meetings; knowledge management/information dissemination. **Events** *General Assembly of Delegates* Brussels (Belgium) / Ghent (Belgium) 2020, *General Assembly of Delegates* Brussels (Belgium) 2019, *General Assembly of Delegates* San Remo (Italy) 2018, *General Assembly of Delegates* Warsaw (Poland) 2017, *Autumn Meeting* Haarlem (Netherlands) 2016. **Publications** *Key Notes* – newsletter.
Members Full; Associate; Affiliate. Full in 14 countries:
Austria, Colombia, Denmark, Ethiopia, Germany, Israel, Italy, Kenya, Morocco, Netherlands, Sweden, Türkiye, Uganda, USA.
Affiliate in 6 countries:
Belgium, France, Germany, Japan, Netherlands, South Africa.
IGO Relations Consultative status with: *European Commission (EC, #06633).* **NGO Relations** Member of (1): FSI – Floriculture Sustainability Initiative. [2021.06.08/XD1283/**D**]

- ♦ Union du fleuve Mano (#16566)
- ♦ Union des foires internationales / see UFI – The Global Association of the Exhibition Industry (#20276)
- ♦ Union foraine européenne (#08483)
- ♦ Union of Foresters of Southern Europe (#20478)
- ♦ Unión Franco-Ibérica para la Coordinación de la Producción y del Transporte de la Electricidad (inactive)
- ♦ Union franco-ibérique pour la coordination de la production et du transport d'électricité (inactive)

♦ Union francophone de l'audit interne (UFAI) 20409

SG c/o Institut Français de l'Audit et du Contrôle Internes (IFACI), 98 bis boulevard Haussmann, 75008 Paris, France. T. +33140084800. Fax +33140084820. E-mail: webmaster@ifaci.com.
Pres Institut des auditeurs internes – Section Montréal, 900 rue Cherrier, Montréal QC H2L 1H7, Canada. E-mail: info@ivim.com.
URL: http://www.ufai.org/

History 1987. **Languages** French. **Events** *Conference / Conferences* Dakar (Senegal) 2014, *Conference* Hammamet (Tunisia) 2012, *Conferences* Bamako (Mali) 2006, *Conference / Conferences* Yaoundé (Cameroon) 2005, *Conference / Conferences* Québec, QC (Canada) 2002.
Members Institutes in 17 countries:
Belgium, Burkina Faso, Cameroon, Canada, Congo DR, Côte d'Ivoire, France, Guinea, Haiti, Lebanon, Luxembourg, Madagascar, Mali, Morocco, Senegal, Switzerland, Tunisia.
Associated institute in 1 country:
Algeria.
Observer institute in 3 countries:
Benin, Mauritania, Niger.
NGO Relations Associated with: *Institute of Internal Auditors (IIA, #11272).* [2015/XM1343/**D**]

♦ Union Francophone des Aveugles (UFA) 20410

SG c/o Chez GIAA, 5 av Daniel Lesueur, 75007 Paris, France. T. +33147349537 – +33123733451251 – +33114388718355.
Pres address not obtained.
URL: https://unionfrancophone-aveugles.org/

History Jun 2001, Casablanca (Morocco). Registration: France. **Aims** Promote cooperation with developing francophone countries by supplying schools with books, teaching aids and scholarships for visually disabled children; encourage international cooperation between editors of French Braille publications, spoken books and numerical works; promote French Braille standardization; facilitate integration of visually disabled children into mainstream classrooms; help set up regional Braille printing units and libraries and ensure coordination of francophone libraries and media libraries. **Structure** Executive Committee. **Languages** French. **Staff** 2.00 FTE, voluntary. **Finance** Sources: donations. Annual budget: 91,500 EUR (2012). **Activities** Advocacy/lobbying/activism; financial and/or material support; training/education. **Publications** *Introduction to Union Francophone des Aveugles* – leaflet.
Members National organizations (47) in 26 countries:
Belgium, Benin, Burkina Faso, Burundi, Cameroon, Canada, Central African Rep, Chad, Congo Brazzaville, Congo DR, Côte d'Ivoire, France, Gabon, Guinea, Haiti, Madagascar, Mali, Mauritania, Mauritius, Morocco, Niger, Romania, Senegal, Switzerland, Togo, Tunisia.
Regional organizations (2):
African Union of the Blind (AFUB, #00489); European Blind Union (EBU, #06350).
NGO Relations Member of (1): *World Blind Union (WBU, #21234).* Links with national organizations. [2022/XD8743/y/**D**]

- ♦ Union of French-Language Publishers (no recent information)
- ♦ Union de Fribourg, 1885 (inactive)
- ♦ Union of the Gas Industries of the Common Market Countries / see MARCOGAZ – Technical Association of the European Natural Gas Industry (#16572)
- ♦ Unión General de Correos / see Universal Postal Union (#20682)
- ♦ Union générale arabe d'assurance (#10104)
- ♦ Union générale des artistes arabes (inactive)
- ♦ Union générale des chambres de commerce, d'industrie et d'agriculture des pays arabes / see Union of Arab Chambers (#20350)
- ♦ Union générale des éditeurs arabes (no recent information)
- ♦ Union générale des étudiants de l'Afrique de l'Ouest (inactive)

- ♦ Union générale des étudiants arabes (no recent information)
- ♦ Union générale des paysans et des coopératives arabes (no recent information)
- ♦ Union générale des postes / see Universal Postal Union (#20682)
- ♦ Union générale des travailleurs d'Afrique noire (inactive)
- ♦ Union der Genossenschaftlichen Einkaufsorganisationen Europas / see Independent Retail Europe (#11154)
- ♦ Union der Genossenschaftlichen Einkaufsorganisationen für Lebensmittel / see Independent Retail Europe (#11154)
- ♦ Union géodésique et géophysique internationale (#15776)
- ♦ Unión Geografica Internacional (#13713)
- ♦ Union géographique internationale (#13713)
- ♦ Union graphique nordique (no recent information)
- ♦ Union des groupements d'achat de l'alimentation / see Independent Retail Europe (#11154)
- ♦ Union des Groupements d'Achat coopératifs de Détaillants de l'Europe / see Independent Retail Europe (#11154)
- ♦ Union des groupements de commerçants détaillants indépendants de l'Europe / see Independent Retail Europe (#11154)
- ♦ Union des groupements de détaillants indépendants de l'Europe / see Independent Retail Europe (#11154)
- ♦ Union des groupements de prévoyance des fonctionnaires européens / see AFILIATYS (#00151)
- ♦ Union des groupements professionnels de l'industrie de la féculerie de pommes de terre de la CEE / see Union des féculeries de pommes de terre de l'Union européenne (#20406)
- ♦ Union of Groups of Independent Retailers of Europe / see Independent Retail Europe (#11154)
- ♦ Union der Handelskammern des Rheingebietes / see Union of European Chambers of Commerce for Transport (#20384)
- ♦ Union hébraïque mondiale (no recent information)
- ♦ Union pour l'héritage anglais (#05482)
- ♦ Union des historiens arabes (no recent information)
- ♦ Union hydroélectrique africaine (inactive)
- ♦ Union ibéroaméricaine des parents (#11035)

♦ Unión Iberoamericana de Colegios y Agrupaciones de Abogados (UIBA) 20411

União-Ibero-americana dos Colégios e Ordens dos Advogados (UIBA) – Ibero-American Lawyers' Union

Pres C/ 48 no 971, Piso 1, 1900 La Plata, Argentina.
URL: http://uiba.org/

History Nov 1976, Madrid (Spain). **Aims** Promote and ensure the following of dignity, independence and freedom in the *legal profession* as essential values for the realization of *justice*; protect the interests of lawyers and students of *law*; promote cooperation among members and the development of legal science. **Structure** Congress of Representatives (every 2 years); Council of Delegates (meets every year); Presidency; Permanent Secretariat. National Secretariats. Working Commissions. Permanent Commission on Freedom of Defence. **Languages** Spanish. **Staff** Part-time, paid and voluntary. **Finance** Members' dues. **Events** *Congress* San José (Costa Rica) 2008, *Meeting on legally strengthening the Latin American and Caribbean coalition of cities against racism and discrimination* Santo Domingo (Dominican Rep) 2007, *Congress* Panama (Panama) 2006, *Congress* Rio Grande (Puerto Rico) 2004, *Congress* Lima (Peru) 2002. **Publications** *Union Iberoamerican de Colegios y Agrupaciones de Abogados* (every 2 years).
Members Colleges of law, associations and other groupings of lawyers in 22 countries:
Argentina, Bolivia, Brazil, Chile, Colombia, Costa Rica, Cuba, Dominican Rep, Ecuador, El Salvador, Guatemala, Honduras, Mexico, Nicaragua, Panama, Paraguay, Peru, Portugal, Puerto Rico, Spain, Uruguay, Venezuela.
IGO Relations Accredited by: *United Nations Office at Vienna (UNOV, #20604)*. Associated with Department of Global Communications of the United Nations. [2021/XD0343/**D**]

- ♦ Unión Iberoamericana de Municipalistas (#11034)
- ♦ Unión Iberoamericana de Padres de Familia y Padres de Alumnos (#11035)
- ♦ Unión Iberoamericana de Sociedades de Fisica / see Federación Iberoamericana de Sociedades de Fisica (#09321)

♦ Union of Ibero-American Capital Cities 20412

Union des capitales ibéroaméricaines – Unión de Ciudades Capitales Iberoamericanas (UCCI) – União de Cidades Capitais Ibero-Americanas (UCCI)

Gen Dir Calle Montalban 1 – 2a planta, 28014 Madrid, Spain. T. +34915889693. E-mail: ucci@madrid.es.
Gen Sec address not obtained.
URL: https://ciudadesiberoamericanas.org/

History 12 Oct 1982, Madrid (Spain). Founded during 2 consecutive meetings in Cadiz (Spain) and Madrid (Spain), where 21 mayors of the Ibero-American capitals signed the twinning between all of them. **Aims** Encourage links, relations and exchange among member cities; study issues affecting lives and activities of associated municipalities; promote rights of neighbourhood, peaceful coexistence and citizen participation in public affairs; promote balanced and harmonious development of Ibero-American capital cities and work for solidarity and cooperation among them. **Structure** Plenary Assembly (every 2 years); Executive Committee; Regions (4); Sectorial Committees (16); Working Groups (5). **Languages** Portuguese, Spanish. **Staff** 12.00 FTE, paid. **Finance** Sources: donations; government support. **Activities** Awards/prizes/competitions; events/meetings; training/education. **Events** *Meeting of Directors of International Relations and UCCI Coordinators* Madrid (Spain) 2020, *Tourism and Innovation in the Ibero-American Space* Madrid (Spain) 2020, *Sectoral Committee on Sustainable and Resilient Cities Meeting* San Juan (Puerto Rico) 2019, *Meeting of the UCCI Mayors – Central America , Mexico and the Caribbean* Santo Domingo (Dominican Rep) 2019, *Ibero-American Meeting of Citizen Innovation and Citizen Laboratories* Madrid (Spain) 2018. **Publications** *Ibero-American Cities* (annual) in Portuguese, Spanish – magazine.
Members Capitals and most important cities (29) of 24 countries:
Andorra (Andorra la Vella), Argentina (Buenos Aires), Bolivia (La Paz – Sucre), Brazil (Brasilia – Sao Paulo – Rio de Janeiro), Chile (Santiago), Colombia (Santa Fé de Bogota), Costa Rica (San José), Cuba (Havana), Dominican Rep (Santo Domingo), Ecuador (Quito), El Salvador (San Salvador), Guatemala (Guatemala), Haiti (Puerto Principe), Honduras (Tegucigalpa), Mexico (Mexico City), Nicaragua (Managua), Panama (Panama), Paraguay (Asunción), Peru (Lima), Portugal (Lisbon), Puerto Rico (San Juan), Spain (Madrid – Barcelona – Cadiz), Uruguay (Montevideo), Venezuela (Caracas).
Consultative Status Consultative status granted from: *ECOSOC (#05331)* (Special). **NGO Relations** Cooperates with (5): *Consejo de Empresarios Iberoamericanos (CEIB, #04708)*; *Federación Iberoamericana de Jóvenes Empresarios (FIJE, #09314)*; *Global Taskforce of Local and Regional Governments (Global Taskforce, #10622)*; *International Association of Public Transport (#12118)*; *Local Governments for Sustainability (ICLEI, #16507)*. Also links with national organizations. [2021.06.24/XD7307/**D**]

- ♦ Union indépendante de l'industrie européenne des lubrifiants / see Union Européenne de l'Industrie des Lubrifiants (#20398)
- ♦ Union of Independent Retailer's Groups in Europe / see Independent Retail Europe (#11154)
- ♦ Union of Industrial and Employers' Confederations of Europe / see BUSINESSEUROPE (#03381)
- ♦ Union des industries de la Communauté européenne / see BUSINESSEUROPE (#03381)
- ♦ Union of Industries of the European Community / see BUSINESSEUROPE (#03381)
- ♦ Union des industries ferroviaires européennes (#02536)
- ♦ Union des industries gazières des pays du Marché commun Union der Gas-Industrie des Gemeinsamen Marktes / see MARCOGAZ – Technical Association of the European Natural Gas Industry (#16572)
- ♦ Union des ingénieurs et des techniciens utilisant la langue française / see Union internationale des ingénieurs et des scientifiques utilisant la langue française (#20427)
- ♦ Union Institute for Cooperation to Development (internationally oriented national body)
- ♦ Union interafricaine des avocats (inactive)
- ♦ Union interafricaine des droits de l'homme (inactive)
- ♦ Union inter-africaine des organisations professionnelles d'éleveurs (no recent information)
- ♦ Union interaméricaine des Caraïbes (inactive)
- ♦ Union interaméricaine des pères de famille (inactive)
- ♦ Unión Interamericana del Caribe (inactive)

♦ Unión Interamericana de Organismos Electorales (UNIORE) 20413

Inter-American Union of Electoral Organizations

Contact c/o CAPEL, Av 8 calles 41 y 43, Casa 222, San José, San José, San José, Costa Rica. T. +50622340404. Fax +50622340955.
URL: http://www.iidh.ed.cr/capel/

History Founded 22 Nov 1991, Caracas (Venezuela), during a joint meeting convened by *Association of Electoral Organizations of Central America and the Caribbean (Tikal Protocol, #02484)* and *Association of South American Electoral Organizations (Quito Protocol, #02919)*. Decisions have the character of recommendations and orientations for the organisms that integrate it. **Aims** Increase cooperation between member associations and individual Electoral Organizations belonging to the Union; promote the sharing of information on electoral systems; foster participation of representatives of member organizations in an observer capacity in electoral processes, at the invitation of the country where they are held which shall provide the necessary facilities as far as is practicable in terms of its own resources; formulate general recommendations for member organizations; promote honest, efficient and *democratic* electoral systems which guarantee universal suffrage and a free and secret ballot; provide support and assistance, as far as practicable, to Electoral Organizations which request it. **Structure** Governing body: Inter-American Conference of Electoral Organizations; Conference (every 2 years) chaired by Host Organization. **Languages** English, Spanish. **Finance** Electoral Organizations; *Centre for Electoral Promotion and Assistance (CAPEL, see: #11334)*. **Activities** Monitoring/evaluation; events/meetings. **Events** *Conference* Dominican Rep 2012, *Conference* Mexico 2010, *Conference* San Salvador (El Salvador) 2008, *Conference* Panama (Panama) 2006, *Conference* Panama (Panama) 2004.
Members Electoral organizations (29) in 24 countries and territories:
Antigua-Barbuda, Argentina, Bolivia, Brazil, Canada, Chile, Colombia, Costa Rica, Dominican Rep, Ecuador, El Salvador, Guatemala, Honduras, Jamaica, Mexico, Nicaragua, Panama, Paraguay, Peru, Puerto Rico, St Lucia, Uruguay, USA, Venezuela. [2020.03.03/XD7319/**D**]

- ♦ Unión Interamericana de Padres de Familia (inactive)
- ♦ Unión Interamericana para la Vivienda (#11433)
- ♦ Union inter-arabe pour l'hôtellerie et le tourisme (inactive)
- ♦ Unión Intercontinental de Amas de Casa (#20378)
- ♦ Unión Internacional de Abogados (#20422)
- ♦ Unión Internacional de Administraciones Locales (inactive)
- ♦ Unión Internacional de los Arquitectos (#20419)
- ♦ Unión Internacional de Artesania y de las Pequeñas y Medianas Empresas (inactive)
- ♦ Unión Internacional de Asociaciones de Ahorros y Préstamo para la Vivienda / see International Union for Housing Finance (#15780)
- ♦ Unión Internacional de Asociaciones de Alpinismo (#20420)
- ♦ Unión Internacional de las Asociaciones de Instaladores de Calefacción, Ventilación y Aire Acondicionado (inactive)
- ♦ Unión Internacional de Asociaciones y Organizaciones Técnicas / see Union internationale des associations et organismes scientifiques et techniques (#20421)
- ♦ Unión Internacional de Asociaciones de Propietarios de Vagones Particulares / see International Union of Wagon Keepers (#15827)
- ♦ Unión Internacional de Asociaciones Técnicas Cinematograficas (inactive)
- ♦ Unión Internacional de Asociaciones de Trabajadores de Alimentos y Bebidas / see International Union of Food, Agricultural, Hotel, Restaurant, Catering, Tobacco and Allied Workers Associations (#15772)
- ♦ Unión Internacional de Asociaciones de Visitadores Médicos (#15791)
- ♦ Unión Internacional de Bioelectrografia Médica y Aplicada (#15792)
- ♦ Unión Internacional de Biofisica Pura y Aplicada (#15808)
- ♦ Unión Internacional de Carreras de Yates / see World Sailing (#21760)
- ♦ Unión Internacional de Ciencias Antropológicas y Etnológicas (#15755)
- ♦ Unión Internacional de Ciencias Biológicas (#15760)
- ♦ Unión Internacional de Ciencias Fisiológicas (#15800)
- ♦ Unión Internacional de Ciencias Geológicas (#15777)
- ♦ Unión Internacional de Ciencias de la Nutrición (#15796)
- ♦ Unión Internacional de Ciencias Prehistóricas y Protohistóricas (#15801)
- ♦ Unión Internacional de Cine Amateur / see Union internationale du cinéma (#20423)
- ♦ Unión Internacional de Cines (#15763)
- ♦ Unión Internacional de Compañias de Seguros de Aviación (#15750)
- ♦ Unión Internacional de Conductores por Carreteras (#15802)
- ♦ Unión Internacional para la Conservación de la Naturaleza y de los Recursos Naturales (#15766)
- ♦ Unión Internacional contra el Cancer (#20415)
- ♦ Unión Internacional contra la Tuberculosis y Enfermedades Respiratorias (#15752)
- ♦ Unión Internacional de Cristalografica (#15768)
- ♦ Unión Internacional Cristiana de Dirigentes de Empresa (#12566)
- ♦ Unión Internacional de Directores de Jardines Zoológicos / see World Association of Zoos and Aquariums (#21208)
- ♦ Unión Internacional de Editores (#14675)
- ♦ Unión Internacional de Educación Antialcohólica (inactive)
- ♦ Unión Internacional de Educación para la Salud / see International Union for Health Promotion and Education (#15778)
- ♦ Unión Internacional de Estudiantes de Arquitectura (inactive)
- ♦ Unión Internacional para el Estudio Cientifico de la Población (#15814)
- ♦ Unión Internacional para el Estudio del Cuaternario (#15811)
- ♦ Unión Internacional para el Estudio de los Insectos Sociales (#15819)
- ♦ Unión Internacional de Explotación Cinematografica / see International Union of Cinemas (#15763)
- ♦ Unión Internacional de Federaciones de Policia (inactive)
- ♦ Unión Internacional de Fisica Pura y Aplicada (#15810)
- ♦ Unión Internacional de Historia y Filosofía de las Ciencias / see International Union of History and Philosophy of Science and Technology (#15779)
- ♦ Unión Internacional Humanista y Etica / see Humanists International (#10972)
- ♦ Unión Internacional para la Imposición de los Bienes Raices y el Comercio Libre / see International Union for Land Value Taxation and Free Trade (#15787)
- ♦ - Unión Internacional pro Impuesto sobre el Valor de la Tierra y el Librecambio (#15787)
- ♦ Unión Internacional de Jóvenes Demócrata Cristianos (inactive)
- ♦ Unión Internacional de Juventudes Socialistas (#15815)
- ♦ Unión Internacional por la Libertad de la Enseñanza (inactive)
- ♦ Unión Internacional de Magistrados (#11978)
- ♦ Unión Internacional de Mecanica Teórica y Aplicada (#15823)
- ♦ Unión Internacional de Medicina Estética (#15771)
- ♦ Unión Internacional de Motonautica / see Union internationale Motonautique (#20431)
- ♦ Unión Internacional de la Navegación Fluvial (inactive)
- ♦ Unión Internacional del Notariado (#15795)
- ♦ Unión Internacional del Notariado Latino / see International Union of Notaries (#15795)
- ♦ Unión Internacional de Oraciones (religious order)
- ♦ Unión Internacional de Organismos Familiares / see World Family Organization (#21399)
- ♦ Unión Internacional de los Organismos Turisticos y Culturales de Correos y Telecomunicaciones (inactive)
- ♦ Unión Internacional de Organizaciones de Investigación Forestal (#15774)
- ♦ Unión Internacional de Panaderos y Pasteleros (#15757)
- ♦ Unión Internacional de Profesores Socialistas Demócratas / see International Social Democratic Union for Education (#14881)

- ♦ Unión Internacional de Promoción de la Salud y de Educación para la Salud (#15778)
- ♦ Unión Internacional de la Propiedad Urbana (#15804)
- ♦ Unión Internacional de Protección a la Infancia (inactive)
- ♦ Unión Internacional para la Protección de las Obras Literarias y Artisticas (#15806)
- ♦ Unión Internacional para la Protección de las Obtenciones Vegetales (#20436)
- ♦ Unión Internacional para la Protección de la Propiedad Industrial (#15805)
- ♦ Unión Internacional de Quimica Pura y Aplicada (#15809)
- ♦ Unión Internacional de Radioaficionados (#11646)
- ♦ Unión Internacional de Radio y Televisión / see International Radio and Television Union (#14689)
- ♦ Unión Internacional Raiffeisen (#13291)
- ♦ Unión Internacional de las Repúblicas Americanas / see OAS (#17629)
- ♦ Unión Internacional de Seguros de Transportes (#15789)
- ♦ Unión Internacional de Servicios Médicos en los Ferrocarriles (#20437)
- ♦ Unión Internacional de los Sindicatos de la Industria Quimica, del Petróleo y Similares (inactive)
- ♦ Unión Internacional de Sindicatos de Trabajadores de la Agricultura, de los Bosques y de las Plantaciones (inactive)
- ♦ Unión Internacional de Sindicatos de los Trabajadores del Comercio (inactive)
- ♦ Unión Internacional de Sindicatos de Trabajadores de la Construcción (#20185)
- ♦ Unión Internacional de los Sindicatos de Trabajadores Energéticos (inactive)
- ♦ Unión Internacional de Sindicatos de Trabajadores de la Energia, el Metal, La Quimica, el Petróleo e Industrias Afines / see Trade Union International of Chemical, Energy, Metal, Oil and Allied Industries (#20188)
- ♦ Unión Internacional de Sindicatos de Trabajadores de las Industrias Alimentaria, Tabacalera, Hotelera y Similares (inactive)
- ♦ Unión Internacional de Sindicatos de Trabajadores de la Metalurgia (inactive)
- ♦ Unión Internacional del Sindicatos de Trabajadores de la Mineria, la Metalurgia y el Metal (unconfirmed)
- ♦ Unión Internacional de Sindicatos de Trabajadores de Servicios Públicos y Similares (#20191)
- ♦ Unión Internacional de Sindicatos de Trabajadores de los Transportes / see Trade Unions International of Transport, Fisheries and Communication (#20192)
- ♦ Union Internacional Socialists de Educación (#14881)
- ♦ Unión Internacional de las Sociedades de Microbiologia (#15794)
- ♦ Unión Internacional de Sociedades de Profesionales Forestales (no recent information)
- ♦ Unión Internacional de Sociedades de Quimicos y Técnicos del Cuero (#15788)
- ♦ Unión Internacional de Socorros (inactive)
- ♦ Unión Internacional de Técnicos de la Industria del Calzado (#20439)
- ♦ Unión Internacional de Telecomunicaciones (#15673)
- ♦ Unión Internacional de Tiro / see International Shooting Sport Federation (#14852)
- ♦ Unión Internacional de Trabajadores de la Alimentación y Afines / see International Union of Food, Agricultural, Hotel, Restaurant, Catering, Tobacco and Allied Workers Associations (#15772)
- ♦ Unión Internacional de Trabajadores de la Alimentación, Agricolas, Hoteles, Restaurantes, Tabaco y Afines (#15772)
- ♦ Unión Internacional de Transportes por Carretera (#14761)
- ♦ Unión Internacional de Transportes Públicos (#12118)
- ♦ Unión Internacional Vegetariana (#15842)

♦ Union of International Associations (UIA) 20414

Union des associations internationales (UAI) – Unión de Asociaciones Internacionales – Union der Internationalen Verbände – Unie van de Internationale Verenigingen

SG Rue Washington 40, 1050 Brussels, Belgium. T. +3226401808. E-mail: uia@uia.org.
Pres/UN Representative CIC Case 20, 1211 Geneva 20, Switzerland. T. +41227336717. Fax +41227347082.
URL: https://www.uia.org/

History 1 Jun 1907, Brussels (Belgium). Founded by Henri La Fontaine (Nobel Peace Prize 1913) and Paul Otlet, Secretary-General of the then *'International Institute of Bibliography – Institut international de bibliographie'*, set up 2 Sep 1895, Brussels, currently *International Federation for Information and Documentation (FID, inactive)*, with which activities were closely associated. Officially founded under patronage of the Belgian government on 29 Jan 1908. Became a federation under present name in 1910, at 1st World Congress of International Organizations. Statutes adopted 1908; modified 1910, 1951, 1955, 1965, 1986, 2007. Worked closely with *Institut international de la paix, Monaco (inactive)*, which had been set up in 1903 and produced the 1905, 1906 and 1907 editions of the *Annuaire de la Vie internationale*; collaborated with the Institute on the 1908-1909 edition of this publication, which subsequently evolved into the *Yearbook of International Organizations*. The work of the UIA contributed to the creation, 10 Jan 1920, of *League of Nations (SDN, inactive)*, and, 9 Aug 1925, of *International Institute of Intellectual Cooperation (IICI, inactive)*. During the 1920s, the UIA created *International University (inactive)*. Former names and other names: *Central Office of International Associations* – former (1 Jun 1907 to 1910); *Office central des institutions internationales* – former (1 Jun 1907 to 1910). Registration: Belgian Royal Decree, Start date: 2 Jul 1920, Belgium; Banque-Carrefour des Entreprises, No/ID: 0408.287.747, Start date: 30 Sep 1965. **Aims** As a platform for global civil society cooperation, collaborate with, provide services to and promote international associations. **Structure** General Assembly (every 2 years); Executive Council; Bureau; Secretariat. **Languages** English, French. **Staff** 9.00 FTE, paid; 2.00 FTE, voluntary. **Finance** Sources: fees for services; members' dues; sale of publications. Annual budget: 550,000 EUR. **Activities** Advocacy/lobbying/activism; events/meetings; knowledge management/information dissemination; networking/liaising; research/documentation. Promoted an international convention on the legal status of international associations which resulted in the signature at the Council of Europe, 1986, of *European Convention on the Recognition of the Legal Personality of International Non-Governmental Organisations (1986)*. **Events** *Associations Round Table – Europe* Lucerne (Switzerland) 2026, *Associations Round Table – Europe* Brussels (Belgium) 2025, *Associations Round Table – Europe* Florence (Italy) 2024, *Associations Round Table – Asia Pacific* 2023, *Associations Round Table – Europe* Brussels (Belgium) 2023. **Publications** *World of Associations News* (12 a year). *International Association Statutes Series* (1986); *International Congress Science Series* in English, French – in 12 vols. *Yearbook of International Organizations* (57th ed 2020) – in 6 vols; *World Guide to Logotypes, Emblems and Trademarks of International Organizations* (1997); *World Guide to Religious and Spiritual Organizations* (1996); *International Biographical Dictionary of Religion* (1994); *Encyclopedia of World Problems and Human Potential* (4th ed 1994) – in 3 vols; *The Identity of African Associations and the Participation of NGOs in Development in the Context of a New World Order* (1985); *African International Organization Directory and African Participation in Other International Organizations* (1984); *Arab, Islamic International Organization Directory and Arab and Islamic Participation in Other International Organizations* (1984); *Intergovernmental Organization Directory* (1984); *International Organization Abbreviations and Addresses* (1984); *World Forum Proceedings: from international to transnational* (1983); *Annuaire des organisations internationales* (4th ed 1980); *Yearbook of International Congress Proceedings* (2nd ed 1962-69); *Documents for the Study of International Non-Governmental Relations* – 20 vols issued. **Information Services** *Encyclopedia of World Problems and Human Potential Online*; *International Congress Calendar Online*; *Yearbook of International Organizations Online*.
Members Active individuals, limited to 250 and subject to election by General Assembly. Currently 86 individuals in 28 countries:
Australia, Austria, Belgium, Brazil, Canada, Chile, Denmark, Finland, France, Germany, India, Italy, Japan, Kenya, Korea Rep, Laos, Mauritania, Netherlands, Norway, Peru, Sweden, Switzerland, Thailand, Tunisia, UK, Ukraine, USA, Vietnam.
Associate (71) corporate bodies or individuals interested in the aims and activities of the UIA and wishing to associate themselves with its work by payment of an annual membership fee. Subject to approval by the Executive Council. Includes 2 organizations listed in this Yearbook:
City Destinations Alliance (CityDNA, #03960); *International Congress and Convention Association (ICCA, #12892)*.
Consultative Status Consultative status granted from: *ECOSOC (#05331)* (Special); *UNESCO (#20322)* (Associate Status); *ILO (#11123)* (Special List). **IGO Relations** Cooperates with (2): *Council of Europe (CE, #04881)*; *UN Environment Programme World Conservation Monitoring Centre (UNEP-WCMC, #20295)*. Associated with Department of Global Communications of the United Nations. **NGO Relations** Member of (3): *Conference of Non-Governmental Organizations in Consultative Relationship with the United Nations (CONGO, #04635)*; *International Conference of NGOs (#12883)*; *Joint Meetings Industry Council (JMIC, #16140)*. Contact maintained with all international nongovernmental organizations eligible for inclusion in the *'Yearbook of International Organizations'*. Proposed, 1949, the setting up of a *International Service Centre for and about Nongovernmental Organizations (inactive)*, which never materialized as such but whose functions are in part fulfilled by *International Association Centre (MAI)*, which UIA was instrumental in setting up, 20 Aug 1982, Brussels (Belgium). Special links with: *Federation of European and International Associations Established in Belgium (FAIB, #09508)*; *Fédération des Institutions Internationales établies à Genève (FIIG, #09599)*; *International Association of Professional Congress Organisers (IAPCO, #12103)*; conferences of consultative status nongovernmental organizations; bodies using the Union's secretariat facilities; those with which it has co-editing or co-publishing arrangements and with Associate Members. [2023/XF3352/y/**F**]

- ♦ Union of International Bakers / see International Union of Bakers and Confectioners (#15757)

♦ Union for International Cancer Control (UICC) 20415

Union internationale contre le cancer (UICC) – Unión Internacional contra el Cancer – Internationale Vereinigung zur Krebsbekämpfung – Unione Internazionale contro il Cancro

CEO 31-33 Avenue Giuseppe Motta, 1202 Geneva, Switzerland. T. +41228091811. Fax +41228091810. E-mail: info@uicc.org.
URL: http://www.uicc.org/

History 22 Mar 1934, Paris (France). Founded following adoption of a decision at a cancer congress, 1933, Madrid (Spain). First General Assembly: 4 May 1935. Current English title adopted at General Assembly, Shenzhen (China). Former names and other names: *Unio Internationalis Contra Cancrum* – former; *International Union Against Cancer (UICC)* – former. Registration: Swiss Civil Code, Switzerland; EU Transparency Register, No/ID: 749441042554-43, Start date: 18 May 2021. **Aims** Eliminate cancer as a life-threatening disease for future generations by connecting, mobilizing and working together with organizations, leading experts, key stakeholders and volunteers in a dynamic community. **Structure** General Assembly (every 2 years, in conjunction with World Cancer Congress); Board of Directors; CEO. **Languages** English, French, Spanish. **Staff** 30.00 FTE, paid. **Finance** Sources: donations; grants; members' dues; revenue from activities/projects; sale of publications. **Activities** Advocacy/lobbying/activism; awards/prizes/competitions; events/meetings; networking/liaising. **Events** *World Cancer Congress* Geneva (Switzerland) 2022, *Biennial World Cancer Congress* Muscat (Oman) 2020, *Biennial World Cancer Congress* Kuala Lumpur (Malaysia) 2018, *International Chinese Conference on Oncology* Shenyang (China) 2018, *World Cancer Leaders Summit* Mexico City (Mexico) 2017. **Publications** *Journal of Surgical Oncology* (12 a year); *UICC News* (4 a year); *UICC International Calendar of Meetings on Cancer* (2 a year); *Association of UICC Fellows Membership Directory* (annual); *UICC Membership Directory* (every 2 years); *International Journal of Cancer, Predictive Oncology and Radiation Oncology Investigations* (36 a year); *Seminars in Surgical Oncology* (8 a year); *The Prostate* (16 a year); *UICC International Directory of Cancer Institutes and Organizations* – electronic. *Control Strategy Planning* – guides. *Global Action Against Cancer*; *Illustrated Guide to the TNM/pTNM Classification of Malignant Tumours*; *Introducing the UICC*; *Manual of Clinical Oncology (8th ed)*; *TNM Atlas (5th ed)*; *TNM Supplement: A Commentary on Uniform Use (3rd ed)*; *Tobacco Control Country Profiles (2nd ed)*; *UICC Handbook for Europe – Evidence-based Cancer Prevention: Strategies for NGOS*; *UICC Tobacco Fact Sheets*. Annual Report; reference books; monographs; booklets.
Members Full: available to organizations substantially engaged in the cancer control, support UICC objectives and have appropriate organizational structures. Associate: available to organizations, networks or entities that support UICC objectives. Organizations (389) in 118 countries and territories:
Afghanistan, Algeria, Argentina, Armenia, Australia, Bahrain, Bangladesh, Belgium, Bermuda, Bolivia, Botswana, Brazil, Bulgaria, Burkina Faso, Burundi, Cameroon, Canada, Chile, China, Colombia, Comoros, Congo DR, Côte d'Ivoire, Croatia, Cuba, Cyprus, Czechia, Denmark, Dominican Rep, Ecuador, Egypt, El Salvador, Estonia, Ethiopia, Fiji, Finland, France, Georgia, Germany, Ghana, Greece, Guatemala, Honduras, Hungary, Iceland, India, Indonesia, Iran Islamic Rep, Iraq, Ireland, Israel, Italy, Japan, Jordan, Kenya, Korea Rep, Kuwait, Kyrgyzstan, Latvia, Lebanon, Libya, Lithuania, Luxembourg, Malaysia, Mali, Malta, Mauritius, Mexico, Moldova, Mongolia, Morocco, Mozambique, Namibia, Nepal, Netherlands, New Zealand, Nicaragua, Niger, Nigeria, Norway, Pakistan, Panama, Paraguay, Peru, Philippines, Poland, Portugal, Qatar, Romania, Russia, Saudi Arabia, Senegal, Serbia, Singapore, Slovakia, Slovenia, South Africa, Spain, Sri Lanka, Sudan, Sweden, Switzerland, Syrian AR, Taiwan, Tanzania UR, Thailand, Trinidad-Tobago, Tunisia, Uganda, UK, Ukraine, United Arab Emirates, Uruguay, USA, Venezuela, Vietnam, Yemen, Zimbabwe.
Included in the above Full Members, 17 organizations listed in this Yearbook:
African Oncology Institute (no recent information); *African Organization for Research and Training in Cancer (AORTIC, #00405)*; *Arab Medical Association Against Cancer (AMAAC, #01006)*; *European Institute of Oncology, Milan (EIO)*; *European Organisation for Research and Treatment of Cancer (EORTC, #08101)*; *European School of Oncology (ESO, #08434)*; *European Society for Medical Oncology (ESMO, #08648)*; *International Extranodal Lymphoma Study Group (IELSG)*; *International Hereditary Cancer Center*; *International Society for Nurses in Cancer Care (ISNCC, #15312)*; *Latin-American and Caribbean Society of Medical Oncology (#16286)*; *Ludwig Institute for Cancer Research (LICR, #16520)*; *Lymphoma Coalition (LC, #16535)*; *Reach to Recovery International (RRI, #18625)*; *Société internationale d'oncologie gériatrique (SIOG, #19493)*; *World Cancer Research Fund International (WCRF)*.
Associate Members – organizations in 61 countries:
Algeria, Armenia, Australia, Bahrain, Bangladesh, Belgium, Bermuda, Bolivia, Bulgaria, Cameroon, Canada, Chile, Congo DR, Croatia, Egypt, Estonia, Ethiopia, Fiji, Honduras, India, Indonesia, Iran Islamic Rep, Italy, Jordan, Kenya, Korea Rep, Kyrgyzstan, Latvia, Lithuania, Malaysia, Mali, Malta, Mexico, Morocco, Nepal, Netherlands, New Zealand, Nicaragua, Nigeria, Pakistan, Paraguay, Peru, Philippines, Russia, Senegal, Slovakia, Slovenia, Spain, Switzerland, Tonga, Trinidad-Tobago, Tunisia, Türkiye, Uganda, UK, Ukraine, Uruguay, USA, Venezuela, Vietnam, Zimbabwe.
Included in the above Associate Members, 7 organizations listed in this Yearbook:
Childhood Cancer International (CCI, #03871); *European Cervical Cancer Association (ECCA, #06512)*; *European SocieTy for Radiotherapy and Oncology (ESTRO, #08721)*; *Instituto Centro Americano de la Salud (ICAS, #11328)*; *International Psycho-Oncology Society (IPOS, #14665)*; *PATH (#18260)*; *Synergies Africaines contre le SIDA et les Souffrances (Synergies Africaines, #20081)*.
Consultative Status Consultative status granted from: *ECOSOC (#05331)* (Special); *WHO (#20950)* (Official Relations). **NGO Relations** Founding member of: *The NCD Alliance (NCDA, #16963)*. Member of: *European Cervical Cancer Association (ECCA, #06512)*; *Fédération des Institutions Internationales établies à Genève (FIIG, #09599)*; *Framework Convention Alliance (FCA, #09981)*. Participates in: *Breast Health Global Initiative (BHGI, #03318)*. Collaborates with: *Association of European Cancer Leagues (ECL, #02500)*. Provides secretariat for: *Organization of European Cancer Institutes (OECI, #17865)*. Joint meetings with: *European Society of Surgical Oncology (ESSO, #08753)*; *European SocieTy for Radiotherapy and Oncology (ESTRO, #08721)*; *International Society of Paediatric Oncology (#15339)*. Partner of: *Global Smokefree Partnership (GSP, #10602)*. Together with: *International Union Against Tuberculosis and Lung Disease (The Union, #15752)*, set up: *International Non Governmental Coalition Against Tobacco (INGCAT, no recent information)*. Together with: *Pasteur Institute*, set up: *International Network for Cancer Treatment and Research (INCTR, #14238)*. Instrumental in setting up: *International Digestive Cancer Alliance (IDCA, #13174)*. Located at: *International Institute of Anticancer Research (IIAR)*. [2020/XB2648/y/**B**]

♦ Union for the International Classification for Industrial Designs (Locarno Union) 20416

Union pour la classification internationale pour les dessins et modèles industriels

Address not obtained.
URL: http://www.wipo.org/

History 27 Apr 1971, on entry into force of *Locarno Agreement Establishing an International Classification for Industrial Design (1968)*, signed 27 Apr 1971, and amended 1979. The countries to which the agreement applies constitute a special union. A union within *World Intellectual Property Organization (WIPO, #21593)*. **Structure** Assembly; Committee of Experts. **Activities** The Agreement establishes a classification for industrial designs. A Committee of Experts, set up under the Agreement, periodically revises this classification.
Members Open to States party to the Locarno Agreement. States party to the Agreement, as of Jan 2012 (52):
Argentina, Armenia, Austria, Azerbaijan, Belarus, Belgium, Bosnia-Herzegovina, Bulgaria, China, Croatia, Cuba, Czechia, Denmark, Estonia, Finland, France, Germany, Greece, Guinea, Hungary, Iceland, Ireland, Italy, Kazakhstan, Korea DPR, Korea Rep, Kyrgyzstan, Latvia, Malawi, Mexico, Moldova, Mongolia, Montenegro, Netherlands, North Macedonia, Norway, Romania, Russia, Serbia, Slovakia, Slovenia, Spain, Sweden, Switzerland, Tajikistan, Trinidad-Tobago, Türkiye, Turkmenistan, UK, Ukraine, Uruguay, Uzbekistan. [2012/XF4436/t/**F***]

♦ Union for the International Deposit of Industrial Designs (The Hague Union) 20417

Union pour le dépôt international des dessins ou modèles industriels

Address not obtained.

URL: http://www.wipo.org/

History 1925, The Hague (Netherlands), by the *The Hague Agreement Concerning the International Deposit of Industrial Designs (1925)*. Revised: 1934, London (UK); 1960, The Hague. Supplemented by: Additional Act of Monaco (1961); Complementary Act of Stockholm (Sweden) (1967); Protocol of Geneva (Switzerland) (1975). Agreement amended 1979. A union administered by *World Intellectual Property Organization (WIPO, #21593)*. **Aims** Facilitate the obtention of *protection* of industrial designs. **Structure** Assembly. **Finance** Financed by fees collected from the users of the system. **Activities** Establishes a system that facilitates securing of protection of industrial designs in the States party to the Agreement, through deposit et the International Bureau of WIPO of industrial designs.

Members Open to States party to the Hague Agreement. States party to the Agreement, as of Jan 2009 (51):
Albania, Armenia, Belgium, Belize, Benin, Bosnia-Herzegovina, Botswana, Bulgaria, Côte d'Ivoire, Croatia, Denmark, Egypt, Estonia, France, Gabon, Georgia, Germany, Ghana, Greece, Hungary, Iceland, Italy, Korea DPR, Kyrgyzstan, Latvia, Liechtenstein, Lithuania, Luxembourg, Mali, Moldova, Monaco, Mongolia, Montenegro, Morocco, Namibia, Netherlands, Niger, North Macedonia, Oman, Romania, Sao Tomé-Principe, Senegal, Serbia, Singapore, Slovenia, Spain, Suriname, Switzerland, Syrian AR, Türkiye, Ukraine.
Regional parties (1), listed in this Yearbook:
European Union (EU, #08967).
States party to the Agreement but not members of the Assembly (3):
Holy See, Indonesia, Tunisia. [2009/XF4440/t/**F***]

- ♦ Union internationale d'action morale et sociale (inactive)
- ♦ Union internationale des agents commerciaux et des courtiers / see Internationally United Commercial Agents and Brokers (#14072)
- ♦ Union internationale agricole pour la fixation du prix des céréales (inactive)
- ♦ Union internationale agricole et horticole des femmes (inactive)
- ♦ Union internationale des agriculteurs français pour le renouveau (internationally oriented national body)
- ♦ Union internationale d'aide à la santé mentale (no recent information)

♦ Union internationale des alsaciens (UIA) 20418

SG 1 place de la Gare, 68000 Colmar, France. T. +33389202020. Fax +33389202121. E-mail: uia@alsacemonde.org.

URL: http://www.alsacemonde.org/

History Founded 1981, as *Union internationale des alsaciens de l'étranger (UIAE)*. **Aims** Promote *friendship* between people from Alsace living outside France; promote the Alsace region abroad. **Structure** General Assembly (annual); Executive Committee. **Languages** English, French, German. **Events** *Journée Annuelle et Assemblée Générale* Rouffach (France) 2015, *Journée Annuelle et Assemblée Générale / General Assembly* Truchtersheim (France) 2014, *Journée Annuelle et Assemblée Générale / General Assembly* Ensisheim (France) 2013, *Journée Annuelle et Assemblée Générale / General Assembly* Pfaffenhoffen (France) 2012, *Journée Annuelle et Assemblée Générale / General Assembly* Wintzenheim (France) 2011. **Publications** *L'Alsace dans le Monde* (3 a year); *Courrier d'Alsace* – electronic newsletter.

Members National organizations (26) in 18 countries and territories:
Belgium, Brazil, Canada, France, Germany, Greece, Lithuania, Luxembourg, North Macedonia, Poland, Romania, Spain, Switzerland, Tahiti Is, Thailand, Tunisia, UK, USA.
Delegates in 6 countries:
Argentina, Australia, China, Lithuania, Poland, Türkiye. [2014.11.05/XE3355/**E**]

- ♦ Union internationale des alsaciens de l'étranger / see Union internationale des alsaciens (#20418)
- ♦ Union internationale des amateurs de télégraphes sans fil / see International Amateur Radio Union (#11646)
- ♦ Union internationale des anciens catholiques (inactive)
- ♦ Union internationale d'angiologie (#15754)
- ♦ Union internationale d'angiologie – société pour la Médecine et la Chirurgie Vasculaire ainsi que les Interventions Endovasculaires / see International Union of Angiology (#15754)
- ♦ Union internationale antiraciste (inactive)
- ♦ Union internationale pour les applications de l'électricité (#15770)
- ♦ Union internationale d'archéologie slave (inactive)

♦ Union internationale des architectes (UIA) 20419

International Union of Architects (UIA) – Unión Internacional de los Arquitectos (UIA) – Internationaler Architekten Union (UIA) – Uniao Internacional dos Arquitetos (UIA)

Acting Managing Dir Tour Maine Montparnasse, 33 av de Maine, BP 158, 75755 Paris CEDEX 15, France. T. +33145243688. Fax +33145240278. E-mail: uia@uia-architectes.org.

URL: http://www.uia-architectes.org/

History 28 Jun 1948, Lausanne (Switzerland). Foundedby merger of *Comité permanent international des architectes (CPIA, inactive)*, set up in 1867, Paris (France), and of *Réunions internationales des architectes (RIA, inactive)*, formed in 1931. Registration: France. **Aims** Unite the architects of the world on a democratic basis; maintain free exchange among architects; represent architects at international and governmental levels; promote architects' creative, technical and cultural talents and the service they provide to the public; defend the rights and status of the architect in every country; ensure the continued development of *professional* methods while respecting the specificity of different communities; promote new technologies and encourage new ideas and concepts in architectural *design*; promote multi-disciplinary exchange; aid in the sustainable development of the built environment; provide the needed assistance to architects' professional structures in developing countries; promote architectural education and facilitate exchange among architects, students and teachers of architecture worldwide. **Structure** General Assembly (every 3 years); Council; Regional Councils (5); General Policy Committee; General Secretariat under the control of Secretary General. Membership open to all national professional organizations. Congresses and Working Group Seminars open; Bureau and Council meetings closed. **Languages** English, French, Mandarin Chinese, Portuguese, Russian, Spanish. **Staff** 6.00 FTE, paid. **Finance** Dues from National Member Sections. **Activities** Member Sections (grouped in 5 geographical regions) constitute the life-force of the Union and the centre of its action. Work Programmes: Public Health; Educational and Cultural Spaces; Sports and Leisure; Architectural Heritage (one representative for each region); Spiritual Places; Architecture and Tourism (one representative for each region); Habitat; Architecture for a Sustainable Future, Renewable Energy Sources, Intermediate Cities Urbanization and Development; Education Programme including 'UIA Charter of Architectural Education'; Professional Practice Commission; UIA Programme International Competitions; Architecture and Children; Architecture for All. The Work Programmes facilitate international contacts between architects with a view to exchange of professional experience; organize international seminars; participate in the studies and work of international bodies dealing in the field of their specificities. Congresses (every 3 years). *'International Competitions'* As mandated by UNESCO since 1956, assists in running international competitions in architecture and town-planning and ensures that UIA/UNESCO recommendations on this matter are respected. *'UIA Prizes'* are honorary distinctions awarded every 3 years by an international jury. Sponsors exhibitions and seminars on architecture, town-planning and construction. Instrumental in setting up: *International College of Expert Architects (no recent information)*. **Events** *Triennial Congress* Copenhagen (Denmark) 2023, *Madrid UIA Forum* Madrid (Spain) 2022, *Triennial Congress* Rio de Janeiro (Brazil) 2021, *Triennial Congress* Rio de Janeiro (Brazil) 2020, *Seminar on Public Health* Paris (France) 2018. **Publications** *UIA e-Newsletter* (twice a month) in English, French. *UIA/UNESCO recommendations on international competitions of architecture and town-planning; instructions and recommendations for international competition promoters* (2021); *UIA-UNESCO Charter for Architectural Education – Charte UIA-UNESCO de la Formation de l'architecte* (revised ed 2019) in English, French.

Members National and Regional Sections; Temporary members; Associate members. National Sections, totalling more than 1 million architects, in 130 countries and territories:
Afghanistan, Albania, Andorra, Angola, Argentina, Armenia, Australia, Austria, Azerbaijan, Bahamas, Bangladesh, Barbados, Belarus, Belgium, Belize, Benin, Bolivia, Bosnia-Herzegovina, Brazil, Brunei Darussalam, Bulgaria, Burkina Faso, Cameroon, Canada, Cape Verde, Central African Rep, Chad, Chile, China, Colombia, Congo Brazzaville, Congo DR, Costa Rica, Côte d'Ivoire, Croatia, Cyprus, Czechia, Denmark, Ecuador, Egypt, Estonia, Ethiopia, Faeroe Is, Fiji, Finland, France, Gabon, Georgia, Germany, Ghana, Greece, Haiti, Honduras, Hong Kong, Hungary, Iceland, India, Indonesia, Iran Islamic Rep, Ireland, Israel, Italy, Jamaica, Japan, Kazakhstan, Kenya, Korea DPR, Korea Rep, Kosovo, Kuwait, Kyrgyzstan, Laos, Latvia, Lebanon, Lithuania, Luxembourg, Macau, Malawi, Malaysia, Mali, Malta, Mauritania, Mauritius, Mexico, Mongolia, Morocco, Namibia, New Zealand, Niger, Nigeria, North Macedonia, Norway, Pakistan, Palestine, Philippines, Poland, Portugal, Puerto Rico, Romania, Russia, Rwanda, Sao Tomé-Principe, Saudi Arabia, Senegal, Serbia, Sierra Leone, Singapore, Slovakia, Slovenia, South Africa, Spain, Sri Lanka, Sudan, Suriname, Sweden, Switzerland, Syrian AR, Tajikistan, Tanzania UR, Thailand, Trinidad-Tobago, Tunisia, Türkiye, Uganda, UK, Ukraine, USA, Uzbekistan, Vietnam, Zambia.
Included in the national sections, countries grouped in 2 regional associations:
Baltic Architects Unions Association (BAUA, #03093); Nordic Section.

Consultative Status Consultative status granted from: *Council of Europe (CE, #04881)* (Participatory Status); *ECOSOC (#05331)* (Special); *UNESCO (#20322)* (Associate Status); *ILO (#11123)* (Special List); *WHO (#20950)* (Official Relations); *UNICEF (#20332)*; *UNIDO (#20336)*; *World Intellectual Property Organization (WIPO, #21593)* (Permanent Observer Status). **IGO Relations** In liaison with technical committees of: *United Nations Human Settlements Programme (UN-Habitat, #20572)*. Associated with Department of Global Communications of the United Nations.

NGO Relations Member of: *NGO Committee on UNICEF (#17120)*. Partner of: *World Urban Campaign (WUC, #21893)*. In liaison with technical committees of: *International Organization for Standardization (ISO, #14473)*.
Agreements with:
- *Africa Union of Architects (AUA, #00529)*;
- *Architects Council of Europe (ACE, #01086)*;
- *Architects Regional Council Asia (ARCASIA, #01087)*;
- *Conselho Internacional dos Arquitetos de Lingua Portuguesa (CIALP)*;
- *Documentation and Conservation of the Modern Movement (DOCOMOMO International, #05110)*;
- *Emergency Architects*;
- *International Council on Monuments and Sites (ICOMOS, #13049)*;
- *International Federation of Landscape Architects (IFLA, #13467)*;
- *International Society of City and Regional Planners (ISOCARP, #15012)*;
- *Pan American Federation of Architects' Associations (#18098)*;
- *Union méditerranéenne des architectes (UMAR, #20459)*;
- *World Green Building Council (WorldGBC, #21544)*. [2022.02.02/XB2689/**B**]

- ♦ Union internationale de l'artisanat et des petites et moyennes entreprises (inactive)
- ♦ Union internationale des artistes (inactive)
- ♦ Union internationale des arts (inactive)

♦ Union internationale des associations d'alpinisme (UIAA) 20420

International Mountaineering and Climbing Federation – Unión Internacional de Asociaciones de Alpinismo – Internationaler Verband der Alpinistenvereine – Unione Internazionale delle Associazioni Alpinistiche

SG Monbijoustrasse 61, 3000 Bern 14, Switzerland. T. +41313701828. E-mail: office@theuiaa.org.

URL: http://www.theuiaa.org/

History 27 Aug 1932, Chamonix (France). Founded during a meeting of representatives from 18 countries in Chamonix. 1st Assembly: 1933, Cortina d'Ampezzo (Italy). Previous statutes approved 11 Oct 1986, Munich (Germany FR); revised Sep 1990. Current statutes adopted 18 Oct 2008, Teheran (Iran Islamic Rep); Revised 9 Oct 2010, Bormio (Italy), 8 Oct 2011, Kathmandu (Nepal) and 13 Oct 2012, Amsterdam (Netherlands). Registered Office in Bern (Switzerland). Former names and other names: *International Union of Alpinist Associations (IUAA)* – former. **Aims** Encourage, develop and support the practice of all forms of mountaineering and mountain *sports* in the international field. **Structure** General Assembly (annual); Management Committee; Executive Board. Mountaineering Commissions; Sports Commissions; Commission Working Groups. Court. Continental Organizations (3): *Confederación Panamericana de Deportes de Montaña y Escalada (UPAME, #04472)*; European Mountaineering Associations (EUMA); *Union of Asian Alpine Associations (UAAA, #20359)*5. Secretariat in Bern (Switzerland). **Languages** English. **Staff** 4.00 FTE, paid. Voluntary. **Finance** Sources: members' dues. **Activities** Networking/liaising; sporting activities. **Events** *Annual General Assembly* Malta 2023, *Annual General Assembly* Banff, AB (Canada) 2022, *Annual General Assembly* Bern (Switzerland) 2021, *Annual General Assembly* Antalya (Turkey) 2020, *Annual General Assembly* Nicosia (Cyprus) 2019. **Publications** *UIAA Electronic Newsletter* (12 a year) in English. Environmental guidelines; resolutions; rules for competitions; standards; media information.

Members National federations in 68 countries and territories:
Afghanistan, Albania, Argentina, Austria, Azerbaijan, Bangladesh, Belgium, Bosnia-Herzegovina, Brazil, Bulgaria, Canada, Chile, China, Costa Rica, Croatia, Cyprus, Czechia, Denmark, Finland, France, Georgia, Germany, Greece, Guatemala, Hong Kong, Hungary, India, Indonesia, Iran Islamic Rep, Ireland, Israel, Italy, Japan, Jordan, Kazakhstan, Korea Rep, Kosovo, Liechtenstein, Lithuania, Luxembourg, Malaysia, Malta, Monaco, Mongolia, Morocco, Nepal, Netherlands, New Zealand, North Macedonia, Norway, Pakistan, Poland, Portugal, Romania, Russia, Serbia, Slovakia, Slovenia, South Africa, Spain, Sri Lanka, Sweden, Switzerland, Taiwan, Türkiye, UK, Ukraine, USA.

IGO Relations *FAO (#09260)*; *UNEP (#20299)*; *United Nations (UN, #20515)* in the *'International Partnership for Sustainable Developments in Mountain Regions'*. **NGO Relations** Member of (2): *Association of the IOC Recognized International Sports Federations (ARISF, #02767)*; *Olympic Movement (#17719)*. Partner of (1): *European Union of Mountaineering Associations (EUMA, #09002)*. Recognized by: *International Olympic Committee (IOC, #14408)*. [2021/XC2684/y/**B**]

- ♦ Union internationale des associations d'annonceurs / see World Federation of Advertisers (#21407)
- ♦ Union internationale des associations de délégués médicaux (#15791)
- ♦ Union internationale d'associations des demeures historiques / see European Historic Houses Association (#07491)
- ♦ Union internationale des associations de guides de montagne (#15756)
- ♦ Union internationale des associations d'installateurs de chauffage, ventilation et conditionnement d'air (inactive)
- ♦ Union internationale des associations d'inventeurs et d'artistes industriels (inactive)
- ♦ Union internationale des associations des langues étrangères (inactive)

♦ Union internationale des associations et organismes scientifiques et techniques (UATI) 20421

International Union of Scientific and Technical Associations and Organizations

SG c/o Maison de l'UNESCO, 1 rue Miollis, 75732 Paris CEDEX 15, France. T. +33145684827. E-mail: uati@uati.info.

URL: https://uati.uisf.fr/

History Founded 12 Oct 1950, Paris (France), as *Union of International Engineering Organizations (UIEO)*, at a Conference of International Technical Associations, convened by *UNESCO (#20322)*, which adopted the Constitution. Subsequently titles: *Union of International Technical Associations – Union des associations techniques internationales*; *Union internationale des associations et organismes techniques (UATI) – International Union of Technical Associations and Organizations*. Statutes entered into effect 2 Mar 1951, when registered in accordance with Belgian law. Statutes subsequently modified: 27 May 1952; 18 Nov 1966; 18 Feb 1981; 1 Mar 1984; 6-7 Mar 1986; 8 May 1987; 29 Dec 1988; 26 Apr 1990; 25 Apr 1991; 5 Apr 1995; 10 Apr 1997; Apr 2007. Registered in accordance with French law on modification of statutes, 10 Jun 2000. Spanish titles *Unión de Asociaciones Técnicas Internacionales* and subsequently *Unión Internacional de Asociaciones y Organizaciones Técnicas* are not considered official. **Aims** Promote and coordinate: educational and training activities and scientific, technical, technological, social and cultural exchange, in particular with *developing countries* and emerging countries; *sustainable development*, in particular as a means of eradicating poverty and improving living standards; reduction of natural and man-made disaster risks. **Structure** General Assembly (every 2 years, in Paris); Board of Directors (meeting twice a year), comprising 25 members; Bureau of the Administrative Board. Technical Committees (10): Environment and Sustainable Development; Higher Education in Technology; Application of Advanced Techniques; Communication, Information and Informatics; Terminology; Integrated Transport; Engineering and Medicine; Health and Hygiene Policy in Arid and Semi-arid Areas; Heritage; Education and Standardization. **Languages** English, French. **Staff** 1.00 FTE, paid; 6.00 FTE, voluntary. **Finance** Sources: donations; gifts, legacies; government support; members' dues;

subsidies. **Activities** Events/meetings; financial and/or material support; projects/programmes; research/documentation; training/education. **Events** *Access to energy for everybody* Paris (France) 2005, *World congress on men's health medicine* Paris (France) 2004, *SIDMED : séminaire itinérant de la décennie internationale pour la réduction des catastrophes naturelles (IDNDR/ISDR) pour la Méditerranée* Marseille (France) 2003, *Transport and social integration in megapoles* Paris (France) 2003, *General Assembly* Paris (France) 2002. **Publications** *Convergence* (3 a year) in English, French – newsletter, jointly with ICET. Reports issued by Committees and Working Groups.
Members Regular international technical associations meeting the following conditions (a) have the aim of developing international cooperation between specialists in technical fields; (b) active in the area of technology as defined in the by-laws; (c) have member organizations in at least 3 countries; (d) executive board of international composition; (e) non-governmental. Associate national bodies competent in technical fields which, due in particular to their multidisciplinary nature, are unlikely to belong regular member. International organizations listed in this Yearbook (4):
Alliance de Villes Euro-méditerranéennes de Culture (AVEC, #00726); Comité transnational des géotechniciens d'Afrique (CTGA, #04199); Union internationale des ingénieurs et des scientifiques utilisant la langue française (UISF, #20427); World Road Association (PIARC, #21754).
National bodies (7) in 4 countries:
France (4), Georgia, Italy, Poland.
Consultative Status Consultative status granted from: *UNIDO (#20336); UNESCO (#20322)* (Associate Status). **IGO Relations** Accredited by (1): *United Nations Office at Vienna (UNOV, #20604).* Cooperates with (1): *United Nations Economic Commission for Europe (UNECE, #20555).* Associated with Department of Global Communications of the United Nations. **NGO Relations** Cooperates with (1): *International Organization for Standardization (ISO, #14473).* [2019/XA3353/y/**A**]

♦ Union internationale des associations et organismes techniques / see Union internationale des associations et organismes scientifiques et techniques (#20421)
♦ Union internationale des associations patronales catholiques / see International Christian Union of Business Executives (#12566)
♦ Union internationale des associations de presse (inactive)
♦ Union internationale des associations pour la prévention de la pollution de l'air et la protection de l'environnement (#15753)
♦ Union internationale des associations de prévention de la pollution atmosphérique / see International Union of Air Pollution Prevention and Environmental Protection Associations (#15753)
♦ Union internationale d'associations de propriétaires de wagons de particuliers / see International Union of Wagon Keepers (#15827)
♦ Union internationale des associations scoutes-guides pluralistes-laïques (no recent information)
♦ Union internationale des associations pour la Société des Nations (inactive)
♦ Union internationale des associations techniques cinématographiques (inactive)
♦ Union internationale d'assurances transports (#15789)
♦ Union internationale des assureurs aéronautiques (#15750)
♦ Union internationale des astronomes amateurs (no recent information)
♦ Union internationale des auberges pour la jeunesse / see Hostelling International (#10950)
♦ Union internationale des automobile-clubs médicaux (no recent information)

♦ Union Internationale des Avocats (UIA) 20422

International Association of Lawyers – Unión Internacional de Abogados
Exec Dir 20 rue Drouot, 75009 Paris, France. T. +33144885566. Fax +33144885577. E-mail: uiacentre@uianet.org.
URL: http://www.uianet.org/
History 8 Jul 1927, Charleroi (Belgium), a previous *Association internationale des avocats (inactive)* having been set up on 10 Mar 1905, Liège (Belgium). New statutes adopted: 14 Dec 1965; 8 Jul 1983; and modified: 16 Oct 1986; 2 Aug 1991; 19 Aug 1994, Paris (France); 3 Sep 1997, Philadelphia PA (USA); Aug 2005, Fez (Morocco). Previously referred to in English as *International Union of Lawyers* and as *Internationale Anwalts-Union – Unione Internazionale degli Avvocati.* Previously registered in accordance with Belgian Law. Since 1 jan 2012, registered in accordance with French law. **Aims** Provide benefits for members including information and idea exchange, legal training and development of productive relationships; advance the fundamental principles of the legal profession; promote the rule of law; defend lawyers' independence and freedom to practice their profession. **Structure** General Assembly (at least annual); Governing Board; Executive Committee; Commissions and Working Groups (43). **Languages** English, French, Spanish. **Staff** 10.00 FTE, paid. **Finance** Sources: meeting proceeds; members' dues. **Activities** Events/meetings; knowledge management/information dissemination; standards/guidelines. **Events** *Congress* Rome (Italy) 2023, *Congress* Dakar (Senegal) 2022, *Congress* Madrid (Spain) 2021, *Annual Business Law Forum* Amsterdam (Netherlands) 2020, *Annual Congress* Paris (France) 2020. **Publications** *Juriste international* in English, French, Spanish – magazine. *L'UIA et la profession d'avocat.* Annual Membership Directory; newsletters; congress and seminar proceedings.
Members Collective: national and local bars, national associations of local bars. Associate: international associations of lawyers, national or international associations of academic lawyers. Collective and/or associate members in 56 countries and territories:
Angola, Argentina, Australia, Austria, Azerbaijan, Belgium, Benin, Bolivia, Bosnia-Herzegovina, Brazil, Bulgaria, Cameroon, Canada, Cape Verde, Chile, China, Croatia, Czechia, Dominican Rep, Egypt, Equatorial Guinea, France, Germany, Greece, Hungary, India, Iran Islamic Rep, Iraq, Italy, Lebanon, Libya, Luxembourg, Malaysia, Mali, Mexico, Morocco, Netherlands, North Macedonia, Palestine, Poland, Portugal, Romania, Rwanda, Senegal, Serbia, Slovenia, Spain, Switzerland, Syrian AR, Togo, Tunisia, Türkiye, UK, USA, Vietnam, Zambia.
Individuals in 91 countries and territories:
Algeria, Andorra, Angola, Argentina, Australia, Austria, Azerbaijan, Bahrain, Belgium, Benin, Bosnia-Herzegovina, Brazil, Bulgaria, Burkina Faso, Burundi, Cambodia, Cameroon, Canada, Cape Verde, Central African Rep, Chile, China, Congo Brazzaville, Congo DR, Côte d'Ivoire, Croatia, Cuba, Czechia, Denmark, Egypt, Equatorial Guinea, Finland, France, Gabon, Germany, Greece, Guatemala, Guinea, Haiti, Hungary, India, Iraq, Ireland, Israel, Italy, Japan, Kazakhstan, Kuwait, Lebanon, Liechtenstein, Lithuania, Luxembourg, Madagascar, Mali, Mauritania, Mexico, Monaco, Morocco, Mozambique, Netherlands, Nigeria, North Macedonia, Norway, Pakistan, Paraguay, Peru, Poland, Portugal, Romania, Russia, San Marino, Saudi Arabia, Senegal, Serbia-Montenegro, Singapore, Slovakia, Slovenia, South Africa, Spain, Sweden, Switzerland, Syrian AR, Togo, Tunisia, Türkiye, UK, Ukraine, United Arab Emirates, USA, Venezuela, Vietnam.
Consultative Status Consultative status granted from: *ECOSOC (#05331)* (Special); *ILO (#11123)* (Special List); *Council of Europe (CE, #04881)* (Participatory Status); *World Intellectual Property Organization (WIPO, #21593)* (Observer Status). **IGO Relations** Accredited by: *United Nations Office at Geneva (UNOG, #20597);* United Nations Office at New York; *United Nations Office at Vienna (UNOV, #20604).* **NGO Relations** Founding member of: *Sport Integrity Global Alliance (SIGA, #19925).* Member of: *International Legal Assistance Consortium (ILAC, #14025); World Union of Professions (WUP, #21882).* Observer to: *Presidents of Law Associations in Asia (POLA, #18486).* Partner of: *Global Forum on Law, Justice and Development (GFLJD, #10373).* [2019.10.03/XC1301/**B**]

♦ Union internationale des bègues éliminant leur bégaiement (no recent information)
♦ Union internationale de biochimie / see International Union of Biochemistry and Molecular Biology (#15759)
♦ Union internationale de biochimie et de biologie moléculaire (#15759)
♦ Union internationale des biologistes du gibier (#15775)
♦ Union internationale de biophysique pure et appliquée (#15808)
♦ Union internationale de la boulangerie et de la boulangerie-pâtisserie / see International Union of Bakers and Confectioners (#15757)
♦ Union internationale des boulangers, confiseurs et métiers similaires (inactive)
♦ Union internationale de bowling amateur (inactive)
♦ Union internationale de boxe (inactive)
♦ Union internationale catholique des classes moyennes (inactive)
♦ Union internationale catholique pour l'étude du droit des gens d'après les principes chrétiens (inactive)
♦ Union internationale des centres du bâtiment (#15761)
♦ Union internationale de chasse / see Fédération Internationale de Tir aux Armes Sportives de Chasse (#09665)
♦ Union internationale des chauffeurs routiers (#15802)
♦ Union internationale des chemins de fer (#15813)
♦ Union internationale des chevaux en équipe / see International Brotherhood of Teamsters
♦ Union internationale de chimie / see International Union of Pure and Applied Chemistry (#15809)
♦ Union internationale de chimie pure et appliquée (#15809)
♦ Union internationale chrétienne des dirigeants d'entreprise (#12566)

♦ Union internationale du cinéma (UNICA) 20423

Chairman Via Balgine 6, 6997 Sessa TI, Switzerland. T. +41919450000. E-mail: info@unica1937.org.
URL: https://unica1937.org
History 1937, Paris (France). Founded as a permanent commission; approved at 4th Congress, 13-19 June 1938, Vienna (Austria). Statutes adopted 15 Aug 1947 Stockholm (Sweden); revised: Salerno (Italy) 1968; Hradec Kralové (Czech Rep) 1994; St Petersburg (Russia) 2015; Suceava (Romania) 2016; Dortmund (Germany) 2017; Blansko (Czech Rep) 2018; Zeist (Nederlands) 2019; Locarno (Switzerland) 2022; Comacchio (Italy) 2023. Former names and other names: *International Union of Amateur Film Makers* – former; *Union internationale du cinéma amateur* – former; *Union des fédérations nationales du cinéma non professionnel* – former; *Fédération internationale du cinéma non professionnel* – former; *International Union of Amateur Cinema* – former; *Unión Internacional de Cine Amateur* – former; *Union internationale du cinéma non professionnel* – former. **Aims** Promote video and film making as a means of international communication; support international cultural cooperation; represent member federations at UNESCO; achieve recognition of independence and freedom of expression for member federations. **Structure** General Assembly (annual), in conjunction with Congress; Committee. **Languages** English, French, German. **Staff** 10.00 FTE, voluntary. **Finance** Sources: donations; grants; members' dues; subsidies. **Activities** Events/meetings; knowledge management/information dissemination. **Events** *Annual Congress* Comacchio (Italy) 2023, *Annual Congress* Locarno (Switzerland) 2022, *Annual Congress* Zeist (Netherlands) 2019, *Annual Congress* Blansko (Czechia) 2018, *Annual Congress* Dortmund (Germany) 2017. **Publications** *Histoire de l'UNICA* by Jean Borel; *UNICA 1931-1981* by Sandór Buglya. Reports and congress proceedings. **Information Services** *Film Library* – established 1938, has over 1,100 works.
Members National film organizations in 29 countries:
Austria, Belgium, Bulgaria, Croatia, Czechia, Estonia, Finland, France, Georgia, Germany, Hungary, Italy, Korea Rep, Liechtenstein, Luxembourg, Netherlands, North Macedonia, Norway, Poland, Romania, Russia, Slovakia, Slovenia, Spain, Sweden, Switzerland, Tunisia, UK, Ukraine.
NGO Relations Member of (1): *International Council for Film, Television and Audiovisual Communication (IFTC, #13022).* [2023.02.19/XC2685/**C**]

♦ Union internationale du cinéma amateur / see Union internationale du cinéma (#20423)
♦ Union internationale du cinéma non professionnel / see Union internationale du cinéma (#20423)
♦ Union internationale des cinémas (#15763)
♦ Union internationale "Les clefs d'or" / see Union Internationale des Concierges d'Hôtels "Les Clefs d'Or" (#20424)
♦ Union internationale des collèges travaillant pour la paix mondiale (inactive)
♦ Union internationale du commerce de gros en fleurs / see UNION FLEURS (#20408)
♦ Union internationale du commerce et de la réparation du cycle et du motocycle (inactive)

♦ Union Internationale des Concierges d'Hôtels "Les Clefs d'Or" (UICH) 20424

International Union of Hotel Concierges "The Golden Keys"
Head Office 12 rue Cambon, 75001 Paris, France. T. +33142607757. E-mail: parisoffice@lesclefsdor.org.
Gen Sec Hilton London Metropole, 225 Edgware Road, London, W2 1JU, UK.
URL: http://www.lesclefsdor.org/
History 1952, Paris (France). Current statutes amended 13 Apr 2015. Former names and other names: *Union internationale des portiers des grands hôtels – "Les clefs d'or" (UIPGH)* – former (1952); *Union internationale "Les clefs d'or"* – former; *Society of the Golden Keys* – former. Registration: No/ID: 20070034, Start date: 25 Aug 2007, France, Paris. **Aims** Group national sections or individual members bearing the name "Les Clefs d'Or". **Finance** Sources: members' dues. **Activities** Awards/prizes/competitions; events/meetings; training/education. **Events** *Annual Congress* Doha (Qatar) 2021, *Annual Congress* Delhi (India) 2020, *Annual Congress* Cannes (France) 2019, *Asian Congress* Singapore (Singapore) 2019, *Annual Congress* Seoul (Korea Rep) 2018. **Publications** *Les clefs d'or* (periodical).
Members National sections and individual members in 44 countries and territories:
Argentina, Australia, Austria, Belgium, Brazil, Canada, Czechia, Denmark, Finland, France, Germany, Greece, Hong Kong, Hungary, India, Ireland, Israel, Italy, Japan, Korea Rep, Luxembourg, Macau, Malaysia, Mexico, Morocco, Netherlands, New Zealand, Norway, Philippines, Poland, Portugal, Qatar, Romania, Russia, Singapore, Spain, Sweden, Switzerland, Taiwan, Thailand, Türkiye, UK, United Arab Emirates, USA. [2022.04.21/XF5347/**F**]

♦ Union internationale des constructeurs d'ascenseurs (internationally oriented national body)
♦ Union internationale des constructeurs d'automobiles (inactive)
♦ Union internationale contre l'alcoolisme / see International Council on Alcohol and Addictions (#12989)
♦ Union internationale contre le cancer (#20415)
♦ Union internationale contre le duel et pour la protection de l'honneur (inactive)
♦ Union internationale contre les maladies vénériennes et les tréponématoses / see International Union against Sexually Transmitted Infections (#15751)
♦ Union internationale contre le péril vénérien / see International Union against Sexually Transmitted Infections (#15751)
♦ Union internationale contre le terrorisme (internationally oriented national body)
♦ Union internationale contre la traite des enfants (inactive)
♦ Union internationale contre la tuberculose / see International Union Against Tuberculosis and Lung Disease (#15752)
♦ Union internationale contre la tuberculose et les maladies respiratoires (#15752)
♦ Union internationale contre la vivisection (inactive)
♦ Union internationale pour la coopération culturelle (inactive)
♦ Union internationale de coopération en matière de brevets (#14530)
♦ Union internationale pour la coopération dans les recherches solaires (inactive)
♦ Union internationale des cordonniers (inactive)
♦ Union internationale de courses de yacht / see World Sailing (#21760)
♦ Union internationale de la couverture et plomberie (inactive)
♦ Union internationale de cristallographie (#15768)
♦ Union internationale de dendrologie (#13148)
♦ Union internationale pour le développement des stations uvales et de la consommation du raisin (inactive)
♦ Union internationale de directeurs de jardins zoologiques / see World Association of Zoos and Aquariums (#21208)
♦ Union internationale des distributeurs de chaleur / see Euroheat and Power (#05694)
♦ Union internationale de droit pénal (inactive)
♦ Union internationale du droit privé (inactive)
♦ Union internationale des ecclésiastiques et pasteurs antimilitaristes (inactive)
♦ Union internationale des écrivains révolutionnaires (inactive)
♦ Union internationale des éditeurs (#14675)
♦ Union internationale pour l'education (#14881)
♦ Union internationale pour l'éducation anti-alcoolique de la jeunesse (inactive)
♦ Union internationale pour l'éducation sanitaire de la population / see International Union for Health Promotion and Education (#15778)
♦ Union internationale d'éducation pour la santé / see International Union for Health Promotion and Education (#15778)
♦ Union internationale d'électrothermie / see International Union for Electricity Applications (#15770)

- ♦ Union internationale pour l'émission de billets à coupons combinés (inactive)
- ♦ Union internationale des employés de services (internationally oriented national body)
- ♦ Union internationale des enseignants socialistes / see International Social Democratic Union for Education (#14881)
- ♦ Union internationale pour l'enseignement des populations rurales par des projections lumineuses scientifiques (inactive)

♦ Union internationale des entrepreneurs de peinture (UNIEP) 20425

SG Rue de Trèves 45, 1040 Brussels, Belgium. T. +3224862512.
Pres Bahngasse 1, 3339 Melk, Austria.
URL: http://www.uniep.org/

History 23 Oct 1953, Zurich (Switzerland), by 8 countries (Belgium, Denmark, Germany, France, Italy, Luxembourg, Netherlands and Switzerland) and 10 national associations. New statutes adopted: 3 Oct 1963, Zurich; Nov 1974, Madrid (Spain); 1983, Århus (Denmark). **Aims** Serve as permanent link between member organizations; collect and diffuse documentation; carry out research on problems of common professional interest; promote information exchange between members and encourage them to exchange experiences and best practices in the context of the *painting* profession. **Structure** General Assembly (annual); Board; Secretariat in Brussels (Belgium). **Languages** English, French, German. **Staff** 2.00 FTE, paid. **Finance** Members' dues. **Activities** Advocacy/lobbying/activism; knowledge management/information dissemination; research and development; training/education; networking/liaising; events/meetings; projects/programmes. **Events** *Annual Delegate Assembly / Delegate Assembly* Frankfurt-Main (Germany) 2014, *Annual Delegate Assembly / Delegate Assembly* Cologne (Germany) 2013, *Annual Delegate Assembly / Delegate Assembly* Lucerne (Switzerland) 2012, *Annual Delegate Assembly / Delegate Assembly* Amsterdam (Netherlands) 2011, *Annual delegate assembly / Delegate Assembly* Munich (Germany) 2010. **Publications** *UNIEP Newsletter* (4 a year). Annual Report.
Members National and Observer associations (18) in 15 countries:
Austria, Belgium, Czechia, Denmark, France, Germany, Hungary, Ireland, Italy, Luxembourg, Slovakia, Slovenia, Sweden, Switzerland, UK.
NGO Relations Member of: *SMEunited (#19327).* [2019.02.14/XD2739/**D**]

- ♦ Union internationale espérantiste catholique (#12455)
- ♦ Union internationale des espérantistes végétariens / see World Esperantist Vegetarian Association (#21389)
- ♦ Union internationale pour l'étude des insectes sociaux (#15819)
- ♦ Union internationale pour l'étude du Quaternaire (#15811)
- ♦ Union internationale pour l'étude scientifique de la population (#15814)
- ♦ Union internationale pour l'étude scientifique des problèmes de la population / see International Union for the Scientific Study of Population (#15814)
- ♦ Union internationale des études orientales et asiatiques (inactive)
- ♦ Union internationale d'études sociales (inactive)
- ♦ Union internationale des étudiants en architecture (inactive)
- ♦ Union internationale des étudiants démocrates-chrétiens et conservateurs / see European Democrat Students (#06901)
- ♦ Union internationale de l'exploitation cinématographique / see International Union of Cinemas (#15763)
- ♦ Union internationale des fabricants d'imperméables (inactive)
- ♦ Union internationale des fédérations et associations nationales de tir / see International Shooting Sport Federation (#14852)
- ♦ Union internationale des fédérations de billard amateurs (inactive)
- ♦ Union internationale des fédérations de détaillants en produits laitiers (inactive)
- ♦ Union internationale des fédérations des ouvriers et ouvrières de l'alimentation / see International Union of Food, Agricultural, Hotel, Restaurant, Catering, Tobacco and Allied Workers Associations (#15772)
- ♦ Union internationale des femmes architectes (#15828)
- ♦ Union internationale des femmes libérales chrétiennes (#11999)
- ♦ Union Internationale des forgerons-constructeurs / see European Metal Union (#07785)
- ♦ Union internationale pour la formation technique et culturelle des adultes (inactive)
- ♦ Union internationale francophone pour la formation des informaticiens et gestionnaires d'entreprise (no recent information)
- ♦ Union Internationale du Gaz (#13700)
- ♦ Union internationale de grands magasins (inactive)
- ♦ Union internationale des groupements professionnels des importateurs et distributeurs grossistes en alimentation (inactive)
- ♦ Union internationale des groupes bibliques universitaires (#13583)

♦ Union Internationale des Guides et Scouts d'Europe – Fédération du Scoutisme Européen (UIGSE-FSE) 20426

International Union of Guides and Scouts of Europe – Federation of European Scouting

Officer Le relais de Poste, Route de Montargis, CS 80594, 77570 Château-Landon, France. T. +33766449638. E-mail: info@uigse-fse.org.
URL: http://www.uigse-fse.org/

History 1 Nov 1956, Cologne (Germany). Religious Directory revised 15 Mar 1963, Paris (France). Former names and other names: *Federation of European Scouting (FES)* – former; *Association des Guides et Scouts d'Europe* – alias; *International Union of European Guides and Scouts* – alias; *Internationale Vereinigung der Pfadfinderschaft Europas* – former; *Internationale Vereniging van Europese Scouts en Gidsen* – former. Registration: Start date: 23 Sep 1977, France, Clamart. **Aims** Train young people through the traditional practice of Baden-Powell scouting, with reference to the *Christian* values which are the basis of European civilization; create an active community in which youth of various European countries can fully participate; at the same time, develop each national culture, which is the manifold expression of their common inheritance. **Structure** Federal Council; Federal Bureau; Federal Commission. **Languages** Albanian, Belarusian, Czech, Dutch, English, French, German, Hungarian, Italian, Lithuanian, Polish, Portuguese, Romanian, Russian, Slovakian, Spanish, Ukrainian. **Staff** 1.00 FTE, paid. **Finance** Sources: members' dues. Annual budget: 120,000 EUR. **Activities** Events/meetings. **Events** *International Meeting* Rome (Italy) 2019, *International Meeting* Metz (France) 2014, *International Meeting* Levoca (Slovakia) 2007, *European jamboree / International Meeting* Zelazko (Poland) 2003, *International congress / International Meeting* Cortina d'Ampezzo (Italy) 1998. **Publications** *Maîtrises* (5 a year) in French; *Die Spur* (4 a year) in German; *Azimut 360* (regular) in Dutch, French; *Gniazdo* (regular) in Polish; *Scout d'Europa* (regular) in Italian; *Scout d'Europe* (7 a year) in French; *Servir/Dienen* (regular) in Dutch, French; *Sois prêt* (regular) in French.
Members National associations. Full in 13 countries:
Austria, Belarus, Belgium, France, Germany, Italy, Poland, Portugal, Romania, Slovakia, Spain, Switzerland, Ukraine.
Candidate and Associated in 9 countries:
Canada, Czechia, Germany, Ireland, Lithuania, Luxembourg, Netherlands, Russia, USA.
Observer in 5 countries:
Albania, Brazil, Hungary, Mexico, UK.
Consultative Status Consultative status granted from: *Council of Europe (CE, #04881)* (Participatory Status). **NGO Relations** Member of (1): *Forum of Catholic Inspired NGOs (#09905).* [2022.10.19/XD3560/**D**]

- ♦ Union internationale d'histoire et de méthodologie des sciences (inactive)
- ♦ Union internationale d'histoire et de philosophie des sciences / see International Union of History and Philosophy of Science and Technology (#15779)
- ♦ Union internationale de l'histoire des sciences (inactive)
- ♦ Union internationale de l'hospitalisation privée (no recent information)
- ♦ Union internationale des hôteliers (inactive)
- ♦ Union internationale des huissiers de justice et officiers judiciaires (#15785)
- ♦ Union internationale humaniste et laïque / see Humanists International (#10972)
- ♦ Union internationale de l'industrie du gaz / see International Gas Union (#13700)
- ♦ Union internationale des infirmières diplômées d'Etat (inactive)
- ♦ Union internationale des ingénieurs de opération (internationally oriented national body)
- ♦ Union Internationale des Ingénieurs Professionnels (#15803)

♦ Union internationale des ingénieurs et des scientifiques utilisant la langue française (UISF) 20427

SG c/o UATI, Maison de l'UNESCO, 1 rue Miollis, 75732 Paris CEDEX 15, France. T. +33689152429.
Pres address not obtained. T. +33145684827.

History 4 Feb 1987. Founded as *Union des ingénieurs et des techniciens utilisant la langue française (UITF) – Union of Engineers and Technicians Utilizing the French Language.* Principal founder: Pierre Aigrain. Current title adopted 2003. Registration: France. **Aims** Maintain worldwide links among communities of scientists and civil *engineers* who make use of the French language in their professional activities; provide them with scientific and technical knowledge within the context of French culture; encourage exchange and transfer of information in a networked structure; promote visibility of their activities through publications. **Structure** General Assembly (every two years); Council; Advisory Council; Technical and Scientific Committee; Higher Education Network. **Languages** French. **Staff** 3.00 FTE, voluntary. **Finance** Members' dues. Contracts. **Activities** Events/meetings; publishing activities; training/education. **Events** *Science and Technology for Development in Africa Conference* Paris (France) 2015, *Conférence Internationale sur l'Eau / Science and Technology for Development in Africa Conference* Algiers (Algeria) 2013, *Colloque sur les Nouvelles Technologies dans la Conception et l'Exécution des Routes* Beirut (Lebanon) 2013, *Seminar* Brazzaville (Congo Brazzaville) 2013, *Colloque sur la Simulation en Hydraulique et Environnement* Casablanca (Morocco) 2013.
Members Individual and organizations using French in their engineering or scientific activities. Members in 28 countries:
Algeria, Belgium, Benin, Burkina Faso, Burundi, Cameroon, Canada, Central African Rep, Chad, Congo Brazzaville, Congo DR, Côte d'Ivoire, Djibouti, France, Gabon, Greece, Italy, Lebanon, Madagascar, Mali, Morocco, Niger, Russia, Senegal, Sweden, Togo, Tunisia, Vietnam.
NGO Relations Member of: *Union internationale des associations et organismes scientifiques et techniques (UATI, #20421).* [2019.02.16/XC0384/**C**]

- ♦ Union internationale des ingénieurs et techniciens des travaux de forage (inactive)
- ♦ Union internationale des instituts d'archéologie, d'histoire et d'histoire de l'art de Rome (#15782)
- ♦ Union internationale des instituts d'essais forestiers / see International Union of Forest Research Organizations (#15774)
- ♦ Union Internationale des Instituts de Recherches Forestières (#15774)
- ♦ Union internationale des jeunes démocrates-chrétiens (inactive)
- ♦ Union internationale des jeunes écrivains et artistes pour la paix, l'amour et la justice (internationally oriented national body)
- ♦ Union internationale des jeunesses radicales, libérales et démocrates (inactive)
- ♦ Union internationale des jeunesses socialistes (#15815)

♦ Union internationale des journalistes africains (UIJA) 20428

Pres 1 allée du 8 mai 1945, 94140 Alfortville, France. T. +33619788417.

History Founded 23 Nov 1974, Kinshasa (Congo DR), following decision at a symposium in 1973, Yamoussoukro (Côte d'Ivoire), and previous efforts commencing with Pan-African meeting of journalists, 1961, Bamako (Mali), under the auspices of *Organization of African Unity (OAU, inactive)*, when *Pan African Journalists' Union, 1961 (PAJU, inactive)* was set up (ceased activities 1965). Also known as *Union of African Journalists (UAJ) – Union des journalistes africains (UJA).* **Aims** Work for the benefit of the continent and African journalists in a spirit of cooperation and African unity; promote cooperation among journalists; coordinate professional activities; defend the right to freedom of expression in the spirit of realistic understanding, especially in the struggle against apartheid; defend African causes in general. **Structure** General Assembly; Bureau; Council; permanent Headquarters in Cairo (Egypt). **Languages** Arabic, English, French. **Staff** Paid by Egyptian government. **Finance** Members' dues. **Activities** Training/education; events/meetings; knowledge management/information dissemination. **Events** *Journalists of Africa; the union challenge of the nineties* Harare (Zimbabwe) 1990, *Humanity and the media* Tunis (Tunisia) 1989, *Congress* Cairo (Egypt) 1987. **Publications** *The African Journalist* (12 a year) in Arabic, English, French; *Le Devoir Africain* – magazine.
Members Syndicates and organizations of African journalists in all member countries of OAU. Members in 50 countries and territories:
Algeria, Angola, Benin, Botswana, Burkina Faso, Burundi, Cameroon, Cape Verde, Central African Rep, Chad, Comoros, Congo Brazzaville, Congo DR, Côte d'Ivoire, Djibouti, Egypt, Equatorial Guinea, Eswatini, Ethiopia, Gabon, Gambia, Ghana, Guinea, Guinea-Bissau, Kenya, Lesotho, Liberia, Libya, Madagascar, Malawi, Mali, Mauritania, Mauritius, Mozambique, Niger, Nigeria, Rwanda, Sahara West, Sao Tomé-Principe, Senegal, Seychelles, Sierra Leone, Somalia, Sudan, Tanzania UR, Togo, Tunisia, Uganda, Zambia, Zimbabwe.
Consultative Status Consultative status granted from: *World Intellectual Property Organization (WIPO, #21593)* (Permanent Observer Status). **NGO Relations** Cooperates with: *Federation of Arab Journalists (FAJ, #09422); Federación Latinoamericana de Periodistas (FELAP, #09359).* [2017.11.25/XD5342/**D**]

- ♦ Union internationale des journalistes et de la presse de langue française / see Union internationale de la presse francophone (#20435)

♦ Union internationale des laboratoires indépendants (UILI) 20429

International Union of Independent Laboratories – Internationale Vereinigung Unabhängiger Laboratorien

Secretariat PO Box 4602, 4803 EP Breda, Netherlands. T. +34625065790. E-mail: secretariat@uili.org.
Pres c/o LabWing BV, PO Box 4975, 4801 DZ Breda, Netherlands. T. +31765645070.
URL: http://www.uili.org/

History Sep 1960, Hamburg (Germany FR), following a preparatory meeting, Mar 1959, Paris (France). Registered in accordance with French law, 1961. **Aims** Promote the international status of laboratories and scientific consultants, emphasizing the importance of their role in international trade. **Structure** General Assembly (every 2 years); Governing Board. **Languages** English. **Staff** 1.00 FTE, paid. **Finance** Sources: members' dues. **Activities** Events/meetings. **Events** *General Assembly* Rotterdam (Netherlands) 2021, *General Assembly* Rotterdam (Netherlands) 2020, *Lab Meeting* Rotterdam (Netherlands) 2020, *Lab Meeting* Singapore (Singapore) 2018, *General Assembly* Bogota (Colombia) 2017. **Publications** *UILI Newsletter* (6 a year) – online; *UILI Directory.*
Members National associations of independent laboratories and consultants in 9 countries (marked "); private laboratories; independent consultants. Members in 22 countries:
Argentina (*), Belgium, Brazil, Canada (*), Chile, Colombia (*), France, Greece, India (*), Ireland, Japan (*), Malaysia, Netherlands (*), Nigeria (*), Paraguay, Portugal (*), Saudi Arabia, Singapore, Spain (*), Türkiye, UK, Uruguay.
Consultative Status Consultative status granted from: *ECOSOC (#05331)* (Ros C). **NGO Relations** In liaison with technical committees of: *International Organization for Standardization (ISO, #14473).* Stakeholder Member of: *African Accreditation Cooperation (AFRAC, #00196).* Affiliate member of: *Asia Pacific Accreditation Cooperation (APAC, #01816).* [2019.02.13/XC2728/**C**]

- ♦ Union internationale pour la liberté d'enseignement (inactive)
- ♦ Union internationale des ligues féminines catholiques / see World Union of Catholic Women's Organisations (#21876)
- ♦ Union internationale pour les livres de jeunesse (#12366)
- ♦ Union internationale des locataires (#15822)
- ♦ Union internationale de logique, méthodologie et philosophie des sciences (inactive)
- ♦ Union internationale des magistrats (#11978)
- ♦ Union internationale des maîtres abstinents (inactive)
- ♦ Union internationale des maîtres-boulangers / see International Union of Bakers and Confectioners (#15757)
- ♦ Union internationale des maîtres d'hôtel (inactive)

♦ Union internationale de la marionnette (UNIMA) 20430

International Puppeteers Union

Secretariat 10 cours Aristide Briand, BP 402, 08107 Charleville-Mézières, France. T. +33324328563. E-mail: contact@unima.org.
URL: http://www.unima.org/

History 20 May 1929, Prague (Czechia). Reorganized 9 Dec 1957, Prague. Former names and other names: *Union mondiale de la marionnette* – alias. **Aims** Foster cooperation between *puppeteers* throughout the world. **Structure** Council (meets every 4 years), comprising Councillors from all member countries; Executive Committee (meets annually) of 18 members; Board of 5 members. Daily functioning of the Association is run by the General Secretary, President and Treasurer. Commissions (16): Professional Training; Scientific Research; Communication; Publication; Statutes; Europe; Asia-Pacific; Africa; Middle East and North Africa; Tree Americas; Social Justice; Heritage; Youth; International Festivals; Cooperation; Puppetry in Education. Congress (every 4 years). **Languages** English, French, Spanish. **Staff** 2.00 FTE, paid. Many voluntary. **Finance** Members' dues. Sponsoring. **Activities** Projects/programmes; events/meetings; research/documentation. **Events** *UNIMA Congress & World Puppetry Festival* Bali (Indonesia) 2021, *Quadrennial Congress* Bali (Indonesia) 2020, *Quadrennial Congress* San Sebastian (Spain) 2016, *Quadrennial Congress* Chengdu (China) 2012, *Quadrennial Congress* Perth, WA (Australia) 2008. **Publications** *Puppets Festivals Directory*; *Researchers Directory*; *World Encyclopaedia of Puppetry Arts*.

Members Associations and individuals in 87 countries:
Albania, Algeria, Argentina, Armenia, Australia, Austria, Azerbaijan, Belarus, Belgium, Bolivia, Bosnia-Herzegovina, Brazil, Bulgaria, Burkina Faso, Burundi, Cambodia, Canada, Chile, China, Colombia, Congo DR, Costa Rica, Côte d'Ivoire, Croatia, Cuba, Cyprus, Czechia, Denmark, Ecuador, Egypt, Estonia, Finland, France, Georgia, Germany, Greece, Hungary, Iceland, India, Indonesia, Iran Islamic Rep, Ireland, Israel, Italy, Japan, Kazakhstan, Korea Rep, Kyrgyzstan, Lebanon, Lithuania, Madagascar, Mali, Mexico, Moldova, Morocco, Myanmar, Netherlands, New Zealand, Nicaragua, North Macedonia, Norway, Pakistan, Peru, Philippines, Poland, Portugal, Romania, Russia, Senegal, Serbia, Slovakia, Slovenia, South Africa, Spain, Sweden, Switzerland, Togo, Tunisia, Türkiye, UK, Ukraine, Uruguay, USA, Uzbekistan, Venezuela, Vietnam, Zambia.

Consultative Status Consultative status granted from: *UNESCO (#20322)* (Consultative Status).
[2017.06.01/XD2240/**D**]

- ♦ Union internationale de mathématique (inactive)
- ♦ Union internationale de mécanique théorique et appliquée (#15823)
- ♦ Union internationale de médecine esthétique (#15771)
- ♦ Union internationale de médecine thermale et de climatothalassothérapie (inactive)
- ♦ Union internationale du métal / see European Metal Union (#07785)
- ♦ Union internationale des métis (inactive)
- ♦ Union internationale pour les micro-algues (no recent information)
- ♦ Union internationale des miroitiers-vitriers / see European Glaziers Association (#07394)
- ♦ Union internationale monarchiste (no recent information)

♦ Union internationale Motonautique (UIM) 20431

International Powerboating Federation – Federación Internacional de Motonautica

SG Stade Louis II – Entrée H, 1 ave des Castelans, 98000 Monte Carlo, Monaco. T. +37792052522. Fax +37792050460. E-mail: uim@uim.sport.
Communications Officer address not obtained.
URL: http://www.uimpowerboating.com/

History 1922, Brussels (Belgium). Transferred to Monaco, Apr 1988. Current statutes adopted, 2004. Former names and other names: *Union internationale du yachting automobile (UIYA)* – former; *International Motor Yachting Union* – former; *Union of International Motorboating* – former; *Union of International Powerboating* – former; *Unión Internacional de Motonautica* – former. Registration: Banque-Carrefour des Entreprises, Start date: 4 Sep 1972. **Aims** Protect and build the future of the *Sport*; create a safe, accessible, unified and thriving world renowned sport. **Structure** General Assembly (annual); Council; Executive Committee. Commissions (5); Committees (8). **Languages** English, French. **Staff** 4.00 FTE, paid; 150.00 FTE, voluntary. **Finance** Sources: members' dues. **Activities** Awards/prizes/competitions; events/meetings; sporting activities. **Events** *General Assembly* 2021, *General Assembly* 2020, *General Assembly* Qingdao (China) 2019, *General Assembly* Beirut (Lebanon) 2018, *General Assembly* Budva (Montenegro) 2017. **Publications** *UIM Newsletter* (6 a year); *UIM Official Yearbook*; *UIM Sporting Calendar*. Sporting rules and regulations in English.

Members Full (46); Corresponding (17). National authorities in 57 countries:
Australia, Austria, Belgium, Bulgaria, Canada, China, Colombia, Croatia, Cyprus, Czechia, Denmark, Estonia, Finland, France, Germany, Hungary, India, Indonesia, Ireland, Italy, Japan, Korea Rep, Kuwait, Latvia, Lebanon, Lithuania, Macau, Maldives, Malta, Mexico, Monaco, Montenegro, Morocco, Netherlands, New Zealand, Norway, Poland, Portugal, Qatar, Russia, Saudi Arabia, Serbia, Slovakia, Slovenia, South Africa, Spain, Sri Lanka, Sweden, Switzerland, Thailand, Trinidad-Tobago, Türkiye, UK, Ukraine, United Arab Emirates, Uruguay, USA.

NGO Relations Member of (2): *Association of the IOC Recognized International Sports Federations (ARISF, #02767)*; *Olympic Movement (#17719)*. Cooperates with (1): *International Testing Agency (ITA, #15678)*. Recognized by: *International Olympic Committee (IOC, #14408)*. [2022.04.28/XC3355/**C**]

- ♦ Union internationale de la navigation fluviale (inactive)
- ♦ Union of International Encounter Centres of France / see Ethic étapes
- ♦ Union of International Engineering Organizations / see Union internationale des associations et organismes scientifiques et techniques (#20421)
- ♦ Union internationale du Notariat (#15795)
- ♦ Union internationale du notariat latin / see International Union of Notaries (#15795)
- ♦ Union der Internationalen Verbände (#20414)

♦ Union internationale des oenologues (UIOE) 20432

International Union of Oenologists

Contact 18 rue d'Aguesseau, 75008 Paris, France. T. +33675257505. E-mail: contact@uioe.eu.
URL: http://www.uioe.eu/

History 23 Feb 1966, Paris (France). **Aims** Establish close links between oenologists in every country, represent them and defend their legitimate interests; standardize their rights and responsibilities on a world scale; facilitate the exchange of knowledge by means of publications and congresses. **Structure** Administrative Council (annual); Executive Committee. Officers: President; 1st and 2nd Vice-Presidents; Secretary-General; Treasurer. **Languages** French. **Staff** Voluntary. **Finance** Sources: members' dues. **Events** *General Assembly* Bordeaux (France) 2014, *General Assembly* Paris (France) 2011, *General Assembly* Bento Gonçalves (Brazil) 2010, *General Assembly* Verona (Italy) 2007, *Congrès mondial sur l'analyse sensorielle des vins / Congress* Barcelona (Spain) 1986.

Members Individuals (about 15,000), grouped in national organizations, in 13 countries:
Brazil, Canada, Chile, Croatia, France, Germany, Greece, Italy, Portugal, Slovenia, Spain, Switzerland, UK.

NGO Relations Observer status with (1): *World Federation of Major International Wine and Spirits Competitions (VinoFed, #21452)*. In liaison with technical committees of: *International Organization for Standardization (ISO, #14473)*. [2015/XD2744/**D**]

- ♦ Union internationale des oeuvres catholiques d'éducation physique / see International Catholic Federation of Physical Education and Sports (#12456)
- ♦ Union internationale des officiers et fonctionnaires de l'état civil (inactive)
- ♦ Union internationale des organisations associatives pro-européennes (no recent information)
- ♦ Union internationale des organisations de détaillants de la branche alimentaire (inactive)
- ♦ Union internationale des organismes familiaux / see World Family Organization (#21399)
- ♦ Union internationale d'ornithologie appliquée (inactive)
- ♦ Union internationale des orphelins de guerre (inactive)
- ♦ Union internationale des ouvriers chapeliers (inactive)
- ♦ Union internationale des ouvriers coiffeurs (inactive)
- ♦ Union internationale pour le pacte Roerich (inactive)
- ♦ Union internationale de la pâtisserie, confiserie et glacerie (inactive)
- ♦ Union internationale des patronages (inactive)
- ♦ Union internationale de pentathlon moderne / see World Penthathlon (#21720)
- ♦ Union internationale de pentathlon moderne et biathlon / see World Penthathlon (#21720)
- ♦ Union internationale du pétrole (inactive)
- ♦ Union internationale de pharmacologie / see International Union of Basic and Clinical Pharmacology (#15758)
- ♦ Union internationale des philologues espérantistes (inactive)
- ♦ Union Internationale de Phlébologie (#15797)
- ♦ Union internationale de photographie (inactive)
- ♦ Union internationale de physique pure et appliquée (#15810)
- ♦ Union internationale des planteurs et producteurs de tabac / see International Tobacco Growers Union (#15695)
- ♦ Union internationale des portiers des grands hôtels – "Les clefs d'or" / see Union Internationale des Concierges d'Hôtels "Les Clefs d'Or" (#20424)
- ♦ Union internationale de la press catholique / see International Christian Organisation of the Media (#12563)

♦ Union internationale de la presse électronique (UIPRE) 20433

CEO Hegnacher Str 30, 71336 Waiblingen, Germany. T. +49715123331. Fax +49715123338. E-mail: ceoffice@uipre-internationalpress.org.
Pres address not obtained.
URL: http://www.uipre-internationalpress.org/

History 20 Aug 1959, Frankfurt-Main (Germany). Statutes adopted and entered into force 1 Jan 1960; most recently revised 30 Aug 1991. **Aims** Work and organize for international and European journalists and experts in all electronic-clusters. **Structure** General Assembly; Executive Committee. **Languages** English, German. **Finance** Sources: members' dues. **Activities** Awards/prizes/competitions; certification/accreditation; events/meetings; knowledge management/information dissemination; networking/liaising; politics/policy/regulatory; publishing activities; research/documentation; standards/guidelines. **Events** *General Meeting* Breisach am Rhein (Germany) 2010, *General Meeting* Berlin (Germany) 2009, *General Meeting* Berlin (Germany) 2009, *General Meeting* Hannover (Germany) 2009, *General Meeting* Schluchsee (Germany) 2009. **Publications** *UIPRE Medienreport*. **Members** Individuals. Membership countries not specified. [2023.02.28/XD9062/v/**D**]

♦ Union internationale de presse ferroviaire (FERPRESS) 20434

International Union of Railway Press – Internationale Eisenbahn-Presse-Vereinigung

Pres Danneckerstrasse 50, 70182 Stuttgart, Germany. T. +49711242554 – +491741522971. E-mail: info@ferpress.ch – info@ferpress.org.
Treas address not obtained.

History 1960, Salzburg (Austria). Launched 1965, Vienna (Austria). **Aims** Unite railway *journalists*. **Structure** General Assembly. **Languages** English, French, German. **Staff** Voluntary. **Finance** Members' dues. **Activities** Events/meetings. **Events** *General Assembly* Blumberg (Germany) 2015, *General Assembly* Germany 2015, *General Assembly* Sinsheim (Germany) 2014, *General Assembly* Berlin (Germany) 2013, *General Assembly* Friedrichshafen (Germany) 2012.

Members in 12 countries:
Austria, Belgium, Denmark, France, Germany, Italy, Netherlands, Norway, Poland, Spain, Switzerland, USA.

NGO Relations Joint meetings with: *Union européenne des modélistes ferroviaires et des amis des chemins de fer (#20400)*. [2015.06.30/XD6840/**D**]

- ♦ Union internationale de la presse filmée (inactive)

♦ Union internationale de la presse francophone (UPF) 20435

SG 3 Cité Bergère, 75009 Paris, France. T. +33147700280. Fax +33148242632. E-mail: union@presse-francophone.org.
URL: http://www.presse-francophone.org/

History Founded Sep 1950, Paris (France), as *Union internationale des journalistes et de la presse de langue française (UIJPLF)*, at 1st Congress, following recommendation of French national union congress, May 1950, Limoges (France). New name adopted, 2001 Beirut (Lebanon). **Aims** Preserve and safeguard the French language and culture; link journalists in all parts of the world who use the French language; develop and coordinate relations among publishers, *radio* and *television* stations, and all other media for *communication* in French; promote technical cooperation in information and professional training. **Structure** Bureau. **Languages** French. **Staff** 7.00 FTE, paid. **Finance** Sources: members' dues. **Activities** Carries out investigations into written and audio-visual French-language publications. Organizes congresses and meetings. Instrumental in setting up *Pressothèque de langue française (#18489)*. **Events** *Assises internationales / International Assize* Bucharest (Romania) 2006, *Assises internationales* Algiers (Algeria) 2005, *International Assize* Yaoundé (Cameroon) / Algiers (Algeria) 2005, *Assises internationales / International Assize* Ouagadougou (Burkina Faso) 2004, *Assises internationales / International Assize* Libreville (Gabon) 2003. **Publications** *La gazette de la presse francophone* (6 a year). **Information Services** *Pressothèque de langue française* – international library and documentation centre of the French-language press.

Members National organizations in 49 countries and territories:
Albania, Algeria, Angola, Armenia, Azerbaijan, Belgium, Benin, Bulgaria, Burkina Faso, Burundi, Cambodia, Cameroon, Canada, Central African Rep, Chad, Comoros, Congo Brazzaville, Congo DR, Côte d'Ivoire, Djibouti, France, Gabon, Georgia, Greece, Guinea, Haiti, Italy, Laos, Lebanon, Luxembourg, Madagascar, Mali, Mauritania, Mauritius, Moldova, Monaco, Morocco, Niger, Palestine, Romania, Rwanda, Senegal, Seychelles, Switzerland, Togo, Tunisia, USA, Vanuatu, Vietnam.
Individuals in 76 countries and territories. Membership countries not specified.

Consultative Status Consultative status granted from: *ECOSOC (#05331)* (Ros A); *UNESCO (#20322)* (Consultative Status). [2022/XC1285/**C**]

- ♦ Union internationale de la presse médicale (no recent information)
- ♦ Union internationale de la presse pour la paix (inactive)
- ♦ Union internationale pour la presse scientifique (inactive)
- ♦ Union internationale pour prévenir l'introduction et la propagation du phylloxéra (inactive)
- ♦ Union Internationale de Prières de Banneux Notre-Dame (religious order)
- ♦ Union internationale des producteurs de plantes vivaces (#13277)
- ♦ Union internationale des producteurs de tabac (#15695)
- ♦ Union internationale des professeurs et maîtres de conférences des universités techniques et scientifiques et des instituts post-universitaires de perfectionnement technique et scientifique (inactive)
- ♦ Union internationale des professeurs de rythmique Jaques-Dalcroze / see International Federation of Eurhythmics Teachers (#13418)
- ♦ Union internationale de promotion de la santé et d'éducation pour la santé (#15778)
- ♦ Union internationale pour la promotion du travail (inactive)
- ♦ Union internationale de la propriété foncière bâtie / see International Union of Property Owners (#15804)
- ♦ Union internationale de la propriété immobilière (#15804)
- ♦ Union internationale pour la protection du commerce en temps de guerre (inactive)
- ♦ Union internationale de protection de l'enfance (inactive)
- ♦ Union internationale pour la protection de l'enfance du premier âge (inactive)
- ♦ Union internationale pour la protection de la nature / see International Union for Conservation of Nature and Natural Resources (#15766)

♦ Union internationale pour la protection des obtentions végétales (UPOV) 20436

International Union for the Protection of New Varieties of Plants – Unión Internacional para la Protección de las Obtenciones Vegetales – Internationaler Verband zum Schutz von Pflanzenzuechtungen

SG Chemin des Colombettes 34, 1211 Geneva 20, Switzerland. T. +41223389111. Fax +41227330336. E-mail: upov.mail@upov.int.
URL: http://www.upov.int/

History 2 Dec 1961, Paris (France). Founded by *International Convention for the Protection of New Varieties of Plants, 1961 (1961)*; the Convention entered into force in 1968 and was revised: 10 Nov 1972, Geneva (Switzerland); 23 Oct 1978, Geneva; 19 Mar 1991, Geneva. *World Intellectual Property Organization (WIPO, #21593)* provides administrative support services. **Aims** Provide and promote an effective system of plant variety protection with the aim of encouraging development of new varieties of plants for the benefit of society. **Structure** Council (meeting annually in Ordinary Session). Office (secretariat) headed by Secretary-General, located in Geneva (Switzerland). UPOV Secretary-General is also Director General of WIPO. **Languages** English, French, German, Spanish. **Staff** 11.00 FTE, paid. *Administrative Tribunal of the International Labour Organization (ILO Tribunal, #00118)* is competent to settle disputes. **Finance** Sources: members' dues. **Activities** Events/meetings; knowledge management/information dissemination; research/documentation. **Events** *Ordinary Session* Geneva (Switzerland) 2021, *Ordinary Session* Geneva (Switzerland) 2020, *Session* Seoul (Korea Rep) 2019, *Meeting of Test Guidelines Harmonisation on Dendrobium* Busan (Korea Rep) 2015, *Meeting* Obihiro (Japan) 2015. **Publications** *UPOV Reports on the Impact of Plant Variety Protection.* Guidance and information materials; seminar and symposium proceedings.

Members The Convention may be ratified, accepted or approved by any State which has signed it. A State which has not signed it and certain intergovernmental organizations may accede to it. Any State which is not a member of the Union and certain intergovernmental organizations shall obtain the positive advice of the UPOV Council in respect of the conformity of its laws with the 1991 Act of the UPOV Convention before depositing the instrument of accession. Members States as of 12 Oct 2022 (76):

Albania, Argentina, Australia, Austria, Azerbaijan, Belarus, Belgium, Bolivia, Bosnia-Herzegovina, Brazil, Bulgaria, Canada, Chile, China, Colombia, Costa Rica, Croatia, Czechia, Denmark, Dominican Rep, Ecuador, Egypt, Estonia, Finland, France, Georgia, Germany, Ghana, Hungary, Iceland, Ireland, Israel, Italy, Japan, Jordan, Kenya, Korea Rep, Kyrgyzstan, Latvia, Lithuania, Mexico, Moldova, Montenegro, Morocco, Netherlands, New Zealand, Nicaragua, North Macedonia, Norway, Oman, Panama, Paraguay, Peru, Poland, Portugal, Romania, Russia, Serbia, Singapore, Slovakia, Slovenia, South Africa, Spain, St Vincent-Grenadines, Sweden, Switzerland, Tanzania UR, Trinidad-Tobago, Tunisia, Türkiye, UK, Ukraine, Uruguay, USA, Uzbekistan, Vietnam.

African Intellectual Property Organization (#00344); *European Union (EU, #08967).*

Observer States (58):

Afghanistan, Algeria, Armenia, Bangladesh, Barbados, Brunei Darussalam, Burkina Faso, Burundi, Cambodia, Côte d'Ivoire, Cuba, Cyprus, Djibouti, Dominica, El Salvador, Fiji, Gabon, Greece, Guatemala, Guyana, Honduras, India, Indonesia, Iran Islamic Rep, Iraq, Jamaica, Kazakhstan, Laos, Lebanon, Libya, Liechtenstein, Luxembourg, Madagascar, Malawi, Malaysia, Mauritius, Mongolia, Myanmar, Nigeria, Pakistan, Philippines, Saudi Arabia, Senegal, Seychelles, Sri Lanka, Sudan, Suriname, Syrian AR, Tajikistan, Thailand, Tonga, Turkmenistan, Uganda, United Arab Emirates, Venezuela, Yemen, Zambia, Zimbabwe.

Intergovernmental observers (17):

African Regional Intellectual Property Organization (ARIPO, #00434); *Andean Community (#00817)*; *Bioversity International (#03262)*; *CGIAR System Organization (CGIAR, #03843)*; *EFTA (#05391)*; *European Patent Office (EPO, #08166)*; *FAO (#09260)*; *International Seed Testing Association (ISTA, #14829)*; *OECD (#17693)*; *South Centre (#19753)*; The Word Conservation Union; *UNDP (#20292)*; *UNEP (#20299)*; *UNIDO (#20336)*; Word Bank; *World Intellectual Property Organization (WIPO, #21593)*; *World Trade Organization (WTO, #21864).*

Non-governmental observers (25):

- *African Seed Trade Association (AFSTA, #00454);*
- *Asia and Pacific Seed Association (APSA, #02023);*
- *Association for Plant Breeding for the Benefit of Society (APBREBES, #02861);*
- *Association of European Horticultural Breeders (AOHE, no recent information);*
- *Biotechnology Innovation Organization (BIO);*
- *BUSINESSEUROPE (#03381);*
- *Committee of National Institutes of Patent Agents (CNIPA, #04274);*
- *COPA – european farmers (COPA, #04829);*
- *CropLife International (#04966);*
- *European Coordination Via Campesina (ECVC, #06795);*
- *European Federation of Agents of Industry in Industrial Property (#07042);*
- *European Federation of Pharmaceutical Industries and Associations (EFPIA, #07191);*
- *European Organization of Agricultural and Rural Contractors (#08105);*
- *Euroseeds (#09179);*
- *Fédération Internationale des Conseils en Propriété Intellectuelle (FICPI, #09624);*
- *General Confederation of Agricultural Cooperatives in the European Union (#10107);*
- *International Association for the Protection of Intellectual Property (#12112);*
- *International Association of Horticultural Producers (#11940);*
- *International Chamber of Commerce (ICC, #12534);*
- *International Commission for the Nomenclature of Cultivated Plants (ICNCP, see: #15760);*
- *International Community of Breeders of Asexually Reproduced Ornamental and Fruit Varieties (#12821);*
- *International Seed Federation (ISF, #14828);*
- *Seed Association of the Americas (SAA, #19214);*
- *Union of European Practitioners in Intellectual Property (UNION, #20392);*
- *World Farmers' Organisation (WFO, #21401).*

IGO Relations Observer status with: *FAO (#09260)*; *International Treaty on Plant Genetic Resources for Food and Agriculture (2001)*; *Secretariat of the Convention on Biological Diversity (SCBD, #19197)*; *World Intellectual Property Organization (WIPO, #21593)*; *World Trade Organization (WTO, #21864).* Honorary member of: *International Tropical Fruits Network (TFNet, #15736).* Member of: *World Farmers' Organisation (WFO, #21401).* [2022.10.12/XF2671/y/**F***]

♦ Union internationale pour la protection des oeuvres littéraires et artistiques (#15806)
♦ Union internationale pour la protection de la propriété industrielle (#15805)
♦ Union internationale du Pruth pour régler la navigation sur le Danube (inactive)
♦ Union internationale de psychologie scientifique / see International Union of Psychological Science (#15807)
♦ Union internationale pour la publication des tarifs douaniers / see International Customs Tariffs Bureau (#13124)
♦ Union internationale des publicitaires (inactive)
♦ Union internationale des radio-amateurs (#11646)
♦ Union internationale de radiodiffusion (inactive)
♦ Union internationale de radioécologie (#15812)
♦ Union internationale des radioécologistes / see International Union of Radioecology (#15812)
♦ Union Internationale des Radiologistes Interventionnels (unconfirmed)
♦ Union internationale de radiotélégraphie scientifique / see Union radio-scientifique internationale (#20475)
♦ Union internationale Raiffeisen (#13291)
♦ Union internationale Raoul Follereau (#18618)
♦ Union internationale pour le règlement concernant les lois et coutumes de la guerre sur terre (inactive)
♦ Union internationale des républiques américaines / see OAS (#17629)
♦ Union internationale de la résistance et de la déportation (no recent information)
♦ Union internationale des Roms (#14765)
♦ Union internationale des sages-femmes / see International Confederation of Midwives (#12863)
♦ Union internationale des salles municipales, des halls de sport et des salles polyvalentes / see European Association of Event Centers (#06032)
♦ Union internationale des sanatoriums privés (inactive)
♦ Union internationale des sciences agricoles (inactive)
♦ Union Internationale des Sciences Anthropologiques et Ethnologiques (#15755)
♦ Union internationale des sciences biologiques (#15760)
♦ Union internationale des sciences de la communication (inactive)
♦ Union internationale des sciences géologiques (#15777)
♦ Union internationale des sciences médicales (inactive)
♦ Union internationale des sciences de la nutrition (#15796)
♦ Union internationale de la science du sol (#15817)
♦ Union internationale des sciences physiologiques (#15800)
♦ Union internationale des sciences physiques et technologiques en médecine (#15799)
♦ Union internationale des sciences préhistoriques et protohistoriques (#15801)
♦ Union internationale pour la science, la technique et les applications du vide (#15826)
♦ Union internationale de science et de technologie alimentaires (#15773)
♦ Union internationales contre le péril vénérien et les tréponématoses / see International Union against Sexually Transmitted Infections (#15751)
♦ Union internationale de secours (inactive)
♦ Union internationale de secours aux enfants (inactive)

♦ Union internationale des services médicaux des chemins de fer (UIMC) 20437

International Union of Railway Medical Services – Unión Internacional de Servicios Médicos en los Ferrocarriles – Internationaler Verband der Bahnärztlichen Dienste

Contact c/o UIC, 16 rue Jean Rey, 75015 Paris, France.
Gen Sec address not obtained.
Chair address not obtained.
URL: https://uic.org/special-groups/uimc/

History 28 Feb 1949, Brussels (Belgium). Statutes adopted, 16 Nov 1951; amended 1955. New statutes adopted 11 Aug 1956; amended 27 Aug 1970, 5 June 1978, 29 Sep 1989. Most recent statutes adopted 27-28 Apr 1995; amended 4 Oct 2002. In 1995, became an autonomous special group of *International Union of Railways (#15813).* Registration: Belgium. **Aims** Promote and disseminate progress made by medicine to railways; encourage professional contacts between railway medical officers in order to exchange information and knowledge; further medical research specific to the rail mode and put results to practice; guarantee the highest possible level of railway operating safety and the best possible care of railway staff. **Structure** General Assembly (annual, at Scientific Congress); Management Committee; Working Parties. **Languages** English, French, German. **Finance** Sources: members' dues. **Activities** Advocacy/lobbying/activism; events/meetings. **Events** *UIMC Congress* Frankfurt-Main (Germany) 2023, *UIMC Congress* Miami, FL (USA) 2022, *UIMC Congress* 2021, *UIMC Congress* 2020, *UIMC Congress* Rome (Italy) 2019. **Publications** UIMC railway medical guidelines.

Members Railway administrations (48) in 24 countries:

Australia, Austria, Belgium, Denmark, France, Germany, Hungary, Ireland, Italy, Japan, Luxembourg, Morocco, Netherlands, Norway, Poland, Portugal, Russia, Slovakia, Slovenia, Spain, Sweden, Switzerland, UK, USA.

NGO Relations Member of (1): *Council for International Organizations of Medical Sciences (CIOMS, #04905)* (Founder). [2023.02.20/XC2771/**C**]

♦ Union internationale de ski nautique / see International Waterski and Wakeboard Federation (#15872)
♦ Union internationale des socialistes antialcooliques (inactive)
♦ Union internationale des socialistes religieux / see International League of Religious Socialists (#14022)
♦ Union internationale des sociétés de chimistes du cuir / see International Union of Leather Technologists and Chemists Societies (#15788)
♦ Union internationale des sociétés coopératives de gros (inactive)
♦ Union internationale des sociétés d'épargne et de prêts immobiliers / see International Union for Housing Finance (#15780)
♦ Union internationale des sociétés éthiques (inactive)
♦ Union internationale des sociétés d'immunologie (#15781)
♦ Union internationale des sociétés d'ingénieurs forestiers (no recent information)

♦ Union internationale des sociétés de lipoplastie (UISL) 20438

International Union of Lipoplastic Surgery Societies

Address not obtained.

Members National organizations (23) in 22 countries:

Argentina, Armenia, Belarus, Belgium, Brazil, Bulgaria, Chile, Colombia, France, Georgia, Germany, Italy, Japan, Peru, Poland, Portugal, Russia, Serbia, Spain, Türkiye, USA. [2010/XD8935/**D**]

♦ Union internationale des sociétés de maîtres de danse (inactive)
♦ Union internationale des sociétés de microbiologie (#15794)
♦ Union internationale des sociétés de la paix (inactive)
♦ Union internationale des sociétés de techniciens et chimistes des industries du cuir (#15788)
♦ Union internationale des sociétés de transport combiné rail – route (#15765)
♦ Union internationale de spéléologie (#15818)
♦ Union internationale sportive, culturelle et touristique des postes et télécommunications (#20483)
♦ Union internationale sportive des PTT (inactive)
♦ Union internationale des stations électriques (inactive)
♦ Union internationale du sucre (inactive)
♦ Union internationale sud-américaine pour le règlement du droit international privé (inactive)
♦ Union internationale des supérieures générales (#15820)
♦ Union internationale syndicale des travailleurs de l'agriculture, alimentation, commerce, textiles et industries similaires (#20190)
♦ Union internationale des syndicats de l'industrie du cuir, de la chaussure, de la fourrure et des articles en cuir (inactive)
♦ Union internationale des syndicats des industries alimentaires / see International Union of Food, Agricultural, Hotel, Restaurant, Catering, Tobacco and Allied Workers Associations (#15772)
♦ Union internationale des syndicats des industries chimiques, du pétrole et similaires (inactive)
♦ Union internationale des syndicats de police (inactive)
♦ Union internationale des syndicats du textile et de l'habillement (inactive)
♦ Union internationale des syndicats des travailleurs de l'agriculture, des forêts et des plantations (inactive)
♦ Union internationale des syndicats des travailleurs du bâtiment, du bois et des matériaux de construction (#20185)
♦ Union internationale des syndicats des travailleurs du commerce (inactive)
♦ Union internationale des syndicats des travailleurs de l'énergie (inactive)
♦ Union internationale de syndicats de travailleurs de l'énergie, du métal, de la chimie, du pétrole et des industries analogues / see Trade Union International of Chemical, Energy, Metal, Oil and Allied Industries (#20188)
♦ Union internationale des syndicats des travailleurs de la fonction publique et assimilés (#20191)
♦ Union internationale des syndicats des travailleurs de l'industrie alimentaire, des tabacs, hôtels et branches connexes (inactive)
♦ Union internationale des syndicats des travailleurs de la métallurgie (inactive)
♦ Union internationale des syndicats des travailleurs des postes, télégraphes, téléphones et radio / see Trade Unions International of Public and Allied Employees (#20191)
♦ Union internationale des syndicats des travailleurs des transports / see Trade Unions International of Transport, Fisheries and Communication (#20192)
♦ Union internationale des syndicats des travailleurs des transports terrestres et aériens (inactive)
♦ Union internationale pour la taxation des biens fonciers et le libre-échange / see International Union for Land Value Taxation and Free Trade (#15787)
♦ Union internationale pour la taxation de la valeur de la terre (#15787)

♦ Union internationale des techniciens de l'industrie de la chaussure (UITIC) 20439

International Union of Shoe Industry Technicians – Unión Internacional de Técnicos de la Industria del Calzado – Internationaler Verband der Schuhtechniker

SG address not obtained.
URL: http://www.uitic.org/

History Jan 1974. Also referred to in English as *International Association of Shoe Industry Technicians* and in German as *Internationale Union der Schuh Industrie Techniker.* **Aims** Develop technical knowledge in the footwear industry. **Structure** General Assembly/Council of Delegates (every 3 years), comprising representatives of member associations. Executive Committee, comprising President, Vice-President, Treasurer, General Secretary and 7 members. **Languages** English, French. **Finance** Members' dues: Associations (groups of 100 members) – euro 65 (maximum euro 195); individuals and technical centres euro 25. **Activities** Organizes International Technical Conference (every 2 years up to 1993, then every 3 years); promotes technical study trips to other countries. **Events** *Triennial conference* China 2021, *Triennial conference* Porto (Portugal) 2018, *Triennial Conference* Chennai (India) 2016, *Triennial Conference* Guangzhou (China) 2013, *Triennial conference* León (Mexico) 2010. **Publications** *UITIC News.*

Members National associations of footwear technicians; individuals; companies; institutes. Associations in 8 countries:
China, Czechia, France, Germany, Hungary, Italy, Spain, Vietnam.
Individuals and technical centres in 17 countries:
Argentina, Belgium, Colombia, France, Germany, Greece, Hungary, India, Mexico, Morocco, Peru, Portugal, Romania, Russia, Spain, Tunisia, UK. [2020/XC0078/t/**C**]

- ♦ Union internationale des télécommunications (#15673)
- ♦ Union internationale des théâtres universitaires (inactive)
- ♦ Union internationale de tir / see International Shooting Sport Federation (#14852)
- ♦ Union internationale de tourisme coopératif et associatif (inactive)
- ♦ Union internationale touristique et culturelle des postes et des télécommunications (inactive)
- ♦ Union internationale de tramways, de chemins de fer d'intérêt local et de transports publics automobiles / see International Association of Public Transport (#12118)
- ♦ Union internationale des transports publics (#12118)
- ♦ Union Internationale des Transports Routiers (#14761)
- ♦ Union internationale des travailleurs de l'alimentation, de l'agriculture, de l'hôtellerie-restauration, du tabac et des branches connexes (#15772)
- ♦ Union internationale des travailleurs de l'alimentation et des branches connexes / see International Union of Food, Agricultural, Hotel, Restaurant, Catering, Tobacco and Allied Workers Associations (#15772)
- ♦ Union internationale des travailleurs du bois (inactive)
- ♦ Union internationale des travailleurs d'hôtels, restaurants et cafés (inactive)
- ♦ Union internationale de travail des partis socialistes (inactive)
- ♦ Union internationale universitaire socialiste et démocratique / see International Social Democratic Union for Education (#14881)
- ♦ Union of International and European Civil Servants / see European Public Service Union (#08303)
- ♦ Union internationale végétarienne (#15842)

♦ Union internationale des vélodromes (UIV) 20440

Pres UIV Secretariat, Ballerup Super Arena, Ballerup Indraetsby 4, 2750 Ballerup, Denmark. T. +4544776199. Fax +4544776198.

History 1956. Former names and other names: *European Union of Winter Cycling Tracks* – former (1956 to 1979); *Union européenne des vélodromes d'hiver (UEVH)* – former (1956 to 1979). **Aims** Promote track cycling. **Structure** General Meeting. Executive Committee, comprising President and 2 Vice-Presidents.
Members Full; associate; passive. Velodromes and organizers of track cycling events (14) in 8 countries:
Austria, Belgium, Denmark, Germany, Italy, Netherlands, Switzerland, USA. [2015/XU3954/**D**]

- ♦ Union internationale des villes et pouvoirs locaux (inactive)
- ♦ Union internationale des virologistes des agrumes (#14441)
- ♦ Union internationale des voitures et fourgons (inactive)
- ♦ Union internationale des voyageurs (unconfirmed)
- ♦ Union internationale des wagons (inactive)
- ♦ Union internationale des wagons-privés (#15827)
- ♦ Union internationale du yachting automobile / see Union internationale Motonautique (#20431)
- ♦ Union of International Fairs / see UFI – The Global Association of the Exhibition Industry (#20276)
- ♦ Union of Internationalist Teachers (inactive)

♦ Union for the International Language Ido 20441

Union pour la langue internationale Ido – Uniono por la Linguo Internaciona Ido

Contact Deutsche Ido-Gesellschaft, c/o ver di Berlin, Köpenicker Str 30, 10179 Berlin, Germany.
Contact Breitscheidstr 22, 90549 Nürburg, Germany.
URL: http://www.ido.li/

History 1909. "Ido" is an improved form of Esperanto. **Aims** Organize the Ido-language movement; guard linguistic qualities of Ido language. **Structure** Directing Committee. Officers: President; Secretary; Treasurer. **Languages** Ido. **Staff** 14.00 FTE, voluntary. **Finance** Members' dues. Budget (annual): euro 1,000. **Events** *Meeting / Annual Meeting* Tallinn (Estonia) / Riga (Latvia) 2009, *Meeting* Paris (France) 2007. **Publications** *Progreso* (3 a year).
Members Individuals in 29 countries:
Argentina, Australia, Belgium, Canada, China, Czechia, Finland, France, Germany, Hungary, Italy, Japan, Korea Rep, Latvia, Mexico, Nepal, Netherlands, New Zealand, Norway, Poland, Romania, Russia, Slovakia, Spain, Sri Lanka, Sweden, Switzerland, UK, USA.
Group societies in 4 countries:
France, Germany, Spain, UK. [2019/XE0249/**E**]

- ♦ Union of International Motorboating / see Union internationale Motonautique (#20431)

♦ Union of International Mountain Leader Associations (UIMLA) 20442

Contact 256 rue de la République, 73000 Chambéry, France. E-mail: secretary@uimla.org.
URL: http://www.uimla.org/

History Constitution signed 27 Nov 2004, Chambéry (France). Current statutes adopted Nov 2020. Registration: France. **Aims** Works towards the social and lawful acknowledgement of International Mountain Leader (IML) in the European Union, the European economic area and in all the countries where required. **Structure** General Assembly; Executive Board. **Languages** English, French. **Events** *Extraordinary General Assembly* 2021, *General Assembly* 2020, *General Assembly* Brasov (Romania) 2019, *General Assembly* Poprad (Slovakia) 2018, *General Assembly* Namur (Belgium) 2017. **Publications** *UIMLA Internal Newsletter*.
Members Country associations in 27 countries:
Andorra, Argentina, Austria, Belgium, Bolivia, Bulgaria, Chile, Croatia, Czechia, France, Germany, Greece, Hungary, Italy, Japan, Nepal, Netherlands, North Macedonia, Peru, Poland, Romania, Slovakia, Slovenia, Spain, Sweden, Switzerland, UK.
NGO Relations Member of (5): *International Commission for Alpine Rescue (ICAR, #12662)*; *International Union of Associations of Mountain Guides (#15756)*; Linking Tourism and Conservation; Mountain Safety Info; *Union internationale des associations d'alpinisme (UIAA, #20420)*. [2021.06.21/XJ5450/**D**]

- ♦ Union international des ornithologues (#14487)

♦ Union for the International Patent Classification (IPC Union) 20443

Union pour la classification internationale des brevets

Address not obtained.
URL: http://www.wipo.org/

History 1975, Strasbourg (France), on entry into force of *Strasbourg Agreement Concerning the International Patent Classification (IPC Agreement, 1971)*. Agreement amended 1979. A union administered by *World Intellectual Property Organization (WIPO, #21593)*. **Aims** Establish a classification of the fields of technology with a view to facilitating searching patent documents and making searches for anticipations. **Structure** Assembly; Committee of Experts. **Finance** Contributions of the member States. **Activities** International Patent Classification (IPC) divides technology into 8 main sections with approximately 64,000 subdivisions. Worldwide uniformity of classification would greatly facilitate retrieval of documents. The IPC is already used by patent offices in more than 70 countries and is designed to achieve such uniformity.
Members Open to States party to the IPC Agreement. States party to the Agreement, as of Feb 2014 (62):
Albania, Argentina, Armenia, Australia, Austria, Azerbaijan, Belarus, Belgium, Bosnia-Herzegovina, Brazil, Bulgaria, Canada, China, Croatia, Cuba, Czechia, Denmark, Egypt, Estonia, Finland, France, Germany, Greece, Guinea, Ireland, Israel, Italy, Japan, Kazakhstan, Korea DPR, Korea Rep, Kyrgyzstan, Luxembourg, Malawi, Mexico, Moldova, Monaco, Mongolia, Montenegro, Netherlands, North Macedonia, Norway, Poland, Portugal, Romania, Russia, Serbia, Slovakia, Slovenia, Spain, Suriname, Sweden, Switzerland, Tajikistan, Trinidad-Tobago, Türkiye, Turkmenistan, UK, Ukraine, Uruguay, USA, Uzbekistan. [2014/XF4433/**F***]

- ♦ Union of International Powerboating / see Union internationale Motonautique (#20431)

♦ Union for the International Registration of Audiovisual Works 20444

Union pour l'enregistrement international des oeuvres audiovisuelles – Unión para el Registro Internacional de Obras Audiovisuales

Address not obtained.
URL: http://www.wipo.org/

History 27 Feb 1991, on entry into force of *Treaty on the International Registration of Audiovisual Works (1989)*, also referred to as *'Film Register Treaty (FRT)'*, which was adopted 18 Apr 1989, Geneva (Switzerland). The Union is also referred to as *Film Register Treaty Union*. Administered by *World Intellectual Property Organization (WIPO, #21593)*. **Aims** Increase *legal security* in transactions relating audiovisual works. **Structure** Assembly. **Activities** The Treaty establishes, under the auspices of WIPO, an international register of audiovisual works. Registration in the International Register, on the basis of applications by persons who have an interest in the work, has the effect that any statement recorded in the said Register has to be considered true (subject to certain exceptions) until the contrary is proved. The *International Film Registry* is an administrative unit of the International Bureau of WIPO.
Members Member States of WIPO having accepted the FRT (13):
Argentina, Austria, Brazil, Burkina Faso, Chile, Colombia, Czechia, France, Hungary, Mexico, Peru, Senegal, Slovakia.
IGO Relations Organizations admitted as observers: *Arab States Broadcasting Union (ASBU, #01050)*; *Council of Europe (CE, #04881)*; *European Commission (EC, #06633)*; *ILO (#11123)*; *UNESCO (#20322)*; *United Nations (UN, #20515)*.
NGO Relations Organizations admitted as observers:
- *African Union of Broadcasting (AUB, #00490)*;
- *Asia-Pacific Broadcasting Union (ABU, #01863)*;
- *Association for the International Collective Management of Audiovisual Works (AGICOA, #02658)*;
- *GIGAEurope AISBL (#10151)*;
- *European Broadcasting Union (EBU, #06404)*;
- *Independent Film Producers International Association (IFPIA, no recent information)*;
- *Independent Film and Television Alliance (IFTA)*;
- *Inter-American Copyright Institute (ICI, #11421)*;
- *International Association of Audiovisual Writers and Directors (AIDAA, no recent information)*;
- *International Association of Authors of Comics and Cartoons (AIAC, inactive)*;
- *International Association of Broadcasting (IAB, #11738)*;
- *International Bureau of the Societies Administering the Rights of Mechanical Recording and Reproduction (#12416)*;
- *International Chamber of Commerce (ICC, #12534)*;
- *International Federation of Actors (#13337)*;
- *International Federation of Film Distributors Associations (#13428)*;
- *International Federation of Film Producers' Associations (#13429)*;
- *International Federation of Musicians (#13486)*;
- *International Literary and Artistic Association (#14058)*;
- *International Union of Cinemas (#15763)*;
- *International Writers Guild (IWG, inactive)*;
- *Media and Entertainment International (MEI, inactive)*;
- *Motion Picture Association (MPA)*;
- *Organización de Telecomunicaciones de Iberoamérica (OTI, #17851)*;
- Sovexportfilm (SEF). [2009/XF5211/**F***]

♦ Union for the International Registration of Marks (Madrid Union) ... 20445

Union pour l'enregistrement international des marques (Union de Madrid)

Address not obtained.
URL: http://www.wipo.int/

History 15 Jul 1892, on the entry into force of *Madrid Agreement Concerning the International Registration of Marks, 1891 (1891)*, signed 14 Apr 1891, Madrid (Spain), and revised: 14 Dec 1900, Brussels (Belgium); 2 Jun 1911, Washington DC (USA); 6 Nov 1925, The Hague (Netherlands); 2 Jun 1934, London (UK); 15 Jun 1957, Nice (France); 14 Jul 1967, Stockholm (Sweden). Amended 1979. The *Protocol to the Madrid Agreement Concerning the International Registration of Marks (1989)*, adopted at Madrid on Jun 27, is open to States party to the Paris Convention and to intergovernmental organizations meeting certain criteria. It will enter into force after the deposit, with the Director General of WIPO, of four instruments of ratification, acceptance, approval or accession, among which at least one must be the instrument of a country party to the Madrid Agreement and one the instrument of a State party to the Agreement or of an intergovernmental organization. A union administered by *World Intellectual Property Organization (WIPO, #21593)*. **Aims** Facilitate registration of marks in several countries. **Structure** Assembly. **Finance** Financed by fees collected from the users of the system. **Activities** Establishes a system for the international registration of marks at the International Bureau of WIPO with effect in the contracting States. **Events** *Session* Geneva (Switzerland) 1996.
Members Open to States party to the Madrid Agreement. States party to the Agreement, as of Jan 2009 (56):
Albania, Algeria, Armenia, Austria, Azerbaijan, Belarus, Belgium, Bhutan, Bosnia-Herzegovina, Bulgaria, China, Croatia, Cuba, Cyprus, Czechia, Egypt, Eswatini, France, Germany, Hungary, Iran Islamic Rep, Italy, Kazakhstan, Kenya, Korea DPR, Kyrgyzstan, Latvia, Lesotho, Liberia, Liechtenstein, Luxembourg, Monaco, Mongolia, Montenegro, Morocco, Mozambique, Netherlands, Poland, Portugal, Romania, Russia, San Marino, Serbia, Sierra Leone, Slovakia, Slovenia, Spain, Sudan, Switzerland, Syrian AR, Tajikistan, Ukraine, Uzbekistan, Vietnam.
Regional organization (1):
European Union (EU, #08967).
Contracting Parties to the Protocol, as of Jan 2009 (77):
Albania, Antigua-Barbuda, Armenia, Australia, Austria, Azerbaijan, Bahrain, Belarus, Belgium, Bhutan, Bosnia-Herzegovina, Botswana, Bulgaria, China, Croatia, Cuba, Cyprus, Czechia, Denmark, Estonia, Eswatini, Finland, France, Georgia, Germany, Ghana, Greece, Hungary, Iceland, Iran Islamic Rep, Ireland, Italy, Japan, Kenya, Korea DPR, Korea Rep, Kyrgyzstan, Latvia, Lesotho, Liechtenstein, Lithuania, Luxembourg, Madagascar, Moldova, Monaco, Mongolia, Montenegro, Morocco, Mozambique, Namibia, Netherlands, North Macedonia, Norway, Oman, Poland, Portugal, Romania, Russia, San Marino, Sao Tomé-Principe, Serbia, Sierra Leone, Singapore, Slovakia, Slovenia, Spain, Sweden, Switzerland, Syrian AR, Türkiye, Turkmenistan, UK, Ukraine, USA, Uzbekistan, Vietnam, Zambia. [2009/XF4439/**F***]

- ♦ Union for the International Registration of Trademarks (inactive)
- ♦ Union of International Technical Associations / see Union internationale des associations et organismes scientifiques et techniques (#20421)
- ♦ Union of International Tenant Associations / see International Union of Tenants (#15822)
- ♦ **The Union** International Union Against Tuberculosis and Lung Disease (#15752)
- ♦ Unión Interparlamentaria (#15961)
- ♦ Union interparlementaire (#15961)
- ♦ Union interparlementaire arabe (#00995)
- ♦ Union interparlementaire nordique (inactive)
- ♦ Unionis Apostolicae Sacerdotum Saecularium / see International Confederation Apostolic Union of Clergy (#12844)
- ♦ Union of Issuers Quoted in Europe (inactive)
- ♦ Union des jeunes démocrates européens (#05037)
- ♦ Union de la jeunesse arabe (no recent information)
- ♦ Union de la jeunesse européenne (inactive)
- ♦ Union de la jeunesse Ouest-Africaine (inactive)

♦ Union of Jewish Congregations in Latin America and the Caribbean (UJCL) 20446

Unión Judia de Congregaciones de Latinoamérica y El Caribe

Sec Carrera 20, No 37-54, Bogota, Bogota DC, Colombia. T. +5712455264. E-mail: mifgashonline@gmail.com.
URL: http://www.ujcl.org/

History Founded Feb 1998, Costa Rica. **Aims** Preserve the continuity of Judaism in Latin America and the Caribbean. **Structure** Board of Directors. **Events** *Conference* Guadalajara (Mexico) 2012, *Conference* Panama (Panama) 2010, *Conference* Kingston (Jamaica) 2008, *Conference* San José (Costa Rica) 2007, *Conference* Guadalajara (Mexico) 2006. **Publications** *UJCL Newsletter*.
Members in 9 countries and territories:
Aruba, Costa Rica, Cuba, Curaçao, El Salvador, Honduras, Jamaica, Panama, Puerto Rico. [2014/XD9124/**D**]

- ♦ Union des journalistes africains / see Union internationale des journalistes africains (#20428)
- ♦ Union des journalistes de l'Afrique de l'Ouest (#20885)

- ♦ Union des journalistes arabes / see Federation of Arab Journalists (#09422)
- ♦ Union des journalistes des Caraïbes (inactive)
- ♦ Union des journalistes socialistes et progressistes de la Méditerranée (inactive)
- ♦ Union des journalistes sportifs africains (inactive)
- ♦ Unión Judia de Congregaciones de Latinoamérica y El Caribe (#20446)
- ♦ Union juridique internationale (inactive)
- ♦ Union des juristes arabes (#20354)
- ♦ Unión de Juventudes Demócratas Europeas (#05037)
- ♦ Unión de Juventudes Democraticas Hispanoamericanas (no recent information)
- ♦ Union der Kartoffelstärkefabriken der Europäischen Union (#20406)
- ♦ Union pour la langue internationale Ido (#20441)
- ♦ Union de la langue néerlandaise (internationally oriented national body)
- ♦ Unión Latina (inactive)

♦ Unión Latina de Economia Politica de la Información, la Comunicación ya la Cultura (ULEPICC) 20447

Sec Fac de Comunicación, Univ de Sevilla, Americo Vespucio s/n, Isla de la Cartuja, 41092 Seville, Sevilla, Spain. T. +349554486061. E-mail: fcompoliticas@gmail.com.
URL: http://ulepicc.com/

History Jul 2002, Seville (Spain). Founded during the 3rd Encuentro Latino de Economia Politica de la Comunicación. **Events** *Congress* Havana (Cuba) 2015, *Congress* Buenos Aires (Argentina) 2013, *Congress* Madrid (Spain) 2009, *Congress* Mexico City (Mexico) 2007, *Congress* Salvador (Brazil) 2005. **Publications** *Economia Politca de las Tecnologias de la Información y la Comunicación* (4 a year) – review. **NGO Relations** Member of: *Confederación Iberoamericana de Asociaciones Cientificas y Académicas de la Comunicación (CONFIBERCOM, #04448).* [2014/XJ7209/**D**]

- ♦ Union of Latin American and Caribbean Museums (inactive)

♦ Union of Latin American Parties (UPLA) 20448

Contact Nueva de Lyon 96, of 401, Providencia, 7510078 Santiago, Santiago Metropolitan, Chile. T. +5623355355. Fax +5622334742.
Exec Dir address not obtained. E-mail: upla@upla.net.
URL: http://www.upla.net/

History Also referred to as *Americas Democrat Union.*
Members Full in 17 countries:
Argentina, Bolivia, Canada, Chile, Colombia, Costa Rica, Dominica, Dominican Rep, Ecuador, El Salvador, Guatemala, Honduras, Nicaragua, Panama, Paraguay, Peru, Venezuela.
NGO Relations Part of: *International Democrat Union (IDU, #13147).* [2013/XJ0259/**D**]

- ♦ Union of Latin American Schools and Faculties of Architecture (#20380)
- ♦ Union of Latin American Universities / see Association of Universities of Latin America and the Caribbean (#02970)
- ♦ Union latine (inactive)
- ♦ Union latinoaméricaine des aveugles (#16256)
- ♦ Union latinoaméricaine et des Caraïbes de radiodiffusion (inactive)
- ♦ Union latinoaméricaine d'emballage (#16358)
- ♦ Union latinoaméricaine des jeunesses oecuméniques (no recent information)
- ♦ Union latinoaméricaine de sociétés de phtisiologie (inactive)
- ♦ Union latinoaméricaine de tennis de table (#20453)
- ♦ Unión Latinoamericana y del Caribe de Radiodifusión (inactive)
- ♦ Unión Latinoamericana de Ciegos (#16256)
- ♦ Unión Latinoamericana del Embalaje (#16358)

♦ Unión Latinoamericana de Entidades de Psicologia (ULAPSI) 20449

Contact Av Prof Mello Moraes 1721, Sao Paulo SP, 05508-030 SP, Brazil. T. +551130914391 – +551130914392. Fax +551130914392.
URL: http://www.ulapsi.bvsalud.org/

History 23 Nov 2002, Puebla (Mexico). **Events** *Congreso* San José (Costa Rica) 2018, *Congreso* Antigua (Guatemala) 2014, *Congress* Montevideo (Uruguay) 2011, *Congress* Mexico City (Mexico) 2009, *Congress* Havana (Cuba) 2007. [2013/XJ6928/**D**]

♦ Unión Latinoamericana de Ergonomía (ULAERGO) 20450

Pres address not obtained.
URL: http://www.ulaergo.com/

History 3 Sep 2020, Santiago (Chile). Registration: Start date: 2019, Colombia. **Structure** Board of Governors. **Events** *Congress* Buenos Aires (Argentina) 2019.
Members Organizations in 12 countries:
Argentina, Brazil, Chile, Colombia, Costa Rica, Cuba, Ecuador, Mexico, Nicaragua, Peru, Uruguay, Venezuela.
[2020/AA0020/**D**]

♦ Unión Latinoamericana de Espeleologia (ULE) 20451

Pres El Payén 1035, Bo Carilauquen, 5613 Malargüe, Argentina. T. +542604094916.
URL: http://www.fade.org.ar/ULE_home.htm

History 12 Oct 2010, Malargüe (Argentina). **Aims** Promote and develop scientific and technical exchange between *speleologists* of Latin America. **Structure** General Assembly; Executive Bureau. **Languages** English, French, Spanish. **Staff** 63.00 FTE, paid. **Finance** Members' dues. **Events** *General Assembly* Malargüe (Argentina) 2012.
Members Full in 5 countries:
Argentina, Brazil, Ecuador, Mexico, Paraguay. [2014.06.18/XJ2952/**D**]

- ♦ Unión Latinoamericana de Juventudes Ecuménicas (no recent information)
- ♦ Unión Latinoamericana de Motociclismo / see FIM Latin America (#09762)

♦ Union Latinoamericana de Mujeres (Red ULAM) 20452

Contact address not obtained. E-mail: secretariaejecutiva@redulam.org.
URL: http://www.facebook.com/UnionLAtinoamericanaMujeres/

History 2008, Cuenca (Ecuador). **Aims** Strengthen the voice, impact and influence of women's groups, so that governments and corporations respond to the concerns of women affected by *mining* projects and policies. **Structure** Board of Directors. **Languages** Spanish. **Staff** None paid. **Activities** Networking/liaising; events/meetings. Resource centre gathers and disseminates environmental information. **Publications** *RedULAM Bulletin* (12 a year).
Members Full in 4 countries:
Bolivia, Ecuador, Peru, Venezuela.
IGO Relations None. [2020.03.03/XM6323/**D**]

- ♦ Unión Latinoamericana de Organismos de Rescate (inactive)
- ♦ Unión Latinoamericana de Sociedades de Tisiologia (inactive)

♦ Unión Latinoamericana de Tenis de Mesa (ULTM) 20453

Latin American Table Tennis Union (LATTU) – Union latinoaméricaine de tennis de table

Exec Sec address not obtained.
SG address not obtained.
URL: http://www.ultmonline.org/

History 31 Aug 1973, Beijing (China). Founded during the celebration of Afro-Asian Latin American International Friendship Table Tennis Tournament. Continental federation of: *International Table Tennis Federation (ITTF, #15650).* **Aims** Give solutions to efforts made to develop table tennis in all countries and regions of Latin America; organize Latin American *championships*; endorse all table tennis competitions and activities. **Structure** Executive Committee. **Languages** English, Portuguese, Spanish. **Staff** Voluntary. **Finance** Sources: members' dues. **Activities** Sporting activities. **Events** *Congress / General Meeting* Guatemala (Guatemala) 1993, *Technical and regional meeting* Ponce (Puerto Rico) 1993, *Annual meeting* Bogota (Colombia) 1988, *General Meeting* Bogota (Colombia) 1988, *Annual meeting / General Meeting* Delhi (India) 1987.

Members National associations in 39 countries and territories:
Anguilla, Antigua-Barbuda, Argentina, Aruba, Barbados, Belize, Bolivia, Bonaire Is, Brazil, Cayman Is, Chile, Colombia, Costa Rica, Cuba, Curaçao, Dominica, Dominican Rep, Ecuador, El Salvador, Grenada, Guatemala, Guyana, Haiti, Honduras, Jamaica, Mexico, Nicaragua, Panama, Paraguay, Peru, Puerto Rico, St Kitts-Nevis, St Lucia, St Maarten, St Vincent-Grenadines, Suriname, Trinidad-Tobago, Uruguay, Venezuela.
NGO Relations Member of (1): *Asociación de Confederaciones Deportivas Panamericanas (ACODEPA, #02119).* [2023/XD1591/**D**]

- ♦ Union Latinoamericana de Visitadores Médicos (no recent information)
- ♦ Unión Latinoamericana de Yoga (#20329)
- ♦ Union of Latin Writers and Artists (inactive)
- ♦ Union libanaise culturelle mondiale (#21622)
- ♦ Union libanesa Cultural Mundial (#21622)
- ♦ Union libérale mondiale / see Liberal International (#16454)
- ♦ Union of Liberal Labour Organizations (no recent information)

♦ Union of Local Authority Chief Executives of Europe 20454

Union des dirigeants territoriaux de l'Europe (UDITE)

Contact County Hall, Atlantic Wharf, Cardiff, CF10 4UW, UK. T. +442920872401. Fax +442920872407.
URL: http://www.udite.eu/

History Mar 1990, Nancy (France), as *Standing Committee of European Local Authority Chief Executives – Commission permanente des dirigeants territoriaux européens.* Registered in accordance with French law. Present name adopted 1991. **Aims** Promote relations between the professional associations of chief executives representing European local authorities; develop exchanges of information; share professional experiences; contribute to the enhancement of the role and functions of local authorities. **Structure** Presidency rotates every 2 years between member countries. **Finance** Members' dues. **Activities** Established the *Public Risk Management Organization (PRIMO).* Grants the 'UDITE Performance Improvement Award'. Organizes biennial congress. **Events** *Congress* Cardiff (UK) 2008, *Congress* Malta 2006. **Publications** *UDITE E-newsletter* (2 a year). **IGO Relations** Member of: *Congress of Local and Regional Authorities of the Council of Europe (#04677).* **NGO Relations** Member of: *Assembly of European Regions (AER, #02316).*
[2014/XJ4240/**D**]

♦ Union of Local and Non Local General Service Staff FAO/WFP 20455

Syndicat du personnel local et non local des services généraux de la FAO – Sindicato del Personal Local y no Local de los Servicios Generale de la FAO – Sindacato del Personale Locale e non Locale dei Servizi Generali della FAO

Gen Sec FAO Headquarters, Via delle Terme di Caracalla, 00153 Rome RM, Italy. T. +39657053530. E-mail: ugss@fao.org – ugss@wfp.org.

History 26 Oct 1976, Rome (Italy), as *Union of Local and Non Local General Service Staff of the Food and Agriculture Organization of the United Nations (UGSS) – Syndicat du personnel local et non local des services généraux de l'Organisation des Nations Unies pour l'alimentation et l'agriculture – Sindicato del Personal Local y no Local de los Servicios Generales de la Organización de las Naciones Unidas para la Agricultura y la Alimentación – Sindacato del Personale Locale e non Locale dei Servizi Generali dell'Organizzazione per l'Alimentazione e l'Agricoltura delle Nazioni Unite,* when recognition agreement with Director-General of FAO came into effect, to represent general service staff members of *FAO (#09260)* and *World Food Programme (WFP, #21510).* **Aims** Safeguard conditions of employment of General Service staff and fight for improvements in a broad range of areas such as career development, health insurance coverage, staff security, work/family arrangements, pensions and matters of general staff welfare. **Structure** Assembly (annual); Executive Committee; Control Board; Secretariat. **Languages** English, Italian. **Staff** 0.50 FTE, paid. **Finance** Members' dues. **Events** *Extraordinary General Assembly* Rome (Italy) 2015. **Publications** *UGSS/WPF Newsletter.* Bulletins. **Members** All general service staff, local and non-local, serving at FAO and WFP headquarters; other such staff in regional offices and the field, as agreed with FAO. Staff not at HQ can become associate members. [2019.02.12/XE1731/v/**E**]

- ♦ Union of Local and Non Local General Service Staff of the Food and Agriculture Organization of the United Nations / see Union of Local and Non Local General Service Staff FAO/WFP (#20455)
- ♦ Union of Luso-Afro-America-Asiatic Capital Cities (#20328)
- ♦ **Union de Madrid** Union pour l'enregistrement international des marques (#20445)
- ♦ Union du Maghreb arabe (#01004)
- ♦ Union maghrébine des associations de volontariat (no recent information)
- ♦ Union of Maghreb Youth and Students (inactive)
- ♦ Union dei Magistrati Amministrativi Europea / see Association of European Administrative Judges (#02497)
- ♦ Union magnétique (inactive)
- ♦ Union Magrébine et Nord Africaine des Agriculteurs (unconfirmed)
- ♦ Union of Maritime Ports of Arab Countries (no recent information)

♦ Unión Matematica de América Latina y el Caribe (UMALCA) 20456

Mathematical Union for Latin America and the Caribbean

Sec c/o SBM, Estrada Dona Castorina 110, sala 109, Rio de Janeiro RJ, 22460-320, Brazil. E-mail: contacto@umalca.org – secretaria@umalca.org.
URL: http://www.umalca.org/

History 26 Jul 1995, Rio de Janeiro (Brazil). Statutes adopted, 1995. Former names and other names: *RELAMA-UMALCA* – former. **Aims** Create a higher level working environment for mathematics across Latin America and the Caribbean by improving academic conditions and promoting exchange of students and researchers of the region. **Structure** General Assembly; Executive Committee; Scientific Committee; EMALCAS Commission. **Languages** Portuguese, Spanish. **Finance** Sources: grants; members' dues. Other sources: cooperation from universities and international organizations including: *UNESCO (#20322).* **Activities** Events/meetings; networking/liaising; training/education. **Events** *CLAM: Congreso Latinoamericano de Matemáticos* Montevideo (Uruguay) 2021, *Congress* Córdoba (Argentina) 2012, *General Assembly* Cancún (Mexico) 2005, *Congress* Cancún (Mexico) 2004, *General assembly / CLAM* Cancún (Mexico) 2004. **Publications** *Boletin de la UMALCA* (2 a year). *Directory of Mathematicians in Latin America and the Caribbean* (1999).
Members National mathematical societies of 9 countries:
Argentina, Brazil, Chile, Colombia, Cuba, Mexico, Peru, Uruguay, Venezuela.
NGO Relations Member of (1): *International Mathematical Union (IMU, #14121)* (Affiliate). Instrumental in setting up (1): *Mathematical Council of the Americas (MCofA, #16600).* Activities coordinated with: *International Commission on Mathematical Instruction (ICMI, #12700); Red de Redes Científicas de América Latina y el Caribe (CCRCLA, no recent information).* [2022/XD5106/**D**]

- ♦ Union mathématique africaine (#00370)
- ♦ Union mathématique internationale (#14121)
- ♦ Union des médecins arabes (#01007)
- ♦ Union médicale balkanique (#03078)
- ♦ Union médicale latine (inactive)
- ♦ Union médicale de la Méditerranée latine / see Surgery Society of the Latin Mediterranean (#20042)
- ♦ Union médicale méditerranéenne (inactive)
- ♦ Unión Mediterranea de Confederaciones Empresariales (#20458)

♦ Union for the Mediterranean (UfM) 20457

Union pour la Méditerranée

SG Palacio de Pedralbes, Pere Duran Farell 11, 08034 Barcelona, Spain. T. +34935214100. Fax +34935214102. E-mail: communication@ufmsecretariat.org – info@ufmsecretariat.org.
URL: http://ufmsecretariat.org/

History 27 Nov 1995, Barcelona (Spain). Established on signature of the *Barcelona Declaration* at an inter-ministerial conference of the 15 member states of *European Union (EU, #08967)* and 12 countries of southern and eastern rim of the Mediterranean. Relaunched 13 Jul 2008, at Paris (France) Summit for the Mediterranean; endorsed, Nov 2008. With *Greater Arab Free-Trade Area (GAFTA, #10700)*, *Euro-Mediterranean Free-Trade Area (EMEFTA)* initially expected to be completed by 2010, but as yet not operational. Former names and other names: *Euro-Mediterranean Partnership (EUROMED)* – full title (27 Nov 1995 to 13 Jul 2008); *The Barcelona Process: Union for the Mediterranean* – former. **Aims** Bring together all countries of the European Union and 15 countries of the Southern and Eastern Mediterranean; enhance regional cooperation, dialogue and implementation of projects and initiatives with tangible impact on citizens. **Structure** Senior Officials' Meeting (SOM); Co-Presidency (one from European Union and one from Mediterranean side); Secretariat. **Languages** Arabic, English, French. **Activities** Preferential access to EU markets through *EU Customs Union (#05579)*, including: *Monitoring Committee for EURO-Mediterranean Cooperation in RTD (MoCo)*; *Network of the Ancient Sites for the Performing Arts (DIONYSOS, no recent information)*; *Techno-Economic Analysis Network for the Mediterranean (TEAM)*. **Events** *Mediterranean Water Forum* Malta 2021, *Euro-Mediterranean Summit of Economic and Social Councils and Similar Institutions* Barcelona (Spain) 2019, *UfM Business Forum* Cairo (Egypt) 2019, *Energy and Climate Business Forum* Lisbon (Portugal) 2019, *Meeting* Brussels (Belgium) 2018. **Publications** *UfM Newsletter* (4 a year).
Members Governments of the 43 EU and Mediterranean Partner Countries (MPCs):
Albania, Algeria, Austria, Belgium, Bosnia-Herzegovina, Bulgaria, Croatia, Cyprus, Czechia, Denmark, Egypt, Estonia, Finland, France, Germany, Greece, Hungary, Ireland, Israel, Italy, Jordan, Latvia, Lebanon, Lithuania, Luxembourg, Malta, Mauritania, Monaco, Montenegro, Morocco, Netherlands, Palestine, Poland, Portugal, Romania, Slovakia, Slovenia, Spain, Sweden, Syrian AR, Tunisia, Türkiye, UK.
IGO Relations Observer status with (1): *United Nations (UN, #20515)* (General Assembly). Member of (2): *Parliamentary Assembly of the Mediterranean (PAM, #18212)*; *United Nations Alliance of Civilizations (UNAOC, #20520)*. Partner of (6): *Assemblée Régionale et Locale Euro-Méditerranéenne (ARLEM, #02313)*; *Center for Mediterranean Integration (CMI, #03649)*; *European Commission (EC, #06633)*; *European Investment Bank (EIB, #07599)*; *European Union (EU, #08967)*; *Parliamentary Assembly – Union for the Mediterranean (PA – UfM, #18216)*. Instrumental in setting up (1): *Anna Lindh Euro-Mediterranean Foundation for the Dialogue between Cultures (Anna Lindh Foundation, #00847)*. Invited to meetings: *League of Arab States (LAS, #16420)*. **NGO Relations** Member of (1): *UNITED for Intercultural Action – European Network Against Nationalism, Racism, Fascism and in Support of Migrants and Refugees (UNITED, #20511)*. Partner of (5): *Asociación de las Camaras de Comercio e Industria del Mediterraneo (ASCAME, #02112)*; *Centre d'études des transports pour la Méditerranée occidentale (CETMO)*; *Intermediterranean Commission (IMC, #11521)*; *International Road Transport Union (IRU, #14761)*; *Observatoire méditerranéen de l'énergie (OME, #17634)*. Cooperates with (1): *Association of Organisations of Mediterranean Businesswomen (#02840)*. [2020/XF4533/F*]

♦ Union of Mediterranean Architects (#20459)

♦ Union of Mediterranean Confederations of Enterprises (BUSINESS-MED) 20458

Union Méditerranéenne des Confédérations d'Entreprises – Unión Mediterranea de Confederaciones Empresariales – Unione Mediterranea delle Confederazioni d'Impresa

Contact Rue des Emeraudes Immeuble Zarrad 2, Appt A2/1, Les Berges du Lac 2, 1053 Tunis, Tunisia. T. +21699908551. E-mail: secretariat@businessmed-umce.org.
URL: http://www.businessmed-umce.org/

History 28 Feb 2002, Istanbul (Türkiye). Registration: EU Transparency Register, No/ID: 865034435102-35. **Aims** As a key platform for multilateral cooperation dedicated to its members: promote foreign direct investment; promote Mediterranean dialogue and socio-economic integration. **Structure** General Assembly; Rotating Presidency (every 3 years). **Languages** Arabic, English, French, Italian, Spanish. **Staff** 21.00 FTE, paid. **Finance** EU and member contributions. **Activities** Advocacy/lobbying/activism; knowledge management/information dissemination; networking/liaising; politics/policy/regulatory. **Events** *Mediterranean economic leaders summit* Barcelona (Spain) 2010, *General Assembly* Cairo (Egypt) 2008, *Mediterranean competitiveness day* Marseille (France) 2008, *Mediterranean competitiveness day* Valencia (Spain) 2007, *Mediterranean competitiveness day* Palermo (Italy) 2006. **Publications** Activity report; documents; studies; leaflet.
Members Founding members in 10 countries:
Algeria, Egypt, Israel, Jordan, Lebanon, Mauritania, Morocco, Palestine, Syrian AR, Tunisia.
Associate members in 10 countries:
Cyprus, France, Germany, Greece, Italy, Mauritania, Portugal, Serbia, Spain, Türkiye.
IGO Relations *ILO (#11123)*; government ministries. **NGO Relations** Memorandum of Understanding with: *Asociación de las Camaras de Comercio e Industria del Mediterraneo (ASCAME, #02112)*; *Union of Black Sea and Caspian Business (BCB, #20369)*. Part of: *MedAlliance consortium (inactive)*. Links with *BUSINESSEUROPE (#03381)*; *International Organisation of Employers (IOE, #14428)*. [2022.02.15/XM1844/D]

♦ Union of Mediterranean Holiday Villages (inactive)
♦ Union of Mediterranean Studies Centres (internationally oriented national body)
♦ Union pour la Méditerranée (#20457)

♦ Union méditerranéenne des architectes (UMAR) 20459

Union of Mediterranean Architects

Contact Engineer Street, 11-3118, Beirut, Lebanon. T. +9611858917. E-mail: info@umar.org.
URL: http://www.umar.org/

History 1 Jan 1994, Rethymnon (Greece). **Structure** General Meeting (annual); Executive Committee. **Languages** English, French.
Members in 17 countries:
Albania, Algeria, Croatia, Cyprus, Egypt, France, Greece, Israel, Italy, Malta, Mauritania, Morocco, Palestine, Portugal, Spain, Tunisia, Türkiye. [2019/XM0546/D]

♦ Union Méditerranéenne des Confédérations d'Entreprises (#20458)

♦ Union Méditerranéenne des Géomètres (UMG) 20460

Mediterranean Union of Surveyors

Contact 8 avenue Michlifen, 1er étage, Agdal, Rabat, Morocco. T. +212537675555. Fax +212537675567. E-mail: unionmedgeometre@gmail.com.
URL: http://www.umgeometres.com/

History 22 Jun 2010, Marseille (France). Registered in accordance with French law. **Aims** Strengthen the links of existing cultural and professional exchanges between surveyors of the Mediterranean Basin within the framework of a platform of exchange, cooperation and partnership. **Structure** General Assembly; Executive Board. Permanent Committees. **Languages** English, French. **Finance** Members' dues. **Events** *Congrès International / Congress* Marrakech (Morocco) 2015.
Members Full; Associate; Observer. Members in 7 countries:
Algeria, Egypt, France, Italy, Lebanon, Morocco, Tunisia.
NGO Relations Cooperates with (1): *International Testing Agency (ITA, #15678)*. *Arab Federation of Surveyors (#00955)*; *Council of European Geodetic Surveyors (#04890)*; *Fédération des géomètres francophone (FGF, #09591)*; *International Federation of Surveyors (FIG, #13561)*. [2015/XJ9413/D]

♦ Union méditerranéenne de pathologie thoracique (inactive)
♦ Union méditerranéenne de voile (#16673)

♦ Union of Middle Eastern and Mediterranean Paediatric Societies (UMEMPS) 20461

Union des sociétés de pédiatrie du Moyen-Orient et de la Méditerranée (USPMOM)

Treas Saint-George Hospital, PO Box 166378, Beirut, Lebanon.
SG Gazi Universitesi, Tip Fakultesi, Besevler, 06500 Ankara/Ankara, Türkiye.
URL: http://www.umemps.org/

History 3 Sep 1966, East Jerusalem (Jordan), at 5th Middle East Mediterranean Paediatric Congress. Statutes amended: Sep 1969; Sep 1970; Mar 1972; Dec 1979; Sep 1981; Dec 1982. **Aims** Promote collaboration among paediatric societies of the Middle East and Mediterranean Basin in order to meet the various paediatric problems in a group action; diffuse knowledge and advances in paediatrics in the above-mentioned regions. **Structure** General Assembly (annual), composed of one officially delegated member from each paediatric member society. Executive Committee (meets annually), consisting of President, Vice-President, General Secretary, Treasurer and 5 Counsellors. **Languages** English, French. **Staff** 1.00 FTE, paid; 1.00 FTE, voluntary. **Finance** Members' dues (annual): US$ 100. **Activities** Organizes seminars, symposia and paediatric days. Congress held annually with the exception of years in which an IPA Congress is organized. **Events** *Congress* Cagliari (Italy) 2019, *Congress* Amman (Jordan) 2018, *Congress* Marrakech (Morocco) 2017, *Congress* Limassol (Cyprus) 2016, *Congress* Athens (Greece) 2015.
Members Paediatric societies in 27 countries:
Albania, Algeria, Bahrain, Bosnia-Herzegovina, Croatia, Cyprus, Egypt, France, Greece, Iran Islamic Rep, Iraq, Italy, Jordan, Kuwait, Lebanon, Libya, Mauritania, Morocco, Saudi Arabia, Slovenia, Spain, Sudan, Syrian AR, Tunisia, Türkiye, United Arab Emirates, Yemen.
IGO Relations Collaborates with: *UNICEF (#20332)*; *WHO (#20950)*. [2015/XD4149/D]

♦ Union monarchiste (inactive)
♦ Union mondiale (#21874)
♦ Union mondiale des anciens et anciennes élèves de la Compagnie de Jésus (#21877)

♦ Union mondiale des anciens élèves Lasalliens (UMAEL) 20462

World Union of Lasallian Former Students

Contact Via Aurelia 476, 00165 Rome RM, Italy. E-mail: umael.secretary@lasalle.org – info@umael.org.
URL: http://www.lasalle.org/

History 1992, when statutes were approved by Brother Superior John Johnston. First General Assembly: Dec 1994. Replaced *World Confederation of Former Students of Christian Brothers Schools – Confédération mondiale des anciens élèves des Frères des écoles chrétiennes – Confederación Mundial de los Antiguos Alumnos de los Hermanos de las Escuelas Cristianas*, set up 1958, referred to from 1976 as *Confédération Lasallienne mondiale* and which ceased to exist in 1989. Previous English title: *World Union of Lasallian Former Pupils (UMAEL)*. **Aims** Unite Lasallian *former pupils*. **Structure** Executive Council, elected by national federations which comprise associations within a country or of each administrative 'District' within a country. **Finance** Members' subscriptions. **Events** *World Congress* Minneapolis, MN (USA) 2019, *World Congress* Manila (Philippines) 2011, *World Congress* Panama 2007, *Asia-Pacific youth assembly* Pattaya (Thailand) 1997, *General Assembly* 1994. **Publications** *Intercom – UMAEL* (4 a year); *Bulletin de l'UMAEL* (annual).
Members Associations and federations in 80 countries and territories:
Argentina, Aruba, Australia, Austria, Belgium, Benin, Bolivia, Brazil, Burkina Faso, Cameroon, Canada, Chile, Colombia, Congo DR, Costa Rica, Côte d'Ivoire, Cuba, Djibouti, Dominican Rep, Ecuador, Egypt, Equatorial Guinea, Eritrea, Ethiopia, France, Germany, Greece, Guatemala, Guinea, Haiti, Honduras, Hong Kong, India, Ireland, Israel, Italy, Japan, Jordan, Kenya, Lebanon, Luxembourg, Madagascar, Malaysia, Malta, Mexico, Mozambique, Myanmar, New Caledonia, New Zealand, Nicaragua, Niger, Nigeria, Pakistan, Palestine, Panama, Papua New Guinea, Paraguay, Peru, Philippines, Poland, Portugal, Puerto Rico, Réunion, Romania, Rwanda, Singapore, Slovakia, South Africa, Spain, Sri Lanka, St Vincent-Grenadines, Switzerland, Thailand, Togo, Türkiye, UK, Ukraine, USA, Venezuela, Vietnam.
NGO Relations Affiliated to: *Organisation mondiale des anciens élèves de l'enseignement catholique (OMAEC, #17816)*. [2019/XE0289/E]

♦ Union mondiale des associations d'anciens parlementaires francophones (inactive)
♦ Union mondiale des aveugles (#21234)
♦ Union mondiale de billard (#21230)
♦ Union mondiale chrétienne des femmes abstinentes (#21840)
♦ Union mondiale des clubs de Saint Bernard (#21887)
♦ Union mondiale pour la conservation de la nature et de ses ressources (#15766)
♦ Union mondiale démocrate chrétienne / see Centrist Democrat International (#03792)
♦ Union mondiale pour l'économie franche (inactive)
♦ Union mondiale des écrivains-médecins (inactive)
♦ Union mondiale des efforts chrétiens (#21768)
♦ Union mondiale des enseignants catholiques / see UMEC-WUCT (#20280)
♦ Union mondiale des études juives (#21879)
♦ Union Mondiale des Etudiants Juifs (#21878)
♦ Union mondiale de la femme pour la concorde internationale (inactive)
♦ Union mondiale des femmes rurales (#02338)
♦ Union mondiale des gitans / see International Romani Union (#14765)
♦ Union mondiale des intellectuels (inactive)
♦ Union mondiale de la jeunesse (inactive)
♦ Union mondiale pour le judaïsme libéral (#21883)
♦ Union mondiale des libres penseurs (inactive)
♦ Union mondiale des marchés de gros (#21889)
♦ Union mondiale des marchés de gros au sein d'IULA / see World Union of Wholesale Markets (#21889)
♦ Union mondiale de la marionnette / see Union internationale de la marionnette (#20430)
♦ Union mondiale des nationaux socialistes (#21880)
♦ Union mondiale pour la nature / see International Union for Conservation of Nature and Natural Resources (#15766)
♦ Union mondiale des organisations féminines catholiques (#21876)
♦ Union mondiale ORT / see World ORT (#21698)
♦ Union mondiale OSE pour la protection de la santé des populations juives et oeuvres de secours aux enfants (inactive)
♦ Union mondiale des professions libérales (#21882)
♦ Union mondiale pour la protection de la vie (inactive)
♦ Union mondiale des revues de droit international et des relations internationales (inactive)
♦ Union mondiale pour la sauvegarde de l'enfance et de l'adolescence (inactive)
♦ Union mondiale des sionistes révisonnistes (inactive)
♦ Union mondiale de ski nautique / see International Waterski and Wakeboard Federation (#15872)
♦ Union mondiale des sociétés catholiques de philosophie (#21875)
♦ Union mondiale des sociétés d'histoire pharmaceutique (inactive)
♦ Union mondiale des sociétés ORT pour la propagation du travail artisanal industriel et agricole parmi les juifs / see World ORT (#21698)
♦ Union mondiale des sociétés de philosophie pythagoricienne (inactive)
♦ Union mondiale St Gabriel (#21885)
♦ Union mondiale des Turcs d'Ahiska (internationally oriented national body)
♦ Union Mondiale des Villes Olympiques (#21881)
♦ Union mondiale des villes de la paix (no recent information)
♦ Union mondiale des voix françaises (inactive)

♦ Union monétaire de l'Afrique centrale (UMAC) 20463

Central African Monetary Union (CAMU)

Contact c/o CEMAC, BP 969, Bangui, Central African Rep. T. +236612185. Fax +236612135.
URL: http://www.cemac.int/institutionsCEMAC.htm

History 22 Nov 1972, Brazzaville (Congo Brazzaville), by 5 member States and by Government of France. 'Convention of Transaction Accounts' signed 13 Mar 1973, Libreville (Gabon). Equatorial Guinea became a member as from 1 Jan 1985. Has also been referred to in English as *Central African Monetary System* and as *Central African Monetary Area (CAMA)*; and in French as *Zone monétaire centrafricaine*. Since the setting up of *Communauté économique et monétaire d'Afrique centrale (CEMAC, #04374)*, 16 Mar 1994, an institution of CEMAC. **Aims** Act as the institution in charge of monetary issues and harmonization of monetary policies of the member countries. **Structure** Monetary Committee (meets at least once a year), comprising Ministers of Finance and Economic Affairs of member states, is a principal organ of CEMAC. Common monetary unit, the

Central African Financial Cooperation Franc (CFA Franc), is issued by *Banque des Etats de l'Afrique centrale (BEAC, #03169)*, whose statutes are annexed to the Convention on Monetary Cooperation. Joint Reserve Fund, deposited in the French Treasury, ensures external convertibility of the CFA Franc. Conditions governing the fund covered by 'Operational Account Convention', signed between France and member countries. *Central African Clearing Arrangement* came into force in 1982 among member countries and Zaire. **Languages** French. **Activities** Harmonizes monetary policies; controls external payments and the general exchange regime. Close cooperation with: *Union économique de l'Afrique centrale (UEAC, #20376)*, the latter replacing *Union douanière et économique de l'Afrique centrale (UDEAC, inactive)*; *Commission bancaire de l'Afrique centrale (COBAC, #04204)*. **Publications** *Etudes et statistiques* (12 a year) – bulletin. Annual report.
Members Governments of 6 countries:
Cameroon, Central African Rep, Chad, Congo Brazzaville, Equatorial Guinea, Gabon.
Non-member participant:
France.
IGO Relations Participates in the activities of: *UNCTAD (#20285)*. [2016/XD6441/**E***]

- ♦ Union monétaire centroaméricaine (inactive)
- ♦ Union monétaire latine (inactive)
- ♦ Union monétaire Ouest africaine (inactive)
- ♦ Union monétaire scandinave (inactive)
- ♦ Unión Monetaria Centroamericana (inactive)
- ♦ Unión de Mujeres Americanas (inactive)
- ♦ Unión Mundial de Antiguos Alumnos de la Compañia de Jesús (#21877)
- ♦ Unión Mundial de Ciegos (#21234)
- ♦ Unión Mundial de Ciudades de la Paz (no recent information)
- ♦ Unión Mundial Demócrata Cristiana / see Centrist Democrat International (#03792)
- ♦ Unión Mundial de Educadores Católicos / see UMEC-WUCT (#20280)
- ♦ Unión Mundial de Estudiantes Judios (#21878)

♦ Union Mundial pro Interlingua (UMI) 20464

Admin Osmankäämintie 44 C, FI-01300 Helsinki, Finland.
URL: http://www.interlingua.com/

History Founded Feb 1954, on adoption of provisional Constitution. Statutes revised: Jul 1955, 1970, 1993. Developed from *International Auxiliary Language Association (IALA, inactive)*, set up 1924. Renewed, 2005, on adoption of new statutes. Registered in accordance with French law. **Aims** Promote the use of the international *language* Interlingua as a means of international communication. **Structure** General Assembly (every 2 years); General Council; Executive Council. **Languages** Interlingua. **Staff** 4.00 FTE, voluntary. **Finance** Sources: members' dues. Other sources: Subventions. **Activities** Encourages and assists organization of courses by Sections; acts as forum for exchange of information and mutual consultation; organizes conferences; carries out joint work on linguistic and terminological problems. **Events** *Biennial Conference* Prague (Czechia) 2019, *Biennial Conference* Las Palmas de Gran Canaria (Spain) 2017, *Biennial Conference* Benidorm (Spain) 2015, *Biennial Conference* Freiburg-Breisgau (Germany) 2013, *Biennial Conference* Chepelare (Bulgaria) 2011. **Publications** *Panorama* (6 a year). Study books; manuals; brochures; reviews. **Information Services** *Servicio de Libros UMI* – books in and on Interlingua.
Members National associations (11); Individuals (about 700), in 40 countries:
Algeria, Andorra, Australia, Austria, Belgium, Brazil, Bulgaria, Canada, China, Colombia, Congo DR, Cyprus, Czechia, Denmark, Estonia, France, Germany, Guatemala, Holy See, Hungary, India, Italy, Japan, Latvia, Lithuania, Netherlands, Norway, Poland, Portugal, Romania, Russia, Slovakia, Spain, Sweden, Switzerland, Tajikistan, Türkiye, UK, Ukraine, USA.
NGO Relations *Association for the Expansion of International Roles of the Languages of Continental Europe (#02589).* [2020/XC4560/**C**]

- ♦ Unión Mundial pro Judaismo Progresista (#21883)
- ♦ Unión Mundial Macabi (#16537)
- ♦ Unión Mundial de Mercados Mayoristas (#21889)
- ♦ Unión Mundial de Mercados Mayoristas dentro la IULA / see World Union of Wholesale Markets (#21889)
- ♦ Unión Mundial de Mujeres Cristianas contra el Alcoholismo (#21840)
- ♦ Unión Mundial para la Naturaleza / see International Union for Conservation of Nature and Natural Resources (#15766)
- ♦ Unión Mundial de las Organizaciones Femeninas Católicas (#21876)
- ♦ Unión Mundial ORT / see World ORT (#21698)
- ♦ Unión Mundial de los Profesiones Liberales (#21882)
- ♦ Unión Mundial para la Protección de la Infancia y la Adolescencia (inactive)
- ♦ Unión Mundial San Gabriel (#21885)
- ♦ Unión Mundial de Sociedades de Historia Farmacéutica (inactive)
- ♦ Union Mundial de Yoga (no recent information)
- ♦ Union des musées d'Amérique latine et des Caraïbes (inactive)
- ♦ Unión de Museos de América Latina y del Caribe (inactive)
- ♦ Union des musiciens nordiques (no recent information)
- ♦ Unión de los Músicos Nórdicos (no recent information)
- ♦ Union musulmane internationale (inactive)
- ♦ Unión de Naciones Suramericanas (#20481)

♦ Union of National African Paediatric Societies and Associations (UNAPSA) 20465

Union des sociétés et des associations africaines de pédiatrie

Contact Dept of Paediatrics and Child Health, Makerere Medical School, PO Box 7072, Kampala, Uganda.
Pres PO 01 Box 2640 RP, Cotonou, Benin. T. +229307242. Fax +229307242.

History Feb 1979, Nairobi (Kenya), taking over the activities of *African Paediatric Club (inactive)*, set up Dec 1973, Zaria (Nigeria). **Aims** Encourage cooperation between paediatric societies and associations in Africa. **Structure** Executive Committee, consisting of President, Secretary-General, 1st Vice-President, 2nd Vice-President, Immediate Past President and 3 ex-officio members. **Languages** English, French. **Staff** 6.00 FTE, paid. **Finance** Levy on members. **Activities** Organizes Congresses. **Events** *Congress* Yaoundé (Cameroon) 2014, *Congress* Cotonou (Benin) 2005, *Congress on malaria in pregnant woman and child* Cotonou (Benin) 1999, *The health of the African child in the next millennium – perspectives and challenges* Cotonou (Benin) 1999, *Child health in a changing African environment* Kampala (Uganda) 1996. **Publications** *UNAPSA Newsletter* (annual). Workshop proceedings.
Members Paediatric societies and associations in 38 countries:
Angola, Benin, Burkina Faso, Burundi, Cameroon, Cape Verde, Central African Rep, Chad, Congo Brazzaville, Congo DR, Côte d'Ivoire, Egypt, Equatorial Guinea, Ethiopia, Gabon, Gambia, Ghana, Guinea, Guinea-Bissau, Kenya, Lesotho, Liberia, Madagascar, Malawi, Mali, Mauritius, Mozambique, Namibia, Niger, Nigeria, Senegal, Sierra Leone, South Africa, Tanzania UR, Togo, Uganda, Zambia, Zimbabwe.
IGO Relations *UNICEF (#20332)*; *WHO (#20950)*. **NGO Relations** Affiliate Society of: *International Pediatric Association (IPA, #14541).* [2014/XD6865/**D**]

- ♦ Union nationale des maisons familiales rurales d'éducation et d'orientation (internationally oriented national body)
- ♦ Union of National European Paediatric Societies and Associations / see European Paediatric Association (#08124)
- ♦ Union of National Federations of Building Materials Merchants in the EEC / see European Association of National Builders' Merchants Associations (#06128)

♦ Union of National Pediatric Societies of Turkic Republics (UNPSTR) 20466

SG Cinnah Caddesi 35/6 Çankaya, 06690 Ankara/Ankara, Türkiye. T. +903124381934. Fax +903124381935.

History 1993, Ankara (Turkey). **Aims** Bring together paediatricians of Turkish speaking areas in order to foster friendship and exchange of scientific experience and knowledge. **Structure** Executive Committee, comprising representatives of national member societies. **Languages** English, Russian, Turkish. **Staff** Voluntary. **Finance** Members' dues. **Events** *International Congress* Baku (Azerbaijan) 2015, *International Congress* Antalya (Turkey) 2014, *International Congress* Teheran (Iran Islamic Rep) 2012, *International Congress* Dushanbe (Tajikistan) 2011, *International Congress* Almaty (Kazakhstan) 2010. **Publications** Congress programmes; abstract books.
Members National paediatric societies in 13 countries and territories:
Afghanistan, Azerbaijan, Bashkortostan, Crimea, Kazakhstan, Kyrgyzstan, Nakhchivan, Northern Cyprus, Tajikistan, Tatarstan, Türkiye, Turkmenistan, Uzbekistan.
NGO Relations Affiliate Society of: *International Pediatric Association (IPA, #14541).* [2015/XD6071/**D**]

- ♦ Union of National Radio and Television Organizations of Africa / see African Union of Broadcasting (#00490)
- ♦ Union des Nations Sud-Américaines (#20481)
- ♦ Union Network International / see UNI Global Union (#20338)
- ♦ Union Network International – Africa Region / see UNI Global Union – Africa Region (#20339)
- ♦ Union Network International Africa Regional Office / see UNI Global Union – Africa Region (#20339)
- ♦ Union Network International Americas Regional Office / see UNI Global Union – Americas Regional Office (#20340)
- ♦ Union Network International Asia and Pacific Regional Office / see UNI Global Union – Asia and Pacific Regional Office (#20341)
- ♦ Union Network International Europa / see UNI Global Union – Europa (#20342)
- ♦ Union Network International Europa Regional Office / see UNI Global Union – Europa (#20342)
- ♦ **Union de Nice** Union particulière pour la classification internationale des produits et des services aux fins de l'enregistrement des marques (#19913)
- ♦ Union de la noblesse russe (#19009)
- ♦ Unión Nórdica de Conductores Abstemios (inactive)
- ♦ Union of Nordic Associations / see Föreningarna Nordens Förbund (#09859)
- ♦ Union nordique de boxe (inactive)
- ♦ Union nordique du café (inactive)
- ♦ Union nordique des cheminots (inactive)
- ♦ Union nordique des cheminots anti-alcooliques (inactive)
- ♦ Union nordique des conducteurs anti-alcooliques (inactive)
- ♦ Union nordique des écoles privées (inactive)
- ♦ Union nordique des éditeurs de musique (no recent information)
- ♦ Union nordique des employés de banque (inactive)
- ♦ Union nordique de l'enseignement de la musique (inactive)
- ♦ Union nordique du film et de la télévision (inactive)
- ♦ Union nordique des fonctionnaires de prison (inactive)
- ♦ Union nordique des grossistes en matériel optique (inactive)
- ♦ Union nordique de gymnastique (inactive)
- ♦ Union nordique de l'industrie de la viande (inactive)
- ♦ Union nordique d'informatique (no recent information)
- ♦ Union nordique des jeunes conservateurs (#17473)
- ♦ Union nordique de journalistes (#17487)
- ♦ Union nordique de judo (inactive)
- ♦ Union Nordique des Musées (#17455)
- ♦ Union nordique des passeports (#17380)
- ♦ Union nordique du personnel des assurances (inactive)
- ♦ Union nordique des pharmaciens (#17456)
- ♦ Union nordique de police criminelle (inactive)
- ♦ Union nordique des postiers (inactive)
- ♦ Union nordique des ramoneurs (inactive)
- ♦ Union nordique des remorqueurs routiers (inactive)
- ♦ Union nordique pour la santé et le travail (inactive)
- ♦ Union nordique des techniciens dentaires (inactive)
- ♦ Union nordique du théâtre (#17448)
- ♦ Union nordique de tir (#17408)
- ♦ Union nordique de tir à l'arc (#17499)
- ♦ Union nordique des travailleurs de l'alimentation, des boissons et des tabacs (no recent information)
- ♦ Union nordique des travailleurs de la construction des routes (inactive)
- ♦ Union nordique des travailleurs des hôtels, des cafés et des restaurants (inactive)
- ♦ Union nordique des travailleurs des télécommunications (inactive)
- ♦ Union nordique des travailleurs textiles (inactive)
- ♦ Union nordique des travailleurs du textile, du vêtement et du cuir (inactive)
- ♦ Union nordique des voyageurs de commerce (inactive)
- ♦ Union novialiste internationale (inactive)
- ♦ Union numismatique nordique (#17370)
- ♦ Union Océanie de judo (#17665)

♦ Union of OIC News AGencies (UNA) 20467

Union des agences de presse de l'OCI

Dir Gen PO Box 5054, Jeddah 21422, Saudi Arabia. T. +96626658561 – +96626652056. Fax +96626659358. E-mail: director.general@una-oic.org – info@una-oic.org.
URL: http://www.una-oic.org/

History Aug 1972, Kuala Lumpur (Malaysia). Established at General Assembly of *Organisation of Islamic Cooperation (OIC, #17813)*, attended by delegates of 19 countries, following decision of 2nd *Council of Foreign Ministers (CFM, see: #17813)*, Dec 1970, Karachi (Pakistan). A specialized organ of OIC. Former names and other names: *Agence islamique internationale de presse* – former; *International Islamic News Agency (IINA)* – former. **Aims** Develop closer and better relations between OIC Member States in the information field; promote contacts and technical cooperation between *news agencies* and member states; work for better understanding of Islamic people and their political, economic and social problems; serve the causes of the Islamic States by providing *information* on their progress and achievements and by explaining their stand to world *public opinion*. **Structure** General Assembly (every 2 years); Executive Board; Director General. **Languages** Arabic, English, French. **Finance** Members' contributions. Other sources: voluntary donations and subsidies from Member States. **Publications** *IINA News Bulletin* (daily) in Arabic, English, French; *IINA News Bulletin* (12 a year) in Arabic, English, French; *Islamic World* (annual). Books; video reports in Arabic, French, English. **Members** News Agencies in all OIC countries. **NGO Relations** Partner of (1): *Fédération Atlantique des Agences de Presse Africaines (FAAPA, #09462).* [2020/XF4325/**F***]

- ♦ Uniono por la Linguo Internaciona Ido (#20441)
- ♦ Union des ordres fiscaux de l'Afrique de l'ouest (#20898)
- ♦ Union d'organisations syndicales libres (no recent information)
- ♦ Union of Organizations of Manufacturers of Pasta Products in the EC / see Union of Organizations of manufacturers of Pasta Products of the EU (#20468)

♦ Union of Organizations of manufacturers of Pasta Products of the EU 20468

Union des associations de fabricants de pâtes alimentaires de l'UE (UNAFPA)

Secretariat Viale del Poggio Fiorito 61, 00144 Rome RM, Italy. T. +3968091071. Fax +3968073186. E-mail: unafpa@pasta-unafpa.org.
URL: http://www.pasta-unafpa.org/

History 15 Mar 1960, as *Union of Associations of Pasta Manufacturers of the EEC – Union des associations de fabricants de pâtes alimentaires de la CEE Vereinigung der Verbände der Teigwarenindustrie in der EWG – Unione delle Associazioni degli Industriali Pastificatori della CEE – Unie van Verenigingen van Fabrikanten van Deegwaren in de EEG.* Subsequently changed to: *Union of Organizations of Manufacturers of Pasta Products in the EC – Union des associations de fabricants de pâtes alimentaires de la CE.* **Aims** Ensure the definition, representation and defence of the interests of the EU pasta industry within the framework of the *European Union.* **Structure** Chairmanship rotates annually. **Events** *World congress* Porlamar (Venezuela) 2000, *World Congress* Rome (Italy) 1995, *World congress* Rome (Italy) 1995. **Publications** Monograph of pasta manufacturing in Europe.
Members Associations in 11 countries:
Austria, Belgium, Czechia, France, Germany, Greece, Italy, Portugal, Spain, Sweden, UK.
IGO Relations Recognized by: *European Commission (EC, #06633).* **NGO Relations** Affiliated member of: *FoodDrinkEurope (#09841).* Supporting member of: *International Pasta Organisation (IPO, #14528).* [2015/XE3344/E]

- ♦ Union ornithologique scandinave (inactive)
- ♦ Union ouest-européenne des chambres de commerce et d'industrie des régions rhénane, rhodanienne et danubienne / see Union of European Chambers of Commerce for Transport (#20384)
- ♦ Unión del Pacifico Democratico (#05035)
- ♦ Unión de Paises Exportadores de Banano (inactive)
- ♦ Union paléontologique internationale / see International Palaeontological Association (#14501)
- ♦ Union panafricaine des étudiants (#00644)
- ♦ Union panafricaine de la jeunesse (#18076)
- ♦ Union panafricaine des journalistes (inactive)
- ♦ Union panafricaine des journalistes, 1961 (inactive)
- ♦ Union panafricaine des postes (#18060)
- ♦ Union panafricaine de la science et de la technologie (inactive)
- ♦ Union panafricaine des télécommunications (inactive)
- ♦ Union panafricaine des travailleurs des banques et institutions financières (inactive)
- ♦ Union panafricaine des travailleurs croyants (inactive)
- ♦ Union panaméricaine d'associations d'ingénieurs (#20469)
- ♦ Union panaméricaine des baptistes (inactive)
- ♦ Union panaméricaine de gymnastique (#20471)
- ♦ Union panaméricaine de judo (#18115)
- ♦ Union panaméricaine de taekwondo (#18136)
- ♦ Union panaméricaine des techniciens et experts en sciences économiques (inactive)

♦ Unión Panamericana de Asociaciones de Ingenieros (UPADI) 20469

Union panaméricaine d'associations d'ingénieurs – Pan American Union of Engineering Societies – União Panamericana de Associações de Engenheiros

Pres Av Dr Dante Pazzanese 120, Sao Paulo SP, 04012-180, Brazil. T. +551134669266. E-mail: upadi@upadi.com.
URL: http://www.upadi.com/

History Founded 1949, Rio de Janeiro (Brazil). Constitution most recently revised, 2000, Panama City. Previously also referred to in English as *Pan American Federation of Engineering Societies.* **Aims** Encourage, promote, expand, guide and standardize the efforts and practices of engineers of the Americas; contribute to promotion of the welfare of society in member organizations countries. **Structure** General Assembly (every 2 years). Board of Directors, comprising one Director and one Alternate Directors for each Member Organization. Consulting Council, comprising former Presidents and other prominent personalities, nominated by Board of Directors. Executive Committee of 6 members. Technical Council, comprising President and representatives of UPADI Technical Committees and specialized engineering organizations. UPADI Foundation, managed by Executive Board, appointed by Board of Directors. Board of Trustees of UPADI Pan American Engineering Award. Board of Trustees of 'Carlos Lopez Rivera' Pan American Award for Integration and Solidarity. Juries for awards and prizes. Committees (12): Engineering Education; Engineering Professional Practice; Historic Heritage, Urban Development and Population Growth; Hydrographic Basins; Chemistry and Petroleum; Information Systems and Telecommunications; Civil Engineering and Seismic Resistant Structures; Energy; Environment and Human Development; Sea and Coastal Engineering; Transportation; Maintenance. **Languages** English, French, Portuguese, Spanish. **Staff** 2.00 FTE, paid; 9.00 FTE, voluntary. **Finance** Members' dues. Other sources: donations; consulting services for third parties. UPADI Foundation, set up 1951, Havana (Cuba), provides a fund to support UPADI development activities. **Activities** Events/meeting; training/education; awards/prizes/competitions. **Events** *Convention and Annual Assembly* Bogota (Colombia) 2022, *Convention* Santa Cruz (Bolivia) 2014, *Convention* Havana (Cuba) 2012, *Convention* Buenos Aires (Argentina) 2010, *International directorate meeting* San Juan (Puerto Rico) 2009. **Publications** *Panamerican Engineering Education Bulletin* (4 a year); *UPADI Newsletter* (4 a year). Abstracts of Conventions and Seminars.
Members National engineering organizations (31) in 27 countries and territories:
Argentina, Aruba, Belize, Bolivia, Brazil, Chile, Colombia, Costa Rica, Cuba, Dominican Rep, Ecuador, El Salvador, Guatemala, Haiti, Honduras, Jamaica, Mexico, Nicaragua, Panama, Paraguay, Peru, Puerto Rico, Spain, Trinidad-Tobago, Uruguay, USA, Venezuela.
Observers in 2 countries:
Portugal, Spain.
IGO Relations Cooperates with: *OAS (#17629); UNESCO (#20322).* **NGO Relations** Member of: *Consejo de las Asociaciones Profesionales de Ingenieros Civiles de Lengua Oficial Portuguesa y Castellana (CECPC-CICPC, #04702); Engineering for the Americas (EftA, no recent information);* WFEO. Cooperates with: *Council of Industrial Research Associations of the Americas (CIRAA, no recent information); Federación Panamericana de Ingenieria Económica y de Costos (FEPIEC, no recent information); Federación Panamericana de Ingenieria Oceanica y Costera (FEPIOC, #09380); Federation of Engineering Organizations of Central America and Panama (#09483); Inter-American Association of Sanitary and Environmental Engineering (#11400); Latin American Organization of Colleges, Councils and Professional Societies of Engineering, Architecture, Surveying and Associated Branches (OLCPIA, no recent information); Panamerican Confederation of Mechanical and Electrical Engineering and Related Fields, San Juan (#18089).* Instrumental in setting up: *World Federation of Engineering Organizations (WFEO, #21433).* [2022/XD3059/y/D]

- ♦ Union Panamericana de Asociaciones de Montañismo / see Confederación Panamericana de Deportes de Montaña y Escalada (#04472)
- ♦ Union Panamericana de Asociaciones de Montañismo y Escalada / see Confederación Panamericana de Deportes de Montaña y Escalada (#04472)

♦ Unión Panamericana de Asociaciones de Valuación (UPAV) 20470

Pan-American Union of Appraisal Associations

Pres PO Box 10537, San Juan PR 00922-0537, USA. Fax +17877746526.
URL: http://www.upav.org/

Structure Executive Committee. **Events** *Congress* Monterrey (Mexico) 2012, *Congress* Miami, FL (USA) 2010, *Congress* Buenos Aires (Argentina) 2002, *The new paradigm of valuation facing the monetary unification* Porlamar (Venezuela) 2000, *Congress* Cusco (Peru) 1998.
Members Individuals in 10 countries:
Argentina, Brazil, Canada, Colombia, Costa Rica, Dominican Rep, Mexico, Peru, Puerto Rico, USA, Venezuela.
NGO Relations Partner of: *Appraisal Institute (AI).* [2012/XD7081/D]

- ♦ Unión Panamericana para el control de las Infecciones Transmitidas Sexualmente (no recent information)
- ♦ Union Panamericana de Fundaciones de Asma y Alergia / see UNASMA – Fundación Internacional de Asma y Alergias (#20282)

♦ Union Panamericana de Gimnasia (UPAG) 20471

Pan American Gymnastics Union (PAGU) – Union panaméricaine de gymnastique

Pres Tenayuca 55, Of 403, Colonia Letrán Valle, Alcaldía Benito Juárez, 03650 Mexico City CDMX, Mexico. T. +525589847848. E-mail: info@upag-pagu.org.
URL: https://upag-pagu.com/

History 1971, Cali (Colombia). Continental affiliated union of: *Fédération internationale de gymnastique (FIG, #09636).* Former names and other names: *Union Panamericana de Ginastica* – former. **Structure** Executive Committee. **Activities** Sporting activities. **Events** *Congress* Cancún (Mexico) 2001, *Congress* Winnipeg, MB (Canada) 1999. **Members** Membership countries not specified. **NGO Relations** Member of (1): *Asociación de Confederaciones Deportivas Panamericanas (ACODEPA, #02119).* [2023/XD2261/D]

- ♦ Union Panamericana de Ginastica / see Union Panamericana de Gimnasia (#20471)
- ♦ Unión Panamericana de Judo (#18115)
- ♦ Unión Panamericana de Taekwondo (#18136)
- ♦ Union panatlantique (inactive)
- ♦ Unión Paneuropea / see International Paneuropean Union (#14509)
- ♦ Union paneuropéenne / see International Paneuropean Union (#14509)
- ♦ Union paneuropéenne internationale (#14509)
- ♦ Union panpacifique (inactive)
- ♦ **Unión de Paris** Unión Internacional para la Protección de la Propiedad Industrial (#15805)
- ♦ **Union de Paris** Union internationale pour la protection de la propriété industrielle (#15805)
- ♦ Unión Parlamentaria Scout Mundial (#21773)
- ♦ Unión de Parlamentarios del Mercosur / see Unión de Parlamentarios Sudamericanos y del MERCOSUR (#20472)

♦ Unión de Parlamentarios Sudamericanos y del MERCOSUR (UPSM) . 20472

Pres Honrable Camara, Calle 53 entre 7 y 8, La Plata, Buenos Aires, Argentina.
History 1999, as *Unión de Parlamentarios del Mercosur (UPM).* **IGO Relations** *Confederación Parlamentaria de las Américas (COPA, #04479).* [2018/XD9370/D*]

- ♦ Union parlementaire africaine (#00412)
- ♦ Union parlementaire d'Asie / see Asian-Pacific Parliamentarians' Union (#01622)
- ♦ Union parlementaire des états membres de l'OCI (#18220)
- ♦ Union parlementaire européenne (inactive)
- ♦ Union parlementaire mondiale du scoutisme (#21773)
- ♦ Union de parlementaires de l'Asie et du Pacifique (#01622)
- ♦ Union des parlements africains / see African Parliamentary Union (#00412)
- ♦ Union particulière pour la classification internationale des produits et des services aux fins de l'enregistrement des marques (#19913)
- ♦ Unión de los Partidos Socialistas de la Comunidad Europea / see Party of European Socialists (#18249)
- ♦ Union des partis africains pour la démocratie et le développement (inactive)
- ♦ Union des partis socialistes de la Communauté européenne / see Party of European Socialists (#18249)
- ♦ Union des pays exportateurs de bananes (inactive)
- ♦ Unión de Pequeños y Medianos Productores de Café de México, Centroamérica y el Caribe (no recent information)
- ♦ Union du personnel des finances en Europe (#20407)
- ♦ Union Pétrolière Européenne Indépendante / see UPEI – The voice of Europe's independent fuel suppliers (#20726)
- ♦ Union des phoniatres européens (#20390)
- ♦ Union phytopathlogique méditerranéenne / see Mediterranean Phytopathological Union (#16672)
- ♦ Union of Pioneer Organizations – Federation of Children's Organizations / see International Union of Children's Organizations (#15762)
- ♦ Union Pontificale Missionnaire (see: #16827)
- ♦ Union des ports maritimes arabes (no recent information)
- ♦ Union of Portuguese-Speaking Capital Cities / see União das Cidades Capitais Luso-Afro-Américo-Asiaticas (#20328)
- ♦ Unión Postal de las Américas y España / see Postal Union of the Americas, Spain and Portugal (#18466)
- ♦ Unión Postal de las Américas, España y Portugal (#18466)
- ♦ Unión Postal Arabe / see Arab Permanent Postal Commission (#01025)
- ♦ Union postale africaine (no recent information)
- ♦ Union postale des Amériques et de l'Espagne / see Postal Union of the Americas, Spain and Portugal (#18466)
- ♦ Union postale des Amériques, de l'Espagne et du Portugal (#18466)
- ♦ Union postale arabe / see Arab Permanent Postal Commission (#01025)
- ♦ Union postale de l'Asie et de l'Océanie / see Asian-Pacific Postal Union (#01625)
- ♦ Union postale de l'Asie et du Pacifique (#01625)
- ♦ Union postale balkanique (inactive)
- ♦ Union postale balte (#03137)
- ♦ Union postale panaméricaine / see Postal Union of the Americas, Spain and Portugal (#18466)
- ♦ Union postale des pays du Nord (#17391)
- ♦ Union postale du Sud et de l'Ouest de l'Asie (inactive)
- ♦ Union postale universelle (#20682)
- ♦ Unión Postal de los Paises del Norte (#17391)
- ♦ Unión Postal Panamericana / see Postal Union of the Americas, Spain and Portugal (#18466)
- ♦ Unión Postal Universal (#20682)
- ♦ Union des postes sud-américaines / see Postal Union of the Americas, Spain and Portugal (#18466)
- ♦ Union of Potato Starch Factories of the European Union (#20406)
- ♦ Union des praticiens européens en propriété industrielle / see Union of European Practitioners in Intellectual Property (#20392)
- ♦ Union des praticiens européens en propriété intellectuelle (#20392)
- ♦ Union de la presse du Commonwealth / see CPU Media Trust (#04941)
- ♦ Union de la presse économique et financière européenne / see European Business Press (#06423)
- ♦ Union de la presse islamique (inactive)
- ♦ Union de prévoyance des fonctionnaires européens / see AFILIATYS (#00151)
- ♦ Union of Producers, Conveyors and Distributors of Electric Power in Africa / see Association of Power Utilities in Africa (#02867)
- ♦ Union of Producers, Transporters and Distributors of Electric Power in Africa / see Association of Power Utilities in Africa (#02867)
- ♦ Union des producteurs, transporteurs et distributeurs d'énergie électrique d'Afrique / see Association of Power Utilities in Africa (#02867)
- ♦ Unión Profesional Internacional de Ginecólogos y Obstétricos (#20473)
- ♦ Union des professeurs internationalistes (inactive)
- ♦ Union of Professional Groups of the Potato-Starch Industry of the EEC / see Union des féculeries de pommes de terre de l'Union européenne (#20406)

♦ Union professionnelle internationale des gynécologues et obstétriciens (UPIGO) 20473

International Professional Union of Gynaecologists and Obstetricians – Unión Profesional Internacional de Ginecólogos y Obstétricos – Internationaler Berufsverband der Frauenärzte und Geburtshelfer

Past Pres/Treas 1 rue de Firminy, 67370 Dingsheim, France. T. +33388561777. Fax +33388561777.
Pres address not obtained.
SG address not obtained.
URL: http://www.upigo.org/

History 23 Jul 1954, Paris (France). registered according to French law. Originally known as *International Liaison Committee of Professional Organizations of Gynaecologists and Obstetricians.* **Aims** Study and represent, at an international level, moral and material interests of practitioners in gynaecology and obstetrics; study and explain ethical, professional and social problems arising in these disciplines; harmonize post-graduate training in gynaecology and obstetrics in Europe; foster transfer of knowledge and skill from Western to Eastern Europe. **Structure** General Assembly; Managing Council; Executive Board. **Languages** English, French, German. **Staff** Voluntary. **Finance** National contributions (based on number of inhabitants, GNP and number of doctors). Other sources: private and public sponsoring. Annual budget: about US$ 40,000. **Activities** Guidance/assistance/consulting; networking/liaising; knowledge management/information dissemination; standards/guidelines; training/education. **Events** *Annual Meeting* Smolenice (Slovakia) 2010, *Meeting / Annual Meeting* Luxembourg (Luxembourg) 2009, *Annual Meeting* Copenhagen (Denmark) 2008, *Annual Meeting* Hammamet (Tunisia) 2007, *Annual Meeting* Paris (France) 2006.
Members Full in 18 countries:
Benin, Congo Brazzaville, Côte d'Ivoire, Denmark, France, Germany, Greece, Italy, Luxembourg, Mali, Niger, Poland, Senegal, Slovakia, Switzerland, Togo, UK, Ukraine.
Consultative Status Consultative status granted from: *Council of Europe (CE, #04881)* (Participatory Status). **NGO Relations** Official relations with: *European Union of Medical Specialists (UEMS, #09001).* Instrumental in setting up *Extended European Board of Gynaecology and Obstetrics (E-EBGO, inactive).*
[2017.06.01/XD2762/**D**]

♦ Union for Progressive Judaism (internationally oriented national body)
♦ Union pour la protection des appellations d'origine et leur enregistrement international (#20474)

♦ Union for the Protection of Appellations of Origin and their International Registration (Lisbon Union) 20474

Union pour la protection des appellations d'origine et leur enregistrement international
Address not obtained.
URL: http://www.wipo.org/

History 1958, Lisbon (Portugal), by *Lisbon Agreement for the Protection of Appellations of Origin and Their International Registration (Lisbon Agreement, 1958).* Revised: 1967, Stockholm (Sweden); amended 1979. A union administered by *World Intellectual Property Organization (WIPO, #21593).* **Aims** Promote the *protection* of appellations of origin. **Structure** Assembly. **Activities** Establishes a system for the protection of appellations of origin, that is, the geographical name of a country, region, or locality, which serves to designate a product originated therein, the quality and characteristics of which are due exclusively or essentially to the geographical environment, including natural and human factors. Such names are registered by the International Bureau of WIPO upon request of the contracting State concerned.
Members Open to States party to the Lisbon Agreement. States party to the Agreement, as of Jan 2012 (27):
Algeria, Bulgaria, Burkina Faso, Congo Brazzaville, Costa Rica, Cuba, Czechia, France, Gabon, Georgia, Haiti, Hungary, Iran Islamic Rep, Israel, Italy, Korea DPR, Mexico, Moldova, Montenegro, Nicaragua, North Macedonia, Peru, Portugal, Serbia, Slovakia, Togo, Tunisia.
State party to the Agreement but not member of the Assembly (1):
Haiti. [2012/XF4437/**F***]

♦ Union for the Protection of the Human Person by International Social and Economic Cooperation (inactive)
♦ Union of Providence of European Officials / see AFILIATYS (#00151)
♦ Union of Provident Associations of Officials of the European Union / see AFILIATYS (#00151)
♦ Union of Public Relations Counsels in Europe (inactive)
♦ Union of Publishers in Central Africa (no recent information)
♦ Unión Radiocientífica Internacional (#20475)
♦ Union de radiodiffusion pour l'Asie et le Pacifique (#01863)
♦ Union de radiodiffusion des Etats arabes (#01050)
♦ Union des radiodiffusions des Caraïbes (#03465)
♦ Union des radiodiffusions et télévisions nationales d'Afrique / see African Union of Broadcasting (#00490)
♦ Unión de Radiodifusión de los Estados Arabes (#01050)
♦ Union radiophonique et télévisuelle internationale (#14689)
♦ Union des radios arabes / see Arab States Broadcasting Union (#01050)

♦ Union radio-scientifique internationale (URSI) 20475

International Union of Radio Science – Unión Radiocientífica Internacional – Internationaler Radio-Wissenschaftlicher Verein
SG c/o Ghent Univ (INTEC), Technologiepark-Zwijnaarde 126, 9052 Ghent, Belgium. T. +3292643320. E-mail: secretary-general@ursi.org.
URL: http://www.ursi.org/

History 1913, Brussels (Belgium). Re-constituted 1919, during Constitutive Assembly of *International Research Council (IRC) – Conseil international des recherches (CIR),* currently *International Council for Science (ICSU, inactive).* Former names and other names: *International Commission on Scientific Radio Telegraphy* – former (1913 to Jul 1919); *Commission internationale de télégraphie sans fil* – former (1913 to Jul 1919); *International Union of Scientific Radiotelegraphy* – former (Jul 1919 to 1928); *Union internationale de radiotélégraphie scientifique* – former (Jul 1919 to 1928); *International Scientific Radio Union* – former (1928 to 1969). **Aims** Stimulate and coordinate, on an international basis, studies, research, applications, scientific exchange and communication in the field of radio science. **Structure** General Assembly and Scientific Symposium (every 3 years); Council; Board of Officers; Standing Committees (3); Coordinating Committees; Secretariat at Ghent University (Belgium). **Languages** English, French. **Staff** 1.60 FTE, paid. **Finance** Sources: members' dues. **Activities** Awards/prizes/competitions; events/meetings; financial and/or material support. **Events** *Asia-Pacific Radio Science Conference* Sydney, NSW (Australia) 2025, *International Symposium on Antennas and Propagation and USNC-URSI Radio Science Meeting* Portland, OR (USA) 2023, *GASS : Triennial General Assembly and Scientific Symposium* Sapporo (Japan) 2023, *Triennial Atlantic Radio Science Conference* Las Palmas de Gran Canaria (Spain) 2022, *VERSIM : Workshop on Linear and Non-Linear Wave Phenomena at Audible Frequencies, their Generation, Propagation and Effects* Sodankylä (Finland) 2022. **Publications** *Radio Science Bulletin* (4 a year). *URSI Radio Science Letters.*
Members Member committees in 44 countries and territories:
Argentina, Australia, Austria, Belgium, Brazil, Bulgaria, Canada, Chile, China, Czechia, Denmark, Egypt, Finland, France, Germany, Greece, Hungary, India, Iraq; Ireland, Israel, Italy, Japan, Korea Rep, Netherlands, New Zealand, Nigeria, Norway, Peru, Poland, Portugal, Russia, Saudi Arabia, Singapore, Slovakia, South Africa, Spain, Sweden, Switzerland, Taiwan, Türkiye, UK, Ukraine, USA.
Consultative Status Consultative status granted from: *World Meteorological Organization (WMO, #21649).* **IGO Relations** Member of (1): *International Committee on Global Navigation Satellite Systems (ICG, #12775).* Working relations with: *International Telecommunication Union (ITU, #15673).* **NGO Relations** Member of: *International Science Council (ISC, #14796)* and its committees: *Committee on Space Research (COSPAR, #04287); Scientific Committee on Antarctic Research (SCAR, #19147); Scientific Committee on Oceanic Research (SCOR, #19149); Scientific Committee on Solar-Terrestrial Physics (SCOSTEP, #19151).* Responsible for: *Scientific Committee on Frequency Allocations for Radio Astronomy and Space Science (IUCAF, #19148).* Informal contacts with: *European Geosciences Union (EGU, #07390).* [2023.02.14/XC2770/**C**]

♦ Union des radios communautaires de l'aire francophone (inactive)
♦ Union radiotélégraphique universelle / see International Telecommunication Union (#15673)
♦ Union radiotélégraphique universelle (inactive)
♦ Union régionale des conférences de supérieurs majeurs d'Afrique de l'Ouest francophone (inactive)
♦ Union région Europe – Chambre européenne d'experts / see European Chamber of Extrajudicial Adjudicators and Experts of Europe
♦ Unión para el Registro Internacional de Obras Audiovisuales (#20444)
♦ Unión de las Repúblicas Americanas / see OAS (#17629)
♦ Union des républiques américaines / see OAS (#17629)
♦ Union des républiques socialistes soviétiques (inactive)
♦ Union of Resistance Veterans for a United Europe (inactive)
♦ Union des résistants pour une Europe unie (inactive)

♦ Union de Responsabilidad Social Universitaria de Latinoamérica (URSULA) 20476

Exec Dir address not obtained. E-mail: comunicaciones@unionursula.org – contacto@unionursula.org.
URL: https://unionursula.org/

Aims Create in Latin America and the Caribbean a common agenda and shared vision on what "University Social Responsibility is. **Activities** Events/meetings; training/education. **Events** *Forum* 2021.
Members Educational institutes in 15 countries:
Argentina, Bolivia, Brazil, Chile, Colombia, Costa Rica, Dominican Rep, Ecuador, El Salvador, Mexico, Paraguay, Peru, Spain, Uruguay, Venezuela.
Included in the above, 1 institute listed in this Yearbook:
Latin American Center for Service Learning (#16291).
IGO Relations *Development Bank of Latin America (CAF, #05055).* [2022/XM8898/**D**]

♦ Union of Risk Management for Preventive Medicine / see International Association of Risk Management in Medicine (#12138)
♦ Union des riziers européens (#09537)

♦ Union of Road Transport Associations in the Black Sea Economic Cooperation Region (BSEC-URTA) 20477

International Secretariat TOBB Plaza Esentepe Mah Harman Sok No 10, Kat 10, Sisli, 34381 Istanbul/Istanbul, Türkiye. T. +902122156005. Fax +902122156003. E-mail: info@bsec-urta.org.
URL: http://www.bsec-urta.org/

History 24 Oct 2001, Antalya (Turkey), by *Organization of Black Sea Economic Cooperation (BSEC, #17857).* **Aims** Promote the development of road transport in the BSEC countries; safeguard the interests of its members vis-à-vis governments and international bodies. **Structure** General Assembly. Management Council, comprising President, Founding President, 2 Vice-Presidents and Secretary-General. Secretariat in Istanbul (Turkey). **Languages** English, Russian. **Staff** 4.00 FTE, paid. **Finance** Members' dues. **Activities** Facilitation of road transport by eliminating barriers and difficulties; Interaction; Good examples; Project development and information; Lobbying and promotion; Combined transportation; Professional training. **Events** *General Assembly* Istanbul (Turkey) 2019, *General Assembly* Bucharest (Romania) 2015, *General Assembly* Geneva (Switzerland) 2014, *General Assembly* Istanbul (Turkey) 2014, *General Assembly* Tbilisi (Georgia) 2013.
Members Associations in 11 countries:
Albania, Armenia, Azerbaijan, Bulgaria, Georgia, Greece, Moldova, Romania, Russia, Türkiye, Ukraine.
Observers in 3 countries:
Romania, Russia, Serbia.
NGO Relations *International Road Transport Union (IRU, #14761).* [2020/XD9429/**D**]

♦ Union des Roms / see International Romani Union (#14765)
♦ Union of Rural Women from West Africa and Chad (internationally oriented national body)
♦ Union Sahel-Benin / see Entente Council (#05491)
♦ Union sanitaire universelle – Conseil sanitaire maritime et quarantenaire d'Egypte (inactive)
♦ Union scandinave des commerçants-détaillants en textiles (inactive)
♦ Union scandinave de golf (inactive)
♦ Union scandinave des musées / see Nordic Union of Museums (#17455)
♦ Union of Scientific and Engineering Associations (internationally oriented national body)
♦ Union of Scientific and Technical Organizations / see International Commission on Glass (#12683)
♦ Union scientifique continentale du verre (no recent information)
♦ Union scientifique mondiale des médecins acupuncteurs et des sociétés d'acupuncture (inactive)
♦ **Union SCIPT** Union for Sports, Culture, Tourism International for Posts and Telecommunications (#20483)
♦ Unión de Seguros y de Créditos Internacionales (#15767)
♦ Union des services routiers des chemins de fer européens (inactive)
♦ Unión de los Servicios por Carretera de los Ferrocarriles Europeos (inactive)

♦ Unión de Silvicultores del Sur de Europa (USSE) 20478

Union of Foresters of Southern Europe – Union des sylviculteurs du Sud de l'Europe (USSE)
Acting Managing Dir Parque tecnológico de Bizkaia, C/Kanala, Edif 103 – 2o Planta, 48170 Zamudio, Biscay, Spain. T. +34944747826. Fax +34944763715. E-mail: usse@usse-eu.org.
URL: https://www.usse-eu.org/

History 1989. A grouping of the type *European Economic Interest Grouping (EEIG, #06960).* **Aims** Provide and circulate between members the technical, economic, tax, law and regulatory information regarding forest issues; unite, economically-speaking the forest cover represented by each member; contribute to the prevention of forest fires by developing silviculture through the spreading of forest techniques and wood market knowledge; develop training for the benefit of the members and promote scientific and economic research by encouraging exchanges. **Structure** General Assembly; Board of Directors. **Languages** English, French, Portuguese, Spanish. **Staff** 4.00 FTE, paid. **Finance** Sources: members' dues. **Activities** Events/meetings; networking/liaising; research and development; training/education. **Events** *Workshop on the assessment of forest fire risks and innovative strategies for fire prevention* Rhodes Is (Greece) 2010, *European meeting of poplar growers* Valladolid (Spain) 2010, *International congress on cultivated forests* Bilbao (Spain) 2006, *International seminar on policies fostering investments innovations in support of rural development* Sliac (Slovakia) 2006, *International conference on prevention strategies for fires in Southern Europe / Conference* Barcelona (Spain) 2005. **Publications** Information Services: Database.
Members Forestry associations in 5 countries:
France, Greece, Italy, Portugal, Spain.
Consultative Status Consultative status granted from: *ECOSOC (#05331)* (Roster). **IGO Relations** Member of (1): *European Forest Institute (EFI, #07297).* **NGO Relations** Member of (2): *International Family Forestry Alliance (IFFA, #13329)* (Associate); *PEFC Council (#18288).* Instrumental in setting up (1): *European Institute of the Cultivated Forest (IEFC).* [2022/XD5367/**D**]

♦ Unión Sindical – Servicio Público Europeo / see Union Syndicale Fédérale (#20485)
♦ Union of the Sisters of the Presentation of the Blessed Virgin Mary (religious order)
♦ Union of Small and Medium Coffee Producers of Mexico, Central America and the Caribbean (no recent information)

♦ Union of Socialist Local and Regional Representatives in Europe (USLRRE) 20479

Union des élus locaux et régionaux socialistes d'Europe (UELRSE) – Union der Sozialdemokratischen Kommunal- und Regionalpolitiker Europas (USKRE)
SG Admin communales, rue de l'Hôtel de Ville 1, 4160 Anthisnes, Belgium.
URL: http://www.uslrre.eu/

History 1979. Previously also referred to in German as *Union der Sozialistischen Kommunal- und Regionalpolitiker Europas.* **Aims** Reinforce local autonomy on the basis of the European charter of local autonomy of 1985; encourage contacts and cooperation between parties and their organizations of elected members; construct a network of elected local and regional socialist representatives so as to develop the exchange of ideas and defend their interests. **Structure** Bureau, consisting of 2 representatives from each of the participating parties/organizations, including President, 5 Vice-President, Secretary-General, Deputy Secretary-General, Treasurer and Deputy Treasurer. **Languages** English, French, German. **Activities** Organizes seminars and conferences. **Members** Member parties of the SI in the European Community. Associated membership open to those parties, or their special organizations, which have observer status with PES. Membership countries not specified. **NGO Relations** Consultative body of: *Party of European Socialists (PES, #18249).*
[2019/XD2357/**D**]

♦ Union of Socialist Parties in the European Community / see Party of European Socialists (#18249)
♦ Union de Sociedades de Cardiologia de América del Sur / see South American Society of Cardiology (#19707)

♦ Union des sociétés arabes de pédiatrie (#20355)
♦ Union des sociétés et des associations africaines de pédiatrie (#20465)
♦ Union des sociétés et des associations nationales européennes de pédiatrie / see European Paediatric Association (#08124)

♦ Union des sociétés de pédiatrie du Maghreb arabe 20480

Contact Hôpital Mustapha, Clinique Médicale Infantile, 16000 Algiers, Algeria.
Members Full in 5 countries:
Algeria, Libya, Mauritania, Morocco, Tunisia.
NGO Relations Regional Society of: *International Pediatric Association (IPA, #14541).* [2015/XD2962/D]

♦ Union des sociétés de pédiatrie du Moyen-Orient et de la Méditerranée (#20461)
♦ Union des Soeurs de la Présentation de la Bienheureuse Vierge Marie (religious order)
♦ Union des solidaristes russes (internationally oriented national body)

♦ Union of South American Nations 20481

Union des Nations Sud-Américaines – Unión de Naciones Suramericanas (UNASUR) – União das Nações Sul-Americanas (UNASUL)
SG Av Manuel Córdova Galarza, Mitad del Mundo, CP 170311, Quito, Ecuador. T. +59323990900. E-mail: secretaria.general@unasursg.org.
URL: http://www.unasursg.org/
History 9 Dec 2004, Cusco (Peru). 9 Dec 2004, Cuzco (Peru), as *South American Community of Nations – Comunidad Sudamericana de Naciones (CSN) – Comunidade Sul-Americana de Nações (CSN),* during 3rd South American Summit, by *Andean Community (#00817)* and *Southern Common Market (#19868),* with the addition of Guyana and Suriname, when Cuzco Declaration was signed. Present name adopted Apr 2007. Constitutive Treaty signed, 23 May 2008, at 3rd Summit of Heads of State, Brasilia (Brazil). Became effective 30 days after 9th member delivered ratification document, 11 Mar 2011. Expected to include the proposed *Bank of the South.* Apr 2018, Argentina, Brazil, Chile, Colombia, Paraguay and Peru suspended membership; Aug 2018, Colombia withdrew; Brazil and Ecuador withdrew Mar 2019, with Ecuador asking bloc to return Quito headquarters. *Foro para el Progreso y Desarrollo de América del Sur (PROSUR, #09888)* was set up, Mar 2019, to counter left-wing direction of UNASUR. **Aims** Build, in a participatory and consensual manner, *integration* and union among peoples in the cultural, social, economic and political fields, prioritizing political dialogue, social policies, education, energy, infrastructure, financing and the environment, among others, with a view to eliminating socio-economic inequality, in order to achieve social inclusion and participation of civil society, to strengthen *democracy* and reduce asymmetries within the framework of strengthening the sovereignty and independence of the States. **Structure** Council of Heads of State and Government; Council of Ministers of Foreign Affairs; Council of Delegates. Ministerial and Sectoral Councils (currently 12): *South American Defense Council (CDS); South American Council of Health of UNASUR (CSS);* Electoral Council of UNASUR (CEU); *South American Energy Council of UNASUR (CES); South American Science, Technology and Innovation Council of UNASUR (COSUCTI); South American Council of Culture of UNASUR (CSC); South American Council of Social Development of UNASUR (CSDS); South American Economy and Finance Council of UNASUR (CSEF); South American Education Council of UNASUR (CSE); South American Council of Infrastructure and Planning of UNASUR (COSIPLAN); World Drug Problem Council (CSPMD); South American Council on Safety, Justice and Coordination of Acion against Transnational Organized Crime (DOT).* General Secretariat. One country exerts the Pro Tempore Presidency of the Union during one year. Headquarters located in Quito (Ecuador). **Languages** Dutch, English, Portuguese, Spanish. **Staff** At General Secretariat: 7, plus 6 Diplomatic Delegates (expected to be 12, one for each member country). **Finance** Currently functions on temporary budget based on voluntary contributions of each Member State. A definitive establishment of rules of procedures for the permanent budget expected soon. **Activities** Politics/policy/regulatory. **Events** *Energy Ministerial Meeting* Abu Dhabi (United Arab Emirates) 2013, *Meeting of Heads of State* Lima (Peru) 2011, *Meeting of Heads of State* Buenos Aires (Argentina) 2010, *South American-Arab countries summit* Doha (Qatar) 2009, *Meeting of Heads of State* Quito (Ecuador) 2009.
Members Governments of 4 countries:
Bolivia, Guyana, Suriname, Venezuela.
IGO Relations Observer status with (1): *United Nations (UN, #20515)* (General Assembly). **NGO Relations** *Centro de Estudios sobre el Esoterismo Occidental de la Unión de Naciones Suramericanas (CEEO-UNASUR, #03798).* [2017/XJ4435/D*]

♦ Union of South American Posts / see Postal Union of the Americas, Spain and Portugal (#18466)
♦ Union of Soviet Socialist Republics (inactive)
♦ Union der Sozialdemokratischen Kommunal- und Regionalpolitiker Europas (#20479)
♦ Union der Sozialistischen Kommunal- und Regionalpolitiker Europas / see Union of Socialist Local and Regional Representatives in Europe (#20479)
♦ Union sportive internationale des cheminots (inactive)
♦ Union sportive internationale des polices (#14614)

♦ Union sportive des polices d'Europe (USPE) 20482

European Police Sports Association
Gen Sec Radelandstrasse 21, 13589 Berlin, Germany. T. +49304664994470. Fax +49304664994490. E-mail: office@uspe.org.
URL: http://www.uspe.org/
History Founded Nov 1950, Paris (France). **Aims** Encourage sport throughout the European police forces; coordinate the preparation, organization and control of international competitions in all sports disciplines; build up social, cooperative and professional relations between the European police forces. **Structure** Executive Committee of 5 officers and 5 members. Technical Committee. **Languages** English, French, German. **Finance** Supported by: Government of Germany; *European Handball Federation (EHF, #07446); International Olympic Committee (IOC, #14408); Union of European Football Associations (UEFA, #20386).* **Activities** Events/meetings; sporting activities. **Events** *Congress* Vienna (Austria) 2022, *Congress* Vienna (Austria) 2020, *Congress* Liberec (Czechia) 2018, *Biennial Congress* Berlin (Germany) 2016, *Biennial Congress* Budapest (Hungary) 2014. **Publications** *USPE Magazine.*
Members in 40 countries:
Albania, Armenia, Austria, Belarus, Belgium, Bulgaria, Croatia, Cyprus, Czechia, Denmark, Estonia, Finland, France, Germany, Greece, Hungary, Iceland, Ireland, Italy, Latvia, Lithuania, Luxembourg, Moldova, Monaco, Netherlands, North Macedonia, Norway, Poland, Portugal, Romania, Russia, Serbia, Slovakia, Slovenia, Spain, Sweden, Switzerland, Türkiye, UK, Ukraine. [2015.09.04/XJ3399/D]

♦ Union for Sports, Culture, Tourism International for Posts and Telecommunications (Union SCIPT) 20483

Union internationale sportive, culturelle et touristique des postes et télécommunications
Pres GO plc, Spencer Hill, Marsa, HMR12, Malta. T. +356232759. Fax +356241410. E-mail: union-scipt@gmail.com.
URL: http://www.unionscipt.com/
History 11 Jun 1992, Malta, by merger of *International Sporting Union of the PTT (UISPTT, inactive)* and *Union internationale touristique et culturelle des postes et des télécommunications (UTC-PTT, inactive).* Also referred to as *Union for Sports, Culture, Tourism International in the Post and Telecommunication Sectors.* **Aims** Contribute to the physical and intellectual well-being of posts and telecommunications *employees* by: promoting sporting, tourist and cultural exchanges among these *staff*; developing reciprocal friendship and understanding between them; communicating information and sharing experience on these matters. **Structure** Congress (every 4 years). Executive Committee (meets once a year), comprising one representative from each Union member. Bureau, consisting of President, Vice-President for Sport, Vice-President for Tourism and Culture, Secretary-General, Assistant Secretary-General and 2 other members. **Languages** English, French. **Staff** Voluntary. **Finance** Members' dues: Swiss Fr 300. Budget (annual): Swiss Fr 12,000. **Activities** Organizes sporting championships, touring exhibitions, cultural trips and holiday programme. Encourages support for developing international contact among artists, etc, as already occurs with their sporting colleagues. **Events** *Quadrennial Congress* Switzerland 2000, *Quadrennial Congress* Stockholm (Sweden) 1996, *Quadrennial Congress* Malta 1992. **Publications** *Bulletin d'informations UNION SCIPT* in English, French; *UNION SCIPT Bulletin* in French.
Members PTT administrations (49) or national PTT sports, cultural and tourism organizations in 37 countries:
Algeria, Austria, Belgium, Burkina Faso, Central African Rep, Chad, Congo Brazzaville, Cyprus, Denmark, Estonia, Finland, France, Gabon, Germany, Greece, Hungary, Ireland, Israel, Italy, Latvia, Luxembourg, Malta, Monaco, Morocco, Netherlands, Norway, Poland, Portugal, Senegal, Slovenia, Spain, Sweden, Switzerland, Thailand, Tunisia, Türkiye, UK. [2021/XE3142/E]

♦ Union for Sports, Culture, Tourism International in the Post and Telecommunication Sectors / see Union for Sports, Culture, Tourism International for Posts and Telecommunications (#20483)
♦ Union Stéréoscopique Internationale (#15606)
♦ Union des stockeurs professionnelle de céréales dans la CEE / see Unistock Europe (#20492)
♦ Union sucrière (inactive)
♦ Union sud-américaine des associations d'ingénieurs (inactive)
♦ Unión Sudamericana de Asociaciones de Ingenieros (inactive)
♦ Union des supérieurs généraux (#20484)
♦ Unión de los Superiores Generales (#20484)

♦ Union of Superiors General 20484

Union des supérieurs généraux (USG) – Unione Superiori Generali – Unión de los Superiores Generales
Secretariat Via dei Penitenzieri 19, 00183 Rome RM, Italy. T. +3966868229. Fax +3966874317. E-mail: segreteria@usgroma.org.
URL: https://www.usgroma.org/
History 23 Jan 1952, Rome (Italy). Statutes officially approved by the Holy See 3 Jan 1955. New Statutes approved: 2 Aug 1962; 27 May 1967; Sep 1989. **Aims** Promote better service to the *Church* and to the world. **Structure** General Assembly; Executive Council; Commissions. Instrumental in setting up, 1971, Rome (Italy), *Agrimissio (no recent information).* **Finance** Members' contributions. **Activities** Holds meetings (twice a year: in May and November; only for members). **Events** *Assembly* Rome (Italy) 2019, *Congress* Rome (Italy) 1993, *Half-yearly general assembly* Rome (Italy) 1991, *Half-yearly general assembly* Rome (Italy) 1990, *Half-yearly general assembly* Rome (Italy) 1990. **Publications** Proceedings of meetings.
Members Superiors General (218) of male Catholic religious orders of pontifical right in 26 countries:
Argentina, Australia, Austria, Belgium, Brazil, Canada, Colombia, France, Germany, Hungary, India, Iraq, Ireland, Italy, Kenya, Lebanon, Malta, Mexico, Netherlands, Poland, Portugal, Rwanda, Spain, Switzerland, USA, Vietnam.
NGO Relations Joint commission, *Commission for Justice, Peace and Integrity of Creation – USG/UISG (#04230),* and joint consultation, *Permanent International Ecumenical Consultation of Religious (PIECR, #18326),* with: *International Union of Superiors General (#15820).* Member of: *Service of Documentation and Studies on Global Mission (#19241).* Instrumental in setting up: *Talitha Kum – International Network against Trafficking in Persons (Talitha Kum, #20090).* [2020/XF5364/v/F]

♦ Union des sylviculteurs du Sud de l'Europe (#20478)
♦ Union syndicale Eurocontrol Maastricht (#20187)
♦ Union Syndicale – European Public Service / see Union Syndicale Fédérale (#20485)
♦ Union syndicale fédérale / see Union Syndicale Fédérale (#20485)

♦ Union Syndicale Fédérale (USF) 20485

Secretariat Ave des Gaulois 36, 1040 Brussels, Belgium. T. +3227339800. Fax +3227330533. E-mail: usf@unionsyndicale.eu.
URL: https://unionsyndicale.eu/
History 16 Nov 1974, Brussels (Belgium). Founded 16-17 Nov 1974, Brussels (Belgium), as *Union of European and International Public Services Unions – Union des syndicats des services publics européens et internationaux (USSPEI),* abbreviation *Union des syndicats (UdS),* following decision at a preliminary meeting, 15-17 Mar 1974, Ispra (Italy). Since Congress in 1994, Florence (Italy), also referred to by abbreviated title *Union syndicale fédérale (USF).* Also officially referred to in a number of European languages as *Union Syndicale – European Public Service – Union syndicale – Service public européen – Unión Sindical – Servicio Público Europeo – Gewerkschaftsbund – Europäischer Öffentlicher Dienst – União Sindical – Serviço Público Europeu – Unione Sindacale – Servizio Pubblico Europeo – Vakbondsvereniging – Europese Overheidsdienst – Fagforening – Europaeiske Offentlig Tjeneste – Sindikalistiki Enosi – Evropaiki Dimosia Ipiresia.* **Aims** Establish major common principles – internal and external *solidarity,* social *rights,* right to *employment,* trade union rights, equality between men and women, stability of employment, human rights; maintain a constant two-way flow of information on these principles between member organizations and their members; coordinate and organize interests of union members and develop resources and collaborative efforts among them; secure and maintain employment opportunities and improve *working conditions* in the interests of all working people and in the face of privately manipulated markets and currency flows; protect interests of workers in the Third World; administer common means for action and consultation, including those of a legal or political nature; represent member organizations before relevant bodies in defence of common interests – *staff* regulations, remuneration, right of negotiation; coordinate and harmonize action of member organizations concerning *European Community* and/or international matters of common interest; deal with inter-trade union and international relations. **Structure** Federal Congress (every 4 years); Federal Committee (meets 3-4 times a year); Federal Bureau (executive body); Disputes Board; Audit Board. **Languages** English, French. **Staff** 3.00 FTE, paid. **Finance** Members' dues according to size of membership. **Activities** Events/meetings. **Events** *Congress* Nivelles (Belgium) 2011, *Congress* Crotone (Italy) 2008, *Congress* Athens (Greece) 2003, *Congress* Brussels (Belgium) 1998, *Congress* Florence (Italy) 1994. **Publications** *AGORA* (4 a year) – magazine.
Members European and International public services unions in 9 countries:
Belgium, France, Germany, Greece, Ireland, Italy, Luxembourg, Netherlands, Spain.
Public service unions representing the following 11 organizations:
Centre for the Development of Enterprise (CDE, inactive); Council of Europe (CE, #04881); European Agency for Safety and Health at Work (EU-OSHA, #05843); European Centre for the Development of Vocational Training (Cedefop, #06474); European Foundation for the Improvement of Living and Working Conditions (Eurofound, #07348); European Patent Office (EPO, #08166); European School Bergen (Netherlands); *European Training Foundation (ETF, #08934); European University Institute (EUI, #09034); International and European Public Services Organisation (IPSO, #13311);* Union Syndicale (Brussels, Luxembourg, Ispra, Karlsruhe, Petten).
IGO Relations Cooperates with: *European Committee of the Regions (CoR, #06665); Court of Justice of the European Union (CJEU, #04938) European Commission (EC, #06633); European Economic and Social Committee (EESC, #06963); European Parliament (EP, #08146).* **NGO Relations** Member of: *European Federation of Public Service Unions (EPSU, #07202); European Trade Union Confederation (ETUC, #08927); Public Services International (PSI, #18572).* Cooperates with: *Union syndicale du service public européen (#20486).* [2022/XD1557/y/E]

♦ Union Syndicale Fédérale of the European and International Public Services / see Union Syndicale Fédérale (#20485)
♦ Union syndicale fédérale des services publics européens et internationaux / see Union Syndicale Fédérale (#20485)
♦ Union syndicale internationale vasculaire (unconfirmed)
♦ Union syndicale de l'Office européen des brevets (#19944)
♦ Union syndicale panafricaine (inactive)
♦ Union syndicale – Service public européen / see Union Syndicale Fédérale (#20485)

♦ Union syndicale du service public européen 20486

European Public Service Union
Contact Avenue des Gaulois 36, 1040 Brussels, Belgium. T. +3227339800.
URL: http://www.unionsyndicale.eu/
History 1973. **Aims** Represent the interests of the *staff* of European Institutions and organizations, having their headquarters or a seat in Brussels; serve and defend the economic, social, professional and moral interests of its members and of the entire staff of the European institutions and organizations. **Structure** General Meeting (annual); Executive Committee; Audit Board; Disputes Board. **Finance** Members' dues. **Activities** Guidance/assistance/consulting. **Publications** *AGORA.* **IGO Relations** Provides staff negotiations for: *Court of Justice of the European Union (CJEU, #04938).* Represents staff of: *European Committee of the Regions (CoR, #06665); Council of Europe (CE, #04881); European Commission (EC, #06633); European Economic and Social Committee (EESC, #06963); European External Action Service (EEAS, #07018); EUROCONTROL (#05667); European Parliament (EP, #08146).* **NGO Relations** Affiliated to: *Union Syndicale Fédérale (USF, #20485).* [2015.09.21/XF4293/E]

♦ Union des syndicats / see Union Syndicale Fédérale (#20485)
♦ Union des syndicats des services publics européens et internationaux / see Union Syndicale Fédérale (#20485)
♦ Union des syndicats de travailleurs du Maghreb arabe (no recent information)
♦ Union tarifaire Balkans-Proche-Orient (inactive)
♦ Union of Technical Assistance for Motor Vehicle and Road Traffic (no recent information)
♦ Union des télécommunications des Caraïbes (#03560)
♦ Union de tennis de table de l'Europe du Nord (#17599)
♦ Union of Thai Sanghas in Europe (unconfirmed)
♦ Union des théâtres de l'Europe (#20487)

♦ Union of the Theatres of Europe 20487

Union des théâtres de l'Europe (UTE)

Contact address not obtained. Fax +4921195421387. E-mail: ute@union-theatres-europe.eu.
URL: https://www.union-theatres-europe.eu/

History Founded Mar 1990, by Jack Lang, French Minister of Culture. Initiative started by 3 theatres in Italy, France and Spain. Registered in accordance with French law. **Aims** In the artistic, political and societal spheres: develop international and transnational collaborations; maintain and transmit Europe's cultural heritage, focusing on its appropriation by young artists; question, develop and renew this heritage through artistic projects, and also through political projects that offer a critical reflection on today's society. **Structure** Board of Directors. **Languages** English, French, German. **Staff** 2.00 FTE, paid. Freelancers. **Finance** Co-funded by the Culture Programme and Creative Europe Programme of the *European Union (EU, #08967)*. **Activities** Events/meetings; training/education.
Members Theatres (17) in 14 countries:
Austria, Bulgaria, Czechia, France, Germany, Greece, Hungary, Israel, Italy, Luxembourg, Portugal, Romania, Russia, Serbia.
Personal and associated members in 10 countries and territories:
France, Georgia, Greece, Hungary, Israel, Palestine, Poland, Portugal, Romania, Russia. [2022/XD8777/**D**]

♦ Union thérapeutique internationale (inactive)
♦ Union des transporteurs routiers de l'Afrique de l'Ouest / see West Africa Road Transport Union (#20901)

♦ Union des travailleurs espérantistes des pays de langue française (SAT-AMIKARO) 20488

Association of French-Language Countries Nationless Esperantist Workers

Contact 132-134 boulevard Vincent Auriol, 75013 Paris, France. T. +33953509958.
URL: http://www.sat-amikaro.org/

History 1937, Paris (France). Registration: Start date: 25 Oct 2003, France. **Aims** Promote the international language *Esperanto*; allow access of persons who speak Esperanto to its practical application in the framework of Sennacieca Asocio Tutmonda (SAT); in particular, put Esperanto at the service of individuals, associations, unions and movements working for social progress, emancipation of peoples, transnational solidarity, peace and the environment. **Languages** Esperanto, French. **Staff** Voluntary. **Finance** Members' dues. **Activities** Specializes in information, education, publication, documentation and research in the French language; offers courses on Esperanto (including correspondence courses); provides library service and press service. **Events** *Congress* Baugé-en-Anjou (France) 2022, *Congress* 2021, *Congress* Baugé-en-Anjou (France) 2020, *Congress* Montluçon (France) 2019, *Congress* Paris (France) 2018. **Publications** *SAT-Amikaro* (10 a year) in Esperanto, French. Brochures; documentation; books; dictionaries.
Members Associations in 38 countries:
Argentina, Australia, Austria, Belgium, Bosnia-Herzegovina, Brazil, Bulgaria, Canada, China, Congo DR, Croatia, Czechia, Denmark, Estonia, Germany, Hungary, Ireland, Israel, Italy, Japan, Korea Rep, Latvia, Luxembourg, Madagascar, Netherlands, Norway, Poland, Portugal, Russia, Slovakia, Slovenia, Spain, Sweden, Switzerland, Togo, UK, Ukraine, Uzbekistan.
NGO Relations *Association of Esperantist Greens (AEG, #02494)*; *Nationless Worldwide Association (#16941)*. [2022/XD5211/**D**]

♦ **UNION** Union of European Practitioners in Intellectual Property (#20392)
♦ Union universelle des littérateurs espérantistes (inactive)
♦ Union universelles des communautés séphardites (inactive)
♦ Union universelle des sociétés d'activité chrétienne / see World's Christian Endeavor Union (#21768)
♦ Unión de Universidades de América Latina / see Association of Universities of Latin America and the Caribbean (#02970)
♦ Unión de Universidades de América Latina y el Caribe (#02970)
♦ Union des universités de l'Amérique latine / see Association of Universities of Latin America and the Caribbean (#02970)
♦ Union des universités de l'Amérique latine et les Caraïbes (#02970)
♦ Union des universités de la Méditerranée (#16687)
♦ Union of Utrecht / see International Old Catholic Bishops' Conference (#14403)
♦ Union d'Utrecht / see International Old Catholic Bishops' Conference (#14403)
♦ Union végétarienne internationale / see International Vegetarian Union (#15842)
♦ Union der Verbundgruppen von Selbständigen Einzelhändlern Europas / see Independent Retail Europe (#11154)
♦ Union der Verbundgruppen selbständiger Einzelhändler Europas / see Independent Retail Europe (#11154)
♦ Union des villages de vacances de la Méditerranée (inactive)
♦ Union des villes africaines (inactive)
♦ Union des villes capitales de langue portugaise / see União das Cidades Capitais Luso-Afro-Américo-Asiaticas (#20328)
♦ Union des villes-capitales luso-afro-américano-asiatiques (#20328)
♦ Union des villes de la Caraïbe (inactive)
♦ Union der Wasserversorgungsvereinigungen von Mitgliedländern der Europäischen Gemeinschaften / see European Federation of National Associations of Water and Waste Water Services (#07170)
♦ Union of the Water Supply Associations from Countries of the European Communities / see European Federation of National Associations of Water and Waste Water Services (#07170)
♦ Union of West African Voluntary Workcamps Associations (inactive)
♦ Union Westeuropäischer Industrie- und Handelskammern des Rhein-, Rhône- und Donaugebietes / see Union of European Chambers of Commerce for Transport (#20384)
♦ Union Yoseikan Europe (no recent information)
♦ Union of Young Latin American Democrats (no recent information)
♦ **UNIORE** Unión Interamericana de Organismos Electorales (#20413)
♦ UNIO – United Nations Information Organization (inactive)
♦ Unio universa sudiorum rerum orientalium (inactive)
♦ UNIPAX – Unione Mondiale per la Pace ed i Diritti Fondamentali dell'Uomo e dei Popoli (internationally oriented national body)
♦ **UNIPAZ** Universidade Internacional da Paz (#20689)
♦ UNIPEDE – Internationale Union der Erzeuger und Verteiler Elektrischer Energie (inactive)
♦ UNIPEDE – International Union of Producers and Distributors of Electrical Energy (inactive)
♦ UNIPEDE – Union internationale des producteurs et distributeurs d'énergie électrique (inactive)
♦ UNIP – Unión Interamericana de Padres de Familia (inactive)
♦ UNIP – Università Internazionale delle Istituzione dei Popoli per la Pace (internationally oriented national body)
♦ UNIQUE – Union of Issuers Quoted in Europe (inactive)
♦ UNIROPE – Union internationale des organisations associatives pro-européennes (no recent information)
♦ Unisa Centre for Latin American Studies (internationally oriented national body)
♦ Unisa Sentrum vir Latyns-Amerikaanse Studies (internationally oriented national body)
♦ **UNISCAPE** European Network of Universities for the Implementation of the European Landscape Convention (#08030)
♦ UNISDR / see United Nations Office for Disaster Risk Reduction (#20595)

♦ UNISEC Europe 20489

Contact Am Hubland, 97074 Würzburg, Germany. T. +499313186647. Fax +499313186679. E-mail: schi@informatik.uni-wuerzburg.de.
URL: http://unisec-europe.eu/

History 2014. UNISEC stands for: *University Space Engineering Consortium*. **Aims** Motivate students of different age classes by *space exploration* related tasks; promote hands-on activities at *universities* to realize systems to complement current more theoretically oriented classes. **Activities** Standards/guidelines.
Members Full in 5 countries:
Germany, Italy, Lithuania, Russia, Türkiye.
NGO Relations Chapter of: *University Space Engineering Consortium (UNISEC-Global, #20704)*. [2018.09.28/XM4720/**D**]

♦ **UNISEC-Global** University Space Engineering Consortium (#20704)

♦ Unis pour l'Equite et la Fin du Racisme (UFER) 20490

United for Equity and Ending Racism (UFER)

Pres Bd Lambermont 392, 1030 Brussels, Belgium. E-mail: mouvement.ufer@gmail.com.
SG 812 Outremont, Outremont, Montréal QC H2V 3N6, Canada.
URL: http://www.ufer-international.org/

History 27 Jan 1952, Paris (France). Former names and other names: *Mouvement international pour l'union fraternelle entre les races et les peuples (UFER)* – former (1952); *International Movement for Fraternal Union among Races and Peoples (UFER)* – former (1952); *Internationale Bewegung für eine Brüderliche Vereinigung der Rassen und Völker* – former (1952); *Mezdunarodnoe Dvizenie za Bratskoe Edinstvo Ras i Narodov* – former (1952). **Aims** Promote mutual *understanding*, dialogue and cooperation among races, peoples and cultural groups in the spirit of the Universal Declaration of the Human Rights. **Languages** English, French. **Finance** Sources: members' dues. **Activities** Events/meetings; knowledge management/information dissemination; training/education. **Publications** *UFER News* in English, French.
Members Individuals in 36 countries:
Argentina, Australia, Austria, Belgium, Benin, Bolivia, Brazil, Burkina Faso, Burundi, Cambodia, Canada, Congo DR, Egypt, France, Germany, Ghana, Haiti, India, Italy, Japan, Kenya, Korea Rep, Lebanon, Nepal, Netherlands, Palestine, Peru, Philippines, Rwanda, South Africa, Spain, Switzerland, Taiwan, Uganda, USA, Vietnam.
Consultative Status Consultative status granted from: *ECOSOC (#05331)* (Special); *UNICEF (#20332)*.
NGO Relations Member of: *Committee of NGOs on Human Rights, Geneva (#04275)*; *Conference of Non-Governmental Organizations in Consultative Relationship with the United Nations (CONGO, #04635)*; *NGO Committee on the Status of Women, Geneva (#17117)*; *NGO Committee on UNICEF (#17120)*. [2020.05.06/XB5103/v/**F**]

♦ **UNISERV** United Nations International Civil Servants Federation (#20579)
♦ **UNISFA** United Nations Interim Security Force for Abyei (#20578)

♦ UNISFÉRA 20491

Manager address not obtained. E-mail: info@unisfera.org.
URL: http://www.unisfera.org/

History Founded 2002. Also referred to as *UNISFERA International Centre*. **Aims** Advance innovation and *sustainable development* by combining *expertise* in public policy and corporate management with consulting experience. **Languages** English, French, Spanish. **Activities** Politics/policy/regulatory; training/education; events/meetings. **Consultative Status** Consultative status granted from: *UNEP (#20299)*. **IGO Relations** Accredited to the Conference of the Parties of: *Secretariat of the United Nations Convention to Combat Desertification (Secretariat of the UNCCD, #19208)*; *United Nations Framework Convention on Climate Change – Secretariat (UNFCCC, #20564)*. Cooperates with: *Global Soil Partnership (GSP, #10608)*. [2019.02.12/XM3691/**F**]

♦ UNISFERA International Centre / see UNISFÉRA (#20491)

♦ Unistock Europe 20492

SG Rue Montoyer 23, 1000 Brussels, Belgium. T. +3225020808. Fax +3225026030. E-mail: info@unistock.be – flora.dewar@coceral.com.
URL: http://www.unistock.be/

History 4 Dec 1969. Founded as the association of professional storekeepers for agri-bulk commodities within EEC. Former names and other names: *Union of Cereal Storage Firms in the EEC* – former; *Union des stockeurs professionnelle de céréales dans la CEE (UNISTOCK)* – former; *Vereinigung der Gewerblichen Getreidelagerhalter in der EWG* – former; *Unione Professionale dei Depositari di Cereali nella CEE* – former; *Vereniging van Particuliere Graanopslagbedrijven in de EEG* – former; *Faglige Sammenslutning af Kornoplagringsvirksomheder i EØF* – former; *Unistock Europe – Association of Professional Portside Storekeepers in the Food and Feed Chain* – former. Registration: Banque-Carrefour des Entreprises, Belgium; EU Transparency Register, No/ID: 81131801106-72. **Aims** Further the interests of professional portside storekeepers for agribulk commodities within the European Union. **Structure** General Assembly (annual); Board of Directors; Secretariat. **Languages** English. **Finance** Sources: members' dues. **Events** *General Meeting* Rouen (France) 2013, *General Meeting* Belfast (UK) 2012, *Annual general meeting / General Meeting* Santander (Spain) 2011, *General Meeting* Dublin (Ireland) 2010, *General Meeting* Rotterdam (Netherlands) 2009.
Members Regular in 10 countries:
Belgium, Finland, France, Germany, Ireland, Netherlands, Poland, Portugal, Spain, UK.
Extraordinary in 4 countries:
Argentina, Germany, Netherlands, Sweden.
NGO Relations Joint secretariat with and member of: *Committee of the Trade in Cereals, Oilseeds, Pulses, Olive Oil, Oils and Fats, Animal Feed and Agrosupply of the EU (COCERAL, #04289)*. [2022.02.06/XE2738/**E**]

♦ Unistock Europe – Association of Professional Portside Storekeepers in the Food and Feed Chain / see Unistock Europe (#20492)
♦ UNISTOCK / see Unistock Europe (#20492)
♦ UNIS – United Nations International School (internationally oriented national body)
♦ **UNITAB** Union internationale des producteurs de tabac (#15695)

♦ Unitaid 20493

Exec Dir Unitaid – Global Health Campus, Chemin du Pommier 40, 5th Floor, 1218 Le Grand-Saconnex GE, Switzerland. T. +41227911200. Fax +41227914890. E-mail: unitaid@who.int.
Contact address not obtained.
URL: http://www.unitaid.org

History 19 Sep 2006, New York, NY (USA). Established by Brazil, Chile, France, Norway and UK. Constitution adopted May 2007. **Aims** Accelerate access to high-quality drugs and diagnostics for *HIV/AIDS*, *tuberculosis* and *malaria* in high-burden countries. **Structure** Executive Board; Secretariat. **Languages** English, French. **Staff** 94.00 FTE, paid. **Finance** Sources: contributions; donations. Levy on airline tickets. **Activities** Healthcare. **IGO Relations** Partner of (2): *Global Fund to Fight AIDS, Tuberculosis and Malaria (Global Fund, #10383)*; *Joint United Nations Programme on HIV/AIDS (UNAIDS, #16149)*. Secretariat hosted by: *WHO (#20950)*. **NGO Relations** Partner of (3): *Medicines for Malaria Venture (MMV, #16634)*; *Roll Back Malaria Partnership (RBM, #18968)*; *Stop TB Partnership (#19999)*. [2022.02.02/XM1974/**E***]

♦ UNITAR Centre for Heavy Crude and Tar Sands (inactive)
♦ Unitarian Mission Cooperation Centre (internationally oriented national body)
♦ Unitarian Service Committee of Canada / see SeedChange

♦ Unitarian Universalist Association (UUA) 20494

Pres 24 Farnsworth St, Boston MA 02210, USA. T. +16179484301 – +16179484302. E-mail: info@uua.org.
URL: http://www.uua.org/

History 1961, by the consolidation of two denominations: the *Universalists*, organized in 1793, and the *Unitarians*, organized in 1825. **Aims** Serve the needs of member congregations; organize new congregations; extend and strengthen Unitarian Universalist institutions and implement its principles. **Structure** Board of Trustees. President. Moderator. **Staff** 150.00 FTE, paid. **Finance** Contributions, donations, endowment funds. Budget (annual): US$ 15 million. **Activities** Provides resources and offers consultation to local congregations; creates religious education curricula; spurs social action efforts; furthers the settlement of professional religious leaders. Includes *'Unitarian Universalists Association's Office of Bisexual, Gay, Lesbian and Transgender Concerns'*. **Publications** *The UU World* – journal online and printed. Pamphlets; devotional material.
Members Congregations (over 1,000) in 7 countries:
Australia, Canada, France, Mexico, New Zealand, Philippines, USA.
Included in the above, 1 associate member listed in this Yearbook:
Unitarian Universalist Women's Federation (UUWF).
Consultative Status Consultative status granted from: *ECOSOC (#05331)* (Special). **IGO Relations** Associated with Department of Global Communications of the United Nations. **NGO Relations** Full member of: *NGO Committee on Financing for Development, New York (#17108).* Member of: *Committee of Religious NGOs at the United Nations (CRNGOs, #04282); Faith and Ethics Network for the International Criminal Court; International Association for Religious Freedom (IARF, #12130).* [2017/XF3041/**F**]

- ♦ Unitarian Universalist Musicians' Network / see Association for Unitarian Universalist Music Ministries
- ♦ Unitarian Universalist Service Committee (internationally oriented national body)
- ♦ Unitarian Universalists in Europe / see European Unitarian-Universalists (#09025)
- ♦ Unitarian Universalist Women's Federation (internationally oriented national body)
- ♦ **UNITAR** United Nations Institute for Training and Research (#20576)
- ♦ Unitas Association (inactive)
- ♦ Unitas Fratrum / see Moravian Church (#16854)

♦ Unitas Malacologica 20495

Sec Dept of Marine Ecosystem Dynamics, AORI, Univ of Tokyo, 5-1-5 Kashiwanoha, Kashiwa CHIBA, 277-8564 Japan.
Pres SNSB, Zoologische Staatssammlung München, Münchhausenstr 21, 81247 Munich, Germany.
URL: http://www.unitasmalacologica.org/

History 17 Sep 1962, London (UK). Founded 1962, at first European Malacological Congress, when constitution was adopted, following recommendations, 1959, Netherlands, that a *European Malacological Union* be formed. Most recent statutes adopted 21 Aug 1977, Amsterdam (Netherlands). Registration: Swiss Civil Code, Switzerland. **Aims** Further the study of *mollusca*, by individual malacologists and by interested societies and institutions; enter into world wide cooperation with all organizations concerned with the study of mollusca. **Structure** General Assembly (normally every 3 years); Council. **Languages** English. **Staff** 5.00 FTE, voluntary. **Finance** Sources: members' dues. **Activities** Events/meetings; financial and/or material support. **Events** *Triennial Congress* Munich (Germany) 2022, *Triennial Congress* Asilomar, CA (USA) 2019, *Triennial Congress* George Town (Malaysia) 2016, *Triennial congress* Ponta Delgada (Portugal) 2013, *Triennial congress* Phuket (Thailand) 2010. **Publications** *UM Newsletter* (2 a year). Congress reports (every 3 years); symposium reports.
Members Societies in 27 countries and territories:
Australia, Austria, Belgium, Brazil, China, France, Germany, Greece, Hungary, Indonesia, Israel, Italy, Japan, Korea Rep, Mexico, Netherlands, Philippines, Portugal, Russia, South Africa, Spain, Taiwan, Türkiye, UK, Uruguay, USA, Venezuela.
NGO Relations Member of: *International Union of Biological Sciences (IUBS, #15760).* [2020.09.04/XC0805/**C**]

- ♦ Unitas Malacologica – International Society for Malacology / see Unitas Malacologica (#20495)
- ♦ Unité – Association Suisse pour l'échange de personnes dans la coopération internationale (internationally oriented national body)
- ♦ **UNITECR IEB** UNITECR International Executive Board (#20496)

♦ UNITECR International Executive Board (UNITECR IEB) 20496

Secretariat Markgrafenstrasse 56, 10117 Berlin, Germany. T. +4930204590. Fax +49302045950. E-mail: unitecr15@mci-group.com.
URL: http://www.unitecr.org/

History to organize biennial *Unified International Technical Conference on Refractories (UNITECR).* **Aims** Contribute to progress and exchange of industrial knowledge and technology concerning *refractories.* **Structure** Board, including representatives from member organizations. **Events** *UNITECR : Unified International Technical Conference on Refractories* Frankfurt-Main (Germany) 2023, *UNITECR : Unified International Technical Conference on Refractories* Chicago, IL (USA) 2021, *UNITECR : Unified International Technical Conference on Refractories* Yokohama (Japan) 2019, *UNITECR : Unified International Technical Conference on Refractories* Vienna (Austria) 2015, *UNITECR : Unified International Technical Conference on Refractories* Victoria, BC (Canada) 2013.
Members Founding organizations (4) in 4 countries:
Brazil, Germany, Japan, USA.
Included in the above, 1 organization listed in this Yearbook:
Latin American Association of Manufacturers of Refractory Materials (#16244).
Principal organizations (3) in 3 countries:
Belgium, China, India.
Included in the above, 1 organization listed in this Yearbook:
European Refractories Producers Federation (#08339). [2014/XM2117/**E**]

- ♦ UNITEC – Universidad Tecnológica Centroamericana (internationally oriented national body)
- ♦ United4Rescue (internationally oriented national body)
- ♦ United Against Hunger (internationally oriented national body)
- ♦ United Ancient Order of Druids (religious order)

♦ United Animal Nations (UAN) 20497

Nations Unies des animaux – Vereinte Tiernationen
SG Case postale, 1820 Montreux VD 1, Switzerland. T. +41219644284 – +41219643737 – +41219642424. Fax +41219645736.
URL: http://www.ffw.ch/

History 8 Nov 1979, Geneva (Switzerland), by *Franz Weber Foundation*, at constituent Assembly when a *Charter of the United Animal Nations – Charte des Nations Unies des Animaux – Charta der Vereinten Tiernationen* was signed. Registered in accordance with Swiss law. **Aims** Promote the fundamental knowledge that animals are not only worthy of protection and conservation because they are profitable to man for economic, aesthetic and ecological reasons, but that animals in their quality as independent parts of Creation have a right to existence and development independent from man and that such right is an expression of the primaeval and fundamental Law which guarantees life on our planet; obtain incorporation of such knowledge into human legislation in the form of clear-cut and unequivocal laws which guarantee conservation of nature and animal species and prevent destruction and torture of animals; obtain legal status for animal populations. **Structure** General Assembly (annual); Board, consisting of 7 to 15 members and presided by Secretary-General; Security Council, composed of 9 members; *International Court of Justice for Animal Rights (#13099)*; Secretariat; an Organ of financial supervision. **Languages** English, French, German. **Finance** Members's dues. Other sources: gifts and donations; legacies; contributions; subsidiaries.
Members Organizations and institutions (120); individuals. Members in 14 countries:
Austria, Belgium, Chile, Dominican Rep, France, Germany, India, Israel, Italy, Lebanon, Spain, Switzerland, UK, USA. [2010.07.05/XF4837/**F**]

- ♦ United Arab Shipping Company (no recent information)

♦ United Bible Societies (UBS) 20498

Alliance biblique universelle (ABU) – Sociedades Bíblicas Unidas (SBU)
Dir-Gen United Bible Societies, UK Hub, Stonehill Green, Westlea, Swindon, SN5 7PJ, UK. T. +441793236200. E-mail: gmagi@biblesocieties.org – communications@biblesocieties.org.
URL: http://www.unitedbiblesocieties.org/

History Founded May 1946, Haywards Heath (UK). Registered in England and Wales: No 2264875. UK Registered Charity: 800058. **Aims** Work towards the day when everyone can access the Bible in the language and medium of their choice. **Structure** World Assembly (every 6 years); Global Mission Team; Global Council (meets twice a year). Meetings closed except for on special invitation. **Languages** English, French, Spanish. **Staff** 100.00 FTE, paid. **Finance** Contributions from member societies. **Activities** Publishing activities; religious activities. **Events** *World Assembly* Brazil 2016, *World assembly* Seoul (Korea Rep) 2010, *World assembly* Newport (UK) 2004, *World Assembly* Midrand (South Africa) 2000, *World Assembly* Mississauga, ON (Canada) 1996. **Publications** *The Bible Translator* (4 a year).
Members Affiliation fully interconfessional (Protestant, Roman Catholic, and Orthodox) and interdenominational. Bible Societies working in more than 200 countries and territories, located in 111 countries and territories:
Argentina, Armenia, Australia, Austria, Bangladesh, Barbados, Belarus, Belgium, Benin, Bolivia, Brazil, Bulgaria, Burkina Faso, Burundi, Cameroon, Canada, Chad, Chile, Colombia, Congo Brazzaville, Congo DR, Costa Rica, Côte d'Ivoire, Croatia, Curaçao, Cyprus, Czechia, Denmark, Dominican Rep, Egypt, El Salvador, England, Eritrea, Estonia, Ethiopia, Fiji, Finland, France, Germany, Ghana, Greece, Guatemala, Haiti, Honduras, Hong Kong, Hungary, Iceland, India, Indonesia, Ireland, Italy, Jamaica, Japan, Jordan, Kazakhstan, Kenya, Korea Rep, Latvia, Lebanon, Lesotho, Lithuania, Madagascar, Malawi, Malaysia, Malta, Mauritius, Mexico, Moldova, Myanmar, Namibia, Nepal, Netherlands, New Zealand, Nicaragua, Nigeria, Northern Ireland, Norway, Pakistan, Panama, Papua New Guinea, Paraguay, Peru, Philippines, Poland, Portugal, Puerto Rico, Romania, Russia, Rwanda, Scotland, Serbia, Singapore, Slovakia, Slovenia, South Africa, Spain, Sri Lanka, Suriname, Sweden, Switzerland, Taiwan, Tanzania UR, Thailand, Togo, Uganda, Ukraine, Uruguay, USA, Venezuela, Zambia, Zimbabwe.
Also members in the Gulf countries. Affiliate offices and partners in 32 countries and territories:
Affiliate offices and partners in 32 countries and territories:
Albania, Algeria, Angola, Azerbaijan, Botswana, Cambodia, Central African Rep, Cuba, Ecuador, Eswatini, Gabon, Gambia, Georgia, Guinea, Iraq, Israel, Kyrgyzstan, Liberia, Mali, Micronesia FS, Morocco, Mozambique, Niger, North Macedonia, Palestine, Senegal, Sierra Leone, Sudan, Syrian AR, Türkiye, Uzbekistan, Vietnam.
Consultative Status Consultative status granted from: *UNESCO (#20322)* (Consultative Status). **NGO Relations** Cooperates with: *SAT-7 (#19056); SIL International (#19278)*; national organizations. Member of: *Forum of Bible Agencies International (#09903).* [2018.09.13/XB3370/**B**]

- ♦ United Board for Christian Colleges in China / see United Board for Christian Higher Education in Asia
- ♦ United Board for Christian Higher Education in Asia (internationally oriented national body)
- ♦ United Central Africa Association (inactive)
- ♦ United Christian Broadcasters (internationally oriented national body)
- ♦ United Christian Missionary Society (internationally oriented national body)
- ♦ United Church Board for World Ministries / see Common Global Ministries Board
- ♦ United Church of God / see United Church of God – International Association (#20499)

♦ United Church of God – International Association (UCGIA) 20499

Head Office PO Box 541027, Cincinnati OH 45254-1027, USA. T. +15135769796. Fax +15135769795. E-mail: info@ucg.org.
URL: http://www.ucg.org/

History 1995, California (USA), as *United Church of God (UCG).* Incorporated 30 Apr – 2 May 1995, Indianapolis IN (USA), by Council of Elders. An offshoot of *Grace Communion International (#10685).* **Aims** Preach the *gospel* worldwide; make disciples in all nations and care for those disciples. **Structure** General Conference of Elders (General Assembly, annual). Council of Elders, comprising 12 elders, acting as Board of Directors. Home Office and Management Team. Corporate Secretary; Corporate Treasurer. Local congregations, each with pastor assisted by elders, deacons and deaconesses. **Finance** Contributions. Budget (annual): US$ 15 million. **Activities** Organizes Bible study courses, united youth camps and annual festival. Maintains Ambassador Bible Center. **Publications** *Good News* (6 a year) – magazine. Booklets; tapes.
Members Congregations in 40 countries and territories:
Argentina, Australia, Bahamas, Barbados, Bolivia, Cameroon, Canada, Chile, Colombia, Costa Rica, Dominica, El Salvador, Estonia, France, Germany, Ghana, Guatemala, Honduras, Italy, Kenya, Malawi, Martinique, Mauritius, Mexico, Netherlands, New Zealand, Nigeria, Peru, Philippines, Rwanda, South Africa, St Lucia, Switzerland, Tonga, Trinidad-Tobago, UK, USA, Venezuela, Zambia, Zimbabwe.
NGO Relations *Caribbean-Atlantic Assembly of the Church of God (no recent information); Church of God – Men International (CGMI, no recent information).* [2010/XF4738/**F**]

♦ United Cities and Local Governments of Africa (UCLG Africa) 20500

Cités et Gouvernements Locaux Unis d'Afrique (CGLU Afrique)
SG 22 rue Essaadyine, Quartier Hassan, 10020 Rabat, Morocco. T. +212537260062. Fax +212537260060.
URL: http://www.afriquelocale.org/

History 6 Dec 2003, Yaoundé (Cameroon). Founded as *Council of Cities and Regions in Africa – Conseil des communes et régions d'Afrique (CCRA)*, during 3rd Africities Summit, by merger of *IULA African Union of Local Authorities (IULA-AULA, inactive)*, African chapter of *União das Cidades Capitais Luso-Afro-Américo-Asiaticas (UCCLA, #20328)* and *Union of African Towns (UAT, inactive).* Formally launched May 2005, Pretoria (South Africa). **Aims** Promote political dialogue with central and local governments, civil societies and the international community with a view to adopting decentralization amongst Africa's priority development issues. **Structure** General Assembly; Pan African Council of Local Governments; Executive Committee; Presidency; General Secretariat. **Finance** Members' dues. Other sources: grants from national governments; support from development partners for program implementation. **Activities** *Académie Africaine des Collectivités Territoriales (ALGA).* **Events** *Africities Summit* Kisumu (Kenya) 2022, *IASIA Conference* Rabat (Morocco) 2022, *Africities Summit* Marrakech (Morocco) 2018, *Africities Summit* Johannesburg (South Africa) 2015, *Africities Summit* Dakar (Senegal) 2012. **Publications** *UCLGA Newsletter.*
Members Active; Associate; Honorary. Members in 42 countries:
Algeria, Benin, Botswana, Burkina Faso, Burundi, Cameroon, Cape Verde, Central African Rep, Chad, Comoros, Congo Brazzaville, Côte d'Ivoire, Egypt, Eswatini, Ethiopia, Gabon, Gambia, Ghana, Guinea-Bissau, Kenya, Lesotho, Libya, Madagascar, Malawi, Mali, Mauritania, Mauritius, Morocco, Mozambique, Namibia, Niger, Nigeria, Rwanda, Sao Tomé-Principe, Senegal, Seychelles, Tanzania UR, Togo, Tunisia, Uganda, Zambia, Zimbabwe.
NGO Relations Founding member of: *World Organization of United Cities and Local Governments (UCLG, #21695).* Member of: *Global Taskforce of Local and Regional Governments (Global Taskforce, #10622); International Institute of Administrative Sciences (IIAS, #13859).* Partner of: *Municipal Development Partnership for West and Central Africa (MDP, #16902); Sanitation and Water for All (SWA, #19051).* Framework Partnership Agreement with: *PLATFORMA (#18397).* [2021/XE4716/**E**]

♦ United Cities and Local Governments Asia Pacific (UCLG ASPAC) .. 20501

SG Jakarta's City Hall Complex, Bldg F 2nd Floor, Jl Medan Merdeka Selatan 8-9, Jakarta 10110, Indonesia. T. +622138901802. Fax +622138901801. E-mail: bernadia@uclg-aspac.org – secretariat@uclg-aspac.org.
URL: http://www.uclg-aspac.org/

History 2004, as a regional association of *World Organization of United Cities and Local Governments (UCLG, #21695).* Continues activities of *International Union of Local Authorities – Asian and Pacific Section (IULA-ASPAC, inactive).* EU Transparency Register: 415938437621-12. **Aims** Provide UCLG World with institutional support in pursuing its mission and objectives within the Asia-Pacific region; implement capacity development programmes according to regional needs; serve as the Asia-Pacific advocate for local government associations and their members. **Structure** Regional General Assembly (every 2 years, with Asia Pacific Congress); Regional Council; Executive Board; Presidency; Secretary General. **Languages** English. **Staff** 9.00 FTE, paid. **Finance** Members' dues. Other sources: support from UN and other agency programmes; donations. **Events** *Seminar on Resilient Livelihoods of the Urban Poor during the Pandemic from a Gender Perspective* Jeju (Korea Rep) 2020, *International Workshop on Sustainable Tourism and Forest Management in the Asia-Pacific Region* Jeju (Korea Rep) 2018, *ASEAN Mayors Forum* Singapore (Singapore) 2018, *Culture Summit* Jeju (Korea Rep) 2017, *Seminar on Sustainable Tourism Management for Coastal Destinations in the Asia Pacific Region* Jeju (Korea Rep) 2017. **Publications** *UCLG ASPAC e-News* (6 a year); *UCLG ASPAC Newsletter* (4 a year). Annual Report. **Members** Categories National Associations of Local Government; Individual Local Governments; International Organizations; Joint members of METROPOLIS (capital cities and those over 1 million); Associate; Honorary; NGOs; Corporate. Membership countries not specified. **NGO Relations** Memorandum of Understanding with: *Commonwealth Local Government Forum (CLGF, #04348).* Member of: *Global Taskforce of Local and Regional Governments (Global Taskforce, #10622).* Formal relationship with: *World Association of the Major Metropolises (Metropolis, #21158).* [2019.11.05/XJ1853/**E**]

♦ United Cities and Local Governments Middle East and West Asia (UCLG-MEWA) 20502

Birlesmis Kentler Ve Yerel Yönetimler Orta Dogu Ve Bati Asya Bölge Teskilati

SG Yerebatan Caddesi No 2, Sultanahmet, 34110 Istanbul/Istanbul, Türkiye. T. +902125111010. Fax +902125190058. E-mail: uclg-mewa@uclg-mewa.org.
URL: http://uclg-mewa.org/

History Set up 2004, as a section of *World Organization of United Cities and Local Governments (UCLG, #21695)*, as a continuation of *IULA-EMME – International Union of Local Authorities, Eastern Mediterranean and Middle East section*. Constitution adopted May 2004, France (Paris). **Aims** Be the united voice and world advocate of democratic local self-government, promoting its values, objectives and interests, through cooperation between local governments, and within the wider international community. **Structure** Management. Committees (7).
Members Full in 20 countries:
Afghanistan, Azerbaijan, Bahrain, Cyprus, Egypt, Iran Islamic Rep, Iraq, Jordan, Kuwait, Lebanon, Libya, Oman, Pakistan, Palestine, Qatar, Saudi Arabia, Syrian AR, Türkiye, United Arab Emirates, Yemen. [2015/XJ9962/**E**]

♦ United Congregational Church of Southern Africa (UCCSA) 20503

Gen Sec PO Box 96014, Birxton, Johannesburg, 2019, South Africa. T. +27118379997. E-mail: tellus.uccsa@gmail.com.
Pres PO Box 30377, Wibsey, Johannesburg, 1717, South Africa. T. +27116485824. E-mail: potozana@yahoo.co.uk – trinitychurch@telkomsa.net.
URL: http://www.uccsa.co.za/

History 1967, by the former London (UK) Missionary Society, the Bantu Congregational Church of the American Mission and the Congregational Union of South Africa. Reconstituted 1972, to include congregations of the South African Association of the Disciples of Christ. **Aims** Proclaim the Gospel, seeking the extension of the Kingdom of God in worship, fellowship, witness and service, by constant reformation according to His Word and participating in the ecumenical movement. **Structure** Assembly. Denominational Officers: President; President-Elect; General Secretary; Honorary Treasurer; Administrator; Media Officer. Regional Councils (19); Synods (5). Secretariat in Johannesburg (South Africa), headed by General Secretary. **Staff** 6.00 FTE, paid. **Finance** Contributions from local churches on the basis of their annual income. Grants for specific projects made by overseas partners. Budget (annual): about South African Rand 1.1 million. **Activities** Programmes: Pastoral Plan for Transformation in Church and Society – coordinated by a Mission Council; Church and Society Department – AIDS Programme in conjunction with ecumenical partners; Participation of Youth in the Training in Mission Programme; Lay Training Programme. Regional Councils (19): Algoa; Free State; Karoo; Kei; Kwazulu-Natal; Outeniqua; Peninsula; Central; Teemande; Northern Cape. Synods (5): Botswana; Mozambique; Namibia; South Africa; Zimbabwe. **Events** *Assembly* Durban (South Africa) 2005, *Assembly* Bulawayo (Zimbabwe) 2003, *Assembly* Windhoek (Namibia) 2001, *Meeting* Tygerkloof Spruit (South Africa) 1999, *Soldiers of Christ conference* Zimbabwe 1999. **Publications** *Congregational Chronicle* (4 a year).
Members Churches (over 350, comprising 400,000 individuals) in 5 countries:
Botswana, Mozambique, Namibia, South Africa, Zimbabwe.
NGO Relations Member of: *Council for World Mission (CWM, #04925)*; *Disciples Ecumenical Consultative Council (DECC, #05100)*; *International Congregational Fellowship (ICF, #12889)*; *Oikocredit International (Oikocredit, #17704)*; *South African Council of Churches (SACC, #19699)*; *World Communion of Reformed Churches (WCRC, #21289)*; *World Council of Churches (WCC, #21320)*. [2013/XF5048/**F**]

- ♦ United Cultures Foundation (internationally oriented national body)
- ♦ United Economic Space (unconfirmed)

♦ United Elvis Presley Society (UEPS) 20504

Contact Pijlstraat 15, 2070 Zwijndrecht, Belgium. T. +3232529222. Fax +3232529222. E-mail: elvispresleysociety@outlook.be.
URL: http://www.ueps.be/

History 1 Jan 1986, Brussels (Belgium), by merger of two sections of *International Elvis Presley Fan Club (IEPFC)*, set up 1961. **Aims** Improve knowledge about Elvis Presley, have him appreciated for his human personality and his *musical* achievements. **Structure** Board, comprising 6 members. **Finance** Members' dues. **Activities** Organizes meetings and travel. **Publications** *Elvis* (4 a year).
Members Individuals in 13 countries:
Australia, Belgium, Canada, France, Germany, Greece, Italy, Luxembourg, Netherlands, Spain, Sweden, Switzerland, USA. [2022/XE5070/v/**E**]

- ♦ United to End Genocide (internationally oriented national body)
- ♦ United for Equity and Ending Racism (#20490)

♦ United Europe 20505

Acting Managing Dir Elbchaussee 359, 22609 Hamburg, Germany. T. +494028406911. E-mail: info@united-europe.eu.
URL: https://www.united-europe.eu/

History 2013. Registration: Hamburg District court, No/ID: VR 21966, Start date: 29 Nov 2013, Germany, Hamburg. **Aims** Build and support a Europe that can ensure peace, liberty and prosperity for the next generations. **Structure** Board of Directors. **Activities** Advocacy/lobbying/activism; events/meetings; networking/liaising. **Members** Personal; Company. Membership countries not specified. [2022/AA2961/**E**]

♦ United European Gastroenterology (UEG) 20506

Exec Dir House of European Gastroenterology, Wickenburggasse 1, 1080 Vienna, Austria. T. +4319971639. Fax +431997163910. E-mail: office@ueg.eu.
Events – Congress Management address not obtained.
URL: http://www.ueg.eu/

History 28 Sep 1992, Athens (Greece). Coordinating Council set up 1988 to identify and establish guidelines for annual scientific European joint meeting. Officially founded at 1st United European Gastroenterology Week (UEGW). Originally registered in accordance with Swiss Civil Code. Former names and other names: *United European Gastroenterology Federation (UEGF)* – former. Registration: Start date: 2012, Austria. **Aims** Improve prevention and care of *digestive diseases* in Europe through providing education, supporting research and improving clinical standards. **Structure** Meeting of Members (annual); National Societies Forum; Council; Committees (6); Young Talent Group; Equality and Diversity Taskforce; E-Learning Team; Secretariat based in Vienna (Austria). **Languages** English. **Staff** 27.00 FTE, paid. **Finance** Sources: fees for services; meeting proceeds; members' dues; sale of publications. **Activities** Events/meetings; training/education. **Events** *UEG Week* Vienna (Austria) 2022, *UEG Week* Vienna (Austria) 2021, *UEG Week* Vienna (Austria) 2020, *UEG Week* Barcelona (Spain) 2019, *UEG Week* Vienna (Austria) 2018. **Publications** *UEG Journal* (10 a year); *UEG Newsletter*. Annual Report; congress proceedings; strategic plan; brochure; abstracts; survey of digestive health. **Information Services** *UEG e-Learning Portal*.
Members Founding ("); Associate. European associations and societies (17):
European Association for Endoscopic Surgery and Other Interventional Techniques (EAES, #06026); *European Association for Gastroenterology, Endoscopy and Nutrition (EAGEN, #06051)*; *European Association for the Study of the Liver (EASL, #06233)*; *European Crohn's and Colitis Organisation (ECCO, #06864)*; *European Digestive Surgery (EDS, #06919)*; *European Federation – International Society for Digestive Surgery (EFISDS, #07148)*; *European Helicobacter and Microbiota Study Group (EHMSG, #07471)*; *European Pancreatic Club (EPC, #08136)*; *European Society for Clinical Nutrition and Metabolism (ESPEN, #08550)*; *European Society for Paediatric Gastroenterology, Hepatology and Nutrition (ESPGHAN, #08680)*; *European Society of Coloproctology (ESCP, #08556)*; *European Society of Digestive Oncology (ESDO, #08582)*; *European Society of Gastrointestinal and Abdominal Radiology (ESGAR, #08605)*; *European Society of Gastrointestinal Endoscopy (ESGE, #08606)*; *European Society of Neurogastroenterology and Motility (ESNM, #08663)*; *European Society of Pathology (ESP, #08689)*; *European Society of Primary Care Gastroenterology (ESPCG, #08715)*.
National societies in 43 countries:
Albania, Algeria, Armenia, Austria, Belgium, Bosnia-Herzegovina, Bulgaria, Croatia, Czechia, Denmark, Egypt, Estonia, Finland, France, Georgia, Germany, Greece, Hungary, Ireland, Israel, Italy, Latvia, Lithuania, Luxembourg, Montenegro, Morocco, Netherlands, North Macedonia, Norway, Poland, Portugal, Romania, Russia, Serbia, Slovakia, Slovenia, Spain, Sweden, Switzerland, Tunisia, Türkiye, UK, Ukraine.
NGO Relations Member of (5): *Associations and Conference Forum (AC Forum, #02909)*; *Biomedical Alliance in Europe (#03251)*; *European Alcohol Policy Alliance (Eurocare, #05856)*; *European Cancer Organisation (ECO, #06432)*; *European Chronic Disease Alliance (ECDA, #06648)*. Instrumental in setting up (1): *International Digestive Cancer Alliance (IDCA, #13174)*. [2022.05.18/XE1882/y/**D**]

- ♦ United European Gastroenterology Federation / see United European Gastroenterology (#20506)
- ♦ United European Tattoo Artists (internationally oriented national body)
- ♦ United Evangelical Lutheran Church in Southern Africa (internationally oriented national body)
- ♦ United Evangelical Mission / see United Evangelical Mission (#20507)

♦ United Evangelical Mission (UEM) 20507

Mission évangélique unie (MEU) – Vereinte Evangelische Mission (VEM)

Gen Sec Rudolfstrasse 137, 42285 Wuppertal, Germany. T. +49202890040. Fax +492028900479. E-mail: info@vemission.org.
URL: http://www.vemission.org/

History 1996. Full title: *United Evangelical Mission (UEM) – Communion of Churches in Three Continents – Mission évangélique unie (MEU) – Communion d'églises dans trois continents – Vereinte Evangelische Mission (VEM) – Gemeinschaft von Kirchen in Drei Erdteilen*. **Aims** To spread the *gospel* through evangelism, diaconia, advocacy, development and partnership. **Structure** General Assembly (every 3 years); Council of Delegates; Management Team, headed by General Secretary; Departments (7). **Languages** English, German. **Finance** Members' dues. Other sources: donations; third party financing. **Activities** Projects/programmes; religious activities. **Events** *General Assembly* Parapat (Indonesia) 2018, *Asia Regional Assembly* Hong Kong (Hong Kong) 2013. **Publications** *VEM-Newsletter* (6 a year) in German; *VEM-Journal* (4 a year) in German; *Mission Echo*; *Mission Sparks*. Annual Report in English and German.
Members Churches (35) and 1 church-owned organization in 12 countries and territories:
Botswana, Cameroon, Congo DR, Germany, Hong Kong, Indonesia, Namibia, Philippines, Rwanda, South Africa, Sri Lanka, Tanzania UR.
NGO Relations Member of: *Ecumenical Advocacy Alliance (EAA, inactive)*; *Oikocredit International (Oikocredit, #17704)*; *Ökumenisches Netz Zentralafrika (ÖNZ)*. [2018.09.05/XG7883/**F**]

- ♦ United Families of America / see United Families International (#20508)
- ♦ United Families International / see United Families International (#20508)

♦ United Families International (UFI) 20508

Pres PO Box 2630, Gilbert AZ 85299-2630, USA. T. +18774357834. Fax +14808924417. E-mail: ufi@unitedfamilies.org.
URL: http://www.unitedfamilies.org/

History 1978, USA, by Susan Roylance and Jan Clark, as *United Families of America*. Expanded to *'United Families International'* in 1995. Registered in accordance with USA law. **Aims** Recognizing the family as the basic unit and cornerstone of successful *civilization*, strengthen families by: encouraging the building of strong family units; educating the public on matters directly affecting the family unit; working for family-friendly public *policy*; recognizing that a strong, stable, caring family is the best advocate for children; advocating the family as a fundamental frontline preventative against economic and social ills such as poverty and crime; working to eliminate the inequality and abuse within a family which leads to family breakdown and to increased economic and social costs in the society as a whole; provide ongoing *humanitarian service* worldwide; support the rule of law, national sovereignty and representative government; protect religious and cultural values and rights of all faiths; seek to establish peace and human dignity through grassroots, personalized heartfelt service and respectful dialogue, keeping international restraints to a minimum in order to allow family, freedom and faith to flourish. **Staff** 12.00 FTE, paid. **Finance** Donations and funds raised from private foundations, organizations and individuals. Budget (annual): US$ 800,000. **Activities** Researches and publishes issues and findings of social and political importance to the family unit. Develops educational programmes for family involvement and participation. Organizes seminars and workshops. **Events** *World Congress of Families* Mexico 2003, *World Congress of Families* Geneva (Switzerland) 1999, *World Congress of Families* Prague (Czech Rep) 1996. **Publications** *UFI Newsletter: The Family Times* (6 a year). *The Traditional Family in Peril* (1996). Guides to family issues.
Members Full in 24 countries:
Brazil, Cameroon, Canada, Congo DR, Costa Rica, Eswatini, France, India, Italy, Kenya, Malaysia, Mali, Nigeria, Philippines, Poland, Portugal, Qatar, South Africa, Spain, Switzerland, UK, Ukraine, USA, Zimbabwe.
Consultative Status Consultative status granted from: *ECOSOC (#05331)* (Special). [2015/XF3983/**F**]

- ♦ United Federation for Peacekeeping and Sustainable Development / see International Federation for Peace and Sustainable Development

♦ United Federation of Travel Agents' Associations (UFTAA) 20509

Union des fédérations des associations d'agences de voyages – Union de Federaciones de las Asociaciones de Agencias de Viajes

Pres Monte Carlo Sun, 74 bd d'Italie, 98000 Monte Carlo, Monaco. E-mail: support@uftaa.org.
URL: http://www.uftaa.org/

History 22 Nov 1966, Rome (Italy). Founded on merger of *Fédération internationale des agences de voyages (FIAV, inactive)* and *Universal Organization of Travel Agents' Associations (UOTAA, inactive)*. Statutes adopted by General Assembly, 23 Nov 1973, Abidjan (Côte d'Ivoire); amended in Nov 1997, Cartagena de Indias (Colombia). Started operation as a confederation, 1 Jan 2003. Former names and other names: *Universal Federation of Travel Agents' Associations* – former; *Fédération universelle des associations d'agences de voyages (FUAAV)* – former; *Federación Universal de las Asociaciones de Agencias de Viajes (FUAAV)* – former. Registration: Monaco. **Aims** Act as an international forum where matters affecting the world travel industry are addressed; represent and defend the interests of incoming and outgoing tour operators, travel and *tourism* agencies before governmental bodies, suppliers and other entities of international scope; strengthen its members' image; enhance the world travel and tourism industry and a sustainable tourism. **Structure** General Assembly (annual, during the World Congress); Board of Directors; Regions (9); Secretariat. **Languages** English, French, Spanish. **Staff** 3.00 FTE, paid. **Finance** Sources: contributions; members' dues. **Activities** Events/meetings; networking/liaising; training/education. **Events** *Midyear Forum* Colombo (Sri Lanka) 2019, *Congress* Tel Aviv (Israel) 2018, *Midyear Forum* Salerno (Italy) 2017, *Congress* Istanbul (Turkey) 2016, *Congress* Brussels (Belgium) 2015. **Publications** *Global Connect* (4 a year). **Members** Association: travel and tourism associations; Affiliate: individual and stand alone organizations; Associate: tourism boards; large travel and hospitality organizations. Membership countries not specified. **IGO Relations** Special links with: *International Civil Aviation Organization (ICAO, #12581)*; *International Maritime Organization (IMO, #14102)*. Affiliated member of: *World Tourism Organization (UNWTO, #21861)*. Accredited by: *United Nations Office at Vienna (UNOV, #20604)*. Associated with Department of Global Communications of the United Nations. **NGO Relations** Conventions with related organizations: *The European Travel Agents' and Tour Operators' Associations (ECTAA, #08942)* – UFTAA/ECTAA Convention; *International Hotel and Restaurant Association (IH&RA, #13813)* – IH and RA/UFTAA Convention of 1979; *International Road Transport Union (IRU, #14761)* – UFTAA/IRU Convention; *Confederación de Organizaciones Turísticas de la América Latina (COTAL, #04466)* – UFTAA/COTAL Convention. Partner of: *International Institute for Peace through Tourism (IIPT)*; Passenger Agency Program Global Joint Council (PAPGJC) of *International Air Transport Association (IATA, #11614)*. [2021.07.02/XB3404/**B**]

- ♦ United Food and Commercial Workers International Union / see United Food and Commercial Workers Union
- ♦ United Food and Commercial Workers Union (internationally oriented national body)

♦ United for Foreign Domestic Workers' Rights (UFDWR) 20510

Contact c/o APWLD, 189/3 Changklan Road, A Muang, Chiang Mai, 50100, Thailand. T. +6653284527. Fax +6653280847. E-mail: apwld@apwld.org.
Contact CARAM Asia Secretariat, Wisma Hamid Arshat No 12 – 5, Jalan Bangsar Utama 9, Bangsar Utama, 59000 Kuala Lumpur, Malaysia. T. +60322827708 – +60322821669. Fax +60322821155. E-mail: info@caram-asia.org.
Blog: http://ufdwrs.blogspot.com/

History following a regional Summit, 2022, Colombo (Sri Lanka), by *Asia Pacific Forum on Women, Law and Development (APWLD, #01912), Asia Pacific Mission for Migrants (APMM), Coordination of Action Research on AIDS and Mobility – Asia (CARAM Asia)* and *Mekong Migration Network (MMN, #16702)*. **Aims** Undertake advocacy activities to ensure that rights of domestic workers are protected at all levels; facilitate the information flow in the region, particularly to and from *migrant* domestic workers; increase awareness of issues.
Members National and international organizations, including the following 7 organizations listed in this Yearbook:
Asian Migrants' Coordinating Body (AMCB); Asia Pacific Forum on Women, Law and Development (APWLD, #01912); Asia Pacific Mission for Migrants (APMM); Committee for Asian Women (CAW, #04243); Coordination of Action Research on AIDS and Mobility – Asia (CARAM Asia); Global Alliance Against Traffic in Women (GAATW, #10184); Mekong Migration Network (MMN, #16702). [2013/XJ4706/y/**F**]

♦ United Garment Workers Union / see United Food and Commercial Workers Union
♦ United Help for International Children (internationally oriented national body)
♦ United HIAS Service / see HIAS
♦ United for Human Rights (internationally oriented national body)

♦ UNITED for Intercultural Action – European Network Against Nationalism, Racism, Fascism and in Support of Migrants and Refugees (UNITED) 20511

Réseau européen contre le nationalisme, le racisme, le fascisme et pour le soutien des réfugiés et des migrants – Europäisches Netzwerk gegen Nationalismus, Rassismus, Faschismus und zur Unterstützung von Migranten und Flüchtlingen – Red Europea contra el Nacionalismo, el Racismo, el Fascismo y por el Apoyo de los Refugiados y Emigrantes

SG Postbus 413, 1000 AK Amsterdam, Netherlands. T. +31206834778. Fax +31206834582.
URL: https://unitedfia.org/

History 1992, Strasbourg (France). Founded by participants of two European seminars. Registration: Handeslregister, No/ID: KVK 41212307, Netherlands. **Aims** Coordinate the networking process of European organizations of various political backgrounds which want to unite their efforts to fight racism and fascism and influence migration and *asylum* policies. **Structure** Board; 'Committee of Recommendation'; International Planning Group. **Languages** English. **Staff** 2.00 FTE, paid. 4-6.5 FTE, voluntary. **Finance** Sources: contributions; members' dues. Supported by: *Council of Europe (CE, #04881); European Commission (EC, #06633); European Youth Foundation (EYF, #09141).* **Activities** Advocacy/lobbying/activism; guidance/assistance/consulting; knowledge management/information dissemination. **Events** *Conference on Best Practices in Integration* Budapest (Hungary) 2018, *Conference on Modern-Day Activism* Lithuania 2018, *Conference on Building up Strategies against Extremism* Prague (Czechia) 2017, *YOUth ACTivism shaping our intercultural Europe* Budapest (Hungary) 2015, *Conference* Malaga (Spain) 2015. **Publications** *European Address Book Against Racism* (annual); *Calendar of Internationalism* (4-6 a year). Annual Report. Information and thematic leaflets; campaign material; conference reports; campaign reports; posters; postcards; stickers. CD-Rom versions also available.
Members A network of over 560 organizations working on a voluntary basis in 47 countries:
Albania, Armenia, Austria, Azerbaijan, Belarus, Belgium, Bosnia-Herzegovina, Bulgaria, Croatia, Cyprus, Czechia, Denmark, Estonia, Finland, France, Georgia, Germany, Greece, Hungary, Iceland, Ireland, Italy, Kazakhstan, Kyrgyzstan, Latvia, Lithuania, Luxembourg, Malta, Moldova, Montenegro, Netherlands, North Macedonia, Norway, Poland, Portugal, Romania, Russia, Serbia, Slovakia, Slovenia, Spain, Sweden, Switzerland, Türkiye, UK, Ukraine, Uzbekistan.
Included in the above, 86 organizations listed in this Yearbook:
- *Africa Centre, Finland;*
- *Amnesty International (AI, #00801);*
- *Association des états généraux des étudiants de l'Europe (AEGEE-Europe, #02495);*
- *Balkan Centre for Regional Development (BCRD);*
- *Bundeskoordination Internationalismus (BUKO);*
- *Caritas Internationalis (CI, #03580)* (Serbia);
- *Comhlamh;*
- *Comitato Internazionale per lo Sviluppo dei Popoli (CISP);*
- *Comité de liaison et d'action des étrangers (CLAE);*
- *Danish Center for Conflict Resolution (DCCR);*
- *Ecumenical Youth Council in Europe (EYCE, #05352);*
- *European Centre for Jewish Students (ECJS, #06487);*
- *European Centre for Minority Issues (ECMI);*
- *European Dialogue (ED);*
- *European Network against Racism (ENAR, #07862);*
- *European Union of Jewish Students (EUJS, #08997);*
- *European Youth for Action (EYFA, #09136);*
- *European Youth Forum (#09140);*
- *European Youth Human Rights Network (EYHR-Net);*
- *Fédération des Agences Internationales pour le Développement (AIDE Fédération, #09414);*
- *Football Against Racism in Europe (FARE Network, #09853);*
- *Forum Afrika;*
- *Forum of European Muslim Youth and Student Organisations (FEMYSO, #09909);*
- *Helsinki Citizens' Assembly (hCa, #10905);*
- *Human Rights Watch (HRW, #10990)* (Europe and Central Asia Division);
- *Human Rights without Frontiers International (HRWF, #10983);*
- *Institut für Migrations- und Rassismusforschung, Hamburg;*
- *Interfaith International;*
- *International Alliance of Iranian Students (IAIS);*
- *International Cultural Youth Exchange (ICYE Federation, #13122);*
- *Internationales Bildungs- und Begegnungswerk (IBB);*
- *International Eurasia-Press Fund (IEPF, #13309);*
- *International Federation of Chemical, Energy, Mine and General Workers' Unions (ICEM, inactive);*
- *International Federation of Liberal Youth (IFLRY, #13469);*
- *International Federation of Red Cross and Red Crescent Societies (#13526);*
- *International Fellowship of Reconciliation (IFOR, #13586);*
- *International Institute of Social History (IISG);*
- *International League Against Racism and Antisemitism (#14014);*
- *International Lesbian, Gay, Bisexual, Transgender, Queer and Intersex Youth and Student Organization (IGLYO, #14032);*
- *International Union of Socialist Youth (IUSY, #15815);*
- *International Young Christian Workers (IYCW, #15927);*
- *International Young Nature Friends (IYNF, #15929);*
- *Jesuit Refugee Service (JRS, #16106);*
- *Jewish Organization of Prisoners of Fascist Concentration Camps, Ghettos 'RUF';*
- *Johannes Wier Foundation for Health and Human Rights, Netherlands (JWS);*
- *Joint Council for the Welfare of Immigrants (JCWI);*
- *Mahatma Gandhi Human Rights Movement;*
- *Martin Luther Federation* (Hungarian Branch);
- *Minorities of Europe (MOE, #16818);*
- *Mirovni inštitut;*
- *Multiethnic Interaction on Xenophobia in Europe (MixEurope);*
- *Norwegian People's Aid (NPA);*
- *Norwegian Refugee Council (NRC);*
- *Open Society Foundations (OSF, #17763);*
- *Organisation suisse d'aide aux réfugiés (OSAR);*
- *PAX;*
- *Peace Research Institute Oslo (PRIO);*
- *People to People International (PTPI, #18300)* (Estonia Branch);
- *Platform for International Cooperation on Undocumented Migrants (PICUM, #18401);*
- *Portuguese Refugee Council (CPR);*
- *Save the Children International (#19058);*
- *Searchlight;*
- *SERVAS International (#19234);*
- *Service Civil International (SCI, #19238);*
- *Simon Wiesenthal Centre-Europe (CSWE);*
- *Society for Threatened Peoples International (STP International, #19654);*
- *Solidarité sans frontières, Liège (SsF, no recent information);*
- *SOS racisme international;*
- *UNHCR (#20327);*
- *Union for the Mediterranean (UfM, #20457);*
- *Universal Alliance (UA, #20671);*
- *Unrepresented Nations and Peoples Organization (UNPO, #20714);*
- *Women's International League for Peace and Freedom (WILPF, #21024);*
- *World Alliance of Young Men's Christian Associations (YMCA, #21090);*
- *World Council of Churches (WCC, #21320);*
- *World Federation of Democratic Youth (WFDY, #21427);*
- *World House, Bielefeld;*
- *World Organization of the Scout Movement (WOSM, #21693);*
- *World University Service (WUS, #21892);*
- *World Uyghur Congress (WUC, #21896);*
- *World Young Women's Christian Association (World YWCA, #21947);*
- *Young European Federalists (#21984);*
- *Young European Socialists (YES, #21989);*
- *Young Humanists International (#21993);*
- *Young Women from Minorities (WFM, no recent information);*
- *Youth for Understanding (YFU, #22027).*

Consultative Status Consultative status granted from: *ECOSOC (#05331)* (Special); *Council of Europe (CE, #04881)* (Participatory Status). **IGO Relations** *European Commission Against Racism and Intolerance (ECRI, see: #04881); European Union Agency for Fundamental Rights (FRA, #08969). European Youth Centres (EYCs, #09138).* **NGO Relations** *Internet Centre Anti-Racism Europe (ICARE).* [2023/XF2719/y/**F**]

♦ United Kingdom Dominions Wool Disposals – Joint Organization (inactive)
♦ United Kingdom Forum for International Education and Training (internationally oriented national body)
♦ United Kingdom Foundation for the Peoples of the South Pacific / see Just World Partners
♦ United Kingdom Foundation for the South Pacific / see Just World Partners
♦ United Kingdom One World Linking Association (internationally oriented national body)
♦ United Kingdom United States Agreement (1947 treaty)

♦ United Lodge of Theosophists (ULT) 20512

Loge unie des théosophes

Contact Theosophy Hall, 40 New Marine Lines, Churchgate – East, Near Nirmala Niketan – Opp American Centre, Mumbai, Maharashtra 400 020, Mumbai MAHARASHTRA 400 020, India. T. +912222039024 – +912222085137.
Contact The Theosophy Company, 347 East 72nd St, New York NY 10021, USA. T. +12125352230. E-mail: ult@ult.org.
URL: http://www.ultindia.org/

History Founded 18 Feb 1909, Los Angeles CA (USA), when the parent lodge was set up. Bombay (India) centre came into being in 1929. **Aims** Disseminate the fundamental principles of the philosophy of Theosophy, and their exemplification in practice, through truer realization of the SELF; form a nucleus of Universal Brotherhood of Humanity without distinction of race, creed, sex, caste or colour; study ancient and modern religions, philosophies and sciences; investigate unexplained laws of nature and psychic powers latent in man. **Structure** No constitution, by-laws or officers. Associates record desire to be enrolled but without obligation other than decided by the individual himself. Centres (25) worldwide. **Languages** Dutch, English, French, Gujarati, Hindi, Italian, Marathi, Spanish, Swedish. **Finance** Voluntary contributions. Each lodge is autonomous and supports its own programme of activities. **Activities** Free public lectures and study classes; public reading room and library; dissemination of theosophical literature. **Publications** *The Theosophical Movement* (12 a year); *Theosophy* (4 a year). *Bhagavad Gita; Dhammapada; Friendly Philosopher* – works of Robert Crosbie; *Ocean of Theosophy, Echoes from the Orient* – works of W Q Judge; *The Secret Doctrine, Isis Unveiled* – works of H P Blavatsky; *Yogasutras* by Patanjali.
Members Individuals of in lodges and study-groups in 14 countries:
Belgium, Cameroon, Canada, Denmark, France, Greece, Haiti, India, Italy, Mexico, Netherlands, Sweden, UK, USA.
Sister Centres in 4 countries:
Cameroon, Haiti, UK, USA. [2016/XD3374/v/**F**]

♦ United Methodist Central Conference of Northern Europe 20513

Contact Rigensgade 21A, 1316 Copenhagen K, Denmark.
Street Address Akersbakken 37, 0172 Oslo, Norway.
URL: http://www.umc-northerneurope.org/

History within the framework of *The United Methodist Church (UMC, #20514).* **Events** *Quadrennial central conference* Lithuania 2013, *Quadrennial central conference* Strandby (Denmark) 2009, *Quadrennial central conference* Moscow (Russia) 2005, *Central Conference* Helsinki (Finland) 2001, *Quadrennial central conference* Karis (Finland) 2001.
Members Representatives of 6 national conferences from 9 countries (Estonia and Latvia together):
Denmark, Estonia, Finland, Latvia, Lithuania, Norway, Russia, Sweden, Ukraine. [2017.07.11/XF3053/**E**]

♦ The United Methodist Church (UMC) 20514

La Iglesia Metodista Unida

United Methodist Communications 810 12th Avenue South, Nashville TN 37203, USA. E-mail: umcom@umcom.org.
URL: https://www.umc.org/

History 1968, USA. Founded on union of the Methodist Church, derived from the Methodist Episcopal Church in America, set up in 1784, with the Evangelical United Brethren Church, set up 1946 on merger of United Brethren and Evangelical churches. **Aims** Make disciples of Jesus Christ for the transformation of the world. **Structure** Internal bodies include: *General Board of Church and Society of the United Methodist Church (GBCS);* Discipleship Ministries (Formerly General Board of Discipleship) *Global Ministries of The United Methodist Church (GM-UMC);* General Board of Higher Education and Ministry (GHEM); The Connectional Table General Commission on Archives and History (GCAH); General Commission on Communication (UMCOM); United Methodist Women (UMW) General Commission on United Methodist Men (UMM); General Commission on the Status and Role of Women (COSROW); General Council on Finance and Administration (GCFA); General Commission on Religion and Race (GCORR) *United Methodist Committee on Relief (UMCOR);* The United Methodist Council of Bishops United Methodist Publishing House (UMPH). **Activities** Advocacy/lobbying/activism; events/meetings; religious activities; training/education. **Events** *Meeting* Berlin (Germany) 2015, *General conference* Fort Worth, TX (USA) 2008, *Conference* Liepaja (Latvia) 2008, *East Africa annual conference* Mukono (Uganda) 2007, *Information conference* Riga (Latvia) 2007. **Members** Membership countries not specified. **NGO Relations** Member of (6): *Churches United In Christ (CUIC); Conference of European Churches (CEC, #04593); Crisis Action (#04957); EarthAction (EA, #05159); NGO Committee on Financing for Development, New York (#17108)* (Full); *NGO Working Group on the Security Council (#17128).* Cooperates with (1): *European Methodist Council (EMC, #07787).* Supports (2): *Forum for African Women Educationalists (FAWE, #09896); IO – Facilitating Space for Feminist Conversations (Io, #16005).* [2022.02.08/XF4425/**F**]

♦ United Methodist Committee on Relief (internationally oriented national body)
♦ United Methodist Volunteers in Mission (internationally oriented national body)
♦ United Mission to Nepal (internationally oriented national body)
♦ United Mission for Relief & Development (internationally oriented national body)
♦ United Muslim Relief / see United Mission for Relief & Development
♦ United National Church of Africa, the People's Church / see Volkskerk van Afrika

♦ United Nations (UN) 20515

Nations Unies (ONU) – Naciones Unidas (ONU)

Contact Office of the Spokesperson for the Secretary-General, United Nations, S-233, New York NY 10027, USA. T. +12129631234. Fax +12129637055. E-mail: haqf@uubdn.org.
SG address not obtained.
Main: http://www.un.org/

History 26 Jun 1945, San Francisco, CA (USA). Established on signature of the *Charter of the United Nations – Charte des Nations Unies*. The Charter had been drawn up by representatives of 50 countries, Aug-Oct 1944, Dumbarton Oaks, Washington DC (USA), at the United Nations Conference on International Organization, on the basis of proposals worked out by representatives of China, the Soviet Union, the United Kingdom and the United States. Poland, not represented at the Conference, signed it later and became one of the original 51 member states. The United Nations officially came into existence on 24 Oct 1945, when the Charter had been ratified by China, France, USSR, UK, USA and a majority of the other signatories. *United Nations Day* is now universally celebrated on 24th October.
The name "United Nations" was devised by US President Franklin D Roosevelt. It was first used in the "Declaration by United Nations" of 1 Jan 1942, when representatives of 26 nations pledged their governments to continue fighting together against the Axis Powers and subscribed themselves to a common programme of purposes and principles embodied in the *Atlantic Charter (1941)*. This was followed by the Moscow Declaration, 30 Oct 1943, in which the signatories recognized "the necessity of establishing at the earliest practicable date a general international organization, based on the principle of the sovereign equality of all peace-loving states, and open to membership by all such states... for the maintenance of international peace and security". The United Nations was sometimes referred to in early official documents as *United Nations Organisation (UNO)*.
The resolution for dissolution of the *League of Nations (SDN, inactive)*, the forerunner of the United Nations, was adopted by the 21st and final session of the Assembly of the League on 18 Apr 1946. The "Common Plan for the Transfer of League of Nations Assets" was drawn up jointly by a United Nations Committee and the Supervisory Commission, acting on behalf of the United Nations and the League of Nations respectively, and was approved by the first General Assembly of the United Nations on 12 Feb 1946, Pursuant to provisions of the Plan, certain material assets of the League were transferred to the United Nations. Since then the Archives of the League of Nations have been maintained at the United Nations Library at Geneva.
The United Nations Charter may be amended by a vote of two thirds of the members of the General Assembly and ratification by two thirds of the members of the United Nations, including the five permanent members of the Security Council. The Charter has been amended five times: in 1965, increasing membership of the Security Council from 11 to 15 (Article 23) and the number of affirmative votes of the Council on procedural matters from seven to nine and on all other matters from seven to nine including the concurring votes of the five permanent members (Article 27); in 1965, increasing membership of the Economic and Social Council (ECOSOC) from 18 to 27 and, in 1973, to 54 (Article 61); in 1968, increasing the number of votes required in the Security Council to convene a General Conference to review the Charter from seven to nine (Article 109).
'Human Rights' On 16 Feb 1946, by resolution 5 (I), ECOSOC established a permanent Commission on Human Rights, consisting of government representatives whose task was to elaborate a Declaration defining the Fundamental Human Rights and Freedoms to which the Charter makes reference seven times. The resultant document, *Universal Declaration of Human Rights (UDHR, 1948)*, was adopted by the General Assembly in Dec 1948 and serves as a statement of principle, morally binding on member states of the United Nations. In Dec 1966, the General Assembly adopted two International Covenants: on Economic, Social and Cultural Rights, and on Civil and Political Rights, Resolution 2200 (XXI). The Covenants entered into force 3 Jan 1976 and 23 Mar 1976 respectively.
'Legal Status' The United Nations is an organization composed of states which have accepted the obligations contained in the UN Charter. Article 104 of the Charter states that "The Organization shall enjoy in the territory of each of its members such legal capacity as may be necessary for the exercise of its functions and the fulfillment of its purposes". Article 105 declares that "The Organization shall enjoy in the territory of each of its members such privileges and immunities as are necessary for the fulfillment of its purposes". It further declares that "Representatives of the members of the United Nations and officials of the Organization shall similarly enjoy such privileges and immunities as are necessary for the independent exercise of their functions in connection with the Organization". In Feb 1946, the General Assembly approved a Convention on the Privileges and Immunities of the United Nations. The Convention provides, among other things, that UN property and assets shall enjoy immunity from legal process and be free from all direct taxes and customs duties and that UN officials and experts shall enjoy such privileges and immunities as are necessary for the independent exercise of their functions. The UN may also issue to its officials laissez-passer (passports), recognized as valid documents by member states.
In Jun 1947, the United Nations concluded an agreement with United States of America on all matters of privileges and immunities in regard to the UN Headquarters. The agreement entered into force in Nov 1947. Section 8 of Article III of the agreement states, inter alia, that the United Nations "shall have the power to make regulations, operative within the headquarters district, for the purpose of establishing therein conditions in all respects necessary for full execution of its functions. No federal, state or local law or regulation of the United States which is inconsistent with a regulation of the United Nations authorized by this section, shall, to the extent of such inconsistency, be applicable within the headquarters district".
Following the assassination of Count Folke Bernadotte and of others serving the United Nations in Palestine, the General Assembly, in Dec 1948, requested an advisory opinion of the International Court of Justice on the question of reparation for injury suffered in the service of the UN. The Court, in April 1949, rendered the unanimous opinion that the UN is an international person – though not a state or a "super-state" – and has the capacity to maintain its rights by bringing international claims against member as well as non-member states to obtain reparation for damages caused to itself or to any of its agents. When the UN was bringing such a claim, it could do so only by basing it upon a breach of obligations due to itself. The Court declared that respect for this rule would usually prevent a conflict between the action of the UN and such rights as the agent's national state might possess. It further held that to ensure the efficient and independent performance of its missions and to afford effective support to its agents, the Organization itself must be able to provide them with adequate protection.
Aims The aims are contained in the Preamble to the Charter of the United Nations, which reads as follows:
"We the peoples of the United Nations determined
to save succeeding generations from the scourge of war, which twice in our lifetime has brought untold sorrow to mankind, and
to reaffirm faith in fundamental *human rights*, in the dignity and worth of the human person, in the equal rights of men and women and of nations large and small, and
to establish conditions under which *justice* and respect for the obligations arising from treaties and other sources of international law can be maintained, and
to promote social *progress* and better standards of life in larger freedom,
and for these ends
to practice *tolerance* and live together in peace with one another as good neighbours, and
to unite our strength to maintain international peace and security, and
to ensure, by the acceptance of principles and the institution of methods, that armed force shall not be used, save in the common interest, and
to employ international machinery for the promotion of the economic and social advancement of all peoples, have resolved to combine our efforts to accomplish these aims.
Accordingly, our respective Governments, through representatives assembled in the city of San Francisco, who have exhibited their full powers found to be in good and due form, have agreed to the present Charter of the United Nations and do hereby establish an international organization to be known as the United Nations".
The four principal *'Purposes'* of the United Nations are:
To maintain international peace and security;
To develop friendly relations among nations;
To cooperate internationally in solving international economic, social, cultural and humanitarian problems and in promoting respect for human rights and fundamental freedoms;
To be a centre for harmonizing the actions of nations in attaining these common ends.
The United Nations acts in accordance with the following *'Principles'*:
It is based on the sovereign equality of all its members.
All members are to fulfil in good faith their Charter obligations.
They are to settle their international disputes by peaceful means without endangering peace, security and justice.
They are to refrain in their international relations from the threat or use of force against any other state.
They are to give the United Nations every assistance in any action it takes in accordance with the Charter, and shall not assist states against which the United Nations is taking preventive or enforcement action.
The United Nations shall ensure that states which are not members act in accordance with these principles in so far as it is necessary for the maintenance of international peace and security.
Nothing in the Charter authorizes the United Nations to intervene in matters which are essentially within the domestic jurisdiction of any state.
Structure Main Organs (6):
(1) *General Assembly* is the main deliberative, policymaking and representative organ of the UN, in which all Member States are represented. Meets annually Sep to Dec, New York NY (USA). Decisions on important questions, such as those on peace and security, admission of new members and budgetary matters, require a two-thirds majority; decisions on other questions are by simple majority. President elected annually for one year.
The Assembly: is empowered to make recommendations to States on international issues within its competence; also initiates political, eonomic, humanitarian, social and legal actions.
Secretariat.
Main Committees (6):
- First Committee – Disarmament & International Security;
- Second Committee – Economic & Financial;
- Third Committee – Social, Humanitarian & Cultural;
- Fourth Committee – Special Political & Decolonization;
- Fifth Committee – Administrative & Budgetary;
- Sixth Commitee – Legal.

Subsidiary Organs of the General Assembly:
Boards:
- Board of auditors;
- Trade and development Board;
- United Nations Joint Staff Pension Board;
- Advisory Board on disarmament matters.

Executive Boards:
- Executive Board of *UNICEF (#20332)*;
- Executive Board of *UNDP (#20292)* and *United Nations Population Fund (UNFPA, #20612)*;
- Executive Board of *World Food Programme (WFP, #21510)*.

Commissions:
- *United Nations Disarmament Commission (#20552)*;
- *International Civil Service Commission (ICSC, #12587)*;
- *International Law Commission (ILC, #14004)*;
- *United Nations Commission on International Trade Law (UNCITRAL, #20531)*;
- *United Nations Conciliation Commission for Palestine (UNCCP, no recent information)*:
- *United Nations Peacebuilding Commission (PBC, #20606)*.

Advisory Commission:
- Advisory Commission on *United Nations Relief and Works Agency for Palestine Refugees in the Near East (UNRWA, #20622)*.

Committees:
- Investments Committee;
- United Nations Staff pension Committee;
- Committee for the United Nations Population Award;
- Committee on Contributions;
- *United Nations Committee for Programme and Coordination (CPC, #20546)*;
- *Committee on Information (COI, #04260)*;
- *United Nations Committee on Relations with the Host Country (#20547)*;
- *United Nations Committee on the Exercise of the Inalienable Rights of the Palestinian People (CEIRPP, #20539)*;
- *Committee on the Peaceful Uses of Outer Space (COPUOS, #04277)*;
- Credentials Committee;
- General Committee;
- *United Nations Scientific Committee on the Effects of Atomic Radiation (UNSCEAR, #20624)*.

Ad hoc Committees; Advisory Committees; Executive Committee; High-level Committee; Special Committees, including: *Special Committee on the Charter of the United Nations and on the Strengthening of the Role of the Organization (#19905)*; *United Nations Special Committee on Peace-keeping Operations (#20628)*; *United Nations Special Committee to Investigate Israeli Practices Affecting the Human Rights of the Palestinian People and Other Arabs of the Occupied Territories (#20627)*.
Assembly:
- United Nations Environment Assembly of *UNEP (#20299)*.

Council:
- *United Nations Human Rights Council (HRC, #20571)*;
- Governing Council of *United Nations Human Settlements Programme (UN-Habitat, #20572)*;
- Council of *United Nations University (UNU, #20642)*.

Working Groups and others, include:
- *Joint Inspection Unit of the United Nations (JIU, #16133)*.

(2) *United Nations Security Council (UNSC, #20625)*.
(3) *ECOSOC (#05331)*.
(4) *United Nations Trusteeship Council (#20639)* – operations formally suspended 1 Nov 1994 but continues to exist.
(5) *International Court of Justice (ICJ, #13098)*.
(6) *'Secretariat'* performs the administrative functions of the United Nations. It services the other organs and administers the programmes and policies laid down by them. It is headed by the Secretary-General, who is appointed by the General Assembly on the recommendation of the Security Council. Article 100 of the Charter states that: "In the performance of their duties the Secretary-General and the staff shall not seek or receive instruction from any government or from any other authority external to the Organization. They shall refrain from any action which might reflect on their position as international officials responsible only to the Organization. Each member of the United Nations undertakes to respect the exclusively international character of the responsibilities of the Secretary-General and the staff and not to seek to influence them in the discharge of their responsibilities".
'Secretary-General' Secretaries-General normally serve for 5 years but may serve further terms. As of 2009, none has served more than 2 terms.
- Trygve Lie (Norway) held office from Feb 1946 to his resignation in Nov 1952;
- Dag Hammarskjöld (Sweden), from Apr 1953 to Sep 1961, when he died in a plane crash;
- U Thant (Burma, now Myanmar), from Nov 1961 (when appointed acting Secretary-General) to Dec 1971, having been formally appointed in Nov 1962;
- Kurt Waldheim (Austria), Jan 1972 to Dec 1981;
- Javier Pérez de Cuéllar (Peru), Jan 1982 to Dec 1991;
- Boutros Boutros-Ghali (Egypt), Jan 1992 to Dec 1996;
- Kofi A Annan (Ghana), Jan 1997 to Dec 2006;
- Ban Ki-moon (Korea Rep), Jan 2007 to Dec 2016;
- António Guterres (Portugal), current Secretary-General, since 1 Jan 2017.

'Deputy Secretary-General' This post was established on 19 Dec 1997, to help manage Secretariat operations, to raise the United Nations profile and leadership in economic and social spheres and to strengthen it as a leading centre for development policy and assistance.
- Ms Louise Fréchette, the first to hold this post, assumed responsibilities in Feb 1998;
- Mark Malloch Brown, 1 Apr 2006 to 31 Jan 2007;
- Dr Asha-Rose Migiro, 1 Feb 2007 to 30 June 2012;
- Jan Eliasson, 1 July 2012 to 31 Jan 2017;
- Amina J Mohammed, since 1 Feb 2017.

Offices and Departments of the Secretariat at Headquarters in New York:
Executive Office of the Secretary General (EOSG):
- Office of the Spokesperson for the Secretary General.

Office of Internal Oversight Services:
- Internal Audit Division;
- Inspection and Evaluation Division;
- Investigations Division.

Office of Legal Affairs (OLA):
- Office of the Legal Counsel;
- General Legal Division;
- Treaty Section;
- Codification Division;
- International Trade Law Division;

- Division for Ocean Affairs and the Law of the Sea.

Department of Political and Peacebuilding Affairs (DPPA):
- Peacebuilding Support Office;
- *United Nations Office on Genocide Prevention and the Responsibility to Protect (#20598)*;
- Africa I and II Divisions;
- Americas Division;
- Asia and the Pacific Division;
- Europe Division;
- Middle East and West Asia Division;
- Electoral Assistance Division;,
- Division for Palestinian Rights;
- Policy and Mediation Division;
- Security Council Affairs Division;
- Decolonization Unit.

Office for Disarmament Affairs (DDA):
- Weapons of Mass Destruction Branch;
- Conventional Arms Branch;
- Information and Outreach Branch;
- Regional Disarmament Branch;
- *Conference on Disarmament (CD, #04590)* Secretariat and Conference Support Branch.

Department of Peace Operations (DPO):
- Office of Operations;
- Office of Military Affairs;
- Office of Rule of Law and Security Institutions, comprising: Police Division; Mine Action Service; Disarmament, Demobilization and Reintegration Section; Criminal Law and Judicial Advisory Services – Justice and Corrections; Security Sector Reform Unit;
- Policy, Evaluation and Training Division.

Department of Operational Support:
- Department of Operational Support (DOS);
- Office of the Under-Secretary-General (OUSG);
- Office of Support Operations (OSO);
- Office of Supply Chain Management (OSCM);
- Division of Administration, New York (DOA);
- Office of Information and Communication Technology.

United Nations Office for the Coordination of Humanitarian Affairs (OCHA, #20593):
- Coordination;
- Policy;
- Information Management;
- Humanitarian Financing.

Office of Counter-Terrorism (OCT).

Department of Economic and Social Affairs (DESA):
- Financing for Sustainable Development Office;
- Office for Intergovernmental Support and Coordination for Sustainable Development;
- Division for Inclusive Social Development;
- Secretariat of the *United Nations Forum on Forests (UNFF, #20562)*;
- Statistics Division;
- Division for Sustainable Development Goals;
- Population Division;
- Economic Analysis and Policy Division;
- Division for Public Institutions and Digital Government;
- Capacity Development Office.

Department for General Assembly and Conference Management:
- Central Planning and Coordination Division;
- Documentation Division;
- General Assembly and ECOSOC Affairs Division
- Meetings and Publishing Division;
- Protocol and Liaison Service.

Department of Global Communications:
- News and Media Division;
- Outreach Division;
- Strategic Communications Division.

Department of Safety and Security:
- Field Support Service;
- Division of Regional Operations;
- Division of Headquarters Security and Safety Services.

Department of Management Strategy, Policy and Compliance:
- Programme Planning, Finance and Budget;
- Office of Human Resources, comprising: HR Portal; Careers Portal;
- Business Transformation & Accountability;
- Office of Information and Communication Technology;
- Umoja.

Internal Justice Bodies:
- Office of the United Nations Ombudsman;
- Office of Administration of Justice;
- UN Dispute Tribunal
- UN Appeals Tribunal.

Other Offices:
- Office of the Victims' Rights Advocate;
- *United Nations Joint Staff Pension Fund (UNJSPF, #20581)*;
- Secretariat of *United Nations System Chief Executives Board for Coordination (CEB, #20636)*;
- Ethics Office;
- *United Nations Global Compact (#20567)* Office;
- United Nations Office for Partnerships (UNOP);
- *United Nations Democracy Fund (UNDEF, #20551)*;
- *United Nations Staff Union (#20630)*.

Special Advisers, Representatives and Envoys:
- *United Nations Office of the High Representative for the Least Developed Countries, Landlocked Developing Countries and Small Island Developing States (UN-OHRLLS, #20599)*;
- *United Nations Office of the Special Advisor on Africa (OSAA, see: #20515)*;
- Office of the Special Advisers to the Secretary-General on the Prevention of Genocide and the Responsibility to Protect;
- Special Representative of the Secretary-General for Children and Armed Conflict;
- office of the Special Representative of the Secretary-General on Sexual Violence in Conflict.

Offices Outside Main Headquarters:

Geneva:
- *United Nations Office at Geneva (UNOG, #20597)*;
- *Office of the United Nations High Commissioner for Human Rights (OHCHR, #17697)*, including the work of the previous *United Nations Centre for Human Rights (CHR, inactive)*;
- *United Nations Office for Disaster Risk Reduction (UNDRR, #20595)*, comprising: Advocacy and Outreach Section; Risk Knowledge Section; DRR Coordination Section;
- *UNCTAD (#20285)*.

Nairobi:
United Nations Office at Nairobi (UNON, #20600).

Vienna:
- *United Nations Office at Vienna (UNOV, #20604)*;
- *United Nations Office on Drugs and Crime (UNODC, #20596)*;
- *United Nations Office for Outer Space Affairs (UNOOSA, #20601)*.

UN Regional Commissions:
- *United Nations Economic Commission for Africa (ECA, #20554)*;
- *United Nations Economic Commission for Europe (UNECE, #20555)*;
- *United Nations Economic Commission for Latin America and the Caribbean (ECLAC, #20556)*;
- *United Nations Economic and Social Commission for Asia and the Pacific (ESCAP, #20557)*;
- *United Nations Economic and Social Commission for Western Asia (ESCWA, #20558)*.

The *United Nations System (#20635)*, also known as 'UN family', is made up of the organizations established by the Charter of the United Nations, that is, the United Nations proper, the specialized agencies provided for in Article 57 of the Charter and a number of programmes established by the General Assembly under its authority derived from Article 22 of the Charter. To this must be added *International Atomic Energy Agency (IAEA, #12294)* which is not a specialized agency in the strict legal sense.

The organizations are referred to collectively as "organizations of the United Nations system" which encompasses those organizations within and outside the "United Nations Common System". The Specialized Agencies and Related Organizations maintain separate legislative and governing bodies which provide the directives for their mandates. These organizations coordinate with the broader work of the United Nations through Inter-Organizational Agreements with the General Assembly and the Economic and Social Council facilitated through *United Nations System Chief Executives Board for Coordination (CEB, #20636)*.

Funds and Programmes within the UN System (6):
- *UNDP (#20292)*;
- *UNEP (#20299)*;
- *United Nations Population Fund (UNFPA, #20612)*;
- *United Nations Human Settlements Programme (UN-Habitat, #20572)*;
- *UNICEF (#20332)*;
- *World Food Programme (WFP, #21510)*.

UN Specialized Agencies within the UN System:
- *FAO (#09260)*;
- *International Civil Aviation Organization (ICAO, #12581)*;
- *International Fund for Agricultural Development (IFAD, #13692)*;
- *ILO (#11123)*;
- *International Monetary Fund (IMF, #14180)*;
- *International Maritime Organization (IMO, #14102)*;
- *International Telecommunication Union (ITU, #15673)*;
- *UNESCO (#20322)*;
- *UNIDO (#20336)*;
- *World Tourism Organization (UNWTO, #21861)*;
- *Universal Postal Union (UPU, #20682)*;
- *WHO (#20950)*;
- *World Intellectual Property Organization (WIPO, #21593)*;
- *The World Bank Group (#21218)*, comprising: *International Bank for Reconstruction and Development (IBRD, #12317)*; *International Centre for Settlement of Investment Disputes (ICSID, #12515)* (not a specialized agency); *International Development Association (IDA, #13155)*; *International Finance Corporation (IFC, #13597)*; *Multilateral Investment Guarantee Agency (MIGA, #16888)* (not an specialized agency).

Other Entities and Bodies within the UN System:
- *Joint United Nations Programme on HIV/AIDS (UNAIDS, #16149)*;
- *UNHCR (#20327)*;
- *United Nations Institute for Disarmament Research (UNIDIR, #20575)*;
- *United Nations Institute for Training and Research (UNITAR, #20576)*;
- *United Nations Office for Project Services (UNOPS, #20602)*;
- *United Nations Relief and Works Agency for Palestine Refugees in the Near East (UNRWA, #20622)*;
- *United Nations System Staff College (UNSSC, #20637)*;
- *UN Women (#20724)*.

Related Organizations within the UN System:
- *Preparatory Commission for the Comprehensive Nuclear-Test-Ban Treaty Organization (CTBTO, #18482)*;
- *International Atomic Energy Agency (IAEA, #12294)*;
- *International Organization for Migration (IOM, #14454)*;
- *Organisation for the Prohibition of Chemical Weapons (OPCW, #17823)*;
- *United Nations Framework Convention on Climate Change – Secretariat (UNFCCC, #20564)*;
- *World Trade Organization (WTO, #21864)*.

Organizations set up by the United Nations and/or functioning within its system:

ECOSOC Subsidiary Bodies:
- *United Nations Statistical Commission (#20633)*;
- *United Nations Commission on Population and Development (CPD, #20533)*;
- *United Nations Commission for Social Development (CSocD, #20535)*;
- *United Nations Commission on the Status of Women (CSW, #20536)*;
- *United Nations Commission on Narcotic Drugs (CND, #20532)*;
- *United Nations Commission on Crime Prevention and Criminal Justice (CCPCJ, #20530)*;
- *United Nations Commission on Science and Technology for Development (CSTD, #20534)*;
- *United Nations Forum on Forests (UNFF, #20562)*;
- *United Nations Committee of Experts on the Transport of Dangerous Goods and on the Globally Harmonized System of Classification and Labelling of Chemicals (Committee of Experts on TDG and GHS, #20543)*;
- *Intergovernmental Working Group of Experts on International Standards of Accounting and Reporting (ISAR, #11503)*;
- *United Nations Group of Experts on Geographical Names (UNGEGN, #20569)*;
- *United Nations Committee of Experts on Global Geospatial Information Management (UN-GGIM, #20540)*;
- *United Nations Committee for Development Policy (CDP, #20537)*;
- *United Nations Committee of Experts on Public Administration (CEPA, #20542)*;
- *United Nations Committee of Experts on International Cooperation in Tax Matters (#20541)*;
- *United Nations Committee on Economic, Social and Cultural Rights (CESCR, #20538)*;
- *United Nations Permanent Forum on Indigenous Issues (UNPFII, #20609)*

OHCHR Bodies:
- *Committee Against Torture (CAT, #04241)*;
- *Committee on the Elimination of Discrimination against Women (CEDAW, #04250)*;
- *Committee on the Elimination of Racial Discrimination (CERD, #04251)*;
- *Committee on Enforced Disappearances (CED, #04252)*;
- *Committee on Migrant Workers (CMW, #04271)*;
- *Committee on the Rights of the Child (#04283)*;
- *Committee on the Rights of Persons with Disabilities (CRPD, #04284)*;
- *Human Rights Committee (CCPR, #10979)*
- *Subcommittee on Prevention of Torture and other Cruel, Inhuman or Degrading Treatment or Punishment (SPT, #20023)*;
- *United Nations Committee on Economic, Social and Cultural Rights (CESCR, #20538)*.

Other bodies:
- *Association of Former International Civil Servants – New York (AFICS New York, #02600)*;
- *European Centre for Social Welfare Policy and Research (European Centre, #06500)*;
- *European Institute for Crime Prevention and Control affiliated with the United Nations (HEUNI, #07550)*;
- *Instituto Latinoamericano de las Naciones Unidas para la Prevención del Delito y Tratamiento del Delincuente (ILANUD, #11347)*;
- *Inter-Governmental Consultations on Migration, Asylum and Refugees (IGC, #11479)*;
- *Intergovernmental Oceanographic Commission (IOC, #11496)*;
- *International Computing Centre (ICC, #12839)*;
- *International Conference on the Great Lakes Region (ICGLR, #12880)*;
- *International Institute on Ageing, United Nations – Malta (INIA, #13860)*;
- *International Search and Rescue Advisory Group (INSARAG, #14816)*;
- *UN Environment Programme World Conservation Monitoring Centre (UNEP-WCMC, #20295)*;
- *United Nations Asia and Far East Institute for the Prevention of Crime and the Treatment of Offenders (UNAFEI, #20521)*;
- *United Nations Centre for Regional Development (UNCRD, #20526)*;
- *United Nations Crime Prevention and Criminal Justice Programme Network (#20549)*;
- *United Nations Fund for International Partnerships (UNFIP, #20565)*
- *United Nations Girls' Education Initiative (UNGEI, #20566)*;
- *United Nations International School (UNIS)*;
- *United Nations Mine Action Service (UNMAS, #20585)* and *United Nations Voluntary Trust Fund for Assistance in Mine Action (UN VTF, #20649)*;
- *United Nations Postal Administration (UNPA, #20613)*;
- *United Nations Programme of Assistance in the Teaching, Study, Dissemination and Wider Appreciation of International Law (#20614)*;
- *United Nations Regional Centre for Peace and Disarmament in Africa (UNREC, #20616)*;
- *United Nations Regional Centre for Peace and Disarmament for Asia and the Pacific (UNRCPD, #20617)*;
- *United Nations Regional Centre for Peace, Disarmament and Development in Latin America and the Caribbean (UNLIREC, #20618)*;
- *United Nations Regional Commissions New York Office (RCNYO, #20620)*;
- *Special Committee on Decolonization (C-24, #19906)*;
- *United Nations Sustainable Development Group (UNSDG, #20634)*;
- *United Nations Voluntary Fund on Disability (#20648)*.

Languages Arabic, Chinese, English, French, Russian, Spanish. **Staff** International staff at Headquarters and in the field derive from over 145 countries but, as international civil servants, they swear not to seek or receive instructions from any government or outside authority. Jurisdiction of the Administrative Tribunal of the United Nations extends to all organs of the UN. Field service staff negotiations through *United Nations Field Staff Union (UNFSU, #20561)*. **Finance** Main source is members' contributions. Additional revenue received from: the assessment levied on salaries of all staff members; sale of UN postage stamps for philatelic purposes; sale of publications and surplus property; income from the rental of office space. *'Regular Programme Budget'* covers expenses relating to substantive programmes, programme support and administrative activities (both Headquarters and worldwide). It is financed by contributions of member states assessed in accordance with a scale specified by the Assembly, based on capacity to pay and primarily determined by total national income in relation to that of other states – but factors such as low per capita income are also taken into account. No contributor may be assessed at more than 25% or less than 0.01% of the budget. The budget is considered and approved by the General Assembly every 2 years. It is initially submitted by the Secretary-General and reviewed by the 16-member expert *'Advisory Committee on Administrative and Budgetary Questions'*. Programme aspects are reviewed by the 34-member *'Committee for Programme and Coordination'*. Outside the regular budget, member states are assessed on a modification of the basic scale to cover costs of peacekeeping missions. A number of other activities outside the regular budget are financed mainly through voluntary contributions from both government and private sources; programmes financed in this way include UNDP, WFP, UNHCR, UNICEF, UNRWA, INSTRAW and UNFPA.

Activities Activities in the following fields:

Maintain International Peace and Security, through:
- Preventive Diplomacy and Mediation;
- Peacekeeping;
- Peacebuilding;
- Countering Terrorism;
- Disarmament.

Peacekeeping missions currently active:
- *United Nations Mission for the Referendum in Western Sahara (MINURSO, #20586)* (Sep 1991 – to present);
- *United Nations Multidimensional Integrated Stabilization Mission in the Central African Republic (MINUSCA, #20588)* (Apr 2014 – to present);
- *United Nations Multidimensional Integrated Stabilization Mission in Mali (MINUSMA, #20589)* (Apr 2013 – to present);
- *United Nations Organization Stabilization Mission in the Democratic Republic of Congo (MONUSCO, #20605)* (Jul 2010 – to present);
- *African Union/United Nations Hybrid Operation in Darfur (UNAMID, inactive)* (July 2007 – to present);
- *United Nations Disengagement Observer Force (UNDOF, #20553)* (June 1974 – to present);
- *United Nations Peace-keeping Force in Cyprus (UNFICYP, #20608)* (Mar 1964 – to present);
- *United Nations Interim Force in Lebanon (UNIFIL, #20577)* (Mar 1978 – to present);
- *United Nations Interim Security Force for Abyei (UNISFA, #20578)* (Jun 2011 – to present);
- *UN Interim Administration Mission in Kosovo (UNMIK, #20343)* (June 1999 – to present);
- *United Nations Mission in South Sudan (UNMISS, #20587)* (Jul 2011 – to present);
- *United Nations Military Observer Group in India and Pakistan (UNMOGIP, #20584)* (Jan 1949 – to present);
- *United Nations Truce Supervision Organization (UNTSO, #20638)* (June 1948 – to present).

Civilian component of peace-keeping forces: *United Nations Police (UNPOL, #20611)*.

United Nations Assistance Mission in Afghanistan (UNAMA, #20522) is a political mission.

List of Past Peacekeeping Operations:

Africa:
- *United Nations Angola Verification Mission (UNAVEM, inactive)* (UNAVEM I: Jan 1989 – May 1991, UNAVEM II: May 1991 – Feb 1995,UNAVEM III: Feb 1995 – June 1997);
- *United Nations Aouzou Strip Observer Group (UNASOG, inactive)* (May 1994 – June 1994);
- *United Nations Assistance Mission for Rwanda (UNAMIR, inactive)* (Oct 1993 – Mar 1996);
- *United Nations Mission in Côte d'Ivoire (MINUCI, inactive)* (May 2003 – Apr 2004);
- *United Nations Mission in Ethiopia and Eritrea (UNMEE, inactive)* (June 2000 – July 2008);
- *United Nations Mission in Sierra Leone (UNAMSIL, inactive)* (Oct 1999 – Dec 2005);
- *United Nations Mission in the Central African Republic (MINURCA, inactive)* (Apr 1998 – Feb 2000);
- *United Nations Mission in the Central African Republic and Chad (MINURCAT, inactive)* (Sep 2007 – Dec 2010);
- *United Nations Observer Mission in Angola (MONUA, inactive)* (July 1997 – Feb 1999);
- *United Nations Observation Mission in Liberia (UNOMIL, inactive)* (Sep 1993 – Sep 1997);
- *United Nations Mission of Observers in Sierra Leone (UNOMSIL, inactive)* (July 1998 – Oct 1999);
- *United Nations Observer Mission in Uganda-Rwanda (UNOMUR, inactive)* (June 1993 – Sep 1994);
- *United Nations Operation in Burundi (ONUB, inactive)* (May 2004 – Dec 2006) and replaced by *United Nations Integrated Office in Burundi (BINUB, inactive)*;
- *United Nations Operation in Côte d'Ivoire (UNOCI, inactive)* (Apr 2004 – Jun 2017);
- *United Nations Operation in Mozambique (UNOMOZ, inactive)* (Dec 1992 – Dec 1994);
- *United Nations Operation in Somalia (UNOSOM, inactive)* (UNOSOM I: Apr 1992 – Mar 1993, UNOSOM II: May 1993 – Mar 1995);
- *United Nations Mission in the Sudan (UNMIS, inactive)* (Mar 2005 – Jul 2011);
- *United Nations Operation in the Congo (inactive)* (July 1960 – June 1964);
- United Nations Organization Mission in the Democratic Republic of the Congo (MONUC) (Feb 2000 – Jul 2010);
- *United Nations Transition Assistance Group (UNTAG, inactive)* (Apr 1989 – Mar 1990);
- *United Nations Mission in Liberia (UNMIL, inactive)* (Sep 2003 – Mar 2018).

Americas:
- *Mission of the Representative of the Secretary-General in the Dominican Republic (DOMREP, inactive)* (May 1965 – Oct 1966);
- *United Nations Civilian Police Mission in Haiti (MIPONUH, inactive)* (28 Nov 1997 – Mar 2000);
- *United Nations Mission in Haiti (UNMIH, inactive)* (Sep 1993 – June 1996);
- *United Nations Observer Group in Central America (ONUCA, inactive)* (Nov 1989 – Jan 1992);
- *United Nations Observer Mission in El Salvador (inactive)* (July 1991 – Apr 1995);
- *United Nations Support Mission in Haiti (UNSMIH, inactive)* (July 1996 – July 1997);
- *United Nations Transition Mission in Haiti (UNTMIH, inactive)* (Aug 1997 – Nov 1997);
- *United Nations Verification Mission in Guatemala (MINUGUA, inactive)* (Jan 1997- May 1997);
- *United Nations Stabilization Mission in Haiti (MINUSTAH, inactive)* (Apr 2004 – Oct 2017);
- *United Nations Mission for Justice Support in Haiti (MINUJUSTH, inactive)* (Oct 2017 – Oct 2019).

Asia and the Pacific:
- *United Nations Advance Mission in Cambodia (UNAMIC, inactive)* (Oct 1991 – Mar 1992);
- *United Nations Good Offices Mission in Afghanistan and Pakistan (UNGOMAP, inactive)* (Apr 1988 – Mar 1990);
- *United Nations India-Pakistan Observation Mission (UNIPOM, inactive)* (Sep 1965 – Mar 1966);
- *United Nations Mission of Observers in Tajikistan (UNMOT, inactive)* (Dec 1994 – May 2000);
- *United Nations Mission of Support in East Timor (UNMISET, inactive)* (May 2002 – May 2005);
- *United Nations Security Force in West New Guinea – West Irian (UNSF, inactive)* (Oct 1962 – Apr 1963);
- *United Nations Transitional Administration in East Timor (UNTAET, inactive)* (Oct 1999 – May 2002);
- *United Nations Transitional Authority in Cambodia (UNTAC, inactive)* (Mar 1992 – Sep 1993);
- *United Nations Integrated Mission in Timor-Leste (UNMIT, inactive)* (Aug 2006 – Dec 2012).

Europe:
- *Croatia – United Nations Civilian Police Support Group (UNPSG, inactive)* (Jan 1998 – Oct 1998);
- *United Nations Confidence Restoration Operation in Croatia (UNCRO, inactive)* (Mar 1995- Jan 1996);
- *United Nations Mission in Bosnia and Herzegovina (UNMIBH, inactive)* (Dec 1995 – Dec 2002);
- *United Nations Mission of Observers in Prevlaka (UNMOP, inactive)* (Jan 1996 – Dec 2002);
- *United Nations Observer Mission in Georgia (UNOMIG, inactive)* (Aug 1993 – June 2009);
- *United Nations Preventive Deployment Force for Macedonia (UNPREDEP, inactive)* (Mar 1995 – Feb 1999);
- *United Nations Protection Force (UNPROFOR, inactive)* (Feb 1992 – Dec 1995);
- *United Nations Transitional Administration for Eastern Slavonia, Baranja and Western Sirmium (UNTAES, inactive)* (Jan 1996 – Jan 1998).

Middle East:
- *United Nations Emergency Force (UNEF, inactive)* (UNEF I: Nov 1956 – June 1967, UNEF II: Oct 1973 – July 1979);
- *United Nations Iran-Iraq Military Observer Group (UNIIMOG, inactive)* (Aug 1988 – Feb 1991);
- *United Nations Iraq-Kuwait Observation Mission (UNIKOM, inactive)* (Apr 1991 – Mar 2003);
- *United Nations Observation Group in Lebanon (UNOGIL, inactive)* (June 1958 – Dec 1958);
- *United Nations Yemen Observation Mission (UNYOM, inactive)* (July 1963 – Sep 1964);

United Nations Supervision Mission in Syria (UNSMIS) (Apr 2012 – Aug 2012).

Protect Human Rights.

Deliver Humanitarian Aid.

Promote Sustainable Development – mainly through the Sustainable Development Goals (SDGs) which will complete the work begun with the Millennium Development Goals:
- Goal 1: No Poverty
- Goal 2: Zero Hunger
- Goal 3: Good Wealth and Well-Being
- Goal 4: Quality Education
- Goal 5: Gender Equality
- Goal 6: Clean Water and Sanitation
- Goal 7: Affordable and Clean Energy
- Goal 8: Decent Work and Economic Growth
- Goal 9: Industries, Innovation and Infrastructure;
- Goal 10: Reduced Inequalities
- Goal 11: Sustainable Cities and Communities
- Goal 12: Responsible Consumption and Production
- Goal 13: Climate Action
- Goal 14: Life Below Water
- Goal 15: Life on Land
- Goal 16: Peace, Justice and Strong Institutions
- Goal 17: Partnerships for the Goals

Uphold International Law, includes:
- UN Treaty Collection (UNTC) contains over 560 multilateral treaties.

Events *Session* New York, NY (USA) 2023, *United Nations Water Conference* New York, NY (USA) 2023, *Permanent Mission of Japan to the United Nations Symposium on the Abductions Issue* 2022, *Session* New York, NY (USA) 2022, *Global Conference on Strengthening Synergies between the Paris Agreement and the 2030 Agenda for Sustainable Development* Tokyo (Japan) 2022.

Publications *UN Chronicle* (4 a year) – up-to-date coverage of United Nations activities; *Official Records of the General Assembly*; *UN Demographic Yearbook* – results of the international demographic survey of statistics for over 250 countries and territories on population trends, marriages, divorces, births, deaths and life expectancy; *UN Disarmament Yearbook*; *UN Statistical Yearbook* – comprehensive collection of international statistics of population, energy, health and housing; *Yearbook of the United Nations* – concise account of the activities of the United Nations and its related agencies during each calendar year. *United Nations Treaty Series (UNTS)* – 1,450 vols, containing over 30,000 treaties and international agreements registered or filed and recorded with and published by the Secretariat since 1946 (pursuant to Article 102 of the Charter) – includes texts of treaties in their authentic languages and also translations into English and French as appropriate – about 60 additional vols annually. *Everyone's United Nations* (10th ed 1986) – covers the whole life of the Organization, focusing on 1978-1985. Books; reports; compilations of statistics; periodicals; films; videos. Information Services: *United Nations Information Centres (UNICs, #20574)* – a network of centres – also referred to as 'United Nations Information Services (UNISs)' – aims to ensure that people everywhere receive as full as possible information about the United Nations.

United Nations and the Yearbook of International Organizations: In a note (E/2808) to ECOSOC dated 17 Nov 1955, the Secretary-General stated that information concerning international intergovernmental organizations (IGOs), including all those on the last list submitted to the Council and describing inter alia the relations between those organizations and the United Nations and specialized agencies, is provided in detail and kept up to date in the "Yearbook of International Organizations", published by the Union of International Associations (UAI), Brussels. The Secretary-General felt that the preparation of the list of IGOs fell within the category of activities which, in the Council's words, "might better be undertaken by such bodies as universities, national, private and public institutions or non-governmental organizations". He therefore proposed not to issue a further list of this kind unless the Council should so desire. The Secretary-General concluded by stating that the discontinuance of the list prepared by the Secretariat would in no way prevent the Council from considering from time to time any specific matter relating to the status of particular IGOs and their relationship with the United Nations and the specialized agencies that might be brought forward by a member of the Council or by the Secretary-General himself. Moreover, should the Council decide at any future date to undertake a comprehensive review of the structure of IGOs, as it did in the past, "Yearbook of International Organizations" could be used as a general background document, while the Secretariat would provide the Council with whatever supplementary information might prove necessary.

Information Services *Audio-Visual Production Libraries Unit* – archives of historic film; *Dag Hammarskjöld Library* – UN HQ New York, main repository of UN documents and publications; *Official Documents System (ODS)* – online database, free to users worldwide since 23 Dec 2003, contains all UN official documents since 1993, in all 6 official languages, plus key documents back to 1945; *ReliefWeb* – global information system of the Department of Humanitarian Affairs to disseminate information on emergencies and natural disasters; *United Nations Archives and Records Centre* – UN documents and declassified Secretariat records; *United Nations Database Information Centre System (UNDICS)* – collection of data maintained by the United Nations on behalf of itself and the specialized agencies; *United Nations Treaty Collection* in English, French; *UN News Centre* – online.

Members The 51 original members are indicated with in the list below. Of these original members: USSR is currently replaced by Russia; Czechoslovakia is replaced by the Czech Republic and Slovakia. Membership is open to all peace-loving states which accept and, in the judgement of the UN, are able and willing to carry out the obligations of the Charter. A state desiring to become a member must submit an application containing a declaration that it accepts the obligations contained in the Charter. New members are admitted by a two-thirds vote of the General Assembly upon recommendation of the Security Council, membership becoming effective on the date on which the Assembly takes this decision. On recommendation of the Security Council, the General Assembly may suspend the exercise of the rights and privileges of membership of a member against which preventive or enforcement action has been taken by the Security Council and may expel a member which has persistently violated the principles of the Charter. In the case of suspension, the exercise of rights and privileges may be restored by the Security Council; the Charter does not cover re-admission of expelled members. Member states (grouped by the United Nations as: African States; Asian and Pacific States; Latin American and Caribbean States; Eastern European States; Western European and other States) total 193:

Afghanistan, Albania, Algeria, Andorra, Angola, Antigua-Barbuda, Argentina (*), Armenia, Australia (*), Austria, Azerbaijan, Bahamas, Bahrain, Bangladesh, Barbados, Belarus (*), Belgium (*), Belize, Benin, Bhutan, Bolivia (*), Bosnia-Herzegovina, Botswana, Brazil (*), Brunei Darussalam, Bulgaria, Burkina Faso, Burundi, Cambodia, Cameroon, Canada (*), Cape Verde, Central African Rep, Chad, Chile (*), China (*), Colombia (*), Comoros, Congo Brazzaville, Congo DR, Costa Rica (*), Côte d'Ivoire, Croatia, Cuba (*), Cyprus, Czechia, Denmark (*), Djibouti, Dominica, Dominican Rep (*), Ecuador (*), Egypt (*), El Salvador (*), Equatorial Guinea, Eritrea, Estonia, Eswatini, Ethiopia (*), Fiji, Finland, France (*), Gabon, Gambia, Georgia, Germany, Ghana, Greece (*), Grenada, Guatemala (*), Guinea, Guinea-Bissau, Guyana, Haiti (*), Honduras (*), Hungary, Iceland, India (*), Indonesia, Iran Islamic Rep (*), Iraq (*), Ireland, Israel, Italy, Jamaica, Japan, Jordan, Kazakhstan, Kenya, Kiribati, Korea DPR, Korea Rep, Kuwait, Kyrgyzstan, Laos, Latvia, Lebanon (*), Lesotho, Liberia (*), Libya, Liechtenstein, Lithuania, Luxembourg (*), Madagascar, Malawi, Malaysia, Maldives, Mali, Malta, Marshall Is, Mauritania, Mauritius, Mexico (*), Micronesia FS, Moldova, Monaco, Mongolia, Montenegro, Morocco, Mozambique, Myanmar, Namibia, Nauru, Nepal, Netherlands (*), New Zealand (*), Nicaragua (*), Niger, Nigeria, North Macedonia, Norway (*), Oman, Pakistan, Palau, Panama (*), Papua New Guinea, Paraguay (*), Peru (*), Philippines (*), Poland (*), Portugal, Qatar, Romania, Russia (*), Rwanda, Samoa, San Marino, Sao Tomé-Principe, Saudi Arabia (*), Senegal, Serbia, Seychelles, Sierra Leone, Singapore, Slovakia, Slovenia, Solomon Is, Somalia, South Africa (*), South Sudan, Spain, Sri Lanka, St Kitts-Nevis, St Lucia, St Vincent-Grenadines, Sudan, Suriname, Sweden, Switzerland, Syrian AR (*), Tajikistan, Tanzania UR, Thailand, Timor-Leste, Togo, Tonga, Trinidad-Tobago, Tunisia, Türkiye (*), Turkmenistan, Tuvalu, Uganda, UK (*), Ukraine (*), United Arab Emirates, Uruguay (*), USA (*), Uzbekistan, Vanuatu, Venezuela (*), Vietnam, Yemen, Zambia, Zimbabwe.

Non-member Observer State:

Palestine.

IGO Relations Separate, autonomous intergovernmental agencies are related to the United Nations by special agreements. They work with the United Nations and each other through the coordinating machinery of the ECOSOC.

Observers to UN General Assembly as of Jan 2020:
- *Organisation of African, Caribbean and Pacific States (OACPS, #17796)*;
- *African Development Bank (ADB, #00283)*;
- *African Union (AU, #00488)*;
- *Agency for the Prohibition of Nuclear Weapons in Latin America and the Caribbean (#00554)*;
- *Andean Community (#00817)*;
- *ASEAN+3 Macroeconomic Research Office (AMRO, #01134)*;
- *Asian-African Legal Consultative Organization (AALCO, #01303)*;
- *Asian Development Bank (ADB, #01422)*;
- *Asian Infrastructure Investment Bank (AIIB, #01512)*;
- *Association of Caribbean States (ACS, #02411)*;
- *ASEAN (#01141)*;
- *Organization of Black Sea Economic Cooperation (BSEC, #17857)*;
- *Caribbean Community (CARICOM, #03476)*;
- *Central American Bank for Economic Integration (CABEI, #03658)*;
- *Central American Integration System (#03671)*;
- *Central European Initiative (CEI, #03708)*;
- *Collective Security Treaty Organization (CSTO, #04103)*;
- *Common Fund for Commodities (CFC, #04293)*;
- *Commonwealth of Independent States (CIS, #04341)*;
- *Commonwealth Secretariat (#04362)*;
- *Comunidade dos Países de Língua Portuguesa (CPLP, #04430)*;
- *Community of Sahel-Saharan States (CEN-SAD, #04406)*;

- *Conferencia de Ministros de Justicia de los Países Iberoamericanos (COMJIB, #04656);*
- *Conference on Interaction and Confidence-Building Measures in Asia (CICA, #04609);*
- *Gulf Cooperation Council (GCC, #10826);*
- *Council of Europe (CE, #04881);*
- Customs Cooperation Council;
- *D-8 Organization for Economic Cooperation (D-8, #04994);*
- *East African Community (EAC, #05181);*
- *Economic Community of Central African States (ECCAS, #05311);*
- *Economic Community of West African States (ECOWAS, #05312);*
- *Economic Cooperation Organization (ECO, #05313);*
- *Energy Charter Conference (#05466);*
- *Eurasian Development Bank (EDB, #05605);*
- Eurasian Economic Community;
- *Eurasian Group on Combating Money Laundering and Financing of Terrorism (EAG, #05608);*
- *European Organization for Nuclear Research (CERN, #08108);*
- *European Public Law Organization (EPLO, #08299);*
- *European Union (EU, #08967);*
- *Fondo para el Desarrollo de los Pueblos Indigenas de América Latina y el Caribe (FILAC, #09832);*
- *Global Fund to Fight AIDS, Tuberculosis and Malaria (Global Fund, #10383);*
- *Global Green Growth Institute (GGGI, #10392);*
- Group of Seven Plus;
- *The Hague Conference on Private International Law (HCCH, #10850);*
- Holy See;
- Ibero-American Conference – *Ibero-American General Secretariat (#11024);*
- *Commission de l'Océan Indien (COI, #04236);*
- *Indian Ocean Rim Association (IORA, #11161);*
- *Inter-American Development Bank (IDB, #11427);*
- *Intergovernmental Authority on Development (IGAD, #11472);*
- *International Anti-Corruption Academy (IACA, #11654);*
- *International Centre for Migration Policy Development (ICMPD, #12503);*
- *International Civil Defence Organization (ICDO, #12582);*
- *International Conference on the Great Lakes Region (ICGLR, #12880);*
- *International Council for the Exploration of the Sea (ICES, #13021);*
- *International Criminal Court (ICC, #13108);*
- *International Criminal Police Organization – INTERPOL (ICPO-INTERPOL, #13110);*
- *International Development Law Organization (IDLO, #13161);*
- *International Fund for Saving the Aral Sea (IFAS, #13694);*
- *International Humanitarian Fact-Finding Commission (IHFFC, #13820);*
- *International Hydrographic Organization (IHO, #13825);*
- *International Institute for Democracy and Electoral Assistance (International IDEA, #13872);*
- *International Institute for the Unification of Private Law (UNIDROIT, #13934);*
- *International Network for Bamboo and Rattan (INBAR, #14234);*
- *International Organization for Migration (IOM, #14454);*
- *Organisation internationale de la Francophonie (OIF, #17809);*
- *International Renewable Energy Agency (IRENA, #14715);*
- *International Seabed Authority (ISBA, #14813);*
- *International Think Tank for Landlocked Developing Countries (ITTLLDC, #15687);*
- *International Tribunal for the Law of the Sea (ITLOS, #15731);*
- *Ibero-American Youth Organization (#11036);*
- *Islamic Development Bank (IsDB, #16044);*
- *Italian-Latin American Institute (ILAI, #16071);*
- *Sistema Económico Latinoamericano (SELA, #19294);*
- *Latin American Integration Association (LAIA, #16343);*
- *Parlamento Latinoamericano (PARLATINO, #18203);*
- *League of Arab States (LAS, #16420);*
- *New Development Bank (NDB, #17081);*
- *OPEC Fund for International Development (OFID, #17745);*
- *Organisation of Eastern Caribbean States (OECS, #17804);*
- *Organization for Democracy and Economic Development (GUAM, #17861);*
- *OECD (#17693);*
- *Organization for Security and Cooperation in Europe (OSCE, #17887);*
- *OAS (#17629);*
- *Organisation of Islamic Cooperation (OIC, #17813);*
- *Pacific Community (SPC, #17942);*
- *Pacific Islands Development Forum (PIDF, #17967);*
- *Pacific Islands Forum (#17968);*
- Pan African Intergovernmental Agency for Water and Sanitation for Africa;
- *Parliamentary Assembly of the Mediterranean (PAM, #18212);*
- *Partners in Population and Development (PPD, #18247);*
- *Permanent Court of Arbitration (PCA, #18321);*
- *Regional Centre on Small Arms and Light Weapons in the Great Lakes Region, the Horn of Africa and Bordering States (RECSA, #18760);*
- *Shanghai Cooperation Organization (SCO, #19256);*
- *South Asian Association for Regional Cooperation (SAARC, #19721);*
- *South Centre (#19753);*
- *Southern African Development Community (SADC, #19843);*
- Sovereign Military Order of Malta;
- State of Palestine;
- *Union for the Mediterranean (UfM, #20457);*
- *Union of South American Nations (#20481);*
- *University for Peace (UPEACE, #20702);*
- *Union économique et monétaire Ouest africaine (UEMOA, #20377).*

NGO Relations Since 1945, NGOs have had a special relationship with the United Nations, one that has become increasingly complex and diversified. Almost every department of the United Nations and its specialized agencies has liaison offices or services for NGOs; and resolutions and legislative mandates of UN bodies call for consultative, operational, programmes and informational relationships with NGOs. A review of operations carried out by UN organizations with NGOs, Apr 1988, produced a number of directions and guidelines. More than 3,000 national and international organizations are formally related to the United Nations either through consultative status with ECOSOC or association with the Department of Global Communciations. *Conference of Non-Governmental Organizations in Consultative Relationship with the United Nations (CONGO, #04635)* and *Global NGO Executive Committee (GNEC, #10507)* channel information and represent the interests of these organizations. Many other NGOs cooperate with United Nations agencies, substantive departments and offices through United Nations Information Centres worldwide. *'Interdepartmental Working Group on Relations between Non-Governmental Organizations and the United Nations'* reviews and makes recommendations to the Secretary-General, monitors compliance and deals on an ad hoc basis with policies and procedures governing the NGO relationship. (See also separate ECOSOC entry). Observers to the General Assembly as of Jan 2020: *International Chamber of Commerce (ICC, #12534); International Committee of the Red Cross (ICRC, #12799); International Federation of Red Cross and Red Crescent Societies (#13526); International Olympic Committee (IOC, #14408); International Union for Conservation of Nature and Natural Resources (IUCN, #15766); Inter-Parliamentary Union (IPU, #15961).* [2023/XA3375/y/**A***]

♦ United Nations Academic Impact (UNAI) 20516

Impact Académique – Impacto Académico – Impacto Acadêmico

Chief Secretariat Outreach Div, UN Dept of Global Communications, 405 East 42nd St, S-09FWS, New York NY 10017, USA. E-mail: academicimpact@un.org.
URL: https://www.un.org/en/academicimpact

History within *United Nations (UN, #20515).* **Aims** Align institutions of higher education with the United Nations in supporting and contributing to the realization of United Nations goals and mandates, including the promotion and protection of human rights, access to education, sustainability and conflict resolution. **Events** *Meeting on Diplomatic Policy in Jamaica* Tokyo (Japan) 2018, *Seminar on Challenges and Opportunities of Language Education in University Globalization* Tokyo (Japan) 2018, *Conference* Seoul (Korea Rep) 2015, *Seoul Forum* Seoul (Korea Rep) 2015, *Global Conference* Seoul (Korea Rep) 2014.
Members Institutes of higher learning in 147 countries. Membership countries not specified.
Included in the above, 35 organizations listed in this Yearbook:
- *APS Europeo Istituto Pegaso (#00883);*
- *Asian Forum on Business Education (AFBE, #01490);*
- *Asian Institute of Technology (AIT, #01519);*
- *Asian University for Women (AUW);*
- *Caribbean Studies Association (CSA, #03559);*
- *China Education Association for International Exchange (CEAIE);*
- *Community of Mediterranean Universities (CMU, #04403);*
- *Danube Programme Coordination Unit (Danube PCU, inactive);*
- *Escuela Superior de Administración y Dirección de Empresas (ESADE);*
- *ESMT Berlin;*
- *Euclid University (EUCLID, #05575);*
- *European Institute of Public Administration (EIPA, #07569);*
- *Foreign Policy Association (FPA);*
- *Geneva School of Diplomacy and International Relations (GSD);*
- *Global Education Motivators (GEM, #10336);*
- *IHE Delft Institute for Water Education (#11110);*
- *Imam Khomeini International University (IKIU, no recent information);*
- *Institut de recherche pour le développement (IRD);*
- *International Association for the Advancement of Innovative Approaches to Global Challenges (IAAI, #11687);*
- *International Culture University (ICU);*
- *International Independent University of Environmental and Political Sciences, Moscow (IIUEPS);*
- *International Institute for Population Sciences (IIPS, #13911);*
- *International Institute of Labour and Social Relations (IILSR);*
- *International School for Social and Business Studies (ISSBS);*
- *International University of Business Agriculture and Technology (IUBAT);*
- *International University of Japan (IUJ);*
- *Middle East Technical University (METU);*
- *Moskovskij Gosudarstvennyj Institut Mezdunarodnyh Otnosenij (MGIMO);*
- *Schiller International University (SIU);*
- *Southeast Asia Interdisciplinary Development Institute (SAIDI, no recent information);*
- *Texas A and M International University;*
- *Universidad Latinoamericana de Ciencia y Tecnologia (ULACIT);*
- *University of the South Pacific (USP, #20703);*
- *World Academy of Art and Science (WAAS, #21065);*
- *World Engagement Institute (WEI).*

IGO Relations Partners include: *Central European Initiative (CEI, #03708).*
NGO Relations Partners include:
- *Academic Council on the United Nations System (ACUNS, #00020);*
- *Asociación Universitaria Iberoamericana de Postgrado (AUIP, #02307);*
- *Association of Arab Universities (AARU, #02374);*
- *Association of Universities of Latin America and the Caribbean (#02970);*
- *Baltic Sea Region University Network (BSRUN, #03149);*
- *Black Sea University Network (BSUN);*
- *Community of Mediterranean Universities (CMU, #04403);*
- *Compostela Group of Universities (#04419);*
- *Federación Latinoamericana de Facultades de Comunicación Social (FELAFACS, #09353);*
- *Hispanic Association of Colleges and Universities (HACU);*
- *Institute of International Education (IIE);*
- *International Association of University Presidents (IAUP, #12248);*
- *International Federation of Catholic Universities (IFCU, #13381);*
- *Mediterranean Universities Union (UNIMED, #16687);*
- *NAFSA – Association of International Educators;*
- *Network of Universities from the Capitals of Europe (UNICA, #17061);*
- *Universitas 21 (#20690);*
- *University Mobility in Asia and the Pacific (UMAP, #20700).* [2021.08.31/XJ1983/y/**E**]

♦ United Nations Action for Cooperation against Trafficking in Persons (UN-ACT) 20517

Management Office UN Bldg 12th Floor, Rajdamnern Nok Ave, Bangkok, 10200, Thailand. T. +6623049100. Fax +662800268. E-mail: unact@undp.org.
URL: http://un-act.org/

History 2014, by *UNDP (#20292),* building upon the work of *United Nations Inter-Agency Project on Human Trafficking (UNIAP, inactive).* **Aims** Ensure a coordinated approach to more strategically and effectively combat trafficking in persons in the Greater Mekong Sub-region (GMS) and beyond. **Structure** Managed by *UNDP (#20292).* **Staff** 25.00 FTE, paid. **Finance** Currently supported primarily by governments of Norway and Sweden. **Activities** Capacity building. Active in: Cambodia, China, Laos, Myanmar, Thailand, Vietnam. **Events** *International Seminar on Mixed Migration in Southeast and East Asia* Nakhon Pathom (Thailand) 2017. **Publications** *UN-ACT Newsletter.* [2017/XM5885/**E***]

♦ United Nations Ad Hoc Group of Experts on International Cooperation in Tax Matters / see United Nations Committee of Experts on International Cooperation in Tax Matters (#20541)

♦ United Nations African Institute for Economic Development and Planning 20518

Institut Africain de Développement Economique et de Planification des Nations Unies (IDEP)

Dir Rue du 18 Juin, PO Box 3186, 18524 Dakar, Senegal. T. +221338231020. Fax +221338222964. E-mail: administration@unidep.org – idep@unidep.org – eca-idep-com@un.org.
URL: http://www.uneca.org/idep/

History 1 Mar 1962. Established by Resolution 58 (VI), adopted at 4th session of the Conference of Ministers of the *United Nations Economic Commission for Africa (ECA, #20554).* Began operations on 21 Nov 1963. First Statutes approved by ECA Resolution 93 (VI) of 27 Feb 1964, and its first Governing Council was elected in Nov 1964. Present Statutes adopted by ECA Resolution 350 (XIV), 27 Mar 1979, and subsequently by the UN General Assembly at its 34th Session. A subsidiary body of ECA. **Aims** Assist policymakers and other stakeholders in enhancing their skills in the areas of policymaking, long-term perspective planning and institutional and regulatory reforms, as well as facilitate the emergence of policy ideas and consensus positions in Africa. **Structure** Governing Council, comprising 12 members, 11 of which are African ministers of finance, economic development, and/or planning, with the 12th member state being the Under Secretary-General of the United Nations/Executive Secretary of UNECA. Technical Advisory Committee. Management, Programmes and Administrative Units, including: Office of the Director; Capacity Development and Training Division; Administration; Library and Knowledge Management Division. Headquarters located in Dakar (Senegal). **Languages** Arabic, English, French, Portuguese. **Staff** 30.00 FTE, paid. **Finance** Sources: members' dues. Core finance also from *United Nations (UN, #20515).* Other sources obtained from multilateral, bilateral and foundation sources. **Activities** Capacity building; events/meetings; guidance/assistance/consulting; research/documentation; training/education. **Events** *International symposium on internal conflicts, peace and development* Dakar (Senegal) 1992, *Workshop* Egypt 1992, *Workshop* Senegal 1992, *Seminar on development of enterpreneurial capacity for cottage and small-scale industries* Dakar (Senegal) 1991, *Workshop* Ghana 1991. **Publications** *IDEP Journal of Development Practice; IDEP Newsletter. IDEP Monthly Development Seminars PaperSeries; IDEP Policy Brief Series.*
Members Governments of 54 African countries:
Algeria, Angola, Benin, Botswana, Burkina Faso, Burundi, Cameroon, Cape Verde, Central African Rep, Chad, Comoros, Congo Brazzaville, Congo DR, Côte d'Ivoire, Djibouti, Egypt, Equatorial Guinea, Eritrea, Eswatini, Ethiopia, Gabon, Gambia, Ghana, Guinea, Guinea-Bissau, Kenya, Lesotho, Liberia, Libya, Madagascar, Malawi, Mali, Mauritania, Mauritius, Morocco, Mozambique, Namibia, Niger, Nigeria, Rwanda, Sao Tomé-Principe, Senegal, Seychelles, Sierra Leone, Somalia, South Africa, South Sudan, Sudan, Tanzania UR, Togo, Tunisia, Uganda, Zambia, Zimbabwe. [2023/XE3628/j/**E***]

♦ United Nations African Institute for the Prevention of Crime and the Treatment of Offenders (UNAFRI) 20519

Institut africain des Nations Unies pour la prévention du crime et le traitement des délinquants

Dir PO Box 10590, Kampala, Uganda. T. +256414221119 – +256414185236. Fax +256312263797. E-mail: unafriu@yahoo.co.uk – unafri@unafri.or.ug.
URL: http://www.unafri.or.ug/

History 14 Jun 1989, Kampala (Uganda). Established at inaugural meeting of the Governing Board. Statute adopted by Resolution 642 (XXXIII) of 14th meeting of the Conference of Ministers of *United Nations Economic Commission for Africa (ECA, #20554),* 14-17 Apr 1988, Niamey (Niger). Secretariat became operational in

Jan 1991. Former names and other names: *African Institute for the Prevention of Crime and the Treatment of Offenders* – alias; *Institut africain pour la prévention du crime et le traitement des délinquants* – alias. **Aims** (a) Assist in formulating policies and programmes for prevention of crime and treatment of offenders, in the context of overall national development planning; (b) provide an empirical basis for *policy* formulation and decision-making by undertaking policy-oriented studies and research on priority problems in the region, including collection of *information* on crime trends and their impact on development and on crime prevention and *criminal justice* policies and programmes; (c) design and conduct training programmes for different categories and levels of criminal justice and related personnel, including policy makers, administrators, judges, prosecutors, lawyers, police and correctional officials, teachers, social workers and researchers, focusing on the *trainers*; upgrade this public service sector and impart new knowledge and skills through special inter-disciplinary courses, workshops, seminars, fellowships, internships and study tours; (d) assist in developing effective policies and programmes for prevention and control of *juvenile crime* and *delinquency* and for the treatment of juvenile offenders; (e) establish the framework for a data bank, promote exchange and transfer of knowledge, expertise and experience and disseminate information to governments, scholars, practitioners, researchers and organizations involved in the field; (f) assist in promoting innovative approaches to crime prevention and criminal justice reforms in accordance with United Nations norms and guidelines, drawing upon African traditions and orientations as well as on new developments in the field; (g) promote collaboration among the governments of the region in formulating common policies and undertaking joint action on matters of mutual concern in crime prevention and control, including appropriate legal agreements and practical arrangements at the regional and subregional levels. **Structure** Governing Board (executive authority), consisting of: 2 representatives from each of the 5 ECA subregions, selected from 2 ECA member states in each region by ECA Conference of Ministers; a representative of the host country; a representative of the Executive Secretary of ECA; one representative each of *United Nations Office at Vienna (UNOV, #20604)*; by invitation of the Governing Board, representatives of *Instituto Latinoamericano de las Naciones Unidas para la Prevención del Delito y Tratamiento del Delincuente (ILANUD, #11347)*, *United Nations Asia and Far East Institute for the Prevention of Crime and the Treatment of Offenders (UNAFEI, #20521)*, *European Institute for Crime Prevention and Control affiliated with the United Nations (HEUNI, #07550)* and *United Nations Interregional Crime and Justice Research Institute (UNICRI, #20580)*, representatives of interested international bodies and donor agencies and eminent experts may also attend as non-voting observers. Chairmanship of the Board is selected on annual rotational basis from amongst members of the Board (no member country holding the Chairmanship longer than 2 years). Secretariat, headed by Executive Director/ Head of Mission, situated in Kampala (Uganda). **Languages** English, French. **Staff** 14.00 FTE, paid. **Finance** Main sources: annual contributions of member states as determined by Governing Board; UN grant; project proposals; voluntary contributions by donors; rental income from available infrastructure. **Activities** Politics/ policy/regulatory; projects/programmes; research/documentation; training/education. **Events** *Congress* Sao Paulo (Brazil) 2010, *Congress* Bangkok (Thailand) 2005, *Congress* Vienna (Austria) 2000, *Congress* Cairo (Egypt) 1995, *Workshop on transnational crime in Africa* Kampala (Uganda) 1995. **Publications** *UNAFRI Newsletter* (4 a year); *African Journal for Criminal Justice (AJCJ)*. Training seminars/workshops and research reports.

Members Governments of 29 countries:
Burkina Faso, Burundi, Cameroon, Congo Brazzaville, Congo DR, Egypt, Equatorial Guinea, Gambia, Ghana, Guinea, Kenya, Libya, Malawi, Morocco, Mozambique, Niger, Nigeria, Rwanda, Senegal, Seychelles, Sierra Leone, Somalia, Sudan, Tanzania UR, Togo, Tunisia, Uganda, Zambia, Zimbabwe.

IGO Relations Member of: *United Nations Crime and Justice Information Network (UNCJIN, inactive)*. **NGO Relations** Represented (in rotation with other UN Institutes) on Executive Board of: *International Scientific and Professional Advisory Council of the United Nations Crime Prevention and Criminal Justice Programme (ISPAC, #14810)*. Memorandum of Understanding with: *Association internationale de lutte contre la cybercriminalité (AILCC, #02714)*. Member of: *International Centre for the Prevention of Crime (ICPC, #12508)*.
[2022/XE6121/j/**E***]

♦ United Nations African Mothers' Association (internationally oriented national body)
♦ United Nations African Mothers for Crisis / see United Nations African Mothers' Association

♦ United Nations Alliance of Civilizations (UNAOC) 20520

Alliance des civilisations des Nations Unies – Alianza de Civilizaciones de las Naciones Unidas

Dir 730 Third Avenue, 20th Floor, New York NY 10017, USA. T. +19292746217. E-mail: contactaoc@unops.org.
URL: http://www.unaoc.org/

History 2005. Established at the initiative of the governments of Spain and Turkey, under the auspices of *United Nations (UN, #20515)*. **Aims** Assist in diminishing hostility and promoting harmony among nations. **Structure** High Representative, supported by Secretariat. Groups of Friends. **Finance** Voluntary Trust Fund. **Activities** Events/meetings. **Events** *World Forum on Intercultural Dialogue* Baku (Azerbaijan) 2019, *World Forum on Intercultural Dialogue* Baku (Azerbaijan) 2017, *Global Forum* Baku (Azerbaijan) 2016, *World Forum on Intercultural Dialogue* Baku (Azerbaijan) 2015, *Global Forum* Bali (Indonesia) 2014.

Members Governments of Group of Friends (127):
Afghanistan, Albania, Algeria, Andorra, Angola, Argentina, Armenia, Australia, Austria, Azerbaijan, Bahrain, Bangladesh, Belarus, Belgium, Benin, Bolivia, Bosnia-Herzegovina, Brazil, Brunei Darussalam, Bulgaria, Burkina Faso, Canada, Cape Verde, Chile, China, Colombia, Congo Brazzaville, Costa Rica, Côte d'Ivoire, Croatia, Cuba, Cyprus, Czechia, Denmark, Dominican Rep, Ecuador, Egypt, El Salvador, Equatorial Guinea, Eritrea, Estonia, Ethiopia, Finland, France, Gambia, Georgia, Germany, Ghana, Greece, Guatemala, Guinea-Bissau, Guyana, Hungary, India, Indonesia, Iran Islamic Rep, Iraq, Ireland, Italy, Japan, Jordan, Kazakhstan, Korea Rep, Kuwait, Kyrgyzstan, Latvia, Lebanon, Libya, Lithuania, Luxembourg, Malaysia, Mali, Malta, Mauritania, Mexico, Mongolia, Montenegro, Morocco, Mozambique, Netherlands, New Zealand, Niger, North Macedonia, Norway, Oman, Pakistan, Palestine, Panama, Paraguay, Peru, Philippines, Poland, Portugal, Qatar, Romania, Russia, San Marino, Sao Tomé-Principe, Saudi Arabia, Senegal, Serbia, Singapore, Slovakia, Slovenia, South Africa, Spain, St Vincent-Grenadines, Sudan, Suriname, Sweden, Switzerland, Syrian AR, Tanzania UR, Thailand, Timor-Leste, Togo, Tunisia, Türkiye, UK, Ukraine, United Arab Emirates, Uruguay, USA, Uzbekistan, Venezuela, Vietnam, Yemen.

Included in the above, international organizations (28) listed in the Yearbook:
- *African Union (AU, #00488)*;
- *Arab League Educational, Cultural and Scientific Organization (ALECSO, #01003)*;
- *Comunidade dos Paises de Lingua Portuguesa (CPLP, #04430)*;
- *Council of Europe (CE, #04881)*;
- *European Union (EU, #08967)*;
- *FAO (#09260)*;
- *Ibero-American General Secretariat (#11024)*;
- *ILO (#11123)*;
- *International Organization for Migration (IOM, #14454)*;
- *Inter-Parliamentary Union (IPU, #15961)*;
- *Islamic World Educational, Scientific and Cultural Organization (ICESCO, #16058)*;
- *King Abdullah Bin Abdulaziz International Centre for Interreligious and Intercultural Dialogue (KAICIID, #16193)*;
- *League of Arab States (LAS, #16420)*;
- *Muslim World League (MWL, #16917)*;
- *Nordic Council (NC, #17256)*;
- *OAS (#17629)*;
- *Organisation internationale de la Francophonie (OIF, #17809)*;
- *Organisation of Islamic Cooperation (OIC, #17813)*;
- *Organization for Democracy and Economic Development (GUAM, #17861)*;
- *Organization for Security and Cooperation in Europe (OSCE, #17887)*;
- *Organization of Black Sea Economic Cooperation (BSEC, #17857)*;
- *Parliamentary Assembly of the Mediterranean (PAM, #18212)*;
- *Research Centre for Islamic History, Art and Culture (IRCICA, #18852)*;
- *UNESCO (#20322)*;
- *UNHCR (#20327)*;
- *Union for the Mediterranean (UfM, #20457)*;
- *World Organization of United Cities and Local Governments (UCLG, #21695)*;
- *World Tourism Organization (UNWTO, #21861)*.

NGO Relations Memorandum of Understanding with: *Euro-Mediterranean University (EMUNI, #05728)*. Key partner of: *G20 Interfaith Forum Association (IF20, #10055)*.
[2022.02.15/XM1270/y/**E***]

♦ United Nations Asia and Far East Institute for the Prevention of Crime and the Treatment of Offenders (UNAFEI) 20521

Institut pour la prévention du crime et le traitement des délinquants en Asie et en Extrême-Orient

Dir 2-1-18 Mokuseinomori, Akishima-shi, Tokyo, 196-8570 Japan. T. +81425005100. Fax +81425005195. E-mail: unafei@i.moj.go.jp.
Contact address not obtained.
URL: https://www.unafei.or.jp/

History 15 Mar 1961, Tokyo (Japan). Established as a United Nations regional institute by an agreement between the *United Nations (UN, #20515)* and the Government of Japan. Government of Japan assumed full administration, 1970. Former names and other names: *Asia and Far East Institute for the Prevention of Crime and the Treatment of Offenders* – former; *Institut d'Asie et de l'Extrême-Orient pour la prévention du délit et le traitement du délinquant* – former; *Institut des Nations Unies d'Asie et de l'Extrême-Orient pour la prévention du délit et le traitement du délinquant* – former. **Aims** Promote regional cooperation in the field of crime prevention and *criminal justice* through training and research, thereby contributing to sound social development in Asia and the *Pacific* Region. **Structure** Director; Deputy Director; Sections (4); Secretariat. **Languages** English, Japanese. **Finance** Staff payroll and operational expenditures borne by the Government of Japan. **Activities** Events/meetings; knowledge management/information dissemination; projects/programmes; research and development; training/education. **Events** *Regional Seminar on Good Governance for Southeast Asian Countries* Tokyo (Japan) 2021, *Regional Seminar on Good Governance for Southeast Asian Countries* Tokyo (Japan) 2021, *Regional Seminar on Good Governance for Southeast Asian Countries* Tokyo (Japan) 2019, *Seminar on the Third Country Training Programme for Development of Effective Community-Based Treatment of Offenders in the CLMV Countries* Tokyo (Japan) 2019, *Regional Seminar on Good Governance for Southeast Asian Countries* Danang (Vietnam) 2018. **Publications** *UNAFEI Newsletter* (3 a year). *UNAFEI Resource Material Series*. Seminar proceedings; resource materials; brochure.

Members Officials (more than 6,200) from 141 countries/territories participated in the Programmes of UNAFEI:
Afghanistan, Albania, Algeria, Antigua-Barbuda, Argentina, Armenia, Australia, Azerbaijan, Bangladesh, Barbados, Belize, Bhutan, Bolivia, Botswana, Brazil, Brunei Darussalam, Bulgaria, Burkina Faso, Burundi, Cambodia, Cameroon, Chad, Chile, China, Colombia, Congo DR, Cook Is, Costa Rica, Côte d'Ivoire, Cuba, Dominican Rep, Ecuador, Egypt, El Salvador, Estonia, Eswatini, Ethiopia, Fiji, Gabon, Gambia, Georgia, Ghana, Grenada, Guatemala, Guinea, Guyana, Haiti, Honduras, Hong Kong, Hungary, India, Indonesia, Iran Islamic Rep, Iraq, Jamaica, Japan, Jordan, Kazakhstan, Kenya, Kiribati, Korea Rep, Kyrgyzstan, Laos, Latvia, Lebanon, Lesotho, Liberia, Lithuania, Madagascar, Malawi, Malaysia, Maldives, Mali, Marshall Is, Mauritania, Mauritius, Mexico, Micronesia FS, Moldova, Mongolia, Montenegro, Morocco, Mozambique, Myanmar, Namibia, Nauru, Nepal, New Zealand, Nicaragua, Niger, Nigeria, North Macedonia, Oman, Pakistan, Palau, Palestine, Panama, Papua New Guinea, Paraguay, Peru, Philippines, Poland, Romania, Samoa, Saudi Arabia, Senegal, Serbia, Seychelles, Sierra Leone, Singapore, Solomon Is, Somalia, South Africa, South Sudan, Sri Lanka, St Kitts-Nevis, St Lucia, St Vincent-Grenadines, Sudan, Taiwan, Tajikistan, Tanzania UR, Thailand, Timor-Leste, Tonga, Trinidad-Tobago, Tunisia, Türkiye, Turkmenistan, Uganda, Ukraine, United Arab Emirates, Uruguay, USA, Uzbekistan, Vanuatu, Venezuela, Vietnam, Yemen, Zambia, Zimbabwe.

IGO Relations Also links with national institutes: Australian Institute of Criminology (AIC); Korean Institute of Criminology and Justice (KICJ); Thailand Institute of Justice (TIJ).
[2022.11.30/XE7809/j/**E***]

♦ United Nations Asian and Pacific Centre for Transfer of Technology / see Asian and Pacific Centre for Transfer of Technology (#01603)

♦ United Nations Assistance Mission in Afghanistan (UNAMA) 20522

Special Representative/Head PO Box 5858, Grand Central Station, New York NY 10163-5858, USA. Fax +12129632669. E-mail: spokesperson-unama@un.org.
Deputy Special Representative address not obtained.
URL: http://unama.unmissions.org/

History Set up, 28 Mar 2002, by resolution 1401 of *United Nations Security Council (UNSC, #20625)*, within *United Nations System (#20635)*, in the framework of *United Nations (UN, #20515)*. Initial period of 1 year; mandate reviewed annually. Latest mandate renewal, 8 Mar 2018, by Resolution 2405 (2018). **Aims** Provide political good offices in Afghanistan; work with and support the government; support the process of peace and reconciliation; monitor and promote human rights and the protection of civilians in armed conflict; promote good governance; encourage regional cooperation. **Structure** Secretary-General's Special Representative for Afghanistan. Field presence across Afghanistan, as well as liaison offices in Pakistan and Iran Islamic Rep. **Staff** 1211.00 FTE, paid. Staff comprising 833 Afghan nationals, 310 international staff and 68 UN volunteers. **Publications** Documents/reports.
[2019.02.12/XE4634/E*]

♦ United Nations Board of Auditors 20523

Comité des commissaires aux comptes de l'Organisation des Nations Unies

Exec Sec 1 United Nations Plaza, Room DC 1-2680, New York NY 10017, USA. T. +12129635623. Fax +12129633684.
URL: http://www.un.org/auditors/board/

History Dec 1946, by Resolution 74 (I) of the General Assembly of *United Nations (UN, #20515)*. **Events** *Special session* Delhi (India) 2011, *Regular session* New York, NY (USA) 2011, *Special session* Geneva (Switzerland) 2010, *Regular session* New York, NY (USA) 2010, *Special session* Bonn (Germany) 2009.
[2019.10.25/XF2087/**F***]

♦ United Nations Capital Development Fund (UNCDF) 20524

Fonds d'équipement des Nations unies (FENU) – Fondo de las Naciones Unidas para el Desarrollo de la Capitalización (FNUDC)

Main Office Two UN Plaza, 26th Floor, New York NY 10017, USA. T. +12129066565. E-mail: info@uncdf.org.
URL: http://www.uncdf.org/

History Dec 1966, New York NY (USA), by resolution 2186 (XXI) of the *United Nations (UN, #20515)* General Assembly, following preparatory meetings from Apr 1961, New York NY. Mandate modified 1973. Became fully operational in 1974. Autonomous, voluntarily funded UN organization, affiliated with *UNDP (#20292)*. **Aims** Offer "last mile" finance models that unlock public and private resources, especially at the domestic level, to reduce poverty and support local economic development. **Structure** UNDP Executive Board serves simultaneously as UNCDF Executive Board. UNDP Administrator serves simultaneously as UNCDF Managing Director. Authority for managing most aspects of UNCDF delegated to Executive Secretary. **Languages** English, French. **Staff** 180.00 FTE, paid. **Finance** Funding separately from UNDP. Funding from UN Member States, foundations and private sector. Annual income: about US$ 60,000,000. **Activities** Financial and/or material support. **Events** *YES : Youth Entrepreneurship and Self-employment Forum* Addis Ababa (Ethiopia) 2019, *Extreme Poverty Conference* Bangkok (Thailand) 2015, *International forum on the eradication of poverty* New York, NY (USA) 2006, *Global forum on reinventing government* Mexico City (Mexico) 2003, *From donations to investments workshop* Kampala (Uganda) 2002. **Publications** Annual Report. **IGO Relations** Cooperates with governments and international agencies in: *Consultative Group to Assist the Poor (CGAP, #04768)*. Support from: *United Nations Peacebuilding Fund (PBF, #20607)*. **NGO Relations** Collaborates with NGOs so as to support self-reliant initiatives; they may provide technical assistance through sub-contracting arrangements. Stakeholder in: *Child and Youth Finance International (CYFI, inactive)*. Founding member of: *Global Water Solidarity (GWS, #10655)*. Signatory to: *International Aid Transparency Initiative (IATI, #11604)*. Member of: *Consultative Group to Assist the Poor (CGAP, #04768)*. Resource partner of: *Better Than Cash Alliance (#03220)*.
[2020/XF5161/f/**F***]

♦ United Nations Central Emergency Response Fund (CERF) 20525

Fonds Central pour les Interventions d'Urgence – Fondo Central para la Acción en Casos de Emergencias

Chief of Secretariat 2 UN Plaza, 44th St DC2-1370, New York NY 10017, USA. T. +12129638205. E-mail: cerf@un.org.
URL: https://cerf.un.org/

History Established 2006, New York NY (USA), by General Assembly of *United Nations (UN, #20515)*, pursuant to UN Resolution 60/124. **Aims** Provide urgent and effective humanitarian aid to regions threatened by, or experiencing, a humanitarian crisis. **Structure** Housed within: *United Nations Office for the Coordination of Humanitarian Affairs (OCHA, #20593)*. **Finance** Contributions from members states and observers of the United Nations, regional and local authorities, private sector and civil society. Funding target: US$ 450,000,000. **Publications** Annual Report. **IGO Relations** Supports: *International Organization for Migration (IOM, #14454)*; United Nations funds, programmes and specialized agencies.
[2019/XM1701/f/**F***]

♦ United Nations Centre for Housing, Building and Planning (inactive)
♦ United Nations Centre for Human Rights (inactive)

♦ United Nations Centre for Human Settlements – UNCHS / see United Nations Human Settlements Programme (#20572)
♦ United Nations Centre for International Crime Prevention, Vienna (inactive)
♦ United Nations Centre for Natural Resources, Energy and Transport (inactive)

♦ United Nations Centre for Regional Development (UNCRD) 20526

Centre des Nations Unies pour le développement régional (CNUDR) – Centro de las Naciones Unidas para el Desarrollo Regional

Dir Nagono 1-47-1, Nakamura-ku, Nagoya AICHI, 450-0001 Japan. T. +81525619377. Fax +81525619375. E-mail: rep@uncrd.or.jp.
URL: http://www.uncrd.or.jp/

History 18 Jun 1971, Nagoya (Japan). Established under an agreement between *United Nations (UN, #20515)* and the Government of Japan, under *ECOSOC (#05331)* resolutions 1086 C (1965), 1141 (1966) and 1582 (L) (1971). **Aims** In regional development and planning and related fields: serve as a training and research centre for *developing countries*; provide advisory services at their request; assist them in promoting the exchange of data on research, practical experience and teaching and other relevant subjects; assist and cooperate with other concerned national or international organizations. **Structure** Administered by Division for Sustainable Development (DSD) of UN Department of Economic and Social Affairs. Director's Office Units: Administration; Economic and Social Development; Environment; Disaster Management Planning; Information Services. Advisory Committee. **Finance** Government of Japan. **Activities** Networking/liaising; research and development; training/education. **Events** *50th Anniversary Commemorative Symposium* Nagoya (Japan) 2022, *Regional 3R Forum in Asia and the Pacific* Nagoya (Japan) 2022, *Sustainable Railways in Asia-Pacific* 2021, *Regional Environmentally Sustainable Transport Forum in Asia* Tokoname (Japan) 2021, *Think SDGs International Conference* Toyota (Japan) 2021. **Publications** *Regional Development Dialogue (RDD)* (annual). Annual Report; selected articles on local/regional development. **IGO Relations** Partner of: *United Nations Public Administration Network (UNPAN, #20615)*. **NGO Relations** Collaborates with: *Regional Network of Local Authorities for the Management of Human Settlements (CITYNET, #18799).* [2020/XE8305/E*]

♦ United Nations Centre for Science and Technology for Development (inactive)

♦ United Nations Centre for Trade Facilitation and Electronic Business (UN/CEFACT) 20527

Centre pour la facilitation du commerce et les transactions électroniques des Nations Unies (CEFACT-ONU)

Sec ECTD, TFS, Palais des Nations, 1211 Geneva, Switzerland. T. +41229171298. E-mail: uncefact@un.org.
URL: http://www.unece.org/cefact/

History Mar 1997, Geneva (Switzerland). Established as an intergovernmental body of *United Nations Economic Commission for Europe (UNECE, #20555).* Replaces Working Party 4 on Facilitation of International Trade Procedures which had been established in the 1950s. Former names and other names: *Centre for Facilitation of Procedures and Practices for Administration, Commerce and Transport (CEFACT)* – former; *Centre pour la facilitation des procédures et des pratiques dans l'administration, le commerce et le transport* – former; *Centr po Uprosceniju Procedur i Praktiki v Upravlenii, Torgovle i na Transporte* – former. **Aims** Improve the ability of business, trade and administrative organizations from developed, developing and transitional economies to exchange products and relevant services effectively; facilitate international transactions by simplifying and harmonizing procedures and information flows, thus contributing to the growth of global commerce. **Structure** Plenary session (annual); Bureau; Forum/Programme Development Areas (PDAs); Domains (17); Project Teams. **Languages** English, French, Russian. **Finance** On regular United Nations Economic Commission for Europe budget. **Activities** Awareness raising; capacity building; events/meetings; knowledge management/information dissemination; politics/policy/regulatory; projects/programmes; standards/guidelines. Active in all member countries. **Events** *UN/CEFACT Forum* Geneva (Switzerland) 2023, *UN/CEFACT Forum* Geneva (Switzerland) 2022, *UN/CEFACT Forum* Geneva (Switzerland) 2022, *UN/CEFACT Forum* Geneva (Switzerland) 2021, *UN/CEFACT Forum* Geneva (Switzerland) 2021. **Publications** *UNECE Journal. A Short History of UNECE (1947-2007).* Annual Report; historical documents; compendium of legal instruments; sustainable development briefs; reports to ECOSOC; discussion papers.

Members Participating countries (192):
Afghanistan, Albania, Algeria, Andorra, Angola, Antigua-Barbuda, Argentina, Armenia, Australia, Austria, Azerbaijan, Bahamas, Bahrain, Bangladesh, Barbados, Belarus, Belgium, Belize, Benin, Bhutan, Bolivia, Bosnia-Herzegovina, Botswana, Brazil, Brunei Darussalam, Bulgaria, Burkina Faso, Burundi, Cambodia, Cameroon, Canada, Cape Verde, Central African Rep, Chad, Chile, China, Colombia, Comoros, Congo Brazzaville, Congo DR, Costa Rica, Côte d'Ivoire, Croatia, Cuba, Cyprus, Czechia, Denmark, Djibouti, Dominica, Dominican Rep, Ecuador, Egypt, El Salvador, Equatorial Guinea, Eritrea, Estonia, Eswatini, Ethiopia, Fiji, Finland, France, Gabon, Gambia, Georgia, Germany, Ghana, Greece, Grenada, Guatemala, Guinea, Guinea-Bissau, Guyana, Haiti, Honduras, Hungary, Iceland, India, Indonesia, Iran Islamic Rep, Iraq, Ireland, Israel, Italy, Jamaica, Japan, Jordan, Kazakhstan, Kenya, Kiribati, Korea DPR, Korea Rep, Kuwait, Kyrgyzstan, Laos, Latvia, Lebanon, Lesotho, Liberia, Libya, Liechtenstein, Lithuania, Luxembourg, Madagascar, Malawi, Malaysia, Maldives, Mali, Malta, Marshall Is, Mauritania, Mauritius, Mexico, Micronesia FS, Moldova, Monaco, Mongolia, Montenegro, Morocco, Mozambique, Myanmar, Namibia, Nauru, Nepal, Netherlands, New Zealand, Nicaragua, Niger, Nigeria, North Macedonia, Norway, Oman, Pakistan, Palau, Panama, Papua New Guinea, Paraguay, Peru, Philippines, Poland, Portugal, Qatar, Romania, Russia, Rwanda, Samoa, San Marino, Sao Tomé-Principe, Saudi Arabia, Senegal, Serbia, Seychelles, Sierra Leone, Singapore, Slovakia, Slovenia, Solomon Is, Somalia, South Africa, Spain, Sri Lanka, St Kitts-Nevis, St Lucia, St Vincent-Grenadines, Sudan, Suriname, Sweden, Switzerland, Syrian AR, Tajikistan, Tanzania UR, Thailand, Timor-Leste, Togo, Tonga, Trinidad-Tobago, Tunisia, Türkiye, Turkmenistan, Tuvalu, Uganda, UK, Ukraine, United Arab Emirates, Uruguay, USA, Uzbekistan, Vanuatu, Venezuela, Vietnam, Yemen, Zambia, Zimbabwe.

Regional organizations listed in this Yearbook:
Eurasian Economic Union (EAEU, #05607); European Commission (EC, #06633).

IGO Relations *International Civil Aviation Organization (ICAO, #12581); International Maritime Organization (IMO, #14102); International Telecommunication Union (ITU, #15673); International Trade Centre (ITC, #15703); Organization for Security and Cooperation in Europe (OSCE, #17887); UNCTAD (#20285); UNIDO (#20336); United Nations Commission on International Trade Law (UNCITRAL, #20531); United Nations Economic Commission for Africa (ECA, #20554); United Nations Economic Commission for Latin America and the Caribbean (ECLAC, #20556); United Nations Economic and Social Commission for Asia and the Pacific (ESCAP, #20557); United Nations Economic and Social Commission for Western Asia (ESCWA, #20558); World Customs Organization (WCO, #21350); World Intellectual Property Organization (WIPO, #21593); World Trade Organization (WTO, #21864).* **NGO Relations** *Alliance africaine pour le commerce électronique (AACE, #00652); Asia Pacific Council for Trade Facilitation and Electronic Business (AFACT, #01877); Comité européen de normalisation (CEN, #04162); European Telecommunications Standards Institute (ETSI, #08897); Fédération internationale des associations de transitaires et assimilés (FIATA, #09610); GS1 (#10809); International Association of Ports and Harbors (IAPH, #12096); International Chamber of Commerce (ICC, #12534); International Electrotechnical Commission (IEC, #13255); International Organization for Standardization (ISO, #14473); International Port Community Systems Association (IPCSA, #14623); International Road Transport Union (IRU, #14761); World Trade Point Federation (WTPF, #21865).* [2020.08.27/XK1552/t/E*]

♦ United Nations Centre on Transnational Corporations (inactive)
♦ United Nations Children's Fund (#20332)
♦ United Nations Civilian Police Force / see United Nations Police (#20611)
♦ United Nations Civilian Police Mission in Haiti (inactive)

♦ United Nations Collaborative Programme on Reducing Emissions from Deforestation and Forest Degradation in Developing Countries (UN-REDD Programme) 20528

Secretariat Intl Environment House, Chemin des Anémones 11-13, Châtelaine, 1219 Geneva, Switzerland. T. +41229178946. E-mail: un-redd@un-redd.org.
URL: http://www.un-redd.org/

History Launched 2008, by *FAO (#09260), UNEP (#20299)* and *UNDP (#20292).* Former names and other names: *REDD+* – former. **Aims** Support nationally led REDD+ processes; promote informed and meaningful involvement of all stakeholders, including indigenous peoples and other forest-dependent communities, in national and international REDD+ implementation. **Structure** Executive Board, consisting of representatives from partner countries, donors to the Multi-Partner Trust Fund, Civil Society and indigenous peoples organizations, and *FAO (#09260), UNDP (#20292)* and *UNEP (#20299).* Technical Secretariat. **Languages** English, French, Spanish. **Finance** Funding from: Governments of Denmark, Japan, Luxembourg, Norway, Spain, Switzerland and the EU. Multi-Partner Trust Fund (currently 2008-2015). Budget approved: US$ 320,000,000. **Activities** Research and development; standards/guidelines; guidance/assistance/consulting; events/meetings. **Events** *Forests Africa International Conference* Nairobi (Kenya) 2013. **Publications** *UN-REDD Newsletter* (4 a year).

Members States receiving support to National Programmes (25):
Argentina, Bangladesh, Bolivia, Cambodia, Chile, Colombia, Congo Brazzaville, Congo DR, Côte d'Ivoire, Ecuador, Honduras, Indonesia, Mongolia, Myanmar, Nigeria, Panama, Papua New Guinea, Paraguay, Peru, Philippines, Solomon Is, Sri Lanka, Tanzania UR, Vietnam, Zambia.

Other partner countries (40):
Argentina, Bangladesh, Benin, Bhutan, Burkina Faso, Cameroon, Chile, Costa Rica, Czechia, Dominican Rep, El Salvador, Equatorial Guinea, Ethiopia, Fiji, Gabon, Ghana, Guatemala, Guinea-Bissau, Guyana, India, Jamaica, Kenya, Laos, Liberia, Madagascar, Malawi, Malaysia, Mexico, Morocco, Nepal, Pakistan, Samoa, Solomon Is, South Sudan, Sudan, Suriname, Togo, Tunisia, Uganda, Zimbabwe.

IGO Relations Partners include: *Collaborative Partnership on Forests (CPF, #04100); Forest Carbon Partnership Facility (FCPF, #09862); Global Environment Facility (GEF, #10346); Green Climate Fund (GCF, #10714); United Nations Forum on Forests (UNFF, #20562); United Nations Framework Convention on Climate Change (UNFCCC, 1992).* [2020.01.20/XJ7645/E*]

♦ United Nations Command Military Armistice Commission (UNCMAC) 20529

Address not obtained.

History 27 Jul 1953, by *United Nations Security Council (UNSC, #20625),* to implement the armistice agreement which brought an end to the Korean War. Also referred to as *Military Armistice Commission in Korea.* Mandate: indefinite, no fixed termination date. **Aims** Settle through negotiation any violation of the agreement; act as intermediary between commanders of opposing sides. **Structure** Commission comprises 10 senior military officers. Intergovernmental member: *United Nations Unified Command in Korea (UNC, #20641).* Headquarters in Seoul (Korea Rep). **Activities** Monitors violations of the agreement along the demilitarized zone (DMZ) between North and South Korea and acts as intermediary between the two sides. **Events** *Seminar* Jeju (Korea Rep) 2017. [2017/XE3328/E*]

♦ United Nations Commission on Crime Prevention and Criminal Justice (CCPCJ) 20530

Commission des Nations Unies pour la prévention du crime et la justice pénale – Comisión de las Naciones Unidas de Prevención del Delito y Justicia Penal

Sec UNODC, Vienna International Centre, PO Box 500, 1400 Vienna, Austria. T. +43126060 ext 4280. E-mail: unodc-sgb@un.org.
URL: http://www.unodc.org/unodc/en/commissions/CCPCJ/index.html

History Feb 1992. Established as a functional commission of *ECOSOC (#05331),* by ECOSOC resolution 1992/1 and pursuant to resolution 46/152 of the General Assembly of *United Nations (UN, #20515),* to replace *United Nations Committee on Crime Prevention and Control (inactive).* Establishment followed Ministerial Meeting, Nov 1991, Versailles (France), and recommendations of an *Intergovernmental Working Group on the Creation of an Effective International Crime and Justice Programme.* 1st Session: 21-30 Apr 1992, Vienna (Austria). Through GA resolution 61/252 (2006), also became a governing body of *United Nations Office on Drugs and Crime (UNODC, #20596).* Based at *Vienna International Centre (VIC)* at *United Nations Office at Vienna (UNOV, #20604).* Former names and other names: *Commission on Crime Prevention and Criminal Justice* – alias; *Commission pour la prévention du crime et la justice pénale* – alias; *Comisión de Prevención del Delito y Justicia Penal* – alias. **Aims** Act as principal *policy-making* body of the United Nations in the field of crime prevention and criminal justice; develop, monitor and review implementation of UN crime prevention programme, act as governing body of United Nations Office on Drugs and Crime and approve budget of the United Nations Crime Prevention and Criminal Fund; act as preparatory body for the quinquennial United Nations Congress on Crime Prevention and Criminal Justice, preparatory events for which may be organized by other agencies. **Structure** Session (regular annual) in Vienna (Austria), with reconvened session to consider budgetary and administrative matters. Pursuant to ECOSOC Decision 2011/259, joint meeting during reconvened sessions with *United Nations Commission on Narcotic Drugs (CND, #20532).* Member states (40), elected by ECOSOC for a 3-year term on the basis of equitable geographical distribution (12 from Africa, 9 from Asia, 8 from Latin America and Caribbean, 7 from Western European and other states and 4 from Eastern Europe). Bureau. **Languages** Arabic, Chinese, English, French, Russian, Spanish. **Staff** Secretariat services provided by the Secretariat to the Governing Bodies (SGB) – *United Nations Office on Drugs and Crime (UNODC, #20596).* **Finance** On the regular budget of the United Nations through assessed contributions of member states. Extra-budgetary funding through voluntary contributions to the United Nations Crime Prevention and Criminal Justice Fund. **Activities** Awareness raising; capacity building; guidance/assistance/consulting; politics/policy/regulatory. Commission serves as preparatory body for the quinquennial *United Nations Congress on Crime Prevention and Criminal Justice.* **Events** *Regular session* Vienna (Austria) 2023, *Intersessional Meeting on the implementation of the Kyoto Declaration* Vienna (Austria) 2022, *Reconvened session* Vienna (Austria) 2022, *Regular session* Vienna (Austria) 2022, *Reconvened Session* Vienna (Austria) 2021. **Publications** *CCPCJ Newsletter.* Technical and specialized publications as required; documents; reports.

Members Governments of 40 countries (term expiry date, 31 Dec of the year in parentheses):
Angola (2023), Armenia (2023), Austria (2024), Bahrain (2024), Belarus (2024), Brazil (2024), Bulgaria (2024), Cameroon (2023), Canada (2024), Chile (2024), China (2023), Colombia (2023), Côte d'Ivoire (2023), Cuba (2024), Dominican Rep (2024), El Salvador (2023), Eritrea (2023), France (2024), Germany (2023), Ghana (2024), India (2024), Italy (2023), Japan (2023), Kenya (2023), Korea Rep (2023), Libya (2024), Mauritius (2023), Morocco (2023), Namibia (2023), Nigeria (2023), Pakistan (2024), Paraguay (2024), Peru (2023), Qatar (2024), Russia (2023), Saudi Arabia (2023), Thailand (2024), Togo (2024), UK (2023), USA (2024).

IGO Relations Formal contacts with several IGOs, several of which attend sessions as observers, including *United Nations Crime Prevention and Criminal Justice Programme Network (#20549).* **NGO Relations** Pursuant to Article 71 of the United Nations Charter and ECOSOC Resolution 1996/31 of 25 Jul 1996, formal contacts with a number of NGOs, many of which attend sessions as observers. [2022.10.14/XE3128/E*]

♦ United Nations Commission on International Trade Law (UNCITRAL) 20531

Commission des Nations Unies pour le droit commercial international (CNUDCI) – Comisión de las Naciones Unidas para el Derecho Mercantil Internacional (CNUDMI) – Komissija Organizacii Obedinennyh Nacij po Pravu Mezdunarodnoj Torgovli

Sec Int Trade Law Div – UN Office of Legal Affairs, Vienna Int Centre, PO Box 500, 1400 Vienna, Austria. T. +431260604060. Fax +431260605813. E-mail: uncitral@un.org.
URL: http://www.uncitral.un.org/

History 17 Dec 1966. Established within the framework of *United Nations (UN, #20515),* by General Assembly Resolution 2205 (XXI). Activities commenced Jan 1968, New York NY (USA). **Aims** Promote modernization and harmonization of the law of international commerce. **Structure** Commission Session (annual, alternately in New York NY – USA and Vienna – Austria); Working Groups; other subsidiary bodies. Secretariat at *Vienna International Centre (VIC).* **Languages** Arabic, Chinese, English, French, Russian, Spanish. **Staff** 20.00 FTE, paid. 3 additional staff in Regional Centre for Asia and Pacific (RCAP), established in 2012, paid from extrabudgetary resources. **Finance** From the overall budget of the United Nations Office of Legal Affairs. Law reform programme and seminars, regional centres and the Transparency Registry financed through trust fund. **Activities** Advocacy/lobbying/activism; knowledge management/information dissemination; politics/policy/regulatory. Management of treaties and agreements:

- *Convention on the Limitation Period in the International Sale of Goods (1974);*
- *Convention on the Recognition and Enforcement of Foreign Arbitral Awards (New York Convention, 1958)* with the recommendation regarding the interpretation of article II, paragraph 2, and article VII, paragraph 1 (adopted in 2006);
- *Protocol Amending the Convention on the Limitation Period in the International Sale of Goods (1980);*
- *Provisions for a Unit of Account and Adjustment of Limitations of Liability (1982);*
- *UNCITRAL Arbitration Rules (1976);*
- *UNCITRAL Conciliation Rules (1980);*
- UNCITRAL Expedited Arbitration Rules;
- UNCITRAL Mediation Rules;

- *UNCITRAL Model Law on Cross-border Insolvency (1997)*;
- *UNCITRAL Model Law on Electronic Commerce (1996)*;
- *UNCITRAL Model Law on Electronic Signatures (2001)*;
- UNCITRAL Model Law on Electronic Transferable Records;
- UNCITRAL Model Law on Enterprise Group Insolvency with Guide to Enactment;
- *UNCITRAL Model Law on International Commercial Arbitration (1985)* (original 1985 text and as amended in 2006);
- *UNCITRAL Model Law on International Commercial Conciliation (2002)*;
- UNCITRAL Model Law on International Commercial Mediation and International Settlement Agreements Resulting from Mediation (amending the Model Law on International Commercial Arbitration)
- *UNCITRAL Model Law on International Credit Transfers (1992)*;
- *UNCITRAL Model Law on Procurement of Goods and Construction (1993)*;
- *UNCITRAL Model Law on Procurement of Goods, Construction and Services (1994)*;
- UNCITRAL Model Law on Public Procurement;
- UNCITRAL Model Law on Recognition and Enforcement of Insolvency-Related Judgments with Guide to Enactment;
- UNCITRAL Model Law on Secured Transactions;
- *United Nations Convention on Transparency in Treaty-based Investor-State Arbitration (Mauritius Convention on Transparency, 2014)*;
- *Uniform Rules on Contract Clauses for an Agreed Sum Due Upon Failure of Performance (1983)*;
- *United Nations Convention on the Assignment of Receivables in International Trade (2001)*;
- *United Nations Convention on the Carriage of Goods by Sea (1978)*;
- *United Nations Convention on Contracts for the International Carriage of Goods Wholly or Partly by Sea (Rotterdam Rules, 2008)*;
- *United Nations Convention on Contracts for the International Sale of Goods (1980)*;
- *United Nations Convention on Independent Guarantees and Stand-by Letters of Credit (1995)*;
- *United Nations Convention on International Bills of Exchange and International Promissory Notes (1988)*;
- *United Nations Convention on the Liability of Operators of Transport Terminals in International Trade (1991)*;
- *United Nations Convention on Transparency in Treaty-based Investor-State Arbitration*;
- *United Nations Convention on the Use of Electronic Communications in International Contracts (2005)*.

A number of other UNCITRAL legislative guides, model legislative provisions and other standards.
Events *Asia Pacific ADR Conference* Seoul (Korea Rep) 2021, *Tokyo Forum on Dispute Resolution* Tokyo (Japan) 2021, *Session* Vienna (Austria) 2021, *Session* Vienna (Austria) 2021, *Session* Vienna (Austria) 2021. **Publications** *UNCITRAL Yearbook* in English, French, Russian, Spanish. Guides; conventions; registers; texts; digests. **Information Services** *Case Law on UNCITRAL Text (CLOUT)* – database; *New York Convention Guide* – database; *Transparency Registry* – database; *UNCITRAL Law Library On-line Catalogue* – database.
Members Member states of the United Nations (60) elected for 6 years by the UN General Assembly (term of office expires on the last day prior to beginning of annual session in the year indicated):
Algeria (2025), Argentina (2022), Australia (2022), Austria (2022), Belarus (2022), Belgium (2025), Brazil (2022), Burundi (2022), Canada (2025), Chile (2022), China (2025), Colombia (2022), Côte d'Ivoire (2025), Croatia (2025), Czechia (2022), Dominican Rep (2025), Ecuador (2025), Finland (2025), France (2025), Germany (2025), Ghana (2025), Honduras (2025), Hungary (2025), India (2022), Indonesia (2025), Iran Islamic Rep (2022), Israel (2022), Italy (2022), Japan (2025), Kenya (2022), Korea Rep (2025), Lebanon (2022), Lesotho (2022), Libya (2022), Malaysia (2025), Mali (2025), Mauritius (2022), Mexico (2025), Nigeria (2022), Pakistan (2022), Peru (2025), Philippines (2022), Poland (2022), Romania (2022), Russia (2025), Singapore (2025), South Africa (2025), Spain (2022), Sri Lanka (2022), Switzerland (2025), Thailand (2022), Türkiye (2022), Uganda (2022), UK (2025), Ukraine (2025), USA (2022), Venezuela (2022), Vietnam (2025), Zimbabwe (2019).
IGO Relations Observer status with (1): *World Trade Organization (WTO, #21864)*.
Links inter alia with:
- *Asian-African Legal Consultative Organization (AALCO, #01303)*;
- *Asian Clearing Union (ACU, #01380)*;
- *Cairo Regional Centre for International Commercial Arbitration (CRCICA, #03398)*;
- *Comisión Centroamericana de Transporte Maritimo (COCATRAM, #04131)*;
- *Common Market for Eastern and Southern Africa (COMESA, #04296)*;
- *Commonwealth Secretariat (#04362)*;
- *Corte Centroamericana de Justicia (CCJ, #04850)*;
- *East African Development Bank (EADB, #05183)*;
- *EFTA (#05391)*;
- *European Bank for Reconstruction and Development (EBRD, #06315)*;
- *European Commission (EC, #06633)*;
- *European Space Agency (ESA, #08798)*;
- *Gulf Cooperation Council (GCC, #10826)*;
- *The Hague Conference on Private International Law (HCCH, #10850)*;
- *Inter-American Development Bank (IDB, #11427)*;
- *Organisation intergouvernementale pour les transports internationaux ferroviaires (OTIF, #17807)*;
- *International Bank for Reconstruction and Development (IBRD, #12317)*;
- *International Cotton Advisory Committee (ICAC, #12979)*;
- *International Development Law Organization (IDLO, #13161)*;
- *International Institute for the Unification of Private Law (UNIDROIT, #13934)*;
- *International Monetary Fund (IMF, #14180)*;
- *NAFTA Secretariat (#16927)* Article 2022 Advisory Committee;
- *OAS (#17629)*;
- *OECD (#17693)*;
- *Office of the United Nations High Commissioner for Human Rights (OHCHR, #17697)*;
- *Permanent Court of Arbitration (PCA, #18321)*;
- *Southeast European Cooperative Initiative (SECI, #19812)*;
- *Southern Common Market (#19868)*;
- *Steering Committee on Trade Capacity and Standards (CTCS, #19979)*;
- *UNCTAD (#20285)*;
- *UNIDO (#20336)*;
- *United Nations Centre for Trade Facilitation and Electronic Business (UN/CEFACT, #20527)*;
- *United Nations Economic Commission for Europe (UNECE, #20555)*;
- *World Intellectual Property Organization (WIPO, #21593)*.

NGO Relations Links with over 200 NGOs, including: *Comité maritime international (CMI, #04192)*; *International Bar Association (IBA, #12320)*; *International Chamber of Commerce (ICC, #12534)*; *International Law Association (ILA, #14003)*. [2022.02.07/XE6309/**E***]

♦ United Nations Commission on Narcotic Drugs (CND) 20532

Commission des stupéfiants des Nations Unies – Comisión de Estupefacientes de las Naciones Unidas

Sec c/o UNODC, Vienna International Centre, PO Box 500, 1400 Vienna, Austria. T. +43126060 ext 4280. E-mail: unodc-sgb@un.org.
URL: http://www.unodc.org/unodc/en/commissions/CND/index.html

History 16 Feb 1946. Established by resolution 9 (I) of *ECOSOC (#05331)*, as a functional commission. Based at *United Nations Office at Vienna (UNOV, #20604)*. Since 1991, also a governing body of *United Nations Office on Drugs and Crime (UNODC, #20596)*. **Aims** Act as the central *policy-making* body within the UN System dealing with drug-related matters; assist the Economic and Social Council in supervising the application of the international drug control treaties; advise the Council on matters pertaining to the control of narcotic drugs, psychotropic substances and their precursors; perform normative functions under the international drug control treaties; serve as the governing body of the United Nations Office on Drugs and Crime (UNODC); monitor political commitments on drug control. **Structure** Session (regular annual) in Vienna (Austria) with reconvened session to consider budgetary and administrative matters; regular intersessional meetings; pursuant to ECOSOC decision 2011/259, joint meetings during reconvened sessions with *United Nations Commission on Crime Prevention and Criminal Justice (CCPCJ, #20530)*. Member States (53), elected by ECOSOC for a 4-year term on the basis of equitable geographical distribution (currently: 11 from Africa, 11 from Asia, 10 from Latin America and the Caribbean, 14 from Western European and other States and 6 from Eastern Europe; one seat to rotate between the Asian and the Latin American and Caribbean States every 4 years). Members are elected from among UN Member States and members of the specialized agencies and the Parties to the international drug control conventions. Subsidiary bodies (5): Subcommission on Illicit Drug Traffic and Related Matters in the Near and Middle East and 4 Meetings of *Heads of National Drug Law Enforcement Agencies (HONLEA)*; HONLEA Asia and the Pacific; HONLEA Africa; HONLEA Latin America and the Caribbean; HONLEA Europe. **Languages** Arabic, Chinese, English, French, Russian, Spanish. **Staff** Secretariat services provided by the Secretariat to the Governing Bodies (SGB) – *United Nations Office on Drugs and Crime (UNODC, #20596)*. **Finance** On the regular budget of the *United Nations (UN, #20515)* through assessed contributions of member states. Extra-budgetary funding through *Fund of the United Nations International Drug Control Programme*. **Activities** Awareness raising; knowledge management/information dissemination; management of treaties and agreements. **Events** *Regular session* Vienna (Austria) 2023, *Reconvened session* Vienna (Austria) 2022, *Regular session* Vienna (Austria) 2022, *Reconvened Session* Vienna (Austria) 2021, *Session* Vienna (Austria) 2021. **Publications** *CND Newsletter*. *Competent National Authorities under the International Drug Control Treaties*; *Manufacture of Narcotic Drugs, Psychotropic Substances and their Precursors*.
Members Representatives of 52 states (term expiry date, 31 Dec of the year in parentheses):
Algeria (2021), Angola (2023), Australia (2021), Austria (2023), Bahrain (2023), Bangladesh (2025), Belgium (2021), Bolivia (2025), Brazil (2021), Canada (2021), China (2023), Colombia (2021), Côte d'Ivoire (2021), Ecuador (2023), Egypt (2023), El Salvador (2023), France (2021), Germany (2023), Ghana (2025), Hungary (2023), Iran Islamic Rep (2025), Italy (2023), Jamaica (2023), Japan (2023), Kazakhstan (2023), Kenya (2023), Libya (2023), Lithuania (2025), Mexico (2023), Morocco (2023), Nepal (2023), Netherlands (2023), Nigeria (2023), Pakistan (2023), Peru (2023), Poland (2023), Russia (2021), Saudi Arabia (2025), Slovenia (2025), South Africa (2023), Spain (2023), Sweden (2023), Switzerland (2021), Thailand (2023), Trinidad-Tobago (2025), Tunisia (2025), Türkiye (2023), Turkmenistan (2023), UK (2023), Ukraine (2023), Uruguay (2023), USA (2023).
IGO Relations Formal contacts with several IGOS, several of which may attend sessions as observers. **NGO Relations** Pursuant to Article 71 of the United Nations Charter and ECOSOC Resolution 1296 (XLIV), and Rules 75 and 76 of the Rules of Procedure of the Functional Commissions of ECOSOC, formal contacts with a number of NGOs, many of which attend sessions as observers. [2022.10.14/XE5951/**E***]

♦ United Nations Commission on Population and Development (CPD) 20533

Commission des Nations Unies de la population et du développement

Dir c/o Population Div, Dept of Economic and Social Affairs, UN Headquarters, 2 United Nations Plaza, Room DC 2-1950, New York NY 10017, USA. T. +12129633209. Fax +12129632147. E-mail: population@un.org.
URL: https://www.un.org/development/desa/pd/

History 10 Aug 1948. Established by resolution 150 (VII) of *ECOSOC (#05331)*. Present title adopted 1995 by General Assembly of *United Nations (UN, #20515)*, resolution 49/128 and ECOSOC resolution 1995/209. Former names and other names: *United Nations Population Commission* – former; *Commission des Nations Unies de la population* – former. **Aims** Study and advise ECOSOC on population trends, consequences, integrating population and development strategies, population and related development policies and programmes and provision of population assistance; monitor, review and assess the implementation of the Programme of Action of the Conference; adopt a topic-oriented and prioritized multi-year work programme, undertaking a quinquennial review and appraisal of the progress made; review on a regular basis the flow of financial resources and the funding mechanism to achieve the goals of the Conference's Plan of Action; maintain and enhance public attention and support; consider the reports of the meetings of inter-agency mechanisms as well as of intergovernmental and non-governmental organizations for the implementation of the Programme of Action; provide recommendations to the Council on the integrated consideration of the reports and issues and review the findings of research and analysis pertaining to the interrelationship between population and development at the national, regional and global levels. **Structure** Annual Session. Members (47) are elected by ECOSOC for 4-year terms on the basis of: 12 from African States; 11 from Asia-Pacific States; 9 from Latin American and Caribbean States; 10 from Western European and other States; 5 from Eastern European States. Representatives from *United Nations Statistical Commission (#20633)* and *United Nations Commission for Social Development (CSocD, #20535)* take part without the right to vote. **Languages** Arabic, Chinese, English, French, Russian, Spanish. **Staff** 40.00 FTE, paid. **Finance** Supported by: *United Nations (UN, #20515)*. **Activities** Events/meetings. Together with UN General Assembly and ECOSOC, plays a primary role in reviewing the implementation of the *'Programme of Action of the International Conference on Population and Development'* adopted at *'International Conference on Population and Development (ICPD)'*, Sep 1994, Cairo (Egypt). **Events** *Session* New York, NY (USA) 2021, *Session* New York, NY (USA) 2020, *Session* New York, NY (USA) 2019, *Session* New York, NY (USA) 2018, *Session* New York, NY (USA) 2017. **Publications** For all publications, see: https://www.un.org/development/desa/pd/
Members Representatives of 46 States (expiry date in brackets) – currently only 11 African states:
Argentina (2022), Australia (2025), Bangladesh (2022), Belarus (2023), Belgium (2025), Botswana (2025), Bulgaria (2022), Burkina Faso (2022), Canada (2024), China (2022), Colombia (2022), Comoros (2025), Congo DR (2023), Costa Rica (2025), Côte d'Ivoire (2022), Cuba (2025), Denmark (2025), Dominican Rep (2024), El Salvador (2023), Ethiopia (2025), Germany (2022), Haiti (2022), India (2025), Iran Islamic Rep, Israel (2023), Jamaica (2023), Japan (2025), Lebanon (2024), Libya (2024), Malaysia (2023), Mauritania (2022), Mexico (2025), Moldova (2025), Nepal (2022), Netherlands (2022), Philippines (2025), Russia (2022), Somalia (2024), Togo (2023), Türkiye (2024), Turkmenistan (2024), UK (2025), Ukraine (2024), USA (2022), Vanuatu (2022), Zambia (2024). [2022.11.29/XE1125/**E***]

♦ United Nations Commission on Science and Technology for Development (CSTD) 20534

Commission des Nations Unies de la science et de la technique au service du développement

Contact Division on Technology and Logistics – UNCTAD, Palais des Nations, Avenue de la Paix 8-14, 1211 Geneva 10, Switzerland. T. +41229171234 – +41229175701. Fax +41229170522. E-mail: stdev@unctad.org.
URL: http://unctad.org/en/Pages/CSTD.aspx

History 30 Apr 1992. Established by resolution 1992/218 of *ECOSOC (#05331)*, and further by resolution A/RES/46/235 of the General Assembly of *United Nations (UN, #20515)*, 20 Jul 1992, as a functional commission of ECOSOC, combining the activities of the previous *United Nations Intergovernmental Committee on Science and Technology for Development (IGCSTD, inactive)* and *Advisory Committee on Science and Technology for Development (ACSTD, inactive)*. First session, Apr 1993, New York NY (USA). Functions revised by ECOSOC, 1998. Since Jul 1993, serviced by Secretariat of *UNCTAD (#20285)*, Geneva (Switzerland). In resolution E/2006/46, adopted Jul 2006, ECOSOC decided that the Commission shall effectively assist the Council as the focal point in the system-wide follow-up to the outcomes of World Summit on the Information Society (WSIS), and agreed to increase the membership of the Commission from 33 to 43 members. Former names and other names: *Commission on Science and Technology for Development* – alias; *Commission de la science et de la technique au service du développement* – alias. **Aims** Provide UN General Assembly and ECOSOC with high-level advice on relevant issues through analysis and appropriate policy recommendations or options, so as to enable them to guide the future work of the UN, develop common policies and agree on appropriate action. Current mandate: (a) Review and assess progress at international and regional levels in implementation of Action Lines, recommendations and commitments contained in the outcome documents of the WSIS; (b) Share best and effective practices and lessons learned, and identify obstacles and constraints encountered, actions and initiatives to overcome them and important measures for further implementation of the Summit outcomes; (c) Promote dialogue and foster partnerships, in coordination with other appropriate UN funds, programmes and specialized agencies, to contribute to attainment of Summit objectives and implementation of its outcomes and to use information and communication technologies for development and achievement of internationally agreed development goals, with participation of governments, private sector, civil society, the UN and other international organizations in accordance with their different roles and responsibilities. **Structure** Commission.(annual sessions, in Geneva, Switzerland), following decision 2006/269, adopted 15 Dec 2006 by ECOSOC, comprises 43 members, elected by ECOSOC for a 4-year term on the basis of: 11 from Africa; 9 from Asia; 8 from Latin America and Caribbean; 5 from Eastern Europe; 10 from Western Europe and other states. Bureau. **Languages** Arabic, Chinese, English, French, Russian, Spanish. **Activities** Events/meetings; knowledge management/information dissemination. **Events** *Session* Geneva (Switzerland) 2023, *Inter-sessional Panel Meeting* Geneva (Switzerland) 2022, *Session* Geneva (Switzerland) 2022, *Inter-sessional Panel Meeting* Geneva (Switzerland) 2021, *Session* Geneva (Switzerland) 2021. **Publications** *Technology and Innovation Report* (every 2 years). *Science and Technology for Development Series*.
Members 43 countries (term expiry date, 31 Dec of the year in parentheses):
Austria (2024), Belarus (2024), Belgium (2022), Botswana (2026), Brazil (2024), Burundi (2024), Cameroon (2024), Canada (2022), China (2026), Cuba (2026), Dominican Rep (2022), Ecuador (2026), Egypt (2026), Ethiopia (2022), Finland (2024), Gambia (2024), Guatemala (2024), Guinea (2024), Hungary (2026), Iran Islamic Rep (2022), Israel (2024), Japan (2024), Kenya (2022), Latvia (2026), Liberia (2022), Madagascar (2022), Nepal (2022), Oman (2026), Panama (2022), Paraguay (2024), Peru (2024), Philippines (2024), Portugal (2024), Romania (2026), Russia (2024), Saudi Arabia (2024), South Africa (2024), Switzerland (2024), Thailand (2022), Türkiye (2026), Turkmenistan (2024), UK (2026), USA (2026).
NGO Relations Pursuant to Article 71 of the United Nations Charter and ECOSOC Resolution 1996/31, formal contacts with a number of NGOs (not specified), many of which act as observers. Also links with NGOs accredited by ECOSOC. [2022.12.23/XE3120/**E***]

♦ United Nations Commission for Social Development (CSocD) 20535

Commission des Nations Unies du développement social

Contact Div for Inclusive Social Dvlpmnt, Dept Economic & Social Affairs, Secretariat Bld – UN Headquarters, 29th Floor, 405 East 42 Street, New York NY 10017, USA. T. +12129632775. Fax +12129633062. E-mail: social@un.org.
URL: http://www.un.org/development/desa/dspd/

History 1946. Established by resolution 10 (II) of *ECOSOC (#05331)*. Following reappraisal of the role of the Commission in 1961 and 1966, current name was adopted to clarify its role as a preparatory and advisory body of ECOSOC. In its resolution 50/161 of 22 Dec 1995, the General Assembly of *United Nations (UN, #20515)* decided that the General Assembly, ECOSOC and the Commission should constitute a three-tiered intergovernmental process in the follow-up to the implementation of the Copenhagen (Denmark) Declaration on Social Development and Programme of Action of the World Summit for Social Development. In ECOSOC resolution 1996/7, additional terms of reference were adopted. Former names and other names: *Social Commission* – former. **Aims** Advise the Council on policies of a general character, in particular on all matters in the social field not covered by the specialized inter-governmental agencies. As of resolution 380J (XXXII) of 1961, priority is given to the establishment of social objectives and programme priorities and social research in areas affecting social and *economic development*. **Structure** Bureau. **Activities** Events/meetings. **Events** *Annual session* New York, NY (USA) 2020, *Annual Session* New York, NY (USA) 2019, *Annual session* New York, NY (USA) 2018, *Annual Session* New York, NY (USA) 2017, *Annual Session* New York, NY (USA) 2016.
Members Representatives of 46 States (term expiry date, 31 Dec of the year in parentheses), as of 2022 – 5 vacancies remaining:
Afghanistan (2025), Argentina (2023), Austria (2023), Brazil (2025), Chad (2023), China (2025), Colombia (2023), Congo DR (2024), Costa Rica (2025), Cuba (2024), Djibouti (2025), Dominican Rep (2024), Ecuador (2025), Ethiopia (2024), Finland (2025), Guatemala (2023), Guinea (2025), Iran Islamic Rep (2024), Iraq (2023), Israel (2023), Japan (2024), Korea Rep (2024), Libya (2024), Morocco (2023), Nigeria (2024), North Macedonia (2024), Paraguay (2024), Poland (2025), Portugal (2023), Qatar (2023), Russia (2024), Sierra Leone (2023), South Africa (2023), Switzerland (2025), Tajikistan (2025), Türkiye (2024), Turkmenistan (2025), Uganda (2025), Ukraine (2023), USA (2024), Zambia (2025).
NGO Relations Pursuant to Article 71 of the United Nations Charter and ECOSOC Resolution 1996 (31), formal contacts with a number of NGOs, many of which act as observers. [2022/XE1126/**E***]

♦ United Nations Commission on the Status of Women (CSW) 20536

Commission des Nations Unies de la condition de la femme – Comisión de la Condición Jurídica y Social de la Mujer

Exec Sec UN-Women, 220 East 42nd St, New York NY 10017, USA. T. +16467814449. Fax +16467814496.
URL: http://www.unwomen.org/en/csw/

History 21 Jun 1946. Established as a functional commission of *ECOSOC (#05331)*, by Council resolution 11 (II), within the framework of *United Nations (UN, #20515)*. Mandate expanded in 1987, by Council resolution 1987/22. In accordance with General Assembly resolution 50/203, together with General Assembly and ECOSOC and in accordance with their respective mandates and with Assembly resolution 48/162 and other relevant resolutions, constitutes a 3-tiered intergovernmental mechanism playing the primary role in overall policy-making and follow-up and in coordinating implementation and monitoring of the Platform for Action adopted at 4th World Conference of Women, 1995, Beijing (China). Terms of reference modified, 1996, in accordance with the Economic and Social Council resolution 1996/6. Since 2011, functions within *UN Women (#20724)*. **Aims** Prepare recommendations and reports to ECOSOC on promoting women's *rights* in political, economic, civil, social and educational fields; make recommendations to ECOSOC on issues requiring immediate attention in the field of *gender* equality, women's empowerment and women's human rights; follow up progress on implementation of the outcomes of the World Conferences on women, including through regularly reviewing the critical areas of concern in the Beijing Platform for Action and develop its catalytic role in mainstreaming a *gender* perspective in United Nations activities. **Structure** Commission, meeting in annual session, always at UN Headquarters, comprises 45 members elected by ECOSOC for a 4-year term on the basis of: 13 from Africa; 11 from Asia; 4 from Eastern Europe; 9 from Latin America and the Caribbean; 8 from Western Europe and from other states. Bureau, comprising Chairperson and 4 Vice-Chairpersons. Secretariat provided by UN Division for the Advancement of Women, New York NY. **Languages** Arabic, Chinese, English, French, Russian, Spanish. **Staff** 3.00 FTE, paid. **Finance** On the regular budget of the United Nations. **Activities** Plays a central role in monitoring implementation of the Beijing Platform for Action adopted at the 4th World Conference on Women, 1995, and of the further actions and initiatives contained in the outcome document of the 23rd special session of the General Assembly and the declaration adopted at the ten-year review of implementation in 2005. In accordance with its new methods of work (Council resolutions 2006/9 and 2009/15), focuses on one priority theme per year and proposes actions addressed to governments, the UN system and civil society. Also evaluates progress in the implementation of agreed conclusions from a previous session. Discusses an emerging issue affecting the situation of women and reviews progress in mainstreaming in gender perspective at national level, with a particular focus on the priority theme. Resolutions and decisions are brought to the attention of ECOSOC; draft resolutions and draft decisions reviewed by ECOSOC for adoption. **Events** *Session* New York, NY (USA) 2022, *Session* New York, NY (USA) 2021, *Session* New York, NY (USA) 2020, *Session* New York, NY (USA) 2019, *Session* New York, NY (USA) 2018.
Members Representatives of 44 States (one vacancy; terms begin at first meeting of Commission's session and expire at close of session in the year in parentheses), as of 2023:
Afghanistan (2025), Algeria (2026), Argentina (2025), Armenia (2023), Australia (2023), Austria (2025), Bangladesh (2023), Belarus (2023), Brazil (2024), Cape Verde (2026), China (2026), Colombia (2024), Costa Rica (2026), Cuba (2023), Denmark (2024), Dominican Rep (2025), Egypt (2026), Equatorial Guinea (2023), Germany (2023), India (2025), Israel (2025), Japan (2026), Latvia (2025), Lebanon (2026), Malaysia (2023), Mauritania (2026), Mexico (2024), Mongolia (2024), Morocco (2025), Nigeria (2025), Pakistan (2026), Panama (2026), Philippines (2024), Russia (2024), Senegal (2024), Somalia (2024), South Africa (2023), Switzerland (2024), Togo (2023), Trinidad-Tobago (2026), Tunisia (2026), Türkiye (2025), USA (2023), Zambia (2025).
IGO Relations Intergovernmental organizations designated by the Economic and Social Council under rule 79 may also attend the sessions of the Commission as observers. **NGO Relations** Pursuant to Article 71 of the United Nations Charter and ECOSOC Resolution 1996 (31), nongovernmental organizations in consultative status with the Council may participate in the sessions of the Commission as observers. [2023/XE1129/**E***]

- ♦ United Nations Commission on Sustainable Development (inactive)
- ♦ United Nations Committee Against Torture / see Committee Against Torture (#04241)
- ♦ United Nations Committee on Crime Prevention and Control (inactive)
- ♦ United Nations Committee for Development Planning / see United Nations Committee for Development Policy (#20537)

♦ United Nations Committee for Development Policy (CDP) 20537

Comité des politiques de développement

Officer in Charge 405 E 42nd St, Room S-2529, New York NY 10017, USA. T. +12129634752. Fax +12129631061. E-mail: cdp@un.org.
URL: http://cdp.un.org/

History 15 Aug 1964. Established by resolution 1035 (XXXVII) of *ECOSOC (#05331)*, of which it is a subsidiary body. Original terms of reference contained in ECOSOC resolution 1079 (XXXIX), 28 Jul 1965, have been modified under subsequent resolutions. Current title adopted 1998, by ECOSOC resolution 1998/46. Former names and other names: *United Nations Committee for Development Planning* – former (15 Aug 1964 to 31 Jul 1998). **Aims** Provide independent expert advice to ECOSOC on a wide range of issues related to the 2030 Agenda for Sustainable Development; review the status of least developed countries (LDCs) and monitor their progress during and after graduation from the LDC category. **Structure** Plenary (annual); Committee of 24 members, nominated by Secretary-General and appointed by ECOSOC for a period of three years; Secretariat, which is part of the Economic Analysis and Policy Division (EAPD) of the Department of Economic and Social Affairs (DESA). **Languages** Arabic, Chinese, English, French, Russian, Spanish. **Staff** 7.00 FTE, paid. Voluntary Committee members. **Finance** Financed through UN Regular Budget. **Activities** Every three years, reviews the least developed country (LDC) category and recommends to ECOSOC and the UN General Assembly which countries should be included into or graduated from the list. The review is based on quantitative criteria developed by the CDP as well as country-specific additional information; monitors countries that are graduating or have graduated from the LDC list and alerts ECOSOC of any sign of deterioration of their development progress; advises ECOSOC on its annual theme and on emerging issues relevant for implementation of the 2030 Agenda for Sustainable Development and presents its findings at the High Level Segment of ECOSOC, the High Level Political Forum and related events. **Events** *Plenary session* New York, NY (USA) 2021, *Session* New York, NY (USA) 2019, *Session* New York, NY (USA) 2018, *Session* New York, NY (USA) 2017, *Session* New York, NY (USA) 2010. **Publications** *CDP Background Paper Series*; *CDP Policy Review Series*. Annual Report to ECOSOC; policy notes; research volumes.
Members 2019-2021, experts from 24 countries:
Bangladesh, Brazil, China, Colombia, Ethiopia, France, Germany, India, Italy, Japan, Korea Rep, Mexico, Netherlands, Nigeria, Papua New Guinea, Russia, Serbia, South Africa, Sudan, Trinidad-Tobago, Uganda, UK, USA, Zambia.
NGO Relations Does not have formal contacts with NGO's but takes on board views stemming from the broad development spectrum (including NGO's) when preparing advice to ECOSOC. [2021.08.30/XE1144/**E***]

♦ United Nations Committee on Economic, Social and Cultural Rights (CESCR) 20538

Comité des droits économiques, sociaux et culturels – Comité de Derechos Económicos, Sociales y Culturales

Secretariat UNOG-OHCHR, 1211 Geneva 10, Switzerland. T. +41229171234. Fax +41229179008. E-mail: cescr@ohchr.org.
URL: http://www.ohchr.org/en/hrbodies/cescr/

History 3 May 1978. Established, by decision 1978/10 of *ECOSOC (#05331)*. Composition, organization and administrative arrangements modified, 6 May 1982, by resolution 1982/33. Current name adopted under ECOSOC resolution 1985/17, 28 May 1985. Comes within the framework of *United Nations (UN, #20515)*, functioning under *International Covenant on Economic, Social and Cultural Rights (ICESCR, 1966)*. Based at *United Nations Office at Geneva (UNOG, #20597)*. A treaty body of *Office of the United Nations High Commissioner for Human Rights (OHCHR, #17697)*. Former names and other names: *Sessional Working Group on the Implementation of the International Covenant on Economic, Social and Cultural Rights* – former (6 May 1982); *Sessional Working Group of Governmental Experts on the Implementation of the International Covenant on Economic, Social and Cultural Rights* – former (6 May 1982 to 28 May 1985). **Aims** Monitor implementation of the International Covenant on Economic, Social and Cultural Rights; examine individual complaints and conduct enquiries under optional protocol procedures; adopt General Comments (interpretations) on articles of the Covenant. **Structure** Committee comprises 18 members serving in their personal capacity, elected by ECOSOC from experts in the field nominated by States Parties to the Covenant, with 15 seats equally distributed among regional groups plus 3 seats in accordance with increases in the number of States Parties to the Covenant per regional group; extraordinary sessions held when workload heavy. Bureau; Pre-sessional Working Group. **Activities** Monitoring/evaluation. **Events** *Session* Geneva (Switzerland) 2021, *Session* Geneva (Switzerland) 2020, *Session* Geneva (Switzerland) 2020, *Session* Geneva (Switzerland) 2019, *Session* Geneva (Switzerland) 2019.
Members Experts (18) from 18 countries (figure in brackets indicates expiry date):
Belgium (2022), Brazil (2022), China (2020), Colombia (2022), Egypt (2020), El Salvador (2022), Germany (2020), India (2022), Jordan (2020), Korea Rep (2022), Mauritius (2022), Nigeria (2022), Poland (2020), Romania (2020), Russia (2022), South Africa (2020), Spain (2020), Suriname (2020).
States Parties to Covenant as of Aug 2020 (171):
Afghanistan, Albania, Algeria, Angola, Antigua-Barbuda, Argentina, Armenia, Australia, Austria, Azerbaijan, Bahamas, Bahrain, Bangladesh, Barbados, Belarus, Belgium, Belize, Benin, Bolivia, Bosnia-Herzegovina, Brazil, Bulgaria, Burkina Faso, Burundi, Cambodia, Cameroon, Canada, Cape Verde, Central African Rep, Chad, Chile, China, Colombia, Congo Brazzaville, Congo DR, Costa Rica, Côte d'Ivoire, Croatia, Cyprus, Czechia, Denmark, Djibouti, Dominica, Dominican Rep, Ecuador, Egypt, El Salvador, Equatorial Guinea, Eritrea, Estonia, Eswatini, Ethiopia, Fiji, Finland, France, Gabon, Gambia, Georgia, Germany, Ghana, Greece, Grenada, Guatemala, Guinea, Guinea-Bissau, Guyana, Haiti, Honduras, Hungary, Iceland, India, Indonesia, Iran Islamic Rep, Iraq, Ireland, Israel, Italy, Jamaica, Japan, Jordan, Kazakhstan, Kenya, Korea DPR, Korea Rep, Kuwait, Kyrgyzstan, Laos, Latvia, Lebanon, Lesotho, Liberia, Libya, Liechtenstein, Lithuania, Luxembourg, Madagascar, Malawi, Maldives, Mali, Malta, Marshall Is, Mauritania, Mauritius, Mexico, Moldova, Monaco, Mongolia, Montenegro, Morocco, Myanmar, Namibia, Nepal, Netherlands, New Zealand, Nicaragua, Niger, Nigeria, North Macedonia, Norway, Oman, Pakistan, Palestine, Panama, Papua New Guinea, Paraguay, Peru, Philippines, Poland, Portugal, Qatar, Romania, Russia, Rwanda, San Marino, Sao Tomé-Principe, Senegal, Serbia, Seychelles, Sierra Leone, Slovakia, Slovenia, Solomon Is, Somalia, South Africa, Spain, Sri Lanka, St Vincent-Grenadines, Sudan, Suriname, Sweden, Switzerland, Syrian AR, Tajikistan, Tanzania UR, Thailand, Timor-Leste, Togo, Trinidad-Tobago, Tunisia, Türkiye, Turkmenistan, Uganda, UK, Ukraine, Uruguay, Uzbekistan, Venezuela, Vietnam, Yemen, Zambia, Zimbabwe. [2021.03.10/XE0199/v/**E***]

- ♦ United Nations Committee on the Elimination of Racial Discrimination / see Committee on the Elimination of Racial Discrimination (#04251)

♦ United Nations Committee on the Exercise of the Inalienable Rights of the Palestinian People (CEIRPP) 20539

Comité des Nations Unies pour l'exercice des droits inaliénables du peuple palestinien – Comité para el Ejercicio de los Derechos Inalienables del Pueblo Palestino

Chairman c/o UN Secretariat, Div for Palestinian Rights, 730 Third Ave, Room TB-08008, New York NY 10017, USA. T. +12129638231. Fax +12129634199.
URL: https://www.un.org/unispal/

History 10 Nov 1975. Established by resolution 3376 (XXX) of the General Assembly of the *United Nations (UN, #20515)*. **Aims** Promote the realization of the inalienable rights of the Palestinian people; support the Middle East peace process; mobilize international support for and assistance to the Palestinian people. **Structure** Committee; Bureau. **Activities** Convenes international meetings and conferences, including meetings with civil society, in all regions of the world, with the participation, inter alia, of political personalities, representatives of Governments and intergovernmental organizations, United Nations officials, parliamentarians, academics and representatives of the media. Guides publications programme and other information activities. Conducts annual training programme for staff of the Palestinian Authority. Organizes International Day of Solidarity with the Palestinian People, 29 Nov. **Events** *International Conference on the Question of Jerusalem* 2021, *United Nations Round Table on Legal Aspects of the Question of Palestine* Amman (Jordan) 2016, *International Conference on the Question of Jerusalem* Dakar (Senegal) 2016, *Session* New York, NY (USA) 2016, *International Conference on the Question of Jerusalem* Jakarta (Indonesia) 2015. **Publications** *CEIRPP Newsletter*. *Studies and Publications on the Question of Palestine* – and other publications – prepared by the Division for Palestinian Rights. Publications prepared by the Department of Public Information (DPI). **Information Services** *United Nations Information System on the Question of Palestine (UNISPAL)* – containing over 18,000 documents.
Members States (25):
Afghanistan, Belarus, Bolivia, Cuba, Cyprus, Ecuador, Guinea, Guyana, India, Indonesia, Laos, Madagascar, Malaysia, Mali, Malta, Namibia, Nicaragua, Nigeria, Pakistan, Senegal, Sierra Leone, South Africa, Tunisia, Türkiye, Venezuela.
Observers (24) – 21 States and 3 international organizations:
Algeria, Bangladesh, Bulgaria, China, Egypt, Iraq, Jordan, Kuwait, Lebanon, Libya, Mauritania, Morocco, Niger, Palestine, Qatar, Saudi Arabia, Sri Lanka, Syrian AR, United Arab Emirates, Vietnam, Yemen.
African Union (AU, #00488); *League of Arab States (LAS, #16420)*; *Organisation of Islamic Cooperation (OIC, #17813)*.
IGO Relations Cooperates with: *African Union (AU, #00488)*; *European Union (EU, #08967)*; *League of Arab States (LAS, #16420)*; *Non-Aligned Movement (NAM, #17146)*; *Organisation of Islamic Cooperation (OIC, #17813)*. **NGO Relations** About 1,000 NGOs accredited with the Committee. [2020/XE0599/y/**E***]

♦ United Nations Committee of Experts on Global Geospatial Information Management (UN-GGIM) 20540

Comité d'experts des Nations Unies sur la gestion de l'information géospatiale à l'échelle mondiale – Comité de Expertos sobre la Gestión Mundial de la Información Geoespacial

Contact UN Statistics Div, Two UN Plaza DC2-1675, New York NY 10017, USA. Fax +12129639851. E-mail: ggim@un.org.
URL: https://ggim.un.org/

History Jul 2011. Established when resolution (2011/24) adopted by *ECOSOC (#05331)* to create UN-GGIM, following report of the Secretary-General (E/2011/89). **Aims** Play a leading role in setting the agenda for the development of global geospatial information and promote its use to address key global challenges; provide a forum to liaise and coordinate among Member States, and among international organizations, civil society and private sector. **Structure** Bureau. Regional entities: *Regional Committee of United Nations Global Geospatial Information Management for Asia and the Pacific (UN-GGIM-AP, #18766)*; *Regional Committee of*

the UN on Global Geospatial Information Management for the Americas (UN-GGIM Americas, #18765); UN-GGIM for Arab States; UN-GGIM for Europe; UN-GGIM AFRICA.Functional Groups. Thematic Networks, include: *UN-GGO: Geospatial Societies (UN-GGIM GS, #20324)*. **Languages** Arabic, Chinese, English, French, Russian, Spanish. **Events** *Session* New York, NY (USA) 2021, *Session* New York, NY (USA) 2020, *Session* New York, NY (USA) 2020, *Plenary Meeting* Brussels (Belgium) 2019, *Session* New York, NY (USA) 2019. **Publications** *Future Trends in Geospatial Information Management – The Five to Ten Year Vision*; *The Global Fundamental Geospatial Data Themes*; *The Global Statistical Geospatial Framework (GSGF)*; *The Integrated Geospatial Information Framework (IGIF)*; *The Strategic Framework on Geospatial Information and Services for Disasters*. **IGO Relations** *United Nations Group of Experts on Geographical Names (UNGEGN, #20569)*; *United Nations Regional Cartographic Conference for the Americas (UNRCCA)*; *United Nations Regional Cartographic Conference for Asia and the Pacific (UNRCC-AP)*. Partner organizations: *Group on Earth Observations (GEO, #10735)*; *International Hydrographic Organization (IHO, #13825)*. UN partner agencies:
- *Statistical Institute for Asia and the Pacific (SIAP, #19972)*;
- *UNEP (#20299)*;
- *UNCTAD (#20285)*;
- *UNDP (#20292)*;
- *UNHCR (#20327)*;
- *UNICEF (#20332)*;
- *United Nations Economic Commission for Africa (ECA, #20554)*;
- *United Nations Economic Commission for Europe (UNECE, #20555)* – Statistics Division;
- *United Nations Economic Commission for Latin America and the Caribbean (ECLAC, #20556)* – Statistics Division;
- *United Nations Economic and Social Commission for Asia and the Pacific (ESCAP, #20557)* – Statistics Division;
- *United Nations Economic and Social Commission for Western Asia (ESCWA, #20558)*;
- *United Nations Human Settlements Programme (UN-Habitat, #20572)*;
- *United Nations Population Fund (UNFPA, #20612)*;
- *United Nations Research Institute for Social Development (UNRISD, #20623)*;
- *World Food Programme (WFP, #21510)*.

NGO Relations Partner organizations: *EuroGeographics (#05684)*; *European Umbrella Organization for Geographical Information (EUROGI, #08964)*; *International Federation of Surveyors (FIG, #13561)*; *International Association of Geodesy (IAG, #11914)*; *International Cartographic Association (ICA, #12446)*; *International Geographical Union (IGU, #13713)*; *International Organization for Standardization (ISO, #14473)*; *International Society for Photogrammetry and Remote Sensing (ISPRS, #15362)*; *UN-GGO: Geospatial Societies (UN-GGIM GS, #20324)*; *Open Geospatial Consortium (OGC, #17752)*. [2022/XJ7860/**E***]

♦ United Nations Committee of Experts on International Cooperation in Tax Matters 20541

Comité d'experts de la coopération internationale en matière fiscale

Contact FFD Office, 2 UN PLaza, DC2-2172, New York NY 10017, USA. T. +19173675734. Fax +12129630443. E-mail: taxffdoffice@un.org – taxcommittee@un.org.

URL: https://www.un.org/development/desa/financing/what-we-do/ECOSOC/tax-committee/tax-committee-home

History 1968. Established within the framework of *United Nations (UN, #20515)*, pursuant to *ECOSOC (#05331)* resolution 1273 (XLIII) of 4 Aug 1967. Name changed under resolution 1980/13. Present title adopted under resolution 2004/69. Former names and other names: *Group of Experts on Tax Treaties between Developed and Developing Countries* – former (1968 to 1980); *United Nations Ad Hoc Group of Experts on International Cooperation in Tax Matters* – former (1980 to Nov 2004). **Aims** Review and update as necessary the *'United Nations Model Double Taxation Convention between Developed and Developing Countries'* and the *'Manual for the Negotiation of Bilateral Tax Treaties between Developed and Developing Countries'*; provide a framework for dialogue with a view to enhancing and promoting international tax cooperation among national tax authorities; consider how new and emerging issues could affect international cooperation in tax matters and develop assessments, commentaries and appropriate recommendations; make recommendations on capacity-building and provision of technical assistance to developing countries and countries with economies in transition; give special attention to developing countries and countries with economies in transition in dealing with all the above issues. **Structure** Committee of 25 experts. Subcommittees. Trust Fund for International Cooperation in Tax Matters (Tax Trust Fund), set up Jul 2006. **Activities** Guidance/assistance/consulting; monitoring/evaluation; networking/liaising. **Events** *Session* New York, NY (USA) 2020, *Session* New York, NY (USA) 2020, *Session* Geneva (Switzerland) 2019, *Session* Geneva (Switzerland) 2011, *Session* Geneva (Switzerland) 2009. [2020/XE1145/**E***]

♦ United Nations Committee of Experts on Public Administration (CEPA) 20542

Contact Division for Public Institutions and Digital Government, UN DESA, Two UN Plaza (DC2-17th floor), New York NY 10017, USA. T. +12129632764. E-mail: dpidg@un.org.

URL: https://publicadministration.un.org/en/Intergovernmental-Support/Committee-of-Experts-on-Public-Administration

History 24 May 1967. Founded by resolution 1199 (XLII) of *ECOSOC (#05331)*. Subsequent resolutions call for convening of meetings. Current name adopted 2002, by resolution 2001/45 of ECOSOC. Former names and other names: *Meeting of the Group of Experts of the United Nations Programme in Public Administration and Finance* – former. **Aims** Study and make recommendations to improve governance and public administration structures and processes for development. **Structure** Committee comprises 24 experts (serving four year terms) nominated by Secretary-General in consultation with Member States, and approved by ECOSOC. Committee meets annually at UN Headquarters in New York. **Languages** Arabic, Chinese, English, French, Russian, Spanish. **Staff** 3.00 FTE, paid. **Activities** Awards/prizes/competitions. **Events** *Session* New York, NY (USA) 2023, *Session* New York, NY (USA) 2022, *Session* New York, NY (USA) 2021, *Session* New York, NY (USA) 2020, *Session* New York, NY (USA) 2019. **Publications** *UNPAN Newsletter* (4 a year); *United Nations Global E-Government Survey* (every 2 years); *World Public Sector Report* (every 3 years). Meeting proceedings; papers; reports; directories; manuals. **Information Services** *Worldwide Directory and Information Service*. **Members** Not a membership organization. **IGO Relations** Observers – UN regional commissions, specialized agencies and Bretton Woods institutions: *FAO (#09260)*; *ILO (#11123)*; *UNESCO (#20322)*; *UNIDO (#20336)*; *United Nations Economic Commission for Africa (ECA, #20554)*; *United Nations Economic Commission for Europe (UNECE, #20555)*; *United Nations Economic Commission for Latin America and the Caribbean (ECLAC, #20556)*; *United Nations Economic and Social Commission for Asia and the Pacific (ESCAP, #20557)*; *United Nations Economic and Social Commission for Western Asia (ESCWA, #20558)*; *UNDP (#20292)*; *UNESCO (#20322)*; *United Nations Interregional Crime and Justice Research Institute (UNICRI, #20580)*; *WHO (#20950)*; *The World Bank Group (#21218)*. **NGO Relations** Observers: selected regional and international NGOs (not specified). [2022.10.27/XF3808/**F***]

♦ United Nations Committee of Experts on the Transport of Dangerous Goods / see United Nations Committee of Experts on the Transport of Dangerous Goods and on the Globally Harmonized System of Classification and Labelling of Chemicals (#20543)

♦ United Nations Committee of Experts on the Transport of Dangerous Goods and on the Globally Harmonized System of Classification and Labelling of Chemicals (Committee of Experts on TDG and GHS) 20543

Comité d'experts du transport des marchandises dangereuses et du Système général harmonisé de classification et d'étiquetage des produits chimiques – Comité de Expertos en Transporte de Mercancias Peligrosas y en el Sistema Globalmente Armonizado de Clasificación y Etiquetado de Productos Quimicos

Chief – Road Safety/Dangerous Goods UNECE, Palais des Nations, Office 418, 1211 Geneva 10, Switzerland. T. +41229172402.

URL: http://www.unece.org/trans/danger/danger.htm

History 15 Apr 1953, as *United Nations Committee of Experts on the Transport of Dangerous Goods*, by resolution 468G (XV) of *ECOSOC (#05331)*. Current title adopted, 2001, on reconfiguration of the Committee and its sub-committees in accordance with ECOSOC Resolution 1999/65. **Aims** Make recommendations to governments and to intergovernmental organizations on ensuring safe and *environmentally* sound conditions of transport of dangerous goods and on facilitating *trade* in such goods, through uniform *legislation* applicable to the various modes of transport worldwide; make available a globally harmonized system for classification and labelling of chemicals for worldwide use and application in all sectors and keep it up to date. **Structure** Committee of Experts (meets every 2 years); Sub-Committees (2). Secretariat services provided by Transport Division of *United Nations Economic Commission for Europe (UNECE, #20555)*. **Languages** Arabic, Chinese, English, French, Russian, Spanish. **Finance** United Nations regular budget. **Events** *Biennial Session* Geneva (Switzerland) 2016, *Biennial Session* Geneva (Switzerland) 2010, *Biennial Session* Geneva (Switzerland) 2008, *Biennial Session* Geneva (Switzerland) 2006, *Biennial Session* Geneva (Switzerland) 2004. **Publications** *Globally Harmonized System of Classification and Labelling of Chemicals (GHS)*; *UN Recommendations on the Transport of Dangerous Goods – Manual of Tests and Criteria*; *UN Recommendations on the Transport of Dangerous Goods – Model Regulations*.

Members Experts designated by governments of 40 countries:
Argentina, Australia, Austria, Belgium, Brazil, Canada, China, Czechia, Denmark, Finland, France, Germany, Greece, India, Iran Islamic Rep, Ireland, Italy, Japan, Kenya, Korea Rep, Mexico, Morocco, Netherlands, New Zealand, Nigeria, Norway, Poland, Portugal, Qatar, Russia, Senegal, Serbia, South Africa, Spain, Sweden, Switzerland, UK, Ukraine, USA, Zambia.
Other participating countries (under Rule 72 of ECOSOC Rules of Procedures) (12):
Algeria, Bahamas, Bulgaria, Gambia, Indonesia, Namibia, Philippines, Romania, Slovakia, Slovenia, Thailand, Tunisia.

IGO Relations Links with: *United Nations Office at Geneva (UNOG, #20597)*. Organizations involved in the work of the Committee:
- *Central Commission for the Navigation of the Rhine (CCNR, #03687)*;
- *Commission du Danube (CD, #04210)*;
- *European Commission (EC, #06633)*;
- *FAO (#09260)*;
- *ILO (#11123)*;
- *Organisation intergouvernementale pour les transports internationaux ferroviaires (OTIF, #17807)*;
- *International Atomic Energy Agency (IAEA, #12294)*;
- *International Civil Aviation Organization (ICAO, #12581)*;
- *International Maritime Organization (IMO, #14102)*;
- *International Programme on Chemical Safety (IPCS, #14650)*;
- *OECD (#17693)*;
- *Organisation for the Prohibition of Chemical Weapons (OPCW, #17823)*;
- *Organisation for Cooperation between Railways (OSJD, #17803)*;
- *UNEP (#20299)*;
- *United Nations Economic Commission for Africa (ECA, #20554)*;
- *United Nations Economic Commission for Latin America and the Caribbean (ECLAC, #20556)*;
- *United Nations Economic and Social Commission for Asia and the Pacific (ESCAP, #20557)*;
- *United Nations Economic and Social Commission for Western Asia (ESCWA, #20558)*;
- *United Nations Institute for Training and Research (UNITAR, #20576)*;
- *Universal Postal Union (UPU, #20682)*;
- *WHO (#20950)*.

NGO Relations Organizations involved in the work of the Committee:
- *Conseil européen de l'industrie chimique (CEFIC, #04687)*;
- *Conseil européen de l'industrie des peintures, des encres d'imprimerie et des couleurs d'art (CEPE, #04688)*;
- *Cosmetics Europe – The Personal Care Association (#04852)*;
- *CropLife International (#04966)*;
- *CTIF International Association of Fire and Rescue Services (#04979)*;
- *Dangerous Goods Advisory Council (DGAC, #05001)*;
- *European Association of Automotive Suppliers (CLEPA, #05948)*;
- *European Biosafety Association (EBSA, #06343)*;
- *European Cylinder Makers Association (ECMA, #06878)*;
- *European Industrial Gases Association (EIGA, #07525)*;
- *European Portable Battery Association (EPBA, #08255)*;
- *Fédération Européenne des Aérosols (FEA, #09557)*;
- *Fédération internationale des associations de transitaires et assimilés (FIATA, #09610)*;
- *Fertilizers Europe (#09738)*;
- *Global Express Association (GEA, #10351)*;
- *Industrial Federation Paints and Coats of Mercosul (IFPCM, #11175)*;
- *International Air Transport Association (IATA, #11614)*;
- *International Association for Soaps, Detergents and Maintenance Products (#12166)*;
- *International Cargo Handling Coordination Association (ICHCA, inactive)*;
- *International Chamber of Commerce (ICC, #12534)*;
- *International Chamber of Shipping (ICS, #12535)*;
- *International Chemical Trade Association (ICTA, #12543)*;
- *International Confederation of Container Reconditioners (ICCR, #12854)*;
- *International Confederation of Drum Manufacturers (ICDM, #12857)*;
- *International Confederation of Plastics Packaging Manufacturers (ICPP)*;
- *International Council of Chemical Associations (ICCA, #13003)*;
- *International Council of Intermediate Bulk Container Associations (ICIBCA)*;
- *International Council on Mining and Metals (ICMM, #13048)*;
- *International Dangerous Goods and Containers Association (IDGCA)*;
- *International Electrotechnical Commission (IEC, #13255)*;
- *International Federation of Air Line Pilots' Associations (IFALPA, #13349)*;
- *International Fibre Drum Institute (IFDI)*;
- *International Occupational Hygiene Association (IOHA, #14391)*;
- *International Organization for Standardization (ISO, #14473)*;
- *International Petroleum Industry Environmental Conservation Association (IPIECA, #14562)*;
- *International Road Transport Union (IRU, #14761)*;
- *International Tank Container Organization (ITCO, #15654)*;
- *International Union of Railways (#15813)*;
- *International Vessel Operators Dangerous Goods Association (IVODGA)*;
- *Liquid Gas Europe (#16488)*;
- National organizations;
- *Oil Companies' European Association for Environment, Health and Safety in Refining and Distribution (CONCAWE, #17708)*;
- *RECHARGE (#18627)*;
- *World Coatings Council (#21283)*;
- *World Federation for Culture Collections (WFCC, #21424)*;
- *World Nuclear Transport Institute (WNTI, #21676)*. [2019.07.29/XE1146/**E***]

♦ United Nations Committee on Negotiations with Intergovernmental Agencies 20544

Comité chargé des négociations avec les institutions intergouvernementales

Contact Office for ECOSOC Support and Coordination, Dept of Economic and Social Affairs, Room DC 1-1428, UN Headquarters, New York NY 10017, USA.

URL: http://www.un.org/en/ecosoc/about/subsidiary.shtml

History Established 16 Feb 1946, by resolution 11 (I) of *ECOSOC (#05331)*. A standing body of ECOSOC. **Aims** Carry out negotiations with intergovernmental agencies with a view to bringing them into relationship with the United Nations in accordance with Articles 57 and 63 of the Charter. **Structure** Membership and composition decided by ECOSOC when it decides that the Committee should enter into negotiations with one or more intergovernmental agencies. [2016/XE2548/**E***]

♦ United Nations Committee on Non-governmental Organizations 20545

Chair Permanent Mission of Uruguay to the UN, 866 United Nations Plaza, Ste 322, New York NY 10017, USA. T. +12127528240. Fax +12129639248.

URL: http://csonet.org/?menu=105/

History 21 Jun 1946, by resolution 3 (II) of *ECOSOC (#05331)*. Current procedures and criteria established by ECOSOC resolution 1996/31, 25 Jul 1996. **Aims** Consider applications for general and special *consultative status* and for listing on the Roster made by *NGOs* to ECOSOC and requests for change in status; make recommendations on these to ECOSOC; monitor the evolving relationships between NGOs and the United Nations; consider referrals from ECOSOC and its commissions on matters concerning NGOs. **Structure** Committee meets annually for 3 weeks and also informally before each session of ECOSOC. **Languages** Arabic, Chinese, English, French, Russian, Spanish. **Activities** Examines the 4-yearly reports submitted by NGOs in consultative status regarding the support their activities make to the work of the United Nations. Consults with these NGOs on matters within their competence which may or may not be on the provisional agenda of ECOSOC. **Events** *Regular Session* New York, NY (USA) 2015, *Resumed Session* New York, NY (USA) 2015, *Regular Session* New York, NY (USA) 2014, *Resumed Session* New York, NY (USA) 2014, *Resumed session* New York, NY (USA) 2010. **Publications** *Calendar of Meetings Open to Participation of NGOs in*

Consultative Status and on the Roster; List of Non-Governmental Organizations in Consultative Status and on the Roster with the Economic and Social Council.
Members For 4-year term commencing 1 Jan 2015, governments of 19 countries:
Azerbaijan, Burundi, China, Cuba, Greece, Guinea, India, Iran Islamic Rep, Israel, Mauritania, Nicaragua, Pakistan, Russia, South Africa, Sudan, Türkiye, Uruguay, USA, Venezuela.
NGO Relations *Global 2000 – 2010 International* is member and consultant. [2017.06.27/XE1138/**E***]

♦ United Nations Committee on the Peaceful Uses of Outer Space / see Committee on the Peaceful Uses of Outer Space (#04277)

♦ United Nations Committee for Programme and Coordination (CPC) . 20546

Comité du programme et de la coordination – Comité del Programa y de la Coordinación
Sec UN Headquarters, First Avenue at 46th St, L-0321, New York NY 10017, USA. T. +12129632021. Fax +12129630360. E-mail: cpc@un.org.
URL: https://www.un.org/en/ga/cpc/
History 1962. Established under resolution 920 (XXXIV) of *ECOSOC (#05331)* of the *United Nations (UN, #20515)*. Resolution 2008 (LX) (1976) defines terms of reference. Reports to UN General Assembly and to ECOSOC. **Aims** Examine the totality of the Secretary-General's work programme giving particular attention to programme changes arising out of decisions adopted by intergovernmental organs and conferences or suggested by the Secretary-General. **Structure** Committee meets every year, once for 4 weeks every budget year and twice (4 weeks and 2 weeks) in plan years. Members (34) are elected for 3-year terms by UN General Assembly based on ECOSOC's recommendations, on the basis of: 9 from Africa; 7 from Asia; 7 from Latin America and the Caribbean; 7 from West Europe and other states; 4 from Eastern Europe. **Finance** On the UN regular budget. Annual budget: 900,000 USD. **Activities** Under resolution 2008 (LX), 1976, functions as main subsidiary organ for planning, programming and coordination of ECOSOC and the UN General Assembly Monitors programme implementation under Article VI of *'Regulations and Rules Governing Programme Planning, the Programme Aspects of the Budget, the Monitoring of Implementation and the Methods of Evaluation'*, cooperating with Advisory Committee on Administrative and Budgetary Questions and *Joint Inspection Unit of the United Nations (JIU, #16133)*. Activities and programmes are considered on a sector-by-sector basis and a periodical review appraises implementation of important legislative decisions. **Events** *Organizational session* New York, NY (USA) 2010, *Session* New York, NY (USA) 2010, *Organizational session* New York, NY (USA) 2009, *Session* New York, NY (USA) 2009, *Session* New York, NY (USA) 2008. **Publications** Annual Report. **Members** Governments of 34 countries. Membership countries not specified. **IGO Relations** *UNESCO (#20322)*; *United Nations System Chief Executives Board for Coordination (CEB, #20636)*; *United Nations Human Settlements Programme (UN-Habitat, #20572)*; *United Nations System-wide Special Initiative on Africa (SIA, inactive)*. [2011/XE1028/**E***]

♦ United Nations Committee on Relations with the Host Country 20547

Comité des relations avec le pays hôte
Permanent Representative Permanent Mission of the Republic of Cyprus to the UN, 15 West 38th Street, 11th Floor, New York NY 10018, USA. T. +12124816023. E-mail: unmission@mfa.gov.cy.
History 15 Dec 1971. Established, by resolution 2819 (XXVI) of General Assembly of the *United Nations (UN, #20515)*, replacing *'Informal Joint Committee on Host Country Relations'* which had been set up under resolution 2618 (XXIV) of 17 Dec 1969. **Aims** Deal with the full range of issues concerning the relationship between the host country and the United Nations community. **Structure** Committee comprises representative from 19 Member States; Bureau. **Languages** Arabic, Chinese, English, French, Russian, Spanish. **Staff** Serviced by officials of UN Secretariat. **Publications** Annual report.
Members Governments of 19 Member States of the United Nations:
Bulgaria, Canada, China, Costa Rica, Côte d'Ivoire, Cuba, Cyprus, France, Honduras, Hungary, Iraq, Libya, Malaysia, Mali, Russia, Senegal, Spain, UK, USA. [2021/XE1415/**E***]

♦ United Nations Committee on the Rights of the Child / see Committee on the Rights of the Child (#04283)
♦ United Nations Communications Group (inactive)

♦ United Nations Compensation Commission (UNCC) 20548

Commission d'indemnisation de l'ONU
Secretariat Villa la Pelouse, Palais des Nations, 1211 Geneva 10, Switzerland. T. +41229173600. Fax +41229170069. E-mail: unccwebmaster@un.org.
URL: http://www.uncc.ch/
History 20 May 1991. Established by resolution of *United Nations Security Council (UNSC, #20625)*, as a subsidiary organ of the Security Council, to administer *United Nations Compensation Fund – Fonds d'indemnisation de l'ONU*. Comes within the framework of *United Nations (UN, #20515)*, based at *United Nations Office at Geneva (UNOG, #20597)*. As a subsidiary organ of the Security Council, operates within the framework of the Council's resolutions, particularly resolutions 687 (1991), 692 (1991), 1483 (2003), 1546 (2004) and 1956 (2010), that together established the Commission, its jurisdiction, its policy guidelines and its financing. Former names and other names: *Commission de compensation de l'ONU* – former. **Aims** Process claims; administer the UN Compensation Fund and ensure payment of successful *claims* for any direct loss, *damage*, including *environmental* damage and the *depletion* of *natural resources*, or *injury* to foreign governments, nationals and corporations, as a result of Iraq's unlawful invasion and occupation of Kuwait in accordance with Security Council resolution 687 (1991). **Structure** Governing Council (currently holds 2 formal sessions a year), consisting of the 15 members of the Security Council (5 permanent and 10 non-permanent), from which a President and 2 Vice-Presidents are elected (2-year terms). Secretariat, headed by Executive Secretary. **Finance** Source: Until Nov 2017, 5 % of proceeds of sales of Iraqi petroleum and petroleum products were paid into the Compensation Fund in accordance with Security Council resolution 1483 (2003), adopted May 2003. Reaffirmed in subsequent resolutions. with adoption of Governing Council decision 276 (2017), percentage set at 0.5 % for 2018; at 1.5 % for 2019; at 3 % for 2020, with rate remaining at 3 % until the outstanding compensation has been paid in full.
Activities The Commission accepted for filing claims of individuals, corporations and governments, submitted by some 100 governments, as well 13 international organizations for individuals who were not in a position to have their claims filed by a government. Since 1991, it received about 2.7 million claims seeking a total of about US$ 325,500 million in compensation. Legal responsibility and liability of Iraq for losses and damage was established by the Security Council and expressly accepted by the Government of Iraq. The Commission is thus neither a court nor a tribunal with an elaborate adversarial process. Rather, it was created as a claims resolution facility that could make determinations on a large number of claims in a reasonable time. As such, it operates more in an administrative manner than in a litigation format. Claims processing procedures were prescribed by the Secretary-General and were further elaborated by the Governing Council in a number of its decisions, which have been implemented by the panels of Commissioners.
Processing of claims concluded mid-2007. Nineteen panels of commissioners reviewed and evaluated submitted claims and reported recommendations to Governing Council. Total compensation awarded: US$ 52,400 million. Since 2007, principal areas of activity: servicing Governing Council; payment of outstanding awards; management of Follow-up Programme for Environmental Awards. As of 2020, paid out about US 49800000000 to successful claimants.
Events *Session* Geneva (Switzerland) 2011, *Session* Geneva (Switzerland) 2010, *Session* Geneva (Switzerland) 2009, *Session* Geneva (Switzerland) 2009, *Session* Geneva (Switzerland) 2007. **Publications** *La Commission d'Indemnisation des Nations Unies et le Droit de la Responsibilité* (2001) by Kolliopoulos Alexandros; *The United Nations Compensation Commission – a Handbook* (1999) by Marco Frigessi di Rattalma and Tullio Treves; *War in the Gulf, 1990-1991: The Iraq-Kuwait Conflict and Its Implications* (1997) by M Khadduri and E Ghareeb; *Nazioni Unite e danni derivanti dalla guerra del Golfo* (1995) by M Frigessi di Rattalma; *The United Nations Compensation Commission* (1995); *The Gulf Conflict 1990-1991: Diplomacy and War in the New World Order* (1992) by L Freedman and E Karsh; *The United Nations and the Iraq-Kuwait Conflict* (1990-1996). International Legal Materials; International Law Reports. [2011.11.17/XK0230/**E***]

♦ United Nations Conciliation Commission for Palestine (no recent information)
♦ United Nations Conference on Disarmament Issues (meeting series)
♦ United Nations Conference on Environment and Development (meeting series)
♦ United Nations Conference on the Law of the Sea (inactive)
♦ United Nations Conference on the Standardization of Geographical Names / see United Nations Group of Experts on Geographical Names (#20569)
♦ United Nations Conference on Trade and Development (#20285)
♦ United Nations Convention Against Corruption (2003 treaty)
♦ United Nations Convention against Illicit Traffic in Narcotic Drugs and Psychotropic Substances (1988 treaty)
♦ United Nations Convention Against Transnational Organized Crime (2000 treaty)
♦ United Nations Convention on the Assignment of Receivables in International Trade (2001 treaty)
♦ United Nations Convention on the Carriage of Goods by Sea (1978 treaty)
♦ United Nations Convention to Combat Desertification (1994 treaty)
♦ United Nations Convention on Conditions for Registration of Ships (1986 treaty)
♦ United Nations Convention on Contracts for the International Carriage of Goods Wholly or Partly by Sea (2008 treaty)
♦ United Nations Convention on Contracts for the International Sale of Goods (1980 treaty)
♦ United Nations Convention on Independent Guarantees and Stand-by Letters of Credit (1995 treaty)
♦ United Nations Convention on International Bills of Exchange and International Promissory Notes (1988 treaty)
♦ United Nations Convention on International Multimodal Transport of Goods (1980 treaty)
♦ United Nations Convention on International Settlement Agreements Resulting from Mediation (2018 treaty)
♦ United Nations Convention on Jurisdictional Immunities of States and Their Property (2004 treaty)
♦ United Nations Convention on the Law of the Sea (1982 treaty)
♦ United Nations Convention on the Liability of Operators of Transport Terminals in International Trade (1991 treaty)
♦ United Nations Convention on the Rights of the Child (1989 treaty)
♦ United Nations Convention on Transparency in Treaty-based Investor-State Arbitration (2014 treaty)
♦ United Nations Convention on the Use of Electronic Communications in International Contracts (2005 treaty)
♦ United Nations Correspondents Association (internationally oriented national body)
♦ United Nations Council for Namibia (inactive)

♦ United Nations Crime Prevention and Criminal Justice Programme Network 20549

Commission pour la Prévention du Crime et la Justice Pénale
Secretariat c/o Office for Drug Control and Crime Prevention, PO Box 500, 1400 Vienna, Austria. T. +431260604269. Fax +431260605898. E-mail: unodc@unodc.org.
URL: https://www.unodc.org/unodc/en/commissions/CCPCJ/PNI/institutes.html
History 18 Dec 1991. Since 1997, implemented within the framework of *United Nations Office on Drugs and Crime (UNODC, #20596)*. Set up under resolution 46/152 of the General Assembly of *United Nations (UN, #20515)*. **Aims** Assist the international community in strengthening cooperation in the crucial area of crime prevention and criminal justice. **Activities** Information exchange; research; training; public education. **IGO Relations** Institutes: CICP; *European Institute for Crime Prevention and Control affiliated with the United Nations (HEUNI, #07550)*; *Instituto Latinoamericano de las Naciones Unidas para la Prevención del Delito y Tratamiento del Delincuente (ILANUD, #11347)*; *Latin American Crime and Justice Research Institute (no recent information)*; *Naif Arab University for Security Sciences (NAUSS, #16929)*; *United Nations African Institute for the Prevention of Crime and the Treatment of Offenders (UNAFRI, #20519)*; *United Nations Interregional Crime and Justice Research Institute (UNICRI, #20580)*. **NGO Relations** Institutes: Australian Institute of Criminology; *International Centre for Criminal Law Reform and Criminal Justice Policy (ICCLR)*; *International Centre for the Prevention of Crime (ICPC, #12508)*; *International Scientific and Professional Advisory Council of the United Nations Crime Prevention and Criminal Justice Programme (ISPAC, #14810)*; National Institute of Justice (USA); *Raoul Wallenberg Institute of Human Rights and Humanitarian Law (RWI)*; *Siracusa International Institute for Criminal Justice and Human Rights (SII, #19289)*. [2009/XK2387/**F***]

♦ United Nations Criminal Tribunals Staff Union (UN-CTSU) 20550

Pres Churchillplein 1, 2517 JW The Hague, Netherlands. T. +31705128119. E-mail: staffunion@un.org.
Gen Sec address not obtained.
URL: https://www.staffunion.org/
History 1993. Founded to represent staff of *International Criminal Tribunal for the former Yugoslavia (ICTY, inactive)*. Since 2013, also represents staff of *International Residual Mechanism for Criminal Tribunals (IRMCT, #14746)* in The Hague (Netherlands), Arusha (Tanzania UR) and Kigali (Rwanda). Former names and other names: *ICTY Staff Union* – former (1993 to 2015). **Aims** Represent, safeguard and promote the rights, interests and welfare of the staff in conformance with the principles laid down in the UN Charter and all relevant staff rules and regulations. **Structure** Executive Committee. **NGO Relations** Member of (1): *Coordinating Committee for International Staff Unions and Associations of the United Nations System (CCISUA, #04818)*. [2020/AA1001/**E**]

♦ United Nations Declaration on the Elimination of Violence Against Women (1993 treaty)

♦ United Nations Democracy Fund (UNDEF) 20551

Fonds des Nations unies pour la démocratie – Fondo de la Naciones Unidas para la Democracia
Contact 405 East 42nd Street, S-1517, New York NY 10017, USA. T. +12129633399. Fax +12129631486. E-mail: democracyfund@un.org.
URL: http://www.un.org/democracyfund/
History Jul 2005. Established by Kofi Annan, Secretary-General of *United Nations (UN, #20515)*. Endorsed by UN member states at 2005 World Summit (A/RES/60/01). **Aims** Support democracy through empowering civil society worldwide with focus on strengthening the voice of civil society, promoting human rights and ensuring participation of all groups in democratic processes; complement and enhance the United Nations more traditional work with governments in order to strengthen democratic governance worldwide by supporting the "demand" rather than the "supply" side of democratization. **Structure** Functions as a trust fund under the UN Secretary-General. Advisory Board. Programme Consultative Group comprises: UN Department of Political Affairs; UN Department Peacekeeping Operations; *Office of the United Nations High Commissioner for Human Rights (OHCHR, #17697)*; *UNDP (#20292)*; *UN Women (#20724)*; *United Nations Office on Drugs and Crime (UNODC, #20596)*; UN Peacebuilding Support Office. **Languages** English, French. **Staff** 7.00 FTE, paid. **Finance** Voluntary contributions from UN member states. **Activities** Funds, helps design, manages, mentors and generates civil society projects that empower civil society and strengthen democracy worldwide. Since its foundation in 2005, the Fund has provided over US$ 226,000,000 to more than 870 projects, the majority conducted by local civil society groups in over 130 countries in Africa, Arab region, Asia, Eastern Europe and Latin America. Projects fall under 6 thematic areas: strengthening civil society interaction with government; women's empowerment; youth engagement; rule of law and human rights; electoral processes; and, media and freedom of information. Organizes International Day of Democracy (15 September). **Events** *Athens Democracy Forum* Athens (Greece) 2022, *Athens Democracy Forum* Athens (Greece) 2016, *Global forum on reinventing government* Vienna (Austria) 2007. **Publications** Available on website. [2022.12.01/XM1968/f/**F***]

♦ United Nations Department of Humanitarian Affairs / see United Nations Office for the Coordination of Humanitarian Affairs (#20593)
♦ United Nations Development Group / see United Nations Sustainable Development Group (#20634)
♦ United Nations Development Programme (#20292)

♦ United Nations Disarmament Commission 20552

Commission du désarmement des Nations Unies
Sec Room S-3061, United Nations, S-30FW 405 E 42nd St, New York NY 10017, USA. T. +12129634238.
URL: http://www.un.org/disarmament/institutions/disarmament-commission/

History Established 1978, when it was revitalized, within the framework of the *United Nations (UN, #20515)*, as a subsidiary forum for deliberation on disarmament issues to the UN General Assembly. Linked with the *United Nations Security Council (UNSC, #20625)*. Successor to the earlier Disarmament Commission, set up 11 Jan 1952, by a Resolution of the General Assembly, and which last met in 1965. **Aims** Make recommendations on various problems in the field of disarmament and follow up the relevant decisions and recommendations of the Special Sessions of the General Assembly devoted to disarmament. **Structure** Plenary; Committee of the Whole; Bureau; Working Groups (2). **Finance** Within the United Nations regular budget. **Activities** Events/meetings; politics/policy/regulatory. **Events** *Annual Session* New York, NY (USA) 2014, *Annual Session* New York, NY (USA) 2013, *Annual Session* New York, NY (USA) 2012, *Organizational Session* New York, NY (USA) 2012, *Annual Session* New York, NY (USA) 2011. **Publications** *The United Nations Disarmament Yearbook*. Reports (annual). Meeting proceedings. **Members** Participants All United Nations Member States and Permanent Observers; specialized international organizations; non-governmental organizations. **IGO Relations** *Conference on Disarmament (CD, #04590)*; *United Nations Office for Disarmament Affairs (UNODA, #20594)*. [2018.06.28/XE6549/E*]

♦ United Nations Disarmament Information Programme (inactive)

♦ United Nations Disengagement Observer Force (UNDOF) 20553

Force des Nations Unies chargée d'observer le dégagement (FNUOD) – Fuerza de las Naciones Unidas para la Observación de la Separación (FNUOS)

Contact c/o Department of Peace-keeping Operations, United Nations, Room S-3260E, New York NY 10017, USA. T. +12129633795. Fax +12123672103.
Contact c/o UNDOF, PO Box 5837, Damascus, Syrian AR.
Postal Address c/-Hq AUSBAT, 1500 Vienna, Austria.
URL: https://undof.unmissions.org/

History 31 May 1974, New York, NY (USA). Established by resolution 350 (1974) of the *United Nations Security Council (UNSC, #20625)*, within *United Nations System (#20635)*, in the framework of the *United Nations (UN, #20515)*. Mandate renewed through resolution 2361 (2017). Current mandate runs until 30 June 2022. **Aims** Supervise the *cease-fire* between *Israel* and *Syria*, the disengagement of Israeli and Syrian forces and supervise the areas of separation and limitation to ensure that there are no military forces within it. **Staff** Deployed personnel (2021): 1,250, of which 125 civilians. Staff negotiations through *United Nations Field Staff Union (UNFSU, #20561)*. **Finance** Annual budget: 65,507,400 USD (2022). **Activities** Supervision is carried out through static positions and observation posts, which are manned 24 hours a day, and by foot and mobile patrols operating along predetermined routes day and night. Temporary outposts and additional patrols are set up to perform specific tasks. Fortnightly inspections of armament and force levels in the area of limitation are carried out with the assistance of liaison officers from the parties, who accompany the inspection teams. In addition to its normal peace-keeping functions, UNDOF carries out humanitarian activities, including transfer of released prisoners and bodies of war dead and assisting the ICRC with facilities for transfer of prisoners and bodies, exchange of parcels and passage of persons and personal effects. It also supplies medical treatment to the local population within the means available.

Members Military contingents provided by 7 countries:
Austria, Canada, Croatia, India, Japan, Philippines, Poland.

IGO Relations *United Nations Mine Action Service (UNMAS, #20585)*; *United Nations Special Committee on Peace-keeping Operations (#20628)*. Cooperates with: *United Nations Truce Supervision Organization (UNTSO, #20638)*, which assists UNDOF though provision of about 80 observers. [2022/XE1538/F*]

♦ United Nations Economic Commission for Africa (ECA) 20554

Commission économique des Nations Unies pour l'Afrique (CEA) – Comisión Económica de las Naciones Unidas para Africa (CEPA)

Exec Sec Menelik II Avenue, PO Box 3001, Addis Ababa, Ethiopia. T. +251115445000. Fax +251115514416. E-mail: ecainfo@uneca.org.
URL: http://www.uneca.org/

History 29 Apr 1958. Established within the framework the *United Nations (UN, #20515)* and under implementation of Resolution 671A (XXV) of *ECOSOC (#05331)*, when members were 8 independent African States (Egypt; Ethiopia; Ghana; Liberia; Libya; Morocco; Sudan; Tunisia), 6 colonial powers (Belgium; France; Italy; Portugal; Spain; the United Kingdom) and the then Union of South Africa. Associate members were: Gambia; Kenya; Nigeria; Sierra Leone; Tanganyika; Uganda; Zanzibar; UK-administered Somaliland Protectorate. 28 Jul 1958, Italian-administered Trust Territory of Somaliland was admitted to associate membership and, 12 Dec 1958, Guinea became a full member. Between 1958 and 1982, 41 other African countries achieved independence and subsequently became full members of the Commission. By 1963, Italy and Belgium had ceased to be members and France, Spain and UK had become associate members, allowing the non-self governing territories still under their administration direct representation as associate members. South Africa was suspended and Portugal expelled from the Commission in 1963. First Session held 29 Dec 1958 – 6 Jan 1959, Addis Ababa (Ethiopia). Former names and other names: *UNECA* – former. **Aims** Promote the economic and social development of its member States; foster intra-regional integration; promote international cooperation for Africa's development; provide advisory services in key thematic fields: Macroeconomic Policy; Regional Integration and Trade; Social Development; Natural Resources; Innovation and Technology; Gender; Governance; Statistic. **Structure** Joint annual *African Union (AU, #00488)* / Economic Commission for Africa Conference of African Ministers of Finance, Planning and Economic Development. Subregional ministerial conferences. Sectoral Committees (7): *'Committee on Food Security and Sustainable Development'*; *'Committee on Governance and Popular Participation'*; *'Committee on Development Information Science and Technology (CODIST)'*; *'Committee on Trade, Regional Cooperation and Integration'*; *'Committee on Women and Development'*; *'Committee on Statistics'*; *'Committee on Human and Social Development'*. Headed by Executive Secretary and assisted by 2 Deputy Executive Secretaries. Substantive Divisions for policy research (5): Macroeconomic Policy; Regional Integration and Trade; Social Policy Development; Special Initiatives; *African Centre for Statistics*. Knowledge delivery pillar: Capacity Development Division; *United Nations African Institute for Economic Development and Planning (#20518)* – ECA's training arm; Division of Administration; Subregional Offices (5): *ECA Sub-Regional Office for Central Africa (ECA/SRO-CA, #05274)*; *ECA Sub-Regional Office for Eastern Africa (SRO-EA Kigali, #05275)*; *ECA Office for North Africa (#05273)*; *ECA Subregional Office for Southern Africa (SRO-SA Lusaka, #05276)*; *ECA Sub-Regional Office for West Africa (SRO-WA, #05277)*. Knowledge generation and knowledge delivery underpinned by: Strategic and operation Quality Division; Public Information and Knowledge Management Division. Substantive Divisions complemented by: ECA Partnerships Office; Joint Secretariat Support Office of ECA, African Union Commission and *African Development Bank (ADB, #00283)*. **Languages** Arabic, English, French. **Staff** 725 staff, excluding part-time. Personnel negotiations through *UNECA Staff Union (#20293)*. **Finance** Regular budget: US$ 94,006,000. **Activities** Knowledge management/information dissemination; research/documentation; advocacy/lobbying/activism; politics/policy/regulatory; capacity building; guidance/assistance/consulting. **Events** *International Forum on Energy for Sustainable Development* Geneva (Switzerland) 2022, *Annual Session* Addis Ababa (Ethiopia) 2021, *AEC : African Economic Conference* Cape Verde 2021, *International Forum on Energy for Sustainable Development* Geneva (Switzerland) 2021, *AEC : African Economic Conference* Addis Ababa (Ethiopia) 2020. **Publications** *African Population and Development Bulletin* (4 a year) in English, French; *Rural Progress* (4 a year); *Economic Report on Africa* (annual); *Survey of Economic and Social Conditions in Africa* (annual); *Investment Africa* (periodical); *Statistical Yearbook*. *African Population Studies* – series. *Demographic Handbook for Africa* (1992); *Compendium of Intra-African and Related Foreign Trade Statistics*; *Directory of Activities of International Voluntary Agencies in Rural Development in Africa*. Information Services: Resources include ECA databases and databases obtained or online from other organizations. *African Information Society Initiative (AISI, inactive)* – based at ECA.

Members Full: independent countries, African members of the United Nations. Governments of 54 countries:
Algeria, Angola, Benin, Botswana, Burkina Faso, Burundi, Cameroon, Cape Verde, Central African Rep, Chad, Comoros, Congo Brazzaville, Congo DR, Côte d'Ivoire, Djibouti, Egypt, Equatorial Guinea, Eritrea, Eswatini, Ethiopia, Gabon, Gambia, Ghana, Guinea, Guinea-Bissau, Kenya, Lesotho, Liberia, Libya, Madagascar, Malawi, Mali, Mauritania, Mauritius, Morocco, Mozambique, Namibia, Niger, Nigeria, Rwanda, Sao Tomé-Principe, Senegal, Seychelles, Sierra Leone, Somalia, South Africa, South Sudan, Sudan, Tanzania UR, Togo, Tunisia, Uganda, Zambia, Zimbabwe.

IGO Relations *World Trade Organization (WTO, #21864)* (Observer Status). Special relations with: *FAO (#09260)*; *UNDP (#20292)*; *UNEP (#20299)*; *UNIDO (#20336)*; *WHO (#20950)*. Liaises with: *United Nations Population Fund (UNFPA, #20612)*. Administers: *Universal Postal Union (UPU, #20682)*. Member of: *Inter-Agency Working Group on Desertification (IAWGD, inactive)*; *United Nations Group on the Information Society (UNGIS, #20570)*; *UN-Water (#20723)*. Observer to: *International Organization for Migration (IOM, #14454)*.
Cooperates with:
- *African Bureau of Educational Sciences (BASE, no recent information)*;
- *African Foundation for Research and Development (AFRAND, no recent information)*;
- *African Statistical Association (AFSA, #00475)*;
- *Association of African Central Banks (AACB, #02352)*;
- *Company for Habitat and Housing in Africa (Shelter-Afrique, #04408)*;
- *Global Action Plan for Environment and Development in the 21st Century (Agenda 21, inactive)*;
- *International Telecommunication Union (ITU, #15673)*;
- *Regional Remote Sensing Centre, Kinshasa (RRSC, inactive)*;
- *Regional Remote Sensing Centre for North African States (#18807)*.

Cooperates in regional integration schemes with:
- *African Organization of Cartography and Remote Sensing (AOCRS, inactive)*;
- *African Union (AU, #00488)*;
- *Communauté économique des pays des Grands Lacs (CEPGL, #04375)*;
- *Economic Community of Central African States (ECCAS, #05311)*;
- *Economic Community of West African States (ECOWAS, #05312)*;
- *Preferential Trade Area for Eastern and Southern African States (PTA, inactive)*, currently *Common Market for Eastern and Southern Africa (COMESA, #04296)*;
- *Southern African Development Community (SADC, #19843)*.

Together with AU, instrumental in setting up: *Port Management Association of West and Central Africa (PMAWCA, #18463)*. Instrumental in elaborating: *United Nations Convention to Combat Desertification (UNCCD, 1994)*.
Together with AU, instrumental in setting up:
- Regional Coordinating Committee for the Implementation of
- *Pan African Telecommunications Network (PANAFTEL, no recent information)*;
- *Port Management Association of Eastern and Southern Africa (PMAESA, #18462)*;
- *Union of African Railways (UAR, #20347)*.

Operating under the aegis of ECA and AU: *Trans-African Highway Bureau (no recent information)*. Other intergovernmental institutions set up or helped into being by ECA include:
- *Africa Rice Center (AfricaRice, #00518)*;
- *African Accounting Council (AAC, no recent information)*;
- *African Centre for Applied Research and Training in Social Development (ACARTSOD, #00237)*;
- *African Development Bank (ADB, #00283)*;
- *African Development Bank Group (ADB Group, #00284)*;
- *African Institute for Higher Technical Training and Research (AIHTTR, inactive)*;
- *African Intellectual Property Organization (#00344)*;
- *African Minerals and Geosciences Centre (AMGC, #00373)*;
- *African Ministerial Conference on the Environment (AMCEN, #00374)*;
- *African Regional Centre for Engineering Design and Manufacturing (ARCEDEM, no recent information)*;
- *African Regional Centre of Technology (ARCT, #00432)*;
- *African Regional Institute for Geospatial Information Science and Technology (AFRIGIST, #00433)*;
- *African Regional Intellectual Property Organization (ARIPO, #00434)*;
- *African Training and Research Centre in Administration for Development (CAFRAD, #00486)*;
- *Association of African Tax Administrators (AATA, no recent information)*;
- *Association of African Trade Promotion Organizations (AATPO, no recent information)*;
- *Central African Clearing House (CACH, no recent information)*;
- *Central African Mineral Resources Development Centre (CAMRDC, no recent information)*;
- *Conference of Ministers of African Least Developed Countries (no recent information)*;
- *FAO Regional Office for Africa (FAO/RAF, #09265)*;
- *Institut de formation et de recherche démographiques (IFORD, #11304)*;
- *Lake Chad Basin Commission (LCBC, #16220)*;
- *Liptako-Gourma Integrated Development Authority (LGA, no recent information)*;
- *Mano River Union (MRU, #16566)*;
- *Niger Basin Authority (NBA, #17134)*;
- *Regional Centre for Mapping of Resources for Development (RCMRD, #18757)*;
- *Regional Institute for Population Studies (RIPS, no recent information)*;
- *Regional Remote Sensing Centre, Ouagadougou (CRTO, inactive)*;
- *Special Action Programme on Administration and Management in Africa (SAPAM, inactive)*;
- *United Nations African Institute for Economic Development and Planning (#20518)*.

NGO Relations Cooperates with:
- *African Academy of Sciences (AAS, #00193)*;
- *African Airlines Association (AFRAA, #00200)*;
- *African Association for Public Administration and Management (AAPAM, #00215)*;
- *African Centre for Monetary Studies (ACMS, inactive)*;
- *African Curriculum Organization (ACO, no recent information)*;
- *African Higher School for Railway Engineers (inactive)*;
- *African Network of Scientific and Technological Institutions (ANSTI, #00395)*;
- *African Science and Technology Information System (ASTIS, no recent information)*;
- *African Union of Broadcasting (AUB, #00490)*;
- *African Women's Development and Communication Network (FEMNET, #00503)*;
- *Association for the Advancement of Agricultural Sciences in Africa (AAASA, no recent information)*;
- *Association for Social Work Education in Africa (ASWEA, inactive)*;
- *Central African Development Information System (CADIS, no recent information)*;
- *Council for the Development of Social Science Research in Africa (CODESRIA, #04879)*;
- *Federation of African Chambers of Commerce (FACC, no recent information)*;
- *Forum of African Voluntary Development Organizations (FAVDO, inactive)*;
- *Geological Society of Africa (GSAf, #10135)*;
- *International Centre of Insect Physiology and Ecology (ICIPE, #12499)*;
- *International Chamber of Commerce (ICC, #12534)*;
- *International Commission on Irrigation and Drainage (ICID, #12694)*;
- *International Planned Parenthood Federation (IPPF, #14589)*;
- *International Statistical Institute (ISI, #15603)*;
- *International Union for Conservation of Nature and Natural Resources (IUCN, #15766)*;
- *International Union for the Scientific Study of Population (IUSSP, #15814)*;
- *The Lutheran World Federation (LWF, #16532)*;
- *Pan Africanist Congress (PAC, no recent information)*;
- *Research and Development Forum for Science-Led Development in Africa (RANDFORUM, no recent information)*;
- *SIFIDA Investment Company (inactive)*;
- *World Federation of Trade Unions (WFTU, #21493)*. [2019/XE4174/E*]

♦ United Nations Economic Commission for Asia and the Far East / see United Nations Economic and Social Commission for Asia and the Pacific (#20557)

♦ United Nations Economic Commission for Europe (UNECE) 20555

Commission économique des Nations Unies pour l'Europe (CEE-ONU) – Comisión Económica de las Naciones Unidas para Europa (CEPE) – Evropejskaja Ekonomiceskaja Komissija OON (EEK)

Contact Palais des Nations, 1211 Geneva 10, Switzerland. T. +41229171234. E-mail: unece_info@un.org.
URL: http://www.unece.org/

History 28 Mar 1947. Established by Resolution 36 (IV) of *ECOSOC (#05331)*. 1st Session held in May 1947, Geneva (Switzerland). Took over the functions of *Emergency Economic Committee for Europe (inactive)*, which had been set up in 1945. In 1951 became a permanent organ (regional commission) of *United Nations (UN, #20515)*; currently one of the 5 regional commissions of the United Nations. Based at *United Nations Office at Geneva (UNOG, #20597)*. Former names and other names: *UNECE* – alias; *CEE-ONU* – alias; *ECE* – alias. **Aims** Promote pan-European economic *integration* by bringing together 56 countries located in the European Union, non-EU, the Caucasus and Central Asia, as well as North America, Turkey and Israel; encourage dialogue and cooperation among members on economic and sectoral issues; provide analysis, policy advice and assistance to governments; give focus to UN global mandates in the economic field, in cooperation with other global players and key stakeholders, notably the business community; set out norms, standards and conventions to facilitate international cooperation within and outside the region. **Structure** Commission operates through Plenary Session (every 2 years) and reports to ECOSOC. Executive Committee. Sectoral Committees: *Committee on Environmental Policy (#04253)*; *Committee on Inland Transport (#04262)*; *Conference of European Statisticians (CES, #04600)*; *Committee on Sustainable Energy (#04288)*; *Steering Committee on Trade Capacity and Standards (CTCS, #19979)*, including *UNECE Committee on Forests and the Forest Industry (COFFI, #20294)*; *Committee on Housing and Land Management (#04259)*; Committee on

Innovation, Competitiveness and Public-Private Partnerships (CICPPP). ECOSOC bodies serviced by UNECE: *United Nations Committee of Experts on the Transport of Dangerous Goods and on the Globally Harmonized System of Classification and Labelling of Chemicals (Committee of Experts on TDG and GHS, #20543)* and its Sub-Committees. Also instrumental in setting up: *Cooperative Programme for Monitoring and Evaluation of the Long-range Transmission of Air Pollutants in Europe (EMEP, #04800)*. **Languages** English, French, Russian. **Staff** 180.00 FTE, paid. **Finance** Annual budget: 61,800,000 USD (2021).

Activities Programme of work currently covers statistics, environment, transport, trade, sustainable energy, forests, housing and land management and economic cooperation and integration. Management of treaties and agreements, including:
- *European Agreement Concerning the International Carriage of Dangerous Goods by Inland Waterways (2000)*;
- *Customs Convention on the International Transport of Goods under Cover of TIR Carnets, 1975 (TIR convention, 1975)*;
- *International Convention on the Harmonization of Frontier Controls of Goods (1982)*;
- *Convention on Customs Treatment of Pool Containers Used in International Transport (1994)*;
- *European Agreement on Main International Traffic Arteries (AGR, 1975)*;
- *European Agreement on Main Inland Waterways of International Importance (AGN, 1996)*;
- *Convention on Civil Liability for Damage Caused During Carriage of Dangerous Goods by Road, Rail and Inland Navigation Vessels (CRTD, 1989)*;
- *Convention on Long-range Transboundary Air Pollution (#04787)*;
- *Convention on the Protection and Use of Transboundary Watercourses and International Lakes (1992)*;
- *Protocol on Water and Health to the 1992 Convention on the Protection and Use of Transboundary Watercourses and International Lakes (1999)*;
- *Convention on Environmental Impact Assessment in a Transboundary Context (Espoo Convention, 1991)*;
- *Convention on the Transboundary Effects of Industrial Accidents (1992)*;
- *Convention on Access to Information, Public Participation in Decision-making and Access to Justice in Environmental Matters (Århus Convention, 1998)*;
- *Protocol on Pollutant Release and Transfer Registers (Kiev protocol, 2003)*.

Events *Biennial Session* Geneva (Switzerland) 2023, *Future-Proof Green Cities Make Future-Proof Countries* Budapest (Hungary) 2022, *International Forum on Energy for Sustainable Development* Geneva (Switzerland) 2022, *Regional Forum on Sustainable Development for the UNECE Region Session* Geneva (Switzerland) 2022, *International Forum on Energy for Sustainable Development* Geneva (Switzerland) 2021. **Publications** Annual Report; newsletter; bulletins; discussion papers; historical documents; sustainable development briefs; reports.

Members Governments of 56 countries:
Albania, Andorra, Armenia, Austria, Azerbaijan, Belarus, Belgium, Bosnia-Herzegovina, Bulgaria, Canada, Croatia, Cyprus, Czechia, Denmark, Estonia, Finland, France, Georgia, Germany, Greece, Hungary, Iceland, Ireland, Israel, Italy, Kazakhstan, Kyrgyzstan, Latvia, Liechtenstein, Lithuania, Luxembourg, Malta, Moldova, Monaco, Montenegro, Netherlands, North Macedonia, Norway, Poland, Portugal, Romania, Russia, San Marino, Serbia, Slovakia, Slovenia, Spain, Sweden, Switzerland, Tajikistan, Türkiye, Turkmenistan, UK, Ukraine, USA, Uzbekistan.

Members of the United Nations not members of the Commission, and European countries not members of the United Nations, may participate in a consultative capacity. Current participant (1):
Holy See.

IGO Relations Member of (1): *UN-Water (#20723)*. Partner of (1): *United Nations Public Administration Network (UNPAN, #20615)*.

Cooperates with (67):
- *Arctic Monitoring and Assessment Programme (AMAP, #01100)*;
- *Asian and Pacific Development Centre (APDC, #01608)*;
- *Baltic Marine Environment Protection Commission – Helsinki Commission (HELCOM, #03126)*;
- *Bank for International Settlements (BIS, #03165)*;
- *Central Commission for the Navigation of the Rhine (CCNR, #03687)*;
- *Central European Initiative (CEI, #03708)*;
- *Centralnoe Dispetcherskoe Upravlenie Obedinennyh Energeticheskih Sistem (CDU OES, no recent information)*;
- *Commission du Danube (CD, #04210)*;
- *Committee on Forest Development in the Tropics (inactive)*;
- *Commonwealth of Independent States (CIS, #04341)*;
- *Commonwealth Secretariat (#04362)*;
- *Congress of Local and Regional Authorities of the Council of Europe (#04677)*;
- *Council of Europe (CE, #04881)*;
- *EFTA (#05391)*;
- *European Bank for Reconstruction and Development (EBRD, #06315)*;
- *European Commission (EC, #06633)*;
- *European Community (inactive)*;
- *European Environment Agency (EEA, #06995)*;
- *European Forestry Commission (EFC, #07299)*;
- *European Foundation for the Improvement of Living and Working Conditions (Eurofound, #07348)*;
- *European Organization for Nuclear Research (CERN, #08108)*;
- *European Population Committee (CAHP, inactive)*;
- *European Union (EU, #08967)*;
- *FAO Regional Office for Europe and Central Asia (FAO/REU, #09267)*;
- *Global Resource Information Database (GRID, #10578)*;
- *Guidance Committee for Road Safety in the Nordic Countries (inactive)*;
- *Inter-American Development Bank (IDB, #11427)*;
- *Inter-Governmental Consultations on Migration, Asylum and Refugees (IGC, #11479)*;
- *Intergovernmental Group on Grains (#11488)*;
- *Intergovernmental Group on Meat and Dairy Products (#11491)*;
- *Intergovernmental Oceanographic Commission (IOC, #11496)*;
- *International Atomic Energy Agency (IAEA, #12294)*;
- *International Centre for Promotion of Enterprises (ICPE, #12509)*;
- *International Council for the Exploration of the Sea (ICES, #13021)*;
- *International Energy Agency (IEA, #13270)*;
- *International Institute for the Unification of Private Law (UNIDROIT, #13934)*;
- *International Institute of Refrigeration (IIR, #13918)*;
- *International Joint Commission (IJC)*;
- *International Organization of Legal Metrology (#14451)*;
- *International Rubber Study Group (IRSG, #14772)*;
- *International Transport Forum (ITF, #15725)*;
- *Interstate Statistical Committee of the Commonwealth of Independent States (CIS-Stat, #15983)*;
- *Islamic University of Technology (IUT, #16055)*;
- *Mediterranean Action Plan (MAP, #16638)*;
- *NAFTA Secretariat (#16927)*;
- *Nordic Council (NC, #17256)*;
- *Nordic Council of Ministers (NCM, #17260)*;
- *OECD (#17693)*;
- *Organisation for Cooperation between Railways (OSJD, #17803)*;
- *Organisation for the Prohibition of Chemical Weapons (OPCW, #17823)*;
- *Organisation intergouvernementale pour les transports internationaux ferroviaires (OTIF, #17807)*;
- *Organization for Security and Cooperation in Europe (OSCE, #17887)*;
- *Organization of Black Sea Economic Cooperation (BSEC, #17857)*;
- *OSPAR Commission for the Protection of the Marine Environment of the North-East Atlantic (OSPAR Commission, #17905)*;
- *Plan Bleu pour l'environnement et le développement en Méditerranée (Plan Bleu, #18379)*;
- *Regional Environmental Centre for Central and Eastern Europe (REC, #18782)*;
- *Secretariat of the Basel Convention (SBC, #19196)*;
- *Statistical Office of the European Union (Eurostat, #19974)*;
- *Trade Electronic Data Interchange System (TEDIS, inactive)*;
- *UN Environment Programme World Conservation Monitoring Centre (UNEP-WCMC, #20295)*;
- UNEP Global Resources Information Database;
- *United Nations Regional Commissions New York Office (RCNYO, #20620)*;
- *WHO European Centre for Environment and Health (ECEH, see: #20945)*;
- *WHO Regional Office for Europe (#20945)*;
- *World Customs Organization (WCO, #21350)*;
- *World Tourism Organization (UNWTO, #21861)*;
- *World Water Assessment Programme (WWAP, #21907)*.

Instrumental in setting up (2): *International E-Road Network (#13296)*; *Trans-European North-South Motorway Project (TEM, #20208)*.

An important feature of activities is cooperation with other UN bodies, with the specialized agencies and with other intergovernmental organizations and their secretariats.

United Nations bodies:
- *International Trade Centre (ITC, #15703)*;
- *UNEP (#20299)*;
- *UNCTAD (#20285)*;
- *UNDP (#20292)*;
- *UNICEF (#20332)*;
- *United Nations Commission on International Trade Law (UNCITRAL, #20531)*;
- *United Nations Commission on Sustainable Development (CSD, inactive)*;
- *United Nations Economic Commission for Africa (ECA, #20554)*;
- *United Nations Economic Commission for Latin America and the Caribbean (ECLAC, #20556)*;
- *United Nations Economic and Social Commission for Asia and the Pacific (ESCAP, #20557)*;
- *United Nations Economic and Social Commission for Western Asia (ESCWA, #20558)*;
- *United Nations Group on the Information Society (UNGIS, #20570)*;
- *United Nations Human Settlements Programme (UN-Habitat, #20572)*;
- *United Nations Institute for Training and Research (UNITAR, #20576)*;
- *United Nations Office at Vienna (UNOV, #20604)*;
- *United Nations University (UNU, #20642)*.

Specialized Agencies:
- *FAO (#09260)*;
- *ILO (#11123)*;
- *International Bank for Reconstruction and Development (IBRD, #12317)*;
- *International Civil Aviation Organization (ICAO, #12581)*;
- *International Fund for Agricultural Development (IFAD, #13692)*;
- *International Maritime Organization (IMO, #14102)*;
- *International Monetary Fund (IMF, #14180)*;
- *International Telecommunication Union (ITU, #15673)*;
- *International Tropical Timber Organization (ITTO, #15737)*;
- *UNESCO (#20322)*;
- *UNIDO (#20336)*;
- *United Nations Population Fund (UNFPA, #20612)*;
- *WHO (#20950)*;
- *World Meteorological Organization (WMO, #21649)*;
- *World Trade Organization (WTO, #21864)* (Observer status).

Working Party on Land Administration is observer to: *Permanent Committee on Cadastre in the European Union (PCC, #18319)*.

Signatory to:
- *Agreement on the Unification of Requirements with Regard to the Formulation and Filing of Patent Applications (1975)*;
- *Protocol to the 1979 Convention on Long Range Transboundary Air Pollution Concerning the Control of Nitrogen Oxides Emissions or Their Transboundary Fluxes (1988 NOx protocol, 1988)*.

Transport agreements concluded under UNECE auspices and not mentioned elsewhere in this text:
- *Convention on Road Traffic, 1949 (1949)*;
- *Protocol on Road Signs and Signals (1949)*;
- *Declaration on the Construction of Main International Traffic Arteries (1950)*;
- *European Agreement on the Application of Article 23 of the 1949 Convention on Road Traffic (1950)*;
- *European Agreement Supplementing the 1949 Convention on Road Traffic and the 1949 Protocol on Road Signs and Signals (1950)*;
- *International Convention to Facilitate the Crossing of Frontiers for Goods Carried by Rail (1952)*;
- *International Convention to Facilitate the Crossing of Frontiers for Passengers and Baggage Carried by Rail (1952)*;
- *Additional Protocol to the Convention Concerning Customs Facilities for Touring, Relating to the Importation of Tourist Publicity Documents and Material (1954)*;
- *Convention Concerning Customs Facilities for Touring (1954)*;
- *Customs Convention on the Temporary Importation of Private Road Vehicles (1954)*;
- *General Agreement on Economic Regulations for International Road Transport (1954)*;
- *Convention on the Contract for the International Carriage of Goods by Road (CMR, 1956)*;
- *Convention on the Taxation of Road Vehicles Engaged in International Goods Transport (1956)*;
- *Convention on the Taxation of Road Vehicles Engaged in International Passenger Transport (1956)*;
- *Convention on the Taxation of Road Vehicles for Private Use in International Traffic (1956)*;
- *Customs Convention on Containers, 1956 (1956)*;
- *Customs Convention on the Temporary Importation of Commercial Road Vehicles (1956)*;
- *Customs Convention on the Temporary Importation for Private Use of Aircraft and Pleasure Boats (1956)*;
- *European Agreement Concerning the International Carriage of Dangerous Goods by Road (ADR, 1957)*;
- *European Agreement on Road Markings (1957)*;
- *Agreement concerning the Adoption of Harmonized Technical United Nations Regulations for Wheeled Vehicles, Equipment and Parts which can be Fitted and/or be Used on Wheeled Vehicles and the Conditions for Reciprocal Recognition of Approvals Granted on the Basis of these United Nations Regulations (1958)*;
- *Customs Convention Concerning Spare Parts Used for Repairing EUROP Wagons (1958)*;
- *Customs Convention on the International Transport of Goods under Cover of TIR Carnets, 1959 (TIR Convention, 1959)*;
- *Convention Relating to the Unification of Certain Rules Concerning Collisions in Inland Navigation (1960)*;
- *European Convention on Customs Treatment of Pallets Used in International Transport (1960)*;
- *Convention on the Registration of Inland Navigation Vessels (1965)*;
- *Convention on the Measurement of Inland Navigation Vessels (1966)*;
- *Convention on Road Signs and Signals (1968)*;
- *Convention on Road Traffic, 1968 (1968)*;
- *European Agreement Concerning the Work of Crews of Vehicles Engaged in International Road Transport, 1970 (AETR, 1970)*;
- *European Agreement Supplementing the Convention on Road Signs and Signals (1971)*;
- *European Agreement Supplementing the Convention on Road Traffic (1971)*;
- *Customs Convention on Containers, 1972 (1972)*;
- *Convention on the Contract for the International Carriage of Passengers and Luggage by Road (CVR, 1973)*;
- *Convention Relating to the Limitation of the Liability of Owners of Inland Navigation Vessels (CLN, 1973)*;
- *Protocol on Road Markings (1973)*;
- *Agreement on Minimum Requirements for the Issue and Validity of Driving Permits (APC, 1975)*;
- *Convention on the Contract for the International Carriage of Passengers and Luggage by Inland Waterway (CVN, 1976)*;
- *Protocol to the Convention on the Contract for the International Carriage of Goods by Road (CMR, 1978)*;
- *Protocol to the Convention on the Contract for the International Carriage of Passengers and Luggage by Inland Waterways (CVN, 1978)*;
- *Protocol to the Convention on the Contract for the International Carriage of Passengers and Luggage by Road (CVR, 1978)*;
- *Protocol to the Convention Relating to the Limitation of Liability of Owners of Inland Navigation Vessels (1978)*;
- *European Agreement on Main International Railway Lines (AGC, 1985)*;
- *European Agreement on Important International Combined Transport Lines and Related Installations (AGTC, 1991)*;
- *Protocol Amending Article 1-a, Article 14-1 and Article 14-3b of the European Agreement of 30 September 1957 Concerning the International Carriage of Dangerous Goods by Road (1993)*;
- *Agreement Concerning the Adoption of Uniform Conditions for Periodical Technical Inspections of Wheeled Vehicles and the Reciprocal Recognition of Such Inspections (1997)*;
- *Agreement Concerning the Establishing of Global Technical Regulations for Wheeled Vehicles, Equipment and Parts Which Can be Fitted And/or be Used on Wheeled Vehicles (1998)*.

NGO Relations Memorandum of Understanding with (1): *Association Européenne des Concessionnaires d'Autoroutes et d'Ouvrages à Péage (ASECAP, #02559)*. Member of (1): *One UN Climate Change Learning Partnership (UN CC:Learn, #17735)*.

Nongovernmental organizations in consultative status with ECOSOC which participate in the work of ECE:
- *Alliance internationale de tourisme (AIT, #00694)*;
- *Bureau international des containers et du transport intermodal (BIC, #03364)*;
- *International Motor Vehicle Inspection Committee (CITA, #14187)*;
- *Conseil européen de l'industrie chimique (CEFIC, #04687)*;
- *Fédération internationale des associations de transitaires et assimilés (FIATA, #09610)*;
- *Fédération Internationale de l'Automobile (FIA, #09613)*;
- *Fédération internationale des professions immobilières (FIABCI, #09653)*;
- *Graduate Women International (GWI, #10688)*;
- *Greenpeace International (#10727)*;
- *International Air Transport Association (IATA, #11614)*;
- *International Association of Public Transport (#12118)*;
- *International Baccalaureate (IB, #12306)*;
- *International Bar Association (IBA, #12320)*;
- *International Chamber of Commerce (ICC, #12534)*;
- *International Chamber of Shipping (ICS, #12535)*;
- *International Council of Environmental Law (ICEL, #13018)*;
- *International Council of Jewish Women (ICJW, #13036)*;
- *International Council for Research and Innovation in Building and Construction (CIB, #13069)*;
- *International Council of Women (ICW, #13093)*;
- *International Electrotechnical Commission (IEC, #13255)*;
- *International Federation for Housing and Planning (IFHP, #13450)*;

- *International Federation for Medical and Biological Engineering (IFMBE, #13477)*;
- *International Federation of Robotics (IFR, #13532)*;
- *International Gas Union (IGU, #13700)*;
- *International Motorcycle Manufacturers Association (IMMA, #14186)*;
- *International Organization of Motor Vehicle Manufacturers (#14455)*;
- *International Organization for Standardization (ISO, #14473)*;
- *International Road Federation (IRF Global, #14759)*;
- *International Road Transport Union (IRU, #14761)*;
- *International Statistical Institute (ISI, #15603)*;
- *International Trade Union Confederation (ITUC, #15708)*;
- *International Transport Workers' Federation (ITF, #15726)*;
- *International Union of Building Centres (#15761)*;
- *International Union for Conservation of Nature and Natural Resources (IUCN, #15766)*;
- *International Union of Forest Research Organizations (IUFRO, #15774)*;
- *International Union of Tenants (IUT, #15822)*;
- *Liquid Gas Europe (#16488)*;
- National Council of German Women's Organizations;
- *Soroptimist International (SI, #19686)*;
- *Union internationale des architectes (UIA, #20419)*;
- *World Coal Association (WCA, #21280)*;
- *World Energy Council (WEC, #21381)*;
- *World Federation of Trade Unions (WFTU, #21493)*;
- *World Federation of United Nations Associations (WFUNA, #21499)*;
- *World LPG Association (WLPGA, #21629)*;
- *World Mining Congress (WMC, #21654)*;
- *World Road Association (PIARC, #21754)*.

Other non-governmental organizations which participate in the work of ECE:
- *Asociación Latinoamericana del Acero (Alacero, #02176)*;
- *Association of Plastics Manufacturers in Europe (Plastics Europe, #02862)*;
- *BirdLife International (#03266)*;
- *Building and Wood Workers' International (BWI, #03355)*;
- *Comité européen de normalisation (CEN, #04162)*;
- *Comité international des transports ferroviaires (CIT, #04188)*;
- *Conseil européen de l'industrie des peintures, des encres d'imprimerie et des couleurs d'art (CEPE, #04688)*;
- *Council of Bureaux (CoB, #04873)*;
- *CropLife International (#04966)*;
- *Dangerous Goods Advisory Council (DGAC, #05001)*;
- *Data for Development International Association (DFD, inactive)*;
- *Eurogas (#05682)*;
- *European Association of Automotive Suppliers (CLEPA, #05948)*;
- *European Association of the Machine tool Industries and related Manufacturing Technologies (CECIMO, #06113)*;
- *European Association of Producers of Steel for Packaging (#06167)*;
- *European Committee for Electrotechnical Standardization (CENELEC, #06647)*;
- *European Construction Industry Federation (#06766)*;
- *European East-West Conferences on Materials and Processes (MatTech)*;
- *European Environmental Bureau (EEB, #06996)*;
- *European Federation of Building Societies (EFBS, #07064)*;
- *European Federation of Chemical Engineering (EFCE, #07074)*;
- *European Federation of Organisations for Medical Physics (EFOMP, #07183)*;
- *European Industrial Gases Association (EIGA, #07525)*;
- *European-Mediterranean Seismological Centre (EMSC, #07774)*;
- *European Network for Housing Research (ENHR, #07924)*;
- *European Potato Trade Association (EUROPATAT, #08257)*;
- *European Regional Industrial Development Organization (ERIDO, inactive)*;
- *European Research Foundation and Institute for Industrial Location and Regional Development (ERFI, no recent information)*;
- *European Steel Association (EUROFER, #08835)*;
- *European Tyre and Rim Technical Organisation (ETRTO, #08962)*;
- *EUROTER – Tourism in Rural Europe (no recent information)*;
- *Fédération Européenne des Aérosols (FEA, #09557)*;
- *GLOBE International (#10668)*;
- *GS1 (#10809)*;
- *Intergas Marketing (inactive)*;
- *International Association of Classification Societies (IACS, #11778)*;
- *International Association of Medicine and Biology of the Environment (IAMBE, inactive)*;
- *International Centre for Trade and Statistical Overview (no recent information)*;
- *International Committee for Economic Reform and Cooperation, Kiev (ICERC, no recent information)*;
- *International Congress for Tropical Medicine and Malaria (ICTMM)*;
- *International Environmental Bureau (IEB, inactive)*;
- *International Federation for Information Processing (IFIP, #13458)*;
- *International Federation of Pedestrians (IFP, #13502)*;
- *International Federation for the Promotion of Mechanism and Machine Science (IFToMM, #13519)*;
- *International Federation of Red Cross and Red Crescent Societies (#13526)*;
- *International Institute on Ageing, United Nations – Malta (INIA, #13860)*;
- *International Institute for Applied Systems Analysis (IIASA, #13861)*;
- *International Institute of Welding (IIW, #13935)*;
- *International Union of Railways (#15813)*;
- *International Urban Development Association (INTA, #15832)*;
- *MARCOGAZ – Technical Association of the European Natural Gas Industry (#16572)*;
- *NGV Global (#17131)*;
- *Oil Companies' European Association for Environment, Health and Safety in Refining and Distribution (CONCAWE, #17708)*;
- *Réunion internationale des laboratoires d'essais et de recherches sur les matériaux et les constructions (RILEM, #18930)*;
- *Society for Worldwide Interbank Financial Telecommunication (SWIFT, #19661)*;
- *South East Asia Iron and Steel Institute (SEAISI, #19756)*;
- *Stockholm Environment Institute (SEI, #19993)*;
- *Transfrigoroute International (TI, #20213)*;
- *Union internationale des associations et organismes scientifiques et techniques (UATI, #20421)*;
- *International Union for Combined Road – Rail Transport (UIRR, #15765)*;
- *International Union of Wagon Keepers (#15827)*;
- *World Association of Girl Guides and Girl Scouts (WAGGGS, #21142)*;
- *World Association of Industrial and Technological Research Organizations (WAITRO, #21145)*;
- *World Resources Institute (WRI, #21753)*;
- *World Wide Fund for Nature (WWF, #21922)*.

Serves as secretariat for: *Population Information Network for Europe (POPIN-Europe, no recent information)*.

[2022.10.13/XE4176/**E***]

♦ United Nations Economic Commission for Latin America / see United Nations Economic Commission for Latin America and the Caribbean (#20556)

♦ United Nations Economic Commission for Latin America and the Caribbean (ECLAC) 20556

Commission économique des Nations Unies pour l'Amérique latine et les Caraïbes (CEPALC) – Comisión Económica de las Naciones Unidas para América Latina y el Caribe (CEPAL)

Contact Av Dag Hammarskjöld 3477, Vitacura, Casilla 179D, 7630412 Santiago, Santiago Metropolitan, Chile. T. +56224712000. Fax +56222080252. E-mail: prensa@cepal.org.
Street Address Av Dag Hammarskjöld 3477, Vitacura, Santiago, Santiago Metropolitan, Chile.
URL: http://www.eclac.org/

History 25 Feb 1948, by Resolution 106 (VI) of *ECOSOC (#05331)*, as a subsidiary organ of ECOSOC, to which it reports periodically, and one of five regional commissions of *United Nations (UN, #20515)*. Original title: *United Nations Economic Commission for Latin America (ECLA) – Commission économique des Nations Unies pour l'Amérique latine – Comisión Económica de las Naciones Unidas para América Latina*. The scope of the Commission was later broadened to include the countries of the Caribbean and by resolution 1984/67 of 27 Jul 1984, adopted its present title as of 1985. **Aims** Original mandate: contribute to economic development of Latin America and the Caribbean, coordinate actions directed towards this end and reinforce economic relationships among the countries and with other nations of the world. Mandate later included promotion of the region's social and sustainable development.
Structure Organizations of ECLAC System:
'Biennial Session of the Commission' (in even-numbered years) – reviews the work of the Secretariat and approves its biennial Work Programme. Includes 2 ad hoc committees: Cooperation among Developing Countries and Regions; Population and Development.
'Committee of the Whole' (meeting if necessary in years when there is no Biennial Session, normally in New York NY) was set up in 1952 and meets with member states' permanent representatives at UN to review the work of the Secretariat and approve the biennial Work Programme.
'Secretariat', based in Santiago (Chile) and headed by the Executive Secretary who is assisted by the Deputy Executive Secretary, oversees: Division of Administration; Programme Planning and Operations Division; Office of the Secretary of the Commission; Subregional Headquarters (2); National Offices (5).
Subsidiary bodies:
- *Committee of High-Level Government Experts (CEGAN, see: #20556)* (meeting as necessary) was set up in 1971 and coordinates among developing country members of the Commission.
- *Regional Conference on Women in Latin America and the Caribbean (#18770)* (session every 3 years), was set up in 1977 by the Regional Action Plan for the Integration of Women into Latin American Economic and Social Development, adopted in 1977, Havana (Cuba), and acts as liaison between member governments and ECLAC Secretariat.
- *Consejo Regional de Planificación (CRP, #04725)* (meeting every 2 years) was set up in 1974 and is the guiding intergovernmental body of ILPES.
- *Conferencia Estadística de las Américas (CEA CEPAL, see: #20556)*, set up 25 Jul 2000;
- *Central American Economic Cooperation Committee (#03667)* was set up in 1952 and acts as a consultative and advisory body for the 5 Central American member countries of ECLAC in matters concerning Central American economic integration;
- *Caribbean Council for Science and Technology (CCST, #03485)* was set up in 1980 and promotes cooperation in the field of science and technology aimed at furthering the social and economic development of member nations.

Languages English, French, Portuguese, Spanish. **Staff** 500.00 FTE, paid. Personnel negotiations through *ECLAC Staff Association (#05285)*. **Finance** For biennium 2010-2011: US$ 110,129,900 from UN budget; estimated voluntary extrabudgetary contributions, about US$ 24.5 million.
Activities Reports periodically to ECOSOC on its economic and social development activities in the region; provides secretariat services and documentation for the Commission and its subsidiary bodies; coordinates ECLAC activities with those of the major departments and offices at UN Headquarters, specialized agencies and intergovernmental organizations with a view to avoiding duplication and ensuring complementarity in the exchange of information; provides advisory services to governments at their request and plans, organizes and executes programmes of technical cooperation; formulates and promotes development cooperation activities and projects of regional and subregional scope commensurate with the needs and priorities of the region and acts as an executing agency for such projects; undertakes studies, research and other support activities within the terms of reference of the Commission; gathers, organizes, interprets and disseminates information and data relating to the economic and social development of the region; promotes economic and social development through regional and subregional cooperation and integration; assists in bringing a regional perspective to global problems and forums and introduces global concerns at the regional and subregional levels; collaborates with governments of the region in the investigation and analysis of regional and national economic and social problems and provides guidance in the formulation of development plans; organizes and convenes regional intergovernmental meetings on topics in the field of economic and social development; organizes regional preparatory meetings prior to global conferences which serve as a basis for discussion and allow the region to reach consensus; contributes to UN-sponsored global conferences and summits, including those on sustainable development, human rights, population and development, social development, women, human settlements, small island developing states and the information society; organizes conferences and intergovernmental and expert group meetings and sponsors training workshops, symposia and seminars.
Work Programmes are executed by the Secretariat through 9 Divisions: Economic Development; Social Development; Productive Development and Management; Sustainable Development and Human Settlements; Natural Resources and Infrastructure; Gender Affairs; Statistics and Economic Projections; Population -*Latin American and Caribbean Demographic Centre (#16273)*; International Trade and Integration.
Events *International Forum on Energy for Sustainable Development* Geneva (Switzerland) 2022, *International Forum on Energy for Sustainable Development* Geneva (Switzerland) 2021, *International Forum on Energy for Sustainable Development* Bangkok (Thailand) 2019, *Biennial Session* Havana (Cuba) 2018, *International Forum on Energy for Sustainable Development* Kiev (Ukraine) 2018. **Publications** *CEPAL Review* in English, Spanish; *Demographic Bulletin* in English, Spanish; *FAL Bulletin* in English, Spanish; *Notas de Población* in Spanish. *Comercio Internacional*; *Mujer y Desarrollo*; *Seminarios y Conferencias*; *Reformas Económics*; *Recursos Naturales e Infraestructura*; *Políticas Sociales*; *Política Fiscal*; *Población y Desarrollo*; *Medio Ambiente y Desarrollo*; *Desarrollo Productive*; *Manuales*; *Macroeconomia del Desarrollo*; *Informes y Estudios Especiales*; *Gestión Pública*; *Financiamiento del Desarrollo*; *Estudios y Perspectives*; *Estudios Estadisticos y Prospectivos*; *Temas de Coyuntura*. Books; institutional periodical reports.
Members Governments of 44 countries:
Antigua-Barbuda, Argentina, Bahamas, Barbados, Belize, Bolivia, Brazil, Canada, Chile, Colombia, Costa Rica, Cuba, Dominica, Dominican Rep, Ecuador, El Salvador, France, Germany, Grenada, Guatemala, Guyana, Haiti, Honduras, Italy, Jamaica, Japan, Korea Rep, Mexico, Netherlands, Nicaragua, Panama, Paraguay, Peru, Portugal, Spain, St Kitts-Nevis, St Lucia, St Vincent-Grenadines, Suriname, Trinidad-Tobago, UK, Uruguay, USA, Venezuela.
Associate Members governments of 8 territories:
Anguilla, Aruba, Cayman Is, Montserrat, Puerto Rico, Turks-Caicos, Virgin Is UK, Virgin Is USA.
IGO Relations Observer to: *International Organization for Migration (IOM, #14454)*; *World Trade Organization (WTO, #21864)*. Works in close cooperation with other organs and specialized agencies of the UN System:
- *Central American Bank for Economic Integration (CABEI, #03658)*;
- *FAO (#09260)*;
- *ILO (#11123)* (Regional Office for Latin America and the Caribbean);
- *International Bank for Reconstruction and Development (IBRD, #12317)* (World Bank);
- *International Maritime Organization (IMO, #14102)*;
- *International Monetary Fund (IMF, #14180)*;
- *International Trade Centre (ITC, #15703)*;
- *Office of the United Nations High Commissioner for Human Rights (OHCHR, #17697)*;
- *Organisation of Eastern Caribbean States (OECS, #17804)*;
- *Pan American Health Organization (PAHO, #18108)*;
- *UNEP (#20299)*;
- *UN Women (#20724)*;
- *UNCTAD (#20285)*;
- *UNDP (#20292)*;
- *UNESCO (#20322)*;
- *UNICEF (#20332)*;
- *UNIDO (#20336)*;
- *United Nations Group on the Information Society (UNGIS, #20570)*;
- *United Nations Human Settlements Programme (UN-Habitat, #20572)*;
- *United Nations Population Fund (UNFPA, #20612)*.

Also cooperates closely with:
- *Association of Caribbean States (ACS, #02411)*;
- *Caribbean Action Plan (CAR, #03432)*;
- *Central American Integration System (#03671)*;
- *Inter-American Development Bank (IDB, #11427)*;
- *Latin American Energy Organization (#16313)*;
- *OAS (#17629)*;
- *OECD (#17693)*;
- *Sistema Económico Latinoamericano (SELA, #19294)*;
- *Southern Common Market (#19868)*;
- *Union of South American Nations (#20481)*;
- *World Food Programme (WFP, #21510)*.

NGO Relations Contacts with the following NGOs in Consultative Status with ECOSOC:
- *Baha'i International Community (#03062)*;
- *Consejo de Educación de Adultos de América Latina (CEAAL, #04707)*;
- *Consejo Latinoamericano de Ciencias Sociales (CLACSO, #04718)*;
- *Consumers International (CI, #04773)*;
- *Indian Council of South America (#11158)*;
- *Inter American Press Association (IAPA, #11444)*;
- *Inter-American Statistical Institute (IASI, #11452)*;
- *International Chamber of Commerce (ICC, #12534)*;
- *International Council for Adult Education (ICAE, #12983)*;
- *International Council on Social Welfare (ICSW, #13076)*;
- *International Federation of Business and Professional Women (BPW International, #13376)*;

- *International Federation of Red Cross and Red Crescent Societies (#13526)*;
- *International Institute of Public Finance (IIPF, #13915)*;
- *International Organisation of Employers (IOE, #14428)*;
- *International Social Science Council (ISSC, inactive)*;
- *International Statistical Institute (ISI, #15603)*;
- *International Trade Union Confederation (ITUC, #15708)*;
- *IPS – Inter Press Service International Association (#16013)*;
- *Society for International Development (SID, #19581)*;
- *World Alliance of Young Men's Christian Associations (YMCA, #21090)*;
- *World Business Council for Sustainable Development (WBCSD, #21254)*;
- *World Economic Forum (WEF, #21367)*;
- *World Federation of Trade Unions (WFTU, #21493)*;
- *World Organization of the Scout Movement (WOSM, #21693)*. [2014/XE4175/**E***]

♦ United Nations Economic Commission for Western Asia / see United Nations Economic and Social Commission for Western Asia (#20558)

♦ United Nations Economic and Social Commission for Asia and the Pacific (ESCAP) 20557

Commission économique et sociale des Nations Unies pour l'Asie et le Pacifique (CESAP) – Comisión Económica y Social de las Naciones Unidas para Asia y el Pacifico (CESPAP)

Exec Sec United Nations Building, Rajadamnern Avenue, Bangkok, 10200, Thailand. T. +6622881234. Fax +6622881000. E-mail: comm_ctr.unescap@un.org – unisbkk.unescap@un.org.
URL: http://www.unescap.org/

History 28 Mar 1947. Established provisionally, by Resolution 37 (IV) of *ECOSOC (#05331)*. Present name adopted by ECOSOC Resolution 1895 (LVII), to reflect the much broader developmental goals and geographical reach that it had by then acquired. Its mandate was broadened further in 1977 by the General Assembly which recognized ESCAP and other regional commissions as the main general economic and social development centres within the United Nations system for their respective regions and as executing agencies for inter-country development projects in their own right. A regional commission of *United Nations (UN, #20515)*. Former names and other names: *United Nations Economic Commission for Asia and the Far East (ECAFE)* – former; *Commission économique des Nations Unies pour l'Asie et l'Extrême-Orient (CEAEO)* – former; *Comisión Económica de las Naciones Unidas para Asia y el Lejano Oriente (CEPALO)* – former; *UNESCAP* – former. **Aims** Original mandate: assist in regional *reconstruction* efforts of countries devastated by *war*. This mandate was subsequently broadened to encompass *development* issues in general. Programmes and projects aim to stimulate growth, improve *socio-economic* conditions and help build the foundations of modern society. Mission Statement: reduce *poverty*, manage *globalization* and address emerging social issues. **Structure** Commission meets annually at ministerial level. Advisory Committee of Permanent Representatives and Other Representatives Designated by Members of the Commission (APCR), composed of members and associate members. Thematic Committees (3): Managing Globalization; Poverty Reduction; Emerging Social Issues. Special Bodies (2): Least Developed and Landlocked Developing Countries; Pacific Island Developing Countries. Secretariat, comprising Office of the Executive Secretary, including United Nations Information Services and LDC Coordination Unit, and 10 Divisions/Centres: Trade and Investment Division (TID); Environment and Sustainable Development Division (ESDD); Poverty and Development Division (PDD); Emerging Social Issues Division (ESID); Transport and Tourism Division (TTD); Information, Communication and Space Technology Division (ICSTD); Statistics Division (SD); Programme Management Division (PMD); Administrative Services Division (ASD); *UNESCAP Pacific Operations Centre (UN/EPOC, see: #20557)*. **Languages** Chinese, English, French, Russian. **Staff** 582.00 FTE, paid. **Finance** Regular budget of the United Nations; extra-budgetary.

Activities Acts as "think-tank" and catalyst for such major regional ventures such as the Asian Development Bank and *Asian Highway Network (#01504)*. In the absence of any other such institutional arrangement for region-wide, high-level political assembly, constitutes a forum for governments in the Asia-Pacific region. At ministerial-level, provides an opportunity for governments to meet every year to review and discuss economic and social issues in order to promote and strengthen regional cooperation. Technical assistance, provided through ESCAP's in-house multidisciplinary capability, focuses chiefly on direct advisory services to governments, training and pooling of regional experience and information through meetings, publications and inter-country networks. Implementing project to form a network of centres of education, training and research in transport planning and policy development and logistics in the region. Divisions/Centres, each conducting its own meetings, projects and publications. Priority areas include: promotion of intra-regional trade and investment; transfer of technology; privatization and entrepreneurship; environment; urbanization; poverty alleviation; drug abuse control; population; social development; labour migration.
Regional research and training institutions (4):
- *Centre for Sustainable Agricultural Mechanization (CSAM, #03789)*;
- *Asian and Pacific Centre for Transfer of Technology (APCTT, #01603)*;
- *Asian and Pacific Training Centre for Information and Communication Technology for Development (APCICT, #01645)*;
- *Statistical Institute for Asia and the Pacific (SIAP, #19972)*.

The work of ESCAP is organized under 3 thematic areas:
- *'Poverty Reduction'*: Poverty and Development Division – helps reduce poverty through research and operational activities, analyses, tests, documents and disseminates innovative policies and practices in poverty reduction; provides practical advice and assistance in adapting and replicating proven good practices and programmes in poverty reduction that target the most vulnerable groups in society, including women; monitors and analyses global, regional and sub-regional economic and social trends and development issues that have an impact on poverty levels.
- Statistics Division – works to strengthen the statistical infrastructure in countries of the region and helps them monitor their progress towards achieving the 'Millennium Development Goals'.

'Managing Globalization': Trade and Investment Division – through a mix of research and operational activities, works to assist developing countries cope with the strains placed on their economies by the increasing pace of globalization and provides training to improve understanding of the complexities of the Doha Development process to officials from countries preparing to apply for WTO membership. Environment and Sustainable Development Division – works to promote regional and sub-regional cooperation and capacity-building for the sustainable development of natural resources, with a focus on energy and water sectors, and to strengthen national capacities for achieving environmentally sound development. Transport and Tourism Division – by providing technical advice and shared knowledge, works to assist Member Governments develop efficient regional and interregional transport linkages, improve infrastructures and promote sustainable tourism at the national, sub-regional and regional levels. Information, Communication and Space Technology Division – promotes regional cooperation and an enabling environment for the development, transfer and application of information, communication and space technology; works to address critical regional issues such as cyber-crime. *'Addressing Emerging Social Issues'*: Emerging Social Issues Division – works to identify emerging social issues, especially those that directly affect the poor and other vulnerable and disadvantaged groups of people in the region; works to increase awareness and understanding of how various issues, like population ageing, lowered fertility rates and HIV/AIDS affect each country and the region as a whole. Special emphasis is also placed on ways to empower women and prevent the stigma and discrimination of persons with disabilities. One centre and 2 programme supports are: ESCAP/POC – provides technical assistance to the Pacific island countries; Programme Management Division; Administrative Services Division.
Annual Session held in Bangkok (Thailand) since 1995 (exceptions in Events).

Events *International Forum on Energy for Sustainable Development* Geneva (Switzerland) 2022, *Forum on Carbon Neutrality Goals of China, Japan and the Republic of Korea* Incheon (Korea Rep) 2021, *International Forum on Low Carbon Cities* Incheon (Korea Rep) 2021, *North-East Asian Multistakeholder Forum on Sustainable Development Goals 2021* Incheon (Korea Rep) 2021, *Regional Environmentally Sustainable Transport Forum in Asia* Tokoname (Japan) 2021. **Publications** *ESCAP Newsletter* (12 a year); *Asia-Pacific Population Journal* (2 a year); *Asia-Pacific Development Journal* (2 a year); *Asia-Pacific Countries with Special Needs Development Report* (annual); *Asia-Pacific Trade and Investment Report* (annual). Directories; conference proceedings; working papers; briefs. Information Services: *ESCAP Bibliographic Information Systems (EBIS, no recent information)*.

Members Governments of 53 countries and territories:
Afghanistan, Armenia, Australia, Azerbaijan, Bangladesh, Bhutan, Brunei Darussalam, Cambodia, China, Fiji, France, Georgia, India, Indonesia, Iran Islamic Rep, Japan, Kazakhstan, Kiribati, Korea DPR, Korea Rep, Kyrgyzstan, Laos, Malaysia, Maldives, Marshall Is, Micronesia FS, Mongolia, Myanmar, Nauru, Nepal, Netherlands, New Zealand, Pakistan, Palau, Papua New Guinea, Philippines, Russia, Samoa, Singapore, Solomon Is, Sri Lanka, Tajikistan, Thailand, Timor-Leste, Tonga, Türkiye, Turkmenistan, Tuvalu, UK, USA, Uzbekistan, Vanuatu, Vietnam.

Associate Members (9), none being a member of the United Nations:
Cook Is, Guam, Hong Kong, Macau, New Caledonia, Niue, Northern Mariana Is, Polynesia Fr, Samoa USA.
In addition, non-member countries which are members of the United Nations may participate in a consultative capacity in discussions of matters of particular concern to them.

IGO Relations Member of: *United Nations Group on the Information Society (UNGIS, #20570)*; *UN-Water (#20723)*.

NGO Relations Links with the following NGOs in Consultative Status with ECOSOC:
- *International Alliance of Women (IAW, #11639)*;
- *International Chamber of Commerce (ICC, #12534)*;
- *International Co-operative Alliance (ICA, #12944)*;
- *International Council on Social Welfare (ICSW, #13076)*;
- *International Council of Voluntary Agencies (ICVA, #13092)*;
- *International Council of Women (ICW, #13093)*;
- *International Federation of Business and Professional Women (BPW International, #13376)*;
- *International Organisation of Employers (IOE, #14428)*;
- *International Planned Parenthood Federation (IPPF, #14589)*;
- *International Social Security Association (ISSA, #14885)*;
- *International Trade Union Confederation (ITUC, #15708)*;
- *International Union of Microbiological Societies (IUMS, #15794)*;
- *Muslim World League (MWL, #16917)*;
- *Organisation of African Trade Union Unity (OATUU, #17798)*;
- *Society for International Development (SID, #19581)*;
- *Women's International Democratic Federation (WIDF, #21022)*;
- *World Assembly of Youth (WAY, #21113)*;
- *World Federation of Democratic Youth (WFDY, #21427)*;
- *World Federation of Trade Unions (WFTU, #21493)*;
- *World Federation of United Nations Associations (WFUNA, #21499)*;
- *World Muslim Congress (WMC, #21664)*;
- *The World Veterans Federation (WVF, #21900)*. [2020/XE4177/**E***]

♦ United Nations Economic and Social Commission for Western Asia (ESCWA) 20558

Commission économique et sociale des Nations Unies pour l'Asie occidentale (CESAO) – Comisión Económica y Social de las Naciones Unidas para el Asia Occidental (CESPAO)

Exec Sec PO Box 11-8575, Riad el-Solh Square, Beirut, Lebanon. T. +9611981301 – +9611978802. Fax +9611981510.
URL: http://www.unescwa.org/

History 9 Aug 1973, by Resolution 1818 (LV) of *ECOSOC (#05331)*, as a regional commission of *United Nations (UN, #20515)*, integrating *United Nations Economic and Social Office in Beirut (UNESOB, inactive)*, set up in 1963. Commenced operations in Jan 1974. Original title: *United Nations Economic Commission for Western Asia (ECWA) – Commission économique des Nations Unies pour l'Asie occidentale (CEAO) – Comisión Económica de las Naciones Unidas para el Asia Occidental (CEPAO)*. Current title adopted 1985. Original membership comprised UN member states which formerly belonged to UNESOB, with further applications for membership decided upon by ECOSOC on recommendation of the Commission. ECOSOC Resolution 2089 (LXIII), 22 Jul 1977, amended terms of reference as recommended by the Commission so as to provide for the membership of Palestine Liberation Organization (PLO); Egypt was admitted to membership at the same time. Sudan was admitted 2008. **Aims** Support economic and social development in the countries of the region; promote cooperation; encourage interaction; promote exchange of experiences, best practices and lessons learned. **Structure** /Policy making organs/: Biennial Meeting provides overall direction to the work of the secretariat. Specialized subsidiary inter-governmental committees (7): Energy; Water Resources; Social Development; Transport; Liberalization of Foreign Trade and Economic Globalization; Statistics; Women. Consultative Committee on Science and Technology – high level technical committee; Advisory Committee of Ambassadors. /Executive direction and management/ Composed of the Office of the Executive Secretary (OES) – provides overall direction and integrated management, programme oversight, planning and coordination, as well as policy guidelines to the substantive divisions, the technical cooperation programme and other support services. /Programme support/ Administrative Services Division and Programme Planning and Technical Cooperation Division provide programme support. **Languages** Arabic, English, French. **Staff** 415.00 FTE, paid. Staff includes 124 professionals. Personnel negotiations through *Staff Union of the United Nations Economic and Social Commission for Western Asia (Staff Union-ESCWA, #19946)*. **Finance** Budget (annual): US$ 28,291,900 million; extra-budgetary: US$ 5,703,134 million. Budget covered by the United Nations. Main funding agencies: *Arab Gulf Programme for United Nations Development Organizations (AGFUND, #00971)*; ESCWA Trust Fund; *UNDP (#20292)*; *United Nations Population Fund (UNFPA, #20612)*. **Activities** Research/documentation; networking/liaising; knowledge management/information dissemination; guidance/assistance/consulting; capacity building. **Events** *International Forum on Energy for Sustainable Development* Geneva (Switzerland) 2022, *International Forum on Energy for Sustainable Development* Geneva (Switzerland) 2021, *Enhancing the Resilience and Sustainability of the Agricultural Sector in the Arab Region* Khartoum (Sudan) 2021, *International Forum on Energy for Sustainable Development* Bangkok (Thailand) 2019, *International Forum on Energy for Sustainable Development* Kiev (Ukraine) 2018. **Publications** *Annual Review of Developments in Globalisation and Regional Integration in the Arab Countries*. *The Economic and Social Survey*; *The Integrated Social Policies Report*; *The Millenium Development Goals in the Arab Region*. Produces over 50 publications every 2 years, more than half of which are recurrent publications and address issues of priority in each sub-programme. Publications can be found via the website.

Members Governments of 18 countries and territories:
Bahrain, Egypt, Iraq, Jordan, Kuwait, Lebanon, Libya, Mauritania, Morocco, Oman, Palestine, Qatar, Saudi Arabia, Sudan, Syrian AR, Tunisia, United Arab Emirates, Yemen.

IGO Relations Member of: *Inter-Agency Working Group on Desertification (IAWGD, inactive)*; *United Nations Group on the Information Society (UNGIS, #20570)*; *UN-Water (#20723)*. Collaborative organization of: *Arab Organization for Agricultural Development (AOAD, #01018)*. Partner of: *United Nations Public Administration Network (UNPAN, #20615)*. Memorandum of Understanding with: *Arab Women Organization (AWO, #01078)*; *International Centre for Migration Policy Development (ICMPD, #12503)*. **NGO Relations** In liaison with technical committees of: *International Organization for Standardization (ISO, #14473)*. Will serve as secretariat for the proposed: *Population Information Network for Western Asia (POPIN Western Asia, no recent information)*. Hosts: *Arab Water Network for Capacity Building (Awarenet, #01076)*. Close relationship with: *International Union for the Scientific Study of Population (IUSSP, #15814)*. [2016.03.02/XE4178/**E***]

♦ United Nations Economic and Social Council (#05331)
♦ United Nations Educational, Scientific and Cultural Organization (#20322)
♦ United Nations Educational and Training Programme for Southern Africa (inactive)
♦ United Nations Emergency Force (inactive)
♦ United Nations Environment Development – UK Committee / see Stakeholder Forum for a Sustainable Future
♦ United Nations Environment Programme (#20299)

♦ United Nations Environment Programme Finance Initiative (UNEP FI) 20559

Head Avenue de la Paix 8-14, 1211 Geneva 10, Switzerland. E-mail: info@unepfi.org.
URL: https://www.unepfi.org/

History Established in the run up to the *United Nations Conference on Environment and Development (UNCED)* – Rio Earth Summit, 1992. A partnership between *UNEP (#20299)* and the global financial sector. A unit with UNEP's Resources & Market Branch, part of the Economy Division. **Aims** Mobilize private sector finance for sustainable development; inspire, inform and enable financial institutions to improve people's quality of life without compromising that of future generations. **Structure** Annual General Meeting; Leadership Council; Global Steering Committee; Secretariat. Industry Committees: Banking; Insurance; Investment. Thematic Advisory Groups; Regional Advisory Groups. **Activities** Events/meetings; knowledge management/information dissemination; projects/programmes. **Events** *Sustainable Investment Forum Europe* London (UK) 2022, *Sustainable Investment Forum Europe* Paris (France) 2021, *Sustainable Investment Forum Europe* London (UK) 2020.

Members Financial institutions in 82 countries and territories:

Andorra, Argentina, Australia, Austria, Bahrain, Bangladesh, Belgium, Bermuda, Brazil, Bulgaria, Canada, Chile, China, Colombia, Costa Rica, Croatia, Cyprus, Czechia, Denmark, Dominican Rep, Ecuador, Egypt, El Salvador, Estonia, Finland, Germany, Ghana, Greece, Guatemala, Hong Kong, Hungary, Iceland, India, Indonesia, Ireland, Italy, Japan, Jordan, Kenya, Korea Rep, Latvia, Liechtenstein, Luxembourg, Malaysia, Mauritius, Mexico, Mongolia, Montenegro, Morocco, Myanmar, Namibia, Netherlands, New Zealand, Nicaragua, Nigeria, North Macedonia, Norway, Pakistan, Panama, Paraguay, Philippines, Poland, Portugal, Romania, Russia, Serbia, Singapore, Slovenia, South Africa, Spain, Suriname, Sweden, Switzerland, Thailand, Togo, Trinidad-Tobago, Türkiye, UK, Ukraine, United Arab Emirates, USA, Venezuela.

Supporting institutions in 50 countries and territories and including 39 organizations listed in this Yearbook: Argentina, Australia, Barbados, Belgium, Bermuda, Brazil, Canada, Chile, China, Colombia, Costa Rica, Ecuador, Egypt, Germany, Ghana, Greece, Guatemala, Guernsey, Hong Kong, Hungary, India, Indonesia, Ireland, Italy, Jordan, Kenya, Korea Rep, Lebanon, Luxembourg, Malawi, Mexico, Mongolia, Morocco, Netherlands, New Zealand, Norway, Panama, Paraguay, Peru, Philippines, Poland, Russia, Senegal, South Africa, Spain, St Lucia, Switzerland, Tanzania UR, UK, USA.

- *Acción Climática*;
- *African Institute of Corporate Citizenship (AICC)*;
- *Association of Development Financing Institutions in Asia and the Pacific (ADFIAP, #02472)*;
- *Association of Insurers and Reinsurers of Developing Countries (AIRDC, #02650)*;
- *Association of Mutual Insurers and Insurance Cooperatives in Europe (AMICE, #02816)*;
- *Caribbean Association of Banks (CAB, #03443)*;
- *Central European University (CEU, #03717)*;
- *Climate Bonds Initiative (#04006)*;
- *Deutsche Gesellschaft für Internationale Zusammenarbeit (GIZ)*;
- *European Association of Co-operative Banks (EACB, #05990)*;
- *European Banking Federation (EBF, #06312)*;
- *European Public Real Estate Association (EPRA, #08301)*;
- *European Savings and Retail Banking Group (ESBG, #08426)*;
- *European Sustainable Investment Forum (EUROSIF, #08865)*;
- *Federación Interamericana de Empresas de Seguros (FIDES, #09331)*;
- *Federación Internacional de Administradoras de Fondos de Pensiones (FIAP, #09334)*;
- *FSD Africa (#10010)*;
- *Institute for Global Environmental Strategies (IGES, #11266)*;
- *Insurance Association of the Caribbean (IAC, #11360)*;
- *Insurance Institute for Asia and the Pacific (IIAP)*;
- *International Actuarial Association (IAA, #11586)*;
- *International Association for the Representation of the Mutual Interests of the Inland Shipping and the Insurance and for Keeping the Register of Inland Vessels in Europe (#12131)*;
- *International Cooperative and Mutual Insurance Federation (ICMIF, #12948)*;
- *International Finance Corporation (IFC, #13597)*;
- *International Institute for Sustainable Development (IISD, #13930)*;
- *International Insurance Society (IIS, #13939)*;
- *International Union of Marine Insurance (IUMI, #15789)*;
- *Latin American Banking Association (#16254)*;
- *Latin American Confederation of Credit Unions (#16302)*;
- *Local Governments for Sustainability (ICLEI, #16507)*;
- *Microinsurance Network (#16747)*;
- *Multilateral Investment Guarantee Agency (MIGA, #16888)*;
- *Nordic Association of Marine Insurers (Cefor, #17198)*;
- *Oceana*;
- *Organization of Eastern and Southern Africa Insurers (OESAI, #17864)*;
- *The Nature Conservancy (TNC)*;
- *Union of Arab Banks (UAB, #20349)*;
- *World Benchmarking Alliance (WBA, #21228)*;
- *World Wide Fund for Nature (WWF, #21922)*. [2022/AA2663/y/**E**]

♦ United Nations Environment Programme Mediterranean Action Plan for the Barcelona Convention / see Mediterranean Action Plan (#16638)

♦ United Nations Evaluation Group (UNEG) 20560

Sec 220 East 42nd Street, Room 2036, New York NY 10017, USA. E-mail: uneg.contact@undp.org.
URL: http://www.unevaluation.org/

History Founded 1984, as *Inter Agency Working Group (IAWG)* by *UNDP (#20292)* Central Evaluation Office. Initially, IAWG was mainly composed of UNDP and its "executing agencies", ie UN specialized agencies through which UNDP implemented its programmes and collaborated for development work. Current name adopted, 2003. **Aims** Promote, strengthen and advocate for a robust, influential, independent and credible evaluation function throughout the UN system for decision-making, accountability and learning. **Structure** Annual General Meeting; Executive Steering Committee; Secretariat. **Languages** UN languages. **Staff** Voluntary. **Finance** Members' dues and contributions. **Activities** Standards/guidelines; guidance/assistance/consulting; advocacy/lobbying/activism; events/meetings. Active in: Africa; America; Asia; Europe. **Publications** *Evaluation Competency Framework* (2016); *Evaluation Changes Lives* (2015); *Integrating Human Rights and Gender Equality in Evaluations* (2014); *Impact Evaluation in UN Agency Evaluation Systems: Guidance on Selection, Planning and Management* (2013); *Resource Pack on Joint Evaluations* (2013); *UNEG Handbook for Conducing Evaluations of Normative Work in the UN System* (2013); *UNEG Guidance on Preparing Management Responses to UNDAF Evaluation* (2012); *UNEG Practical Tips on How to Strengthen National Evaluation Systems* (2012); *UNEG Code of Conduct for Evaluation in the UN System* (2008); *Norms for Evaluation in the UN System* (2005); *Standards for Evaluation in the UN System* (2005).

Members UN departments and organizations (50), including UN Secretariat Departments and Offices and Regional Commissions (14):

Department for General Assembly and Conference Management (DGACM), Monitoring, Evaluation, Risk Management and Statistical Verification Unit (MERS); Department for Peacekeeping Operations (DPKO); Department of Economic and Social Affairs (DESA), Development Cooperation Policy Branch; Department of Public Information (DPI), Evaluation and Communications Research Unit; Department of Safety and Security (DSS) – temporary member; Office of Internal Oversight Services (OIOS), Inspection and Evaluation Division; *Office of the United Nations High Commissioner for Human Rights (OHCHR, #17697)* (Policy, Planning, Monitoring and Evaluation Service); Peace Building Support Office (PBSO) Financing for Peacebuilding Branch; *United Nations Economic and Social Commission for Asia and the Pacific (ESCAP, #20557)* (Evaluation Unit); *United Nations Economic and Social Commission for Western Asia (ESCWA, #20558)* (Strategic Directions & Partnerships Section); *United Nations Economic Commission for Africa (ECA, #20554)* (Programme Planning and Monitoring and Evaluation Section); *United Nations Economic Commission for Europe (UNECE, #20555)* (Programme Management Unit); *United Nations Economic Commission for Latin America and the Caribbean (ECLAC, #20556)* (Programme Planning and Evaluation Unit); *United Nations Office for the Coordination of Humanitarian Affairs (OCHA, #20593)*.

UN Programmes and Funds established by the General Assembly (15):

International Trade Centre (ITC, #15703) (Evaluation and Monitoring Unit); *Joint United Nations Programme on HIV/AIDS (UNAIDS, #16149)* (Evaluation Unit); *UNCTAD (#20285)* (Evaluation and Monitoring Unit); *UNDP (#20292)* (Independent Evaluation Office); *UNEP (#20299)* (Evaluation Office); *UNHCR (#20327)* (Policy Development and Evaluation Service); *UNICEF (#20332)* (Evaluation Office); *United Nations Capital Development Fund (UNCDF, #20524)* (Evaluation Unit); *United Nations Human Settlements Programme (UN-Habitat, #20572)* (Evaluation Unit); *United Nations Office on Drugs and Crime (UNODC, #20596)* (Independent Evaluation Unit); *United Nations Population Fund (UNFPA, #20612)* (Evaluation Office); *United Nations Relief and Works Agency for Palestine Refugees in the Near East (UNRWA, #20622)* (Evaluation Division); *United Nations Volunteers (UNV, #20650)* (Evaluation Unit); *UN Women (#20724)* (Evaluation Office); *World Food Programme (WFP, #21510)*.

UN Specialized Agencies working through the Economic and Social Council (10):

FAO (#09260) (Office of Evaluation); *ILO (#11123)* (Evaluation Unit); *International Civil Aviation Organization (ICAO, #12581)* (Evaluation and Internal Audit Office); *International Fund for Agricultural Development (IFAD, #13692)* (Independent Office of Evaluation); *International Maritime Organization (IMO, #14102)* (Internal Oversight and Ethics Office and the Technical Co-operation Division); *UNESCO (#20322)* (Evaluation Section); *UNIDO (#20336)* (Evaluation Group); *WHO (#20950)* (Office of Internal Oversight Service); *World Intellectual Property Organization (WIPO, #21593)* (Evaluation Section); *World Meteorological Organization (WMO, #21649)*.

Related Organizations and Funds (7):

Comprehensive Nuclear-Test-Ban Treaty Organization (CTBTO, #04420) (Evaluation Section); *Global Environment Facility (GEF, #10346)* (Independent Evaluation Office); *International Atomic Energy Agency (IAEA, #12294)* (Programme Evaluation Function); *International Organization for Migration (IOM, #14454)* (Office of the Inspector General); *Organisation for the Prohibition of Chemical Weapons (OPCW, #17823)* (Office of Internal Oversight); *Pan American Health Organization (PAHO, #18108)* (Office of Internal Oversight and Evaluation Services); *World Trade Organization (WTO, #21864)*.

Research and training institutes (2):

United Nations Institute for Training and Research (UNITAR, #20576) (Planning, Performance and Results Section); *United Nations Interregional Crime and Justice Research Institute (UNICRI, #20580)* (Monitoring and Evaluation Unit).

Observers (3):

International Bank for Reconstruction and Development (IBRD, #12317) (World Bank Independent Evaluation Group IEG); *Joint Inspection Unit of the United Nations (JIU, #16133)*; SDG Achievement Fund (SDG-F).

IGO Relations Cooperates with: *Active Learning Network for Accountability and Performance in Humanitarian Action (ALNAP, #00101)*; Evaluation Cooperation Group (ECG); *International Organisation for Cooperation in Evaluation (IOCE, #14426)*; *OECD Development Assistance Committee (DAC, see: #17693)*. **NGO Relations** Cooperates with: *EvalPartners (#09208)*; *International Organisation for Cooperation in Evaluation (IOCE, #14426)*. [2020/XJ8546/y/**E**]

♦ United Nations Fellowship of Rotarians / see United Nations Friends in Rotary

♦ United Nations Field Staff Union (UNFSU) 20561

Syndicat du personnel de l'Organisation des Nations Unies

Secretariat c/o UNGSC/UNLB, Piazza Del Vento, 1 Casale, 72011 Brindisi BR, Italy. T. +39831056280. E-mail: fsu@un.org.
URL: http://www.unfsu.org/

History 1980, Israel. Founded within the framework of *United Nations (UN, #20515)*. Former names and other names: *Field Service Staff Union (FSSU)* – former (1 Mar 1980 to 1 Mar 2000); *UNFSU* – alias. **Aims** Defend the rights and supports the welfare and well-being of internationally recruited United Nations staff who are assigned to, and work in, UN Field Entities. **Structure** Executive; Council; Committee. **NGO Relations** Member of (1): *United Nations International Civil Servants Federation (UNISERV, #20579)*. [2022.10.19/XE4242/v/**E**]

♦ United Nations Forum on Forests (UNFF) 20562

Forum des Nations Unies sur les forêts – Foro de las Naciones Unidas sobre los Bosques

Dir DESA – UN Secretariat Bldg – 26th floor, 405 E 42nd Street, New York NY 10017, USA. T. +12129633401. Fax +19173673186. E-mail: unff@un.org.
URL: http://www.un.org/esa/forests/index.html

History 18 Oct 2000. Established by *ECOSOC (#05331)* by resolution 2000/35. A functional commission and subsidiary body of ECOSOC, based on the Rio Declaration, the Forest Principles, Chapter 11 of *Global Action Plan for Environment and Development in the 21st Century (Agenda 21, inactive)* and the outcome of *Intergovernmental Panel on Forests (IPF, inactive)* / *Intergovernmental Forum on Forests (IFF)* Processes and other key milestones of international forest policy. **Aims** Promote management, conservation and sustainable development of all types of forest; strengthen long-term political commitment to this end. **Structure** Forum (meets biennially); Bureau, comprising Chairperson and 4 Vice-Chairpersons. Secretariat, headed by Director. **Languages** Arabic, Chinese, English, French, Russian, Spanish. **Activities** Advocacy/lobbying/activism; policy/politics/regulatory; networking/liaising. **Events** *Session* New York, NY (USA) 2022, *Session* New York, NY (USA) 2019, *Session* New York, NY (USA) 2018, *Session* New York, NY (USA) 2017, *Session* New York, NY (USA) 2015. **Publications** Session reports; reports of the Secretary-General on topics for discussion at sessions. **Members** Open to all UN Member States and Member States of specialized agencies. **Consultative Status** Observer Status (11): *African Forest Forum (AFF, #00318)*; *Amazon Cooperation Treaty Organization (ACTO, #00766)*; *ASEAN (#01141)*; *Center for International Forestry Research (CIFOR, #03646)*; *Commission des forêts d'Afrique centrale (COMIFAC, #04214)*; *International Network for Bamboo and Rattan (INBAR, #14234)*; *International Tropical Timber Organization (ITTO, #15737)*; *Ministerial Conference on the Protection of Forests in Europe (FOREST EUROPE, #16817)*; *Pacific Community (SPC, #17942)*; *Working Group on Criteria and Indicators for the Conservation and Sustainable Management of Temperate and Boreal Forests (Montreal Process, #21058)*; *World Agroforestry Centre (ICRAF, #21072)*. **IGO Relations** Member of and acts as secretariat of: *Collaborative Partnership on Forests (CPF, #04100)*. **NGO Relations** Major Group Focal Point system with focal points from each of the major groups: Business and Industry; Children and Youth; Indigenous People; Local Authorities; Non-governmental Organizations; Scientific and Technological Communities; Small Forest Landowners / Farmers; Women; Workers and Trade Unions. Participating networks include: *Asia-Pacific Association of Forestry Research Institutions (APAFRI, #01841)*; *Building and Wood Workers' International (BWI, #03355)*; *Global Alliance of Community Forestry (GACF, #10190)*; *International Forestry Students' Association (IFSA, #13628)*; *Women Organizing for Change in Agriculture and Natural Resource Management (WOCAN)*. [2022/XF6300/**F***]

♦ United Nations Foundation (UNF) 20563

Pres/CEO 320 East 43rd Street, 3rd Floor, New York NY 10017, USA. T. +12126973315.
Contact 1750 Pennsylvania Ave NW, Ste 300, Washington DC 20006, USA. T. +12028879040. Fax +12028879021.
URL: http://www.unfoundation.org/

History 20 May 1998. Founded to administer the gift of US$ 1,000 million announced by R E Turner, Sep 1997. Not legally constituted as a foundation but as a public charity. **Aims** Fund projects focusing on *prevention*, mainly in the areas of: *population* and *women's* issues; *environment* and *climate change*; *children's health*. **Structure** International Board of Directors, chaired by R E Turner. Administered through *United Nations Fund for International Partnerships (UNFIP, #20565)*. **Finance** Sources: original donation, 90%: other donors, 10%. **Activities** Closely collaborates with UNFIP. Leads *Clean Cooking Alliance (#03987)*. **Events** *Social Good Summit* New York, NY (USA) 2018, *Social Good Summit* New York, NY (USA) 2017, *Annual Solutions Summit* New York, NY (USA) 2016, *Social Good Summit* New York, NY (USA) 2016, *Australia Social Good Summit* Sydney, NSW (Australia) 2015. **Members** Not a membership organization. **Consultative Status** Consultative status granted from: *ECOSOC (#05331)* (Ros B); *UNEP (#20299)*. **IGO Relations** Accredited by: *United Nations Framework Convention on Climate Change – Secretariat (UNFCCC, #20564)*. Member of: *Global Bioenergy Partnership (GBEP, #10251)*. Cooperates with: *Caribbean Action Plan (CAR, #03432)*. Supports: *WMO Resource Mobilization Office (RMO, see: #21649)*. Sustainable Development Programme is Affiliate member of: *World Tourism Organization (UNWTO, #21861)*. Most likely recipients: *UNEP (#20299)*; *UNICEF (#20332)*; *United Nations Population Fund (UNFPA, #20612)*.

NGO Relations Member of: *Africa Grantmakers' Affinity Group (AGAG)*; *Alliance for Malaria Prevention (AMP, #00706)*; *GEF CSO Network (GCN, #10087)*; *InsideNGO (inactive)*; *Paediatric Radiation Oncology Society (PROS, #18019)*; *Planetary Health Alliance (PHA, #18383)*; *Reproductive Health Supplies Coalition (RHSC, #18847)*. Associate member of: *Globalization Studies Network (GSN, #10440)*. Partner of: *World Leadership Alliance – Club de Madrid (WLA-CdM, #21619)*; *Global Innovation Exchange (The Exchange, inactive)*. Hosts: *Family Planning 2020 (FP2020, inactive)*. Supports:

- *Conectas Human Rights*;
- *The Elders Foundation (#05413)*;
- *Every Woman Every Child (EWEC, #09215)*;
- *International Centre for Trade and Sustainable Development, Geneva (ICTSD, #12524)*;
- *International Initiative for Impact Evaluation (3ie, #13851)*;
- *International Planned Parenthood Federation (IPPF, #14589)*;
- *Many Strong Voices (MSV, #16568)*;
- *Partnership for African Social and Governance Research (PASGR, #18230)*;
- *Tostan (#20176)*;
- *Transparency International (TI, #20223)*;
- *UNEP Copenhagen Climate Centre (#20296)*. [2020/XG7799/f/**F**]

♦ United Nations Framework Convention on Climate Change (1992 treaty)

♦ United Nations Framework Convention on Climate Change – Secretariat (UNFCCC) 20564

Convention-cadre des nations unies sur les changements climatiques – Secrétariat (CCNUCC)

Exec Sec PO Box 260-124, 53153 Bonn, Germany. T. +492288151000. Fax +492288151999. E-mail: secretariat@unfccc.int.
Street Address UN Campus, Platz der Vereinten Nationen 1, 53113 Bonn, Germany.
URL: http://unfccc.int/
History 1995, Geneva (Switzerland). Established as permanent secretariat to *United Nations Framework Convention on Climate Change (UNFCCC, 1992)*, having previously acted as secretariat to *Climate Convention Information Exchange Programme (CC:INFO, inactive)* in the run-up to implementing the Convention. Set up by the Conference of the Parties to, and under the terms of, the Convention. Relocated to Bonn (Germany), Aug 1996. Former names and other names: *UNFCCC Climate Change Secretariat* – former. **Aims** According to Article 8 of the Convention: (a) make arrangements for sessions of the Conference of the Parties and its subsidiary bodies established under the Convention and provide them with services as required; (b) compile and transmit reports submitted to it; (c) facilitate assistance to the Parties, particularly *developing countries*, on request, in compilation and communication of information required in accordance with the provisions of the Convention; (d) prepare reports on its activities and present them to the Conference of the Parties; (e) ensure the necessary coordination with secretariats of other relevant international bodies; (f) under the overall guidance of the Conference of the Parties, enter into such administrative and contractual arrangements as may be required for the effective discharge of its functions; (g) perform the other secretariat functions specified in the Convention and its protocols and such other functions as may be determined by the Conference of the Parties. **Structure** Institutionally linked to the United Nations and administered under UN rules and regulations. Headed by Executive Secretary, appointed by UN Secretary-General in consultation with the Bureau of the Conference of Parties (COP). Secretariat is a neutral body of civil servants responding to COP through the Executive Secretary; work of the Secretariat is guided by Bureaux of the Convention bodies and includes the following: Executive Division; Legal Affairs Division; Intergovernmental Support and Collective Progress Division; Adaptation Division; Conference Affairs Division; Administrative Services, Human Resources, and Information and Communication Technology Division; Communications and Engagement Division; Operations Coordination; Means of Implementation Division; Mitigation Division; Transparency Division. **Languages** Arabic, Chinese, English, French, Russian, Spanish. **Staff** 500.00 FTE, paid. **Activities** Guidance/assistance/consulting; management of treaties and agreements. Manages the following treaties/agreements: *Kyoto Protocol to the United Nations Framework Convention on Climate Change (1997)*; *Paris Agreement (2015)*; *United Nations Framework Convention on Climate Change (UNFCCC, 1992)*. **Events** *Annual Session of the Conference of the Parties* Sharm el Sheikh (Egypt) 2022, *Climate and SDGs Conference* Tokyo (Japan) 2022, *Global Conference on Strengthening Synergies between the Paris Agreement and the 2030 Agenda for Sustainable Development* Tokyo (Japan) 2022, *Annual Session of the Conference of the Parties* Glasgow (UK) 2021, *Asia-Pacific Climate Week Thematic Session* Tokyo (Japan) 2021.
Members State Parties (197) as of Feb 2022:
Afghanistan, Albania, Algeria, Andorra, Angola, Antigua-Barbuda, Argentina, Armenia, Australia, Austria, Azerbaijan, Bahamas, Bahrain, Bangladesh, Barbados, Belarus, Belgium, Belize, Benin, Bhutan, Bolivia, Bosnia-Herzegovina, Botswana, Brazil, Brunei Darussalam, Bulgaria, Burkina Faso, Burundi, Cambodia, Cameroon, Canada, Cape Verde, Central African Rep, Chad, Chile, China, Colombia, Comoros, Congo Brazzaville, Congo DR, Cook Is, Costa Rica, Côte d'Ivoire, Croatia, Cuba, Cyprus, Czechia, Denmark, Djibouti, Dominica, Dominican Rep, Ecuador, Egypt, El Salvador, Equatorial Guinea, Eritrea, Estonia, Eswatini, Ethiopia, Fiji, Finland, France, Gabon, Gambia, Georgia, Germany, Ghana, Greece, Grenada, Guatemala, Guinea, Guinea-Bissau, Guyana, Haiti, Honduras, Hungary, Iceland, India, Indonesia, Iran Islamic Rep, Iraq, Ireland, Israel, Italy, Jamaica, Japan, Jordan, Kazakhstan, Kenya, Kiribati, Korea DPR, Korea Rep, Kuwait, Kyrgyzstan, Laos, Latvia, Lebanon, Lesotho, Liberia, Libya, Liechtenstein, Lithuania, Luxembourg, Madagascar, Malawi, Malaysia, Maldives, Mali, Malta, Marshall Is, Mauritania, Mauritius, Mexico, Micronesia FS, Moldova, Monaco, Mongolia, Montenegro, Morocco, Mozambique, Myanmar, Namibia, Nauru, Nepal, Netherlands, New Zealand, Nicaragua, Niger, Nigeria, Niue, North Macedonia, Norway, Oman, Pakistan, Palau, Palestine, Panama, Papua New Guinea, Paraguay, Peru, Philippines, Poland, Portugal, Qatar, Romania, Russia, Rwanda, Samoa, San Marino, Sao Tomé-Principe, Saudi Arabia, Senegal, Serbia, Seychelles, Sierra Leone, Singapore, Slovakia, Slovenia, Solomon Is, Somalia, South Africa, South Sudan, Spain, Sri Lanka, St Kitts-Nevis, St Lucia, St Vincent-Grenadines, Sudan, Suriname, Sweden, Switzerland, Syrian AR, Tajikistan, Tanzania UR, Thailand, Timor-Leste, Togo, Tonga, Trinidad-Tobago, Tunisia, Türkiye, Turkmenistan, Tuvalu, Uganda, UK, Ukraine, United Arab Emirates, Uruguay, USA, Uzbekistan, Vanuatu, Venezuela, Vietnam, Yemen, Zambia, Zimbabwe.
Included, 1 regional entity:
European Union (EU, #08967).
IGO Relations Accredited bodies attending COP sessions:
- *Adaptation Fund (AF, #00109)* Board;
- *Organisation of African, Caribbean and Pacific States (OACPS, #17796)*;
- *African Centre of Meteorological Applications for Development (ACMAD, #00242)*;
- *African Development Bank (ADB, #00283)*;
- *African Regional Centre of Technology (ARCT, #00432)*;
- *African Union (AU, #00488)* Commission;
- *Amazon Cooperation Treaty Organization (ACTO, #00766)*;
- *Andean Community (#00817)*;
- *Arab Maghreb Union (AMU, #01004)*;
- *Arctic Athabaskan Council (AAC)*;
- *ASEAN (#01141)*;
- *Asian-African Legal Consultative Organization (AALCO, #01303)*;
- *Asian Development Bank (ADB, #01422)*;
- *Asian-Pacific Parliamentarians' Conference on Environment and Development (APPCED, #01621)*;
- *Asian Productivity Organization (APO, #01674)*;
- *Banque ouest africaine de développement (BOAD, #03170)*;
- *Black Sea Trade and Development Bank (BSTDB, #03278)*;
- *CABI (#03393)*;
- *Caribbean Community (CARICOM, #03476)* Secretariat;
- *Caribbean Community Climate Change Centre (CCCCC, #03477)*;
- *Caribbean Development Bank (CDB, #03492)*;
- *Caribbean Meteorological Organization (CMO, #03524)*;
- *Central American Bank for Economic Integration (CABEI, #03658)*;
- *Centre de coopération internationale en recherche agronomique pour le développement (CIRAD, #03733)*;
- *Comisión Centroamericana de Ambiente y Desarrollo (CCAD, #04129)*;
- *Comisión Permanente del Pacífico Sur (CPPS, #04141)*;
- *Comité permanent inter-Etats de lutte contre la sécheresse dans le Sahel (CILSS, #04195)*;
- *Commission for Environmental Cooperation (CEC, #04211)*;
- *Commonwealth Secretariat (#04362)*;
- *Communauté économique et monétaire d'Afrique centrale (CEMAC, #04374)*;
- *Congress of Local and Regional Authorities of the Council of Europe (#04677)*;
- *Council of Europe (CE, #04881)*;
- *Development Bank of Latin America (CAF, #05055)*;
- *EFTA (#05391)*;
- *Energy Charter Conference (#05466)*;
- *European Bank for Reconstruction and Development (EBRD, #06315)*;
- *European Space Agency (ESA, #08798)*;
- *European University Institute (EUI, #09034)*;
- *Independent World Commission on the Oceans (IWCO, inactive)*;
- *Inter-American Development Bank (IDB, #11427)*;
- *Inter-American Institute for Global Change Research (IAI, #11437)*;
- *International Development Research Centre (IDRC, #13162)*;
- *International Energy Agency (IEA, #13270)*;
- *International Institute of Biological Control (IIBC, inactive)*;
- *International Institute of Refrigeration (IIR, #13918)*;
- *International Organization for Migration (IOM, #14454)*;
- *International Transport Forum (ITF, #15725)*;
- *International Tropical Timber Organization (ITTO, #15737)*;
- *Latin American Energy Organization (#16313)*;
- *League of Arab States (LAS, #16420)*;
- *Nordic Council of Ministers (NCM, #17260)*;
- *Nordic Environment Finance Corporation (NEFCO, #17281)*;
- *OAS (#17629)*;
- *Organization of African Unity (OAU, inactive)*;
- *Observatoire du Sahara et du Sahel (OSS, #17636)*;
- *OECD (#17693)*;
- *OIC Ministerial Standing Committee on Scientific and Technological Cooperation (COMSTECH, #17702)*;
- *Organisation internationale de la Francophonie (OIF, #17809)*, replacing *Agence intergouvernementale de La Francophonie (inactive)*;
- *Organization of Arab Petroleum Exporting Countries (OAPEC, #17854)*;
- *Organization of the Petroleum Exporting Countries (OPEC, #17881)*;
- *Pacific Islands Forum Secretariat (#17970)*;
- *Parlamento Latinoamericano (PARLATINO, #18203)*;
- *Permanent Court of Arbitration (PCA, #18321)*;
- *Regional Environmental Centre for Central and Eastern Europe (REC, #18782)*;
- *Regional Organization for the Protection of the Marine Environment (ROPME, #18805)*;
- *Secretariat of the Pacific Regional Environment Programme (SPREP, #19205)*;
- *Secretariat of the Convention of Wetlands (#19200)*;
- *South Centre (#19753)*;
- *Southern African Development Community (SADC, #19843)*;
- *Tropical Agriculture Research and Higher Education Center (#20246)*.

Member of: *Collaborative Partnership on Forests (CPF, #04100)*; *UN-Water (#20723)*. Participates in: *Group on Earth Observations (GEO, #10735)*. Partner of: *United Nations Forum on Forests (UNFF, #20562)*; *World Water Assessment Programme (WWAP, #21907)*. Supports: *Intergovernmental Panel on Climate Change (IPCC, #11499)*.
NGO Relations Accredited bodies attending COP sessions (over 2,000) including the following organizations listed in this Yearbook:
- *Action for Solidarity, Equality, Environment and Diversity (A SEED, #00098)*;
- *African Centre for Technology Studies (ACTS, #00243)*;
- *Air Conditioning and Refrigeration European Association (AREA, #00601)*;
- *Airlines for America (A4A)*;
- *Aleut International Association (AIA)*;
- *Alliance internationale de tourisme (AIT, #00694)*;
- *Alliance to Save Energy (ASE)*;
- *American Nuclear Society (ANS)*;
- *American Society of International Law (ASIL)*;
- *Asian Institute of Technology (AIT, #01519)*;
- *Asociación Regional de Empresas del Sector Petróleo, Gas y Biocombustibles en Latinoamérica y el Caribe (ARPEL, #02296)*;
- *European Automobile Manufacturers' Association (ACEA, #06300)*;
- *Association internationale forêts méditerranéennes (AIFM, #02699)*;
- *Bariloche Foundation (FB)*;
- *Battelle Memorial Institute (BMI, #03187)*;
- *Biomass Users' Network (BUN, no recent information)*;
- *BirdLife International (#03266)*;
- *Brot für die Welt*;
- *Building and Wood Workers' International (BWI, #03355)*;
- *Business and Industry Advisory Committee to the OECD (BIAC, #03385)*;
- *BUSINESSEUROPE (#03381)*;
- *Carl Duisberg Gesellschaft (CDG, inactive)*;
- *CEE Bankwatch Network (#03624)*;
- *CEMBUREAU – The European Cement Association (CEMBUREAU, #03634)*;
- *Centre for Applied Studies in International Negotiations (CASIN, no recent information)*;
- *Centre for European Policy Studies (CEPS, #03741)*;
- *Centre for International Climate and Environmental Research, Oslo (CICERO)*;
- *Center for International Environmental Law (CIEL)*;
- *Center for International Forestry Research (CIFOR, #03646)*;
- *Center for International Relations/Peace and Conflict Studies*;
- *Centre for International Sustainable Development Law (CISDL)*;
- *Center for Sustainable Development in the Americas (CSDA)*;
- *Church of the Brethren*;
- *Circumpolar Conservation Union (CCU)*;
- *Citizens' Alliance for Saving the Atmosphere and the Earth (CASA)*;
- *Climate Action Network (CAN, #03999)*;
- *Climate Action Network Europe (CAN Europe, #04001)*;
- *Climate Action Network Latin America (CANLA, #04002)*;
- *Climate Action Network South East Asia (CANSEA, #04004)*;
- *Climate Group (#04013)*;
- *Climate Institute*;
- *COGEN Europe (#04085)*;
- *Community of European Railway and Infrastructure Companies (CER, #04396)*;
- *Community Forestry International (CFI)*;
- *Confederation of European Forest Owners (CEPF, #04525)*;
- *Confederation of European Paper Industries (CEPI, #04529)*;
- *Confédération européenne des industries du bois (CEI Bois, #04545)*;
- *Conseil européen de l'industrie chimique (CEFIC, #04687)*;
- *Conservation International (CI)*;
- *Coordinadora de las Organizaciones Indígenas de la Cuenca Amazónica (COICA, #04811)*;
- *Counterpart International (FSP)*;
- *Earth Council Alliance (ECA, inactive)*;
- *Earth Island Institute (EII)*;
- *EarthAction (EA, #05159)*;
- *Ecologic Institut (#05303)*;
- *Entreprise Works / VITA*;
- *Environmental Defense Fund (EDF)*;
- *Environmental Investigation Agency (EIA)*;
- *Environnement et développement du Tiers-monde (enda, #05510)*;
- *Equiterre*;
- *Eurogas (#05682)*;
- *Euroheat and Power (EHP, #05694)*;
- *nucleareurope (#17616)*;
- *European Business Council for a Sustainable Energy Future (e5, #06417)*;
- *European Committee of the Manufacturers of Fire Protection Equipment and Fire Fighting Vehicles (#06659)*;
- *European Consortium for the Responsible Application of Refrigerants (EUCRAR, inactive)*;
- *European Council for an Energy Efficient Economy (ECEEE, #06818)*;
- *European Environmental Bureau (EEB, #06996)*;
- *European Federation of Agencies and Regions for Energy and the Environment (FEDARENE, #07041)*;
- *European Federation of Allergy and Airways Diseases Patients' Associations (EFA, #07045)*;
- *European Federation for Transport and Environment (T and E, #07230)*;
- *European Insulation Manufacturers Association (EURIMA, #07577)*;
- *European Landowners' Organization (ELO, #07639)*;
- *European Nuclear Society (ENS, #08059)*;
- *European Partnership for Energy and the Environment (EPEE, #08157)*;
- *European Round Table for Industry (ERT, #08407)*;
- *European Science and Environment Forum (no recent information)*;
- *European Trade Union Confederation (ETUC, #08927)*;
- *European Union of Medical Specialists (UEMS, #09001)*;
- *EUROSOLAR – European Association for Renewable Energy (#09183)*;
- *FACE Foundation (no recent information)*;
- *FARMAPU-INTER and CECOTRAP-RCOGL*;
- *Federación de Organizaciones para el Futuro de Orinoquia y Amazonia (FEDEORAMA)*;
- *Ford Foundation (#09858)*;
- *Forest Stewardship Council (FSC, #09869)*;
- *Foundation for International Development Economics (IDE, no recent information)*;
- *Franciscans International (FI, #09982)*;
- *Free World Foundation (FWF)*;
- *Fridtjof Nansen Institute (FNI)*;
- *Friends of the Earth International (FoEI, #10002)*;
- *Fundación Ecológica Universal (FEU, no recent information)*;
- *GenderCC – Women for Climate Justice (GenderCC, #10095)*;
- *General Board of Church and Society of the United Methodist Church (GBCS)*;
- *Global Climate Change Institute, Tsinghua University (GCCI)*;
- *Global Climate Coalition (GCC, inactive)*;
- *Global Commons Institute, London*;
- *Global Cooperation Council (GCC)*;
- *Global Environment Centre (GEC)*;
- *Global Environmental Action (GEA)*;
- *Global Environmental Forum (GEF)*;
- *Global Forest Coalition (GFC, #10368)*;
- *Global Industrial and Social Progress Research Institute (GISPRI)*;

- *GLOBE International (#10668);*
- *Global Public Policy Institute (GPPi);*
- *Green Earth Organization (GEO, inactive);*
- *Greenpeace International (#10727);*
- *Gwich'in Council International (GCI);*
- *Heinrich Böll Foundation;*
- *HELIO International (inactive);*
- *IFOAM – Organics International (IFOAM, #11105);*
- *Information, Alternatives and Opposition Network International (IAO, no recent information);*
- *Institute of Electrical and Electronics Engineers (IEEE, #11259);*
- *Institute for European Environmental Policy (IEEP, #11261);*
- *Institute for Resource and Security Studies (IRSS, no recent information);*
- *Instituto de Pesquisa Ambiental da Amazônia (IPAM);*
- *International Academy of Technological Sciences (IATS, no recent information);*
- *International Air Transport Association (IATA, #11614);*
- *International Alliance of the Indigenous Tribal Peoples of the Tropical Forests (IAITPTF, #11629);*
- *International Aluminium Institute (IAI, #11643);*
- *International Association for the Advancement of Innovative Approaches to Global Challenges (IAAI, #11687);*
- *International Association of Public Transport (#12118);*
- *International Center for Environmental Technology Transfer (ICETT);*
- *International Centre for Trade and Sustainable Development, Geneva (ICTSD, #12524);*
- *International Chamber of Commerce (ICC, #12534);*
- *International Climate Change Partnership (ICCP);*
- *International Council for Capital Formation;*
- *International Council of Environmental Law (ICEL, #13018);*
- *International Council for Science (ICSU, inactive);*
- *International Council of Women (ICW, #13093);*
- *International Emissions Trading Association (IETA, #13262);*
- *International Federation of Building and Wood Workers (IFBWW, inactive);*
- *International Federation of Industrial Energy Consumers (IFIEC, inactive);*
- *International Federation of Institutes for Advanced Study (IFIAS, inactive);*
- *International Federation of Red Cross and Red Crescent Societies (#13526);*
- *International Fertilizer Association (IFA, #13589);*
- *International Food Policy Research Institute (IFPRI, #13622);*
- *International Forestry Students' Association (IFSA, #13628);*
- *International Gas Union (IGU, #13700);*
- *International Global Change Institute, Hamilton (IGCI);*
- *International Hydropower Association (IHA, #13828);*
- *International Institute for Applied Systems Analysis (IIASA, #13861);*
- *International Institute for Energy Conservation (IIEC, #13875);*
- *International Institute for Energy Conservation – Europe (IIEC-Europe, see: #13875);*
- *International Institute for Sustainable Development (IISD, #13930);*
- *International Lake Environment Committee Foundation (ILEC, #13998);*
- *International-Lawyers.Org (INTLawyers, #14008);*
- *International Network for Environmental Management (INEM, #14263);*
- *International Network for Sustainable Energy (INFORSE, #14331);*
- *International Organization of Motor Vehicle Manufacturers (#14455);*
- *International Organization for Standardization (ISO, #14473);*
- *International Peace Research Association (IPRA, #14537);*
- *International Petroleum Industry Environmental Conservation Association (IPIECA, #14562);*
- *International Polar Foundation (IPF);*
- *International Policy Network (IPN);*
- *International Project for Sustainable Energy Paths (IPSEP, no recent information);*
- *International Research Centre on Environment and Development (CIRED);*
- *International Risk Governance Council (IRGC, #14756);*
- *International Rivers;*
- *International Society of Biometeorology (ISB, #14969);*
- *International Society of Doctors for the Environment (ISDE, #15065);*
- *OWLS Society (#17921);*
- *International Solar Energy Society (ISES, #15564);*
- *International Studies Association, University of Wyoming;*
- *International Trade Union Confederation (ITUC, #15708);*
- *International Union for Conservation of Nature and Natural Resources (IUCN, #15766);*
- *International Union of Railways (#15813);*
- *International Water Management Institute (IWMI, #15867);*
- *International Youth and Student Movement for the United Nations (ISMUN, inactive);*
- *Inuit Circumpolar Council (ICC, #15995);*
- *INZET – Association for North South Campaigns (inactive);*
- *Japan International Forestry Promotion and Cooperation Center (JIFPRO);*
- *JIN Climate and Sustainability;*
- *KIST Europe (no recent information);*
- *Kontaktstelle für Umwelt-und Entwicklung (KATE);*
- *Local Governments for Sustainability (ICLEI, #16507);*
- *Maastrichts Europees Instituut voor Transnationaal Rechtswetenschappelijk Onderzoek (METRO);*
- *Middlebury Institute of International Studies, Monterey (MIIS);*
- *The Nature Conservancy (TNC);*
- *Network for Environment and Sustainable Development in Africa (NESDA, inactive);*
- *NGV Global (#17131);*
- *NGVA Europe (#17130);*
- *Northern Forum, The (#17592);*
- *Observatoire méditerranéen de l'énergie (OME, #17634);*
- *Organization for Industrial, Spiritual and Cultural Advancement International (OISCA International, #17872);*
- *Overseas Development Institute (ODI);*
- *Oxfam GB;*
- *Pacific Rim Consortium in Energy, Combustion, and the Environment (PARCON, inactive);*
- *Panos Network (#18183);*
- *Paul H Nitze School of Advanced International Studies (SAIS);*
- *PEFC Council (#18288);*
- *Perimart International (no recent information);*
- *Pew Center on Global Climate Change;*
- *Potsdam Institute for Climate Impact Research (PIK);*
- *Pro-Natura International (#16951);*
- *Religions for Peace (RfP, #18831);*
- *Renewable Energy and Energy Efficiency Partnership (REEEP, #18837);*
- *Resource Renewal Institute (RRI);*
- *The Rockefeller Foundation (#18966);*
- *Royal Institute of International Affairs (RIIA);*
- *Scientists for Global Responsibility (SGR);*
- *Society for Development Alternatives;*
- *Society for Threatened Peoples International (STP International, #19654);*
- *SolarPower Europe (#19676);*
- *Southern Centre for Energy and the Environment (SCEE, no recent information);*
- *Sovereignty International;*
- *Stockholm Environment Institute (SEI, #19993);*
- *Tearfund, UK;*
- *Third World Network (TWN, #20151);*
- *Third World Solidarity Action (ASTM);*
- *Transnational Institute (TNI, #20219);*
- *Union of Concerned Scientists (UCS);*
- *Union of the Electricity Industry – Eurelectric (#20379);*
- *United Nations Foundation (UNF, #20563);*
- *Verification Research, Training and Information Centre (VERTIC);*
- *VIVAT International (#20801);*
- *Wetlands International (#20928);*
- *Wildlife Conservation Society (WCS);*
- *WindEurope (#20965);*
- *Winrock International;*
- *Women Engage for a Common Future (WECF, #20992);*
- *World Agroforestry Centre (ICRAF, #21072);*
- *World Alliance for Decentralized Energy (WADE, #21081);*
- *World Business Council for Sustainable Development (WBCSD, #21254);*
- *World Coal Association (WCA, #21280);*
- *World Conservation Trust (IWMC, #21312);*
- *World Council of Churches (WCC, #21320);*
- *World Economic Forum (WEF, #21367);*
- *World Environment Center (WEC, #21386);*
- *World Federation of United Nations Associations (WFUNA, #21499);*
- *World LPG Association (WLPGA, #21629);*
- *World Nuclear Association (WNA, #21674);*
- *World Petroleum Council (WPC, #21722);*
- *World Resources Institute (WRI, #21753);*
- *World Sustainable Energy Coalition (WSEC, inactive);*
- *World Wide Fund for Nature (WWF, #21922);*
- *World Wind Energy Association (WWEA, #21937);*
- *ZEW – Leibniz-Zentrum für Europäische Wirtschaftsforschung;*
- *Zonta International (#22038).*

Observer members: *All India Women's Conference (AIWC, #00737); Green Cross International (GCI, #10715).* Working relationship with: *Asian Disaster Preparedness Center (ADPC, #01426).* Participant: *World Climate Research Programme (WCRP, #21279).* Instrumental in setting up: *Community Development Carbon Fund (CDCF, #04395).* [2022.02.21/XK1561/**F***]

♦ United Nations Friends in Rotary (internationally oriented national body)

♦ United Nations Fund for International Partnerships (UNFIP) 20565

Fonds des nations unies pour les partenariats internationaux (FNUPI) – Fondo de las Naciones Unidas para la Colaboración Internacional

Main Office UNOP, 1 United Nations Plaza, Room DC1-1330, New York NY 10017, USA. T. +12129631000. Fax +12129631486. E-mail: partnerships@un.org.
URL: http://www.un.org/partnerships/

History 1 Mar 1998. Founded by Kofi Annan, Secretary General of *United Nations (UN, #20515),* to administer, jointly with *United Nations Foundation (UNF, #20563),* the gift of US$ 1,000 million announced by R E Turner, Sep 1997. **Aims** Serve as the interface between the UN Foundation (UNF) and the United Nations system; facilitate development of high-impact programmes and projects for channelling UNF funds into the UN system; encourage innovative partnerships between the UN and civil society. **Structure** Comes under the leadership of UN Deputy Secretary-General. Advisory Board, chaired by UN Deputy Secretary-General. Managed by the United Nations Office for Partnerships (UNOP). **Activities** Advocacy/lobbying/activism. **IGO Relations** UN bodies involved in programmes include: *ECOSOC (#05331); International Bank for Reconstruction and Development (IBRD, #12317); Office of the United Nations High Commissioner for Human Rights (OHCHR, #17697); UNDP (#20292); UNEP (#20299); UNESCO (#20322); UNICEF (#20332).* Basic Implementation Agreement with: *International Fund for Agricultural Development (IFAD, #13692).* Member of: *United Nations Sustainable Development Group (UNSDG, #20634).* Cooperates with: *United Nations Institute for Training and Research (UNITAR, #20576).* Works with secretariat of Advisory Group for a United Nations Information and Communication Technologies Task Force. **NGO Relations** Instrumental in setting up: *Digital Diaspora Network – Latin American and Caribbean (no recent information).* [2015/XK1877/f/**F***]

♦ United Nations Fund for Population Activities / see United Nations Population Fund (#20612)
♦ United Nations Fund for Science and Technology for Development (inactive)
♦ United Nations Geographic Information Working Group (unconfirmed)

♦ United Nations Girls' Education Initiative (UNGEI) 20566

Initiative des Nations Unies pour l'éducation des filles

Head of Secretariat c/o UNICEF, Programme Division, Education Section, 3 UN Plaza, 7th Floor, New York NY 10017, USA. Fax +6173267129. E-mail: ungei@unicef.org.
URL: http://www.ungei.org/

History Apr 2000, Dakar (Senegal). Established at the World Education Forum, by the *United Nations (UN, #20515),* as a partnership of institutions with the aim of bringing more girls to school. In 2010, UNGEI partners reaffirmed their commitment through the Dakar Declaration on Accelerating Girls' Education and Gender Equality. **Aims** In accordance with the Millennium Development Goals (MDG 2 and MDG 3): work to narrow the gender gap in primary and secondary education by empowering all girls and boys through quality education to realize their full potential and contribute to transforming societies; ensure that, by 2015, all children complete primary schooling, with girls and boys having equal access to free, quality education. **Structure** Global Advisory Committee, composed of all partners, chaired by 2 partners on a rotational basis; Steering Committee. *UNICEF (#20332)* serves as lead agency and secretariat. Regional Focal Points (RFPs) in: East Asia and the Pacific; Eastern and Southern Africa; the Middle East and North Africa; South Asia; West and Central Africa. **Languages** English, French. **Activities** Advocacy/lobbying/activism. **Publications** Papers; studies; reports; brochures.

Members Partners (32):
- *Africa Network Campaign on Education for All (ANCEFA, #00302);*
- *Aga Khan Foundation (AKF, #00545);*
- *Asia South Pacific Association for Basic and Adult Education (ASPBAE, #02098);*
- *CamFed International;*
- *Canadian International Development Agency (CIDA, inactive);*
- *CARE International (CI, #03429);*
- Cisco;
- *Commonwealth Secretariat (#04362);*
- Comparative, International and Development Education Centre (CIDEC);
- *DANIDA;*
- *Department for International Development (DFID, inactive);*
- *Education Development Center (EDC);*
- *FHI 360;*
- Foreign Affairs, Trade and Development Canada (DFATD);
- *Forum for African Women Educationalists (FAWE, #09896);*
- *ILO (#11123);*
- *International Bank for Reconstruction and Development (IBRD, #12317)* (World Bank);
- *International Rescue Committee (IRC, #14717);*
- *Norwegian Agency for Development Cooperation (Norad);*
- *Oxfam International (#17922);*
- *Plan International (#18386);*
- *Save the Children International (#19058);*
- *Swedish International Development Cooperation Agency (Sida);*
- *UNESCO (#20322);*
- *UNICEF (#20332);*
- *United Nations Population Fund (UNFPA, #20612);*
- *United States Agency for International Development (USAID);*
- *World Education (WE);*
- *World Food Programme (WFP, #21510);*
- *World Learning;*
- *World Vision International (WVI, #21904);*
- Youth Advisory Group (YAG) of the Global Education First Initiative.

NGO Relations Supports: *Forum for African Women Educationalists (FAWE, #09896).* [2020/XF6503/**F***]

♦ United Nations Global Compact 20567

Main Office 2 United Nations Plaza, DC2-612, New York NY 10017, USA. T. +1212907-1301.
URL: http://www.unglobalcompact.org/

History Founded 26 Jul 2000, New York NY (USA), following a proposal by Kofi Annan, Secretary-General of *United Nations (UN, #20515),* at *World Economic Forum (WEF, #21367),* 31 Jan 1999, Davos (Switzerland). Mandate renewed and expanded by UN General Assembly, 1 Dec 2011. Also referred to as the *Global Compact.* **Aims** Call for companies to voluntarily align their operations and strategies with universally accepted principles in the areas of *human rights,* labour, environment and anti-corruption, and take actions in support of UN goals, including the Millennium Development Goals; act as a platform for the development, implementation, and disclosure of responsible corporate policies and practices. **Structure** Governance shared by 7 entities: Global Compact Leaders Summit; Local Networks; Annual Local Networks Forum; Global Compact Board; Global Compact Office; Inter-Agency Team, consisting of *ILO (#11123), Office of the United*

Nations High Commissioner for Human Rights (OHCHR, #17697), UNDP (#20292), UNEP (#20299), UNIDO (#20336), UN Women (#20724) and *United Nations Office on Drugs and Crime (UNODC, #20596)*; Global Compact Donor Group, consisting of Governments that voluntarily contribute to a UN Trust Fund. **Languages** Arabic, Chinese, English, French, German, Portuguese, Russian, Spanish. **Staff** 40.00 FTE, paid. **Finance** Staff salaries and operating expenses paid through trust fund to which governments and business participants make annual voluntary contributions. **Activities** Advocacy/lobbying/activism. **Events** *Anti-Corruption Forum* Seoul (Korea Rep) 2019, *Energy, Natural Resources and Chemistry Seminar* Seoul (Korea Rep) 2019, *SDGs Forum* Seoul (Korea Rep) 2019, *Corporate Anti-Corruption Management Cooperation Forum* Seoul (Korea Rep) 2018, *Global Corporate Sustainability Management Forum* Seoul (Korea Rep) 2018. **Publications** Bulletin (12 a year). Books; guides; case studies.

Members Business participants and other stakeholders in over 130 countries. Participants include the following organizations listed in this Yearbook (116):
- *Advocates for International Development (A4ID);*
- *Africa-America Institute (AAI);*
- *Africa Clean Energy Group (AFRICLEG);*
- *African Institute of Corporate Citizenship (AICC);*
- *Agency for Technical Cooperation and Development (ACTED);*
- *AIESEC (#00593);*
- *ANIMA Investment Network (#00833);*
- *Arab International Women's Forum (AIWF, #00994);*
- *Arab Organization for Human Resource Management (AOHRM, no recent information);*
- *AVI;*
- *AVSI Foundation;*
- *Basel Institute on Governance;*
- *Bonsucro (#03302);*
- *bon't worry;*
- *Catholic Organization for Relief and Development (Cordaid);*
- *Caucasus Environmental NGO Network (CENN, #03613);*
- *Caux Round Table, The (CRT, #03614);*
- *CDP (#03621);*
- *Chamber of Computer Logistics People Worldwide (CCLP Worldwide, #03847);*
- *Child Legacy International;*
- *Code REDD;*
- *Convergences;*
- *Creative Associates International (Creative);*
- *DEVNET International (#05059);*
- *Earth Child Institute (ECI, #05162);*
- *EDU (#05363);*
- *EUROMIC (#05735);*
- *European Institute for Asian Studies (EIAS, #07545);*
- *European Landowners' Organization (ELO, #07639);*
- *Femmes chefs d'entreprises mondiales (FCEM, #09733);*
- *Fundación Agreste;*
- *Fundación de Comunicaciones Latinoamericanas David Livingston (Fundalivingston);*
- *Fundación para las Comunidades Internacionales (FU.CO.IN.);*
- *Glasswing International;*
- *Global CCS Institute (#10274);*
- *Global Competitiveness Empowerment Forum (GCEF);*
- *Global Forum on Human Settlements (GFHS, #10372);*
- *Global Health Council (GHC, #10402);*
- *Global Impact;*
- *Global Initiative for Positive Change (GIPC);*
- *Global Reporting Initiative (GRI, #10567);*
- *Global Sourcing Council (GSC);*
- *Global Sustain;*
- *Global Women Social Enterprise (GWSE);*
- *Green Project Management (GPM);*
- *Help the Poor International (HPI);*
- *Human Rights at Sea (HRAS);*
- *IBREA Foundation;*
- *Indigenous Peoples' Center for Documentation, Research and Information (DOCIP);*
- *Initiative for Global Development (IGD);*
- *Institute for Economics and Peace (IEP, #11257);*
- *Institute for Multi-Track Diplomacy (IMTD);*
- *Institute of International Social Development (IISD, no recent information);*
- *Institut zur Cooperation bei Entwicklungs-Projekte (ICEP);*
- *International Academy for Quality (IAQ, #11573);*
- *International Administrative Science Association (IASA);*
- *International Association for Political Science Students (IAPSS, #12095);*
- *International Businesses Standards Organization (IBSO);*
- *International Centre for Environmental Education and Community Development (ICENECDEV);*
- *International Centre for Hydropower (ICH);*
- *International Centre for Sport Security (ICSS, #12518);*
- *International City Leaders;*
- *International Co-operative Alliance (ICA, #12944);*
- *International Council for Small Business (ICSB, #13075);*
- *International Culture University (ICU);*
- *International Emergency Management Organization (IEMO, #13260);*
- *International Eurasia-Press Fund (IEPF, #13309);*
- *International Federation of Business and Professional Women (BPW International, #13376);*
- *International Federation of Training and Development Organizations (IFTDO, #13573);*
- *International Planned Parenthood Federation (IPPF, #14589);*
- *International Road Transport Union (IRU, #14761);*
- *International Society for Small and Medium Enterprises (ISSME, #15446);*
- *International Sustainability and Carbon Certification (ISCC);*
- *International Young Professionals Foundation (IYPF, #15930);*
- *Interregional Union of Life Help for Mentally Handicapped Persons (Sail of Hope);*
- *ISEAL (#16026);*
- *Japanese NGO Center for International Cooperation (JANIC);*
- *Junior Chamber International (JCI, #16168);*
- *Latin American Council for Peace Research (#16310);*
- *LEAP Africa;*
- *Management for Development Foundation (MDF Training and Consultancy);*
- *Mediators Beyond Borders International (MBB);*
- *New World Hope Organization (NWHO);*
- *Organización de Entidades Mutuales de las Américas (ODEMA, #17836);*
- *Organization for International Economic Relations (OiER, #17873);*
- *Organization for Poverty Alleviation and Development (OPAD);*
- *Pacific Institute;*
- *Pan African Institute for Development (PAID, #18053)* (West Africa);
- *Peace and Life Enhancement Initiative International (PLEII);*
- *Peace Without Limits – PWL – International Organization (PWL);*
- *People's Movement for Human Rights Learning (PDHRE, #18307);*
- *Responsible Jewellery Council (RJC, #18920);*
- *Right to Energy – SOS Future;*
- *Roundtable on Sustainable Palm Oil (RSPO, #18986);*
- *Sedex (#19211);*
- *Service and Research Institute on Family and Children (SERFAC, #19243);*
- *SOCHAIR Organization (Europe) (#19331);*
- *Social Development International (SDI);*
- *SOLIDARIDAD Network (#19681);*
- *STUF United Fund;*
- *Sustainable Development Solutions Network (SDSN, #20054);*
- *Transparency International (TI, #20223);*
- *Universal Peace Federation (UPF International, #20681);*
- *WeForest (#20852);*
- *World Association of Former United Nations Internes and Fellows (WAFUNIF, #21141);*
- *World Association of Girl Guides and Girl Scouts (WAGGGS, #21142);*
- *World Bamboo Organization (WBO, #21214);*
- *World Business Council for Sustainable Development (WBCSD, #21254);*
- *World Economic Forum (WEF, #21367);*
- *World Federation of United Nations Associations (WFUNA, #21499);*
- *WorldLoop;*
- *World Mediation Organization (WMO, #21645);*
- *World Sustainability Fund (WSF);*
- *World Union of Small and Medium Enterprises (WUSME, #21886);*
- *World Vision International (WVI, #21904);*
- *World Youth Bank Network (WYB, #21954).*

IGO Relations Cooperates with (1): *Global Green Growth Forum (3GF)*. Core agency: *UNIDO (#20336)*. Adheres to: *Global Partnership for Effective Development Co-operation (GPEDC, #10532)*. **NGO Relations** Member of (3): *Global Open Data for Agriculture and Nutrition (GODAN, #10514); Science Based Targets Network; World Benchmarking Alliance (WBA, #21228)*. Partner of (1): *UNLEASH*. Cooperates with (3): *Global Initiative for Inclusive Information and Communication Technologies (G3ict, #10425); Principles for Responsible Investment Initiative (PRI Initiative, #18499); Principles for Responsible Management Education (PRME, #18500)*. Supports (1): *SEED (#19213)*. Instrumental in setting up (3): *Foundation for the Global Compact; Globally Responsible Leadership Initiative (GRLI, #10462); Higher Education Sustainability Initiative (HESI)*. [2020/XF6051/y/**F**]

♦ United Nations Global Programme Against Money Laundering / see United Nations Global Programme Against Money Laundering, Proceeds of Crime and the Financing of Terrorism (#20568)

♦ United Nations Global Programme Against Money Laundering, Proceeds of Crime and the Financing of Terrorism (GPML) 20568

Programme mondial des nations unies contre le blanchiment de l'argent – Programa Mundial de las Naciones Unidas Contra el Blanqueo de Dinero

Secretariat c/o UNODC, PO Box 500, 1400 Vienna, Austria. T. +431260604269. Fax +431260606878. E-mail: gpml@unodc.org.

URL: http://www.unodc.org/unodc/en/money-laundering/index.html

History 1997, by *United Nations Office on Drugs and Crime (UNODC, #20596)*, within the framework of *United Nations (UN, #20515)*, in response to mandate established by *United Nations Convention against Illicit Traffic in Narcotic Drugs and Psychotropic Substances (1988)*. Mandate strengthened by *'Political Declaration and Action Plan Against Money Laundering'* adopted by special session of UN General Assembly, Jun 1998, which requires signatories to the Convention to put in place a number of specific measures, particularly with reference to activities of financial institutions, and by *United Nations Convention Against Transnational Organized Crime (2000)* and the *United Nations Convention Against Corruption (UNCAC, 2003)*. Functions within the Implementation Support Section of the Organized Crime and Illicit Trafficking Branch. Original title: *United Nations Global Programme Against Money Laundering*. Also referred to as *Global Programme Against Money Laundering*. **Aims** Strengthen the ability capacity of Member States to counter money laundering and the *financing* of *terrorism* (AML/CFT) by improving legal, institutional and regulatory frameworks; assist Member States in depriving *criminals* of the proceeds of their activity. **Languages** English, French. **Finance** Extra-budgetary funding; donor funding. **Activities** Assists legal, financial and law enforcement authorities to develop the infrastructure and expertise to combat money laundering and terrorist financing in accordance with UN instruments and international standards; assists governments in developing and introducing legislation in the field, developing AML/CFT policy and sharing best practices; helps lay the groundwork for creation of financial intelligence units; provides a basis for UN action in money laundering and terrorism financing matters. Group: Research and Analysis – including web administration of *International Money Laundering Information Network (IMoLIN, #14181)* / AMLID. **Publications** *Russian Capitalism and Money Laundering* (2000); *Financial Havens, Banking Secrecy and Money Laundering* (1999). Country briefings on Central Asian states. **Members** UN Membership (192). [2019.10.22/XE3748/**E***]

♦ United Nations Group of Experts on Geographical Names (UNGEGN) 20569

Groupe d'experts des Nations Unies sur les noms géographiques (GENUNG) – Grupo de Expertos de las Naciones Unidas en Nombres Geograficos

Secretariat UN Statistics Div, Two UN Plaza DC2-1678, New York NY 10017, USA. T. +12129635823. Fax +12129639851. E-mail: geoinfo_unsd@un.org.

URL: http://unstats.un.org/unsd/geoinfo/UNGEGN/default.html

History 23 Apr 1959, by resolution 715 A (XXVII) of *ECOSOC (#05331)*, followed by resolution 1314 (XLIV) of 31 May 1968. Current name adopted 4 May 1973. Current statutes and rules of procedure adopted by ECOSOC on 12 Jul 1993. Through ECOSOC resolution 2018/2 of 10 Nov 2017, *United Nations Conference on the Standardization of Geographical Names (UNCSGN)* and UNGEGN discontinued in their current format with mandates retained by UNGEGN. New Rules of Procedure adopted at ECOSOC plenary meeting, 24 Jul 2018. **Aims** Emphasize the importance of, and demonstrate benefits arising from, *standardization* of geographical names; collect results of the work of national and international bodies dealing with such standardization and disseminate these results to UN member countries; study and propose principles and means of resolving problems in the field; provide a vehicle for liaison and coordination in the field among UN member states and between them and relevant international organizations. **Structure** Bureau; Working Groups (8); Task Teams (2); Geographical/Linguistic Divisions (24). **Languages** Arabic, Chinese, English, French, Russian, Spanish. **Finance** Secretariat financed by the United Nations. **Activities** Events/meetings; knowledge management/information dissemination; research and development; training/education; standards/guidelines. **Events** *Biennial Session* New York, NY (USA) 2023, *Biennial Session* New York, NY (USA) 2021, *Biennial Session* New York, NY (USA) 2019, *Session* New York, NY (USA) 2017, *UN Conference on the Standardization of Geographical Names* New York, NY (USA) 2017. **Publications** *Information Bulletin of the United Nations Group of Experts on Geographical Names* (2 a year). Session reports; technical standardization and training manuals. **Members** All UN Member States may assign representatives to UNGEGN, although not all do so. **IGO Relations** Observers at recent UNGEGN sessions: *International Hydrographic Organization (IHO, #13825); Pan American Institute of Geography and History (PAIGH, #18113)*. **NGO Relations** Observers at recent UNGEGN sessions: *International Cartographic Association (ICA, #12446)*; International Consortium of Universities for Toponymic Education (ICUTE); *International Geographical Union (IGU, #13713); Internet Corporation for Assigned Names and Numbers (ICANN, #15949)*. [2022/XE0198/**E***]

♦ United Nations Group on the Information Society (UNGIS) 20570

Secretariat c/o ITU, Place des Nations, 1211 Geneva 20, Switzerland. T. +41227306039 – +41227305111. Fax +41227305939 – +41227337256. E-mail: contact@ungis.org.

URL: http://www.ungis.org/

History Apr 2006, when endorsed by *United Nations System Chief Executives Board for Coordination (CEB, #20636)*, as requested by the Tunis Agenda of Nov 2005, to set up a UN group consisting of the relevant UN bodies and organizations with the mandate to facilitate the implementation of WSIS outcomes. **Aims** As an interagency mechanism, coordinate substantive policy issues facing the United Nations system's implementation of the Geneva Plan of Action and Tunis Agenda for the Information Society adopted by the World Summit on the Information Society, thereby contributing to improving policy coherence in the UN system, as requested by the 2005 World Summit. **Events** *Meeting* Geneva (Switzerland) 2009, *Meeting* Geneva (Switzerland) 2009, *Meeting* Geneva (Switzerland) 2008, *Meeting* Paris (France) 2007, *Meeting* Geneva (Switzerland) 2006.

Members Organizations (29):
- *FAO (#09260);*
- *ILO (#11123);*
- *International Atomic Energy Agency (IAEA, #12294);*
- *International Bank for Reconstruction and Development (IBRD, #12317);*
- *International Telecommunication Union (ITU, #15673);*
- *OECD (#17693);*
- *UNCTAD (#20285);*
- *UNDP (#20292);*
- *UNESCO (#20322);*
- *UNHCR (#20327);*
- *UNICEF (#20332);*
- *UNIDO (#20336);*
- United Nations Department of Economic and Social Affairs (UNDESA);

- *United Nations Economic and Social Commission for Asia and the Pacific (ESCAP, #20557);*
- *United Nations Economic and Social Commission for Western Asia (ESCWA, #20558);*
- *United Nations Economic Commission for Africa (ECA, #20554);*
- *United Nations Economic Commission for Europe (UNECE, #20555);*
- *United Nations Economic Commission for Latin America and the Caribbean (ECLAC, #20556);*
- *United Nations Human Settlements Programme (UN-Habitat, #20572);*
- *United Nations Institute for Training and Research (UNITAR, #20576);*
- *United Nations Office on Drugs and Crime (UNODC, #20596);*
- *United Nations Relief and Works Agency for Palestine Refugees in the Near East (UNRWA, #20622);*
- *Universal Postal Union (UPU, #20682);*
- *WHO (#20950);*
- *World Food Programme (WFP, #21510);*
- *World Intellectual Property Organization (WIPO, #21593);*
- *World Meteorological Organization (WMO, #21649);*
- *World Tourism Organization (UNWTO, #21861);*
- *World Trade Organization (WTO, #21864).* [2009/XJ0813/y/**E***]

♦ United Nations Habitat and Human Settlements Foundation (inactive)
♦ United Nations High Commissioner for Refugees (#20327)

♦ United Nations Human Rights Council (HRC) 20571

Conseil des droits de l'homme des Nations Unies

Contact Human Rights Council Branch, OHCHR, Avenue Giuseppe Motta 48, 1202 Geneva, Switzerland. T. +41229179220. Fax +41229179011. E-mail: ohchr-infodesk@un.org.
URL: http://www.ohchr.org/

History 15 Mar 2006. Established within *United Nations (UN, #20515)* system, as a subsidiary body of the UN General Assembly, by GA Resolution 60/251. Replaces *United Nations Commission on Human Rights (inactive)*. **Aims** Promote universal respect for the protection of all human rights and fundamental freedoms for all, without distinction of any kind and in a fair and equal manner; contribute, through dialogue and cooperation, towards the prevention of human rights violations and respond promptly to human rights emergencies; address situations of violations of human rights, including gross and systematic violations, and make recommendations thereon; promote the effective coordination and the mainstreaming of human rights within the United Nations system. **Structure** Council of 47 Member States, elected by a majority of members of the General Assembly of the United Nations through direct and secret ballot, with distribution of seats in accordance with equitable geographical representation: African States – 13; Asia-Pacific States – 13; Eastern European States – 6; Latin American and Caribbean States – 8; Western European and Other States – 7. Members elected for 3-year terms, not eligible for immediate re-election after serving 2 consecutive terms. Bureau. *Advisory Committee* serves as think tank. Participation open to observers, including NGOs, IGOs, national human rights institutions and specialized agencies. Based in Geneva (Switzerland). **Languages** Arabic, Chinese, English, French, Russian, Spanish. **Activities** Awareness raising; capacity building; events/meetings; guidance/assistance/consulting. Helps Members States meet their human rights obligations through dialogue, capacity building and technical assistance; serves as a forum for dialogue on thematic issues on all human rights; makes recommendations to the General Assembly for further development of international law in the field of human rights; undertakes a universal periodic review of the fulfilment by each State of its human rights obligations and commitments; works in close cooperation in the field of human rights with Governments, regional organizations, national human rights institutions and civil society; makes recommendations with regard to the promotion and protection of human rights. **Events** *Session* Geneva (Switzerland) 2022, *Session* Geneva (Switzerland) 2022, *Session* Geneva (Switzerland) 2022, *World Human Rights Cities Forum* Gwangju (Korea Rep) 2022, *Session* Geneva (Switzerland) 2021. **Publications** Annual Report; official records.

Members Composition of Council, with representatives from 47 governments (date indicates date of expiry at end of year) – * Russia's rights of membership were suspended by the General Assembly on 7 April 2022, following which it relinquished its membership on the same day. On 10 May 2022, the General Assembly elected Czechia for the remainder of the term of office of the Russian Federation beginning on 10 May 2022 and ending on 31 December 2023.
Algeria (2025), Argentina (2024), Bangladesh (2025), Belgium (2025), Benin (2024), Bolivia (2023), Cameroon (2024), Chile (2025), China (2023), Costa Rica (2025), Côte d'Ivoire (2023), Cuba (2023), Czechia (as of 10 May 2022 until 2023*), Eritrea (2024), Finland (2024), France (2023), Gabon (2023), Gambia (2024), Georgia (2025), Germany (2025), Honduras (2024), India (2024), Kazakhstan (2024), Kyrgyzstan (2025), Lithuania (2024), Luxembourg (2024), Malawi (2023), Malaysia (2024), Maldives (2025), Mexico (2023), Montenegro (2024), Morocco (2025), Nepal (2023), Pakistan (2023), Paraguay (2024), Qatar (2024), Romania (2025), Senegal (2023), Somalia (2024), South Africa (2025), Sudan (2025), UK (2023), Ukraine (2023), United Arab Emirates (2024), USA (2024), Uzbekistan (2023), Vietnam (2025).

NGO Relations Links with ECOSOC status NGOs and others. [2022.12.15/XM1098/**E***]

♦ United Nations Human Settlements Programme / see United Nations Human Settlements Programme (#20572)

♦ United Nations Human Settlements Programme (UN-Habitat) 20572

Programme des Nations Unies pour les établissements humains (ONU-Habitat)

Exec Dir PO Box 30030, GPO, Nairobi, 00100, Kenya. T. +25420762555. E-mail: unhabitat-info@un.org – unhabitat-oed@un.org.
URL: http://www.unhabitat.org/

History 12 Oct 1978. Absorbed the former *United Nations Centre for Housing, Building and Planning (CHBP, inactive)*. Set up under resolution 32/162 of the General Assembly of *United Nations (UN, #20515)*, in the framework of *United Nations System (#20635)*, following recommendations of the United Nations Conference on Human Settlements – Habitat I – 1976, Vancouver BC (Canada). At 2nd conference, Habitat II, 1996, Istanbul (Turkey), progress was assessed and new goals set, with "Habitat Agenda" containing over 100 commitments and 600 recommendations, adopted by 171 countries. Upgraded under current title under resolution 56/206, so as to strengthen the role and status of the Centre and its governing body. Former names and other names: *United Nations Centre for Human Settlements – UNCHS (Habitat)* – former (1978 to 21 Dec 2001); *Centre des Nations Unies pour les établissements humains (CNUEH)* – former (1978 to 21 Dec 2001); *Centro de las Naciones Unidas para los Asentamientos Humanos (CNUAH)* – former (1978 to 21 Dec 2001); *United Nations Human Settlements Programme (UN-HABITAT)* – alias. **Aims** Work with partners to build inclusive, safe, resilient and sustainable cities and communities; promote urbanization as a positive transformative force for people and communities, reducing inequality, discrimination and poverty; promote socially and environmentally sustainable *towns* and *cities*. **Structure** UN-Habitat Assembly (meets every 4 years), composed of the 193 member states of the United Nations; Executive Board (meets 3 times a year); Committee of Permanent Representatives – CPR (meets twice every 4 years). See: https://unhabitat.org/governance. **Languages** Arabic, Chinese, English, French, Russian, Spanish. **Staff** 100.00 FTE, paid. **Finance** Voluntary contributions from governmental and intergovernmental donors, with UN General Assembly providing part of regular budget. **Activities** New strategic plan 2020-2023: https://unhabitat.org/our-strategy Programmes, initiatives and networks listed in this Yearbook include: *Global Land Tool Network (GLTN, #10452)*; *Global Network for Sustainable Housing (GNSH, #10502)*; *Global Water Operators' Partnerships Alliance (GWOPA, #10652)*; *World Urban Campaign (WUC, #21893)*. **Events** *World Urban Forum* Katowice (Poland) 2022, *Spatial Planning Platform Meeting* Tokyo (Japan) 2021, *World Urban Forum* Abu Dhabi (United Arab Emirates) 2020, *Seoul Urban Regeneration International Conference* Seoul (Korea Rep) 2020, *International Leaders in Urban Governance Programme Meeting* Singapore (Singapore) 2019. **Publications** *World Cities Report* (every 2 years); *Urban Insight* (regular) – newsletter. Books; technical publications; monographs; seminar reports; bibliographic notes. **Information Services** *Best Practices and Local Leadership Programme* – best practices database.

Members Member States elected by the UN-Habitat Assembly (36):
Angola, Argentina, Bahrain, Brazil, Cameroon, Canada, Chile, China, Congo DR, Costa Rica, Egypt, Ethiopia, France, Germany, India, Iran Islamic Rep, Japan, Kenya, Korea Rep, Malawi, Mexico, Morocco, Nigeria, Pakistan, Poland, Portugal, Romania, Russia, Senegal, Serbia, Spain, Sri Lanka, Sweden, Türkiye, Uruguay, USA.

IGO Relations Maintains relations with all relevant international organizations within and outside the United Nations System. Cooperation inside the United Nations also includes:
- *Committee on Housing and Land Management (#04259);*
- *FAO (#09260);*
- *Global Programme of Action for the Protection of the Marine Environment from Land-Based Activities (GPA, see: #20299);*
- *Global Resource Information Database (GRID, #10578);*
- *ILO (#11123);*
- *International Bank for Reconstruction and Development (IBRD, #12317);*
- *International Environmental Technology Centre (IETC, #13282);*
- *International Fund for Agricultural Development (IFAD, #13692);*
- *International Maritime Organization (IMO, #14102);*
- *Joint Inspection Unit of the United Nations (JIU, #16133);*
- *Management of Social Transformations (MOST, #16562);*
- *Office of the United Nations High Commissioner for Human Rights (OHCHR, #17697);*
- *Office of the United Nations Special Coordinator for the Middle East Process (UNSCO, #17698);*
- *Regional Centre for Mapping of Resources for Development (RCMRD, #18757);*
- *UNEP (#20299);*
- *UN System Network on Rural Development and Food Security (no recent information);*
- *UNCTAD (#20285);*
- *UNDP (#20292);*
- *UNESCO (#20322);*
- *UNHCR (#20327);*
- *UNICEF (#20332);*
- *UNIDO (#20336);*
- *United Nations Centre for Regional Development (UNCRD, #20526);*
- *United Nations Committee for Programme and Coordination (CPC, #20546);*
- *United Nations Economic Commission for Africa (ECA, #20554);*
- *United Nations Economic Commission for Europe (UNECE, #20555);*
- *United Nations Economic Commission for Latin America and the Caribbean (ECLAC, #20556);*
- *United Nations Economic and Social Commission for Asia and the Pacific (ESCAP, #20557);*
- *United Nations Economic and Social Commission for Western Asia (ESCWA, #20558);*
- *United Nations Framework Convention on Climate Change – Secretariat (UNFCCC, #20564);*
- *United Nations Group on the Information Society (UNGIS, #20570);*
- *United Nations Institute for Training and Research (UNITAR, #20576);*
- *United Nations Population Fund (UNFPA, #20612);*
- *United Nations Research Institute for Social Development (UNRISD, #20623);*
- United Nations Secretariat;
- *United Nations Standing Committee on Youth for the Asia-Pacific Region (no recent information);*
- *United Nations Sustainable Development Group (UNSDG, #20634);*
- *United Nations System Chief Executives Board for Coordination (CEB, #20636);*
- *United Nations University (UNU, #20642);*
- *United Nations Volunteers (UNV, #20650);*
- *WHO (#20950);*
- *WHO Regional Office for Europe (#20945);*
- *World Food Programme (WFP, #21510);*
- *World Meteorological Organization (WMO, #21649);*
- *World Water Assessment Programme (WWAP, #21907).*

Functions as UN Task Manager for the human settlements chapter of: *Global Action Plan for Environment and Development in the 21st Century (Agenda 21, inactive)*. Member of: *UN-Water (#20723)*. Memorandum of Understanding with: *Mediterranean Action Plan (MAP, #16638)*. Together with other UN agencies, comprises: *Joint WHO/FAO/UNEP/UNCHS Panel of Experts on Environmental Management for Vector Control (PEEM, no recent information)*. Maintains Joint Section on Human Settlements with ESCAP. Governing Council attends sessions of the Conference of Parties of *United Nations Framework Convention on Climate Change (UNFCCC, 1992)* and its subsidiary bodies.
Cooperation outside the United Nations includes:
- *Arab Fund for Economic and Social Development (AFESD, #00965);*
- *ASEAN (#01141);*
- *Asian Development Bank (ADB, #01422);*
- *Caribbean Community (CARICOM, #03476);*
- *Caribbean Development Bank (CDB, #03492);*
- *Centre for Environment and Development for the Arab Region and Europe (CEDARE, #03738);*
- *Commonwealth Science Council (CSC, #04361);*
- *Commonwealth Secretariat (#04362);*
- *Company for Habitat and Housing in Africa (Shelter-Afrique, #04408);*
- *Council of Europe (CE, #04881);*
- *Economic Community of West African States (ECOWAS, #05312);*
- *European Commission (EC, #06633);*
- *Inter-American Development Bank (IDB, #11427);*
- *League of Arab States (LAS, #16420);*
- *OAS (#17629);*
- *OECD (#17693);*
- *Organisation of Islamic Cooperation (OIC, #17813);*
- *Sistema Económico Latinoamericano (SELA, #19294).*

In collaboration with Commonwealth Science Council, instrumental in setting up: *Network of African Countries on Local Building Materials and Technologies (no recent information)*.

NGO Relations Memorandum of Understanding with (6): *Global Parliamentarians on Habitat (GPH, #10525)*; *Habitat International Coalition (HIC, #10845)*; *Huairou Commission (#10960)*; *International Federation of Surveyors (FIG, #13561)*; *World Associations of Cities and Local Authorities Coordination (WACLAC, no recent information)*; *Youth for Habitat International Network (YFHIN, #22018)*. Member of (1): *Cities Alliance (#03950)*. Instrumental in setting up (1): *Cities Alliance (#03950)*.
Rotary International (RI, #18975) has Observer status. In liaison with technical committees of: *International Organization for Standardization (ISO, #14473)*.
Collaborates with:
- *Arab Urban Development Institute (AUDI, #01071);*
- *Asian Institute of Technology (AIT, #01519);*
- *Association européenne pour le développement socio-culturel de la ville (Eurocultures, no recent information);*
- *Building and Wood Workers' International (BWI, #03355);*
- *Commonwealth Human Ecology Council (CHEC, #04339);*
- *Environment Liaison Centre International (ELCI, no recent information);*
- *Environnement et développement du Tiers-monde (enda, #05510);*
- *European Forum for Urban Security (Efus, #07340);*
- *Ford Foundation (#09858);*
- *Franciscans International (FI, #09982);*
- *Grassroots Organizations Operating Together in Sisterhood (GROOTS);*
- *Habitat for Humanity International (HFHI);*
- *HIC Women and Shelter Network (WAS, no recent information);*
- *Institute for Housing and Urban Development Studies (IHS);*
- *International Centre for the Prevention of Crime (ICPC, #12508);*
- *International Council of Women (ICW, #13093);*
- *International Institute for Environment and Development (IIED, #13877);*
- *International Society of City and Regional Planners (ISOCARP, #15012);*
- *International Trade Union Confederation (ITUC, #15708);*
- *International Union of Tenants (IUT, #15822);*
- *Local Governments for Sustainability (ICLEI, #16507);*
- *NGO Committee on Human Settlements (#17110);*
- *Parliamentarians for Global Action (PGA, #18208);*
- *Plan International (#18386);*
- *The Prince of Wales International Business Leaders Forum (PWIBLF, inactive);*
- *Realf;*
- *Together Foundation (no recent information);*
- *Trades Union International of Workers in the Building, Wood, Building Materials and Allied Industries (UITBB, #20185);*
- *Union internationale des architectes (UIA, #20419);*
- *Women's Environment and Development Organization (WEDO, #21016);*
- *World Federation of Trade Unions (WFTU, #21493);*
- *World Organization of United Cities and Local Governments (UCLG, #21695);*
- *Youth for Unity and Voluntary Action (YUVA).* [2021.09.01/XE6809/**E***]

♦ United Nations Industrial Development Fund / see Industrial Development Fund (#11173)
♦ United Nations Industrial Development Organization (#20336)

♦ United Nations Informal Regional Network of Non-Governmental Organizations (UN-NGO-IRENE) 20573

Réseau informel régional des organisations non gouvernementales des Nations Unies

Contact address not obtained. T. +12129636207. Fax +12129631265. E-mail: nkaraborni@yahoo.com.
URL: http://www.unpan.org/NGO.asp

History Apr 2001, Aracaju (Brazil), within *ECOSOC (#05331)*, with support of *World Family Organization (WFO, #21399)*. **Aims** Bridge the gap between developed and developing countries; build ngo capacity; reinforce networking among ngos from the North and the South; increase cooperation and promote partnerships between ngos to enhance the implementation of the Millennium Declaration and the Millennium Development Goals particularly for the people in the Caribbean region. **Languages** English, French. **Staff** 2.00 FTE, paid. Voluntary. **Finance** Income from voluntary trust fund set up by ECOSOC; contributions from ngos. **Activities** Organizes conferences and meetings. **Events** *World family summit +6* Paris (France) 2010, *World family summit +5* Istanbul (Turkey) 2009, *World family summit +4 / World Family Summit* Cairo (Egypt) 2008, *World family summit +3* Warsaw (Poland) 2007. **Publications** *UN-NGO-IRENE Update* – electronic newsletter.
Members Ngos in consultative status with ECOSOC (not specified). **IGO Relations** Partners: *Group of 77 (G-77, #10732)*; *UNIDO (#20336)*; *United Nations Institute for Training and Research (UNITAR, #20576)*; *United Nations Non-Governmental Liaison Service (NGLS, #20591)*. **NGO Relations** Partners: *Conference of Non-Governmental Organizations in Consultative Relationship with the United Nations (CONGO, #04635)*; *Euro-Arab Network of NGOs for Development and Integration (READI)*; *International Association of Economic and Social Councils and Similar Institutions (IAESCSI, #11858)*; *World Federation of United Nations Associations (WFUNA, #21499)*; national organizations. [2010/XM0509/**F**]

♦ United Nations Information Centres (UNICs) 20574

Centres d'Information des Nations Unies

Secretariat Information Centres Service, Dept of Global Communications, United Nations, S-1060A, New York NY 10017, USA. Fax +12129637330. E-mail: dpi_dis_unit@un.org.
URL: http://unic.un.org/

History As branch offices of *Department of Public Information (DPI)* – currently *Department of Global Communiations*, and became the first field offices of *United Nations (UN, #20515)*. Among the first cities where UNICs were established, 1946-1947, were: Geneva (Switzerland); Mexico City (Mexico); Moscow (Russia); Delhi (India); Prague (Czech Rep); Rio de Janeiro (Brazil); Washington DC (USA). Among most recent UNICs set up are: Pretoria (South Africa) and Warsaw (Poland), 1995; Sanaa (Yemen), 1994; Windhoek (Namibia), 1992. The *United Nations Regional Information Centre for Western Europe (UNRIC, #20621)*, Brussels (Belgium), was established in 2004, and services Western Europe; it replaces 9 UN Information Centres based in Europe. **Aims** Promote greater public understanding of, and support for, the aims and activities of the United Nations by disseminating information on the work of the Organization to people everywhere, especially in *developing countries*. **Languages** Arabic, Chinese, English, French, Russian, Spanish. Also local languages. **Staff** 300.00 FTE, paid. **Finance** Regular budget of the United Nations; contributions from host countries. **Activities** UNICs: serve as local focal point in their countries for information outreach programmes. They: organize press conferences, educational seminars, and exhibits to promote special UN observances and campaigns, major reports and global conferences; arrange for translation and adaptation of UN information materials into local languages; build local partnerships with government offices, national and local media, NGOs, educational institutions and national library services to promote public awareness and support for the UN; organize Model United Nations Conferences and media training programmes; support education curriculum development; disseminate UN information material, posting local language publications and information on the Internet; maintain UN reference libraries providing access to UN print and audio-visual materials; provide feedback on national and regional media coverage of UN activities and developments; provide communication support and handle media liaison for UN Secretary-General and other UN officials during visits. UNICs are active members of *United Nations Country Teams (UNCT)*, composed of agencies of the UN family in the field. They often play a leading role in coordinating joint information and communication activities and in creation and functioning of inter-agency UN Communications Groups, thus reinforcing the projection of a unified and coherent image of the UN to the public at the national and regional levels. UNICs receive administrative and programme support from the Information Centres Service (ICS), Department of Public Information. **Events** *International Symposium on Responsible Business, Responsible Supply Chain Contributing SDGs* Tokyo (Japan) 2018, *Climate Change Symposium* Tokyo (Japan) 2017, *International Conference on the Impacts of International Criminal Courts/Tribunals and Law on Human Rights and International Humanitarian Law* Teheran (Iran Islamic Rep) 2016, *International Conference on Evolution of Legal Concepts in Light of Evolution of International Criminal Courts and Tribunals* Teheran (Iran Islamic Rep) 2014. **Publications** Newsletters.
Members Information centres, services and offices in 62 countries:
Algeria, Argentina, Armenia, Australia, Austria, Azerbaijan, Bahrain, Bangladesh, Belarus, Belgium, Bolivia, Brazil, Burkina Faso, Burundi, Cameroon, Colombia, Congo Brazzaville, Czechia, Egypt, Eritrea, Georgia, Ghana, India, Indonesia, Iran Islamic Rep, Japan, Kazakhstan, Kenya, Lebanon, Lesotho, Libya, Madagascar, Mexico, Morocco, Myanmar, Namibia, Nepal, Nigeria, Pakistan, Panama, Paraguay, Peru, Philippines, Poland, Romania, Russia, Senegal, South Africa, Sri Lanka, Sudan, Switzerland, Tanzania UR, Togo, Trinidad-Tobago, Tunisia, Türkiye, Ukraine, USA, Uzbekistan, Yemen, Zambia, Zimbabwe.
NGO Relations UNICs work in partnership with members of civil society who are actively involved with issues of concern to the United Nations. NGOs count on UNICs as partners in organizing seminars, exhibits and commemorative events, focusing on such key issues as the promotion of human rights and peace and security, the eradication of poverty and protection of the environment. NGOs have worked with the Department of Public Information since 1946, and are indispensable partners for UN efforts at the country level. There are currently over 1,500 NGOs associated with DPI. [2018/XE3516/**E***]

♦ United Nations Information Organization (inactive)

♦ United Nations Institute for Disarmament Research (UNIDIR) 20575

Institut des Nations Unies pour la recherche sur le désarmement

Dir Palais des Nations, Bureau A-525, Av de la Paix 8-14, 1211 Geneva 10, Switzerland. T. +41229171141. E-mail: unidir@un.org.
URL: http://www.unidir.org/

History 1 Oct 1980, as an autonomous institution within the framework of the *United Nations (UN, #20515)*, following resolution 34/83 M adopted 11 Dec 1979 by UN General Assembly. By resolution 37/99 K of 13 Dec 1982, the General Assembly decided that UNIDIR should function as an autonomous institution working in close relationship with UN Department for Disarmament Affairs. Statute, approved by General Assembly resolution 39/148 H of 17 Dec 1984, became effective 1 Jan 1985. Based at *United Nations Office at Geneva (UNOG, #20597)*. **Aims** Support Members States, the UN and policy and research communities in advancing ideas and actions that contribute to a more sustainable and peaceful world. **Structure** Director reports to Board of Trustees, which also functions as UN Secretary-General's Advisory Board on Disarmament Matters (meeting twice a year). **Languages** English, French. **Staff** 25.00 FTE, paid. **Finance** Voluntary contributions from States, public and private organizations. **Activities** Knowledge management/information dissemination; guidance/assistance/consulting; research/documentation. **Events** *United Nations Workshop on Space Law* Vienna (Austria) 2016, *Forum on civil society and outer space* Vienna (Austria) 2007, *Conference on information technology and international security* Geneva (Switzerland) 1996, *Workshop on fissile materials and tritium* Geneva (Switzerland) 1995, *Meeting on security and economic considerations of arms and technology transfers among exporting and importing states* Geneva (Switzerland) 1994. **Publications** *UNIDIR Newsletter* (12 a year). **Members** Not a membership organization. **NGO Relations** Member of: *Asia-Pacific Regional Space Agency Forum (APRSAF, #02010)*; *Geneva Forum*. [2019.02.12/XE6904/j/**E***]

♦ United Nations Institute for Training and Research (UNITAR) 20576

Institut des Nations Unies pour la Formation et la Recherche – Instituto de las Naciones Unidas para la Formación Profesional e Investigaciones

Exec Dir Av de la Paix 7 bis, 1211 Geneva CH-1202, Switzerland. T. +41229178400. Fax +41229178047. E-mail: info@unitar.org.
URL: http://www.unitar.org/

History Proposed in a 1962 resolution of the UN General Assembly – resolution 1827 (XVII), 18 Dec 1962. Established following recommendation of *ECOSOC (#05331)* to the General Assembly which commissioned the Secretary-General with the establishment of a United Nations Institute for Training and Research as an autonomous body within the *United Nations System (#20635)* (General Assembly resolution 1934 (XVIII) of 11 Dec 1963). Commenced functioning Mar 1965. Headquarters originally based in New York NY (USA), with a European office in Geneva (Switzerland). In 1993, headquarters were transferred to Geneva. **Aims** Develop capacities to enhance global decision-making; support country level action for shaping a better future; empower individuals and institutions through knowledge and learning. **Structure** Board of Trustees (meets at least annually); headed by Executive Director. Headquarters: Geneva (Switzerland). Out-posted offices: New York NY (USA); Hiroshima (Japan). Project Office: Port Harcourt (Nigeria). **Languages** Arabic, Chinese, English, French, Japanese, Portuguese, Russian, Spanish. **Staff** 250.00 FTE, paid. **Finance** Sources: contributions; contributions of member/participating states; government support; grants; international organizations; revenue from activities/projects. Project-based organization without funds from regular UN budget. Annual budget: 28,900,000 USD (2019). **Activities** Capacity building; events/meetings; knowledge management/information dissemination; research and development; training/education. **Events** *Preventing Violent Extremism – Good Practices for Engaging Youth through Sports Programs* 2020, *Seminar on Resilient Livelihoods of the Urban Poor during the Pandemic from a Gender Perspective* Jeju (Korea Rep) 2020, *E-mobility and Sustainable Urban Transport* Seogwipo (Korea Rep) 2020, *Enhancing a Victim-Centered Approach Identification, Assistance and Protection of Trafficking Victims in the Asia-Pacific Region* Seogwipo (Korea Rep) 2020, *Workshop on Jeju Human Security* Jeju (Korea Rep) 2019. **Publications** *A Manual for UN Mediators: Advice from UN Representatives and Envoys*; *A More Strategic Partnership for the Prevention and Resolution of Conflict*; *Environmental Law Courses*; *Environnement et Commerce – Perspectives pour l'Afrique de l'Ouest*; *International Environmental Law: Atmosphere, Freshwater and Soil*; *International Environmental Negotiations*; *Introduction to International Environmental Law – Introduction au Droit International de l'Environnement*; *Manual for UN Delegates – Conference Process, Procedure and Negotiation*; *Multilateral Conferences and Diplomacy – glossary of terms for UN Delegates – Multilateral Conferences and Diplomacy – Glosario Para Delegados de la ONU*; *Multilateral Diplomacy: the United Nations System at Geneva: A Working Guide*; *Organizations and Cooperation in Conflict Prevention: Strategic Management and Coordination*; *The International Criminal Court: the Making of the Rome Statute – Issues, Negotiations, Results*; *The Law of Cyber-Space – An Invitation to the Table of Negotiations*; *The Nexus between Peacekeeping and Peace-building: Debriefing and Lessons*; *Training and Human Capacity-Building in Post-Conflict*.
IGO Relations Partnerships and networks -
/United Nations Bodies/:
– Dag Hammarskjöld Library (DHL);
– Department of Peace-Keeping Operations (DKPO);
– Department of Political Affairs (DPA);
– *ECOSOC (#05331)*;
– *FAO (#09260)*;
– *Global Environment Facility (GEF, #10346)*;
– *ILO (#11123)*;
– Inter-Agency Support Group on Indigenous Issues (IASG);
– *International Programme on Chemical Safety (IPCS, #14650)*;
– *International Telecommunication Union (ITU, #15673)*;
– *International Trade Centre (ITC, #15703)*;
– *Joint United Nations Programme on HIV/AIDS (UNAIDS, #16149)*;
– Office for Outer Space Affairs (UN/OOSA);
– *Office of the United Nations High Commissioner for Human Rights (OHCHR, #17697)*;
– *Organisation for the Prohibition of Chemical Weapons (OPCW, #17823)*;
– *Secretariat of the United Nations Convention to Combat Desertification (Secretariat of the UNCCD, #19208)*;
– *UN-Water (#20723)*;
– *UNCTAD (#20285)*;
– *UNDP (#20292)*;
– *UNESCO (#20322)*;
– *UNHCR (#20327)*;
– *UNICEF (#20332)*;
– *UNIDO (#20336)*;
– *United Nations Assistance Mission in Afghanistan (UNAMA, #20522)*;
– *United Nations Compensation Commission (UNCC, #20548)*;
– *United Nations Economic Commission for Africa (ECA, #20554)*;
– *United Nations Economic Commission for Europe (UNECE, #20555)*;
– *United Nations Framework Convention on Climate Change – Secretariat (UNFCCC, #20564)*;
– *United Nations Fund for International Partnerships (UNFIP, #20565)*;
– *United Nations Group on the Information Society (UNGIS, #20570)*;
– *United Nations Human Settlements Programme (UN-Habitat, #20572)*;
– United Nations Library Geneva;
– United Nations Mission of Support in East Timor (UNMISET);
– *United Nations Office for the Coordination of Humanitarian Affairs (OCHA, #20593)*;
– *United Nations Office on Drugs and Crime (UNODC, #20596)*;
– United Nations Office Geneva (UNOG);
– United Nations Office of Legal Affairs (OLA);
– *United Nations Office at Nairobi (UNON, #20600)*;
– *United Nations Office for Project Services (UNOPS, #20602)*;
– *United Nations Office at Vienna (UNOV, #20604)*;
– *United Nations Operation in Burundi (ONUB, inactive)*;
– *United Nations Permanent Forum on Indigenous Issues (UNPFII, #20609)*;
– *United Nations Population Fund (UNFPA, #20612)*;
– United Nations Secretariat;
– United Nations Stabilization Mission in Haiti (MINUSTAH);
– *United Nations University (UNU, #20642)*;
– *United Nations Volunteers (UNV, #20650)*;
– *WHO (#20950)*;
– *The World Bank Group (#21218)*;
– *World Food Programme (WFP, #21510)*;
– *World Intellectual Property Organization (WIPO, #21593)*;
– *World Trade Organization (WTO, #21864)*.
/Other International Organizations/:
– Secretariat of
– *Convention on Access to Information, Public Participation in Decision-making and Access to Justice in Environmental Matters (Århus Convention, 1998)*;
– *International Monetary Fund (IMF, #14180)*;
– *International Organization for Migration (IOM, #14454)*;
– *OECD (#17693)*;
– *Organisation internationale de la Francophonie (OIF, #17809)*;
– *Organization for Security and Cooperation in Europe (OSCE, #17887)*;
– *Secretariat of the Basel Convention (SBC, #19196)*;
– *Secretariat of the Convention on Biological Diversity (SCBD, #19197)*;
– *Secretariat of the Convention of Wetlands (#19200)*;
– *Secretariat of the Rotterdam Convention (#19206)*;
– *Secretariat of the Stockholm Convention on Persistent Organic Pollutants (Secretariat of the Stockholm Convention, #19207)*.
/Regional Organizations/:
– *African Commission on Human and Peoples' Rights (ACHPR, #00255)*;
– *African Development Bank (ADB, #00283)*;
– *African Union (AU, #00488)*;
– *Andean Community (#00817)*;
– *ASEAN (#01141)*;
– *Asia-Pacific Economic Cooperation (APEC, #01887)*;
– *Asian Development Bank (ADB, #01422)*;
– *Comisión Centroamericana de Ambiente y Desarrollo (CCAD, #04129)*;
– *Commonwealth Secretariat (#04362)*;
– *Comunidade dos Países de Língua Portuguesa (CPLP, #04430)*;
– *Council of Europe (CE, #04881)*;
– EC-ASEAN Intellectual Property Rights Cooperation Programme (ECAP II);
– *European Commission (EC, #06633)* – DG Development and DG Environment;
– *European Organization for Nuclear Research (CERN, #08108)*;
– *European Space Agency (ESA, #08798)*;
– European Union Space Centre;
– GEF/UNDP/IMO Regional Programme on Building Partnerships in Environmental Management for the Seas of East Asia (PEMSEA);
– *Joint Research Centre (JRC, #16147)*;
– *Macroeconomic and Financial Management Institute of Eastern and Southern Africa (MEFMI, #16539)*;
– *New Partnership for Africa's Development (NEPAD, #17091)*;
– Pôle régional de formation en gestion de la dette en Afrique du centre et de l'ouest (Pôle-Dette);

- Region Rhône-Alpes;
- Regional Trade Facilitation Programme, Gaborone (Botswana);
- *Southern African Development Community (SADC, #19843)*;
- *West African Institute for Financial and Economic Management (WAIFEM, #20883)*.

/National Governments and Local Authorities/: numerous partnerships, including with the following organizations that are listed in this Yearbook:
- *Banque centrale des Etats de l'Afrique de l'Ouest (BCEAO, #03167)*;
- *Banque des Etats de l'Afrique centrale (BEAC, #03169)*;
- *Deutsche Gesellschaft für Internationale Zusammenarbeit (GIZ)*;
- *Japan International Cooperation Agency (JICA)*;
- *Swedish International Development Cooperation Agency (Sida)*.

NGO Relations /Partnerships and networks
Cooperates with a number of nongovernmental organizations, societies, centres of excellence and academic institutions, including the following listed in this Yearbook:
- *Asian Disaster Reduction Center (ADRC, #01427)*;
- *Association internationale des Maires et responsables des capitales et métropoles partiellement ou entièrement Francophones (AIMF, #02715)*;
- *Centre for Conflict Resolution, Cape Town (CCR)*;
- *Centre for International Courts and Tribunals (CICT)*;
- *Federación Latinoamericana de Ciudades, Municipios y Asociaciones de Gobiernos Locales (FLACMA, #09350)*;
- *Fondation pour l'économie et le développement durable des régions d'Europe (FEDRE, #09817)*;
- *Global Change System for Analysis, Research and Training (START, #10278)*;
- *Global Ecovillage Network (GEN, #10331)*;
- *The Hague Academy of International Law*;
- *Hiroshima Peace Institute*;
- *Institute for Policy Studies, Singapore (IPS)*;
- *International Centre for Tropical Agriculture (#12527)*;
- *International Christian University (ICU)*;
- *International Committee of the Red Cross (ICRC, #12799)*;
- *International Council on Monuments and Sites (ICOMOS, #13049)*;
- *International Law Institute – African Centre for Legal Excellence (ILI – ACLE, #14005)*;
- *International Ocean Institute (IOI, #14394)*;
- *International Peace Institute (IPI, #14536)*;
- *International Physicians for the Prevention of Nuclear War (IPPNW, #14578)*;
- *International Union for Conservation of Nature and Natural Resources (IUCN, #15766)*;
- *Interpeace (#15962)*;
- *International Pollutants Elimination Network (IPEN, #14616)*;
- *Japan Bank for International Cooperation (JBIC)*;
- *MapAction*;
- *Rädda Barnen – Save the Children Sweden*;
- *Regional Network of Local Authorities for the Management of Human Settlements (CITYNET, #18799)*;
- *Ritsumeikan Asia Pacific University (APU)*;
- Centre for International Studies and Diplomacy of *School of Oriental and African Studies (SOAS)*;
- *Singapore International Foundation (SIF)*;
- *Thomson Reuters Foundation (TRF)*;
- *Union of the Baltic Cities (UBC, #20366)*;
- *World Organization of United Cities and Local Governments (UCLG, #21695)*;
- *World Wide Fund for Nature (WWF, #21922)*.

Also cooperates with companies in the private sector. [2020.09.12/XE3387/j/**E***]

♦ United Nations Integrated Mission in Timor-Leste (inactive)
♦ United Nations Integrated Office in Burundi (inactive)
♦ United Nations Inter-Agency Project on Human Trafficking (inactive)

♦ United Nations Interim Force in Lebanon (UNIFIL) 20577

Force intérimaire des Nations Unies au Liban (FINUL) – Fuerza Provisional de las Naciones Unidas en el Libano (FPNUL)

Contact PO Box 199, Tyre SOUTH LEBANON, Lebanon.
URL: https://unifil.unmissions.org/

History 19 Mar 1978. Established by resolutions 425 (1978) and 426 (1978) of the *United Nations Security Council (UNSC, #20625)*, for an initial period of 6 months, subject to extension. Comes within *United Nations System (#20635)*, in the framework of *United Nations (UN, #20515)*. The first UNIFIL troops arrived in the area on 23 Mar 1978. **Aims** Confirm the withdrawal of Israeli forces from Southern Lebanon and the return of the area under effective Lebanese authority; restore international peace and security; assist the Government of Lebanon and the Lebanese armed forces in securing the borders against hostile activities and unauthorized entry of arms or related materials; help ensure protection of and humanitarian access to civilian populations, as well as voluntary and safe return of displaced persons; protect United Nations personnel, facilities, installations and equipment. **Structure** Force Commander Reserve; Sectors (2); field battalions (9); administrative and logistics UNIFIL House, located in Beirut (Lebanon). **Staff** Authorized personnel (2021): 13,000. Deployed personnel (2021): 10,638 of which 809 civilians. Shares military observers from: *United Nations Truce Supervision Organization (UNTSO, #20638)*. **Finance** Annual budget: 510,251,500 USD (2022). **Activities** Conflict resolution; capacity building; monitoring/evaluation; guidance/assistance/consulting; training/education.
Members Contributors of military personnel of 43 countries:
Armenia, Austria, Bangladesh, Belarus, Brazil, Brunei Darussalam, Cambodia, China, Colombia, Croatia, Cyprus, El Salvador, Estonia, Fiji, Finland, France, Germany, Ghana, Greece, Guatemala, Hungary, India, Indonesia, Ireland, Italy, Kazakhstan, Kenya, Korea Rep, Malaysia, Malta, Nepal, Netherlands, Nigeria, North Macedonia, Qatar, Serbia, Sierra Leone, Slovenia, Spain, Sri Lanka, Tanzania UR, Türkiye, Uruguay.
IGO Relations *United Nations Special Committee on Peace-keeping Operations (#20628)*. [2022/XF7577/**F***]

♦ United Nations Interim Security Force for Abyei (UNISFA) 20578

Address not obtained.
URL: https://unisfa.unmissions.org/

History Jun 2011. Established by resolution 1990 of *United Nations Security Council (UNSC, #20625)* of *United Nations (UN, #20515)*. Current mandate runs until 15 Nov 2022. **Aims** Monitor the flashpoint border between north and south; facilitate the delivery of humanitarian aid; use force in protecting civilians and humanitarian workers in Abyei. **Staff** Authorized personnel (2021): 4,190. Deployed personnel (2021): 3,801 of which 217 civilians. **Finance** Annual budget: 280,581,200 USD (2022). **IGO Relations** *United Nations Special Committee on Peace-keeping Operations (#20628)*. [2022/AA1006/**F***]

♦ United Nations International Children's Emergency Fund / see UNICEF (#20332)

♦ United Nations International Civil Servants Federation (UNISERV) . . 20579

Fédération des Fonctionnaires Internationaux des Nations Unies (FFINU)

Address not obtained.
URL: https://uniserv-federation.com/

History Current statutes approved 30 Sep 2019. **Structure** Annual General Meeting; Executive.
Members Staff bodies (4):
International Staff Association of UNESCO (ISAU, #15597); *UNDP/UNFPA/UNOPS/UN Women Staff Association (Staff Council, #20291)*; *United Nations Field Staff Union (UNFSU, #20561)*; *United Nations Staff Union (#20630)* (New York). [2021/AA2043/y/**E**]

♦ United Nations International Computing Centre / see International Computing Centre (#12839)
♦ United Nations International Drug Control Programme (inactive)
♦ United Nations International Institute on Ageing / see International Institute on Ageing, United Nations – Malta (#13860)
♦ United Nations International School (internationally oriented national body)
♦ United Nations International Strategy for Disaster Reduction / see United Nations Office for Disaster Risk Reduction (#20595)

♦ United Nations Interregional Crime and Justice Research Institute (UNICRI) 20580

Institut interrégional de recherche des Nations Unies sur la criminalité et la justice – Instituto Interregional de las Naciones Unidas para Investigaciones sobre la Delincuencia y la Justicia

Communications Officer Viale Maestri del Lavoro 10, 10127 Turin TO, Italy. T. +39116537111. Fax +39116313368. E-mail: unicri.publicinfo@un.org.
Liaison Office Palazzetto Venezia, Piazza San Marco 50, 00186 Rome RM, Italy. T. +3966789907. Fax +3966780668. E-mail: unicri.romeoffice@un.org.
URL: http://www.unicri.it/

History 15 Jan 1968, Rome (Italy). Established following Resolution 1086 B (XXXIX) of *ECOSOC (#05331)*, 30 Jul 1965, urging an expanded United Nations Programme in Crime Prevention and Criminal Justice. Operates within the framework of *United Nations Crime Prevention and Criminal Justice Programme Network (#20549)*, as an autonomous institution of *United Nations (UN, #20515)*. New statutes and present name adopted by Resolution 1989/56 of ECOSOC, 24 May 1989. Former names and other names: *United Nations Social Defence Research Institute (UNSDRI)* – former; *Institut de recherche des Nations Unies sur la défense sociale* – former; *Instituto de Investigaciones de las Naciones Unidas para la Defensa Social* – former. **Aims** Deal with crime and justice issues within broader policies for socio-economic change and development, and protection of human rights. **Structure** Board of Trustees; Director. **Languages** English, French. **Staff** 34.00 FTE, paid. **Finance** Funded by *United Nations Crime Prevention and Criminal Justice Fund*, to which contributions are made on a voluntary basis by United Nations Member States, NGOs, academic institutions and private foundations. No funding from regular UN budget. **Activities** Guidance/assistance/consulting; knowledge management/information dissemination; politics/policy/regulatory; research/documentation; training/education. **Events** *COVID-19 Disinformation and Biotechnology* Geneva (Switzerland) 2021, *Meeting on Supply Chain Security and Trafficking of Precious Metals* Geneva (Switzerland) 2020, *Supply Chain Security and Trafficking of Precious Metals* Geneva (Switzerland) 2020, *COVID-19 – Crime Prevention and Criminal Justice Priorities – A Spotlight on Vulnerable Groups* Turin (Italy) 2020, *Interregional Seminar on COVID-19 Inter-Agency Coordination for Central Asia and South-East and Eastern Europe* Turin (Italy) 2020. **Publications** *F3 – Freedom From Fear Magazine*. *UNICRI Series*. Reports. Information Services: Provides library services through its Documentation Centre and Criminological Library. **IGO Relations** Cooperates with (1): *University for Peace (UPEACE, #20702)*. **NGO Relations** Member of (1): *Basel Institute on Governance*. Cooperates with (1): *International Centre for Counter-Terrorism – The Hague (ICCT)*. [2021.03.12/XE4069/j/**E***]

♦ United Nations Joint Staff Pension Fund (UNJSPF) 20581

Caisse commune des pensions du personnel des Nations Unies – Caja Común de Pensiones del Personal de las Naciones Unidas

CEO PO Box 5036, United Nations, New York NY 10017, USA. T. +12129636931. Fax +12129633146.
Geneva Office c/o Palais des Nations, 1211 Geneva 10, Switzerland. Fax +41229289099.
URL: http://www.unjspf.org/

History 1949, by resolution 248 (III) of the General Assembly of *United Nations (UN, #20515)* effective 23 Jan 1949; and amended by: resolution 680 (VII) effective 1 Jan 1953; resolution 772 (VIII) effective 1 Jan 1954 and 1 Jan 1955; resolution 874 (IX) effective 4 Dec 1954; resolution 955 (X) effective 3 Nov 1955; resolution 1073 (XI) effective 7 Dec 1956; resolution 1201 (XII) effective 1 Jan 1958; resolution 1309 (XIII) dated 10 Dec 1958; resolutions 1561 (XV) and 1614 (XV) effective 1 Apr 1961; resolution 1799 (XVII) effective 1 Jan 1963; resolution 2524 (XXIV) effective 1 Jan 1970; resolution 2887 (XXVI) effective 1 Jan 1972; resolution 3354 (XXIX) effective 1 Jan 1975; resolution 3526 (XXX) effective 1 Jan 1976; resolution 31/196 effective 1 Jan 1977; resolution 32/74 effective 1 Jan 1978; resolution 34/221 effective 1 Jan 1980; resolution 35/215 effective 1 Jan 1981; resolution 37/131 effective 1 Jan 1983; resolution 38/233 effective 1 Jan 1984; resolution 39/246 effective 1 Jan 1985; resolution 40/245 effective 1 Jan 1986; resolution 41/208 effective 1 Apr 1987; resolution 42/222 effective 1 Jan 1988 and 1 Jan 1989; resolution 44/199 effective 1 Jan 1990; resolution 45/242 effective 1 Jan 1991; resolution 46/192 effective 1 Jan 1992; resolution 47/203 effective 1 Jan 1993; resolution 48/225 effective 1 Jan 1994; resolution 49/224 effective 1 Jan 1995; resolution 51/217 effective 1 Jan 1997; resolution 53/210 effective 1 Jan 1999; resolution 55/224 effective 1 Jan 2001; resolution 57/286 effective 1 Jan 2003; resolution 59/269 effective 1 Jan 2005; resolution 61/240 effective 1 Jan 2007; resolution 62/252 effective 1 Jan 2009; resolution 63/252 effective 1 Jan 2010. **Aims** Provide retirement, death, disability and related benefits for staff of the United Nations, Specialized Agencies and the other organizations admitted to membership in the Fund. **Structure** Jointly administered by member organizations through *United Nations Joint Staff Pension Board (UNJSPB)*, consisting of 33 members, one third chosen by General Assembly or corresponding body of member organizations, one third by their executive heads and on third by their participants, with 4 additional representatives of retirees. United Nations Joint Staff Pension Board Standing Committee; Investments Committee; United Nations Joint Staff Pension Fund Senior Management; Committee of Actuaries; Emergency Fund. Officers: Chairman; 1st and 2nd Vice-Chairmen; Rapporteur. **Languages** English, French. **Staff** 252.00 FTE, paid. **Finance** The assets of the Fund derive from: (a) contributions of the participants; (b) contributions of the member organizations; (c) the yield from the investments of the Fund; (d) deficiency payments, if any (under article 26); (e) receipts from any other source. **Events** *Session / Board Session* Paris (France) 2012, *Session / Board Session* Geneva (Switzerland) 2011, *Board Session* London (UK) 2010, *Board Session* Vienna (Austria) 2009, *Board Session* Rome (Italy) 2008. **Publications** Annual Report.
Members International organizations (23) representing 121,000 active participants:
- *European and Mediterranean Plant Protection Organization (EPPO, #07773)*;
- *FAO (#09260)*;
- *ILO (#11123)*;
- *International Atomic Energy Agency (IAEA, #12294)*;
- *International Centre for Genetic Engineering and Biotechnology (ICGEB, #12494)*;
- *International Centre for the Study of the Preservation and Restoration of Cultural Property (ICCROM, #12521)*;
- *International Civil Aviation Organization (ICAO, #12581)*;
- *International Criminal Court (ICC, #13108)*;
- *International Fund for Agricultural Development (IFAD, #13692)*;
- *International Maritime Organization (IMO, #14102)*;
- *International Organization for Migration (IOM, #14454)*;
- *International Seabed Authority (ISBA, #14813)*;
- *International Telecommunication Union (ITU, #15673)*;
- *International Tribunal for the Law of the Sea (ITLOS, #15731)*;
- *Inter-Parliamentary Union (IPU, #15961)*;
- *Special Tribunal for Lebanon (STL, #19911)*;
- *UNESCO (#20322)*;
- *UNIDO (#20336)*;
- United Nations;
- *WHO (#20950)*;
- *World Intellectual Property Organization (WIPO, #21593)*;
- *World Meteorological Organization (WMO, #21649)*;
- *World Tourism Organization (UNWTO, #21861)*.

NGO Relations *Federation of Associations of Former International Civil Servants (FAFICS, #09457)* sends 6 representatives to sessions of the Board of the Fund. Member of: *International Council on Archives (ICA, #12996)*. [2018/XF5941/fy/**F***]

♦ United Nations of Ju Jitsu (UNJJ) 20582

Vice-Chairman address not obtained.
Chair address not obtained.
URL: http://www.un-jj.net/

History 21 Sep 1991, Chiny (Belgium). Registered in accordance with Belgian law. **Aims** Disseminate, promote and develop the scientific understanding and teaching contained in the *philosophy* of ju-jitsu *martial art*. **Structure** General Assembly. Council (meets at least once a year), consisting of 3 to 5 members. Officers: President, Secretary, Treasurer, and possibly one or more Vice-Presidents. **Finance** Members' dues. **Activities** Events/meetings; training/education. **Events** *Congress* Copenhagen (Denmark) 2015, *Congress* Southend-on-Sea (UK) 2014, *Congress* South Africa 2013, *Congress* Willingen (Germany) 2012, *Congress* New York, NY (USA) 2011.
Members Full national associations; Associate. Founder members (12) in 8 countries:

Belgium, Denmark, Germany, Italy, Malta, South Africa, Spain, UK.
Associate members in 17 countries:
Austria, Belgium, Denmark, Egypt, France, Germany, Iceland, Ireland, Italy, Kenya, Malta, Netherlands, Saudi Arabia, Spain, Sweden, UK, Zimbabwe. [2017/XF5316/F]

♦ United Nations Latin American Institute for the Prevention of Crime and the Treatment of Offenders (#11347)

♦ United Nations Liaison Office for Peace and Security (UNLOPS) 20583

Head address not obtained. E-mail: unlops@un.org.
URL: https://unlops.unmissions.org/

History 2011. Established to represent the entities of the *United Nations (UN, #20515)* Secretariat, in New York NY (USA), that support Member States and the Secretary-General in maintaining international peace and security: #the Departments of Peace Operations (DPO), Political and Peacebuilding Affairs (DPPA), Operational Support (DOS) and the Office of Counter-Terrorism (OCT). **Aims** Support the partnership between the United Nations and the European Union (EU) and other Brussels-based organizations on peace and security matters across the spectrum from conflict prevention to crisis management, peace operations and counter-terrorism. **Publications** *UNLOPS Brussels Bulletin*. **IGO Relations** Cooperates with (1): *European Union (EU, #08967)*. **NGO Relations** Member of (1): *Brussels Dialogue on Climate Diplomacy (BDCD, #03341)*. [2022/AA2445/**E***]

♦ United Nations – Mandated University for Peace / see University for Peace (#20702)

♦ United Nations Military Observer Group in India and Pakistan (UNMOGIP) 20584

Groupe d'observateurs militaires des Nations Unies dans l'Inde et le Pakistan

Contact Dept of Peace-Keeping Operations DPKA, UN Headquarters, Room S-1005 I, United Nations, New York NY 10017, USA. T. +12129636846. Fax +12129631186. E-mail: seblewongel@un.org – geekie@un.org.
Head address not obtained.
URL: https://unmogip.unmissions.org/

History 24 Jan 1949. Established by the *United Nations Security Council (UNSC, #20625)*, within, *United Nations System (#20635)*, in the framework of the *United Nations (UN, #20515)*. **Aims** Acting as part of UN *Peacekeeping* Operations, observe, to the extent possible, developments pertaining to the strict observance of the *ceasefire* of 17 Dec 1971 and report thereon to the Secretary-General. **Structure** Field mission manned by military observers and supported by Chief Administrative Officer and UN Field Service personnel; assisted by local staff; headed by Chief Military Observer appointed by and responsible to the Secretary-General of the United Nations. Headquarters: May-Oct – Srinagar (India); Nov-Apr – Rawalpindi (Pakistan). Liaison Office in Delhi (India). Field Stations (11): 7 in Pakistan (Bhimber – Domel – Gilgit – Kotli – Rawalakot – Sialkot – Skardu); 4 in India (Baramulla – Jammu – Poonch – Rajouri). **Staff** Deployed personnel (2021): 111, of which 68 civilians. Staff negotiations through *United Nations Field Staff Union (UNFSU, #20561)*. **Finance** Financed from the regular budget of the United Nations. Annual budget: 10,519,800 USD (2022). **Activities** Observers are currently stationed on both sides of the Line of Control agreed upon by India and Pakistan under the Simla agreement of Jul 1972. Despite some disagreement between Pakistan and India as to UNMOGIP mandate, UNMOGIP observers report developments pertaining to observance of the ceasefire along the line of control and assist both sides in keeping the peace, subject to restrictions on the activities of military observers on the Indian side of the Line of Control.
Members Military observers from 8 participating countries:
Chile, Croatia, Finland, Italy, Korea Rep, Philippines, Sweden, Uruguay.
IGO Relations *United Nations Mine Action Service (UNMAS, #20585)*; *United Nations Special Committee on Peace-keeping Operations (#20628)*. [2022/XE1153/**F***]

♦ United Nations Military Observer Mission to Congo / see United Nations Organization Stabilization Mission in the Democratic Republic of Congo (#20605)

♦ United Nations Mine Action Service (UNMAS) 20585

Service de l'action contre les mines des Nations Unies

Officer-in-charge c/o UN Headquarters, 1 United Nations Plaza, New York NY 10017, USA. T. +12129634710.
URL: http://www.mineaction.org/

History Oct 1997. Established by Kofi Annan, Secretary General of *United Nations (UN, #20515)*. Recognized as a Division, 2002. Currently a specialized service of the UN located within the Department of Peace Operations. Former names and other names: *MINAS* – former. **Aims** Eliminate the threat posed by mines, explosive remnants of war and improvised explosive devices by coordinating United Nations mine action, leading operational responses at the country level, and supporting the development of standards, policies and norms. **Structure** Deputy Director/Officer-in-Charge. **Languages** English. **Staff** 31.00 FTE, paid. **Finance** Supported by: *United Nations Voluntary Trust Fund for Assistance in Mine Action (UN VTF, #20649)*. **Activities** Advocacy/lobbying/activism; capacity building; guidance/assistance/consulting; humanitarian/emergency aid; politics/policy/regulatory. **Publications** *Portfolio of Mine Action Projects* (annual). *Gender Guidelines for Mine Action Programmes*; *Mine Action and Effective Coordination: The United Nations Inter-Agency Policy*; *United Nations Inter-Agency Mine Action Strategy*. Annual Report. **NGO Relations** Links with several organizations, including: *CARE International (CI, #03429)*; *Clear Path International (CPI)*; *Folkekirkens Nødhjaelp (FKN)*; *Help International, UK*; *Humanity and Inclusion (HI, #10975)*; *International Campaign to Ban Landmines (ICBL, inactive)*; *International Mine Initiative (IMI)*; *INTERSOS*; *Landmine Survivors Network (LSN)*; *Norwegian People's Aid (NPA)*; *Rädda Barnen – Save the Children Sweden*; *Response International (inactive)*; *World Rehabilitation Fund (WRF, #21749)*. [2020/XE2286/**E***]

♦ United Nations Mission in the Central African Republic and Chad (inactive)
♦ United Nations Mission in Côte d'Ivoire (inactive)
♦ United Nations Mission in East Timor (inactive)
♦ United Nations Mission for Justice Support in Haiti (inactive)
♦ United Nations Mission in Liberia (inactive)
♦ United Nations Mission of Observers in Prevlaka (inactive)
♦ United Nations Mission of Observers in Tajikistan (inactive)

♦ United Nations Mission for the Referendum in Western Sahara (MINURSO) 20586

Mission des Nations Unies pour l'organisation d'un referendum au Sahel occidental (MINURSO) – Misión de las Naciones Unidas para la Organización del Referéndum en el Sahara Occidental

Contact c/o Dept of Peace-keeping Operations, UN – Room S-3260E, New York NY 10017, USA. T. +12129631234. Fax +12129634879. E-mail: minursoinformationofficer@un.org.
URL: http://minurso.unmissions.org/

History 29 Apr 1991. Established by resolution 690 (1991) of *United Nations Security Council (UNSC, #20625)*, within *United Nations System (#20635)*, in the framework of *United Nations (UN, #20515)*. Budget approved 17 May 1991. Operational Sep 1991. Mandate repeatedly extended, with latest resolutions: 27 Apr 2011, by resolution S/RES1979 (2001), mandate extended until 30 apr 2012; 16 apr 2012, by resolution S/RES2/2044 (2012), mandate extended until 30 Apr 2013. Mandate currently extended until 31 Oct 2022. **Aims** Implement the settlement plan agreed upon by both parties in the conflict, namely: maintain and monitor the *cease-fire* between forces of Morocco and those of the Frente Popular para la Liberación de Sagiuia al Hamra y de Rio de Oro (Front POLISARIO); implement *peace* solution endorsed by the Security Council and agreed upon by both parties; provide logistical assistance to UNHCR for Confidence Building Measures (CBMs) programme which includes family visits and setting up telephone lines between *refugee* camps in Tindouf (Southwest Algeria) and Western Sahara; enlarge family visit programme by road; establish postal services; meetings between representatives of civil societies of both sides are under negotiation. **Structure** Components (3): military personnel; police; civilians. **Languages** Arabic, English, French, Spanish. **Staff** Autohorised number of personnel (2021): 245. Deployed personnel (2021): 488 of which 230 civilians. **Finance** Annual budget: 60,908,900 USD (2022). **Activities** Military component is dedicated to monitoring the cease-fire. Concerted efforts are made by Special Representative (SRSG) to support PESG action to move political process forward through talks with the parties, neighbouring countries and other member states. Staff is involved in logistics and support for continuation of the Confidence Building Measures.

Members States contributing military personnel, as of Oct 2012 (31):
Argentina, Austria, Bangladesh, Brazil, China, Croatia, Djibouti, Egypt, El Salvador, France, Ghana, Greece, Guinea, Honduras, Hungary, Ireland, Italy, Korea Rep, Malaysia, Mongolia, Nepal, Nigeria, Pakistan, Paraguay, Peru, Poland, Russia, Sri Lanka, Togo, Uruguay, Yemen.
States contributing troops, as of Oct 2012 (2):
Bangladesh, Ghana.
States contributing police personnel, as of Oct 2012 (4):
Chad, Egypt, Jordan, Yemen. [2022/XF2272/**F***]

♦ United Nations Mission in South Sudan (UNMISS) 20587

Address not obtained.
URL: https://unmiss.unmissions.org/

History Jul 2011. Established by resolution 1996 (2011) of *United Nations Security Council (UNSC, #20625)* of *United Nations (UN, #20515)*. Following crisis Dec 2013, resolution 2155 (2014) mandate reinforced. Current mandate runs until 15 Mar 2022. **Staff** Authorized personnel (2021): 19,101. Deployed personnel (2021): 17,982, of which 2,268 civilians. **Finance** Annual budget: 1,201,887,500 USD (2022). **IGO Relations** *United Nations Special Committee on Peace-keeping Operations (#20628)*. [2022/AA1007/**F***]

♦ United Nations Mission in the Sudan (inactive)
♦ United Nations Mission of Support in East Timor (inactive)

♦ United Nations Multidimensional Integrated Stabilization Mission in the Central African Republic (MINUSCA) 20588

Mission Multidimensionnelle Intégrée des Nations Unies pour la Stabilisation en République Centrafricaine (MINUSCA)

Address not obtained.
URL: https://peacekeeping.un.org/en/mission/minusca

History 10 Apr 2014. Established by *United Nations (UN, #20515)* General Assembly resolution 2149 (2014), when African-led International Support Mission in the Central African Republic (MISCA) transferred its authority over to MINUSCA. Current mandate extended until 15 Nov 2022. **Staff** Total personnel (2021): 15,663, of which 1,230 civilians. Authorized personnel (2021): 17,420. **Finance** Annual budget: 1,115,738,700 USD (2021). **IGO Relations** *United Nations Special Committee on Peace-keeping Operations (#20628)*. [2022/AA1005/**F***]

♦ United Nations Multidimensional Integrated Stabilization Mission in Mali (MINUSMA) 20589

Mission Multidimensionnelle Intégrée des Nations Unies pour la Stabilisation au Mali (MINUSMA)

Address not obtained.
URL: https://peacekeeping.un.org/en/mission/minusma

History Established by *United Nations Security Council (UNSC, #20625)* resolution 2100, 25 Apr 2013; altered by resolution 2164, 25 Jun 2014. Current mandate extended until 30 June 2022, by resolution 2584 (2021). **Staff** Authorised personnel (2021): 15,209. Deployed personnel (2021): 18,108, of which 3,384 civilians. **Finance** Annual budget: 1,262,194,200 USD (2022). **IGO Relations** *United Nations Special Committee on Peace-keeping Operations (#20628)*. [2022/AA1004/**F***]

♦ United Nations Network on Migration 20590

Secretariat c/o IOM, Route des Morillons 17, CP 71, 1211 Geneva 19, Switzerland. E-mail: unmignet@iom.int.

History Established 23 May 2018, as successor to *Global Migration Group (GMG, inactive)*. Functions within *United Nations (UN, #20515)*. **Aims** Ensure effective, coordinated system-wide support to the implementation of the Global Compact on Safe, Orderly and Regular Migration (GCM), adopted 2018. **Structure** Executive Committee. *International Organization for Migration (IOM, #14454)* serves as Coordinator and Secretariat. Working Groups.
Members UN agencies (37):
– Department of Economic and Social Affairs (DESA);
– Department of Global Communications;
– *FAO (#09260)*;
– *ILO (#11123)*;
– *Inter-Agency Standing Committee (IASC, #11393)*;
– *International Bank for Reconstruction and Development (IBRD, #12317)* (World Bank);
– *International Fund for Agricultural Development (IFAD, #13692)*;
– *International Maritime Organization (IMO, #14102)*;
– *International Organization for Migration (IOM, #14454)*;
– *Joint United Nations Programme on HIV/AIDS (UNAIDS, #16149)*;
– Multi-Partner Trust Fund Office (MPTFO);
– Office of the Special Representative of the Secretary-General for International Migration (OSRSG);
– *Office of the United Nations High Commissioner for Human Rights (OHCHR, #17697)*;
– Peacebuilding Support Office (PBSO);
– *UNCTAD (#20285)*;
– *UNDP (#20292)*;
– *UNEP (#20299)*;
– *UNESCO (#20322)*;
– *UNHCR (#20327)*;
– *UNICEF (#20332)*;
– *UNIDO (#20336)*;
– *United Nations Alliance of Civilizations (UNAOC, #20520)*;
– *United Nations Economic and Social Commission for Asia and the Pacific (ESCAP, #20557)*;
– *United Nations Economic and Social Commission for Western Asia (ESCWA, #20558)*;
– *United Nations Economic Commission for Africa (ECA, #20554)*;
– *United Nations Economic Commission for Europe (UNECE, #20555)*;
– *United Nations Economic Commission for Latin America and the Caribbean (ECLAC, #20556)*;
– *United Nations Human Settlements Programme (UN-Habitat, #20572)*;
– *United Nations Institute for Training and Research (UNITAR, #20576)*;
– *United Nations Office for the Coordination of Humanitarian Affairs (OCHA, #20593)*;
– *United Nations Office on Drugs and Crime (UNODC, #20596)*;
– *United Nations Sustainable Development Group (UNSDG, #20634)*;
– *United Nations System Chief Executives Board for Coordination (CEB, #20636)*;
– *United Nations University (UNU, #20642)*;
– *UN Women (#20724)*;
– *WHO (#20950)*;
– *World Food Programme (WFP, #21510)*. [2018/XM7576/**F***]

♦ United Nations NGO Committee on Narcotics and Substance Abuse, New York NY / see New York NGO Committee on Drugs (#17097)
♦ United Nations NGO Committee on Youth / see NGO Committee on Youth (#17121)

♦ United Nations Non-Governmental Liaison Service (NGLS) 20591

Service de liaison des Nations Unies avec les organisations non gouvernementales (SLNG) – Servicio de Enlace No Gubernamental de las Naciones Unidas

Main Office UN-NGLS, Dept Global Comms, 1 United Nations Plaza, New York NY 10017, USA.
URL: https://www.un.org/en/civilsociety/

History 1975. An inter-agency programme of *United Nations System (#20635)*; role and work endorsed by the Administrative Committee on Coordination in 1992 and by the UN General Assembly in 1993. As of 2018, comes within United Nations *Department for Global Communications*. Former names and other names: *UN-NGLS* – alias. **Aims** Promote dynamic partnerships between the United Nations and non-governmental organizations by: providing information, advice, expertise and support services; being part of the UN's efforts to strengthen dialogue and win public support for economic and social *development*; being concerned with the entire UN development agenda, including *human development*, *environment* and development, global *economy*, African recovery and development. **Structure** Officer in Charge; 3 Programme Officers; Programme Associate; JPO; 2 Administrative Assistants. **Languages** English, French. **Staff** 7.00 FTE, paid. **Finance** Main source: voluntary contributions by agencies, programmes, funds and departments of the UN system, currently: *FAO (#09260)*; *ILO (#11123)*; UN Department for Economic and Social Affairs; *UNEP (#20299)*;

UNCTAD (#20285) – Administering Agency; *UNDP (#20292)*; *United Nations Population Fund (UNFPA, #20612)*. Other sources: a number of bilateral donors, foundations and, on occasion, NGOs. **Activities** Guidance/assistance/consulting; knowledge management/information dissemination. **Events** *Annual Solutions Summit* New York, NY (USA) 2016, *Annual Solutions Summit* New York, NY (USA) 2015, *Meeting on Advancing Regional Recommendations on Post-2015* New York, NY (USA) 2013, *Symposium on responding to global crises* Geneva (Switzerland) 2010, *Meeting on COP 15 and climate justice* New York, NY (USA) 2010. **Publications** *Infolettre* (12 a year) in French – electronic newsletter; *Civil Society Observer* (5-6 a year) – e-bulletin; *NGLS Update* (twice a month) – electronic newsletter; *NGLS Roundup* – information bulletins. *Development Dossiers*; *NGLS Guide to Intergovernmental Negotiations and Decision Making*; *NGLS Handbook*; *The Road to Rio*; *The United Nations System: A Guide for NGOs*. Publications on topical issues, including: climate change and climate justice; decent and fair globalization; multilateralism. **Members** Not a membership organization but works with the NGO community on an informal basis. [2018/XE7655/**E***]

♦ United Nations – Nuclear Young Generation (UN-NYG) 20592

Contact address not obtained. E-mail: united-nations.nuclear-young-generation@iaea.org.
URL: https://unnyg.org/

History 2013. **Aims** Provide opportunities for the young generation of nuclear professionals at Vienna-based UN organizations; broaden their views on global, peaceful nuclear activities. **IGO Relations** Partner of (1): *African Commission on Nuclear Energy (AFCONE, #00256)*. Recognized by (1): *Vienna International Centre (VIC)*. [2021/AA3158/v/**E**]

♦ United Nations Nutrition / see UN Nutrition (#20710)

♦ United Nations Office for the Coordination of Humanitarian Affairs (OCHA) 20593

Bureau de la coordination des affaires humanitaires (BCAH)

New York Office UN Secretariat, 405 East 42nd St, New York NY 10017, USA. T. +12129631234. E-mail: ochany@un.org.
URL: http://www.unocha.org/

History Apr 1992, New York NY (USA), by the Secretary-General of *United Nations (UN, #20515)*, as *United Nations Department of Humanitarian Affairs (DHA)*, pursuant to resolution 46/182, Dec 1991, of the UN General Assembly, when post of Emergency Relief Coordinator (ERC) was established. Reorganized under current title, 1998, in accordance with reform plan of the UN Secretary-General. Previously also referred to as *Office for the Coordination of Humanitarian Affairs*. **Aims** Coordinate the global emergency response to save lives and protect people in humanitarian crises; advocate for effective and principled humanitarian action by all, for all. **Structure** Leadership; Senior Leadership Team; Senior Management Team. Also includes: *International Search and Rescue Advisory Group (INSARAG, #14816)*. **Staff** 2300.00 FTE, paid. **Finance** Sources: 5% from UN regular budget; 95% from voluntary contributions. Annual budget: 340,000,000 USD. **Activities** Humanitarian/emergency aid; knowledge management/information dissemination; networking/liaising; financial and/or material support; advocacy/lobbying/activism. **Events** *Conference on Ending Sexual and Gender-based Violence in Humanitarian Crises* Oslo (Norway) 2019, *World Humanitarian Summit* Istanbul (Turkey) 2016, *Round Table on Disaster Preparedness* Bangkok (Thailand) 2015, *North and South East Asia Regional Consultation for the World Humanitarian Summit* Tokyo (Japan) 2014, *Symposium* Tokyo (Japan) 2014. **Information Services** *ReliefWeb* – online portal to information on humanitarian emergencies and disasters, updated daily from offices in Geneva (Switzerland), New York NY (USA) and Kobe (Japan), publishing daily over 150 new documents and maps from over 2,500 sources. **IGO Relations** Works closely with UN operational agencies, governments, regional organizations and intergovernmental humanitarian organizations (not specified). Arrangement with: *UNEP (#20299)*. Strategic coordination for: *White Helmets (#20933)*. Member of: *United Nations Sustainable Development Group (UNSDG, #20634)*. Participates in: *Open Partial Agreement on the Prevention of, Protection against and Organization of Relief in Major Natural and Technological Disasters (EUR-OPA Major Hazards Agreement, #17762)*. **NGO Relations** Works closely with several consortia of NGOs, as well as with a wide variety of individual NGOs. At Headquarters level, consortia with which OCHA works include: *American Council for Voluntary International Action (InterAction)*; *International Council of Voluntary Agencies (ICVA, #13092)*; *Steering Committee for Humanitarian Response (SCHR, #19978)*. At field level, works with a variety of NGO consortia and individual NGOs on a country-by-country basis. Instrumental in setting up: *Asian Disaster Preparedness Center (ADPC, #01426)*. [2019.11.01/XE3242/**E***]

♦ United Nations Office for Disarmament Affairs (UNODA) 20594

Bureau des affaires de désarmement des Nations Unies – Oficina de Asuntos de Desarmede las Naciones Unidas

High Representative c/o Information and Outreach Branch, UN Plaza, Room S-3024, New York NY 10017, USA. Fax +12129634066 – +1212(19173671755. E-mail: unoda-web@un.org.
URL: http://www.un.org/disarmament/

History 1982. Originally established upon recommendation of *United Nations (UN, #20515)* General Assembly's 2nd special session on disarmament (SSOD II). Established as *Department for Disarmament Affairs*, Jan 1998. Former names and other names: *Centre for Disarmament Affairs* – former. **Aims** Promote: nuclear disarmament and non-proliferation; strengthening of disarmament regimes in respect to other weapons of mass destruction, and chemical and biological weapons; disarmament efforts in the area of conventional weapons, especially landmines and small arms, which are the weapons of choice in contemporary conflicts. **Structure** Branches (5): CD Secretariat and Conference Support (Geneva – Switzerland); Weapons of Mass Destruction (WMD); Conventional Arms Branch (CAB); Regional Disarmament Branch (RDB); Information and Outreach (IOB). Other offices: Office in Vienna (Austria); *United Nations Regional Centre for Peace, Disarmament and Development in Latin America and the Caribbean (UNLIREC, #20618)*, Lima (Peru); *United Nations Regional Centre for Peace and Disarmament for Asia and the Pacific (UNRCPD, #20617)*, Kathmandu (Nepal); *United Nations Regional Centre for Peace and Disarmament in Africa (UNREC, #20616)*, Lomé (Togo). **Languages** English, French. **Staff** 90.00 FTE, paid. **Finance** Financed from regular budget of UN with supplementary support through voluntary contributions from governments and private contributors. **Activities** Guidance/assistance/consulting; advocacy/lobbying/activism; knowledge management/information dissemination; events/meetings. **Events** *Joint Conference on Disarmament and Non-Proliferation Issues* Seoul (Korea Rep) 2021, *Joint Conference on Disarmament and Non-Proliferation Issues* Seoul (Korea Rep) 2020, *Joint Conference on Disarmament and Non-Proliferation Issues* Seoul (Korea Rep) 2019, *Joint Conference on Disarmament and Non-Proliferation Issues* Jeju (Korea Rep) 2018. **Publications** *UNODA Update* (4 a year); *Fact Sheets on Disarmament Issues* (2 a year); *Civicl Societyand Disarmament* (annual); *United Nations Disarmament Yearbook* (annual); *UNODAProgrammes Financed from Voluntary Contributions* (annual); *UNODA Occasional Papers*. *Disarmament Study Series*. Guides; reports. **NGO Relations** *International Action Network on Small Arms (IANSA, #11585)*; *Women's International League for Peace and Freedom (WILPF, #21024)*. [2022/XM6677/**E***]

♦ United Nations Office for Disaster Risk Reduction (UNDRR) 20595

Oficina de las Naciones Unidas para la Reducción del Riesgo de Desastres

Secretariat Rue de Varembé 9-11, 1202 Geneva, Switzerland. T. +41229178907 – +41229178908. Fax +41227339531 – +41227339855. E-mail: isdr@un.org.
URL: https://www.undrr.org/

History Established by decision of General Assembly of *United Nations (UN, #20515)*, based on the experience of *International Decade for Natural Disaster Reduction (IDNDR, inactive)*, the 1994 Yokohama Strategy and the 1999 strategy *'A Safer World in the 21st Century: Disaster and Risk Reduction'*, and the *'Geneva Mandate on Disaster Reduction'* adopted Jul 1999 at IDNDR Programme Forum. Mandate extended 2001 (GA Res 56/195). *'Hyogo Declaration'* and *'Hyogo Framework for Action 2005-2015'* endorsed, 2005. Succeeded by *'Sendai Framework for Disaster Risk Reduction 2015-2030'*, adopted 18 Mar 2015. Former names and other names: *United Nations International Strategy for Disaster Reduction (UNISDR)* – former; *Estrategia Internacional para la Reducción de Desastres (ESRD)* – former. **Aims** Serve as the focal point in the UN system for the coordination of disaster reduction; ensure synergies among the disaster reduction activities of the UN system and regional organizations and activities in socio-economic and humanitarian fields. **Structure** Office of the Special Representative of the Secretary-General for Disaster Risk Reduction; Executive Office. Sections (3): Advocacy and Outreach; Risk Knowledge; Coordination and Regional Programming. Headquarters in Geneva (Switzerland). Regional offices (5): Asia – Bangkok (Thailand); Africa – Nairobi (Kenya); Europe – Brussels (Belgium); Arab States – Cairo (Egypt); Americas and the Caribbean – Panama (Panama). Liaison offices in: New York NY (USA); Bonn (Germany). **Finance** Voluntary and purpose-designated contributions. **Activities** Networking/liaising; knowledge management/information dissemination; events/meetings. **Events** *International Recovery Forum* Kobe (Japan) 2022, *COVID-19 Safe Hospital Seminar* Incheon (Korea Rep) 2021, *Green Bond Basics* Incheon (Korea Rep) 2021, *Integrated Research on Disaster Risk International Conference* Japan 2021, *World Landslide Forum* Kyoto (Japan) 2021. **Publications** *Evidence* (12 a year) – newsletter; *UN/ISDR Highlights* – electronic newsletter. **IGO Relations** *Open Partial Agreement on the Prevention of, Protection against and Organization of Relief in Major Natural and Technological Disasters (EUR-OPA Major Hazards Agreement, #17762)*. Regional Unit hosted by: *Pan American Health Organization (PAHO, #18108)*. Member of: *Global Facility for Disaster Reduction and Recovery (GFDRR, #10352)*; *UN-Water (#20723)*. Memorandum of Understanding with: *Economic Cooperation Organization (ECO, #05313)*. Cooperative agreement with: *Islamic World Educational, Scientific and Cultural Organization (ICESCO, #16058)*. Agreement with: *Council of Europe (CE, #04881)*; *United Nations University (UNU, #20642)*. Other main regional partners and counterparts include: *Association of Caribbean States (ACS, #02411)*; *Caribbean Disaster Emergency Management Agency (CDEMA, #03493)*; *Central American Integration System (#03671)*; *OAS (#17629)*. Observer to: *Sistema Económico Latinoamericano (SELA, #19294)*. Participates in: *Global Framework for Climate Services (GFCS, #10380)*; *Group on Earth Observations (GEO, #10735)*. Adheres to: *Global Partnership for Effective Development Co-operation (GPEDC, #10532)*. Cooperates with: *International Civil Defence Organization (ICDO, #12582)*; *South Asian Association for Regional Cooperation (SAARC, #19721)*. **NGO Relations** Member of: *Global Gender and Climate Alliance (GGCA, no recent information)*. Regional partner: *Centro de Coordinación para la Prevención de los Desastres Naturales en América Central (CEPREDENAC, #03795)*. Partner of: *ProAct (#18506)*; *One UN Climate Change Learning Partnership (UN CC:Learn, #17735)*; *UN Climate Resilience Initiative (A2R, #20284)*. Memorandum of Understanding with: *Local Governments for Sustainability (ICLEI, #16507)*. Supports: *International Consortium on Landslides (ICL, #12917)*. Cooperates with: *Fundación Henry Dunant América Latina (FuHD – AL, #10024)*. Instrumental in setting up: *Global Fire Monitoring Centre (GFMC)*; *Global Network of Civil Society Organizations for Disaster Reduction (GNDR, #10485)*. Close links with: *Regional Disaster Information Center for Latin America and the Caribbean (#18778)*. [2020/XK2002/**E***]

♦ United Nations Office for Drug Control and Crime Prevention, Vienna / see United Nations Office on Drugs and Crime (#20596)

♦ United Nations Office on Drugs and Crime (UNODC) 20596

Office des Nations Unies contre la drogue et le crime (ONUDC) – Oficina de las Naciones Unidas contra la Droga y el Delito (ONUDD)

Exec Dir Vienna Intl Centre, PO Box 500, 1400 Vienna, Austria. T. +431260600. Fax +431260605866. E-mail: unodc-registry@un.org.
Street Address Vienna International Centre, Wagramer Strasse 5, 1400 Vienna, Austria.
URL: http://www.unodc.org/

History 1 Nov 1997, Vienna (Austria). Established on merger of *United Nations International Drug Control Programme (UNDCP, inactive)* and *United Nations Centre for International Crime Prevention, Vienna (CICP, inactive)*, within the framework of *United Nations (UN, #20515)*. Based at *United Nations Office at Vienna (UNOV, #20604) – Vienna International Centre (VIC)*. Former names and other names: *United Nations Office for Drug Control and Crime Prevention, Vienna (ODCCP)* – former; *Office for Drug Control and Crime Prevention* – alias. **Aims** Work to achieve health, security and justice for all by tackling global threats produced by illicit drugs and transnational organized crime, and by delivering legal and technical assistance to prevent *terrorism*. **Structure** Headed by Executive Director, assisted by Deputy Executive Director. Office of the Executive Director combines functions with those of the Office of the Director-General of UNOV. Divisions (4): Operations; Treaty Affairs; Policy Analysis and Public Affairs; Management. Includes: Secretariat of *International Narcotics Control Board (INCB, #14212)*; Secretariat to the Governing Bodies. Governing bodies: *United Nations Commission on Narcotic Drugs (CND, #20532)*; *United Nations Commission on Crime Prevention and Criminal Justice (CCPCJ, #20530)*. Also covers: *United Nations Crime Prevention and Criminal Justice Programme Network (#20549)*. Headquarters; Liaison Offices (2); Liaison and Partnership Offices (2); Regional Offices (8); Country Offices (7): Programme Offices (94); Office of the Gulf Cooperation Council Region. **Languages** Arabic, Chinese, English, French, Russian, Spanish. **Staff** 2400.00 FTE, paid.

Activities Advocacy/lobbying/activism; events/meetings; knowledge management/information dissemination; management of treaties and agreements; politics/policy/regulatory; research/documentation; training/education. Normative areas of activity:
- Strengthening Member States' capacities to confront threats from transnational organized crime;
- Tackling corruption and its catastrophic impact on societies;
- Strengthening crime prevention and building effective criminal justice systems;
- Supporting Member States in implementing a balanced, comprehensive and evidence-based approach to the world drug problem that addresses both supply and demand;
- Countering terrorism.

Topics:
- Alternative development;
- Corruption;
- Crime prevention and criminal justice;
- Cybercrime;
- Drug prevention, treatment and care;
- Drug trafficking;
- Firearms;
- Falsified medical products;
- HIV and AIDS;
- Trafficking in persons and smuggling of migrants;
- Maritime crime and piracy;
- Money-laundering;
- Organized crime;
- Terrorism prevention;
- Wildlife and forest crime.

Programmes include: *United Nations Global Programme Against Money Laundering, Proceeds of Crime and the Financing of Terrorism (GPML, #20568)* which manages *International Money Laundering Information Network (IMoLIN, #14181)*.

Conventions and related protocols underpinning the operational work of UNODC:
- *United Nations Convention Against Transnational Organized Crime (2000)*, with the following protocols: *Protocol to Prevent, Suppress and Punish Trafficking in Persons, Especially Women and Children (2000)*, *Protocol Against the Smuggling of Migrants by Land, Sea and Air (2000)* and *Protocol Against the Illicit Manufacturing of and Trafficking in Firearms, Their Parts and Components and Ammunition (2001)*;
- *United Nations Convention Against Corruption (UNCAC, 2003)*.

Drug-related treaties:
- *Single Convention on Narcotic Drugs, 1961, as amended by the Protocol amending the Single Convention on Narcotic Drugs, 1961 (1975)*;
- *Convention on Psychotropic Substances (1971)*;
- *United Nations Convention against Illicit Traffic in Narcotic Drugs and Psychotropic Substances (1988)*.

Events *Criminal Justice Forum for Asia and the Pacific (Crim-AP)* Tokyo (Japan) 2022, *Global Youth Forum for a Culture of Lawfulness* Tokyo (Japan) 2022, *Global Parliamentary Summit on Counter-Terrorism* Vienna (Austria) 2021, *Session* Vienna (Austria) 2021, *Session* Vienna (Austria) 2021. **Publications** *Perspectives* (4 a year) – newsletter; *World Drug Report* (annual). *Directory of Nongovernmental Organizations Working in Drug Demand Reduction* (2001). Surveys. **Information Services** *Databank on Transnational Organized Crime*. **Members** All UN member states are considered members of UNODC. **IGO Relations** Memorandum of Understanding with (9): *European Monitoring Centre for Drugs and Drug Addiction (EMCDDA, #07820)*; *FAO (#09260)*; *International Centre for Migration Policy Development (ICMPD, #12503)*; *Joint United Nations Programme on HIV/AIDS (UNAIDS, #16149)*; *UNDP (#20292)*; *UNESCO (#20322)*; *Universal Postal Union (UPU, #20682)*; *WHO (#20950)*; *World Customs Organization (WCO, #21350)*. Member of (5): *Asia/Pacific Group on Money Laundering (APG, #01921)*; *Middle East and North Africa Financial Action Task Force (MENAFATF, #16779)*; *United Nations Group on the Information Society (UNGIS, #20570)*; *United Nations Sustainable Development Group (UNSDG, #20634)*; *United Nations System Chief Executives Board for Coordination (CEB, #20636)*. Instrumental in setting up (1): *International Anti-Corruption Academy (IACA, #11654)*. Cooperation agreement with: *UNHCR (#20327)*. Part of Consultative Group of: *United Nations Democracy Fund (UNDEF, #20551)*. Cooperates closely with: *Budapest Process (#03344)*; *United Nations Institute for Training and Research (UNITAR, #20576)*; *United Nations Interregional Crime and Justice Research Institute (UNICRI, #20580)*. Panel member of: *Interagency Panel on Juvenile Justice (IPJJ, #11390)*. Observer member of: *Eurasian Group on Combating Money Laundering and Financing of Terrorism (EAG, #05608)*; *Global Initiative to Combat Nuclear Terrorism (GICNT, #10424)*; *International Fund for Agricultural Development (IFAD, #13692)*. Official observer of: *Pacific Islands Law Officers' Network (PILON, #17972)*. Through Programme Against Corruption, works with: *United Nations Commission on Crime Prevention and Criminal Justice (CCPCJ, #20530)*. Participates in: *Committee of Experts on the Evaluation of Anti-Money Laundering Measures and the Financing of Terrorism (MONEYVAL, #04257)*. Liaises with: *International Civil Aviation Organization (ICAO, #12581)*. **NGO Relations** Cooperations with thousands NGOs through headquarters Civil Society Team as well as field offices. Key umbrella organizations: Non-Governmental Organizations Committee on Narcotic Drugs; *Alliance of NGOs on Crime Prevention and Criminal Justice (#00709)*; Coalition of Civil Society Friends of the UN Convention on Corruption. [2022/XE3574/**E***]

♦ United Nations Office at Geneva (UNOG) 20597

Office des Nations Unies à Genève

Dir Gen Palais des Nations, Avenue de la Paix 8-14, 1211 Geneva 10, Switzerland. T. +41229172100 – +41229172102. Fax +41229170002. E-mail: unog.ngo@un.org.
NGO Liaison Office Office of the Director-General, Room 151, Palais des Nations, 1211 Geneva 10, Switzerland. T. +41229172127 – +41229171304. Fax +41229170583. E-mail: ungeneva.ngoliaison@unog.ch.
URL: https://www.ungeneva.org/

History as the second largest headquarters of the *United Nations (UN, #20515)*. Located at the 'Palais des Nations', Geneva (Switzerland), the former headquarters of *League of Nations (SDN, inactive)*. **Staff** Representation through *UNOG Staff Coordinating Council (#20712)*. Staff at UNOG: 1,570. **Activities** For 2016, serviced 11,800 international conferences and meetings. (See also separate United Nations entry). Engages with high-level political representatives who come to the UN premises in Geneva (Switzerland) to take part in international discussions, exchange views, identify priorities and formulate strategies to tackle current, interconnected challenges; organizes information programmes in order to provide a better understanding of the work of the UN and its specialized agencies, funds and programmes, based in Geneva, to the public; provides support services to some 20 United Nations offices and 22 Geneva-based entities of the United Nations common system. **Events** *Geneva Peace Week* Geneva (Switzerland) 2021, *Strategies for Transformative Global Leadership* 2020, *Geneva Peace Week* Geneva (Switzerland) 2020, *Global Leadership for the 21st Century* Geneva (Switzerland) 2020, *Geneva Peace Week* Geneva (Switzerland) 2019. **Publications** Annual Report in English/French. **Information Services** *United Nations Information Service (UNIS)* – Geneva; *UNOG Library*. **IGO Relations** See separate United Nations entry. **NGO Relations** IN 2016, 4,277 representatives of 864 nongovernmental organizations in consultative status with the Economic and Social Council of the United Nations (ECOSOC) were accredited to UNOG to take part in UN activities at the Palais des Nations. (See separate United Nations entry). [2022.12.16/XE3343/**E***]

♦ United Nations Office on Genocide Prevention and the Responsibility to Protect 20598

Special Advisor of the SG on Genocide Prevention address not obtained. T. +19173672589. E-mail: osapg@un.org.
Special Adviser of the SG on the Responsiblity to Protect address not obtained.
URL: https://www.un.org/en/genocideprevention

History An Office within the *United Nations (UN, #20515)* Secretariat, Department of Political and Peacebuilding Affairs. Mandates of the 2 Special Advisers are distinct but complementary. Mandate of the Special Adviser on the Prevention of Genocide mainly outlined in a 2004 letter (S/2004/567). Mandate of the Special Adviser on the Responsibility to Protect outlined in a 2007 letter (S/2007/721). **Aims** Raise awareness of the causes and dynamics of genocide; alert relevant actors where there is a risk of genocide; advocate and mobilize for appropriate action. **Structure** Special Adviser on the Prevention of Genocide; Special Adviser on the Responsibility to Protect. **Activities** Awareness raising; capacity building; guidance/assistance/consulting. **Events** *Global Summit on Religion , Peace and Security* Geneva (Switzerland) 2019, *Global Summit on Religion , Peace and Security* Geneva (Switzerland) 2016. **NGO Relations** Partner of (4): *Asia-Pacific Centre for the Responsibility to Protect (#01868)*; *Auschwitz Institute for the Prevention of Genocide and Mass Atrocities*; *Global Centre for the Responsibility to Protect (GCR2P, #10277)*; *International Coalition for the Responsibility to Protect (ICRtoP, #12620)*. [2020/AA1000/**E***]

♦ United Nations Office of the High Representative for the Least Developed Countries, Landlocked Developing Countries and Small Island Developing States (UN-OHRLLS) 20599

Bureau du Haut Représentant des Nations Unies pour les pays les moins avancés, les pays en développement sans littoral et les petits États insulaires en développement

Public Information Officer United Nations Secretariat, Room DC1-1228, New York NY 10017, USA. T. +12129635370 – +12129639078. E-mail: ohrlls-unhq@un.org.
Acting High Representative address not obtained.
URL: http://un.org/ohrlls

History 24 Dec 2001, New York, NY (USA). Founded by the Secretary-General of *United Nations (UN, #20515)*. **Aims** Mobilize international support for the three most vulnerable groups of countries (Least Developed, Landlocked Developing Countries and Small Island Developing States) and ensure effective coordination, monitoring and review of the implementation of internationally agreed programmes of action. **Activities** Advocacy/lobbying/activism; monitoring/evaluation; projects/programmes. . **Events** *United Nations Conference on the Least Developed Countries* New York, NY (USA) / Doha (Qatar) 2022, *High-Level Meeting on Sustainable Transport of Landlocked Developing Countries* Santa Cruz (Bolivia) 2016, *United Nations conference on the least developed countries* Istanbul (Turkey) 2011, *International forum on the eradication of poverty* New York, NY (USA) 2006. **IGO Relations** Member of (2): *United Nations Sustainable Development Group (UNSDG, #20634)*; *UN-OCEANS (#20711)*. [2022/XM0663/**E***]

♦ United Nations Office at Nairobi (UNON) 20600

Office des Nations unies à Nairobi (ONUN)

Dir Gen PO Box 67578, Nairobi, 00200, Kenya. T. +254207621234. Fax +254207623933. E-mail: unon-nairobiunic@un.org.
URL: http://www.unon.org/

History Jan 1996, Nairobi (Kenya), by Secretary General of *United Nations (UN, #20515)*. The UN presence in Nairobi was put on a par with *United Nations Office at Geneva (UNOG, #20597)* and *United Nations Office at Vienna (UNOV, #20604)* in 1998. **Staff** Personnel negotiations through *Nairobi Staff Union (#16930)*. **Activities** Acts as the administrative body for the various United Nations offices based in Nairobi (Kenya). Based at UNON: *UNEP (#20299)*; *United Nations Human Settlements Programme (UN-Habitat, #20572)*. Services: Budget and financial management; Human resources management; Support services; Information technology; Conference services; Security Services. **Events** *Fire wardens meeting* Nairobi (Kenya) 2009, *Pan-African conference on the training of translators, conference interpreters and public service interpreters in Africa* Nairobi (Kenya) 2009, *IAMLADP : international annual meeting on language arrangements, documentation and publications* Nairobi (Kenya) 2005. **IGO Relations** Cooperates with: *United Nations Institute for Training and Research (UNITAR, #20576)*. [2017/XE3872/**E***]

♦ United Nations Office for Outer Space Affairs (UNOOSA) 20601

Bureau des Nations Unies pour les affaires spatiales

Contact UN Office at Vienna, PO Box 500, 1400 Vienna, Austria. T. +431260604950. Fax +431260605830. E-mail: oosa@unoosa.org.
URL: http://www.unoosa.org/

History 13 Dec 1958. Initially created as a small expert unit within *United Nations (UN, #20515)* Secretariat to service the ad hoc *Committee on the Peaceful Uses of Outer Space (COPUOS, #04277)*, established by the UN General Assembly in its resolution 1348 (XIII). Unit moved to work under the Department of Political and Security Council Affairs, 1962 and transformed into Outer Space Affairs Division of that Department, 1968. 1992, Division transformed into Office for Outer Space Affairs within Department for Political Affairs. 1993, Office relocated to *United Nations Office at Vienna (UNOV, #20604)*, where it assumed responsibility for substantive secretariat services to the Legal Subcommittee, which had previously been provided by the Office of Legal Affairs in New York. **Aims** Promote international cooperation in exploration and peaceful uses of outer space, and use of space science, technology and applications for sustainable development. **Structure** Office of the Director (OD); Space Applications Section (SAS); Committee, Policy and Legal Affairs Section (CPLA); United Nations Platform for Space-based Information for Disaster Management and Emergency Response (UN-SPIDER); Executive Secretariat of the International Committee on Global Navigation Satellite Systems (ICG). Headed by Director. Based at: *Vienna International Centre (VIC)*. **Languages** Arabic, Chinese, English, French, Russian, Spanish. **Staff** 31.00 FTE, paid. **Finance** Sources: contributions. Funded by UN regular budget. **Activities** Events/meetings; knowledge management/information dissemination; research/documentation.
'Committee, Policy and Legal Affairs Section (CPLA)' – facilitates intergovernmental discussions within framework of *Committee on the Peaceful Uses of Outer Space (COPUOS, #04277)*, its 2 Subcommittees (Scientific and Technical; Legal), and related working Group. Office also provides secretariat services to Special Political and Decolonization Committee (Fourth Committee) of General Assembly when it considers the item on international cooperation in the peaceful uses of outer space.
'Space Applications Section (SAS)' – promotes practical applications of space technology and its use for economic and social development. Programmes include:
Programme on Space Applications (PSA) – aims to enhance understanding and subsequent use of space technology for peaceful purposes in general, and for national development, in particular, in response to expressed needs in different geographic regions of the world.
Regional Centres for Space Science and Technology Education – aims to develop national capacities for research and applications in remote sensing and geographic information systems, meteorological satellite applications, satellite communications and geopositioning systems, and space and atmospheric sciences. Regional centres have been set up in: *Centre for Space Science and Technology Education in Asia and the Pacific /Affiliated to the United Nations/ (CSSTEAP, see: #04277)*, India (1995); *Centre régional africain des sciences et technologies de l'espace en langue française /Affilié à l'Organisation des nations unies/ (CRASTE-LF, see: #04277)*, Morocco (1998); *African Regional Centre for Space Science and Technology Education – English (ARCSSTE-E, #00431)* Nigeria (1998); *Centre for Space Science and Technology Education in Latin America and the Caribbean /Affiliated to the United Nations/ (CSSTE-LAC, see: #04277)*, Mexico and Brazil (2003); *Regional Centre for Space Science and Technology Education for Western Asia (see: #04277)*, Jordan (2012); *Centre for Space Science and Technology Education in Asia and the Pacific /Affiliated to the United Nations/ (CSSTEAP, see: #04277)*.
United Nations Platform for Space-based Information for Disaster Management and Emergency Response (UN-SPIDER, #20610) – aims to ensure that all countries and international and regional organizations have access to and develop the capacity to use all types of space-based information to support the full disaster management cycle.
Events *United Nations/Austria Symposium on Space for Climate Action* 2022, *International Conference on the Use of Space Technology for Water Resources Management* Accra (Ghana) 2022, *Space for Women Meeting* Daejeon (Korea Rep) 2022, *UN/Republic of Korea Space for Women Expert Meeting* Daejeon (Korea Rep) 2022, *United Nations/Mongolia Workshop on the Applications of Global Navigation Satellite Systems* Ulaanbaatar (Mongolia) 2021. **Publications** Reports. [2022.10.11/XJ7585/**E***]

♦ United Nations Office for Project Services (UNOPS) 20602

Bureau des Nations Unies pour les services d'appui aux projets – Oficina de las Naciones Unidas de Servicios para Proyectos

Acting Exec Dir Marmorvej 51, PO Box 2695, 2100 Copenhagen, Denmark. T. +4545337500. E-mail: info@unops.org.
URL: http://www.unops.org/

History 1973. Established within the framework of *UNDP (#20292)*. Became a separate, self-financing entity within the UN development system, 1 Jan 1995, by decision of the *United Nations (UN, #20515)* General Assembly. Former names and other names: *Office for Project Services* – former. **Aims** Serve people in need by expanding the ability of the United Nations, governments and other partners to manage projects, infrastructure and procurement in a sustainable and efficient manner. **Structure** The Executive Board, created by resolution 48/162 of 20 Dec 1993, of the United Nations Development Programme, the United Nations Population Fund and the United Nations Office for Project Services is mandated to support and supervise the activities of the 3 organizations, and provides UNOPS with support and oversight functions. At the 65th session, Dec 2010, the General Assembly adopted the decision to include UNOPS in the Board's title (resolution A/RES/65/176), in accordance with the recommendations of the Economic and Social Council and wishes of the 192 member states of the United Nations. The Executive Director of UNOPS reports directly to the UN Secretary-General and the Executive Board, and has the authority to sign host country agreements and appoint UNOPS representatives in the field. **Languages** English, French, Spanish. **Finance** Self-financing. **Activities** Capacity building; conflict resolution; events/meetings; guidance/assistance/consulting; training/education. **Events** *Smart Technology for Sustainable Development and Procurement Conference* Suwon (Korea Rep) 2019, *Smart Technology for Sustainable Development and Procurement Conference* Goyang (Korea Rep) 2018, *EMDS : Meeting of Municipalities with Sustainable Development* Brasilia (Brazil) 2017, *East Asian seas congress* Manila (Philippines) 2009, *Annual international aid and trade conference* New York, NY (USA) 2000. **Publications** *Annual Statistical Report on UN Procurement*. Brochures, strategic plan; fact sheets; videos. https://www.unops.org/news-and-stories?type%5B%5D=PublicationArticle **IGO Relations** Member of (1): *United Nations Sustainable Development Group (UNSDG, #20634)*. Cooperates with (1): *United Nations Institute for Training and Research (UNITAR, #20576)*. [2023.02.13/XK0972/**E***]

♦ United Nations Office for South-South Cooperation (UNOSSC) 20603

Contact c/o UNDP, One United Nations Plaza, New York NY 10017, USA. T. +12129066392. E-mail: unossc@unossc.org.
URL: http://www.unsouthsouth.org/

History Established 1974, by *United Nations (UN, #20515)* General Assembly resolution A/3251 (XXIX), as a special unit within *UNDP (#20292)*. Current title adopted 2 Apr 2012 by High-level Committee decision 17/1, and endorsed by General Assembly resolution 67/39. **Aims** Promote, coordinate and support South-South and triangular cooperation globally and within the United Nations system. **Activities** Networking/liaising; advocacy/lobbying/activism; guidance/assistance/consulting. Manages several funds including: *United Nations Fund for South-South Cooperation*; *Pérez-Guerrero Trust Fund for South-South Cooperation*. **Events** *Symposium on South-South and Triangular Cooperation* Brussels (Belgium) 2020, *High-level Conference* Buenos Aires (Argentina) 2019, *Regional Networking Forum on South-South and Triangular Cooperation* New York, NY (USA) 2018. [2020/XM6825/**E***]

♦ United Nations Office of the Special Advisor on Africa (see: #20515)
♦ United Nations Office of the Special Coordinator for Africa and the Least Developed Countries (inactive)
♦ United Nations Office for Sustainable Development (internationally oriented national body)

♦ United Nations Office at Vienna (UNOV) 20604

Office des Nations Unies à Vienne – Oficina de las Naciones Unidas en Viena

Dir-Gen PO Box 500, 1400 Vienna, Austria. T. +431260600. Fax +4312633389.
Street Address VIC, Wagramer Str 5, 1400 Vienna, Austria.
URL: http://www.unvienna.org/

History 1979, as one of the headquarters of the *United Nations (UN, #20515)*, to provide the services necessary to facilitate transfer of a number of United Nations offices to Vienna (Austria) and later to combine some administrative and common services previously performed separately by other organizations established in Vienna. In 1993, most units dealing with social development and humanitarian affairs, including *United Nations Centre for Social Development and Humanitarian Affairs (UNCSDHA, inactive)*, were transferred to the Department of Economic and Social Affairs, New York NY (USA), but responsibility for executive direction and management of the programme on crime prevention and criminal justice was maintained with the Director-General and extended to cover the Programme on Peaceful Uses of Outer Space, transferred from New York in the same year. Since 2002, closely associated with *United Nations Office on Drugs and Crime (UNODC, #20596)* through which additional common services are provided. The Office includes *United Nations*

Commission on Crime Prevention and Criminal Justice (CCPCJ, #20530) and *United Nations Commission on Narcotic Drugs (CND, #20532).* **Structure** Office of the Director-General, which runs parallel with that of the Office of the Executive Director of UNODC. Based at: *Vienna International Centre (VIC).* **Languages** English, French. **Staff** Personnel negotiations through *Staff Council of the United Nations Staff Union at Vienna (UNOV Staff Council).* **Activities** Serves as the representative office of the Secretary-General in Vienna (Austria) and performs representation and liaison functions with permanent missions, the host Government as well as governments, IGOs and NGOs in Vienna. Services meetings of *Committee on the Peaceful Uses of Outer Space (COPUOS, #04277)* and hosts *United Nations Office for Outer Space Affairs (UNOOSA, #20601)*; provides administrative and other support services to United Nations Secretariat units located in Vienna and certain common services to other organizations of the United Nations system in Vienna; provides conference services for its own meetings and those of other United Nations Secretariat entities and UNIDO, held in Vienna and elsewhere, and interpretation for IAEA meetings; provides public information on United Nations activities and conferences in Vienna. **Events** *IAMLADP : international annual meeting on language arrangements, documentation and publications* Vienna (Austria) 2002, *International conference on the use of military and civil defence assets in disaster relief* Oslo (Norway) 1994, *United Nations Asia and the Pacific preparatory meeting for the international year of the family* Beijing (China) 1993, *United Nations Latin America and the Caribbean preparatory meeting for the international year of the family* Bogota (Colombia) 1993, *Conference of European ministers responsible for social affairs and family matters* Bratislava (Slovakia) 1993. **Publications** Reports of COPUOS; Reports of the Experts on Space Applications; Highlights; guidelines; seminar, conference and other reports; directories. **IGO Relations** Maintains close links with most of the entities of the United Nations system, in particular: *International Atomic Energy Agency (IAEA, #12294)*; *UNIDO (#20336)*; and with sister offices *United Nations Office at Geneva (UNOG, #20597)*; *United Nations Office at Nairobi (UNON, #20600).* Also with several other intergovernmental organizations (unspecified). Cooperates with: *United Nations Institute for Training and Research (UNITAR, #20576).* **NGO Relations** Maintains a network of national, regional and international nongovernmental organizations in consultative status with ECOSOC, as provided for in ECOSOC resolution 1996/31 of 25 Jul 1999, which updates ECOSOC Resolution 1296 of 23 May 1968. Brings together NGOs at conferences and meetings for exchange of information and contributions to intergovernmental bodies on a global basis. [2008.09.12/XE7552/**E***]

♦ United Nations Operation in Côte d'Ivoire (inactive)
♦ United Nations Operation Lifeline Sudan (inactive)
♦ United Nations Organisation / see United Nations (#20515)
♦ United Nations Organization Mission in the Democratic Republic of Congo / see United Nations Organization Stabilization Mission in the Democratic Republic of Congo (#20605)

♦ United Nations Organization Stabilization Mission in the Democratic Republic of Congo (MONUSCO) 20605

Mission de l'Organisation des Nations Unies pour la Stabilisation en République démocratique du Congo – Misión de Estabilización de la Naciones Unidas en la República Democratica del Congo

Contact 12 av des Aviateurs, Kinshasa, Congo DR. T. +243128906000. Fax +2431289056208.
New York Office PO Box 4653, Grand Central Station, New York NY 10163-4653, USA. T. +12129630103. Fax +12129630205.
URL: https://monusco.unmissions.org/

History Feb 2000. Established by resolution 1258 of the *United Nations Security Council (UNSC, #20625)*, within *United Nations System (#20635)*, in the framework of *United Nations (UN, #20515).* An *Interim Emergency Multinational Force in Bunia* (May 2003 – Sep 2003) was set up by resolution 1484. UN Security Council Resolution 1493 of 30 Jul 2003 extended mandate until 30 Jul 2004, increased military strength and provided a new mandate. Security Council resolution 1925 (2010) extended mandate until 30 Jun 2010. Current mandate until 20 Dec 2022. Former names and other names: *United Nations Military Observer Mission to Congo (MONUC)* – former; *Interim Emergency Multinational Force in Bunia* – former; *United Nations Organization Mission in the Democratic Republic of Congo (MONUC)* – former; *Mission des Nations Unies en République démocratique du Congo* – former; *Misión de las Naciones Unidas en la República Democratica del Congo* – former. **Aims** Use all necessary means to carry out its mandate relating, among other things, to the protection of civilians, humanitarian personnel and human rights defenders under imminent threat of physical violence and to support the Government of the DRC in its stabilization and peace consolidation efforts. **Staff** Authorized personnel (2021): 16,316. Deployed personnel (2021): 17,783 of which 2,970 civilians. **Finance** Annual budget: 1,123,346,000 USD (2022).
Members As at 31 Oct 2010, states contributing military personnel (52):
Algeria, Bangladesh, Belgium, Benin, Bolivia, Bosnia-Herzegovina, Burkina Faso, Cameroon, Canada, China, Czechia, Denmark, Egypt, France, Ghana, Guatemala, India, Indonesia, Ireland, Jordan, Kenya, Malawi, Malaysia, Mali, Mongolia, Morocco, Mozambique, Nepal, Niger, Nigeria, Norway, Pakistan, Paraguay, Peru, Poland, Romania, Russia, Senegal, Serbia, South Africa, Spain, Sri Lanka, Sweden, Switzerland, Tanzania UR, Tunisia, UK, Ukraine, Uruguay, USA, Yemen, Zambia.
As at 31 Oct 2010, states contributing police personnel (24):
Bangladesh, Benin, Burkina Faso, Cameroon, Central African Rep, Chad, Côte d'Ivoire, Egypt, France, Guinea, India, Jordan, Madagascar, Mali, Niger, Nigeria, Romania, Russia, Senegal, Sweden, Togo, Türkiye, Ukraine, Yemen.
IGO Relations *United Nations Special Committee on Peace-keeping Operations (#20628).*
[2022/XF5668/**F***]

♦ United Nations Parliamentary Assembly (unconfirmed)

♦ United Nations Peacebuilding Commission (PBC) 20606

Commission de consolidation de la paix (CCP) – Comisión de Consolidación de la Paz

Chair UN Headquarters, New York NY 10017, USA. T. +12129631234 – +12129634475. Fax +12129634879. E-mail: inquiries@un.org – ecu@un.org.
URL: http://www.un.org/en/peacebuilding/

History Dec 2005, by *United Nations (UN, #20515)* General Assembly and *United Nations Security Council (UNSC, #20625)*, as an intergovernmental advisory body. **Aims** Support peace efforts in countries emerging from conflict. **Structure** Organizational Committee (OC); Country Specific Configurations (CSC); Working Group on Lessons Learned. Peacebuilding Support Office (PBSO) acts as secretariat. **Activities** Advises, supports and represents interests of countries on its agenda (Burundi, Central African Rep, Guinea, Guinea-Bissau, Liberia, Sierra Leone); helps ensure predictable financing for early recovery and sustained financial engagement over the longer term; brings relevant stakeholders together in support of shared peacebuilding goals, to avoid duplication and fill gaps. *United Nations Peacebuilding Fund (PBF, #20607)*, launched 2006, supports activities, actions, programmes and organizations (about US$ 200 million) that seek to build lasting peace in countries emerging from conflict. Organizes meetings. **Events** *Annual Session* New York, NY (USA) 2015, *Annual Session* New York, NY (USA) 2014.
Members Member States (31) elected by the General Assembly (7), Security Council (7), Economic and Social Council (7), top providers of military personnel and civilian police to UN missions (5), and top providers of assessed contribution to UN budgets and of voluntary contributions to UN Funds, programmes and agencies, including a standing peacebuilding fund:
Argentina, Bangladesh, Bosnia-Herzegovina, Brazil, Canada, Chad, China, Croatia, Denmark, Dominican Rep, Egypt, Ethiopia, France, Germany, Guatemala, India, Indonesia, Japan, Kenya, Malaysia, Nepal, Nigeria, Pakistan, Peru, Russia, South Africa, Spain, Sweden, Tunisia, UK, USA.
Regional participants (4):
European Union (EU, #08967); *International Bank for Reconstruction and Development (IBRD, #12317)* (World Bank); *International Monetary Fund (IMF, #14180)*; *Organisation of Islamic Cooperation (OIC, #17813).*
IGO Relations Advisory body to: UN General Assembly; *United Nations Security Council (UNSC, #20625).*
[2018/XM0878/y/**E***]

♦ United Nations Peacebuilding Fund (PBF) 20607

Fonds de consolidation de la paix des Nations Unies

Contact Peacebuilding Support Office, UN Headquarters, 405 East 42nd Street, 34th Floor, New York NY 10017, USA. E-mail: williamsbj@un.org – marcus.lenzen@un.org.
URL: https://www.un.org/peacebuilding/fund

History 2006. Established by General Assembly resolution of the Security Council of *United Nations (UN, #20515)*, to stand alongside the *United Nations Peacebuilding Commission (PBC, #20606)* and the Peacebuilding Support Office. **Aims** Sustain peace in countries or situations at risk or affected by violent conflict; work across pillars and support integrated UN responses to fill critical gaps; respond quickly and with the flexibility to peacebuilding opportunities and catalyze processes and resources in a risk-tolerant fashion. **Structure** Managed by Peacebuilding Support Office. **Languages** English, French, Spanish. **Finance** Sources: contributions of member/participating states; international organizations. **Activities** Financial and/or material support. **Publications** *Consolidated Annual PBF Progress Report*; *Synthesis Review.* Secretary-General Reports; brochure.
IGO Relations Supports:
– *FAO (#09260)*;
– *ILO (#11123)*;
– *International Organization for Migration (IOM, #14454)*;
– Multi-Partner Trust Fund Office (MPTFO);
– *Office of the United Nations High Commissioner for Human Rights (OHCHR, #17697)*;
– *UN Women (#20724)*;
– *UNDP (#20292)*;
– *UNESCO (#20322)*;
– *UNICEF (#20332)*;
– *UNIDO (#20336)*;
– *United Nations Capital Development Fund (UNCDF, #20524)*;
– *United Nations Human Settlements Programme (UN-Habitat, #20572)*;
– *United Nations Office on Drugs and Crime (UNODC, #20596)*;
– *United Nations Office for Project Services (UNOPS, #20602)*;
– *United Nations Peacebuilding Commission (PBC, #20606)*;
– *United Nations Population Fund (UNFPA, #20612)*;
– *World Food Programme (WFP, #21510).*
NGO Relations NGOs may receive financing if they are partnered with an eligible UN organization or through the Gender and Youth Promotion Initiative (GYPI). [2022.02.11/XM0920/f/**F***]

♦ United Nations Peace Keepers Federal Council / see United Peace Keepers Federal Council (#20655)

♦ United Nations Peace-keeping Force in Cyprus (UNFICYP) 20608

Force des Nations Unies chargée du maintien de la paix à Chypre – Fuerza de las Naciones Unidas para el Mantenimiento de la Paz en Chipre

Contact PO Box 21642, CY-1590 Nicosia, Cyprus. T. +35722864401. Fax +35722864752.
URL: https://unficyp.unmissions.org/

History 4 Mar 1964. Established by resolution 186 (1964) of the *United Nations Security Council (UNSC, #20625)*, within *United Nations System (#20635)*, in the framework of *United Nations (UN, #20515).* Mandate periodically extended, usually for periods of 6 months. In connection with the hostilities in Jul and Aug 1974, the Security Council adopted a number of resolutions requiring the Force to perform additional functions relating, in particular, to maintenance of the cease-fire. **Aims** Maintain the *cease-fire* and the status quo; promote restoration of normal conditions; carry out *humanitarian* functions. **Structure** Chief of Mission; Force Commander; Chief of Staff; Senior Advisor; Spokesperson; Chief Administrative Officer; Chief Civil Affairs Officer; Military Units and UNCIVPOL. **Staff** Deployed personnel (2021): 1,005 of which 151 civilians. Staff negotiations through *United Nations Field Staff Union (UNFSU, #20561).* **Finance** Previously financed in total by troop-contributing governments, the Government of Cyprus and voluntary contributions. Since 15 Jun 1993, in line with Security Council resolution 831 of 27 May 1993, costs not covered by voluntary contributions are financed from assessed contributions in the same manner as other peacekeeping operations. Annual budget: 57,567,300 USD (2022). **Activities** Following a de facto cease-fire, which came into effect on 16 Aug 1974, UNFICYP inspected the deployment of the Cyprus National Guard and the Turkish forces, and cease-fire lines and a buffer zone were established between the areas controlled by the opposing parties. Maintains constant surveillance from 41 permanently manned observation posts, 2 observation posts manned during daylight hours and from 118 temporarily manned observation posts as well as through vehicle, foot and air patrols and maintains surveillance of the seaward extension of the cease-fire lines. Maintains a patrol track for surveillance, monitoring of agricultural activities, the resupply of observation posts and rapid reaction to any incidents. As a result of the absence of a formal cease-fire agreement, UNFICYP is confronted with hundreds of incidents each year. It investigates and acts upon all violations of the cease-fire and the status quo. Action depends upon the nature of the incident and may include the deployment of troops, verbal and written protests and follow-up action to ensure that the violation has been rectified or will not recur. In the framework of humanitarian activities, UNFICYP is entrusted to encourage the fullest possible resumption of normal civilian activity in the buffer zone.
Members As of 30 Nov 2009, military personnel from 11 countries:
Argentina, Austria, Brazil, Canada, Chile, Croatia, Hungary, Paraguay, Peru, Slovakia, UK.
As of 30 Nov 2009, police personnel from 10 countries:
Australia, Bosnia-Herzegovina, Croatia, El Salvador, India, Ireland, Italy, Montenegro, Netherlands, Ukraine.
[2022/XE2070/**F***]

♦ United Nations Peace Keeping Forces Council / see United Peace Keepers Federal Council (#20655)

♦ United Nations Permanent Forum on Indigenous Issues (UNPFII) 20609

Instance permanente sur les questions autochtones – Foro Permanente para las Cuestiones Indigenas

Secretariat IPDB DISD DESA, United Nations Secretariat, Room S-2555, New York NY 10017, USA. T. +19173675100. Fax +19173675102. E-mail: indigenous_un@un.org.
URL: https://www.un.org/development/desa/indigenouspeoples/

History 28 Jul 2000. Established by resolution 2000/22 of *ECOSOC (#05331)*, as a subsidiary organ of ECOSOC within the framework of *United Nations (UN, #20515)*, having been proposed during the World Conference on Human Rights. Former names and other names: *Permanent Forum of the World's Indigenous People* – former; *Permanent Forum on Indigenous Issues (SPFII)* – former. **Aims** Provide expert advice and recommendations to ECOSOC and, through ECOSOC, to *United Nations* programmes, funds and agencies; raise awareness and promote integration and coordination of activities relating to indigenous issues within the UN system; prepare and disseminate information on indigenous issues. **Structure** Forum (meeting for 10 days annually, usually in New York NY – USA), comprises 16 members: 8 nominated by Governments and elected by ECOSOC and 8 nominated by Indigenous Peoples' Organizations and appointed by President of ECOSOC following consultation with the Bureau and regional groups though their coordinators. States, United Nations bodies and organs, intergovernmental organizations and non-governmental organizations in consultative status with the Council may participate as observers; organizations of indigenous people may equally participate as observers in accordance with the procedures which have been applied in the Working Group on Indigenous Populations of the Subcommission on the Promotion and Protection of Human Rights. **Languages** Arabic, Chinese, English, French, Russian, Spanish. **Staff** 10.00 FTE, paid. **Finance** Meetings financed from the regular budget of the United Nations. Other activities financed through voluntary contributions. **Activities** Advocacy/lobbying/activism; awareness raising; events/meetings; guidance/assistance/consulting; monitoring/evaluation; politics/policy/regulatory. **Events** *Annual Session* New York, NY (USA) 2022, *Annual Session* New York, NY (USA) 2021, *Annual Session* New York, NY (USA) 2020, *Annual Session* New York, NY (USA) 2019, *Annual Session* New York, NY (USA) 2018. **Publications** *State of the World's Indigenous Peoples (SOWIP)* (5th ed). Session studies and reports. **Information Services** *UNPFII Recommendations Database.* **IGO Relations** Designates representatives to: *United Nations Commission on Sustainable Development (CSD, inactive)*; other relevant functional commissions of ECOSOC (not specified); UN General Assembly. Cooperates with: *United Nations Institute for Training and Research (UNITAR, #20576).* Members of: Inter-Agency Support Group (IASG). **NGO Relations** Links with over 1,000 indigenous peoples' organizations and non-governmental organizations worldwide. [2022/XE4327/**E***]

♦ United Nations Philatelists (internationally oriented national body)

♦ United Nations Platform for Space-based Information for Disaster Management and Emergency Response (UN-SPIDER) 20610

Programme des nations unies pour l'exploitation de l'information d'origine spatiale aux fins de gestion des catastrophes et des interventions d'urgence – Plataforma de las Naciones Unidas de información obtenida desde el espacio para la gestión de desastres y la respuesta de emergencia (ONU-SPIDER)

Vienna Office UN Office for Outer Space Affairs, Vienna Intl Ctr, PO Box 500, 1400 Vienna, Austria. T. +431260604951. Fax +431260605830. E-mail: un-spider@unoosa.org.
Bonn Office UN Office for Outer Space Affairs, UN Campus, Platz der Vereinten Nationen 1, 53113 Bonn, Germany. T. +492288150682. Fax +492288150699.
Beijing Office Room 514, No 6 Guangbai East Road, Chaoyang District, 100124 Beijing, China. T. +861052811371.
URL: http://www.un-spider.org/

History 2006. Set up through Resolution 61/110 of 14 Dec 2006 of *United Nations (UN, #20515)* General Assembly, as part of UN Programme on Space Applications, within *United Nations Office for Outer Space Affairs (UNOOSA, #20601).* **Aims** Ensure that all countries and international and regional organizations have access to and develop the capacity to use all types of space-based information to support the full disaster management cycle. **Structure** Regional Support Offices (regional or national centres of expertise): Europe – Russia, Hungary, Romania, Ukraine; Africa – Algeria, Nigeria, *Regional Centre for Mapping of Resources for Development (RCMRD, #18757)*; Latin America and Caribbean – Argentina, Colombia, West Indies – *University of the West Indies (UWI, #20705), Water Center for the Humid Tropics of Latin America and the Caribbean (#20824)*; Asia Pacific – *Asian Disaster Reduction Center (ADRC, #01427)*, Indonesia, *International Centre for Integrated Mountain Development (ICIMOD, #12500), European Federation of Associations of Locks and Builders Hardware Manufacturers (ARGE, #07054)*, Iran Islamic Rep, Pakistan. National Focal Points. Communities of Practice. **Activities** Networking/liaising; capacity building; guidance/assistance/consulting; knowledge management/information dissemination. **Events** *United Nations/Islamic Republic of Iran Workshop on the Space Technology Applications for Drought, Flood and Water Resource Management* Teheran (Iran Islamic Rep) 2021, *Regional Workshop for the Utilization of Space-Based and Geospatial Information for Achieving the Targets of the Sendai Framework for Disaster Risk Reduction* Ahmedabad (India) 2018, *Mitch+20 : Seminar on Twenty Years After Hurricane Mitch* Antigua (Guatemala) 2018, *United Nations International Conference on Space-Based Technologies for Disaster Risk Reduction* Beijing (China) 2018, *International Meeting on Towards Big (Space) Data in Support of Disaster Risk Reduction and Emergency Response in Africa* Bonn (Germany) 2018. **Publications** *UN-SPIDER Updates* (12 a year); *UN-SPIDER Newsletter*.
Members National Focal Points in 46 countries:
Algeria, Armenia, Austria, Belarus, Belize, Bolivia, Bosnia-Herzegovina, Burkina Faso, Burundi, Chile, China, Côte d'Ivoire, Croatia, Egypt, El Salvador, India, Iraq, Jordan, Kenya, Korea Rep, Lebanon, Malawi, Malta, Mauritius, Morocco, Myanmar, New Zealand, Nigeria, Panama, Philippines, Qatar, Senegal, Singapore, Spain, Syrian AR, Tajikistan, Tanzania UR, Thailand, Togo, Trinidad-Tobago, Tunisia, Türkiye, Ukraine, United Arab Emirates, Venezuela, Zambia.
NGO Relations Participates in: *International Working Group on Satellite-Based Emergency Mapping (IWG-SEM, #15911).* [2016.06.17/XJ6560/**F***]

♦ United Nations Pledging Conference for Development Activities (meeting series)

♦ United Nations Police (UNPOL) 20611

Commissioner United Nations Police Division, UN Secretariat, 405 East 1st Ave, S-2264, New York NY 10017, USA. T. +12129631293. Fax +19173672012.
URL: https://police.un.org/en/

History Established within the framework of *United Nations (UN, #20515)* Department of Peace-keeping Operations, within *United Nations System (#20635).* Deployed as a component of UN Peacekeeping Missions, for example in Cambodia, the former Yugoslavia, Rwanda and (previously) in Namibia. Former names and other names: *United Nations Civilian Police Force (UNCIVPOL)* – former; *CIVPOL* – former. **Aims** Enhance international peace and security by supporting Member States in conflict, post conflict and other crisis situations to realize effective, efficient, representative, responsive and accountable police services that serve and protect the population. **Languages** UN languages. **Staff** Authorized: 17616. Employed (2019): over 12000. **Finance** United Nations Peacekeeping Support Account; United Nations Regular Budget; extra-budgetary funds. **Activities** Conflict resolution; capacity building; events/meetings. **Publications** *United Nations Police Magazine.* Security Council resolutions; reports.
Members Current United Nations police contributing countries (96):
Argentina, Austria, Bangladesh, Belgium, Benin, Bhutan, Bosnia-Herzegovina, Brazil, Bulgaria, Burkina Faso, Burundi, Cameroon, Canada, Chad, Chile, China, Colombia, Congo Brazzaville, Costa Rica, Côte d'Ivoire, Croatia, Czechia, Djibouti, Dominican Rep, Egypt, El Salvador, Estonia, Ethiopia, Fiji, Finland, France, Gambia, Germany, Ghana, Greece, Grenada, Guinea, Iceland, India, Indonesia, Ireland, Italy, Jamaica, Jordan, Kenya, Korea Rep, Kyrgyzstan, Lithuania, Madagascar, Malawi, Malaysia, Mali, Mauritania, Mexico, Mongolia, Montenegro, Namibia, Nepal, Netherlands, New Zealand, Niger, Nigeria, Norway, Pakistan, Palau, Paraguay, Philippines, Poland, Portugal, Romania, Russia, Rwanda, Samoa, Senegal, Serbia, Sierra Leone, Singapore, Slovakia, South Africa, Spain, Sri Lanka, Sweden, Switzerland, Tajikistan, Tanzania UR, Thailand, Togo, Tunisia, Türkiye, Uganda, Ukraine, Uruguay, USA, Vanuatu, Zambia, Zimbabwe.
IGO Relations Partners with all relevant United Nations entities and organs, many international and professional policing organizations, including: *African Union (AU, #00488); Collective Security Treaty Organization (CSTO, #04103); European Union (EU, #08967); International Criminal Police Organization – INTERPOL (ICPO-INTERPOL, #13110); Organisation internationale de la Francophonie (OIF, #17809); Organization for Security and Cooperation in Europe (OSCE, #17887).* **NGO Relations** Partners with many think tanks and civil society organizations, including: *International Association of Peacekeeping Training Centres (IAPTC, #12072); International Centre for Criminal Law Reform and Criminal Justice Policy (ICCLR); International Forum for the Challenges of Peace Operations (Challenges Forum, #13632).* [2019.07.15/XF5133/**F***]

♦ United Nations Population Commission / see United Nations Commission on Population and Development (#20533)

♦ United Nations Population Fund (UNFPA) 20612

Fonds des Nations Unies pour la population – Fondo de Población de las Naciones Unidas

Exec Dir 605 Third Ave, 4th/5th/6th Floors, New York NY 10158, USA. T. +12122975020. Fax +12125576416. E-mail: hq@unfpa.org.
URL: http://www.unfpa.org/

History Established Jul 1967, as *Trust Fund for Population Activities.* Became operational and name changed to *United Nations Fund for Population Activities – Fonds des Nations Unies pour les activités en matière de population – Fondo de las Naciones Unidas para Actividades en Materia de Población* in 1969. UN General Assembly resolution 3019 (XXVII), 18 Dec 1972, placed the Fund under its own authority, designating as governing body the Governing Council of *UNDP (#20292)* (changed in 1993 to UNDP/UNFPA Executive Board). Resolution 34/104, 14 Dec 1979, affirmed UNFPA as a subsidiary organ of the General Assembly of *United Nations (UN, #20515)*, linked to *ECOSOC (#05331)*, in the framework of *United Nations System (#20635).* Current title adopted 11 Dec 1987, when UN General Assembly adopted ECOSOC decision 1987/175 of 8 Jul 1987, retaining the abbreviation UNFPA. **Aims** Promote the right of every woman, man and child to enjoy a life of health and equal opportunity; support countries in using population data for policies and programmes to reduce poverty and ensure that every pregnancy is wanted, every childbirth is safe, every young person's potential is fulfilled; advance the Programme of Action endorsed by the 1994 International Conference on Population and Development, emphasizing interdependence of population and development focusing on meeting individual needs rather than demographic targets; promote cooperation and coordination among UN system organizations, bilateral agencies, governments, non-governmental organizations and the private sector in addressing issues of population and development *reproductive health*, gender equality and women's empowerment. **Structure** Joint Executive Board with UNDP, under policy supervision of ECOSOC. Headquarters in New York NY (USA). **Languages** Arabic, Chinese, English, French, Russian, Spanish. **Staff** More than 2,600, in 132 offices. Staff negotiations through *UNDP/UNFPA/UNOPS/UN Women Staff Association (Staff Council, #20291).* **Finance** Voluntary contributions from governments and private donors. Annual budget (2016): US$ 900,300,000. **Events** *Meeting on the Impact of COVID-19 on Declining Birthrate* Tokyo (Japan) 2021, *AidEx : Europe's Leading Humanitarian and Development Aid Conference* Brussels (Belgium) 2019, *Conference on Ending Sexual and Gender-based Violence in Humanitarian Crises* Oslo (Norway) 2019, *Joint Conference on Women's Fistula* Seongnam (Korea Rep) 2018, *Open Seminar* Seongnam (Korea Rep) 2018. **Publications** *State of World Population* (annual); *UNFPA Report* (annual); *Global Review Report*; *Maternal Health Thematic Fund Annual Report 2015*; *The World Confirms Cairo: Official Outcomes of the ICPD at Ten Review. A Guide for Global Policy Action*; *Prevention is for Life*; *The State of the World's Midwifery*; *The ICPD Vision: How Far Has the 11-Year Journey Taken Us ?*; *Technical Guidance for Prioritizing Adolescent Health*; *Sexual and Reproductive Health Needs of Women and Adolescent Girls Living with HIV*; *Seventeen Ways to End FGM/C*; *Reproductive Health of Women in Thailand: Progress and Challenges Towards Attainment of International Development Goals*; *Reducing Poverty and Achieving the Millennium Development Goals: Argument for Investing in Reproductive Health and Rights*; *Preventing HIV/AIDS in Young People*; *Ending Child Marriage: Meeting the Need – Strengthening Family Planning Programmes*; *Our Voice, Our Future: Young People Report on Progress Made on the UNFASS Declaration of the Commitment on HIV/AIDS*; *Moving Young*; *Into Good Hands: Progress Reports from the Field*; *International Migration and the Millennium Development Goals: Selected Papers of the UNFPA Expert Group Meeting*; *ICPD Beyond 2014*; *Humanitarian Action 2017 Overview*; *Focusing on Gender*; *Female Condom: A Powerful Tool for Protection*; *Women are the Fabric: Reproductive Health for Communities in Crisis.* Papers; reports; updates. **IGO Relations** Member of: *Inter-Agency Standing Committee (IASC, #11393); United Nations Sustainable Development Group (UNSDG, #20634); United Nations System Chief Executives Board for Coordination (CEB, #20636).* Instrumental in setting up: *Inter-Agency Task Force on Employment and Sustainable Livelihoods for All (inactive); Inter-Agency Task Force on Enabling Environment for Economic and Social Development (inactive); Joint Consultative Group on Policies (JCGP, no recent information).* Supports: *Latin American and Caribbean Demographic Centre (#16273); Swedish International Development Cooperation Agency (Sida).* Cooperates with: *United Nations Girls' Education Initiative (UNGEI, #20566); United Nations Institute for Training and Research (UNITAR, #20576); United Nations University (UNU, #20642).*
NGO Relations Organizations approved for consultative status:
- Action Health Incorporated (Nigeria);
- *Advocates for Youth, Washington DC*;
- *Africa-America Institute (AAI)*;
- *African Society for Environmental Studies Programme (ASESP, no recent information)*;
- *African Women's Development and Communication Network (FEMNET, #00503)*;
- *Agence universitaire de La Francophonie (AUF, #00548)*;
- Al-Azhar Centre for Reproductive Health and Population Studies (Egypt);
- *Amref Health Africa (#00806)*;
- *Asian Forum of Parliamentarians on Population and Development (AFPPD, #01493)*;
- *Asian Institute for Development Communication (Aidcom, #01515)*;
- *Asian-Pacific Resource and Research Centre for Women (ARROW, #01629)*;
- *Associazione per la Partecipazione allo Sviluppo (APS, no recent information)*;
- *Centre for African Family Studies (CAFS, #03726)*;
- *CIVICUS: World Alliance for Citizen Participation (#03962)*;
- *Coalition for Sexual and Bodily Rights in Muslim Societies (CSBR, #04068)*;
- *Deutsche Stiftung Weltbevölkerung (DSW)*;
- *EarthAction (EA, #05159)*;
- *EngenderHealth*;
- *Inspire – the European Partnership for Sexual and Reproductive Health and Rights (Inspire, #11232)*;
- *FHI 360*;
- *Forum for African Women Educationalists (FAWE, #09896)*;
- *Girls not Brides (#10154)*;
- *Global Fund for Women (GFW, #10384)*;
- *HelpAge International (#10904)*;
- *Inter-African Committee on Traditional Practices Affecting the Health of Women and Children (IAC, #11384)*;
- *International Center for Research on Women (ICRW)*;
- *International Commission of Jurists (ICJ, #12695)*;
- *International Council on the Management of Population Programs (ICOMP, #13043)*;
- *International Institute for Population Sciences (IIPS, #13911)*;
- *International Institute for Vital Registration and Statistics (IIVRS, inactive)*;
- *International Union for the Scientific Study of Population (IUSSP, #15814)*;
- *International Women's Health Coalition (IWHC)*;
- *IntraHealth International*;
- *Latin American and Caribbean Women's Health Network (LACWHN, #16288)*;
- *Latin American Women's Press Agency (no recent information)*;
- *London School of Hygiene and Tropical Medicine (LSHTM)*;
- *Panos Network (#18183)*;
- *PATH (#18260)*;
- *Pathfinder International (#18261)*;
- *PCI Media*;
- *Society for International Development (SID, #19581)*;
- *Union for African Population Studies (UAPS, #20346)*;
- *Women's Environment and Development Organization (WEDO, #21016)*;
- *World Young Women's Christian Association (World YWCA, #21947).*

Cooperates with:
- *Adventist Development and Relief Agency International (ADRA, #00131)*;
- *Asian Population and Development Association (APDA)*;
- *Catholics for Choice (#03609)*;
- *Center for Reproductive Rights*;
- *Commonwealth Medical Association (CMA, #04351)*;
- *European Parliamentary Forum for Sexual & Reproductive Rights (EPF, #08149)*;
- *Global Health Cluster (GHC, #10401)*;
- *Inter-American Parliamentary Group on Population and Development (IAPG, inactive)*;
- *International Foundation for Population and Development (IFPD, #13674)*;
- *International Planned Parenthood Federation (IPPF, #14589)*;
- *IPS – Inter Press Service International Association (#16013)*;
- *Japanese Organization for International Cooperation in Family Planning (JOICFP)*;
- *MSI Reproductive Choices*;
- *Parliamentarians for Global Action (PGA, #18208)*;
- *PAI (#18025)*;
- *Population Institute (PI)*;
- *Rutgers (#19011).*

Member of: *Global Gender and Climate Alliance (GGCA, no recent information).* Supports: *Tostan (#20176).* Instrumental in setting up: *Education for All Network (EFA Network, inactive); Latin American Feature Service on Women and Population (no recent information); Women's Feature Service (WFS, #21017).* [2020/XF5606/f/**F***]

♦ United Nations Postal Administration (UNPA) 20613

Administration postale des Nations Unies (APNU) – Postverwaltung der Vereinten Nationen (UNPA)

European Office Internationales Zentrum Vienna, Postfach 900, 1400 Vienna, Austria. T. +431260604032 – +431260604025. Fax +431260605825. E-mail: unpa-europe@un.org.
USA Office PO Box 5900, Grand Central Station, New York NY 10163-5900, USA. T. +12129631282. Fax +12129639854.
URL: http://unstamps.org/

History 16 Nov 1950. Established when the General Assembly of the *United Nations (UN, #20515)* unanimously decided to establish UNPA in response to an idea first proposed by Argentina in 1947. The first postage stamps were issues on 24 Oct 1951 following an agreement with the Government of USA to issue stamps in US currency. Similar agreements were concluded with the Governments of Switzerland and Austria in 1969 and 1979 respectively. **Aims** Use UN stamps to reflect the work of the world organization; draw attention to significant world problems and serve as a reminder of the UNs commitment to its goals. **Languages** English, French, German, Italian, Spanish. **Activities** Awareness raising. **Publications** *Fascination* (3 a year) – journal.
Members Sales locations in 13 countries and territories:
Argentina, Australia, Botswana, Brazil, China, Egypt, Hong Kong, Israel, Japan, New Zealand, Pakistan, Singapore, Uganda. [2022.10.11/XF0951/**F***]

♦ United Nations Programme of Assistance in the Teaching, Study, Dissemination and Wider Appreciation of International Law 20614

Programme d'assistance des Nations Unies aux fins de l'enseignement, de l'étude, de la diffusion et d'une compréhension plus large du droit international

Contact Codification Div, Office of Legal Affairs, Room DC2-0554, 323 East 44th St, New York NY 10017, USA. Fax +12129631963.
URL: http://legal.un.org/poa/

History 20 Dec 1965. Established by resolution 2099 (XX) of the General Assembly of the *United Nations (UN, #20515).* Its continuation was subsequently authorized by the Assembly through adoption of resolutions at its annual sessions until its 26th session, and thereafter biennially. At its 64th session, the General Assembly decided to consider this agenda item on an annual basis (resolution 64/113). Latest relevant resolution 70/116, 14 Dec 2015. **Aims** Contribute to a better knowledge of international law as a means for strengthening international peace and security and promoting friendly relations and cooperation among states. **Structure** Advisory Committee, comprising 25 members appointed by United Nations General Assembly. Secretary General reports on past and future implementation of the Programme: to the Advisory Committee every year; to 6th (Legal) Committee every year. Administered and coordinated by Codification Division of United Nations Office of Legal Affairs (OLA). **Languages** Arabic, Chinese, English, French, Russian, Spanish. **Staff** Provided by OLA. **Finance** UN regular budget; voluntary contributions. **Activities** Projects/programmes; training/education; knowledge management/information dissemination; publishing activities. **Events** *Session* New York, NY (USA) 2005, *Session* New York, NY (USA) 2004, *Session* New York, NY (USA) 2002, *Session* New York, NY (USA) 2001, *Session* New York, NY (USA) 1999. **Publications** *International Law Handbook: Collection of Instruments – Recueil de droit international: Collection d'instruments.* **Information Services** *United Nations Audiovisual Library of International Law.*

Members Advisory Committee 1 Jan 2020 – 31 Dec 2023 comprises representatives of 25 countries:
Argentina, Canada, Chile, Ethiopia, France, Ghana, Iran Islamic Rep, Israel, Italy, Kenya, Lebanon, Malaysia, Mexico, Nigeria, Pakistan, Poland, Portugal, Russia, Singapore, Slovakia, Sudan, Tanzania UR, Trinidad-Tobago, Uruguay, USA.
[2019.09.03/XF0919/**E***]

♦ United Nations Programme on Space Applications / see African Regional Centre for Space Science and Technology Education – English (#00431)

♦ United Nations Public Administration Network (UNPAN) 20615

Address not obtained.
URL: http://www.unpan.org/

History Set up 1999 as a programme by Division for Public Institutions and Digital Government of the Department of Economic and Social Affairs of *United Nations (UN, #20515)*. **Aims** Promote the sharing of knowledge, experiences and best practices worldwide in sound public policies, effective public administration and efficient civil services, through capacity-building and cooperation among United Nations member states, with emphasis on south-south cooperation. **Languages** Arabic, Chinese, English, French, Russian, Spanish. **Finance** Sponsored by UN Dept of Economic and Social Affairs. **Activities** Meetings/events; awards/prizes/competitions. **Events** *Digital-5 Summit* Busan (Korea Rep) 2016. **Publications** *Governance World Watch* (12 a year); *UN E-governemnt Survey* (every 2 years); *UNPAN Newsletter*. World Public Sector Reports. **IGO Relations** Partners: *African Civil Service Observatory (ACSO, #00249)*; *African Training and Research Centre in Administration for Development (CAFRAD, #00486)*; *Arab Administrative Development Organization (ARADO, #00893)*; *Caribbean Centre for Development Administration (CARICAD, #03468)*; *Central American Institute of Public Administration (#03670)*; *Cooperation Committee of High-Level Forum on City Informatization in the Asia-Pacific Region (RCCHFCI, no recent information)*; *Latin American Centre for Development Administration (#16294)*; *Regional School of Public Administration (ReSPA, #18810)*; *United Nations African Institute for Economic Development and Planning (#20518)*; *United Nations Centre for Regional Development (UNCRD, #20526)*; *United Nations Economic Commission for Africa (ECA, #20554)*; *United Nations Economic Commission for Europe (UNECE, #20555)*; *United Nations Economic Commission for Latin America and the Caribbean (ECLAC, #20556)*; *United Nations Economic and Social Commission for Asia and the Pacific (ESCAP, #20557)*; *United Nations Economic and Social Commission for Western Asia (ESCWA, #20558)*. **NGO Relations** *African Association for Public Administration and Management (AAPAM, #00215)*; *Eastern Regional Organization for Public Administration (EROPA, #05249)*; *International Centre of Innovation and Exchange in Public Administration (CIAP)*; *International Centre for Parliamentary Studies (ICPS)*; *International Institute of Administrative Sciences (IIAS, #13859)*; *International Public Management Association for Human Resources (IPMA-HR)*; *Network of Institutes and Schools of Public Administration in Central and Eastern Europe (NISPAcee, #17039)*; *World e-Governments Organization of Cities and Local Governments (WeGO, #21542)*.
[2014.10.27/XJ3321/**F***]

♦ United Nations Refugees Emergency Fund (inactive)
♦ United Nations Regional Cartographic Conference for the Americas (meeting series)
♦ United Nations Regional Cartographic Conference for Asia and the Pacific (meeting series)

♦ United Nations Regional Centre for Peace and Disarmament in Africa (UNREC) 20616

Centre régional des Nations Unies pour la paix et le désarmement en Afrique

Contact BP 2705, Lomé, Togo. T. +2282535000. Fax +2282504315. E-mail: jtatrabor@unrec.org – mail@unrec.org.
URL: http://www.unrec.org/

History 1 Jan 1986. Established in the framework of the *United Nations (UN, #20515)* Secretariat, pursuant to resolution 40/151 G adopted by consensus, 16 Dec 1985, at 40th session of the United Nations General Assembly and, pursuant to resolution SHG/Res 138 XXI adopted at the 21st ordinary session of the Head of State and Government of *Organization of African Unity (OAU, inactive)*, held in Addis Ababa (Ethiopia) 16-20 Jul 1985. Officially inaugurated on 24 Oct 1986. Former names and other names: *UNRCPDA* – former. **Aims** Provide substantive support for initiatives and other efforts of Member States of the African region towards realization of measures of peace, arms limitation and disarmament. **Structure** Functions within Regional Disarmament Branch of *United Nations Office for Disarmament Affairs (UNODA, #20594)*. **Finance** Sources: existing United Nations resources; voluntary contributions from Member States; contributions from interested organizations and individuals. **Activities** Conflict resolution; guidance/assistance/consulting; capacity building. **Events** *Conference on confidence-building, security and development* Lomé (Togo) 1988, *Conference on the relationship between human rights, peace and development* Lomé (Togo) 1988. **Publications** Surveys; papers; reports; guides; training manuals. **Information Services** *Arms Register and Database on Small Arms and Light Weapons*. **IGO Relations** Close cooperation with: *African Union (AU, #00488)*; *East African Community (EAC, #05181)*; *Economic Community of Central African States (ECCAS, #05311)*; *Economic Community of West African States (ECOWAS, #05312)*; *Intergovernmental Authority on Development (IGAD, #11472)*; *Southern African Development Community (SADC, #19843)*.
[2020/XE0621/**E***]

♦ United Nations Regional Centre for Peace and Disarmament in Asia and the Pacific / see United Nations Regional Centre for Peace and Disarmament for Asia and the Pacific (#20617)

♦ United Nations Regional Centre for Peace and Disarmament for Asia and the Pacific (UNRCPD) 20617

Centre régional des Nations Unies pour la paix et le désarmement en Asie et dans le Pacifique

Contact KSK Bldg – 4th Floor, Ward No 5 Lagankhel, Lalitpur, PO Box 107, Kathmandu, Nepal. E-mail: unrcpd-info@un.org.
URL: http://unrcpd.org/

History 1987. Established by the General Assembly of the *United Nations (UN, #20515)*. A Regional Centre of *United Nations Office for Disarmament Affairs (UNODA, #20594)*. Former names and other names: *Centre for Peace and Disarmament for Asia and the Pacific* – alias; *United Nations Regional Centre for Peace and Disarmament in Asia and the Pacific* – alias. **Aims** Assist countries in the region to achieve peace, security and disarmament goals through provision of substantive support, coordination of activities at sub-regional, regional and international levels, and information sharing on global and regional activities. **Activities** Knowledge management/information dissemination; guidance/assistance/consulting; events/meetings. **Events** *Joint Conference on Disarmament and Non-Proliferation Issues* Seoul (Korea Rep) 2021, *Joint Conference on Disarmament and Non-Proliferation Issues* Seoul (Korea Rep) 2020, *Joint Conference on Disarmament and Non-Proliferation Issues* Seoul (Korea Rep) 2019, *Joint Conference on Disarmament and Non-Proliferation Issues* Jeju (Korea Rep) 2018, *United Nations Conference on Disarmament Issues* Hiroshima (Japan) 2017.

Members Countries covered by the UNRCPD mandate (43):
Afghanistan, Australia, Bangladesh, Bhutan, Brunei Darussalam, Cambodia, China, Fiji, India, Indonesia, Japan, Kazakhstan, Kiribati, Korea DPR, Korea Rep, Kyrgyzstan, Laos, Malaysia, Maldives, Marshall Is, Micronesia FS, Mongolia, Myanmar, Nauru, Nepal, New Zealand, Pakistan, Palau, Papua New Guinea, Philippines, Samoa, Singapore, Solomon Is, Sri Lanka, Tajikistan, Thailand, Timor-Leste, Tonga, Turkmenistan, Tuvalu, Uzbekistan, Vanuatu, Vietnam.
[2019.11.01/XE0897/**E***]

♦ United Nations Regional Centre for Peace, Disarmament and Development in Latin America / see United Nations Regional Centre for Peace, Disarmament and Development in Latin America and the Caribbean (#20618)

♦ United Nations Regional Centre for Peace, Disarmament and Development in Latin America and the Caribbean (UNLIREC) 20618

Centre régional des Nations Unies pour la paix, le désarmement et le développement en Amérique latine et les Caraïbes – Centro Regional de las Naciones Unidas para la Paz, el Desarme y el Desarrollo en América Latina y el Caribe

Dir Av Jorge Chávez 275 – piso 3, Miraflores, 15818, Lima, Peru. T. +516259114. Fax +5116259100. E-mail: information@unlirec.org.
URL: http://www.unlirec.org/

History 1 Jan 1987. Established by *United Nations (UN, #20515)* General Assembly resolution 41/60J of 3 Dec 1986. Present name adopted in accordance with resolution A/C1/43/L73. Re-opened and re-inaugurated, 1 Dec 1999. Former names and other names: *United Nations Regional Centre for Peace, Disarmament and Development in Latin America* – former; *Centre régional des Nations Unies pour la paix, le désarmement et le développement en Amérique latine* – former; *Centro Regional de las Naciones Unidas para la Paz, el Desarme y el Desarrollo en América Latina* – former. **Aims** Translate the decisions, instruments and commitments of Member States in the field of disarmament, arms and non-proliferation into action, at the national, sub-regional and regional levels; support Latin American and Caribbean States in achieving and maintaining peace and security through disarmament. **Structure** Overseen and coordinated by the United Nations Office for Disarmament Affairs (ODA) Regional Disarmament, Information and Outreach Branch (RDIOB), in New York NY (USA). UNLIREC headquarters in Lima (Peru). **Languages** English, French, Portuguese, Spanish. **Staff** 20.00 FTE, paid; 5.00 FTE, voluntary. Staff include paid in situ experts, internal and external consultants and non-paid interns. **Finance** Operations: voluntary contributions of UN member states, funds and the donor community to UNLIREC Voluntary Trust Fund. Peru annually provides US$ 30,000. UN regular budget covers the salaries of the Director, Executive Office Coordinator and Political Affairs Officer and limited operating costs. **Activities** Awareness raising; capacity building; events/meetings; financial and/or material support; guidance/assistance/consulting; knowledge management/information dissemination; politics/policy/regulatory; projects/programmes; research and development; research/documentation; standards/guidelines; training/education. **Publications** *UNLIREC Bulletin*.

Members Covers 33 UN Member States in the region:
Antigua-Barbuda, Argentina, Bahamas, Barbados, Belize, Bolivia, Brazil, Chile, Colombia, Costa Rica, Cuba, Dominica, Dominican Rep, Ecuador, El Salvador, Grenada, Guatemala, Guyana, Haiti, Honduras, Jamaica, Mexico, Nicaragua, Panama, Paraguay, Peru, St Kitts-Nevis, St Lucia, St Vincent-Grenadines, Suriname, Trinidad-Tobago, Uruguay, Venezuela.
[2021.08.31/XE1055/**E***]

♦ United Nations Regional Centre for Preventive Diplomacy for Central Asia (UNRCCA) 20619

Head 43 Archabil Avenue, 744036 Ashgabat, Turkmenistan. T. +99312481612 – +99312481613 – +99312481614. Fax +99312481607. E-mail: unrcca-dpa@un.org.
URL: http://unrcca.unmissions.org/

History Inaugurated 10 Dec 2007, Ashgabat (Turkmenistan), on initiative of 5 Central Asian states. **Aims** Liaise with the Governments of the region on issues relevant to preventive diplomacy; provide monitoring and analysis; maintain contact with regional organizations and facilitate coordination and information exchange. **Activities** Training/education; events/meetings; networking/liaising.

Members Governments of 5 countries:
Kazakhstan, Kyrgyzstan, Tajikistan, Turkmenistan, Uzbekistan.

IGO Relations *UN Special Programme for the Economies of Central Asia (SPECA, #20715)*.
[2021/XM6341/**E***]

♦ United Nations Regional Centre for Research on Human Settlements (no recent information)

♦ United Nations Regional Commissions New York Office (RCNYO) . . . 20620

Dir Room S-1508, United Nations Headquarters, New York NY 10017, USA. T. +12129635565. Fax +19173671102. E-mail: rcnyo1@un.org.
URL: http://www.regionalcommissions.org/

History 1 Jan 1981, New York, NY (USA). Established within the framework of *United Nations (UN, #20515)*. **Aims** Serve as a focal point for work concerning substantive and operational activities of the secretariats of the five United Nations regional commissions with the concerned offices, programmes and departments at Headquarters, as well as with relevant intergovernmental and non-governmental organizations in New York; provide executive secretaries, permanent missions of States Members of the UN and observer missions at Headquarters with information on selected activities and decisions of the regional commissions; inform Headquarters of relevant activities and decisions of the regional commissions; follow up with Headquarters offices, including UNDP, UNFPA and UNICEF, concerning matters which are of interest to regional commissions; represent executive secretaries at intergovernmental, interagency and intersecretariat meetings at Headquarters and keep them informed of relevant decisions adopted at these meetings; facilitate coordination and cooperation among regional commissions in planning and implementation of programmes and on issues of common interest to regional commissions; provide technical services for meetings of executive secretaries; maintain document reference services for technical reports issued by regional commissions and for UN Headquarters; promote effective cooperation between secretariats of the regional commissions and Headquarters services, especially in respect to the provisions by regional commissions of inputs for the global policy-making processes of the central UN organs; facilitate communications between regional commissions, relevant committees, bodies of the General Assembly and the Economic and Social Council. **Structure** Not an international organization; an office representing the 5 regional economic commissions of the United Nations: *United Nations Economic Commission for Africa (ECA, #20554)*; *United Nations Economic Commission for Europe (UNECE, #20555)*; *United Nations Economic Commission for Latin America and the Caribbean (ECLAC, #20556)*; *United Nations Economic and Social Commission for Asia and the Pacific (ESCAP, #20557)*; *United Nations Economic and Social Commission for Western Asia (ESCWA, #20558)*. **Events** *International Forum on Energy for Sustainable Development* Yerevan (Armenia) 2015. **Publications** *Regional Commissions Development Update* (2 a year) – newsletter. **NGO Relations** Accredited associations: *International Association of Educators for World Peace (IAEWP)*; *International Association of University Presidents (IAUP, #12248)*; *Pathways To Peace (PTP, #18262)*; *Zonta International (#22038)*.
[2020/XE4065/**E***]

♦ United Nations Regional Information Centre for Western Europe (UNRIC) 20621

Centre régional d'information des Nations Unies pour l'Europe occidentale – Centro Regional de Información de las Naciones Unidas – Regionales Informationszentrum der Vereinten Nationen – Centro Regional de Informação das Nações Unidas – Centro Regionale d'Informazione delle Nazioni Unite – Regionaal Informatiecentrum van de Verenigde Naties – FN's Regionale Informationskontor

Dir Residence Palace, Bloc C, Rue de la Loi 155, 7th Floor, 1040 Brussels, Belgium. T. +3227888484. Fax +3227888465. E-mail: info@unric.org.
URL: http://www.unric.org/

History 1 Jan 2004, Brussels (Belgium). Established within the framework of *United Nations (UN, #20515)*. Replaces the 9 centres of *United Nations Information Centres (UNICs, #20574)* in the countries of the European Union which closed, 31 Dec 2003, following a decision by the UN General Assembly at its 58th session. Former names and other names: *Regional United Nations Information Centre for Western Europe (RUNIC)* – former. **Aims** Communicate the values, history and mandate of the United Nations and its actions in building a more peaceful, fair and sustainable world; represent the UN's Department of Global Communications in Western Europe and engage with partners, civil society, media, public institutions, the academic community, the private sector, think tanks and the creative community; provide support to United Nations agencies located in Brussels and work together with the European Union institutions. **Structure** Director; Deputy Director; Staff. **Languages** Danish, Dutch, English, Finnish, French, German, Greek, Icelandic, Italian, Norwegian, Portuguese, Spanish, Swedish. **Staff** 20.00 FTE, paid. **Finance** through United Nations. **Activities** Events/meetings; projects/programmes. **Publications** *UNRIC Info Point & Library Newsletter* (12 a year) – newsletter; *Brèves: l'actualité onusienne en Europe. L'ONU et la Belgique, la France, le Luxembourg, Monaco, l'Union européenne* in French. *UNRIC Library Backgrounders* in English, French, Spanish – information sheets covering various countries/regions or specific topics and list relevant URLs within the UN system.

Members Serves 22 countries:
Andorra, Belgium, Cyprus, Denmark, Finland, France, Germany, Greece, Holy See, Iceland, Ireland, Italy, Luxembourg, Malta, Monaco, Netherlands, Norway, Portugal, San Marino, Spain, Sweden, UK. [2022.10.11/XE4669/**E***]

♦ United Nations Relief and Rehabilitation Administration (inactive)

♦ United Nations Relief and Works Agency for Palestine Refugees in the Near East (UNRWA) 20622

Office de secours et de travaux des Nations Unies pour les réfugiés de Palestine dans le Proche-Orient – Organismo de Obras Públicas y Socorro de las Naciones Unidas para los Refugiados de Palestina en el Cercano Oriente (OOPS)

Amman Office PO Box 140157, Amman 11814, Jordan.
Gaza Office PO Box 338, IL-78100 Ashkelon, Israel. T. +97282287701. Fax +97282887699.
URL: http://www.unrwa.org/

History 8 Dec 1949. Established by General Assembly Resolution 302 (IV), as a subsidiary organ of *United Nations (UN, #20515)* within the *United Nations System (#20635)*, linked to the General Assembly, to carry out direct relief and works programmes for Palestine refugees and to prepare for the time when the relief assistance was no longer needed. Operations commenced on 1 May 1950. Although not originally envisaged as a permanent organization, in the absence of a solution to the Palestine refugee problem the UN General Assembly has repeatedly extended the mandate. **Aims** In cooperation with host authorities, provide registered Palestine refugees with essential *humanitarian* assistance in the areas of: education; health; relief and social services; microfinance and *microenterprise*; projects; emergency operations. **Structure** *'Governance'*: no official governing body; activities are reviewed annually by Advisory Commission, comprised of representatives from 10 countries, with Palestinian Liberation Organization (PLO) as observer. Commissioner-General, appointed by UN Secretary-General with the endorsement of the Advisory Commission, reports directly to UN General Assembly. UNRWA also meets at least twice yearly with host authorities and donor governments to address issues of mutual concern and review activities. *'Structure and Headquarters'*: Field operations handled by field offices (5): Jordan; Lebanon; Syrian Arab Republic; West Bank; Gaza Strip. Headquarters: 1950-1978 in Beirut (Lebanon); 1978-Jun 1996 in Vienna (Austria); since Jul 1996, divided between Gaza and Amman (Jordan). Liaison offices at the United Nations, New York NY (USA) and Palais des Nations, Geneva (Switzerland). Office in Cairo (Egypt). **Languages** English. **Staff** International staff: 103. Total staff: over 30,000 (2015), of whom over 99% are locally-recruited Palestinians, mostly Palestine refugees. Most staff are directly involved in providing services, for example teachers, doctors, social workers, sanitation labourers. Field staff negotiations through: *UNRWA Area Staff Union (no recent information)*; international staff negotiations through: *UNRWA International Staff Association (ISA, no recent information)*. **Finance** No system of assessed contributions. Budget approved by UN General Assembly. Main source (95%): voluntary contributions from governments and *European Community (inactive)*, mostly in cash although 7% in kind – mainly food commodities for distribution to needy refugees. By UN General Assembly Mandate, receives selective technical and financial support from: *UNESCO (#20322)*; *WHO (#20950)*. Other sources: contributions from other UN bodies to cover staffing costs, including funding of 103 international posts by UN Secretariat. Additional contributions cover projects and other extrabudgetary activities, such as the Emergency Appeal.
Activities Areas of operation comprise Jordan, Lebanon, Syrian Arab Republic, West Bank and Gaza Strip. Works in cooperation with governing authorities in the occupied Palestinian territory, West Bank and Gaza, and with governments of the host countries for Palestine refugees – Jordan, Syria and Lebanon – serving a refugee population of over 4 million, of whom 1.2 million live in 59 official refugee camps. Provides services direct to beneficiaries, planning and executing activities and projects and building and administering facilities such as schools and clinics. Flexible mandate enables provision of different types of assistance as conditions in the region change. Main Programmes (3):
– *'Education'* – provides: basic elementary and preparatory schooling free of charge to all Palestine refugee children and youth in accordance with local government school systems; university level, pre-service teacher education for young Palestinian refugees and in-service training for UNRWA teachers, through *UNRWA/UNESCO Institute of Education (IUNRWA/UNESCO IE, no recent information)*; technical education and vocational training for young Palestinian refugees.
– *'Health Care'* – offers primary health care through 122 facilities. Services include: outpatient medical care; disease prevention and control; maternal and child health care; family planning; special non-communicable disease care; dental care.
– *'Relief and Social Services'* – provides a range of assistance to low-income refugees. This includes: food support; shelter reconstruction and repair; youth activities; skills training for women; assistance for mentally and physically challenged individuals; micro-credit to small entrepreneurs.
Other current activities:
– *'Emergency Operations'* – since Oct 2000, has provided ongoing humanitarian assistance on an emergency basis to some 317,000 families affected by the strife in the occupied Palestinian territory. Assistance includes: food aid; job creation; post-injury medical care and rehabilitation; psychological counselling for youth; remedial education for schooling interrupted by the conflict.
– *'Microfinance and Micro-enterprise Programme'* – helps to reduce poverty and stimulate economic growth, supporting development of the micro-enterprise and small business sector by providing working capital and areas of operation comprise Jordan, Lebanon, Syrian Arab Republic, West Bank and Gaza Strip. Works in cooperation with governing authorities in the occupied Palestinian territory, West Bank and Gaza, and with governments of the host countries for Palestine refugees – Jordan, Syria and Lebanon – serving a refugee population of over 4 million, of whom 1.2 million live in 59 official refugee camps. Provides services direct to beneficiaries, planning and executing activities and projects and building and administering facilities such as schools and clinics. Flexible mandate enables provision of different types of assistance as conditions in the region change. Main Programmes (3):
– *'Education'* – provides: basic elementary and preparatory schooling free of charge to all Palestine refugee children and youth in accordance with local government school systems; university level, pre-service teacher education for young Palestinian refugees and in-service training for UNRWA teachers, through *UNRWA/UNESCO Institute of Education (IUNRWA/UNESCO IE, no recent information)*; technical education and vocational training for young Palestinian refugees.
– *'Health Care'* – offers primary health care through 122 facilities. Services include: outpatient medical care; disease prevention and control; maternal and child health care; family planning; special non-communicable disease care; dental care.
– *'Relief and Social Services'* – provides a range of assistance to low-income refugees. This includes: food support; shelter reconstruction and repair; youth activities; skills training for women; assistance for mentally and physically challenged individuals; micro-credit to small entrepreneurs.
Other current activities:
– *'Emergency Operations'* – since Oct 2000, has provided ongoing humanitarian assistance on an emergency basis to some 317,000 families affected by the strife in the occupied Palestinian territory. Assistance includes: food aid; job creation; post-injury medical care and rehabilitation; psychological counselling for youth; remedial education for schooling interrupted by the conflict.
– *'Microfinance and Micro-enterprise Programme'* – helps to reduce poverty and stimulate economic growth, supporting development of the micro-enterprise and small business sector by providing working capital and capital investment loans.
Events *Symposium on Conflict and Crisis in the Near East* Tokyo (Japan) 2018, *Meeting* Vienna (Austria) 1993, *Major donors meeting* Amman (Jordan) 1992, *Pledging conference* New York, NY (USA) 1992, *NGO meeting* Vienna (Austria) 1991. **Publications** *Report of the Commissioner-General to the General Assembly* (annual). Public information materials, including brochures and maps. Information Services: Photo and film library chronicling activities since 1950. Recent UNRWA videos available on request.
Members Advisory Commission representatives of governments of 10 countries:
Belgium, Egypt, France, Japan, Jordan, Lebanon, Syrian AR, Türkiye, UK, USA.
Observer (1):
Palestine Liberation Organization (PLO).
IGO Relations Cooperates with: *UNHCR (#20327)*. Member of: *United Nations Group on the Information Society (UNGIS, #20570)*. Represented on: *United Nations System Chief Executives Board for Coordination (CEB, #20636)*. Participates in: *Joint Inspection Unit of the United Nations (JIU, #16133)*.
Links with:.
– *Arab Fund for Economic and Social Development (AFESD, #00965)*;
– *Arab Gulf Programme for United Nations Development Organizations (AGFUND, #00971)*;
– *ECOSOC (#05331)*;
– *Islamic Development Bank (IsDB, #16044)*;
– *League of Arab States (LAS, #16420)*;
– *Office of the United Nations Special Coordinator for the Middle East Process (UNSCO, #17698)*;
– *OPEC Fund for International Development (OFID, #17745)*;
– *Organisation of Islamic Cooperation (OIC, #17813)*;
– *Refugee Working Group (RWG, #18741)*;
– *Swedish International Development Cooperation Agency (Sida)*;
– *UNDP (#20292)*;
– *UNESCO Regional Office for Education in the Arab States (UNEDBAS, #20320)*;
– *UNICEF (#20332)*;
– *United Nations Office for the Coordination of Humanitarian Affairs (OCHA, #20593)*;
– *United Nations Office at Vienna (UNOV, #20604)*;
– *United Nations Population Fund (UNFPA, #20612)*.
NGO Relations Member of: *Association for Human Resources Management in International Organizations (AHRMIO, #02634)*. Cooperates with: *ICDL Europe (#11052)*; *International Council of Voluntary Agencies (ICVA, #13092)*; *The Lutheran World Federation (LWF, #16532)*. [2022/XE1325/**E***]

♦ United Nations of Religious Groups (unconfirmed)

♦ United Nations Research Institute for Social Development (UNRISD) 20623

Institut de recherche des Nations Unies pour le développement social – Instituto de Investigación de las Naciones Unidas para el Desarrollo Social

Headquarters Palais des Nations, 1211 Geneva 10, Switzerland. T. +41229173060. Fax +41229170650. E-mail: info@unrisd.org
URL: http://www.unrisd.org/

History 1963. Operates as an autonomous body within the framework of *United Nations (UN, #20515)*. Based at *United Nations Office at Geneva (UNOG, #20597)*. Reports to *United Nations Commission for Social Development (CSocD, #20535)*. **Aims** Ensure that social equity, inclusion and justice are central to development thinking, policy and practice. **Structure** Board comprises: Chair appointed by UN Secretary-General; 10 members nominated by UN Commission for Social Development and confirmed by *ECOSOC (#05331)*; representative of UN Secretary-General; Executive-Secretary of *United Nations Economic and Social Commission for Western Asia (ESCWA, #20558)*; Directors of *United Nations African Institute for Economic Development and Planning (#20518)*, *Latin American and Caribbean Institute for Economic and Social Planning (#16279)* and *Asian and Pacific Development Centre (APDC, #01608)*; representatives of 2 of the following UN specialized agencies, appointed in rotation – *ILO (#11123)*, *UNESCO (#20322)*, *FAO (#09260)*, *WHO (#20950)*; UNRISD Director (ex-officio). **Languages** English, French, Spanish. **Staff** 21.00 FTE, paid. **Finance** Voluntary contributions, grants and material assistance from governments and UN bodies. **Activities** Research/documentation; monitoring/evaluation; politics/policy/regulatory; events/meetings. **Events** *People's Global Online Summit* Geneva (Switzerland) 2022, *Religion revisited conference* Berlin (Germany) 2009, *Conference on social and political dimensions of the global crisis* Geneva (Switzerland) 2009, *Conference on the political and social economy of care* New York, NY (USA) 2009, *Workshop on poverty reduction and policy regimes* Malaysia 2007. **Publications** *UNRISD eBulletin*. Research papers; working papers; briefs. **NGO Relations** Instrumental in setting up: *Interpeace (#15962)*. [2020/XE3388/jv/**E***]

♦ United Nations Revolving Fund for Natural Resources Exploration (inactive)
♦ United Nations Rwanda Emergency Office, Kigali (inactive)

♦ United Nations Scientific Committee on the Effects of Atomic Radiation (UNSCEAR) 20624

Comité scientifique des Nations Unies pour l'étude des effets des rayonnements ionisants

Sec Vienna International Ctr, PO Box 500, 1400 Vienna, Austria. T. +431260604331. Fax +431260605902.
Information Officer address not obtained. T. +431260604122.
URL: http://www.unscear.org/

History Established 1955, by resolution 913 (X) of the General Assembly of *United Nations (UN, #20515)*. **Aims** Assess and report on exposures of humans and the *environment* to ionizing radiation from natural and man-made sources and accidental releases of *radioactive* materials derived from measurements made worldwide; evaluate the effects and *risks* of radiation exposures through *epidemiological* and research findings. **Structure** Scientific Committee; Secretariat administered by *UNEP (#20299)* – DEWA. **Languages** English. **Staff** 4.00 FTE, paid. **Finance** Appropriations through Programme Budget of the United Nations. Annual budget: US$ 800,000. **Activities** Events/meetings. **Events** *Session* Vienna (Austria) 2021, *Session* Vienna (Austria) 2019, *Session* Vienna (Austria) 2018, *Session* Vienna (Austria) 2017, *Session* Vienna (Austria) 2016. **Publications** Reports.
Members Representatives of 27 countries:
Argentina, Australia, Belarus, Belgium, Brazil, Canada, China, Egypt, Finland, France, Germany, India, Indonesia, Japan, Korea Rep, Mexico, Pakistan, Peru, Poland, Russia, Slovakia, Spain, Sudan, Sweden, UK, Ukraine, USA.
IGO Relations *International Atomic Energy Agency (IAEA, #12294)*; *International Nuclear Information System (INIS, #14378)*. *Vienna International Centre (VIC)*; *WHO (#20950)*. **NGO Relations** *Information System on Occupational Exposure (ISOE, #11199)*; *International Commission on Radiation Units and Measurements (ICRU, #12722)*; *International Commission on Radiological Protection (ICRP, #12724)*. [2019.02.11/XE5946/**E***]

♦ United Nations Security Council (UNSC) 20625

Conseil de sécurité des Nations Unies – Consejo de Seguridad de las Naciones Unidas

Chief of Secretariat c/o United Nations – Room DC2-0852, New York NY 10017, USA. T. +12129635248.
URL: https://www.un.org/securitycouncil/

History 24 Oct 1945, New York, NY (USA). Established by the *Charter of the United Nations – Charte des Nations Unies*. Officially constituted, 12 Jan 1946. A principal organ of *United Nations (UN, #20515)* within *United Nations System (#20635)*, on which Member States have conferred primary responsibility for maintaining peace and security. In performing its functions, the Security Council acts on behalf of the Member States, all of whom have agreed to accept and carry out its decisions in accordance with the Charter. **Aims** Maintain international peace and security; develop friendly relations among nations; cooperate in solving international problems and in promoting respect for human rights; be a centre for harmonizing the actions of nations.
Structure Comprises 15 members (in accordance with an amendment to the Charter, in force since 31 Aug 1965, the Security Council was enlarged from 11 to 15 members), each entitled to one vote, including: 5 permanent members; 10 elected by the General Assembly for 2-year terms, ineligible for immediate re-election, the 10 non-permanent seats are distributed on a regional basis as follows: 5 for African and Asian States; one for Eastern European States; 2 for the Latin American and Caribbean States; and 2 for Western European and other States. Presidency is held monthly in turn by Member States, in English alphabetical order. A decision on any matter other than a question of procedure is by an affirmative vote of 9 members, including concurring votes of permanent members, in accordance with the rule of 'Great Power Unanimity', popularly known as the 'veto' privilege. In practice, an abstention by one of the permanent members is not regarded as a veto. Any member, whether permanent or non-permanent, must abstain from voting in any decision in a dispute to which it is a party. On questions of procedure, a decision is by an affirmative vote of any nine members. Because the maintenance of peace requires constant vigilance and may call for prompt action, the Security Council is so organized as to be able to function continuously. Meetings are held periodically, and, should it so decide, the Council may hold its meetings at places other than headquarters.
Secretariat. Standing Committees and Working Groups are comprised of the 15 members of the Council.
Committees:
– *Counter-Terrorism Committee (CTC, #04928)*;
– Non-Proliferation Committee;
– *United Nations Security Council Military Staff Committee (MSC, #20626)*;
– Sanctions Committees.
Standing Committees and Ad hoc Bodies, including:

– *United Nations Compensation Commission (UNCC, #20548).*
International Courts and Tribunals:
– *International Residual Mechanism for Criminal Tribunals (IRMCT, #14746).*
Security Council Affairs Division (SCAD), part of Political and Peacebuilding Affairs (DPPA), provides substantive and secretariat support to Security Council. Includes:
– Security Council Secretariat Branch;
– Security Council Subsidiary Organs, including *United Nations Peacebuilding Commission (PBC, #20606)*;
– Security Council Practices and Charter Research Branch;
– Military Staff Committee Secretariat.
Activities Functions and powers:
– maintain international peace and security in accordance with the principles and purposes of the United Nations;
– investigate any dispute or situation which might lead to international friction;
– recommend methods of adjusting such disputes or the terms of settlement;
– formulate plans for the establishment of a system to regulate armaments;
– determine the existence of a threat to the peace or act of aggression and to recommend what action should be taken;
– call on Members to apply economic sanctions and other measures not involving the use of force to prevent or stop aggression;
– take military action against an aggressor;
– recommend the admission of new Members;
– exercise the trusteeship functions of the United Nations in "strategic areas";
– recommend to the General Assembly the appointment of the Secretary-General and, together with the Assembly, elect the Judges of *International Court of Justice (ICJ, #13098)*.
Events *Meeting on the situation in the Sudan* Nairobi (Kenya) 2004, *Summit* New York, NY (USA) 1992.
Members Permanent members (5), designated by Charter and irrespective of region:
China, France, Russia, UK, USA.
Non-permanent members (10) according to equitable geographical distribution (term expires 31 Dec of year in parentheses):
Belgium (2020), Dominican Rep (2020), Estonia (2021), Germany (2020), Indonesia (2020), Niger (2021), South Africa (2020), St Vincent-Grenadines (2021), Tunisia (2021), Vietnam (2021).
IGO Relations *International Atomic Energy Agency (IAEA, #12294)*. May instigate warrants for cases to be decided by: *International Criminal Court (ICC, #13108)*, set up 2 Jul 2002. Associated with: *Agreement on a Comprehensive Political Settlement of the Cambodia Conflict (Paris Agreement, 1991)*. Instrumental in setting up:
– *African Union/United Nations Hybrid Operation in Darfur (UNAMID, inactive)*;
– *Bureau intégré des Nations Unies pour le Cambodge (BINUC, no recent information)*;
– *Commission de démarcation de la frontière entre l'Iraq et le Koweït (no recent information)*;
– *International Security Assistance Force (ISAF, inactive)*;
– *Office of the High Representative in Bosnia and Herzegovina (OHR, #17696)*;
– *UN Interim Administration Mission in Kosovo (UNMIK, #20343)*;
– *United Nations Assistance Mission in Afghanistan (UNAMA, #20522)*;
– *United Nations Command Military Armistice Commission (UNCMAC, #20529)*;
– *United Nations Disengagement Observer Force (UNDOF, #20553)*;
– *United Nations Integrated Mission in Timor-Leste (UNMIT, inactive)*;
– *United Nations Integrated Office in Burundi (BINUB, inactive)*;
– *United Nations Interim Force in Lebanon (UNIFIL, #20577)*;
– *United Nations Military Observer Group in India and Pakistan (UNMOGIP, #20584)*;
– *United Nations Mission in the Central African Republic and Chad (MINURCAT, inactive)*;
– *United Nations Mission in Liberia (UNMIL, inactive)*;
– *United Nations Mission for the Referendum in Western Sahara (MINURSO, #20586)*;
– *United Nations Mission in the Sudan (UNMIS, inactive)*;
– *United Nations Observer Mission in Angola (MONUA, inactive)*;
– *United Nations Observer Mission in Georgia (UNOMIG, inactive)*;
– *United Nations Operation in Burundi (ONUB, inactive)*;
– *United Nations Operation in Côte d'Ivoire (UNOCI, inactive)*;
– *United Nations Organization Stabilization Mission in the Democratic Republic of Congo (MONUSCO, #20605)*;
– *United Nations Peace-keeping Force in Cyprus (UNFICYP, #20608)*;
– *United Nations Special Committee on Peace-keeping Operations (#20628)*;
– *United Nations Stabilization Mission in Haiti (MINUSTAH, inactive)*;
– *United Nations Truce Supervision Organization (UNTSO, #20638)*;
– *United Nations Unified Command in Korea (UNC, #20641)*. [2020/XE3376/E*]

♦ United Nations Security Council Counter-Terrorism Committee / see Counter-Terrorism Committee (#04928)

♦ United Nations Security Council Military Staff Committee (MSC) . . . 20626

Comité d'état-major du Conseil de sécurité des Nations Unies (CEM)

Liaison Officer United Nations, Room S-3540, New York NY 10017, USA. T. +12129635278. Fax +12129631156.

History 1946, New York NY (USA), by Article 47 of the Charter of *United Nations (UN, #20515)*, as the military organ of *United Nations Security Council (UNSC, #20625)*. Previously also referred to in French as *Comité des chefs d'état-major du Conseil de sécurité des Nations Unies (CEM)*. **Aims** Advise and assist the Security Council on all questions relating to its military requirements for the maintenance of international *peace* and *security*, employment and command of forces, the regulation of *armaments* and possible *disarmament*; responsible for the *strategic* direction of any armed forces placed at the Council's disposal. **Structure** Delegations are headed by officers of the rank of Lieutenant-General or Major-General, and are usually represented at meetings (held at the call of the Chairman in closed session in New York NY) by officers of the rank of Colonel. The Chairmanship rotates monthly. **Languages** Chinese, English, French, Russian. **Activities** The Chairman personally performs liaison between MSC and the Secretary-General. Liaison Officer acts under the authority of both the Chairman of the MSC and the Secretary-General for the purpose of exchanging information, transmitting pertinent documents and arranging for conferences between them.
Members Chiefs of Staff of the permanent members (5) of the Security Council or their representatives:
China, France, Russia, UK, USA. [2003.07.22/XE0146/E*]

♦ United Nations Social Defence Research Institute / see United Nations Interregional Crime and Justice Research Institute (#20580)
♦ United Nations Society of Mohicans (inactive)

♦ United Nations Special Committee to Investigate Israeli Practices Affecting the Human Rights of the Palestinian People and Other Arabs of the Occupied Territories 20627

Comité spécial chargé d'enquêter sur les pratiques israéliennes affectant les droits de l'homme du peuple palestinien et des autres Arabes des territoires occupés – Comité Especial encargado de investigar las practicas israelies que afecten a los derechos humanos del pueblo palestino y otros habitantes arabes de los territorios ocupado

Contact OHCHR, 1211 Geneva 10, Switzerland.
URL: http://www.un.org/ga/

History 19 Dec 1968, as *United Nations Special Committee to Investigate Israeli Practices affecting the Human Rights of the Population of the Occupied Territories*, by Resolution 2443 (XXIII) of General Assembly of the *United Nations (UN, #20515)*. Based at *Office of the United Nations High Commissioner for Human Rights (OHCHR, #17697)*, *United Nations Office at Geneva (UNOG, #20597)*. **Aims** Investigate Israeli practices affecting the human rights of the Palestinian people and other Arabs of the occupied territories. **Structure** A sub-organ of the United Nations General Assembly. Currently composed of representatives of 3 Member States, namely Sri Lanka (Chairman), Malaysia and Senegal (Members). **Activities** Annual visit to various countries of the Middle East to collect first hand information from witnesses of the occupied territories and the occupied Syrian Golan. Consultations in Geneva (Switzerland) during the debate on Palestine issues at the Commission on Human Rights; presentation of the report and participation in the related debate on Palestine. **Events** *Meeting* Geneva (Switzerland) 2007, *Meeting* Geneva (Switzerland) 2003, *Meeting* Geneva (Switzerland) 2002, *Meeting* Geneva (Switzerland) 2002, *Meeting* Geneva (Switzerland) 2002.
Members Member States (3):
Malaysia, Senegal, Sri Lanka. [2019/XE0585/E*]

♦ United Nations Special Committee to Investigate Israeli Practices affecting the Human Rights of the Population of the Occupied Territories / see United Nations Special Committee to Investigate Israeli Practices Affecting the Human Rights of the Palestinian People and Other Arabs of the Occupied Territories (#20627)

♦ United Nations Special Committee on Peace-keeping Operations . . 20628

Comité spécial des opérations de maintien de la paix

Contact United Nations, c/o Dept of Peacekeeping Operations, 405 East 42nd Street, New York NY 10017, USA. T. +12129631234. Fax +12129634879.
URL: https://peacekeeping.un.org/en

History 1965. Established by *United Nations (UN, #20515)* General Assembly resolution 2006 (XIX). **Aims** Review comprehensively issues relating to peacekeeping and report on findings to UN General Assembly. **Activities** UN methods and machinery for preventing or controlling conflicts have taken many forms – peace-keeping forces, observer missions, fact-finding missions, supervision of plebiscites, missions of good offices, conciliation panels, mediators and special representatives. Current operations (12):
– *United Nations Mission for the Referendum in Western Sahara (MINURSO, #20586)* (Sep 1991 – present);
– *United Nations Multidimensional Integrated Stabilization Mission in the Central African Republic (MINUSCA, #20588)* (Apr 2014- present);
– *United Nations Multidimensional Integrated Stabilization Mission in Mali (MINUSMA, #20589)* (Apr 2013 – present);
– *United Nations Organization Stabilization Mission in the Democratic Republic of Congo (MONUSCO, #20605)* (Feb 2000 – present);
– *United Nations Disengagement Observer Force (UNDOF, #20553)* (Jun 1974 – present);
– *United Nations Peace-keeping Force in Cyprus (UNFICYP, #20608)* (Mar 1964 – present);
– *United Nations Interim Force in Lebanon (UNIFIL, #20577)* (Mar 1978 – present);
– *United Nations Interim Security Force for Abyei (UNISFA, #20578)* (Jun 2011 – present);
– *UN Interim Administration Mission in Kosovo (UNMIK, #20343)* (Jun 1999 – present);
– *United Nations Mission in South Sudan (UNMISS, #20587)* (Jul 2011 – present);
– *United Nations Military Observer Group in India and Pakistan (UNMOGIP, #20584)* (Jan 1949 – present);
– *United Nations Truce Supervision Organization (UNTSO, #20638)* (Jun 1948 – present).
Past peacekeeping operations:
'Africa':
– *African Union/United Nations Hybrid Operation in Darfur (UNAMID, inactive)* (Jul 2007 – Dec 2020);
– *United Nations Angola Verification Mission (UNAVEM, inactive)* (UNAVEM I: Jan 1989 – May 1991, UNAVEM II: May 1991 – Feb 1995, UNAVEM III: Feb 1995 – Jun 1997);
– *United Nations Aouzou Strip Observer Group (UNASOG, inactive)* (May 1994 – Jun 1994);
– *United Nations Assistance Mission for Rwanda (UNAMIR, inactive)* (Oct 1993 – Mar 1996);
– *United Nations Mission in Ethiopia and Eritrea (UNMEE, inactive)* (Jun 2000 – Jul 2008);
– *United Nations Mission in Sierra Leone (UNAMSIL, inactive)* (Oct 1999 – Dec 2005), replacing *United Nations Mission of Observers in Sierra Leone (UNOMSIL, inactive)* (Jul 1998 – Oct 1999);
– *United Nations Mission in the Central African Republic (MINURCA, inactive)* (Apr 1998 – Feb 2000);
– *United Nations Mission in the Central African Republic and Chad (MINURCAT)* (Sep 2007 – Dec 2010);
– *United Nations Observer Mission in Angola (MONUA, inactive)* (Jul 1997 – Feb 1999);
– *United Nations Observation Mission in Liberia (UNOMIL, inactive)* (Sep 1993 – Sep 1997);
– *United Nations Observer Mission in Uganda-Rwanda (UNOMUR, inactive)* (Jun 1993 – Sep 1994);
– *United Nations Operation in Burundi (ONUB, inactive)* (May 2004 – Dec 2006) and succeeded by *United Nations Integrated Office in Burundi (BINUB, inactive)* (2006-2014);
– *United Nations Operation in Côte d'Ivoire (UNOCI, inactive)* (Apr 2004 – present), replacing *United Nations Mission in Côte d'Ivoire (MINUCI, inactive)* (May 2003 – Apr 2004);
– *United Nations Operation in Mozambique (UNOMOZ, inactive)* (Dec 1992 – Dec 1994);
– *United Nations Operation in Somalia (UNOSOM, inactive)* (UNOSOM I: Apr 1992 – Mar 1993, UNOSOM II: May 1993 – Mar 1995);
– *United Nations Mission in the Sudan (UNMIS, inactive)* (Mar 2005 to present);
– *United Nations Operation in the Congo (inactive)* (Jul 1960 – Jun 1964);
– *United Nations Transition Assistance Group (UNTAG, inactive)* (Apr 1989 – Mar 1990);
– *United Nations Mission in Liberia (UNMIL, inactive)* (Sep 2003 – Mar 2018).
'Americas':
– *Mission of the Representative of the Secretary-General in the Dominican Republic (DOMREP, inactive)* (May 1965 – Oct 1966);
– *United Nations Civilian Police Mission in Haiti (MIPONUH, inactive)* (28 Nov 1997 – Mar 2000), replacing *United Nations Transition Mission in Haiti (UNTMIH, inactive)* (Aug 1997 – Nov 1997), which replaced *United Nations Support Mission in Haiti (UNSMIH, inactive)* (Jul 1996 – Jul 1997);
– *United Nations Mission in Haiti (UNMIH, inactive)* (Sep 1993 – Jun 1996);
– *United Nations Observer Group in Central America (ONUCA, inactive)* (Nov 1989 – Jan 1992);
– *United Nations Observer Mission in El Salvador (inactive)* (Jul 1991 – Apr 1995);
– *United Nations Verification Mission in Guatemala (MINUGUA, inactive)* (Jan 1997- May 1997);
– *United Nations Stabilization Mission in Haiti (MINUSTAH, inactive)* (Jun 2004 – Oct 2017).
'Asia and the Pacific':
– *United Nations Transitional Authority in Cambodia (UNTAC, inactive)* (Mar 1992 – Sep 1993), absorbing *United Nations Advance Mission in Cambodia (UNAMIC, inactive)* (Oct 1991 – Mar 1992);
– *United Nations Good Offices Mission in Afghanistan and Pakistan (UNGOMAP, inactive)* (Apr 1988 – Mar 1990);
– *United Nations India-Pakistan Observation Mission (UNIPOM, inactive)* (Sep 1965 – Mar 1966);
– *United Nations Mission of Observers in Tajikistan (UNMOT, inactive)* (Dec 1994 – May 2000);
– *United Nations Integrated Mission in Timor-Leste (UNMIT, inactive)* (Aug 2006 to 31 Dec 2012), replacing *United Nations Mission of Support in East Timor (UNMISET, inactive)* (May 2002 – May 2005), which replaced *United Nations Transitional Administration in East Timor (UNTAET, inactive)* (Oct 1999 – May 2002) and *United Nations Mission in East Timor (UNAMET, inactive)* (Jun 1999 – Sep 1999);
– *United Nations Security Force in West New Guinea – West Irian (UNSF, inactive)* (Oct 1962 – Apr 1963).
'Europe':
– *United Nations Protection Force (UNPROFOR, inactive)* (Feb 1992 – Dec 1995), from 31 Mar 1995 including *United Nations Confidence Restoration Operation in Croatia (UNCRO, inactive)* (Mar 1995 – Jan 1996) and *United Nations Preventive Deployment Force for Macedonia (UNPREDEP, inactive)* (Mar 1995 – Feb 1990); subsequently followed up by: *United Nations Mission in Bosnia and Herzegovina (UNMIBH, inactive)* (Dec 1995 – Dec 2002); *United Nations Transitional Administration for Eastern Slavonia, Baranja and Western Sirmium (UNTAES, inactive)* (Jan 1996 – Jan 1998), *Croatia – United Nations Civilian Police Support Group (UNPSG, inactive)* (Jan 1998 – Oct 1998) and *United Nations Mission of Observers in Prevlaka (UNMOP, inactive)* (Jan 1996 – Dec 2002);
– *United Nations Observer Mission in Georgia (UNOMIG, inactive)* (Aug 1993 – Jun 2009).
'Middle East':
– *United Nations Emergency Force (UNEF, inactive)* (UNEF I: Nov 1956 – Jun 1967, UNEF II: Oct 1973 – Jul 1979);
– *United Nations Iran-Iraq Military Observer Group (UNIIMOG, inactive)* (Aug 1988 – Feb 1991);
– *United Nations Iraq-Kuwait Observation Mission (UNIKOM, inactive)* (Apr 1991 – Mar 2003);
– *United Nations Observation Group in Lebanon (UNOGIL, inactive)* (Jun 1958 – Dec 1958);
– *United Nations Yemen Observation Mission (UNYOM, inactive)* (Jul 1963 – Sep 1964);
– *United Nations Supervision Mission in Syria (UNSMIS)* (Apr 2012 – Aug 2012).
Civilian component is jointly referred to as *United Nations Police (UNPOL, #20611)*.
Events *Substantive session* New York, NY (USA) 2005, *Substantive session* New York, NY (USA) 2004, *Substantive session* New York, NY (USA) 2000, *Substantive session* New York, NY (USA) 1998, *Substantive session* New York, NY (USA) 1997.
Members Representatives of 151 UN Member States:
Afghanistan, Albania, Algeria, Angola, Argentina, Armenia, Australia, Austria, Azerbaijan, Bangladesh, Belarus, Belgium, Benin, Bhutan, Bolivia, Bosnia-Herzegovina, Brazil, Bulgaria, Burkina Faso, Burundi, Cambodia, Cameroon, Canada, Central African Rep, Chad, Chile, China, Colombia, Congo Brazzaville, Congo DR, Costa Rica, Côte d'Ivoire, Croatia, Cuba, Cyprus, Czechia, Denmark, Djibouti, Dominican Rep, Ecuador, Egypt, El Salvador, Eritrea, Estonia, Eswatini, Ethiopia, Fiji, Finland, France, Gabon, Gambia, Georgia, Germany, Ghana, Greece, Grenada, Guatemala, Guinea, Guyana, Haiti, Honduras, Hungary, Iceland, India, Indonesia, Iran Islamic Rep, Iraq, Ireland, Israel, Italy, Jamaica, Japan, Jordan, Kazakhstan, Kenya, Korea Rep, Kuwait, Kyrgyzstan, Laos, Lebanon, Lesotho, Liberia, Libya, Lithuania, Luxembourg, Madagascar, Malawi, Malaysia, Mali, Mauritania, Mauritius, Mexico, Moldova, Mongolia, Montenegro, Morocco, Mozambique, Myanmar, Namibia, Nepal, Netherlands, New Zealand, Nicaragua, Niger, Nigeria, North Macedonia, Norway, Pakistan, Palau, Papua New Guinea, Paraguay, Peru, Philippines, Poland, Portugal, Qatar, Romania, Russia, Rwanda, Samoa, Saudi Arabia, Senegal, Serbia, Sierra Leone, Singapore, Slovakia, Slovenia, South Africa, Spain, Sri Lanka, Sudan, Sweden, Switzerland, Syrian AR, Tanzania UR, Thailand, Timor-Leste, Togo, Tunisia, Türkiye, Uganda, UK, Ukraine, Uruguay, USA, Vanuatu, Venezuela, Vietnam, Yemen, Zambia, Zimbabwe.
Observers (4):
Holy See, Latvia, Panama, South Sudan.
International observers (7):
African Union (AU, #00488); *European Union (EU, #08967)*; *International Committee of the Red Cross (ICRC, #12799)*; *International Criminal Police Organization – INTERPOL (ICPO-INTERPOL, #13110)*; *Organisation internationale de la Francophonie (OIF, #17809)*; *Organisation of Islamic Cooperation (OIC, #17813)*; *Sovereign Military Hospitaller Order of St John of Jerusalem, of Rhodes and of Malta (SMOM)*. [2022/XE1131/y/E*]

♦ United Nations Special Committee on the Situation with Regard to the Implementation of the Declaration on the Granting of Independence to Colonial Countries and Peoples / see Special Committee on Decolonization (#19906)
♦ United Nations Special Fund (inactive)

♦ United Nations Special Fund, 1974 (no recent information)
♦ United Nations Stabilization Mission in Haiti (inactive)
♦ United Nations Staff College Project / see United Nations System Staff College (#20637)
♦ United Nations Staff Council at Vienna / see United Nations Staff Union, Vienna (#20631)

♦ United Nations Staff Mutual Insurance Society Against Sickness and Accident (UNSMIS) 20629

Société d'assurance mutuelle du personnel contre la maladie

Main Office Palais des Nations, Av de la Paix 8-14, 1202 Geneva, Switzerland. E-mail: unsmis@unog.ch – unsmis@un.org.

URL: https://medical-insurance.unog.ch

History 1949, under the 'Staff Rules' of *United Nations (UN, #20515)*. **Activities** Provides insurance services to current and retired staff of: *United Nations Office at Geneva (UNOG, #20597)*. Also serves staff of the following organizations which have concluded agreements with UNOG: *UNHCR (#20327)*; *UNICEF (#20332)*; *World Meteorological Organization (WMO, #21649)*. **Members** Individuals (15,000). Membership countries not specified. [2021/XE1981/**E**]

♦ United Nations Staff Union 20630

Syndicat du personnel des Nations Unies

Pres Room L-0300, 405 E 42nd St, New York NY 10017, USA. T. +12129637075. E-mail: staffunionu@un.org.

URL: http://u-seek.org/

History 1946, New York, NY (USA). Founded to represent staff members of *United Nations (UN, #20515)*, New York offices. **Aims** Represent New York Secretariat Staff, Locally Recruited Staff in the field and Staff Members of UN Information Centers. **Structure** Council; Executive Board. **Languages** English, French, Spanish. **Finance** Sources: members' dues. Dues are optional. **Activities** Events/meetings. **Events** *Annual General Meeting* Delhi (India) 1986. **Members** Staff members of the United Nations (11,000). **NGO Relations** Member of (2): *Coordinating Committee for International Staff Unions and Associations of the United Nations System (CCISUA, #04818)*; *United Nations International Civil Servants Federation (UNISERV, #20579)*. [2020/XE0225/v/**E**]

♦ United Nations Staff Union at Nairobi / see Nairobi Staff Union (#16930)

♦ United Nations Staff Union, Vienna 20631

Pres Room E1112/13, PO Box 500, 1400 Vienna, Austria. T. +431260605534 – +431260603588. Fax +4312633771.

URL: http://staffunion.unov.org/

History 1980. Former names and other names: *Staff Union of the UN Office at Vienna* – former; *United Nations Staff Council at Vienna* – former. **Aims** Protect the rights and well-being of all UN staff in Vienna and its associated field offices by representing and empowering staff within the framework of the values and objectives embodied in the UN Charter. **Structure** Council; Committee. **Languages** English. **Finance** Voluntary contributions. **Publications** *UN Staff Committee Vienna Newsletter*. **IGO Relations** *Vienna International Centre (VIC)*. **NGO Relations** Member of: *Coordinating Committee for International Staff Unions and Associations of the United Nations System (CCISUA, #04818)*. [2020/XE0806/v/**E**]

♦ United Nations Standards Coordinating Committee (inactive)

♦ United Nations Standing Advisory Committee on Security Questions in Central Africa (UNSAC) 20632

Comité consultatif permanent des Nations Unies chargé des questions de sécurité en Afrique centrale

Secretariat Africa II Div, Dept of Political Affairs, S-3402, UNHQ, New York NY 10017, USA. T. +12129634943. Fax +19173674148.

URL: https://www.un.org/disarmament/disarmsec/unsac/

History 28 May 1992, New York NY (USA), by Secretary-General of *United Nations (UN, #20515)*, pursuant to General Assembly resolution 46/37 B of 6 Dec 1991, following a request by the Central African States for the creation of an advisory committee under the auspices of the UN. **Aims** Promote peace and security in the Central African region through confidence-building measures, including *arms limitation* and *disarmament*. **Structure** Meeting at Ministerial level (twice a year); Meeting at Expert level (twice a year). Bureau, consisting of President, 2 Vice-Presidents, Rapporteur and Secretary. UN Regional Office for Central Africa (UNOCA) serves as secretariat. **Languages** French. **Finance** UN regular budget and voluntary contributions to the Trust Fund of the Standing Advisory Committee. **Activities** Organizes conferences, seminars and workshops. Meeting reports are circulated as General Assembly and Security Council document after each ministerial meeting. Adopted *Central African Convention for the Control of Small Arms and Light Weapons, Their Ammunition, Parts and Components That Can be Used for Their Manufacture, Repair and Assembly (Kinshasa Convention, 2010)*. **Events** *Ministerial Meeting* Libreville (Gabon) 2015, *Ministerial Meeting* Luanda (Angola) 2015, *Ministerial Meeting* Bujumbura (Burundi) 2014, *Ministerial Meeting* Malabo (Equatorial Guinea) 2014, *Ministerial Meeting* Ndjamena (Chad) 2013. **Publications** *United Nations Concern for Peace and Security in Central Africa* in English, French – reference document. Secretary-General's report on the Committee (annual); meeting reports.

Members Governments of 11 countries:
Angola, Burundi, Cameroon, Central African Rep, Chad, Congo Brazzaville, Congo DR, Equatorial Guinea, Gabon, Rwanda, Sao Tomé-Principe.

IGO Relations Formal contacts with: *Economic Community of Central African States (ECCAS, #05311)*. [2017.10.16/XE1885/**E***]

♦ United Nations Statistical Commission 20633

Commission des Nations Unies de statistique

Contact Statistics Div, Dept Economic and Social Affairs, United Nations HQ, DC 2 Bldg Room 1670, New York NY 10017, USA. T. +12129634849. Fax +12129639851. E-mail: statistics@un.org – statcom@un.org.

URL: http://unstats.un.org/unsd/statcom/commission.htm

History 16 Feb 1946. Established by resolution 8 (I) of *ECOSOC (#05331)*, within the framework of *United Nations (UN, #20515)*. Terms of reference set out in resolutions 8 (I), 8 (II) of 21 Jun 1946, and 1566 (L) of 3 May 1971. A Functional Commission of ECOSOC; oversees the work of the UN Statistics Division (UNSD). **Aims** Assist ECOSOC: in promoting development of national statistics and improving their comparability; in coordinating statistical work of specialized agencies; in developing central statistical services of UN Secretariat; in advising UN organs on general questions relating to collection, analysis and dissemination of statistical information; in promoting the improvement of statistics and statistical methods generally. Ultimate goal as set out in ECOSOC resolution 1566 (L), 1971: achievement of an integrated system in the collection, *data processing* and dissemination of international statistics by the organs and agencies of the United Nations System, with special regard to the requirements of reviewing and appraising economic and social progress, taking into account the needs of *developing countries*. **Structure** Annual Session, always in New York NY (USA). Members (24) are elected by ECOSOC for 4-year terms on the basis of: 5 from African States; 4 from Asian States; 4 from Eastern European States; 4 from Latin American and Caribbean States; 7 from Western European and other States. Bureau. **Languages** Arabic, Chinese, English, French, Russian, Spanish. **Events** *Session* New York, NY (USA) 2023, *Session* New York, NY (USA) 2022, *Session* New York, NY (USA) 2021, *Session* New York, NY (USA) 2020, *Session* New York, NY (USA) 2019. **Publications** All documents, final reports for each session and other related information available on website.

Members Representatives of 24 UN Member States (term expiry date, 31 Dec of the year in parentheses):
Australia (2025), Brazil (2023), Burundi (2025), Colombia (2024), Cuba (2025), Czechia (2023), Finland (2025), Georgia (2023), Germany (2024), Hungary (2024), Japan (2024), Korea Rep (2023), Kuwait (2023), Madagascar (2023), Mexico (2024), Netherlands (2025), Russia (2025), Samoa (2024), Sierra Leone (2023), Switzerland (2024), Tunisia (2025), UK (2024), USA (2023), Zambia (2025). [2022/XE1124/**E***]

♦ United Nations Statistical Office (inactive)
♦ United Nations Sustainable Building and Construction Initiative (unconfirmed)

♦ United Nations Sustainable Development Group (UNSDG) 20634

Assistant SG c/o Development Coordination Office, 405 East 42nd Street, 25th Floor, New York NY 10017, USA. T. +12129065500. Fax +12129063609. E-mail: dcocommunications@un.org.

URL: https://unsdg.un.org/

History 1997. Established as one of 3 pillars of *United Nations System Chief Executives Board for Coordination (CEB, #20636)*, within the framework of *United Nations (UN, #20515)*, to deal with operational activities for development with a focus on country-level work. Former names and other names: *United Nations Development Group (UNDG)* – former; *Groupe des Nations Unies pour le développement (GNUD)* – former. **Aims** Bring together the United Nations operational agencies working on development; advance a common agenda based on key *reforms* in the development sector, while maintaining and reinforcing the distinctive identities of members, to promote greater operational coherence and to build a more effective resident coordinator system. **Structure** Chaired by UN Deputy Secretary-General (on behalf of the UN Secretary-General). *UNDP (#20292)* Administrator serves as Vice-Chair. Development Coordination Office (DCO) serves as Secretariat. **Activities** Advocacy/lobbying/activism; monitoring/evaluation; politics/policy/regulatory.

Members Entities (36):
- *FAO (#09260)*;
- *ILO (#11123)*;
- *International Fund for Agricultural Development (IFAD, #13692)*;
- *International Organization for Migration (IOM, #14454)*;
- *International Telecommunication Union (ITU, #15673)*;
- *International Trade Centre (ITC, #15703)*;
- *Joint United Nations Programme on HIV/AIDS (UNAIDS, #16149)*;
- *Office of the United Nations High Commissioner for Human Rights (OHCHR, #17697)*;
- *UNCTAD (#20285)*;
- *UNDP (#20292)*;
- *UNEP (#20299)*;
- *UNESCO (#20322)*;
- *UNHCR (#20327)*;
- *UNICEF (#20332)*;
- *UNIDO (#20336)*;
- *United Nations Capital Development Fund (UNCDF, #20524)*;
- United Nations Department of Economic and Social Affairs (UN DESA);
- United Nations Department of Political and Peacebuilding Affairs (DPPA);
- *United Nations Economic and Social Commission for Asia and the Pacific (ESCAP, #20557)*;
- *United Nations Economic and Social Commission for Western Asia (ESCWA, #20558)*;
- *United Nations Economic Commission for Africa (ECA, #20554)*;
- *United Nations Economic Commission for Europe (UNECE, #20555)*;
- *United Nations Economic Commission for Latin America and the Caribbean (ECLAC, #20556)*;
- *United Nations Human Settlements Programme (UN-Habitat, #20572)*;
- *United Nations Office for Disaster Risk Reduction (UNDRR, #20595)*;
- *United Nations Office for Project Services (UNOPS, #20602)*;
- *United Nations Office for the Coordination of Humanitarian Affairs (OCHA, #20593)*;
- *United Nations Office on Drugs and Crime (UNODC, #20596)*;
- United Nations Peacebuilding Support Office;
- *United Nations Population Fund (UNFPA, #20612)*;
- *United Nations Relief and Works Agency for Palestine Refugees in the Near East (UNRWA, #20622)*;
- *United Nations Volunteers (UNV, #20650)*;
- *UN Women (#20724)*;
- *WHO (#20950)*;
- *World Food Programme (WFP, #21510)*;
- *World Meteorological Organization (WMO, #21649)*.

IGO Relations Cooperation with: *UNIDO (#20336)*. Adheres to: *Global Partnership for Effective Development Co-operation (GPEDC, #10532)*. **NGO Relations** Supports: *Economic Research Forum (ERF, #05318)*. [2011.12.01/XE4205/**E***]

♦ United Nations Sustainable Development Solutions Network / see Sustainable Development Solutions Network (#20054)

♦ United Nations System 20635

Système des Nations Unies – Sistema de las Naciones Unidas

Headquarters United Nations, 405 East 42nd St, New York NY 10017, USA. T. +12129631234. Fax +12127582718.

URL: http://www.un.org/

Structure UN System is made up of the organizations established by the Charter of the United Nations, that is, the United Nations proper, the specialized agencies provided for in Article 57 of the Charter and a number of programmes established by the General Assembly under its authority derived from Article 22 of the Charter. To this must be added the International Atomic Energy Agency (IAEA) which is not a specialized agency in the strict legal sense. The organizations are referred to collectively as "organizations of the United Nations system" which encompasses those organizations within and outside the "United Nations Common System". The Specialized Agencies and Related Organizations maintain separate legislative and governing bodies which provide the directives for their mandates. These organizations coordinate with the broader work of the United Nations through Inter-Organizational Agreements with the General Assembly and the Economic and Social Council facilitated through *United Nations System Chief Executives Board for Coordination (CEB, #20636)*.

Alphabetical Listing of UN System Organizations and Entities:
- *FAO (#09260)*;
- *International Atomic Energy Agency (IAEA, #12294)*;
- *International Civil Aviation Organization (ICAO, #12581)*;
- *International Civil Service Commission (ICSC, #12587)*;
- *International Fund for Agricultural Development (IFAD, #13692)*;
- *ILO (#11123)*;
- *International Maritime Organization (IMO, #14102)*;
- *International Monetary Fund (IMF, #14180)*;
- *International Organization for Migration (IOM, #14454)*;
- *International Telecommunication Union (ITU, #15673)*;
- *International Trade Centre (ITC, #15703)*;
- *Joint Inspection Unit of the United Nations (JIU, #16133)*;
- *Joint United Nations Programme on HIV/AIDS (UNAIDS, #16149)*;
- *Office of the United Nations High Commissioner for Human Rights (OHCHR, #17697)*;
- *UNHCR (#20327)*;
- *Organisation for the Prohibition of Chemical Weapons (OPCW, #17823)*;
- *Preparatory Commission for the Comprehensive Nuclear-Test-Ban Treaty Organization (CTBTO, #18482)*;
- *UN Women (#20724)*;
- *United Nations (UN, #20515)*;
- *UNICEF (#20332)*;
- *UNCTAD (#20285)*;
- *UNDP (#20292)*;
- *United Nations Economic and Social Commission for Asia and the Pacific (ESCAP, #20557)*;
- *United Nations Economic and Social Commission for Western Asia (ESCWA, #20558)*;
- *United Nations Economic Commission for Africa (ECA, #20554)*;
- *United Nations Economic Commission for Europe (UNECE, #20555)*;
- *United Nations Economic Commission for Latin America and the Caribbean (ECLAC, #20556)*;
- *UNESCO (#20322)*;
- *UNEP (#20299)*;
- *United Nations Framework Convention on Climate Change (UNFCCC, 1992)*;
- *United Nations Human Settlements Programme (UN-Habitat, #20572)*;
- *UNIDO (#20336)*;
- *United Nations Institute for Disarmament Research (UNIDIR, #20575)*;
- *United Nations Institute for Training and Research (UNITAR, #20576)*;
- *International Computing Centre (ICC, #12839)*;
- *United Nations Office for Disaster Risk Reduction (UNDRR, #20595)*;
- *United Nations Interregional Crime and Justice Research Institute (UNICRI, #20580)*;
- *United Nations Office for Project Services (UNOPS, #20602)*;
- *United Nations Office on Drugs and Crime (UNODC, #20596)*;
- *United Nations Population Fund (UNFPA, #20612)*;
- *United Nations Relief and Works Agency for Palestine Refugees in the Near East (UNRWA, #20622)*;
- *United Nations Research Institute for Social Development (UNRISD, #20623)*;

- *United Nations System Staff College (UNSSC, #20637)*;
- *United Nations University (UNU, #20642)*;
- *Universal Postal Union (UPU, #20682)*;
- *The World Bank Group (#21218)*;
- *World Food Programme (WFP, #21510)*;
- *WHO (#20950)*;
- *World Intellectual Property Organization (WIPO, #21593)*;
- *World Meteorological Organization (WMO, #21649)*;
- *World Tourism Organization (UNWTO, #21861)*;
- *World Trade Organization (WTO, #21864)*.

Events *Youth Forum* Dakar (Senegal) 2001, *Youth Forum* Vienna (Austria) 1991. **Members** Not applicable. [2020/XF1000/**F***]

♦ United Nations System Chief Executives Board / see United Nations System Chief Executives Board for Coordination (#20636)

♦ United Nations System Chief Executives Board for Coordination (CEB) 20636

Conseil des chefs de secrétariat des organismes des Nations Unies (CCS)

Sec CEB New York Office, 2 UN Plaza, DC2-0610, New York NY 10017, USA.
Geneva Office Palais des Nations, Bureau A-503/C-553, 1211 Geneva 10, Switzerland.
URL: http://www.unsceb.org/

History 1946. Established at the request of *ECOSOC (#05331)* in Resolution 13 (III). An inter-organization body of the *United Nations (UN, #20515)*, part of the *United Nations System (#20635)*. Assumed many functions of *Inter-Agency Task Force on Basic Social Services for All (BSSA, inactive)*. Former names and other names: *Administrative Committee on Coordination (ACC)* – former; *Comité administrative de coordination (CAC)* – former; *United Nations System Chief Executives Board (CEB)* – former; *Conseil des chefs de secrétariat des organismes des Nations Unies pour la coordination* – former. **Aims** As the highest level inter-agency body in the UN system, foster cooperation and coordination among the organizations of the UN system across a wide range of policy, programme and management issues in the pursuit of the common goals of the Member States; promote inter-agency dialogue and develop a coordinated and integrated approach to major international developments and trends. **Structure** Board comprises Executive Heads, chaired by UN Secretary-General, and meets twice a year. Secretariat, co-located in New York NY (USA) and Geneva (Switzerland). Carries out its role through 2 mechanisms: High-Level Committee on Programmes; High-Level Committee on Management. **Activities** Focuses on the review and follow-up to the Millennium Declaration and the preparations and follow-up to the 2005 World Summit. HLCP work focus includes the future of multilateralism, curbing transnational crime, bridging the digital divide, conflict prevention, financing for development, HIV/AIDS and its linkages with food security and governance, the follow-up to the World Summit on Sustainable Development (WSSD), support for *New Partnership for Africa's Development (NEPAD, #17091)*, implementation of the development agenda at the country level, enhancing the role of the UN system in the field of economic development, gender mainstreaming and knowledge management. HLCM has addressed issues that include security and safety of the UN staff, the impact on management and programme of the changing relationship between regular and voluntary funding, measures to improved UN system-wide mobility, managing for results in the UN system, UN system collaboration on accountability and transparency, strengthening of the International Civil Service, the UN system contingency plan for an influenza pandemic, as well as various information and communication technology, finance and budget and human resources issues. **Events** *Meeting* New York, NY (USA) 2018, *Meeting* Rome (Italy) 2018, *Meeting* Geneva (Switzerland) 2017, *Annual Meeting* The Hague (Netherlands) 2017, *Regular session* New York, NY (USA) 2011. **Publications** *CEB Annual Overview Reports*; *CEB Summary of Conclusions*; *One United Nations: Catalyst for Progress and Change – How the Millennium Declaration is changing the way the UN system works*. Meeting reports.

Members Organizations (31) of the United Nations system:
- *FAO (#09260)*;
- *ILO (#11123)*;
- *International Atomic Energy Agency (IAEA, #12294)*;
- *International Civil Aviation Organization (ICAO, #12581)*;
- *International Fund for Agricultural Development (IFAD, #13692)*;
- *International Maritime Organization (IMO, #14102)*;
- *International Monetary Fund (IMF, #14180)*;
- *International Organization for Migration (IOM, #14454)*;
- *International Telecommunication Union (ITU, #15673)*;
- *The World Bank Group (#21218)*;
- *UNCTAD (#20285)*;
- *UNDP (#20292)*;
- *UNEP (#20299)*;
- *UNESCO (#20322)*;
- *UNHCR (#20327)*;
- *UNICEF (#20332)*;
- *UNIDO (#20336)*;
- *United Nations Human Settlements Programme (UN-Habitat, #20572)*;
- *United Nations Office for Project Services (UNOPS, #20602)*;
- *United Nations Office on Drugs and Crime (UNODC, #20596)*;
- *United Nations Population Fund (UNFPA, #20612)*;
- *United Nations Relief and Works Agency for Palestine Refugees in the Near East (UNRWA, #20622)*;
- *United Nations (UN, #20515)*;
- *Universal Postal Union (UPU, #20682)*;
- *UN Women (#20724)*;
- *WHO (#20950)*;
- *World Food Programme (WFP, #21510)*;
- *World Intellectual Property Organization (WIPO, #21593)*;
- *World Meteorological Organization (WMO, #21649)*;
- *World Tourism Organization (UNWTO, #21861)*;
- *World Trade Organization (WTO, #21864)*. [2020/XE4062/**E***]

♦ United Nations System Staff College (UNSSC) 20637

Dir Viale Maestri del Lavoro 10, 10127 Turin TO, Italy. T. +39116535911. Fax +39116535901. E-mail: info@unssc.org.
URL: http://www.unssc.org

History Jan 1996, as part of *United Nations (UN, #20515)*, as *United Nations Staff College Project (UNSCP)*. Following initial project phase, the UN General Assembly adopted resolution A/RES/55/278 approving the United Nations System Staff College with its own legal status as an innovative instrument to enhance cooperation and coherence throughout the United Nations System. **Aims** Serve as a distinct, system-wide, knowledge-management and learning institution; contribute to a more effective, results-oriented and agile United Nations. **Structure** Board of Governors (meets annually). **Languages** English. **Finance** Sources: course fees; learning services' contracts; contribution from UN agencies; voluntary contributions from members and foundations. **Activities** Training/education; knowledge management/information dissemination; guidance/assistance/consulting; standards/guidelines; capacity building. [2018.06.18/XK1600/**F***]

♦ United Nations System Standing Committee on Nutrition (inactive)
♦ United Nations Transitional Administration in East Timor (inactive)

♦ United Nations Truce Supervision Organization (UNTSO) 20638

Organisme des Nations Unies chargé de la surveillance de la trève (ONUST)

Chief of Staff Government House, PO Box 490, 91004 Jerusalem, Israel. T. +97225687444. Fax +97225687400.
USA Office UNTSO, PO Box 5854, Grand Central Station, New York NY 10163-5854, USA.
URL: https://untso.unmissions.org/

History Jun 1948. Established by the *United Nations Security Council (UNSC, #20625)*, within *United Nations System (#20635)*, in the framework of the *United Nations (UN, #20515)*. In 1949 its military observers (UNMOs) remained to supervise the Armistice Agreements between Israel and its Arab neighbours and have been for many years the main basis of the uneasy truce in the whole area. The body of staff officers and its communications system were instrumental in setting up: the first *United Nations Emergency Force (UNEF, inactive) – UNEF I* – at short notice during the time of Suez crisis; *United Nations Operation in the Congo (inactive)* (Congo, Congo DR) in 1960; the observer group in Lebanon during the crisis of 1958; the United Nations Yemen observer group in 1963; *UNEF II* in Sinai in 1973; UNDOF in 1974; UNIFIL in 1978; *United Nations Good Offices Mission in Afghanistan and Pakistan (UNGOMAP, inactive)* – now replaced by the *Office of the Secretary-General in Afghanistan and Pakistan (OSGAP)* – in 1988; *United Nations Iran-Iraq Military Observer Group (UNIIMOG, inactive)* in 1988 (UNTSO had a small number of Observers attached to UMIIMOG and had observers posted in Baghdad (Iraq) and Teheran (Iran Islamic Rep), during the period 1984-1988); *United Nations Iraq-Kuwait Observation Mission (UNIKOM, inactive)* (1991-2003). Former names and other names: *United Nations Truce Supervision Organization in Palestine* – former; *Organisme des Nations Unies chargé de la surveillance de la trève en Palestine* – former.

Aims Observe and report on the unconditional *ceasefire* ordered by the UN Security Council in 1948 and assist the parties in the implementation of the agreements of 1949 between Israel and 4 neighbouring Arab countries.

Structure Head of the Mission is the Chief of Staff. He is assisted by a body of 3 staff elements: Advisory staff, comprising Senior Adviser and Senior Legal Adviser; Military staff, comprising Deputy Chief of Staff, Chief Joint Operations Centre, Chief Military Personnel Officer, Chief Plans Officer, Chiefs of Field Stations, Liaison Officers, and observers assigned to operations or observation duties; Administrative staff, comprising Chief Administrative Officer, Senior Administrative Officer, Field Service Officers and other staff, recruited internationally and locally.

Operates from 7 duty stations in the 5 countries of the mission area:
- Jerusalem – Headquarters Government House and Mixed Armistice Commission (MAC) House;
- Beirut (Lebanon) – United Nations Liaison Office in Beirut (UNLOB);
- Naqoura – Headquarters Observer Group Lebanon (OGL).
- Camp Faouar (Golan Heights) – Headquarters Observer Group Golan (OGG);
- Damascus (Syrian AR) – Observer Group Golan-Damascus (OGG-D) and Observer Detachment Damascus (ODD);
- Tiberias – Headquarters Observer Group Golan-Tiberias (OGG-T);
- Ismailia – Liaison Office Cairo (LOC).

Also maintains 3 Patrol Bases in southern Lebanon and 11 Observation Posts on the Golan, and conducts regular patrols in southern Lebanon, Golan and Sinai.

Staff Deployed personnel (2021): 388 of which 232 civilians. Staff negotiations through *United Nations Field Staff Union (UNFSU, #20561)*. **Finance** Financed from the regular budget of the United Nations. Annual budget: 36,501,000 USD (2021). **Activities** Activities are spread over territory within the 5 states. Groups of United Nations Military Observers (UNMOs) monitor cease-fire arrangements and assist parties in supervising the Armistice Agreements. UNTSO reports to the UN Security Council, through UN Secretary-General, on violations such as firing, overflights, incidents and other military movements. The function of UNMOs has changed in the light of changing circumstances following the wars of 1956, 1967 and 1973, but they remain in the area, acting as go-between for the hostile parties and as a means by which isolated incidents can be contained and prevented from escalating into major conflicts. They also conduct patrolling, inspections liaison, negotiations and representational duties. UNMOs and UN civilian support staff are also available at short notice to form the nucleus of other peace-keeping operations and remain to assist such operations, their rapid deployment being the initial deterrent to renewed fighting. In particular, contributes to the activities of *United Nations Disengagement Observer Force (UNDOF, #20553)* and *United Nations Interim Force in Lebanon (UNIFIL, #20577)* in the implementation of their respective mandates. Military observers are unarmed and carry out their functions with absolute impartiality. They operate with the consent of the parties and are dependent on cooperation with the parties for their effectiveness. Although their presence may deter violations of the truce and their acting on the basis of UN resolutions means they exercise a degree of moral persuasion, there is no element of enforcement in their functioning. When an outbreak of violence threatens, the Chief of Staff may, on his own initiative, appeal to the parties for restraint and, if a firing incident actually occurs, he may attempt to arrange an immediate ceasefire; he may bring the matter to the attention of the Security Council through the Secretary General. In cases requiring investigation, inquiries are carried out by observers at the scene whenever possible.

Members As of 30 Nov 2009, military personnel provided by 23 countries:
Argentina, Australia, Austria, Belgium, Canada, Chile, China, Denmark, Estonia, Finland, France, Ireland, Italy, Nepal, Netherlands, New Zealand, Norway, Russia, Slovakia, Slovenia, Sweden, Switzerland, USA.

IGO Relations *United Nations Special Committee on Peace-keeping Operations (#20628)*. Relations with the 5 host countries: Egypt; Israel; Jordan; Lebanon; Syrian AR. [2021/XE1048/**F***]

♦ United Nations Truce Supervision Organization in Palestine / see United Nations Truce Supervision Organization (#20638)

♦ United Nations Trusteeship Council 20639

Conseil de tutelle des Nations Unies – Consejo de Administración Fiduciaria de las Naciones Unidas

Address not obtained.
URL: http://www.un.org/documents/tc.htm

History under Chapter XIII of the Charter of the United Nations, as a principal organ of *United Nations (UN, #20515)* within the *United Nations System (#20635)*; Member States administering Trust Territories are accountable to the United Nations for the discharge of their responsibilities and obligations in the administration of the Territories. On 28 May 1986, referring to the last of the 11 Trust Territories originally placed under the International Trusteeship System – *Trust Territory of the Pacific Islands (inactive)* (a strategic area in accordance with Article 83 of the United Nations Charter) administered by the USA, the Council considered – resolution 2183 (LIII) – that the Administering Authority had satisfactorily discharged its obligations under the Trusteeship Agreement and that it was appropriate for that agreement to be terminated. It also requested the Administering Authority to agree to a date for the full entry into force of the Compacts of Free Association and the Commonwealth Covenant. Subsequently, the USA informed the Secretary-General that the Compact of Free Association with the Marshall Islands would enter into force on 21 Oct 1986 and the Compact of Free Association with the Federated States of Micronesia and the Commonwealth Covenant with the Northern Mariana Islands on 3 Nov 1986.

By its resolutions 683 (1990) adopted 22 Dec 1990, the Security Council determined that, in the light of the entry of the new status agreements for the Federated States of Micronesia, the Marshall Islands and the Northern Mariana Islands, the objectives of the Trusteeship Agreement had been fully attained, and the applicability of the Trusteeship Agreement had terminated, with respect to those entities. Palau, therefore, remained the only entity under the 1947 Trusteeship Agreement. The Security Council expressed the hope that the people of Palau would be able in due course to complete the process of freely exercising their right to self-determination and the Trusteeship Council continued to review the situation in Palau at its regular annual sessions.

At its 57 session, May 1990, the Trusteeship Council noted that the Compact of Free Association did not obtain the 75% majority necessary for ratification at the plebiscite held in Palau on 6 Feb 1990; and the statement of the representative of the Government of Palau in the Trusteeship Council, 21 May 1990, that the leadership of Palau was currently reviewing possible options with respect to the resolution of Palau's future political status. On 4 Nov 1992, Palau held a Constitutional amendment referendum and changed to simple majority (50 plus 1%), the approval requirement for the Compact of Free Association. Thereafter, the 8th plebiscite was held on 9 Nov 1993 and the Compact was approved by 68% voting in favour and 32% voting against. In Jan 1994, at the end of the 60th session of the Trusteeship Council, USA informed the Council that its Government and the Government of Palau intended to implement the Compact of Free Association as quickly as practicable. Planning for the smooth transition to Palau's new status was thus underway.

In May 1994, at its 61st session, the Council considered the annual report of the Administering Authority and made recommendations to the Security Council on the future status of the Territory. It adopted the report of the drafting committee (comprising representatives of China, France, Russia and UK) that the Trusteeship Council welcomed the holding of a plebiscite in Palau and its result and congratulated the people of Palau. The Council expressed the hope that, in the near future, the Administering Authority would take up the matter of the termination of the Trusteeship Agreement with the Security Council, in accordance with Article 83 of the Charter of the United Nations. At the same session, by adopting resolution 2199 (LXI) entitled "Attainment of self-government of independence by Trust Territories", the Council, *'inter alia'*, requested USA, in consultation with the Government of Palau, to agree on a date for the full entry into force of the Compact of Free Association,

and to inform the Secretary-General of the United Nations of that date. The Council considered that USA had satisfactorily discharged its obligations under the terms of the Trusteeship Agreement to be terminated with effect from the date referred to above, as agreed upon by the two Governments.
With the independence of Palau, the last remaining United Nations trust territory, the Council formally suspended operation on 1 Nov 1994. By a resolution adopted on that day, it amended its rules of procedure to drop the obligation to meet annually and agreed to meet as occasion required – by its decision or the decision of its President, or at the request of a majority of its members or the General Assembly or the Security Council. Suspended operations on 1 Nov 1994.
Aims *'Non-Self-Governing Territories'* A declaration on all non-self-governing Territories forms part of the United Nations Charter, and through it the Members of the United Nations accept as a sacred trust the obligation to promote the wellbeing and advancement of dependent peoples and their progressive development towards self-government, to ensure their just treatment and protection against abuse, to promote international peace and security, and to promote development measures and encourage research. The States administering colonies and other dependencies are requested to transmit regularly to the Secretary-General statistical and other information on economic, social and educational conditions in the territories which they administer. **Structure** Council comprises one Administering Authority, namely the USA (Trust Territory of the Pacific Islands) and 4 non-administering members (China, France, UK and Russia – previously USSR), which are members by virtue of their being permanent members of the Security Council. After Nauru attained independence in Jan 1968, the General Assembly decided that, because it was no longer possible to ensure parity between administering and non-administering members, the Council would consist of members automatically appointed under sub-paragraphs 1 (a) and 1 (b) of Article 86 until all Trusteeship Agreements have been terminated or, in the case of an amendment to the Charter, until the amendment comes into force. *Special Committee on Decolonization (C-24, #19906) – Special Committee of 24* – established by the General Assembly on 27 Nov 1961, following adoption by the General Assembly, 14 Dec 1960, of the Declaration on the Granting of Independence to Colonial Countries and Peoples, in response to growing concern over the slowness of progress towards independence of many peoples and lands outside the Trusteeship system and still under colonial rule. The Special Committee is the main body in the United Nations dealing with the progress of peoples in dependent territories towards self-determination and independence. It looks regularly into conditions in non-self-governing territories and, with the approval of the General Assembly, it also considers whether additional territories should be brought within its purview. **Finance** Source: Regular Budget of the United Nations. **Activities** The Trusteeship Council, in supervising the administration of the Trust Territories on behalf of the General Assembly, or, in the case of the strategic area, on behalf of the Security Council, examines the annual reports submitted by the Administering Authorities. It also examines petitions affecting the Trust Territories, reports of visiting missions, and observations on conditions in the Territories which may have been submitted by specialized agencies, and which are within their sphere of competence. **Events** *Annual Session* New York, NY (USA) 1994, *Annual Session* New York, NY (USA) 1993, *Annual Session* New York, NY (USA) 1992, *Annual Session* New York, NY (USA) 1991, *Annual Session* New York, NY (USA) 1990. **Publications** *Report of the Trusteeship Council to the Security Council on the Trust Territory of the Pacific Islands* (annual). Other special reports.
Members Administering countries (1):
USA.
Non-administering countries – permanent members of the Security Council – (4):
China, France, Russia, UK. [2010/XE3378/d/**E***]

♦ United Nations Trust Fund for African Development (UNTFAD) 20640

Fonds d'affectation spéciale des Nations Unies pour le développement de l'Afrique (FASNUDA)

Contact address not obtained. T. +251115517200. Fax +251115510365. E-mail: ecainfo@uneca.org.
URL: http://www.uneca.org/

History 1977. Established within the framework of *United Nations (UN, #20515)* and administered by *United Nations Economic Commission for Africa (ECA, #20554)*. No activities reported since 2014. **Aims** Mobilize resources for African development. Priorities: promote Africa's economic and social transformation through regional economic cooperation and integration for accelerated attainment of individual and collective self-reliance and *sustainability*; address the growing importance of the social dimensions of economic development of the African countries and of the interrelationship between economic and social factors in the development process; strengthen and develop capacities for socio-economic and human development; promote popular participation; improve the management of environmental factors for sustainable development; improve the management and coordination of emergency, humanitarian and rehabilitation assistance. **Finance** Pledged contributions of African governments and interested non-African governments, mobilized biennially through a Pledging Conference of *Conference of African Ministers Responsible for Economic and Social Development and Planning (inactive)*. Pledged contributions up to 1992: US$ 12.5 million. Contribution to ECA's operational activities for 1992: US$ 1,679,591. *'UNTFAD Specific'* receives resources pledged by ECA Member States and donors for specific projects. *'UNTFAD General'* pools unspecified contributions for use in developing and implementing regional projects and programmes. **Activities** Finances small-scale technical assistance projects an initial phases of major development projects and pilot projects. Provides seed money to help build up and mobilize substantive additional resources from foreign donors. In line with the work programme of ECA for 1993-1994, areas of major focus (as available funding allows) are: transport and communication; regional cooperation and integration; women in development; enhancing long-term strategic planning and institutional capacity; food and agriculture; environmental and natural resource management. Proposed portfolio of projects for 1994-1995 includes *Second United Nations Industrial Development Decade for Africa (IDDA II)* and *Second United Nations Transport and Communications Decade for Africa (UNTACDA II)*, the latter through UNTACDA Trust Funds. **IGO Relations** Instrumental in setting up and close cooperation with: *African Regional Centre of Technology (ARCT, #00432)*. [2014/XF0810/df/**F***]

♦ United Nations Trust Fund for Sudano-Sahelian Activities (no recent information)
♦ United Nations Trust Fund in Support of Actions to Eliminate Violence Against Women / see UN Trust Fund to End Violence against Women (#20716)

♦ United Nations Unified Command in Korea (UNC) 20641

Address not obtained.

History 7 Jul 1950, pursuant to resolution 84 (1950) of the *United Nations Security Council (UNSC, #20625)*, to command the armed forces sent to the Korean war. Not a subsidiary organ of the United Nations but established under the authority of the United States. **IGO Relations** 7 Jul 1950, pursuant to resolution 84 (1950) of the *United Nations Security Council (UNSC, #20625)*, to command the armed forces sent to the Korean war. Not a subsidiary organ of the United Nations but established under the authority of the United States. Sits on: *United Nations Command Military Armistice Commission (UNCMAC, #20529)*. [2017/XE4397/**E***]

♦ United Nations University (UNU) 20642

Université des Nations Unies (UNU) – Universidad de las Naciones Unidas

Main Office 5-53-70 Jingumae, Shibuya-ku, Tokyo, 150-8925 Japan. T. +81354671212. Fax +81334992828.
UNU Office at the UN 2 UN Plaza, Room DC2-2060 United Nations, New York NY 10017, USA. T. +12129636387. Fax +12123719454.
UNU Office at UNESCO c/o UNESCO, Bureau 7B 4-06, 1 rue Miollis, 75732 Paris CEDEX 15, France. T. +33145684642. Fax +33140659186.
URL: http://www.unu.edu/

History 6 Dec 1973. Established by resolution 3081 (XXVIII) of the General Assembly of the United Nations, approving the Charter of the University. Originally proposed in 1969 by UN Secretary-General U Thant (1909-1974). Commenced operations Sep 1975. An organ of *United Nations (UN, #20515)* in the framework of *United Nations System (#20635)*, linked to the General Assembly and to *ECOSOC (#05331)*. **Aims** Contribute, through collaborative research and education, to efforts to resolve pressing global problems of human survival, development and welfare that are the concern of the UN, its Peoples and Member States.
Structure Council composed of 13 appointed members (serving a 3-year term, in an individual capacity), 3 ex-officio members (UN Secretary-General, UNESCO Director-General and UNITAR Executive Director) and UNU Rector. Rector, based at UNU Headquarters in Tokyo (Japan), assisted by 2 Vice-Rectors at headquarters and one Vice-Rector, based in Bonn (Germany). Liaison offices: UN Secretariat – New York NY (USA); UNESCO – Paris (France). Institutes and programmes (13), coordinated by *UNU Centre*:
- *UNU Institute on Comparative Regional Integration Studies (UNU-CRIS, #20717)*, Bruges (Belgium), set up 2011;
- *United Nations University Institute for Environment and Human Security (UNU-EHS, #20645)*, Bonn (Germany), set up 2003;
- *UNU Institute for Integrated Management of Material Fluxes and of Resources (UNU-FLORES, see: #20642)*, Dresden (Germany), set up 2012;
- *United Nations University Institute on Globalization, Culture and Mobility (UNU-GCM, #20646)*, Barcelona (Spain), set up 2012;
- *United Nations University Institute for the Advanced Study of Sustainability (UNU-IAS, #20643)*, Tokyo (Japan), set up 2014;
- *UNU International Institute for Global Health (UNI-IIGH, #20719)*, Kuala Lumpur (Malaysia), set up 2007;
- *United Nations University Institute on Computing and Society (UNU-CS, #20644)*, Macau, set up 1992;
- *UNU Institute for Natural Resources in Africa (UNU-INRA, #20718)*, Accra (Ghana), set up 1990;
- *United Nations University – Institute for Water, Environment and Health (UNU-INWEH, see: #20642)*, Hamilton (Canada), set up 1996;
- *United Nations University – Maastricht Economic and Social Research Institute on Innovation and Technology (UNU-MERIT, #20647)*, Maastricht (Netherlands), set up 1990;
- *UNU World Institute for Development Economics Research (UNU-WIDER, #20722)*, Helsinki (Finland), set up 1985;
- *UNU Programme for Biotechnology in Latin America and the Caribbean (UNU/BIOLAC, see: #20642)*, Caracas (Venezuela), commenced 1988;
- Iceland-Based Programme, consisting of 4 components: UNU Fisheries Training Programme (UNU-FTP); UNU Geothermal Training Programme (UNU-GTP); UNU Land Restoration Training Programme (UNU-LRT); UNU Gender Equality Studies and Training Programme (UNU-GEST).

Languages English, French, Spanish. **Staff** 679.00 FTE, paid. Negotiations through *UNU Staff Council (#20721)*. **Finance** No funds from UN regular budget, but entirely financed through voluntary contributions made by governments, agencies, international organizations, foundations and other donors, as well as from investment income. Budget (2012): US$ 71.4 million. **Activities** Training/education; capacity building; research/documentation; knowledge management/information dissemination. **Events** *Climate and SDGs Conference* Tokyo (Japan) 2022, *Global Conference on Strengthening Synergies between the Paris Agreement and the 2030 Agenda for Sustainable Development* Tokyo (Japan) 2022, *Seminar on Gender Activism, Politics, and Intersectionality in the Era of COVID-19* Tokyo (Japan) 2022, *Seminar on Working Local, Thinking Global Seminar UNDP's Work in Malaysia Towards Advancing the SDGs* Tokyo (Japan) 2022, *Worlds of Blue – Tokyo Blue Talk* Tokyo (Japan) 2022. **Publications** *Food and Nutrition Bulletin* (4 a year); *Global Environmental Change: Human and Policy Dimensions* (4 a year); *Journal of Food Composition and Analysis* (4 a year); *Mountain Research and Development* (4 a year) – jointly with International Mountain Society (IMS); *Global Governance* (3 a year) – journal; *UNU Update* – electronic newsletter. Books in social sciences, humanities, and pure and applied natural sciences based on or related to UNU research. Annual Report. Information Services: UNU has its own printing press producing academic publications and cooperating in production of journals (UNU Press). **Information Services** *Global Environment Information Centre (GEIC)*.
Members Associated institutions (20) in 15 countries:
Australia, Brazil, Chile, China, Egypt, Germany, India, Japan, Kenya, Korea Rep, Mexico, Netherlands, Thailand, UK, USA.
IGO Relations Agreements with:
- *ASEAN (#01141)*;
- *Asian-African Legal Consultative Organization (AALCO, #01303)*;
- *Caribbean Regional Fisheries Mechanism (CRFM, #03547)*;
- *Common Market for Eastern and Southern Africa (COMESA, #04296)*;
- *FAO (#09260)*;
- *International Center for Agricultural Research in the Dry Areas (ICARDA, #12466)*;
- *International Centre for Genetic Engineering and Biotechnology (ICGEB, #12494)*;
- *International Organization for Migration (IOM, #14454)*;
- *OAS (#17629)*;
- *Secretariat of the Pacific Regional Environment Programme (SPREP, #19205)*;
- *Southeast Asian Ministers of Education Organization (SEAMEO, #19774)*;
- *UNEP (#20299)*;
- *UNCTAD (#20285)*;
- *UNDP (#20292)*;
- *UNESCO (#20322)*;
- *UNHCR (#20327)*;
- *United Nations Economic Commission for Africa (ECA, #20554)*;
- *United Nations Office for the Coordination of Humanitarian Affairs (OCHA, #20593)*;
- *United Nations Office for Disaster Risk Reduction (UNDRR, #20595)*;
- *United Nations Office of the Special Advisor on Africa (OSAA, see: #20515)*;
- *University for Peace (UPEACE, #20702)*;
- *WHO (#20950)*;
- *World Intellectual Property Organization (WIPO, #21593)*.

Cooperates with:
- *African Development Bank (ADB, #00283)*;
- *Arab Gulf Programme for United Nations Development Organizations (AGFUND, #00971)*;
- *Asian Development Bank (ADB, #01422)*;
- *Commonwealth Secretariat (#04362)*;
- *Federation of Arab Scientific Research Councils (FASRC, no recent information)*;
- *Global Environment Facility (GEF, #10346)*;
- *ILO (#11123)*;
- *Institute of Nutrition of Central America and Panama (INCAP, #11285)*;
- *Inter-American Development Bank (IDB, #11427)*;
- *Intergovernmental Panel on Climate Change (IPCC, #11499)*;
- *International Bank for Reconstruction and Development (IBRD, #12317)*;
- *International Development Research Centre (IDRC, #13162)*;
- *International Fund for Agricultural Development (IFAD, #13692)*;
- *International Monetary Fund (IMF, #14180)*;
- *International Trade Centre (ITC, #15703)*;
- *Joint United Nations Programme on HIV/AIDS (UNAIDS, #16149)*;
- *Latin American Faculty of Social Sciences (#16316)*;
- *Office of the United Nations High Commissioner for Human Rights (OHCHR, #17697)*;
- *OPEC Fund for International Development (OFID, #17745)*;
- *Organisation for the Prohibition of Chemical Weapons (OPCW, #17823)*;
- *Pan American Health Organization (PAHO, #18108)*;
- *Secretariat of the Basel Convention (SBC, #19196)*;
- *Secretariat of the Convention on Biological Diversity (SCBD, #19197)*;
- *Secretariat of the United Nations Convention to Combat Desertification (Secretariat of the UNCCD, #19208)*;
- *UNICEF (#20332)*;
- *UNIDO (#20336)*;
- *United Nations Economic and Social Commission for Asia and the Pacific (ESCAP, #20557)*;
- *United Nations Economic and Social Commission for Western Asia (ESCWA, #20558)*;
- *United Nations Framework Convention on Climate Change – Secretariat (UNFCCC, #20564)*;
- *United Nations Human Settlements Programme (UN-Habitat, #20572)*;
- *United Nations Institute for Disarmament Research (UNIDIR, #20575)*;
- *United Nations Institute for Training and Research (UNITAR, #20576)*;
- *United Nations International Research and Training Institute for the Advancement of Women (UN-INSTRAW, inactive)*;
- United Nations Office of Legal Affairs (UNOLA);
- United Nations Office for Outer Space Affairs (UNOOSA);
- United Nations Department of Peace-keeping Operations;
- *United Nations Population Fund (UNFPA, #20612)*;
- *United Nations Research Institute for Social Development (UNRISD, #20623)*;
- *United Nations Special Committee on Peace-keeping Operations (#20628)*;
- *United Nations Volunteers (UNV, #20650)*;
- *World Food Programme (WFP, #21510)*;
- *World Meteorological Organization (WMO, #21649)*;
- *World Trade Organization (WTO, #21864)*.

Member of: *UN-OCEANS (#20711)*; *UN-Water (#20723)*. Instrumental in setting up: *United Nations University Food and Nutrition Programme for Human and Social Development (UNU/FNP, inactive)*.
NGO Relations Member of: *Regional Energy Resources Information Center (RERIC, #18780)*; *Sustainable Development Solutions Network (SDSN, #20054)*. Agreements with: *African Academy of Sciences (AAS, #00193)*; *African Centre for the Constructive Resolution of Disputes (ACCORD)*; *Association of African Universities (AAU, #02361)*; *Consortium on Science, Technology and Innovation for the South (COSTIS, no recent information)*; *International Cell Research Organization (ICRO, #12463)*; *International Foundation for Science (IFS, #13677)*; *International Ocean Institute (IOI, #14394)*; *International Union for Conservation of Nature and Natural Resources (IUCN, #15766)*.

Instrumental in setting up: *Higher Education Sustainability Initiative (HESI)*; *United Nations University Institute for Sustainability and Peace (UNU-ISP, inactive)*; *UNU International Institute for the Alliance of Civilizations (UNU-IIAOC, inactive)*; *UNU Institute of Advanced Studies (UNU/IAS, inactive)*; *International Conflict Research Institute (INCORE, see: #20642)*, Coleraine (Northern Ireland), jointly with the University of Ulster. [2021/XF2488/**F***]

♦ United Nations University Food and Nutrition Programme for Human and Social Development (inactive)

♦ United Nations University Institute for the Advanced Study of Sustainability (UNU-IAS) 20643

Main Office 5-53-70 Jingumae, Shibuya-ku, Tokyo, 150-8925 Japan.
URL: http://ias.unu.edu/

History 1 Jan 2014, as one of 13 institutes within *United Nations University (UNU, #20642)*, on the merger of *UNU Institute of Advanced Studies (UNU/IAS, inactive)* and *United Nations University Institute for Sustainability and Peace (UNU-ISP, inactive)*. **Aims** Advance efforts towards a more sustainable future, through policy-oriented research and capacity development focused on sustainability and its social, economic and environmental dimensions. **Activities** Training/education. **Events** *Catalyzing Nature-based Solutions for Biodiversity, Climate Change and Sustainable Development through Ecosystem Restoration* Tokyo (Japan) 2022, *Interlinkages between Paris Agreement and SDGs: Global and Local Initiatives* Tokyo (Japan) 2022, *Seminar on Community-based Activities and Governance for Seascape Restoration* Tokyo (Japan) 2022, *The Role of Multi-Stakeholder Partnerships to Accelerate Local Action on Climate and Sustainable Society* Tokyo (Japan) 2022, *Working Together for Everyone's Well-being: The Satoyama Initiative and Building Back Better* Tokyo (Japan) 2022. **NGO Relations** Participant in: *Global Partnership on Local and Subnational Action for Biodiversity (#10536)*. Partner of: *Asian Co-Benefits Partnership (ACP, #01382)*. Member of: *Institute for Global Environmental Strategies (IGES, #11266)*. Hosts: *International Partnership for the Satoyama Initiative (IPSI, #14525)*. [2020/XJ8611/j/**E**]

♦ United Nations University Institute on Computing and Society (UNU-CS) 20644

Dir UN University, Casa Silva Mendes, Est do Engenheiro Trigo No 4, Macau, Macau. T. +85328712930. E-mail: cs-info@unu.edu.
URL: http://cs.unu.edu/

History Dec 1989, within the framework of *United Nations University (UNU, #20642)*, on approval by UNU Council, as *UNU International Institute for Software Technology (UNU-IIST) – Institut international de l'UNU pour la technologie des logiciels (UNU-IITL)*. Formally came into being 12 Mar 1991, with the signing in Macau of agreements between UNU, the Governor of Macau and the Governments of Portugal and the People's Republic of China. Activities started Jul 1992. Previously known as *UNU Computing and Society (UNU-CS)*. Present title adopted 2015. **Aims** Focus on key challenges faced by developing societies through high-impact innovations in computing and communication technologies. **Structure** International Advisory Board; Director. **Languages** English. **Staff** 10-30. **Finance** Endowment fund of US$ 20,000,000 by governments of China, Macau and Portugal; annual contributions from Macau Foundation. **Activities** Training/education; research and development; projects/programmes; events/meetings; publishing activities. **Events** *International Workshop on Formal Aspects of Component Software* Oslo (Norway) 2011, *ICS : international conference on software development process / Biennial World Computer Congress / General Assembly* Beijing (China) 2000, *International symposium on software industry in developing countries* Beijing (China) 2000, *Conference on mathematics and its role in civilization* Macau 2000, *Global Chinese conference on computer in education* Macau 1999. **Publications** Reports; conference papers; journal articles; white papers; book chapters.

Members Individuals and institutions in 50 countries and territories:
Argentina, Australia, Azerbaijan, Bangladesh, Belarus, Botswana, Brazil, Bulgaria, Burkina Faso, Cameroon, China, Côte d'Ivoire, Cuba, Czechia, Denmark, Egypt, Ethiopia, France, Gabon, Germany, Hong Kong, India, Indonesia, Japan, Kazakhstan, Korea DPR, Korea Rep, Malawi, Malaysia, Mongolia, Nepal, Netherlands, Nigeria, Pakistan, Paraguay, Philippines, Poland, Portugal, Romania, Russia, Senegal, Singapore, South Africa, Tajikistan, Thailand, Tunisia, UK, Ukraine, Uruguay, Vietnam.

NGO Relations Member of: *Alliance for Affordable Internet (A4AI, #00651)*. [2018.09.06/XE3096/j/**E**]

♦ United Nations University Institute for Environment and Human Security (UNU-EHS) 20645

Institut de l'Environnement et de la Sécurité Humaine de l'Université des Nations Unies – Instituto de Medio Ambiente y Seguridad Humana de la Universidad de las Naciones Unidas

Dir UN Campus, Platz der Vereinten Nationene 1, 53113 Bonn, Germany. T. +492288150202. Fax +492288150299. E-mail: info@ehs.unu.edu.
URL: http://www.ehs.unu.edu/

History Founded Dec 2003, as an institute of *United Nations University (UNU, #20642)*. **Aims** Advance human security through knowledge-based approaches to reducing vulnerability and environmental risks. **Languages** English. **Finance** Supported by the German Federal Ministry of Education and Research and the Ministry of Science and Research of the State of North Rhine-Westphalia. **Activities** Research/documentation; training/education. **Events** *Workshop on Earth Observation-Based Information Products for Drought Risk on a National Basis* Bonn (Germany) 2017, *International conference on environment, forced migration and social vulnerability* Bonn (Germany) 2008, *Policy dialogue on environmentally induced migration* Brussels (Belgium) 2008, *Workshop on migration, social vulnerability, and environmental research* Munich (Germany) 2008, *Queer Asian sites* Sydney, NSW (Australia) 2007. **Publications** All publications available online. **IGO Relations** Partner of: *Group on Earth Observations (GEO, #10735)*; *West African Science Service Center on Climate Change and Adapted Land Use (WASCAL, #20897)*. **NGO Relations** Member of (1): *Global Alliance of Disaster Research Institutes (GADRI, #10194)*. Partner of: *Global Forum on Law, Justice and Development (GFLJD, #10373)*. [2019.07.11/XM1096/j/**E**]

♦ United Nations University Institute on Globalization, Culture and Mobility (UNU-GCM) 20646

Dir Sant Manual Pavilion, 1st Floor, Sant Pau Art Nouveau Site, C/Sant Antoni Maria Claret 167, 08025 Barcelona, Spain. T. +34935565991.
URL: http://gcm.unu.edu/

History Set up 2012, as one of 13 institutions within *United Nations University (UNU, #20642)*. **Aims** Contribute to good governance, cultural diversity, democracy and human rights through a better understanding of cultural mobility and diversity in the context of globalization. **Languages** English. **Staff** 10.00 FTE, paid. **Publications** *Mosaics* (12 a year) – newsletter. [2016.10.19/XJ8613/j/**E**]

♦ United Nations University Institute for Natural Resources in Africa / see UNU Institute for Natural Resources in Africa (#20718)
♦ United Nations University – Institute for Water, Environment and Health (see: #20642)

♦ United Nations University – Maastricht Economic and Social Research Institute on Innovation and Technology (UNU-MERIT) 20647

Dir Boschstraat 24, 6211 AX Maastricht, Netherlands. T. +31433884400. Fax +31433884499. E-mail: info@merit.unu.edu.
URL: http://www.merit.unu.edu/

History Set up May 1989, Maastricht (Netherlands), as *UNU Institute for New Technologies (UNU/INTECH) – Institut de l'UNU pour les technologies nouvelles*, as a research and training centre of the *United Nations University (UNU, #20642)*. Became operational Oct 1990. Subsequently changed title to *United Nations University – Maastricht Economic and Social Research and Training Centre on Innovation and Technology*, 1 Jan 2006, when merged with Maastricht Economic Research Institute on Innovation and Technology (MERIT). Since Dec 2010, includes Maastricht Graduate School of Governance. **Aims** Explore how countries can catch up in the unequal global playing field of the 21st century, without increasing inequality and social exclusion; analyse knowledge flows at regional and global levels, and their impact on local development, employment and productivity; train specialists in order to strengthen democratic governance in domestic and international organizations. **Structure** Board; UN Staff; Contractors. **Languages** English. **Staff** 74.00 FTE, paid. **Finance** Financed by income from endowment granted by Dutch Government, which also provides annual operating contribution. Project funds from international funding bodies, including: *European Commission (EC, #06633)*; *Fundación Andina para el Desarrollo Tecnológico (Tecnos, no recent information)*; *International Institute of Social Studies, The Hague (ISS)*; *Inter-American Development Bank (IDB, #11427)*; *International Development Research Centre (IDRC, #13162)*; *UNIDO (#20336)*. **Activities** Research/documentation; training/education; events/meetings. **Events** *Base of the Pyramid Symposium* Tokyo (Japan) 2013, *DIME Final Conference* Maastricht (Netherlands) 2011, *ICIM : international conference on innovation and management* Maastricht (Netherlands) 2008, *Global seminar* Jeju (Korea Rep) 2006, *Conference on hydrogen fuel cells and alternatives in the transport sector* Maastricht (Netherlands) 2005. **Publications** Books; articles; briefs; working/discussion papers; theses; proceedings; conference presentations. **Members** Not a membership organization. **IGO Relations** Collaborates with: *FAO (#09260)*; *ILO (#11123)*; *International Bank for Reconstruction and Development (IBRD, #12317)* (World Bank); *UNCTAD (#20285)*; *UNICEF (#20332)*; *UNIDO (#20336)*; *World Intellectual Property Organization (WIPO, #21593)*. **NGO Relations** Associate member of: *European Association of Development Research and Training Institutes (EADI, #06012)*. Collaborations/partnerships with: *Brookings Institution (BI)*; *Research Policy Institute, Lund (RPI)*; *United Nations University Institute on Computing and Society (UNU-CS, #20644)*; *UNU Institute on Comparative Regional Integration Studies (UNU-CRIS, #20717)*; UNU Media Centre; UNU Office at UNESCO; UNU Press; UNU Vice Rectorate in Europe. [2017.10.11/XE3003/j/**E**]

♦ United Nations University – Maastricht Economic and Social Research and Training Centre on Innovation and Technology / see United Nations University – Maastricht Economic and Social Research Institute on Innovation and Technology (#20647)

♦ United Nations Voluntary Fund on Disability 20648

Fonds de contributions volontaires des Nations Unies pour les handicapés

Contact Secretariat Convention Rights op Persons with Disabilities, Div for Social Policy and Development – DESA, 2 United Nations Plaza, Room DC2-1372, New York NY 10017, USA. T. +12129631996. Fax +12129630111. E-mail: enable@un.org.
URL: https://www.un.org/development/desa/disabilities/about-us/united-nations-voluntary-fund-on-disability.html

History 1978. Established within the framework of *United Nations (UN, #20515)*, pursuant to General Assembly resolution 32/133 of 16 Dec 1977, which, inter alia, called upon UN member States to make contributions for the *International Year of the Disabled Persons (IYDP)* in 1981. Became operational 1980. Administered by the Secretariat of *Convention on the Rights of Persons with Disabilities (CRPD, 2006)*, within United Nations Department of Economic and Social Affairs. Former names and other names: *Trust Fund for the International Year of Disabled Persons* – former (1978 to 1985); *Voluntary Fund for the United Nations Decade of Disabled Persons* – former (1985 to 1992). **Aims** Provide governments and organizations of persons with disabilities with support for catalytic and innovative projects of direct benefit to disabled persons, especially in *developing countries*. **Events** *Inter-agency meeting on the United Nations decade of disabled persons* Vienna (Austria) 1991, *Inter-agency meeting on the United Nations decade of disabled persons* Vienna (Austria) 1988. **Publications** *Disabled Persons Bulletin* (3 a year). **IGO Relations** *ECOSOC (#05331)*; *United Nations Commission for Social Development (CSocD, #20535)*. [2020/XF2096/f/**F***]

♦ United Nations Voluntary Trust Fund for Assistance in Mine Action (UN VTF) 20649

Contact United Nations, New York NY 10017, USA. T. +12129631234. Fax +12127582718.

History 1994. Established as an inter-agency mechanism by *United Nations (UN, #20515)* General Assembly (A/RES/49/215). Former names and other names: *UN Voluntary Trust Fund for Assistance to Mine Clearance* – former; *United Nations Voluntary Trust Fund for Assistance to Mine Clearance* – former; *Fonds d'affectation spéciale pour l'assistance à la lutte antimines* – former. **Aims** Support a coherent multilateral response to risks posed by mines and explosive remnants of war, including cluster munitions as well as by other conventional explosive hazards. **Structure** Managed by *United Nations Mine Action Service (UNMAS, #20585)*. **Finance** Sources: government support. Annual budget: 71,622,723 USD (2019). [2019/XK0968/f/**F***]

♦ United Nations Voluntary Trust Fund for Assistance to Mine Clearance / see United Nations Voluntary Trust Fund for Assistance in Mine Action (#20649)

♦ United Nations Volunteers (UNV) 20650

Volontaires des Nations Unies (VNU) – Voluntarios de las Naciones Unidas (VNU) – Freiwilligen Programm der Vereinten Nationen

Postal address Postfach 260 111, 53153 Bonn, Germany.
Street address UN Campus, Platz der Vereinten Nationen 1, 53113 Bonn, Germany. T. +49228815. Fax +492288152001.
URL: http://www.unv.org/

History 1 Jan 1971. Established by authority of General Assembly of *United Nations (UN, #20515)* Resolution 2659 (XXV) of 7 Dec 1970, and at the request of UN member countries in order to be a development partner of the UN system. Declaration of Sanaa (Yemen) adopted 7-13 Mar 1982. Declaration of Maseru adopted 16-21 Nov 1986. Kathmandu (Nepal) Statement, 1-6 Dec 1991. UNV headquarters moved from Geneva (Switzerland) to Bonn (Germany) in 1996. **Aims** Contribute to peace and development through volunteerism worldwide. **Structure** Based in Bonn (Germany). Regional Offices (5); Field Units (about 60). Administered by UNDP. **Languages** English, French, Spanish. **Staff** 150.00 FTE, paid. **Finance** Main sources: UNDP; contributions from donor governments through UNV Special Voluntary Fund (SVF). **Activities** Advocacy/lobbying/activism; networking/liaising; events/meetings; awareness raising. **Events** *International Volunteer Conference* Busan (Korea Rep) 2017, *Joint Forum on Volunteering for Peace and Development* Seoul (Korea Rep) 2015, *International symposium on volunteering* Geneva (Switzerland) 2001, *Seminar on urban poverty and environment in Latin America* Villa de Leiva (Colombia) 1993, *UNV high-level intergovernmental meeting* Maseru (Lesotho) 1986. **Publications** Annual Report; thematic booklets; promotional flyers; evaluations and project reports; news releases; fact sheets; videos.

IGO Relations Close cooperation with:
- *Arab Gulf Programme for United Nations Development Organizations (AGFUND, #00971)*;
- Asian Development Bank;
- *ECOSOC (#05331)*;
- *FAO (#09260)*;
- *ILO (#11123)*;
- *International Bank for Reconstruction and Development (IBRD, #12317)*;
- *International Civil Aviation Organization (ICAO, #12581)*;
- *International Fund for Agricultural Development (IFAD, #13692)*;
- *International Maritime Organization (IMO, #14102)*;
- *International Organization for Migration (IOM, #14454)*;
- *International Telecommunication Union (ITU, #15673)*;
- *International Trade Centre (ITC, #15703)*;
- *UNEP (#20299)*;
- *UNCTAD (#20285)*;
- *UNDP (#20292)*;
- *UNESCO (#20322)*;
- *UNHCR (#20327)*;
- *UNICEF (#20332)*;
- *UNIDO (#20336)*;
- *United Nations Capital Development Fund (UNCDF, #20524)*;
- *United Nations Economic Commission for Africa (ECA, #20554)*;
- *United Nations Economic Commission for Latin America and the Caribbean (ECLAC, #20556)*;
- *United Nations Economic and Social Commission for Asia and the Pacific (ESCAP, #20557)*;
- *United Nations Framework Convention on Climate Change – Secretariat (UNFCCC, #20564)*;
- *United Nations Human Settlements Programme (UN-Habitat, #20572)*;
- *United Nations Institute for Training and Research (UNITAR, #20576)*;
- *United Nations Office at Vienna (UNOV, #20604)*;
- *United Nations Population Fund (UNFPA, #20612)*;
- *Universal Postal Union (UPU, #20682)*;
- *WHO (#20950)*;
- *World Food Programme (WFP, #21510)*;
- *World Meteorological Organization (WMO, #21649)*;
- *World Tourism Organization (UNWTO, #21861)*.

[2021/XF4104/**F***]

♦ United Nations Watch (internationally oriented national body)
♦ United Nations Women's Guild – Geneva (internationally oriented national body)

♦ United Nations Women's Guild – New York (UNWG – New York) ... 20651

Cercle féminin des Nations Unies – New York – Circulo femenino de Naciones Unidas – Nueva York

Dir One UN Plaza, Room DC1 0775, New York NY 10017, USA. T. +12129638279. Fax +12129633121. E-mail: unwg@un.org.
URL: http://www.unwg.org/

History 28 Apr 1948, Great Neck, NY (USA). Current constitution and bylaws adopted 2013. **Aims** Assist children in need and/or mother-child care programmes throughout the world; serve as a mutual bond and center of interest for women connected with the United Nations Organizations around the world. **Structure** General Meeting (annual); Board; Secretariat. **Finance** Sources: members' dues. **NGO Relations** Close contact with: *United Nations Women's Guild – Geneva (UNWG – Geneva)*; *United Nations Women's Guild of Vienna (UNWG-Vienna).* [2020/XG6794/v/**E**]

♦ United Nations Women's Guild of Vienna (internationally oriented national body)
♦ United Nations of Youth / see United Network of Young Peacebuilders (#20653)

♦ United Nations Youth Associations Network (UNYANET) 20652

Réseau des associations de la jeunesse pour les nations unies – Internationales Jugendnetzwerk für die Vereinten Nationen

Pres Johannesgasse 2-2-32, 1010 Vienna, Austria.
URL: http://unyanet.org/

History Founded 5 Aug 2011, Vienna (Austria), at *United Nations Office at Vienna (UNOV, #20604).* **Aims** Facilitate cooperation between UNY(S)As; promote the idea of UNY(S)As among political institutions and civil society in general; support the establishment of UNY(S)As in countries without such institutions; facilitate fundraising; exchange ideas, know-how and best practices; establish common projects, programmes and initiatives. **Structure** General Assembly; Executive Board; Working Groups. **Languages** English. **Staff** Voluntary. **Finance** Members' dues. Project funding. **Activities** Events/meetings; training/education; advocacy/lobbying/activism. **Events** *General Assembly* Bucharest (Romania) 2015, *General Assembly* Rome (Italy) 2014, *General Assembly* Rome (Italy) 2014, *Summit* Ljubljana (Slovenia) 2013.
Members Associations (17) in 17 countries:
Austria, Bangladesh, Canada, Denmark, Finland, Germany, Ghana, Italy, Norway, Romania, Russia, Serbia, Slovenia, Spain, Switzerland, Türkiye, Uganda.
Observers in 3 countries:
Cameroon, Indonesia, Poland.
Included in the above, 1 organization listed in this Yearbook:
United Nations Youth and Student Association of Austria – Academic Forum for Foreign Affairs (UNYSA-AUSTRIA-AFA). [2017.05.09/XJ5753/**E**]

♦ United Nations Youth and Student Association of Austria – Academic Forum for Foreign Affairs (internationally oriented national body)
♦ United Nation World Peace Association (internationally oriented national body)
♦ United Networks of International Corporate Events Organizers (unconfirmed)

♦ United Network of Young Peacebuilders (UNOY) 20653

Sec Intl Coordinator, Laan van Meerdervoort 70, 2517 AN The Hague, Netherlands. T. +31703647799. Fax +31703622633. E-mail: info@unoy.org.
URL: http://www.unoy.org/

History Jun 1989, Netherlands. Founded Jun 1989, Handel (Netherlands), at a meeting of 35 young people from 5 continents when Charter was drawn up, under the title *United Nations of Youth (UNOY Foundation).* Also referred to as *UNOY Peacebuilders.* Registered in accordance with Dutch law. **Aims** Work towards establishing peaceful societies; facilitate capacity development and support advocacy work of members. **Structure** International Steering Group; Board; International Secretariat, based in The Hague (Netherlands). **Languages** English, French. **Finance** Institutional and project funding from national and international donors, including: *Anna Lindh Euro-Mediterranean Foundation for the Dialogue between Cultures (Anna Lindh Foundation, #00847)*; *Catholic Organization for Relief and Development (Cordaid)*; *Council of Europe (CE, #04881)* – North South Centre; *European Youth Foundation (EYF, #09141)*; *European Commission (EC, #06633)* – Erasmus+; Haella Stichting; Manpower Group; *Open Society Foundations (OSF, #17763)*; *Oxfam Novib.* **Activities** Advocacy/lobbying/activism; capacity building; networking/liaising; research/documentation; training/education. **Events** *Young Peacebuilders Forum* Bogota (Colombia) 2019, *Forum* The Hague (Netherlands) 2018, *Annual African Students conference* The Hague (Netherlands) 2010, *Annual African Students conference* The Hague (Netherlands) 2009, *Annual African Students conference* The Hague (Netherlands) 2008. **Publications** *Peaceful Digests* (weekly); *Peace it Together Newsletter* (12 a year) – electronic; *UNOY Newsletter* (12 a year). *Guiding Principles Youth Participation in Peacebuilding* (2014); *Mainstreaming Peace Education: Methodologies, Approaches and Visions – A Practitioner's Manual* (2014); *Young and Green Peace* (2014); *Recipeace for Dialogue* (2013); *Looking at Collaboration in North-South Networks* (2011); *New Fundraising Trends Guide* (2011); *20 years of UNOY* (2009); *Youth Advocacy for a Culture of Peace – A Reflective Guide for Action in Europe* (2008); *UNOY's Post-2015 Report.*
Members Active; Associate. Organizations (58) in 36 countries:
Afghanistan, Argentina, Armenia, Bangladesh, Belarus, Belgium, Benin, Burundi, Cameroon, Cape Verde, Colombia, Congo DR, Egypt, Eritrea, Estonia, Georgia, Germany, Ghana, Hungary, India, Italy, Kenya, Liberia, Mexico, Nepal, Nigeria, Northern Ireland, Pakistan, Palestine, Peru, Philippines, Romania, Sierra Leone, Somalia, Spain, Sweden.
Consultative Status Consultative status granted from: *ECOSOC (#05331)* (Special). [2014.11.20/XF1203/**F**]

♦ United Paintball Federation (UPBF) 20654

Gen Sec address not obtained. E-mail: info@upbf.net.
Pres address not obtained.
URL: https://upbf.net/

History France. Registration: No/ID: 2070, Start date: 20 Apr 2019, France. **Aims** Unite, promote and support all the national paintball federations worldwide, coordinate their common interests and goals while preserving their autonomy, promoting their values. **Structure** Executive Committee; Commissions. **Activities** Sporting activities.
Members Full in countries:
Belgium, Brazil, Bulgaria, Canada, Croatia, Estonia, Finland, France, Gabon, Germany, India, Italy, Latvia, Malaysia, Moldova, Netherlands, Norway, Poland, Portugal, Russia, Singapore, South Africa, Spain, Sweden, Türkiye, UK, Ukraine, USA.
NGO Relations Member of (1): *International Federation for Sports Officials (IFSO, #13555).* Represented confederations: *African Paintball Federation (AFPBF, #00408)*; Asian and Pacific Paintball Federation; *European Paintball Federation (EPBF, #08132)*; Middle Eastern Paintball Federation; North Central American Paintball Federation; South American Paintball Federation. [2022.06.14/AA1939/**C**]

♦ United Parent Projects Muscular Dystrophy / see World Duchenne Organization (#21366)
♦ United for Peace and Justice (internationally oriented national body)

♦ United Peace Keepers Federal Council (UNPKFC) 20655

President 88/1-9 Moo, Khu Fang Nuea Sub-district, Nong Chok District, Bangkok, 10530, Thailand. T. +66021700198 – +66992626288 – +66930810521. E-mail: info@unpkfc.org.
URL: http://unpkfc.org/

History 13 Jan 2020, Bangkok (Thailand). Established with the objectives of collaborating with the Government of Thailand, UN Agencies and other International Organizations for supporting the Peacekeeping missions and mandates of the United Nations. Former names and other names: *United Nations Peace Keeping Forces Council (UNPKFC)* – former (13 Jan 2020 to Jun 2021); *United Nations Peace Keepers Federal Council (UNPKFC)* – former (Jun 2021 to Jan 2022). Registration: EU Transparency Register, No/ID: 444434744465-79, Start date: 22 Oct 2021. **Aims** Support, promote, and implement the United Nations mandate on "Peacebuilding" in accordance with the Universal Declaration of Human Rights and UN SDG Goals in all 17 fields. **Structure** Executive Council; Advisory Board; Regional Directors; Goodwill and Peace Ambassadors. **Languages** English, Thai. **Activities** Conflict resolution; events/meetings; financial and/or material support; humanitarian/emergency aid; religious activities; training/education. Active in: Argentina, Bangladesh, Brunei Darussalam, Cambodia, Georgia, India, Indonesia, Laos, Malaysia, Myanmar, Nepal, Oman, Philippines, Singapore, Thailand, Timor-Leste, Vietnam. **Events** *UNPKFC MUN2021 Model United Nations* Bangkok (Thailand) 2021, *World Humanitarian Day Meeting* Bangkok (Thailand) 2021, *World Youth Skills Day Annual Conference* Bangkok (Thailand) 2021, *International Day of UN Peacekeepers Conference* Mueang Samut Prakan (Thailand) 2021. **IGO Relations** Partner of (5): Europolice Federation; *Internet Governance Forum (IGF, #15950)*; *UNHCR (#20327)*; United Forces International Organization; World Inter-Religious Council. [2022.03.11/XM8954/**E**]

♦ United Plastics Distributors Association / see International Association of Plastics Distribution

♦ United Poets Laureate International 20656

Main Office 64 Vienna St, Merville Park, 1709 Parañaque METRO MANILA, Philippines.
Facebook: https://www.facebook.com/unitedpoetslaureateinternational/

History 1963, by Dr Amado M Yuzon. **Aims** Promote friendly relations through the exchange and cultivation of poetry. **Structure** President, Executive Vice-President and Regional Vice-Presidents, elected for two year terms. Secretary-Treasurer, appointed by President. Territories (8), some sub-divided into regions: North America (Canada, Western USA, Eastern USA); Europe (Western, Eastern); Poets-in-Exile; British Isles; Oceania; Asia (Mainland, Islands); South America; Africa. **Finance** Annual members' dues: US$25. **Activities** Awards, laureateships. *World Congress of Poets.* **Events** *World Congress of Poets* Rohnert Park, CA (USA) 2016, *World Congress of Poets* Osaka (Japan) 2014, *World Congress of Poets* Sydney, NSW (Australia) 2013, *World congress of poets* Larissa (Greece) 2011, *World congress of poets* Managua (Nicaragua) 2009. **Publications** *World Brotherhood and Peace Through Poetry* – journal. *Laurel Leaves.* **Members** Regular, Associate, Honorary.Membership countries not specified. **NGO Relations** *World University (WU).* [2019/XD8908/**D**]

♦ United Presbyterian Frontier Fellowship / see Presbyterian Frontier Fellowship
♦ United Press International (internationally oriented national body)
♦ United Purpose (internationally oriented national body)

♦ United Regions Organisation/FOGAR 20657

Organisation des Régions Unies (ORU/FOGAR) – Organización de Regiones Unidas (ORU/FOGAR)

SG Rocafort 242 bis, 3rd Floor, 08029 Barcelona, Spain. T. +34607050705. E-mail: secretariat@regionsunies-fogar.org.
General Coordinator address not obtained.
URL: http://www.regionsunies-fogar.org/

History 2007, Marseille (France). Current articles of association adopted 1 Oct 2013, Rabat (Morocco). Former names and other names: *United Regions Organization/ Forum of Global Association of Regional Governments and Regions Associations* – full title; *Global Regions Forum* – former. Registration: Spain. **Aims** Ensure that the voice of regional governments and federal states is heard in globalization as well as promote the participation of regional governments in the design and management of education and health policies, together with the construction of social infrastructure; promote sustainable development, which takes account of the environment; organize new strategic governance rules, including at the sub-state level of government; advocate new governance based on the recognition of the diversity of cultures and lifestyles; promote initiatives for mutual knowledge and cooperation between regional governments and federal states worldwide. **Structure** General Assembly; Bureau; Presidency; Secretary General. Financial Committee. **Finance** Sources: members' dues. **Activities** Awards/prizes/competitions; events/meetings; projects/programmes. **Events** *General Assembly* 2021, *General Assembly* 2020, *General Assembly* 2019, *General Assembly* Rabat (Morocco) 2018, *General Assembly* San Sebastian (Spain) 2017. **Publications** *ORU Newsletter.* **Members** Geographical or thematic networks of regional governments and federal states; regional governments and federal states on an individual basis. Membership countries not specified. [2022.10.13/XJ9757/**C**]

♦ United Regions Organization/ Forum of Global Association of Regional Governments and Regions Associations / see United Regions Organisation/FOGAR (#20657)

♦ United Religions Initiative (URI) 20658

Exec Dir PO Box 29242, San Francisco CA 94129, USA. T. +14155612300. Fax +14155612313. E-mail: info@uri.org – ed@uri.org.
Street Address 1009 General Kennedy Ave, San Francisco CA 94129, USA.
URL: http://www.uri.org/

History Jun 1993, San Francisco, CA (USA). Founded by a group led by Bishop William Swing. Expected to lead to a *United Religions Organization.* Former names and other names: *People of the United Religions Initiative* – alias. Registration: 501(c)(3) organization, No/ID: EIN: 68-0369482, Start date: 1996, USA, San Francisco. **Aims** Promote enduring, daily interfaith cooperation to end religiously motivated violence and to create cultures of peace, justice and healing for the Earth and all living beings. **Structure** Global Council; President's Council; Global Support Office; Regions (8): Africa; *United Religions Initiative Europe (URI Europe, #20659)*; Latin America and the Caribbean; Middle East and North Africa; Multi-Region; North America; Southeast Asia and the Pacific. **Finance** Sources: donations. **Activities** Events/meetings. **Events** *Accelerate Peace Conference* Palo Alto, CA (USA) 2019, *Quest for global healing conference* Ubud (Indonesia) 2006, *Europe and Middle East regional assembly* Berlin (Germany) 2002, *Latin America regional assembly / Latin America and Caribbean Regional Assembly* Oaxtepec (Mexico) 2002, *Global assembly* Rio de Janeiro (Brazil) 2002. **Publications** *You Are I* (bi-weekly); *InterAction* (4 a year) – newsletter; *Organizational Review* (annual). **Members** Membership countries not specified. **Consultative Status** Consultative status granted from: *ECOSOC (#05331)* (Special). **IGO Relations** *UNESCO (#20322).* Associated with Department of Global Communications of the United Nations. **NGO Relations** Cooperates with (1): *G20 Interfaith Forum Association (IF20, #10055).* Organizations involved: *Brahma Kumaris World Spiritual University (BKWSU, #03311)*; *Centro pro Unione*; *Parliament of the World's Religions (PoWR, #18222)*; *Global AIDS Interfaith Alliance (GAIA)*; *Dialogue Institute*; *North American Interfaith Network (NAIN)*; *Temple of Understanding (ToU, #20124).* [2022/XF4552/**F**]

♦ United Religions Initiative Europe (URI Europe) 20659

Verenigde Religies Initiatief Europa

Regional Coordinator Ahornweg 3, 53177 Bonn, Germany. E-mail: info@urieurope.org – rceurope@uri.org – urieurope@gmail.com.
Chair Rijnweg 166, 2681 ST Monster, Netherlands.
URL: https://www.urieurope.org/

History Set up as a regional organization of *United Religions Initiative (URI, #20658).* Registration: Start date: 2001, Belgium. **Aims** Promote enduring, daily interfaith cooperation; end religiously motivated violence; create cultures of peace, justice and healing. **Structure** General Meeting; Board. **Languages** English. **Staff** 1.50 FTE, paid. Several voluntary. **Activities** Advocacy/lobbying/activism; conflict resolution; events/meetings; networking/liaising; training/education. **Events** *European URI Conference and Regional Assembly* Ohrid (North Macedonia) 2019, *European URI Conference and Regional Assembly* Damme (Belgium) 2018, *European URI Conference and Regional Assembly* Damme (Belgium) 2016, *European URI Conference and Regional Assembly* Plovdiv (Bulgaria) 2015, *European URI Conference and Regional Assembly* Istanbul (Turkey) 2010. **Publications** *URI Europe Dialogue Letter* – electronic newsletter.
Members Cooperation Circles (62) in 22 countries and territories:
Austria, Basque Country, Belgium, Bosnia-Herzegovina, Bulgaria, Catalunya, Denmark, Finland, France, Germany, Hungary, Italy, Kosovo, Netherlands, North Macedonia, Poland, Romania, Russia, Serbia, Tajikistan, Türkiye, UK.
IGO Relations Affiliated to: *ECOSOC (#05331).* Associated with Department of Global Communications of the United Nations. **NGO Relations** Relations with stakeholders in interfaith relations, peace, justice and healing, including: *Parliament of the World's Religions (PoWR, #18222)*; *Religions for Peace (RfP, #18831).* [2022.05.30/XE4269/**E**]

♦ United Schools International (USI) 20660

Fédération internationale des écoles unies – Federación Internacional de las Escuelas Unidas – Internationale Föderation der Vereinten Schulen

SG c/o USO House, USO Road, Jeet Singh Marg, Delhi 110067, DELHI 110067, India. T. +911126561103. Fax +911126856283. E-mail: usousiindia@gmail.com.

URL: http://www.uso-usi-india.org/
History 7 Aug 1961, Delhi (India), at an international Conference sponsored by the United Schools Organization of India (USO), set up in 1951. Sometimes referred to in French as: *Fédération Internationale des Ecoles Unies*. **Aims** Promote education about the various aspects of United Nations in the schools of the world; educate pupils in the activities of the United Nations with particular emphasis on its role in promoting international peace, cooperation and good-will through friendly relations without discrimination of race, sex, language or religion; encourage exchange of views, information and correspondence between school- children of different countries with the object of strengthening international understanding. **Structure** General Council; Executive Council. **Languages** English, Hindi. **Staff** 20.00 FTE, paid. **Finance** Members' dues. **Activities** Training/education; events/meetings. **Events** *Asian regional seminar on peaceful uses of atomic energy* Delhi (India) 2010, *General Conference* Delhi (India) 2010, *Asian regional seminar* Delhi (India) 1998, *Asian regional seminar* Delhi (India) 1993, *Triennial general conference* Delhi (India) 1993. **Publications** *United Schools International Newsletter* (periodical). Conference and seminar reports; source books for Tests on UN, UNESCO, General Knowledge.
Members Regular associations or branches of USI; Corporate secondary schools where there is no national organization; Associate national organizations which want to cooperate with USI; Life individuals who support the activities and programmes of USI. Members in 46 countries:
Afghanistan, Armenia, Australia, Bahrain, Bangladesh, Belgium, Bhutan, Bulgaria, Canada, Cyprus, Denmark, Ecuador, Egypt, Ethiopia, Fiji, Georgia, Greece, India, Indonesia, Ireland, Italy, Japan, Korea Rep, Laos, Lebanon, Malaysia, Malta, Mauritius, Nepal, Netherlands, Nigeria, Norway, Pakistan, Philippines, Romania, Russia, Rwanda, Senegal, Sierra Leone, Singapore, Sri Lanka, Thailand, Tunisia, Ukraine, United Arab Emirates, Vietnam.
Consultative Status Consultative status granted from: *ECOSOC (#05331)* (Ros A); *FAO (#09260)* (Liaison Status); *UNICEF (#20332)*. **IGO Relations** Accredited by: *United Nations Office at Vienna (UNOV, #20604)*. Associated with Department of Global Communications of the United Nations. **NGO Relations** Member of: *Conference of Non-Governmental Organizations in Consultative Relationship with the United Nations (CONGO, #04635)*. Instrumental in setting up *United Schools International Arab Regional Office (no recent information)*.
[2017/XC3389/**F**]

♦ United Scientist for Projects and Development / see International Scientists Association (#14811)

♦ United Seamen's Service (USS) 20661

Service unifié pour les marins – Servicio Unificado para Marinos
Exec Dir 104 Broadway, Ground Floor, Jersey City NJ 07306, USA. E-mail: ussam-mla@ix.netcom.com.
URL: http://www.unitedseamensservice.org/
History Aug 18 1942, New York NY (USA). **Aims** Provide health, welfare and recreational services to seafarers of all nations in its club-like centers across the globe; promote the welfare of American seafarers and their dependents, seafarers of all nations, US government military and civilian personnel and other persons engaged in the maritime industry. **Structure** Board of Directors; Council of Trustees; International Council; Executive Committee. **Finance** Seamen's Centre user fees; fundraising. Annual budget: about US$ 5,000,000. **Activities** Events/meetings; guidance/assistance/consulting; knowledge management/information; humanitarian/emergency aid; projects/programmes. **Events** *Annual meeting* New York, NY (USA) 2009, *Annual meeting* New York, NY (USA) 2008, *Annual meeting* New York, NY (USA) 2007, *Annual meeting* New York, NY (USA) 2006, *Annual meeting* New York, NY (USA) 2005. **Publications** Annual Report.
Members USS Headquarters and USS International Centers (6) in 6 countries and territories:
British Indian Ocean Terr, Germany, Japan, Korea Rep, Morocco, USA.
Seafarers from over 70 countries and territories received service and aid from USS.
Consultative Status Consultative status granted from: *ECOSOC (#05331)* (Ros C); *ILO (#11123)* (Special List). **NGO Relations** Member of: *Global Impact*; *International Council on Social Welfare (ICSW, #13076)*; *International Seafarers' Welfare and Assistance Network (ISWAN, #14815)*. [2018.09.05/XF3390/**F**]

♦ United Society for Christian Literature (internationally oriented national body)
♦ United Society for the Propagation of the Gospel / see USPG (#20736)
♦ United Through Sport (unconfirmed)
♦ United States of Africa (unconfirmed)
♦ United States Agency for International Development (internationally oriented national body)
♦ United States Air Force School for Latin American / see Inter-American Air Forces Academy
♦ United States and Canadian Academy of Pathology (internationally oriented national body)
♦ United States Center for World Mission (internationally oriented national body)
♦ United States Committee for Refugees and Immigrants (internationally oriented national body)
♦ United States Committee for UNICEF / see United States Fund for UNICEF
♦ United States European Command (internationally oriented national body)
♦ United States Fund for UNICEF (internationally oriented national body)
♦ United States Ice Patrol / see International Ice Patrol (#13832)
♦ United States Institute of Peace (internationally oriented national body)
♦ United States International Council on Disabilities (internationally oriented national body)
♦ United States International Foundation for Studies in Reproduction / see World Foundation for Medical Studies in Female Health
♦ United States/Pacific Island Nations Joint Commercial Commission (internationally oriented national body)
♦ United States Peace Corps / see Peace Corps
♦ United States Trademark Association / see International Trademark Association (#15706)
♦ UnitedSuccess (unconfirmed)
♦ United Support of Artists for Africa / see USA for Africa
♦ United Textile Workers of America / see United Food and Commercial Workers Union

♦ United Theological College of the West Indies (UTCWI) 20662

Pres UTCWI Secretariat, 7 Golding Avenue, Mona, Kingston, Jamaica. T. +18769272868. Fax +18769770812. E-mail: unitheol@cwjamaica.com.
URL: http://www.utcwi.edu.jm/
History 1965, within the framework of *Church in the Province of the West Indies (CPWI, #03921)*. **Aims** Prepare men and women for *ministry* in the *Church* and society; promote spiritual formation and academic excellence. **Structure** Board, including President. **Languages** English, French, Spanish. **Staff** 15.00 FTE, paid. **Finance** Sponsoring; grants; fundraising. **Activities** Training/education. **Publications** *Caribbean Journal of Religious Studies (CJRS)* (2 a year).
Members Covers 18 countries:
Antigua-Barbuda, Bahamas, Barbados, Belize, Costa Rica, Dominica, Grenada, Guyana, Haiti, Honduras, Jamaica, Panama, St Kitts-Nevis, St Lucia, St Vincent-Grenadines, Suriname, Trinidad-Tobago, Turks-Caicos.
NGO Relations *Caribbean Conference of Churches (CCC, #03479)*. [2017.06.28/XE2019/**E**]

♦ **UNITED** UNITED for Intercultural Action – European Network Against Nationalism, Racism, Fascism and in Support of Migrants and Refugees (#20511)
♦ United Villages (unconfirmed)
♦ United Way International / see United Way Worldwide (#20663)

♦ United Way Worldwide 20663

Contact 701 North Fairfax St, Alexandria VA 22314-2045, USA. T. +17035190092 – +17038367112. Fax +17035190097. E-mail: worldwide@unitedway.org.
URL: https://www.unitedway.org/
History May 1974, as *United Way International (UWI)*, by *United Way of America*. The 'United Way' concept was originally founded in Colorado (USA), 1887. Previously known as *International Council on United Fund Raising*. UWI merged with United Way of America in May 2009 to form current structure. **Aims** Promote *philanthropy* and *volunteerism* worldwide. **Structure** Board of Directors, comprising Chairman, 2 Vice-Chairs, Secretary, Treasurer, 3 members and 14 members at large. **Staff** 16.00 FTE, paid. **Finance** Members' dues: US$ 200. Financial support from corporations, foundations and individuals, of which the following body is included in this Yearbook: *Bill and Melinda Gates Foundation (BMGF)*. **Activities** Training in fund raising, planning and allocations. 6-Point Programme: Technical Assistance; Feasibility Studies; Corporate Involvement; Training of Volunteers and Professionals; Information Exchange; Coordination; Disaster Relief Programmes. **Events** *Round Table on Philanthropy* Seoul (Korea Rep) 2015, *Asia Pacific Meeting* Seoul (Korea Rep) 2007, *Biennial Conference* Melbourne, VIC (Australia) 2006, *Community indicators conference* Burlington, VT (USA) 2005, *Biennial Conference* San Juan (Puerto Rico) 2004. **Publications** *Global Perspectives* (4 a year) – newsletter. Annual Report.
Members Organizations in 46 countries and territories:
Australia, Belarus, Belgium, Brazil, Canada, Chile, China, Colombia, Costa Rica, Ecuador, Ghana, Greece, Guatemala, Hong Kong, Hungary, India, Indonesia, Israel, Jamaica, Japan, Jordan, Kazakhstan, Kenya, Korea Rep, Malaysia, Mauritius, Mexico, New Zealand, Nicaragua, Nigeria, Peru, Philippines, Poland, Puerto Rico, Romania, Russia, Singapore, South Africa, Taiwan, Thailand, Trinidad-Tobago, Uganda, UK, USA, Venezuela, Virgin Is USA.
Consultative Status Consultative status granted from: *ECOSOC (#05331)* (Ros A); *UNICEF (#20332)*. **IGO Relations** Associated with Department of Global Communications of the United Nations. **NGO Relations** Member of: *American Council for Voluntary International Action (InterAction)*; *CIVICUS: World Alliance for Citizen Participation (#03962)*. [2016/XF4401/**F**]

♦ United Women of the Americas (inactive)
♦ United World College of the Adriatic (internationally oriented national body)
♦ United World College of the Atlantic / see UWC Atlantic College

♦ United World Colleges (UWC International) 20664

Exec Dir Third Floor, 55 New Oxford Street, London, WC1A 1BS, UK. T. +442072697800. E-mail: info@uwcio.uwc.org.
URL: http://www.uwc.org/
History First college – UWC Atlantic College – opened 1962, Glamorgan (UK). Former names and other names: *United World Colleges International* – alias; *United World Colleges International Organisation* – alias. Registration: Charity Commission, No/ID: 313690, England and Wales. **Aims** Make *education* a force to unite people, nations and cultures for peace and a sustainable future.
Structure UWC International Congress (meets every 6 years); UWC Council; International Board of Directors; International Office, London (UK), headed by Executive Director. UWC schools and colleges (currently 16) are accountable to the International Board through the Chairpersons of their governing bodies:
– *UWC Atlantic College*, Cardiff (UK);
– *Lester B Pearson United World College of the Pacific*, Victoria BC (Canada);
– *United World College of South East Asia (UWCSEA)*, Singapore (Singapore);
– *Waterford KaMhlaba United World College of Southern Africa*, Mbabane (Eswatini);
– UWC-USA, Montezuma NM (USA);
– *Collegio del Mondo Unito dell'Adriatico (UWC Adriatic)*, Trieste (Italy);
– Li Po Chun United World College of Hong Kong (LPCUWC), Hong Kong;
– *UWC Red Cross Nordic (RCNUWC)*, Flekke (Norway);
– UWC Mahindra College, Pune (India);
– UWC Costa Rica, Santa Ana (Costa Rica);
– UWC Mostar, Mostar (Bosnia-Herzegovina);
– UWC Maastricht, Maastricht (Netherlands);
– UWC Dilijan (Armenia);
– UWC Changshu (China);
– UWC Robert Bosch College (Germany);
– UWC Thailand (Thailand);
– UWC ISAK Japan (Japan).
Languages English, Spanish. **Staff** 22.00 FTE, paid. **Finance** Funds for students' scholarships raised by national committees, colleges and International Office. Funds raised worldwide from UWC alumni, friends and supporters, foundations and trusts, companies, NGOs, governments and individuals. **Activities** Events/meetings; training/education. **Events** *South East Asia Regional Rethinking Learning Conference* Singapore (Singapore) 2018, *Congress* Trieste (Italy) 2016, *International Council Meeting* Cardiff (UK) 2013, *Latin American and Caribbean regional meeting* San José (Costa Rica) 2007, *Regional conference* Madrid (Spain) 2006. **Publications** *International Council Report*; *UWC IMPACT*. College prospectuses; promotional materials.
Members Full membership comprises: Officers; International Board members; College Boards members; National Committees members; UWC graduates, staff and former staff; supporters and friends. National Committees in 152 countries and territories:
Afghanistan, Åland, Albania, Angola, Argentina, Armenia, Australia, Austria, Bahamas, Bangladesh, Barbados, Belarus, Belgium, Belize, Benin, Bermuda, Bhutan, Bolivia, Bosnia-Herzegovina, Botswana, Bulgaria, Burkina Faso, Cambodia, Cameroon, Canada, Cayman Is, Chile, China, Colombia, Congo Brazzaville, Congo DR, Costa Rica, Côte d'Ivoire, Croatia, Cuba, Cyprus, Czechia, Denmark, Dominican Rep, Ecuador, Egypt, El Salvador, Estonia, Eswatini, Ethiopia, Faeroe Is, Fiji, Finland, France, Georgia, Germany, Ghana, Great Britain, Greece, Greenland, Guatemala, Guyana, Haiti, Honduras, Hong Kong, Hungary, India, Indonesia, Iran Islamic Rep, Iraq, Ireland, Israel, Italy, Jamaica, Japan, Jordan, Kazakhstan, Kenya, Kiribati, Korea Rep, Kosovo, Kyrgyzstan, Laos, Latvia, Lebanon, Lesotho, Liberia, Libya, Lithuania, Luxembourg, Madagascar, Malawi, Malaysia, Malta, Marshall Is, Mauritius, Mexico, Micronesia FS, Moldova, Mongolia, Montenegro, Morocco, Mozambique, Myanmar, Namibia, Nepal, Netherlands, New Zealand, Nicaragua, Niger, North Macedonia, Northern Ireland, Norway, Pakistan, Palestine, Panama, Paraguay, Peru, Philippines, Poland, Portugal, Romania, Russia, Rwanda, Sahara West, Senegal, Serbia, Sierra Leone, Singapore, Slovakia, Slovenia, Somalia, South Africa, South Sudan, Spain, Sri Lanka, Sudan, Sweden, Switzerland, Syrian AR, Taiwan, Tajikistan, Tanzania UR, Thailand, Timor-Leste, Trinidad-Tobago, Tunisia, Türkiye, Uganda, Ukraine, Uruguay, USA, Venezuela, Vietnam, Yemen, Zambia, Zimbabwe.
Also National Committee of:
Gulf Cooperation Council (GCC, #10826).
Consultative Status Consultative status granted from: *UNESCO (#20322)* (Consultative Status). **IGO Relations** Cooperates with (2): *UNHCR (#20327)*; *United Nations Relief and Works Agency for Palestine Refugees in the Near East (UNRWA, #20622)*. **NGO Relations** Supports (1): *Alliance for International Education (AIE)*.
[2022.10.13/XC4504/**B**]

♦ United World Colleges International / see United World Colleges (#20664)
♦ United World Colleges International Organisation / see United World Colleges (#20664)
♦ United World College of South East Asia (internationally oriented national body)
♦ United World Haedong Kumdo Federation (unconfirmed)
♦ United World Mission (internationally oriented national body)
♦ United World Philharmonic Foundation (internationally oriented national body)
♦ United World Philharmonic Youth Orchestra (internationally oriented national body)

♦ United World Wrestling (UWW) 20665

Secretariat Rue du Château 6, 1804 Corsier-sur-Vevey VD, Switzerland. T. +41213128426. E-mail: info@uww.org – info@unitedworldwrestling.org.
URL: https://uww.org/
History 1912, Stockholm (Sweden). Founded at the Olympic Games, by a committee appointed to work out proposals for rules and statutes of an international federation to comprise wrestling, weightlifting, tug-of-war, throwing events and shot-putting. Reconstituted 1921, Lausanne (Switzerland). First printed Rules, 1937. New Rules adopted in 1950, Stockholm. Most recent edition of Rules: 2003. Former names and other names: *International Amateur Wrestling Federation* – former; *Fédération internationale de lutte amateur* – former; *Fédération internationale des luttes associées (FILA)* – former; *International Federation of Associated Wrestling Styles* – former. **Aims** Encourage development of all wrestling styles (Greco-Roman, freestyle, women's, traditional, grappling, belt wrestling, Pankration Athlima, etc); promote the *sport* in all countries; bring support and technical assistance to developing countries; contribute to development of friendly relations among all wrestlers and between national federations; establish and distribute international rules for different wrestling styles; exercise control over wrestling throughout affiliated national federations and associate members; supervise application of wrestling rules and regulations at Olympic Games, world championships, world cups, continental competitions and all international events held under FILA control; designate, select, train, improve and coordinate international referees; represent the sport and protect interests at the International Olympic Committee and at other meetings; arbitrate and take all necessary decisions in any case of litigation or disputes arising between national federations. **Structure** Congress (every 2 years); Bureau (meeting at least annually); Executive Committee. Committees; Commissions. Continental Councils (5): UWW African Council; *United World Wrestling Asia (UWWA, #20667)*; *UWW-Europe (#20739)*; UWW Oceania; *United World Wrestling Americas (UWW Americas, #20666)*. **Languages** Arabic, English, French, German, Russian, Spanish. **Staff** 6.00 FTE, paid. **Finance** Sources: members' dues. Other sources: championship and international meet fees; sponsors; course fees; bequests and gifts; TV licence fees. **Activities** Sporting activities; training/education. **Events** *Congress* Belgrade (Serbia) 2021, *Congress* Budapest (Hungary) 2018, *Congress* London (UK) 2012, *Congress* Moscow (Russia) 2010, *Congress* Athens (Greece) 2004. **Publications** *Revue de lutte – Wrestling*

Review (periodical). *The Roots of Wrestling – The Traditional Wrestling Styles* (2000); *The Wrestler's Diet – A Guide to Healthy Weight Control* in English, French.
Members Affiliate – national federations competent in all styles of wrestling; Associate. National federations in 176 countries and territories:
Afghanistan, Albania, Algeria, Angola, Argentina, Armenia, Australia, Austria, Azerbaijan, Bahamas, Bangladesh, Barbados, Belarus, Belgium, Benin, Bolivia, Bosnia-Herzegovina, Botswana, Brazil, Bulgaria, Burkina Faso, Burundi, Cambodia, Cameroon, Canada, Cayman Is, Central African Rep, Chad, Chile, China, Colombia, Comoros, Congo Brazzaville, Congo DR, Costa Rica, Côte d'Ivoire, Croatia, Cuba, Cyprus, Czechia, Denmark, Dominican Rep, Ecuador, Egypt, El Salvador, Eritrea, Estonia, Finland, France, Gabon, Gambia, Georgia, Germany, Ghana, Greece, Guam, Guatemala, Guinea, Guinea-Bissau, Haiti, Honduras, Hong Kong, Hungary, Iceland, India, Indonesia, Iran Islamic Rep, Iraq, Ireland, Israel, Italy, Jamaica, Japan, Jordan, Kazakhstan, Kenya, Kiribati, Korea DPR, Korea Rep, Kyrgyzstan, Laos, Latvia, Lebanon, Liberia, Libya, Lithuania, Luxembourg, Madagascar, Malawi, Malaysia, Mali, Malta, Marshall Is, Mauritania, Mauritius, Mexico, Micronesia FS, Moldova, Monaco, Mongolia, Montenegro, Morocco, Mozambique, Myanmar, Namibia, Nauru, Nepal, Netherlands, New Zealand, Nicaragua, Niger, Nigeria, Niue, North Macedonia, Northern Mariana Is, Norway, Pakistan, Palau, Palestine, Panama, Paraguay, Peru, Philippines, Poland, Portugal, Puerto Rico, Qatar, Romania, Russia, Rwanda, Samoa, Samoa USA, San Marino, Sao Tomé-Principe, Saudi Arabia, Senegal, Serbia, Seychelles, Sierra Leone, Singapore, Slovakia, Slovenia, Solomon Is, Somalia, South Africa, Spain, Sri Lanka, St Vincent-Grenadines, Sudan, Suriname, Sweden, Switzerland, Syrian AR, Taiwan, Tajikistan, Tanzania UR, Thailand, Togo, Tonga, Trinidad-Tobago, Tunisia, Türkiye, Turkmenistan, Tuvalu, Uganda, UK, Ukraine, United Arab Emirates, Uruguay, USA, Uzbekistan, Venezuela, Vietnam, Virgin Is USA, Yemen, Zimbabwe.
NGO Relations Member of (5): *Association of Summer Olympic International Federations (ASOIF, #02943); International Committee for Fair Play (#12769); International Council of Sport Science and Physical Education (ICSSPE, #13077); Olympic Movement (#17719); The Association for International Sport for All (TAFISA, #02763).* Cooperates with (1): *International Testing Agency (ITA, #15678).* Recognized by: *International Olympic Committee (IOC, #14408).* Agreement of cooperation with: *International Federation of Celtic Wrestling (IFCW, #13383).* [2020.03.10/XB1163/**B**]

♦ United World Wrestling Americas (UWW Americas) 20666

Confederación Panamericana de Lucha Olímpica
Pres 12 Avenida y Calle 26, Zona 5, 2° Nivel, Edificio Polideportivo, 01005 Guatemala, Guatemala. T. +50222961092. E-mail: info@uwwamericas.org.
URL: http://uwwamericas.org/
History A continental council of *United World Wrestling (UWW, #20665).* **Structure** Executive Committee.
Members Federations in 29 countries and territories:
Argentina, Bahamas, Barbados, Bolivia, Brazil, Canada, Chile, Colombia, Costa Rica, Cuba, Dominican Rep, El Salvador, Guatemala, Guyana, Haiti, Honduras, Jamaica, Mexico, Nicaragua, Panama, Paraguay, Peru, Puerto Rico, St Vincent-Grenadines, Suriname, Uruguay, USA, Venezuela, Virgin Is USA.
NGO Relations Member of (1): *Asociación de Confederaciones Deportivas Panamericanas (ACODEPA, #02119).* [2022/AA3101/**E**]

♦ United World Wrestling Asia (UWWA) 20667

Gen Sec address not obtained. E-mail: office@uww.asia.
URL: https://uww.asia/
History A continental council of *United World Wrestling (UWW, #20665).* **Structure** Executive Committee.
Activities Sporting activities.
Members National federations in 38 countries and territories:
Afghanistan, Bahrain, Bangladesh, Cambodia, China, Hong Kong, India, Indonesia, Iran Islamic Rep, Iraq, Kazakhstan, Korea DPR, Korea Rep, Kuwait, Kyrgyzstan, Laos, Lebanon, Macau, Malaysia, Mongolia, Myanmar, Nepal, Pakistan, Palestine, Philippines, Qatar, Saudi Arabia, Singapore, Sri Lanka, Syrian AR, Taiwan, Tajikistan, Thailand, Turkmenistan, United Arab Emirates, Uzbekistan, Vietnam, Yemen. [2022/AA3100/**E**]

- ♦ UNITEE – New European Business Confederation (unconfirmed)
- ♦ UNITE Global Parliamentarians Network to end HIV/AIDS, Viral Hepatitis and other Infectious Diseases / see Global Parliamentarians Network to End Infectious Diseases (#10526)
- ♦ **UNITE** Global Parliamentarians Network to End Infectious Diseases (#10526)
- ♦ Unité de recherche sur la surveillance de la tuberculose (#20256)
- ♦ Unité spirituelle des nations (inactive)
- ♦ Uniting Church in Australia World Mission / see UnitingWorld
- ♦ Uniting Church Overseas Aid / see UnitingWorld
- ♦ Uniting Church Unity and International Mission / see UnitingWorld
- ♦ Uniting International Mission / see UnitingWorld
- ♦ Uniting for Peace (internationally oriented national body)

♦ Uniting Presbyterian Church in Southern Africa (UPCSA) 20668

Gen Sec PO Box 12355, Aston Manor, 1630, South Africa.
URL: https://unitingpresbyterian.org/
History Sep 1999. Founded on merger of *Presbyterian Church of Southern Africa (PCSA, inactive)* and *Reformed Presbyterian Church in Southern Africa (inactive).* **Aims** Bear witness to the Gospel of Jesus Christ to all non-believers; build up the believers in faith, hope and love through the ministry of the Holy Spirit; be faithful through our teaching and practice in proclaiming the sovereign rule of God in all social, economic, political and ecological relations. **Structure** General Assembly (biennial). **Finance** Contributions from congregations. **Events** *Biennial General Assembly* South Africa 2008, *Biennial General Assembly* Johannesburg (South Africa) 2004, *Biennial General Assembly* 2002. **Publications** Papers and proceedings.
Members Presbyteries (20) in 4 countries:
Namibia, South Africa, Zambia, Zimbabwe.
NGO Relations Member of: *Council for World Mission (CWM, #04925); Oikocredit International (Oikocredit, #17704); South African Council of Churches (SACC, #19699); World Communion of Reformed Churches (WCRC, #21289); World Council of Churches (WCC, #21320).* [2022/XF5566/**F**]

- ♦ Uniting Reformed Church in Southern Africa (internationally oriented national body)
- ♦ UnitingWorld (internationally oriented national body)
- ♦ UNITIS – European Organization of Cosmetic Ingredients Industries and Services (internationally oriented national body)
- ♦ Unitive Society (inactive)
- ♦ Unit for Research and Education on the UN Convention on the Rights of the Child / see International Institute for Child Rights and Development
- ♦ Unit for the Study of Wars, Armaments and Development (internationally oriented national body)
- ♦ UNITWIN Network / see UNITWIN/UNESCO Chairs Programme (#20669)

♦ UNITWIN/UNESCO Chairs Programme 20669

Coordinator UNESCO – Div of Higher Education, 7 place de Fontenoy, 75352 Paris 07 SP, France. T. +33145681074 – +33145680986. Fax +33145685626 – +33145685628. E-mail: unitwin@unesco.org.
URL: https://en.unesco.org/unitwin-unesco-chairs-programme/
History Founded 13 May 1992, Paris (France), as *UNITWIN Network – Réseau UNITWIN*, pursuant the recommendations of 25th General Conference of *UNESCO (#20322).* **Aims** Promote international inter-university cooperation and networking to enhance institutional capacities through knowledge sharing and collaborative work. **Structure** Board, consisting of Vice-Chancellors or Rectors of participating institutions. Utrecht University (Netherlands) is responsible for General Secretariat. Includes: *UNITWIN Network for Southern Africa; UNITWIN Student Network.* **Finance** Regular University budget; national government funding; donor agencies. **Events** *Arts Education in and Through a Time of Crisis* Seoul (Korea Rep) 2021, *Seminar on Culture, Tourism and Development* Paris (France) 2018, *Networking workshop* Seoul (Korea Rep) 2017, *Work Conference* Seoul (Korea Rep) 2017, *Gender Summit North and Latin America* Mexico City (Mexico) 2016. **Information Services** *UNITWIN/UNESCO Chairs* – database. **Members** Higher education and research institutions (over 700) in 126 countries (not specified). **NGO Relations** Agreement with: *Community of Mediterranean Universities (CMU, #04403); Nouvelles orientations pour l'écotechnique (NOE)* of *Cousteau Society.* Supports: *Institutional Development Programme between European and Latin American Universities (COLUMBUS Association, #11316); COPERNICUS Alliance – European Network on Higher Education for Sustainable Development (CA, #04830). Refugee Studies Centre, Oxford (RSC)* is member. Instrumental in setting up: *ORBICOM – International Network of UNESCO Chairs in Communication (#17785); Network of UNESCO Chairs and Training Centres in Cultural Policy and Management (NETCULT, no recent information); Programme for Palestinian-European-American Cooperation in Education (PEACE Programme, #18527).* [2017/XF5362/**F**]

♦ Unity-and-Diversity World Council (UDC) 20670

Contact PO Box 661401, Los Angeles CA 90066-9201, USA. T. +14242282087. Fax +14248279187. E-mail: udcworld@gmail.com.
URL: http://udcworld.org/
History 1965, during International Cooperation Year, as *International Cooperation Council (ICC).* Present name adopted 1980. Registered in the State of California (USA). **Aims** Establish and sustain a local-to-global cooperating body of individuals, groups and networks for the pursuit of peace, justice and an environmentally sustainable civilization for all races, cultures and religions based on universal ethical and spiritual principles. **Structure** Head office in Los Angeles CA (USA). **Languages** English. **Staff** 2.00 FTE, paid. **Finance** Members' dues. Other sources: income from regular programs, special events, publications and fund-raisers. **Activities** Events/meetings; publishing activities. **Events** *GPA session* Mumbai (India) 2002, *GPA official world session* Apia (Samoa) 2000, *Annual world convergence* Los Angeles, CA (USA) 2000, *Special millennium world convergence* Los Angeles, CA (USA) 2000, *Annual world congress* Los Angeles, CA (USA) 1999. **Publications** *Science and Spirituality* by Mary Mann and Leland Stewart; *The Art of Peace* by Stephen L Fiske; *There are No Enemies* by Mary Mann; *World Scriptures – in 2 vols* by Leland Stewart. **Members** Individuals, groups and networks. Membership countries not specified. **NGO Relations** *United Religions Initiative (URI, #20658).* Links with over 200 groups, faith and interfaith organizations. [2018/XF4993/**F**]

- ♦ Unity of Nations Action for Climate Change Council (internationally oriented national body)
- ♦ Uniunea Europeana (#08967)
- ♦ Uniunea Latina (inactive)
- ♦ UNI / see UNI Global Union (#20338)
- ♦ Universala Blanka Frataro (#20684)
- ♦ Universal Action Fund for Excellence / see Intergovernmental Collaborative Action Fund for Excellence
- ♦ Universala deklaracio de homaj rajtoj (1948 treaty)
- ♦ Universala Esperanto-Asocio (#20676)
- ♦ Universala Islama Esperanto-Asocio (internationally oriented national body)
- ♦ Universala Ligo (inactive)

♦ Universal Alliance (UA) 20671

Alliance universelle (AU)
Int Coordinator UA Head Office, 12 Place Rd, Fowey, PL23 1EL, UK.
History 12 Aug 1949, Algeria. Dissolved Aug 1957. Reborn 1989. **Aims** Through philosophical and moral teachings based on modern spiritualism – karmic progress and *reincarnation* – promote non-violence and spirituality without dogma or inflexible creeds. **Structure** Comprises separate national organizations whose international aspects are coordinated through the UK organization. Planetary Council. **Languages** English, French. **Staff** 40.00 FTE, paid. **Finance** Voluntary donations. **Activities** Networking/liaising; events/meetings; knowledge management/information dissemination. **Events** *Conference / Global Conference* Athens (Greece) 2001, *Annual global or pankosmic conference* Kalamata (Greece) 1998, *Conference* London (UK) 1998, *Annual global or pankosmic conference* Kalamata (Greece) 1997, *Global Conference* Kalamata (Greece) 1997. **Publications** *Phoenix New Life Poetry and New World Creation Project News and Reviews* (4 a year) – journal. *Précis of the Universal Alliance* in English, French – booklet. **Information Services** *Vision Quester Information Service.*
Members Individuals and organizations, in 17 countries and territories:
Canada, Cuba, France, India, Israel, Italy, Jordan, Pakistan, Palestine, Romania, Russia, South Africa, Switzerland, UK, Ukraine, USA, Uzbekistan.
NGO Relations Cooperates with: *Universal Esperanto Association (UEA, #20676).* Member of: *EarthAction (EA, #05159); UNITED for Intercultural Action – European Network Against Nationalism, Racism, Fascism and in Support of Migrants and Refugees (UNITED, #20511).* Links with many networks and organizations including: *International Association of Educators for World Peace (IAEWP); International Peace Research Association (IPRA, #14537);* national organizations and grass-roots action centres, networks and movements. [2019.04.23/XF4593/**F**]

- ♦ Universal Alliance of Diamond Workers (inactive)
- ♦ Universal Alliance for a New and Better Humanity / see New Humanity Group

♦ Universala Medicina Esperanto-Asocio (UMEA) 20672

Association médicale espérantiste universelle – Universal Medical Esperanto Association
SG Krankenhaus der Barmherzigen Brüder, Abteilung für Neurologie und Neurophysiologie, Nordallee 1, 54292 Trier, Germany. T. +496512081751. E-mail: umea@uea.org.
URL: http://umea.fontoj.net/
History 1908, Dresden (Germany). Former names and other names: *World Medical Esperantist Association* – former (1908 to 1964); *Tutmonda Esperantista Kuracista Asocio* – former (1908 to 1964); *International Association of Medical Esperantists* – alias. **Aims** Spread and use the international language Esperanto in the medical sphere. **Structure** National branches in member countries. **Languages** English, Esperanto. **Staff** Voluntary. **Finance** Sources: members' dues. **Activities** Events/meetings; networking/liaising. **Events** *International Medical Esperanto Congress (IMEK)* Hódmezővásárhely (Hungary) 2022, *Biennial International Congress* Hódmezővásárhely (Hungary) 2020, *Biennial International Congress* Nitra (Slovakia) 2016, *International Congress* Budapest (Hungary) 2014, *Annual meeting* Tel Aviv (Israel) 2000. **Publications** *Medicina Internacia Revuo (MIR)* (2 a year); *Presidential Bulletin* (2 a year).
Members Individuals (about 110): doctors, dentists, veterinarians, nurses and pharmacists in 32 countries:
Albania, Argentina, Austria, Belgium, Benin, Brazil, China, Congo DR, Croatia, Cuba, Czechia, Finland, France, Germany, Hungary, Iran Islamic Rep, Italy, Japan, Korea Rep, Lithuania, Luxembourg, Poland, Romania, Russia, Serbia, Slovakia, Spain, Sweden, Togo, UK, Ukraine, USA.
NGO Relations Member of (1): *Universal Esperanto Association (UEA, #20676).* Cooperates with (10): *Akademio Internacia de la Sciencoj, San Marino (AIS, #00617); Comité permanent des congrès d'espéranto (inactive); Esperanto Academy (#05543); International Association of Esperanto Pharmacists (inactive); International Association of Esperanto Railway Employees (IAEF, inactive); International Esperanto Institute (IEI, #13302); International Esperanto Museum, Vienna (no recent information); Rotaria Amikaro de Esperanto (RADE, #18973); Rotary International (RI, #18975); Tutmonda Esperantista Junulara Organizo (TEJO, #20268).* Supports (1): *Healthcare Information For All (HIFA, #10878).* [2021/XD3555/v/**C**]

- ♦ Universal Association of Esperanto Good Templars (inactive)
- ♦ Universal Association of Professional Colleges and Universities (internationally oriented national body)
- ♦ Universal Biosophical Association (inactive)

♦ Universal Boxing Organization (UBO) 20673

Pres Akazienweg 6, 32584 Lohne, Germany. T. +491708319964.
Vice-Pres / Gen Sec address not obtained.
URL: http://www.uboboxing.com/
History 2004. **Structure** Regional Offices (5). [2022/XM4068/**C**]

- ♦ Universal Christian Council for Life and Work (inactive)
- ♦ Universal Church / see Universal Church of the Kingdom of God (#20674)

♦ Universal Church of the Kingdom of God (UCKG) 20674

Contact UCKG HelpCentre, 232 Seven Sisters Road, London, N4 3NX, UK.
URL: http://universal.org/
History 1977, Rio de Janeiro (Brazil), by Edir Macedo, a convert of Bishop Robert McAlister, a Canadian missionary in the Pentecostal tradition. Also referred to as *Universal Church.* **Aims** Reach out to *needy, less privileged* people, often excluded by established religions.
Members Churches in 76 countries:
Angola, Argentina, Australia, Barbados, Belgium, Bolivia, Botswana, Brazil, Cameroon, Canada, Cape Verde, Chile, China, Colombia, Congo Brazzaville, Costa Rica, Côte d'Ivoire, Dominican Rep, Ecuador, El Salvador, Equatorial Guinea, Eswatini, Ethiopia, France, Gabon, Germany, Ghana, Greece, Guatemala, Guinea-Bissau, Guyana, Honduras, India, Ireland, Israel, Italy, Jamaica, Japan, Kenya, Lesotho, Luxembourg, Madagascar, Malawi, Mauritius, Mexico, Mozambique, Namibia, Netherlands, New Zealand, Nicaragua, Nigeria, Panama, Paraguay, Peru, Philippines, Poland, Portugal, Puerto Rico, Romania, Russia, Sao Tomé-Principe, Senegal, South Africa, Spain, Sweden, Switzerland, Tanzania UR, Togo, Trinidad-Tobago, Uganda, UK, Uruguay, USA, Venezuela, Zambia, Zimbabwe. [2011/XM7445/**F**]

- ♦ Universal Copyright Convention, 1952 (1952 treaty)

♦ Universal Copyright Convention, 1971 (1971 treaty)

♦ Universal Decimal Classification Consortium (UDC Consortium) . . . 20675

Administrator PO Box 90407, 2509 LK The Hague, Netherlands. T. +31703140509. Fax +31703140450.
URL: http://www.udcc.org/

History 1991, by *International Federation for Information and Documentation (FID, inactive)*. **Aims** Maintain and develop the Universal Decimal Classification in its various language versions. **Structure** Advisory Board of 26 members. Executive Committee, comprising Chairman, Editor-in-Chief and 5 members. **Languages** English. **Staff** 2.00 FTE, paid. **Finance** Members' dues. Sales of publications and licenses to UDC. **Activities** Organizes conferences and seminars. **Events** *Expanding resource discovery* Lisbon (Portugal) 2015, *Conference* The Hague (Netherlands) 2011, *Seminar* The Hague (Netherlands) 2011, *Conference* Prague (Czech Rep) 2009, *Classification at a crossroads-multiple directions to usability* The Hague (Netherlands) 2009. **Publications** *Extensions and Corrections to the UDC* (annual); *UDC Dutch Tables* (annual). Guides.
Members National organizations in 5 countries:
Belgium, Czechia, Russia, Spain, UK. [2011.08.10/XF5268/**F**]

♦ Universal Declaration on Bioethics and Human Rights (2005 treaty)
♦ Universal Declaration on Civil Protection / see International Civil Defence Organization (#12582)
♦ Universal Declaration on the Human Genome and Human Rights (1997 treaty)
♦ Universal Declaration of Human Rights (1948 treaty)
♦ Universal Education Foundation / see Learning for Well-being Foundation (#16431)
♦ Universal Esperantist League (inactive)

♦ Universal Esperanto Association (UEA) 20676

Association universelle de l'espéranto – Asociación Universal del Esperanto – Esperanto Weltbund – Universala Esperanto-Asocio

Dir Gen Nieuwe Binnenweg 176, 3015 BJ Rotterdam, Netherlands. T. +31104361044. Fax +4930364280169. E-mail: info@uea.org – direktoro@co.uea.org – sekretario@co.uea.org.
Contact address not obtained.
URL: http://uea.org/

History 28 Apr 1908, Switzerland. Took over the activities of *Central Esperantist Office (inactive)*, set up Aug 1905, and *Comité permanent des congrès d'espéranto (inactive)*, formed 28 Aug 1906. I *Universal Esperantist League (inactive)*, created in 1936, merged with UEA in Apr 1947. Former names and other names: *Internacia Ligo* – former; *Association espérantiste universelle* – former. **Aims** Promote Esperanto; stimulate discussion of the world language problem; call attention to the necessity of equality among languages. **Structure** Committee; Board of Directors. **Languages** Esperanto. **Staff** 8.00 FTE, paid. Several voluntary. **Finance** Sources: donations; meeting proceeds; members' dues; sale of publications. **Activities** Events/meetings; networking/liaising; research/documentation. **Events** *Annual World Congress* Turin (Italy) 2023, *Annual World Congress* Montréal, QC (Canada) 2022, *Annual World Congress* Belfast (UK) 2021, *Annual World Congress* Montréal, QC (Canada) 2020, *Annual World Congress* Lahti (Finland) 2019. **Publications** *Esperanto* (12 a year); *Kontakto* (6 a year); *Jarlibro* (annual). Congress handbooks; catalogues; records.
Members National organizations (72); Individuals. Total membership (18,500), in 116 countries and territories:
Albania, Algeria, Angola, Argentina, Armenia, Australia, Austria, Azerbaijan, Bangladesh, Belarus, Belgium, Belize, Benin, Bolivia, Bosnia-Herzegovina, Brazil, Bulgaria, Burundi, Cambodia, Cameroon, Canada, Chad, Chile, China, Colombia, Congo Brazzaville, Congo DR, Costa Rica, Côte d'Ivoire, Croatia, Cuba, Cyprus, Czechia, Denmark, Dominican Rep, Ecuador, Egypt, El Salvador, Estonia, Ethiopia, Finland, France, Georgia, Germany, Ghana, Greece, Guatemala, Haiti, Hungary, Iceland, India, Indonesia, Iran Islamic Rep, Ireland, Israel, Italy, Japan, Kazakhstan, Kenya, Korea Rep, Latvia, Lithuania, Luxembourg, Madagascar, Malaysia, Malta, Mexico, Moldova, Mongolia, Morocco, Nepal, Netherlands, New Zealand, Nicaragua, Nigeria, North Macedonia, Norway, Pakistan, Panama, Paraguay, Peru, Philippines, Poland, Portugal, Puerto Rico, Romania, Russia, Rwanda, Saudi Arabia, Senegal, Serbia, Singapore, Slovakia, Slovenia, South Africa, Spain, Sri Lanka, Sweden, Switzerland, Taiwan, Tajikistan, Tanzania UR, Thailand, Timor-Leste, Togo, Tunisia, Türkiye, Uganda, UK, Ukraine, Uruguay, USA, Uzbekistan, Venezuela, Vietnam, Zimbabwe.
Affiliated international organizations (6):
ESPERANTO + EDUKADO (ILEI, #05544); Internacia Komerca kaj Ekonomia Fakgrupo (IKEF, #11522); International Esperantist Scientific Association (#13301); International Federation of Esperantist Railwaymen (#13415); International League of Blind Esperantists (#14017); Universala Medicina Esperanto-Asocio (UMEA, #20672).
International members (29), listed in this Yearbook:
- *Association of Esperantist Greens (AEG, #02494);*
- *Association of Handicapped Esperantists with International Club (no recent information);*
- *Ateista Tutmonda Esperanto-Organizo (ATEO, #03001);*
- *Bahaa Esperanto-Ligo (BEL, #03061);*
- *Christian Esperanto International Association (#03901);*
- *Esperantista Internacia Centro de la Mondcivitana Registraro (no recent information);*
- *Esperantist Law Association (EJA, no recent information);*
- *Esperantist Music League (MEL, no recent information);*
- *Esperanto-Ligo Filatelista (ELF, #05545);*
- *Europa Klubo (EK);*
- *European Esperanto Union (#07006);*
- *Filozofia Asocio Tutmonda (FAT, no recent information);*
- *Internacia Asocio de Bibliistoj kaj Orientalistoj (IABO, inactive);*
- *Internacia Asocio de Esperantistaj Matematikistoj (IAdEM, no recent information);*
- *Internacia Komitato por Etnaj Liberecoj (IKEL, #11523);*
- *Internacia Ligo de Esperantistaj Radio-Amatoroj (ILERA, #11524);*
- *Internacia Poastista kaj Telekomunikista Esperanto-Asocio (IPTEA, no recent information);*
- *International Catholic Esperantists Union (#12455);*
- *International Communist Esperantist Collective (#12819);*
- *International Naturist Organization for Esperanto (INOE, #14220);*
- *Ligo de Samseksamaj Geesperantistoj (LSG, #16475);*
- *Literary Academy of Esperanto (no recent information);*
- *Movado sen Nomo;*
- *Oomoto;*
- *Organiza Societo de Internaciaj Esperanto Konferencoj (OSIEK);*
- *Skolta Esperanto-Ligo (SEL, #19309);*
- *Veterana Esperantista Klubo (VEK, #20758);*
- *World Association of Esperanto Journalists (#21138);*
- *World Esperantist Vegetarian Association (#21389).*

Consultative Status Consultative status granted from: *ECOSOC (#05331)* (Special); *UNESCO (#20322)* (Consultative Status); *UNICEF (#20332)*; *OAS (#17629)*. **IGO Relations** Accredited by (1): *United Nations Office at Vienna (UNOV, #20604)*. Associated with Department of Global Communications of the United Nations.
NGO Relations Member of (4): *Campaign for a More Democratic United Nations (CAMDUN, inactive); Conference of Non-Governmental Organizations in Consultative Relationship with the United Nations (CONGO, #04635); European Language Council (ELC, #07646); NGO Committee on UNICEF (#17120).* Instrumental in setting up (4): *Centre for Research and Documentation on World Language Problems (CeD, #03780); Foundation Africa (see: #20676); Foundation Asia (see: #20676); NGO Coalition for an International Auxiliary Language (CIAL, inactive).*
In liaison A with *International Organization for Standardization (ISO, #14473)* Technical Committee 37.
Associated organizations:
- *Akademio Internacia de la Sciencoj, San Marino (AIS, #00617);*
- *Asocio por Eŭropa Konscio;*
- *Budhana Ligo Esperantista (BLE, #03348);*
- *Centre for Documentation and Exploration of the International Language (CDELI);*
- *Esperanto Academy (#05543);*
- *Esperanto Cultural Centre (KCE);*
- *Espermenso (no recent information);*
- *Fonds mondial de solidarité contre la faim (FMSCF, #09836);*
- *Hejmoj de Internacia Kulturo (HIK, no recent information);*
- *Hilelista Esperanto-Komunumo (HEK);*
- *Infanoj Chirkaw la Mondo (ICLM);*
- *Internacia Agrikultura Esperanto-Asocio (IAEA, no recent information);*
- *Internacia Scienca Instituto Ivo Lapenna (ISIIL, #11525);*
- *International Association of Esperanto-Speaking Cyclists (#11878);*
- *International Cultural Centre (IKS);*
- *International Esperanto Institute (IEI, #13302);*
- *International Esperanto Museum, Vienna (no recent information);*
- *International Science Academy Comenius (#14795);*
- *International Working Group of Esperanto-speaking Foresters (no recent information);*
- *Nationless Worldwide Association (#16941);*
- *Rotaria Amikaro de Esperanto (RADE, #18973);*
- *Tutmonda Agado de Esperantistaj Nefumantoj (TAdEN, #20265);*
- *Tutmonda Asocio de Konstruistoj Esperantistaj (TAKE, #20266);*
- *Tutmonda Ekumena Ligo (TEL, #20267);*
- *Tutmonda Esperantista Junulara Organizo (TEJO, #20268);*
- *Tutmonda Ortodoksa Esperanto Ligo (no recent information);*
- *Universal Alliance (UA, #20671);*
- *Universala Artista Ligo de Esperantistoj (UALE, no recent information);*
- *Universala Islama Esperanto-Asocio (UIEA).* [2023/XA3399/y/**A**]

♦ Universal Federation of Hotel-Keepers' Societies (inactive)
♦ Universal Federation of Pedagogical Societies (inactive)
♦ Universal Federation of Students Against Alcoholism (inactive)
♦ Universal Federation of Travel Agents' Associations / see United Federation of Travel Agents' Associations (#20509)
♦ UniversalGiving (internationally oriented national body)

♦ Universal Great Brotherhood (UGB) 20677

Grande fraternité universelle – Gran Fraternidad Universal (GFU) – Gran Fratellanza Universale

SG Apartado Postal 3987, Caracas 1010-A DF, Venezuela. T. +582128643956. Fax +582128630906. E-mail: c.supremo@granfraternidaduniversal.org – sec.general@granfraternidaduniversal.org.
Street Address Consejo Supremo, Calle Nueva Agua Salud No 5B, de Guamito a Minerva, 1010A Apartado Postal 3987, Caracas DF, Venezuela.
URL: http://www.granfraternidaduniversal.org/

History 1948, Caracas (Venezuela), by Dr Serge Raynaud de la Ferrière, as *Universal Great Brotherhood Foundation – Gran Fraternidad Universal Fundación*. Full title: *Universal Great Brotherhood, Foundation Dr Serge Raynaud de la Ferrière – Grande fraternité universelle, Fondation Dr Serge Raynaud de la Ferrière – Gran Fraternidad Universal, Fundación Dr Serge Raynaud de la Ferrière – Gran Fratellanza Universale, Fundación Dr Serge Raynaud de la Ferrière*. **Aims** As a cultural and civil institution, work on an intellectual and spiritual re-education of humans and establish peace among all human beings working on science for living. **Structure** Supreme Council, comprising General Secretary, Treasurer, Lawyer and 9 secretaries. Countries directed internally by Executive Council, consisting of President, Vice-President, Treasurer, Lawyer and 5 secretaries. Towns are directed by a Subsidiary Council, dependent on Supreme Council. Organisms (4): Servicio Centralizador de la Literatura (Central Department of Literature); Servicio de Brigadas Misionales (Missionary Brigades); Servicio de Representaciones Oficiales (Official Representation Service); Servicio Iniciatico Esotérico (Esoteric Initiatory Service). **Languages** English, French, Italian, Portuguese, Spanish. **Staff** Voluntary. **Finance** Voluntary member collaboration; income from social and cultural activities. **Activities** Organizes cultural and social activities. **Events** *International Congress* Mexico City (Mexico) 2013, *International Congress* Jauja (Peru) 2011, *International Congress* Brasilia (Brazil) 2010, *International Congress* Mexico City (Mexico) 2009, *International Congress* Seville (Spain) 2007. **Publications** *Circular Letters*. *Great Messages* – series; *Psychological Propositions* – series. Books; booklets.
Members Active; Sympathetic. Members in 21 countries:
Argentina, Australia, Bolivia, Brazil, Chile, Colombia, Costa Rica, Ecuador, El Salvador, Honduras, Italy, Mexico, Nicaragua, Panama, Paraguay, Peru, Puerto Rico, Spain, Uruguay, USA, Venezuela.
Consultative Status Consultative status granted from: *ECOSOC (#05331)* (Special). **IGO Relations** Associated with the Department of Global Communications of the United Nations. [2013.11.19/XF4479/f/**F**]

♦ Universal Great Brotherhood Foundation / see Universal Great Brotherhood (#20677)
♦ Universal Great Brotherhood, Foundation Dr Serge Raynaud de la Ferrière / see Universal Great Brotherhood (#20677)
♦ Universal House of Sephardis (inactive)
♦ Universal Human Rights Network (internationally oriented national body)
♦ Universalis Matter (internationally oriented national body)
♦ Universal League for Sexual Reform (inactive)

♦ Universal Love and Brotherhood Association (ULBA) 20678

Association pour l'amour et la fraternité universelles – Jinrui Aizen Kai

Headquarters Ten'on-kyo, Kameoka-shi, Kyoto, 621-8686 Japan. T. +81771232145. Fax +81771250061. E-mail: k-kimura@oomoto.or.jp – mail@jinruiaizenkai.jp.
URL: http://www.jinruiaizenkai.jp/

History Founded 1925, by Onisaburo Deguchi (1871-1948). **Aims** Promote the ideals of universal unity, brotherhood, and peace. **Activities** Events/meetings; financial and/or material support; knowledge management/information dissemination. **Publications** *Aizen Shinbun* (12 a year); *Oomoto* (6 a year).
Members Individuals (30,000) in 7 countries and territories:
Brazil, India, Japan, Micronesia FS, Nepal, Philippines, Sri Lanka. [2015/XD4997/v/**D**]

♦ Universal Medical Assistance International Centre (inactive)
♦ Universal Medical Esperanto Association (#20672)

♦ Universal Movement for Scientific Responsibility (UMSR) 20679

Mouvement universel de la responsabilité scientifique (MURS)

Pres MURS France, 4 rue Théophile Roussel, 75012 Paris, France.
URL: http://murs.fr/

History 24 Sep 1974, Paris (France), following symposium on 'Biology and the Future of Many'. Registered in accordance with French law. **Aims** Follow the progress of knowledge through impartiality and cooperation in a permanent forum of researchers, highly qualified educators and decision-makers focusing attention on and discussing problems which may arise for mankind from scientific development and its applications; promote general awareness of questions facing society and each of its individual members by confronting and comparing potential benefits and risks resulting from such development and making such knowledge available in a manner comprehensible to the public at large; alert decision-makers to positive and negative effects that might involve man's future; stimulate reflection on the future of man and of the planet, and on urgent measures necessary for safeguarding that future; encourage adaptation to the mutations which humanity is undergoing. **Structure** Board of Management, consisting of President, Vice-President, General Secretary, Honorary (founding) President, Honorary Vice-Presidents, Honorary Member and members. **Languages** English, French, Spanish. **Staff** 1.00 FTE, paid; 2.00 FTE, voluntary. **Finance** Members' dues. Grants. **Activities** Organizes: integrated activities of multidisciplinary teams; national and international symposia and seminars; public lectures; public courses (3-4 a year) at the Sorbonne, Paris (France) and at the College de France, Paris (France). **Events** *International symposium* Cairo (Egypt) 1986. **Publications** *Cahiers du MURS* (4 a year); *Lettres aux générations 2000* (3 a year); *Bulletin de liaison du MURS* (periodical). Synoptic papers.
Members Individuals; Voluntary Associations; Companies. Members in 25 countries:
Algeria, Argentina, Australia, Austria, Belgium, Brazil, Canada, Egypt, France, Germany, Greece, India, Italy, Japan, Luxembourg, Mexico, Poland, Portugal, Romania, Spain, Switzerland, Tunisia, UK, Uruguay, USA.
IGO Relations *UNESCO (#20322).* [2018/XC4360/**F**]

♦ Universal Negro Improvement Association and African Communities League / see Universal Negro Improvement Association and African Communities League of the World
♦ Universal Negro Improvement Association and African Communities League of the World (internationally oriented national body)

♦ Universal Networking Digital Language Foundation (UNDL Foundation) 20680

Contact address not obtained. T. +41228798090. Fax +41228798091. E-mail: info@undlfoundation.org.
URL: http://www.undlfoundation.org/

History 17 Jan 2001. Registration: Switzerland. **Aims** Increase research and development in the Universal Networking Language (UNL) and its applications in all areas of human knowledge and activities. **Structure** Council of 7 to 12 members. **Consultative Status** Consultative status granted from: *ECOSOC (#05331)* (Special). [2016/XJ4118/f/**F**]

♦ Universal Organization of Travel Agents' Associations (inactive)
♦ Universal Outreach Foundation (internationally oriented national body)
♦ Universal Pantheist Society (internationally oriented national body)
♦ Universal Pantheon (internationally oriented national body)
♦ Universal Pantheon Press Agency / see Universal Pantheon

♦ Universal Peace Federation (UPF International) 20681

Dir Executive Office 220 White Plains Rd, FL 5, Tarrytown NY 10591, USA. T. +19146311331. Fax +19143321582. E-mail: info@upf.org.
Chairman address not obtained.
URL: http://www.upf.org/

History 3 Feb 1999, Seoul (Korea Rep). Based on the founding vision of Rev Dr and Mrs Sun Myung Moon. Previously referred to as *Interreligious and International Federation for World Peace (IIFWP)*. Current title adopted Sep 2005. Registration: 501(c)(3) organization, No/ID: EIN: 52-2199888, Start date: 2000, USA, NY. **Aims** Promote *interfaith* dialogue and cooperation for peace and human development; strengthen marriage and family, leadership and good governance, peace education and service; revitalize the United Nations; promote a culture of peace through education, sports, arts, media and service; develop a framework for interreligious cooperation, conflict prevention and resolution. **Structure** Board of Directors; International Administrative Headquarters, located in New York NY (USA); Committees (5); Regional offices (10); National Chapters (145). **Languages** Arabic, Chinese, English, French, Japanese, Korean, Russian, Spanish. **Staff** 8.00 FTE, paid. Thousands of volunteers worldwide. **Finance** Annual budget (average): US$ 2,000,000 – 3,000,000. **Activities** Conflict resolution; events/meetings; training/education. **Events** *International Leadership Conference* 2021, *International Leadership Conference* Seoul (Korea Rep) 2021, *International Conference on the Unity of Sciences* Goyang (Korea Rep) 2020, *International University President Conference* Goyang (Korea Rep) 2020, *World Summit* Goyang (Korea Rep) 2020. **Publications** *Dialogue and Alliance* – journal; *UPF Today* – magazine. **Consultative Status** Consultative status granted from: *ECOSOC (#05331)* (General). **IGO Relations** Partnership with: *African Union (AU, #00488)*. **NGO Relations** Member of (1): *Conference of Non-Governmental Organizations in Consultative Relationship with the United Nations (CONGO, #04635)*. Participant of: *United Nations Global Compact (#20567)*. Co-sponsors programmes with other organizations, including: *Geneva Interfaith Intercultural Alliance (GiiA)*; *Inter-Religious Federation for World Peace (IRFWP, inactive)*; *World Association of Non-Governmental Organizations (WANGO, #21167)*. [2022/XF6610/**F**]

♦ Universal Peace and Violence Amelioration Centre (internationally oriented national body)
♦ Universal Postal Convention, 1906 (1906 treaty)
♦ Universal Postal Convention, 1920 (1920 treaty)
♦ Universal Postal Convention, 1924 (1924 treaty)
♦ Universal Postal Convention, 1929 (1929 treaty)
♦ Universal Postal Convention, 1952 (1952 treaty)
♦ Universal Postal Convention, 1957 (1957 treaty)
♦ Universal Postal Convention, 1964 (1964 treaty)
♦ Universal Postal Convention, 1974 (1974 treaty)
♦ Universal Postal Convention, 1979 (1979 treaty)
♦ Universal Postal Convention, 1984 (1985 treaty)

♦ Universal Postal Union (UPU) 20682

Union postale universelle (UPU) – Unión Postal Universal (UPU)

Dir Gen PO Box 312, 3000 Bern 12, Switzerland. T. +41313503111. Fax +41313503110. E-mail: info@upu.int.
URL: http://www.upu.int/

History 9 Oct 1874, Bern (Switzerland), as *General Postal Union – Union générale des postes – Unión General de Correos*, on signature by 22 countries of *Treaty concerning the establishment of a General Postal Union (Bern Treaty) – Traité concernant la création d'une Union générale des postes (Traité de Berne) – Tratado concerniente a la creación de una Unión General de Correos (Tratado de Berna)*. The Treaty came into force 1 Jul 1875 (in the case of France, 1 Jan 1876). Present name adopted in 1878. Since 1 Jul 1948, UPU is a Specialized Agency of *United Nations (UN, #20515)* within the framework of *United Nations System (#20635)*, linked to *ECOSOC (#05331)*. UPU Constitution (incorporating the General Regulations, the Convention and its Detailed Regulations) is a diplomatic convention ratified by the appropriate authority in each member country. Amendments may only be made at Congress and are recorded in an Additional Protocol, which is also subject to ratification. Resolutions, decisions, recommendations and formal opinions, together with UPU Acts proper, make up the Decisions of Congress. To these is added the Agreement making the UPU a specialized agency of the UN and defining relations between the two organizations. This Agreement is annexed to the Constitution and determines the conditions of any amendment to it. The current Constitution, was adopted by 15th Congress, 1964, Vienna (Austria), and has been in force since 1 Jan 1966. There have been 7 Additional Protocols, adopted at the following Congresses: 1969, Tokyo (Japan); 1974, Lausanne (Switzerland); 1984, Hamburg (Germany FR); 1989, Washington DC (USA); 1994, Seoul (Korea Rep); 1999, Beijing (China); 2004, Bucharest (Romania). The 1999 protocol came into force on 1 Jan 2001; 2004 protocol came into force on 1 Jan 2006; 2008 protocol comes into force on 1 Jan 2010. Constitution registered in *'UNTS 1/8844'*. EU Transparency Register: 81947973709-24. **Aims** Ensure organization and development of *postal services*; promote development of communication among peoples by efficient operation of postal services; contribute to international collaboration in the cultural, social and economic fields; ensure that all postal users/customers enjoy the right to a universal postal service; participate in the provision of technical assistance as requested by member countries; ensure the interoperability of postal networks by implementing a suitable policy of standardization; meet the changing needs of postal customers; improve the quality of postal services.

Structure *'Universal Postal Congress'* (every 4 years) is the supreme authority, focusing on broad policy issues and comprising representatives of all member countries. Regulatory power is increasingly being delegated to *UPU Council of Administration (CA, see: #20682)*, meeting annually at UPU headquarters, Bern (Switzerland), comprises 41 members elected by Congress, plus Chairman appointed by the host country of the previous Congress. It ensures continuity of UPU work between Congresses, supervises Union activities and studies regulatory, administrative, legislative and legal issues of interest to the Union. In order to ensure UPU's ability to react quickly to changes in the postal environment, CA has power to approve proposals from the Postal Operations Council for adoption of regulations or new procedures until the next Congress has taken a decision on the matter. It may also take measures within its competence that it considers necessary to resolve urgent affairs. CA approves the UPU biennial budget, accounts and the yearly update of strategic planning.

In addition to the Management Committee, which prepares and coordinates the CA sessions, and the Strategic Planning Group, which advises the CA as well as the POC on strategic planning, there are: /CA Committees/ (4): *'Committee 1 – Governance Issues'*, including: Reform of the Union; Acts of the Union; Universal Postal Service; Interconnectivity; Terminal Dues Governance; *'Committee 2 – Joint CA/POC Committee – Development and Cooperation'*, including: Sustainable Development; Postal Economics; Technical Cooperation and Postal Reform and E-Commerce Development; *'Committee 3 – Finance and Administration'*; *'Committee 4 – Joint CA/POC Committee – UPU Strategy'*, including: Strategy Planning; Strategy Implementation; Strategy Reporting.

Postal Operations Council (POC, see: #20682) (meeting annually, at UPU Headquarters in Bern) is the technical and operational body, comprising national postal administrations of 40 countries, elected by Congress. It deals with operational, economic and commercial aspects of international postal services. The first POC meeting after each Congress revises the Detailed Regulations. POC aims to help postal services to modernize and upgrade their postal products, including letter post, EMS, postal parcels and postal financial services. It promotes introduction of new postal products by collecting, analysing and publicizing results of postal services' experiments and prepares, and issues recommendations to member countries concerning standards for technological, operational or other processes within its competence where practice of uniformity is essential.

'Strategic Planning Group' – advises CA and POC.

/POC Committees/ (4): *'Letter Post'*, including: Product Development and Marketing Group; Remuneration Group; *World Association for the Development of Philately (WADP, #21132)*; Direct Mail Advisory Board; Quality Improvement Group; Transport Group; Quality of Service Link User Group. *'Parcels'*, including: Product Development and Marketing Group; Quality Improvement Group; Remuneration Group; Customs Group. *'Postal Financial Services'*, including: Development Group; Multilateral Framework Group; Financial Relations Group. *'Standards and Technology'*, including Standards Board; Addressing Group; E-Services Group; Operations and Accounting Review Group. *'Direct Reporting Bodies'*: Postal Security Group; QSF Board; UPU Clearing Group; EMS Cooperative; Telematics Cooperative.

Consultative Committee, created 16 Sep 2004, gives postal stakeholders other than public postal operators and regulators a voice in the organization's deliberations. It consists of NGOs representing customers, suppliers of goods and services to the postal sector and other organizations that have an interest in international postal services, including direct marketers, private operators, international mailers and printers.

'International Bureau (IB)', established in 1874 by the Treaty of Bern, is based in Bern. It provides secretariat and support facilities for UPU bodies, acting as organ of liaison, information and consultation and promoting technical cooperation among UPU members. It also acts as clearinghouse for settlement of accounts between postal administrations for inter-administration charges related to exchange of postal items and international reply coupons and is responsible for ensuring UPU representation in external relations, notably with international organizations. It does not intervene between designated postal operators and their customers.

/Directorates and Units under the supervision of the Director-General/:
– Directorate – Director General's Office, Strategic Planning and Communication;
– Legal Affairs Directorate and Ethics Office (DAJ);
– Environment and Sustainable Development (PEDD);
– Internal Audit;
– Operations and Technology Directorate;
– Economic and Regulatory Affairs Directorate;
– Markets Development Directorate;
– Finance Directorate;
– Logistics Directorate;
– Human Resources and Social Relations Directorate;
– Development Cooperation Directorate.

Languages Arabic, Chinese, English, French, Portuguese, Russian, Spanish. **Staff** International Bureau: about 250 from about 50 countries. The *Administrative Tribunal of the International Labour Organization (ILO Tribunal, #00118)* is competent in case of dispute. **Finance** Members' contributions, in 10 classes from 1 to 50 units. Each new member country selects its contribution class, although an additional contribution class of one half unit is reserved for least developed countries. Since 1992, annual budget increases are maintained at or below the level of inflation.

Activities Basic activity is the adoption of provisions for the various international postal services carried out by member postal administrations. Fundamental rules are introduced by the Bern Treaty of 1874, as they still appear in the UPU Constitution concluded in 1964, Vienna (Austria), and subsequent amendments. Provisions relating to application of the Constitution and operation of the Union are contained in UPU General Regulations and are revised at each Quadrennial Congress. These Regulations are agreements concluded by the Postal Operations Council, which has authority to amend them at its annual sessions. Both the Convention and Regulations are binding on all member countries and include common rules applicable to the international postal service and provisions concerning letter post and parcel post services. The Convention provides for: formation among all member countries of a single postal territory for the reciprocal exchange of letter-post items; guaranteed freedom of transit within the territory of the Union; standardization of charges to be collected by each country for letter-post items addressed to any part of the Union's territory; promotion of better quality, development and modernization of postal services; remuneration as compensation for the delivery of mail received from abroad; arbitration procedure to settle disputes between administrations. The 1999 Beijing Congress introduced a new text concerning the universal postal service at the beginning of the Convention, stating that postal users and customers are entitled to quality basic postal services at all points in their territory and at affordable prices.

'Activities within the United Nations System': Under an agreement concluded between the United Nations and the Union in 1947, which came into force 1 Jul 1948, the UN recognized the Universal Postal Union as a specialized agency and the UPU legally became a member of the United Nations system of organizations. In 1968, UNDP gave favourable reception to important postal projects for setting up or expanding national or multinational training schools in Africa, Asia, Latin America and the Middle East. The provisions of the UPU Constitution therefore authorize countries to establish Restricted Unions and conclude special agreements concerning the postal service, provided conditions are not introduced which are less favourable for the public than those laid down in the Union's Acts. There are currently 17 such Restricted Unions.

'Cooperation to enhance postal development': The principle of technical cooperation was first introduced into the UPU Constitution at the 1964 Vienna Congress, resulting from the need to provide assistance to the many newly-formed countries that had become members of the UPU during the early 1960s. Funding for these activities typically came from the UNDP or other international development agencies, or was given on a bilateral basis. Currently the major portion of funding for technical cooperation activities comes from contributions of member countries to UPU budget or to a special voluntary fund. A principal goal of the *'Postal Development Action Group (PDAG)'*, a special working group set up within the UPU, is to increase the level of outside financial resources (notably from international financial institutions) devoted to reform and modernization of postal services. PDAG also actively encourages the continued use of bilateral and multilateral assistance between postal administrations themselves. A crucial element in selecting beneficiary countries is their own motivation to participate actively in the technical cooperation projects to be undertaken. Once commitment has been secured, development contracts covering multi-year integrated projects are concluded between these countries and the Union. UPU also conducts short projects which may include study cycles, training fellowships and the services of development consultants who carry out on-the-spot studies concerning training, management or postal operations.

In addition to the work indicated under "Structure", the International Bureau undertakes enquiries at the request of Postal Administrations and delivers international reply coupons to them. It may serve as an office for compensation and as an intermediary for the regulation of different accounts relating to the international postal service. A *'Universal Postal Union Customs Contact Committee'* has been set up to seek methods of accelerating and simplifying customs formalities. The Bureau's ability to assist postal services of developing countries in the most effective manner is strengthened by the presence of UPU Regional Coordinators in the field, established by the Washington Congress in 1989 and expanded to the present number of 7 at the Beijing Congress in 1999. The Regional Coordinator's principal responsibilities are for the programming, preparation, implementation and follow-up of postal development projects within their regions.

'Quality of service': Since postal services are under constant pressure to make further improvements in the quality of their postal products, each Congress since 1984 has adopted a policy aimed at reinforcing the quality of the international service. In 1999, the 22nd UPU Congress approved creation of a *'Quality of Service Fund'* with the aim to finance projects for improving the quality of postal services in developing countries. The fund is maintained by terminal dues payments made by postal administrations in industrialized countries.

'Technology': Global Electronic Data Interchange (EDI) project aims to spread the use of advanced information technology systems to the postal services of developing countries. Member postal administrations are able to track mail shipments end to end using computer applications that facilitate processing and allow exchange of electronic data.

'Philately': The Philatelic industry is represented in the UPU-World Association for the Development of Philately (WADP). UPU Congresses set guidelines and recommended postage stamp themes likely to contribute to strengthening bonds of international friendship, although policies regarding the issue, sale and marketing of postage stamps are a matter for each member country. 'Philatelic code of ethics for use by UPU member countries' adopted 1999, Beijing.

'Security': Postal Security Action Group (PSAG) aims to help postal services fulfil their obligation to customers by ensuring the integrity of mail and protecting those involved in its handling.

'Customer Focus and Market Development': Industry groups promote closer ties with postal customers, including publishing, direct mail and private operators.

'UPU Agreements': *Postal Payment Service Agreement (1999)* and its Regulations were adopted in 1999, Beijing, and replace *Cash-on-delivery Agreement (1984), Giro Agreement, 1984 (1984)* and *Money Orders and Postal Travellers Cheques Agreement, 1984 (1984)*. They are binding only on parties to the Agreement

Other agreements concluded under UPU auspices:
- *Agreement Concerning Postal Money Orders and Postal Travellers' Cheques, 1952 (1952)*;
- *Agreement Concerning Cash-on-delivery Items, 1952 (1952)*;
- *Agreement Concerning Cash-on-delivery Items, 1957 (1957)*;
- *Agreement Concerning Postal Money Orders and Postal Travellers' Cheques, 1964 (1964)*;
- *Agreement Concerning Cash-on-delivery Items, 1964 (1964)*;
- *Agreement Concerning Postal Money Orders and Postal Travellers' Cheques, 1969 (1969)*;
- *Agreement Concerning Giro Transfers (1969)*;
- *Agreement Concerning Cash-on-delivery Items, 1969 (1969)*;
- *Money Orders and Postal Travellers Cheques Agreement, 1979 (1979)*;
- *Giro Agreement, 1979 (1979)*;
- *Collection of Bills Agreement (1984)*;
- *International Savings Agreement (1984)*;
- *Postal Parcels Agreement, 1984 (1984)*;
- *Subscriptions to Newspapers and Periodicals Agreement (1984)*.

Events *Extraordinary Congress* Geneva (Switzerland) 2019, *World Summit on the Information Society (WSIS) Forum* Geneva (Switzerland) 2016, *Quadrennial Congress* Istanbul (Turkey) 2016, *Quadrennial postal congress* Doha (Qatar) 2012, *Annual meeting* Bern (Switzerland) 2011. **Publications** *Union postale* (4 a year) in Arabic, Chinese, English, French, German, Russian, Spanish – magazine. Annual Report. Biennial Report; Congress and Council reports; postal statistics; vocabularies; glossaries; brochures.

Members According to current provisions, accession to the Union is open to any member of the UN; sovereign countries which do not belong to the UN may also request admission and are admitted if the request is approved by at least two-thirds of member countries, which represent and/or include the following territories: Australia: Norfolk Islands. China: Hong Kong and Macau. Denmark: Faeroe Islands, Greenland. France: French Overseas Departments: French Guiana, Guadeloupe (including St Barthélémy and St Martin), Martinique, Réunion; Territorial Community of Mayotte; Territorial Community of St Pierre and Miquelon; French Overseas Territories coming within the Union's jurisdiction by virtue of article 23 of the Constitution: French Polynesia (including Clipperton Island), French Southern and Antarctic Territories (St Paul and Amsterdam Islands, Crozet Islands, Kerguelen Islands, Terre Adélie), New Caledonia, Scattered islands (Bassas da India, Europa, Juan de Nova, Glorieuses, Tromelin), Wallis and Futuna Islands. Great Britain: United Kingdom of Great Britain and Northern Ireland, Guernsey, Jersey, Isle of Man; Overseas Territories (United Kingdom of Great Britain and Northern Ireland): Anguilla, Ascension, Bermuda, British Indian Ocean Territory, Cayman Islands, Falkland Islands (Malvinas), Gibraltar, Montserrat, Pitcairn Islands (Pitcairn, Henderson, Ducie and Oeno), South Georgia and the South Sandwich Islands, St Helena (Dependencies – Islands), Tristan da Cunha, Turks and Caicos Islands, Virgin Is UK. Netherlands: Aruba and Netherlands Antilles (Bonaire, Curaçao, Saba, St Eustatius, St Maarten). New Zealand (including the Ross Dependency): Cook Islands, Niue, Tokelau. United States of America: Territories of the United States of America coming within the Union's jurisdiction by virtue of article 23 of the Constitution: Guam, Puerto Rico, Samoa, Virgin Islands of the United States of America; Trust Territory of the Pacific Islands, comprising the Mariana Islands (including Saipan and Tinian, but not the United States Possession of Guam). Member countries, 192 – UK Overseas Territories are included in conformity with UPU's 'Official List of Members', St Kitts-Nevis is officially referred to by UPU as 'St Christopher (St Kitts) and Nevis':
Member countries, 192 – UK Overseas Territories are included in conformity with UPU's 'Official List of Members', St Kitts-Nevis is officially referred to by UPU as 'St Christopher (St Kitts) and Nevis':
Afghanistan, Albania, Algeria, Angola, Antigua-Barbuda, Argentina, Armenia, Australia, Austria, Azerbaijan, Bahamas, Bahrain, Bangladesh, Barbados, Belarus, Belgium, Belize, Benin, Bhutan, Bolivia, Bosnia-Herzegovina, Botswana, Brazil, Brunei Darussalam, Bulgaria, Burkina Faso, Burundi, Cambodia, Cameroon, Canada, Cape Verde, Central African Rep, Chad, Chile, China, Colombia, Comoros, Congo Brazzaville, Congo DR, Costa Rica, Côte d'Ivoire, Croatia, Cuba, Cyprus, Czechia, Denmark, Djibouti, Dominica, Dominican Rep, Ecuador, Egypt, El Salvador, Equatorial Guinea, Eritrea, Estonia, Eswatini, Ethiopia, Fiji, Finland, France, Gabon, Gambia, Georgia, Germany, Ghana, Greece, Grenada, Guatemala, Guinea, Guinea-Bissau, Guyana, Haiti, Holy See, Honduras, Hungary, Iceland, India, Indonesia, Iran Islamic Rep, Iraq, Ireland, Israel, Italy, Jamaica, Japan, Jordan, Kazakhstan, Kenya, Kiribati, Korea DPR, Korea Rep, Kuwait, Kyrgyzstan, Laos, Latvia, Lebanon, Lesotho, Liberia, Libya, Liechtenstein, Lithuania, Luxembourg, Madagascar, Malawi, Malaysia, Maldives, Mali, Malta, Mauritania, Mauritius, Mexico, Moldova, Monaco, Mongolia, Montenegro, Morocco, Mozambique, Myanmar, Namibia, Nauru, Nepal, Netherlands, New Zealand, Nicaragua, Niger, Nigeria, North Macedonia, Norway, Oman, Pakistan, Panama, Papua New Guinea, Paraguay, Peru, Philippines, Poland, Portugal, Qatar, Romania, Russia, Rwanda, Samoa, San Marino, Sao Tomé-Principe, Saudi Arabia, Senegal, Serbia, Seychelles, Sierra Leone, Singapore, Slovakia, Slovenia, Solomon Is, Somalia, South Africa, South Sudan, Spain, Sri Lanka, St Kitts-Nevis, St Lucia, St Vincent-Grenadines, Sudan, Suriname, Sweden, Switzerland, Syrian AR, Tajikistan, Tanzania UR, Thailand, Timor-Leste, Togo, Tonga, Trinidad-Tobago, Tunisia, Türkiye, Turkmenistan, Tuvalu, Uganda, UK, UK Overseas Territories, Ukraine, United Arab Emirates, Uruguay, USA, Uzbekistan, Vanuatu, Venezuela, Vietnam, Yemen, Zambia, Zimbabwe.

Independent countries whose situation with regard to UPU has not yet been settled (4):
Andorra, Marshall Is, Micronesia FS, Palau.

Restricted Unions (16), listed in this Yearbook:
African Postal Union (APU, no recent information); *Arab Permanent Postal Commission (APPC, #01025)*; *Asian-Pacific Postal Union (APPU, #01625)*; *Associação dos Operadores de Correios e Telecomunicações dos Paises e Territórios de Lingua Oficial Portuguesa (AICEP, #02333)*; *Association of European Public Postal Operators (PostEurop, #02534)*; *Baltic Postal Union (BPU, #03137)*; *Caribbean Postal Union (CPU, #03541)*; *Communications Regulators' Association of Southern Africa (CRASA, #04384)*; *Conférence européenne des administrations des postes et des télécommunications (CEPT, #04602)*; *Conference of Posts and Telecommunications of Central Africa (#04642)*; *Nordic Postal Union (NPU, #17391)*; *Pan African Postal Union (PAPU, #18060)*; *Postal Union for the Mediterranean (PUMed, #18467)*; *Postal Union of the Americas, Spain and Portugal (PUASP, #18466)*; *Regional Commonwealth in the Field of Communications (RCC, #18767)*; *Southern Africa Postal Operators Association (SAPOA, #19866)*; *West African Postal Conference (WAPCO, #20893)*.

IGO Relations Observer to: *International Organization for Migration (IOM, #14454)*; *World Trade Organization (WTO, #21864)*. Special relations with: *UNESCO (#20322)* (special reduced rates for books and printed matters); *UNDP (#20292)*; *International Atomic Energy Agency (IAEA, #12294)* (transport of radio-active material); *International Civil Aviation Organization (ICAO, #12581)* (air mail); *WHO (#20950)* (transport of perishable substances); *International Bank for Reconstruction and Development (IBRD, #12317)* (financial problems). Member of: *United Nations Group on the Information Society (UNGIS, #20570)*. Represented on: *United Nations System Chief Executives Board for Coordination (CEB, #20636)*. Permanent observer status with: *World Intellectual Property Organization (WIPO, #21593)*. Cooperates in joint technical assistance projects, especially in the vocational training field, with: *European Aviation Security Training Institute (EASTI, #06304)*; *International Telecommunication Union (ITU, #15673)*. Memorandum of Understanding signed with: *Economic Cooperation Organization (ECO, #05313)*; *World Customs Organization (WCO, #21350)*; *UNEP (#20299)*; *United Nations Office on Drugs and Crime (UNODC, #20596)*. Agreement with: *International Criminal Police Organization – INTERPOL (ICPO-INTERPOL, #13110)*. Participates in: *Inter-Agency Task Force on Employment and Sustainable Livelihoods for All (inactive)*.

NGO Relations Contact Committees with: *International Air Transport Association (IATA, #11614)*. In liaison with technical committees of: *International Organization for Standardization (ISO, #14473)*. Memorandum of Understanding with: *International Post Corporation (IPC, #14624)*. In liaison with technical committees of: *Comité européen de normalisation (CEN, #04162)*. Founding Member of Direct Mail Advisory Board: *Direct Marketing Association (DMA)*. Member of: *Better Than Cash Alliance (#03220)*. Links with Contact Committee UPU/Publishers, with private operators and with:
- *SITA (#19299)*;
- *European Express Association (EEA, #07017)*;
- *Federation of International Civil Servants' Associations (FICSA, #09603)*;
- *Fédération internationale de philatélie (FIP, #09650)*;
- *FIPP (#09776)*;
- *Global Express Association (GEA, #10351)*;
- *International Chamber of Commerce (ICC, #12534)*;
- *International Electrotechnical Commission (IEC, #13255)*;
- *International Federation of Air Line Pilots' Associations (IFALPA, #13349)*;
- *International Publishers Association (IPA, #14675)*;
- *One UN Climate Change Learning Partnership (UN CC:Learn, #17735)*;
- *Organisation internationale des experts (ORDINEX, #17808)*;
- *World Savings Banks Institute (WSBI, #21764)*. [2017.12.11/XB3408/y/**B***]

♦ Universal Radio-Telegraph Union (inactive)

♦ Universal Rights Group (URG) 20683

Exec Dir Maison de la Paix, Chemin Eugène-Rigot 2E, Bldg 5, 1202 Geneva, Switzerland. T. +41225550960. E-mail: info@universal-rights.org.
URL: http://www.universal-rights.org/

History Founded 2013, Versoix (Switzerland). **Aims** Support and strengthen policy-making, implementation and impact across the international human rights system. **Structure** Board of Trustees; Advisory Group; Secretariat. **Languages** English, French, Spanish. **Finance** Financed by voluntary contributions. **Activities** Research/documentation; knowledge management/information dissemination; events/meetings. **Publications** *URG Insights* (12 a year). Reports.
Members Operational members in 3 countries:
Colombia, Switzerland, USA.
Consultative Status Consultative status granted from: *ECOSOC (#05331)* (Special). **NGO Relations** National organizations. [2019.12.11/XM7281/**F**]

♦ Universal Sanitary Union – Marine Health and Quarantine Council of Egypt (inactive)
♦ Universal Scientific Alliance (inactive)
♦ Universal Society of Hinduism (unconfirmed)
♦ Universal Syrian Orthodox Church / see Greek Orthodox Patriarchate of Antioch and All the East (#10710)
♦ Universal Theatre Society (inactive)
♦ Universal Union for Consumer Protection and Civil Abuse (internationally oriented national body)
♦ Universal Union of Esperantist Men of Letters (inactive)
♦ Universal Union of Sephardi Communities (inactive)

♦ Universal White Brotherhood (UWB) 20684

Fraternité blanche universelle (FBU) – Fraternidad Blanca Universal – Universelle Weisse Bruderschaft (UWB) – Fraternidade Branca Universal – Fratellanza Bianca Universale – Universele Witte Broederschap – Det Universelle Hvite Broderskap – Universala Blanka Frataro – Fraternitatea Albà Universalà – Vesmírné Bílé Bratrstvo – Visuotnės Baltosios Brolijos – Powszechne Biale Bractwo

Contact 2 rue du Belvédère de la Ronce, 92310 Sèvres, France. T. +33145340885. Fax +33146230926. E-mail: fbu@fbu.org.
Contact FBU Center USA, PO Box 932, Locust Valley, New York NY 11560, USA.
URL: http://www.fbu.org/

History 15 Feb 1947, Sèvres (France). Registered in accordance with French law. **Aims** Propagate the teaching of Omraam Mikhaël Aïvanhov to bring about a harmonious life where each race, religion and nationality is respected. **Activities** Easter and Summer Holidays (annually) at 'Domaine du Bonfin' in Fréjus (France); Summer and Winter congresses in Québec (Canada); Christmas Holidays at Sèvres (France). **Events** *Easter congress* Fréjus (France) 1988, *Summer congress* Fréjus (France) 1988, *Easter congress* 1987, *Summer congress* Fréjus (France) 1987. **Publications** Books; brochures; cassettes, all by Omraam Mikhaël Aïvanhov, in Arabic, Armenian, Bulgarian, Chinese, Czech, Danish, Dutch, English, Esperanto, French, German, Greek, Hebrew, Hindi, Hungarian, Italian, Japanese, Korean, Latvian, Lithuanian, Malagasy, Norwegian, Polish, Portuguese, Romanian, Russian, Serb, Slovak, Spanish, Swahili.
Members Registered organizations in 34 countries:
Austria, Belgium, Benin, Bolivia, Burkina Faso, Cameroon, Canada, Colombia, Congo Brazzaville, Congo DR, Côte d'Ivoire, Czechia, France, Gabon, Germany, Ghana, Greece, Haiti, Italy, Lebanon, Madagascar, Netherlands, New Zealand, Norway, Peru, Portugal, Romania, Russia, Spain, Switzerland, Togo, UK, USA, Venezuela. [2012.07.12/XF8516/**F**]

♦ Universal Women's Alliance for Peace by Education (inactive)

♦ Universal Zulu Nation (UZN) 20685

Contact PO Box 510, Bronx NY 10475-9998, USA. T. +17183034375.
URL: http://www.zulunation.com

History 12 Nov 1973, Bronx NY (USA), by Afrika Bambaataa. **Aims** Promote peace and unity, knowledge, wisdom, understanding, and inner-standing for all people worldwide. **Activities** Training/education; awareness raising.
Members National chapters in 18 countries:
Australia, Belgium, Brazil, Canada, Colombia, Croatia, Denmark, Finland, France, Germany, Italy, Japan, Nigeria, Norway, South Africa, Switzerland, UK, USA.
Also members in the West Indies. Membership countries not specified.
NGO Relations Works with: *International Society of Indigenous Sovereigns (ISIS, no recent information)* through *'Universal Zulu Kemetic Muurs'*. [2018.07.16/XD6836/**D**]

♦ Universele verklaring van menseregte (1948 treaty)
♦ Universele verklaring van de rechten van de mens (1948 treaty)
♦ Universele Witte Broederschap (#20684)
♦ Det Universelle Hvite Broderskap (#20684)
♦ Universelle Weisse Bruderschaft (#20684)

♦ Universeum 20686

Contact Oude Turfmarkt 129, 1012 GC Amsterdam, Netherlands. E-mail: contact@universeum-network.eu.
URL: http://www.universeum-network.eu/

History 16 Apr 2000, Wittenberg (Germany). Full title: *Universeum – European Academic Heritage Network*. Current statutes approved 18 Jun 2010, Uppsala (Sweden). Registered in accordance with French law. **Aims** Preserve, study, provide access to and promote university collections, *museums*, archives, libraries, botanical gardens, astronomical *observatories*, etc. **Structure** Ordinary General Assembly (at least annual). Executive Committee, comprising President, 2 Vice-Presidents, Secretary and Treasurer. Scientific Committee. **Languages** English. **Finance** Members' dues. Other sources: subsidies; donations and legacies; proceeds from events. **Activities** Organizes annual meeting; offers scholarships and grants; organizes annual European University Heritage Day (18 Nov). **Events** *Annual Meeting* Utrecht (Netherlands) 2016, *Annual meeting* Trondheim (Norway) 2012, *Annual meeting* Padua (Italy) 2011, *Annual meeting* Uppsala (Sweden) 2010, *Annual meeting* Toulouse (France) 2009.
Members Individual; Institutional; Student; Founding; Honorary; Supporting. Founding members in 7 countries:
France, Germany, Italy, Netherlands, Portugal, Sweden, UK. [2018/XJ2100/**D**]

♦ Universeum – European Academic Heritage Network / see Universeum (#20686)
♦ Universidad Abierta Interamericana (internationally oriented national body)
♦ Universidad de las Américas (internationally oriented national body)
♦ Universidad de los Andes (internationally oriented national body)

♦ Universidad Andina Simón Bolivar (UASB) 20687

Simón Bolivar Andean University

Central Campus Calle Real Audiencia No 73, Casilla Postal 545, Sucre, Bolivia. T. +59146460265. Fax +59146460833. E-mail: info@uasb.edu.bo.
URL: http://www.uasb.edu.ec/

History 11 Dec 1985, La Paz (Bolivia). 11-16 Dec 1985, La Paz (Bolivia), during 5th Session of *Andean Parliament (#00820)*. Bylaws approved Mar 1987. Registered in accordance with Bolivian law. An institution of *Sistema Andino de Integración (SAI, #19292)* within the framework of *Andean Community (#00817)*. **Aims** Promote and carry out research, teaching, post-university training and the provision of services; promote a spirit of cooperation and coordination among universities of the region. **Structure** Main campus in Sucre (Bolivia). Branches in Quito (Ecuador), La Paz (Bolivia), Caracas (Venezuela) and Cali (Colombia). **Activities** Prepares and carries out teaching, theoretical and practical training and refresher training programs, primarily for professionals who are university graduates with qualified experience; prepares and performs high-level scientific research and studies; provides consulting and technical cooperation services. **Events** *Seminar* Quito (Ecuador) 1994. **Publications** *Andean R and D Newsletter*. **NGO Relations** Member of: *Asociación Universitaria Iberoamericana de Postgrado (AUIP, #02307)*. [2015/XF4590/**F***]

♦ Universidad Biblica Latinoamericana (internationally oriented national body)
♦ Universidad Centroamericana José Simeón Cañas (internationally oriented national body)
♦ Universidad Centroamericana, Managua (internationally oriented national body)

♦ Universidad CLAEH **20688**

Headquarters Zelmar Michelini 1220, 11100 Montevideo, Uruguay. T. +59829007194. Fax +59829007194. E-mail: info@claeh.edu.uy.
Northeast Regional Office General Flores 185, 45000 Tacuarembó, Uruguay. T. +5986324438. Fax +59863224438. E-mail: regionalne@claeh.edu.uy.
URL: http://claeh.edu.uy/

History 1957, Montevideo (Uruguay). 1997, created the *Instituto Universitario CLAEH*. 2017, recognized as a university. Former names and other names: *Latin American Centre of Human Economy* – former; *Centre latinoaméricain d'économie humaine* – former; *Centro Latinoamericano de Economia Humana (CLAEH)* – former. **Aims** Promote and organize national and regional interdisciplinary research teams within the *social sciences* field; approach training in the social area from a *humanistic* viewpoint; publicize contents of projects; stimulate collective reflection on problems of *social transformation*; promote and carry out activities supporting *grass roots development*. **Structure** Executive Structure: Direction; Social Policies Program; Local Development Program; Government and Political System Program; Entrepreneurship Program. Regional headquarters in Tacuarembó (Uruguay). **Languages** Spanish. **Finance** Funds provided by: international agencies of cooperation for development; organizations related to the United Nations, especially *UNDP (#20292)*; Latin American Social Sciences Council (CLACSO). members of the institution. Also: profits from technical advice and consultancy services; profits from the sale of publications, enrolment fees for courses and seminars, etc. Annual budget: about US$ 300,000. **Activities** Research/documentation; advocacy/lobbying/activism; training/education; guidance/assistance/consulting; monitoring/evaluation. **Events** *Seminar* Montevideo (Uruguay) 1991, *Perspectives and alternatives for the next 20 years* Montevideo (Uruguay) 1990, *Rio de la Plata comparative history* Montevideo (Uruguay) 1989, *Seminar on local development* Montevideo (Uruguay) 1987. **Publications** *Cuadernos del CLAEH* (2 a year) – journal. *Argumentos* – books. Working papers; research aids; promotion aids; articles; training booklets. **Members** Individuals. Membership countries not specified. **IGO Relations** *UNICEF (#20332)*. Member of: *Latin American and Caribbean Research Network (#16284)*. **NGO Relations** Member of: *Asociación Latinoamericana de Organizaciones de Promoción (ALOP, inactive)*; *Consejo Latinoamericano de Ciencias Sociales (CLACSO, #04718)*; *The Reality Of Aid (ROA, #18626)*.
[2018.01.22/XE7536/v/**E**]

- ♦ Universidad Cooperativa Internacional (#12952)
- ♦ Universidade Holistica Internacional de Brasilia / see Universidade Internacional da Paz (#20689)

♦ Universidade Internacional da Paz (UNIPAZ) **20689**

Rector Luiz Boiteux Piazza 1302, Sapiens Parque, Ed InovaLab, Florianópolis SC, SC 88056-000, Brazil. T. +554832341864. E-mail: contato@unipazsc.org.br – adm.funcipaz@unipazdf.org.br – unipaz@unipazdf.org.br.
URL: http://unipazsc.org.br/

History 1987. Previously referred to as *International Holistic University, Brasilia – Universidade Holistica Internacional de Brasilia*. **Structure** Includes *UNIPAZ Europe (no recent information)*. **Events** *International holistic conference* Findhorn (UK) 1999.
Members Campuses in 7 countries:
Argentina, Belgium, Brazil, Ecuador, France, Honduras, Portugal.
IGO Relations *UNDP (#20292)*; *UNESCO (#20322)*; *UNICEF (#20332)*. **NGO Relations** Managed by: *City of Peace Foundation (no recent information)*. [2019/XN5162/**F**]

- ♦ Universidade Radiofónica e Televisiva Internacional / see International Radio and Television Union (#14689)
- ♦ Universidades en Busca de la Paz (inactive)
- ♦ Universidades Caribe (#20694)
- ♦ Universidad Europea de Voluntariado (see: #02978)
- ♦ Universidad de Iberoamérica (internationally oriented national body)
- ♦ Universidad Iberoamericana, México (internationally oriented national body)
- ♦ Universidad Iberoamericana de Postgrado / see Asociación Universitaria Iberoamericana de Postgrado (#02307)
- ♦ Universidad Interamericana de Puerto Rico (internationally oriented national body)
- ♦ Universidad Internacional del Desarrollo Sostenible (internationally oriented national body)
- ♦ Universidad Internacional de Estudios Sociales, Pro Deo / see Libera Università Internazionale degli Studi Sociali, Guido Carli
- ♦ Universidad Internacional de Estudios Sociales 'Guido Carli' (internationally oriented national body)
- ♦ Universidad Internacional de Radio y Televisión / see International Radio and Television Union (#14689)
- ♦ Universidad Latinoamericana de Ciencia y Tecnologia (internationally oriented national body)
- ♦ Universidad Maritima Mundial (#21633)
- ♦ Universidad de las Naciones Unidas (#20642)
- ♦ Universidad para la Paz (#20702)
- ♦ Universidad de la Paz (internationally oriented national body)
- ♦ Universidad de Relaciones y Estudios Internacionales (internationally oriented national body)
- ♦ Universidad Técnica Latinoamericana, San Salvador (internationally oriented national body)
- ♦ Universidad Tecnológica Centroamericana (internationally oriented national body)
- ♦ Universidad Tecnológica Intercontinental (internationally oriented national body)
- ♦ Universidad Virtual Africana (#00496)
- ♦ Università Internazionale delle Istituzione dei Popoli per la Pace (internationally oriented national body)
- ♦ Universitair Centrum voor Ontwikkelingssamenwerking, Brussel (internationally oriented national body)
- ♦ Universitaires Sans Frontières (internationally oriented national body)
- ♦ Universitaire Stichting voor Ontwikkelingssamenwerking (internationally oriented national body)
- ♦ Universitaires pour le Tiers-monde / see Món-3 – Universitaris pel Tercer Món
- ♦ Università Pontificia Salesiana (#19038)

♦ Universitas 21 . . . . **20690**

Contact c/o Strathcona 109, Univ of Birmingham, Edgbaston, Birmingham, B15 2TT, UK. T. +441214149596. E-mail: u21@universitas21.com.
URL: http://www.universitas21.com/

History 1997, Melbourne, VIC (Australia). Founded 1997 at inaugural meeting. Registration: UK, Guernsey. **Aims** Inspire international collaboration across the network's membership through empowering staff, researchers and students of all U21 universities to share excellence, collaborate across borders and nurture global knowledge exchange. **Structure** General Meeting (annual); Board. **Languages** English. **Staff** 5.50 FTE, paid. **Finance** Sources: members' dues. **Activities** Advocacy/lobbying/activism; knowledge management/information dissemination; networking/liaising; research/documentation; training/education. **Events** *Seniors Leaders Group Meeting* Auckland (New Zealand) 2019, *Annual General Meeting* College Park, MD (USA) 2019, *Annual General Meeting* Melbourne, VIC (Australia) 2018, *Seniors Leaders Group Meeting* Santiago (Chile) 2018, *Seniors Leaders Group Meeting* Seoul (Korea Rep) 2017. **Publications** *U21 Newsletter* (12 a year); *U21 Annual Review*. Impact report; position papers.
Members Universities (27) in 19 countries and territories:
Australia, Belgium, Canada, Chile, China, Hong Kong, India, Ireland, Japan, Korea Rep, Mexico, Netherlands, New Zealand, Singapore, South Africa, Sweden, Switzerland, UK, USA.
Consultative Status Consultative status granted from: *ECOSOC (#05331)* (Special). [2021.06.09/XF6120/**F**]

- ♦ Universitas Asiae et Pacificarum (internationally oriented national body)
- ♦ Universitatea Libera Internationala din Moldova (internationally oriented national body)
- ♦ Università del Teatro Eurasiano (internationally oriented national body)
- ♦ Università Telematica Internazionale UNINETTUNO (internationally oriented national body)
- ♦ Universitätszentrum für Friedensforschung, Wien (internationally oriented national body)
- ♦ Université africaine de développement coopératif (#00494)
- ♦ Université de l'Afrique de l'Est (inactive)
- ♦ Université d'Amérique centrale José Simeón Cañas (internationally oriented national body)
- ♦ Université des Amériques (internationally oriented national body)
- ♦ Université des Andes (internationally oriented national body)
- ♦ Université arabe Nayef des sciences de sécurité (#16929)
- ♦ Université catholique d'Afrique centrale (unconfirmed)
- ♦ Université Catholique de l'Afrique de l'Est (#03610)
- ♦ Université coopérative internationale (#12952)
- ♦ Université européenne d'écriture / see Institut Européen d'Ecriture
- ♦ Université européenne d'écriture créative et audiovisuelle / see Institut Européen d'Ecriture
- ♦ Université Européenne Jean Monnet (internationally oriented national body)
- ♦ Université européenne du volontariat (see: #02978)
- ♦ Université fédéraliste mondiale (inactive)
- ♦ Université francophone d'Alexandrie / see Université internationale de langue française au service du développement africain à Alexandrie d'Egypte (#20691)
- ♦ Université humanitaire européenne, Minsk / see European Humanities University
- ♦ Université ibéroaméricaine d'études post-universitaires / see Asociación Universitaria Iberoamericana de Postgrado (#02307)
- ♦ Université ibéroaméricaine, México (internationally oriented national body)
- ♦ Université des Indes occidentales (#20705)
- ♦ Université interaméricaine (inactive)
- ♦ Université interaméricaine de Porto Rico (internationally oriented national body)
- ♦ Université internationale (inactive)
- ♦ Université internationale du développement durable (internationally oriented national body)
- ♦ Université internationale d'études sociales 'Guido Carli' (internationally oriented national body)
- ♦ Université internationale islamique Malaisie (#13961)

♦ Université internationale de langue française au service du développement africain à Alexandrie d'Egypte (Université Senghor) **20691**

Rector 1 Place Ahmed Orabi, BP 415, El Mancheya, Alexandria, 21111, Egypt. T. +2034843374. Fax +2034843479. E-mail: rectorat@usenghor.org – info@usenghor.org.
URL: http://www.usenghor-francophonie.org/

History 26 May 1989, Dakar (Senegal). Founded by Summit of Heads of State and Government of Francophone countries. Since 1997, an operating institution of *Organisation internationale de la Francophonie (OIF, #17809)*. Officially opened 4 Nov 1990. Former names and other names: *Université Léopold Sedar Senghor – Université internationale de langue française au service du développement africain* – former; *Université francophone d'Alexandrie* – former. **Aims** Become a major player in the training and capacity building of executives in and for Africa. **Structure** General Assembly; High Council; Board of Directors; Academic Council; Departments; 12 Campuses outside Egypt. **Languages** Egyptian Arabic, English, French. Teaching in French; learning in French and Arabic. **Staff** 75.00 FTE, paid. **Finance** Sources: contributions; government support; grants; international organizations; private foundations; subscriptions. Annual budget: 2,500,000 EUR (2022). **Activities** Events/meetings; research/documentation; training/education. **Publications** *Collections Université Senghor*. **IGO Relations** Memorandum of Understanding with (1): *Secretariat of the Convention of Wetlands (#19200)*. Cooperates with (2): *Conférence au sommet des chefs d'Etat et de gouvernement des pays ayant le français en partage (Sommet de la Francophonie, #04648)*; *Organisation internationale de la Francophonie (OIF, #17809)*. [2022.10.18/XF2205/**F**]

- ♦ Université international de l'espace (#15575)
- ♦ Université internationale de théâtre (inactive)
- ♦ Université islamique de l'Afrique de l'Ouest / see Islamic University in Niger (#16054)
- ♦ Université islamique au Niger (#16054)
- ♦ Université islamique de technologie (#16055)
- ♦ Université Léopold Sedar Senghor – Université internationale de langue française au service du développement africain / see Université internationale de langue française au service du développement africain à Alexandrie d'Egypte (#20691)
- ♦ Université libre internationale de Bruxelles (internationally oriented national body)
- ♦ Université libre international de Moldavie (internationally oriented national body)
- ♦ Université libre des pays des Grands Lacs (internationally oriented national body)
- ♦ Université libre de science spirituelle (#19134)
- ♦ Université maritime mondiale (#21633)
- ♦ Université de la Méditerranée / see Mediterranean Universities Union (#16687)
- ♦ Université de la Méditerranée, Marseille (internationally oriented national body)
- ♦ Université mobile méditerranéenne de mastologie (#16836)
- ♦ Université mondiale
- ♦ Université mondiale du développement durable / see International University on Sustainable Development
- ♦ Université des Nations Unies (#20642)
- ♦ Université nordique d'été (#17535)
- ♦ Université Numérique Francophone Mondiale (internationally oriented national body)
- ♦ Université Numérique Francophone des Sciences de la Santé et du Sport (internationally oriented national body)
- ♦ Université du Pacifique Sud (#20703)
- ♦ Université pour la Paix (#20702)
- ♦ Université de paix, Namur (internationally oriented national body)
- ♦ Université Panafricaine (unconfirmed)
- ♦ Université radiophonique internationale / see International Radio and Television Union (#14689)
- ♦ Université radiophonique et télévisuelle internationale / see International Radio and Television Union (#14689)
- ♦ Université et la recherche de la paix (inactive)
- ♦ Université de relations et des études internationales (internationally oriented national body)
- ♦ Université des réseaux d'expression française (inactive)
- ♦ Université rurale européenne / see Association for European Rural Universities (#02541)
- ♦ Université sans frontière (internationally oriented national body)
- ♦ Universités Caraïbe (#20694)
- ♦ **Université Senghor** Université internationale de langue française au service du développement africain à Alexandrie d'Egypte (#20691)
- ♦ Université spirituelle internationale des Brahma Kumaris (#03311)
- ♦ Université technique du Moyen-Orient (internationally oriented national body)
- ♦ Université virtuelle africaine (#00496)

♦ Universities Allied for Essential Medicines (UAEM) **20692**

Exec Dir address not obtained. E-mail: info@essentialmedicine.org.
URL: http://www.essentialmedicine.org/

History USA. Registered in accordance with US law. **Events** *Europe Conference* Maastricht (Netherlands) 2018, *Europe Conference* Berlin (Germany) 2016, *Europe Conference* Basel (Switzerland) 2014.
Members Chapters in 5 countries:
Canada, Germany, Uganda, UK, USA.
Consultative Status Consultative status granted from: *ECOSOC (#05331)* (Special). **NGO Relations** Member of: *European Alliance for Responsible R and D and Affordable Medicines (#05879)*. [2017/XJ8091/**F**]

♦ Universities of Applied Sciences Network (UASNET) **20693**

SG Vlaamse Hogescholenraad, Ravensteingalerij 27, bus 3, 1000 Brussels, Belgium. T. +3222111006. E-mail: bruno@uasnet.eu – post@uasnet.eu.
URL: http://www.uasnet.eu/

History Developed out of the EDUPROF project (2008-2011). Current title adopted, 20 Jan 2011. Also known as: *European Network for Universities of Applied Sciences (UASNET)*. Current statutes into force 1 Jan 2012. **Aims** Function as an informal peer learning community for national associations for universities of applied sciences (UAS) that want to work together on strengthening the profile of professionally oriented higher education and applied sciences within Europe. **Structure** General Assembly (biannual); Steering Committee; Secretariat. **Languages** English. **Finance** Members' dues. **Activities** Events/meetings. **Publications** Positions papers; reports.

Members Representatives of national or regional associations of universities of applied sciences in 8 countries:
Belgium, Denmark, Estonia, Finland, Ireland, Lithuania, Netherlands, Portugal. [2019.02.12/XJ1574/**F**]

♦ Universities Association of the Union of Soviet Socialist Republics / see Euroasian Universities Association (#05641)
♦ Universities Bureau of the British Empire / see Association of Commonwealth Universities, The (#02440)

♦ Universities Caribbean 20694

Universités Caraïbe – Universidades Caribe

Secretariat c/o Latin American Caribbean Centre, Vice Chancellery, Univeristy of the West Indies, Kingston 7, Jamaica. T. +18767024721. Fax +18769777525. E-mail: universitiescaribbean@gmail.com.
URL: http://www.universitiescaribbean.com/

History Nov 1967, San Juan (Puerto Rico). Founded at inaugural meeting attended by heads of 16 Caribbean universities, following recommendations of meeting 1967, Tobago. Former names and other names: *Association of Caribbean Universities and Research Institutes (UNICA)* – former (Nov 1967 to Nov 2018); *Association des Universités et Centres de Recherche de la Caraïbe* – former (Nov 1967 to Nov 2018); *Asociación de Universidades e Institutos de Investigación del Caribe* – former (Nov 1967 to Nov 2018). Registration: Jamaica. **Aims** Promote positive, carefully directed efforts for Caribbean development; encourage contact, communication and collaboration among universities and research institutes of the greater Caribbean region, through meetings, joint undertakings in teaching and research, publications, staff and student exchange; work with national associations of universities to achieve excellence in teaching and research and to develop advanced level studies. **Structure** General Assembly; Executive Committee of 12 members. Finance Sub-Committee; Standing Committee of Directors of Research Institutes; Standing Research Liaison Committee. **Languages** English, French, Spanish. **Staff** 1.00 FTE, paid. **Finance** Members' dues: US$ 1,000 (universities and research institutes); US$ 4,000 (large universities). **Activities** Organizes: meetings; workshops; conferences; seminars; Assembly of UNICA Presidents. Program areas: agriculture – increased food production of the small farmer; science – new sources/alternative forms of energy; education – audio-visual material related to Caribbean region for classroom use. Includes *UNICA Consortium for the Training of Administrators of Natural Areas in the Lesser Antilles. Caribbean and Latin American Studies Library.* **Events** *Conference* Mayagüez (Puerto Rico) 2007, *Biennial Conference* Jamaica 1996, *Assembly of university presidents* San Juan (Puerto Rico) 1995, *Biennial Conference* San Juan (Puerto Rico) 1994, *Biennial Conference* Santo Domingo (Dominican Rep) 1992. **Publications** *Regional Sample Survey of Studies on Urbanism.* Conference proceedings. Information Services: *Caribbean and Latin American Studies Library.* **Members** Voting universities and research institutes in 20 countries and territories of the greater Caribbean region:
Antigua-Barbuda, Barbados, Cuba, Dominica, Dominican Rep, Guatemala, Guyana, Haiti, Honduras, Jamaica, Mexico, Neth Antilles, Nicaragua, Panama, Peru, Puerto Rico, Suriname, Trinidad-Tobago, Venezuela, Virgin Is USA.
Regional affiliate:
Association of Caribbean University, Research and Institutional Libraries (ACURIL, #02413).
IGO Relations Cooperative program with: *OAS (#17629).* **NGO Relations** Member of: *Consejo Universitario Iberoamericano (CUIB, #04727); Inter-American Organization for Higher Education (IOHE, #11442).* Working with: *Caribbean Natural Resources Institute (CANARI, #03525)* in setting up *Consortium of Caribbean Universities for Natural Resource Management (CCUNRM, no recent information).* Cooperates with: *International Council for Adult Education (ICAE, #12983).* [2021/XD4170/y/**D**]

♦ Universities Federation for Animal Welfare (internationally oriented national body)
♦ Universities Federation for Animal Welfare – Science in the Service of Animal Welfare / see Universities Federation for Animal Welfare
♦ Universities Field Staff International / see Institute of World Affairs
♦ Universities Fighting World Hunger (unconfirmed)
♦ Universities and the Quest for Peace (inactive)

♦ Universities Space Research Association (USRA) 20695

Pres and CEO 7178 Columbia Gateway Dr, Columbia MD 21046, USA. T. +14107302656. E-mail: info@usra.edu.
URL: http://www.usra.edu/

History Founded 12 Mar 1969. **Aims** Advance space- and aeronautics-related sciences exploration through innovative research, technology, and education programmes; promote space and aeronautics policy; develop and operate premier facilities and programmes by involving universities, governments ad the private sector for the benefit of humanity. **Structure** Council of Institutions (COI); Board of Trustees; Science Councils. **Staff** 500.00 FTE, paid. **Events** *Symposium* Washington, DC (USA) 2003. **Publications** Annual Report.
Members Colleges and universities (97) in 5 countries:
Canada, Germany, Israel, UK, USA. [2016.10.20/XD7497/**D**]

♦ Universiti Islam Antarabangsa Malaysia (#13961)
♦ Universiti Perubatan Antarabangsa Malaysia (internationally oriented national body)
♦ University of the Americas (internationally oriented national body)

♦ University of the Arctic (UArctic) 20696

International Secretariat Univ of Lapland, Box 122, FI-96101 Rovaniemi, Finland. T. +358405010209. Fax +35816362941. E-mail: secretariat@uarctic.org.
Pres GRID/Arendal, Box 183, 4802 Arendal, Norway. T. +4790870099. E-mail: president@uarctic.org.
URL: http://www.uarctic.org/

History Jun 2001, Rovaniemi (Finland). Created through the *Arctic Council (#01097).* Registration: Finland; EU Transparency Register, No/ID: 672801740172-77, Start date: 3 Nov 2020. **Aims** Develop knowledge to address local and global challenges of relevance to Arctic peoples and societies by providing unique educational, research, and innovation opportunities through collaboration within a powerful network of member institutions; uphold principles of sustainable development as well as the United Nations Sustainable Development Goals. **Structure** Assembly; Board; Strategic leadership; Senior Leadership Team. International Secretariat, located in Rovaniemi (Finland). Decentralized leadership and administration with offices, programmes and other functions hosted at member institutions in the Circumpolar North. **Languages** English, Russian. **Staff** 12.00 FTE, paid. **Finance** Sources: contributions; fundraising; gifts, legacies; government support; in-kind support; members' dues; private foundations; revenue from activities/projects. Membership fees and in-kind support from members makes up the largest part of finances. Annual budget: 845,000 EUR (2022). **Activities** Advocacy/lobbying/activism; capacity building; events/meetings; knowledge management/information dissemination; networking/liaising; research/documentation; training/education. **Events** *Congress* Moscow (Russia) 2022, *Annual Members Meeting* Portland, ME (USA) 2022, *Congress* Reykjavik (Iceland) 2021, *Rectors Forum* Peterborough, ON (Canada) 2019, *Annual Council Meeting* Stockholm (Sweden) 2019. **Publications** *Shared Voices* (12 a year) – newsletter; *UArctic News.* Calendar; online tools.
Members Universities, colleges, research institutes and indigenous people's organizations (over 200) in 24 countries and territories:
Austria, Belgium, Canada, China, Czechia, Denmark, Faeroe Is, Finland, France, Germany, Greenland, Iceland, India, Ireland, Italy, Japan, Korea Rep, Mongolia, Netherlands, Norway, Svalbard, Sweden, UK, USA.
Russian membership paused.
Consultative Status Consultative status granted from: *UNESCO (#20322)* (Consultative Status). **IGO Relations** Observer status with (2): *Arctic Council (#01097); UNESCO (#20322).* Memoranda of Understanding (MoU) with all permanent participant indigenous organizations of the Arctic Council. **NGO Relations** Cooperates with (1): *Association of Polar Early Career Scientists (APECS, #02864).* Also links with national organizations. [2022.05.11/XD7508/**D**]

♦ University of Asia and the Pacific (internationally oriented national body)

♦ University Association for Contemporary European Studies (UACES) 20697

Exec Dir Idea Space 83, 83 Lavender Hill, London, SW11 5QL, UK. T. +442045244294. E-mail: admin@uaces.org.
URL: http://www.uaces.org/

History 1968, London (UK). England and Wales registered Charitable Incorporated Organisation: 1163773. **Aims** Advance education for the public benefit through promotion of teaching and research in contemporary European Studies. **Structure** Committee of Trustees. **Languages** English. **Staff** 3.00 FTE, paid. **Finance** Members' dues. Sale of publications. **Activities** Events/meetings; research/documentation. **Events** *Annual Conference* Belfast (UK) 2023, *Annual Conference* Lisbon (Portugal) 2019, *Annual Conference* Bath (UK) 2018, *European Conference on Teaching and Learning Politics, International Relations and European Studies* Prague (Czechia) 2018, *Annual Conference* Krakow (Poland) 2017. **Publications** *UACES Newsletter* (4 a year); *JCER – Journal of Contemporary European Research; Journal of Common Market Studies (JCMS). Contemporary European Studies* – series. Books. **Members** Individuals (over 1,000) in over 50 countries. Membership countries not specified. **NGO Relations** *International Studies Association (ISA, #15615).* [2023/XD3870/**D**]

♦ University Center for the Euro-Mediterranean Studies / see Euro-Mediterranean University (#05728)
♦ University Center for International Studies, Pittsburgh (internationally oriented national body)

♦ University of Central Asia (UCA) 20698

Central Admin Office 138 Toktogula Street, 720001 Bishkek, Kyrgyzstan. T. +996312910822. Fax +996312910831.
URL: http://www.ucentralasia.org/

History Founded 2000, by International treaty signed by the Presidents of Kazakhstan, Kyrgyzstan and Tajikistan and His Highness the Aga Khan. **Aims** Promote social and economic development of Central Asia, particularly its mountain societies, while helping different peoples of the region to preserve and draw upon their rich cultural traditions and heritages as assets for the future. **Languages** English, Kazakh, Kirghiz, Russian, Tajik. **Activities** Training/education.
Members Universities (3) in 3 countries:
Kazakhstan, Kyrgyzstan, Tajikistan.
NGO Relations *Aga Khan Development Network (AKDN, #00544); Mountain Partnership (MP, #16862).* Founding member of: *Global Research Consortium on Economic Structural Transformation (GReCEST).* [2016.01.13/XM2204/**D**]

♦ University Centre for Development Cooperation, Brussels (internationally oriented national body)
♦ University Centre for Peace Research, Vienna (internationally oriented national body)
♦ University College for Aspiring Missionary Doctors / see CUAMM – Medici con l'Africa
♦ University College of the West Indies / see University of the West Indies (#20705)
♦ University Consortium / see Southeast Asian University Consortium for Graduate Education in Agriculture and Natural Resources (#19786)
♦ University Council for Educational Administration (internationally oriented national body)
♦ University of East Africa (inactive)
♦ University of Eurasian Theatre (internationally oriented national body)
♦ University Foundation for Development Cooperation (internationally oriented national body)
♦ University Foundation for International Development Cooperation (internationally oriented national body)
♦ University of Global Education / see Institute of Global Education
♦ University of Hawai'i Institute for Peace / see Spark M Matsunaga Institute for Peace and Conflict Resolution

♦ University Industry Innovation Network (UIIN) 20699

CEO Science Park 400, 1098 XH Amsterdam, Netherlands. T. +31208950182. E-mail: office@uiin.org.
URL: http://www.uiin.org/

History 2012. **Aims** Contribute to the improvement of the relationships between university and industry. **Structure** Board of Directors. **Finance** Members' dues. **Activities** Awards/prizes/competitions; events/meetings; training/education. **Events** *University-Industry Interaction Conference* Budapest (Hungary) 2020, *University-Industry Interaction Conference* Helsinki (Finland) 2019, *University-Industry Interaction Conference* London (UK) 2018, *Asia-Pacific Conference on University-Industry Engagement* Adelaide, SA (Australia) 2017, *University-Industry Interaction Conference* Dublin (Ireland) 2017. **Publications** *University-Industry Innovation Magazine.*
Members Organizational in 27 countries:
Australia, Belgium, Colombia, Czechia, Denmark, Finland, Germany, Hungary, Iceland, India, Italy, Latvia, Lithuania, Malaysia, Netherlands, New Zealand, Norway, Portugal, Romania, Russia, South Africa, Spain, Sweden, Thailand, Türkiye, UK, USA.
Included in the above, 2 organizations listed in this Yearbook:
EFMD – The Management Development Network (#05387); EIT Digital (#05404).
NGO Relations Member of: *EFMD – The Management Development Network (#05387).* [2020/XJ7909/y/**F**]

♦ University Institute of European Studies (internationally oriented national body)
♦ University Institute of European Studies, Torino (internationally oriented national body)
♦ University Institute on International Studies / see Centre for International Information and Documentation, Barcelona
♦ University Institute of Oriental Studies (internationally oriented national body)
♦ University of International Business and Economics (internationally oriented national body)
♦ University of the Mediterranean / see Mediterranean Universities Union (#16687)

♦ University Mobility in Asia and the Pacific (UMAP) 20700

SG Fu Jen Catholic Univ Office of Int Education, No 510 Zhongzheng Rd, Xinzhuang Dist, New Taipei City 24205, Taiwan. T. +886229056358. Fax +886229017174. E-mail: umaptaiwan@gmail.com.
URL: http://140.136.202.112/

History Founded 1993. International Secretariat managed by Japan from 2000 to 2005; transferred to Thailand from 2006 to 2010; transferred to Fu Jen Catholic University in Taiwan since 2011, under the commission of authority from MOE (Ministry of Education) in Taiwan. **Aims** Achieve a better understanding of cultural, economic and social systems of the other countries and territories in Asia and the Pacific region through enhanced cooperation among *higher education* institutions and increased mobility of university students and staff. **Structure** Board (meets at least twice a year); Committees; International Secretariat. **Languages** English. **Staff** 4.00 FTE, paid. **Finance** Grants and income classified into different funds: (a) General Fund, comprising membership fees and interest income; (b) Trust Fund, from Japan's UMAP Student Support Trust Fund Account and UMAP Scholarship Program Fund Account; (c) Extra-Budgetary Funds – members and others may make additional contributions or provide facilities or other resources "in kind". **Activities** Training/education; events/meetings. **Events** *Board Meeting* Philippines 2011, *Board Meeting* Taiwan 2011, *Meeting* Seoul (Korea Rep) 1999, *Biennial reference group meeting* Bangkok (Thailand) 1998, *Biennial reference group meeting* Auckland (New Zealand) 1996. **Publications** *2012 UMAP International Conference-Scross-Cultural Exchang ein Global Education* (2012). Annual Report; Committee and Board meeting reports.
Members Governmental and non-governmental representatives of the higher education sector in the region. Full in 19 countries and territories:
Australia, Bangladesh, Cambodia, Fiji, Hong Kong, India, Indonesia, Japan, Kazakhstan, Korea Rep, Macau, Malaysia, Mexico, Mongolia, Papua New Guinea, Philippines, Taiwan, Thailand, Vietnam.
NGO Relations Cooperates with: *United Nations Academic Impact (UNAI, #20516).* [2014.11.10/XF3048/y/**F**]

♦ University Mobility in the Indian Ocean Region (internationally oriented national body)

♦ University Network of the European Capitals of Culture (UNeECC) . . 20701

SG ULBS, Bd-ul Victoriei Nr 10, 550024 Sibiu, Romania.
URL: http://www.uneecc.org/

History Founded Dec 2006, Pécs (Hungary), by 15 founding members. Registered in accordance with Hungarian law. **Aims** Ensure recognition of the role and contribution of universities to success of the cities conferred the title "European Capital of Culture"; provide member universities with possibility of continuous and full participation in the European Capitals of Culture movement enhanced by "Universities of the Year"; foster inter-university cooperation to develop and reshape the universities' regional position to create new activities for city and university collaboration. **Structure** General Assembly; Board; Presidency; Secretariat. **Languages** English. **Finance** Members' dues. **Activities** Events/meetings; training/education. **Events** *Transatlantic Dialogue* Esch-sur-Alzette (Luxembourg) 2017, *Annual Conference* Pilsen (Czech Rep)

2015, *Transatlantic Dialogue* Luxembourg (Luxembourg) 2014, *General Assembly and Conference / Annual Conference* Umeå (Sweden) 2014, *General Assembly and Conference / Annual Conference* Marseille (France) 2013. **Publications** Conference proceedings.
Members Universities and colleges (47) in 25 countries:
Austria, Belgium, Bulgaria, Czechia, Denmark, Estonia, France, Germany, Greece, Hungary, Ireland, Italy, Lithuania, Luxembourg, Malta, Netherlands, Norway, Poland, Portugal, Romania, Slovenia, Spain, Sweden, Türkiye, UK.
Included in the above, one college listed in this Yearbook:
College of Europe (#04105). [2018.06.01/XJ3759/**E**]

♦ University of the Pacific Research Centre (internationally oriented national body)

♦ University for Peace (UPEACE) 20702

Université pour la Paix – Universidad para la Paz (UPAZ)

Rector PO Box 138-6100, Ciudad Colón, San José, San José, 10701, Costa Rica. T. +50622059000. Fax +50622491929. E-mail: info@upeace.org.
URL: http://www.upeace.org/

History 5 Dec 1980. Established on the initiative of the Government of Costa Rica, under *United Nations (UN, #20515)* Resolution 35/55 of the 35th Session of the General Assembly, which called for a treaty organization to "support the central Peace and Security Objectives of the United Nations through a World-Wide Movement of Education of Peace." Proposed by President of Costa Rica, Rodrigo Carazo, Sep 1978; resolutions, 19 Dec 1978 and 14 Dec 1979, of UN General Assembly; preliminary work of *International Association of University Presidents (IAUP, #12248).* Inaugural meeting of Council: 6 Mar 1982. Headquarters in Costa Rica. Statutes registered in *'UNTS 1/19735'.* Former names and other names: *United Nations – Mandated University for Peace* – alias. **Aims** Promote among all human beings the spirit of understanding, tolerance and peaceful coexistence; stimulate cooperation among peoples; help lessen obstacles and threats to world peace and progress, in keeping with the noble aspirations proclaimed in the Charter of the United Nations. **Structure** Council (governing body) comprises 17 members, 10 of whom are appointed by UN Secretary-General in consultation with the Director-General of UNESCO and 7 ex-officio members as follows: the Chancellor of the University; the Rector; 2 members nominated by the Government of Costa Rica; a representative of the UN Secretary-General; a representative of the Director General of UNESCO; the Rector of the United Nations University. **Languages** English, Spanish. **Staff** 76.00 FTE, paid; 10.00 FTE, voluntary. **Finance** Student tuition and voluntary contributions by governments, intergovernmental bodies, foundations and other nongovernmental organizations (not specified). **Activities** Capacity building; events/meetings; research/documentation; training/education. Active in: China, Colombia, Costa Rica, Ethiopia, Germany, Honduras, Italy, Netherlands, Philippines, Serbia, Somalia, Switzerland, USA. **Events** *Launch of White Paper on Illicit Economies and Organized Crime in Africa* Geneva (Switzerland) 2022, *International Seminar on Access to Justice for Afro-descendants in Latin America and the Caribbean* San José (Costa Rica) 2022, *Journalism in Times of Crisis* San José (Costa Rica) 2021, *Latin America – Crisis and Convulsions in an Unstable Global Context* San José (Costa Rica) 2020, *Model UN conference* San José (Costa Rica) 2005. **Publications** *Ideas for Peace* (weekly); *Africa Peace and Conflict Journal.* Maintains a library, which includes books, journals, interdisciplinary documentary collection and computer-based information services.
Members Governments signatory to the International Agreement – 42 countries:
Argentina, Bangladesh, Bosnia-Herzegovina, Cambodia, Cameroon, Chile, Colombia, Costa Rica, Cuba, Cyprus, Dominican Rep, Ecuador, El Salvador, Guatemala, Guyana, Honduras, India, Italy, Korea Rep, Liberia, Mexico, Monaco, Montenegro, Nepal, Nicaragua, Pakistan, Panama, Peru, Philippines, Russia, Senegal, Serbia, Slovenia, Somalia, Spain, Sri Lanka, St Lucia, Suriname, Togo, Türkiye, Uruguay, Venezuela.
IGO Relations Observer status with (1): *United Nations (UN, #20515)* (General Assembly). *ECOSOC (#05331).* Agreement of cooperation with the United Nations, as proposed by ECOSOC, 21 May 1986. Special agreement with: *UNESCO (#20322)*; UN Department for Disarmament Affairs (UN/DDA); *United Nations Human Settlements Programme (UN-Habitat, #20572)*: *United Nations Interregional Crime and Justice Research Institute (UNICRI, #20580)*; *United Nations Institute for Disarmament Research (UNIDIR, #20575)*; *United Nations Institute for Training and Research (UNITAR, #20576)*; *United Nations University (UNU, #20642).* **NGO Relations** Agreements with other institutions and national universities, including: *Instituto Interamericano de Derechos Humanos (IIDH, #11334).* Instrumental in setting up: *Centro Internacional de Investigación e Información para la Paz (CIIIP-UPAZ, no recent information)*; *European Centre for Peace and Development (ECPD, #06496).* [2022.10.12/XF8239/**F***]

♦ University of Peace, Namur (internationally oriented national body)
♦ University Platform for Research on Islam in Europe and Lebanon (#18396)
♦ University of Relations and International Studies (internationally oriented national body)
♦ University Research Corporation International (internationally oriented national body)
♦ University Royal Oriental Institute of Naples / see University Institute of Oriental Studies
♦ University of Southern Europe / see International University of Monaco

♦ University of the South Pacific (USP) 20703

Université du Pacifique Sud

Contact The Registrar, Laucala Campus, Suva, Fiji. T. +6793231000. Fax +6793231531 – +6793231539. E-mail: library@usp.ac.fj.
URL: http://www.usp.ac.fj/

History 1967, Suva (Fiji), by Royal Charter, following consultations by the *'Interim Council of the University of the South Pacific'* with governments in the Pacific region (Cook Is, Fiji, Kiribati, Marshall Is, Nauru, Niue, Samoa, Solomon Is, Tokelau, Tonga, Tuvalu, Vanuatu). **Aims** Serve the needs of governments in the Pacific by providing *education* and *training*, research and consultancy services geared to regional needs. **Structure** Council, comprising Pro-Chancellor, Vice-Chancellor, Deputy Vice-Chancellor, 3 Pro Vice-Chancellors, 28 appointed members; one appointed by Privy Council, 4 appointed by Senate, 2 appointed by Statute 11 (1) (b) (xv), 3 elected by the Court of Convocation, 2 elected by academic staff, 4 elected by students associations and 2 co-opted members. In attendance: 4 Deans; Director Finance; Director Planning and Development. Senate, comprising (all ex-officio) Vice-Chancellor (Chair), Deputy Vice-Chancellor, Pro Vice-Chancellors, Deans, USP Professors, University Librarian and Appointed Members. Officers: Chancellor; Pro-Chancellor; Vice-Chancellor; Deputy Vice-Chancellor; 3 Pro-Chancellors; Registrar. Council Committees (6): Audit; Finance and General Purpose; Tender Board; Budget and Strategic Planning; Staff Policy; Staff Conduct. Committees of the Senate (10): Academic Standards and Quality; Faculty Boards of Studies; Distance and Flexible Learning; Library Advisory; Student Development; Campus Directors Conference; University Open Day Organizing; MBA Advisory Board; MSP Advisory; University Research. Joint Committees of Council and Senate (4): Appointments; Honorary Degrees; Staff Review; Students Discipline Appeals. Campuses (14): Alufa, Apia (Samoa); Cook Islands, Ratoronga (Cook Is); Kiribati, Tarawa (Kiribati); Niue, Alofi (Niue); Tonga, Nuku'alofa (Tonga); Emalus, Port Vila (Vanuatu); Labasa (Fiji); Marshall Islands, Majuro (Marshall Is); Solomon Islands, Honiara (Solomon Is); Tuvalu, Funafuti (Tuvalu); Laucala, Suva (Fiji); Lautoka (Fiji); Nauru; Tokelau, Alafua (Tokelau). **Languages** English. **Staff** 524.00 FTE, paid. **Finance** Grants from member countries (about 35% of total); student fees (30%); aid and donations (20%); balance – trading and miscellaneous receipts; capital development and other projects – grants from countries and organizations outside USP region (especially Australia, European Union, UK, Japan). Budget (annual): about Fiji Dollars 120 million. **Activities** Education programmes. Centers and institutes include: *Oceania Centre for Arts, Culture and Pacific Studies (OCACPS, #17655)*; *Pacific Centre for Environment and Sustainable Development (PaCE-SD, #17940)*; *Chemical Society of the South Pacific (CSSP, #03862)*; *Pacific Islands Legal Information Institute (PacLII).* Meeting activities. **Events** *PacINET : INET Pacific Regional Conference* Suva (Fiji) 2012, *International conference on chemistry, environment and climate change / Conference* Suva (Fiji) 2011, *Science of the Pacific peoples conference* Suva (Fiji) 1992, *Global community forum* 1990, *Global community forum on Pacific cooperation and development* Apia (Samoa) 1987. **Publications** *USP Beat* (bi-weekly) – news magazine; *Oceanian Wave* (4 a year) – magazine; *USP Calendar* (annual). Annual Report; Enrolment Guide; Orientation Guide (for new students).
Members Governments of 12 countries and territories:
Cook Is, Fiji, Kiribati, Marshall Is, Nauru, Niue, Samoa, Solomon Is, Tokelau, Tonga, Tuvalu, Vanuatu.
IGO Relations Under Lomé Conventions, links with: *European Commission (EC, #06633).* Observer member of: *Western and Central Pacific Fisheries Commission (WCPFC, #20912).* Official observer of: *Pacific Islands Law Officers' Network (PILON, #17972).* **NGO Relations** Institutional member of: *Regional Energy Resources Information Center (RERIC, #18780).* Member of: *Asian and Pacific Energy-Environment Planning Network (APENPLAN, no recent information)*; *Asia-Pacific Quality Network (APQN, #02004)*; *International Science Council (ISC, #14796)*; *International Union for Conservation of Nature and Natural Resources (IUCN, #15766)*; *Pacific Islands Telecommunications Association (PITA, #17979).* Library is member of: *International Federation of Library Associations and Institutions (IFLA, #13470).* Student body: *University of South Pacific Students' Association (USPSA, no recent information).* Set up: *Pacific Writing Forum.* Instrumental in setting up: *Oceania Sport Information Centre (OSIC).* Member of: *International Association of Universities (IAU, #12246).* [2010/XF8052/**F***]

♦ University Space Engineering Consortium / see UNISEC Europe (#20489)

♦ University Space Engineering Consortium (UNISEC-Global) 20704

SG Central Yayoi 2F, 2-3-2 Yayoi, Bunkyo, Tokyo, 113-0032 Japan. T. +81358006645. Fax +81368263988. E-mail: secretariat@unisec-global.org.
URL: http://www.unisec-global.org/

History 24 Nov 2013, Tokyo (Japan). Set up 24 Nov 2013, at end of 1st UNISEC-Global Meeting. Registration: Japan. **Aims** Create a world where space science and technology is used by individuals and institutions in every country and offers opportunities across the whole structure of society for peaceful purposes and for the benefit of humankind. **Structure** Steering Committee; Secretary-General; Local Chapters (24). **Languages** English. **Staff** 4.00 FTE, paid. Several voluntary. **Finance** Sources: donations; revenue from activities/projects; sponsorship. Annual budget: 40,000,000 JPY (2022). **Activities** Awards/prizes/competitions; events/meetings; research and development; training/education. **Events** *APRSAF Space Education for All Working Group – Higher Education* Hanoi (Vietnam) 2022, *Meeting* Istanbul (Turkey) 2022, *Meeting* Tokyo (Japan) 2019, *Meeting* Strasbourg (France) 2018, *Meeting* Rome (Italy) 2017. **Publications** *UNISEC Space Takumi Journal.*
Members Full in 28 countries and territories:
Algeria, Angola, Bangladesh, Bulgaria, Canada, Chile, Costa Rica, Egypt, Germany, India, Italy, Japan, Lithuania, Malaysia, Mexico, Mongolia, Namibia, Nepal, Nigeria, Peru, Philippines, Russia, South Africa, Taiwan, Thailand, Tunisia, Türkiye, Vietnam.
Included in the above, 2 organizations listed in this Yearbook:
International Space University (ISU, #15575); *UNISEC Europe (#20489).*
IGO Relations Observer status with (1): *Committee on the Peaceful Uses of Outer Space (COPUOS, #04277).* [2023.02.17/XJ7920/y/**C**]

♦ University Students for the Third World (internationally oriented national body)
♦ University Surgeons of South-East Asia / see Association of University Surgeons of Asia (#02974)
♦ University Without Walls International Council / see International Council for Innovation in Higher Education

♦ University of the West Indies (UWI) 20705

Université des Indes occidentales

St Augustine Campus address not obtained. T. +18686622002. Fax +18686639684. E-mail: marketing.communications@sta.uwi.edu.
URL: http://www.uwi.tt/

History 1948, Mona (Jamaica), as *University College of the West Indies*, when it was a College of the University of London. Present name and status adopted 2 Apr 1962, when it achieved full university status. *Imperial College of Tropical Agriculture (inactive)* was converted into the St Augustine (Trinidad-Tobago) Campus, 1961. A 3rd campus was established at Cave Hill (Barbados), 1963. Open Campus opened, 2008. **Aims** Unlock West Indian potential for economic and cultural growth through high quality *teaching* and research aimed at meeting critical regional needs, by providing West Indian society with an active intellectual centre and by linking the West Indian community with distinguished centres of research and teaching in the Caribbean and overseas. **Structure** Steering Committee for International Offices (meets annually, usually in Jan). Campuses (4): Cave Hill (Barbados); Mona (Jamaica); St Augustine (Trinidad-Tobago); Open Campus with 16 Centres (Anguilla; Antigua-Barbuda; Bahamas; Barbados; Belize; Virgin Is UK; Cayman Is; Dominica; Grenada; Jamaica; Montserrat; St Kitts-Nevis; St Lucia; St Vincent-Grenadines; Trinidad-Tobago; Turks-Caicos). Faculties (7): Engineering; Humanities and Education; Law; Medical Sciences; Science and Agriculture; Social Sciences; Pure and Applied Science. Management with Vice-Chancellor as Chief Executive and Chancellor chairing University Council. Former students: *UWI Medical Alumni Association (UWIMAA, #20738).* **Languages** English. **Staff** St Augustine (Trinidad-Tobago) Campus: 689 academic staff and 2,231 non-academic staff. **Finance** Arranged by Government of Trinidad and Tobago in consultation with other CARICOM countries. **Activities** Institutions include: *Caribbean Agricultural Research and Development Institute (CARDI, #03436)*; Institute of Business; *Institute of Caribbean Studies, Kingston*; *Institute of International Relations, St Augustine*; Institute of Social and Economic Research; School of Continuing Studies (previously Extra Mural department), including *Women and Development Unit (WAND, #20990)*; Institute of Gender and Development Studies; Centre for Resource Management Environmental Studies (CERMES); *UWI Centre for Environment and Development, Mona (UWICED, see: #20705)*; UWI Creative Arts Centre, St Augustine (Trinidad-Tobago); *Caribbean Landslide Working Group (see: #20705).* Organizes regional conferences on university-industry cooperation in the Caribbean. Instrumental in setting up: *Association of Caribbean Higher Education Administrators (ACHEA, #02406)*; *Caribbean Centre for Money and Finance (#03469)*; *Caribbean Law Institute (CLI, #03523)*, a joint project with Florida State University College of Law. Provides educational certification programme for *Association of Caribbean Commissioners of Police (ACCP, #02403).* **Events** *Caribbean emergency medicine congress* Barbados 2009, *Biennial international conference on colorectal cancer* Bridgetown (Barbados) 2008, *Sub-regional meeting regarding higher education in the Caribbean* Kingston (Jamaica) 2005, *Conference on re-mapping the Americas* St Augustine (Trinidad-Tobago) 2005, *Conference on evaluation in education* St Michael (Barbados) 2003. **Publications** *UWI Today* (12 a year) – newspaper; *STAN – St Augustine News* (4 a year) – magazine; *Business, Finance and Economics in Emerging Economies* (2 a year); *Pelican* (2 a year) – magazine; *Caribbean Dialogue* – policy bulletin of Caribbean affairs; *Caribbean Journal of Social Sciences*; *Journal of Tropical Agriculture.* Annual reports; faculty reports; calendar; department reports; faculty brochures.
Members Supported by and serves 16 countries and territories:
Anguilla, Antigua-Barbuda, Bahamas, Barbados, Belize, Cayman Is, Dominica, Grenada, Jamaica, Montserrat, St Kitts-Nevis, St Lucia, St Vincent-Grenadines, Trinidad-Tobago, Turks-Caicos, Virgin Is UK.
IGO Relations Recognized by the Community Treaty as an Institution of: *Caribbean Community (CARICOM, #03476).* Observer to: *Caribbean Regional Fisheries Mechanism (CRFM, #03547)*; *Regional Nursing Body, CARICOM Community (RNB, no recent information).* Contracting party to the Agreement establishing: *Council of Legal Education (CLE, #04908).* Coordinates: *Caribbean Information System for the Agricultural Sciences (CAGRIS, #03518).* Partner with: *European Union – Latin America and the Caribbean Foundation (EU-LAC Foundation, #08999).* Member of: *Latin American and Caribbean Research Network (#16284).* Under Lomé Conventions, links with: *European Commission (EC, #06633).* **NGO Relations** Library is member of: *International Federation of Library Associations and Institutions (IFLA, #13470).* Member of: *International Association of Universities (IAU, #12246).* Cooperates with: *Caribbean Regional Network of People Living with HIV/AIDS (CRN+, #03549)*; *West India Committee (WIC, #20920).* Mona Campus provides secretariat for: *Caribbean Cardiac Society (CCS, #03467)*; *Caribbean HIV/AIDS Regional Training Network (CHART, #03515).* Member of: *Engineering for the Americas (EftA, no recent information)*; *Caribbean Association for Distance and Open Learning (CARADOL, no recent information)*; *International Council on Archives (ICA, #12996)*; *International Council for Research and Innovation in Building and Construction (CIB, #13069)*; *North American and Caribbean Association of Schools of Social Work (NACASSW, #17562)*; *Talloires Network (#20093).* Partner of: *Blue Finance (#03283).* [2013.10.22/XF7988/**F***]

♦ University Women of Asia (UWA) 20706

Pres University Women's Asn, SCWO Centre, Mail Box No 8, 96 Waterloo Street, Singapore 187967, Singapore. E-mail: info@uwas.org.
Contact KAUW, 423-44 Ssangmoon-dong, Dobong-ku, Seoul 132-885, Korea Rep. T. +8229932378. Fax +8229807272.
URL: http://www.ifuw.org/uwa/

History 1986, as a regional grouping of *Graduate Women International (GWI, #10688).* **Aims** Create opportunities for members to achieve IFUW objectives in IFUW framework; promote understanding of similarities and differences in sociological, economic and historical background; further cooperation and encourage participation in solving problems in individual and *family* life and all levels of *public* life; encourage members to reach decision-making positions at national, regional and international level. **Structure** Council (meets annually). Secretariat at residence of current President. **Languages** English. **Finance** Members' dues. **Events**

Meeting on climate change Singapore (Singapore) 2010, *Meeting on impressionism and beyond* Singapore (Singapore) 2010, *Meeting on ingredients for emotional wellness* Singapore (Singapore) 2010, *Triennial Conference* Singapore (Singapore) 2009, *International conference / Triennial Conference* Seoul (Korea Rep) 2002.
Members National organizations in 9 countries and territories:
Bangladesh, Hong Kong, India, Japan, Korea Rep, Nepal, Pakistan, Philippines, Sri Lanka. [2014/XD2813/**E**]

♦ University Women of Europe (UWE) 20707

Groupe européen des femmes diplômées des universités (GEFDU)
Pres Reid Hall, 4 rue de Chevreuse, 75006 Paris, France. E-mail: boarduwe@gmail.com.
Registered Office P.O. Box 7922, 1008 AC Amsterdam, Netherlands.
URL: http://universitywomenofeurope.org/
History 1981. Founded as a regional grouping of *Graduate Women International (GWI, #10688)*. Registration: Swiss Civil Code, Start date: 1981, Switzerland. **Aims** Ensure and promote women's interests; put forward qualified women for posts at *decision-making* level; promote in Europe the aims of International Federation of University Women. **Structure** Annual General Meeting; Executive Board. **Languages** English, French. **Staff** Voluntary. **Finance** Sources: members' dues. **Activities** Advocacy/lobbying/activism; awareness raising; monitoring/evaluation; projects/programmes; training/education. **Events** *Annual Conference and General Assembly* Paris (France) 2020, *Meet and Greet Event* Dundee (UK) 2019, *Annual Conference and General Assembly* Geneva (Switzerland) 2019, *Annual Conference and General Assembly* Rome (Italy) 2018, *Annual Conference and General Assembly* Graz (Austria) 2017. **Publications** Colloquia reports; circular letters.
Members National associations or federations of university women of European countries which are affiliated to GWI. Full members in 17 countries and territories:
Austria, Cyprus, England, Finland, France, Germany, Ireland, Italy, Netherlands, Romania, Scotland, Slovenia, Spain, Sweden, Switzerland, Türkiye, Wales.
Consultative Status Consultative status granted from: *Council of Europe (CE, #04881)* (Participatory Status).
NGO Relations Member of (1): *European Women's Lobby (EWL, #09102)* (Executive Board).
[2020.06.04/XD1482/**E**]

♦ Universo Audiovisual del Niño Latinoamericano (internationally oriented national body)
♦ **UNJJ** United Nations of Ju Jitsu (#20582)
♦ Unjoni Ewropea (#08967)
♦ **UNJSPF** United Nations Joint Staff Pension Fund (#20581)
♦ UNLEASH (internationally oriented national body)
♦ **UNLIREC** United Nations Regional Centre for Peace, Disarmament and Development in Latin America and the Caribbean (#20618)
♦ **UNLOPS** United Nations Liaison Office for Peace and Security (#20583)
♦ UN Major Group of Children and Youth / see Children and Youth International (#03882)
♦ Unmanned Aircraft Systems Traffic Management / see Global UTM Association (#10644)
♦ Unmanned Aviation Association (internationally oriented national body)

♦ Unmanned Vehicle Systems International (UVS International) 20708

Contact 86 rue Michel Ange, 75016 Paris, France. T. +33146518865. Fax +33146510522.
History 1995, as *European Unmanned Vehicle Systems Association (EURO UVS)*. Present name adopted 2004. **Aims** Promote unmanned vehicle systems (air, ground, naval) worldwide; establish standards, certification procedures, air traffic management regulations for unmanned aircraft systems; increase cooperation in the field. **Structure** General Assembly. Board of Directors, including President, Treasurer and Secretary. **Languages** English. **Finance** Members' dues. **Activities** Organizes annual conferences and photo competition. **Events** *Annual Conference* Bangalore (India) 2009, *Annual Conference* Beijing (China) 2009, *Annual Conference* Moscow (Russia) 2009, *Annual Conference* Paris (France) 2009, *Annual Conference* Paris (France) 2008. **Publications** *UVS News Flash* (bi-weekly). *UAS: The global perspective* (7th ed 2009); *Acronyms and Abbreviations* (7th ed 2007); *Terms and Definitions* – book. Documents. **Members** Associate; corporate; honorary. Corporations and institutions (256) in 34 countries. Membership countries not specified. **IGO Relations** Recognized by: *European Union Aviation Safety Agency (EASA, #08978)*; *European Commission (EC, #06633)*; *European Defence Agency (EDA, #06895)*; *EUROCONTROL (#05667)*; *European Space Agency (ESA, #08798)*; *International Civil Aviation Organization (ICAO, #12581)*; *Joint Aviation Authorities Training Organisation (JAA TO, #16122)*; *NATO (#16945)*; national governments. [2009.06.01/XM3117/**F**]

♦ **UNMAS** United Nations Mine Action Service (#20585)
♦ UNMFREO – Union nationale des maisons familiales rurales d'éducation et d'orientation (internationally oriented national body)
♦ **UNMIK** UN Interim Administration Mission in Kosovo (#20343)

♦ UN Millennium Campaign 20709

Campaña del Milenio
Dir FF Bldg – Room 617, 304 East 45th St, 6th Floor, New York NY 10017, USA. T. +12129066324. Fax +12129066057.
URL: http://endpoverty2015.org/
History Oct 2002, by UN Secretary General Kofi Anan. Sub-title: *Voices Against Poverty*. Also referred to as *End Poverty 2015*. **Aims** Inform, inspire and encourage public involvement and action in realizing United Nations Millennium Development Goals, a set of 8 time-bound targets to end extreme *poverty* worldwide.
Members Campaigns in 54 countries:
Argentina, Australia, Austria, Bangladesh, Brazil, Burkina Faso, Canada, Chile, Colombia, Costa Rica, Denmark, El Salvador, Ethiopia, Finland, Germany, Ghana, India, Indonesia, Ireland, Italy, Japan, Kenya, Luxembourg, Mexico, Morocco, Mozambique, Namibia, Nepal, Netherlands, New Zealand, Nigeria, Norway, Pakistan, Paraguay, Peru, Philippines, Poland, Senegal, Sierra Leone, South Africa, Spain, Sudan, Sweden, Tanzania UR, Thailand, Tunisia, Uganda, UK, Uruguay, USA, Vietnam, Zambia, Zimbabwe.
NGO Relations Supports: *Global Call for Action Against Poverty (GCAP, #10263)*. [2014/XM0665/**F**]

♦ UNMIL – United Nations Mission in Liberia (inactive)
♦ UNMISET – United Nations Mission of Support in East Timor (inactive)
♦ **UNMISS** United Nations Mission in South Sudan (#20587)
♦ UNMIS – United Nations Mission in the Sudan (inactive)
♦ UNMIT – United Nations Integrated Mission in Timor-Leste (inactive)
♦ **UNMOGIP** United Nations Military Observer Group in India and Pakistan (#20584)
♦ UNMOP – United Nations Mission of Observers in Prevlaka (inactive)
♦ UNMOT – United Nations Mission of Observers in Tajikistan (inactive)
♦ UnMundo América Latina (see: #17738)
♦ UNM – Ung Nordisk Musik (inactive)
♦ UN-NGLS / see United Nations Non-Governmental Liaison Service (#20591)
♦ UN NGO Committee on the Family, New York NY / see NGO Committee on the Family, New York NY (#17107)
♦ **UN-NGO-IRENE** United Nations Informal Regional Network of Non-Governmental Organizations (#20573)

♦ UN Nutrition 20710

ONU Nutrition – ONU Nutrición
Exec Sec viale delle Terme di Caracalla, 00153 Rome RM, Italy. T. +390657051. E-mail: info@unnutrition.org – unnutrition@fao.org.
Secretariat Contact address not obtained.
URL: https://www.unnutrition.org/
History 29 Feb 2020. Founded on merger of UN Network for the Scaling up Nutrition Movement and *United Nations System Standing Committee on Nutrition (UNSCN, inactive)*. Formally annouced at *ECOSOC (#05331)* Management Segment, July 2020. Secretariat operational from 1 Jan 2021. One of 4 networks of *Scaling Up Nutrition Movement (SUN Movement, #19064)*. Former names and other names: *United Nations Nutrition* – alias. **Aims** Overcome fragmentation, increase harmonization on nutrition and provide coordinated and aligned support to governments for greater impact on children, women and people everywhere. **Structure** Steering Committee; Chair; Secretariat. **Languages** Arabic, Chinese, English, French, Russian, Spanish. **Staff** 9.50 FTE, paid. **Finance** Sources: contributions of member/participating states. Contributions to a multi-donor trust fund managed by *FAO (#09260)*. Annual budget: 1,000,000 USD (2021). **Activities** Advocacy/lobbying/activism; awareness raising; capacity building; events/meetings; guidance/assistance/consulting; knowledge management/information dissemination; networking/liaising; politics/policy/regulatory; publishing activities; standards/guidelines. **Publications** Discussion papers.
Members Organizations (15):
CGIAR System Organization (CGIAR, #03843); *FAO (#09260)*; *ILO (#11123)*; *International Atomic Energy Agency (IAEA, #12294)*; *International Fund for Agricultural Development (IFAD, #13692)*; *UNEP (#20299)*; *UNHCR (#20327)*; *UNICEF (#20332)*; *UNIDO (#20336)*; United Nations Department of Economic and Social Affairs (UN-DESA); *United Nations Office for the Coordination of Humanitarian Affairs (OCHA, #20593)*; *United Nations Population Fund (UNFPA, #20612)*; *UN Women (#20724)*; *WHO (#20950)*; *World Food Programme (WFP, #21510)*.
Associate members (2):
Bioversity International (#03262); *International Centre for Tropical Agriculture (#12527)*.
Observers (2):
Committee on World Food Security (CFS, see: #09260); Global Nutrition Cluster. [2021.05.19/AA1802/y/**E**]

♦ **UN-NYG** United Nations – Nuclear Young Generation (#20592)
♦ UNO-CARA-PEN – International Union for Cultural Cooperation (inactive)

♦ UN-OCEANS 20711

Contact The United Nations Legal Counsel, c/o Div for Ocean Affairs and the Law of the Sea, Office of Legal Affairs, DC2-450, New York NY 10017, USA. E-mail: doalos@un.org.
URL: http://www.unoceans.org/
History Established as a coordinating mechanism within the framework of *United Nations (UN, #20515)*, when endorsed by *United Nations System Chief Executives Board for Coordination (CEB, #20636)* (CEB/2003/7), as *Oceans and Coastal Areas Network*, building on *Sub-Committee on Oceans and Coastal Areas of the Administrative Committee on Coordination (ACC SOCA)* (1993-2001). In 2013, the General Assembly of the United Nations, in paragraph 279 of resolution 68/70, recognized the work undertaken so far by UN-Oceans, approved the revised terms of reference for the work of UN-Oceans, with a revised mandate, as annexed to the resolution, and decided to review these terms of reference at its 72nd session in light of the work of UN-Oceans. **Aims** Enhance coordination, coherence and effectiveness of competent organizations of the United Nations system and the International Seabed Authority, within existing resources, in conformity with the United Nations Convention on the Law of the Sea, the respective competences of each of its participating organizations and the mandates and priorities approved by their respective governing bodies. **Structure** Focal Point – United Nations Legal Counsel/Division for Ocean Affairs and the Law of the Sea, Office of Legal Affairs. Chair, elected for each meeting from among UN-Oceans participants present at the meeting. **Languages** English. **Staff** Work necessary for the performance of the functions of the Focal point carried out by staff of the Division for Ocean Affairs and the Law of the Sea. **Finance** Sources: contributions of member/participating states. Member states and others in a position to do so make financial earmarked contributions to the trust fund established by the Secretary-General for the Office of Legal Affairs to support promotion of international law (A/RES/69/245, para 303). **Activities** Capacity building; events/meetings; knowledge management/information dissemination; networking/liaising. **Events** *Taking Stock of Ongoing Ocean-Related Initiatives in Light of the COVID-19 Pandemic* 2020, *Meeting on One Ocean, One Climate, One UN* Paris (France) 2015. **Publications** Mandates; leaflet.
Members Competent organizations, programmes and bodies of the United Nations system, as well as the International Seabed Authority (24):
– *Counter-Terrorism Committee (CTC, #04928)* (Executive Directorate);
– Department of Economic and Social Affairs;
– Division for Ocean Affairs and Law of the Sea (UN-DOALOS);
– *FAO (#09260)*;
– *ILO (#11123)*;
– *Intergovernmental Oceanographic Commission (IOC, #11496)*;
– *International Atomic Energy Agency (IAEA, #12294)*;
– *International Bank for Reconstruction and Development (IBRD, #12317)* (World Bank);
– *International Maritime Organization (IMO, #14102)*;
– *International Seabed Authority (ISBA, #14813)*;
– Office for Disarmament Affairs;
– *Secretariat of the Convention on Biological Diversity (SCBD, #19197)*;
– *Secretariat of the Convention on International Trade in Endangered Species of Wild Fauna and Flora (CITES Secretariat, #19199)*;
– *Secretariat of the Convention on the Conservation of Migratory Species of Wild Animals (UNEP/CMS, #19198)*;
– *UNCTAD (#20285)*;
– *UNDP (#20292)*;
– *UNEP (#20299)*;
– *UNESCO (#20322)*;
– *UNHCR (#20327)*;
– *UNIDO (#20336)*;
– United Nations Convention on the Protection of the Underwater Cultural Heritage;
– *United Nations Economic and Social Commission for Asia and the Pacific (ESCAP, #20557)*;
– *United Nations Framework Convention on Climate Change – Secretariat (UNFCCC, #20564)*;
– *United Nations Institute for Training and Research (UNITAR, #20576)*;
– *United Nations Office for Project Services (UNOPS, #20602)*;
– *United Nations Office of the High Representative for the Least Developed Countries, Landlocked Developing Countries and Small Island Developing States (UN-OHRLLS, #20599)*;
– *United Nations University (UNU, #20642)*;
– *World Meteorological Organization (WMO, #21649)*;
– *World Tourism Organization (UNWTO, #21861)*.
NGO Relations None. [2021.03.22/XJ5752/y/**E***]

♦ UNOCI – United Nations Operation in Côte d'Ivoire (inactive)
♦ **UNODA** United Nations Office for Disarmament Affairs (#20594)
♦ **UNODC** United Nations Office on Drugs and Crime (#20596)

♦ UNOG Staff Coordinating Council 20712

Conseil de Coordination du Personnel d'ONUG
Exec Sec Palais des Nations 8-14, Ave de la Paix, 1211 Geneva 10, Switzerland. T. +41229173614. E-mail: coord_council@unog.ch.
URL: http://www.staffcoordinatingcouncil.org/
History Founded 1982. **Aims** Represent staff members of the United Nations office at Geneva (UNOG). **Structure** Executive Bureau; Presidency. **Members** Individuals (25). **NGO Relations** Member of: *Coordinating Committee for International Staff Unions and Associations of the United Nations System (CCISUA, #04818)*.
[2016/XE4153/**E**]

♦ **UNOG** United Nations Office at Geneva (#20597)
♦ **UN-OHRLLS** United Nations Office of the High Representative for the Least Developed Countries, Landlocked Developing Countries and Small Island Developing States (#20599)
♦ UNON Staff Union / see Nairobi Staff Union (#16930)
♦ **UNON** United Nations Office at Nairobi (#20600)
♦ **UNOOSA** United Nations Office for Outer Space Affairs (#20601)
♦ **UNOPS** United Nations Office for Project Services (#20602)
♦ UNOSD – United Nations Office for Sustainable Development (internationally oriented national body)
♦ **UNOSSC** United Nations Office for South-South Cooperation (#20603)
♦ UNO / see United Nations (#20515)
♦ **UNOV** United Nations Office at Vienna (#20604)
♦ UNOY Foundation / see United Network of Young Peacebuilders (#20653)
♦ UNOY Peacebuilders / see United Network of Young Peacebuilders (#20653)
♦ **UNOY** United Network of Young Peacebuilders (#20653)
♦ **UNPA Campaign** Campaign for a UN Parliamentary Assembly (#03406)
♦ **UNPAN** United Nations Public Administration Network (#20615)
♦ **UNPA** Postverwaltung der Vereinten Nationen (#20613)

♦ UNPA – United Nations Parliamentary Assembly (unconfirmed)
♦ **UNPA** United Nations Postal Administration (#20613)
♦ **UNPFII** United Nations Permanent Forum on Indigenous Issues (#20609)
♦ UNPI – United Nations Philatelists (internationally oriented national body)
♦ UNPKFC / see United Peace Keepers Federal Council (#20655)
♦ **UNPKFC** United Peace Keepers Federal Council (#20655)

♦ UN Plus 20713

Co-Founder Avenue Appia 20, 1211 Geneva, Switzerland. T. +41227911034. Fax +41227914162. E-mail: unplus@unaids.org.
URL: http://www.unplus.org/

History Mar 2005. Full title: *UN Plus – UN System HIV Positive Staff Group.* Also known under the acronym *UN+.* **Aims** Unite for solidarity, equality and acceptance for people living with *HIV* within the *United Nations* system through awareness raising, policy change and advocacy. **Structure** Global Advisory Group. Global Coordinator. **Publications** *UN+ Position Papers.* **Members** Individuals (over 100) representing 37 countries and 37 agencies. Membership countries not specified. **NGO Relations** Partner of: *Global Coalition on Women and AIDS (GCWA, #10297).* [2014/XJ2920/**E**]

♦ UN Plus – UN System HIV Positive Staff Group / see UN Plus (#20713)
♦ **UNPOL** United Nations Police (#20611)
♦ **UNPO** Unrepresented Nations and Peoples Organization (#20714)
♦ **UNPSTR** Union of National Pediatric Societies of Turkic Republics (#20466)
♦ UNRCC-AP – United Nations Regional Cartographic Conference for Asia and the Pacific (meeting series)
♦ UNRCCA – United Nations Regional Cartographic Conference for the Americas (meeting series)
♦ **UNRCCA** United Nations Regional Centre for Preventive Diplomacy for Central Asia (#20619)
♦ UNRCPDA / see United Nations Regional Centre for Peace and Disarmament in Africa (#20616)
♦ **UNRCPD** United Nations Regional Centre for Peace and Disarmament for Asia and the Pacific (#20617)
♦ **UNREC** United Nations Regional Centre for Peace and Disarmament in Africa (#20616)
♦ **UN-REDD Programme** United Nations Collaborative Programme on Reducing Emissions from Deforestation and Forest Degradation in Developing Countries (#20528)
♦ UNREF – United Nations Refugees Emergency Fund (inactive)
♦ UNREO – United Nations Rwanda Emergency Office, Kigali (inactive)

♦ Unrepresented Nations and Peoples Organization (UNPO) 20714

Organisation des peuples et des nations non représentés

Exec Dir Rue de Trèves 49/51, Box 18, 1040 Brussels, Belgium. E-mail: unpo@unpo.org.
SG address not obtained.
URL: https://www.unpo.org/

History 11 Feb 1991, The Hague (Netherlands). Founded by 15 indigenous peoples, nations and minorities at the 'Peace Palace' (location of the International Court of Justice), following a preliminary meeting Sep 1990, Tartu (Estonia). Registration: No/ID: KVK 41156820, Netherlands; Sweden; USA; EU Transparency Register, No/ID: 80014376860-01, Start date: 3 Oct 2011. **Aims** Support indigenous peoples, minorities and unrepresented territories in expressing their positions, needs and grievances in legitimate forums. **Structure** General Assembly (at least every 18 months); Presidency; Secretariat. **Languages** English, French, German, Italian, Portuguese. **Staff** 7.00 FTE, paid.
Finance Sources: donations; government support; in-kind support; members' dues; revenue from activities/projects; subsidies. UNPO was assisted by many funders and contributors, who supported the organization upon its foundation and many of whom have continued to do so, including the following listed in this Yearbook:
- *European Commission (EC, #06633);*
- *European Cultural Foundation (ECF, #06868);*
- *Ford Foundation (#09858);*
- *Friedrich Naumann Foundation for Freedom;*
- *German Catholic Bishops' Organisation for Development Cooperation (MISEREOR);*
- *Heinrich Böll Foundation;*
- *Humanistisch Instituut voor Ontwikkelingssamenwerking (Hivos);*
- *ICCO – Interchurch Organization for Development Cooperation;*
- *International Campaign for Tibet (ICT, #12429);*
- *Konrad Adenauer Foundation (KAF);*
- *MacArthur Foundation;*
- *McKnight Foundation;*
- *Nando Peretti Foundation (NPF);*
- *Nonviolent Radical Party, Transnational and Transparty (PRNTT, #17154);*
- *Oxfam Novib;*
- *Swedish International Development Cooperation Agency (Sida);*
- *World Council of Churches (WCC, #21320).*

Activities Advocacy/lobbying/activism; awareness raising; capacity building; events/meetings; guidance/assistance/consulting; knowledge management/information dissemination; training/education. **Events** *General Assembly* Brussels (Belgium) 2015, *General Assembly* Geneva (Switzerland) 2012, *General Assembly* Rome (Italy) 2010, *Meeting* The Hague (Netherlands) 2010, *UN seminar on UN ideas that changed the world* The Hague (Netherlands) 2010. **Publications** *UNPO Newsletter.* Reports.
Members Full (44), representing indigenous peoples, minorities, unrecognized States and occupied territories. Membership countries not specified. Founding members include:
World Uyghur Congress (WUC, #21896).
NGO Relations Member of (6): *Advocacy Network for Africa (ADNA); Coalition for the International Criminal Court (CICC, #04062); Global Partnership for the Prevention of Armed Conflict (GPPAC, #10538); Hague Appeal for Peace (HAP, #10848); Nonviolent Peaceforce (NP, #17153); UNITED for Intercultural Action – European Network Against Nationalism, Racism, Fascism and in Support of Migrants and Refugees (UNITED, #20511).*
Cooperates with:
- *Amnesty International (AI, #00801);*
- *Assyrian Universal Alliance (AUA);*
- *Bureau du Tibet – Bureau de représentation de sa Sainteté le Dalaï Lama (#03374);*
- *Catholic Organization for Relief and Development (Cordaid);*
- *Commonwealth Lawyers for Cooperation in Asia-Pacific (no recent information);*
- *Cultural Survival;*
- *Escarre International Centre for the Ethnic Minorities and Nations (#05535);*
- *European Centre for Minority Issues (ECMI);*
- *European Language Equality Network (ELEN, #07647);*
- *Federal Union of European Nationalities (FUEN, #09396);*
- *Federation of West Thrace Turks in Europe (ABTTF);*
- *Fourth World General Council (#09978);*
- *Friends of the Earth International (FoEI, #10002);*
- *Global Partnership for the Prevention of Armed Conflict Foundation (GPPAC Foundation);*
- *Greenpeace International (#10727);*
- *Hands Off Cain – Citizens' and Parliamentarians' League for the Abolition of the Death Penalty Worldwide (Hands Off Cain, #10857);*
- *Hudson Institute;*
- *Human Rights Watch (HRW, #10990);*
- *Indigenous Peoples' Center for Documentation, Research and Information (DOCIP);*
- *International Alert (#11615);*
- *International Campaign for Tibet (ICT, #12429);*
- *International Centre for Human Rights and Democratic Development (Rights and Democracy, inactive);*
- *International Centre for Reproductive Health (ICRH);*
- *International Federation for Human Rights (#13452);*
- *International Federation of Red Cross and Red Crescent Societies (#13526)* (Netherlands Society);
- *International Fellowship of Reconciliation (IFOR, #13586);*
- *International Human Rights Association of American Minorities (IHRAAM);*
- *International Scientific Conference Minorities for Europe of Tomorrow (ISCOMET, #14808);*
- *Linguapax International (#16482);*
- *Minority Rights Group International (MRG, #16820);*
- *Naga International Support Centre, Amsterdam (NAGALIM);*
- *National Endowment for Democracy (NED);*
- *National Movements and Intermediary Structures in Europe (NISE, #16938);*
- *Netherlands Centre for Indigenous Peoples (NCIV);*
- *Netherlands Institute of Human Rights (SIM);*
- *No Peace Without Justice (NPWJ, #17155);*
- *Pax Christi – International Catholic Peace Movement (#18266);*
- *Society for Threatened Peoples International (STP International, #19654);*
- *South Asia Democratic Forum (SADF, #19715);*
- *Survival International (#20047);*
- *Taiwan Foundation for Democracy (TFD);*
- *Tibet Justice Center (#20159);*
- *Tribus sans Frontières (TSF, no recent information);*
- *World Council of Churches (WCC, #21320);*
- *World Uyghur Congress (WUC, #21896).* [2023/XF1794/**F**]

♦ UNRFNRE – United Nations Revolving Fund for Natural Resources Exploration (inactive)
♦ **UNRIC** United Nations Regional Information Centre for Western Europe (#20621)
♦ **UNRISD** United Nations Research Institute for Social Development (#20623)
♦ UNRRA – United Nations Relief and Rehabilitation Administration (inactive)
♦ **UNR** Ungdomens Nordiska Råd (#17474)
♦ **UNR** Ungdommens Nordiske Råd (#17474)
♦ **UNR** Union de la noblesse russe (#19009)
♦ UNRWA/UNESCO Institute of Education (no recent information)
♦ **UNRWA** United Nations Relief and Works Agency for Palestine Refugees in the Near East (#20622)
♦ **UNSAC** United Nations Standing Advisory Committee on Security Questions in Central Africa (#20632)
♦ **UNSCEAR** United Nations Scientific Committee on the Effects of Atomic Radiation (#20624)
♦ UNSCN – United Nations System Standing Committee on Nutrition (inactive)
♦ **UNSCO** Office of the United Nations Special Coordinator for the Middle East Process (#17698)
♦ UNSCP / see United Nations System Staff College (#20637)
♦ **UNSC** United Nations Security Council (#20625)
♦ **UNSDG** United Nations Sustainable Development Group (#20634)
♦ UNSDRI / see United Nations Interregional Crime and Justice Research Institute (#20580)
♦ Unsere Kleinen Brüder und Schwestern (internationally oriented national body)
♦ UNSF – United Nations Special Fund, 1974 (no recent information)
♦ **UNSMIS** United Nations Staff Mutual Insurance Society Against Sickness and Accident (#20629)

♦ UN Special Programme for the Economies of Central Asia (SPECA) . 20715

Dep Coordinator at UNECE Palais des Nations, 1211 Geneva 10, Switzerland. T. +41229171134. Fax +41229170178.
Dep Coordinator at ESCAP ESCAP Subregional Office for North and Central Asia, 68A Amangeldy Street, Almaty, Kazakhstan. T. +77273384401. Fax +77273384417.
URL: http://www.unece.org/speca/

History Established Mar 1998, by governments of Kazakhstan, Kyrgyzstan, Tajikistan and Uzbekistan with support of *United Nations Economic Commission for Europe (UNECE, #20555)* and *United Nations Economic and Social Commission for Asia and the Pacific (ESCAP, #20557)*, by the Tashkent Declaration. Governments of Turkmenistan, Azerbaijan and Afghanistan joined the programme later. **Aims** Support regional economic cooperation among the countries of Central Asia; facilitate *economic development* and *integration* into the world economy. **Structure** Governing Council; SPECA Economic Forums; Thematic Working Groups (6). **Languages** English, Russian. **Staff** No dedicated secretariat; supported as necessary by UNECE and ESCAP secretariats. **Finance** Programme implementation financed from UN Regular Programme of Technical Cooperation, UN Development Account and extrabudgetary resources. **Activities** Research and development; knowledge management/information dissemination; capacity building. **Events** *Economic Forum* Dushanbe (Tajikistan) 2015, *Economic Forum* Ashgabat (Turkmenistan) 2014, *Economic Forum* Almaty (Kazakhstan) 2013, *Economic Forum* Bangkok (Thailand) 2012, *Economic Forum* Ashgabat (Turkmenistan) 2011.
Members Full in 7 countries:
Afghanistan, Azerbaijan, Kazakhstan, Kyrgyzstan, Tajikistan, Turkmenistan, Uzbekistan. [2019/XE3921/**E***]

♦ **UN-SPIDER** United Nations Platform for Space-based Information for Disaster Management and Emergency Response (#20610)
♦ Unspoken Smiles Foundation (internationally oriented national body)
♦ **UNSSC** United Nations System Staff College (#20637)
♦ UNSTAT – United Nations Statistical Office (inactive)
♦ UNTAET – United Nations Transitional Administration in East Timor (inactive)
♦ **UNTFAD** United Nations Trust Fund for African Development (#20640)
♦ Unto (internationally oriented national body)

♦ UN Trust Fund to End Violence against Women (UN Trust Fund) ... 20716

Fonds d'affectation spéciale des Nations Unies pour l'élimination de la violence à l'égard des femmes

Headquarters c/o UN Women, 405 East 42nd St, New York NY 10017, USA. T. +16467814400. Fax +16467814444.
Street Address 220 East 42nd St, 21st Floor, New York NY, USA. T. +16467814805.
URL: http://www.unwomen.org/en/trust-funds/un-trust-fund-to-end-violence- against-women/

History 1996, within the framework of *United Nations (UN, #20515)*, pursuant to General Assembly resolution 50/166. Originally managed by *United Nations Development Fund for Women (UNIFEM, inactive)* and currently by *UN Women (#20724).* Operations commenced 1997. Original title: *United Nations Trust Fund in Support of Actions to Eliminate Violence Against Women.* **NGO Relations** Supports: *Equality Now (#05518).* [2014.01.23/XM0931/f/**F***]

♦ **UN Trust Fund** UN Trust Fund to End Violence against Women (#20716)
♦ **UNTSO** United Nations Truce Supervision Organization (#20638)
♦ UNU/BIOLAC – UNU Programme for Biotechnology in Latin America and the Caribbean (see: #20642)
♦ UNU Computing and Society / see United Nations University Institute on Computing and Society (#20644)
♦ UNUCOPCA – Universal Union for Consumer Protection and Civil Abuse (internationally oriented national body)
♦ **UNU-CRIS** UNU Institute on Comparative Regional Integration Studies (#20717)
♦ UNU-CS / see United Nations University Institute on Computing and Society (#20644)
♦ **UNU-CS** United Nations University Institute on Computing and Society (#20644)
♦ **UNU-EHS** United Nations University Institute for Environment and Human Security (#20645)
♦ UNU-FLORES – UNU Institute for Integrated Management of Material Fluxes and of Resources (see: #20642)
♦ UNU/FNP – United Nations University Food and Nutrition Programme for Human and Social Development (inactive)
♦ **UNU-GCM** United Nations University Institute on Globalization, Culture and Mobility (#20646)
♦ **UNU-IAS** United Nations University Institute for the Advanced Study of Sustainability (#20643)
♦ UNU-IIST / see United Nations University Institute on Computing and Society (#20644)
♦ UNU-IITL / see United Nations University Institute on Computing and Society (#20644)
♦ UNU/INRA Programme / see UNU Institute for Natural Resources in Africa (#20718)
♦ **UNU-INRA** UNU Institute for Natural Resources in Africa (#20718)

♦ UNU Institute on Comparative Regional Integration Studies (UNU-CRIS) 20717

Dir Potterierei 72, 8000 Bruges, Belgium. T. +3250471100. Fax +3250471309. E-mail: pvantorre@cris.unu.edu.
URL: http://www.cris.unu.edu/

History 2001, as an institute of *United Nations University (UNU, #20642)*. **Aims** Contribute to achieving the universal goals of the UN and UN through comparative and interdisciplinary research and training for a better understanding of the processes and consequences of intra- and inter-regional integration; act as a think-tank that generates policy-relevant knowledge about new forms of governance and cooperation; contribute to capacity building on issues of integration and cooperation, particularly in developing countries. **Structure** Advisory Committee. **Finance** Core funding from: Flemish Government and Province of West-Flanders (Belgium). **Events** *International Symposium on Latin America in the Pacific Rim* Tokyo (Japan) 2015. **Publications** *UNU-CRIS Newsletter. BRIGG Working Papers; Chinese Book Series; UNU-CRIS Working Papers*. Annual Report. Books; articles. **NGO Relations** Collaborates with: *College of Europe (#04105)*, Bruges (Belgium). [2016/XJ6120/j/**E**]

- ♦ UNU Institute for Governance, State and Society (internationally oriented national body)
- ♦ UNU Institute for Integrated Management of Material Fluxes and of Resources (see: #20642)

♦ UNU Institute for Natural Resources in Africa (UNU-INRA) 20718

Institut de l'UNU pour les ressources naturelles en Afrique (UNU-IRNA)

Contact Intl House, Annia Jage Road, Univ of Ghana – Legon Campus, Accra, Ghana. T. +233302213850ext6318. E-mail: inra@unu.edu.

URL: http://inra.unu.edu/

History Dec 1986, under the auspices of *United Nations University (UNU, #20642)*. From 1990 to 1993, operated as *UNU Programme on Natural Resources in Africa* or *UNU/INRA Programme*. Became an institute, 1 Dec 1993, when transferred from Nairobi (Kenya) to Accra (Ghana). UNU/INRA office formally opened 1 Dec 1994. Alternative title: *United Nations University Institute for Natural Resources in Africa*. Has also been referred to as: *Institute for Natural Resources in Africa (INRA)*; *International Institute for Natural Resources in Africa*. **Aims** Emphasizing *food security*, respond to the problem of *sustainable development* in Africa by improving the capacity of Africa's existing universities and training institutions to produce well-trained, well-equipped and motivated individuals capable of developing, adapting and disseminating technology that promotes sustainable use of *natural resources*. **Structure** Operational Units; College of Research Associates; Main Office in Accra (Ghana). **Languages** English, French. **Finance** Core funding: endowment fund contributed by governments of Cameroon, Ghana and Zambia. Funds contributed to UNU by government of Japan and donations from governments and private individuals. **Activities** Research and development; capacity building; politics/policy/regulatory; guidance/assistance/consulting; knowledge management/ information dissemination. **Events** *Biennial meeting of college of research associates* Accra (Ghana) 2003, *Workshop on national soil fertility action plans* Ouagadougou (Burkina Faso) 1997, *Regional workshop on environment, biodiversity and agricultural change in West Africa* Accra (Ghana) 1994. **Publications** Books; reports; newsletters.

Members Membership covers 53 countries:
Algeria, Angola, Benin, Botswana, Burkina Faso, Burundi, Cameroon, Cape Verde, Central African Rep, Chad, Comoros, Congo Brazzaville, Congo DR, Côte d'Ivoire, Djibouti, Egypt, Equatorial Guinea, Eritrea, Eswatini, Ethiopia, Gabon, Gambia, Ghana, Guinea, Guinea-Bissau, Kenya, Lesotho, Liberia, Libya, Madagascar, Malawi, Mali, Mauritania, Mauritius, Morocco, Mozambique, Namibia, Niger, Nigeria, Rwanda, Sao Tomé-Principe, Senegal, Seychelles, Sierra Leone, Somalia, South Africa, Sudan, Tanzania UR, Togo, Tunisia, Uganda, Zambia, Zimbabwe.

IGO Relations *UNEP (#20299)*; *UNESCO (#20322)*; *United Nations Economic Commission for Africa (ECA, #20554)*. [2017.03.09/XE5942/j/**E**]

- ♦ UNU Institute for New Technologies / see United Nations University – Maastricht Economic and Social Research Institute on Innovation and Technology (#20647)
- ♦ UNU/INTECH – Institut de l'UNU pour les technologies nouvelles / see United Nations University – Maastricht Economic and Social Research Institute on Innovation and Technology (#20647)

♦ UNU International Institute for Global Health (UNI-IIGH) 20719

Institut international pour la santé global de l'UNU

Dir UNU-IIGH Bldg, UKM Medical Ctr, Jalan Yaacob Latiff, Cheras, 56000 Kuala Lumpur, Malaysia. T. +60391715394. Fax +60391715402. E-mail: iigh-info@unu.edu.

URL: http://www.iigh.unu.edu/

History 2007, Kuala Lumpur (Malaysia), following an agreement signed between *United Nations University (UNU, #20642)* and the Government of Malaysia. **Aims** Undertake research, capacity-development and dissemination of knowledge related to key issues of human health; contribute to development and strengthening of health services policy frameworks and management actions, particularly for people in developing countries; support implementation of a preventive and promotive approach to human health. **Structure** Board of Advisors. **Events** *International Public Health Conference* Kuala Lumpur (Malaysia) 2015. **NGO Relations** Associate partner of: *World Urban Campaign (WUC, #21893)*. [2015.08.28/XM3373/j/**E**]

- ♦ UNU International Institute for Software Technology / see United Nations University Institute on Computing and Society (#20644)
- ♦ UNU-INWEH – United Nations University – Institute for Water, Environment and Health (see: #20642)
- ♦ **UNU-IRNA** Institut de l'UNU pour les ressources naturelles en Afrique (#20718)
- ♦ **UNU-MERIT** United Nations University – Maastricht Economic and Social Research Institute on Innovation and Technology (#20647)
- ♦ Unum Omnes / see UNUM OMNES International Council of Catholic Men (#20720)

♦ UNUM OMNES International Council of Catholic Men (ICCM) 20720

Fédération internationale des hommes catholiques (FIHC) – Federación Internacional de los Hombres Católicos – Internationale Vereinigung Katholischer Männer

SG Palazzo San Calisto 16, 00120 Vatican City, Vatican. T. +39669887382. Fax +39669887382. E-mail: unum-omnes@libero.it – secretarygeneral@unum-omnes.org.

URL: http://unum-omnes.org/

History 19 Sep 1948, Lourdes (France). Founded on the initiative of *'Italian Union of Men of Catholic Action'* and in conjunction with similar associations from other countries. Statutes approved by the Holy See, 1951. New statutes approved by the Holy See, 1978. Former names and other names: *Fédération internationale des d'hommes d'action catholique (FIHAC)* – former (1948 to 1950); *Unum Omnes* – alias. **Aims** Help men realize their potential in life as Catholics; encourage them to assume their rightful role in the church and society; promote family as a source of human life and the sphere of their responsibility and action; promote establishment of, and dialogue between, catholic men organizations; promote relations with national and international organizations; represent hopes and expectations of men in all fields of life. **Structure** General Assembly (normally every 3 years); Executive Committee; Secretariat in Rome (Italy). **Languages** English, French, German, Spanish. **Staff** Voluntary. **Finance** Sources: donations; members' dues. **Activities** Events/ meetings; knowledge management/information dissemination; networking/liaising; projects/programmes. **Events** *General Assembly* Vienna (Austria) 2015, *General Assembly* Rome (Italy) 2012, *General assembly* Maynooth (Ireland) 2003, *Regional Meeting* Luxembourg (Luxembourg) 2000, *Regional meeting* Rome (Italy) 1998. **Publications** *Unum Omnes Newsletter* (annual). Congress reports; brochures.

Members Organizations in 25 countries:
Argentina, Austria, Croatia, Czechia, France, Germany, Ghana, India, Ireland, Italy, Kenya, Korea Rep, Liberia, Lithuania, Luxembourg, Madagascar, Malta, Mexico, Nigeria, Poland, Romania, Spain, Uganda, Ukraine, USA.

Associate in 9 countries:
Australia, Chad, Ethiopia, Hungary, Paraguay, South Africa, Tanzania UR, Uganda, Zambia.

Consultative Status Consultative status granted from: *ECOSOC (#05331)* (Ros C); *FAO (#09260)* (Liaison Status). **IGO Relations** Cooperates with (1): *UNICEF (#20332)*. **NGO Relations** Member of (1): *Forum of Catholic Inspired NGOs (#09905)*. [2023.02.19/XB1736/**C**]

- ♦ **UN** United Nations (#20515)
- ♦ UNU Programa de Biotecnologia para América Latina y el Caribe (see: #20642)
- ♦ UNU Programme for Biotechnology in Latin America and the Caribbean (see: #20642)
- ♦ UNU Programme on Natural Resources in Africa / see UNU Institute for Natural Resources in Africa (#20718)
- ♦ UNU/SCN Network for Capacity Development in Nutrition in Central and Eastern Europe / see Capacity Development Network in Nutrition in Central and Eastern Europe (#03418)

♦ UNU Staff Council 20721

Contact c/o United Nationals Univ 53-70, Jingumae 5-chome, Shibuya-ku, Tokyo, 150-8925 Japan. T. +81354671212. Fax +81334992828. E-mail: staffcouncil@unu.edu.

History 29 Jul 1982, Tokyo (Japan). Acts as in house staff association for *United Nations University (UNU, #20642)*. **Aims** Represent staff members; serve for all personnel of the UNU throughout the UNU-wide system; assist the Rector in identifying, examining and resolving issues relating to staff welfare, including conditions of work, general conditions of life and other personnel policies. **Structure** Council; Advisory Group; Officers (3). **Languages** English. **Staff** 450.00 FTE, paid. **Finance** Voluntary contributions by staff members. **Activities** Staff Welfare Fund activities.

Members Individuals in 13 countries and territories:
Belgium, Canada, Finland, France, Germany, Ghana, Japan, Jordan, Macau, Malaysia, Netherlands, USA, Venezuela.

NGO Relations Member of (1): *Coordinating Committee for International Staff Unions and Associations of the United Nations System (CCISUA, #04818)*. [2022.02.02/XE0081/v/**E**]

- ♦ **UNU** United Nations University (#20642)
- ♦ **UNU** Université des Nations Unies (#20642)
- ♦ UNU-WIDER / see UNU World Institute for Development Economics Research (#20722)
- ♦ **UNU-WIDER** UNU World Institute for Development Economics Research (#20722)

♦ UNU World Institute for Development Economics Research (UNU-WIDER) 20722

Institut mondial de recherche sur l'économie du développement – Instituto Mundial de Investigaciones de Economia del Desarrollo

Dir Katajanokanlaituri 6B, FI-00160 Helsinki, Finland. T. +35896159911. Fax +358961599333. E-mail: wider@wider.unu.edu.

URL: http://www.wider.unu.edu/

History 1984. Established within the framework of *United Nations University (UNU, #20642)*. Started work, Mar 1985, Helsinki (Finland). Former names and other names: *World Institute for Development Economics Research of the United Nations University (UNU-WIDER)* – alias. **Aims** Provide economic analysis and policy advice to governments as well as freely available original research to promote sustainable and equitable development for all. **Structure** Board of up to 10 members, appointed by the Rector of UNU in consultation with the Chairman of the Council of UNU and with other members of the Council designated by the Chairman. Director (chief academic and administrative officer), appointed by the Rector in consultation with the Board of UNU-WIDER and the Chairman of the UNU Council. **Languages** English, Finnish, Portuguese. **Staff** 65.00 FTE, paid. **Finance** Endowment fund; additional contributions from: *European Union (EU, #08967)*; governments of Finland, Norway, South Africa, Sweden and UK. **Activities** Capacity building; knowledge management/information dissemination; research/documentation; training/education. **Events** *WIDER Development Conference* Bogota (Colombia) 2022, *WIDER Development Conference* Helsinki (Finland) 2022, *WIDER Development Conference* 2021, *WIDER Development Conference* Helsinki (Finland) 2020, *Nordic Conference on Development Economics* Helsinki (Finland) 2018. **Publications** *WIDER Angle* (12 a year) – newsletter. *WIDER Studies in Development Economics* – book series; *WIDER Working Paper Series*. Studies; special issues; policy and research briefs. **IGO Relations** *African Development Bank (ADB, #00283)*; *ILO (#11123)*; *International Bank for Reconstruction and Development (IBRD, #12317)* (World Bank); *International Organization for Migration (IOM, #14454)*; *UN Women (#20724)*; *UNCTAD (#20285)*; UNDESA; *UNDP (#20292)*; *UNICEF (#20332)* Mozambique; *United Nations Economic and Social Commission for Asia and the Pacific (ESCAP, #20557)*; *WHO (#20950)*. **NGO Relations** *African Economic Research Consortium (AERC, #00292)*; *International Food Policy Research Institute (IFPRI, #13622)*; research institutes; universities. [2022.10.24/XE2758/j/**E**]

- ♦ Unversitarios por el Tercer Mundo / see Món-3 – Universitaris pel Tercer Món
- ♦ UN Voluntary Trust Fund for Assistance to Mine Clearance / see United Nations Voluntary Trust Fund for Assistance in Mine Action (#20649)
- ♦ **UN VTF** United Nations Voluntary Trust Fund for Assistance in Mine Action (#20649)
- ♦ **UNV** United Nations Volunteers (#20650)
- ♦ UN Watch – United Nations Watch (internationally oriented national body)

♦ UN-Water 20723

ONU-Eau

Secretariat c/o United Nations, Dept of Economic and Social Affairs, Room DC2-2310, New York NY 10017, USA. E-mail: unwater@un.org.

URL: http://www.unwater.org/

History 2003, by *United Nations (UN, #20515)* High Level Committee on Programmes, evolving out of several close collaborations among UN agencies. **Aims** Provide information, policy briefs and other communication materials for policy-makers and managers who work directly with water issues, other decision-makers that have an influence on how water is used, and the general public; build the knowledge base on water issues through efficient monitoring and reporting systems and facilitating access to this knowledge through regular reports and the Internet; provide a platform for system-wide discussions to identify challenges in global water management, analyse options for meeting these challenges and ensure that reliable information and sound analysis informs the global policy debate on water. **Structure** Chair and Vice-Chair, rotating among UN agencies (usually every 2 years). Permanent Secretariat, hosted by UN Department for Economic and Social Affairs (UNDESA). **Activities** and programmes are hosted by individual member agencies on behalf of UN-Water. Sets up regional UN-Water Initiatives, such as "UN-Water Africa". Reporting: World Water Development Report (WWDR); WHO/UNICEF Joint Monitoring Programme on Water Supply and Sanitation reports; Global Annual Assessment on Sanitation and Drinking-Water (GLAAS). Task Forces deal with: indicators, monitoring and reporting; gender and water; sanitation; transboundary waters; climate change and water; country-level coordination.

Members UN organizations (28):
- *FAO (#09260)*;
- *ILO (#11123)*;
- *International Atomic Energy Agency (IAEA, #12294)*;
- *International Bank for Reconstruction and Development (IBRD, #12317)*;
- *International Fund for Agricultural Development (IFAD, #13692)*;
- *Secretariat of the Convention on Biological Diversity (SCBD, #19197)*;
- *Secretariat of the United Nations Convention to Combat Desertification (Secretariat of the UNCCD, #19208)*;
- *UNCTAD (#20285)*;
- UN DESA;
- *UNDP (#20292)*;
- *UNEP (#20299)*;
- *UNESCO (#20322)*;
- *UNHCR (#20327)*;
- *UNICEF (#20332)*;
- *UNIDO (#20336)*;
- *United Nations Economic and Social Commission for Asia and the Pacific (ESCAP, #20557)*;
- *United Nations Economic and Social Commission for Western Asia (ESCWA, #20558)*;
- *United Nations Economic Commission for Africa (ECA, #20554)*;
- *United Nations Economic Commission for Europe (UNECE, #20555)*;
- *United Nations Economic Commission for Latin America and the Caribbean (ECLAC, #20556)*;
- *United Nations Framework Convention on Climate Change – Secretariat (UNFCCC, #20564)*;
- *United Nations Human Settlements Programme (UN-Habitat, #20572)*;
- *United Nations Institute for Training and Research (UNITAR, #20576)*;
- *United Nations Office for Disaster Risk Reduction (UNDRR, #20595)*;
- *United Nations University (UNU, #20642)*;
- *WHO (#20950)*;
- *World Meteorological Organization (WMO, #21649)*;
- *World Tourism Organization (UNWTO, #21861)*.

IGO Relations Special partners: UN Secretary General's Advisory Board on Water and Sanitation. UN Office for Outer Space Affairs. Partner: *Secretariat of the Convention of Wetlands (#19200)*. Cooperates with: *UNIDO (#20336)*.

NGO Relations Special partners: *UN Global Impact (#20325)*; *Water Supply and Sanitation Collaborative Council (WSSCC, inactive)*. Member of: *Youth and United Nations Global Alliance (YUNGA, #22028)*. Partners:

- *International Association for Water Law (#12263)*;
- *Gender and Water Alliance (GWA, #10102)*;
- *Global Water Partnership (GWP, #10653)*;
- *International Association of Hydrogeologists (IAH, #11953)*;
- *International Association of Hydrological Sciences (IAHS, #11954)*;
- *International Commission on Irrigation and Drainage (ICID, #12694)*;
- *International Federation of Private Water Operators (AquaFed, #13517)*;
- *International Hydropower Association (IHA, #13828)*;
- *International Union for Conservation of Nature and Natural Resources (IUCN, #15766)*;
- *International Water Association (IWA, #15865)*;
- *International Water Management Institute (IWMI, #15867)*;
- *International Water Resources Association (IWRA, #15871)*;
- *Public Services International (PSI, #18572)*;
- *Stakeholder Forum for a Sustainable Future (SF)*;
- *Stockholm International Water Institute (SIWI)*;
- *WaterLex (inactive)*;
- *Women for Water Partnership (WfWP, #21041)*;
- *World Business Council for Sustainable Development (WBCSD, #21254)*;
- *World Water Council (WWC, #21908)*;
- *World Wide Fund for Nature (WWF, #21922)*. [2011/XJ2271/y/**E***]

♦ UNWFPA – UN Women for Peace Association (internationally oriented national body)
♦ UNWG – Geneva – United Nations Women's Guild – Geneva (internationally oriented national body)
♦ **UNWG – New York** United Nations Women's Guild – New York (#20651)
♦ UNWG-Vienna – United Nations Women's Guild of Vienna (internationally oriented national body)

♦ UN Women 20724

ONU Femmes – ONU Mujeres

Exec Dir 220 East 42nd St, New York NY 10017, USA. T. +16467814400. Fax +16467814444. E-mail: media.team@unwomen.org.
URL: http://www.unwomen.org/

History 2 Jul 2010. Established under resolution 64/289 of the General Assembly of the *United Nations (UN, #20515)* within *United Nations System (#20635)*, on merger of *'Division for the Advancement of Women (DAW)', United Nations International Research and Training Institute for the Advancement of Women (UN-INSTRAW, inactive), 'Office of the Special Adviser on Gender Issues and Advancement of Women (OSAGI)'* and *United Nations Development Fund for Women (UNIFEM, inactive)*. Officially launched 24 Feb 2011, New York NY (USA). Former names and other names: *UN Women – United Nations Entity for Gender Equality and the Empowerment of Women* – full title; *ONU Femmes – Entité des Nations Unies pour l'égalité des sexes et l'autonomisation des femmes* – full title; *ONU Mujeres – Entidad de las Naciones Unidad para la Igualdad de Género y el Empoderamiento de la Mujer* – full title. **Aims** Support Member States to advance gender equality, in line with national priorities and international norms and policies; build effective partnerships with civil society and mobilize support, both political and financial, for the achievement of international goals for women. regular monitoring of system-wide progress. **Structure** UN General Assembly, *ECOSOC (#05331)* and *United Nations Commission on the Status of Women (CSW, #20536)* constitute multi-tiered intergovernmental governance structure for normative support functions and provide normative policy guidance. UN General Assembly, ECOSOC and UN Women Executive Board constitute multi-tiered intergovernmental governance structure for operational activities and provide operational policy guidance. Executive Board, consisting of representatives of 41 countries worldwide, serving on a rotating basis: 10 from Africa, 10 from Asia, 4 from Eastern Europe, 6 from Latin America and Caribbean, 5 from Western Europe and 6 from contributing countries. Bureau, comprising President and 4 regional Vice-Presidents (Asia; Eastern European; Latin America and Caribbean; Western European and Others). Regional Centres (2): Cairo (Egypt); Panama (Panama). Liaison Offices (4): Brussels (Belgium); Japan; African Union; Madrid (Spain). Sub-regional Offices Central Africa – Kigali (Rwanda); East and Horn of Africa – Nairobi (Kenya); South Africa – Johannesburg (South Africa); West Africa – Dakar (Senegal); Andean – Quito (Ecuador); Caribbean – Christ Church (Barbados); Mexico, Central America, Cuba and the Dominican Republic – Mexico City (Mexico); Southern Cone – Brasilia (Brazil); Arab States – Amman (Jordan); North Africa – Rabat (Morocco); East and South-East Asia – Bangkok (Thailand); Pacific – Suva (Fiji); South Asia – Delhi (India); Central and South Eastern Europe – Bratislava (Slovakia); Eastern Europe and Central Asia – Almaty (Kazakhstan). **Languages** Arabic, Chinese, English, French, Russian, Spanish. **Staff** As of 31 Aug 2012: headquarters – 246; field – 279. **Finance** Large funded by voluntary contributions and regular UN budget. **Activities** *'Programme and Technical Assistance'* – to countries requesting assistance. *'Grant-making Funds'* – to fuel innovative, high-impact programmes by government agencies and civil society groups through *Fund for Gender Equality* and *UN Trust Fund to End Violence against Women (UN Trust Fund, #20716)*. *United Nations Commission on the Status of Women (CSW, #20536)* – dedicated exclusively to gender equality and the advancement of women. *'Other Intergovernmental Processes'* – information on women's rights issues to General Assembly, ECOSOC and Security Council. Maintains UN Secretary General's database on violence against women. *'Capacity Development and Training'* – training programmes for national governments. *'Expert Group Meetings'*. *'UN System Coordination'* – to obtain full realization of women's rights and opportunities. **Events** *International Conference on Women, Peace and Security (ICWPS)* Abu Dhabi (United Arab Emirates) 2022, *Generation Equality Forum – Part 1* Mexico City (Mexico) 2021, *Generation Equality Forum – Part 2* Paris (France) 2021, *SNOW (Say No to the Oppression of Women) Seminar* Singapore (Singapore) 2019, *Symposium on HeForShe Engaging Youth to Achieve a Society where Everyone Shines* Tokyo (Japan) 2018.
Members Executive Board 41 governments (date of expiry between brackets):
Algeria (2015), Angola (2013), Australia (2015), Austria (2015), Belgium (2015), Brazil (2015), Cape Verde (2013), China (2013), Congo Brazzaville (2013), Djibouti (2015), Dominican Rep (2013), Ethiopia (2013), Gabon (2015), Gambia (2015), Grenada (2013), Hungary (2013), Indonesia (2013), Ireland (2015), Japan (2013), Kazakhstan (2013), Korea Rep (2013), Latvia (2015), Malawi (2015), Maldives (2015), Mexico (2013), Nigeria (2013), Norway (2013), Peru (2013), Philippines (2015), Russia (2015), Saudi Arabia (2013), Solomon Is (2015), Spain (2013), Switzerland (2015), Thailand (2015), UK (2015), Ukraine (2013), United Arab Emirates (2015), Uruguay (2015), USA (2015), Venezuela (2015). [2022/XJ2621/**F***]

♦ UN Women for Peace Association (internationally oriented national body)
♦ UN Women – United Nations Entity for Gender Equality and the Empowerment of Women / see UN Women (#20724)
♦ UNWPA – United Nation World Peace Association (internationally oriented national body)
♦ UNWTO / see World Tourism Organization (#21861)
♦ UNWTO Commission for Africa (see: #21861)
♦ UNWTO Commission for the Americas (see: #21861)
♦ UNWTO Commission for East Asia and the Pacific (see: #21861)
♦ UNWTO Commission for Europe (see: #21861)
♦ UNWTO Commission for the Middle East (see: #21861)
♦ UNWTO Commission for South Asia (see: #21861)
♦ UNWTO Staff Association, Madrid (internationally oriented national body)
♦ **UNWTO ST-EP Foundation** UNWTO Sustainable Tourism for Eliminating Poverty Foundation (#20725)

♦ UNWTO Sustainable Tourism for Eliminating Poverty Foundation (UNWTO ST-EP Foundation) 20725

Secretariat 8F KNTO Bldg, 10 Da-dong, Jung-gu, Seoul 100-180, Korea Rep. T. +8223181862 – +8223181867. Fax +8223182163. E-mail: contact@unwtostep.org.
URL: http://www.unwtostep.org/

History 2004, Seoul (Korea Rep), when Memorandum of Understanding was signed between Republic of Korea and *World Tourism Organization (UNWTO, #21861)*, of which it became a cornerstone of its ST-EP (Sustainable Tourism for Eliminating Poverty) initiative. Constitution approved at 16th UNWTO General Assembly, 2005, Dakar (Senegal). Since 2013, in process of becoming an Independent International Organization called *International ST-EP Organization*. **Aims** Harness the power of tourism to generate new opportunities for development and empowerment in least developed and developing countries, and particularly in Sub-Saharan Africa. **Structure** Board of Directors. **Activities** Capacity building; knowledge management/information exchange; awareness raising. [2017/XM4428/f/**F***]

♦ **UNWTO** World Tourism Organization (#21861)
♦ **UNYANET** United Nations Youth Associations Network (#20652)
♦ UNYSA-AUSTRIA-AFA – United Nations Youth and Student Association of Austria – Academic Forum for Foreign Affairs (internationally oriented national body)
♦ UOF – Universal Outreach Foundation (internationally oriented national body)
♦ UOM / see FIM Oceania
♦ UOSL – Union d'organisations syndicales libres (no recent information)
♦ UOTAA – Universal Organization of Travel Agents' Associations (inactive)
♦ UPA / see African Parliamentary Union (#00412)
♦ UPA / see Arab Permanent Postal Commission (#01025)
♦ UPACITS – Unión Panamericana para el control de las Infecciones Transmitidas Sexualmente (no recent information)
♦ **UPADI** Unión Panamericana de Asociaciones de Ingenieros (#20469)
♦ UPA DI – UPA International Development (internationally oriented national body)
♦ UPAE / see Postal Union of the Americas, Spain and Portugal (#18466)
♦ **UPAEP** Unión Postal de las Américas, España y Portugal (#18466)
♦ **UPAG** Union Panamericana de Gimnasia (#20471)
♦ UPA International Development (internationally oriented national body)
♦ UPAJ – Union panafricaine des journalistes, 1961 (inactive)
♦ UPAM / see Confederación Panamericana de Deportes de Montaña y Escalada (#04472)
♦ **UPAME** Confederación Panamericana de Deportes de Montaña y Escalada (#04472)
♦ UPAO / see Asian-Pacific Postal Union (#01625)
♦ **UPAP** Union panafricaine des postes (#18060)
♦ UPAT – Union panafricaine des télécommunications (inactive)
♦ **UPA** Union parlementaire africaine (#00412)
♦ UPA – Union postale africaine (no recent information)
♦ UPA – Université Panafricaine (unconfirmed)
♦ UPA / see User Experience Professionals Association (#20735)
♦ **UPAV** Unión Panamericana de Asociaciones de Valuación (#20470)
♦ **UPAZ** Universidad para la Paz (#20702)
♦ **UPBF** United Paintball Federation (#20654)
♦ **UPB** Union postale balte (#03137)
♦ **UPCI** Union parlementaire des états membres de l'OCI (#18220)
♦ **UPCSA** Uniting Presbyterian Church in Southern Africa (#20668)
♦ UPDEA / see Association of Power Utilities in Africa (#02867)
♦ **UPEACE** University for Peace (#20702)
♦ UPEB – Unión de Paises Exportadores de Banano (inactive)
♦ UPEFE / see European Business Press (#06423)
♦ UPEI / see UPEI – The voice of Europe's independent fuel suppliers (#20726)

♦ UPEI – The voice of Europe's independent fuel suppliers 20726

Pres Av de la Renaissance 1, 1000 Brussels, Belgium. T. +3227402020. Fax +3227402028. E-mail: info@upei.org.
SG address not obtained.
URL: http://www.upei.org/

History 18 May 1962. Former names and other names: *Union Pétrolière Européenne Indépendante (UPEI)* – former; *Union of European Petroleum Independents* – former. Registration: Préfecture Police de Paris, No/ID: W751056460, Start date: 25 Jun 1962, France. **Aims** Represent European importers and wholesale/retail distributors of energy for the transport and heating sectors, supplying Europe's consumers independently of the major energy producers. **Structure** Presidential Board. **Languages** English. **Staff** 2.00 FTE, paid. **Finance** Sources: members' dues. **Activities** Advocacy/lobbying/activism; events/meetings. **Events** *Low carbon mobility – what's in the policy toolbox?* Brussels (Belgium) 2019, *Future fuels in Europe: the Finnish perspective* Helsinki (Finland) 2019, *Transport in Transition Conference* Ljubljana (Slovenia) 2018, *Towards a Cleaner Society Fuels Conference* Tallinn (Estonia) 2017, *Future of Automotive Fuels Conference* Prague (Czech Rep) 2016. **Publications** Annual Report; statements; studies.
Members National organizations and companies (24) in 20 countries:
Belgium, Bulgaria, Croatia, Czechia, Estonia, Finland, France, Germany, Hungary, Ireland, Italy, Latvia, Lithuania, Netherlands, Portugal, Slovakia, Slovenia, Spain, Switzerland, UK.
IGO Relations EU institutions. [2022.05.10/XD3409/**D**]

♦ **UPE** Union des phoniatres européens (#20390)
♦ UPFE / see AFILIATYS (#00151)
♦ **UPF International** Universal Peace Federation (#20681)
♦ **UPF** Union internationale de la presse francophone (#20435)
♦ **UPIGO** Union professionnelle internationale des gynécologues et obstétriciens (#20473)
♦ UPI – Ulkopoliittinen Instituutti (internationally oriented national body)
♦ UPI – United Press International (internationally oriented national body)
♦ **UPJ** Union panafricaine de la jeunesse (#18076)
♦ **UPJ** Unión Panamericana de Judo (#18115)
♦ UPJ – Union for Progressive Judaism (internationally oriented national body)
♦ **UPLA** Union of Latin American Parties (#20448)
♦ UPMOCI / see Parliamentary Union of the OIC Member States (#18220)
♦ **UPMS** Union parlementaire mondiale du scoutisme (#21773)
♦ UPM / see Unión de Parlamentarios Sudamericanos y del MERCOSUR (#20472)
♦ UPM – Union Pontificale Missionnaire (see: #16827)
♦ **UPO-FCO** International Union of Children's Organizations (#15762)
♦ **UPOV** Union internationale pour la protection des obtentions végétales (#20436)
♦ **UPPN** Union postale des pays du Nord (#17391)

♦ UPR Info 20727

Exec Dir Rue de Varembé 3, 4th Floor, 1202 Geneva, Switzerland. T. +41223217770. Fax +41223217770. E-mail: info@upr-info.org.
URL: http://www.upr-info.org/

History Feb 2008. Founded to strengthen and raise awareness on *Universal Periodic Review* (UPR), a human rights mechanism of *United Nations (UN, #20515)*, started in Apr 2008. Registration: Swiss Civil Code, Switzerland. **Aims** Support engagement of all UPR stakeholders to improve the *human rights* situation of all segments of society so they can achieve their full potential. **Structure** Executive Board; Secretariat; Honorary Members. **Languages** English, French, Spanish. **Staff** 9.00 FTE, paid. **Finance** Sources: government support. Supported by: Canton of Geneva; City of Geneva; Federal Department of Foreign Affairs of Switzerland; Foreign and Commonwealth Office of the United Kingdom of Great Britain and Northern Ireland; *Irish Aid*; Kingdom of the Netherlands; Ministry for Foreign Affairs of Sweden; Norwegian Ministry of Foreign Affairs; *Organisation internationale de la Francophonie (OIF, #17809)*. **Activities** Events/meetings; guidance/assistance/consulting; monitoring/evaluation; projects/programmes; publishing activities; training/education. **Publications** *Italy and the Universal Periodic Review of the United Nations Human Rights Council: Playing the two-level game* (2017) by Andrea Cofelice; *Understanding the UPR: Methods of assessing its functioning* (2017) by Edward McMahon; *Evolution Not Revolution* (2016) by Edward McMahon et al; *Minority Issues in the First Cycle of the UPR* (2015) by Rita Izsak; *The Implacable Ritual: A study examining the inertia of death penalty abolition within the Universal Periodic Review* (2015) by John Riordan; *UPR: A Platform for Dialogue, Accountability, and Change on Sexual and Reproductive Health and Rights* (2015) by Kate Gilmore et al; *Acknowledging the SOGI norm: the politics of its recognition in the HRC and the politics for its recognition through the UPR* (2013) by Aengus Carroll; *Do Civil Society Organization-Suggested Recommendations Matter?* (2013) by Edward McMahon et al; *SOGI Rights in the UPR* (2013) by Mari Dahl Schlanbusch; *A study of the Universal Periodic Review (UPR) from the perspective of Children's Rights* (2012) by James Jolley; *The UPR: A Work in Progress* (2012) by Edward McMahon; *Cultural Relativism in the Universal Periodic Review of the Human Rights Council* (2011) by Roger Lloret Blackburn; *Evaluating the Implementation of UPR Recommendations: A Quantitative Analysis of the Implementation Efforts of Nine UN Member States* (2011) by David Frazier; *Herding Cats and Sheep: Assessing State and Regional Behavior in the Universal Periodic Review Mechanism of the United Nations*

Human Rights Council (2010) by Prof Edward McMahon; *Opportunities for Nongovernmental Organization Advocacy in the Universal Periodic Review Process at the UN Human Rights Council* (2010) by Lawrence Moss. Studies; reports; analysis and recommendation documents; guidelines. **Consultative Status** Consultative status granted from: *ECOSOC (#05331)* (Special). [2022/XJ4938/**E**]

- ♦ UPROCAFE – Unión de Pequeños y Medianos Productores de Café de México, Centroamérica y el Caribe (no recent information)
- ♦ **UPSM** Unión Parlamentaria Scout Mundial (#21773)
- ♦ **UPSM** Unión de Parlamentarios Sudamericanos y del MERCOSUR (#20472)
- ♦ UPSOA – Union postale du Sud et de l'Ouest de l'Asie (inactive)
- ♦ UPST – Union panafricaine de la science et de la technologie (inactive)
- ♦ **UPS** Università Pontificia Salesiana (#19038)
- ♦ UPTC – Union panafricaine des travailleurs croyants (inactive)
- ♦ UPU Council of Administration (see: #20682)
- ♦ UP – United Purpose (internationally oriented national body)
- ♦ UP – Université de paix, Namur (internationally oriented national body)
- ♦ **UPU** Union postale universelle (#20682)
- ♦ **UPU** Unión Postal Universal (#20682)
- ♦ **UPU** Universal Postal Union (#20682)
- ♦ UPVAC – Universal Peace and Violence Amelioration Centre (internationally oriented national body)
- ♦ UQP – Universities and the Quest for Peace (inactive)
- ♦ Urad pre vydavanie Publikacii Európskej únie (#18562)
- ♦ Urad pro Publikace Evropské unie (#18562)
- ♦ Urad za Publikacije Evropske unije (#18562)
- ♦ Urad Skupnosti za Rastlinske Sorte (#04404)
- ♦ Urad Spolocenstva pre Odrody Rastlin (#04404)
- ♦ **URAM** International Society for the Study of Human Ideas on Ultimate Reality and Meaning (#15474)
- ♦ Uranium Institute / see World Nuclear Association (#21674)
- ♦ URBAMA / see Centre d'études et de recherches sur l'urbanisation du monde arabe – Equipe monde arabe et méditerranée

♦ Urban Affairs Association (UAA) 20728

Exec Dir c/o Urban Studies Program, PO Box 413, 2200 E Kenwood Blvd, Milwaukee WI 53201-0413, USA. T. +14142293025. E-mail: info@uaamail.org.
URL: http://urbanaffairsassociation.org/

History 1969, Boston, MA (USA). Former names and other names: *Council of University Institutes for Urban Affairs* – former (1969 to 1981). **Aims** Create interdisciplinary spaces for engaging in intellectual and practical discussions about urban life. **Structure** Governing Board. **Activities** Events/meetings; awards/prizes/competitions. **Events** *Conference* Nashville, TN (USA) 2023, *Conference* Washington, DC (USA) 2022, *Annual Conference* Nashville, TN (USA) 2021, *Annual Conference* Washington, DC (USA) 2020, *EURA-UAA joint conference* Dublin (Ireland) 2019. **Publications** *Journal of Urban Affairs* (10 a year); *Journal of Race, Ethnicity and the City* (2 a year). [2016/XM4126/**D**]

♦ Urban Biodiversity and Design (URBIO) 20729

Co-Pres address not obtained.
Co-Pres address not obtained.
URL: https://www.urbionetwork.com/

History 2008. Also referred to as *URBIO – International Network for Education and Applied Research.* **Aims** Promote urban biodiversity through continuing dialogue. **Structure** Advisory Board. President; Secretary-General. **Activities** Events/meetings. **Events** *Conference* Berlin (Germany) 2021, *Conference* Berlin (Germany) 2020, *International Conference of Urban Biodiversity and Design / Conference* Incheon (Korea Rep) 2014, *International Conference on Urban Biodiversity and Design / Conference* Mumbai (India) 2012, *International conference on urban biodiversity and design / Conference* Nagoya (Japan) 2010. **Publications** *URBIO Newsletter.* **NGO Relations** Participant in: *Global Partnership on Local and Subnational Action for Biodiversity (#10536).* [2017/XJ4718/**F**]

- ♦ Urban Climate Change Research Network (internationally oriented national body)

♦ Urban Data Management Society (UDMS) 20730

Pres c/o Steinbeis Centre, Schellingstr 24, 70174 Stuttgart, Germany.
Treas address not obtained.
URL: http://www.udms.net/

History 1971. Former names and other names: *European Urban Data Management Society* – alias. **Aims** Promote the development of information systems in local government. **Structure** Board, comprising President, Vice-President, Treasurer, Programme Coordinator and Past President. **Events** *International Conference on Smart Data and Smart Cities* Stuttgart (Germany) 2021, *Symposium* Ghent (Belgium) 2015, *Symposium* London (UK) 2013, *Symposium* Delft (Netherlands) 2011, *Symposium* Ljubljana (Slovenia) 2009. **Publications** Proceedings.
Members Organizations in 10 countries:
Austria, Czechia, Denmark, France, Italy, Netherlands, Norway, Portugal, UK, USA.
NGO Relations Member of: *European Geographic Information Network (EGIN, #07387).* [2021/XD3677/**D**]

♦ Urban Economics Association (UEA) 20731

Contact address not obtained. E-mail: uea@urbaneconomics.org.
URL: http://www.urbaneconomics.org/

Structure Council; Executive Committee, Programme Committee. **Activities** Events/meetings; training/education; awards/prizes/competitions. **Events** *European Meeting* London (UK) 2022, *North American Meeting* Washington, DC (USA) 2022, *North American Meeting* Berkeley, CA (USA) 2021, *European Meeting* London (UK) 2021, *North American Meeting* Berkeley, CA (USA) 2020. **Publications** *Journal of Economic Geography, Regional Science and Urban Economics*; *Journal of Urban Economics.*
Members Individuals in 56 countries and territories:
Afghanistan, Argentina, Australia, Austria, Belgium, Brazil, Canada, Chile, China, Colombia, Croatia, Czechia, Denmark, Finland, France, Georgia, Germany, Hong Kong, India, Iran Islamic Rep, Ireland, Israel, Italy, Japan, Jordan, Korea Rep, Latvia, Lebanon, Luxembourg, Mexico, Morocco, Netherlands, New Zealand, Nigeria, Norway, Pakistan, Philippines, Poland, Portugal, Qatar, Romania, Singapore, Slovakia, South Africa, Spain, Sweden, Switzerland, Taiwan, Thailand, Türkiye, Uganda, UK, United Arab Emirates, Uruguay, USA, Zimbabwe. [2017/XM6271/**D**]

♦ Urban Environmental Accords (UEA) 20732

Contact No 181 Chunbyunwooha-ro, Seo-gu, Gwangju 61954, Korea Rep. T. +8262601 1331 – +82626011332. Fax +82626011313. E-mail: uea@ueama.org.
URL: http://www.ueama.org/

History 2012, Gwangju, Korea Rep, when Secretariat was set up. Accords signed by 53 city representatives, May 2005, San Francisco CA (USA). **Aims** Promote cooperative relationships between cities and international organizations in the field of global *environment* protection; develop policies and programs to contribute to creation of low-carbon *green* cities. **Structure** Executive Committee. Secretariat. **Languages** English, Korean. **Staff** 12.00 FTE, paid. **Finance** Financed by Local Government (Gwangju Metropolitan City). Annual budget: US$ 500,000. **Activities** Awards/prizes/competitions; capacity building; knowledge management/information dissemination; events/meetings; networking/liaising; research and development. **Events** *Summit* Yeosu (Korea Rep) 2021, *Summit* Palembang (Indonesia) 2019, *Forum on City Heatways* Gwangju (Korea Rep) 2018, *Seminar on Low Carbon Green Living for Adults* Gwangju (Korea Rep) 2018, *Workshop of Policy Research* Gwangju (Korea Rep) 2018. **Publications** *UEA Newsletter.* Studies.
Members Cities (157) in 53 countries and territories:
Afghanistan, Argentina, Australia, Austria, Bangladesh, Benin, Brazil, Cambodia, Cameroon, Canada, China, Colombia, Costa Rica, Cyprus, Denmark, Ecuador, Fiji, France, Germany, Greece, India, Indonesia, Iran Islamic Rep, Iraq, Ireland, Israel, Italy, Japan, Kenya, Korea Rep, Malaysia, Mexico, Mongolia, Mozambique, Nepal, Netherlands, Panama, Peru, Philippines, Romania, Russia, Senegal, South Africa, Spain, Sri Lanka, Sweden, Switzerland, Taiwan, Türkiye, Uganda, UK, Ukraine, USA.
IGO Relations *European Union (EU, #08967)*; *UNEP (#20299)*; *United States Agency for International Development (USAID).* **NGO Relations** City-Net; *Local Governments for Sustainability (ICLEI, #16507).* [2017.10.11/XJ9518/**F**]

- ♦ Urban Future global conference (meeting series)
- ♦ **URBANICOM** International Association Town Planning and Distribution (#12232)
- ♦ Urbanisation, réseaux urbains et régionalisation au Maghreb / see Centre d'études et de recherches sur l'urbanisation du monde arabe – Equipe monde arabe et méditerranée
- ♦ Urban Knowledge Network Asia (unconfirmed)
- ♦ Urban Land Institute (internationally oriented national body)
- ♦ Urban and Regional Information Systems Association (internationally oriented national body)
- ♦ Urban Saints (internationally oriented national body)
- ♦ URBIO – International Network for Education and Applied Research / see Urban Biodiversity and Design (#20729)
- ♦ **URBIO** Urban Biodiversity and Design (#20729)
- ♦ URCAF – Union des radios communautaires de l'aire francophone (inactive)
- ♦ URCAO – Union régionale des conférences de supérieurs majeurs d'Afrique de l'Ouest francophone (inactive)
- ♦ URC-CHS – Center for Human Services (internationally oriented national body)
- ♦ URCI – University Research Corporation International (internationally oriented national body)
- ♦ URCSA – Uniting Reformed Church in Southern Africa (internationally oriented national body)
- ♦ URC / see UNEP Copenhagen Climate Centre (#20296)
- ♦ URE / see Association for European Rural Universities (#02541)
- ♦ Ured za publikacije Europske unije (#18562)
- ♦ Ured Zajednice za Zastitu Biljnih Sorti (#04404)
- ♦ UREF – Université des réseaux d'expression française (inactive)
- ♦ UREI – Universidad de Relaciones y Estudios Internacionales (internationally oriented national body)
- ♦ URF – Union des services routiers des chemins de fer européens (inactive)
- ♦ Urgences sans frontières / see Global Emergency Medical Net (#10339)
- ♦ Urgent Action Fund for Women's Human Rights (internationally oriented national body)
- ♦ Urgewald (internationally oriented national body)
- ♦ Urgewald – Kampagne für den Regenwald / see Urgewald
- ♦ **URG** Universal Rights Group (#20683)
- ♦ **URI Europe** United Religions Initiative Europe (#20659)
- ♦ URI / see International Radio and Television Union (#14689)
- ♦ URISA – Urban and Regional Information Systems Association (internationally oriented national body)
- ♦ **URI** United Religions Initiative (#20658)
- ♦ URMPM / see International Association of Risk Management in Medicine (#12138)
- ♦ **UR Network** Understanding Risk Network (#20287)
- ♦ UroGynaecological Society of Australasia (internationally oriented national body)
- ♦ **UROLA** Latin-American Uro-oncology Association (#16391)

♦ Urological Association of Asia (UAA) 20733

Main Office 20 College Road, Academia Level 5, Singapore 169856, Singapore. E-mail: secretar-iat.uaa@gmail.com.
URL: http://www.uaanet.org/

History 1990, Fukuoka (Japan). **Aims** Promote urology in Asia; encourage research and clinical practice among the urologists of Asia. **Structure** Executive Committee. Includes: *Asian School of Urology (ASU, see: #20733).* **Languages** English. **Staff** 1.00 FTE, paid. **Finance** Congress proceeds. **Activities** Events/meetings. **Events** *UAA Congress* 2025, *UAA Congress* Bali (Indonesia) 2024, *UAA Congress* Dubai (United Arab Emirates) 2023, *UAA Congress* Sydney, NSW (Australia) 2022, *UAA Congress* Singapore (Singapore) 2021. **Publications** *Asian Urology Newsletter* (annual).
Members Full in 26 countries and territories:
Australia, Bahrain, Bangladesh, Cambodia, China, Hong Kong, India, Indonesia, Iran Islamic Rep, Japan, Korea Rep, Kuwait, Macau, Malaysia, Myanmar, Nepal, New Zealand, Pakistan, Philippines, Singapore, Sri Lanka, Taiwan, Thailand, Türkiye, United Arab Emirates, Vietnam.
Affiliated members (4):
Asian Association of UTI and STI (AAUS, #01343); *Asian Society for Female Urology (no recent information)*; *Asian Society of Endourology (ASE, #01719)*; *Asian Society of Uro-Oncology (APSU, #01746).* [2022/XD8723/y/**D**]

- ♦ Urological Society of Latin Mediterranean Countries (inactive)
- ♦ Uroterapeutisk Förening (internationally oriented national body)
- ♦ URPE – Union des résistants pour une Europe unie (inactive)
- ♦ **URSI** Union radio-scientifique internationale (#20475)
- ♦ URSS – Union des républiques socialistes soviétiques (inactive)
- ♦ **URSULA** Union de Responsabilidad Social Universitaria de Latinoamérica (#20476)
- ♦ Ursulinas de Jesús (religious order)
- ♦ Ursulinenkongregation (religious order)
- ♦ Ursuline Nuns (religious order)
- ♦ Ursulines of the Canadian Union (religious order)
- ♦ Ursulines Filles de Marie-Immaculée (religious order)
- ♦ Ursuline Sisters of Mount St Joseph (religious order)
- ♦ Ursulines de Jésus (religious order)
- ♦ Ursulines of Jesus (religious order)
- ♦ Ursulines of the Roman Union (religious order)
- ♦ Ursulines de Tildonk (religious order)
- ♦ Ursulines de l'Union Canadienne (religious order)
- ♦ Ursulines de l'Union Romaine (religious order)
- ♦ URTI / see International Radio and Television Union (#14689)
- ♦ **URTI** Union radiophonique et télévisuelle internationale (#14689)
- ♦ URTNA / see African Union of Broadcasting (#00490)
- ♦ URUPABOL – Comisión Mixta Permanente Uruguay, Paraguay, Bolivia (inactive)
- ♦ Urzad Miedzy Narodowy Obywateli Swiata / see Registre des Citoyens du Monde (#18822)
- ♦ Urzad Publikacji Unii Europejskiej (#18562)
- ♦ USA for Africa (internationally oriented national body)
- ♦ Usability Professionals Organization / see User Experience Professionals Association (#20735)
- ♦ USAFA / see USA for Africa

♦ USAID/SADC/IITA/CIP Southern Africa Root Crops Research Network (SARRNET) 20734

IITA Country Rep IITA-Mozambique, Av FPLM 8km, via Corrane, Muhala Expansão, Nampula, Mozambique. T. +25826216381.
URL: http://www.iita.org/

History 1993, as a follow-up of the *East and Southern Africa Rootcrops Research Network (ESARRN)*, established 1984 and evolving into SARRNET and *Eastern Africa Root Crops Research Network (EARRNET, inactive)*; a joint initiative of *International Institute of Tropical Agriculture (IITA, #13933)*; *International Potato Center (#14627)*; *Southern African Development Community (SADC, #19843)* and *United States Agency for International Development (USAID).* **Aims** Engage in applied market-led research and development on *cassava* and *sweet potato*, including demand-led processing and utilization, commercialization and such aspects as training, information and technology exchange and institutional capacity building in order to improve food security and income generating process of rural households and emerging farmers. **Structure** Steering Committee (meets annually), including Coordinator serving as Secretary. **Staff** 8.00 FTE, paid. **Finance** Donor: USAID. **Activities** Organizes meetings, workshops and regional training courses. Applied market-led participatory research in the fields of development and/or introduction and evaluation of improved germplasm, managing pests and diseases through an ecologically sustainable plant protection approach, surveying production systems, development and dissemination of post harvest technologies and establishment of multiplication and distribution systems for improved planting materials, fostering private sector participation in commercialization of cassava and sweet potato. **Events** *Regional scientific workshop on cassava and sweetpotato* Lusaka (Zambia) 1998. **Publications** *ROOTS* (2 a year) – newsletter. Annual Report; reports; scientific papers; workshop proceedings.

Members SADC member countries (14):
Angola, Congo DR, Eswatini, Madagascar, Malawi, Mauritius, Mozambique, Namibia, South Africa, Tanzania UR, Zambia, Zimbabwe. [2017/XF3253/**F**]

- ♦ USAID – United States Agency for International Development (internationally oriented national body)
- ♦ USAI – Unión Sudamericana de Asociaciones de Ingenieros (inactive)
- ♦ **USAP** Union des sociétés arabes de pédiatrie (#20355)
- ♦ USAR / see Organisation suisse d'aide aux réfugiés
- ♦ US-Arab Chamber of Commerce / see National US-Arab Chamber of Commerce
- ♦ US-ASEAN Business Council (internationally oriented national body)
- ♦ US-ASEAN Council for Business and Technology / see US-ASEAN Business Council
- ♦ US/Canada Hydrographic Commission (see: #13825)
- ♦ USCAP – United States and Canadian Academy of Pathology (internationally oriented national body)
- ♦ USCAS / see South American Society of Cardiology (#19707)
- ♦ USC Canada / see SeedChange
- ♦ US-Central American Free Trade Agreement (2004 treaty)
- ♦ US/CHC – US/Canada Hydrographic Commission (see: #13825)
- ♦ US Civil Defence Council / see International Association of Emergency Managers
- ♦ US Civilian Research and Development Foundation / see CRDF Global
- ♦ US Civilian Research and Development Foundation for the Independent States of the Former Soviet Union / see CRDF Global
- ♦ USCL – United Society for Christian Literature (internationally oriented national body)
- ♦ US Committee for Refugees and Immigrants / see United States Committee for Refugees and Immigrants
- ♦ US Committee for Refugees and Immigrants (internationally oriented national body)
- ♦ US Committee for UNICEF / see United States Fund for UNICEF
- ♦ US Consortium of APEC Study Centers (internationally oriented national body)
- ♦ USCRI – United States Committee for Refugees and Immigrants (internationally oriented national body)
- ♦ USCRI – US Committee for Refugees and Immigrants (internationally oriented national body)
- ♦ USC Shoah Foundation Institute for Visual History and Education (internationally oriented national body)
- ♦ USCV – Union scientifique continentale du verre (no recent information)
- ♦ USCWM – United States Center for World Mission (internationally oriented national body)
- ♦ USE / see International University of Monaco
- ♦ USEA – Union of Scientific and Engineering Associations (internationally oriented national body)

♦ User Experience Professionals Association (UXPA) 20735

Exec Dir address not obtained. T. +14703338972. E-mail: office@uxpa.org – uxpaofficemanager@gmail.com.
URL: http://uxpa.org/

History 1991, as *Usability Professionals Organization (UPA)*. Current title adopted 2012. Incorporated in the State of Texas (USA). **Structure** Membership Meeting (annual); Board of Directors; Executive Committee. **Finance** Sources: members' dues. **Activities** Events/meetings; knowledge management/information dissemination. **Events** *Conference* Seattle, WA (USA) 2016, *Conference* Coronado, CA (USA) 2015. **Publications** *Journal of Usability Studies*; *User Experience Magazine*.
Members Chapters in 23 countries and territories:
Argentina, Australia, Austria, Belgium, Brazil, Canada, Chile, China, Germany, Hong Kong, India, Iran Islamic Rep, Israel, Mexico, Netherlands, New Zealand, Peru, Spain, Switzerland, Türkiye, UK, United Arab Emirates, USA.
Regional chapter (1): [2018/XW0226/t/**C**]

- ♦ USE – Symposium on UltraSonic Electronics (meeting series)
- ♦ US Federation for Middle East Peace / see International Federation for Peace and Sustainable Development
- ♦ USFMEP / see International Federation for Peace and Sustainable Development
- ♦ USFSPEI / see Union Syndicale Fédérale (#20485)
- ♦ USF / see Union Syndicale Fédérale (#20485)
- ♦ **USF** Union Syndicale Fédérale (#20485)
- ♦ USF – Universitaires Sans Frontières (internationally oriented national body)
- ♦ USF – Université sans frontière (internationally oriented national body)
- ♦ US Global Change Research Information Office (internationally oriented national body)
- ♦ **USG** Union des supérieurs généraux (#20484)
- ♦ Usher Study Group (internationally oriented national body)
- ♦ Ushirika La Yatima Na Watoto Fukara (internationally oriented national body)
- ♦ USICD – United States International Council on Disabilities (internationally oriented national body)
- ♦ USIC – Union sportive internationale des cheminots (inactive)
- ♦ US Institute of Peace / see United States Institute of Peace
- ♦ **USIP** Union sportive internationale des polices (#14614)
- ♦ USIP – United States Institute of Peace (internationally oriented national body)
- ♦ **USI** United Schools International (#20660)
- ♦ USIV – Union syndicale internationale vasculaire (unconfirmed)
- ♦ **USKRE** Union der Sozialdemokratischen Kommunal- und Regionalpolitiker Europas (#20479)
- ♦ **USLRRE** Union of Socialist Local and Regional Representatives in Europe (#20479)
- ♦ USMMASA – Union scientifique mondiale des médecins acupuncteurs et des sociétés d'acupuncture (inactive)
- ♦ **USOEB** Union syndicale de l'Office européen des brevets (#19944)
- ♦ USOS – Universitaire Stichting voor Ontwikkelingssamenwerking (internationally oriented national body)
- ♦ US Overseas Cooperative Development Council (internationally oriented national body)
- ♦ USPA – Union syndicale panafricaine (inactive)
- ♦ USPD / see International Scientists Association (#14811)
- ♦ US Peace Corps / see Peace Corps
- ♦ US Peace Council (internationally oriented national body)
- ♦ **USPE** Union sportive des polices d'Europe (#20482)

♦ USPG 20736

Gen Sec 5 Trinity Street, London, SE1 1DB, UK. T. +442079212200. E-mail: info@uspg.org.uk – communications@uspg.org.uk.
URL: http://www.uspg.org.uk/

History 1701, London (UK). 1965, merged with *Universities' Mission to Central Africa (UMCA)*. Former names and other names: *Society for the Propagation of the Gospel in Foreign Parts (SPG)* – former (1701 to 1965); *United Society for the Propagation of the Gospel (USPG)* – former (1965); *USPG – Anglicans in World Mission* – former (1965). Registration: Charity Commission, No/ID: 234518, UK, England and Wales. **Aims** Support churches of the Anglican Communion in their mission; sustain relationships between churches; support partners in growing the church's capacity for mission, particularly through leadership development and health work. **Languages** English. **Staff** 28.00 FTE, paid. **Activities** Religious activities; training/education. Active in over 50 countries by sharing people and resources. Education and training in mission in England, Wales, Ireland and Scotland. **Publications** *Koinonia* (4 a year); *USPG Prayer Diary* (4 a year). **NGO Relations** Member of (4): *ECHO – International Health Services*; *International Partnership on Religion and Sustainable Development (PaRD, #14524)*; *Joint Learning Initiative on Faith and Local Communities (JLI, #16139)*; *Partnership for World Mission (PWM)*. [2022.05.04/XF2090/**F**]

- ♦ USPG – Anglicans in World Mission / see USPG (#20736)
- ♦ **USPMOM** Union des sociétés de pédiatrie du Moyen-Orient et de la Méditerranée (#20461)
- ♦ **USP** University of the South Pacific (#20703)
- ♦ **USRA** Universities Space Research Association (#20695)
- ♦ USSA – UNAIDS Secretariat Staff Association (see: #16149)
- ♦ **USSE** Unión de Silvicultores del Sur de Europa (#20478)
- ♦ **USSE** Union des sylviculteurs du Sud de l'Europe (#20478)
- ♦ USSPEI / see Union Syndicale Fédérale (#20485)
- ♦ USSR Aikido Federation / see International Euro-Asian Aikido Federation (#13310)
- ♦ USSR – Union of Soviet Socialist Republics (inactive)
- ♦ **USS** United Seamen's Service (#20661)
- ♦ USTA / see International Trademark Association (#15706)
- ♦ Ustav Mezinarodnich Vztahu, Praha (internationally oriented national body)
- ♦ USTMA – Union des syndicats de travailleurs du Maghreb arabe (no recent information)
- ♦ US Travel Association (internationally oriented national body)
- ♦ USUARIOS – Asociación de Usuarios del Transporte Maritimo, Terrestre y Aéreo del Istmo Centroamericano (no recent information)
- ♦ UT – Conférence internationale pour l'unité technique des chemins de fer (inactive)
- ♦ UT – Convention relative à 'unité technique dans le domaine des chemins de fer (1882 treaty)
- ♦ UTC-PTT – Union internationale touristique et culturelle des postes et des télécommunications (inactive)
- ♦ **UTCWI** United Theological College of the West Indies (#20662)
- ♦ **UTE** Union des théâtres de l'Europe (#20487)
- ♦ UTF – Uroterapeutisk Förening (internationally oriented national body)
- ♦ UTIC – Universidad Tecnológica Intercontinental (internationally oriented national body)
- ♦ Utility Economic Development Association (internationally oriented national body)
- ♦ UTI – Union thérapeutique internationale (inactive)
- ♦ UT-LANIC – Latin American Network Information Center, University of Texas (internationally oriented national body)
- ♦ UTLA – Universidad Técnica Latinoamericana, San Salvador (internationally oriented national body)
- ♦ UTO – World Federation of United Cities (inactive)
- ♦ UTRAO / see West Africa Road Transport Union (#20901)
- ♦ Utrecht Centre for International Legal Studies (internationally oriented national body)
- ♦ Utrechter Union / see International Old Catholic Bishops' Conference (#14403)

♦ Utrecht Network 20737

Address not obtained.
Registered Office c/o Univ of Bologna, Via Zamboni, 33, 40126 Bologna BO, Italy.
URL: http://www.utrecht-network.org/

History 1987. Registration: Netherlands. **Aims** Encourage contacts between *universities* on matters related to academic, educational, social and technological developments through cooperation in the area of *internationalization* and mobility. **Structure** General Meeting (annual); Steering Committee; Task Forces; Rectors and Presidents Meeting. **Languages** English. **Staff** 0.50 FTE, paid. **Finance** Annual budget: 120,000 EUR. **Activities** Training/education. **Events** *Annual Meeting* Brussels (Belgium) 2022, *Annual Meeting* 2021, *Annual Meeting* 2020, *Annual Meeting* Riga (Latvia) 2019, *Annual Meeting* Bratislava (Slovakia) 2018.
Members Universities (30) in 26 countries:
Austria, Belgium, Czechia, Denmark, Estonia, Finland, France, Germany, Greece, Hungary, Ireland, Italy, Latvia, Lithuania, Malta, Netherlands, Norway, Poland, Portugal, Romania, Slovakia, Slovenia, Spain, Switzerland, Türkiye, UK.
[2022.07.22/XF6767/**F**]

- ♦ Utredningsinstituttet for forskning og høyere utdanning / see Nordisk Institutt for Studier av Innovasjon, Forskning og Utdanning
- ♦ Utrikespolitiska Institutet, Helsinki (internationally oriented national body)
- ♦ Utrikespolitiska Institutet, Stockholm (internationally oriented national body)
- ♦ UTSE – Union of Thai Sanghas in Europe (unconfirmed)
- ♦ UTSS – Under The Same Sun (internationally oriented national body)
- ♦ UTS – United Through Sport (unconfirmed)
- ♦ Utviklingsfondet (internationally oriented national body)
- ♦ UTWA / see United Food and Commercial Workers Union
- ♦ **UUA** Unitarian Universalist Association (#20494)
- ♦ UUMN / see Association for Unitarian Universalist Music Ministries
- ♦ UUSC – Unitarian Universalist Service Committee (internationally oriented national body)
- ♦ UUWF – Unitarian Universalist Women's Federation (internationally oriented national body)
- ♦ UVA – Union des villes africaines (inactive)
- ♦ UVISP-Assisi – Unione Volontariato Internazionale per lo Sviluppo e La Pace (internationally oriented national body)
- ♦ UVO-ROSTE / see UNESCO Office in Venice – UNESCO Regional Bureau for Science and Culture in Europe (#20316)
- ♦ **UVS International** Unmanned Vehicle Systems International (#20708)
- ♦ UVVM – Union des villages de vacances de la Méditerranée (inactive)
- ♦ **UWA** University Women of Asia (#20706)
- ♦ UWAVWA – Union of West African Voluntary Workcamps Associations (inactive)
- ♦ **UWB** Universal White Brotherhood (#20684)
- ♦ **UWB** Universelle Weisse Bruderschaft (#20684)
- ♦ UWC Adriatic – Collegio del Mondo Unito dell'Adriatico (internationally oriented national body)
- ♦ UWC Atlantic College (internationally oriented national body)
- ♦ **UWC International** United World Colleges (#20664)
- ♦ UWC Red Cross Nordic (internationally oriented national body)
- ♦ UWCSEA – United World College of South East Asia (internationally oriented national body)
- ♦ UWC / see World Congress of Free Ukrainians (#21305)
- ♦ **UWE** University Women of Europe (#20707)
- ♦ UWHKF – United World Haedong Kumdo Federation (unconfirmed)
- ♦ UWICED – UWI Centre for Environment and Development, Mona (see: #20705)
- ♦ UWI Centre for Environment and Development, Mona (see: #20705)
- ♦ **UWIMAA** UWI Medical Alumni Association (#20738)

♦ UWI Medical Alumni Association (UWIMAA) 20738

Exec Officer PO Box 226, Mona, Kingston, Jamaica. T. +18769775800. Fax +18769775800. E-mail: medalum@uwimona.edu.jm.
URL: http://www.uwimedicalalumni.org/

History to bring together alumni of *University of the West Indies (UWI, #20705)*. **Aims** Provide on an ongoing basis support for the Faculty of Medical Sciences of the University of the West Indies in the areas of fundraising, personnel training and exchange, to the acquisition and distribution of equipment and materials to the support of research in the area and through all of the above to the betterment of medical care of the people in the Caribbean basin. **Structure** Secretariat, comprising Board of Directors and Executive Officer. **Events** *International Medical Conference* Jamaica 2013, *International medical conference* Jamaica 2008, *International Medical Conference* Nassau (Bahamas) 2007, *International Medical Conference* Grenada 2005, *International medical conference* Nassau (Bahamas) 2003. **Publications** *UWIMAA Newsletter* (4 a year).
Members Chapters in 6 countries:
Bahamas, Barbados, Canada, Jamaica, Trinidad-Tobago, USA. [2012/XE4636/**E**]

- ♦ UWI / see United Way Worldwide (#20663)
- ♦ **UWI** University of the West Indies (#20705)
- ♦ UWM – United World Mission (internationally oriented national body)
- ♦ **UWPIAA** Up With People International Alumni Association (#18299)
- ♦ **UWP** Up With People (#18296)
- ♦ **UWW Americas** United World Wrestling Americas (#20666)
- ♦ **UWWA** United World Wrestling Asia (#20667)

♦ **UWW-Europe** **20739**
Sec address not obtained.
Pres address not obtained.
Facebook: https://www.facebook.com/unitedworldwrestling.europe/
History 1978, Oulu (Finland). Founded as a support organ of *United World Wrestling (UWW, #20665)*. Former names and other names: *Comité européen des luttes associées* – former; *Conseil européen des luttes associées (CELA)* – former. **Aims** Promote wrestling in Europe. **Structure** General Assembly (every 4 years); Bureau. **Languages** English, French. **Staff** 1.00 FTE, paid; 1.00 FTE, voluntary. **Finance** International transfer taxes of wrestlers in Europe. Annual budget: 150,000 CHF. **Events** *Annual Conference* Vantaa (Finland) 2014, *General Assembly* Tbilisi (Georgia) 2013, *Annual Conference* Belgrade (Serbia) 2012, *Annual Conference* Baku (Azerbaijan) 2010, *General Assembly* Vilnius (Lithuania) 2009.
Members National federations in 47 countries:
Albania, Armenia, Austria, Azerbaijan, Belarus, Belgium, Bosnia-Herzegovina, Bulgaria, Croatia, Cyprus, Czechia, Denmark, Estonia, Finland, France, Georgia, Germany, Greece, Hungary, Iceland, Ireland, Israel, Italy, Latvia, Lithuania, Luxembourg, Malta, Moldova, Monaco, Montenegro, Netherlands, North Macedonia, Norway, Poland, Portugal, Romania, Russia, San Marino, Serbia, Slovakia, Slovenia, Spain, Sweden, Switzerland, Türkiye, UK, Ukraine. [2020/XM3858/**E**]

♦ UWWIC / see International Council for Innovation in Higher Education
♦ **UWW** United World Wrestling (#20665)
♦ **UXPA** User Experience Professionals Association (#20735)
♦ UZF – Universitätszentrum für Friedensforschung, Wien (internationally oriented national body)
♦ **UZN** Universal Zulu Nation (#20685)
♦ V4 / see Visegrad Group (#20794)
♦ **VAC4EU** Vaccine monitoring Collaboration for Europe (#20740)
♦ Vaccine Congress (meeting series)

♦ **Vaccine monitoring Collaboration for Europe (VAC4EU)** **20740**
SG Rue Washington 40, 1050 Brussels, Belgium. E-mail: secretariat@vac4eu.org.
Administrator address not obtained.
URL: https://vac4eu.org/
History Founded as the sustainability solution of the ADVANCE project (2013-2019). Registration: Banque-Carrefour des Entreprises, No/ID: 0741.674.866, Start date: 17 Jan 2020, Belgium. **Aims** Implement the ADVANCE vision, system and blueprint; enable robust and timely evidence-generation on the effects of vaccines in a collaborative manner in Europe for use by citizens, health care professionals, public health organizations and regulatory agencies. **Structure** General Assembly; Executive Board; Secretariat. **Activities** Research/documentation; training/education.
Members Institutions in 9 countries:
Belgium, Denmark, France, Germany, Italy, Netherlands, Norway, Spain, UK.
NGO Relations Member of (1): *Federation of European and International Associations Established in Belgium (FAIB, #09508)*. Partner of (3): *Active Citizenship Network (ACN)*; *Global Vaccine Data Network (GVDN, #10645)*; *SIGMA Consortium (#19271)*. [2023/AA3229/**E**]

♦ Vaccines for Africa Initiative (internationally oriented national body)

♦ **Vaccines Europe (VE)** **20741**
Exec Dir Rue du Trône 108B, 1050 Brussels, Belgium.
URL: https://www.vaccineseurope.eu/
History 1991. A specialist group within *European Federation of Pharmaceutical Industries and Associations (EFPIA, #07191)*. Former names and other names: *European Vaccines Manufacturers (EVM)* – former. Registration: EU Transparency Register, No/ID: 53073567234-18, Start date: 23 Nov 2011. **Aims** Drive a sustainable and resilient vaccines environment in Europe, protecting people against infectious diseases at all stages of life. **Structure** Board; Executive Office. Working Groups. **Activities** Networking/liaising; politics/policy/regulatory. **Members** Companies. Membership countries not specified. **NGO Relations** Supports (1): *Steering Group on Influenza Vaccination (#19980)*. [2022/XE3593/**E**]

♦ VACFA – Vaccines for Africa Initiative (internationally oriented national body)

♦ **Vacuum Insulation Panel Association (VIPA International)** **20742**
Global Office Av de Tervueren 188A – bte 4, 1150 Brussels, Belgium. T. +3227611681. E-mail: vipa-international@kellencompany.com.
URL: http://vipa-international.com/
History Aug 2014. Registration: USA, Delaware. **Aims** Act as the global voice of the vacuum insulation panel industry; promote quality and raise awareness about the potential of saving space and energy costs and reducing carbon dioxide emissions in a wide range of applications and industries. **Structure** General Assembly; Board of Directors; Executive Committee; Working Groups; Secretariat. **Languages** English. **Staff** 1.00 FTE, paid. **Finance** Sources: members' dues. **Activities** Awareness raising; standards/guidelines.
Members Manufacturer; Material Supplier; Equipment Supplier; Associate. Members in 10 countries:
Belgium, Czechia, Denmark, France, Germany, Israel, Japan, Korea Rep, UK, USA.
NGO Relations Liaison Member of: *Comité européen de normalisation (CEN, #04162)*.
[2021.02.17/XM4814/**C**]

♦ VAHA – Value Health Africa (internationally oriented national body)
♦ VAIS – Vlaams Agentschap voor International Samenwerking (internationally oriented national body)
♦ **VAI** Vida Ascendente Internacional (#20769)
♦ VAKA / see Hand in Hand tegen Racisme
♦ VAKA – Vereniging voor Vrede en Verdraagzaamheid / see Hand in Hand tegen Racisme
♦ Vakbondsvereniging – Europese Overheidsdienst / see Union Syndicale Fédérale (#20485)
♦ Valdivia Group – Group of Temperate Southern Hemisphere Countries on the Environment (no recent information)
♦ Valid International (internationally oriented national body)
♦ Validity Alapitvany – Központ a Mentalis Sérültek Jogaiért (#20743)

♦ **Validity Foundation** **20743**
Validity Alapitvany – Központ a Mentalis Sérültek Jogaiért
Contact Impact Hub, Ferenciek Tere 2, Budapest 1053, Hungary. E-mail: validity@validity.ngo.
Contact PO Box 68543, London, SW15 9FP, UK.
URL: http://validity.ngo/
History as *Mental Disability Advocacy Center (MDAC)* by *Open Society Foundations (OSF, #17763)*. Registered in accordance with Hungarian law, Nov 2002. UK Registered Charity: 1104456. **Aims** Use the law to secure equality, inclusion and justice for people with mental disabilities. **Structure** Board of Trustees. **Languages** English. **Staff** 10.00 FTE, paid. **Finance** Support from: *European Commission (EC, #06633)*; *Open Society Foundations (OSF, #17763)*; private philanthropists. Annual budget: about euro 800,000. **Activities** Advocacy/lobbying/activism; politics/policy/regulatory; monitoring/evaluation; capacity building. **Consultative Status** Consultative status granted from: *Council of Europe (CE, #04881)* (Participatory Status); *ECOSOC (#05331)* (Special). **IGO Relations** *Council of Europe (CE, #04881)*; *European Union (EU, #08967)*; *Office of the United Nations High Commissioner for Human Rights (OHCHR, #17697)*; *UNICEF (#20332)*; *United Nations (UN, #20515)*; *WHO (#20950)*. **NGO Relations** Links with various international and national organizations.
[2019/XE4702/**E**]

♦ **VALID Nutrition** **20744**
Contact Cuibin Farm, Derry Duff, Bantry, CO. CORK, Ireland. T. +353867809541. E-mail: office@validnutrition.org.
Contact 9 Hollywood Mews, London, SW10 9HU, UK.
URL: http://www.validnutrition.org/
History 2005. Registration: Charity, No/ID: CHY 17583, Ireland; Charity Register, No/ID: 1141922, England and Wales; 501(c)(3) not-for-profit, USA. **Aims** Make highly nutritious "ready-to-use food" products more accessible and affordable to those who need them most, while also increasing awareness of their benefits and therefore generating demand. **Structure** Directors; Trustees; Management Team. **Languages** English. **Finance** Sources: fees for services; sale of products. **Activities** Advocacy/lobbying/activism; research and development. **IGO Relations** Partners include: *Department for International Development (DFID, inactive)*; *Irish Aid*; *UNICEF (#20332)*; *United States Agency for International Development (USAID)*; *World Food Programme (WFP, #21510)*. **NGO Relations** Partners include: *1,000 Days*; *Advocates for International Development (A4ID)*; *Ashoka – Innovators for the Public (#01248)*; *Concern Worldwide*; *Global Innovation Fund (GIF)*; *Scaling Up Nutrition Movement (SUN Movement, #19064)*; *Valid International*. [2023.02.15/XM5392/**F**]

♦ Välinen työympäristöä koskeva sopimus (1989 treaty)
♦ VALP – Variation and Language Processing Conference (meeting series)
♦ Valtion Rakennustoiminnan Pohjoismainen Kontaktielin (#17252)
♦ Value Health Africa (internationally oriented national body)

♦ **Values Caucus at the United Nations** **20745**
Main Office 866 UN Plaza, Ste 120, New York NY 10017, USA. T. +12128032531. Fax +12128032566.
URL: http://www.valuescaucus.org/
History Aug 1994, during 1st Preparatory Conference of the World Summit on Social Development. Also referred to as *Values Caucus at the United Nations*. **Aims** Promote examination of the values guiding *human behaviour* at individual, family, professional, organizational, national, international and spiritual level; develop in-depth participatory, multidisciplinary and cross-cultural dialogue to promote positive values, transcending differences; participate in the work of the United Nations. **Structure** Coordinating Council; 2 Chairmen.
[2017/XM2328/**F**]

♦ **VAMAS** Versailles Project on Advanced Materials and Standards (#20757)
♦ VaMoS – International Workshop on Variability Modelling of Software-Intensive Systems (meeting series)
♦ VAM – Voices of African Mothers (internationally oriented national body)

♦ **Vanadium International Technical Committee (VANITEC)** **20746**
Comité technique international du vanadium – Comité Técnico Internacional del Vanadio – Internationaler Technischer Vanadium Ausschuss
Main Office Hildenbrook House, The Slade, Tunbridge Wells, TN9 1HR, UK. T. +441892530448. E-mail: info@vanitec.org.
URL: http://www.vanitec.org/
History 1972. Registration: Companies House, No/ID: 06490949, Start date: 2008, England and Wales. **Aims** Promote the use of vanadium and vanadium containing products. **Events** *Meeting* London (UK) 2014, *Meeting* Perth, WA (Australia) 2014, *Meeting* Beijing (China) 2013, *Meeting* Lugano (Switzerland) 2013, *Meeting* Venice (Italy) 2012. **NGO Relations** Member of: *Association européenne des métaux (EUROMETAUX, #02578)*.
[2021/XM1244/**E**]

♦ Vance Center – Cyrus R Vance Center for International Justice (internationally oriented national body)
♦ Vanguard Africa Foundation (unconfirmed)
♦ Vanguards of Conquest / see Al-Jihad (#00637)
♦ Van Hall Larenstein University of Applied Sciences (internationally oriented national body)
♦ **VANITEC** Vanadium International Technical Committee (#20746)
♦ Van Leer Jerusalem Institute (internationally oriented national body)
♦ Van Tienhoven Foundation for International Nature Protection (internationally oriented national body)
♦ Van Tienhoven Stichting tot Internationale Natuurbescherming (internationally oriented national body)
♦ The Vanunu Trust / see Campaign for a Nuclear-Free Middle East
♦ Van Vollenhoven Institute for Law and Administration in Non-Western Countries / see Van Vollenhoven Institute for Law, Governance and Development
♦ Van Vollenhoven Institute for Law, Governance and Development (internationally oriented national body)
♦ Van Vollenhoven Instituut voor Recht, Bestuur en Ontwikkeling (internationally oriented national body)
♦ VAO – Vision Aid Overseas (internationally oriented national body)
♦ Variation and Language Processing Conference (meeting series)
♦ VASA / see Anthropology Southern Africa (#00851)
♦ VASAB 2010 / see Vision and Strategies around the Baltic Sea (#20798)
♦ **VASAB** Vision and Strategies around the Baltic Sea (#20798)
♦ Vasco da Gama – European Institute of Diplomacy and International Relations (unconfirmed)
♦ **Vas-Cog** International Society for Vascular, Behavioural and Cognitive Disorders (#15534)

♦ **Vascular Access Society (VAS)** **20747**
Secretariat Pauwels PCO, Avenue Ceramique 222, 6221 KX Maastricht, Netherlands. T. +31433218180. Fax +31433214370.
URL: http://www.vascularaccesssociety.com/
History 30 Oct 1997, Maastricht (Netherlands). Founded during 3rd International Congress on Access for Dialysis. **Aims** Raise interest in the field of hemodialysis vascular access; promote and conducts basic and clinical research. **Structure** Council; Board; Secretariat. **Activities** Training/education; events/meetings; awards/prizes/competitions. **Events** *International Congress* Mestre (Italy) 2025, *International Congress* Porto (Portugal) 2023, *International Congress* Berlin (Germany) 2021, *Biennial Congress* Rotterdam (Netherlands) 2019, *Biennial Congress* Ljubljana (Slovenia) 2017. **Publications** *Journal of Vascular Access* (4 a year); *VAS Newsletter*. **Members** Individuals. Membership countries not specified. [2022/XM8106/**D**]

♦ Vascular and Endovascular Research Group in Europe (no recent information)
♦ Vascular Society of Southern Africa (internationally oriented national body)

♦ **VAS-European Independent Foundation in Angiology/Vascular Medicine (VAS)** **20748**
Headquarters c/o Research Ctr on Vascular Diseases, Dept Biomedical Science- Univ of Milan/L Sacco Hosp, Via G B Grassi 74, 20157 Milan MI, Italy. T. +390250319813. E-mail: vas@unimi.it.
URL: http://www.vas-int.net/
History Set up 1998 as *VAS-Vascular-Independent Research and Education-European Organisation (VAS)*. Also in 1998, joined by *European Working Group on Medical Angiology (EWGMA)*, which was set up 1991. **Aims** Fight against vascular *disease* for its prevention and for the benefit of *patients* and society; harmonize European Education and Training in Europe; enforce collaborative research; propose new effective and equitable approaches in health care. **Structure** Board; Advisory Board; Committees; Teams and Working Groups. **Languages** English. **Finance** Sources: donations; revenue from activities/projects. **Activities** Awareness raising; healthcare; projects/programmes; research/documentation; training/education. **Events** *European Angiology Days* Milan (Italy) 2021, *European Angiology Days* Busto Arsizio (Italy) 2018. **Publications** Documents. **Members** Individuals (around 600): medical professors, clinicians, researchers, technicians and nurses in the field of Angiology/Vascular Medicine; Institutions: universities, scientific societies, centers, patients organizations. Members in 45 countries. Membership countries not specified. **NGO Relations** Member of (1): *European Public Health Alliance (EPHA, #08297)*. Recognized by: *European Union of Medical Specialists (UEMS, #09001)*. [2022/XM5790/**D**]

♦ VASSA – Vascular Society of Southern Africa (internationally oriented national body)
♦ VASTA – Voice and Speech Trainers Association (internationally oriented national body)
♦ Västerländska Buddhistordens Vänner / see Triratna Buddhist Community (#20243)
♦ Västnordensamarbetet / see Nordic Atlantic Cooperation (#17209)
♦ **VAS** Vascular Access Society (#20747)
♦ VAS-Vascular-Independent Research and Education-European Organisation / see VAS-European Independent Foundation in Angiology/Vascular Medicine (#20748)
♦ VAS / see VAS-European Independent Foundation in Angiology/Vascular Medicine (#20748)
♦ **VAS** VAS-European Independent Foundation in Angiology/Vascular Medicine (#20748)

♦ **VAT Forum** **20749**
Contact Prinsenstraat 40, 1850 Grimbergen, Belgium. T. +32475794574. E-mail: info@vatforum.com.
URL: http://www.vatforum.com/
Aims Gather, manage and distribute information on indirect taxation from around the world. **Structure** Board. **Activities** Events/meetings; research/documentation; training/education. **Events** *Annual VAT Summit* Barcelona (Spain) 2023, *Annual Summit* Limassol (Cyprus) 2019, *Annual Summit* Barcelona (Spain) 2018. **Information Services** *VAT Forum online courses*. [2023.02.13/XM8349/**F**]

♦ Vatican Foundation "International Center Family of Nazareth" 20750

Fondation Vaticane "Centre International Famille de Nazareth" – Fundación Vaticana "Centro Internacional Familia de Nazaret" – Fondazione Vaticana "Centro Internazionale Famiglia di Nazareth

Gen Sec Palazzo San Calisto Piazza San Calisto 16, 00120 Vatican City, Vatican. T. +39669887187. Fax +39669887162.

History 15 Oct 2012. Founded on the initiative of Pope Benedict XVI. **Aims** Promote the spiritual formation and evangelization of the family; support pastoral care for families around the world, especially in the Holy Land. **Structure** Administrative Board; Board of Statutory Auditors. **Events** *Gathering of the Renewal for a New Evangelization of the Family* Philadelphia, PA (USA) 2015. [2016.06.21/XJ9686/f/**F**]

- ♦ Vatican Radio / see Radio Vaticana – Vatican News
- ♦ Vatican-WCC Joint Working Group / see Joint Working Group between the Roman Catholic Church and the World Council of Churches (#16152)
- ♦ **VATSIM** Virtual Air Traffic Simulation Network (#20786)
- ♦ **VBA** Volta Basin Authority (#20808)
- ♦ **VBBW** Vereinigung der Bergbevölkerungen der Welt (#21658)
- ♦ VBC – Virtual Biosecurity Centre (unconfirmed)
- ♦ VBW – Verein für Europäische Binnenschiffahrt und Wasserstrassen (internationally oriented national body)
- ♦ VCDNP – Vienna Center for Disarmament and Non-Proliferation (internationally oriented national body)
- ♦ **VCH-International** Internationaler Verband Christlicher Hotels (#13298)
- ♦ VCI – Veritas College International (internationally oriented national body)
- ♦ VCRS – Veterinary Comparative Respiratory Society (internationally oriented national body)
- ♦ VDQS – Vineyard Data Quantification Society (unconfirmed)
- ♦ VDSIC – Visible Seal International Council (internationally oriented national body)
- ♦ VDSM / see European Association of Event Centers (#06032)
- ♦ VDW – Vitamin D Workshop (meeting series)
- ♦ VEAWI – Vereinigung der Europäischen Aluminiumwaren-Industrie (inactive)
- ♦ VECAM – Veille européenne et citoyenne sur les autoroutes de l'information et le multimédia (internationally oriented national body)
- ♦ VECH / see European Federation of Campingsite Organisations and Holiday Park Assocations (#07066)
- ♦ Vecinos Mundiales (internationally oriented national body)
- ♦ **VECONAC** Veterans Confederation of ASEAN Countries (#20759)
- ♦ VECoS – International Conference on Verification and Evaluation of Computer and Communication Systems (meeting series)
- ♦ VECO – VredesEilanden Country Offices / see Rikolto
- ♦ VECPAR – International Meeting on High Performance Computing for Computational Science (meeting series)
- ♦ **VEC** Vienna Energy Club (#20771)
- ♦ **VEF** Vienna Economic Forum (#20770)
- ♦ VEGA – Volunteers for Economic Growth Alliance (internationally oriented national body)

♦ Vegetable Science International Network (VEGINET) 20751

Chairperson 9 – 1st Cross – 1st Main, 1st Block, Rajmahal Vilas (RMV) Extension 2nd Stage, Bangalore, Bangalore, Karnataka 560 094, Bangalore KARNATAKA 560 094, India. T. +918023415188. Fax +918023511555.

URL: https://pnasf.in/veginet.html

History Nov 2002, Bangalore (India). Founded at General Assembly of the International Conference on Vegetables (ICV-2002). **Aims** Strengthen partnership and inter-institutional cooperation among member organizations of the vegetable sector towards improved production and utilization of vegetables. **Structure** General Assembly; Executive Council; Finance Committee; Conference/Congress Advisory Committees; Scientific Activities Committee/Commission; Secretariat. **Languages** English. **Activities** Events/meetings. **Events** *International conference on horticulture* Bangalore (India) 2009. **Publications** *E-VEGINET NEWS* (periodical). **Members** in about 50 countries of Asia, the Americas and Africa. Membership countries not specified. [2018/XJ1485/**E**]

- ♦ Vegetara Ligo Esperantista / see World Esperantist Vegetarian Association (#21389)
- ♦ **VEGINET** Vegetable Science International Network (#20751)
- ♦ Veille européenne et citoyenne sur les autoroutes de l'information et le multimédia (internationally oriented national body)
- ♦ Veille météorologique mondiale (#21910)
- ♦ VEK – Vereniging van Ecologen voor Kernenergie (internationally oriented national body)
- ♦ **VEK** Veterana Esperantista Klubo (#20758)
- ♦ velafrica (internationally oriented national body)
- ♦ VELB / see European Lactation Consultants Alliance (#07638)
- ♦ Vellore Rural Communities Trust / see Friends of Vellore
- ♦ Velo-city (meeting series)

♦ Vélo mondial 20752

Exec Dir Kleine-Gartmanplantsoen, 1017 RR Amsterdam, Netherlands. T. +310627055688. E-mail: operations@velomondial.net.

URL: http://www.velomondial.net/

History 2000. Registration: Handelsregister, No/ID: KVK 41266195, Netherlands; EU Transparency Register, No/ID: 719697743496-64, Start date: 12 Jul 2021. **Aims** Enhance the contribution sustainable mobility can have towards CO2 emission reduction, climate change control, improvement of air quality, road safety, poverty relief, sustainable economic development and health promotion. **Structure** Executive Board; Non-Executive Board. **Languages** English. **Staff** 1.00 FTE, paid. **Finance** Private and public contracts. **Activities** Advocacy/lobbying/activism; awareness raising; projects/programmes. **Events** *Regional Conference* New York, NY (USA) 2009, *Velo mondial world cycle conference / Conference* Cape Town (South Africa) 2006, *Regional Conference* Doha (Qatar) 2005, *Regional Conference* Dublin (Ireland) 2005, *Regional conference* Osaka (Japan) 2005. **Publications** *Enabling Cycling Cities: Ingredients for Success..* [2022.02.08/XF6634/**F**]

- ♦ velos für afrika / see velafrica
- ♦ VEM – Gemeinschaft von Kirchen in Drei Erdteilen / see United Evangelical Mission (#20507)
- ♦ **VEM** Vereinte Evangelische Mission (#20507)
- ♦ Venezuelan Investment Fund / see Economic and Social Development Bank
- ♦ Venice Commission of the Council of Europe / see European Commission for Democracy through Law (#06636)
- ♦ **Venice Commission** European Commission for Democracy through Law (#06636)
- ♦ Venice European Centre for the Skills of Architectural Heritage Conservation / see European Centre for Heritage Crafts and Professions (#06484)
- ♦ Venice European Centre for the Trades and Professions of the Conservation of Architectural Heritage / see European Centre for Heritage Crafts and Professions (#06484)
- ♦ Venice Regional Seapower Symposium for the Navies of the Mediterranean and Black Sea Countries (meeting series)
- ♦ Venice RSS – Venice Regional Seapower Symposium for the Navies of the Mediterranean and Black Sea Countries (meeting series)
- ♦ Vennskap Nord-Sør (internationally oriented national body)
- ♦ VENRO – Verband Entwicklungspolitik und Humanitäre Hilfe e.V. (internationally oriented national body)
- ♦ Venue Management Association – Asia and Pacific (internationally oriented national body)
- ♦ Verband der Bäckereigrundstoff- und Backmittelhersteller in der EWG / see Federation of European Manufacturers of Ingredients to the Bakery, Confectionery and Patisserie Industries (#09513)
- ♦ Verband der Bäckmittel- und Backgrundstoffhersteller im EWR / see Federation of European Manufacturers of Ingredients to the Bakery, Confectionery and Patisserie Industries (#09513)
- ♦ Verband der in Belgien Niedergelassenen Europäischen und Internationalen Vereinigungen (#09508)
- ♦ Verband der in Belgien Niedergelassenen Internationalen Vereinigungen / see Federation of European and International Associations Established in Belgium (#09508)
- ♦ Verband Binationaler Familien und Partnerschaften (internationally oriented national body)
- ♦ Verband der Diätetischen Lebensmittelindustrie der EU / see Specialised Nutrition Europe (#19909)
- ♦ Verband der Diätetischen Lebensmittelindustrie der EWG / see Specialised Nutrition Europe (#19909)
- ♦ Verband für die Taxonomische Untersuchung der Flora des Tropischen Afrikas (#02948)
- ♦ Verband Entwicklungspolitik deutscher Nichtregierungsorganisationen / see Verband Entwicklungspolitik und Humanitäre Hilfe e.V.
- ♦ Verband Entwicklungspolitik und Humanitäre Hilfe e.V. (internationally oriented national body)
- ♦ Verband der Europäischen Angelgerätehersteller / see European Fishing Tackle Trade Association (#07267)
- ♦ Verband der Europäischen Arbeitsgemeinschaften von Werkschriftleitern / see European Association for Internal Communication (#06091)
- ♦ Verband der Europäischen Bauwirtschaft (#06766)
- ♦ Verband der Europäischen Beamtem / see European Public Service Union (#08303)
- ♦ Verband der Europäischen Bettfedern- und Bettwarenindustrie / see European Down and Feather Association (#06941)
- ♦ Verband der Europäischen Dachziegel- und Mauerziegelfabrikanten / see Tiles and Bricks Europe (#20163)
- ♦ Verband der Europäischen Eisenbahn-Industrien (#02536)
- ♦ Verband der Europäischen Elektrowerkzeug-Hersteller (#08264)
- ♦ Verband der Europäischen Fiberfassindustrie (#06038)
- ♦ Verband der europäischen Fußballnationalmannschaften der Winzer (#20388)
- ♦ Verband von Europäischen Geographischen Gesellschaften (#02512)
- ♦ Verband der Europäischen Gipsindustrien / see European Association of Plaster and Plaster Product Manufacturers (#06152)
- ♦ Verband des Europäischen Gross- und Aussenhandels (inactive)
- ♦ Verband der Europäischen Hersteller Elektronischer Bauelemente (#06974)
- ♦ Verband der Europäischen Hersteller von Fahrzeugrädern (#02552)
- ♦ Verband der Europäischen Hersteller von Lehren, Feinmesswerkzeugen, -geräten und Maschinen für die Langmesstechnik (no recent information)
- ♦ Verband der Europäischen Hersteller von Polyurethan-Weichblockschaum (#06042)
- ♦ Verband der europäischen Hersteller und Verteiler von Kühl- und Klimatisierungsanlagen (#00601)
- ♦ Verband der Europäischen Jute-Industrien (inactive)
- ♦ Verband der Europäischen Kaliproduzenten (#02872)
- ♦ Verband der Europäischen Laminatfussbodenhersteller (#02533)
- ♦ Verband der Europäischen Landwirtschaft (inactive)
- ♦ Verband der Europäischen Möbelindustrie (#07370)
- ♦ Verband der europäischen Online-Apotheken / see European Association of E-Pharmacies (#06029)
- ♦ Verband der Europäischen Otorhinolaryngologie, Kopf- und Halschirurgie (#04528)
- ♦ Verband der Europäischen Porenbetonindustrie (#06297)
- ♦ Verband der Europäischen Produzenten von Kraftsackpapieren / see European Kraft Paper Producers for the Flexible Packaging Industry (#07630)
- ♦ Verband der Europäischen Sozialen Apoteken (#20401)
- ♦ Verband der Europäischen Sozialen und Genossenschaftlichen Apoteken / see Union européenne des Pharmacies sociales (#20401)
- ♦ Verband der Europäischen Stahlfassindustrie (#06222)
- ♦ Verband der Europäischen Stickstoffproduzenten (inactive)
- ♦ Verband der Europäischen Zigaretten Papier Verarbeitenden Industrie / see European Rolling Paper Association (#08399)
- ♦ Verband der europäischen Zuckerfabrikanten (#04159)
- ♦ Verband Europäischer Campingplatzhalter / see European Federation of Campingsite Organisations and Holiday Park Assocations (#07066)
- ♦ Verband Europäischer Dämmstoffhersteller (#07577)
- ♦ Verband Europäischer Expresskuriere (inactive)
- ♦ Verband Europäischer Filmregisseure (#09541)
- ♦ Verband Europäischer Freilichtmuseen (#02527)
- ♦ Verband Europäischer Gartenbauzüchter (no recent information)
- ♦ Verband Europäischer Gaskontrollgerätehersteller / see Association des fabricants européens d'appareils de contrôle et de régulation (#02592)
- ♦ Verband Europäischer Geigen- und Bogenbau Meister (#06273)
- ♦ Verband Europäischer Hersteller von Nahrungsmittel Emulgatoren (#07281)
- ♦ Verband Europäischer Klebstoffindustrien / see Fédération européenne des industries de colles et adhésifs (#09572)
- ♦ Verband Europäischer Kleinwasserkraftwerke (#08495)
- ♦ Verband Europäischer Kontrollgerätehersteller / see Association des fabricants européens d'appareils de contrôle et de régulation (#02592)
- ♦ Verband Europäischer Kunststoffverarbeiter (#08216)
- ♦ Verband Europäischer Laktationsberaterinnen IBCLC / see European Lactation Consultants Alliance (#07638)
- ♦ Verband Europäischer Lehrmittelfirmen / see Worlddidac Association (#21361)
- ♦ Verband Europäischer Rechtsanwaltkammern (#06320)
- ♦ Verband Europäischer Regionen der Fluglinien (#08347)
- ♦ Verband Europäischer Schreib- und Zeichengeräte-Hersteller (#09125)
- ♦ Verband der Geometer Europas (inactive)
- ♦ Verband Güteschutz Horizontalbohrungen (#05133)
- ♦ Verband Industrieller Metalldeckenhersteller (#02641)
- ♦ Verband der Internationalen und Europäischen Beamtem / see European Public Service Union (#08303)
- ♦ Verband der Internationalen Schulen (#14789)
- ♦ Verband internationaler Messen / see UFI – The Global Association of the Exhibition Industry (#20276)
- ♦ Verband Krankenschwestern im Norden (#17371)
- ♦ Verband für Krisenhilfe und Solidarische Entwicklungszusammenarbeit (internationally oriented national body)
- ♦ Verband für Kulturelle Zusammenarbeit (inactive)
- ♦ Verband der Latein-amerikanischen Fremdenverkehrsorganisationen (#04466)
- ♦ Verband der Maisverarbeiter in den EWG-Ländern / see Euromaisiers (#05709)
- ♦ Verband für Marketing im Hotelwesen / see Hospitality Sales and Marketing Association International (#10948)
- ♦ Verband der mehrschichtig modularen Fussbodenbeläg (internationally oriented national body)
- ♦ Verband der Messen und Fachausstellungen der Benelux-Länder (inactive)
- ♦ Verband der Modelleisenbahner und Eisenbahnfreunde Europas (#20400)
- ♦ Verband der Naturnah Dekenden Forstleute in Europe / see PRO SILVA (#18543)
- ♦ Verband des Nordischen Bankpersonals (inactive)
- ♦ Verband der Nordischen Landwirtschaftsforscher / see Nordiska Jordbruksforskares Förening (#17486)
- ♦ Verband der Olivenölindustrie der EWG (#09596)
- ♦ Verband der Patentwirtschaftler (inactive)
- ♦ Verband der Schokolade-, Dauerbackwaren- und Zuckerwarenindustrien der EWG / see Association of the Chocolate, Biscuit and Confectionery Industries of the EU (#02427)
- ♦ Verband der Strassenverkehrsdienste der Europäischen Eisenbahnen (inactive)
- ♦ Verband Technischer Veröffentlichungen auf dem Gebiet der Eisenhüttenkunde (inactive)

- Verband der Verkehrsgewerkschaften in der Europäischen Union / see European Transport Workers' Federation (#08941)
- Verband der Wild- und Geflügeleinzelhändler der EWG-Länder / see European Poultry, Egg and Game Association (#08258)
- Verbindingscentrum van Vleesverwerkende Industrieën van de EEG / see Liaison Centre for the Meat Processing Industry in the EU (#16452)
- Verbindingscomité voor de Bouw van Uitrustingen en Onderdelen / see European Association of Automotive Suppliers (#05948)
- Verbindingscomité voor de Carrosserie- en Aanhangwagenbouw / see International Association of the Body and Trailer Building Industry (#11727)
- Verbindingscomité voor de Industrie van Onderdelen Uitrustingen voor Voertuigen / see European Association of Automotive Suppliers (#05948)
- Verbindungsausschuss der Aufbauten- und Anhängerindustrie / see International Association of the Body and Trailer Building Industry (#11727)
- Verbindungs-Ausschuss der Diplom-Landwirte der Mitgliedstaaten der Europäischen Wirtschaftsgemeinschaften / see Confédération européenne des associations d'ingénieurs agronomes (#04538)
- Verbindungsausschuss der Kraftfahrzeugteile- und Zubehörindustrie / see European Association of Automotive Suppliers (#05948)
- Verbindungsbüro der Kautschukindustrien der Europäischen Union / see European Tyre and Rubber Manufacturers' Association (#08963)
- Verbindungsbüro der Kautschukindustrien der Europäischen Wirtschaftsgemeinschaft / see European Tyre and Rubber Manufacturers' Association (#08963)
- Verbindungs-Komitee der Internationalen Frauen-Organisationen (inactive)
- Verbindungsstelle der Europäischen Berufsverbände EWG / für Aromatische Erzeugnisse / see European Flavour Association (#07269)
- Verbiti – Società del Verbo Divino (religious order)
- Verbond van Europese en Internationale in België Gevestigde Verenigingen (#09508)
- Verbond van Europese Organisaties voor de Groot- en Buitenlandse Handel (inactive)
- Verbond van Fabrikanten van Diepvrieslevensmiddelen in de EEG (inactive)
- Verbond van Internationale in België Gevestigde Verenigingen / see Federation of European and International Associations Established in Belgium (#09508)
- Verbond van Organisaties uit de EEG-Landen op het Gebied van het Verduurzamen van Vis / see European Union Fish Processors Association (#08989)
- Verbond van Organisaties uit de Europese Unie op het Gebied van het Verduurzamen van Vis (#08989)
- Verbond van Verenigingen van in het Buitenland Woonachtige Landgenoten uit de Europese Gemeenschap / see Europeans throughout the World (#08839)
- Verbruikersunie Derde Wereld / see Association for the Advancement of Consumerism in the World (#02347)
- Verdenserklaringen om menneskerettighederne (1948 treaty)
- Verdensorganisationen for unge mod klimaforandringer (inactive)
- Verdens Skove (internationally oriented national body)
- Verdens ungdoms organisasjon mot klimatiske endringer (inactive)
- Verdrag van Amsterdam (1997 treaty)
- Verdrag Betreffende de Europese Unie (1992 treaty)
- Verdrag voor grensoverschrijdende samenwerking (2005 treaty)
- Verdrag inzake de bescherming van de Maas (1994 treaty)
- Verdrag Inzake de Bescherming van de Schelde, 1994 (1994 treaty)
- Verdrag van Nice (2001 treaty)
- Verdrag tot oprichting van de Europese Gemeenschap voor Kolen en Staal (1951 treaty)
- Verdrag tot vaststelling van een Grondwet voor Europa (2004 treaty)
- Vereenigd Nasionale Kerk van Afrika, Onze Volkskerk / see Volkskerk van Afrika

♦ Verein Alpenstadt des Jahres 20753

Alpine Town of the Year Association – Association Ville des Alpes de l'Année – Associazione Città alpina dell'anno – Društvo Alpsko mesto leta

Acting Managing Dir Rathausplatz 1, 87527 Sonthofen, Germany. E-mail: office@alpenstaedte.org.
French Website: https://www.villedesalpes.org/

History 1997, Villach (Austria). Registration: Bavaria District court, No/ID: VR 201321, Start date: 25 Mar 2020, Germany, Kempten. **Aims** Strengthen awareness of the Alps; involve the population; consolidate ties with the region; shape the future sustainably; develop cooperation. **Structure** Members Assembly; Board; Secretariat. **Activities** Advocacy/lobbying/activism; events/meetings. **Events** *AlpWeek* Brig (Switzerland) 2022. **NGO Relations** Secretariat provided by: *CIPRA International (#03930)*. [2023/AA3115/E]

- Verein Barmherzigkeit (internationally oriented national body)
- Vereinbarung zur anwendung des Europäischen übereinkommens vom 17 oktober 1980 über die gewährung ärztlicher betreuung an personen bei vorübergehendem aufenthalt (1988 treaty)
- Vereinbarung über die anwendung des Europäischen übereinkommens über die internationale handelsschiedsgerichtsbarkeit (1962 treaty)
- Verein Deutscher Eisenbahnverwaltungen (inactive)
- Verein der Elefantenpfleger und -Manager Europas (inactive)
- Verein zur Entwicklung und Förderung des Global Democracy Award (#02470)
- Verein für Europäische Binnenschiffahrt und Wasserstrassen (internationally oriented national body)
- Verein der europäischen Bürgerwissenschaften (#06557)
- Verein der Europäischen Gesundheitsapothekerinspektoren (no recent information)
- Verein für ein Europäisches Kulturparlament (#06870)
- Verein der Flusswasserwerke (#02895)
- Verein zur Fördering kosmetischer Chirurgie (#21068)
- Verein zur Förderung der Entwicklung und Implementierung von Ausbildungsstandards in der Humangenetik / see European Board of Medical Genetics (#06361)
- Verein zur Förderung der Europäischen Akademie für Lebensforschung, Integration und Zivilgesellschaft / see European Academy for Life Research, Integration and Civil Society (#05799)
- Verein zur Förderung der europäischen Sojaproduktion – Donau Soja / see Donau Soja (#05116)
- Verein zur Förderung Internationaler Bildungschancen (internationally oriented national body)
- Verein zur Förderung internationaler Produktdatennormen / see ProSTEP iViP Association
- Verein der Freunde Robert Schumans / see Association Robert Schuman (#02896)
- Vereinigtes Institut für Kernforschung / see Joint Institute for Nuclear Research (#16134)
- Vereinigung Bedeutender Friedhöfe in Europa (#02915)
- Vereinigung der Bergbevölkerungen der Welt (#21658)
- Vereinigung der Berufsorganisationen des Zuckerhandels für die Länder der EU / see European Association of Sugar Traders (#06239)
- Vereinigung der Biologen der Europäischen Gemeinschaften / see European Countries Biologists Association (#06852)
- Vereinigung der Commonwealth Universitäten (#02440)
- Vereinigung für die Entwicklung und die Zusammenstellung des Europäischen Touristen Austausches (inactive)
- Vereinigung für die internationalen Fahrvergünstigungen des Eisenbahnpersonals (#02465)
- Vereinigung für die Kultur und die Berufliche Zukunft in Europe (#20373)
- Vereinigung für die Verhütung der Folter (#02869)
- Vereinigung für die Verteidigung der Religionsfreiheit (#02681)
- Vereinigung der Erfrischungsgetränke in den EU-Ländern / see UNESDA Soft Drinks Europe (#20323)
- Vereinigung Europa – Dritte Welt / see eu can aid (#05570)
- Vereinigung der Europäischen Aluminiumwaren-Industrie (inactive)
- Vereinigung der Europäischen Astronauten (inactive)
- Vereinigung der Europäischen Automatenverbände / see European Vending and Coffee Service Association (#09049)
- Vereinigung der Europäischen Büromöbel Hersteller (#08109)
- Vereinigung der Europäischen Dental-Industrie (#09595)
- Vereinigung der Europäischen Elektrowerkzeug-Hersteller / see European Power Tool Association (#08264)
- Vereinigung der europäischen ergonomischen Gesellschaften eV / see Federation of European Ergonomics Societies (#09504)
- Vereinigung der Europäischen Fachverbände der Floristen / see International Florist Organisation (#13616)
- Vereinigung der Europäischen Faltschachtel- Industrie (#06453)
- Vereinigung der Europäischen Gaszähler-Hersteller / see Association of European Manufacturers of Gas Meters, Gas Pressure Regulators, Safety Devices and Stations (#02521)
- Vereinigung der Europäischen Gesellschaften für Zytologie (#07097)
- Vereinigung der Europäischen Hersteller von Durchlauf-Gas-Wasserheizern und -Badeöfen sowie - Umlauf Gas-Wasserheizern (inactive)
- Vereinigung der Europäischen Hersteller von Gasbeheizten Speicherwasserheizern (inactive)
- Vereinigung der Europäischen Hersteller von Lichtkuppeln, Lichtbändern und RWA (#07434)
- Vereinigung der Europäischen Hersteller von Technischer Keramik für Elektronische, Elektrische, Mechanische und andere Anwendungen / see European Technical Ceramics Federation (#08878)
- Vereinigung der Europäischen Industrie und Handelskammern (#02423)
- Vereinigung der Europäischen Polyurethan-Hartschaum-Verbände (#09538)
- Vereinigung der Europäischen Unabhängigen Stahlerzeuger (inactive)
- Vereinigung der Europäischen Verbände der Automatenwirtschaft / see European Gaming and Amusement Federation (#07374)
- Vereinigung der Europäischen Verbände der Holzindustrie im Baubereich (inactive)
- Vereinigung der Europäischen Verbände der Techniker der Farb-, Email- und Druckfarben-Industrien des Europäischen Festlandes / see Federation of Associations of Technicians for Industry of Paints in European Countries (#09461)
- Vereinigung Europäischer Akkumulatoren-Hersteller (#02498)
- Vereinigung Europäischer Baustoffhersteller / see Construction Products Europe AISBL (#04761)
- Vereinigung Europäischer Fachverbände der Lieferanten für Laboratorien (no recent information)
- Vereinigung Europäischer Giessereiverbände / see European Foundry Association, The (#07352)
- Vereinigung Europäischer Hersteller von Alarmanlagen für Brand, Einbruch und Überfall / see Association of European Manufacturers of Fire and Security Systems (#02520)
- Vereinigung Europäischer Hersteller von Eisenbahnausrüstungen (inactive)
- Vereinigung Europäischer Hersteller und Errichter von Sicherheitsanlagen (#02520)
- Vereinigung Europäischer Hohlglas- und Kramik-Gorsshandels-Verbände (inactive)
- Vereinigung Europäischer Journalisten (#02516)
- Vereinigung Europäischer Konjunktur-Institute (#02506)
- Vereinigung Europäischer Markeninhaber / see MARQUES (#16588)
- Vereinigung Europäischer Polizeiakademien (#02531)
- Vereinigung Europäischer Studentenverbände (inactive)
- Vereinigung Europäischer Trockenbatterie-Hersteller / see European Portable Battery Association (#08255)

♦ Vereinigung Europäischer Verbände des Kachelofenbauer/Hafner-Handwerks (VEUKO) 20754

Union of European Association of Stove-Fitters Trade

Contact Dassanowskyweg 8, 1220 Vienna, Austria. T. +43125658850. Fax +431256588520. E-mail: office@veuko.com.
URL: http://www.veuko.com/

History 2003, but having existed since 1966 as a meeting. **Events** *Annual Congress* Budapest (Hungary) 2004. **Members** Full in 14 countries and territories:
Austria, Czechia, Estonia, Germany, Hungary, Italy, Lithuania, Luxembourg, Poland, Russia, Slovakia, Slovenia, Switzerland, Trentino-South Tyrol.
NGO Relations Member of: *SMEunited (#19327)*. [2019/XM2713/t/E]

- Vereinigung Europäischer Verwaltungsrichter (#02497)
- Vereinigung der Fischgrosshändler, Importeure und Exporteure von Fischen der Europäischen Union / see Comité des organisations nationales des importateurs et exportateurs de poisson de l'UE (#04194)
- Vereinigung der Fischgrosshändler, Importeure und Exporteure von Fischen der EWG / see Comité des organisations nationales des importateurs et exportateurs de poisson de l'UE (#04194)
- Vereinigung der Fischindustrie in der Europäischen Gemeinschaft / see European Union Fish Processors Association (#08989)
- Vereinigung der Fischindustrie in der Europäischen Union (#08989)
- Vereinigung der Fischindustrie in der EWG / see European Union Fish Processors Association (#08989)
- Vereinigung der Fischmehl- und Fischölhersteller in der Europäischen Gemeinschaft / see European Fismeal and Fish Oil Producers (#07268)
- Vereinigung zur Förderung der Chirurgie in Entwicklungsländern / see Deutsche Gesellschaft für Globale- und Tropenchirurgie
- Vereinigung zur Förderung des Internationalen Pressevertriebes (#02876)
- Vereinigung der Geflügelschlächtereien des Geflügelimport- und Exporthandels der EG-Länder / see Association de l'aviculture, de l'industrie et du commerce de volailles dans les pays de l'Union européenne (#02390)
- Vereinigung der Geflügelschlächtereien des Geflügelimport- und Exporthandels der Europäischen Union (#02390)
- Vereinigung der Genossenschaftsbanken der EG / see European Association of Co-operative Banks (#05990)
- Vereinigung der Gewerblichen Getreidelagerhalter in der EWG / see Unistock Europe (#20492)
- Vereinigung von Halbamtlichen und Privaten in Genf Niedergelassenen Internationalen Organisationen / see Fédération des Institutions Internationales établies à Genève (#09599)
- Vereinigung der Hersteller von Johannisbrotkernmehl (#11183)
- Vereinigung der Hersteller von Technischer Keramik in der EWG für Elektronische, Elektrische, Mechanische und andere Anwendungen / see European Technical Ceramics Federation (#08878)
- Vereinigung der Institute für Europäische Studien (inactive)
- Vereinigung des Internationalen Handels in Blumenzwiebeln und Pflanzen (no recent information)
- Vereinigung für Internationale Zusammenarbeit (internationally oriented national body)
- Vereinigung Junger Europäischer Beamter (#02772)
- Vereinigung Junger RechtshistorikerInnen (#02987)
- Vereinigung der Jura-Regionen / see Conférence TransJurassience
- Vereinigung der Keramikfliesenhersteller des Gemeinsamen Markts / see European Ceramic Tile Manufacturers' Federation (#06508)
- Vereinigung der Kohlesaürehaltigen Getränke in den EG-Ländern / see UNESDA Soft Drinks Europe (#20323)
- Vereinigung der Kohlesaürehaltigen Getränke in den EU-Ländern / see UNESDA Soft Drinks Europe (#20323)
- Vereinigung der Margarine-Industrie der EG-Länder / see European Margarine Association (#07736)
- Vereinigung für Menschenrechte und Demokratie in Afrika (internationally oriented national body)
- Vereinigung der Militärpresse Europas (#07803)
- Vereinigung der Nationalen Europäischen und Mittelländischen Gesellschaften für Darm- und Magenheilkunde (inactive)

- Vereinigung der Nationalen Verbände von Fischereiunternehmen in der EU (#02841)
- Vereinigung der Nationalen Verbände von Fischereiunternehmen in der EWG / see Association des organisations nationales d'entreprises de pêche de l'UE (#02841)
- Vereinigung Nationaler Stuck-Putz-Trockenbauverbände in Europa (inactive)
- Vereinigung der Obst- und Fruchtweinindustrie der EWG / see Association des Industries des Cidres et Vins de Fruits de l'UE (#02643)
- Vereinigung für Öffentliche Fernseh Information über Europa-Angelegenheiten (inactive)
- Vereinigung der Ölmühlenindustrie der EG / see FEDIOL – The EU Vegetable Oil and Proteinmeal Industry (#09718)
- Vereinigung von Pensionären der Sparkassen, Banken und Ähnlichen Einrichtungen / see Group of European Retired Staff and Pensioners from Savings Banks, Banks and Related Institutions (#10777)
- Vereinigung der Schmelzkäse-Industrie in der EU (#02642)
- Vereinigung der Schmelzkäse-Industrie in der EWG / see Association de l'industrie de la fonte de fromage de l'UE (#02642)
- Vereinigung von Schulen für den Öffentlichen Gesundheitswesen in der Europäische Region (#02904)
- Vereinigung der Skandinavischen Farben und Lacktechniker (#09702)
- Vereinigung der Spar- und Kreditgenossenschaften der EWG / see European Association of Co-operative Banks (#05990)
- Vereinigung des Speiseeisindustrie der EU / see EUROGLACES – European Ice Cream Association (#05688)
- Vereinigung des Speiseeisindustrie der EWG / see EUROGLACES – European Ice Cream Association (#05688)
- Vereinigung der Steuerberaterverbände in Europa / see CFE Tax Advisers Europe (#03842)
- Vereinigung für das Studium der Deutschen Politik / see International Association for the Study of German Politics (#12200)
- Vereinigung der Verbände der Fischmehlhersteller in der Europäischen Wirtschaftsgemeinschaft / see European Fismeal and Fish Oil Producers (#07268)
- Vereinigung der Verbände und Hersteller Kulinarischer Lebensmittel in Europa / see CULINARIA EUROPE (#04980)
- Vereinigung zur Wissenschaftlichen Erforschung des Planens und Bauens in der Dritten Welt (internationally oriented national body)
- Vereinigung der Zivilflug-Gesellschaften (inactive)
- Verein Internationales AK Laienforum / see Internationales Altkatholische Forum (#13299)
- Verein der Kirchlichen Archivare (#05279)
- Verein Nordischer Papierhistoriker (#02831)
- Verein Robert Schuman (#02896)
- Verein für Sprach- und Kulturaustausch in Mittel-, Ost- und Südosteuropa (internationally oriented national body)
- Verein für Technische Holzfragen / see International Association for Technical Issues Related to Wood
- Vereinte Evangelische Mission (#20507)
- Vereinte Tiernationen (#20497)
- Verein zur Wahrung der Schiffahrtsintressen / see Association for European Inland Navigation and Waterways
- Verein für Zivile Konfliktbearbeitung eV / see German Platform for Peaceful Conflict Management
- Verenigde Religies Initiatief Europa (#20659)
- Verenigende Geref Kerk in Suider-Afrika (internationally oriented national body)
- Vereniging van Beroepsorganisaties van de Suikerhandel in de Landen van de EU / see European Association of Sugar Traders (#06239)
- Vereniging van de Chocolade-, Biscuit-, Beschuit- en Suikerwerkindustrieen in de EEG / see Association of the Chocolate, Biscuit and Confectionery Industries of the EU (#02427)
- Vereniging van de Cider- en Vruchtenwijnindustrie van de EEG / see Association des Industries des Cidres et Vins de Fruits de l'UE (#02643)
- Vereniging van Consumptieijsfabrikanten in de EEG / see EUROGLACES – European Ice Cream Association (#05688)
- Vereniging van Consumptieijsfabrikanten in de EU / see EUROGLACES – European Ice Cream Association (#05688)
- Vereniging van Ecologen voor Kernenergie (internationally oriented national body)
- Vereniging voor de Eenmaking van het Wereldchristendom (religious order)
- Vereniging Europa – Derde Wereld / see eu can aid (#05570)
- Vereniging Europeana Network (#05899)
- Vereniging European Society of Veterinary Oncology / see European Society of Veterinary Oncology (#08782)
- Vereniging voor Europese Binnenscheepvaart en Waterwegen (internationally oriented national body)
- Vereniging van de Europese Fabrikanten van Badgeisers en Gaswandketels (inactive)
- Vereniging van de Europese Fabrikanten van Gasgestookte Warmwatervoorraadtoestellen (inactive)
- Vereniging van de Europese Fabrikanten van Levensmiddelenemulgatoren (#07281)
- Vereniging van de Europese Industrie van Stalen Vaten / see European Association of Steel Drum Manufacturers (#06222)
- Vereniging van Europese Journalisten (#02516)
- Vereniging van Europese Lagere Scholen (inactive)
- Vereniging voor Europese Publieke Informatieverstrekking via Televisie (inactive)
- Vereniging van Fabrikanten van Lactose (inactive)
- Vereniging voor Gebarentaal en Gebarentaalkunde (internationally oriented national body)
- Vereniging der Gepensioneerden van Europese Spaarbanken / see Group of European Retired Staff and Pensioners from Savings Banks, Banks and Related Institutions (#10777)
- Vereniging voor Internationale Culturele Betrekkingen / see Dutch Centre for International Cooperation
- Vereniging van de Internationale Handel in Bloembollen en Planten (no recent information)
- Vereniging voor Latijns-Amerikaanse en Caraïbische Studies (internationally oriented national body)
- Vereniging van de Margarine-Industrie der EG Landen / see European Margarine Association (#07736)
- Vereniging der Nationale Organisaties van Visserijondernemingen in de EEG / see Association des organisations nationales d'entreprises de pêche de l'UE (#02841)
- Vereniging der Nationale Organisaties van Visserijondernemingen in de EU (#02841)
- Vereniging van Nederlandse Gemeenten – Internationaal (internationally oriented national body)
- Vereniging van Organisaties van Vismeelfabrikanten in de Europese Economische Gemeenschap / see European Fismeal and Fish Oil Producers (#07268)
- Vereniging Parkinsonism and Related Disorders / see International Association of Parkinsonism and Related Disorders (#12068)
- Vereniging van Particuliere Graanopslagbedrijven in de EEG / see Unistock Europe (#20492)
- Vereniging van Rivierwaterbedrijven (#02895)
- Vereniging Robert Schuman (#02896)
- Vereniging van Steden voor Recyclage / see Association of Cities and Regions for Sustainable Resource Management (#02433)
- Vereniging van Steden en Regio's voor Recyclage / see Association of Cities and Regions for Sustainable Resource Management (#02433)
- Vereniging voor Taalkunde van het Caraibisch Gebied (#19530)
- Vereniging van Tafelrondes in Suidelike Afrika / see Round Table Southern Africa (#18984)
- Vereniging Tropische Bossen (internationally oriented national body)
- Vereniging voor Uitwisseling van Cultuur en Wetenschap tussen Oost en West (no recent information)
- Vereniging van Vismeel- en Visoliefabrikanten in de Europese Gemeenschap / see European Fismeal and Fish Oil Producers (#07268)
- Vereniging VluchtelingenWerk Nederland / see Dutch Refugee Council
- Vereniging der Vrienden van Robert Schuman / see Association Robert Schuman (#02896)
- VERF / see Exit International (#09224)
- VERGE – Vascular and Endovascular Research Group in Europe (no recent information)
- Verification Research, Training and Information Centre (internationally oriented national body)
- Verified Carbon Standard Association / see Verra (#20756)
- Veritas College International (internationally oriented national body)
- Verkehrsgesellschaft für den Pazifik (#17932)
- Verkstadsindustrins Inter-Nordiske Forskningskommitté (inactive)

♦ Vermiculite Association (TVA) 20755

Contact Whitegate Acre, Metheringham Fen, Lincoln, LN4 3AL, UK. T. +441526323990. Fax +441526323181. E-mail: tva@vermiculite.org.
URL: http://www.vermiculite.org/

History 1948. **Aims** Promote knowledge and use of vermiculite worldwide. **Events** *Annual Meeting* Amsterdam (Netherlands) 2016, *Annual Meeting and Vermiculite Conference* Stockholm (Sweden) 2010, *Annual Meeting and Vermiculite Conference* Big Sky, MT (USA) 2009, *Annual meeting and conference / Annual Meeting and Vermiculite Conference* Amsterdam (Netherlands) 2008, *Annual meeting and conference* St Petersburg (Russia) 2007.
Members Companies in 17 countries:
Australia, Brazil, Canada, China, Denmark, France, Germany, Israel, Japan, Netherlands, Russia, South Africa, Spain, Sweden, UK, USA, Zimbabwe.
NGO Relations Instrumental in setting up: *European Vermiculite Association (EVA, no recent information).*
[2010/XD9256/**D**]

♦ Verra 20756

Communications Manager One Thomas Circle NW, Suite 1050, Washington DC 20005, USA. T. +12024802282. E-mail: info@verra.org.
URL: https://verra.org/

History 2005. Founded by environmental and business leaders. Bylaws amended May 2019. Former names and other names: *Verra – Standards for a Sustainable Future* – former; *Verified Carbon Standard Association* – former. Registration: Section 501(c)(3), USA, District of Columbia. **Aims** Catalyze tangible climate action and sustainable development outcomes; drive large-scale investment towards high-impact activities that tackle pressing environmental and social issues. **Structure** Board of Directors; Advisory Groups; Committees. **Activities** Projects/programmes; standards/guidelines. **NGO Relations** Subscriber to: *ISEAL (#16026).*
[2021.09.09/XM8970/**F**]

- Verra – Standards for a Sustainable Future / see Verra (#20756)
- Le verre dans la construction (inactive)

♦ Versailles Project on Advanced Materials and Standards (VAMAS) . 20757

Sec Materials Division, National Physical Laboratory, Hampton Road, Teddington, TW11 0LW, UK. T. +442089436174. Fax +442086140497.
Chair Head – Materials and Engineering Sciences, Research and International Directorate, National Physical Laboratory, Hampton Road, Teddington, TW11 0LW, UK. T. +442089436564. Fax +442086140433.
URL: http://www.vamas.org/

History 1982, following an economic summit meeting, Versailles (France), of the *'Group of Seven (G-7)'*, now *Group of Eight (G-8, #10745)*, Heads of State and representatives from the European Community (EC). Continuation Agreement signed 1997 and 2007. **Aims** Promote world *trade* by innovation and adoption of advanced materials through international collaborations that provide the technical basis for harmonization of measurement methods, leading to best practices and standards. **Structure** Steering Committee; Technical Working Areas. **Finance** Members' dues. **Activities** Works on pre-standards in rapidly developing technical areas; establishes the basis of new standards technical committees; transfers results to standards bodies leading directly to international standards; contributes to development of reference materials; develops test methods and procedures; increases proficiency of laboratories, including industrial laboratories; establishes agreement of nomenclature; generates high quality data via inter-laboratory comparison exercises; delivers precision data statements; provides reliable material properties.
Members Governments of 15 countries:
Australia, Brazil, Canada, China, France, Germany, India, Italy, Japan, Korea Rep, Mexico, South Africa, Taiwan, UK, USA.
Regional organization (1):
European Commission (EC, #06633).
IGO Relations Memorandum of Understanding with: *Bureau international des poids et mesures (BIPM, #03367).* **NGO Relations** Memoranda of Understanding with: *International Electrotechnical Commission (IEC, #13255); International Organization for Standardization (ISO, #14473); World Materials Research Institutes Forum (WMRIF, #21642).*
[2019.04.24/XM1776/**F***]

- Versammlung der Europäischen Weinbauregionen (#02317)
- Versammlung der Regionen Europas (#02316)
- VERTECH CITY / see Réseau VERTECH CITY (#18908)
- VERTECH CITY Network (#18908)
- VERTIC – Verification Research, Training and Information Centre (internationally oriented national body)
- Vertrag betreffend die regelung der lachsfischerei im stromgebiet des Rheins (1995 treaty)
- Vertrag von Nizza (2001 treaty)
- Vertrag über die Europäische Union (1992 treaty)
- Vertrag über die gründung der Europäischen Gemeinschaft für Kohle und Stahl (1951 treaty)
- Vertrag über eine Verfassung für Europe (2004 treaty)
- Vertrag zur vertiefung der grenzüberschreitenden zusammenarbeit (2005 treaty)
- Verts européens / see European Green Party (#07409)
- Very Large Data Base Endowment / see Very Large Databases Endowment
- Very Large Databases Endowment (internationally oriented national body)
- Very Large Power Grid Operators Association / see GO15 (#10672)
- Very Small Aperture Terminal / see GVF (#10842)
- Very Special Arts International / see VSA
- **VESA** Verband der Europäischen Sozialen Apoteken (#20401)
- Vesmirné Bilé Bratrstvo – Visuotnés Baltosios Brolijos (#20684)
- **Vestnordenfonden** Nordiska Utvecklingsfonden för Västnorden (#20926)
- Vestnordisk Råd (#20925)

♦ Veterana Esperantista Klubo (VEK) 20758

Veteran Esperantists Club – Club des vétérans de l'espéranto

Contact Nieuwe Binnenweg 176, 3015 BJ Rotterdam, Netherlands. T. +31104361044.
URL: http://uea.org/agadoj/

History 1949, Vienna (Austria). **Aims** Link speakers of Esperanto who have been loyal to the movement for over 40 years. **Languages** Esperanto. **Activities** Meetings (irregular) in conjunction with UEA World Congress. **Events** *General Meeting* Buenos Aires (Argentina) 2014, *General Meeting* Reykjavik (Iceland) 2013, *General Meeting* Hanoi (Vietnam) 2012, *General Meeting* Copenhagen (Denmark) 2011, *General Meeting* Havana (Cuba) 2010.
Members Individuals (240) in 46 countries:
Albania, Argentina, Australia, Austria, Belgium, Brazil, Bulgaria, Canada, China, Croatia, Cuba, Czechia, Denmark, Estonia, Finland, France, Germany, Greece, Hungary, Iceland, India, Ireland, Israel, Italy, Japan, Korea Rep, Latvia, Lithuania, Luxembourg, Malta, Netherlands, Norway, Poland, Portugal, Romania, Russia, Serbia, Slovakia, Slovenia, Spain, Sweden, Switzerland, UK, Ukraine, USA, Vietnam.
NGO Relations Member of: *Universal Esperanto Association (UEA, #20676).*
[2014.03.10/XF1858/**F**]

- Veteran Esperantists Club (#20758)

♦ Veterans Confederation of ASEAN Countries (VECONAC) 20759

Pres The War Veterans Organization of Thailand, 420/3 Ratchavithi Road, Rachthewi, Bangkok, 10400, Thailand. T. +6623548620. Fax +6623548620. E-mail: wvoprd@thaiveterans.mail.go.th.
Sec address not obtained.
URL: http://www.veconac.org/

History 19 Dec 1980, Jakarta (Indonesia). **Aims** Promote and improve the quality of life and evaluate fully the influence of ageing and the effects of war on the health and social conditions of war victims; promote better understanding among peoples in order to intensify cooperation in the endeavours to attain prosperity, social justice and peace; promote a better universal understanding of the aspirations, sentiments, appreciation and interests of the countries of the region. **Structure** General Assembly (every 2 years). Executive Board (meets annually). **Finance** Sources: members' dues. **Activities** Knowledge management/information dissemination; projects/programmes. **Events** *General Assembly* Bangkok (Thailand) 2022, *General Assembly* Hanoi (Vietnam) 2021, *General Assembly* Hanoi (Vietnam) 2020, *General Assembly* Phnom Penh (Cambodia) 2019, *General Assembly* Vientiane (Laos) 2018. **Publications** *The Veterans Confederation of ASEAN Countries – Its History and Development* (1992). General Assembly proceedings.
Members Full in 8 countries:
Brunei Darussalam, Indonesia, Malaysia, Myanmar, Philippines, Singapore, Thailand, Vietnam.
Consultative Status Consultative status granted from: *ASEAN (#01141)*. [2022/XD1980/**E**]

♦ Veterans International / see International Veterans Table Tennis Society (#15845)
♦ Veterans for Peace (internationally oriented national body)
♦ Veterans of Safety International (internationally oriented national body)
♦ Vétérinaires sans frontières Europa / see Vétérinaires Sans Frontières International (#20760)

♦ Vétérinaires Sans Frontières International (VSF International) 20760

Secretariat Av des Arts 7-8, 1210 Brussels, Belgium. E-mail: info@vsf-international.org.
URL: http://www.vsf-international.org/
History 1989. Former names and other names: *Vétérinaires sans frontières Europa (VSF Europa)* – former (1989 to Dec 2014); *Veterinarios sin Fronteras Europea* – former; *Dierenartsen zonder Grenzen Europa* – former; *Veterinaris sense Fronteres Europea* – former. Registration: Start date: 2002, Belgium. **Aims** Reduce poverty, contribute to food and nutrition security and improve the livelihoods and well-being of vulnerable populations by supporting smallholder *farmers* and *livestock* keepers, promoting food sovereignty and implementing the One Health approach. **Structure** General Assembly; Board; Headquarters in Brussels (Belgium). **Languages** Czech, Dutch, English, French, German, Italian, Portuguese, Swedish. **Staff** 1.00 FTE, paid. **Finance** Sources: contributions; international organizations; members' dues; private foundations. **Activities** Advocacy/lobbying/activism; awareness raising; capacity building; networking/liaising; training/education. **Events** *Développement – il y a urgence* Lyon (France) 1993.
Members Organizations in 12 countries:
Austria, Belgium, Canada, Czechia, France, Germany, Ireland, Italy, Netherlands, Portugal, Sweden, Switzerland.
Representatives in 37 countries and territories:
Algeria, Bolivia, Burkina Faso, Burundi, Cambodia, Cape Verde, China, Colombia, Congo DR, Dominican Rep, Ecuador, Ethiopia, Ghana, Guatemala, Haiti, Honduras, Kenya, Laos, Madagascar, Malawi, Mali, Mauritania, Mongolia, Morocco, Nicaragua, Niger, Peru, Rwanda, Sahara West, Senegal, Somalia, South Sudan, Sudan, Tanzania UR, Togo, Uganda, Vietnam. [2020.05.06/XF5035/**F**]

♦ Veterinarios sin Fronteras Europea / see Vétérinaires Sans Frontières International (#20760)
♦ Veterinaris sense Fronteres Europea / see Vétérinaires Sans Frontières International (#20760)
♦ Veterinary Comparative Respiratory Society (internationally oriented national body)

♦ Veterinary Education Worldwide (ViEW) 20761

Sec Bristol Veterinary School, Langford House, Langford, Bristol, BS40 5DU, UK.
URL: https://vetedworldwide.com/
History Sep 2004, Edinburgh (UK). Founded during a workshop organized by *Association for Medical Education in Europe (AMEE, #02797)*. **Aims** Promote and support excellence in veterinary education at an international level. **Structure** An informal organization without secretariat. Officers: President; Secretary. **Languages** English. **Staff** 3.00 FTE, voluntary. **Finance** Members' dues. **Events** *Annual meeting* Prague (Czech Rep) 2008, *Annual meeting* Trondheim (Norway) 2007, *Annual meeting* Genoa (Italy) 2006, *Annual meeting* Amsterdam (Netherlands) 2005, *Annual meeting* Edinburgh (UK) 2004.
Members Individuals (70) in 19 countries:
Belgium, Canada, Denmark, France, Germany, Greece, India, Ireland, Nepal, Netherlands, Nigeria, Pakistan, Sweden, Switzerland, Türkiye, UK, Ukraine, Uruguay, USA. [2020/XM0097/**D**]

♦ Veterinary European Transnational Network for Nursing Education and Training (VETNNET) 20762

Coordinator address not obtained. E-mail: jmesquita@esav.ipv.pt.
Sec address not obtained.
URL: http://www.vetnnet.com/
Aims Bring together colleges, veterinary associations, veterinary nurse associations, accreditation bodies and other organizations with an active interest in veterinary nurse training. **Structure** Board. **Events** *Conference* Bruges (Belgium) 2019, *Conference* Porto (Portugal) 2015, *Conference* Lipica (Slovenia) 2014. **Publications** *VETNNET Newsletter*.
Members Full in 17 countries:
Belgium, Croatia, Czechia, Denmark, Finland, France, Ireland, Italy, Lithuania, Netherlands, Norway, Portugal, Slovenia, Spain, Sweden, UK, USA.
NGO Relations Member of: *Federation of European Companion Animal Veterinary Associations (FECAVA, #09497)*. [2015/XJ8340/**F**]

♦ The Vetiver Network / see The Vetiver Network International (#20763)

♦ The Vetiver Network International (TVNI) 20763

Pres 149 E Rosewood, San Antonio TX 78212, USA. T. +12107327138. E-mail: information@vetiver.org.
URL: http://www.vetiver.org/
History 1989. Became an international NGO, 1994. Former names and other names: *The Vetiver Network (TVN)* – former (1989 to 1994). **Aims** Promote the Vetiver System, a concept integrating simple scientific principals of hydrology, soil mechanics and similar natural processes to manage *soil* and *water* on a *landscape* scale. **Structure** National and regional networks include: *Latin American Vetiver Network (LAVN, no recent information)*; *Pacific Rim Vetiver Network (PRVN, #18002)*. **Languages** English, French, Mandarin Chinese, Portuguese, Spanish, Swahili, Vietnamese. **Staff** Voluntary. **Finance** Sources: donations. Annual budget: 20,000 USD. **Activities** Certification/accreditation; events/meetings. **Events** *International Conference on Vetiver (ICV-7)* Chiang Mai (Thailand) 2021, *International Conference on Vetiver (ICV-7)* Chiang Mai (Thailand) 2020, *International conference on vetiver* Cebu City (Philippines) 2018, *International conference on vetiver* Danang (Vietnam) 2015, *International conference on vetiver* Lucknow (India) 2011. **Publications** *Vetiver Systems Applications – Technical Reference Manual* (2008); *Vetiver Grass – The Hedge against Erosion* (5th ed 2000).
Members Individuals in 61 countries and territories:
Australia, Bangladesh, Belize, Bolivia, Botswana, Burkina Faso, Burundi, Cameroon, China, Colombia, Congo Brazzaville, Congo DR, Costa Rica, Ecuador, El Salvador, Eswatini, Ethiopia, Fiji, Guatemala, Haiti, Honduras, India, Indonesia, Israel, Italy, Jamaica, Kenya, Madagascar, Malawi, Malaysia, Mali, Mexico, Mozambique, Namibia, New Zealand, Nicaragua, Nigeria, Pakistan, Panama, Papua New Guinea, Paraguay, Peru, Philippines, Portugal, Puerto Rico, Rwanda, Senegal, South Africa, Spain, Sri Lanka, St Lucia, Taiwan, Tanzania UR, Thailand, Uganda, Uruguay, USA, Venezuela, Vietnam, Zambia, Zimbabwe.
NGO Relations Links with many NGOs and commercial organizations working with communities in developing and developed countries. [2022/XG7109/**F**]

♦ **VETNNET** Veterinary European Transnational Network for Nursing Education and Training (#20762)
♦ VETOMAC – International Conference on Vibration Engineering and Technology of Machinery (meeting series)
♦ **VEUKO** Vereinigung Europäischer Verbände des Kachelofenbauer/Hafner-Handwerks (#20754)
♦ **VE** Vaccines Europe (#20741)
♦ **VFDM** Vsemirnaja Federacija Demokraticeskoj Molodezi (#21427)
♦ VFP – Veterans for Peace (internationally oriented national body)
♦ VFP – Volunteers for Peace (internationally oriented national body)
♦ **VFP** Vsemirnaja Federacija Profsojuzov (#21493)
♦ **VFSE** Vinyl Films and Sheets Europe (#20779)

♦ VGB PowerTech (VGB) 20764

Contact Postfach 10 39 32, 45039 Essen, Germany. T. +492018128213. Fax +492018128350.
Street address Deilbachtal 173, 45257 Essen, Germany.
URL: http://www.vgb.org/
History Founded 1920. Registered in accordance with German law, at the District Court of Registry, Essen (Germany). **Aims** Support business activities of member companies for generation, storage and *power plant* internal utilization of electricity and heat, and of the by-products resulting therefrom. **Structure** General Assembly; Board of Directors; Technical Advisory Board; Scientific Advisory Board; Executive Board. **Languages** English, German. **Staff** 50.00 FTE, paid. **Finance** Members' dues. **Activities** Advocacy/lobbying/activism; events/meetings; standards/guidelines; networking/liaising; research and development; knowledge management/information dissemination; guidance/assistance/consulting. **Events** *Conference on Maintenance of Wind Power Plants* Bremen (Germany) 2019, *Conference on Thermal Waste Utilization and Fluidized Bed Firing Systems* Hamburg (Germany) 2019, *Conference on Gas Turbines and Operation of Gas Turbines* Mainz (Germany) 2019, *Innovation in Power Generation* Salzburg (Austria) 2019, *Conference on Chemistry in Power Plants* Würzburg (Germany) 2019. **Publications** *PowerTech Journal* (11 a year). Annual Report; VGB Standards. **Members** Ordinary; Sponsoring; Extraordinary. Companies (450) in 35 countries. Membership countries not specified. **NGO Relations** Cooperates with: *Comité européen de normalisation (CEN, #04162)*. [2018.10.01/XJ1175/**D**]

♦ **VGB** VGB PowerTech (#20764)
♦ VGG – Vereniging voor Gebarentaal en Gebarentaalkunde (internationally oriented national body)
♦ VGIFUW / see Women First International Fund (#20996)
♦ VGKSA – Verenigende Geref Kerk in Suider-Afrika (internationally oriented national body)
♦ **VGT** Virtual Global Taskforce (#20788)
♦ VHEMT – Voluntary Human Extinction Movement (unconfirmed)
♦ VHI – Vision Health International (internationally oriented national body)
♦ **VHL-Europa** European VHL (von Hippel-Lindau) Federation (#09060)
♦ **VHPB** Viral Hepatitis Prevention Board (#20782)
♦ VHP – Vishva Hindu Parishad (internationally oriented national body)

♦ La Via Campesina 20765

International Secretariat Number 5 Gloucester Drive, Eastlea, Harare, HARARE, Zimbabwe. T. +263242746552. E-mail: viacampesina@viacampesina.org.
URL: http://www.viacampesina.org/
History 1993, Mons (Belgium). Former names and other names: *La Via Campesina – International Peasant's Movement* – full title. **Aims** As an international movement of peasants, small and medium-size farmers, landless people, women farmers, indigenous people, migrants and agricultural workers from around the world, defend small-scale sustainable agriculture as a way to promote social justice and dignity. **Events** *Meeting* Seoul (Korea Rep) 2018, *International Conference* Derio (Spain) 2017, *International Conference* Jakarta (Indonesia) 2013, *International Conference* Maputo (Mozambique) 2008, *International conference* Sao Paulo (Brazil) 2004.
Members Organizations (182) in 66 countries:
Angola, Argentina, Austria, Belgium, Bolivia, Brazil, Burkina Faso, Cambodia, Canada, Chile, Colombia, Congo Brazzaville, Congo DR, Cuba, Denmark, Dominica, Dominican Rep, Ecuador, Finland, France, Georgia, Germany, Greece, Grenada, Haiti, India, Indonesia, Italy, Japan, Korea Rep, Madagascar, Malaysia, Mali, Malta, Mexico, Morocco, Mozambique, Nepal, Netherlands, Niger, Norway, Pakistan, Paraguay, Peru, Philippines, Portugal, Romania, Senegal, South Africa, Spain, St Lucia, St Vincent-Grenadines, Sweden, Switzerland, Tanzania UR, Thailand, Timor-Leste, Togo, Tunisia, Türkiye, Uganda, UK, Uruguay, USA, Venezuela, Vietnam.
Included in the above, 2 organizations listed in this Yearbook:
Mouvement international de la jeunesse agricole et rurale catholique (MIJARC, #16865); *Windward Islands Farmers' Association (WINFA, #20966)*.
NGO Relations Member of: *Climate Justice Now ! (CJN!, inactive)*; *Global Coalition on Migration (GCM, #10293)*; *World Social Forum (WSF, #21797)*. Member of the Coordinating Committee of: *More and Better (#16855)*. *European Coordination Via Campesina (ECVC, #06795)* is a member. Endorses: *Ban Terminator Campaign (#03172)*. Cooperates with: *Transnational Institute (TNI, #20219)*. [2020/XF3985/**F**]

♦ La Via Campesina – International Peasant's Movement / see La Via Campesina (#20765)
♦ VIAC – Vienna International Arbitral Centre (internationally oriented national body)
♦ VIAC – Vietnam International Arbitration Centre (internationally oriented national body)

♦ VIA Don Bosco 20766

Dir Av du Val d'Or 90, 1150 Brussels, Belgium. T. +3224274720. Fax +3224259031. E-mail: info@viadonbosco.org.
URL: http://www.viadonbosco.org
History 1 Jan 1969, Brussels (Belgium). Current statutes adopted 1995. Effective members are delegates of the general councils of *Society of St Francis of Sales (Salesians of Don Bosco)* or *Daughters of Mary Help of Christians (Salesian Sisters)* or are responsible for Salesian provinces in Europe. Former names and other names: *Centre de coordination des oeuvres sociales au Tiers monde* – former; *Service for Mission and Development* – former; *Service de coopération missionnaire au développement (Don Bosco-Comide International)* – former; *Dienst Missie en Ontwikkelingssamenwerking (DMOS)* – former; *COMIDE* – former. Registration: Banque-Carrefour des Entreprises, No/ID: 0413.119.733, Start date: 17 Aug 2006, Belgium. **Aims** Integrate vulnerable young people through vocational education and employment in Africa and Latin-America; develop global citizenship competencies within youth in Belgium. **Structure** General Assembly (annual); Administrative Council; Management Council; Departments (3). **Languages** Dutch, French. **Finance** Sources: donations; gifts, legacies; private foundations. Supported by: *European Union (EU, #08967)*; *Flemish International Cooperation Agency (FICA)*; *World Bank Institute (WBI, #21220)*. **Activities** Active in: Belgium, Benin, Bolivia, Cameroon, Congo DR, Ecuador, El Salvador, Haiti, Madagascar, Mali, Peru, Tanzania UR. **IGO Relations** Accredited by (1): *Organisation internationale de la Francophonie (OIF, #17809)*. **NGO Relations** Member of (9): *Belgian Platform for Education and Development (Educaid.be)*; *CNCD Opération 11 11 11*; *Coalition of the Flemish North South Movement – 11 11 11*; *Corporate Funding Programme (CFP)*; *Don Bosco International (DBI, #05117)*; *Don Bosco Network (DBN, #05118)*; *Fédération francophone et germanophone des associations de coopération au développement (ACODEV, #09587)*; *Vlaamse Federatie van NGO's voor Ontwikkelingssamenwerking (ngo-federatie)*; *Wereldmediahuis*. Collaboration agreement with: *Dienst voor Internationale Samenwerking aan Ontwikkelingsprojecten (DISOP)*; *Broederlijk Delen*; *Studio Globo*; *TRIAS*; *Rikolto*. Links with national organizations. [2020.05.06/XE1957/**E**]

♦ VIAKL / see Internationales Altkatholische Forum (#13299)
♦ Viatorians – Clerics of St Viator (religious order)
♦ VIA – Vision africa (internationally oriented national body)
♦ Vibrio – International Conference on the Biology of Vibrios (meeting series)
♦ VIC / see KIYO
♦ VICB / see Dutch Centre for International Cooperation
♦ VIC Children's Rights NGO / see KIYO
♦ Vicentian Congregation (religious order)
♦ Vicentinos – Congregazione della Missione (religious order)
♦ **VICH** International Cooperation on Harmonization of Technical Requirements for the Registration of Veterinary Medicinal Products (#12941)
♦ VICS – Volunteer International Christian Service (internationally oriented national body)
♦ Pro Victimis Foundation (internationally oriented national body)

♦ Victim Support Europe (VSE) 20767

Exec Dir Rue Froissart 123-133, 1040 Brussels, Belgium. T. +32023460455. Fax +32023460455. E-mail: info@victimsupporteurope.eu.
URL: https://victim-support.eu/

History 1989. Former names and other names: *European Forum for Victim Services* – former; *Forum européen de secours aux victimes* – former. Registration: Swiss Civil Code, Start date: 1990, End date: 2010, Switzerland; Banque-Carrefour des Entreprises, No/ID: 0828.549.254, Start date: 18 Aug 2010, Belgium; EU Transparency Register, No/ID: 83945428894-94, Start date: 5 Jun 2012. **Aims** Promote development of effective services for victims of *crime* throughout Europe; promote fair and equal compensation for victims of crime in Europe, regardless of the nationality of the victim; promote *rights* of victims of crime in Europe in their involvement in the criminal justice system and with other agencies; exchange experience and information between member organizations to share best practices and knowledge. **Structure** General Meeting (annual); Executive Board; Secretariat in Brussels (Belgium). **Languages** English. **Staff** 17.00 FTE, paid; 3.00 FTE, voluntary. **Finance** Sources: donations; fees for services; grants; members' dues. Supported by: *European Union (EU, #08967)*. **Activities** Advocacy/lobbying/activism; guidance/assistance/consulting. **Events** *Annual Conference* Berlin (Germany) 2023, *Annual Conference* San Gwann (Malta) 2022, *Annual Conference* Brussels (Belgium) 2021, *Annual Conference* Berlin (Germany) 2020, *Annual Conference* Brussels (Belgium) 2020. **Publications** *VSE Newsletter*. *Handbook for Implementation of Legislation and Best Practice for Victims of Crime in Europe* (2013); *For a Good Implementation of the 116006 Helpline – handbook* (2012); *Victims of Crime in the EU – training manual* (2012); *Manifesto for Europe* (2008); *Statement of Victims' Rights to Standards of Service* (1999); *Statement of the Social Rights of Victims of Crime* (1998); *Statement of Victims' Rights in the Process of Criminal Justice* (1996). *Manifesto 2014-2019*.
Members National and regional organizations (70) in 30 countries:
Austria, Belgium, Bulgaria, Croatia, Cyprus, Czechia, Denmark, Estonia, Finland, France, Germany, Hungary, Ireland, Italy, Latvia, Lithuania, Malta, Netherlands, New Zealand, Poland, Portugal, Romania, Russia, Serbia, Slovakia, Spain, Sweden, Switzerland, UK, USA.
International Cruise Victims (ICV).
Consultative Status Consultative status granted from: *ECOSOC (#05331)* (Special); *Council of Europe (CE, #04881)* (Participatory Status). **NGO Relations** Member of (1): *Federation of European and International Associations Established in Belgium (FAIB, #09508)*. [2022.09.02/XJ1377/**D**]

♦ Victoria International Development Education Association (internationally oriented national body)
♦ Victoria League for Commonwealth Friendship (internationally oriented national body)

♦ Victory Outreach International 20768

Head Office PO Box 210068, Chula Vista CA 91921, USA. T. +16192167400. E-mail: info@victoryoutreach.org.
URL: http://www.victoryoutreach.org/

History 1967, USA, as a Pentecostal denomination. **Aims** As an international church-oriented network of inner city *ministries* and *Pentecostal* denominations worldwide: evangelize the hurting people of the world with the message of hope and plan of Jesus Christ; meet the needs of people from all walks of life; introduce the lost to Christ; restore broken *families*; effectively train and nurture believers to reach their full potential; plant and develop churches, *rehabilitation* homes and training centres in strategic cities worldwide; inspire and instil within people the desire to fulfill their potential in life with a sense of dignity, belonging and destiny. **Structure** A worldwide network of churches and ministries. **Finance** Main source: members fund their own local Victory Outreach Church. **Activities** *'Victory Outreach International Intercessory Prayer Network'* – worldwide prayer partners respond to requests for intercessory prayer. *'God's Anointed Now Generation'* – youth television and radio programmes. *'Victory Education Training Institute'* – main campus in California (USA) services 500 students and 42 extensions worldwide, totalling 6000 students annually. *'Evangelism'* – Gospel preached to over 300,000 people annually in live audiences, with evangelistic crusades held in over 28 countries and territories in cooperation with local Victory Outreach Churches and other local church fellowships. *'United We Can'* – missions provide clothing, food and shelter and establishes churches and homes to serve adults and children in desperate need, while giving them the hope of Jesus Christ. *'Training and Conferences'*: Annual Victory Outreach International World Conference; Men's and Women's Leadership Training Conference; Annual Leadership Conference; general education programme – designed to invite self-growth, personal and educational development and nurture a positive environment for learning; Bible Institute – prepares Christian believers for life and ministry; Urban Training Centers (UTC) – based in Los Angeles CA (USA) Bridgeport CT (USA) and Tijuana (Mexico), train young people with practical, hands-on experience in church planting, missions outreach and church leadership. **Events** *European Conference* Amsterdam (Netherlands) 2012, *European conference* Amsterdam (Netherlands) 2009.
Members Churches (245) and ministries reaching over 100,000 worshippers, mainly in the USA (162 churches) but in a total of 26 countries and territories:
Aruba, Australia, Brazil, Canada, Chile, Colombia, Cuba, El Salvador, India, Indonesia, Ireland, Israel, Italy, Liberia, Mexico, Netherlands, New Zealand, Nigeria, Philippines, Puerto Rico, Spain, Suriname, UK, USA, Venezuela. [2010/XM4000/**F**]

♦ VIC – Vienna International Centre (internationally oriented national body)
♦ **VIC** Vineyard International Consortium (#20778)
♦ VID / see Peaceworkers USA
♦ Vida Ascendente Internacional (#20769)
♦ Vida Humana Internacional (#10977)
♦ Vidal Sassoon Centro Internacional de Estudio del Antisemitismo (internationally oriented national body)
♦ Vidal Sassoon International Center for the Study of Antisemitism (internationally oriented national body)
♦ VIDA – Voluntariado Internacional para o Desenvolvimento Africano (internationally oriented national body)
♦ VIDA – Volunteers for Inter-American Development Assistance (internationally oriented national body)
♦ VIDC / see Vienna Institute for International Dialogue and Cooperation
♦ VIDC – Vienna Institute for International Dialogue and Cooperation (internationally oriented national body)
♦ VIDEA – Victoria International Development Education Association (internationally oriented national body)
♦ VIDES International / see Volontariato Internazionale Donna Educazione Sviluppo (#20806)
♦ **VIDES** Volontariato Internazionale Donna Educazione Sviluppo (#20806)
♦ Vieh- und Fleischhandelsunion (#20394)
♦ Vie humaine internationale (#10977)

♦ Vie montante internationale (VMI) 20769

Vida Ascendente Internacional (VAI) – Life Ascending International (LAI)
Sec Rue Sarrette 15, 75014 Paris, France. E-mail: vminternationale@gmail.com.
URL: https://vmi-vai-lai.org/

History 1985, Rome (Italy). Also referred to as *Life Ascending International (LAI)*. 25 Mar 1996, recognized by *Pontifical Council for the Laity (inactive)*. Former names and other names: *International Ascent* – former. **Aims** Bring together on a world level those national lay organizations which exercise their apostolate among retired and elderly people, who in their turn hear the Word and pass it on to others. **Structure** General Assembly (every 4 years). International Committee, consisting of President, Secretary, Continental Representatives and an Ecclesiastical Assistant. **Finance** Members' dues. **Events** *Regional Conference on Bridging the Gaps in Mental Health and Psychological Support in Emergencies in Asia* Bangkok (Thailand) 2015, *Meeting* Rome (Italy) 2000, *Meeting* Prague (Czech Rep) 1998, *European congress* Leuven (Belgium) 1996, *Meeting* Rome (Italy) 1996. **Publications** Newsletter (2 a year).
Members Active national organizations; Associate individuals and organizations. Members in 67 countries and territories:
Algeria, Angola, Argentina, Australia, Austria, Belarus, Belgium, Benin, Botswana, Brazil, Burundi, Cameroon, Canada, Central African Rep, Chile, Colombia, Congo Brazzaville, Congo DR, Costa Rica, Côte d'Ivoire, Czechia, Dominican Rep, Ecuador, El Salvador, Finland, Germany, Ghana, Greece, Guatemala, Holy See, Honduras, Iceland, Ireland, Italy, Japan, Korea Rep, Lebanon, Malta, Mexico, Monaco, Morocco, Netherlands, New Zealand, Nicaragua, Norway, Panama, Paraguay, Peru, Poland, Portugal, Puerto Rico, Romania, Rwanda, Senegal, Serbia, Spain, Switzerland, Taiwan, Tanzania UR, Thailand, Togo, Tunisia, Türkiye, UK, Uruguay, USA, Venezuela.
Consultative Status Consultative status granted from: *ECOSOC (#05331)* (Special). **NGO Relations** Member of: *Crescendo Worldwide Network (#04950)*; *Forum of Catholic Inspired NGOs (#09905)*. [2021/XF0452/**F**]

♦ Viên Liên Hiệp Nghiên Cú'u Nguyên Tú / see Joint Institute for Nuclear Research (#16134)
♦ Vienna Agreement Establishing an International Classification of the Figurative Elements of Marks (1973 treaty)
♦ Vienna Agreement for the Protection of Type Faces and Their International Deposit (1973 treaty)
♦ Vienna Agreement – Vienna Agreement Establishing an International Classification of the Figurative Elements of Marks (1973 treaty)
♦ Vienna Agreement – Vienna Agreement for the Protection of Type Faces and Their International Deposit (1973 treaty)
♦ Vienna Center for Disarmament and Non-Proliferation (internationally oriented national body)
♦ Vienna Centre – European Coordination Centre for Research and Documentation in Social Sciences (inactive)
♦ Vienna Club / see Club of Vienna (#04039)
♦ Vienna Convention on Civil Liability for Nuclear Damage (1963 treaty)
♦ Vienna Convention on Consular Relations (1963 treaty)
♦ Vienna Convention on Diplomatic Relations (1961 treaty)
♦ Vienna Convention on the Law of Treaties (1969 treaty)
♦ Vienna Convention on the Law of Treaties between States and International Organizations or between International Organizations (1986 treaty)
♦ Vienna Convention for the Protection of the Ozone Layer (1985 treaty)
♦ Vienna Convention on the Representation of States in Their Relations with International Organizations of a Universal Character (1975 treaty)
♦ Vienna Convention on Succession of States in Respect of State Property, Archives and Debts (1983 treaty)
♦ Vienna Convention on Succession of States in Respect of Treaties (1978 treaty)

♦ Vienna Economic Forum (VEF) 20770

Main Office Prinz Eugen Strasse 58/4-5, 1040 Vienna, Austria. T. +4317141014. Fax +4317141019. E-mail: office@vienna-economic-forum.com.
URL: http://www.vienna-economic-forum.com/

History Apr 2004. Registration: No/ID: 467074752, Austria; EU Transparency Register, No/ID: 927885415117-52. **Aims** Promote economic cooperation between the countries from the Adriatic to the Black Sea. **Structure** Board. Committees (5): Ambassadors; Patrons; Minister of Economy; Governors; Culture. **Events** *Vienna Economic Forum* Vienna (Austria) 2021, *Vienna Economic Forum* Vienna (Austria) 2018, *Vienna Economic Forum* Vienna (Austria) 2017, *Vienna Economic Forum* Vienna (Austria) 2016, *Vienna Economic Forum* Vienna (Austria) 2014.
Members Full in 14 countries:
Albania, Austria, Bosnia-Herzegovina, Bulgaria, Croatia, Kosovo, Lithuania, Moldova, Montenegro, North Macedonia, Romania, Slovenia, Türkiye, Ukraine.
Consultative Status Consultative status granted from: *ECOSOC (#05331)* (Special). **IGO Relations** Cooperates with: *Southeast European Cooperative Initiative (SECI, #19812)*. **NGO Relations** Memorandum of understanding with: *Union of Black Sea and Caspian Business (BCB, #20369)*. [2020.05.04/XJ0657/**F**]

♦ Vienna Energy Club (VEC) 20771

Information Officer c/o Energy Community, Am Hof 4, Level 5-6, 1010 Vienna, Austria.
URL: http://www.vienna-energy-club.at/

History At the initiative of Slavtcho Neykov, then Director of *Energy Community (#05468)*, representatives of 8 Vienna-based international organizations dealing with energy topics met, Sep 2009. **Aims** Provide an informal platform for discussions and exchange of views regarding key energy issues. **Events** *Meeting* Vienna (Austria) 2019, *Meeting* Vienna (Austria) 2018, *Meeting* Vienna (Austria) 2018, *Meeting* Vienna (Austria) 2016, *Meeting* Vienna (Austria) 2015.
Members Vienna-based international organizations (10):
Energy Community (#05468); *International Atomic Energy Agency (IAEA, #12294)*; *International Institute for Applied Systems Analysis (IIASA, #13861)*; *International Peace Institute (IPI, #14536)*; *OPEC Fund for International Development (OFID, #17745)*; *Organization for Security and Cooperation in Europe (OSCE, #17887)*; *Organization of the Petroleum Exporting Countries (OPEC, #17881)*; *Renewable Energy and Energy Efficiency Partnership (REEEP, #18837)*; *Sustainable Energy for All (SEforALL, #20056)*; *UNIDO (#20336)*. [2019/XM4474/y/**E**]

♦ Vienna Institute for Comparative Economic Studies, The / see Wiener Institut für Internationale Wirtschaftsvergleiche
♦ Vienna Institute for Development and Cooperation / see Vienna Institute for International Dialogue and Cooperation
♦ Vienna Institute for International Dialogue and Cooperation (internationally oriented national body)
♦ Vienna Institute for International Economic Studies (internationally oriented national body)
♦ Vienna International Arbitral Centre (internationally oriented national body)
♦ Vienna International Arbitral Centre of the Austrian Federal Economic Chamber / see Vienna International Arbitral Centre
♦ Vienna International Centre (internationally oriented national body)
♦ Vienna International Plant Conference Association / see Vienna International Science Conferences and Events Association (#20772)

♦ Vienna International Science Conferences and Events Association (VISCEA) 20772

Sec/Treas Dietrichgasse 33/3, 1030 Vienna, Austria. T. +4319677202. E-mail: l_ryazan@hotmail.com.
Pres address not obtained.
URL: http://www.viscea.org/

History 2006. Originally referred to as *Vienna International Plant Conference Association (VIPCA)*. **Aims** Initiate and assist in organizing professional and high quality scientific conferences and events in Vienna. **Structure** Advisory Board. **Activities** Meeting activities. **Events** *Conference on Plant Abiotic Stress Tolerance* Vienna (Austria) 2020, *Conference on Plant Biotic Stresses and Resistance Mechanisms* Vienna (Austria) 2020, *Conference on Plant Nutrition, Growth and Environment Interactions* Vienna (Austria) 2020, *International Conference on Plant Hormones and Other Growth Regulators* Vienna (Austria) 2020, *International Conference on Plant Genome Editing and Genome Engineering* Vienna (Austria) 2019. [2014/XJ7968/**E**]

♦ Vienna NGO Committee on Drugs (VNGOC) 20773

Comité de Vienne des ONG sur les stupéfiants
Chairperson PO Box 14, Wagramerstr 5, 1040 Vienna, Austria. E-mail: info@vngoc.org.
Main Website: http://www.vngoc.org/

History 31 May 1983, Vienna (Austria). Founded originally in the framework of *Conference of Non-Governmental Organizations in Consultative Relationship with the United Nations (CONGO, #04635)* and in cooperation with *United Nations Office at Vienna (UNOV, #20604)*. Former names and other names: *NGO Committee on Narcotic Drugs and Psychotropic Substances* – former; *CONGO Committee on Narcotic, Drugs and Psychotropic Substances* – former; *Vienna NGO Committee on Narcotic Drugs* – former. Registration: Austrian Registry of Association (Vereinsregister, Landespolizeidirektion Wien), No/ID: 995552988, Start date: 9 Dec 2011, Austria, Vienna. **Aims** Support and facilitate non-governmental organizations (NGOs) to work with the UN system on international drug policy, strategy and practice; improve policy, strategy and practice in the UN drug control system. **Structure** General Assembly (every 2 years); Executive Board. Not an international organization but a grouping of NGOs worldwide. **Languages** English, French, German, Spanish. **Staff** 0.50 FTE, paid. **Finance** Sources: meeting proceeds; members' dues; sponsorship. Annual budget: 12,000 EUR (2019). **Activities** Advocacy/lobbying/activism; awareness raising; capacity building; events/meetings. **Events** *Annual General Assembly – Part 1* Vienna (Austria) 2021, *Annual General Assembly – Part 2* Vienna (Austria) 2021, *NGO global forum Vienna* Vienna (Austria) 2008, *Meeting* Vienna (Austria) 2004, *Meeting* Vienna (Austria) 1996. **Publications** Annual Report; Annual Guide to the Commission on Narcotic Drugs; Strategic Plan; declarations; reports.
Members in 76 countries and territories:

Afghanistan, Albania, Argentina, Australia, Austria, Azerbaijan, Bangladesh, Belgium, Bolivia, Bosnia-Herzegovina, Brazil, Bulgaria, Canada, Chile, Colombia, Congo Brazzaville, Congo DR, Costa Rica, Croatia, Cyprus, El Salvador, Finland, France, Georgia, Germany, Greece, Hungary, India, Indonesia, Iran Islamic Rep, Ireland, Italy, Jordan, Kenya, Kosovo, Kyrgyzstan, Lebanon, Lithuania, Macau, Malawi, Malaysia, Mauritius, Mexico, Montenegro, Morocco, Nepal, Netherlands, New Zealand, Niger, Nigeria, Norway, Pakistan, Palestine, Peru, Philippines, Poland, Portugal, Russia, Serbia, Singapore, Slovakia, Slovenia, South Africa, Spain, Sri Lanka, Sudan, Sweden, Switzerland, Thailand, Tunisia, Türkiye, Uganda, UK, Ukraine, USA, Zimbabwe.

International organizations include the following 34 listed in this Yearbook:
- *African Action on AIDS (AAA);*
- *Association DIOGENIS – Initiative for Drug Policy Dialogue in South East Europe (Association DIOGENIS);*
- *DIANOVA International (#05068);*
- *Europe Against Drugs (EURAD, #05774);*
- *European Cities Against Drugs (ECAD, #06553);*
- *European Federation of Therapeutic Communities (EFTC, #07225);*
- *European Union of Women (EUW, #09022);*
- *Foundation for a Drug-Free Europe (FDFE, #09946);*
- *Graduate Women International (GWI, #10688);*
- *ICOS (#11086);*
- *International Agency for Crime Prevention, Criminal Law and Jurisdiction;*
- *International AIDS Society (IAS, #11601);*
- *International Association of Applied Psychology (IAAP, #11705);*
- *International Council of Women (ICW, #13093);*
- *International Council on Alcohol and Addictions (ICAA, #12989);*
- *International Federation of Business and Professional Women (BPW International, #13376);*
- *International Federation of Social Workers (IFSW, #13544);*
- *International Inner Wheel (IIW, #13855);*
- *International Narcotic and Antiterrorist Enforcement Officers Association (NATEA);*
- *International Police Association (IPA, #14612);*
- *International Society of Addiction Medicine (ISAM, #14896);*
- *Lions Clubs International (LCI, #16485);*
- *Mentor International (MI, #16716);*
- *Movendi International (#16871);*
- *Organization of the Families of Asia and the Pacific (OFAP, #17867);*
- *Pax Romana, International Catholic Movement for Intellectual and Cultural Affairs (ICMICA, #18267);*
- *Pax Romana, International Movement of Catholic Students (IMCS, #18268);*
- *Rotary International (RI, #18975);*
- *Salvation Army (#19041);*
- *Soroptimist International (SI, #19686);*
- *Transnational Institute (TNI, #20219);*
- *Women's Federation for World Peace International (WFWPI);*
- *World Association of Girl Guides and Girl Scouts (WAGGGS, #21142);*
- *Zonta International (#22038).*

Consultative Status Consultative status granted from: *ECOSOC (#05331)* (Special). **IGO Relations** Cooperates with (1): *United Nations Office on Drugs and Crime (UNODC, #20596).* **NGO Relations** Links with many leading NGOs in the field of drugs abuse and many NGOs accredited to the United Nations Economic and Social Council (ECOSOC). [2021/XE4053/y/E]

♦ Vienna NGO Committee on the Family 20774

Comité de Vienne des ONG sur les questions de la famille

Contact c/o Kolping Austria, Paulanergasse 11, 1040 Vienna, Austria. E-mail: contact@viennafamilycommittee.org.

URL: http://www.viennafamilycommittee.org/

History Founded with the support of the then *United Nations Centre for Social Development and Humanitarian Affairs (UNCSDHA, inactive)*, and following informal meetings of organizations to discuss the family, convened by *United Nations Office at Vienna (UNOV, #20604)*, and held in 1984 and 1985. Former names and other names: *NGO Committee on the Family* – former; *Comité des ONG sur les questions de la famille* – former; *NGO Committee on the Family – Vienna* – former; *Committee of Non-governmental Organizations on the Family* – former. **Aims** As a platform for exchange of information on family issues, offer coordination, facilitation and promotion of the activities of Non-Governmental Organisations (NGOs) represented at the United Nations, who are interested in questions relating to families; convene meetings, and facilitate liaison with United Nations agencies, governments, other Civil Society Organisations (CSOs), research institutions etc.; form a bridge between families-oriented Civil Society Organisations, the United Nations, Member States of the United Nations, and their governments, and Academic Institutions. **Structure** Committee (full Committee meeting twice a year) operates from Vienna (Austria), at United Nations' *Vienna International Centre (VIC).* Board; Executive Secretariat; Office of Chairperson; Working Groups (involved with a specific task). **Languages** English. **Staff** Voluntary by Board Members. **Finance** Sources: fundraising; in-kind support; members' dues. **Activities** Events/meetings; guidance/assistance/consulting; knowledge management/information dissemination; networking/liaising; publishing activities. **Events** *Status of Food and Nutrition in Europe and Central Asia* Vienna (Austria) 2021, *Child & Youth Media Protection from the Perspective of Parents* Vienna (Austria) 2019, *Feed the Child and Save the World* Vienna (Austria) 2019, *Internet Use and Domestic Communication Cultures – Families Online* Vienna (Austria) 2017, *30 Years Vienna NGO Committee on the Family – Outlook to the Future* Vienna (Austria) 2015. **Publications** *Families International* (4 a year) – online bulletin. Annual Report. **Information Services** *Interactive Internet Forum* – Online network resources; *Online archive of the 10th anniversary*; *Online archive of the 20th anniversary.*

Members International NGOs and national organizations with humanitarian objectives (65) in 91 countries and territories:

Albania, Algeria, Argentina, Australia, Austria, Bangladesh, Belarus, Belgium, Bolivia, Bosnia-Herzegovina, Brazil, Bulgaria, Cameroon, Canada, Chile, China, Colombia, Congo Brazzaville, Costa Rica, Croatia, Czechia, Denmark, Ecuador, Egypt, Estonia, Ethiopia, Finland, France, Germany, Ghana, Greece, Guatemala, Holy See, Hong Kong, Hungary, Iceland, India, Indonesia, Ireland, Israel, Italy, Japan, Jordan, Kenya, Kuwait, Latvia, Liechtenstein, Lithuania, Luxembourg, Madagascar, Malawi, Malaysia, Mali, Malta, Mauritius, Morocco, Nepal, Netherlands, New Zealand, Nigeria, North Macedonia, Norway, Pakistan, Philippines, Poland, Portugal, Romania, Russia, Serbia, Singapore, Slovakia, Slovenia, South Africa, Spain, Sri Lanka, St Lucia, Sudan, Sweden, Switzerland, Tanzania UR, Thailand, Trinidad-Tobago, Tunisia, Türkiye, Uganda, UK, Ukraine, USA, Venezuela, Zambia, Zimbabwe.

Included in the above, 35 organizations listed in this Yearbook:
- *Associated Country Women of the World (ACWW, #02338);*
- *Association Internationale des Charités (AIC, #02675);*
- *Brahma Kumaris World Spiritual University (BKWSU, #03311);*
- *Caritas Internationalis (CI, #03580);*
- *Consumers International (CI, #04773);*
- *European Union of Women (EUW, #09022);*
- *Fédération européenne des femmes actives en famille (FEFAF, #09568);*
- *Fundación pro Derechos de la Familia – Secretariado Internacional (PRODEFA, no recent information);*
- *HelpAge International (#10904);*
- *International Association for Counselling (IAC, #11821);*
- *International Catholic Child Bureau (#12450);*
- *International Confederation of Christian Family Movements (ICCFM, #12851);*
- *International Council of Jewish Women (ICJW, #13036);*
- *International Council of Psychologists (ICP, #13065);*
- *International Council of Women (ICW, #13093);*
- *International Council on Alcohol and Addictions (ICAA, #12989);*
- *International Council on the Management of Population Programs (ICOMP, #13043);*
- *International Federation for Family Development (IFFD, #13423);*
- *International Federation for Home Economics (IFHE, #13447);*
- *International Federation for Parent Education (IFPE, #13499);*
- *International Federation of Business and Professional Women (BPW International, #13376);*
- *International Federation on Ageing (IFA, #13345);*
- *International Trade Union Confederation (ITUC, #15708);*
- *Italian Centre of Solidarity (CeIS);*
- *KOLPING INTERNATIONAL (#16203);*
- Latter Day Saints Charities;
- *Make Mothers Matter (#16554);*
- *Pax Romana, International Catholic Movement for Intellectual and Cultural Affairs (ICMICA, #18267);*
- *Pax Romana, International Movement of Catholic Students (IMCS, #18268);*
- *Salvation Army (#19041);*
- *World Association of Girl Guides and Girl Scouts (WAGGGS, #21142);*
- *World Family Organization (WFO, #21399);*
- *World Federation of Methodist and Uniting Church Women (WFM and UCW, #21457);*
- *World Vision International (WVI, #21904);*
- *Zonta International (#22038).* [2021.09.04/XE0615/y/E]

♦ Vienna NGO Committee on Narcotic Drugs / see Vienna NGO Committee on Drugs (#20773)

♦ Vienna NGO Committee on the Status of Women 20775

Contact address not obtained. E-mail: ngocswvienna@gmail.com.

URL: http://www.ngocswvienna.org/

History 1982. Founded within the framework of *Conference of Non-Governmental Organizations in Consultative Relationship with the United Nations (CONGO, #04635).* Former names and other names: *NGO Committee on the Status of Women, Vienna* – alias; *NGO CSW Vienna* – alias. **Aims** Facilitate the activities of NGOs represented at the UN in Vienna with special focus on issues relating to gender equality and the status of women; act as a forum for exchange of information and views on matters of common interest; facilitate liaison with UN Women and initiate discussions leading to statements submitted to the United Nations Commission on the Status of Women. **Structure** Board; ad hoc Working Groups. **Languages** English. **Staff** Voluntary. **Finance** Sources: members' dues. **Activities** Advocacy/lobbying/activism; events/meetings; networking/liaising. **Events** *Meeting* Vienna (Austria) 2010, *Meeting* Vienna (Austria) 2004, *Meeting* Vienna (Austria) 2004, *Meeting* Vienna (Austria) 2004, *Meeting* Vienna (Austria) 2004.

Members NGOs (25) listed in this Yearbook:
- *African Action on AIDS (AAA);*
- *Associated Country Women of the World (ACWW, #02338);*
- *Dominicans for Justice and Peace (OP, #05113);*
- *European Union of Women (EUW, #09022);*
- *Federation of American Women's Clubs Overseas (FAWCO, #09416);*
- *Graduate Women International (GWI, #10688);*
- *International Alliance of Women (IAW, #11639);*
- *International Association of Democratic Lawyers (IADL, #11837);*
- *International Council of Jewish Women (ICJW, #13036);*
- *International Council of Women (ICW, #13093);*
- *International Federation for Home Economics (IFHE, #13447);*
- *International Federation of Business and Professional Women (BPW International, #13376);*
- *International Federation of Social Workers (IFSW, #13544);*
- *International Federation on Ageing (IFA, #13345);*
- *International Inner Wheel (IIW, #13855);*
- *Pan Pacific and South East Asia Women's Association (PPSEAWA, #18186);*
- *Pax Romana, International Catholic Movement for Intellectual and Cultural Affairs (ICMICA, #18267);*
- *SERVAS International (#19234);*
- *Socialist International Women (SIW, #19341);*
- *Soka Gakkai International (SGI, #19672);*
- *Soroptimist International (SI, #19686);*
- *Women's Federation for World Peace International (WFWPI);*
- *Women's International Zionist Organization (WIZO, #21030);*
- *World Union for Progressive Judaism (WUPJ, #21883);*
- *Zonta International (#22038).*

NGO Relations Liaises with: *NGO Committee on the Status of Women, Geneva (#17117); NGO Committee on the Status of Women, New York NY (see: #04635); NGO Committee on Sustainable Development, Vienna (#17119).* [2021.05.26/XE1386/y/E]

♦ **Vienna Union** International Union for an International Classification of the Figurative Elements of Marks (#15784)

♦ Vienna Wiestenthal Institute for Holocaust Studies (internationally oriented national body)

♦ Vier Pfoten International 20776

Four Paws International

Contact Linke Wienzeile 236, 1150 Vienna, Austria. T. +43154550200. Fax +431545502099. E-mail: office@vier-pfoten.org.

URL: https://www.four-paws.org/

History Registered in accordance with Austrian law: FN 227934y. EU Transparency Register: 69150873293-75. **Aims** Be the strong, global and independent voice for *animals* under human control. **Structure** Board. **Activities** Advocacy/lobbying/activism. **Consultative Status** Consultative status granted from: *ECOSOC (#05331)* (Special). **NGO Relations** Member of (3): *Asia for Animals Coalition (AfA, #01250); International Companion Animal Management Coalition (ICAM, #12828); OECD Watch (#17694).* [2019/XM6709/F]

♦ Viertes protokoll zum Allgemeinen abkommen über die vorrechte und befreiungen des Europarats (1961 treaty)
♦ Viessmann European Research Centre (internationally oriented national body)
♦ Viessmann Research Centre on Modern Europe / see Viessmann European Research Centre
♦ Vietnam International Arbitration Centre (internationally oriented national body)
♦ **ViEW** Veterinary Education Worldwide (#20761)
♦ VIF / see Economic and Social Development Bank
♦ VIF – Verkstadsindustrins Inter-Nordiske Forskningskommitté (inactive)
♦ Vigdis International Centre for Multilingualism and Intercultural Understanding (internationally oriented national body)
♦ Vigilancia Meteorológica Mundial (#21910)
♦ Vihreät – Euroopan Vapaa Allianssi – Ryhmä (#10781)
♦ Vijece Europske Unije (#04895)
♦ Vikingarna som kör NonStop (#20777)
♦ Viking Congress (meeting series)
♦ Viking Fund / see Wenner-Gren Foundation for Anthropological Research

♦ Viking NonStop User Group (VNUG) 20777

Vikingarna som kör NonStop

Chairman c/o Swedbank, Brunkebergstorg 8, SE-105 34 Stockholm, Sweden. T. +46703901253.

URL: http://www.vnug.biz/

History Former names and other names: *Nordic Tandem Users' Group (NTUG)* – alias; *Nordic NonStop Users' Group* – alias. **Aims** Unite users of Tandem *computers* in the Nordic countries.

Members Full in 3 countries:

Denmark, Norway, Sweden. [2013.07.24/XF0894/E]

♦ Vilagpolgarok Nemzetközi Nyilvantartasi Könyve (#18822)
♦ Viljely-ja Puutarhakasvien Pohjoismainen Geenipankki / see Nordic Genetic Resource Centre (#17303)
♦ Village Earth (internationally oriented national body)
♦ Village Monde (internationally oriented national body)
♦ VillageReach (internationally oriented national body)
♦ Villages of Hope-Africa (internationally oriented national body)
♦ Villages internationaux d'enfants / see CISV International (#03949)
♦ Villages Unis (unconfirmed)
♦ Villes Atlantiques (#03008)
♦ Viña del Mar acuerdo – Acuerdo Latinoamericano sobre control de buques por el estado rector del puerto (1992 treaty)
♦ Viña del Mar agreement – Latin American Agreement on Port State Control of Vessels (1992 treaty)
♦ Vincentians – Congregation of the Mission (religious order)
♦ Vineyard Benelux (internationally oriented national body)
♦ Vineyard DACH (internationally oriented national body)
♦ Vineyard Data Quantification Society (unconfirmed)

♦ Vineyard International Consortium (VIC) 20778

Group Coordinator The Vineyard Centre, Vulcan Street, Hull, HU6 7PS, UK. E-mail: office@vineyard.org.

Benelux Office Postbus 1557, 3500 BN Utrecht, Netherlands. T. +31306051500. Fax +31302340958.

URL: http://www.vineyard.org/
History May 1983, USA. Also known as *International Christian Fellowship*. Formerly also known as *Vineyard Ministries International (VMI)*. **Aims** Facilitate a network of local churches seeking to preach the *gospel* among all nations by and through local *churches*. **Structure** Regional or national groupings (9): Australia; Benelux; Canada; Germany, Austria, Switzerland; New Zealand; Denmark, Finland, Iceland, Norway, Sweden; South Africa; UK and Ireland; USA. Includes *Mouvement africaine Vineyard Europe (MAVE, see: #20778)*. **Activities** Training/education; networking/liaising.
Members National organizations in 6 countries:
Australia, Canada, New Zealand, South Africa, UK, USA.
Regional organizations (3):
Nordic Association of Vineyard Churches (#17207); Vineyard Benelux; Vineyard DACH.
NGO Relations Member of: *EarthAction (EA, #05159).* [2018.07.26/XN8107/y/F]

♦ Vineyard Ministries International / see Vineyard International Consortium (#20778)
♦ Vineyard Norden (#17207)
♦ Vineyard Nordic / see Nordic Association of Vineyard Churches (#17207)
♦ **VinoFed** World Federation of Major International Wine and Spirits Competitions (#21452)

♦ Vinyl Films and Sheets Europe (VFSE) 20779

Contact c/o Polymer Comply Europe, Avenue de Cortenbergh 71, 1000 Brussels, Belgium. T. +3227324124. Fax +3227324218. E-mail: info@pceu.eu.
URL: https://www.vfse.org/
History Set up following merger of *European Decorative and Stationery Plastics Foils Association (EDEFA, inactive), European Polyvinyl Film Manufacturers Association (EPFMA, inactive)* and *European Automotive Trim Suppliers (EATS, inactive)*, following discussions starting 2016. **Aims** Represent and defend the interests of the European suppliers of *plastics* sheets and foils. **Structure** Working Groups (3): Packaging; Automotive; Decoration. **Activities** Research/documentation; advocacy/lobbying/activism; events/meetings.
NGO Relations Sector Group of: *European Plastics Converters (EuPC, #08216).* [2022/XM7653/D]

♦ VinylPlus 20780

Contact Avenue de Cortenbergh 71, 1000 Brussels, Belgium. T. +3222395105. E-mail: info@vinylplus.eu.
URL: http://www.vinylplus.eu/
Aims Provide the organizational infrastructure to manage and monitor the implementation of the programme built around the renewed Voluntary Commitment of the *European* PVC *industry*. **Structure** Board; Monitoring Committee. **Activities** Events/meetings. **Events** *VinylPlus Sustainability Forum* Brussels (Belgium) 2020, *VinylPlus Sustainability Forum* Prague (Czechia) 2019, *VinylPlus Sustainability Forum* Prague (Czechia) 2019, *VinylPlus Sustainability Forum* Madrid (Spain) 2018, *VinylPlus Sustainability Forum* Madrid (Spain) 2018.
Members Founding partners (4):
European Council of Vinyl Manufacturers (ECVM, #06849); European Plasticisers (#08214); European Plastics Converters (EuPC, #08216); European Stabiliser Producers Association (ESPA, #08827).
Partners (companies) in 22 countries:
Austria, Belgium, Czechia, Denmark, Estonia, Finland, France, Germany, Greece, Hungary, Ireland, Italy, Lithuania, Luxembourg, Netherlands, Norway, Poland, Portugal, Spain, Sweden, Switzerland, UK. [2019/XM7696/y/F]

♦ Vinzenzgemeinschaft / see International Confederation of the Society of St Vincent-de-Paul (#12870)
♦ Violence and Harassment Convention, 2019 (2019 treaty)

♦ Violence Prevention Alliance (VPA) 20781

Technical Officer Dept for Management of Noncommunicable Diseases/Violence and Injury Prevention/Disability, WHO, Av Appia 20, 1211 Geneva 27, Switzerland. T. +41227912111. Fax +41227914332. E-mail: violenceprevention@who.int.
URL: http://www.who.int/violenceprevention/en/
History Jan 2004, as a network of *WHO (#20950)* Member States, international agencies and civil society organizations. **Aims** Prevent interpersonal violence (eg child maltreatment, youth violence, intimate partner violence, sexual violence and elder abuse) and self-directed violence (eg suicide) using a public health approach. **Activities** Project/programmes; events/meetings. **Events** *Annual Meeting / Meeting* Munich (Germany) 2012, *Meeting* Rome (Italy) 2010, *Meeting* Washington, DC (USA) 2008. **Publications** *Prevent* – newsletter.
Members Participating organizations (50) in 12 countries:
Australia, Belgium, Canada, Germany, Jamaica, Malaysia, Norway, Philippines, South Africa, Thailand, UK, USA.
Included in the above, 13 organizations listed in this Yearbook:
Center for Global Nonkilling (#03642); DIGNITY – Danish Institute Against Torture; Education Development Center (EDC); International Bank for Reconstruction and Development (IBRD, #12317) (Conflict, Crime and Violence Team); *International Centre for the Prevention of Crime (ICPC, #12508); International Physicians for the Prevention of Nuclear War (IPPNW, #14578); International Society for Prevention of Child Abuse and Neglect (ISPCAN, #15385); Men's Resources International (MRI); UNDP (#20292); UNICEF (#20332); United Nations Office on Drugs and Crime (UNODC, #20596); WAVE Trust – Worldwide Alternatives to Violence; World Council of Churches (WCC, #21320).* [2017.06.21/XJ1675/y/E]

♦ **VIPA International** Vacuum Insulation Panel Association (#20742)
♦ VIPCA / see Vienna International Science Conferences and Events Association (#20772)

♦ Viral Hepatitis Prevention Board (VHPB) 20782

Exec Sec Ctr for the Evaluation of Vaccination – VAXINFECTIO, Fac of Medicine and Health Sciences – Univ of Antwerp, Universiteitsplein 1, 2610 Antwerp, Belgium. T. +3232652523 – +3232652640. Fax +3232652640. E-mail: info@vhpb.org.
URL: http://www.vhpb.org/
History 1992. Founded under the auspices of the Society for Occupational Medicine. **Aims** Eliminate transmission of hepatitis B in all workers at risk in the industrialized world. **Structure** Board; Permanent Scientific Secretariat. **Activities** Events/meetings. **NGO Relations** Member of (1): *ACHIEVE (#00068).* Cooperates with (1): *European Liver Patients 'Association (ELPA, #07706).* [2021/XM4243/v/D]

♦ Virgil Society 20783

Sec c/o 8 Purley Oaks Road, Sanderstead, CR2 0NP, UK. T. +442086602924.
URL: http://www.virgilsociety.org.uk/
History Founded 1943, London (UK). UK Registered Charity. **Aims** Unite all those who cherish the central *educational tradition* of Western *Europe*, of which Virgil is the symbol. **Structure** General Assembly (annual); Council. **Staff** Voluntary. **Finance** Members' dues. **Activities** Events/meetings. **Events** *Annual general meeting* London (UK) 1993. **Publications** *Members' Newsletter* (2 a year). Proceedings (every 3 years).
Members Individuals and institutions in 9 countries:
Australia, Canada, France, Germany, Netherlands, Norway, Spain, UK, USA. [2020.01.10/XN4565/E]

♦ Virginia Gildersleeve International Fund / see Women First International Fund (#20996)
♦ Virginia Gildersleeve International Fund for University Women / see Women First International Fund (#20996)

♦ VIRGO Collaboration 20784

Spokesperson c/o EGO, Via E Amaldi, I-56021 S Stefano a Macerata, Cascina PI, Italy. T. +3950752345.
URL: http://public.virgo-gw.eu/.the-virgo-collaboration/
History Jun 1994. **Aims** Produce high-quality data. **Publications** *h – The Gravitational Voice* – newsletter.
Members Individuals (over 300); institutions. Full in 6 countries:
France, Hungary, Italy, Netherlands, Poland, Spain.
NGO Relations *European Gravitational Observatory (EGO); LIGO Scientific Collaboration (LSC).* [2016/XM5294/F]

♦ Virgo Consortium for Cosmological Supercomputer Simulations (Virgo Consortium) 20785

Contact Inst for Computational Cosmology, Dept of Physics, Durham Univ, South Road, Durham, DH1 3LE, UK. T. +441913343631.
URL: http://www.virgo.dur.ac.uk/
History 1994. **Aims** Carry out state-of-the-art cosmological simulations. **Events** *Meeting* Durham (UK) 2020, *Meeting* Leiden (Netherlands) 2018.
Members Institutes; Core members; Associates; Students. Members in 6 countries:
Canada, China, Germany, Netherlands, UK, USA. [2021/XF5748/F]

♦ **Virgo Consortium** Virgo Consortium for Cosmological Supercomputer Simulations (#20785)

♦ Virtual Air Traffic Simulation Network (VATSIM) 20786

Pres address not obtained. E-mail: president@vatsim.net.
URL: http://www.vatsim.net/
History Founded Jul 2001. **Aims** Create a global community for learning, sharing experiences and pursuing new opportunities in the virtual world. **Structure** Board of Governors; Executive Committee. **Events** *Global Conference* Vienna (Austria) 2014. [2015/XJ9586/v/F]

♦ Virtual Biosecurity Centre (unconfirmed)

♦ Virtual Educa 20787

SG Virtual Educa, c/ Rio Bidasoa 16, 28803 Alcala de Henares, Madrid, Spain. T. +34918837189. Fax +34918800254. E-mail: info@virtualeduca.org.
URL: http://www.virtualeduca.org/
History 2000. **Aims** As a multilateral cooperation initiative for the realization of *innovative* projects in the areas of education and training for *human development*, serve as a forum for exchange of experience and for realization of projects linked to *knowledge* society. **Structure** Governing Council, comprising one representative of each member institution. Executive Committee; Permanent Committee; Consultative Council; Advisory Council; Scientific and Programme Committee. National offices in: Argentina; Bolivia; Brazil; Chile; Colombia; Costa Rica; Ecuador; El Salvador; Spain; USA, Honduras; Nicaragua; mexico; Panama; Paraguay; Peru; Dominican Rep; Venezuela. **IGO Relations** Secretariat hosted by: *Ibero-American General Secretariat (#11024).* [2010/XJ0760/F]

♦ Virtual Global Taskforce (VGT) 20788

Secretariat c/o HSI-ICE, 500 12th St SW, Washington DC 20536, USA. E-mail: vgtsecretariat@ice.dhs.gov.
URL: http://www.virtualglobaltaskforce.com/
History 2003. **Aims** Build an effective, international partnership of law enforcement agencies, non government organisations and industry to help protect children from *online child abuse*. **Structure** Board of Management of 9 members. **Activities** Rescues children worldwide; conducts targeted law enforcement operations into online and offline offending; identifies and holds to account child sex offenders worldwide. **Events** *Biennial International Conference / International Conference* Abu Dhabi (United Arab Emirates) 2012, *Biennial international conference / International Conference* Sydney, NSW (Australia) 2010, *International Conference* Vancouver, BC (Canada) 2008, *International Conference* Washington, DC (USA) 2007, *International Conference* Belfast (UK) 2005. **Publications** Factsheets.
Members Law enforcement agencies (9). National members (7):
Australia, Canada, Italy, New Zealand, UK, United Arab Emirates, USA.
International agencies (2):
European Police Office (Europol, #08239); International Criminal Police Organization – INTERPOL (ICPO-INTERPOL, #13110).
NGO Relations Partners include: *End Child Prostitution, Child Pornography and Trafficking of Children for Sexual Purposes (ECPAT, #05456); International Association of Internet Hotlines (INHOPE, #11970).* [2014/XJ4045/F*]

♦ Virtual Institute for Artificial Electromagnetic Materials and Metamaterials / see Virtual Institute for Artificial Electromagnetic Materials and Metamaterials (#20789)

♦ Virtual Institute for Artificial Electromagnetic Materials and Metamaterials (METAMORPHOSE VI) 20789

SG "Roma Tre" Univ – Dept of Engineering, Bldg B – Room 3-13, Via Vito Volterra 62, 00146 Rome RM, Italy. E-mail: contact@metamorphose-vi.org.
Registered Address c/o UCL/Laboratoire d'Hyperfréquences, Place du Levant 3, 1348 Louvain-la-Neuve, Belgium.
URL: https://www.metamorphose-vi.org/
History 2007. Founded by the partners of the FP-6 Network of Excellence "METAMaterials ORganized for radio, millimetre wave, and PHOtonic Superlattice Engineering" – METAMORPHOSE NoE. Former names and other names: *Virtual Institute for Artificial Electromagnetic Materials and Metamaterials (METAMORPHOSE VI AISBL)* – legal name. Registration: Banque-Carrefour des Entreprises, No/ID: 0891.977.059, Start date: 10 May 2007, Belgium. **Aims** Research, study and promote artificial electromagentic materials and metamaterials. **Structure** General Assembly; Board of Directors. **Finance** Sources: members' dues. **Activities** Events/meetings; networking/liaising; training/education. **Events** *Metamaterials: International Congress on Artificial Materials for Novel Wave Phenomena* Siena (Italy) 2022, *Metamaterials: International Congress on Artificial Materials for Novel Wave Phenomena* New York, NY (USA) 2021, *International Congress on Engineered Material Platforms for Novel Wave Phenomena (Metamaterials)* New York, NY (USA) 2020, *METAMATERIALS : International Congress on Engineered Material Platforms for Novel Wave Phenomena* Rome (Italy) 2019, *METAMATERIALS : International Congress on Engineered Material Platforms for Novel Wave Phenomena* Espoo (Finland) 2018.
Members Individual; Institutional. Institutions in 12 countries:
Belgium, Finland, France, Germany, Greece, Italy, Poland, Russia, Spain, Sweden, UK, USA. [2022/AA2694/D]

♦ Virtual Physiological Human Institute for Integrative Biomedical Research (VPH Institute) 20790

Manager KU Leuven, Sportsecretariaat, Campus Arenberg II, Celestijnenlaan 300c, 3001 Leuven, Belgium. E-mail: manager@vph-institute.org – director@vph-institute.org.
Exec Dir address not obtained.
URL: http://www.vph-institute.org/
History Proposed Sep 2007; set up 2010; formally opened 2011. Registration: Banque-Carrefour des Entreprises, Start date: May 2011, Belgium. **Aims** Ensure that the Virtual Physiological Human is fully realized, universally adopted, and effectively used both in research and clinic. **Structure** General Assembly; Board of Directors; Board of Trustees. **Languages** English. **Staff** 3.00 FTE, paid. **Finance** Sources: members' dues. Other sources: European Funded projects **Activities** Events/meetings; research/documentation. communication, stakeholder engagement. **Events** *International Conference on the Virtual Physiological Human* Porto (Portugal) 2022, *International Conference on the Virtual Physiological Human* Paris (France) 2020, *International Conference on the Virtual Physiological Human* Amsterdam (Netherlands) 2016, *International Conference on the Virtual Physiological Human* Trondheim (Norway) 2014. **Publications** *VPH Institute Newsletter*.
Members Institutions (54); Individuals (28). Members in 20 countries:
Austria, Belgium, Bulgaria, Cuba, France, Germany, Greece, Italy, Korea Rep, Netherlands, New Zealand, Norway, Poland, Romania, Serbia, Singapore, Spain, Switzerland, UK, USA.
Included in the above, 1 organization listed in this Yearbook:
European Medical Association (EMA, #07761).
IGO Relations *European Commission (EC, #06633).* **NGO Relations** Founding member of: *Avicenna Alliance (#03047).* [2022.11.24/XJ9301/jy/D]

♦ Virtual Reality Industry Forum (VRIF) 20791

Contact 5177 Brandin Court, Fremont CA 94538, USA. T. +15104924055. Fax +15104924001. E-mail: info@vr-if.org.
URL: https://www.vr-if.org/
History Former names and other names: *VR Industry Forum* – alias. **Aims** Further the widespread availability of high quality audiovisual VR experiences, for the benefit of consumers. **Structure** Board of Directors. **Finance** Sources: members' dues. **Activities** Events/meetings. **Publications** *VR Industry Forum Newsletter.* [2020/AA0288/t/F]

♦ **Virtual University of the Adriatic-Ionic Basin (UniAdrion)** **20792**
Secretariat Univ Politcenica delle Marche, Piazza Roma 22, 30121 Ancona AN, Italy. T. +39712202293. Fax +39712202303. E-mail: info@uniadrion.net.
URL: http://www.uniadrion.net/
History Set up within the framework of *Adriatic and Ionian Initiative (AII, #00121)*. **Aims** Promote cooperation among universities and research centres. **Structure** General Assembly; Board of Advisors; Executive Secretariat; President. **Activities** Training/education; research/documentation. **Events** *Forum of the Adriatic and Ionian Chambers of Commerce, Cities and Universities* Budva (Montenegro) 2019, *Forum of the Adriatic and Ionian Chambers of Commerce, Cities and Universities* Split (Croatia) 2018, *General Assembly* Sarajevo (Bosnia-Herzegovina) 2015, *General Assembly* Ancona (Italy) 2014.
Members Regular; Associate. Regular in 8 countries:
Albania, Bosnia-Herzegovina, Croatia, Greece, Italy, Montenegro, Serbia, Slovenia.
Associate in 3 countries:
Croatia, North Macedonia, Serbia. [2016/XM4554/**F**]

♦ Virtus Global Center for Corporate Governance (internationally oriented national body)

♦ **Virtus: World Intellectual Impairment Sport** **20793**
Exec Dir PO Box 4972, Sheffield, S25 9EQ, UK.
URL: https://www.virtus.sport/
History Feb 1986, Netherlands, as *International Sports Federation for Persons with Mental Handicap (INAS-FMH) – Federación Internacional de Deportes para Personas con Deficiencias Mentales*. Also previously referred to as *International Sports Federation for the Intellectually Disabled – Fédération internationale des sports pour les personnes handicapées mentales*. 1994, name changed to *International Sports Federation for Persons with an Intellectual Disability (INAS-FID) – Fédération internationale de sports pour personnes ayant une déficience intellectuelle – Federación Internacional de Deportes para Personas con Discapacidad Intelectual*. 2010, present name adopted. UK Registered Charity: 1144903. Registration: Charity Commission, No/ID: 1173901, Start date: 2017, England and Wales. **Aims** Further development of sports for persons with intellectual disability in an international movement. **Structure** General Assembly (every 2 years). Executive Committee, consisting of President, Vice-President, Secretary General, Treasurer. Eligibility Officer; Technical Officer. Regional Representatives (5): Africa; Americas; Asia and South Pacific; Europe; North Africa and Middle East. **Languages** English. **Staff** Voluntary. **Finance** Sources: members' dues. Member nations are main organizers for regional and world championships. Annual budget: 150,000 USD. **Activities** Organizes: world and regional championships; educational seminars for national sports organizations for mentally handicapped in underdeveloped countries. Participates in IPC Paralympics (summer and winter) and in other IPC competitions. Sports specific matters are dealt with by directors per sport. Individual sports covered: athletics; cycling; nordic skiing; swimming; tennis; table tennis. Team sports covered: basketball; football. **Events** *General Assembly* Vichy (France) 2022, *General Assembly* Brisbane, QLD (Australia) 2019, *General Assembly* Brisbane, QLD (Australia) 2017, *General Assembly* Sheffield (UK) 2015, *General Assembly* Rio de Janeiro (Brazil) 2013. **Publications** *INAS-FMH Magazine* (6 a year).
Members Sports federations for persons with mental handicap in 86 countries and territories:
Algeria, Argentina, Australia, Austria, Bangladesh, Belgium, Benin, Brazil, Burkina Faso, Cameroon, Canada, Central African Rep, Chile, Colombia, Côte d'Ivoire, Croatia, Czechia, Denmark, Dominican Rep, Ecuador, Egypt, Estonia, Faeroe Is, Finland, France, Germany, Ghana, Greece, Guatemala, Guinea, Honduras, Hong Kong, Hungary, Iceland, India, Iran Islamic Rep, Italy, Japan, Jordan, Kenya, Korea Rep, Kuwait, Lebanon, Libya, Lithuania, Macau, Madagascar, Mali, Mexico, Morocco, Namibia, Netherlands, New Zealand, Niger, Nigeria, Norway, Peru, Philippines, Poland, Portugal, Puerto Rico, Romania, Russia, Saudi Arabia, Senegal, Serbia, Sierra Leone, Singapore, Slovakia, South Africa, Spain, Suriname, Sweden, Taiwan, Togo, Tunisia, Türkiye, Turkmenistan, Uganda, UK, Ukraine, United Arab Emirates, Uruguay, Venezuela, Vietnam, Zimbabwe.
NGO Relations Maintains relations with: *World Athletics (#21209)*; *Fédération internationale de basketball (FIBA, #09614)*; *International Federation of Association Football (#13360)*. Member of: *International Paralympic Committee (IPC, #14512)*. [2021/XD0462/**C**]

♦ **VISCEA** Vienna International Science Conferences and Events Association (#20772)
♦ Visegrad Four / see Visegrad Group (#20794)

♦ **Visegrad Group** **20794**
Groupe de Visegrad
Address not obtained.
URL: http://www.visegradgroup.eu/
History Established 1991, Visegrad (Hungary). Unofficially referred to as *Visegrad Four* or *V4* since Czech Rep and Slovakia became independent. Previously also referred to as *Countries of Visegrad – Pays de Visegrad – Visegradlanden*. **Aims** Promote *political cooperation* in *Central Europe*. **Structure** Not an institutionalized entity, but a meeting of representatives – from high-leve meetings of prime ministers and heads of states to expert consultations. Annual official summits of prime ministers. Rotating presidency. *International Visegrad Fund (#15859)*, (jointly-funded) based in Bratislava (Slovakia). **Languages** Czech, English, Hungarian, Polish, Slovakian. **Staff** 13.00 FTE, paid. **Finance** Annual contributions to *International Visegrad Fund (#15859)*0. Annual budget (2014): euro 8,000,000. **Activities** Set up: *International Visegrad Fund (#15859)*. **Events** *Conference on Digital Transformation* Brussels (Belgium) 2019, *Prime Ministers Summit* Warsaw (Poland) 2013, *V4 and Japan foreign ministers meeting* Gödöllö (Hungary) 2011, *Meeting of justice ministers* Hungary 2011, *Prime ministers summit* Slovakia 2011. **Publications** *Visegrad Bulletin*.
Members Governments of 4 countries:
Czechia, Hungary, Poland, Slovakia. [2019/XF5264/**E***]

♦ Visegradlanden / see Visegrad Group (#20794)

♦ **Visegrad Patent Institute (VPI)** **20795**
Dir I Janos Pal papa tér 7, Budapest 1081, Hungary. T. +3616135130. Fax +3617990188. E-mail: director@vpi.int – secretariat@vpi.int.
URL: http://www.vpi.int/
History Operations started 1 Jul 2019, as an IGO established by *Visegrad Group (#20794)*. **Aims** Cooperate in the field of patents. **Structure** Administrative Board; Secretariat.
Members Governments of 4 countries:
Czechia, Hungary, Poland, Slovakia.
Consultative Status Consultative status granted from: *World Intellectual Property Organization (WIPO, #21593)* (Observer Status). **IGO Relations** *Patent Cooperation Treaty (PCT, 1970)*. [2018/XM8476/**E***]

♦ VISES – Associazione Volontari Iniziative di Sviluppo Economico e Sociale (internationally oriented national body)
♦ Vishva Hindu Parishad (internationally oriented national body)
♦ Vishwa Hindu Mahasangh (#21569)
♦ Visible Evidence (meeting series)
♦ Visible Seal International Council (internationally oriented national body)
♦ Vision africa (internationally oriented national body)
♦ Vision Aid Overseas (internationally oriented national body)

♦ **Vision Alliance** **20796**
SG No 3 Professors' Colony, Palamalai Road, SRK Vidyalaya Post, Coimbatore, Tamil Nadu 641 020, Coimbatore TAMIL NADU 641 020, India. T. +914222469104. Fax +914222693414. E-mail: ceo201922@gmail.com.
URL: https://www.iapb.org/vision-alliance/
History 7 Dec 2009, Bensheim (Germany), by *International Agency for the Prevention of Blindness (IAPB, #11597)*, *World Blind Union (WBU, #21234)* and *International Council for Education of People with Visual Impairment (ICEVI, #13015)*. **Aims** Create greater synergy and collaboration between member organizations at global, regional and national levels so as to improve programmes of each organization. [2012/XJ5215/y/**E**]

♦ **VisionFund International** **20797**
CEO 5th Floor, 11 Belgrave Road, London, SW1V 1RB, UK. T. +442078023464. E-mail: weare@visionfund.org.
International Headquarters c/o WVI, 800 West Chestnut Avenue, Monrovia CA 91016-3198, USA. T. +1626303881.
URL: http://www.visionfund.org/
History Set up as the microfinance subsidiary of *World Vision International (WVI, #21904)*. **Aims** Empower families to create incomes and jobs; unlock economic potential for communities to thrive. **Structure** Board of Directors; Senior Management Team. **Activities** Financial and/or material aid. **NGO Relations** Member of: *Partnership for Responsible Financial Inclusion (PRFI, #18241)*. [2018/XM6434/f/**E**]

♦ Vision GRAM-International (internationally oriented national body)
♦ Vision Health International (internationally oriented national body)
♦ Vision International Development and Educational Organization (internationally oriented national body)
♦ Visión Mundial Internacional (#21904)

♦ **Vision and Strategies around the Baltic Sea (VASAB)** **20798**
Secretariat Alberta iela 10, Riga LV-1010, Latvia. T. +37167350630. E-mail: info@vasab.org.
URL: https://vasab.org/
History 21 Aug 1992, Karlskrona (Sweden). Founded at meeting of Ministers for spatial planning and development of Baltic Sea states. Former names and other names: *Vision and Strategies around the Baltic Sea 2010 (VASAB 2010)* – former. **Aims** Prepare policy options for territorial development of the Baltic Sea Region; provide a forum for exchange of know-how on spatial planning and development between the Baltic Sea countries. **Structure** Conference of Ministers responsible for spatial planning in BSR countries (meets every 2-5 years); Steering Committee – *Committee on Spatial Development of the Baltic Sea Region* – meets every 4-5 months, comprises national representatives under rotating Chairmanship, currently Denmark (from Jul 2019). Secretariat located in Riga (Latvia). **Languages** English. **Activities** Events/meetings; politics/policy/regulatory. **Events** *Joint HELCOM-VASAB Maritime Spatial Planning Working Group Meeting* Helsinki (Finland) 2022, *Conference of Ministers for Spatial Planning* Tallinn (Estonia) 2014, *Conference of Ministers for Spatial Planning* Vilnius (Lithuania) 2009, *Conference of Ministers for Spatial Planning* Gdansk (Poland) 2005, *Meeting* Helsinki (Finland) 2003. **Publications** *Accessibility of the Baltic Sea Region – Past and future dynamics* (2019); *Development of Cities in the Baltic Sea Region* (2016); *Urban Revitalisation in the Baltic Sea Region* (2016); *Long-Term Perspective for the Territorial Development of the Baltic Sea Region* (2009); *VASAB 2010 PLUS Spatial Development Action Programme* (2001); *Compendium of Spatial Planning Systems in the Baltic Sea Region* (2000); *Towards a Framework for Spatial Development in the Baltic Sea Region* (1994). Conference proceedings; occasional publications; reports.
Members Representatives of national and regional governments in 9 countries:
Belarus, Estonia, Finland, Germany, Latvia, Lithuania, Poland, Russia, Sweden. [2021.02.25/XF3820/**F***]

♦ Vision and Strategies around the Baltic Sea 2010 / see Vision and Strategies around the Baltic Sea (#20798)
♦ visionSynergy (internationally oriented national body)
♦ Visitandines – Visitation Sainte-Marie (religious order)
♦ Visitation Nuns – Order of the Visitation of the Blessed Virgin Mary (religious order)
♦ Visitation Sainte-Marie (religious order)
♦ VISPE – Volontari Italiani per la Solidarietà ai Paesi Emergenti (internationally oriented national body)
♦ VIS – Volontariato Internazionale per lo Sviluppo (internationally oriented national body)
♦ Vitae Civilis – Institute for Development, Environment and Peace (internationally oriented national body)
♦ Vital Strategies (internationally oriented national body)
♦ Vital Voices Global Partnership (internationally oriented national body)
♦ Vitamin Angels (internationally oriented national body)
♦ Vitamin D Workshop (meeting series)
♦ Vita et Pax in Christo Jesu (religious order)
♦ Vita Umana Internazionale (#10977)

♦ **Vitiligo Research Foundation (VR Foundation)** **20799**
CEO 1 Penn Plaza Ste 6205, New York NY 10119, USA. E-mail: info@vrfoundation.org.
URL: http://vrfoundation.org/
History 2010. A US non-profit organization. **Aims** Develop effective *treatments* for people worldwide who suffer from vitiligo. **Structure** Board of Directors; Management Team; Scientific Advisory Team. **Activities** Healthcare; research and development. **Consultative Status** Consultative status granted from: *ECOSOC (#05331)* (Special). [2019.12.11/XM6710/f/**F**]

♦ Viva Africa (internationally oriented national body)

♦ **Viva Network** **20800**
Chief Exec Unit 8 The Gallery, 54 Marston Street, Oxford, OX4 1LF, UK. T. +441865811660. Fax +441865811661. E-mail: enquiries@viva.org.
URL: http://www.viva.org/
History Founded 1996. Registered as a charity in England: 1053389. Registered as a charity in Hong Kong: 1657942. **Aims** Release *children* from *poverty* and abuse. **Structure** Boards (3): International; Hong Kong; US. **Events** *Forum in Pediatric Oncology* Singapore (Singapore) 2012. **Consultative Status** Consultative status granted from: *ECOSOC (#05331)* (Ros A). **NGO Relations** Member of: *Global Connections*; *Global Partnership to End Violence Against Children (End Violence Against Children, #10533)*; *Keeping Children Safe*; *Micah Global (#16741)*. [2020/XQ5382/**F**]

♦ Viva Salud (internationally oriented national body)

♦ **VIVAT International** **20801**
Contact 777 United Nations Plaza, Ste 6-H, New York NY 10017, USA. T. +16464870003. E-mail: viny@vivatinternational.org.
Contact address not obtained.
URL: https://www.vivatinternational.org/
History 18 Nov 2000. Founding Congregations: *Missionarie Serve dello Spirito Santo (SSpS)* and *Società del Verbo Divino (Verbiti)*. **Aims** Focus on issues dealing with *human rights*, particularly in the areas of *women, poverty* eradication, *sustainable development* and the culture of *peace*. **Structure** Board of Trustees; Executive Board; Offices in New York NY (USA) and Geneva (Switzerland); National Branches and National Groups. **Languages** English, French, German, Indonesian, Portuguese, Spanish. **Staff** New York Central Office: 2; Geneva Office: 1. **Activities** Advocacy/lobbying/activism; awareness raising; networking/liaising. **Publications** *VIVAT E-Newsletter* (4 a year) in English, Spanish. *May All Have Life in its Fullness and Dignity*. **Information Services** *VIVAT E-Information* in English, Spanish. **Members** Founding Congregations (2); Member Congregations (9). Individuals (over 25,000) in over 120 countries. Membership countries not specified. **Consultative Status** Consultative status granted from: *ECOSOC (#05331)* (Special). **IGO Relations** Accredited by (1): *United Nations Framework Convention on Climate Change – Secretariat (UNFCCC, #20564)*. **NGO Relations** Member of (14): Justice Coalition of Religious; *Mining Working Group at the UN (MWG, #16813)*; *NGO Committee on Financing for Development, New York (#17108)*; NGO Committee on Language and Languages; *NGO Committee on Migration, New York (#17112)*; *NGO Committee on Sustainable Development, New York (#17118)*; *NGO Committee on the Rights of Indigenous Peoples (#17114)*; *NGO Committee on the Status of Women, New York NY (see: #04635)*; *NGO Committee to Stop Trafficking in Persons (NGO CSTIP)*; NGO Major Group; NGO Working Group on Girls; NGO Working Group to End Homelessness; Religious at the United Nationa; Working Group to End Homelessness. [2023.02.25/XE4329/**E**]

♦ VIWOS – Vlamingen in de Wereld – Ontwikkelingssamenwerking (internationally oriented national body)
♦ VIZ – Vereinigung für Internationale Zusammenarbeit (internationally oriented national body)
♦ **VJEB** Vereinigung Junger Europäischer Beamter (#02772)
♦ Vjemirnaja Organizacija Veterinarov-Konevcov (#21388)
♦ **VJR** Vereinigung Junger RechtshistorikerInnen (#02987)
♦ VKIFD / see Von Karman Institute for Fluid Dynamics (#16182)
♦ **VKI** Von Karman Institute for Fluid Dynamics (#16182)
♦ **VKP** Vseobscaja Konfederacija Profsojuzov (#10108)
♦ Vlaams Agentschap voor International Samenwerking (internationally oriented national body)
♦ Vlaams Aktiekomitee tegen Atoomwapens / see Hand in Hand tegen Racisme

♦ Vlaamse Federatie van NGO's voor Ontwikkelingssamenwerking (internationally oriented national body)
♦ Vlaamse Vereniging voor Ontwikkelingssamenwerking en Technische Bijstand (internationally oriented national body)
♦ Vlaamse Vereniging voor Opleidingsprogramma's in het Buitenland / see Vlaamse Vereniging voor Ontwikkelingssamenwerking en Technische Bijstand
♦ Vlaamse Vredeskoepel VAKA-OCV / see Hand in Hand tegen Racisme
♦ Vlaams Instituut voor Vrede en Geweldpreventie (internationally oriented national body)
♦ Vlaams Internationaal Centrum / see KIYO
♦ Vlaams Vredesinstituut – Vlaams Instituut voor Vrede en Geweldpreventie (internationally oriented national body)
♦ Vlamingen in de Wereld – Ontwikkelingssamenwerking (internationally oriented national body)
♦ VLDB Endowment / see Very Large Databases Endowment
♦ VLDB – Very Large Databases Endowment (internationally oriented national body)
♦ VLE / see World Esperantist Vegetarian Association (#21389)
♦ VLPGO / see GO15 (#10672)
♦ VLSI – International Symposium on VLSI Technology and Circuits (meeting series)
♦ VluchtelingenWerk Nederland (internationally oriented national body)
♦ VMA – International Association for Voice Mail and Voice Processing Services (inactive)
♦ VMA – Venue Management Association – Asia and Pacific (internationally oriented national body)
♦ VMI – Forschungsinstitut für Verbands- und Genossenschafts-Management (internationally oriented national body)
♦ **VMI** Vie montante internationale (#20769)
♦ VMI / see Vineyard International Consortium (#20778)
♦ **VMI** Visión Mundial Internacional (#21904)
♦ **VMM** Veille météorologique mondiale (#21910)
♦ **VMM** Vigilancia Meteorológica Mundial (#21910)
♦ VMPT – International Conference on Virtual Machining Process Technology (meeting series)
♦ **VMUG** VMware User Group (#20802)

♦ VMware User Group (VMUG) 20802

Exec Dir 113 Seaboard Ln, Ste C-250, Franklin TN 37067, USA. T. +13123216886. E-mail: info@vmug.com.
URL: https://www.vmug.com/

History Officially launched Aug 2010. Registered under the laws of the State of Illinois (USA). **Aims** Maximize members' use of VMware and partner solutions. **Structure** Board of Directors. **Activities** Events/meetings; knowledge management/information dissemination; training/education. [2019/XM7857/**C**]

♦ V-Net / see Network of Associations of Victims of Terrorism (#16998)
♦ VNG International – International Agency of the Association of Netherlands Municipalities (internationally oriented national body)
♦ VNG International – Vereniging van Nederlandse Gemeenten – Internationaal (internationally oriented national body)
♦ **VNGOC** Vienna NGO Committee on Drugs (#20773)
♦ VNIKI – All-Russia Market Research Institute (internationally oriented national body)
♦ **VNUG** Viking NonStop User Group (#20777)
♦ **VNU** Volontaires des Nations Unies (#20650)
♦ **VNU** Voluntarios de las Naciones Unidas (#20650)

♦ Vocal Europe 20803

Registered Address Rue de la Science 14B, 1040 Brussels, Belgium. T. +328803650. E-mail: office@vocaleurope.eu.
URL: https://www.vocaleurope.eu/

History 2013. Registration: Banque-Carrefour des Entreprises, No/ID: 0699.685.051, Start date: 6 Jul 2018, Belgium. **Aims** Engage in research and communication on EU Diplomatic Actions, Enlargement Policy and Democracy. **Structure** Advisory Board. **Activities** Advocacy/lobbying/activism; events/meetings; research/documentation; training/education. [2021/AA1442/j/**F**]

♦ Vocationistes – Société des Vocations Divines (religious order)
♦ Vocationist Fathers – Society of Divine Vocations (religious order)
♦ Vocationist Sisters – Sisters of the Society of the Divine Vocations (religious order)
♦ Voces Sin Fronteras (#20805)
♦ **VOCTECH** SEAMEO Regional Centre for Vocational and Technical Education (#19180)
♦ Vodafone Group Foundation (internationally oriented national body)
♦ Voeding Derde Wereld (internationally oriented national body)
♦ VOHMA / see International Vessel Operators Dangerous Goods Association
♦ VOICA / see Fondazione Canossiana Voica

♦ The Voice of the Martyrs (VOM) 20804

La Voz De Los Martires – A Voz Dos Martires – Pomoc Pronasledovane Cirkvi – Martyrernes Rost – Stefanus-Lahetys Ry – Missionen Martyrernas Rost

Head Office PO Box 443, Bartlesville OK 74005-0443, USA. T. +19183370302. Fax +19187470085. E-mail: thevoice@vom-usa.org.
URL: http://www.persecution.com/

History 1969, as *Jesus to the Communist World*, by Rev Richard Wurmbrand. Subsequently, name changed to *Christian Missions to the Communist World International* or *Christian Missions to the Communist World (CMCW)*. Present name adopted 1992. **Aims** Minister to *persecuted Christians* in communist, Islamic and other countries closed to the *gospel* of Christ and in countries emerging from communism, by providing *Bibles* and Christian literature and making *evangelical broadcasts* in their own languages; give relief to families of Christian martyrs in these countries; bring non-Christians in the free world to Christ; educate Christians in the West about atrocities committed against Christians in communist, Islamic and other countries opposed to the gospel of Christ. **Structure** *International Christian Association (ICA, #12556)* coordinates worldwide ministries through country offices established in about 38 countries as a result of Pastor Richard and Sabina Wurmbrand's international travels following their arrival in USA from Romania. Belgian branch: *Hulp aan de Verdrukte Kerk (HVK)*. **Finance** Donations. Annual budget: about US$ 58,000,000. **Events** *Annual conference* Indianapolis, IN (USA) 1997. **Publications** *The Voice of the Martyrs* (12 a year). Books; pamphlets.
Members Works in 88 countries and territories:
Afghanistan, Albania, Angola, Argentina, Armenia, Australia, Austria, Bahrain, Bangladesh, Belgium, Bhutan, Bolivia, Bosnia-Herzegovina, Botswana, Brazil, Bulgaria, Cambodia, Cameroon, Canada, Central African Rep, Chad, China, Colombia, Congo Brazzaville, Congo DR, Costa Rica, Croatia, Cuba, Czechia, Denmark, Egypt, El Salvador, Estonia, Ethiopia, Finland, Germany, Ghana, Guatemala, Haiti, Honduras, Hong Kong, Hungary, India, Indonesia, Iran Islamic Rep, Israel, Japan, Kenya, Korea Rep, Kuwait, Latvia, Lithuania, Madagascar, Malawi, Malaysia, Mexico, Moldova, Mozambique, Myanmar, Nepal, Netherlands, New Zealand, Nicaragua, Nigeria, Pakistan, Paraguay, Peru, Philippines, Portugal, Romania, Rwanda, Saudi Arabia, Slovakia, Somalia, South Africa, Sudan, Sweden, Switzerland, Tanzania UR, Türkiye, Uganda, UK, Ukraine, Uruguay, USA, Vietnam, Zambia, Zimbabwe.
NGO Relations Associate Member of: *World Evangelical Alliance (WEA, #21393)*. Instrumental in setting up: *Release International*. [2017.03.10/XF1331/**F**]

♦ Voices of African Mothers (internationally oriented national body)
♦ Voices Against Poverty / see UN Millennium Campaign (#20709)

♦ Voices Without Frontiers (VWF) 20805

Voix sans frontières (VSF) – Voces Sin Fronteras

International Secretariat 2 Sainte-Catherine East Street, Ste 102, Montréal QC H2X 1K4, Canada. T. +15149820351. Fax +15148497129. E-mail: secretariat@si.amarc.org.

History Founded Oct 1996, Copenhagen (Denmark), under the umbrella of European section of *Association mondiale des radiodiffuseurs communautaires (AMARC, #02810)*. **Aims** Promote equal *rights*; campaign against *racial discrimination*. [2015.06.01/XE4483/**E**]

♦ Voice and Speech Trainers Association (internationally oriented national body)
♦ **VOICE** Voluntary Organisations in Cooperation in Emergencies (#20809)
♦ Voice of Women / see Canadian Voice of Women for Peace
♦ Voie infinie (#11188)
♦ Voir Ensemble (unconfirmed)
♦ VOIR – Organisation internationale pour la recherche sur les associations et l'action volontaire (inactive)
♦ La voix européenne des Autorités Locals et Régionales pour le développement / see PLATFORMA (#18397)
♦ Voix des femmes / see Canadian Voice of Women for Peace
♦ Voix des femmes canadiennes pour la paix (internationally oriented national body)
♦ La Voix du patrimoine culturel / see Europa Nostra (#05767)
♦ Voix sans frontières (#20805)
♦ Volens – Volontariat et coopération internationale – Volontaires de l'enseignement (internationally oriented national body)
♦ Volkenrechtelijk Instituut, Utrecht / see Utrecht Centre for International Legal Studies
♦ Volkshilfe Österreich (internationally oriented national body)
♦ Volkskerk van Afrika (internationally oriented national body)
♦ Volkswagen Foundation (internationally oriented national body)
♦ VolkswagenStiftung (internationally oriented national body)
♦ Volontaires des Nations Unies (#20650)
♦ Volontariaat en Internationale Samenwerking – Vrijwilligers voor het Onderwijs (internationally oriented national body)
♦ Volontariat et coopération internationale – Volontaires de l'enseignement (internationally oriented national body)
♦ Volontariat international femmes éducation développement (#20806)
♦ Volontariato Internazionale Canossiano / see Fondazione Canossiana Voica

♦ Volontariato Internazionale Donna Educazione Sviluppo (VIDES) ... 20806

Volontariat international femmes éducation développement – International Volunteerism Organization for Women, Education, Development

Gen Dir via Gregorio VII, 133, 00165 Rome RM, Italy. T. +39066390196 – +39639379861. Fax +396632001 – +396632006. E-mail: ufficioprogetti@vides.org.
Registered Office Rue Victor Lowet 12, 1083 Brussels, Belgium. T. +3224680546. Fax +3224680602.
Main Website: http://www.vides.org/

History 30 Nov 1987, Italy. Former names and other names: *VIDES International* – alias. Registration: Banque-Carrefour des Entreprises, No/ID: 0445.306.016, Start date: 23 Apr 1991, Belgium. **Aims** Defend human rights, especially of women, children and young people; promote volunteering at local and international level; support children and their families; promote leadership of young people as active and responsible citizens. **Structure** General Assembly; Directive Council; Presidential Council; Commissions (2). **Languages** English, French, Italian, Portuguese, Spanish. **Staff** 2.50 FTE, paid; 2.00 FTE, voluntary. **Finance** Sources: donations; gifts, legacies; grants; members' dues. **Activities** Advocacy/lobbying/activism; events/meetings; networking/liaising; projects/programmes; training/education. Active in all member countries. **Events** *Asian Seminar* Ho Chi Minh City (Vietnam) 2019, *African Seminar* Lusaka (Zambia) 2019, *European Seminar* Rome (Italy) 2019, *Round Table* Rome (Italy) 2019, *Seminar* Santo Domingo (Dominican Rep) 2019. **Publications** *VIDES* (4 a year). *VIDES: un progetto per i giovani. Una storia che contagia* (2020) by MariaGrazia Caputo in Italian; *For a Civilization of Love: 25 Years of Youth Volunteering for the Young* (2012); *La Vita a Passo di Donna* (2010); *Essere Donna in Asia: Dai Diritti Violati a una Nuova Cultura di Pace* (2004); *A Model to Evaluate Actions and Policies on Social Inclusion* (2001) by Liliana Leone Leone. Leaflet; reports; papers.
Members Organizations and individuals in 48 countries:
Argentina, Austria, Belgium, Brazil, Cambodia, Cameroon, Canada, Chile, Colombia, Congo Brazzaville, Congo DR, Costa Rica, Czechia, Dominican Rep, El Salvador, Equatorial Guinea, France, Gabon, Germany, Guatemala, Haiti, Honduras, Hungary, India, Ireland, Italy, Japan, Kenya, Korea Rep, Lesotho, Mexico, Nicaragua, Panama, Philippines, Poland, Portugal, Slovakia, Slovenia, South Africa, Spain, Switzerland, Thailand, UK, Uruguay, USA, Venezuela, Vietnam, Zambia.
Consultative Status Consultative status granted from: *ECOSOC (#05331)* (Special). **IGO Relations** Associated with the Department of Global Communications of the United Nations. **NGO Relations** Member of (4): *Conference of Non-Governmental Organizations in Consultative Relationship with the United Nations (CONGO, #04635)*; *Federation of European and International Associations Established in Belgium (FAIB, #09508)*; *Forum of Catholic Inspired NGOs (#09905)*; *International Catholic Centre of Geneva (ICCG, #12449)*. [2021/XF1813/**F**]

♦ Volontariato Internazionale per lo Sviluppo (internationally oriented national body)
♦ Volontarie di Don Bosco (religious order)
♦ Volontari Italiani per la Solidarietà ai Paesi Emergenti (internationally oriented national body)
♦ Volontari nel Mondo – FOCSIV – Federazione Organismi Cristiani Servizio Internazionale Volontario (internationally oriented national body)

♦ Volonteurope 20807

SG Mundo-j, Rue de l'Industrie 10, 1000 Brussels, Belgium. T. +442037805878. E-mail: info@volonteurope.eu.
URL: http://www.volonteurope.eu/

History 21 May 1981, Utrecht (Netherlands). Former names and other names: *International Network Promoting Volunteer Action Across Europe* – former; *Réseau international pour la promotion du volontariat* – former; *Red Internacional para la Promoción del Voluntariado en Europa* – former; *Internationale Netzwerk für die Verbreitung von Voluntäraktivitäten in Europa* – former; *Rete Internazionale per la Promozione del Volontariato in Europa* – former; *Committee to encourage Unpaid Volunteer Action in Countries of Europe* – former; *Comité de promotion de l'action volontaire dans les pays d'Europe* – former. Registration: Banque-Carrefour des Entreprieses, No/ID: 0743.517.173, Start date: 11 Feb 2020, Belgium; Netherlands; EU Transparency Register, No/ID: 834514818751-23, Start date: 11 Sep 2015. **Aims** Promote the values and principles of volunteering, active citizenship and social justice at local, regional, national and European level. **Structure** Board; Secretariat. **Languages** English, French, Spanish. **Staff** 4.00 FTE, paid. **Finance** Subsidies; grants; participants' contributions. **Events** *Annual Conference* Brussels (Belgium) 2019, *Annual Conference* Gdansk (Poland) 2018, *Annual Conference* Brussels (Belgium) 2017, *Annual Conference* Nantes (France) 2016, *Annual Conference* Seville (Spain) 2015. **Publications** *Journal No 7*; *Volonteurope Newsletter*. Reports.
Members Member or associate organizations in 21 countries:
Albania, Belgium, Bulgaria, Czechia, Denmark, France, Germany, Greece, Hungary, Ireland, Italy, Lithuania, Malta, Netherlands, North Macedonia, Poland, Portugal, Romania, Slovenia, Spain, UK.
Consultative Status Consultative status granted from: *Council of Europe (CE, #04881)* (Participatory Status). **IGO Relations** Partner of: *European Commission (EC, #06633)* Europe for Citizens Programme. Member of: *European Economic and Social Committee (EESC, #06963)* Liaison Group. **NGO Relations** Member of (4): *Civil Society Europe*; *European Council for Non-Profit Organizations (#06834)*; *Lifelong Learning Platform – European Civil Society for Education (LLLP, #16466)*; *Social Platform (#19344)*. Supports (1): *Association pour le volontariat en Europe (AVE, #02978)*. [2021/XE0094/**F**]

♦ Volta Basin Authority (VBA) 20808

Autorité du Bassin de la Volta (ABV)

Acting Exec Dir 10 PO Box 13621, Ouagadougou, Burkina Faso. T. +22650376067. Fax +22650376486. E-mail: secretariat.abv@gmail.com.
URL: http://abv.int/

History Volta Basin Technical Committee (VBTC) set up Jul 2004. Draft convention approved Jul 2006. Convention signed 19 Jan 2007, Ouagadougou (Burkina Faso). Statutes signed 16 Nov 2007 and into force 14 Aug 2009. **Aims** Promote permanent consultation and sustainable development of the water and related resources of the Volta basin for equitable distribution of benefits towards poverty alleviation and better socio-economic integration. **Structure** Assembly of Heads of State and Government; Council of Ministers in charge of Water Resources; Forum of the Parties; Committee of Experts; Executive Directorate, located in Ouagadougou (Burkina Faso). **Languages** English, French. **Staff** 32.00 FTE, paid. **Finance** Funding from Member States and Technical and Financial Partners, including: *African Development Bank (ADB, #00283)*; *Economic Community*

of West African States (ECOWAS, #05312) – Water Resources Coordination; *European Union (EU, #08967)*; *Facilité africaine de l'eau (FAE, #09233)*; *FAO Regional Office for Africa (FAO/RAF, #09265)*; Government of France; *International Union for Conservation of Nature and Natural Resources (IUCN, #15766)* – West and Central Africa Programme; *Swedish International Development Cooperation Agency (Sida)*. **Activities** Events/meetings; projects/programmes. **Events** *Forum of Parties* Ouagadougou (Burkina Faso) 2012. **Publications** Reports.
Members Governments of 6 countries:
Benin, Burkina Faso, Côte d'Ivoire, Ghana, Mali, Togo.
IGO Relations Partners include: *International Network of Basin Organizations (INBO, #14235)*; *Niger Basin Authority (NBA, #17134)*; *Organisation pour la mise en valeur du fleuve Sénégal (OMVS, #17815)*; *Volta River Authority (VRA)*; *West African Science Service Center on Climate Change and Adapted Land Use (WASCAL, #20897)*; *World Hydrological Cycle Observing System (WHYCOS, #21573)*; *World Meteorological Organization (WMO, #21649)*. **NGO Relations** Partners include: *Global Water Partnership (GWP, #10653)*.
[2022.10.11/XM1735/**F***]

- ♦ Voltaire Foundation (internationally oriented national body)
- ♦ Volta River Authority (internationally oriented national body)
- ♦ Volubilis – Réseau euro-méditerranéen pour la ville et les paysages (internationally oriented national body)
- ♦ Volubilis – Réseau européen pour l'environnement et les paysages / see Volubilis – Réseau euro-méditerranéen pour la ville et les paysages
- ♦ Volubilis – Volubilis – Réseau euro-méditerranéen pour la ville et les paysages (internationally oriented national body)
- ♦ Voluntariado Internacional para o Desenvolvimento Africano (internationally oriented national body)
- ♦ Voluntarios de las Naciones Unidas (#20650)
- ♦ Voluntarios Optometristas al Servicio de la Humanidad (internationally oriented national body)
- ♦ Voluntary Euthanasia Research Foundation / see Exit International (#09224)
- ♦ Voluntary Fund for the United Nations Decade of Disabled Persons / see United Nations Voluntary Fund on Disability (#20648)
- ♦ Voluntary Human Extinction Movement (unconfirmed)
- ♦ Voluntary Organisations Cooperation in Emergencies / see Voluntary Organisations in Cooperation in Emergencies (#20809)

♦ Voluntary Organisations in Cooperation in Emergencies (VOICE) . . . 20809

Main Office Rue Royale 71, 1000 Brussels, Belgium. T. +3225411360. Fax +3225349953. E-mail: voice@voiceeu.org.
URL: https://voiceeu.org/
History Jun 1992, Brussels (Belgium), as *Voluntary Organisations Cooperation in Emergencies*, as part of the *Liaison Committee of Development NGOs to the European Union (NGDO-EU Liaison Committee, inactive)*, to follow EU humanitarian aid under *ECHO (inactive)*. Independent network as of 2001. Registered in accordance with Belgian law since 2001. EU Transparency Register: 47126711656-13. Registration: ASBL/VZW, No/ID: BE0475213787, Belgium. **Aims** Assist members with donor requirements (EC DG Humanitarian Aid); prepare and facilitate dialogue between NGOs and the European Union; monitor EU humanitarian policies and procedures and explore lobby opportunities; influence other European institutions; defend and promote humanitarian principles, such as impartiality and independence. **Structure** General Assembly (Forum); Board; Executive Committee; Secretariat, based in Brussels (Belgium). **Languages** English. **Staff** 4.00 FTE, paid. 1 intern. **Finance** Members' dues. **Activities** Networking/liaising; knowledge management/information dissemination; events/meetings; training/education; advocacy/lobbying/activism. **Events** *Charter4Change Annual Meeting* Copenhagen (Denmark) 2019, *World Humanitarian Summit* Brussels (Belgium) 2016, *General Assembly* Brussels (Belgium) 2009, *General Assembly* Brussels (Belgium) 2008, *Field security and perception: experiences from crisis situations* Brussels (Belgium) 2007. **Publications** *VOICE FLASH* (12 a year) – e-newsletter, members only; *VOICE OUT LOUD* (2 a year) – newsletter. Annual reports; press releases; position statements; policy briefings; papers on humanitarian aid in the European framework.
Members Professional humanitarian NGOs in 19 European countries:
Austria, Belgium, Czechia, Denmark, Finland, France, Germany, Greece, Ireland, Italy, Luxembourg, Netherlands, Norway, Poland, Slovakia, Spain, Sweden, Switzerland, UK.
Included in the above, 48 organizations listed in this Yearbook:
- *Action Against Hunger (#00086)* (UK-France-Spain);
- *ActionAid (#00087)* (UK);
- *Adventist Development and Relief Agency International (ADRA, #00131)* (Denmark-Germany-UK);
- *Agency for Technical Cooperation and Development (ACTED)*;
- *CARE International (CI, #03429)* (Austria-France-Germany-Netherlands-UK);
- *Caritas Europa (#03579)* (Austria-Germany-Italy-Luxembourg-Spain);
- *Catholic Agency for Overseas Development (CAFOD)*;
- *Catholic Organization for Relief and Development (Cordaid)*;
- *CESVI Fondazione*;
- *Christian Aid* (UK);
- *Comitato Internazionale per lo Sviluppo dei Popoli (CISP)*;
- *Concern Worldwide*;
- *Danish Refugee Council (DRC)*;
- *Diakonie Katastrophenhilfe*;
- *Fida International*;
- *Finn Church Aid (FCA)*;
- *Folkekirkens Nødhjaelp (FKN)*;
- *Hilfswerk International*;
- *Humanity and Inclusion (HI, #10975)* (Belgium-France);
- *ICCO – Interchurch Organization for Development Cooperation*;
- *INTERMON OXFAM*;
- *International Medical Corps (IMC)* (UK);
- *International Relief Service of Caritas Catholica, Belgium (CSI)* (Caritas Secours International);
- *International Rescue Committee (IRC, #14717)* (UK);
- *Islamic Relief Worldwide (IRWW, #16048)*;
- *Malteser International*;
- *MEDAIR*;
- *Médecins du Monde – International (MDM, #16613)* (Belgium-France-Greece-Portugal-Spain);
- *Medico International*;
- *Mercy Corps International (MCI)*;
- *Mission East*;
- *MSI Reproductive Choices*;
- *Norwegian Refugee Council (NRC)*;
- *Oxfam GB*;
- *Oxfam International (#17922)* (Oxfam Solidarité – Solidariteit Belgium of);
- *Oxfam Novib* (Oxfam Netherlands);
- *Plan International (#18386)* (Germany, UK);
- *PMU Interlife*;
- *Projection Europe (no recent information)*;
- *Secours catholique – Caritas France*;
- *Solidarités International*;
- *Tearfund, UK*;
- *Télécoms sans frontières (TSF)*;
- *Triangle génération humanitaire (TGH)*;
- *Trocaire – Catholic Agency for World Development*;
- *Welthungerhilfe*;
- *World Vision International (WVI, #21904)* (Austria-Finland-Germany-Netherlands-UK);
- *ZOA*.

NGO Relations Members of VOICE Board: *Action Against Hunger (#00086)*; *Agency for Technical Cooperation and Development (ACTED)*; *Concern Worldwide*; *Humanity and Inclusion (HI, #10975)*; *ICCO – Interchurch Organization for Development Cooperation*; *Malteser International*; *Norwegian Refugee Council (NRC)* Europe; *Plan International (#18386)*. Member of: *Active Learning Network for Accountability and Performance in Humanitarian Action (ALNAP, #00101)*. On Steering Committee of: *Global Humanitarian Platform (GHP, #10413)*.
[2020/XE1881/y/**E**]

- ♦ Voluntary Service International (internationally oriented national body)
- ♦ Voluntary Service Overseas (internationally oriented national body)
- ♦ Voluntas Dei Institute (religious order)
- ♦ Volunteer Africa (internationally oriented national body)
- ♦ Volunteering Matters (internationally oriented national body)
- ♦ Volunteer International Christian Service (internationally oriented national body)
- ♦ Volunteer Optometric Services to Humanity International (internationally oriented national body)
- ♦ Volunteers Centre for Development Cooperation, Gorizia (internationally oriented national body)
- ♦ Volunteers for Economic Growth Alliance (internationally oriented national body)
- ♦ Volunteer Service Abroad (internationally oriented national body)
- ♦ Volunteers for Inter-American Development Assistance (internationally oriented national body)
- ♦ Volunteers for International Development / see Peaceworkers USA
- ♦ Volunteers for Peace (internationally oriented national body)
- ♦ **VOM** The Voice of the Martyrs (#20804)

♦ Voorburg Group on Service Statistics 20810

Co-Chair c/o Statistics Norway, Akersveien 26, 0177 Oslo, Norway. T. +4762885000.
Sec Service Sector Statistics Div, US Census Bureau, Dept of Commerce, Washington DC 20233-6100, USA. T. +13017632683. Fax +13017636843.
URL: http://www.voorburggroup.org/
History 1986, at the request from *United Nations Statistical Office (UNSTAT, inactive)*. Name derives from Voorburg (Netherlands) where the first meeting was held, Jan 1987. **Aims** Establish an internationally comparable methodology for measuring the constant *dollar* outputs of the service industries. **Structure** Bureau of 5. **Languages** English. **Staff** Voluntary. Meetings staffed by host country. **Finance** Financed by member organizations. Meetings financed by host country. **Activities** Develops concepts, methods and best practices in the area of services, centred on producer price indices for services, turnover by products and classifications. **Events** *Annual Meeting* Paris (France) 2019, *Annual Meeting* Rome (Italy) 2018, *Annual Meeting* Delhi (India) 2017, *Annual Meeting* Zagreb (Croatia) 2016, *Annual Meeting* Sydney, NSW (Australia) 2015. **Publications** Reports; papers.
Members in 29 countries:
Australia, Austria, Canada, China, Czechia, Fiji, Finland, France, Germany, Greece, Hungary, India, Ireland, Israel, Italy, Japan, Latvia, Lithuania, Mexico, Netherlands, New Zealand, Norway, Poland, Slovenia, Spain, Sweden, UK, USA, Vietnam.
IGO Relations *European Central Bank (ECB, #06466)*; *OECD (#17693)*; *Statistical Institute for Asia and the Pacific (SIAP, #19972)*; *Statistical Office of the European Union (Eurostat, #19974)*; *United Nations (UN, #20515)* Statistics Division.
[2017/XM3083/**E***]

- ♦ Voorzieningsagentschap van Euratom (#05617)
- ♦ Vorläufiges europäisches abkommen über die systeme der sozialen sicherheit für den fall des alters, der invalidität und zugunsten der hinterbliebenen (1953 treaty)
- ♦ Vorläufiges europäisches abkommen über soziale sicherheit unter ausschluss der systeme für den fall des alters, der invalidität und zugunsten der hinterbliebenen (1953 treaty)
- ♦ VOSH International – Volunteer Optometric Services to Humanity International (internationally oriented national body)
- ♦ VOS – Veterans of Safety International (internationally oriented national body)

♦ VoteWatch Europe 20811

Contact Av de Tervueren 32-34, Box 1, 1040 Brussels, Belgium. T. +3223181191. E-mail: secretariat@votewatcheurope.eu.
URL: http://www.votewatch.eu/
History Launched early 2009. **Aims** Provide visibility to issues that affect all *EU* countries, both smaller and bigger, and all societal sectors. **Structure** General Assembly; Board; Coordinating Team. **Finance** Main funding sources: Adessium Foundation; *Joseph Rowntree Charitable Trust*; *Open Society Foundations (OSF, #17763)*; subscription fees and other paid services; individual donations. Annual budget (2015): euro 220,000. **NGO Relations** Member of: *European Policy Centre (EPC, #08240)*.
[2017/XM5708/**F**]

- ♦ VOW / see Canadian Voice of Women for Peace
- ♦ VOW – Canadian Voice of Women for Peace (internationally oriented national body)
- ♦ La voz europea de las autoridades Locales y Regionales para el desarrollo / see PLATFORMA (#18397)
- ♦ VOZ Evropejskoe Regionalnoe Bjuro / see WHO Regional Office for Europe (#20945)
- ♦ La Voz De Los Martires (#20804)
- ♦ A Voz Dos Martires (#20804)
- ♦ **VPA** Violence Prevention Alliance (#20781)
- ♦ **VPH Institute** Virtual Physiological Human Institute for Integrative Biomedical Research (#20790)
- ♦ **VPI** Visegrad Patent Institute (#20795)
- ♦ Vrabio Ginekes tis Evropis (#20993)
- ♦ Pour un vrai développement durable (internationally oriented national body)
- ♦ VRA – Volta River Authority (internationally oriented national body)
- ♦ Vredeseilanden / see Friends of the Islands of Peace
- ♦ Vredeseilanden / see Rikolto
- ♦ Vredeseilanden – Coopibo / see Rikolto
- ♦ Vredeseilanden – Vrienden van de Vredeseilanden (internationally oriented national body)
- ♦ Vredespaleis (internationally oriented national body)
- ♦ VREDE – Studie- en Informatiecentrum voor Vredes- en Ontwikkelingsproblematie (internationally oriented national body)
- ♦ VREDE – Study and Information Centre for Peace and Development Problems (internationally oriented national body)
- ♦ Vredesuniversiteit (internationally oriented national body)
- ♦ **VRE** Versammlung der Regionen Europas (#02316)
- ♦ **VR Foundation** Vitiligo Research Foundation (#20799)
- ♦ Vrienden van de Vredeseilanden (internationally oriented national body)
- ♦ Vrienden van de Vredeseilanden en de Aktie Vredesbrood / see Friends of the Islands of Peace
- ♦ **VRIF** Virtual Reality Industry Forum (#20791)
- ♦ VR Industry Forum / see Virtual Reality Industry Forum (#20791)
- ♦ VRML Consortium / see Web3D Consortium (#20844)
- ♦ Vrouwen in de Euregio Maas-Rijn (#09734)
- ♦ Vrouwen van Europa / see Association femmes d'Europe
- ♦ Vrouwen in techniek en exact (#06276)
- ♦ VSA / see VSA
- ♦ VSA (internationally oriented national body)
- ♦ VSA arts / see VSA
- ♦ VSA – Volunteer Service Abroad (internationally oriented national body)
- ♦ Vsemirnaja Akademija Iskusstva i Nauki (#21065)
- ♦ Vsemirnaja Associacija Institutov i Obscestv po Izuceniju Istorii i Socialnyh Problem Rabocego Dvizenija (inactive)
- ♦ Vsemirnaja Federacija Demokraticeskoj Molodezi (#21427)
- ♦ Vsemirnaja Federacija Obedinennyh Gorodov (inactive)
- ♦ Vsemirnaja Federacija Profsojuzov (#21493)
- ♦ Vsemirnaja Psihiatriceskaja Associacija (#21741)
- ♦ Vsemirnaja Veterinarnaja Associacija (#21901)
- ♦ Vsemirnaya Turistskaya Organizatsiya (#21861)
- ♦ Vsemirnyj Centr Informacii po Dvuhjazycnomu Obrazovaniju / see Information Centre for Bilingual and Plurilingual Education (#11195)
- ♦ Vsemirnyj Gornyj Kongress (#21654)
- ♦ Vsemirnyj Sojuz Evrejskih Studentov / see World Union of Jewish Students (#21878)
- ♦ Vsemirnyj Sovet Mira (#21717)
- ♦ Vseobscaja Konfederacija Profsojuzov (#10108)

♦ Vsesoyuznoye Obshchestvo Aviastroiteley (inactive)
♦ **VSE** Victim Support Europe (#20767)
♦ VSF-CICDA / see Agronomes et vétérinaires sans frontières
♦ VSF Europa / see Vétérinaires Sans Frontières International (#20760)
♦ **VSF International** Vétérinaires Sans Frontières International (#20760)
♦ VSF-Int / see Vétérinaires Sans Frontières International (#20760)
♦ **VSF** Voix sans frontières (#20805)
♦ VSI – Voluntary Service International (internationally oriented national body)
♦ **VSMM Society** International Society on Virtual Systems and Multimedia (#15544)
♦ **VSM** Vsemirnyj Sovet Mira (#21717)
♦ VSO International / see Voluntary Service Overseas
♦ VSO – Voluntary Service Overseas (internationally oriented national body)
♦ VTB – Vereniging Tropische Bossen (internationally oriented national body)
♦ Vues d'Afrique (internationally oriented national body)
♦ Vulgo de Lourdes – Congregatio Missionariorum Immaculatae Conceptionis Beatae Mariae Virginis (religious order)
♦ VVGP – Vital Voices Global Partnership (internationally oriented national body)
♦ VVI / see Vlaams Instituut voor Vrede en Geweldpreventie
♦ VVOB – Vlaamse Vereniging voor Ontwikkelingssamenwerking en Technische Bijstand (internationally oriented national body)
♦ VWC – Vereniging voor de Eenmaking van het Wereldchristendom (religious order)
♦ **VWF** Voices Without Frontiers (#20805)
♦ VWI – Vienna Wiesenthal Institute for Holocaust Studies (internationally oriented national body)
♦ **W3C** World Wide Web Consortium (#21935)
♦ W4B Alliance / see Wood Sector Alliance for the New European Bauhaus (#21046)
♦ W4RA – Web alliance for Regreening in Africa (internationally oriented national body)
♦ **W4** Women's WorldWide Web (#21039)
♦ W4W – Waves for Water (internationally oriented national body)
♦ **WAAA** West African Archeological Association (#20866)
♦ WAACLALS – West African Association for Commonwealth Literature and Language Studies (inactive)
♦ **WAAC** World Academy of Arts and Culture (#21066)
♦ WAADS – World Association of Alzheimer's Disease Scientists (inactive)
♦ **WAAEA** West African Association for Environmental Assessment (#20868)
♦ **WAAE** World Alliance for Arts Education (#21078)
♦ **WAAFoST** West African Association of Food Science and Technology (#20869)
♦ Waakzaamheidscomité voor de Europese Raden (internationally oriented national body)
♦ WAALD – West African Association of Agricultural Librarians and Documentalists (inactive)
♦ WAAME – West African Association for Marine Environment (internationally oriented national body)
♦ WAAM Network Configuration / see Workarea Art-Ambient (#21050)
♦ **WAAM** Workarea Art-Ambient (#21050)
♦ **WAANSA** West Africa Action Network on Small Arms (#20863)
♦ **WAAP** World Association for Animal Production (#21117)
♦ **WAAS** World Academy of Art and Science (#21065)
♦ WAATI – West African Association of Theological Institutions (no recent information)
♦ **WAAVP** World Association for the Advancement of Veterinary Parasitology (#21114)
♦ WAA – World Allium Association (inactive)
♦ **WAA** World Apheresis Association (#21097)
♦ **WAA** World Archery Asia (#21107)
♦ **WAA** World Association of Agronomists (#21115)
♦ **WAA** World Atlatl Association (#21210)
♦ WABA – West African Bankers' Association (no recent information)
♦ **WABA** West African Bar Association (#20870)
♦ **WABA** World Alliance for Breastfeeding Action (#21079)
♦ **WABCG** World Association of Beet and Cane Growers (#21120)
♦ **WABC** World Association of Basketball Coaches (#21119)
♦ **WABF** World Anti-Bullying Forum (#21094)
♦ **WABIL** World Ahlul Baytas Islamic League (#21073)
♦ **WABIP** World Association for Bronchology and Interventional Pulmonology (#21121)
♦ WABSE – World Associates for Biosystem Science and Engineering (internationally oriented national body)
♦ WABT – World Academy of Biomedical Technologies (internationally oriented national body)
♦ WAB / see World Association for Bronchology and Interventional Pulmonology (#21121)
♦ **WAB** World Association for Buiatrics (#21122)
♦ WAC / see WACI Health
♦ WACAF – West and Central African Action Plan (no recent information)
♦ **WACAHRI** West and Central Africa Human Rights Training Institute (#20906)
♦ WACANOR – West and Central African Operational Research Society (inactive)
♦ **WACAP** World Alliance of Cities Against Poverty (#21080)
♦ WACAP – World Association for Children and Parents (internationally oriented national body)
♦ WACA – World Affairs Councils of America (internationally oriented national body)
♦ **WACA** World Airlines Clubs Association (#21075)
♦ **WACB** West African Central Bank (#20871)
♦ WACB – West African Currency Board (inactive)
♦ WACB – World Association for Christian Broadcasting (inactive)
♦ WACC Network / see Women Against Cervical Cancer (#20985)
♦ WACCS – World Association of Chinese Character Studies (unconfirmed)
♦ **WACC** Women Against Cervical Cancer (#20985)
♦ **WACC** World Association for Christian Communication (#21126)
♦ WACC / see World Federation of Chinese Catering Industry (#21418)
♦ **WACEM** World Academic Council of Emergency Medicine (#21063)
♦ WACE – World Association of Chinese Epileptologists (unconfirmed)
♦ **WACE** World Association for Cooperative Education (#21128)
♦ WACH – West African Clearing House (inactive)
♦ WACI / see WACI Health
♦ WACI Health (internationally oriented national body)
♦ **WACIPAC** West African Centre for International Parasite Control (#20872)
♦ **WAC-I** We Are Church International (#20841)
♦ WACL / see World League for Freedom and Democracy (#21621)
♦ **WACN** West African College of Nursing (#20874)
♦ WACO System / see World Air Cargo Organization (#21074)
♦ **WACO** World Air Cargo Organization (#21074)
♦ WACPF – West Africa Centre for Peace Foundation (internationally oriented national body)
♦ **WACP** West African College of Physicians (#20875)
♦ **WACP** World Association of Cultural Psychiatry (#21130)
♦ WACRACT – West African Centre for Rural and Agricultural Credit Training (meeting series)
♦ **WACRAL** World Association of Christian Radio Amateurs and Listeners (#21127)
♦ **WACRA** World Association for Case Method Research and Application (#21123)
♦ **WACRA** Worldwide Airline Customer Relations Association (#21912)
♦ **WACREN** West and Central African Research and Education Network (#20908)
♦ WACSI – West Africa Civil Society Institute (internationally oriented national body)
♦ **WACSOF** West African Civil Society Forum (#20864)
♦ **WACS** West African College of Surgeons (#20876)
♦ WACS / see World Association of Chefs Societies (#21124)
♦ **WACS** World Association of Chefs Societies (#21124)
♦ **WAC** World Academy of Ceramics (#21067)
♦ **WAC** World Archaeological Congress (#21103)
♦ WAC – World Armenian Congress (meeting series)
♦ **WAC** World Association of Copepodologists (#21129)
♦ **WADAF** West African Association for the Development of Artisanal Fisheries (#20867)
♦ **WADA** World Anti-Doping Agency (#21096)
♦ **WADB** West African Development Bank (#03170)
♦ **WADC** West African Commission on Drugs (#20877)
♦ Wadden Sea Conference (meeting series)

♦ Wadden Sea Forum (WSF) 20812

Contact Virchowstrasse 1, 26382 Wilhelmshaven, Germany. T. +494421910818. Fax +494421910830.
URL: http://www.waddensea-forum.org/

History 2002, following decision by 9th Governmental Conference of the Trilateral Wadden Sea Cooperation (TWSC). 'Integrated Coastal Zone Management (ICZM)' adopted 2005; new ICZM strategy launched end 2013. Originally set up as an independent platform of stakeholder organizations in Denmark, Germany and Netherlands. Became a non-profit association, Apr 2011. **Aims** Foster *sustainable development* in the Wadden Sea Region. **Structure** General Assembly; Executive Board; Working Groups (5); Secretariat. **Languages** English. **Staff** 2.00 FTE, paid. **Finance** Financed by: Trilateral Wadden Sea Cooperation: Governments and regional authorities of Denmark, Germany and Netherlands. **Activities** Knowledge management/information dissemination; networking/liaising; projects/programmes; guidance/assistance/consulting. **Publications** Meeting documents; reports and studies; conference and symposium proceedings.
Members Representatives of local and regional user groups and organizations from 3 countries:
Denmark, Germany, Netherlands. [2018.08.07/XF6991/**F***]

♦ Waddenzee Conferentie (meeting series)
♦ **WADD** World Association on Dual Disorders (#21134)
♦ WADEA – West African Distance Education Association (inactive)
♦ **WADEM** World Association for Disaster and Emergency Medicine (#21133)
♦ **WADE** World Alliance for Decentralized Energy (#21081)
♦ WADE – World Association of Document Examiners (inactive)
♦ WADI – Association for Emergency Aid and Solidarity Development Cooperation (internationally oriented national body)
♦ WADI – Verband für Krisenhilfe und Solidarische Entwicklungszusammenarbeit (internationally oriented national body)

♦ Wado International Karate-Do Federation (WIKF) 20813

Wado Kokusai Karatedo Renmei

Sec 105 Vista Bay Drive, Campbell River BC V9W 6L5, Canada.
URL: http://www.wikf.com/

History 1991, by Tatsuo Suzuki. **Aims** Promote Wado Ryu Karate-Do as developed by Hironori Ohtsuka. **Structure** Regions (3): Asia; Europe; Pan America.
Members Clubs in 29 countries and territories:
Armenia, Australia, Belgium, Canada, Chile, Curaçao, Cyprus, Dominican Rep, France, Greece, India, Indonesia, Ireland, Italy, Japan, Malaysia, Morocco, Netherlands, Norway, Pakistan, Panama, Peru, Philippines, Portugal, Puerto Rico, Sweden, UK, USA, Venezuela. [2013.10.01/XD9300/**D**]

♦ Wado Kokusai Karatedo Renmei (#20813)
♦ **WADP** World Association for the Development of Philately (#21132)
♦ **WADP** World Association for Dynamic Psychiatry (#21135)
♦ **WAD** World Association of Detectives (#21131)
♦ **WAEC** West African Examinations Council (#20879)
♦ WAEDM / see World Association for Disaster and Emergency Medicine (#21133)
♦ **WAEH** World Association of Eclectic Hypnotherapists (#21137)
♦ **WAEH** World Association of Eye Hospitals (#21139)
♦ **WAEON** West Africa Election Observers Network (#20865)
♦ WAEO – World Aerospace Education Organization (no recent information)
♦ WAEP – World Association for Element-Building and Prefabrication (inactive)
♦ **WAER** World Association for Educational Research (#02811)
♦ **WAE** World Archery Europe (#21108)
♦ WAF / see International Federation of Armsports
♦ WAFAH – West African Federation of Associations for the Advancement of Handicapped Persons (no recent information)
♦ WAFA – World Association of Festivals and Artists (unconfirmed)
♦ **WAFA** World Association of Floral Artists (#21140)
♦ **WAFF** West Asian Football Federation (#20904)
♦ WAFI / see Aglow International (#00561)
♦ **WAFSRN** West African Farming Systems Research Network (#20880)
♦ **WAFUNIF** World Association of Former United Nations Internes and Fellows (#21141)
♦ WAF – World Agricultural Forum (internationally oriented national body)
♦ WAF / see World Armwrestling Federation (#21110)
♦ **WAF** World Armwrestling Federation (#21110)
♦ WAGC / see International Golf Federation (#13727)
♦ Wages Due Lesbians / see International Wages Due Lesbians
♦ **WAGF** West Asian Games Federation (#20905)
♦ **WAGF** World Assemblies of God Fellowship (#21111)
♦ **WAGGGS** World Association of Girl Guides and Girl Scouts (#21142)
♦ Waging Peace (internationally oriented national body)
♦ **WAGNET** Women and Gender in Chinese Studies Network (#20997)
♦ Wagon africain de gestion de nouvelles électroniques (see: #12575)
♦ WAGRA – World Assemblies of God Relief and Development Agency (see: #21111)
♦ **WAHA** Women and Health Alliance International (#21001)
♦ WAHC – West African Health Community (inactive)
♦ wahlbeobachtung.org (internationally oriented national body)
♦ **WAHO** West African Health Organization (#20881)
♦ **WAHO** World Arabian Horse Organization (#21102)
♦ **WAHRDN** West African Human Rights Defenders' Network (#20882)
♦ WAHS – World Association for Hallyu Studies (internationally oriented national body)
♦ **WAHTT** World Association for Hospitality and Tourism Education and Training (#21144)
♦ **WAHVM** World Association for the History of Veterinary Medicine (#21143)
♦ **WAICA** West African Insurance Companies Association (#20884)
♦ WAICENT – World Agricultural Information Centre (see: #09260)
♦ **WAidid** World Association for Infectious Diseases and Immunological Disorders (#21147)
♦ **WAIFEM** West African Institute for Financial and Economic Management (#20883)
♦ WAIFI – International Workshop on the Arithmetic of Finite Fields (meeting series)
♦ WAIFTR – World Alliance for International Friendship through the Churches (inactive)
♦ Waigani convention – Convention to Ban the Importation into Forum Island Countries of Hazardous Wastes and Radioactive Wastes and to Control the Transboundary Movement and Management of Hazardous Wastes within the South Pacific (1995 treaty)
♦ WAILA – West African Institute for Legal Aid (internationally oriented national body)
♦ **WAIMH** World Association for Infant Mental Health (#21146)
♦ **WAIM** World Association of Integrated Medicine (#21148)
♦ **WAINOVA** World Alliance for Innovation (#21082)
♦ Wainwright House (internationally oriented national body)
♦ WAIPAD – World Association for Infant Psychiatry and Allied Disciplines (inactive)

- ♦ **WAIPA** World Association of Investment Promotion Agencies (#21149)
- ♦ WAIS – West African Immunology Society (no recent information)
- ♦ WAIS – World Association of International Studies (internationally oriented national body)
- ♦ WAIS – World Association for Island Studies (internationally oriented national body)
- ♦ **WAITRO** World Association of Industrial and Technological Research Organizations (#21145)
- ♦ WAITS – World Artificial Organ, Immunology and Transplantation Society (no recent information)
- ♦ WAI – WASH Alliance International (internationally oriented national body)
- ♦ WAI – Weltverband der Arbeitnehmer in Industriebetrieben (inactive)
- ♦ WAI – Wire Association International (internationally oriented national body)
- ♦ WAJA / see West African Journalists' Union (#20885)
- ♦ **WAJ** World Association of Judges (#21150)
- ♦ **WAKO** World Association of Kickboxing Organizations (#21151)
- ♦ WALA – West African Library Association (no recent information)
- ♦ **WALA** World Airport Lawyers Association (#21076)
- ♦ **WALA** World Association for Laser Applications (#21152)
- ♦ WALCC – World Alliance for Low Carbon Cities (unconfirmed)
- ♦ WALCE – Women against Lung Cancer in Europe (internationally oriented national body)

♦ Walk21 Foundation (Walk21) 20814

CEO 24 Moorend Road, Cheltenham, GL5 0HD, UK. E-mail: network@walk21.com.
URL: https://www.walk21.com/

History 2000. Former names and other names: *Walk21 – Leading the Walking Movement* – full title. Registration: Charity Commission, No/ID: 1174564, England and Wales. **Aims** Ensure the right to walk and opportunity to enjoy is supported and encouraged for everyone worldwide. **Structure** Board of Trustees; Advisory Council; Team. **Activities** Advocacy/lobbying/activism; events/meetings; guidance/assistance/consulting; knowledge management/information dissemination; networking/liaising; training/education. **Events** *International Walk21 Conference on Walking and Liveable Communities* Dublin (Ireland) 2022, *International Walk21 Conference on Walking and Liveable Communities* Seoul (Korea Rep) 2021, *Walk21: International Conference on Walking and Liveable Cities* Seoul (Korea Rep) 2020, *Walk21: International Conference on Walking and Liveable Cities* Rotterdam (Netherlands) 2019, *Walk21: International Conference on Walking and Liveable Cities* Bogota (Colombia) 2018. [2022.10.19/AA0537/f/**F**]

- ♦ Walk21 – Leading the Walking Movement / see Walk21 Foundation (#20814)
- ♦ **Walk21** Walk21 Foundation (#20814)
- ♦ Walk Free Foundation (internationally oriented national body)
- ♦ Walking Tree Travel (internationally oriented national body)
- ♦ Wallace Global Fund (internationally oriented national body)
- ♦ Walled Towns Friendship Circle / see European Walled Towns (#09079)
- ♦ **WALN** World Association of Lebanese Neurosurgeons (#21156)
- ♦ **WALP** World Association of Law Professors (#21154)
- ♦ **WALS** West African Linguistics Society (#19506)
- ♦ **WALS** World Association of Lesson Studies (#21157)

♦ Walter E Dandy Neurosurgical Society (WEDNS) 20815

Headquarters 3635 Vista Ave, 5th Fl FDT, St Louis MO 63110, USA. T. +13145778716. Fax +13145778720.
URL: http://wedns.org/

History 19 Nov 2011, St Louis MO (USA). Named in honour of Walter E Dandy (1886-1946). **Aims** Be the premier neurosurgical society representing all neurosurgeons from across the globe, working collaboratively to enhance the field of neurosurgery and achieve better patient outcomes. **Structure** Executive Committee. *Dandy College of Neurosurgery (FCDN)*. Divisions (8): Cerebrovascular; Functional; Pediatric; Peripheral Nerve; Skull Base; Spine; Trauma; Tumor. Chapters on 4 continents. **Events** *Annual Meeting* Santa Monica, CA (USA) 2016. [2019/XM4597/**E**]

- ♦ Walter H Shorenstein Asia-Pacific Research Center (internationally oriented national body)
- ♦ Walther-Schücking-Institut de droit international (internationally oriented national body)
- ♦ Walther-Schücking-Institute for International Law (internationally oriented national body)
- ♦ Walther-Schücking-Institut für Internationales Recht (internationally oriented national body)
- ♦ **WALT** World Association for Laser Therapy (#21153)
- ♦ **WAL** World Association of Lawyers (#21155)
- ♦ **WAMA** West African Monetary Agency (#20887)
- ♦ **WAMA** World Alliance of Martial Arts (#21083)
- ♦ WAMA – World Anti-Aging Medical Association (inactive)
- ♦ WAMBA – World Aviation MBA Association (internationally oriented national body)
- ♦ **WAMDEVIN** West African Management Development Institutes Network (#20886)
- ♦ **WAME** World Association of Medical Editors (#21162)
- ♦ **WAMHF** World Association of Medical and Health Films (#21163)
- ♦ **WAM International** Women Advancing Microfinance International (#20983)
- ♦ WAMIP – World Alliance of Mobile Indigenous Peoples (unconfirmed)
- ♦ **WAMI** West African Monetary Institute (#20888)
- ♦ WAMI – World Association for Medical Informatics (inactive)
- ♦ WAMLA – West African Modern Language and Literature Association (inactive)
- ♦ **WAML** World Association for Medical Law (#21164)
- ♦ WAMM – Commonwealth Women's Affairs Ministers Meeting (meeting series)
- ♦ **WAMP** West African Museums Programme (#20890)
- ♦ WAMRAC / see World Association of Christian Radio Amateurs and Listeners (#21127)
- ♦ **WAMSB** World Association of Marching Show Bands (#21160)
- ♦ WAMSRA – Women's Association for Multidisciplinary Studies and Research in Africa (inactive)
- ♦ WAMS – World Academy of Medical Sciences (unconfirmed)
- ♦ **WAMS** World Association of Marine Stations (#21161)
- ♦ WAMS – World Association for Medical Sexology (unconfirmed)
- ♦ **WA-MS** World Association of Membrane Societies (#21165)
- ♦ WAMT – World Association of Majorette-sport and Twirling (unconfirmed)
- ♦ WAMU – West African Monetary Union (inactive)
- ♦ **WAM** World Anticancer Movement (#21095)
- ♦ **WAMY** World Assembly of Muslim Youth (#21112)
- ♦ **WAMZ** West African Monetary Zone (#20889)
- ♦ **WANAHR** World Alliance for Nutrition and Human Rights (#21084)
- ♦ WANA Institute – West Asia-North Africa Institute (internationally oriented national body)
- ♦ WANASO – Western African Network of AIDS Service Organizations (see: #00272)
- ♦ WANDA – World Alliance of Neuromuscular Disorder Associations (inactive)
- ♦ **WAND** Women and Development Unit (#20990)
- ♦ **WANEP** West Africa Network for Peacebuilding (#20878)
- ♦ WANGONeT – West African NGO Network (internationally oriented national body)
- ♦ **WANGO** World Association of Non-Governmental Organizations (#21167)
- ♦ **WAN-IFRA** World Association of Newspapers and News Publishers (#21166)
- ♦ **WANO** World Association of Nuclear Operators (#21168)
- ♦ **WANSED** West African Network on Security and Democratic Governance (#20892)
- ♦ **WANS** World Academy of Nursing Science (#21069)
- ♦ WAN – World Association of Navigation (inactive)
- ♦ WAN – World Association of Newspapers (inactive)

♦ WAO-Afrique 20816

Dir Rue des Frères Franciscains, BP 80242, Lomé, Togo. T. +2282258990. Fax +2282257345.
URL: http://waoafrique.org/

History 1989, as an autonomous organization within the framework of *World Association for Orphans and Abandoned Children (WAO, inactive)*. Became autonomous, 1990. **Aims** Promote the *rights* of *children* in Africa; give children in difficult situations equal opportunities in life by mobilizing resources necessary to satisfy their basic needs and providing them with a secure and stimulating environment; promote, monitor and evaluate application of children's rights such as recognized by the United Nations convention; encourage a response to conscience and create a common platform on questions of children's and *human rights* in Africa. **Structure** Board of Directors. **NGO Relations** Member of: *Child Rights Connect (#03884)*. Cooperates with: *International Bureau for Children's Rights (IBCR, #12412)*. [2010/XE2498/**E**]

- ♦ **WAOCS** World Academy of Cosmetic Surgery (#21068)
- ♦ **WAOE** World Association for Online Education (#21169)
- ♦ WAO – Workshop on Accelerator Operations (meeting series)
- ♦ **WAO** World Allergy Organization – IAACI (#21077)
- ♦ **WAO** World Alliance of Organizations for the Prevention and Treatment of Genetic and Congenital Conditions (#21085)
- ♦ **WAO** World Archery Oceania (#21109)
- ♦ **WAO** World Autism Organisation (#21211)
- ♦ **WAPA** World Apple and Pear Association (#21098)
- ♦ WAPBD / see World Alliance of Organizations for the Prevention and Treatment of Genetic and Congenital Conditions (#21085)
- ♦ WAPCCP / see World Association for Person-Centered and Experiential Psychotherapy and Counseling (#21172)
- ♦ **WAPCEPC** Weltverband für Personzentrierte und Experienzielle Psychotherapie und Beratung (#21172)
- ♦ **WAPCEPC** World Association for Person-Centered and Experiential Psychotherapy and Counseling (#21172)
- ♦ **WAPCO** West African Postal Conference (#20893)
- ♦ WAPCP – West African Postgraduate College of Pharmacists (internationally oriented national body)
- ♦ **WAPC** World Association of Press Councils (#21175)
- ♦ WAPDAA – World Association for Prevention of Drug and Alcohol Abuse (inactive)
- ♦ **WAPES** World Association of Public Employment Services (#21179)
- ♦ **WAPE** World Association for Political Economy (#21173)
- ♦ WAPF – West African Pharmaceutical Federation (no recent information)
- ♦ WAPMERR – World Agency of Planetary Monitoring and Earthquake Risk Reduction (internationally oriented national body)
- ♦ **WAPM** World Association of Perinatal Medicine (#21170)
- ♦ **WAPOR** World Association for Public Opinion Research (#21180)
- ♦ **WAPO** World Alliance of Pituitary Organizations (#21087)
- ♦ **WAPP** West African Power Pool (#20894)
- ♦ **WAPP** World Association for Personality Psychology (#21171)
- ♦ WAPP / see World Association for Positive and Transcultural Psychotherapy (#21174)
- ♦ **WAPP** World Association for Positive and Transcultural Psychotherapy (#21174)
- ♦ **WAPR** World Association for Psychosocial Rehabilitation (#21178)
- ♦ WAPS – World Academy of Productivity Science (internationally oriented national body)
- ♦ WAPS / see World Association of Societies of Pathology and Laboratory Medicine (#21191)
- ♦ **WAPTE** World Alliance for Pentecostal Theological Education (#21086)
- ♦ WAPTT / see World Association for Hospitality and Tourism Education and Training (#21144)
- ♦ **WAP** World Association of Psychoanalysis (#21177)
- ♦ WARA – West African Research Association (internationally oriented national body)
- ♦ WARBICA – West African Regional Branch of the International Council on Archives (see: #12996)
- ♦ WARC European Area Council / see Council of the World Communion of Reformed Churches in Europe (#04924)

♦ War Child International 20817

War Child Holland Helmholtzstraat 61-G, 1098 LE Amsterdam, Netherlands. T. +31204227777. Fax +31204204716. E-mail: info@warchild.nl.
War Child UK Studio 320, Highgate Studios, 53-97 Highgate Road, London, NW5 1TL, UK. T. +442071122556. E-mail: info@warchild.org.uk.
URL: http://www.warchild.org/

History Feb 1993, London (UK). Founded by social entrepreneur Willemijn Verloop and British film-makers Bill Leeson and David Wilson, as a result of the war in former Yugoslavia. Registration: Charities Commission, No/ID: 1071659, England and Wales. **Aims** Strengthen the resilience and well-being of children living with violence and armed conflict. **Structure** Implementing Offices – War Child Canada; War Child Holland; War Child UK – operate independently. Offices in Australia, Ireland, Sweden, USA. **Languages** Dutch, English, French, German, Spanish, Swedish. **Staff** 496.00 FTE, paid. **Finance** Sources: donations; fundraising; government support; international organizations; revenue from activities/projects. Support from European Commission; United Nations agencies and funds; War Child UK; foundations; educational and religious institutions; associations. Other sources: periodical donations from Business Friend, one-off gifts from actions, donations in kind and restricted subsidies from companies. Annual budget: 51,045,098 EUR (2021). **Activities** Capacity building; conflict resolution; events/meetings; humanitarian/emergency aid. Active in: Afghanistan, Bangladesh, Burundi, Chad, Colombia, Congo DR, Germany, Iraq, Jordan, Lebanon, Netherlands, Palestine, Sierra Leone, South Sudan, Sri Lanka, Sudan, Sweden, Uganda, Yemen. **Events** *International Conference on Mental Health and Psychosocial Support in Crisis Situations* Amsterdam (Netherlands) 2019, *International conference* London (UK) 2005. **Publications** Annual Report. **IGO Relations** Member of (1): *Department for International Development (DFID, inactive)* (CSO Youth Working Group and Child Rights Working Group). Cooperates with (4): *European Union (EU, #08967)*; *FAO (#09260)*; *UNICEF (#20332)*; *United Nations Population Fund (UNFPA, #20612)*. **NGO Relations** Partner of (10): BRAC International; Center for Children's Happiness; ChildFund; Collateral Repair Project; *Defence for Children International (DCI, #05025)*; *Mercy Corps International (MCI)*; *NetHope (#16979)*; *Save the Children International (#19058)*; SOS Children's Villages; World Vision US. Collaborates with organizations across the world. [2022.06.28/XF4002/**F**]

- ♦ WARCS – West African Regional Computer Society (inactive)
- ♦ WARC – West Africa Research Centre, Dakar (internationally oriented national body)
- ♦ WARC – World Alliance of Reformed Churches (inactive)
- ♦ WARDA / see Africa Rice Center (#00518)
- ♦ WAREG – European Water Regulators (unconfirmed)
- ♦ **WARFSA** Water Research Fund of Southern Africa (#20834)
- ♦ **WARF** West Africa Rural Foundation (#20902)
- ♦ **WARIMA** West African Research and Innovation Management Association (#20895)
- ♦ WAR – Movement for the Abolition of War (internationally oriented national body)
- ♦ **WARMTH** World Association of Radiopharmaceutical and Molecular Therapy (#21181)
- ♦ WARM – World Association of Reproductive Medicine (no recent information)
- ♦ WARN-CC – West Asia Regional Network on Climate Change (unconfirmed)
- ♦ WARN – World Against Racism Network (unconfirmed)
- ♦ War and Peace Foundation (internationally oriented national body)
- ♦ War Relief Services / see Catholic Relief Services (#03608)

♦ War Resisters' International (WRI) 20818

Internationale des résistants/résistantes à la guerre (IRG) – Internacional de Resistentes a la Guerra (IRG) – Internationale der Kriegsdienstgegner/innen/ (IdK) – Internationale van Oorlogstegenstanders (IOT) – Internacio de Militgerezistantoj

Main Office 5 Caledonian Road, London, N1 9DX, UK. T. +442072784040. E-mail: office@wri-irg.org – info@wri-irg.org.
URL: http://www.wri-irg.org/

History 1921, Netherlands. Movement reorganized and Headquarters moved to UK in 1923. Constitution revised: 1957, 1960, 1963, 1969, 1972, 1982, 1991, 2002. Former names and other names: *Paco* – former (1921 to 1923). **Aims** Help *pacifists* and their national organizations wage the nonviolent struggle for peace on a world scale; encourage creation of new peace organizations in countries where none exist; help conscientious objectors legally, financially and in other ways; provide an information service for dissemination of news about peace and social change activities everywhere; work for *disarmament* and abolition of conscription; provide a link among peace organizations and persons sincerely wishing (and working) for the abolition of war; promote nonviolence as an instrument of social change. **Structure** Conference (every 3-4 years). International Council, comprising 12 members (plus representatives from sections). Executive Committee of 4. **Languages** English, French, German, Spanish. **Staff** 2.50 FTE, paid. Some voluntary; volunteer translators. **Finance** Contributions from individuals and affiliated organizations; grants. **Activities** Works for legal recognition of conscientious objection to military service and the abolition of conscription. Organizes: training sessions in nonviolent direct action; protest and demonstrations against the arms race, militarism, military service. Established *'International Prisoners for Peace Day'*, organized each 1st December. Coordinates *'International Conscientious Objectors' Day'*, each 15th May. **Events** *Quadrennial Conference* Cape Town (South Africa) 2014, *Quadrennial Conference* Ahmedabad (India) 2010, *International working conference on no to war, no to NATO* Berlin (Germany) 2009, *Seminar* Neve Shalom (Israel) 2007, *Quadrennial Conference* Paderborn (Germany) 2006. **Publications** *Co-Update* (12 a year) in English, French, Spanish – e-newsletter; *War Profiteers' News* (6 a year) in English, Spanish – e-newsletter; *The Broken Rifle* (4 a year) in English, French, German, Spanish; *WRI Women* (annual); *Co-Alert* (on demand) – e-newsletter; *WRI-Info* (irregular) in English, French, German, Spanish – e-newsletter. Leaflets and pamphlets in various languages.
Members Sections; Associate; Associated Publications. Sections in 21 countries:
Australia, Belgium, Canada, Chile, Denmark, Finland, France, Georgia, Germany, Greece, Hungary, India, Italy, Japan, Netherlands, Norway, Spain, Sri Lanka, Sweden, UK, USA.
Included in the above, 2 organizations listed in this Yearbook:
Peace Pledge Union (PPU); *War Resisters League (WRL)*.
Associated organizations in 34 countries:
Austria, Belgium, Bosnia-Herzegovina, Canada, Chad, Colombia, Croatia, Ecuador, Finland, France, Georgia, Germany, India, Ireland, Israel, Italy, Japan, Korea Rep, Nepal, Nigeria, North Macedonia, Norway, Pakistan, Paraguay, Portugal, Romania, Serbia, Spain, Sudan, Switzerland, Türkiye, Uganda, UK, USA, Zimbabwe.
Included in the above, 1 organization listed in this Yearbook:
International Nonviolent Initiatives (INI).
Associated Publications in 2 countries:
Germany, UK.
IGO Relations *UNESCO (#20322)*. Associated with Department of Global Communications of the United Nations. [2020/XC3421/y/**C**]

♦ War Resisters League (internationally oriented national body)
♦ Warsaw Pact – Warsaw Treaty of Friendship, Cooperation and Mutual Assistance (1955 treaty)
♦ Warsaw Treaty of Friendship, Cooperation and Mutual Assistance (1955 treaty)
♦ Warsaw Treaty Organization (inactive)
♦ WARSE – World Academy of Research in Science and Engineering (unconfirmed)
♦ **WARSO** West African Road Safety Organisation (#20896)
♦ War-torn Societies Project / see Interpeace (#15962)
♦ War Trauma Foundation (internationally oriented national body)
♦ WARTU / see West Africa Road Transport Union (#20901)
♦ **WARTU** West Africa Road Transport Union (#20901)
♦ War on Want (internationally oriented national body)
♦ War on Want – Campaign Against World Poverty / see War on Want
♦ Warwick HRI (internationally oriented national body)
♦ Wasa Committee (inactive)
♦ WASAD – World Association for Stress Related and Anxiety Disorders (internationally oriented national body)
♦ WASAE – West Africa Society of Agricultural Engineering (unconfirmed)
♦ **WAS&AF** World Aerial Sports & Arts Federation (#21071)
♦ WASAPS – West Asia Society of Aesthetic Plastic Surgery (no recent information)
♦ WASA – West African Science Association (no recent information)
♦ **WASBE** World Association for Symphonic Bands and Ensembles (#21197)
♦ **WASCAL** West African Science Service Center on Climate Change and Adapted Land Use (#20897)
♦ WASCU – World Association for the Senior Citizens Union (inactive)
♦ WA/SDRC Niamey / see ECA Sub-Regional Office for West Africa (#05277)
♦ **WASD** World Association for Sustainable Development (#21196)
♦ Waseda Institute of Asia-Pacific Studies / see Institute of Asia-Pacific Studies Waseda University
♦ **WASER** World Association for Sedimentation and Erosion Research (#21186)
♦ **WASE** World Association for Supported Employment (#21195)
♦ WASH Alliance International (internationally oriented national body)
♦ WASH / see Global WASH Cluster (#10651)
♦ Washington Center of Foreign Policy Research / see Johns Hopkins Foreign Policy Institute, Washington DC
♦ Washington Global Health Alliance (internationally oriented national body)
♦ Washington Institute for Near East Policy (internationally oriented national body)
♦ Washington Office on Africa (internationally oriented national body)
♦ Washington Office on Latin America (internationally oriented national body)
♦ WASH United (internationally oriented national body)
♦ WASH / see World Action on Salt, Sugar & Health (#21070)
♦ WASKO – World All Styles Kickboxing Organization (no recent information)
♦ WASL – European Syrian Civil Society Exchange (unconfirmed)
♦ **WASLI** World Association of Sign Language Interpreters (#21188)
♦ WASME / see World Association for Small and Medium Enterprises (#21189)
♦ **WASME** World Association for Small and Medium Enterprises (#21189)
♦ **WASMQ** World Academic Society of Medical Qigong (#21064)
♦ WASM – World Association of Sleep Medicine (inactive)
♦ **WASM** World Association for Sport Management (#21194)
♦ WASOG – West African Society of Gastroenterology (inactive)
♦ **WASOG** World Association of Sarcoidosis and other Granulomatous Disorders (#21183)
♦ **WASPaLM** World Association of Societies of Pathology and Laboratory Medicine (#21191)
♦ WASP – West African Society for Pharmacology (inactive)
♦ **WASP** World Association for Social Psychiatry (#21190)
♦ WASP / see World Association of Societies of Pathology and Laboratory Medicine (#21191)

♦ Wassenaar Arrangement on Export Controls for Conventional Arms and Dual-Use Goods and Technologies (Wassenaar Arrangement) 20819

Arrangement de Wassenaar sur le contrôle des exportations d'armes conventionnelles et de biens et technologies à double usage – Wassenaar Arrangement Zu Exportkontrollen für konventionelle Rüstungsgüter und Dual-Use-Güter – Arreglo de Wassenaar Sobre Control de Exportaciones de Armas Convencionales y Productos y Tecnología de Doble Uso

Secretariat Mahlerstrasse 12, Stg 5, 1010 Vienna, Austria. T. +43196003. E-mail: secretariat@wassenaar.org.
URL: http://www.wassenaar.org/

History Jul 1996, Vienna (Austria). Established following agreement, Dec 1995, Wassenaar (Netherlands), by former members of *Coordinating Committee for Multilateral Strategic Export Controls (CoCom, inactive)*, the former COCOM cooperating countries and a number of other countries including Russia and several East and Central European countries. Negotiation process which preceded the establishment of the Wassenaar Arrangement referred to as *New Forum*. **Aims** Contribute to regional and international security and stability by promoting transparency and greater responsibility in transfers of conventional arms and dual-use goods and technologies, thus preventing destabilizing accumulations, as well as acquisition of these items by terrorists. **Structure** Plenary; Subsidiary Bodies; Secretariat in Vienna (Austria). **Languages** English. **Staff** 13.00 FTE, paid. **Finance** Sources: contributions of member/participating states. **Activities** Events/meetings; knowledge management/information dissemination; monitoring/evaluation; networking/liaising; standards/guidelines. **Events** *Plenary Meeting* Vienna (Austria) 2022, *Plenary meeting* Vienna (Austria) 2021, *Plenary meeting* Vienna (Austria) 2020, *Plenary Meeting* Vienna (Austria) 2019, *Plenary Meeting* Vienna (Austria) 2018.
Members Governments of 42 countries:
Argentina, Australia, Austria, Belgium, Bulgaria, Canada, Croatia, Czechia, Denmark, Estonia, Finland, France, Germany, Greece, Hungary, India, Ireland, Italy, Japan, Korea Rep, Latvia, Lithuania, Luxembourg, Malta, Mexico, Netherlands, New Zealand, Norway, Poland, Portugal, Romania, Russia, Slovakia, Slovenia, South Africa, Spain, Sweden, Switzerland, Türkiye, UK, Ukraine, USA. [2022.11.29/XF4482/**F***]

♦ Wassenaar Arrangement Zu Exportkontrollen für konventionelle Rüstungsgüter und Dual-Use-Güter (#20819)
♦ **Wassenaar Arrangement** Wassenaar Arrangement on Export Controls for Conventional Arms and Dual-Use Goods and Technologies (#20819)
♦ Wasser Solidarität / see Programme Solidarité eau (#18529)
♦ **WASSH** World Action on Salt, Sugar & Health (#21070)
♦ Wassu-UAB Foundation (internationally oriented national body)
♦ WASTE (internationally oriented national body)
♦ WASTE – advisers on urban environment and development / see WASTE
♦ waste electrical and electronic equipment / see WEEELABEX Organisation (#20851)
♦ waste electrical and electronic equipment / see European Association of Electrical and Electronic Waste Take Back Systems (#06022)
♦ WasteEng – International Conference on Engineering for Waste and Biomass Valorisation (meeting series)

♦ Waste Free Oceans (WFO) 20820

Contact Av Cortenbergh 71, 1000 Brussels, Belgium. T. +3227396379. Fax +3227324218. E-mail: contact@wastefreeoceans.org.
URL: http://www.wastefreeoceans.org/

History Registration: EU Transparency Register, No/ID: 063093925179-42, Start date: 20 Dec 2016. **Aims** Collect and transform ocean plastic; partner with business and organisations to collect plastic in oceans and recycle the collected plastic to create new products. **Structure** Headquarters: Brussels (Belgium). Offices (3): Americas; Asia; Turkey and MEA. **Activities** Advocacy/lobbying/activism; awareness raising. **IGO Relations** Partners: *Baltic Marine Environment Protection Commission – Helsinki Commission (HELCOM, #03126)*; *European Parliament (EP, #08146)*; *UNEP (#20299)*; *UNIDO (#20336)*. **NGO Relations** Partners: *Association des organisations nationales d'entreprises de pêche de l'UE (EUROPECHE, #02841)*; *Diplomatic Council (DC)*; *World Wide Fund for Nature (WWF, #21922)*. Member of: *Reloop Platform (Reloop, #18835)*. [2020.05.05/XM6096/**F**]

♦ Waste Free Waters (internationally oriented national body)
♦ **WASWAC** World Association of Soil and Water Conservation (#21192)
♦ **WAS** World Aquaculture Society (#21099)
♦ **WAS** World Archaeological Society (#21104)
♦ WAS / see World Association for Sexual Health (#21187)
♦ **WAS** World Association for Sexual Health (#21187)

♦ WATA 20821

SG Tranchepied 25, 1278 La Rippe VD, Switzerland. T. +41792397279. Fax +41793620753. E-mail: infos@wata-dmc.net.
URL: https://www.wata-dmc.net

History 5 May 1949, Geneva (Switzerland). Founded as *World Association of Travel Agencies (WATA)*. Now known only by acronym. Registration: Swiss Civil Code, Switzerland. **Aims** Contribute to profits of member agencies and their protection, by: assisting in development and organization of *tourism* and providing appropriate information to foster such development; reducing risks through collective action. **Structure** General Assembly; Executive Committee. **Languages** English. **Staff** 1.00 FTE, paid. **Finance** Members' dues. **Activities** Knowledge management/information dissemination; projects/programmes. **Events** *General Assembly* Armenia 2012, *General Assembly* Yerevan (Armenia) 2012, *General Assembly* Cyprus 2011, *General Assembly* Delhi (India) 2010, *General Assembly* Barcelona (Spain) 2009.
Members Independent travel agencies (one per metropolitan area unit). Members in 46 countries.
Armenia, Austria, Bhutan, Brazil, Bulgaria, Cape Verde, Chile, China, Croatia, Czechia, Egypt, Estonia, Ethiopia, France, Georgia, Germany, Ghana, Greece, India, Israel, Italy, Kenya, Lebanon, Madagascar, Mongolia, Morocco, Namibia, Nepal, Peru, Poland, Romania, Russia, Serbia, Slovakia, South Africa, Spain, Sri Lanka, Sudan, Switzerland, Syrian AR, Tanzania UR, Türkiye, Uganda, UK, United Arab Emirates, Vietnam. [2021/XF5043/**F**]

♦ **WATA** World Association of Arab Translators and Linguists (#21118)
♦ Watchlist on Children and Armed Conflict (internationally oriented national body)
♦ Watchlist – Watchlist on Children and Armed Conflict (internationally oriented national body)
♦ Watchman International Network (internationally oriented national body)
♦ **WATCH Society** International Society for Wearable Technology in Healthcare (#15546)
♦ Watch Tower Bible and Tract Society / see Jehovah's Witnesses (#16096)
♦ Watch Tower Bible and Tract Society of Pennsylvania / see Jehovah's Witnesses (#16096)
♦ WATCH – World Assembly on Tobacco Counters Health (meeting series)
♦ **WATCH** World Association for the Protection of Tangible and Intangible Cultural Heritage (#21176)
♦ WATD – World Association of Trainers in Development (no recent information)
♦ WATEF – World Association for Triple Helix and Future Strategy Studies (internationally oriented national body)
♦ Water 1st International (internationally oriented national body)

♦ WaterAid 20822

Exec Dir 2nd Floor, 47-49 Durham Street, London, SE11 5JD, UK. T. +442077934500. Fax +442077934545. E-mail: wateraid@wateraid.org.
URL: http://www.wateraid.org/

History 1981. Registration: Charity, No/ID: 288701, England and Wales; Charity, No/ID: SC039479, Start date: 3 Apr 2008, Scotland; No/ID: ABN 99 700 687 141, Australia; No/ID: 119288934, Canada; No/ID: 802426-1268, Sweden; No/ID: 30 018 1674, USA; EU Transparency Register, No/ID: 48655305058-87, Start date: 21 Jan 2011. **Aims** Transform lives by improving access to safe water, *hygiene* and sanitation in the world's *poorest* communities. **Structure** Board of Trustees. **Staff** 1000.00 FTE, paid. **Publications** *Oasis* (2 a year). Annual Review.
Members Offices in 7 countries:
Australia, Canada, India, Japan, Sweden, UK, USA.
Consultative Status Consultative status granted from: *African Commission on Human and Peoples' Rights (ACHPR, #00255)* (Observer); *ECOSOC (#05331)* (Special); *WHO (#20950)* (Official). **IGO Relations** Accredited organization of: *Green Climate Fund (GCF, #10714)*. **NGO Relations** Member of (12): *British Overseas NGO's for Development (BOND)* (Full); *End Water Poverty (EWP, #05464)*; *European Network on Debt and Development (EURODAD, #07891)*; *InsideNGO (inactive)*; *International Coalition for Trachoma Control (ICTC, #12624)*; *Millennium Water Alliance (MWA)*; *Neglected Tropical Diseased NGO Network (NNN, #16969)*; *NetHope (#16979)*; *PMNCH (#18410)*; *Think Global – Development Education Association (DEA)*; *Transparency, Accountability and Participation Network (TAP Network, #20222)*; *Water and Sanitation for the Urban Poor (WSUP)*. Partner of: *1,000 Days*; *African Civil Society Network on Water and Sanitation (ANEW, #00250)*; *Every Woman Every Child (EWEC, #09215)*; *Sanitation and Water for All (SWA, #19051)*. Supports: *Rural Water Supply Network (RWSN, #19006)*. Represented on council of *Freshwater Action Network (FAN, inactive)*. [2020/XG6455/**F**]

♦ Waterbird Society (internationally oriented national body)

♦ **WATERBORNE** **20823**

Secretariat c/o SEA Europe, Rue de la Loi 67, 1000 Brussels, Belgium. E-mail: info@waterborne.eu.
URL: http://www.waterborne.eu/

History Dec 2003, when process was initiated to set *Advisory Council for Waterborne Transport Research in Europe*. Technology Platform under current title launched, Jan 2005, Bremen (Germany). **Aims** Bundle efforts of European waterborne actors to remain champions in maritime transport, production of efficient and safe vessels as well as the related systems and equipment, providing infrastructure and logistics for ports and waterways, and offshore technology and leisure craft; continue to create value and high qualification employment opportunities in Europe. **Structure** General Assembly (annual); Support Group; Working Groups. **Languages** English. **Staff** No FTE. **Finance** Voluntary work; in-kind contributions. **Activities** Guidance/assistance/consulting; networking/liaising; events/meetings. **Events** *TRA European Transport Research Arena Conference* Paris (France) 2014, *TRA European Transport Research Arena Conference* Athens (Greece) 2012, *TRA European Transport Research Arena Conference* Brussels (Belgium) 2010, *TRA European Transport Research Arena Conference* Ljubljana (Slovenia) 2008, *TRA European Transport Research Arena Conference* Gothenburg (Sweden) 2006.

Members Participants (11):

European Barge Union (EBU, #06318); European Community Shipowners' Associations (ECSA, #06683); European Conference of Transport Research Institutes (ECTRI, #06737); European Council for Maritime Applied R and D (ECMAR, #06829); European Dredging Association (EuDA, #06946); European Sea Ports Organisation (ESPO, #08453); European Shipyards' and Maritime Equipment Association (SEA Europe, #08479); Federation of European Private Port Companies and Terminals (FEPORT, #09531); Inland Navigation Europe (INE, #11216); International Council of Marine Industry Associations (ICOMIA, #13044).

IGO Relations *Council of Europe (CE, #04881); European Commission (EC, #06633); European Parliament (EP, #08146)*; INEA. [2020/XJ0498/y/**F**]

♦ WaterCan (internationally oriented national body)

♦ **Water Center for the Humid Tropics of Latin America and the Caribbean** **20824**

Centro del Agua del Trópico Húmedo para América Latina y el Caribe (CATHALAC)

Dir Freddy Picado Traña, Edificio/Bldg 111, Ciudad del Saber – Clayton, Panama, Panamá, Panama PANAMá, Panama. T. +5073173200. Fax +5073173299. E-mail: cathalac@cathalac.int.
URL: http://www.cathalac.int/

History Nov 1992, Panama (Panama). Established on signature of an agreement by the Government of Panama and *UNESCO (#20322)*, and recognized as an intergovernmental entity through Law No. 45 of Sep 16, 2010. **Aims** Promote sustainable development through applied research and project development, education and technology transfer in the field of water resources and the environment; promote water security through Integrated Water Resources Management; establish visionary actions for greater resilience in vulnerable groups to climate change; support institutional capacities through the use of state-of-the-art technologies; contribute to decision makers, in the formation of intergovernmental policies in development sectors and consolidate territorial planning through observation of territorial changes and evaluation of natural resources. **Structure** Directing Council ad honorem composed of a Representative of the Government of Panama, and a representative of the Ministries of Environment or similar Institutions of each Member State of the Center: El Salvador, Nicaragua, Honduras, Dominican Republic. Head office: Panama. **Languages** English, Spanish. **Staff** 20.00 FTE, paid. **Finance** Other sources: government of Panama. Currently self-sufficient. Supported by: *UNESCO (#20322)*. **Activities** Events/meetings; knowledge management/information dissemination; politics/policy/regulatory; training/education. **Events** *International workshop on urban studies* Havana (Cuba) 2001, *Water information summit* Panama (Panama) 2001, *Inter-American Dialogue on Water Management* Panama (Panama) 1999, *Symposium on hydrology in the humid tropics environment* Panama (Panama) 1999, *International symposium on hydrology in the humid tropics environment* Kingston (Jamaica) 1996. **Publications** Proceedings.

Members Participating countries and territories (32):

Antigua-Barbuda, Bahamas, Barbados, Belize, Bermuda, Bolivia, Brazil, Colombia, Costa Rica, Cuba, Dominica, Dominican Rep, Ecuador, El Salvador, Grenada, Guatemala, Guyana, Haiti, Honduras, Jamaica, Mexico, Neth Antilles, Nicaragua, Panama, Peru, Puerto Rico, St Kitts-Nevis, St Lucia, St Vincent-Grenadines, Suriname, Trinidad-Tobago, USA.

IGO Relations Represented on Governing Board: UNESCO; OAS; *International Hydrological Programme (IHP, #13826)*. Functions as Regional Support Office of: *United Nations Platform for Space-based Information for Disaster Management and Emergency Response (UN-SPIDER, #20610)*. Participates in: *Group on Earth Observations (GEO, #10735)* and *AmeriGEOSS (#00796)*. Joint activities with: IAI; *IOC Sub-Commission for the Caribbean and Adjacent Regions (IOCARIBE, #16003)*.. **NGO Relations** Partner of (3): *Consejo Latinoamericano de Ciencias Sociales (CLACSO, #04718); Rainwater Partnership (no recent information)*; *UNLEASH*. [2021.09.06/XE1852/**E***]

♦ Water Center for Latin America and the Caribbean (unconfirmed)
♦ Water for Children Africa (internationally oriented national body)

♦ **Watercoolers Europe** **20825**

Dir Gen 1 Place de Barricades, 1000 Brussels, Belgium. T. +3228802034. E-mail: info@watercoolerseurope.eu.
URL: http://www.watercoolerseurope.eu/

History 1993. Founded as European section of *International Bottled Water Association (IBWA)*. Became independent, 1999, and previous name adopted. Former names and other names: *European Bottled Watercooler Association (EBWA)* – former (1999 to May 2011). Registration: Belgium. **Aims** Act as the authoritative source of information for the Watercooler industry in Europe, Bottled Water Coolers (BWC) and Point of Use Watercoolers (POU); define, promote and maintain quality and hygiene standards in the watercooler industry while maintaining ethical and professional practices. **Structure** General Meeting; Executive Council; Director General. **Languages** English. **Finance** Members' dues. **Activities** Events/meetings. **Events** *Annual Convention* Lisbon (Portugal) 2022, *Annual Convention* Lisbon (Portugal) 2021, *Annual Convention* Berlin (Germany) 2019, *Annual Convention* Dublin (Ireland) 2018, *Annual Convention* Krakow (Poland) 2017.

Members National associations in 21 countries:

Austria, Belgium, Czechia, Denmark, Estonia, France, Germany, Hungary, Italy, Latvia, Lithuania, Netherlands, Norway, Poland, Portugal, Romania, Slovakia, Spain, Sweden, Switzerland, UK. [2022/XD8739/**D**]

♦ **Water and Development Information for Arid Lands Global Network (G-WADI)** **20826**

Réseau global sur la gestion des ressources en eau en zones arides et semi-arides

Contact UNESCO Div of Water Sci, 1 rue Miollis, 75762 Paris, France. T. +33145684001. Fax +33145685811.
URL: http://www.g-wadi.org/

History 2004, within *UNESCO (#20322)*. **Aims** Strengthen the capacity to manage the water resources of arid and semi-arid areas around the world through a network of international and regional cooperation. **Structure** Steering Committee. Secretariat. **Staff** 8.00 FTE, paid. **Finance** Basic funding from UNESCO. Contributions from: *Department for International Development (DFID, inactive)*; in-kind contributions from member organizations. Administrative support from *International Hydrological Programme (IHP, #13826)*. **Activities** Facilitation of networking and exchange of experience; organization of workshops and training-of-trainers courses; distribution of case studies, tutorials and software tools. **Events** *Workshop on water* Dakar (Senegal) 2010, *Meeting* Paris (France) 2003. **Publications** Information Services: Electronic water news service.

Members Centres (5):

IHE Delft Institute for Water Education (#11110); Regional Centre for Training and Water Studies of Arid and Semiarid Zones, Cairo (RCTWS); Regional Centre on Urban Water Management, Teheran (RCUWM, #18761); Regional Water Centre for Arid and Semi-Arid Regions of Latin America and the Caribbean (CAZALAC); Sustainability of Semi-Arid Hydrology and Riparian Areas (SAHRA).

Individuals (mainly researchers, governments officials from water administration, engineers and consultants). Membership countries not specified.

IGO Relations Secretariat provided by IHP. [2016/XM1326/y/**F**]

♦ Water, Engineering and Development Centre (internationally oriented national body)
♦ Water Engineers for the Americas (internationally oriented national body)
♦ Water Environment Federation (internationally oriented national body)

♦ **Water Environment Partnership in Asia (WEPA)** **20827**

Secretariat c/o IGES, Natural Resources and Ecosystem Services Area, 2108-11 Kamiyamaguchi, Hayama KANAGAWA, 240-0115 Japan. T. +81468553865. Fax +81468553809. E-mail: wepa-secretariat@iges.or.jp.
URL: http://www.wepa-db.net/

History Proposed 2003, by Ministry of the Environment, Japan. Officially founded 2004. First phase: Apr 2004-Mar 2009; 2nd Phase: Apr 2009-Mar 2014; 3rd Phase: Apr 2014-Mar 2019; 4th Phase: started Apr 2019. **Aims** Improve the water environment in Asia by strengthening water environmental governance. **Structure** Annual Meeting; Working Groups; Secretariat. **Languages** English. **Activities** Capacity building; events/meetings; guidance/assistance/consulting; knowledge management/information dissemination. **Publications** *WEPA Outlook*.

Members Ministries of 13 countries:

Cambodia, China, Indonesia, Japan, Korea Rep, Laos, Malaysia, Myanmar, Nepal, Philippines, Sri Lanka, Thailand, Vietnam.

NGO Relations Located at: *Institute for Global Environmental Strategies (IGES, #11266)*. [2022.02.11/XJ7853/**F***]

♦ **Water Europe (WE)** **20828**

Exec Dir Bd Reyers 80, 1030 Brussels, Belgium. T. +3227068291. E-mail: info@watereurope.eu.
URL: https://watereurope.eu/

History 2004. Founded by *European Commission (EC, #06633)*. ETP status renewed by EC, 2013. Transformed into a member-based multistakeholder platform, 2007. Former names and other names: *European Water Platform (WssTP)* – former (2004); *Water supply and sanitation Technology Platform* – former. Registration: Banque-Carrefour des Entreprises, No/ID: 0893.349.907, Start date: 9 Nov 2007, Belgium; EU Transparency Register, No/ID: 43176485302-45, Start date: 15 Feb 2011. **Aims** Improve coordination and collaboration in the water sector and water using sectors in the EU and beyond; enhance the performance and competitiveness of the European water sector and water using sectors; contribute to solving global challenges through research and innovation. **Structure** General Meeting; Board of Directors; Executive Committee; Secretariat; Vision Leadership Teams (WE VLTs); Working Groups (WE WG); Policy Advisory Committee (WE PAC). **Staff** 10.00 FTE, paid. **Activities** Advocacy/lobbying/activism; events/meetings; knowledge management/information dissemination; networking/liaising; politics/policy/regulatory; projects/programmes. **Events** *Water Innovation Europe Meeting* Brussels (Belgium) 2022, *Water Knowledge Europe Meeting* Brussels (Belgium) 2022, *Water Market Europe Meeting* Brussels (Belgium) 2022, *International Water Dialogues Days* Brussels (Belgium) 2020, *Water Knowledge Europe Meeting* Brussels (Belgium) 2019.

Members Multinational corporations (5); Research and Technology Developers (96); Utilities (23); Supplies and SMEs (70); Large Water Users (5); Public Authorities (2); Civil Society Organizaions (6). CSOs (6):

CSOs (6):

CDP (#03621); Hydropolitics Association; *International Union for Conservation of Nature and Natural Resources (IUCN, #15766); Join For Water; The Nature Conservancy (TNC); Wetlands International (#20928).*

Members in 13 countries:

Austria, Belgium, Denmark, France, Germany, Italy, Netherlands, Norway, Portugal, Spain, Sweden, Switzerland, UK.

Included in the above, 5 organizations listed in this Yearbook:

COPA – european farmers (COPA, #04829); European Federation of National Associations of Water and Waste Water Services (#07170); European Membrane House (EMH, #07776); General Confederation of Agricultural Cooperatives in the European Union (#10107); International Water Association (IWA, #15865). [2023.02.14/XJ1669/y/**E**]

♦ **Water Footprint Network (WFN)** **20829**

Exec Dir Horst Building, Drienerlolaan 5, 7522 NB Enschede, Netherlands. T. +315348943200. E-mail: info@waterfootprint.org.
URL: http://www.waterfootprint.org/

History by University of Twente (Netherlands), *World Wide Fund for Nature (WWF, #21922), IHE Delft Institute for Water Education (#11110)*, Water Neutral Foundation (South Africa), *World Business Council for Sustainable Development (WBCSD, #21254), International Finance Corporation (IFC, #13597)* and Netherlands Water Partnership. **Aims** Use the water footprint concept to promote the transition toward sustainable, fair and efficient use of fresh water resources worldwide. **Structure** Executive Board; Supervisory Board. **Languages** Dutch, English. **Finance** Donations. **Activities** Networking/liaising; awareness raising; capacity building; knowledge management/information dissemination; politics/policy/regulatory.

Members Academic institutions; Government agencies; non-governmental organizations; businesses; international organizations. Members in 29 countries:

Argentina, Australia, Austria, Belgium, Brazil, Chile, China, Cyprus, Ecuador, Finland, France, Germany, Greece, India, Italy, Japan, Kenya, Mexico, Netherlands, New Zealand, Philippines, Portugal, South Africa, Spain, Sri Lanka, Sweden, Switzerland, UK, USA.

NGO Relations Partner of: Planetary Accounting Network. [2020/XJ0688/y/**E**]

♦ Waterford KaMhlaba United World College of Southern Africa (internationally oriented national body)
♦ Waterforeveryone (internationally oriented national body)
♦ Water Governance Facility (internationally oriented national body)

♦ **Water Integrity Network (WIN)** **20830**

Communications Coordinator Alt Moabit 91b, 10559 Berlin, Germany. T. +4930809246130. Fax +493034703912. E-mail: info@win-s.org.
URL: http://www.waterintegritynetwork.net/

History Aug 2006, Stockholm (Sweden). Founded during Stockholm Water Week. An independent association. Registration: Start date: 2014, Germany. **Aims** Increase integrity levels to reduce corruption in, and improve performance of, the water sector with a focus on pro-poor and equitable service; promote transparency, accountability and participation as pillars of integrity in the water sector. **Structure** Supervisory Board; Coordinating Secretariat. **Languages** English, French, German, Spanish. **Staff** 12.00 FTE, paid. **Finance** Sources: donations. Annual budget: 1,500,000 EUR. **Activities** Advocacy/lobbying/activism; capacity building; research and development. Africa; Latin America; South Asia. **Events** *World Water Week* Stockholm (Sweden) 2021, *East African Forum* Addis Ababa (Ethiopia) 2017, *Africa Forum* Lusaka (Zambia) 2014, *Water Forum* Delft (Netherlands) 2013.

Members Institutional members (6):

Global Water Partnership (GWP, #10653); IHE Delft Institute for Water Education (#11110); International Federation of Private Water Operators (AquaFed, #13517); IRC (#16016); Stockholm International Water Institute (SIWI); Transparency International (TI, #20223).

NGO Relations Partner of (2): *Transparency International (TI, #20223); Water Supply and Sanitation Collaborative Council (WSSCC, inactive).* [2021.09.10/XM2032/y/**F**]

♦ Waterkeeper Alliance (internationally oriented national body)
♦ Waterlines (internationally oriented national body)
♦ Water – Melk – Koeien, Melkstructuren / see Enfance Tiers Monde
♦ Water Mission International (internationally oriented national body)
♦ Water Missions International (internationally oriented national body)
♦ Water Mission – Water Mission International (internationally oriented national body)

♦ **Water Monitoring Alliance (WMA)** **20831**

Alliance pour un mécanisme mondial d'observation sur l'eau

Contact World Water Council, Espace Gaymard, 2/4 place d'Arvieux, 13002 Marseille, France. T. +33491994100. Fax +33491994101. E-mail: wwc@worldwatercouncil.org.
URL: http://www.watermonitoringalliance.net/

History 2005, by *World Water Council (WWC, #21908)* and the French Government. **Aims** Facilitate information and knowledge exchange; enhance monitoring capacities at all levels; provide a better access to data needed for a better water resource and service management. **Finance** Supported by: French Ministry of Ecology and Sustainable Development; French Ministry of Foreign Affairs. **Activities** Facilitates inter-linkages of monitoring programmes. **Information Services** *WMA Database*. [2013/XM0210/**F**]

♦ WaterNet 20832

Manager PO Box MP 600, Mount Pleasant, Harare, HARARE, Zimbabwe. T. +2634336725 – +2634333248. Fax +2634336740.
URL: http://www.waternetonline.org/

History Mar 2000, Victoria Falls (Zimbabwe) by 18 university departments and training institutes from 9 countries in Southern and Eastern Africa. Constitution approved during first Annual General Meeting, Nov 2000, Maputo (Mozambique). **Aims** Enhance regional capacity in integrated water *resources* management. **Structure** General Meeting (annual); Board of Trustees; Secretariat hosted by University of Zimbabwe. **Languages** English, French, Portuguese. **Staff** 7.00 FTE, paid. **Finance** Support from Supporting Members, including: the governments of Sweden and Netherlands; *Global Water Partnership (GWP, #10653)*. UNESCO – IHE facilitates establishment. **Activities** Events/meetings; training/education; research and development; networking/liaising; financial and/or material support. **Events** *IWRM – harnessing the rivers of knowledge for socio-economic development, climate adaptation and environmental sustainability* Maputo (Mozambique) 2011, *Annual General Meeting and Symposium* Ezulwini (Swaziland) 2005, *Annual general meeting and symposium* Windhoek (Namibia) 2004, *Annual general meeting and symposium* Gaborone (Botswana) 2003, *Annual general meeting and symposium* Dar es Salaam (Tanzania UR) 2002.
Members Full: institutions and university departments (41) in 16 countries:
Angola, Botswana, Congo DR, Eswatini, Kenya, Lesotho, Malawi, Mauritius, Mozambique, Namibia, Rwanda, South Africa, Tanzania UR, Uganda, Zambia, Zimbabwe.
Included in the above, 1 organization listed in this Yearbook:
International Water Management Institute (IWMI, #15867).
Supporting (4): organizations and governments, including 2 organizations listed in this Yearbook:
Global Water Partnership (GWP, #10653); *IHE Delft Institute for Water Education (#11110)*.
IGO Relations *Southern African Development Community (SADC, #19843)*. **NGO Relations** Member of: *Network for Capacity Building in Integrated Water Resources Management (CAP-Net, #17000)*. Partner in: *Africa-EU Innovation Alliance for Water and Climate (AfriAlliance, #00169)*. Joint symposia with: *Water Research Fund of Southern Africa (WARFSA, #20834)*; *Global Water Partnership (GWP, #10653)* – Southern Africa. [2017.03.09/XF6566/y/**F**]

♦ Water Network / see Programme Solidarité eau (#18529)
♦ Water.org (internationally oriented national body)
♦ WaterPartners International / see Water.org
♦ Water for People (internationally oriented national body)
♦ Water Pollution Control Federation / see Water Environment Federation

♦ Waterpreneurs 20833

Managing Partner c/o Impact Hub Geneva, Rue Fendt 1, 1201 Geneva, Switzerland. E-mail: info@waterpreneurs.net.
URL: https://www.waterpreneurs.net/

History Registration: Switzerland. **Aims** Help solve the problems raised by the 17 Sustainable Development Goals (SDGs) with a focus on SDG 6: clean *water* and *sanitation*. **Structure** Partners' Meeting; Management. **Languages** English, French, Spanish. **Activities** Projects/programmes; events/meetings. **Publications** White paper. **IGO Relations** *Facilité africaine de l'eau (FAE, #09233)*; *International Bank for Reconstruction and Development (IBRD, #12317)* (World Bank); *OECD (#17693)*; *UN-Water (#20723)*; *UNDP (#20292)*; *UNICEF (#20332)*; *World Intellectual Property Organization (WIPO, #21593)*. **NGO Relations** *Climate Technology Centre and Network (CTCN, #04023)*; *International Centre for Water Management Services (cewas)*; *Sanitation and Water for All (SWA, #19051)*; *Toilet Board Coalition (TBC, #20171)*. [2021/XM6749/**F**]

♦ Water Quality Association (internationally oriented national body)

♦ Water Research Fund of Southern Africa (WARFSA) 20834

Contact Institute of Water and Sanitation Development, Box MP422, Mount Pleasant, Harare, HARARE, Zimbabwe. T. +2634250522. Fax +2634738120.
Street Address 7 Maasdorp Avenue, Alexandra Park, Harare, HARARE, Zimbabwe.
URL: http://www.waternetonline.org/

History 1999. **Aims** Support research projects addressing sustainable utilization of water resources in the SADC region. **Finance** Funded by *Swedish International Development Cooperation Agency (Sida)*. **Events** *Symposium* Lilongwe (Malawi) 2014, *IWRM – harnessing the rivers of knowledge for socio-economic development, climate adaptation and environmental sustainability* Maputo (Mozambique) 2011, *Symposium* Entebbe (Uganda) 2009, *Symposium* Ezulwini (Swaziland) 2005, *Symposium* Windhoek (Namibia) 2004. **NGO Relations** Joint symposia with: *WaterNet (#20832)*. [2014/XF6567/f/**F**]

♦ Water Reuse Europe (WRE) 20835

Sec Vincent Bldg 52a – 1st Fl, Central Avenue, Cranfield, MK43 0AL, UK. T. +441234754330. E-mail: info@water-reuse-europe.org.
URL: https://www.water-reuse-europe.org/

History 2016. Registration: Companies House, No/ID: 09998708, Start date: 16 Feb 2016, England. **Aims** Create a collective identity for the water reuse sector across Europe; share good practices, knowledge, techniques, research, and experiences on water reuse to promote the safe and effective use of recycled water in Europe. **Structure** Board; CEO. **Languages** English. **Finance** Members' dues. **Activities** Events/meetings; knowledge management/information dissemination. **Events** *Conference on Innovations in Water Reuse* Girona (Spain) 2022, *Conference on Innovations in Water Reuse* Girona (Spain) 2021, *Conference on Innovations in Water Reuse* Girona (Spain) 2020, *Conference on Innovations in Water Reuse* Bruges (Belgium) 2017. **Publications** *Water Reuse Europe Newsletter* (4 a year).
Members Companies; public bodies; research organizations; trade and professional associations. Members in 12 countries:
Belgium, France, Germany, Greece, Italy, Luxembourg, Netherlands, Portugal, Spain, Sweden, Switzerland, USA.
IGO Relations *European Commission (EC, #06633)*. **NGO Relations** None. [2023/XM6024/**D**]

♦ Water and Sanitation for Africa (WSA) 20836

Eau et Assainissement pour l'Afrique (EAA)

Contact 03 BP – 7112, Ouagadougou 03, Burkina Faso. T. +22625366210 – +22625366211. Fax +22625366208. E-mail: contact@ws-africa.org.
URL: http://www.ws-africa.org/

History 1988, as a regional centre for *International Training Network for Water and Waste Management (ITN, no recent information)*, and jointly hosted by: *Inter-African Committee for Hydraulic Studies (ICHS, inactive)*; *Inter-State School of Hydraulic and Rural Engineering for Senior Technicians (#15981)*. Original title: *Centre régional pour l'eau potable et l'assainissement à faible coût (CREPA) – Regional Centre for Low-Cost Water Supply and Sanitation*. **Aims** Forward scientific methods for obtaining sanitation and *drinkable water* through a popular message directed to *rural* and *peri-urban* populations throughout Africa. **Structure** Ministerial Council; Technical Advisory Committee. CEO. Foundation acts as charity arm. Research and Policy Centre; Social Enterprise Group as profit-making arm. **Languages** English, French. **Staff** 70.00 FTE, paid. **Finance** Donors: *African Development Bank (ADB, #00283)*; *Agence française de développement (AFD)*; *Conseil Wallonie Bruxelles de la coopération internationale (CWBCI)*; *European Union (EU, #08967)*; *Swiss Agency for Development and Cooperation (SDC)*; *UNICEF (#20332)*; *Union économique et monétaire Ouest africaine (UEMOA, #20377)*; *United States Agency for International Development (USAID)*. **Activities** Events/meetings. Francophone Telematics Centre, Ouagadougou, in conjunction with IOW. **Events** *Symposium on Monitoring Sustainable WASH Service Delivery* Addis Ababa (Ethiopia) 2013, *Session* Ouagadougou (Burkina Faso) 2010, *Session* Brazzaville (Congo Brazzaville) 2007, *Session* Dakar (Senegal) 2004, *Research forum* Ouagadougou (Burkina Faso) 2004. **Publications** *Info WSA* (4 a year); *Bulletin de liaison WSA* (annual). Manuals; conference proceedings; documentary films.
Members Countries (35):
Benin, Burkina Faso, Burundi, Cameroon, Central African Rep, Chad, Comoros, Congo Brazzaville, Congo DR, Côte d'Ivoire, Djibouti, Egypt, Eswatini, Ethiopia, Gabon, Gambia, Ghana, Guinea, Guinea-Bissau, Kenya, Liberia, Libya, Madagascar, Mali, Mauritania, Mozambique, Niger, Nigeria, Rwanda, Senegal, Sierra Leone, Sudan, Togo, Uganda, Zimbabwe.
IGO Relations Partners with: *African Ministers' Council on Water (AMCOW, #00376)*; *UN-Water (#20723)*. Links with a large number of organizations, including: *African Union (AU, #00488)*; *Comité permanent inter-Etats de lutte contre la sécheresse dans le Sahel (CILSS, #04195)*; *Economic Community of West African States (ECOWAS, #05312)* – Water Resources Coordination Center (WRCC/ECOWAS); *International Bank for Reconstruction and Development (IBRD, #12317)*; *International Development Research Centre (IDRC, #13162)*; *Institut International d'Ingénierie de l'Eau et de l'Environnement (2iE, #11313)*; *UNDP (#20292)*. **NGO Relations** Partners include: *African Water Association (AfWA, #00497)*; *Conrad N Hilton Foundation (CNHF)*; *Global Water Partnership (GWP, #10653)*; *International Institute for Environment and Development (IIED, #13877)*; *IRC (#16016)*; *Reall*; *Sanitation and Water for All (SWA, #19051)*; *Stockholm Environment Institute (SEI, #19993)*; *Sustainable Sanitation Alliance (SuSanA, #20066)*; *Water Supply and Sanitation Collaborative Council (WSSCC, inactive)*. Founding member of: *Global Water Solidarity (GWS, #10655)*. Member of: *People in Aid (inactive)*. Cooperates with: *International Office for Water (IOW, #14399)*. Instrumental in setting up: *Réseau francophone sur l'eau et l'assainissement (RéFEA, no recent information)*. [2020.03.04/XE1527/**E**]

♦ Water, Sanitation and Hygiene / see Global WASH Cluster (#10651)

♦ Water and Sanitation Programme (WSP) 20837

Programme pour l'eau et l'assainissement – Programa de Agua y Saneamienta

Contact Water Supply and Sanitation Division, 1818 H St NW, Washington DC 20433, USA. T. +12024739785. Fax +12025223313.
URL: http://www.wsp.org/

History as *UNDP-World Bank Water and Sanitation Programme*. **Aims** Alleviate poverty by helping the *poor* gain sustained access to improved water and sanitation services. **Structure** Regional offices (5): Africa; Andean Region; East Asia and Pacific; South Asia; Washington. **Finance** Support from multilateral and bilateral organizations, including: *Asian Development Bank (ADB, #01422)*; *Australian Aid (inactive)*; *Canadian International Development Agency (CIDA, inactive)*; *DANIDA*; *Department for International Development (DFID, inactive)*; *Department for International Development Cooperation*; *Deutsche Gesellschaft für Technische Zusammenarbeit (GTZ, inactive)*; *Directorate-General for Development Cooperation (DGDC)*; *Japan International Cooperation Agency (JICA)*; *Norwegian Agency for Development Cooperation (Norad)*; *Swedish International Development Cooperation Agency (Sida)*; *Swiss Agency for Development and Cooperation (SDC)*; *UNDP (#20292)*; World Bank. **Events** *Meeting* Vienna (Austria) 2009. **Publications** *ACCESS* – online E-J newsletter. Annual report. **IGO Relations** Administered by: *International Bank for Reconstruction and Development (IBRD, #12317)*. **NGO Relations** Founding member of: *Water Integrity Network (WIN, #20830)*. Member of: *Global Handwashing Partnership (GHP, #10396)*; *Global Water Operators' Partnerships Alliance (GWOPA, #10652)*. Participates in: *Sustainable Sanitation Alliance (SuSanA, #20066)*. Partners: *Global Water Partnership (GWP, #10653)*; *International Training Network for Water and Waste Management (ITN, no recent information)*; *Sanitation and Water for All (SWA, #19051)*. [2009/XE4467/**E***]

♦ Water and Sanitation for the Urban Poor (internationally oriented national body)

♦ Water Science and Technology Association (WSTA) 20838

Sec PO Box 20018, Manama, Bahrain. T. +97317311351. Fax +97317311352. E-mail: info@wstagcc.org.
Pres address not obtained.
Vice-Pres address not obtained.
URL: http://www.wstagcc.org/

History resulting from individual efforts of some of those concerned with water affairs in *Gulf Cooperation Council (GCC, #10826)* countries. Registered in accordance with the law of Bahrain, Sep 1987. **Aims** Encourage and promote interest in water science and strengthen scientific ties among water professionals in countries of GCC countries; encourage scientific research, training programmes and development of local capabilities in the different fields of water sciences and technology; cooperate with universities and research centres in different fields of water sciences and technology; exchange information and expertise between water professionals in GCC countries and the world; encourage usage of scientific means in developing water resources in GCC countries, such as desalination and waste water treatment and reuse for agricultural and industrial purposes. **Structure** Board of 11 members, one from each of the 6 GCC member states, with additional elected members. Executive Committee, comprising President, Vice-President, Secretary and Treasurer. **Languages** Arabic, English. **Staff** 1.00 FTE, paid. **Finance** Budget (annual): Bahrain Dinars 100,000. **Activities** Conducts biennial conference, seminars, symposia and workshops. **Events** *Gulf Water Conference* Muscat (Oman) 2014, *Annual General Assembly* Manama (Bahrain) 2013, *Gulf Water Conference* Doha (Qatar) 2012, *Gulf water conference* Muscat (Oman) 2010, *Gulf water conference* Bahrain 2008. **Publications** *Arabic Encyclopedia of Desalination and Water Reuse*; *Introduction to Desalination* in Arabic; *Water* in Arabic; *Water Desalination and Treatment* in Arabic. Conference proceedings.
Members Individuals (about 750) in 6 countries:
Bahrain, Kuwait, Oman, Qatar, Saudi Arabia, United Arab Emirates.
NGO Relations Affiliated with international societies and associations in the field of water sciences, including: *European Desalination Society (EDS, #06908)*; *International Desalination Association (IDA, #13152)*; *World Water Council (WWC, #21908)*. [2014/XD7091/v/**D**]

♦ Water Security Management, Assessment, Research & Technology (unconfirmed)
♦ Water Solidarity Network (#18529)
♦ Water Solidarity Programme / see Programme Solidarité eau (#18529)
♦ Water-Sp / see Programme Solidarité eau (#18529)
♦ Water Supply and Sanitation Collaborative Council (inactive)
♦ Water supply and sanitation Technology Platform / see Water Europe (#20828)
♦ Water Witness International (internationally oriented national body)
♦ **WATOC** World Association of Theoretical and Computational Chemists (#21198)
♦ **WATOG** World Association of Trainees in Obstetrics & Gynecology (#21199)
♦ WATO – West Africa Tourism Organisation (internationally oriented national body)
♦ **WATRA** West Africa Telecommunications Regulators Association (#20903)
♦ **WATUN** World Alliance to Transform the United Nations (#21088)
♦ Watu Wa Miti / see International Tree Foundation
♦ WAT – World Airport Technology (inactive)
♦ WAUC – World Association of Universities and Colleges (internationally oriented national body)
♦ WAUDC – West African Union Development Council (unconfirmed)
♦ WAUNNGO / see World Association of Non-Governmental Organizations (#21167)
♦ **WAUTI** West African Union of Tax Institutes (#20898)
♦ **WAU** World Anthropological Union (#21093)
♦ **WAVA** World Association of Veterinary Anatomists (#21202)
♦ WAVA / see World Masters Athletics (#21640)
♦ **WAVD** World Association for Veterinary Dermatology (#21203)
♦ Waves – International Conference on Mathematical and Numerical Aspects of Wave Propagation (meeting series)
♦ Waves for Water (internationally oriented national body)
♦ **WAVES** World Association for Vedic Studies (#21201)
♦ WAVE Trust – Worldwide Alternatives to Violence (internationally oriented national body)
♦ **WAVE** Women Against Violence Europe (#20986)
♦ WAVE – World Association of Veterinary Educators (inactive)
♦ WAVE – World Association of Video-Makers and Editions (inactive)
♦ WAVE – World Association of Visioneers and Entreprenologists (internationally oriented national body)
♦ **WAVFH** World Association of Veterinary Food Hygienists (#21204)
♦ **WAVLD** World Association of Veterinary Laboratory Diagnosticians (#21205)
♦ **WAVMA** World Aquatic Veterinary Medical Association (#21101)
♦ WAVMI – World Association of Veterinary Microbiologists, Immunologists and Specialists in Infectious Diseases (no recent information)
♦ **WAVO** World Association of Valuation Organizations (#21200)
♦ WAVPPBT – World Association of Veterinary Physiologists, Pharmacologists, Biochemists and Toxicologists (no recent information)

- ♦ WAVP – World Association of Veterinary Pathologists (no recent information)
- ♦ WAVSFD – World Association of Veterinarians Specialists in Fish Diseases (no recent information)
- ♦ **WAWA** West African Women's Association (#20900)
- ♦ WAWE / see Femmes chefs d'entreprises mondiales (#09733)
- ♦ **WAWFE** Worldwide Association of Women Forensic Experts (#21915)
- ♦ WAWF / see World Federalist Movement – Movement for a Just World Order through a Strengthened United Nations (#21404)
- ♦ WAW – International Wellbeing at Work Conference (meeting series)
- ♦ **WAWLC** World Alliance for Wound and Lymphedema Care (#21089)
- ♦ WAWO – World Asian Workers Organization (inactive)
- ♦ **WAWSS** West African Weed Science Society (#20899)
- ♦ WAWV – World Association of Wildlife Veterinarians (inactive)
- ♦ WaW – Women in Action Worldwide (internationally oriented national body)
- ♦ **WAYEB** Asociación Europea de Mayistas (#02126)

♦ Wayfarer International Committee (WIC) 20839

Sec 19 Highland Road, Oakville ON L6K 1S8, Canada.
URL: http://www.wayfarer-international.org/

History 14 Apr 1972, London (UK). **Aims** Ensure adherence to the one-design nature of the Wayfarer *boat*; coordinate international Wayfarer events; promote the Wayfarer worldwide. **Structure** Committee comprises: voting representatives for each National Class Association; Rules and Technical representatives from each National Class Association (non-voting); International Secretary (non-voting). Interests of copyright holders, Richard and Mark Hartley, Hartley Laminates, as well as Wayfarer builders also represented. **Languages** Danish, Dutch, English. **Staff** Voluntary. **Finance** Members' dues. Budget (annual): about US$ 1,000.
Members National Class Associations (5) in 4 countries:
Canada, Netherlands, UK, USA.
Regional association (1), listed in this Yearbook:
Scandinavian Wayfarer Association (#19128). [2011.06.01/XE4568/**E**]

- ♦ The Way to Happiness Foundation International (internationally oriented national body)
- ♦ **WAYS** World Association of Young Scientists (#21207)
- ♦ WAYU – West African Youth Union (inactive)
- ♦ **WAY** World Assembly of Youth (#21113)
- ♦ **WAZA** World Association of Zoos and Aquariums (#21208)
- ♦ WBAA – World Business Angels Association (no recent information)
- ♦ **WBAF** World Business Angels Investment Forum (#21252)
- ♦ **WBAT** World Bank Administrative Tribunal (#21216)
- ♦ **WBA** Wireless Broadband Alliance (#20969)
- ♦ **WBA** World Backgammon Association (#21212)
- ♦ **WBA** World Bearing Association (#21227)
- ♦ **WBA** World Benchmarking Alliance (#21228)
- ♦ **WBA** World Bioenergy Association (#21231)
- ♦ WBA – World Biogas Association (unconfirmed)
- ♦ **WBA** World Birdstrike Association (#21232)
- ♦ WBA – World Bodyguards Association (internationally oriented national body)
- ♦ **WBA** World Boxing Association (#21241)
- ♦ **WBA** World Business Associates (#21253)
- ♦ WBA / see World Organization of Workers (#21697)
- ♦ **WBA** Worldwide Brewing Alliance (#21917)
- ♦ WBB – World Bowls Board (inactive)
- ♦ WBC / see World President's Organization
- ♦ **WBCA** Weltbewegung der Christlichen Arbeiter (#21660)
- ♦ **WBCPC** World Bladder Cancer Patient Coalition (#21233)
- ♦ **WBCSD** World Business Council for Sustainable Development (#21254)
- ♦ **WBC** World Boxing Council (#21242)
- ♦ WBC – World Budo Confederation (unconfirmed)
- ♦ WBC – World Budokan Council (unconfirmed)
- ♦ **WBDJ** Weltbund der Demokratischen Jugend (#21427)
- ♦ **WBFF** World Bonsai Friendship Federation (#21239)
- ♦ **WBFSH** World Breeding Federation for Sport Horses (#21245)
- ♦ **WBF** World Banana Forum (#21215)
- ♦ WBF – World Boxing Forum (unconfirmed)
- ♦ **WBF** World Brahman Federation (#21244)
- ♦ **WBF** World Bridge Federation (#21246)
- ♦ **WBF** World Budo Federation (#21249)
- ♦ **WBF** Worldwide Backgammon Federation (#21916)
- ♦ **WBGF** World Backgammon Federation (#21213)
- ♦ **WBIF** Western Balkans Investment Framework (#20910)
- ♦ **WBI** World Bank Institute (#21220)
- ♦ WBL – World Boxing League (unconfirmed)
- ♦ **WBMA** World Beard and Moustache Association (#21226)
- ♦ **WBMS** World Bureau of Metal Statistics (#21250)
- ♦ **WBMT** Worldwide Network for Blood and Marrow Transplantation (#21929)
- ♦ **WBN** Worldwide Broker Network (#21918)
- ♦ WBO / see Triratna Buddhist Community (#20243)
- ♦ **WBO** World Bamboo Organization (#21214)
- ♦ **WBO** World Boxing Organization (#21243)
- ♦ WBPF / see World Bodybuilding and Physique Sports Federation (#21237)
- ♦ **WBPF** World Bodybuilding and Physique Sports Federation (#21237)
- ♦ **WBP** Women's Brain Project (#21014)

♦ WBSC Americas Softball 20840

Pres PO Box 721086, Orlando FL 32872, USA. E-mail: conpasa@conpasa.org.
URL: https://www.softballamericas.org/

History 3 Jul 1979, San Juan (Puerto Rico). Regional federation of *World Baseball Softball Confederation (WBSC, #21222)*. Former names and other names: *Pan American Softball Confederation* – former; *Confederación Panamericana de Softbol Amateur (CONPASA)* – former. **Aims** Organize, develop and promote female and male softball in a coordinated manner, in all countries of the American continent; regulate the Pan American Softball competitions. **Structure** Assembly; Board of Directors. Commissions (8): Umpiring; Athletes; Development; Disciplinary; Statutes; Women's; Rules and Technical Code; Hall of Fame. **Activities** Sporting activities. **Events** *Extraordinary Assembly* Valencia (Venezuela) 2016, *General Assembly* Valencia (Venezuela) 2016, *General Assembly* Oklahoma City, OK (USA) 2015, *Extraordinary Assembly* Valencia (Venezuela) 2012, *General Assembly* Valencia (Venezuela) 2012. **Publications** *CONPASA e-Magazine*; *WBSC Americas Softball Magazine* – electronic.
Members Federations in 28 countries and territories:
Argentina, Aruba, Bahamas, Belize, Bermuda, Brazil, Canada, Cayman Is, Colombia, Costa Rica, Cuba, Curaçao, Dominican Rep, Ecuador, El Salvador, Guatemala, Honduras, Jamaica, Mexico, Nicaragua, Panama, Peru, Puerto Rico, Turks-Caicos, USA, Venezuela, Virgin Is UK, Virgin Is USA.
NGO Relations Member of (1): *Asociación de Confederaciones Deportivas Panamericanas (ACODEPA, #02119).* [2022/XM4062/**D**]

- ♦ **WBSC Europe** World Baseball Softball Confederation Europe (#21223)
- ♦ **WBSC Oceania** Oceania Baseball Softball Confederation (#17652)
- ♦ **WBSC** World Baseball Softball Confederation (#21222)
- ♦ **WBSC** World Buddhist Sangha Council (#21248)
- ♦ WBSTF – World Buddhist Supreme Tathagata Followers (religious order)
- ♦ WBS – Waterbird Society (internationally oriented national body)
- ♦ **WBTF** World Baton Twirling Federation (#21225)
- ♦ WBTF – World Business Transformation Forum (internationally oriented national body)
- ♦ WBT International – Wycliffe Bible Translators International (internationally oriented national body)
- ♦ **WBT** World Association of Manufacturers of Bottles and Teats (#21159)
- ♦ **WBU** World Blind Union (#21234)
- ♦ WBU – World Boxing Union (no recent information)
- ♦ **WBU** World Broadcasting Unions (#21247)
- ♦ **WB** World Bowls (#21240)
- ♦ **WB – WWF Forest Alliance** World Bank – WWF Alliance for Forest Conservation and Sustainable Use (#21221)
- ♦ WBW – Women for a Better World (internationally oriented national body)
- ♦ **WC2 University Network** World Cities World Class University Network (#21276)
- ♦ WCA / see Association of World Citizens (#02982)
- ♦ WCAASS – West and Central African Association of Soil Science (no recent information)
- ♦ **WCAA** World Council of Anthropological Associations (#21317)
- ♦ WCACA – World Christian Anti-Communist Association (no recent information)
- ♦ WCAF – World Combat Arts Federation (internationally oriented national body)
- ♦ WCAI – Wireless Communications Association International (internationally oriented national body)
- ♦ WCARGA / see Strategies for Peace (#20008)
- ♦ WCA – Water for Children Africa (internationally oriented national body)
- ♦ **WCA** World Cargo Alliance (#21259)
- ♦ **WCA** World Cement Association (#21265)
- ♦ **WCA** World Cetacean Alliance (#21268)
- ♦ **WCA** World Coal Association (#21280)
- ♦ WCA – World Coffee Alliance (unconfirmed)
- ♦ **WCA** World Communication Association (#21288)
- ♦ **WCA** World Council of Arameans – Syriacs (#21318)
- ♦ **WCA** World Cube Association (#21346)
- ♦ **WCBS** World Confederation of Billiards Sports (#21291)
- ♦ **WCB** World Council for Biomechanics (#21319)
- ♦ WCC AISBL / see World Crafts Council AISBL (#21342)
- ♦ **WCCBT** World Confederation of Cognitive and Behavioural Therapies (#21292)
- ♦ WCCB – World Committee for Christian Broadcasting (inactive)
- ♦ WCCC / see World Centers of Compassion for Children International
- ♦ WCCCI – World Centers of Compassion for Children International (internationally oriented national body)
- ♦ **WCCC** World Convention of Churches of Christ (#21315)
- ♦ WCCD – World Commission on Culture and Development (inactive)
- ♦ WCCD – World Council on City Data (unconfirmed)
- ♦ **WCCES** World Council of Comparative Education Societies (#21322)
- ♦ WCCE – World Conference on Computers in Education (meeting series)
- ♦ WCCE – World Congress of Chemical Engineering (meeting series)
- ♦ WCCE – World Council of Christian Education (inactive)
- ♦ **WCCE** World Council of Civil Engineers (#21321)
- ♦ WCCF – World Cities Culture Forum (meeting series)
- ♦ WCC / see Global Confederation for Interprofessional Education and Collaborative Practice (#10305)
- ♦ **WCC International** World Crafts Council AISBL (#21342)
- ♦ **WCCI** World Council for Curriculum and Instruction (#21325)
- ♦ **WCCJ** World Conference on Constitutional Justice (#21298)
- ♦ WCCL – World Council for Colonial Freedom (inactive)
- ♦ **WCCO** World Historic and Cultural Canal Cities Cooperation Organization (#21570)
- ♦ WCCP / see International Council of Coloproctology (#13009)
- ♦ WCCS – World Congress on Cancers of the Skin (meeting series)
- ♦ **WCCS** World Congress of Chiropractic Students (#21303)
- ♦ **WCC** World Cat Congress (#21262)
- ♦ **WCC** World Chlorine Council (#21274)
- ♦ **WCC** World Council of Churches (#21320)
- ♦ WCC – World Cycling Centre (internationally oriented national body)
- ♦ WCDES – World Community Development Education Society (internationally oriented national body)
- ♦ **WCDN** World Christian Doctors Network (#21275)
- ♦ WCEA – World Continuing Education Alliance (internationally oriented national body)
- ♦ **WCEC** World Chemical Engineering Council (#21271)
- ♦ WCED – World Commission on Environment and Development (inactive)
- ♦ WCER / see European Congress of Ethnic Religions (#06740)
- ♦ **WCET** World Council of Enterostomal Therapists (#21327)
- ♦ **WCEU** World's Christian Endeavor Union (#21768)
- ♦ WCFBA / see Catholic Biblical Federation (#03600)
- ♦ WCFFM – World Council of Former Foreign Ministers (no recent information)
- ♦ WCFIA – Weatherhead Center for International Affairs (internationally oriented national body)
- ♦ WCFLCR – World Congress on Family Law and the Rights of Children and Youth (meeting series)
- ♦ WCFS – World Conference on Floating Solutions (meeting series)
- ♦ WCFS – World Council of Fisheries Societies (internationally oriented national body)
- ♦ **WCFU** World Congress of Free Ukrainians (#21305)
- ♦ WCF – Wild Chimpanzee Foundation (internationally oriented national body)
- ♦ **WCF** World Carillon Federation (#21260)
- ♦ **WCF** World Cat Federation (#21263)
- ♦ **WCF** World Chambers Federation (#21269)
- ♦ WCF – World Citizenship Foundation (internationally oriented national body)
- ♦ **WCF** World Civic Forum (#21277)
- ♦ WCF – World Climate Foundation (unconfirmed)
- ♦ WCF – World Cocoa Foundation (internationally oriented national body)
- ♦ **WCF** World Congress of Faiths (#21304)
- ♦ **WCF** World Croquet Federation (#21344)
- ♦ WCF – World Culture Forum (internationally oriented national body)
- ♦ **WCF** World Curling Federation (#21348)
- ♦ WCGALP – World Congress on Genetics Applied to Livestock Production (meeting series)
- ♦ **WCGCS** World Commission on Global Consciousness and Spirituality (#21285)
- ♦ WCG / see Grace Communion International (#10685)
- ♦ **WCGLBTJ** World Congress of Gay, Lesbian, Bisexual and Transgender Jews (#21306)
- ♦ WCGLJO / see World Congress of Gay, Lesbian, Bisexual and Transgender Jews (#21306)
- ♦ **WCGTC** World Council for Gifted and Talented Children (#21328)
- ♦ WCG – WomanCare Global (internationally oriented national body)
- ♦ WCHR – World Court of Human Rights (unconfirmed)
- ♦ **WCH** World Congress of Herpetology (#21307)
- ♦ WCI / see Wildlife Conservation Society
- ♦ WCIA – Welsh Centre for International Affairs (internationally oriented national body)
- ♦ **WCICC** World Council of Independent Christian Churches (#21330)
- ♦ WCIDF – Women and Children International Development Foundation (internationally oriented national body)
- ♦ WCIP – World Council of Indigenous Peoples (inactive)
- ♦ WCIS / see Wildlife Conservation Society
- ♦ WCISTCO – World City Ice and Snow Tourism Cooperation Organization (unconfirmed)
- ♦ WCI – Women's Climate Initiative (internationally oriented national body)

- ♦ **WCI** World Capital Institute (#21257)
- ♦ WCI / see World Certification Institute (#21267)
- ♦ **WCI** World Certification Institute (#21267)
- ♦ WCI / see World Coal Association (#21280)
- ♦ **WCI** World Council of Isotopes (#21331)
- ♦ **WCJA** World Council of Jain Academies (#21332)
- ♦ WCJCC / see JCC Global (#16093)
- ♦ **WCJJO** World Council of Ju-Jitsu Organisations (#21333)
- ♦ **WCJLN** World Criminal Justice Library Network (#21343)
- ♦ WCK – World Central Kitchen (internationally oriented national body)
- ♦ WCLLL – World Committee for Lifelong Learning (unconfirmed)
- ♦ WCL – World Confederation of Labour (inactive)
- ♦ WCMB – World Conference on Marine Biodiversity (meeting series)
- ♦ WCMC Europe (unconfirmed)
- ♦ **WCMCI** World Committee of Maritime Culture Institutes (#21286)
- ♦ WCMC / see UN Environment Programme World Conservation Monitoring Centre (#20295)
- ♦ WCME – World Council on Media Education (no recent information)
- ♦ **WCMF** World Council of the Marianist Family (#21334)
- ♦ WCMJ – World Congress of Mountain Jews (unconfirmed)
- ♦ **WCMP** World Congress of Muslim Philanthropists (#21308)
- ♦ WCM – Wider Church Ministries (internationally oriented national body)
- ♦ WCM – World Citizenship Movements (inactive)
- ♦ WCNT – World Centre for New Thinking (internationally oriented national body)
- ♦ WCN – Wildlife Conservation Network (internationally oriented national body)
- ♦ **WCN** World Chambers Network (#21270)
- ♦ **WCOE** World Council of Elders of the Ancient Traditions and Cultures (#21326)
- ♦ WCOI – World Congress of Oral Implantology (meeting series)
- ♦ WCoP – World Conference on Pharmacometrics (meeting series)
- ♦ WCOSM – World Council of Orthopaedic Sports Medicine (no recent information)
- ♦ WCOTP – World Confederation of Organizations of the Teaching Profession (inactive)
- ♦ **WCO** World Containerboard Organization (#21314)
- ♦ **WCO** World Corrosion Organization (#21316)
- ♦ **WCO** World Council of Optometry (#21335)
- ♦ WCO – World Culture Open (unconfirmed)
- ♦ **WCO** World Customs Organization (#21350)
- ♦ **WCPA** World Constitution and Parliament Association (#21313)
- ♦ WCPD – World Congress on Prevention of Diabetes and its Complications (meeting series)
- ♦ **WCPFC** Western and Central Pacific Fisheries Commission (#20912)
- ♦ WCPOC / see Western and Central Pacific Fisheries Commission (#20912)
- ♦ WCPP – World Council of Professional Photographers (inactive)
- ♦ **WCPS** World Confederation of Productivity Science (#21294)
- ♦ WCPT Trading Limited / see World Confederation for Physical Therapy (#21293)
- ♦ **WCPT** World Confederation for Physical Therapy (#21293)
- ♦ WCPUN – World Council of Peoples for the United Nations (internationally oriented national body)
- ♦ **WCPU** World Council of Power Utilities (#21336)
- ♦ WCP – World Congress of Poets (see: #21066)
- ♦ WCP – World Conscious Pact (unconfirmed)
- ♦ **WCP** World Council for Psychotherapy (#21337)
- ♦ WCRB – World Congress of Reproductive Biology (meeting series)
- ♦ WCRC European Area Council / see Council of the World Communion of Reformed Churches in Europe (#04924)
- ♦ **WCRC Europe** Council of the World Communion of Reformed Churches in Europe (#04924)
- ♦ **WCRC** World Carpet and Rug Council (#21261)
- ♦ **WCRC** World Communion of Reformed Churches (#21289)
- ♦ **WCRDE** World Council for Regular and Distance Education (#21338)
- ♦ **WCRE** World Council for Renewable Energy (#21340)
- ♦ WCRF / see World Cancer Research Fund International
- ♦ WCRF – World Cancer Research Fund International (internationally oriented national body)
- ♦ **WCRI** World Conferences on Research Integrity Foundation (#21300)
- ♦ **WCRL** World Council of Religious Leaders (#21339)
- ♦ WCRP / see Religions for Peace (#18831)
- ♦ WCRPL – World Congress on Recurrent Pregnancy Loss (meeting series)
- ♦ **WCRP** World Climate Research Programme (#21279)
- ♦ WCRWC / see Women's Refugee Commission
- ♦ WCSA – World Class Soaring Association (internationally oriented national body)
- ♦ WCSA – World Complexity Science Academy (internationally oriented national body)
- ♦ **WCSA** World Crossbow Shooting Association (#21345)
- ♦ WCSE – International Workshop on Computer Science and Engineering (meeting series)
- ♦ **WCSFP** World Congress of Science and Factual Producers (#21309)
- ♦ **WCSF** World Civil Society Forum (#21278)
- ♦ **WC** Southeast Asia Women's Caucus on ASEAN (#19800)
- ♦ WCS – Wildlife Conservation Society (internationally oriented national body)
- ♦ WCS – World Sport Council (unconfirmed)
- ♦ **WCTA** World Cultural Tourism Association (#21347)
- ♦ **WCTC** World Coalition for Trauma Care (#21282)
- ♦ **WCTE** World Committee on Tourism Ethics (#21287)
- ♦ WCTE – World Conference on Timber Engineering (meeting series)
- ♦ **WCTF** World Ceramic Tiles Forum (#21266)
- ♦ WCTOH – World Conference on Tobacco or Health (meeting series)
- ♦ WCTR Society / see World Conference on Transport Research Society (#21301)
- ♦ **WCTRS** World Conference on Transport Research Society (#21301)
- ♦ WCT – WIPO Copyright Treaty (1996 treaty)
- ♦ WCT – World Confederation of Teachers (inactive)
- ♦ WCVDA / see World Association for Veterinary Dermatology (#21203)
- ♦ WCVM – World Council for Venue Management (inactive)
- ♦ WCWB – World Council for the Welfare of the Blind (inactive)
- ♦ **WCW** World Council of Whalers (#21341)
- ♦ WDA-AP – World Dance Alliance – Asia Pacific (see: #21352)
- ♦ **WDA** Wildlife Disease Association (#20959)
- ♦ **WDA** World Dodgeball Association (#21365)
- ♦ **WDA** Worldwide Dragonfly Association (#21920)
- ♦ WDC / see World Development Federation
- ♦ WDCA – World Diving Coaches Association (inactive)
- ♦ WDC-C for Sunspot Index / see Solar Influences Data Analysis Centre (#19675)
- ♦ WDCGG – WMO World Data Centre for Greenhouse Gases (see: #21649)
- ♦ WDCM / see WFCC-MIRCEN World Data Centre for Microorganisms (#20929)
- ♦ **WDCM** WFCC-MIRCEN World Data Centre for Microorganisms (#20929)
- ♦ WDCS / see Whale and Dolphin Conservation
- ♦ WDC – Whale and Dolphin Conservation (internationally oriented national body)
- ♦ **WDC** World Dance Council (#21353)
- ♦ **WDC** World Diamond Council (#21360)
- ♦ WD and DSC Centre / see World Dance Council (#21353)
- ♦ WDEF – World Development Endowment Foundation (internationally oriented national body)
- ♦ **WDF** World Darts Federation (#21355)
- ♦ WDF – World Development Federation (internationally oriented national body)
- ♦ WDF – World Development Foundation (internationally oriented national body)
- ♦ **WDF** World Diabetes Foundation (#21359)
- ♦ **WDGF** World Deaf Golf Federation (#21356)
- ♦ **WDK** Weltbund der Kochverbände (#21124)
- ♦ WDM / see Global Justice Now
- ♦ WDN / see Gaian Democracy Network
- ♦ **WDO** World Design Organization (#21358)
- ♦ **WDO** World Doctors Orchestra (#21364)
- ♦ **WDO** World Duchenne Organization (#21366)
- ♦ **WDSF** World DanceSport Federation (#21354)
- ♦ **WDSI** World Deaf Squash Inc (#21357)
- ♦ WDU – World Disability Union (unconfirmed)
- ♦ WdW / see World Federalist Movement – Movement for a Just World Order through a Strengthened United Nations (#21404)
- ♦ WEAAP / see European Association for Aviation Psychology (#05950)
- ♦ WEAA – Western European Airports Association (inactive)
- ♦ WEAI / see Western Economic Association International
- ♦ WEA International – Western Economic Association International (internationally oriented national body)
- ♦ **WEAll** Wellbeing Economy Alliance (#20856)
- ♦ **WEA in the Nordic Countries** Nordic Organization of Workers' Educational Associations (#17377)
- ♦ WeAreBamboo / see Bamboo Foundation

♦ We Are Church International (WAC-I) 20841

Wir sind Kirche International

Chair address not obtained.
Communications Officer address not obtained.
URL: http://www.we-are-church.org/413/

History Founded 23 Nov 1996, Rome (Italy). Former names and other names: *International Movement We Are Church (IMWAC)* – former; *Internationale Bewegung Wir sind Kirche* – former. Registration: Association Loi de 1901; Repertoire National des Associations, No/ID: W751245938, France, Paris. **Aims** Coordinate activities of national and regional groups to work and pray for the reform and renewal of the *Roman Catholic* Church. **Structure** Council; Coordination Team. **Languages** English, Spanish. **Finance** Sources: donations; members' dues. **Activities** Events/meetings; networking/liaising; religious activities. **Publications** Press releases.
Members National organizations in 18 countries:
Austria, Belgium, Brazil, Canada, Chile, Denmark, France, Germany, Ireland, Italy, Netherlands, Norway, Portugal, South Africa, Spain, Sweden, UK, USA. [2022.10.25/XF6045/**F**]

- ♦ We Are Europe! (internationally oriented national body)
- ♦ WEA Sustainability Center – World Evangelical Alliance Sustainability Center (internationally oriented national body)
- ♦ Weatherhead Center for International Affairs (internationally oriented national body)

♦ Weather Risk Management Association (WRMA) 20842

Main Office 1000 Westgate Dri, Ste 252, St Paul MN 55114, USA. E-mail: info@wrma.org.
URL: http://www.wrma.org/

History 1999. **Aims** Be the industry association for weather risk management professionals to enhance public awareness of the weather risk industry and promote the growth and general welfare of the weather risk market. **Structure** Board of Directors, comprising President, Vice-President, Secretary/Treasurer, Past-President and 7 Directors. **Events** *Annual Meeting* Miami Beach, FL (USA) 2022, *European Fall Meeting* Paris (France) 2022, *European Meeting* Madrid (Spain) 2019, *Annual Meeting* New York, NY (USA) 2019, *European Meeting* London (UK) 2017.
Members Companies (46) in 6 countries:
Australia, Germany, Netherlands, Switzerland, UK, USA. [2022/XJ4469/**C**]

♦ Weavers Committee 20843

Coordinator c/o SPATS, PO Box 2426, Government Buildings, Suva, Fiji. Fax +679303924. E-mail: info@spatsfj.org.
URL: http://spatsfj.org/

History 1989, Tonga, at workshop jointly sponsored by *South Pacific Association of Theological Schools (SPATS, #19882)* and *Pacific Conference of Churches (PCC, #17943)*. Functions as the *Women in Theological Education Committee* of SPATS. The Weavers' Coordinator is a member of the SPATS Council. **Aims** Promote *theological education* for *women* among *Pacific churches*. In particular: promote inclusion of women students in all theological schools and inclusion of theological studies from women's perspectives in their *curricula*; encourage schools to recruit women faculty and *teachers*. **Finance** Support from: PCC; *World Council of Churches (WCC, #21320)*; Evangelisches Missionswerk (Germany); Methodist Church of the USA. Additional grants from: *Folkekirkens Nødhjaelp (FKN)*; *MISSIO (#16827)*; Anglican Church of Canada; Reformed Church of the Netherlands. **Activities** Awareness raising; fostering better relationships with church leaders and principals; listening to and advising on needs of women in churches and schools; establishing Weavers' national branches. Currently expanding work through a multi-denominational network of Christian women. Hopes to develop a resource centre and seeks scholarship opportunities for Pacific women to pursue theological studies. **Events** *Women theology – Pacific perspectives* Suva (Fiji) 1995. **Publications** *Weaving* (4 a year) – newsletter.
Members Schools (19) in 12 countries and territories:
Cook Is, Fiji, Kiribati, Marshall Is, New Caledonia, Polynesia Fr, Samoa, Samoa USA, Solomon Is, Tahiti Is, Tonga, Vanuatu. [2016/XE2252/y/**E**]

- ♦ WEA – Women's Earth Alliance (internationally oriented national body)
- ♦ **WEA** World Economics Association (#21369)
- ♦ **WEA** World Evangelical Alliance (#21393)

♦ Web3D Consortium 20844

Mailing address 650 Castro St, Ste 120-490, Mountain View CA 94041, USA. T. +12483427662 – +1248(18447686886. E-mail: contact@web3d.org.
Treas San Mateo Medical Center, Emergency Dept, 222 West 39th Avenue, San Mateo CA 94403, USA.
URL: http://www.web3d.org/

History Dec 1996, as *VRML Consortium*. Present name adopted, Dec 1998. **Aims** Create and develop *specifications* and *standards* for 3D *graphics* for *internet* applications; foster the adoption of these by developers of related products and services. **Structure** Board of Directors. Executive Committee. Officers: President, Vice-President, Secretary, Treasurer. **Finance** Members' dues. **Activities** Working teams (4): Specification; Communication; Commercialization; Implementation. Working groups on specific technical objectives. Organizes symposia, conferences and meetings. **Events** *Annual Symposium* Perugia (Italy) 2007, *Annual Symposium* Columbia, MD (USA) 2006, *Annual member meeting* Los Angeles, CA (USA) 2004, *Annual Web3D symposium / Annual Symposium* Monterey, CA (USA) 2004, *Annual international conference* London (UK) 2003. **Publications** *Web3D News*.
Members Charter; Corporate; Academic; Professional. Members (125) in 23 countries and territories:
Austria, Brazil, Canada, China, Finland, France, Germany, Honduras, India, Ireland, Israel, Japan, Korea Rep, Netherlands, Norway, Romania, Singapore, Spain, Sweden, Switzerland, Taiwan, UK, USA. [2016/XF4795/**F**]

- ♦ Web alliance for Regreening in Africa (internationally oriented national body)

♦ Webb Society 20845

Pres Inst of Astronomy, Madingley Road, Cambridge, CB3 OHA, UK. E-mail: rwa@ast.cam.ac.uk.
URL: http://www.webbdeepsky.com/

History in honour of Rev Thomas William Webb (1807-1885), an amateur astronomer. **Aims** Encourage amateur observations of double *stars* and 'deep-sky' objects such as star-clusters and *nebula*; serve as a forum for communication and exchange of information. **Structure** Committee, comprising President/Director, Secretary/Treasurer, Editor, Business Manager, 4 Directors and 2 further members. **Events** *Annual Meeting* Cambridge (UK) 2019, *Annual Meeting* Cambridge (UK) 2018, *Annual Meeting* Cambridge (UK) 2017, *Annual Meeting* Cambridge (UK) 2016, *Annual Meeting* Cambridge (UK) 2015. **Publications** *Deep Sky Observer* (4 a year). [2016.03.07/XE3806/**E**]

♦ **WEBBS** World Elite Black Belt Society (#21375)

♦ Web Information Systems Engineering Society (WISE Society) 20846

Chairman Ctr for Applied Informatics, Victoria Univ, PO Box 14428, Melbourne VIC 8001, Australia.
URL: http://www.wise-conferences.org/

History First conference held, Jun 2000. **Aims** Promote and exchange scholarly work in Web Information Systems and related fields worldwide. **Structure** Steering/Executive Committee, comprising Chairman, Deputy Chairman/Secretary, Treasurer and 6 members. **Events** *International Conference on Web Information Systems Engineering* Dubai (United Arab Emirates) 2018, *International Conference on Web Information Systems Engineering* Pushchino (Russia) 2017, *International Conference on Web Information Systems Engineering* Miami, FL (USA) 2016, *International Conference on Web Information Systems Engineering* Shanghai (China) 2016, *International Conference on Web Information Systems Engineering* Thessaloniki (Greece) 2014. **Publications** *World Wide Web: Internet and Web Information Systems (WWW)* – journal. [2018/XJ6631/c/E]

♦ Web Intelligence Consortium (WIC) 20847

Co-Chairman Information Systems Laboratory-Dept of Information Engineering, Maebashi Inst of Technology, 460-1 Kamisadori-Cho, Maebashi GUNMA, 371-0816 Japan. T. +81272657366. Fax +81272657366.
URL: http://wi-consortium.org/

Aims Advance worldwide scientific research and industrial development in the field of web intelligence. **Events** *International Conference on Web Intelligence and Intelligent Agent Technology (WI-AT 2021)* Melbourne, VIC (Australia) 2021, *International Conference on Web Intelligence and Intelligent Agent Technology* Singapore (Singapore) 2015, *International Conference on Web Intelligence and Intelligent Agent Technology* Lyon (France) 2011, *International conference on intelligent agent technology* Sydney, NSW (Australia) 2008, *International conference on web intelligence* Sydney, NSW (Australia) 2008. **Publications** *Web Intelligence and Agent Systems: An International Journal. Annual Review of Intelligent Informatics* – series.
Members Centres (13) in 13 countries and territories:
Australia, Canada, China, France, Hong Kong, India, Japan, Korea Rep, Mexico, Poland, Spain, UK, USA. [2014/XF7147/F]

♦ Web Science Trust (WST) 20848

Exec Dir Room 3015 – Bldg 32, Univ of Southampton, Univ Road, Southampton, SO17 1BJ, UK.
Registered Office c/o Skadden, Arps – Slate – Meagher and Fom LLP, 40 Bank Str, Canary Wharf, London, E14 5DS, UK.
URL: http://webscience.org/

History Originated in *Web Science Research Initiative (WSRI)*, set up 2006. Registration: Charity Commission, No/ID: 1133507, England and Wales. **Aims** Support global development of web science. **Structure** Board of Trustees. **Events** *Web Science Conference* Austin, TX (USA) 2023, *Web Science Conference* Barcelona (Spain) 2022, *Web Science Conference* Southampton (UK) 2021, *Web Science Conference* Southampton (UK) 2020, *Web Science Conference* Boston, MA (USA) 2019. [2022/XM4687/F]

♦ **WECAFC** Western Central Atlantic Fishery Commission (#20911)
♦ WECAN – Women's Earth and Climate Action Network, International (internationally oriented national body)
♦ **WECAN** Workgroup of European Cancer Patient Advocacy Networks (#21054)
♦ **WECARD** West and Central African Council for Agricultural Research and Development (#20907)
♦ WECC / see Women's Earth and Climate Action Network, International
♦ WECC – World Electronics Circuits Council (no recent information)
♦ WECF / see Women Engage for a Common Future (#20992)
♦ **WECF** Women Engage for a Common Future (#20992)

♦ WE Charity 20849

Exec Dir 339 Queen St E, Toronto ON M5A 1S9, Canada. T. +14169255894. Fax +14169258242. E-mail: info@we.org.
URL: http://www.wecharity.org/

History 1995, as *Free the Children (FTC)*, by Craig Kielburger. **Aims** Empower communities to lift themselves out of *poverty*. **Structure** Boards of Directors in Canada, USA and UK Executive Team. **Finance** Donations. **Activities** Projects/programmes; advocacy/lobbying/activism. **NGO Relations** Member of: *Ontario Council for International Cooperation (OCIC)*. [2018.06.25/XN9493/F]

♦ WEC International (WEC) 20850

Action d'évangélisation mondiale (AEM) – Corporación Pro-Cruzada Mundial (CPM) – Weltweiter Evangelisations-Kreuzzug (WEK) – Missão AMEM (AMEM)

UK Headquarters WEC International, PO Box 6461, Coventry, CV3 9NR, UK. T. +441753884631. E-mail: hello@wec-uk.org.
USA Headquarters WEC International, PO Box 1707, Fort Washington PA 19034, USA. T. +12156462322. Fax +12156466202. E-mail: contact.us@wec-usa.org.
URL: https://www.wecinternational.org/

History 1913. Founded initially as *Heart of Africa Mission* as an interdenominational mission agency. Former names and other names: *Worldwide Evangelization Crusade (WEC)* – former; *Worldwide Evangelization for Christ International* – full title. Registration: Charity Commission, No/ID: 237005, Start date: 6 Jan 1965, England and Wales. **Aims** Find new, creative and culturally-relevant ways of taking the good news of Jesus to the peoples and nations who have yet to hear it. **Structure** Leaders' Council; International Director; Deputy International Directors. HQ Offices in Australia, Brazil, Canada, UK, USA. **Languages** Arabic, Dutch, English, French, German, Korean, Portuguese, Spanish. **Staff** Voluntary. **Finance** Sources: gifts, legacies. **Activities** Events/meetings; healthcare; humanitarian/emergency aid; networking/liaising; religious activities; research and development; research/documentation; training/education. **Publications** *Operation World* (2010) by Jason Mandryk in Amharic, Arabic, English, French, German, Greek, Indonesian, Korean, Mandarin Chinese, Portuguese, Russian, Spanish – a prayer handbook for the world.
Members Individuals (over 1,800) in 88 countries and territories:
Albania, Australia, Austria, Belgium, Brazil, Bulgaria, Burundi, Cambodia, Canada, Chad, Colombia, Costa Rica, Czechia, Dominican Rep, Ecuador, Egypt, El Salvador, England, Equatorial Guinea, Ethiopia, Fiji, Finland, France, Gambia, Germany, Ghana, Greece, Guatemala, Guinea-Bissau, Haiti, Hong Kong, Hungary, India, Indonesia, Ireland, Israel, Italy, Japan, Jordan, Kazakhstan, Kenya, Korea Rep, Latvia, Lithuania, Luxembourg, Malaysia, Mexico, Moldova, Mongolia, Mozambique, Nepal, Netherlands, New Zealand, Nicaragua, Nigeria, North Macedonia, Northern Ireland, Philippines, Poland, Portugal, Romania, Russia, Rwanda, Sao Tomé-Principe, Scotland, Senegal, Singapore, Slovakia, Slovenia, Solomon Is, South Africa, Spain, Sri Lanka, Sweden, Switzerland, Taiwan, Thailand, Timor-Leste, Tuvalu, Uganda, UK, Ukraine, USA, Vanuatu, Venezuela, Vietnam, Wales, Zimbabwe.

NGO Relations Member of (4): *Arbeitsgemeinschaft Evangelikaler Missionen (AEM)*; *Association of Evangelicals in Africa (AEA, #02587)*; *Fédération de missions évangéliques francophones (FMEF, #09688)*; *Global Connections*. Instrumental in setting up (1): *Radio Worldwide*. see above [2022.05.04/XF3807/v/F]

♦ WEConnect International (internationally oriented national body)
♦ WECP – World Energy Cities Partnership (unconfirmed)
♦ WEC / see WEC International (#20850)
♦ **WEC** WEC International (#20850)
♦ **WEC** World Employment Confederation (#21376)
♦ **WEC** World Energy Council (#21381)
♦ **WEC** World Environment Center (#21386)
♦ WEC – World Ethnosport Confederation (internationally oriented national body)
♦ **WEDA** Western Dredging Association (#20913)
♦ WEDC – Water, Engineering and Development Centre (internationally oriented national body)
♦ **WEDNS** Walter E Dandy Neurosurgical Society (#20815)
♦ **WEDO** Women's Environment and Development Organization (#21016)
♦ WEEC International Association / see World Environmental Education Congress Network (#21385)
♦ WEEC International Environmental Education Network / see World Environmental Education Congress Network (#21385)
♦ Weed Science Society of America (internationally oriented national body)
♦ Weed Science Society for Eastern Africa (inactive)
♦ WEED – World Economy, Ecology and Development (internationally oriented national body)
♦ **WEEE Forum** European Association of Electrical and Electronic Waste Take Back Systems (#06022)

♦ WEEELABEX Organisation 20851

Managing Dir U Habrovky 11/247, 140 00 Prague 4, Czechia. T. +420225852802. E-mail: office@weeelabex.org.
URL: http://www.weeelabex.org/

History 17 Apr 2013, Prague (Czech Rep). Culminated from the *WEEE label of excellende (WEEELABEX)* project (2009-2012). WEEELABEX standards introduced, Apr 2011. WEEE stands for: *waste electrical and electronic equipment*. Registered in accordance with Czech law. **Aims** Train auditors in the WEEELABEX standards; promote adoption of these standards by operators and member states as a means to improve WEEE management practices in Europe. **Structure** General Assembly; Government Council; Office (Secretariat). **Finance** Members' dues.
Members Producer compliance schemes (25) in 15 countries:
Austria, Belgium, Czechia, Denmark, France, Ireland, Italy, Netherlands, Norway, Portugal, Romania, Slovenia, Spain, Sweden, UK.
Included in the above, 1 organization listed in this Yearbook:
European Recycling Platform (ERP, #08336).
NGO Relations *European Association of Electrical and Electronic Waste Take Back Systems (WEEE Forum, #06022)*. [2015/XM4096/E]

♦ We Effect (internationally oriented national body)

♦ WeForest 20852

CEO Cantersteen 47, 1000 Brussels, Belgium. T. +3223084943. E-mail: contact@weforest.org.
URL: http://www.weforest.org/

History Originally set up 2008, Switzerland; transferred to Belgium, May 2010. Registration: Belgium; Incorporated, USA. **Aims** Conserve and restore the ecological integrity of forests and landscapes, engaging communities to implement and deliver lasting solutions for climate, nature and people. **Structure** Board of Directors; Advisory Board; Scientific Advisors; Executive Team. **Languages** Dutch, English, French, German, Portuguese, Spanish. **Staff** 70.00 FTE, paid; 10.00 FTE, voluntary. **Finance** Sources: donations; grants; investments; sponsorship. Annual budget: 10,000,000 EUR (2023). **Activities** Projects/programmes. Active in: Argentina, Brazil, Ethiopia, Indonesia, Malawi, Senegal, Tanzania UR, Zambia. **Publications** *Forests: Reasons to be Hopeful* (2013) by Bill Liao. **IGO Relations** Observer status with (1): *United Nations Framework Convention on Climate Change (UNFCCC, 1992)*. **NGO Relations** Member of (3): *Club of Rome (COR, #04038)*; *King Baudouin Foundation (KBF)*; *United Nations Global Compact (#20567)*. Partner of (1): *Tropical Forest Alliance (TFA, #20249)*. [2023.02.13/XJ5481/F]

♦ WE Foundation – World Education Foundation (unconfirmed)
♦ WEFTA – Water Engineers for the Americas (internationally oriented national body)
♦ **WEFTA** West European Fish Technologists Association (#20919)
♦ WEF – Water Environment Federation (internationally oriented national body)
♦ WEF – World Eatology Forum (unconfirmed)
♦ **WEF** World Economic Forum (#21367)
♦ **WEF** World Education Fellowship (#21370)
♦ WEF – World Electronics Forum (unconfirmed)
♦ WEF / see World Evangelical Alliance (#21393)

♦ WEGEMT 20853

Mailing Address c/o RINA, 8-9 Northumberland St, London, WC2N 5DA, UK. E-mail: info@wegemt.eu.
Registered Office Mekelweg 2, 2682 CD Delft, Netherlands.
URL: http://www.wegemt.com/

History 1978. Founded by European marine technology universities. Former names and other names: *WEGEMT – European Association of Universities in Marine Technology and Related Sciences* – full title. Registration: Netherlands. **Aims** Update and extend the skills, knowledge and competence in *Europe* of practising *engineers* and advanced level postgraduate students in *marine technology* and related sciences. **Structure** General Assembly (annual). Executive Committee. **Events** *Annual Meeting* Hamburg (Germany) 2007, *Annual Meeting* Helsinki (Finland) 2003. **Publications** Proceedings of meetings. **Members** Universities (42) in 17 countries. Membership countries not specified. **IGO Relations** *European Commission (EC, #06633)*. **NGO Relations** Participant in: *WATERBORNE (#20823)*. [2022/XD8841/D]

♦ WEGEMT – European Association of Universities in Marine Technology and Related Sciences / see WEGEMT (#20853)
♦ **WeGO** World e-Governments Organization of Cities and Local Governments (#21542)
♦ Wegvervoerakkoord tussen de Benelux et de Baltische staten (1992 treaty)
♦ WEI / see European Institute for Wood Preservation (#07575)

♦ Weightlifting Federation of Africa (WFA) 20854

Fédération africaine d'haltérophilie

Gen Sec 18 avenue des Martyrs El Mourouj I, 2074 Tunis, Tunisia. T. +21671362315. E-mail: newwfa@hotmail.com.
Pres address not obtained.
URL: http://www.wfa.com.ly/

History 1978, Alexandria (Egypt), on the occasion of international tournament in Egypt. **Aims** Organize, control and develop weightlifting on a continental scale; develop and intensify friendship and cooperation among national federations and lifters from all African countries; assist the African national weightlifting federations in their activities; as the highest authority in weightlifting in Africa, resolve disputes in regard to this sport that may arise between affiliated federations; control and regulate all African weightlifting events; verify African records. **Structure** Annual Congress (organized every year at Senior or Junior African Championships). Electoral Congress (every 4 years). Executive Board, consisting of President, General-Secretary-Treasurer, 5 Vice-Presidents and 5 members. Committees (4): Technical Committee; Medical Committee; Scientific and Research Committee; Media Committee. Auditor. Coaching and Refereeing Clinics. **Languages** Arabic, English, French. **Staff** Voluntary. **Finance** Members' dues. Subsidies from Egyptian government. Budget (annual): US$ 10,000. **Activities** Organizes African Junior and Senior Championships. Coaching and refereeing centres. **Events** *Congress* Entebbe (Uganda) 2015, *Congress* Uganda 2005, *African electoral congress* Cairo (Egypt) 1991, *Annual Congress* Cairo (Egypt) 1988, *Annual Congress* Nairobi (Kenya) 1987. **Publications** African records and rules.
Members Organizations in 30 countries:
Algeria, Cameroon, Comoros, Congo Brazzaville, Congo DR, Egypt, Eswatini, Ethiopia, Ghana, Kenya, Lesotho, Liberia, Libya, Madagascar, Malawi, Mali, Mauritius, Morocco, Mozambique, Nigeria, Seychelles, Sierra Leone, Somalia, South Africa, Sudan, Tanzania UR, Tunisia, Uganda, Zambia, Zimbabwe. [2016/XD9213/D]

♦ **WEI-IEO** Europäisches Institut für Holzimprägnierung (#07575)
♦ **WEI-IEO** European Institute for Wood Preservation (#07575)
♦ **WEI-IEO** Institut de l'Europe pour l'imprégnation du bois (#07575)

♦ Weimar Triangle 20855

Groupe de Weimar

Address not obtained.

History 1991, Weimar (Germany), by Foreign Ministers of France, Germany and Poland, as an informal discussion group. **Aims** Promote cooperation among founding members. **Activities** Foreign ministers meet annually. **Events** *Summit Meeting* Weimar (Germany) 2006, *Summit Meeting* Nancy (France) 2005, *Summit Meeting* Wroclaw (Poland) 2003, *Summit Meeting* Paris (France) 2002, *Summit Meeting* Hambach (France) 2001.
Members Governments of 3 countries:
France, Germany, Poland. [2010/XE2745/E*]

♦ WEInstitute / see World Engagement Institute
♦ Weitz Center for Development Studies (internationally oriented national body)

- **WEI** Women Enabled International (#20991)
- WEI – Women's Enterprises International (internationally oriented national body)
- WEI – World Engagement Institute (internationally oriented national body)
- **WEK** Weltweiter Evangelisations-Kreuzzug (#20850)
- WELG – Western European Logistics Group (inactive)
- WELG – Women's Ecumenical Liaison Group (inactive)

♦ Wellbeing Economy Alliance (WEAll) 20856

Address not obtained.
URL: https://wellbeingeconomy.org/

Aims Transform the economic system into one that delivers human and ecological wellbeing. **Structure** Global Council.

Members Organizations and institutes in 25 countries:
Argentina, Australia, Bhutan, Brazil, Canada, Chile, Costa Rica, Denmark, Ethiopia, Finland, Germany, Greece, India, Ireland, Japan, Namibia, Netherlands, New Zealand, Norway, South Africa, Spain, Sweden, Trinidad-Tobago, UK, USA.
- *African Transformative Leapfrogging Advisory Services (ATLAS);*
- *Asamblea de Cooperación por la Paz (ACPP);*
- *Club of Rome (COR, #04038);*
- *Earth Charter International (ECI, #05161);*
- *Economy for the Common Good (ECG, #05323);*
- *European Environmental Bureau (EEB, #06996);*
- *European Forest Institute (EFI, #07297);*
- *European Health Futures Forum (EHFF, #07456);*
- *European Youth Forum (#09140);*
- *Finance Watch (#09764);*
- *Global Alliance for Banking on Values (GABV, #10186);*
- *Global Ecovillage Network (GEN, #10331);*
- *Globally Responsible Leadership Initiative (GRLI, #10462);*
- *Green Economy Coalition (GEC, #10717);*
- *International Humanistic Management Association (IHMA);*
- *Local Futures (#16506);*
- *r3.0 (#18597);*
- *Social Enterprise World Forum (SEWF, #19336);*
- *Social Progress Imperative (#19345);*
- *Social Value International (SVI, #19348);*
- *Sustainable Consumption Research and Action Initiative (SCORAI, #20053);*
- *Swedish Organization for Global Health (SOGH);*
- *Tellus Institute;*
- *World Fair Trade Organization (WFTO, #21396).* [2020/AA1056/y/**C**]

- Wellbeing Foundation Africa (internationally oriented national body)
- Wellcome Trust (internationally oriented national body)
- Wellshare International (internationally oriented national body)
- WELLSTART International (internationally oriented national body)

♦ WELMEC – European Cooperation in Legal Metrology 20857

Sec p/a Verispect, Thijsseweg 11, 2629 JA Delft, Netherlands. E-mail: secretary@welmec.org.
URL: http://www.welmec.org/

History Founded Jun 1990, Bern (Switzerland), on signature of a Memorandum of Understanding. Original title: *Western European Legal Metrology Cooperation*. Current title adopted Jan 1995. **Aims** Establish a harmonized and consistent approach to legal metrology in the light of: the European Economic Area (EEA) Agreement extending the *single market* of the European Union to most of EFTA; development of closer cooperation between EU and EFTA; political changes in Central and Eastern Europe; increased international trade in *measuring instruments*; the different coverage of legal metrology in various countries. **Structure** Committee (meets annually), comprising delegates of national bodies and observers. Chairman's Group; Working Groups (97): Weighing Instruments; General Aspects of Legal Metrology; Review of Enforcement Activities; Prepackages; Software; MID; Measuring Instruments for Liquids Other Than Water. Ad hoc Working Groups; Secretariat in Vienna (Austria). **Finance** Members' contributions. **Activities** Politics/policy/regulatory. **Events** *Meeting* Vienna (Austria) 2015, *Meeting* Bratislava (Slovakia) / Cast Papiernicka (Slovakia) 2004, *Meeting* Ljubljana (Slovenia) 2004, *Meeting* Oslo (Norway) 2004, *Meeting* Prague (Czech Rep) 2004. **Publications** *European Legal Metrology Directory* (1997). Directives; guides; brochures. Information Services: Library and information service. **Information Services** *European Metrological Type Approval Database (EMeTAS); Library and information service.*

Members National bodies having signed the memorandum. Full countries of the European Union and EFTA (28):
Austria, Belgium, Cyprus, Czechia, Denmark, Estonia, Finland, France, Germany, Greece, Hungary, Iceland, Ireland, Italy, Latvia, Lithuania, Luxembourg, Malta, Netherlands, Norway, Poland, Portugal, Slovakia, Slovenia, Spain, Sweden, Switzerland, UK.
Associate countries having signed agreements with EU (3):
Bulgaria, Romania, Türkiye.

NGO Relations Observer status with: *European Cooperation for Accreditation (EA, #06782)*. Member of: *European Accreditation Advisory Board (EAAB, see: #06782)*. Cooperates with: *Association européenne de fabricants de compteurs d'eau et d'énergie thermique (AQUA, #02567).* [2015/XF2664/**F**]

- Welsh Centre for International Affairs (internationally oriented national body)
- Weltakademie für Kunst und Wissenschaft (#21065)
- Weltarbeitsgruppe für Greifvögel und Eulen (#21945)
- Weltausschuss für Gehörlosenschach / see International Chess Committee of the Deaf (#12544)
- Weltbergbau-Kongress (#21654)
- Weltbewegung der Christlichen Arbeiter (#21660)
- Weltbewegung der Mütter / see Make Mothers Matter (#16554)
- Weltbund der Angestellten / see World Organization of Workers (#21697)
- Weltbund der Angestelltengewerkschaften / see World Organization of Workers (#21697)
- Weltbund der Christlichen Vereine Junger Männer (#21090)
- Weltbund Christlicher Abstinenter Frauen (#21840)
- Weltbund Christlicher Verbände Junger Frauen / see World Young Women's Christian Association (#21947)
- Weltbund der Demokratischen Jugend (#21427)
- Weltbund für Erneuerung der Erziehung (#21370)
- Weltbund Junger Esperantisten / see Tutmonda Esperantista Junulara Organizo (#20268)
- Weltbund der Katholischen Frauenjugend (inactive)
- Weltbund der Katholischen Jugend (inactive)
- Weltbund der Kochverbände (#21124)
- Weltbund für Psychische Hygiene (#21455)
- Weltbund für Religiöse Freiheit (#12130)
- Weltbund der Rosenvereine (#21478)
- Weltbund zum Schutze des Lebens (inactive)
- Weltbund von Schwesternschaften und Verbänden der Diakonie / see World Federation of Diaconal Associations and Diaconal Communities (#21429)
- Weltbund St Gabriel (#21885)
- Weltbund von Verbänden und Gemeinschaften der Diakonie (#21429)
- Weltbund der Vereinte Städte (inactive)
- Weltbund der Weltföderalisten / see World Federalist Movement – Movement for a Just World Order through a Strengthened United Nations (#21404)
- Weltbürger-Register (#18822)
- Weltbürger Stiftung (internationally oriented national body)
- Weltdatenzentrum Abfluss (#10584)
- Welt-Esperanto-Jugend (#20268)
- Weltfernschachbund (#12971)
- Weltföderation Agrarischer Arbeiter (inactive)
- Weltföderation der Agrar- und Lebensmittelarbeiter (inactive)
- Weltföderation von Arbeitern in Lebensmittel-, Tabak- und Hotelindustrien-WVA (inactive)
- Weltföderation der Methodistinnen / see World Federation of Methodist and Uniting Church Women (#21457)
- Weltföderation der Wissenschaftler (#21480)
- Weltfond der Solidarität gegen Hunger (#09836)
- Weltfrauen Sicherheits Rat (unconfirmed)
- Weltfreundschaft Föderation (inactive)
- Weltfriedensdienst (internationally oriented national body)
- Weltfriedensrat (#21717)
- Weltfrontkämpferverband / see The World Veterans Federation (#21900)
- Weltgemeinschaft Reformierter Kirchen (#21289)
- Welt-Gesellschaft für Buiatrik (#21122)
- Welt-Gesellschaft für Geschichte der Veterinärmedizin (#21143)
- Weltgesellschaft der Pferdetierärzte (#21388)
- Welt-Gesellschaft der Tierärztlichen Ausbilder (inactive)
- Weltgesellschaft der Veterinärspezialisten auf dem Gebiete der Mikrobiologie, Immunologie und Infektionskrankheiten (no recent information)
- Weltgewerkschaftsbund (#21493)
- Welthaus Bielefeld (internationally oriented national body)
- Welthilfsverband (inactive)
- Welt Hugenotten Zentrum (internationally oriented national body)
- Welthungerhilfe (internationally oriented national body)
- Welt-Informationszentrum für Zweisprachige Erziehung / see Information Centre for Bilingual and Plurilingual Education (#11195)
- Welt-Informationszentrum für Zweisprachige und Mehrsprachige Erziehung / see Information Centre for Bilingual and Plurilingual Education (#11195)
- Weltinstitut für fortgeschrittene phänomenologische Forschung und Bildung / see World Phenomenology Institute (#21725)
- Welt-Institut der Freunden / see Global College, Long Island University
- Weltinstitut der Sparkassen (#21764)
- Welt Interessen Gemeinschaft Alterer Langstvecken Läufer (inactive)
- Weltjugendchor (#21955)
- Weltjugendorganisation gegen Klimaveränderung (inactive)
- Weltkoalition zur Abschaffung der Versuche an Mensch und Tier (inactive)
- Weltkonferenz der Religionen für den Frieden / see Religions for Peace (#18831)
- Weltkongress Alternativen und Umwelt (meeting series)
- Weltkongress der Freien Ukrainer (#21305)
- Weltkongress der Uiguren (#21896)
- Weltkreis des Konsens / see Consensus for Sustainable People, Organisations and Communities
- Weltlandfrauenverband (#02338)
- Weltlautschrift Verein (#14573)
- Welt Natur Fonds (#21922)
- Weltnatürliche Gesundheit Organisation (internationally oriented national body)
- Weltnotwerk der KAB (internationally oriented national body)
- Welt-Organisation Agudath Israel (#00584)
- Weltorganisation der Arbeitnehmer (#21697)
- Welt-Organisation Bild und Ton (inactive)
- Weltorganisation gegen die Folter (#21685)
- Weltorganisation für Familien (no recent information)
- Weltorganisation für Gastroenterologie (#21536)
- Welt-Organisation der konzertanten Blasorchester und Bläser-Ensembles (#21197)
- Welt Organisation für Schiffsmodellbau und Schiffsmodellsport (#21691)
- Welt Organisation des Thermalismus (#17820)
- Weltorganisation für Vorschulische Erziehung (#21689)
- Welt ORT (#21698)
- WeltPartner (internationally oriented national body)
- Weltrat für Bildung (#21325)
- Weltrat des Kunsthandwerks (#21342)
- Weltrat für Sport und Leibeserziehung / see International Council of Sport Science and Physical Education (#13077)
- Weltrat für Sportwissenschaft und Leibes-/Körpererziehung (#13077)
- Weltschachverband (#09627)
- Welt Simmental-Fleckvieh Vereinigung (#21785)
- Weltstiftung für Pathologie (#21714)
- Weltstiftung für Pathologie und Laboratoriumsmedizin der WASPaLM / see World Pathology Foundation (#21714)
- Welt-Tierärztegesellschaft (#21901)
- Welttierschutzbund (inactive)
- Welttierschutz-Gesellschaft (#21092)
- Welt Union der Frauen für internationale Eintracht (inactive)
- Welt-Union der Freidenker (inactive)
- Weltunion der Freien Berufe (#21882)
- Weltunion der Grossmärkte (#21889)
- Weltunion der Grossmärkte im IULA / see World Union of Wholesale Markets (#21889)
- Weltunion der Katholischen Frauen Organisationen (#21876)
- Weltunion der Katholischen Philosophischen Gesellschaften (#21875)
- Weltunion Katholischer Lehrer / see UMEC-WUCT (#20280)
- Welt Union der St Bernards-Klubs (#21887)

♦ Weltunion der Vereine für Deutsche Schäferhunde (WUSV) 20858

World Union of German Shepherd Associations

Secretariat Steinerne Furt 71, 86167 Augsburg, Germany. T. +498217400215. Fax +49821740029915. E-mail: wusv@schaeferhunde.de.
URL: https://www.wusv.org/

History 1968. Former names and other names: *Europa-Union der Vereine für Deutsche Schäferhunde (EUSV)* – former (1968 to 1974). Registration: Bavaria District court, No/ID: VR 2404, Start date: 9 Dec 1999, Germany, Augsburg. **Structure** Board of Directors; General Secretariat. **Activities** Advocacy/lobbying/activism; awards/prizes/competitions; training/education. [2022.01.03/AA2146/**C**]

- Weltverband der Anaesthesisten-Gesellschaften (#21482)
- Weltverband der Angestellten der Kernindustrie (inactive)
- Weltverband der Arbeitnehmer (inactive)
- Weltverband der Arbeitnehmer in Industriebetrieben (inactive)
- Weltverband für Balneologie und Klimatologie (#09692)
- Weltverband der Bärte (#21226)
- Weltverband der Bau- und Holzarbeiterorganisationen (inactive)
- Weltverband zur Bekämfung des Hungers (inactive)
- Weltverband Deutschsprachiger Medien (no recent information)
- Weltverbandes für das Skilehrwesen / see Interski International (#15975)
- Weltverband zur Förderung der Veterinärpasitologie (#21114)
- Weltverband der Friseure (#21550)
- Weltverband der Gemeinschaften Christlichen Lebens / see Christian Life Community (#03905)
- Weltverband der Gesellschaften für Biologische Psychiatrie (#21483)
- Weltverband der Gesellschaften für Geschichte der Pharmazie (inactive)
- Weltverband der Jersey Vienzüchter (#21598)

- ♦ Weltverband Jüdischer Studenten / see World Union of Jewish Students (#21878)
- ♦ Weltverband Katholischer Pädagogen / see UMEC-WUCT (#20280)
- ♦ Weltverband der Kinderfreunde (#02808)
- ♦ Weltverband der Lehrer (inactive)
- ♦ Weltverband der Lehrerorganisationen (inactive)
- ♦ Weltverband der Lehrmittelfirmen / see Worlddidac Association (#21361)
- ♦ Weltverband der Massschneider (#21453)
- ♦ Weltverband der Metallindustrie (inactive)
- ♦ Weltverband für Öffentliche Meinungs-Forschung (#21180)
- ♦ Weltverband ORT / see World ORT (#21698)
- ♦ Weltverband für Personzentrierte und Experienzielle Psychotherapie und Beratung (#21172)
- ♦ Weltverband für Psychiatrie (#21741)
- ♦ Weltverband für Psychotherapie (#21337)
- ♦ Weltverband für Religiös-Liberales Judentum (#21883)
- ♦ Weltverband der Schwebefähren (#21869)
- ♦ Weltverband der Skatspieler (#14866)
- ♦ Weltverband der Sportartikel-Industrie (#21487)
- ♦ Weltverband der Vereinigungen für Personalführung / see World Federation of People Management Associations (#21474)
- ♦ Weltverband der Zeitungen (inactive)
- ♦ Weltverbund der Diamantbearbeiter (inactive)
- ♦ Weltvereinigung der Braunviehzüchter (unconfirmed)
- ♦ Weltvereinigung der Geflügeltierärzte (#21902)
- ♦ Weltvereinigung für Geflügelwissenschaft (#21825)
- ♦ Weltvereinigung der Gesellschaften für Pathologie und für Laboratoriumsmedizin (#21191)
- ♦ Weltvereinigung der Jüdischen Gesellschaftlichen Zentren / see JCC Global (#16093)
- ♦ Weltvereinigung der Kaninchenwissenschaften (#21744)
- ♦ Weltvereinigung Kosmopolit (inactive)
- ♦ Weltvereinigung der Lotterien (#21628)
- ♦ Weltvereinigung der Tierärztlichen Lebensmittelhygieniker (#21204)
- ♦ Weltvereinigung für Tierproduktion (#21117)
- ♦ Welt-Vereinigung von Unternehmerinnen (#09733)
- ♦ Weltvereinigung der Veterinäranatomen (#21202)
- ♦ Weltvereinigung der Veterinärpathologen (no recent information)
- ♦ Weltverkehrsforum (#15725)
- ♦ Weltweite Aktion gegen den 'Frei' handel und die WTO (#18304)
- ♦ Weltweiter Energie Informationsdienst (#21582)
- ♦ Weltweiter Evangelisations-Kreuzzug (#20850)
- ♦ Weltwirtschaft, Oekologie und Entwicklung (internationally oriented national body)
- ♦ WEM / see Council of European Employers of the Metal, Engineering and Technology-Based Industries (#04887)
- ♦ **WEMC** World Energy & Meteorology Council (#21383)
- ♦ We Mean Business (unconfirmed)
- ♦ WEMOS (internationally oriented national body)
- ♦ WEMOS – Health Unlimited / see WEMOS
- ♦ WeMove Europe / see We Move Europe (#20859)

♦ We Move Europe (WeMove.EU) 20859

Exec Dir Liegnitzer Str 14, 10999 Berlin, Germany. E-mail: info@wemove.eu.
URL: https://www.wemove.eu/

History Owned and operated by *WeMove Europe SCE*. Registration: No/ID: HRB 175639, Start date: 5 Apr 2016, Germany, Charlottenburg. **Aims** Build a *community* towards better decisions in Europe. **Structure** Board. **Finance** External and community funding. **Activities** Advocacy/lobbying/activism; awareness raising. [2022/XM4922/F]

- ♦ **WeMove.EU** We Move Europe (#20859)
- ♦ WEMT / see Confederation of European Maritime Technology Societies (#04526)
- ♦ WENDOV / see European Network on Volunteer Development (#08032)
- ♦ Wendy and Emery Reves Center for International Studies (internationally oriented national body)
- ♦ WENMISS – World Society for Endoscopic, Navigated and Minimal Invasive Spine Surgery (inactive)
- ♦ Wenner-Gren Foundation for Anthropological Research (internationally oriented national body)
- ♦ Wenner-Gren Foundations (internationally oriented national body)
- ♦ Wenner-Gren Foundation – Wenner-Gren Foundation for Anthropological Research (internationally oriented national body)
- ♦ Wenner-Gren Stiftelserna (internationally oriented national body)
- ♦ **WENRA** Western European Nuclear Regulators Association (#20914)
- ♦ WEN – Women's Environmental Network (internationally oriented national body)
- ♦ **WEN** Work and Economy Research Network in the European Churches (#21051)
- ♦ WEO – World Egg Organisation (unconfirmed)
- ♦ **WEO** World Endoscopy Organization (#21380)
- ♦ **WEPA** Water Environment Partnership in Asia (#20827)
- ♦ **WEPF** World Eightball Pool Federation (#21373)
- ♦ WEP International / see Atria – Institute for Gender Equality and Women's History

♦ WePROTECT Global Alliance 20860

Contact Piustuin 20, 2161 HA Lisse, Netherlands. E-mail: info@weprotectga.org.
URL: https://www.weprotect.org/

History 5 Dec 2012, Brussels (Belgium). Launched by former US Attorney General Eric Holder and *European Commission (EC, #06633)* Commissioner Cecilia Malmström. WePROTECT Children Online Global Summit, set up Dec 2014, London (UK). Merger of separate entities, May 2016. Former names and other names: *Global Alliance Against Child Sexual Abuse Online* – former (5 Dec 2012 to May 2016). Registration: EU Transparency Register, No/ID: 834646340101-36, Start date: 27 Oct 2020. **Aims** Ensure that the online world is designed and regulated to keep children safe; bring together experts to break down complex problems into bite-sized pieces and work together to solve them; develop and promote strategic frameworks and innovative approaches to protect children from sexual exploitation and abuse online. **Structure** Board. **Activities** Advocacy/lobbying/activism; politics/policy/regulatory.
Members As of March 2021, governments (98), private sector companies (50), civil society organisations (49) and international organisations (9) in 90 countries:
Albania, Angola, Armenia, Australia, Austria, Bahrain, Belarus, Belgium, Bosnia-Herzegovina, Bulgaria, Burundi, Cambodia, Canada, Central African Rep, China, Colombia, Costa Rica, Croatia, Cyprus, Czechia, Denmark, Dominican Rep, El Salvador, Estonia, Ethiopia, Finland, France, Georgia, Germany, Ghana, Greece, Guatemala, Honduras, Hungary, Indonesia, Ireland, Israel, Italy, Japan, Jordan, Kenya, Korea Rep, Kosovo, Kuwait, Latvia, Lithuania, Luxembourg, Madagascar, Malta, Mexico, Moldova, Mongolia, Montenegro, Namibia, Nepal, Netherlands, New Zealand, Nigeria, North Macedonia, Norway, Oman, Pakistan, Paraguay, Peru, Philippines, Poland, Portugal, Qatar, Romania, Rwanda, San Marino, Saudi Arabia, Serbia, Slovakia, Slovenia, Spain, Sri Lanka, Sudan, Sweden, Switzerland, Tanzania UR, Thailand, Trinidad-Tobago, Türkiye, Uganda, UK, United Arab Emirates, USA, Vietnam, Zambia. [2021.03.24/XM8729/B]

- ♦ **WEPZA** World Economic Processing Zones Association (#21368)
- ♦ **WERA** World Education Research Association (#21372)
- ♦ WERC / see Center for the Study of Global Christianity
- ♦ WERC – World Environment and Resources Council (inactive)
- ♦ Wereldassociatie voor de Wetenschappelijke Studie van de Konijnenteelt (#21744)
- ♦ Wereldbamd (#09690)
- ♦ Wereldfederatie van Agrarische Arbeiders (inactive)
- ♦ Wereldfederatie van Arbeiders in Voedings-, Tabaks, en Hotelbedrijven-WVA (inactive)
- ♦ Wereld Federatie der Diamantbeurzen (#21430)
- ♦ Wereldfederatie van Landbouw- en Voedingsarbeiders (inactive)
- ♦ Wereldfederatie der Leiders van de Schooheidsinstituten en van Esthetiek (no recent information)
- ♦ Wereldfederatie van Meester Kleermakers (#21453)
- ♦ Wereldfederatie voor de Metaalindustrie (inactive)
- ♦ Wereldfederatie der Vrienden van de Musea (#21435)
- ♦ Wereldfederatie van Werknemers uit Industriële Bedrijven (inactive)
- ♦ Wereldjongerenorganisatie tegen Klimaatverandering (inactive)
- ♦ Wereldmediahuis (internationally oriented national body)
- ♦ Wereldsolidariteit / see WSM
- ♦ Wereldvakbond van Onderwijspersoneel (inactive)
- ♦ Wereldverbond van de Arbeid (inactive)
- ♦ Wereldverbond van Beambten / see World Organization of Workers (#21697)
- ♦ Wereldverbond van Beambtenvakorganisaties / see World Organization of Workers (#21697)
- ♦ Wereldverbond van Bouwvakarbeiders- en Houtbewerkersorganisaties (inactive)
- ♦ Wereldverbond van Diamantbewerkers (inactive)
- ♦ Wereldverbond van Katholieke Onderwijsgevenden / see UMEC-WUCT (#20280)
- ♦ Wereldvereniging der Kindervrienden (#02808)
- ♦ Wereldwijd Mediahuis / see Wereldmediahuis
- ♦ WERF – World Endometriosis Research Foundation (internationally oriented national body)
- ♦ WERI – World Economy Research Institute, Warsaw (internationally oriented national body)
- ♦ Das Werk (religious order)
- ♦ Het Werk (religious order)
- ♦ Werkcomité van de Mouterijen in de EEG / see Working Committee of the Malting Industry of the EU (#21055)
- ♦ Werkcomité van de Mouterijen in de EU (#21055)
- ♦ Werkgemeenschap van Europese Grensgebieden (#02499)
- ♦ Werkgroep Inheemse Volken / see Netherlands Centre for Indigenous Peoples
- ♦ Werkgroep Medische Ontwikkelingssamenwerking / see WEMOS
- ♦ Werkstatt 3 – Kommunikations- und Informationszentrum für Entwicklung, Frieden und Menschenrechte (internationally oriented national body)
- ♦ Werk Unserer Lieben Frau von Montligeon (religious order)
- ♦ Werner Lamberz International Institute of Journalism, College of Solidarity / see International Institute of Journalism, Berlin – Brandenburg
- ♦ WER – World Emergency Relief (internationally oriented national body)
- ♦ **WESA** World ESports Association (#21390)
- ♦ **WESCO** World Esports Consortium (#21391)
- ♦ **WES** European Network to Promote Women's Entrepreneurship (#07975)
- ♦ WESIB / see European Students' Union (#08848)

♦ Wesleyan Church Headquarters 20861

Gen Sec PO Box 50434, Indianapolis IN 46250-0434, USA. T. +13177747338. Fax +13177743924. E-mail: communications@wesleyan.org – information@wesleyan.org – info@wesleyan.org.
Street Address 13300 Olio Road, Fishers IN 46037, USA.
URL: http://www.wesleyan.org/

History 26 Jun 1968, as *Wesleyan World Headquarters*. **Aims** Preach *gospel* to all nations; make *disciples* of all who follow *Christ*. **Finance** Voluntary offerings. **Activities** Religious activities. **Events** *General Conference* Lexington, KY (USA) 2012, *Women's ministry summit* Galloway, OH (USA) 2011, *General Conference* Orlando, FL (USA) 2008, *General Conference* Grand Rapids, MI (USA) 2004, *General conference* Greensboro, NC (USA) 2000. **Publications** *Wesleyan Life* (4 a year).
Members Organizations in 31 countries:
Australia, Brazil, Canada, Chile, Colombia, Costa Rica, Egypt, Ghana, Guyana, Haiti, Honduras, India, Indonesia, Korea Rep, Liberia, Mexico, Mozambique, Myanmar, New Zealand, Nicaragua, Peru, Philippines, Puerto Rico, Sierra Leone, South Africa, Suriname, UK, USA, Venezuela, Zambia, Zimbabwe.
Also members in the Caribbean. Membership countries not specified. [2016.11.02/XE3899/E]

- ♦ Wesleyan World Headquarters / see Wesleyan Church Headquarters (#20861)
- ♦ **WesleyMen** World Fellowship of Methodist and Uniting Church Men (#21503)
- ♦ WESP / see European Studies Center, Pittsburgh PA
- ♦ **WESPAC** Western Pacific Commission for Acoustics (#20918)
- ♦ WESPRAC / see Western Pacific Commission for Acoustics (#20918)

♦ WESSA Share-Net 20862

Contact PO Box 394, Howick, 3290, South Africa. T. +27333303931ext2124 – +27333303931 ext2144. Fax +27333304576. E-mail: sharenet@wessa.co.za.
URL: http://www.wessa.org.za/

History Founded 1989, Howick (South Africa), as a collaborative resource development network by: WWF-South Africa; *Wildlife and Environment Society of South Africa (WESSA, inactive)*; *Environmental Education Association of Southern Africa (EEASA, #05501)*; the Natal Parks Board (now Ezemvelo KZN Wildlife). **Aims** Support *environmental education* in the Southern *African* Development Community (SADC) region. **Structure** Informal environmental resource development and networking project. Coordinated by: *Wildlife and Environment Society of South Africa (WESSA, inactive)*. **Languages** English. **Staff** 4.50 FTE, paid; 2.00 FTE, voluntary. **Finance** Self funding mainly through: sale of environmental learning support materials; development and co-development of environmental teaching and learning support materials; printing of environmental and community resources; some outside funding from organizations for specific projects. Budget (annual): over South African Rand 1 million. **Activities** Training/education; capacity building; guidance/assistance/consulting; networking/liaising; financial and/or material support. **Publications** *Beginners Guides Series*; *Hands-On Series*; *Taking Action Series*. Education for Sustainable Development (ESD) publications; environmental education resources; Enviro picture building games and puzzles; indigenous knowledge resources; teachers guides; water quality resources. **Members** Covers the SADC region and beyond. Membership countries not specified. [2014.06.01/XF4994/E]

- ♦ WESS – World Education System Society (no recent information)

♦ West Africa Action Network on Small Arms (WAANSA) 20863

Pres House No 1, Nene Oboade Street, East Legon, Accra, Ghana. T. +233302542059. Fax +233302542058.
URL: http://www.waansa.org/

History May 2002, Accra (Ghana). A regional affiliate of *International Action Network on Small Arms (IANSA, #11585)*. **Aims** Serve as a forum for the exchange of information, experiences and strategies in combating the proliferation of small arms and light weapons in West Africa. **Structure** General Assembly. Steering Committee. Executive Committee, comprising President and 6 members. Secretariat. **Languages** English, French, Portuguese. **Staff** 3.00 FTE, paid. **Finance** Sources: funding from NGOs; donors. **Activities** include: advocacy and sensibilization; capacity building; communication and coordination. **Publications** Book.
Members West African organizations in 15 countries:
Benin, Burkina Faso, Cape Verde, Côte d'Ivoire, Gambia, Ghana, Guinea, Guinea-Bissau, Liberia, Mali, Niger, Nigeria, Senegal, Sierra Leone, Togo.
NGO Relations Member of: *Control Arms (#04782)*; *International Action Network on Small Arms (IANSA, #11585)*. Affiliated with: Control Arms Campaign. [2016/XM0212/E]

- ♦ West Africa Centre for Peace Foundation (internationally oriented national body)

♦ West Africa Civil Society Forum (WACSOF) 20864

Forum de la société civile de l'Afrique de l'ouest (FOSCAO)

Gen Sec address not obtained. T. +2349033939809. E-mail: info@wacsof-foscao.org.
URL: https://www.wacsof-foscao.org/index.php/en/

Aims Promote democratization, conflict prevention, economic development and poverty eradication through citizens' participation in the West African region; promote permanent dialogue with ECOWAS. **Structure** Peoples' Forum (annual); Executive Committee; Working Committees (10); Secretariat in Abuja (Nigeria). **Finance** Sources: members' dues. **Activities** Networking/liaising; research and development. **Events** *Annual meeting* Cotonou (Benin) 2008, *Annual Meeting* Dakar (Senegal) 2003.

Members Organizations in the 15 ECOWAS member states:
Benin, Burkina Faso, Cape Verde, Côte d'Ivoire, Gambia, Ghana, Guinea, Guinea-Bissau, Liberia, Mali, Niger, Nigeria, Senegal, Sierra Leone, Togo.
IGO Relations *Economic Community of West African States (ECOWAS, #05312).* **NGO Relations** Member of (1): *International Coalition for the Responsibility to Protect (ICRtoP, #12620).* Partner of (1): *Actions for Genuine Democratic Alternatives (AGENDA, #00097).* [2019.02.11/XM0387/**F**]

♦ West Africa Civil Society Institute (internationally oriented national body)
♦ West Africa Economic and Monetary Union (#20377)

♦ West Africa Election Observers Network (WAEON) 20865

Contact PO Box LG 404, Legon, Accra, Ghana. T. +2333027842934 – +233302777214. E-mail: info@waeon.org.
Street address No 95 Nortei Ababio Loop, North Airport Residential Area, Accra, Ghana.
URL: http://www.waeon.org/
History 2010. French acronym *ROASE.* **Aims** Strengthen and support citizens' election observation groups to participate effectively in electoral and democratic processes in West Africa. **Structure** General Assembly; Executive Council; Secretariat hosted by Ghana Center for Democratic Development (CDD-Ghana). **Languages** English. **Staff** 4.00 FTE, paid. **Finance** Donor support; grants. **Activities** Monitoring/evaluation; research/documentation; networking/liaising; capacity building.
Members Organizations in 13 countries:
Benin, Burkina Faso, Côte d'Ivoire, Gambia, Ghana, Guinea, Liberia, Mali, Niger, Nigeria, Senegal, Sierra Leone, Togo.
Included in the above, 1 organization listed in this Yearbook: [2017.09.12/XJ7571/y/**F**]

♦ West Africa Journalists' Association / see West African Journalists' Union (#20885)
♦ West African Accreditation System (unconfirmed)

♦ West African Archeological Association (WAAA) 20866

Association ouest africaine d'archéologie (AOAA)
Gen Sec Dept Archaeology and Heritage Studies, PO Box LG 3, Univ of Ghana, Legon, Ghana. T. +233207888875. E-mail: waaaghana@gmail.com.
URL: https://www.ug.edu.gh/waaaagh/
History Founded Dec 1976, Enugu (Nigeria). **Aims** Promote the study of West African archaeology; disseminate archaeological knowledge to the West African public and stimulate a general awareness of the subject. **Structure** General Meeting (every 2 years); Executive (meets at least once a year). **Languages** English, French. **Finance** Member's dues. Colloquium financed by hosting university and government, possible additional funding from foreign foundations and through sponsorship of local companies. **Events** *Biennial Colloquium* Lomé (Togo) 2015, *Biennial colloquium* Ouagadougou (Burkina Faso) 2006, *Biennial Colloquium* Porto-Novo (Benin) 2005, *Biennial Colloquium* Nigeria 1996, *Biennial colloquium* Cotonou (Benin) 1994. **Publications** *The West African Journal of Archaeology/La revue ouest africaine d'archéologie* (annual). Colloquium proceedings; books.
Members Institutional; Ordinary; Student. Members in 18 countries:
Benin, Burkina Faso, Cameroon, Cape Verde, Chad, Côte d'Ivoire, France, Germany, Guinea, Kenya, Mali, Mauritania, Morocco, Niger, Nigeria, Senegal, Spain, Togo.
IGO Relations Observer status with: *Economic Community of West African States (ECOWAS, #05312).* [2017/XD2809/**D**]

♦ West African Association of Agricultural Economists (no recent information)
♦ West African Association of Agricultural Librarians and Documentalists (inactive)
♦ West African Association for Commonwealth Literature and Language Studies (inactive)

♦ West African Association for the Development of Artisanal Fisheries (WADAF) 20867

Association ouest africaine pour le développement de la pêche artisanale (ADEPA)
Exec Sec Cité Lobatt Fall, BP 958, Dakar, Senegal. T. +221338549813 – +221766841382. E-mail: adepa.wadaf@gmail.com.
Pres 08 BP 7432, Abidjan 01, Côte d'Ivoire.
URL: https://www.adepawadaf.org/
History Founded 1992, Abidjan (Côte d'Ivoire). Registered in accordance with Ivorian law, 1994. Registration in Senegal currently pending approval. **Aims** Contribute to the strengthening of professional organizations of artisanal fishery (OPPA) for their autonomy; promote sustainable artisanal fisheries by influencing decision making in terms of public policy of fisheries. **Structure** General Assembly; Board; Executive Secretariat. **Languages** English, French. **Staff** 3.00 FTE, paid. Voluntary; consultants. **Finance** Subsidies from national, regional and international financiers. Budget (annual): euro 150,000-200,000. **Activities** Projects/programmes; research/documentation; training/education; advocacy/lobbying/activism; capacity building. **Publications** *ADEPA-INFOS* (4 a year) – bulletin. *Advocacy Handbook for Women Processors of Fish Products* in English, French, Portuguese.
Members Associations and individuals in 13 countries:
Benin, Côte d'Ivoire, France, Gambia, Ghana, Guinea, Guinea-Bissau, Mali, Mauritania, Nigeria, Senegal, Sierra Leone, Togo. [2018/XJ8157/**D**]

♦ West African Association for Environmental Assessment (WAAEA) . 20868

Association ouest africaine pour l'évaluation environnementale (AOEE)
Exec Secretariat Immeuble ENEAM – Appt B4, Cotonou, Benin. T. +22921036387.
URL: http://www.aoaee-waaea.com/
History Oct 2002. **Aims** Promote Environmental Assessment capacity throughout the West African region. **Languages** English, French. **Members** in 14 countries. Membership countries not specified. **NGO Relations** Member of: *Capacity Development and Linkages for Environmental Assessment in Africa (CLEAA, no recent information).* [2011/XJ0191/**D**]

♦ West African Association of Food Science and Technology (WAAFoST) 20869

Contact c/o IUFoST, Univ of Guelph, Dept of Food Science, Room 106 50, Stone Road E, Guelph ON N1G 2M7, Canada. T. +16128018315. E-mail: secretariat@iufost.org.
URL: http://www.iufost.org/waafost/
History Oct 2008, as a regional grouping of *International Union of Food Science and Technology (IUFoST, #15773).* [2018/XM2928/**D**]

♦ West African Association for Marine Environment (internationally oriented national body)
♦ West African Association of Theological Institutions (no recent information)
♦ West African Bankers' Association (no recent information)

♦ West African Bar Association (WABA) 20870

Programme Lawyer address not obtained. E-mail: wabaafrica@yahoo.com.
Pres address not obtained.
History Founded 2004, Ghana. **Aims** Enhance professional and commercial interests of lawyers and bar associations in West Africa so as to promote democracy, access to justice, rule of law and human rights. **Structure** General Meeting; Executive Committee of 5 members; Secretariat located in Abuja (Nigeria). **Languages** English, French. **Finance** Members' dues. Donations from funders, main funders including: Open Society Initiative for West Africa (OSIWA); *MacArthur Foundation.* **Activities** Advocacy/lobbying/activism; training/education; events/meetings; projects/programmes. **Publications** Activity reports; judgements of the ECOWAS Court of Justice; compendium of human right instruments of ECOWAS; Strategic Plan Document.
Members Honorary; Institutional; Individual. Members in 15 countries:
Benin, Burkina Faso, Cape Verde, Côte d'Ivoire, Gambia, Ghana, Guinea, Guinea-Bissau, Liberia, Mali, Niger, Nigeria, Senegal, Sierra Leone, Togo.
Consultative Status Consultative status granted from: *African Commission on Human and Peoples' Rights (ACHPR, #00255)* (Observer). **IGO Relations** Cooperates with: *Economic Community of West African States (ECOWAS, #05312); Intergovernmental Action Group against Money Laundering in West Africa (#11471);* embassies. **NGO Relations** Cooperates with: *Centre for Human Rights, Pretoria; Coalition for an Effective African Court on Human and Peoples' Rights (African Court Coalition, #04055); Coalition for the International Criminal Court (CICC, #04062); East Africa Law Society (EALS, #05173); Human Rights Watch (HRW, #10990); International Bar Association (IBA, #12320); International Commission of Jurists (ICJ, #12695)* – African Section; *MacArthur Foundation; Media Foundation for West Africa (MFWA, #16617);* National Bar Associations in West Africa; *Pan-African Lawyers Union (PALU, #18054); Southern African Development Community Lawyers Association (#19845); West Africa Civil Society Forum (WACSOF, #20864).* [2015.09.02/XM8111/**D**]

♦ West African Botanists Association (no recent information)

♦ West African Central Bank (WACB) 20871

Address not obtained.
History 15 Dec 2000, Bamako (Mali), by *Economic Community of West African States (ECOWAS, #05312),* following setting up of *West African Monetary Zone (WAMZ, #20889). West African Monetary Institute (WAMI, #20888)* started operations Mar 2001 to prepare the establishment of WACB; intends to commence operations in 2014. Headquarters will be located in Ghana. **Finance** Initial capital: US$ 100 million. [2009/XJ0413/p/**F***]

♦ West African Centre for International Parasite Control (WACIPAC) . . 20872

Contact Noguchi Memorial Inst Medical Research (NMIMR), College of Health Sciences, Univ of Ghana, PO Box LG 58, Legon, Ghana. T. +23321501233. Fax +23321501233. E-mail: dboakye@noguchi.mimcom.org – wacipac@noguchi.mimcom.org.
URL: http://www.noguchimedres.org/wacipac/
History A regional centre of *Collaborative International Pesticides Analytical Council (CIPAC, #04099)* under the Global Parasite Control Initiative, also referred to as Hashimoto Initiative. **Aims** Promote parasite control in the West African sub-region through a school-based approach. **Activities** International training workshops for programme managers in health and education sectors; in-country training.
Members Full in 10 countries:
Benin, Burkina Faso, Cameroon, Côte d'Ivoire, Ghana, Mali, Niger, Nigeria, Senegal, Togo.
IGO Relations Formal contacts with: *Japan International Cooperation Agency (JICA); WHO (#20950); World Food Programme (WFP, #21510).* **NGO Relations** Formal contacts with: *Asian Centre of International Parasite Control (ACIPAC, #01373); Eastern and Southern Africa Centre of International Parasite Control (ESACIPAC, #05250).* [2008/XM0681/**E**]

♦ West African Centre for Rural and Agricultural Credit Training (meeting series)

♦ West African Chemical Society 20873

Address not obtained.
Members in 8 countries:
Benin, Burkina Faso, Côte d'Ivoire, Guinea, Mali, Niger, Senegal, Togo.
NGO Relations Member of: *Federation of African Societies of Chemistry (FASC, #09411).* [2010/XJ1622/**D**]

♦ West African Clearing House (inactive)

♦ West African College of Nursing (WACN) 20874

Exec Sec 6 Taylor Drive, Off Edmond Cresc, PMB 2023, Yaba, Lagos, Nigeria. T. +23414729865. E-mail: westafricancollegeofnursing@gmail.com – westafricancollegenursing@yahoo.co.uk.
URL: http://www.wacn-online.com/
History 24 Oct 1980, Accra (Ghana), on signature of constitution following decision, 24 Oct 1978, Lagos (Nigeria), at 9th Session of the Assembly of West African Health Ministers, within the framework of *West African Health Community (WAHC, inactive)* and recommendations, 1977, Benin City (Nigeria), of *'Special Committee on Nursing Education in West Africa'.* Provisional Council (3 committees) carried out preparatory work 1978-1980. Officially inaugurated, 1981, Banjul (Gambia). **Aims** Promote excellence in nursing education, at both basic and post-basic levels; maintain standards of nursing within the West African Health Community; accredit institutions for programmes of the college; design and provide facilities for educational and training programmes; establish Code of Ethics; influence government policy decisions. **Structure** General Meeting (every 2 years). Officers: President, Vice-President and other officers elected from among the members (Fellows) of 5 constituent faculties. Council, including representatives of WHO and WAHC. Finance and General Purpose Committee; Joint Committee on Higher Professional Nursing Education. **Finance** Subventions from member countries. Also donations from international organizations. **Activities** Faculties (5): Medical and Surgical; Maternal and Child Health; Mental Health and Psychiatry; Community Health; Nursing Administration, Management and Education. Provides continuing education for nurses; awards post-study fellowships through governments. **Events** *Scientific session* Banjul (Gambia) 2011, *Scientific Session* Gambia 2011, *Scientific Session* Cotonou (Benin) 2009, *Regional workshop* Abuja (Nigeria) 2004, *Scientific session* Monrovia (Liberia) 2001. **Publications** *West African Journal of Nursing. Human Ressources Management: Skills Acquisitions for Senor Nurses* (1997); *Technological Advancement in Nursing – The Way Forward* (1995); *Society and the Nurse in the Twenty First Century* (1993); *A Decade of West African College of Nursing, Past, Present and Future* (1991). Biennial General Meeting and Scientific Session Proceedings.
Members Fellows, Foundation Fellows, Honorary Fellows, in 6 countries:
Benin, Gambia, Ghana, Liberia, Nigeria, Sierra Leone. [2015/XF2524/v/**F**]

♦ West African College of Physicians (WACP) 20875

Collège ouest africain des médecins
Contact 6 Taylor Drive, Edmond Crescent, PMB 2023 Yaba, Lagos, Nigeria. T. +23418737092 – +23418737093. E-mail: ha@wacpcoam.org.
URL: https://wacpcoam.org/
History Oct 1976. Constituent College, together with *West African College of Surgeons (WACS, #20876),* of *West African Postgraduate Medical College (WAPMC, no recent information),* an agency of *West African Health Community (WAHC, inactive).* On coming into force of a treaty, signed 7-9 Jul 1987, Abuja (Nigeria), WAHC is *West African Health Organization (WAHO, #20881),* covering both English and French-speaking West Africa. **Aims** Promote professional training of physicians, standards of professional practice, ethical and moral standards of physicians, and health and healthcare in West Africa. **Structure** Faculty/Faculty Board; Committee Structure; Administration Structure; National Chapters. **Languages** English, French, Portuguese. **Staff** Paid; voluntary. **Finance** Members' dues. Other sources: grants; funding from WAHC. Biennial budget: US$ 1,000,000. **Activities** Training/education; guidance/assistance/consulting. **Events** *Annual General and Scientific Meeting* Accra (Ghana) 2022, *Annual General Meeting* Gambia 2021, *Annual General Meeting* Abidjan (Côte d'Ivoire) 2013, *Annual general meeting* Abidjan (Côte d'Ivoire) 2011, *Annual General Meeting* Calabar (Nigeria) 2010. **Publications** *West African Journal of Medicine (WAJM)* (4 a year).
Members National Chapters in tries:
Benin, Burkina Faso, Cape Verde, Côte d'Ivoire, Gambia, Ghana, Guinea, Guinea-Bissau, Liberia, Mali, Nigeria, Senegal, Sierra Leone, Togo.
IGO Relations Medical bodies of: *WHO (#20950);* [2022/XD5992/**D**]

♦ West African College of Surgeons (WACS) 20876

Collège ouest africain des chirurgiens
Secretariat PMB 1067, Yaba, Lagos, Nigeria. T. +23418846024. E-mail: info@wacscoac.org.
URL: http://www.wacscoac.org
History 3 Dec 1960, Ibadan (Nigeria), as *Association of Surgeons of West Africa – Association des chirurgiens d'Afrique occidentale.* Present name adopted Jan 1973. Constitution revised 29 Jan 1975 when it became a Constituent College, together with *West African College of Physicians (WACP, #20875)* of *West African Postgraduate Medical College (WAPMC, no recent information),* under the auspices of *West African Health Community (WAHC, inactive).* Constitution again revised 25 Jan 1984, Freetown (Sierra Leone). Also referred to in French as *Collège des chirurgiens de l'Afrique de l'Ouest.* On coming into force of a treaty, signed 7-9 Jul 1987, Abuja (Nigeria), WAHC will be replaced by *West African Health Organization (WAHO, #20881),* covering both English and French-speaking West Africa. **Aims** Promote and organize postgraduate education and training in surgery, obstetrics and gynaecology, anaesthesia, otorhinolaryngology, ophthalmology and dental surgery in West Africa; foster and coordinate education, study and research in surgery and allied

disciplines and encourage friendship and free exchange of ideas among surgeons working in the region. **Structure** General Meeting (annual); Council. Executive Committee, comprising President, 1st and 2nd Vice-Presidents, Secretary General, Honorary Treasurer, Assistant Secretary General and Assistant Honorary Treasurer. Committees (3): Finance and General Purposes; Higher Professional Medical Education; Grants and Awards. Faculty Boards (7). Meeting; Officers; Executive Council. **Languages** English, French. **Staff** 17.00 FTE, paid; 7.00 FTE, voluntary. **Finance** Admission fees; profit from examinations and courses; sales of memorabilia. **Activities** Training/education; awards/prizes/competitions; events/meetings. **Events** *Conference* Cotonou (Benin) 2021, *Annual Conference* Abidjan (Côte d'Ivoire) 2015, *Annual Conference* Kumasi (Ghana) 2014, *Annual conference* Abidjan (Côte d'Ivoire) 2011, *Annual Conference* Calabar (Nigeria) 2010. **Publications** *WACS Newsletter* (4 a year); *West African Journal of Medicine* (4 a year). *Neither Sleep nor Wake* (1980); *Care of the Injured* (1977). Proceedings of annual conferences; lecture series; papers.
Members Fellows of College – nationals and residents – (Fellows as residents only) in 32 countries:
Bangladesh, Belgium, Benin, Burkina Faso, Cameroon, Central African Rep, Chad, Congo Brazzaville, Congo DR, Côte d'Ivoire, France, Gabon, Gambia, Ghana, Guinea, India, Ireland (*), Jamaica (*), Liberia, Mali, Niger, Nigeria, Pakistan, Qatar (*), Saudi Arabia (*), Senegal, Sierra Leone, Togo, Trinidad-Tobago (*), UK (*), United Arab Emirates (*), USA.
NGO Relations Member of: *Global Alliance for Surgical, Obstetric, Trauma and Anaesthesia Care (G4 Alliance, #10229)*; *International Federation of Surgical Colleges (IFSC, #13560).* [2021/XD0167/v/F]

♦ West African Commission on Drugs (WADC) 20877
Commission Ouest-Africaine de Drogues
Contact KAIPTC, PMB CT 210 Cantonments, Accra, Ghana. T. +233302718200ext1075. Fax +233302718201. E-mail: wacd@kofiannanfoundation.org.
URL: http://www.wacommissionondrugs.org/
History Set up following a meeting Apr 2012, Dakar (Senegal). **Aims** Mobilize public awareness and political commitment; develop evidence-based policy recommendations; develop local and regional capacities and ownership. **Structure** Commission, comprising President and 10 members. **NGO Relations** Located at: *Kofi Annan International Peacekeeping Training Centre (KAIPTC).* [2014/XJ7193/**D**]

- ♦ West African Committee of Peasant Seeds (unconfirmed)
- ♦ West African Council (inactive)
- ♦ West African Currency Board (inactive)
- ♦ West African Customs Union (inactive)
- ♦ West African Development Bank (#03170)
- ♦ West African Distance Education Association (inactive)
- ♦ West African Economic Community (inactive)
- ♦ West African Economic Community School of Mining and Geology / see School of Mining Industry and Geology (#19132)
- ♦ West African Economics Association (inactive)

♦ West Africa Network for Peacebuilding (WANEP) 20878
Exec Dir PO Box CT 4434, Cantonments, Accra, Ghana. T. +233302411638 – +233302406340. E-mail: wanep@wanep.org.
Admin Dir Hse No ANT 174 Trinity Ave, off Mile 7 Road, Achimota, Ghana.
URL: http://www.wanep.org/
History 1998. Operational since 1999. **Aims** Enable and facilitate mechanisms for cooperation among civil society-based peacebuilding practitioners and organizations in West Africa by promoting cooperative responses with State actors to address the root causes of violent conflicts; provide the structure through which these practitioners and institutions regularly exchange experiences and information on issues and influence policy on peacebuilding and conflict transformation; promote West Africa's social and cultural values as resources for peacebuilding. **Structure** General Assembly; Regional Board; Regional Office in Accra (Ghana); National Offices across West Africa (15). **Languages** English, French, Portuguese. **Staff** Head Office: 25; National Offices: 70. **Finance** Donors; *DANIDA*; *Swedish International Development Cooperation Agency (Sida).* Supported by: Africa Regional Programme, UNDP; *Austrian Development Agency (ADA)*; *European Union (EU, #08967)*; Ministry of Foreign Affairs, Netherlands; Wellspring Philanthropic Fund, US; *WOTRO Science for Global Development.* **Activities** Capacity building; conflict resolution; events/meetings; monitoring/evaluation; networking/liaising; projects/programmes; research/documentation. **Events** *Regional Youth Summit on Political Transitions in the ECOWAS Sub-Region* Accra (Ghana) 2022. **Publications** *Strides and Strains of Civil Society Organizations in Africa: The WANEP Story* (2017). Annual Report; activity reports; topical papers.
Members National offices in 15 countries:
Benin, Burkina Faso, Cape Verde, Côte d'Ivoire, Gambia, Ghana, Guinea, Guinea-Bissau, Liberia, Mali, Niger, Nigeria, Senegal, Sierra Leone, Togo.
Organizations (over 700) across West Africa, including 1 organization listed in this Yearbook:
Pro-Hope International (PHIN).
Consultative Status Consultative status granted from: *African Commission on Human and Peoples' Rights (ACHPR, #00255)* (Observer); *ECOSOC (#05331)* (Special). **IGO Relations** Member of (1): *African Union (AU, #00488)* (Peace and Security Cluster – ECOSOCC). **NGO Relations** Member of (9): *Civil Society Platform for Peacebuilding and Statebuilding (CSPPS, #03970)*; *Control Arms (#04782)*; *Global Partnership for the Prevention of Armed Conflict (GPPAC, #10538)*; *International Campaign to Ban Landmines – Cluster Munition Coalition (ICBL-CMC, #12427)*; *International Coalition for the Responsibility to Protect (ICRtoP, #12620)*; *International Fellowship of Reconciliation (IFOR, #13586)*; *Mediation Support Network (MSN, #16622)*; *Nonviolent Peaceforce (NP, #17153)*; Southern Voice Network. Partner of: *NPI Africa.* [2022.05.17/XF5770/y/F]

♦ West African Examinations Council (WAEC) 20879
Registrar/CEO Nelson Mandela Avenue, Off Guf Street, Okponglo, PO Box 125, Accra, Ghana. T. +233302237784 – +233302248967. Fax +233302222905. E-mail: waechqrs@africaonline.com.gh.
URL: http://www.waecheadquartersgh.org/
History 1952. Established on the initiative of Cambridge and London Universities (UK) and West African Departments of Education. **Aims** Conduct prescribed examinations in member countries and issue certificates; harmonize examination procedures and standards. **Structure** Council; International Committees; Country-specific Committees; State Committees (Nigeria only); Headquarters in Accra (Ghana); National, Zonal and Branch Offices in all member countries. **Languages** English. **Staff** 4000.00 FTE, paid. **Finance** Candidates' fees; subventions and contributions from governments of member countries. **Activities** Standards/guidelines; training/education; research/documentation; financial and/or material support; awards/prizes/competitions. **Events** *Annual Council Meeting* Abuja (Nigeria) 2022, *Annual Council Meeting* Accra (Ghana) 2021, *Annual Council Meeting* Accra (Ghana) 2021, *Annual Council Meeting* Monrovia (Liberia) 2020, *Annual Council Meeting* Freetown (Sierra Leone) 2019. **Publications** *Registrar's Bulletin.* Annual Report; regulations and syllabuses; research reports; seminar papers; statistics on examinations.
Members Governments of 5 West African countries:
Gambia, Ghana, Liberia, Nigeria, Sierra Leone.
NGO Relations Member of: *Association of Commonwealth Examination and Accreditation Bodies (ACEAB, #02438)*; *Association for Educational Assessment in Africa (AEAA, #02482)*; *International Association for Educational Assessment (IAEA, #11861).* [2022/XD4624/**D***]

♦ West African Farming Systems Research Network (WAFSRN) 20880
Réseau d'étude des systèmes de production en Afrique de l'Ouest (RESPAO)
Contact c/o IITA, Oyo Road, PMB 5320, Ibadan, Oyo, Nigeria.
History Mar 1986, Dakar (Senegal), following initiatives 1982, Ibadan (Nigeria), at a workshop of *International Institute of Tropical Agriculture (IITA, #13933)*, when Officers and Steering Committee were elected. Administered through *Semi-Arid Food Grain Research and Development (AU SAFGRAD, #19226).* Currently inactive. **Aims** Promote and facilitate cooperation amongst national, international and external scientists, programmes and institutions working in West and Central Africa in the area of farming systems and other related areas of research; through this cooperation, enhance support for researchers and strengthen national programmes through information dissemination, training, exchange of methodological experiences, comparison of results and collaborative research. **Structure** Steering Committee, consisting of Chairman, Coordinator, representatives of international research centres operating in the region, representatives of collaborative research groups under the umbrella of WAFSRN, and OUA/SAFGRAD representative. from SAFGRAD and the Coordinator (who heads the Secretariat). Permanent Secretariat, headed by Coordinator. **Staff** 3.00 FTE, paid. **Activities** Collection, processing and dissemination of information on farming systems research through a Documentation unit. Training courses. Maintains Collaborative Research groups. Workshops, seminars, biennial symposia, monitoring tours. **Publications** *Agricultural Systems in Africa/Systèmes agricoles en Afrique* (2 a year) in English, French; *WAFSRN Bulletin/Bulletin du RESPAO* (2 a year) in English, French. Special papers; monographs.
Members Covers 17 countries:
Benin, Burkina Faso, Cameroon, Cape Verde, Côte d'Ivoire, Gambia, Ghana, Guinea, Guinea-Bissau, Liberia, Mali, Mauritania, Niger, Nigeria, Senegal, Sierra Leone, Togo. [2008/XF0031/d/**F**]

- ♦ West African Federation of Associations for the Advancement of Handicapped Persons (no recent information)
- ♦ West African Health Community (inactive)

♦ West African Health Organization (WAHO) 20881
Organisation Ouest Africaine de la santé (OOAS) – Organização Oest Africana da Saúde (OOAS)
Dir Gen 01 BP 153, Bobo Dioulasso 01, Burkina Faso. T. +22620975772 – +22620975775. Fax +22620975772. E-mail: wahooas@wahooas.org – wahooas@fasonet.bf.
URL: http://www.wahooas.org/
History 7 Jul 1987, Abuja (Nigeria). following a proposal 7-9 Jul 1987, Abuja (Nigeria), on adoption and signing of a Protocol at 10th meeting of Authority of Heads of State and Government of *Economic Community of West African States (ECOWAS, #05312)*, as a merger of the two existing health institutions in the sub-region, *West African Health Community (WAHC, inactive)* and *Coordination and Cooperation Organization for the Control of the Major Endemic Diseases (OCCGE, inactive).* Organization came into effect on ratifying of protocol by parliaments of ECOWAS member states. **Structure** Heads of State and Member States Governments Authority; Council of Ministers; Assembly of Ministers of Health; General Directorate, headed by General Director. Departments (5): Development of Human Resources; Planification and Technical Assistance; Primary Health Care and Fight against Diseases; Research and Information System of the Sanitary Management; Administration and Finances.
Members Governments of 16 countries:
Benin, Burkina Faso, Cape Verde, Côte d'Ivoire, Gambia, Ghana, Guinea, Guinea-Bissau, Liberia, Mali, Mauritania, Niger, Nigeria, Senegal, Sierra Leone, Togo.
Associate Government (1):
France.
IGO Relations Cooperates in related fields of interest with:
- *African and Malagasy Council for Higher Education (#00364)*;
- *Caribbean Community (CARICOM, #03476)*;
- *Commonwealth Fund for Technical Cooperation (CFTC, #04331)*;
- *Commonwealth Secretariat (#04362)*;
- *Deutsche Gesellschaft für Technische Zusammenarbeit (GTZ, inactive)*;
- *East, Central and Southern African Health Community (ECSA-HC, #05216)*;
- *Entente Council (#05491)*;
- *European Commission (EC, #06633)*;
- *European Development Fund (EDF, #06914)*;
- *Institut de recherche pour le développement (IRD)*;
- *International Development Research Centre (IDRC, #13162)*;
- *Organisation internationale de la Francophonie (OIF, #17809)*;
- *Organization of Coordination for the Control of Endemic Diseases in Central Africa (#17860)*;
- *UNDP (#20292)*;
- *UNESCO (#20322)*;
- *UNICEF (#20332)*;
- *United States Agency for International Development (USAID)*;
- *WHO (#20950)*;
- *WHO Regional Office for Africa (AFRO, #20943).*

NGO Relations Partner with: *Every Woman Every Child (EWEC, #09215)*; *Helen Keller International (HKI, #10902)*; *Réseau africain des formations sur le VIH et le SIDA (RAF-VIH, #18863).* Member of: *Reproductive Health Supplies Coalition (RHSC, #18847).* [2016/XE5978/**E***]

♦ West African Human Rights Defenders' Network (WAHRDN) 20882
Réseau Ouest Africain des Défenseurs des Droits Humains (ROADDH)
Contact 14BP152, Rue Assahoun, Quartier Novissi, Tokoin Protestant, Lomé, Togo. T. +22890300285. E-mail: roaddh@gmail.com.
URL: https://westafricadefenders.org/
History May 2005, Dakar (Senegal). **Aims** Defend and protect the rights of human rights defenders in the West Africa sub-region. **Languages** English, French. **Staff** 5.00 FTE, paid. **Finance** Support from national, regional and international institutions, including: *Brot für die Welt*; *Human Rights Information and Documentation Systems, International (HURIDOCS, #10985)*; *International Service for Human Rights (ISHR, #14841)*; United Nations Office for West Africa (UNOWA). **Activities** Advocacy/lobbying/activism; guidance/assistance/consulting; monitoring/evaluation; research/documentation; training/education.
Members Full in 16 countries:
Benin, Burkina Faso, Cape Verde, Côte d'Ivoire, Gambia, Ghana, Guinea, Guinea-Bissau, Liberia, Mali, Mauritania, Niger, Nigeria, Senegal, Sierra Leone, Togo.
Consultative Status Consultative status granted from: *African Commission on Human and Peoples' Rights (ACHPR, #00255)* (Observer). **NGO Relations** Member of: *Coalition for an Effective African Court on Human and Peoples' Rights (African Court Coalition, #04055).* Sub-regional member of: *Pan-African Human Rights Defenders Network (AfricanDefenders, #18052).* [2022.05.11/XJ6559/**D**]

- ♦ West African Immunology Society (no recent information)
- ♦ West African Industrial Forum (meeting series)

♦ West African Institute for Financial and Economic Management (WAIFEM) 20883
Dir Gen Central Bank Learning Ctr, PMB 2001, Satellite Town, Lagos, Nigeria. T. +23417400588. Fax +23416211909. E-mail: capacity@waifem-cbp.org.
URL: http://www.waifem-cbp.org/
History Jul 1996. Activities started Jan 1997. **Aims** Strengthen capacity for macro-economic and financial management in the member countries. **Structure** Board of Governors of 6 members. Directorate, comprising Director General and 3 Directors (Financial Sector Management; Administration and Finance; Macroeconomic Management). **Finance** Funding. Contributions from central banks. Core donors: *The African Capacity Building Foundation (ACBF, #00233)*; *Debt Relief International (DRI)*; *Swedish International Development Cooperation Agency (Sida).* Donor project funding from: *International Monetary Fund (IMF, #14180)*; *United Nations Institute for Training and Research (UNITAR, #20576).* **Activities** Organizes courses and workshops. **Publications** *WAIFEM News* (4 a year) – newsletter. Annual Report.
Members Governments of 5 countries:
Gambia, Ghana, Liberia, Nigeria, Sierra Leone.
IGO Relations *West African Monetary Agency (WAMA, #20887).* [2010/XE4534/j/**E***]

- ♦ West African Institute for Legal Aid (internationally oriented national body)

♦ West African Insurance Companies Association (WAICA) 20884
SG & CEO No 337 Independence Avenue, Natl Insurance Commission Bldg, PMB CT 356, Accra, Ghana. T. +23321271034. Fax +23321271036.
History 4 May 1973. Former names and other names: *West African Insurance Consultative Association* – former (4 May 1973). **Aims** Promote cooperation in every respect amongst all the insurers and reinsurers operating in the West African sub-region. **Structure** General Assembly. Executive Committee, comprising President, Vice-President, 5 representatives from Nigeria, 3 representatives from Ghana, 2 representatives each from Gambia, Sierra Leone and Liberia, and Immediate Past President. Secretariat, headed by Secretary General. **Languages** English. **Staff** 3.00 FTE, paid. **Finance** Sources: meeting proceeds; members' dues. Other sources: journal advertisement income. **Activities** Events/meetings. Two main annual events: Annual General Meeting and Educational Conference **Events** *Educational Conference* Monrovia (Liberia) 2022,

Professional and ethical behaviour in the insurance industry Banjul (Gambia) 2012, *Meeting* Monrovia (Liberia) 2009, *Meeting* Monrovia (Liberia) 2006, *Meeting* Lagos (Nigeria) 2005. **Publications** *The WAICA Journal* (2 a year).
Members Governments of 5 countries:
Gambia, Ghana, Liberia, Nigeria, Sierra Leone. [2022/XD8994/**D***]

- ♦ West African Insurance Consultative Association / see West African Insurance Companies Association (#20884)
- ♦ West African Insurance Institute (no recent information)
- ♦ West African Inter-Territorial Research Organization (inactive)
- ♦ West African Investment Fund (see: #03170)

♦ West African Journalists' Union 20885

Union des journalistes de l'Afrique de l'Ouest (UJAO)
Contact address not obtained. T. +221338424256. Fax +221338420269. E-mail: info@ujaowaja.net – wajauja@yahoo.fr.
History Founded 21 Jun 1986, Dakar (Senegal). Also referred to as *West Africa Journalists' Association (WAJA) – Association des journalistes d'Afrique occidentale.* **Events** *Forum on how regional human rights mechanisms can strengthen freedom of expression* Banjul (Gambia) 2006, *Conference* Banjul (Gambia) 1999, *Annual congress* Dakar (Senegal) 1998, *Réunion sur la liberté d'expression* Montréal, QC (Canada) 1992, *Towards pluralism in the francophone African press colloquium* Paris (France) 1991. **Members** Membership countries not specified. **NGO Relations** Member of: *African Freedom of Expression Exchange (AFEX); Federation of African Journalists (FAJ, #09404); Global Forum for Media Development (GFMD, #10375); IFEX (#11100).* Houses: *Surveillance et défense de la liberté de presse en Africa de l'Ouest (SDPL, no recent information).* Supports: *International News Safety Institute (INSI, #14364).* [2016/XD2548/**D**]

- ♦ West African Library Association (no recent information)
- ♦ West African Linguistics Society (#19506)

♦ West African Management Development Institutes Network (WAMDEVIN) 20886

Pres ASCON Phase II, PMB 1004, Topo-Badagry, Lagos, Nigeria. T. +2348034087451 – +2348037264580.
URL: http://www.wamdevin.org/
History 2 Nov 1987, Lagos (Nigeria). Previously also referred to as *West African Management Development Institutions Network.* **Aims** Harness the potential which member institutions could derive from pooling and sharing of the expertise in management development, training, research and consultancy available in the sub-region, so as to enhance socio-economic prosperity of member countries. **Structure** General Assembly; Executive Committee. **Finance** Members' dues. Support from Nigerian government. Annual budget: US$ 100,000. **Activities** Networking/liaising; financial and/or material support; guidance/assistance/consulting; events/meetings. **Events** *Global forum on management education* Chicago, IL (USA) 1998. **Publications** *WAMDEVIN Newsletter* (4 a year). *Occasional Papers Series (OPS).* Handbooks; directories; WINET-INFO.
Members Full; Corporate; Institutional Associate. Member institutions (19) in 6 countries:
Cameroon, Gambia, Ghana, Liberia, Nigeria, Sierra Leone.
IGO Relations *Commonwealth Secretariat (#04362).* **NGO Relations** Member of: *International Association of Schools and Institutes of Administration (IASIA, #12147); International Management Development Network (INTERMAN, no recent information).* [2017.03.15/XF2261/**F**]

- ♦ West African Management Development Institutions Network / see West African Management Development Institutes Network (#20886)
- ♦ West African Modern Language and Literature Association (inactive)

♦ West African Monetary Agency (WAMA) 20887

Agence Monétaire de l'Afrique de l'Ouest (AMAO)
Dir Gen 1 Scan Drive, Off Spur Road, PMB 218, Freetown, Sierra Leone. T. +23225232482. Fax +23225223943. E-mail: wamao@amao-wama.org.
URL: http://www.amao-wama.org/
History Established 8 Mar 1996, Freetown (Sierra Leone), as an autonomous specialized Agency of *Economic Community of West African States (ECOWAS, #05312),* following ECOWAS proposal, 1992, as a first step towards rationalization of regional monetary cooperation. Replaced *West African Clearing House (WACH, inactive),* which had been set up on 25 Jun 1975, Lagos (Nigeria), and commenced channelling transactions in Jul 1976. *West African Monetary Zone (WAMZ, #20889)* was confirmed on 20 Dec 2000, Bamako (Mali), following proposals of 10th Summit Meeting of ECOWAS, Jul 1987, Abuja, and of 13th Summit Meeting, May 1990, Banjul (Gambia). **Aims** Monitor, coordinate and implement the ECOWAS Monetary Cooperation Programme (EMCP), geared towards the creation of the ECOWAS single currency. **Structure** Committee of Governors; Technical Committees. **Languages** English, French. **Staff** 36.00 FTE, paid. **Finance** Annual contributions from member Central Banks. **Activities** Research/documentation; projects/programmes; events/meetings. Research geared towards establishment of a single monetary zone with a single currency in West Africa. Cooperates on: ECOWAS Monetary Cooperation Programme (EMCP); harmonization of payment systems, balance of payments and statistics. **Events** *Annual Meeting* Accra (Ghana) 2003, *Annual Meeting* Freetown (Sierra Leone) 2002, *Annual Meeting* Dakar (Senegal) 2001, *Annual Meeting* Bamako (Mali) 2000, *Annual Meeting* Lomé (Togo) 1999. **Publications** *WAMA Bulletin* (2 a year); *The West African Economic Review. ECOWAS Monetary Cooperation Programme Report.* Reports.
Members Central banks of 15 countries – " indicates part of Banque centrale des Etats de l'Afrique de l'Ouest:
Benin (*), Burkina Faso (*), Cape Verde, Côte d'Ivoire (*), Gambia, Ghana, Guinea, Guinea-Bissau (*), Liberia, Mali (*), Niger (*), Nigeria, Senegal (*), Sierra Leone, Togo (*).
IGO Relations Cooperates with: *African Development Bank (ADB, #00283); Association of African Central Banks (AACB, #02352); Bank for International Settlements (BIS, #03165); Economic Community of West African States (ECOWAS, #05312); Economic and Statistical Observatory for Sub-Saharan Africa (AFRISTAT, #05321); International Bank for Reconstruction and Development (IBRD, #12317)* (World Bank); *International Monetary Fund (IMF, #14180); Mano River Union (MRU, #16566); UNCTAD (#20285); UNDP (#20292); Union économique et monétaire Ouest africaine (UEMOA, #20377); United Nations Economic Commission for Africa (ECA, #20554); West African Institute for Financial and Economic Management (WAIFEM, #20883); West African Monetary Institute (WAMI, #20888).* [2023/XF5070/**F***]

♦ West African Monetary Institute (WAMI) 20888

Institut monétaire de l'Afrique de l'ouest (IMAO)
Contact Gulf House – Tetteh Quarshie Interchange, PMB CT 75, Accra, Ghana. T. +233302743801. Fax +233302743807. E-mail: info@wami-imao.org.
URL: http://www.wami-imao.org/
History 15 Dec 2000, Bamako (Mali), by *Economic Community of West African States (ECOWAS, #05312),* as a transitional preparatory institution of the *West African Monetary Zone (WAMZ, #20889).* Operations commenced Mar 2001, to prepare for establishment of *West African Central Bank (WACB, #20871)* in 2005 and launching of a single currency. **Aims** Establish a common central bank with a single *currency* for the economic prosperity of the West African Monetary Zone. **Structure** Board. **Languages** English, French. **Staff** Personnel from Member States. **Finance** Member States' contributions. **Activities** Events/meetings. **Publications** *Macro-Economic Convergence Report* (2 a year); *West African Journal of Monetary and Economic Integration (WAJMEI)* (2 a year). *WAMI Occasional Paper Series.* Annual Report; reports.
Members Central Banks of 6 countries:
Gambia, Ghana, Guinea, Liberia, Nigeria, Sierra Leone.
IGO Relations Sister organizations: *West African Institute for Financial and Economic Management (WAIFEM, #20883); West African Monetary Agency (WAMA, #20887).* [2018.08.01/XE4257/j/**E***]

- ♦ West African Monetary Union (inactive)

♦ West African Monetary Zone (WAMZ) 20889

Zone monétaire de l'Afrique de l'ouest (ZMAO)
Contact c/o WAMI, Gulf House, Tetteh Quarshie Interchange, PMB CT 75, Accra, Ghana. T. +233302743801. Fax +233302743807. E-mail: info@wami-imao.org.
URL: http://www.wami-imao.org/
History 20 Dec 2000, Bamako (Mali), following adoption of Accra (Ghana) Declaration, Apr 2000. Grew out of a proposal Jul 1987, Abuja (Nigeria), at 10th Summit Meeting of *Economic Community of West African States (ECOWAS, #05312),* and again in May 1990, Banjul (Gambia), at 13th Summit Meeting. Decision at the 22nd Summit of ECOWAS Heads of State and Government, Lomé (Togo), 9 Dec 1999, facilitated integration process through a fast track approach. Following convergence process, merger would be negotiated between the first monetary zone *Union économique et monétaire Ouest africaine (UEMOA, #20377)* and WAMZ to create ECOWAS single monetary zone. *West African Monetary Agency (WAMA, #20887),* proposed 1992, by ECOWAS as a transformation of *West African Clearing House (WACH, inactive),* would be pivotal to such a merger negotiation as the umbrella agency implementing ECOWAS Monetary Cooperation Programme (EMCP). May 2005, Convergence Council of Ministers and Central Bank Governors agreed to extend commencement of WAMZ monetary union to Dec 2009 and then to or before Jan 2015. In response to exogenous reasons, convergence council further extended commencement to 2020. **Aims** Promote monetary cooperation and integration through the establishment of a common central *bank* that will issue a common *currency.* **Structure** Institutions: Authority of Heads of State and Government – supreme body; Convergence Council of Ministers of Finance, Foreign Affairs, Trade and Regional Integration and Governors of Central Banks – supervisory body (meets 2 times a year); Technical Committee – expert advisory body (meets 2 times a year, prior to meetings of the Convergence Council); transitional preparatory institution *West African Monetary Institute (WAMI, #20888),* which commenced operations in Mar 2001, in preparation for the establishment of *West African Central Bank (WACB, #20871)* in 2005; Stabilization and Cooperation Fund – solidarity fund to provide balance of payments support to members in temporary economic difficulty. **Languages** English, French. **Activities** Organizes: Conference of Heads of State held annually, usually in December, during Summit of Heads of State of ECOWAS; annual Trade and Finance Ministers Forum; economic research to aid monetary integration. **Publications** *West African Journal of Monetary and Economic Integration* (2 a year). Annual Report; Convergence Report.
Members Governments of 6 countries:
Gambia, Ghana, Guinea, Liberia, Nigeria, Sierra Leone. [2017.12.18/XF6262/**F***]

♦ West African Museums Programme (WAMP) 20890

Programme des musées de l'Afrique de l'Ouest
Exec Dir 11 BP 861, Ouagadougou 11, Burkina Faso. T. +22650483966.
History Founded 1982, Abidjan (Côte d'Ivoire), under the auspices of the *International African Institute (IAI, #11596)* and the initiative of the late Philip Ravenhill. Headquarters transferred: to Dakar (Senegal), 1987; Niamey (Niger), 2008; Ouagadougou (Burkina Faso), 2011. Autonomous since 1992. **Aims** Enhance conceptual and intellectual approach of museum work and promote new models of museums relevant to the development of society; promote good museum practice in terms of management, research, documentation, collection development, preservation, exhibition, education and outreach; help strengthen the professional museum network in West Africa and links with the international museum-related network; contribute to the preservation and enrichment of the African *cultural heritage.* **Structure** Board of Directors of 7 members (museum professionals, academicians and financial experts, mainly citizens of African countries) recruits Executive Director and senior technical experts. **Languages** English, French. **Staff** 5.50 FTE, paid. **Finance** Members' dues. Grants and contributions. **Activities** Promotes innovative and/or priority museum and museum-related programmes; encourages training of West African museum professionals; stimulates creation of representative collections and exhibitions; promotes educational activities; helps in funding or fund-raising for such programmes and promotes relationships with funding institutions; provides facilities for interchange and dissemination of information, ideas, experiences and findings and the coordination of activities by and among persons and institutions concerned with museum development in West Africa, both within and beyond West Africa; organizes international workshops and regional seminars. **Events** *Musées et histoire* Ouidah (Benin) 1995, *Museums and history* Ouidah (Benin) 1994, *Museums and archaeology* Abidjan (Côte d'Ivoire) 1993. **Publications** *WAMP Bulletin* (annual). *Directory of Museums in West Africa* (2007); *Directory of Photographic Archives in West Africa* (2001); *Museums and Urban Culture* (2001); *Directory of Museums in West Africa* (2000); *Museums and History in West Africa* (2000); *Museums and Archaeology in West Africa* (1997); *Museums and the Community* (1994); *Directory of Museum Professionals in Africa* (1993). Workshop proceedings.
Members Institutions (over 200 museums) and individuals from 17 countries:
Benin, Burkina Faso, Cameroon, Cape Verde, Côte d'Ivoire, Gambia, Ghana, Guinea, Guinea-Bissau, Liberia, Mali, Mauritania, Niger, Nigeria, Senegal, Sierra Leone, Togo. [2014/XK1052/v/**F**]

♦ West African Network of Farmers' Organizations and Agricultural Producers 20891

Réseau des organisations paysannes et des producteurs agricoles de l'Afrique de l'Ouest (ROPPA)
Main Office BP 884, Ouagadougou 09, Burkina Faso. T. +22650360825. Fax +22650362613.
URL: http://roppa-afrique.org/
History Jul 2000, Cotonou (Benin), by *Sahel and West Africa Club (SWAC, #19034).* **Aims** Promote and defend the values of a sustainable and performing rural agriculture une agriculture serving familial enterprises and agricultural producers. **Events** *Regional forum on food sovereignty* Niamey (Niger) 2006, *Ordinary Meeting* Saint Louis (Senegal) 2006, *Ordinary convention* Saint Louis (Senegal) 2006, *Ordinary convention* Lomé (Togo) 2004, *Ordinary convention* Labé (Guinea) 2001.
Members Organisations in 10 countries:
Benin, Burkina Faso, Côte d'Ivoire, Gambia, Guinea, Guinea-Bissau, Mali, Niger, Senegal, Togo.
IGO Relations *Global Agriculture and Food Security Program (GAFSP, #10174).* **NGO Relations** Memorandum of Understanding with: *European Centre for Development Policy Management (ECDPM, #06473).* Cooperates with: *Alliance Against Hunger and Malnutrition (AAHM, no recent information).* Member of: Coordinating Committee of *More and Better (#16855); PanAfrican Farmers' Organization (PAFO, #18049).* [2018/XF6376/**F**]

♦ West African Network on Security and Democratic Governance (WANSED) 20892

Réseau ouest africain pour la sécurité et la gouvernance démocratique
Project Manager Friedrich Ebert Stifting, 12 Marrakesh Off Kumasi Crescent, Wuse II, Abuja, Federal Capital Territory, Nigeria. T. +23494137977. E-mail: info@fes-nigeria.org.
Aims Facilitate exchange of information in democratic security sector governance; promote research, training and advocacy in security governance. **Languages** English, French.
Members National think tanks in 15 countries:
Benin, Burkina Faso, Cape Verde, Côte d'Ivoire, Gambia, Ghana, Guinea, Guinea-Bissau, Liberia, Mali, Niger, Nigeria, Senegal, Sierra Leone, Togo.
IGO Relations *Economic Community of West African States (ECOWAS, #05312).* **NGO Relations** Nigerian office of: *Friedrich-Ebert-Stiftung (FES)* serves as secretariat. [2008.06.01/XM2768/**F**]

- ♦ West African NGO Network (internationally oriented national body)
- ♦ West African Parliament / see Parliament of the Economic Community of West African States (#18221)
- ♦ West African Pharmaceutical Federation (no recent information)

♦ West African Postal Conference (WAPCO) 20893

Conférence des Postes des Etats de l'Afrique de l'Ouest (CPEAO)
Exec Sec Wuse POst Office, Former 1 Network Office, Wuse Zone 3, Abuja 900283, Federal Capital Territory, Nigeria. T. +2348109448719. E-mail: wapco.cpeao@yahoo.com – info@wapco-cpeao.com.
URL: http://wapco-cpeao.com/index.html
History 13 Apr 2012, Grand-Bassam (Côte d'Ivoire). Replaces *West African Postal Conference (WAPCO, inactive).* A restricted union of *Universal Postal Union (UPU, #20682).*
Members Postal services of 15 countries:
Benin, Burkina Faso, Cape Verde, Côte d'Ivoire, Gambia, Ghana, Guinea, Guinea-Bissau, Liberia, Mali, Niger, Nigeria, Senegal, Sierra Leone, Togo. [2021/XM4918/**D**]

♦ West African Postgraduate College of Pharmacists (internationally oriented national body)

♦ West African Power Pool (WAPP) 20894

Système d'échanges d'énergie électrique ouest africain (EEEOA)

Information and Coordination Ctr 06 BP 2907, Zone des Ambassades, Akpakpa, Cotonou, Benin. T. +22921374195. Fax +22921374196.
URL: http://www.ecowapp.org/

History 5 Dec 1999. Restructured 18 Jan 2006. A Specialized Institution of *Economic Community of West African States (ECOWAS, #05312)*. **Aims** Address the issue of power supply deficiency within West Africa. **Structure** General Assembly. Executive Board. Organizational Committees. General Secretariat, based in Cotonou (Benin). **Events** *General Assembly* Cotonou (Benin) 2008, *General Assembly* Cotonou (Benin) 2006.
Members Utilities in 12 countries:
Benin, Burkina Faso, Côte d'Ivoire, Gambia, Ghana, Guinea, Liberia, Mali, Nigeria, Senegal, Sierra Leone, Togo.
NGO Relations *Association of Power Utilities in Africa (APUA, #02867)* is member and supporting partner. [2009/XM2992/**F**]

♦ West African Regional Branch of the International Council on Archives (see: #12996)
♦ West African Regional Computer Society (inactive)
♦ West African Regional Group (inactive)
♦ West African Research Association (internationally oriented national body)

♦ West African Research and Innovation Management Association (WARIMA) 20895

Admin Dir First Floor, Advancement Office, Univ of Ibadan, Oyo Road, Ibadan, Oyo, Nigeria. Fax +23428103043.
URL: https://warima.org/

History 2007. **Aims** Serve as the professional body for research management staff in the West Africa region. **Structure** Steering Committee, comprising Chair and 7 members. Advisers. Administrator. **Activities** cover: professional development and capacity building; promotion of best practice; increasing awareness of research and innovation issues in academic and public fora; advocacy of appropriate national and institutional policy in support of research and innovation and participation in development and testing of policy; advancement of science, technology and innovation; advancement of a code of professional standards; enhancement of the profile of the profession. **Events** *Managing research and innovation for sustainable development* Ile Ife (Nigeria) 2012. **Publications** *Current Approaches in Research Management* – series of guides to good practice. Reports.
Members in 4 countries:
Cameroon, Ghana, Nigeria, Sierra Leone.
NGO Relations Member of: *International Network of Research Management Societies (INORMS, #14317)*. Sister organization: *Southern African Research and Innovation Management Association (SARIMA)*. Cooperates with: *European Association of Research Managers and Administrators (EARMA, #06195)*. [2021/XJ0181/**D**]

♦ West African Road Safety Organisation (WARSO) 20896

Organisation Ouest africaine de la sécurité routière (OSRAO)

Address not obtained.

History 7 May 2008, under the auspices of *Economic Community of West African States (ECOWAS, #05312)*. **Structure** Officers: President; 1st and 2nd Vice-Presidents; Secretary General; Assistant Secretary-General; Treasurer; 2 Public Relations Officers. **Events** *General Assembly* Ouagadougou (Burkina Faso) 2013, *General Assembly* Banjul (Gambia) 2011, *Meeting of directors general* Abuja (Nigeria) 2009, *Meeting* Benin 2009, *General Assembly* Conakry (Guinea) 2009. [2013/XJ0270/**D**]

♦ West African Road Transporters Union / see West Africa Road Transport Union (#20901)
♦ West African Science Association (no recent information)

♦ West African Science Service Center on Climate Change and Adapted Land Use (WASCAL) 20897

Exec Dir c/o CSIR Office Complex, Agostino Neto Road, Airport Residential Area, PMB CT 504, Contonments, Accra, Ghana. T. +233302740668. E-mail: info@wascal.org – press@wascal.org.
Competence Centre Blvd Mouammar Kadhafi 6, BP 9507, Ouagadougou, Burkina Faso. E-mail: secretariat_cc@wascal.org.
URL: https://wascal.org/

History Establishment of Regional Science Service Centers (RSSC) initiated by German Federal Ministry of Education and Research (BMBF), 2010. Constitution and Cooperation Agreement of WASCAL signed and adopted 10 Feb 2012, Lomé (Togo), by Council of Ministers. Officially recognized by ECOWAS, 1 Jun 2013. Headquarters Agreement signed, 4 Apr 2014, by HE the President of Republic of Ghana, giving full recognition as an international organization based in Ghana. **Aims** Develop effective adaptation and mitigation measures; enhance resilience of human-environmental systems to climate change and increased variability; collect necessary data to assess climate change and improve climate change impact models and provision of relevant and consistent ecosystem and climate services to stakeholders; contribute to educate the next generation of scientists and policy makers that can help the region in developing suitable coping strategies; participate with evidence based strength in international climate change policy discussions. **Structure** Council of Ministers; Governing Board; Executive Committee; Headquarters in Accra (Ghana); Headquarters of Competence Centre in Ouagadougou (Burkina Faso); Scientific Advisory Committee. Coordinated by: *Center for Development Research, Bonn (ZEF)*. **Languages** English, French. **Staff** 36 FTE, direct staff; 50 FTE, affiliated staff. **Finance** Funded by German Federal Ministry of Education and Research. **Activities** Research and development; guidance/assistance/consulting; training/education; events/meetings.
Members Governments (11):
Benin, Burkina Faso, Côte d'Ivoire, Gambia, Germany, Ghana, Mali, Niger, Nigeria, Senegal, Togo.
Observer (1):
Economic Community of West African States (ECOWAS, #05312).
IGO Relations Cooperates with: *African Centre of Meteorological Applications for Development (ACMAD, #00242)*; *AGRHYMET Regional Centre (#00565)*; *Comité permanent inter-Etats de lutte contre la sécheresse dans le Sahel (CILSS, #04195)*; Climate Change Agriculture and Food Security (CCAFS) of *CGIAR System Organization (CGIAR, #03843)*; *Institut International d'Ingénierie de l'Eau et de l'Environnement (2iE, #11313)*; *Niger Basin Authority (NBA, #17134)*; *Union économique et monétaire Ouest africaine (UEMOA, #20377)*; *Volta Basin Authority (VBA, #20808)*. **NGO Relations** Partner in: *Africa-EU Innovation Alliance for Water and Climate (AfriAlliance, #00169)*. Cooperates with: *Africa Adaptation Knowledge Network (AAKNet)*; *Alliance for a Green Revolution in Africa (AGRA, #00685)*; *Forum for Agricultural Research in Africa (FARA, #09897)*; *Global Change System for Analysis, Research and Training (START, #10278)*; *INDEPTH Network (#11156)*; *International Food Policy Research Institute (IFPRI, #13622)*; *International Water Management Institute (IWMI, #15867)*; *United Nations University Institute for Environment and Human Security (UNU-EHS, #20645)*; *West and Central African Council for Agricultural Research and Development (WECARD, #20907)*. [2021/XJ7857/**D***]

♦ West African Society of Gastroenterology (inactive)
♦ West African Society of Ophthalmology / see Société Africaine Francophone d'Ophtalmologie (#19453)
♦ West African Society for Pharmacology (inactive)
♦ West African Society of Plastic Surgeons (no recent information)
♦ West African Students Confederation (inactive)
♦ West African Subregional Development Centre / see ECA Sub-Regional Office for West Africa (#05277)
♦ West African Union Development Council (unconfirmed)

♦ West African Union of Tax Institutes (WAUTI) 20898

Union des ordres fiscaux de l'Afrique de l'ouest (UDOFAO)

Hon Sec 1 Bechar Str, off Mambolo Str, Wuse Zone 2, Abuja, Federal Capital Territory, Nigeria. T. +23417741237. E-mail: info@wauti.org – secretary@wauti.org.
URL: http://www.wauti.org/

Aims Harmonize taxation practice in West Africa. **Structure** General Assembly; Council; Executives; Secretariat. **Events** *Annual International Tax Conference* Niamey (Niger) 2015, *Annual International Tax Conference* Accra (Ghana) 2014, *Annual International Tax Conference* Lagos (Nigeria) 2013, *Annual International Tax Conference* Lagos (Nigeria) 2012.
Members Tax institutes in 10 countries:
Benin, Burkina Faso, Côte d'Ivoire, Ghana, Liberia, Mali, Niger, Nigeria, Senegal, Togo. [2015/XJ9527/**D**]

♦ West African Weed Science Society (WAWSS) 20899

Société Ouest africaine de malherbologie (SOAM)

Address not obtained.

History Founded Apr 1979, Dakar (Senegal), following resolution of First International Weed Science Conference, Ibadan (Nigeria) under the auspices of *International Weed Science Society (IWSS, #15875)*. **Aims** Encourage and promote the development of weed science and weed control technology throughout West Africa; promote communication among weed scientists in West Africa; promote and encourage research, extension and training in weed science. **Structure** Presidency and conferences alternate between anglophone and francophone. **Staff** 0.50 FTE, paid. **Finance** Members' dues. Company donations. **Activities** Knowledge management/information dissemination; events/meetings; training/education. **Events** *Biennial Conference* Cape Coast (Ghana) 1990, *Biennial Conference* Ibadan (Nigeria) 1985, *Biennial Conference* Abidjan (Côte d'Ivoire) 1983, *Biennial Conference* Monrovia (Liberia) 1981. **Publications** Conference proceedings.
Members Individual (40) and corporate (agrochemical companies). Individuals in 8 countries (" indicates national society is affiliate):
Benin, Côte d'Ivoire, Ghana (*), Liberia, Nigeria (*), Senegal (*), Sierra Leone, Togo. [2014/XD2812/**D**]

♦ West African Women's Association (WAWA) 20900

Association des femmes de l'Afrique de l'Ouest (AFAO)

Contact SICAP FOIRE No 10665, BP 45177 Dakar, Senegal. T. +221338646491. E-mail: afaowawa@afaowawa.org.
URL: http://afaowawa.org/

History Mar 1984, Conakry (Guinea). Statutes adopted 9 Jul 1987, Abuja (Nigeria), at 10th meeting of the Authority of Heads of State and Government of *Economic Community of West African States (ECOWAS, #05312)*, as part of ECOWAS Social Programme to mobilize all sections of the West African population for the socio-economic integration of the sub-region. **Aims** Mobilize and involve women of the sub-region in the Community-building process; initiate Community (ECOWAS) projects in priority sectors, inter alia *agricultural development*, trade, *water supply* schemes, *desertification control* and *education*; urge and encourage by all possible means private initiative on the part of women, through, among other things, access to credit for women and the improvement of *distribution channels*; initiate and develop research programmes on *living conditions* and *working conditions* of women and urge Member States of ECOWAS to accord greater attention and a more effective support to the implementation of such programmes; promote peace, gender equality and sustainable development of women and children. **Structure** General Assembly (every 2 years). Bureau (meets twice a year), consisting of President, 1st Vice-President, 2nd Vice-President, Secretary-General and Treasurer. External Auditors (2). **Languages** English, French, Portuguese. **Finance** Annual subsidy from ECOWAS. **Activities** Participates in different ECOWAS programmes. Runs programmes on: economic and social cooperation; environmental protection; socio-cultural cooperation. Organizes meetings and seminars. Works towards the establishment of a financial institution for West-African women. Other priorities: mobilization of resources; fight against poverty; information and training; peace and security. **Events** *General assembly* Abidjan (Côte d'Ivoire) 1998, *General Assembly* Accra (Ghana) 1996.
Members National WAWA chapters and National Women's Machineries already established in 15 ECOWAS member states:
Benin, Burkina Faso, Cape Verde, Côte d'Ivoire, Gambia, Ghana, Guinea, Guinea-Bissau, Liberia, Mali, Niger, Nigeria, Senegal, Sierra Leone, Togo.
IGO Relations *African Development Bank (ADB, #00283)*; *International Bank for Reconstruction and Development (IBRD, #12317)*; *Banque ouest africaine de développement (BOAD, #03170)*. **NGO Relations** Cooperates with: *Global Forum on Agricultural Research (GFAR, #10370)*. Cooperates with institutions and organizations working for the advancement of women. [2020/XE5982/**E**]

♦ West African Youth Union (inactive)
♦ West African Research Centre, Dakar (internationally oriented national body)
♦ West Africa Rice Development Association / see Africa Rice Center (#00518)

♦ West Africa Road Transport Union (WARTU) 20901

Exec Sec c/o Nigerian Shippers' Council, No 4 Otunba Ayodele Soyode Lane, NSC Postal Box PMB 5016, Ikoyi, Lagos, Nigeria. E-mail: nsc@shipperscouncil.gov.ng.

History Sep 1989, Accra (Ghana). Original title: *West African Road Transporters Union (WARTU) – Union des transporteurs routiers de l'Afrique de l'Ouest (UTRAO)*. **Aims** Ensure practical realization of ECOWAS protocol on free movement of *goods* and persons within roads of the sub-region; evolve harmonization of conflicting highway *legislation* of countries in the sub-region; assist member organizations to defend their economic and social interests, boost their *professional* training and research activities in related fields. **Structure** General Assembly. Executive Committee. Sub-Committees. Following decision of 3rd General Assembly, 1992, Cotonou (Benin), local units have been set up in Benin, Ghana and Nigeria. **Finance** Members' dues. **Activities** Events/meetings.
Members Organizations in 16 countries:
Benin, Burkina Faso, Cape Verde, Côte d'Ivoire, Gambia, Ghana, Guinea, Guinea-Bissau, Liberia, Mali, Mauritania, Niger, Nigeria, Senegal, Sierra Leone, Togo.
IGO Relations *Economic Community of West African States (ECOWAS, #05312)*. **NGO Relations** *Federation of West African Manufacturers Associations (FEWAMA, #09714)*. [2017/XD3739/**D**]

♦ West Africa Rural Foundation (WARF) 20902

Fondation rurale de l'Afrique de l'ouest (FRAO) – Fundação Rural da Africa do Oeste

Exec Dir Sacré Coeur 3, VDN – Villa, 10075 Dakar, Senegal.
URL: http://www.frao.info/

History 1993, Dakar (Senegal). **Aims** Enhance capacity building of local organizations (NGO, farmers' organizations) and promote participatory methods for research and action. **Structure** Board, comprising 6 members. **Finance** Grants from: *Ford Foundation (#09858)*; *International Development Research Centre (IDRC, #13162)*. Budget (annual): about US$ 1,250,000. **Activities** Focuses on capacity building of local organizations (NGOs, farmers organizations) and participatory methods for research and action. Organizes annual training courses and workshops. **Publications** *L'Atelier* in English, French, Portuguese. Annual Report.
Members Individuals in 5 countries:
Gambia, Guinea, Guinea-Bissau, Mali, Senegal.
IGO Relations *Africa Rice Center (AfricaRice, #00518)*. **NGO Relations** Member of: *CIVICUS: World Alliance for Citizen Participation (#03962)*. [2015/XF3279/fv/**F**]

♦ West Africa Society of Agricultural Engineering (unconfirmed)

♦ West Africa Telecommunications Regulators Association (WATRA) . 20903

Exec Sec WAEC Bldg, 10 Zambezi Street, off Aguiyi Ironsi Street, Maitama, Abuja, Federal Capital Territory, Nigeria.
URL: http://www.watra.org/

Aims Coordinate dialogue of telecommunications policy and regulations in the region. **Structure** Conference (annual); Executive Committee; Secretariat. **Languages** English, French. **Events** *Annual General Meeting* Abuja (Nigeria) 2021, *Annual General Meeting* Ouagadougou (Burkina Faso) 2019.
Members in 11 countries:
Benin, Burkina Faso, Côte d'Ivoire, Gambia, Ghana, Guinea, Guinea-Bissau, Mali, Nigeria, Senegal, Sierra Leone.
IGO Relations Secretariat provided by: *Economic Community of West African States (ECOWAS, #05312)*. Cooperation agreement with: *Commonwealth Telecommunications Organisation (CTO, #04365)*. **NGO Relations** Member of (1): *Alliance for Affordable Internet (A4AI, #00651)*. [2021/XM2240/**D**]

♦ West Africa Tourism Organisation (internationally oriented national body)

♦ West Asian Football Federation (WAFF) 20904

Exec Dir PO Box 5222, Amman 11953, Jordan. T. +96265563601 – +96265563602. Fax +96265563600. E-mail: info@the-waff.com.
URL: http://www.the-waff.com/

History Original statutes approved 14 May 2011, Amman (Jordan). Current statues adopted 30 Jun 2012. **Aims** Improve the game of football; promote, regulate and control it in the region in the light of fair play and its unifying, educational, cultural and humanitarian values, particularly through youth and development programmes. **Structure** Congress; Executive Committee; Standing Committees; Judicial Committees; General Secretariat. **Languages** Arabic, English. **Staff** 6.00 FTE, paid. **Activities** Awards/prizes/competitions.
Members Federations in 13 countries:
Bahrain, Iran Islamic Rep, Iraq, Jordan, Kuwait, Lebanon, Oman, Palestine, Qatar, Saudi Arabia, Syrian AR, United Arab Emirates, Yemen.
NGO Relations Regional zone of *Asian Football Confederation (AFC, #01487)*. [2015/XJ9406/**D**]

♦ West Asian Games Federation (WAGF) 20905

Contact PO Box 4020 Hawalli, 32071 Kuwait, Kuwait. T. +96525355474. Fax +96525355464.
Structure General Assembly. **Events** *Games* Doha (Qatar) 2005, *Games* Kuwait 2002, *Games* Teheran (Iran Islamic Rep) 1997.
Members Full in 13 countries:
Bahrain, Iran Islamic Rep, Iraq, Jordan, Kuwait, Lebanon, Oman, Palestine, Qatar, Saudi Arabia, Syrian AR, United Arab Emirates, Yemen. [2013/XJ6382/**D**]

♦ West Asia-North Africa Forum / see West Asia-North Africa Institute
♦ West Asia-North Africa Institute (internationally oriented national body)
♦ West Asia Regional Network on Climate Change (unconfirmed)
♦ West Asia Society of Aesthetic Plastic Surgery (no recent information)

♦ West and Central Africa Human Rights Training Institute (WACAHRI) 20906

Contact address not obtained. T. +23321242470. Fax +23321221084.
URL: http://www.wacahri.org/

History 2004. **NGO Relations** *Media Foundation for West Africa (MFWA, #16617)* houses secretariat. [2009/XM3477/j/**E**]

♦ West and Central African Action Plan (no recent information)
♦ West and Central African Association of Soil Science (no recent information)

♦ West and Central African Council for Agricultural Research and Development (WECARD) 20907

Conseil Ouest et Centre Africain pour la Recherche et le Développement Agricoles (CORAF)

Contact 7 Avenue Bourguiba, BP 48, Dakar, Senegal. T. +221338699618. Fax +221338699631. E-mail: secoraf@coraf.org.
URL: http://www.coraf.org/

History 1987, as *Conférence des responsables de la recherche agronomique africains et français*. Officially created 15 Mar 1995. Previously referred to as *Conference of African Agricultural Research Managers – Conférence des responsables de recherche agronomique africains (CORAF)*. Current statutes adopted 19 May 2005, Dakar (Senegal). Registered in accordance with Senegalese law. **Aims** Promote cooperation, consultation and information exchange between member institutions on one hand and partners on the other; define joint sub-regional and regional research objectives and priorities; serve as a consultative body for research carried out by regional and international organizations operating at the sub-regional level; develop joint research programmes in order to strengthen complementary activities of the Council and its partners; harmonize the activities of existing research networks and facilitate the creation of new regional networks or other operational research units with a regional character. **Structure** General Assembly (annual). Governing Council of 9 members, comprising 6 representatives of the National Agricultural Research Systems (NARS) and 3 representatives from agricultural research partners recognized by CORAF/WECARD, including 1 representative each of NGOs, the private sector and professional agricultural organizations. Scientific and Technical Committee of 8 experts, consisting of 6 representatives of NARS, 1 representative of advanced research institutions and 1 representative of regional and international organizations. Includes: *Centre d'étude régional pour l'amélioration de l'adaptation à la sécheresse (CERAAS, see: #20907)*, Senegal. **Languages** English, French. **Staff** 37.50 FTE, paid. **Finance** Members' dues. Other sources: contributions from scientific and financial partners; gifts and legacies; contracts; sale of publications. **Activities** Advocacy/lobbying/activism; research and development. teams; promote the training and supervision of young researchers. **Events** *Agriculture Science Week* Niamey (Niger) 2014, *International Plant Virus Epidemiology Symposium* Arusha (Tanzania UR) 2013, *Workshop* Kano (Nigeria) 2005, *Information and communication technology meeting* Dakar (Senegal) 2000, *Atelier international sur l'igname* Montpellier (France) 1997. **Publications** *Coraf Action* (4 a year) – newsletter; *Sahel Agro-forestry Newletter* (2 a year). Annual report; conference proceedings.
Members Scientific institutions in 22 countries:
Benin, Burkina Faso, Cameroon, Cape Verde, Central African Rep, Chad, Congo Brazzaville, Congo DR, Côte d'Ivoire, Gabon, Gambia, Ghana, Guinea, Guinea-Bissau, Liberia, Mali, Mauritania, Niger, Nigeria, Senegal, Sierra Leone, Togo.
IGO Relations Partner of: *Global Soil Partnership (GSP, #10608)*; *West African Science Service Center on Climate Change and Adapted Land Use (WASCAL, #20897)*. Cooperative research programme with: *Conseil permanent de la Francophonie (CPF, #04697)*. Supports: *Africa Rice Center (AfricaRice, #00518)*; *Bioversity International (#03262)*; *Centre Africain de Recherches sur Bananiers et Plantains (CARBAP, #03725)*. Member of: *Congo Basin Forest Partnership (CBFP, #04662)*. **NGO Relations** Member of: *Global Forum on Agricultural Research (GFAR, #10370)*; *Inland Valley Consortium (IVC, no recent information)*; *International Foundation for Science (IFS, #13677)*. Partner of: *European Cooperative for Rural Development (EUCORD, #06788)*; *International Centre for Tropical Agriculture (#12527)*. Expected to coordinate the proposed: *Cereals Network*. Instrumental in setting up: *Forum for Agricultural Research in Africa (FARA, #09897)*. Supports: *Réseau ouest et centre africain du riz (ROCARIZ, no recent information)*. Cooperates with: *International Centre of Insect Physiology and Ecology (ICIPE, #12499)*; *International Fertilizer Development Center (IFDC, #13590)*. [2013.08.01/XF3083/**F**]

♦ West and Central African Operational Research Society (inactive)

♦ West and Central African Research and Education Network (WACREN) 20908

CEO VCG Office Complex, IPS Road, P. O. Box LG 1279, Accra, Ghana. T. +233302942873. E-mail: info@wacren.net.
URL: http://www.wacren.net/

History 2010, Accra (Ghana). Set up with the help of *Association of African Universities (AAU, #02361)*. **Aims** Build and operate a world class network infrastructure; develop state of the art services; promote collaboration among national, regional, international research and education communities; build the capacity of the REN community. **Structure** General Assembly; Board of Directors; Secretariat. **Languages** English, French. **Finance** Sources: members' dues; revenue from activities/projects. Supported by: *European Commission (EC, #06633)*. **Activities** Capacity building; research and development; research/documentation. Active in all member countries. **Events** *Annual Conference* Accra (Ghana) 2019.
Members Full in 13 countries:
Benin, Burkina Faso, Cameroon, Chad, Côte d'Ivoire, Ghana, Guinea, Liberia, Mali, Niger, Nigeria, Sierra Leone, Togo.
Premium Associate in 1 country:
France.
Associate in 1 country:
Nigeria.
Ongoing initiatives in 2 countries:
Gabon, Senegal.
NGO Relations Cooperates with (5): *African Network Operators Group (AfNOG, #00392)*; *Confederation of Open Access Repositories (COAR, #04573)*; *Electronic Information for Libraries (EIFL, #05425)*; *GÉANT Association (#10086)*; National Institute of Informatics Japan. [2020.05.06/XM6275/**F**]

♦ West-East Bridges Foundation 20909

Contact Marius van Bouwdijk Bastiaansestr 44, 1054 SP Amsterdam, Netherlands. E-mail: main@west-east-fund.com.
URL: http://www.west-east-fund.com/

History 21 Jun 2011, Amsterdam (Netherlands). Former names and other names: *Stichting Respect International West-East Bridges Foundation* – full title. **Aims** Promote cooperation between countries of Western and *Eastern Europe*, exchange of experience and new technologies and support for intercultural dialogue; promote integration and socialization of *migrants* and *refugees*; train young leaders able to support and promote European *values*. **Structure** Community Council; Youth Board. **Languages** English. **Staff** 5.00 FTE, paid; 18.00 FTE, voluntary. **Finance** Sources: donations; grants. Annual budget: 120,000 EUR. **Activities** Events/meetings; networking/liaising; publishing activities; research/documentation; training/education.
Members Full in 11 countries:
Albania, Armenia, Belgium, France, Germany, Jordan, Morocco, Netherlands, Russia, Sweden, UK.
NGO Relations Member of (1): *Eastern Partnership Civil Society Forum (EaP CSF, #05247)*. [2021.09.30/XM5656/f/**F**]

♦ Western African Network of AIDS Service Organizations (see: #00272)

♦ Western Balkans Investment Framework (WBIF) 20910

Secretariat DG NEAR, Directorate D – Western Balkans Unit D5, Rue de la Loi 15, 1000 Brussels, Belgium. E-mail: near-wbif@ec.europa.eu.
URL: http://www.wbif.eu/

History Set up as a joint initiative of *European Commission (EC, #06633)*, international financing institutions – *European Bank for Reconstruction and Development (EBRD, #06315)*; *European Investment Bank (EIB, #07599)*; *Council of Europe Development Bank (CEB, #04897)*; *Kreditanstalt für Wiederaufbau (KfW)*; *The World Bank Group (#21218)*; *Agence française de développement (AFD)*; *International Finance Corporation (IFC, #13597)*; *European Investment Fund (EIF, #07601)* bilateral donors and the governments of Albania, Bosnia-Herzegovina, Kosovo, Macedonia, Montenegro and Serbia. **Aims** Support socio-economic development and EU accession across the Western Balkans through finance and technical assistance for strategic investments. **Structure** Strategic and Operational Board; Project Financiers' Group; Secretariat. **Languages** English. **Finance** Sources: contributions; grants. Other sources: bilateral donors. Supported by: *Agence française de développement (AFD)*; *Council of Europe Development Bank (CEB, #04897)*; *European Bank for Reconstruction and Development (EBRD, #06315)*; *European Commission (EC, #06633)* (Instrument for Pre-Accession); *European Investment Bank (EIB, #07599)*; *Kreditanstalt für Wiederaufbau (KfW)*; *The World Bank Group (#21218)*. **Publications** Annual Report; reports.
Members Governments (6):
Albania, Bosnia-Herzegovina, Kosovo, Montenegro, North Macedonia, Serbia.
IGO Relations Supports (1): *Energy Community (#05468)*. [2023.02.15/XJ8436/**E***]

♦ Western Buddhist Order / see Triratna Buddhist Community (#20243)

♦ Western Central Atlantic Fishery Commission (WECAFC) 20911

Commission des pêches pour l'Atlantique centre-Ouest (COPACO) – Comisión de Pesca para el Atlantico Centro-Occidental (COPACO)

Contact FAO Subregional Office for the Caribbean, 2nd Floor – United Nations House, Marine Gardens – Hastings, Bridgetown, St Michael BB11000, Bridgetown ST MICHAEL BB11000, Barbados. T. +12464267110 – +12464267111ext249. Fax +12464276075. E-mail: wecafc-secretariat@fao.org.
URL: http://www.fao.org/fishery/rfb/wecafc/en

History Established 1973, by Resolution 4/61 of the Council of *FAO (#09260)*, under Article VI(1) of the FAO Constitution. States amended by FAO Council at its 74th Session, Dec 1978, and by the 131st Session, Nov 2006. **Aims** Promote the effective *conservation*, management and development of living marine resources of the area of competence of the Commission, in accordance with the FAO Code of Conduct for Responsible Fisheries; address common problems of fisheries management and development faced by members. **Structure** Commission (meets every 2 years), comprising all members. Scientific Advisory Group (SAG) of 5 scientists. Working Groups (4): Shrimp and Groundfish Fisheries in the Brazil-Guianas Shelf Large Marine Ecosystem; Caribbean Spiny Lobster; Queen Conch and Flying Fish; Anchored Fish Attracting Devices in the Lesser Antilles. Secretariat provided by FAO Subregional Office for the Caribbean (SLC). **Languages** English, French, Spanish. **Activities** Promotes application of the provisions of the FAO Code of Conduct on Responsible Fisheries and its related instruments, including the precautionary approach and the ecosystem approach to fisheries management; ensures adequate attention to small-scale, artisanal and subsistence fisheries; coordinates and cooperates closely with other relevant international organizations on matters of common interest; contributes to improved governance through institutional arrangements that encourage cooperation amongst members; assists members in implementing relevant international fisheries instruments, in particular the FAO Code of Conduct for Responsible Fisheries and its related International Plans of Action; promote, coordinates and, as appropriate, undertakes collection, exchange and dissemination of statistical, biological, environmental and socio-economic data and other marine fishery information as well as its analysis or study; promotes, coordinates and, as appropriate, strengthens development of institutional capacity and human resources, particularly through education, training and extension activities in the areas of competence of the Commission; promotes and facilitates harmonizing of relevant national laws and regulations, and compatibility of conservation and management measures; assists members in and facilitates, as appropriate and upon their request, the conservation, management and development of transboundary and straddling stocks under their respective national jurisdictions; serves as a conduit of independent funding to members for initiatives related to conservation, management and development of the living resources in the area of competence of the Commission. **Events** *Session* Gosier (Guadeloupe) 2016, *Session* Port-of-Spain (Trinidad-Tobago) 2014, *Session* Panama (Panama) 2012, *Session* Cartagena de Indias (Colombia) 2008, *Session* Port-of-Spain (Trinidad-Tobago) 2005. **Publications** Reports; technical papers; circulars.
Members Open to coastal states whose territories are situated wholly or partly within the area of the Commission or states whose vessels engage in fishing in the area of competence of the Commission that notify in writing to the Director-General of the Organization of their desire to be considered as members of the Commission. Governments of 32 countries:
Antigua-Barbuda, Bahamas, Barbados, Belize, Brazil, Colombia, Cuba, Dominica, Dominican Rep, France, Grenada, Guatemala, Guinea, Guyana, Haiti, Honduras, Jamaica, Japan, Korea Rep, Mexico, Netherlands, Nicaragua, Panama, Spain, St Kitts-Nevis, St Lucia, St Vincent-Grenadines, Suriname, Trinidad-Tobago, UK, USA, Venezuela.
Regional Organization:
European Commission (EC, #06633). [2011.10.18/XE3487/**E***]

♦ Western and Central Pacific Fisheries Commission (WCPFC) 20912

Secretariat Kaselehlie St, PO Box 2356, Kolonia FM 96941, USA. T. +6913201992. Fax +6913201108. E-mail: wcpfc@wcpfc.int.
URL: http://www.wcpfc.int/

History Established under the terms of *Convention on the Conservation and Management of Highly Migratory Fish Stocks in the Western and Central Pacific Ocean (Pacific tuna convention, 2000)*, done 5 Sep 2000, Honolulu HI (USA). Headquarters in Micronesia FS. Also referred to as *Tuna Commission* and as *Commission for the Conservation and Management of Highly Migratory Fish Stocks in the Western and Central Pacific Ocean (WCPOC)*. Inaugural session 9-10 Dec 2004, Pohnpei (Micronesia FS). **Structure** Annual Meeting; Committees (4). **Languages** English. **Staff** 32.00 FTE, paid. **Finance** Members' dues. Annual budget: US$ 8,000,000. **Activities** Events/meetings. **Events** *Regular Session* Busan (Korea Rep) 2018, *CDS Technical Meeting* Fukuoka (Japan) 2018, *Regular Session* Fukuoka (Japan) 2018, *Regular Session* Honolulu, HI (USA) 2018, *Regular session* Majuro (Marshall Is) 2018. **Publications** *WCPFC Secretariat Quarterly* (4 a year) – newsletter. Summary reports.
Members Governments of 25 countries and territories:
Australia, China, Cook Is, Fiji, Indonesia, Japan, Kiribati, Korea Rep, Marshall Is, Micronesia FS, Nauru, New Caledonia, New Zealand, Niue, Palau, Papua New Guinea, Philippines, Polynesia Fr, Samoa, Solomon Is, Taiwan, Tonga, Tuvalu, Vanuatu, Wallis-Futuna.
Regional organization (1):
European Union (EU, #08967).
Observers Governments of 3 countries:

Canada, France, USA.
International organizations (12):
Agreement on the Conservation of Albatrosses and Petrels (ACAP, 2001); FAO (#09260); Greenpeace International (#10727); Indian Ocean Tuna Commission (IOTC, #11162); Inter-American Tropical Tuna Commission (IATTC, #11454); International Commission for the Conservation of Atlantic Tunas (ICCAT, #12675); International Game Fish Association (IGFA); Pacific Community (SPC, #17942); Pacific Islands Forum Fisheries Agency (FFA, #17969); Pacific Islands Forum Secretariat (#17970); Secretariat of the Pacific Regional Environment Programme (SPREP, #19205); University of the South Pacific (USP, #20703).
NGO Relations *BirdLife International (#03266); Greenpeace International (#10727); Pacific International Maritime Law Association (PIMLA, #17956); World Wide Fund for Nature (WWF, #21922).*
[2023/XE4655/y/**E***]

♦ Western Dredging Association (WEDA) 20913
Association occidentale de dragage
Exec Dir PO Box 1393, Bonsall CA 92003, USA. T. +19494228231.
URL: http://www.westerndredging.org/
History 1978, as one of the regional groupings associated with *World Organization of Dredging Associations (WODA, #21688).* **Aims** Promote the exchange of knowledge in fields related to dredging, *navigation, marine engineering* and construction by sponsoring or co-sponsoring technical conferences, seminars and symposia, including publication and dissemination of proceedings. **Structure** Board of Directors. Executive Director. **Languages** English. **Activities** Annual technical conference in North America. Co-sponsors triennial World Dredging Congress. **Events** *Dredging Summit* Chicago, IL (USA) 2019, *Fall Conference* Honolulu, HI (USA) 2018, *Dredging Summit* Norfolk, VA (USA) 2018, *Fall Conference* Portland, OR (USA) 2017, *Dredging Summit* Vancouver, BC (Canada) 2017. **Publications** *International Dredging Review. World Dredging Mining and Construction.* Annual membership directory; conference proceedings.
Members Individuals (1028); sustaining members (30). Members in 7 countries:
Argentina, Brazil, Canada, Colombia, Mexico, USA, Venezuela. [2016/XE1212/**E**]

- ♦ Western Economic Association International (internationally oriented national body)
- ♦ Western European Airports Association (inactive)
- ♦ Western European Association for Aviation Psychology / see European Association for Aviation Psychology (#05950)
- ♦ Western European Institute for Wood Preservation / see European Institute for Wood Preservation (#07575)
- ♦ Western European Legal Metrology Cooperation / see WELMEC – European Cooperation in Legal Metrology (#20857)
- ♦ Western European Logistics Group (inactive)
- ♦ Western European Metal Trades Employers' Organization / see Council of European Employers of the Metal, Engineering and Technology-Based Industries (#04887)
- ♦ Western European Network on Volunteer Development / see European Network on Volunteer Development (#08032)

♦ Western European Nuclear Regulators Association (WENRA) 20914
Chair c/o French Nuclear Safety Authority, 15 rue Louis Lejeune, CS 70013, 92541 Montrouge, France. E-mail: info@asn.fr – bordeaux.asn@asn.fr.
URL: https://www.wenra.eu/
History Feb 1999, London (UK). **Aims** Develop a common approach to nuclear safety and regulation, in particular in Europe; provide an independent capability to examine nuclear safety and regulation in applicant countries; evaluate and achieve a common approach to nuclear safety and regulatory issues which arise. **Structure** Plenary Meeting; Chairman; Technical Secretariat. **Languages** English. **Finance** Members' dues. **Events** *Autumn Meeting* Madrid (Spain) 2015.
Members Full in 18 countries:
Belgium, Bulgaria, Czechia, Finland, France, Germany, Hungary, Italy, Lithuania, Netherlands, Romania, Slovakia, Slovenia, Spain, Sweden, Switzerland, UK, Ukraine.
Observers in 13 countries:
Armenia, Austria, Belarus, Canada, Cyprus, Denmark, Ireland, Japan, Luxembourg, Norway, Poland, Russia, Serbia.
[2022/XD8003/**D**]

- ♦ Western European Union (inactive)

♦ Western European Volleyball Zonal Association (WEVZA) 20915
Secretariat Avenida de França 549, 4050-279 Porto, Portugal. T. +351228349570. E-mail: wevza.secretariat@gmail.com.
URL: http://wevza.com/
Aims Encourage the development of Volleyball and Beach Volleyball. **Structure** General Assembly; Executive Committee; Secretariat. **Languages** English.
Members National federations in 8 countries:
Belgium, France, Germany, Italy, Netherlands, Portugal, Spain, Switzerland.
NGO Relations Affiliated with: *European Volleyball Confederation (#09078); Fédération internationale de volleyball (FIVB, #09670).* [2020/XJ8516/**D**]

- ♦ Western Foundation for Raptor Conservation / see HawkWatch International
- ♦ Western Hemisphere Institute for Security Cooperation (internationally oriented national body)
- ♦ Western Humor and Irony Membership / see International Society for Humor Studies (#15184)

♦ Western Indian Ocean Marine Science Association (WIOMSA) 20916
Association des sciences de la mer d'océan Indien occidental
Exec Sec PO Box 3298, Zanzibar Zanzibar Urban/West, Tanzania UR. T. +255242233472 – +255242234597. Fax +255242233852. E-mail: secretary@wiomsa.org.
Pres Kenya Marine and Fisheries Research Institute (KMFRI), PO Box 81651, Mombasa, 80100, Kenya.
URL: http://www.wiomsa.org/
History Dec 1993, Maputo (Mozambique). Registered in accordance with the law of Tanzania. Current constitution adopted Oct 2013. **Aims** Advance regional cooperation in all aspects of *coastal* and marine sciences and management; support sustainable development in the Western Indian Ocean Region, while promoting interdisciplinary and multi-disciplinary approaches. **Structure** General Assembly (every 3 years); Board of Trustees (meets annually); Secretariat; Country Coordinators. **Languages** English. **Staff** 6.00 FTE, paid. **Finance** Members' dues. Other sources: donor funded projects; rentals; book sales. Annual budget: US$ 1,500,000 – 2,000,000. **Activities** Events/meetings; training/education; awards/prizes/competitions; knowledge management/information dissemination. **Events** *Scientific Symposium* Réduit (Mauritius) 2019, *Scientific Symposium* Dar es Salaam (Tanzania UR) 2017, *Scientific Symposium* Port Edward (South Africa) 2015, *Scientific Symposium* Maputo (Mozambique) 2013, *Scientific Symposium* Mombasa (Kenya) 2011. **Publications** *WIOMSA News Brief* (4 a year); *Western Indian Ocean Journal of Marine Sciences* (2 a year); *WIOMSA Magazine – People and the Environment* (2 a year). *WIOMSA Book Series.*
Members Institutional; Individuals; Associate; Fellow; Student; Honorary. Individuals (1,182) in 54 countries and territories:
Australia, Bangladesh, Belgium, Bermuda, Cameroon, Canada, Colombia, Comoros, Côte d'Ivoire, Eritrea, France, Germany, Ghana, India, Ireland, Israel, Italy, Japan, Kenya, Kuwait, Madagascar, Malawi, Maldives, Mauritius, Mayotte, Mexico, Morocco, Mozambique, Namibia, Netherlands, Niger, Nigeria, Norway, Oman, Pakistan, Philippines, Portugal, Qatar, Réunion, Senegal, Seychelles, South Africa, Spain, Sweden, Switzerland, Tanzania UR, Thailand, Tunisia, Uganda, UK, Ukraine, USA, Zambia, Zimbabwe.
Institutional (about 50) in 17 countries and territories:
Comoros, Eritrea, France, Kenya, Madagascar, Mauritius, Mozambique, Pakistan, Philippines, Réunion, Seychelles, South Africa, Sri Lanka, Sweden, Tanzania UR, Ukraine, USA.
Consultative Status Consultative status granted from: *UNEP (#20299).* **NGO Relations** Member of: *International Foundation for Science (IFS, #13677); International Union for Conservation of Nature and Natural Resources (IUCN, #15766); Consortium on Science, Technology and Innovation for the South (COSTIS, no recent information).* Participates in: *Global Island Partnership (GLISPA, #10436).* Supports: *Coastal Oceans Research and Development – Indian Ocean (CORDIO East Africa, #04073).* [2017.01.13/XD6629/**D**]

- ♦ Western Indian Ocean Tuna Organization (no recent information)
- ♦ Western Pacific Association of Critical Care Medicine / see Asia Pacific Association of Critical Care Medicine (#01838)

♦ Western Pacific Association for Medical Education (WPAME) 20917
Pres NUS CenMED, Block MD 11 05-10, Clinical Research Centre, 10 Medical Drive, Singapore 117597, Singapore.
URL: http://www.wpame.org.au/
History 11 Mar 1988, Kuala Lumpur (Malaysia), as *Association for Medical Education in the Western Pacific Region (AMEWPR).* **Aims** Promote and develop medical education in the Western Region; provide a forum and mechanism for exchange of information among members; establish and maintain a resource centre for educational materials. **Structure** Executive Board, consisting of President, Vice President, Secretary/Treasurer, Honorary President and 2 founder members. Advisory Board of 11 members. Includes *Australian and New Zealand Association for Health Professional Educators (ANZAHPE).* **Finance** Support from *WHO Regional Office for the Western Pacific (WPRO, #20947).* **Events** *Annual Meeting* Seoul (Korea Rep) 2013, *Congress* Australia 2000, *Biennial meeting / Congress* Manila (Philippines) 1998, *Biennial Meeting* Kuala Lumpur (Malaysia) 1990. **Publications** *Association for Medical Education in the Western Pacific Region Secretariat News* (periodical). *WHO Guidelines of Quality Assurance of Medical Education for Western Pacific Region* – with WHO/WPRO.
Members In the Western Pacific Region national associations; medical schools; other bodies concerned with medical education. National associations in the Southeast Asian Region. Institutional Membership and Corresponding Members – Focal Points in 15 countries and territories:
Australia, Cambodia, China, Fiji, Hong Kong, Japan, Korea Rep, Laos, Malaysia, Mongolia, New Zealand, Papua New Guinea, Philippines, Singapore, Vietnam.
IGO Relations *WHO (#20950).* **NGO Relations** Member of: *World Federation for Medical Education (WFME, #21454).* [2018/XD8680/**D**]

- ♦ Western Pacific Association for Transactional Analysis (internationally oriented national body)

♦ Western Pacific Commission for Acoustics (WESPAC) 20918
SG c/o Hanyang University ERICA, Dept of Marine Science, 55 Hanyangdaehak-ro, Ansan GYEONGGI 15588, Korea Rep.
URL: http://wespac.hanyang.ac.kr/WESPAC_Acoustics_Commission/Home.html
History 1982, Singapore (Singapore). Founded on the initiative of Prof Kido. Former names and other names: *Western Pacific Regional Commission for Acoustics (WESPRAC)* – former (1982 to 2000). **Aims** Promote international research, development and collaboration in all fields of acoustics in the region. **Events** *WESPAC: Western Pacific Acoustics Conference* Beijing (China) 2021, *WESPAC: Western Pacific Acoustics Conference* Delhi (India) 2018, *WESPAC: Western Pacific Acoustics Conference* Singapore (Singapore) 2015, *WESPAC: Western Pacific Acoustics Conference* Hong Kong (Hong Kong) 2012, *WESPAC: Western Pacific Acoustics Conference* Beijing (China) 2009.
Members National organizations (12) in 9 countries and territories:
Australia, China, Hong Kong, India, Japan, Korea Rep, New Zealand, Russia, Singapore.
NGO Relations Affiliate member of: *International Commission for Acoustics (ICA, #12658).*
[2020/XM3141/**E**]

- ♦ Western Pacific Naval Symposium (meeting series)
- ♦ Western Pacific Orthopaedic Association / see Asia Pacific Orthopaedic Association (#01987)
- ♦ Western Pacific Regional Commission for Acoustics / see Western Pacific Commission for Acoustics (#20918)
- ♦ Western Pacific Regional Fishery Management Council (internationally oriented national body)
- ♦ Western Pacific Society of Chemotherapy / see Asia-Pacific Society of Clinical Microbiology and Infection (#02032)
- ♦ Western Plumbing Officials Association / see International Association of Plumbing and Mechanical Officials
- ♦ Westerwelle Foundation (internationally oriented national body)
- ♦ Westerwelle Foundation for International Understanding / see Westerwelle Foundation
- ♦ Westerwelle Foundation – Stiftung für Internationale Verständigung / see Westerwelle Foundation
- ♦ Westeuropäische Autorenvereinigung "DIE KOGGE" / see Europäische Autorenvereinigung "DIE KOGGE" (#05749)
- ♦ Westeuropäische Gesellschaft für Luftfahrt-Psychologie / see European Association for Aviation Psychology (#05950)
- ♦ West-Europäisches Institut für Holzimprägnierung / see European Institute for Wood Preservation (#07575)
- ♦ West European Center / see West European Studies Center, Bloomington IN
- ♦ West European Confederation of Maritime Technology Societies / see Confederation of European Maritime Technology Societies (#04526)
- ♦ West European Federation of National Socialists (inactive)

♦ West European Fish Technologists Association (WEFTA) 20919
Contact IMARES, PO Box 68, 1970 AB Ijmuiden, Netherlands. T. +31255564722. Fax +31255564644.
URL: http://www.wefta.org/
History 1970. Current bylaws adopted, 1999; amended 2012. **Aims** Improve quality of fish and seafood on and from the European and other markets through research within this area. **Structure** Plenary Meeting (annual). No permanent secretariat. **Activities** Permanent working groups (2): Analytical Methods for Fish and Fishery Products; Microbiology for Fish and Fishery Products. **Events** *Annual Meeting* Rotterdam (Netherlands) 2022, *Annual Meeting* Rotterdam (Netherlands) 2020, *Annual Meeting* Thórshavn (Faeroe Is) 2019, *Annual Meeting* Lisbon (Portugal) 2018, *Annual Meeting* Split (Croatia) 2016.
Members Institutes (21) in 20 countries and territories;:
Belgium, Croatia, Denmark, Estonia, Faeroe Is, Finland, France, Germany, Greece, Iceland, Ireland, Italy, Netherlands, Norway, Poland, Portugal, Spain, Sweden, Türkiye, UK. [2021/XD7483/**D**]

- ♦ West European Network on Work, Unemployment and the Churches / see Work and Economy Research Network in the European Churches (#21051)
- ♦ West European Student Information Bureau / see European Students' Union (#08848)
- ♦ West European Studies Center, Bloomington IN (internationally oriented national body)
- ♦ West European Studies Centre / see European Studies Centre, Oxford
- ♦ West European Studies Program / see European Studies Center, Pittsburgh PA

♦ West India Committee (WIC) 20920
Comité des Indes occidentales
CEO Clutha House, 10 Storey's Gate, London, SW1P 3AY, UK. T. +442077995441. E-mail: enquiries@westindiacommittee.org.
URL: http://westindiacommittee.org/
History Founded 1735. Granted Royal Charter by King Edward VII, 1904. **Aims** Develop sustainable *prosperity* amongst the West Indian community both in the Caribbean and within the societies in which they live and work globally by promoting the interests of *agriculture, manufacturing* industries and *trade.* **Structure** General meeting (annual); Executive Council; Executive Committee; Headquarters in London. Acts as umbrella organization for: *Caribbean Trade Advisory Group (CARITAG, no recent information).* **Languages** English, French, Spanish. **Staff** 5.00 FTE, paid. **Finance** Members' dues. Subventions; grants. Annual budget: about pounds250,000. **Activities** Training/education; advocacy/lobbying/activism; guidance/assistance/consulting; networking/liaising; projects/programmes; politics/policy/regulatory. **Events** *Annual Europe-Caribbean conference* Paris (France) 1999, *Annual Europe-Caribbean conference* Havana (Cuba) 1997, *Annual Europe-Caribbean conference* Port-of-Spain (Trinidad-Tobago) 1995, *Joint conference* London (UK) 1988. **Publications** White papers; circulars; videos.
Members Individuals in 30 countries and territories:
Antigua-Barbuda, Bahamas, Barbados, Belize, Canada, Costa Rica, Cuba, Dominica, Dominican Rep, France, Germany, Grenada, Guadeloupe, Guyana, Haiti, Honduras, Hong Kong, Jamaica, Martinique, Netherlands, Panama, Puerto Rico, St Kitts-Nevis, St Lucia, St Vincent-Grenadines, Suriname, Trinidad-Tobago, UK, USA.
Consultative Status Consultative status granted from: *UNESCO (#20322)* (Consultative Status). **IGO Relations** Cooperates with (2): *Commonwealth Secretariat (#04362); University of the West Indies (UWI, #20705).* **NGO Relations** Instrumental in setting up: *The Caribbean Council (CC, #03482).* [2018.06.01/XF5302/v/**F**]

♦ West Indian ACLALS / see West Indian Association for Commonwealth Literature and Language Studies (#20921)

♦ **West Indian Association for Commonwealth Literature and Language Studies (WIACLALS)** **20921**

Contact Dept of Literatures in English, Univ of West Indies, Mona, Kingston 7, Jamaica. T. +18769272217ext2396. Fax +18769770622.
Journal: https://www.jwilonline.org/

History 1977. Founded as a regional association of *Association for Commonwealth Literature and Language Studies (ACLALS, #02439)*. Former names and other names: *West Indian ACLALS* – former alias; *Caribbean Association for Commonwealth Literature and Language Studies (CACLALS)* – former alias. **Aims** Encourage, foster, promote, disseminate the study of Commonwealth and post-colonial literatures and languages. **Languages** English. **Activities** Events/meetings. **Publications** *Journal of West Indian Literature* (2 a year) in English; *CARIB* (irregular).
Members Full in 11 countries:
Australia, Bahamas, Barbados, Canada, Guyana, Jamaica, St Kitts-Nevis, St Lucia, St Vincent-Grenadines, Trinidad-Tobago, USA. [2018.06.01/XE5282/**E**]

♦ West Indian Limes Association (inactive)
♦ West Indian Sea Island Cotton Association (no recent information)
♦ West Indies Associated States Council of Ministers (inactive)
♦ West Indies Associated States Supreme Court / see Eastern Caribbean Supreme Court (#05236)

♦ **West Indies Central Sugar Cane Breeding Station (CBS)** **20922**

Dir Groves, St George BB19073, ST GEORGE BB19073, Barbados. T. +12464331308. Fax +12464335568. E-mail: wicscbs@caribsurf.com.
URL: http://wicscbs.org/

History 1962, Barbados. Founded under *'West Indies Sugar Association'*, later *Sugar Association of the Caribbean (SAC, #20033)*, having existed since 1932 as *Cane Breeding Station*, a regional organization under the Barbados Department of Agriculture. Incorporated as a non-for profit company, 2015. **Aims** Carry out breeding, *pathology* and related research into sugarcane varieties for the sugar industries of the *Caribbean* and some members in *Central America* and *Africa*. **Structure** Board of Directors. **Languages** English. **Staff** 3.00 FTE, paid. **Finance** Sources: members' dues. Annual budget: 1,000,000 USD. **Activities** Events/meetings; guidance/assistance/consulting; knowledge management/information dissemination. **Events** *Breeding and germplasm workshop* St Michael (Barbados) 2000, *Workshop* St George (Barbados) 1992. **Publications** Technical bulletins (occasional). Annual Report.
Members Full in 16 countries and territories (" indicates member of WISBEN):
Barbados (*), Belize (*), Congo DR, Costa Rica (*), Dominican Rep (*), Guadeloupe (*), Guyana (*), Jamaica (*), Mali, Martinique (*), Nicaragua, Nigeria, Panama (*), Papua New Guinea, Senegal, Sudan (*). [2022.02.04/XE1097/**E**]

♦ West Indies Cricket Board / see Cricket West Indies (#04953)
♦ West Indies Cricket Board of Control / see Cricket West Indies (#04953)
♦ West Indies Farmers' Association / see Windward Islands Farmers' Association (#20966)
♦ West Indies Federation (inactive)
♦ West Indies Netball Board of Control / see Caribbean Netball Association (#03526)

♦ **West Indies Rum and Spirits Producers' Association Inc (WIRSPA)** . **20923**

CEO Mars House, 13 Pine Road, Belleville, St Michael BB11113, ST MICHAEL BB11113, Barbados. T. +12462288033. E-mail: wirspa@wirspa.com.
Chairman Plantation Diamond, East Bank, Georgetown, Guyana.
URL: http://www.wirspa.com/

History Founded late 1960s. **Aims** Promote and protect interests of those concerned with the distillation, export and marketing of rum; develop the Caribbean rum category in international drinks markets with development of the ACR (Authentic Caribbean Rum) Marque. **Structure** Board of Directors; Programme Management Unit – Integrated Development Programme for the Caribbean Rum Sector and Caribbean Rum Sector Support Programme. **Languages** English, Spanish. **Staff** 3.00 FTE, paid. **Activities** Networking/liaising. **Publications** Programme Implementation Report.
Members National associations in 11 countries and territories:
Antigua, Barbados, Belize, Dominican Rep, Grenada, Guyana, Haiti, Jamaica, St Lucia, Suriname, Trinidad-Tobago.
Associate in 3 countries:
Dominica, St Kitts-Nevis, St Vincent-Grenadines.
IGO Relations Cooperates with (2): *Caribbean Community (CARICOM, #03476)*; *Forum of Caribbean States (CARIFORUM, #09904)*. [2021.09.21/XD2408/**D**]

♦ West Indies School of Theology (internationally oriented national body)
♦ West Indies Sugar Association / see Sugar Association of the Caribbean (#20033)
♦ West Indies Sugarcane Breeding and Evaluation Network (see: #20922)
♦ Westminster Foundation for Democracy (internationally oriented national body)

♦ **West Network** **20924**

Dir address not obtained. E-mail: westnetwork@jyu.fi.
URL: https://thewestnetwork.org/

Aims Study the West as a concept, idea, narrative, political and rhetoric tool, and as an imagined or real community with shared values, worldviews, culture, political agendas, and economic and military ties. **Structure** Coordination Group. **Activities** Events/meetings; research/documentation. **Events** *International Conference* Jyväskylä (Finland) 2019, *International Conference* Jyväskylä (Finland) 2016.
Members Individuals in 21 countries:
Austria, Belgium, Brazil, Canada, Finland, Germany, Hungary, Israel, Kyrgyzstan, Morocco, Norway, Poland, Portugal, Russia, Saudi Arabia, Slovakia, Spain, Sweden, Türkiye, UK, USA. [2021/AA0421/v/**F**]

♦ West Nordic Committee / see Nordic Atlantic Cooperation (#17209)

♦ **West Nordic Council** **20925**

Vestnordisk Råd – Länsi-Pohjolan Neuvosto – Nunat Avannarliit Killiit Siunnersuisoqatigiiffiata

Contact c/o Althingi, Kirkjustræti 12, 150 Reykjavik, Iceland. T. +3545630731. Fax +3545630435. E-mail: vestnordisk@althingi.is.
URL: http://www.vestnordisk.is/

History 24 Sep 1985, Nuuk (Greenland). Established as a regional cooperation between the parliaments of Iceland, the Faroe Islands and Greenland. Other language titles also in Icelandic and Faroese. Secretariat established 1997, located in the Icelandic Parliament. **Aims** Promote West Nordic interests; be guardians of *North Atlantic resources* and North Atlantic *culture* and help promote West Nordic interests through the West Nordic governments; follow up on governments' West Nordic cooperation; work with the Nordic Council and act as West Nordic link in Nordic cooperation; act as the parliamentary link for inter-West Nordic organizations. **Structure** General Assembly. Council of 6 representatives of each parliament; Presidium. **Languages** Danish. **Events** *Conference on fishing policy and the EU* Faeroe Is 2005, *Annual conference* 2003, *Annual conference* Thórshavn (Faeroe Is) 2002, *Annual conference* 2001, *Annual conference* 2000.
Members Parliaments of 3 countries and territories:
Faeroe Is, Greenland, Iceland.
IGO Relations *European Parliament (EP, #08146)*; *Nordic Committee of Senior Officials for Regional Policy (EK-R)*; *Nordic Council (NC, #17256)*; *Nordic Council of Ministers (NCM, #17260)*; *Standing Committee of Parliamentarians of the Arctic Region (SCPAR, #19958)*. [2021/XK2130/**F***]

♦ **West-Nordic Foundation** **20926**

Nordiska Utvecklingsfonden för Västnorden (Vestnordenfonden) – Länsipohjolan Pohjoismainen Kehittämisrahasto – Norourlendski Menninggargrunnurin fyri Utnordur – Norraeni Tróunarsjóðurinn fyrir hin Vestlaegu Nordurlönd (Lanasjódur Vesturnordurlanda) – Nunanut Avannarlernut Killernut Tunngatitamik Nunat Avannarliit Ineriartortitsinermut Aninggaasaateqarfiannik

Dir Postbox 8096, 128 Reykjavik, Iceland. T. +298316336. Fax +2985302109. E-mail: vestnorden@vestnorden.is.
URL: http://www.vestnorden.is/

History 17 Sep 1987, on coming into force of an agreement signed, 19 Aug 1986, by the governments of the 5 Nordic countries and the Home Governments of the Faeroe Is and Greenland. Commenced operations Nov 1987. **Aims** Support development of a comprehensive and competitive economy in the West Nordic countries of Faeroe Is, Greenland and Iceland by providing loans, grants and guarantees to projects in connection with or for the benefit of small and medium *enterprises*; by this means encourage *industrial* and *technical* cooperation within the region and with other Nordic countries. **Structure** Board of Directors of 7 members representing each of the 5 Nordic governments as well as the Faeroese and Greenland governments. Members from the Faeroe Islands, Greenland and Iceland form an advisory group. General Manager. **Staff** 3.00 FTE, paid. **Finance** Founding capital comprises annual contributions of the 5 Nordic countries plus Faeroe Is and Greenland up to 1995, when it reached the equivalent of US$ 14.1 million. **Activities** Grants credit and guarantees on normal banking terms or, if circumstances require, on more favourable terms. A loan depreciation fund covers the threat of possible losses. **Publications** Annual report.
Members Governments of 7 countries and territories:
Denmark, Faeroe Is, Finland, Greenland, Iceland, Norway, Sweden.
IGO Relations A cooperation body of: *Nordic Council of Ministers (NCM, #17260)*. [2016/XD0812/f/**F***]

♦ West Pacific Dialogue / see South-West Pacific Dialogue (#19895)
♦ West Pacific Forum / see South-West Pacific Dialogue (#19895)
♦ WESTPAC – IOC Sub-Commission for the Western Pacific (see: #11496)
♦ West Virginia Consortium for Faculty and Course Development in International Studies (internationally oriented national body)
♦ WES – World Education Services (internationally oriented national body)
♦ **WES** World Endometriosis Society (#21379)
♦ Wetenschappelijk-Technische Groep voor Aanbevelingen inzake Bouwenrenovatie en Monumentenzorg (#12152)

♦ **Wetland Link International (WLI)** **20927**

Head WWT Slimbridge Wetland Ctr, Slimbridge, GL2 7BT, UK. T. +441453891214. E-mail: wli@wwt.org.uk.
URL: http://www.wli.org.uk/

History 1991. **Aims** Meet the need for wetland centres to share best practice, provide moral support and develop the approach of using on-site wetland education and awareness-raising activities. **Structure** Global network of wetland education centres; programme of the *'Wildfowl and Wetlands Trust'* (WWT). **Languages** English, French, Spanish. **Finance** Funded through WWT; regional partnership projects. **Activities** Networking/liaising; knowledge management/information dissemination; awareness raising; training/education; events/meetings. **Events** *Asia Conference* Bangkok (Thailand) 2015, *Asia Conference* Suncheon (Korea Rep) 2013. **Publications** *WLI Update* (12 a year) – electronic; *WLI Newsletter* (2 a year). *Wetland Centre Manual.*
Members Wetland centres (350) in 62 countries and territories:
Argentina, Australia, Austria, Bangladesh, Belgium, Botswana, Brazil, Bulgaria, Canada, Chile, China, Colombia, Costa Rica, Cyprus, Czechia, Denmark, Ecuador, France, Ghana, Greece, Hong Kong, Hungary, India, Indonesia, Iran Islamic Rep, Ireland, Italy, Japan, Kazakhstan, Kenya, Korea Rep, Latvia, Malaysia, Mexico, Mongolia, Nepal, Netherlands, New Zealand, Norway, Pakistan, Panama, Paraguay, Poland, Portugal, Russia, Rwanda, Samoa, Senegal, Seychelles, Singapore, Slovakia, Slovenia, Spain, Sri Lanka, Sweden, Syrian AR, Tanzania UR, Thailand, Trinidad-Tobago, UK, USA, Vanuatu.
IGO Relations Memorandum of Cooperation with: *Convention on Wetlands of International Importance Especially as Waterfowl Habitat (Convention on Wetlands, 1971)*. [2020/XJ3630/**F**]

♦ **Wetlands International** **20928**

CEO PO Box 471, 6700 AL Wageningen, Netherlands. T. +31318660933. Fax +31318660950. E-mail: post@wetlands.org.
Street address Horapark 9, 6717 LZ Ede, Netherlands.
URL: http://www.wetlands.org/

History 9 Oct 1995, Kuala Lumpur (Malaysia). 9-13 Oct 1995, Kuala Lumpur (Malaysia), at International Conference on Wetlands and Development, by merger of *Asian Wetland Bureau (AWB, inactive)*, *International Waterfowl and Wetlands Research Bureau (IWRB, inactive)* and *Wetlands for the Americas (WA, inactive)*. Establishment followed several years of planning. Officially launched Mar 1996, with headquarters in Netherlands. **Aims** Conserve and restore wetlands. **Structure** Global Board; Supervisory Council; Management Team. **Languages** English, French, Spanish. **Staff** 150.00 FTE, paid. **Finance** Sources: donations; international organizations; members' dues; revenue from activities/projects. Supported by over 120 government agencies, national NGOs, foundations, development agencies and private sector groups. Supported by governments of Canada, China, Germany, India, Japan, Netherlands, Norway and USA. Supported by: *Asian Development Bank (ADB, #01422)*; *Catholic Organization for Relief and Development (Cordaid)*; *Deutsche Gesellschaft für Internationale Zusammenarbeit (GIZ)*; *European Commission (EC, #06633)*; *International Climate Initiative (ICI)*; *International Committee of the Red Cross (ICRC, #12799)*; *International Food Policy Research Institute (IFPRI, #13622)*; *International Investment Bank (IIB, #13951)*; *International Union for Conservation of Nature and Natural Resources (IUCN, #15766)* (Asia Regional Office); *Japan Fund for Global Environment (JFGE)*; *Kreditanstalt für Wiederaufbau (KfW)*; *Roundtable on Sustainable Palm Oil (RSPO, #18986)*; *UNDP (#20292)*; *UNEP (#20299)*; *United States Agency for International Development (USAID)*; *World Wide Fund for Nature (WWF, #21922)*. **Activities** Advocacy/lobbying/activism; awareness raising; events/meetings; knowledge management/information dissemination; networking/liaising. **Events** *European Rivers Summit* Brussels (Belgium) 2022, *European Rivers Summit* Lisbon (Portugal) 2021, *European River Symposium* Vienna (Austria) 2021, *Atelier International sur la Mise en Oeuvre de Solutions Fondées sur la Nature pour Lutter contre le Changement Climatique* Marseille (France) 2019, *Symposium on Wetlands and Climate Change* Tokyo (Japan) 2019. **Publications** *Global Newsletter* (12 a year). Reports; assessments; policy briefs.
Members Governments (25):
Austria, Bangladesh, Belgium, Benin, Bulgaria, Chile, China, Denmark, Ecuador, Estonia, Finland, Germany, Hungary, India, Ireland, Japan, Kenya, Malaysia, Netherlands, Norway, Pakistan, Slovakia, Slovenia, Sweden, Switzerland.
Non-governmental organizations in 9 countries:
Bulgaria, Denmark, Germany, Ireland, Netherlands, Nigeria, Sweden, Switzerland, UK.
Included in the above, 2 organizations listed in this Yearbook:
Federation of Associations for Hunting and Conservation of the EU (#09459).
Consultative Status Consultative status granted from: *UNEP (#20299)*. **IGO Relations** Partners: *Convention for Cooperation in the Protection and Development of the Marine and Coastal Environment of the West and Central African Region (Abidjan convention, 1981)*; *Permanent Secretariat to the Agreement on the Conservation of African-Eurasian Migratory Waterbirds (#18330)*; *FAO (#09260)*; *Niger Basin Authority (NBA, #17134)*; *Nile Basin Initiative (NBI, #17140)*; *Secretariat of the Convention of Wetlands (#19200)*; *Convention on the Conservation of Migratory Species of Wild Animals (Bonn Convention, 1979)*; *Global Alliances for Water and Climate (GAfWaC, #10230)*; *Niger Basin Authority (NBA, #17134)*; *Secretariat of the Convention on the Conservation of Migratory Species of Wild Animals (UNEP/CMS, #19198)*; UNEP. Close working relations with: *Secretariat of the Convention on Biological Diversity (SCBD, #19197)*. Signature to: *Memorandum of Understanding Concerning the Conservation of the Manatee and Small Cetaceans of Western Africa and Macaronesia (2008)*. Accredited by: *United Nations Framework Convention on Climate Change – Secretariat (UNFCCC, #20564)*.
NGO Relations Partners:
- *BirdLife International (#03266)*;
- *Both ENDS (#03307)*;
- *Catholic Organization for Relief and Development (Cordaid)*;
- *Climate Action Network (CAN, #03999)*;
- *Commonland Foundation*;
- *Conservation International (CI)*;
- *East Asian – Australasian Flyway Partnership (EAAFP, #05198)*;
- *Environmental Paper Network (EPN, #05507)*;
- *EuroNatur – European Nature Heritage Fund (#05738)*;
- *Forest Peoples Programme (FPP, #09865)*;
- *Greenpeace International (#10727)*;
- *Horn of Africa Regional Environment Centre and Network (HoA-REN, #10946)*;
- *IHE Delft Institute for Water Education (#11110)*;

- *International Federation of Red Cross and Red Crescent Societies (#13526);*
- *International Mire Conservation Group (IMCG, #14169);*
- *International Peatland Society (IPS, #14538);*
- *International Union for Conservation of Nature and Natural Resources (IUCN, #15766);*
- *International Water Management Institute (IWMI, #15867);*
- *IRC (#16016);*
- *The Mediterranean Wetlands Initiative (MedWet, #16688);*
- *Michael Succow Foundation for the Protection of Nature (Succow Foundation);*
- *The Nature Conservancy (TNC);*
- *Rainforest Action Network (RAN, #18614);*
- *Red Cross Red Crescent Climate Centre (Climate Centre);*
- *Round Table on Responsible Soy Association (RTRS, #18983);*
- *Roundtable on Sustainable Biomaterials (RSB, #18985);*
- *SIMAVI;*
- *WASH Alliance International (WAI);*
- *WASTE;*
- *Wildfowl and Wetlands Trust (WWT);*
- *Wildlife Conservation Society (WCS);*
- *World Wide Fund for Nature (WWF, #21922).*

Member of: *SDG Watch Europe (#19162).* Instrumental in setting up: *International Wader Study Group (IWSG, see: #15766); North East Asian Crane Site Network (NEACSN, #17579); Programme régional de Conservation de la zone Côtière et Marine en Afrique de l'Ouest (PRCM, #18528).* [2019.03.22/XB0004/**B**]

♦ WETPOL – International Symposium on Wetland Pollutant Dynamics and Control (meeting series)
♦ WEU Parliamentary Assembly – European Security and Defence Assembly (inactive)
♦ WEU – Western European Union (inactive)
♦ **WEVA** World Electric Vehicle Association (#21374)
♦ **WEVA** World Equine Veterinary Association (#21388)
♦ **WEVZA** Western European Volleyball Zonal Association (#20915)
♦ **WE** Water Europe (#20828)
♦ We Will Speak Out (unconfirmed)
♦ We – The World (internationally oriented national body)
♦ WE – World Education (internationally oriented national body)
♦ WE – World ENABLED (internationally oriented national body)
♦ **WEW** Women's Education Worldwide (#21015)
♦ WFAA-WVA – Weltföderation Agrarischer Arbeiter (inactive)
♦ WFAA-WVA – Wereldfederatie van Agrarische Arbeiders (inactive)
♦ **WFAD** World Federation Against Drugs (#21408)
♦ **WFAE** World Forum for Acoustic Ecology (#21512)
♦ WFAFW – World Federation of Agriculture and Food Workers (inactive)
♦ WFAIGH – World Federation of Academic Institutions for Global Health (inactive)
♦ WFA International / see World Fashion Organization (#21403)
♦ WFALA – Weltföderation der Agrar- und Lebensmittelarbeiter (inactive)
♦ **WFAO** World Federation of Amateur Orchestras (#21409)
♦ **WFAS** World Federation of Acupuncture-Moxibustion Societies (#21405)
♦ **WFATE** World Federation of Associations of Teacher Education (#21412)
♦ WFATOD / see World Federation for the Treatment of Opioid Dependence (#21495)
♦ **WFATT** World Federation of Athletic Training and Therapy (#21413)
♦ WFAW-CMT – World Federation of Agricultural Workers (inactive)
♦ **WFA** Weightlifting Federation of Africa (#20854)
♦ **WFA** World Farriers' Association (#21402)
♦ **WFA** World Federation of Advertisers (#21407)
♦ **WFA** World Federation for Animals (#21410)
♦ **WFA** World Forum for Alternatives (#21513)
♦ WFA – World Freight Alliance (unconfirmed)
♦ **WFA** Wushu Federation of Asia (#21964)
♦ **WFBSC** World Federation of Building Service Contractors (#21416)
♦ WFBS – World Finance Banking Symposium (meeting series)
♦ **WFB** Weltrat für Bildung (#21325)
♦ **WFB** World Fellowship of Buddhists (#21501)
♦ WFBWU – World Federation of Building and Woodworkers Unions (inactive)
♦ **WFBY** World Fellowship of Buddhist Youth (#21502)
♦ WFC / see World Friendship Center
♦ **WFCCI** World Federation of Chinese Catering Industry (#21418)

♦ WFCC-MIRCEN World Data Centre for Microorganisms (WDCM) . . . 20929

Dir No 1-3 Beichen West Road, Chaoyang District, 100101 Beijing, China. T. +861064807422. Fax +861064807426.
URL: http://www.wdcm.org/

History Proposed 1966, with title *WFCC World Data Centre for Microorganisms (WDCM).* Under the auspices of *World Federation for Culture Collections (WFCC, #21424).* Relocated to RIKEN, Japan, and Apr 1997 to National Institute of Genetics (NIG), Japan. Inauguration ceremony of centre under current title, 17 May 2011, Beijing (China). Currently under the auspices of WFCC and *UNESCO World Network of Microbiological Resources Centres MIRCEN (no recent information).* **Aims** Establish a data-sharing platform of global microbial resources. **Languages** English. **Staff** 4.00 FTE, paid. **Activities** Knowledge management/ information dissemination; training/education; research/documentation; events/meetings. **Events** *Workshop* Beijing (China) 2018, *Workshop* Beijing (China) 2017, *Workshop* Beijing (China) 2016, *Workshop* Beijing (China) 2014, *Workshop* Shanghai (China) 2013. **Publications** *World Directory of Collections of Cultures of Microorganisms* (4th ed 1993); *Guide to World Data Centre on Microorganisms with a List of Culture Collections in the World* (1989); *World Catalogue of Algae* (1989). **Information Services** *Analyzer of Bio-resource Citations (ABC)* – database; *Culture Collections Information Worldwide (CCINFO)* – database; *Global Catalogue of Microorganisms (GCM)* – database; *Reference Strain Catalogue* – database. **Members** Resource centers (715) in 74 countries. Membership countries not specified. **IGO Relations** *UNEP (#20299);* UNESCO. **NGO Relations** Acts as the data centre for WFCC and: *UNESCO World Network of Microbiological Resources Centres MIRCEN (no recent information).* Regular member of: *ISC World Data System (ISC-WDS, #16024).* [2017.06.01/XF1377/**E**]

♦ **WFCCN** World Federation of Critical Care Nurses (#21423)
♦ WFCC World Data Centre for Microorganisms / see WFCC-MIRCEN World Data Centre for Microorganisms (#20929)
♦ WFCC – World Federation for Cancer Care (inactive)
♦ **WFCC** World Federation for Chess Composition (#21417)
♦ **WFCC** World Federation for Culture Collections (#21424)
♦ WFCI / see World Future Council Foundation (#21533)
♦ WFCLC / see Christian Life Community (#03905)
♦ **WFCMS** World Federation of Chinese Medicine Societies (#21419)
♦ WFCN – World Forum on Community Networking (internationally oriented national body)
♦ WFCPC – World Federation of Christian Pastoral Counselors (see: #21330)
♦ **WFCP** World Federation of Colleges and Polytechnics (#21421)
♦ WFCRC – World Federation for Coral Reef Conservation (internationally oriented national body)
♦ **WFC** World Federation of Chiropractic (#21420)
♦ WFC – World Finance Conference (meeting series)
♦ WFC – World Forestry Center, Portland (internationally oriented national body)
♦ **WFC** World Forum of CSDs (#21514)
♦ **WFC** World Franchise Council (#21529)
♦ WFC – World Friendship Center (internationally oriented national body)
♦ **WFC** World Future Council Foundation (#21533)
♦ WFCW / see World Organization of Workers (#21697)
♦ WFCYWG – World Federation of Catholic Young Women and Girls (inactive)
♦ WFCY – World Federation of Catholic Youth (inactive)
♦ **WFDA** World Forum for Democratization in Asia (#21515)
♦ **WFDB** World Federation of the Deafblind (#21426)
♦ **WFDB** World Federation of Diamond Bourses (#21430)
♦ WFDD – World Faiths Development Dialogue (internationally oriented national body)
♦ **WFDFI** World Federation of Development Financing Institutions (#21428)
♦ **WFDF** World Flying Disc Federation (#21509)
♦ **WFDP** World Fund for Development and Planning (#21531)
♦ **WFDSA** World Federation of Direct Selling Associations (#21431)
♦ WFD – Weltfriedensdienst (internationally oriented national body)
♦ WFD – Westminster Foundation for Democracy (internationally oriented national body)
♦ **WFD** World Federation of the Deaf (#21425)
♦ **WFDWRHL** World Federation of Doctors who Respect Human Life (#21432)
♦ **WFDY** World Federation of Democratic Youth (#21427)
♦ WFEA – World Federation of Education Associations (inactive)
♦ **WFEB** World Forum for Ethics in Business (#21516)
♦ **WFEO** World Federation of Engineering Organizations (#21433)
♦ **WFE** World Federation of Exchanges (#21434)
♦ WFFH – World Foundation for Medical Studies in Female Health (internationally oriented national body)
♦ **WFFL** World Federation of Free Latvians (#18250)
♦ **WFFM** World Federation of Friends of Museums (#21435)
♦ **WFFP** World Forum of Fisher Peoples (#21517)
♦ WFFTH-WCL – World Federation of Workers in Food, Tobacco and Hotel Industries – WCL (inactive)
♦ WFF – Walk Free Foundation (internationally oriented national body)
♦ WFF – World Foresight Forum (internationally oriented national body)
♦ **WFF** World Forum of Fish Harvesters and Fishworkers (#21518)
♦ WFF – World Future Foundation (internationally oriented national body)
♦ **WFGT** World Federation of Great Towers (#21436)
♦ WFHA-AVSC – World Federation of Health Agencies for the Advancement of Voluntary Surgical Contraception (inactive)
♦ WFHHS – World Federation of Holistic Health Sciences (no recent information)
♦ WFHI – Women and Film History International (unconfirmed)
♦ **WFHJ** World Federation of Hungarian Jews (#21439)
♦ **WFHSS** World Federation for Hospital Sterilisation Sciences (#21438)
♦ WFH – World Federation of Healing (inactive)
♦ **WFH** World Federation of Hemophilia (#21437)
♦ **WFICC** World Federation of Intensive and Critical Care (#21444)
♦ WFIC / see World Federation of Investors (#21447)
♦ **WFII** World Federation of Insurance Intermediaries (#21443)
♦ **WFIMC** World Federation of International Music Competitions (#21445)
♦ WFIM – World Federation of Islamic Missions (no recent information)
♦ **WFIPP** World Federation for Incontinence and Pelvic Problems (#21440)
♦ **W-FIRA** World Federation of Industrial Research Associations (#21442)
♦ WFIRC – World Fellowship of Inter-Religious Councils (internationally oriented national body)
♦ **WFIS** World Federation of Independent Scouts (#21441)
♦ WFITA / see International Network for Information Technology in Agriculture (#14287)
♦ **WFITN** World Federation of Interventional and Therapeutic Neuroradiology (#21446)
♦ **WFI** World Federation of Investors (#21447)
♦ WFI – World Forest Institute (internationally oriented national body)
♦ WFIW – World Federation of Industry Workers (inactive)
♦ **WFJCSHD** World Federation of Jewish Child Survivors of the Holocaust and Descendants (#21448)
♦ **WFKA** World Federation of Kowat Alrami and Self Defense (#21450)
♦ WFKO – World Federation of Karate Do Organizations (no recent information)
♦ **WFLD** World Federation for Laser Dentistry (#21451)
♦ WFLO – World Food Logistics Organization (internationally oriented national body)
♦ WFLTH-WVA – Weltföderation von Arbeitern in Lebensmittel-, Tabak- und Hotelindustrien-WVA (inactive)
♦ WFLVA – Wereldfederatie van Landbouw- en Voedingsarbeiders (inactive)
♦ **WFMB** World Federation of Merino Breeders (#21456)
♦ **WfMC** Workflow Management Coalition (#21053)
♦ WFME Ltd / see World Federation for Medical Education (#21454)
♦ **WFME** Federación Mundial de Educación Médica (#21454)
♦ **WFME** Fédération mondiale pour l'enseignement médical (#21454)
♦ **WFME** World Federation for Medical Education (#21454)
♦ **WFMH** World Federation for Mental Health (#21455)
♦ **WFMISS** World Federation of Minimally Invasive Spine Surgery (#21458)
♦ WFMIWSC / see World Federation of Major International Wine and Spirits Competitions (#21452)
♦ **WFMT** World Federation of Master Tailors (#21453)
♦ **WFMT** World Federation of Music Therapy (#21459)
♦ **WFM and UCW** World Federation of Methodist and Uniting Church Women (#21457)
♦ WFM/WCL – World Federation for the Metallurgic Industry (inactive)
♦ **WFM** World Federalist Movement – Movement for a Just World Order through a Strengthened United Nations (#21404)
♦ WFM/WVA – Wereldfederatie voor de Metaalindustrie (inactive)
♦ WFMW / see World Federation of Methodist and Uniting Church Women (#21457)
♦ WFNDEC – World Federation of Non-Destructive Evaluation Centers (internationally oriented national body)
♦ **WFNMB** World Federation of Nuclear Medicine and Biology (#21467)
♦ **WFNMC** World Federation of National Mathematical Competitions (#21460)
♦ **WFNN** World Federation of Neuroscience Nurses (#21465)
♦ **WFNOS** World Federation of Neuro-Oncology Societies (#21462)
♦ **WFNRS** World Federation of Neuroradiological Societies (#21463)
♦ **WFNR** World Federation for NeuroRehabilitation (#21464)
♦ **WFNS** World Federation of Neurosurgical Societies (#21466)
♦ **WFNS** World Foundation of Natural Science (#21527)
♦ **WFN** Water Footprint Network (#20829)
♦ **WFN** World Federation of Neurology (#21461)
♦ WFN – World Freight Network (internationally oriented national body)
♦ WFO – Pan-African Regional Office (see: #21399)
♦ WFOTAA – World Federation of Taiwan Alumni Associations (unconfirmed)
♦ **WFOT** World Federation of Occupational Therapists (#21468)
♦ **WFO** Waste Free Oceans (#20820)
♦ **WFO** World Family Organization (#21399)
♦ **WFO** World Farmers' Organisation (#21401)
♦ **WFO** World Fashion Organization (#21403)
♦ **WFO** World Forum Offshore Wind (#21520)
♦ WFO / see World Foundry Organization (#21528)
♦ **WFO** World Foundry Organization (#21528)
♦ WFPA – World Federation for the Protection of Animals (inactive)
♦ WFPF – World Freerunning Parkour Federation (unconfirmed)
♦ **WFPHA** World Federation of Public Health Associations (#21476)
♦ **WFPIA** World Federation of Pipe Line Industry Associations (#21475)

- ♦ **WFPICCS** World Federation of Pediatric Intensive and Critical Care Societies (#21473)
- ♦ **WFPIST** World Forum for Proximity of Islamic Schools of Thought (#21521)
- ♦ **WFPI** World Federation of Pediatric Imaging (#21472)
- ♦ WFPI – World Free Press Institute (internationally oriented national body)
- ♦ WFPMA / see World Federation of People Management Associations (#21474)
- ♦ **WFPMA** World Federation of People Management Associations (#21474)
- ♦ WFPMM / see Global Self-Care Federation (#10588)
- ♦ WFPM / see World Association of Perinatal Medicine (#21170)
- ♦ WFPPA – World Forensic Psychiatry and Psychology Association (no recent information)
- ♦ WFPU / see World Network of Users and Survivors of Psychiatry (#21672)
- ♦ WFP – Water for People (internationally oriented national body)
- ♦ WFP – Witness for Peace (internationally oriented national body)
- ♦ WFP – Women for Peace, Sweden (internationally oriented national body)
- ♦ **WFP** World Federation of Parasitologists (#21471)
- ♦ **WFP** World Food Programme (#21510)
- ♦ WFRC – World Foundation for Renal Care (no recent information)
- ♦ **WFRS** World Federation of Rose Societies (#21478)
- ♦ **WFRtDS** World Federation of Right to Die Societies (#21477)
- ♦ **WFR** Weltfriedensrat (#21717)
- ♦ **WFSA** World Federation of Societies of Anaesthesiologists (#21482)
- ♦ WFSA / see World Forum on Shooting Activities (#21523)
- ♦ **WFSA** World Forum on Shooting Activities (#21523)
- ♦ WFSA / see Worldwide Ferry Safety Association (#21921)
- ♦ **WFSA** Worldwide Ferry Safety Association (#21921)
- ♦ **WFSBP** World Federation of Societies of Biological Psychiatry (#21483)
- ♦ **WFSBS** World Federation of Skull Base Societies (#21481)
- ♦ **WFSC** World Federation of Societies of Chronobiology (#21484)
- ♦ **WFSD** World Forum on Science and Democracy (#21522)
- ♦ **WFSEC** World Fellowship of Slavic Evangelical Christians (#21505)
- ♦ **WFSF** World Futures Studies Federation (#21535)
- ♦ **WFSGI** World Federation of the Sporting Goods Industry (#21487)
- ♦ WFSICCM / see World Federation of Intensive and Critical Care (#21444)
- ♦ **WFSJ** World Federation of Science Journalists (#21479)
- ♦ **WFSLMS** World Federation of Societies for Laser Medicine and Surgery (#21485)
- ♦ **WFSOS** World Federation of Surgical Oncology Societies (#21488)
- ♦ **WFSO** World Food Safety Organization (#21511)
- ♦ **WFS** Women's Feature Service (#21017)
- ♦ WFS – World Federation of Scientists (internationally oriented national body)
- ♦ WFS – World Federation of Sonographers (inactive)
- ♦ WFS – World Fertility Survey (inactive)
- ♦ **WFS** World Future Society (#21534)
- ♦ **WFSW** World Federation of Scientific Workers (#21480)
- ♦ **WFTAO** World Federation of Technical Assessment Organizations (#21489)
- ♦ WFTA – World Federation of Trading House Associations (no recent information)
- ♦ WFTA – World Food Travel Association (internationally oriented national body)
- ♦ **WFTC** World Federation of Therapeutic Communities (#21491)
- ♦ WFTGA / see World Federation of Tourist Guide Associations (#21492)
- ♦ **WFTGA** World Federation of Tourist Guide Associations (#21492)
- ♦ WFTGLA / see World Federation of Tourist Guide Associations (#21492)
- ♦ **WFTL** World Forum on Theology and Liberation (#21524)
- ♦ **WFTO-Asia** World Fair Trade Organization, Asia (#21398)
- ♦ **WFTOD** World Federation for the Treatment of Opioid Dependence (#21495)

♦ WFTO-Europe 20930

Coordinator Rue Washington 40, 1050 Brussels, Belgium. T. +3226406386. E-mail: info@wfto-europe.org – projects@wfto-europe.org.

URL: https://wfto-europe.org/

History Founded as a regional branch of *World Fair Trade Organization (WFTO, #21396)*. Registration: Banque-Carrefour des Entreprises, No/ID: 0888.374.005, Start date: 29 Mar 2007; EU Transparency Register, No/ID: 452862736936-07, Start date: 9 Jan 2020. **Aims** Enable producers to improve their *livelihoods* and communities through *Fair Trade*. **Structure** Annual General Meeting (AGM); Board of Directors; Coordinator; Committees. **Languages** English. **Staff** 2.00 FTE, paid; 2.00 FTE, voluntary. **Finance** Members' dues. Other Sources: Project grants. Annual budget: about euro 100,000. **Activities** Advocacy/lobbying/activism; monitoring/evaluation; events/meetings. **Events** *Annual General Meeting* Brussels (Belgium) 2019, *Connect and Act Members Meeting* Brussels (Belgium) 2019, *Annual General Meeting* Brussels (Belgium) 2018, *Europe Biennial Conference* Brussels (Belgium) 2018, *Europe Biennial Conference* Wuppertal (Germany) 2016.
Members Full (over 100) in 17 countries:
Austria, Belgium, Bosnia-Herzegovina, Czechia, Denmark, Finland, France, Germany, Greece, Italy, Netherlands, Poland, Romania, Spain, Sweden, Switzerland, UK.
Associate:
IFOAM – Organics International (IFOAM, #11105). [2022/XM8573/**D**]

- ♦ **WFTO-LA** World Fair Trade Latin America (#21395)
- ♦ **WFTO** World Fair Trade Organization (#21396)
- ♦ **WFTO** World Federation of Technology Organizations (#21490)
- ♦ **WFTU** World Federation of Trade Unions (#21493)
- ♦ WFT – World Fisheries Trust (internationally oriented national body)
- ♦ **WFUCA** World Federation of UNESCO Clubs, Centres and Associations (#21498)
- ♦ **WFUMB** World Federation for Ultrasound in Medicine and Biology (#21497)
- ♦ **WFUNA** World Federation of United Nations Associations (#21499)
- ♦ **WFUWO** World Federation of Ukrainian Women's Organizations (#21496)
- ♦ WFVS / see World Federation of Vascular Societies (#21500)
- ♦ **WFVS** World Federation of Vascular Societies (#21500)
- ♦ WFVTH-WVA – Wereldfederatie van Arbeiders in Voedings-, Tabaks, en Hotelbedrijven-WVA (inactive)
- ♦ WfWfW / see Women for Water Partnership (#21041)
- ♦ WFWI – Women for Women International (internationally oriented national body)
- ♦ **WF** World Family of Radio Maria (#21400)
- ♦ WFWO – World for World Organization (internationally oriented national body)
- ♦ WFWPI – Women's Federation for World Peace International (internationally oriented national body)
- ♦ **WfWP** Women for Water Partnership (#21041)
- ♦ **WFW** Weltföderation der Wissenschaftler (#21480)
- ♦ WFYI – World Federation of Young Investors (unconfirmed)
- ♦ WFZC – World Free Zone Convention (meeting series)
- ♦ **WGA** World Glaucoma Association (#21540)
- ♦ **WGB** Welt-Gesellschaft für Buiatrik (#21122)
- ♦ **WGB** Weltgewerkschaftsbund (#21493)
- ♦ **WGCF** World Guernsey Cattle Federation (#21547)
- ♦ WGC / see International World Games Association (#15914)
- ♦ WGC – World Giftedness Center (internationally oriented national body)
- ♦ **WGC** World Gold Council (#21541)
- ♦ WGDO – World Green Design Organization (unconfirmed)
- ♦ WGEO – World Green Economy Organization (unconfirmed)
- ♦ WGF – Water Governance Facility (internationally oriented national body)
- ♦ WGF – World Golf Foundation (internationally oriented national body)
- ♦ **WGGVM** Welt-Gesellschaft für Geschichte der Veterinärmedizin (#21143)
- ♦ WGHA – Washington Global Health Alliance (internationally oriented national body)
- ♦ **WGH** Women in Global Health (#20998)
- ♦ **WGIC** World Geospatial Industry Council (#21538)
- ♦ **WGIN** World Green Infrastructure Network (#21545)
- ♦ **WGI** Whole Grain Initiative (#20939)
- ♦ WGI – World Gastronomy Institute (internationally oriented national body)
- ♦ WGI – World Government Institute (internationally oriented national body)
- ♦ **WGMS** World Glacier Monitoring Service (#21539)
- ♦ WGMWG / see Women in Migration Network (#21008)
- ♦ WGM – World Gospel Mission (internationally oriented national body)
- ♦ **WGNRR** Women's Global Network for Reproductive Rights (#21019)
- ♦ WGO Regionalbüro für Europa / see WHO Regional Office for Europe (#20945)
- ♦ **WGO** World Gastroenterology Organisation (#21536)
- ♦ **WGPAT** Working Group on Prolamin Analysis and Toxicity (#21060)
- ♦ **WGRF** World Greyhound Racing Federation (#21546)
- ♦ WGSRP / see European Parliament Platform for Secularism in Politics (#08152)
- ♦ **WGWC** World Government of World Citizens (#21543)
- ♦ **WH4C** Workers Hub For Change (#21052)
- ♦ WHAHC – World Hospital at Home Congress (meeting series)
- ♦ Whale Conservation Society / see Whale and Dolphin Conservation
- ♦ Whale and Dolphin Conservation (internationally oriented national body)
- ♦ Whale and Dolphin Conservation Society / see Whale and Dolphin Conservation
- ♦ Whales Alive (internationally oriented national body)
- ♦ WHAO – World Human Accountability Organization (internationally oriented national body)
- ♦ WHA – Women's Hospitals Australasia (internationally oriented national body)
- ♦ **WHA** World Haiku Association (#21548)
- ♦ **WHA** World Headache Alliance (#21555)
- ♦ WHA – World Health Academy (unconfirmed)
- ♦ **WHA** World Hepatitis Alliance (#21564)
- ♦ WHA – World History Association (internationally oriented national body)
- ♦ WHCA / see International Hobie Class Association (#13801)
- ♦ WHCO / see Organization of World Heritage Cities (#17891)
- ♦ WHC System / see World Humanity Commission
- ♦ WHC – World Halal Council (unconfirmed)
- ♦ WHC – World Hapkido Confederation (unconfirmed)
- ♦ **WHC** World Harp Congress (#21553)
- ♦ **WHC** World Hereford Council (#21565)
- ♦ **WHC** World Heritage Centre (#21566)
- ♦ WHC – World Humanity Commission (internationally oriented national body)
- ♦ WHD – World Human Dimension (internationally oriented national body)

♦ Wheat Initiative 20931

Secretariat Königin-Luise-Straße 19, 14195 Berlin, Germany. E-mail: wheat.initiative@julius-kuehn.de.

URL: http://www.wheatinitiative.org/

History Launched 15 Sep 2001, Paris (France), as *Research Initiative for Wheat Improvement (IRIWI)*, following endorsement from the *Group of Twenty (G20, #10793)* Agriculture Ministries. **Aims** Encourage and support development of a vibrant global public-private research community sharing resources, capabilities, data and ideas to improve wheat productivity, quality and sustainable production worldwide. **Structure** Research Committee; Institutions' Coordination Committee; Scientific Board; Thematic Expert Working Groups; Secretariat. **Finance** Members' dues. **Events** *International Wheat Congress* Beijing (China) 2022, *International Wheat Congress* Beijing (China) 2021, *International Wheat Congress* Saskatoon, SK (Canada) 2019, *International Wheat Conference* Sydney, NSW (Australia) 2015.
Members Representatives of countries and international research centres; private companies. Members in 14 countries:
Argentina, Australia, Brazil, France, Germany, Hungary, India, Ireland, Italy, Japan, Spain, Türkiye, UK, USA.
International research centres (2):
International Center for Agricultural Research in the Dry Areas (ICARDA, #12466); *International Maize and Wheat Improvement Center (#14077).* [2022/XM4498/**E**]

- ♦ Wheat Trade Convention, 1967 (1967 treaty)
- ♦ Wheat Trade Convention, 1971 (1971 treaty)
- ♦ WHEA – World Heavy Events Association (internationally oriented national body)
- ♦ Wheelchair Sports Worldwide (see: #15881)
- ♦ **WHEN** World Health Editors Network (#21556)
- ♦ Wherever the Need (internationally oriented national body)
- ♦ Where water speaks / see Circle of Blue
- ♦ WHES – World Hunger Education Service (internationally oriented national body)
- ♦ **WHFF** World Holstein Friesian Federation (#21571)
- ♦ **WHFS** World Heart Failure Society (#21561)
- ♦ WHF – World Hapkido Federation (internationally oriented national body)
- ♦ **WHF** World Happiness Forum (#21551)
- ♦ **WHF** World Heart Federation (#21562)
- ♦ **WHF** World Hindu Federation (#21569)
- ♦ **WHF** World Hovercraft Federation (#21572)
- ♦ WHGF / see Global Hapkido Federation (#10397)
- ♦ WHIM / see International Society for Humor Studies (#15184)
- ♦ WHINSEC – Western Hemisphere Institute for Security Cooperation (internationally oriented national body)

♦ Whistleblowing International Network (WIN) 20932

Exec Dir Brunswick House, 51 Wilson Street, Glasgow, G1 1UZ, UK. E-mail: info@whistleblowingnetwork.org.

URL: https://whistleblowingnetwork.org/

History 2013. Registration: OSCR, No/ID: SC048595, Start date: 1 Aug 2018, Scotland. **Aims** Share NGO expertise and solidarity across national, legal, social and cultural boundaries to promote and protect public interest whistleblowing. **Structure** Board of Trustees. **Languages** English, French. **Staff** 3.00 FTE, paid. **Members** National organizations. Membership countries not specified. [2021.09.03/AA0491/**F**]

- ♦ Whitaker Peace and Development Initiative (internationally oriented national body)
- ♦ White Fathers – Society of Missionaries of Africa (religious order)

♦ White Helmets 20933

Casques blancs – Cascos Blancos – Capacetes Brancos

Humanitarian Assistance Specialist White Helmets Commission Headquarters, Esmeralda 1212, 10th floor – Office 1001, C1007 Buenos Aires, Argentina. T. +541155558938. E-mail: acd@mrecic.gov.ar – comca@mrecic.gov.ar.

URL: http://www.cascosblancos.gov.ar/

History Established Dec 1995, when officially sanctioned under resolution 50-19 of the General Assembly of *United Nations (UN, #20515)*, following proposal, 16 Oct 1993, by President Carlos Saúl Menem of Argentina and endorsement, Dec 1994, by General Assembly resolution 49-139-B. Strategic coordination the responsibility of *United Nations Office for the Coordination of Humanitarian Affairs (OCHA, #20593)*. Adopted by *OAS (#17629)*, 1995, under resolution AG/RES 1351 XXV-0/95. Both resolutions adopted again, Jun 2018 (OAS) and December 2018 (UN). **Aims** Design and implement *humanitarian assistance*; provide a supporting role within the framework of post-crisis missions of the United Nations; respond to socio-natural disasters, conflicts, and emergency situations; take part in associated restoration, reconstruction and development

tasks; promote risk prevention and management. **Structure** A unit of the Argentine Ministry of Foreign Affairs and Worship. Comprises civilian units recruited and funded on a national basis, trained and deployed by White Helmets and, in some cases, by the United Nations. **Languages** English, French, Portuguese, Spanish. **Staff** 44.00 FTE, paid; 3000.00 FTE, voluntary. **Finance** Most resources from the Government of Argentina and Ministry of Foreign Affairs and Worship regular budget. Also voluntary contributions administered by UNOPS and OAS projects. **Activities** Humanitarian/emergency aid; training/education. **Publications** *Report on the Global Humanitarian Situation* (weekly); *White Helmets Newsletter*.
Members Active in 71 countries and territories:
Albania, Angola, Antigua-Barbuda, Argentina, Armenia, Belize, Bolivia, Bosnia-Herzegovina, Brazil, Burkina Faso, Cape Verde, Chile, China, Colombia, Costa Rica, Croatia, Cuba, Czechia, Dominica, Dominican Rep, Ecuador, El Salvador, Equatorial Guinea, Grenada, Guatemala, Guyana, Haiti, Honduras, India, Indonesia, Iran Islamic Rep, Iraq, Jamaica, Laos, Lebanon, Libya, Maldives, Mali, Mozambique, Myanmar, Namibia, Nepal, Nicaragua, Niger, Nigeria, North Macedonia, Pakistan, Palestine, Panama, Paraguay, Peru, Philippines, Rwanda, Serbia, Sierra Leone, South Africa, South Sudan, Sri Lanka, St Kitts-Nevis, St Lucia, St Vincent-Grenadines, Suriname, Syrian AR, Thailand, Timor-Leste, Trinidad-Tobago, Tunisia, Ukraine, Uruguay, USA, Venezuela.
[2018.06.01/XF5611/**F***]

♦ White Ribbon Alliance for Safe Motherhood (WRA) 20934

Exec Dir 1100 17th Street NW, Suite 800, Washington DC 20036, USA. T. +12027421214. E-mail: info@whiteribbonalliance.org.
URL: http://www.whiteribbonalliance.org/

Aims Promote increased public awareness of the need to make pregnancy and *childbirth* safe for all women and *newborns* worldwide. **Structure** Board of Directors; National Alliances.
Members Organizations in 112 countries and territories:
Afghanistan, Argentina, Australia, Austria, Azerbaijan, Bahamas, Bangladesh, Barbados, Belarus, Belgium, Benin, Bosnia-Herzegovina, Botswana, Brazil, Burkina Faso, Cambodia, Cameroon, Canada, Chile, China, Congo Brazzaville, Congo DR, Côte d'Ivoire, Croatia, Cyprus, Czechia, Denmark, Dominican Rep, Ecuador, Egypt, Estonia, Ethiopia, Fiji, Finland, France, Gambia, Georgia, Germany, Ghana, Greece, Guatemala, Haiti, Hong Kong, Hungary, Iceland, India, Indonesia, Iran Islamic Rep, Ireland, Israel, Italy, Jamaica, Japan, Jordan, Kenya, Korea Rep, Latvia, Lebanon, Liberia, Libya, Luxembourg, Malawi, Malaysia, Mali, Malta, Mauritania, Mexico, Morocco, Mozambique, Nepal, Netherlands, New Zealand, Niger, Nigeria, North Macedonia, Norway, Pakistan, Palestine, Papua New Guinea, Paraguay, Peru, Philippines, Poland, Portugal, Romania, Russia, Rwanda, Senegal, Sierra Leone, Slovenia, Somalia, South Africa, Spain, Sri Lanka, Sudan, Suriname, Sweden, Switzerland, Syrian AR, Tajikistan, Tanzania UR, Togo, Trinidad-Tobago, Uganda, UK, Uruguay, USA, Vietnam, Yemen, Zambia, Zimbabwe.
NGO Relations Member of (6): *CORE Group*; *Girls not Brides (#10154)*; *Global Alliance for Maternal Mental Health (GAMMH, #10208)*; *InsideNGO (inactive)*; *International Childbirth Initiative (ICI, #12547)*; *PMNCH (#18410)*. Partner of (3): *Every Woman Every Child (EWEC, #09215)*; *Healthy Newborn Network (HNN, #10894)*; *International Confederation of Midwives (ICM, #12863)*. [2021/XM2110/**F**]

- ♦ White Sisters – Missionary Sisters of Our Lady of Africa (religious order)
- ♦ WHITH – International Symposium on Women's Health Issues in Thrombosis and Haemostasis (meeting series)
- ♦ Whitney and Betty MacMillan Center for International and Area Studies at Yale / see MacMillan Center for International and Area Studies
- ♦ Whitney R Harris World Ecology Center (internationally oriented national body)
- ♦ WHITRAP – World Heritage Institute of Training and Research – Asia and Pacific (internationally oriented national body)
- ♦ **WHI** Wolf Haven International (#20980)
- ♦ WHI – World Hope International (internationally oriented national body)
- ♦ **WHL** World Hypertension League (#21574)
- ♦ WHO/AFRO / see WHO Regional Office for Africa (#20943)

♦ WHO Alliance for the Global Elimination of Trachoma (GET 2020) . . 20935

Alliance de l'OMS pour l'elimination du trachoma
Sec c/o WHO, Prevention of Blindness and Deafness, Avenue Appia 20, 1211 Geneva 27, Switzerland. E-mail: trachoma@who.int.
URL: http://www.who.int/blindness/causes/priority/en/index2.html

History 25 Nov 1996, Geneva (Switzerland). 25-26 Nov 1996, Geneva (Switzerland), at first Global Scientific Meeting on Trachoma, convened by the *'Programme for the Prevention of Blindness and Deafness'* of *WHO (#20950)*. **Aims** Develop international policies, strategies and tools to support countries and NGOs in the global elimination of blinding trachoma. **Structure** WHO Secretariat; Expert Committee (ad hoc); Technical Scientific Working Group. **Languages** English, French, Spanish. **Staff** 2.00 FTE, paid. **Activities** Expected to include: epidemiological assessment, including rapid assessment and mapping; project implementation, coordination and monitoring; disease surveillance; project evaluation; resource mobilization. **Events** *Meeting* Geneva (Switzerland) 1997. **Members** Open to governments, international organizations and nongovernmental organizations. Membership not specified. [2013.07.15/XF3937/**F**]

- ♦ WHO Barcelona Office for Health Systems Strengthening (see: #20945)
- ♦ WHO Centre for Health Development, Kobe (see: #20950)
- ♦ WHO Clearinghouse on Smoking and Health Information / see WHO Tobacco Free Initiative (#20949)
- ♦ WHO/EMRO / see WHO Regional Office for the Eastern Mediterranean (#20944)
- ♦ WHO/EURO / see WHO Regional Office for Europe (#20945)
- ♦ WHO/Europe / see WHO Regional Office for Europe (#20945)
- ♦ WHO European Centre for Environment and Health (see: #20945)

♦ WHO European Healthy Cities Network (WHO Healthy Cities) 20936

Contact Div Policy and Governance for Health and Well-being, WHO Regional Office for Europe UN City, Marmorvej 51, 2100 Copenhagen Ø, Denmark. Fax +4545337001. E-mail: eurohealthycities@who.int.
URL: http://www.healthycities.org.uk/

History 1988, within *WHO (#20950)*. First phase completed 1992; 2nd phase 1993-1997; 3rd phase launched 1998; 4th phase 2003-2007; 5th phase 2008-2013; 6th phase 2014-2018. Originally known as *Healthy Cities Project (HCP) – Programme Villes-santé – Proyecto de Ciudades Saludables (PCS) – Gesunde-Städte-Projekt*. **Aims** Put health high on the social, economic and political agenda of city governments. **Structure** Working groups. **Staff** Equivalent of 2.5 professional and 4 support staff, paid. Secondments from various countries. **Finance** Secretariat financed by WHO. Additional financial input from voluntary donations and resource development for special activities including project evaluation and city based projects. Budget (regional budget) for programmatic activities (annual): US$ 100,000. **Activities** Events/meetings; monitoring/evaluation; guidance/assistance/consulting; knowledge management/information dissemination. **Events** *European conference on sustainable cities and towns* Aalborg (Denmark) 2004, *European conference on sustainable cities and towns* Hannover (Germany) 2000, *Symposium* Athens (Greece) 1998, *Regional conference on sustainable cities and towns* Sofia (Bulgaria) 1998, *Symposium* Dublin (Ireland) 1996.
Members Phase 6 Healthy Cities, part of the European National Healthy Cities Network, in 32 countries:
Austria, Belarus, Belgium, Bosnia-Herzegovina, Croatia, Czechia, Denmark, Finland, France, Germany, Greece, Hungary, Ireland, Israel, Italy, Kazakhstan, Latvia, Lithuania, Montenegro, Netherlands, North Macedonia, Norway, Poland, Portugal, Romania, Russia, Serbia, Slovenia, Spain, Sweden, Türkiye, UK.
Phase 6 WHO accredited national networks in 21 countries:
Austria, Belgium, Croatia, Czechia, Denmark, Finland, France, Germany, Greece, Hungary, Ireland, Israel, Italy, Norway, Poland, Portugal, Russia, Spain, Sweden, Türkiye, UK.
Phase 6 Non-WHO accredited national networks in 9 countries:
Belarus, Bosnia-Herzegovina, Cyprus, Estonia, Kazakhstan, Kyrgyzstan, Latvia, Slovenia, Ukraine.
Also a network in the Baltic region. Membership countries not specified.
IGO Relations Secretariat provided by: *WHO Regional Office for Europe (#20945)*. Formal contacts with: *Council of Europe (CE, #04881)*; Ecological Cities Project of *OECD (#17693)*; *European Commission (EC, #06633)*. **NGO Relations** Partner of: *European Sustainable Cities and Towns Campaign (#08863)*. Instrumental in setting up: *International Healthy Cities Foundation (IHCF, no recent information)*. [2019/XF3238/**E**]

- ♦ WHO European Office for Investment for Health and Development, Venice (see: #20945)
- ♦ WHO/EUR Staff Association, Copenhagen / see Staff Association of the WHO Regional Office for Europe (#19941)

♦ WHO Global Network for Age-friendly Cities and Communities (GNAFCC) 20937

Réseau Mondial de l'OMS des Villes et Communautés Amies des Aînés – Red Mundial de la OMS de Ciudades y Comunidades Amigables con las Personas Mayores – Rede Global da OMS de Cidades e Comunidades Amigas das Pessoas Idosas
Contact WHO – Demographic Change and Healthy Ageing Unit, Dept for Social Determinants of Health, Avenue Appia 20, 1211 Geneva, Switzerland. E-mail: gnafcc@who.int – hello@decadeofhealthyageing.org.
URL: https://extranet.who.int/agefriendlyworld/who-network/

History 2010. Founded by *WHO (#20950)*. **Aims** Stimulate and enable cities and communities around the world to become increasingly age-friendly. **Structure** Coordinated by Department of Social Determinants of Health (SDH) at *WHO (#20950)* Headquarters, in collaboration with the 6 WHO Regional Offices and country offices in WHO Member States. Secretariat, coordinated at WHO Headquarters, with administrative support from *International Federation on Ageing (IFA, #13345)*. **Languages** English, French, Spanish.
Members Cities and communities (over 1,400) in 45 countries and territories:
Andorra, Argentina, Australia, Belgium, Bolivia, Brazil, Canada, Chile, China, Colombia, Costa Rica, Cuba, Denmark, Finland, Germany, Hong Kong, Iceland, Iran Islamic Rep, Ireland, Israel, Italy, Japan, Korea Rep, Lithuania, Malaysia, Mexico, Moldova, Netherlands, New Zealand, Norway, Peru, Poland, Portugal, Russia, Singapore, Slovenia, Spain, Sri Lanka, Sweden, Switzerland, Türkiye, UK, United Arab Emirates, Uruguay, USA.
Affiliate programmess (17) at sub-national, national and internationbal levels. [2022.10.11/AA2847/y/**F**]

- ♦ **WHO Healthy Cities** WHO European Healthy Cities Network (#20936)
- ♦ **WHO-HQ SA** WHO-HQ Staff Association, Geneva (#20938)

♦ WHO-HQ Staff Association, Geneva (WHO-HQ SA) 20938

Association du personnel de siège l'OMS, Genève
Contact WHO/HQ, Office 4139, 20 Avenue Appia, 1211 Geneva 27, Switzerland. T. +41227914638. E-mail: staffassociation@who.int.

History 1951. Founded to represent staff members of *WHO (#20950)* based in Geneva (Switzerland). **Structure** General Assembly (annual); Staff Committee. **Languages** English, French. **Staff** 2.00 FTE, paid. **Events** *Annual General Meeting* Geneva (Switzerland) 1997. **Publications** Annual Report.
[2021.09.03/XE1599/v/**E**]

- ♦ WHO Immunology Research and Training Centre (no recent information)
- ♦ Whole Child International (internationally oriented national body)

♦ Whole Grain Initiative (WGI) 20939

Contact c/o ICC, Stubenring 12, 1010 Vienna, Austria. T. +43170772020. E-mail: office@wholegraininitiative.org.
URL: http://www.wholegraininitiative.org/

History 2017, Vienna (Austria). Arose from 6th International Whole Grain Summit. **Aims** Increase the whole grain intake worldwide. **Structure** Governing Board; Scientific Committee; Stakeholder Forum; Working Groups (6). Coordinated by *ICC – International Association for Cereal Science and Technology (#11048)*. **Languages** English. **Activities** Advocacy/lobbying/activism; events/meetings; knowledge management/information dissemination. **Events** *Whole Grain Summit* 2021, *Whole Grain Summit* Rome (Italy) 2020, *Whole Grain Summit* Vienna (Austria) 2017. **Publications** *Global Definition of Whole Grain as Food Ingredient* – May 2019 rev; *Vienna Whole Grain Declaration*.
Members Partners in 21 countries and territories:
Argentina, Australia, Belgium, China, Croatia, Finland, Germany, Greece, Italy, Latvia, Malaysia, Mexico, Netherlands, South Africa, Spain, Sweden, Switzerland, Taiwan, Türkiye, UK, USA.
Cereals and Grains Association (#03830); *European Breakfast Cereal Association (CEEREAL, #06399)*; *Fundación Dieta Mediterranea (FDM)*; *HEALTHGRAIN Forum (HGF, #10882)*; *ICC – International Association for Cereal Science and Technology (#11048)*; *International Maize and Wheat Improvement Center (#14077)*; *ISEKI-Food Association (#16027)*; National institutes and universities. [2021.02.09/AA1295/y/**E**]

- ♦ WHOMS – Women's Home and Overseas Missionary Society (internationally oriented national body)
- ♦ WHO Pan African Emergency Training Centre (no recent information)

♦ WHO Patient Safety 20940

OMS Sécurité des patients
Contact Patient Safety and Risk Management, Service Delivery and Safety Health Systems and Innovation, WHO, Avenue Appia 20, 1211 Geneva 27, Switzerland. E-mail: patientsafety@who.int.
URL: http://www.who.int/patientsafety/en/index.html

History Oct 2004, as *World Alliance for Patient Safety – Alliance mondiale pour la sécurité des patients*, within *WHO (#20950)*. Also referred to as *Patient Safety Programme*. **Aims** Coordinate, disseminate and accelerate improvements in patient safety worldwide; provide a vehicle for international collaboration and action between WHO Member States, WHO's Secretariat, technical experts and consumers, as well as professionals and industry groups. **Finance** Country contributions; grants. **Activities** Programme areas: Clean Care is Safer Care; Safe Surgery Saves Lives; Tackling Antimicrobial Resistance; Patients for Patient Safety; Research for Patient Safety; Taxonomy – International Patient Safety Classification; Reporting and Learning; Solutions for Patient Safety; High 5s; Technology for Patient Safety; Knowledge Management; Eliminating Central Line-Associated Blood Infections; Small Grants; WHO Patient Safety Curriculum Medical Guide; Multi-Professional Curriculum Guide; Patient Safety Checklists. **Publications** *PSP Newlsetter*, *WHO Hand Hygiene Guidelines*; *WHO Safe Surgery Guidelines*. **IGO Relations** Formal contact with: *United Nations (UN, #20515)*.
[2020/XM1553/**E***]

- ♦ WHO Programme on Tobacco or Health / see WHO Tobacco Free Initiative (#20949)

♦ WHO Radiation Emergency Medical Preparedness and Assistance Network (WHO/REMPAN) 20941

Contact WHO, Radiation Programm, Dept of Public Health, Avenue Appia 20, 1211 Geneva, Switzerland. T. +41227914312. Fax +41227914123. E-mail: rempan@who.int – ionizingradiation@who.int.
URL: https://www.who.int/groups/rempan

History by *WHO (#20950)*. **Aims** Promote medical preparedness for radiation accidents among WHO member states; provide advice and assistance in the case of a nuclear accident and radiological emergency; assist in training staff, follow-up studies and rehabilitation. **Events** *Meeting* Geneva (Switzerland) 2021, *Meeting* Nagasaki (Japan) 2011, *Meeting* Oak Ridge, TN (USA) 2004, *Meeting* Moscow (Russia) 2002, *Meeting* Chilton (UK) 2000. **Publications** *Radiation Emergency Response: Internal Guidance* (2002) by G Souchkevitch and I Turai. Meeting proceedings.
Members Collaborating centres in 10 countries:
Armenia, Australia, Brazil, France, Germany, Japan, Russia, UK, Ukraine, USA.
Liaison Institutions in 7 countries:
Argentina, Canada, China, Finland, Hungary, India, USA. [2022/XF5638/**F**]

- ♦ WHO-Regionalbüro für Europa (#20945)

♦ WHO Regional Centre for Environmental Health Activities (CEHA) . . 20942

OMS Centre régional pour les activités d'hygiène de l'environnement
Dir PO Box 926967, Amman 11190, Jordan. T. +96265524655 – +96265531657. Fax +96265516591. E-mail: emceha@who.int.
URL: http://www.emro.who.int/ceha/

History 1985, by *WHO Regional Office for the Eastern Mediterranean (EMRO, #20944)*. Also referred to as *Regional Centre for Environmental Health Activities – Centre régional pour les activités d'hygiène de l'environnement*. **Aims** Provide information, programmatic support, advisory consultations and technical services to Member States to heighten the leadership role of the public health sector in regulating, surveillance and management of environmental risks. **Structure** Director; Administrative Unit; Technical Units (3). **Languages** Arabic, English, French. **Staff** 15.00 FTE, paid. **Finance** Regular funds provided by: *WHO (#20950)*. Extrabudgetary funds from external agencies such as: *Arab Fund for Economic and*

Social Development (AFESD, #00965); *Arab Gulf Programme for United Nations Development Organizations (AGFUND, #00971)*; *Global Environment Facility (GEF, #10346)*; *International Bank for Reconstruction and Development (IBRD, #12317)* (World Bank); *International Development Research Centre (IDRC, #13162)*; *Islamic Development Bank (IsDB, #16044)*; *Islamic World Educational, Scientific and Cultural Organization (ICESCO, #16058)*; *UNEP (#20299)*; *United Nations Office for Project Services (UNOPS, #20602)*. **Activities** Areas covered: (A) Human Resources Development: convenes workshops, short training courses, seminars and conferences at national (85), intercountry (4) and regional levels; assists development of those national institutions and centres involved in training in environmental health fields. (B) Research and Technical Advice: provides short-term consultants to advise and strengthen national environmental health institutions; assists identification and preparation of research proposals in appropriate fields. (C) Information Exchange: provides access to CEHANET's technical information obtained from the Region and elsewhere; promotes concept of Technical Cooperation among Developing Countries (TCDC). Documentation Unit; Demonstration. **Events** *Regional conference on water conservation approaches and technologies* Amman (Jordan) 1993, *Consultation on regional network for education and training* Cairo (Egypt) 1993, *Meeting on appropriate technologies for water supply and sanitation related to rural areas* Amman (Jordan) 1992. **Publications** *CEHA News* (occasional). Management Documents; CEHANET Documents; selected presentations; special studies. Information Services: Index of articles available at CEHA. Audiovisuals. **Information Services** *CEHA Library Catalogue*; *Environmental Health Regional Bibliography*; *Environmental Health Regional Information Network (CEHANET)*; *Environmental Health Terminology* – Thesaurus; *Regional Directory of Environmental Health Institutions*; *Regional Directory of Environmental Health Professionals*; *Union List of Environmental Health Journals* – held in CEHANET National Focal Agencies.
Members EMRO member states (22):
Afghanistan, Bahrain, Djibouti, Egypt, Iran Islamic Rep, Iraq, Jordan, Kuwait, Lebanon, Libya, Morocco, Oman, Pakistan, Palestine, Qatar, Saudi Arabia, Somalia, Sudan, Syrian AR, Tunisia, United Arab Emirates, Yemen. [2018.08.05/XF1193/**E***]

♦ WHO Regional Office for Africa (AFRO) 20943

Bureau régional de l'OMS pour l'Afrique – Sede Regional Africana da OMS
Main Office Cité du Djoué, PO Box 06, Brazzaville, Congo Brazzaville. T. +4724139100 – +47241472427700202. Fax +4724139503. E-mail: afrgocom@who.int.
URL: http://www.afro.who.int/
History 1952, Brazzaville (Congo Brazzaville). Established as part of *WHO (#20950)*. Former names and other names: *WHO/AFRO* – alias. **Aims** Attain the highest possible level of health for all people. **Structure** Mutually supportive organizational layers (3): Regional Office (AFRO Executive Management Team, consisting of Regional Director and 3 Programme Directors); Subregional Health Development Teams (Subregion I – 17 countries, Subregion II – 13 countries, Subregion III – 16 countries); network of WHO country offices in the region. **Staff** Represented by *Staff Association of the WHO Regional Office for Africa (no recent information)*. **Finance** Contributions from member countries; extra-budgetary sources. Regular budget (every 2 years): US$ 154 million.
Activities Regional priority areas: malaria; HIV/AIDS and tuberculosis; safe motherhood; child survival, including integrated management of childhood illness and eradication of poliomyelitis; mental health; preparedness and response to emergencies, including epidemics and disasters; health sector reform and development of sustainable health systems focusing on management, capacity building, research and resource mobilization; poverty reduction through better health.
'General Programme Development and Management' encompasses -
Technical Divisions (6): Health Systems and Services Development; Family and Reproductive Health; Communicable Diseases Prevention and Control; Healthy Environments and Sustainable Development; Non-Communicable Diseases; Administration and Finance.
Major Programmes (3):
- Health, Science and Public Policy (HSP), including Health in Sustainable Development (HSD), Technical Cooperation with Countries (TCC), Research Policy and Strategy Coordination (RPS), Inter-Agency Resource Mobilization (IRM) and Emergency and Humanitarian Action (EHA);
- Human Resources for Health;
- Oral Health.

'Subregional Health Development Teams' – accelerate health development by strengthening implementation at the local/district level; provide support for creation and/or functioning of national health development centres and for creation and/or functioning of multidisciplinary teams for technical cooperation within the sub-region/region.
'Country Offices' – support speedy implementation of "Health for All" strategies; manage WHO technical cooperation activities using the Programme Operations Coordination programme (budget monitoring system); assist governments in identifying and coordinating available and potential internal and external resources for health development.
Events *Session* Lomé (Togo) 2022, *Session* Brazzaville (Congo Brazzaville) 2021, *Session* Brazzaville (Congo Brazzaville) 2020, *Health Forum* Praia (Cape Verde) 2019, *Health Forum* Kigali (Rwanda) 2017. **Publications** Biennial Report.
Members Governments in the 3 WHO/AFRO Subregions – 46 countries:
Algeria, Angola, Benin, Botswana, Burkina Faso, Burundi, Cameroon, Cape Verde, Central African Rep, Chad, Comoros, Congo Brazzaville, Congo DR, Côte d'Ivoire, Equatorial Guinea, Eritrea, Eswatini, Ethiopia, Gabon, Gambia, Ghana, Guinea, Guinea-Bissau, Kenya, Lesotho, Liberia, Madagascar, Malawi, Mali, Mauritania, Mauritius, Mozambique, Namibia, Niger, Nigeria, Rwanda, Sao Tomé-Principe, Senegal, Seychelles, Sierra Leone, South Africa, Tanzania UR, Togo, Uganda, Zambia, Zimbabwe.
IGO Relations Supports: *Organization of Coordination for the Control of Endemic Diseases in Central Africa (#17860)*; *Special Health Fund for Africa (SHFA, no recent information)*. [2021/XE9915/**E***]

♦ WHO Regional Office for the Americas / see Pan American Sanitary Bureau (#18129)

♦ WHO Regional Office for the Eastern Mediterranean (EMRO) 20944

Bureau régional de l'OMS pour la Méditerranée orientale – Oficina Regional de la OMS para el Mediterraneo Oriental
Regional Dir PO Box 7608, Nasr City, Cairo, 11371, Egypt. E-mail: emrgoegp@who.int – emrgoas-urms@who.int.
URL: http://www.emro.who.int/
History 1948. Established as part of *WHO (#20950)*. Former names and other names: *WHO/EMRO* – alias. **Aims** Stimulate and advance work to eradicate *epidemic*, *endemic* and other *diseases*; propose international conventions and agreements in *health*; promote improved *nutrition*, *sanitation*, *working conditions* and other aspects of *environmental hygiene*; promote and conduct research in the field of health; foster cooperation among scientific and professional groups which contribute to advancement of health; develop international *standards* for food, biological and pharmaceutical products; assist in developing an informed public opinion among all peoples on matters of health. **Structure** Regional Committee; Regional Office. *WHO Regional Centre for Environmental Health Activities (CEHA, #20942)* is part of EMRO. **Languages** Arabic, English, French. **Staff** 752 permanent; 428 temporary; 173 non-staff holding Special Services Agreements. **Finance** Base programmes funded through assessed contributions by Member States and voluntary contributions; emergency and polio eradication programmes funded by voluntary contributions only. Annual budget (2018-2019): Base programmes – US$ 336,000,000; emergency programme – US$ 650,905,000; polio eradication programme – US$ 356,700,000. **Activities** Knowledge management/information dissemination; awareness raising; training/education; events/meetings. **Events** *Annual Session* Cairo (Egypt) 2022, *Annual Session* Cairo (Egypt) 2021, *Annual Session* Cairo (Egypt) 2020, *Annual Session* Teheran (Iran Islamic Rep) 2019, *Annual Session* Khartoum (Sudan) 2018. **Publications** *Eastern Mediterranean Health Journal* in Arabic, English, French; *World Health Report* – Arabic version. *EMRO Technical Publications Series*; *Health Education through Religious Series*; *WHO Regional Publications, Eastern Mediterranean Series*. Regional and country profiles.
Members Governments of 22 countries and territories:
Afghanistan, Bahrain, Djibouti, Egypt, Iran Islamic Rep, Iraq, Jordan, Kuwait, Lebanon, Libya, Morocco, Oman, Pakistan, Palestine, Qatar, Saudi Arabia, Somalia, Sudan, Syrian AR, Tunisia, United Arab Emirates, Yemen.
IGO Relations All links through WHO. **NGO Relations** All links through WHO. [2022/XE9802/**E***]

♦ WHO Regional Office for Europe 20945

Bureau régional de l'OMS pour l'Europe – WHO-Regionalbüro für Europa
Regional Director UN City, Marmorvej 51, 2100 Copenhagen, Denmark. T. +4545337000. Fax +4545337001. E-mail: eurocontact@who.int.
URL: http://www.euro.who.int/
History 1951. Founded as part of *WHO (#20950)*. Former names and other names: *OMS Bureau régional de l'Europe* – former; *OMS Oficina Regional para Europa* – former; *WGO Regionalbüro für Europa* – former; *VOZ Evropejskoe Regionalnoe Bjuro* – former; *WHO/EURO* – former; *WHO/Europe* – alias. **Aims** Support Member States in developing and sustaining their own *health* policies, health systems and public health programmes, working to prevent and overcome threats to health, anticipating future challenges and advocating public health. **Structure** Regional Committee for Europe (meeting annually) and attended by high-level policy makers from all 53 member states. Divisions and programmes. **Languages** English, French, German, Russian. **Staff** As of Jan 2008: fixed-term staff: 420; short-term staff: 254. **Finance** Sources: contributions of member/participating states; donations. Annual budget: 27,000,000 USD.
Activities Regional targets were developed in 1984 and updated in 1991 and 1998. Progress in achieving the goals of the health policy and targets for region is evaluated regularly. Country strategy for 2005-2009 focuses on strengthening health systems: all the organizations, institutions and resources that are devoted to producing action principally aimed at improving, maintaining or restoring health. Programmes on: country policies, systems and services; health intelligence; communicable and noncommunicable diseases; family and community health; investment in health; health environment.
Work includes helping countries adapt and implement at local level the agreements, strategies and frameworks developed for global use. These deal with the full spectrum of global health problems: from NCDs to communicable diseases, such as HIV/AIDS or tuberculosis, to improving mental health to transport policies. The Regional Office's role as assistant and coordinator at the local level is increasingly vital in helping countries meet their global commitments. Organizes and contributes to several policy events and technical trainings in the field.
'Centres':
- *European Centre for Health Policy (ECHP, see: #20945)*;
- *WHO European Office for Investment for Health and Development, Venice (see: #20945)*;
- *WHO Barcelona Office for Health Systems Strengthening (see: #20945)*.

Organizes Conferences on Environment and Health in connection with: *European Charter on Environment and Health (1989)*. Provides secretariat for WHO's overall *Regions for Health Network (RHN, #18821)*.
European Observatory on Health Systems and Policies (#08072) supports and promotes evidence-based health policy-making through the comprehensive and rigorous analysis of health care systems in the European region.
Events *Session* Copenhagen (Denmark) 2019, *Annual Meeting* Lisbon (Portugal) 2019, *Workshop on Strategic Procurement of Medicines* Copenhagen (Denmark) 2018, *Session* Rome (Italy) 2018, *High-Level Regional Meeting on Health Systems Respond to NCDs (Noncommunicable Diseases)* Sitges (Spain) 2018. **Publications** Catalogue. Information Services: Statistical databases; data sets; library services. *WHO European Centre for Environment and Health (ECEH, see: #20945)* – gathers data on health and the environment in Europe. **Information Services** *Institutional Repository for Information Sharing* – bibliographic database.
Members Member states (53):
Albania, Andorra, Armenia, Austria, Azerbaijan, Belarus, Belgium, Bosnia-Herzegovina, Bulgaria, Croatia, Cyprus, Czechia, Denmark, Estonia, Finland, France, Georgia, Germany, Greece, Hungary, Iceland, Ireland, Israel, Italy, Kazakhstan, Kyrgyzstan, Latvia, Lithuania, Luxembourg, Malta, Moldova, Monaco, Montenegro, Netherlands, North Macedonia, Norway, Poland, Portugal, Romania, Russia, San Marino, Serbia, Slovakia, Slovenia, Spain, Sweden, Switzerland, Tajikistan, Türkiye, Turkmenistan, UK, Ukraine, Uzbekistan.
IGO Relations Official relations with: *Council of Europe (CE, #04881)*; *European Commission (EC, #06633)*; *Nordic Council (NC, #17256)*; *Nordic Council of Ministers (NCM, #17260)*; *OECD (#17693)*; *Organization for Security and Cooperation in Europe (OSCE, #17887)*. Instrumental in setting up: *South-Eastern European Health Network (SEE Health Network, #19807)*. **NGO Relations** In liaison with technical committees of: *International Organization for Standardization (ISO, #14473)*. Member of: *European Civil Society Forum on HIV/AIDS (CSF, #06568)*; *European Forum for Primary Care (EFPC, #07326)*; *EU Platform for Action on Diet, Physical Activity and Health (inactive)*. Instrumental in setting up: *European Forum of Nursing and Midwifery Associations (#07324)*; *International Network of Health Promoting Hospitals and Health Services (HPH, #14277)*; *European Network for Mental Health Service Evaluation (ENMESH, #07946)*; *Health Evidence Network (HEN, #10880)*. [2021.03.11/XE9798/**E***]

♦ WHO Regional Office for South-East Asia (SEARO) 20946

Office régional de l'OMS pour l'Asie du Sud-Est – Oficina Regional de OMS para Asia Sudoriental
Secretariat World Health House, Indraprastha Estate, Mahatma Gandhi Road, Delhi 1100 002, DELHI 1100 002, India. T. +911123370804. Fax +911123370197. E-mail: sereg@who.int.
URL: http://www.searo.who.int/
History 1948, as part of *WHO (#20950)*. Also referred to by acronym *WHO/SEARO*. **Events** *Session* Kathmandu (Nepal) 2021, *Session* Bangkok (Thailand) 2020, *Session* Delhi (India) 2019, *Session* Delhi (India) 2018, *Regional Consultation for Networking and Coordination of Health Partners for Emergency Response* Bangkok (Thailand) 2017.
Members Governments of 11 countries:
Bangladesh, Bhutan, India, Indonesia, Korea DPR, Maldives, Myanmar, Nepal, Sri Lanka, Thailand, Timor-Leste.
[2018/XE9896/**E***]

♦ WHO Regional Office for the Western Pacific (WPRO) 20947

Bureau régional du Pacifique occidental de l'OMS – Oficina Regional para el Pacifico Occidental de la OMS
Regional Dir United Nations Avenue, PO Box 2932, 1000 Manila, Philippines. T. +6325288001. Fax +6325211036 – +6325260279. E-mail: wprocom@who.int.
URL: http://www.wpro.who.int/
History 7 Apr 1948. 7 April 1948, as a part of *WHO (#20950)*. Also referred to by initials *WHO/WPRO*. **Aims** Coordinate efforts on *health* problems in the region; assure timely, expert technical information needed by countries to build and strengthen their comprehensive national *health care* services. **Structure** Regional Committee (annual meeting). Regional Office in Manila (Philippines). WHO Representatives (9); WHO Country Liaison Officers (5) in: Tarawa (Kiribati), Seoul (Korea Rep), Honiara (Solomon Is), Nuku'alofa (Tonga) and Port Vila (Vanuatu). **Languages** Chinese, English, French. **Staff** 370.00 FTE, paid. **Finance** Regular budget which is provided by member states and from extrabudgetary sources. **Activities** At the Regional Office in Manila (Philippines), health specialists – including Regional Advisers, Intercountry staff, and support staff – coordinate efforts on health problems. In order to assist governments in the planning and implementation of national health programmes, WPRO provides expert consultants to investigate specific health problems, helps train health workers and facilitates the exchange of health information on such health concerns as outbreaks of communicable diseases. **Events** *Annual Session* Himeji (Japan) 2021, *Annual Session* Manila (Philippines) 2020, *Annual Session* Manila (Philippines) 2019, *Annual Session* Manila (Philippines) 2018, *Annual Session* Brisbane, QLD (Australia) 2017. **Publications** *WHO in Action* (4 a year) in English – newsletter. Press releases.
Members Areas, countries and territories (37). Member states with seat of government in the region (27):
Australia, Brunei Darussalam, Cambodia, China, Cook Is, Fiji, Japan, Kiribati, Korea Rep, Laos, Malaysia, Marshall Is, Micronesia FS, Mongolia, Nauru, New Zealand, Niue, Palau, Papua New Guinea, Philippines, Samoa, Singapore, Solomon Is, Tonga, Tuvalu, Vanuatu, Vietnam.
Associate member – 1 territory:
Tokelau.
Member states responsible for areas in the region (3):
France, UK, USA.
Areas (9) governed by other member states:
Guam, Hong Kong, Macau, New Caledonia, Northern Mariana Is, Pitcairn, Polynesia Fr, Samoa USA, Wallis-Futuna.
IGO Relations Links with a large number of IGOs, including: *Global Alliance to Eliminate Lymphatic Filariasis (GAELF, #10195)*. **NGO Relations** Member of: *Federation of International Civil Servants' Associations (FICSA, #09603)*. Supports: *Western Pacific Association for Medical Education (WPAME, #20917)*. Also links with a large number of NGOs (not specified). [2022/XE6238/**E***]

♦ **WHO/REMPAN** WHO Radiation Emergency Medical Preparedness and Assistance Network (#20941)
♦ WHO/SEAR-HELLIS / see WHO South-East Asia Region Health Literature, Library and Information Services Network (#20948)
♦ WHO/SEARO / see WHO Regional Office for South-East Asia (#20946)

♦ WHO South-East Asia Region Health Literature, Library and Information Services Network (HELLIS) 20948

Head Office SEARO Library WHO, World Health House, Indraprastha Estate, Mahatma Gandhi Marg, Delhi 1100 002, DELHI 1100 002, India. E-mail: searolibrary@who.int.
URL: http://hellis.org/

History 1980, as a regional network, part of *WHO (#20950)*. Also referred to by acronyms *WHO/SEAR-HELLIS* and *SEAR-HELLIS*. **Aims** Coordinate national and regional libraries in interacting and cooperating on resource sharing.
Members Libraries (350) in 10 countries:
Bangladesh, Bhutan, India, Indonesia, Korea DPR, Maldives, Myanmar, Nepal, Sri Lanka, Thailand. [2015/XF9616/**F***]

♦ WHO Tobacco Free Initiative (TFI) 20949

OMS initiative pour un monde sans tabac

Contact WHO/Noncommunicable Disease and Mental Health, Avenue Appia 20, 1211 Geneva 27, Switzerland. T. +41227914426. Fax +41227914832. E-mail: tfi@who.int.
URL: http://tobacco.who.int/

History 1980, Geneva (Switzerland), as *WHO Clearinghouse on Smoking and Health Information*, within the framework of *WHO (#20950)*, following on from activities on tobacco control of WHO's Noncommunicable Diseases Cluster. In 1988, title changed to *WHO Programme on Tobacco or Health (WHO-TOH Programme) – Programme OMS tabac ou santé*. Current title adopted in 1998. **Aims** Coordinate an improved global strategic response to tobacco as an important *public health* issue and thus prevent and reduce *death* and *disease* caused by tobacco use. **Structure** WHO Executive Board and World Health Assembly provide policy guidance. **Activities** Builds national capacity for tobacco control at country level through: assessment of country and global needs to expedite tobacco control; performance enhancement in media advocacy, legislation and economics. Group on *Framework Convention on Tobacco Control (FCTC, 2003)* works to build consensus, mobilize support and encourage adoption of the Convention and related protocols. External liaison group emphasizes: interaction with communications media and journalists; UN coordination for tobacco control; development of strong links with NGOs and private sector groups including, in particular, the pharmaceutical industry, entertainment, media and leisure groups. Information management covers: development of a solid evidence base; ensuring that a global surveillance system becomes operational and is used at country level as a policy tool; support for internet-based approaches to maximize global connectivity between tobacco control policy, researchers and advocates. **Events** *Meeting* Maastricht (Netherlands) 2016, *International conference on global tobacco control law* Delhi (India) 2000, *International conference on advancing knowledge on regulating tobacco products* Oslo (Norway) 2000, *International conference on tobacco and health* Kobe (Japan) 1999, *International consultation on tobacco and youth* Singapore (Singapore) 1999. **Publications** *Tobacco Alert* (4 a year). *Framework Convention on Tabocco Control Series*. Reports; guidelines; pamphlets; press and advisory kits for World No-Tobacco Days. **Members** All WHO Member States. **IGO Relations** *FAO (#09260)*; *ILO (#11123)*; *International Bank for Reconstruction and Development (IBRD, #12317)*; *International Monetary Fund (IMF, #14180)*; *UNCTAD (#20285)*; *UNICEF (#20332)*. **NGO Relations** Official relations include: *World Medical Association (WMA, #21646)*; *Union for International Cancer Control (UICC, #20415)*; *International Council of Nurses (ICN, #13054)*; *International Federation of Medical Students' Associations (IFMSA, #13478)*; *World Federation of Public Health Associations (WFPHA, #21476)*. [2009.01.05/XF0660/**F***]

♦ WHO-TOH Programme / see WHO Tobacco Free Initiative (#20949)

♦ WHO – World Health Organization 20950

Organisation mondiale de la santé (OMS) – Organización Mundial de la Salud (OMS)

Dir Gen Avenue Appia 20, 1211 Geneva 27, Switzerland. T. +41227912111. Fax +41227913111. E-mail: publications@who.int.
URL: http://www.who.int/

History 22 Jul 1946, New York, NY (USA). Established on adoption of the Constitution signed by 61 states, 51 of which were also members of the United Nations. *WHO Interim Commission – Commission intérimaire de l'OMS* was set up at the same time. Constitution entered into force on 7 Apr 1948, having been ratified by 26 UN member states, since which time 7th April each year is celebrated as *World Health Day*. First World Health Assembly met from 24 Jun to 24 Jul 1948, Geneva (Switzerland), and adopted an agreement whereby the World Health Organization, already a specialized agency established by intergovernmental agreement, was brought into relationship with the United Nations. The Interim Commission was superseded as from 1 Sep 1948. WHO is a a specialized agency of *United Nations (UN, #20515)* within *United Nations System (#20635)*, linked to *ECOSOC (#05331)*.

WHO continues the movement for international cooperation in health commenced in the 19th century with the first *International Sanitary Conference (inactive)*, 1851, and subsequent similar conferences, at which international conventions were agreed. It took over: the peace-time aspects of the work of the Health Division of *United Nations Relief and Rehabilitation Administration (UNRRA, inactive)*, set up in 1943; the functions of *Office international d'hygiène publique (OIHP, inactive)*, set up 9 Dec 1907, Paris (France); the functions of *Organisation d'hygiène de la Société des Nations (inactive)*, which had ceased to exlst in 1939. *World Health Declaration*, adopted at the 51st Session, May 1998, to celebrate the 50th Anniversary of WHO, includes recommitment to primary health care as defined in the *'Declaration of Alma Ata'*, adopted at International Conference on Primary Health Care, 6-12 Sep 1978, Alma Ata (USSR), and endorsed by resolution WHA 32.30 of the 32nd World Health Assembly, May 1979.

Aims Constitution defines health as a state of complete physical, mental and social *well-being* and not merely the absence of disease or infirmity. Article 1 of the Constitution states: 'The objective of WHO shall be the attainment by all peoples of the highest possible level of health'. Consequent functions devolving from this aim to: (a) act as the directing and coordinating authority on international health work; (b) establish and maintain effective collaboration with the UN, specialized agencies, governmental health administrations, professional groups and other organizations as may be deemed appropriate; (c) upon request, assist governments in strengthening health services; (d) furnish appropriate technical assistance and, in emergencies, necessary aid, upon request or acceptance of governments; (e) provide or assist in providing, upon the request of the UN, health services and facilities to special groups, such as the people of trust territories; (f) establish and maintain such administrative and technical services as may be required, including epidemiological and statistical services; (g) stimulate and advance work to eradicate or control epidemic, endemic and other diseases; (h) in cooperation with other specialized agencies where necessary, promote the prevention of accidental injuries; (i) in cooperation with other specialized agencies where necessary, promote the improvement of nutrition, housing, sanitation, recreation, economic or working conditions and other aspects of environmental hygiene; (j) promote cooperation among scientific and professional groups which contribute to advancement of health; (k) propose conventions, agreements and regulations and make recommendations with respect to international health matters and perform such duties as may be assigned thereby to the Organization and are consistent with its objective; (l) promote maternal and child health and welfare and foster the ability to live harmoniously in a changing total environment; (m) foster activities in the field of mental health, especially those affecting the harmony of human relations; (n) promote and conduct research in the field of health; (o) promote improved standards of teaching and training in the health, medical and related professions; (p) in cooperation with other specialized agencies where necessary, study and report on administrative and social techniques affecting public health and medical care from preventive and curative points of view, including hospital services and social security; (q) provide information, counsel and assistance in the field of health; (r) assist in developing an informed public opinion among all peoples on matters of health; (s) establish and revise as necessary international nomenclatures of diseases, of causes of death and of public health practices; (t) standardize diagnostic procedures as necessary; (u) develop, establish and promote international standards with respect to food, biological, pharmaceutical and similar products; (v) in general, take all necessary action to attain the objective of the Organization.

Structure World Health Assembly (annual, normally in Geneva – Switzerland) comprises delegates representing member states and is attended by such observers as intergovernmental organizations and nongovernmental organizations in official relations with WHO. Executive Board (2 sessions a year, normally in January and May, both normally in Geneva) is composed of 32 persons, each designated by a member state. Officers: Director-General, appointed by the Assembly on a nomination made by Executive Board; Regional Directors appointed by Executive Board in agreement with the respective regional committees. All other staff members are appointed by the Director-General. Secretariat comprises the Director-General and technical and administrative personnel.

/Headquarters Structure/:
'Director-General's Office (DGO)':
– Director-General (DG) with Advisers;
– Media and Communications (MAC);
– Office of Internal Oversight Services (IOS), comprising: Evaluation and Performance Audits (AEP); Operational Audits (AOP);
– Office of the Legal Counsel (LEG), comprising: Commercial and Contractual Matters (CCM); Governing Bodies and Public International Law (GBI); Personnel and Administrative Matters (PAM);
– Office of the Ombudsmen (OMB).
'Director-General's Representatives (DGR)':
– Health Action in Crises (HAC), comprising; Emergency Health Intelligence and Capacity Building (EHC); Emergency Health Partnerships (EHP); Polio Eradication Initiative (POL);
– Representatives of the Director-General.
CLUSTERS (9) -
'Communicable Diseases (CDS)':
– Communicable Diseases Control, Prevention and Eradication (CPE), comprising: Strategy Development and Monitoring for Eradication and Elimination (CEE); Strategy Development and Monitoring for Parasitic Diseases and Vector Control (PVC); Strategy Development and Monitoring of Zoonoses, Foodborne Diseases and kinetoplastidae (ZFK).
– Communicable Disease Surveillance and Response (CSR), comprising: CSR Office for Alert and Response Operations (ARO), consisting of Risk Assessment and Field Operations (AFO), Emerging and Dangerous Pathogens (EDP) and Epidemic Readiness and Intervention (ERI); Global Influenza Programme (GIP); CSR Office in Lyon (France) (LYO), consisting of Epidemiology Strengthening (EPS) and Laboratory Training and Capacity Strengthening (LAB).
– Public Health Mapping and Geographic Information Systems (GIS) – *UNICEF/UNDP/World Bank/WHO Special Programme for Research and Training in Tropical Diseases (TDR, #20331)* (TDR), comprising: Intervention Development and Evaluation (IDE); Programme Planning and Management (PPM); Product Research and Development (PRD); Research Capability Strengthening (RCS); Basic and Strategic Research (STR).
– WHO Mediterranean Centre for Vulnerability Reduction (WMC), comprising: Social Mobilization and Training (SMT).
'External Relations and Governing Bodies (EGB)':
– Governance (GOV), comprising: Documentation and Communications (DCM); Coordination with the UN and other Intergovernmental Agencies (UNI); Word Processing Centre (WPC).
– Government, Civil Society and Private Sector Relations (GPR), comprising: Civil Society Initiative (CSI); Governmental Agencies and Foundations (GVF); Private Sector (PVS).
'Evidence and Information for Policy (EIP)':
– Health Systems Financing, Expenditure and Resource Allocation (FER), comprising: Choosing Interventions – Effectiveness, Quality, Costs, Gender and Ethics (EQC); Designing Policy Options – Financing, Resource Allocation, Regulation and legislation (FAR);
– Human Resources for Health (HRH), comprising: Bulletin of the WHO (BLT);
– Knowledge Management and Sharing (KMS), comprising: Library and Information Networks for Knowledge (LNK); WHO Press (WHP); Knowledge Communities and Strategy (KCS); WHO Web Team (WEB); e-Health (EHL);
– Measurement and Health Information Systems (MHI), comprising; Classification, Assessment, Surveys and Terminology (CAS); Assessing Health Needs – Epidemiology and Burden of Disease (EBD); Research Policy and Cooperation (RPC); Health System Policies and Operations (SPO).
'Family and Community Health (FCH)':
– Gender (GMS);
– Child and Adolescent Health and Development (CAH), comprising; Adolescent Health and Development (ADH); Child Health and Development (CHD); Neonatal and Infant Health and Development (HNI); Technical Support Team (TST);
– Immunization, Vaccines and Biologicals (IVB), comprising: Access to Technologies (ATT); Expanded Programme on Immunization (EPI); Initiative for Vaccine Research (IVR), consisting of Research on Bacterial Vaccines (BAC), Parasitic and other Pathogens Vaccine Research (POP) and WHO-UNAIDS HIV Vaccine Initiative (HVI); Quality Assurance and Safety – Biologicals (QSB); Vaccine Assessment and Monitoring (VAM);
– Reproductive Health and Research (RHR):
– Communication, Advocacy and Information (CAI); Clinical Trials and Informatics Support (CTI); Gender Issues and Reproductive Rights (GRR); Implementing Best Practices (IBP); Monitoring and Evaluation (MAE); Promoting Family Planning (PFP); Policy and Programmatic Issues (PPI); Preventing Unsafe Abortion (PUA); Controlling Sexually Transmitted and Reproductive Tract Infections (STI); Technical Support Team (TCC).
– Gender and Women's Health (GWH).
'General Management (GMG)':
– Management Reform;
– Headquarters Board of Appeal (HBA);
– International Computing Centre (ICC);
– Staff Association (STF);
– Office of the Comptroller (CBF), comprising:
– Accounts (ACT); Administration and Finance Information Support (AFI); Budget Implementation (BUI); Treasury and Risk Management (TSY), consisting of Treasury Operations (TSO) and Treasury Services (TSS);
– Human Resources Services (HRS), comprising; Policy Development (HPD); Recruitment, Placement and Classification (HRC); Staff Development and Training (SDL);
– Infrastructure and Logistics Services (ILS), comprising;
– Contracting and Procurement Services (CPS), consisting of Computer and Office Supplies (COP), Drugs and Biological Procurement (DBP), Environmental and Medical Procurement (ESP), Laboratory Supplies (LSP) and Hospital and Teaching Supplies (THP);
– Infrastructure Support Services (ISS), consisting of Building and Premises Management (BPM), Records and Archives (RAS) and Space Planning and Accommodation (SPA);
– Logistics Support Services (LSS), consisting of: Conference and Events Coordination (CEC), including Conference and Meeting Planning (CMP), Special Events and Exhibitions (SEE) and Usher Services (USS); Pre-Press and Print Production Services (PPS), including Document Production Services (DPS), Graphic Design and Layout (GRA) and Printing Services (PRT); Travel;
– Transportation and Despatch Services (TDS), including Distribution Service (DST), Goods Receipt and Despatch (GRD), Mailing (MLG), Transportation (TRN) and Travel (TRV);
– Premises Security (PSS);
– Information Technology and Telecommunications (ITT), comprising; Management Information System (MIS); Networking and Telecommunications (NTS); Security, Web and Architecture (SWA); Telecommunications (TMS), including Audiovisual and Training Team (AVT); User Support and Training (USP);
– Planning, Resource Coordination and Performance Monitoring (PRP);
– Security and Staff Services (SES), comprising; Health and Medical Services (HMS), including Staff Counsellor (SCO); Personnel Support Services (PSU), consisting of Contact Administration Support (CSA), Pension (PEN) and Staff Orientation Service (SOS); Staff Security (SEC); Staff Financial Services (SFS), consisting of Claims Examination (CLX); Staff Insurance (INS) and Payroll (PAY);
– Management Support Unit (MSU – CDS and HTM);
– Management Support Unit (MSU – EGB and SDE);
– Management Support Unit (MSU – EIP and NMH);
– Management Support Unit (MSU – FCH and HTP);
– Management Support Unit (MSU – GMG).
'HIV/AIDS, TB and Malaria (HTM)':
– HIV/AIDS (HIV), comprising: AIDS Medicine and Diagnostics Service (AMD); Partnerships, External Relations and Communication (PEC); Strategic Information and Research (SIR), Treatment and Prevention Scale-up (TPS);
– Roll Back Malaria (RBM), comprising: Monitoring and Evaluation Team (RME); Roll Back Malaria Partnership Secretariat (RPS); Strategy and Operations Team (RSO);
– Stop TB Department (STB), comprising: Stop TB Partnership Secretariat (TBP); TB Strategy and Operations (TBS); TB/HIV and Drug Resistance (THD); Tuberculosis Monitoring and Evaluation (TME);
– Strategic Planning and Innovation (SPI).
'Health Technology and Pharmaceuticals (HTP)':
– Essential Drugs and Other Medicines (EDM), comprising: Drug Action Programme (DAP); Policy, Access and Rational Use (PAR); Quality Assurance and Safety – Medicines (QSM); Traditional Medicine (TRM);
– Essential Health Technologies (EHT), comprising: Blood Transfusion Safety (BTS); Clinical Procedures (CPR); Devices and Clinical Technology (DCT); Diagnostic Imaging and Laboratory Technology (DIL); Quality and Safety of Plasma Derivatives and Related Substances (QSD).
'Noncommunicable Diseases and Mental Health (NMH)':
– Chronic Diseases and Health Promotion (CHP), comprising: Health Promotion (HPR); Chronic Diseases Prevention and Management (CPM); Surveillance and Information for Policy (SIP);
– Management of Noncommunicable Diseases (MNC), comprising: Health Care (CCH); Chronic Respiratory Diseases and Arthritis (CRA); Cardiovascular Diseases (CVD); Diabetes Mellitus (DIA); Human Genetics (HGN); Blindness and Deafness (PBD); Programme on Cancer Control (PCC);
– Mental Health and Substance Abuse (MSD), comprising: Management of Mental and Brain Disorders (MBD); Mental Health – Evidence and Research (MER); Mental Health Policy and Service Development (MPS); Management of Substance Abuse (MSB);
– Nutrition for Health and Development (NHD), comprising: Food Aid for Development (FAD);
– Standing Committee on Nutrition (SCN);
– Tobacco Free Initiative (TFI), comprising: *Framework Convention on Tobacco Control (FCTC, 2003)* and *Protocol to Eliminate Illicit Trade in Tobacco Products (2012)*; National Capacity (NAC);
– Injuries and Violence Prevention (VIP), comprising: Disability and Rehabilitation (DAR); Prevention of Violence (PVL); Unintentional Injuries Prevention (UIP).

'Sustainable Development and Healthy Environments (SDE)':
- Cooperation and Country Focus (CCO), including: Country Analysis and Support (ASC);
- Coordination of Macroeconomics and Health support unit (CMH);
- Ethics, Trade, Human Rights and Health Law (ETH);
- Food Safety (FOS);
- MDGs, Health and Development Policy (HDP), including: Pro-Poor Health Policies (PHP);
- Protection of the Human Environment (PHE), comprising: Occupational and Environmental Health (OEH); ILO, UNEP and WHO programme *International Programme on Chemical Safety (IPCS, #14650)* (PCS); Radiation and Environmental Health (RAD); Water, Sanitation and Health (WSH).

/Regional Organizations/:

As provided for in the Constitution, 6 regional organizations are responsible for cooperation with governments and with areas geographically defined by the Assembly. Each comprises a Regional Committee (usually meeting once a year), composed of representatives of members and associate member states in the region, and a Regional Office headed by a Regional Director.
- *WHO Regional Office for Africa (AFRO, #20943)*;
- *WHO Regional Office for the Eastern Mediterranean (EMRO, #20944)*;
- *WHO Regional Office for Europe (#20945)*;
- *WHO Regional Office for South-East Asia (SEARO, #20946)*;
- *WHO Regional Office for the Western Pacific (WPRO, #20947)*;
- *WHO Regional Office for the Americas (AMRO)* through *Pan American Sanitary Bureau (PASB, #18129)*, set up in 1902, currently Secretariat of *Pan American Health Organization (PAHO, #18108)*, which has served as WHO Regional Office since 1949.

/Technical Advice/:

'Advisory Committee on Health Research', comprising 15 members. It is the highest level scientific advisory body in the WHO and provides the Director-General with the scientific advice in relation to WHO's research programmes.

'Expert Advisory Panels' (54), comprising a total of about 950 members. These are groups of experts conversant with all branches of knowledge and form of experience needed to cover adequately particular subjects relevant to the Organization.

WHO Centre for Health Development, Kobe (WKC, see: #20950) – the first of a network of centres undertaking research in close collaboration with other institutes in both developed and developing countries, results being widely disseminated.

International Agency for Research on Cancer (IARC, #11598) – coordinates and conducts research on the causes of human cancer, the mechanisms of carcinogenesis and develops scientific strategies for cancer control. It is engaged in both epidemiological and laboratory research and disseminates scientific information through publications, meetings, courses and fellowships.

VISION 2020 – The Right to Sight (inactive) – launched 16 Feb 1999, Geneva, by WHO Director-General, unites intergovernmental, nongovernmental and private organizations in making an international concerted effort to significantly reduce blindness worldwide, in particular to eliminate preventable blindness by the year 2020.

WHO Collaborating Centres – scientific institutions, such as universities and national health institutes (currently over 800), which provide research, training and assessment support on specific topics.

Languages Arabic, Chinese, English, French, Russian, Spanish. **Staff** 4000.00 FTE, paid. Personnel negotiations through WHO Staff Association at Headquarters and in the various Regional Offices: *WHO-HQ Staff Association, Geneva (WHO-HQ SA, #20938)*; *WHO Staff Association for South-East Asia Region (no recent information)*; *WHO/WPR Staff Association (no recent information)*; *Staff Association of the WHO Regional Office for Europe (EURSA, #19941)*; *PAHO/WHO Staff Association (#18024)*; *WHO Eastern Mediterranean Region Staff Association, Cairo (EMRSA, no recent information)*. The *Administrative Tribunal of the International Labour Organization (ILO Tribunal, #00118)* is competent in case of disputes. **Finance** Regular budget: assessed contributions of member states and associate members. Other funding: voluntary contributions from member states and other sources. Working programme budget of US$ 3,300 million for the biennium 2006-2007, adopted May 2004, at 56th World Health Assembly.

Activities 'General Programme of Work (GPW)' provides the framework for activities. Biennial programme budget sets out strategic focus. Priorities 2006-2007, linked to organizational structure comprising DGR and the following work areas:
- *'Representatives of the Director-General (DGR)'* – Representative for Health Action in Crises – represents the WHO in health issues in global emergencies and humanitarian needs; – Representative for Polio Eradication provides overall technical direction and strategic planning for management and coordination of *Global Polio Eradication Initiative (GPEI, #10553)*; – Representative responsible for the Commission on Intellectual Property Rights, Innovation and Public Health.
- 1. *'Communicable Disease Prevention and Control'* – works to reduce morbidity, mortality and disability due to endemic tropical diseases which concern people's health and social and economic well-being worldwide, through prevention, control and, where appropriate, eradication or elimination of selected endemic tropical diseases using, where possible, a synergetic approach taking into consideration recent Health Assembly resolutions. Diseases covered include: Buruli ulcer; dengue fever/dengue haemorrhagic fever; enteric diseases; intestinal parasitoses; leishmaniasis; schistosomiasis; trypanosomiasis; zoonoses. Aims to eradicate dracunculiasis and to eliminate leprosy, lymphatic filariasis, onchocerciasis and Chagas diseases at global or regional level.
- 2. *'Communicable Disease Research'* – researches, generates knowledge and improves and develops essential tools and approaches for developing countries to prevent, diagnose, treat and control neglected infectious diseases; strengthens capacity of disease-endemic countries to research the development and implementation of new and improved approaches to disease control.
- 3. *'Epidemic Alert and Response'* – detects, identifies and responds rapidly to threats to national, regional and global health security due to epidemic-prone, pandemic and emerging infectious diseases of known or unknown etiology; integrates these activities with strengthened communicable disease surveillance and response systems, national health information systems and public health programmes and services.
- 4. *'Malaria'* – Millennium Development Goal 6, target 8 aims to halve the incidence of malaria by 2010 compared to 2000 and reduce it further by 2015. WHO facilitates access of populations at risk to effective treatment of malaria and promotes application of preventive measures against malaria for these populations; it builds capacity for malaria control, strengthens malaria-surveillance systems and monitors and evaluates control.
- 5. *'Tuberculosis'* – aims for every country to reach global control targets of 70% detection and 85% treatment success rates and to sustain this achievement so as to halve TB prevalence and associated death rates by 2015; expands implementation of DOTS strategy and strengthens tuberculosis control, including strategies and policies on tuberculosis/HIV co-infection and multidrug-resistant tuberculosis and increased involvement of communities, health-care providers, nongovernmental organizations and corporate partners, increased country support and nurturing of the Stop TB Partnership; strengthens surveillance, monitoring and evaluation; promotes and facilitates research on new diagnostic tools, drugs and vaccines.
- 6. *'HIV/AIDS'* – aims to effectively control HIV/AIDS and mitigate its socioeconomic impact by accelerating prevention and providing universal access to HIV/AIDS care, including antiretroviral therapy, thus contributing to achieving health-related Millennium Development Goals; rapidly expanding access to treatment and care and accelerating prevention and strengthening health systems to make health-sector response to HIV/AIDS more effective and comprehensive.
- 7. *'Surveillance, Prevention and Management of Chronic, Noncommunicable Diseases'* – aims to: build surveillance systems; reduce exposure to major risk factors; help health systems respond appropriately to rising premature mortality and morbidity related to chronic, noncommunicable diseases.
- 8. *'Health Promotion'* – aims to: improve equity in health, reduce health risks, promote healthy lifestyles and settings and respond to underlying determinants of health; develop and implement multisectoral public policies for health, integrated gender- and age-sensitive approaches facilitating community empowerment; promote life-long health, self-care and health protection in cooperation with relevant national and international partners.
- 9. *'Mental Health and Substance Abuse'* – aims to: ensure that mental health and the consequences of substance abuse are taken fully into account in considerations of health and development; formulate and implement cost-effective responses to mental and neurological disorders and those related to substance use; promote mental health.
- 10. *'Tobacco'* – works to protect present and future generations from health, social, environmental and economic consequences of tobacco consumption and exposure to tobacco smoke, by continuous and substantial reduction in use of tobacco and exposure to tobacco smoke – puts effective tobacco-control measures in place and provides support to Member States in implementing the WHO Framework Convention on Tobacco Control.
- 11. *'Nutrition'* – promotes life-long healthy diet and optimal nutrition, particularly women and children, through implementing, monitoring and evaluating national policies and programmes, contributing to achievement of Millennium Development Goals.
- 12. *'Health and Environment'* – works to: achieve safe, sustainable and health-enhancing human environments, protected from biological, chemical and physical hazards and secure from effects of global and local environmental threats; ensure effective incorporation of health dimensions into national policies and action for environment and health, including legal and regulatory frameworks governing management of the human environment, and into regional and global policies affecting health and environment.
- 13. *'Food Safety'* – works to: reduce the health effect of food contamination; reform and strengthen existing food-safety systems so as to reduce foodborne disease; enable the health sector, in cooperation with other sectors and partners, to assess, communicate and manage foodborne risks effectively and promptly.
- 14. *'Violence, Injuries and Disabilities'* – formulates and implements cost-effective, age- and gender-specific strategies to prevent and mitigate consequences of violence and unintentional injuries and disabilities; promotes and strengthens rehabilitation services.
- 15. *'Reproductive Health'* – through primary health-care systems, aims to make reproductive health accessible to all individuals of appropriate ages no later than the year 2015; aims to provide the widest possible range of safe and effective reproductive and sexual health services across the health system and integrate them into primary health care.
- 16. *'Making Pregnancy Safer'* – aims to: achieve the Millennium Development Goal for maternal health by reducing maternal mortality by 75% from 1990 levels by the year 2015; contribute to lowering infant mortality rate to below 35 per 100,000 live births in all countries by 2015 by reducing perinatal mortality; strengthen national efforts to implement cost-effective interventions so as to provide all women and newborn infants with continuing care throughout pregnancy, childbirth and the postnatal period.
- 17. *'Gender, Women and Health'* – works to: achieve health equity by promoting equal access to, and use of, quality health services by women and men, girls and boys; integrate gender considerations into health policies, programmes and research so as to address issues of gender inequality and inequity and to alleviate their impact on health.
- 18. *'Child and Adolescent Health'* – reduce by two thirds the rate of infant and child mortality by the year 2015 from the 1990 rate; promote physical and mental health of adolescents; reduce by 25% HIV prevalence among young people aged 15 to 24 years by the year 2010; enable countries to pursue evidence-based strategies in order to reduce health risks, morbidity and mortality along the life course; promote health and development of newborn infants, children and adolescents; create mechanisms to measure the impact of those strategies.
- 19. *'Immunization and Vaccine Development'* – protect all people at risk against vaccine-preventable diseases; promote development of new vaccines and innovation in biologicals and immunization-related technologies; ensure greater impact of immunization services, as a component of health delivery systems; accelerate control of high-priority vaccine-preventable diseases; ensure that full humanitarian and economic benefits of such initiatives are realized.
- 20. *'Essential Medicines'* – help save lives and improve health by: framing, implementing and monitoring national medicine policies aiming at increasing equitable access to essential medicines, particularly for high-priority health problems and for poor and disadvantaged populations and at ensuring the quality, safety, efficacy and rational use of medicines, including traditional medicines; developing international standards and supporting implementation of effective regulation in countries; improving rational use of medicines by health professionals and consumers.
- 21. *'Essential Health Technologies'* – strengthen ability of national health systems to resolve health problems through use of essential health technologies; establish safe and reliable services that apply essential health technologies and use biological products through adoption of basic operational frameworks covering policy, quality, safety, access and use.
- 22. *'Policy-Making for Health in Development'* – maximize positive impact of processes related to socioeconomic development, poverty reduction and globalization on health outcomes; raise awareness and advocate the role of better health, particularly of the poor, in achieving overall development objectives; bring ethical, legal and human rights norms into the formulation of national and international health-related programmes, policies and laws; maintain and further secure centrality both of health to a wide range of development processes at national, regional and international levels, and of ethical, economic and human-rights analysis to achievement of just and coherent policies and laws at national, regional and international levels.
- 23. *'Health System Policies and Service Delivery'* – improve availability, quality, equity and efficiency of health services by strengthening their links with the broader public health functions and by strengthening governance, organization and management of health systems; strengthen health-system leadership and capability for effective policy-making in countries; enhance planning and provision of health services that are of good technical quality, responsive to users, contribute to improved equity through greater coverage and make better use of available resources.
- 24. *'Human Resources for Health'* – improve the performance of health systems through strengthening development and management of the health workforce in order to achieve greater equity, coverage, access and quality of care; contribute to managing effectively and creatively the interaction between the supply and demand for health workers.
- 25. *'Health Financing and Social Protection'* – develop systems of health financing that are equitable, efficient, protect against financial risk, promote social protection and can be sustained over time; formulate health-financing strategies that ensure universal coverage and are based on principles of equity, efficiency and social protection, and on the best available information and knowledge; develop capacity to obtain key information and to use it to improve health financing and organizational arrangements as part of national policy.
- 26. *'Health Information, Evidence and Research Policy'* – maximize potential of health systems to improve health and to respond to health needs in a way that is equitable, effective and efficient on the basis of sound health information and scientific knowledge; improve availability, quality, and use of health information at country level strengthen evidence base at regional and global levels in order to monitor and reduce inequalities in health; develop health-research systems, build research capacity and use research findings to strengthen national health systems.
- 27. *'Emergency Preparedness and Response'* – reduce avoidable loss of life, burden of disease and disability among populations affected by crises, emergencies and disasters; optimize health at times of post-crisis transition; contribute to recovery and development; develop and implement policies, programmes and partnerships that increase capacity to prepare, respond and mitigate the risks to health during crises; support recovery and sustainable development.
- 28. *'WHO's Core Presence in Countries'* – provide effective support to, and ensure relevance and effectiveness of WHO's work and accountability to Member States for reaching their national health and development goals and ensure; allocate technical and financial resources accordingly; ensure that country inputs guide WHO policy, technical and advocacy work; contribute to achievement of the health-related Millennium Development Goals through an adequate core presence of WHO at country level.
- 29. *'Knowledge Management and Information Technology'* – foster, equip and support an environment that encourages the generation, sharing, effective application and dissemination of knowledge in Member States and within the Organization in order to promote health, using appropriate knowledge management and information and communication technology.
- 30. *'Planning, Resource Coordination and Oversight'* – apply consistently across the Organization the principles of results-based management and related processes, namely, strategic and operational planning, resource planning and coordination, performance monitoring, quality assurance and evaluation, in support of WHO's leadership role in international health and its programme development and operations; implement fully functional Organization-wide systems and mechanisms for results-based management that provide effective support for WHO's accountability policy and country focus.
- 31. *'Human Resources Management in WHO'* – apply best practice in all aspects of human resources management at all organizational levels; provide the strategic direction, policies and procedures necessary to ensure that human resources services are delivered in a timely and effective manner.
- 32. *'Budget and Financial Management'* – apply best practice in all aspects of budget and financial management, combined with integrity and transparency, at all organizational levels with a sound internal control framework, including relevant financial reporting at all levels, both internally and externally.
- 33. *'Infrastructure and Logistics'* – apply best practice in all aspects of infrastructure and logistics support at all organizational levels; frame an enabling policy and create an institutional environment to support timely implementation of WHO's programmes in Member States.
- 34. *'Governing Bodies'* – ensure sound policy on international public health and development that responds to the needs of Member States; assure good governance of WHO through efficient preparation and conduct of regional and global governing body sessions and effective policy-making processes.
- 35. *'External Relations'* – ensure health goals are incorporated in overall development policies and that resources for health are increased; negotiate, sustain and expand partnerships for health globally; strengthen WHO's collaboration with intergovernmental and governmental bodies, civil society organizations, the private sector and foundations; secure the Organization's resource base.
- 36. *'Direction'* – advance global public health and contribute to attainment of the Millennium Development Goals, particularly directing efforts at country level.

Agreements and other instruments adopted by WHO:
- *Regulations no 1 Regarding Nomenclature of Diseases and Causes of Death (1948)*;
- *Regulations Regarding Nomenclature with Respect to Diseases and Causes of Death (1949)*;
- *International Sanitary Regulations, 1951 (1951)*;
- *WHO nomenclature regulations, 1967*;
- *International Health Regulations, 1969 (1969)*;
- *International Code of Marketing of Breast-milk Substitutes (1981)*;
- *Convention on Assistance in the Case of Nuclear Accident or Radiological Emergency (1986)*;
- *Convention on Early Notification of a Nuclear Accident (1986)*;
- *Ljubljana Charter on Reforming Health Care in Europe (1996)*.

Events *World Conference on Injury Prevention and Safety Promotion* Adelaide, SA (Australia) 2022, *ITU/WHO Workshop on Artificial Intelligence for Health* Helsinki (Finland) 2022, *Meeting of the Focus Group on Artificial Intelligence for Health (ITU-T FG-AI4H)* Helsinki (Finland) 2022, *International AIDS Conference* Montréal, QC (Canada) 2022, *World Bio Summit* Seoul (Korea Rep) 2022. **Publications** *Bulletin of the World Health Organization: The International Journal of Public Health* (12 a year) in English, French, Spanish; *Pan American Journal of Public Health* (12 a year) in English, Portuguese, Spanish; *Eastern Mediterranean Health Journal* (6 a year); *WHO Drug Information* (4 a year) in English; *International Travel and Health* (annual); *World Health Report* (annual); *Weekly Epidemiological Record* in English, French. *Concise International Chemical Assessment Documents (CICADS) Series* – about 6 a year; *Environmental Health Criteria Series*; *WHO Technical Report Series* – about 5 a year. Books, reports, guides and manuals cover medical and public health fields, with emphasis on HIV/AIDS, health systems, environmental health, essential medicines, maternal and child health, communicable and noncommunicable diseases, mental health and international health-related standards and guidelines.

Members All UN member countries may become members of WHO by accepting its Constitution. Other countries may be admitted on approval of their application by a simple majority vote of the World Health Assembly. The Assembly may admit as associate members those territories not responsible for the conduct of their own international relations, following application on their behalf made by the member or other authority responsible for their international relations. Members according to WHO regional distribution:
Members according to WHO regional distribution: 'Regional Office for Africa' (47):

'Regional Office for Africa' (47):
Algeria, Angola, Benin, Botswana, Burkina Faso, Burundi, Cameroon, Cape Verde, Central African Rep, Chad, Comoros, Congo Brazzaville, Congo DR, Côte d'Ivoire, Equatorial Guinea, Eritrea, Eswatini, Ethiopia, Gabon, Gambia, Ghana, Guinea, Guinea-Bissau, Kenya, Lesotho, Liberia, Madagascar, Malawi, Mali, Mauritania, Mauritius, Mozambique, Namibia, Niger, Nigeria, Rwanda, Sao Tomé-Principe, Senegal, Seychelles, Sierra Leone, South Africa, South Sudan, Tanzania UR, Togo, Uganda, Zambia, Zimbabwe.
'Regional Office for the Americas' (35):
Antigua-Barbuda, Argentina, Bahamas, Barbados, Belize, Bolivia, Brazil, Canada, Chile, Colombia, Costa Rica, Cuba, Dominica, Dominican Rep, Ecuador, El Salvador, Grenada, Guatemala, Guyana, Haiti, Honduras, Jamaica, Mexico, Nicaragua, Panama, Paraguay, Peru, St Kitts-Nevis, St Lucia, St Vincent-Grenadines, Suriname, Trinidad-Tobago, Uruguay, USA, Venezuela.
'Regional Office for South-East Asia' (11):
Bangladesh, Bhutan, India, Indonesia, Korea DPR, Maldives, Myanmar, Nepal, Sri Lanka, Thailand, Timor-Leste.
'Regional Office for Europe' (53):
Albania, Andorra, Armenia, Austria, Azerbaijan, Belarus, Belgium, Bosnia-Herzegovina, Bulgaria, Croatia, Cyprus, Czechia, Denmark, Estonia, Finland, France, Georgia, Germany, Greece, Hungary, Iceland, Ireland, Israel, Italy, Kazakhstan, Kyrgyzstan, Latvia, Lithuania, Luxembourg, Malta, Moldova, Monaco, Montenegro, Netherlands, North Macedonia, Norway, Poland, Portugal, Romania, Russia, San Marino, Serbia, Slovakia, Slovenia, Spain, Sweden, Switzerland, Tajikistan, Türkiye, Turkmenistan, UK, Ukraine, Uzbekistan.
'Regional Office for the Eastern Mediterranean' (21):
Afghanistan, Bahrain, Djibouti, Egypt, Iran Islamic Rep, Iraq, Jordan, Kuwait, Lebanon, Libya, Morocco, Oman, Pakistan, Qatar, Saudi Arabia, Somalia, Sudan, Syrian AR, Tunisia, United Arab Emirates, Yemen.
'Regional Office for the Western Pacific' (27):
Australia, Brunei Darussalam, Cambodia, China, Cook Is, Fiji, Japan, Kiribati, Korea Rep, Laos, Malaysia, Marshall Is, Micronesia FS, Mongolia, Nauru, New Zealand, Niue, Palau, Papua New Guinea, Philippines, Samoa, Singapore, Solomon Is, Tonga, Tuvalu, Vanuatu, Vietnam.

IGO Relations Observer to: *World Trade Organization (WTO, #21864)*. Permanent observer status with: *World Intellectual Property Organization (WIPO, #21593)*. Formal contact with: *East, Central and Southern African Health Community (ECSA-HC, #05216)*. Member of: *United Nations Group on the Information Society (UNGIS, #20570)*; *UN-Water (#20723)*. Organizations which have a formal agreement or collaborative links with WHO:
- *African Development Bank (ADB, #00283)*;
- African Union;
- *Arab Gulf Programme for United Nations Development Organizations (AGFUND, #00971)*;
- *Asian Development Bank (ADB, #01422)*;
- *Colombo Plan for Cooperative Economic and Social Development in Asia and the Pacific (CPS, #04120)*;
- *Commonwealth Secretariat (#04362)*;
- *Council of Europe (CE, #04881)*;
- *European Bank for Reconstruction and Development (EBRD, #06315)*;
- *European Commission (EC, #06633)*;
- *FAO (#09260)*;
- *Gulf Health Council (GHC, #10830)*;
- *ILO (#11123)*;
- *Inter-American Development Bank (IDB, #11427)*;
- *International Atomic Energy Agency (IAEA, #12294)*;
- *International Bank for Reconstruction and Development (IBRD, #12317)*;
- *International Civil Aviation Organization (ICAO, #12581)*;
- *International Civil Defence Organization (ICDO, #12582)*;
- *International Committee of Military Medicine (ICMM, #12785)*;
- *International Court of Justice (ICJ, #13098)*;
- *International Fund for Agricultural Development (IFAD, #13692)*;
- *International Maritime Organization (IMO, #14102)*;
- *International Monetary Fund (IMF, #14180)*;
- *International Organization for Migration (IOM, #14454)*;
- *International Telecommunication Union (ITU, #15673)*;
- *Islamic Development Bank (IsDB, #16044)*;
- *Joint United Nations Programme on HIV/AIDS (UNAIDS, #16149)*;
- *League of Arab States (LAS, #16420)*;
- *OAS (#17629)*;
- *OECD (#17693)*;
- *OIE – World Organisation for Animal Health (#17703)*;
- *Organisation of Islamic Cooperation (OIC, #17813)*;
- *Pacific Community (SPC, #17942)*;
- *UNEP (#20299)*;
- *UNCTAD (#20285)*;
- *UNDP (#20292)*;
- *UNESCO (#20322)*;
- *UNHCR (#20327)*;
- *UNICEF (#20332)*;
- *UNIDO (#20336)*;
- *United Nations Economic Commission for Europe (UNECE, #20555)*;
- *United Nations Economic Commission for Latin America and the Caribbean (ECLAC, #20556)*;
- *United Nations Economic and Social Commission for Asia and the Pacific (ESCAP, #20557)*;
- *United Nations Economic and Social Commission for Western Asia (ESCWA, #20558)*;
- *United Nations Institute for Training and Research (UNITAR, #20576)*;
- *United Nations Office for Project Services (UNOPS, #20602)*;
- *United Nations Population Fund (UNFPA, #20612)*;
- *United Nations Relief and Works Agency for Palestine Refugees in the Near East (UNRWA, #20622)*;
- *United Nations Research Institute for Social Development (UNRISD, #20623)*;
- *Universal Postal Union (UPU, #20682)*;
- WIPO;
- *World Food Programme (WFP, #21510)*;
- *World Meteorological Organization (WMO, #21649)*.

/Joint bodies/ – With FAO, include: *Codex Alimentarius Commission (CAC, #04081)*; *Codex Committee on Milk and Milk Products*; *Joint FAO/WHO Expert Committee on Food Additives (JECFA, #16129)*. With FAO and UNEP: *Joint WHO/FAO/UNEP/UNCHS Panel of Experts on Environmental Management for Vector Control (PEEM, no recent information)*. With ILO: *Joint ILO/WHO Committee on Health of Seafarers (no recent information)*; *Global Coalition for Occupation Safety and Health (#10294)*. WHO/UNICEF/UNFPA Coordinating Committee on Health (CCH). With various other UN agencies: *African Programme for Onchocerciasis Control (APOC, no recent information)*; *Joint Group of Experts on the Scientific Aspects of Marine Environmental Protection (GESAMP, #16131)*; *Onchocerciasis Elimination Program for the Americas (OEPA, #17726)*. Includes: *WHO Patient Safety (#20940)*. Cooperation with: *European Atomic Energy Community (Euratom, inactive)*. Member of: *United Nations Sustainable Development Group (UNSDG, #20634)*; *Inter-Agency Standing Committee (IASC, #11393)*. Represented on: *United Nations System Chief Executives Board for Coordination (CEB, #20636)*. In addition, the following United Nations and other intergovernmental bodies, institutions and centres quote relations with WHO:
- *African and Malagasy Council for Higher Education (#00364)*;
- *African Training and Research Centre in Administration for Development (CAFRAD, #00486)*;
- *AGRHYMET Regional Centre (#00565)*;
- *Arab Centre for Medical Literature (ACML, no recent information)*;
- *Arab Company for Drug Industries and Medical Appliances (ACDIMA, #00926)*;
- *ASEAN (#01141)*;
- *Caribbean Food and Nutrition Institute (CFNI, inactive)*;
- *Center for Information on Migration in Latin America (#03643)*;
- *Centre Muraz (#03773)*;
- *Centro Panamericano de Ingenieria Sanitaria y Ciencias del Ambiente (CEPIS, no recent information)*;
- *Comisión Sudamericana para la Lucha contra la Fiebre Aftosa (COSALFA, #04143)*;
- *Commission du Danube (CD, #04210)*;
- *Commonwealth Health Development Programme (CHDP, inactive)*;
- *Communauté économique des pays des Grands Lacs (CEPGL, #04375)*;
- *Conference of European Statisticians (CES, #04600)*;
- *Convention on Long-range Transboundary Air Pollution (#04787)*;
- *Co-operation Group to Combat Drug Abuse and Illicit Trafficking in Drugs (Pompidou Group, #04796)*;
- *Coordination and Cooperation Organization for the Control of the Major Endemic Diseases (OCCGE, inactive)*;
- *Council of Arab Ministers of Health (#04861)*;
- *Eastern and Southern African Management Institute (ESAMI, #05254)*;
- *European Centre for Disaster Medicine (#06475)*;
- *European Centre for Social Welfare Policy and Research (European Centre, #06500)*;
- *European Health Committee (CDSP, inactive)*;
- *European and Mediterranean Plant Protection Organization (EPPO, #07773)*;
- *European Pharmacopoeia Commission (#08198)*;
- *Institute of Nutrition of Central America and Panama (INCAP, #11285)*;
- *Institute for Research, Extension and Training in Agriculture (IRETA, #11291)*;
- *Inter-Agency Working Group on Desertification (IAWGD, inactive)*;
- *Inter-American Conference on Social Security (ICSS, #11419)*;
- *ICDDR,B (#11051)*;
- *International Centre for Genetic Engineering and Biotechnology (ICGEB, #12494)*;
- *International Civil Service Commission (ICSC, #12587)*;
- *International Computing Centre (ICC, #12839)*;
- *International Criminal Police Organization – INTERPOL (ICPO-INTERPOL, #13110)*;
- *International Development Association (IDA, #13155)*;
- *International Development Research Centre (IDRC, #13162)*;
- *International Fund for Saving the Aral Sea (IFAS, #13694)*;
- *International Institute for Adult Education Methods (IIAEM, no recent information)*;
- *International Narcotics Control Board (INCB, #14212)*;
- *International Nuclear Information System (INIS, #14378)*;
- *International Olive Council (IOC, #14405)*;
- *International Organisation of Vine and Wine (OIV, #14435)*;
- *International Programme for the Development of Communication (IPDC, #14651)*;
- *International Trade Centre (ITC, #15703)*;
- *International Union for the Protection of Industrial Property (Paris Union, #15805)*;
- *IOC Sub-Commission for the Western Pacific (WESTPAC, see: #11496)*;
- *Joint Inspection Unit of the United Nations (JIU, #16133)*;
- *Marine Emergency Mutual Aid Centre (MEMAC, #16578)*;
- *Mediterranean Action Plan (MAP, #16638)*;
- *The Mediterranean Science Commission (CIESM, #16674)*;
- *Middle Eastern Regional Radioisotope Centre for the Arab Countries (MERRCAC, #16761)*;
- *Nordic Council (NC, #17256)*;
- *Nordic Council for Arctic Medical Research (NCAMR, inactive)*;
- *Nordic School of Public Health (NHV, inactive)*;
- *OPEC Fund for International Development (OFID, #17745)*;
- *Organization of Coordination for the Control of Endemic Diseases in Central Africa (#17860)*;
- *PAHO/WHO Health Emergencies Department (PHE, #18023)*;
- *Pan Arab Project for Child Development (PAPCHILD, no recent information)*;
- *Pierre Richet Institute (IPR, no recent information)*;
- *Programme on Man and the Biosphere (MAB, #18526)*;
- *Regional Organization for the Protection of the Marine Environment (ROPME, #18805)*;
- *Regional Wood Energy Development Programme in Asia (RWEDP, inactive)*;
- *SEAMEO TROPMED Regional Centre for Microbiology, Parasitology and Entomology (#19185)*;
- *SEAMEO TROPMED Regional Centre for Public Health, Hospital Administration, Environmental and Occupational Health (#19186)*;
- *Sistema Económico Latinoamericano (SELA, #19294)*;
- *Southeast Asian Ministers of Education Organization (SEAMEO, #19774)*;
- *UNESCO Regional Office for Education in the Arab States (UNEDBAS, #20320)*;
- *United Nations Economic Commission for Africa (ECA, #20554)*;
- *United Nations Framework Convention on Climate Change – Secretariat (UNFCCC, #20564)*;
- *United Nations International Emergency Network (UNIENET, no recent information)*;
- *United Nations Interregional Crime and Justice Research Institute (UNICRI, #20580)*;
- *United Nations Joint Staff Pension Fund (UNJSPF, #20581)*;
- *United Nations Office at Vienna (UNOV, #20604)*;
- *United Nations Scientific Committee on the Effects of Atomic Radiation (UNSCEAR, #20624)*;
- *United Nations Standing Committee on Youth for the Asia-Pacific Region (no recent information)*;
- *United Nations University (UNU, #20642)*;
- *United Nations Volunteers (UNV, #20650)*;
- *West and Central African Action Plan (WACAF, no recent information)*;
- *World Tourism Organization (UNWTO, #21861)*.

NGO Relations Maintains a wide variety of contacts and exchanges with NGOs. Informal relations may lead to development of collaboration on the basis of which an NGO may apply for admission into official relations. Principles governing relations between WHO and NGOs set out, inter alia: types of relations at global level; their development, criteria and procedure for admission of NGOs into official relations; relations with NGOs at regional and national levels; privileges and responsibilities of NGOs in their relationship with WHO. WHO Regional Offices have established similar arrangements. As of Feb 2020, 217 NGOs in official relations:
- *Action Against Hunger (#00086)*;
- *Aga Khan Foundation (AKF, #00545)*;
- *Alliance for Health Promotion (A4HP, #00687)*;
- *Alzheimer's Disease International (ADI, #00762)*;
- American Society for Reproductive Medicine (ASRM);
- *Amref Health Africa (#00806)*;
- *Association africaine des centrales d'achats de médicaments essentiels (ACAME, #02348)*;
- *Bill and Melinda Gates Foundation (BMGF)*;
- *Bloomberg Philanthropies*;
- *Bureau international des Médecins sans frontières (MSF International, #03366)*;
- *Caritas Internationalis (CI, #03580)*;
- *Christian Blind Mission (CBM)*;
- *Childhood Cancer International (CCI, #03871)*;
- *Cochrane Collaboration (#04078)*;
- *Commonwealth Pharmacists Association (CPA, #04357)*;
- *Consumers International (CI, #04773)*;
- *Corporate Accountability International*;
- *Council on Health Research for Development (COHRED, no recent information)*;
- *Council for International Organizations of Medical Sciences (CIOMS, #04905)*;
- *CropLife International (#04966)*;
- *Drugs for Neglected Diseases initiative (DNDi, #05137)*;
- *European Association for Injury Prevention and Safety Promotion (EuroSafe, #06083)*;
- *European Society for Medical Oncology (ESMO, #08648)*;
- *FDI – World Dental Federation (#09281)*;
- *Fédération internationale de Gynécologie et d'Obstétrique (FIGO, #09638)*;
- *Fédération mondiale du thermalisme et du climatisme (FEMTEC, #09692)*;
- *FHI 360*;
- *Framework Convention Alliance (FCA, #09981)*;
- *Fred Hollows Foundation*;
- *Global Alliance for Improved Nutrition (GAIN, #10202)*;
- *Global Alliance for Rabies Control (GARC)*;
- *Global Diagnostic Imaging, Healthcare IT, and Radiation Therapy Trade Association (DITTA, #10319)*;
- *Global Health Council (GHC, #10402)*;
- *Global Medical Technology Alliance (GMTA, #10470)*;
- *Global Network of People Living with HIV/AIDS (GNP+, #10494)*;
- *Global Self-Care Federation (GSCF, #10588)*;
- Grand Challenges Canada (GCC);
- *Health Action International (HAI, #10868)*;
- *Health On the Net Foundation (HON, #10887)*;
- *Health Technology Assessment International (HTAi, #10889)*;
- *Helen Keller International (HKI, #10902)*;
- *HelpAge International (#10904)*;
- *Human Rights in Mental Health (FGIP, #10988)*;
- *Humanity and Inclusion (HI, #10975)*;
- Humatem;
- *ICCBBA (#11042)*;
- *International Agency for the Prevention of Blindness (IAPB, #11597)*;
- *International AIDS Society (IAS, #11601)*;
- *International Air Transport Association (IATA, #11614)*;
- *International Alliance for Biological Standardization (IABS, #11622)*;
- *International Alliance of Patients' Organizations (IAPO, #11633)*;
- *International Alliance of Women (IAW, #11639)*;
- *Association Internationale des Technologistes Biomédicaux (ASSITEB-BIORIF, #02747)*;
- *International Association of Cancer Registries (IACR, #11753)*;
- *International Association for Child and Adolescent Psychiatry and Allied Professions (IACAPAP, #11766)*;
- *International Association for Dental Research (IADR, #11838)*;

– *International Association for Hospice and Palliative Care (IAHPC, #11941)*;
– *International Association of Logopedics and Phoniatrics (IALP, #12005)*;
– *International Association for the Scientific Study of Intellectual and Developmental Disabilities (IASSIDD, #12153)*;
– *International Association for the Study of Pain (IASP, #12206)*;
– *International Association for Suicide Prevention and Crisis Intervention (IASP, #12213)*;
– *International Baby Food Action Network (IBFAN, #12305)*;
– *International Bureau for Epilepsy (IBE, #12414)*;
– *International Catholic Committee of Nurses and Medico-social Assistants (#12451)*;
– *International Clearinghouse for Birth Defects Surveillance and Research (ICBDSR, #12594)*;
– *International College of Surgeons (ICS, #12650)*;
– *International Commission on Non-Ionizing Radiation Protection (ICNIRP, #12707)*;
– *International Commission on Occupational Health (ICOH, #12709)*;
– *International Commission on Radiological Protection (ICRP, #12724)*;
– *International Committee Monitoring Assisted Reproductive Technologies (ICMART, #12787)*;
– *International Confederation of Midwives (ICM, #12863)*;
– *International Council of Nurses (ICN, #13054)*;
– *International Council of Ophthalmology (ICO, #13057)*;
– *International Council for Standardization in Haematology (ICSH, #13078)*;
– *International Diabetes Federation (IDF, #13164)*;
– *International Epidemiological Association (IEA, #13287)*;
– *International Ergonomics Association (IEA, #13294)*;
– *International Eye Foundation (IEF, #13324)*;
– *International Federation on Ageing (IFA, #13345)*;
– *International Federation of Anti-Leprosy Associations (ILEP, #13355)*;
– *International Federation of Biomedical Laboratory Science (IFBLS, #13372)*;
– *International Federation of Clinical Chemistry and Laboratory Medicine (IFCC, #13392)*;
– *International Federation of Fertility Societies (IFFS, #13426)*;
– *International Federation of Health Information Management Associations (IFHIMA, #13441)*;
– *International Federation of Healthcare Engineering (IFHE, #13439)*;
– *International Federation for Medical and Biological Engineering (IFMBE, #13477)*;
– *International Federation of Medical Students' Associations (IFMSA, #13478)*;
– *International Federation of Oto-Rhino-Laryngological Societies (IFOS, #13496)*;
– *International Federation of Pharmaceutical Manufacturers and Associations (IFPMA, #13505)*;
– *International Federation of Surgical Colleges (IFSC, #13560)*;
– *International Food Policy Research Institute (IFPRI, #13622)*;
– *International Hospital Federation (IHF, #13812)*;
– *International Insulin Foundation (IIF, #13937)*;
– *International Lactation Consultant Association (ILCA)*;
– *International League Against Epilepsy (ILAE, #14013)*;
– *International Leprosy Association (ILA, #14029)*;
– *International Life Saving Federation (ILS, #14040)*;
– *International Medical Corps (IMC)*;
– *International Medical Informatics Association (IMIA, #14134)*;
– *International Network for Cancer Treatment and Research (INCTR, #14238)*;
– *International Network on Children's Health, Environment and Safety (INCHES, #14240)*;
– *International Network of Women Against Tobacco (INWAT, #14343)*;
– *International Occupational Hygiene Association (IOHA, #14391)*;
– *International Organization for Medical Physics (IOMP, #14453)*;
– *International Organization for Standardization (ISO, #14473)*;
– *International Pediatric Association (IPA, #14541)*;
– *International Pharmaceutical Federation (#14566)*;
– *International Pharmaceutical Students' Federation (IPSF, #14568)*;
– *International Physicians for the Prevention of Nuclear War (IPPNW, #14578)*;
– *International Planned Parenthood Federation (IPPF, #14589)*;
– *International Psycho-Oncology Society (IPOS, #14665)*;
– *International Rescue Committee (IRC, #14717)*;
– *International Society of Andrology (ISA, #14918)*;
– *International Society of Audiology (ISA, #14948)*;
– *International Society for Biomedical Research on Alcoholism (ISBRA, #14968)*;
– *International Society of Blood Transfusion (ISBT, #14979)*;
– *International Society for Burn Injuries (ISBI, #14986)*;
– *International Society of Doctors for the Environment (ISDE, #15065)*;
– *International Society for Environmental Epidemiology (ISEE, #15092)*;
– *International Society of Nephrology (ISN, #15294)*;
– *International Society of Orthopaedic Surgery and Traumatology (#15335)*;
– *International Society of Paediatric Oncology (#15339)*;
– *International Society of Physical and Rehabilitation Medicine (ISPRM, #15366)*;
– *International Society for Prevention of Child Abuse and Neglect (ISPCAN, #15385)*;
– *International Society for Prosthetics and Orthotics (ISPO, #15390)*;
– *International Society for Quality in Health Care (ISQua, #15405)*;
– *International Society of Radiographers and Radiological Technologists (ISRRT, #15410)*;
– *International Society of Radiology (ISR, #15412)*;
– *International Society for Telemedicine and e-Health (ISfTeH, #15504)*;
– *International Society on Thrombosis and Haemostasis (ISTH, #15511)*;
– *International Solid Waste Association (ISWA, #15567)*;
– *International Spinal Cord Society (ISCoS, #15581)*;
– *International Union against Sexually Transmitted Infections (IUSTI, #15751)*;
– *International Union Against Tuberculosis and Lung Disease (The Union, #15752)*;
– *International Union of Basic and Clinical Pharmacology (IUPHAR, #15758)*;
– *International Union for Health Promotion and Education (IUHPE, #15778)*;
– *International Union of Immunological Societies (IUIS, #15781)*;
– *International Union of Microbiological Societies (IUMS, #15794)*;
– *International Union of Nutritional Sciences (IUNS, #15796)*;
– *International Union of Psychological Science (IUPsyS, #15807)*;
– *International Union of Toxicology (IUTOX, #15824)*;
– *International Water Association (IWA, #15865)*;
– *International Women's Health Coalition (IWHC)*;
– *IntraHealth International*;
– *Iodine Global Network (IGN, #16004)*;
– *Movendi International (#16871)*;
– Italian Association of Friends of Raoul Follereau;
– KNCV Tuberculosis Foundation;
– *Knowledge Ecology International (KEI, #16200)*;
– *Lifting The Burden (#16469)*;
– *Lions Clubs International (LCI, #16485)*;
– March of Dimes Foundation;
– *Médecins du Monde – International (MDM, #16613)*;
– *Medical Women's International Association (MWIA, #16630)*;
– *Medicines for Europe (#16633)*;
– *Medicines for Malaria Venture (MMV, #16634)*;
– *Medicines Patent Pool (MPP, #16635)*;
– *Medicus Mundi International – Network Health for All (MMI, #16636)*;
– *Multiple Sclerosis International Federation (MSIF, #16899)*;
– *The Network: Towards Unity for Health (The Network: TUFH, #17060)*;
– *Nutrition International (#17627)*;
– *ORBIS International (#17786)*;
– *Organisation pour la prévention de la cécité (OPC)*;
– *Osteopathic International Alliance (OIA, #17910)*;
– *Oxfam GB*;
– *PATH (#18260)*;
– *Population Council (#18458)*;
– *Public Services International (PSI, #18572)*;
– *RAD-AID International*;
– *Pasteur Network (#18256)*;
– *Rotary International (RI, #18975)*;
– *Save the Children UK (SC UK)*;
– *Sightsavers International (#19270)*;
– *Thalassaemia International Federation (#20139)*;
– *The Transplantation Society (TTS, #20224)*;
– *Tropical Health and Education Trust (THET)*;
– *Union for International Cancer Control (UICC, #20415)*;
– *Union internationale des architectes (UIA, #20419)*;
– United States Pharmacopeial Convention (USP);
– *WaterAid (#20822)*;
– *Wellcome Trust*;
– World Association of Echinococcosis;
– *World Association of Societies of Pathology and Laboratory Medicine (WASPaLM, #21191)*;
– *World Blind Union (WBU, #21234)*;
– *World Cancer Research Fund International (WCRF)*;
– *World Confederation for Physical Therapy (WCPT, #21293)*;
– *World Council of Churches (WCC, #21320)*;
– *World Council of Optometry (WCO, #21335)*;
– *World Federation of Acupuncture-Moxibustion Societies (WFAS, #21405)*;
– *World Federation of Chinese Medicine Societies (WFCMS, #21419)*;
– *World Federation of Chiropractic (WFC, #21420)*;
– *World Federation of the Deaf (WFD, #21425)*;
– *World Federation of Hemophilia (WFH, #21437)*;
– *World Federation for Medical Education (WFME, #21454)*;
– *World Federation for Mental Health (WFMH, #21455)*;
– *World Federation of Neurology (WFN, #21461)*;
– *World Federation of Neurosurgical Societies (WFNS, #21466)*;
– *World Federation of Occupational Therapists (WFOT, #21468)*;
– *World Federation of Public Health Associations (WFPHA, #21476)*;
– *World Federation of Societies of Anaesthesiologists (WFSA, #21482)*;
– *World Federation for Ultrasound in Medicine and Biology (WFUMB, #21497)*;
– *World Heart Federation (WHF, #21562)*;
– *World Hepatitis Alliance (WHA, #21564)*;
– *World Hypertension League (WHL, #21574)*;
– *World Medical Association (WMA, #21646)*;
– *World Obesity (#21678)*;
– *World Organization of Family Doctors (WONCA, #21690)*;
– *World Plumbing Council (WPC, #21732)*;
– *World Psychiatric Association (WPA, #21741)*;
– *World Stroke Organization (WSO, #21831)*;
– *World Veterinary Association (WVA, #21901)*;
– *World Vision International (WVI, #21904)*;
– *Worldwide Hospice Palliative Care Alliance (WHPCA, #21924)*;
– *Worldwide Network for Blood and Marrow Transplantation (WBMT, #21929)*. [2022/XB3548/**B***]

♦ **WHO** World Hypnosis Organization (#21575)
♦ WHO/WPRO / see WHO Regional Office for the Western Pacific (#20947)
♦ **WHPA** World Health Professions Alliance (#21557)
♦ **WHPCA** Worldwide Hospice Palliative Care Alliance (#21924)
♦ WHP – World Health Partners (internationally oriented national body)
♦ WHRDIC / see Women Human Rights Defenders International Coalition (#21002)
♦ **WHRD** Women Human Rights Defenders International Coalition (#21002)
♦ WHRIA – Women's Human Rights International Association (internationally oriented national body)
♦ **WHRIN** Women and Harm Reduction International Network (#21000)
♦ **WHRMC** World Health Risk Management Centre (#21558)
♦ **WHSA** World Health Students' Alliance (#21559)
♦ **WHS Foundation** World Health Summit Foundation (#21560)
♦ WH – World Help (internationally oriented national body)
♦ WHW – Women Help Women (unconfirmed)
♦ WHW – World Heritage Watch (internationally oriented national body)
♦ **WHYCOS** World Hydrological Cycle Observing System (#21573)
♦ WHY – World Hunger Year (internationally oriented national body)
♦ **WIACLALS** West Indian Association for Commonwealth Literature and Language Studies (#20921)
♦ **WIACO** World Insulation and Acoustics Congress Organization (#21591)
♦ **WIA Europe** Women in Aerospace Europe (#20984)
♦ WIAMH – World Islamic Association for Mental Health (no recent information)
♦ WIAPS – Institute of Asia-Pacific Studies Waseda University (internationally oriented national body)
♦ **WIA** World Iodine Association (#21596)
♦ WIBC / see International Indoor Bowls Council (#13839)
♦ WIB – Wereldfederatie van Werknemers uit Industriële Bedrijven (inactive)
♦ **WIB** Women in Black (#20987)
♦ WICBE / see Information Centre for Bilingual and Plurilingual Education (#11195)
♦ WICBPE / see Information Centre for Bilingual and Plurilingual Education (#11195)
♦ WICE – World Industry Council for the Environment (inactive)
♦ WICS – World Islamic Call Society (inactive)
♦ **WIC** Wayfarer International Committee (#20839)
♦ **WIC** Web Intelligence Consortium (#20847)
♦ **WIC** West India Committee (#20920)
♦ WIC – World Igbo Congress (internationally oriented national body)
♦ WIDA – World Inclusive Dance Association (unconfirmed)

♦ WIDE+ 20951

Coordination WIDE Office, Rue de la Sablonnière 18, 1000 Brussels, Belgium. T. +3225459070. Fax +3225127342. E-mail: info@wide-network.org – wide-info@gn.apc.org.
URL: https://wideplus.org/

History 1985, Amsterdam (Netherlands). Founded in response to the 1985 UN Women's Conference in Nairobi (Kenya). Dissolved 2011; reestablished as a formal network, 2015, Brussels (Belgium). Former names and other names: *Network Women in Development Europe (WIDE)* – former; *Mujeres en el Desarrollo en Europa* – former. Registration: Banque-Carrefour des Entreprises, No/ID: 631932333, Belgium, Brussels. **Aims** Promote collective *feminist* movement building in Europe. **Structure** Caucus; Board; Working Groups. **Languages** Dutch, English, French, German, Spanish. **Staff** 2.00 FTE, paid; 15.00 FTE, voluntary. **Activities** Advocacy/lobbying/activism; awareness raising; capacity building; networking/liaising. **Events** *Annual general assembly and conference / Annual General Assembly* Brussels (Belgium) 2011, *Annual general assembly and conference / Annual General Assembly* Bucharest (Romania) 2010, *Annual general assembly and conference / Annual General Assembly* Basel (Switzerland) 2009, *Annual General Assembly* The Hague (Netherlands) 2008, *Annual general assembly and conference* The Hague (Netherlands) 2008. **Publications** *WIDE E-newsletter* (4 a year). *WIDE Policy Papers* – series. Briefing and position papers; reports; manuals; information sheets. **Members** Individuals (40); Organizations (16). Membership countries not specified. **NGO Relations** Member of (5): *Association for Women's Rights in Development (AWID, #02980)*; *GLOBAL RESPONSIBILITY – Austrian Platform for Development and Humanitarian Aid*; *Informal Working Group on Gender and Trade (IWGGT, no recent information)*; *Women in Migration Network (WIMN, #21008)*; *Women's Working Group on Financing for Development (WWG on FfD, #21036)*. Supports (1): *Global Call for Action Against Poverty (GCAP, #10263)*. [2021.09.01/XF0769/y/**F**]

♦ WiDEN – WIne Distilleries European Network (unconfirmed)
♦ Wider Church Ministries (internationally oriented national body)
♦ Wider Quaker Fellowship (see: #10004)
♦ WIDE / see WIDE+ (#20951)
♦ **WIDF** Women's International Democratic Federation (#21022)
♦ WIDOT – World Information For Donation of Organs and Tissues Donation (inactive)
♦ Widows Rights International (internationally oriented national body)
♦ WID – World Institute on Disability (internationally oriented national body)
♦ **WIEF Foundation** World Islamic Economic Forum Foundation (#21597)
♦ **WIEGO** Women in Informal Employment: Globalizing and Organizing (#21003)
♦ WIELD Foundation / see Moremi Initiative for Women's Leadership in Africa
♦ Wiener Institut für Entwicklungsfragen und Zusammenarbeit / see Vienna Institute for International Dialogue and Cooperation

- ♦ Wiener Institut für Internationalen Dialog und Zusammenarbeit (internationally oriented national body)
- ♦ Wiener Institut für Internationale Wirtschaftsvergleiche (internationally oriented national body)
- ♦ Wiener Wiesenthal Institut für Holocaust-Studies (internationally oriented national body)
- ♦ **WIETE** World Institute for Engineering and Technology Education (#21587)
- ♦ WIFE – Women's International Fund for Education (internationally oriented national body)

♦ Wi-Fi Alliance 20952

CEO 10900-B Stonelake Boulevard, Ste 126, Austin TX 78759, USA. T. +15124989434. Fax +15124989435.
URL: http://www.wi-fi.org/

History 1999, USA. Current bylaws approved Jun 2016. Registered in the State of California (USA), 2012. **Aims** Provide a highly-effective collaboration forum; support growth of the Wi-Fi industry; lead industry growth with *new technology* specifications and programs; support industry-agreed standards; deliver great product connectivity through testing and certification. **Structure** Board of Directors; Executive Team. **Finance** Sources: members' dues. **Activities** Certification/accreditation; events/meetings. **Events** *Member Meeting* Chicago, IL (USA) 2022, *Member Meeting* Singapore (Singapore) 2022, *Member Meeting* Lisbon (Portugal) 2020, *Asia-Pacific Meeting* Bangkok (Thailand) 2017, *Member Meeting* Madrid (Spain) 2016. **Members** Companies. Membership countries not specified. [2020/XJ5232/**C**]

- ♦ WIFLAC – Writers International and Friends of Literature and Culture Association (see: #11102)
- ♦ **WIFSA** World Inline Figure Skating Association (#21584)
- ♦ **WIFT International** Women in Film and Television International (#20995)
- ♦ **WIF** Women in Film (#20994)
- ♦ **WIF** Women's International Forum (#21023)
- ♦ **WIF** World Intellectual Forum (#21592)
- ♦ **WIF** Worldview International Foundation (#21903)
- ♦ WIGJ / see Women's Initiatives for Gender Justice (#21021)
- ♦ **WIGOS** WMO Integrated Global Observing System (#20978)
- ♦ WIGSAT / see Women in Global Science and Technology Network (#20999)
- ♦ Wihuri Foundation for International Prizes (internationally oriented national body)
- ♦ Wihurin kansainvälisten palkintojen rahasto (internationally oriented national body)
- ♦ **WIIS** Women In International Security (#21004)
- ♦ WIIW – Wiener Institut für Internationale Wirtschaftsvergleiche (internationally oriented national body)
- ♦ **WIKF** Wado International Karate-Do Federation (#20813)

♦ Wikileaks 20953

Founder BOX 4080, Australia Post Office, Univ of Melbourne Branch, Melbourne VIC 3052, Australia.
URL: http://wikileaks.ch/

History 2007. **Aims** Bring important *news* and *information* to the public, based on principles including defence of *freedom* of speech and *media* publishing, the improvement of our common historical record and the support of the *rights* of all people to create new history. **Finance** Donations. **Activities** Provides an innovative, secure and anonymous way for sources to leak information to Wikileaks journalists; develops and adapts technologies to support these activities. Work procedure: accepts (but does not solicit) anonymous sources of information; analyzes and verifies the material and write a news piece about it describing its significance to society; publishes both the news story and the original material in order to enable readers to analyse the story in the context of the original source material; does not censor news, but may remove or significantly delay publication of some identifying details from original documents to protect innocent people. [2010/XJ2166/**F**]

♦ WikiRate Project 20954

Chairman address not obtained. E-mail: info@wikirate.org.
URL: https://wikirateproject.org/

History Launched 2013. Registered in accordance with German law; Registered as a UK Registered Charity – 1155894; Registered in the US as a 501(c)(3) nonprofit organization. **Aims** Spur *corporations* to be transparent and responsive by making *data* about their social and *environmental* impacts accessible, comparable and free for all. **Activities** Knowledge management/information dissemination. **NGO Relations** Member of: *World Benchmarking Alliance (WBA, #21228)*. [2018/XM8562/**F**]

- ♦ WILA – Workshop on Immigrant Languages in the Americas (meeting series)
- ♦ WILCIC – Women's International Liaison Committee for International Cooperation (inactive)
- ♦ **WiLDAF-AO** Women in Law and Development in Africa-Afrique de l'Ouest (#21005)
- ♦ WildAid / see Wildlife Alliance (#20957)
- ♦ WildAid (internationally oriented national body)
- ♦ Wildcare Africa Trust (internationally oriented national body)
- ♦ Wildcat Foundation (internationally oriented national body)
- ♦ Wild Chimpanzee Foundation (internationally oriented national body)
- ♦ WiLDCOAST (internationally oriented national body)
- ♦ Wilderness Foundation Africa (internationally oriented national body)
- ♦ Wilderness Medical Society (internationally oriented national body)
- ♦ Wilderness Society (internationally oriented national body)

♦ Wild Europe Foundation 20955

Secretariat 1 Pembridge Crescent, London, W11 3DT, UK. T. +447793551542. E-mail: info@wildeurope.org.
URL: http://www.wildeurope.org/

History 2005. Formally recognized in a Resolution of *European Parliament (EP, #08146)*, Feb 2009, as a Foundation. **Aims** Promote a coordinated strategy for protection and restoration of large natural *ecosystems*. **Structure** Executive Committee. **Activities** Advocacy/lobbying/activism. **NGO Relations** Member of (1): *Global Rewilding Alliance (GRA, #10579)*. [2022.10.23/XM5050/f/**F**]

♦ WILD Foundation (WILD) 20956

Pres 717 Poplar Ave, Boulder CO 80304, USA. T. +13034428811. Fax +13034428877. E-mail: info@wild.org.
URL: http://www.wild.org/

History 1974, New York, NY (USA). Former names and other names: *IWLF* – former; *International Wilderness Leadership Foundation (WILD)* – former. **Aims** Expand and empower global coalitions that defend Earth's life-saving wilderness. **Structure** Board of Directors; Advisors (11); Congress Advisory Boards and Officers (appointed for each Congress). **Languages** English. **Staff** 6.00 FTE, paid. Several part-time, paid; several contracted, paid. **Finance** Sources: fundraising. **Activities** Events/meetings; projects/programmes. **Events** *WILD – World Wilderness Congress* Jaipur (India) 2020, *World Wilderness Congress – WILD* Salamanca (Spain) 2013, *World Congressw / World Wilderness Congress – WWC* Mérida (Mexico) 2009, *World congress / World Wilderness Congress – WWC* Anchorage, AK (USA) 2005, *World congress / World Wilderness Congress – WWC* Port Elizabeth (South Africa) 2001. **Publications** *E-leaf* (4 a year) – electronic newsletter; *International Journal of Wilderness* (3 a year). *Wilderness Management* (1990, 2002, 2009). Congress proceedings.
Members Associates in 21 countries:
Australia, Botswana, Canada, Finland, Germany, India, Italy, Mexico, Mozambique, Namibia, Nepal, New Zealand, Norway, Pakistan, Philippines, Russia, South Africa, UK, USA, Zambia, Zimbabwe.
NGO Relations Partner of (1): *Global Rewilding Alliance (GRA, #10579)*. Special links with: *Conservation International (CI)*. Also cooperates with many of national and international organizations interested in the field. Member of: *International Union for Conservation of Nature and Natural Resources (IUCN, #15766)* Wilderness Task Force. [2022.05.04/XF0690/f/**F**]

- ♦ Wildfowl and Wetlands Trust (internationally oriented national body)

♦ Wildlife Alliance 20957

Contact 1441 Broadway, Fifth Floor, New York NY 10018, USA. T. +16465695860. E-mail: info@wildlifealliance.org.
URL: https://www.wildlifealliance.org/

History 1994. Founded on the initiative of Suwanna Gauntlett. Former names and other names: *Global Survival Network (GSN)* – former (1994 to 1999); *WildAid* – former (1999 to 2007). **Aims** Combat *deforestation*, wildlife *extinction*, *climate change* and poverty in the Southeast Asian tropical belt by partnering with local communities and governments. **Structure** Headquarters in New York NY (USA); regional office in Phnom Penh (Cambodia). **Languages** English, Mon-Khmer languages. **Staff** Headquarters: 3 FTE, paid; voluntary. Cambodia: about 180 FTE. **Finance** Donations; grants; individual contributions; government contracts. Annual budget: about US$ 4,100,000. **Activities** Projects/programmes; training/education; awareness raising. **Publications** *Wildlife Alliance Electronic Newsletter*. Annual Report. **NGO Relations** Member of: *International Tiger Coalition (ITC)*; *International Union for Conservation of Nature and Natural Resources (IUCN, #15766)*; *NGO Forum on Cambodia (#17124)*. [2018.09.04/XF6899/**F**]

♦ Wild for Life Campaign (Wild for Life) 20958

Address not obtained.
URL: http://wildfor.life/

History Launched Jun 2016. **Aims** Raise awareness, enact and enforce stronger laws, and step up support to local communities' efforts to stop the illegal trade in wildlife.
Members Founding Partners (4):
Secretariat of the Convention on International Trade in Endangered Species of Wild Fauna and Flora (CITES Secretariat, #19199); *UNDP (#20292)*; *UNEP (#20299)*; *United Nations Office on Drugs and Crime (UNODC, #20596)*.
Collaborators include:
Connect4Climate (#04680); *Global Environment Facility (GEF, #10346)*; *Great Apes Survival Project (GRASP, #10699)*; *International Union for Conservation of Nature and Natural Resources (IUCN, #15766)*; *Save the Elephants (STE)*; *Secretariat of the Convention on the Conservation of Migratory Species of Wild Animals (UNEP/CMS, #19198)*; *The Nature Conservancy (TNC)*; *The World Bank Group (#21218)*; *TRAFFIC International (#20196)*; *UNICEF (#20332)*; UN Sustainable Development Goals (UNSDG). [2020/XM5104/y/**F**]

- ♦ Wildlife Conservation Global (internationally oriented national body)
- ♦ Wildlife Conservation International / see Wildlife Conservation Society
- ♦ Wildlife Conservation International Society / see Wildlife Conservation Society
- ♦ Wildlife Conservation Network (internationally oriented national body)
- ♦ Wildlife Conservation Society (internationally oriented national body)
- ♦ WildlifeDirect (internationally oriented national body)

♦ Wildlife Disease Association (WDA) 20959

Exec Manager 8333 Waters Road, Moorpark CA 93021-9759, USA. T. +17858659233. E-mail: exec.manager@wildlifedisease.org.
URL: http://www.wildlifedisease.org/

History 1951, Milwaukee, WI (USA). Founded during the 16th North American Wildlife Conference. Formal constitution adopted, 1959. Former names and other names: *Wildlife Disease Committee* – former (1951 to 1952). **Aims** Promote healthy wildlife and ecosystems, biodiversity conservation and environmentally sustainable solutions to One Health challenges. **Structure** Parent body includes Sections (7). **Languages** English. **Staff** None. **Finance** Sources: members' dues; sale of publications. **Events** *Annual International Conference* Madison, WI (USA) 2022, *Conference* Cuenca (Spain) 2021, *Conference* Tahoe City, CA (USA) 2019, *Annual Conference* Cortland, NY (USA) 2016, *Biennial Latin America Conference* Bogota (Colombia) 2015. **Publications** *Journal of Wildlife Diseases* (4 a year).
Members Individuals in 80 countries and territories:
Algeria, Andorra, Antigua-Barbuda, Argentina, Australia, Austria, Bangladesh, Belgium, Belize, Bhutan, Bolivia, Botswana, Brazil, Canada, Chile, China, Colombia, Costa Rica, Croatia, Cyprus, Czechia, Denmark, Ecuador, Egypt, Estonia, Finland, France, Germany, Greece, Grenada, Guatemala, Hong Kong, Hungary, Iceland, India, Indonesia, Iran Islamic Rep, Ireland, Israel, Italy, Jamaica, Japan, Kenya, Korea Rep, Malaysia, Mexico, Myanmar, Nepal, Netherlands, New Zealand, Nigeria, Norway, Peru, Philippines, Poland, Portugal, Qatar, Réunion, Romania, Russia, Serbia, Singapore, Slovakia, Slovenia, South Africa, Spain, Sri Lanka, St Kitts-Nevis, Sweden, Switzerland, Syrian AR, Taiwan, Thailand, Tunisia, Uganda, UK, United Arab Emirates, Uruguay, USA, Vietnam. [2022.02.02/XD4719/v/**C**]

- ♦ Wildlife Disease Committee / see Wildlife Disease Association (#20959)

♦ Wildlife Justice Commission (WJC) 20960

Exec Dir Johan de Wittlaan 7, 2517 JR The Hague, Netherlands. T. +31702051050. E-mail: info@wildlifejustice.org.
URL: http://wildlifejustice.org/

History 2015, Netherlands. Registered in accordance with Dutch law. **Aims** Disrupt and help dismantle transnational criminal networks trading in wildlife, timber and fish by collecting evidence and turning it into accountability. **Structure** Supervisory Board; Management Team; Advisory Council. **Staff** 56.00 FTE, paid. **Activities** Advocacy/lobbying/activism; networking/liaising; research/documentation. **Consultative Status** Consultative status granted from: *UNEP (#20299)*. **NGO Relations** Partners include: *Adessium Foundation*; *Fondation Segré*; *Oak Foundation*; *Wildcat Foundation*; *World Wide Fund for Nature (WWF, #21922)*. [2021.09.07/XM7218/**C**]

- ♦ Wildlife Preservation Trust International / see EcoHealth Alliance
- ♦ Wildlife Protection Solutions (internationally oriented national body)
- ♦ Wildlife Rehabilitation Council / see International Wildlife Rehabilitation Council, The (#15885)
- ♦ Wildlife Trust / see EcoHealth Alliance
- ♦ **Wild for Life** Wild for Life Campaign (#20958)
- ♦ Wild Migration – Migratory Wildlife Network (internationally oriented national body)

♦ Wild Salmon Center 20961

Pres/CEO Jean Vollum Natural Capital Center, 721 NW Ninth Ave, Ste 300, Portland OR 97209, USA. T. +15032221804. Fax +15032221805. E-mail: info@wildsalmoncenter.org.
URL: http://www.wildsalmoncenter.org/

History Founded 1992. **Aims** Protect Pacific salmon, steelhead, char and trout stocks and their ecosystems; identify the last, best Pacific salmon habitat; devise practical and scientifically sound strategies to protect forever these places and their biodiversity. **Structure** Board. Regional offices (5): Forks WA (USA); Seattle WA (USA); Kamchatka (Russia); Moscow (Russia); Magadan (Russia). **Activities** Projects/programmes; events/meetings. **Publications** *International Journal of Salmon Conservation*. Annual report.
Members in 4 countries:
Canada, Japan, Russia, USA. [2018/XE4506/**E**]

- ♦ Wildscreen (internationally oriented national body)
- ♦ Wild Welfare (internationally oriented national body)
- ♦ WILD / see WILD Foundation (#20956)
- ♦ **WILD** WILD Foundation (#20956)
- ♦ **WIL** European Network for Women in Leadership (#08034)

♦ Wilfried Martens Centre for European Studies (Martens Centre) ... 20962

Main Office Rue du Commerce 20, 1000 Brussels, Belgium. T. +3223008004. Fax +3223008011. E-mail: info@martenscentre.eu.
URL: http://www.martenscentre.eu/

History 2007. Set up as the political foundation of *European People's Party (EPP, #08185)*. Current title adopted in honour of Belgian and EPP politician Wilfried Martens (1936-2013). Former names and other names: *Centre for European Studies (CES)* – former; *WMCES* – alias. Registration: No/ID: 0881.780.973, Belgium. **Aims** Advance centre-right thought; contribute to formulation of EU and national policies; serve as a framework for national political foundations and academics; stimulate public debate about the EU. **Structure** General Assembly; Executive Board; Academic Council; Fundraising Committee. **Languages** English. **Staff** 20.00 FTE, paid. **Finance** Grant from *European Parliament (EP, #08146)*; fundraising. **Activities** Events/meetings. **Events** *European Ideas Forum* Brussels (Belgium) 2022, *Transatlantic Think Tank Conference (TTTC)* 2021, *Conference on 15 years after accession: the Visegrad countries in the European Union* Brussels (Belgium) 2019, *Conference on Decoded Democracy : Today's Challenges in the Cyber Domain* Brussels (Belgium) 2019, *High-Level Workshop on Towards a Decentralised Eurozone* Brussels (Belgium) 2019. **Publications** *The European View* (2 a year) – policy journal; *European Factbook* (regular). Policy briefs; research papers; collaborative publications.

Members Project partners in 35 countries:
Albania, Austria, Belarus, Belgium, Bosnia-Herzegovina, Bulgaria, Croatia, Cyprus, Czechia, Estonia, Finland, France, Germany, Greece, Hungary, Ireland, Italy, Lebanon, Lithuania, Malta, Netherlands, North Macedonia, Norway, Poland, Portugal, Romania, Serbia, Slovakia, Slovenia, Spain, Sweden, Switzerland, UK, Ukraine, USA.
Included in the above, 3 organizations listed in this Yearbook:
Hanns Seidel Foundation; *Jarl Hjalmarson Foundation*; *Konrad Adenauer Foundation (KAF)*.
NGO Relations Member of (1): *European Policy Centre (EPC, #08240)*. Cooperates with (1): *Robert Schuman Institute for Developing Democracy in Central and Eastern Europe (RSI, #18958)*. [2022/XJ1823/y/**E**]

♦ The William and Flora Hewlett Foundation (internationally oriented national body)
♦ William J Clinton Foundation (internationally oriented national body)
♦ William R Hewlett Foundation / see The William and Flora Hewlett Foundation
♦ Williamsburg Meetings (meeting series)
♦ Willing Workers on Organic Farms / see World-Wide Opportunities on Organic Farms (#21931)

♦ Willis Research Network (WRN) 20963

Chairman 51 Lime Str, London, EC3M 7DQ, UK. T. +442031248345.
URL: http://www.willisresearchnetwork.com/
History 2006. **Aims** Lead the science and understanding of extreme events through focused, transparent and collaborative research. **Activities** Funds long-term research into natural and manmade catastrophes across various disciplines. **Events** *Workshop on metrics and methodologies of estimation of extreme climate events* Paris (France) 2010. **Publications** Academic research papers and reports. **Members** Institutions (40) in 10 countries. Membership countries not specified. [2010.11.24/XJ1756/**F**]

♦ Wilmington College Peace Resource Center (internationally oriented national body)
♦ **WILPF** Women's International League for Peace and Freedom (#21024)
♦ WIMA / see Pacific Women in Maritime Association (#18011)
♦ WIM Association / see Wine in Moderation (#20967)
♦ **WIMA** Women's International Motorcycle Association (#21026)

♦ WiMAX Forum 20964

Pres/CEO 9009 SE Adams St, Ste 2259, Clackamas OR 97015-2259, USA. T. +18586050978. Fax +18584616041. E-mail: alessandra.rocha@wimaxforum.org – membership@wimaxforum.org.
URL: http://www.wimaxforum.org/
History Jun 2001. **Aims** Accelerate the adoption, deployment and expansion of WiMAX, AeroMACS, and WiGRID technologies across the globe while facilitating roaming agreements, sharing best practices and certifying products. **Structure** Board of Directors; Officers; Working Groups; Technical Steering Committee. **Activities** Certification/accreditation; events/meetings; knowledge management/information dissemination. **Events** *Global Congress* Amsterdam (Netherlands) 2010, *Global congress* Amsterdam (Netherlands) 2009, *Forum Americas* Fort Lauderdale, FL (USA) 2009, *Congress Asia* Singapore (Singapore) 2009, *Congress Asia* Singapore (Singapore) 2008. **Members** Operators, component and equipment companies (over 580). Membership countries not specified. [2021.08.31/XJ0129/**E**]

♦ WIM Network / see Red de Mujeres Latinoamericanas y del Caribe en Gestion de Organizaciones (#18723)
♦ **WIMN** Women in Migration Network (#21008)
♦ **WIMRA** Women's International Match Racing Association (#21025)
♦ **WIM** Wine in Moderation (#20967)
♦ **WINA** World Instant Noodles Association (#21586)
♦ WINBAN – Windward Island Banana Growers Association (inactive)
♦ WIN Consortium / see Worldwide Innovative Networking (#21927)

♦ WindEurope 20965

CEO Rue Belliard 40, 1040 Brussels, Belgium. T. +3222131811. Fax +3222131890. E-mail: info@windeurope.org.
URL: http://windeurope.org/
History 1982. Former names and other names: *European Wind Energy Association (EWEA)* – former (1982 to 2016); *Association européenne de l'énergie éolienne* – former (1982 to 2016); *Asociación Europea para la Energia Eólica* – former (1982 to 2016); *Europäischer Windenergieverband* – former (1982 to 2016). Registration: Banque-Carrefour des Entreprises, No/ID: 0476.915.445, Start date: 12 Dec 2001, Belgium; EU Transparency Register, No/ID: 19920706471-21, Start date: 24 Aug 2011. **Aims** Facilitate national and international policies and initiatives that strengthen the development of European and global wind energy markets, infrastructure and technology in order to achieve a more *sustainable* and cleaner energy future. **Structure** General Assembly; Board of Directors; Secretariat. **Languages** English, French. **Staff** 26.00 FTE, paid. **Finance** Members' dues. **Activities** Events/meetings; research/documentation. **Events** *WINDEUROPE Annual Event* Copenhagen (Denmark) 2023, *WINDEUROPE Annual Event* Bilbao (Spain) 2022, *Technology Workshop* Brussels (Belgium) 2022, *Electric City Conference* Copenhagen (Denmark) 2021, *Global Summit* Hamburg (Germany) 2020. **Publications** *Wind Directions* (6 a year) – magazine. Annual Report. Reports.
Members Corporate; Affiliate; Individual. Members in 45 countries and territories:
Argentina, Austria, Belgium, Bulgaria, Canada, China, Croatia, Cyprus, Czechia, Denmark, Estonia, Finland, France, Germany, Greece, Ireland, Isle of Man, Israel, Italy, Japan, Kazakhstan, Kenya, Korea Rep, Kuwait, Latvia, Lithuania, Luxembourg, Mexico, Monaco, Netherlands, New Zealand, Norway, Poland, Portugal, Romania, Russia, Spain, Sweden, Switzerland, Tajikistan, Türkiye, UK, Ukraine, United Arab Emirates, USA.
Consultative Status Consultative status granted from: *UNEP (#20299)*. **IGO Relations** Accredited by (1): *United Nations Framework Convention on Climate Change – Secretariat (UNFCCC, #20564)*. Cooperates with (2): *International Bank for Reconstruction and Development (IBRD, #12317)*; *International Energy Agency (IEA, #13270)*. Associated with Department of Global Communications of the United Nations. **NGO Relations** Member of (5): *Associations and Conference Forum (AC Forum, #02909)*; *Global Wind Energy Council (GWEC, #10656)*; *Industry4Europe (#11181)*; *International Network for Sustainable Energy (INFORSE, #14331)*; *RE-Source Platform (RE-Source, #18916)* (Founding). Instrumental in setting up (2): *Alliance for Rural Electrification (ARE, #00719)*; *European Technology and Innovation Platform on Wind Energy (ETIPWind, #08885)*. Sponsoring Supportive member of: *European Forum for Renewable Energy Sources (EUFORES, #07329)*. [2021/XD7070/**D**]

♦ Winds of Hope Foundation (internationally oriented national body)
♦ Windsor International, University of Windsor (internationally oriented national body)
♦ Windward Island Banana Growers Association (inactive)

♦ Windward Islands Farmers' Association (WINFA) 20966

Pres PO Box 817, Kingstown, St Vincent-Grenadines. T. +18094562704. Fax +18094561383.
URL: http://www.winfacaribbean.org/
History 1987, St Vincent-Grenadines. Also referred to as *West Indies Farmers' Association*. **Aims** Create links between farmers' organizations at regional level; promote democratic participation of farmers at all levels of the *development* process; collaborate with national organizations to improve the socio-economic well-being of farmers; contribute to the building of awareness and solidarity on farming issues amongst farming communities and organizations. **Structure** Board of Directors; Operations Committee. **Finance** Funded mainly through grants from international funding agencies. Budget (annual): between US$ 400,000 and US$ 600,000. **Activities** Training workshops; orientation workshops; inter-island exchange programme; regional meetings; television and radio programmes. **Events** *Negociations between Caribbean Community and Lome* Trinidad-Tobago 1997. **Publications** *WINFA Bulletin* (3 a year).
Members National farmers associations in 5 countries and territories:
Dominica, Grenada, Martinique, St Lucia, St Vincent-Grenadines.
NGO Relations Member of: *Caribbean Policy Development Centre (CPDC, #03540)*; *La Via Campesina (#20765)*. [2009/XF2745/**F**]

♦ WinD – Women in Dialogue (internationally oriented national body)
♦ WINE – Conference on Web and Internet Economics (meeting series)
♦ WIne Distilleries European Network (unconfirmed)

♦ Wine in Moderation (WIM) 20967

Secretary General Av des Arts 43, 5th floor, 1040 Brussels, Belgium. T. +3222309970. Fax +3225130218. E-mail: info@wineinmoderation.eu.
Communication and Project manager address not obtained.
Community Manager address not obtained.
URL: http://www.wineinmoderation.eu/
History 2011. Founded by European wine sector. Former names and other names: *Wine in Moderation – Art de Vivre (WIM Association)* – full title. Registration: AISBL/IVZW, Belgium. **Aims** Coordinate Wine in Moderation programme and expand its reach and impact throughout the world. **Structure** Board; Working Committees; Advisory Groups; Secretariat. **Languages** English. **Staff** 2.50 FTE, paid. **Finance** Sources: members' dues; revenue from activities/projects; sponsorship. Supported by: *European Union (EU, #08967)*. **Activities** Events/meetings; knowledge management/information dissemination. **Publications** Reports; leaflets; brochures; postcards.
Members Effective; Observer. National coordinators (16) in 15 countries:
Argentina, Austria, Chile, Colombia, France, Germany, Greece, Hungary, Italy, Lithuania, Netherlands, Portugal, Spain, Sweden, Uruguay.
Effective European federation:
Comité européen des entreprises vins (CEEV, #04157).
Observer members (4):
European Confederation of Independent Winegrowers (ECIW, #06706); Fédération Française des Vins d'Apéritif (FFVA); *General Confederation of Agricultural Cooperatives in the European Union (#10107)*; University of Reims – Programme Vin and Droit.
NGO Relations Associated Partners: *Confederation of National Associations of Hotels, Restaurants, Cafés and Similar Establishments in the European Union and European Economic Area (HOTREC, #04569)*; *European Advertising Standards Alliance (EASA, #05829)*; *Fédération européenne du verre d'emballage (FEVE, #09583)*; *Fédération Internationale des Confréries Bachiques (FICB, #09623)*; *Fundación Dieta Mediterranea (FDM)*; *International Federation of Wine and Spirits Journalists and Writers (#13577)*; *Réseau Européen des Villes du Vin (RECEVIN, #18881)*; *Euro-Toques International (ETI, #09190)*; *FIVS (#09789)*. [2022.02.21/XJ8691/y/**F**]

♦ Wine in Moderation – Art de Vivre / see Wine in Moderation (#20967)
♦ **WINE** Women's Information Network of Europe (#21020)
♦ **WINFA** Windward Islands Farmers' Association (#20966)

♦ WINFOCUS 20968

Gen Sec Via degli Olivetani 10/12, 20123 Milan MI, Italy. Fax +39256561788. E-mail: secretariat@winfocus.org.
Headquarters Via Appiani 12, 20121 Milan MI, Italy. E-mail: admin@winfocus.org.
URL: http://www.winfocus.org/
History Previous full title: *World Interactive Network Focuses on Critical UltraSound*. **Aims** Promote and spread point-of-care ultrasound into clinical practice, so as to improve primary, emergency and critical care provided in all extra-hospital and in-hospital scenarios. **Structure** Board of Directors. **Activities** National and world congresses. **Events** *World Congress* Dubai (United Arab Emirates) 2019, *World Congress* Madrid (Spain) 2018, *World Congress* Kuala Lumpur (Malaysia) 2014, *World Congress* Hong Kong (Hong Kong) 2013, *World Congress* Barcelona (Spain) 2012. [2017/XJ7842/**F**]

♦ Wings of Hope (internationally oriented national body)
♦ WINGS – Women's International News Gathering Service (internationally oriented national body)
♦ **WINGS** Worldwide Initiatives for Grantmaker Support (#21926)
♦ **WINHEC** World Indigenous Nations Higher Education Consortium (#21578)
♦ WIN International Associates – World in Need (internationally oriented national body)
♦ WIN International – Women in Need International (internationally oriented national body)
♦ WIN – International Workshop on Weak Interactions and Neutrinos (meeting series)
♦ **WINIR** World Interdisciplinary Network for Institutional Research (#21594)
♦ WINNET Europe – European Association of Women Resource Centres (no recent information)
♦ Winrock International (internationally oriented national body)
♦ Winrock International Institute for Agricultural Development / see Winrock International
♦ WINS – Women in Neurosurgery (internationally oriented national body)
♦ **WINS** World Institute for Nuclear Security (#21588)
♦ **WINTA** World Indigenous Tourism Alliance (#21581)
♦ Winter Cities Institute (unconfirmed)
♦ Winter Cycling Federation (internationally oriented national body)
♦ WinVisible – Women With Visible and Invisible Disabilities (internationally oriented national body)
♦ WIN – Watchman International Network (internationally oriented national body)
♦ **WIN** Water Integrity Network (#20830)
♦ **WIN** Whistleblowing International Network (#20932)
♦ WinWin Afrique (unconfirmed)
♦ **WIN** Women in Nuclear (#21009)
♦ WIN – Women's Intercultural Network (internationally oriented national body)
♦ **WIN** Women's International Network (#21027)
♦ **WIN** Women's International Networking (#21028)
♦ WIN / see World Network of Indigenous Peoples and Local Community Land and Sea Managers (#21670)
♦ **WIN** World Network of Indigenous Peoples and Local Community Land and Sea Managers (#21670)
♦ WIN / see Worldwide Independent Network (#21925)
♦ **WIN** Worldwide Independent Network (#21925)
♦ **WIN** Worldwide Innovative Networking (#21927)
♦ **WIOA** World Implant Orthodontic Association (#21577)
♦ **WIOMSA** Western Indian Ocean Marine Science Association (#20916)
♦ WIP / see Netherlands Centre for Indigenous Peoples
♦ **WIPCE International Council** World Indigenous Peoples Conference on Education International Council (#21579)
♦ WIPCS – Wisconsin Institute for Peace and Conflict Studies (internationally oriented national body)
♦ WIPO Copyright Treaty (1996 treaty)
♦ WIPO Performances and Phonograms Treaty (1996 treaty)
♦ **WIPO Staff Association** Staff Association of the World Intellectual Property Organization (#19942)
♦ **WIPO** World Immunopathology Organization (#21576)
♦ **WIPO** World Intellectual Property Organization (#21593)
♦ **WIP** Women in Parliaments Global Forum (#21010)
♦ **WIP** Women in Payments (#21011)
♦ **WIP** World Institute of Pain (#21589)
♦ Wire Association / see Wire Association International
♦ Wire Association International (internationally oriented national body)
♦ WIRED – Nordic Center of Excellence for Research in Water Imbalance Related Disorders (inactive)

♦ Wireless Broadband Alliance (WBA) 20969

Registered Office 8 Eu Tong Sen Street 14-94, The Central, Singapore 059818, Singapore.
URL: http://www.wballiance.com/
History 2003. **Aims** Secure an outstanding user experience through the global deployment of next generation Wi-Fi. **Structure** Board of Directors; Officers. Workgroups. **Activities** Awards/prizes/competitions; events/meetings. **Events** *Wireless Global Congress Asia PAC* Singapore (Singapore) 2023, *Wireless Global Congress* London (UK) 2017, *Wi-Fi Global Congress* Liverpool (UK) 2016, *Wi-Fi Global Congress* London (UK) 2015, *Wi-Fi Global Congress* San Jose, CA (USA) 2015. [2018/XJ8753/**C**]

♦ Wireless Cable Association International / see Wireless Communications Association International
♦ Wireless Communications Association International (internationally oriented national body)

♦ **Wireless Power Consortium (WPC)** **20970**
Contact c/o IEEE-ISTO, 445 Hoes Lane, Piscataway NJ 08854, USA. T. +17324655843.
URL: https://www.wirelesspowerconsortium.com/
History 2008. **Aims** Obtain worldwide compatibility of all wireless chargers and wireless power sources. **Structure** Board. **Activities** Advocacy/lobbying/activism; events/meetings; standards/guidelines. **Events** *Conference* Yokohama (Japan) 2019. **Members** Companies (over 500). Membership countries not specified. [AA0090/**C**]

♦ **Wireless World Research Forum (WWRF)** **20971**
Sec 15 rue Poliveau, 75005 Paris, France. T. +33611181622. E-mail: ramukdoniv@outlook.com.
Chair Huwai Technologies UK, 300 South Oak Way, Green Park, Reading, RG2 6UF, UK. T. +441189208952.
Office c/o Format A AG, Pfingstweidstr 102b, 8005 Zurich ZH, Switzerland.
URL: http://www.wwrf.ch/
History Articles of Association approved 14 Aug 2001; revised 7 Jul 2005, Apr 2006, Apr 2008, Nov 2010 and Jul 2012. Registered in accordance with Swiss Civil Code. **Aims** Encourage research to achieve unlimited *communications* to address key societal challenges for the future. **Structure** General Assembly; Steering Board; Executives; Secretariat. **Languages** English. **Staff** 2-3 voluntary. **Finance** Members' dues. Annual budget: about euro 140,000. **Activities** Events/meetings; networking/liaising; research/documentation. **Events** *Meeting* Abu Dhabi (United Arab Emirates) 2022, *Meeting* Kuala Lumpur (Malaysia) 2021, *Meeting* London (UK) 2019, *Fifth Generation Mobile Communication Promotion Forum* Tokyo (Japan) 2019, *Meeting* Tokyo (Japan) 2019. **Publications** *WWRF Newsletter. WWRF Outlook* – white papers. Articles; book series. **Members** Organizations; Individuals. Members in 20 countries:
Australia, Canada, China, Denmark, Finland, France, Germany, India, Korea Rep, Malaysia, Netherlands, Qatar, Russia, South Africa, Spain, Sweden, Taiwan, Uganda, UK, USA. [2017.10.12/XJ8751/**F**]

♦ Wir sind Kirche International (#20841)
♦ **WIRSPA** West Indies Rum and Spirits Producers' Association Inc (#20923)
♦ Wirtschafts- und Sozialausschuss / see European Economic and Social Committee (#06963)
♦ Wirtschafts- und Sozialausschuss der Europäischen Gemeinschaften / see European Economic and Social Committee (#06963)
♦ **WISAT** Women in Global Science and Technology Network (#20999)
♦ WISA – West Indies Associated States Council of Ministers (inactive)
♦ WISBEN – West Indies Sugarcane Breeding and Evaluation Network (see: #20922)
♦ WISCOMP – Women in Security, Conflict Management and Peace (internationally oriented national body)
♦ Wisconsin Institute for Peace and Conflict Studies (internationally oriented national body)
♦ Wisconsin Institute for the Study of War, Peace, and Global Cooperation / see Wisconsin Institute for Peace and Conflict Studies
♦ **WISC** World International Studies Committee (#21595)
♦ WiseEuropa (internationally oriented national body)
♦ WISE – Foundation for Worldwide International Student Exchange (internationally oriented national body)
♦ WISE Initiative (internationally oriented national body)
♦ WISE International / see World Information Service on Energy (#21582)
♦ **WISE Society** Web Information Systems Engineering Society (#20846)
♦ **WISE** World Information Service on Energy (#21582)
♦ WISE – World Institute of Scientology Enterprises (see: #03922)
♦ WISHH – World Initiative for Soy in Human Health (internationally oriented national body)
♦ WISICA – West Indian Sea Island Cotton Association (no recent information)
♦ WISPA / see Women's Squash Association (#21034)
♦ WISRF / see Women's Squash Association (#21034)
♦ Wissenschaftliche Vereinigung des Pazifischen Ozeans / see Pacific Science Association (#18003)
♦ Wissenschaftlich-Technische Arbeitsgemeinschaft für Bauwerkserhaltung und Denkmalpflege (#12152)
♦ **WISTA** Women's International Shipping and Trading Association (#21029)
♦ WIST – West Indies School of Theology (internationally oriented national body)
♦ **WIS** World Institute of Science (#21590)
♦ **WITBN** World Indigenous Television Broadcasters Network (#21580)
♦ **WITEC** European Association for Women in Science, Engineering and Technology (#06276)
♦ Withuis-Volontariaat / see Studio Globo
♦ Withuis Voluntary Services / see Studio Globo
♦ Witness (internationally oriented national body)
♦ Witness for Peace (internationally oriented national body)
♦ WITSA / see World Innovation, Technology and Services Alliance (#21585)
♦ **WITSA** World Innovation, Technology and Services Alliance (#21585)
♦ **WIT** World Information Transfer (#21583)
♦ **WIWO** Foundation Working Group International Waterbird and Wetland Research (#09976)
♦ **WIZO** Women's International Zionist Organization (#21030)
♦ **WJA** World Jurist Association (#21604)
♦ **WJCB** World Jersey Cattle Bureau (#21598)
♦ **WJC** Wildlife Justice Commission (#20960)
♦ **WJC** World Jewish Congress (#21599)
♦ WJC – World Journalists Conference (meeting series)
♦ WJC – World Judicial Commission (see: #21543)
♦ **WJEC** World Journalism Education Council (#21602)
♦ **WJF** World Judo Federation (#21603)
♦ WJJC – World Jiu Jitsu Confederation (unconfirmed)
♦ WJMC – World Jewish Migration Council (inactive)
♦ **WJP** The World Justice Project (#21605)
♦ WJRF – World Jump Rope Federation (inactive)
♦ **WJRO** World Jewish Restitution Organization (#21601)
♦ **WJR** World Jewish Relief (#21600)
♦ WJYO / see World Organization for Education, Science and Development
♦ **WKA** World Kickboxing and Karate Association (#21612)
♦ WKC – WHO Centre for Health Development, Kobe (see: #20950)
♦ **WKC** World Karate Confederation (#21607)

♦ **WKF Africa** **20972**
Continental Dir Féderation Malgache de Kickboxing et Disciplines Associatés, BP 4148, Antaninarenina, Antananarivo, Madagascar. T. +261320231981.
URL: http://africa.wkfworld.com/
History Original title: *African Kickboxing Federation (AKF).* A continental federation of *World Kickboxing Federation (WKF, #21611).* **Activities** Events/meetings. **Events** *Africa Championship* Johannesburg (South Africa) 2015. [2015/XM2568/**D**]

♦ **WKF Asia** **20973**
Pres PO Box 850, Tripoli NORTH LEBANON, Lebanon. T. +9616220771. Fax +9616444112. E-mail: office@wkfworld.com.
URL: http://asia.wkfworld.com/
History Original title: *Asian Kickboxing Federation.* Also known as *Asian Federation of Kickboxing (AFK).* A continental federation of *World Kickboxing Federation (WKF, #21611).* **Structure** General Assembly; Headquarters in Iran Islamic Rep. **Activities** Events/meetings; sporting activities. **Events** *General Assembly* Dushanbe (Tajikistan) 2007, *General Assembly* Bangalore (India) 2006, *General Assembly* Hamadan (Iran Islamic Rep) 2005, *General Assembly* Hamadan (Iran Islamic Rep) 2005, *General Assembly* Tashkent (Uzbekistan) 2005. **Members** National organizations (23) in 20 countries:
Afghanistan, Bangladesh, Bhutan, China, India, Iran Islamic Rep, Iraq, Kazakhstan, Korea Rep, Mongolia, Nepal, Pakistan, Palestine, Philippines, Russia, Syrian AR, Tajikistan, Turkmenistan, United Arab Emirates, Uzbekistan. [2022/XJ4275/**D**]

♦ **WKF Australia and Oceania** **20974**
Pres PO Box 3290, Mandurah WA 6210, Australia. T. +61451140770. E-mail: admin@wkf.org.au.
URL: http://www.wkf.org.au/
History A continental federation of *World Kickboxing Federation (WKF, #21611).* Former names and other names: *Oceanian Federation of Kickboxing (OFK)* – former. **Aims** Bring credibility, honesty and integrity to the kickboxing, MMA and martial arts industry around the world. **Structure** General Assembly. **Languages** English. **Staff** Voluntary. **Activities** Sporting activities. [2021.02.18/XM2569/**D**]

♦ **WKF Europe** **20975**
Chief Coordinator Newark Martial Arts, 49 Castlegate, Newark, NG24 1BE, UK. E-mail: europe@wkfworld.com.
URL: http://europe.wkfworld.com/
History Original title: *European Federation of Kickboxing (EFK).* A continental federation of *World Kickboxing Federation (WKF, #21611).* **Aims** Promote kickboxing in Europe. **Languages** English, Irish Gaelic. **Staff** 9.50 FTE, paid. **Finance** Sponsorship. **Activities** Advocacy/lobbying/activism; events/meetings. [2015/XM0891/**D**]

♦ **WKFM** World Kashmir Freedom Movement (#21610)
♦ **WKFO** Weltunion der Katholischen Frauen Organisationen (#21876)
♦ **WKF** World Kabaddi Federation (#21606)
♦ WKF – World Kalaripayattu Federation (unconfirmed)
♦ **WKF** World Karate Federation (#21608)
♦ **WKF** World Kickboxing Federation (#21611)
♦ WKF – World Knowledge Forum (meeting series)
♦ **WKF** World Kobudo Federation (#21614)
♦ WKF – World Kobudokan Federation (internationally oriented national body)
♦ WKJ – Weltbund der Katholischen Jugend (inactive)
♦ W K Kellogg Foundation (internationally oriented national body)
♦ WKKF – W K Kellogg Foundation (internationally oriented national body)
♦ **WKL** International Wernicke-Kleist-Leonhard Society (#15878)
♦ WKL – World Kickboxing League (unconfirmed)
♦ **WKM** World Kindness Movement (#21613)
♦ **WKO** World Karate Organization (#21609)
♦ WKSF – World Kettlebell Sport Federation (unconfirmed)
♦ **WLA-CdM** World Leadership Alliance – Club de Madrid (#21619)
♦ **WLA** World Lottery Association (#21628)
♦ WLBSA / see World Womens' Snooker (#21943)
♦ WLBS / see World Womens' Snooker (#21943)
♦ **WLCU** World Lebanese Cultural Union (#21622)
♦ WLC – World Literacy Council (internationally oriented national body)
♦ WLF / see Vital Strategies
♦ **WLFD** World League for Freedom and Democracy (#21621)
♦ **WLF** World Lupus Federation (#21630)
♦ **WLG** World Law Group (#21618)
♦ **WLI** Wetland Link International (#20927)
♦ WLI – World Labour Institute (internationally oriented national body)
♦ **WLO** World Leisure Organization (#21624)
♦ WLPA – World League for the Protection of Animals (inactive)
♦ **WLPGA** World LPG Association (#21629)
♦ WLPGF / see World LPG Association (#21629)
♦ **WLP** Women's Learning Partnership for Rights, Development and Peace (#21031)
♦ WLRA / see World Leisure Organization (#21624)
♦ WLSA Foundation / see World Leading Schools Association (#21620)
♦ **WLSA** Women and Law in Southern Africa Research Trust (#21006)
♦ **WLSA** World Leading Schools Association (#21620)
♦ **WLS** World Lagomorph Society (#21617)
♦ WLT – World Land Trust (internationally oriented national body)
♦ **WLUML** Women Living under Muslim Laws (#21007)
♦ **WLZM** World Labour Zionist Movement (#21615)
♦ **WMAC** World Martial Arts Committee (#21636)
♦ WMAGC / see World Martial Arts Committee (#21636)
♦ **WMAGC** World Martial Arts Games Committee (#21637)
♦ WMAGM / see World Martial Arts Games Committee (#21637)
♦ **WMA** International Association for Word and Music Studies (#12277)
♦ **WMA** Water Monitoring Alliance (#20831)
♦ WMA – Women Mentor Association (unconfirmed)
♦ WMA – World Marketing Association (inactive)
♦ **WMA** World Masters Athletics (#21640)
♦ **WMA** World Media Association (#21644)
♦ **WMA** World Medical Association (#21646)
♦ WMA – World Mission Associates (internationally oriented national body)
♦ **WMCCC** World Mayors Council on Climate Change (#21643)
♦ **WMCCSA** World Masters Cross-Country Ski Association (#21641)
♦ WMCES / see Wilfried Martens Centre for European Studies (#20962)
♦ **WMC** World Malayalee Council (#21631)
♦ WMC – World Martial Arts Masterships Committee (internationally oriented national body)
♦ **WMC** World Methodist Council (#21650)
♦ **WMC** World Mining Congress (#21654)
♦ **WMC** World Muslim Congress (#21664)
♦ **WMCW** World Movement of Christian Workers (#21660)
♦ **WMDA** World Marrow Donor Association (#21635)
♦ WMEI – World Methodist Evangelism Institute (see: #21650)
♦ **WME** World Missionary Evangelism (#21655)
♦ WMF – World Mercy Fund (internationally oriented national body)
♦ **WMF** World Minifootball Federation (#21652)
♦ **WMF** World Minigolf Sport Federation (#21653)
♦ **WMF** World Monuments Fund (#21657)
♦ **WMF** World Muay Federation (#21662)
♦ **WMF** World Mycotoxin Forum (#21665)
♦ WMGA / see International Masters Games Association (#14117)
♦ WMGD – World Movement for Global Democracy (internationally oriented national body)
♦ **WMHS** World Methodist Historical Society (#21651)
♦ WMIA – World Society of Micro-Implant Anchorage (unconfirmed)
♦ **WMIS** World Molecular Imaging Society (#21656)
♦ WMI – Water Missions International (internationally oriented national body)
♦ WMM / see Make Mothers Matter (#16554)
♦ WMO Applications of Meteorology Programme (see: #21649)
♦ WMO Atmospheric Research and Environment Programme (see: #21649)
♦ WMO Climate Data Information Referral Service (see: #21649)
♦ WMO Disaster Risk Reduction Programme (see: #21649)

♦ **WMO/ESCAP Panel on Tropical Cyclones (PTC)** **20976**
Groupe d'experts OMM/CESAP des cyclones tropicaux
Secretariat c/o Meteorological HQ, Pitras Bukhari Road, Sector H-8/2, Islamabad 44000, Pakistan. T. +92519250367. Fax +92519250368. E-mail: ptc.sectt@yahoo.com.

URL: http://www.wmo.int/pages/prog/www/tcp/ESCAP-Trop-cyc-panel.html
History 1972, under the auspices of *World Meteorological Organization (WMO, #21649)* and *United Nations Economic and Social Commission for Asia and the Pacific (ESCAP, #20557)*. **Aims** Promote and coordinate the planning and implementation of measures to minimize loss of life and material damage caused by *tropical cyclones* and associated *floods* and *storm surges* in the *Bay of Bengal* and the *Arabian Sea*. **Structure** Secretariat. **Languages** English. **Staff** provided by Pakistan Meteorological Department. **Finance** Trust Fund (contributions from Member countries). **Events** *Session* Bangkok (Thailand) 2015, *Session* Phuket (Thailand) 2010, *Session* Thailand 2010, *Session* Muscat (Oman) 2009, *Session* Manama (Bahrain) 2008. **Publications** *Panel News* (2 a year); *Panel on Tropical Cyclones* (annual) – review.
Members Covers 8 countries:
Bangladesh, India, Maldives, Myanmar, Oman, Pakistan, Sri Lanka, Thailand.
IGO Relations *International Civil Aviation Organization (ICAO, #12581).* [2009.10.28/XE0529/**E***]

- ♦ WM – Oeuvre de Marie / see Focolare Movement (#09806)
- ♦ WMO Global Runoff Data Centre / see Global Runoff Data Centre (#10584)

♦ WMO Hydrology and Water Resources Programme (HWRP) 20977

Programme d'hydrologie et de mise en valeur des ressources en eau de l'OMM – Programa de Hidrologia y Recursos Hidricos de la OMM

Contact Case Postale 2300, 7 bis ave de la Paix, 1211 Geneva 2, Switzerland. T. +41227308355. Fax +41227308043.
URL: http://www.wmo.int/pages/prog/hwrp/index_en.html

History Established within the framework of *World Meteorological Organization (WMO, #21649).* **Aims** Promote world-wide cooperation in evaluation of water resources and in development of these resources through coordinated establishment of hydrological networks and services, including data collection and processing, hydrological forecasts and warnings and the supply of *meteorological* and *hydrological* data for design purposes. **Structure** Comprises 4 mutually supporting programmes: Basis Systems in Hydrology; Forecasting and Applications in Hydrology; Capacity Building in Hydrology and Water Resources; Water-related Issues. **Events** *International congress of flatlands hydrology* Azul (Argentina) 2010, *Workshop on WMO Flood Forecasting Initiative* Australia 2007, *Regional planning meeting on ARAL-HYCOS* Almaty (Kazakhstan) 2006, *Meeting of climate change and water resources* Geneva (Switzerland) 2006, *FRIEND : international conference on flow regimes from international experimental and network data* Havana (Cuba) 2006. **IGO Relations** *Commission du Danube (CD, #04210); International Commission for the Hydrology of the Rhine Basin (#12693); Niger Basin Authority (NBA, #17134); Permanent Joint Technical Commission for Nile Waters (PJTC, #18327); WMO Resource Mobilization Office (RMO, see: #21649).* **NGO Relations** *International Association of Hydrological Sciences (IAHS, #11954); International Groundwater Resources Assessment Centre (IGRAC, #13739).* [2013.11.20/XF9900/**F***]

♦ WMO Integrated Global Observing System (WIGOS) 20978

Contact c/o WMO, 7bis av de la Paix, Case Postale 2300, 1211 Geneva 2, Switzerland. T. +41227308222. Fax +41227308021. E-mail: wwwmail@wmo.int.
URL: http://www.wmo.int/pages/prog/www/wigos/

History as a programme of *World Meteorological Organization (WMO, #21649).* **Aims** Provide a single focus for the operational and management functions of all WMO observing systems, as well as a framework and mechanism for interactions with WMO co-sponsored observing systems enabling integration, cooperation and coordination. [2010/XJ1595/**E***]

- ♦ WMO-IOC-UNEP-ISC Global Climate Observing System / see Global Climate Observing System (#10289)
- ♦ WMO Resource Mobilization Office (see: #21649)
- ♦ WMO Space Programme (see: #21649)

♦ WMO Staff Association 20979

SA President c/o WMO, Av de la Paix 7bis, Case Postale 2300, 1211 Geneva 2, Switzerland. T. +41227308056. Fax +41227308009. E-mail: staff-association@wmo.int.
SA Secretary address not obtained.
URL: http://www.wmo.int/

History Set up to represent staff members of *World Meteorological Organization (WMO, #21649).* **Aims** Ensure that conditions of employment conform with WMO Convention principles and Staff Regulations and Internal Staff Rules; cooperate in fostering WMO Convention aims; safeguard the rights and defend all WMO staff members and promote their welfare; collaborate in developing a spirit of solidarity and understanding. **Structure** General Assembly (annual); Staff Committee. **Languages** English, French, Spanish. **Staff** 280.00 FTE, paid. **Finance** Sources: contributions; fundraising. Annual budget: 50,000 CHF (2016). **Activities** Events/ meetings; training/education. [2020.05.07/XE1600/v/**E**]

- ♦ WMO World Data Centre for Greenhouse Gases (see: #21649)
- ♦ **WMO** World Mediation Organization (#21645)
- ♦ **WMO** World Memom Organisation (#21648)
- ♦ **WMO** World Meteorological Organization (#21649)
- ♦ WMO World Ozone and Ultra-Violet Data Centre (see: #21649)
- ♦ WMO World Radiation Data Centre, St Petersburg (see: #21649)
- ♦ **WMPA** World Mountain People Association (#21658)
- ♦ WMPL – World Mission Prayer League (internationally oriented national body)
- ♦ **WMRA** World Mountain Running Association (#21659)
- ♦ **WMRIF** World Materials Research Institutes Forum (#21642)
- ♦ WMSC – World Memory Sports Council (unconfirmed)
- ♦ WMS' / see European Aquaculture Society (#05909)
- ♦ WMS – Wilderness Medical Society (internationally oriented national body)
- ♦ WMS – Women's Missionary Society – African Methodist Episcopal Church (internationally oriented national body)
- ♦ WMS / see World Aquaculture Society (#21099)
- ♦ **WMS** World Marketing Summit (#21634)
- ♦ **WMS** World Muscle Society (#21663)
- ♦ WMTC – World Maritime Technology Congress (unconfirmed)
- ♦ **WMTS** World Medical Tennis Society (#21647)
- ♦ WMU – Woman's Missionary Union (internationally oriented national body)
- ♦ **WMU** World Maritime University (#21633)
- ♦ WMWFG / see World Federalist Movement – Movement for a Just World Order through a Strengthened United Nations (#21404)
- ♦ **WMW** World March of Women (#21632)
- ♦ **WNA** World Nuclear Association (#21674)
- ♦ **WNBA** World Ninepin Bowling Association (#21673)
- ♦ **WNBR** World Network of Biosphere Reserves (#21669)
- ♦ **WNFM** World Nuclear Fuel Market (#21675)
- ♦ **WNF** World Naturopathic Federation (#21666)
- ♦ WNF – World Ninja Federation (internationally oriented national body)
- ♦ WNHO – World Natural Health Organization (internationally oriented national body)
- ♦ WNMF – World Natural Medicine Foundation (internationally oriented national body)
- ♦ **WNTI** World Nuclear Transport Institute (#21676)
- ♦ **WNUSP** World Network of Users and Survivors of Psychiatry (#21672)
- ♦ **WNU** World Nuclear University (#21677)
- ♦ WN – World Neighbors (internationally oriented national body)
- ♦ **WN** World Netball (#21668)
- ♦ WOA – Washington Office on Africa (internationally oriented national body)
- ♦ WOA – Workshop on Aggression (meeting series)
- ♦ **WOA** World Olympians Association (#21682)
- ♦ WOA – World Orthopaedic Alliance (unconfirmed)
- ♦ **WOA** World Ostrich Association (#21701)
- ♦ **WOBO** World Organization of Building Officials (#21687)
- ♦ WOBT – Welt-Organisation Bild und Ton (inactive)
- ♦ WOCAAM – World College of Aesthetic and Antiageing Medicine (internationally oriented national body)
- ♦ **WOCAL** World Congress of African Linguistics (#21302)
- ♦ WOCAN – Women Organizing for Change in Agriculture and Natural Resource Management (internationally oriented national body)
- ♦ WOCATE – World Council of Associations for Technology Education (no recent information)
- ♦ **WOCATI** World Conference of Associations of Theological Institutions (#21296)
- ♦ WOCAT – World Overview of Conservation Approaches and Technologies (see: #21192)
- ♦ **WOCCU** World Council of Credit Unions (#21324)
- ♦ WOCOMOCO – World Collaborative Mobility Congress (meeting series)
- ♦ **WoCoVA** World Congress on Vascular Access (#21311)
- ♦ WOCO – World Council of Service Clubs (no recent information)
- ♦ WOCSOC – World Civil Society Conference (meeting series)
- ♦ **WOC Trust** World Orchid Conference Trust (#21683)
- ♦ WOC – World of Children (internationally oriented national body)
- ♦ **WOC** World Ocean Council (#21680)
- ♦ **WOC** World Orthopaedic Concern (#21699)
- ♦ **WODA** World Organization of Dredging Associations (#21688)
- ♦ WODIM – Workshop on Dielectrics in Microelectronics (meeting series)
- ♦ **WOFAPS** World Federation of Associations of Pediatric Surgeons (#21411)
- ♦ WOF – World Organization for the Family (inactive)
- ♦ WOF – World Oriental Federation (inactive)
- ♦ **WOF** World O-Sport Federation (#21700)
- ♦ WOGSC / see World Organisation of Systems and Cybernetics (#21686)
- ♦ WOHI – World of Hope International (internationally oriented national body)
- ♦ WOHO – World Osteopathic Health Organization (inactive)
- ♦ WOHP / see Institutes for Achievement of Human Potential (#11292)
- ♦ WoH – Wings of Hope (internationally oriented national body)
- ♦ WOJD – World Organization of Jewish Deaf (inactive)
- ♦ WOLA – Oficina en Washington para Asuntos Latinoamericanos (internationally oriented national body)
- ♦ WOLA – Washington Office on Latin America (internationally oriented national body)

♦ Wolf Haven International (WHI) 20980

Contact 3111 Offut Lake Rd SE, Tenino WA 98589, USA. T. +13602644695. Fax +13602644639. E-mail: info@wolfhaven.org.
URL: http://www.wolfhaven.org/

History 1982. **Aims** Rescue and provide sanctuary to captive-born wolves; through sanctuary, education and conservation, conserve and protect wolves and their habitat. **Structure** Board of Directors, comprising President, Vice President, Treasurer, Secretary, Executive Director and 4 members. Standing Committee: Finance. **Languages** English. **Staff** 15.00 FTE, paid. **Finance** Annual budget: 800,000 USD. **Activities** Develops programs and materials to be used on and off-site; conducts seminars; organizes workshops and classes for children and adults; participates in wolf management groups and provides testimony at hearings; advocates for conservation at outreach events; partners with state, federal and other nonprofit organizations. **Publications** *WolfTracks* (4 a year) – magazine.
Members Individuals – especially in USA and Canada – in 43 countries and territories:
Argentina, Australia, Belgium, Bermuda, Brazil, Canada, Cayman Is, Chile, China, Costa Rica, Cyprus, Czechia, Denmark, Egypt, Finland, France, Germany, Greece, Guam, Hong Kong, Hungary, Ireland, Italy, Japan, Luxembourg, Mexico, Netherlands, New Caledonia, New Zealand, Norway, Panama, Philippines, Poland, Puerto Rico, Saudi Arabia, Singapore, Spain, Sweden, Switzerland, Thailand, UK, USA, Venezuela. [2023/XF3513/v/**F**]

♦ The Wolfsberg Group 20981

Contact address not obtained. E-mail: info@wolfsberg-principles.com.
URL: http://www.wolfsberg-principles.com/

History 2000, Wolfsberg (Switzerland). Founded by 12 leading financial institutions. **Aims** Develop frameworks and guidance for the management of financial crime risks, particularly with respect to Know Your Customer, Anti-Money Laundering and Counter Terrorist Financing policies. **Activities** Capacity building; knowledge management/information dissemination; standards/guidelines. **NGO Relations** Partner of (1): *Basel Institute on Governance.* [2022.05.04/XJ3292/**E**]

- ♦ WoLLIC – Workshop on Logic, Language, Information and Computation (meeting series)
- ♦ WomanCare Global (internationally oriented national body)
- ♦ Woman and Earth Global Eco-Network (internationally oriented national body)

♦ Womankind Worldwide 20982

Contact Wenlock Studios, 50-52 Wharf Road, London, N1 7EU, UK. T. +442035675930. E-mail: info@womankind.org.uk.
URL: http://www.womankind.org.uk/

History 8 Mar 1989, London (UK). Former names and other names: *Women at Risk* – former (8 Mar 1989). Registration: Charity Commission, No/ID: 328206, England and Wales. **Aims** Achieve a world where the rights of all women and girls are respected, valued and realised. **Structure** Chair of Trustees; Vice Chair of Trustees; Treasurer. **Languages** English. **Staff** 22.00 FTE, paid; 1.00 FTE, voluntary. **Finance** Sources: contributions; donations; fundraising; gifts, legacies; government support; grants; in-kind support; international organizations; private foundations. Supported by: *Bill and Melinda Gates Foundation (BMGF); Comic Relief*; Foreign, Commonwealth and Development Office UK; *The William and Flora Hewlett Foundation; We Effect; World Lottery Association (WLA, #21628).* Annual budget: 5,000,000 GBP (2019). **Activities** Advocacy/lobbying/activism; events/meetings; financial and/or material support. Active in: Ethiopia, Kenya, Nepal, Uganda, Zimbabwe. **Publications** *Womankind Worldwide Newsletter.* **Members** Invites supporters. **Consultative Status** Consultative status granted from: *ECOSOC (#05331)* (Special). **NGO Relations** Member of (8): *Association for Women's Rights in Development (AWID, #02980); British Overseas NGO's for Development (BOND); CHS Alliance (#03911); CIVICUS: World Alliance for Citizen Participation (#03962)*; CORE Coalition; *Council for Education in the Commonwealth (CEC); Global Alliance for Tax Justice (GATJ); Philanthropy Impact.* Also links with national organizations active in the field. [2020.10.13/XF0188/**F**]

- ♦ Woman's Missionary Union (internationally oriented national body)
- ♦ Woman's Union Missionary Society of America for Heathen Lands / see Interserve (#15974)
- ♦ A Woman's Voice International (internationally oriented national body)
- ♦ WOMAN – World Organization of Mothers of All Nations (inactive)
- ♦ **WoMAU** World Martial Arts Union (#21638)
- ♦ Women in Action Worldwide (internationally oriented national body)

♦ Women Advancing Microfinance International (WAM International) 20983

Contact 402 Constitution Avenue NE, Washington DC 20002, USA. T. +12025474546. E-mail: wam.international.president@gmail.com.
URL: http://www.wam-international.org/

History 2003. Registered in accordance with US law. **Aims** Advance and support women working in microfinance and microenterprise development through education and training, by promoting leadership opportunities, and by increasing visibility of women's participation and talent while maintaining a work/life balance. **Structure** Board of Directors of 9 members. Executive Committee, comprising President, Secretary and Treasurer.
Members Chapters in 9 countries:
Canada, Ecuador, India, Kenya, Netherlands, Tunisia, Uganda, UK, USA. [2012/XJ5097/**F**]

♦ **Women in Aerospace Europe (WIA Europe)** **20984**
Contact Huygenstraat 44, Floor 2A, Space Business Park Noordwijk, 2201 DK Noordwijk-aan-Zee, Netherlands. E-mail: info@wia-europe.org.
URL: http://www.wia-europe.org/
History Current statutes adopted Jun 2011. Registered in accordance with Dutch law. **Aims** Expand women's opportunities for leadership; increase their visibility in the aerospace community. **Structure** Board of Directors, including President, Chair, Secretary and Treasurer. **Activities** Training/education; awards/prizes/competitions; financial and/or material support. **Events** *General Assembly* Noordwijk (Netherlands) 2012, *General Assembly* Bremen (Germany) 2011. **NGO Relations** Partnerships with: *Committee on Space Research (COSPAR, #04287)*; *International Space University (ISU, #15575)*; *Space Generation Advisory Council in Support of the United Nations Programme on Space Applications (SGAC, #19898)*. Member of: *International Astronautical Federation (IAF, #12286)*. [2012/XJ6226/**D**]

♦ **Women Against Cervical Cancer (WACC)** **20985**
Secretariat 174 rue de Courcelles, 75017 Paris, France. T. +33144400120. Fax +33147667470.
URL: http://www.wacc-network.org/
History Also referred to as *Women Against Cervical Cancer Network (WACC Network)*. **Aims** Improve awareness of human papillomavirus (HPV) and cervical diseases; make cervical cancer prevention a top priority on women's and public health agendas. **Structure** Executive Board, comprising President, Secretary and Treasurer. Taskforce. **Events** *Forum* Lisbon (Portugal) 2011, *Forum* Monte Carlo (Monaco) 2010, *Meeting* Monte Carlo (Monaco) 2010, *Forum / Meeting* Paris (France) 2009, *Forum* Nice (France) 2008. **Publications** *WACC Newsletter*.
Members Organizations in 17 countries:
Austria, Belgium, Bulgaria, Estonia, Finland, France, Germany, Greece, Italy, Jordan, Lebanon, Morocco, Norway, Portugal, Spain, Sweden, UK.
IGO Relations Partners: *European Centre for Disease Prevention and Control (ECDC, #06476)*; *International Agency for Research on Cancer (IARC, #11598)*; *WHO (#20950)*. **NGO Relations** Partners include: *Asia-Oceania Research Organization in Genital Infection and Neoplasia (AOGIN, #01805)*; *European Cervical Cancer Association (ECCA, #06512)*; *Association of European Cancer Leagues (ECL, #02500)*; *European Cancer Patient Coalition (ECPC, #06433)*; *European Research Organization on Genital Infection and Neoplasia (EUROGIN, #08378)*; *Fédération Internationale de Gynécologie et d'Obstétrique (FIGO, #09638)*; *International Planned Parenthood Federation (IPPF, #14589)*; *Union for International Cancer Control (UICC, #20415)*; national organizations. [2016/XJ4459/**D**]

♦ Women Against Cervical Cancer Network / see Women Against Cervical Cancer (#20985)
♦ Women against Lung Cancer in Europe (internationally oriented national body)

♦ **Women Against Violence Europe (WAVE)** **20986**
Office Administrator Bacherplatz 10/6, 1050 Vienna, Austria. T. +4315482720. Fax +431272027. E-mail: office@wave-network.org.
Exec Manager address not obtained.
URL: http://www.wave-network.org/
History 1994. Registration: No/ID: 601608559, Austria, Vienna. **Aims** Promote and strengthen the *human rights* of *women* and children in general and prevent *violence against women and children* in particular. **Structure** Coordination Office in Vienna (Austria). **Languages** English, German. **Staff** 10.00 FTE, paid. **Finance** Support from: Austrian Ministry for Work and Social Affairs and Consumer Protection; Austrian Association of Cities and Towns; Austrian Ministry for Education and Women's Affairs, and Social Affairs; Women's Department City of Vienna; Vienna Culture Department. Supported by: *European Commission (EC, #06633)*; *Oak Foundation*; *United Nations Population Fund (UNFPA, #20612)*. **Activities** Advocacy/lobbying/activism; capacity building; knowledge management/information dissemination; networking/liaising; research/documentation. **Events** *Conference* Prague (Czechia) 2022, *Annual WAVE Conference* Vienna (Austria) 2021, *Annual WAVE Conference* Vienna (Austria) 2020, *Annual WAVE Conference* Tallinn (Estonia) 2019, *Annual WAVE Conference* Valletta (Malta) 2018. **Publications** *WAVE Newsletter* (6 a year); *FEMPOWER* (annual) in English; *WAVE Country Report* (every 2 years).
Members Organizations (over 100) in 46 countries:
Albania, Armenia, Austria, Azerbaijan, Belarus, Belgium, Bosnia-Herzegovina, Bulgaria, Croatia, Cyprus, Czechia, Denmark, Estonia, Finland, France, Georgia, Germany, Greece, Hungary, Iceland, Ireland, Italy, Kosovo, Latvia, Liechtenstein, Lithuania, Luxembourg, Malta, Moldova, Montenegro, Netherlands, North Macedonia, Norway, Poland, Portugal, Romania, Russia, Serbia, Slovakia, Slovenia, Spain, Sweden, Switzerland, Türkiye, UK, Ukraine.
Consultative Status Consultative status granted from: *ECOSOC (#05331)* (Special). **IGO Relations** Cooperates with (4): *European Institute for Gender Equality (EIGE, #07557)*; *European Union Agency for Fundamental Rights (FRA, #08969)*; *Organization for Security and Cooperation in Europe (OSCE, #17887)*; United National agencies. **NGO Relations** Associate member of: *Social Platform (#19344)*. [2022.02.09/XF5604/**F**]

♦ Women of the Americas (see: #10689)
♦ Women for a Better World (internationally oriented national body)

♦ **Women in Black (WIB)** **20987**
Mujeres de Negro (MDN) – Zene u crnom (ZUC)
Address not obtained.
URL: http://www.womeninblack.org/
History 1988, Jerusalem (Israel). **Aims** As a worldwide movement of women dressed in black: protest against violence; promote *peace* worldwide. **Events** *Conference* Bogota (Colombia) 2010, *Conference* Valencia (Spain) 2007, *Biennial international conference* Jerusalem (Israel) 2005, *Biennial international conference* Italy 2003, *Biennial international conference* Novi Sad (Yugoslavia) 2001. **Publications** *Women in Black Newsletter* (4 a year).
Members Full in 12 countries:
Australia, Canada, Germany, India, Israel, Italy, Netherlands, Serbia, Sweden, Switzerland, UK, USA. [2013/XF6525/**F**]

♦ Women without Borders (internationally oriented national body)
♦ Women and Children International Development Foundation (internationally oriented national body)
♦ Women in Cities International (internationally oriented national body)

♦ **Women Cross DMZ** **20988**
International Coordinator address not obtained. E-mail: info@womencrossdmz.org.
URL: https://www.womencrossdmz.org/
History Founded 24 May 2015, when the De-Militarized Zone (DMZ) in Korea was crossed as a symbolic act of peace. **Aims** End the Korean War; reunite families; ensure women's leadership in peace building. **Structure** Steering Committee; Executive Committee; Advisory Board. **Activities** Awareness raising; networking/liaising; advocacy/lobbying/activism; capacity building. **NGO Relations** *Women's International League for Peace and Freedom (WILPF, #21024)*. [2019/XM8506/v/**E**]

♦ **Women Deliver** **20989**
Main Office 588 Broadway, Ste 905, New York NY 10012, USA. T. +16466959100. Fax +16466959145. E-mail: info@womendeliver.org.
URL: http://www.womendeliver.org/
History 2007, London (UK). **Aims** Promote and advance the *health* of *girls*, women and *mothers* as a core element of the global *development* agenda; serve as a global source of information for advocacy and action; develop and disseminate messages, tools, solutions, and advocacy resources to support a broad community of stakeholders. **Structure** Board, comprising Chair, President and members. Advisory Group. **Events** *Global Conference* Vancouver, BC (Canada) 2019, *Global Conference* Copenhagen (Denmark) 2016, *Global Conference* Kuala Lumpur (Malaysia) 2013, *Global Conference* Washington, DC (USA) 2010, *Women deliver global conference* London (UK) 2007. **Consultative Status** Consultative status granted from: *ECOSOC (#05331)* (Special). **NGO Relations** Member of: *Girls not Brides (#10154)*; *PMNCH (#18410)*. Partner of: *Every Woman Every Child (EWEC, #09215)*; *UNLEASH*. [2019/XJ5482/**F**]

♦ Women and Development (internationally oriented national body)

♦ **Women and Development Unit (WAND)** **20990**
Head of Dept UWI Open Campus Country Site Office, 1 Pine East-West Blvd, The Pine, Bridgetown, St Michael BB11000, Bridgetown ST MICHAEL BB11000, Barbados. T. +12464301130 – +12464301132 – +12316850. E-mail: wand@open.uwi.edu.
URL: https://www.open.uwi.edu/wand/about-wand#:~:text=The%20Women%20and%20Development%20Unit,of%20the%20UWI%20Open%20Campus.
History Aug 1978, Barbados. Established 1978, in the context of the UN Decade for Women. Joined the UWI Open Campus in 2008 as one of the Units in the Consortium for Social Development & Research (CSDR). Rebranded and reshaped direction, 2018. **Aims** Centre women and their families in Caribbean development through public discourse, applied research, online learning and policy development. **Structure** Head; Consultants; Secretary; Office Assistant. **Languages** English, Spanish. **Staff** 2.50 FTE, paid. **Finance** Sources: international organizations; revenue from activities/projects. Supported by: *University of the West Indies (UWI, #20705)*. **Activities** Advocacy/lobbying/activism; awareness raising; capacity building; events/meetings; knowledge management/information dissemination; projects/programmes; publishing activities; religious activities; research and development. Active in: Barbados, Jamaica, St Lucia, Trinidad-Tobago. **Publications** Journal articles; peer-reviewed articles; book chapters. **Members** Not a membership organization. [2020.10.13/XF1608/**F**]

♦ Women in Dialogue (internationally oriented national body)

♦ **Women Enabled International (WEI)** **20991**
Exec Dir 200 Massachusetts Ave NW, Suite 700, Washington DC 20001, USA. T. +12026303818. E-mail: info@womenenabled.org.
URL: http://www.womenenabled.org/
Aims Advance human rights at the intersection of gender and disability. **Structure** Board of Directors. **Languages** English, Portuguese, Spanish. **Finance** Funders and supporters include: *Open Society Foundations (OSF, #17763)*; *Translators without Borders (#20216)*; *UN Women (#20724)*; *United Nations Population Fund (UNFPA, #20612)*; national organizations. **Activities** Advocacy/lobbying/activism; networking/liaising; training/education. **Consultative Status** Consultative status granted from: *ECOSOC (#05331)* (Special). **IGO Relations** UN Department of Economic and Social Affairs. **NGO Relations** Partner of: *Global Forum on Law, Justice and Development (GFLJD, #10373)*. [2022.03.08/XM5044/**F**]

♦ **Women Engage for a Common Future (WECF)** **20992**
International Dir Korte Elisabethstr 6, 3511 JG Utrecht, Netherlands. T. +31302310300. Fax +31302340878. E-mail: wecf@wecf.eu.
URL: https://www.wecf.org/
History 1994, Netherlands. Resulting from *United Nations Conference on Environment and Development (UNCED)*, 1992, Rio de Janeiro (Brazil). Former names and other names: *Women in Europe for a Common Future (WECF)* – former. **Aims** Work for sustainable development; protect human *health* and *environment*; reduce *poverty*. **Structure** Steering Committee; Board of Directors; Board of Trustees. Coordinating Offices (3): Utrecht (Netherlands); Munich (Germany); Annemasse (France). **Languages** Bulgarian, Dutch, English, French, German, Russian. **Staff** 25.00 FTE, paid. **Finance** Supported by: Dutch and German governments; European Union. Private funding. **Activities** Advocacy/lobbying/activism; research/documentation. **Events** *Environment for Europe conference* Kiev (Ukraine) 2003, *Women from West and East Europe conference for the world summit on sustainable development* Celakovice (Czech Rep) 2002, *Workshop on women, sustainable consumption and commercial advertising* Vienna (Austria) 1994. **Publications** *The Review of the EU SDS* in English, German; *WECF News* – electronic newsletter. *A Health Climate ?*; *Chemicals and Health Toolkit*; *Cooperation for Sustainable Rural Development in the Ukraine*; *Ecologocal Sanitation and Associated Hygienic Risk*; *Eine Postkarte an Bundeskanzler Schröder*; *Experience in Rome District*; *Gender Tools and Gender Checklist* in English, Russian; *Protecting Future Generations*; *Reducing the Effects of Polluted Water on Children's Health in Rural Romania*; *Women's Request After the Kyoto Water Forum*; *Working Towards a Toxic Free Future*. Annual Report; reports; statements; conference reports/results; fact sheets; flyers; leaflets; CD-Roms; various downloadable documents.
Members Organizations and individuals in 39 countries:
Afghanistan, Albania, Armenia, Austria, Azerbaijan, Belarus, Belgium, Bulgaria, Czechia, Estonia, Finland, France, Georgia, Germany, Greece, Hungary, Ireland, Italy, Kazakhstan, Kyrgyzstan, Latvia, Lithuania, Moldova, Netherlands, North Macedonia, Poland, Portugal, Romania, Russia, Serbia, Slovakia, Slovenia, Spain, Sweden, Tajikistan, Türkiye, UK, Ukraine, Uzbekistan.
Members include 1 organization listed in this Yearbook:
International Environmental Association of River Keepers (Eco-TIRAS).
Consultative Status Consultative status granted from: *ECOSOC (#05331)* (Special); *UNEP (#20299)*. **IGO Relations** Accredited by (1): *United Nations Framework Convention on Climate Change – Secretariat (UNFCCC, #20564)*. Official partner of: *WHO European Centre for Environment and Health (ECEH, see: #20945)*. Member of: Taskforce on Health and Environment – *WHO Regional Office for Europe (#20945)*. **NGO Relations** Member of (14): *Climate Action Network Europe (CAN Europe, #04001)*; *EDC Free Europe (#05355)*; *European ECO Forum (#06955)*; *European Environmental Bureau (EEB, #06996)*; *European Water Partnership (EWP, #09083)*; *European Women's Lobby (EWL, #09102)*; *Global Call for Climate Action (GCCA, inactive)*; *Global Gender and Climate Alliance (GGCA, no recent information)*; *Health and Environment Alliance (HEAL, #10879)*; *Health Care Without Harm (HCWH, #10875)*; *International Pollutants Elimination Network (IPEN, #14616)*; *Pesticide Action Network Europe (#18338)*; *SDG Watch Europe (#19162)*; *The Butterfly Effect (BE, #03389)*. Cooperates with (3): *European Public Health Alliance (EPHA, #08297)*; *Sustainable Sanitation Alliance (SuSanA, #20066)*; *Women's Environment and Development Organization (WEDO, #21016)*. [2022/XF3476/y/**F**]

♦ Women of the EPP/EUCD / see EPP Women (#05516)

♦ **Women of Europe Award** **20993**
Prix Femmes d'Europe – Premio Mujeres de Europa – Preis Europäische Frauen – Prêmio Mulheres da Europa – Premio Donne d'Europa – Prijs Vrouwen van Europa – Europeiska Kvinnopriset – Euroopan Vuoden Nainen – Duais Mhna na hEorpa – Vrabio Ginekes tis Evropis
Contact c/o European Movement International, Place du Luxembourg 2, 1050 Brussels, Belgium. T. +3225083088. Fax +3225083089.
URL: https://europeanmovement.eu/women-of-europe/
History 1987, under the auspices of *European Commission (EC, #06633)*, *European Movement International (EMI, #07825)* and *European Parliament (EP, #08146)*. In English also referred to as *Women of Europe Prize*. Registered in accordance with Belgian law. **Aims** Stimulate participation of women in development of the *European Union*; promote their engagement in *political*, *economic* and *social* life and make their presence felt; create a network of women who are high achievers in different sectors of national political, economic and social life; be responsible for the award at national level. **Structure** General Assembly (annual). Administrative Council, comprising European President and the Presidents of National Committees, which in turn elect from amongst themselves up to 3 Vice-Presidents and a Treasurer. Secretary-General. **Languages** English, French. **Staff** None. **Finance** Members' dues. **Activities** Each member country organizes annual or biannual presentation of the 'Woman of Europe' Award in that country. Every 2 years, an international jury chooses one national winner. Member countries organize conferences. **Events** *International conference* Brussels (Belgium) 2004, *Intereuropean networking conference* Gotland (Sweden) 1997. **Members** Covers 27 countries. Membership countries not specified. [2019/XE2644/**E**]

♦ Women in Europe for a Common Future / see Women Engage for a Common Future (#20992)
♦ Women of Europe Prize / see Women of Europe Award (#20993)

♦ **Women in Film (WIF)** **20994**
Address not obtained.
URL: https://womeninfilm.org/
History 1973, Los Angeles CA (USA). **Aims** Promote the visions of women in the global communications industry.
Members Affiliated organizations in 14 countries:
Australia, Canada, France, Germany, Ireland, Jamaica, Japan, Kenya, Poland, South Africa, Spain, UK, USA, Zimbabwe.
NGO Relations *Women in Film and Television International (WIFT International, #20995)*. [2020/XF4693/**F**]

♦ Women and Film History International (unconfirmed)

♦ **Women in Film and Television International (WIFT International)** .. **20995**
Contact c/o NYWIFT, 6 East 39th St, New York NY 10016, USA. E-mail: membership@wifti.net.
URL: https://www.wifti.net/
Aims Advance professional development and achievement for women working in all areas of film, video, and other screen-based media. **Structure** Board, comprising Chair, Vice-Chair, Treasurer, Secretary and 5 members. **Activities** Organizes online courses. Annual general meeting; International Short Film Showcase. **Events** *Mini summit* Copenhagen (Denmark) 2008, *European conference for women in film and television* Copenhagen (Denmark) 2006, *Summit* Los Angeles, CA (USA) 2005, *Summit* Auckland (New Zealand) 2004, *Summit* Montego Bay (Jamaica) 2002.
Members Chapters (37) in 12 countries:
Australia, Canada, Denmark, Ireland, Italy, Jamaica, Mexico, New Zealand, Russia, Sweden, UK, USA.
NGO Relations *Women in Film (WIF, #20994).* [2010/XM0707/F]

♦ Women first! / see Féminin Pluriel

♦ **Women First International Fund** **20996**
Contact 11 Broadway Ste 510, New York NY 10004, USA. T. +12122130622. Fax +12122130684. E-mail: vgif@vgif.org.
URL: http://www.womenfirstfund.org/
History 1969. Founded by 11 members of *Graduate Women International (GWI, #10688).* Former names and other names: *Virginia Gildersleeve International Fund for University Women (VGIFUW)* – former (1969 to 1999); *Fonds international Virginia Gildersleeve pour les femmes diplômées des universités* – former (1969 to 1999); *Virginia Gildersleeve International Fund* – former (10 Apr 1999 to 2019). **Aims** Provide grants globally to fund locally generated projects that advance the *rights* and social justice of *women* and *girls.* **Structure** Board of Directors (governance board); Committees; Office. **Staff** 5.00 FTE, paid. Several voluntary. **Finance** Sources: donations; members' dues. **Activities** Events/meetings; financial and/or material support; networking/liaising; projects/programmes. **Events** *Conference* Kolkata (India) 2009, *Mid-year meeting* New York, NY (USA) 2009, *Annual meeting* New York, NY (USA) 2002, *Annual meeting* New York, NY (USA) 2001, *Annual meeting* New York, NY (USA) 2000. **Publications** *Flash* (12 a year); *The Update* (3 a year).
Members Supported by over 1,200 members (mainly in USA). Individuals and organizations in 20 countries:
Argentina, Australia, Canada, El Salvador, Finland, France, Germany, Iceland, India, Ireland, Israel, Japan, Kenya, Netherlands, New Zealand, Rwanda, Sri Lanka, Switzerland, UK, USA.
Consultative Status Consultative status granted from: *ECOSOC (#05331)* (Special). **IGO Relations** Associated with Department of Global Communications of the United Nations. **NGO Relations** Member of: *Conference of Non-Governmental Organizations in Consultative Relationship with the United Nations (CONGO, #04635); NGO Committee on Financing for Development, New York (#17108).* [2020.04.29/XF0318/f/F]

♦ WomenforWomen Reconstructive Surgery / see Reconstructing Women International (#18629)

♦ **Women and Gender in Chinese Studies Network (WAGNET)** **20997**
Acad Adminstrator Queen Elizabeth House, 3 Mansfield Road, Oxford, OX1 3TB, UK.
History 12 Aug 2001, Berlin (Germany). **Aims** Unite scholars in women and gender in Chinese studies. **Structure** General Meeting. Steering Committee of 9 members, including Academic Administrator. **Languages** Chinese, English. **Staff** Voluntary. **Finance** Occasional grants. **Activities** Organizes workshops; facilitates research and academic projects; provides updates on events and news pertinent to membership. **Events** *Workshop* London (UK) 2011, *Workshop* Bristol (UK) 2009, *General Meeting* Bristol (UK) 2008, *General meeting / Workshop* Bremen (Germany) 2007, *Workshop* Prague (Czech Rep) 2005. **Publications** *Women and Gender in Chinese Studies (WAGREV)* – electronic review journal.
Members Individuals in 36 countries and territories:
Australia, Austria, Belgium, Canada, China, Czechia, Denmark, Finland, France, Germany, Grenada, Hong Kong, India, Ireland, Israel, Italy, Japan, Korea Rep, Malaysia, Malta, Netherlands, New Zealand, Norway, Philippines, Poland, Portugal, Russia, Singapore, Spain, Sweden, Switzerland, Taiwan, Thailand, UK, USA, Vietnam.
NGO Relations Formal contact with: *European Association for Chinese Studies (EACS, #05973); International Gender Studies Centre, Oxford (IGS).* [2013/XF6638/F]

♦ Women for Genuine Security (internationally oriented national body)

♦ **Women in Global Health (WGH)** **20998**
Exec Dir address not obtained. E-mail: info@womeningh.org.
URL: http://www.womeningh.org/
History 2015. Launched on the initiative of four early career women as a not-for-profit virtually based organization related to the health sector, and powered by volunteers. Chapters (44) developed worldwide, with 100 expected by 2023. Registration: Start date: 2017, USA.
Aims Strengthen health systems and health security; advance women's empowerment; boost national and global economic growth by developing four core advocacy priorities:
1. Gender equal leadership in global health and going beyond gender parity to Gender Transformative Leadership
2. Gender equity in the health and care workforce: including equal representation of women in leadership and decision-making; fair pay and an end to unpaid work in health systems; protection of women health workers from sexual exploitation, abuse and harassment; and protection from harm via effective PPE (personal protective equipment), vaccines and mental health support
3. Gender responsive health systems including for Universal Health Coverage (UHC) and pandemic preparedness and response
4. Building the WGH movement and alliances for women's leadership and gender equality in global health

Structure Board of Directors. **Activities** Advocacy/lobbying/activism; capacity building. Active in: Argentina, Austria, Bangladesh, Benin, Bolivia, Brazil, Burkina Faso, Cameroon, Canada, Chile, China, Denmark, Egypt, Finland, Georgia, Germany, Guinea, India, Iraq, Ireland, Kenya, Malawi, Mali, Mexico, Niger, Nigeria, Norway, Pakistan, Philippines, Portugal, Senegal, Somalia, South Africa, Spain, Sweden, Switzerland, Togo, Uganda, UK, United Arab Emirates, USA, Washington, Zambia, Zimbabwe. **Publications** *WGH Newsletter. Gender Equity Hub Report.* Research publications. **Members** Nurses, midwives, doctors, public health professionals, health policy makers, community health workers, researchers, pharmacists and private sector health workers. Members (5,500) and supporters (80,000) in over 90 countries. Membership countries not specified. [2023.02.14/XM7599/F]

♦ Women and Global Migration Working Group / see Women in Migration Network (#21008)

♦ **Women in Global Science and Technology Network (WISAT)** **20999**
SG 204 Ventress Road, Brighton ON K0K 1H0, Canada. T. +14164790601. Fax +14164790263. E-mail: info@wisat.org.
URL: http://wisat.org/
History by *International Federation of Institutes for Advanced Study (IFIAS, inactive).* Originally known with the acronym *WIGSAT.* Present acronym adopted, 2012. **Aims** Support global networking on critical issues in science and technology for development. **Structure** Board of Directors. **Activities** Research/documentation; advocacy/lobbying/activism; knowledge management/information dissemination; networking/liaising. **Events** *International symposium on women and information and communication technology* Baltimore, MD (USA) 2005, *Regional Africa conference* Lilongwe (Malawi) 1997. **Publications** *National Assessments on Gender and STI.* **NGO Relations** Member of: *Alliance for Affordable Internet (A4AI, #00651); Gender in science, innovation, technology and engineering (GenderInSITE, #10100).* [2017.06.01/XG5875/F]

♦ **Women and Harm Reduction International Network (WHRIN)** **21000**
Sec address not obtained. E-mail: accessiblejudah@hotmail.com – whrin-request@drugsense.org.
Aims Reduce harm for women who use *drugs*; develop an enabling environment for the implementation and expansion of harm reduction resources for women. **Structure** Board, including Chair, 2 Vice-Chairs and Secretary. **NGO Relations** Member of: *International Drug Policy Consortium (IDPC, #13205).* [2014/XJ8495/F]

♦ **Women and Health Alliance International (WAHA)** **21001**
General Manager 160 bis rue du Temple, 75003 Paris, France. T. +33140290556.
Facebook: https://www.facebook.com/wahainternational
History Registration: France. **Aims** Partner with African and Asian midwife associations, university teaching hospitals, medical specialists and health authorities so as to implement innovative solutions which address the most immediate problems women face when trying to access healthcare services. **NGO Relations** Member of: *Gavi – The Vaccine Alliance (Gavi, #10077)* CSO Constituency; *PMNCH (#18410); Reproductive Health Supplies Coalition (RHSC, #18847).* [2018/XJ7501/D]

♦ Women Help Women (unconfirmed)

♦ **Women Human Rights Defenders International Coalition (WHRD)** .. **21002**
Contact c/o Women's Global Network for Reproductive Rights, Tulpstraat 11, 4101 GJ Culemborg, Netherlands. E-mail: whrd@apwld.org.
URL: http://www.defendingwomen-defendingrights.org/
Members Membership countries not specified. [2019/XJ0762/F]

♦ **Women in Informal Employment: Globalizing and Organizing (WIEGO)** **21003**
Femmes dans l'Emploi Informel: Globalisation et Organisation – Mujeres en Empleo Informal: Globalizando y Organizando – Mulheres no Emprego Informal: Globalizando e Organizando
Operations Office 521 Royal Exchange, Manchester, M2 7EN, UK. T. +441618191200. E-mail: wiego@wiego.org.
URL: http://www.wiego.org/
History Founded 1997. Registration: Charity Commission, No/ID: 1143510, England and Wales. **Aims** Increase the voice, visibility and validity of the working poor, especially women, in the informal sector of the economy. **Structure** Board of Directors; Committees (2); Operations Team. **Languages** English, French, Portuguese, Spanish. **Staff** 43.00 FTE, paid. **Activities** Awareness raising; capacity building. **Events** *Asia-Pacific urban forum* Bangkok (Thailand) 2011, *European seminar on organising in the informal economy* Soesterberg (Netherlands) 2003, *Regional policy seminar on women workers in the informal sector in South Asia* Kathmandu (Nepal) 2000, *Workshop on social protection for women in the informal sector* Geneva (Switzerland) 1999.
Members Individuals (139) in 29 countries:
Argentina, Australia, Brazil, Canada, Chile, China, Colombia, France, Germany, Ghana, India, Indonesia, Kenya, Malaysia, Mexico, Nepal, Netherlands, North Macedonia, Peru, Philippines, South Africa, Spain, Switzerland, Tanzania UR, Thailand, Uganda, UK, Uruguay, USA.
Organizations (34) in 25 countries:
Argentina, Bangladesh, Bulgaria, Burundi, Chile, Colombia, Congo DR, Eswatini, Ghana, Guinea, India, Kenya, Malawi, Mozambique, Nepal, Niger, Philippines, Senegal, South Africa, Switzerland, Thailand, Togo, Venezuela, Zambia, Zimbabwe.
Included in the above, 4 organizations listed in this Yearbook:
HomeNet South Asia (HNSA, #10940); HomeNet South-East Asia (HNSEA, #10941); International Union of Food, Agricultural, Hotel, Restaurant, Catering, Tobacco and Allied Workers Associations (IUF, #15772); StreetNet International (#20010).
Consultative Status Consultative status granted from: *ECOSOC (#05331)* (Special). **IGO Relations** Accredited by: *Green Climate Fund (GCF, #10714).* **NGO Relations** Member of: *Global Call for Climate Action (GCCA, inactive).* Cooperates with: *World Urban Campaign (WUC, #21893).* [2020/XN8993/y/F]

♦ Women International Association for Communication – Mediterranean Media (internationally oriented national body)

♦ **Women In International Security (WIIS)** **21004**
Pres 1301 Connecticut Ave NW, Ste 750, Washington DC 20036, USA. T. +12026846010. E-mail: info@wiisglobal.org.
URL: http://wiisglobal.org/
History Founded 1987. **Aims** Advance the *leadership* and *professional* development of women in the field of international peace and security. **Structure** Advisory Board. **Languages** Dutch, English, French, German. **Staff** 10.00 FTE, paid. **Finance** Members' dues; grants. Financing organizations include: *NATO (#16945)*; UN Office for Disarmament Affairs (UNODA). **Activities** Training/education; guidance/assistance/consulting, networking/liaising; events/meetings; research/documentation; projects/programmes; politics/policy/regulatory. **Events** *Seminar on Peace and Security in the 21st Century* Singapore (Singapore) 2016, *Annual Workshop for Women in International Security* Ottawa, ON (Canada) 2014, *Conference on Women in Combat Units* Washington, DC (USA) 2014, *Annual Workshop for Women in International Security* Toronto, ON (Canada) 2013, *Men, Peace and Security International Symposium* Washington, DC (USA) 2013. **Publications** Public Policy Briefs.
Members Individuals (7,000) in 31 countries:
Albania, Australia, Austria, Belgium, Canada, China, Croatia, Denmark, France, Germany, Greece, Hungary, India, Israel, Italy, Japan, Nepal, Netherlands, New Zealand, North Macedonia, Norway, Philippines, Russia, Serbia, South Africa, Spain, Sweden, Türkiye, UK, Ukraine, USA.
Also in the Horn of Africa. Membership countries not specified.
NGO Relations Cooperates with: Harvard Humanitarian Initiative; Human Rights Center, University of California Berkeley; *Promundo; United States Institute of Peace (USIP).* [2020/XG1602/v/F]

♦ Women and Land Rights in Southern Africa, Zimbabwe (unconfirmed)

♦ **Women in Law and Development in Africa-Afrique de l'Ouest (WiLDAF-AO)** **21005**
Femmes, droit et développement en Afrique-Afrique de l'Ouest (FeDDAF-AO)
Sub-regional Coordinator address not obtained. T. +22822612679. Fax +22822617390. E-mail: wildaf_ao@yahoo.com – wildaf@cafe.tg – wildaf@wildaf-ao.org.
URL: http://www.wildaf-ao.org/
History Feb 1990, Harare (Zimbabwe). **Aims** Promote and strengthen regional and local strategies that link law and development to improve women's status in Africa; increase women's participation and influence at community, national and international levels. **Structure** General Assembly (every 4 years); Board; Executive Committee; Regional Secretariat; Sub-regional Offices; National Networks. **Languages** English, French. **Staff** 16.00 FTE, paid. **Finance** Sources: fees for services; international organizations. OXFAM- BURKINA. Supported by: *African Women's Development Fund (AWDF, #00504); Diakonia; International Development Research Centre (IDRC, #13162); International Land Coalition (ILC, #13999);* OXFAM Burkina; OXFAM Panafrica; *Save the Children International (#19058).* Annual budget: 375,727,291 XOF (2018). **Activities** Advocacy/lobbying/activism; awareness raising; capacity building; events/meetings; guidance/assistance/consulting; knowledge management/information dissemination; monitoring/evaluation; networking/liaising; publishing activities; training/education. Active in: Benin, Burkina Faso, Côte d'Ivoire, Ghana, Guinea, Liberia, Mali, Niger, Nigeria, Senegal, Togo. **Events** *Meeting on the struggle against impunity in Africa / Ordinary Session* Ouagadougou (Burkina Faso) 1996. **Publications** *WILDAF Newsletter* (4 a year). Annual Report; training manuals; information packages; studies; documentaries.
Members Organizations and institutions; individuals. Members in 27 countries:
Benin, Botswana, Burkina Faso, Cameroon, Côte d'Ivoire, Eswatini, Ethiopia, Ghana, Guinea, Kenya, Lesotho, Liberia, Malawi, Mali, Mauritius, Mozambique, Namibia, Niger, Nigeria, Senegal, South Africa, Sudan, Tanzania UR, Togo, Uganda, Zambia, Zimbabwe.
Consultative Status Consultative status granted from: *African Commission on Human and Peoples' Rights (ACHPR, #00255)* (Observer). **IGO Relations** Accredited by (1): *Organisation internationale de la Francophonie (OIF, #17809).* Special Consultative Status with: *ECOSOC (#05331).* **NGO Relations** Member of (2): *International Network for Economic, Social and Cultural Rights (ESCR-Net, #14255); Social Watch (#19350).* [2022/XF5369/F]

♦ Women and Law in Southern Africa Research Project / see Women and Law in Southern Africa Research Trust (#21006)

♦ **Women and Law in Southern Africa Research Trust (WLSA)** **21006**
Contact Plot No 14022 off Katimamulilo Road, Olympia Extenstion, Lusaka, Zambia. T. +2601290512 – +2601291888. Fax +2601290512. E-mail: wlsazam@zamnet.zm.
URL: http://www.wlsa.org.mz/
History 1987, as *Women and Law in Southern Africa Research Project.* **Aims** Improve legal status of women in Southern Africa; develop research skills of women's laws researchers; conduct research on gender issues in Southern Africa, particularly those related to *legal rights*; provide information on gender and the law and influencing policy and law reform in each country and exchange this information among member countries; explore and develop new methodologies and perspectives for the study of gender and the law; cooperate and liaise with other organizations in each country, regionally and internationally. **Structure** Regional Office in Lusaka (Zambia). **Languages** English. **Staff** 4.00 FTE, paid. **Finance** Funds from: *Canadian*

International Development Agency (CIDA, inactive); DANIDA; Ford Foundation (#09858); Humanistisch Instituut voor Ontwikkelingssamenwerking (Hivos); Norwegian Agency for Development Cooperation (Norad); Swedish International Development Cooperation Agency (Sida); United States Agency for International Development (USAID); Government of the Netherlands. **Activities** Development of a regional network of women and men researching women's legal rights. Regional seminars. Studies for all 7 member countries. Programmes of action (6): Activist Research (core programme); Information Dissemination and Documentation; Legal Advice and Services; Lobbying and Advocacy for Policy, Legal Reform and Change; Networking; Training and Education on Women's Rights. **Events** *Conference* Harare (Zimbabwe) 1991, *Research methodology* Harare (Zimbabwe) 1990, *Workshop* Harare (Zimbabwe) 1990, *Workshop* Harare (Zimbabwe) 1990. **Publications** *WLSA Newsletter.* Monographs; bibliographies; working papers. **Information Services** *Database on Women in Southern Africa.*
Members Research teams and national coordinators in 7 countries:
Botswana, Eswatini, Lesotho, Malawi, Mozambique, Zambia, Zimbabwe.
Consultative Status Consultative status granted from: *African Commission on Human and Peoples' Rights (ACHPR, #00255)* (Observer). **NGO Relations** Member of: *African Books Collective (ABC, #00226).* Supports: *Global Call for Action Against Poverty (GCAP, #10263).* [2012/XF1143/F]

♦ Women Living under Muslim Laws (WLUML) 21007
Femmes sous lois musulmanes
Int Coordination Office PO Box 28445, London, N19 5NZ, UK. E-mail: wluml@wluml.org.
Asia Coordination Office Shirkat Gah Women's Resource Centre, PO Box 5192, Lahore, Pakistan. E-mail: sgah@sgah.org.pk.
Africa and Middle East Coordination Office c/o Groupe de Recherche sur les Femmes et les Lois au Senegal, PO Box 5330, Dakar Fann, Dakar, Senegal. E-mail: grefels@gmail.com.
URL: http://www.wluml.org/
History 1984. Former names and other names: *Women Living under Muslim Laws – International Solidarity Network* – alias; *Femmes sous lois musulmanes – Réseau international de solidarité* – alias. Registration: Charity Commission, No/ID: 1144519, England and Wales; Companies House, No/ID: 04117440, Start date: 30 Nov 2000, End date: 3 Nov 2020, England and Wales. **Aims** Provide information, support and a collective space for women whose lives are shaped, conditioned or governed by laws and customs said to derive from Islam. **Structure** Board; Council. **Languages** Arabic, English, French, Indonesian, Persian, Urdu. **Activities** Networking/liaising; capacity building; awareness raising. **Publications** *WLUML Newsletter* (2 a year). Dossiers; occasional journal; occasional papers. **Members** Not a membership organization. Extends to over 70 countries. [2022/XF0636/F]

- ♦ Women Living under Muslim Laws – International Solidarity Network / see Women Living under Muslim Laws (#21007)
- ♦ **Women in Management** Red de Mujeres Latinoamericanas y del Caribe en Gestion de Organizaciones (#18723)
- ♦ Women Mentor Association (unconfirmed)

♦ Women in Migration Network (WIMN) 21008
Contact address not obtained. E-mail: wimninfo@womeninmigration.org.
URL: http://womeninmigration.org/
History Apr 2012, at a pre-meeting of *Association for Women's Rights in Development (AWID, #02980).* Former names and other names: *Women and Global Migration Working Group (WGMWG)* – former. **Aims** Strengthen a gender analysis within the migrant rights movement globally; lift up the particular concerns of migrant women within the global women's movement.
Members Organizations (15), including 10 listed in this Yearbook:
Building and Wood Workers' International (BWI, #03355); Global Alliance Against Traffic in Women (GAATW, #10184); Global Migration Policy Associates (GMPA, #10473); International Trade Union Confederation (ITUC, #15708); Migrant Forum in Asia (MFA, #16798); Pan-African Network in Defense of Migrants' Rights (PANiDMR); Platform for International Cooperation on Undocumented Migrants (PICUM, #18401); Public Services International (PSI, #18572); WIDE+ (#20951); World Young Women's Christian Association (World YWCA, #21947).
NGO Relations Member of: *Global Coalition on Migration (GCM, #10293).* [2020/XJ8933/y/E]

- ♦ Women in Need International (internationally oriented national body)
- ♦ Women in Neurosurgery (internationally oriented national body)

♦ Women in Nuclear (WIN) 21009
Contact Franz Siegel Gasse 26, 2380 Perchtoldsdorf, Austria. E-mail: win@win-global.net.
URL: http://www.win-global.org/
History 1989, by *European Nuclear Society (ENS, #08059).* Currently an independent group. Previously referred to as *Women in Nuclear Group.* **Aims** Develop an international *network* for professional women in *nuclear energy* for exchange of information. **Structure** General Assembly (annual). Board, including Executive of at least 5 and maximum 15 members. Secretariat. **Languages** English. **Finance** Through the work of members. **Activities** Organizes workshops, seminars, debates and study tours. **Events** *Annual Conference* Tokyo (Japan) 2022, *Annual Meeting* Japan 2021, *Annual Meeting* Toronto, ON (Canada) 2021, *Annual Meeting* Niagara Falls, ON (Canada) 2020, *Annual Meeting* Madrid (Spain) 2019. **Publications** *WINFO* (4 a year) – newsletter. **Members** Full (over 4,000) in 91 countries and territories. Membership countries not specified. **NGO Relations** Member of: *European Platform of Women Scientists (EPWS, #08235).* [2020/XK1070/F]

- ♦ Women in Nuclear Group / see Women in Nuclear (#21009)
- ♦ Women Organizing for Change in Agriculture and Natural Resource Management (internationally oriented national body)

♦ Women in Parliaments Global Forum (WIP) 21010
CEO Austurstræti 10a, 101 Reykjavik, Iceland. E-mail: mail@womenleaders.global.
Brussels Office Blvd Charlemagne 96, 1000 Brussels, Belgium. T. +3227331344. E-mail: mail@wpleaders.org.
URL: http://www.womeninparliaments.org/
Structure Advisory Board; Board; Executive Board. **Activities** Advocacy/lobbying/activism; events/meetings; awards/prizes/competitions. **Events** *WIP Global Summit* Amman (Jordan) 2016. **Publications** *WIP News.*
Members Country ambassadors in 39 countries:
Albania, Algeria, Burkina Faso, Burundi, Cameroon, Central African Rep, Congo Brazzaville, Côte d'Ivoire, Czechia, Djibouti, Ecuador, Eritrea, Eswatini, Ethiopia, Gabon, Ghana, Italy, Kenya, Liberia, Malawi, Mali, Mauritania, Mexico, Moldova, Morocco, Namibia, Niger, Norway, Peru, Rwanda, Senegal, Serbia, Sierra Leone, Slovakia, Somalia, South Sudan, Sudan, Tunisia, Zimbabwe.
IGO Relations Partners include: *African Union (AU, #00488); European Commission (EC, #06633); Ibero-American General Secretariat (#11024); International Bank for Reconstruction and Development (IBRD, #12317)* (World Bank); *OECD (#17693); United Nations (UN, #20515).* **NGO Relations** Partners include: *Council of Women World Leaders (CWWL, #04923); United Nations Foundation (UNF, #20563); Women Thrive Alliance; World Economic Forum (WEF, #21367).* [2021/XM4819/F]

♦ Women in Payments (WIP) 21011
CEO 1698 Flambourough Circle, Mississauga ON L5M 3M7, Canada. T. +14166292871. E-mail: info@womeninpayments.org.
URL: https://www.womeninpayments.org/
History Former names and other names: *Global Association of Women in Payments* – full title. **Aims** Connect, inspire and champion women in the payments industry. **Structure** Global Community Council. **Activities** Awards/prizes/competitions; events/meetings. [2021/AA1657/C]

- ♦ Women PeaceMakers Program (internationally oriented national body)
- ♦ Women Peacemakers Program-Africa / see African Women's Active Nonviolence Initiatives for Social Change (#00502)
- ♦ Women for Peace, Sweden (internationally oriented national body)
- ♦ Women for Peace, Switzerland (internationally oriented national body)

♦ Women Political Leaders (WPL) 21012
Pres and Founder Blvd Charlemagne 96, 1000 Brussels, Belgium. T. +3227331344. E-mail: mail@wpleaders.org.
Reykjavik Office Austurstræti 10a, 101 Reykjavik, Iceland. E-mail: mail@womenleaders.global.
URL: https://www.womenpoliticalleaders.org/
Aims Increase both the number and the influence of women in political leadership positions. **Structure** Global Advisory Board; Board. **Activities** Events/meetings. **Events** *Women Political Leaders Summit* 2021, *Women Political Leaders Summit* Tokyo (Japan) 2019, *Women Political Leaders Summit* Vilnius (Lithuania) 2018, *Women Political Leaders Summit* Reykjavik (Iceland) 2017, *Women Political Leaders Summit* Amman (Jordan) 2016. [2021/AA1846/v/F]

- ♦ Women in Politics, Wives of Presidents and Vice Presidents in Africa / see Coalition of Women in Africa for Peace and Development (#04070)
- ♦ Women Presidents Organization (internationally oriented national body)
- ♦ Women Professional Golfers Association / see Ladies European Tour (#16218)
- ♦ Women at Risk / see Womankind Worldwide (#20982)
- ♦ Women's Action Network / see Equality Now (#05518)
- ♦ Women's Aglow Fellowship International / see Aglow International (#00561)
- ♦ Women's Agricultural and Horticultural International Union (inactive)

♦ Women's Alliance for Democracy 21013
Alliance des femmes pour la démocratie
Main Office 33-35 rue Jacob, 75006 Paris, France.
URL: http://www.alliancedesfemmes.fr/
History 1989, France, by Antoinette Fouque (1936-2014). **Aims** Promote women's access to the decision-making process; promote solidarity between men and women; fight against violence against women. **Members** in 25 countries. Membership countries not specified. [2017/XF3217/F]

- ♦ Women's Association for Multidisciplinary Studies and Research in Africa (inactive)

♦ Women's Brain Project (WBP) 21014
Contact address not obtained. E-mail: info@womensbrainproject.com.
URL: http://womensbrainproject.com/
History Launched 2016, St Gallen (Switzerland). **Aims** Advocate for women's brain and *mental health*; stimulate a global discussion on *gender* and sex determinants of female *vulnerability* to brain and mental disease. **Structure** Board of Directors; Executive Committee; Advisory Board. **Activities** Research and development; events/meetings; advocacy/lobbying/a activism; research/documentation. **Publications** *WBP Bulletin.* [2018/XM6625/F]

- ♦ Women's Caucus / see Southeast Asia Women's Caucus on ASEAN (#19800)
- ♦ Women's Caucus for Gender Justice in the International Criminal Court / see Women's Initiatives for Gender Justice (#21021)
- ♦ Women's Climate Initiative (internationally oriented national body)
- ♦ Women's Commission for Refugee Women and Children / see Women's Refugee Commission
- ♦ Women's Corona Club / see Corona Worldwide (#04836)
- ♦ Women's Corona Society / see Corona Worldwide (#04836)
- ♦ Women's Earth Alliance (internationally oriented national body)
- ♦ Women's Earth and Climate Action Network, International (internationally oriented national body)
- ♦ Women's Earth and Climate Caucus / see Women's Earth and Climate Action Network, International
- ♦ Women's Ecumenical Liaison Group (inactive)
- ♦ Women in Security, Conflict Management and Peace (internationally oriented national body)
- ♦ Women's Edge Coalition / see Women Thrive Alliance

♦ Women's Education Worldwide (WEW) 21015
Coordinator Mount Holyoke College, 50 College St, South Hadley MA 01075, USA.
URL: http://www.mtholyoke.edu/proj/wew/
History Founded 2003. **Aims** Share best practices; collect and disseminate data about women's colleges; foster exchange among institutions; advocate for women's education worldwide. **Structure** Executive Committee of 7 institutions. **Activities** Organizes: biennial meeting; Student Leadership Conference; Faculty Conference. **Events** *Biennial Conference* Nanjing (China) 2012, *Student leadership conference* Pavia (Italy) 2011, *Faculty conference* South Hadley, MA (USA) / Northampton, MA (USA) 2011, *Biennial conference* Sydney, NSW (Australia) 2010, *Student leadership conference* USA 2008.
Members Institutions in 17 countries:
Australia, Bahrain, Bangladesh, China, France, India, Italy, Japan, Korea Rep, Pakistan, Peru, Saudi Arabia, Sudan, UK, United Arab Emirates, USA, Zimbabwe. [2013.08.20/XJ4519/C]

- ♦ Women's Enterprises International (internationally oriented national body)
- ♦ Women's Environmental Network (internationally oriented national body)

♦ Women's Environment and Development Organization (WEDO) 21016
Head of Office 147 Prince St, New York NY 11201, USA. T. +12129730325. Fax +12129730335. E-mail: wedo@wedo.org.
URL: http://www.wedo.org/
History Oct 1990, by Bella Abzug; incorporated in Washington DC (USA). Includes activities of the former *Women's Foreign Policy Council (inactive)* and Women USA Fund. **Aims** Ensure that women's rights, social, economic and environmental justice, and sustainable development principles, as well as the linkages between them, are at the heart of global and national policies, programs and practices. **Structure** International Board of Directors, consisting of Chair, 3 Vice Chairs, Secretary, Treasurer and members from various regions of the world. Executive Director. **Finance** Sources: foundations; UN agencies; government grants; individual donors. **Events** *International conference for the reform of international institutions* Geneva (Switzerland) 2006, *Women from West and East Europe conference for the world summit on sustainable development* Celakovice (Czech Rep) 2002, *World conference on breast cancer* Ottawa, ON (Canada) 1999, *World conference on breast cancer* Kingston, ON (Canada) 1997, *Workshop on holding governments and international agencies accountable* New York, NY (USA) 1996. **Publications** *WEDO News and Views* (3-4 a year) – electronic newsletter. Briefing packets; primers; fact sheets; research – all online. **Members** Not a membership organization; part of an international network of women. **Consultative Status** Consultative status granted from: *ECOSOC (#05331)* (Ros B); *UNEP (#20299); United Nations Population Fund (UNFPA, #20612).* **IGO Relations** Accredited to the Conference of the Parties of: *Secretariat of the United Nations Convention to Combat Desertification (Secretariat of the UNCCD, #19208).* Accredited by: *Green Climate Fund (GCF, #10714).* Associated with Department of Global Communications of the United Nations. **NGO Relations** Member of: *Association for Women's Rights in Development (AWID, #02980); Climate Action Network (CAN, #03999); Conference of Non-Governmental Organizations in Consultative Relationship with the United Nations (CONGO, #04635); EarthAction (EA, #05159); Global Call for Climate Action (GCCA, inactive); Global Gender and Climate Alliance (GGCA, no recent information).* Links with numerous organizations worldwide, including: *African Women's Development and Communication Network (FEMNET, #00503); Center for Women's Global Leadership (CWGL); Development Alternatives with Women for a New Era (DAWN, #05054); Equality Now (#05518); International Network on Gender and Sustainable Energy (ENERGIA, #14272); International Women's Health Coalition (IWHC)*; National Council for Research on Women; *Social Watch (#19350); Women Engage for a Common Future (WECF, #20992); Women in Law and Development in Africa-Afrique de l'Ouest (WiLDAF-AO, #21005).* [2018/XF1829/F]

- ♦ Women's Exchange Programme International / see Atria – Institute for Gender Equality and Women's History

♦ Women's Feature Service (WFS) 21017
Contact C-205 – Third Floor, Lajpat Nagar I, Delhi 110024, DELHI 110024, India. T. +911140574336.
URL: http://www.wfsnews.org/

History 1978, by *UNESCO (#20322)* and *United Nations Population Fund (UNFPA, #20612)*, within *Inter Press Service (IPS, #15964)*, an organ of *IPS – Inter Press Service International Association (#16013)*, as an autonomous Third World network of women journalists. Independent since 1991. Registered in accordance with Indian law. **Aims** Make women's voices heard in mainstream media by placing articles in newspapers, magazines, journals and websites in India and abroad; produce features written from a progressive perspective by women journalists; cover development issues with a view to informing public policy. **Structure** Board of Governors of 5 members, including Chairperson and Treasurer. Management Committee. Units (4): Editorial; Marketing; Technical; Administration and Finance. **Languages** English, Hindi. **Staff** 10.00 FTE, paid. **Finance** Proceeds from projects and sale of features. **Activities** Produces about 300 features annually (in English) for publication in mainstream media and as reference material for conferences, workshops and projects and translates selected features into Hindi. **Publications** *Beijing – UN Fourth World Conference on Women* (1998); *Measuring the Immeasurable: Planning, Monitoring and Evaluation of Networks* (1998); *Power to Change: Third World Women Redefine their Environment* (1992) in English, Finnish, German, Japanese. Over 250 theme files for archival search and retrieval of WFS articles on website.
Members Journalists (mostly women) in 22 countries:
Afghanistan, Australia, Austria, Bangladesh, Brazil, Canada, China, France, India, Israel, Italy, Kenya, Nepal, Oman, Pakistan, Philippines, Singapore, Sri Lanka, Uganda, UK, United Arab Emirates, USA.
NGO Relations Member of: *OneWorld International Foundation (OWIF, #17738)*. Instrumental in setting up: *Latin American Feature Service on Women and Population (no recent information)*. [2014/XF5182/v/F]

♦ Women's Federation for World Peace International (internationally oriented national body)

♦ Women's Fund Asia 21018

Exec Dir 30/62A Longden Place, Colombo, 00700, Sri Lanka. T. +94114324541. E-mail: info@wf-asia.org.
URL: https://womensfundasia.org/

History 2004. Region expanded to Southeast Asia and Mongolia, 2018. Former names and other names: *South Asia Women's Fund (SAWF)* – former. Registration: Registrar-General of Companies, No/ID: GA139, Start date: 18 Feb 2018, Sri Lanka, Western Province. **Aims** Support the human rights of all women, girls, trans, and intersex people in Asia. **Structure** Board of Directors, including Chair. **Staff** 2.00 FTE, paid. **Finance** Sources: contributions; donations; fundraising; grants. Annual budget: 600,000,000 LKR (2021). **Activities** Advocacy/lobbying/activism; financial and/or material support; networking/liaising. Promotes feminist philanthropy. Active in: Afghanistan, Bangladesh, Bhutan, Cambodia, India, Indonesia, Laos, Malaysia, Maldives, Mongolia, Myanmar, Nepal, Pakistan, Philippines, Sri Lanka, Thailand, Timor-Leste, Vietnam. **Publications** *Newsletter*. Annual Report. **NGO Relations** Member of (1): *Prospera – International Network of Women's Funds (INWF, #18545)*. [2023.02.20/XM5747/f/F]

♦ Women's Funding Network (internationally oriented national body)

♦ Women's Global Network for Reproductive Rights (WGNRR) 21019

Réseau mondial des femmes pour les droits sur la reproduction – Red Mundial de Mujeres por los Derechos Reproductivos

Exec Dir 3 Marunong Street, Barangay Central, Diliman, 1100 Quezon City, Philippines. T. +6329287785. Fax +6329287992. E-mail: office@wgnrr.org.
URL: http://www.wgnrr.org/

History 1978, London (UK). Founded as *International Campaign for Abortion Rights (ICAR)*, subsequently *International Contraception, Abortion and Sterilization Campaign (ICASC) – Campagne internationale pour la contraception, l'avortement et la stérilisation – Campaña Internacional sobre la Contracepción, el Aborto y la Esterilización*. Current name adopted 1984. **Aims** Promote, in every country and for all women equally, a woman's right to decide whether, when and how to have children – regardless of nationality, class, race, ethnicity, age, religion, disability, sexuality or marital status – in the social, economic and political conditions that make such decisions possible. Reproductive rights means the right to: safe, effective contraception and sterilization; safe, legal abortion; safe, women-controlled pregnancy and childbirth; full information about sexuality and reproduction, about reproductive health and health problems and about benefits and risks of drugs, devices, medical treatments and interventions, without which informed choice is impossible; good quality, comprehensive reproductive health services that meet women's need and are accessible to all women. **Structure** Members' meeting (every 3 years). Board of 7 members. Network coordinated by Office in Amsterdam (Netherlands). Members and supporters work independently in their own countries. **Languages** English, French, Spanish. **Staff** 8.00 FTE, paid. **Finance** Sources: subscriptions and donations. Financial support from a number of organizations, including the following listed in this Yearbook: *DANIDA*; *Humanistisch Instituut voor Ontwikkelingssamenwerking (Hivos)*; *ICCO – Interchurch Organization for Development Cooperation*; *Oxfam Novib*; *World Council of Churches (WCC, #21320)*. **Activities** Major priorities and areas of work at international level are decided at members' meeting. Networking: builds links and exchanges between new and existing groups and individuals. Attends, supports and initiates meetings on women's health and reproductive rights at regional and international level. Organizes and participates in international actions and campaigns. Responds to requests from members for international solidarity. Collects and exchanges information on reproductive health issues, medical and social research and laws, policies and services in every country. **Events** *People's health assembly* Dhaka (Bangladesh) 2000, *International action meeting to stop the research on anti-fertility vaccines / International Women's Health and Meeting* Ottawa, ON (Canada) 1995, *International Women's Health and Meeting* Chennai (India) 1993, *International members meeting* Kampala (Uganda) 1993, *International women and health tribunal and meeting* Kampala (Uganda) 1993. **Publications** *WGNRR Newsletter* (4 a year) in English, French, Spanish. Reports (periodical).
Members Individuals, groups and subscribers (1,650) in 83 countries and territories:
Albania, Algeria, Argentina, Australia, Austria, Bahamas, Bangladesh, Barbados, Belgium, Bolivia, Brazil, Burkina Faso, Cameroon, Canada, Chile, Colombia, Costa Rica, Croatia, Cuba, Denmark, Dominican Rep, Ecuador, Egypt, El Salvador, Fiji, Finland, France, Germany, Greece, Guam, Guatemala, Haiti, Honduras, India, Indonesia, Israel, Italy, Kenya, Malawi, Malaysia, Mauritius, Mexico, Morocco, Namibia, Nepal, Netherlands, New Caledonia, New Zealand (Aotearoa), Nicaragua, Nigeria, Norway, Pakistan, Panama, Paraguay, Peru, Philippines, Poland, Portugal, Puerto Rico, Romania, Senegal, Serbia, Sierra Leone, Singapore, South Africa, Spain, Sri Lanka, Sudan, Suriname, Sweden, Switzerland, Tanzania UR, Thailand, Togo, Trinidad-Tobago, Tunisia, Uganda, UK, Uruguay, USA, Venezuela, Zambia, Zimbabwe.
Consultative Status Consultative status granted from: *ECOSOC (#05331)* (Special). **NGO Relations** Member of: *People's Health Movement (PHM, #18305)*; *World Social Forum (WSF, #21797)*. Supports: *Global Call for Action Against Poverty (GCAP, #10263)*. [2022/XF0198/F]

♦ Women's Home and Foreign Missionary Society / see Women's Missionary Society – African Methodist Episcopal Church
♦ Women's Home and Overseas Missionary Society (internationally oriented national body)
♦ Women's Hospitals Australasia (internationally oriented national body)
♦ Women's Human Rights International Association (internationally oriented national body)

♦ Women's Information Network of Europe (WINE) 21020

Dir Humboldt Univ Gender Library, Unter den Linden 6, 10099 Berlin, Germany.
URL: http://winenetworkeurope.wordpress.com/

Aims Provide a common platform for specialists in *libraries*, *archives* and information/documentation to help facilitate discussion and information-sharing in the areas of *gender*, *feminist* and women's studies and research. **Events** *Members' Meeting* Barcelona (Spain) 2014, *Members Meeting / Members' Meeting* Gothenburg (Sweden) 2013.
Members Full in 25 countries:
Albania, Austria, Belgium, Czechia, Denmark, Estonia, Finland, France, Germany, Hungary, Ireland, Italy, Lithuania, Luxembourg, Netherlands, Norway, Romania, Russia, Serbia, Slovenia, Spain, Sweden, Switzerland, Türkiye, UK.
NGO Relations Cooperates with: *The European Association for Gender Research, Education and Documentation (ATGENDER, #06052)*; *International Federation of Library Associations and Institutions (IFLA, #13470)*. [2019.06.27/XJ6308/F]

♦ Women's Initiative for Empowerment and Leadership Development / see Moremi Initiative for Women's Leadership in Africa

♦ Women's Initiatives for Gender Justice (Women's Initiatives) 21021

Exec Dir Saturnusstraat 9, 2516 AD The Hague, Netherlands. E-mail: admin@4genderjustice.org – info@4genderjustice.org.
URL: http://www.4genderjustice.org/

History 2004, Netherlands. Operated as *Women's Caucus for Gender Justice in the International Criminal Court*, 1997-2003. After *International Criminal Court (ICC, #13108)* was properly set up, Caucus concluded its work, Mar 2003. Registration: Handelsregister, No/ID: 27264260, Netherlands. **Aims** Advocate for gender justice through the *International Criminal Court (ICC)* and other justice mechanisms. **Structure** Board; Executive Director. **Languages** English, French. **Staff** 3.00 FTE, paid. **Finance** Annual budget: 300,000 EUR (2021). **Activities** Advocacy/lobbying/activism; guidance/assistance/consulting; monitoring/evaluation. Active in: Congo DR, Netherlands, Uganda, Ukraine. **Publications** *Gender Report Card on the International Criminal Court*. Expert papers; reports. **NGO Relations** Cooperates with (12): *Amnesty International (AI, #00801)*; *Coalition for the International Criminal Court (CICC, #04062)*; *European Center for Constitutional and Human Rights (ECCHR)*; *Global Justice Center (GJC)*; *IMPACT (#11136)*; *MADRE*; *No Peace Without Justice (NPWJ, #17155)*; *Parliamentarians for Global Action (PGA, #18208)*; *REDRESS*; *Sexual Violence Research Initiative (SVRI, #19251)*; *TRIAL International*; *Women's Link Worldwide*. [2022.10.19/XG9946/F]

♦ **Women's Initiatives** Women's Initiatives for Gender Justice (#21021)
♦ Women's Intercultural Network (internationally oriented national body)
♦ Women's International Artistic Union (inactive)
♦ Women's International Cultural Federation (#09625)
♦ Women's International Cycling Association (inactive)

♦ Women's International Democratic Federation (WIDF) 21022

Fédération démocratique internationale des femmes (FDIF) – Federación Democratica Internacional de Mujeres (FDIM) – Internationale Demokratische Frauenföderation (IDFF) – Mezdunarodnaja Demokraticeskaja Federacija Zenscin (MDFŽ)

Contact Avenida Bernal, Pasaje Jiboa, Avenida Cuchumatanes, casa 12, Urbanización Metrópolis, Mejicanos, CP 1120 San Salvador, El Salvador. E-mail: presidencia.fdim@gmail.com.

History 1 Dec 1945, Paris (France). Statutes modified, Apr 1994, Paris. **Aims** Unite women regardless of race, nationality, religion and political opinion, so that they may work together to win, implement and defend their *rights* as mothers, workers and citizens; defend the rights of *children* to life, *well-being* and education; win and defend national independence and democratic freedoms, eliminate apartheid, racial discrimination and fascism; work for peace and universal disarmament. **Structure** Congress; Executive Committee. **Languages** Arabic, English, French, German, Spanish. **Finance** Sources: donations; members' dues. **Activities** Works for: (1) women's rights in society and in the family and for their right to work, to receive equal pay for equal work, to receive education at all levels and for recognition of their social and cultural life – supports women suffering oppression, racial discrimination, apartheid, any form of fascism, colonialism or neocolonialism, through solidarity activities, study trips, seminars, round-table meetings and publications; (2) the right to health care and adequate nutrition, so children do not die of hunger; (3) children's, especially girls', right to education, protection of children from violence and respect for their individual rights. With respect to peace, works: (1) for preservation and consolidation of peace; against the arms race (including weapons of mass destruction and nuclear weapons); (2) against constantly increasing military expenditure. With respect to NGO activities: was an initiator of the proclamation by the United Nations of *'International Women's Year'* and contributed to the implementation of *'United Nations Decade for Women: Equality, Development, Peace'*. **Events** *Congress* Brasilia (Brazil) 2012, *Congress* Caracas (Venezuela) 2007, *Congress* Rome (Italy) 2006, *International women solidarity conference* Havana (Cuba) 1998, *Congress* Paris (France) 1998. **Publications** *WIDF Letter* (4 a year). *Planète femmes* (1996) by Sylvie Jan.
Members National organizations (151) in 89 countries and territories:
Albania, Algeria, Angola, Argentina, Austria, Azerbaijan, Bangladesh, Belgium, Benin, Bolivia, Brazil, Bulgaria, Burkina Faso, Burundi, Cameroon, Cape Verde, Chile, Colombia, Congo Brazzaville, Costa Rica, Cuba, Cyprus, Djibouti, Dominican Rep, Ecuador, Egypt, El Salvador, France, Gambia, Germany, Ghana, Greece, Guadeloupe, Guatemala, Guinea-Bissau, Guyana, Haiti, Iceland, India, Iraq, Israel, Jamaica, Japan, Jordan, Kurdish area, Laos, Lebanon, Luxembourg, Madagascar, Mali, Martinique, Mauritania, Mauritius, Mexico, Mongolia, Morocco, Mozambique, Netherlands, Nicaragua, Niger, Norway, Palestine, Panama, Paraguay, Peru, Philippines, Portugal, Puerto Rico, Réunion, Romania, Russia, Rwanda, Sahara West, Senegal, Somalia, South Africa, Spain, Sri Lanka, Suriname, Sweden, Syrian AR, Tunisia, Türkiye, UK, Uruguay, USA, Venezuela, Vietnam, Zimbabwe.
Consultative Status Consultative status granted from: *ECOSOC (#05331)* (General); *ILO (#11123)* (Special List); *UNICEF (#20332)*; *UNIDO (#20336)*. **IGO Relations** *UNESCO (#20322)*; *United Nations Economic and Social Commission for Asia and the Pacific (ESCAP, #20557)*. Accredited by: *United Nations Office at Vienna (UNOV, #20604)*. Associated with Department of Global Communications of the United Nations. **NGO Relations** Member of the Board of the: *Conference of Non-Governmental Organizations in Consultative Relationship with the United Nations (CONGO, #04635)* and member of CONGO's ongoing Committees. Links with NGOs in the framework of CONGO activities. Member of: *NGO Committee on the Status of Women, Geneva (#17117)*; *NGO Committee on Disarmament, Peace and Security, New York NY (#17106)* and *NGO Committee for Disarmament, Geneva (#17105)*; *NGO Committee on UNICEF (#17120)*. [2018/XB3438/B]

♦ Women's International Forum (WIF) 21023

Contact UN, Room DC1-0648, New York NY 10017, USA. T. +12129633112. E-mail: briefing@womensinternationalforum.org.
URL: http://womensinternationalforum.org/

History 1975. **Aims** Provide a forum for briefings and discussions on international affairs, so as to promote understanding and mutual appreciation among members of the diplomatic community, the United Nations Secretariat and the UN community at large; network and promote knowledge and raise awareness about current international issues, particularly those related to the UN; uphold the purpose and the principles of the UN Charter. **Structure** Honorary Board; Executive Board. **Activities** Events/meetings. **Members** Individuals (over 300). Membership countries not specified. [2016/XM5118/F]

♦ Women's International Fund for Education (internationally oriented national body)
♦ Women's International Information and Communication Service / see Isis Women's International Cross Cultural Exchange (#16031)
♦ Women's International Information and Communication Service / see IO – Facilitating Space for Feminist Conversations (#16005)

♦ Women's International League for Peace and Freedom (WILPF) . . . 21024

SG Geneva Office, 1 rue de Varembé, Case Postale 28, 1211 Geneva 20, Switzerland. T. +41229197080. Fax +41229197081. E-mail: secretariat@wilpf.org.
New York Office 777 UN Plaza, 6th Floor, New York NY 10017, USA. T. +12126821265. Fax +12122868211.
URL: http://www.wilpf.org/

History 28 Apr 1915, The Hague (Netherlands). Founded at the International Women's Congress, whose president was Jane Addams (Nobel Peace Prize 1931), following activities of *Ligue des femmes pour le désarmement universel*, set up in 1896. Organizers of the founding Congress were members of *International Suffrage Alliance*, currently *International Alliance of Women (IAW, #11639)*. Present title adopted at 2nd Congress, 1919. Constitution last amended in Brisbane (Australia) & online, Jul 2022. Former names and other names: *International Women's Committee for a Durable Peace* – former; *International Committee of Women for Permanent Peace* – former; *Pour la paix par l'éducation* – former; *Ligue internationale de femmes pour la paix et la liberté (LIFPL)* – alias; *Liga Internacional de Mujeres pro la Paz y la Libertad (LIMPAL)* – alias; *Internationale Frauenliga für Frieden und Freiheit (IFFF)* – alias; *Internationella Kvinnoförbundet för Fred och Frihet (IKFF)* – alias. **Aims** Promote a world of permanent peace built on feminist foundations of freedom, justice, nonviolence, human rights, and equality for all, where people, the planet, and all its other inhabitants coexist and flourish in harmony; transform militarized mindsets; prevent violence through peaceful and gender-responsive means that address causes of conflict; replace systems of oppression with feminist alternatives that champion human rights, demilitarization, accountability, and restitution; promote a future where a just, ecological transition has been achieved; promote a powerful, inclusive, and intersectional feminist movement that connects peace activists and other social justice movements on a global scale as we pursue collective action for change. **Structure** Triennial International Congress; International Board (IB); International Secretariat; National Sections and Groups. **Languages** Arabic, English, French, Spanish. **Staff** 40.00 FTE, paid. Several voluntary. **Finance** Sources: government support; members' dues; private foundations; revenue

from activities/projects. **Activities** Advocacy/lobbying/activism; events/meetings. **Events** *Triennial Congress* Brisbane, QLD (Australia) 2022, *Triennial Congress* Brisbane, QLD (Australia) 2021, *Triennial Congress* Accra (Ghana) 2018, *Triennial Congress* The Hague (Netherlands) 2015, *Meeting* Madrid (Spain) 2013. **Publications** Annual Report; reports; case studies; press releases; statements.
Members National Sections in 41 countries and territories:
Afghanistan, Argentina, Australia, Austria, Burkina Faso, Burundi, Cameroon, Canada, Central African Rep, Chad, Colombia, Congo DR, Costa Rica, Côte d'Ivoire, Denmark, Finland, Germany, Ghana, Guinea, India, Italy, Japan, Kenya, Lebanon, Mexico, Netherlands, New Zealand, Niger, Nigeria, Norway, Pakistan, Palestine, Spain, Sudan, Sweden, Switzerland, Togo, Uganda, UK, USA, Zimbabwe.
National Groups in 5 countries:
Senegal, Sierra Leone, South Africa, Sri Lanka, Yemen.
Consultative Status Consultative status granted from: *ECOSOC (#05331)* (Special); *UNEP (#20299)*; *UNESCO (#20322)* (Consultative Status); *ILO (#11123)* (Special List); *FAO (#09260)* (Special Status); *UNCTAD (#20285)* (General Category); *UNICEF (#20332)*. **NGO Relations** Member of (12): *Campaign to Stop Killer Robots (#03405)*; *Committee of NGOs on Human Rights, Geneva (#04275)*; *Conference of Non-Governmental Organizations in Consultative Relationship with the United Nations (CONGO, #04635)*; *International Campaign to Ban Landmines – Cluster Munition Coalition (ICBL-CMC, #12427)*; *International Coalition to Ban Uranium Weapons (ICBUW, #12609)*; *International Network on Explosive Weapons (INEW, #14266)*; *NGO Committee for Disarmament, Geneva (#17105)*; *NGO Committee on Disarmament, Peace and Security, New York NY (#17106)*; *NGO Committee on the Status of Women, Geneva (#17117)*; *NGO Working Group for Women, Peace and Security (NGOWG, #17129)*; Women and Gender Constituency; Women's Major Group.
[2022.10.12/XC3439/**C**]

♦ Women's International Liaison Committee for International Cooperation (inactive)

♦ Women's International Match Racing Association (WIMRA) 21025

Exec Dir 15 Margarita Dr, San Rafael CA 94901-2325, USA. E-mail: execdir@wimra.org – northamerica@wimra.org.
URL: http://www.wimra.org/
History Registed in accordance with USA law. **Aims** Promote and supervise women's match-race *sailing*. **Finance** Members' dues. **Activities** Administers "Women's International Match Race Ranking System".
[2019/XK1872/**E**]

♦ Women's International Motorcycle Association (WIMA) 21026

International Pres 1 Grande Rue, Creuse, 23400 Bosmoreau-les-Mines, France. T. +33555647630. E-mail: president@wimaworld.com.
Main Website: http://www.wimaworld.com/
History 1950, USA. Carried to Europe, 1958. **Aims** Improve and promote activities, advancement, goodwill and friendship among women motorcycle enthusiasts from around the world. **Structure** Divisions are autonomous, but must agree with WIMA International Constitution. **Languages** English, French, German. **Staff** 6.00 FTE, voluntary. **Finance** Sources: donations; members' dues; sale of products. **Activities** Events/meetings; networking/liaising; sporting activities. Active in all member countries. **Events** *International Council of National Presidents (ICNP) Annual Meeting* Melchtal (Switzerland) 2022, *WIMA International Rally General Assembly* Melchtal (Switzerland) 2022, *International Council of National Presidents (ICNP) Annual Meeting* Castleton (UK) 2019, *WIMA International Rally Annual General Assembly* Castleton (UK) 2019, *WIMA International Rally General Assembly* Pietermaai (Curaçao) 2019. **Publications** *WIMA Newsletter*. Rally reports.
Members Divisions in 40 countries and territories:
Australia, Austria, Bangladesh, Belgium, Bulgaria, Canada, Curaçao, Denmark, Estonia, Finland, France, Germany, Ghana, Great Britain, Greece, Iceland, India, Italy, Japan, Korea Rep, Liechtenstein, Lithuania, Luxembourg, Malaysia, Mexico, Morocco, Nepal, Netherlands, New Zealand, Nicaragua, Norway, Pakistan, Panama, Poland, Romania, Sweden, Switzerland, Ukraine, United Arab Emirates, USA.
[2023.02.07/XD0279/**D**]

♦ Women's International Network (WIN) 21027

Contact address not obtained. T. +17818629431. Fax +17818621734.
URL: http://www.feminist.com/win.htm
History Jan 1975, Lexington MA (USA), on the initiative of Fran Hosken, as an open participatory network. **Publications** *WIN NEWS* (4 a year).
[2011/XF4367/**F**]

♦ Women's International Networking (WIN) 21028

Dir c/o CBC-L, Rue de Simplon 37, 1006 Lausanne VD, Switzerland. T. +41216120354. Fax +41216120351. E-mail: info@winconference.net.
URL: http://www.winconference.net/
History 1997, Milan (Italy). Founded by Kristin Engvig. Registration: Start date: 2002, Switzerland. **Aims** Model, develop, empower and connect leaders in a feminine, authentic and global way. **Languages** English. **Activities** Events/meetings; guidance/assistance/consulting; networking/liaising. **Events** *Global Leadership Conference* Rome (Italy) 2022, *Global WIN Conference* Dubai (United Arab Emirates) 2021, *Annual Global Forum* Athens (Greece) 2019, *Annual Global Forum* Rome (Italy) 2018, *Annual Global Forum* Oslo (Norway) 2017. **NGO Relations** Affiliated with (1): *Global Citizen Forum (GCF)*.
[2022/XM3338/**F**]

♦ Women's International News Gathering Service (internationally oriented national body)

♦ Women's International Shipping and Trading Association (WISTA) . 21029

Pres c/o Management Facilities Group, Hogelandsterweg 14, 9936 BH Farmsum, Netherlands.
URL: http://www.wista.net/
History 1974. **Aims** Offer networking for women in shipping. **Structure** General Assembly (annual); Executive Committee. **Languages** English. **Staff** None. **Finance** Members' dues. **Events** *Collaboration for Sustainability – Cross-Industry Solutions for the Future* Geneva (Switzerland) 2022, *Shipping 2025 – Today's Actions for Tomorrow's Business* Hamburg (Germany) 2021, *Conference* Hamburg (Germany) 2020, *Conference* Grand Cayman Is (Cayman Is) 2019, *Meeting on Women, Ports and Facilitation* London (UK) 2019. **Publications** *WISTA Newsletter*.
Members National WISTAs in 39 countries and territories:
Argentina, Australia, Belgium, Canada, Cayman Is, China, Cyprus, Denmark, Dominican Rep, Finland, France, Germany, Ghana, Greece, Hong Kong, India, Ireland, Italy, Japan, Malta, Netherlands, New Zealand, Nigeria, Norway, Panama, Peru, Philippines, Poland, Russia, Singapore, Spain, Sri Lanka, Sweden, Switzerland, Türkiye, UK, Ukraine, United Arab Emirates, USA.
[2020/XD5784/**D**]

♦ Women's International Squash Players Association / see Women's Squash Association (#21034)
♦ Women's International Squash Rackets Federation / see Women's Squash Association (#21034)

♦ Women's International Zionist Organization (WIZO) 21030

Organisation internationale des femmes sionistes – Organización Internacional de Mujeres Sionistas – Internationaler Zionistischer Frauenbund
Chair WIZO House, 38 King David Blvd, 6423711 Tel Aviv, Israel. T. +97236923706. Fax +97236951202. E-mail: infodep@wizo.org.
Pres address not obtained. T. +97236923716. Fax +97236960506.
URL: http://www.wizo.org/
History 11 Jul 1920, London (UK). **Aims** Provide social welfare and educational facilities and programmes for women, senior citizens and children. **Structure** World Conference (every 4 years); World Executive. Meetings closed. Includes *European Council of WIZO Federations (ECWF, #06850)*. **Languages** Arabic, English, French, German, Hebrew, Russian, Spanish. **Finance** Sources: donations; government support; members' dues. **Activities** Financial and/or material support; guidance/assistance/consulting; projects/programmes; training/education. **Events** *Enlarged General Meeting* Tel Aviv (Israel) 2020, *Quadrennial Conference* Tel Aviv (Israel) 1996, *International seminar* Ramat Gan (Israel) 1995, *Quadrennial Conference* Tel Aviv (Israel) 1992, *Quadrennial Conference* Tel Aviv (Israel) 1986. **Publications** *WIZO Review* (annual); *Bamat Haisha*. *L* – leaflets. Leaflets; booklets; Facts and Figures.
Members Federations and representation in 42 countries and territories:
Argentina, Australia, Austria, Belgium, Bolivia, Brazil, Bulgaria, Canada, Chile, Colombia, Costa Rica, Curaçao, Czechia, Denmark, Finland, France, Germany, Guatemala, Honduras, Hong Kong, Hungary, India, Italy, Jamaica, Latvia, Lithuania, Luxembourg, Mexico, Netherlands, New Zealand, Norway, Panama, Paraguay, Peru, South Africa, Spain, Sweden, Switzerland, UK, Uruguay, USA, Venezuela.

Consultative Status Consultative status granted from: *ECOSOC (#05331)* (Special); *UNICEF (#20332)*. **IGO Relations** Accredited by (1): *United Nations Office at Vienna (UNOV, #20604)*. Associated with Department of Global Communications of the United Nations. **NGO Relations** Member of (5): *Committee of NGOs on Human Rights, Geneva (#04275)*; *Conference of Non-Governmental Organizations in Consultative Relationship with the United Nations (CONGO, #04635)*; *NGO Committee on Sustainable Development, Vienna (#17119)*; *NGO Committee on the Status of Women, Geneva (#17117)*; *Vienna NGO Committee on the Status of Women (#20775)*.
[2022.03.04/XE3441/**F**]

♦ Women's League for Conservative Judaism (internationally oriented national body)

♦ Women's Learning Partnership for Rights, Development and Peace (WLP) 21031

Pres/Founder/CEO 4343 Montgomery Ave, Ste 201, Bethesda MD 20814, USA. T. +13016542774. Fax +13016542775. E-mail: wlp@learningpartnership.org.
URL: http://www.learningpartnership.org/
History 1999. **Aims** Advance communication and cooperation among and between the women of the world in order to protect human rights, facilitate sustainable development and promote peace. **Structure** Board, comprising President, Treasurer, Secretary and 4 further members. Expert Advisory Council. Partner Program Advisors. **Languages** Arabic, Assamese, English, French, Hausa, Indonesian, Kirghiz, Malay, Manipuri, Persian, Portuguese, Russian, Shona, Spanish, Swahili, Turkish, Urdu, Uzbek. **Finance** Budget (annual): US$ 2 million. **Activities** Establishes partnerships with women's NGOs in Africa, Asia, Latin America, and the Middle East; produces culture-specific training materials that are tested, evaluated and modified by partner NGOs. Programmes: Young Women's Learning Partnership (YWLP); Leadership, Human Rights and Political Participation Training; Human Rights Campaigns; Technology Capacity-Building; Translation Series. Programmes are designed and adapted by women and men of all ages and economic and educational backgrounds. **Publications** Annual Report; training manuals; guides, videos and CD-Roms in 20 languages; e-learning portal.
Members National and regional partner organizations (20) in the Global South. Members in 20 countries and territories:
Afghanistan, Bahrain, Brazil, Egypt, India, Indonesia, Iran Islamic Rep, Jordan, Kazakhstan, Kyrgyzstan, Lebanon, Malaysia, Mauritania, Morocco, Nicaragua, Nigeria, Pakistan, Palestine, Türkiye, Zimbabwe.
Consultative Status Consultative status granted from: *ECOSOC (#05331)* (Special). **NGO Relations** Instrumental in setting up: *International Women's Democracy Network (IWDN, #15897)*.
[2012.10.26/XM0848/**F**]

♦ Women's Link Worldwide (internationally oriented national body)
♦ Women's Missionary Society – African Methodist Episcopal Church (internationally oriented national body)
♦ Women's Network of the Council for Adult Education in Latin America / see Red de Educación Popular entre Mujeres de América Latina y el Caribe (#18647)
♦ Women's Network for Peace (internationally oriented national body)

♦ Women's Ordination Worldwide (WOW) 21032

Exec Dir address not obtained. T. +16077251364.
Communications address not obtained. T. +447970926910.
Office 111a High Street, Rickmansworth, WD3 1AN, UK.
URL: http://womensordinationcampaign.org/
History 1996, Gmunden (Austria), at 1st *European Women's Synod*. Initially a loose network of organizations. **Aims** Work towards admission of Roman Catholic women to all ordained ministries. **Structure** Steering Committee. **Activities** Advocacy/lobbying/activism; events/meetings. **Events** *Conference* Ottawa, ON (Canada) 2005, *Conference* Dublin (Ireland) 2001.
Members Groups in 11 countries:
Australia, Austria, Canada, Colombia, France, Germany, India, Ireland, Portugal, UK, USA.
International members include 1 organization listed in this Yearbook:
St Joan's International Alliance (SJIA, #19992).
[2020/XJ7103/**F**]

♦ Women's Organization of Hapoel Hamizrachi / see World Emunah Religious Zionist Women's Organization (#21378)
♦ Women's Peace Network / see MADRE

♦ WomenSport International (WSI) 21033

SG 8601 Nightingale Drive, Lanham MD 20706, USA. E-mail: info@womensportinternational.org.
URL: http://womensportinternational.org/
History 1994, Australia. **Aims** Ensure that sport and physical activity receive attention and priority in the lives of girls and women; meet the need for an international umbrella organization that can bring about increased opportunities and positive change for girls and women in these important areas of their lives. **Structure** Advisory Board; Executive Board; Standing Committees; Task Forces. **Languages** English. **Staff** Voluntary. **Finance** Sources: members' dues. **Activities** Advocacy/lobbying/activism; guidance/assistance/consulting; knowledge management/information dissemination; networking/liaising; research/documentation; training/education. **Events** *Gender Equality on Tokyo Olympics and Paralympics* 2021, *Town Hall Forum* Northampton, MA (USA) 2021. **Publications** Advocacy brochures; position statements.
Members Individuals; Students; Organizations. Members in 44 countries:
Argentina, Australia, Austria, Bangladesh, Barbados, Belgium, Botswana, Brazil, Canada, China, Congo Brazzaville, Denmark, Ecuador, Egypt, Ethiopia, Finland, Germany, Ghana, Greece, Hungary, India, Ireland, Israel, Italy, Japan, Kenya, Madagascar, Mexico, Namibia, Nepal, Netherlands, New Zealand, Nigeria, Norway, Pakistan, Palau, Portugal, Singapore, South Africa, Sweden, Switzerland, Uganda, UK, Zimbabwe.
Consultative Status Consultative status granted from: *ECOSOC (#05331)* (Special). **IGO Relations** Member of (1): *Intergovernmental Committee for Physical Education and Sport (#11475)* (Permanent Consultative Council (PCC)). **NGO Relations** Member of (1): *International Council of Sport Science and Physical Education (ICSSPE, #13077)*.
[2021.09.03/XC3230/v/**C**]

♦ Women and Sport in the Mediterranean Countries (no recent information)
♦ Women's Professional Golf Association / see Ladies European Tour (#16218)
♦ Women's Refugee Commission (internationally oriented national body)

♦ Women's Squash Association (WSA) 21034

Address not obtained.
URL: http://wsaworldtour.com/
History Apr 1984, as a women's committee of *World Squash Federation (WSF, #21826)*. Original title: to as *Women's International Squash Rackets Federation (WISRF)*. Subsequently referred to as *Women's International Squash Players Association (WISPA)*. Current title adopted 1 Jan 2012. **Aims** Promote women's professional squash globally through organizational excellence, providing members with the opportunity to maximize their career potential. **Structure** General Meeting (annual); Board of Directors. **Languages** English. **Staff** 2.00 FTE, paid. **Finance** Members' dues. Other sources: tournament registration fees; tournament levies. **Activities** Sporting events. **Events** *Annual General Meeting* Singapore (Singapore) 2009, *Annual General Meeting* Liverpool (UK) 2008, *Annual General Meeting* Doha (Qatar) 2007, *Annual General Meeting* Poughkeepsie, NY (USA) 2006, *Annual General Meeting* Dallas, TX (USA) 2005.
Members Full; Regional; Rising Star. Individuals in 57 countries and territories:
Argentina, Australia, Austria, Barbados, Belgium, Brazil, Canada, Cayman Is, China, Colombia, Czechia, Denmark, Ecuador, Egypt, Estonia, Finland, France, Germany, Greece, Guatemala, Guyana, Hong Kong, Hungary, Iceland, India, Indonesia, Iran Islamic Rep, Ireland, Italy, Japan, Jordan, Korea Rep, Kuwait, Macau, Malaysia, Mexico, Netherlands, New Zealand, Nigeria, Norway, Pakistan, Philippines, Poland, Qatar, Russia, Singapore, Slovakia, Slovenia, South Africa, Spain, Sweden, Switzerland, Türkiye, UK, USA, Uzbekistan, Zambia.
[2015/XE1420/**E**]

♦ Women's Supreme Council / see Jewish Women International (#16114)
♦ WomenStrong International (internationally oriented national body)
♦ Women's University in Africa (internationally oriented national body)

♦ **Women's UN Report Network (WUNRN)** **21035**
Address not obtained.
URL: http://wunrn.com/
History Based on a UN Study on the Status of Women, Religion or Belief, and Traditions. Registered in the USA. In Europe known as *WUNRN Europe*, which is registered in accordance with Belgian law. WUNRN Europe is on the EU Transparency Register: 585360818421-71. **Aims** Address human rights, oppression, and empowerment of women and *girls* worldwide. **Activities** Research/documentation; advocacy/lobbying/activism. [2018/XM6828/**F**]

♦ Women's Voices Now (internationally oriented national body)

♦ **Women's Working Group on Financing for Development (WWG on FfD)** **21036**
Contact c/o DAWN, Women and Gender Institute, Miriam College, Katipunan Road, Loyola Heights, 1108 Quezon City, Philippines. T. +6324359240ext221. Fax +6324346440. E-mail: info@dawnnet.org.
URL: http://www.ffdngo.org/gender-financing-development
History Oct 2007. **Aims** Advance *gender* equality, women's empowerment and human rights in the FfD-related UN processes. **Events** *Civil society forum* Doha (Qatar) 2008, *Women's consultation on financing for development* New York, NY (USA) 2008. **Publications** Statements; reviews; proposals; other documents.
Members Organizations (8):
African Women's Development and Communication Network (FEMNET, #00503); Association for Women's Rights in Development (AWID, #02980); Development Alternatives with Women for a New Era (DAWN, #05054); Global Call for Action Against Poverty (GCAP, #10263) (Feminist Task Force); *International Gender and Trade Network (IGTN, #13707); International Trade Union Confederation (ITUC, #15708);* Network for Women's Rights in Ghana (NETRIGHT); *WIDE+ (#20951).* [2010.06.01/XJ0379/y/**E**]

♦ **Women's World Banking (WWB)** **21037**
Banque Mondiale des Femmes – Banco Mundial de la Mujer
Pres/CEO 122 East 42nd St, 42nd Floor, New York NY 10168, USA. T. +12127688513. Fax +12127688519. E-mail: communications@swwb.org.
URL: https://www.womensworldbanking.org/
History 1976, following suggestion at 1st UN World Conference on Women, 1975, Mexico City (Mexico). Registered in accordance with Dutch law, 1979, Amsterdam (Netherlands). **Aims** Expand economic assets, participation and power of low-income women and their households by helping them access financial services, knowledge and markets. **Structure** Board of Trustees, headed by Chairperson and President. Committees (3): Executive Nominating; Finance; Audit. **Staff** 40.00 FTE, paid. **Finance** Major donors: Norwegian, Dutch, Spanish, Swiss, Irish and Austrian governments; foundations, including: *Bill and Melinda Gates Foundation (BMGF); Starr International Foundation (SIF).* Capital Fund (Dec 2009): US$ 15.8 million. **Activities** Guidance/assistance/consulting. **Events** *Global Meeting* New York, NY (USA) 2009, *Bankers seminar* Acapulco (Mexico) 2007, *Rural finance workshop* Monterrey (Mexico) 2007, *Goldman Sachs capital markets workshop* New York, NY (USA) 2007, *Global Meeting* Morocco 2005. **Publications** E-newsletter. Manuals; reports; working papers; videos.
Members Network members in 28 countries:
Bangladesh, Benin, Bolivia, Bosnia-Herzegovina, Brazil, Burundi, Chile, Colombia, Dominican Rep, Egypt, Ethiopia, Gambia, Ghana, India, Jordan, Kenya, Mexico, Mongolia, Morocco, Nigeria, Pakistan, Paraguay, Peru, Philippines, Russia, Sri Lanka, Tunisia, Uganda.
Consultative Status Consultative status granted from: *ECOSOC (#05331)* (Special). **IGO Relations** Accredited by: *United Nations Office at Vienna (UNOV, #20604).* Collaborates with: *ILO (#11123).* Associated with Department of Global Communications of the United Nations. **NGO Relations** Associated member of, and also instrumental in setting up: *Africa Microfinance Network (AFMIN, #00189).* Member of: *Better Than Cash Alliance (#03220); European Microfinance Platform (E-MFP, #07793); Financial Inclusion Equity Council (CIEF, #09766); Microinsurance Network (#16747); Partnership for Responsible Financial Inclusion (PRFI, #18241).* [2016/XF0030/**F**]

♦ Women's World Day of Prayer, Central Committee / see International Committee for World Day of Prayer (#12811)
♦ Women's World Fellowship (inactive)
♦ Women's World Organization for Rights, Literature and Development (inactive)

♦ **Women's World Summit Foundation (WWSF)** **21038**
Fondation Sommet mondial des femmes (FSMF) – Fundación Cumbre Mundial de la Mujer (FCMM)
CEO PO Box 1504, 1211 Geneva, Switzerland. T. +41227386619. Fax +41227388248. E-mail: wwsf@wwsf.ch.
URL: http://www.woman.ch/
History 8 Mar 1991, Geneva (Switzerland). Founded in response to the UN Secretary-General's call for action at the World Summit for Children, Sep 1990, New York NY (USA). Registration: Switzerland. **Aims** Forward implementation of women's and *children's rights* and the UN *development* agenda. **Structure** Board; Secretariat. **Languages** English, French, German, Spanish. **Staff** 2-3 FTE, paid; mainly voluntary. **Finance** Contributions from members, organizations, international institutions, foundations, businesses and government bodies. **Activities** Advocacy/lobbying/activism; events/meetings; awards/prizes/competitions; capacity building; training/education; monitoring/evaluation; networking/liaising. **Events** *Round table* Geneva (Switzerland) 2010, *Geneva conference* Geneva (Switzerland) 2009, *Round table* 1998, *Geneva summit / Annual Geneva Summit for Women and Children* Geneva (Switzerland) 1998, *Geneva summit / Annual Geneva Summit for Women and Children* Geneva (Switzerland) 1997. **Publications** *Empowering Women and Children* (annual) – newsletter. Kits for prevention of child abuse, in 4 languages; guides; brochures; posters; reports; statements for the UN; press releases. **Members** Individuals; sponsors. Membership countries not specified.
Consultative Status Consultative status granted from: *ECOSOC (#05331)* (Special). **IGO Relations** Associated with Department of Global Communications of the United Nations. **NGO Relations** Member of: *CIVICUS: World Alliance for Citizen Participation (#03962); Child Rights Connect (#03884); Committee of NGOs on Human Rights, Geneva (#04275); Conference of Non-Governmental Organizations in Consultative Relationship with the United Nations (CONGO, #04635); Global Partnership to End Violence Against Children (End Violence Against Children, #10533); International Peace Bureau (IPB, #14535); NGO Committee on the Status of Women, Geneva (#17117).* [2023/XF1453/f/**F**]

♦ Women's World Union for Peace (inactive)

♦ **Women's WorldWide Web (W4)** **21039**
Pres 77 rue de Turbigo, 75003 Paris, France. T. +33175505253.
URL: http://www.w4.org/
History 2012, as on online collaborative platform. **Aims** Empower girls and women around the world, in cities and in rural areas, in both developing and developed countries, by enabling social investors to contribute – either financially through crowdfunding, or in-kind through mentoring and sharing of skills – to innovative, grassroots girls and women's empowerment projects. **Structure** Board; Management Team. **Languages** English, French. **Staff** 5.00 FTE, paid. **Finance** Donations; grants. [2019.08.06/XJ6108/**F**]

♦ Women's WORLD – Women's World Organization for Rights, Literature and Development (inactive)
♦ The Women's Zionist Organization of America / see Hadassah
♦ Women in Technology in the European Community / see European Association for Women in Science, Engineering and Technology (#06276)
♦ Women in Theological Education Committee / see Weavers Committee (#20843)
♦ Women@theTable (unconfirmed)
♦ Women Thrive Alliance (internationally oriented national body)
♦ Women Today International (internationally oriented national body)
♦ Women for Union of the Free (inactive)
♦ Women With Visible and Invisible Disabilities (internationally oriented national body)
♦ Women with Vision in Africa (internationally oriented national body)
♦ Women Waging Peace Network (internationally oriented national body)

♦ **WomenWatch** **21040**
Contact c/o Inter-Agency Network on Women and Gender Equality, 2 UN Plaza, 12th Floor, New York NY 10017, USA. E-mail: womenwatch@un.org.
URL: http://www.un.org/womenwatch/
History Mar 1997, by *Inter-Agency Network on Women and Gender Equality (IANWGE, #11388), United Nations Development Fund for Women (UNIFEM, inactive), United Nations International Research and Training Institute for the Advancement of Women (UN-INSTRAW, inactive)* and the United Nations Division for the Advancement of Women (DAW). An Internet-based organization. **Finance** Members' dues. Supported by: Spanish Government; *ILO (#11123); International Bank for Reconstruction and Development (IBRD, #12317); Sustainable Development Networking Programme – UNDP (SDNP, no recent information); UNDP (#20292); UNESCO (#20322).* [2011/XF6288/**F***]

♦ Women Watch Afrika (internationally oriented national body)

♦ **Women for Water Partnership (WfWP)** **21041**
Chair Ridderbuurt 57, 2402 NH The Hague, Netherlands. T. +31633746164. E-mail: secretariat@womenforwater.org – president@womenforwater.org.
URL: https://womenforwater.org/
History Apr 2004. Former names and other names: *Women for Water, Water for Women (WfWfW)* – former (2004). Registration: Netherlands; Tanzania UR; EU Transparency Register, No/ID: 108487223077-45, Start date: 19 Aug 2016. **Aims** Position women as active leaders, experts, partners and agents of change to realize access to safe water for all, including gender responsive sanitation. **Structure** General Assembly; Steering Committee; Secretariat. **Languages** English. **Finance** Sources: donations; government support; in-kind support; private foundations. **Activities** Advocacy/lobbying/activism; capacity building; events/meetings; knowledge management/information dissemination; politics/policy/regulatory; projects/programmes; training/education. **Events** *Meeting on Measuring Progress in Achieving Equitable Access to Water and Sanitation* Geneva (Switzerland) 2016, *Gender Equity for a Water-Secure Future Conference* Gyeongju (Korea Rep) 2015, *Women for water conference* Soesterberg (Netherlands) 2005. **Publications** Annual Report.
Members Organizations (28) in about 134 countries and territories. Membership countries not specified. Included in the above, 3 organizations listed in this Yearbook:
International Federation of Business and Professional Women (BPW International, #13376); Soroptimist International of Europe (SI/E, #19689); Soroptimist International (SI, #19686).
Consultative Status Consultative status granted from: *ECOSOC (#05331)* (Special); *UNESCO (#20322)* (Consultative Status). **IGO Relations** Partner of: *UNEP (#20299);* United Nations Department for Economic and Social Affairs; *UN-Water (#20723); UN Women (#20724).* **NGO Relations** Partners include: *Akvo Foundation; The Butterfly Effect (BE, #03389); Global Water Challenge (GWC); International Federation of Private Water Operators (AquaFed, #13517); International Water Association (IWA, #15865); United Nations University – Institute for Water, Environment and Health (UNU-INWEH, see: #20642); World Water Council (WWC, #21908).* [2022.10.18/XJ4432/**F**]

♦ Women for Water, Water for Women / see Women for Water Partnership (#21041)
♦ Women on Waves (internationally oriented national body)

♦ **Women Win** **21042**
Exec Dir Rapenburgerstraat 173, 1011 VM Amsterdam, Netherlands. T. +312022177441. E-mail: info@womenwin.org.
Contact 44 Halifax Str, Jamaica Plain MA 02130, USA.
URL: http://womenwin.org/
History 15 Feb 2007, Amsterdam (Netherlands). Registration: Netherlands; USA. **Aims** Advance girls' and women's rights. **Structure** Board of Directors; Advisory Council. **Languages** Dutch, English, Spanish. **Activities** Capacity building; financial and/or material support; knowledge management/information dissemination; networking/liaising; sporting activities; training/education. **Publications** Annual Report. **NGO Relations** Member of (1): *Prospera – International Network of Women's Funds (INWF, #18545).* Affiliated with (1): *streetfootballworld (#20009).* [2022.05.16/XM4478/**F**]

♦ Women for Women International (internationally oriented national body)
♦ Women Working Worldwide (internationally oriented national body)
♦ Women Worldwide Advancing Freedom and Equality (unconfirmed)
♦ **WOMESA** Association of Women Managers in the Maritime Sector in Eastern and Southern Africa (#02979)
♦ WOM – Foundation World Without Mines (internationally oriented national body)

♦ **WoMin** **21043**
Dir Office 902 – floor 9, Southpoint Corner, 87 De Korte Street, Johannesburg, 2001, South Africa. T. +27113391024. E-mail: info@womin.org.za.
URL: https://womin.africa/
History Former names and other names: *African Women Unite Against Destructive Extractivism* – former. **Aims** Support women's organizing; build a movement aimed at challenging the destructive large-scale extraction of natural resources and propose developmental alternatives that respond to the needs of the majority of African women. **Structure** Board of Trustees. [2021/AA1759/**F**]

♦ **WOMP** World Order Models Project (#21684)
♦ Won Buddhism International (internationally oriented national body)
♦ **WONCA Europe** European Society of General Practice/Family Medicine (#08609)
♦ WONCA Region Europe / see European Society of General Practice/Family Medicine (#08609)
♦ WONCA / see World Organization of Family Doctors (#21690)
♦ **WONCA** World Organization of Family Doctors (#21690)

♦ **Wonderland** **21044**
Contact Marxergasse 24/4-03, 1070 Vienna, Austria. E-mail: office@wonderland.cx.
URL: http://www.wonderland.cx/
History 2002. Full title: *Wonderland – platform for european architecture.* **Aims** Offer a network and activities to exchange experience and strengthen the impact of young designers in our built environment. **Structure** Operating Board; Advisory Board. **Languages** English. **Staff** As required for projects. **Finance** Members' dues. Public funds. **Activities** Networking/liaising; research/documentation; events/meetings. **Publications** Newsletter; magazines. Books. **Members** Individuals. Membership countries not specified, but focus is on Europe. **NGO Relations** Member of: Platform für Baukultur. [2019.12.11/XJ5868/v/**F**]

♦ Wonderland – platform for european architecture / see Wonderland (#21044)
♦ WONIPA – Worldwide Nitrocellulose Producers Association (internationally oriented national body)
♦ WONUC – World Council of Nuclear Workers (inactive)
♦ **WON** World Ocean Network (#21681)
♦ **Wood4Bauhaus** Wood Sector Alliance for the New European Bauhaus (#21046)
♦ Woodenfish Foundation (internationally oriented national body)

♦ **Woodrise Alliance** **21045**
Address not obtained.
URL: https://en.woodrise.org/
History 14 Sep 2017. Founded during 1st international Woordrise Congress, when 6 research and innovations centres became the "Signatories" of the Multilateral Co-operation Memorandum for the International Development of Wood and Bio-Sourced Material Usage for the Construction or Renovation of Zero-Carbon, Efficient and Resilient Buildings. **Activities** Events/meetings. **Events** *Woodrise Congress* Bordeaux (France) 2023, *Woodrise Congress* Portoroz (Slovenia) 2022, *International Congress* Kyoto (Japan) 2021, *International Congress* Québec, QC (Canada) 2019, *International Congress* Bordeaux (France) 2017.
Members Research and innovation centres in countries:
Brazil, Canada, China, Finland, France, Germany, Japan, Slovenia, Spain, Sweden, Switzerland.
Confédération européenne des industries du bois (CEI Bois, #04545); European Organization of the Sawmill Industry (EOS, #08114); InnovaWood (IW, #11224). [2023/AA1553/y/**E**]

♦ Woodrow Wilson International Center for Scholars (internationally oriented national body)
♦ Woodrow Wilson School of Public and International Affairs / see Princeton School of Public and International Affairs
♦ Wood Sector Alliance for the NEB / see Wood Sector Alliance for the New European Bauhaus (#21046)

♦ Wood Sector Alliance for the New European Bauhaus (Wood4Bauhaus) 21046

Contact c/o InnovaWood, Rue du Luxembourg 66, 1000 Brussels, Belgium. E-mail: info@wood4bauhaus.eu.
URL: https://wood4bauhaus.eu/

History Initiated by several umbrella organizations: *InnovaWood (IW, #11224)*; *European Panel Federation (EPF, #08137)*; *Confédération européenne des industries du bois (CEI Bois, #04545)*; *European Federation of Building and Woodworkers (EFBWW, #07065)*; *European Organization of the Sawmill Industry (EOS, #08114)*. Former names and other names: *Wood Sector Alliance for the NEB* – alias; *W4B Alliance* – alias. **Aims** Contribute to shaping a better and sustainable future with beautiful, healthy and inclusive living spaces as part of a sustainable, low carbon-built environment. **Activities** Advocacy/lobbying/activism; knowledge management/information dissemination.
Members Organizations (5):
Confédération européenne des industries du bois (CEI Bois, #04545); *European Federation of Building and Woodworkers (EFBWW, #07065)*; *European Organization of the Sawmill Industry (EOS, #08114)*; *European Panel Federation (EPF, #08137)*; *InnovaWood (IW, #11224)*. [2023/AA3127/y/**D**]

♦ Wood Technology Club 21047

Contact Taiwan Woodworking Machinery Assn, 7F-2, No 155 Hsin-yi St, Feng Yuang, Taichung, Taiwan. T. +886425250229. Fax +886425250240. E-mail: service@twma.org.tw.

History Mar 1993. Incorporated activities of *ProWood Club (inactive)*, 20 May 2001, Hannover (Germany). **Languages** Chinese, English. **Activities** Organizes annual meeting. **Publications** Annual Directory.
Members Organizations (20) in 18 countries and territories:
Argentina, Austria, Brazil, China, Czechia, Denmark, Finland, France, Germany, Italy, Japan, Poland, Portugal, Spain, Switzerland, Taiwan, UK, USA.
Included in the above, 1 international organization:
Comité européen des constructeurs de machines à bois (EUMABOIS, #04152). [2010.08.06/XF6732/**F**]

♦ Woodworkers International (inactive)
♦ **WOOMB-International** World Organization – Ovulation Method – Billings (#21692)
♦ **WOO** World Out of Home Organization (#21702)
♦ WOPHIC / see Hearing International (#10895)
♦ **WOPP** World Organization of the Periodical Press (#17819)
♦ WOPS International – International Organization for Water Operators Partnerships (unconfirmed)
♦ WORA – World Organization for the Rights of Animals (inactive)
♦ WORC – World Organization for Respiratory Care (no recent information)
♦ WordNet Association / see Global Wordnet Association (#10661)

♦ Word for the World, The (TWFTW International) 21048

Main Office PO Box 53, Kleinmond, 7195, South Africa. E-mail: info@twftw.org.
URL: http://www.twftw.org/

History 1981. **Aims** Empower nationals to translate the entire *Bible* for their own people. **Structure** Offices in: South Africa; Slovakia; Congo DR; Ethiopia; Malawi; Tanzania UR; UK; USA; Zambia; Zimbabwe. **NGO Relations** Member of: *Forum of Bible Agencies International (#09903).* [2018/XM3643/**F**]

♦ The Work (religious order)

♦ Workability International 21049

Gen Sec GPO Box 2687, Sydney NSW 2001, Australia. T. +61292563168. E-mail: secretariat@workability-international.org.
URL: http://www.workability-international.org/

History 1987, Sweden. Founded as an informal group of organizations from around the world with direct responsibility for employing people with disabilities. Present name adopted at World AGM, San Diego CA (USA). Former names and other names: *International Organization for the Provision of Work for Persons with Disabilities and Who are Occupationally Handicapped (IPWH)* – former; *International Group on Sheltered and Special Employment* – former; *Organization for the Provision of Work for Handicapped Persons* – former. Registration: Companies House, No/ID: 04230009, Start date: 6 Jun 2001, England and Wales. **Aims** On a global basis, champion the right to *work* of anyone with a *disability* or is otherwise *marginalized*; work for legal *rights* to *equal opportunities* and non-discrimination in all aspects of their lives, especially in the world of work. **Structure** General Meeting (annual). Board of Directors, elected by members to represent Americas, Asia, Europe, Oceania and developing regions. Regional Groups (4): Americas; Asian; Europe; Oceania. **Languages** English. **Staff** 1.00 FTE, paid. **Finance** Sources: members' dues. Annual budget: 100,000 USD. **Activities** *'Practical Cooperation'*: Profiling, assessment, training, personal and career development; Funding, licensing, franchising and intertrading; Practical uses of technology and workplace adaptations; Commercial matters and marketing; Production methods and opportunities in service industries; Integration, progression and placements; Socio-economic costing. *'International Affairs'* – partnerships with other bodies and authorities. *'Commercial Initiatives'* – promotes commercial interests of member organizations with companies, governments and authorities. **Events** *Annual Conference* Sydney, NSW (Australia) 2020, *Annual Conference* Anaheim, CA (USA) 2019, *Annual Conference* Stockholm (Sweden) 2018, *Annual Conference* Auckland (New Zealand) 2016, *Asia Conference* Pattaya (Thailand) 2015. **Publications** *WI Newsletter* (4 a year). *Europe's Undervalued Workforce* (1999); *Paid Jobs for People with Disabilities* (1999); *The Case for Supported Employment for People with Disabilities within the European Union* (1998); *How to Integrate Persons With Disabilities into Working Like within the European Union* (1997). Reports of conferences, seminars and workshops.
Members Full; Associate; Special. Corporate or unincorporated associations and ministries at national level or with knowledge and experience of how work is provided for people with disabilities in their respective countries. Members (119) in 32 countries and territories:
Australia, Austria, Belgium, Brazil, Bulgaria, Canada, Finland, France, Georgia, Germany, Hungary, Iceland, India, Ireland, Japan, Korea Rep, Lithuania, Malawi, Nepal, Netherlands, New Zealand, Norway, Poland, Romania, Spain, Sri Lanka, Sweden, Switzerland, Taiwan, UK, USA, Vietnam.
Consultative Status Consultative status granted from: *ILO (#11123)* (Special List). **IGO Relations** Member of: *United Nations Economic and Social Commission for Asia and the Pacific (ESCAP, #20557)*. **NGO Relations** Member of (2): *Conference of Non-Governmental Organizations in Consultative Relationship with the United Nations (CONGO, #04635)*; *European Disability Forum (EDF, #06929)* (Founding). Networking partner with: *RI Global (#18948)*. Close cooperation with: *European Group for the Employment of Persons with Mental Disabilities (GEEPHM, no recent information)*. *Goodwill Industries International (GII)* is a member. [2021/XF0933/**D**]

♦ Workable World Trust (internationally oriented national body)

♦ Workarea Art-Ambient (WAAM) 21050

Promoter Via Bertolotti 58, 17014 Cairo Montenotte GE, Italy.
Latin America WAAM Council Clemente Padin, Casilla de Correo Central 1211, Montevideo, Uruguay.

History 1980, Milan (Italy). Previously also known as *WAAM Network Configuration*. Registered in accordance with Italian law, 1984. **Aims** Promote *environmental* and *artistic* activities worldwide; develop contacts with the international network of *mail-art*. **Structure** Officers: President; Vice-President; Secretary; Keeper; Eco-Advisor; Promoter; Directors. **Languages** English, Italian. **Staff** 3.00 FTE, paid. **Finance** Members' dues. Annual budget: euro 2,000. **Activities** Events/meetings; publishing activities. **Publications** *Direct Mail* (weekly); *Notiziario* (12 a year); *Minus* (4 a year). *Ob No Fluxus.*
Members WAAM organizations (15) in 14 countries:
Brazil, Denmark, Estonia, Germany, Hungary, Italy, Nigeria, Russia, Serbia, Spain, Switzerland, UK, Uruguay, USA. [2019.07.02/XF5308/**F**]

♦ Work and Economy Research Network in the European Churches (WEN) 21051

Réseau travail et économie dans les Eglises européennes – Netzwerk Arbeit und Wirtschaft in den Europäischen Kirchen

Contact address not obtained. T. +420222211799. Fax +420222211799.

History as *West European Network on Work, Unemployment and the Churches – Réseau d'Europe occidentale sur le travail, le chômage et les Eglises*. **Aims** Analyse economic change locally, nationally and regionally, and identify common issues from the perspective of excluded and marginalized people and communities; develop theological reflection in the context of changing economic and political realities; promote mutual learning to strengthen churches' action locally, nationally and internationally; enable churches to strengthen their impact on European institutions through a more integrated approach to issues of unemployment, poverty, women and economy, regional disparities, migration, inequality and marginalization, especially focusing on globalization and Central and Eastern Europe. **Structure** General Meeting (every 2 years). Executive of 5. **Languages** English. **Staff** 1.00 FTE, paid; 10.00 FTE, voluntary. **Finance** Members' dues. Grants for specific projects. **Activities** Encourages cross-national collaborative consultation and sharing of experience on specific themes. Publishes findings. Main theme: Alternatives to Competitive Globalization; with a special focus on issues of economy and work in Central and Eastern Europe. **Events** *Biennial consultation* Prague (Czech Rep) 2005, *Facing up to globalisation consultation / European Consultation* Prague (Czech Rep) 2005, *Biennial consultation* Yarmouth (UK) 2003, *Biennial consultation* Most (Czech Rep) 2001, *Biennial consultation* Nürburg (Germany) 1999. **Publications** Consultation reports; conference reports; resource booklet.
Members Organizations and individuals (about 250) in 28 countries:
Albania, Austria, Belgium, Czechia, Denmark, Estonia, Finland, France, Germany, Greece, Hungary, Iceland, Ireland, Italy, Latvia, Lithuania, Luxembourg, Netherlands, Norway, Poland, Portugal, Romania, Russia, Slovakia, Spain, Sweden, Switzerland, UK.
NGO Relations Close ties with: *European Contact Group – Ecumenical Network for Economic and Social Action (ECG, #06773)*. Collaboration with: *Conference of European Churches (CEC, #04593).* [2013/XF1066/**F**]

♦ Worker Rights Consortium (internationally oriented national body)
♦ Workers of Divine Love (religious order)

♦ Workers Hub For Change (WH4C) 21052

Coordinator Lot 3585, Kampung Lubuk Layang, Batu 3, Jalan Mentakab, 28000 Neusiedl am See, Burgenland, Malaysia. T. +60192371100. E-mail: easytocall@gmail.com.

History Founded 2007, as a collective of human rights defenders. **Aims** Protect and protect human rights, defending human rights defenders; campaign with special emphasis on worker, trade union and migrant worker rights. **Structure** Board. **Languages** Burmese, English, Malay, Thai. Others languages when relevant. **Staff** 4.00 FTE, voluntary. **Finance** Donations; crowdfunding. **Activities** Advocacy/lobbying/activism; awareness raising; capacity building; guidance/assistance/consulting; knowledge management/information dissemination; events/meetings; networking/liaising; politics/policy/regulatory; publishing activities; research/documentation; training/education. Active in: Cambodia, Indonesia, Malaysia, Myanmar, Thailand. **IGO Relations** *ASEAN (#01141)*; *European Union (EU, #08967)*; *ILO (#11123)*; UN bodies. **NGO Relations** Member of: *Clean Clothes Campaign (CCC, #03986)*; *GoodElectronics (#10679).* [2019.02.26/XM7604/**F**]

♦ Workers' International Centre of Latin American Solidarity (inactive)
♦ Workers International League (inactive)
♦ Workers International Struggles Initiative (unconfirmed)

♦ Workflow Management Coalition (WfMC) 21053

Exec Dir 759 CJC, Ste 363, Cohasset MA 02025, USA. T. +17817199209. Fax +17817350491.

History 1993. **Aims** Create and contribute to process related standards; educate the market on related issues; concentrate purely on process. **Structure** Committees (3): Steering; Technical; External Relations.
Members Full in 10 countries:
China, Ireland, Italy, Japan, Korea Rep, Poland, Singapore, Taiwan, UK, USA.
Included in the above, 1 organization listed in this Yearbook:
Association for Intelligent Information Management (AIIM, #02652). [2017/XJ2178/y/**C**]

♦ Workgroup of European Cancer Patient Advocacy Networks (WECAN) 21054

Coordinator address not obtained.
URL: https://wecanadvocate.eu/

History 2015. Initiated when 15 European cancer patient organizations came together to form the informal network. It was born out of the need to work together and share experiences throughout the European cancer community and with member organizations. **Aims** Act as a well-coordinated cancer patient community towards all stakeholders by building levels of trust, collaboration, alignment, and mutual support between pan-European cancer patient umbrella organizations by: collaborating, aligning, and developing joint projects/actions; providing education to grow the skills and expertise of patient advocates; sharing workload when contributing to different stakeholder initiatives; providing resources for cancer patient organizations. **Structure** Informal network of leaders from 23 cancer patient umbrella organizations active in Europe. Rotating Chairmanship (annual), open to any member. **Languages** English. **Finance** Funding for projects, initiatives, work groups, or programs comes from individual organizations associated with WECAN. **Activities** Advocacy/lobbying/activism; awareness raising; capacity building; guidance/assistance/consulting; knowledge management/information dissemination; networking/liaising; politics/policy/regulatory; projects/programmes; publishing activities; research/documentation; standards/guidelines; training/education. Active in: Albania, Austria, Belarus, Belgium, Bulgaria, Croatia, Czechia, Denmark, Estonia, Finland, France, Germany, Greece, Hungary, Ireland, Italy, Latvia, Liechtenstein, Lithuania, Luxembourg, Moldova, Netherlands, Norway, Poland, Portugal, Romania, Slovakia, Slovenia, Spain, Sweden, Switzerland, UK, Ukraine.
Members Organizations (22):
– *Acute Leukemia Advocates Network (ALAN, #00107)*;
– *Childhood Cancer International Europe (CCI Europe, #03872)*;
– *CLL Advocates Network (CLLAN, #04026)*;
– *CML Advocates Network (#04041)*;
– *Digestive Cancers Europe (DiCE, #05070)*;
– *Europa Donna – The European Breast Cancer Coalition (#05745)*;
– *Europa Uomo (#05770)*;
– *EURORDIS – Rare Diseases Europe (#09175)*;
– *International Brain Tumour Alliance (IBTA, #12393)*;
– *International Kidney Cancer Coalition (IKCC, #13983)*;
– *International Neuroendocrine Cancer Alliance (INCA, #14348)*;
– *Lung Cancer Europe (LuCE, #16523)*;
– Lymphoma Coalition Europe;
– *MDS Alliance (#16608)*;
– *Melanoma Patient Network Europe (MPNE)*;
– *MPN Advocates Network (#16876)*;
– *Myeloma Patients Europe (MPE, #16924)*;
– *Pancreatic Cancer Europe (PCE, #18172)*;
– *Sarcoma Patients EuroNet (SPAEN, #19054)*;
– *Thyroid Cancer Alliance (TCA, #20157)*;
– *World Bladder Cancer Patient Coalition (WBCPC, #21233)*;
– *Youth Cancer Europe (YCE, #22008).* [2022.02.11/AA1440/y/**F**]

♦ Work of the Holy Angels (religious order)
♦ Working Committee for Collaboration in Geomorphology / see International Association of Geomorphologists (#11917)
♦ Working Committee of Common Market Brewers / see The Brewers of Europe (#03324)
♦ Working Committee of the EEC Malting Industry / see Working Committee of the Malting Industry of the EU (#21055)
♦ Working Committee of the EU Malting Industry / see Working Committee of the Malting Industry of the EU (#21055)

♦ Working Committee of the Malting Industry of the EU 21055

Comité de travail des malteries de l'UE – Comité de Trabajo de las Malterias de la UE – Arbeitskomitee der Mälzereien in der EU – Comitato di Lavoro delle Malterie della UE – Werkcomité van de Mouterijen in de EU – Arbejdskomiten for Malterier i EU – Arbetsgruppen för Mälterier i EU – Euroopan Uionin Mallasteollisuuden Yhteistyökomitea

Secretariat EUROMALT, Rue Montoyer 23, 5th Floor, 1000 Brussels, Belgium. T. +3225020808. E-mail: euromalt@graininindustry.com.
URL: http://www.euromalt.be/

History 14 Apr 1959, Brussels (Belgium). Former names and other names: *Working Committee of the EEC Malting Industry* – former; *Comité de travail des malteries de la CEE (EUROMALT)* – former; *Arbeitskomitee der Mälzereien in der EWG* – former; *Comitato di Lavoro delle Malterie della CEE* – former; *Werkcomité van de Mouterijen in de EEG* – former; *Working Committee of the EU Malting Industry* – former; *Comité de travail des malteries de l'UE (EUROMALT)* – former; *Arbeitskomitee der Mälzereien in der EU* – former; *Comitato di Lavoro delle Malterie della UE* – former; *Werkcomite van de Mouterijen in de EU* – former; *Arbejkomiteen for EU Malterier* – former. Registration: EU Transparency Register, No/ID: 58967214515-43; Belgium. **Events** *Meeting* Brussels (Belgium) 1992.
Members National maltsters organizations in 13 countries:
Austria, Belgium, Denmark, Finland, France, Germany, Hungary, Ireland, Italy, Netherlands, Spain, Sweden, UK.
IGO Relations Recognized by: *European Commission (EC, #06633)*. **NGO Relations** Member of: *Committee of the Trade in Cereals, Oilseeds, Pulses, Olive Oil, Oils and Fats, Animal Feed and Agrosupply of the EU (COCERAL, #04289)*. [2020.05.06/XE3448/t/**E**]

♦ Working Community of Cantons, Länder, Counties, Regions and Republics of the Eastern Alpine Regions / see Alps-Adriatic-Alliance (#00747)

♦ Working Community of the Danube Regions 21056

Communauté de travail des pays du Danube – Arbeitsgemeinschaft Donauländer (ARGE) – Pracovni Spolecenstvi Podunajskych Zemi – Pracovné Spoločenstvo Podunajskych Krajin – Dunamenti Tartomanyok Munkaközössége – Radna Zajednica Podunavskih Regija – Radna Zajednica Podunavskih Zemalja – Comunitatea de Lucru a Statelor Dunarene – Rabotna Obstnost Dunavski Strani

SG Office of the Lower Austrian Federal Government, Land Niederösterreich, Landhausplatz 1 – Haus 3, 3109 St Pölten, Austria. T. +432742900512475. Fax +432742900513610. E-mail: post.lad1@noel.gv.at.
URL: http://www.argedonau.at/

History 17 May 1990, Austria. 17 May 1990, Wachau (Austria), on signature of the *'Joint Declaration'* on the ship *'Prinz Eugen'* in the Danube. *Procedural Rules of the Working Community of the Danube Regions* adopted 14 Oct 1993. **Aims** Promote *cooperation* among members for the *development* of the Danube area to serve the interests of its inhabitants and to foster peaceful cooperation in Europe. **Structure** Conference of Heads of Government with chairmanship rotating every two years; Working Group of Senior Officials, permanently chaired by chief Executive for Lower Austria; Office; Working Groups (4). **Languages** English, German. **Finance** No members' dues. Each member bears costs of activities; interpreters paid by host region. For joint projects, groups elaborate a financing plan and submit it for approval. **Activities** Projects/programmes. **Events** *Conference of Heads of Government* Bratislava (Slovakia) 2016, *Conference of Heads of Government* Ulm (Germany) 2015, *Conference of Heads of Government* Stuttgart (Germany) 2014, *Conference of Heads of Government* St Pölten (Austria) 2013, *Conference on Heads of Government* St Pölten (Austria) 2012. **Publications** Books; procedures; brochures.
Members Regions (or whole countries) (38) in a total of 8 countries:
Austria (Upper Austria; Lower Austria; Vienna; Burgenland; Slovak Rep; Trnava; Bratislava), Bulgaria (Vidin; Montana; Vratsa; Pleven; Veliko Tarnovo; Rousse; Silistra), Croatia (Zupanija Osjecko-Baranjska; Zupanija Vukovarsko-Srijemska; Serb Rep), Germany (Baden Württemberg; Bavaria – until 2005), Hungary (Györ-Moson-Sopron County; Komarom-Esztergom County; Pest County; Fejér County; Bacs-Kiskún County; Tolna County; Baranya County; Budapest), Moldova, Romania (Danube Regions – Caras Severin; Mehedinti; Dolj; Olt; Teleorman; Giurgiu; Calarasi; Ialomita; Braila; Galati; Tulcea und Constanta), Ukraine (Odessa Region).
Observer (2):
Czechia (South Moravia Region), Slovakia (Nitra).
IGO Relations Observer member and cooperates with: *Central European Initiative (CEI, #03708)*. Regional initiatives with: *Southeast European Cooperative Initiative (SECI, #19812)*. **NGO Relations** Observer member of: *Assembly of European Regions (AER, #02316)*. Contacts with: *Alps-Adriatic-Alliance (#00747)*. [2019.12.19/XF3180/**F***]

♦ Working Community of the European Gypsum Industries / see European Association of Plaster and Plaster Product Manufacturers (#06152)

♦ Working Community of the Pyrenees 21057

Communauté de travail des Pyrénées (CTP) – Comunidad de Trabajo de los Pirineos – Comunitat de Treball dels Pirineus – Pirinioetako lan Elkartea – Comunautat de Trabalh dels Pirenèus

SG 22 boulevard du Maréchal Juin, CP 31406, Toulouse CEDEX 4, France. T. +33534459640. Fax +33561396106.
Pres address not obtained.
URL: http://www.ctp.org/

History 1983. **Aims** Act as an *interregional* body of *transborder cooperation* to become a laboratory of for *European integration*. **Structure** Council, consisting of 8 representatives of each member. Presidency (in alphabetical order). Coordination Committee, comprising the President of each member collectivity or his representative and Secretary General of the Community. Working Commissions. Secretariat, headed by Secretary General. **Languages** Basque, Catalan, French, Occitan, Spanish. **Activities** Economic development; improvement of communications; research and protection of the environment. **Events** *Meeting* Jaca (Spain) 1994. **Publications** *Boletín de Informaciones Transfronterizas*. Plenary Council proceedings. **Members** Member collectivities (8) 3 French Regions (Aquitaine, Languedoc-Roussillon, Midi-Pyrénées); 4 Spanish Autonomies (Aragón, Cataluña, Euskadi, Navarra); Principality of Andorra. **NGO Relations** Founding organization of: *Conference of Peripheral Maritime Regions of Europe (CPMR, #04638)* and *Assembly of European Regions (AER, #02316)*. [2011.06.01/XE0418/**E**]

♦ Working Conference of Baltic Sea Countries, Norway and Iceland (meeting series)
♦ Working Group for Advertising, Market and Opinion Research (inactive)
♦ Working Group for the Archaeology of the Saxons and their Neighbours in north-western Europe / see Internationales Sachsensymposion – Arbeitsgemeinschaft zur Archäologie der Sachsen und ihrer Nachbarvölker in Nordwesteuropa (#13305)
♦ Working Group for an ASEAN Human Rights Mechanism (unconfirmed)

♦ Working Group on Criteria and Indicators for the Conservation and Sustainable Management of Temperate and Boreal Forests (Montreal Process) 21058

Groupe de travail sur les critères et les indicateurs de la conservation et de l'aménagement durable des forêts des régions tempérées et boréales (le Processus de Montréal) – Grupo de Trabajo sobre Criterios e Indicadores para la Conservación y el Manejo Sustentable de los Bosques Templados y Boreales (Proceso de Montreal)

Liaison Office Forestry Agency, 1-2-1 Kasumigaseki, Chiyoda-ku, Tokyo, 100-8952 Japan. T. +81335918449. Fax +81335939565.
URL: http://www.montrealprocess.org/

History Founded 1994, Geneva (Switzerland). Feb 1995, agreed the "Santiago Declaration" which set out scope and key definitions covering 7 criteria and 67 associated indicators as guidelines for policy-makers to use in assessing national forest trends and progress toward sustainable forest management in temperate and boreal forests. By 2003, the Montreal Process member countries had published their first Country Forest Reports using the agreed MP criteria and indicators. The illustrative trends of these where consolidated into the First Forest Overview Report 2003. The Working Group approved a revised set of indicators and the member countries used the improved indicators to prepare their second round of Country Forest Reports in 2009. In agreeing to the updated set of indicators, the Working Group underscored the relevance of Criteria and Indicators to decision making within their countries and international comparability. **Aims** Develop and implement internationally agreed criteria and indicators for the conservation and sustainable management of temperate and boreal forests. **Structure** Working Group (meeting annually); Technical Advisory Committee (meeting at the request of the Working Group). **Languages** English, French, Spanish. **Staff** Initiatives undertaken by member countries of the Montréal Process Working Group are carried out as part of their regular programmes. **Finance** Member countries pay own participation costs and also sometimes make contributions to facilitate participation of other less-developed countries. **Activities** In 2007, agreed on the conceptual framework for the Montréal Process Strategic Action Plan (SAP) 2009-2015 which established 5 strategic directions for the Montréal Process: 1. Enhance the relevance of the Montréal Process criteria and indicators for policymakers, practitioners and others; 2. Strengthen member country capacity to monitor, assess and report on forest trends and progress toward sustainable forest management using the Montréal Process criteria and indicators; 3. Enhance collaboration and cooperation with forest related regional and international organizations and instruments and other criteria and indicator processes; 4. Enhance communication on the value of criteria and indicators and the accomplishments of the Montréal Process. **Events** *International Symposium* Kumamoto (Japan) 2019, *Working Group Meeting* Adelaide, SA (Australia) 2013, *Technical Advisory Committee Meeting* Moscow (Russia) / Suzdal (Russia) 2012, *Technical Advisory Committee Meeting* Tokyo (Japan) 2012, *Working Group Meeting* Victoria, BC (Canada) 2011. **Publications** *Second Montréal Process Overview Report* (2009); *Criteria and Indicators for the Conservation and Sustainable Management of Temperate and Boreal Forests* (4th ed 2009); *Technical Notes of the Montréal Process Criteria and Indicators Criteria 1-7* (3rd ed 2009); *Scaling National Criteria and Indicators to the Local Level* (2001); *Progress and Innovation in Implementing Criteria and Indicators for the Conservation and Sustainable Management of Temperate and Boreal Forests* (2000); *Forests for the Future: Montréal Process Criteria and Indicators* (1999); *First Approximation Report of the Montréal Process* (1997); *Québec City Declaration*. Reports; progress reports; brochures; recordings.
Members Governments of countries representing 49% of the world's forests, 83% of the world's temperate and boreal forests, 33% of the world's population and 45% of the world's wood products. Governments of 12 countries:
Argentina, Australia, Canada, Chile, China, Japan, Korea Rep, Mexico, New Zealand, Russia, Uruguay, USA.
IGO Relations Observer to: *Intergovernmental Negotiating Committee for a Legally Binding Agreement on Forests in Europe (INC-Forests, inactive)*; *Ministerial Conference on the Protection of Forests in Europe (FOREST EUROPE, #16817)*. Accredited at 5th Session of *United Nations (UN, #20515)* Forum on Forests. [2013.09.24/XE4190/**E**]

♦ Working Group on Development and Peace / see Arbeitsgemeinschaft Frieden und Entwicklung

♦ Working Group of European Mint Directors for the Technical Study of the European Single Coinage System (MDWG) 21059

Pres c/o Monnaie de Paris, 11 Quai de Conti, 75006 Paris, France. T. +33140465666.
Secretariat c/o EC – ECFIN-C-5/MDWG Secretariat, Rue de la Loi 200, 1049 Brussels, Belgium. T. +3222953333. Fax +3222993505.

History Feb 1994, after running on free initiative for 2 years. Also referred to as *Mint Directors Working Group*. **Aims** Coordinate and study the common topics of the European coinage system. **Structure** Officers: President; 2 Vice-Presidents; Chairmen of 3 Sub-Groups; Secretary. Secretariat held by European Commission. **Languages** English. **Finance** Members finance own costs. **Activities** Carries out technical studies – notably under the mandate of *Council of the European Union (#04895)* and *Economic and Financial Committee (EFC)*, in collaboration with the European Commission. Sub-Groups (3): Collector Coin; Technical; Quality Assurance Control.
Members Full in 27 countries:
Austria, Belgium, Bulgaria, Cyprus, Czechia, Denmark, Estonia, Finland, France, Germany, Greece, Hungary, Ireland, Italy, Latvia, Lithuania, Luxembourg, Malta, Netherlands, Poland, Portugal, Romania, Slovakia, Slovenia, Spain, Sweden, UK.
Regional organization (1), listed in this Yearbook:
European Commission (EC, #06633). [2019/XE2249/**E**]

♦ Working Group of German-speaking Myriapodologists (unconfirmed)
♦ Working Group Indigenous Peoples / see Netherlands Centre for Indigenous Peoples
♦ Working Group on Medical Development Cooperation / see WEMOS
♦ Working Group on Peace and Development (internationally oriented national body)

♦ Working Group on Prolamin Analysis and Toxicity (WGPAT) 21060

Chair biotask AG, Schelztorstr 54-56, 73728 Esslingen, Germany. T. +4971131059068. Fax +4971131059070.
URL: http://www.wgpat.com/

History 1985. **Aims** Perform and coordinate research on analysis of *gluten* in food and on evaluation of clinical and *nutritional* aspects of *coeliac* disease. **Structure** Executive. **Languages** English. **Activities** Events/meetings; research and development. **Events** *Annual Meeting* Wageningen (Netherlands) 2023, *Annual Meeting* Munich (Germany) 2022, *Annual Meeting* Burgstall (Italy) 2020, *Annual Meeting* Urbino (Italy) 2019, *Annual Meeting* Ayr (UK) 2018. **Publications** Proceedings. **Members** in 8 countries. Membership countries not specified. **IGO Relations** Observer status with (1): *Codex Alimentarius Commission (CAC, #04081)*. [2022.10.13/XM7046/**D**]

♦ Working Group on Rainforests and Biodiversity (internationally oriented national body)

♦ Working Group on Sustainable Development (SDWG) 21061

Exec Sec Fram Centre, Postboks 6606, Stakkevollan, 9296 Tromsø, Norway. E-mail: secretariat@sdwg.org.
URL: https://sdwg.org/

History Sep 1998, Iqaluit, NU (Canada). Established by *Arctic Council (#01097)*, at 1st Arctic Council Ministerial meeting. **Aims** Protect and enhance economies, culture and health of the inhabitants of the Arctic, in an environmentally sustainable manner. **Events** *Meeting* Tromsø (Norway) 2007, *Meeting* Oulu (Finland) 2002, *Meeting* Espoo (Finland) 2001, *Meeting* Rovaniemi (Finland) 2001. **IGO Relations** Member of: *Arctic Monitoring and Assessment Programme (AMAP, #01100)*. Cooperates with: *Conservation of Arctic Flora and Fauna (CAFF, #04728)*. [2021/XE4116/**E***]

♦ Working Group on Tourism and Development (internationally oriented national body)
♦ Working Group – Working Group for an ASEAN Human Rights Mechanism (unconfirmed)
♦ **Workingonsafety.net** International Network on the Prevention of Accidents and Trauma at Work (#14306)
♦ Working Party North Sea / see North Sea Foundation

♦ Working Time Society (WTS) 21062

Pres US DOT Volpe Ctr, 55 Broadway, Cambridge MA 02142, USA.
URL: http://www.workingtime.org/

History 2001. A parallel organization to the Shiftwork Scientific Committee of the ICOH. Previously also referred to as *International Society for Working Time and Health Research (ISWTHR)*. **Aims** Discuss basic and applied problems associated with *shiftwork*; act as an advisory committee for national and international bodies; promote cooperative efforts for the solution of *occupational* work problems in this area. **Structure** General Meeting; Executive Board; Committees (6). **Languages** English. **Staff** 20.00 FTE, voluntary. **Finance** Members' dues. **Activities** Events/meetings; publishing activities; knowledge management/information dissemination; networking/liaising. **Events** *Biennial Symposium* Coeur d'Alene, ID (USA) 2019, *Biennial Symposium* Ayers Rock, NT (Australia) 2017, *International Symposium on Shiftwork and Working Time* Helsingør (Denmark) 2015, *International Symposium on Shiftwork and Working Time* Sao Paulo (Brazil) 2013, *International symposium on shiftwork and working times* Stockholm (Sweden) 2011. **Publications** *Consensus Papers* – series. **Information Services** *Shiftwork International Network (SINET)* – electronic network for exchange of scientific information and consultations.
Members Individuals (350) in 49 countries:
Argentina, Australia, Austria, Belgium, Brazil, Bulgaria, Canada, Chile, China, Croatia, Cuba, Denmark, Egypt, Finland, France, Germany, India, Indonesia, Iran Islamic Rep, Ireland, Israel, Italy, Japan, Kenya, Korea Rep, Kuwait, Malaysia, Monaco, Netherlands, New Zealand, Norway, Pakistan, Philippines, Poland, Portugal, Russia, Singapore, Slovakia, Slovenia, South Africa, Spain, Sweden, Switzerland, Thailand, Tunisia, UK, Ukraine, USA, Vietnam.
NGO Relations Cooperates with: *International Commission on Occupational Health (ICOH, #12709)* (Scientific Committee on Shiftwork and Working Time). [2020.03.08/XD9188/**D**]

- ♦ Working Together for Health Development / see SIMAVI
- ♦ Working Together for Human Rights (internationally oriented national body)
- ♦ Working Weekends on Organic Farms / see World-Wide Opportunities on Organic Farms (#21931)
- ♦ WORKiNS – Workers International Struggles Initiative (unconfirmed)
- ♦ Work of Mary / see Focolare Movement (#09806)
- ♦ Workshop 3 – Centre for Communication and Information on Development, Peace and Human Rights (internationally oriented national body)
- ♦ Workshop on Accelerator Operations (meeting series)
- ♦ Workshop on Aggression (meeting series)
- ♦ Workshop on Dielectrics in Microelectronics (meeting series)
- ♦ Workshop on Elliptic Curve Cryptography (meeting series)
- ♦ Workshop "Higgs Hunting" (meeting series)
- ♦ Workshop on Immigrant Languages in the Americas (meeting series)
- ♦ Workshop on Logic, Language, Information and Computation (meeting series)
- ♦ Workshop on Method of Fundamental Solutions (meeting series)
- ♦ Workshop on Relational Contracts (meeting series)
- ♦ Workshop on Scattering of Atoms and Molecules from Surfaces (meeting series)
- ♦ Workshop on the Semantics and Pragmatics of Dialogue (meeting series)

♦ World Academic Council of Emergency Medicine (WACEM) 21063

Contact address not obtained. E-mail: wacem.org@gmail.com.
URL: https://wacem.org/

History 2014. Originally a meeting series called "INDUSEM". Congress renamed WACEM Congress when WACEM was founded. **Aims** Improve quality of patient care for the critically ill and injured; connect academicians, academies and academic organizations worldwide; advance academic emergency medicine and acute care sciences worldwide. **Structure** World Governing Council of Academicians; Secretary General. **Events** *World Academic Congress of Emergency Medicine (WACEM2019)* Dubai (United Arab Emirates) 2019, *World Academic Congress of Emergency Medicine (WACEM2018)* Doha (Qatar) 2018, *World Academic Congress of Emergency Medicine (WACEM2017)* Colombo (Sri Lanka) / Galle (Sri Lanka) 2017, *World Academic Congress of Emergency Medicine (WACEM2016)* Bangalore (India) 2016, *World Academic Congress of Emergency Medicine (WACEM2015)* Delhi (India) 2015. [2020/AA0473/**E**]

♦ World Academic Society of Medical Qigong (WASMQ) 21064

Main Office Beijing Univ of Chinese Medicine, 11 Bei San Huan Dong Lu, Chaoyang District, 100029 Beijing, China.
URL: http://www.wasmq.org/

History 1989, Beijing (China). Also referred to as *World Society of Medical Qigong.* **Aims** Promote the use of *deep breathing* exercises as a medical practice; promote the study of medical qigong. **Events** *Conference* Beijing (China) 2016, *Conference* Beijing (China) 2012. **Publications** *World Qigong* (periodical) in Chinese. **Members** Individuals (577) in 19 countries. Membership countries not specified. [2015/XE3154/v/**E**]

♦ World Academy of Art and Science (WAAS) 21065

Académie mondiale des arts et des sciences – Academia Mundial de Arte y Ciencia – Weltakademie für Kunst und Wissenschaft – Vsemirnaja Akademija Iskusstva i Nauki

CEO 5 Pudavai Sivam St, Venkata Nagar, Puducherry, Pondicherry 605011, Puducherry PONDICHERRY 605011, India. Fax +914132212338.
Registered Office 4225 Solano Ave, Suite 631, Napa CA 94558, USA.
URL: http://www.worldacademy.org/

History 24 Dec 1960. Founded in 1960 by eminent intellectuals including Albert Einstein; Robert Oppenheimer, Father of Manhattan Project; Bertrand Russell, Joseph Needham, co-Founder of UNESCO; Lord Boyd Orr, first Director General of FAO; Brock Chisholm, first Director General of WHO and many others. Former names and other names: *World University of the World Academy of Art and Science* – former; *World University of the Science* – former. Registration: Start date: 2010, USA, State of California. **Aims** Contribute to the progress of global *civilization*, enhancement of world order and realization of human dignity through transnational studies, operational projects, appraisals and recommendations; function as a world university to promote global higher education and a transnational forum for *interdisciplinary* discussion; establish foundations for a human-centred paradigm of global social development; examine social consequences and policy implications of knowledge. **Structure** Plenum (annual); Board of Trustees; Executive Committee; Standing Committees. Regional Centers (7): Institute for Advanced Studies in Levant Culture and Civilization (Romania); Dag Hammarskjöld University College (Zagreb); Serbian Association of Economists International Centre for Sustainable Development of Energy, Water and Environment Systems (Zagreb); Montenegrin Academy of Sciences and Art (Podgorica); Mother's Service Society (India); Person-Centered Approach Institute (Rome). **Languages** English. **Staff** 8.00 FTE, paid; 2.00 FTE, voluntary. **Finance** Sources: grants; members' dues. Annual budget: 615,000 USD (2022). **Activities** Awareness raising; events/meetings; guidance/assistance/consulting; knowledge management/information dissemination; networking/liaising; politics/policy/regulatory; projects/programmes; publishing activities; research and development; research/documentation; training/education. **Events** *Human Security & Multilateralism* Baku (Azerbaijan) 2022, *World Conference on Basic Sciences and Sustainable Development* Belgrade (Serbia) 2022, *Education for Human Security* Bucharest (Romania) 2022, *International Conference on Future Education* Puducherry (India) 2022, *Global Leadership Challenges in Higher Education for Effective Multilateralism and Sustainable Human Security* 2021. **Publications** *Cadmus Journal* (2 a year); *Eruditio Journal* (2 a year); *World Academy of Art and Science Newsletter* (2 a year); *World University Consortium (WUC) Newsletter.* Future of Education Reports. Books.

Members Fellows (800) in 84 countries and territories:
Albania, Andorra, Argentina, Australia, Austria, Azerbaijan, Belgium, Bosnia-Herzegovina, Brazil, Bulgaria, Canada, Chile, China, Colombia, Croatia, Czechia, Denmark, Ecuador, Egypt, Eritrea, Estonia, Finland, France, Georgia, Germany, Ghana, Greece, Guatemala, Hungary, India, Indonesia, Iran Islamic Rep, Ireland, Israel, Italy, Jamaica, Japan, Jordan, Kazakhstan, Kenya, Korea Rep, Kuwait, Lebanon, Malaysia, Malta, Mexico, Moldova, Monaco, Montenegro, Morocco, Nepal, Netherlands, New Zealand, Niger, Nigeria, North Macedonia, Norway, Pakistan, Palestine, Peru, Philippines, Poland, Portugal, Qatar, Romania, Russia, Serbia, Singapore, Slovenia, South Africa, Spain, Sri Lanka, Sweden, Switzerland, Syrian AR, Thailand, Türkiye, UK, Ukraine, United Arab Emirates, Uruguay, USA, Venezuela, Zambia.

Associate Fellows in 11 countries:
Albania, Belgium, Brazil, Canada, Croatia, France, India, Montenegro, North Macedonia, Slovenia, USA.

Junior Fellows in 8 countries:
Andorra, Azerbaijan, Belgium, Canada, Croatia, India, Switzerland, USA.

Consultative Status Consultative status granted from: *ECOSOC (#05331)* (Special); *UNESCO (#20322)* (Consultative Status). **IGO Relations** Associated with Department of Global Communications of the United Nations. **NGO Relations** Member of (4): *Environment Liaison Centre International (ELCI, no recent information)*; *InterAcademy Partnership (IAP, #11376)*; *Inter-University Centre for Advanced Studies (IUC, #15986)*; *United Nations Academic Impact (UNAI, #20516).* [2022.10.17/XB3449/v/**B**]

♦ World Academy of Arts and Culture (WAAC) 21066

Treas 4423 Pitch Pine Court, San Jose CA 95136, USA. T. +14082818041.
SG address not obtained. E-mail: eugenia_sn@hotmail.com.
URL: http://www.worldacademyofartsandculture.com/

History 1969. Registered 1985, in the State of California (USA). **Aims** Substitute peace for war in the minds of men; promote world *brotherhood*; engender exchange of culture for mutual understanding of peoples striving for excellence in uplifting mankind through *poetry* and culture. **Structure** Board of Trustees. Executive Board, comprising President, Secretary General, Treasurer, 6 Vice-Presidents and PR Officer. International Committee. Set up, 1973, the *World Congress of Poets (WCP, see: #21066)*, for which WAAC is the Governing Body. **Languages** Arabic, Chinese, English, French, German, Irish Gaelic, Korean, Spanish. **Staff** 18.00 FTE, paid. **Finance** Financed through dues from poets. **Activities** World Congress of Poets: 5-day symposia; poetry readings; poetry workshops; cultural exchange through museums, art exhibits, dance/music. Sponsors educational and research papers; bestows awards; maintains library in Taipei (Taiwan) and biographical archives. **Events** *World Congress of Poets* Taipei (Taiwan) / Hualien (Taiwan) 2015, *World Congress of Poets* Seoul (Korea Rep) 2014, *World Congress of Poets* Trujillo (Peru) 2014, *World Congress of Poets* Ipoh (Malaysia) 2013, *World Congress of Poets* Kfar Saba (Israel) 2012. **Publications** *Messenger for World Poets* (annual); *World Academy of Arts and Culture Newsletter* (annual).

Members Literary organizations and poets in 69 countries and territories:
Argentina, Australia, Austria, Belgium, Benin, Bolivia, Bosnia-Herzegovina, Brazil, Bulgaria, Canada, Chile, China, Colombia, Croatia, Cyprus, Czechia, Denmark, Egypt, Finland, France, Germany, Greece, Hong Kong, Iceland, India, Indonesia, Ireland, Israel, Italy, Japan, Kenya, Korea Rep, Kuwait, Luxembourg, Malaysia, Malta, Mexico, Morocco, Netherlands, New Zealand, Nigeria, Norway, Pakistan, Peru, Philippines, Puerto Rico, Qatar, Romania, Russia, Saudi Arabia, Senegal, Serbia, Singapore, Slovakia, South Africa, Spain, Sri Lanka, Sweden, Switzerland, Taiwan, Thailand, Tunisia, Türkiye, UK, Ukraine, United Arab Emirates, Uruguay, USA, Venezuela. [2014/XF0350/**F**]

- ♦ World Academy of Biomedical Technologies (internationally oriented national body)

♦ World Academy of Ceramics (WAC) 21067

Chairman Corso Mazzini 52, 48018 Faenza RA, Italy. T. +3954622461. E-mail: info@waceramics.org – secretariat@waceramics.org.
URL: http://www.waceramics.org/

History Founded 1987. **Aims** Promote progress in the field of ceramics; foster better understanding of the social impact and cultural interactions of ceramic science, technology, history and art. **Structure** General Assembly; Advisory Board. **Languages** English. **Staff** 4.00 FTE, voluntary. **Events** *Forum* Perugia (Italy) 2012, *Forum* Chianciano Terme (Italy) 2008, *Forum* Faenza (Italy) / Cesenatico (Italy) 2004, *Forum* Ravello (Italy) 2000, *Forum* Krakow (Poland) 1996. **Publications** Meeting proceedings.

Members Individuals in 29 countries:
Australia, Austria, Belgium, Brazil, Canada, China, Czechia, France, Germany, Hungary, India, Ireland, Italy, Japan, Korea Rep, Netherlands, New Zealand, Poland, Russia, Serbia, Singapore, Slovakia, Slovenia, Spain, Switzerland, Taiwan, UK, Ukraine, USA.

NGO Relations Member of: *International Ceramic Federation (ICF, #12530).* [2018.09.10/XM2194/v/**E**]

♦ World Academy of Cosmetic Surgery (WAOCS) 21068

Verein zur Förderung kosmetischer Chirurgie

Exec Dir address not obtained. T. +18477783636. E-mail: info@waocs.org.
URL: https://waocs.org/

History Registration: No/ID: ZVR 14709696410, Austria. **Aims** Train and educate doctors in cosmetic surgery. **Structure** Board. **Activities** Events/meetings; training/education. **Events** *Scientific Meeting* London (UK) 2020, *Annual Scientific Meeting* London (UK) 2019, *Annual Scientific Meeting* Vienna (Austria) 2018. [2020/XM7995/**F**]

- ♦ World Academy of Medical Sciences (unconfirmed)

♦ World Academy of Nursing Science (WANS) 21069

Contact 88/20 Nagarindrasri Bldg, Amphur Mueng, Nonthaburi, 11000, Thailand. T. +6625967500. E-mail: secretarywans@gmail.com.
URL: https://wansglobal.org/

History 18 Sep 2009. **Aims** Contribute to the health and welfare of people worldwide through the promotion of international academic exchanges and collaborative research in the fields of nursing. **Structure** Board of Directors. **Activities** Organizes academic conference. **Events** *International Nursing Research Conference* Taipei (Taiwan) 2022, *International Nursing Research Conference* Osaka (Japan) 2020, *International Nursing Research Conference* Bangkok (Thailand) 2017, *International Nursing Research Conference* Hannover (Germany) 2015, *International Nursing Conference / Conference* Seoul (Korea Rep) 2013.

Members Founding members in 7 countries:
Germany, Indonesia, Japan, Korea Rep, Singapore, Thailand, USA.

Included in the above, 1 regional organization:
East Asian Forum of Nursing Scholars (EAFONS, #05205). [2022/XJ5527/**C**]

- ♦ World Academy of Productivity Science (internationally oriented national body)
- ♦ World Academy of Research in Science and Engineering (unconfirmed)
- ♦ The World Academy of Sciences for the advancement of science in developing countries / see TWAS (#20270)
- ♦ World Accord (internationally oriented national body)
- ♦ The World According to Women (internationally oriented national body)
- ♦ World Accordion Organization (inactive)
- ♦ World Acoustics Society (inactive)
- ♦ World Action on Salt and Health / see World Action on Salt, Sugar & Health (#21070)

♦ World Action on Salt, Sugar & Health (WASSH) 21070

Chair c/o Wolfson Institute, Queen Mary Univ of London, Charterhouse Square, London, EC1M 6BQ, UK. T. +442078826217 – +442078825941. E-mail: wash@qmul.ac.uk.
URL: http://www.worldactiononsalt.com/

History 2005. Founded following the success of a UK national programme (Action on Salt / Consensus Action Salt for Health). Former names and other names: *World Action on Salt and Health (WASH)* – former (2005). Registration: Charity Commission, No/ID: 1098818, England and Wales. **Aims** Improve the health of populations throughout the world by achieving a gradual reduction in salt intake. **Activities** Events/meetings.

Members Individuals (598) in 94 countries and territories:
Algeria, Angola, Argentina, Australia, Austria, Azerbaijan, Bahrain, Bangladesh, Barbados, Belgium, Botswana, Brazil, Bulgaria, Cameroon, Canada, Chile, China, Colombia, Congo DR, Costa Rica, Croatia, Cuba, Cyprus, Czechia, Denmark, Ecuador, Egypt, Ethiopia, Fiji, Finland, France, Gabon, Georgia, Germany, Ghana, Greece, Guam, Hong Kong, Hungary, India, Iran Islamic Rep, Ireland, Israel, Italy, Jamaica, Japan, Jordan, Kenya, Korea Rep, Kuwait, Lebanon, Libya, Lithuania, Malawi, Malaysia, Malta, Mauritius, Mexico, Monaco, Nepal, Netherlands, New Zealand, Nigeria, North Macedonia, Norway, Oman, Pakistan, Paraguay, Peru, Poland, Portugal, Qatar, Russia, Rwanda, Sao Tomé-Principe, Saudi Arabia, Serbia, Slovakia, Slovenia, South Africa, Spain, Sri Lanka, Sweden, Switzerland, Taiwan, Thailand, Türkiye, UK, Ukraine, United Arab Emirates, USA, Venezuela, Vietnam, Zimbabwe.

Also members in West Indies. Membership countries not specified.

IGO Relations *WHO (#20950).* [2021/XJ1727/v/**F**]

♦ World Aerial Sports & Arts Federation (WAS&AF) 21071

Pres address not obtained.
URL: http://www.aerialart.org/

History 2019, Switzerland. **Aims** Provide the opportunity to all the performers to perform without limits, in a security place, in the proper environment. **Structure** Executive Committee; Technical Commissions. **Languages** English. **Activities** Sporting activities; training/education.

Members National federations in 9 countries:
Greece, Hungary, Italy, Malta, Pakistan, Poland, Russia, Switzerland, Ukraine.

Delegates in 13 countries:
Bulgaria, China, Estonia, Lithuania, Monaco, Morocco, Netherlands, Nigeria, Portugal, San Marino, South Africa, Spain, UK.

NGO Relations Member of (2): *General Association of Asia Pacific Sports Federations (GAAPSF, #10106)*; *International Sport Network Organization (ISNO, #15592).* [2021.09.03/AA1086/**D**]

- ♦ World Aerospace Education Organization (no recent information)
- ♦ World Affairs Center for the United States / see Foreign Policy Association
- ♦ World Affairs Councils of America (internationally oriented national body)
- ♦ World Affairs Institute (internationally oriented national body)
- ♦ World Against Racism Network (unconfirmed)
- ♦ World Agency of Planetary Monitoring and Earthquake Risk Reduction (internationally oriented national body)
- ♦ World Agricultural Forum (internationally oriented national body)
- ♦ World Agricultural Information Centre (see: #09260)
- ♦ World Agriculture Society (inactive)

♦ World Agroforestry Centre (ICRAF) 21072

Exec Dir United Nations Ave, Gigiri, PO Box 30677, Nairobi, 00100, Kenya. T. +254207224000. Fax +254207224001. E-mail: worldagroforestry@cgiar.org.
URL: http://www.worldagroforestry.org/

History Jul 1977, Nairobi (Kenya). Founded following the initiative of *International Development Research Centre (IDRC, #13162)*. Commenced operations in 1978, Nairobi, on agreement with the Government of Kenya. Became an international agricultural research centre organized under the auspices of *CGIAR System Organization (CGIAR, #03843)*, 1991. Former names and other names: *International Council for Research in Agroforestry* – former; *Conseil international pour la recherche en agroforesterie* – former (1991); *Consejo Internacional para Investigación en Agrosilvicultura* – former (1991); *International Centre for Research in Agroforestry (ICRAF)* – former (1991); *Centre international pour la recherche en agroforesterie* - – former (1991); *Centro Internacional de Investigación en Agroforesteria* – former (1991); *CIRAF* – former; *Centro Internacional para Investigación en Agrosilvicultura* – former. **Aims** Mitigate *tropical deforestation, land depletion* and *rural poverty* through improved agroforestry systems, focusing on strategic and applied research in partnership with national institutions. **Structure** International Board of Trustees (meets annually); Permanent Secretariat. Coordinates: *African Network for Agriculture, Agroforestry and Natural Resources Education (ANAFE, #00380)*; *Agency for Forestry Research Networks for Africa (AFRD, no recent information)*; *Plant Resources for Tropical Africa (PROTA, inactive)*. **Languages** English, French. **Staff** 370.00 FTE, paid. **Finance** Direct contributions from: Governments of Belgium, France, Germany, Italy, Japan, Kenya, Spain; Netherlands Ministry of Development Cooperation; Royal Norwegian Ministry of Development Cooperation; donor agencies, including:
- *African Development Bank (ADB, #00283)*;
- *Australian Aid (inactive)*;
- *Canadian International Development Agency (CIDA, inactive)*;
- *Department for International Development (DFID, inactive)*;
- *Department for International Development Cooperation*;
- *Ford Foundation (#09858)*;
- IDRC;
- *International Bank for Reconstruction and Development (IBRD, #12317)*;
- *International Fund for Agricultural Development (IFAD, #13692)*;
- *The Rockefeller Foundation (#18966)*;
- *Swedish International Development Cooperation Agency (Sida)*;
- *Swiss Agency for Development and Cooperation (SDC)*;
- *Tinker Foundation*;
- *UNDP (#20292)*;
- *United States Agency for International Development (USAID)*.

Provision of facilities and privileges by Government of Kenya.
Activities Knowledge management/information dissemination; training/education; research/documentation. Main work is in 6 ecologically-distinct regions: Subhumid highlands of Eastern and Central Africa; Subhumid plateau of Southern Africa; Semi-arid lowlands of West Africa; Humid tropics of Southeast Asia; Humid tropics of West Africa. **Events** *World Congress on Agroforestry* Québec, QC (Canada) 2022, *World Congress of Agroforestry* Montpellier (France) 2019, *Pedometrics Conference* Nairobi (Kenya) 2013, *International Conference on Forests for Food Security and Nutrition* Rome (Italy) 2013, *ASEAN conference on biodiversity* Singapore (Singapore) 2009. **Publications** *Agroforestry Systems* (12 a year) – jointly with Kluwer; *Agroforestry Abstracts* (4 a year). Monographs; proceedings; working papers; annotated bibliographies; field manuals; brochures; slide series; computer programs. Information Services: *Agroforestry Abstracts* is jointly with *CABI (#03393)*. Monographs; proceedings; working papers; annotated bibliographies; field manuals; brochures; slide series; computer programs. Information Services: Library; documentation and publication service; agroforestry video; selective dissemination of information (SDI). **Information Services** *DATA CHAIN*; *Multipurpose Trees Database*; *Soil Changes under Agroforestry (SCUAF)*.
Members Regional Offices (15) in 14 countries:
Cameroon, Indonesia, Kenya (2), Malawi, Mali, Mexico, Niger, Peru, Philippines, Tanzania UR, Thailand, Uganda, Zambia, Zimbabwe.
Public and private institutions in 19 countries:
Brazil, Burkina Faso, Burundi, Cameroon, Indonesia, Kenya, Malawi, Mali, Mexico, Niger, Peru, Philippines, Rwanda, Senegal, Tanzania UR, Thailand, Uganda, Zambia, Zimbabwe.
Consultative Status Consultative status granted from: *UNEP (#20299)*.
IGO Relations Accredited to the Conference of the Parties of: *Secretariat of the United Nations Convention to Combat Desertification (Secretariat of the UNCCD, #19208)*. Accredited by: *United Nations Framework Convention on Climate Change – Secretariat (UNFCCC, #20564)*. Partner of: *United Nations Forum on Forests (UNFF, #20562)*. Member of: *Collaborative Partnership on Forests (CPF, #04100)*; *Congo Basin Forest Partnership (CBFP, #04662)*; *International Information System for the Agricultural Sciences and Technology (AGRIS, #13848)*. Observer to: *Global Bioenergy Partnership (GBEP, #10251)*. Cooperates with other CGIAR supported IGO centres:
- *Africa Rice Center (AfricaRice, #00518)*;
- *Bioversity International (#03262)*;
- *International Center for Agricultural Research in the Dry Areas (ICARDA, #12466)*;
- *International Crops Research Institute for the Semi-Arid Tropics (ICRISAT, #13116)*;
- *International Livestock Research Institute (ILRI, #14062)*;
- *International Rice Research Institute (IRRI, #14754)*.

Collaborating institutions:
- *African Union Scientific Technical Research Commission (AU STRC, #00493)*;
- *AGRHYMET Regional Centre (#00565)*;
- *Asian Development Bank (ADB, #01422)*;
- *Australian Centre for International Agricultural Research (ACIAR)*;
- *Centre de coopération internationale en recherche agronomique pour le développement (CIRAD, #03733)*;
- *Comité permanent inter-Etats de lutte contre la sécheresse dans le Sahel (CILSS, #04195)*;
- *Deutsche Gesellschaft für Technische Zusammenarbeit (GTZ, inactive)*;
- *FAO (#09260)*;
- *Institut de recherche pour le développement (IRD)*;
- *Institut du Sahel (INSAH, #11357)*;
- *Institute of Agricultural and Zootechnical Research (IRAZ, no recent information)*;
- *Inter-American Institute for Cooperation on Agriculture (IICA, #11434)*;
- *International Network for Bamboo and Rattan (INBAR, #14234)*;
- *Norwegian Agency for Development Cooperation (Norad)*;
- *Programa Cooperative de Investigación, Desarrollo e Innovación Agricolo para los Trópicos Suramericanos (PROCITROPICOS, #18521)*;
- *Programme on Man and the Biosphere (MAB, #18526)*;
- *Regional Centre for Mapping of Resources for Development (RCMRD, #18757)*;
- *Southeast Asian Regional Center for Graduate Study and Research in Agriculture (SEARCA, #19781)*;
- *Southeast Asian Regional Centre for Tropical Biology (SEAMEO BIOTROP, #19782)*;
- *Southern African Development Community (SADC, #19843)*;
- *Tropical Agriculture Research and Higher Education Center (#20246)*;
- *UNEP (#20299)*;
- *UN Environment Programme World Conservation Monitoring Centre (UNEP-WCMC, #20295)*;
- *UNESCO (#20322)*;
- *World Meteorological Organization (WMO, #21649)*.

NGO Relations Member of (12): *Environment Liaison Centre International (ELCI, no recent information)*; *Global Alliance for Climate-Smart Agriculture (GACSA, #10189)*; *Global Diplomatic Forum (GDF, #10321)*; *Global Landscapes Forum (GLF, #10451)* (Charter member); *InsideNGO (inactive)*; *International Council for Medicinal and Aromatic Plants (ICMAP, #13047)*; *International Foundation for Science (IFS, #13677)*; *International Land Coalition (ILC, #13999)*; *International Partnership for the Satoyama Initiative (IPSI, #14525)*; *International Society of Tropical Foresters (ISTF, #15522)*; *Natural Capital Coalition (NCC, #16952)*; *ORCID (#17790)*. Instrumental in setting up (3): *Alley Farming Network for Tropical Africa (AFNETA, no recent information)*; *International Union of Agroforestry (IUAF)*; *Tree Pest Management Network for Central, Eastern and Southern Africa (no recent information)*.
Cooperates with other CGIAR supported NGO centres:
- *Center for International Forestry Research (CIFOR, #03646)*;
- *International Centre for Tropical Agriculture (#12527)*;
- *International Food Policy Research Institute (IFPRI, #13622)*;
- *International Institute of Tropical Agriculture (IITA, #13933)*;
- *International Maize and Wheat Improvement Center (#14077)*;
- *International Potato Center (#14627)*;
- *International Water Management Institute (IWMI, #15867)*;
- *WorldFish (#21507)*.

Also close working links with: *CARE International (CI, #03429)*; and with a number of national non-governmental organizations. Supports: *Asia Network for Sustainable Agriculture and Bioresources (ANSAB, #01445)*. Partner of: *Climate Technology Centre and Network (CTCN, #04023)*; *Global Partnership on Forest and Landscape Restoration (GPFLR, #10535)*; *Rights and Resources Initiative (RRI, #18947)*; *Rainwater Partnership (no recent information)*. Provides secretariat for: *Southern and Eastern Africa Rainwater Network (SearNet, #19876)*; *Tropical Forest Alliance (TFA, #20249)*. Works with: *Young Professionals for Agricultural Development (YPARD, #21996)*.
Collaborating institutions:
- *Africa University, Mutare*;
- *African Research Utilization Network (ARUNET, no recent information)*;
- *Association for Strengthening Agricultural Research in Eastern and Central Africa (ASARECA, #02933)*;
- *Commonwealth Scientific and Industrial Research Organization (CSIRO)*;
- *Institut de recherche en biologie et ecologie tropical (IRBET, no recent information)*;
- *International Centre of Insect Physiology and Ecology (ICIPE, #12499)*;
- *International Circle for the Promotion of the Creation (#12575)*;
- *International Fertilizer Development Center (IFDC, #13590)*;
- *International Institute of Rural Reconstruction (IIRR, #13921)*;
- *International Union of Biological Sciences (IUBS, #15760)*;
- *International Union of Forest Research Organizations (IUFRO, #15774)*;
- *International Union of Soil Sciences (IUSS, #15817)*;
- *Overseas Development Institute (ODI)*;
- *Pan African Institute for Development (PAID, #18053)*;
- *Plant Resources of South-East Asia (PROSEA Association, #18391)*;
- *RECOFTC – The Center for People and Forests (RECOFTC, #18628)*;
- *Soil Fertility Initiative for Africa (SFI, no recent information)*;
- *West and Central African Association of Soil Science (WCAASS, no recent information)*;
- *Winrock International*. [2021/XD6784/**E**]

♦ World Ahlul Baytas Islamic League (WABIL) 21073

SG 19 Chelmsford Square, London, NW10 3AP, UK. T. +442084598475. Fax +442084517059.
URL: http://www.wabil.com/

History Founded 1983, England. A charitable organization. **Aims** Provide educational, social and humanitarian services and promote human rights. **Languages** Arabic, English. **Finance** Members' donations. **Activities** Events/meetings. **Publications** *Ahlul Bayt* (12 a year) – magazine.
Members Offices in approx 80 countries. Members in 105 countries and territories:
Afghanistan, Albania, Algeria, Argentina, Austria, Azerbaijan, Bahrain, Bangladesh, Belgium, Benin, Bosnia-Herzegovina, Brazil, Burkina Faso, Burundi, Cameroon, Canada, China, Comoros, Congo Brazzaville, Congo DR, Côte d'Ivoire, Cuba, Denmark, Djibouti, Egypt, Equatorial Guinea, Eswatini, Ethiopia, Finland, France, Germany, Ghana, Guinea, Guinea-Bissau, Guyana, Hong Kong, India, Indonesia, Iran Islamic Rep, Iraq, Ireland, Israel, Italy, Japan, Jordan, Kenya, Korea Rep, Kuwait, Lebanon, Lesotho, Liberia, Libya, Madagascar, Malawi, Malaysia, Mali, Mauritania, Mauritius, Morocco, Mozambique, Myanmar, Namibia, Nepal, Netherlands, New Zealand, Niger, Nigeria, Norway, Oman, Pakistan, Palestine, Paraguay, Philippines, Poland, Portugal, Romania, Russia, Rwanda, Saudi Arabia, Senegal, Sierra Leone, Singapore, Somalia, South Africa, Spain, Sri Lanka, Sudan, Sweden, Switzerland, Syrian AR, Tanzania UR, Thailand, Trinidad-Tobago, Tunisia, Türkiye, Turkmenistan, Uganda, UK, Ukraine, United Arab Emirates, USA, Uzbekistan, Venezuela, Yemen, Zimbabwe. [2017.06.21/XF4653/**F**]

♦ World AIDS Campaign / see WACI Health
♦ World AIDS Campaign International / see WACI Health

♦ World Air Cargo Organization (WACO) 21074

Registered Office St. Peterstr 1, 8001 Zurich ZH 8001, Switzerland. E-mail: admin@waco-system.com.
Operations Office 6-9 The Square, Stockley Park, Uxbridge, UB11 1FW, UK.
URL: https://www.waco-system.com/

History 1973. Founded as an association of freight forwarding companies. Former names and other names: *WACO System* – alias. Registration: No/ID: CH-020.6.000.394-5, Switzerland. **Structure** Annual General Meeting; Extraordinary General Meeting; Executive Board. **Events** *Annual General Meeting* Nice (France) 2021, *Annual General Meeting and Conference* Dubai (United Arab Emirates) 2016. **Members** Companies (119) in 115 countries and territories. Membership countries not specified. [2020/XN3841/**C**]

♦ World Airlines Clubs Association (WACA) 21075

Association mondiale des airlines clubs

Manager c/o IATA, 800 Place Victoria, PO Box 113, Montréal QC H4Z 1M1, Canada. T. +14382583243. E-mail: info@waca.org.
URL: http://www.waca.org/

History 26 Apr 1966, Cannes (France), following a meeting of airline club representatives. Officially constituted Mar 1967. **Aims** Unite and promote the activities of interline clubs throughout the world. **Structure** Annual General Assembly; Council; Regional Coordinators. **Languages** English. **Staff** 1.00 FTE, voluntary. **Finance** Sources: donations; members' dues. Other sources: entrance fees; revenues; raffles. **Activities** Awareness raising; networking/liaising. **Events** *Annual General Assembly* Budapest (Hungary) 2013, *Annual General Assembly* Cairo (Egypt) 2012, *Africa, Indian Ocean Islands regional meeting* Mauritius 2011, *Annual General Assembly* Phuket (Thailand) 2011, *Annual General Assembly* Recife (Brazil) 2010. **Publications** *WACA World News*. *WACA Contact Directory*. Programme brochures.
Members Interline Clubs and Members-at-Large in 26 countries and territories:
Australia, Austria, Bahamas, Bangladesh, Canada, Finland, Germany, Hong Kong, Hungary, Iceland, Israel, Italy, Jordan, Lebanon, Mauritius, New Zealand, Norway, Portugal, Seychelles, Singapore, South Africa, Sri Lanka, Sweden, Switzerland, UK, USA.
NGO Relations Partner of: *International Institute for Peace through Tourism (IIPT)*. [2019.10.23/XC3451/**C**]

♦ World Airport Lawyers Association (WALA) 21076

Asociación Mundial de Abogados Aeroportuarios

Exec Dir c/o Abiax Air, Blanco Encalada 197, Of 24, B1642ABB San Isidro, Argentina. E-mail: wala@abiaxair.com.
Registered Address 2800 Park Place, 666 Burrard St, Vancouver BC V6C 2X8, Canada.
URL: https://www.abiaxair.com/wala/

History Apr 2008. Former names and other names: *Worldwide Airports Lawyers Association* – alias. **Aims** Promote cooperation among legal affairs departments and legal advisors of worldwide airports and other public and private sectors of the worldwide and regional *aeronautical* industry. **Structure** Assembly. Board. **Events** *Conference and AGM* Bogota (Colombia) 2019, *Annual Conference* London (UK) 2018, *Conference and AGM* Bologna (Italy) 2017, *Conference and AGM* Athens (Greece) 2015, *Conference and AGM* Buenos Aires (Argentina) 2014. **Members** Membership countries not specified. [2020/XJ1064/**D**]

♦ World Airport Technology (inactive)
♦ World Airway Management Alliance (unconfirmed)

♦ World Allergy Organization – IAACI (WAO) 21077

Main Office 555 E Wells St, Ste 1100, Milwaukee WI 53202, USA. T. +14142761791. Fax +14142763349. E-mail: info@worldallergy.org.
URL: http://www.worldallergy.org/

History 1945, Minneapolis MN (USA), as *International Association of Allergists – Association internationale des allergistes*. Name changed to *International Association of Allergology – Association internationale d'allergologie*, Sep 1951, Zurich (Switzerland), at First International Congress of Allergology, when Constitution was amended. Constitution further amended Nov 1967, Montréal (Canada). Subsequently changed name to *International Association of Allergology and Clinical Immunology (IAACI) – Association internationale d'allergologie et d'immunologie clinique – Asociación Internacional de Alergologia e Inmunologia Clinica – Internationale Gesellschaft der Allergologie und Klinische Immunologie*, 1980. 1980. Current title adopted at Congress, 2000, Sydney (Australia). Registered in accordance with the law of the State of Wisconsin (USA). **Aims** Be a global resource and advocate in the field of allergy, advancing excellence in clinical care through education, research and training as a world-wide alliance of allergy and *clinical immunology* societies. **Structure** Congress (every 2 years); Board of Directors; Executive Committee; House of Delegates. **Languages** English. **Activities** Events/meetings; guidance/assistance/consulting; research and development; training/education. **Events** *Congress* Warsaw (Poland) 2024, *Congress* Bangkok (Thailand) 2023, *Congress* Istanbul (Türkiye) 2022, *Congress* Kyoto (Japan) 2020, *Congress* Lyon (France) 2019. **Publications** *WAO Journal*.

Members National and Regional Affiliate Organizations representing 35,000 individuals in 77 countries and territories:
Albania, Argentina, Armenia, Australia, Austria, Azerbaijan, Bangladesh, Belarus, Belgium, Brazil, Bulgaria, Canada, Chile, China, Colombia, Croatia, Cuba, Cyprus, Denmark, Ecuador, Egypt, Finland, France, Georgia, Germany, Greece, Guatemala, Honduras, Hong Kong, Hungary, Iceland, India, Indonesia, Iran Islamic Rep, Israel, Italy, Japan, Jordan, Kenya, Korea Rep, Kuwait, Latvia, Lebanon, Malaysia, Mexico, Moldova, Mongolia, Morocco, Netherlands, Norway, Panama, Paraguay, Peru, Philippines, Poland, Portugal, Romania, Russia, Serbia, Singapore, Slovenia, South Africa, Spain, Sri Lanka, Sweden, Switzerland, Taiwan, Thailand, Tunisia, Türkiye, UK, Ukraine, Uruguay, USA, Venezuela, Vietnam, Zimbabwe.
[2021/XC1251/y/**C**]

♦ World Alliance for Arts Education (WAAE) 21078

Chair address not obtained.
Main Website: https://www.waae.online/

History Mar 2006, Lisbon (Portugal). Founded during 1st *UNESCO (#20322)* World Congress on Arts Education. Joint declaration signed at InSEA world congress in Viseu (Portugal). **Aims** Advocate for arts education action, research and networks. **Structure** Presidential Council; Rotating Chair. **Languages** English. **Staff** Voluntary. **Activities** Advocacy/lobbying/activism; events/meetings; research/documentation. **Events** *Summit* Funchal (Portugal) 2023, *Seminar* 2021, *Summit* Frankfurt-Main (Germany) 2019, *Summit* Auckland (New Zealand) 2017, *Summit* Hangzhou (China) 2016.
Members Organizations (4):
International Drama/Theatre and Education Association (IDEA, #13198); International Society for Education through Art (INSEA, #15074); International Society for Music Education (ISME, #15287); World Dance Alliance (#21352).
IGO Relations *UNESCO (#20322).* [2022.10.19/XJ2016/y/**E**]

♦ World Alliance for Breastfeeding Action (WABA) 21079

Alliance mondiale pour l'allaitement maternel

Programme Coordinator PO Box 1200, 10850 Penang, Malaysia. T. +6046584816. Fax +6046572655. E-mail: waba@waba.org.my.
URL: https://waba.org.my/

History 14 Feb 1991, New York, NY (USA). Registration: Companies Commission of Malaysia, No/ID: 847762P, Start date: 24 Feb 2009, Malaysia, Penang. **Aims** Protect, promote and support breastfeeding worldwide in the framework of the Innocenti Declarations (1990 and 2005) and the Global Strategy for *Infant* and Young Child Feeding. **Structure** International Advisory Council; Steering Committee; Secretariat; Affiliates. **Languages** English. **Staff** 10.00 FTE, paid. **Activities** Advocacy/lobbying/activism; awareness raising; capacity building; events/meetings; knowledge management/information dissemination; networking/liaising; training/education. **Events** *Global forum* Penang (Malaysia) 2016, *Global forum* Penang (Malaysia) 2010, *Global forum* Arusha (Tanzania UR) 2002, *Global forum* Bangkok (Thailand) 1996. **Publications** *World Breastfeeding Week (WBW) action folder.* Books; information brochure; postcards. Information Services: General breastfeeding information and referral service to taskforce expertise. Organizational database on breastfeeding groups in a particular country or region.
Members Participants in 117 countries. Membership countries not specified. International founding members (7):
International founding members (7):
Consumers International (CI, #04773); International Baby Food Action Network (IBFAN, #12305); International Lactation Consultant Association (ILCA); La Leche League International (LLLI, #16433); WELLSTART International; World Council of Churches (WCC, #21320).
Participating international organizations listed in this Yearbook (14):
Asian Community Health Action Network (ACHAN, #01393); Asia Pacific Forum on Women, Law and Development (APWLD, #01912); Asia Pacific Public Health Nutrition Association (no recent information); ChildFund International (#03869); Corporate Accountability International; Fédération Internationale de Gynécologie et d'Obstétrique (FIGO, #09638); International Confederation of Midwives (ICM, #12863); International Union for Health Promotion and Education (IUHPE, #15778); People's Health Movement (PHM, #18305); Pesticide Action Network (PAN, #18336); Plan International (#18386); Religions for Peace (RfP, #18831); Soroptimist International (SI, #19686); World Organization of Family Doctors (WONCA, #21690).
Consultative Status Consultative status granted from: *ECOSOC (#05331)* (Special); *UNICEF (#20332).* **IGO Relations** *FAO (#09260);* United Nations System Standing Committee on Nutrition; *WHO (#20950).* Close cooperation with UNICEF. Associated with Department of Global Communications of the United Nations. **NGO Relations** Member of: *Child Rights International Network (CRIN, #03885); Right to Food and Nutrition Watch Consortium (#18943).* [2021.10.20/XF2699/y/**B**]

♦ World Alliance of Cities Against Poverty (WACAP) 21080

Alliance mondiale des villes contre la pauvreté (AMVCP)

Contact UN Capital Development Fund, Two UN Plaza – 26th Floor, New York NY 10017, USA. T. +12129066565. Fax +12129066479.
URL: https://www.wacapnet.org

History 17 Oct 1997, as a programme within *UNDP (#20292),* during the International Year for the Eradication of Poverty. Since 2014, housed at UN Office for South-South Cooperation. **Aims** Fight against poverty through social inclusion and access to basic services for the poor in *developing* cities. **Structure** A network of city governments. Coordinator. **Languages** English, French, Spanish. **Staff** 1.00 FTE, paid. **Finance** Grants from governments, municipalities and foundations. **Activities** Networking/liaising; knowledge management/information dissemination; advocacy/lobbying/activism. **Events** *Forum* Dublin (Ireland) 2013, *Confronting the crisis collectively – working together to end poverty* Rotterdam (Netherlands) 2010, *Forum* Rotterdam (Netherlands) 2009, *Local democratic governance to achieve the millennium development goals and eradicate poverty* Athens (Greece) 2008, *Forum* Valencia (Spain) 2006. **Publications** Case studies; forum reports; brochures.
Members Cities in 146 countries:
Afghanistan, Albania, Algeria, Angola, Argentina, Armenia, Austria, Azerbaijan, Bahrain, Bangladesh, Belarus, Belgium, Benin, Bhutan, Bolivia, Brazil, Bulgaria, Burkina Faso, Burundi, Cameroon, Canada, Cape Verde, Central African Rep, Chile, Colombia, Comoros, Congo Brazzaville, Congo DR, Costa Rica, Côte d'Ivoire, Croatia, Cyprus, Denmark, Djibouti, Dominican Rep, Ecuador, Egypt, El Salvador, Equatorial Guinea, Eritrea, Ethiopia, Finland, France, Gabon, Gambia, Georgia, Germany, Ghana, Greece, Guatemala, Guinea, Guinea-Bissau, Guyana, Haiti, Honduras, Hungary, India, Indonesia, Iran Islamic Rep, Ireland, Israel, Italy, Jamaica, Japan, Jordan, Kenya, Kiribati, Korea Rep, Kosovo, Kuwait, Kyrgyzstan, Laos, Latvia, Lebanon, Lesotho, Liberia, Lithuania, Luxembourg, Madagascar, Malawi, Malaysia, Maldives, Mali, Marshall Is, Mauritania, Mauritius, Mexico, Moldova, Monaco, Mongolia, Morocco, Mozambique, Namibia, Nepal, Netherlands, Nicaragua, Niger, Nigeria, North Macedonia, Northern Mariana Is, Norway, Pakistan, Palestine, Panama, Peru, Philippines, Poland, Portugal, Qatar, Romania, Russia, Rwanda, Samoa, Sao Tomé-Principe, Senegal, Serbia, Seychelles, Sierra Leone, Slovakia, Somalia, South Africa, Spain, Sri Lanka, St Lucia, Sudan, Suriname, Sweden, Switzerland, Tajikistan, Tanzania UR, Timor-Leste, Togo, Trinidad-Tobago, Tunisia, Türkiye, Uganda, UK, Ukraine, United Arab Emirates, USA, Uzbekistan, Vanuatu, Venezuela, Yemen, Zambia, Zimbabwe.
IGO Relations Partners: *UNDP (#20292); UN Women (#20724); United Nations Institute for Training and Research (UNITAR, #20576).* **NGO Relations** Associate partner of: *World Urban Campaign (WUC, #21893).* [2018/XF6573/**F**]

♦ World Alliance for Clean Technologies (unconfirmed)

♦ World Alliance for Decentralized Energy (WADE) 21081

Contact 1620 Eye St NW, Suite 700, Washington DC 20006, USA. T. +12026675600. E-mail: info@localpower.org.
Contact UK Edinburgh Quay, 133 Fountainbridge, Edinburgh, EH3 9BA, UK.
URL: http://www.localpower.org/

History Sep 1998. Former names and other names: *International Cogeneration Alliance (ICA)* – former (1998 to 2002). Registration: Company, No/ID: SC189700, Start date: 1998, End date: 2020, Scotland. **Aims** Promote *sustainable economic development* and energy market modernization through wider use of high efficiency cogeneration systems and on-site renewably; justify and advocate reform of outdated energy policies and regulations. **Structure** Board of Directors of 10 members, including Chairman. **Finance** Supported by corporate leaders in various energy industries, national cogeneration and decentralized energy associations and of private and public institutions. **Activities** Advocacy/lobbying/activism; research/documentation; events/meetings. **Events** *Annual Power and Electricity World Asia Conference* Singapore (Singapore) 2012, *China International Smart Grid Construction, Distributed Energy and Energy Storage Technology and Equipment Summit* Beijing (China) 2011, *Annual decentralized energy and cogeneration conference* Beijing (China) 2004. **Publications** *Cogeneration and On-Site Power Production* (6 a year). *WADE Market Analyses.*
Members Associations and companies in 14 countries:
Australia, Belgium, Brazil, Canada, Czechia, Finland, Germany, India, Indonesia, Netherlands, Norway, Portugal, UK, USA.
Included in the above, 1 organization listed in this Yearbook:
COGEN Europe (#04085).
IGO Relations Accredited by: *United Nations Framework Convention on Climate Change – Secretariat (UNFCCC, #20564).* **NGO Relations** Member of: *Global Methane Initiative (GMI, #10471)* Project Network. Observer member of: *World Wind Energy Association (WWEA, #21937).* [2020/XF5976/d/**F**]

♦ World Alliance for Efficient Solutions (unconfirmed)

♦ World Alliance for Innovation (WAINOVA) 21082

Coordinator c/o IASP Headquarters, C/ Maria Curie 35, Campanillas, 29590 Malaga, Málaga, Spain. T. +34952028303. Fax +34952020464. E-mail: wainova@wainova.org.
URL: http://www.wainova.org/

History Founded 2005. **Aims** Contribute to the world's economic and social development by promoting innovation, technology transfer and the establishment of technology- and innovation-based companies. **Events** *General Assembly* Bordeaux (France) 2010. **Publications** *Atlas of Innovation.*
Members Associations (28). National and regional organizations in 17 countries:
Argentina, Australia, Belgium, Brazil, Canada, Finland, France, Germany, Italy, Peru, Portugal, Spain, Sweden, Thailand, Türkiye, UK, Uruguay.
International organizations (5):
Asian Science Park Association (ASPA, #01693); Association of University Research Parks (AURP, #02973); Baltic Association of Science/Technology Parks and Innovation Centres (BASTIC, #03101); European Business and Innovation Centre Network (EBN, #06420); International Association of Science Parks and Areas of Innovation (IASP, #12151). [2020/XJ2637/y/**C**]

♦ World Alliance for International Friendship through the Churches (inactive)
♦ World Alliance for Low Carbon Cities (unconfirmed)

♦ World Alliance of Martial Arts (WAMA) 21083

Sec address not obtained.
URL: http://waofma.com/

Structure Officers include: President; Future President; Past-President; Administrative Coordinator; Secretary; Webmaster. **Events** *Congress* Cuxhaven (Germany) 2014, *Congress* Kazan (Russia) 2013.
Members Individuals in 10 countries:
Bosnia-Herzegovina, Croatia, Denmark, Germany, Kazakhstan, Russia, Serbia, Sweden, UK, USA. [2013/XJ7399/v/**D**]

♦ World Alliance of Mobile Indigenous Peoples (unconfirmed)
♦ World Alliance of Neuromuscular Disorder Associations (inactive)

♦ World Alliance for Nutrition and Human Rights (WANAHR) 21084

Contact address not obtained. T. +31703504278.

History 1992, Oslo (Norway), at meeting of *Norwegian Centre for Human Rights (NCHR).* Formally established, 1994, Florence (Italy), at meeting of UNICEF Innocenti Research Centre (IRC). **Aims** Promote human rights approach to *food* and *nutrition* problems, focusing on advocacy and outreach work. **Members** Institutions; individuals. Membership countries not specified. [2008.06.01/XF6543/**F**]

♦ World Alliance of Organizations for the Prevention of Birth Defects / see World Alliance of Organizations for the Prevention and Treatment of Genetic and Congenital Conditions (#21085)

♦ World Alliance of Organizations for the Prevention and Treatment of Genetic and Congenital Conditions (WAO) 21085

Secretariat Helios, Gerstkamp 130, 2592 CV The Hague, Netherlands. T. +31356831920. Fax +31356027440.

History 5 Apr 1994, New York, NY (USA). Founded on the initiative of the 'March of Dimes' (USA). First meeting 27 May 1995, Berlin (Germany), in conjunction with *EGAN – Patients Network for Medical Research and Health (EGAN, #05394)* and *European Society of Human Genetics (ESHG, #08624).* Former names and other names: *World Alliance of Organizations for the Prevention of Birth Defects (WAPBD)* – former (5 Apr 1994). Registration: Netherlands. **Aims** Promote respect for persons with disabilities; promote protection from stigmatization of and discrimination against those affected with birth defects, as well as those at risk for transmission of birth defects to their children; increase dissemination of knowledge about prevention to parents effected. **Structure** Board, comprising President, Vice-President, Secretary/Treasurer, Past-President and 7 members. **Languages** English. **Activities** Involved in major multi-national projects and organization of regional and international congresses. **Events** *International conference on birth defects and disabilities in the developing world* Delhi (India) 2009, *Central and Eastern European summit on preconception health and prevention of birth defects* Budapest (Hungary) 2008, *Meeting* Rio de Janeiro (Brazil) 2007, *Meeting* Beijing (China) 2005, *Annual meeting / Meeting* Matsue (Japan) 2000. **IGO Relations** *WHO (#20950).* [2009.09.03/XE2742/**E**]

♦ World Alliance for Patient Safety / see WHO Patient Safety (#20940)

♦ World Alliance for Pentecostal Theological Education (WAPTE) 21086

Chair c/o Trinity Bible College and Graduate School, 50 Sixth Ave S, Ellendale ND 58436, USA.
URL: http://www.wapte.org/

History 28 Jul 2009, Springfield, MO (USA). **Aims** Assist and encourage pentecostal/charismatic theological associations in their endeavour to promote the development of pentecostal theological education and leadership training. **Structure** Board of Directors; Officers. **Publications** *The Pentecostal Educator* (2 a year).
Members Organizations include 4 organizations listed in this Yearbook:
Asia Pacific Theological Association (APTA, see: #10110); Asociación Teológica de América Latina (ATAL, no recent information); European Pentecostal Theological Association (EPTA, #08184); International Church of the Foursquare Gospel (ICFG).
NGO Relations Serves as Education Commission of *Pentecostal World Fellowship (#18295).*
[2020/XJ2787/**B**]

♦ World Alliance of Pituitary Organizations (WAPO) 21087

Exec Dir Nonnenhof 4, 5411 BM Zeeland, Netherlands. T. +31653865700. E-mail: mail@wapo.org.
URL: http://www.wapo.org/

History 2014. Registration: Start date: May 2016, Netherlands. **Aims** Unite the international pituitary *patient* community to push for optimal treatment and care for all patients with pituitary and related conditions worldwide. **Structure** Board of Directors. **Languages** English, Spanish. Languages of members. **Finance** Sources: donations; fundraising; members' dues. **Activities** Advocacy/lobbying/activism; events/meetings; knowledge management/information dissemination. **Events** *WAPO Summit* Netherlands 2022, *WAPO e-Summit* 2021, *WAPO e-Summit* 2020, *WAPO Summit* Lyon (France) 2019, *WAPO Summit* Venice (Italy) 2018. **Publications** *Global Pituitary Voice* (bi-weekly) in English.
Members Full: organizations (43) in 35 countries and territories:
Argentina, Australia, Belgium, Brazil, Bulgaria, Canada, Chile, China, Denmark, Ecuador, England, France, Gambia, Greece, Guatemala, Ireland, Italy, Lithuania, Malaysia, Mexico, Netherlands, New Zealand, Norway, Panama, Peru, Poland, Russia, South Africa, Spain, Switzerland, Taiwan, UK, Ukraine, Uruguay, USA.
NGO Relations Member of (3): *EURORDIS – Rare Diseases Europe (#09175); Rare Diseases International (RDI, #18621); World Patients Alliance (WPA).* Partner of (2): *European Society of Endocrinology (ESE, #08594); International Society of Endocrinology (ISE, #15086).* [2023/XM7439/**C**]

♦ World Alliance of Reformed Churches (inactive)

♦ World Alliance to Transform the United Nations (WATUN) 21088

Exec Dir Secretariat, 2606 Córdoba St, Providencia Colony, PC 44630, Guadalajara JAL, Mexico. T. +523338173475.

Aims Urge and promote a Review of the UN Charter as a first step in reforming or transforming the United Nations. **Structure** Executive Committee, including Chair, 1st and 2nd Vice-Chairs, Secretary and Treasurer. **Events** *World parliament model* Mexico City (Mexico) 2010.
Members Organizations (4), including the following listed in this Yearbook:
Democratic World Federalists; World Federalist Movement – Movement for a Just World Order through a Strengthened United Nations (WFM, #21404). [2010/XJ1834/**E**]

♦ **World Alliance for Wound and Lymphedema Care (WAWLC)** **21089**

SG address not obtained. E-mail: wawlcjm@aol.com – info@wawlc.org.
URL: http://www.wawlc.org/

Aims Advance sustainable prevention and care of wounds and lymphoedema in settings with limited resources. **Structure** Advisory Committee; Secretariat; Working Groups (4). **Languages** English. **Activities** Events/meetings. **Members** Organizations. Membership countries not specified. **NGO Relations** *Bureau international des Médecins sans frontières (MSF International, #03366); European Wound Management Association (EWMA, #09121); International Lymphoedema Framework (ILF, #14070); WHO (#20950)*; national associations. [2019.04.03/XJ7752/y/**C**]

♦ **World Alliance of Young Men's Christian Associations (YMCA)** **21090**

Alliance universelle des unions chrétiennes de jeunes gens (UCJG) – Alianza Mundial de Asociaciones Cristianas de Jóvenes (ACJ) – Weltbund der Christlichen Vereine Junger Männer (CVJM)

Secretariat Chemin de Mouille-Galand 5, 1214 Vernier GE, Switzerland. T. +41228495100. E-mail: office@ymca.int.
URL: http://www.ymca.int/

History 23 Aug 1855, Paris (France). Statutes modified 1955, 1985, 1991, 1994, 1998, 2002, 2006, 2010. **Aims** Work for social justice for all youth, regardless of religion, race, gender or culture. **Structure** World Council (held every 4 years), consists of representatives of member movements (numbers according to a given scale). Executive Committee of 31 members (meets annually). Regional organizations (4): *Africa Alliance of Young Men's Christian Associations (#00155); Asia and Pacific Alliance of YMCAs (APAY, #01826); YMCA Europe (#21977); Latin American and Caribbean Alliance of YMCAs (LACA, #16264)*. Also includes: *Middle East Committee of YMCAs (#16755)*; YMCA of the USA; National Council of the YMCAs in Canada. **Languages** English, French, German, Spanish. **Staff** 7.00 FTE, paid. **Finance** Regular budget: contributions of member movements on the basis of a scale determined by the World Council. Other programmes: special appeals. **Activities** Addresses issues affecting each community by developing programs and activities with special focus on young people in order to build a "human community of justice with love, peace and reconciliation for the fullness of life for all creation". **Events** *World Council Meeting* Aarhus (Denmark) 2022, *Meeting* Geneva (Switzerland) 2022, *Meeting* Geneva (Switzerland) 2022, *Meeting* Vernier (Switzerland) 2021, *Meeting* Vernier (Switzerland) 2021. **Publications** Annual Report.

Members National YMCAs. Full and Associate members in 118 countries and territories:
Albania, Angola, Argentina, Armenia, Aruba, Australia, Austria, Azerbaijan, Bahamas, Bangladesh, Barbados, Belarus, Belgium, Belize, Bolivia, Bosnia-Herzegovina, Brazil, Bulgaria, Cambodia, Cameroon, Canada, Cayman Is, Chile, China, Colombia, Costa Rica, Cuba, Czechia, Denmark, Dominican Rep, Ecuador, Egypt, El Salvador, England, Estonia, Ethiopia, Fiji, Finland, France, Gambia, Georgia, Germany, Ghana, Greece, Guatemala, Guyana, Haiti, Honduras, Hong Kong, Hungary, Iceland, India, Indonesia, Ireland, Israel, Italy, Jamaica, Japan, Jordan, Kenya, Korea Rep, Kosovo, Latvia, Lebanon, Liberia, Lithuania, Madagascar, Malaysia, Malta, Mexico, Moldova, Montenegro, Myanmar, Nepal, Netherlands, New Zealand, Nicaragua, Nigeria, North Macedonia, Norway, Pakistan, Palestine, Panama, Paraguay, Peru, Philippines, Poland, Portugal, Romania, Russia, Scotland, Senegal, Serbia, Sierra Leone, Singapore, Slovakia, South Africa, Spain, Sri Lanka, St Vincent-Grenadines, Suriname, Sweden, Switzerland, Taiwan, Tanzania UR, Thailand, Timor-Leste, Togo, Trinidad-Tobago, Türkiye, Ukraine, Uruguay, USA, Venezuela, Vietnam, Wales, Zambia, Zimbabwe.

Consultative Status Consultative status granted from: *ECOSOC (#05331)* (Special); *UNESCO (#20322)* (Consultative Status); *ILO (#11123)* (Special List); *UNICEF (#20332)*. **IGO Relations** Associated with Department of Global Communications of the United Nations.

NGO Relations Member of:
– *Committee of NGOs on Human Rights, Geneva (#04275); Conference of INGOs of the Council of Europe (#04607); Conference of Non-Governmental Organizations in Consultative Relationship with the United Nations (CONGO, #04635); Ecumenical Advocacy Alliance (EAA, inactive); Fédération des Institutions Internationales établies à Genève (FIIG, #09599); Global Call for Climate Action (GCCA, inactive); International Conference of NGOs (#12883); Movimiento Mundial por la Infancia de Latinoamérica y El Caribe (MMI-LAC, #16873); NGO Committee on Disarmament, Peace and Security, New York NY (#17106)* and *NGO Committee for Disarmament, Geneva (#17105); NGO Committee on the Status of Women, Geneva (#17117); NGO Committee on UNICEF (#17120)*. [2020/XB3453/**B**]

♦ World Allium Association (inactive)
♦ World All Style Karate Organization / see World Association of Kickboxing Organizations (#21151)
♦ World All Styles Kickboxing Organization (no recent information)
♦ World Amateur Baseball Federation (inactive)
♦ World Amateur Golf Council / see International Golf Federation (#13727)
♦ World Amateur Kickboxing Organization / see World Association of Kickboxing Organizations (#21151)
♦ **World AMN** Academy for Multidisciplinary Neurotraumatology (#00042)
♦ World Angus Forum / see World Angus Secretariat (#21091)

♦ **World Angus Secretariat** **21091**

Contact Aberdeen-Angus Cattle Soc, 6 Kings Place, Perth, PH2 8AD, UK. T. +441738622477. Fax +441738636436. E-mail: info@aberdeen-angus.co.uk.
Permanent Secretariat c/o American Angus Assn, 3201 Frederick Avenue, St Joseph MO 64506, USA. T. +18163835100. Fax +18162339703.
URL: http://www.worldangussecretariat.com/

History 1969, at *World Angus Forum*. **Aims** Facilitate information sharing of Angus societies/associations worldwide. **Structure** General Meeting (every 2 years); Chairman; Secretariat. **Finance** Members' dues. **Activities** Events/meetings. **Events** *Forum* Kansas City, MO (USA) 2025, *Forum* Sydney, NSW (Australia) 2021, *Forum* Edinburgh (UK) 2017, *Forum* Rotorua (New Zealand) 2013, *Forum* Calgary, AB (Canada) 2009.

Members Organizations in 20 countries:
Argentina, Australia, Brazil, Canada, Chile, Denmark, Germany, Ireland, Japan, Mexico, New Zealand, Norway, Paraguay, Portugal, South Africa, Sweden, UK, Uruguay, USA, Zimbabwe. [2017/XF3887/c/**F**]

♦ **World Animal Protection** **21092**

Société mondiale pour la protection des animaux – Sociedad Mundial Protectora de Animales – Welttierschutz-Gesellschaft

Headquarters 222 Grays Inn Road, 5th Floor, London, WC1X 8HB, UK. T. +442072390500. Fax +442072390653. E-mail: info@worldanimalprotection.org.uk.
URL: http://www.worldanimalprotection.org/

History 1 Jan 1981, London (UK). Founded on the amalgamation of *World Federation for the Protection of Animals (WFPA, inactive)*, set up 31 Aug 1950, Scheveningen (Netherlands), and *International Society for the Protection of Animals (ISPA, inactive)*, formed in 1959, Washington DC (USA). *International Council Against Bullfighting (ICAB, inactive)*, created 1958, London, merged with WSPA which is continuing the work of ICAB. Former names and other names: *World Society for the Protection of Animals (WSPA)* – former; *Société mondiale pour la protection des animaux* – former; *Sociedad Mundial Protectora de Animales* – former; *Welttierschutz-Gesellschaft* – former. Registration: Charity Commission, No/ID: 1081849, UK, England and Wales. **Aims** Promote effective means for protection of animals and relief of suffering worldwide; maintain effective liaison between, and seek cooperation with, local organizations having similar objectives; provide facilities for membership of all approved *animal welfare* societies and individuals interested in animal welfare; organize international and regional conferences; seek recognition and representation on suitable international bodies; study international and national legislation relating to animal welfare and promote international efforts for protection of animals; provide means of informing members concerning international aspects of animal welfare, including humane education; mount animal rescue operations in the event of man-made or natural disaster. **Structure** Meeting (annual); Board of Directors; Committees. **Languages** English, French, German, Spanish. **Staff** 250.00 FTE, paid. **Finance** Sources: donations; fundraising; members' dues. **Activities** Advocacy/lobbying/activism. **Events** *Conference on global trade and farm animal welfare* Brussels (Belgium) 2009, *International advancing bear care conference* San Francisco, CA (USA) 2009, *International forum on global aspects of farm animal welfare* Brussels (Belgium) 2008, *Biennial Congress* London (UK) 2000, *Biennial Congress* Boston, MA (USA) 1998. **Publications** *Eurolink* (4 a year); *Animals International* (2 a year); *Libearty News* (2 a year). Annual Report.

Members Voting membership; Associate membership. Members in 76 countries and territories:
Argentina, Australia, Austria, Bahamas, Bahrain, Belgium, Brazil, Bulgaria, Canada, Chile, Colombia, Costa Rica, Croatia, Cuba, Cyprus, Czechia, Denmark, Ecuador, Egypt, Estonia, Fiji, Finland, France, Georgia, Germany, Ghana, Greece, Guyana, Hungary, Iceland, India, Ireland, Israel, Italy, Jamaica, Japan, Kenya, Korea Rep, Lithuania, Luxembourg, Malaysia, Malta, Mexico, Montenegro, Morocco, Namibia, Netherlands, New Zealand, Nigeria, Norway, Peru, Poland, Portugal, Romania, Russia, Senegal, Serbia, Sierra Leone, Singapore, Slovakia, Slovenia, South Africa, Spain, Sri Lanka, Sweden, Switzerland, Taiwan, Trinidad-Tobago, Tunisia, Türkiye, UK, Ukraine, Uruguay, USA, Venezuela, Zimbabwe.

Consultative Status Consultative status granted from: *ECOSOC (#05331)* (General); *FAO (#09260)* (Liaison Status); *UNEP (#20299)*. **IGO Relations** Associated with: *OIE – World Organisation for Animal Health (#17703)*. Accredited by: *International Whaling Commission (IWC, #15879)*. Formal association agreements: *FAO (#09260); UNEP (#20299); United Nations Office on Drugs and Crime (UNODC, #20596); World Food Programme (WFP, #21510)*. Associated with Department of Global Communications of the United Nations. **NGO Relations** Observer status with (1): *World Veterinary Association (WVA, #21901)*. Member of (12): *Climate Action Network Europe (CAN Europe, #04001); Conference of Non-Governmental Organizations in Consultative Relationship with the United Nations (CONGO, #04635); Fur Free Alliance (FFA, #10043); International Association of Human-Animal Interaction Organizations (IAHAIO, #11944); International Coalition for Animal Welfare (ICFAW, #12607); International Companion Animal Management Coalition (ICAM, #12828); International Tiger Coalition (ITC); OECD Watch (#17694); Ontario Council for International Cooperation (OCIC); Seas at Risk (SAR, #19189); Species Survival Network (SSN, #19916); World Cetacean Alliance (WCA, #21268)*. In liaison with technical committee of: *International Organization for Standardization (ISO, #14473)*. Special relationship with: *International Union for Conservation of Nature and Natural Resources (IUCN, #15766)*. Partner of: *Global Call for Climate Action (GCCA, inactive)*. [2021.09.01/XB2515/**B**]

♦ **World Anthropological Union (WAU)** **21093**

WCAA Sec address not obtained.
URL: https://www.waunet.org/

History Founded 2018, as a single bicameral organization, incorporating *International Union of Anthropological and Ethnological Sciences (IUAES, #15755)* and *World Council of Anthropological Associations (WCAA, #21317)*, which continue to exist as 2 distinctly separate but constituent chambers. **Aims** Represent anthropologies and ethnologies at a global and international level. **Structure** WAU Constituency; Steering Committee. **Finance** Sources: members' dues. **Members** Individual; Associational; Scientific Commissions: Group/corporate. Membership countries not specified. **NGO Relations** Member of (2): *International Council for Philosophy and Human Sciences (CIPSH, #13061); International Science Council (ISC, #14796)*. [2021/XM9007/**B**]

♦ World Anti-Aging Medical Association (inactive)

♦ **World Anti-Bullying Forum (WABF)** **21094**

Managing Dir Västra Norrlandsgatan 22b, SE-903 29 Umeå, Sweden. E-mail: wabf@friends.se – info@worldantibullyingforum.com.
Chair address not obtained.
Main Website: https://www.worldantibullyingforum.com

History 1997. Former names and other names: *Friends* – alias; *Friends International Center against Bullying (FICAB)* – former. **Aims** Unite researchers and practitioners in the work against bullying; end violence against and between children in accordance with the UN's sustainable development goals. **Activities** Events/meetings; guidance/assistance/consulting; research/documentation; training/education. **Events** *World Anti-Bullying Forum* Chapel Hill, NC (USA) 2023, *World Anti-Bullying Forum* Stockholm (Sweden) 2021, *World Anti-Bullying Forum* Dublin (Ireland) 2019, *World Anti-Bullying Forum* Stockholm (Sweden) 2017. **NGO Relations** Member of: *Global Partnership to End Violence Against Children (End Violence Against Children, #10533)*. [2022/XM6926/**D**]

♦ **World Anticancer Movement (WAM)** **21095**

Antikrebs Weltbewegung

Contact Billrothstr 78, 1190 Vienna, Austria. T. +431360365205. Fax +431360365805. E-mail: wam@cryosurgery.at.
URL: http://wam.cryosurgery.at/

History 4 Apr 2012, Vienna (Austria). Full title: *World Anticancer Movement "21st Century: Humanity versus Cancer" – Antikrebs Weltbewegung "21 Jahrhundert: Menschheit gegen Krebs"*. Registered in accordance with Austrian law. **Structure** Assembly. **NGO Relations** *International Society of Cryosurgery (ISC, #15040)*. [2014/XJ8466/**F**]

♦ World Anticancer Movement "21st Century: Humanity versus Cancer" / see World Anticancer Movement (#21095)
♦ World Anti-Communist League / see World League for Freedom and Democracy (#21621)

♦ **World Anti-Doping Agency (WADA)** **21096**

Agence Mondiale Antidopage (AMA)

Dir-Gen 800 rue du Square-Victoria, Bureau 1700, Montréal QC H4Z 1B7, Canada. T. +15149049232. Fax +15149048650. E-mail: media@wada-ama.org.
Dir – European Regional Office address not obtained.
URL: http://www.wada-ama.org/

History 10 Nov 1999, Lausanne (Switzerland). Founded by *International Olympic Committee (IOC, #14408)*. Inaugural meeting 13 Jan 2000, Lausanne (Switzerland). Registration: EU Transparency Register, No/ID: 057050117687-88, Start date: 4 Jun 2015. **Aims** Promote, coordinate and monitor the fight against doping in *sport* in all its forms. **Structure** Foundation Board, composed of 38 members. Executive Committee of 12 members. Headquarters in Montréal QC (Canada). Regional offices in: Lausanne (Switzerland); Cape Town (South Africa); Tokyo (Japan); Montevideo (Uruguay). **Languages** English, French. **Staff** 60.00 FTE, paid. **Finance** Funded equally by sports movement (through IOC) and governments of the world. **Activities** Key activities: scientific research; education; development of anti-doping capacities; monitoring World Anti-Doping Code. **Events** *World Conference on Doping in Sport* Busan (Korea Rep) 2025, *Therapeutic Use Exemption Symposium* Incheon (Korea Rep) 2023, *Annual Symposium* Lausanne (Switzerland) 2023, *Annual Symposium* Lausanne (Switzerland) 2022, *Global Education Conference* Sydney, NSW (Australia) 2022. **Publications** *PlayTrue* – magazine. *List of Prohibited Substances and Methods – Athlete Guide*.

Members Membership countries not specified. Included in members, 2 organizations listed in this Yearbook: Included in members, 2 organizations listed in this Yearbook:
Fédération internationale d'escrime (FIE, #09629); International Fistball Association (IFA, #13609).

Consultative Status Consultative status granted from: *UNESCO (#20322)* (Foundations). **IGO Relations** Partner of: *Enlarged Partial Agreement on Sport (EPAS, #05487)*. **NGO Relations** Memorandum of Understanding with (1): *Central European Anti-Doping Organization (CEADO, #03703)*. Member of (1): *Olympic Movement (#17719)*. Partner of (3): *Oceania Regional Anti-Doping Organization (ORADO, #17670); Panamerican Regional Antidoping Organization (PAN-RADO, #18125); Southeast Asia Regional Anti-Doping Organisation (SEARADO, #19792)*. Cooperates with (1): *International Testing Agency (ITA, #15678)*. [2022/XF5737/**F**]

♦ World Antinuclear Alliance of Citizens and Legislators Nevada – Semipalatinsk – Mururoa / see International Antinuclear Movement 'Nevada-Semipalatinsk'

♦ **World Apheresis Association (WAA)** **21097**

Operations Office c/o Canadian Apheresis Group, 435 St Laurent Blvd, Ste 199, Ottawa ON K1K 2Z8, Canada. T. +16137489613. Fax +16137489613. E-mail: cag@cagcanada.ca – waa@worldapheresis.org.
URL: http://www.worldapheresis.org/

History 1984. **Aims** Foster global scientific investigation, encourage clinical applications and facilitate international exchange of information and ideas regarding apheresis and all associated fields of clinical and laboratory medicine; stimulate and encourage worldwide availability of safe and effective apheresis techniques for the collection of donor cells and plasma or the therapeutic removal of blood constituents. **Structure** Board of Directors, consisting of President, Immediate Past-President, President-Elect, 3 Vice-Presidents, General Secretary, Assistant Secretary General, Treasurer, and District Councillors (14), representing: America; Eastern Mediterranean; Europe; South East Asia and Western Pacific. **Languages** English. **Staff** 1.00 FTE, voluntary. **Finance** Sources: members' dues. **Events** *International Congress* Istanbul (Turkey) 2021, *International Congress* Istanbul (Turkey) 2020, *International Congress* Paris (France) 2016, *International Congress* San Francisco, CA (USA) 2014, *International Congress* Istanbul (Turkey) 2012. **Publications** *WAA Newsletter* (annual); *Transfusion Science* – journal. Congress proceedings.

Members National associations in 18 countries:
Argentina, Australia, Brazil, Canada, China, France, Germany, Greece, India, Italy, Japan, Korea Rep, Mexico, New Zealand, Philippines, Sweden, Türkiye, USA.

Included in the above, 4 organizations listed in this Yearbook:
Asociación Latinoamericana de Aféresis y Terapias celulares (ALAyTeC, #02178); European Society for Artificial Organs (ESAO, #08525); European Society for Haemapheresis and Haemotherapy (ESFH, #08614); International Society for Apheresis (ISFA, #14927). [2021/XD0988/y/**C**]

♦ World Apostolate of Fatima (religious order)

♦ World Apple and Pear Association (WAPA) 21098

SG Rue de Trèves 49-51, Boîte 8, 1040 Brussels, Belgium. T. +3227771580. Fax +3227771581. E-mail: wapa@wapa-association.org.
URL: http://www.wapa-association.org/

History 2001. Registration: EU Transparency Register, No/ID: 78070741455-29. **Aims** Improve countries' business activities; increase demand for apples and pears, while ensuring a fair return for *producers*. **Structure** President; Secretariat.
Members Full in 22 countries:
Argentina, Australia, Austria, Belgium, Brazil, Chile, China, Croatia, Denmark, France, Germany, Italy, Moldova, Netherlands, New Zealand, Poland, Russia, Slovenia, South Africa, UK, Ukraine, USA. [2021.09.16/XM3886/**C**]

♦ World Aquaculture Society (WAS) 21099

Société mondiale de mariculture

Dir PO Box 397, Sorrento LA 70778-0397, USA. T. +12253475408.
Events – Conference Management PO Box 2302, Valley Center CA 92082, USA. T. +17607515005.
URL: http://www.was.org/

History Sep 1970. Former names and other names: *World Mariculture Society (WMS)* – former (1970 to 1986). **Aims** Secure promotion and evaluation of educational, scientific and technological advancement of aquaculture and mariculture throughout the world. **Structure** Annual Meeting; Board of Directors; Chapters (4). **Languages** English. **Staff** 2.00 FTE, paid. **Finance** Sources: meeting proceeds; members' dues; sale of publications. **Activities** Events/meetings; knowledge management/information dissemination. **Events** *World Aquaculture (WA2023)* Darwin, NT (Australia) 2023, *Aquaculture America* New Orleans, LA (USA) 2023, *Latin American & Caribbean Aquaculture (LACQUA23)* Panama (Panama) 2023, *Annual Conference* San Diego, CA (USA) 2022, *World Aquaculture Session* Singapore (Singapore) 2022. **Publications** *Journal of the World Aquaculture Society* (6 a year); *World Aquaculture, the magazine* (4 a year). *Advances in World Aquaculture Series*; *Workshops Series*.
Members Lifetime; Individual; Student; Corporate; Sustaining; E-Member. Members in 82 countries and territories:
Algeria, Argentina, Australia, Austria, Bahamas, Barbados, Belgium, Belize, Bermuda, Bhutan, Bolivia, Brazil, Canada, Chile, China, Colombia, Costa Rica, Côte d'Ivoire, Czechia, Denmark, Dominican Rep, Ecuador, Egypt, El Salvador, Finland, France, Germany, Greece, Guatemala, Guyana, Haiti, Honduras, Hong Kong, Hungary, Iceland, India, Indonesia, Ireland, Israel, Italy, Jamaica, Japan, Kenya, Kuwait, Luxembourg, Malaysia, Mexico, Monaco, Morocco, Netherlands, New Zealand, Norway, Pakistan, Panama, Papua New Guinea, Paraguay, Peru, Philippines, Poland, Portugal, Puerto Rico, Romania, San Marino, Saudi Arabia, Serbia, Singapore, South Africa, Spain, Sri Lanka, Sudan, Sweden, Switzerland, Syrian AR, Taiwan, Tanzania UR, Trinidad-Tobago, Türkiye, UK, Uruguay, USA, Venezuela. [2021.02.24/XD5909/**C**]

♦ World Aquatics 21100

Exec Dir Chemin de Bellevue 24a/24b, 1005 Lausanne VD, Switzerland. T. +41213104710. Fax +41213126610. E-mail: media@fina.org.
URL: https://www.fina.org/

History 1908, London (UK). Former names and other names: *International Amateur Swimming Federation* – former; *Fédération internationale de natation amateur* – former; *Fédération internationale de natation (FINA)* – former (2001); *International Swimming Federation* – former (2001). **Aims** Enable everyone in the world to swim; increase participation in all aquatic sports. **Structure** General Congress (every 4 years); Technical Congress; Bureau; Technical Committees (7); Commissions (8); Doping Panel and DCRB (Doping Control Review Board); Ad-hoc Committees; Arbitration Court; Disciplinary Panel. **Languages** English, French. **Staff** 37.00 FTE, paid. **Finance** World Championships (commercial rights); IOC television rights share; sponsorship; partnerships. **Activities** Awards/prizes/competitions; events/meetings; sporting activities. **Events** *Bureau Meeting* Gwangju (Korea Rep) 2019, *General Congress* Gwangju (Korea Rep) 2019, *World Sports Medicine Congress* Toronto, ON (Canada) 2016, *Extraordinary Congress* Doha (Qatar) 2014, *World Aquatics Convention* Doha (Qatar) 2014. **Publications** *FINA Aquatics World* (12 a year); *Official Handbook* (every 4 years). Circulars; manuals.
Members National federations in 210 countries and territories:
Afghanistan, Albania, Algeria, Andorra, Angola, Anguilla, Antigua-Barbuda, Argentina, Armenia, Aruba, Australia, Austria, Azerbaijan, Bahamas, Bahrain, Bangladesh, Barbados, Belarus, Belgium, Belize, Benin, Bermuda, Bhutan, Bolivia, Bosnia-Herzegovina, Botswana, Brazil, Brunei Darussalam, Bulgaria, Burkina Faso, Burundi, Cambodia, Cameroon, Canada, Cape Verde, Cayman Is, Central African Rep, Chad, Chile, China, Colombia, Comoros, Congo Brazzaville, Congo DR, Cook Is, Costa Rica, Côte d'Ivoire, Croatia, Cuba, Curaçao, Cyprus, Czechia, Denmark, Djibouti, Dominica, Dominican Rep, Ecuador, Egypt, El Salvador, Equatorial Guinea, Eritrea, Estonia, Eswatini, Ethiopia, Faeroe Is, Fiji, Finland, France, Gabon, Gambia, Georgia, Germany, Ghana, Gibraltar, Great Britain, Greece, Grenada, Guam, Guatemala, Guinea, Guinea-Bissau, Guyana, Haiti, Honduras, Hong Kong, Hungary, Iceland, India, Indonesia, Iran Islamic Rep, Iraq, Ireland, Israel, Italy, Jamaica, Japan, Jordan, Kazakhstan, Kenya, Korea DPR, Korea Rep, Kosovo, Kuwait, Kyrgyzstan, Laos, Latvia, Lebanon, Lesotho, Liberia, Libya, Liechtenstein, Lithuania, Luxembourg, Macau, Madagascar, Malawi, Malaysia, Maldives, Mali, Malta, Marshall Is, Mauritania, Mauritius, Mexico, Micronesia FS, Moldova, Monaco, Mongolia, Montenegro, Morocco, Mozambique, Myanmar, Namibia, Nepal, Netherlands, New Zealand, Nicaragua, Niger, Nigeria, North Macedonia, Northern Mariana Is, Norway, Oman, Pakistan, Palau, Palestine, Panama, Papua New Guinea, Paraguay, Peru, Philippines, Poland, Portugal, Puerto Rico, Qatar, Romania, Russia, Rwanda, Saba, Samoa, Samoa USA, San Marino, Saudi Arabia, Senegal, Serbia, Seychelles, Sierra Leone, Singapore, Slovakia, Slovenia, Solomon Is, Somalia, South Africa, Spain, Sri Lanka, St Kitts-Nevis, St Lucia, St Maarten, St Vincent-Grenadines, Sudan, Suriname, Sweden, Switzerland, Syrian AR, Taiwan, Tajikistan, Tanzania UR, Thailand, Timor-Leste, Togo, Tonga, Trinidad-Tobago, Tunisia, Türkiye, Turkmenistan, Turks-Caicos, Uganda, Ukraine, United Arab Emirates, Uruguay, USA, Uzbekistan, Vanuatu, Venezuela, Vietnam, Virgin Is UK, Virgin Is USA, Yemen, Zambia, Zimbabwe.
Continental Associations (5), listed in this Yearbook:
Asia Swimming Federation (AASF, #02099); Confédération africaine de natation amateur (CANA, #04502); Ligue européenne de natation (LEN, #16477); Oceania Swimming Association (#17677); PanAm Aquatics (#18077).
NGO Relations Member of (2): *Association of Summer Olympic International Federations (ASOIF, #02943); Olympic Movement (#17719).* Cooperates with (1): *International Testing Agency (ITA, #15678).* Recognized by: *International Olympic Committee (IOC, #14408).* [2022/XB1161/y/**B**]

♦ World Aquatic Veterinary Medical Association (WAVMA) 21101

Administrator 25871 Duran Ave, Conifer CO 80433, USA. E-mail: administrators@wavma.org.
URL: http://www.wavma.org/

History 2007. Registration: Illinois Secretary of State/US Internal Revenue Service, No/ID: EIN: 20-8500089, Start date: 17 Mar 2007, USA. **Aims** Serve the discipline of aquatic veterinary medicine in enhancing aquatic animal health and welfare, public health and seafood safety in support of the veterinary profession, aquatic animal owners and industries and other stakeholders. **Structure** Annual General Meeting; Board of Directors. **Languages** English. **Staff** 2.00 FTE, paid. **Finance** Sources: fees for services; members' dues. **Activities** Guidance/assistance/consulting. **Events** *Annual General Meeting* Basseterre (St Kitts-Nevis) 2018, *Annual Meeting* Targu-Mures (Romania) 2017, *Annual Meeting* Istanbul (Turkey) 2015, *Annual Meeting* Denver, CO (USA) 2014, *Annual Meeting* Chicago, IL (USA) 2013. **Publications** *The Aquatic Veterinarian* (4 a year).
Members in 82 countries. Membership countries not specified. **NGO Relations** Member of (2): *World Small Animal Veterinary Association (WSAVA, #21795); World Veterinary Association (WVA, #21901).* [2022.01.04/XM3357/**D**]

♦ World Arabian Horse Organization (WAHO) 21102

Organisation mondiale du cheval arabe

Exec Sec Newbarn Farmhouse, Forthampton, GL19 4QD, UK. T. +441684274455. Fax +441684274422. E-mail: wahoexecsec@gmail.com.
URL: http://www.waho.org/

History 1970, London (UK). Founded by a meeting of fourteen Arabian horse societies. Constitution adopted at 1st Conference, May 1972, Seville (Spain). Registration: Charity Commission, No/ID: 278988, England and Wales. **Aims** Preserve, improve and maintain purity of blood horses of the Arabian breed; promote public interest in the science of breeding Arabian horses by continuing the introduction of Arabian blood into breeding of light horses. **Structure** General Meeting; Executive Committee; Executive Committee Emeritus; Executive Secretary. **Languages** English. **Staff** 2.00 FTE, paid. **Finance** Sources: donations; members' dues. **Activities** Events/meetings; knowledge management/information dissemination. **Events** *Biennial Conference* Amman (Jordan) 2022, *Biennial Conference* Amman (Jordan) 2021, *Biennial Conference* Terrigal, NSW (Australia) 2019, *Biennial Conference* Manama (Bahrain) 2017, *Biennial Conference* Doha (Qatar) 2014. **Publications** *Membership Directory*; *WAHO Newsletter*.
Members Members (Voting Members); Associate; Individual Associate; Honorary Life Individual Associate. Members in 100 countries and territories:
Albania, Algeria, Andorra, Argentina, Australia, Austria, Azerbaijan, Bahrain, Belgium, Belize, Bolivia, Bosnia-Herzegovina, Botswana, Brazil, Brunei Darussalam, Bulgaria, Canada, Chile, China, Colombia, Croatia, Cuba, Czechia, Denmark, Ecuador, Egypt, England, Estonia, Finland, France, Germany, Greece, Hungary, India, Indonesia, Iran Islamic Rep, Iraq, Ireland, Israel, Italy, Japan, Jordan, Kazakhstan, Kenya, Korea Rep, Kuwait, Lebanon, Libya, Lithuania, Luxembourg, Malaysia, Malta, Mexico, Montenegro, Morocco, Namibia, Netherlands, New Zealand, North Macedonia, Northern Ireland, Norway, Oman, Pakistan, Palestine, Panama, Paraguay, Peru, Philippines, Poland, Portugal, Qatar, Romania, Russia, Saudi Arabia, Scotland, Serbia, Slovakia, Slovenia, South Africa, Sovereign Military Order of Malta, Spain, Sudan, Sweden, Switzerland, Syrian AR, Taiwan, Thailand, Tunisia, Türkiye, UK, Ukraine, United Arab Emirates, Uruguay, USA, Vanuatu, Venezuela, Vietnam, Wales, Yemen, Zimbabwe. [2021.03.02/XD5305/**C**]

♦ World Archaeological Congress (WAC) 21103

Pres SCS-Kyushu Univ, 744 Moto'oka, Nishi-ku, Fukuoka, 819-0395 Japan.
Vice Pres IU Anthropology Dept, 701 E Kirkwood Ave, Bloomington IN 47405-7100, USA.
Sec UEA School of Art History, Norwich Research Park, Norwich, NR4 7TJ, UK.
URL: http://www.worldarchaeologicalcongress.org/

History 1987. Statutes adopted 1990. Registered in accordance with USA law. **Aims** Promote interest in the past in all countries; encourage the development of regionally-based histories; foster international interaction; promote scientific investigation of the past, ethical archaeological practice and protection of cultural heritage worldwide; support empirical investigation and appreciation of the political contexts within which research is conducted and interpreted and promote dialogue and debate among advocates of different views of the past. **Structure** Assembly. Council comprising Officers, one Senior and one Junior representative from each Regional Electoral College, 8 representatives of indigenous peoples/Fourth World, WAC members and one student representative. Executive, comprising President, Vice-President, Secretary, Treasurer, 3 Council members (from different electoral regions), one indigenous member and one Student representative. **Languages** Arabic, Chinese, English, French, Russian, Spanish. **Finance** Members' dues: US$ 50 – US$ 25. **Activities** Organizes quadrennial Congress and one or more Inter-Congress between these. Conducts scholarly programs. **Events** *Quadrennial Congress* Kyoto (Japan) 2016, *Quadrennial Congress* Sweimeh (Jordan) 2013, *Quadrennial Congress* Dublin (Ireland) 2008, *Cultural heritage and indigenous cultural and intellectual property rights* Burra, SA (Australia) 2006, *Quadrennial Congress* Washington, DC (USA) 2003. **Publications** *Archaeologies* (3 a year) – journal. *One World Archaeology* – book series.
Members Archaeologists, heritage managers, students, members of the public. Members in 75 countries:
Algeria, Argentina, Australia, Austria, Belgium, Benin, Botswana, Brazil, Burkina Faso, Cameroon, Canada, Chile, China, Colombia, Côte d'Ivoire, Croatia, Czechia, Denmark, Egypt, Finland, France, Germany, Ghana, Greece, Guatemala, Hungary, Iceland, India, Indonesia, Ireland, Israel, Italy, Japan, Jordan, Kenya, Lebanon, Madagascar, Marshall Is, Mexico, Moldova, Namibia, Netherlands, New Zealand, Nicaragua, Nigeria, Norway, Panama, Papua New Guinea, Poland, Portugal, Romania, Russia, Saudi Arabia, South Africa, Spain, Sri Lanka, Sweden, Switzerland, Syrian AR, Tajikistan, Tanzania UR, Thailand, Togo, Tunisia, Türkiye, Turkmenistan, Uganda, UK, Ukraine, Uruguay, USA, Uzbekistan, Venezuela, Vietnam, Zimbabwe. [2016/XF3697/v/**F**]

♦ World Archaeological Society (WAS) 21104

Association mondiale d'archéologie

Address not obtained.
URL: http://www.worldarchaeologicalsociety.com/

History 1971, Hollister MO (USA). **Aims** Promote scientific study and circulation of knowledge in all fields and periods covered by archaeology, *anthropology* and *art history* and apply such knowledge to the present in practical, creative ways. **Structure** Director; Advisors; Special Correspondents. **Languages** English. **Staff** 1.00 FTE, voluntary. **Finance** Members' dues: for USA – US$ 16; for all other countries – US$ 20. Corresponding: free. **Activities** Runs Information Centre and referral system for members and others. Promotes research and archaeology-related projects. Projects to promote reading, writing and art: (1) Most Interesting Old Book Find Contest /any field/ (continuous – no deadline); (2) WAS Commendations for Books – Journals – Newsletters – Papers – Art – Photography /fields of Archaeology, Anthropology, Art History/ (continuous – no deadline); (3) Old Bible Repair Project. **Publications** *WAS Newsletter* (occasional); *WAS Special Publications* (occasional).
Members Individuals (mainly USA membership) in 21 countries and territories:
Argentina, Australia, Canada, Colombia, Costa Rica, Cyprus, Denmark, Germany, Israel, Italy, Japan, Jordan, Mexico, Nigeria, Philippines, Russia, South Africa, Taiwan, UK, USA, Venezuela. [2012.06.29/XF5541/v/**F**]

♦ World Archery 21105

Fédération Mondiale de Tir à l'Arc

SG Maison du Sport Intl, Avenue de Rhodanie 54, 1007 Lausanne VD, Switzerland. T. +41216143050. E-mail: info@archery.sport.
URL: http://www.worldarchery.sport/

History 1931, Lvow (Poland). Former names and other names: *International Archery Federation* – former; *Fédération internationale de tir à l'arc (FITA)* – former; *World Archery Federation* – full title (2011). **Aims** Promote and regulate archery worldwide. **Structure** Congress (every 2 years); Executive Board; Executive Committee; Permanent Committees (9). Meetings closed. **Languages** English. **Staff** 14.00 FTE, paid. **Finance** Sources: meeting proceeds; members' dues. Olympic revenue. **Activities** Events/meetings; sporting activities. **Events** *World Archery Congress* Berlin (Germany) 2023, *International Judge Seminar* Singapore (Singapore) 2023, *World Archery Congress* Yankton, SD (USA) 2021, *World Archery Congress*'s Hertogenbosch (Netherlands) 2019, *World Archery Congress* Mexico City (Mexico) 2017. **Publications** *World Archery News* (12 a year); *Judges Newsletter* (2 a year). Annual Report; Constitution and Rules (every 2 years).
Members National amateur and recognised associations in 173 countries and territories:
Afghanistan, Albania, Algeria, Andorra, Argentina, Armenia, Australia, Austria, Azerbaijan, Bahamas, Bahrain, Bangladesh, Barbados, Belarus, Belgium, Benin, Bermuda, Bhutan, Bolivia, Brazil, Bulgaria, Cameroon, Canada, Central African Rep, Chad, Chile, China, Colombia, Comoros, Congo DR, Costa Rica, Côte d'Ivoire, Croatia, Cuba, Curaçao, Cyprus, Czechia, Denmark, Djibouti, Dominican Rep, Ecuador, Egypt, El Salvador, Estonia, Faeroe Is, Falklands/Malvinas, Fiji, Finland, France, Georgia, Germany, Ghana, Great Britain, Greece, Guadeloupe, Guatemala, Guinea, Guyana, Haiti, Honduras, Hong Kong, Hungary, Iceland, India, Indonesia, Iran Islamic Rep, Iraq, Ireland, Israel, Italy, Jamaica, Japan, Jordan, Kazakhstan, Kenya, Korea DPR, Korea Rep, Kosovo, Kuwait, Kyrgyzstan, Laos, Latvia, Lebanon, Lesotho, Libya, Liechtenstein, Lithuania, Luxembourg, Macau, Madagascar, Malawi, Malaysia, Mali, Malta, Martinique, Mauritius, Mexico, Moldova, Monaco, Mongolia, Montenegro, Morocco, Myanmar, Namibia, Nepal, Netherlands, New Caledonia, New Zealand, Niger, Nigeria, Niue, Norfolk Is, North Macedonia, Norway, Pakistan, Palau, Palestine, Panama, Papua New Guinea, Paraguay, Peru, Philippines, Poland, Portugal, Puerto Rico, Qatar, Romania, Russia, Rwanda, Samoa, San Marino, Saudi Arabia, Senegal, Serbia, Sierra Leone, Singapore, Slovakia, Slovenia, Solomon Is, Somalia, South Africa, Spain, Sri Lanka, St Kitts-Nevis, St Vincent-Grenadines, Sudan, Sweden, Switzerland, Syrian AR, Tahiti Is, Taiwan, Tajikistan, Thailand, Timor-Leste, Togo, Tonga, Trinidad-Tobago, Tunisia, Türkiye, Turkmenistan, Uganda, Ukraine, United Arab Emirates, Uruguay, USA, Uzbekistan, Vanuatu, Venezuela, Vietnam, Virgin Is UK, Virgin Is USA, Yemen, Zimbabwe.
Sponsors (4), Providers (2), Partners (5) and Associates (24) in 14 countries:
Belgium, China, Denmark, France, Germany, Italy, Japan, Korea Rep, Netherlands, Singapore, Switzerland, Türkiye, UK, USA.
Continental members (5):
Federation of African Archery (FAA, #09400); World Archery Americas (COPARCO, #21106); World Archery Asia (WAA, #21107); World Archery Europe (WAE, #21108); World Archery Oceania (WAO, #21109).
NGO Relations Member of (6): *Association of Paralympic Sports Organisations (APSO, #02850); Association of Summer Olympic International Federations (ASOIF, #02943); International Masters Games Association (IMGA, #14117); International Paralympic Committee (IPC, #14512); International World Games Association (IWGA, #15914); Olympic Movement (#17719).* Cooperates with (1): *International Testing Agency (ITA, #15678).* Recognized by: *International Olympic Committee (IOC, #14408).* [2022.10.11/XB1170/y/**B**]

♦ World Archery Africa / see Federation of African Archery (#09400)

♦ World Archery Americas (COPARCO) 21106

Pres Cra 66B, No 31a-15, Medellín, Antioquia, Colombia. T. +5742659510. E-mail: worldarcheryamericas@gmail.com.

URL: https://www.worldarcheryamericas.com/
History Former names and other names: *Pan American Archery Confederation* – former; *Confederación Panamericana de Tiro con Arco* – former; *COPANARCO* – former. **Structure** Council. **Activities** Sporting activities.
Members Full in 32 countries and territories:
Argentina, Bahamas, Barbados, Bermuda, Bolivia, Brazil, Canada, Chile, Colombia, Costa Rica, Cuba, Dominican Rep, Ecuador, El Salvador, Falklands/Malvinas, Guatemala, Guyana, Haiti, Honduras, Mexico, Panama, Paraguay, Peru, Puerto Rico, St Kitts-Nevis, St Vincent-Grenadines, Trinidad-Tobago, Uruguay, USA, Venezuela, Virgin Is UK, Virgin Is USA.
Associate in 2 territories:
Guadeloupe, Martinique.
NGO Relations Member of (3): *Asociación de Confederaciones Deportivas Panamericanas (ACODEPA, #02119)*; *Asociación de Confederaciones Deportivas Sudamericanas (ACODESU, no recent information)*; *World Archery (#21105)*. [2023/XD5073/**D**]

♦ World Archery Asia (WAA) 21107

Contact 199 Gangdong-daero, Dasung Bldg 6F, Gandong-gu, Seoul, Korea Rep. E-mail: asian-archery@sports.or.kr.
URL: http://www.asianarchery.com/
History Set up as *Asian Archery Federation (AAF)*. **Structure** Executive Board. **Events** *International Judge Seminar* Singapore (Singapore) 2023, *Judges Seminar* Sharjah (United Arab Emirates) 2022, *Judges Seminar* Dubai (United Arab Emirates) 2021, *Judge Committee Meeting* Incheon (Korea Rep) 2018, *Judge Conference* Incheon (Korea Rep) 2018.
Members Federations in 37 countries and territories:
Afghanistan, Bangladesh, Bhutan, Cambodia, China, Hong Kong, India, Indonesia, Iran Islamic Rep, Iraq, Japan, Kazakhstan, Korea DPR, Korea Rep, Kuwait, Kyrgyzstan, Laos, Lebanon, Macau, Malaysia, Mongolia, Myanmar, Nepal, Pakistan, Philippines, Qatar, Saudi Arabia, Singapore, Sri Lanka, Syrian AR, Taiwan, Tajikistan, Thailand, Turkmenistan, United Arab Emirates, Uzbekistan, Vietnam.
NGO Relations Member of: *World Archery (#21105)*. [2023/XD9334/**D**]

♦ World Archery Europe (WAE) 21108

SG Via Vitorchiano 113/115, 00189 Rome RM, Italy. E-mail: rapportinternazionali@fitarco-italia.org.
URL: http://www.archeryeurope.org/
History Founded 17 Apr 1988, Paris (France), as *European and Mediterranean Archery Union (EMAU)*. Present name adopted, 2012. **Aims** Promote and encourage archery throughout Europe. **Structure** Congress; Executive Board. **Languages** English. **Staff** 1.00 FTE, paid; 1.00 FTE, voluntary. **Finance** Members' dues. Sponsors. **Activities** Sporting events; training/education; events/meetings. **Events** *Congress* Munich (Germany) 2022, *Congress* 2021, *Congress* Legnica (Poland) 2018, *Congress* Nottingham (UK) 2016, *Congress* Etchmiadzin (Armenia) 2014.
Members Associations in 50 countries:
Albania, Andorra, Armenia, Austria, Azerbaijan, Belarus, Belgium, Bulgaria, Croatia, Cyprus, Czechia, Denmark, Estonia, Faeroe Is, Finland, France, Georgia, Germany, Great Britain, Greece, Hungary, Iceland, Ireland, Israel, Italy, Kosovo, Latvia, Liechtenstein, Lithuania, Luxembourg, Malta, Moldova, Monaco, Montenegro, Netherlands, North Macedonia, Norway, Poland, Portugal, Romania, Russia, San Marino, Serbia, Slovakia, Slovenia, Spain, Sweden, Switzerland, Türkiye, Ukraine.
NGO Relations Continental member of: *World Archery (#21105)*. [2021/XD6198/**D**]

♦ World Archery Federation / see World Archery (#21105)

♦ World Archery Oceania (WAO) 21109

SG 3 Mudgway Place, Riverdale, Palmerston North 4412, New Zealand. T. +6463543707. E-mail: secretary@worldarcheryoceania.org.
URL: http://www.worldarcheryoceania.org/
Aims Ensure development of the *sport* in the Oceania region; provide the infrastructure advice and know-how for member nations to develop the sport. **Structure** Council.
Members Federations in 13 countries and territories:
Australia, Fiji, New Caledonia, New Zealand, Niue, Norfolk Is, Palau, Papua New Guinea, Samoa, Solomon Is, Tahiti Is, Tonga, Vanuatu.
NGO Relations Member of (2): *Organisation of Sports Federations of Oceania (OSFO, #17828)*; *World Archery (#21105)*. [2021/XM4691/**D**]

♦ World Armenian Congress (meeting series)
♦ World Armsport Federation / see World Armwrestling Federation (#21110)
♦ World Armsport Federation / see International Federation of Armsports
♦ World Armwrestling Federation / see World Armwrestling Federation (#21110)

♦ World Armwrestling Federation (WAF) 21110

Contact Sofia Park Trading Zone, Building 16V – F1-1, Office 1-2, 1766 Sofia, Bulgaria. T. +359888968541. E-mail: contact@waf-armwrestling.com.
URL: http://www.waf-armwrestling.com/
History 1967. Former names and other names: *World Armwrestling Federation* – former; *World Armsport Federation (WAF)* – former. **Aims** Promote the *sport* of armwrestling; organize International Armwrestling Championships. **Structure** Executive Committee, comprising 6 Continental representatives. **Languages** English, Russian. **Staff** 6.00 FTE, paid; 4.00 FTE, voluntary. **Finance** Annual budget: 100,000 USD. **Activities** Events/meetings; sporting activities. **Events** *Asia congress* Dibrugarh (India) 2003, *Annual congress* Alexandria (Egypt) 2002, *Annual meeting / Asia Congress* Gardone Riviera (Italy) 2001, *Asia congress* Mirik (India) 2000, *Annual meeting / Annual Congress* Virginia Beach, VA (USA) 2000. **Publications** *Arm Bender* – official journal. *WAF Book of Armsport*. Books.
Members National armwrestling organizations in 80 countries and territories:
Afghanistan, Argentina, Armenia, Australia, Austria, Azerbaijan, Belarus, Belgium, Bolivia, Bosnia-Herzegovina, Brazil, Bulgaria, Cameroon, Canada, Chile, China, Colombia, Costa Rica, Croatia, Czechia, Denmark, Dominican Rep, Egypt, England, Estonia, Finland, France, Georgia, Ghana, Greece, Greenland, Hungary, Iceland, India, Indonesia, Iran Islamic Rep, Iraq, Israel, Italy, Japan, Kazakhstan, Korea Rep, Kyrgyzstan, Latvia, Lebanon, Lithuania, Malaysia, Mali, Moldova, Mongolia, Morocco, Nepal, Netherlands, New Zealand, Nigeria, Norway, Pakistan, Palestine, Poland, Romania, Russia, Scotland, Serbia, Singapore, Slovakia, South Africa, Spain, Sweden, Switzerland, Syrian AR, Taiwan, Tajikistan, Tunisia, Türkiye, Turkmenistan, Uganda, Ukraine, United Arab Emirates, USA, Uzbekistan.
NGO Relations Member of (2): *Alliance of Independent recognised Members of Sport (AIMS, #00690)*; *Olympic Movement (#17719)*. Recognized by: *International Olympic Committee (IOC, #14408)*. [2021/XD3980/**B**]

♦ World Artifex Society (inactive)
♦ World Artificial Organ, Immunology and Transplantation Society (no recent information)
♦ World Asian Workers Organization (inactive)

♦ World Assemblies of God Fellowship (WAGF) 21111

Fraternidad Mundial de las Asambleas de Dios
Chairman 1445 N Boonville Ave, Springfield MO 65802, USA. Fax +14178636614. E-mail: chairman@worldagfellowship.org.
URL: http://worldagfellowship.org/
History Founded 1988, derived from missionary work of the USA-based *'Assemblies of God'*, set up 1914, and establishment of relationships with other Pentecostal churches Commonly referred to as *Assemblies of God (AG)*. The largest of several international fellowships of Pentecostal churches. **Aims** As an international fellowship of autonomous *Pentecostal churches*: fulfil the Lord's command to *evangelize* the lost, providing them the opportunity to hear and respond to the gospel; encourage and assist one another; promoting harmonious relationships; seek the most effective means of accomplishing this under the dynamic leadership of the Holy Spirit. **Structure** General Assembly; Executive Council; National Councils. Includes *World Assemblies of God Relief and Development Agency (WAGRA, see: #21111)*. **Activities** Awareness raising. **Events** *Triennial General Assembly* Madrid (Spain) 2021, *Triennial General Assembly* Madrid (Spain) 2020, *World Missions Congress* Madrid (Spain) 2018, *Triennial General Assembly* Singapore (Singapore) 2017, *World Missions Congress* Bangkok (Thailand) 2015. **Members** Comprises over 150 autonomous but loosely associated national groupings of churches serving about 66.4 million members in over 212 countries. Membership countries not specified. [2018.07.31/XJ8312/**F**]

♦ World Assemblies of God Relief and Development Agency (see: #21111)

♦ World Assembly Against Racism / see International League Against Racism and Antisemitism (#14014)

♦ World Assembly of Muslim Youth (WAMY) 21112

Contact 86 Whitechapel High Street, London, E1 7QX, UK. T. +442076367010. E-mail: info@wamy.co.uk.
URL: http://www.wamy.co.uk/
History 1972. **Aims** Infuse *Islamic* spirit of unity, confidence and resolution among Islamic young people; gather together Islamic thinkers and functionaries to contribute to the growth of Islamic *Dawah*. **Activities** Organizes world conferences on Islamic economics, science and technology. **Events** *International Conference* Seoul (Korea Rep) 1996, *Conference* Seoul (Korea Rep) 1995, *Conference / International Conference* Kuala Lumpur (Malaysia) 1993, *Conference* Melbourne, VIC (Australia) 1993, *International Conference* Granada (Spain) 1992. **IGO Relations** Cooperates with: *Islamic World Educational, Scientific and Cultural Organization (ICESCO, #16058)*. Associated with Department of Global Communications of the United Nations. **NGO Relations** Member of: *International Federation of Non-Government Organizations for the Prevention of Drug and Substance Abuse (IFNGO, #13490)*. [2015/XF8664/**F**]

♦ World Assembly of Small and Medium Enterprises / see World Association for Small and Medium Enterprises (#21189)
♦ World Assembly on Tobacco Counters Health (meeting series)

♦ World Assembly of Youth (WAY) 21113

Assemblée mondiale de la jeunesse (AMJ) – Asamblea Mundial de la Juventud (AMJ)
SG World Youth Complex, Jalan Lebuh Raya, 75450 Melaka, Malacca, Malaysia. T. +6062321871 – +6062322711. Fax +6062327271. E-mail: info@way.org.my – office@way.org.my.
URL: http://www.way.org.my/
History 24 Aug 1949, London (UK). Founded following an initiative undertaken by youth leaders from national youth councils of all member countries of the United Nations at international conference. Draft charter prepared Feb 1949, Ashbridge (UK); ratified at first official meeting of WAY, 1950, Brussels (Belgium). The charter was ratified by 29 of the national youth councils present. Amendments to Charter: 1950; 1951; 1952; 1953; 1956; 1958; 1962; 1964; 1966; 1969; 1972; 1976; 1983; 1988; 1993; 1995. Registration: No/ID: 0411.044.131, Start date: 26 Nov 1995, Belgium. **Aims** Coordinate national youth councils and youth organisations; bring people from different societies, communities and countries together to share ideas, thoughts and actions on how to improve cooperation on a global level and among youth. **Structure** General Assembly (every 4 years); Bureau; Executive Committee; Headquarters located in Melaka (Malaysia). **Languages** English, French, Spanish. **Staff** 12.00 FTE, paid; 2000.00 FTE, voluntary. **Finance** Sources: fundraising; grants; members' dues. Annual budget: 350,000 USD. **Activities** Advocacy/lobbying/activism; events/meetings; guidance/assistance/consulting; networking/liaising; politics/policy/regulatory; projects/programmes; publishing activities; research and development; training/education. **Events** *International Teenage Pregnancy Prevention Conference* Malaysia 2019, *Annual Melaka International Youth Dialogue* Melaka (Malaysia) 2019, *Quadrennial General Assembly* Melaka (Malaysia) 2019, *International Youth Forum* Seoul (Korea Rep) 2019, *International Youth Forum* Goyang (Korea Rep) 2018. **Publications** *Youth Round-Up* (6 a year); *WAY Information* (6 a year); *WAY Forum* (4 a year). Monthly youth press service; monthly bulletins; press releases; books.
Members Full; Observer; Associate; Consultative. Full in 79 countries and territories:
Angola, Anguilla, Argentina, Armenia, Australia, Bahamas, Bangladesh, Barbados, Belize, Bolivia, Botswana, Brunei Darussalam, Cameroon, Canada, Chile, Colombia, Comoros, Cook Is, Côte d'Ivoire, Croatia, Czechia, Dominica, Ecuador, El Salvador, Eswatini, Fiji, Gambia, Germany, Ghana, Greece, Guinea-Bissau, Guyana, India, Indonesia, Iraq, Jamaica, Jordan, Kenya, Korea Rep, Latvia, Lesotho, Libya, Luxembourg, Malaysia, Mali, Mauritius, Mongolia, Montserrat, Namibia, Nepal, Nicaragua, Nigeria, Niue, North Macedonia, Norway, Pakistan, Papua New Guinea, Peru, Puerto Rico, Rwanda, Samoa, Senegal, Sierra Leone, Slovakia, Solomon Is, Somalia, Sri Lanka, St Kitts-Nevis, Suriname, Thailand, Tonga, Trinidad-Tobago, Uganda, UK, USA, Vanuatu, Yemen, Zambia, Zimbabwe.
Observer in 28 countries and territories:
Albania, Algeria, Benin, Burkina Faso, Central African Rep, China, Congo Brazzaville, Congo DR, Cuba, Ethiopia, Kuwait, Madagascar, Mexico, Morocco, Paraguay, Philippines, Portugal, Russia, Sahara West, Sao Tomé-Principe, Seychelles, Singapore, South Africa, Sudan, Syrian AR, Türkiye, United Arab Emirates, Vietnam.
Associate in 8 countries:
Azerbaijan, Bhutan, Cambodia, Guatemala, Mozambique, Poland, Tanzania UR, Tunisia.
Consultative members (11):
Arab African Youth Council (AAYC, #00894); *Arab Youth Union (AYU, no recent information)*; *Asian Youth Council (AYC, #01788)*; Better Community For All (ABC4All); Caribbean Youth Forum; *European Youth Forum (#09140)*; Forum for the Integration of Andean Youth; *Global Youth Innovation Network (GYIN)*; *Pacific Youth Council (Youthlink, #18013)*; *Pan African Youth Union (#18076)*; SADC Youth Movement.
Consultative Status Consultative status granted from: *ECOSOC (#05331)* (Special); *FAO (#09260)* (Special Status); *ILO (#11123)* (Special List); *UNESCO (#20322)* (Associate Status); *UNICEF (#20332)*; *UNCTAD (#20285)* (General Category). **IGO Relations** Accredited by (1): *United Nations Office at Vienna (UNOV, #20604)*. Associated with Department of Global Communications of the United Nations. **NGO Relations** Member of (4): *Child Rights International Network (CRIN, #03885)*; *EarthAction (EA, #05159)*; *Framework Convention Alliance (FCA, #09981)*; *NGO Committee on UNICEF (#17120)*. Partner of (1): *UNLEASH*. Instrumental in setting up (1): *World Youth Bank Network (WYB, #21954)*. [2022.11.30/XB3456/y/**B**]

♦ World Assistance Corps / see Corps mondial de secours (#04845)
♦ World Associates for Biosystem Science and Engineering (internationally oriented national body)
♦ World Association for Adult Education (inactive)

♦ World Association for the Advancement of Veterinary Parasitology (WAAVP) 21114

Association mondiale pour l'avancement de parasitologie vétérinaire – Asociación Mundial para el Avance de la Parasitologia Veterinaria – Weltverband zur Förderung der Veterinärparasitologie
Sec/Treas Life Sciences Bldg, 24 Tyndall Avenue, Bristol, BS8 1TQ, UK. E-mail: contact.waavp@gmail.com.
Pres address not obtained.
URL: http://www.waavp.org/
History Set up 17 Aug 1963, Hannover (Germany FR). **Aims** Encourage research in veterinary parasitology and promote exchange of information and material among researchers, veterinary practitioners and animal health investigators. **Structure** Executive Committee; Standing Committees (8). **Languages** English. **Staff** Voluntary. **Finance** Sources: members' dues. **Activities** Awards/prizes/competitions; events/meetings. **Events** *Biennial Conference* Madison, WI (USA) 2019, *Biennial Conference* Kuala Lumpur (Malaysia) 2017, *Biennial Conference* Liverpool (UK) 2015, *Biennial Conference* Perth, WA (Australia) 2013, *Biennial Conference* Buenos Aires (Argentina) 2011. **Publications** Guidelines; symposia proceedings. **Members** Regular veterinarians and non-veterinarians who are university or college graduates and directly engaged in research advisory work or teaching concerned with parasites of veterinary importance; Associate; at the discretion of Executive Committee for those not qualifying as Regular member; Honorary nominated by members and approved by Executive Committee. Membership countries not specified. **NGO Relations** Instrumental in setting up: *European Veterinary Parasitology College (EVPC, #09058)*. [2019.04.24/XB3463/**B**]

♦ World Association of Agrologists / see World Association of Agronomists (#21115)

♦ World Association of Agronomists (WAA) 21115

Asociación Mundial de Ingenieros Agrónomos (AMIA)
Contact c/o CONAF, Via Po 22, 00198 Rome RM, Italy. E-mail: generalsecretary@worldagronomistsassociation.org.
URL: http://www.worldagronomistsassociation.org/
History 8 Sep 1994, Santiago (Chile). Founded following First World Congress of Professionals in Agronomy. Former names and other names: *World Association of Agrologists* – alias. **Aims** Unite and represent associations of agrologists from around the world so as to encourage the practice of the profession; promote academic excellence, know-how and professionalism amongst those practising the profession; promote social and rural economic development; represent and defend the interests of the agronomic community in international forums and before governments. **Structure** Board, comprising President, Vice-President,

Regional Vice-Presidents (America; Europe; Africa and Asia), General Secretary and 3 Technical Secretaries. **Events** *World Congress* Milan (Italy) 2015, *World Congress* Québec, QC (Canada) 2012, *World congress of agronomists and professionals in agronomy* Madrid (Spain) 2008, *World congress of agronomists and professionals in agronomy* Fortaleza (Brazil) 2004, *World congress of agronomists and professionals in agronomy* Mexico 2000.
Members Continental; National; Associate; Honorary; Cooperators. Continental members (2):
Asociación Panamericana de Ingenieros Agrónomos (APIA, #02289); Confédération européenne des associations d'ingénieurs agronomes (CEDIA, #04538).
National organizations in 19 countries:
Argentina, Bolivia, Brazil, Canada, Chile, Colombia, Costa Rica, Ecuador, Guatemala, Honduras, Italy, Mexico, Nicaragua, Panama, Paraguay, Peru, Puerto Rico, Spain, Uruguay.
Associate in 7 countries:
Argentina, Bolivia, Brazil, Chile, El Salvador, India, Paraguay.
Included in the above, 1 organization listed in this Yearbook:
International Maize and Wheat Improvement Center (#14077).
Cooperators in 2 countries:
Brazil, Chile.
Included in the above, 1 organization listed in this Yearbook:
Inter-American Institute for Cooperation on Agriculture (IICA, #11434).
NGO Relations *Confédération européenne des associations d'ingénieurs agronomes (CEDIA, #04538).* [2021/XJ4970/y/**C**]

♦ World Association of Alumnae of the Sacred Heart 21116

Association mondiale des anciennes et anciens du Sacré Coeur (AMASC) – Asociación Mundial de Antiguas e Antiguos del Sagrado Corazón

Pres 6441 W Eugie Ave, Glendale AZ 85304, USA. E-mail: mae13@shaw.ca.
URL: http://www.amasc-sacrecoeur.org/

History 1960, Brussels (Belgium), at the request of the then Mother General, Mother de Valon. Previously also referred to as *Association Mundial de Antiguas del Sagrado Corazón.* Registered in accordance with Belgian law. **Aims** Create and maintain friendship and solidarity between all national federation and associations of former pupils of the Sacre Coeur so as to bring about true international collaboration; actively and effectively cooperate with the society of the Sacre Coeur. **Structure** Officers: President, Vice-President, 11 Directors, Treasurer-General, Secretary General. Secretariat located in Brussels (Belgium). **Languages** English, French, Spanish. **Staff** None. **Finance** From National Associations to World Secretariat. **Activities** Social Solidarity in supporting projects in Africa and South America. **Events** *World Congress* Mérida (Mexico) 2018, *European Meeting* Madrid (Spain) 2016, *World Congress* Phoenix, AZ (USA) 2014, *World Conference* Malta 2010, *World congress* Valletta (Malta) 2010. **Publications** *AMASC Newsletter* (annual).
Members National associations in 35 countries and territories:
Argentina, Australia, Austria, Belgium, Brazil, Canada, Chile, Colombia, Congo DR, Costa Rica, Cuba, Egypt, England, France, Germany, Hungary, India, Ireland, Italy, Japan, Korea Rep, Lebanon, Malta, Mexico, Netherlands, New Zealand, Peru, Philippines, Poland, Puerto Rico, Scotland, Spain, Uruguay, USA, Venezuela.
Individuals in 5 countries:
Chad, Cuba, Kenya, Portugal, Uganda.
NGO Relations Affiliated to: *Organisation mondiale des anciens élèves de l'enseignement catholique (OMAEC, #17816).* [2010/XE6179/**E**]

♦ World Association of Alzheimer's Disease Scientists (inactive)
♦ World Association of Anatomic and Clinical Pathology Societies / see World Association of Societies of Pathology and Laboratory Medicine (#21191)

♦ World Association for Animal Production (WAAP) 21117

Association mondiale de zootechnie (AMZ) – Asociación Mundial para la Producción Animal (AMPA) – Weltvereinigung für Tierproduktion (WVT)

SG Via G Tomassetti 3 A/1, 00161 Rome RM, Italy. T. +39644202639. Fax +39644266798. E-mail: waap@waap.it.
Pres address not obtained.
URL: https://waap.it/

History 24 May 1965, Rome (Italy). **Aims** Consider scientific, technical and educational problems as well as overall policies related to animal production. **Structure** Council; Officers. **Languages** English. **Staff** 3.00 FTE, paid. **Finance** Sources: members' dues. **Activities** Events/meetings. **Events** *Joint International Congress on Animal Science* Lyon (France) 2023, *World Conference* Vancouver, BC (Canada) 2018, *World Conference* Beijing (China) 2013, *SAPT : sustainable animal production in the tropics conference* Gosier (Guadeloupe) 2010, *World Congress* Cape Town (South Africa) 2008. **Publications** *News Items* (irregular).
Members National societies (15) in 15 countries:
Canada, China, India, Japan, Kenya, Korea Rep, Malaysia, Nigeria, Peru, Philippines, South Africa, Tanzania UR, Thailand, Uganda, USA.
Regional associations (2):
Asociación Latinoamericana para la Producción Animal (ALPA, #02257); European Federation of Animal Science (EAAP, #07046).
Consultative Status Consultative status granted from: *ECOSOC (#05331)* (Ros C); *FAO (#09260)* (Special Status). **IGO Relations** Participates as observer in the activities of: *Codex Alimentarius Commission (CAC, #04081).* [2021/XC3458/y/**C**]

♦ World Association of Arab Translators and Linguists (WATA) 21118

Association internationale des traducteurs et des linguistes arabes – Internationale Vereinigung der arabischen Ubersetzer und Sprachwissenschaftler

Contact address not obtained.
URL: http://www.wata.cc/

History 2003, Doha (Qatar). **Members** Membership countries not specified. [2008/XJ8056/**D**]

♦ World Association of Basketball Coaches (WABC) 21119

SG Route Suisse 5, PO Box 29, 1295 Mies VD, Switzerland. T. +41225450000. Fax +41225450099. E-mail: info@fiba.com.
Pres Australian Inst of Sport, Leverrier Crescent, Bruce ACT 2617, Australia. T. +61262141111.

History Founded in the framework of *Fédération internationale de basketball (FIBA, #09614).* **Events** *Meeting* Noordwijk (Netherlands) 2007.
Members National federations (members of FIBA) in 206 countries and territories:
Afghanistan, Albania, Algeria, Andorra, Angola, Antigua-Barbuda, Argentina, Armenia, Aruba, Australia, Austria, Azerbaijan, Bahamas, Bahrain, Bangladesh, Barbados, Belarus, Belgium, Belize, Benin, Bhutan, Bolivia, Bosnia-Herzegovina, Botswana, Brazil, Brunei Darussalam, Bulgaria, Burkina Faso, Burundi, Cambodia, Cameroon, Canada, Cape Verde, Cayman Is, Central African Rep, Chad, Chile, China, Colombia, Comoros, Congo Brazzaville, Congo DR, Cook Is, Costa Rica, Côte d'Ivoire, Croatia, Cuba, Cyprus, Czechia, Denmark, Djibouti, Dominica, Dominican Rep, Ecuador, Egypt, El Salvador, England, Equatorial Guinea, Eritrea, Estonia, Ethiopia, Fiji, Finland, France, Gabon, Gambia, Georgia, Germany, Ghana, Gibraltar, Greece, Grenada, Guam, Guatemala, Guinea, Guinea-Bissau, Guyana, Haiti, Honduras, Hong Kong, Hungary, Iceland, India, Indonesia, Iran Islamic Rep, Iraq, Ireland, Israel, Italy, Jamaica, Japan, Jordan, Kazakhstan, Kenya, Kiribati, Korea DPR, Korea Rep, Kuwait, Kyrgyzstan, Laos, Latvia, Lebanon, Lesotho, Liberia, Libya, Lithuania, Luxembourg, Macau, Madagascar, Malawi, Malaysia, Maldives, Mali, Malta, Marshall Is, Mauritania, Mauritius, Mexico, Micronesia FS, Moldova, Monaco, Montserrat, Morocco, Mozambique, Myanmar, Namibia, Nauru, Netherlands, New Caledonia, New Zealand, Nicaragua, Niger, Nigeria, Norfolk Is, North Macedonia, Northern Mariana Is, Norway, Oman, Pakistan, Palau, Palestine, Panama, Papua New Guinea, Paraguay, Peru, Philippines, Poland, Portugal, Puerto Rico, Qatar, Romania, Russia, Rwanda, Samoa, Samoa USA, San Marino, Sao Tomé-Principe, Saudi Arabia, Scotland, Senegal, Serbia, Seychelles, Sierra Leone, Singapore, Slovakia, Slovenia, Solomon Is, Somalia, South Africa, Spain, Sri Lanka, St Kitts-Nevis, St Lucia, St Vincent-Grenadines, Sudan, Suriname, Sweden, Switzerland, Syrian AR, Tahiti Is, Taiwan, Tajikistan, Tanzania UR, Thailand, Togo, Tonga, Trinidad-Tobago, Tunisia, Türkiye, Tuvalu, Uganda, Ukraine, United Arab Emirates, Uruguay, USA, Uzbekistan, Vanuatu, Venezuela, Vietnam, Virgin Is UK, Virgin Is USA, Wales, Yemen, Zambia, Zimbabwe. [2014.06.01/XD7353/**E**]

♦ World Association of Beet and Cane Growers (WABCG) 21120

Association mondiale des planteurs de betteraves et de canne à sucre – Asociación Mundial de Productores de Caña y Remolacha Azucareras

Exec Sec 29 rue du General Foy, 75008 Paris, France. T. +33144694112.
URL: http://www.wabcg.org/

History Oct 1984, Paris (France), at 2nd World Sugar Farmers Conference, as a specialized body *International Federation of Agricultural Producers (IFAP, inactive).* Initially proposed May 1981, Guadalajara (Mexico), at 1st World Sugar Farmers Conference. Provisional constitution approved Nov 1982, under the name *Association mondiale des producteurs de betteraves et de canne à sucre.* **Aims** Contribute to economic, technical and social progress of beet and cane growers in member countries. **Structure** World Sugar Farmers Council; Executive Board, includes: *International Confederation of European Beet Growers (CIBE, #12860)* and *Ibero-American and Filipino Confederation of Sugar Cane Growers (CIFPCA, no recent information);* World Sugar Farmers Conference Organizing Committee; Budget and Finance Committee; Secretariat provided by IFAP. **Finance** Members' dues. **Events** *Meeting* Rotterdam (Netherlands) 2018, *Congress* Paris (France) 2016, *Meeting* Paris (France) 2016, *Meeting* Guadalajara (Mexico) 2015, *Meeting* Brussels (Belgium) 2014. **Publications** *World Sugar Farmer News* (4 a year).
Members Sugar farmers in 28 countries and territories:
Australia, Belgium, Belize, Brazil, Canada, Colombia, Denmark, Eswatini, Fiji, France, Germany, India, Jamaica, Japan, Kenya, Malawi, Mauritius, Mexico, Netherlands, Pakistan, South Africa, Spain, Sweden, Switzerland, Trinidad-Tobago, UK, USA, Zimbabwe. [2019.07.01/XE9602/**E**]

♦ World Association for Bronchology / see World Association for Bronchology and Interventional Pulmonology (#21121)

♦ World Association for Bronchology and Interventional Pulmonology (WABIP) 21121

Gen Manager Ebisu Prime Square 1F MBE 501, 1-1-39 Hiroo, Shibuya, Tokyo, 150-0012 Japan. E-mail: contact@wabip.com.
URL: http://www.wabip.com/

History 15 Jul 1979. Former names and other names: *World Association for Bronchology (WAB)* – former (15 Jul 1979 to 2010). Registration: No/ID: 0111-05-001776, Japan. **Aims** Connect a growing network of specialized medical doctors, health care professionals and industry/technology experts devoted to the art and science of airway, *lung* and *esophageal diseases.* **Structure** Board of Regents; Executive Officers; Committees; Taskforce. **Languages** English. **Staff** 4.00 FTE, paid. **Finance** Sources: meeting proceeds; members' dues. **Activities** Awards/prizes/competitions; events/meetings; training/education. **Events** *World Congress for Bronchology and Interventional Pulmonology* Bali (Indonesia) 2024, *World Congress for Bronchology and Interventional Pulmonology* Marseille (France) 2022, *Biennial Congress* Shanghai (China) 2020, *Biennial Congress* Rochester, MN (USA) 2018, *Biennial Congress* Florence (Italy) 2016. **Publications** *WABIP Newsletter* (3 a year); *Journal of Bronchology and Interventional Pulmonology; Respiration* – journal; *Respirology* – journal.
Members Medical professionals (over 7,200) representing over 50 regional and national societies in 45 countries and territories:
Argentina, Australia, Bolivia, Brazil, Canada, China, Colombia, Ecuador, Egypt, El Salvador, France, Greece, Hungary, India, Indonesia, Israel, Italy, Japan, Jordan, Korea Rep, Malaysia, Mexico, Moldova, Netherlands, New Zealand, North Macedonia, Paraguay, Peru, Philippines, Romania, Russia, Scotland, Senegal, Serbia, Singapore, Slovenia, South Africa, Spain, Sudan, Thailand, Türkiye, UK, United Arab Emirates, USA, Vietnam.
Regional organizations (4):
Asian-Pacific Association on Bronchology and Interventional Pulmonology; *Asian Pediatric Interventional Pulmonology Association (APIPA); Asociación Sudamericana de Endoscopia Respiratoria (ASER); European Association for Bronchology and Interventional Pulmonology (EABIP, #05959).* [2022.02.02/XD4674/**C**]

♦ World Association for Buiatrics (WAB) 21122

Société mondiale de buiatrie (AMB) – Asociación Mundial de Buiatria (AMB) – Welt-Gesellschaft für Buiatrik (WGB)

SG Dept Veterinary Medical Sciences, Univ of Bologna, Via Tolara di Sopra 50, 40064 Ozzano dell'Emilia BO, Italy. T. +39512097582.
URL: http://www.buiatrics.com/

History 17 May 1962, Vienna (Austria). Founded at 2nd International Congress on Cattle Diseases, preliminary meeting having been held 6-10 Oct 1960, Hannover (Germany FR). Statutes amended 6-10 July 1998, Sydney (Australia). New statutes adopted, July 2008, Budapest (Hungary). **Aims** Propagate scientific and practical knowledge of the diseases, management and production of both *dairy* and *beef cattle;* improve competitiveness of the *bovine* practitioner by contributing to a high standard of basic *veterinary* education in all aspects of bovine medicine and production and ensuring continuous retraining; promote such practitioners as essential partners for animal health and welfare, optimal and profitable production and consumer safety; anticipate and adapt speedily to changes in consumer requirements and available production techniques. **Structure** General Assembly (every 2 years, at Congress); Board of Governors; Executive Committe; National Correspondents. **Languages** English, French, German, Spanish. **Staff** Voluntary. **Finance** Sources: meeting proceeds; sponsorship. **Activities** Events/meetings. **Events** *Biennial Congress* Madrid (Spain) 2022, *Biennial Congress* Madrid (Spain) 2021, *Biennial Congress* Sapporo (Japan) 2018, *Biennial Congress* Dublin (Ireland) 2016, *Biennial Congress* Cairns, QLD (Australia) 2014.
Members Full: national buiatrics associations; Associate: multi-national associations or federations; Observer: veterinarians or scientists working with cattle where no national buiatrics association exists. National associations in 60 countries:
Argentina, Australia, Austria, Belgium, Brazil, Canada, Chile, China, Colombia, Costa Rica, Croatia, Czechia, Denmark, Ecuador, Egypt, Estonia, Ethiopia, Finland, France, Germany, Greece, Hungary, India, Iran Islamic Rep, Ireland, Israel, Italy, Japan, Korea Rep, Kosovo, Lithuania, Malaysia, Mexico, Moldova, Morocco, Netherlands, New Zealand, Nigeria, North Macedonia, Norway, Pakistan, Paraguay, Peru, Poland, Portugal, Romania, Serbia, Slovakia, Slovenia, South Africa, Spain, Sweden, Switzerland, Tunisia, Türkiye, UK, Ukraine, Uruguay, USA, Zimbabwe.
Associate members (4):
Association vétérinaire Euro-Arabe (AVEA, #02975); Mediterranean Federation for Health and Production of Ruminants (FEMESPRUM); *Sociedad Latinoamericana de Buiatria (#19394); Union of Arabian Veterinarians (no recent information).* [2023.02.14/XC3459/y/**C**]

♦ World Association for Case Method Research and Application (WACRA) 21123

Exec Dir 23 Mackintosh Ave, Needham MA 02492-1218, USA. T. +17814448982. Fax +17814441548. E-mail: wacra@rcn.com – denise.smith@wacra.org.
URL: http://www.wacra.org/

History 14 Apr 1984, London (UK), at 2nd International Conference on Case Method Research and Case Method Application, evolving from informal contacts among professors, researchers, policy-makers, professionals and business executives. Original title: *World Association for Case Method Research and Case Method Application.* Legally registered Mar 1989, Boston MA (USA). 'WACRA' registered as a trademark, Mar 1997. **Aims** Advance use of the case method in teaching, training and planning; encourage research using the case method; coordinate case writing and case application activities; encourage cooperation among the public sector, the business community and other case-oriented professions; widen focus to include games, simulation, other interactive learning, teaching methods and distance education. **Structure** Executive Board; International Advisory Board. **Languages** English, French, German, Spanish. **Staff** Voluntary. **Finance** Sources: meeting proceeds. **Activities** Events/meetings; guidance/assistance/consulting; networking/liaising; publishing activities; training/education. **Events** *Conference* Florence (Italy) 2021, *Conference* Florence (Italy) 2020, *Creative Teaching Conference* Monaco (Monaco) 2020, *Creative Teaching Conference* Lisbon (Portugal) 2019, *Annual International Conference* Rotterdam (Netherlands) 2018. **Publications** *International Journal of Case Method Research Application (IJCRA)* (4 a year). *Art of Interactive Teaching; Forging New Partnerships; Innovation Through Cooperation; Interactive Teaching and Emerging Technologies; Interactive Teaching and Learning; Managing Change; Teaching and Interactive Methods.*
Members Individual academics and professionals and organizations in 62 countries and territories:
Argentina, Australia, Austria, Belarus, Belgium, Bosnia-Herzegovina, Botswana, Brazil, Bulgaria, Canada, Chile, China, Colombia, Croatia, Cuba, Czechia, Denmark, Egypt, El Salvador, Estonia, Fiji, Finland, France, Georgia, Germany, Greece, Hong Kong, Hungary, India, Indonesia, Ireland, Italy, Japan, Kuwait, Latvia, Lebanon, Lithuania, Malaysia, Mauritius, Mexico, Moldova, Netherlands, New Zealand, Nigeria, Peru, Poland, Portugal, Romania, Russia, Serbia, Singapore, Slovakia, Slovenia, South Africa, Spain, Sweden, Switzerland, UK, Ukraine, USA, Venezuela, Zimbabwe. [2019.12.14/XD4038/**C**]

♦ World Association for Case Method Research and Case Method Application / see World Association for Case Method Research and Application (#21123)

♦ World Association of Center Associates / see World Business Associates (#21253)

♦ World Association of Chefs Societies (WACS) 21124
Fédération mondiale des sociétés de cuisiniers (FMSC) – Asociación Mundial de Sociedades de Cocineros (AMSC) – Weltbund der Kochverbände (WDK)
Main Office 15 rue Tiquetonne, 75002 Paris, France. T. +33664223321. E-mail: office@worldchefs.org.
URL: http://www.worldchefs.org/
History Oct 1928, Paris (France). 1939-1945 activities suspended. 1949, Geneva (Switzerland), re-established. Most recent statutes adopted 2006. Based in Lucerne (Switzerland). Former names and other names: *World Association of Cooks Societies (WACS)* – former. **Aims** Maintain and improve *culinary* standards of global *cuisines*. **Structure** Congress (every 2 years); Advisory Committee; Executive Committee; Central Committee; Continental Directors (5); Committees (14). Includes: *Worldchefs Global Education Network*. **Languages** English, French, German, Spanish. **Staff** 10.00 FTE, paid. **Finance** Sources: grants; members' dues; sponsorship. **Activities** Events/meetings; projects/programmes. **Events** *Congress* St Petersburg (Russia) 2026, *Worldchefs Congress* Singapore (Singapore) 2024, *Worldchefs Congress* Abu Dhabi (United Arab Emirates) 2022, *Biennial Congress* St Petersburg (Russia) 2020, *Biennial Congress* Kuala Lumpur (Malaysia) 2018. **Publications** *Die Küche* in English, French, German.
Members National; Affiliate. Culinary associations, one per country, representing about 5 million professional cooks in 106 countries and territories:
Argentina, Australia, Austria, Azerbaijan, Bahamas, Belarus, Belgium, Bolivia, Bosnia-Herzegovina, Bulgaria, Cambodia, Canada, Chile, China, Colombia, Cook Is, Costa Rica, Croatia, Cuba, Cyprus, Czechia, Denmark, Dominican Rep, Ecuador, Egypt, England, Fiji, Finland, France, Germany, Ghana, Greece, Guatemala, Hong Kong, Hungary, Iceland, India, Indonesia, Ireland, Israel, Italy, Japan, Jordan, Kazakhstan, Kenya, Korea DPR, Korea Rep, Kyrgyzstan, Latvia, Lebanon, Liberia, Lithuania, Luxembourg, Macau, Malaysia, Maldives, Malta, Mauritius, Moldova, Mongolia, Montenegro, Morocco, Myanmar, Namibia, Nepal, Netherlands, New Zealand, North Macedonia, Norway, Pakistan, Palestine, Panama, Peru, Philippines, Poland, Portugal, Puerto Rico, Qatar, Romania, Russia, Samoa, Saudi Arabia, Scotland, Serbia, Singapore, Slovakia, Slovenia, South Africa, Spain, Sri Lanka, Sweden, Switzerland, Syrian AR, Taiwan, Thailand, Togo, Tunisia, Türkiye, Ukraine, United Arab Emirates, USA, Uzbekistan, Vanuatu, Venezuela, Vietnam, Wales. [2021/XD0304/**C**]

♦ World Association for Children and Parents (internationally oriented national body)
♦ World Association of Children's Friends (#02808)
♦ World Association of Chinese Character Studies (unconfirmed)

♦ World Association for Chinese Church Music 21125
Secretariat 67-2A OG Business Park, Jalan Datuk Tan Yew Lai, 58200 Kuala Lumpur, Malaysia. T. +60162039504. E-mail: yapteckchong@gmail.com.
URL: http://www.waccm.org/
History Founded 1972, as *South East Asia Association for the Promotion of Church Music*. Current name adopted 1982. **Aims** Promote Church Music among Chinese churches worldwide. **Structure** Board of Directors; Managing/Executive Committee. **Languages** Chinese. **Staff** Voluntary. **Finance** Members' dues. **Activities** Events/meetings. **Events** *Biennial Conference* Bangkok (Thailand) 2018, *Biennial Conference* Medan (Indonesia) 2014, *Biennial Conference* Auckland (New Zealand) 2012, *Biennial Conference* Kuala Lumpur (Malaysia) 2010, *Biennial conference* Kuching (Malaysia) 2008. **Publications** *Choral Anthem Collections* (every 2 years); *Voice of Sacred Music* – newsletter. *Enhancement of Church Music Ministry*.
Members Organizations (25) in 12 countries and territories:
Australia, Canada, China, Hong Kong, Indonesia, Malaysia, New Zealand, Philippines, Singapore, Taiwan, Thailand, USA. [2018.06.01/XD5999/**D**]

♦ World Association of Chinese Cuisine / see World Federation of Chinese Catering Industry (#21418)
♦ World Association of Chinese Epileptologists (unconfirmed)
♦ World Association for Christian Broadcasting (inactive)

♦ World Association for Christian Communication (WACC) 21126
Association mondiale pour la communication chrétienne (AMCC) – Asociación Mundial para la Comunicación Cristiana (AMCC)
Gen Sec 308 Main St, Toronto ON M4C 4X7, Canada. T. +14166911999. E-mail: wacc@waccglobal.org.
London Office 100 Church Road, Teddington, TW11 8QE, UK. T. +442081425851.
Main: http://www.waccglobal.org/
History 12 May 1975, London (UK). Founded by uniting: the former *'World Association for Christian Communication'*, set up 1968, Oslo (Norway), on merger of *World Association for Christian Broadcasting (WACB, inactive)* with the *'Coordinating Committee for Christian Broadcasting'*; *World Committee for Christian Broadcasting (WCCB, inactive)*, formed 1956, Königstein (Germany FR), by merger of *Informal International Conference of Christian Broadcasting (IICCB, inactive)* with a group of missionary societies; *Agency for Christian Literature Development (ACLD, inactive)*, set up 1970. Most recent constitution adopted 1987. Registration: Charities Commission, No/ID: 296073, England and Wales, ON; Companies House, No/ID: 2082273, England and Wales; Corporations Canada, No/ID: 438311-7, Canada; Canada Revenue Agency, No/ID: 83970 9524 RR0001, Canada. **Aims** Promote communication as a basic human right by working with those denied the right to communicate because of status, identity or gender; advocate full access to information and communication; promote open and diverse media. **Structure** General Meeting (annual); Boards of Directors; Executive Committee; General Secretary; Officers. **Languages** English, French, Spanish. **Staff** 10.50 FTE, paid. **Finance** Sources: grants; members' dues. Grants from church-related and secular funding organizations, in particular Protestant churches of Europe and North America, and government development agencies. Annual budget: 2,100,000 CAD (2022). **Activities** Advocacy/lobbying/activism; events/meetings; financial and/or material support; knowledge management/information dissemination; networking/liaising; projects/programmes. Active in: Africa; Asia; Caribbean; Europe; Latin America; Middle East; North America; Pacific. **Events** *International Symposium for Peaceful Unification on the Korean Peninsula* Seoul (Korea Rep) 2017, *Symposium on Communication Rights for All* Erlangen (Germany) 2013, *International congress* Cape Town (South Africa) 2008, *International ecumenical film conference / International Film Meeting* Edinburgh (UK) 2007, *International women summit on HIV and AIDS* Nairobi (Kenya) 2007. **Publications** *The Hub* (12 a year); *Media Development* (4 a year); *Media and Gender Monitor* (2 a year); *No-Nonsense Guides* (2 a year).
Members Corporate (voting): churches; boards and agencies of churches; councils of churches; publishing, printing and distribution houses; publications; broadcasting stations, film makers and programming agencies that disseminate Christian material; educational institutions; secular communication organizations; other organizations sympathetic to the objectives of the Association. Personal (non-voting): individuals sympathetic to the objectives of the Association. Affiliate (non-voting): those who support the work of the Association. As of 2018, Corporate (200), Personal (450) and Affiliate (2,000) in 130 countries worldwide. Membership countries not specified. **Consultative Status** Consultative status granted from: *ECOSOC (#05331)* (Ros A). **IGO Relations** Accredited by (1): *United Nations Office at Vienna (UNOV, #20604)*. **NGO Relations** Member of (4): *ACT Alliance (#00081)*; *Federación Latinoamericana de Facultades de Comunicación Social (FELAFACS, #09353)*; *International Association for Media and Communication Research (IAMCR, #12022)*; *UK Consortium on AIDS and International Development*. Cooperates with (3): *Globethics.net Foundation (#10669)*; *International Federation of Journalists (IFJ, #13462)*; *World Catholic Association for Communication (SIGNIS, #21264)*. [2022.10.25/XC3461/y/**B**]

♦ World Association of Christian Radio Amateurs and Listeners (WACRAL) 21127
Address not obtained.
URL: http://www.WACRAL.org/
History 20 Nov 1957, Huddersfield (UK), as *World Association of Methodist Radio Amateurs and Clubs (WAMRAC)*, by Rev Arthur W Shepherd. Until 1966, in association with *World Methodist Council (WMC, #21650)*. Present name adopted 1978. Current Constitution adopted Oct 2009. **Aims** Further the interests of members in all aspects of amateur radio and directly associated activities and promote and encourage Christian fellowship and friendship among radio amateurs and listeners worldwide. **Structure** General Meeting (annual). Executive Committee, comprising President, Vice-President, General Secretary, Treasurer, Membership Secretary, Publicity Officer, Conference Organizer, Datacoms Coordinator, Awards Manager, Newsletter Editor and 3 membership representatives. **Languages** English, German. **Staff** 13.00 FTE, voluntary. **Finance** Members' dues. Other sources: grants; donations. Budget (annual): pounds4,000. **Activities** Organizes: *World Christian Radio Fellowship* for radio amateurs and short wave listeners – weekly on Amateur bands; special radio activities; Fellowship weekends and get-togethers. **Events** *Conference* Malvern (UK) 2010, *Conference* Bognor Regis (UK) 2009, *Conference* Forest of Dean (UK) 2008, *Conference* Forest of Dean (UK) 2007, *Annual Conference* Theddingworth (UK) 2006. **Publications** *WACRAL Newsletter* (3 a year); *Membership Register* (annual). Members' handbook.
Members Individuals and clubs (600) in 43 countries and territories:
Australia, Austria, Belgium, Brazil, China, Czechia, England, Estonia, Eswatini, Finland, Germany, Guyana, Iceland, India, Indonesia, Ireland, Isle of Man, Italy, Jersey, Kazakhstan, Latvia, Luxembourg, Malaysia, Netherlands, New Zealand, Nigeria, Northern Ireland, Norway, Poland, Romania, Russia, Scotland, Slovakia, South Africa, Spain, Sri Lanka, Switzerland, Uganda, Ukraine, Uruguay, USA, Wales, Zimbabwe. [2019/XD3471/**F**]

♦ World Association of Community Broadcasters / see Association mondiale des radiodiffuseurs communautaires (#02810)
♦ World Association of Community Radio Broadcasters (#02810)
♦ World Association of Community Radios / see Association mondiale des radiodiffuseurs communautaires (#02810)
♦ World Association of Cooks Societies / see World Association of Chefs Societies (#21124)

♦ World Association for Cooperative Education (WACE) 21128
CEO 600 Suffolk St, Wannalancit Business Center, Ste 125, Univ of Massachusetts Lowell, Lowell MA 01854, USA. T. +19789341868. Fax +19789344084.
URL: http://www.waceinc.org/
History 1983. Also referred to as *World Council and Assembly on Cooperative Education*. **Aims** Develop an awareness in education, business, government and employing organizations of cooperative education as a means to achieve a better relationship between education and work and as a strategy for *human development* which will benefit the community through *improved productivity* and increased *competitiveness*. **Structure** Council, consisting of President, Deputy President and 35 members. **Finance** Members' dues: US$ 85 individual; US$ 255 organizational. Other sources: grants from member organizations, corporations and foundations. **Activities** Fosters the development of cooperative education in new regions as well in those regions where it is already established or emerging; provides an international network of members from employing organizations and educational institutions; conducts regular world and regional conferences; encourages the development of international cooperative education programs and placements; operates a clearing house for information on cooperative education at the international level. **Events** *International Research Symposium* Kanazawa (Japan) 2022, *World Conference* Cincinnati, OH (USA) 2019, *World Conference* Chiang Mai (Thailand) 2017, *World Conference* Kyoto (Japan) 2015, *World Conference* Durban (South Africa) 2013. **Publications** *Global Newslink* (3 a year). Membership directory (annual).
Members Individual; Institutional/Organizational. Members in 35 countries and territories:
Australia, Austria, Bangladesh, Belarus, Belgium, Brazil, Canada, China, Egypt, El Salvador, France, Germany, Ghana, Hong Kong, India, Indonesia, Ireland, Italy, Jamaica, Japan, Kenya, Malaysia, Mexico, Namibia, Netherlands, New Zealand, Paraguay, Philippines, Saudi Arabia, South Africa, Spain, Sweden, Thailand, UK, USA. [2018/XF1821/**F**]

♦ World Association of Copepodologists (WAC) 21129
Gen Sec Dept of Marine Sciences, Univ of Connecticut, Groton CT 06340-6048, USA. T. +18604059098. Fax +18604059151.
URL: http://www.monoculus.org/
History 1987, London (UK). Founded during 3rd International Conference on Copepoda. **Aims** Promote and support interest in all aspects of research on copepoda. **Structure** Executive Council. **Languages** English. **Finance** Members' dues. **Activities** Events/meetings. **Events** *International Conference on Copepoda (ICOC)* Hiroshima (Japan) 2024, *International Conference on Copepoda (ICOC)* 2022, *Triennial Conference* Skukuza (South Africa) 2021, *Triennial Conference* Skukuza (South Africa) 2020, *Triennial Conference* Los Angeles, CA (USA) 2017. **Publications** *Monoculus* (annual).
Members Individuals in 69 countries and territories:
Algeria, Argentina, Australia, Austria, Bangladesh, Barbados, Belgium, Brazil, Bulgaria, Canada, Chile, China, Colombia, Costa Rica, Croatia, Czechia, Denmark, Ecuador, Egypt, Estonia, Finland, France, Germany, Greece, Hong Kong, Hungary, India, Indonesia, Ireland, Israel, Italy, Japan, Kazakhstan, Korea Rep, Kuwait, Lebanon, Malaysia, Mexico, Myanmar, Netherlands, New Zealand, Norway, Pakistan, Peru, Philippines, Poland, Portugal, Puerto Rico, Romania, Russia, Serbia, Singapore, Slovenia, South Africa, Spain, Sweden, Switzerland, Taiwan, Thailand, Tunisia, Türkiye, UK, Ukraine, Uruguay, USA, Uzbekistan, Venezuela, Vietnam. [2019.02.12/XJ3032/v/**D**]

♦ World Association of Cultural Psychiatry (WACP) 21130
Sec address not obtained.
URL: http://www.waculturalpsy.org/
History 2006, Beijing (China). **Aims** Promote awareness of the need to improve the cultural competence of mental health care; provide reliable psychiatric care to every patient regardless of cultural background; promote international cooperation in research, training and education in cultural psychiatry. **Structure** Board of Directors. Officers: President; President-Elect; Secretary; Treasurer. Working Committees. **Finance** Sources: members' dues. **Activities** Awareness raising; events/meetings; knowledge management/information dissemination; publishing activities; training/education. **Events** *World Congress* Rotterdam (Netherlands) 2022, *World Congress* New York, NY (USA) 2018, *Global challenge and cultural psychiatry* Puerto Vallarta (Mexico) 2015, *Symposium* Puerto Vallarta (Mexico) 2015, *World Congress* London (UK) 2012. **Publications** *WACP Newsletter*, *World Cultural Psychiatry Research Review* – journal.
Members Individuals with a professional background in psychiatry, health-related care (physicians, nurses, social workers) and social and behavioral science (cultural psychologists, medical anthropologists, sociologists). Membership countries not specified.
Includes the following organization:
International Association of Ethnopsychologists and Ethnopsychotherapists (IAEE, #11880). [2022.10.15/XM0888/**C**]

♦ World Association of Cybernetics, Computer Science, and System Theory (inactive)

♦ World Association of Detectives (WAD) 21131
Association mondiale des détectives
Admin Manager PO Box 200030, Evans CO 80620, USA. T. +14439824586. Fax +19704807794.
Exec Dir address not obtained.
URL: http://www.wad.net/
History Founded 1925, as World Association of Detectives. Merged in 1950 with *International Secret Service Association (inactive)*, formed in 1921, when it adopted the title: *World Secret Service Association*. Present name adopted 1966. US non-profit corporation. **Aims** Promote and maintain the highest ethical practices in the profession; foster and perpetuate a spirit of cooperation among members and similar organizations; endeavour to establish and further mutual feelings of trust, goodwill and friendship among agencies throughout the free world. **Languages** English. **Staff** 2.00 FTE, paid. **Finance** Sources: members' dues. Annual budget: US$ 100,000 – 120,000. **Events** *Annual Conference* Aruba 2022, *Mid-Term Board Meeting* Prague (Czechia) 2021, *Annual Convention* Vancouver, BC (Canada) 2021, *Annual Convention* Aruba 2020, *Mid-Term Board Meeting* Panama (Panama) 2020. **Publications** *WAD Newsletter* (6 a year); *WAD Membership Directory* (annual).
Members Principals of agencies or firms legally qualified to practise the profession of private investigator, detective, security agent or consultant. Individuals in 69 countries and territories:
Argentina, Australia, Austria, Belgium, Bermuda, Brazil, Canada, Channel Is, Chile, China, Colombia, Costa Rica, Cyprus, Czechia, Denmark, Ecuador, England, Finland, France, Germany, Greece, Guadeloupe, Guam, Hong Kong, India, Indonesia, Ireland, Israel, Italy, Japan, Kazakhstan, Korea Rep, Lebanon, Luxembourg, Malaysia, Mexico, Moldova, Netherlands, New Zealand, Nigeria, Norway, Pakistan, Paraguay, Philippines, Poland, Portugal, Puerto Rico, Romania, Russia, Scotland, Singapore, Slovenia, South Africa, Spain, Sweden, Switzerland, Syrian AR, Tahiti Is, Taiwan, Thailand, Trinidad-Tobago, Türkiye, Ukraine, United Arab Emirates, Uruguay, USA, Venezuela, Wales, Zimbabwe.
NGO Relations Member of: *International Federation of Associations of Private Detectives (#13364)*. [2022/XC0196/v/**C**]

♦ World Association for the Development of Philately (WADP) 21132

Association mondiale pour le développement de la philatélie (AMDP)

Secretariat UPU International Bureau, PO Box 312, 3000 Bern 15, Switzerland. T. +41313503111. Fax +41313503110. E-mail: philately@upu.int.
URL: http://www.upu.int/en/activities/philately/world-association-for-the-developme nt-of-philately.html/

History as UPU Contact Committee for Philately. **Aims** Develop and promote philately through ongoing positive dialogue between philatelic industry partners and designated operators. **IGO Relations** *Universal Postal Union (UPU, #20682)* and its *Postal Operations Council (POC, see: #20682).* **NGO Relations** *Association internationale des journalistes philatéliques (AIJP, #02709)* is a member. In partnership with: *International Federation of Stamp Dealers' Associations (IFSDA, #13557).* [2019/XD8031/**D**]

♦ World Association for Disaster and Emergency Medicine (WADEM) 21133

Association mondiale pour la médecine de catastrophe et d'urgence

Exec Officer 3330 University Ave, Ste 130, Madison WI 53705, USA. T. +16088196604. Fax +16088196604. E-mail: info@wadem.org.
URL: http://www.wadem.org/

History 2 Oct 1976, Mainz (Germany). Former names and other names: *Club of Mainz* – former (1976 to 1985); *Club de Mayence* – former (1976 to 1985); *Club of Mainz for Emergency and Disaster Medicine Worldwide* – former (1976 to 1985); *Club de Mayence pour la propagation de la médecine d'urgence et des soins intensifs* – former (1976 to 1985); *World Association for Emergency and Disaster Medicine (WAEDM)* – former (1985 to 1993); *Association mondiale pour la médecine d'urgence et de catastrophe* – former (1985 to 1993). **Aims** Foster evidence-based improvement, education and advocacy of emergency and disaster health care and disaster risk reduction. **Structure** Board of Directors. **Languages** English. **Staff** 2.50 FTE, paid. **Finance** Sources: donations; meeting proceeds; members' dues; sale of publications. **Activities** Events/meetings; knowledge management/information dissemination; networking/liaising; publishing activities; training/education. **Events** *Congress* Tokyo (Japan) 2025, *Congress* Killarney (Ireland) 2023, *Congress* Tokyo (Japan) 2022, *Biennial Congress* Tokyo (Japan) 2021, *Virtual Forum* Tokyo (Japan) 2021. **Publications** *Prehospital and Disaster Medicine* (6 a year).

Members Individuals in 55 countries and territories:
Argentina, Australia, Austria, Barbados, Belgium, Brazil, Bulgaria, Canada, China, Colombia, Czechia, Denmark, Egypt, Finland, France, Germany, Ghana, Greece, India, Indonesia, Ireland, Israel, Italy, Japan, Kenya, Korea Rep, Luxembourg, Malaysia, Mexico, Moldova, Netherlands, New Zealand, Nigeria, Norway, Papua New Guinea, Peru, Poland, Portugal, Qatar, Russia, Saudi Arabia, Senegal, Singapore, Slovakia, South Africa, Spain, Sri Lanka, St Lucia, Sweden, Switzerland, Taiwan, Thailand, Türkiye, UK, USA.

NGO Relations Cooperates with: *Global Health Cluster (GHC, #10401).* [2020.10.12/XF8297/v/**F**]

♦ World Association of Document Examiners (inactive)

♦ World Association on Dual Disorders (WADD) 21134

Secretariat Londres 17, 28028 Madrid, Spain. T. +34913612600. E-mail: secretariat@worlddualdisorders.org.
URL: http://www.worlddualdisorders.org/

History Apr 2015. Registered in accordance with Spanish law. **Aims** Increase the study, research and divulgation of dual pathology from a bio-psycho-social perspective. **Structure** General Assembly; Board of Directors; Executive Committee; Secretariat. **Activities** Events/meetings. **Events** *World Congress* Portoroz (Slovenia) 2023, *World Congress* Mexico City (Mexico) 2022, *World Congress* Paris (France) 2021, *World Congress* Marrakech (Morocco) 2020, *World Congress* Madrid (Spain) 2019. **Publications** *Dual Disorders Newsletter.* [2019/XM5060/**C**]

♦ World Association for Dynamic Psychiatry (WADP) 21135

Association mondiale de psychiatrie dynamique

Gen Sec Kantstr 120, 10625 Berlin, Germany. T. +49303132698. Fax +49303136959. E-mail: dapberlin@t-online.de.
URL: http://wadpinternational.com/

History 9 Dec 1980, Munich (Germany). Registration: Swiss Civil Code, Switzerland. **Aims** Disseminate the theory and practice of the Berlin School of dynamic psychiatry of Günter Ammon. **Structure** Board of Governors; Executive Council. **Languages** English. **Staff** 50.00 FTE, paid. **Finance** Sources: meeting proceeds; members' dues. **Activities** Events/meetings; knowledge management/information dissemination; research/documentation; training/education. **Events** *Congress* Berlin (Germany) 2021, *Peace and agression – a social challenge for psychiatry and psychotherapy* Berlin (Germany) 2020, *Congress* Florence (Italy) 2017, *Congress / World Congress* St Petersburg (Russia) 2014, *Research, Pathology and treatment* Berlin (Germany) 2011. **Publications** *Dynamische Psychiatrie/Dynamic Psychiatry* (periodical). *Handbook of Dynamic Psychiatry – Vols 1-2* (1984).

Members Individuals in 26 countries:
Austria, Brazil, China, Cuba, Dominican Rep, Egypt, France, Germany, Ghana, Greece, Hungary, India, Indonesia, Israel, Italy, Japan, Netherlands, Poland, Portugal, Russia, Serbia, Slovenia, Switzerland, Türkiye, UK, USA.

NGO Relations Affiliated member of: *World Psychiatric Association (WPA, #21741).* [2021/XD4653/v/**F**]

♦ World Association of Early Childhood Educators (AMEI-WAECE) ... 21136

Asociación Mundial de Educadores Infantiles (AMEI-WAECE) – Associação Mundial de Educadores Infantis (AMEI-WAECE)

Main Office Calle Estrella Polar no 7, 28007 Madrid, Spain. T. +34915018754. Fax +34915018746. E-mail: consultas@waece.org.
URL: http://www.waece.org/

History 1991, Madrid (Spain). Bylaws approved 20 May 1992; became fully operational 1994. By-laws amended, Oct 2004. Registration: Registry of Association, No/ID: 109-157, Start date: Oct 2004, Spain. **Aims** Foster and coordinate the pedagogical renovation of early childhood education; conduct studies and research to help educators in their work; promote pedagogical research; conduct studies on the status of early childhood education; foster the union and collaboration of early childhood educators on grounds of mutual interest; develop and foster exchanges of experiences among early childhood educators around the world. **Structure** General Assembly; Governing Board; Presidency. **Languages** English, Portuguese, Spanish. **Staff** 8.00 FTE, paid. **Finance** Sources: grants; members' dues; revenue from activities/projects. **Activities** Events/meetings; networking/liaising; research and development; research/documentation; training/education. **Events** *International Congress* Madrid (Spain) 2021, *International Congress* Madrid (Spain) 2020, *International Congress* Madrid (Spain) 2018, *International Congress* Madrid (Spain) 2016, *International Congress* Madrid (Spain) 2015. **Publications** *WAECE Newsbulletin* (weekly) in English, Spanish.

Members Full in 40 countries:
Argentina, Australia, Bolivia, Brazil, Canada, Chile, China, Colombia, Costa Rica, Croatia, Cuba, Dominican Rep, Ecuador, El Salvador, France, Germany, Guatemala, Honduras, Ireland, Israel, Italy, Japan, Malaysia, Mexico, Netherlands, Nicaragua, Nigeria, Panama, Paraguay, Peru, Portugal, Puerto Rico, South Africa, Spain, Sweden, Switzerland, UK, Uruguay, USA, Venezuela.

IGO Relations Associated with the Department of Global Communications of the United Nations. [2021.02.17/XD7484/**D**]

♦ World Association of Eclectic Hypnotherapists (WAEH) 21137

Pres and Chairman 1495 E San Marcelo Blvd, Brownsville TX 78526, USA. T. +19565446383. Fax +19565740576. E-mail: eoowaeh@yahoo.com.
URL: https://www.facebook.com/WAEHMX/

History 1993, by Dr Emmanuel O Olukotun. **Aims** Contribute to the psychological wellbeing of humanity by: promoting and advancing the contribution of hypnotherapy to the health sciences; encouraging scientific investigation and clinical utilization of hypnotherapy at the highest professional level. **Activities** Training programmes; biennial congress; code of professional standards. **Events** *Congress* Colima (Mexico) 2009, *International congress on integrative and eclectic psychotherapy* Morelia (Mexico) 2007, *World congress of eclectic hypnotherapy in psychology, psychiatry and medicine* Morelia (Mexico) 2007, *Congress* Mazatlan, SIN (Mexico) 2006, *Congress* Morelia (Mexico) 2003. **Publications** *Eclectic Hypnotherapy* – journal; *Hypnotherapy Bulletin.*

Members Student; Associate; Fellows; Honorary. Members in 27 countries:
Argentina, Australia, Austria, Belgium, Brazil, Canada, Croatia, Cuba, Denmark, Ecuador, Estonia, France, Germany, Hong Kong, Israel, Italy, Japan, Mexico, New Zealand, Nigeria, Poland, South Africa, Spain, Switzerland, Türkiye, Ukraine, USA.

NGO Relations Administrative office at and joint congresses with: *International Academy of Eclectic Psychotherapists (IAEP, no recent information).* [2019/XF3884/v/**F**]

♦ World Association for Ecology / see AME World Ecology Foundation
♦ World Association for Educational Research (#02811)
♦ World Association for Element-Building and Prefabrication (inactive)
♦ World Association for Emergency and Disaster Medicine / see World Association for Disaster and Emergency Medicine (#21133)
♦ World Association of Esperantist Teachers (inactive)

♦ World Association of Esperanto Journalists 21138

Association mondiale des journalistes espérantistes – Tutmonda Esperantista Jurnalista Asocio (TEJA)

Contact Rygos 26-66, LT-05222 Vilnius, Lithuania.
URL: http://www.tejha.org/

History 1948, Malmö (Sweden). **Aims** Provide support for, and raise standards of, journalists and other writers contributing to the Esperanto press, whether at regional, national or international level; promote awareness of the international language among non-Esperanto journalists as an effective, efficient and equitable means of disseminating news and information. **Structure** President, Vice-President, General Secretary. **Languages** Esperanto. **Staff** Part-time, voluntary. **Finance** Sources: contributions; members' dues. **Activities** Develops training by correspondence programme for Esperanto contributors to Esperanto publications. **Events** *Annual General Assembly* Rotterdam (Netherlands) 2008, *Annual General Assembly* Vilnius (Lithuania) 2005, *Annual General Assembly* Gothenburg (Sweden) 2003, *Annual General Assembly* Fortaleza (Brazil) 2002, *Annual General Assembly* Zagreb (Croatia) 2001.

Members Individuals (94) in 38 countries:
Australia, Austria, Belgium, Brazil, Bulgaria, China, Croatia, Cuba, Czechia, Denmark, Estonia, Finland, France, Germany, Hungary, India, Iran Islamic Rep, Italy, Japan, Latvia, Lithuania, Luxembourg, Mexico, Nepal, Netherlands, Norway, Pakistan, Poland, Russia, Serbia, Slovakia, Spain, Sweden, Switzerland, Taiwan, UK, Ukraine, USA.

NGO Relations Member of: *Universal Esperanto Association (UEA, #20676).* [2018/XC3468/**C**]

♦ World Association of Eye Hospitals (WAEH) 21139

Contact c/o Oogziekenhuis, Schiedamse Vest 180, 3011 BH Rotterdam, Netherlands. T. +31104017777.
URL: http://www.waeh.org/

History 2007, Rotterdam (Netherlands). **Structure** Board. **Events** *Annual Meeting* Baltimore, MD (USA) / San Francisco, CA (USA) 2022, *Annual Meeting* Stockholm (Sweden) 2021, *Annual Meeting – PHASE I* Singapore (Singapore) 2020, *Annual Meeting – PHASE II* Singapore (Singapore) 2020, *Annual Meeting* London (UK) 2019.

Members Founding; Full; Associate. Hospitals (26) in 23 countries:
Australia, Bangladesh, Belgium, Chile, China, India, Indonesia, Ireland, Israel, Korea Rep, Malaysia, Mexico, Nepal, Netherlands, Philippines, Singapore, Suriname, Sweden, Switzerland, Thailand, UK, USA, Vietnam. [2020/XM3879/**D**]

♦ World Association of Festivals and Artists (unconfirmed)

♦ World Association of Floral Artists (WAFA) 21140

Contact c/o NAFAS, Osborne House, 12 Devonshire Square, London, EC2M 4TE, UK. E-mail: info@nafas.org.uk.
URL: https://www.nafas.org.uk/about-us/wafa/

History Jun 1981, London (UK). **Aims** Enhance the diversity of the floral art form by transcending international cultural barriers and bringing together fresh ideas. **Structure** General Assembly (held in the last year of the 3-year term of the World Executive Committee). World Executive Committee (elected for 3 years by host country). Committee rotated among national association member countries every 3 years. **Languages** English. **Staff** 10.00 FTE, voluntary. **Finance** Members' dues on a per capita basis. **Activities** Events/meetings. **Events** *World Association of Floral Artists World Show and Conference* Auckland (New Zealand) 2023, *Triennial International Seminar* Dublin (Ireland) 2014, *Triennial International Seminar* Ireland 2014, *Triennial International Seminar* Boston, MA (USA) 2011, *Triennial international seminar* Chicago, IL (USA) / Washington, DC (USA) / Wilmington, DE (USA) 2009.

Members Floral associations in 29 countries and territories:
Argentina, Australia, Barbados, Belgium, Bermuda, Canada, France, Hong Kong, India, Ireland, Italy, Jamaica, Japan, Kenya, Korea Rep, Malta, Mexico, Netherlands, New Zealand, Oman, Pakistan, Peru, Russia, South Africa, Switzerland, Trinidad-Tobago, UK, Uruguay, Zimbabwe. [2021/XD0509/**C**]

♦ World Association of Food Grade Biopolymer Producers / see Biopolymer International (#03256)

♦ World Association of Former United Nations Internes and Fellows (WAFUNIF) 21141

Association mondiale des anciens stagiaires et boursiers de l'Organisation des Nations Unies – Asociación Mundial de Antiguos Internistas y Becarios de la Organización de la Naciones Unidas

Pres 2 United Nations Plaza, DC2-0370, New York NY 10017-4403, USA. T. +12129633110. Fax +12129634609. E-mail: wafunif@wafunif.org.
URL: https://wafunif.org/

History 14 Jun 1978, New York NY (USA). **Aims** Be an alumni organization for UN internes and fellows; be a channel of communication between the UN and those it has services through internships and fellowships; rekindle interest of people in the UN and international affairs worldwide; give expression to the views of adherents on pertinent issues; use individual and collective member resources to promote, at international, regional, national and local levels through research, information and education to help improve public understanding of the principles, aims, purposes, activities and potentialities of the UN; support and encourage maintenance and further development of internship, fellowship and training programmes within the UN system. **Structure** General Assembly; Board of Directors of 21 members; Advisory Council; Executive Committee. Secretariat. Chapters. **Languages** Arabic, Chinese, English, French, Russian, Spanish. **Staff** 24.00 FTE, paid. **Finance** Individual and institutional contribution. Budget (annual) US$ 500,000. **Activities** Awards/prizes/competitions; advocacy/lobbying/activism; events/meetings. **Events** *International Conference on Global Environment, Carbon Reduction, and Eco-Drive as a Solution towards Sustainability* New York, NY (USA) 2014, *World alliance forum* Awaji (Japan) 2009, *Forum on issues of diversity in Europe and European citizenship* Paris (France) 2006, *Symposium of the challenges of Agenda 21 for international cooperation* Rio de Janeiro (Brazil) 1992, *Symposium on financing and managing environmentally sound technologies for development* Rio de Janeiro (Brazil) 1992. **Publications** *WAFUNIF Journal*; *WAFUNIF Newsletter.* Thematic studies; policy guides; session reports; special memoranda. **Members** Individuals; national chapters; regional All UN member countries. **Consultative Status** Consultative status granted from: *ECOSOC (#05331)* (Special); *UNCTAD (#20285)* (General Category). **IGO Relations** Accredited by: *United Nations (UN, #20515)*; *United Nations Office at Geneva (UNOG, #20597)*; *United Nations Office at Vienna (UNOV, #20604).* Associated with Department of Global Communications of the United Nations. **NGO Relations** Member of: *United Nations Global Compact (#20567).* [2021/XE9256/**E**]

♦ World Association for Free Time and for Human and Social Well-being (inactive)
♦ World Association of French-Speaking Doctors (no recent information)

♦ World Association of Girl Guides and Girl Scouts (WAGGGS) 21142

Association mondiale des guides et des éclaireuses (AMGE) – Asociación Mundial de las Guias Scouts (AMGS)

Pres World Bureau – Olave Ctr, 12c Lyndhurst Road, London, NW3 5PQ, UK. T. +442077941181. Fax +442074313764. E-mail: wagggs@wagggs.org.
Europe Region Office Rue des Poissonniers 13, 1000 Brussels, Belgium. T. +3228932420. E-mail: europe@wagggs.org.
URL: http://www.wagggs.org/

History 17 May 1928, Budapest (Hungary). Founded at 5th International Conference. Previously an International Council functioned from Feb 1919 for 9 years. Constitution first drafted 1928 and adopted 1936. Registration: No/ID: 0457.323.425, Start date: 29 Feb 1996, Belgium; EU Transparency Register, No/ID: 07410725016-32, Start date: 17 Jan 2011; Charity, No/ID: 306125, Start date: 3 May 1963, End date: 11 Nov 2017, England and Wales; Charity, No/ID: 1159255, England and Wales. **Aims** Enable girls and young women to develop their fullest potential as responsible citizens of the world; provide girls and young women with opportunities for self-training in development of character, responsible citizenship and service in their own and world communities; advocate on behalf of girls and young women on issues that affect them. **Structure** World Conference (every 3 years), consisting of 2 delegates (maximum) per Member Organization. World Board, comprising 17 Voting Members, CEO (and Treasurer). World Bureau, situated in London (UK), is the secretariat of the World Association. Committees of the World Board: Chairman's Coordinating Group; Development of Girl Guides and Girl Scouts; Communications and Finance and Business Management. World Centres (4): Pax Lodge (London); Sangam (India); Our Cabaña (Mexico); Our Chalet (Switzerland). United Nations Representatives based in Geneva (Switzerland), Nairobi (Kenya), New York, Paris (France), Rome (Italy) and Vienna (Austria). Regions (5) elect their own Regional Committees: Africa; Arab; Asia Pacific; Europe; Western Hemisphere. *World Guide and Scout Consultative Committee* is the means of liaising with World Organization of the Scout Movement (WOSM). **Languages** Arabic, English, French, Spanish. **Staff** 84.00 FTE, paid. Occasional voluntary. **Finance** Sources: contributions; donations; gifts, legacies; grants; investments; members' dues; revenue from activities/projects. Supported by: *Olave Baden-Powell Society (OB-PS, #17715)*. **Activities** Awards/prizes/competitions; events/meetings; projects/programmes; training/education. **Events** *Triennial World Conference* London (UK) 2021, *Triennial World Conference* Kampala (Uganda) 2020, *Triennial European Guide and Scout Conference* Split (Croatia) 2019, *Triennial World Conference* Delhi (India) 2017, *Triennial European Guide and Scout Conference* Melsomvik (Norway) 2016. **Publications** *Our World News* (4 a year) in English, French, Spanish; *Annual Review* in English, French, Spanish. *Book-Trefoil Round the World* in English. Reports; Fundraising and partnership leaflets in English, French, Spanish; leaflets; charts and posters; WAGGGS projects; additional kits; various charts, pamphlets and leaflets to meet pecific needs; flags; badges; postcards and notecards.

Members National Girl Guide/Girl Scout Organizations (145), with a total membership of 10 million. Members in 144 countries and territories:

Antigua-Barbuda, Argentina, Armenia, Aruba, Australia, Austria, Bahamas, Bahrain, Bangladesh, Barbados, Belarus, Belgium, Belize, Benin, Bolivia, Botswana, Brazil, Brunei Darussalam, Burkina Faso, Burundi, Cambodia, Cameroon, Canada, Central African Rep, Chad, Chile, Colombia, Congo Brazzaville, Congo DR, Cook Is, Costa Rica, Côte d'Ivoire, Curaçao, Cyprus, Czechia, Denmark, Dominica, Dominican Rep, Ecuador, Egypt, El Salvador, Estonia, Eswatini, Fiji, Finland, France, Gambia, Georgia, Germany, Greece, Grenada, Guatemala, Guinea, Guyana, Haiti, Honduras, Hong Kong, Hungary, Iceland, India, Ireland, Israel, Italy, Jamaica, Japan, Jordan, Kenya, Kiribati, Korea Rep, Kuwait, Latvia, Lebanon, Lesotho, Liberia, Libya, Liechtenstein, Lithuania, Luxembourg, Madagascar, Malawi, Malaysia, Maldives, Malta, Mauritania, Mauritius, Mexico, Monaco, Mongolia, Namibia, Nepal, Netherlands, New Zealand, Nicaragua, Nigeria, Norway, Oman, Pakistan, Panama, Papua New Guinea, Paraguay, Peru, Philippines, Poland, Portugal, Qatar, Romania, Russia, Rwanda, San Marino, Senegal, Sierra Leone, Singapore, Slovakia, Slovenia, Solomon Is, South Africa, Spain, Sri Lanka, St Kitts-Nevis, St Lucia, St Vincent-Grenadines, Sudan, Suriname, Sweden, Switzerland, Syrian AR, Taiwan, Tanzania UR, Thailand, Togo, Tonga, Trinidad-Tobago, Tunisia, Türkiye, Uganda, UK, Ukraine, United Arab Emirates, Uruguay, USA, Venezuela, Yemen, Zambia, Zimbabwe.

Consultative Status Consultative status granted from: *Council of Europe (CE, #04881)* (Participatory Status); *ECOSOC (#05331)* (Special); *UNESCO (#20322)* (Consultative Status); *FAO (#09260)* (Liaison Status); *ILO (#11123)* (Special List); *UNICEF (#20332)*; *UNEP (#20299)*. **IGO Relations** Accredited by (1): *United Nations Office at Vienna (UNOV, #20604)*. Member of (1): *European Youth Centres (EYCs, #09138)*. Participates in the work of: *United Nations Economic Commission for Europe (UNECE, #20555)*. Associated with Department of Global Communications of the United Nations. **NGO Relations** Member of (18): *Child Rights Connect (#03884)*; *Child Rights International Network (CRIN, #03885)*; *CIVICUS: World Alliance for Citizen Participation (#03962)*; *Committee of NGOs on Human Rights, Geneva (#04275)*; *Conference of Non-Governmental Organizations in Consultative Relationship with the United Nations (CONGO, #04635)*; *Espacio Iberoamericano de Juventud (EIJ, no recent information)*; *Foro Latinoamericano de Juventud (FLAJ, #09881)*; *Global Campaign for Education (GCE, #10264)*; *New York NGO Committee on Drugs (NYNGOC, #17097)*; *NGO Committee on Financing for Development, New York (#17108)* (as Full member); *NGO Committee on the Status of Women, Geneva (#17117)*; *NGO Committee on UNICEF (#17120)*; *NGO-UNESCO Liaison Committee (#17127)*; *Philanthropy Impact*; *United Nations Global Compact (#20567)*; *Vienna NGO Committee on Drugs (VNGOC, #20773)*; *Vienna NGO Committee on the Family (#20774)*; *Youth and United Nations Global Alliance (YUNGA, #22028)*. Partner of (2): *Every Woman Every Child (EWEC, #09215)*; *Global Call for Climate Action (GCCA, inactive)*. Cooperates with (1): *Alliance Against Hunger and Malnutrition (AAHM, no recent information)*. Close links with: *World Organization of the Scout Movement (WOSM, #21693)*. European Region is member of: Children's Rights Action Group; *European Women's Lobby (EWL, #09102)*; *European Youth Forum (#09140)*; *Federation of European and International Associations Established in Belgium (FAIB, #09508)*. Founding member of: *NGO Forum on Environment (FOE, #17125)*. [2021/XB3469/**B**]

♦ World Association for Gynecological Cancer Prevention (inactive)
♦ World Association for Hallyu Studies (internationally oriented national body)

♦ World Association for the History of Veterinary Medicine (WAHVM) 21143

Association mondiale de l'histoire de la médecine vétérinaire (AMHMV) – Welt-Gesellschaft für Geschichte der Veterinärmedizin (WGGVM) – Asociación Mundial de Historia de la Medicina Veterinaria (AMHMV)

Sec Royal Dick School of Veterinary Studies, Univ of Edinburgh, Easter Bush Campus, Midlothian, EH25 9RG, UK.
Pres Dept of History, Kings College London, Strand, London, WC2R 2LS, UK.
URL: http://www.wahvm.co.uk/

History Founded 9 May 1969, Hannover (Germany FR). **Aims** Encourage, promote and coordinate research and education in the history of veterinary medicine. **Structure** Executive Board of Directors; Extended Board; Working Groups; Head Office at address of President. **Languages** English. **Finance** Sources: donations; subscriptions. **Activities** Awards/prizes/competitions; events/meetings; knowledge management/information dissemination; research/documentation; training/education. **Events** *Biennial Congress* Tshwane (South Africa) 2020, *Biennial Congress* Bergen (Norway) 2018, *Biennial Congress* Vienna (Austria) 2016, *Biennial Congress / Congress* London (UK) 2014, *Biennial congress / Congress* Utrecht (Netherlands) 2012. **Publications** *WAHVM Newsletter*. *Guide to Veterinary Museums*.

Members Veterinarians and non-veterinarians in following categories National Societies for the History of Veterinary Medicine; Individual; Associate; Affiliate. Members in 36 countries:

Argentina, Austria, Belgium, Brazil, Bulgaria, Canada, Croatia, Cuba, Czechia, Denmark, Egypt, Estonia, Finland, France, Germany, Greece, Hungary, Ireland, Italy, Luxembourg, Mexico, Netherlands, Norway, Panama, Poland, Portugal, Romania, South Africa, Spain, Sweden, Switzerland, Türkiye, UK, Ukraine, USA, Venezuela.

Paying members (1,079) in 36 countries. Membership countries not specified. [2019.02.13/XC6574/**C**]

♦ World Association for Hospitality and Tourism Education and Training (WAHTT) 21144

Association mondiale pour la formation hôtelière et touristique (AMFORHT) – Asociación Mundial para la Formación Hotelera y Turistica

Permanent SG 10 rue Jean Moulin, 24750 Trelissac, France.
URL: https://amforht.groupment.com/platform/welcome/

History 10 Sep 1969, Nice (France). Restructured 29 May 1998, Nice (France). Former names and other names: *World Association for Professional Training in Tourism (WAPTT)* – former (10 Sep 1969 to 29 May 1998); *Association mondiale pour la formation professionelle touristique (AMFORT)* – former (10 Sep 1969 to 29 May 1998); *Asociación Mundial para la Formación Profesional Turistica* – former (10 Sep 1969 to 29 May 1998); *Nueva Asociación Mundial para la Formación Hotelera y Turistica* – former. Registration: France. **Aims** Act as a platform for meetings, exchanges, concertation between the 3 categories that can shape the future of hospitality and tourism education and training, namely international organizations, industry and academia. **Structure** General Assembly; Board of Directors; Executive Committee; Committees (5): Training – Employment; Conferences and Forum; Economic Research Institute and Research; International Development; Communication. **Languages** English, French, Spanish. **Staff** None. **Finance** Sources: donations; members' dues. **Activities** Events/meetings. **Events** *World Forum on Tourism and Hospitality Education* Seoul (Korea Rep) 2021, *World Forum on Tourism and Hospitality Education* Seoul (Korea Rep) 2020, *World Forum on Tourism and Hospitality Education* Paris (France) 2019, *World Forum on Tourism and Hospitality Education* Luxembourg (Luxembourg) 2018, *World Forum on Tourism and Hospitality Education* Montréal, QC (Canada) 2017. **Publications** *AMFORHT News* (4 a year) in English, French.

Members Institutional – international organizations; industry; academia; Individual. Members in 52 countries and territories:

Algeria, Argentina, Aruba, Australia, Belgium, Brazil, Cameroon, Canada, Czechia, Estonia, France, Gabon, Germany, Hong Kong, India, Indonesia, Ireland, Israel, Italy, Japan, Jordan, Kazakhstan, Kenya, Lebanon, Lithuania, Luxembourg, Malaysia, Marshall Is, Mexico, Monaco, Montenegro, Netherlands, Palestine, Poland, Polynesia Fr, Portugal, Réunion, Romania, Russia, Serbia, Slovakia, Spain, Switzerland, Syrian AR, Tanzania UR, Thailand, Tunisia, Türkiye, Uganda, UK, Ukraine, USA.

IGO Relations Member of (1): *World Tourism Organization (UNWTO, #21861)*. **NGO Relations** Member of (1): *World Tourism Network (WTN, #21860)*. [2021.06.17/XD1402/y/**C**]

♦ World Association of Industrial and Technological Research Organizations (WAITRO) 21145

Gen Sec Internationale Forschungsprogramme & Netzwerke (P32), Fraunhofer Headquarters, Schloss Birlinghoven, 53757 St Augustin, Germany. T. +492241141470. Fax +492241142256.
URL: http://www.waitro.org/

History 28 Oct 1970, Vienna (Austria). Established under the sponsorship of UNIDO, at a meeting attended by representatives of industrial research organizations, United Nations agencies and other international organizations, following a recommendation by a UNIDO Interregional Workshop and International Symposium on Industrial Development, 1967, Athens (Greece), of which the latter was attended by delegates from 79 countries. Original Constitution and By-Laws approved by the Meeting of the Founding Members, 29 Oct 1970, Vienna. By-Laws revised by 8th biennial meeting of the General Assembly, 26 Sep 1986, Århus (Denmark). Last revision of Constitution and By-Laws adopted by 20th biennial meeting of the General Assembly, 14 Oct 2010, Dubai (United Arab Emirates). **Aims** Promote and encourage cooperation among industrial and technological research and development organizations (RTOs) to contribute to sustainable developement. **Structure** General Assembly (every 2 years, during Congress); Executive Committee; Secretariat, headed by Secretary General; Regional Focal Points (5). Representatives of UN and international agencies: UNCTAD; UNESCO (Permanent Observer); UNIDO. **Languages** English. **Staff** 8.00 FTE, paid. **Finance** Sources: contributions; grants; members' dues. **Activities** Events/meetings; knowledge management/information dissemination; networking/liaising; research/documentation; training/education. **Events** *Virtual Summit and General Assembly* St Augustin (Germany) 2020, *Biennial Congress and General Assembly* Penang (Malaysia) 2018, *Biennial Congress and General Assembly* Medellin (Colombia) 2016, *Networking Conference* Bangkok (Thailand) 2015, *Biennial General Assembly* Copenhagen (Denmark) 2014. **Publications** *WAITRO News* (4 a year); *Directory of Membership* (annual); *Pictorial Report* (every 4 years). *R and D Institutes and Local Industry Interaction: An International Perspective* by Moses D Mengu; *WAITRO Journey Through Time 1970-2014*. Conference and seminar reports and proceedings; brochures; technical papers. **Members** Technical Membership: open to organizations (national bodies or institutes) and universities actively engaged in industrial or technical research and development; Sustaining Membership: open to organizations (public and private) active in encouraging and promoting research and development activities and desirous of assisting the Association by financial or other means of advancing its aims. Over 100 member organizations in more than 50 countries and territories. **Consultative Status** Consultative status granted from: *ECOSOC (#05331)* (Special); *UNESCO (#20322)* (Consultative Status); *UNIDO (#20336)*; *UNCTAD (#20285)* (Special Category). **IGO Relations** Accredited by: *United Nations Office at Vienna (UNOV, #20604)*. Participates in the work of: *United Nations Economic Commission for Europe (UNECE, #20555)*. Associated with Department of Global Communications of the United Nations. **NGO Relations** Member of: *Conference of Non-Governmental Organizations in Consultative Relationship with the United Nations (CONGO, #04635)*; *World Federation of Industrial Research Associations (W-FIRA, #21442)*; *World Federation of Technology Organizations (WFTO, #21490)*. [2022/XB3950/ty/**B**]

♦ World Association for Infant Mental Health (WAIMH) 21146

Central Office Univ of Tampere, Fac Medicine & Life Sciences, Arvo Ylpön katu 34, FI-33014 Tampere, Finland. T. +358504627379. E-mail: office@waimh.org.
URL: http://www.waimh.org/

History 1992. Founded on merger of *World Association for Infant Psychiatry and Allied Disciplines (WAIPAD, inactive)*, set up 1980 as *'World Association for Infant Psychiatry (WAIP)'*, with *International Association for Infant Mental Health (inactive)*. Former names and other names: *Association mondiale de santé mentale du nourrisson* – former alias; *Asociación Mundial para la Salud Mental Infantil* – former alias; *Internationale Gesellschaft für Seelische Gesundheit in der Frühen Kindheit* – former alias. Registration: USA, Washington DC. **Aims** Promote the mental wellbeing and healthy development of infants throughout the world, taking into account cultural, regional, and environmental variations; generate and disseminate scientific knowledge. **Structure** Board of Directors; Executive Committee. **Languages** English. **Staff** 1.00 FTE, paid. **Finance** Sources: members' dues. **Activities** Awards/prizes/competitions; events/meetings; research/documentation; training/education. **Events** *World Congress* Dublin (Ireland) 2023, *World Congress* Brisbane, QLD (Australia) 2021, *World Congress* Brisbane, QLD (Australia) 2020, *World Congress* Rome (Italy) 2018, *World Congress* Prague (Czech Rep) 2016. **Publications** *Infant Mental Health Journal* (6 a year); *Perspectives on Infant Mental Health* (4 a year). *WAIMH Handbook on Infant Mental Health* – 4 vols. Meeting, workshop, institute, symposia, conference and congress proceedings; newsletters; books; monographs; reports; studies; other periodicals.

Members Affiliates in 24 countries:

Argentina, Australia, Belgium, Brazil, Canada, Estonia, Finland, France, Greece, Ireland, Israel, Italy, Japan, Korea Rep, Latvia, Luxembourg, Netherlands, New Zealand, Portugal, South Africa, Spain, Türkiye, UK, USA.

Regional affiliates (2):

German Speaking Association for Infant Mental Health (GAIMH, #10139); *Nordisk Förening för Spädbarns Utveckling (NFSU, #17509)*.

NGO Relations Member of: *Global Alliance for Maternal Mental Health (GAMMH, #10208)*. [2022/XC0093/**C**]

♦ World Association for Infant Psychiatry and Allied Disciplines (inactive)

♦ World Association for Infectious Diseases and Immunological Disorders (WAidid) 21147

Secretariat c/o AIM Congress, Via Ripamonti 129, 20141 Milan MI, Italy. T. +39256601847. Fax +39256609045. E-mail: waidid.secretariat@aimgroup.eu.
URL: http://www.waidid.org/

History Founded Jul 2014, Italy. Registered in accordance with Italian law. **Aims** Advance the scientific research in the field of infectious diseases and immunology; disseminate information on the related pathologies both at national and international level. **Structure** General Assembly; Board of Directors. Working Groups. **Activities** Events/meetings. **Events** *Biennial Congress* Milan (Italy) 2020, *Biennial Congress* Milan (Italy) 2018, *Biennial Congress* Milan (Italy) 2016. [2019.06.04/XM7752/**C**]

♦ World Association of Integrated Medicine (WAIM) 21148

Pres N10/60 C-1, Kakarmatta, PO Bazardeeha, Varanasi, Uttar Pradesh 221106, Varanasi UTTAR PRADESH 221106, India. T. +915422300928. E-mail: integratedmedicine@yahoo.com.
URL: http://www.integratedmedicineindia.org/

History 30 Nov 1993, Colombo (Sri Lanka). **Aims** Promote and establish teaching, training, treatment, research and national implementation of integrated medicine worldwide. **Structure** Board of Governors of 6 officers and 5 executive members. **Finance** Sources: donations; members' dues. **Activities** Events/meetings. **Events** *Global conference on integrated medicine* Delhi (India) 2001. **Publications** *International Journal of Integrated Medicine*. Books.

Members Organizations in 4 countries:

Bangladesh, India, Iran Islamic Rep, USA. [2022.05.31/XF4823/sy/**F**]

♦ World Association of International Studies (internationally oriented national body)
♦ World Association of Inventors and Researchers (inactive)
♦ World Association for Investment in Building and Construction (inactive)

♦ World Association of Investment Promotion Agencies (WAIPA) 21149

Exec Dir World Trade Center, Bldg A1 8th Fl, No 297 Yesilkoy, Istanbul/Istanbul, Türkiye. T. +902124686980.
Geneva office c/o MEI2, Chemin de Balexert 9, Châtelaine, 1219 Geneva, Switzerland. E-mail: info@waipa.org.
URL: http://www.waipa.org/

History 25 Apr 1995, Geneva (Switzerland). 25-27 Apr 1995, Geneva (Switzerland), by representatives of Investment Promotion Agencies (IPAs) of 60 countries, at founding meeting under the auspices of *UNCTAD (#20285)*. Also referred to as *World Association of IPAs*. Registered in accordance with Swiss Civil Code. **Aims** Provide the opportunity for investment promotion agencies (IPAs) to network and exchange best practices in investment promotion. **Structure** General Assembly (annual, at session of UNCTAD's Commission on Investment Technology and Related Financial Issues); Steering Committee; Consultative Committee; Secretariat, located in Geneva (Switzerland). **Languages** English. **Staff** 7.00 FTE, paid. **Finance** Sources: donations; fees for services; members' dues. **Activities** Events/meetings; guidance/assistance/consulting; knowledge management/information dissemination; training/education. **Events** *Annual Investment Meeting* Dubai (United Arab Emirates) 2019, *Conference* Warsaw (Poland) 2019, *A new era in foreign direct investment* Xiamen (China) 2018, *Conference* Dubai (United Arab Emirates) 2017, *Annual Conference* Istanbul (Turkey) 2016. **Publications** *WAIPA Newsletter* (4 a year); *WAIPA Electronic Bulletin* (24 a year). Annual Report; surveys; research papers.
Members Agencies promoting national or regional investment (128) in 99 countries and territories:
Afghanistan, Algeria, Argentina, Azerbaijan, Bahrain, Bangladesh, Barbados, Bosnia-Herzegovina, Botswana, Brazil, Bulgaria, Burkina Faso, Cameroon, Cape Verde, Cayman Is, Chile, China, Colombia, Comoros, Congo Brazzaville, Congo DR, Costa Rica, Côte d'Ivoire, Cuba, Curaçao, Cyprus, Djibouti, Dominican Rep, Ecuador, Egypt, El Salvador, Eswatini, Fiji, Finland, Gabon, Gambia, Ghana, Greece, Guatemala, Guinea, India, Iran Islamic Rep, Iraq, Italy, Japan, Jordan, Kazakhstan, Kenya, Korea Rep, Kosovo, Kuwait, Lebanon, Lesotho, Macau, Madagascar, Malaysia, Maldives, Mali, Malta, Marshall Is, Mauritius, Moldova, Mongolia, Morocco, Namibia, Nepal, Nigeria, Pakistan, Palestine, Panama, Peru, Poland, Polynesia Fr, Portugal, Qatar, Romania, Russia, Samoa, Saudi Arabia, Senegal, Sierra Leone, Slovenia, South Africa, Spain, St Kitts-Nevis, St Lucia, Switzerland, Tajikistan, Tanzania UR, Tonga, Tunisia, Türkiye, Uganda, UK, United Arab Emirates, Uzbekistan, Vanuatu, Venezuela, Zambia.
Consultative Status Consultative status granted from: *UNCTAD (#20285)* (Special Category). **IGO Relations** *ILO (#11123)*; *OECD (#17693)*; *UNIDO (#20336)*; *The World Bank Group (#21218)*. **NGO Relations** *International Chamber of Commerce (ICC, #12534)*; *International Economic Development Council (IEDC)*.
[2019.12.12/XD3944/C]

- World Association of IPAs / see World Association of Investment Promotion Agencies (#21149)
- World Association for Island Studies (internationally oriented national body)

♦ World Association of Judges (WAJ) 21150

Association mondiale de juges – Asociación Mundial de Magistrados

Pres address not obtained. E-mail: wja@worldjurist.org.
URL: http://www.worldjurist.org/

History 13 Mar 1966, Geneva (Switzerland), as *World Association of Judges of the World Peace through Law Center*, by *'World Peace Through Law Center (WPLTC)'*, now *World Jurist Association (WJA, #21604)*, to which it is affiliated. **Aims** Advance the administration of *judicial justice* through cooperation and communication among ranking judicial officials of all nations in an effort to bring to bear upon the common problems of humankind the universally accepted processes, procedures, principles and institutions of the *rule of law*. **Structure** Executive Committee of 16 members; Secretariat General. Sections: High Courts; Appellate Courts; Trial Courts. **Languages** English. **Finance** Members' dues. Foundation grants. **Events** *Biennial Meeting* Adelaide, SA (Australia) / Sydney, NSW (Australia) 2003, *Biennial Meeting* Belfast (UK) / Dublin (Ireland) 2001, *Biennial Meeting* Vienna (Austria) 1999, *Biennial Meeting* Doha (Qatar) 1997, *World conference* Montréal, QC (Canada) 1995. **Publications** *Law/Technology* (4 a year) – journal; *World Jurist* (at least 7 a year) – newsletter. **Members** Supreme and High Court Justices eligible on individual basis. Other judges eligible in appropriate categories. Since membership in WAJ includes membership in WJA, same members as WJA.
[2020/XE3471/v/E]

- World Association of Judges of the World Peace through Law Center / see World Association of Judges (#21150)
- World Association of Kickboxing Organizations / see World Association of Kickboxing Organizations (#21151)

♦ World Association of Kickboxing Organizations (WAKO) 21151

Admin Office Via A Manzoni 18, 20052 Monza MB, Italy. T. +39335286388. E-mail: administration@wako.sport.
Legal address Bahnhofstr 23, 6300 Zug, Switzerland.
URL: https://wako.sport/

History 14 Dec 1985. Founded in Borgworm (Belgium) and Zurich (Switzerland) (simultaneously). Merged with *International Amateur Kickboxing Sport Association (IAKSA, inactive)*, 27 Sep 2006. Former names and other names: *World All Style Karate Organization* – former; *World Association of Kickboxing Organizations* – former; *World Amateur Kickboxing Organization* – former. **Structure** Includes professional division 'WAKO-PRO', formerly known as 'Professional Kickboxing Organization' and then 'International Kickboxing League'. **Members** Membership countries not specified. **NGO Relations** Member of (4): *Alliance of Independent recognised Members of Sport (AIMS, #00690)* (Associate); *Association of the IOC Recognized International Sports Federations (ARISF, #02767)*; *International World Games Association (IWGA, #15914)*; *Olympic Movement (#17719)*. Cooperates with (1): *International Testing Agency (ITA, #15678)*. Recognized by: *International Olympic Committee (IOC, #14408)*; *World Martial Arts Committee (WMAC, #21636)*. [2022/XD4563/D]

- World Association of Labour History Institutions (inactive)

♦ World Association for Laser Applications (WALA) 21152

Pres address not obtained.
URL: https://waltza.co.za/

History 2007, after discussions in 2004. **Aims** Promote research, education, clinical applications and procedures in medicine, surgery, dentistry, physical therapy, neuroscience, veterinary medicine, safety, new instrumentation and optical diagnostics; serve as a catalyst in developing a regional hub for Photonics-Optoelectronic Industries in Gulf countries and neighbours, including the Far East. **Events** *Annual Dubai congress on anti-ageing and aesthetic medicine* Dubai (United Arab Emirates) 2010. **NGO Relations** Affiliated with: *Afro-Asian Society for Cosmetic Dermatology and Laser (ASCDL, no recent information)*; *Asian Pacific Association for Lasers in Medicine and Surgery (APALMS, #01599)*; *International Academy of Laser Medicine and Surgery (IALMS, #11553)*; *International Society for Laser Surgery and Medicine (ISLSM, #15229)*; *International Society for Medical Laser Applications (ISLA, #15256)*; *New European Surgical Academy (NESA, #17084)*; *European Medical Laser Association (EMLA, #07763)*; *World Society of Anti-Aging Medicine (WOSAAM, #21798)*. [2016/XJ1106/D]

♦ World Association for Laser Therapy (WALT) 21153

Pres Bergen Univ College, Postboks 7030, 5020 Bergen, Norway. E-mail: info@waltza.co.za.
SG address not obtained.
URL: http://waltza.co.za/

History 7 May 1994, Barcelona (Spain), by merger of *International Laser Therapy Association (ILTA, inactive)* and *International Society for Lower-Power Laser Applications in Medicine (inactive)*. Also referred to as *World Association for Low Density Laser Therapy*. **Aims** Stimulate high quality research in photobiomodulation; offer evidence-based guidance, education and standards for best practice in low level laser therapy; contribute to the promotion of health and quality of life. **Structure** Executive Council. **Activities** Events/meetings. **Events** *Joint Photobiomodulation Conference* Arlington, VA (USA) 2021, *Joint Photobiomodulation Conference* Arlington, VA (USA) 2020, *Biennial Congress* Nice (France) 2018, *Biennial Congress* São Sebastião (Brazil) 2016, *Biennial Congress / Congress* Washington, DC (USA) 2014. **Publications** *WALT eNewsletter* (3 a year); *Photomedicine and Laser Surgery* – journal. [2017/XD3816/D]

♦ World Association of Law Professors (WALP) 21154

Pres address not obtained. E-mail: wja@worldjurist.org.
URL: http://www.worldjurist.org/

History 1975, Washington DC (USA), as an independent association, by *'World Peace Through Law Center (WPTLC)'*, now *World Jurist Association (WJA, #21604)*, to which it is affiliated. **Aims** Utilize the talents and energies of the world's outstanding scholars and teachers of law and bring them to bear on important *transnational law* issues; endeavour to improve the effectiveness of scholarship and education in dealing with problems related to international *legal matters*, including, but not limited to, training for law, practice, the administration of *justice*, *human rights*, the environment, and coordination among law systems. **Languages** English. **Finance** Members' dues. **Events** *Biennial Meeting* Adelaide, SA (Australia) / Sydney, NSW (Australia) 2003, *Biennial Meeting* Belfast (UK) / Dublin (Ireland) 2001, *Biennial Meeting* Vienna (Austria) 1999, *Biennial Meeting* Doha (Qatar) 1997, *Seminar* San Francisco, CA (USA) 1995. **Publications** *World Jurist* (6 a year) – newsletter; *Law/Technology* (4 a year) – journal. **Members** Individual members. Membership equals that of WJA. [2020/XE3576/v/E]

♦ World Association of Lawyers (WAL) 21155

Contact World Jurist Assn, 51 Monroe St, Ste 404, Rockville MD 20850, USA. T. +12024665428. Fax +12024528540. E-mail: wja@worldjurist.org.
URL: http://www.worldjurist.org/

History 1975, Washington DC (USA), by *'World Peace Through Law Center (WPTLC)'*, now *World Jurist Association (WJA, #21604)*. **Aims** Mobilize the talents and energies of the world's outstanding *legal practitioners* and bring them to bear on important *transnational legal* issues; endeavour to improve the lawyer's effectiveness in dealing with the numerous problems resulting from a practice which is increasingly international. **Languages** English. **Finance** Members' dues. **Activities** Research/education; publishing activities. **Events** *Biennial Meeting* Prague (Czech Rep) 2011, *Biennial Meeting* Kiev (Ukraine) 2009, *Biennial Meeting* Lisbon (Portugal) 2007, *Biennial Meeting* Beijing (China) / Shanghai (China) 2005, *Biennial Meeting* Sydney, NSW (Australia) / Adelaide, SA (Australia) 2003. **Members** Individual members. Since membership in WAL includes membership in WJA, same members as WJA. [2018/XE5362/v/E]

♦ World Association of Lebanese Neurosurgeons (WALN) 21156

Pres Dept of Neurosurgery, Thomas Jefferson Univ Hosp, 909 Walnut St, Philadelphia PA 19107, USA. T. +12159557000. Fax +12155037038.
Sec Dept Neurosurgery, Univ of Illinois at Chicago, 912 S Wood St MC-799, Chicago IL 60612, USA.
URL: http://www.waln.org/

History 1993. Incorporated in the State of Illinois (USA). **Aims** Foster Lebanese neurosurgical heritage; promote bridges of professional brotherhood among neurosurgeons of Lebanese descent and/or education. **Structure** Members' Meeting; Board of Directors (meeting at least twice a year); Regional Representatives from Brazil, Europe and Lebanon. **Languages** English. **Staff** None. **Finance** Members' dues. **Activities** Training/education; financial and/or material support; guidance/assistance/consulting. **Events** *Congress* Natal (Brazil) 2010, *Congress* Beirut (Lebanon) 2009, *Congress* Beirut (Lebanon) 2007, *Congress* Beirut (Lebanon) 2006, *Into the third millennium* Beirut (Lebanon) 2004. **Publications** *WALN Newsletter*.
Members Categories – Eligible; Active; Resident; Associate; individuals in 18 countries:
Argentina, Australia, Brazil, Canada, Colombia, Egypt, France, India, Iraq, Jamaica, Jordan, Lebanon, Saudi Arabia, Sweden, Syrian AR, UK, United Arab Emirates, USA.
NGO Relations *Arab College of Neurosurgery (#00923)*; *Pan Arab Neurosurgical Society (PANS, #18151)*; national organizations. [2016.10.19/XD9255/v/D]

♦ World Association of Lesson Studies (WALS) 21157

Pres NIE-NTU, 1 Nanyang Walk, Singapore 637616, Singapore.
URL: http://www.walsnet.org/

Aims Facilitate communication between research groups in different countries to share their knowledge. **Structure** General Meeting (annual). Council, comprising President, Chairperson Web Communications Committee, Chairperson Organizing Committee of Annual Conference, Honorary Treasurer, Honorary Treasurer and 45 members. **Events** *International Conference* Kuala Lumpur (Malaysia) 2022, *International Conference* 2021, *International Conference* 2020, *International Conference* Amsterdam (Netherlands) 2019, *International Conference* Beijing (China) 2018. **Publications** *The Journal of Lesson Studies and Learning*.
Members Founding in 8 countries and territories:
Australia, China, Hong Kong, Japan, Singapore, Sweden, UK, USA. [2014/XJ5523/D]

- World Association for Low Density Laser Therapy / see World Association for Laser Therapy (#21153)
- World Association of Majorette-sport and Twirling (unconfirmed)

♦ World Association of the Major Metropolises (Metropolis) 21158

Association mondiale des grandes métropoles – Asociación Mundial de las Grandes Metrópolis

SG c/ Avinyó 15, 08002 Barcelona, Spain. T. +34933429460. Fax +34933429466. E-mail: metropolis@metropolis.org.
URL: http://www.metropolis.org/

History Apr 1985. Registration: France. **Aims** Foster the performance of metropolises in addressing local and global challenges and advocate metropolitan interests through the connection of political leaders, policy makers and practitioners worldwide; promote the vision of metropolitan spaces for and by people, where participatory and effective metropolitan governance fosters economic development, sustainability, social cohesion, gender equality and quality of life. **Structure** General Assembly; (every 3 years at Metropolis Congress); Board of Directors; Regional Offices; General Secretariat, headed by Secretary General. **Languages** English, French, Spanish. **Staff** 17.00 FTE, paid. **Finance** Sources: grants; members' dues. Other sources: administration grants and partnerships. **Activities** Awards/prizes/competitions; events/meetings; networking/liaising; projects/programmes; research/documentation; training/education. Three areas of action: strengthen global leadership on metropolitan diplomacy and advocacy; build adaptive capacities for metropolitan governance; foster within Metropolis an accountable and sustainable internal governance culture. **Events** *Triennial Congress* Guangzhou (China) 2021, *Meeting* Barcelona (Spain) 2020, *Triennial Congress* Guangzhou (China) 2020, *Meeting* Montevideo (Uruguay) 2019, *Meeting* Johannesburg (South Africa) 2018. **Members** Major cities and metropolitan areas (143). Membership countries not specified. **IGO Relations** Accredited by (1): *United Nations Office at Vienna (UNOV, #20604)*. Affiliated with (1): *Regions of Climate Action (R20, #18820)*. **NGO Relations** Partner of (1): *World Urban Campaign (WUC, #21893)*. Instrumental in setting up (1): *FMDV (#09804)*. Cooperation agreement with: *World Organization of United Cities and Local Governments (UCLG, #21695)*. [2022.02.14/XD0472/B]

♦ World Association of Manufacturers of Bottles and Teats (WBT) ... 21159

Contact 122 avenue Charles de Gaulle, 92522 Neuilly-sur-Seine, France. E-mail: enquiries@thewbt.org.
Registered Office 194 rue de Rivoli, 75001 Paris, France.
URL: http://www.thewbt.org/

History 1991. Registered in accordance with French law. EU Transparency Register: 204651515772-21. **Aims** Represent interests of the industry to media, national and international institutions; promote ethical manufacturing and marketing of infant bottles and teats adhering to relevant national and international standards. **Structure** General Assembly (annual); Executive Committee. **Activities** Research and development; knowledge management/information dissemination; networking/liaising.
Members Full in 10 countries:
Austria, France, Germany, Italy, Japan, Netherlands, Poland, Switzerland, Türkiye, UK.
NGO Relations Liaison Organization of: *Comité européen de normalisation (CEN, #04162)*. Cooperates with: *European Nursery Products Confederation (ENPC, #08061)*; *International Association of Infant Food Manufacturers (IFM, #11961)*; *Association of Plastics Manufacturers in Europe (Plastics Europe, #02862)*.
[2018/XM4804/D]

♦ World Association of Marching Show Bands (WAMSB) 21160

Pres and CEO address not obtained. E-mail: wamsb@wamsb.org.
URL: http://www.wamsb.org/

History Jul 1993. Incorporated in the State of Delaware (USA). Registration: Non-profit organization, Start date: 1995, USA. **Aims** Promote international development and communication of marching show bands worldwide. **Structure** International Board; Regional and National Chapters; Affiliates; Executive Council; Advisory Council; Judges Bureau; Working Committees. **Languages** English. **Staff** Voluntary. **Finance** Sources: donations; members' dues; sponsorship. **Activities** Awards/prizes/competitions; events/meetings; publishing activities. **Events** *Annual Championship* Rastede (Germany) 2024, *Annual Championship* Buckhannon, WV (USA) 2023, *Annual Championship* Bangkok (Thailand) 2022, *Annual Championship* Rastede (Germany) 2021, *Annual Championship* Bangkok (Thailand) 2020. **Publications** *WAMSB Newsletter* (2 a year). *Judging System and Contest Manual*. Association, chapter and project reports; certificates; score sheets; symposium and project documents.
Members Band and educational associations and individuals in 54 countries and territories:

Argentina, Australia, Austria, Belgium, Bolivia, Brazil, Canada, Chile, China, Colombia, Costa Rica, Croatia, Cuba, Czechia, Denmark, Finland, France, Germany, Ghana, Hong Kong, Hungary, Iceland, Indonesia, Ireland, Israel, Italy, Japan, Korea Rep, Malaysia, Mexico, Netherlands, New Zealand, Nigeria, Norway, Pakistan, Peru, Philippines, Poland, Puerto Rico, Russia, Scotland, Singapore, South Africa, Spain, Sweden, Switzerland, Taiwan, Thailand, Tonga, Uganda, UK, Uruguay, USA, Venezuela. [2022/XD6416/D]

♦ World Association of Marine Stations (WAMS) 21161

Chair address not obtained. E-mail: worldmarinestations@mba.ac.uk.
Sec address not obtained.
URL: https://www.worldmarinestations.org/

History Apr 2010. Formally established by *European Network of Marine Research Institutes and Stations (MARS Network, #07941)* and *Intergovernmental Oceanographic Commission (IOC, #11496)*. Following a period of inactivity, a joint communiqué on the establishment of WAMS was agreed at the 2021 conference. **Aims** Provide a forum for marine stations worldwide to establish inclusive partnerships and strengthen collaboration among marine scientists to foster marine scientific research internationally. **Structure** Steering Group. **Activities** Training/education; capacity building; networking/liaising; research/documentation; knowledge management/information dissemination. **Events** *World Congress of Marine Stations* 2021, *Meeting* 2010.

Members Founding members (10):
Association of Marine Laboratories of the Caribbean (AMLC, #02794); *European Network of Marine Research Institutes and Stations (MARS Network, #07941)*; *Global Ocean Observing System for Africa (GOOS Africa, #10512)*; *Intergovernmental Oceanographic Commission (IOC, #11496)*; Japanese Association for Marine Biology, Japan (JAMBIO); National Association of Marine Laboratories USA (NAML); Pacific Institutes of Marine Science (PIMS); *Partnership for Observation of the Global Oceans (POGO, #18239)*; *Programme on Man and the Biosphere (MAB, #18526)*; Tropical Marine Network, Australia. [2021/XJ9240/y/E]

♦ World Association of Medical Editors (WAME) 21162

Sec address not obtained.
URL: http://wame.org/

History 16 Mar 1995, Bellagio (Italy). Inaugural meeting 19 Sep 1997, Prague (Czech Rep). Registered in the USA. **Aims** Facilitate worldwide cooperation and communication among editors of peer-reviewed medical *journals*; improve editorial standards; promote professionalism in medical editing through education, self-criticism and self-regulation; encourage research on the principles and practice of medical editing. **Structure** Executive Board. Standing Committees (7): Editorial Policy; Education; Ethics; Finance; Membership; Research; Web. Small Journals Task Force. **Languages** English. **Staff** Part-time, voluntary. **Finance** Sources: contributions; grants. Other sources: Sponsored by medical journals and foundations. **Activities** Provides resources for editors; discusses topics. **Events** *Conference* Delhi (India) 2015, *Meeting* Vancouver, BC (Canada) 2009, *Meeting* Chicago, IL (USA) 2005, *Meeting* Barcelona (Spain) 2001, *Inaugural Meeting* Prague (Czech Rep) 1997.

Members (over 1,500) in 55 countries and territories:
Argentina, Armenia, Australia, Belgium, Brazil, Burundi, Canada, China, Colombia, Croatia, Cuba, Czechia, Denmark, Egypt, Fiji, Finland, France, Germany, Hong Kong, Hungary, Iceland, India, Indonesia, Iran Islamic Rep, Israel, Italy, Korea Rep, Kuwait, Libya, Malawi, Malaysia, Malta, Mexico, Netherlands, New Zealand, Nigeria, Norway, Pakistan, Peru, Poland, Portugal, Romania, Saudi Arabia, Serbia, Singapore, Slovenia, South Africa, Spain, Sweden, Switzerland, Tanzania UR, Türkiye, UK, USA, Venezuela.

NGO Relations Member of: *International Committee of Medical Journal Editors (ICMJE)*. [2014/XD6354/v/C]

♦ World Association of Medical and Health Films (WAMHF) 21163

Association mondiale du cinéma médical et de la santé – Asociación Mundial del Cine Médico y de la Salud

Gen Sec c/o WAMHF Secretariat, Demmerik 12, 3645 EC Vinkeveen, Netherlands.
URL: http://www.wamhf.com/

History 1990, Badajoz (Spain), during the 6th International Medical and Health Film Festival. **Aims** Promote production, documentation, preservation, distribution and utilization of the use and exchange of medical and health *audiovisual* productions. **Structure** General Assembly (annual). Executive Committee, comprising President, Vice-President, Secretary, Treasurer and 2 members. **Languages** English, French, Spanish. **Finance** Members' dues.

Members Individuals, associations and institutions in 26 countries:
Argentina, Belgium, Brazil, Canada, Chile, Colombia, Costa Rica, Cuba, Denmark, Ecuador, Finland, France, Germany, Italy, Japan, Mexico, Netherlands, Portugal, Senegal, Spain, Sweden, Switzerland, Uganda, UK, Uruguay, USA.

IGO Relations *WHO (#20950)*. [2011.10.07/XD7887/D]

♦ World Association for Medical Informatics (inactive)

♦ World Association for Medical Law (WAML) 21164

Communications Manager address not obtained.
URL: http://www.wafml.memberlodge.org/

History 1967, Ghent (Belgium). Former names and other names: *World Medical Law Association* – former (1967); *Association mondiale de droit médical* – former (1967); *Asociación Mundial de Derecho Médico* – former (1967). **Aims** Encourage the study and discussion of health law, legal medicine and ethics for the benefit of society and advancement of human rights. **Structure** General Assembly (every 2 years); Board of Governors; Executive Committee; Council of Presidents; Committees (4). **Languages** English. **Finance** Members' dues. **Events** *World Congress* Istanbul (Türkiye) 2025, *World Congress* Toronto, ON (Canada) 2024, *World Congress* Vilnius (Lithuania) 2023, *World Congress* Gold Coast, QLD (Australia) 2022, *World Congress* Istanbul (Turkey) 2021. **Publications** *Medicine and Law* (4 a year) – peer reviewed journal. Newsletter (4 a year). **NGO Relations** Member of: *Council for International Organizations of Medical Sciences (CIOMS, #04905)*. [2022/XD5405/D]

♦ World Association for Medical Sexology (unconfirmed)

♦ World Association of Membrane Societies (WA-MS) 21165

Contact Dept Chemical Engineering, Fac of Engineering – KUL, Celestijnenlaan 200F – bus 2424, 3001 Leuven, Belgium. T. +3216322340.
URL: http://www.wa-ms.org/

History 2017, San Francisco, CA (USA). Founded during International Congress on Membranes and Membrane Processes, by *Aseanian Membrane Society (AMS, #01196)*, *European Membrane Society (EMS, #07777)* and North American Membrane Society (NAMS). **Aims** Enhance the use of membrane technology and collaborations between professional societies on membrane science and technology worldwide. **Structure** General Assembly; Steering Committee. Working Groups. **Languages** English. **Staff** 18.00 FTE, voluntary. **Finance** Through founding societies.

Members Founding organizations (3):
Aseanian Membrane Society (AMS, #01196); *European Membrane Society (EMS, #07777)*; North American Membrane Society (NAMS).
Other members in 5 countries:
Belgium, Mexico, Netherlands, Poland, Russia.
African Membrane Society (AMSIC, #00371). [2021/XM7527/y/C]

♦ World Association of Methodist Radio Amateurs and Clubs / see World Association of Christian Radio Amateurs and Listeners (#21127)
♦ World Association of Navigation (inactive)
♦ World Association of Newspapers (inactive)

♦ World Association of Newspapers and News Publishers (WAN-IFRA) 21166

Exec Dir c/o APIG, 69 Rue du Chevaleret, 75013 Paris, France. E-mail: info@wan-ifra.org.
German Office Rotfeder-Ring 11, 60327 Frankfurt-Main, Germany. T. +49692400630. Fax +4969240063300. E-mail: info@wan-ifra.org.
URL: http://www.wan-ifra.org/

History Jul 2009. Founded on merger of *World Association of Newspapers (WAN, inactive)* and *IFRA (inactive)*. Registration: Swiss Civil Code, Switzerland. **Aims** Act as partner of newspapers and the news publishing industry worldwide; defend and promote press freedom, quality *journalism* and editorial integrity; provide the industry with applied research in the fields of technology and business. **Structure** Board; Advisory Council Executive Committee; Technical Committees (3); Regional Committees (4); Regional Offices (3); Headquarters in Frankfurt-Main (Germany) and Paris (France). **Activities** Awards/prizes/competitions; events/meetings. Operates: *African Press Network for the 21st Century (RAP 21, #00423)*; *Arab Press Network (APN, #01031)*. **Events** *World News Media Congress* Saragossa (Spain) 2022, *World News Media Congress* 2021, *Asian Media Leaders eSummit* Singapore (Singapore) 2021, *Digital Media Asia Conference* Singapore (Singapore) 2021, *Science in the Newsroom Global Summit* Singapore (Singapore) 2020. **Publications** *Trends in Newsrooms*; *WAN-IFRA World News Publishing Focus*; *World Digital Media Trends*; *World Press Trends*.

Members National Associations (nearly 80); Press Agencies (17); Affiliates (21); Companies (over 3,000).
National associations in 67 countries and territories:
Albania, Algeria, Argentina, Austria, Belgium, Bolivia, Bosnia-Herzegovina, Brazil, Bulgaria, Burkina Faso, Canada, Chile, Colombia, Cyprus, Czechia, Denmark, Dominican Rep, Ecuador, Estonia, Finland, France, Gabon, Germany, Ghana, Greece, Hungary, India, Indonesia, Ireland, Italy, Japan, Korea Rep, Kyrgyzstan, Latvia, Luxembourg, Mali, Mauritius, Mexico, Moldova, Mongolia, Netherlands, New Zealand, North Macedonia, Norway, Pakistan, Paraguay, Peru, Philippines, Poland, Portugal, Romania, Russia, Serbia, Slovakia, South Africa, Spain, Sri Lanka, Sweden, Switzerland, Taiwan, Türkiye, Uganda, UK, Ukraine, Uruguay, USA, Venezuela.
Press Agencies in 13 countries:
Austria, Belgium, Denmark, Finland, France, Greece, Japan, Netherlands, Qatar, Russia, Sweden, UK, USA.
Affiliates in 16 countries and territories:
Australia, Belgium, Denmark, France, Hong Kong, Italy, Netherlands, Philippines, Saudi Arabia, Singapore, Spain, Sweden, Switzerland, UK, United Arab Emirates, USA.
Included in the above, 7 organizations listed in this Yearbook:
Association for the Promotion of the International Circulation of the Press (DISTRIPRESS, #02876); *European Association of Daily Newspapers in Minority and Regional Languages (Midas, #06002)*; *European Newspaper Publishers' Association (ENPA, #08048)*; *Inter American Press Association (IAPA, #11444)*; *International Classified Marketplace Association (ICMA, #12592)*; *Middle East Publishers' Association (MEPA, #16788)*.

Consultative Status Consultative status granted from: *UNESCO (#20322)* (Associate Status); *Council of Europe (CE, #04881)* (Participatory Status); *World Intellectual Property Organization (WIPO, #21593)* (Observer Status). **NGO Relations** Member of (1): *Ethical Journalism Network (EJN, #05554)*. [2022/XJ2814/y/B]

♦ World Association of NGOs / see World Association of Non-Governmental Organizations (#21167)

♦ World Association of Non-Governmental Organizations (WANGO) . . 21167

Chair 220 White Plains Rd, Fifth Floor, Tarrytown NY 10591, USA. T. +19146318990. E-mail: secretariat@wango.org.
UN Affairs Office 866 United Nations Plaza, Suite 529, New York NY 10017, USA. T. +12128268999. Fax +12128263352. E-mail: unoffice@wango.org.
URL: http://www.wango.org/

History 1 Aug 2000. Former names and other names: *World Association of United Nations Non-Governmental Organizations (WAUNNGO)* – former (1 Aug 2000 to Oct 2000); *World Association of NGOs* – alias. Registration: 501(c)(3) organization, No/ID: EIN: 13-4142142, Start date: 2001, USA, New York. **Aims** Serve member organizations; strengthen and encourage the NGO sector as a whole; increase public understanding of the NGO community; provide ways and support needed for NGOs to connect, partner and multiply their contributions to solve humanity's basic problems. **Structure** International Council; International Executive Committee; Secretariat. **Languages** English, French, Spanish. **Staff** 4.00 FTE, paid; 1.00 FTE, voluntary. **Finance** Sources: grants; members' dues; private foundations. **Activities** Awards/prizes/competitions; events/meetings; projects/programmes. **Events** *Symposium* New York, NY (USA) 2016, *Africa Conference* Nairobi (Kenya) 2010, *Africa Conference* Accra (Ghana) 2008, *Annual Conference* Toronto, ON (Canada) 2007, *World Congress of NGOs* Toronto, ON (Canada) 2007. **Publications** *WANGO E-News* (12 a year). Codes of ethics; conference proceedings; handbook.

Members Organization (Regular; Senior; Affiliate) and Individual (Associate; Fellow). Individuals and organizations in 46 countries and territories:
Armenia, Australia, Bahamas, Bangladesh, Belgium, Canada, Dominican Rep, Ecuador, Finland, France, Georgia, Germany, Ghana, Hong Kong, Hungary, India, Iran Islamic Rep, Italy, Kenya, Korea Rep, Lebanon, Liberia, Malawi, Malaysia, Mauritius, Nepal, Netherlands, Niger, Nigeria, Norway, Philippines, Puerto Rico, South Africa, Spain, St Vincent-Grenadines, Switzerland, Taiwan, Tajikistan, Tanzania UR, Thailand, Trinidad-Tobago, Türkiye, Uganda, UK, USA, Vietnam.

IGO Relations Cooperates with (2): *United States Agency for International Development (USAID)*; *World Intellectual Property Organization (WIPO, #21593)*. **NGO Relations** Partner of (3): Cecilia Attias Foundation for Women; *Global Forum on Human Settlements (GFHS, #10372)*; *World Information Transfer (WIT, #21583)*. Links with: *Universal Peace Federation (UPF International, #20681)* [2023.02.23/XD8357/C]

♦ World Association of Nuclear Operators (WANO) 21168

CEO Level 35, 25 Canada Square, Canary Wharf, London, E14 5LQ, UK. T. +442074789200.
URL: http://www.wano.info/

History Founded 9 May 1989, UK, on adoption of a Charter. Registered under UK law. **Aims** Maximize safety and reliability of the operation of *nuclear power* plants by exchanging information and encouraging communication, comparison and emulation among members. **Structure** General Assembly (every 2 years). President; Chairman. Regional Centres (4) in Atlanta GA (USA), Moscow (Russia), Paris (France), Tokyo (Japan), each a legal entity with its own Governing Board and supporting staff of about 10. Governing Board (meets 3 times a year) comprising Chairman and one other member of each regional Governing Board, serviced by Coordinating Centre in London (UK). **Languages** English. **Staff** About 20 full-time in each regional centre and 13 in coordinating centre. **Finance** Sources: members' dues. **Activities** Major programmes: exchange of information on nuclear events via *WANO Network*, Peer Reviews; exchange visits among members of each centre and between centres; collection of good practices in all centres; collection of performance indicators for all member nuclear power plants. **Events** *Biennial General Meeting* Prague (Czechia) 2022, *Biennial General Meeting* London (UK) 2019, *Seminar on Gori-2 Nuclear Power Plant* Busan (Korea Rep) 2017, *Biennial General Meeting* Gyeongju (Korea Rep) 2017, *Seminar* Busan (Korea Rep) 2016. **Publications** *Inside WANO* (3 a year) – magazine. Reports. Information Services: Database of event reports, good practices and performance indicators collected from members.

Members Ordinary (one per country where there is a nuclear operator), Joint (140 nuclear utilities), Associate (4 regional centres). Members ("A" indicates Atlanta Centre, "M" Moscow Centre, "P" Paris Centre, "T" Tokyo Centre) in 35 countries and territories:
Argentina (P), Armenia (M), Belgium (P), Brazil (AP), Bulgaria (M), Canada (A), China (PT), Cuba (M), Czechia (M), Finland (MP), France (P), Germany (P), Hungary (M), India (T), Iran Islamic Rep (M), Japan (T), Kazakhstan (M), Korea Rep (T), Lithuania (M), Mexico (A), Netherlands (P), Pakistan (AT), Poland (M), Romania (A), Russia (M), Slovakia (M), Slovenia (P), South Africa (A), Spain (P), Sweden (P), Switzerland (P), Taiwan (T), UK (P), Ukraine (M), USA (A).

IGO Relations Affiliated with: *International Atomic Energy Agency (IAEA, #12294)*. **NGO Relations** Formal contacts with: *Union of the Electricity Industry – Eurelectric (#20379)*. In liaison with technical committees of: *International Organization for Standardization (ISO, #14473)*. Supports: *World Nuclear University (WNU, #21677)*. [2015/XD2065/C]

♦ World Association for Online Education (WAOE) 21169

Pres Nomi-cho 5-26, Takatsuki, Osaka, 569-0077 Japan.
Main Website: http://www.waoe.org/

History 1998. **Aims** Advance development, implementation, evaluation and administration of online education. **Structure** Virtual organization; Officers. **Languages** English. **Staff** None. **Finance** Privately supported. **Activities** Networking/liaising. **Members** Widely distributed geographically. Membership countries not specified. [2021.06.08/XD9482/D]

♦ World Association of Opinion and Marketing Research Professionals – The World Association of Research Professionals / see World Association of Research Professionals (#21182)
♦ World Association of Pastoral Care and Counselling / see International Council on Pastoral Care and Counselling (#13059)

♦ World Association of Perinatal Medicine (WAPM) 21170

Pres Cumhuriyet cad 30/5, Elmadağ (Divan Otel Yani), Taksim, Istanbul/Istanbul, Türkiye. T. +905424428736. E-mail: office@worldperinatal.org – wapminfo@gmail.com.
SG address not obtained.
Main Website: https://www.worldperinatal.org/

History 11 Apr 1988, Rome (Italy). Founded during 11th Congress of *European Association of Perinatal Medicine (EAPM, #06148)*, when constitution was adopted. New name and new constitution suggested, Oct 1988, Brazil, at 12th Congress of *Fédération Internationale de Gynécologie et d'Obstétrique (FIGO, #09638)*. Current name and new constitution and by-laws adopted at 1st World Congress, Tokyo (Japan). Current constitution approved by the General Assembly, 16 Sep 2003, Osaka (Japan). Former names and other names: *World Federation of Perinatal Medicine (WFPM)* – former. **Aims** Promote research in all aspects of perinatal medicine in order to attain a higher level of physical and mental health for women, mothers and their fetal patients and children. **Structure** General Assembly (every 2 years at World Congress); Council; Committees (4). **Languages** English. **Staff** 1.00 FTE, paid. **Finance** Sources: members' dues. **Activities** Awards/prizes/competitions; events/meetings; networking/liaising; training/education. **Events** *World Congress of Perinatal Medicine* Milan (Italy) 2023, *World Congress of Perinatal Medicine in Developing Countries* Punta Cana (Dominican Rep) 2022, *World Congress of Perinatal Medicine* 2021, *World Congress of Perinatal Medicine* Istanbul (Turkey) 2019, *World Congress of Perinatal Medicine* Belgrade (Serbia) 2017. **Publications** *Journal of Perinatal Medicine* – official journal.

Members Individuals, groups and national societies in 105 countries and territories:
Albania, Algeria, Andorra, Argentina, Armenia, Australia, Austria, Bahamas, Belgium, Bosnia-Herzegovina, Brazil, Bulgaria, Cambodia, Canada, Chile, China, Colombia, Congo Brazzaville, Congo DR, Costa Rica, Croatia, Cuba, Cyprus, Czechia, Denmark, Dominican Rep, Ecuador, Egypt, El Salvador, Estonia, Ethiopia, Finland, France, Georgia, Germany, Greece, Guatemala, Hong Kong, Hungary, Iceland, India, Indonesia, Ireland, Israel, Italy, Japan, Jordan, Korea DPR, Korea Rep, Latvia, Lebanon, Libya, Lithuania, Luxembourg, Malta, Mexico, Monaco, Morocco, Myanmar, Nepal, Netherlands, New Zealand, Niger, North Macedonia, Norway, Pakistan, Panama, Paraguay, Peru, Philippines, Poland, Portugal, Romania, Russia, San Marino, Saudi Arabia, Senegal, Serbia, Singapore, Slovakia, Slovenia, Somalia, South Africa, Spain, Sri Lanka, Sudan, Sweden, Switzerland, Syrian AR, Taiwan, Thailand, Timor-Leste, Togo, Tunisia, Türkiye, Uganda, UK, Ukraine, United Arab Emirates, Uruguay, USA, Venezuela, Yemen, Zambia, Zimbabwe.

NGO Relations Instrumental in setting up (1): *International Academy of Perinatal Medicine (IAPM, #11568)*. Sister societies include: Ian Donald Inter-University School of Ultrasound in Obstetrics and Gynecology; *International Society – The Fetus as a Patient (#15118)*; *International Cooperation Agency for Maternal and Infant Health (Matres Mundi International)*. [2022/XD6328/**C**]

♦ World Association for Personality Psychology (WAPP) 21171

Sec address not obtained.
Registered Address address not obtained.
URL: https://www.perpsy.org/

History Founded 2013, Stellenbosch (South Africa). Registration: Start date: 10 Oct 2013, Netherlands. **Aims** Foster and develop empirical and theoretical personality psychology worldwide. **Structure** Executive Committee. **Languages** English. **Finance** Sources: members' dues. **Activities** Awards/prizes/competitions; events/meetings; knowledge management/information dissemination; research/documentation. **Events** *World Conference on Personality* Hanoi (Vietnam) 2019, *World Conference on Personality* Rio de Janeiro (Brazil) 2016, *World Conference on Personality* Stellenbosch (South Africa) 2013. **Publications** *International Journal of Personality Psychology (IJPP)* – online. [2020.01.15/XM8617/**C**]

♦ World Association for Person-Centered and Experiential Psychotherapy and Counseling (WAPCEPC) 21172

Association mondiale pour le counseling et la psychothérapie centrés-sur-la-personne – Associação Mundial de Counselling e Psicoterapia Centrados-na-Pessoa (AMCPCP) – Weltverband für Personzentrierte und Experienzielle Psychotherapie und Beratung (WAPCEPC)

Chair Diefenbachgasse 5/2, 1150 Vienna, Austria. Fax +441989763901. E-mail: chair@pce-world.org – office@pce-world.org.
URL: http://www.pce-world.org/

History 8 Jul 1997, Lisbon (Portugal). Statutes agreed by consensus at General Assembly, 2000; amended at General Assembly, 2006. Most recent bylaws adopted, July 2008; amended: 2020, 2022. Former names and other names: *World Association for Person-Centred Counselling and Psychotherapy (WAPCCP)* – former. Registration: Gemeinnütziger Verein, Start date: 2021, Austria. **Aims** Further cooperation among person-centred associations, institutes and individuals in the field of psychotherapy and counselling. **Structure** General Assembly (every 2 years); Executive Board; Scientific Committee. Chapters: *Network of the European Associations for Person-Centred and Experiential Psychotherapy and Counselling (PCE Europe, #17013)*; Australia and New Zealand; Maghreb; North America. **Languages** English. **Staff** 0.50 FTE, paid; 9.00 FTE, voluntary. **Finance** Sources: members' dues. **Events** *World PCE Conference* Athens (Greece) 2024, *World PCE Conference* Copenhagen (Denmark) 2022, *World PCE Conference* Auckland (New Zealand) 2021, *World PCE Conference* Auckland (New Zealand) 2020, *World PCE Conference* Vienna (Austria) 2018. **Publications** *Person-Centered and Experiential Psychotherapies* (4 a year); *WA Newsletter* (3 a year).

Members Individuals and associations in 33 countries and territories:
Argentina, Australia, Austria, Belgium, Brazil, Canada, China, Cyprus, Czechia, Denmark, France, Germany, Greece, Hong Kong, Hungary, India, Ireland, Israel, Italy, Japan, Luxembourg, Mexico, Netherlands, New Zealand, Norway, Poland, Portugal, Slovakia, Spain, Sweden, Switzerland, UK, USA. [2022.10.30/XD7585/**D**]

♦ World Association for Person-Centred Counselling and Psychotherapy / see World Association for Person-Centered and Experiential Psychotherapy and Counseling (#21172)

♦ World Association for Political Economy (WAPE) 21173

Secretariat Rm 303, Hongwa Bldg, 777 Guoding Rd, 200433 Shanghai, China. E-mail: wapember@vip.163.com – hpjjx@vip.163.com.
Sec address not obtained.
URL: http://www.wape2015.com/

History 24 Dec 2004, Hong Kong. **Aims** Pass down, develop and carry forward Marxian economics; utilize modern Marxian economics to analyse and study world economy, reveal the law of development and its mechanism, offer proper policies to promote the economic and social improvement on national and global levels, so as to improve the welfare of people worldwide. **Structure** General Assembly; Council; Secretariat; Advisory Committee. **Languages** Chinese, English. **Staff** Part-time, voluntary. **Finance** Financed by: donations; universities; research institutes. Budget (annual): US$ 100,000. **Activities** Awards/prizes/competitions. **Events** *Forum* Johannesburg (South Africa) 2015, *Forum* Hanoi (Vietnam) 2014, *Forum* Florianópolis (Brazil) 2013, *Forum* Mexico City (Mexico) 2012, *Forum* Amherst, MA (USA) 2011. **Publications** *Journal of Economics of Shanghai School* (4 a year) in Chinese; *World Review of Political Economy* (4 a year) in English.

Members Full in 32 countries:
Argentina, Australia, Austria, Belgium, Brazil, Bulgaria, Canada, China, Congo Brazzaville, Cuba, France, Germany, Greece, India, Israel, Italy, Japan, Korea Rep, Laos, Luxembourg, Mexico, Netherlands, Peru, Portugal, Russia, South Africa, Sri Lanka, Türkiye, UK, Ukraine, USA, Vietnam. [2015.06.29/XM3596/**D**]

♦ World Association for Positive Psychotherapy / see World Association for Positive and Transcultural Psychotherapy (#21174)

♦ World Association for Positive and Transcultural Psychotherapy (WAPP) 21174

Chair Luisenstrasse 28, 65185 Wiesbaden, Germany. T. +496114503440. Fax +496114503424. E-mail: wapp@positum.org.
URL: http://www.positum.org/

History 1994, Wiesbaden (Germany). Former names and other names: *International Centre for Positive Psychotherapy (ICPP)* – former (1994 to 2008); *International Centre for Positive Psychotherapy, Transcultural Family Therapy and Psychosomatic Medicine* – former (1994 to 2008); *International Centre for Positive Family Therapy and Positive Psychotherapy* – former (1994 to 2008); *World Association for Positive Psychotherapy (WAPP)* – former (2008 to 2016). Registration: Start date: 1996, Germany. **Aims** Promote physical, *mental*, social and spiritual *health* of individuals, families and groups; promote theory, method and practice of Positive Psychotherapy and its application under the transcultural and interdisciplinary point of view; develop programmes in the field of prevention and rehabilitation regarding families and members. **Structure** Board. **Languages** English, Russian. **Activities** Events/meetings; training/education. **Events** *World Congress* Crete (Greece) 2022, *World Congress* Kemer (Turkey) 2019, *World Congress* Antalya (Turkey) 2014, *World congress* Istanbul (Turkey) 2010, *World congress* Famagusta (Cyprus) 2007. **Publications** *Positum* (2 a year). Primary books (27 to date), translated into 24 languages.

Members Organizations in 20 countries:
Armenia, Austria, Azerbaijan, Belarus, Bolivia, Bulgaria, China, Cyprus, Ethiopia, Georgia, Germany, Kosovo, Latvia, North Macedonia, Poland, Romania, Russia, Türkiye, UK, Ukraine.

Individuals in 41 countries:
Albania, Armenia, Austria, Azerbaijan, Belarus, Bolivia, Bulgaria, Canada, China, Cyprus, Denmark, Estonia, Ethiopia, Finland, France, Georgia, Germany, Greece, India, Kazakhstan, Korea Rep, Kosovo, Lithuania, Luxembourg, Moldova, Mongolia, Netherlands, North Macedonia, Norway, Poland, Romania, Russia, South Africa, Spain, Sweden, Switzerland, Türkiye, UK, Ukraine, United Arab Emirates, USA.

NGO Relations Instrumental in setting up (1): *European Federation of Centres for Positive Psychotherapy (EFCPP, #07071)*. Board member of: *European Association for Psychotherapy (EAP, #06176)*. [2022.05.04/XE3904/**E**]

♦ World Association of Press Councils (WAPC) 21175

SG Halaskargazi Cad No 110, 7 Osmanbey, 34255 Istanbul/Istanbul, Türkiye. T. +902122249513. Fax +902122249514. E-mail: thewapc@gmail.com – berguna@tm.net.my.
URL: https://www.thewapc.com/tiki-index.php

History 1992. Also referred to as *World Association of Press – Media Councils*. **Aims** Strengthen implementation of press freedoms; ensure members of media pursue their profession as "responsible journalists". **Structure** General Meetings. **Languages** English. **Finance** Members' dues. **Activities** Advocacy/lobbying/activism. **Events** *International Conference* Tanzania UR 2004, *International Conference* Dhaka (Bangladesh) 2001.

Members Press councils in 16 countries and territories:
Azerbaijan, Bangladesh, Eswatini, India, Kenya, Malawi, Nepal, Northern Cyprus, Pakistan, Sri Lanka, Tanzania UR, Türkiye, Uganda, USA, Zambia, Zimbabwe. [2022/XD7743/**D**]

♦ World Association of Press – Media Councils / see World Association of Press Councils (#21175)
♦ World Association for Prevention of Drug and Alcohol Abuse (inactive)
♦ World Association of Probiotics, Prebiotics, Postbiotics in Pediatrics (unconfirmed)
♦ World Association for Professional Training in Tourism / see World Association for Hospitality and Tourism Education and Training (#21144)
♦ World Association for the Promotion of Culture (inactive)

♦ World Association for the Protection of Tangible and Intangible Cultural Heritage (WATCH) 21176

Associazione Mondiale per la Protezione del Patrimonio Culturale, Tangibile ed Intangibile in Tempo di Conflitti Armati

Registered Office Via Francesco Dall'Ongaro 62, 00152 Rome RM, Italy. T. +39658334359. Fax +3965819114. E-mail: info@eyeonculture.net.
URL: http://www.eyeonculture.net/

History Full title in English: *World Association for the Protection of Tangible and Intangible Cultural Heritage in Times of Armed Conflicts*. **Aims** Enhance, assist and support all activities aimed at safeguarding cultural heritage from the dangers cause by armed conflicts. **Structure** Annual General Assembly; Board of Trustees. **Languages** English. **Activities** Advocacy/lobbying/activism; events/meetings. **Members** Categories Founder; Ordinary; Supporting; Honorary. Membership countries not specified. **IGO Relations** Partner of: *International Centre for the Study of the Preservation and Restoration of Cultural Property (ICCROM, #12521)*. Observer at meetings of: International Committee of *Convention for the Protection of Cultural Property in the Event of Armed Conflict (The Hague Convention, 1954, 1954)*. **NGO Relations** National organizations. Member of: *World Heritage Watch (WHW)*. [2017.12.06/XM3840/**E**]

♦ World Association for the Protection of Tangible and Intangible Cultural Heritage in Times of Armed Conflicts / see World Association for the Protection of Tangible and Intangible Cultural Heritage (#21176)

♦ World Association of Psychoanalysis (WAP) 21177

Association mondiale de psychanalyse (AMP) – Asociación Mundial de Psicoanalisis – Associazione Mondiale di Psicoanalisi

Pres address not obtained. E-mail: amp.wapol@gmail.com.
URL: http://www.wapol.org/

History Jan 1992. Former names and other names: *Association Mondiale de Psychanalyse du Champ freudien* – alias. Registration: France. **Aims** Promote Lacan-oriented psychoanalysis. **Languages** English, French, Italian, Spanish. **Finance** Sources: members' dues. **Events** *Congress* Paris (France) 2022, *International Congress* Buenos Aires (Argentina) 2020, *Congrès International* Barcelona (Spain) 2018, *Congrès International* Rio de Janeiro (Brazil) 2016, *Congrès International* Paris (France) 2014.

Members Full in 43 countries:
Algeria, Argentina, Armenia, Australia, Austria, Belarus, Belgium, Bolivia, Brazil, Canada, Chile, Colombia, Cuba, Denmark, Ecuador, France, Germany, Greece, Guatemala, Hungary, Israel, Italy, Japan, Korea Rep, Lebanon, Mexico, Moldova, Monaco, Nicaragua, Peru, Poland, Portugal, Romania, Russia, Slovenia, Spain, Sweden, Switzerland, UK, Ukraine, USA, Venezuela, Vietnam.

Consultative Status Consultative status granted from: *ECOSOC (#05331)* (Special). **NGO Relations** *EuroFédération de psychanalyse (EFP)*; *Federación Americana de Psicoanalisis de la Orientación Lacaniana (FAPOL)*. [2020/XD4315/**C**]

♦ World Association for Psychosocial Rehabilitation (WAPR) 21178

Association mondiale pour la réadaptation psychosociale (AMRP) – Asociación Mundial para la Rehabilitación Psicosocial

Pres "USHAKIRANA" 406-A/10, 7TH Main II, Block Jayanagar, Bangalore, Karnataka 560011, Bangalore KARNATAKA 560011, India. Fax +919449523983 – +919663002121.
URL: http://www.wapr.info/

History 18 Oct 1986, Vienne (France). Founded as *Psychosocial Rehabilitation International*, when statutes were adopted; extensive planning meetings having taken place, Apr 1979 and Jan 1980, Geneva (Switzerland), under the auspices of *International Committee Against Mental Illness (ICAMI, #12742)* at the offices of the World Health Organization, where a number of key international agencies – International Labour Office, Council of Europe – were represented. In 1980 an informal organization, *World Rehabilitation Association for the Psycho-Socially Disabled (WRAPSD)*, was set up, being responsible for the founding congress of the present organization. Legal recognition in: Chennai (India); Edinburgh (UK); New York State (USA). Registration: France; No/ID: G87433769, Start date: Dec 2015, Spain. **Aims** Disseminate principles and practices of psychosocial rehabilitation. **Structure** Assembly (at least every 2 years); Board; Executive Committee. **Languages** English, French, Spanish. **Staff** Voluntary. **Finance** Sources: contributions; government support; members' dues. Supported by: *International Committee Against Mental Illness (ICAMI, #12742)*; *WHO (#20950)*; *World Rehabilitation Fund (WRF, #21749)*. **Activities** Guidance/assistance/consulting; networking/liaising. **Events** *World Congress* Abu Dhabi (United Arab Emirates) 2021, *World Congress* Madrid (Spain) 2018, *Abu Dhabi International Congress* Abu Dhabi (United Arab Emirates) 2017, *Asia Pacific Meeting* Bangkok (Thailand) 2017, *European Conference* Cesena (Italy) 2017. **Publications** *WAPR Bulletin* (4 a year) – electronic. Editorial; educational activities; proceedings of regional symposia; other data.

Members National secretaries in 85 countries:
Argentina, Austria, Belgium, Bhutan, Botswana, Brazil, Burkina Faso, Burundi, Cambodia, Cameroon, Canada, Chile, Colombia, Congo DR, Costa Rica, Cuba, Cyprus, Denmark, Dominican Rep, Ecuador, Egypt, El Salvador, Equatorial Guinea, Ethiopia, France, Georgia, Germany, Greece, Guatemala, Honduras, Hungary, India, Indonesia, Ireland, Israel, Italy, Kenya, Korea Rep, Lebanon, Liberia, Lithuania, Luxembourg, Madagascar, Malaysia, Mali, Mauritius, Mexico, Morocco, Mozambique, Myanmar, Nepal, Netherlands, Nicaragua, Niger, Nigeria, Norway, Pakistan, Panama, Paraguay, Peru, Philippines, Poland, Portugal, Romania, Russia, Rwanda, Senegal, Serbia, Singapore, Slovenia, South Africa, Spain, Sri Lanka, Sudan, Sweden, Switzerland, Tanzania UR, Thailand, Tunisia, Türkiye, UK, Uruguay, USA, Venezuela, Vietnam.

Consultative Status Consultative status granted from: *ILO (#11123)* (Special List). **IGO Relations** Accredited by (1): *United Nations Office at Vienna (UNOV, #20604)*. Associated with Department of Global Communications of the United Nations. **NGO Relations** Member of (2): *Conference of Non-Governmental Organizations in Consultative Relationship with the United Nations (CONGO, #04635)*; *Standing Committee of Presidents of International NGOs Concerned with Mental Health Issues (no recent information)*. Instrumental in setting up (1): *Asian Federation of Psychiatric Associations (AFPA, #01470)*. In addition, foundation also sponsored by: *ASEAN Federation for Psychiatry and Mental Health (AFPMH, #01184)*; national organizations; several French ministries. [2022/XD2756/**B**]

♦ World Association of Public Employment Services (WAPES) 21179

Association mondiale des services d'emploi publics (AMSEP) – Asociación Mundial de Servicios Públicos de Empleo (AMSPE)

Exec Sec VDAB Bld, Bd de l'Empereur 11, 1000 Brussels, Belgium. T. +3222357250. Fax +3222357259. E-mail: management.assistant@wapes.org – wapes@wapes.org.
URL: http://www.wapes.org/

History May 1989. Founded following initiatives by Directors-General of employment services in Canada, France, Germany, Netherlands, Sweden and USA and of ILO. Registration: Banque-Carrefour des Entreprises, No/ID: 0827.036.846, Start date: 29 Jun 2010, Belgium. **Aims** Encourage contacts among member institutions; promote exchange of information and experience on members' activities; encourage cooperation of more developed bodies with those less developed; provide services of common interest; stimulate technical assistance to members. **Structure** General Assembly (annual); Managing Board; Executive Committee; Executive Secretariat in Brussels (Belgium). **Languages** English, French, Spanish. **Staff** 3.00 FTE, paid. **Finance** Sources: members' dues. **Activities** Events/meetings; guidance/assistance/consulting; knowledge management/information dissemination; research/documentation; training/education. **Events** *Conference* Ankara (Turkey) 2019, *Conference* Siem Reap (Cambodia) 2019, *Workshop on Organisational Learning* Stockholm (Sweden) 2019, *World Congress and General Assembly* Marrakech (Morocco) 2018, *Workshop on Social Protection and Roles of Public Employment Services* Seoul (Korea Rep) 2017. **Publications** Reports; articles; studies.

Members National public or governmental bodies representing public employment services in 78 countries:
Algeria, Argentina, Armenia, Austria, Azerbaijan, Belgium, Benin, Bosnia-Herzegovina, Bulgaria, Burkina Faso, Cambodia, Cameroon, Canada, Cape Verde, Central African Rep, Chad, Chile, China, Congo Brazzaville, Congo DR, Côte d'Ivoire, Croatia, Cyprus, Czechia, Denmark, Djibouti, Dominican Rep, Estonia, Finland, France, Gabon, Germany, Guatemala, Guinea, Honduras, Hungary, Iceland, India, Israel, Italy, Japan, Kenya, Korea Rep, Luxembourg, Malaysia, Mali, Malta, Mauritania, Moldova, Montenegro, Morocco, Netherlands, Niger, North Macedonia, Norway, Panama, Peru, Philippines, Portugal, Romania, Russia, Saudi Arabia, Senegal, Slovenia, Spain, Sri Lanka, Sweden, Switzerland, Thailand, Togo, Tunisia, Türkiye, UK, Ukraine, Uruguay, USA, Vietnam, Zimbabwe.

Consultative Status Consultative status granted from: *ILO (#11123)* (Special List). [2021.02.28/XC0019/**C**]

♦ World Association for Public Opinion Research (WAPOR) 21180

Association mondiale de recherches sur l'opinion publique (AMROP) – Asociación Mundial para el Estudio de la Opinión Pública – Weltverband für Öffentliche Meinungs-Forschung

Gen Sec Department of Political Science, Univ of Nebraska-Lincoln, 1019 Oldfather Hall, Lincoln NE 68588-0367, USA. T. +14024727720. E-mail: waporoffice@gmail.com.
URL: http://wapor.org/

History Founded 1947, Williamstown MA (USA), at 2nd International Meeting for Public Opinion Research. **Aims** Establish and promote contacts between persons and institutions in the field of qualitative and quantitative scientific research on opinions, attitudes and behaviour of people in the various countries of the world; improve and protect the use of such research in national and international affairs; assist in the promotion of development of public opinion research in the emerging democracies of the world. **Structure** Conference (annual); Executive Council; Regional representatives (27). **Languages** English. **Staff** 0.50 FTE, paid. **Finance** Sources: meeting proceeds; members' dues. Other sources: journal subscriptions. **Activities** Awards/prizes/competitions; events/meetings. **Events** *Annual Conference* Lincoln, NE (USA) 2020, *Annual Conference* Toronto, ON (Canada) 2019, *Annual Conference* Marrakech (Morocco) 2018, *Annual Conference* Lisbon (Portugal) 2017, *Annual Conference* Austin, TX (USA) 2016. **Publications** *International Journal of Public Opinion Research* (4 a year); *WAPOR Newsletter* (4 a year). *WAPOR Directory of Members* – online, members only. Code of Professional Ethics and Practices.

Members Individuals (about 480) using sample surveys and related social science methods in 64 countries and territories:
Argentina, Armenia, Australia, Austria, Bangladesh, Barbados, Belarus, Belgium, Bosnia-Herzegovina, Brazil, Canada, Chile, China, Congo DR, Costa Rica, Croatia, Cyprus, Czechia, Denmark, Egypt, El Salvador, Estonia, Finland, France, Germany, Greece, Hong Kong, Hungary, India, Indonesia, Iran Islamic Rep, Ireland, Israel, Italy, Japan, Kazakhstan, Korea Rep, Lithuania, Luxembourg, Malaysia, Mexico, Netherlands, New Zealand, Nigeria, Norway, Philippines, Poland, Portugal, Romania, Russia, Serbia, Singapore, Slovenia, South Africa, Spain, Sweden, Switzerland, Thailand, Tunisia, Türkiye, UK, Ukraine, USA, Venezuela.

IGO Relations *UNESCO (#20322)*. **NGO Relations** Member of: *International Science Council (ISC, #14796)*. Associate member of: *International Association for Media and Communication Research (IAMCR, #12022)*. Represented in: *International Federation of Social Science Organizations (IFSSO, #13543)*. Has organized joint conferences with: *International Association of Political Consultants (IAPC, #12094)*; *International Communication Association (ICA, #12814)*; *International Society of Political Psychology (ISPP, #15374)*; *International Sociological Association (ISA, #15553)*; *World Association of Research Professionals (ESOMAR, #21182)*. [2022/XC3462/v/**C**]

♦ World Association of Publishers, Manufacturers and Distributors of Educational Materials / see Worlddidac Association (#21361)

♦ World Association of Radiopharmaceutical and Molecular Therapy (WARMTH) 21181

Treas Dept of Nuclear Medicine, Max Heart and Vascular Inst/Superspeciality Hosp, 2 Press Enclave Road, Saket, Delhi, DELHI, India.
URL: https://warmth.org/

History 1998, Berlin (Germany), as a subsidiary of *World Federation of Nuclear Medicine and Biology (WFNMB, #21467)*. Original title: *World Radiopharmaceutical Therapy Council (WRPTC)*. Restructured under current title, Nov 2009, when constitution was adopted. **Aims** Bring together professionals working with radionuclides for therapeutic uses. **Structure** General Assembly. Governing Body, comprising President, President-Elect, Secretary, Treasurer, Past-Chairman and 13 members. **Finance** Sources: members' dues. **Activities** Organizes: International Conference on Radiopharmaceutical Therapy (ICRT); International Symposium on Radiopharmaceutical Therapy (ISRT). **Events** *International Symposium on Radiopharmaceutical Therapy* Delhi (India) 2021, *International Symposium on Radiopharmaceutical Therapy* Delhi (India) 2020, *International Symposium on Radiopharmaceutical Therapy* Helsinki (Finland) 2018, *International Conference* Vienna (Austria) 2017, *International Conference* Kochi (India) 2016. **Members** Ordinary; Associate; Corporate. Membership countries not specified. [2018/XQ5352/**C**]

♦ World Association of Reproductive Medicine (no recent information)

♦ World Association of Research Professionals (ESOMAR) 21182

Main Office Atlas Arena, Azië Bldg – 5th Floor, Hoogoorddreef 5, 1101 BA Amsterdam, Netherlands. T. +31206642141. Fax +31205897885. E-mail: info@esomar.org.
URL: http://www.esomar.org/

History Founded 17 Sep 1948, Amsterdam (Netherlands), as *European Society for Opinion and Marketing Research (ESOMAR) – Association européenne pour les études d'opinion et de marketing – Asociación Europea para la Investigación de Mercados y de Opinion – Europäische Gesellschaft für Meinungs- und Marketing-Forschung*. Previous full title: *World Association of Opinion and Marketing Research Professionals – The World Association of Research Professionals (ESOMAR)*. Registered in accordance with Swiss Civil Code. EU Transparency Register: 29952722795-07. **Aims** Bring together the research community to share knowledge and safeguard the future of the industry by promoting the value of marketing, and social and opinion research, based on the common principles of ethical practice and professional development. **Structure** General Meeting (annual, at Congress); International Council; Management Team; National representatives liaise with individual members. Head Office in Amsterdam (Netherlands). **Languages** English, French, German, Spanish. **Staff** 32.00 FTE, paid. **Finance** Members' dues. **Activities** Networking/liaising; events/meetings; standards/guidelines; guidance/assistance/consulting; capacity building. **Events** *Insights Festival Seminar* Amsterdam (Netherlands) 2021, *Asia Pacific Conference* Amsterdam (Netherlands) 2020, *Annual Congress* Toronto, ON (Canada) 2020, *Annual Congress* Edinburgh (UK) 2019, *Global Qualitative Conference* Berlin (Germany) 2018. **Publications** *Research World* (12 a year) – international reference magazine. *The ESOMAR 2006 Excellence Book*; *The ESOMAR Best Practice Book*; *The ESOMAR Directory of Market Research Organisations – vols I and II*; *The ESOMAR Handbook of Market Research*; *What is Market Research ?* – guide book. ESOMAR Industry Reports – Industry and Prices Studies.

Members Individuals (over 4,900) in 99 countries and territories:
Argentina, Australia, Austria, Azerbaijan, Bahrain, Bangladesh, Barbados, Belgium, Bolivia, Bosnia-Herzegovina, Brazil, Bulgaria, Canada, Chile, China, Colombia, Costa Rica, Côte d'Ivoire, Croatia, Cyprus, Czechia, Denmark, Dominican Rep, Ecuador, Egypt, El Salvador, Estonia, Fiji, Finland, France, Georgia, Germany, Greece, Guatemala, Honduras, Hong Kong, Hungary, Iceland, India, Indonesia, Iran Islamic Rep, Ireland, Israel, Italy, Japan, Jordan, Kazakhstan, Kenya, Korea DPR, Korea Rep, Kuwait, Kyrgyzstan, Latvia, Lebanon, Lithuania, Luxembourg, Malaysia, Malta, Mauritius, Mexico, Morocco, Netherlands, New Zealand, Nicaragua, Nigeria, North Macedonia, Norway, Pakistan, Panama, Paraguay, Peru, Philippines, Poland, Portugal, Puerto Rico, Qatar, Romania, Russia, Saudi Arabia, Serbia, Singapore, Slovakia, Slovenia, South Africa, Spain, Sri Lanka, Sweden, Switzerland, Thailand, Trinidad-Tobago, Tunisia, Türkiye, UK, Ukraine, United Arab Emirates, Uruguay, USA, Venezuela, Vietnam.

NGO Relations Cooperates with: Advertising Research Foundation (in USA); *International Chamber of Commerce (ICC, #12534)*; *World Association for Public Opinion Research (WAPOR, #21180)*; *World Federation of Advertisers (WFA, #21407)*; a number of national organizations active in the field. Instrumental in setting up: *Foundation for Information (FI, no recent information)*; *World Industry Network (WIN, inactive)*. [2017/XD0853/tv/**D**]

♦ World Association of Sarcoidosis and other Granulomatous Disorders (WASOG) 21183

Sec Lung Research Lab L4 01, Karolinska Institute, SE-171 76 Stockholm, Sweden. T. +46851775117. Fax +46851775451.
Pres Emeritus Pulmonary Medicine, 1200 N State St, GNH 11900, Los Angeles CA 90033, USA.
URL: http://www.wasog.org/

History 1958, London (UK), as *International Committee on Sarcoidosis*, during 1st Congress. Reconstituted under current title at World Congress, 1987, Milan (Italy), when numbering of congresses recommenced at 1. **Aims** Bring together investigators in biological and medical sciences and others interested in and dedicated to advancing and promoting knowledge of sarcoidosis and other granulomatous diseases worldwide; amalgamate existing sarcoidosis societies and provide an international link and forum for national societies founded in the future; foster, facilitate and carry out research and clinical activities in the field, focusing attention on damage to brain, heart, lungs, eyes and skin; provide a helpline for patients. **Structure** Executive Committee, comprising President, 2 Vice Presidents, General Secretary, Treasurer, Archivist and 10 members. **Languages** English. **Activities** Members meet every 2 years to keep abreast of advances and hypotheses. **Events** *International Conference on Sarcoidosis and Interstitial Lung Diseases* Yokohama (Japan) 2019, *International Conference on Diffuse Parenchymal Lung Diseases* Gdansk (Poland) 2016, *International Conference on Diffuse Lung Diseases* Sao Paulo (Brazil) 2015, *Biennial Meeting* Kusadasi (Turkey) 2014, *Conference* Maastricht (Netherlands) 2011. **Publications** *Sarcoidosis, Vasculitis and Diffuse Lung Diseases* (3 a year) – official journal, formerly 'Sarcoidosis' and 'Sarcoidosis and other Granulomatous Disorders'. **Members** Physicians (over 300) in 30 countries. Membership countries not specified. [2013/XD9277/v/**D**]

♦ World Association for the School as an Instrument of Peace 21184

Association mondiale pour l'école instrument de paix (EIP) – Asociación Mundial por la Escuela Instrumento de Paz – Associazione Mondiale per la Scuola Strumento di Pace

SG Rue du Simplon 5, 1207 Geneva, Switzerland. T. +41227352422 – +41227364452. Fax +41227364863.
URL: https://www.portail-eip.org

History 19 Sep 1967, Geneva (Switzerland). Registration: Switzerland. **Aims** Promote human rights and peace in formal and informal education, notably by: encouraging cooperative behaviour and peace among people, groups and nations; non-violent resolution of conflict; encouraging personal development and expansion favourizing acceptance of others; transmitting the knowledge required to improve understanding of peace and human rights in the educational field. Combat all forms of inequity and injustice, sources of breakdown and exclusion; be aware of the role which the school should play in the service of humanity so that children of today and citizens of tomorrow benefit from such an education and are able to live in a world at peace. **Structure** General Assembly. Board of Directors; National Sections. Includes: *International Training Centre on Human Rights and Peace Teaching, Geneva (CIFEDHOP, see: #21184)*. **Languages** English, French, Spanish. **Staff** 1 FTE, paid; others part-time, paid and voluntary. **Finance** Members' dues (annual): Active/Individual, euro 30 – euro 50; Benefactor, euro 130 – euro 200; School or Association, euro 160 – euro 250. Public grants; donations and grants from international organizations and governmental agencies. **Activities** Advocacy/lobbying/activism; events/meetings; knowledge management/information dissemination; research/documentation; training/education. **Events** *Session* Geneva (Switzerland) 1994, *Peace and human rights* Geneva (Switzerland) 1987. **Publications** *Ecole et paix* (annual) in English, French, Spanish – bulletin. *100 et 1 mots pour l'éducation aux droits de l'homme* (2001); *Comprendre pour agir et vivre ensemble* (2001); *Sites et liens* (2001); *La Convention des droits de l'enfant* (1999); *Eduquer aux droits humains* (1998); *Un demi-siècle de droits de l'homme* (1998); *La Convention des droits de l'enfant* (1993); *Dessine-moi un droit de l'homme* (1984); *Version simplifiée de la Déclaration universelle des droits de l'homme* (1978); *History and Purpose of EIP*. Simplified version of the Declaration of Human Rights in English, Spanish, French, Hindi, Urdu, Thai strip cartoon version of *United Nations Convention on the Rights of the Child (CRC, 1989)*; albums; collections; DVD.

Members Organizations, individuals and schools. National sections in 40 countries:
Argentina, Belgium, Benin, Burkina Faso, Cameroon, Canada, Chile, Colombia, Congo DR, France, Germany, Ghana, Greece, Guinea, Hungary, India, Japan, Jordan, Madagascar, Mali, Mauritius, Mexico, Morocco, Niger, Palestine, Panama, Portugal, Russia, Senegal, Slovenia, Spain, Switzerland, Syrian AR, Thailand, Togo, Tunisia, UK, Ukraine, Uruguay, USA.

Consultative Status Consultative status granted from: *ECOSOC (#05331)* (Ros C); *UNESCO (#20322)* (Consultative Status); *ILO (#11123)* (Special List). **IGO Relations** Consultative Status with: *African Commission on Human and Peoples' Rights (ACHPR, #00255)*. Accredited by: *United Nations Office at Vienna (UNOV, #20604)*. Cooperates with: *International Bureau of Education (IBE, #12413)*. Associated with Department of Global Communications of the United Nations. [2018/XD3464/**C**]

♦ World Association of Seaweed Processors (MARINALG International) 21185

Association mondiale des industries de traitement des algues marines

Contact Avenue de Tervueren 188a, Box 4, 1150 Brussels, Belgium. T. +3227611600. E-mail: info@marinalg.org.
URL: http://www.marinalg.org/

History 30 Mar 1976, as *Association mondiale des producteurs d'extraits d'algues*. Registered in accordance with French law. **Aims** Deal with regulatory matters and *food additive* legislation; promote the image of seaweed-derived products. **Structure** General Assembly (annual); Board of Directors. **Languages** English, French. **Finance** Members' dues. **Activities** Coordinates and sponsors studies. **Events** *Annual General Assembly* Paris (France) 1995, *Annual General Assembly* Paris (France) 1994, *Annual General Assembly* Paris (France) 1990, *Annual General Assembly* Vancouver, BC (Canada) 1989.

Members Companies in 11 countries:
Chile, China, Denmark, France, Indonesia, Ireland, Korea Rep, Morocco, Philippines, Spain, USA.

IGO Relations Participates as observer in the activities of: *Codex Alimentarius Commission (CAC, #04081)*. Contacts with: *Joint FAO/WHO Expert Committee on Food Additives (JECFA, #16129)*. **NGO Relations** Member of: *EU Specialty Food Ingredients (#09200)*. Close cooperation with: *International Food Additives Council (IFAC)*. [2018/XD2719/t/**D**]

♦ World Association for Sedimentation and Erosion Research (WASER) 21186

Contact c/o IRTCES, 20 West Chegongzhuang Rd, PO Box 366, Beijing, China. T. +861068786413. Fax +861068411174. E-mail: liuxy@iwhr.com.
URL: http://www.waser.cn/

History by *International Research and Training Centre on Erosion and Sedimentation (IRTCES, #14745).* **Aims** Promote study and development of the science of erosion and sedimentation; foster the application and dissemination of knowledge in the field. **Structure** Assembly. Council of 17 members, including President, 2 Vice-Presidents and Secretary-General. **Languages** Chinese, English. **Staff** 14.00 FTE, paid. 3 advisors; 6 invited experts. **Finance** Members' dues (small amount). Other sources: mainly financed by governmental organizations; also financed by *UNESCO (#20322)* and other donors. Budget (annual): US$ 300,000. **Activities** Organizes symposia and training courses; sponsors international symposia, conferences and workshops. **Events** *International Symposium on River Sedimentation (ISRS)* 2025, *International Symposium on River Sedimentation* Florence (Italy) 2023, *International Symposium on River Sedimentation* Florence (Italy) 2022, *International Symposium on River Sedimentation* Chengdu (China) 2019, *CONSOWA : World Conference on Soil and Water Conservation under Global Change* Lleida (Spain) 2017. **Publications** *WASER Journal.*
Members in over 40 countries, including international organizations. Membership countries not specified. Included in the above, 2 international organizations listed in this Yearbook:
Included in the above, 2 international organizations listed in this Yearbook:
International Association for Hydro-Environment Engineering and Research (IAHR, #11950); UNESCO (#20322).
NGO Relations Member of: *International Water-Related Associations' Liaison Committee (IWALC, #15869).* [2014/XM1835/D]

♦ World Association for the Senior Citizens Union (inactive)
♦ World Association for Sexology / see World Association for Sexual Health (#21187)

♦ World Association for Sexual Health (WAS) 21187

Association mondiale pour la santé sexuelle – Asociación Mundial para la Salud Sexual

SG/Treas 1300 S 2nd St, Suite 180, Minneapolis MN 55454, USA. E-mail: secretariat@worldsexualhealth.net.
URL: http://www.worldsexualhealth.net/

History 24 Oct 1978, Rome (Italy). Former names and other names: *World Association for Sexology (WAS)* – former; *Société mondiale de sexologie* – former; *Asociación Mundial de Sexologia* – former. **Aims** Promote and advocate for sexual health and sexual rights throughout the lifespan and across the world by advancing the field of sexology, sexuality research, comprehensive sexuality education and clinical care and services, all of these informed by evidence and scientific enquiry. **Structure** General Assembly; Advisory Committee; Executive Committee; Statutory Committees (5); Ad-hoc Committees (9). **Languages** English, Spanish. **Finance** Sources: contributions; donations; members' dues. **Activities** Advocacy/lobbying/activism; events/meetings; guidance/assistance/consulting; networking/liaising; publishing activities; research/documentation; training/education. **Events** *Biennial Congress* Antalya (Türkiye) 2023, *Biennial Congress* Cape Town (South Africa) 2021, *Biennial Congress* Mexico City (Mexico) 2019, *Biennial Congress* Prague (Czechia) 2017, *Biennial Congress* Singapore (Singapore) 2015. **Publications** *International Journal of Sexual Health; WAS Newsletter. Declaration on Sexual Pleasure* (2019); *Declaration of Sexual Rights* (2014); *Millennium Declaration* (2008). Guidance and international standards documents; recommendations papers.
Members Individual supporting members: professional sexologists; national and continental federations, organizations and NGOs. Members in 63 countries and territories:
Argentina, Armenia, Australia, Austria, Bahrain, Bangladesh, Belgium, Brazil, Canada, Chile, China, Colombia, Costa Rica, Croatia, Cuba, Czechia, Denmark, Ecuador, Egypt, Estonia, Finland, France, Germany, India, Indonesia, Iran Islamic Rep, Ireland, Israel, Italy, Japan, Korea Rep, Lebanon, Malaysia, Mexico, Netherlands, Nigeria, North Macedonia, Norway, Oman, Pakistan, Panama, Papua New Guinea, Paraguay, Peru, Poland, Portugal, Puerto Rico, Romania, Russia, Senegal, Singapore, South Africa, Spain, Sweden, Switzerland, Taiwan, Thailand, Tunisia, Türkiye, UK, Uruguay, USA, Venezuela.
Regional continental federations (5):
African Federation for Sexual Health and Rights (AFSHR, #00312); Asia-Oceania Federation of Sexology (AOFS, #01798); European Federation of Sexology (EFS, #07213); Latin American Federation of Sexology and Sexual Education Societies (#16331); North American Federation of Sexuality Organization (NAFSO).
Sexological organizations, institutes and foundations (over 100), including the following 3 organizations listed in this Yearbook:
International Academy of Sex Research (IASR, #11575); Society for the Scientific Study of Sexuality (SSSS); World Professional Association For Transgender Health (WPATH, #21739).
IGO Relations *Pan American Health Organization (PAHO, #18108); WHO (#20950).* [2023/XD8944/y/B]

♦ World Association of Sign Language Interpreters (WASLI) 21188

Main Office c/o IDA, 150 Route de Ferney, PO Box 2100, 1211 Geneva 2, Switzerland.
URL: https://wasli.org/

History 23 Jul 2003, Montréal, QC (Canada). Founded during 14th World Congress of *World Federation of the Deaf (WFD, #21425)*, following discussions begun in 1975 during WFD congresses. **Aims** Develop the profession of sign language interpreting worldwide. **Structure** General Meeting (every 4 years). Executive Board, comprising President, Vice-President, Secretary, Treasurer and 8 regional representatives (Africa; Asia; Australasia/Oceania; Balkans; Europe; Latin America; North America; Transcaucasia and Central Asia). **Languages** English, International Sign Language. **Finance** Members' dues. **Events** *Conference* Incheon (Korea Rep) 2023, *Conference* Geneva (Switzerland) 2021, *Conference* Paris (France) 2019, *Conference* Istanbul (Turkey) 2015, *Conference* Durban (South Africa) 2011. **Publications** Conference proceedings.
Members in 25 countries:
Australia, Canada, Chile, Colombia, Denmark, Finland, France, Gambia, Ghana, India, Italy, Japan, Korea Rep, Malaysia, Nepal, New Zealand, Nigeria, Norway, Panama, Peru, Philippines, Spain, Uganda, UK, USA. [2021/XM1366/D]

♦ World Association of the Ski Teaching System / see Interski International (#15975)
♦ World Association of Sleep Medicine (inactive)

♦ World Association for Small and Medium Enterprises (WASME) ... 21189

Association mondiale des petites et moyennes entreprises – Asociación Mundial de Empresas Pequeñas y Medianas

Exec Sec WASME House, Plot No 4 – Sector 16-A – Institutional Area, Gautam Budh Nagar, Noida, Uttar Pradesh 201301, Noida UTTAR PRADESH 201301, India. T. +911204216283 – +911204216284. E-mail: wasme@wasmeinfo.org – info@wasmeinfo.org.
URL: https://www.wasmeinfo.org/

History 1980, Delhi (India). Former names and other names: *World Assembly of Small and Medium Enterprises (WASME)* – former; *Assemblée mondiale des petites et moyennes entreprises* – former; *Asamblea Mundial de Empresas Pequeñas y Medianas* – former. Registration: India. **Aims** Build a cohesive community of micro, small and medium enterprises; take necessary action to strengthen them and positively impact the overall global economy. **Structure** Council; Governing Body; Bureau; Secretariat, headed by Secretary General. **Languages** English, Hindi. **Staff** 35.00 FTE, paid. **Finance** Members' dues and admission fees. Other sources: special contributions for specific purposes; conferences and training courses proceeds; sale of reports and documents; research studies; incidental income generated from activities. **Activities** Advocacy/lobbying/activism; awards/prizes/competitions; capacity building; events/meetings; financial and/or material support; knowledge management/information dissemination; projects/programmes; research and development; research/documentation; training/education. **Events** *International Conference on SMEs* Noida (India) 2019, *International Conference on SMEs* Dubai (United Arab Emirates) 2018, *International Conference on SMEs* Delhi (India) 2017, *International Conference on SMEs* Yenagoa (Nigeria) 2014, *International Conference on Small and Medium Enterprises / International Conference on SMEs* Durban (South Africa) 2013. **Publications** *World SME News; World SME Update.*
Members General members: enterprise promotion agencies; banks and financial institutions; governmental organizations; chambers of commerce and industry; associations of SMEs; training, consultancy and research organizations. Associate members: individual firms and corporate bodies engaged in small and medium business activities in any country. Members in 65 countries and territories:
Algeria, Argentina, Bahrain, Bangladesh, Bolivia, Botswana, Brazil, Bulgaria, Burkina Faso, Burundi, Cambodia, Cameroon, Canada, China, Colombia, Côte d'Ivoire, Cyprus, Czechia, Egypt, Eswatini, Ethiopia, France, Germany, Ghana, Greece, Hong Kong, Hungary, India, Indonesia, Israel, Italy, Kazakhstan, Kenya, Korea Rep, Malawi, Malaysia, Mauritius, Mexico, Morocco, Namibia, Nepal, Netherlands, Nigeria, Oman, Pakistan, Philippines, Poland, Portugal, Romania, San Marino, Saudi Arabia, Senegal, Singapore, Sri Lanka, Tanzania UR, Thailand, Tunisia, Türkiye, Uganda, UK, United Arab Emirates, USA, Vietnam, Zambia, Zimbabwe.

Consultative Status Consultative status granted from: *UNESCO (#20322)* (Consultative Status); *ILO (#11123)* (Special); *UNCTAD (#20285)* (General Category); *UNIDO (#20336).* **IGO Relations** Contacts with: *OECD (#17693)* and with UN regional commissions *United Nations Economic Commission for Africa (ECA, #20554); United Nations Economic Commission for Europe (UNECE, #20555); United Nations Economic and Social Commission for Asia and the Pacific (ESCAP, #20557).* Accredited by: *United Nations Office at Vienna (UNOV, #20604).* Permanent Observer status with: *UNDP (#20292); United Nations Commission on International Trade Law (UNCITRAL, #20531); United Nations Economic and Social Commission for Asia and the Pacific (ESCAP, #20557); World Customs Organization (WCO, #21350); World Intellectual Property Organization (WIPO, #21593).* **NGO Relations** Honorary member of: *Association of African Development Finance Institutions (AADFI, #02353).* Maintains contacts with: *Association of Development Financing Institutions in Asia and the Pacific (ADFIAP, #02472); International Association of Crafts and Small and Medium-Sized Enterprises (IACME, inactive); International University of Entreprenology (IUE)*; national organizations. [2019/XD2160/B]

♦ World Association for Social Psychiatry (WASP) 21190

Association mondiale de psychiatrie sociale

SG Dept of Psychiatry, All India Institute of Medical Sciences, Ansari Nagar, New Delhi, Delhi 110016, New Delhi DELHI 110016, India. E-mail: sec.gen.wasp@gmail.com.
Pres address not obtained.
URL: https://www.socialpsychiatry.org/wasp

History 1964, London (UK). Founded by Joshua Bierer, as *International Association for Social Psychiatry.* Reorganized in 1970. Present name adopted 1978. Registered in accordance with Swiss Civil Code and domiciled in Zurich (Switzerland). Registration: Start date: 22 Sep 2003, France. **Aims** Study the nature of man and his cultures and the prevention and treatment of his vicissitudes and *behaviour disorders*; advance the physical, social and philosophical *wellbeing* of *mankind.* **Languages** English. **Activities** Events/meetings. **Events** *Asia Pacific Hybrid Congress* Delhi (India) 2021, *Congress* Bucharest (Romania) 2019, *Social psychiatry in a rapidly changing world* Delhi (India) 2016, *European Congress for Social Psychiatry* Geneva (Switzerland) 2015, *World Congress* Lisbon (Portugal) 2013. **Publications** *World Social Psychiatry (WSP)* (3 a year) in English.
Members Individuals: Fellows, Members, Associates, in 79 countries and territories:
Argentina, Australia, Austria, Bahamas, Bahrain, Bangladesh, Belgium, Bolivia, Bosnia-Herzegovina, Brazil, Bulgaria, Canada, Chile, China, Colombia, Costa Rica, Croatia, Cuba, Cyprus, Czechia, Denmark, Estonia, Finland, France, Georgia, Germany, Greece, Hong Kong, Hungary, Iceland, India, Indonesia, Ireland, Israel, Italy, Japan, Kenya, Korea Rep, Latvia, Liechtenstein, Lithuania, Luxembourg, Malta, Mexico, Monaco, Montenegro, Netherlands, New Zealand, Nigeria, North Macedonia, Norway, Pakistan, Papua New Guinea, Peru, Philippines, Poland, Portugal, Puerto Rico, Romania, Russia, Saudi Arabia, Serbia, Singapore, Slovenia, South Africa, Spain, Sri Lanka, Sweden, Switzerland, Taiwan, Thailand, Tonga, Türkiye, UK, Ukraine, Uruguay, USA, Venezuela. [2022/XC4154/v/B]

♦ World Association of Societies of Pathology – Anatomic and Clinical / see World Association of Societies of Pathology and Laboratory Medicine (#21191)

♦ World Association of Societies of Pathology and Laboratory Medicine (WASPaLM) 21191

Association mondiale des societés de pathologie et biologie médicale – Asociación Mundial de Sociedades de Patologia y Medicina Laboratorial – Weltvereinigung der Gesellschaften für Pathologie und für Laboratoriumsmedizin

Exec Dir c/o JSLM, 2F UI Building, 2-2 Kanda Ogawa-machi, Chiyoda-ku, Tokyo, 101-0052 Japan. T. +81332950351. Fax +81332950352. E-mail: waspalm@jslm.org.
Secretariat Office c/o MZ Congressi, Via Carlo Farini 81, 20159 Milan MI, Italy. T. +39266802323. E-mail: waspalm@mzcongressi.com.
URL: http://www.waspalm.com/

History 21 Nov 1947, Paris (France). Founded as *International Society of Clinical Pathology (ISCP) – Société internationale de biologie clinique (SIBC)*, by merger of *European Association of Clinical Pathologists (inactive)*, set up in 1943, and Société française de biologie clinique. Name changed, 1969, Montréal (Canada), to *World Association of Anatomic and Clinical Pathology Societies (WAPS) – Association mondiale des sociétés de pathologie anatomique et clinique* and 1972, Munich (Germany FR), to *World Association of Societies of Pathology – Anatomic and Clinical (WASP) – Association mondiale des sociétés de pathologie – anatomie pathologique et biologie médicale – Asociación Mundial de las Sociedades de Patologia – Anatómica y Clinica – Weltvereinigung der Gesellschaften für Pathologie und für Laboratoriumsmedizin.* Current title adopted in 1999. Statutes amended 29 Sep 1981; 11 Oct 1983; 24 Jun 1987; 18 May 1989; 26 Jun 1991; 12 Oct 1995; 17 Sep 1999. New statutes adopted 22 Nov 2001; amended: 1 Sep 2003; 29 May 2005; 22 Aug 2007. **Aims** Improve health worldwide by promoting the teaching and practice of pathology/laboratory medicine. Promote: education, research and international quality standards; high quality, cost effective medical laboratory services; exchange of information among pathologists and laboratory scientists worldwide. Support constituent societies through: communication; facilitation of standard setting; leadership in establishing international standards for laboratory accreditation and certification of pathologists and pathologist assistants; creation of global opportunities for cooperation in education, research, practice and commerce. Encourage formation of, and cooperation between, societies of pathology and laboratory medicine worldwide; foster cooperation with other international health organizations. **Structure** Board. Association Committees (5); Board Committees (2); Special Committees. Include: *World Pathology Foundation (WPF, #21714).* **Languages** English, Italian. **Staff** Voluntary. **Finance** Member's dues from Constituent Societies. Other sources: corporate sponsorship. **Activities** Awards/prizes/competitions; events/meetings; publishing activities; research/documentation. **Events** *Biennial Congress* Punta del Este (Uruguay) 2022, *Biennial Congress* Xian (China) 2019, *Biennial Congress* Kyoto (Japan) 2017, *Biennial Congress* Cancún (Mexico) 2015, *Biennial Congress* Québec, QC (Canada) 2013. **Publications** *WASPaLM Newsletter.*
Members Constituent Societies (about 40) in 32 countries and territories:
Austria, Bolivia, Brazil, Bulgaria, China, Cuba, Ecuador, France, Germany, Hong Kong, India, Indonesia, Ireland, Italy, Japan, Jordan, Korea Rep, Malaysia, Mexico, Peru, Portugal, Romania, South Africa, Sri Lanka, Sudan, Switzerland, Taiwan, Thailand, Türkiye, UK, Uruguay, USA.
Included in the above, 1 organization listed in this Yearbook:
Consultative Status Consultative status granted from: *ECOSOC (#05331)* (Ros C); *WHO (#20950)* (Official Relations). **IGO Relations** Accredited by: *United Nations Office at Vienna (UNOV, #20604).* **NGO Relations** International member of: *Council for International Organizations of Medical Sciences (CIOMS, #04905).* Member of: Standardization Committee of *International Union of Immunological Societies (IUIS, #15781).* Policy of cooperation with (USA) National Committee for Clinical Laboratory Standards (NCCLS). In liaison with technical committees of: *International Organization for Standardization (ISO, #14473).* [2020/XC3466/B]

♦ World Association of Soil and Water Conservation (WASWAC) 21192

Association mondiale pour la conservation du sol et de l'eau

Pres 402 – IRTCES Bldg, No 20 Chegongzhuang Road West, 100048 Beijing, China. T. +861068786579. Fax +861068411174. E-mail: waswac@foxmail.com – waswac@vip.163.com.
SG address not obtained.
URL: http://www.waswac.org.cn/

History Jan 1983, Honolulu, HI (USA). Founded at International Soil Conservation Conference held by *International Soil Conservation Organization (ISCO, #15560)*, to allow continuing contact between participants of ISCO Conferences. **Aims** Promote wise use of management practices that will improve and safeguard the quality of land and water resources so they continue to meet the needs of agriculture, society and nature. **Structure** Council; Committees (7); Secretariat, headed by Secretary General. Associated body: *World Overview of Conservation Approaches and Technologies (WOCAT, see: #21192).* **Languages** English. **Staff** 12.00 FTE, voluntary. **Finance** Sources: members' dues. Administrative and financial support from International Research and Training Center on Erosion and Sedimentation (IRTCES), China. **Activities** Awards/prizes/competitions; events/meetings; knowledge management/information dissemination; publishing activities; research and development; research/documentation; training/education. **Events** *WASWAC World Conference* Delhi (India) 2019, *IYFSWC : International Youth Forum of Soil and Water Conservation* Moscow (Russia) 2018, *CONSOWA : World Conference on Soil and Water Conservation under Global Change* Lleida (Spain) 2017, *WASWAC World Conference* Belgrade (Serbia) 2016, *ARCO Satellite International Workshop* Tsukuba (Japan) 2015. **Publications** *WASWAC Hot News* (12 a year); *International Soil and Water Conservation Research* (4 a year).
Members Individuals and organizations in 84 countries and territories:

Albania, Argentina, Australia, Austria, Belgium, Bhutan, Bolivia, Brazil, Bulgaria, Burkina Faso, Burundi, Cambodia, Cameroon, Canada, Chile, China, Colombia, Costa Rica, Czechia, Denmark, Djibouti, Ecuador, Egypt, Ethiopia, Fiji, France, Germany, Ghana, Hungary, India, Indonesia, Iran Islamic Rep, Iraq, Israel, Italy, Jamaica, Japan, Kenya, Korea Rep, Laos, Lesotho, Malawi, Malaysia, Mali, Mexico, Morocco, Nepal, Netherlands, New Zealand, Niger, Nigeria, Pakistan, Paraguay, Peru, Philippines, Poland, Puerto Rico, Romania, Russia, Rwanda, Serbia, Sierra Leone, Slovakia, South Africa, Spain, Sri Lanka, St Lucia, Sudan, Sweden, Switzerland, Syrian AR, Tanzania UR, Thailand, Timor-Leste, Tunisia, Uganda, UK, Ukraine, United Arab Emirates, USA, Venezuela, Vietnam, Zambia, Zimbabwe. [2022/XD1172/**B**]

♦ World Association of Special Education 21193

Asociación Mundial de Educación Especial (AMEE)

Pres address not obtained.

Structure Officers: President; 2 Vice-Presidents; Secretary-General. **Events** *Meeting* Santo Domingo (Dominican Rep) 2009. [2008/XM0225/**D**]

♦ World Association for Sport Management (WASM) 21194

Exec Dir Dept of Sport Management, Aletheia Univ, No 32 Zhenli St, Danshui Dist, New Taipei City 25103, Taiwan. T. +886226291721. Fax +886226237335.

URL: https://wasmorg.com/

History 27 Apr 2012, Taiwan, by representatives of the 6 continental associations: North American Society for Sport Management (NASSM); Sport Management Association of Australia and New Zealand (SMAANZ); *European Association for Sport Management (EASM, #06219)*; *Asociación Latinoamericana de Gerencia Deportiva (ALGEDE, #02227)*; *Asian Association for Sport Management (AASM, #01340)*; *African Sport Management Association (ASMA, #00473)*. Successor to *International Sport Management Alliance (inactive)*. **Aims** Facilitate sport management research, teaching and learning excellence and professional practice. **Structure** Board; Executive; Secretariat. **Events** *Conference* Doha (Qatar) 2023, *Conference* Santiago (Chile) 2019, *Conference* Kaunas (Lithuania) 2017, *Conference* Madrid (Spain) 2014, *Global Sport Management Summit* Taipei (Taiwan) 2013. **Publications** *Global Sport Management News*.

Members Continental federations (6):

African Sport Management Association (ASMA, #00473); *Asian Association for Sport Management (AASM, #01340)*; *Asociación Latinoamericana de Gerencia Deportiva (ALGEDE, #02227)*; *European Association for Sport Management (EASM, #06219)*; North American Society for Sport Management (NASSM); Sport Management Association of Australia and New Zealand (SMAANZ).

NGO Relations Member of: *International Council of Sport Science and Physical Education (ICSSPE, #13077)*. [2020/XJ9554/y/**B**]

♦ World Association for Stress Related and Anxiety Disorders (internationally oriented national body)
♦ World Association for the Struggle Against Hunger (inactive)

♦ World Association for Supported Employment (WASE) 21195

Secretariat Steenpad 3, 4797 SG Willemstad, Netherlands. T. +311687472711. Fax +311687472255.

URL: https://www.wase.ca/

History 1995. **Aims** Promote vocational integration of people with *disabilities* using the principle and technology of Supported Employment throughout the world. **Structure** Board. **Languages** English. **Staff** None. **Finance** Sources: members' dues. **Events** *World Supported Employment Conference* Vancouver, BC (Canada) 2023, *International forum on work, information society and employment* Vienna (Austria) 1998. **Publications** Handbook; DVD. **Members** Organizations and individuals. Membership countries not specified. **Consultative Status** Consultative status granted from: *ECOSOC (#05331)* (Special). [2017.10.16/XD5472/**C**]

♦ World Association for Sustainable Development (WASD) 21196

Main Office Queen Mary University of London, Enterprise Zone, The QMB Innovation Centre, 5 Walden St, London, E1 2EF, UK. T. +447772851284. E-mail: admin@wasd.org.uk.

URL: https://www.wasd.org.uk/

History 11 Nov 2003, London (UK). **Aims** Promote exchange of knowledge, experience, information and ideas among academicians, scholars, professionals, policy and decision makers, industry, executives and students; improve mutual understanding of the roles of science and technology in achieving sustainable development worldwide; provide professionals, researchers and policymakers with the best available scientific evidence when contributing to better technological and economic development for all within the populations they serve. **Structure** General Assembly; Advisory Board. **Languages** Arabic, English. **Activities** Events/meetings; projects/programmes; publishing activities. **Events** *Transforming Universities – Making an Impact on the Implementation of the United Nations 2030 Agenda* London (UK) 2022, *Annual International Conference* Rabat (Morocco) 2022, *Annual International Conference* London (UK) 2019, *Annual International Conference* London (UK) 2016, *Annual International Conference* Istanbul (Türkey) 2015. **Publications** *International Journal of Food, Nutrition and Public Health (IJFNPH)*; *International Journal of Innovation and Knowledge Management in Middle East and North Africa*; *International Journal of Sudan Research*; *Middle Eastern Journal of Entrepreneurship, Leadership and Sustainable Development*; *World Journal of Entrepreneurship, Management and Sustainable Development*; *World Journal of Science, Technology and Sustainable Development (WJSTSD)*. *Globalization, Technology and Sustainable Development*; *Middle East and North Africa*; *Outlook*. [2023.03.04/XJ8415/**C**]

♦ World Association for Symphonic Bands and Ensembles (WASBE) . 21197

Organisation mondiale des orchestres d'harmonie et ensembles à vents – Asociación Mundial de Bandas y Ensambles – Welt-Organisation der konzertanten Blasorchester und Bläser-Ensembles

Exec Dir Ulrich-Schmitt-Str 16, 76467 Bietigheim-Bissingen, Germany. T. +4915127526818. E-mail: office@wasbe.org – wasbeoffice@gmail.com.

URL: http://wasbe.org/

History 1981. **Aims** Enhance the quality of the wind band throughout the world and expose members to new worlds of repertoire, musical culture, people and places. **Structure** Board of Directors; International Artistic Advisory Committee; Executive Director. **Languages** English, French, German, Japanese, Spanish. **Staff** None. **Finance** Members' dues. Annual budget: US$ 80,000. **Activities** Networking/liaising; events/meetings; awareness raising. **Events** *WASBE Conference* Gwangju (Korea Rep) 2024, *WASBE Conference* Prague (Czechia) 2022, *Biennial Conference* Buñol (Spain) 2019, *Biennial Conference* Utrecht (Netherlands) 2017, *Biennial Conference* San Jose, CA (USA) 2015. **Publications** *WASBE Magazine* (4 a year); *WASBE Journal* (annual). Members Directory.

Members Sections in 8 countries:

Austria, Finland, France, Germany, Japan, Singapore, South Africa, Switzerland.

Individuals (over 1,000) in 61 countries and territories:

Argentina, Australia, Austria, Bahrain, Barbados, Belarus, Belgium, Brazil, Canada, Chile, China, Colombia, Costa Rica, Croatia, Cyprus, Czechia, Denmark, Ecuador, Finland, France, Germany, Greece, Hong Kong, Hungary, Iceland, Ireland, Israel, Italy, Japan, Jordan, Korea DPR, Korea Rep, Latvia, Liechtenstein, Lithuania, Luxembourg, Malaysia, Malta, Montenegro, Netherlands, New Zealand, Nigeria, Norway, Oman, Panama, Poland, Portugal, Russia, Serbia, Singapore, Slovenia, South Africa, Spain, Sweden, Switzerland, Taiwan, UK, Ukraine, Uruguay, USA, Venezuela.

Honorary Life Members (6) in 5 countries:

France, Japan, Netherlands, Norway, USA. [2022/XF2498/**F**]

♦ World Association of Theoretical and Computational Chemists (WATOC) 21198

Pres Univ of Sydney, Camperdown NSW 2006, Australia. T. +61286279486.

Sec-Treas Institut für Organische Chemie, Justus-Liebig-Universität, Heinrich-Buff-Ring 17, 35392 Giessen, Germany.

URL: http://watoc.net

History 1982. Former names and other names: *World Association of Theoretical Organic Chemists* – former (1982); *World Association of Theoretically Oriented Chemists* – former. **Aims** Promote the field of theoretical and computational chemistry; advance interactions between scientists working in this field worldwide. **Structure** Board (meets every 3 years). **Languages** English. **Staff** None. **Finance** Sources: members' dues. No allocated budget. **Activities** Events/meetings; networking/liaising. **Events** *Triennial Congress* Vancouver, BC (Canada) 2022, *Triennial Congress* Vancouver, BC (Canada) 2021, *Triennial Congress* Vancouver, BC (Canada) 2020, *Triennial Congress* Munich (Germany) 2017, *Triennial Congress* Santiago (Chile) 2014. **Members** Individuals (345). Membership countries not specified. [2022.02.14/XD4946/**D**]

♦ World Association of Theoretically Oriented Chemists / see World Association of Theoretical and Computational Chemists (#21198)
♦ World Association of Theoretical Organic Chemists / see World Association of Theoretical and Computational Chemists (#21198)

♦ World Association of Trainees in Obstetrics & Gynecology (WATOG) 21199

Secretariat 35 rue Berger, 75001 Paris, France. T. +33661143924. E-mail: watog-secretariat@watog.org.

URL: http://www.watog.org/

History 7 Oct 2012. Founded under the auspices of *Fédération Internationale de Gynécologie et d'Obstétrique (FIGO, #09638)*. **Aims** Help every obstetrician and gynecologist (OB/GYN) trainee in the world to access the highest level of education, overcome cultural and gender barriers and facilitate contact and exchange between members from different countries. **Structure** Executive Board. Regional Executive Boards: Asia; Latin America; Africa; Europe; North America; Oceania. **Members** Trainees (over 100000) worldwide. Membership countries not specified. **NGO Relations** Partner of (2): *Fédération Internationale de Gynécologie et d'Obstétrique (FIGO, #09638)*; *International Society of Ultrasound in Obstetrics and Gynaecology (ISUOG, #15527)*. [2021/AA1814/**B**]

♦ World Association of Trainers in Development (no recent information)
♦ World Association for Transport Animal Welfare and Studies (internationally oriented national body)
♦ World Association of Travel Agencies / see WATA (#20821)
♦ World Association for Triple Helix and Future Strategy Studies (internationally oriented national body)
♦ World Association of United Nations Non-Governmental Organizations / see World Association of Non-Governmental Organizations (#21167)
♦ World Association of Universities and Colleges (internationally oriented national body)
♦ World Association of University Professors / see International Association of University Professors and Lecturers (#12250)

♦ World Association of Valuation Organizations (WAVO) 21200

Contact 110 Middle Road, 09-00 Chiat Hong Bldg, Singapore 188968, Singapore. T. +6562223030. Fax +6562252453.

URL: http://www.wavoglobal.org/

History 2005, Australia, having informally existed since 2000. Relocated to Singapore (Singapore), 2008. **Aims** Develop and enhance the practice of property valuation, so as to ensure that valuation services of consistently high quality are provided with professional integrity, across the development world and to developing countries and countries in transition. **Structure** Council, consisting of 1 representative per Full Member. Executive Committee, headed by Chairman. **Languages** English. **Staff** 2.00 FTE, paid. **Events** *IVSC-WAVO Global Valuation Conference* Seoul (Korea Rep) 2020, *Congress* Gold Coast, QLD (Australia) 2019, *Valuation Congress* Daegu (Korea Rep) 2016, *Valuation Congress* Beijing (China) 2015, *Valuation Congress* Chennai (India) 2013.

Members National organizations (16) in 13 countries and territories:

Australia, Canada, China, Hong Kong, India, Italy, Korea Rep, New Zealand, Romania, Singapore, UK, USA, Vietnam. [2013/XM3106/**D**]

♦ World Association for Vedic Studies (WAVES) 21201

Chairman c/o MET Intl, 1900 Surveyor Rd, Carrollton TX 75006, USA.

Treas 780 Ullswater Cove, Alpharetta GA 30022, USA. T. +17706648779. Fax +17706648780. E-mail: treasurer@wavesinternational.net.

URL: https://thewavesinternational.com/

History 6 Oct 1996, Atlanta GA (USA). **Aims** Promote Vedic and ancient Indian studies. **Structure** Council, comprising President, 4 Vice Presidents, General Secretary, 4 Secretaries, 4 Joint Secretaries, Treasurer, Deputy Treasurer and 10 further members. Standing Committees. **Finance** Members' dues. **Events** *Biennial Conference* Fairfield, IA (USA) 2014, *Biennial Conference* Port-of-Spain (Trinidad-Tobago) 2010, *Biennial Conference* Trinidad-Tobago 2008, *Biennial Conference* Houston, TX (USA) 2006, *Biennial conference* Rockville, MD (USA) 2004. **Publications** *Journal of Studies on Ancient India* (4 a year). [2022/XD7744/**D**]

♦ World Association of Veteran Athletes / see World Masters Athletics (#21640)
♦ World Association of Veteran Long-Distance Runners (inactive)
♦ World Association of Veterinarians Specialists in Fish Diseases (no recent information)

♦ World Association of Veterinary Anatomists (WAVA) 21202

Association mondiale des anatomistes vétérinaires (AMAV) – Asociación Mundial de Anatomistas Veterinarios (AMAV) – Weltvereinigung der Veterinäranatomen (WVVA)

SG NMBU Veterinary Med, Ullevålsveien 72, 0454 Oslo, Norway.

URL: http://www.wava-amav.org/

History 23 Sep 1957, Freiburg-Breisgau (Germany). Founded following initiative of 6th Congress of Anatomy, 28 Jul 1955, Paris (France). Constitution adopted at 5th General Assembly, 1961, Vienna (Austria), and modified: 1967, Paris; 1975, Thessaloniki (Greece); 1985, London (UK). Former names and other names: *International Association of Veterinary Anatomists* – former (23 Sep 1957 to 1961); *Association internationale des anatomistes vétérinaires* – former (23 Sep 1957 to 1961); *Internationale Vereinigung der Veterinäranatomen* – former (23 Sep 1957 to 1961). Registration: France. **Aims** Bring together individuals and associations (collective members) interested in the study and teaching of domestic animal anatomy and their development by organizing meetings, encouraging research work, multiplying contacts and exchanging information and material; promote comparative gross, microscopic and developmental anatomy of domestic, laboratory and zoo animals. **Structure** General Assembly (at International Congress of Anatomy or at World Veterinary Congress). Executive Committee. Officers: President; 3 Vice-Presidents; Secretary-General; Treasurer. Committees (5). Regions (4). **Languages** English, French, German, Spanish. **Staff** Voluntary. **Finance** Sources: members' dues. **Activities** International Congress alternates with Federative International Congress of Anatomists (IFAA) and World Veterinary Congress (WVA). **Events** *General Assembly and International Congress* Stara Zagora (Bulgaria) 2012, *General assembly and international congress* Paris (France) 2010, *General assembly and international congress* Cape Town (South Africa) 2009, *General Assembly and International Congress* Vancouver, BC (Canada) 2008, *General assembly and congress* Knoxville, TN (USA) 2003. **Publications** *Anatomia, Histologia, Embryologia* (6 a year) – journal; *WAVA Newsletter* (annual). *Nomina Anatomica Veterinaria* (4th ed 1994) – nomenclatures (3) in one volume; *Nomina Embryologica* (1992); *Nomina Histologica* (2nd ed, 2nd revised ed 1994 1983). Information Services: Information centres.

Members Individual: active; associated; honorary. Collective: national or regional associations of veterinary anatomists. Members in 55 countries:

Argentina, Australia, Austria, Belgium, Brazil, Bulgaria, Canada, Croatia, Cuba, Czechia, Denmark, Egypt, Estonia, Finland, France, Germany, Greece, Hungary, India, Iran Islamic Rep, Ireland, Italy, Japan, Kenya, Korea Rep, Lithuania, Mexico, Netherlands, New Zealand, Nigeria, North Macedonia, Norway, Pakistan, Peru, Philippines, Poland, Portugal, Romania, Russia, Slovakia, Slovenia, South Africa, Spain, Sudan, Switzerland, Thailand, Türkiye, Uganda, UK, Ukraine, Uruguay, USA, Venezuela, Zambia, Zimbabwe.

NGO Relations Member of: *International Federation of Associations of Anatomists (IFAA, #13361)*; *World Veterinary Association (WVA, #21901)*. [2019/XB3472/**B**]

♦ World Association for Veterinary Dermatology (WAVD) 21203

Sec c/o UCD Vet Med, 1 Garrod Drive, Davis CA 95616, USA.

URL: http://www.wavd.org/

History 1986. Former names and other names: *World Congress of Veterinary Dermatology Association (WCVDA)* – former. Registration: Companies House, Scotland. **Aims** Organize the World Congress of Veterinary Dermatology; advance the science of veterinary dermatology on a global basis. **Structure** Board. **Activities** Awards/prizes/competitions; events/meetings; research/documentation; training/education. **Events** *World Congress of Veterinary Dermatology* Boston, MA (USA) 2024, *World Congress of Veterinary Dermatology* Sydney, NSW (Australia) 2020, *World Congress* Bordeaux (France) 2016, *World Congress* Vancouver, BC (Canada) 2012, *World congress* Hong Kong (Hong Kong) 2008. **Publications** *Advances in Veterinay Dermatology*.

Members National organizations (4) in 3 countries:

Australia, Canada, USA.

Regional organizations (3):

Asian Society of Veterinary Dermatology (AiSVD, #01749); European College of Veterinary Dermatology (ECVD, #06622); European Society of Veterinary Dermatology (ESVD, #08777).
Affiliate members (2):
International Committee on Allergic Diseases of Animals (ICADA, #12744); International Society of Veterinary Dermatopathology (ISVD, #15539).
Provisional member (1):
Sociedad Latinoamericana de Dermatologia Veterinaria (SLDV, #19399). [2021/XF0672/y/**C**]

♦ World Association of Veterinary Educators (inactive)

♦ World Association of Veterinary Food Hygienists (WAVFH) 21204

Association vétérinaire mondiale d'hygiène alimentaire – Asociación Mundial de Veterinarios Higienistas de los Alimentos (AMVHA) – Weltvereinigung der Tierärztlichen Lebensmittelhygieniker

Sec-Treas Fed Inst for Risk Assessment BfR, Diedersdorfer Weg 1, 12277 Berlin, Germany. T. +493084122121.
URL: http://www.wavfh.com/

History 1955, Utrecht (Netherlands). Statutes adopted 1 Sep 1956. Present Statutes adopted 1980, Bilthoven (Netherlands). Former names and other names: *International Association of Veterinary Food Hygienists (IAVFH)* – former (1955). **Aims** Exchange on international level the results of scientific research pertaining to the safety and quality of food products of animal origin; act as a forum for exchange of information on teaching and on provision of services relating to the safety and quality of foods from animals. **Structure** General Assembly; Executive Board. Meetings closed. **Languages** English, French, German. **Staff** 3.00 FTE, voluntary. **Finance** Sources: members' dues. **Activities** Events/meetings; guidance/assistance/consulting. **Events** *International World Veterinary Congress* Lyon (France) 1999, *Symposium* The Hague (Netherlands) 1997, *International World Veterinary Congress* Yokohama (Japan) 1995, *Healthy animals – safe food – healthy man* Bangkok (Thailand) 1993, *Roundtable Conference* Dublin (Ireland) 1990. **Publications** Proceedings of symposia and roundtable conferences.
Members National veterinary associations in 46 countries and territories:
Argentina, Australia, Austria, Brazil, Bulgaria, Canada, Chile, China, Cuba, Czechia, Denmark, Finland, France, Germany, Greece, Hungary, India, Indonesia, Iraq, Ireland, Israel, Italy, Japan, Jordan, Kenya, Luxembourg, Mexico, Namibia, Netherlands, New Zealand, Nigeria, Norway, Pakistan, Peru, Poland, Portugal, Russia, Serbia, Spain, Sweden, Switzerland, Taiwan, Thailand, Türkiye, Uruguay, USA.
IGO Relations Consultations ('observers') with: *WHO (#20950).* **NGO Relations** Observer status with (1): *Union européenne des vétérinaires hygiénistes (UEVH, #20404).* Member of (1): *World Veterinary Association (WVA, #21901).* [2012/XC3473/**C**]

♦ World Association of Veterinary Laboratory Diagnosticians (WAVLD) 21205

Exec Dir 2503 Eisenhower Ave, Ames IA 50010, USA. T. +15157085622.
URL: http://www.wavld.org/

History Founded 1977, following organizational meeting, coinciding with the dedication of a new Veterinary Research and Diagnostic Laboratory at Palo Alto (Mexico). Decision to adopt current name made at second meeting, Lucerne (Switzerland), 1980. Constitution and bylaws approved at third meeting, Ames IA (USA) 1983. **Aims** Improve animal and human *health* by facilitating availability of quality laboratory testing provided through veterinary diagnostic laboratories around the world. **Structure** Board of Directors; Officers. **Languages** English. **Staff** 1.00 FTE, voluntary. **Finance** Annual budget: US$ 1,000. **Activities** Knowledge management/information dissemination; training/education; guidance/assistance/consulting; events/meetings. **Events** *International Symposium* Lyon (France) 2023, *International Symposium* Lyon (France) 2021, *International Symposium* Chiang Mai (Thailand) 2019, *International Symposium* Sorrento (Italy) 2017, *International Symposium* Saskatoon, SK (Canada) 2015. **Publications** Symposium proceedings. **Members** No official membership. [2019.02.13/XD2041/v/**D**]

♦ World Association of Veterinary Microbiologists, Immunologists and Specialists in Infectious Diseases (no recent information)
♦ World Association of Veterinary Pathologists (no recent information)
♦ World Association of Veterinary Physiologists, Pharmacologists, Biochemists and Toxicologists (no recent information)
♦ World Association of Video-Makers and Editions (inactive)
♦ World Association of Visioneers and Entreprenologists (internationally oriented national body)
♦ World Association of Wildlife Veterinarians (inactive)
♦ World Association of Women Business Owners / see Femmes chefs d'entreprises mondiales (#09733)
♦ World Association of Women Entrepreneurs (#09733)

♦ World Association of Women Journalists and Writers 21206

Asociación Mundial de Mujeres Periodistas y Escritoras (AMMPE)

Pres c/o Fundesur, Coronel Rodhe 1471, General Roca, Argentina.
URL: http://www.ammpe.org/

History Founded May 1969, Mexico City (Mexico) at the First Global Meeting, attended by representatives of 36 countries. Refounded 2010, Argentina. **Aims** Ensure respect for human rights as set forth by the United Nations; promote gender equity in all areas; promote equal access to new technologies of information and communication; promote professional development of members; promote joint efforts in communications between different countries; promote networking and coordination between networks of communications professionals; support professional development opportunities for members; promote exchange of knowledge, experiences, ideas and cultural values; promote organization of national and regional journalism competitions; promote recognition of personalities in the field of communication; promote freedom of expression; promote protection and care of the environment. **Structure** President; Founder and Honorary President for Life; 18 Vice-Presidents; 2 substitutes. **Languages** English, Spanish. **Finance** Members' dues. **Events** *Congress* London (UK) 2018, *Congress* Santiago (Chile) 2016, *Congress* Santiago de Querétaro (Mexico) 2014, *Congress* Taichung (Taiwan) 2012, *Congress* Buenos Aires (Argentina) 2010.
Members Full in 27 countries and territories:
Argentina, Belgium, Brazil, Canada, Chile, Congo DR, Egypt, El Salvador, Finland, France, Guatemala, Honduras, Hong Kong, Israel, Japan, Korea Rep, Mexico, Nigeria, Philippines, Portugal, Puerto Rico, Spain, Sudan, Sweden, Taiwan, Uruguay, USA.
IGO Relations Associated with Department of Global Communications of the United Nations. **NGO Relations** Affiliated with: *Red de Escritoras Latinoamericanas (RELAT, #18649).* [2014/XD6410/**D**]

♦ World Association of World Federalists / see World Federalist Movement – Movement for a Just World Order through a Strengthened United Nations (#21404)

♦ World Association of Young Scientists (WAYS) 21207

Pres Dept – Science and Technology, Bldg 53 – CSIR Campus, Meiring Naude Road, Brummeria, Pretoria, 0001, South Africa. E-mail: webmaster@dst.gov.za.

History Launched following conference organized by *UNESCO (#20322)* and with the help of *TWAS (#20270), Islamic World Educational, Scientific and Cultural Organization (ICESCO, #16058)* and Moroccan Ministry of National Education, 2004. **Aims** Empower young scientists worldwide; promote scientific excellence and collaborative practices. **Structure** Board; Secretariat. Offices (2): Alexandria (Egypt); Pretoria (South Africa). **Finance** Project related support; donations. **Events** *General conference / Conference* Marrakech (Morocco) 2004. **Publications** *WAYS Newsletter*. Information Services: Develops online toolbox.
Members Individuals (about 1,000) in 122 countries and territories:
Albania, Algeria, Argentina, Armenia, Australia, Austria, Azerbaijan, Bahamas, Bangladesh, Belarus, Belgium, Benin, Bhutan, Bolivia, Bosnia-Herzegovina, Botswana, Brazil, Bulgaria, Burkina Faso, Cameroon, Canada, Chile, China, Colombia, Congo DR, Costa Rica, Croatia, Cuba, Czechia, Denmark, Ecuador, Egypt, Estonia, Eswatini, Ethiopia, Finland, France, Gabon, Gambia, Georgia, Germany, Ghana, Greece, Hong Kong, Hungary, Iceland, India, Indonesia, Iran Islamic Rep, Ireland, Israel, Italy, Japan, Jordan, Kazakhstan, Kenya, Korea Rep, Kyrgyzstan, Latvia, Lebanon, Lesotho, Lithuania, Luxembourg, Madagascar, Malawi, Malaysia, Maldives, Malta, Mauritius, Mexico, Mongolia, Morocco, Mozambique, Nepal, Netherlands, New Zealand, Niger, Nigeria, North Macedonia, Oman, Pakistan, Papua New Guinea, Peru, Philippines, Poland, Portugal, Romania, Russia, Rwanda, Saudi Arabia, Senegal, Serbia, Sierra Leone, Singapore, Slovakia, Somalia, South Africa, Spain, Sri Lanka, Sudan, Sweden, Switzerland, Syrian AR, Taiwan, Tanzania UR, Thailand, Togo, Trinidad-Tobago, Tunisia, Türkiye, Uganda, UK, Ukraine, United Arab Emirates, Uruguay, USA, Uzbekistan, Venezuela, Vietnam, West Bank-Gaza, Zambia, Zimbabwe.
IGO Relations *UNESCO (#20322).* **NGO Relations** Works with: *Young Professionals for Agricultural Development (YPARD, #21996).* Hosts: *Permafrost Young Researcher Network (PYRN, #18318).* [2019/XJ4115/**E**]

♦ World Association of Zoos and Aquariums (WAZA) 21208

CEO Carrer de Roger de Llúria, 2, 2-2, 08010 Barcelona, Spain. T. +34607842011. E-mail: secretariat@waza.org.
Coordinator address not obtained. E-mail: communications@waza.org.
URL: http://www.waza.org/

History 1946, Rotterdam (Netherlands). Follows up from the earlier *'International Association of Directors of Zoological Gardens'*, founded 1935, Basel (Switzerland). Former names and other names: *International Union of Directors of Zoological Gardens (IUDZG)* – former (1946 to 2000); *Union internationale de directeurs de jardins zoologiques* – former (1946 to 2000); *Unión Internacional de Directores de Jardines Zoológicos* – former (1946 to 2000); *Internationaler Verband von Direktoren Zoologischer Gärten* – former (1946 to 2000). **Aims** Guide, encourage and support zoos, aquariums and like-minded organizations of the world in animal care and welfare, environmental education and global conservation. **Structure** General Meeting (annual); Council; Committees (8). **Languages** English. **Staff** 7.00 FTE, paid. **Activities** Advocacy/lobbying/activism; events/meetings. **Events** *Annual Conference* Puerto de la Cruz (Spain) 2022, *Annual Conference* Barcelona (Spain) 2021, *Annual Conference* Barcelona (Spain) 2020, *Annual Conference* Buenos Aires (Argentina) 2019, *Annual Conference* Bangkok (Thailand) 2018. **Publications** *WAZA Magazine*; *WAZA News*. *Social Change for Conservation – The World Zoo and Aquarium Conservation Education Strategy* (2020) in Chinese, English, French, German, Hindi, Japanese, Russian, Spanish; *Protecting our Planet – The WAZA Sustainability Strategy 2020-2030* (2020) in Catalan, English, French, German, Italian, Japanese, Portuguese, Russian, Spanish; *International Zoological Studbooks*; *World Zoo and Aquarium Conservation Strategy* in Chinese, English, French, German, Japanese, Polish, Russian, Spanish – jointly with Conservation Breeding Specialist Group of IUCN/SSC. *77 Years: The History of the World Association of Zoos And Aquariums 1935-2012* (2012); *Building a Future for Wildlife: Zoos and Aquariums Committed to Biodiversity Conservation* (2010); *WAZA Aquarium Strategy for Conservation and Sustainability* (2009) in Chinese, English, Japanese, Portuguese, Spanish; *Zoo Future 2005* (1995). Conference proceedings.
Members Associations (23) in 15 countries:
Canada, Colombia, Czechia, Denmark, France, Germany, Ireland, Italy, Japan, Mexico, Slovakia, Spain, Sweden, UK, USA.
Included in the above, 8 organizations listed in this Yearbook:
Asociación Latinoamericana de Parques Zoológicos y Acuarios (ALPZA, #02252); Eurasian Regional Association of Zoos and Aquariums (EARAZA, #05614); European Association of Zoos and Aquaria (EAZA, #06283); Meso-American and Caribbean Zoo and Aquarium Association (#16730); Pan-African Association of Zoos and Aquaria (PAAZA, #18039); South Asian Zoo Association for Regional Cooperation (SAZARC, #19746); Southeast Asian Zoos and Aquariums Association (SEAZA, #19788); Zoo and Aquarium Association Australasia (#22039).
Affiliate (15) in 8 countries:
China, Germany, India, Türkiye, UK, United Arab Emirates, Uruguay, USA.
Included in the above, 3 organizations listed in this Yearbook:
European Association of Zoo and Wildlife Veterinarians (EAZWV, #06284); International Zoo Educators Association (IZE, #15944); Species360 (#19915).
Corporate (14) in 6 countries:
Australia, Denmark, Germany, Italy, UK, USA.
IGO Relations Cooperates with (1): *Secretariat of the Convention of Wetlands (#19200).* **NGO Relations** Member of (2): *International Tiger Coalition (ITC); International Union for Conservation of Nature and Natural Resources (IUCN, #15766).* Partner of (1): *International Congress of Zookeepers (ICZ, #12902).* [2022.06.30/XD0191/y/**C**]

♦ World Athletics 21209

CEO 6-8 Quai Antoine 1er, BP 359, 98000 Monte Carlo, Monaco. T. +37793108888. Fax +37793159515. E-mail: info@worldathletics.org.
Pres address not obtained.
URL: https://www.worldathletics.org/

History 17 Jul 1912, Stockholm (Sweden). Founded at congress following the Olympic Games. Constitution accepted at 2nd Congress, 1913, Berlin (Germany). First Technical Rules for international competitions presented at 3rd Congress, 1914, Lyon (France). Headquarters moved from Stockholm to London (UK), 1946; moved to Monaco, 1993. Constitution amended 1968, to provide for setting up Continental Area Associations. Most recent amendments to Constitution: Rome (Italy); 1982, Athens (Greece); 1984, Los Angeles CA (USA); 1986, Stuttgart (Germany FR); 1987, Rome; 1989 Barcelona (Spain); 1991, Tokyo (Japan); 1993, Stuttgart (Germany); 1995, Gothenburg (Sweden); 1997, Athens; 1999, Seville (Spain); 2001, Edmonton (Canada); 2003, Paris (France); 2005, Helsinki (Finland); 2007, Osaka (Japan); 2009, Berlin (Germany); 2011 Daegu (Korea Rep). Former names and other names: *International Amateur Athletic Federation* – former; *Fédération internationale d'athlétisme amateur* – former; *Federación Internacional Atletismo Aficionada* – former; *Internationaler Leichtathletik Verband* – former; *International Association of Athletics Federations (IAAF)* – former (2001). **Aims** Further enhance athletics to offer new and exciting prospects for athletes and spectators alike; ensure that every area of athletics is reviewed, tested and encouraged to strive for excellence. **Structure** Congress (every 2 years); Council; Executive Board; Committees. **Languages** English, French. **Staff** 75.00 FTE, paid. **Finance** Sources: members' dues. Other sources: sale of official books; marketing and television rights; fees from competitions. **Activities** Events/meetings; monitoring/evaluation; sporting activities. **Events** *Congress* Eugene, OR (USA) 2021, *Congress* Doha (Qatar) 2019, *International Pole Vault Meeting* Busan (Korea Rep) 2017, *Congress* London (UK) 2017, *Meeting* Vienna (Austria) 2016. **Publications** *IAAF News* (12 a year) in English; *New Studies in Athletics – Scientific and Coaching Journal* (4 a year); *IAAF Magazine* (annual) in English; *IAAF Directory/Calendar* (annual); *IAAF Competition Rules* (every 2 years) in English, French, Spanish. *IAAF Scoring Tables for Men's and Women's Track and Field Events.* Coaching books. Statistics handbooks.
Members National associations in 213 countries and territories:
Afghanistan, Albania, Algeria, Andorra, Angola, Anguilla, Antigua-Barbuda, Argentina, Armenia, Aruba, Austria, Azerbaijan, Bahamas, Bahrain, Bangladesh, Barbados, Belarus, Belgium, Belize, Benin, Bermuda, Bhutan, Bolivia, Bosnia-Herzegovina, Botswana, Brazil, Brunei Darussalam, Bulgaria, Burkina Faso, Burundi, Cambodia, Cameroon, Canada, Cape Verde, Cayman Is, Central African Rep, Chad, Chile, China, Colombia, Comoros, Congo Brazzaville, Congo DR, Cook Is, Costa Rica, Côte d'Ivoire, Croatia, Cuba, Cyprus, Czechia, Denmark, Djibouti, Dominica, Dominican Rep, Ecuador, Egypt, El Salvador, Equatorial Guinea, Eritrea, Estonia, Eswatini, Ethiopia, Fiji, Finland, France, Gabon, Gambia, Georgia, Germany, Ghana, Gibraltar, Great Britain, Greece, Grenada, Guatemala, Guinea, Guinea-Bissau, Guyana, Haiti, Honduras, Hong Kong, Hungary, Iceland, India, Indonesia, Iran Islamic Rep, Iraq, Ireland, Israel, Italy, Jamaica, Japan, Jordan, Kazakhstan, Kenya, Kiribati, Korea DPR, Korea Rep, Kosovo, Kuwait, Kyrgyzstan, Laos, Latvia, Lebanon, Lesotho, Liberia, Libya, Liechtenstein, Lithuania, Luxembourg, Macau, Madagascar, Malawi, Malaysia, Maldives, Mali, Malta, Marshall Is, Mauritania, Mauritius, Mexico, Micronesia FS, Moldova, Monaco, Mongolia, Montenegro, Montserrat, Morocco, Mozambique, Myanmar, Namibia, Nauru, Nepal, Netherlands, New Zealand, Nicaragua, Niger, Nigeria, Norfolk Is, North Macedonia, Northern Ireland, Northern Mariana Is, Norway, Oman, Pakistan, Palau, Palestine, Panama, Papua New Guinea, Paraguay, Peru, Philippines, Poland, Polynesia Fr, Portugal, Puerto Rico, Qatar, Romania, Russia, Rwanda, Samoa, Samoa USA, San Marino, Sao Tomé-Principe, Saudi Arabia, Senegal, Serbia, Seychelles, Sierra Leone, Singapore, Slovakia, Slovenia, Solomon Is, Somalia, South Africa, South Sudan, Spain, Sri Lanka, St Kitts-Nevis, St Lucia, St Vincent-Grenadines, Sudan, Suriname, Sweden, Switzerland, Syrian AR, Taiwan, Tajikistan, Tanzania UR, Thailand, Timor-Leste, Togo, Tonga, Trinidad-Tobago, Tunisia, Türkiye, Turkmenistan, Turks-Caicos, Tuvalu, Uganda, Ukraine, United Arab Emirates, Uruguay, USA, Uzbekistan, Vanuatu, Venezuela, Vietnam, Virgin Is UK, Virgin Is USA, Yemen, Zambia, Zimbabwe.
Continental associations (6):
Asian Athletics Association (AAA, #01348); Confederation of African Athletics (CAA, #04504); European Athletics (#06291); North American, Central American and Caribbean Athletic Association (NACAC, #17563); Oceania Athletics Association (OAA, #17651); South American Athletic Confederation (#19701).
NGO Relations Member of (5): *Association of Summer Olympic International Federations (ASOIF, #02943); International Council of Sport Science and Physical Education (ICSSPE, #13077); International Masters Games Association (IMGA, #14117); Olympic Movement (#17719); Sports Rights Owners Coalition (SROC, #19929).* Recognized by: *International Olympic Committee (IOC, #14408).* Summer Olympic International Federation of: *International Committee for Fair Play (#12769).*
Close cooperation with:
- *Academia de Ciencias de América Latina (ACAL, #00010);*
- *Association internationale de la presse sportive (AIPS, #02729);*
- *Asociación Panamericana de Atletismo (APA, #02284);*
- *Association of Track and Field Statisticians (ATFS, #02957);*
- *Central American and Caribbean Sports Organization (CACSO, #03665);*
- *Commonwealth Games Federation (CGF, #04332);*

– *Confederación Atlética del Istmo Centroamericano (CADICA, #04441)*;
– *European Athletics Coaches Association (EACA, #06292)*;
– *International University Sports Federation (FISU, #15830)*;
– *International Association of Ultrarunners (IAU, #12244)*;
– *International Athletics Foundation (IAF, #12290)*;
– *Panam Sports Organization (Panam Sports, #18138)*;
– *World Masters Athletics (WMA, #21640)*;
– *World Mountain Running Association (WMRA, #21659)*. [2021/XB1153/**B**]

♦ World Atlatl Association (WAA) 21210

Exec Sec 611 Broken Wheel Court, Cheyenne WY 82007, USA. T. +13074210834.
URL: http://www.worldatlatl.org/

History 17 Sep 1987, by individuals and organizations interested in the ancient hunting weapon – the atlatl. Incorporated in in the State of Colorado (USA). **Aims** Encourage the use, practice, competition, promotion, manufacture and perpetuation of the atlatl *spear thrower* as an ancient *hunting weapon* and as a modern *sporting device*; cooperate with anthropologists and archaeologists to discover, record and preserve material and information that establishes or illustrates the presence of the atlatl; provide for the maintenance and preservation of archaeological and anthropological materials and information relating to the atlatl and for making such information available for study; maintain records, rules and standards of good sportsmanship for contests using the atlatl. **Structure** Annual Meeting; Board of Directors. **Languages** English. **Finance** Members' dues. **Activities** Events/meetings. **Events** *Annual Meeting* Collinsville, IL (USA) 2015, *Symposium on Linking Science and Policy for Implementing the 2030 Agenda for Sustainable Development* Tokyo (Japan) 2015, *Annual Meeting* Cheyenne, WY (USA) 2014, *Annual Meeting* Madison, CT (USA) 2013, *Annual Meeting* Fond du Lac, WI (USA) 2012. **Publications** *The Atlatl* (4 a year).
Members Individuals; groups of individuals; organizations and institutions (362, mostly in USA). Individuals in 10 countries:
Belgium, Canada, France, Germany, Italy, Netherlands, Philippines, Switzerland, UK, USA. [2015.06.01/XF1488/v/**F**]

♦ World Autism Organisation (WAO) 21211

Organisation mondiale de l'autisme (OMA) – Organización Mundial del Autismo – Organização Mundial de Autismo – Organizzazione Mondiale per l'Autismo
Contact PO Box 33425, Al-Rawda, 73455 Kuwait, Kuwait. T. +96599771757. E-mail: info@worldautismorganisation.com.
URL: https://worldautismorganisation.com/

History 21 Nov 1998, Luxembourg. Founded by *Autism-Europe (AE, #03040)*. Registration: Belgium. **Aims** Encourage and foster the development of services appropriate to the needs of people with autism throughout the world; share knowledge and experience, and encourage resourcing in all parts of the world where it is needed. **Structure** General Assembly; Executive Committee. **Languages** Arabic, English, German, Spanish. **Staff** 4.00 FTE, voluntary. **Finance** Sources: members' dues. **Activities** Events/meetings. **Events** *World Congress* Kuching (Malaysia) 2022, *World Congress* Houston, TX (USA) 2018, *World Congress* Herning (Denmark) 2016, *World Congress* Kuwait (Kuwait) 2014, *World congress* Monterrey (Mexico) 2010.
Members Full; Affiliated; Individual. Members in 15 countries:
Argentina, Canada, Denmark, Germany, Ireland, Kenya, Kuwait, Mexico, Namibia, Qatar, South Africa, Spain, Sudan, UK, USA.
IGO Relations Cooperates with: *UNESCO (#20322)*; *WHO (#20950)*. [2020.03.06/XC0113/**C**]

♦ World Aviation MBA Association (internationally oriented national body)

♦ World Backgammon Association (WBA) 21212

Pres Vincenti Buildings, Strait Street 12-13, Valletta, VLT-05, Malta. T. +12345707010. Fax +12345707010. E-mail: ckt@world-backgammon-association.com – info@world-backgammon-association.com.
WBA Munich Hofmillerstr 3, 81245 Munich, Germany. T. +491715422222. Fax +491715422222.
URL: http://www.world-backgammon-association.com/

History 2001, Beverly Hills, CA (USA). **Aims** Promote the *game* of backgammon worldwide. **Structure** Regional offices (8): Istanbul (Turkey); Lima (Peru); Munich (Germany); Zurich (Switzerland); Bucharest (Romania); Johannesburg (South Africa); Chandigarh (India); Athens (Greece). **Activities** Organizes: Backgammon Nations World Cup; European Backgammon Doubles Championships; Backgammon Davis Doubles; European Backgammon Tour; national Backgammon Opens. [2018/XJ3138/**D**]

♦ World Backgammon Federation (WBGF) 21213

Pres Franz-Jozef Str 27, 6130 Schwaz, Austria. T. +436648792959. E-mail: contact@wbgf.info.
URL: https://wbgf.info/

History 2014. Former names and other names: *European Backgammon Federation (EUBGF)* – former (2014 to 2018). Registration: Austria. **Aims** Develop, improve, expand and promote backgammon as a mind sport according to principles of Olympic and sports rules. **Structure** Executive Board; Committees (3). **Activities** Advocacy/lobbying/activism; sporting activities. Active in: Bosnia-Herzegovina, Croatia, Denmark, France, Germany, Greece, Hungary, Iceland, Italy, Montenegro, North Macedonia, Sweden, USA.
Members Full in 35 countries and territories:
Argentina, Australia, Austria, Belgium, Bulgaria, Cyprus, Czechia, Denmark, Egypt, France, Germany, Gibraltar, Greece, Hungary, Iceland, Ireland, Italy, Jamaica, Japan, Korea Rep, Montenegro, New Zealand, Norway, Peru, Romania, Russia, Serbia, South Africa, Sweden, Switzerland, Türkiye, UK, Ukraine, United Arab Emirates, USA.
NGO Relations Partner of (1): *Worldwide Backgammon Federation (WBF, #21916)*. [2022.12.07/AA3043/**C**]

♦ World Bamboo Organization (WBO) 21214

Chairperson 9 Bloody Pond Rd, Plymouth MA 02360, USA. E-mail: info@worldbamboo.net.
URL: http://www.worldbamboo.net/

History 1992, Japan. Statutes adopted Jun 1993; amended 2004 and 2007. Former names and other names: *International Bamboo Association (IBA)* – former. Registration: USA. **Aims** Promote and support the use of bamboo as a sustainable and alternative natural resource through the development of partnerships and alliances, and the creation of mechanisms for global communication, information exchange and technology transfer. **Structure** Ambassadors, appointed by Executive Director. **Languages** English. **Staff** Voluntary. **Finance** Sources: donations; sponsorship. **Activities** Events/meetings; financial and/or material support; guidance/assistance/consulting. **Events** *World Bamboo Workshop* Binh Duong (Vietnam) / Vietnam 2022, *World Bamboo Congress* Taoyuan (Taiwan) 2021, *World Bamboo Congress* Taoyuan (Taiwan) 2020, *World Bamboo Congress* Xalapa (Mexico) 2018, *World Bamboo Congress* Korea Rep 2015. **Publications** *WBO Newsletter* (periodic) – online; *WBO Journal* – online. Congress proceedings. **Members** Over 3,500 members worldwide. Membership countries not specified. **NGO Relations** Member of (1): *United Nations Global Compact (#20567)*. [2022.06.14/XD8047/**C**]

♦ World Banana Forum (WBF) 21215

Forum mondial de la banane – Foro Mundial Bananero
Secretariat Trade and Markets Division, FAO, Via delle Termi di Caracalla, 00153 Rome RM, Italy. T. +39657052218 – +39657055810. Fax +39657054495. E-mail: wbf@fao.org.
URL: http://www.fao.org/world-banana-forum/

History 2009. Founded when Trade and Markets Division of *FAO (#09260)* organized the first forum. **Aims** Promote worldwide adoption of best practices for sustainable banana production and trade; provide a space where farmer organizations, exporter groups, trading companies, worker unions, fresh produce companies, retailers, governments, research institutions and civil society organizations can discuss the various problems facing the banana sector and jointly seek solutions through collaboration. **Structure** Steering Committee; Executive Board; Secretariat. Task Forces. Working Groups (3): Sustainable Production Systems and Environmental Impact; Distribution of Value, Labour Rights. **Activities** Events/meetings; networking/liaising. **Events** *Conference* Geneva (Switzerland) 2017, *Conference* Geneva (Switzerland) 2017, *Conference* Guayaquil (Ecuador) 2012. **Members** Retailers; importers; producers; exporters; consumer associations; governments: research institutions; trade unions; civil society organizations. Membership countries not specified. **IGO Relations** *Intergovernmental Group on Bananas and on Tropical Fruits (#11486)*. [2022/XM6126/**F**]

♦ World Bank / see International Bank for Reconstruction and Development (#12317)

♦ World Bank Administrative Tribunal (WBAT) 21216

Tribunal administratif de la Banque mondiale
Secretariat 1800 G Street NW, U11-1101, Washington DC 20006, USA. T. +12024580271. Fax +12025223581. E-mail: tribunal@worldbank.org.
URL: http://www.worldbank.org/tribunal/

History 1 Jul 1980, Washington, DC (USA). Covers *International Bank for Reconstruction and Development (IBRD, #12317)*, *International Development Association (IDA, #13155)* and *International Finance Corporation (IFC, #13597)* within the *The World Bank Group (#21218)*. Statutes adopted 30 Apr 1980; amended 31 Jul 2001. Rules adopted 26 Sep 1980; amended 8 Oct 1982, 15 Oct 1995, 1 Jun 1998 and 1 Jan 2002. Former names and other names: *Administrative Tribunal of the International Bank of Reconstruction and Development, International Development Association and International Finance Corporation* – full title; *Tribunal de la Banque internationale pour la reconstruction et le développement, de l'Association internationale de développement et de la Société financière internationale* – full title. **Aims** Decide on applications submitted by *staff* members of the World Bank Group alleging non-observance of their contracts or terms of appointment. **Structure** Tribunal comprises 7 judges, nationals of different member States of the World Bank, appointed by Executive Directors of the Bank from candidates drawn up by the Bank's President. President and 2 Vice-Presidents are elected from among Tribunal members. Administered by Secretariat. **Languages** English. **Staff** 7.00 FTE, paid. **Activities** Conflict resolution. Up to June 2022, the Tribunal had rendered 678 decisions. **Publications** *The Bench: Newsletter of the World Bank Administrative Tribunal* (2 a year); *World Bank Administrative Tribunal Reports* (annual). *Case-Law of the World Bank Administrative Tribunal – vols 1-3* (1997); *Index of Decisions of the World Bank Administrative Tribunal* (5th ed 1996).
Members Judges (7) from 7 countries:
Barbados, Canada, France, Iran Islamic Rep, Ireland, Liberia, USA. [2022.11.29/XF4459/**F***]

♦ World Bank – Civil Society Joint Facilitation Committee (JFC) 21217

Contact address not obtained. T. +12023318518. Fax +12023318774. E-mail: civilsociety@worldbank.org.
URL: http://www.worldbank.org/

History 22 Apr 2005, Washington DC (USA), during World Bank – Civil Society Global Policy Forum. Comes within the framework of *The World Bank Group (#21218)*, specifically *International Bank for Reconstruction and Development (IBRD, #12317)* (popularly referred to as 'World Bank'). Successor to *NGO-World Bank Committee (NGOWB, inactive)*. **Aims** Facilitate the creation of transparent and democratic mechanisms for more effective engagement between civil society organizations and the World Bank at the global level.
Members Organizations involved:
Alliance Sud, Swiss Alliance of Development Organisations Swissaid – Catholic Lenten Fund – Bread for All – Helvetas – Caritas – Interchurch Aid; *Asociación Latinoamericana de Organizaciones de Promoción (ALOP, inactive)*; *Caribbean Policy Development Centre (CPDC, #03540)*; *Center for Development Studies and Promotion (DESCO)*; *Freedom from Debt Coalition (FDC)*; *Institut Africain pour le Développement Economique et Social – Centre Africain de Formation (INADES-Formation, #11233)*; *Inter-Africa Group – Centre for Dialogue on Humanitarian, Peace and Development Issues in the Horn of Africa (IAG, #11381)*; *Oxfam Australia*; *Pacific Asia Resource Centre (PARC)*; *Save the Children International (#19058)*; *Society for Participatory Research in Asia (PRIA)*; *World Education (WE)*.
NGO Relations Located at: *CIVICUS: World Alliance for Citizen Participation (#03962)*. [2010/XM1466/y/**E**]

♦ The World Bank Group 21218

Groupe Banque mondiale – Grupo del Banco Mundial
Pres 1818 H St NW, Washington DC 20433, USA. T. +12024731000. Fax +12024736391.
URL: http://www.worldbank.org/

History to link the agencies comprising the Group. A specialized agency of *United Nations (UN, #20515)*, linked to *ECOSOC (#05331)*, to which the four agencies comprising the Group submit a common report. Comes within *United Nations System (#20635)*. Formal relationships between the World Bank and the United Nations are governed by an agreement approved by the Bank's Board of Governors, Sep 1947, and by the UN General Assembly, Nov 1947. Previously also referred to as *Groupe de la Banque mondiale*. **Aims** Raise living standards in poorer developing countries by conveying financial resources from the developed world; to this end, strengthen capacities in human resource development, environmentally sustainable development and private sector development. **Structure** Consists of 5 closely associated institutions, all owned by member countries that carry ultimate decision-making power: *International Bank for Reconstruction and Development (IBRD, #12317)*, established Jul 1944; *International Development Association (IDA, #13155)*, established 24 Sep 1960; *International Finance Corporation (IFC, #13597)*, established 24 Jul 1956; *Multilateral Investment Guarantee Agency (MIGA, #16888)*, established 12 Apr 1988; *International Centre for Settlement of Investment Disputes (ICSID, #12515)*, established 14 Oct 1966. The term "World Bank Group" encompasses all 5 institutions; the term "World Bank" refers specifically to IBRD and IDA. **Finance** Resources for development projects and programs come from member countries' capital subscriptions and borrowings (IBRD and IFC), or from replenishments from more industrialized and developed members (IDA), from special contributions and from transfers from IBRD net earnings. **Activities** Guiding principles (currently 6) are to: increase selectivity of activities; strengthen partnerships with others; emphasize client-orientation; increase results orientation; ensure cost effectiveness; maintain strong commitment to financial integrity. IBRD makes loans and provides economic and sector analytical work for the economic development and reconstruction of developing countries. IDA makes loans on softer terms than IBRD, for important development projects in developing countries. IFC promotes economic development in less developed areas through investments in private enterprise, without government guarantee of repayment, seeking to stimulate the flow of private capital into productive business. MIGA promotes private investment in developing countries through providing guarantees on investments to protect investors from non-commercial risks. The Group is responsible for *Africa Transport Policy Program (SSATP, #00527)*, set up in 1987 on the initiative of IBRD and reconstituted 5 Nov 2001, Stockholm (Sweden). An independent inspection panel reviews complaints from parties negatively affected by Bank projects. Instrumental in setting up: *Cities Alliance (#03950)*; *IFC Global Corporate Governance Forum (GCGF, inactive)*; *Global Road Safety Partnership (GRSP, #10581)*. **Events** *Board of Governors Annual Meeting* Marrakech (Morocco) 2022, *Launch of the Twentieth Cycle of the International Development Association (IDA20) Meeting of Donor and Recipient Countries* Tokyo (Japan) 2022, *Roundtable on Tackling the Zero Carbon Challenge in Cities* Tokyo (Japan) 2022, *Seminar on Finance for an Equitable Recovery* Tokyo (Japan) 2022, *Seminar on Translating community-led vision into practice* Tokyo (Japan) 2022. **Publications** *Commodity Markets and the Developing Countries* (4 a year); *Financial Flows and the Developing Countries* (4 a year); *World Bank Group Directory* (4 a year); *World Bank Economic Review* (3 a year); *World Bank Research Observer* (2 a year); *World Bank Annual Report*. *Global Development Finance*; *World Debt Tables*; *World Development Report*. Numerous reports, studies, books, anthologies and other documents. **Information Services** *Environmental Assessment Reports* – review potential environmental impact of individual projects; *Public Information Centre* – provides information, via the Internet, about projects under preparation for financing; *Small Grants Programme* – supports activities promoting dialogue and information exchange, including conferences, seminars, publications and other activities, with special emphasis on vulnerable populations such as women, youth, indigenous populations. **IGO Relations** Member of (1): *Infrastructure Consortium for Africa (ICA, #11206)*. Cooperates with (3): *International Monetary Fund (IMF, #14180)*; *Nordic Development Fund (NDF, #17271)*; *United Nations Institute for Training and Research (UNITAR, #20576)*. **NGO Relations** Member of (2): *Donor Committee for Enterprise Development (DCED, #05122)*; *International Association of Professional Congress Organisers (IAPCO, #12103)*. Cooperates with (1): *International Hotel and Restaurant Association (IH&RA, #13813)*. Supports (4): *ACCION International*; *Communities and Small-Scale Mining (CASM, inactive)*; *Institute for International Urban Development (I2UD)*; *Robert S McNamara Fellowships Program (RSM)*. [2020/XF6841/**F***]

♦ World Bank Group Staff Association 21219

Chair 1818 H St NW, MSN MC 1-106, Washington DC 20433, USA. T. +12024739000. E-mail: staffassociation@worldbank.org.

History 25 Feb 1972. Founded as the staff association of *International Bank for Reconstruction and Development (IBRD, #12317)*, *International Development Association (IDA, #13155)* and *International Finance Corporation (IFC, #13597)*, and, subsequently of *Multilateral Investment Guarantee Agency (MIGA, #16888)*. **Aims** Create a platform to advocate for staff rights and to opine on institutional policies that may impact staff. **Structure** Delegate Assembly; Executive Committee; Administrative Office headed by Chairperson; Country Office Staff Associations (COSAs); Working Groups; ad hoc Committees; Task Forces and Resource Groups. **Languages** English. **Staff** 10.00 FTE, paid. Additional consultants, on a needs-basis. **Finance** Sources: members' dues. **Activities** Advocacy/lobbying/activism; awards/prizes/competitions; awareness raising; conflict resolution; financial and/or material support; guidance/assistance/consulting; knowledge management/information dissemination; projects/programmes; standards/guidelines. Active in: Middle East and North Africa; East Asia and Pacific; Sub-Saharan Africa; Eastern and Central Europe; Latin America and Caribbean; South Asia. **Events** *Reimagining the World Bank Group Workplace: A Vision for Tomorrow* Washington, DC (USA) 2022, *Reimagining the WBG Workplace (post COVID)* 2021, *Focus on Goma: A Volcano, an Earthquake and an Pandemic* Washington, DC (USA) 2021, *Things You Need to Know During this Time of Change Seminar* Washington, DC (USA) 2015, *Things You Need to Know During this Time of Change Seminar* Washington, DC (USA) 2015. **Publications** *Staff Updates* (about 24 a year) – newsletter. Biennial Report; Statement to the Board of Directors.

Members Membership open to all members of the staff of the World Bank Group, on one of the following types of appointments: open-ended, term, local non-regular. Currently members in 135 countries and territories:
Afghanistan, Albania, Algeria, Angola, Argentina, Armenia, Australia, Austria, Azerbaijan, Bangladesh, Belarus, Belgium, Benin, Bhutan, Bolivia, Bosnia-Herzegovina, Botswana, Brazil, Bulgaria, Burkina Faso, Burundi, Cambodia, Cameroon, Central African Rep, Chad, Chile, China, Colombia, Comoros, Congo Brazzaville, Congo DR, Costa Rica, Côte d'Ivoire, Croatia, Djibouti, Dominican Rep, Ecuador, Egypt, El Salvador, Equatorial Guinea, Ethiopia, Fiji, France, Gabon, Gambia, Georgia, Germany, Ghana, Guatemala, Guinea, Guinea-Bissau, Guyana, Haiti, Honduras, Hungary, India, Indonesia, Iraq, Italy, Jamaica, Japan, Jordan, Kazakhstan, Kenya, Kiribati, Korea Rep, Kosovo, Kuwait, Kyrgyzstan, Laos, Lebanon, Lesotho, Liberia, Libya, Madagascar, Malawi, Malaysia, Maldives, Mali, Mauritania, Mauritius, Mexico, Moldova, Mongolia, Montenegro, Morocco, Mozambique, Myanmar, Nepal, Nicaragua, Niger, Nigeria, North Macedonia, Pakistan, Panama, Papua New Guinea, Paraguay, Peru, Philippines, Poland, Romania, Russia, Rwanda, Saudi Arabia, Senegal, Serbia, Sierra Leone, Singapore, Solomon Is, South Africa, South Sudan, Sri Lanka, Sudan, Switzerland, Tajikistan, Tanzania UR, Thailand, Timor-Leste, Togo, Tonga, Tunisia, Türkiye, Uganda, UK, Ukraine, United Arab Emirates, Uruguay, USA, Uzbekistan, Vanuatu, Vietnam, West Bank-Gaza, Yemen, Zambia, Zimbabwe.

NGO Relations Consultative status with: *Federation of International Civil Servants' Associations (FICSA, #09603).* [2022.05.04/XE4078/v/**E**]

♦ World Bank Institute (WBI) 21220

Institut de la banque mondiale – Instituto del Banco Mundial

Vice-Pres 1818 H St NW, Washington DC 20433, USA. T. +12024731000. Fax +12026760858.
URL: http://wbi.worldbank.org/

History 1955, by *International Bank for Reconstruction and Development (IBRD, #12317)* (popularly referred to as 'World Bank') as *Economic Development Institute (EDI) – Institut de développement économique (IDE) – Instituto de Desarrollo Económico (IDE)* to train government officials from developing countries in economic analysis and implementation of development projects. EDI was also referred to as *IBRD Economic Development Institute – Institut de la BIRD pour le développement économique.* Reorganized in 1995 and again in 1998. EDI merged with the World Bank's 'Learning and Leadership Center' in 1999, expanding its work programme to the training of World Bank staff. Current name adopted 1999. Became a vice-presidency in 2000. **Aims** Evolving from a training institute to a capacity development institute, enable the Bank's clients to acquire, share and apply global and local knowledge to solve problems, make informed choices, order priorities and plan and implement policies, projects and programmes; build capacity for development in response to specific country needs; engage with policymakers, academics, development practitioners, parliamentarians, journalists, teachers, youth and civil society leaders worldwide; help clients apply knowledge to development challenges; work in partnership with other organizations to promote multi-directional sharing of local and global knowledge.

Structure /Office of the Vice-President/ oversees work of:
- 1. Human Resources;
- 2. Director Operations;
- 3. Communications;
- 4. Director Regional Coordination;
- 5. Director Global Programmes, including Manager Governance;
- 6. Director Capacity Development and Sector and Thematic Programmes, comprising:
  - Sector Manager Human Development and Education;
  - Sector Manager Poverty Reduction and Economic Management;
  - Sector Manager Environmentally and Socially Sustainable Development;
  - Sector Manager Finance and Private Sector Development;
  - Technical Coordinator Capacity Development;
- 7. Trade;
- 8. Director Staff Learning (HRS);
- 9. Manager Global Development Learning Network (GDLN) and Multimedia;
- 10. Manager Institute Evaluation Group;
- 11. Chief Administrative Officer, Partnerships and Scholarships Administrator.

/External Advisory Council/, established in 1997, currently comprises 14 members, based at World Bank headquarters in Washington DC (USA).
/Country Offices/ – Abuja (Nigeria); Accra (Ghana); Addis Ababa (Ethiopia); Beijing (China); Cairo (Egypt); Dakar (Senegal); Dar es Salaam (Tanzania UR); Marseilles (France); Delhi (India); Ouagadougou (Burkina Faso); Paris (France).

Languages Arabic, Chinese, English, French, Portuguese, Russian, Spanish. **Staff** 212.00 FTE, paid. **Finance** Funded by the World Bank. Contributions of resource partners represent nearly half of the working capital, and include bilateral aid agencies, foundations, private sector and other organizations. Main contributors include Japan, the governments of Austria, Belgium, Finland, France, Germany, Italy, Korea Rep, Netherlands, Norway, Spain, and the following organizations listed in this Yearbook: *Canadian International Development Agency (CIDA, inactive); DANIDA; Department for International Development (DFID, inactive); The William and Flora Hewlett Foundation; Irish Aid; Swedish International Development Cooperation Agency (Sida); Swiss Agency for Development and Cooperation (SDC); United States Agency for International Development (USAID).*

Activities Provides learning programmes and policy advice on economic management and poverty reduction, environmentally and socially sustainable development, financial and private sector development, governance, human development, infrastructure and knowledge for development; organizes courses, seminars, knowledge networks, communities of practice and expert advice; uses both interactive technology and blended applications of new and traditional educational methods – video conferencing, the web and the classroom – to take knowledge worldwide.
- *'Learning Programmes'* include designing and delivery of courses, seminars, policy consultations and other events. Programmes: Business Competitiveness and Development; Community Empowerment and Social Inclusion; Education; Environment and Natural Resources Management; Financial Sector; Governance and Anti-Corruption; Health and AIDS; Investment Climate; Knowledge for Development; Poverty and Growth; Public-Private Partnership in Infrastructure; Rural Poverty and Development; Social Protection and Risk Management; Trade; Urban and Local Government; Water.
- *'Country Programmes'* – Regional Coordination Team (RCT), founded 2005, works with regional teams to develop a strategic approach to capacity development at the country level.
- *Global Development Learning Network (GDLN, #10317)*, initiated 2000, is a global partnership of over 100 learning centers (GDLN Affiliates) offering the use of advanced information and communication technology to people working in development worldwide.
- *'Knowledge Sharing'* – 'Knowledge Management for Organizational Capacity' aims to enhance the capacity of development-oriented organizations in World Bank client countries to achieve greater impact through the application of knowledge management tools and practices.
- 'Knowledge Bank' page acts as a repository for some of the key documents related to the World Bank's "Knowledge Bank" strategy.
- *'Scholarships'* Scholarship Program and Fellowships Program aim to share knowledge sharing and build capacity in the developing world: Robert S McNamara Fellowships Program (RSM Fellowships); Joint Japan/World Bank Graduate Scholarship Program (JJ/WBGSP).
- *'Institute Evaluation Group (IEG)'* evaluates learning and capacity development programmes implemented under the auspices of WBI and the World Bank's Knowledge and Learning Board; provides training on evaluation methods in cooperation with the Bank's Operations Evaluation Department and IFC's Operations Evaluation Group; facilitates Quality Enhancement Reviews of WBI's capacity development programs.

Events *ASEAN+3 HRD Forum* Seoul (Korea Rep) 2016, *Global Water and Environment Forum* Seoul (Korea Rep) 2016, *Korea-World Bank Cooperation Forum on Transportation Infrastructure* Seoul (Korea Rep) 2016, *Meeting on the Fourth Industrial Revolution and its Impact on Learning* Seoul (Korea Rep) 2016, *Meeting* Seoul (Korea Rep) 2016. **Publications** *WBI News* (12 a year) – electronic newsletter; *Development Outreach* (4 a year) – magazine; *Global Links* – yearbook. Annual Report. Books; case studies; working papers. **Members** Not a membership organization but has 75,000 direct training participants. [2013/XE7670/j/**E***]

♦ World Bank – WWF Alliance for Forest Conservation and Sustainable Use (WB – WWF Forest Alliance) 21221

Contact World Wildlife Fund, 1250 Twenty-Fourth Str NW, PO Box 97180, Washington DC 20090-7180, USA. T. +12022934800. E-mail: forestalliance@wwfus.org.
URL: http://www.worldwildlife.org/alliance/index.cfm

History 1998, by *International Bank for Reconstruction and Development (IBRD, #12317)* (World Bank) and *World Wide Fund for Nature (WWF, #21922).* **Aims** Significantly reduce rate of loss and degradation of all forest types. [2007/XM1097/**E**]

♦ World Baseball Softball Confederation (WBSC) 21222

Confederación Mundial de Béisbol Softbol

Headquarters Avenue Général-Guisan 45, 1009 Pully VD, Switzerland. T. +41213188240. Fax +41213188241. E-mail: office@wbsc.org.
URL: http://www.wbsc.org/

History Apr 2013. Founded on merger of *International Softball Federation (ISF, inactive)* and *International Baseball Federation (IBAF, inactive)*, with both federations becoming divisions within WBSC. Articles adopted 2013; revised and adopted 2014. Registration: Swiss Civil Code, Switzerland. **Aims** Provide a unified voice and governance of all disciplines of the *sports* of Baseball and Softball worldwide. **Structure** General Meeting (biennial); Executive Board; Baseball Executive Committee; Softball Executive Committee; Departments (3); Joint Commissions (8). Baseball Commissions (4); Softball Commissions (5). **Languages** English, Spanish. **Events** *Congress* Sakai (Japan) 2019. **Publications** *WBSC Newsletter.*

Members Federations in 141 countries and territories:
Afghanistan, Antigua-Barbuda, Argentina, Armenia, Aruba, Australia, Austria, Azerbaijan, Bahamas, Barbados, Belarus, Belgium, Belize, Bermuda, Bolivia, Botswana, Brazil, Brunei Darussalam, Bulgaria, Burkina Faso, Cameroon, Canada, Cayman Is, Chile, China, Colombia, Cook Is, Costa Rica, Côte d'Ivoire, Croatia, Cuba, Curaçao, Cyprus, Czechia, Denmark, Dominican Rep, Ecuador, El Salvador, Estonia, Fiji, Finland, France, Gambia, Georgia, Germany, Ghana, Great Britain, Greece, Guam, Guatemala, Guernsey, Guinea, Guinea-Bissau, Guyana, Haiti, Honduras, Hong Kong, Hungary, Iceland, India, Indonesia, Iran Islamic Rep, Iraq, Ireland, Israel, Italy, Jamaica, Japan, Jordan, Kazakhstan, Kenya, Korea DPR, Korea Rep, Latvia, Lesotho, Liberia, Lithuania, Malaysia, Mali, Malta, Marshall Is, Mexico, Micronesia FS, Moldova, Mongolia, Morocco, Myanmar, Namibia, Nauru, Nepal, Netherlands, New Caledonia, New Zealand, Nicaragua, Nigeria, Northern Mariana Is, Norway, Pakistan, Palau, Panama, Papua New Guinea, Peru, Philippines, Poland, Portugal, Puerto Rico, Romania, Russia, Samoa, Samoa USA, San Marino, Senegal, Serbia, Sierra Leone, Singapore, Slovakia, Slovenia, Solomon Is, South Africa, Spain, Sri Lanka, Sweden, Switzerland, Taiwan, Thailand, Togo, Trinidad-Tobago, Tunisia, Türkiye, Turks-Caicos, Uganda, Ukraine, Uruguay, USA, Uzbekistan, Venezuela, Vietnam, Virgin Is UK, Virgin Is USA, Zambia, Zimbabwe.
Continental federations (7):
Africa Baseball and Softball Association (ABSA, #00158); Baseball Federation of Asia (BFA, #03181); Confederación Panamericana de Béisbol (COPABE, #04468); Oceania Baseball Softball Confederation (WBSC Oceania, #17652); Softball Confederation of Asia (SCA, #19669); WBSC Americas Softball (#20840); World Baseball Softball Confederation Europe (WBSC Europe, #21223).

NGO Relations Member of (3): *Association of the IOC Recognized International Sports Federations (ARISF, #02767); International World Games Association (IWGA, #15914); Olympic Movement (#17719).* Recognized by: *International Olympic Committee (IOC, #14408).* [2022/XJ9416/**B**]

♦ World Baseball Softball Confederation Europe (WBSC Europe) 21223

Headquarters Av Général-Guisan 45, 1009 Pully VD, Switzerland. E-mail: office@wbsceurope.org.
URL: https://www.wbsceurope.org/

History 10 Feb 2018, France. Founded during joint congress of *Confederation of European Baseball (CEB, #04518)* and *European Softball Federation (ESF, #08792)*, following the merge of *World Baseball Softball Confederation (WBSC, #21222)* earlier. Officially launched, Feb 2019, when constitution adopted. **Structure** Congress; Executive Board. Commissions (2): Baseball; Softball. Commissions organized through: *Confederation of European Baseball (CEB, #04518); European Softball Federation (ESF, #08792).* **Activities** Events/meetings; sporting activities. **Events** *Congress* 2022, *Congress* Vilnius (Lithuania) 2020.

Members Baseball confederations in 40 countries and territories:
Armenia, Austria, Belarus, Belgium, Bulgaria, Croatia, Cyprus, Czechia, Denmark, Estonia, Finland, France, Georgia, Germany, Great Britain, Greece, Hungary, Ireland, Israel, Italy, Kosovo, Latvia, Lithuania, Malta, Moldova, Netherlands, Norway, Poland, Portugal, Romania, Russia, San Marino, Serbia, Slovakia, Slovenia, Spain, Sweden, Switzerland, Türkiye, Ukraine.
Softball confederations in 36 countries and territories:
Austria, Belgium, Bulgaria, Croatia, Cyprus, Czechia, Denmark, Finland, France, Georgia, Germany, Great Britain, Greece, Guernsey, Hungary, Ireland, Israel, Italy, Kosovo, Lithuania, Malta, Moldova, Netherlands, Norway, Poland, Romania, Russia, San Marino, Serbia, Slovakia, Slovenia, Spain, Sweden, Switzerland, Türkiye, Ukraine. [2022/XM7777/**D**]

♦ World Batik Council 21224

CEO 3rd Floor, Wisma Penyayang, No 6, Jalan Equine, Taman Enquine Bandar Putra Permai, 43300 Seri Kembangan, Selangor, Malaysia. T. +6389460222. Fax +6389460233.
URL: http://www.worldbatikcouncil.com/

Aims Develop an international network of batik practitioners and enthusiasts; foster closer ties among batik-producing countries worldwide; create a global forum for the batik craft and industry to impart knowledge, views and ideas, new trends and challenges; share techniques, innovative technology, research input and marketing strategies for the betterment of the *craft* and industry; develop the long-term growth, expansion and interest in the craft and industry internationally. **Structure** Council of 25 members. **Events** *Kuala Lumpur international batik convention* Kuala Lumpur (Malaysia) 2007, *Kuala Lumpur international batik convention* Kuala Lumpur (Malaysia) 2005. [2012/XM2270/**C**]

♦ World Baton Twirling Federation (WBTF) 21225

Fédération mondiale de twirling bâton

Pres 2429 7th St, Clay Center KS 67432, USA. T. +17853042919. Fax +18666789612.
URL: http://www.wbtf.org/

History Founded 1977, London (UK). **Aims** Encourage and develop the sport of baton twirling worldwide. **Structure** Board of Directors; Executive Officers; Committees. **Languages** English. **Finance** Members' Dues. **Activities** Events/meetings. **Events** *Board Meeting* Amsterdam (Netherlands) 2013, *Meeting* Spain 1978. **Publications** *WBTF Record Book* (annual).

Members Full in 25 countries and territories:
Australia, Belgium, Brazil, Canada, Croatia, England, France, Germany, Hungary, India, Ireland, Italy, Japan, Kazakhstan, Netherlands, Norway, Puerto Rico, Russia, Scotland, Slovenia, South Africa, Spain, Sweden, Switzerland, USA.

NGO Relations Member of: *The Association for International Sport for All (TAFISA, #02763).* [2021/XM1902/**D**]

♦ World Beard and Moustache Association (WBMA) 21226

Weltverband der Bärte – Associazione Mondiale Barbe e Baffi

Address not obtained.
URL: https://www.worldbeardandmoustacheassociation.org/

Aims Encourage the worldwide appreciation of beards and moustaches. **Structure** Board. **Activities** Events/meetings.

Members Full in 15 countries:
Australia, Belgium, Canada, France, Germany, Hungary, Mongolia, Netherlands, New Zealand, Norway, Sri Lanka, Sweden, Switzerland, UK, USA. [2021/AA1584/**C**]

♦ World Bearing Association (WBA) 21227

Contact c/o ABMA, 2025 M St NW, Ste 800, Washington DC 20036, USA. T. +12023671155. Fax +12023672155.
URL: http://stopfakebearings.com/

History Sep 2006, by *Federation of European Bearing Manufacturers Associations (FEBMA, #09493)*, the American Bearing Manufacturers Association and the Japan Bearing Industrial Association. **Aims** Promote the common, lawful interests of the world bearing industry, such as open economic engagement, sustainable development and the protection of legal rights of companies. **Events** *Annual Meeting* Tokyo (Japan) 2009. [2018/XM3974/**C**]

♦ **World Benchmarking Alliance (WBA)** **21228**
Exec Dir Rhijnspoorplein 10-38, 1018 TX Amsterdam, Netherlands. E-mail: hello@worldbenchmarkingalliance.org.
URL: https://www.worldbenchmarkingalliance.org/
History Founded by Aviva, Index Initative and *United Nations Foundation (UNF, #20563)*. **Aims** Build a movement to measure and incentivize business impact towards a sustainable future for everyone. **Structure** Supervisory Board; Executive Board. **Staff** 80.00 FTE, paid. **Activities** Advocacy/lobbying/activism. **Publications** *ALLY Voices* – Blog series. Reports. **Members** Organizations (over 240). Membership countries not specified. [2021.06.16/XM8557/y/**C**]

♦ **World BEYOND War** **21229**
Dir 513 E Main St, Suite 1484, Charlottesville VA 22902, USA. E-mail: info@worldbeyondwar.org.
URL: http://worldbeyondwar.org/
Aims End war; establish a just and sustainable *peace*. **Structure** Coordinating Committee. **Finance** Donations. **Events** *Annual Global Conference* Ottawa, ON (Canada) 2020, *Annual Global Conference* Limerick (Ireland) 2019, *Annual Global Conference* Toronto, ON (Canada) 2018. **Members** in 175 countries. Membership countries not specified. **NGO Relations** Member of: *International Peace Bureau (IPB, #14535)*. [2020.04.29/XM6358/**F**]

♦ World Bicycle Relief (internationally oriented national body)
♦ World Billiards and Snooker Council / see International Billiards and Snooker Federation (#12340)

♦ **World Billiards Union** **21230**
Union mondiale de billard (UMB)
SG Lavantgasse 18/324, 1210 Vienna, Austria.
Pres 64 Mossadak Street, Dokki GIZA, 12311, Egypt.
URL: http://www.umb-carom.org/cm/PG56L23/Union-Mondiale-de-Billard.aspx
History Founded 1 Jun 1959, Madrid (Spain), having existed since 1926 as *UIFAB*. United since Jan 1992 in an umbrella organization, *World Confederation of Billiards Sports (WCBS, #21291)*, which also includes *World Pool-Billiard Association (WPA, #21733)* and *World Professional Billiards and Snooker Association (WPBSA, #21740)*. **Aims** Ensure permanent and stable liaison between member federations and confederations; act as ruling authority for world *championships*. **Structure** Congress; Continental Confederation Committees; Committee. **Languages** English, French, German, Spanish. **Staff** 3.50 FTE, voluntary. **Activities** Events/meetings. **Events** *Biennial Congress* Terneuzen (Netherlands) 2014, *Biennial Congress* Madrid (Spain) 2010, *Biennial Congress* Colombia 2000, *Biennial Congress* Valencia (Spain) 1998, *Biennial Congress* Saint-Vincent (Italy) 1996. **Publications** *Le billard mondial* (4-5 a year) in English, French, German, Spanish. [2020/XD3479/y/**C**]

♦ **World Bioenergy Association (WBA)** **21231**
Contact Kammakargatan 22, SE-111 40 Stockholm, Sweden. T. +4684417084. E-mail: info@worldbioenergy.org.
URL: https://worldbioenergy.org/
History 2008. Registration: Skatteverket, No/ID: 802444-7958, Start date: 7 Apr 2008, Sweden. **Aims** Promote increasing utilization of bioenergy globally to support the business environment for bioenergy companies. **Structure** General Assembly; Board; Steering Committee. **Languages** English, Swedish. **Staff** 1.00 FTE, paid. **Finance** Sources: members' dues; sale of products. **Activities** Events/meetings; networking/liaising; publishing activities. **Events** *Biogas and Waste to Energy Forum* Bangkok (Thailand) 2017, *Workshop* Brussels (Belgium) 2014, *Bioenergy from Forest Conference* Helsinki (Finland) 2014, *Nordic Baltic Bioenergy Conference* Oslo (Norway) 2013. **Publications** *Global Bioenergy Statistics Report*; *WBA Bioenergy Magazine*. Fact sheets; mission reports; press releases; policy paperzs. **Members** Individuals (over 250) in over 60 countries. Membership countries not specified. **IGO Relations** Accredited by (1): *Green Climate Fund (GCF, #10714)*. Observer status with (1): *Global Bioenergy Partnership (GBEP, #10251)*. Observer to: *International Renewable Energy Agency (IRENA, #14715)*; *United Nations Framework Convention on Climate Change – Secretariat (UNFCCC, #20564)*. **NGO Relations** Member of (1): *REN21 (#18836)* (as Steering Committee Member of). Together with *International Geothermal Association (IGA, #13717)*, *International Hydropower Association (IHA, #13828)*, *International Solar Energy Society (ISES, #15564)* and *World Wind Energy Association (WWEA, #21937)*, instrumental in setting up: *International Renewable Energy Alliance (Ren Alliance, #14716)*. [2021.06.18/XJ1664/**C**]

♦ World Biogas Association (unconfirmed)

♦ **World Birdstrike Association (WBA)** **21232**
Chair Hanna Kunath Str 18, 28199 Bremen, Germany. E-mail: boardwba@worldbirdstrike.com.
Sec address not obtained.
URL: https://www.worldbirdstrike.com/
History Jun 2012, Stavanger (Norway). Successor to *International Bird Strike Committee (IBSC, inactive)*. Current constitution adopted Nov 2012; revised Dec 2016. **Aims** Improve flight *safety* regarding all aspects of the bird/wildlife strike risk to *aviation*, including measures for its mitigation and reduction. **Structure** General Assembly (every 2 years); Board of Directors; Advisory Group; Task Groups. **Finance** Sources: members' dues. **Activities** Events/meetings; training/education. **Events** *Conference* 2021, *Conference* Warsaw (Poland) 2018, *Conference* Amsterdam (Netherlands) 2016. **Members** Founder; Active; Institutional; Sponsor; Honourable. Membership countries not specified. [2022.02.02/XM6766/**C**]

♦ **World Bladder Cancer Patient Coalition (WBCPC)** **21233**
Exec Dir Square de Meeûs 38-40, 1000 Brussels, Belgium. T. +3223003345. E-mail: info@worldbladdercancer.org.
URL: http://worldbladdercancer.org/
History Jan 2019. Registration: Banque-Carrefour des Entreprises, No/ID: 0720.618.047, Start date: 12 Feb 2019, Belgium; EU Transparency Register, No/ID: 337323338117-73, Start date: 11 May 2020. **Aims** Foster an international community of people affected by bladder cancer; advocate for access to the best possible bladder cancer information, support and care; build alliances with health professionals, policy makers, academics, researchers and industry. **Structure** Board of Directors; Executive Committee; Secretariat. **Events** *World Bladder Cancer Patient Forum* 2022.
Members Full; Affiliate. Organizations in 6 countries:
Australia, Canada, France, Italy, UK, USA.
NGO Relations Member of (3): *All.Can (#00645)*; *Global Cancer Coalitions Network (GCCN, #10270)*; *Workgroup of European Cancer Patient Advocacy Networks (WECAN, #21054)*. Partner of (5): *European Association of Urology (EAU, #06264)*; *European Cancer Organisation (ECO, #06432)*; *European Cancer Patient Coalition (ECPC, #06433)*; *Société Internationale d'Urologie (SIU, #19499)*; *Union for International Cancer Control (UICC, #20415)*. [2022/AA0141/**C**]

♦ **World Blind Union (WBU)** **21234**
Union mondiale des aveugles (UMA) – Unión Mundial de Ciegos (UMC)
CEO 1929 Bayview Ave, Toronto ON M4G 3E8, Canada. T. +14164869698. Fax +14164868107. E-mail: info@wbu.ngo.
Pres 200 E Wells St, Baltimore MD 21230, USA. E-mail: president@wbu.ngo.
URL: http://www.worldblindunion.org/
History 26 Oct 1984, Riyadh (Saudi Arabia). Founded as one united world body composed of representatives of national associations of the blind and agencies serving the blind, successor body to both *World Council for the Welfare of the Blind (WCWB, inactive)*, set up 20 Jul 1951, Paris (France), and *International Federation of the Blind (IFB, inactive)*, formed in Aug 1964, New York NY (USA). Constitution adopted 26 Oct 1984; amended at: 3rd General Assembly, 2-6 Nov 1992, Cairo (Egypt); 26-30 Aug 1996, Toronto (Canada); 20-24 Nov 2000, Melbourne (Australia); 22-26 Nov 2004, Cape Town (South Africa); 18-22 Aug 2008, Geneva (Switzerland); 12-16 Nov 2012, Bangkok (Thailand). Registration: Start date: 20 Dec 1984, France; Start date: 16 Mar 2007, Canada. **Aims** Protect and promote the human, civil, political, economic, social and cultural rights of blind and partially sighted people worldwide; contribute to a world in which blind and partially sighted persons can participate fully in any aspect of life they choose; advocate for equal opportunities, protection and promotion of fundamental human rights of all blind and partially sighted persons, to ensure that their voice is heard. **Structure** General Assembly (every 4 years); Executive Committee; Regional (Geographical) Unions: *African Union of the Blind (AFUB, #00489)*; *Asian Blind Union (#01360)*; *European Blind Union (EBU, #06350)*; *Latin American Blind Union (#16256)*; East Asia/Pacific; North America/Caribbean. Geographical Unions serve as bridges between national members and the Union at world level, and further the work of the Union at regional level. Working Groups (10); Ad-hoc Committees (3); Standing Committees (8); Other Groups (2). **Languages** English, French, Spanish. **Staff** 4.00 FTE, paid. **Finance** Sources: donations; members' dues. **Activities** Advocacy/lobbying/activism; capacity building; events/meetings; healthcare; networking/liaising. **Events** *Joint General Assembly* Madrid (Spain) 2021, *Asia-Pacific Regional Seminar on Massage* Tokyo (Japan) 2021, *Joint General Assembly* Madrid (Spain) 2020, *Asia-Pacific Regional Seminar on Massage* Fuzhou (China) 2018, *Quadrennial General Assembly* Orlando, FL (USA) 2016. **Publications** *WBU Electronic Bulletin* (4 a year).
Members Categories: National; Special; International; Associate; Honorary Life. National members (over 250) in 178 countries and territories:
Afghanistan, Albania, Algeria, Angola, Anguilla, Antigua-Barbuda, Argentina, Armenia, Australia, Austria, Azerbaijan, Bahamas, Bahrain, Bangladesh, Barbados, Belarus, Belgium, Belize, Benin, Bolivia, Bosnia-Herzegovina, Brazil, Brunei Darussalam, Bulgaria, Burkina Faso, Burundi, Cambodia, Cameroon, Canada, Cape Verde, Central African Rep, Chad, Chile, China, Colombia, Congo Brazzaville, Congo DR, Costa Rica, Côte d'Ivoire, Croatia, Cuba, Cyprus, Czechia, Denmark, Djibouti, Dominica, Dominican Rep, Ecuador, Egypt, El Salvador, Equatorial Guinea, Eritrea, Estonia, Eswatini, Ethiopia, Fiji, Finland, France, Gabon, Gambia, Georgia, Germany, Ghana, Greece, Grenada, Guatemala, Guinea, Guinea-Bissau, Guyana, Haiti, Honduras, Hong Kong, Hungary, Iceland, India, Indonesia, Iraq, Ireland, Israel, Italy, Jamaica, Japan, Jordan, Kazakhstan, Kenya, Korea Rep, Kuwait, Kyrgyzstan, Laos, Latvia, Lebanon, Lesotho, Liberia, Libya, Lithuania, Luxembourg, Macau, Madagascar, Malawi, Malaysia, Mali, Malta, Martinique, Mauritania, Mauritius, Mexico, Moldova, Mongolia, Montenegro, Montserrat, Morocco, Mozambique, Myanmar, Namibia, Nepal, Netherlands, New Zealand, Nicaragua, Niger, Nigeria, North Macedonia, Norway, Pakistan, Panama, Paraguay, Peru, Philippines, Poland, Portugal, Qatar, Romania, Russia, Rwanda, Sao Tomé-Principe, Senegal, Serbia, Seychelles, Sierra Leone, Singapore, Slovakia, Slovenia, Somalia, South Africa, South Sudan, Spain, Sri Lanka, St Kitts-Nevis, St Lucia, St Vincent-Grenadines, Sudan, Sweden, Switzerland, Syrian AR, Taiwan, Tajikistan, Tanzania UR, Thailand, Timor-Leste, Togo, Tonga, Trinidad-Tobago, Tunisia, Türkiye, Turkmenistan, Turks-Caicos, Uganda, UK, Ukraine, United Arab Emirates, Uruguay, USA, Uzbekistan, Venezuela, Vietnam, Virgin Is UK, Yemen, Zambia, Zimbabwe.
Special members in 5 countries:
Bhutan, Iran Islamic Rep, Oman, Papua New Guinea, Samoa.
International members (12):
CBM Global Disability Inclusion (CBM Global); *DAISY Consortium (#04996)*; Hadley Institute for the Blind and Visually Impaired; *International Agency for the Prevention of Blindness (IAPB, #11597)*; *International Blind Sports Federation (IBSA, #12363)*; *International Council for Education of People with Visual Impairment (ICEVI, #13015)*; *International Federation of Library Associations and Institutions (IFLA, #13470)* (Libraries for the Blind Section); *International Guide Dog Federation (IGDF, #13763)*; *Lions Clubs International (LCI, #16485)*; *Perkins International*; *Sightsavers International (#19270)*; *Union Francophone des Aveugles (UFA, #20410)* (currently inactive).
Honorary Life members (38) in 23 countries:
Australia, Brazil, Canada, Denmark, Germany, India, Japan, Malaysia, New Zealand, Nigeria, Norway, Pakistan, Russia, Saudi Arabia, Singapore, South Africa, Spain, Sweden, Uganda, UK, Uruguay, USA, Venezuela.
Associate members (15) in 9 countries and territories:
Bangladesh, Central African Rep, France, India, Malaysia, Netherlands, South Africa, Sweden, USA.
Included in the above Associate members, 3 organizations listed in this Yearbook:
Helen Keller International (HKI, #10902); *International Federation for Catholic Associations of the Blind (#13377)*; *World Services for the Blind (WSB)*.
Consultative Status Consultative status granted from: *ECOSOC (#05331)* (General); *ILO (#11123)* (Special List); *WHO (#20950)* (Official Relations); *FAO (#09260)* (Liaison Status); *UNICEF (#20332)*; *World Intellectual Property Organization (WIPO, #21593)* (Permanent Observer Status). **IGO Relations** Accredited by (1): *United Nations Office at Vienna (UNOV, #20604)*. Associated with Department of Global Communications of the United Nations. **NGO Relations** Member of (2): *Conference of Non-Governmental Organizations in Consultative Relationship with the United Nations (CONGO, #04635)*; *Vision Alliance (#20796)*. Cooperates with (1): *International Organization for Standardization (ISO, #14473)*. Member of the Board of: *International Agency for the Prevention of Blindness (IAPB, #11597)*; *International Council for Education of People with Visual Impairment (ICEVI, #13015)*; *International Disability Alliance (IDA, #13176)*. Consultative status with: *International Federation of Library Associations and Institutions (IFLA, #13470)*. [2022/XB8500/y/**B**]

♦ **World Blue Chain: for the Protection of Animals and Nature** **21235**
Chaîne bleue mondiale: pour la protection des animaux et de la nature (CBM) – Cadena Azul Mundial – Blaue Weltkette – Catena Blue Mondiale – Adeia Azul Mundial – Blauwe Wereldketen: voor de Bescherming van de Dieren en de Natuur
Pres Av de Visé 39, 1170 Brussels, Belgium. T. +3226735230. E-mail: contact@bwk-cbm.be – info@chaine-bleue-mondiale.be.
URL: http://www.chaine-bleue-mondiale.be/
History 1962, Brussels (Belgium). Statutes most recently modified 17 June 2021. Registration: Banque-Carrefour des Entreprises, Start date: 15 Jul 1964, Belgium; Start date: 23 Nov 1966, France. **Aims** Promote world-wide education in order to: protect animals against bad treatment and cruelty; protect nature and environment. **Structure** General Assembly; Executive Board. *Centre international de rencontres et de documentation pour la protection des animaux et la conservation de la nature* in Brussels (Belgium). **Languages** Dutch, English, French. **Staff** 2.00 FTE, paid; 2.00 FTE, voluntary. **Finance** Sources: donations; members' dues. Annual budget: 400,000 EUR. **Activities** Financial and/or material support; knowledge management/information dissemination; monitoring/evaluation; research/documentation. **Events** *Annual Meeting* Brussels (Belgium) 1990, *Annual meeting / Triennial International Congress* Paris (France) 1990, *Annual meeting* Brussels (Belgium) 1988, *Triennial congress / Triennial International Congress* London (UK) 1987, *Annual Meeting* Geneva (Switzerland) 1986. **Publications** *La chaîne* (4 a year). Films; cassettes.
Members Individuals (about 6,000). Centres in 12 countries:
Austria, Belgium, France, Germany, Ireland, Italy, Luxembourg, Netherlands, Portugal, Spain, Switzerland, UK. [2022.05.04/XC4465/**F**]

♦ **World Boccia** **21236**
Registered Office 101 New Cavendish Street, London, W1W 6XH, UK. E-mail: admin@bisfed.com – info@bisfed.com.
URL: http://www.bisfed.com/
History Former names and other names: *Boccia International Sports Federation (BISFed)* – legal name. Registration: Companies House, No/ID: 08199521, Start date: 3 Sep 2012, England and Wales. **Aims** Promote, enhance and support Boccia as a sport for all people and help promote its activities; govern the sport of Boccia internationally; promote Boccia amongst those who make decisions that directly impact upon the sport; promote and represent members' interests. **Structure** General Assembly; Board. Committees (6): Referees; Development; Rules; Competitions; Anti-doping; Classification. **Activities** Sporting activities.
Members Full; Affiliate. Full national organizations in 59 countries and territories:
Argentina, Australia, Azerbaijan, Bahrain, Belgium, Bermuda, Brazil, Canada, Chile, China, Colombia, Costa Rica, Croatia, Czechia, Denmark, Ecuador, El Salvador, England, Faeroe Is, Finland, France, Germany, Greece, Hong Kong, Hungary, India, Iran Islamic Rep, Iraq, Ireland, Israel, Italy, Japan, Korea Rep, Kuwait, Macau, Malaysia, Mexico, Netherlands, New Zealand, Norway, Peru, Poland, Portugal, Puerto Rico, Russia, Singapore, Slovakia, Slovenia, South Africa, Spain, Sweden, Taiwan, Thailand, Tunisia, Türkiye, UK, Ukraine, United Arab Emirates, Venezuela.
Affiliate in 3 countries and territories:
Russia, Scotland, Spain.
NGO Relations Member of (2): *Association of Paralympic Sports Organisations (APSO, #02850)*; *International Paralympic Committee (IPC, #14512)*. [2022/XM5702/**C**]

♦ **World Bodybuilding and Physique Sports Federation (WBPF)** **21237**
SG 32D Jalan Tani, Singapore 417876, Singapore. T. +6596163203. E-mail: wbpfpresident@yahoo.com – abbfasia@yahoo.com.sg.
URL: http://www.wbpsf.org/
History 13 Aug 2009, Pattaya (Thailand). Former names and other names: *WBPF* – trading name. Registration: UK. **Aims** Steward, modernise and develop the sporting disciplines of bodybuilding, men's athletic and women's model physique globally. **Structure** Headquarters based in Bangkok (Thailand). **Languages** English. **Staff** 4.00 FTE, paid. **Activities** Sporting activities.
Members Affiliate (10), including 2 organizations listed in this Yearbook:

Asian Bodybuilding and Physique Sports Federation (ABBF, #01361); South Pacific Bodybuilding Federation (SPBBF, #19883).
NGO Relations Member of (4): *General Association of Asia Pacific Sports Federations (GAAPSF, #10106); Pacific Games Council (PGC, #17951); The Association for International Sport for All (TAFISA, #02763); World Leisure Organization (WLO, #21624).* [2022.10.12/XM7402/**B**]

♦ World Body Cursillos in Christianity 21238

Organisation mondiale de cours chrétiens – Organismo Mundial de Cursillos de Cristianidad (OMCC)

Pres Rua do Farol 6, 2520-401 Peniche, Portugal. T. +351914771314. E-mail: omcc.president@gmail.com.
URL: http://www.orgmcc.org/

History Founded 1980, as the central office of a worldwide movement which originated in Spain in the 1940s. Also referred to in English as *World Cursillo Body.* **Aims** Represent the Cursillos in Christianity Movement in the Pontifical Council for the Laity. **Structure** Executive Committee; International Groups, each with their own Executive Committee; National and Diocesan Secretariats; World Secretariat rotates every 4 years between 4 International Groups. **Languages** English, Spanish. **Staff** None. **Finance** International Groups share expenses of OMCC. **Activities** Events/meetings. **Events** *World Encounter* Fatima (Portugal) 2017. **Publications** *Bi-monthly OMCC Bulletin.*
Members Full in 62 countries and territories:
Antigua-Barbuda, Argentina, Australia, Austria, Barbados, Belgium, Benin, Bolivia, Brazil, Canada, Chile, Colombia, Costa Rica, Croatia, Cuba, Czechia, Dominica, Dominican Rep, Ecuador, El Salvador, Germany, Gibraltar, Grenada, Guam, Guatemala, Guyana, Honduras, Hungary, Ireland, Italy, Jamaica, Japan, Korea Rep, Mexico, Montserrat, Netherlands, Nicaragua, Northern Mariana Is, Panama, Paraguay, Peru, Philippines, Portugal, Puerto Rico, Samoa USA, Slovakia, South Africa, Spain, Sri Lanka, St Lucia, St Vincent-Grenadines, Switzerland, Taiwan, Thailand, Togo, Trinidad-Tobago, Uganda, UK, Uruguay, USA, Venezuela, Vietnam.
Also members in the Caribbean. Membership countries not specified. [2015.06.01/XF7833/**F**]

♦ World Bodyguards Association (internationally oriented national body)

♦ World Bonsai Friendship Federation (WBFF) 21239

Chairman 6912 Ely Rd, Solebury, New Hope PA 18938-9634, USA. T. +12158625925. E-mail: takasagoan@gmail.com – info@bonsaikyokai.or.jp.
URL: http://wbff-bonsai.com/

History 6 Apr 1989, Omiya (Japan). **Aims** Promote and diffuse throughout the world bonsai, a living art that can be appreciated by the people; exchange actively knowledge, technology and information related to the *art* of bonsai among countries of the world, thus advancing international friendship and goodwill. **Structure** Board of Directors (meets at least once a year), consisting of Chairman, Vice Chairman and 5 members. President; Honorary Members (2). Consultants: International Consultants (2); Special Adviser; Legal Consultant. Honorary Members (2). Latin-American Region: *Latin American and Caribbean Bonsai Federation (FELAB, #16266).* **Languages** English. **Finance** Annual dues from Regional Organizations. Donations. **Events** *World Convention* Perth, WA (Australia) 2021, *World Convention* Saitama (Japan) 2017, *World Convention* Jintan (China) 2013, *World Convention* San Juan (Puerto Rico) 2009, *World convention* Washington, DC (USA) 2005. **Publications** *The Bonsai of the World* (every 4 years). **Members** Membership comprised of regional members (Regional Organizations) representing 9 geographical regions of the world (1) Africa; (2) Australia/New Zealand; (3) China (including Taiwan); (4) Europe; (5) India; (6) Japan; (7) Asian Subcontinent (excluding China, India and Japan); (8) Latin America; (9) North America (Canada/USA/Mexico). **NGO Relations** *Bonsai Clubs International (BCI, #03301).* [2016/XF1258/**F**]

♦ World Border Organization / see BORDERPOL (#03304)
♦ World Bowling / see International Bowling Federation (#12384)

♦ World Bowls (WB) 21240

Chief Exec Sportscotland, Caledonia House, 1 Redheughs Rigg, South Gyle, Edinburgh, EH12 9DQ, UK. T. +441313179764. E-mail: worldbowls@btconnect.com.
URL: http://www.worldbowls.com/

History 1 Jul 2001. Founded by merger of *International Women's Bowling Board (IWBB, inactive)* and *World Bowls Board (WBB, inactive).* **Aims** Promote, foster and safeguard the flat green *game* of bowls; settle disputes; uphold the laws of the *sport* as currently adopted. **Structure** General Meeting (every 2 years); Council; Board; Chief Executive. **Languages** English. **Staff** 1.00 FTE, paid. **Finance** Sources: members' dues; sponsorship. Other sources: approval/accreditation fees; endorsement fees. **Events** *Biennial Council Meeting* Birmingham (UK) 2022, *Biennial general meeting* Helensvale, QLD (Australia) 2020, *Biennial general meeting* Manchester (UK) 2002.
Members Organizations in 57 countries and territories:
Argentina, Australia, Botswana, Brazil, Brunei Darussalam, Canada, China, Cook Is, Cyprus, Czechia, England, Falklands/Malvinas, Fiji, France, Germany, Ghana, Guernsey, Hong Kong, Hungary, India, Iran Islamic Rep, Ireland, Isle of Man, Israel, Jamaica, Japan, Jersey, Kenya, Korea Rep, Macau, Malawi, Malaysia, Malta, Namibia, Netherlands, New Zealand, Nigeria, Niue, Norfolk Is, Pakistan, Papua New Guinea, Philippines, Portugal, Samoa, Scotland, Singapore, South Africa, Spain, Sri Lanka, Switzerland, Thailand, Tonga, Türkiye, USA, Wales, Zambia, Zimbabwe.
International Bowls for the Disabled; *International Indoor Bowls Council (IIBC, #13839).* [2022.10.19/XF6344/**F**]

♦ World Bowls Board (inactive)

♦ World Boxing Association (WBA) 21241

Asociación Mundial de Boxeo (AMB)

Pres Av Aquilino de la Guardia y Calle 47, Ocean Business Plaza – 14th Fl – Office 14-05, Marbella, Panama, Panamá, Panama PANAMá, Panama. T. +5072037680 – +5072037681.
URL: http://www.wbaboxing.com/

History 1921, USA. 1921, Rhode Island (USA), as (USA) *'National Boxing Association (NBA)'.* Listed title adopted, 23 Aug 1962, when became international. Constitution amended: 1978, Cartagena de Indias (Colombia); 1980, Puerto Rico; 1991, Panama. Offshoots include: *World Boxing Council (WBC, #21242),* set up Feb 1963, Mexico City (Mexico); *International Boxing Federation (IBF, #12386),* set up 1982; *World Boxing Organization (WBO, #21243),* set up 28 Oct 1988, San Juan (Puerto Rico); *World Boxing Union (WBU, no recent information),* set up 1995, UK. **Structure** General Assembly (annual). Executive Committee, comprising: President; 4 Vice-Presidents; Regional Development Coordinators for Africa (WBAA) and Europe (WBAE); Presidents and Vice-Presidents of *Latin American Boxing Federation (#16259), Pan Asian Boxing Association (PABA, #18161),* and World Boxing Association North America (WBANA); International Coordinator; International Commissioner; Executive Secretary, currently President of *Federación Latinoamericana de Comisiones de Boxeo Profesional (FEDECENTRO, #09351);* Treasurer; Legal Adviser; Administrative Adviser; General Adviser, currently President of FEDEBOL – Bolivia. President's advisers (5). Regional Development Committees (5): Africa; Europe (Zones 1 and 2); Latin America; Orient and Pacific. Other committees (7): World Championships; Ratings; Legislative; Credentials; International Officials; Medical Advisory; Appeals. **Activities** Current concerns include: *'KO Drugs World Campaign',* including organization of special games events. **Events** *Annual Convention* Panama (Panama) 2020, *Annual Convention* Fuzhou (China) 2019, *Annual Convention* Medellin (Colombia) 2017, *Annual Convention* Chengdu (China) 2007, *Annual Convention* Yalta, Crimea (Ukraine) 2004.
Members Affiliated commissions (30) in 21 countries:
Argentina, Belarus, Belgium, Brazil, Canada, China, Colombia, Denmark, France, Italy, Japan, Korea Rep, Nicaragua, Panama, Russia, South Africa, Thailand, Trinidad-Tobago, UK, Ukraine, Venezuela. [2020/XC0092/**C**]

♦ World Boxing Council (WBC) 21242

Conseil mondial de la boxe (CMB) – Consejo Mundial de Boxeo (CMB)

Contact Riobamba 835, Col Lindavista, 07300 Mexico City CDMX, Mexico. T. +525551195274. Fax +525551195294. E-mail: contact@wbcboxing.com.
URL: http://www.wbcboxing.com/

History Feb 1963, Mexico City (Mexico). Founded at a meeting attended by representatives of Boxing Commissions from 11 countries. An offshoot of *World Boxing Association (WBA, #21241).* **Aims** Ensure uniform control and supervision of boxing; encourage boxing as *sport* and public appreciation of it; promote clean, fair and equitable *competition;* promote boxing safety; certify and recognize championship bouts and champions; promote competition in boxing; promote health protection and welfare of boxers; mediate for controversy solving. **Structure** World Convention (annual). Board of Governors, including: President; Permanent Vice-President; Honorary Lifetime Vice-President; Senior Vice-President; Executive Vice-President; 4 further Vice-Presidents; Vice-President at large; General Secretary; Executive Secretary; Treasurer; Legal Counsellor; Special Advisers to the President (7); Continental Federations (9). Championship Committees (2); Continental Americas Championships; WBC International Championships. Other World Committees (15): AIBA-WBC Liaison Committee; Anti-Doping Programme; Boxing Personalities; Finance Committee; Human Equality; International Boxer Passport; International Press; Promoter Liaison; Planning Committee; Ratings Committee; Rules and Regulations; WBC Ring Officials Board; WBC Legal Committee; *World Boxing School (no recent information); WBC World Medical Advisory Board (no recent information).* Sports Technical Adviser. International Ambassador. World Representatives (11) covering: Argentina; Caribbean; Central America; England; Guatemala (Guatemala); Hong Kong; Mid-Atlantic East USA; Pakistan; Panama; USA. **Languages** English, Spanish. **Staff** 8.00 FTE, paid; 200.00 FTE, voluntary. 50 honorary. **Finance** Income from promoters, boxing champions and challengers, affiliate members. Annual budget: 750,000 USD. **Activities** Events/meetings; standards/guidelines. **Events** *Annual Convention* Acapulco (Mexico) 2022, *Annual Convention* Mexico City (Mexico) 2021, *Annual Convention* Mexico City (Mexico) 2020, *Annual Convention* Cancún (Mexico) 2019, *Annual Convention* Kiev (Ukraine) 2018. **Publications** *WBC Bulletin* (6 a year); *WBC Magazine* (annual).
Members Continental boxing federations (9):
African Boxing Union (ABU, #00229); American Boxing Confederation (AMBC, #00776); Asian Boxing Council (#01364); CIS and Slovenian Boxing Bureau (CISBB, no recent information); European Boxing Union (EBU, #06388); North American Boxing Federation (NABF, #17560); Oriental and Pacific Boxing Federation (OPBF, #17894); South Continent Boxing Federation (FECONSUR). [2021/XD5220/y/**B**]

♦ World Boxing Forum (unconfirmed)
♦ World Boxing League (unconfirmed)

♦ World Boxing Organization (WBO) 21243

Organización Mundial de Boxeo (OMB)

Pres Condominium First Federal, 1056 Muñoz Rivera Ave, Ste 711-714, San Juan PR 00927, USA. T. +17877654444 – +17877650938 – +17877654781. Fax +17877589053.
URL: http://www.wboboxing.com/

History 28 Oct 1988, San Juan (Puerto Rico), by members of the previous sanctioning body, the *World Boxing Association (WBA, #21241),* which had existed since 1962, deriving from a national body set up 1920. **Aims** Encourage and assist the sport of boxing throughout the world; strive to improve public relations through educational means; encourage use of the sport as a conditioner and developer of physical fitness and as an effective offset to the increase of passive activities and entertainment; ensure greater efficiency and uniformity in the supervision of professional boxing, regulate it and obtain more effective control. **Structure** Annual Meeting; Executive Committee; World Championships Committee. Regions (7): Africa; Americas; Asia-Pacific; Europe. **Languages** English, Spanish. **Staff** 4.00 FTE, paid. **Finance** Sources: members' dues. Other sources: bouts; merchandise sales; international official dues; sanction fees; promoter licence fees; championship belts. **Activities** Awards/prizes/competitions; certification/accreditation; events/meetings; sporting activities. **Events** *Annual Convention* Tokyo (Japan) 2019, *Annual Convention* Panama (Panama) 2018, *Annual Convention* Miami, FL (USA) 2017, *Annual Convention* San Juan (Puerto Rico) 2016, *Annual Convention* Orlando, FL (USA) 2015. **Publications** *Ratings* (12 a year); *WBO Bulletin* (12 a year); *WBO Convention Magazine.*
Members Regular: athletic commissions of any duly authorized body legally organized to regulate, control or supervise boxing in any country, territorial or political subdivision, province or city; Associate; Special Associate; Honorary. Members in 49 countries:
Argentina, Australia, Belarus, Belgium, Belize, Brazil, Canada, Colombia, Costa Rica, Cyprus, Denmark, Dominican Rep, El Salvador, France, Germany, Ghana, Guatemala, Hungary, Ireland, Italy, Kazakhstan, Kenya, Korea DPR, Korea Rep, Latvia, Mexico, Mongolia, Netherlands, New Zealand, Nicaragua, Nigeria, North Macedonia, Norway, Panama, Philippines, Puerto Rico, Russia, San Marino, Serbia, South Africa, Spain, Tanzania UR, Thailand, Uganda, UK, Ukraine, USA, Uzbekistan. [2019.07.19/XD4530/**C**]

♦ World Boxing Union (no recent information)

♦ World Brahman Federation (WBF) 21244

Contact 3003 South Loop West, Ste 520, Houston TX 77054, USA. T. +17133490854. Fax +17133499795. E-mail: abba@brahman.org.
URL: http://www.worldbrahman.org/

History 6 Oct 1981. **Aims** Preserve, improve and enhance the status of the Brahman breed around the world; foster better relations between member associations; promote the Brahman *breed* and its use in all areas of the world; exchange scientific and technical information. **Structure** President; Secretary General. **Finance** Sources: members' dues. **Events** *World Congress* Asunción (Paraguay) 2022, *World Congress* Asunción (Paraguay) 2020, *World Congress* Bucaramanga (Colombia) 2018, *World Congress* Rockhampton, QLD (Australia) 2016, *World Congress* Parys (South Africa) 2014.
Members Federations in 10 countries:
Argentina, Australia, Brazil, Colombia, Ecuador, Panama, Philippines, South Africa, USA, Venezuela. [2013/XJ6458/**C**]

♦ World Breeding Federation for Sport Horses (WBFSH) 21245

Sec Dansk Varmblod, Vilhelmsborg Allé 1, 8320 Mårslet, Denmark. T. +4587475400. E-mail: varmblod@varmblod.dk.
URL: http://www.wbfsh.org/

History 1994, Berlin (Germany). Reorganized Oct 1999. **Aims** Stimulate the development of sport-horse breeding worldwide; coordinate stimulate cooperation among member studbooks; represent the common interests of the sport-horse breeding world internationally; cooperate with other relevant organizations to promote horse breeding generally, better integrate sport and breeding and to advance interests of member studbooks and individuals. **Structure** Board, comprising President and 5 Vice-Presidents. Executive Committee. Committees (3): Audit; Board of Appeal; Disciplinary. Departments (5): Promotion; Development; Breeding; Finance; Cooperation. **Events** *General Assembly* Mårslet (Denmark) 2022, *General Assembly* Mårslet (Denmark) 2021, *General Assembly* UK 2020, *General Assembly* Saumur (France) 2019, *General Assembly* Budapest (Hungary) 2018.
Members Full in 30 countries:
Argentina, Australia, Austria, Belgium, Brazil, Canada, Croatia, Denmark, Estonia, Finland, France, Germany, Hungary, Ireland, Italy, Latvia, Luxembourg, Mexico, Morocco, Netherlands, Norway, Poland, Portugal, Slovenia, South Africa, Spain, Sweden, Switzerland, UK, USA.
NGO Relations Founding Member of: *European Horse Network (EHN, #07499).* [2012/XJ5798/**C**]

♦ World Bridge Federation (WBF) 21246

Fédération mondiale de bridge

Pres WBF Secretariat, Maison du Sport International, Av de Rhodanie 54, 1007 Lausanne VD, Switzerland. T. +41215447218. E-mail: secretariat@worldbridgefed.com – president@worldbridgefed.com.
Assistant to Pres Via Moscova 46/5, 20121 Milan MI, Italy. T. +39236704987.
URL: http://www.worldbridge.org/

History 18 Aug 1958, Oslo (Norway). Original By-Laws and Constitution revised 2010, Philadelphia PA (USA). New By-Laws and Constitution adopted 2018, Orlando FL (USA). Registration: Start date: Aug 1977, USA, Stat of New York; Swiss Civil Code, Start date: Oct 2002, Switzerland. **Aims** Promote, foster, promulgate, develop and govern the *sport* of Bridge internationally. **Structure** Congress (every 2 years); Executive Council; Management Committee; Committees; Secretariat. Geographical zones (8): *European Bridge League (EBL, #06402);* North American Bridge Federation; *Confederación Sudamericana de Bridge (CSB, #04484); Bridge Federation of Asia & the Middle East (BFAME, #03328); Central American & Caribbean Bridge Federation (CAC, #03662); Asia Pacific Bridge Federation (APBF, #01862); South Pacific Bridge Federation (SPBF, #19884); African Bridge Federation (ABF, #00230).* **Languages** English. **Staff** 2.00 FTE, paid. **Finance** Sources: meeting

proceeds; members' dues. **Activities** Events/meetings; knowledge management/information dissemination; sporting activities; training/education. **Events** *Congress* Wroclaw (Poland) 2022, *Congress* Lausanne (Switzerland) 2020, *Congress* Orlando, FL (USA) 2018, *Congress* Wroclaw (Poland) 2016, *Congress* Sanya (China) 2014. **Publications** *WBF Directory* (every 2 years). *WBF Anti-Doping Regulations*; *WBF General Conditions of Contest*. Books of the World Championships.
Members National bridge organizations (103) grouping over 700,000 players in 102 countries and territories:
Albania, Argentina, Australia, Austria, Bangladesh, Barbados, Belarus, Belgium, Bermuda, Bolivia, Bosnia-Herzegovina, Botswana, Brazil, Bulgaria, Canada, Chile, China, Colombia, Costa Rica, Croatia, Cuba, Cyprus, Czechia, Denmark, Ecuador, Egypt, England, Estonia, Faeroe Is, Finland, France, Georgia, Germany, Greece, Grenada, Guadeloupe, Guatemala, Haiti, Hong Kong (China Hong Kong), Hungary, Iceland, India, Indonesia, Ireland, Israel, Italy, Jamaica, Japan, Jordan, Kenya, Korea Rep, Kuwait, Latvia, Lebanon, Lithuania, Macau (China Macau), Malaysia, Malta, Martinique, Mexico, Monaco, Morocco, Netherlands, New Zealand, Norway, Pakistan, Palestine, Panama, Paraguay, Peru, Philippines, Poland, Portugal, Réunion, Romania, Russia, San Marino, Saudi Arabia, Scotland, Serbia, Singapore, Slovakia, Slovenia, South Africa, Spain, Sri Lanka, Suriname, Sweden, Switzerland, Syrian AR, Taiwan (Chinese Taipei), Thailand, Trinidad-Tobago, Tunisia, Türkiye, Ukraine, United Arab Emirates, Uruguay, USA, Venezuela, Wales, Zambia.
NGO Relations Member of (3): *Association of the IOC Recognized International Sports Federations (ARISF, #02767)*; *International Bridge Press Association (IBPA, #12399)*; *Olympic Movement (#17719)*. Cooperates with (1): *International Testing Agency (ITA, #15678)*. Instrumental in setting up (1): *International Mind Sports Association (IMSA, #14164)*. Recognized by: *International Olympic Committee (IOC, #14408)*.
[2022/XB3952/**B**]

♦ World Broadcasting Unions (WBU) 21247

Secretariat PO Box 500, Station A, Toronto ON M5W 1E6, Canada. T. +14165989877. Fax +14165989774.
URL: http://www.worldbroadcastingunions.org/
History 1992, by *North American Broadcasters Association (NABA, #17561)*. **Aims** Act as coordinating body at international broadcasting level. **Structure** Working Committees (4): *International Satellite Operations Group (ISOG)*; Technical Committee; Sports Committee; WIPO Broadcaster Treaty Group. Inter-Union Legal Committee. **Languages** English, French, Spanish. **Staff** 5.00 FTE, paid. **Finance** Members' dues. Annual budget: US$ 1,000,000. **Activities** Events/meetings. **Events** *Meeting* Tokyo (Japan) 2014, *World electronic media forum* 2011, *Annual meeting* Copenhagen (Denmark) 2009, *World electronic media forum* Mexico City (Mexico) 2009, *Meeting* Tokyo (Japan) 2009.
Members International organizations (8):
African Union of Broadcasting (AUB, #00490); *Arab States Broadcasting Union (ASBU, #01050)*; *Asia-Pacific Broadcasting Union (ABU, #01863)*; *Caribbean Broadcasting Union (CBU, #03465)*; *European Broadcasting Union (EBU, #06404)*; *International Association of Broadcasting (IAB, #11738)*; NABA; *Organización de Telecomunicaciones de Iberoamérica (OTI, #17851)*.
NGO Relations NABA serves as secretariat. [2018.06.27/XD6922/y/**D**]

♦ World Brotherhood Federation (inactive)

♦ World Buddhist Sangha Council (WBSC) 21248

SG – English Section 6 Shaoshing North Street, Taipei, Taiwan. T. +88622395564. Fax +886223913770. E-mail: wbsc5564@ms64.hinet.net.
URL: http://www.wbsc886.org/
History 1966. Constitution adopted 16 May 1966, Colombo (Sri Lanka); amended at: 3rd International Congress, 4 Dec 1981, Taipei (Taiwan); 4th International Congress, 8 Jan 1986, Bangkok (Thailand); 5th International Congress, 31 Oct 1989, Taipei; 6th International Congress, 8 Nov 1995; 7th International Congress, 12 Nov 2000. **Aims** Promote better relationships amongst the Sangha; promote *Dhammaduta* activities throughout the world, particularly in countries from which requests for such activities are made; promote cordiality of relationship between the laity and the Sangha; uphold the *freedom* and *peace* in the world through the Sangha. **Structure** General Council followed by General Assembly (every 4 years). Executive Committee (meets every 2 years), consisting of President, 2 (or more) Vice-Presidents, Secretary-General (English section), Secretary-General (Chinese section), Assistant Secretary-General (English section), Assistant Secretary-General (Chinese section), General Treasurer, Assistant General Treasurer and 11 Committee members in charge (as Directors) of the following activities: (1) Propagation of the Dhamma; (2) Education of the Sangha and laity; (3) Social affairs: (4) Healthy relationship between the Sangha and the laity; (5) Youth organizations; (6) Finance; (7) Culture; (8) Membership; (9) Rituals; (10) Liaison; (11) Bhikshuni. **Languages** Chinese, English. **Events** *General Conference* Kuala Lumpur (Malaysia) 2005, *General Conference* Taipei (Taiwan) 2000, *International Congress* Taiwan 2000, *General Conference / International Congress* Penang (Malaysia) 1995, *Youth conference* Singapore (Singapore) 1993.
Members Full Sangha of the countries accepting the terms and conditions of WBSC Constitution. Associate members of the Buddhist laity. Branch Organizations Sangha organizations throughout the world accepting WBSC Constitution. Members in 26 countries and territories:
Australia, Bangladesh, Canada, France, Germany, Hong Kong, India, Indonesia, Japan, Korea Rep, Macau, Malaysia, Mongolia, Myanmar, Nepal, Netherlands, New Zealand, Philippines, Russia, Singapore, Sri Lanka, Sweden, Taiwan, Thailand, UK, USA.
NGO Relations Associate Member Unit of: *World League for Freedom and Democracy (WLFD, #21621)*.
[2012/XF0147/**F**]

♦ World Buddhist Supreme Tathagata Followers (religious order)
♦ World Buddhist University (internationally oriented national body)
♦ World Budo Confederation (unconfirmed)

♦ World Budo Federation (WBF) 21249

International Pres Murat Reis Mah, Silahtar Bahce Sok No 24/1, Uskudar, Istanbul/Istanbul, Türkiye. T. +902163428046. Fax +902163428046.
URL: http://www.worldbudo.com/
Aims Promote and popularize martial arts. **Structure** Council (elected for 4-year term); Secretariat location changes according to the location of the current International President. **Languages** Dutch, English, Turkish. **Finance** Sources: members' dues. **Activities** Events/meetings; training/education.
Members in 30 countries:
Australia, Austria, Azerbaijan, Bangladesh, Belarus, Belgium, Bulgaria, Canada, Croatia, Egypt, Germany, Greece, India, Iran Islamic Rep, Iraq, Israel, Italy, Kazakhstan, Lebanon, Netherlands, Portugal, Russia, Saudi Arabia, Serbia, Sri Lanka, Türkiye, UK, Ukraine, United Arab Emirates, USA.
NGO Relations Includes and works through many other organizations and federations worldwide.
[2015.01.07/XJ0529/**C**]

♦ World Budokan Council (unconfirmed)
♦ World Budo Martial Arts Federation (unconfirmed)

♦ World Bureau of Metal Statistics (WBMS) 21250

Office mondial des statistiques du métal – Oficina Mundial de Estadisticas del Metal (OMEM)
Managing Director 31 Star Street, Ware, SG12 7AA, UK. T. +4401920461274. E-mail: enquiries@world-bureau.co.uk.
URL: http://www.world-bureau.com/
History 1946. **Aims** Offer publications and services which are essential for metals specialists. **Languages** English. **Staff** 7.00 FTE, paid. **Finance** Sources: sale of publications. **Publications** *World Metal Statistics* (12 a year); *Annual Stainless Steel Statistics* (annual); *Metallstatistik* (annual); *World Metal Statistics Yearbook*. *Long Term Production/Consumption*; *World Flow Charts*. Bespoke reports. **Information Services** *Crude Steel Database*; *Database Service*; *Stainless Steel Database*. **Consultative Status** Consultative status granted from: *UNCTAD (#20285)* (Special Category). [2022.05.04/XE4953/**E**]

♦ World Business Academy 21251

Founder/Pres/CEO 2020 Alameda Padre Serra, Ste 135, Santa Barbara CA 93103, USA. T. +18058924600. Fax +18058840900. E-mail: info@worldbusiness.org.
URL: http://www.worldbusiness.org/
History Founded 1986, as a result of a series of discussions and projects at *SRI International*. **Aims** Inspire business to assume *responsibility* for the whole of society by changing the consciousness of leaders, students and the public. **Structure** Board of Directors, consisting of President, Chairman and 9 members. Fellows (78). **Staff** 3.00 FTE, paid. **Finance** Members' dues. Other sources: grants; contributions. **Activities** Carries out research and promotes educational materials to business leaders in the areas of new business paradigms, sustainable business strategies and the development of human potential at work; organizes global and regional conferences. **Events** *Fellows conference / Fellows' Conference* Evanston, IL (USA) 2006, *Fellows conference / Fellows' Conference* Santa Barbara, CA (USA) 2005, *Annual members meeting* Santa Barbara, CA (USA) 2004, *Fellows conference / Fellows' Conference* Santa Barbara, CA (USA) 2004, *Annual members meeting* London (UK) 2003. **Publications** *Currents in Commerce* (12 a year) – online newsletter. *Freedom from Mid-East Oil* (2007).
Members Organizations (248) in 23 countries:
Australia, Belgium, Brazil, Canada, China, Croatia, Czechia, Denmark, Finland, France, Germany, India, Ireland, Japan, Netherlands, Russia, South Africa, Sweden, Switzerland, Tanzania UR, Thailand, UK, USA.
IGO Relations *ILO (#11123)*. **NGO Relations** Links with a large number of organizations active in the field (not specified). Instrumental in setting up: *Foundation for Global Community – Global Initiatives Team for the CSCE*; *KVK Raju International Leadership Academy, Hyderabad (no recent information)*. [2015/XF2897/**F**]

♦ World Business Angels Association (no recent information)

♦ World Business Angels Investment Forum (WBAF) 21252

SG address not obtained.
URL: https://www.wbaforum.org/
Aims Ease access to finance for businesses from start up to scale up, so s to generate more jobs and more social justice worldwide. **Structure** Executive Council; Board. **Events** *World Congress of Angel Investors* Antalya (Türkiye) 2022, *World Congress of Angel Investors* 2021, *World Congress of Angel Investors* 2021, *World Congress* Istanbul (Turkey) 2021, *World Congress* Istanbul (Turkey) 2020. **IGO Relations** Affiliated with (1): *Global Partnership for Financial Inclusion (GPFI, #10534)*. **NGO Relations** *Asociación de las Camaras de Comercio e Industria del Mediterraneo (ASCAME, #02112)*. [2022/XM8730/**F**]

♦ World Business Associates (WBA) 21253

Pres 7910 Woodmont Avenue – Ste 1440, Bethesda MD 20814, USA. T. +12024665428. Fax +12024528540. E-mail: wja@worldjurist.org.
URL: http://www.worldjurist.org/
History 1979, as *World Association of Center Associates (WACA) – Association mondiale des associés du Centre (AMAC)*, by *'World Peace Through Law Center (WPTLC)'*, now *World Jurist Association (WJA, #21604)*, to which it is affiliated. **Aims** Mobilize individuals, non-legal and business-legal professionals interested in the work of WJA; promote the objectives of WJA; promote interest, activities and research in the field of international *law*. **Languages** English. **Staff** 3.00 FTE, paid. 2 interns. **Events** *Biennial Meeting* Adelaide, SA (Australia) / Sydney, NSW (Australia) 2003, *Biennial Meeting* Belfast (UK) / Dublin (Ireland) 2001, *Biennial Meeting* Vienna (Austria) 1999, *Biennial Meeting* Doha (Qatar) 1997, *Biennial Meeting* Manila (Philippines) 1993. **Publications** *Law/Technology* (4 a year) – journal; *The World Jurist* (at least 6 a year) – newsletter.
Members Individual members. Membership equals that of WJA. [2012.07.24/XE6510/v/**E**]

♦ World Business Council / see World President's Organization

♦ World Business Council for Sustainable Development (WBCSD) . . . 21254

Pres/CEO Maison de la Paix, Chemin Eugène-Rigot 2B, CP 2075, 1211 Geneva 1, Switzerland. T. +41228393100. Fax +41228393131. E-mail: info@wbcsd.org.
URL: http://www.wbcsd.org/
History 1 Jan 1995, Geneva (Switzerland). Founded upon merger of *Business Council for Sustainable Development (BCSD, inactive)* and *World Industry Council for the Environment (WICE, inactive)*. **Aims** Accelerate the transition to a sustainable world by making more sustainable businesses more successful. **Structure** Council (meets annually); Executive Committee; Regional Offices (2); Regional Network; Secretariat in Geneva (Switzerland). **Languages** English. **Staff** 90.00 FTE, paid. 90. **Finance** Sources: members' dues. **Activities** Events/meetings; guidance/assistance/consulting; politics/policy/regulatory; projects/programmes. **Events** *Annual General Meeting* Tokyo (Japan) 2022, *Annual Council Meeting* Tokyo (Japan) 2021, *Annual General Meeting* Tokyo (Japan) 2021, *Annual Council Meeting* Tokyo (Japan) 2020, *Annual General Meeting* Tokyo (Japan) 2020. **Publications** Case studies; recommendations; videos.
Members International companies (200) in over 20 major industrial sectors in 53 countries and territories:
Algeria, Argentina, Australia, Austria, Belgium, Bolivia, Brazil, Canada, China, Colombia, Costa Rica, Croatia, Denmark, Ecuador, Egypt, El Salvador, France, Germany, Greece, Guatemala, Honduras, Hungary, India, Japan, Kazakhstan, Korea Rep, Malaysia, Mexico, Mongolia, Mozambique, Neth Antilles, New Zealand, Nicaragua, Norway, Pakistan, Panama, Paraguay, Peru, Philippines, Poland, Portugal, Russia, South Africa, Spain, Sri Lanka, Taiwan, Thailand, Türkiye, UK, United Arab Emirates, Uruguay, USA, Zimbabwe.
Consultative Status Consultative status granted from: *ECOSOC (#05331)* (Ros A); *UNEP (#20299)*; *United Nations Commission on Sustainable Development (CSD, inactive)*; *World Trade Organization (WTO, #21864)*.
IGO Relations Accredited to the Conference of the Parties of: *Secretariat of the United Nations Convention to Combat Desertification (Secretariat of the UNCCD, #19208)*. Partners include: *Inter-American Development Bank (IDB, #11427)*; *International Bank for Reconstruction and Development (IBRD, #12317)* (World Bank); *International Energy Agency (IEA, #13270)*; *International Finance Corporation (IFC, #13597)*; *Round Table on Sustainable Development at the OECD (see: #17693)*; *UN-Water (#20723)*; *UNDP (#20292)*; *UNEP (#20299)*; *United Nations Forum on Forests (UNFF, #20562)*; *United Nations Framework Convention on Climate Change – Secretariat (UNFCCC, #20564)*.
NGO Relations Instrumental in setting up: *Greenhouse Gas Protocol (GHG Protocol, #10721)*; *International Emissions Trading Association (IETA, #13262)*; *Low Carbon Technology Partnerships Initiative (LCTPi, #16516)*. Member of: *Global Alliance for Buildings and Construction (GlobalABC, #10187)*; *Natural Capital Coalition (NCC, #16952)*; *We Mean Business*. Founding partner of: *Water Footprint Network (WFN, #20829)*. Partners include:
- *Arab Union for Cement and Building Materials (AUCBM, #01065)*;
- *BUSINESSEUROPE (#03381)*;
- *Confederation of European Paper Industries (CEPI, #04529)*;
- *Energy Poverty Action (EPA, #05474)*;
- *Global Enabling Sustainability Initiative (GeSI, #10340)*;
- *Green Economy Coalition (GEC, #10717)*;
- *International Aluminium Institute (IAI, #11643)*;
- *International Chamber of Commerce (ICC, #12534)*;
- *International Federation of Private Water Operators (AquaFed, #13517)*;
- *International Institute for Environment and Development (IIED, #13877)*;
- *International Institute for Sustainable Development (IISD, #13930)*;
- *International Union for Conservation of Nature and Natural Resources (IUCN, #15766)*;
- *LatinoAméricaPosible (LAP, #16402)*;
- *Library Assembly of Eurasia (LAE, #16458)*;
- *The Nature Conservancy (TNC)*;
- *SNV Netherlands Development Organisation (SNV)*;
- *Oxfam International (#17922)*;
- *Peterson Institute for International Economics, Washington (PIIE)*;
- *SEED (#19213)*;
- *Stockholm International Water Institute (SIWI)*;
- *United Nations Global Compact (#20567)*;
- *World Economic Forum (WEF, #21367)*;
- *World Energy Council (WEC, #21381)*;
- *World Resources Institute (WRI, #21753)*;
- *World Steel Association (worldsteel, #21829)*;
- *World Wide Fund for Nature (WWF, #21922)*. [2020/XD4162/**C**]

♦ World Business Organization / see International Chamber of Commerce (#12534)
♦ World Business Transformation Forum (internationally oriented national body)
♦ World Calendar Association (inactive)

♦ The World Calendar Association – International (TWCA) 21255
Dir PO Box 456, Ellinwood KS 67526, USA.
History 11 Jun 1947, New York NY (USA), as successor to *World Calendar Association (inactive)*, set up Oct 1930. 1955, name changed to *International World Calendar Association (IWCA) – Association internationale pour le calendrier mondial*. Present name adopted, 2005. **Aims** Conduct scientific research and organize international non-governmental support for adoption of a perpetual calendar, namely four equal quarters of 91 days each plus one World Day. **Structure** Congress (annual); World Consultative Committee. **Languages** English. **Finance** Members' dues. Gifts. **Publications** *Calendar Contrasts*; *World Calendar Reform*. **Members** National committees and affiliated individuals in various countries.Membership countries not specified. [2017/XD2821/**D**]

♦ WorldCALL 21256
Contact UPV Ling Aplicada, Camino de Vera 14, 46022 Valencia, Spain.
URL: http://www.worldcall.org/
Aims Enhance *computer-assisted language teaching* and learning in the global community by bringing together educators worldwide. **Structure** Steering Committee of 7. **Events** *Conference* Kazan (Russia) 2023, *CALLing all the CALLers worldwide* Concepción (Chile) 2018, *Sustainability and CALL* Glasgow (UK) 2013, *Conference* Fukuoka (Japan) 2008, *Conference* Banff, AB (Canada) 2003.
Members Organizations (8), including the following 3 listed in this Yearbook:
Confédération européenne des centres de langues de l'enseignement supérieur (CercleS, #04540); European Association for Computer Assisted Language Learning (EUROCALL, #05985); International Association for Language Learning Technology (IALLT). [2017/XJ6085/y/**C**]

♦ World Cancer Research Fund / see World Cancer Research Fund International
♦ World Cancer Research Fund International (internationally oriented national body)

♦ World Capital Institute (WCI) 21257
Technical Secretariat Tecnológico de Monterrey, Campus Monterrey, Edificio CETEC 3N, Eugenio Garza Sada 2501, Sur 64849, 64849 Monterrey NL, Mexico. T. +528183284049. E-mail: worldcapitalinstitutewci@gmail.com – info@worldcapitalinstitute.org.
Exec Dir – Events c/o Science and Engineering Fac, Civil Engineering and The Built Environment Property and Planning, Queensland Univ of Technology, 2 George Street, Brisbane QLD 4001, Australia. T. +61731382418. Fax +61731381170.
URL: http://www.worldcapitalinstitute.org/
History Former names and other names: *World Capitalist Institute* – former. **Aims** Further the understanding and application of knowledge as the most powerful leverage of development. **Structure** Executive Board; International Advisory Board. Technical Secretariat. **Activities** Awards/prizes/competitions; events/meetings; research/documentation. **Events** *Knowledge Cities World Summit* Caxias do Sul (Brazil) 2021, *Knowledge Cities World Summit* 2020, *Knowledge Cities World Summit* Florianópolis (Brazil) 2019, *Knowledge Cities World Summit* Vienna (Austria) 2016, *Knowledge Cities World Summit* Daegu (Korea Rep) 2015. [2021/XJ2306/j/**C**]

♦ World Capitalist Institute / see World Capital Institute (#21257)
♦ World Care (internationally oriented national body)

♦ World Carfree Network 21258
Contact address not obtained.
Main: http://www.worldcarfree.net/
History 1997. Founded growing out of the activities of *Car Busters*. Functions as a virtual network. *World Carfree Network Europe (WCN Europe)*, set up 2 Oct 2006, and dissolved 16 Mar 2012. **Aims** Promote alternatives to car dependence and automobile-based planning at the international level; reduce the human impact on the natural *environment* while improving the *quality of life* for all. **Languages** English. **Staff** 2.00 FTE, paid; 3.00 FTE, voluntary. **Finance** Grants; donations; sales of resource materials. **Activities** Organizes Towards Carfree Cities Conference. Acts a information and networking centre for organizations working in the field of sustainable transport worldwide. **Events** *Towards Carfree Cities Conference* Guadalajara (Mexico) 2011, *Towards Carfree Cities Conference* York (UK) 2010, *Towards Carfree Cities Conference* Portland, OR (USA) 2008, *Towards carfree cities conference* Istanbul (Turkey) 2007, *Towards carfree cities conference* Bogota (Colombia) 2006. **Publications** *World Carfree news* (12 a year) – bulletin; *Carbusters Online*. *The Towards Carfree Cities* – conference series.
Members Full organizations (50) in 20 countries:
Australia, Bangladesh, Brazil, Canada, Colombia, Czechia, Estonia, France, Germany, Greece, Hungary, Italy, Peru, Poland, Russia, Serbia, Spain, UK, USA, Venezuela.
Included in the above, 1 organization listed in this Yearbook:
United Nations Human Settlements Programme (UN-Habitat, #20572). [2017/XJ4517/**F**]

♦ World Cargo Alliance (WCA) 21259
Headquarters 10795 W Twain Ave, Ste 110, Las Vegas NV 89135, USA. E-mail: info@wcaworld.com.
China Room 503 Building B, Guangqi Cultural Plaza, 2899A Xietu Road, Xuhui District, 200030 Shanghai, China. T. +862164879050. Fax +862164879071. E-mail: dwang@wcaworld.com.
URL: http://www.wcaworld.com/
History 1998. **Aims** Provide independent international *freight forwarders* with effective means of communicating with each other to establish and maintain *business* partnerships that would benefit *shippers* and buyers worldwide. **Events** *Worldwide Conference* Singapore (Singapore) 2023, *Projects Network Conference* Amsterdam (Netherlands) 2019, *Sino-European Freight Forwarders Conference* Barcelona (Spain) 2019, *Worldwide Conference* Singapore (Singapore) 2019, *Sino-European Freight Forwarders Conference* Barcelona (Spain) 2018. **Members** 1119 in 165 countries. Membership countries not specified. [2017/XJ0680/**D**]

♦ World Carillon Federation (WCF) 21260
Fédération mondiale du carillon (FMC) – Beiaard Wereld Federatie (BWF)
Vice-Pres Broekstraat 23, 3271 Averbode, Belgium. T. +3213782022.
URL: http://www.carillon.org/
History 1974, Douai (France). Statutes adopted, 8 Aug 1978, Amersfoort (Netherlands). **Aims** Serve as a link among carillon associations in order to defend and promote interests of carillonneurs and develop the art of the carillon, including: its improvement from a musical point of view as well as from construction; creation and maintenance of relations among carillonneurs worldwide; establishment of artistic and musical exchanges. **Structure** Committee of Delegates. Executive Committee of 7 members. **Languages** Dutch, English, French. **Staff** Voluntary. **Finance** Members' dues. **Activities** Organizes triennial world congress, establishes world standards. **Events** *World Congress* Utrecht (Netherlands) 2023, *World Congress and Joint Congress* Hartford, CT (USA) 2021, *Biennial World Congress* USA 2020, *Biennial World Congress* Barcelona (Spain) 2017, *Biennial World Congress* Antwerp (Belgium) 2014. **Publications** *WCF Bulletin* (2 a year).
Members Organizations in 20 countries and territories:
Australia, Belgium, Canada, Denmark, Finland, France, Germany, Iceland, Ireland, Lithuania, Mexico, Netherlands, New Zealand, Northern Ireland, Norway, Poland, Sweden, Switzerland, UK, USA.
Included in the above, 1 regional organization listed in this Yearbook:
Nordisk Selskab for Campanologi og Klokkespil (NSCK, #17533). [2021/XD8115/**D**]

♦ World Carpet and Rug Council (WCRC) 21261
Secretariat 730 College Drive, PO Box 2048, Dalton GA 30722-2048, USA. T. +17064282104. Fax +17064283104.
Chairman Rue Montoyer 24 – Bte 6, 1000 Brussels, Belgium. T. +3222801813. Fax +3222801809. E-mail: ecra@euratex.org.
URL: http://www.wcrc-net.org/
Aims Promote areas of common interest that will facilitate the growth of the carpet industry worldwide and regionally. **Structure** Chairman; Vice-President; Secretariat.
Members Organizations in 5 countries:
Australia, Canada, China, Japan, USA.
Regional organization:
European Carpet and Rug Association (ECRA, #06452). [2018/XJ0288/**E**]

♦ World Cat Congress (WCC) 21262
Sec/Treas 2316 Beechmont Road, Beechmont QLD 4211, Australia. E-mail: secretary@worldcatcongress.org.
URL: http://www.worldcatcongress.org/
History Founded following the World Congress of Feline Associations, 1994, Venice (Italy). Charter accepted, Mar 1999; Constitution drawn up, Sep 2003 and amended Jun 2005, Mar 2014, Apr 2015, Apr 2017, Apr 2018, Jul 2019. **Aims** Promote better understanding and cooperation among the world's various cat associations in matters of mutual interest and concern such as cat legislation and feline welfare which affects all cat lovers, from the pedigree breeder to the pet owner. **Structure** General Meeting (annual). **Languages** English. **Staff** 0.5 FTE, honorary. **Finance** Sources: members' dues. **Activities** Events/meetings; publishing activities. **Events** *Annual Congress* Launceston, TAS (Australia) 2023, *Annual Congress* Cape Town (South Africa) 2019, *Annual Congress* Milan (Italy) 2018, *Annual Congress* Las Vegas, NV (USA) 2017, *Annual Congress* Bangkok (Thailand) 2016.
Members Organizations (9) including the following 3 international organizations listed in this Yearbook:
Fédération internationale féline (FIFe, #09632); The International Cat Association (TICA); World Cat Federation (WCF, #21263). [2022/XM3693/y/**C**]

♦ World Cat Federation (WCF) 21263
SG Hapsalas 15-31, Riga LV-1005, Latvia. E-mail: wcf@wcf-online.de.
Pres Geisbergstr 2, 45139 Essen, Germany. T. +49201555724. Fax +49201555747.
URL: https://wcf.de
History 1988, Rio de Janeiro (Brazil). Registration: Germany. **Aims** Standardize rules regarding shows, judges and awards; define breeds and uniform standards; acknowledge and adjust pedigree registration of the clubs; introduce and regulate an international registration list of kennels; produce an official list of all WCF educated or recognized judges. **Structure** General Assembly (every 2 years); Board; Extended Board; Panels (3). **Languages** English, French, German. **Finance** Members' dues. **Events** *General Assembly* Essen (Germany) 2010, *General Assembly* Essen (Germany) 2008, *General Assembly* Essen (Germany) 2006, *General Assembly* Essen (Germany) 2004, *General Assembly* Milan (Italy) 2002.
Members Full in 29 countries:
Argentina, Australia, Austria, Belarus, Belgium, Brazil, Chile, Cyprus, Czechia, Estonia, France, Germany, Hungary, India, Israel, Italy, Latvia, Lithuania, Malta, New Zealand, Poland, Romania, Russia, South Africa, Spain, Switzerland, Ukraine, United Arab Emirates, USA.
Patronage membership in 12 countries:
Belgium, Colombia, France, Germany, Israel, Italy, Monaco, Poland, Russia, Switzerland, Türkiye, Ukraine.
NGO Relations Founding member of: *World Cat Congress (WCC, #21262).* [2021/XD6863/**D**]

♦ World Catholic Association for Communication (SIGNIS) 21264
Association catholique mondiale pour la communication – Asociación Católica Mundial para la Comunicación
SG Rue Royale 310, 1210 Brussels, Belgium. T. +3227349708. Fax +3227347018. E-mail: news@signis.net – sg@signis.net.
URL: http://www.signis.net/
History Nov 2001, Rome (Italy). Set up by merger of *Unda, International Catholic Association for Radio and Television (inactive)*, founded 19 Jun 1928, Cologne (Germany) as *'International Catholic Bureau for Broadcasting – Bureau catholique international de radiodiffusion'*, and *International Catholic Organization for Cinema and Audiovisual (OCIC, inactive)*, founded 1928, The Hague (Netherlands). Officially recognized as an International Association of the Faithful by the Holy See thorough approval of its Canonical Statutes, 24 Oct 2014. Registration: Banque-Carrefour des Entreprises, No/ID: 0876.462.801, Start date: 4 Oct 2005, Belgium. **Aims** Engage with *media* professionals and support Catholic communicators; transform cultures in the light of the Gospel by promoting human dignity, justice and reconciliation. **Structure** Assembly of Delegates; Board of Management. Regional secretariats: *Asociación Católica Latinoamericana y Caribeña de Comunicación (SIGNIS ALC, see: #21264); SIGNIS Africa (see: #21264); SIGNIS Asia (see: #21264); SIGNIS Europe (see: #21264); SIGNIS Middle East (no recent information); SIGNIS North America (no recent information); SIGNIS Pacific (see: #21264).* Also includes: *SIGNIS Services Rome (SSR, #19274).* **Languages** English, French, Spanish. **Staff** 16.00 FTE, paid. **Finance** by Catholic aid agencies worldwide, Belgian government, and OPPF (Vatican). **Activities** Advocacy/lobbying/activism; awards/prizes/competitions; capacity building; events/meetings; projects/programmes; training/education. **Events** *World Congress* Seoul (Korea Rep) 2022, *World Congress* Seoul (Korea Rep) 2021, *TV Seminar* Dublin (Ireland) 2018, *The situation of the Catholic Church and society in the digital age* Rome (Italy) 2018, *World Congress* Québec, QC (Canada) 2017. **Publications** *SIGNIS Media* (4 a year) in English, French, Spanish – magazine in; *SIGNIS Web News*. Annual Report; specialized books; brochures.
Members Full Member – national Catholic associations that bring together institutions and persons that are active in audiovisual media and international Catholic organizations for communications; Associate (non-voting) – institutions and individuals active in the field of communications. Members in in 147 countries and territories:
Angola, Antigua-Barbuda, Argentina, Australia, Austria, Bahamas, Bangladesh, Barbados, Belgium/Flemish Region, Belgium/Wallonia Region, Belize, Benin, Bermuda, Bolivia, Botswana, Brazil, Burkina Faso, Burundi, Cameroon, Canada, Caroline Is, Central African Rep, Chad, Chile, Colombia, Congo Brazzaville, Congo DR, Cook Is, Costa Rica, Côte d'Ivoire, Croatia, Cuba, Curaçao, Czechia, Denmark, Dominica, Dominican Rep, Ecuador, Egypt, El Salvador, England, Equatorial Guinea, Eswatini, Ethiopia, Fiji, Finland, France, Gabon, Gambia, Germany, Ghana, Grenada, Guadeloupe, Guam, Guatemala, Guinea, Guyana, Haiti, Holy See, Honduras, Hong Kong, Hungary, India, Indonesia, Ireland, Israel, Italy, Jamaica, Japan, Kenya, Kiribati, Korea Rep, Lebanon, Lesotho, Liberia, Lithuania, Luxembourg, Macau, Madagascar, Malawi, Malaysia, Mali, Malta, Marshall Is, Martinique, Mauritius, Mexico, Micronesia FS, Monaco, Mozambique, Myanmar, Netherlands, New Caledonia, New Zealand, Nicaragua, Niger, Nigeria, Northern Mariana Is, Norway, Pakistan, Panama, Papua New Guinea, Paraguay, Peru, Philippines, Poland, Portugal, Puerto Rico, Réunion, Romania, Rwanda, Samoa, Samoa USA, Scotland, Senegal, Seychelles, Sierra Leone, Singapore, Slovakia, Slovenia, Solomon Is, South Africa, Spain, Sri Lanka, St Lucia, Sudan, Suriname, Sweden, Switzerland, Syrian AR, Tahiti Is, Taiwan, Tanzania UR, Thailand, Togo, Tonga, Trinidad-Tobago, Tuvalu, Uganda, UK, Uruguay, USA, Vanuatu, Venezuela, Wallis-Futuna, Zambia, Zimbabwe.
National, international or internationally-oriented organizations and other bodies, including 18 organizations listed in this Yearbook:
Asian Communication Network (ACN, #01391); Asociación Latinoamericana de Comunicación Grupal (no recent information); Catholic Foreign Missionary Society of America (Maryknoll Fathers) (Social Communication Department); *Centre for the Study of Communication and Culture (CSCC, #03788); Centro Internazionale Salesiano per le Communicazioni Sociali (CISCOM, no recent information); Centro Orientamento Educativo, Barzio (COE); Communication Foundation for Asia (CFA, #04380); Franciscan Media; Missionary Oblates of Mary Immaculate (OMI); Multimedia International (MI, #16893); Order of Preachers (Dominicans); Organización Católica Latinoamericana y Caribeña de Comunicación (OCLACC, #17833); Pious Society of the Daughters of St Paul (Daughters of St Paul); Radio Veritas Asia (#18604); Secrétariat International Spiritain de Communications Sociales par l'Audio-visuel (SISCOMS, no recent information); Società del Verbo Divino (Verbiti); Société des Missions Etrangères de la Province de Québec (SMEPQ); Society of St Francis of Sales (Salesians of Don Bosco).*
Consultative Status Consultative status granted from: *ECOSOC (#05331)* (Ros C); *UNESCO (#20322)* (Consultative Status); *Council of Europe (CE, #04881)* (Participatory Status). **IGO Relations** Accredited by: *United Nations Office at Vienna (UNOV, #20604).* Invited to sessions of Intergovernmental Council of: *International Programme for the Development of Communication (IPDC, #14651).* Associated with Department of Global Communications of the United Nations.
NGO Relations Member of: *Crescendo Worldwide Network (#04950); Federation of European and International Associations Established in Belgium (FAIB, #09508); Forum of Catholic Inspired NGOs (#09905); International Centre of Films for Children and Young People (#12493); International Council for Film, Television and Audiovisual Communication (IFTC, #13022); International Network for a Culture of Nonviolence and Peace (#14247).*
Partner organizations:
- *Asociación Latinoamericana de Educación y Comunicación Popular (ALER, #02207);*
- *Association mondiale des radiodiffuseurs communautaires (AMARC, #02810);*
- *Caritas Internationalis (CI, #03580);*
- *Catholic Media Council (CAMECO, #03605);*
- *Catholic Radio and Television Network (#03607);*
- *International Catholic Centre of Geneva (ICCG, #12449);*

– *International Catholic Cooperation Centre for UNESCO (CCIC, #12454)*;
– *International Catholic Organizations Information Center (ICO Center)*;
– *International Interchurch Film Organization (INTERFILM, #13943)*;
– *International Federation of Catholic Universities (IFCU, #13381)*;
– *Pax Christi – International Catholic Peace Movement (#18266)*;
– *Symposium of Episcopal Conferences of Africa and Madagascar (SECAM, #20077)*;
– *World Association for Christian Communication (WACC, #21126)*. [2021/XB0012/y/**B**]

♦ World Catholic Federation for the Biblical Apostolate / see Catholic Biblical Federation (#03600)
♦ **WorldCC** World Commerce and Contracting (#21284)

♦ World Cement Association (WCA) 21265

CEO 19 Eastbourne Terrace, Paddington Station, London, W2 6LG, UK. E-mail: info@worldcementassociation.org.
URL: https://worldcementassociation.org/

History 2016. Registration: Companies House, No/ID: 10187292, England and Wales. **Aims** Bring together the capabilities of cement producers worldwide with equal rights for all, regardless of size, nationality or group. **Events** *Annual Conference* Dubai (United Arab Emirates) 2023, *International Cement Conference on Global Trade* Istanbul (Türkiye) 2023, *Annual Conference* Dubai (United Arab Emirates) 2022, *Annual Conference* 2021, *Annual Conference* Shanghai (China) 2019. [2023/AA3067/**C**]

♦ World Centers of Compassion for Children / see World Centers of Compassion for Children International
♦ World Centers of Compassion for Children International (internationally oriented national body)
♦ World Central Kitchen (internationally oriented national body)
♦ World Centre of Excellence for Destinations (internationally oriented national body)
♦ World Centre for Information and Applied Research on Urban Pollution (inactive)
♦ World Centre for New Thinking (internationally oriented national body)
♦ World Centre for Peace, Freedom and Human Rights (internationally oriented national body)
♦ World Centre of Women's Organizations (inactive)

♦ World Ceramic Tiles Forum (WCTF) 21266

Contact Rue Belliard 12, 1040 Brussels, Belgium. T. +3228083880. E-mail: events@cerameunie.eu.
URL: http://www.worldceramictiles.org/

Aims Organize an annual meeting of ceramic tiles manufacturers worldwide. **Activities** Events/meetings. **Events** *Annual Forum* Berlin (Germany) 2019, *Annual Forum* Sao Paulo (Brazil) 2018, *Annual Forum* Guangzhou (China) 2017, *Annual Forum* Delhi (India) 2016, *Annual Forum* Seville (Spain) 2015.
Members Full in 32 countries and territories:
Argentina, Australia, Austria, Brazil, Bulgaria, China, Czechia, Finland, France, Germany, Hungary, India, Indonesia, Ireland, Israel, Italy, Japan, Malaysia, Mexico, Morocco, Netherlands, Poland, Portugal, Romania, Russia, Spain, Taiwan, Thailand, Türkiye, UK, Ukraine, USA.
Included in the above, 1 organization listed in this Yearbook:
European Ceramic Tile Manufacturers' Federation (CET, #06508). [2018/XM7058/cy/**F**]

♦ World Certification Institute (WCI) 21267

Vice-Pres address not obtained. E-mail: info@worldcertification.org.
URL: http://www.worldcertification.org/

History 2000, USA. Task Group set up Oct 1999; officially set up 2000. Former names and other names: *World Certification Institute – Global Authority on Occupational Certification (WCI)* – full title. Registration: USA. **Aims** Assess and certify globally accepted experiential work practices, skills, competencies and professional management. **Structure** Council; Board. **Languages** English. **Finance** Self-funding. **Activities** Certification/accreditation. **Members** Individual Membership: Associate (AWCI); Full (MWCI); Associate Fellow (AFWCI); Fellow (FWCI); Senior Fellow (FWCI Senior). Institutional Affiliation: Authorized Center; Accredited Center. Membership countries not specified. [2023.01.31/XM4207/v/**C**]

♦ World Certification Institute – Global Authority on Occupational Certification / see World Certification Institute (#21267)
♦ World Cervicogenic Headache Society (no recent information)

♦ World Cetacean Alliance (WCA) 21268

Secretariat Studio 3, Lower Promenade, Madira Drive, Brighton, BN2 1ET, UK. T. +441273355011.
URL: http://worldcetaceanalliance.org/

History Proposed Nov 2012, Brighton (UK), at World Whale Conference. Launched 8 Jun 2013. UK Registered Charity: 1160484. **Aims** Conserve and protect cetaceans and their habitats. **Structure** Interim Global Council; Trustees; Working Groups; Secretariat. **Languages** English. **Staff** 2.00 FTE, paid; 20.00 FTE, voluntary. **Activities** Events/meetings; projects/programmes. **Events** *World Whale Conference and Whale Heritage Sites Summit* Hervey Bay, QLD (Australia) 2019, *Whale Heritage Sites Summit* Durban (South Africa) 2017, *World Whale Conference* Durban (South Africa) 2017, *Whale Heritage Sites Summit* Horta (Portugal) 2015, *World Whale Conference* Horta (Portugal) 2015.
Members Non-profit organizations; Whale or dolphin watching tour operators; Individual partners. Organizations in 12 countries:
Argentina, Australia, Canada, Greece, Italy, Malta, Netherlands, New Zealand, Slovenia, Spain, UK, USA.
Included in the above, 6 organizations listed in this Yearbook:
Born Free Foundation; *Cetacean Society International (CSI)*; *Change For Animals Foundation (CFAF)*; *Earthrace Conservation (#05168)*; *Ocean Futures Society*; *World Animal Protection (#21092)*.
Business in 14 countries:
Argentina, Australia, Costa Rica, Dominican Rep, Iceland, Maldives, Mexico, Portugal, South Africa, Spain, Thailand, Tonga, UK, USA.
Individuals in 6 countries:
France, Germany, Nepal, Spain, UK, USA.
NGO Relations *Dolphinaria-Free Europe (DFE, #05112)*; *Global Ghost Gear Initiative (GGGI, #10390)*. [2016.06.29/XM4231/y/**C**]

♦ World Challenge – Don Wilkerson / see Global Teen Challenge
♦ World Chambers Consortium / see World Chambers Network (#21270)

♦ World Chambers Federation (WCF) 21269

Contact 33-43 Avenue du President Wilson, 75116 Paris, France. T. +33149532944. Fax +33149533079. E-mail: wcf@iccwbo.org.
URL: https://iccwbo.org/chamber-services/world-chambers-federation/

History Founded 1950, Paris (France), as *International Bureau of Chambers of Commerce (IBCC) – Bureau international des chambres de commerce (BICC)*, to function within *International Chamber of Commerce (ICC, #12534)*, as a liaison bureau for chambers of commerce in all parts of the world. Current name adopted 1 Jun 2001. **Aims** Unite the worldwide network of chambers of *commerce* and *industry*; facilitate exchange of best practice and development of new global products and services for chambers; foster international partnerships between chambers and other stakeholders to help local businesses grow; administer global trade service chains by chambers. **Structure** General Council; Executive Committee; Specialized Working Groups. **Languages** English, French. **Activities** Events/meetings; standards/guidelines; awards/prizes/competitions. **Events** *World Chambers Congress* 2025, *World Chambers Congress* Geneva (Switzerland) 2023, *World Chambers Congress* Dubai (United Arab Emirates) 2021, *World Chambers Congress* Rio de Janeiro (Brazil) 2019, *World Chambers Congress* Sydney, NSW (Australia) 2017. **Publications** *Governance Principles for Chambers and Business Associations*; *International Certificate of Origin Guidelines*. Information Services: Together with Regional and Paris Chamber of Commerce and Industry, joint operator of *World Chambers Network (WCN, #21270)* – global electronic network of chambers of commerce providing Internet information services to assist chambers in facilitating trade, investment and strategic business cooperation for their member companies.
Members Chambers of commerce and national associations of chambers of commerce in 143 countries and territories:
Afghanistan, Albania, Algeria, Argentina, Armenia, Australia, Austria, Azerbaijan, Bahamas, Bahrain, Bangladesh, Barbados, Belarus, Belgium, Benin, Bosnia-Herzegovina, Brazil, Bulgaria, Burkina Faso, Burundi, Cambodia, Cameroon, Canada, Central African Rep, Chad, Chile, China, Colombia, Congo DR, Congo Brazzaville, Costa Rica, Côte d'Ivoire, Croatia, Cyprus, Czechia, Denmark, Djibouti, Dominican Rep, Egypt, El Salvador, Eritrea, Estonia, Ethiopia, Finland, France, Gabon, Gambia, Georgia, Germany, Ghana, Greece, Guatemala, Honduras, Hong Kong, Hungary, Iceland, India, Indonesia, Iran Islamic Rep, Ireland, Israel, Italy, Jamaica, Japan, Jordan, Kazakhstan, Kenya, Korea DPR, Korea Rep, Kuwait, Latvia, Lebanon, Lesotho, Liberia, Libya, Liechtenstein, Lithuania, Luxembourg, Macau, Madagascar, Malaysia, Mali, Malta, Mauritania, Mauritius, Mexico, Mongolia, Montenegro, Morocco, Mozambique, Namibia, Nepal, Netherlands, New Zealand, Niger, Nigeria, North Macedonia, Norway, Oman, Pakistan, Panama, Papua New Guinea, Peru, Philippines, Poland, Portugal, Qatar, Romania, Russia, Rwanda, Saudi Arabia, Senegal, Serbia, Singapore, Slovakia, Slovenia, South Africa, Spain, Sri Lanka, Sudan, Suriname, Sweden, Switzerland, Syrian AR, Taiwan, Tajikistan, Tanzania UR, Thailand, Togo, Trinidad-Tobago, Tunisia, Türkiye, Uganda, UK, Ukraine, United Arab Emirates, Uruguay, USA, Uzbekistan, Venezuela, Vietnam, Zambia, Zimbabwe.
Also members in islands of the Pacific. Membership countries not specified.
NGO Relations Memorandum of Understanding with: *Asociación de las Camaras de Comercio e Industria del Mediterraneo (ASCAME, #02112)*. [2018.07.31/XE5098/**E**]

♦ World Chambers Network (WCN) 21270

Chairman address not obtained. T. +33149532944. Fax +33149533079. E-mail: wcf@iccwbo.org.
URL: http://www.worldchambers.com/

History Paris (France), as *World Network of Chambers of Commerce and Industry*, within the framework of *International Chamber of Commerce (ICC, #12534)*; operated by a consortium of 2 bodies: *World Chambers Federation (WCF, #21269)*; Paris Chamber of Commerce and Industry. Previously also operated by: *G77 Trade Information Network (TIN, inactive)* of *Group of 77 (G-77, #10732)*. Previous titles: *Consortium for Global Commerce (The Consortium)*; *World Chambers Consortium*. **Aims** Promote and develop *electronic international trade* by implementing trust tools, thereby facilitating increased participation in global trade for small and medium-sized enterprises (SMEs) worldwide. **Structure** Run by consortium of *World Chambers Federation (WCF, #21269)* and Paris Chamber of Commerce and Industry. Reports to Global Council of WCF. **Languages** English, French, Spanish. **Activities** Provides: international online business opportunity service (Global business Exchange – GBX); worldwide chamber of commerce directory of over 12,000 chambers; Chamber Trust directory of verified companies; Chamber e-Vault secure repository. Participates in regional chamber events and congresses. **Publications** *Global Business Exchange (GBX)* – online directory. **Members** Chambers of commerce and industry (12,000) which operate international business development programmes worldwide. Membership countries not specified. **IGO Relations** Strategic partners: *European Commission (EC, #06633)*. **NGO Relations** Strategic partners include: *Asociación de las Camaras de Comercio e Industria del Mediterraneo (ASCAME, #02112)*; *Association des chambres de commerce et d'industrie européennes (EUROCHAMBRES, #02423)*; *Confederation of Asia-Pacific Chambers of Commerce and Industry (CACCI, #04512)*; *Conférence Permanente des Chambres Consulaires Africaines et Francophones (CPCCAF, #04639)*; *Federation of Central American Chambers of Commerce (#09470)*; *Junior Chamber International (JCI, #16168)*; *SAARC Chamber of Commerce and Industry (SAARC CCI, #19015)*. [2017/XK1547/**F**]

♦ World Chemical Engineering Council (WCEC) 21271

Secretariat DECHEMA, Theodor Heuss Allee 25, 60486 Frankfurt-Main, Germany.
URL: https://wcec-online.org/

History 27 Sep 2001, Melbourne, VIC (Australia). Founded during 6th World Congress of Chemical Engineering. **Aims** Ensure a high standard of chemical engineering and related science and technology. **Structure** Council. Executive Committee. **Events** *World Congress of Chemical Engineering* Beijing (China) 2025, *World Congress of Chemical Engineering* Buenos Aires (Argentina) 2023, *World Congress of Chemical Engineering* Buenos Aires (Argentina) 2022, *World Congress of Chemical Engineering* Buenos Aires (Argentina) 2021, *World Congress of Chemical Engineering* Barcelona (Spain) 2017.
Members in 10 countries and territories:
Australia, China, France, Germany, Hong Kong, India, Japan, Russia, South Africa, UK, USA.
International organizations (3):
Asian Pacific Confederation of Chemical Engineering (APCChE, #01605); *European Federation of Chemical Engineering (EFCE, #07074)*; *Inter-American Confederation of Chemical Engineering (IACChE, #11417)*.
NGO Relations Related conference series: *World Congress of Chemical Engineering (WCCE)*. [2022/XM1837/y/**D**]

♦ World Chess Federation (#09627)

♦ World Childhood Foundation 21272

Swedish Office Wennergren Center, Sveavägen 166, SE-113 46 Stockholm, Sweden. T. +46855117500. Fax +468200302. E-mail: info@childhood.org.
USA Office 183 Madison Ave, Suite 715, New York NY 10016, USA. T. +12128676088. Fax +12128676099. E-mail: info@childhood-usa.org.
URL: http://www.childhood.org/

History 1999, by Queen Silvia of Sweden. **Aims** Prevent and address *child abuse* around the world. **Structure** Offices in 4 countries: Brazil; Germany; Sweden; USA. **Activities** Projects/programmes. **Consultative Status** Consultative status granted from: *ECOSOC (#05331)* (Special). **NGO Relations** *Early Childhood Peace Consortium (ECPC, #05156)*. [2016.02.24/XJ7896/f/**F**]

♦ World of Children (internationally oriented national body)

♦ World Chinese Kung Fu Association (World CKA) 21273

Contact Via Bariletti 31, Ponte Felcino, 06077 Perugia PG, Italy. T. +39756919600. Fax +39755919238.
URL: http://www.worldcka.org/

History 1996. Also referred to as *World Wushu Association*. **Aims** Develop and promote traditional Chinese *martial arts*. **Activities** Organized championships.
Members National organizations in 15 countries:
Azerbaijan, Bangladesh, Brazil, Bulgaria, Cuba, Germany, Hungary, Iran Islamic Rep, Italy, Korea Rep, Lebanon, Peru, Romania, Russia, UK. [2010/XM2809/**D**]

♦ World Chlorine Council (WCC) 21274

Contact c/o Euro Chlor – CEFIC, Av E Van Nieuwenhuyse 4 – Box 2, 1160 Brussels, Belgium. T. +3226767351. E-mail: dcn@cefic.be.
URL: http://worldchlorine.org/

History Founded 1993. **Aims** Be a global forum to promote health, safety and environmental best practices in order to provide society with the benefits of the chlor-alkali industry. **Structure** General Assembly; Governing Council; Management Committee; Secretariat; Global Teams; Task Forces. **Finance** Project funding. **Activities** Advocacy/lobbying/activism. **Events** *General Assembly* Delhi (India) 2015. **Publications** Policy papers; reports; safety procedures.
Members Organizations in 8 countries:
Canada, China, India, Japan, Korea Rep, Mexico, Russia, USA.
Included in the above, 4 organizations listed in this Yearbook:
Chlorine Institute; *Euro Chlor (#05659)*; *European Network of Red Cross Societies Against Violence (ENAV, inactive)*; *Latin American Chlor-Alkali and Derivatives Industry Association (CLOROSUR, #16295)*.
Consultative Status Consultative status granted from: *ECOSOC (#05331)* (Ros A). **NGO Relations** *International Council of Chemical Associations (ICCA, #13003)*. [2021/XG6112/**F**]

♦ World Christian Anti-Communist Association (no recent information)

♦ World Christian Doctors Network (WCDN) 21275

Address not obtained.
URL: http://www.wcdn.org/

History Founded as part of the *Manmin Central Church*. **Events** *International Christian Medical Conference* Valencia (Spain) 2016, *International Christian Medical Conference* Sofia (Bulgaria) 2014, *International Christian Medical Conference* Toluca (Mexico) 2013, *International Christian Medical Conference* Nairobi (Kenya) 2012, *International Christian Medical Conference* Brisbane, QLD (Australia) 2011. [2014/XJ8972/**F**]

♦ World Chromatography Conference (meeting series)
♦ World Circle of the Consensus / see Consensus for Sustainable People, Organisations and Communities

♦ World Circle of Survival Consensus / see Consensus for Sustainable People, Organisations and Communities
♦ World Cities Culture Forum (meeting series)

♦ World Cities World Class University Network (WC2 University Network) 21276

Contact Intl Relations, City Univ London, Northampton Square, London, EC1V 0HB, UK. T. +442070400113.
URL: http://www.wc2network.org/

History Sep 2010. Founded by City University London (UK). **Aims** Bring together top universities located in the heart of major world cities so as to address cultural, environmental and political issues of common interest to world cities and their universities. **Events** *Symposium* St Petersburg (Russia) 2019, *Symposium* Toronto, ON (Canada) 2018, *Symposium* Sao Paulo (Brazil) 2017, *Symposium* Berlin (Germany) 2016, *Meeting* Hong Kong (Hong Kong) 2016.
Members Universities in 12 countries:
Brazil, China, Germany, Hong Kong, India, Italy, Japan, Mexico, Russia, South Africa, UK, USA. [2015/XJ9133/**F**]

♦ World Citizen Foundation (internationally oriented national body)
♦ World Citizen Party (inactive)
♦ World Citizens / see Association of World Citizens (#02982)
♦ World Citizens Assembly / see Association of World Citizens (#02982)
♦ World Citizenship Foundation (internationally oriented national body)
♦ World Citizenship Movements (inactive)
♦ World City Ice and Snow Tourism Cooperation Organization (unconfirmed)

♦ World Civic Forum (WCF) 21277

Forum mondial de la participation citoyenne – Foro Civico Mundial

Contact address not obtained. T. +2129635318. Fax +2129639681.

History By Kyung Hee University (Korea Rep) and the Dept of Economic and Social Affairs of *United Nations (UN, #20515)*. **Aims** Act as a venue for global reflection and dialogue to enhance future civilizations; address internationally agreed development goals, including the Millennium Development Goals from various perspectives of education, research and practice. **Structure** Plenary; Global university network; International Board; Secretariat. **Languages** English. **Activities** Roundtables; Plenary and Thematic sessions; Institutional Partner Sessions; session on key issues. **Events** *Building our humanitarian planet* Seoul (Korea Rep) 2009. **IGO Relations** *UNESCO (#20322)*; *World Tourism Organization (UNWTO, #21861)*. [2009.09.07/XM8220/**F**]

♦ World Civil Society Conference (meeting series)

♦ World Civil Society Forum (WCSF) 21278

Forum mondial de la société civile – Foro Mundial de la Sociedad Civil

Pres c/o Mandat International, Chemin du Champ-Baron, 3, 1209 Geneva, Switzerland. T. +41227744222. E-mail: contact@mandint.org.
URL: http://www.worldcivilsociety.org/

History May 2000, New York NY (USA). Full title: *Association for the World Civil Society Forum – Association pour le forum mondial de la société civile – Asociación del Foro Mundial de la Sociedad Civil*. Statutes adopted, 22 May 2001, Geneva (Switzerland). Registered in accordance with Swiss Civil Code. **Aims** Facilitate cooperation between organizations of civil society and the *United Nations*; promote cooperation among civil society organizations worldwide. **Structure** General Assembly. Executive Committee. Steering Committee, comprising President, Treasurer, Secretary and 8 further members. Preparatory Working Group. **Languages** English, French, Spanish. **Finance** Members' dues. Other sources: donations and legacies; private and official subsidies; contributions; sales items. **Events** *Forum* 2006, *Forum* Geneva (Switzerland) 2006, *Promoting the role of civil society in global governance* Geneva (Switzerland) 2002, *Preparatory meeting of the world civil society forum* Geneva (Switzerland) 2001. **Members** Active; Supporting/Consultative. Membership countries not specified. **NGO Relations** Located at: *Mandat International*. Member of: *EarthAction (EA, #05159)*. [2010/XE4252/**E**]

♦ **World CKA** World Chinese Kung Fu Association (#21273)
♦ World Class Soaring Association (internationally oriented national body)
♦ World Climate Foundation (unconfirmed)

♦ World Climate Research Programme (WCRP) 21279

Programme mondial de recherches sur le climat (PMRC) – Programa Mundial de Investigaciones Climaticas (PMIC)

Address not obtained.
URL: http://www.wcrp-climate.org/

History 1979. Established as a joint programme of *World Meteorological Organization (WMO, #21649)* and *International Council for Science (ICSU, inactive)*. Contribution of *Scientific Committee on Oceanic Research (SCOR, #19149)* managed by *Joint SCOR/IOC Committee on Climatic Changes and the Ocean (CCCO, inactive)*, which ceased to exist in 1992, when *Intergovernmental Oceanographic Commission (IOC, #11496)* joined WMO and ICSU in co-sponsoring WCRP under a revised Agreement, which came into effect on 1 Jan 1993. WCRP had taken over activities of *Global Atmospheric Research Programme (GARP, inactive)*, which ceased to exist on 1 Jan 1980, when WMO/ICSU Agreement came into effect.
Since Jul 2018, *International Science Council (ISC, #14796)* replaced ICSU as sponsoring organization. Scientific guidance is provided by the *Joint Scientific Committee for the World Climate Research Programme (JSC/WCRP) – Comité scientifique mixte pour le programme mondial de recherches climatiques*, also referred to as *Joint WMO/ICSU/IOC Scientific Committee (JSC) – Comité scientifique mixte OMM/CIUS/COI*.
Aims Increase humankind's ability to understand and predict climate; help the global climate research community create a scientific foundation for meeting the increasing demand in several socio-economic sectors for relevant climate information; develop fundamental scientific understanding of the physical climate, of its temporal variations; assess indications from past records of significant regional and global trends and the extent of human influence on climate; investigate the basic physical processes that play a fundamental role in the climate system; develop physical/mathematical models to simulate the climate system and provide quantitative prediction of climate variations and long-term change; observe and monitor components of the climate system, especially by means of satellite systems; draw together national scientific activities to provide a global perspective on aspects of the climate system which would otherwise not be available. **Structure** Joint Scientific Committee (annual session) works with the international climate research community. Programme implemented through Joint Planning Staff in Geneva (Switzerland) and 4 International Project Offices. Includes *Global Precipitation Climatology Centre (GPCC)*. **Languages** English. **Staff** 7.00 FTE, paid. **Finance** Supported through the Joint Climate Research Fund, held by WMO, on behalf of the 3 sponsors, being WMO, IOC and *International Science Council (ISC, #14796)*. Budget (annual): Swiss Fr 2 million. **Events** *WCRP Open Science Conference* Kigali (Rwanda) 2023, *SPARC General Assembly* Boulder, CO (USA) / Reading (UK) / Qingdao (China) 2022, *WCRP Sea Level Conference* Singapore (Singapore) 2022, *Climate Obervation Conference* 2021, *Hydroclimatology Panel Meeting* Sydney, NSW (Australia) 2019. **Publications** *WCRP e-zine*. Annual Report; activity reports; brochures; CD-ROMs; DVDs. **IGO Relations** Participates in: *Group on Earth Observations (GEO, #10735)*. Observer to: *Global Runoff Data Centre (GRDC, #10584)*. **NGO Relations** Also sponsors: *Global Change System for Analysis, Research and Training (START, #10278)*. Close links with: *International Global Atmospheric Chemistry Project (IGAC, #13721)* of IGBP. [2013/XF9983/**F**]

♦ World Coal Association (WCA) 21280

Main Office The Clubhouse, Holborn Circus, 20 St Andrew Street, London, EC4A 3AG, UK. T. +442078510052. Fax +442037452760. E-mail: info@worldcoal.org.
URL: http://www.worldcoal.org/

History 1985. Former names and other names: *International Coal Development Institute* – former (1985 to 1988); *World Coal Institute (WCI)* – former (1988 to 2010). **Aims** Build a sustainable future for global coal and play an active role in achieving clean coal usage, technology and innovation. **Structure** General Meeting (annual); Board of Directors (meets twice a year). **Languages** English. **Finance** Sources: members' dues. **Activities** Advocacy/lobbying/activism; events/meetings. **Events** *Asia Pacific clean coal forum* Beijing (China) 2011, *Workshop on Sustainable Development, Energy Access and Climate Policies* Brussels (Belgium) 2011, *Conference* 1995, *Coal for development* London (UK) 1993, *Coal in the environment* London (UK) 1991. **Publications** *Coal – Energy for Sustainable Development* (2012). *Coal Matters* (2012) – factsheet series.
Members Corporate in 10 countries:
Australia, China, Colombia, India, Indonesia, New Zealand, Russia, South Africa, Switzerland, USA.
Associate in 10 countries:
Australia, Brazil, Canada, China, Colombia, Indonesia, Japan, New Zealand, South Africa, USA.
Consultative Status Consultative status granted from: *ECOSOC (#05331)* (Special); *UNIDO (#20336)*. **IGO Relations** Working relations with: *International Bank for Reconstruction and Development (IBRD, #12317)*; *International Energy Agency (IEA, #13270)*; *United Nations Economic Commission for Europe (UNECE, #20555)*. Accredited by: *United Nations Framework Convention on Climate Change – Secretariat (UNFCCC, #20564)*; *United Nations Office at Vienna (UNOV, #20604)*. Associated with Department of Global Communications of the United Nations. **NGO Relations** Founding member of: *Global CCS Institute (#10274)*. Member of: *Climate Technology Centre and Network (CTCN, #04023)*. Working relations with: *International Chamber of Commerce (ICC, #12534)*; *World Economic Forum (WEF, #21367)* Global Agenda Council on Energy Security; *World Energy Council (WEC, #21381)*. [2021.09.08/XF1825/**F**]

♦ World Coal Institute / see World Coal Association (#21280)
♦ World Coalition for the Abolition of Experimentation on Mankind and Animals (inactive)

♦ World Coalition Against the Death Penalty 21281

Coalition mondiale contre la peine de mort

Contact Mundo M, 47 av Pasteur, 93100 Montreuil, France. T. +33180877043. E-mail: contact@worldcoalition.org.
URL: http://www.worldcoalition.org/

History May 2002, Rome (Italy). Registration: EU Transparency Register, No/ID: 609857635030-40. **Aims** Fight against the death penalty at an international level. **Structure** General Assembly; Steering Committee; Executive Board; Secretariat. **Languages** English, French. **Staff** 3.00 FTE, paid. **Finance** Sources: members' dues. **Activities** Advocacy/lobbying/activism; events/meetings. **Events** *World Congress against the Death Penalty* Berlin (Germany) 2022, *World Congress against the Death Penalty* Brussels (Belgium) 2019, *World Congress against the Death Penalty* Oslo (Norway) 2016, *World Congress against the Death Penalty* Madrid (Spain) 2013, *World Congress against the Death Penalty* Geneva (Switzerland) 2010. **Publications** Reports.
Members Organizations, cities and foundations (over 150) in 34 countries and territories:
Australia, Bahrain, Belarus, Belgium, Burundi, Canada, Congo DR, Côte d'Ivoire, Fiji, France, India, Indonesia, Iran Islamic Rep, Iraq, Italy, Japan, Jordan, Malta, Morocco, Nigeria, Pakistan, Palestine, Puerto Rico, Spain, Switzerland, Taiwan, Tanzania UR, Togo, Tunisia, Uganda, UK, Ukraine, USA, Uzbekistan.
Included in the above, 14 organizations listed in this Yearbook:
Amnesty International (AI, #00801); *Anti-Death Penalty Asia Network (ADPAN)*; *Arab Coalition Against the Death Penalty (Arab Coalition, #00921)*; *Conférence internationale des barreaux de tradition juridique commune (CIB, #04612)*; *Death Watch International*; *Forum Africain contra la peine de mort (FACPM)*; *Human Rights Watch (HRW, #10990)*; *International Federation for Human Rights (#13452)*; *International Federation of ACATs – Action by Christians for the Abolition of Torture (#13334)*; *Lawyers for Human Rights International (LFHRI)*; *Movement Against Racism and for Friendship between Peoples (MRAP)*; *Parliamentarians for Global Action (PGA, #18208)*; *Penal Reform International (PRI, #18290)*; *World Organisation Against Torture (OMCT, #21685)*.
Consultative Status Consultative status granted from: *African Commission on Human and Peoples' Rights (ACHPR, #00255)* (Observer). **IGO Relations** Observer status with (1): *OAS (#17629)*. **NGO Relations** Member of (2): *Human Rights and Democracy Network (HRDN, #10980)* (as Full member); *International Drug Policy Consortium (IDPC, #13205)*. [2022.05.05/XF7017/y/**F**]

♦ World Coalition of Disabled / see Disabled Peoples' International (#05097)

♦ World Coalition for Trauma Care (WCTC) 21282

Contact address not obtained.
URL: https://www.world-coalition-trauma-care.org/

History Aug 2012, Rio de Janeiro (Brazil). **Aims** Increase awareness of the importance of trauma as a disease worldwide; promote trauma education at all levels worldwide; develop trauma systems wordwide. **Structure** Board of Directors. **Activities** Awareness raising; events/meetings; training/education. **Events** *World Trauma Congress* Tokyo (Japan) 2023, *World Trauma Congress* Tokyo (Japan) 2022, *World Trauma Congress* 2021, *World Trauma Congress* New Delhi (India) 2018, *World Trauma Congress* New Delhi (India) 2016.
Members Societies in countries:
Australia, Austria, Brazil, Canada, China, Germany, India, Japan, Korea Rep, Portugal, South Africa, USA.
Australasian Trauma Society (ATS); *European Society for Trauma and Emergency Surgery (ESTES, #08768)*; *International Society of Surgery (ISS, #15496)*; *Sociedad Panamericana de Trauma (SPT, #19436)*; *World Society of Emergency Surgery (WSES, #21802)*. [2021/AA1217/y/**C**]

♦ World Coatings Council 21283

Secretariat c/o ACA, 901 New York Ave NW, Ste 300 W, Washington DC 20001, USA. T. +12024626272. Fax +12024628549. E-mail: worldcoatings@paint.org.
URL: https://worldcoatingscouncil.org/

History 1992, as *International Paint and Printing Ink Council (IPPIC)*. Current title adopted 2019. **Aims** Provide a forum for information exchange and cooperation on the major issues and priorities facing paint and printing ink industries worldwide; promote development of product stewardship and environmental responsibility through implementation of the principles and practices of Coatings Care (copyright) by paint and printing ink industries' companies and associations on a worldwide basis. **Structure** Meeting (annual); Secretariat. **Languages** English. **Staff** 20.00 FTE, paid. **Finance** Sources: members' dues. **Activities** Events/meetings; knowledge management/information dissemination. **Events** *Coatings Summit* Miami, FL (USA) 2022, *Coatings Summit* Miami, FL (USA) 2021, *Coatings Summit* Paris (France) 2019, *Meeting* Busan (Korea Rep) 2017, *Meeting* Tokyo (Japan) 2016. **Publications** *Coatings Yearbook*.
Members Major trade associations in 13 countries:
Australia, Brazil, Canada, China, France, Germany, Japan, Mexico, New Zealand, South Africa, Türkiye, UK, USA.
Regional member (1):
Conseil européen de l'industrie des peintures, des encres d'imprimerie et des couleurs d'art (CEPE, #04688).
Consultative Status Consultative status granted from: *ECOSOC (#05331)* (Ros A); *International Maritime Organization (IMO, #14102)*; *UNEP (#20299)*. [2020/XD5027/y/**C**]

♦ WORLDCOB – World Confederation of Businesses (internationally oriented national body)
♦ World Cocoa Foundation (internationally oriented national body)
♦ World Coffee Alliance (unconfirmed)
♦ World Coffee Producers Forum (meeting series)
♦ World Collaborative Mobility Congress (meeting series)
♦ World College of Aesthetic and Antiageing Medicine (internationally oriented national body)
♦ World Combat Arts Federation (internationally oriented national body)

♦ World Commerce and Contracting (WorldCC) 21284

CEO 90 Grove St, Ste 01, Ridgefield CT 06877, USA. T. +12034318741. Fax +12034319305. E-mail: info@iaccm.com.
URL: https://www.worldcc.com/

History 1999. Former names and other names: *International Association for Contract and Commercial Management (IACCM)* – former (1999 to 2020). **Aims** Increase organizational and professional excellence in contracting and commercial management; promote the role of contracts and negotiation professionals in industry and commerce; increase education and training in the field. **Structure** Council; Board of Directors; Advisory Council; Management Team. Offices (4): Americas; Europe/Africa; Australia/New Zealand; Asia. **Finance** Sources: members' dues. **Activities** Awards/prizes/competitions; certification/accreditation; events/meetings; training/education. **Events** *EMEA Americas Vibe Summit* 2022, *Vibe Summit – Asia Pacific Conference* 2022, *EMEA Americas Vibe Summit* 2021, *Vibe Summit – Asia Pacific Conference* 2021, *European Conference* Madrid (Spain) 2019. **Members** Individual (over 49,000); Corporate (over 17,000). Membership countries not specified. [2022/XM0623/**C**]

♦ World Commission for Cerebral Palsy / see International Cerebral Palsy Society (#12531)
♦ World Commission on Culture and Development (inactive)
♦ World Commission on Environment and Development (inactive)

♦ **World Commission on Global Consciousness and Spirituality (WCGCS)** **21285**

Contact Dept of Philosophy, Haverford College, Haverford PA 19041, USA. T. +16108961030. Fax +16108964926. E-mail: agangade@haverford.edu.
URL: http://www.globalspirit.org/

Aims Promote global wisdom, vision and values by cultivating a growing community of people from diverse cultural, religious, disciplinary and spiritual orientations. **Structure** Executive Committee, comprising 3 Co-Chairmen and 3 Co-Convenors. **NGO Relations** Together with: *Club of Budapest (#04032)*, instrumental in setting up: *World Wisdom Council (#21941)*. [2009/XM0923/**E**]

♦ World Committee Against War and Fascism (inactive)
♦ World Committee for Biomechanics / see World Council for Biomechanics (#21319)
♦ World Committee for Christian Broadcasting (inactive)
♦ World Committee for Comparative Leukemia Research / see International Association for Comparative Research on Leukemia and Related Diseases (#11799)
♦ World Committee for Lifelong Learning (unconfirmed)

♦ **World Committee of Maritime Culture Institutes (WCMCI)** **21286**

Contact 1 Dongsam-dong, Yeongdo-Gu, Busan 606-791, Korea Rep. T. +82514105262 – +82514105263 – +82514105264. Fax +82514059809.
URL: https://www.ima.ac.kr/kr/

History Founded 29 May 2010, at the Director Meeting of the foremost 10 research institutions in Korea Rep, China and Japan, as an academic consortium of research institutes for maritime culture in East Asia. **Aims** Collectively formulate an alternative in order to build a new maritime culture of peace and coexistence through academic collaboration of world standard institutions, crossing the boundaries of individuals researchers, institutes and nation states; serve as a central repository for developing joint research between member institutes. **Structure** Headquarters at Institute of International Maritime Affairs in Busan (Korea Rep). **Languages** Chinese, English, Japanese, Korean. **Finance** Funded by National Research Foundation of Korea. **Activities** Research/documentation; events/meetings; networking/liaising. **Events** *International Conference* Busan (Korea Rep) 2021, *International Conference* Busan (Korea Rep) 2018, *International Conference* Perth, WA (Australia) 2016, *International Conference* Taipei (Taiwan) 2015, *International Conference* Busan (Korea Rep) 2014.
Members Research institutions (10) in 5 countries and territories:
China, Hong Kong, Japan, Korea Rep, Taiwan.
Included in the above, 1 organization listed in the above:
Institute of International Maritime Affairs (IMA). [2016.08.07/XJ4879/y/**D**]

♦ **World Committee on Tourism Ethics (WCTE)** **21287**

Comité mondial d'éthique du tourisme – Comité Mundial de Etica del Turismo

Contact WCTE Secretariat, c/o UNWTO, Calle Capitan Haya 42, 28020 Madrid, Spain. T. +34915678172. Fax +34915713733. E-mail: ecsr@unwto.org.
URL: https://www.unwto.org/world-committee-tourism-ethics

History Founded 2003, as a subsidiary body to the General Assembly of the *World Tourism Organization (UNWTO, #21861)*. **Aims** Ensure adherence to principles governing responsible and sustainable development of world tourism; interpret, apply and evaluate the provision of the Global Code of Ethics for Tourism (GCET), a comprehensive set of principles designed to guide key players in tourism development, adopted by the UNWTO General Assembly in 1999. **Structure** Chair, 8 members and 3 alternate members, elected by the UNWTO General Assembly for 4-year terms. **Languages** English. **Activities** Monitoring/evaluation; research/documentation. Priority areas (2013-2017): the exploitation of children in all its forms; trafficking; poaching and illegal trading of wildlife; accessible tourism for all; promotion of fair models of all inclusive holidays; unfounded rating on travel portals which may impact the reputation of companies and destinations. **Events** *Meeting* Chengdu (China) 2017, *Meeting* Madrid (Spain) 2017, *Meeting* Madrid (Spain) 2016, *Meeting* Rovinj (Croatia) 2015, *Meeting* Rome (Italy) 2014. **Members** Independent experts serving in their personal capacities. Membership countries not specified. **NGO Relations** Cooperates with: *OITS/ European Commission for Social Tourism (CETS, #17713)*. [2018/XJ3711/**E**]

♦ World Committee of Women Against War and Fascism (inactive)
♦ World Committee of the World Congress of the Partisans of Peace (inactive)
♦ World Committee for a World Constitutional Convention / see World Constitution and Parliament Association (#21313)

♦ **World Communication Association (WCA)** **21288**

SG Dept of Communication, North Dakota State University, PO Box 6050, Fargo ND 58108, USA.
Pres School of Communication, Journalism, and Marketing, Massey University, PO Box 756, Wellington 6140, New Zealand.
URL: http://wcaweb.org/

History Aug 1983, continuing the work of *Communication Association of the Pacific (CAP)*, formed 1968. **Aims** Encourage and support research, teaching and practice of communication in all forms and circumstances; further public understanding and support of academic inquiry and training in communication; sustain the concept of free, responsible and effective communication by and among all peoples. **Structure** Board of Directors. **Languages** English. **Staff** Voluntary. **Finance** Sources: grants; members' dues. **Events** *Biennial Conference* 2021, *ABC Asia-Pacific Conference* Wellington (New Zealand) 2019, *Biennial Conference* Lisbon (Portugal) 2015, *Biennial Conference* Seoul (Korea Rep) 2013, *Biennial Conference* Lima (Peru) 2011. **Publications** *Journal of Intercultural Communication Research* (3 a year); *WCA Newsletter* (2 a year).
Members Regular; Student; Sustaining; Institutional. Regional associations in 26 countries and territories:
Argentina, Australia, Brazil, Canada, China, Congo DR, Finland, Germany, Guam, Hong Kong, Japan, Korea Rep, Malaysia, Mexico, New Zealand, Nigeria, Philippines, Puerto Rico, Singapore, South Africa, Taiwan, Thailand, UK, USA, Venezuela, Zimbabwe.
Individuals in 18 countries and territories:
Australia, Chile, China, Finland, Hong Kong, India, Japan, Malaysia, Peru, Philippines, Poland, Russia, Singapore, Spain, Sri Lanka, Sweden, Türkiye, USA. [2022/XD0474/**C**]

♦ **World Communion of Reformed Churches (WCRC)** **21289**

Communion mondiale d'église réformées (CMER) – Comunión Mundial de Iglesias Reformadas (CMIR) – Weltgemeinschaft Reformierter Kirchen (WRK)

Exec Sec Communications/Operations Calvin Centre, Knochenhauerstr 42, 30159 Hannover, Germany. T. +4951189738310. E-mail: wcrc@wcrc.eu – gs@wcrc.eu.
URL: http://www.wcrc.ch/

History Jun 2010. Founded on merger of *Reformed Ecumenical Council (REC, inactive)* and *World Alliance of Reformed Churches (WARC, inactive)*. **Aims** Respond to God's call to meet spiritual needs and foster justice for all in the transformation of the world through the love of Jesus Christ. **Structure** General Council (every 7 years); Executive Committee (annual). Regional structure include: Africa Communion of Reformed Churches *(ACRC)*; Northeast Asia Area Council; Caribbean and North American Area Council; *Council of the World Communion of Reformed Churches in Europe (WCRC Europe, #04924)*; *Alliance of Presbyterian and Reformed Churches in Latin America (#00713)*; *Global Institute of Theology (GIT, see: #21289)*. **Languages** English, French, German, Spanish. **Staff** 8.00 FTE, paid. **Finance** Annual budget: 3,400,000 EUR. **Activities** Advocacy/lobbying/activism; projects/programmes; religious activities. **Events** *Meeting* Leipzig (Germany) 2017, *Meeting* Grand Rapids, MI (USA) 2010. **Publications** *Reformed Communiqué* (3 a year); *Reformed World* (2 a year).
Members Represents over 100 million Christians in 233 Congregational, Presbyterian, Reformed, United, Uniting and Waldensian churches in 108 countries and territories:
Algeria, Angola, Argentina, Australia, Austria, Bangladesh, Belgium, Bolivia, Botswana, Brazil, Bulgaria, Burkina Faso, Cameroon, Canada, Cayman Is, Central African Rep, Chile, China, Colombia, Congo Brazzaville, Congo DR, Costa Rica, Croatia, Cuba, Czechia, Denmark, Dominican Rep, Egypt, El Salvador, Equatorial Guinea, Eswatini, Ethiopia, France, Germany, Ghana, Greece, Grenada, Guatemala, Guyana, Honduras, Hong Kong, Hungary, India, Indonesia, Iran Islamic Rep, Ireland, Italy, Jamaica, Japan, Kenya, Kiribati, Korea Rep, Latvia, Lebanon, Lesotho, Liberia, Lithuania, Luxembourg, Madagascar, Malawi, Malaysia, Marshall Is, Mauritius, Mexico, Morocco, Mozambique, Myanmar, Netherlands, New Caledonia, New Zealand, Niger, Nigeria, Pakistan, Philippines, Poland, Portugal, Romania, Rwanda, Samoa, Senegal, Serbia, Singapore, Slovakia, Slovenia, Solomon Is, South Africa, South Sudan, Spain, Sri Lanka, Sudan, Sweden, Switzerland, Tahiti Is, Taiwan, Thailand, Togo, Trinidad-Tobago, Tuvalu, Uganda, UK, Ukraine, Uruguay, USA, Vanuatu, Venezuela, Vietnam, Zambia, Zimbabwe.
Included in the above, 10 organizations listed in this Yearbook:
African Protestant Church (EPA); *Presbyterian Church of Africa (PCA, #18485)*; *Presbyterian Church of East Africa (PCEA)*; *Reformed Church in Africa*; *Reformed Church of East Africa (no recent information)*; *Union of Armenian Evangelical Churches in the Near East (UAECNE, #20358)*; *United Congregational Church of Southern Africa (UCCSA, #20503)*; *Uniting Presbyterian Church in Southern Africa (UPCSA, #20668)*; *Uniting Reformed Church in Southern Africa (URCSA)*; *Volkskerk van Afrika*.
NGO Relations Member of (3): *ACT Alliance (#00081)*; *We Will Speak Out (WWSO)*; *World Council of Churches (WCC, #21320)*. Cooperates with (4): *G20 Interfaith Forum Association (IF20, #10055)*; Global Christian Forum; *World Association for Christian Communication (WACC, #21126)*; *World Student Christian Federation (WSCF, #21833)*. Also links with national organizations. [2023.03.03/XJ1229/y/**B**]

♦ World Community Development Education Society (internationally oriented national body)
♦ World Community Fund Against Hunger (#09836)
♦ World Complexity Science Academy (internationally oriented national body)
♦ World Computer Exchange (internationally oriented national body)
♦ World Computing Services Industry Congress (meeting series)
♦ World Computing Services Industry Forum / see World Innovation, Technology and Services Alliance (#21585)
♦ World Concern / see World Concern International (#21290)

♦ **World Concern International** **21290**

Main Office 19303 Fremont Ave N, Seattle WA 98133, USA. E-mail: info@worldconcern.org.
URL: http://www.worldconcern.org/

History 1955, Seattle, WA (USA). Founded by Wilbert Saunders and Jim McCoy. Joined *CRISTA Ministries* – then known as *King's Garden*, 1973. Former names and other names: *Medicine for Missions* – former (1955 to 1973); *World Concern* – former (1973). **Aims** Provide life, opportunity and hope to all; support poor and rural families with clean water, medicine, food, farm animals and seeds for crops; provide care and education for vulnerable children and orphans; provide critical disaster response services in case of natural and man-made disasters. **Structure** Board of Directors. **Staff** 875.00 FTE, paid. **Finance** Sources: contributions. Annual budget: 81,676,323 USD. **Activities** Active in over 30 countries, struggling with extreme poverty, HIV/AIDS, malnutrition, hunger, drought, natural disasters, war and disease. Instrumental in setting up: #G4185. **Publications** *Solutions* – official newsletter.
Members Countries and territories served (14):
Bangladesh, Bolivia, Burkina Faso, Chad, Haiti, Kenya, Laos, Myanmar, Somalia, Sri Lanka, Sudan, Tibet, Uganda, Vietnam.
NGO Relations Member of (7): *Accord Network*; *Association of Evangelicals in Africa (AEA, #02587)* (Associate); *Christian Connections for International Health (CCIH)*; *Global Relief Alliance*; *InsideNGO (inactive)*; *Neglected Tropical Diseased NGO Network (NNN, #16969)*; *World Evangelical Alliance (WEA, #21393)* (Associate). Instrumental in setting up: *ONE (#17728)*. Partner of: *1,000 Days*. [2022/XF1896/**F**]

♦ **World Confederation of Billiards Sports (WCBS)** **21291**

SG La Serraliere, 38610 Venon, France.
Pres 75 Whiteladies Road, Clifton, Bristol, BS8 2NT, UK.
URL: https://www.wcbs.sport/

History Founded Jan 1992, Lausanne (Switzerland), at 1st official General Assembly, following recommendations of a meeting, 1990, Bristol (UK). **Aims** As umbrella organization for every kind of billiards, unite in one world confederation the different billiards organizations; adopt a sports policy in conformity with the IOC rules as defined in the Olympic Charter; promote billiards sports as based on human and social values and as developing human fraternity and solidarity through international *competitions*; introduce guidelines to standardize the worldwide sports calendar; develop contacts with public authorities and the media; achieve and maintain recognition and affiliation by and with the multiple sports federations; achieve and organize participation in multiple sports events. **Structure** General Assembly (every 4 years). Committee of 10, including 3 members from each of the 3 member divisions: *'Pool'*, represented by *World Pool-Billiard Association (WPA, #21733)* (3 members – 4 votes) and including *Asian Pocket Billiards Union (APBU, #01668)*, *European Pocket Billiard Federation (EPBF, #08237)*, *Oceania Pocket Billiard Association (OPBA, #17668)* and *Billiard Congress of America (BCA)*; *'Carom'*, represented by *World Billiards Union (#21230)* (3 members – 4 votes); *'Snooker'*, represented by *World Professional Billiards and Snooker Association (WPBSA, #21740)* (2 members – 2 votes) and including *Asian Confederation of Billiards Sports (ACBS, #01396)*, and by *International Billiards and Snooker Federation (IBSF, #12340)* (2 members – 2 votes). **Languages** English. **Staff** 9 officers, voluntary. **Finance** Sources: members' dues. **Activities** Organizes and/or sanctions: world championships in all disciplines and divisions of billiards sports on an annual or biennial basis; all intercontinental events organized with participation from more than one division of billiards sports. Organizes congresses to promote billiards sports and fellowship. **Events** *Biennial General Assembly* Wroclaw (Poland) 2017, *Biennial General Assembly* Wroclaw (Poland) 2015, *Biennial General Assembly* Duisburg (Germany) 2005, *Biennial General Assembly* Cardiff (UK) 2002, *Biennial General Assembly* Antalya (Turkey) 2000.
Members National organizations (164) in 99 countries and territories:
Algeria, Argentina, Aruba, Australia, Austria, Bahrain, Bangladesh, Belgium, Bolivia, Brunei Darussalam, Bulgaria, Cambodia, Canada, Chile, China, Colombia, Costa Rica, Croatia, Cyprus, Czechia, Denmark, Ecuador, Egypt, England, Fiji, Finland, France, Germany, Greece, Hong Kong, Hungary, Iceland, India, Indonesia, Iran Islamic Rep, Ireland, Isle of Man, Israel, Italy, Japan, Jordan, Kenya, Korea Rep, Kuwait, Latvia, Lebanon, Liechtenstein, Lithuania, Luxembourg, Macau, Malaysia, Malta, Mauritius, Mexico, Mongolia, Myanmar, Namibia, Nepal, Netherlands, New Zealand, Nicaragua, Nigeria, Northern Ireland, Norway, Pakistan, Panama, Papua New Guinea, Peru, Philippines, Poland, Portugal, Puerto Rico, Qatar, Russia, Saudi Arabia, Scotland, Serbia, Singapore, Slovakia, Slovenia, South Africa, Spain, Sri Lanka, Sweden, Switzerland, Syrian AR, Taiwan, Thailand, Türkiye, Ukraine, United Arab Emirates, Uruguay, USA, Venezuela, Vietnam, Wales, Zambia, Zimbabwe.
NGO Relations Member of (3): *Association of the IOC Recognized International Sports Federations (ARISF, #02767)*; *International World Games Association (IWGA, #15914)*; *Olympic Movement (#17719)*. Recognized by: *International Olympic Committee (IOC, #14408)*. Regional/specialist organizations: *African Billiards and Snooker Confederation (ABSC, #00221)*; APA; APBU; BCA; *Confederación Panamericana de Billar (CPB, #04469)*; *Confédération Européenne de Billard (CEB, #04539)*; EPBF; *European 8-Ball Pool Federation (EEPF, #05777)*; *European Billiards and Snooker Association (EBSA, #06330)*; *European Blackball Association (#06349)*; *International Professional Pool Players' Association (IPA, #14648)*; *South East Asia Games Federation (SEAGF, no recent information)*; UMB; WPA; WSF. [2018/XB0059/**B**]

♦ World Confederation of Boules Sport (inactive)
♦ World Confederation of Businesses (internationally oriented national body)

♦ **World Confederation of Cognitive and Behavioural Therapies (WCCBT)** **21292**

Pres address not obtained. E-mail: admin@wccbt.org.
Pres Elect address not obtained.
URL: https://wccbt.org/

History 7 Jan 2019. Founded by 6 founding member associations, who were previously members of the World Congress Committee (WCC): *Association for Behavioural and Cognitive Therapies (ABCT)*; *Asociación Latinoamericana de Analisis y Modificación del Comportamiento (ALAMOC, #02179)*; Australian Association for Cognitive and Behavioural Therapies; *European Association for Behavioural and Cognitive Therapies (EABCT, #05953)*; *Asian Cognitive Behaviour Therapy Association (ACBTA, #01383)*; *International Association of Cognitive Behavioral Therapy (IACBT, #11781)*. Registration: New York State Registration Board, Start date: 2021, USA, New York State. **Aims** Promote health and well-being through the scientific development and implementation of evidence-based cognitive behavioral strategies designed to evaluate, prevent, and treat mental conditions and illnesses. **Structure** General Meeting (every 3 years); Board of Directors. **Activities** Events/meetings. **Events** *World Congress of Cognitive and Behavioral Therapies* USA 2025, *World Congress of Cognitive and Behavioral Therapies* Seoul (Korea Rep) 2023, *World Congress of Cognitive and Behavioral Therapies* Seoul (Korea Rep) 2022, *World Congress of Cognitive and Behavioral Therapies* Berlin (Germany) 2019.
Members Regional associations (6):
Australia.
Asian Cognitive Behaviour Therapy Association (ACBTA, #01383); *Asociación Latinoamericana de Analisis y Modificación del Comportamiento (ALAMOC, #02179)*; *Association for Behavioural and Cognitive Therapies (ABCT)*; *European Association for Behavioural and Cognitive Therapies (EABCT, #05953)*; *International Association of Cognitive Behavioral Therapy (IACBT, #11781)*. [2022.06.14/AA0741/y/**C**]

- ♦ World Confederation for Diplomatic and Press Relations (inactive)
- ♦ World Confederation of Education (#04464)
- ♦ World Confederation for Existential Therapy (unconfirmed)
- ♦ World Confederation for Gastronomy (no recent information)
- ♦ World Confederation of General Zionists / see World Confederation of United Zionists (#21295)
- ♦ World Confederation of Jewish Community Centres / see JCC Global (#16093)
- ♦ World Confederation of Labour (inactive)
- ♦ World Confederation of Manipulative Therapists / see International Federation of Orthopaedic Manipulative Physical Therapists (#13495)
- ♦ World Confederation of Organizations of the Teaching Profession (inactive)

♦ World Confederation for Physical Therapy (WCPT) 21293

Confédération mondiale pour la thérapie physique

CEO Victoria Charity Centre, 11 Belgrave Road, London, SW1V 1RB, UK. E-mail: info@world.physio.
Congress Manager address not obtained.
URL: https://world.physio/

History 8 Sep 1951, Copenhagen (Denmark). Founded when Articles of Association were agreed, a Provisional Committee having been set up in 1948 and a draft constitution drawn up in Apr 1950, Paris (France). Former names and other names: *World Physiotherapy* – trading name; *WCPT Trading Limited* – legal name. Registration: Charity Register, No/ID: 234307, England and Wales; Companies House, No/ID: 08322671, England and Wales. **Aims** Further the physical therapy profession and improve global health. **Structure** General Meeting (every 4 years, at Congress); Executive Board; International Scientific Committee; Sub-committees, sub-groups and special interest sub-groups. Regions (5): Africa; Asia Western Pacific; *Europe Region World Physiotherapy (ER-WPT, #09167)*; North America Caribbean; South America. Secretariat in London (UK), headed by CEO. Meetings open to accredited delegates and observers. **Languages** English. **Staff** 8.00 FTE, paid. **Finance** Sources: members' dues. **Activities** Events/meetings; guidance/assistance/consulting; networking/liaising; projects/programmes; standards/guidelines; training/education. **Events** *World Physiotherapy Congress* Tokyo (Japan) 2025, *World Physiotherapy Congress* Dubai (United Arab Emirates) 2023, *Africa Congress* Cotonou (Benin) 2021, *World Physiotherapy Congress* London (UK) 2021, *European Congress – Physiotherapy Education* Brussels (Belgium) 2020. **Publications** *WCPT e-update* (12 a year); *WCPT News* (4 a year); *Congress Update. Keynotes.* Quadrennial report; annual report; briefing papers; policy documents; guidelines; standards; articles.

Members National organizations in 128 countries and territories:
Afghanistan, Albania, Angola, Argentina, Australia, Austria, Bahamas, Bahrain, Bangladesh, Barbados, Belgium, Benin, Bermuda, Bhutan, Bolivia, Bosnia-Herzegovina, Brazil, Bulgaria, Cambodia, Cameroon, Canada, Chile, Colombia, Congo DR, Costa Rica, Côte d'Ivoire, Croatia, Curaçao, Cyprus, Czechia, Denmark, Dominican Rep, Ecuador, Estonia, Eswatini, Ethiopia, Fiji, Finland, France, Georgia, Germany, Ghana, Greece, Guatemala, Guyana, Haiti, Hong Kong, Hungary, Iceland, India, Indonesia, Iran Islamic Rep, Ireland, Israel, Italy, Jamaica, Japan, Jordan, Kenya, Korea Rep, Kosovo, Kuwait, Latvia, Lebanon, Liechtenstein, Lithuania, Luxembourg, Macau, Madagascar, Malawi, Malaysia, Mali, Malta, Mauritius, Mexico, Mongolia, Montenegro, Morocco, Myanmar, Namibia, Nepal, Netherlands, New Zealand, Niger, Nigeria, Norway, Oman, Pakistan, Palestine, Panama, Papua New Guinea, Peru, Philippines, Portugal, Puerto Rico, Romania, Rwanda, Saudi Arabia, Senegal, Singapore, Slovakia, Slovenia, South Africa, Spain, Sri Lanka, St Lucia, Sudan, Suriname, Sweden, Switzerland, Syrian AR, Taiwan, Tanzania UR, Thailand, Togo, Trinidad-Tobago, Türkiye, Uganda, UK, Ukraine, United Arab Emirates, Uruguay, USA, Venezuela, Vietnam, Yemen, Zambia, Zimbabwe.

Subgroups: independent organizations in their own right (14):
International Acupuncture Association of Physical Therapists (IAAPT, #11587); International Association for Physical Therapists Working with Older People (IPTOP, #12083); International Confederation of Cardiorespiratory Physical Therapists (ICCrPT, #12850); International Federation of Orthopaedic Manipulative Physical Therapists (IFOMPT, #13495); International Federation of Physical Therapists working in Occupational Health and Ergonomics (IFPTOHE, #13511); International Federation of Sports Physical Therapy (IFSPT, #13556); International Neurological Physical Therapy Association (INPA, #14353); International Organisation of Aquatic Physical Therapists (IOAPT, #14423); International Organisation of Physical Therapists in Paediatrics (IOPTP, #14433); International Organization of Physical Therapists in Mental Health (IOPTMH, #14461); International Organization of Physical Therapists in Pelvic and Women's Health (IOPTPWH, #14462); International Physiotherapists for HIV/AIDS, Oncology, Palliative Care Empowerment (IPT-HOPE, #14580); International Private Physical Therapy Association (IPPTA, #14644); International Society for Electrophysical Agents in Physical Therapy (ISEAPT, #15080).

Consultative Status Consultative status granted from: *ECOSOC (#05331)* (Ros A); *WHO (#20950)* (Official Relations); *UNICEF (#20332)*. **IGO Relations** Accredited by (1): *United Nations Office at Vienna (UNOV, #20604)*. Associated with Department of Global Communications of the United Nations. **NGO Relations** Founding member of: *Global Rehabilitation Alliance (#10565)*. European Region is member of: *European Forum for Primary Care (EFPC, #07326); EU Platform for Action on Diet, Physical Activity and Health (inactive); European Public Health Alliance (EPHA, #08297); Guidelines International Network (GIN, #10817)*. Member of: *Associations and Conference Forum (AC Forum, #02909); Global Health Workforce Alliance (GHWA, inactive); International Institute on Ageing, United Nations – Malta (INIA, #13860); International Society for Quality in Health Care (ISQua, #15405); NGO Committee on UNICEF (#17120)*. Consultative status with: *World Health Professions Alliance (WHPA, #21557)*. Collaborates with: *World Medical Association (WMA, #21646)*.
[2023/XC3489/y/**B**]

- ♦ World Confederation of Private Education / see Confederación Mundial de Educación (#04464)
- ♦ World Confederation of Private Teaching / see Confederación Mundial de Educación (#04464)

♦ World Confederation of Productivity Science (WCPS) 21294

Confédération mondiale de la science sur la productivité

Exec Sec 500 Sherbrooke St West, Ste 900, Montréal QC H3A 3C6, Canada. E-mail: wcps@gestionpga.com.
URL: http://www.wcps.info/

History 1969, UK, as a fraternal association of national productivity services societies. **Aims** Promote the science of productivity and the quality of life worldwide and in all spheres of activity. **Structure** International Assembly. Board of Directors, comprising President, Chairman, Vice-Chairman, Treasurer and Executive Secretary. World Academy of Productivity Science, comprising Fellow having made a contribution to productivity science and to the work of the Confederation. World Network of Productivity Organizations (WNPO), comprising WCPS Network Partners and other affiliated bodies. **Languages** English. **Staff** 2.00 FTE, paid. **Finance** No dues or subscriptions. **Activities** Exchange of information at seminars, international congress and international assembly. **Events** *World Productivity Congress* Bangalore (India) 2020, *World Productivity Congress* Manama (Bahrain) 2017, *World Productivity Congress* Halifax, NS (Canada) 2015, *World Productivity Congress* Québec, QC (Canada) 2013, *World productivity congress* Antalya (Turkey) 2010. **Publications** *International Journal of Productivity and Performance Management.*

Members Individuals and associations devoted to management of productivity in 36 countries and territories:
Australia, Botswana, Canada, China, Costa Rica, Ethiopia, Finland, France, Germany, Ghana, Greece, Hong Kong, Iceland, India, Indonesia, Israel, Japan, Latvia, Malaysia, Mexico, Nepal, Netherlands, New Zealand, Nigeria, Norway, Philippines, Poland, Singapore, South Africa, Spain, Sweden, Tanzania UR, Türkiye, UK, USA, Zambia.

NGO Relations *World Academy of Productivity Science (WAPS).* [2021/XD3956/y/**C**]

- ♦ World Confederation of Teachers (inactive)

♦ World Confederation of United Zionists 21295

Contact c/o 8th Fl, 40 Wall St, New York NY 10005, USA.

History 1946, as *World Confederation of General Zionists*; reorganized in 1958. Registration: USA. **Aims** Strive for Israel-centred creative *Jewish* survival in Diaspora. **Languages** English, Hebrew, Polish, Yiddish. **Staff** 1.00 FTE, paid. **Finance** Supported from Israeli sources. **Activities** Promotes Zionist education, information and welfare activities on behalf of Israel in all countries throughout the Diaspora; encourages private and collective agriculture and industry in Israel. **Events** *Congress* Israel 2010, *Congress* Israel 2009. **Publications** *Zionist Information News* (12 a year) in English, Spanish.

Members Full in 40 countries:
Argentina, Australia, Austria, Belgium, Brazil, Canada, Chile, Colombia, Costa Rica, Czechia, Denmark, Dominican Rep, Ecuador, France, Germany, Greece, Guatemala, Hungary, India, Ireland, Israel, Italy, Mexico, Netherlands, New Zealand, Norway, Panama, Peru, Poland, Portugal, Puerto Rico, Russia, South Africa, Spain, Sweden, Switzerland, UK, Uruguay, USA, Venezuela.
[2014/XE4519/**C**]

♦ World Conference of Associations of Theological Institutions (WOCATI) 21296

Pres address not obtained.
Consultant address not obtained.
URL: https://www.wocati.org/

History 19 Jun 1989, Yogyakarta (Indonesia). Founded when statutes were adopted. Former names and other names: *International Network of Theological Associations* – former (1989). **Aims** Identify and advocate excellence in theological *education* and ministerial practice; encourage full compliance with standards and purposes established by members; provide leadership and understanding of purposes, role and needs of theological education. **Structure** Meeting; Executive Committee. **Languages** English. **Staff** Voluntary. **Finance** Sources: members' dues. on a voluntary basis. **Events** *World congress* Nairobi (Kenya) 1996, *Congress / World Congress* Pittsburgh, PA (USA) 1992.

Members Full: national and regional confessional theological associations; Affiliate: interested organizations, consortia or networks. Members in 78 countries and territories:
Argentina, Australia, Barbados, Bermuda, Brazil, Bulgaria, Cameroon, Canada, Chile, China, Colombia, Congo Brazzaville, Congo DR, Costa Rica, Cyprus, Denmark, Eswatini, Fiji, Finland, France, Germany, Ghana, Greece, Hong Kong, India, Indonesia, Italy, Jamaica, Japan, Kenya, Kiribati, Korea Rep, Lesotho, Malawi, Malaysia, Marshall Is, Mexico, Mozambique, Myanmar, Namibia, Netherlands, New Zealand, Nicaragua, Nigeria, Norway, Pakistan, Panama, Papua New Guinea, Paraguay, Peru, Philippines, Puerto Rico, Russia, Rwanda, Samoa, Sierra Leone, Singapore, Solomon Is, South Africa, Spain, Sri Lanka, St Kitts-Nevis, St Lucia, Sweden, Switzerland, Taiwan, Tanzania UR, Thailand, Tonga, Trinidad-Tobago, Uganda, UK, Uruguay, USA, Venezuela, Vietnam, Zambia, Zimbabwe.

Included in the above, the following international and regional organizations (12) listed in this Yearbook:
Association for Theological Education in South East Asia (ATESEA, #02952); Association of Seminaries and Theological Institutions (#02912); Association of Theological Institutions in Southern and Central Africa (ATISCA, no recent information); Association of Theological Institutions of Eastern Africa (ATIEA, #02953); Association of Theological Seminaries and Institutes in the Middle East (ATIME, #02954); Australian and New Zealand Association of Theological Schools (ANZATS, no recent information); Caribbean Association of Theological Schools (CATS, #03461); Conference of African Theological Institutions (CATI, #04580); Melanesian Association of Theological Schools (MATS); North East Asia Association of Theological Schools (NEAATS, no recent information); South Pacific Association of Theological Schools (SPATS, #19882); West African Association of Theological Institutions (WAATI, no recent information). [2020.09.17/XF5294/y/**F**]

- ♦ World Conference of Banking Institutes (meeting series)
- ♦ World Conference of The Boys' Brigade / see Global Fellowship of Christian Youth (#10357)
- ♦ World Conference of Broadcasting Unions (meeting series)
- ♦ World Conference on Carbon (meeting series)

♦ World Conference of Catholic University Institutions of Philosophy . 21297

Conférence Mondiale des Institutions Universitaires Catholiques de Philosophie (COMIUCAP)

Pres Pontificia Univ Gregoriana, Piazza della Pilotta 3, 00187 Rome RM, Italy. T. +39667011. Fax +39667015413. E-mail: comiucap@unigre.it.
URL: http://www.comiucap.net/

History Set up Apr 1999, Rome (Italy). Officially inaugurated, Mar 2000, Paris (France), at *UNESCO (#20322)*. **Aims** Promote teaching and research in the different fields of philosophy. **Structure** General Assembly (every 4 years, at World Congress); Officers from 5 regions: Africa; Asia/Oceania; Europe; Latin-America; North America. **Languages** English, French, Spanish. **Staff** 6.00 FTE, voluntary. **Finance** Sources: members' dues. **Activities** Events/meetings; research/documentation. **Events** *World Congress* Manila (Philippines) 2022, *World Congress* Manila (Philippines) 2020, *World Congress* Bogota (Colombia) 2017, *Latin-America Meeting* Cusco (Peru) 2015, *Asia-Oceania Meeting* Melbourne, VIC (Australia) 2015. **Publications** *COMIUCAP Journal.* Books.

Members Institutional; Individual. Institutional in 26 countries:
Argentina, Australia, Austria, Belgium, Brazil, Chile, Colombia, Congo DR, France, India, Ireland, Italy, Japan, Kenya, Korea Rep, Lebanon, Macau, Peru, Philippines, Poland, Portugal, South Africa, Spain, Ukraine, USA, Venezuela.

Included in the above, 1 organization listed in this Yearbook:
Catholic University of Eastern Africa, The (CUEA, #03610).

NGO Relations *International Federation of Catholic Universities (IFCU, #13381).* [2019/XJ9559/**B**]

- ♦ World Conference on Computers in Education (meeting series)
- ♦ World Conference on Congenital Disorders of Glycosylation (CDG) for Families and Professionals (meeting series)

♦ World Conference on Constitutional Justice (WCCJ) 21298

Sec Gen The Venice Commission, Council of Europe – DG I, 67075 Strasbourg CEDEX, France. T. +33388412067. Fax +33388413738. E-mail: venice@coe.int.
URL: https://www.venice.coe.int/WebForms/pages/?p=02_WCCJ

History First Congress organized by *European Commission for Democracy through Law (Venice Commission, #06636)* of *Council of Europe (CE, #04881)*, Jan 2009, Cape Town (South Africa), when declaration was adopted. Established as a permanent body, Apr 2009. Statutes adopted 23 May 2011 and entered into force 24 Sep 2011. **Aims** Promote constitutional justice – understood as constitutional review including human rights case-law – as a key element for democracy, the protection of human rights and the rule of law. **Structure** General Assembly (at Congress); Bureau, composed of representatives of regional and linguistic groups, Host Court of the previous and next Congresses, and 3 Courts elected by General Assembly; Secretariat provided by *European Commission for Democracy through Law (Venice Commission, #06636)*. **Languages** Arabic, English, French, German, Portuguese, Russian, Spanish. **Staff** 1.50 FTE, paid. **Finance** Sources: contributions; government support; international organizations; members' dues. **Activities** Politics/policy/regulatory. **Events** *World Congress on Constitutional Justice* Bali (Indonesia) 2022, *World Congress on Constitutional Justice* Vilnius (Lithuania) 2017, *World Congress on Constitutional Justice* Seoul (Korea Rep) 2014, *World Congress on Constitutional Justice* Rio de Janeiro (Brazil) 2011, *World Congress on Constitutional Justice* Cape Town (South Africa) 2009.

Members Constitutional Courts and Councils and Supreme Courts (118) of 113 countries and Palestine*. (*This designation shall not be construed as recognition of a State of Palestine and is without prejudice to the individual positions of Council of Europe member States on this issue.)
Albania, Algeria, Andorra, Angola, Armenia, Australia, Austria, Azerbaijan, Bahrain, Belarus, Belgium, Benin, Bosnia-Herzegovina, Brazil, Bulgaria, Burkina Faso, Burundi, Cambodia, Cameroon, Canada, Cape Verde, Central African Rep, Chad, Chile, Colombia, Comoros, Congo Brazzaville, Congo DR, Costa Rica, Côte d'Ivoire, Croatia, Cyprus, Czechia (Czech republic), Denmark, Djibouti, Dominican Rep, Ecuador, Egypt, Equatorial Guinea, Estonia, Eswatini, Ethiopia, Finland, France, Gabon, Georgia, Germany, Ghana, Guinea, Guinea-Bissau, Hungary, India, Indonesia, Ireland, Israel, Italy, Jordan, Kazakhstan, Kenya, Korea Rep, Kosovo, Kuwait, Kyrgyzstan, Latvia, Lebanon, Lithuania, Luxembourg, Madagascar, Malaysia, Mali, Mauritania, Mauritius, Mexico, Moldova, Monaco, Mongolia, Montenegro, Morocco, Mozambique, Namibia, Netherlands, Nicaragua, Niger, North Macedonia, Norway, Pakistan, Palestine (*), Panama, Peru, Poland, Portugal, Romania, Samoa, Sao Tomé-Principe, Senegal, Serbia, Seychelles, Slovakia, Slovenia, Somalia, South Africa, Spain, Sweden, Switzerland, Tajikistan, Tanzania UR, Thailand, Togo, Türkiye, Uganda, Ukraine, Uzbekistan, Zambia, Zimbabwe.

IGO Relations Invited to participate in the Bureau: *Association of Asian Constitutional Courts and Equivalent Institutions (ACC, #02378)*; Commonwealth Courts; *Conference of European Constitutional Courts (CECC, #04594); Conferencia Iberoamericana de Justicia Constitucional (CIJC, #04652); Conferência das Jurisdições Constitucionais dos Paises de Lingua Portuguesa (CJCPLP, #04653); Conference of Constitutional Jurisdictions of Africa (CCJA, #04585)*. **NGO Relations** Invited to participate in the Bureau: *Association des cours constitutionnelles Francophone (ACCF, #02459); Eurasian Association of Contitutional Review Bodies (EACRB, #05602)*; Southern African Chief Justices Forum (SACJF); *Union of Arab Constitutional Courts and Councils (UACCC, #20351).* [2022.12.02/XJ9010/c/**E***]

- ♦ World Conference – a Family of Christian Youth Organizations / see Global Fellowship of Christian Youth (#10357)
- ♦ World Conference on Floating Solutions (meeting series)
- ♦ World Conference of Historical Cities Council / see The League of Historical Cities (#16424)
- ♦ World Conference on Injury Control (meeting series)
- ♦ World Conference on Marine Biodiversity (meeting series)
- ♦ World Conference Mass Customization, Personalization & Co-Creation (meeting series)
- ♦ World Conference of Mayors for Peace through Inter-city Solidarity / see Mayors for Peace (#16605)

♦ World Conference on Movement: Brain, Body, Cognition (meeting series)
♦ World Conference on Pharmacometrics (meeting series)
♦ World Conference on Religion and Peace / see Religions for Peace (#18831)
♦ World Conference on Religion and Peace / see European Council of Religious Leaders – Religions for Peace (#06840)
♦ World Conference of Religions for Peace / see Religions for Peace (#18831)

♦ World Conference of Secular Institutes 21299

Conférence mondiale des instituts séculiers – Conferenza Mondiale degli Istituti Secolari (CMIS)

Main Office Piazzo San Calisto 16, 00153 Rome RM, Italy. T. +39669887100. Fax +39669887285. E-mail: cmisroma@gmail.com.
URL: http://www.cmis-int.org/

History Founded 23 May 1974, as an association of secular institutes. **Aims** Organize collaboration between Secular Institutes. **Structure** General Assembly (every 4 years); Executive Council (annual). Closed meetings. **Languages** English, French, German, Italian, Polish, Portuguese, Spanish. **Staff** Voluntary. **Finance** Members' dues. **Activities** Research/documentation; networking/liaising. **Events** *Quadrennial World Convention* Assisi (Italy) 2012, *Quadrennial World Convention* Mexico 2008, *Quadrennial world convention and general assembly / Quadrennial World Convention* Poland 2004, *Quadrennial World Convention* Rome (Italy) 2000, *Quadrennial world convention and general assembly* Rome (Italy) 2000.
Members Organizations in 38 countries:
Argentina, Austria, Belgium, Brazil, Burundi, Canada, Colombia, Congo DR, Costa Rica, Croatia, Czechia, Dominican Rep, Ecuador, Eritrea, France, Germany, Hungary, India, Italy, Japan, Korea Rep, Laos, Malta, Mexico, Morocco, Netherlands, New Zealand, Philippines, Poland, Portugal, Slovakia, Spain, Sri Lanka, Switzerland, Thailand, UK, Uruguay, USA.
Individuals in 60 countries and territories:
Albania, Algeria, Argentina, Austria, Belgium, Benin, Brazil, Burundi, Canada, Chile, Colombia, Congo DR, Costa Rica, Croatia, Czechia, Dominican Rep, Ecuador, Eritrea, France, Germany, Hong Kong, Hungary, India, Israel, Italy, Japan, Kenya, Korea Rep, Laos, Latvia, Lithuania, Luxembourg, Madagascar, Malta, Mexico, Moldova, Morocco, Netherlands, New Zealand, Pakistan, Peru, Philippines, Poland, Portugal, Russia, Rwanda, Senegal, Singapore, Slovakia, Spain, Sri Lanka, Switzerland, Syrian AR, Taiwan, Thailand, Uganda, UK, Uruguay, USA, Vietnam. [2020/XF3686/**F**]

♦ World Conference on Soviet Jewry (meeting series)

♦ World Conferences on Research Integrity Foundation (WCRI) 21300

Chair c/o VUA – Humanities, Dept of Philosophy, De Boelelaan 1105, 1081 HV Amsterdam, Netherlands.
URL: https://wcrif.org/

History Jul 2017. Originally a conference series organized since 2007. Registration: No/ID: KVK 69154481, Netherlands. **Aims** Promote research integrity through support for the ongoing organization and development of the World Conferences and all related activities. **Structure** Governing Board; Executive Committee. **Activities** Awards/prizes/competitions; events/meetings. **Events** *World Conference on Research Integrity* 2024, *World Conference on Research Integrity* Cape Town (South Africa) 2022, *World Conference on Research Integrity* Hong Kong (Hong Kong) 2019, *World Conference on Research Integrity* Amsterdam (Netherlands) 2017, *World Conference on Research Integrity* Rio de Janeiro (Brazil) 2015. **NGO Relations** *Committee on Publication Ethics (COPE, #04281)*; *European Science Foundation (ESF, #08441).* [2022/XS1501/cf/**F**]

♦ World Conference of Therapeutic Communities (meeting series)
♦ World Conference on Timber Engineering (meeting series)
♦ World Conference on Titanium (meeting series)
♦ World Conference on Tobacco or Health (meeting series)

♦ World Conference on Transport Research Society (WCTRS) 21301

Association de la Conférence mondiale sur la recherche dans les transports (CMRT)

SG Inst for Transport Studies, Univ of Leeds, 34-40 University Road, Leeds, LS2 9JT, UK. T. +441133430961. E-mail: wctrs@leeds.ac.uk.
URL: http://www.wctrs-society.com/

History 1986, Vancouver, BC (Canada). Founded during the World Conference on Transportation Research. Began as a forum for bridging transport researchers and practitioners, 1977, Rotterdam (Netherlands). Former names and other names: *WCTR Society* – former. Registration: Switzerland. **Aims** Provide a forum for interchange of ideas among *transport* researchers, managers, policy makers and educators from all over the world, from a perspective which is multimodal, multi-disciplinary and multi-sectoral. **Structure** General Assembly (every 3 years); Steering Committee; Special Interest Groups. **Languages** English. **Staff** 1.00 FTE, paid. **Finance** Members' dues. **Activities** Events/meetings; politics/policy/regulatory; knowledgement management/information dissemination. **Events** *World Conference on Transport Research* Montréal, QC (Canada) 2023, *High-Speed Rail and Spatial Scenarios for Europe 2050* Singapore (Singapore) 2020, *World Conference on Transport Research* Mumbai (India) 2019, *World Conference* Shanghai (China) 2016, *World Conference* Rio de Janeiro (Brazil) 2013. **Publications** *WCTRS Newsletter* (usually 3 a year); *Case Studies on Transport Policy* – journal; *Transport Policy* – journal. Conference proceedings.
Members Individuals in 80 countries and territories:
Albania, Algeria, Argentina, Australia, Austria, Bangladesh, Belgium, Bolivia, Brazil, Canada, Chile, China, Colombia, Costa Rica, Croatia, Cyprus, Czechia, Denmark, Ecuador, Egypt, Estonia, Ethiopia, Finland, France, Germany, Ghana, Greece, Hong Kong, Hungary, Iceland, India, Indonesia, Iran Islamic Rep, Ireland, Israel, Italy, Japan, Kazakhstan, Kenya, Korea Rep, Lebanon, Luxembourg, Malaysia, Malta, Mexico, Montenegro, Netherlands, New Zealand, Nigeria, Norway, Palestine, Peru, Philippines, Poland, Portugal, Qatar, Romania, Russia, Saudi Arabia, Serbia, Singapore, Slovenia, South Africa, Spain, Sri Lanka, Sweden, Switzerland, Taiwan, Tanzania UR, Thailand, Togo, Türkiye, Uganda, UK, United Arab Emirates, Uruguay, USA, Venezuela, Vietnam, Zimbabwe.
NGO Relations Observer status with: *Eastern Asia Society for Transportation Studies (EASTS, #05229)*; *European Transport Research Alliance (ETRA, #08939).* [2020/XF1807/cv/**F**]

♦ World Conference on Urine Therapy (meeting series)
♦ World Congress of Accounting Historians (meeting series)
♦ World Congress of Acupuncture (meeting series)

♦ World Congress of African Linguistics (WOCAL) 21302

Pres PN van Eyckhof 3, Room 3-04b, 2311 BV Leiden, Netherlands. T. +31715272243.
URL: http://www.wocal.rutgers.edu/

History 1991, Pretoria (South Africa). **Aims** Act as a forum for scholars in African linguistics; stimulate research and studies on African languages; disseminate knowledge about African languages. **Structure** General Meeting (every 3 years, in conjunction with World Congress); Standing Committee. **Languages** Arabic, English, French. **Staff** Voluntary. **Finance** Congress funded by organizing institution and voluntary sources. **Events** *Congress* Leiden (Netherlands) 2021, *Congress* Rabat (Morocco) 2018, *Congress* Kyoto (Japan) 2015, *Language description and documentation for development, education and the preservation of cultural heritage in Africa* Buea (Cameroon) 2012, *African linguistics for understanding and progress* Cologne (Germany) 2009. **Publications** Congress proceedings. **Members** No formal membership. **IGO Relations** *African Union (AU, #00488)* – Academy of African Languages (ACALAN). **NGO Relations** *SIL International (#19278).* [2019/XM2303/**F**]

♦ World Congress Alternatives and Environment (meeting series)
♦ World Congress on Cancers of the Skin (meeting series)
♦ World Congress of Chemical Engineering (meeting series)

♦ World Congress of Chiropractic Students (WCCS) 21303

Contact 160 Eglinton Ave East, Suite 601, Toronto ON M4P 3B5, Canada. E-mail: info@wccsworldwide.org – secretary@wccsworldwide.org – publicrelations@wccsworldwide.org.
Pres address not obtained.
URL: http://www.wccsworldwide.org/

History 1980. **Aims** Advance and unite the global chiropractic profession through inspiration, integrity and leadership. **Structure** Board of Directors (6); Regional Coordinators (4); Legislative Committee (3). **Languages** English. **Staff** Voluntary. **Finance** Sources: meeting proceeds; sponsorship. **Activities** Events/meetings. **Events** *Western Pacific Regional Meeting* Murdoch, WA (Australia) 2020, *Annual General Meeting* Toronto, ON (Canada) 2020, *Annual General Meeting* Brisbane, QLD (Australia) 2019, *Africa Regional Meeting* Durban (South Africa) 2019, *Americas Regional Meeting* Logan, UT (USA) 2019. **Publications** *Quarterly Report.*
Members Full in 15 countries:
Australia, Brazil, Canada, Denmark, France, Germany, Japan, Malaysia, Mexico, New Zealand, South Africa, Spain, Switzerland, UK, USA. [2023.02.22/XM5705/cy/**C**]

♦ World Congress on Controversies to Consensus in Diabetes, Obesity and Hypertension (meeting series)
♦ World Congress on Controversies, Debates and Consensus in Bone, Muscle and Joint Diseases (meeting series)
♦ World Congress on Controversies in Multiple Myeloma (meeting series)
♦ World Congress on Controversies in Neurology (meeting series)
♦ World Congress on Controversies in Obstetrics, Gynecology and Infertility (meeting series)
♦ World Congress on Controversies in Preconception, Preimplantation and Prenatal Genetic Diagnosis (meeting series)
♦ World Congresses and Conferences for Peace (meeting series)
♦ World Congress of Ethnic Religions / see European Congress of Ethnic Religions (#06740)

♦ World Congress of Faiths (WCF) 21304

Exec Sec 21 Maple Street, London, W1T 4BE, UK. T. +447747612327. E-mail: admin@worldfaiths.org.
URL: http://www.worldfaiths.org/

History 1936, London (UK). Founded by Sir Francis Younghusband. Former names and other names: *Interfaith Fellowship – World Congress of Faiths* – former. Registration: Charity Commission, No/ID: 244096, England and Wales. **Aims** Bring people of different faiths and commitments together, in mutual respect and trust; promote better *understanding* between *religious communities*; further dialogue between people of different convictions about religious truth and practice. **Structure** General Meeting; Executive Committee. **Languages** English. **Staff** 0.50 FTE, paid. **Finance** Sources: members' dues. **Activities** Events/meetings; networking/liaising. **Events** *Seeking the transformation of a fractured world* Birmingham (UK) 2006, *Annual General Meeting* London (UK) 2006, *The future of multi-faith Britain* Leicester (UK) 2003, *Annual General Meeting* London (UK) 2003, *The religions of Egypt – past, present and future* London (UK) 2003. **Publications** *Interreligious Insight* (2 a year).
Members Branches; Individuals. Members in 34 countries and territories:
Australia, Bangladesh, Barbados, Belgium, Canada, China, Denmark, France, Germany, Hong Kong, India, Iran Islamic Rep, Ireland, Israel, Italy, Japan, Kenya, Malaysia, Netherlands, New Zealand, Nigeria, Norway, Pakistan, Papua New Guinea, Sierra Leone, Singapore, South Africa, Spain, Sri Lanka, Switzerland, Taiwan, UK, Uruguay, USA.
NGO Relations Member of (1): *International Interfaith Organizations Network (IION, #13945).* Associated with: *International Association for Religious Freedom (IARF, #12130).* [2023.02.28/XF3494/**F**]

♦ World Congress on Family Law and the Rights of Children and Youth (meeting series)

♦ World Congress of Free Ukrainians (WCFU) 21305

Congrès mondial des ukrainiens libres – Congreso Mundial de Ucranios Libres – Weltkongress der Freien Ukrainer – Congresso Mundial dos Ucranianos Livres

Head Office 145 Evans Ave, Suite 207, Toronto ON M8Z 5X8, Canada. T. +14163233020. Fax +14163233250. E-mail: uwc@ukrainianworldcongress.org.
Contact 72 Blvd Charlemagne, 1040 Brussels, Belgium. T. +32489629049.
URL: http://www.ukrainianworldcongress.org/

History 1967, New York, NY (USA). Former names and other names: *Ukrainian World Congress (UWC)* – alias. **Aims** Act as a spokesman for the Ukrainian communities in the *diaspora* (over 3 million people); represent all facets of religious, social, political, economic, cultural and educational life of Ukrainians outside the Ukraine. **Structure** Executive, comprising Executive Committee, 5 Ukrainian Churches Representatives, 2 WFUWO Representatives, 8 Vice-Presidents and 10 Chairpersons of UWC Councils and Commissions. Executive Committee, consisting of President, 1st and 2nd Vice-Presidents, Secretary-General, Financial Officer and Treasurer. Board of Directors, comprising Executive and 25 Ukrainian National (Regional) Representatives, European Congress of Ukrainians Representative, 11 representatives of Ukrainian international organizations and Councils and Commissions' representatives. Councils and Commissions (10): World Educational Coordinating Council; World Council of Ukrainian Social Services; World Scholarly Council; World Council on Cultural Affairs; Conference of Ukrainian Youth Organizations; Commission on Human and Civil Rights; Sport Commission; World Council of Ukrainian Cooperatives; Ukrainian World Congress United Nation Committee; Media Council. **Languages** English, Ukrainian. **Staff** 3.50 FTE, paid. **Finance** Donations. **Activities** Advocacy/lobbying/activism; events/meetings. **Events** *Annual General Meeting* Berlin (Germany) 2019, *Annual General Meeting* Madrid (Spain) 2015, *Quinquennial congress* Toronto, ON (Canada) 1993, *Congress* 1988, *Quinquennial Congress* Toronto, ON (Canada) 1983. **Publications** *UWC Newsletter* (12 a year); *Presidium* (4 a year); *Ukrainian Newsletter* in English; *Visnyk* in Ukrainian. Congress proceedings.
Members Organizations (130) and individuals () in 20 countries:
Argentina, Australia, Austria, Belgium, Brazil, Canada, Croatia (*), Czechia, Denmark (*), France, Germany, Italy (*), Poland, Romania, Slovakia, Sweden (*), Switzerland (*), UK, Ukraine, USA.
Consultative Status Consultative status granted from: *Council of Europe (CE, #04881)* (Participatory Status).
NGO Relations *World Federation of Ukrainian Women's Organizations (WFUWO, #21496).* [2021/XF2587/**F**]

♦ World Congress of Gay, Lesbian and Bisexual Jewish Organizations / see World Congress of Gay, Lesbian, Bisexual and Transgender Jews (#21306)

♦ World Congress of Gay, Lesbian, Bisexual and Transgender Jews (WCGLBTJ) 21306

Keshet Ga'avah

Pres PO Box 1096, Alexandria VA 22313-1096, USA. E-mail: president@glbtjews.org.
URL: https://glbtjews.org/

History 1980, San Francisco, CA (USA). Founded following meetings held in the USA since 1975. Former names and other names: *World Congress of Gay and Lesbian Jewish Organizations* – former; *World Congress of Gay, Lesbian and Bisexual Jewish Organizations (WCGLJO)* – former (1998). Registration: State of California, DOJ, No/ID: C1543485, Start date: 1986, USA. **Aims** Establish a network of communication among members; provide mutual assistance in members' activities; challenge homophobia and sexism within the Jewish community; respond to anti-semitism at large; educate the public and raise consciousness about homosexuality in general, and about gay, lesbian, bisexual and transgender (GLBT) Jews in particular; build a coalition between the GLBT world and the Jewish community. **Structure** Board of Directors (meets once a year); Steering Committee; Officers. **Languages** Dutch, English, French, Hebrew, Italian, Spanish. **Staff** Voluntary. **Finance** Sources: grants; members' dues. Annual budget: 5,000 USD. **Activities** Events/meetings; training/education. Active in all member countries. **Events** *European Dialog about Anti-Semitism and Homophobia in Europe* Rome (Italy) 2020, *World Conference* Sydney, NSW (Australia) 2019, *World Conference* Rome (Italy) 2018, *World Conference* Paris (France) 2017, *World Conference* Tel Aviv (Israel) 2015. **Publications** *World Congress Newsletter* (6 a year).
Members Organizations of Rainbow Jews in 13 countries:
Argentina, Australia, Brazil, Canada, France, Germany, Israel, Italy, Mexico, Netherlands, South Africa, UK, USA.
NGO Relations Member of (2): *Global Interfaith Network for People of All Sexes, Sexual Orientation, Gender Identity and Expression (GIN-SSOGIE, #10431)*; *ILGA World (International Lesbian, Gay, Bisexual, Trans and Intersex Association, #11120).* Instrumental in setting up (1): *Pink Triangle Coalition (PTC, inactive).* [2021.03.18/XD0051/**D**]

♦ World Congress of Gay and Lesbian Jewish Organizations / see World Congress of Gay, Lesbian, Bisexual and Transgender Jews (#21306)
♦ World Congress on Genetics Applied to Livestock Production (meeting series)

♦ World Congress of Herpetology (WCH) 21307

SG c/o Hungarian Natural History Museum, Dept of Zoology, Baross u. 13, Budapest 1082, Hungary. T. +3612101085.
Treas c/o USU, College of Science, Department of Biology, Logan UT 84322, USA.
URL: http://www.worldcongressofherpetology.org/

History 1982, Raleigh, NC (USA). Acts as a Section of *International Union of Biological Sciences (IUBS, #15760).* **Aims** Promote international interest, collaboration and cooperation in herpetology. **Structure** Executive Committee, consisting of not less than 16 and not more than 20 members. International Herpetological Committee, comprising not fewer than 40 and not more than 50 members. Secretary-General, Secretary-General-Elect and Treasurer elected amongst the members of the Executive Committee. **Finance** Sources: donations; fundraising. Other sources: registration fees. **Activities** Events/meetings. Holds

periodic international congresses of herpetology; establishes specialist committees; serves as the Section of Herpetology of IUBS. **Events** *World Congress* Kuching (Malaysia) 2024, *World Congress* Dunedin (New Zealand) 2020, *World Congress* Hangzhou (China) 2016, *World Congress* Vancouver, BC (Canada) 2012, *World Congress* Manaus (Brazil) 2008.
Members Delegates from 69 countries and territories:
Algeria, Argentina, Australia, Austria, Bahamas, Bangladesh, Belgium, Bolivia, Botswana, Brazil, Canada, Cayman Is, Chile, China, Colombia, Costa Rica, Czechia, Denmark, Ecuador, Egypt, Fiji, Finland, France, Germany, Greece, Guatemala, Hungary, India, Indonesia, Iran Islamic Rep, Ireland, Israel, Italy, Jamaica, Japan, Kenya, Madagascar, Malaysia, Mexico, Montenegro, Netherlands, New Zealand, Nicaragua, Nigeria, Norway, Pakistan, Panama, Papua New Guinea, Peru, Philippines, Poland, Portugal, Russia, Serbia, Singapore, Slovenia, Solomon Is, South Africa, Spain, Sri Lanka, Sweden, Switzerland, Taiwan, Thailand, Türkiye, UK, Uruguay, USA, Venezuela. [2022.02.15/XE6005/cv/F]

♦ World Congress on Hydrogen Sulfide in Biology and Medicine (meeting series)
♦ World Congress on Leishmaniasis (meeting series)
♦ World Congress on Leishmaniosis (meeting series)
♦ World Congress of Mountain Jews (unconfirmed)

♦ World Congress of Muslim Philanthropists (WCMP) 21308

CEO PO Box 3654, Oak Brook IL 60522, USA. T. +16308899512. Fax +16308899511. E-mail: info@thewcmp.org.
URL: http://www.thewcmp.org/
History Formally launched 23 Mar 2008, Istanbul (Turkey). **Aims** Advance impact giving and investing by leveraging the most effective use of knowledge, wealth, and influence among Muslim philanthropists; build a culture of enduring engagement where Muslim donors collaborate with each other, and emerge as a significant, distinctive and vital component of the global philanthropic community. **Structure** Board of Directors. **Languages** Arabic, English. **Finance** Sources: members' dues; sponsorship. Annual budget: 350,000 USD. **Activities** Awards/prizes/competitions; events/meetings; training/education. **Events** *Global Donors Forum* Washington, DC (USA) 2022, *Global Donors Forum* London (UK) 2018, *Annual Global Donors Forum* Kuala Lumpur (Malaysia) 2012, *Annual Global Donors Forum / Global Donors Forum* Dubai (United Arab Emirates) 2011, *Annual Global Donors Forum / Global Donors Forum* Doha (Qatar) 2010. **Publications** *Journal of Muslim Philanthropy*. **Members** Membership countries not specified. **IGO Relations** Sponsors and partners include: *ECOSOC (#05331)*; *International Bank for Reconstruction and Development (IBRD, #12317)*; *Islamic Development Bank (IsDB, #16044)*; *Islamic World Educational, Scientific and Cultural Organization (ICESCO, #16058)*; *United Nations Alliance of Civilizations (UNAOC, #20520)*; *UNDP (#20292)*; UN Office for Partnerships; *WHO (#20950)*. **NGO Relations** Sponsors and partners include: *ActionAid (#00087)*; *Arab Foundations Forum (AFF, #00963)*; Dubai Cares; *Islamic Relief Worldwide (IRWW, #16048)*; *Reach Out to Asia (ROTA)*. Member of: *PMNCH (#18410)*. Supports: *SDG Philanthropy Platform (SDGfunders)*. [2019/XJ4982/C]

♦ World Congress of Oral Implantology (meeting series)
♦ World Congress of Paediatric Gastroenterology, Hepatology and Nutrition / see Federation of International Societies for Pediatric Gastroenterology, Hepatology and Nutrition (#09678)
♦ World Congress of Pediatric Cardiology and Cardiac Surgery (meeting series)
♦ World Congress of Poets (see: #21066)
♦ World Congress on Prevention of Diabetes and its Complications (meeting series)
♦ World Congress on Probation and and Parole (meeting series)
♦ World Congress on Recurrent Pregnancy Loss (meeting series)
♦ World Congress of Reproductive Biology (meeting series)

♦ World Congress of Science and Factual Producers (WCSFP) 21309

Dir c/o Hot Docs, 720 Spadina Ave, Suite 402, Toronto ON M5S 2T9, Canada. T. +14162032155. Fax +14162030446.
URL: https://www.wcsfp.com/
Structure Board of Directors. **Activities** Events/meetings. **Events** *Congress* Strasbourg (France) 2021, *Congress* Toronto, ON (Canada) 2020, *Congress* Tokyo (Japan) 2019. [2021.05.18/AA0152/F]

♦ World Congress on Sheep and Cattle Breeding (meeting series)
♦ World Congress on Sleep Apnea (meeting series)
♦ World Congress on Superconductivity (meeting series)

♦ World Congress of Tatars (BTK) 21310

Chairman Karla Marksa 38/5, Kazan TATARSTAN, Russia, 420111. T. +78432365916. Fax +78432646337. E-mail: tatar-congress@mail.ru.
URL: http://tatar-congress.org/
History Also referred to as *World Tatar Congress*. **Aims** Promote solidarity among those of Tatar *culture*. **Structure** Executive Committee. [2022/XM2091/F]

♦ World Congress on Twin Pregnancy (meeting series)

♦ World Congress on Vascular Access (WoCoVA) 21311

Events Manager PO Box 675, 3720 AR Bilthoven, Netherlands. T. +31612053880. E-mail: secretariat@wocova.com.
CEO address not obtained.
URL: http://www.wocova.com/
History 2009. Initially organized as an independent foundation; currently within *Global Vascular Access Network (GloVANet)*. Registration: Netherlands. **Aims** Organize worldwide congresses on vascular access. **Structure** Board; Global Committee; Scientific Committee. **Languages** Dutch, English, German. **Activities** Events/meetings. **Events** *Congress* Athens (Greece) 2022, *Congress* Athens (Greece) 2021, *Congress* Copenhagen (Denmark) 2018, *Congress* Lisbon (Portugal) 2016, *Congress* Berlin (Germany) 2014. **Publications** Consensus and scientific publications. [2020.11.16/XM6296/c/E]

♦ World Congress of Veterinary Dermatology Association / see World Association for Veterinary Dermatology (#21203)
♦ World Connect (internationally oriented national body)
♦ World Connect – Just Imagine / see World Connect
♦ World Conscience (inactive)
♦ World Conscious Pact (unconfirmed)
♦ World Conservation Monitoring Centre / see UN Environment Programme World Conservation Monitoring Centre (#20295)

♦ World Conservation Trust (IWMC) 21312

Exec Vice-Pres Head Office – Europe, Passage Montriond 3, 1006 Lausanne VD, Switzerland. T. +41216165000. Fax +41216165000. E-mail: iwmcch@bluewin.ch.
Pres 1470 Heather Ridge Blvd, Unit 104, Dunedin FL 34698, USA. T. +17277344949. Fax +17277344949. E-mail: iwmc@iwmc.org.
URL: http://www.iwmc.org/
History 1994, Switzerland. Former names and other names: *International Wildlife Management Consortium* – former (1994). Registration: Switzerland; Canada. **Aims** Promote sustainable use of wildlife resources – terrestrial and aquatic – as a conservation mechanism. **Structure** Board of Directors. **Events** *Symposium* Chengdu (China) 2000, *Symposium* Bali (Indonesia) 1997. **Publications** *IWMC Conservation Tribune* (12 a year) – newsletter. Reports.
Members Full in 44 countries and territories:
Antigua-Barbuda, Argentina, Australia, Belgium, Botswana, Cameroon, Canada, China, Cuba, Denmark, Dominica, France, Gabon, Germany, Grenada, Iceland, Indonesia, Italy, Japan, Kenya, Malaysia, Mexico, Monaco, Namibia, Nepal, Netherlands, New Zealand, Norway, Panama, Papua New Guinea, Philippines, Russia, Singapore, South Africa, St Lucia, St Vincent-Grenadines, Switzerland, Taiwan, Thailand, Trinidad-Tobago, UK, USA, Venezuela, Zimbabwe.
IGO Relations Accredited by: *FAO (#09260)*; *International Tropical Timber Organization (ITTO, #15737)*; *International Whaling Commission (IWC, #15879)*. [2022/XE2826/E]

♦ World Conservation Union / see International Union for Conservation of Nature and Natural Resources (#15766)
♦ World Constitution Fund (internationally oriented national body)

♦ World Constitution and Parliament Association (WCPA) 21313

Association pour une constitution mondiale et un parlement mondial
Pres 313 7th Ave, Radford VA 24141, USA.
SG address not obtained. E-mail: govt_rules@yahoo.com.
Main: http://www.earth-constitution.org
History Founded 1958, USA, by Philip and Margaret Isely, as *World Committee for a World Constitutional Convention*. Current name adopted, 1960. Organized 4 World Constituent Assemblies through which hundreds of world citizens wrote the Constitution for the Federation of Earth, also known as the Earth Constitution: Aug-Sep 1968, Interlaken (Switzerland) and Wolfach (Germany FR); 1977, Innsbruck (Austria); 1979, Colombo (Sri Lanka); 1991, Troia (Portugal). Since 1991 the Earth Constitution is considered a finished document and the *'Earth Federation Movement (EFM)'* has been launched to ratify the Constitution. **Aims** Work toward a global *democracy* embracing all nations and peoples under the Constitution for the Federation of Earth; ratify the Earth Constitution; develop the World Parliament and enforceable global laws disarming the nations and protecting our planetary environment. **Structure** Executive Council; Steering Committee for *Provisional World Parliament (see: #21313)*; National Chapters. **Languages** English, Esperanto, French, Spanish. **Staff** 18.00 FTE, paid. **Finance** Donations. **Activities** Advocacy/lobbying/activism; politics/policy/regulatory; events/meetings. **Events** *Session of Provisional World Parliament* Kolkata (India) 2015, *Session* Kolkata (India) 2015, *Session / Session of Provisional World Parliament* Lucknow (India) 2013, *Session of Provisional World Parliament* Kolkata (India) 2012, *Session* Kolkata (India) 2010. **Publications** *Across Frontiers* – bulletin. *A Constitution for the Federation of Earth, with Historical Introduction, Commentary, and Conclusion* by Glen T Martin; *Earth Federation Now* by Errol E Harris; *Emerging World Law: Key Documents and Decisions of the Global Constituent Assemblies and the Provisional World Parliament* by Eugenia Almand and Glen T Martin; *One World Renaissance: Holistic Planetary Transformation Through a Global Social Contract* by Glen T Martin; *The Anatomy of a Sustainable World: Our Choice between Climate Change or System Change* by Glen T Martin; *Triumph of Civilization: Democracy, Nonviolence, and the Piloting of Spaceship Earth* by Glen T Martin. Web blogs.
Members Executive Cabinet Members and World Trustees in 118 countries:
Albania, Angola, Argentina, Australia, Bangladesh, Belarus, Belgium, Benin, Bermuda, Bolivia, Brazil, Bulgaria, Burkina Faso, Burundi, Cambodia, Cameroon, Canada, Cape Verde, Central African Rep, Chad, Chile, China, Colombia, Comoros, Congo Brazzaville, Congo DR, Costa Rica, Côte d'Ivoire, Croatia, Cyprus, Czechia, Denmark, Dominican Rep, Ecuador, Egypt, El Salvador, Eritrea, Estonia, Ethiopia, Finland, France, Gambia, Georgia, Germany, Ghana, Greece, Guinea, Guyana, Haiti, Hungary, India, Indonesia, Iran Islamic Rep, Iraq, Ireland, Israel, Italy, Jamaica, Japan, Jordan, Kenya, Korea Rep, Kyrgyzstan, Latvia, Liberia, Libya, Lithuania, Madagascar, Malaysia, Maldives, Mali, Mauritania, Mauritius, Mexico, Morocco, Mozambique, Nepal, Netherlands, New Zealand, Nicaragua, Niger, Nigeria, North Macedonia, Pakistan, Panama, Papua New Guinea, Peru, Philippines, Poland, Romania, Russia, Rwanda, Sao Tomé-Principe, Senegal, Serbia, Sierra Leone, Slovakia, Slovenia, South Africa, Spain, Sri Lanka, St Vincent-Grenadines, Sudan, Switzerland, Tanzania UR, Togo, Tunisia, Türkiye, Uganda, UK, Ukraine, Uruguay, USA, Uzbekistan, Venezuela, Vietnam, Zambia, Zimbabwe.
NGO Relations Member of: *EarthAction (EA, #05159)*. [2018.06.01/XC3495/F]

♦ World Containerboard Organization (WCO) 21314

Main Office Ave Louise 250, 1050 Brussels, Belgium. T. +3226474157. Fax +3226471724.
URL: http://www.wco-containerboard.org/
History Nov 2001, Brussels (Belgium). **Aims** Promote the interests of producers of corrugated case materials (containerboard). **Structure** Board of Directors, comprising President and 11 members. **Languages** English. **Events** *WCO / ICCA Global Summit* 2021, *Biennial Summit* Palm Beach, FL (USA) 2019, *Biennial Summit* Guajará (Brazil) 2017, *Biennial Summit* Taipei (Taiwan) / Shanghai (China) 2015, *Biennial Summit* Paris (France) 2013. **Publications** News bulletin.
Members Full in 21 countries:
Australia, Austria, Brazil, Canada, Finland, France, Germany, Ireland, Japan, Mexico, Netherlands, Portugal, Russia, South Africa, Spain, Sweden, Taiwan, Thailand, Türkiye, UK, USA.
NGO Relations Cooperates with (1): *International Corrugated Case Association (ICCA, #12974)*. [2021/XD3398/D]

♦ World Continuing Education Alliance (internationally oriented national body)

♦ World Convention of Churches of Christ (WCCC) 21315

Convention mondiale des Eglises du Christ
Exec Dir PO Box 43514, Louisville KY 40253, USA. E-mail: office@worldconvention.org.
URL: http://www.worldconvention.org/
History Founded 1930, Washington DC (USA). One of 20 world organizations referred to as *'Christian World Communions or Church Family Groups'*, meeting separately every 4 years. **Aims** Show the essential oneness of the churches in the Lord Jesus Christ; impart inspiration; cultivate the spirit of fellowship; cooperate with Christians everywhere toward the unity of the Church on the basis of the New Testament. **Structure** Officers: President, Past President, 1st Vice President, 5 further Vice Presidents and Treasurer. Committee, comprising 20 members. **Languages** English. **Staff** 2.00 FTE, paid. **Finance** Annual budget: US$ 158,000. Permanent Endowment Fund. **Activities** Events/meetings; religious activities. **Events** *Global Gathering* Warsaw (Poland) 2022, *Quadrennial Assembly* Seoul (Korea Rep) 2016, *Quadrennial Assembly* Goiânia (Brazil) 2012, *Quadrennial assembly / Quadrennial Meeting* Nashville, TN (USA) 2008, *Quadrennial assembly / Quadrennial Meeting* Brighton (UK) 2004. **Publications** *ChristiaNet* (12 a year) – newsletter.
Members A Christian fellowship of individuals and churches worldwide. Members in 179 countries and territories:
Afghanistan, Albania, Angola, Anguilla, Antigua-Barbuda, Argentina, Aruba, Australia, Austria, Bahamas, Bangladesh, Barbados, Belarus, Belgium, Belize, Benin, Bermuda, Bolivia, Bosnia-Herzegovina, Botswana, Brazil, Bulgaria, Burkina Faso, Cambodia, Cameroon, Canada, Cayman Is, Central African Rep, Chad, Chile, China, Colombia, Congo DR, Cook Is, Costa Rica, Côte d'Ivoire, Croatia, Cuba, Cyprus, Czechia, Denmark, Dominica, Dominican Rep, Ecuador, Egypt, El Salvador, Equatorial Guinea, Estonia, Eswatini, Ethiopia, Fiji, Finland, France, Gabon, Gambia, Georgia, Germany, Ghana, Gibraltar, Greece, Grenada, Guadeloupe, Guam, Guatemala, Guiana Fr, Guinea, Guinea-Bissau, Guyana, Haiti, Honduras, Hong Kong, Hungary, Iceland, India, Indonesia, Iran Islamic Rep, Ireland, Israel, Italy, Jamaica, Japan, Jordan, Kazakhstan, Kenya, Kiribati, Korea Rep, Kuwait, Laos, Latvia, Lebanon, Lesotho, Liberia, Libya, Lithuania, Luxembourg, Madagascar, Malawi, Malaysia, Mali, Malta, Marshall Is, Mauritius, Mexico, Micronesia FS, Moldova, Montserrat, Morocco, Mozambique, Myanmar, Namibia, Nepal, Netherlands, New Caledonia, New Zealand, Nicaragua, Niger, Nigeria, Northern Mariana Is, Norway, Pakistan, Panama, Papua New Guinea, Paraguay, Peru, Philippines, Poland, Portugal, Puerto Rico, Romania, Russia, Rwanda, Samoa, Samoa USA, Saudi Arabia, Senegal, Serbia, Seychelles, Sierra Leone, Singapore, Slovakia, Slovenia, Solomon Is, South Africa, Spain, Sri Lanka, St Kitts-Nevis, St Lucia, St Maarten, St Vincent-Grenadines, Sudan, Suriname, Sweden, Switzerland, Tahiti Is, Taiwan, Tanzania UR, Thailand, Togo, Tonga, Trinidad-Tobago, Tunisia, Türkiye, Turks-Caicos, Tuvalu, Uganda, UK, Ukraine, United Arab Emirates, Uruguay, USA, Uzbekistan, Vanuatu, Venezuela, Vietnam, Virgin Is UK, Virgin Is USA, Zambia, Zimbabwe. [2020/XD3496/F]

♦ World Corrosion Organization (WCO) 21316

Dir Gen PO Box 2544, New York NY 10116-2544, USA. E-mail: info@corrosion.org – wco@corrosion.org.
Pres address not obtained.
URL: http://www.corrosion.org/
History Founded 2006, as an umbrella organization. **Aims** Promote education and best practices in corrosion control for the socio-economic benefit of society, preservation of resources, and protection of the environment. **Structure** General Assembly; Board of Administrators; Board. **Languages** English. **Staff** Voluntary. **Finance** Sources: donations; members' dues. **Activities** Awareness raising; events/meetings. **Events** *Annual Meeting* Phoenix, AZ (USA) 2018, *Annual Meeting* New Orleans, LA (USA) 2017, *General Assembly* New Orleans, LA (USA) 2017, *Annual Meeting* Vancouver, BC (Canada) 2016, *General Assembly* Vancouver, BC (Canada) 2016. **Publications** *Materials and Corrosion* – official journal. *Study on Global Needs for Knowledge Dissemination, Research and Development in Materials Deterioration and Corrosion Control* (2009).
Members Membership is limited to non-for-profit organizations with interest/activity in the fields of corrosion research and mitigation. Founder members (3):
Chinese Society for Corrosion and Protection (CSCP); *European Federation of Corrosion (EFC, #07090)*; *The Australasian Corrosion Association (ACA, #03023)*.
Partner member:
Materials Technology Institute.
General members in 28 countries:
Australia, Austria, Canada, China, Croatia, Czechia, Egypt, France, Germany, Hungary, Israel, Japan, Korea Rep, Kuwait, Libya, Lithuania, Netherlands, New Zealand, Poland, Portugal, Saudi Arabia, South Africa, Spain, Sweden, Türkiye, UK, USA, Venezuela.
IGO Relations Affiliated with Department of Global Communications of the United Nations. [2015.06.24/XM2911/C]

♦ **World Council of Anthropological Associations (WCAA)** **21317**

Sec address not obtained.
Chair address not obtained.
URL: https://www.waunet.org/wcaa/

History Founded 2004, Recife (Brazil). Together with *International Union of Anthropological and Ethnological Sciences (IUAES, #15755)*, became one of 2 distinctly separate but constituent chambers within *World Anthropological Union (WAU, #21093)*, 2018. **Aims** Promote the discipline of anthropology in an international context; increase cooperation and the sharing of information among world anthropologists through scientific debate, cooperation in research activities and dissemination of anthropological knowledge. **Structure** Council; Organizing Committee; Task Forces. **Languages** English. **Staff** None. **Finance** Supported by: *Wenner-Gren Foundations*; voluntary contributions from member associations. Annual budget: about US$ 20,000. **Activities** Events/meetings; research/documentation; knowledge management/information dissemination. **Events** *Biennial Meeting* Florianópolis (Brazil) 2018, *Interim Delegates Meeting* Ottawa, ON (Canada) 2017, *Biennial Meeting* Dubrovnik (Croatia) 2016, *Interim Delegates Meeting* Minneapolis, MN (USA) 2016, *Interim Delegates Meeting* Bangkok (Thailand) 2015. **Publications** *Déjà Lu* – electronic journal.

Members National and regional organizations (52) in 35 countries and territories:
Argentina, Australia, Brazil, Canada, Chile, China, Croatia, Czechia, Finland, France, Germany, Hong Kong, India, Indonesia, Ireland, Israel, Italy, Japan, Korea Rep, Latvia, Mexico, New Zealand, Norway, Philippines, Poland, Portugal, Russia, Serbia, Spain, Sweden, Taiwan, Tunisia, UK, Uruguay, USA.
International organizations listed in this Yearbook (9):
Anthropology Southern Africa (#00851); Association of Social Anthropologists of the UK (ASA, #02917); European Association of Social Anthropologists (EASA, #06209); International Association for Southeast European Anthropology (InASEA, #12173); International Union of Anthropological and Ethnological Sciences (IUAES, #15755); Latin American Anthropological Association (#16234); Pan African Association of Anthropologists (PAAA, #18036); Société internationale d'ethnologie et de folklore (SIEF, #19481); Wenner-Gren Foundations. [2020/XM1075/y/**D**]

♦ **World Council of Arameans – Syriacs (WCA)** **21318**

Sec Mozartlaan 161, 7557 DN Hengelo, Netherlands.
URL: http://www.wca-ngo.org/

History 1983, as *Syriac Universal Alliance (SUA)*. **Aims** Protect and secure the *rights*, liberty and equality of the Aramean people; safeguard and promote the *cultural heritage* of its ancestors, ensuring justice, and uniting all its people as a *self-determined* and internationally recognized Aramean nation. **Structure** Board.
Members Federations in 9 countries:
Australia, Austria, Belgium, Germany, Netherlands, Sweden, Switzerland, UK, USA.
Consultative Status Consultative status granted from: *ECOSOC (#05331)* (Special). **NGO Relations** Member of: *Conference of Non-Governmental Organizations in Consultative Relationship with the United Nations (CONGO, #04635).* [2015/XQ0191/**E**]

♦ World Council and Assembly on Cooperative Education / see World Association for Cooperative Education (#21128)
♦ World Council of Associations for Technology Education (no recent information)
♦ World Council for Automobile Mobility and Tourism (see: #09613)

♦ **World Council for Biomechanics (WCB)** **21319**

Chair c/o Uniservices House – Bldg 439, Level 6, Room 613, 70 Symonds Street, Auckland 1010, New Zealand. T. +6499238395.
URL: http://www.wc-biomechanics.org/

History 3 Sep 1990. Former names and other names: *World Committee for Biomechanics* – former (1990 to 1994). Registration: Start date: 2015, Netherlands. **Aims** Provide permanence and stability for periodic meetings of the World Congress of Biomechanics; communicate information about the World Congress and any associate satellite meetings, as well as about the scientific priorities in Biomechanics, to people interested in the subject. **Structure** Council; Executive Committee. **Languages** English. **Finance** Congress proceeds. **Activities** Events/meetings. **Events** *World Congress of Biomechanics (WCB)* 2026, *World Congress of Biomechanics (WCB)* Taipei (Taiwan) 2022, *World Congress of Biomechanics* Dublin (Ireland) 2018, *World Congress of Biomechanics* Boston, MA (USA) 2014, *World Congress on Biomechanics* Singapore (Singapore) 2010.
Members Individuals in 19 countries and territories:
Australia, Austria, Brazil, China, Czechia, France, Hong Kong, Ireland, Israel, Japan, Korea Rep, Netherlands, New Zealand, Russia, Singapore, Spain, Taiwan, UK, USA.
NGO Relations Affiliated organization of: *International Union of Theoretical and Applied Mechanics (IUTAM, #15823).* [2022/XF5282/**F**]

♦ World Council of Christian Education (inactive)

♦ **World Council of Churches (WCC)** **21320**

Conseil oecuménique des Eglises (COE) – Consejo Mundial de Iglesias (CMI) – Ökumenischer Rat der Kirchen (ÖRK)

Acting Gen Sec Route de Ferney 150, CP 2100, 1211 Geneva 2, Switzerland. T. +41227916111. Fax +41227910361. E-mail: media@wcc-coe.org.
Street Address Ecumenical Centre, Route des Morillons 1, Grand-Saconnex, 1218 Geneva, Switzerland.
URL: http://www.oikoumene.org/

History Aug 1948, Amsterdam (Netherlands). Founded by 147 churches, carrying on the activity of *Life and Work Movement (inactive)* and of *Faith and Order Movement (inactive)*, two bodies which, prior to World War II, proposed the setting up of a such a Council. Originally European/North American centred, the Council steadily became more world-oriented in fact as well as in inspiration. In Dec 1961, Delhi (India), at WCC 3rd Assembly, *International Missionary Council (IMC, inactive)* merged with WCC to become *Commission on World Mission and Evangelism of the World Council of Churches (CWME, inactive)*; CWME ceased to exist in the late 1980s, when it merged into WCC programme. *World Council of Christian Education (WCCE, inactive)* merged with WCC in Jan 1972; it had been set up in 1907 as *'World's Sunday School Association'* and from 1947 was referred to as *'World Council of Christian Education and Sunday School Association'* before receiving its final title. WCC constitution was most recently revised in Dec 1998, Harare (Zimbabwe). Registration: Swiss Civil Code, Switzerland. **Aims** As a fellowship of churches which confess the Lord Jesus Christ as God and Saviour according to the scriptures, seek to fulfil together the common calling to the glory of the one God, Father, Son and Holy Spirit. **Structure** Assembly (every 8 years); Central Committee; Executive Committee; Commissions and Working Groups (7). **Languages** English, French, German, Spanish. **Staff** 110.00 FTE, paid. **Finance** Sources: contributions; fees for services; sale of publications. Contributions from member churches; funds from church-related organizations, foundations and individuals; income from investments, rental of offices. **Activities** Networking/liaising; projects/programmes; religious activities. **Events** *Assembly* Karlsruhe (Germany) 2022, *Assembly* Karlsruhe (Germany) 2021, *International Symposium for Korean Peninsula Peace and Reunification* Seoul (Korea Rep) 2017, *Assembly* Busan (Korea Rep) 2013, *Delegation Conference* Busan (Korea Rep) 2013. **Publications** *Ecumenical Review* (4 a year) in English; *International Review of Mission* (2 a year) in English; *Current dialogue* (annual) in English. Annual Review; brochures. **Information Services** *WCC News* in English, French, German, Spanish; *WCC Publications.*

Members Churches (349) from 121 countries and territories, representing over 580 million Christians worldwide.
Albania, Algeria, Angola, Antigua-Barbuda, Argentina, Armenia, Australia, Austria, Bangladesh, Belgium, Benin, Bolivia, Botswana, Brazil, Burundi, Cameroon, Canada, Chile, China, Congo Brazzaville, Congo DR, Cook Is, Costa Rica, Côte d'Ivoire, Cuba, Cyprus, Czechia, Denmark, Egypt, El Salvador, Equatorial Guinea, Eritrea, Estonia, Eswatini, Ethiopia, Fiji, Finland, France, Gabon, Gambia, Germany, Ghana, Greece, Hong Kong, Hungary, Iceland, India, Indonesia, Iran Islamic Rep, Iraq, Ireland, Israel, Italy, Jamaica, Japan, Kenya, Kiribati, Korea Rep, Latvia, Lebanon, Lesotho, Liberia, Madagascar, Malawi, Malaysia, Marshall Is, Mexico, Mozambique, Myanmar, Namibia, Netherlands, New Caledonia, New Zealand, Nicaragua, Nigeria, Niue, Norway, Pakistan, Papua New Guinea, Peru, Philippines, Poland, Polynesia Fr, Portugal, Puerto Rico, Romania, Russia, Rwanda, Samoa, Samoa USA, Serbia, Seychelles, Sierra Leone, Singapore, Slovakia, Solomon Is, South Africa, Spain, Sri Lanka, St Vincent-Grenadines, Sudan, Suriname, Sweden, Switzerland, Syrian AR, Taiwan, Tanzania UR, Thailand, Timor-Leste, Togo, Tonga, Trinidad-Tobago, Türkiye, Tuvalu, Uganda, UK, Uruguay, USA, Vanuatu, Zambia, Zimbabwe.
Included in the above, the following churches listed in this Yearbook:
- *African Christian Church and Schools (ACCS, no recent information);*
- *African Church of the Holy Spirit (ACHS);*
- *African Israel Nineveh Church (AINC);*
- *African Methodist Episcopal Church (AME);*
- *African Methodist Episcopal Zion Church (AME Zion);*
- *African Protestant Church (EPA);*
- *Anglican Church of Southern Africa (ACSA, #00826);*
- *Church of the Brethren;*
- *Church of the Province of Central Africa (#03917);*
- *Church of the Province of West Africa (CPWA, #03920);*
- *Council of African Instituted Churches (no recent information);*
- *Ecumenical Patriarchate of Constantinople (#05349);*
- *European Continental Province of the Moravian Church (#06777);*
- *Fellowship of Christian Councils in Southern Africa (FOCCISA);*
- *International Council of Community Churches (ICCC);*
- *Methodist Church of Southern Africa;*
- *Organization of African Instituted Churches (OAIC, #17853);*
- *Presbyterian Church of Africa (PCA, #18485);*
- *Presbyterian Church of East Africa (PCEA);*
- *The Conference of the Methodist Church in the Caribbean and the Americas (MCCA, #04629);*
- *United Congregational Church of Southern Africa (UCCSA, #20503);*
- *United Evangelical Lutheran Church in Southern Africa (UELCSA);*
- *Uniting Presbyterian Church in Southern Africa (UPCSA, #20668);*
- *Uniting Reformed Church in Southern Africa (URCSA).*

Consultative Status Consultative status granted from: *ILO (#11123)* (Special List); *UNICEF (#20332); UNEP (#20299); WHO (#20950)* (Official). **IGO Relations** Observer to: *International Organization for Migration (IOM, #14454).*
NGO Relations Full member of: *NGO Committee on Financing for Development, New York (#17108).* Member of: *Global Call for Climate Action (GCCA, inactive); Global Partnership to End Violence Against Children (End Violence Against Children, #10533); International Network for a Culture of Nonviolence and Peace (#14247); International NGO Platform on the Migrant Workers' Convention (IPMWC, #14367); NGO Committee for Disarmament, Geneva (#17105); UNITED for Intercultural Action – European Network Against Nationalism, Racism, Fascism and in Support of Migrants and Refugees (UNITED, #20511); NGO Working Group on the Security Council (#17128).* Partner of: *International Campaign to Abolish Nuclear Weapons (ICAN, #12426).* Since 1965, cooperates with *Pontifical Council for Promoting Christian Unity (PCPCU, #18446)* through *Joint Working Group between the Roman Catholic Church and the World Council of Churches (JWG, #16152).* Close links with national councils of churches in 56 countries and the following regional ecumenical organizations: *All Africa Conference of Churches (AACC, #00640); Caribbean Conference of Churches (CCC, #03479); Christian Conference of Asia (CCA, #03898); Conference of European Churches (CEC, #04593); Latin American Council of Churches (LACC, #16309); Middle East Council of Churches (MECC, #16756); Pacific Conference of Churches (PCC, #17943).*
Working relations with international organizations comprising churches of the same tradition or confession:
- *Anglican Communion (#00827);*
- *Disciples Ecumenical Consultative Council (DECC, #05100);*
- *Friends World Committee for Consultation (FWCC, #10004);*
- *General Conference of Seventh-Day Adventists (SDA, #10109);*
- *International Old Catholic Bishops' Conference (IBC, #14403);*
- *The Lutheran World Federation (LWF, #16532);*
- *Mennonite World Conference (MWC, #16713);*
- *Moravian Church (#16854);*
- *Salvation Army (#19041);*
- *World Communion of Reformed Churches (WCRC, #21289);*
- *World Convention of Churches of Christ (WCCC, #21315);*
- *World Evangelical Alliance (WEA, #21393);*
- *World Methodist Council (WMC, #21650).*

Working relations with international ecumenical organizations:
- *CEVAA – Communauté d'églises en mission (#03840);*
- *Council for World Mission (CWM, #04925);*
- *Ecumenical Association of Third World Theologians (EATWOT, #05344);*
- *Fellowship of the Least Coin (FLC, #09728);*
- *Frontier Internship in Mission (FIM);*
- *International Committee for World Day of Prayer (#12811);*
- *International Cultural Youth Exchange (ICYE Federation, #13122);*
- *International Federation of ACATs – Action by Christians for the Abolition of Torture (#13334);*
- *International Forum of Associations of Christian Higher Education (IFACHE, inactive);*
- *Life and Peace Institute (LPI, #16467);*
- *Oikocredit International (Oikocredit, #17704);*
- *United Bible Societies (UBS, #20498);*
- *United Evangelical Mission (UEM, #20507);*
- *World Alliance of Young Men's Christian Associations (YMCA, #21090);*
- *World Federation of Diaconal Associations and Diaconal Communities (DIAKONIA, #21429);*
- *World Student Christian Federation (WSCF, #21833);*
- *World Vision International (WVI, #21904).*

Links with the following organizations or their representatives housed at the Ecumenical Centre: *ACT Alliance (#00081); Brethren Volunteer Service (BVS, #03321);* Ecumenical Patriarchate of Constantinople; Fondation pour l'aide au protestantisme réformé (FAP); Moscow (Russia) Patriarchate (representation).
Instrumental in setting up:
- *CONOSUR – Network of Ecumenical Lay Centres – OIKOSNET Latin America (no recent information); Ecumenical Pharmaceutical Network (EPN, #05350); Ecumenical Youth Council in Europe (EYCE, #05352); European Contact Group – Ecumenical Network for Economic and Social Action (ECG, #06773);* Global Christian Forum; *HelpAge International – Europe (inactive); International Interchurch Film Organization (INTERFILM, #13943); OIKOSNET (no recent information).*

[2022.02.02/XB3501/y/**B**]

♦ World Council on City Data (unconfirmed)

♦ **World Council of Civil Engineers (WCCE)** **21321**

Secretariat Colegio de Ingenieros, C/ Almagro 42, 28010 Madrid, Spain. T. +34917006422. E-mail: wcce@ciccp.es.
Facebook: https://www.facebook.com/World-Council-of-Civil-Engineers-WCCE-115858305092823/

History 13 Nov 2005, Istanbul (Türkiye). Founded 2005, during a meeting of *European Council of Civil Engineers (ECCE, #06810).* Registration: Spain. **Aims** Create and foster a global platform of civil engineering societies, civil engineering related companies, non-governmental organizations related to civil engineering, academic institutions and individual professional civil engineers. **Structure** General Assembly; Executive Committee; Standing Committees (6). **Languages** English. **Staff** 1.00 FTE, paid. **Events** *General Assembly* Lisbon (Portugal) 2019, *General Assembly* Sucre (Bolivia) 2018, *General Assembly* Victoria Falls (Zimbabwe) 2015, *General Assembly* Lisbon (Portugal) 2014, *General Assembly* Santiago (Cuba) 2013. **Publications** *Journal of Applied Water Engineering and Research* – Joint publication with IAHR; *Revista Iberoamericana del Agua* – Joint Publication with IAHR; *World Annual Civil Engineering Report. Water Monographies Volume I* – Joint Publication with UN-Water.

Members Ordinary (national and international); Associate (sectoral, NGOs and academic institutions, corporate, individual). National associations in 23 countries:
Bolivia, Brazil, Cape Verde, Colombia, Costa Rica, Cuba, Cyprus, Dominican Rep, Georgia, Greece, Honduras, Italy, Kenya, Kuwait, Mexico, Montenegro, Nigeria, Portugal, Puerto Rico, Spain, Tanzania UR, Türkiye, Zambia, Zimbabwe.
International members (4):
African Engineers Forum (AEF, #00300); European Council of Civil Engineers (ECCE, #06810); Federation of African Engineering Organisations (FAEO, #09402); Unión Panamericana de Asociaciones de Ingeniería.
Associate in 2 countries:
Brazil, Spain.
Universidad de Granada.
IGO Relations Memorandum of Understanding with (1): *International Network of Basin Organizations (INBO, #14235).* Partner of: *Global Alliances for Water and Climate (GAfWaC, #10230).* **NGO Relations** Member of: *Consejo de las Asociaciones Profesionales de Ingenieros Civiles de Lengua Oficial Portuguesa y Castellana (CECPC-CICPC, #04702); World Federation of Engineering Organizations (WFEO, #21433).*

[2020.08.25/XJ6403/y/**C**]

♦ World Council for Colonial Freedom (inactive)

♦ World Council of Coloproctology / see International Council of Coloproctology (#13009)

♦ World Council of Comparative Education Societies (WCCES) 21322
Conseil mondial des associations d'éducation comparée (CMAEC) – Consejo Mundial de Sociedad de Educación Comparada (CMSEC)
Mailing Address c/o UNESCO International Bureau of Education, PO Box 199, 1211 Geneva 20, Switzerland. T. +41225550600. Fax +41225550646. E-mail: contact@wcces-online.org.
Pres African Studies and Research Center, Cornell Univ, 310 Triphammer Rd, Ithaca NY 14850, USA. T. +16072557839. Fax +16072550784.
URL: http://www.wcces-online.org/
History 1970. Founded with the assistance of *International Bureau of Education (IBE, #12413)*. Statutes adopted in 1972; revised 1984, 1996, 2017, 2019 and 2020. Registration: Art 60ff ZGB, Switzerland; Title 26 Section 501(c)(3), USA. **Aims** Promote study of comparative and international education throughout the world and enhance the academic status of this field; bring comparative education to bear on the major problems of the day by fostering cooperative action by specialists from different parts of the world. **Structure** World Congress (normally every 3 years); Executive Committee; Bureau; Standing Committees; Task Forces. **Languages** Arabic, Chinese, English, French, Russian, Spanish. **Staff** 100.00 FTE, voluntary. **Finance** Sources: donations; meeting proceeds; members' dues; sale of publications. **Activities** Events/meetings; knowledge management/information dissemination; networking/liaising; projects/programmes. **Events** *World Congress* Bangalore (India) 2024, *World Congress* Bangalore (India) 2022, *Symposium* Geneva (Switzerland) 2022, *Symposium* Geneva (Switzerland) 2021, *Symposium* Lisbon (Portugal) 2020. **Publications** *World Voices Nexus: The WCCES Chronicle* (3 a year) in Arabic, Chinese, English, French, Russian, Spanish – Publishes peer-reviewed short articles (about 3000 words); *Global Comparative Education: Journal of the WCCES* in Arabic, Chinese, English, French, Russian, Spanish – Publishes full-length articles of about 6000 words. *WCCES-Brill Book Series: Comparative and International Education: Diversity of Voices* (2019) in English – Publishes peer-reviewed full-length articles of about 6000-8000 words.
Members Societies in 35 countries and territories:
Argentina, Australia, Brazil, Canada, China, Cuba, Czechia, Egypt, France, Greece, Haiti, Hong Kong, Hungary, India, Israel, Italy, Japan, Kazakhstan, Korea Rep, Mexico, Nepal, Netherlands, Nigeria, Philippines, Portugal, Russia, South Africa, Spain, Taiwan, Türkiye, UK, Ukraine, Uruguay, USA, Venezuela.
Included in the above, 12 organizations listed in this Yearbook:
Africa for Research in Comparative Education Society (AFRICE); Association francophone d'éducation comparée (AFEC, #02610); British Association for International and Comparative Education (BAICE); Comparative and International Education Society (CIES); Comparative and International Education Society of Canada (CIESC); Comparative Education Society of Asia (CESA, #04409); Gulf Comparative Education Society (GCES, #10825); Indian Ocean Comparative Education Society (IOCES, #11159); International Society of Comparative Education, Science and Technology (ISCEST Nigeria); Nederlandstalig Genootschap voor Vergelijkende Studie van Opvoeding en Onderwijs (NGVO); Oceania Comparative and International Education Society (OCIES); Southern African Comparative and History of Education Society (SACHES, #19839).
Consultative Status Consultative status granted from: *UNESCO (#20322)* (Consultative Status).
[2022.11.19/XC4490/y/**C**]

♦ World Council Congress Diplomatic Chaplains for Peace, Universal Human Rights and Justice (unconfirmed)

♦ World Council of Conservative/Masorti Synagogues 21323
Conseil mondial des synagogues massort – Consejo Mundial de Synagogas Masorti
Deputy Dir c/o Masorti Olami, 32 Pierre Koenig St, 93426 Jerusalem, Israel. T. +97226247106. Fax +97226247677. E-mail: mail@masortiolami.org.
Head Office 3080 Broadway, New York NY 10027, USA. T. +12122806039. Fax +12126785321.
URL: http://masortiolami.org/
History 1957. Current statutes adopted 26 Apr 2010, New York NY (USA). Former names and other names: *World Council of Synagogues* – former. **Aims** Build, renew and strengthen *Jewish* life through the Conservative/Masorti movement, working with existing and developing communities in Europe, Latin America, the Former Soviet Union, Africa, Asia and Australia; support the development of congregations; develop young leadership; provide educational and spiritual leadership to communities in these localities. **Structure** Assembly; Board of Directors. **Languages** English, French, German, Hebrew, Portuguese, Russian, Spanish. **Staff** 5.50 FTE, paid. **Finance** Sources: contributions; grants; private foundations. **Activities** Events/meetings; religious activities; training/education. **Events** *Biennial international conference* Jerusalem (Israel) 1989, *Biennial international conference* Jerusalem (Israel) 1987. **Publications** *Monthly E-Zine*. Annual Review.
Members Organizations in 32 countries and territories:
Argentina, Australia, Belgium, Brazil, Canada, Chile, Colombia, Cuba, Czechia, Ecuador, France, Germany, Honduras, Hungary, India, Israel, Mexico, Netherlands, Paraguay, Peru, Portugal, Puerto Rico, Russia, South Africa, Spain, Sweden, Switzerland, Uganda, UK, Ukraine, Uruguay, USA.
IGO Relations Associated with Department of Global Communications of the United Nations. **NGO Relations** Associated with: *Jewish Agency for Israel (#16111); World Zionist Organization (WZO, #21961)*. Member of: *Committee of Religious NGOs at the United Nations (CRNGOs, #04282)*. Instrumental in setting up: *World Jewish Congress (WJC, #21599)*.
[2020.07.23/XD2546/**D**]

♦ World Council of Credit Unions (WOCCU) 21324
Conseil mondial des coopératives d'épargne et de crédit – Consejo Mundial de Cooperativas de Ahorro y Crédito
Communications Officer PO Box 2982, Madison WI 53701-2982, USA. T. +16083952000. Fax +16083952001. E-mail: mail@woccu.org – communications@woccu.org.
Washington DC Office 99 M Street SE, Suite 300, Washington DC 20003-3799, USA. T. +12026380205.
URL: http://www.woccu.org/
History Derives from the (US) 'Credit Union National Extension Bureau', set up 1921, Boston MA (USA); this was replaced, Aug 1934, by 'Credit Union National Association – USA', which expanded in 1940 to service credit union leagues of Canada and the Western Hemisphere and was registered, 8 Oct 1940, in the State of New York (USA). Became a worldwide association in 1958. Corporate name changed to *CUNA International* in 1965. The World Council was set up following CUNA decision of 1970, specifically to address the needs of all credit union movements. Annual board meeting replaced by General Assembly, first held Jun 1995, followed by major structural changes. Incorporated in the State of Wisconsin, 10 Nov 1970. Officially started operations 1 Jan 1971. Registration: USA. **Aims** Expand financial inclusion worldwide through the global credit union community. **Structure** General Assembly; Board of Directors; Executive Committee. Charitable arm: *Worldwide Foundation for Credit Unions*. **Languages** English, French, Spanish. **Staff** 32.00 FTE, paid. Variable field staff. **Finance** Sources: contributions; fees for services; grants; members' dues. **Activities** Advocacy/lobbying/activism; events/meetings; guidance/assistance/consulting; networking/liaising; projects/programmes; training/education. **Events** *World Credit Union Conference* Vancouver, BC (Canada) 2023, *World Credit Union Conference* Glasgow (UK) 2022, *World Credit Union Conference* 2021, *Annual World Conference* Paradise Is (Bahamas) 2019, *Annual World Conference* Singapore (Singapore) 2018. **Publications** Annual Report; Annual Statistical Report; technical guides; electronic newsletters.
Members Direct Members (52); Affiliate Members (4); Associate Members (11). Direct members in 49 countries and territories:
Afghanistan, Antigua-Barbuda, Australia, Bahamas, Barbados, Belize, Bermuda, Brazil, Cameroon, Canada, Cayman Is, Colombia, Costa Rica, Curaçao, Dominica, Dominican Rep, El Salvador, Estonia, Ghana, Great Britain, Grenada, Guatemala, Guyana, Ireland, Jamaica, Kenya, Korea Rep, Malawi, Mexico, Moldova, Montenegro, New Zealand, North Macedonia, Panama, Papua New Guinea, Paraguay, Peru, Poland, Romania, Russia, Seychelles, Singapore, St Kitts-Nevis, St Lucia, St Vincent-Grenadines, Suriname, Ukraine, USA, Virgin Is UK.
Included in the above, 1 regional member:
Caribbean Confederation of Credit Unions (CCCU, #03478).
Affiliate in 2 countries:
Liberia, Netherlands.
Associate (national) in 2 countries:
Poland, USA.
Associate (international – 5):
African Confederation of Cooperative Savings and Credit Associations (ACCOSCA, #00261); Association of Asian Confederation of Credit Unions (ACCU, #02377); International Cooperative and Mutual Insurance Federation (ICMIF, #12948); International Cooperative Banking Association (ICBA, #12945); Internationale Raiffeisen Union e.V. (IRU, #13291).
According to the recent Statistical Report, the international credit union system serves over 235,000,000 individuals and comprises 68,882 credit unions in 109 countries and territories:
Afghanistan, Albania, Antigua-Barbuda, Australia, Azerbaijan, Bahamas, Bangladesh, Barbados, Belarus, Belize, Benin, Bermuda, Bolivia, Brazil, Burkina Faso, Cambodia, Cameroon, Canada, Cayman Is, Chile, Colombia, Costa Rica, Côte d'Ivoire, Curaçao, Dominica, Dominican Rep, Ecuador, El Salvador, Estonia, Eswatini, Ethiopia, Fiji, Gambia, Ghana, Great Britain, Grenada, Guatemala, Guinea-Bissau, Guyana, Haiti, Honduras, Hong Kong, India, Indonesia, Iran Islamic Rep, Ireland, Jamaica, Kenya, Kiribati, Korea Rep, Kyrgyzstan, Laos, Latvia, Lesotho, Liberia, Lithuania, Malawi, Malaysia, Mali, Mauritius, Mexico, Micronesia FS, Moldova, Mongolia, Montserrat, Myanmar, Nepal, Netherlands, New Zealand, Nicaragua, Niger, North Macedonia, Palau, Panama, Papua New Guinea, Paraguay, Peru, Philippines, Poland, Romania, Russia, Rwanda, Samoa, Senegal, Seychelles, Singapore, Solomon Is, South Africa, Sri Lanka, St Kitts-Nevis, St Lucia, St Vincent-Grenadines, Suriname, Taiwan, Tanzania UR, Thailand, Timor-Leste, Togo, Tonga, Trinidad-Tobago, Tuvalu, Uganda, Ukraine, Uruguay, USA, Vanuatu, Vietnam, Zambia, Zimbabwe.
Consultative Status Consultative status granted from: *FAO (#09260)* (Special Status); *ILO (#11123)* (Special List). **NGO Relations** Instrumental in setting up (1): *European Network of Credit Unions*.
[2022.11.30/XB0461/y/**B**]

♦ World Council for Curriculum and Instruction (WCCI) 21325
Conseil mondial d'éducation (CME) – Consejo Mundial de Educación – Weltrat für Bildung (WFB)
Exec Dir Hufstedler School of Education, HSOE Room 306, 11630, 10455 Pomerado Rd, San Diego CA 92131, USA. T. +18586354718. Fax +18586354714. E-mail: wcci@alliant.edu.
URL: http://www.wcci-international.org/
History Mar 1970, Asilomar, CA (USA). Constitution adopted 1 Aug 1971; amended: 1 Aug 1975; 1 Jul 1983; 1 Jan 1987; 1 Dec 1998; ratified, Mar 2007. **Aims** Provide opportunity for individuals in different parts of the world to work together to improve curricula and instruction in the schools and universities of the world; stimulate cross-cultural and cross-national *educational* endeavours; facilitate dissemination of existing and new professional knowledge. **Structure** Board of Directors; Executive Committee. **Languages** English. **Staff** Voluntary. **Finance** Sources: gifts, legacies; grants; members' dues. **Activities** Events/meetings; projects/programmes. **Events** *World conference* San Diego, CA (USA) 2020, *World Conference* Rome (Italy) 2018, *World Conference* Budapest (Hungary) 2016, *World Conference* San Diego, CA (USA) 2014, *World Conference* Kaohsiung (Taiwan) 2012. **Publications** *WCCI Newsletter* (2 a year). Conference proceedings.
Members Individual; Institutional. Members in 37 countries and territories:
Argentina, Australia, Bahrain, Bangladesh, Botswana, Canada, Chile, China, Colombia, Egypt, Fiji, Hong Kong, Hungary, India, Indonesia, Iran Islamic Rep, Jamaica, Japan, Latvia, Lesotho, Malaysia, New Zealand, Nigeria, Philippines, Saudi Arabia, Sierra Leone, Slovakia, Spain, Sri Lanka, Taiwan, Thailand, Türkiye, Ukraine, United Arab Emirates, USA, Vietnam, Yemen.
Included in the above, 3 organizations listed in this Yearbook:
Equitas – International Centre for Human Rights Education; International Center for the Advancement of Scientific Literacy (no recent information); International Institute on Peace Education (IIPE).
Consultative Status Consultative status granted from: *ECOSOC (#05331)* (Special). **IGO Relations** Accredited by (1): *United Nations Office at Vienna (UNOV, #20604)*. Associated with Department of Global Communications of the United Nations.
[2021/XB4622/y/**B**]

♦ World Council of Elders / see World Council of Elders of the Ancient Traditions and Cultures (#21326)

♦ World Council of Elders of the Ancient Traditions and Cultures (WCOE) 21326
Contact PO Box 7915, Boulder CO 80306, USA. Fax +18777504162. E-mail: worldcouncilofelders@gmail.com.
URL: http://www.worldcouncilofelders.org/
History Also referred to as *World Council of Elders*. **Aims** Support the educational, *healing* and unifying work of traditional indigenous elders worldwide. **Events** *International conference of the elders / Conference* Mumbai (India) 2003. **Members** Individuals in 37 countries (membership countries not specified). **NGO Relations** *International Centre for Cultural Studies (ICCS)*.
[2010/XF6681/**F**]

♦ World Council of Enterostomal Therapists (WCET) 21327
Main Office 4 Lan Drive, Suite 310, Westford MA 01886, USA. T. +19782747167. E-mail: admin@wcetn.org.
Pres address not obtained. E-mail: president@wcetn.org.
URL: http://wcetn.org/
History 1975. First conference held in 1978. Constitution adopted 14 Aug 1980; amended Jul 1996 and Jun 2008. Former names and other names: *World Council of Enterostomal Therapy Nurses* – former (1975). **Aims** Lead the global advancement of specialized professional *nursing* care for people with ostomy, wound or continence needs. **Structure** General Meeting (every 2 years, normally at Congress). Board, consisting of the Executive Board and International Delegates of countries where there are full members. Executive Board, comprising the officers – and Chairpersons of the Standing Committees and Congress and Meetings Coordinator. Standing Committees (4): Education; Norma N Gill Foundation (NNGF); Editorial Board; Publications. National and regional affiliate groups. Sub-group: *Asia Pacific Enterostomal Therapy Nurses Association (APETNA, see: #21327)*. **Languages** English. **Staff** 0.50 FTE, paid. **Finance** Sources: members' dues. **Activities** Financial and/or material support; networking/liaising; training/education. **Events** *Biennial Congress* Fort Worth, TX (USA) 2022, *Biennial Congress* Fort Worth, TX (USA) 2022, *Biennial Congress* Glasgow (UK) 2020, *Biennial Congress* Kuala Lumpur (Malaysia) 2018, *Biennial Congress* Cape Town (South Africa) 2016. **Publications** *WCET Journal* (4 a year). *Enterostomal Therapy Nursing: Growth and Evoloution of a Nursing Specialty Worldwide*; *WCET International Ostomy Guideline*. Educational aids.
Members Full; Associate; Commercial; Honorary; Life. Individuals in 58 countries and territories:
Australia, Austria, Bahrain, Belgium, Brazil, Canada, Chile, China, Colombia, Costa Rica, Czechia, Denmark, Estonia, Finland, France, Germany, Hong Kong, Hungary, India, Indonesia, Iran Islamic Rep, Ireland, Israel, Italy, Japan, Kenya, Korea Rep, Macau, Malaysia, Mexico, Nepal, Netherlands, New Zealand, Norway, Oman, Philippines, Poland, Portugal, Puerto Rico, Qatar, Russia, Saudi Arabia, Serbia, Singapore, Slovenia, South Africa, Spain, Sri Lanka, Sweden, Switzerland, Taiwan, Tanzania UR, Thailand, Togo, Türkiye, UK, United Arab Emirates, USA.
[2022/XD6219/v/**C**]

♦ World Council of Enterostomal Therapy Nurses / see World Council of Enterostomal Therapists (#21327)
♦ World Council of Fine Arts (no recent information)
♦ World Council of Fisheries Societies (internationally oriented national body)
♦ World Council of Former Foreign Ministers (no recent information)

♦ World Council for Gifted and Talented Children (WCGTC) 21328
Consejo Mundial del Niño Dotado y Talentoso
Exec Admin Western Kentucky Univ, 1906 College Heights Blvd, Ste 11030, Bowling Green KY 42101, USA. T. +12707454123. Fax +12707454124. E-mail: headquarters@world-gifted.org.
URL: https://world-gifted.org/
History Founded Sep 1975, London (UK). Headquarters moved to Bowling Green KY (USA) in 2011. Registration: Start date: 1976, USA, Delaware. **Aims** Advocate for gifted and talented children by fostering international exchange of information on research and programmes in gifted education, promoting educational programmes for gifted and talented children, and creating a climate of acceptance for gifted children. **Structure** Executive Committee; Headquarters. **Languages** English. **Staff** 1.00 FTE, paid. **Finance** Sources: donations; meeting proceeds; members' dues. **Activities** Advocacy/lobbying/activism; events/meetings; knowledge management/information dissemination; networking/liaising; research/documentation; training/education. **Events** *World Conference for Gifted and Talented Children* 2023, *World Conference for Gifted and Talented Children* Dubai (United Arab Emirates) 2021, *Biennial Conference* Nashville, TN (USA) 2019, *Biennial Conference* Sydney, NSW (Australia) 2017, *Biennial World Conference* Odense (Denmark) 2015. **Publications** *Gifted and Talented International* (2 a year); *World Gifted* (2-3 a year). Conference proceedings.
Members Individuals interested in gifted education. Membership countries not specified. Affiliated federations (5):
Affiliated federations (5):

African Federation for the Gifted and Talented (AFGT, #00308); Asia-Pacific Federation on Giftedness (APFG, #01899); European Committee Promoting the Education of Gifted and Talented Young People (EUROTALENT, #06664); European Council for High Ability (ECHA, #06822); Ibero-American Federation of the World Council for Gifted and Talented Children (#11023). [2022/XD0805/y/**C**]

♦ World Council of Hellenes Abroad (World SAE) 21329

Headquarters SAE Central, Maria Kallas 23, 546 55 Thessaloniki, Greece. T. +302310411955. Fax +302310411886. E-mail: saeinfo@sae.gr.
URL: http://www.sae.gr/

History 8 Dec 1995. Also referred to as *Council of Hellenes Abroad (SAE)*. **Aims** Unite, enhance and promote Hellenism as an influential power worldwide; improve economic, social and political status of Hellenes. **Structure** Board, comprising President, Alternate President, 4 Vice-Presidents and 4 Secretaries. Divisions (4): Asia and Africa; Europe; North and South America; Oceania. **Events** *World Convention* Thessaloniki (Greece) 2003, *World Convention* Thessaloniki (Greece) 2001, *World Convention* Thessaloniki (Greece) 1999, *World Convention* Thessaloniki (Greece) 1997. [2018/XM0299/**D**]

♦ World Council of Hindus / see Vishva Hindu Parishad
♦ World Council for Imamiah Affairs (no recent information)

♦ World Council of Independent Christian Churches (WCICC) 21330

Concilio Mundial de Iglesias Cristianas Independientes (CMICI)

Headquarters Bowling Green Station, PO Box 76, New York NY 10274-0076, USA. E-mail: info@wcicc.org.
Contact 1643 Savannah Hwy, Ste B194, Charleston SC 29407, USA. T. +16462019823. E-mail: ngo@wcicc.org.
URL: http://www.wcicc.org/

History 24 Mar 1993, USA. Since Jul 1994, a US Federally Approved Tax Exempt Religious Organization. **Aims** Promote, on an international level, Christian humanitarian *relief* projects: for alleviation of *poverty*, especially in economically depressed nations; on religious freedom and *human rights* violations, especially on the effects of churches and congregations of member nations. **Structure** Ruling Body of member-elected delegates (meets every 3 years at World Congress Convention); Executive Council; Executive Board of Elders; International Board of Commissioners. Annex divisions (5): WCICC College of Bishops; *Global Accrediting Group (GAG, see: #21330); Mount Sinai International Seminary (see: #21330); World Federation of Christian Pastoral Counselors (WFCPC, see: #21330); World Wide Alliance for Christian Education (WWACE, see: #21330).* **Languages** English, Punjabi. **Staff** Paid; voluntary. **Finance** Sources: contributions; grants. **Activities** Events/meetings; humanitarian/emergency aid; training/education. **Events** *World conference* Delhi (India) 2018, *World congress* Naples (Italy) 2018, *World congress* Naples (Italy) 2017, *Conference* Delhi (India) 2016, *World Congress* Naples (Italy) 2014. **Publications** *Crosswinds* (12 a year).

Members Pastors, churches, ministries, medical clinics, schools and colleges, totalling 380,000 members, in 85 countries and territories:
Anguilla, Argentina, Armenia, Australia, Austria, Bangladesh, Belgium, Benin, Bhutan, Botswana, Brazil, Burkina Faso, Burundi, Cameroon, Canada, Chile, China, Colombia, Congo DR, Costa Rica, Côte d'Ivoire, Cuba, Denmark, Dominican Rep, Ethiopia, Finland, France, Gambia, Germany, Ghana, Greece, Guyana, Haiti, Hong Kong, Iceland, India, Indonesia, Iran Islamic Rep, Iraq, Ireland, Israel, Italy, Jamaica, Japan, Kenya, Korea Rep, Kosovo, Liberia, Luxembourg, Malawi, Malaysia, Mozambique, Myanmar, Nepal, Netherlands, Nigeria, Norway, Pakistan, Peru, Philippines, Portugal, Puerto Rico, Romania, Russia, Rwanda, Seychelles, Sierra Leone, Singapore, South Africa, Spain, Sri Lanka, St Kitts-Nevis, Sudan, Sweden, Switzerland, Taiwan, Tanzania UR, Togo, Trinidad-Tobago, Uganda, UK, USA, Vietnam, Zambia, Zimbabwe.

Consultative Status Consultative status granted from: *ECOSOC (#05331)* (Special). **IGO Relations** Invited to Governing Council sessions of: *International Fund for Agricultural Development (IFAD, #13692); United Nations Permanent Forum on Indigenous Issues (UNPFII, #20609); United Nations Commission on the Status of Women (CSW, #20536).* Associated with Department of Global Communications of the United Nations. **NGO Relations** Instrumental in setting up (1): *International Institute of Pneumiatrics (see: #21330).* [2021/XF4095/**F**]

♦ World Council of Indigenous Peoples (inactive)
♦ World Council of Institutes Paulo Freire (unconfirmed)

♦ World Council of Isotopes (WCI) 21331

Secretariat 18F Seoul Forest IT Valley, 77 Seoungsuil-ro, Seongdong-gu, Seoul, Korea Rep. E-mail: secretary@wci-ici.org.
URL: http://www.wci-ici.org/

History Sep 2008, Vienna (Austria). Formation approved, Sep 2008, at 6th International Conference on Isotopes (ICI), as successor to its International Monitoring and Steering Committee. Original bylaws adopted 30 Sep 2008; Revised 17 Jun 2009 and 24 Aug 2014. **Aims** Promote safe and environmentally sound isotope technologies to serve the needs for global wellbeing. **Structure** General Meeting/Executive Committee; President; Special Committees; Standing Committees; Secretariat. **Activities** Events/meetings; training/education. **Events** *International Conference on Isotopes* Saskatoon, SK (Canada) 2022, *International Conference on Isotopes* Kuala Lumpur (Malaysia) 2020, *International Conference on Isotopes* Doha (Qatar) 2017, *International Conference on Isotopes* Chicago, IL (USA) 2014, *International Conference on Isotopes (ICI)* Moscow (Russia) 2011. **Publications** *WCI Newsletter* (12 a year).

Members Organizations; Individuals. Organizations in 50 countries:
Argentina, Australia, Austria, Bangladesh, Belarus, Belgium, Brazil, Canada, China, Czechia, Ethiopia, France, Germany, Ghana, Hungary, India, Indonesia, Iran Islamic Rep, Italy, Japan, Jordan, Kenya, Korea Rep, Kyrgyzstan, Malaysia, Mauritius, Mexico, Mongolia, Morocco, Netherlands, Nigeria, Pakistan, Philippines, Poland, Qatar, Romania, Russia, Saudi Arabia, Singapore, South Africa, Sri Lanka, Thailand, Tunisia, Uganda, UK, United Arab Emirates, USA, Uzbekistan, Vietnam, Yemen.
Included in the above, 6 organizations listed in this Yearbook:
Asia and Oceania Federation of Nuclear Medicine and Biology (AOFNMB, #01795); Asian Regional Cooperative Council for Nuclear Medicine (ARCCNM, #01683); Asian School of Nuclear Medicine (ASNM, #01692); Forum for Nuclear Cooperation in Asia (FNCA, #09926); International Committee on Non-Destructive Testing (ICNDT, #12793); World Nuclear Association (WNA, #21674).
Individuals in 22 countries:
Australia, Bangladesh, Belgium, Brazil, Canada, China, Hungary, India, Indonesia, Italy, Japan, Jordan, Korea Rep, Lebanon, Pakistan, Poland, Qatar, Russia, South Africa, Switzerland, UK, USA.

NGO Relations *International Isotope Society (IIS, #13964).* [2020/XM4815/y/**C**]

♦ World Council of Jain Academies (WCJA) 21332

SG c/o Jain Academy, 20 James Close, London, NW11 9QX, UK. T. +442084555573. Fax +442089227619.

History Jan 1999, by Jain Academy (UK) and Jain Academic Foundation of North America. UK Registered Charity. **Aims** Carry out the academic study of Jain culture and society; provide resources to the academic institutions that teach Jainism. **Structure** Headquarters in UK; Secretary General is Chief Executive (elected every 4 years). Chapters (4): American; European; Indian; Other Countries. **Finance** Community donations; raises money for projects as required. **Activities** Organizes courses, lectures and seminars, including fast tract of study courses for Western students and professors for Jain studies and research; provides occasional consultative services to UK Education authorities; provides resources for the Jain Academy and Research Centre at Mumbai University, India, and advises the Centre for the teaching of Jain Curriculum; provides resources for the International Summer School for Jain Studies in India, and provides scholarships to the students interested in joining the summer school. Has sponsored (initially for a period of 5 years) the Department of Jain Studies at the Faculty of Comparative Religions, Antwerp (Belgium). **Publications** *Jainism: World of Conquerors* (2004) by Natubhai Shah.

Members Individuals and organizations in 9 countries and territories:
Belgium, Canada, Hong Kong, India, Kenya, Switzerland, UK, United Arab Emirates, USA. [2010.06.01/XE4279/**E**]

♦ World Council of Ju-Jitsu Organisations (WCJJO) 21333

Pres 128 Junction Road, Andover, SP10 3JB, UK. T. +441264400737.
Vice-Pres 9 Saint Paul Crescent, Varsity Lakes, Gold Coast QLD 4227, Australia. T. +61755761064. E-mail: roger@wcjjo.org.
URL: http://wcjjo.org/

History 1977. **Aims** Guide and assist the growth of ju-jitsu internationally. **Structure** Executive Team. **Languages** English. **Finance** Sources: members' dues. **Activities** Sporting activities. **NGO Relations** Member of: *The Association for International Sport for All (TAFISA, #02763).* [2017/XM5482/**C**]

♦ World Council of Management (inactive)

♦ World Council of the Marianist Family (WCMF) 21334

Conseil mondial de la famille marianiste – Consejo Mundial de la Familia Marianista

Contact Curia Generalizia dei Marianisti, Via Latina 22, 00179 Rome RM, Italy. T. +39670475892 – +39677209956. Fax +3967000406. E-mail: moulincharli@gmail.com.
URL: http://www.marianist.org/

History 10 Jun 1996, Rome (Italy). **Aims** Bear witness to the *gospel* through our lives and through our service characterized by simplicity, dialogue, discernment and enablement for mission; in alliance with Mary, work together in faith and hope to service the needs of persons for dignity, liberation and justice. **Structure** Comprises 4 branches: *Congregation of the Daughters of Mary Immaculate (Daughters of Mary); Society of Mary (Marianists); Marian Alliance (AM, see: #21334); Marianist Lay Communities (MLC, see: #21334).* **Languages** English, French, Spanish. **Finance** Donations from the 4 branches. **Activities** Organizes annual meeting (always in Rome) of leadership teams of each of the branches.

Members Full; Individual. Full national organizations in 25 countries:
Argentina, Australia, Austria, Belgium, Brazil, Canada, Chile, Colombia, Congo Brazzaville, Congo DR, Côte d'Ivoire, France, Haiti, India, Italy, Japan, Kenya, Korea Rep, Mexico, Peru, Philippines, Poland, Spain, Togo, USA.
Individuals in 35 countries:
Albania, Argentina, Australia, Austria, Belgium, Benin, Brazil, Canada, Chile, Colombia, Congo Brazzaville, Congo DR, Côte d'Ivoire, Cuba, Ecuador, France, Germany, Haiti, India, Ireland, Italy, Japan, Kenya, Korea Rep, Malawi, Mexico, Nepal, Peru, Philippines, Poland, Spain, Togo, Tunisia, USA, Zambia.

NGO Relations Full member of: *NGO Committee on Financing for Development, New York (#17108).* [2012.07.23/XE4548/**E**]

♦ World Council on Media Education (no recent information)
♦ World Council of Muslim Communities (internationally oriented national body)
♦ World Council for New Thinking (unconfirmed)
♦ World Council of Nuclear Workers (inactive)

♦ World Council of Optometry (WCO) 21335

Managing Dir 243 N Lindbergh Blvd, St Louis MO 63141-7881, USA. T. +13149834197. E-mail: enquiries@worldoptometry.org.
URL: http://worldcouncilofoptometry.info/

History 1927, Cologne (Germany). Reconstituted 1951, London (UK). Previous Constitution and Statutes adopted May 1975; amended: 1978; 1980; 1981; 1985; 1986. New Memorandum and Articles adopted Jun 2009; amended 2011; 2017. Former names and other names: *International Optical League* – former (1927 to 1970); *Ligue internationale d'optique* – former (1927 to 1970); *International Optometric and Optical League (IOOL)* – former (1970). **Aims** Facilitate development of optometry around the world; support optometrists in promoting eye health and vision care as a human right accessible to all people. **Structure** General Assembly Meeting (annual); Executive Committee; Standing Committees. **Languages** English. **Staff** 2.00 FTE, paid. **Finance** Sources: members' dues. **Activities** Certification/accreditation; events/meetings; guidance/assistance/consulting; knowledge management/information dissemination; training/education. **Events** *World Congress of Optometry* Melbourne, VIC (Australia) 2023, *World Congress of Optometry* Melbourne, VIC (Australia) 2021, *World Congress* Orlando, FL (USA) 2019, *World Congress* Hyderabad (India) 2017, *World Congress* Medellin (Colombia) 2015. **Publications** *WCO E-News* (6 a year); *WCO Report* (every 2 years); *World Focus Magazine* (every 2 years).

Members Country; Affiliate. Members in 52 countries and territories:
Argentina, Australia, Brazil, Cameroon, Canada, Chile, China, Colombia, Costa Rica, Fiji, France, Guyana, Hong Kong, India, Iran Islamic Rep, Ireland, Israel, Italy, Jamaica, Japan, Jordan, Korea Rep, Lebanon, Malaysia, Mexico, Morocco, Nepal, Netherlands, New Zealand, Nigeria, Norway, Palestine, Peru, Philippines, Portugal, Puerto Rico, Saudi Arabia, Singapore, South Africa, Spain, Sri Lanka, Sudan, Suriname, Sweden, Switzerland, Tanzania UR, Thailand, Trinidad-Tobago, Uganda, UK, USA, Zimbabwe.
Volunteer Optometric Services to Humanity International (VOSH International).
Regional groups (7):
African Council of Optometry (AFCO, #00275); American Optometric Association (AOA); *Asia Pacific Council of Optometry (APCO, #01876); Asociación Latinoamericana de Optometria y Optica (ALDOO, #02247);* Canadian Association of Optometrists (CAO); *Eastern Mediterranean Council of Optometry (EMCO, #05243); European Council of Optometry and Optics (ECOO, #06835).*

Consultative Status Consultative status granted from: *WHO (#20950)* (Official Relations). **NGO Relations** Instrumental in setting up: *Common Market Opticians' Group (inactive)* – currently merged with *Pan European Group of Optometrists (inactive)* to form European Council of Optometry and Optics (ECOO). [2021/XC2305/y/**B**]

♦ World Council of Orthopaedic Sports Medicine (no recent information)
♦ World Council of Peoples for the United Nations (internationally oriented national body)
♦ World Council for the Peoples World Convention (inactive)

♦ World Council of Power Utilities (WCPU) 21336

SG-Treas Council of Power Utilities, A-2/158, Janakpuri, Delhi 110058, DELHI 110058, India. T. +91115618472 – +911155545626. Fax +91115611622.
URL: http://www.indiapower.org/wcpuprofile.php

History 1995. **Aims** Increase information exchange between power generating utilities, manufacturers of *power plant* equipment, engineering consultants, power planners, power financiers and environmentalists. **Structure** General Assembly; Governing Council, including President, 2 Vice-Presidents, Secretary-General-Treasurer. **Languages** English. **Staff** 7.00 FTE, paid. **Finance** Members' dues. **Events** *Annual Gentech World Asia Conference* Singapore (Singapore) 2012, *Annual LNG Outlook Asia Conference* Singapore (Singapore) 2012, *Annual Smart Electricity World Asia Conference* Singapore (Singapore) 2012, *Annual Transmission and Distribution World Asia Conference* Singapore (Singapore) 2012, *Utility Revenue and Customer Management World Asia Conference* Singapore (Singapore) 2012. **Publications** *WCPU Newsletter.*

Members Individuals in 4 countries:
China, India, Nepal, Zambia.
Organizations in 4 countries:
India, Nepal, South Africa, Zambia. [2011/XD6021/**D**]

♦ World Council of Professional Photographers (inactive)

♦ World Council for Psychotherapy (WCP) 21337

Fédération mondiale de psychothérapie – Asociación Mundial de Psicoterapia – Weltverband für Psychotherapie (WVP) – Associazione Mondiale di Psicoterapia

Main Office Freudplatz 1, 1020 Vienna, Austria.
URL: http://www.worldpsyche.org/

History Founded 25 Jun 1995, Zurich (Switzerland), during annual congress of *European Association for Psychotherapy (EAP, #06176).* Registered in accordance with Austrian law. **Aims** Promote psychotherapy in all continents, in accordance with the 'Strasbourg Declaration on Psychotherapy', 1990; enhance conditions of psychotherapy patients; cooperate with national and international organizations in peacekeeping and conflict management measures; establish ethical guidelines for psychotherapists; support efforts to achieve and maintain human rights; exchange *training* standards worldwide; consult with authorities in different countries on issues concerning the emotional and psychic sphere of individuals and groups. **Structure** General Meeting (every 3 years); Governing Board; Court of Arbitration. Continental organizations: Australia/Pacific Islands; Africa; Asia (*Asian Federation for Psychotherapy (AFP, #01471)*); Latin America (*Latin American Federation for Psychotherapy (#16329)*); North America; Europe (EAP). Office and Secretary in Vienna (Austria). **Languages** English, German. **Staff** 287.00 FTE, paid. **Finance** Sources: contributions; members' dues; subsidies. Annual budget: USD. **Activities** Conflict resolution; guidance/assistance/consulting; knowledge management/information dissemination; standards/guidelines. **Events** *Triennial World Congress* Vienna (Austria) 2025, *Children, Society and Future – the Planet of Psychotherapy* Moscow (Russia) 2022, *Triennial World Congress* Moscow (Russia) 2021, *Triennial World Congress* Moscow (Russia) 2020, *Triennial World Congress* Paris (France) 2017. **Publications** *International Development of Psychotherapy. Psychotherapy in Africa – First Investigations; Traditional Healing in Africa.*

Members Ordinary; Extraordinary; Honorary. Individuals and organizations in 62 countries and territories:

Algeria, Argentina, Australia, Austria, Belgium, Bosnia-Herzegovina, Brazil, Bulgaria, Burkina Faso, Cameroon, Canada, China, Colombia, Côte d'Ivoire, Croatia, Cuba, Czechia, Denmark, Egypt, Estonia, Finland, France, Georgia, Germany, Greece, Hong Kong, Hungary, India, Indonesia, Ireland, Israel, Italy, Japan, Kenya, Korea DPR, Korea Rep, Kuwait, Madagascar, Mexico, Namibia, Netherlands, New Zealand, Nigeria, Norway, Peru, Poland, Portugal, Romania, Russia, Serbia, Slovakia, Slovenia, Spain, Sweden, Switzerland, Taiwan, Türkiye, UK, Ukraine, United Arab Emirates, Uruguay, USA.
Consultative Status Consultative status granted from: *ECOSOC (#05331)* (Special). [2021/XC0052/**B**]

♦ World Council for Regular and Distance Education (WCRDE) 21338

Contact 3/106 – 1st Floor, Vivek Khand-3, Gomti Nagar, Lucknow, Uttar Pradesh 226010 UP, Lucknow UTTAR PRADESH 226010 UP, India. T. +915222303663 – +915222303664. Fax +915222397710. E-mail: info@wcrde-edu.org.
URL: http://www.wcrde-edu.org/

History 2012. Legally controlled by *International Non-Olympic Committee (INOC, #14374)*. Registered in accordance with Indian law. **Aims** Promote distance education throughout the world. **Structure** Supervisory Committee. **Finance** Members' dues. **Publications** *WCRDE Newsletter*.
Members Universities, educational institutions and authorities; individuals engaged in the field. Universities in 8 countries:
Belize, Dominica, India, Iran Islamic Rep, Japan, Panama, Spain, USA.
Institutional members in 3 countries:
Canada, India, Japan.
Included in the above, 2 organizations listed in this Yearbook:
International Super-Cricket Committee (ISCC, #15626); *World Sports Karate Federation (WSKF, #21824)*.
Individuals in 5 countries:
Canada, Iran Islamic Rep, Malaysia, Singapore, USA.
NGO Relations Partners include: *International Nobel Peace Prize Recommendation Forum (INPRRF, #14373)*; *International Non-Olympic Committee (INOC, #14374)*. [2019.12.12/XJ7936/y/**E**]

♦ World Council of Religious Leaders (WCRL) 21339

Secretariat 5A Nai Lert Tower,, 2/4 Wireless Road, Patumwan, Bangkok, 10330, Thailand. T. +6622521748. Fax +6626550382. E-mail: secretariat@wcorl.org.
Headquarters Empire State Bldg, 350 Fifth Ave, 59th Floor, New York NY 10118, USA. T. +12129672891. Fax +12129672898. E-mail: hq@wcorl.org.
URL: http://www.wcorl.org/

History 14 Jun 2002, Bangkok (Thailand). Evolved out of Millennium World Peace Summit, 28-31 Aug 2000, New York NY (USA). **Aims** Build an integrated framework for peace; serve as a model and guide for the creation of a community of world religions; assist the United Nations and its agencies in the prevention, resolution and healing of conflicts, in the eradication of their causes and in addressing social and environmental problems. **Structure** Secretariat in New York NY (USA); Regional Councils; National Councils. **Activities** Events/meetings. **Events** *World religious leaders summit for peace* Sapporo (Japan) 2008. **NGO Relations** Member of (1): *International Interfaith Organizations Network (IION, #13945)*. Advocacy and networking with: *Pax Christi – International Catholic Peace Movement (#18266)*. [2011.06.01/XM0251/**D**]

♦ World Council for Renewable Energy (WCRE) 21340

Exec Chairman Fed Environment Agency of Germany, Wörlitzer Platz 1, 06844 Dessau, Germany. T. +4934021032649.
Contact c/o EUROSOLAR, Kaiser-Friedrich-Str 11, 53113 Bonn, Germany. T. +49228362373 – +49228362375.
URL: http://www.wcre.de/

History 10 Jun 2001, Berlin (Germany), during the International Impulse Conference for the Creation of an International Renewable Energy Agency. **Aims** Serve as the global voice for renewable energy. **Structure** Chairmen Committee of 5 members, including President of *World Wind Energy Association (WWEA, #21937)*. Advisory Committee. **Activities** Events/meetings. Involved in setting up: *International Renewable Energy Agency (IRENA, #14715)*. **Events** *European Biomass Conference* Bologna (Italy) 2023, *European Biomass Conference* Marseille (France) 2022, *IRES : International Renewable Energy Storage Conference* Bonn (Germany) 2021, *European Biomass Conference* Marseille (France) 2021, *European Biomass Conference* 2020. **Publications** *World Renewable Energy Outlook*. **IGO Relations** Member of: *Global Bioenergy Partnership (GBEP, #10251)*. Cooperates with: *UNESCO Office, Jakarta – Regional Bureau for Sciences in Asia and the Pacific (#20313)*. **NGO Relations** Secretariat provided by: *EUROSOLAR – European Association for Renewable Energy (#09183)*. Instrumental in setting up: *World Renewable Energy Parliamentary Network (WREPN, inactive)*; *World Wind Energy Institute (WWEI, #21938)*. Supports: *Global 100% RE (#10160)*. [2014/XC0132/**C**]

♦ World Council of Service Clubs (no recent information)
♦ World Council of Synagogues / see World Council of Conservative/Masorti Synagogues (#21323)
♦ World Council for Venue Management (inactive)
♦ World Council for the Welfare of the Blind (inactive)

♦ World Council of Whalers (WCW) 21341

Contact address not obtained. E-mail: whaling@shaw.ca.

History Jan 1997, following a series of meetings since 1992. **Aims** Promote sustainable use of living marine resources; protect the rights of whaling peoples. **Structure** General Assembly (annual). **Languages** English. **Staff** 3.00 FTE, paid. **Finance** Members' dues. Budget (annual): Canadian $ 12,000. **Events** *Assembly* Thorshavn (Faeroe Is) 2002, *Assembly* Nelson (New Zealand) 2000, *Assembly* Reykjavik (Iceland) 1999, *Assembly* Victoria, BC (Canada) 1998. **Publications** *Issues Related to Indigenous Whaling: Tonga*; *Whaling Around the World*. Assembly and conference reports.
Members Organizational; Sustaining; Individual. Members in 20 countries:
Antigua-Barbuda, Australia, Canada, Denmark, Dominica, Germany, Iceland, Indonesia, Japan, New Zealand, Norway, Philippines, Russia, St Kitts-Nevis, St Lucia, St Vincent-Grenadines, Switzerland, Tonga, UK, USA.
IGO Relations Accredited by: *International Whaling Commission (IWC, #15879)*. [2012/XD8305/**D**]

♦ World Court of Human Rights (unconfirmed)
♦ World Crafts Council / see World Crafts Council AISBL (#21342)

♦ World Crafts Council AISBL (WCC International) 21342

Conseil mondial de l'artisanat (CMA) – Consejo Mundial de Artesanias – Weltrat des Kunsthandwerks

Pres PO Box 29550, 13156 Safat, Kuwait. E-mail: wcc.international.sect.ku@gmail.com.
URL: http://www.wccinternational.org/

History 12 Jun 1964, New York, NY (USA). Founded by Ms Aileen Osborn Vanderbuilt Webb, Ms Margaret M Patch and Smt Kamaladevi Chattopadhyay at 1st World Crafts Council General Assembly at the University of Colombia, New York City (USA). Former names and other names: *Consejo Mundial de Artes y Oficios (CMAO)* – alias; *World Crafts Council (WCC AISBL)* – former. Registration: Banque-Carrefour des Entreprises, No/ID: 0502.557.196, Start date: 8 Nov 2021, Belgium, Mons. **Aims** Strengthen the status of crafts in cultural and economic life; promote fellowship among craftspeople by offering them encouragement, help and advice; foster and assists cultural exchange; further wider knowledge and recognition of the craftspeople's works with due regard to the separate cultural and national backgrounds and traditions of its members. **Structure** Executiver Board; Regions (5): Africa, Asia-Pacific, Europe, North America, Latin America, each holding regional General Assembly, electing regional President and Vice-President, and each with its own Secretariat. **Languages** English, French, German, Irish Gaelic, Spanish. **Staff** 3.00 FTE, paid. **Finance** Annual budget: 100,000 USD. **Activities** Events/meetings; guidance/assistance/consulting. **Events** *International Workshop Series* 2021, *Extraordinary General Assembly* Safat (Kuwait) 2021, *International Workshop Series* 2020, *General Assembly* Safat (Kuwait) 2020, *Craft City Networking Forum* Kuching (Malaysia) 2019. **Publications** Annual Report; WCC brochure; Event Catalogues. **Information Services** *EASYCRAFT* – System – offers information, communication tools, online system exhibition and e-shopping.
Members National Entities in 89 countries and territories:
Algeria, Argentina, Australia, Bangladesh, Barbados, Belgium, Benin, Bolivia, Brazil, Brunei Darussalam, Burkina Faso, Burundi, Cameroon, Canada, Central African Rep, Chad, Chile, China, Colombia, Congo DR, Côte d'Ivoire, Cuba, Cyprus, Denmark, Dominican Rep, Ecuador, Finland, France, Gabon, Georgia, Germany, Guatemala, Guinea, Guinea-Bissau, Indonesia, Iran Islamic Rep, Ireland, Italy, Jordan, Kazakhstan, Korea DPR, Korea Rep, Kuwait, Kyrgyzstan, Lebanon, Liberia, Libya, Luxembourg, Madagascar, Malaysia, Mali, Malta, Mauritania, Mauritius, Mexico, Nepal, Netherlands, New Zealand, Niger, Nigeria, Norway, Oman, Palestine, Paraguay, Peru, Portugal, Rwanda, Saudi Arabia, Scotland, Senegal, Slovakia, South Africa, Spain, Sri Lanka, Sweden, Switzerland, Thailand, Togo, Trinidad-Tobago, Tunisia, Uganda, UK, Ukraine, United Arab Emirates, Uruguay, Uzbekistan, Venezuela, Zambia, Zimbabwe.
Associate members in 32 countries and territories:
Argentina, Australia, Bangladesh, Brazil, Chile, China, Cuba, Ecuador, El Salvador, India, Iran Islamic Rep, Kazakhstan, Korea DPR, Kuwait, Lebanon, Malaysia, Morocco, Nepal, Oman, Pakistan, Palestine, Paraguay, Philippines, Qatar, Saudi Arabia, South Africa, Sri Lanka, Taiwan, Tajikistan, Uzbekistan, Vietnam, Zimbabwe.
International and Regional NGO members in 6 countries:
India, Indonesia, Iran Islamic Rep, Namibia, Thailand, Uzbekistan.
Individual members in 31 countries:
Australia, Bahrain, Brazil, Canada, Chile, China, Ecuador, Egypt, India, Indonesia, Iran Islamic Rep, Jordan, Kazakhstan, Korea Rep, Kuwait, Kyrgyzstan, Laos, Lebanon, Nepal, Peru, Qatar, Rwanda, Singapore, South Africa, Sri Lanka, United Arab Emirates, Uruguay, USA, Uzbekistan, Venezuela, Vietnam.
Honorary members in 16 countries:
Argentina, Australia, Bangladesh, Canada, China, Colombia, Denmark, India, Ireland, Japan, Malaysia, South Africa, Thailand, UK, Uruguay, USA.
Consultative Status Consultative status granted from: *ECOSOC (#05331)* (Ros C); *UNESCO (#20322)* (Consultative Status); *UNICEF (#20332)*. **NGO Relations** Member of (2): *Conference of Non-Governmental Organizations in Consultative Relationship with the United Nations (CONGO, #04635)*; *International Federation of Interior Architects / Designers (IFI, #13460)*. [2022.03.04/XB3504/**B**]

♦ World Criminal Justice Library Network (WCJLN) 21343

Co-Chairman Rutgers CLJ Gottfredson Lib, 123 Washington St, Newark NJ 07102, USA. T. +19733535522. Fax +19733531275. E-mail: pschultz@andromeda.rutgers.edu.
URL: http://andromeda.rutgers.edu/~wcjlen/WCJ/

History Apr 1991, Newark NJ (USA), at a meeting of librarians and criminal justice information specialists. **Aims** Provide a comprehensive coverage of criminal justice information and avoid duplication of effort by pooling *information* and services, sharing acquisition lists, collecting development policies, identifying data sets and foreign language document servicing. **Structure** Steering Committee of 5. **Languages** English. **Staff** Voluntary. **Finance** No budget. **Activities** Disseminates, through on-line data bases and other means, national and international crime statistics and criminal justice profiles. **Events** *Conference* Solna (Sweden) 2008, *Conference* Montréal, QC (Canada) 2006, *Biennial conference / Conference* Ljubljana (Slovenia) 2004, *Biennial conference / Conference* Canberra, ACT (Australia) 2003, *Biennial conference / Conference* Zutphen (Netherlands) 2001. **Publications** None.
Members Libraries, institutes, centers and academies in 22 countries:
Australia, Canada, Czechia, Denmark, Finland, France, Germany, Hungary, Italy, Japan, Korea Rep, Lithuania, Netherlands, New Zealand, Norway, Slovenia, South Africa, Spain, Sweden, Uganda, UK, USA.
Included in the above, 4 founding members listed in this Yearbook:
European Institute for Crime Prevention and Control affiliated with the United Nations (HEUNI, #07550); *International Centre for Comparative Criminology (ICCC, #12482)*; *Siracusa International Institute for Criminal Justice and Human Rights (SII, #19289)*; *United Nations Commission on Crime Prevention and Criminal Justice (CCPCJ, #20530)*. [2011.06.01/XF2701/y/**F**]

♦ World Croquet Federation (WCF) 21344

SG Witherden, Weydown Road, Haslemere, GU27 1DT, UK.
URL: http://www.worldcroquet.org.uk/

History Founded 1986. **Aims** Encourage, promote and develop the game itself and the teaching of it internationally; promote international individual and team championships; uphold and enforce the Laws of Croquet; make and uphold regulations for international championships; assist information exchange between individual national associations. **Structure** Council; Management Committee. **Languages** English. **Staff** 1.00 FTE, paid. **Finance** Members' dues. **Activities** Events/meetings. **Publications** *WCF Newsletter* (12 a year).
Members National croquet associations in 29 countries and territories:
Australia, Austria, Belgium, Canada, Czechia, Denmark, Egypt, England, Finland, France, Germany, India, Ireland, Isle of Man, Italy, Japan, Jersey, Latvia, New Zealand, Norway, Palestine, Russia, Scotland, South Africa, Spain, Sweden, Switzerland, USA, Wales. [2018/XD6601/**D**]

♦ World Crossbow Shooting Association (WCSA) 21345

SG 33 Cadell Street, Goolwa SA 5214, Australia. T. +61885555888. Fax +61885555999. E-mail: secretarygeneral@worldcrossbow.com.
URL: http://www.worldcrossbow.com/

History Founded 10 Jan 2003, Cambridge (New Zealand). Registered in accordance with Australian law, 11 Feb 2003. **Aims** Foster development of international crossbow shooting. **Structure** Council (meets every 2 years, in conjunction with World Outdoor Target Championship); Technical Committee. **Languages** English. **Staff** 1.00 FTE, voluntary. **Finance** Members' dues. Budget (annual): US$ 2,500. **Activities** Events/meetings; standards/guidelines; advocacy/lobbying/activism. **Events** *Meeting / WCSA Crossbow Championship and Council* Bloomfield, NJ (USA) 2007, *Meeting / WCSA Crossbow Championship and Council* Perth, WA (Australia) 2005, *Meeting / WCSA Crossbow Championship and Council* Lilleshall (UK) 2003. **Publications** *Basic Coaching Manual* – CD-ROM. Tournament and shooting rules.
Members Founding; national organizations in 18 countries and territories:
Australia, Austria, Brazil, Czechia, Estonia, Finland, Germany, India, Ireland, Japan, Malta, New Zealand, Poland, Portugal, Sweden, Taiwan, UK, USA. [2015.01.08/XD8771/**D**]

♦ World Cube Association (WCA) 21346

Contact address not obtained. E-mail: communication@worldcubeassociation.org – contact@worldcubeassociation.org.
URL: http://www.worldcubeassociation.org/

History Aug 2004. Registration: 501(c)(3) Nonprofit Organization, No/ID: 82-3825954, Start date: 19 Oct 2019, USA. **Aims** Bring opportunities for community membership and leadership to young people around the world through increasing the accessibility of 'twisty puzzle' competitions. **Structure** Board; Delegates; Committees; Teams. **Languages** English. **Activities** Awards/prizes/competitions. [2022.06.18/XM4330/**C**]

♦ World Cultural Council (#04705)

♦ World Cultural Tourism Association (WCTA) 21347

Pres 512-1205 – 710 Gil, 20 Hanam-daero, Seo-gu, Gwangju 61903, Korea Rep. T. +82629618958.
URL: http://www.worldculturaltourismassociation.org/

History 2000, Gwangju (Korea Rep). **Aims** Explore, analyse and evaluate the state of art in cultural tourism; bring together researchers, policy makers and practitioners. **Structure** Directorial Board; Bureau; Committees (4). **Languages** English. **Staff** 5.00 FTE, paid; 22.00 FTE, voluntary. **Finance** Sources: meeting proceeds; members' dues; sale of publications. Annual budget: 50,000 USD. **Activities** Awards/prizes/competitions; awareness raising; capacity building; events/meetings; guidance/assistance/consulting; knowledge management/information dissemination; monitoring/evaluation; research/documentation; training/education. Active in all member countries. **Events** *Conference* Kuala Lumpur (Malaysia) 2020, *Conference* Chiang Mai (Thailand) 2019, *Conference* Bangkok (Thailand) 2018, *Conference* Hyderabad (India) 2018, *Conference* Tokyo (Japan) 2017. **Publications** *International Journal of Culture and Tourism Research*.
Members Organizations in 18 countries and territories:
Australia, Canada, China, Greece, India, Indonesia, Japan, Kazakhstan, Korea Rep, Philippines, Serbia, Spain, Taiwan, Tanzania UR, Thailand, Türkiye, USA, Vietnam.
Individuals in 136 countries and territories:
Argentina, Australia, Austria, Azerbaijan, Bahamas, Bahrain, Barbados, Belarus, Belgium, Bolivia, Brazil, Brunei Darussalam, Bulgaria, Burkina Faso, Burundi, Cambodia, Cameroon, Canada, Central African Rep, Chile, China, Colombia, Congo DR, Costa Rica, Côte d'Ivoire, Croatia, Cuba, Cyprus, Czechia, Denmark, Dominica, Dominican Rep, Ecuador, Egypt, El Salvador, Estonia, Fiji, Finland, France, Gambia, Georgia, Germany, Ghana, Greece, Guatemala, Guinea, Haiti, Honduras, Hungary, Iceland, India, Indonesia, Iran Islamic Rep, Iraq, Ireland, Israel, Italy, Jamaica, Japan, Jordan, Kazakhstan, Kenya, Kosovo, Kuwait, Kyrgyzstan, Laos, Latvia, Lebanon, Lithuania, Luxembourg, Malawi, Malaysia, Maldives, Mali, Malta, Mauritius, Mexico, Micronesia FS, Mongolia, Montenegro, Morocco, Mozambique, Myanmar, Namibia, Nepal, Netherlands, New Zealand, Nicaragua, Niger, Nigeria, North Macedonia, Norway, Oman, Pakistan, Panama, Paraguay, Peru, Philippines, Poland, Portugal, Qatar, Romania, Russia, Rwanda, Saudi Arabia, Senegal, Serbia, Sierra Leone, Singapore, Slovakia, Slovenia, Somalia, South Africa, South Sudan, Spain, Sri Lanka, Sudan, Sweden, Taiwan, Tanzania UR, Thailand, Togo, Trinidad-Tobago, Tunisia, Türkiye, Uganda, UK, Ukraine, United Arab Emirates, Uruguay, USA, Uzbekistan, Venezuela, Vietnam, Zambia, Zimbabwe. [2020.12.24/XM3630/**D**]

♦ World Culture Forum (internationally oriented national body)
♦ World Culture Open (unconfirmed)

♦ World Culture Project (internationally oriented national body)
♦ World Cultures Institute (internationally oriented national body)

♦ World Curling Federation (WCF) 21348

SG 3 Atholl Crescent, Perth, PH1 5NG, UK. T. +441738451630. E-mail: info@worldcurling.org.
URL: https://worldcurling.org/

History 1 Apr 1966. Constitution ratified 1967. The rules for international competitions approved in 1968; subsequently revised on several occasions. Former names and other names: *International Curling Federation (ICF)* – former. **Aims** Represent curling internationally; facilitate growth of the sport through member associations and federations. **Structure** General Assembly (annual; biannual if necessary); Board; Commissions (9). **Languages** English. **Staff** 22.00 FTE, paid. **Finance** Sources: members' dues; sponsorship. Supported by: *International Olympic Committee (IOC, #14408)*. **Activities** Sporting activities. **Events** *World Curling Congress* St Petersburg (Russia) 2021, *World Curling Congress* St Petersburg (Russia) 2020, *Annual General Assembly* Stockholm (Sweden) 2016, *World Curling Congress* Stockholm (Sweden) 2016, *World Curling Congress* Belgrade (Serbia) 2015. **Publications** Rules.

Members National Curling Associations in 70 countries and territories:
Afghanistan, Andorra, Australia, Austria, Belarus, Belgium, Bolivia, Bosnia-Herzegovina, Brazil, Bulgaria, Canada, China, Croatia, Czechia, Denmark, Dominican Rep, England, Estonia, Finland, France, Georgia, Germany, Greece, Guyana, Hong Kong, Hungary, Iceland, India, Ireland, Israel, Italy, Jamaica, Japan, Kazakhstan, Kenya, Korea Rep, Kosovo, Kuwait, Kyrgyzstan, Latvia, Liechtenstein, Lithuania, Luxembourg, Mexico, Mongolia, Netherlands, New Zealand, Nigeria, Norway, Poland, Portugal, Qatar, Romania, Russia, Saudi Arabia, Scotland, Serbia, Slovakia, Slovenia, Spain, Sweden, Switzerland, Taiwan, Thailand, Türkiye, Turkmenistan, Ukraine, USA, Virgin Is USA, Wales.

NGO Relations Member of (4): *Association of Paralympic Sports Organisations (APSO, #02850)*; *Association of the International Olympic Winter Sports Federations (AIOWF, #02757)*; *International Paralympic Committee (IPC, #14512)*; *Olympic Movement (#17719)*. Cooperates with (1): *International Testing Agency (ITA, #15678)*. Recognized by: *International Olympic Committee (IOC, #14408)*. [2023.02.15/XD7790/**C**]

♦ World Curriculum by Comparative Education Societies (World Curriculum) 21349

Pres 4950 Cherry Ave Ste 84, San Jose CA 95118, USA. T. +16692968896. E-mail: contact@worldcurriculum.org.
URL: https://www.worldcurriculum.org/

History 2020, Geneva (Switzerland). Founded by Council on Comparative Education in Kazakhstan (CCEK), Haitian Association for the Development of Comparative Education (HADCE), Hungarian Educational Research Association – History of Education and Comparative Education Section (HERA-HECES), *Indian Ocean Comparative Education Society (IOCES, #11159)*, Nederlandstalig Genootschap voor de Vergelijkende studie (NGVO), Sociedad Uruguaya de Educación Comparada y Internacional (SUECI) and Ukrainian Comparative Education Society (UCES). Registration: Switzerland; 501(c)(3), USA. **Aims** Create a world curriculum on the principles of equality, social justice, peace, harmony, and cooperation; conduct omparative education research with a focus on curriculum and assessment for continual revision of the world curriculum; disseminate the world curriculum and associated assessments to the people worldwide. **Structure** Advisory Board; Executive Board. **Languages** English. **Staff** 25.00 FTE, voluntary. **Finance** Sources: donations. **Activities** Research and development; research/documentation. Active in: Canada, China, Germany, Hungary, India, Kazakhstan, Netherlands, Switzerland, Ukraine, Uruguay, USA. [2022.11.10/AA3023/**F**]

♦ **World Curriculum** World Curriculum by Comparative Education Societies (#21349)
♦ World Cursillo Body / see World Body Cursillos in Christianity (#21238)

♦ World Customs Organization (WCO) 21350

Organisation mondiale des douanes (OMD) – Organización Mundial de Aduanas (OMA)
Address not obtained.
URL: http://www.wcoomd.org/

History 15 Dec 1950, Brussels (Belgium), as *Customs Co-operation Council (CCC) – Conseil de coopération douanière (CCD)*, on signature of 3 conventions resulting from the work of *European Customs Union Study Group (inactive)*, set up 12 Sep 1947: Convention establishing a Customs Co-operation Council (entered into force 4 Nov 1952); *Convention on the Nomenclature for the Classification of Goods in Customs Tariffs (1950)* (entered into force 11 Sep 1959), subsequently replaced by *International Convention on the Harmonized Commodity Description and Coding System (1983)* (entered into force 1 Jan 1988); *Convention on the Valuation of Goods for Customs Purposes (1950)* (entered into force 28 Jul 1953), no longer widely applied, following the establishment of the Agreement on Implementation of Article VII of GATT. Present working name adopted 1994. **Aims** Enhance effectiveness and efficiency of customs administrations in areas of compliance with *trade regulations*, protection of society and revenue collection, thereby contributing to economic and social well-being of nations; establish, maintain, support and promote international instruments for harmonization and uniform application of simplified and effective customs systems and procedures governing the movement of commodities, people and conveyances across customs frontiers; reinforce members' efforts to secure compliance with their legislation; maximize the level and effectiveness of members' cooperation with each other and with international organizations in order to combat customs and other transnational offences; assist members in their efforts to meet the challenges of the modern business environment and adapt to changing circumstances, by promoting communication and cooperation among members and with other international organizations, and by fostering integrity, human resource development, transparency, improvements in the management and working methods of customs administrations and the sharing of best practice. **Structure** Council (meets once a year in Jun in Brussels). General Secretariat, headed by Secretary General. Policy Commission. Committees (4): Finance; Audit; Harmonized System; Enforcement. Technical Committees (3): Permanent; Rules of Origin; Customs Valuation. Administrative Committees (2): Customs Convention on Containers, 1972; Istanbul Convention. Contact Committees (2): WCO/IATA/ICAO Guidelines on Advanced Passenger Information (API); UPU/WCO. Management Committees (1): Revised Kyoto Convention. Sub-Committees (4): Integrity; Harmonized System Review; Scientific; Information Management. High Level Working Group (1): Capacity Building, Training and Technical Assistance. Working Groups (2): Commercial Fraud; SAFE. Project Groups (2): Global Information and Intelligence Strategy (GIIS Project Group); Global Information and Intelligence Strategy. Harmonized System Working Party. Electronic Crime Expert Group (ECEG). Customs Enforcement Network Management Team (CENMat). Contracting Parties to the ATA Convention. Private Sector Consultative Group. **Languages** English, French. **Staff** 194.00 FTE, paid. The *Administrative Tribunal of the International Labour Organization (ILO Tribunal, #00118)* is competent to settle disputes. **Finance** Sources: members' dues. Other sources: voluntary contributions from donors for projects. Annual budget (2017/2018): euro 15,900,000 (members' contributions); euro 20,900,000 (voluntary contributions).

Activities Management of treaties and agreements: *General Agreement on Tariffs and Trade, 1994 (GATT 1994, 1994)*, forming part of the *'Marrakech Agreement'* setting up *World Trade Organization (WTO, #21864)*, which superseded the original *General Agreement on Tariffs and Trade, 1947 (GATT 1947, 1947)* while including the text of GATT 1947; *International Convention on the Simplification and Harmonization of Customs Procedures (Kyoto convention, 1973)*, revised Jun 1999. Guidance/assistance/consultancy; politics/policy/regulatory; monitoring/evaluation; standards/guidelines; advocacy/lobbying/activism.
Agreements concluded under CCC/WCO auspices:
- *Customs Convention Regarding ECS Carnets for Commercial Samples (1956)*;
- *Customs Convention on the Temporary Importation of Packings (1960)*;
- *Customs Convention on the ATA Carnet for the Temporary Admission of Goods (ATA Convention, 1961)*;
- *Customs Convention Concerning Facilities for the Importation of Goods for Display or Use at Exhibitions, Fairs, Meetings or Similar Events (1961)*;
- *Customs Convention on the Temporary Importation of Professional Equipment (1961)*;
- *Customs Convention Concerning Welfare Material for Seafarers (1964)*;
- *Customs Convention on the Temporary Importation of Scientific Equipment (1968)*;
- *Customs Convention on the Temporary Importation of Pedagogic Material (1970)*;
- *Customs Convention on the International Transit of Goods (ITI Convention, 1971)*;
- *Customs Convention on Containers, 1972 (1972)*;
- International convention on the simplification and harmonization of customs procedures (Kyoto convention);
- *International Convention on Mutual Administrative Assistance for the Prevention, Investigation and Repression of Customs Offences (Nairobi convention, 1977)*;
- *Convention on Temporary Admission (Istanbul convention, 1990)*.

Events *Green Customs Global Conference* Brussels (Belgium) 2022, *Human Capital Management Global Conference* Brussels (Belgium) 2022, *WCO Technology Conference* Maastricht (Netherlands) 2022, *Global Authorized Economic Operator Conference* Dubai (United Arab Emirates) 2021, *Global Free Zone Conference* Brussels (Belgium) 2020. **Publications** *WCO News* (periodical).

Members Customs administrations (182), including Contracting Parties in 166 countries and territories:
Albania, Algeria, Andorra, Angola, Antigua-Barbuda, Argentina, Armenia, Australia, Austria, Azerbaijan, Bahamas, Bahrain, Bangladesh, Barbados, Belarus, Belgium, Benin, Bermuda, Bhutan, Bolivia, Botswana, Brazil, Brunei Darussalam, Bulgaria, Burkina Faso, Burundi, Cambodia, Cameroon, Canada, Cape Verde, Central African Rep, Chile, China, Colombia, Comoros, Congo Brazzaville, Congo DR, Costa Rica, Côte d'Ivoire, Croatia, Cuba, Curaçao, Cyprus, Czechia, Denmark, Ecuador, Egypt, Eritrea, Estonia, Eswatini, Ethiopia, Fiji, Finland, France, Gabon, Gambia, Georgia, Germany, Ghana, Greece, Guatemala, Guinea, Guyana, Haiti, Hong Kong, Hungary, Iceland, India, Indonesia, Iran Islamic Rep, Iraq, Ireland, Israel, Italy, Jamaica, Japan, Jordan, Kazakhstan, Kenya, Korea Rep, Kosovo, Kuwait, Kyrgyzstan, Latvia, Lebanon, Lesotho, Liberia, Libya, Lithuania, Luxembourg, Macau, Madagascar, Malawi, Malaysia, Maldives, Mali, Malta, Mauritania, Mauritius, Mexico, Moldova, Mongolia, Morocco, Mozambique, Myanmar, Namibia, Nepal, Netherlands, New Zealand, Nicaragua, Niger, Nigeria, North Macedonia, Norway, Oman, Pakistan, Palestine, Panama, Papua New Guinea, Paraguay, Peru, Philippines, Poland, Portugal, Qatar, Romania, Russia, Rwanda, Samoa, Saudi Arabia, Senegal, Serbia, Seychelles, Sierra Leone, Singapore, Slovakia, Slovenia, Somalia, South Africa, South Sudan, Spain, Sri Lanka, Sudan, Sweden, Switzerland, Syrian AR, Tajikistan, Tanzania UR, Thailand, Togo, Trinidad-Tobago, Tunisia, Türkiye, Turkmenistan, Uganda, UK, Ukraine, United Arab Emirates, Uruguay, USA, Uzbekistan, Venezuela, Vietnam, Yemen, Zambia, Zimbabwe.

IGO Relations Cooperates with: *International Transport Forum (ITF, #15725)*; *Union of African Shippers' Councils (UASC, #20348)*. Observer to: *Codex Alimentarius Commission (CAC, #04081)*; *Global Forum on Transparency and Exchange of Information for Tax Purposes (#10379)*. Memorandum of Understanding with:
- *Caribbean Customs Law Enforcement Council (CCLEC, #03487)*;
- *Communauté économique et monétaire d'Afrique centrale (CEMAC, #04374)*;
- *Economic Cooperation Organization (ECO, #05313)*;
- *Eurasian Economic Union (EAEU, #05607)* – Eurasian Economic Commission;
- *European Police Office (Europol, #08239)*;
- *Inter-American Development Bank (IDB, #11427)*;
- *Inter-American Drug Abuse Control Commission (#11429)*;
- *International Atomic Energy Agency (IAEA, #12294)*;
- *International Centre for Migration Policy Development (ICMPD, #12503)*;
- *International Civil Aviation Organization (ICAO, #12581)*;
- *International Criminal Police Organization – INTERPOL (ICPO-INTERPOL, #13110)*;
- *International Maritime Organization (IMO, #14102)*;
- *International Narcotics Control Board (INCB, #14212)*;
- *Islamic Development Bank (IsDB, #16044)*;
- *OECD (#17693)*;
- *OIE – World Organisation for Animal Health (#17703)*;
- *Organisation for the Prohibition of Chemical Weapons (OPCW, #17823)*;
- *Secretariat of the Basel Convention (SBC, #19196)*;
- *Secretariat of the Convention on International Trade in Endangered Species of Wild Fauna and Flora (CITES Secretariat, #19199)*;
- *Southeast European Law Enforcement Center (SELEC, #19815)*;
- *UNEP (#20299)*;
- *UNCTAD (#20285)*;
- *UNESCO (#20322)*;
- *United Nations Office for the Coordination of Humanitarian Affairs (OCHA, #20593)*;
- United Nations Office for Disarmament Affairs (UNODA);
- *United Nations Office on Drugs and Crime (UNODC, #20596)*;
- *Universal Postal Union (UPU, #20682)*;
- *WHO (#20950)*.

Relations with the United Nations, including specialized agencies and bodies having special status, such as:
- *ECOSOC (#05331)*;
- *FAO (#09260)*;
- *Financial Action Task Force (FATF, #09765)*;
- *International Monetary Fund (IMF, #14180)*;
- *UNDP (#20292)*;
- *UNIDO (#20336)*;
- *United Nations Commission on Narcotic Drugs (CND, #20532)*;
- *United Nations Economic Commission for Africa (ECA, #20554)*;
- *United Nations Economic Commission for Europe (UNECE, #20555)*, especially *'Working Party on Facilitation of International Trade Procedures'*;
- *United Nations Economic Commission for Latin America and the Caribbean (ECLAC, #20556)*;
- *United Nations Economic and Social Commission for Asia and the Pacific (ESCAP, #20557)*;
- *United Nations Economic and Social Commission for Western Asia (ESCWA, #20558)*;
- WIPO;
- *World Trade Organization (WTO, #21864)*.

Member of: *Asia/Pacific Group on Money Laundering (APG, #01921)*; *Eastern and Southern African Anti-Money Laundering Group (ESAAMLG, #05252)*; Southeast European Law Enforcement Center (SELEC).
Relations with:
- *Organisation of African, Caribbean and Pacific States (OACPS, #17796)*;
- *African Union (AU, #00488)*;
- *Andean Community (#00817)*;
- *ASEAN (#01141)*;
- *Caribbean Community (CARICOM, #03476)*;
- *Common Market for Eastern and Southern Africa (COMESA, #04296)*;
- *Communauté économique des pays des Grands Lacs (CEPGL, #04375)*;
- *Co-operation Group to Combat Drug Abuse and Illicit Trafficking in Drugs (Pompidou Group, #04796)*;
- *Council of Arab Economic Unity (CAEU, #04859)*;
- *Economic Community of West African States (ECOWAS, #05312)*;
- *EFTA (#05391)*;
- *EU Customs Union (#05579)*;
- *European Monitoring Centre for Drugs and Drug Addiction (EMCDDA, #07820)*;
- *Intergovernmental Committee for Promoting the Return of Cultural Property to its Countries of Origin or its Restitution in case of Illicit Appropriation (#11476)*;
- *International Customs Tariffs Bureau (#13124)*;
- *International Olive Council (IOC, #14405)*;
- *League of Arab States (LAS, #16420)*;
- *Nordiska Tulladministrativa Rådet (NTR, #17497)*;
- *OAS (#17629)*;
- *Postal Operations Council (POC, see: #20682)*;
- *Secretaria Permanente del Convenio Multilateral sobre Cooperación y Asistencia Mutua entre las Direcciones Nacionales de Aduanas de América Latina, España y Portugal (COMALEP, #19194)*;
- *Secretaria Permanente del Tratado General de Integración Económica Centroamericana (SIECA, #19195)*;
- *Southeast European Cooperative Initiative (SECI, #19812)*;
- *Southern African Customs Union (SACU, #19842)*;
- *Steering Committee on Trade Capacity and Standards (CTCS, #19979)*;
- *Union économique et monétaire Ouest africaine (UEMOA, #20377)*;
- *United Nations Centre for Trade Facilitation and Electronic Business (UN/CEFACT, #20527)*;
- *World Intellectual Property Organization (WIPO, #21593)*;
- World Trade Organization (WTO).

NGO Relations Memorandum of Understanding with:
- *Airports Council International (ACI, #00611)*;
- Asociación Nacional para la Defensa de la Marcas (ANDEMA);
- *BIMCO (#03236)*;
- *Business Software Alliance (BSA, #03387)*;
- *Federation of European Movers Associations (FEDEMAC, #09519)*;
- *Federation of the European Sporting Goods Industry (FESI, #09552)*;
- *Fédération internationale des associations de transitaires et assimilés (FIATA, #09610)*;
- *Federation of National Associations of Shipbrokers and Agents (FONASBA, #09694)*;
- *Global Express Association (GEA, #10351)*;
- *ICC Commercial Crime Services (CCS, see: #12534)*;
- *The International Air Cargo Association (TIACA, #11608)*;
- *International Air Transport Association (IATA, #11614)*;
- *International Association of Ports and Harbors (IAPH, #12096)*;
- *International Banking Security Association (IBSA, #12312)*;
- *International Bureau of the Societies Administering the Rights of Mechanical Recording and Reproduction (#12416)*;
- *International Chamber of Commerce (ICC, #12534)*;

- *International Chamber of Shipping (ICS, #12535);*
- *International Council of Chemical Associations (ICCA, #13003);*
- *International Council of Museums (ICOM, #13051)* and its *ICOM International Committee for University Museums and Collections (UMAC, #11058);*
- *International Federation of Customs Brokers Associations (IFCBA, #13400);*
- *International Road Transport Union (IRU, #14761);*
- *Motion Picture Association (MPA);*
- *Piracy Reporting Centre, Kuala Lumpur (#18373);*
- *TradeMark East Africa (TMEA, #20183);*
- *TRAFFIC International (#20196).*

In liaison with technical committees of: *International Organization for Standardization (ISO, #14473).* Technical collaboration and exchange of observers with all international nongovernmental organizations having an interest in customs matters, including:
- *Aviation Research and Development Institute (ARDI, no recent information);*
- *Bureau international des containers et du transport intermodal (BIC, #03364);*
- *Bureau of International Recycling (BIR, #03368);*
- *DIGITALEUROPE (#05073);*
- *EDANA, the voice of nonwovens (EDANA, #05353);*
- *European Express Association (EEA, #07017);*
- *Fédération européenne du commerce chimique (Fecc, #09563);*
- *ICC Counterfeiting Intelligence Bureau (CIB, #11043);*
- *ICC – International Association for Cereal Science and Technology (#11048);*
- *Imaging Consumables Coalition of Europe, Middle-East and Africa (ICCE, #11124);*
- *International Anticounterfeiting Coalition (IACC, #11656);*
- *International Electrotechnical Commission (IEC, #13255);*
- *International Exhibition Logistics Association (IELA, #13322);*
- *International Maritime Bureau (IMB, #14097);*
- *International Union of Railways (#15813);*
- *World Chambers Federation (WCF, #21269);*
- *World Shipping Council (WSC, #21781).*

Member of: *International Network for Environmental Compliance and Enforcement (INECE, #14261).*
[2020/XB0462/**B***]

♦ World Cycling Centre (internationally oriented national body)

♦ WorldDAB 21351

Dir 55 New Oxford Street, London, WC1A 1BS, UK.
URL: http://www.worlddab.org/

History Founded to succeed *EuroDAB Forum*, set up Oct 1995. "DMB" is an acronmym of Digital Multimedia Broadcasting; "DAB" is an acronym of Digital Audio Broadcasting. Former names and other names: *World DAB Forum* – former alias; *WorldDMB Forum* – former. Registration: EU Transparency Register, No/ID: 313735017680-60. **Aims** Coordinate implementation of digital *radio* systems using the Eureka-147-based technologies such as *Digital* Audio Broadcasting (DAB, DAB+) and Digital Multimedia Broadcasting (DMB); enable commercial marketing of the system to the economic and social benefit of all concerned. **Structure** General Assembly. Project headquarters in Geneva (Switzerland). Project Office in London (UK). **Languages** English. **Staff** 4.00 FTE, paid. **Finance** Members' dues. **Activities** Workshops; conferences. **Events** *WorldDAB Summit* London (UK) 2022, *WorldDAB Summit* 2021, *General Assembly* Brussels (Belgium) 2019, *General Assembly* Berlin (Germany) 2018, *General Assembly* Paris (France) 2017. **Publications** *Eureka Newsletter* (4 a year); *Global Update Brochure* (2 a year).
Members National DAB bodies, broadcasters or DAB service providers, manufacturers, network providers, regulatory bodies, research agencies. Organizations (84) in 22 countries:
Australia, Belgium, China, Czechia, Denmark, France, Germany, Hungary, India, Italy, Japan, Korea Rep, Luxembourg, Malaysia, Netherlands, Norway, Romania, Singapore, Sweden, Switzerland, UK, USA.
Included in the above, the following 6 organizations listed in this Yearbook:
Asia-Pacific Broadcasting Union (ABU, #01863); Association of European Radios (AER, #02535); European Broadcasting Union (EBU, #06404); European Commission (EC, #06633); European Telecommunications Standards Institute (ETSI, #08897); Radio France internationale (RFI). [2022/XE3531/y/**E**]

♦ World DAB Forum / see WorldDAB (#21351)

♦ World Dance Alliance 21352

SG c/o Nusantara Performing Arts Research Ctr (NusParc) 30A – First Floor, Jaan Datuk Sulaiman Taman Tun Ismail, 60000 Kuala Lumpur, Malaysia. T. +60377331331. Fax +60377321331.
Pres School of Arts and Aesthetics, Jawaharlal Nehru Univ, Delhi 110067, DELHI 110067, India. T. +919830008458. E-mail: urmimala.sarkar@gmail.com.
URL: http://www.worlddancealliance.org/

History Jul 1990, Hong Kong, at Hong Kong International Dance Conference. **Aims** Serve as a primary voice for dance and dancers throughout the region; encourage exchange of ideas a awareness of dance in all its forms. **Structure** Board; Regional centres (3): *World Dance Alliance – Americas Center (no recent information); World Dance Alliance – Asia Pacific (WDA-AP, see: #21352); World Dance Alliance European (see: #21352).* **Languages** English, French, Spanish. **Activities** Publishing activities; events/meetings. **Events** *Congress* Angers (France) 2014, *World conference on arts education* Seoul (Korea Rep) 2010, *Congress* Philadelphia, PA (USA) 1999, *Congress* Düsseldorf (Germany) 1997, *Congress* Melbourne, VIC (Australia) 1995. **Publications** *Asia-Pacific Channels* (2 a year) – magazine; *Journal of Emerging Dance Scholarship (JEDS).* **NGO Relations** Affiliated Member of: *International Council for Traditional Music (ICTM, #13087); International Theatre Institute (ITI, #15683); World Alliance for Arts Education (WAAE, #21078).* [2019.02.13/XF2887/**F**]

♦ World Dance Alliance – Asia Pacific (see: #21352)
♦ World Dance Alliance European (see: #21352)

♦ World Dance Council (WDC) 21353

Head Office Guldenstrasse 9, 4614 Marchtrenk, Austria. T. +436648720145. E-mail: gensec@wdcdance.com.
Registered Address Ibex House, 162-164 Arthur Road, London, SW19 8AQ, UK.
URL: http://www.wdcdance.com/

History Sep 1950, Edinburgh (UK). Former names and other names: *International Council of Ballroom Dancing (ICBD)* – former (1950 to 1993); *Conseil international pour la danse de salon* – former (1950 to 1993); *World Dance and Dance Sport Council (WD and DSC Centre)* – former (May 1993 to 2006). **Aims** Promote, encourage, publicize and facilitate all dancing, both for professionals and amateurs in all its forms. **Structure** Meeting (annual); Company Directors. **Languages** English. **Staff** 2.00 FTE, paid. **Finance** Sources: members' dues. **Activities** Awards/prizes/competitions; events/meetings; training/education. **Events** *Annual General Meeting* Blackpool (UK) 2011, *World ballroom dancing congress* Blackpool (UK) 1997, *World ballroom dancing congress* Blackpool (UK) 1995.
Members National associations of fully professional dancers in 59 countries and territories:
Armenia, Australia, Austria, Barbados, Belgium, Bulgaria, Canada, China, Croatia, Cyprus, Czechia, Denmark, England, Estonia, Finland, France, Georgia, Germany, Greece, Hong Kong, Hungary, Iceland, Indonesia, Ireland, Israel, Italy, Japan, Kazakhstan, Korea Rep, Latvia, Lebanon, Lithuania, Macau, Malaysia, Malta, Mexico, Moldova, Monaco, Netherlands, New Zealand, Norway, Philippines, Poland, Portugal, Romania, Russia, Scotland, Serbia, Singapore, Slovakia, Slovenia, South Africa, Spain, Sweden, Switzerland, Taiwan, Thailand, Ukraine, USA.
International member:
Asian Dance Council (ADC, #01418).
NGO Relations Formal contact with: *European Association for Dance History (EADH, #06004).* Member of: *The Association for International Sport for All (TAFISA, #02763); International Dance Council (#13130).*
[2021.02.24/XC1734/y/**C**]

♦ World Dance and Dance Sport Council / see World Dance Council (#21353)

♦ World DanceSport Federation (WDSF) 21354

Gen Sec Maison du Sport Intl, Avenue de Rhodanie 54, 1007 Lausanne VD, Switzerland. E-mail: office@wdsf.org.
URL: http://www.worlddancesport.org/

History 1957, as *International Council of Amateur Dancers (ICAD).* 1990, name changed to *International Dance Sport Federation (IDSF).* 2011, present name adopted. **Aims** Advance, promote and protect the character, status and interests of dance practised as sport on the world level. **Structure** General Meeting (annual); Praesidium; Managing Committee. **Languages** English. **Staff** 4.00 FTE, paid. **Finance** Annual budget: 1,500,000 CHF. **Activities** Knowledge management/information dissemination; standards/guidelines; training/education. **Events** *Annual General Meeting* Budapest (Hungary) 2019, *Annual General Meeting* Lausanne (Switzerland) 2018, *Annual General Meeting* Singapore (Singapore) 2017, *Adjudicators Congress* Helsinki (Finland) 2016, *Adjudicators Congress* Oslo (Norway) 2015. **Publications** Magazines; videos.
Members National associations in 90 countries and territories:
Albania, Andorra, Armenia, Australia, Austria, Azerbaijan, Belarus, Belgium, Bolivia, Bosnia-Herzegovina, Botswana, Brazil, Bulgaria, Cambodia, Cameroon, Canada, Chile, China, Colombia, Croatia, Czechia, Denmark, Dominican Rep, Ecuador, England, Estonia, Finland, France, Georgia, Germany, Greece, Guatemala, Hong Kong, Hungary, Iceland, India, Indonesia, Ireland, Israel, Italy, Japan, Kazakhstan, Korea Rep, Kyrgyzstan, Latvia, Lebanon, Lesotho, Liechtenstein, Lithuania, Luxembourg, Macau, Malaysia, Malta, Mexico, Moldova, Monaco, Mongolia, Montenegro, Netherlands, New Zealand, North Macedonia, Northern Ireland, Norway, Philippines, Poland, Portugal, Romania, Russia, Scotland, Serbia, Singapore, Slovakia, Slovenia, South Africa, Spain, Sweden, Switzerland, Syrian AR, Taiwan, Thailand, Trinidad-Tobago, Türkiye, Turkmenistan, Ukraine, Uruguay, USA, Uzbekistan, Vietnam, Wales, Zimbabwe.
International associate members (3), listed in this Yearbook:
International Dance Organization (IDO, #13131); International Federation of Cheerleading (IFC, #13386); World Rock'n'Roll Confederation (WRRC, #21755).
NGO Relations Member of (4): *Association of Summer Olympic International Federations (ASOIF, #02943)* (Associate); *Association of the IOC Recognized International Sports Federations (ARISF, #02767); International World Games Association (IWGA, #15914); Olympic Movement (#17719).* Cooperates with (1): *International Testing Agency (ITA, #15678).* Recognized by: *International Olympic Committee (IOC, #14408).* Collaborates with: *International Paralympic Committee (IPC, #14512).* [2017.11.30/XC0021/**C**]

♦ World Darts Federation (WDF) 21355

Contact British Darts Organisation, Unit 4 Glan-y-Lyn Industrial Estate, Taffs Well, Cardiff, CF15 7JD, UK. T. +442920811815. E-mail: wdfpres@dartswdf.com.
URL: http://www.dartswdf.com/

History 1976, by representatives of 15 countries. **Aims** Promote the *sport* of darts. **Structure** Officers: President; Vice-President; Secretary General; Treasurer; Coordinator; Communications Officer. **Languages** English. **Finance** Members' dues (annual), according to individual membership. **Activities** Organizes: World Cup (alternate even years); Americas Cup plus Asia-Pacific Cup plus Europe Cup (alternate odd years). Holds: General Membership Meetings (every 2 years), in conjunction with World Cup events; Conference (every 2 years, during alternate years), following the Winmau World Championships, always in England. **Events** *General Membership Meeting* Ireland 2011, *Conference / General Membership Meeting* Charlotte, NC (USA) 2009, *General Membership Meeting* 's Hertogenbosch (Netherlands) 2007, *Conference* The Hague (Netherlands) 2007, *Conference / General Membership Meeting* Perth, WA (Australia) 2005.
Members National darts bodies in 67 countries and territories:
Australia, Austria, Bahamas, Barbados, Belgium, Belize, Bermuda, Botswana, Brazil, Brunei Darussalam, Bulgaria, Canada, Cayman Is, Cyprus, Czechia, Denmark, England, Estonia, Faeroe Is, Finland, France, Germany, Gibraltar, Greece, Guyana, Hong Kong, Hungary, Iceland, India, Iran Islamic Rep, Ireland, Isle of Man, Italy, Jamaica, Japan, Korea Rep, Latvia, Lithuania, Luxembourg, Malaysia, Malta, Nepal, Netherlands, New Zealand, Northern Ireland, Norway, Pakistan, Philippines, Poland, Portugal, Romania, Russia, Scotland, Serbia, Singapore, Slovakia, Slovenia, South Africa, Spain, St Lucia, Sweden, Switzerland, Trinidad-Tobago, Türkiye, Turks-Caicos, USA, Wales.
NGO Relations Member of (2): *Alliance of Independent recognised Members of Sport (AIMS, #00690); Olympic Movement (#17719).* Recognized by: *International Olympic Committee (IOC, #14408).* [2017/XF1270/**C**]

♦ World Data Center for Human Interactions in the Environment / see Center for International Earth Science Information Network

♦ World Deaf Golf Federation (WDGF) 21356

Sec 2 Holly Court, Mitcham VIC 3132, Australia. E-mail: secretary@worlddeafgolf.com.
URL: http://www.worlddeafgolf.com/

History Set up following meeting held 13 Jul 1994, Battle Creek MI (USA). Officially setup 8 Aug 1995. **Structure** General Meeting; Board. **Activities** Sporting activities.
Members Full in 15 countries and territories:
Australia, Canada, Denmark, England, Finland, Germany, Ireland, Japan, Netherlands, Norway, Scotland, South Africa, Sweden, USA, Wales. [2016/XN8487/**C**]

♦ World Deaf Squash Inc (WDSI) 21357

Address not obtained.

History Oct 2003. **Aims** Develop opportunities for deaf people to participate into a game of squash, including participation, coaching, officials and spectators; coordinate World Deaf Squash Championships, with support from both Deaflympic and WSF; support Deaf Squash nations with their national development and needs. **Structure** Directors (3): Finance; Technical; Media and Public Relations.
Members National organizations in 6 countries and territories:
Australia, England, Netherlands, Pakistan, Scotland, South Africa.
NGO Relations Member of: *World Squash Federation (WSF, #21826).* [2017/XJ0692/**E**]

♦ World Debating Championships / see World Schools Debating Championships (#21767)
♦ World Democratic Organizations Federation (internationally oriented national body)
♦ World Deserts Foundation (#09816)
♦ World Design Consortium / see International Association of Designers (#11844)

♦ World Design Organization (WDO) 21358

Organisation mondiale de design (OMD)

Main Office 455 St-Antoine Street West, Suite SS10, Montréal QC H2Z 1J1, Canada. T. +15144484949. E-mail: office@wdo.org.
URL: http://www.wdo.org/

History 29 Jun 1957, London (UK). Founded following proposal 1953. Constitution adopted at 1st General Assembly, Sep 1959, Stockholm (Sweden); amended 30 Sep 1999, Sydney (Australia). Secretariat based in Montréal QC (Canada) since 2005; previously based in Brussels (Belgium) 1974-1985, and Helsinki (Finland) 1985-2005. Former names and other names: *International Council of Societies of Industrial Designers* – former (1957 to 1959); *Conseil international d'esthétique industriel* – former (1957 to 1959); *Conseil international de design industriel* – former (1957 to 1959); *Consejo Internacional de Sociedades de Diseño Industrial* – former (1957 to 1959); *Internationaler Rat der Gesellschaften für Industrielle Formgebung und Formgestaltung* – former (1957 to 1959); *International Council of Societies of Industrial Design (Icsid)* – former (1959 to 2017); *Conseil international des sociétés de design industriel* – former (1959 to 2017). **Aims** Advocate, promote and share knowledge of industrial design driven innovation that has the power to create a better world. **Structure** World Design Assembly (every 2 years); Board of Directors; Secretariat. **Languages** English. **Staff** 10.00 FTE, paid. **Finance** Annual budget: 1,000,000 CAD. **Activities** Awards/prizes/competitions; events/meetings; knowledge management/information dissemination; networking/liaising; projects/programmes; standards/guidelines; training/education. **Events** *Biennial General Assembly* Hyderabad (India) 2019, *Biennial General Assembly* Turin (Italy) 2017, *Biennial General Assembly* Gwangju (Korea Rep) 2015, *Biennial General Assembly / Biennial International Congress* Montréal, QC (Canada) 2013, *Biennial General Assembly / Biennial International Congress* Taipei (Taiwan) 2011. **Publications** *Design 360* (4 a year). *WDO Code of Professional Ethics.* Guidelines; seminar and conference reports; register of members.
Members Voting members Professional; Promotional; Corporate; Educational; Cities. Non-voting members Associate. Members (190) in 41 countries and territories:
Australia, Austria, Belgium, Botswana, Brazil, Canada, Chile, China, Colombia, Denmark, Estonia, Finland, France, Germany, Ghana, Hong Kong, Hungary, India, Ireland, Italy, Japan, Korea Rep, Latvia, Malaysia, Mexico, Netherlands, New Zealand, Norway, Philippines, Russia, Singapore, Slovenia, South Africa, Spain, Sweden, Switzerland, Taiwan, Thailand, Türkiye, UK, USA.
Consultative Status Consultative status granted from: *ECOSOC (#05331)* (Special); *ILO (#11123)* (Special List); *World Intellectual Property Organization (WIPO, #21593)* (Permanent Observer Status); *UNIDO (#20336)* (signed Apr 1977). **IGO Relations** Accredited by (1): *United Nations Office at Vienna (UNOV, #20604).* Cooperates with (1): *European Union Intellectual Property Office (EUIPO, #08996).* **NGO Relations** Cooperates with (1): *International Organization for Standardization (ISO, #14473).* [2023.02.19/XC1755/y/**C**]

♦ World Development Council / see World Development Federation
♦ World Development Endowment Foundation (internationally oriented national body)
♦ World Development Federation (internationally oriented national body)
♦ World Development Foundation (internationally oriented national body)
♦ World Development Movement / see Global Justice Now

♦ World Diabetes Foundation (WDF) 21359

Managing Dir KrogshØjvej 30A, 2800 Bagsvaerd, Denmark. T. +4544422556. E-mail: contact@worlddiabetesfoundation.org.
URL: http://www.worlddiabetesfoundation.org/
History 14 Nov 2002, on World Diabetes Day, by Novo Nordisk AS. Registered in accordance with Danish law. **Aims** Alleviate human suffering related to diabetes and its complications in developing countries. **Structure** Board of Directors. **Staff** 18.00 FTE, paid. **Finance** Budget (2001-2024): US$ 274,000,000. **Activities** Financial and/or material support; projects/programmes; advocacy/lobbying/activism; awareness raising; training/education; capacity building; events/meetings. **Events** *Rencontres africaines francophones de diabétologie* Brazzaville (Congo Brazzaville) 2011, *Meeting on the burden of chronic diseases and its impact on developing countries* Copenhagen (Denmark) 2010. **Publications** Newsletter. Brochure; impact folder; focus area reviews. **NGO Relations** Collaborates with: *International Diabetes Federation (IDF, #13164).* Project partnerships with: *Asian-Pacific Resource and Research Centre for Women (ARROW, #01629); Fédération Internationale de Gynécologie et d'Obstétrique (FIGO, #09638); Folkekirkens Nødhjaelp (FKN); International Committee of the Red Cross (ICRC, #12799); International Union Against Tuberculosis and Lung Disease (The Union, #15752).* [2019.03.28/XJ2362/f/**F**]

♦ World Diamond Council (WDC) 21360

Exec Dir 580 Fifth Ave, Ste 613, New York NY 10036, USA. T. +17605259393. Fax +12125758187. E-mail: ed@worlddiamondcouncil.org – communications@worlddiamondcouncil.org.
Pres address not obtained. E-mail: president@worlddiamondcouncil.org.
URL: http://www.worlddiamondcouncil.com/
History 19 Jul 2000, Antwerp (Belgium), by *International Diamond Manufacturers Association (IDMA, #13171)* and *World Federation of Diamond Bourses (WFDB, #21430).* **Aims** Prevent exploitation of diamonds for *illicit* purposes such as war and inhumane acts by developing, implementing and overseeing a tracking system for the *export* and import of rough diamonds. **Structure** Steering Committee, including Chairman, 4 Vice-Chairmen, Executive Director, Secretary and General Counsel. **Activities** Committees (10): Banking; Finance; Information and Research; International Government and United Nations Liaison; Legal; Membership; Producers; Steering; Technical; United States Legislative. **Events** *Annual Meeting* Mumbai (India) 2018, *Annual Meeting* Dubai (United Arab Emirates) 2017, *Annual Meeting* Antwerp (Belgium) 2014, *Annual Meeting* Tel Aviv (Israel) 2013, *Annual Meeting* Vicenza (Italy) 2012.
Members Charter members and government observers in 13 countries:
Angola, Australia, Belgium, Botswana, Canada, India, Israel, Italy, Namibia, Russia, South Africa, UK, USA.
[2015/XE4286/**E**]

♦ Worlddidac Association 21361

Acting Gen Dir Industrie Baennli 3a, 4628 Wolfwil SO, Switzerland. T. +41313117682. Fax +41313121744. E-mail: info@worlddidac.org.
URL: http://www.worlddidac.org/
History 1 Sep 1952, Germany FR. Current statutes adopted 21 Dec 2020. Former names and other names: *EURODIDAC* – former; *Association européenne de matériel didactique* – former; *Europäischer Lehrmittelverb-and* – former; *European Association of Manufacturers and Distributors of Educational Materials* – former; *Association européenne de fabricants et de revendeurs de matériel didactique* – former; *Verband Europäischer Lehrmittelfirmen* – former; *World Association of Publishers, Manufacturers and Distributors of Educational Materials* – full title (1983); *Association mondiale des éditeurs, fabricants et revendeurs de matériels didactiques* – full title (1983); *Weltverband der Lehrmittelfirmen* – full title (1983). Registration: Swiss Civil Code, Switzerland. **Aims** Further improvement in education and encourage creation of better educational materials and their production by industry suppliers, while simultaneously facilitating sales of educational and training materials throughout the world. **Structure** General Assembly (annual); Presidium; Secretariat, headed by Director General. **Languages** English, French, German. **Staff** 1.70 FTE, paid; 1.00 FTE, voluntary. **Finance** Sources: meeting proceeds; members' dues. **Activities** Advocacy/lobbying/activism; awards/prizes/competitions; capacity building; certification/accreditation; events/meetings; guidance/assistance/consulting; knowledge management/information dissemination; networking/liaising; projects/programmes; research/documentation; training/education. **Events** *Conference* Bern (Switzerland) 2023, *Worlddidac Asia Meeting* Bangkok (Thailand) 2021, *Future Talk* Bern (Switzerland) 2021, *Worlddidac Asia Meeting* Bangkok (Thailand) 2020, *Worlddidac Asia Meeting* Bangkok (Thailand) 2018. **Publications** *Education Market Journal* (3-4 a year); *Worlddidac Newsletter.* Members' online directory; award brochure (every 2 years). **Information Services** *Members Market Place* – newsletter about Member's activities and new developments.
Members Full companies active in the field of education and training; Associate individuals, national and international associations active in these fields. Full members in 48 countries and territories:
Argentina, Austria, Bahrain, Belgium, Brazil, Canada, Chile, China, Colombia, Congo DR, Czechia, Denmark, Finland, France, Germany, Greece, Guinea-Bissau, Hong Kong, Hungary, India, Indonesia, Ireland, Israel, Italy, Japan, Kazakhstan, Korea Rep, Mexico, Netherlands, Norway, Peru, Poland, Portugal, Romania, Russia, Singapore, Slovakia, Slovenia, Spain, Sri Lanka, Sweden, Switzerland, Taiwan, Thailand, Tunisia, UK, USA, Vietnam.
Included in the above, 2 organizations listed in this Yearbook:
Audiovisual and Integrated Experience Association (AVIXA); International Vocational Education and Training Association (IVETA, #15861).
Consultative Status Consultative status granted from: *UNESCO (#20322)* (Consultative Status).
[2022.06.15/XC4259/y/**C**]

♦ World Digital Solidarity Agency (DSA) 21362

Agence mondiale de solidarité numérique (ASN)
Dir Villa Créatis, 2 rue des Mûriers, 69009 Lyon, France. T. +33426234105. Fax +33426234109.
History Jul 2006. Registered in accordance with French law. **Aims** Provide expertise, analysis, surveillance, promotion and technical support. **Structure** Board, comprising President and Vice-President. Advisory Board. Executive Secretariat, headed by Director. **Events** *International conference for digital solidarity* Lyon (France) 2008. [2009/XM2957/**D**]

♦ World Disability Union (unconfirmed)
♦ World Diving Coaches Association (inactive)
♦ WorldDMB Forum / see WorldDAB (#21351)

♦ World of DMCs 21363

Exec Officer address not obtained. T. +447739170073. E-mail: info@world-of-dmcs.com.
Assn Headquarters PO Box 32062, Dubai, United Arab Emirates.
URL: http://world-of-dmcs.com/
History 2007. **Aims** As an association of Destination Management Companies (DMCs) worldwide, bring together professional accredited DMCs to form a marketing association to promote events, MICE groups and incentives worldwide; offer cost effective umbrella under which members can participate in key international trade shows targeting MICE. **Structure** Board of Directors; Executive Director. **Languages** English. **Staff** 1.00 FTE, paid. **Finance** Sources: members' dues. **Activities** Awareness raising; knowledge management/information dissemination; networking/liaising. **Publications** None.
Members DMCs in 40 countries and territories:
Armenia, Aruba, Australia, Austria, Azerbaijan, Brazil, Bulgaria, Croatia, Cuba, Curaçao, Czechia, Denmark, Finland, France, Germany, Greece, Iceland, India, Italy, Jordan, Kenya, Lebanon, Malta, Mauritius, Morocco, Oman, Poland, Portugal, Russia, Singapore, Slovenia, South Africa, Spain, Switzerland, Thailand, Türkiye, Uganda, United Arab Emirates, Vietnam, Zimbabwe.
[2018.09.19/XJ7069/**C**]

♦ World Doctors Orchestra (WDO) 21364

Musical Dir/Pres c/o Inst for Social Medicine, Campus Charité Mitte, Luisenstrasse 57, 10117 Berlin, Germany. T. +491772131825. E-mail: office@world-doctors-orchestra.org.
Corporate Office USA 9306 Grand Ave, Manassas VA 20110, USA. T. +15712299899.
URL: http://www.world-doctors-orchestra.org/
History 2008. Registered in accordance with German and US laws. **Aims** Raise awareness that *healthcare* is a human right and the precondition for human development. **Structure** International Orchestra Committee; Advisory Board. **Languages** English. **Staff** 0.50 FTE, paid. **Finance** Sponsorship; donations.
[2019.12.11/XJ7203/**F**]

♦ World Dodgeball Association (WDA) 21365

Registered Address Sport City, Gate 13, Rowsley St, Manchester, M11 3FF, UK. E-mail: info@planetdodgeball.com.
URL: https://www.dodgeball.sport/
History 22 Oct 2013. Founded through the amalgation of 3 continental bodies. Registration: Limited Company, No/ID: 08918471, England and Wales. **Structure** World Council; Executive Board; Senior Management Team.
Members National federations in 47 countries and territories:
Afghanistan, Angola, Argentina, Australia, Belarus, Bhutan, Brunei Darussalam, Bulgaria, Cambodia, Chile, Costa Rica, Dominican Rep, Egypt, Hong Kong, India, Indonesia, Iran Islamic Rep, Italy, Japan, Korea Rep, Malaysia, Malta, Mexico, Nepal, New Zealand, Nigeria, Pakistan, Peru, Philippines, Qatar, Russia, Saudi Arabia, Singapore, South Africa, Sudan, Switzerland, Taiwan, Thailand, Tunisia, Türkiye, Uganda, Ukraine, United Arab Emirates, USA, Vietnam, Zambia, Zimbabwe.
NGO Relations Member of (3): *Alliance of Independent recognised Members of Sport (AIMS, #00690)* (Observer); *General Association of Asia Pacific Sports Federations (GAAPSF, #10106); International Sport Network Organization (ISNO, #15592).* [2020/AA1087/**C**]

♦ World Draughts Federation (#09690)
♦ World Dredging Association / see World Organization of Dredging Associations (#21688)

♦ World Duchenne Organization (WDO) 21366

Administration Landjuweel 34, 3905 PG Veenendaal, Netherlands. T. +31206275062. E-mail: info@worldduchenne.org – admin@worldduchenne.org.
URL: https://www.worldduchenne.org/
History Current statutes adopted Dec 2021. Former names and other names: *United Parent Projects Muscular Dystrophy* – former (Dec 2021). Registration: Handelsregister, No/ID: KVK 30226334, Netherlands; EU Transparency Register, No/ID: 051535245114-08, Start date: 10 Jan 2022. **Aims** Find a cure and viable treatments for Duchenne and Becker Muscular Dystrophy; promote good standards of care; inform parents and people living with the condition around the globe. **Structure** Board. **Activities** Advocacy/lobbying/activism; research/documentation. **Events** *International Conference on Duchenne and Becker Muscular Dystrophy* Rome (Italy) 2022. **Publications** *Journal of Neuromuscular Diseases.*
Members Organizations in 35 countries:
Argentina, Australia, Belgium, Bolivia, Brazil, Canada, Chile, Cyprus, Czechia, Finland, France, Greece, India, Ireland, Israel, Italy, Kenya, Lebanon, Lithuania, Mexico, Netherlands, North Macedonia, Romania, Russia, Serbia, Slovakia, Slovenia, South Africa, Spain, Sweden, Switzerland, Türkiye, UK, Ukraine, USA.
NGO Relations Member of (3): *European Patients' Forum (EPF, #08172); EURORDIS – Rare Diseases Europe (#09175); Rare Diseases International (RDI, #18621).* [2022/AA2322/f/**C**]

♦ World Eatology Forum (unconfirmed)
♦ World-Ecology Research Network (unconfirmed)
♦ World Economic Development Congress (meeting series)

♦ World Economic Forum (WEF) 21367

Founder/Executive Chairman Route de la Capite 91-93, 1223 Cologny GE, Switzerland. T. +41228691212. Fax +41227862744. E-mail: contact@weforum.org.
URL: http://www.weforum.org/
History 1971, Geneva (Switzerland). Founded by Prof Klaus Schwab. Former names and other names: *European Management Symposium* – former (1971 to 1972); *European Management Forum (EMF)* – former (1972 to 1987); *Forum européen de management* – former (1972 to 1987); *Europäisches Management Forum* – former (1972 to 1987). Registration: Switzerland; EU Transparency Register, No/ID: 049060636194-17, Start date: 14 Oct 2019. **Aims** Integrate leaders from business, governments, academia, media and civil society in a partnership committed to improving the state of the world; create opportunities for leaders worldwide to address key economic, social and political issues on the global, regional and industry agendas. **Structure** Foundation Board; International Business Council. Managing Board of 4 Managing Directors; Global Agenda; Regional Agenda; Industry Agenda, Centre for Global Industries; Multistakeholder Initiatives. Offices in: Geneva, (Switzerland); Beijing (China); New York NY (USA); Tokyo (Japan). Includes: *Centre for the Fourth Industrial Revolution.* **Languages** English. **Staff** Geneva (Switzerland): 313, representing 56 nationalities. **Finance** Membership fees; partnership fees. Cost contributions for different activities. **Activities** Events/meetings; networking/liaising. **Events** *World Economic Forum Annual Meeting* Davos (Switzerland) 2023, *World Economic Forum Annual Meeting* Davos (Switzerland) 2022, *Special Annual Meeting* Singapore (Singapore) 2021, *World Economic Forum* Singapore (Singapore) 2021, *Global Technology Governance Summit* Tokyo (Japan) 2021. **Publications** *Global Agenda Council Report*; *Global Competitiveness Report*; *Global Risks Report.* Regional competitiveness reports.
Members Companies (over 1,000) located in 72 countries and territories:
Angola, Argentina, Australia, Austria, Bahrain, Belgium, Bermuda, Brazil, Bulgaria, Canada, Chile, China, Colombia, Denmark, Egypt, Finland, France, Germany, Greece, Hong Kong, Hungary, India, Indonesia, Ireland, Israel, Italy, Japan, Jordan, Kazakhstan, Kenya, Korea Rep, Kuwait, Lebanon, Liechtenstein, Luxembourg, Malaysia, Mauritius, Mexico, Monaco, Morocco, Netherlands, Nigeria, Norway, Oman, Pakistan, Palestine, Peru, Philippines, Poland, Portugal, Qatar, Russia, Saudi Arabia, Senegal, Singapore, Slovenia, South Africa, Spain, Sri Lanka, Sweden, Switzerland, Syrian AR, Taiwan, Thailand, Tunisia, Türkiye, UK, Ukraine, United Arab Emirates, USA, Venezuela, Vietnam.
NGO Relations Instrumental in setting up (6): *Disaster Resource Partnership (DRP, #05099); Energy Poverty Action (EPA, #05474); Global Battery Alliance (GBA, #10249); International Women's Partnership for Peace and Justice (IWP); United Nations Global Compact (#20567); World Social Forum (WSF, #21797).* Collaborates with a wide range of NGOs in its various activities and initiatives. [2021/XF0463/c/**F**]

♦ World Economic Processing Zones Association (WEPZA) 21368

Secretariat The Manor, Hull Place, Sholden, Deal, CT14 0AQ, UK.
URL: http://www.wepza.org/
History 1978, as *World Export Processing Zones Association – Association mondiale des zones franches industrielles (AMZFI)*, following proposals made by UNIDO in 1974. Final draft of statutes approved 1978, Manila (Philippines). Statutes amended 1985, Flagstaff AZ (USA), when organization ceased to be inter-governmental, instead grouping Economic Processing Zones, Free Zones and Export Industrial Parks, whether public or private, as well as associated professionals and advisors, throughout the world. Also referred to in French as *Association mondiale des zones industrielles d'exportation (AMZIE)* and as *Association mondiale des zones industrielles libres.* **Aims** Assist *developing countries* in obtaining the greatest possible benefit from Industrial Parks, Special Economic Zones (SEZs), Free Zones, Free Ports, and Export Processing Zones (EPZs); improve international business and *distribution* through the use of such zones. **Structure** General Assembly of members; Officers; Board of Advisors. **Languages** English, French. **Staff** 13.00 FTE, paid. **Finance** Members' dues. **Activities** Events/meetings; research/documentation; knowledge management/information idssemination; training/education. **Events** *Conference* Antalya (Turkey) 2007, *Conference* Cape Town (South Africa) 2004, *Conference* Delhi (India) 2004, *General Assembly* Johannesburg (South Africa) 2004, *Conference* Istanbul (Turkey) 2003. **Publications** *Journal of The Flagstaff Institute*; *WEPZA Newsletter.* Data diskettes on exports and imports by USA and the European Community of product groups interesting to EPZs; conference proceedings. **Information Services** *SEZ Knowledge Bank.*
Members Public and private export processing zones and export industrial parks in 36 countries and territories:
Australia, Bangladesh, Bulgaria, Chile, China, Croatia, Ecuador, Egypt, England, Hong Kong, Hungary, Indonesia, Iran Islamic Rep, Japan, Jordan, Kazakhstan, Kenya, Korea Rep, Malaysia, Mexico, Neth Antilles, Nigeria, Pakistan, Philippines, Romania, Russia, Saudi Arabia, Serbia, Spain, Sudan, Taiwan, Tanzania UR, Türkiye, United Arab Emirates, USA, Vietnam.
Consultative Status Consultative status granted from: *ECOSOC (#05331)* (Ros C); *UNCTAD (#20285)* (General Category); *UNIDO (#20336).* [2018.06.15/XC7371/**F**]

♦ World Economics Association (WEA) 21369

Contact 12 Maurice Road, Bristol, BS6 5BZ, UK. E-mail: info@worldeconomicsassociation.org.
URL: http://www.worldeconomicsassociation.org/

History Launched 16 May 2011. **Aims** Increase the relevance, breadth and depth of economic thought. **Structure** Executive Committee. **Activities** Events/meetings; publishing activities. **Publications** *WEA Commentaries* (4 a year); *Economic Thought* – journal; *Real-World Economics Review*; *World Economic Review*. Books. [2018/XM7528/**C**]

- ♦ World Economy, Ecology and Development (internationally oriented national body)
- ♦ World Economy Research Institute, Warsaw (internationally oriented national body)
- ♦ World Education (internationally oriented national body)

♦ World Education Fellowship (WEF) 21370

Ligue mondiale pour l'éducation nouvelle (LIEN) – Liga Mundial pro Educación Nueva – Weltbund für Erneuerung der Erziehung

Gen Sec 54 Fox Lane, London, N13 4AL, UK.
Chair 20 Melrose Road, Merton Park, London, SW19 3HG, UK.
URL: http://www.wef-international.org/

History 1921, Calais (France). Founded on the initiative of Beatrice Ensor (1885-1974) and Adolphe Ferrière (1879-1960) and Elisabeth Rotten (1882-1964) in succession to *International Bureau of New Schools (inactive)*, set up in 1899. Former names and other names: *New Education Fellowship* – former; *Compagnons de l'éducation nouvelle* – former; *Ligue Internationale d'Education Nouvelle (LIEN)* – former. Registration: Charities Act 1960, No/ID: 314112, UK. **Aims** Promote high standards of education for all groups worldwide. **Structure** Guiding Committee; Sections (20). **Languages** English, French, German. **Staff** 0.50 FTE, paid. **Finance** Sources: contributions; donations; investments. **Activities** Knowledge management/information dissemination; research/documentation; training/education. **Events** *International Conference* Sofia (Bulgaria) 2009, *Conference / International Conference* Gangwon (Korea Rep) 2008, *Education for full humanity – education in a technological society* Sofia (Bulgaria) 2006, *Biennial conference / International Conference* Mumbai (India) 2004, *Youth conference / International Conference* Sun City (South Africa) 2001. **Publications** *The New Era in Education* (3 a year). Monographs; conference reports. Sections produce their own journals and newsletters.

Members National Sections (including French-Speaking Group and German-Speaking Group) and Representatives in 13 countries:
Australia, Belgium, Bhutan, France, Germany, India, Japan, Netherlands, Nigeria, South Africa, Sri Lanka, UK, USA.

Consultative Status Consultative status granted from: *ECOSOC (#05331)* (Ros C). **IGO Relations** Associated with Department of Global Communications of the United Nations. [2021/XC3507/**F**]

♦ World Education Forum 21371

Forum mondial de l'éducation – Foro Mondial de Educación – Fórum Mundial de Educação

Address not obtained.
URL: http://www.forummundialeducacao.org/

Structure International Council; Organizing Committee. **Activities** Organizes meetings. [2008/XM4648/**F**]

- ♦ World Education Foundation (unconfirmed)

♦ World Education Research Association (WERA) 21372

SG c/o Plaza Euskadi 5, 48009 Bilbao, Biscay, Spain. E-mail: wera@aera.net.
USA Office 1430 K St NW, Ste 1200, Washington DC 20008, USA.
URL: http://www.weraonline.org/

History 18 Apr 2009, San Diego, CA (USA). **Aims** Advance education research as a scientific and scholarly field. **Structure** Council; Executive Committee; Secretariat; International Research Networks. **Languages** English. **Finance** Sources: members' dues. **Activities** Capacity building; events/meetings; knowledge management/information dissemination; networking/liaising; projects/programmes; publishing activities. **Events** *Focal Meeting* Singapore (Singapore) 2023, *Focal Meeting* San Diego, CA (USA) 2022, *WERA-IRN Extended Education Conference* Reykjavik (Iceland) 2021, *Focal Meeting* Santiago de Compostela (Spain) 2021, *WERA-IRN Extended Education Conference* Reykjavik (Iceland) 2020. **Publications** *WERA 2015 Yearbook*; *WERA 2018 Annual Volume*. Book series.

Members Education research associations in 24 countries and territories:
Brazil, Chile, Cyprus, Ecuador, Germany, Ghana, Hong Kong, Japan, Korea Rep, Malaysia, Mexico, Netherlands, Pakistan, Peru, Poland, Russia, Scotland, Singapore, South Africa, Spain, Sweden, Taiwan, Türkiye, USA.
Regional organization: [2022/XJ6407/**C**]

- ♦ World Education Services (internationally oriented national body)
- ♦ World Education System Society (no recent information)
- ♦ World Egg Organisation (unconfirmed)

♦ World Eightball Pool Federation (WEPF) 21373

Sec 12 Helston Grove, Hemel Hempstead, HP2 6NU, UK. T. +441442244776.
Pres 10 Crittenden Road, Findon SA 5023, Australia. T. +61883474400. Fax +61883474996.
URL: http://www.wepf.org/

History Founded 14 Nov 1992, Perth (Australia). **Aims** Govern the playing of 'UK 8-Ball Pool' worldwide. **Activities** Sporting activities. **Publications** *World Pool Magazine*.

Members Regional bodies (3):
African Eight-Ball Pool Federation; English Pool Association (EPA); *European 8-Ball Pool Federation (EEPF, #05777)*.

NGO Relations Links with national federations. [2018.06.15/XD6959/y/**D**]

♦ World Electric Vehicle Association (WEVA) 21374

Fédération mondiale de promotion des véhicles électriques (FMPVE)

Vice-Pres c/o EDTA, 1250 Eye St NW, Ste 902, Washington DC 20005, USA. T. +12024080774.
URL: http://www.wevaonline.net/

History 2 Dec 1990, Hong Kong, during 10th Electric Vehicle Symposium (EVS), a memorandum of understanding having been signed, 15-16 Nov 1988, Toronto (Canada), during 9th Symposium. **Aims** Facilitate exchange of information encouraging development of electric vehicles. **Structure** Steering Committee of representatives of regional zones. Chairman and central secretariat provided in a rotational basis by regional associations. **Languages** English. **Staff** Voluntary. **Activities** Coordinates schedule of biennial symposium organized in rotation by regional associations. **Events** *International Electric Vehicle Symposium* Sacramento, CA (USA) 2023, *International Electric Vehicle Symposium* Oslo (Norway) 2022, *International Electric Vehicle Symposium* Nanjing (China) 2021, *International Electric Vehicle Symposium* Portland, OR (USA) 2020, *International Electric Vehicle Symposium* Lyon (France) 2019.

Members Regional associations (3):
Electric Drive Transportation Association (EDTA); *Electric Vehicle Association of Asia Pacific (EVAAP, #05418)*; *European Association for Electromobility (AVERE, #06024)* (also covers Africa). [2013/XD2104/y/**D**]

- ♦ World Electronics Circuits Council (no recent information)
- ♦ World Electronics Forum (unconfirmed)
- ♦ World Elevator Federation (unconfirmed)

♦ World Elite Black Belt Society (WEBBS) 21375

Headquarters 71 Lancaster Road, Enfield, EN2 0DW, UK. T. +442083638822.
URL: https://www.webbsinternational.com/

History 2001, UK, by Bryan Cheek. **Aims** Provide *Martial Artists* from around the world a platform to display their skills and enable contact with like-minded people world wide. **Structure** President; 4 Vice-Presidents. **Events** *World Congress* Bielsko-Biala (Poland) 2015, *World Congress* Barcelona (Spain) 2014, *World Congress* Lisbon (Portugal) 2013, *World Congress* Montréal, QC (Canada) 2012, *World Congress* Cancún (Mexico) 2005. [2021/XJ6727/**C**]

- ♦ World Emergency Relief / see Emerge Poverty Free
- ♦ World Emergency Relief (internationally oriented national body)

♦ World Employment Confederation (WEC) 21376

Managing Dir Av du Port 86c, Boîte 302, 1000 Brussels, Belgium. T. +3224211585. Fax +3222034268. E-mail: info@wecglobal.org.
URL: http://www.wecglobal.org/

History 17 May 1967, Paris (France). Constitution revised in June 2020. Former names and other names: *International Confederation of Temporary Work Organizations* – former (17 May 1967); *International Confederation of Temporary Work Businesses* – former; *Confédération internationale des entreprises de travail temporaire* – former; *Confederación Internacional de Empresas de Trabajo Temporal* – former; *Confédération internationale des agences privées pour l'emploi (Ciett)* – former; *International Confederation of Private Employment Agencies* – former; *Confédération internationale des agences d'emploi privé* – former; *World Employment Confederation – The voice of labour market enablers* – full title (2016). Registration: Banque-Carrefour des Entreprises, No/ID: 0882.145.120, Start date: 28 Jun 2006, Belgium. **Aims** As the voice of the private employment services industry at the global level, represent national federations as well as workforce solutions companies from across the world; broaden recognition of the positive economic and social role which the private employment services industry plays in enabling work, adaptation, security and prosperity. **Structure** General Assembly; Board; Standing Committees. **Languages** English. **Staff** 7.00 FTE, paid. **Finance** Sources: members' dues. **Activities** Advocacy/lobbying/activism; capacity building; events/meetings; knowledge management/information dissemination; networking/liaising; politics/policy/regulatory; publishing activities; standards/guidelines. **Events** *World Employment Conference* Brussels (Belgium) 2022, *World Employment Conference* Madrid (Spain) 2021, *Annual Conference* Madrid (Spain) 2020, *Annual Conference* Gold Coast, QLD (Australia) 2019, *Annual Conference* Dublin (Ireland) 2018. **Publications** Activity Report, Economic Report, Social Impact Report, position papers, internal publications.

Members National Federations in 45 countries:
Argentina, Australia, Austria, Belgium, Brazil, Canada, Chile, China, Colombia, Croatia, Czechia, Denmark, Estonia, Finland, France, Germany, Greece, Hungary, India, Indonesia, Ireland, Italy, Japan, Latvia, Lithuania, Luxembourg, Mexico, Netherlands, New Zealand, Norway, Peru, Philippines, Poland, Portugal, Romania, Russia, Slovakia, Slovenia, South Africa, Spain, Sweden, Switzerland, Türkiye, UK, USA.
Regional Federation (1):
World Employment Federation Europe (#21377).
Corporate members (7):
Gi Group; House of HR; Kelly; ManpowerGroup; Randstad; RGF Staffing; The Adecco Group.

IGO Relations Participates in conferences of: *ILO (#11123)*; *International Organization for Migration (IOM, #14454)*; *OECD (#17693)*. **NGO Relations** Member of (1): *Federation of European and International Associations Established in Belgium (FAIB, #09508)*. Associate expert of: *Business and Industry Advisory Committee to the OECD (BIAC, #03385)*. [2021.03.26/XC4198/**C**]

- ♦ World Employment Confederation Latin America (#04457)
- ♦ World Employment Confederation – The voice of labour market enablers / see World Employment Confederation (#21376)

♦ World Employment Federation Europe 21377

Managing Dir Tour et Taxis, Av du Port 86c, Box 302, 1000 Brussels, Belgium. T. +3222033803. Fax +3222034268. E-mail: info@wecglobal.org.
URL: http://www.weceurope.org/

History Founded 2005, Belgium, as *European Confederation of Private Employment Agencies (Eurociett) – Confédération européenne des agences privées pour l'emploi*. Current title adopted Sep 2016. Regional federation of *World Employment Confederation (WEC, #21376)*. Registered in accordance with Belgian law, 2006. **Aims** Protect and promote the interests of private employment agencies in Europe. **Structure** Governing Body; Executive Committee; Standing Committees; Head Office. **Languages** English. **Staff** 6.00 FTE, paid. **Finance** Members' dues. **Publications** *Agency Work Business Indicator* (12 a year); *Economic Report* (annual).

Members National federations and companies in 30 countries:
Austria, Belgium, Bulgaria, Croatia, Czechia, Denmark, Estonia, Finland, France, Germany, Greece, Hungary, Ireland, Italy, Latvia, Lithuania, Luxembourg, Netherlands, Norway, Poland, Portugal, Romania, Serbia, Slovakia, Slovenia, Spain, Sweden, Switzerland, Türkiye, UK.

IGO Relations *European Commission (EC, #06633)*; *European Union (EU, #08967)*; *OECD (#17693)*. **NGO Relations** Member of: *Centre for European Policy Studies (CEPS, #03741)*; *European Business Services Alliance (EBSA, #06426)*; *European Policy Centre (EPC, #08240)*. [2019.12.12/XM3386/**D**]

♦ World Emunah Religious Zionist Women's Organization 21378

Main Office Rechov Arlozorov 6, PO Box 7788, 9219301 Jerusalem, Israel. T. +97225660414. Fax +97225662811. E-mail: info@worldemunah.org.
URL: http://www.worldemunah.org/

History 1977, Israel. Original organization, set up 1948, USA. All founding members of the World organization either changed their former names to Emunah or added Emunah to their names. Former names and other names: *Hapoel Hamizrachi Women's Organization* – former (1948); *Women's Organization of Hapoel Hamizrachi* – former; *World Religious Women's Zionist Organization* – former. **Aims** Encourage, motivate and assist member organizations abroad in their endeavours to raise funds for EMUNAH projects in Israel; strengthen through the commitment to Israel in communities abroad and reinforce the Jewish identity of the family through the teaching of Jewish values and traditions. **Structure** Officers: Founding President, President, Honorary Chairperson, Chairperson, 2 Vice-Chairpersons, 2 Secretaries, Financial Secretary, Treasurer, Public Affairs Officer, 2 Liaison Officers, 2 Honorary Vice-Presidents, 25 Vice-Presidents. **Languages** English, French, Hebrew, Spanish. **Staff** Voluntary. **Finance** Sources: members' dues. **Activities** Events/meetings; religious activities. **Publications** Educational material.

Members Organizations in 27 countries and territories:
Argentina, Australia, Austria, Belgium, Brazil, Canada, Costa Rica, France, Georgia, Gibraltar, Hong Kong, Ireland, Israel, Italy, Mexico, Panama, Peru, Russia, South Africa, Spain, Sweden, Switzerland, UK, Ukraine, Uruguay, USA, Venezuela.

NGO Relations Member of (1): *World Zionist Organization (WZO, #21961)*. [2022.02.15/XD7792/**F**]

- ♦ World ENABLED (internationally oriented national body)
- ♦ World Endodontics Confederation (inactive)
- ♦ World Endometriosis Research Foundation (internationally oriented national body)

♦ World Endometriosis Society (WES) 21379

CEO 1201 West Pender St, Suite 300, Vancouver BC V6E 2V2, Canada. T. +16046812153. E-mail: office@endometriosis.ca – wes@endometriosis.ca.
URL: http://endometriosis.ca/

History 1998. Registration: Canada. **Aims** Promote the exchange of clinical experience, scientific thought, and investigation among gynaecologists, endocrinologists, scientists, biologists and other qualified individuals interested in advancing the field of endometriosis. **Structure** Board of Trustees of 6 officers, 3 ex-officios and up to 7 representatives. **Languages** English. **Staff** 0.50 FTE, paid. **Finance** Sources: meeting proceeds; members' dues. **Events** *World Congress on Endometriosis* Edinburgh (UK) 2023, *World Congress on Endometriosis* Dubai (United Arab Emirates) 2021, *Meeting on the Limits and Limitations of Surgery and Endometriosis* Melbourne, VIC (Australia) 2019, *World Congress on Endometriosis* Vancouver, BC (Canada) 2017, *World Congress on Endometriosis* Sao Paulo (Brazil) 2014. **Publications** *WES e-Journal*. **NGO Relations** *World Endometriosis Research Foundation (WERF)*. [2022/XM3581/**C**]

♦ World Endoscopy Organization (WEO) 21380

Project Manager c/o Hamilton Services GmbH, Landwehr Str 9, 80336 Munich, Germany. T. +4989907793612. Fax +4989907793620. E-mail: secretariat@worldendo.org.
URL: http://www.worldendo.org/

History 1962, Munich (Germany). Founded during World Congress of Gastroenterology. Most recent statutes adopted 2018. Former names and other names: *International Society for Endoscopy (ISE)* – former (1962 to 1976); *Association internationale d'endoscopie* – former (1962 to 1976); *International Gesellschaft für Endoskopie* – former (1962 to 1976); *Organisation mondiale d'endoscopie digestive (OMED)* – former (3 Jul 1976 to 2018); *World Organization for Digestive Endoscopy* – former (3 Jul 1976 to 2018); *Organización Mundial de Endoscopia Digestiva* – former (3 Jul 1976 to 2018). **Aims** Develop and implement quality education in digestive endoscopy; increase access and knowledge of endoscopy in underserved areas of the world; support international cooperation to achieve optimal practices in endoscopy; inform the public of the many benefits from high quality and safe endoscopy. **Structure** General Assembly (every 2 years, at Congress); Governing Council; Executive Committee; Standing Committees (8); Ad hoc Committees (9). Geographic zones represented by: *Asian-Pacific Society for Digestive Endoscopy (APSDE, #01633); European Society of Gastrointestinal Endoscopy (ESGE, #08606); Sociedad Interamericana de Endoscopia Digestiva (SIED, #19384).* **Languages** English. **Staff** 5.00 FTE, paid. **Finance** Sources: donations; members' dues. **Activities** Events/meetings; knowledge management/information dissemination; networking/liaising; research/documentation; training/education. **Events** *World Congress of GI Endoscopy* Seoul (Korea Rep) 2024, *World Congress of GI Endoscopy* Kyoto (Japan) 2022, *World Congress of GI Endoscopy* Rio de Janeiro (Brazil) 2020, *International Conference on Gastroenterology and Therapeutic Gastrointestinal Endoscopy* Abu Dhabi (United Arab Emirates) 2018, *Asia Pacific Digestive Week* Hong Kong (Hong Kong) 2017. **Publications** *Digestive Endoscopy (DEN)* – journal; *WEO Newsletter.* **Members** National digestive endoscopy societies or endoscopy sections of gastroenterology societies within the 3 regional zones of ASPDE, ESGE and SIED. Membership countries not specified. **NGO Relations** Endorses: *International Symposium on Endoscopic Ultrasonography.* [2022.10.12/XD6003/y/**C**]

♦ World Energy Cities Partnership (unconfirmed)
♦ World Energy Conference / see World Energy Council (#21381)

♦ World Energy Council (WEC) 21381

Conseil mondial de l'énergie (CME) – Consejo Mundial de la Energia

SG/CEO 62-64 Cornhill, London, EC3V 3NH, UK. T. +442077345996. Fax +442077345926. E-mail: info@worldenergy.org.
URL: http://www.worldenergy.org/

History 1923. Founded by energy experts aiming to rebuild the electricity grid in Europe following World War I. Structure reconstituted, 1968. Original purpose widened. Former names and other names: *World Power Conference* – former (1923 to 1968); *World Energy Conference* – former (1968 to 1990); *Conférence mondiale de l'énergie* – former (1968 to 1990). Registration: Charity Commission, No/ID: 1086559, Start date: 2001, England and Wales; Companies House, No/ID: 04184478, Start date: 21 Mar 2001, England and Wales. **Aims** Promote the *sustainable supply* and use of energy for the greatest benefit of all people. **Structure** Executive Assembly (annual, hosted by a different country each year); Officers Council. Permanent Standing Committees (3). Secretariat, located in London (UK). **Languages** Arabic, Chinese, English, French, German, Spanish. **Finance** Sources: members' dues. Other sources: interest earned from WEC Foundation charitable trust and income from WEC Services Limited (WSL), which manages revenues from the World Energy Congress. Budget covers the work programme, regional programmes, service to members, and operating costs for the London office. **Activities** Events/meetings; knowledge management/information dissemination; monitoring/evaluation; politics/policy/regulatory; projects/programmes; standards/guidelines. **Events** *World Energy Congress* Rotterdam (Netherlands) 2025, *World Energy Congress* St Petersburg (Russia) 2022, *Asia Clean Energy Forum* Manila (Philippines) 2021, *Nordic Energy Forum* Helsinki (Finland) 2019, *Round Table on Natural Gas and LNG Market Dynamics in Asia* Singapore (Singapore) 2019. **Publications** *World Energy Focus* (annual); *World Energy Issues Monitor* (annual); *World Energy Scenario* (annual); *World Energy Trilemma* (annual); *World Energy Trilemma Index* (annual). *World Energy Perspectices* – report series; *World Energy Resources* – report series. *Biofuels: Policies, Standards and Technologies* (2010); *Energy and Urban Innovation* (2010); *Energy Efficiency: A Recipe for Success* (2010); *Interconnectivity: Benefits and Challenges* (2010); *Logistics Bottlenecks* (2010); *Performance of Generating Plant* (2010); *Roadmap towards a Competitive European Energy Market* (2010); *Shale Gas* (2010); *Water for Energy* (2010). Other publications.
Members Autonomous national Member Committees representing over 3,000 member organizations reflecting a range of local and national energy companies, government departments and organizations. Committees in 100 countries and territories:
Albania, Algeria, Argentina, Armenia, Austria, Belgium, Bolivia, Botswana, Brazil, Bulgaria, Cameroon, Canada, Chad, Chile, China, Colombia, Congo DR, Côte d'Ivoire, Croatia, Cyprus, Czechia, Denmark, Ecuador, Egypt, Estonia, Eswatini, Ethiopia, Finland, France, Gabon, Germany, Ghana, Greece, Hong Kong, Hungary, Iceland, India, Indonesia, Iran Islamic Rep, Iraq, Ireland, Israel, Italy, Japan, Jordan, Kazakhstan, Kenya, Korea Rep, Kuwait, Latvia, Lebanon, Libya, Lithuania, Luxembourg, Malaysia, Mexico, Monaco, Mongolia, Morocco, Namibia, Nepal, Netherlands, New Zealand, Niger, Nigeria, North Macedonia, Pakistan, Paraguay, Peru, Philippines, Poland, Portugal, Qatar, Romania, Russia, Saudi Arabia, Senegal, Serbia, Singapore, Slovakia, Slovenia, South Africa, Spain, Sri Lanka, Sweden, Switzerland, Syrian AR, Taiwan, Tajikistan, Tanzania UR, Thailand, Trinidad-Tobago, Tunisia, Türkiye, UK, Ukraine, United Arab Emirates, Uruguay, USA, Zimbabwe.
Consultative Status Consultative status granted from: *UNESCO (#20322)* (Consultative Status).
IGO Relations Maintains relations with:
- *African Development Bank (ADB, #00283)*;
- *African Energy Commission (AFREC, #00298)*;
- *African Union (AU, #00488)*;
- *Asian Development Bank (ADB, #01422)*;
- *Black Sea Regional Energy Centre (BSREC, inactive)*;
- *Canadian International Development Agency (CIDA, inactive)*;
- *Carbon Sequestration Leadership Forum (CSLF, #03425)*;
- *Committee on Sustainable Energy (#04288)*;
- *Energy Charter Treaty (ECT, 1994)*;
- *European Commission (EC, #06633)*;
- *Group of Twenty (G20, #10793)*;
- *Inter-American Development Bank (IDB, #11427)*;
- *International Atomic Energy Agency (IAEA, #12294)*;
- *International Bank for Reconstruction and Development (IBRD, #12317)* (World Bank);
- *International Energy Agency (IEA, #13270)*;
- *International Partnership for Energy Efficiency Cooperation (IPEEC, #14520)*;
- *Latin American Energy Organization (#16313)*;
- *OECD (#17693)*;
- *Organization of Arab Petroleum Exporting Countries (OAPEC, #17854)*;
- *Organization of the Petroleum Exporting Countries (OPEC, #17881)*;
- UN Advisory Group on Energy and Climate Change (UN AGECC);
- UN Department of Public Information (DPI);
- UN Energy;
- *UNEP (#20299)*;
- *UNDP (#20292)*;
- *UNIDO (#20336)*;
- *United Nations (UN, #20515)*;
- United Nations Department of Economic and Social Affairs (UNDESA);
- *United Nations Economic Commission for Europe (UNECE, #20555)*;
- *United Nations Framework Convention on Climate Change (UNFCCC, 1992)*;
- *World Trade Organization (WTO, #21864)*.

NGO Relations Maintains relations with:
- *Arab Thought Forum (ATF, #01055)*;
- *Association of Power Utilities in Africa (APUA, #02867)*;
- *EarthAction (EA, #05159)*;
- Edison Electric Institute – USA;
- *Energy Poverty Action (EPA, #05474)*;
- *Global CCS Institute (#10274)*;
- *International Chamber of Commerce (ICC, #12534)*;
- *International Council on Large Electric Systems (#13040)*;
- *International Emissions Trading Association (IETA, #13262)*;
- *International Hydropower Association (IHA, #13828)*;
- *International Institute for Applied Systems Analysis (IIASA, #13861)*;
- *International Organization for Standardization (ISO, #14473)*;
- *International Peatland Society (IPS, #14538)*;
- *Sustainable Energy for All (SEforALL, #20056)*;
- *Union of the Electricity Industry – Eurelectric (#20379)*;
- *VGB PowerTech (VGB, #20764)*;
- *World Business Council for Sustainable Development (WBCSD, #21254)*;
- *World Coal Association (WCA, #21280)*;
- *World Economic Forum (WEF, #21367)*;
- *World LPG Association (WLPGA, #21629)*;
- *World Petroleum Council (WPC, #21722)*;
- *World Wide Fund for Nature (WWF, #21922)*. [2021/XB3510/**B**]

♦ World Energy Forum 21382

Pres 866 United Nations Plaza, Ste 422, New York NY 10017, USA. T. +12127593185. Fax +16466664349. E-mail: info@worldeforum.org.
URL: http://worldeforum.org/en/

Aims Lead a global conversation on energy issues and educate and campaign for accessible and *sustainable* energy that can benefit all nations and peoples; facilitate political will as well as research, technological advancement and capacity-building so as to achieve an energy-secure world. **Structure** President/Chairman; Presidential Advisory Council; Executive Office. Offices (8): Research; Strategic Planning; Development; Technology; Financial Affairs; Media; Administration; International Affairs. *World Energy Fund*; World Energy Press. **Finance** Members' dues. **Activities** Events/meetings; awards/prizes/competitions. **Events** *World Energy Youth Forum* New York, NY (USA) 2015, *America Middle East Energy Summit* Washington, DC (USA) 2015, *Annual Meeting* Barcelona (Spain) 2014, *Forum* Spain 2014, *Annual Meeting* Dubai (United Arab Emirates) 2012. **Publications** *World Energy Monitor.* **Members** Categories Regular; Not-for-Profit Organization; Corporate; Student; Introductory. Membership countries not specified. [2015/XJ1882/**F**]

♦ World Energy & Meteorology Council (WEMC) 21383

Managing Dir The Enterprise Ctr, Univ Drive, Univ of East Anglia, Norwich, NR4 7TJ, UK. T. +442032863250. E-mail: info@wemcouncil.org.
URL: https://www.wemcouncil.org/

History 2015, UK. Convenes the International Conference Energy & Meteorology series (ICEM), which had been organised since 2011. Registration: Companies House, No/ID: 09889302, Start date: 25 Nov 2015, England and Wales. **Aims** Promote and enhance interaction between the energy industry and the weather, climate and broader environmental sciences community. **Structure** Advisory Board. **Activities** Events/meetings; networking/liaising; projects/programmes; training/education. **Events** *International Conference Energy and Meteorology* Copenhagen (Denmark) 2019, *International Conference Energy & Meteorology* Shanghai (China) 2018, *International Conference Energy & Meteorology* Bari (Italy) 2017, *International Conference Energy & Meteorology* Boulder, CO (USA) 2015, *International Conference Energy & Meteorology* Toulouse (France) 2013. **IGO Relations** Cooperates with (2): *European Centre for Medium-Range Weather Forecasts (ECMWF, #06490); World Meteorological Organization (WMO, #21649).* [2022/AA2375/**C**]

♦ World Engagement Institute (internationally oriented national body)

♦ World Entertainment Technology Federation (World-ETF) 21384

Federación Mundo de Tecnologia del Entretenimiento y el Espectaculo (Mundo-ETF)

Contact c/o VPLT, Fuhrenkamp 3-5, 30851 Langenhagen, Germany. T. +4951127074750. Fax +4951127074777.
Contact c/o PLASA, Redoubt House, 1 Edward Road, Eastbourne, BN23 8AS, UK. T. +441323524120. Fax +441323524121.
URL: http://www.esta.org/about/worldetf.html

History Sep 1995, by national organizations in UK, Germany, USA and Italy. **Aims** Provide a forum for discussion of common issues, such as technical standards, trading methods, training and education; enhance the prospects for industry growth internationally. **Languages** English, German, Italian, Japanese, Spanish. **Members** Associations in 7 countries:
Canada, Germany, Italy, Japan, Spain, UK, USA. [2017.11.27/XD5869/**D**]

♦ World Environmental Education Congress Network 21385

Secretariat Ist per l'Ambiente, Corso Moncalieri 18, 10131 Turin TO, Italy. T. +391143666522. Fax +39114366522. E-mail: secretariat@weecnetwork.org.
URL: http://www.weecnetwork.org/

History 2003, when first World Environmental Education Congress (WEEC) was organized. Previously also referred to as *WEEC International Environmental Education Network* and *WEEC International Association.* **Aims** Facilitate mutual cooperation and improve the level of cultural and scientific debate; ensure continuity of the World *Environmental Education* Congress. **Structure** Scientific Committee; Honour Committee; Organizing Committee. **Languages** English, French, Italian, Spanish. **Finance** Donations; funding from foundations; EU projects; congress local partners; sponsorships. **Activities** Events/meetings. **Events** *World Environmental Education Congress (WEEC)* Prague (Czechia) 2022, *World Environmental Education Congress* Prague (Czechia) 2021, *World Environmental Education Congress* Bangkok (Thailand) 2019, *World Environmental Education Congress* Vancouver, BC (Canada) 2017, *World Environmental Education Congress* Gothenburg (Sweden) 2015. **Publications** Newsletter; congress proceedings.
Members Full in 137 countries and territories:
Afghanistan, Albania, Algeria, Angola, Argentina, Armenia, Australia, Austria, Azerbaijan, Bahamas, Bahrain, Bangladesh, Belgium, Benin, Bhutan, Bolivia, Botswana, Brazil, Bulgaria, Burkina Faso, Burundi, Cameroon, Canada, Chad, Chile, China, Colombia, Congo DR, Costa Rica, Côte d'Ivoire, Croatia, Cuba, Cyprus, Czechia, Denmark, Dominican Rep, Ecuador, Egypt, El Salvador, Equatorial Guinea, Eswatini, Ethiopia, Fiji, Finland, France, Gambia, Georgia, Germany, Ghana, Greece, Guatemala, Guinea, Guinea-Bissau, Haiti, India, Indonesia, Iran Islamic Rep, Iraq, Ireland, Israel, Italy, Jamaica, Japan, Jordan, Kazakhstan, Kenya, Korea Rep, Kyrgyzstan, Laos, Latvia, Lebanon, Lesotho, Libya, Madagascar, Malawi, Malaysia, Mali, Malta, Marshall Is, Mauritania, Mauritius, Mexico, Mongolia, Morocco, Mozambique, Namibia, Nepal, Netherlands, New Zealand, Nicaragua, Niger, Nigeria, North Macedonia, Norway, Oman, Pakistan, Palestine, Panama, Paraguay, Peru, Philippines, Poland, Portugal, Puerto Rico, Qatar, Romania, Russia, Saudi Arabia, Senegal, Singapore, Solomon Is, South Africa, Spain, Sri Lanka, St Maarten, Sudan, Sweden, Switzerland, Syrian AR, Taiwan, Tanzania UR, Thailand, Togo, Trinidad-Tobago, Tunisia, Türkiye, Uganda, UK, Ukraine, United Arab Emirates, Uruguay, USA, Uzbekistan, Venezuela, Yemen, Zambia, Zimbabwe. [2019.12.11/XM0404/**F**]

♦ World Environment Center (WEC) 21386

Pres/CEO 734 15th St NW, Ste 720, Washington DC 20005, USA. T. +12023121370. Fax +12026372411. E-mail: info@wec.org.
WEC Europe Bodenseestrasse 4, 81241 Munich, Germany. T. +498918920563. Fax +498918920565.
URL: http://www.wec.org/

History 1974, New York NY (USA), as *Center for International Environment Information (CIEI).* Independent since 1981. **Aims** Advance *sustainable development* through business practices of member companies and in partnership with governments, multi-lateral organizations, NGOs and other stakeholders. **Structure** Head Office in Washington DC (USA); Regional Offices in Munich (Germany) and San Salvador (El Salvador). **Languages** English, French, German, Spanish, Vietnamese. **Activities** Knowledge management/information dissemination; capacity building; awards/prizes/competitions; events/meetings. **Events** *Annual Colloquium* 2018, *Annual Colloquium* Washington, DC (USA) 2017, *International environment forum* Madrid (Spain) 1998, *Meeting* The Hague (Netherlands) 1996, *International environment forum* New York, NY (USA) 1990. **Publications** *Business Skills for a Changing World.*
Members Corporations in 6 countries:
Germany, Mexico, Netherlands, Switzerland, UK, USA.
Consultative Status Consultative status granted from: *UNEP (#20299).* **IGO Relations** Accredited by: *United Nations Framework Convention on Climate Change – Secretariat (UNFCCC, #20564).* **NGO Relations** Member of: *International Union for Conservation of Nature and Natural Resources (IUCN, #15766).* [2018/XE2872/**E**]

♦ World Environment and Resources Council (inactive)

♦ World EOD Foundation 21387

Fundación Mundial de EOD

UK Office 33 A Church Road, Watford, WD17 4PY, UK. T. +447785555540. E-mail: jw@eod.org.
Asia-Pacific Office 4 Soi Intamara 3, Suthisarn Road, Phayathai, Bangkok, 10400, Thailand. T. +6622795105. Fax +6622714814.
URL: http://www.eod.org/

History as *World EOD Organization – Organización Mundial de EOD.* Full title: *World Explosive Ordnance Disposal Foundation – Fundación Mundial de Destrucción Estatutaria de Explosivos.* UK Registered Charity: 1062814. **Aims** Bring together those involved in EOD – *explosive ordnance disposal*, other *bomb* technicians and related intelligence operatives in a professionally organized and secure environment for exchange of experience and skills. **Events** *Conference* Madrid (Spain) 2014, *Conference* Bangkok (Thailand) 2006, *Conference* Singapore (Singapore) 2000, *Conference* Esher (UK) 1999, *Conference* Washington, DC (USA) 1999.
Members Full in 98 countries and territories:

Algeria, Argentina, Australia, Austria, Bahamas, Bahrain, Belgium, Belize, Bosnia-Herzegovina, Bulgaria, Cambodia, Canada, Chile, China, Colombia, Congo Brazzaville, Congo DR, Costa Rica, Côte d'Ivoire, Croatia, Cuba, Cyprus, Czechia, Denmark, Dominica, Egypt, Ethiopia, Fiji, Finland, France, Gambia, Germany, Ghana, Greece, Haiti, Hong Kong, Hungary, Iceland, India, Indonesia, Iran Islamic Rep, Iraq, Ireland, Israel, Italy, Jamaica, Japan, Jordan, Korea Rep, Kuwait, Laos, Lebanon, Luxembourg, Malawi, Malaysia, Malta, Mauritius, Monaco, Netherlands, New Zealand, Nicaragua, Nigeria, Norway, Oman, Pakistan, Panama, Peru, Philippines, Poland, Portugal, Qatar, Romania, Russia, Rwanda, Saudi Arabia, Serbia, Sierra Leone, Singapore, Somalia, South Africa, Spain, Sri Lanka, Sweden, Switzerland, Syrian AR, Taiwan, Thailand, Tunisia, Türkiye, Uganda, UK, Ukraine, USA, Venezuela, Vietnam, Yemen, Zambia, Zimbabwe. [2018/XD3766/f/**F**]

♦ World EOD Organization / see World EOD Foundation (#21387)
♦ World Equine Airway Symposium (meeting series)

♦ World Equine Veterinary Association (WEVA) 21388

Association mondiale des vétérinaires équins – Asociación Mundial Veterinaria Equina – Weltgesellschaft der Pferdetierärzte – Vjemirnaja Organizacija Veterinarov-Konevcov

Exec Assistant VetMed Phase II 0442, 205 Duck Pond Dr, Blacksburg VA 24061, USA.
Sec Oniris, La Chantrerie, CS-40307, Nantes CEDEX 3, France.
URL: http://wevaonline.org/

History 1985, within the framework of *World Veterinary Association (WVA, #21901)*. Most recent statutes adopted 1997. **Aims** Unify the equine veterinary profession throughout the world by providing a common forum for national and international equine veterinary organizations and other equine interest associations; provide a central body to coordinate and exchange information related to the horse; encourage equine veterinary practitioners to attain a degree of excellence by provision of high-level education by competent scientists, ongoing retraining, development of specializations in medicine, surgery and all aspects of production, care for all equines used in agriculture, sport and leisure, and promotion of the equine practitioner as an essential partner in all aspects of equine health, production and welfare. **Structure** General Assembly (every 2 years). Executive Committee, consisting of President, 2 Vice-Presidents, Secretary-Treasurer and up to 7 other members. Secretariat in Abu Dhabi (United Arab Emirates). **Languages** English. **Staff** 5.00 FTE, voluntary. **Finance** Sources: members' dues. **Activities** Holds/promotes national and international meetings, seminars and conferences on health, breeding and welfare of the horse. Topics of concern: research; national and international exhibitions, shows, racing and other equine sporting events; international transport; management and control of disease. Awards Schering-Plough Award for outstanding research. **Events** *Biennial Congress* Verona (Italy) 2019, *Biennial Congress* Beijing (China) 2018, *Biennial Congress* Guadalajara (Mexico) 2015, *Congress* Istanbul (Turkey) 2014, *Biennial Congress / Congress* Budapest (Hungary) 2013. **Publications** *WEVA Newsletter* (2 a year); *Journal of Equine Veterinary Science* – official journal.
Members National and regional associations in 28 countries:
Argentina, Australia, Belgium, Brazil, Chile, Colombia, Denmark, France, Hungary, India, Ireland, Italy, Japan, Mexico, Morocco, New Zealand, Nigeria, Peru, Portugal, Russia, South Africa, Spain, Sweden, Switzerland, Thailand, UK, Uruguay, USA.
International associations listed in this Yearbook (1):
Individuals in 4 countries:
Korea Rep, Kuwait, Sudan, United Arab Emirates.
NGO Relations Associate member of WVA and represented on its Permanent Committee (which is entitled to be represented at all WEVA meetings). [2019/XD0139/y/**C**]

♦ World Esperantist Educational Service (inactive)

♦ World Esperantist Vegetarian Association 21389

Association mondiale des végétariens espérantistes – Tutmonda Esperantista Vegetarana Asocio (TEVA)

Contact Assebroeklaan 2, 8310 Bruges, Belgium. T. +3250675178. E-mail: teva@ivu.org.
URL: http://vegetarismo.info/

History Founded Aug 1908, Dresden (Germany), at 4th Universal Esperanto Congress, as *International Union of Esperanto Vegetarians – Union internationale des espérantistes végétariens – Internacia Unuigo de Esperantistaj Vegetaranoj (IUEV)*, under the initiative of R de Ladevèze and Zamenhof and the honorary presidency of Leo Tolstoy. Previously also referred to as *Vegetara Ligo Esperantista (VLE)*. **Aims** Spread a knowledge of Esperanto among vegetarians, and of vegetarianism among Esperantists; promote in a friendly collaboration respect for nature and for all living creatures. **Structure** Annual Assembly. **Languages** Esperanto. **Staff** 4.00 FTE, voluntary. **Finance** Sources: contributions; members' dues. **Activities** Events/meetings. **Events** *Assembly* Nitra (Slovakia) 2016, *Assembly* Lille (France) 2015, *Assembly* Buenos Aires (Argentina) 2014, *Assembly* Reykjavik (Iceland) 2013, *Assembly* Hanoi (Vietnam) 2012. **Publications** *Esperantista Vegetarano*.
Members Individuals in 29 countries:
Argentina, Australia, Belgium, Brazil, Cameroon, Canada, China, Colombia, Croatia, Cuba, Denmark, France, Hungary, Iran Islamic Rep, Ireland, Israel, Italy, Japan, Netherlands, Norway, Pakistan, Poland, Portugal, Russia, Spain, Sweden, Switzerland, UK, Uruguay. [2018.08.08/XC2715/v/**C**]

♦ World Esperanto Youth Organization (#20268)

♦ World ESports Association (WESA) 21390

Exec Chairman Baarerstr 2, 6300 Zug, Switzerland. E-mail: info@wesa.gg.
URL: http://www.wesa.gg/

History Registration: No/ID: CHE-378.271.319, Switzerland, Zug. **Aims** Further professionalize esports by introducing elements of player representation, standardized regulations, and revenue shares for teams. **Structure** Executive Board. [2020/AA1025/**C**]

♦ World E-sports Consortium / see World Esports Consortium (#21391)

♦ World Esports Consortium (WESCO) 21391

Headquarters Paulista Avenue 854 – 10th floor, Sao Paulo SP, 01310-100, Brazil. E-mail: contact@wescoesport.com.
Contact 553 Rangel Pestana Street, Jundiaí SP, 13201-000, Brazil.
URL: https://wescoesport.com/

History 2016, Yinchuan (China). Former names and other names: *World E-sports Consortium* – alias. **Aims** Improve electronic sports constantly and promote it globally in the light of its unifying, educational, cultural and humanitarian values, particularly through youth and development programmes. **Structure** Presidency; Board of Directors; Executive Secretariat. Commissions; Court of Arbitration; Advisory Board. Main Headquarters in Brazil. Regional Headquarters: Asian; European; Middle-East; African; Oceania. Branch Offices: Western Europe; Eastern Europe; United Arab Emirates; North American; South American. **Languages** Chinese, English, French, Italian, Portuguese, Russian, Spanish. **Staff** 12.00 FTE, paid; 38.00 FTE, voluntary. **Finance** Sources: contributions; donations; fees for services; government support; investments; private foundations; revenue from activities/projects; sale of products; sponsorship. Annual budget: 12,500,000 USD (2022). **Activities** Awards/prizes/competitions; awareness raising; events/meetings; knowledge management/information dissemination; networking/liaising; sporting activities; training/education.
Members Continental; National; Private associations; Private companies. Members in 66 countries and territories:
Albania, Algeria, Andorra, Argentina, Australia, Bahamas, Belgium, Bolivia, Brazil, Burkina Faso, Cameroon, Central African Rep, Chile, China, Colombia, Congo DR, Côte d'Ivoire, Dominica, Dominican Rep, Ecuador, El Salvador, Estonia, France, Gabon, Ghana, Guadeloupe, Guatemala, Guinea, Haiti, Honduras, Hong Kong, India, Indonesia, Iran Islamic Rep, Ireland, Italy, Jamaica, Libya, Mauritania, Mexico, Mongolia, Morocco, Namibia, Netherlands, Nigeria, North Macedonia, Panama, Peru, Portugal, Rwanda, Scotland, Senegal, Serbia, St Lucia, Tanzania UR, Togo, Turkmenistan, UK, Ukraine, USA, Uzbekistan, Venezuela, Zambia, Zimbabwe.
Africa Electric Sport Association (AESA, #00167); Asian Electronic Sports Federation (AESF, #01435); General Association of Asia Pacific Sports Federations (GAAPSF, #10106); International Esports Federation (IESF, #13303); Pan American Electronic Sports Confederation (PAMESCO, #18096).
NGO Relations Partner of (8): *Africa Electric Sport Association (AESA, #00167); Asian Electronic Sports Federation (AESF, #01435); Central American and Caribbean Confederation of Esports (CACESCO); General Association of Asia Pacific Sports Federations (GAAPSF, #10106); International Esports Federation (IESF, #13304); Pan American Electronic Sports Confederation (PAMESCO, #18096); South American Esports Confederation (SAESCO); World O-Sport Federation (WOF, #21700).* [2022.11.30/AA1091/y/**B**]

♦ **World-ETF** World Entertainment Technology Federation (#21384)
♦ World Ethanol & Biofuels (meeting series)
♦ World Ethnosport Confederation (internationally oriented national body)

♦ World Ethnosport Society 21392

Pres Aptiekas iela 6-57, Riga LV-1005, Latvia. T. +37123668188. E-mail: to@ethnosport.org.
URL: http://ethnosport.org/

History 2012, Montréal, QC (Canada). Registration: Start date: 2018, Latvia. **Aims** Develop ethnosport for the preservation of *traditional sports* and games. **Structure** General Meeting; Board; Council. **Languages** English, Latvian, Russian. **Staff** 2.00 FTE, paid; 200.00 FTE, voluntary. **Finance** Sources: donations; grants; members' dues; revenue from activities/projects. Annual budget: 80,000 USD (2018). **Activities** Events/meetings; sporting activities.
Members Organizations in 46 countries:
Afghanistan, Armenia, Australia, Azerbaijan, Belarus, Benin, Bolivia, Brazil, Bulgaria, Cameroon, Canada, Chile, China, Colombia, Congo DR, Croatia, Estonia, Ghana, Greece, Guatemala, Hungary, India, Iran Islamic Rep, Jordan, Kazakhstan, Kenya, Kuwait, Latvia, Lithuania, Madagascar, Malaysia, Moldova, Morocco, Netherlands, Niger, Pakistan, Poland, Russia, Sri Lanka, Togo, Türkiye, Uganda, Ukraine, Uruguay, USA, Uzbekistan.
IGO Relations *Intergovernmental Committee for Physical Education and Sport (#11475) UNESCO (#20322).*
NGO Relations Memorandum of Understanding with (1): *The Association for International Sport for All (TAFISA, #02763).* Member of (2): *General Association of Asia Pacific Sports Federations (GAAPSF, #10106); International Sport Network Organization (ISNO, #15592).* [2019.12.15/XM7390/**C**]

♦ World Evangelical Alliance (WEA) 21393

Alliance évangélique universelle (AEM) – Alianza Evangélica Mundial (AEM)

Main Office Church Street Station, PO Box 3402, New York NY 10008-3402, USA. E-mail: wea@worldea.org.
URL: http://www.worldea.org/

History 1951. Founded on re-organization of *World's Evangelical Alliance (inactive)*, set up 19 Aug 1846, London (UK). Current title adopted at General Assembly of May 2001, Kuala Lumpur (Malaysia). Former names and other names: *World Evangelical Fellowship (WEF)* – former (1951 to 1 Jan 2002); *Union évangélique mondiale (UEM)* – alias. **Aims** Foster *Christian* unity; provide a worldwide identity, voice and platform to Evangelical Christians; proclaim the Gospel to all nations; promote Christ-centred transformation within society. **Structure** General Assembly (every 6 years); International Council; North American Council; Senior Leadership Team; Commissions (6); Initiatives and branches include: *International Institute for Religious Freedom (IIRF, #13919); World Evangelical Alliance Sustainability Center (WEA Sustainability Center).* **Languages** Chinese, English, French, German, Japanese, Korean, Portuguese, Spanish. **Staff** 12.00 FTE, paid. **Finance** Members services; financial contributions. **Activities** Advocacy/lobbying/activism; networking/liaising; religious activities. **Events** *General Asembly* Bogor (Indonesia) 2019, *General Assembly* Seoul (Korea Rep) 2014, *Conference* Thailand 2011, *General Assembly* Pattaya (Thailand) 2008, *General Assembly* Kuala Lumpur (Malaysia) 2001. **Publications** *Religious Liberty Prayer Bulletin* (weekly) – electronic; *WEA Newlsetter* (12 a year) – electronic; *Evangelical Review of Theology* (4 a year); *Theological News* (4 a year); *The Geneva Report to the UN* (annual). *Directory of Evangelical Associations* (1991-1992).
Members Regional organizations (6):
Asia Evangelical Alliance (AEA, #01275); Association of Evangelicals in Africa (AEA, #02587); European Evangelical Alliance (EEA, #07010); Evangelical Association of the Caribbean (EAC, #09210); Latin Evangelical Alliance (#16397); South Pacific Evangelical Alliance (SPEA, #19886).
National evangelical alliances (127) in 126 countries and territories:
Albania, Angola, Antigua-Barbuda, Argentina, Australia, Austria, Azerbaijan, Bangladesh, Barbados, Belgium (2), Benin, Bolivia, Bosnia-Herzegovina, Botswana, Brazil, Bulgaria, Burkina Faso, Cambodia, Canada, Central African Rep, Chad, Chile, Colombia, Costa Rica, Côte d'Ivoire, Croatia, Cyprus, Czechia, Denmark, Dominica, Dominican Rep, Ecuador, Egypt, El Salvador, England, Eritrea, Estonia, Eswatini, Ethiopia, Fiji, Finland, France, Gambia, Germany, Ghana, Greece, Guatemala, Guinea, Guinea-Bissau, Guyana, Haiti, Honduras, Hungary, India, Indonesia, Ireland, Israel, Italy, Jamaica, Japan, Jordan, Kazakhstan, Kenya, Korea Rep, Kosovo, Latvia, Lesotho, Liberia, Luxembourg, Madagascar, Malawi, Malaysia, Mali, Mauritius, Mexico, Mongolia, Morocco, Mozambique, Myanmar, Namibia, Nepal, Netherlands, New Zealand, Nicaragua, Nigeria, North Macedonia, Norway, Pakistan, Panama, Papua New Guinea, Paraguay, Peru, Philippines, Poland, Portugal, Romania, Rwanda, Samoa, Senegal, Serbia, Sierra Leone, Singapore, Slovakia, Solomon Is, South Africa, Spain, Sri Lanka, St Croix Is, St Kitts-Nevis, St Lucia, St Vincent-Grenadines, Sudan, Sweden, Switzerland (2), Tanzania UR, Thailand, Tonga, Trinidad-Tobago, Türkiye, Uganda, UK, Uruguay, USA, Venezuela, Zambia, Zimbabwe.
National alliances not affiliated with regional bodies (4) in 5 countries and territories:
Algeria, Egypt, Jordan, Palestine.
Associate: international evangelical agencies (101) in 15 countries and territories:
Australia, Brazil, Canada, China, Cyprus, Finland, Hong Kong, India, Japan, Netherlands, Nicaragua, Norway, Taiwan, UK, USA.
Included in the above Associate members, 86 organizations listed in this Yearbook:
- *Advancing the Ministries of the Gospel International (AMG International);*
- *Africa Inland Mission International (AIM International, #00182);*
- Apostolos Campus Ministry International (ACMI);
- *Arab World Evangelical Ministers Association (AWEMA);*
- *Asia Missions Association (AMA);*
- Asian Access;
- *Asia Theological Association (ATA, #02101);*
- *Associação Evangélica de Educação Teológica na América Latina (AETAL, #02326);*
- *Association of Christian Schools International (ACSI, #02430);*
- *Association of Christians Ministering Among Internationals (ACMI);*
- *Barnabas International;*
- Barnabas Relief Fund;
- Biblica;
- *Campus Crusade for Christ International (CCCI);*
- Campus Missions International;
- *CEDAR Fund;*
- *Christian Communications International (CCI);*
- *Christopher Sun Evangelistic Association;*
- *Church Mission Society (CMS);*
- *Church of God World Missions;*
- *Compassion International (CI, #04413);*
- *Cooperación Misionera Iberoamericana (COMIBAM, #04791);*
- Creatio International;
- Diakonos International;
- *EFCA ReachGlobal;*
- Elim Center International;
- *Engineering Ministries International (EMI);*
- Evangelical Environmental Network (EEN);
- *Every Home for Christ International (EHCI, #09214);*
- *Finnish Lutheran Overseas Mission;*
- *Food for the Hungry (fh, #09845);*
- *General Baptist Foreign Mission Society;*
- Global AIDS Prayer Partnership (GAPP);
- *Global Mapping International (GMI);*
- *Global Scholars;*
- Gospel & Information Technology (G and IT);
- *Greater Europe Mission (GEM);*
- *Healthcare Christian Fellowship International (HCFI, #10873);*
- *Holy Bible Society (HBS);*
- *International Aid;*
- *International Association of Evangelical Chaplains (IAEC);*
- *International Friendship Evangelism (IFE);*
- *International Needs (IN, #14222);*
- *International Students (ISI);*
- *International Teams;*
- *Jews for Jesus (JFJ);*
- Jubilee World;
- *Latin America Mission (LAM, inactive);*
- Lexis Dei Fellowship;
- *Literacy and Evangelism International (LEI);*
- Luis Palau Association;
- *Middle East Media;*
- *Mission Aviation Fellowship (MAF, #16829);*

- *Mission Covenant Church of Norway*;
- *Mission to Unreached Peoples (MUP)*;
- *Navigators*;
- *Norsk Luthersk Misjonssamband (NLM)*;
- *OC International (OCI, #17688)*;
- One Mission Society (OMS);
- *Open Doors International (#17749)*;
- *Operation Mobilisation (#17772)*;
- *Overseas Council International (OCI)*;
- *Overseas Radio and Television*;
- *Partners International*;
- *Pioneers International*;
- *Project Partner with Christ (no recent information)*;
- *Ravi Zacharias International Ministries (RZIM)*;
- *Scripture Union International Council (#19161)*;
- *SEND International*;
- *SIM International*;
- *South America Mission (SAM)*;
- *The Evangelical Alliance Mission (TEAM)*;
- *The Voice of the Martyrs (VOM, #20804)*;
- *United States Center for World Mission (USCWM)*;
- *United World Mission (UWM)*;
- *Veritas College International (VCI)*;
- *visionSynergy*;
- *World Concern International (#21290)*;
- *World Mission*;
- *World Mission Prayer League (WMPL)*;
- *World Team (WT, #21849)*;
- *World Thrust International (no recent information)*;
- *WorldVenture*;
- Young Disciples of Jesus;
- Youth Evangelical Fellowship International;
- *Youth for Christ International (YFCI, #22009)*.

Affiliate: international organizations serving as non-structured ministry partners of WEA in a specialized field in 2 countries:
UK, USA.
Included in the above Affiliate members, 2 organizations listed in this Yearbook:
Dawn Ministries (no recent information); ICMC.
Consultative Status Consultative status granted from: *ECOSOC (#05331)* (Special); *UNEP (#20299)*. **NGO Relations** Sponsors: *South Pacific Association of Evangelical Colleges (SPAEC, inactive)*. Member of: *Fédération de missions évangéliques francophones (FMEF, #09688)*; *Joint Learning Initiative on Faith and Local Communities (JLI, #16139)*; *Side by Side (#19265)*. Associate member of: *Conference of Non-Governmental Organizations in Consultative Relationship with the United Nations (CONGO, #04635)*. Instrumental in setting up: *Great Commission Global Roundtable (GCGR, inactive)*. Missions Commission is partner of: *Global Connections*. Global partners include: *Advocates International*; *International Council for Evangelical Theological Education (ICETE, #13020)*; *Micah Global (#16741)*; *World Vision International (WVI, #21904)*; *Wycliffe Global Alliance (#21965)*. [2022/XC3511/y/**B**]

♦ World Evangelical Alliance Sustainability Center (internationally oriented national body)
♦ World Evangelical Fellowship / see World Evangelical Alliance (#21393)

♦ World Evangelism Committee 21394

Mailing address PO Box 8142, Lafayette IN 47903, USA. T. +17654132966. E-mail: info@worldmethodist.org.
URL: http://www.worldmethodist.org/

History 1971, Denver, CO (USA). Founded within the framework of *World Methodist Council (WMC, #21650)*. **Aims** Offer resources and events to strengthen discipleship and equip Christ followers to share their faith. **Structure** Board of Directors; Committee; Regional Secretaries (19). **Finance** Sources: contributions. Annual budget: 1,300,000 USD. **Activities** Networking/liaising. **Publications** *Embrace*; *Faith-Sharing New Testament*.
Members Associations in 131 countries and territories:
Albania, Algeria, Angola, Antigua-Barbuda, Argentina, Australia, Austria, Bahamas, Bangladesh, Belgium, Belize, Benin, Bermuda, Bolivia, Botswana, Brazil, Bulgaria, Burundi, Cambodia, Cameroon, Canada, Cape Verde, Chile, Colombia, Congo DR, Costa Rica, Côte d'Ivoire, Croatia, Cuba, Czechia, Denmark, Dominica, Dominican Rep, Ecuador, Egypt, El Salvador, Equatorial Guinea, Estonia, Eswatini, Fiji, Finland, France, Gambia, Germany, Ghana, Grenada, Guadeloupe, Guam, Guatemala, Guiana Fr, Guyana, Haiti, Honduras, Hong Kong, Hungary, India, Indonesia, Ireland, Israel, Italy, Jamaica, Japan, Jordan, Kazakhstan, Kenya, Korea Rep, Kyrgyzstan, Lebanon, Leeward Is, Lesotho, Liberia, Malawi, Malaysia, Mexico, Mozambique, Myanmar, Namibia, Netherlands, New Zealand, Nicaragua, Niger, Nigeria, North Macedonia, Norway, Pakistan, Palestine, Panama, Papua New Guinea, Paraguay, Peru, Philippines, Poland, Portugal, Puerto Rico, Romania, Russia, Rwanda, Samoa, Senegal, Serbia, Sierra Leone, Singapore, Slovakia, Solomon Is, South Africa, Spain, Sri Lanka, St Kitts-Nevis, St Lucia, St Vincent-Grenadines, Suriname, Sweden, Switzerland, Syrian AR, Taiwan, Tajikistan, Tanzania UR, Thailand, Togo, Tonga, Trinidad-Tobago, Tunisia, Uganda, UK, Uruguay, USA, Venezuela, Virgin Is USA, Windward Is, Zambia, Zimbabwe.
NGO Relations Instrumental in setting up (1): *World Methodist Evangelism Institute (WMEI, see: #21650)*. [2023.02.28/XK0804/**E**]

♦ World Evangelization Research Center / see Center for the Study of Global Christianity
♦ World Exchange (internationally oriented national body)
♦ World Explosive Ordnance Disposal Foundation / see World EOD Foundation (#21387)
♦ World Export Processing Zones Association / see World Economic Processing Zones Association (#21368)
♦ World Eye Surgeons Society (no recent information)
♦ WORLDEYES – World Eye Surgeons Society (no recent information)

♦ World Fair Trade Latin America (WFTO-LA) 21395

Secretariat Km 38-600 – Ruta Aregua-Ypacarai, Urbanización Paraiso al Lago, Ypacarai, Central, Paraguay. T. +595971739166. E-mail: secretaria@wfto-la.org.
URL: http://www.wfto-la.org/

History Founded as a regional office of *World Fair Trade Organization (WFTO, #21396)*. **Aims** Strengthen the advocacy, marketing and monitoring capacities of member organizations; promote cooperative relationships among them and with other social actors, so s to contribute to the improvement of the living conditions of small producers in Latin America, according to the principles of Fair Trade. **Structure** Annual General Meeting; Regional Board of Directors; Regional Secretariat. **Languages** English, Portuguese, Spanish. **Staff** 1.00 FTE, paid; 2.00 FTE, voluntary.
Members Full in 13 countries:
Bolivia, Brazil, Chile, Colombia, Ecuador, El Salvador, Guatemala, Honduras, Mexico, Nicaragua, Paraguay, Peru, Uruguay. [2020.01.15/XM8575/t/**D**]

♦ World Fair Trade Organization (WFTO) 21396

Main Office Godfried Bomansstr 8-3, 4103 WR Culemborg, Netherlands. T. +31345536487. E-mail: info@wfto.com.
URL: http://www.wfto.com/

History May 1989. Former names and other names: *International Federation for Alternative Trade* – former; *Fédération internationale de commerce alternatif* – former; *International Fair Trade Association (IFAT)* – former; *Fédération internationale de commerce equitable* – former. Registration: No/ID: 40536675, Netherlands. **Aims** Improve *livelihoods* of *marginalized* producers and workers, especially in the South; change unfair structures of international trade, mainly by means of Fair Trade; improve and coordinate cooperation of member organizations; promote the interests of, and provide services to, member organizations and individuals. **Structure** General Meeting (annual); Board of Directors; Global Office; Fair Trade Advocacy Office; Regional Offices (5): *World Fair Trade Organization – Africa (#21397)*; *World Fair Trade Organization, Asia (WFTO-Asia, #21398)*; *WFTO-Europe (#20930)*; *World Fair Trade Latin America (WFTO-LA, #21395)*; WFTO Pacific. **Languages** English, French, Spanish. **Staff** 7.00 FTE, paid. **Finance** Sources: members' dues. **Activities** Events/meetings; standards/guidelines. **Events** *IFTTC : International Fair Trade Towns Conference* Cardiff (UK) 2019, *Biennial Summit* Lima (Peru) 2019, *Europe Biennial Conference* Brussels (Belgium) 2018, *Asia Summit* Kathmandu (Nepal) 2018, *Biennial Summit* Delhi (India) 2017. **Publications** *WFTO Newsletter* (12 a year). *The Charter of Fair Trade Principles*. Annual Report. Information Services: General information service for members and associates.
Members Full (over 400) – fair trade organizations, networks and support organizations in 72 countries and territories:
Argentina, Australia, Austria, Bangladesh, Belgium, Bolivia, Bosnia-Herzegovina, Brazil, Cambodia, Cameroon, Canada, Chile, China, Colombia, Costa Rica, Czechia, Denmark, Ecuador, Egypt, Ethiopia, Finland, France, Germany, Ghana, Greece, Guatemala, Honduras, Hong Kong, India, Indonesia, Ireland, Israel, Italy, Japan, Kenya, Laos, Lebanon, Madagascar, Malta, Mauritius, Mexico, Micronesia FS, Mongolia, Namibia, Nepal, Netherlands, New Zealand, Nigeria, Northern Ireland, Norway, Pakistan, Palestine, Paraguay, Peru, Philippines, Poland, Romania, Rwanda, Senegal, South Africa, Spain, Sri Lanka, Sweden, Switzerland, Tanzania UR, Thailand, Uganda, UK, Uruguay, USA, Vietnam, Zimbabwe.
NGO Relations Member of (3): *European Inter-Network of Ethical and Responsible Initiatives (#07593)*; *Wellbeing Economy Alliance (WEAll, #20856)*; *World Social Forum (WSF, #21797)*. WFTO – Europe is instrumental in setting up: *Fair Trade Advocacy Office (FTAO, #09238)*. [2019/XD2389/ty/**B**]

♦ World Fair Trade Organization – Africa 21397

Head Office PO Box Box 46337, GPO 00100, Nairobi, Kenya. T. +254203866005 – +254203866006 – +254203866007. Fax +25420866008. E-mail: info@wfto-africa.org.
URL: http://www.wfto-africa.org/

History Founded as *Cooperation for Fair Trade in Africa (COFTA)*. Regional chapter of *World Fair Trade Organization (WFTO, #21396)*. **Aims** Improve the sustainable livelihoods of African producers through partnerships that advocate for fair trade.
Members Organizations (over 70) in 21 countries:
Botswana, Burkina Faso, Burundi, Cameroon, Egypt, Eswatini, Ethiopia, Ghana, Kenya, Malawi, Mauritius, Morocco, Namibia, Nigeria, Rwanda, Senegal, South Africa, Tanzania UR, Uganda, Zambia, Zimbabwe. [2014/XJ1533/t/**E**]

♦ World Fair Trade Organization, Asia (WFTO-Asia) 21398

Secretariat Support Coordinator 219/84 (Baan Thanawan), Moo 8, San Phi Suea, Muang, Chiang Mai, 50300, Thailand. T. +660932345374. E-mail: gee@wfto-asia.com – fah@wfto-asia.com.
URL: https://wfto-asia.com/

History Founded as a regional organization of *World Fair Trade Organization (WFTO, #21396)*. **Aims** Enable dedicated producers, co-ops and organizations in Asia to seek greater equity in international trade. **Structure** Board of Directors. **Publications** *WFTO-Asia Newsletter*.
Members Full in 19 countries and territories:
Armenia, Bangladesh, Cambodia, China, Hong Kong, India, Indonesia, Japan, Korea Rep, Laos, Malaysia, Mongolia, Nepal, Pakistan, Philippines, Sri Lanka, Taiwan, Thailand, Vietnam. [2022/XM8574/t/**D**]

♦ World Faiths Development Dialogue (internationally oriented national body)

♦ World Family Organization (WFO) 21399

Organisation mondiale de la famille (OMF)

Headquarters 28 place St Georges, 75009 Paris, France. T. +33148780759. Fax +33142829524. E-mail: info@worldfamilyorganization.org.
Secretariat Rua Duque de Caxias 831, São Francisco, Curitiba PR, 80530-040, Brazil. T. +554132545678. Fax +554130496263. E-mail: media@worldfamilyorganization.org.
URL: http://www.worldfamilyorganization.org/

History Jun 1947, Paris (France). First Constitution adopted by General Assembly by 20 nations, 3 July 1948, Geneva (Switzerland); amended 6 Dec 1985, Delhi (India), 19-20 Sep 1993, Cairo (Egypt), 25-26 Nov 1998, Vienna (Austria) and 8 Dec 2006, at the Dead Sea (Jordan). Former names and other names: *International Union of Family Organizations (IUFO)* – former; *Union internationale des organismes familiaux (UIOF)* – former; *Unión Internacional de Organismos Familiares* – former; *Internationale Union der Familienverbände* – former; *Unione Internazionale degli Organismi Familiari* – former; *Internationale Unie van Gezinsorganisaties* – former. Registration: France. **Aims** Represent families of the world at all levels; defend their interests; act with them and for them vis-à-vis governments and the international community; in cooperation with specialized agencies where necessary, promote policies for improvement of housing, health, sanitation, nutrition, education, recreation, work conditions, welfare systems, social protection and benefits, family relationships and environmental issues affecting families; in cooperation with members, experts and advisory groups, promote scientific studies concerning family structures, concepts and terminology. **Structure** General Assembly (annual since 1998, formerly every 4 years); Executive Board; Presidency Office; Regional Offices. Commissions and Committee; World Family University and Research Centre; WFO Office for Project Services. **Languages** Arabic, English, French, Portuguese, Spanish. **Staff** 16.00 FTE, paid. **Finance** Sources: donations; donations; fees for services; fees for services; gifts, legacies; gifts, legacies; members' dues; members' dues. Special funds. **Activities** With respect to the United Nations and the consultative process, acts as the link between both the aspirations and achievements of the families and the work done for them at the level of the UN; acts as the promoter and organizer on international efforts among governmental, non-governmental organizations as well as the private sector in increasing awareness of family issues and policy formulation; promotes and/or sponsors conferences, seminars, international, regional, national and local meetings and training to discuss major family concerns; establishes and maintains collaboration with the UN, specialized agencies, professional groups and other organizations as well as other governmental and non-governmental family institutions administration, as may be deemed appropriate. Work carried out through Technical Commissions (13): Condition of the Woman; Economic; Education; Family Action among the Working Class; Family Income and Social Security; Family Life and Population; Family Policies and the Role of Public Authorities; Family Rights; Health and Nutrition; Family Housing and the Environment; *International Commission on Couple and Family Relations (ICCFR, #12676)*; Rural Families; Youth. Leading in 2004, in partnership with the UN and the UN System, the celebration of the 10th anniversary of the International Year of the Family. Instrumental in setting up *COFACE Families Europe (#04084)*. **Events** *World Family Summit* Lisbon (Portugal) 2019, *World Family Summit* Geneva (Switzerland) 2017, *World Family Summit* Sao Paulo (Brazil) 2016, *World Family Summit +9* Zhuhai (China) 2014, *World Family Summit + 8* Berlin (Germany) 2013. **Publications** Electronic newsletter; activity reports.
Members NGOs, governmental bodies, universities, academic and research centres interested in family matters, in 134 countries:
Afghanistan, Albania, Algeria, Angola, Argentina, Armenia, Australia, Austria, Azerbaijan, Bahrain, Bangladesh, Belgium, Benin, Bhutan, Bolivia, Botswana, Brazil, Bulgaria, Burkina Faso, Burundi, Cambodia, Cameroon, Canada, Cape Verde, Central African Rep, Chile, China, Colombia, Congo Brazzaville, Congo DR, Costa Rica, Côte d'Ivoire, Cuba, Cyprus, Czechia, Denmark, Dominican Rep, Ecuador, Egypt, El Salvador, Ethiopia, Finland, France, Gabon, Gambia, Germany, Ghana, Greece, Guatemala, Guinea, Guinea-Bissau, Haiti, Hungary, India, Indonesia, Iran Islamic Rep, Iraq, Ireland, Israel, Italy, Japan, Jordan, Kenya, Korea DPR, Korea Rep, Kuwait, Lebanon, Liberia, Libya, Liechtenstein, Lithuania, Luxembourg, Madagascar, Malaysia, Mali, Malta, Mauritania, Mauritius, Mexico, Monaco, Mongolia, Morocco, Mozambique, Namibia, Nepal, Netherlands, New Zealand, Nicaragua, Nigeria, North Macedonia, Norway, Oman, Pakistan, Palestine, Panama, Paraguay, Peru, Philippines, Poland, Portugal, Puerto Rico, Qatar, Romania, Russia, Rwanda, Sao Tomé-Principe, Saudi Arabia, Senegal, Sierra Leone, Singapore, Slovakia, Somalia, South Africa, Spain, Sri Lanka, Sudan, Sweden, Switzerland, Syrian AR, Tanzania UR, Thailand, Timor-Leste, Tunisia, Türkiye, Uganda, UK, Ukraine, United Arab Emirates, Uruguay, USA, Venezuela, Yemen, Zambia, Zimbabwe.
Consultative Status Consultative status granted from: *ECOSOC (#05331)* (General); *UNESCO (#20322)* (Consultative Status); *ILO (#11123)* (Special List); *FAO (#09260)*; *UNICEF (#20332)*. **IGO Relations** Accredited by: *United Nations Office at Vienna (UNOV, #20604)*. Official representation with: *United Nations Economic Commission for Africa (ECA, #20554)*; *United Nations Economic Commission for Europe (UNECE, #20555)*; *United Nations Economic Commission for Latin America and the Caribbean (ECLAC, #20556)*; *United Nations Economic and Social Commission for Western Asia (ESCWA, #20558)*. Permanent relations with: *African Union (AU, #00488)*; *League of Arab States (LAS, #16420)*; *OAS (#17629)*. Associated with Department of Global Communications of the United Nations. **NGO Relations** Member of (3): *Committee of NGOs on Human Rights, Geneva (#04275)*; *Conference of Non-Governmental Organizations in Consultative Relationship with the United Nations (CONGO, #04635)*; *World Organization for Early Childhood Education (OMEP, #21689)*. Instrumental in setting up (1): *United Nations Informal Regional Network of Non-Governmental Organizations (UN-NGO-IRENE, #20573)*. [2023/XB2717/**B**]

♦ World Family of Radio Maria (WF) 21400

Administrative Headquarters Via Mazzini 12, 21020 Casciago MB, Italy. T. +39332229500. Fax +39332826920. E-mail: info.wf@radiomaria.org.
URL: http://www.radiomaria.org/

History 1998, by Italian Association Radio Maria. Registered in accordance with Italian law. **Aims** Spread the Gospel message in keeping with the doctrine and pastoral instruction of the Catholic Church and in allegiance with the Holy Father, using all the potential of the radio. **Publications** *WF Magazine*.
Members Associations in 58 countries:
Albania, Argentina, Austria, Belgium, Bolivia, Bosnia-Herzegovina, Brazil, Burkina Faso, Burundi, Cameroon, Canada, Central African Rep, Chile, Colombia, Congo Brazzaville, Congo DR, Costa Rica, Croatia, Dominican Rep, Ecuador, El Salvador, France, Gabon, Germany, Guatemala, Hungary, India, Indonesia, Italy, Kenya, Lebanon, Lithuania, Malawi, Malta, Mexico, Mozambique, Netherlands, Nicaragua, Panama, Papua New Guinea, Paraguay, Peru, Philippines, Romania, Russia, Rwanda, Serbia, Sierra Leone, Spain, Switzerland, Tanzania UR, Togo, Uganda, Ukraine, Uruguay, USA, Venezuela, Zambia.
Consultative Status Consultative status granted from: *ECOSOC (#05331)* (Special). **NGO Relations** Supporting member of: *Digital Radio Mondiale Consortium (DRM, #05082).* [2011.11.28/XJ1167/**F**]

♦ World Farmers' Organisation (WFO) 21401
Organizzazione Mondiale Degli Agricoltori (OMA)
Secretariat Via del Tritone 102, 00187 Rome RM, Italy. T. +396421291. E-mail: info@wfo-oma.org.
URL: http://www.wfo-oma.org/
History 12 Jul 2011, Rome (Italy). Founded when draft statutes were adopted, following the dissolution of *International Federation of Agricultural Producers (IFAP, inactive)*. Registration: Italy. **Aims** As a member-based organisation representing a community of geographically balanced entrepreneurial farmers, see that their rights as food producers and role as economic actors are globally recognized regardless of their size (small, medium and large- scale), gender, and age; advocate for the worldwide farming community in international processes impacting the agricultural sector, scaling the local to the global, replicating successes and inspiring producers from one country to another. **Structure** General Assembly; Board of Directors; President; Working Groups and Committees; International Secretariat. **Languages** English, French, Italian, Spanish. **Staff** 13.00 FTE, paid. **Finance** Sources: contributions; members' dues. **Activities** Events/meetings. **Events** *General Assembly* Budapest (Hungary) 2022, *General Assembly* 2021, *General Assembly* Minneapolis, MN (USA) 2020, *General Assembly* Luxembourg (Luxembourg) 2019, *General Assembly* Moscow (Russia) 2018.
Members Farmers' organizations and cooperatives (70) in 48 countries:
Argentina, Austria, Belgium, Botswana, Burundi, Cambodia, Canada, Congo Brazzaville, Côte d'Ivoire, Croatia, Cyprus, Denmark, Ethiopia, Finland, France, Germany, Ghana, Haiti, Iceland, Ireland, Italy, Jamaica, Japan, Jordan, Kenya, Korea Rep, Luxembourg, Malawi, Malaysia, Mauritius, Mozambique, Netherlands, New Zealand, Norway, Paraguay, Poland, Russia, Rwanda, South Africa, Sweden, Switzerland, Thailand, Tunisia, Uganda, UK, USA, Zambia, Zimbabwe.
Included in the above, 1 organization listed in this Yearbook:
Conseil européen des jeunes agriculteurs (CEJA, #04689).
Consultative Status Consultative status granted from: *ECOSOC (#05331)* (Special); *UNEP (#20299)*. **NGO Relations** Member of (1): *Global Landscapes Forum (GLF, #10451)* (as Charter member of).
[2022.06.30/XJ4561/**C**]

♦ World Farriers' Association (WFA) 21402
President PO Box 6564, Albuquerque NM 87197-6564, USA. T. +15053456338. E-mail: wfassoc@msn.com.
History 1984, by Walt Taylor in conjunction with associations in Japan and the UK. **Aims** Promote exchange of information and education of farriers worldwide; foster and promote liaison between the farriery and *veterinary* professions; assist interested parties in founding and running farrier associations, organizations or societies; provide assistance to fledgling organizations through an adoption scheme; develop educational standards in farriery for students, instructors and schools; encourage international trade of materials used by and available to farriers, especially in developing countries; encourage international farriery competitions for all skill levels. **Activities** Collaborative programme *'Working Together for Equines'* launched, Jun 1989.
Members Membership countries not specified. [2015/XG0337/**D**]

♦ World Fashion Associations International / see World Fashion Organization (#21403)

♦ World Fashion Organization (WFO) 21403
Chairman and CEO WHO Headquarters, Ronald Reagan and International Trade Building, 1200 Pennsylvania Ave NW, PO Box 7889, Washington DC 20004, USA.
URL: http://www.wfoi.org/
History Functions under the title *World Fashion Associations International (WFA International)*. **Aims** Further the development of world fashion. **Structure** Council, comprising Executive Board and Advisory Board. Chairmanship, consisting of Chairman and 2 Vice-Chairmen. **Events** *Meeting* Seoul (Korea Rep) 2011.
[2015/XJ5583/**C**]

♦ World Federalist Movement – Movement for a Just World Order through a Strengthened United Nations (WFM) 21404
Mouvement fédéraliste mondial (MFM) – Stichting Wereldverbond van Wereld Federalisten
Main Office c/o WFBN, Laan van Nieuw Oost-Indië 252, 2593 CD The Hague, Netherlands. E-mail: info@wfm-igp.org.
USA Office c/o Citizens for Global Solutions, 5 Thomas Cir NW, Third Floor, Washington DC 20005, USA.
URL: http://www.wfm-igp.org/
History Sep 1946, Luxembourg. Established when plans were also made which led to the setting up of *Union of European Federalists, The (UEF, #20385)*, 15 Dec 1946, Paris (France). 1st Congress held 1947, Montreux (Switzerland).
For a period from 1976, *World Federalist Movement, 1954 (WFM, inactive)* comprised WAWF together with the then *'Parliamentarians for World Order (PWO)'*, currently *Parliamentarians for Global Action (PGA, #18208)* and the then *'Young World Federalists'*, subsequently *'World Federalist Youth Movement for a New International Order (WFM/NIO Youth)'*, currently *Youth for Development and Cooperation (YDC, inactive)*. The 1954 Movement was replaced by WAWF on 12 Aug 1987.
Statutes of the World Federalist Movement adopted at 6th Congress, 3 Sep 1954, London (UK); and amended: 9 Aug 1956, Stockport (UK); 17-22 Aug 1959; 20-27 Jun 1965, San Francisco CA (USA); 30 Jul – 5 Aug 1967, Oslo (Norway); 29 Jul – 3 Aug 1968, Helsingør (Denmark); 27 Aug 1970, Ottawa (Canada); 18 Aug 1972, Brussels (Belgium); 17 Jan 1975, Delhi (India); 30 Jul 1980, Tokyo (Japan); 14 Jul 1985, London (UK). New statutes adopted 1987, Philadelphia PA (USA). Former names and other names: *World Movement for World Federal Government (WMWFG)* – former (1947 to 1956); *Mouvement universel pour une fédération mondiale* – former (1947 to 1956); *World Association of World Federalists (WAWF)* – former (1956 to 1991); *Association mondiale des fédéralistes mondiaux (AMFM)* – former (1956 to 1991); *Asociación Universal de Federalistas Mundiales (AUFM)* – former (1956 to 1991); *Weltbund der Weltföderalisten (WdW)* – former (1956 to 1991); *Stichting Wereld Verbond van Wereld Federalisten* – former (1956 to 1991). Registration: Netherlands.
Aims Realize global peace and justice through development of democratic institutions and application of international law. **Structure** Congress (every 2 years), comprising representatives of member organizations based on size and status. Executive Committee/Board (meets twice a year) of 9 members. Other committees (5): Credentials; Finance; Outreach; Publications; Religion and Peace. Acts as secretariat for *Coalition for the International Criminal Court (CICC, #04062)* in the framework of setting up *International Criminal Court (ICC, #13108)*. **Languages** English. **Staff** 22.00 FTE, paid. **Finance** Sources: donations; grants; members' dues; private foundations. Annual budget: 1,500,000 USD. **Activities** Events/meetings; knowledge management/information dissemination; networking/liaising; projects/programmes. **Events** *International conference for the reform of international institutions* Geneva (Switzerland) 2006, *World congress* The Hague (Netherlands) 2004, *World congress* Copenhagen (Denmark) 2003, *World congress* London (UK) 2002, *The Hague appeal for peace conference* The Hague (Netherlands) 1999. **Publications** Congress reports; study conference reports and various special reports on the United Nations and other subjects. Information Services: Institute for Global Policy provides information/website on the International Criminal Court; Responsibility to Protect; UN reform; UN elections.
Members National organizations; associated organizations; youth; parliamentary organizations; individual supporters. Members in 20 countries:
Argentina, Australia, Bangladesh, Belgium, Denmark, Dominican Rep, France, Germany, India, Italy, Japan, Netherlands, New Zealand, Norway, Philippines, Spain, Switzerland, Uganda, UK, USA.
Associate members: organizations supporting the work of WFM, including 3 organizations listed in this Yearbook:
Democracia Global; *Democratic World Federalists*; *Workable World Trust (WWT).*
Consultative Status Consultative status granted from: *Council of Europe (CE, #04881)* (Participatory Status); *ECOSOC (#05331)* (Special); *UNEP (#20299)*; *African Commission on Human and Peoples' Rights (ACHPR, #00255)* (Observer). **IGO Relations** *UNESCO (#20322)*; *United Nations Conference on Environment and Development (UNCED)*. Associated with Department of Global Communications of the United Nations. **NGO Relations** Founding member of: *International Coalition for the Responsibility to Protect (ICRtoP, #12620)*. Member of: *Abolition 2000 – Global Network to Eliminate Nuclear Weapons (Abolition 2000, #00006)*; *Conference of Non-Governmental Organizations in Consultative Relationship with the United Nations (CONGO, #04635)*; *Corps mondial de secours (CMS, #04845)*; *EarthAction (EA, #05159)*; *NGO Committee on Disarmament, Peace and Security, New York NY (#17106)* and *NGO Committee for Disarmament, Geneva (#17105)*; *World Alliance to Transform the United Nations (WATUN, #21088)*. Institute for Global Policy is member of: *UBUNTU – World Forum of Civil Society Networks (inactive)*. Affiliated youth organization: *Asian Youth Centre (AYC, #01787)*. Involved in: *Hague Appeal for Peace (HAP, #10848)*. Cooperates with: *Global Action to Prevent War (GAWP).* [2022/XC3477/**F**]

♦ World Federalist Press Association (inactive)
♦ World Federalist University (inactive)
♦ World Federation of Academic Institutions for Global Health (inactive)

♦ World Federation of Acupuncture-Moxibustion Societies (WFAS) . . 21405
Fédération mondiale des sociétés d'acupuncture
SG F7- B Dongjiu Mansion, Xizhaosi Street, Dong Cheng District, 100061 Beijing, China. T. +861087194973. Fax +861087194952. E-mail: office@wfas.org.cn.
URL: http://www.wfas.org.cn/
History Founded Nov 1987, Beijing (China), as *World Federation of Acupuncture Societies*. **Aims** Promote understanding and cooperation among acupuncture-moxibustion groups worldwide; encourage academic exchange on acupuncture science and thus contribute to health of mankind; strive for legal status of acupuncture in all countries; develop acupuncture education and training. **Structure** General Assembly (every 4 years, usually at World Conference); Executive Committee; Sub-Committees (7); Secretariat in Beijing (China), headed by Secretary General. **Languages** Chinese, English. **Staff** 6.00 FTE, paid. **Finance** Sources: members' dues. **Activities** Events/meetings; training/education. **Events** *International Symposium on Acupuncture-Moxibustion* Zhuhai (China) 2021, *International Symposium on Acupuncture-Moxibustion* Antalya (Turkey) 2019, *World Scientific and Cultural Meeting on Acupuncture* Paris (France) 2018, *General Assembly* Beijing (China) 2017, *World Conference* Daegu (Korea Rep) 2017. **Publications** *WFAS Communication* (12 a year); *World Journal of Acupuncture-Moxibustion* (4 a year); *Commerative Album* (on occasion of big event).
Members Members and Associate Members. Societies representing acupuncture workers in 46 countries and territories:
Argentina, Australia, Austria, Belgium, Bolivia, Brazil, Canada, Chile, China, Colombia, Egypt, France, Germany, Hong Kong, Hungary, India, Indonesia, Iran Islamic Rep, Ireland, Israel, Italy, Japan, Korea Rep, Macau, Malaysia, Mexico, Netherlands, New Zealand, Norway, Philippines, Poland, Portugal, Russia, Singapore, Slovenia, South Africa, Spain, Sweden, Switzerland, Thailand, Türkiye, UK, Ukraine, USA, Venezuela, Vietnam.
Included in the above, 2 organizations listed in this Yearbook:
European Foundation of Traditional Chinese Medicine; *Hispano-American Association of Acupuncture.*
Consultative Status Consultative status granted from: *WHO (#20950)* (Official Relations). **NGO Relations** In the process of establishing: *World Foundation of Acupuncture (no recent information).*
[2019.08.28/XC0075/y/**C**]

♦ World Federation of Acupuncture Societies / see World Federation of Acupuncture-Moxibustion Societies (#21405)

♦ World Federation of ADHD 21406
Global Head Office c/o Wartmann & Merker, Kirchgasse 48, 8001 Zurich ZH, Switzerland. T. +49406708820. Fax +49406703283. E-mail: adhd@cpo-hanser.de.
URL: http://www.adhd-federation.org/
History 2007, Würzburg (Germany). Founded at the 1st International Congress. Former names and other names: *World Federation of Attention Deficit Hyperactivity Disorder* – alias. Registration: Swiss Civil Code, Switzerland. **Aims** Support and promote worldwide clinical and scientific study projects, including training activities in the field of ADHD; support information exchange between scientists, physicians, health experts, ADHD lay organisations, self-help groups and the public; collaborate with other related professional and lay organizations. **Structure** Board. **Languages** English, German, Spanish. **Staff** 2.00 FTE, paid. **Finance** Sources: members' dues. **Activities** Awards/prizes/competitions; events/meetings; publishing activities; standards/guidelines. **Events** *From Child to Adult Disorder* Amsterdam (Netherlands) 2023, *From Child to Adult Disorder* Zurich (Switzerland) 2021, *From Child to Adult Disorder* Lisbon (Portugal) 2019, *From Child to Adult Disorder* Vancouver, BC (Canada) 2017, *From Child to Adult Disorder* Glasgow (UK) 2015. **Publications** *The WF ADHD International Consensus Statement* in Arabic, Catalan, Chinese, English, French, German, Italian, Russian, Spanish, Turkish; *The World Federation of ADHD Guide* in Chinese, English, Spanish. Scientific papers.
Members Full in 30 countries:
Australia, Austria, Belgium, Brazil, Canada, Chile, Croatia, Denmark, France, Germany, Guatemala, Iceland, India, Israel, Italy, Japan, Mexico, Netherlands, New Zealand, Norway, Pakistan, Philippines, Poland, South Africa, Spain, Sweden, Switzerland, Türkiye, UK, USA. [2022.02.02/XJ0654/**C**]

♦ World Federation of Advertisers (WFA) 21407
Fédération mondiale des annonceurs (FMA)
CEO Av Louise 140, 1050 Brussels, Belgium. T. +3225025740. Fax +3225025666. E-mail: info@wfanet.org.
URL: https://wfanet.org/
History 28 Oct 1953, Brussels (Belgium). Present title adopted, Brussels, following decision of meeting 1984, Rio de Janeiro (Brazil), when organization was expanded to include major companies and individuals in countries not having national associations. Former names and other names: *International Union of Advertisers Associations (IUAA)* – former; *Union internationale des associations d'annonceurs (UIAA)* – former. Registration: Banque-Carrefour des Entreprises, No/ID: 0408.292.301, Start date: 11 Sep 1961, Belgium; EU Transparency Register, No/ID: 6440918199-49, Start date: 15 Jul 2008. **Aims** Ensure conditions worldwide to enable members to improve their effectiveness and efficiency; enable advertisers to conduct activities in conditions of free speech and free market, especially in common markets and free trade areas; defend and, where possible, extend freedom of commercial expression and advertising; challenge over-*regulation* of advertising through legislation enacted by national or international authorities; ensure recognition by governments, opinion leaders and supranational bodies of the contribution of advertising to economic growth and improved standards of living; assist advertisers' associations in their contacts with public authorities or other professional organizations; advocate self-regulation of the industry worldwide, based on the principle that advertising should be legal, honest, decent and truthful; carry out studies and collect documentation on problems regarding advertising in all its forms; promote advertising in the economy of each country; allow exchange of information among member groups and with government bodies which regulate, limit or prohibit commercial expression. **Structure** General Assembly (annual); Executive Committee; Officers; National Advertisers Council (NAC) (annual); European Action Group; Committees (5); International Secretariat based in Brussels (Belgium). **Languages** Dutch, English, French, German, Italian, Spanish. **Staff** 22.00 FTE, paid. **Finance** Sources: members' dues. **Activities** Advocacy/lobbying/activism; knowledge management/information dissemination; politics/policy/regulatory. **Events** *Global Marketer Week Conference* Istanbul (Türkiye) 2023, *Global Marketer Week Conference* Athens (Greece) 2022, *Global Marketer Week Conference* 2021, *Chief Marketing Officers Forum* Singapore (Singapore) 2020, *Media Forum Asia Pacific* Singapore (Singapore) 2020. **Publications** *Global Newsletter*. Annual Report; brief.
Members National associations in 55 countries. Membership countries not specified.
Corporate (56 international companies). Membership countries not specified.
Consultative Status Consultative status granted from: *World Intellectual Property Organization (WIPO, #21593)* (Permanent Observer Status). **IGO Relations** Observer status with (1): *Codex Alimentarius Commission (CAC, #04081)*. Cooperates with (8): *ECOSOC (#05331)*; *European Commission (EC, #06633)*; *European Economic and Social Committee (EESC, #06963)*; *European Parliament (EP, #08146)*; *FAO (#09260)*; *International Telecommunication Union (ITU, #15673)*; *UNEP (#20299)*; *WHO (#20950).*

NGO Relations Member of (2): *European Interactive Digital Advertising Alliance (EDAA, #07582); International Council for Advertising Self-Regulation (ICAS, #12984).* Instrumental in setting up (1): *Global Alliance for Responsible Media (GARM, #10224).*
Associate expert group of *Business and Industry Advisory Committee to the OECD (BIAC, #03385).*
Close relationship with:
- *Association of Commercial Television in Europe (ACT, #02436);*
- *Commercial Film Producers Europe (CFP-E, #04202);*
- *Cosmetics Europe – The Personal Care Association (#04852);*
- *egta – association of television and radio sales houses (#05397);*
- *European Advertising Standards Alliance (EASA, #05829);*
- *European Association of Communications Agencies (EACA, #05983);*
- *European Broadcasting Union (EBU, #06404);*
- *European Newspaper Publishers' Association (ENPA, #08048);*
- *Federation of European Data & Marketing (FEDMA, #09499);*
- *FIPP (#09776);*
- *FoodDrinkEurope (#09841);*
- *International Advertising Association (IAA, #11590);*
- *International Chamber of Commerce (ICC, #12534);*
- *International Federation of Audit Bureaux of Certification (IFABC, #13366);*
- *World Association of Research Professionals (ESOMAR, #21182).* [2023/XC2680/**B**]

♦ World Federation Against Drugs (WFAD) 21408

SG PO Box 10136, SE-100 55 Stockholm, Sweden. T. +4686442174. E-mail: info@wfad.se.
URL: http://www.wfad.se/

History 2009. Founded following first Forum held 2008, Stockholm (Sweden). Registration: EU Transparency Register, No/ID: 82494487698-33. **Aims** Work for a drug-free world. **Structure** Board, comprising President, Vice-President, Regional Representatives (Africa, Asia, Europe, Latin America, North America) and 2 Special Advisors. **Activities** Organizes *World Forum Against Drugs.* **Events** *Forum* Vienna (Austria) 2020, *Forum* Gothenburg (Sweden) 2018, *Forum* Vienna (Austria) 2016, *Meeting* Vienna (Austria) 2015, *Forum* Stockholm (Sweden) 2014. **Members** Full (organizations); Individual. Membership countries not specified. **Consultative Status** Consultative status granted from: *ECOSOC (#05331)* (Special). **NGO Relations** Member of: *Civil Society Forum on Drugs (CSFD, #03968).* [2021/XJ8272/**C**]

- ♦ World Federation of Agricultural Workers (inactive)
- ♦ World Federation of Agriculture and Food Workers (inactive)
- ♦ World Federation of Air Line Pilots / see International Federation of Air Line Pilots' Associations (#13349)

♦ World Federation of Amateur Orchestras (WFAO) 21409

Chairperson Koyo Building 3F, 46 Tachibana, Toyohashi, Aichi, 441-8028 Japan. T. +81532336885. Fax +81532336875.
Vice-Chairman Bachmanstraat 7, 2596 JA The Hague, Netherlands. T. +31703462658. Fax +31703462658.
URL: http://www.wfao.org/

History Aug 1998. **NGO Relations** *European Association of Amateur Orchestras (EAAO, inactive)* is founding member. [2010/XD8493/**D**]

♦ World Federation for Animals (WFA) 21410

Address not obtained.
URL: https://wfa.org/

History Registration: 501(c)(3) non-profit, USA; EU Transparency Register, No/ID: 403197145826-48, Start date: 15 Mar 2022. **Aims** Improve the well-being of all animals and end exploitation and suffering. **Structure** General Assembly; Board. **Finance** Sources: members' dues. **Activities** Advocacy/lobbying/activism; knowledge management/information dissemination; research/documentation.
Members Founding organizations in countries:
Australia, Belgium, Denmark, France, Germany, Sweden, UK, USA.
Africa Network for Animal Welfare (ANAW, #00301); Asia for Animals Coalition (AfA, #01250); Compassion in World Farming (CIWF, #04414); Cruelty Free International; Eurogroup for Animals (#05690); Vier Pfoten International (#20776); World Animal Net (WAN, inactive); World Animal Protection (#21092); World Horse Welfare. [2021/AA2147/y/**C**]

- ♦ World Federation of Arab-Islamic International Schools (inactive)

♦ World Federation of Associations of Pediatric Surgeons (WOFAPS) . 21411

Fédération mondiale des associations de chirurgiens pédiatres – Foederatio Mundialis Associationum Nationalium Internationalium Pediatricae Scientiae Chirurgicae

SG/Treas Goethe University Frankfurt, Dept of Pediatric Surgery and Pediatric Urology, 60323 Frankfurt-Main, Germany. E-mail: info@wofaps.org.
Pres Alexandria University, 22 El-Guish Rd, El-Shatby, Alexandria, 21526, Egypt.
Registered Address Rue du Rhône 96-98, 1211 Geneva, Switzerland. E-mail: info@wofaps.org.
URL: http://www.wofaps.org/

History 15 Oct 1974, Sao Paulo (Brazil). Former names and other names: *International Society of Pediatric Surgeons* – alias. Registration: Switzerland. **Aims** Promote paediatric surgery throughout the world. **Structure** General Meeting (every 3 years); Executive Committee. **Languages** English, French, Spanish. **Staff** 1.00 FTE, paid; 1.00 FTE, voluntary. **Finance** Sources: meeting proceeds; members' dues. **Events** *World Congress of Pediatric Surgery* Prague (Czechia) 2022, *World Congress* Doha (Qatar) 2019, *World Congress* Washington, DC (USA) 2016, *World Congress* Berlin (Germany) 2013, *World congress* Delhi (India) 2010.
Members Associations (Scandinavian countries being grouped in a single organization) in 43 countries:
Argentina, Australia, Austria, Belgium, Brazil, Canada, Chile, Colombia, Croatia, Czechia, Denmark, Egypt, Finland, France, Germany, Greece, Hungary, India, Indonesia, Israel, Italy, Japan, Lebanon, Mexico, Netherlands, New Zealand, Norway, Pakistan, Peru, Poland, Portugal, Serbia, South Africa, Spain, Sweden, Switzerland, Tunisia, Türkiye, UK, United Arab Emirates, Uruguay, USA, Venezuela.
CDH International.
Corresponding members in 6 countries:
Algeria, China, Germany, Iraq, Panama, Philippines.
NGO Relations Affiliate Society of: *International Pediatric Association (IPA, #14541).* Speciality member of: *International Federation of Surgical Colleges (IFSC, #13560).* Instrumental in setting up: *International Charitable Fund for Children in Disasters (no recent information).* [2022/XC4487/**C**]

- ♦ World Federation of Associations of Poison Centres and Clinical Toxicology Centres (inactive)

♦ World Federation of Associations of Teacher Education (WFATE) . . . 21412

Exec Sec 35 Brevoort Rd, Columbus OH 43214, USA. T. +14186510227. E-mail: execsecretary@worldfate.org.
URL: http://www.worldfate.org/

History Founded 2010, Chicago IL (USA), at the first World Congress. Incorporated in the State of Ohio (USA). **Aims** Establish a worldwide community for teacher education; promote the development of teacher education associations throughout the world; represent the interests of teacher education associations to international bodies and organizations; provide equitable educational opportunities by promoting quality teacher education throughout the world. **Structure** Directorate, consisting of up to 3 representatives from each participating organization; Board. Officers (3). **Languages** English. **Staff** 3.00 FTE, voluntary. **Finance** Sources: donations; meeting proceeds; members' dues. Annual budget: 5,000 USD. **Activities** Events/meetings; knowledge management/information dissemination; publishing activities; research/documentation; training/education. Active in: China, Kenya, Spain, USA. **Events** *Biennial Conference* Houston, TX (USA) 2021, *Biennial Conference* Houston, TX (USA) 2020, *Biennial Conference* Melbourne, VIC (Australia) 2018, *Biennial Conference* Barcelona (Spain) 2016, *Biennial Conference / World Congress* Beijing (China) 2014. **Publications** *Journal of the World Federation of Associations of Teacher Education.*
Members Organizations in 2 countries:
Australia, USA.
Individuals in 22 countries and territories:
Australia, Austria, Belgium, Canada, China, Croatia, Czechia, Finland, France, Germany, Hong Kong, Hungary, India, Ireland, Kenya, Mongolia, Philippines, South Africa, Spain, Sweden, Türkiye, USA.
IGO Relations *UNESCO (#20322).* [2021/XM8174/**C**]

- ♦ World Federation of the Associations for the Treatment of Opioid Dependence / see World Federation for the Treatment of Opioid Dependence (#21495)

♦ World Federation of Athletic Training and Therapy (WFATT) 21413

Pres Dept Kinesiology and Applied Health, Univ of Winnipeg, 515 Portage Ave, Winnipeg MB R3B 2E9, Canada. T. +12047869190.
URL: http://www.wfatt.org/

History Founded 1997. **Aims** Provide leadership to advance international interests of members for the common goal of optimal health care for physically active populations. **Structure** Board of Directors; Executive Committee. **Languages** English. **Staff** None. **Finance** Members' dues. Annual budget: about Canadian $ 38,000. **Activities** Events/meetings. **Events** *World Congress* Tokyo (Japan) 2019, *World Congress* Madrid (Spain) 2017, *World Congress* St Louis, MO (USA) 2015, *World Congress* Dublin (Ireland) 2013, *World congress* Banff, AB (Canada) 2011. **Publications** *WFATT Action.*
Members National organizations (11) in 8 countries and territories:
Canada, Ireland, Japan, Korea Rep, South Africa, Taiwan, UK, USA.
NGO Relations Member of: *International Council of Sport Science and Physical Education (ICSSPE, #13077).* [2019/XD8769/**D**]

- ♦ World Federation of Attention Deficit Hyperactivity Disorder / see World Federation of ADHD (#21406)

♦ World Federation of Ayrshire Breed Societies 21414

Gen Manager Westburn House, McNee Road, Prestwick, KA9 2PB, UK. T. +447771826403. E-mail: society@ayrshirescs.org.
URL: http://www.worldayrshirefederation.com/

History Also known as *Ayrshires-International.* **Aims** Promote and organize semen, livestock and embryo exchange between countries; represent the field to governments and other bodies on matters concerning Ayrshire *cattle*; promote Ayrshire cattle to member and non-member countries as part of breed development. **Structure** Executive. **Languages** English, French. **Staff** Voluntary. **Finance** Members' dues. **Activities** Events/meetings. **Events** *Ayrshire World Conference* Adelaide, SA (Australia) / Melbourne, VIC (Australia) 2020, *Ayrshire World Conference* Springfield, MA (USA) 2016, *Ayrshire World Conference* Cape Town (South Africa) 2012, *Ayrshire World Conference* Hämeenlinna (Finland) 2008.
Members Full in 8 countries:
Australia, Canada, Finland, New Zealand, South Africa, Sweden, UK, USA.
Associate in one country:
Colombia. [2020/XM0932/**F**]

♦ World Federation of the Bergen Belsen Associations 21415

Contact PO Box 288, Lenox Hill Station, New York NY 10021, USA.

History Founded Apr 1945. **Aims** Perpetuate memory of the victims of the concentration camp Bergen Belsen and all other victims of the *Nazi Holocaust*; maintain memorials; support research and publications. **Events** *Meeting* Hannover (Germany) / Bergen-Belsen (Germany) 2014, *Meeting* Hannover (Germany) / Bergen-Belsen (Germany) 2013, *Meeting* Hannover (Germany) / Bergen-Belsen (Germany) 2012, *Meeting* Hannover (Germany) / Bergen-Belsen (Germany) 2011, *Meeting* Hannover (Germany) / Bergen-Belsen (Germany) 2010.
Members Groups in several countries, mainly in 3 countries:
Canada, Israel, USA. [2014.12.25/XE3421/**E**]

♦ World Federation of Building Service Contractors (WFBSC) 21416

Fédération mondiale des entreprises de nettoyage

Headquarters 330 N Wabash Ave, Ste 2000, Chicago IL 60611, USA.
URL: http://www.wfbsc.org/

History 1979, Bern (Switzerland). Registered in accordance with UK law. **Aims** Promote worldwide recognition of the size, scope, role and value of the professional building service contractor; increase knowledge and improve professional competence of members; generate and maintain professional and social relations between manufacturing companies (associate members) and contractors (other members); provide an international forum for contractors to address problems of common concern; represent member associations of building service and *cleaning* service contractors at international level. **Structure** Board of Directors. Administered by BSCA International. **Languages** English. **Staff** 3.00 FTE, paid. **Finance** Members' dues based on annual budget. **Activities** World Congress (every 2 years). Worldwide educational fora. **Events** *Global Executive Summit* Berlin (Germany) 2019, *World Congress* Berlin (Germany) 2017, *World Congress* Tokyo (Japan) 2016, *World Congress* New York, NY (USA) 2014, *World congress* Curitiba (Brazil) 2012. **Publications** *International Dimensions* (4 a year).
Members Full national building service contractors' associations; cleaning contractors' associations. Associate firms supplying the industry. Affiliate associations of allied industries. Subscribing educational organizations. Honorary. Full members in 18 countries and territories:
Argentina, Australia, Belgium, Brazil, Canada, France, Germany, India, Italy, Japan, Korea DPR, Netherlands, New Zealand, Portugal, Sweden, Taiwan, UK, USA.
Associate members in 4 countries:
Australia, Netherlands, UK, USA.
Included in the above, 1 organization listed in this Yearbook:
Building Service Contractors Association International (BSCAI).
IGO Relations *WHO (#20950)* (Liaison Status). **NGO Relations** Instrumental in setting up: *Asian Building Maintenance Association (ABMA, #01368).* [2018/XC0112/y/**C**]

- ♦ World Federation of Building and Woodworkers Unions (inactive)
- ♦ World Federation for Cancer Care (inactive)
- ♦ World Federation of Cataract and Refractive Surgeons (inactive)
- ♦ World Federation of Catholic Therapeutic Communities (inactive)
- ♦ World Federation of Catholic Young Women and Girls (inactive)
- ♦ World Federation of Catholic Youth (inactive)
- ♦ World Federation for Central Service in Hospitals (inactive)

♦ World Federation for Chess Composition (WFCC) 21417

Treas address not obtained.
Pres address not obtained. E-mail: loyaldragon@gmail.com.
URL: http://www.wfcc.ch/

History Successor to *Fédération internationale des échecs (FIDE, #09627)* Permanent Commission for Chess Composition (PCCC), set up 1954. **Aims** Disseminate and encourage chess composition throughout the world. **Structure** Meeting; Presidium; Delegates; Committees. **Activities** Awards/prizes/competitions; events/meetings; knowledge management/information dissemination; sporting activities; standards/guidelines. **Events** *World Congress* Geneva (Switzerland) 2014, *World Congress / Congress* Batumi (Georgia) 2013, *World Congress* Kobe (Japan) 2012, *Congress* Jesi (Italy) 2011, *Congress* Crete (Greece) 2010.
Members Full in 41 countries:
Argentina, Austria, Azerbaijan, Belarus, Belgium, Bosnia-Herzegovina, Brazil, Bulgaria, Croatia, Czechia, Denmark, Estonia, Finland, France, Georgia, Germany, Great Britain, Greece, Hungary, Israel, Italy, Japan, Kazakhstan, Latvia, Lithuania, Moldova, Mongolia, Morocco, Netherlands, North Macedonia, Poland, Romania, Russia, Serbia, Slovakia, Slovenia, Spain, Sweden, Switzerland, Ukraine, USA. [2018/XJ6752/**C**]

♦ World Federation of Chinese Catering Industry (WFCCI) 21418

SG 45 Fuxingmennei Street, Xicheng District, 100801 Beijing, China. T. +861066094199 – +861066094184. Fax +861066094151. E-mail: wacc1991@sina.com.
URL: http://www.wacc.cn/

History Founded 1991, as *World Association of Chinese Cuisine (WACC)*, by China Cuisine Association. **Aims** Organize academic research and discussion on Chinese cuisine theory and culture worldwide; promote China's catering culture. **Activities** Events/meetings; training/education; networking/liaising. **Events** *Congress* Beijing (China) 2008, *Congress* Guangzhou (China) 2004, *Congress* Tokyo (Japan) 2000, *Congress* Toronto, ON (Canada) 1995, *Congress* Beijing (China) 1991. **Members** Full (80) in 9 countries. Membership countries not specified. [2016/XD3270/t/**D**]

♦ **World Federation of Chinese Medicine Societies (WFCMS)** **21419**

Fédération mondiale des sociétés de médecine chinoise

SG Room 505 – Bldg A, Wealth Garden, No 19 Xiaoying Street, Chaoyang District, 100101 Beijing, China. T. +861058650240 – +861058650036. Fax +861058650018 – +861058650041. E-mail: tcm_forum@vip.163.com – wfcms.hyj518@vip.163.com.

URL: http://en.wfcms.org/

History Founded 25 Sep 2003, Beijing (China). **Aims** Promote international exchange, dissemination and development of traditional Chinese medicine (TCM); develop into the base of strategic research on the internationalization of TCM, the base for the research, formulating and implementation of the international standards of TCM and the base for Chinese Medicine science, information, talents and products exchange. **Structure** Council Board; Supervision Board; Committee for Senior Advisors; Advisory Committee for Working; Specialty Committee. **Languages** Chinese, English. **Staff** 60.00 FTE, paid. **Finance** Sources: donations; members' dues. **Activities** Events/meetings; knowledge management/information dissemination; standards/guidelines; training/education. **Events** *World Congress of Chinese Medicine* Sao Paulo (Brazil) 2022, *World Congress of Chinese Medicine* Hong Kong (Hong Kong) 2021, *World Congress of Chinese Medicine* Beijing (China) 2020, *World Congress of Chinese Medicine* Budapest (Hungary) 2019, *World Congress of Chinese Medicine* Rome (Italy) 2018. **Publications** *World Chinese Medicine* (12 a year) – journal. *International Standard Chinese-English Basic Nomenclature of Chinese Medicine*; *International Standard Chinese-French Basic Nomenclature of Chinese Medicine*; *International Standard Chinese-Italian Basic Nomenclature of Chinese Medicine*; *International Standard Chinese-Portuguese Basic Nomenclature of Chinese Medicine*; *International Standard Chinese-Spanish Basic Nomencla ture of Chinese Medicine*; *World Classification Standard for Professional Titles of Chinese Medicine Doctors*; *World Core Courses of Chinese Medicine Specialty*; *World Standard of Chinese Medicine Undergraduate (pre-CMD) Education*; *World Standard of Establishment and Service CM Clinic*.

Members Organizations (251) in 67 countries. Membership countries not specified. Included in the above 7 organizations listed in this Yearbook:

Included in the above 7 organizations listed in this Yearbook:

Balkan Su Jok Therapy Centre (no recent information); *European Foundation of Traditional Chinese Medicine*; *International Institute of Holistic Medicine*; *Nordic Modern Natural Therapeutics Society (no recent information)*; *Southern Africa Traditional Chinese Medicine Academy (no recent information)*; *World Natural Medicine Foundation (WNMF)*; *World Union of Traditional Medicine, USA (no recent information)*.

Consultative Status Consultative status granted from: *WHO (#20950)* (Official). **IGO Relations** *UNESCO (#20322)* – Intangible Heritage Culture. **NGO Relations** Liaison organization of: *International Organization for Standardization (ISO, #14473)*. [2019/XC0137/y/C]

♦ **World Federation of Chiropractic (WFC)** **21420**

Fédération mondiale de chiropratique – Federación Mundial de Quiropractica

SG 2 St Clair Ave West, 18th Floor, Toronto ON M4V 1L5, Canada. T. +16472558030. Fax +18888376748. E-mail: info@wfc.org.

URL: https://www.wfc.org

History 2 Oct 1988, Sydney, NSW (Australia). Founded at World Chiropractic Congress. **Aims** Advance awareness, utilization and integration of chiropractic internationally. **Structure** Annual Members Meeting; Board of Directors; Executive Committee. **Languages** English, French, Spanish. **Staff** 5.00 FTE, paid. **Finance** Sources: donations; members' dues. **Events** *WFC Biennial Congress* Gold Coast, QLD (Australia) 2023, *Education Conference* St Louis, MO (USA) 2022, *Biennial Congress* 2021, *Biennial Congress* Berlin (Germany) 2019, *Education Conference* London (UK) 2018. **Publications** *Quarterly World Report*.

Members National associations in 93 countries and territories:

Argentina, Australia, Austria, Azerbaijan, Bahamas, Bahrain, Barbados, Belgium, Belize, Bermuda, Bolivia, Botswana, Brazil, Canada, Cayman Is, Chile, Colombia, Congo Brazzaville, Costa Rica, Croatia, Cyprus, Denmark, Ecuador, Egypt, El Salvador, Estonia, Ethiopia, Finland, France, Germany, Ghana, Greece, Guatemala, Honduras, Hong Kong, Hungary, Iceland, India, Indonesia, Iran Islamic Rep, Ireland, Israel, Italy, Japan, Jordan, Kenya, Korea Rep, Lebanon, Libya, Liechtenstein, Luxembourg, Malaysia, Malta, Mauritius, Mexico, Morocco, Namibia, Netherlands, New Zealand, Norway, Pakistan, Panama, Peru, Philippines, Poland, Portugal, Qatar, Russia, Rwanda, Saudi Arabia, Serbia, Singapore, Slovakia, South Africa, Spain, Sri Lanka, St Kitts-Nevis, Sweden, Switzerland, Syrian AR, Taiwan, Thailand, Trinidad-Tobago, Türkiye, Turks-Caicos, Uganda, UK, Ukraine, United Arab Emirates, USA, Virgin Is UK, Zambia, Zimbabwe.

Consultative Status Consultative status granted from: *WHO (#20950)* (Official Relations). **NGO Relations** Founding member of: *Global Rehabilitation Alliance (#10565)*. Member of: *Council for International Organizations of Medical Sciences (CIOMS, #04905)*. Accrediting agencies include: *Councils on Chiropractic Education International (CCEI, #04916)*. [2022.12.07/XD1950/y/B]

♦ World Federation of Christian Life Communities / see Christian Life Community (#03905)

♦ World Federation of Christian Pastoral Counselors (see: #21330)

♦ World Federation of Clerical Workers / see World Organization of Workers (#21697)

♦ **World Federation of Colleges and Polytechnics (WFCP)** **21421**

Coordinator Colleges and Institutes Canada, Ste 701, 1 Rideau Street, Ottawa ON K1N 8S7, Canada. T. +16137462222. Fax +16137466721. E-mail: secretariat@wfcp.org.

URL: http://www.wfcp.org/

History Founded 24 Mar 2002, Melbourne (Australia), during 2nd World Congress of Colleges and Polytechnics, when adopted first constitution, prior to which it existed as an informal network. In 1999, the Association of Canadian Community Colleges (now known as Colleges and Institutes Canada) hosted the 1st World Congress of Colleges and Polytechnics in Québec QC (Canada). The Congress was planned by an International Planning Committee, with partners from the USA, Canada, New Zealand, Colombia, South Africa, Commonwealth Africa, India and South East Asia. **Aims** Be the international voice of colleges, institutes and polytechnics; link members, offering them quality services, networking and collective action; advocate for colleges, institutes and polytechnics in public debate and to outside partners; provide a platform for members to learn from each other and work on collaborative projects; foster linkages between employers and colleges, institutes and polytechnics. **Structure** Congress (every 2 years); Board; Regions (4); Affinity Groups (7); Secretariat in Ottawa ON (Canada). **Languages** English. **Staff** 0.50 FTE, paid. **Finance** Members' dues. **Activities** Events/meetings; knowledge management/information dissemination; politics/policy/regulatory; research/documentation; training/education; awards/prizes/competitions. **Events** *World Congress* San Sebastian (Spain) 2020, *World Congress* Melbourne, VIC (Australia) 2018, *World Congress* Vitória (Brazil) 2016, *World Congress* Beijing (China) 2014, *World Congress* Halifax, NS (Canada) 2012. **Publications** *WFCP Newsletter* (3-4 a year).

Members Organizations, colleges and polytechnics (38) in 42 countries and territories:

Australia, Basque Country, Botswana, Brazil, Cambodia, Canada, Chile, China, Croatia, Eswatini, Gambia, Ghana, Hong Kong, India, Kazakhstan, Kenya, Latvia, Lesotho, Malawi, Mauritius, Mexico, Mozambique, Namibia, Netherlands, Nigeria, Peru, Portugal, Russia, Saudi Arabia, Senegal, Seychelles, Sierra Leone, Singapore, South Africa, Spain, Tunisia, UK, United Arab Emirates, USA, Vietnam, Zambia, Zimbabwe.

Included in the above, 2 organizations listed in this Yearbook:

Association of Caribbean Tertiary Institutions (ACTI, #02412); *Commonwealth Association of Polytechnics in Africa (CAPA, #04308)*.

IGO Relations None. [2016.12.19/XM2659/y/D]

♦ World Federation of Coloproctology / see International Council of Coloproctology (#13009)

♦ The World Federation of Consuls / see World Federation of Consuls (#21422)

♦ **World Federation of Consuls (FICAC)** **21422**

Permanent Secretary IT TOWER, Av Louise 480, 1050 Brussels, Belgium. T. +32472330955. E-mail: permanent.secretariat@ficacworld.org.

Pres address not obtained. E-mail: president@ficacworld.org – president.office@ficacworld.org.

URL: http://www.ficacworld.org/

History 2 Oct 1982, Copenhagen (Denmark). Founded under the *Copenhagen Consular Declaration*, being originally restricted to European Consular Corps and Associations. Opened internationally under revised constitution adopted 1986, taking note of *Vienna Convention on Consular Relations (1963)* and other conventions. Constitution revised, 11 May 1998, Eilat (Israel); most recently revised, 2018. Former names and other names: *Fédération internationale des corps et associations consulaires (FICAC)* – full title; *The World Federation of Consuls* – full title; *International Federation of Consular Corps and Associations* – full title. Registration: Banque-Carrefour des Entreprises, No/ID: 0882.537.672, Start date: 1 Jul 2006, Belgium. **Aims** Act as a forum to share experiences and coordinate efforts to enhance the status and effectiveness of Consuls; bring together Consular Associations and Corps from around the globe. **Structure** General Assembly (every 3 years); Executive Committee; Regional Committees; Central Committees; Secretariat. **Languages** English. **Staff** Voluntary. **Finance** Sources: members' dues. **Activities** Events/meetings. Active in all member countries. **Events** *World Congress of Consuls* Limassol (Cyprus) 2022, *HCCN-FICAC Regional Conference* Kathmandu (Nepal) 2019, *Central and Eastern Europe Conference* Sofia (Bulgaria) 2019, *Triennial Congress and General Assembly* Brussels (Belgium) 2018, *Conference* Tel Aviv (Israel) 2017. **Publications** *FICAC Newsletter*. *FICAC Who's Who* by K S Bhalla; *Introduction to International Consular Cooperation*; *Privileges and Obligations for Honorary Consuls*.

Members Consular associations and bodies having signed the Consular Declaration of 2 Oct 1982, in 68 countries and territories:

Albania, Argentina, Aruba, Bahamas, Bangladesh, Barbados, Belarus, Belgium, Benin, Brazil, Bulgaria, Chile, Colombia, Croatia, Curaçao, Cyprus, Czechia, Dominican Rep, Ecuador, France, Georgia, Ghana, Greece, Haiti, Honduras, Hong Kong, Hungary, India, Indonesia, Israel, Italy, Jamaica, Jordan, Kazakhstan, Korea Rep, Kyrgyzstan, Lithuania, Macau, Malaysia, Mali, Malta, Mauritania, Monaco, Montenegro, Morocco, Mozambique, Nepal, Nigeria, Norway, Pakistan, Philippines, Romania, Russia, Saudi Arabia, Serbia, Slovenia, Sri Lanka, St Kitts-Nevis, Suriname, Thailand, Trinidad-Tobago, Tunisia, Türkiye, Uganda, Ukraine, USA, Vietnam, Zambia.

Consultative Status Consultative status granted from: *United Nations (UN, #20515)* (Consultative Status – ECOSOC). **IGO Relations** Accredited by (3): *European Community (inactive)*; *OAS (#17629)*; *United Nations (UN, #20515)*. Associated with Department of Global Communications of the United Nations. **NGO Relations** Memorandum of Understanding with (3): *Asociación de las Camaras de Comercio e Industria del Mediterraneo (ASCAME, #02112)*; Fondation Prince Albert II de Monaco; *Interlegal (#11517)*. International Associate of: *World Federation of United Nations Associations (WFUNA, #21499)*. [2023.02.21/XD1019/C]

♦ World Federation for Coral Reef Conservation (internationally oriented national body)

♦ **World Federation of Critical Care Nurses (WFCCN)** **21423**

Pres c/o The Prince Charles Hosp, 627 Rode Road, Chermside QLD, Brisbane QLD 4032, Australia. T. +61731394000.

Mailing Address PO Box 50, Dayboro QLD 4521, Australia. E-mail: info@wfccn.org.

URL: http://www.wfccn.org/

History 30 Oct 2001, Sydney, NSW (Australia). **Aims** Assist critical care nurses and nursing organizations. **Structure** Council of Representatives; Board of Directors. **Languages** English. **Staff** Voluntary. **Finance** Members' dues. Other sources: donations; corporate sponsorship. **Activities** Projects/programmes; events/meetings. **Events** *World Congress* Philippines 2022, *World Congress* Dubai (United Arab Emirates) 2021, *World Congress* Dubai (United Arab Emirates) 2020, *Congress* Belgrade (Serbia) 2018, *Council Meeting and General Assembly* Rio de Janeiro (Brazil) 2017. **Publications** *CONNECT* (4 a year) – journal.

Members Critical care nursing organizations (45) in 39 countries and territories:

Argentina, Australia, Bolivia, Brazil, Cameroon, Canada, Chile, China, Colombia, Croatia, Cyprus, Denmark, Ghana, Hong Kong, Iceland, India, Italy, Japan, Korea Rep, Mexico, Netherlands, New Zealand, Nigeria, Norway, Peru, Philippines, Poland, Serbia, Slovenia, South Africa, Spain, Sri Lanka, Sweden, Taiwan, Türkiye, UK, United Arab Emirates, USA, Zambia.

NGO Relations Founding member of: *Global Sepsis Alliance (GSA, #10590)*. Affiliate member of: *International Council of Nurses (ICN, #13054)*. Instrumental in setting up: African Federation of Critical Care Nurses (AFCCN); *Federación Latinoamericana de Enfermeria en Cuidado Intensivo (FLECI)*. Collaborate partnerships with: *Asia Pacific Federation of Critical Care Nurses (APFCCN, no recent information)*; *European Federation of Critical Care Nursing Associations (EfCCNa, #07094)*; *European Society of Intensive Care Medicine (ESICM, #08632)*; *Society of Critical Care Medicine (SCCM)*; *World Federation of Pediatric Intensive and Critical Care Societies (WFPICCS, #21473)*; *World Federation of Intensive and Critical Care (WFICC, #21444)*. [2022/XD8762/D]

♦ **World Federation for Culture Collections (WFCC)** **21424**

Sec Westerdijk Fungal Biodiversity Inst, Uppsalalaan 8, 3584 CT Utrecht, Netherlands. T. +31302122614. Fax +31302512097.

Permanent Secretariat Belgian Coordinated Collection of Micro-organisms – BCCM, c/o Belgian Science Policy Office, 231 Av Louise, 1050 Brussels, Belgium. T. +3222383713. Fax +3222305912.

URL: http://www.wfcc.info/

History 1970, Mexico City (Mexico), at 10th International Congress of *International Union of Microbiological Societies (IUMS, #15794)*, of which it is a federation. **Aims** Promote and support establishment of culture collections and related services; provide liaison and set up an information network between the collections and their users. **Structure** Executive Board; Committees (8). Maintains *WFCC-MIRCEN World Data Centre for Microorganisms (WDCM, #20929)*. **Languages** English. **Staff** 12.00 FTE, voluntary. **Finance** Members' financial support. **Activities** Capacity building; events/meetings; knowledge management/information dissemination; research/documentation; standards/guidelines; training/education. **Events** *International Conference on Culture Collections* Pucón (Chile) 2019, *Quadrennial congress* Singapore (Singapore) 2017, *Quadrennial Congress* Beijing (China) 2013, *Quadrennial congress* Florianópolis (Brazil) 2010, *Quadrennial Congress* Goslar (Germany) 2007. **Publications** *WFCC Newsletter* (2 a year). *Living Resources for Biotechnology*. *World Directory of Collections of Cultures of Microorganisms*. Guides; guidelines; technical information sheets; congress proceedings.

Members Ordinary; Sustaining; Affiliate Collection; Affiliate Organization; Honorary. Members in 68 countries and territories:

Argentina, Armenia, Australia, Austria, Belarus, Belgium, Brazil, Bulgaria, Canada, Chile, China, Colombia, Cuba, Czechia, Denmark, Egypt, Estonia, Finland, France, Germany, Greece, Hong Kong, Hungary, India, Indonesia, Iran Islamic Rep, Ireland, Israel, Italy, Japan, Kazakhstan, Korea Rep, Latvia, Malaysia, Mexico, Morocco, Netherlands, New Zealand, Nigeria, Norway, Pakistan, Papua New Guinea, Philippines, Poland, Portugal, Romania, Russia, Senegal, Serbia, Singapore, Slovakia, Slovenia, South Africa, Spain, Sri Lanka, Sweden, Switzerland, Taiwan, Thailand, Türkiye, Uganda, UK, Ukraine, USA, Uzbekistan, Venezuela, Vietnam, Zimbabwe.

International organization:

IUMS Division of Virology (see: #15794).

Consultative Status Consultative status granted from: *World Intellectual Property Organization (WIPO, #21593)* (Permanent Observer Status). **NGO Relations** Multidisciplinary commission within: *International Union of Biological Sciences (IUBS, #15760)*. Co-opted Delegate of: *Committee on Data for Science and Technology (CODATA, #04247)*. [2020/XD3396/C]

♦ World Federation of Deaconess Associations / see World Federation of Diaconal Associations and Diaconal Communities (#21429)

♦ **World Federation of the Deaf (WFD)** **21425**

Exec Dir PO Box 65, FI-00401 Helsinki, Finland. E-mail: info@wfdeaf.org.

Contact Light House, Ilkantie 4, Haaga, FI-00401 Helsinki, Finland.

URL: http://wfdeaf.org/

History Founded at 1st World Congress of the Deaf. First Statutes adopted 23 Sep 1951, Rome (Italy); amended: Aug 1963, Stockholm (Sweden); 11 Aug 1967, Warsaw (Poland); Jul 1987, Espoo (Finland); 3 Jul 1991, Tokyo (Japan); 8 Jul 1995, Vienna (Austria); 18 Jul 2003, Montréal QC (Canada); 15 Jul 2007, Madrid (Spain); Jul 2011, Durban (South Africa); July-Aug 2015, Istanbul (Turkey); Jul 2019, Paris (France). Former names and other names: *Fédération mondiale des sourds (FMS)* – former. Registration: No/ID: 2276868-6, Start date: 15 Dec 2008, Finland, Europe. **Aims** Improve the lives of deaf people who face inequality by promoting human rights and access to sign languages. **Structure** General Assembly; Board; Secretariat; Regional Secretariats (9); Expert Groups; Youth Section. **Languages** English. International Signs. **Staff** 6.00 FTE, paid; 9.00 FTE, voluntary. **Finance** Sources: contributions; donations; gifts, legacies; government support; members' dues; sale of publications; sponsorship. Annual budget: 80,000 EUR (2021). **Activities** Advocacy/lobbying/activism; events/meetings; knowledge management/information dissemination; management of treaties and agreements; networking/liaising. Manages the following treaties/agreements: *Convention on the Rights of Persons with Disabilities (CRPD, 2006)*. **Events** *Quadrennial World Congress* Jeju (Korea Rep) 2023, *International Conference* Bangkok (Thailand) 2022, *International Conference* Bangkok (Thailand) 2021, *Asia-Pacific Representatives Meeting* Paris (France) 2019, *Quadrennial World Congress* Paris (France) 2019. **Publications** *WFD Newsletter*. *WFD Position Papers and Statements*. Congress and conference proceedings.

Members Categories (5): Ordinary; Associate; International; Honorary; Individual. National associations of the deaf in 131 countries and territories:

Albania, Algeria, Argentina, Armenia, Australia, Austria, Azerbaijan, Bangladesh, Belarus, Belgium, Benin, Bolivia, Bosnia-Herzegovina, Botswana, Brazil, Bulgaria, Burkina Faso, Burundi, Cameroon, Canada, Chad, Chile, China, Colombia, Congo Brazzaville, Congo DR, Côte d'Ivoire, Croatia, Cuba, Czechia, Denmark, Dominican Rep, Ecuador, El Salvador, Eritrea, Eswatini, Ethiopia, Fiji, Finland, France, Gambia, Georgia, Germany, Ghana, Greece, Guatemala, Guinea, Haiti, Honduras, Hong Kong, Hungary, Iceland, India, Indonesia, Iran Islamic Rep, Ireland, Italy, Japan, Jordan, Kazakhstan, Kenya, Korea DPR, Korea Rep, Kosovo, Kuwait, Laos, Latvia, Lebanon, Lesotho, Liberia, Lithuania, Macau, Madagascar, Malawi, Mali, Malta, Mauritania, Mexico, Moldova, Mongolia, Morocco, Namibia, Nepal, Netherlands, New Zealand, Nicaragua, Niger, Nigeria, Norway, Pakistan, Palestine, Panama, Paraguay, Peru, Philippines, Poland, Portugal, Qatar, Romania, Russia, Rwanda, Samoa, Senegal, Serbia, Singapore, Slovakia, Slovenia, Somalia, South Africa, Spain, Sri Lanka, Sudan, Sweden, Switzerland, Syrian AR, Tajikistan, Tanzania UR, Thailand, Togo, Tunisia, Türkiye, Uganda, UK, Ukraine, United Arab Emirates, Uruguay, USA, Uzbekistan, Venezuela, Zambia, Zimbabwe.

Consultative Status Consultative status granted from: *ECOSOC (#05331)* (Special); *UNESCO (#20322)* (Consultative Status); *ILO (#11123)* (Special List); *WHO (#20950)* (Official Relations); *Council of Europe (CE, #04881)* (Participatory Status). **NGO Relations** Member of (1): *International Disability Alliance (IDA, #13176)*. Partner of (5): Deaf Kidz International; DeafSkills; *Nippon Foundation*; *Sign Language Linguistics Society (SLLS)*; VTC. The following functions as regional secretariat: *European Union of the Deaf (EUD, #08985)*. [2022.10.11/XB3536/**B**]

♦ World Federation of the Deafblind (WFDB) 21426

Pres c/o FNDB, Postboks 5922 Majorstua, 0308 Oslo, Norway. T. +4722933350.
URL: http://www.wfdb.org/

History Sep 1997, Paipa (Colombia), informally by delegates of the 6th Helen Keller World Conference for deafblind people of *Helen Keller International (HKI, #10902)*. Formally founded Oct 2001, Auckland (New Zealand), at the 7th Helen Keller World Conference and 1st founding General Assembly of WFDB. **Aims** Promote human rights of deafblind persons and advance their economic, educational and social welfare. **Structure** General Assembly (every 4 years, usually in conjunction with Helen Keller World Conference); Executive Council; Regional Representatives (6). **Languages** Danish, Dutch, English, French, German, Norwegian, Spanish, Swedish. **Staff** Voluntary. **Finance** Subsidies from: *Swedish International Development Cooperation Agency (Sida)* through *MyRight – Empower People with Disabilities*. Budget (annual): about euro 30,000 to 50,000. **Events** *Helen Keller World Conference on Services to Deaf-Blind Persons* Nairobi (Kenya) 2022, *General Assembly* Benidorm (Spain) 2018, *Helen Keller World Conference on Services to Deaf-Blind Persons* Benidorm (Spain) 2018, *General Assembly* Tagaytay (Philippines) 2013, *Helen Keller World conference on services to deaf-blind persons* Tagaytay (Philippines) 2013. **Publications** *WFDB News* – online.

Members As of May 2012, National and Associate members in 64 countries:
Argentina, Australia, Bangladesh, Belgium, Bolivia, Brazil, Bulgaria, Burkina Faso, Canada, Chile, Colombia, Congo Brazzaville, Côte d'Ivoire, Croatia, Cuba, Czechia, Denmark, Dominican Rep, Ecuador, Ethiopia, Finland, France, Georgia, Germany, Greece, Guatemala, Guinea, Honduras, Hungary, Iceland, India, Israel, Italy, Japan, Kazakhstan, Kenya, Liberia, Malawi, Mali, Nepal, Netherlands, New Zealand, Nicaragua, Nigeria, Norway, Pakistan, Peru, Poland, Romania, Russia, Slovenia, South Africa, Spain, Sri Lanka, Sweden, Tanzania UR, Türkiye, Uganda, UK, Ukraine, Uruguay, USA, Venezuela, Zambia.

Consultative Status Consultative status granted from: *ECOSOC (#05331)* (Special). **IGO Relations** *African Union (AU, #00488)*; *European Commission (EC, #06633)*; *International Bank for Reconstruction and Development (IBRD, #12317)* (World Bank); *United Nations (UN, #20515)*. **NGO Relations** Member of: *International Disability Alliance (IDA, #13176)*; IDA CPRD Forum. Cooperates with: *Deafblind International (DbI, #05014)*; *European Deafblind Network (EDbN, #06890)*; *European Deafblind Union (EDBU, #06891)*; *Latin American Federation of the Deafblind*; *RI Global (#18948)*; *World Blind Union (WBU, #21234)*. [2019/XD7556/**D**]

♦ World Federation of Democratic Youth (WFDY) 21427

Fédération mondiale de la jeunesse démocratique (FMJD) – Federación Mundial de la Juventud Democratica (FMJD) – Weltbund der Demokratischen Jugend (WBDJ) – Vsemirnaja Federacija Demokraticeskoj Molodezi (VFDM)

Pres Frangepan útca 16, Budapest 1139, Hungary. T. +3613502202. Fax +3613501204. E-mail: wfdy@wfdy.org.
URL: http://www.wfdy.org/

History 1945, London (UK), succeeding to *International Bureau of the Association of Socialist Youth Leagues (inactive)*. Based in Hungary since 1951. New statutes adopted: 1957, Kiev (USSR); 1962, Warsaw (Poland); 1966, Sofia (Bulgaria); 1970, Budapest (Hungary), 5-10 Dec 1991, Athens (Greece). **Aims** Work for *peace, freedom*, democracy, independence and *equality*. **Structure** Assembly (every 4 years); General Council; Coordinating Council; Commissions. Attached bureaux: *International Bureau for Youth Tourism and Exchanges (BITEJ, inactive)*; *Service international volontaire de solidarité et de l'amitié de la jeunesse (SIVSAJ, no recent information)*. **Languages** English, French, Spanish. **Staff** 7.00 FTE, paid. **Finance** Members' dues. Other sources: donations; payment for services rendered. **Activities** Events/meetings; research/documentation. **Events** *World Festival* Quito (Ecuador) 2013, *Quadrennial General Assembly* Lisbon (Portugal) 2011, *World Festival* Tschwane (South Africa) 2010, *Quadrennial General Assembly* Hanoi (Vietnam) 2007, *World Festival* Caracas (Venezuela) 2005. **Publications** *WFDY News* (12 a year) in English, French, Spanish; *World Youth* (12 a year) in English, French, Spanish. Bulletins, brochures, folders.

Members Full; Observer; Associate. Organizations (over 270) in 109 countries and territories:
Afghanistan, Angola, Argentina, Australia, Austria, Bahrain, Bangladesh, Belgium, Benin, Bolivia, Botswana, Brazil, Bulgaria, Burundi, Cambodia, Canada, Cape Verde, Chile, China, Colombia, Congo Brazzaville, Costa Rica, Cuba, Cyprus, Czechia, Denmark, Dominican Rep, Ecuador, Egypt, El Salvador, Ethiopia, Fiji, Finland, France, Germany, Ghana, Greece, Grenada, Guadeloupe, Guatemala, Guinea-Bissau, Haiti, Honduras, Hungary, Iceland, India, Indonesia, Iran Islamic Rep, Iraq, Ireland, Israel, Italy, Jamaica, Japan, Jordan, Korea DPR, Kuwait, Laos, Lebanon, Libya, Liechtenstein, Luxembourg, Madagascar, Mali, Malta, Martinique, Mauritius, Mexico, Mongolia, Morocco, Mozambique, Namibia, Nepal, Netherlands, New Zealand, Nicaragua, Nigeria, Norway, Oman, Pakistan, Palestine, Panama, Paraguay, Peru, Philippines, Poland, Portugal, Puerto Rico, Romania, San Marino, Sao Tomé-Principe, Sierra Leone, Somalia, South Africa, Spain, Sri Lanka, St Vincent-Grenadines, Sudan, Sweden, Switzerland, Syrian AR, Türkiye, UK, Uruguay, USA, Venezuela, Vietnam, Yemen, Zimbabwe.
Members also in the former USSR; countries not specified.

Consultative Status Consultative status granted from: *ILO (#11123)* (Special List); *FAO (#09260)* (Liaison Status); *UNICEF (#20332)*. **IGO Relations** Cooperates with: *UNEP (#20299)*; *United Nations Office at Vienna (UNOV, #20604)*. Associated with Department of Global Communications of the United Nations.

NGO Relations Member of:
- *Conference of Non-Governmental Organizations in Consultative Relationship with the United Nations (CONGO, #04635)*;
- *EarthAction (EA, #05159)*;
- *Environment Liaison Centre International (ELCI, no recent information)*;
- *Espacio Iberoamericano de Juventud (EIJ, no recent information)*;
- *Foro Latinoamericano de Juventud (FLAJ, #09881)*;
- *NGO Committee on Disarmament, Peace and Security, New York NY (#17106)* and *NGO Committee for Disarmament, Geneva (#17105)*;
- *UNITED for Intercultural Action – European Network Against Nationalism, Racism, Fascism and in Support of Migrants and Refugees (UNITED, #20511)*;
- *World Social Forum (WSF, #21797)*.

Instrumental in setting up: *World Youth Rainforest Action (WYRA, no recent information)* [2019/XB3519/**F**]

♦ World Federation of Development Financing Institutions (WFDFI) . . 21428

Fédération mondiale des institutions financières de développement – Federación Mundial de Instituciones Financieras de Desarrollo (FEMIDE)

Secretariat 06 BP 321, Immeuble AIAFD, Boulevard Latrille rue J61, Cocody-Deux Plateaux, Abidjan 06, Côte d'Ivoire. T. +22522527940. Fax +22522522584. E-mail: info@adfi-ci.org.
URL: http://wfdfi.net/

History 24 Sep 1979, Madrid (Spain). **Aims** As an institutional club of professional bankers, enhance the profession of development *banking*; as a forum, lead the objectives of development financing activities by means of discussions or negotiations with international development agencies; as a body, promote investment opportunities in the world by holding international conferences to help potential *investors*. **Structure** Board of Governors. Rotating Secretariat, agreed in 1992. **Languages** English, French, Spanish. **Staff** 5.00 FTE, paid. **Finance** Sources: members' dues. Budget (annual): Peruvian soles 120,000. **Activities** Coordinates joint cooperative actions, liaison activities and communications between members and other institutions. Conducts surveys, carries out research and maintains information exchange. Provides and encourages professional training. **Events** *International CEO Forum* Kyrenia (Cyprus) 2018, *General Assembly* Singapore (Singapore) 2006, *General Assembly* Santiago (Chile) 2002, *General Assembly* Washington, DC (USA) 1992, *General Assembly* Bangkok (Thailand) 1991.

Members Institutions Ordinary Regional; Temporary Regional; Special; Individual Associations; Honorary. Ordinary over 300 development banks and development financing institutions in over 140 countries. Membership countries not specified.
Ordinary over 300 development banks and development financing institutions in over 140 countries. Membership countries not specified.
Regional development financing institutions (DFIs) (4):
Asociación Latinoamericana de Instituciones Financieras para el Desarrollo (ALIDE, #02233); *Association of African Development Finance Institutions (AADFI, #02353)*; *Association of Development Financing Institutions in Asia and the Pacific (ADFIAP, #02472)*; *Association of National Development Finance Institutions in Member Countries of the Islamic Development Bank (ADFIMI, #02817)*.

Consultative Status Consultative status granted from: *ECOSOC (#05331)* (Ros C); *UNIDO (#20336)*. **IGO Relations** Cooperation agreement with: *UNCTAD (#20285)*. Accredited by: *United Nations Office at Vienna (UNOV, #20604)*. [2019/XC9152/y/**C**]

♦ World Federation of Diaconal Associations and Diaconal Communities (DIAKONIA) 21429

Fédération mondiale d'associations et de communautés diaconales – Weltbund von Verbänden und Gemeinschaften der Diakonie

Sec Malanchthonstr 12, 72116 Mössingen, Germany.
Pres PO Box 506, Marleston, Adelaide SA 5033, Australia.
Registered Address Wilhelm-Löhe-Str 16, 91564 Neuendettelsau, Germany. E-mail: rfl@diakonia-world.org.
URL: https://diakonia-world.org/

History Oct 1947, Copenhagen (Denmark). Founded following discussions, 31 Aug-6 Sep 1946, Amsterdam/Utrecht (Netherlands), when an interim committee was formed, and a meeting of this committee was held Apr 1947, Riehen (Switzerland). Constitution adopted 1947, Copenhagen; revised: 1966, Edinburgh (UK); 1979, Manila (Philippines); 1992, Wolfville NS (Canada); 2005, Durham (UK); 2009, Atlanta GA (USA). Former names and other names: *World Federation of Deaconess Associations* – former (Oct 1947 to 1979); *World Federation of Diaconal Associations and Sisterhoods* – former (1979); *Alliance oecuménique des communautés et des associations de diaconesses* – former (1979); *Weltbund von Schwesternschaften und Verbänden der Diakonie* – former (1979); *Foundation DIAKONIA World Federation of Diaconal Associations and Diaconal Communications (Foundation Diakonia)* – full title; *Stiftung DIAKONIA Weltbund von Verbänden und Gemeinschaften der Diakonie (Stiftung DIAKONIA)* – full title; *DIAKONIA World Federation* – alias. Registration: Start date: 2018, Germany, Ansbach; Netherlands. **Aims** Called by Jesus Christ to the service of reconciliation in the world with the world of faith and the action of love: further ecumenical relationships between diaconal associations and diaconal communities; reflect on the nature and task of diakonia in the New Testament sense; further a sense of diakonia in Churches and congregations; strengthen a sense of community among the associations, render mutual aid, and undertake common tasks. **Structure** Assembly of Delegates of all member bodies (every 4 years, at World Conference); Executive Committee. Regional bodies (3): *DIAKONIA of the Americas and the Caribbean (DOTAC, #05063)*; *DIAKONIA of Asia-Pacific (DAP, #05064)*; *DIAKONIA Region Africa/Europe (DRAE, see: #21429)*, the latter including *'European Association of Diaconal Institutions of the Free Churches'*. **Languages** English, German. **Staff** 1.00 FTE, paid; 1.00 FTE, voluntary. **Finance** Sources: donations; members' dues. **Activities** Events/meetings; financial and/or material support. **Events** *World Conference* Darwin, NT (Australia) 2021, *World Conference* Chicago, IL (USA) 2017, *World conference* Berlin (Germany) 2013, *World conference* Atlanta, GA (USA) 2009, *World conference* Durham (UK) 2005. **Publications** *DIAKONIA News* (periodical); *DIAKONIA Nachrichten*.

Members Associations and communities of diaconesses, diaconal sisterhoods and brotherhoods, organizations of diaconal ministers and church workers in 32 countries:
Australia, Austria, Brazil, Cameroon, Canada, Denmark, Egypt, Fiji, Finland, France, Germany, Hungary, India, Indonesia, Japan, Kenya, Korea Rep, Madagascar, Malawi, Netherlands, New Zealand, Nigeria, Norway, Philippines, Rwanda, South Africa, Sweden, Switzerland, Tanzania UR, UK, USA, Zambia.
Included in the above, 1 organization listed in this Yearbook:
European Association of Diaconal Institutions of the Free Churches (#06013).

NGO Relations Cooperates with: *Ecumenical Group of Women (KAIRE, #05348)*. Member of: *GLOBAL RESPONSIBILITY – Austrian Platform for Development and Humanitarian Aid*, through Australian Branch. Supports: *Global Call for Action Against Poverty (GCAP, #10263)*. [2020/XC1316/y/**C**]

♦ World Federation of Diaconal Associations and Sisterhoods / see World Federation of Diaconal Associations and Diaconal Communities (#21429)

♦ World Federation of Diamond Bourses (WFDB) 21430

Fédération mondiale des bourses de diamants – Wereld Federatie der Diamantbeurzen

SG Pelikaanstraat 62, 2018 Antwerp, Belgium. T. +3232349121. Fax +3232264073.
URL: http://www.wfdb.com/

History 1947, Antwerp (Belgium). **Aims** Protect the interests of the affiliated bourses and their individual members; further amicable settlement or arbitration of differences and disputes between the individual members of the affiliated bourses and between affiliated bourses; promote understanding and closer cooperation between people all over the world who earn their living from the diamond trade; participate in promotion of the world trade and encourage the establishment of bourses, in view of an affiliation in all centres where diamonds are actively traded. **Languages** English. **Activities** Organizes: together with IDMA, World Diamond Congress (every 2 years); Presidents' Meeting (on alternate year). **Events** *Biennial World Congress* Dubai (United Arab Emirates) 2016, *Asia-Pacific Presidents Summit* Seoul (Korea Rep) 2016, *Biennial World Congress / Biennial World Diamond Congress* Antwerp (Belgium) 2014, *WFDB Asian Summit* Singapore (Singapore) 2014, *Presidents Meeting / Presidents' Meeting* Istanbul (Turkey) 2013. **Publications** *Connections – A Profile of Diamond People and their History* by Russel Shor.

Members Affiliated bourses (28) in 20 countries and territories:
Australia, Austria, Belgium, China, Germany, Hong Kong, India, Israel, Italy, Japan, Netherlands, Panama, Russia, Singapore, South Africa, Thailand, Türkiye, UK, United Arab Emirates, USA.

NGO Relations Together with: *International Diamond Manufacturers Association (IDMA, #13171)*, set up: *International Diamond Council (IDC, #13170)*; *World Diamond Council (WDC, #21360)*. [2015/XD3520/**D**]

♦ World Federation of Direct Selling Associations (WFDSA) 21431

Fédération mondiale de vente directe

Main Office 1667 K St NW, Ste 1100, Washington DC 20006, USA. T. +12024528866. Fax +12024539010.
URL: http://www.wfdsa.org/

History 1972, Montréal, QC (Canada). **Aims** Support direct selling associations in the areas of governance, education and communication; promote personal interaction among direct selling executives, especially regarding developments in specific markets; encourage adherence to a high standard of business practices; advocate policies that protect and advance consumer rights; promote international strategies that are beneficial to all countries concerned. **Structure** CEO Council. Board of Directors, consisting of 1 representative per national DSA plus one seat for *European Direct Selling Association (SELDIA, #06928)*. CEO Advisory Group of 8. Association Advisory Council, consisting of 2 representatives from the following regions: Asia/Pacific; Europe/Africa; Latin America; North America. Operating Group, comprising Chairman, Vice-Chairman, Treasurer, Assistant Treasurer, Secretary, Executive Director and 4 Committee Chairmen (Advocacy; Association Services; Ethics; Global Regulatory Affairs). Board of Directors. Executive Committee. Long Range Planning Committee. **Languages** English. **Staff** 4.00 FTE, paid. **Finance** Sources: meeting proceeds; members' dues. **Events** *World Congress* Dubai (United Arab Emirates) 2023, *World Congress* 2021, *World Congress* Bangkok (Thailand) 2020, *World Congress* Paris (France) 2017, *Congress* Singapore (Singapore) 2008. **Publications** *World Federation News* (6 a year).

Members Trade associations, all having ratified and accepted the World Codes of Conduct for Direct Selling, in 55 countries and territories:
Argentina, Australia, Austria, Belgium, Brazil, Canada, Chile, Colombia, Costa Rica, Czechia, Denmark, Ecuador, El Salvador, Estonia, Finland, France, Germany, Guatemala, Honduras, Hong Kong, Hungary, India, Indonesia, Ireland, Israel, Italy, Japan, Korea Rep, Lithuania, Malaysia, Mexico, Netherlands, New Zealand, Norway, Panama, Peru, Philippines, Poland, Portugal, Romania, Russia, Singapore, Slovenia, South Africa, Spain, Sweden, Switzerland, Taiwan, Thailand, Türkiye, UK, Ukraine, Uruguay, USA, Venezuela. [2022/XD1494/**C**]

♦ World Federation of Doctors / see World Medical Association (#21646)

♦ World Federation of Doctors who Respect Human Life (WFDWRHL) . 21432

Fédération mondiale des médecins pour le respect de la vie humaine – Federación Mundial de Médicos que respetan la Vida Humana – Svjetska Federacija Lijecnika i Drugih Zdravstvenih Radnika Koji Postuju Ljudski Zivot

SG Serruyslaan 64, 8400 Ostend, Belgium. T. +3259800860. E-mail: ps@ouardye.org.
Coordination Center for East Europe Kaptol 3, Zagreb, Croatia. T. +3841570571 – +3841570572. Fax +3841272622.

History 13 May 1974, Noordwijkerhout (Netherlands). **Aims** Further the practice of medicine according to the *'Declaration of Geneva (Switzerland), 1948'*; uphold this Declaration publicly; give moral and public support to medical doctors and health personnel who suffer discrimination because they persist in upholding the Declaration; further legal protection for all members of the human species, from conception to natural death, in accordance with the *'United Nations Declaration of Human Rights, 1948'*, the *'Declaration of the Rights of the Child, 1959'* and the *'WMA Declaration on Human Experimentation, 1975'*, Helsinki (Finland). **Structure** General Assembly; Council. Executive Committee, comprising President, Vice-President, Treasurer and Secretary General, 4 Honorary Vice-Presidents and 4 Regional Coordinators: East Asia; Africa; Latin America; Europe. **Languages** English, French, Spanish. **Staff** 1.00 FTE, paid; 2.00 FTE, voluntary. **Finance** Sources: contributions. **Activities** Organizes meetings and congresses; maintains contacts with the Holy See. **Events** *Congress* Helvoirt (Netherlands) 1995, *Triennial congress / Congress* Pamplona (Spain) 1992, *Congress* Merano (Italy) 1989, *Congress* Rome (Italy) 1988, *Congress* Rome (Italy) 1988. **Publications** *News Exchange of the WFDWRHL* (4 a year).

Members National or local medical associations; Individuals. Members in 74 countries and territories:
Albania, Argentina, Australia, Austria, Bangladesh, Belgium, Benin, Bosnia-Herzegovina, Brazil, Canada, Chile, Colombia, Congo DR, Costa Rica, Croatia, Cyprus, Czechia, Denmark, Dominican Rep, Ecuador, El Salvador, Faeroe Is, Finland, France, Germany, Guatemala, Haiti, Holy See, Honduras, Hong Kong, Hungary, India, Indonesia, Ireland, Italy, Japan, Kenya, Kuwait, Lithuania, Luxembourg, Malaysia, Mauritius, Mexico, Netherlands, New Zealand, Nigeria, Norway, Pakistan, Paraguay, Peru, Philippines, Poland, Portugal, Puerto Rico, Russia, Serbia, Singapore, Slovakia, Slovenia, South Africa, Spain, Sudan, Sweden, Switzerland, Tanzania UR, Thailand, Trinidad-Tobago, UK, Ukraine, United Arab Emirates, Uruguay, USA, Venezuela, Zambia.

IGO Relations Maintains contacts with: *Council of Europe (CE, #04881)*. **NGO Relations** Member of: *European Working Group 'Courage to Take a Moral Stance' (#09109).* [2012/XD7273/**C**]

♦ World Federation of Education Associations (inactive)
♦ World Federation for Education and Research in Public Health (inactive)
♦ World Federation of Energy, Chemical and Various Industry Workers' Unions (inactive)

♦ World Federation of Engineering Organizations (WFEO) 21433

Fédération Mondiale des Organisations d'Ingénieurs (FMOI)

Exec Dir Maison de l'UNESCO, 1 rue Miollis, 75015 Paris, France. T. +33145684846. Fax +33145684865. E-mail: secretariat@wfeo.org – executivedirector@wfeo.net.
URL: http://www.wfeo.net/

History 4 Mar 1968, Paris (France). Founded under the auspices of *UNESCO (#20322)*, following the setting up of an international working group in 1966, Paris. Constitution adopted 28 Jun 1971. **Aims** Provide information and leadership to the engineering *profession* on issues of concern to the public or the profession; serve society and be recognized by national and international organisations and the public, as a source of advice and guidance on the policies, interests and concerns that relate engineering and *technology* to the human and natural *environment*; include the engineering dimension in solving current challenges facing the world, such as water and food security issues, energy challenges and green growth; foster peace, socio-economic security and sustainable development among all countries through the proper application of technology; facilitate relationships between governments, business and people by contributing an engineering dimension to discussion of policies and investment. **Structure** General Assembly (every 2 years); Executive Council (meets annually); Executive Board. Standing Technical Committees (10): Disaster Risk Management; Engineering for Innovative Technologies; Engineering and the Environment; Energy; Young Engineers/Future Leaders; Education in Engineering; Anti Corruption; Women in Engineering; Engineering Capacity Building; Information and Communication. Working Group on Water; Working Group for the Development of a Global Infrastructure Report; WFEO-UN Relations Committee. **Languages** English, French, Spanish. **Staff** 3.00 FTE, paid. **Finance** Sources: members' dues. Annual budget: 300,000 USD. **Activities** Advocacy/lobbying/activism; awards/prizes/competitions; events/meetings; healthcare; projects/programmes; research/documentation; standards/guidelines; training/education. **Events** *World Landslide Forum* Kyoto (Japan) 2021, *World Landslide Forum* Kyoto (Japan) 2020, *World Engineers Conference and Convention* Melbourne, VIC (Australia) 2019, *World Landslide Forum* Ljubljana (Slovenia) 2017, *World Engineering Conference and Convention* Kyoto (Japan) 2015. **Publications** E-newsletter; STCs Studies; guidelines; reports.

Members National and Affiliate: engineering organizations (one per country), in 93 countries and territories:
Algeria, Argentina, Australia, Bahrain, Bangladesh, Belize, Bolivia, Brazil, Bulgaria, Cameroon, Canada, Chile, China, Colombia, Congo DR, Costa Rica, Côte d'Ivoire, Croatia, Cuba, Cyprus, Czechia, Ecuador, Egypt, Fiji, France, Ghana, Greece, Honduras, Hong Kong, Hungary, India, Iraq, Italy, Japan, Jordan, Kenya, Korea Rep, Kuwait, Lebanon, Libya, Madagascar, Malawi, Malaysia, Malta, Mauritius, Mexico, Moldova, Mongolia, Montenegro, Morocco, Myanmar, Nepal, New Zealand, Nigeria, North Macedonia, Oman, Pakistan, Palestine, Peru, Philippines, Poland, Portugal, Puerto Rico, Qatar, Romania, Russia, Rwanda, Saudi Arabia, Senegal, Serbia, Sierra Leone, Singapore, Slovakia, Slovenia, South Africa, Spain, Sri Lanka, Sudan, Switzerland, Syrian AR, Taiwan, Tanzania UR, Tunisia, Türkiye, Uganda, UK, Ukraine, United Arab Emirates, Uruguay, USA, Yemen, Zambia, Zimbabwe.

International members (10):
Commonwealth Engineers Council (CEC, #04324); Engineering Association of Mediterranean Countries (EAMC, #05480); Fédération Européenne d'Associations Nationales d'Ingénieurs (FEANI, #09558); Federation of African Engineering Organisations (FAEO, #09402); Federation of Arab Engineers (FAE, #09420); Federation of Engineering Institutions of Asia and the Pacific (FEIAP, #09480); Federation of Engineering Institutions of South and Central Asia (FEISCA, #09482); Union of Scientific and Engineering Associations (USEA); Unión Panamericana de Asociaciones de Ingenieros (UPADI, #20469); World Council of Civil Engineers (WCCE, #21321).

Associates (14), including 2 organizations listed in this Yearbook:
European Council of Engineers Chambers (ECEC, #06819); World Geospatial Industry Council (WGIC, #21538).

Consultative Status Consultative status granted from: *ECOSOC (#05331)* (Ros C); *FAO (#09260)* (Liaison Status); *World Intellectual Property Organization (WIPO, #21593)* (Permanent Observer Status); *UNESCO (#20322)* (Associate Status); *UNIDO (#20336)*; *UNEP (#20299)*. **IGO Relations** Cooperation Agreement with: *International Science, Technology and Innovation Centre for South-South Cooperation under the auspices of UNESCO (ISTIC, #14799)*. **NGO Relations** Member of (1): *Consejo de las Asociaciones Profesionales de Ingenieros Civiles de Lengua Oficial Portuguesa y Castellana (CECPC-CICPC, #04702)*. Cooperates with (1): *Federation of Engineering Institutions of Asia and the Pacific (FEIAP, #09480)*. Cooperation agreement with: *International Federation of Engineering Education Societies (IFEES, #13412); International Federation of Consulting Engineers (#13399); International Network of Women Engineers and Scientists (INWES, #14345).* [2022.02.02/XA3522/y/**A**]

♦ World Federation of Exchanges (WFE) 21434

CEO 125 Old Broad St, London, EC2N 1AR, UK. T. +442071514150. E-mail: contact@world-exchanges.org.
URL: http://www.world-exchanges.org/

History Founded Oct 1961, Paris (France), as *Fédération internationale des bourses de valeurs (FIBV) – International Federation of Stock Exchanges*, to succeed *Association of European Stock Exchanges (inactive)*, set up 1957. Current title adopted in 2002. Registered in accordance with French law. **Aims** Demonstrate the role, functioning and integrity of regulated markets; maintain a platform for professionals in the industry to discuss issues of common interest and to identify new approaches and solutions which enhance the competitive position of regulated *markets*; act as a central reference point for the industry by offering members guidance in the process of international harmonization of business practices; create, develop and maintain cooperative relationships with *regulators* so as to advocate the benefits of exchange self-regulation within the total regulatory framework in both national and international environments; support emerging exchanges in their efforts to develop markets which function according to member standards, thus contributing to global respect for the norms of a well-regulated industry. **Structure** General Assembly (annual). Board of Directors, comprising 17 elected members. Chairmanship – Chairman and Vice-Chairman – rotates every 2 years among Board members. Working Committee open to all Federation members. Permanent Office in Paris (France), headed by CEO, assisted by COO. **Languages** English. **Staff** 9.00 FTE, paid. **Finance** Sources: members' dues. **Activities** Working Committee handles topics of transnational interest. Services to members include: advice; advocacy; establishment of industry statistics and business news; business and thematic studies; surveys; organization of topical conferences and workshops. **Events** *General Assembly and Annual Meeting* Shenzhen (China) 2020, *General Assembly and Annual Meeting* Singapore (Singapore) 2019, *General Assembly and Annual Meeting* Athens (Greece) 2018, *General Assembly and Annual Meeting* Bangkok (Thailand) 2017, *General Assembly and Annual Meeting* Cartagena de Indias (Colombia) 2016. **Publications** *Focus* (12 a year) – newsletter and statistics. Annual report and statistics; workshop reports; studies.

Members Member exchanges in 58 countries and territories:
Argentina, Australia, Austria, Belgium, Bermuda, Brazil, Canada, Chile, China, Colombia, Cyprus, Denmark, Egypt, Finland, France, Germany, Greece, Hong Kong, Hungary, Iceland, India, Indonesia, Ireland, Israel, Italy, Japan, Jordan, Korea Rep, Latvia, Lithuania, Luxembourg, Malaysia, Malta, Mauritius, Mexico, Morocco, Netherlands, Norway, Oman, Peru, Philippines, Poland, Portugal, Russia, Saudi Arabia, Singapore, Slovenia, South Africa, Spain, Sri Lanka, Sweden, Switzerland, Taiwan, Thailand, Türkiye, UK, United Arab Emirates, USA.

Affiliate in 17 countries and territories:
Bahrain, China, Côte d'Ivoire, Kazakhstan, Kenya, Lebanon, Namibia, Nigeria, Pakistan, Palestine, Papua New Guinea, Qatar, Romania, Tunisia, Ukraine, United Arab Emirates, Vietnam.

Correspondent in 30 countries and territories:
Argentina, Australia, Azerbaijan, Bahrain, Bangladesh, Barbados, Belarus, Bosnia-Herzegovina, Bulgaria, Canada, Cayman Is, China, Costa Rica, Croatia, Czechia, Ghana, India, Jamaica, Japan, Kuwait, Libya, Mauritius, Pakistan, Panama, Singapore, Slovakia, Ukraine, United Arab Emirates, Vietnam, Zambia.

NGO Relations Together with: *International Bar Association (IBA, #12320)* – through *International Federation of Accountants (IFAC, #13335)*, set up: *International Capital Markets Group (ICMG, inactive).* [2020/XC2018/**C**]

♦ World Federation of Foreign-Language Teachers' Associations / see International Federation of Language Teacher Associations (#13468)
♦ World Federation of Free Latvians (#18250)
♦ World Federation of Free Zones (#09693)

♦ World Federation of Friends of Museums (WFFM) 21435

Fédération mondiale des amis des musées (FMAM) – Federación Mundial de Amigos de los Museos (FMAM) – Wereldfederatie der Vrienden van de Musea

Contact Rue du Musée 9, 1000 Brussels, Belgium.
URL: http://www.museumsfriends.com/

History 15 Jun 1975, Brussels (Belgium). Founded at second Congress, the first Congress having been held 1972, Barcelona (Spain). Registration: Crossroads Bank for Enterprises, No/ID: 0416.131.483, Start date: 15 Jun 1975, Belgium. **Aims** Unite friends of museums in order to facilitate exchange of ideas and experiences in conservation of cultural heritage; promote establishment and development of national federations and associations of friends of museums and support initiatives towards enrichment of museums; foster highest ethical standards among friends and volunteers of museums using the precepts of the WFFM Code of Ethics; encourage ties between museum professional and volunteers, young people and the general public; generate public and government awareness of museums worldwide. **Structure** General Assembly (annual); Council; Executive Committee. **Languages** English, French, Spanish. **Staff** Voluntary. **Finance** Sources: grants; members' dues; subsidies. **Activities** Events/meetings; knowledge management/information dissemination; politics/policy/regulatory; projects/programmes; research/documentation; training/education. Organizes: International Congress (every 3 years); regional meetings; colloquia. Exchanges mainly with European countries. **Events** *General Assembly* Marseille (France) 2022, *Triennial Congress* Canberra, ACT (Australia) 2020, *General Assembly* Montréal, QC (Canada) 2019, *Meeting* Montréal, QC (Canada) 2019, *Meeting* Lisbon (Portugal) 2018. **Publications** *Lettre d'information FMAM* in English, French. Regular chronicle in *Museum*, the quarterly review of UNESCO. Annual Report. Congress proceedings.

Members Active (18 national federations) in 17 countries:
Argentina, Australia, Belgium, Brazil, Canada, Denmark, France, Greece, Italy, Korea Rep, Mexico, Norway, Portugal, Spain, Sweden, UK, USA.

Associate (33) in 25 countries:
Brazil, Canada, Chile, Colombia, Czechia, Estonia, Hungary, Indonesia, Ireland, Israel, Korea Rep, Lithuania, Luxembourg, New Zealand, Peru, Philippines, Romania, Russia, Singapore, South Africa, Spain, Switzerland, Thailand, Uruguay, USA. [2022/XD0115/**C**]

♦ World Federation of Great Towers (WFGT) 21436

Fédération des grandes tours du monde

Exec Dir c/o TV Turm Alexanderplatz Gastronomieges mbH, Panoramastrasse 1a, 10178 Berlin, Germany. T. +493024757511.
URL: http://www.great-towers.com/

History 1989, Paris (France). **Aims** Promote dialogue amongst the towers on issues such as improving tower management and generating more traffic and revenue. **Languages** English, French. **Staff** 2.00 FTE, paid. **Finance** Members' dues. **Events** *Annual Conference* Guangzhou (China) 2019, *Annual Conference* Mexico City (Mexico) 2018, *Annual Conference* Moscow (Russia) 2017, *Annual Conference* Tokyo (Japan) 2016, *Annual Conference* Cape Town (South Africa) 2014. **Publications** *Tower2Tower Newsletter* (12 a year).

Members Full in 21 countries and territories:
Australia, Austria, Canada, China, Czechia, Egypt, Germany, Japan, Korea Rep, Macau, Malaysia, Mexico, Netherlands, New Zealand, Russia, Slovakia, Spain, UK, United Arab Emirates, USA, Uzbekistan. [2020/XD4202/**D**]

♦ World Federation of Hainanese Associations / see International Federation of Hainan Associations (#13434)
♦ World Federation of the Heads of Beauty Institutes and Aesthetics (no recent information)
♦ World Federation of Healing (inactive)
♦ World Federation of Health Agencies for the Advancement of Voluntary Surgical Contraception (inactive)

♦ World Federation of Hemophilia (WFH) 21437

Fédération mondiale de l'hémophilie – Federación Mundial de Hemofilia

CEO 1425 bv René Lévesque Ouest, Bureau 1200, Montréal QC H3G 1T7, Canada. T. +15148757944. Fax +15148758916. E-mail: wfh@wfh.org.
URL: http://www.wfh.org/

History 1963, Copenhagen (Denmark). Founded on the initiative of Frank Schnabel. **Aims** Provide global leadership to improve and sustain care for people with inherited bleeding disorders, including hemophilia, von Willebrand disease, rare factor deficiencies, and inherited platelet disorders. **Structure** General Assembly (at International Congress); Board of Directors; Medical Advisory Board (MAB); Committees, including: *International Association for Musculoskeletal Problems in Haemophilia and Related Disorders (inactive)*. Regional groups: *European Haemophilia Consortium (EHC, #07444)*; South-East Asian Regional Group (ASEAN). **Languages** English, French, Spanish. **Staff** 39.00 FTE, paid. **Finance** Sources: donations; members' dues; sponsorship. **Activities** Capacity building; research and development; training/education. **Events** *International Congress and General Assembly* Kuala Lumpur (Malaysia) 2024, *International Conference on Hemophilia and Rare Bleeding Disorder* Abu Dhabi (United Arab Emirates) 2022, *Gene Therapy Round Table* Montréal, QC (Canada) 2022, *International Congress and General Assembly* Montréal, QC (Canada) 2022, *Global Forum* Montréal, QC (Canada) 2021. **Publications** *Hemophilia World* (3 a year) – magazine, in print and online; *WFH eNews*. Annual Report; guidelines; monographs. **Members** Associate/Organizational; Professional; Sustaining; Individual. National Member Organizations (NMOs) in 127 countries. Membership countries not specified. **Consultative Status** Consultative status granted from: *WHO (#20950)* (Official Relations). **NGO Relations** Member of: *International Alliance of Patients' Organizations (IAPO, #11633)*. Official relations with: *International Society of Hematology (ISH, #15159); International Society on Thrombosis and Haemostasis (ISTH, #15511); Rare Diseases International (RDI, #18621).* [2020/XB3523/**B**]

♦ World Federation of Holistic Health Sciences (no recent information)

♦ World Federation for Hospital Sterilisation Sciences (WFHSS) 21438

Publication Officer c/o Graf under Partner AG, Tribschenstr 7, Postfach 3065, 6002 Lucerne, Switzerland. E-mail: info@wfhss.com.
Pres address not obtained.

URL: http://www.wfhss.com/
History 1999, as *European Forum for Hospital Sterile Supply (EFHSS)*. Subsequently changed title to *World Forum for Hospital Sterile Supply* and in 2006 to *World Forum for Hospital Sterilisation Sciences*. Since 2015, registered in accordance with Swiss Civil Code. **Aims** Promote harmonization of sterilization departments and decontamination practices worldwide. **Structure** General Assembly (annual); Executive Committee. **Languages** English. **Staff** 9.00 FTE, voluntary. **Finance** Members' dues. Other sources: advertisements; exhibitions. **Activities** Events/meetings. **Events** *World Sterilization Congress* Barcelona (Spain) 2022, *World Sterilization Congress* Geneva (Switzerland) 2021, *Annual Conference* Hong Kong (Hong Kong) / Macau (Macau) 2020, *Annual Conference* The Hague (Netherlands) 2019, *Annual Conference* Mexico City (Mexico) 2018. **Publications** *Central Service* (12 a year) in French – journal.
Members Organizations (56) in 50 countries and territories:
Argentina, Australia, Austria, Belgium, Brazil, Bulgaria, Chile, Colombia, Croatia, Czechia, Denmark, Finland, France, Germany, Greece, Hong Kong, Hungary, India, Iran Islamic Rep, Ireland, Israel, Italy, Japan, Korea Rep, Kuwait, Latvia, Lithuania, Malaysia, Malta, Mexico, Morocco, Netherlands, New Zealand, North Macedonia, Norway, Oman, Poland, Portugal, Romania, Saudi Arabia, Slovakia, Slovenia, South Africa, Spain, Sweden, Switzerland, Türkiye, UK, United Arab Emirates, USA.
Included in the above, 3 organizations listed in this Yearbook:
Infection Control Africa Network (ICAN, #11184); International Association of Healthcare Central Service Material Management (IAHCSMM); Sociedad Latinoamericana de Esterilización (SOLAES, #19403).
[2022/XF5381/y/F]

♦ World Federation of Hungarian Jews (WFHJ) 21439

Fédération mondiale des juifs originaires de Hongrie – Magyar Zsidók Vilagszövetsége
Contact address not obtained. T. +12126835377.
History as *World Federation of Jews of Hungarian Descent*. **Aims** Present the Hungarian Jewish cultural heritage by issuing publications.
Members Individuals in 19 countries:
Argentina, Australia, Austria, Belgium, Brazil, Canada, Chile, Ecuador, France, Greece, Hungary, Israel, Italy, Mexico, Sweden, Switzerland, UK, USA, Venezuela.
[2011/XE4767/E]

♦ World Federation of Hydrotherapy and Climatotherapy (#09692)

♦ World Federation for Incontinence and Pelvic Problems (WFIPP) . . . 21440

Communications Officer c/o FINCO, Viale Orazio Flacco 24, 70124 Bari BA, Italy. E-mail: communicationsofficer@wfipp.org.
URL: http://www.wfipp.org/
History Dec 2005, Bari (Italy). Former names and other names: *World Federation of Incontinent Patients* – former. Registration: Italy. **Aims** Improve the quality of life of citizens who suffer from incontinence and related problems. **Structure** Executive Council.
Members Organizations in 14 countries:
Australia, Brazil, Canada, India, Italy, Japan, Lithuania, Malta, Poland, Slovakia, Sweden, Uganda, UK, USA.
NGO Relations Member of (2): *EU Health Coalition; International Alliance of Patients' Organizations (IAPO, #11633)*. Associate member of: *EURORDIS – Rare Diseases Europe (#09175)*. Provisional member of: *European Patients' Forum (EPF, #08172).*
[2021.09.01/XM1081/D]

♦ World Federation of Incontinent Patients / see World Federation for Incontinence and Pelvic Problems (#21440)

♦ World Federation of Independent Scouts (WFIS) 21441

Pres Angelstrasse 15, 65558 Heistenbach, Germany. T. +49643284399. E-mail: office@wfis-worldwide.org.
URL: http://www.wfis.world/
History 1996, Laubach (Germany). Registration: Goverment, Start date: 2014, Germany; United Nations, USA. **Aims** Act as an umbrella association for regional and national Scout organizations. **Structure** Committee; Regional Councils (6). **Languages** English, French, Hindi, Spanish. **Staff** Voluntary. **Finance** Councils have their own fees. **Activities** Events/meetings; training/education. **Events** *World Jamboree* India 2017, *World Jamboree* Spain 2013, *World jamboree* Zacatlan, ZAC (Mexico) 2011, *World jamboree* Medellin (Colombia) 2007, *World Conference* Canada 2004. **Publications** *Scouting for Boys*; *Wolf Cub Handbook*. Education handbooks. Publications from individual Regional Councils.
Members Recognized Scout organizations (168) in 75 countries and territories.
Argentina, Aruba, Australia, Austria, Bangladesh, Belgium, Belize, Bolivia, Brazil, Burkina Faso, Burundi, Cameroon, Canada, Central African Rep, Chile, China, Colombia, Comoros, Congo Brazzaville, Costa Rica, Côte d'Ivoire, Curaçao, Cyprus, Czechia, Denmark, Dominican Rep, Ecuador, El Salvador, England, Ethiopia, France, Germany, Ghana, Guatemala, Honduras, India, Ireland, Italy, Japan, Kenya, Korea Rep, Kosovo, Latvia, Libya, Liechtenstein, Malaysia, Mali, Malta, Mexico, Morocco, Nepal, Nicaragua, Nigeria, Northern Cyprus, Pakistan, Panama, Paraguay, Portugal, Puerto Rico, Romania, Russia, Rwanda, Sahrawi ADR, Scotland, Spain, Suriname, Switzerland, Türkiye, Uganda, UK, Ukraine, United Arab Emirates, USA, Venezuela, Wales.
IGO Relations Associated with Department of Global Communications of the United Nations.
[2022.05.02/XC0138/C]

♦ World Federation of Industrial Research Associations (W-FIRA) . . . 21442

Contact c/o EIRMA, Rue de la Loi 81 A, 1040 Brussels, Belgium.
Contact address not obtained.
History 21 May 2013, Washington DC (USA), by national associations in Australia, New Zealand, Brazil, USA, Japan, Korea and by *European Industrial Research Management Association (EIRMA, #07531)*. **NGO Relations** *World Association of Industrial and Technological Research Organizations (WAITRO, #21145).*
[2019/XJ7029/t/C]

♦ World Federation of Industry Workers (inactive)
♦ World Federation for Information Technology in Agriculture / see International Network for Information Technology in Agriculture (#14287)

♦ World Federation of Insurance Intermediaries (WFII) 21443

Secretariat Ave Albert-Elisabeth 40, 1200 Brussels, Belgium. T. +3227379581. E-mail: wfii@wfii.net.
URL: https://www.wfii.org/
History 30 Jan 1999, Washington, DC (USA). Registration: Banque-Carrefour des Entreprises, No/ID: BE0467874649, Start date: 1 Jun 1999, Belgium. **Aims** Promote the role of insurance intermediaries in the economy. **Structure** World Council; Executive CSE Committee; Secretariat. **Languages** English. **Activities** Advocacy/lobbying/activism. **Events** *Annual Meeting* Rome (Italy) 2019, *World Council and Executive Committee Meeting* Sydney, NSW (Australia) 2014, *Seminar on services in the new economy / Conference* Brussels (Belgium) 2001.
Members National associations (over 100) of insurance agents and brokers in over 80 countries. Membership countries not specified.
Founding insurance organizations (8), including 3 bodies listed in this Yearbook:
Association of African Insurance Brokers (AAIB, #02358); BIPAR – European Federation of Insurance Intermediaries (#03263); Pan American Confederation of Insurance Producers (#18088).
Observer national organization (1) in 1 country:
Japan.
[2019/XD7738/y/D]

♦ World Federation of Intensive and Critical Care (WFICC) 21444

CEO Rue Washington 40, 1050 Brussels, Belgium. T. +447702285271.
President address not obtained.
Main Website: http://www.wficc.com
History 21 Jun 1981, Washington, DC (USA). Founded following initial groundwork after 1st world congress, 1974, London (UK) and 2nd world congress, 1977, Paris (France). Former names and other names: *World Federation of Societies of Intensive and Critical Care Medicine (WFSICCM)* – former; *Fédération mondiale des sociétés de soins intensifs et de réanimation* – former; *Federación Mundial de Sociedades de Medicina Intensiva* – former. **Aims** Promote the highest standards of intensive and critical care medicine for humankind, without discrimination. **Structure** Elected Council; Executive Committee; Chief Executive Officer. **Languages** English, French, Spanish. **Staff** 0.50 FTE, paid. **Finance** Sources: meeting proceeds; members' dues. **Activities** Research/documentation; standards/guidelines; training/education. **Events** *World Congress of Intensive and Critical Care* Delhi (India) 2025, *World Congress of Intensive and Critical Care* Istanbul (Türkiye) 2023, *World Congress of Intensive and Critical Care* Vancouver, BC (Canada) 2021, *Biennial Congress* Melbourne, VIC (Australia) 2019, *Biennial Congress* Rio de Janeiro (Brazil) 2017. **Publications** *Journal of Critical Care.*

Members National scientific societies (over 80) in 80 countries and territories:
Argentina, Australia, Austria, Bangladesh, Belgium, Belize, Bolivia, Bosnia-Herzegovina, Botswana, Brazil, Canada, Chile, China, Colombia, Costa Rica, Croatia, Czechia, Dominican Rep, Ecuador, Egypt, El Salvador, Finland, France, Georgia, Germany, Guatemala, Honduras, Hong Kong, Hungary, India, Indonesia, Ireland, Israel, Italy, Japan, Kenya, Korea Rep, Kuwait, Latvia, Lebanon, Malaysia, Mexico, Mongolia, Namibia, Nepal, Netherlands, New Zealand, Nigeria, Norway, Oman, Pakistan, Panama, Paraguay, Peru, Philippines, Portugal, Puerto Rico, Romania, Russia, Saudi Arabia, Serbia, Singapore, Slovakia, Slovenia, South Africa, Spain, Sri Lanka, Sudan, Sweden, Switzerland, Taiwan, Tanzania UR, Thailand, Tunisia, Türkiye, UK, United Arab Emirates, Uruguay, USA, Venezuela.
NGO Relations Member of (1): *Federation of European and International Associations Established in Belgium (FAIB, #09508)*. Founding member of: *Global Sepsis Alliance (GSA, #10590).*
[2023.02.15/XC0334/C]

♦ World Federation of International Juridical Institutions (inactive)

♦ World Federation of International Music Competitions (WFIMC) . . . 21445

Fédération mondiale des concours internationaux de musique (FMCIM)
Gen Sec Rue de Carouge 104, 1204 Geneva, Switzerland. T. +41223213620. E-mail: fmcim@fmcim.org.
URL: http://www.wfimc.org/
History 17 Feb 1957, Geneva (Switzerland). Former names and other names: *Federation of International Music Competitions* – former (1957 to 1986); *Fédération des concours internationaux de musique (FCIM)* – former (1957 to 1986). Registration: Swiss Civil Code, Switzerland. **Aims** Establish a global network of internationally recognized organizations that, through public competition, discover the most promising young talents in the great tradition of classical music and further their careers by presenting them before distinguished juries, general audiences, the media and the rest of the music community. **Structure** General Assembly (annual); Board; Secretariat. **Languages** English, French. **Staff** 3.00 FTE, paid. **Finance** Sources: government support; members' dues. Support from Department of Culture of the Canton of Geneva (Switzerland). **Activities** Advocacy/lobbying/activism; guidance/assistance/consulting; networking/liaising. **Events** *Annual General Assembly* Bydgoszcz (Poland) 2022, *Annual General Assembly* Reggio Emilia (Italy) 2021, *Annual General Assembly* Hamamatsu (Japan) 2020, *Annual General Assembly* Norrköping (Sweden) 2019, *Annual General Assembly* Glasgow (UK) 2018. **Publications** *WFIMC Yearbook* (annual).
Members Permanent international competitions (120) in 42 countries:
Andorra, Armenia, Australia, Austria, Belgium, Brazil, Canada, Chile, China, Croatia, Czechia, Denmark, Finland, France, Georgia, Germany, Greece, Hong Kong, Hungary, Ireland, Israel, Italy, Japan, Korea Rep, Lithuania, Luxembourg, Netherlands, New Zealand, Norway, Poland, Portugal, Romania, Russia, Serbia, Singapore, Slovakia, South Africa, Spain, Switzerland, UK, Ukraine, USA.
IGO Relations *UNESCO (#20322)*. **NGO Relations** Member of: *International Artist Managers' Association (IAMA, #11673); International Music Council (IMC, #14199)*. Associated organizations: *European Broadcasting Union (EBU, #06404); European Union of Music Competitions for Youth (EMCY, #09003)*; Fédération française des festivals internationaux de musique (FFFIM); *International Society for the Performing Arts Foundation (ISPA, #15350); Jeunesses Musicales International (JMI, #16110).*
[2022.06.14/XC0948/C]

♦ World Federation of Inter-Religious Councils / see World Fellowship of Inter-Religious Councils

♦ World Federation of Interventional and Therapeutic Neuroradiology (WFITN) 21446

Fédération mondiale de neuroradiologie interventionnelle
Exec Dir address not obtained.
Registered Office 7 rue de Castellane, 75008 Paris, France.
URL: http://www.wfitn.org/
History 1990. Registration: France. **Languages** English. **Events** *Congress* Kyoto (Japan) 2022, *Congress* Kyoto (Japan) 2021, *Biennial Congress* Naples (Italy) 2019, *Biennial Congress* Budapest (Hungary) 2017, *Biennial Congress* Gold Coast, QLD (Australia) 2015.
Members Individuals in 26 countries:
Argentina, Australia, Austria, Belgium, Brazil, Canada, Chile, China, Denmark, France, Germany, Hungary, India, Italy, Japan, Luxembourg, Mexico, Netherlands, Portugal, Russia, Spain, Sweden, Switzerland, Türkiye, UK, USA.
[2021/XD3850/v/D]

♦ World Federation of Investment Clubs / see World Federation of Investors (#21447)

♦ World Federation of Investors (WFI) 21447

SG/Pres Prinsenhof 39, 9000 Ghent, Belgium. T. +3292231043. E-mail: secgeneral@wfic.org.
Chairman address not obtained.
URL: http://www.wfic.org/
History 1960, London (UK). Former names and other names: *World Federation of Investment Clubs (WFIC)* – former (1960 to 1966). **Aims** Promote wider *share ownership* through investment education. **Structure** Executive Committee; Advocacy Commitee. **Languages** English. **Staff** Voluntary. **Finance** Sources: members' dues. Annual budget: 10,000 USD. **Activities** Advocacy/lobbying/activism; events/meetings; training/education. **Events** *Annual Meeting* Ghent (Belgium) 2022, *Meeting* Bled (Slovenia) 2021, *Annual Meeting* Beirut (Lebanon) 2019, *Executive Committee Meeting* Ghent (Belgium) 2018, *Annual Meeting* Paris (France) 2018.
Members National investors associations (53) in 45 countries and territories:
Andorra, Austria, Belgium, Brazil, Cameroon, Canada, Croatia, Denmark, Finland, France, Georgia, Germany, Greece, Guatemala, Hong Kong, Iceland, India, Italy, Japan, Kenya, Korea Rep, Lebanon, Lithuania, Malta, Moldova, Netherlands, Nigeria, North Macedonia, Norway, Philippines, Poland, Portugal, Romania, Russia, Serbia, Singapore, Slovenia, South Africa, Spain, Sweden, Thailand, Türkiye, UK, USA, Zimbabwe.
NGO Relations Cooperates with (2): *International Financial Litigation Network (IFLN, #13602); World Federation of Young Investors (WFYI).*
[2022.11.29/XD8120/B]

♦ World Federation of Islamic Missions (no recent information)
♦ World Federation of Jewish Child Survivors of the Holocaust / see World Federation of Jewish Child Survivors of the Holocaust and Descendants (#21448)

♦ World Federation of Jewish Child Survivors of the Holocaust and Descendants (WFJCSHD) 21448

Contact 67 South Bedford St, Ste 400W, Burlington MA 01803, USA. E-mail: mxalez@gmail.com.
URL: http://www.holocaustchild.org/
History 1987, as *Federation of Jewish Child Survivors of the Holocaust (FJCSH)*. Subsequently changed title to *World Federation of Jewish Child Survivors of the Holocaust*. **Aims** Join hands and hearts to keep Holocaust memory alive, fighting hatred and genocide. **Structure** Board. **Languages** English. **Staff** None. **Finance** Members' dues. Other sources: contributions; grants. **Activities** Advocacy/lobbying/activism; training/education; awareness raising. **Events** *International Conference* Houston, TX (USA) 2015, *International Conference* Berlin (Germany) 2014, *International Conference* Las Vegas, NV (USA) 2013, *International Conference* Cleveland, OH (USA) 2012, *International Conference* Warsaw (Poland) 2011. **Publications** *World Federation News Updates (WFNU)* (periodical); *Mishpocha Newsletter*.
Members Groups (55, of which 25 in USA) comprising about 10,000 individuals. Members in 23 countries:
Argentina, Australia, Belgium, Bosnia-Herzegovina, Canada, Croatia, Czechia, Germany, Hungary, Israel, Italy, Lithuania, Montenegro, Netherlands, Poland, Russia, Serbia, Slovakia, South Africa, Sweden, Switzerland, Ukraine, USA.
Also members in the Caribbean. Membership countries not specified.
NGO Relations Member of: *Association of Holocaust Organizations (AHO).*
[2017.10.11/XD8040/E]

♦ World Federation of Jewish Community Centres / see JCC Global (#16093)
♦ World Federation of Jewish Fighters, Partisans and Camp Inmates (no recent information)
♦ World Federation of Jews of Hungarian Descent / see World Federation of Hungarian Jews (#21439)
♦ World Federation of Karate Do Organizations (no recent information)

♦ World Federation of Khoja Shia Ithna-Asheri Muslim Communities (World Federation of KSIMC) 21449

Secretariat Wood Lane, Stanmore, HA7 4LQ, UK. T. +442089549881. Fax +442089549034. E-mail: secretariat@world-federation.org.
URL: http://www.world-federation.org/

History Founded 1976, London (UK), at constitutional conference. Registered UK Charity: 282303. **Aims** Promote the Shia Ithna Asheri faith worldwide; alleviate poverty, disease and dependence; educate community members; facilitate funding and support communal endeavours. **Structure** Conference (every 3 years); Office. **Languages** English, French, Gujarati, Urdu. **Staff** 10.00 FTE, paid; 100.00 FTE, voluntary. **Finance** Donations. **Activities** Guidance/assistance/consulting; financial and/or material support; humanitarian/emergency aid. **Events** *Triennial Conference* Dubai (United Arab Emirates) 2003, *Triennial Conference* London (UK) 2000, *Triennial Conference* Birmingham (UK) 1982. **Publications** *Shia World* (occasional). *Laws of Islam on the Internet. Islamic Concepts* – audio-cassette series. Press releases; books; teaching aids; audio-cassettes.
Members Organizations, consisting of about about 125,000 community members, in 21 countries:
Australia, Burundi, Canada, Congo DR, France, India, Kenya, Kuwait, Madagascar, Mauritius, Mozambique, Pakistan, Portugal, Réunion, Sweden, Switzerland, Tanzania UR, Uganda, UK, United Arab Emirates, Yemen.
Included in the above, one organization listed in this Yearbook:
Federation of Khoja Shia Ithna-Asheri Jamaats of Africa (#09683).
Consultative Status Consultative status granted from: *ECOSOC (#05331)* (Special). **NGO Relations** Member of: *Conference of Non-Governmental Organizations in Consultative Relationship with the United Nations (CONGO, #04635)*; *End Water Poverty (EWP, #05464).* [2018.10.02/XD6403/**D**]

♦ World Federation of Kowat Alrami and Self Defense (WFKA) 21450

Pres PO Box 850, Tripoli NORTH LEBANON, Lebanon. T. +9616220771. Fax +9616444112. E-mail: samurai2@inco.com.lb.
URL: http://www.kowatalrami.org/
Structure Board of Directors.
Members Full in 63 countries and territories:
Afghanistan, Albania, Algeria, Armenia, Australia, Austria, Belgium, Bosnia-Herzegovina, Brazil, Burkina Faso, Cameroon, Canada, Côte d'Ivoire, Croatia, Egypt, England, Finland, Georgia, Germany, Ghana, Greece, Hong Kong, Hungary, India, Iran Islamic Rep, Iraq, Italy, Jordan, Kuwait, Lebanon, Libya, Mauritania, Moldova, Morocco, Netherlands, New Zealand, Nigeria, Pakistan, Palestine, Philippines, Poland, Portugal, Puerto Rico, Qatar, Saudi Arabia, Scotland, Senegal, Serbia, Sierra Leone, Spain, Sri Lanka, Sudan, Sweden, Syrian AR, Tunisia, Türkiye, Uganda, Ukraine, United Arab Emirates, USA, Uzbekistan, Wales, Yemen.
NGO Relations Member of (2): *International Council of Traditional Sports and Games (ICTSG, #13088)*; *International Martial Art Games Committee (IMGC, #14107).* [2017.07.24/XM5474/**C**]

♦ **World Federation of KSIMC** World Federation of Khoja Shia Ithna-Asheri Muslim Communities (#21449)

♦ World Federation for Laser Dentistry (WFLD) 21451

Main Office Rue Paul Spaak 3, 1000 Brussels, Belgium.
URL: https://wfldlaser.com/
History 1988. Former names and other names: *International Society for Lasers in Dentistry (ISLD)* – former (1988 to 2006). **Aims** Share knowledge in the dental laser field. **Structure** Executive Committee, including President, Past-President, President-Elect, Secretary, Treasurer and 7 members. **Languages** English. **Staff** Voluntary. **Activities** Organizes international congress (every 2 years). **Events** *Congress* Krakow (Poland) 2022, *European Congress* Montpellier (France) 2021, *General Assembly* Brussels (Belgium) 2020, *Asia Pacific Conference* Beijing (China) 2019, *European Congress* Plovdiv (Bulgaria) 2019.
Members Full in 37 countries and territories:
Argentina, Australia, Austria, Belgium, Brazil, Canada, Chile, Egypt, Finland, France, Germany, Greece, Hong Kong, Hungary, India, Iran Islamic Rep, Iraq, Israel, Italy, Japan, Korea Rep, Lebanon, Libya, Luxembourg, Malaysia, Mauritius, Mexico, Portugal, Romania, Saudi Arabia, Singapore, Spain, Taiwan, Thailand, Türkiye, UK, USA. [2021/XD7636/**D**]

♦ World Federation of Major International Wine and Spirits Competitions (VinoFed) 21452

Fédération mondiale des grands concours internationaux de vins et spiritueux (FMGCIVS)
Pres Rue Beausite 4, 3960 Sierre VS, Switzerland. T. +41274563144. Fax +41274562144. E-mail: info@vinofed.com.
URL: http://www.vinofed.com/
History Also referred to by acronym *WFMIWSC*. **Aims** Promote wine and spirits competitions and encourage exchange of information regarding their economic and technical administration. **Structure** General Meeting (annual); Board of Directors; Executive Board. **Languages** French, Italian. **Staff** Voluntary. **Finance** Competitions. **Activities** Awards/prizes/competitions. **Events** *Meeting* Paris (France) 2001.
Members Competition organizers in 9 countries:
Argentina, Canada, France, Germany, Hungary, Italy, Slovenia, Spain, Switzerland.
Observer members (2):
International Organisation of Vine and Wine (OIV, #14435); *Union internationale des oenologues (UIOE, #20432).*
IGO Relations Observer to: *International Organisation of Vine and Wine (OIV, #14435).*
[2018.06.13/XD5185/**D**]

♦ World Federation of Master Tailors (WFMT) 21453

Fédération mondiale des maîtres-tailleurs – Weltverband der Massschneider – Wereldfederatie van Meester Kleermakers
Dir c/o Drottningholms Palace Theatre, Drottningens paviljong, SE-178 93 Drottningholm, Sweden.
URL: http://www.wfmastertailors.com/
History 1910, Brussels (Belgium). Previously existing as a Belgian federation, set up 1865. Former names and other names: *Fédération internationale des maîtres-tailleurs* – former (1910). **Aims** Promote the culture of fine clothing by safeguarding quality and passing down skills and expertise relevant to this sector to new generations. **Structure** Congress (every 2 years). Executive Committee, including President. **Languages** English, French, German. **Staff** 3.00 FTE, voluntary. **Finance** Sources: members' dues. Annual budget: 5,680 EUR. **Activities** Events/meetings. **Events** *Biennial Congress* Osaka (Japan) 2021, *Biennial Congress* Verona (Italy) 2019, *Biennial Congress* Taipei (Taiwan) 2017, *Biennial Congress* Tampere (Finland) 2015, *Biennial Congress* Seoul (Korea Rep) 2013. **Publications** Conference proceedings.
Members National federations in 24 countries:
Argentina, Austria, Brazil, Denmark, Egypt, Finland, France, Germany, Greece, Indonesia, Italy, Japan, Korea Rep, Malaysia, Netherlands, Portugal, Singapore, Spain, Sweden, Switzerland, Taiwan, Thailand, Türkiye, USA. [2020/XC3527/**C**]

♦ World Federation for Medical Education (WFME) 21454

Fédération mondiale pour l'enseignement médical (WFME) – Federación Mundial de Educación Médica (WFME)
Main Office 13A chemin du Levant, 01210 Ferney-Voltaire, France. E-mail: admin@wfme.org.
Registered Address Mildenham Mill, Egg Lane, Claines, Worcester, WR3 7SA, UK.
URL: http://www.wfme.org/
History 30 Sep 1972, Copenhagen (Denmark). Founded when constitution was signed, resulting from recommendations of meeting held in 1966, Delhi (India). Founders include: *WHO (#20950)*; *World Medical Association (WMA, #21646)*. Also has official titles in Arabic, Chinese and Russian. Previously had offices in: the Americas; Edinburgh (UK); Copenhagen (Denmark). Former names and other names: *Fédération mondiale de l'éducation médicale* – alias; *WFME Ltd* – legal name. Registration: Companies House, No/ID: 08994665, England and Wales. **Aims** Enhance quality of medical education worldwide; promote highest standards in medical education. **Structure** Executive Council. Regional Associations (6): Africa, Americas; Europe; the Middle East; South-East Asia; Western Pacific. **Languages** English. **Finance** Sources: revenue from activities/projects. **Activities** Certification/accreditation; events/meetings; standards/guidelines. **Events** *World Conference on Medical Education* Seoul (Korea Rep) 2019, *UNESCO World Conference on Bioethics, Medical Ethics and Health Law* Jerusalem (Israel) 2018, *Joint Conference* Istanbul (Turkey) 2014, *World Conference on Medical Education* Malmö (Sweden) 2012, *Geneva conference on person-centered medicine* Geneva (Switzerland) 2009. **Publications** Monographs; reports; conference proceedings.
Members Full: regional associations (6):
Association for Medical Education in Europe (AMEE, #02797); *Association for Medical Education in the Eastern Mediterranean Region (AMEEMR, #02796)*; *Association of Medical Schools in Africa (AMSA, #02798)*; *Pan American Federation of Associations of Medical Schools (PAFAMS, #18100)*; *South-East Asian Regional Association for Medical Education (SEARAME, #19780)*; *Western Pacific Association for Medical Education (WPAME, #20917).*
Founding members:
WHO (#20950); *World Medical Association (WMA, #21646).*
Executive members:
Educational Commission for Foreign Medical Graduates (ECFMG); *International Federation of Medical Students' Associations (IFMSA, #13478)*; Junior Doctor's Network (JDN).
Consultative Status Consultative status granted from: *ECOSOC (#05331)* (Ros C); *WHO (#20950)* (Official Relations). [2023.03.01/XD1261/y/**C**]

♦ World Federation for Mental Health (WFMH) 21455

Fédération mondiale pour la santé mentale (FMSM) – Federación Mundial de Salud Mental – Weltbund für Psychische Hygiene
Sec 6800 Park Ten Blvd, Suite 220-N, San Antonio TX 78218, USA. E-mail: info@wfmh.global.
URL: http://www.wfmh.global/
History 19 Aug 1948, London (UK). Founded during 3rd International Congress on Mental Health, as successor body to *International Committee for Mental Hygiene (inactive)*, set up 1931. Registration: USA, Colombia. **Aims** Promote among all peoples and nations the highest possible standard of mental health, defined in the broadest biological, medical, educational, social and cultural terms. **Structure** Assembly of voting members (annual); World Congress (every 2 years); Board of Directors; Executive Committee. **Languages** English. **Staff** 2.00 FTE, paid. **Finance** Sources: fees for services; gifts, legacies; grants; members' dues; private foundations. **Activities** Advocacy/lobbying/activism; events/meetings; guidance/assistance/consulting; research/documentation; training/education. **Events** *Biennial World Congress* London (UK) 2022, *Biennial World Congress* London (UK) 2021, *Biennial World Congress* Buenos Aires (Argentina) 2019, *Biennial World Congress* Delhi (India) 2017, *Biennial World Congress* Cairo (Egypt) 2015. **Publications** *WFMH Bulletin* (3 a year). *The Search for Mental Health: A History and Memoir of WFMH* (1998). Annual Report. World Congress proceedings; WMH Day Packet; monographs on special topics. **Information Services** *Clearing House for Information on Mental Health.*
Members Member (Voting) Associations (56) national and international organizations concerned with the enhancement and maintenance of health, mental health and human development; Affiliate Organizations (35) organizations interested in supporting the work of the Federation. Members in 95 countries and territories:
Afghanistan, Argentina, Australia, Austria, Azerbaijan, Belgium, Bolivia, Botswana, Brazil, Bulgaria, Canada, Chile, China, Croatia, Cyprus, Czechia, Denmark, Egypt, El Salvador, Finland, France, Georgia, Germany, Ghana, Greece, Hong Kong, Hungary, Iceland, India, Indonesia, Iran Islamic Rep, Iraq, Ireland, Israel, Italy, Jamaica, Japan, Jordan, Kazakhstan, Kenya, Kuwait, Lebanon, Lesotho, Lithuania, Malawi, Malaysia, Mauritius, Mexico, Mongolia, Morocco, Namibia, Nepal, Netherlands, New Zealand, Nigeria, Norway, Pakistan, Palau, Palestine, Papua New Guinea, Peru, Philippines, Poland, Portugal, Puerto Rico, Qatar, Romania, Russia, Rwanda, Saudi Arabia, Senegal, Serbia, Sierra Leone, Singapore, Slovenia, South Africa, Spain, Sri Lanka, St Kitts-Nevis, St Lucia, Sweden, Switzerland, Taiwan, Thailand, Trinidad-Tobago, Türkiye, Uganda, UK, Ukraine, United Arab Emirates, Uruguay, USA, Yemen, Zambia, Zimbabwe.
Included in the above, 1 organization listed in this Yearbook:
International Council of Psychologists (ICP, #13065).
Consultative Status Consultative status granted from: *ECOSOC (#05331)* (Special); *ILO (#11123)* (Special List); *WHO (#20950)* (Official Relations); *UNICEF (#20332)*. **IGO Relations** Accredited by (1): *United Nations Office at Vienna (UNOV, #20604).* Associated with Department of Global Communications of the United Nations. [2022/XA3514/y/**A**]

♦ World Federation of Merino Breeders (WFMB) 21456

Fédération mondiale des éleveurs de mérinos
CEO PO Box 320, Condobolin NSW 2877, Australia. T. +61268952274.
URL: http://www.merinoworldfederation.com/
History Apr 1986, Madrid (Spain), during 2nd World Merino Conference, when Constitution was adopted. **Aims** Facilitate and promote the breeding of Merino sheep and the use of Merino wool, meat and other products throughout the world. **Structure** World Executive. **Finance** Sources: members' dues. **Activities** Awareness raising; events/meetings; knowledge management/information dissemination. **Events** *Quadrennial Conference / World Conference* Stellenbosch (South Africa) 2014, *World Conference* France 2010, *Quadrennial Conference* Rambouillet (France) 2010, *Quadrennial Conference / World Conference* Australia 2006, *Quadrennial Conference* Budapest (Hungary) 2002. **Publications** *Merino World* – newsletter.
Members Full in 12 countries:
Argentina, Australia, France, Hungary, Lesotho, New Zealand, Portugal, Russia, South Africa, Spain, Uruguay, USA.
[2019.03.22/XU6805/**C**]

♦ World Federation for the Metallurgic Industry (inactive)

♦ World Federation of Methodist and Uniting Church Women (WFM and UCW) 21457

World Sec 20 Calvert Road, New Plymouth 4310, New Zealand. T. +6467695856. E-mail: world.secretary@wfmucw.org.
URL: http://wfmucw.org/
History Founded 26 Oct 1939, Pasadena CA (USA), as *World Federation of Methodist Women (WFMW) – Fédération mondiale de femmes méthodistes – Weltföderation der Methodistinnen*. Reorganized 1956, becoming a World Federation officially recognized by *World Methodist Council (WMC, #21650)*. Current constitution adopted 2001. **Aims** Be a support group for women acting as a catalyst in their faith and actions so as to promote women's interests in all areas of life, in spiritual growth, equality, development and peace; work towards the recognition of the *equal* status of women; facilitate, encourage and actively promote leadership training for women; be a voice for Methodist, United and Uniting Church Women. **Structure** Assembly (every 5 years, normally preceding World Methodist Council and Conference); Executive Committee; Regional Areas, each with Area President and Area Vice-Presidents: Southern and East Africa; West Africa; Latin America – *Confederación Femenina Metodista América Latina y El Caribe (CFMAL and El Caribe, no recent information)*; North America; East Asia and West Asia; Europe – Britain and Ireland; Europe – Continental; South Pacific. Areas comprise several national organizations (71 Units) each with its own constitution and bylaws. UN representatives (3) in New York NY (USA) and Santiago (Chile); Consultant on Ageing in New York NY (USA). 1 rep UN in Geneva (Switzerland). **Languages** English. **Staff** 25.00 FTE, voluntary. **Finance** Contributions based on Unit membership; special gifts; offerings. **Activities** Events/meetings; projects/programmes; training/education. **Events** *Quinquennial Assembly* Gothenburg (Sweden) 2021, *Quinquennial Assembly* Houston, TX (USA) 2016, *Quinquennial Assembly* Jeju (Korea Rep) 2006, *Quinquennial Assembly* Loughborough (UK) 2001, *West Africa regional seminar* Ghana 1998. **Publications** *Tree of Life* (4 a year) – international newsletter; *Handbook of the World Federation of Methodist and Uniting Church Women* (every 5 years). *From Memory to Hope – A Narrative History of the Areas of the World Federation of Methodist Women*; *Methodist Women: A World Sisterhood*; *Women and Leadership – Responding to the Call*; *Women and Spiritual Growth – Responding to the Call*. Resource leaflets; annual study material; training/development manuals. **Information Services** *World Federation Archives* – at WMC HQ, Lake Junaluska NC (USA).
Members National Units (representing about 3 million members) and individuals, in 77 countries and territories:
Angola, Argentina, Australia, Austria, Bahamas, Barbados, Benin, Botswana, Brazil, Bulgaria, Canada, Chile, Congo DR, Costa Rica, Cuba, Czechia, Denmark, Estonia, Eswatini, Fiji, Finland, Gambia, Germany, Ghana, Haiti, Hong Kong, Hungary, India, Indonesia, Ireland, Italy, Jamaica, Kenya, Korea Rep, Latvia, Lesotho, Malaysia, Mexico, Mozambique, Myanmar, New Zealand, Nigeria, North Macedonia, Norway, Pakistan, Panama, Papua New Guinea, Paraguay, Philippines, Poland, Portugal, Russia, Rwanda, Samoa, Serbia-Montenegro, Sierra Leone, Singapore, Slovakia, Slovenia, Solomon Is; South Africa, Spain, Sri Lanka, St Kitts-Nevis, St Lucia, St Vincent-Grenadines, Sweden, Switzerland, Taiwan, Togo, Tonga, Uganda, UK, Uruguay, USA, Zambia, Zimbabwe.
Consultative Status Consultative status granted from: *ECOSOC (#05331)* (Special); *ILO (#11123)* (Special List); *UNICEF (#20332)*. **IGO Relations** Represented at: *United Nations Economic Commission for Latin America and the Caribbean (ECLAC, #20556).* Associated with Department of Global Communications of the United Nations. **NGO Relations** Affiliated with World Methodist Council. Related to: *European Methodist Council (EMC, #07787)*; *World Council of Churches (WCC, #21320)*. Member of: *Conference of Non-Governmental Organizations in Consultative Relationship with the United Nations (CONGO, #04635).*
[2018.09.14/XC3528/**B**]

♦ World Federation of Methodist Women / see World Federation of Methodist and Uniting Church Women (#21457)

♦ World Federation of Minimally Invasive Spine Surgery (WFMISS) .. 21458

Contact R Martiniano de Carvalho 951, Bela Vista, Sao Paulo SP, Brazil. T. +551135056687.
Seat Rua Conselheiro Brotero 1486, Higienópolis, Sao Paulo SP, Brazil.
URL: http://www.wfmiss.com/

History 16 Aug 2012, Praia do Forte (Brazil), during 3rd World Congress of Minimally Invasive Spine Surgery and Techniques (WCMISST), when constitution was adopted. Registered in accordance with Brazilian law. **Aims** Congregate and connect all societies worldwide dedicated to minimally invasive spine surgeries and techniques (MISST) so as to promote scientific exchange among professionals in the field, foster development of this clinical endeavour, and disseminate relevant knowledge as widely and effectively as possible. **Structure** Administrative Council; Executive Committee. **Finance** Sources: members' dues. **Events** *World Congress* Mexico City (Mexico) 2016, *World Congress* Istanbul (Turkey) 2014, *World Congress of Minimally Invasive Spine Surgery and Techniques (WCMISST)* Praia do Forte (Brazil) 2012, *World Congress of Minimally Invasive Spine Surgery and Techniques (WCMISST)* Las Vegas, NV (USA) 2010, *World Congress of Minimally Invasive Spine Surgery and Techniques (WCMISST)* Hawaii (USA) 2008. **NGO Relations** *Sociedad Interamericana de Cirugia de Columa Minimamente Invasiva (SICCMI, #19383).* [2015/XJ9720/**C**]

♦ World Federation of Modern Language Associations / see International Federation of Language Teacher Associations (#13468)

♦ World Federation of Moroccan Jewry (unconfirmed)

♦ World Federation of Music Therapy (WFMT) 21459

Federación Mundial de Musicoterapia

Sec address not obtained. E-mail: secretary@wfmt.info – president@wfmt.info.
Treas address not obtained. E-mail: treasurer@wfmt.info.
URL: http://www.wfmt.info/

History 1985, Genoa (Italy). **Aims** Promote development and recognition of the profession of music therapy throughout the world. **Structure** Council; Commissions (8); Regional Liaisons (8). **Languages** English. **Staff** None. **Finance** Sources: members' dues. Patronage. **Activities** Certification/accreditation; events/meetings; networking/liaising; publishing activities; research and development; training/education. **Events** *World Congress* Vancouver, BC (Canada) 2023, *World Congress* Tshwane (South Africa) 2020, *World Congress* Tsukuba (Japan) 2017, *World Congress* Vienna (Austria) / Krems (Austria) 2014, *World congress* Seoul (Korea Rep) 2011. **Publications** *Music Therapy Today* – journal.

Members Organizational (Full and Associate); Individual (Professional and Associate); Student (Organizational and Individual). Members in 40 countries and territories:
Argentina, Australia, Austria, Bahrain, Brazil, Canada, Chile, China, Colombia, Czechia, Dominican Rep, Egypt, France, Germany, Ghana, Greece, Hong Kong, India, Indonesia, Iran Islamic Rep, Italy, Japan, Korea Rep, Kuwait, Lebanon, Mexico, New Zealand, Philippines, Poland, Puerto Rico, Qatar, Singapore, South Africa, Spain, Switzerland, Taiwan, Tunisia, Türkiye, UK, USA.

NGO Relations Also links with national associations. [2022.05.11/XD6826/**D**]

♦ World Federation of National Mathematical Competitions (WFNMC) 21460

Sec ul Pivchenkova 5-69, Moscow MOSKVA, Russia, 121108. E-mail: turnirgorodov@gmail.com.
URL: http://www.wfnmc.org/

History 1984, Adelaide (Australia), during the 5th International Congress for Mathematical Education (ICME). Constitution approved, 1996; revised, 2004. **Aims** Provide a focal point for those interested in, and concerned with, conducting national mathematics competitions for the purpose of stimulating the learning of mathematics; serving as a resource for exchange of information and ideas on mathematics competitions and related activities; assist with development and improvement of mathematics competitions and related activities; increase public awareness of the role of mathematics competitions and related activities in the education of all students and assuring that the importance of that role is properly recognized in academic circles; create and enhance professional links between mathematicians involved in competitions and related activities around the world. **Structure** Formal General Meeting (every 4 years); Executive Committee; Regional Representatives (7); Programme Committee; Awards Committee; Editorial Panel. **Languages** English. **Finance** Members' dues. **Activities** Events/meetings; awards/prizes/competitions. **Events** *Congress* Sofia (Bulgaria) 2022, *Congress* Graz (Austria) 2018, *Congress* Barranquilla (Colombia) 2014, *General Meeting* Seoul (Korea Rep) 2012, *Congress* Riga (Latvia) 2010. **Publications** *Mathematics Competitions* (2 a year) – journal. **Members** Individuals and organizations. Membership countries not specified. **NGO Relations** An affiliated international study group of: *International Commission on Mathematical Instruction (ICMI, #12700).* [2017.03.08/XD5514/**D**]

♦ World Federation of Neurology (WFN) 21461

Management Dir Chester House, Fulham Green, 81-83 Fulham High St, London, SW6 3JA, UK. T. +442035421657 – +442035421658. E-mail: info@wfneurology.org.
URL: http://www.wfneurology.org/

History 1931, Bern (Switzerland), as *International Neurological Congress – Congrès neurologique international*; reconstituted 1955, Brussels (Belgium). Present title adopted 1957. Previous French title *Fédération mondiale de neurologie (FMN)* no longer used. Most recent statutes adopted 19 Sep 2000. UK Registered Charity: 1068673. **Aims** Foster quality neurology and brain health worldwide. **Structure** General Meeting (annual); Council of Delegates; Trustees; Committees (13); Applied Research Groups (15). Regional body: *Asian and Oceanian Association of Neurology (AOAN, #01574).* **Languages** English. **Staff** 2.00 FTE, paid. **Finance** Sources: members' dues. Contributions from national societies, foundations and industry. **Activities** Events/meetings; knowledge management/information dissemination; research/documentation; training/education. **Events** *International Congress on Neuromuscular Diseases* Brussels (Belgium) 2022, *International Congress on Neuromuscular Diseases* 2021, *Meeting* Nara (Japan) 2021, *Biennial Congress* Rome (Italy) 2021, *Biennial Congress* Dubai (United Arab Emirates) 2019. **Publications** *Journal of Neurological Sciences* (6 a year); *World Neurology – The Newsletter of the WFN* (6 a year). Research Group reports; seminar proceedings.

Members National neurological societies, groups and individuals in 116 countries and territories:
Albania, Algeria, Argentina, Armenia, Australia, Austria, Azerbaijan, Bahrain, Bangladesh, Belgium, Bolivia, Brazil, Bulgaria, Burkina Faso, Cameroon, Canada, Chile, China, Colombia, Congo DR, Costa Rica, Côte d'Ivoire, Croatia, Cuba, Cyprus, Czechia, Denmark, Dominican Rep, Ecuador, Egypt, El Salvador, Estonia, Ethiopia, Finland, France, Georgia, Germany, Greece, Guatemala, Guinea, Honduras, Hong Kong, Hungary, Iceland, India, Indonesia, Iran Islamic Rep, Iraq, Ireland, Israel, Italy, Japan, Jordan, Kazakhstan, Kenya, Korea Rep, Kuwait, Kyrgyzstan, Latvia, Lebanon, Libya, Lithuania, Luxembourg, Malaysia, Mexico, Moldova, Mongolia, Morocco, Myanmar, Netherlands, New Zealand, Nicaragua, Nigeria, North Macedonia, Norway, Oman, Pakistan, Palestine, Panama, Paraguay, Peru, Philippines, Poland, Portugal, Puerto Rico, Qatar, Romania, Russia, Saudi Arabia, Senegal, Serbia, Singapore, Slovakia, Slovenia, South Africa, Spain, Sri Lanka, Sudan, Sweden, Switzerland, Syrian AR, Taiwan, Tanzania UR, Thailand, Tunisia, Türkiye, Uganda, UK, United Arab Emirates, Uruguay, USA, Uzbekistan, Venezuela, Vietnam, Yemen, Zambia.

Consultative Status Consultative status granted from: *WHO (#20950)* (Official Relations). [2020/XB3529/y/**B**]

♦ World Federation of Neuro-Oncology Societies (WFNOS) 21462

Contact c/o Society for Neuro-Oncology, PO Box 273297, Houston TX 77277-3296, USA. T. +17135260269. E-mail: shelley@soc-neuro-onc.org.
URL: https://wfnos.org/

Structure Includes: *Asian Society for Neuro-Oncology (ASNO, #01731)*; *European Association for Neuro-Oncology (EANO, #06132)*; (US) Society for Neuro-Oncology. **Activities** Events/meetings. **Events** *Quadrennial Meeting* Seoul (Korea Rep) 2022, *Quadrennial Meeting* Seoul (Korea Rep) 2021, *Quadrennial Meeting* Zurich (Switzerland) 2017, *Quadrennial Meeting* San Francisco, CA (USA) 2013, *Quadrennial meeting* Yokohama (Japan) 2009. **Publications** *Neuro-Oncology* – journal. **NGO Relations** Instrumental in setting up: *International Brain Tumour Alliance (IBTA, #12393).* [2019.12.12/XD8921/**D**]

♦ World Federation of Neuroradiological Societies (WFNRS) 21463

Exec Dir 800 Enterprise Dr, Ste 205, Oak Brook IL 60523, USA.
URL: http://www.wfnrs.org/

History 1993. **Structure** Officers: President; Vice-President; Secretary-General; Treasurer; President, Symposium Neuroradiologicum; Historian. Staff: Executive Director; Project Coordinator. **Events** *Quadrennial Neuroradiologicum Symposium* New York, NY (USA) 2022, *Quadrennial Neuroradiologicum Symposium* Taipei (Taiwan) 2018, *Quadrennial Neuroradiologicum Symposium / Quadrennial Symposium* Istanbul (Turkey) 2014, *Quadrennial Neuroradiologicum Symposium* Bologna (Italy) 2010, *Quadrennial Neuroradiologicum Symposium* Adelaide, SA (Australia) 2006.

Members National and regional societies (15) in 15 countries and territories:
Australia, Austria, France, Germany, Japan, Korea Rep, Norway, Saudi Arabia, Spain, Sweden, Switzerland, Taiwan, Thailand, UK, USA.

Included in the above, 3 organizations listed in this Yearbook:
Asian and Oceanian Society of Neuroradiology and Head and Neck Radiology (AOSNHNR, #01582); *European Society of Neuroradiology (ESNR, #08664)*; *Pan-Arab NeuroRadiology Society (PANRS, #18150).* [2018/XD5979/**D**]

♦ World Federation for NeuroRehabilitation (WFNR) 21464

Exec Dir 14 Rake House Farm, Rake Lane, North Shields, NE29 8EQ, UK. T. +441912595547.
Pres address not obtained.
URL: http://www.wfnr.co.uk/

History 1996, Newcastle upon Tyne (UK). **Aims** Advance development and improve quality of neurological *rehabilitation* worldwide; stimulate collaboration between clinicians and others interested in neurological rehabilitation; facilitate exchange of knowledge and scientific research. **Structure** General Assembly (during World Congress); Council; Management Presidium. **Languages** English. **Staff** 1.00 FTE, paid. **Finance** Sources: subscriptions. **Events** *World Congress for NeuroRehabilitation (WCNR)* Daegu (Korea Rep) 2026, *World Congress for NeuroRehabilitation (WCNR)* Vancouver, BC (Canada) 2024, *World Congress for NeuroRehabilitation (WCNR)* Vienna (Austria) 2022, *World Congress* North Shields (UK) 2020, *World Congress for NeuroRehabilitation* Mumbai (India) 2018. **Publications** *Neurorehabilitation and Neural Repair* (4 a year); *WFNR Update* (2 a year).

Members Affiliated organizations in 40 countries:
Albania, Australia, Austria, Belarus, Belgium, Benin, Cameroon, Chile, China, Croatia, Czechia, Denmark, Egypt, Finland, France, Germany, Greece, India, Indonesia, Italy, Japan, Korea Rep, Mauritius, Moldova, Mongolia, Netherlands, Philippines, Poland, Romania, Russia, Siberia, South Africa, Spain, Sweden, Switzerland, Thailand, Türkiye, UK, Ukraine, USA.

Also members in Latin America and Pan Arabic region. Membership countries not specified.

NGO Relations Founding member of: *Global Rehabilitation Alliance (#10565).* Member of: *World Federation of Neurology (WFN, #21461).* Associate member of: *International Industry Society in Advanced Rehabilitation Technology (IISART, #13840).* [2023/XJ3126/**C**]

♦ World Federation of Neuroscience Nurses (WFNN) 21465

Fédération mondiale des infirmiers en neurochirurgie

Pres 1405 W 50th Terrace, Kansas City MO 64112, USA. T. +15736739358. E-mail: charmaine.gust@gmail.com.
URL: http://www.wfnn.org/

History 1973. Founded following activities initiated by Agnes Marshall in 1969. **Aims** Encourage and provide the opportunity for association of neuroscience nurses throughout the world; aid the exchange and dissemination of knowledge and ideas in the field; foster high standards in patient care; promote growth in the specialty; encourage clinical nursing research; encourage establishment of national societies. **Languages** English. **Staff** Voluntary. **Finance** Sources: members' dues. **Activities** Awards/prizes/competitions; events/meetings. **Events** *Quadrennial International Meeting* Darwin, NT (Australia) 2025, *Quadrennial International Meeting* Darwin, NT (Australia) 2021, *Sydney Neuroscience Symposium* Sydney, NSW (Australia) 2021, *Sydney Neuroscience Symposium* Sydney, NSW (Australia) 2020, *Quadrennial International Meeting* Opatija (Croatia) 2017. **Publications** *World Federation of Neuroscience Nursing Newsletter.*

Members National societies in 14 countries:
Australia, Austria, Belgium, Canada, Denmark, Finland, France, Germany, Italy, Japan, Korea Rep, Netherlands, UK, USA.

Individuals in 8 countries:
Cuba, Estonia, Ghana, Greece, India, Israel, Romania, Russia. [2022.10.19/XD6206/**D**]

♦ World Federation of Neurosurgical Societies (WFNS) 21466

Fédération mondiale des sociétés de neurochirurgie – Federación Mundial de Sociedades de Neurocirugia

Office Manager Rue du Marché 5, 1260 Nyon VD, Switzerland. T. +41223624304. Fax +41223624352. E-mail: centraloffice@wfns.org.
URL: http://www.wfns.org/

History 1955. Constitution adopted during 1st International Congress of Neurological Surgery, 1957, Brussels (Belgium). **Aims** Advance neurological surgery in all its aspects by facilitating personal association of neurosurgeons throughout the world. **Structure** Congress (every 4 years); Executive Committee; Administrative Council. *Ad hoc* Committees: Cerebrovascular Diseases & Therapy; Education & Training; Global Neurosurgery; Honorary Presidents; Liaison Committee WFNS/WHO; Medal of Honour; Neuroendoscopy; Neuro-Oncology; Neurosurgical Anatomy; Neurotraumatology; Pediatric Neurosurgery; Peripheral Nerve Surgery; Skull-Base Surgery; Spine; Stereotactic and Functional Neurosurgery; William Scoville Award; Women in Neurosurgery; Young Neurosurgeons Award Committee (Atos Alves de Souza); Young Neurosurgeons Forum. **Languages** English. **Staff** 2.00 FTE, paid. **Finance** Sources: meeting proceeds; members' dues. **Activities** Events/meetings; knowledge management/information dissemination; research and development; standards/guidelines; training/education. **Events** *World Congress of Neurosurgery* Cape Town (South Africa) 2023, *International Conference on Recent Advances in Neurotraumatology (ICRAN)* Santa Cruz (Bolivia) 2023, *World Congress of Neurosurgery* Bogota (Colombia) 2022, *Quadrennial Congress* Bogota (Colombia) 2021, *Congress of the International Society of Minimally Invasive Neurosurgery* Surabaya (Indonesia) 2021. **Publications** *WFNS Bulletin* (2-4 a year). Congress proceedings.

Members Continental, national, regional and multinational general neurosurgical societies (137). Full in 95 countries and territories:
Albania, Algeria, Argentina, Armenia, Australia, Austria, Bangladesh, Belgium, Bolivia, Brazil, Bulgaria, Cambodia, Canada, Chile, China, Colombia, Costa Rica, Croatia, Cuba, Cyprus, Czechia, Dominican Rep, Ecuador, Egypt, El Salvador, Finland, France, Georgia, Germany, Ghana, Greece, Honduras, Hong Kong, Hungary, India, Indonesia, Iran Islamic Rep, Israel, Italy, Japan, Jordan, Kazakhstan, Korea Rep, Kuwait, Kyrgyzstan, Latvia, Lebanon, Libya, Lithuania, Malaysia, Mexico, Moldova, Mongolia, Morocco, Myanmar, Nepal, Netherlands, Nigeria, North Macedonia, Norway, Pakistan, Palestine, Panama, Paraguay, Peru, Philippines, Poland, Portugal, Qatar, Romania, Russia, Saudi Arabia, Serbia, Singapore, Slovakia, Slovenia, South Africa, Spain, Sudan, Sweden, Switzerland, Syrian AR, Taiwan, Thailand, Tunisia, Türkiye, UK, Ukraine, United Arab Emirates, Uruguay, USA, Uzbekistan, Venezuela, Vietnam, Yemen.

Consultative Status Consultative status granted from: *ECOSOC (#05331)* (Ros C); *WHO (#20950)* (Official Relations). [2022/XC3530/y/**B**]

♦ World Federation of Non-Destructive Evaluation Centers (internationally oriented national body)

♦ World Federation of Nuclear Medicine and Biology (WFNMB) 21467

Fédération mondiale de médecine et de biologie nucléaires – Federación Mundial de Medicina y Biologia Nucleares

Permanent Secretariat WFNMB Office, Schmalzhofgasse 26, 1060 Vienna, Austria. T. +4318904427. E-mail: office@wfnmb.org.
Pres address not obtained.
URL: http://www.wfnmb.org/

History 1970. **Aims** Assist national and nuclear medical services in the development, organization and quality control of nuclear medicine. **Structure** Officers: President, Secretary-General, Treasurer and Scientific Chairman. **Languages** English. **Staff** None. **Finance** Members' dues: US$ 1, per full member, per year. Budget (annual): about US$ 10,000. **Activities** *World Association of Radiopharmaceutical and Molecular Therapy (WARMTH, #21181)* is a subsidiary. International committees on radiation protection and education are at the planning stage. **Events** *Quadrennial Congress* Kyoto (Japan) 2022, *Symposium* Cairns, QLD (Australia) 2018, *Quadrennial Congress* Melbourne, VIC (Australia) 2018, *Quadrennial Congress* Cancún (Mexico) 2014, *Quadrennial Congress* Cape Town (South Africa) 2010. **Publications** *Alasbimn Journal*; *European Journal of Nuclear Medicine.* Conference proceedings.

Members National societies in 79 countries and territories:
Algeria, Argentina, Australia, Austria, Bangladesh, Belgium, Bolivia, Brazil, Bulgaria, Canada, Chile, China, Colombia, Costa Rica, Côte d'Ivoire, Croatia, Cuba, Czechia, Denmark, Ecuador, Egypt, Ethiopia, Finland, France, Germany, Greece, Guatemala, Hong Kong, Hungary, India, Indonesia, Iran Islamic Rep, Iraq, Ireland, Israel, Italy, Japan, Korea Rep, Kuwait, Malaysia, Mauritius, Mexico, Mongolia, Morocco, Netherlands, New Zealand, Nigeria, North Macedonia, Norway, Pakistan, Paraguay, Peru, Philippines, Poland, Portugal, Puerto Rico, Romania, Saudi Arabia, Senegal, Sierra Leone, Singapore, Slovakia, South Africa, Spain, Sri Lanka, Sweden, Switzerland, Taiwan, Thailand, Tunisia, Türkiye, Uganda, UK, United Arab Emirates, Uruguay, USA, Venezuela, Zambia, Zimbabwe.

Also members in the Caribbean and in the former USSR. Member countries not specified.
Consultative Status Consultative status granted from: *ECOSOC (#05331)* (Ros C). **IGO Relations** Affiliated with: *International Atomic Energy Agency (IAEA, #12294)*. **NGO Relations** Affiliated organization: *African Association of Nuclear Medicine (AANM, #00210)*. [2020/XD0946/C]

♦ World Federation of Occupational Therapists (WFOT) 21468
Fédération mondiale des ergothérapeutes – Federación Mundial de Ergoterapeutas
Exec Dir PO 53187, London, E18 9DF, UK. E-mail: admin@wfot.org.
Pres address not obtained.
Official address c/o Avocat Mentha and Associés, Rue de l'Athénée 4, 1211 Geneva 12, Switzerland.
URL: http://www.wfot.org/
History 7 Apr 1952, Liverpool (UK). **Aims** Promote occupational therapy as an art and science internationally; support development, use and practice of occupational therapy worldwide, demonstrating its relevance and contribution to society. **Structure** Council (meets every 2 years). **Languages** English, French, German, Spanish. **Staff** 6.00 FTE, paid. Several voluntary. **Finance** Sources: donations; members' dues. **Activities** Events/meetings; research and development; standards/guidelines; training/education. **Events** *Congress* Paris (France) 2022, *Council Meeting* Paris (France) 2022, *Council Meeting* 2021, *Congress* Cape Town (South Africa) 2018, *Council Meeting* Medellin (Colombia) 2016. **Publications** *WFOT Bulletin* (2 a year). Position statements; resources guidelines; manuals.
Members Organizations (105) and individuals (over 580,000). Full in 74 countries and territories:
Argentina, Australia, Austria, Bangladesh, Belgium, Brazil, Bulgaria, Canada, Chile, China, Colombia, Cyprus, Czechia, Denmark, Estonia, Finland, France, Georgia, Germany, Ghana, Greece, Haiti, Hong Kong, Iceland, India, Indonesia, Iran Islamic Rep, Ireland, Israel, Italy, Japan, Jordan, Kenya, Korea Rep, Kosovo, Latvia, Lithuania, Madagascar, Malawi, Malaysia, Malta, Mauritius, Mexico, Morocco, Netherlands, New Zealand, Norway, Pakistan, Palestine, Peru, Philippines, Portugal, Romania, Russia, Rwanda, Saudi Arabia, Singapore, Slovenia, South Africa, Spain, Sri Lanka, Sweden, Switzerland, Taiwan, Tanzania UR, Thailand, Trinidad-Tobago, Türkiye, Uganda, UK, USA, Venezuela, Zambia, Zimbabwe.
Associate in 24 countries and territories:
Armenia, Bahamas, Bermuda, Bosnia-Herzegovina, Botswana, Costa Rica, Croatia, Dominican Rep, Faeroe Is, Guyana, Jamaica, Kazakhstan, Lebanon, Luxembourg, Macau, Mongolia, Namibia, Nigeria, Panama, Poland, Serbia, Seychelles, Tunisia, Ukraine.
Regional members (7):
Arabic Occupational Therapists Regional Group (AOTRG); *Asia Pacific Occupational Therapists Regional Group (APOTRG, #01982)*; *Association of Caribbean Occupational Therapists (#02409)*; *Council of Occupational Therapists for the European Countries (COTEC, #04912)*; Kuwait Group; *Latin American Occupational Therapists Confederation (#16356)*; *Occupational Therapy African Region Group (OTARG, #17646)*.
Consultative Status Consultative status granted from: *ECOSOC (#05331)* (Ros C); *WHO (#20950)* (Official Relations). **IGO Relations** Accredited by (1): *United Nations Office at Vienna (UNOV, #20604)*. Associated with Department of Global Communications of the United Nations. **NGO Relations** Member of (1): *Global Rehabilitation Alliance (#10565)* (as Founding member). [2022.06.21/XC3531/y/C]

♦ World Federation of Orthodontists 21469
Executive Secretariat 401 North Lindbergh Bld, St Louis MO 63141, USA. E-mail: wfo@wfo.org.
SG 830 West End Court, Suite 175, Vernon Hills IL 60060-1382, USA. T. +18473674920. Fax +18479496396.
URL: http://www.wfo.org/
History 15 May 1995, San Francisco CA (USA), at 4th International Orthodontic Congress. **Aims** Advance the art and science of, and encourage high standards in, orthodontics worldwide. **Structure** General Assembly (every 5 years, at Congress); Council; Executive Committee. **Activities** Certification/accreditation; events/meetings; guidance/assistance/consulting; knowledge management/information dissemination; standards/guidelines. **Events** *Quinquennial Congress* Yokohama (Japan) 2020, *Quinquennial Congress / International Orthodontic Congress* London (UK) 2015, *General Assembly* Sydney, NSW (Australia) 2010, *Quinquennial Congress* Sydney, NSW (Australia) 2010, *General assembly / International Orthodontic Congress* Paris (France) 2005. **Publications** *WFO Gazette* (2 a year).
Members Organizations (104) in 82 countries and territories:
Argentina, Australia, Azerbaijan, Bangladesh, Belgium, Bolivia, Brazil, Bulgaria, Canada, Chile, Colombia, Costa Rica, Cyprus, Czechia, Denmark, Dominican Rep, Ecuador, Egypt, El Salvador, France, Germany, Greece, Guatemala, Honduras, Hong Kong, Hungary, Iceland, India, Indonesia, Iran Islamic Rep, Iraq, Ireland, Israel, Italy, Japan, Jordan, Korea Rep, Kuwait, Latvia, Lebanon, Lithuania, Luxembourg, Macau, Malaysia, Mexico, Moldova, Morocco, Namibia, Netherlands, New Zealand, Nicaragua, Nigeria, Norway, Palestine, Panama, Paraguay, Peru, Philippines, Poland, Portugal, Romania, Russia, Saudi Arabia, Serbia, Singapore, Slovakia, Slovenia, South Africa, Spain, Sri Lanka, Sudan, Sweden, Syrian AR, Taiwan, Thailand, Tunisia, Türkiye, UK, Ukraine, United Arab Emirates, USA, Venezuela.
Individuals in 16 countries and territories:
Algeria, Armenia, Aruba, Austria, Bahrain, Barbados, Belize, China, Croatia, Ghana, Kenya, Myanmar, Nepal, Pakistan, Qatar, Uruguay.
Regional affiliates (6):
Arab Orthodontic Society (AOS, #01022); *Asociación Iberoamericana de Ortodoncistas (AIO, #02151)*; *Caribbean Society of Orthodontists*; *European Orthodontic Society (EOS, #08118)*; *Foederatio Europea Orthodontica (FEO, #09811)*; *Latin American Odontological Federation (#16357)*. [2020/XE0975/y/B]

♦ World Federation of Overseas Korean Traders Associations (World OKTA) 21470
Headquarters Secretariat Kintex Road 217-59, Office Building No 1002 – Kintex 2, Seo-gu, Ilsan, Goyang GYEONGGI 10390, Korea Rep. T. +82216449033. Fax +8225715381.
URL: http://www.okta.net/
History Apr 1981, Los Angeles CA (USA). **Aims** Develop and expand Korean export markets. **Structure** Executive Committee. Officers: President; 4 Vice-Presidents; Chairman. Committees (8). Sub-Committees (4). **Activities** Organizes conventions, seminars and trade school. **Events** *International Leaders Meeting* Daejeon (Korea Rep) 2021, *Convention* Seoul (Korea Rep) 2021, *International Leaders Meeting* Daejeon (Korea Rep) 2020, *Convention* Seoul (Korea Rep) 2020, *Convention* Las Vegas, NV (USA) 2019. [2018/XM2893/t/D]

♦ World Federation of Parasitologists (WFP) 21471
Fédération mondiale des parasitologues
Exec Sec University of Kent, School of Biosciences, Ingram Building, Room 220, Canterbury, CT2 7NH, UK.
Pres Statens Serum Institut, Artillerivej 5, 2300 Copenhagen, Denmark.
URL: http://www.wfpnet.org/
History 1960, Warsaw (Poland). **Aims** Unite those engaged in the study of parasites and to present forums for international exchange of information and ideas. **Structure** Congress (every 4 years); Permanent Council; Executive Board. **Languages** English. **Staff** None. **Finance** Sources: members' dues. **Activities** Events/meetings; knowledge management/information dissemination. **Events** *International Congress of Parasitology (ICOPA)* Canada 2026, *International Congress of Parasitology* Copenhagen (Denmark) 2022, *International Congress of Parasitology* Daegu (Korea Rep) 2018, *International Congress of Parasitology* Mexico City (Mexico) 2014, *International Congress of Parasitology* Melbourne, VIC (Australia) 2010. **Publications** *Parasite Epidemiology and Control* (3 a year).
Members National organizations in 63 countries and territories:
Algeria, Argentina, Australia, Austria, Belgium, Brazil, Bulgaria, Canada, Chile, China, Colombia, Costa Rica, Cuba, Czechia, Denmark, Ecuador, Egypt, Estonia, Finland, France, Georgia, Germany, Greece, Guatemala, Hungary, Iceland, India, Indonesia, Iran Islamic Rep, Ireland, Israel, Italy, Japan, Kenya, Korea Rep, Lithuania, Malaysia, Mexico, Montenegro, Morocco, Netherlands, New Zealand, Nigeria, Norway, Pakistan, Peru, Philippines, Poland, Romania, Russia, Senegal, Serbia, Slovakia, South Africa, Spain, Sweden, Switzerland, Thailand, Türkiye, UK, USA, Uzbekistan, Venezuela.
Included in the above, 8 organizations listed in this Yearbook:
American Society of Tropical Medicine and Hygiene (ASTMH); *East African Society for Parasitology*; *European Federation of Parasitologists (EFP, #07186)*; *International Commission on Trichinellosis (#12735)*; *Latin American Federation of Parasitologists (#16327)*; *Parasitological Society of Southern Africa (PARSA)*; *Scandinavian-Baltic Society for Parasitology (SBSP, #19081)*; *Southeastern and Eastern European Parasitologists (SEEEP, #19803)*.
Consultative Status Consultative status granted from: *ECOSOC (#05331)* (Ros C); *FAO (#09260)* (Special Status). **NGO Relations** Member of (1): *International Union of Biological Sciences (IUBS, #15760)* (as Scientific member). [2023/XC3532/y/B]

♦ World Federation of Pediatric Imaging (WFPI) 21472
Pres Children's Natl Med Ctr, 111 Michigan Ave NW, Washington DC 20010, USA. E-mail: wfpi-office@gmail.com.
URL: http://www.wfpiweb.org/
History 2011. Founded by *Asian and Oceanic Society for Pediatric Radiology (AOSPR, #01587)*, *Sociedad Latinoamericana de Radiologia Pediatrica (SLARP, #19424)*, *European Society of Paediatric Radiology (ESPR, #08686)* and *Society for Pediatric Radiology (SPR)*. Currently run under the auspices of SPR. **Aims** Provide an international platform for paediatric radiology organizations united to address challenges in global paediatric imaging training and the delivery of services. **Structure** Council. **Languages** English. **Staff** 0.50 FTE, paid. **Finance** Members' dues. Contributions from regional organization members, mainly Europe and USA. **Activities** Advocacy/lobbying/activism; knowledge management/information dissemination; networking/liaising; research/documentation; training/education. **Events** *Annual General Meeting* Washington, DC (USA) 2021, *Annual General Meeting* Washington, DC (USA) 2020, *Annual General Meeting* San Francisco, CA (USA) 2019, *Annual General Meeting* Berlin (Germany) 2018, *Annual General Meeting* Vancouver, BC (Canada) 2017. **Publications** *Small World* – newsletter. *Mini-Symposium – World Federation of Pediatric Imaging: Outreach in the Developing World* (2014).
Members Regional, national and supranational. Included in the above, 3 organizations listed in this Yearbook:
Asian and Oceanic Society for Pediatric Radiology (AOSPR, #01587); *European Society of Paediatric Radiology (ESPR, #08686)*; *Sociedad Latinoamericana de Radiologia Pediatrica (SLARP, #19424)*.
Allied membership to groups/societies associated with paediatric imaging. [2019/XJ9137/y/C]

♦ World Federation of Pediatric Intensive and Critical Care Societies (WFPICCS) 21473
Admin Office c/o Kenes Intl, Rue François Versonnex 7, PO Box 6053, 1211 Geneva 6, Switzerland. T. +41229089160. Fax +41227322607. E-mail: wfpiccsoffice@kenes.com.
URL: http://www.wfpiccs.org/
History Sep 1997, Paris (France). **Aims** Disseminate and make available high standards of pediatric intensive and critical care to children worldwide. **Languages** English. **Activities** Advocacy/lobbying/activism; events/meetings; research/documentation; training/education. **Events** *Congress* Cape Town (South Africa) 2022, *Biennial World Congress* Geneva (Switzerland) 2020, *World Congress* Singapore (Singapore) 2018, *World Congress* Toronto, ON (Canada) 2016, *Biennial World Congress* Istanbul (Turkey) 2014. **Publications** *Pediatric Critical Care Medicine* in German – journal.
Members Societies (over 40) in 24 countries and territories:
Australia, Cameroon, Canada, China, France, Ghana, India, Indonesia, Ireland, Italy, Japan, Korea Rep, Malaysia, New Zealand, Philippines, Singapore, South Africa, Spain, Sri Lanka, Taiwan, Thailand, Türkiye, UK, USA.
International organization:
International Pediatric Simulation Society (IPSS, #14546).
Regional organizations (4):
African Paediatric Critical Care Association (no recent information); *Association for European Paediatric and Congenital Cardiology (AEPC, #02529)*; *European Society of Paediatric and Neonatal Intensive Care (ESPNIC, #08683)*; *Sociedad Latinoamericana de Cuidados Intensives Pediatricos (SLACIP)*.
NGO Relations Journal produced with: *Society of Critical Care Medicine (SCCM)*. Founding member of: *Global Sepsis Alliance (GSA, #10590)*. [2022/XD7088/y/B]

♦ World Federation of People Management Associations (WFPMA) . . 21474
Secretariat c/o SHRM, 1800 Duke St, Alexandria VA 22314, USA. T. +17035356035. E-mail: wfpma.secretariat@shrm.org.
URL: http://www.wfpma.org/
History Founded Jun 1976, San Diego CA (USA), as *World Federation of Personnel Management Associations (WFPMA) – Fédération mondiale des associations de direction de personnel – Federación Mundial de Asociaciones de Dirección de Personal – Weltverband der Vereinigungen für Personalführung*, by 3 regional personnel organizations – *European Association for People Management (EAPM, #06146)*, *Federación Interamericana de Asociaciones de Gestión Humana (FIDAGH, #09329)*, and *Society for Human Resource Management (SHRM)* – at annual conference of the latter. Has also been referred to as: *Federación Mundial de Asociaciones de Administración de Personal*. Present name adopted, Sep 2008. Registered in Geneva (Switzerland) in accordance with the Swiss Civil Code. **Aims** Aid the development and improve the effectiveness of *professional* people management all over the world; demonstrate the importance of the HR role in all employing organizations, both public and private. **Structure** Board. Rotating Presidency among Full Members. **Languages** English, French, German, Spanish. **Staff** Voluntary. **Finance** Sources: members' dues. **Activities** Awards/prizes/competitions; events/meetings; guidance/assistance/consulting; research/documentation. **Events** *Exalting People Professionals Amidst a Planetary Pandemic* Colombo (Sri Lanka) 2021, *World Congress* Colombo (Sri Lanka) 2020, *Biennial World Congress* Chicago, IL (USA) 2018, *Biennial World Congress* Istanbul (Turkey) 2016, *Biennial World Congress* Santiago (Chile) 2014. **Publications** *WorldLink* (5 a year) – electronic newsletter.
Members Full continental and regional federations made up of over 90 national human resource associations, representing over 600,000 people management professionals (5):
African Human Resource Confederation (AHRC); *Asian Pacific Federation of Human Resource Management (APFHRM, #01611)*; *European Association for People Management (EAPM, #06146)*; *Federación Interamericana de Asociaciones de Gestión Humana (FIDAGH, #09329)*; *North American Human Resource Management Association (NAHRMA)*.
Affiliate national professional people management associations from a continent or region where no federation currently exists. Membership countries not specified.
Consultative Status Consultative status granted from: *ILO (#11123)* (Special List). [2020/XD5570/y/C]

♦ World Federation of Perinatal Medicine / see World Association of Perinatal Medicine (#21170)
♦ World Federation of Personnel Management Associations / see World Federation of People Management Associations (#21474)

♦ World Federation of Pipe Line Industry Associations (WFPIA) 21475
Contact Chemin des Papillons 4, Cointrin, 1216 Geneva, Switzerland. T. +41223060230. Fax +41223060239.
URL: https://www.iploca.com/about-us/world-federation
History 1 Jun 2016. Founded when Heads of Agreement was finalized. **Aims** Provide a platform for collaboration among associations related to the onshore and offshore construction of international and regional oil, gas, water and slurry pipelines. **Languages** English.
Members Organizations in 4 countries and including 2 international organizations listed in this Yearbook:
Australia, Canada, UK, USA.
IMCA International Marine Contractors Association (IMCA, #11127); *International Pipe Line and Offshore Contractors Association (IPLOCA, #14586)*. [2020/AA2829/ty/C]

♦ World Federation of Proprietary Medicine Manufacturers / see Global Self-Care Federation (#10588)
♦ World Federation for the Protection of Animals (inactive)
♦ World Federation of Psychiatric Users / see World Network of Users and Survivors of Psychiatry (#21672)

♦ World Federation of Public Health Associations (WFPHA) 21476
Fédération mondiale des associations de santé publique – Federación mundial de las asociaciones de salud pública
Exec Dir c/o Inst of Global Health, c/o Campus Biotech, Chemin des Mines 9, 1202 Geneva, Switzerland. T. +41223790466.
Exec Manager address not obtained.
URL: https://www.wfpha.org/
History 20 May 1967, Geneva (Switzerland). Founded with 16 core member associations, following meeting of a group of delegates representing 32 national public health associations during the 20th World Health Assembly, also in May 1967. **Aims** Promote and protect global public health worldwide by supporting establishment and organizational development of public health associations and societies of public health. **Structure** Executive Board. **Languages** English, French, German, Spanish. **Staff** 1.00 FTE, paid. Voluntary. **Finance**

Sources: donations; members' dues. **Activities** Advocacy/lobbying/activism; events/meetings; knowledge management/information dissemination; projects/programmes; research/documentation; training/education. **Events** *World Congress on Public Health* Rome (Italy) 2023, *World Congress on Public Health* Geneva (Switzerland) 2020, *World Congress on Public Health* Melbourne, VIC (Australia) 2017, *Asia-Pacific Conference on Public Health* Bangkok (Thailand) 2016, *World Congress on Public Health* Kolkata (India) 2015. **Publications** *Journal of Public Health Policies*; *WFPHA Newsletter*. Annual Report; articles.
Members Multidisciplinary national public health associations. Full (Individual or Sustaining) in 88 countries and territories:
Afghanistan, Albania, Algeria, Armenia, Australia, Austria, Bangladesh, Belgium, Bolivia, Bosnia-Herzegovina, Brazil, Bulgaria, Burkina Faso, Cameroon, Canada, Chad, Chile, China, Colombia, Congo DR, Costa Rica, Croatia, Cuba, Czechia, Denmark, Egypt, Estonia, Ethiopia, Finland, France, Gambia, Georgia, Germany, Ghana, Haiti, Hong Kong, India, Indonesia, Iran Islamic Rep, Israel, Italy, Japan, Kazakhstan, Kenya, Korea Rep, Latvia, Lebanon, Lithuania, Malawi, Malta, Mauritania, Mexico, Mongolia, Mozambique, Nepal, Netherlands, New Zealand, Nicaragua, Niger, Nigeria, North Macedonia, Norway, Panama, Poland, Portugal, Romania, Rwanda, Senegal, Serbia, Sierra Leone, Slovakia, Slovenia, Somalia, South Africa, Spain, Sudan, Sweden, Switzerland, Taiwan, Tanzania UR, Thailand, Tunisia, Uganda, UK, United Arab Emirates, USA, Vietnam, Yemen.
Regional member associations (5):
African Federation of Public Health Associations (AFPHA, #00310); Alianza de Asociaciones de Salud Pública de las Americas (AASPA); *Association of Schools of Public Health in Africa (ASPHA, #02903)*; *Association of Schools of Public Health in the European Region (ASPHER, #02904)*; *European Public Health Association (EUPHA, #08298)*.
Sustaining Members (16), include national associations the following 7 organizations listed in this Yearbook:
European Association of Dental Public Health (EADPH, #06007); *European Healthcare Fraud and Corruption Network (EHFCN, #07453)*; *European Public Health Alliance (EPHA, #08297)*; *Federation of African Medical Students' Associations (FAMSA, #09407)*; *Institut de hautes études internationales et du développement (IHEID)*; *International Federation of Medical Students' Associations (IFMSA, #13478)*; *International Pharmaceutical Students' Federation (IPSF, #14568)*.
Consultative Status Consultative status granted from: *ECOSOC (#05331)* (Ros C); *WHO (#20950)* (Official Relations); *UNEP (#20299)*. **NGO Relations** Member of (6): *European Forum for Primary Care (EFPC, #07326)* (Associated); *Framework Convention Alliance (FCA, #09981)*; *Geneva Global Health Hub (G2H2, #10122)*; *NGO Committee on UNICEF (#17120)*; *Planetary Health Alliance (PHA, #18383)*; *World Patients Alliance (WPA)*. Partner of (1): *International Campaign to Abolish Nuclear Weapons (ICAN, #12426)*. [2023/XC3870/y/**B**]

♦ World Federation of Right to Die Societies (WFRtDS) 21477
Fédération mondiale des associations pour le droit de mourir dans la dignité

Exec Dir Zeeburgerkade 230, 1019 HK Amsterdam, Netherlands. T. +31653647585.
Main Website: http://www.wfrtds.org

History 1980, Oxford (UK). Founded at 3rd international conference of Right to Die Societies. Statutes most recently adopted 6 Sep 2018, Cape Town (South Africa). **Aims** Provide an international link for organizations working to secure or protect the rights of individuals to self-determination at the end of their lives. **Structure** General Assembly (every 2 years); Committee; Headquarters, located in Geneva (Switzerland). **Languages** English. **Staff** 3.00 FTE, voluntary. **Finance** Sources: members' dues. Annual budget: 35,000 USD (2021). **Activities** Events/meetings; knowledge management/information dissemination. **Events** *World Conference* Toronto, ON (Canada) 2022, *Biennial Conference* Mexico City (Mexico) 2020, *Biennial Conference* Cape Town (South Africa) 2018, *Biennial Conference* Amsterdam (Netherlands) 2016, *Biennial Conference* Chicago, IL (USA) 2014. **Publications** Online updates.
Members Member societies 59 in 30 countries and territories:
Australia, Austria, Belgium, Canada, Catalunya, Colombia, Finland, France, Germany, Hong Kong, Iceland, Ireland, Israel, Italy, Japan, Korea Rep, Luxembourg, Mexico, Nepal, Netherlands, New Zealand, Norway, Portugal, South Africa, Spain, Sweden, Switzerland, UK, USA, Zimbabwe. [2022.06.14/XC0349/**C**]

♦ World Federation of Rose Societies (WFRS) 21478
Fédération mondiale des sociétés pour la culture de la rose – Weltbund der Rosenvereine

Exec Dir 76 Bennetts Court, Yate, BS37 4XH, UK. T. +441454310148. E-mail: info@worldrose.org.
URL: http://www.worldrose.org/

History 1968, London (UK). First conference, 12 Nov 1971, Hamilton (New Zealand). **Aims** Encourage and facilitate interchange of information about and knowledge of the rose between national rose societies; encourage and sponsor research into problems concerning the rose; establish common standards for judging new seedling roses; assist in coordinating the registration of rose names; establish uniform system of rose classification. **Structure** Council (meets every 3 years at World Rose Convention); Executive Committee; Regional Vice-Presidents. **Languages** English. **Staff** 15.00 FTE, voluntary. **Finance** Sources: members' dues. **Activities** Events/meetings. **Events** *World Rose Convention* Fukuyama (Japan) 2025, *Regional Rose Conference* Kalmar (Sweden) 2024, *International Heritage Rose Conference* Brussels (Belgium) 2023, *World Rose Convention* Adelaide, SA (Australia) 2022, *World Rose Convention* Adelaide, SA (Australia) 2021. **Publications** *World Rose News* (3 a year).
Members National societies in 39 countries and territories:
Argentina, Australia, Austria, Belgium, Bermuda, Canada, Chile, China, Czechia, Denmark, Finland, France, Germany, Greece, Hungary, Iceland, India, Israel, Italy, Japan, Luxembourg, Monaco, Netherlands, New Zealand, Northern Ireland, Norway, Pakistan, Poland, Romania, Russia, Slovakia, Slovenia, South Africa, Spain, Sweden, Switzerland, UK, Uruguay, USA. [2022.10.12/XD2787/**C**]

♦ World Federation of Science Journalists (WFSJ) 21479
Fédération mondiale des journalistes scientifiques

Pres 1195 Wellington St, Bureau 301, Montréal QC H3C 1W1, Canada. T. +16139797227. E-mail: info@wfsj.org.
Sec address not obtained.
URL: http://www.wfsj.org/

History 24 Nov 2002, São José dos Campos (Brazil). Founded at 3rd World Conference of Science Journalists (WCSJ). Registration: Charitable Organization, No/ID: 831911748RR0001, Canada. **Aims** Raise quality standards in science and technology reporting worldwide. **Structure** General Assembly (annual, at WCSJ); Board. **Languages** English. **Staff** 4.00 FTE, paid. **Finance** Members' dues. Projects. **Events** *World Conference of Science Journalists* Medellin (Colombia) 2023, *World Conference of Science Journalists* Medellin (Colombia) 2022, *World Conference of Science Journalists* Lausanne (Switzerland) 2019, *World Conference* San Francisco, CA (USA) 2017, *World Conference* Seoul (Korea Rep) 2015.
Members National, regional and international associations (62) in 50 countries. Membership countries not specified. International organizations (4):
International organizations (4):
African Federation of Science Journalists (#00311); *Arab Science Journalists Association (ASJA, #01038)*; *European Union of Science Journalists' Associations (EUSJA, #09017)*; *International Science Writers' Association (ISWA, #14800)*.
Associate member (1) in 1 country:
USA. [2022/XJ3283/y/**D**]

♦ World Federation of Scientific Workers (WFSW) 21480
Fédération mondiale des travailleurs scientifiques (FMTS) – Federación Mundial de Trabajadores Cientificos – Weltföderation der Wissenschaftler (WFW)

Pres 13 rue Victor Morin, 76130 Mont-Saint-Aignan, France. T. +33255828014. E-mail: president@fmts-wfsw.org.
Treas 263 rue de Paris, 93516 Montreuil CEDEX, France. E-mail: treasurer@fmts-wfsw.org.
URL: http://www.fmts-wfsw.org/

History 21 Jul 1946, London (UK). Founded on the initiative of British Association of Scientific Workers. Charter adopted 21-25 Sep 1948, Prague (Czechoslovakia). Constitution amended at 10th General Assembly, 1973, Varna (Bulgaria). New constitution adopted at 21st General Assembly, 8-12 Sep 2013, Moscow/Nizhny Novgorod (Russia). **Aims** Contribute to placing science and technology at the service of the well-being of mankind. **Structure** General Assembly; Executive Council; International Secretariat. **Languages** English, French. **Staff** None. **Finance** Sources: donations; members' dues; sale of publications. Other sources: funds from UNESCO and scientific foundations. **Activities** Events/meetings; knowledge management/information dissemination; publishing activities. **Events** *World Forum Science and Democracy* Belém (Brazil) 2009, *Scientific work and the researcher's condition* Marne-la-Vallée (France) 2009, *International Symposium* Paris (France) 2009, *International Symposium* Berlin (Germany) 2007, *Symposium / International Symposium* Lisbon (Portugal) 2004. **Publications** *Scientific World* (3 a year) – newsletter. Conference proceedings.
Members National organizations in 19 countries:
Algeria, Argentina, Belarus, Canada, China, Cuba, Egypt, France, India, Japan, Madagascar, Mongolia, Morocco, Portugal, Romania, Russia, Senegal, Spain, USA.
Individuals in 27 countries:
Algeria, Argentina, Australia, Austria, Belgium, Benin, Bulgaria, Cameroon, Canada, Côte d'Ivoire, Cuba, Czechia, France, Germany, Greece, Hungary, Ireland, Italy, Japan, Kenya, Mali, Poland, Romania, Switzerland, Tunisia, Ukraine, USA.
Consultative Status Consultative status granted from: *ECOSOC (#05331)* (Ros C); *UNESCO (#20322)* (Consultative Status). **IGO Relations** Regular contacts with: *ILO (#11123)*. Accredited by: *United Nations Office at Vienna (UNOV, #20604)*. Associated with Department of Global Communications of the United Nations. **NGO Relations** Member of: *Conference of Non-Governmental Organizations in Consultative Relationship with the United Nations (CONGO, #04635)*; *NGO-UNESCO Liaison Committee (#17127)*. Cooperates with various other NGOs in the framework of the "World Forum Science and Democracy" (beside the *World Social Forum (WSF, #21797)*). [2020/XC3533/**C**]

♦ World Federation of Scientists (internationally oriented national body)
♦ World Federation of Sephardi Communities (inactive)

♦ World Federation of Skull Base Societies (WFSBS) 21481
Address not obtained.

History 9 Nov 2000, Foz do Iguaçu (Brazil). Continues the activities of *International Skull Base Society (inactive)* and *International Skull Base Study Group (no recent information)*. **Events** *World Federation of Skull Base Societies Meeting* Rio de Janeiro (Brazil) 2022, *International Skull Base Congress* Osaka (Japan) 2016, *International Skull Base Congress* Brighton (UK) 2012, *International Skull Base Congress* Vancouver, BC (Canada) 2008, *International Skull Base Congress* Sydney, NSW (Australia) 2004. [2020/XM3556/**C**]

♦ World Federation of Sleep Research and Sleep Medicine Societies (inactive)

♦ World Federation of Societies of Anaesthesiologists (WFSA) 21482
Fédération mondiale des sociétés d'anesthésiologistes – Federación Mundial de Sociedades de Anestesiólogos – Weltverband der Anaesthesisten-Gesellschaften

Address not obtained.
URL: http://www.wfsahq.org/

History 9 Sep 1955, Scheveningen (Netherlands). Revised Statutes and Bylaws adopted: Sep 1968, London (UK); Jan 1984, Manila (Philippines); May 1988, Washington DC (USA); 2004, Paris (France); 2008, Cape Town (South Africa); 2012 Buenos Aires (Argentina); 2016, Hong Kong (Hong Kong). Registered in USA as a 501(c)(3) organization: EIN 13-3211128. Also registered as a charity in England and Wales: 1166545. **Aims** Improve patient care and access to safe anaesthesia. **Structure** General Assembly (every 4 years, at World Congress); Board; Council; Permanent Committees (6). Regional Sections: *European Society of Anaesthesiology and Intensive Care (ESAIC, #08518)*; *Latin American Confederation of Societies of Anesthesiology (#16305)*; Asian and Australasian Regional Section (AARS); African Regional Section (ARS); Pan Arab Section. **Languages** English, French, Spanish. **Staff** 8.00 FTE, paid. **Finance** Sources: donations; gifts, legacies; members' dues; subsidies. **Activities** Advocacy/lobbying/activism; events/meetings; research/documentation; training/education. Instrumental in setting up: *African Federation for the Study of Pain (AFSP, no recent information)*; *Asian and Oceanic Society of Regional Anaesthesia and Pain Medicine (AOSRA-PM, #01588)*; *Society of Anaesthesiologists of East Africa (SAEA, see: #21482)*. **Events** *Quadrennial World Congress* Singapore (Singapore) 2024, *Quadrennial Asian Australasian Congress* Seoul (Korea Rep) 2022, *Quadrennial World Congress* Prague (Czechia) 2021, *Quadrennial World Congress* Prague (Czechia) 2020, *All African Congress* Marrakech (Morocco) 2019. **Publications** *Anaesthesia Tutorial of the Week (ATOTW)*; *ATOTW Newsletter*; *Update in Anaesthesia* in English, French, Mandarin Chinese, Russian, Spanish – journal. *Primary Trauma Core Manual* (2001); *Anaesthesia at the District Hospital* (2nd ed 2000) – jointly with WHO; *WFSA 50 Years*. Annual Report.
Members National Societies from 136 countries and territories:
Albania, Algeria, Angola, Argentina, Australia, Austria, Bangladesh, Belarus, Belgium, Benin, Bolivia, Bosnia-Herzegovina, Botswana, Brazil, Brunei Darussalam, Bulgaria, Burkina Faso, Burundi, Cambodia, Cameroon, Canada, Chile, China, Colombia, Congo Brazzaville, Congo DR, Costa Rica, Côte d'Ivoire, Croatia, Cuba, Cyprus, Czechia, Denmark, Dominican Rep, Ecuador, Egypt, El Salvador, Estonia, Ethiopia, Finland, France, Gabon, Georgia, Germany, Ghana, Greece, Guatemala, Guyana, Haiti, Honduras, Hong Kong, Hungary, Iceland, India, Indonesia, Iran Islamic Rep, Iraq, Ireland, Israel, Italy, Japan, Jordan, Kazakhstan, Kenya, Korea Rep, Kosovo, Laos, Latvia, Lebanon, Lithuania, Madagascar, Malawi, Malaysia, Maldives, Mali, Malta, Mauritius, Mexico, Micronesia FS, Moldova, Mongolia, Morocco, Mozambique, Myanmar, Nepal, Netherlands, New Zealand, Nicaragua, Niger, Nigeria, North Macedonia, Norway, Oman, Pakistan, Palestine, Panama, Papua New Guinea, Paraguay, Peru, Philippines, Poland, Portugal, Romania, Russia, Rwanda, Saudi Arabia, Senegal, Serbia, Singapore, Slovakia, Slovenia, South Africa, Spain, Sri Lanka, Srpska, Sudan, Sweden, Switzerland, Syrian AR, Taiwan, Tanzania UR, Thailand, Trinidad-Tobago, Tunisia, Türkiye, Uganda, UK, Ukraine, United Arab Emirates, Uruguay, USA, Uzbekistan, Venezuela, Vietnam, Zambia, Zimbabwe.
Regional association:
Pacific Society of Anaesthetists (#18004).
Consultative Status Consultative status granted from: *ECOSOC (#05331)* (Ros C); *WHO (#20950)* (Official Relations). **IGO Relations** Accredited by: *United Nations Office at Vienna (UNOV, #20604)*. **NGO Relations** Member of: *Global Alliance for Surgical, Obstetric, Trauma and Anaesthesia Care (G4 Alliance, #10229)*; *PMNCH (#18410)*. Affiliated to: *Fédération Internationale de Gynécologie et d'Obstétrique (FIGO, #09638)*. In liaison with technical committees of: *International Electrotechnical Commission (IEC, #13255)*; *International Organization for Standardization (ISO, #14473)*. [2019.04.24/XB3534/y/**B**]

♦ World Federation of Societies of Biological Psychiatry (WFSBP) . . . 21483
Fédération mondiale des sociétés de psychiatrie biologique – Federación Mundial de Sociedades de Psiquiatrica Biológica – Weltverband der Gesellschaften für Biologische Psychiatrie

Pres Zum Ehrenhain 34, 22885 Barsbüttel, Germany. T. +494067088290. Fax +494067088291. E-mail: info@wfsbp.org.
URL: http://www.wfsbp.org/

History Sep 1974, Buenos Aires (Argentina). Founded during 1st Congress of Biological Psychiatry. Constitution ratified at 2nd congress, 1978, Barcelona (Spain). **Aims** Promote, in all countries, education and attainment of the highest level of knowledge and understanding in the field of biological psychiatry. **Structure** Executive Committee. **Languages** English, French, German, Spanish. **Staff** 2.00 FTE, paid. **Finance** Sources: members' dues. **Activities** Events/meetings; publishing activities; training/education. **Events** *World Congress of Biological Psychiatry* Barsbüttel (Germany) 2021, *World Congress of Biological Psychiatry* Vancouver, BC (Canada) 2019, *Asia-Pacific Regional Congress* Kobe (Japan) 2018, *World Congress of Biological Psychiatry* Copenhagen (Denmark) 2017, *Latin American Regional Congress* Lima (Peru) 2016. **Publications** *World Journal of Biological Psychiatry* – scientific journal.
Members National societies in 63 countries and territories:
Argentina, Armenia, Austria, Belgium, Bolivia, Bosnia-Herzegovina, Brazil, Bulgaria, Canada, Chile, Colombia, Costa Rica, Croatia, Czechia, Denmark, Dominican Rep, Ecuador, Egypt, El Salvador, Estonia, France, Germany, Greece, Guatemala, Honduras, Hong Kong, Hungary, India, Indonesia, Israel, Italy, Japan, Kazakhstan, Korea Rep, Latvia, Lebanon, Lithuania, Malaysia, Mexico, Morocco, Netherlands, North Macedonia, Norway, Pakistan, Panama, Paraguay, Peru, Poland, Portugal, Romania, Russia, Serbia, Slovakia, South Africa, Spain, Sweden, Switzerland, Taiwan, Thailand, Türkiye, Ukraine, Uruguay, Venezuela.
Individuals in 6 countries:
Australia, Ireland, New Zealand, Tunisia, UK, USA. [2023/XC6620/**C**]

♦ World Federation of Societies of Chronobiology (WFSC) 21484
Address not obtained.

History 10 Nov 2001. **Aims** Strive, in all countries, to promote education and the attainment of the highest level of knowledge and understanding in the field of chronobiology. **Structure** Council (meets at congress), composed of one delegate from each of the member societies. Executive Committee, comprising President, Vice-President and Secretary-Treasurer. **Languages** English. **Staff** Voluntary. **Finance** Registration fees; grants. **Activities** Organizes quadrennial world congress. **Events** *World Congress of Chronobiology* Suzhou (China) 2019, *World Congress of Chronobiology* Manchester (UK) 2015, *World Congress of Chronobiology* Puebla (Mexico) 2011, *World congress* Chicago, IL (USA) 2007, *World Congress* Tokyo (Japan) 2007.
Members National and regional organizations (13), including 5 organizations listed in this Yearbook:

European Biological Rhythms Society (EBRS, #06337); European Society of Chronobiology (ESC, no recent information); International Society for Chronobiology (ISC, #15010); Latin American Chronobiology Group (LACG, #16296); Mediterranean Society for Chronobiology (MSC). [2019/XD8836/y/**D**]

♦ World Federation of Societies of Intensive and Critical Care Medicine / see World Federation of Intensive and Critical Care (#21444)

♦ World Federation of Societies for Laser Medicine and Surgery (WFSLMS) 21485

SG Japan Medical Laser Laboratory, Shinanomachi Rengakan 4F, Shinanomachi 35, Shinjuku, Tokyo, 160-0016 Japan. E-mail: wfslms@jmll.co.jp.
URL: http://www.jmll.co.jp/wfslms/index.htm

Aims Contribute to the health and welfare of mankind through minimum tissue damage and high efficacy of haemostasis in laser medicine; create a worldwide education and training system of laser medicine and educate medical staff in developing countries. **Languages** Japanese. **Events** *LASER FLORENCE : International Congress on Laser Medicine and Surgery* Florence (Italy) 2019, *LASER FLORENCE : International Congress on Laser Medicine and Surgery* Florence (Italy) 2017, *LASER FLORENCE : International Congress on Laser Medicine and Surgery* Florence (Italy) 2015, *Future of laser in medicine* France 2013, *Congress* Lithuania 2013. [2017.06.06/XM1721/**D**]

♦ World Federation of the Sodalities of Our Lady / see Christian Life Community (#03905)

♦ World Federation on Soft Computing 21486

Chair School Mathematics, Computer Science and Engineering, University of London, Nothampton Square, London, EC1V 0HB, UK. T. +442070408422.
Contact Dept of Computational Science and Engineering, Nagoya Univ, Furo-cho, Chikusa-ku, Nagoya AICHI, 464-8603 Japan.
URL: http://www.wfsc.de/

Activities *World Conference on Soft Computing* held online. **Events** *International Conference on Intelligence Networking and Collaborative Systems* Fukuoka (Japan) 2011, *International symposium on advances in artificial intelligence and applications* Wisla (Poland) 2010, *International conference on intelligent systems design and applications* Pisa (Italy) 2009, *International conference on intelligent systems design and applications* Kaohsiung (Taiwan) 2008, *International conference on intelligent systems design and applications* Rio de Janeiro (Brazil) 2007. **Publications** *Applied Soft Computing* (4 a year). [2019/XD8283/**D**]

♦ World Federation of Sonographers (inactive)
♦ World Federation of Spine Surgeons and Spondyliatrists (no recent information)

♦ World Federation of the Sporting Goods Industry (WFSGI) 21487

Fédération mondiale de l'industrie d'articles de sport – Weltverband der Sportartikel-Industrie

SG Haus des Sports, Talgut-Zentrum 27, 3063 Ittigen BE, Switzerland. T. +41319396061. E-mail: info@wfsgi.org.
URL: http://www.wfsgi.org/

History Nov 1978, on constitution of the first Board in Munich (Germany), a Committee having existed since 1977, Chicago IL (USA). Also referred to as *International Sports Goods Organization*. Registered in accordance with Swiss Civil Code. Statutes most recently revised: 5 Feb 2011. **Aims** Support and promote the sporting goods industry by providing a platform where members can promote fair trade in order to increase sport participation; keep members updated on law and regulations; act as the voice of the sporting goods industry. **Structure** General Assembly (annual) in Munich (Germany); Board of Directors; Committees (7). **Languages** English. **Staff** 8.00 FTE, paid. **Finance** Sources: members' dues. **Activities** Events/meetings; knowledge management/information dissemination. **Events** *World Cycling Forum* Rotterdam (Netherlands) 2019, *Annual meeting* Munich (Germany) 2010, *Annual meeting* Munich (Germany) 2009, *Biennial General Assembly* Munich (Germany) 1999, *General Assembly* Paris (France) 1994. **Publications** *WFSGI Magazine* (annual); *News Alert*.

Members Full (national and regional organizations, industry suppliers and industry supporters); Associate. Members in 31 countries:
Australia, Austria, Belgium, Brazil, Canada, China, Czechia, Denmark, France, Germany, Hong Kong, Hungary, India, Indonesia, Italy, Japan, Korea Rep, Netherlands, New Zealand, Pakistan, Poland, Romania, Russia, Singapore, Slovakia, Switzerland, Taiwan, UK, United Arab Emirates, USA, Vietnam.

IGO Relations Registered NGO with: *ILO (#11123) WHO (#20950); World Trade Organization (WTO, #21864)*. **NGO Relations** Member of (1): *Olympic Movement (#17719)*. Recognized by: *International Olympic Committee (IOC, #14408)*. In liaison with technical committees of: *Comité européen de normalisation (CEN, #04162); International Organization for Standardization (ISO, #14473)*. [2019.02.25/XD0565/t/**C**]

♦ World Federation of Surgical Oncology Societies (WFSOS) 21488

Pres Dept. of Thoracic Surgery, Harefield Hospital, Hill End Road, Harefield, UB9 6JH, UK.
Dir of WFSOS School 3 2nd Botkinsky Passage, Moscow Fed State Intitution, P A Herzen Scientific Research Oncological Inst, Dep of Microsurgery, Moscow MOSKVA, Russia, 125284.

History 1992, London (UK). Registration: Private company limited by guarantee, No/ID: 09489624, Start date: 13 Mar 2015, England. **Aims** Promote surgical oncology internationally, stressing its major importance in the treatment of cancer; encourage and assist the formation of new surgical oncology societies and recognized surgical oncology groups; assist collaboration among members; disseminate information; cooperate with and advise non-surgical national and international oncological societies and recognized groups; develop standards of education, training, practice and research. **Structure** Council (meets annually); Executive Committee (meets twice a year); Committee on Education and Training; International Chapter (individual members); Executive Secretariat. **Languages** English. **Finance** Sources: members' dues. Other sources. **Activities** Events/meetings; training/education. **Events** *World congress* Rio de Janeiro (Brazil) 2009, *International congress of oncosurgery* Krasnodar (Russia) 2008, *World congress* Los Angeles, CA (USA) 2003, *World congress* Naples (Italy) 2001, *World congress* San Diego, CA (USA) 1998. **Publications** *Journal of Surgical Oncology*; *WFSOS Newsletter*.

Members National Societies in 34 countries:
Argentina, Australia, Austria, Belgium, Brazil, Canada, Czechia, Egypt, Estonia, France, Germany, Greece, Hungary, India, Indonesia, Ireland, Israel, Italy, Japan, Korea Rep, Lebanon, Montenegro, Nepal, Netherlands, Philippines, Poland, Portugal, Russia, Serbia, Slovenia, Switzerland, Türkiye, UK, USA.

Regional associations (1):
Royal Australasian College of Surgeons (RACS).

NGO Relations Member of: *International Federation of Surgical Colleges (IFSC, #13560).* [2020/XC0120/y/**C**]

♦ World Federation of Taiwan Alumni Associations (unconfirmed)
♦ World Federation of Teachers' Unions (#09662)

♦ World Federation of Technical Assessment Organizations (WFTAO) 21489

SG c/o ETA-Danmark A/S, Göteborg Plads 1, 2150 Copenhagen, Denmark. T. +4572245900. E-mail: tb@etadanmark.dk.
URL: http://www.wftao.com/

History 1996. **Aims** Enhance and promote the role of technical assessments of innovative and non-standardized systems and products in the *construction* field worldwide; develop mutual confidence on technical assessments made by members. **Structure** General Assembly (at least every 2 years). Coordinating Committee, elected by General Assembly and chaired by the General Secretary, manages business activities. **Languages** English. **Events** *Meeting* Copenhagen (Denmark) 2010, *Meeting* Calgary, AB (Canada) 2009, *Meeting* Johannesburg (South Africa) 2008, *Meeting* Surfers Paradise, QLD (Australia) 2007, *Meeting* Pasadena, CA (USA) 2006.

Members in 21 countries:
Australia, Brazil, Canada, Czechia, Denmark, Finland, France, Germany, Hungary, Ireland, Israel, Italy, Japan, New Zealand, Norway, Portugal, Romania, South Africa, Spain, UK, USA. [2018/XD5895/**D**]

♦ World Federation of Technology Organizations (WFTO) 21490

SG 10767 – 148th Street, Surrey BC V3R 0S4, Canada. T. +16045852788. Fax +16045852790.

History 13 Jun 1995, Vancouver (Canada). **Aims** Promote and enhance the recognition and careers of technicians and technologists; support technology education and training and the transfer of credentials; encourage continuing education and professional development; enhance opportunities in science and technology for women; promote a maintenance culture particularly as it applies to developing countries. **Structure** General Assembly (every 3 years). Executive Board. Country representatives in 18 locations. **Languages** English. **Finance** Members' dues: US$ 200. **Activities** Organizes (every 3 years) an *'International Symposium on Technology Education and Training'*. Special task force works on developing an international standard and defining a process for recognizing equivalent technology education and certification. **Events** *International symposium* 2001, *World congress of colleges and polytechnics* Québec, QC (Canada) 1999, *General Assembly* 1998, *International symposium on technology education and training / Triennial Symposium* Cape Town (South Africa) 1998, *Triennial Symposium* Vancouver, BC (Canada) 1995. **Publications** *WTO NEWS* (3 a year); *Global Connexion* – newsletter. Working on a glossary of common terms.

Members Categories Professional Association; Education; Nongovernmental Organization; Corporate; Government institution. Members in 21 countries:
Australia, Canada, France, Germany, Hong Kong, India, Iraq, Ireland, Kenya, Malaysia, Namibia, New Zealand, Philippines, Poland, Singapore, South Africa, Switzerland, UK, United Arab Emirates, USA, Zambia.

IGO Relations *Commonwealth Secretariat (#04362); Commonwealth Foundation (CF, #04330).* [2012.08.14/XD5114/**C**]

♦ World Federation of Therapeutic Communities (WFTC) 21491

Fédération mondiale des communautés thérapeutiques – Federación Mundial de Communidades Terapéuticas – Federazione Mondiale delle Comunità Terapeutiche

Pres 135 Paul Drive, San Rafael CA 94903, USA. T. +15267820. E-mail: wftc@cpinc.org.
Sec address not obtained.
URL: http://www.wftc.org/

History 1979, New York NY (USA), from recommendations, 1975, Bangkok (Thailand), of a conference of *International Council on Alcohol and Addictions (ICAA, #12989)*. Registered in the State of New York (USA). Statutes most recently revised: Sep 1990, Athens (Greece). By-Laws most recently revised: Feb 1998, Cartagena de Indias (Colombia); 2000, San Francisco CA (USA); 2002, Melbourne (Australia); 2004, Spain; 2006, New York NY (USA); 2009, Lima (Peru). **Aims** Join together in a worldwide association of sharing, understanding and cooperation within the global Therapeutic Community (TC) movement as well as widen recognition and acceptance of TC among health organizations and health delivery systems of international and national bodies; call for a *holistic* approach to healing. **Structure** Executive Council, consisting of Officers (President; Deputy President; 1st, 2nd and 3rd Vice Presidents; Secretary; Treasurer), 6 Standing Committee Chairpersons (International Organizing; International Concerns; Scientific and Professional Advisory; Standards and Goals; Mowrer and Sholl Awards; Operations) and Presidents of Regional TC Chapters. Board of Directors (meets during World Conference), comprising representatives of all Regular Member Agencies and Regional TC Chapter Associations. **Languages** English. **Staff** Voluntary. **Finance** Sources: members' dues. **Events** *Evolution and innovation* Delhi (India) 2020, *Conference* Bangkok (Thailand) 2018, *Conference* Cancún (Mexico) 2014, *Conference* Bali (Indonesia) 2012, *Conference* Lima (Peru) 2009. **Publications** *WFTC Bulletin* (4 a year).

Members Board; Corresponding; Individuals; Organizations. Members in 40 countries and territories:
Argentina, Bangladesh, Bolivia, Brazil, Canada, Chile, China, Colombia, Costa Rica, Dominican Rep, Ecuador, El Salvador, Germany, Greece, Guatemala, Honduras, Hong Kong, India, Indonesia, Ireland, Italy, Malaysia, Malta, Mexico, New Zealand, Nicaragua, Norway, Panama, Papua New Guinea, Paraguay, Peru, Philippines, Poland, Puerto Rico, Spain, Thailand, Uruguay, USA, Venezuela, Virgin Is USA.

Individuals in 20 countries and territories:
Argentina, Australia, Bangladesh, Barbados, Belgium, Brazil, Finland, Germany, Hong Kong, India, Italy, Malaysia, Netherlands, Papua New Guinea, Philippines, Singapore, Sri Lanka, Thailand, UK, USA.

Regional Therapeutic Community Chapter Associations (6):
Asian Federation of Therapeutic Communities (AFTC, #01476); Australasian Therapeutic Communities Association (ATCA); European Federation of Therapeutic Communities (EFTC, #07225); Federación Latinoamericana de Comunidades Terapéuticas (FLACT, #09352); Federation of Therapeutic Communities of Central and Eastern Europe (FTCCEE, #09707); Therapeutic Communities of America.

Consultative Status Consultative status granted from: *ECOSOC (#05331)* (Special). **IGO Relations** Associated with Department of Global Communications of the United Nations. **NGO Relations** *DIANOVA International (#05068)* is member. [2021/XD0802/y/**C**]

♦ World Federation of Tourist Guide Associations / see World Federation of Tourist Guide Associations (#21492)

♦ World Federation of Tourist Guide Associations (WFTGA) 21492

Pres c/o Wiener Wirtschaftskammer, Lothringer Str 4, No 254, 1040 Vienna, Austria. E-mail: president@wftga.org – info@wftga.org.
URL: http://www.wftga.org/

History Feb 1985, Israel. Founded during 1st International Convention of Tourist Guide Associations. Officially registered at 2nd Convention, 1987, Vienna (Austria). Former names and other names: *World Federation of Tourist Guide Lecturers' Associations (WFTGLA)* – former (1985); *World Federation of Tourist Guide Associations (WFTGA)* – former (1987). Registration: No/ID: ZVR 679385413, Austria. **Aims** Establish contact with tourist guide associations worldwide and reinforce their professional ties; represent *professional* tourist guides internationally and promote and protect their interests; promote high standards of training and ethics within the profession and enhance its reputation. **Structure** General Assembly (every 2 years, at International Convention); Executive Board; Area Representatives (16). **Languages** English. **Staff** 1.00 FTE, paid. **Finance** Sources: members' dues; revenue from activities/projects; sponsorship. **Activities** Events/meetings; knowledge management/information dissemination; training/education. **Events** *Biennial International Convention* Siracusa (Italy) 2024, *Biennial International Convention* Madrid (Spain) 2022, *Biennial International Convention* Novi Sad (Serbia) 2022, *Biennial International Convention* Novi Sad (Serbia) 2021, *Biennial International Convention* Tbilisi (Georgia) 2019. **Publications** *Guidelines International* (2 a year) – electronic newsletter. Reports; handbook; reference book; manuals; training material in 7 languages; presentations for international panels. Information Services: Access to tourist guides worldwide; website information on the tourist guide industry.

Members Full members (associations of professional tourist guides) in 67 countries and territories:
Albania, Andorra, Argentina, Armenia, Australia, Austria, Belize, Bhutan, Botswana, Brazil, Cameroon, Canada, Chile, Colombia, Costa Rica, Cyprus, Czechia, Denmark, Dominican Rep, Ecuador, Egypt, Estonia, Finland, Gambia, Georgia, Germany, Greece, Hong Kong, India, Indonesia, Iran Islamic Rep, Iraq, Israel, Italy, Japan, Kyrgyzstan, Latvia, Macau, Malaysia, Malta, Montenegro, Morocco, Myanmar, Nepal, Netherlands, New Zealand, Panama, Peru, Philippines, Puerto Rico, Romania, Russia, Serbia, Singapore, Slovakia, South Africa, Spain, Sri Lanka, Sweden, Tanzania UR, Thailand, Türkiye, UK, Ukraine, USA, Zimbabwe.

Individual members (tourist guides in countries where there is no association of professional tourist guides) in 25 countries:
Azerbaijan, Barbados, Belarus, Belgium, China, Ethiopia, Ghana, Kazakhstan, Kyrgyzstan, Malawi, Malaysia, Mexico, Morocco, Mozambique, New Zealand, North Macedonia, Poland, Romania, Saudi Arabia, Slovenia, Tonga, Ukraine, United Arab Emirates, Uruguay, Zimbabwe.

Affiliate members (tourism-related organizations, whether governmental, local authority, international organization or other bodies involved at the city, regional, national or international level with tourism and travel related activities, educational institutes of tourism partners, etc) in 24 countries and territories:
Albania, Azerbaijan, Bangladesh, Bosnia-Herzegovina, Curaçao, Cyprus, Czechia, Dominican Rep, Ecuador, Egypt, Ghana, Hong Kong, Iran Islamic Rep, Ireland, Kenya, Libya, Mauritius, Nepal, North Macedonia, Pakistan, Poland, Saudi Arabia, South Africa, Thailand.

Consultative Status Consultative status granted from: *UNESCO (#20322)* (Consultative Status). **IGO Relations** Affiliate member of: *World Tourism Organization (UNWTO, #21861)*. **NGO Relations** Member of (1): *World Tourism Network (WTN, #21860).* [2023.02.17/XC0020/**C**]

♦ World Federation of Tourist Guide Lecturers' Associations / see World Federation of Tourist Guide Associations (#21492)

♦ World Federation of Trade Unions (WFTU) 21493

Fédération syndicale mondiale (FSM) – Federación Sindical Mundial (FSM) – Weltgewerkschaftsbund (WGB) – Vsemirnaja Federacija Profsojuzov (VFP)

Gen Sec 6 Florinis Street, Moschato, 183 46 Athens, Greece. T. +302109214417 – +302109236700. Fax +302109214517. E-mail: secretariat@wftucentral.org – info@wftucentral.org.

URL: http://www.wftucentral.org/

History 3 Oct 1945, Paris (France), by the World Trade Union Congress, a preliminary Conference having been held 6-17 Feb 1945, London (UK). Constitution adopted Oct 1945, Paris (France), and amended: 1949, Milan (Italy); 1957, Leipzig (German DR); 1965, Warsaw (Poland); 1969, Budapest (Hungary); 1973, Varna (Bulgaria); 1978, Prague (Czechoslovakia); 1990, Moscow (Russia); 1994, Damascus (Syrian AR); 2011, Athens (Greece). **Aims** Prime objective is *emancipation* of workers by means of:
(a) combating all forms of exploitation of people and obtaining and guaranteeing *living conditions* and *working conditions* for all workers which would allow them the widest possible benefits from the fruits of their labour, including:
– the right to work for all and the guarantee of this right;
– full and adequate *social security* legislation to protect workers and their families in the event of sickness and old age and every other type of assistance and social security;
– training, education and culture for all workers, thus enabling them to gain access to any responsibility or position within their capabilities.
(b) fighting for: final elimination of all forms of exploitation, domination or expansionism in the political, economic, social, cultural or racial spheres; assurance of the freedom and security of all peoples; elimination of underdevelopment; assurance of the economic and political independence of all peoples; establishment of a new, just, international economic order;
(c) achieving social, economic and political democracy, the defence and development of workers' and trade unions' *rights* and freedoms, respect for human rights and the implementation of the Universal Declaration of Trade Union Rights;
(d) international detente, establishment of a just and lasting peaceful coexistence amongst all states, mutually advantageous cooperation amongst all peoples, an end to the arms race, especially in nuclear arms and progressive arms reduction leading to general and complete disarmament.
Structure *World Trade Union Congress (WTUC)* (initially every 4 years, now every 5); General Council (meets once between Congresses); Presidential Council (governing body between sessions of General Council), consisting of President, Vice-Presidents, General Secretary and representatives of the 6 Trade Union Internationals (TUIs) formed within WFTU. Secretariat, headed by General Secretary. **Languages** Arabic, English, French, Spanish. **Staff** 38.00 FTE, paid. **Finance** Affiliation fees. **Activities** Instrumental in setting up: *International Trade Union Centre for Labour Research and Studies (inactive).* **Events** *World congress* Durban (South Africa) 2016, *World congress* Athens (Greece) 2011, *International trade union symposium* Athens (Greece) 2008, *European trade union conference on the truth about Darfur* Athens (Greece) 2007, *International trade union conference of working women* Brussels (Belgium) 2007. **Publications** *Flashes* (12 a year) in Arabic, Russian. Press communiqués; documents of congress and conferences; pamphlets; leaflets; posters.
Members Organizations whose total membership, including those represented through TUIs, is 90 million individuals in 126 countries and territories:
Afghanistan, Albania, Angola, Antigua-Barbuda, Argentina, Armenia, Australia, Austria, Azerbaijan, Bahrain, Bangladesh, Barbados, Belarus, Benin, Bolivia, Botswana, Brazil, Bulgaria, Burkina Faso, Cambodia, Cameroon, Canada, Chile, Colombia, Congo Brazzaville, Congo DR, Costa Rica, Côte d'Ivoire, Cuba, Cyprus, Czechia, Djibouti, Dominican Rep, Ecuador, Egypt, El Salvador, Eritrea, Ethiopia, Fiji, Finland, France, Gambia, Ghana, Greece, Guadeloupe, Guatemala, Guiana Fr, Guinea, Guinea-Bissau, Guyana, Haiti, Honduras, Hungary, India, Indonesia, Iran Islamic Rep, Iraq, Jamaica, Japan, Jordan, Kazakhstan, Korea DPR, Kuwait, Kyrgyzstan, Laos, Lebanon, Lesotho, Liberia, Libya, Madagascar, Malawi, Malaysia, Mali, Martinique, Mauritius, Mexico, Mozambique, Nepal, New Caledonia, New Zealand, Niger, Nigeria, Oman, Pakistan, Palestine, Panama, Papua New Guinea, Peru, Philippines, Poland, Portugal, Puerto Rico, Réunion, Romania, Russia, Saudi Arabia, Senegal, Sierra Leone, Slovakia, Solomon Is, Somalia, South Africa, Sri Lanka, St Lucia, St Pierre-Miquelon, St Vincent-Grenadines, Sudan, Sweden, Syrian AR, Tajikistan, Tanzania UR, Thailand, Togo, Trinidad-Tobago, Tunisia, Türkiye, Turkmenistan, Uganda, Ukraine, Uruguay, Uzbekistan, Vanuatu, Venezuela, Vietnam, Yemen, Zimbabwe.
Trade Union Internationals (TUIs) – 10:
Fédération internationale syndicale de l'enseignement (FISE, #09662); Trades Union International of Workers in the Building, Wood, Building Materials and Allied Industries (UITBB, #20185); Trade Union International of Chemical, Energy, Metal, Oil and Allied Industries (TUI CHEMISTRY-ENERGY, #20188); Trade Union International of Mining, Metallurgy and Metal (TUI Metal); Trade Union International (TUI) of Workers in Hotels and Tourism (HOTOUR); *Trade Unions International of Agriculture, Food, Commerce, Textile and Allied Industries (#20190); Trade Unions International of Public and Allied Employees (#20191); Trade Unions International of Transport, Fisheries and Communication (TUI Transport, #20192);* TUI Banks, Insurance and Financial Unions (BIFU); TUI Pensioners and Retires (TUI P and R).
Consultative Status Consultative status granted from: *ECOSOC (#05331)* (General); *UNESCO (#20322)* (Consultative Status); *ILO (#11123)* (General); *UNCTAD (#20285)* (General Category); *UNIDO (#20336); FAO (#09260); UNICEF (#20332).* **IGO Relations** Participates in the work of: *United Nations Economic Commission for Europe (UNECE, #20555).* Associated with Department of Global Communications of the United Nations. **NGO Relations** Member of the Board of: *Conference of Non-Governmental Organizations in Consultative Relationship with the United Nations (CONGO, #04635); NGO Committee on Disarmament, Peace and Security, New York NY (#17106).* [2023/XA3537/ty/**A**]

♦ World Federation of Trade Unions of Non Manual Workers / see World Organization of Workers (#21697)
♦ World Federation of Trading House Associations (no recent information)
♦ World Federation of Traditional Medicine (no recent information)

♦ World Federation of Travel Journalists and Writers 21494

Fédération internationale des journalistes et écrivains du tourisme (FIJET) – Federación Mundial de Periodistas y Escritores de Turismo

Pres address not obtained. E-mail: contact@fijet.net.

URL: http://www.fijet.net/

History 4 Dec 1954, Paris (France), at the suggestion of French and Belgian travel journalists' and writers' associations. Previously also referred to in English as *International Federation of Travel Journalists and Writers.* By-laws adopted 30 No 2006, Karlovy Vary (Czech Rep). Registered in accordance with Czech law. **Aims** Promote expansion of *tourism* worldwide as a powerful reconciliation factor between peoples; defend the right of all people to travel vacations; conserve human, natural, cultural and historical resources with concern over their ecology; preserve and popularize monuments; disseminate information about nations and their history, habits, traditions and culture; develop new forms of tourism and new destinations to provide holidays at all social levels; encourage tourism organizations worldwide and the international exchange of experiences. **Structure** General Assembly (annual). Board of Directors, consisting of Representatives of national member associations. Executive Committee, comprising President, Vice-President, Secretary General, Treasurer and 5 members. **Languages** English, French, Spanish. **Staff** 1.50 FTE, voluntary. **Finance** Sources: members' dues. **Activities** Exchange of members; study tours; documentation centre and library. 'Golden Apple Award'. Seminars. Research on tourism in developing countries. **Events** *Annual Congress and General Assembly* Budapest (Hungary) 2014, *Annual Congress and General Assembly / Congress and Annual General Assembly* Cairo (Egypt) 2012, *Annual Congress and General Assembly / Congress and Annual General Assembly* Bucharest (Romania) 2011, *Annual Congress and General Assembly* Istanbul (Turkey) 2010, *Annual Congress and General Assembly / Congress and Annual General Assembly* Shanghai (China) 2009. **Publications** E-newsletter (12 a year). Membership directory.
Members National associations in 28 countries:
Belgium, Bulgaria, Croatia, Czechia, Egypt, France, Germany, Greece, Israel, Italy, Lebanon, Libya, Mexico, Netherlands, Panama, Poland, Romania, Russia, Serbia, Slovakia, Slovenia, Spain, Sweden, Switzerland, Tunisia, Türkiye, Ukraine, USA.
IGO Relations Affiliate member of: *World Tourism Organization (UNWTO, #21861).* **NGO Relations** Member of: *International Federation of Communication Associations.* [2016/XC2033/**C**]

♦ World Federation for the Treatment of Opioid Dependence (WFTOD) 21495

Pres 225 Varick St, Ste 402, New York NY 10014, USA. E-mail: info@wftod.org.

URL: http://www.wftod.org/

History Jul 2007, Ljubljana (Slovenia), by *European Opiate Addiction Treatment Association (EUROPAD, #08090)* and American Association for the Treatment of Opioid Dependence. Also referred to as *World Federation of the Associations for the Treatment of Opioid Dependence (WFATOD).* **Aims** Ensure that patients receive good quality care in addition to the medications that they are receiving, which involves medical and psychological support. **Structure** Officers: President; Vice-President; Treasurer; Corporate Secretary. **Events** *Inaugural meeting* Ljubljana (Slovenia) 2007. **Consultative Status** Consultative status granted from: *ECOSOC (#05331)* (Special). **NGO Relations** *South Eastern European-Adriatic Addiction Treatment Network (SEEAN, #19806).* [2017/XM3178/**E**]

♦ World Federation of Ukrainian Women's Organizations (WFUWO) .. 21496

Fédération mondiale des organisations des femmes ukrainiennes – Federación Mundial de Organizaciones Femeninas Ucranias – Svitova Federacija Ukrainskih Zinocih Organizacij (SFUZO)

Pres 145 Evans Avenue, Ste 206, Etobicoke ON M8Z 5X8, Canada. T. +14165462491. E-mail: wfuwo.office@gmail.com.

URL: http://wfuwo.org/

History Nov 1948, Philadelphia PA (USA), a *World Union of Ukrainian Women* having been set up in 1937. **Aims** Represent member organizations internationally; coordinate their activities at the national level according to Congress resolutions; promote cultural and educational programmes advancing the status of women; foster the development of the Ukrainian language, literature, history and fine arts; maintain charitable programmes which maintain the principles of political and religious tolerance, recognizing and respecting universal human rights; support the new democratic Ukrainian nation. **Structure** World Congress (every 5 years). President; Executive Members. Board of Directors (meets annually), representing member organizations. Standing Committees. **Languages** English, Ukrainian. **Staff** 0.50 FTE, paid. **Finance** Members' dues. Donations. **Activities** Issues and concerns dealt with via Standing Committees (9): The Arts; Cultural Affairs; Education; International Relations; Organization; Press and Publications; Programming; Social Welfare; Women's Studies. Organizes: World Congress (every 5 years); Annual Board Meeting in Toronto (Canada); annual and regional conferences. **Events** *Annual General Meeting* Stockholm (Sweden) 2015, *Annual Summit* Stockholm (Sweden) 2015, *Annual General Meeting* Paris (France) 2014, *Annual General Meeting* Lviv (Ukraine) 2013, *Annual Conference European Conference* Poland 2010. **Publications** *Ukrainian Women in the World* (4 a year) in Ukrainian; *Ukrainian Women in the World* (annual) in English. Multilingual resource material on human rights and on cultural, social and educational topics.
Members Organizations (27) in 17 countries:
Argentina, Australia, Belgium, Brazil, Canada, Czechia, Estonia, France, Germany, Italy, Lithuania, Poland, Spain, Sweden, Switzerland, UK, USA.
Consultative Status Consultative status granted from: *ECOSOC (#05331)* (Special); *UNICEF (#20332).* **IGO Relations** Associated with Department of Global Communications of the United Nations. **NGO Relations** Member of: *Conference of Non-Governmental Organizations in Consultative Relationship with the United Nations (CONGO, #04635); General Federation of Women's Clubs (GFWC); NGO Committee on the Status of Women, Geneva (#17117); NGO Committee on UNICEF (#17120); World Congress of Free Ukrainians (WCFU, #21305).* Cooperates with: *International Council of Women (ICW, #13093).* [2017/XF0040/**E**]

♦ World Federation for Ultrasound in Medicine and Biology (WFUMB) 21497

Fédération mondiale de médecine et biologie des ultra-sons

Admin Office PO Box 72719, London, SW19 9HD, UK. E-mail: admin@wfumb.org.

URL: http://www.wfumb.org/

History Jun 1969, Vienna (Austria). **Aims** Encourage research in the field and promote international cooperation; disseminate scientific information. **Structure** General Assembly. Officers: President; Past President; President-elect; 2 Vice-Presidents; Secretary; Treasurer; 6 Administrative Councillors; 3 Coopted Councillors; Editor-in-Chief; Newsletter Editor. **Languages** English. **Staff** 1.00 FTE, paid; 17.00 FTE, voluntary. **Finance** Sources: meeting proceeds; members' dues. Other sources: subscriptions to Journal. **Activities** Sponsors meetings; cooperates with other societies and organizations in specific learning, education and training; appoints commissions on special problems; awards prizes and distinctions. **Events** *WFUMB Congress* Kyoto (Japan) 2025, *Congress* Muscat (Oman) 2023, *Congress* Timisoara (Romania) 2022, *Congress* Timisoara (Romania) 2021, *Congress* Melbourne, VIC (Australia) 2019. **Publications** *Ultrasound in Medicine and Biology* – journal. Other official documents.
Members Affiliated national or regional organizations in 65 countries and territories:
Algeria, Argentina, Austria, Bangladesh, Belgium, Brazil, Bulgaria, Cameroon, Canada, Chile, China, Congo DR, Côte d'Ivoire, Croatia, Czechia, Denmark, Ecuador, Egypt, Finland, France, Gambia, Germany, Ghana, Greece, Hungary, India, Indonesia, Iran Islamic Rep, Israel, Italy, Japan, Kenya, Korea Rep, Libya, Lithuania, Malaysia, Marshall Is, Netherlands, Nigeria, Norway, Paraguay, Peru, Poland, Portugal, Russia, Senegal, Sierra Leone, Slovakia, Slovenia, Somalia, Spain, Sudan, Sweden, Switzerland, Syrian AR, Taiwan, Thailand, Togo, Tunisia, Türkiye, Uganda, UK, Uruguay, USA, Venezuela.
Included in the above, 6 regional organization:
American Institute of Ultrasound in Medicine (AIUM); *Asian Federation of Societies for Ultrasound in Medicine and Biology (AFSUMB, #01473); Australasian Society for Ultrasound in Medicine (ASUM, #03030); European Federation of Societies for Ultrasound in Medicine and Biology (EFSUMB, #07217); Latin American Federation of Societies of Ultrasound in Medicine and Biology (#16333); Mediterranean and African Society of Ultrasound (MASU, #16640).*
Consultative Status Consultative status granted from: *WHO (#20950)* (Official Relations). [2021/XD4075/y/**C**]

♦ World Federation of UNESCO Clubs, Centres and Associations (WFUCA) 21498

Fédération mondiale des associations, centres et clubs UNESCO (FMACU) – Federación Mundial de Asociaciones, Centros y Clubs UNESCO (FMACU)

SG Vinh Phuc Lane – D3 Building, Ba Dinh Dist, Hanoi, Vietnam. T. +8437616880. Fax +8437616879.

URL: http://wfuca.org/

History 2 Jul 1981, Paris (France), at 2nd World Congress of UNESCO clubs and associations held at *UNESCO (#20322)* headquarters, Paris. **Aims** Further the ideals, objectives and programmes of UNESCO and, to that end, further, strengthen and encourage the development of UNESCO clubs, centres and associations; promote international understanding and *education*, particularly with a view to the effective exercice of human rights, the endogenous development of every people, and the construction of a new world economic and social order, and pursue these aims also in nations and peoples, particularly in order to advance mutual understanding among the different cultures in the world; involve people in UNESCO work, particularly at the grass roots level; promote utilization of science and technology for peaceful purposes, for the welfare of humanity, and, in particular, of the developing countries; promote in all societies the right of every person and every people to a *cultural identity.* **Structure** World Congress (every 4 years). Executive Board, consisting of 12 members, including President and Treasurer. Secretariat, headed by Secretary General. Regional branches: *European Federation of UNESCO Clubs, Centres and Associations (EFUCA, #07231); Asian Pacific Federation of UNESCO Clubs and Associations (AFUCA, #01614).* **Languages** English, French, Spanish. **Staff** Voluntary. **Finance** Members' dues. Other sources: UNESCO punctual financing of projects; donations. **Activities** Plan of Action: *'Friends of the Treasures of the World'* (preservation of heritage), including *Friends of the World Treasures (FWT, no recent information)*; promotion of books and reading (partnership between rich and poor countries); development of 'community development centres' (with the Japanese federation). *Centre for Studies, Research and Training in International Understanding and Cooperation (CERFCI, no recent information)* – programme focusing mainly on: development; communication; cultural heritage; environment; literacy; human rights. Organizes study sessions, workshops and seminars on various topics within this framework. Organizes youth meetings and ad-hoc meetings. **Events** *Asia-Europe Forum on Education* Bucharest (Romania) 2015, *Regional forum of Arab clubs* Beirut (Lebanon) 2011, *Quadrennial world congress* Hanoi (Vietnam) 2011, *World forum of clubs* Paris (France) 2011, *Forum of Latin America and the Caribbean clubs* San José (Costa Rica) 2010. **Publications** *Confluences – The World in your Pocket* (4 a year); *Confluences Arts et Culture* (annual). *Confluences – Notebooks.* Documents and other publications. All in English, French, Spanish.
Members Full; Corresponding; Associate; Honorary. National associations of UNESCO clubs in 73 countries and territories:

Algeria, Angola, Armenia, Bangladesh, Belarus, Belgium, Benin, Bosnia-Herzegovina, Bulgaria, Burkina Faso, Burundi, Cameroon, Central African Rep, China, Congo Brazzaville, Congo DR, Costa Rica, Côte d'Ivoire, Cyprus, Egypt, Estonia, France, Gabon, Gambia, Germany, Ghana, Greece, Guinea, Guinea-Bissau, India, Indonesia, Italy, Jamaica, Japan, Korea Rep, Kuwait, Latvia, Libya, Lithuania, Madagascar, Malaysia, Mali, Malta, Mauritania, Mauritius, Mongolia, Morocco, Nepal, Netherlands, Pakistan, Paraguay, Poland, Portugal, Puerto Rico, Romania, Russia, Sao Tomé-Principe, Senegal, Sierra Leone, Spain, Sri Lanka, St Lucia, Thailand, Togo, Trinidad-Tobago, Tunisia, Ukraine, Uruguay, USA, Venezuela, Vietnam, Yemen, Zambia.
Consultative Status Consultative status granted from: *UNESCO (#20322)* (Associate Status). **IGO Relations** Accredited to the Conference of the Parties of: *Secretariat of the United Nations Convention to Combat Desertification (Secretariat of the UNCCD, #19208).* Accredited by: *United Nations Office at Vienna (UNOV, #20604).* Associated with Department of Global Communications of the United Nations. **NGO Relations** Member of: *International Conference of NGOs (#12883); EarthAction (EA, #05159); UNESCO Network of Associated Libraries (UNAL, #20311).* Instrumental in setting up: *African Confederation of UNESCO Clubs, Centres and Associations (CACU, #00264).* [2012/XE6342/y/E]

♦ World Federation of United Cities (inactive)

♦ World Federation of United Nations Associations (WFUNA) 21499

Fédération mondiale des associations pour les Nations Unies (FMANU) – Federación Mundial de Asociaciones pro Naciones Unidas

SG One UN Plaza, Room 240, New York NY 10017, USA. T. +12129635611 – +12129635610. Fax +12129630447. E-mail: info@wfuna.org.
Geneva Office Palais des Nations, Villa Bocage VB-3, 1211 Geneva 10, Switzerland. T. +41229173213. Fax +41229170185.
URL: http://www.wfuna.org/

History 2 Aug 1946, Luxembourg, taking over the functions of *International Federation of League of Nations Societies (inactive).* Registered in accordance with US law; Registered in accordance with Swiss Civil Code. EU Transparency Register: 412066335513-72. **Aims** Act as a peoples' movement for the United Nations; coordinate and further activities of members and promote establishment of new United Nations Associations; cooperate with other organizations which support the United Nations and its development; promote *tolerance, understanding, solidarity* and *cooperation* among men, women and children throughout the world without distinction as to race, sex, language, religion or political orientation; contribute to removal of obstacles to peace, work for *justice, security* and *disarmament* and promote development of *peaceful co-existence* and cooperation among nations; strive for recognition of and respect for *human rights* and fundamental *freedoms* throughout the world and for recognition of the *responsibilities* and duties which these rights involve for individuals, groups and states; promote economic *development*, enhancement of social progress and better *living standards*; promote research, information and education about the goals of the United Nations Charter and the work of the United Nations system. **Structure** Plenary Assembly (every 2-3 years), consisting of delegates from national associations, elects President, 6 Vice-Presidents, Secretary-General/Treasurer and Executive Committee of 18 members. Honorary Presidents (11). Secretariat, headed by Secretary-General. **Languages** English, French, Spanish. **Finance** Members' dues. Other sources: grants for special projects; donations. **Activities** Strategic framework includes: building a global network of United Nations Associations (UNAs); facilitate communication and information sharing with and between UNAs; sustain the global network of UNAs; energize the global network of UNAs; help shape the UN Agenda. **Events** *Plenary Assembly* Vancouver, BC (Canada) 2015, *Plenary Assembly* Rio de Janeiro (Brazil) 2012, *UN-Connecting the world conference* Geneva (Switzerland) 2010, *Plenary assembly* Seoul (Korea Rep) 2009, *APMUN : Asia Pacific model United Nations conference* Incheon (Korea Rep) 2008. **Publications** *Human Rights Nexus Newsletter* (24 a year); *News from UNAs; UN Connections.* Annual Report. Reports on projects, seminars and conferences.
Members Full: National Associations in 110 countries and territories:
Afghanistan, Albania, Antigua-Barbuda, Argentina, Armenia, Australia, Austria, Bangladesh, Barbados, Belarus, Belgium, Benin, Bhutan, Bolivia, Brazil, Bulgaria, Burundi, Cambodia, Cameroon, Central African Rep, Chile, China, Congo DR, Côte d'Ivoire, Croatia, Cuba, Cyprus, Czechia, Denmark, Dominican Rep, Ecuador, Egypt, Estonia, Ethiopia, Finland, France, Georgia, Germany, Ghana, Greece, Guatemala, Guinea, Guyana, Haiti, Hungary, Iceland, India, Indonesia, Iran Islamic Rep, Ireland, Israel, Italy, Jamaica, Japan, Kenya, Korea Rep, Kyrgyzstan, Latvia, Lebanon, Lesotho, Liberia, Lithuania, Luxembourg, Malaysia, Mali, Mauritius, Mexico, Mongolia, Mozambique, Nepal, Netherlands, New Zealand, Nicaragua, Nigeria, North Macedonia, Norway, Pakistan, Panama, Peru, Philippines, Poland, Romania, Russia, Samoa, Senegal, Serbia, Sierra Leone, Singapore, Slovakia, Slovenia, South Africa, Spain, Sri Lanka, Sudan, Suriname, Sweden, Switzerland, Syrian AR, Tanzania UR, Thailand, Trinidad-Tobago, Tunisia, Türkiye, Uganda, UK, USA, Venezuela, Yemen, Zambia.
Consultative Status Consultative status granted from: *ECOSOC (#05331)* (General); *UNESCO (#20322)* (Associate Status); *ILO (#11123)* (Special List); *UNCTAD (#20285)* (General Category); *FAO (#09260); International Atomic Energy Agency (IAEA, #12294); UNICEF (#20332); World Meteorological Organization (WMO, #21649).* **IGO Relations** Cooperates with: UN Information Centres; UN bodies and agencies. Maintains relations with: *United Nations Population Fund (UNFPA, #20612).* Accredited by: *United Nations Framework Convention on Climate Change – Secretariat (UNFCCC, #20564); United Nations Office at Vienna (UNOV, #20604).* Associated with Department of Global Communications of the United Nations.
NGO Relations Secretary-General is member of the Board of: *Conference of Non-Governmental Organizations in Consultative Relationship with the United Nations (CONGO, #04635).* Member of:
- *Academic Council on the United Nations System (ACUNS, #00020);*
- *Committee of NGOs on Human Rights, Geneva (#04275);*
- *Fédération des Institutions Internationales établies à Genève (FIIG, #09599);*
- *International Campaign to Abolish Nuclear Weapons (ICAN, #12426);*
- *International Coalition for the Responsibility to Protect (ICRtoP, #12620);*
- *International Forum for the Challenges of Peace Operations (Challenges Forum, #13632);*
- *NGO Committee on Disarmament, Peace and Security, New York NY (#17106)* and *NGO Committee for Disarmament, Geneva (#17105);*
- *NGO Committee on the Status of Women, Geneva (#17117);*
- *NGO Committee on Sustainable Development, Vienna (#17119);*
- *NGO Working Group on the Security Council (#17128);*
- *NGO Committee on UNICEF (#17120).*

Supporting partner of: *World Tourism Forum (#21859).* Supports: *Global Call for Action Against Poverty (GCAP, #10263).* Partner of: *United Nations Informal Regional Network of Non-Governmental Organizations (UN-NGO-IRENE, #20573).* Participant of: *United Nations Global Compact (#20567).* [2019/XE3539/E]

♦ World Federation of Vascular Societies (WFVS) 21500

Main Office 9400 W Higgins Rd, Ste 315, Rosemont IL 60018-4975, USA. E-mail: secretarywfvs@gmail.com – info@worldfvs.org.
URL: https://worldfvs.org/

History 2007. Also referred to as *World Federation for Vascular Specialties (WFVS).* **Aims** Provide a forum for the international exchange of scientific, educational and political issues related to the diagnosis, treatment and prevention of vascular diseases. **Structure** Council, including President, Vice-President and Secretary-General. **Activities** Annual Meeting. **Events** *Congress* Stellenbosch (South Africa) 2014, *Joint Annual Scientific Meeting* Melbourne, VIC (Australia) 2012, *Annual Meeting* Chicago, IL (USA) 2011, *Annual Meeting* Kyoto (Japan) 2010, *Annual Meeting* Oslo (Norway) 2009.
Members Organizations in 6 countries:
Australia, India, Japan, New Zealand, South Africa, USA.
Organizations listed in this Yearbook (2):
European Society for Vascular Surgery (ESVS, #08772); Vascular Society of Southern Africa (VASSA).
[2022/XM8277/y/C]

♦ World Federation for Vascular Specialties / see World Federation of Vascular Societies (#21500)
♦ World Federation of Workers in Food, Tobacco and Hotel Industries – WCL (inactive)
♦ World Federation of YMHA's and Jewish Community Centres / see JCC Global (#16093)
♦ World Federation of Young Investors (unconfirmed)

♦ World Fellowship of Buddhists (WFB) 21501

Organisation mondiale des bouddhistes

Hon SG 616 Benjasiri Park, Sukhumvit 24 off Soi Medhinivet – Sukhumvit Road, Klong Toey, Bangkok, 10110, Thailand. T. +662661128487. Fax +6626610555.
URL: http://wfbhq.org/

History Founded 25 May 1950, Colombo (Ceylon). **Aims** Propagate the doctrine of the Buddha and promote among members strict observance and practice of his teachings; secure unity, solidarity and brotherhood amongst Buddhists; work in the field of social, educational, cultural and other *humanitarian* services; work to secure peace and harmony among men and happiness for all beings; collaborate with other organizations working for the same ends. **Structure** General Conference (every 2 years); General Council; Executive Council; Standing Committees (11); Regional Centres. **Languages** English, Thai. **Staff** 14.00 FTE, paid; 15.00 FTE, voluntary. **Finance** Annual contributions. Grants from Thai Government. **Events** *Biennial General Conference* Narita (Japan) 2018, *Biennial General Conference* Seoul (Korea Rep) 2016, *Biennial General Conference* Baoji (China) 2014, *Biennial General Conference* Yeosu (Korea Rep) 2012, *Biennial General Conference* Colombo (Sri Lanka) 2010. **Publications** *WFB Review* (4 a year). Book series in English, Thai.
Members Regional centres (191) in 40 countries and territories:
Australia, Austria, Bangladesh, Belgium, Bhutan, Brazil, Cambodia, Canada, China, Czechia, Finland, France, Germany, Ghana, Hong Kong, Hungary, India, Indonesia, Japan, Korea DPR, Korea Rep, Laos, Malaysia, Mongolia, Myanmar, Nepal, Netherlands, New Zealand, Norway, Philippines, Russia, Singapore, Sri Lanka, Sweden, Taiwan, Tanzania UR, Thailand, UK, USA, Vietnam.
Consultative Status Consultative status granted from: *ECOSOC (#05331)* (General); *UNESCO (#20322)* (Consultative Status). [2018.08.03/XC3541/C]

♦ World Fellowship of Buddhist Youth (WFBY) 21502

Association mondiale des jeunes bouddhistes

Contact c/o WFB, 616 Benjasir Park, Soi Methinivet off Soi Sukhumvit 24, Sukhumvit Road, Bangkok, 10110, Thailand. T. +6626611284. Fax +6626610555. E-mail: wfbyhq@gmail.com.
URL: http://www.wfbytoday.org/

History May 1972, Colombo (Sri Lanka), during 10th Conference of the *World Fellowship of Buddhists (WFB, #21501).* **Aims** Promote and strengthen among the younger generations the observance and practice of the teachings of the Buddha; secure unity and solidarity among Buddhist youth; organize activities in the field of the various humanitarian services, working to secure peace and harmony. **Structure** General Conference (every 2 years). Officers: President, 8 Vice-Presidents, Secretary-General and Treasurer-General. **Languages** English, Thai. **Staff** 1.00 FTE, paid; 5.00 FTE, voluntary. **Finance** Members' dues. **Activities** Seminars; Research; training; information exchange. **Events** *International Buddhist Youth Forum* Colombo (Sri Lanka) 2010, *General conference* Kaohsiung (Taiwan) 2006, *International Buddhist youth forum* Seoul (Korea Rep) 2004, *International Buddhist youth forum* Auckland (New Zealand) 2002, *General Conference* Kuala Lumpur (Malaysia) 2002. **Publications** *WFBY Communication* (12 a year). Conference proceedings.
Members Regional centres (37) in 14 countries and territories:
Bangladesh, Hong Kong, India, Indonesia, Japan, Korea Rep, Malaysia, Nepal, Russia, Singapore, Sri Lanka, Taiwan, Thailand, USA.
NGO Relations *World Buddhist University.* [2014/XD2327/D]

♦ World Fellowship of Inter-Religious Councils (internationally oriented national body)

♦ World Fellowship of Methodist and Uniting Church Men (WesleyMen) 21503

Pres c/o World Methodist Council, 585 N Lakeshore Drive, Lake Junaluska NC 28745, USA. E-mail: info@wesleymen.org.
URL: http://wesleymen.org/

History Jul 2001, Brighton (UK), at a meeting of *World Methodist Council (WMC, #21650).* Also known under the acronym *UFMUCM.* **Aims** End world *hunger.* **Structure** President; Vice-President. Includes *World Wesleyan Hunger Fund.* **Staff** 3.00 FTE, paid. **Events** *Meeting* Houston, TX (USA) 2016, *Meeting* Seoul (Korea Rep) 2006. **NGO Relations** Affiliate of: *World Methodist Council (WMC, #21650).* [2015.10.12/XJ5133/E]

♦ World Fellowship of Orthodox Youth (Syndesmos) 21504

Fraternité mondiale de la jeunesse orthodoxe

Secretariat c/o ACER-MJO, 91 rue Olivier de Serres, 75015 Paris, France. E-mail: syndesmos@syndesmos.org.
URL: http://www.syndesmos.org/

History Founded 1953, Paris (France), to foster contacts and promote cooperation among Orthodox youth movements in Western Europe, Greece and the Middle East and to engage with one voice in the ecumenical dialogue. Extended, 1968, to include theological schools. New Constitution adopted at: 10th General Assembly, 1980, Valamo (Finland); 14th General Assembly, 1992, Moscow (Russia). Amended and revised at 15th General Assembly, 1995, Kykko (Cyprus) and 17th General Assembly, 2003, Durrës (Albania). Previously referred to as *World Fellowship of Orthodox Youth Organizations – Fraternité mondiale des organisations de la jeunesse orthodoxe.* Also known as *Fédération mondiale de la jeunesse orthodoxe.* **Aims** Serve as a bond of unity among Orthodox youth movements, organizations and theological schools around the world, promoting a consciousness of the catholicity of the Orthodox faith; foster relations, coordination and mutual aid among them; promote among young people a full understanding of the Orthodox faith and the mission of the Church in the contemporary world and an active participation of youth in ecclesial life; promote a way of life founded in eucharistic communion, in the Gospel and in patristic teaching, for witness and service to the world; assist and promote Orthodox efforts for visible *Christian* unity and for positive relations with people of other faiths; encourage reflection and action on issues affecting the lives of Orthodox Christians and the local churches; be an instrument for furthering cooperation and deeper communion between the Orthodox Church and the Oriental Orthodox Churches. **Structure** General Assembly (every 4 years), composed of 1-2 delegates of each member movement. Standing Board of Administration, consisting of Executive Committee (President, 3 Vice-Presidents, 1 Federated Vice-President), Secretary-General, 10 Regional Representatives (Africa, America, Asia, Balkan, Central Europe, Eastern Europe, Middle East, Northern Europe, Southern Europe, Western Europe) and 1 Federated Members' Representative. Programmes implemented by General Secretariat. **Languages** English, Irish Gaelic, Russian. **Staff** 4.00 FTE, paid; 1.00 FTE, voluntary. **Finance** Funded by: *European Youth Foundation (EYF, #09141); World Council of Churches (WCC, #21320);* Orthodox Church sources; donations – 'Friends of SYNDESMOS'; subscriptions. **Activities** come under the headings: communications and cooperation; international youth events; study and reflection; training; education; mission; Christian unity; media and publishing. Organizes annual international Orthodox youth camps, conferences, study seminars and exchanges between Orthodox youth throughout the world. World Day of Orthodox Youth – 2nd February (15th February old calendar). Mission projects in catechesis, youth leadership, organization and theological education in Africa, Asia, Eastern Europe and North America. International cooperation in Orthodox religious education. **Events** *Quadrennial general assembly / General Assembly* Athens (Greece) 2009, *Conference on woman and ministries in the church* France 2007, *Mission in Eastern Europe in orthodox context* Moscow (Russia) 2007, *General Assembly* Durrës (Albania) 2003, *Intercultural youth encounter* Novi Sad (Yugoslavia) 2001. **Publications** *SYNDESMOS News* (2 a year). *The Bond of Unity: SYNDESMOS – fifty years of work for Orthodox youth and unity* (2003); *For the Peace from Above: an Orthodox Resource Book on War, Peace and Nationalism* (1999); *Orthodox Youth and Ecumenism: Resource Book* (1998); *Orthodoxy and Ecology: Resource Book* (1996); *Orthodox Youth Camp Manual* (1995); *Our Faith* (1995); *Orthodox Icons and Line Drawings* (1993). Reports of Conferences, Assemblies and Seminars; directories of Orthodox Churches and youth movements.
Members Orthodox youth organizations and theological schools (121) in 43 countries:
Albania, Argentina, Armenia, Belarus, Belgium, Bosnia-Herzegovina, Bulgaria, Cameroon, Canada, Chile, Congo Brazzaville, Cyprus, Czechia, Egypt, Estonia, Ethiopia, Finland, France, Georgia, Germany, Ghana, Greece, India, Indonesia, Israel, Japan, Jordan, Kenya, Korea Rep, Lebanon, Lithuania, Netherlands, Nigeria, Poland, Romania, Russia, Serbia, Slovakia, South Africa, Uganda, UK, USA, Zimbabwe.
IGO Relations *UNESCO (#20322).* **NGO Relations** *Conference of European Churches (CEC, #04593); Ecumenical Youth Council in Europe (EYCE, #05352);* World Council of Churches; *World Student Christian Federation (WSCF, #21833).* [2020/XC2571/C]

♦ World Fellowship of Orthodox Youth Organizations / see World Fellowship of Orthodox Youth (#21504)

♦ World Fellowship of Slavic Evangelical Christians (WFSEC) 21505

Address not obtained.

Publications *Evangelskoye Slovo-The Gospel Word* (4 a year). **Members** Primarily North American membership. [2008/XF0943/F]

♦ World Ferry Safety Association / see Worldwide Ferry Safety Association (#21921)

♦ World Fertility Survey (inactive)
♦ World Filtration Congress (meeting series)
♦ World Finance Banking Symposium (meeting series)
♦ World Finance Conference (meeting series)

♦ World Fintech Association 21506

SG 258 (2F), Seokchonhosu-ro, Songpa-Gu, Seoul 05624, Korea Rep. T. +82221402787. Fax +82221402701.
LinkedIn: https://www.linkedin.com/company/world-fintech-forum/

History 2016, Seoul (Korea Rep). **Aims** Foster the FinTech industry through analysis and research; contribute to the economic development of countries around the world. **Structure** Organizing Committee. **Languages** English, Korean. **Staff** 5.00 FTE, paid; 10.00 FTE, voluntary. **Finance** Sponsorship. **Activities** Awareness raising; events/meetings; networking/liaising; research/documentation; standards/guidelines. **Events** *Seminar on Brussels your Gateway to Europe* Seoul (Korea Rep) 2019, *Future Finance Forum* Seoul (Korea Rep) 2018, *Block chain on business and entrepreneurship* Seongnam (Korea Rep) 2017, *Forum* Seoul (Korea Rep) 2016. **Publications** Daily newsletters.
Members Full in 20 countries and territories:
Brazil, Canada, China, Czechia, Denmark, France, Germany, Hong Kong, Indonesia, Ireland, Korea Rep, Luxembourg, Mexico, Netherlands, Russia, Singapore, Spain, Switzerland, UK, USA. [2017.02.02/XM5551/**E**]

♦ WorldFish 21507

Main Office Jalan Batu Maung, Batu Maung, 11960 Bayan Lepas, Penang, Malaysia. T. +6046286888. Fax +6046265530. E-mail: worldfishcenter@cgiar.org.
URL: http://www.worldfishcenter.org/

History Jan 1975, Honolulu, HI (USA). Founded with sponsorship from the *The Rockefeller Foundation (#18966)*, as part of its Conquest of Hunger Programme. Incorporated in the Philippines, 1977. Since 1992, a research centre of *CGIAR System Organization (CGIAR, #03843)*. Former names and other names: *International Centre for Living Aquatic Resources Management (ICLARM)* – former; *Centre international de gestion des resources aquatiques biologiques* – former; *WorldFish Center* – former. Registration: Start date: 1977, Philippines. **Aims** Reduce poverty and hunger by improving fisheries and aquaculture. **Structure** Board of Trustees; Executive Team; Science Leadership Team; Country Directors. **Languages** English. **Staff** 460.00 FTE, paid.
Finance Sources: government support; international organizations; private foundations. Support from: universities; advanced research institutions; financing institutions; international agricultural research centres; national agricultural research systems; NGOs; private sector.
Supported by:
- *African Development Bank (ADB, #00283)*;
- *Asian Development Bank (ADB, #01422)*;
- *Australian Centre for International Agricultural Research (ACIAR)*;
- *AVRDC – The World Vegetable Center (#03051)*;
- *Bill and Melinda Gates Foundation (BMGF)*;
- *CARE International (CI, #03429)* (Bangladesh);
- *CGIAR System Organization (CGIAR, #03843)*;
- *Department for International Development (DFID, inactive)*;
- *Deutsche Gesellschaft für Internationale Zusammenarbeit (GIZ)*;
- *European Commission (EC, #06633)*;
- *FAO (#09260)*;
- *International Bank for Reconstruction and Development (IBRD, #12317)* (World Bank);
- *International Fund for Agricultural Development (IFAD, #13692)*;
- *International Institute for Environment and Development (IIED, #13877)*;
- *Japan International Cooperation Agency (JICA)*;
- *New Zealand Ministry of Foreign Affairs and Trade – New Zealand Aid Programme*;
- *Norwegian Agency for Development Cooperation (Norad)*;
- *Oak Foundation*;
- *OIKOS International Foundation for Ecological Economics (inactive)*;
- *Plan International (#18386)*;
- *Save the Children International (#19058)*;
- *Swedish International Development Cooperation Agency (Sida)*;
- *Swiss Agency for Development and Cooperation (SDC)*;
- *Synergos (#20082)*;
- *UNEP (#20299)*;
- *United States Agency for International Development (USAID)*;
- *Winrock International*;
- *World Food Programme (WFP, #21510)*.

Activities Advocacy/lobbying/activism; capacity building; humanitarian/emergency aid; projects/programmes; research and development; research/documentation; training/education. Active in: Bangladesh, Cambodia, Colombia, Egypt, Ghana, Honduras, India, Kenya, Malawi, Malaysia, Mexico, Myanmar, Peru, Sierra Leone, Solomon Is, Tanzania UR, Timor-Leste, Vietnam, Zambia. **Events** *Annual International Conference* Alexandria (Egypt) 2021, *Global symposium on gender and fisheries* Penang (Malaysia) 2004, *Regional workshop on fisheries co-management* Mangochi (Malawi) 1997, *Workshop on aquaculture data and fishbase* Manila (Philippines) 1997, *Conference for environmental issues in third-world aquaculture development* Bellagio (Italy) 1990. **Publications** *The benefits of aquaculture* (2015). Annual Report. **Information Services** *Coral Triangle Atlas*; *FishBase*; *ReefBase*. **Members** Not a membership organization.
IGO Relations Member of: CGIAR. Observer to: *International Council for the Exploration of the Sea (ICES, #13021)*. Associate member of: *Asia-Pacific Association of Agricultural Research Institutions (APAARI, #01830)*. Invited to Governing Council sessions of: *International Fund for Agricultural Development (IFAD, #13692)*. Cooperates with: *Asia-Pacific Fishery Commission (APFIC, #01907)*. Observer to: *Regional Commission for Fisheries (RECOFI, #18763)*. Links with other CGIAR bodies: *International Center for Agricultural Research in the Dry Areas (ICARDA, #12466)*; *International Livestock Research Institute (ILRI, #14062)*; *International Rice Research Institute (IRRI, #14754)*; *Africa Rice Center (AfricaRice, #00518)*.
Partners include:
- *Agence française de développement (AFD)*;
- *Arab Organization for Agricultural Development (AOAD, #01018)*;
- *Centre de coopération internationale en recherche agronomique pour le développement (CIRAD, #03733)*;
- *Deutsche Gesellschaft für Technische Zusammenarbeit (GTZ, inactive)*;
- *ECOSOC (#05331)*;
- *Lake Chad Basin Commission (LCBC, #16220)*;
- *Lake Victoria Fisheries Organization (LVFO, #16222)*;
- *Network of Aquaculture Centres in Asia-Pacific (NACA, #16991)*;
- *New Partnership for Africa's Development (NEPAD, #17091)*;
- *Pacific Community (SPC, #17942)*;
- *Regional Organization for the Conservation of the Environment of the Red Sea and Gulf of Aden (PERSGA, #18804)*;
- *Secretariat of the Pacific Regional Environment Programme (SPREP, #19205)*;
- *Southeast Asian Fisheries Development Center (SEAFDEC, #19767)*;
- *Southern African Development Community (SADC, #19843)*;
- *UN Environment Programme World Conservation Monitoring Centre (UNEP-WCMC, #20295)*;
- *UNICEF (#20332)*;
- *University of the South Pacific (USP, #20703)*. [2020.11.18/XE5021/**E**]

♦ WorldFish Center / see WorldFish (#21507)
♦ World Fisheries Trust (internationally oriented national body)
♦ World Fish Migration Foundation (internationally oriented national body)

♦ World Flower Council 21508

Main Office 1608 Tyler St, Hollywood FL 33020, USA. T. +19544446445. Fax +18885067808. E-mail: info@worldflowercouncil.com.
URL: http://www.worldflowercouncil.org/

History 1983, Gifu (Japan), as *Pacific Flower Culture Promotional Conference*. Current title adopted, Jan 1984. **Aims** Promote world peace by sharing beauty of flowers and promote education about flowers with floral industry. **Structure** Council, including International Chairman, Chairman Emeritus, International Vice-Chairperson and Assistant Vice-Chairperson representing Asia and the Pacific Rim and International Vice-Chairpersons representing the Americas, Europe and Africa. Board of Directors of 5. **Languages** English. **Staff** 2.00 FTE, paid; 2.00 FTE, voluntary. **Finance** Members' dues (annual): Individual – US$ 50; Corporate – US$ 150. Grants. **Activities** Sponsors and participates in summits and exhibitions. **Events** *Annual Summit* Sapporo (Japan) 2013, *Annual Summit* Cabo San Lucas (Mexico) 2012, *Annual Summit* Heathrow (UK) / London (UK) 2011, *Annual Summit* London (UK) 2011, *Annual Summit* Auckland (New Zealand) 2010. **Publications** *WFC Newsletter* (4 a year); *Annual Summit Newsletter*.
Members Full in 30 countries and territories:
Australia, Azerbaijan, Brunei Darussalam, Cambodia, Canada, China, England, France, Hong Kong, India, Indonesia, Italy, Japan, Kenya, Korea Rep, Latvia, Macau, Malaysia, Netherlands, New Zealand, Philippines, Russia, Singapore, South Africa, St Kitts-Nevis, Sweden, Taiwan, Thailand, USA, Vietnam. [2017/XF2661/**F**]

♦ World Flying Disc Federation (WFDF) 21509

Exec Dir Enggasse 2a, 55296 Harxheim, Germany. T. +4961389020868. Fax +4961389020869.
Legal Seat 5825 Delmonico Drive, Suite 350, Colorado Springs CO 80919, USA.
URL: http://www.wfdf.org/

History 12 Jul 1984, Örebro (Sweden). Founded by European Flying Disc Federation, taking over from *International Frisbee Association (IFA)*, set up 1967, subsequently (1978) *International Frisbee Disc Association (IFDA)*. **Aims** Develop and promote worldwide the *sport* of Flying Disc. **Structure** Congress (annual); Board of Directors; Executive Committee. Committees for different events; regional committees; rules and public relations committees. **Languages** English. **Staff** 1.50 FTE, paid. **Finance** Annual budget: 75,000 USD. **Events** *Annual Congress* Harxheim (Germany) 2020, *Annual Congress* Ida-Viru (Estonia) 2019, *Annual Congress* Cincinnati, OH (USA) 2018, *Annual Congress* Royan (France) 2017, *Annual Congress* London (UK) 2016. **Publications** *WFDF Newsletter*.
Members National associations in 76 countries and territories:
Afghanistan, Argentina, Australia, Austria, Bahrain, Belarus, Belgium, Bolivia, Brazil, Brunei Darussalam, Canada, Chile, China, Colombia, Congo DR, Costa Rica, Croatia, Czechia, Denmark, Dominican Rep, Egypt, Estonia, Finland, France, Georgia, Germany, Guam, Hong Kong, Hungary, Iceland, India, Indonesia, Iran Islamic Rep, Ireland, Israel, Italy, Japan, Jordan, Kenya, Korea Rep, Latvia, Lebanon, Lithuania, Luxembourg, Malaysia, Mexico, Morocco, Netherlands, New Zealand, Norway, Palestine, Panama, Philippines, Poland, Portugal, Qatar, Russia, Rwanda, Singapore, Slovakia, Slovenia, South Africa, Spain, Sweden, Switzerland, Taiwan, Tanzania UR, Thailand, Türkiye, Uganda, UK, Ukraine, United Arab Emirates, Uruguay, USA, Venezuela.
International organization:
Beach Ultimate Lovers Association (BULA, #03190).
NGO Relations Member of (6): *Alliance of Independent recognised Members of Sport (AIMS, #00690)* (Associate); *Association of the IOC Recognized International Sports Federations (ARISF, #02767)*; *International Council of Sport Science and Physical Education (ICSSPE, #13077)*; *International World Games Association (IWGA, #15914)*; *Olympic Movement (#17719)*; *The Association for International Sport for All (TAFISA, #02763)*. Recognized by: *International University Sports Federation (FISU, #15830)*; *International Olympic Committee (IOC, #14408)*; *International Paralympic Committee (IPC, #14512)*. [2020/XC0377/y/**C**]

♦ World Food Conference (meeting series)
♦ World Food Logistics Organization (internationally oriented national body)
♦ World Food Prize Foundation (internationally oriented national body)

♦ World Food Programme (WFP) 21510

Programme alimentaire mondial (PAM) – Programa Mundial de Alimentos (PMA)

Exec Dir Via Cesare Giulio Viola 68, Parco dei Medici, 00148 Rome RM, Italy. T. +39665131. E-mail: wfpinfo@wfp.org.
URL: http://www.wfp.org/

History 24 Nov 1961. Established as part of *United Nations System (#20635)*, jointly by the United Nations General Assembly resolution 1714 (XVI) of 19 Dec 1961 and resolution 1/61 of the 1961 Conference of *FAO (#09260)*. Initially established on a 3-year experimental basis, with operations starting Jan 1963 and extended by General Assembly resolution 2095 (XX) of 20 Dec 1965, on a continuing basis for as long as multilateral food aid is found feasible and desirable. The General Assembly and the FAO Conference endorsed resolution XXII of 16 Nov 1976 at the World Food Conference, by which the *United Nations/FAO Intergovernmental Committee (IGC)*, which provided guidance on policy, administration and operations of the Programme, reconstituted as the *Committee on Food Aid Policies and Programmes of the UN/FAO World Food Programme (inactive)*. In line with the provisions of General Assembly resolution 48/162, WFP was restructured in 1995. WFP is an organ of *United Nations (UN, #20515)* linked to the General Assembly and to *ECOSOC (#05331)*. Was awarded the Nobel Peace Prize in 2020. **Aims** Save and change lives in pursuit of zero hunger by 2030: respond to emergencies and save lives and livelihoods; mitigate the impact of mainly conflict and climate change-driven disasters, through emergency preparedness and resilience building among communities; seek long-term solutions to hunger and undernutrition by focusing on sustainable development and in partnership with governments, private companies and humanitarian sector. **Structure** Executive Board; Secretariat, with headquarters in Rome (Italy), headed by Executive Director. **Languages** Arabic, Chinese, English, French, Portuguese, Russian, Spanish. **Staff** More than 22,000, of whom over 87% work in the field. **Finance** Voluntary contributions. Funding from: governments; private sector organizations; individual donors. Annual budget: 9,600,000,000 USD (2019). **Activities** Humanitarian/emergency aid; knowledge management/information dissemination. **Events** *Global Humanitarian Aviation Conference* Sharm el Sheikh (Egypt) 2019, *Global Humanitarian Aviation Conference* Sharm el Sheikh (Egypt) 2018, *Asia Pacific Symposium on Sustainable Food Systems for Healthy Diets and Improved Nutrition* Bangkok (Thailand) 2017, *Global Humanitarian Aviation Conference* Lisbon (Portugal) 2017, *Global Humanitarian Aviation Conference* Madrid (Spain) 2016. **Publications** Annual Performance Report.
Members In 2022, Executive Board Members (36) (date of expiry between brackets):
Argentina (2023), Australia (2022), Bangladesh (2024), Brazil (2023), Burundi (2022), Canada (2022), China (2023), Cuba (2022), Denmark (2023), Dominican Rep (2022), France (2024), Germany (2022), Ghana (2024), Hungary (2023), India (2024), Iran Islamic Rep (2024), Japan (2023), Korea Rep (2024), Lesotho (2023), Madagascar (2022), Mexico (2023), Morocco (2023), Netherlands (2024), Norway (2023), Peru (2024), Poland (2023), Russia (2024), Saudi Arabia (2022), Senegal (2024), Somalia (2022), South Africa (2022), Spain (2022), Sweden (2024), Turkmenistan (2022), UK (2023), USA (2024).
IGO Relations Reports annually to: *ECOSOC (#05331)*; *FAO (#09260)* Council. Observer to: *World Trade Organization (WTO, #21864)*. Member of: *Agricultural and Land and Water Use Commission for the Near East (ALAWUC, #00570)*; *Committee of International Development Institutions on the Environment (CIDIE, no recent information)*; *Inter-Agency Standing Committee (IASC, #11393)*; *Inter-Agency Working Group on Desertification (IAWGD, inactive)*; *Intergovernmental Organizations Conference (IGO Conference, #11498)*; *United Nations Sustainable Development Group (UNSDG, #20634)*. Protocol Agreement with: FAO and *International Fund for Agricultural Development (IFAD, #13692)*. Represented on: *United Nations System Chief Executives Board for Coordination (CEB, #20636)*. Participates in: *Inter-Agency Task Force on Employment and Sustainable Livelihoods for All (inactive)*. Co-sponsor of: *Joint United Nations Programme on HIV/AIDS (UNAIDS, #16149)*. Memoranda of Understanding or other agreements with: *Global Information and Early Warning System on Food and Agriculture (GIEWS, #10416)*; *UNHCR (#20327)*; *UNICEF (#20332)*; *United Nations Volunteers (UNV, #20650)*. Key partner of: *United Nations Girls' Education Initiative (UNGEI, #20566)*. Member of: *United Nations Group on the Information Society (UNGIS, #20570)*. Close cooperation with: *ILO (#11123)*; *International Bank for Reconstruction and Development (IBRD, #12317)*; *UNDP (#20292)*; *UNESCO (#20322)*; *United Nations Economic Commission for Latin America and the Caribbean (ECLAC, #20556)*; *United Nations Institute for Training and Research (UNITAR, #20576)*; *WHO (#20950)*. Cooperation agreement with: *Islamic World Educational, Scientific and Cultural Organization (ICESCO, #16058)*. Participates in: *Joint Inspection Unit of the United Nations (JIU, #16133)*. Support from: *United Nations Peacebuilding Fund (PBF, #20607)*. **NGO Relations** Works with more than 1,000 NGOs around the globe, from small grassroots groups to large international aid agencies. Member of: *Active Learning Network for Accountability and Performance in Humanitarian Action (ALNAP, #00101)*; *Association for Human Resources Management in International Organizations (AHRMIO, #02634)*; *Better Than Cash Alliance (#03220)*; *Inter-Agency Task Team on Children affected by AIDS (IATT, #11394)*; *Permanent Conference of Mediterranean Audiovisual Operators (COPEAM, #18320)*. Partner of: *Global Health Cluster (GHC, #10401)*. Supporting organization of: *Scaling Up Nutrition Movement (SUN Movement, #19064)*. Supports: *Africare (#00516)*; *Development Training International (DTI)*; *Humanitarian Practice Network (HPN, #10973)*; *Ockenden International*. Signatory to: *International Aid Transparency Initiative (IATI, #11604)*. [2022.11.30/XE3543/**F***]

♦ World Food Safety Organization (WFSO) 21511

Contact address not obtained. E-mail: admin@worldfoodsafety.org.

URL: http://www.worldfoodsafety.org/
History 16 Jun 2001, Malta. UK Registered Company: 4581661. **Aims** Promote safety of food products, representing the interests of consumers, producers, retailers and wholesalers. **Structure** Executive Committee. **Events** *Food safety and hygiene conference / Conference* Frankfurt-Main (Germany) 2003.
[2010/XD9005/D]

♦ World Food Travel Association (internationally oriented national body)
♦ World Forensic Psychiatry and Psychology Association (no recent information)
♦ World Foresight Forum (internationally oriented national body)
♦ World Forest Institute (internationally oriented national body)
♦ World Forestry Center, Portland (internationally oriented national body)
♦ World Forestry Congress (meeting series)

♦ World Forum for Acoustic Ecology (WFAE) 21512

Chair PO Box 268, Fairfield VIC 3078, Australia. E-mail: wfae.organization@gmail.com.
URL: http://www.wfae.net/
History Founded 1993. **Aims** Promote: education in listening to the soundscope, sharpening aural awareness and deepening listeners' understanding of environmental sounds and their meanings; research and study of all aspects of the soundscope; publishing and distributing information and research on acoustic ecology; protecting and preserving existing natural soundscopes and times and places of quiet; designing and creating health and acoustically balanced *sonic* environments. **Structure** Board, including Chairman. **Languages** English, French, German. **Staff** 25.00 FTE, voluntary. **Finance** Members' dues, set by individual affiliate organizations. **Events** *International Conference* Corfu (Greece) 2011, *International Conference* Finland 2010, *International conference* Koli (Finland) 2010, *International conference* Mexico City (Mexico) 2009, *International conference* Hirosaki (Japan) 2006. **Publications** *The WFAE Newsletter* (4 a year) – online; *Soundscope – The Journal of Acoustic Ecology* (annual).
Members Affiliated organizations and individuals in 9 countries:
Australia, Canada, Finland, Germany, Italy, Japan, Mexico, UK, USA.
[2013.06.17/XF6182/F]

♦ World Forum on Advanced Materials (meeting series)

♦ World Forum for Alternatives (WFA) 21513

Forum mondial des alternatives (FMA) – Foro Mundial de las Alternativas (FMA)
Pres CP 3501, Dakar, Senegal. T. +221338211144. Fax +221338211144.
SG Av Sainte Gertrude 5, 1348 Louvain-la-Neuve, Belgium. T. +3210489570. Fax +3210489570. E-mail: cetri@cetri.be.
History Mar 1997, Cairo (Egypt). **Aims** Mobilize individuals suffering under current international *economic policy*; promote humanistic, democratic and pro-people alternatives. **Structure** Executive Committee. **Events** *Assembly* Caracas (Venezuela) 2008. **Publications** *Globalization of Resistance – the State of Struggles* (annual). *Directory of Social Movements.*
Members Full; Associate; Collaborators. Members in 80 countries. (not specified). International organizations (7):
International organizations (7):
Alternatives – Action and Communication Network for International Development; *Arab and African Research Centre (AARC)*; *Asian Regional Exchange for New Alternatives (ARENA, #01684)*; *Centre d'études et initiatives de solidarité internationale (CEDETIM)*; *Consejo Latinoamericano de Ciencias Sociales (CLACSO, #04718)*; *Europe – Third World Centre (CETIM)*; *Third World Forum (TWF, #20149)*.
NGO Relations Member of: *World Social Forum (WSF, #21797)*. [2015.06.01/XF4631/y/F]

♦ World Forum on China Studies (internationally oriented national body)
♦ World Forum on Community Networking (internationally oriented national body)

♦ World Forum of CSDs (WFC) 21514

Secretariat address not obtained.
URL: http://worldcsds.wordpress.com/
History 15 Apr 2011, Cape Town (South Africa), at CSD11 Conference. **Aims** Further enhance inter-association communications. **Structure** Board, comprising Chairs and Vice-Chairs of regional associations. Secretariat. **Languages** English. **Staff** Part-time, voluntary. **Finance** No budget. **Events** *Global Conference of Central Securities Depositories* Cancún (Mexico) 2015, *Meeting* Boston, MA (USA) 2014, *Meeting* Zurich (Switzerland) 2014, *Meeting* Dubai (United Arab Emirates) 2013. **Publications** *WFC Newsletter.*
Members Federations (5):
Africa and Middle East Depositories Association (AMEDA, #00190); *Americas' Central Securities Depositories Association (ACSDA, #00792)*; *Asia Pacific Central Securities Depository Group (ACG, #01866)*; *Association of Eurasian Central Securities Depositories (AECSD, #02496)*; *European Central Securities Depositories Association (ECSDA, #06468)*. [2019/XJ8700/y/F]

♦ World Forum for Democratization in Asia (WFDA) 21515

Contact c/o Taiwan Foundation for Democracy, No 4/Alley 17, Lane 147/Section 3, Sinyi Road, Taipei 106, Taiwan. T. +886227080100. Fax +886227081148. E-mail: tfd@tfd.org.tw.
Facebook: https://www.facebook.com/wfda.net/
History 15 Sep 2005, Taipei (Taiwan). 15-17 Sep 2005, Taipei (Taiwan), by *Alliance for Reform and Democracy in Asia (ARDA, #00716)*, *Alternative ASEAN Network on Burma (ALTSEAN Burma)*, *Forum Asia Democracy (FAD, #09900)*, *Initiatives for International Dialogue* and Taiwan Foundation for Democracy. **Aims** Support democracy activists in Asia; focus attention of the Asian people on the democratization process in the region and encourage participation in it; seek international support for the democratization effort in Asia; stimulate and facilitate overall coordination of democracy programmes. **Structure** Steering Committee. **Languages** English. **Staff** 1.00 FTE, paid. **Finance** Main funding from Taiwan Foundation for Democracy. **Activities** Framework for Action includes following core activities: communicating Asia's commitment to democracy; regional standard-setting; action for defence of human rights; promoting political accountability; promoting the role of women in democracy and the political process; promoting dialogue and cooperation on issues of peace and conflict resolution; supporting free and fair elections. **Events** *Biennial Conference* Seoul (Korea Rep) 2009, *Biennial Conference* Manila (Philippines) 2007, *Biennial Conference* Taipei (Taiwan) 2005.
Members Organizations and individuals in 23 countries and territories:
Bangladesh, Bhutan, Cambodia, China, Hong Kong, India, Indonesia, Japan, Korea DPR, Korea Rep, Laos, Malaysia, Mongolia, Myanmar, Nepal, Pakistan, Philippines, Singapore, Sri Lanka, Taiwan, Thailand, Timor-Leste, Vietnam.
IGO Relations Formal contacts with: *Community of Democracies (CD, #04394)*. [2017.07.05/XM0817/c/F]

♦ World Forum for Ethics in Business (WFEB) 21516

Main Office Av des Courses 16, B-11, 1050 Brussels, Belgium. T. +497804973966. Fax +497804973967. E-mail: office@wfeb.org.
URL: http://wfeb.org/
History Founders include: Sri Sri Ravi Shankar. Registered in accordance with Belgian law: 822.216.342. **Aims** Provide a platform for the promotion and defence of ethical approaches to business enterprise and corporate governance; facilitate global dialogue and foster cooperation among the private sector, academic world, government agencies, international organizations, media, spiritual as well as secular communities and all other stakeholders so as to foster decency; recruit support for trends, initiatives and projects encouraging or enhancing ethical and/or spiritual motivations, practices, norms and goals in the business world. **Structure** Board of Directors, comprising President and 5 members. Advisory Committee. **Activities** Events/meetings; awards/prizes/competitions. **Events** *Munich Conference on Ethics in Innovation* Munich (Germany) 2017, *International Leadership Symposium* Delhi (India) 2016, *World Summit on Ethics and Leadership in Sports* Zurich (Switzerland) 2016, *International Leadership Symposium* Brussels (Belgium) 2015, *World Summit on Ethics in Sports* Zurich (Switzerland) 2014. **Consultative Status** Consultative status granted from: *ECOSOC (#05331)* (Special). **NGO Relations** Founder is also founder of: *International Association for Human Values (IAHV, #11947)*. [2017/XJ6254/s/F]

♦ World Forum of Fisher Peoples (WFFP) 21517

Forum mondial des populations de pêcheurs – Foro Mundial Comunidades Pesqueras
Gen Sec address not obtained.
Coordinator address not obtained.
URL: http://worldfishers.org/
History 21 Nov 1997, Delhi (India). **Aims** Protect, defend and strengthen the communities that depend on fishery for their livelihood; represent the small-scale, artisanal fishers' interest at international level; act as the global political organ for the fishers' communities. **Structure** General Assembly; Coordination Committee; Continental Committees. **Languages** English, French, Spanish. **Staff** 2.00 FTE, voluntary. **Finance** Members' dues (annual): US$ 250. Donations. **Activities** Organizes annual global campaign on world fisheries (21 Nov). **Events** *General Assembly* Delhi (India) 2017.
Members Organizations (36) in 24 countries and territories:
Bangladesh, Benin, Canada, France, Guadeloupe, Guinea, Honduras, India, Kenya, Madagascar, Malaysia, Mali, Martinique, Mauritania, Nepal, New Zealand, Pakistan, Philippines, Senegal, South Africa, Spain, Sri Lanka, Thailand, Uganda.
IGO Relations Contacts with: *FAO (#09260)*; *International Fund for Agricultural Development (IFAD, #13692)*. **NGO Relations** Member of: *Deep Sea Conservation Coalition (DSCC, #05024)*; *International NGO/CSO Planning Committee for Food Sovereignty (IPC, #14365)*. Member of the Coordinating Committee of: *More and Better (#16855)*. Cooperates with: *Transnational Institute (TNI, #20219)*. [2020/XF6624/F]

♦ World Forum of Fish Harvesters and Fishworkers (WFF) 21518

Exec Dir PO Box 33929, Kampala, Uganda. T. +256414348774. Fax +256414348774. E-mail: info@worldfisherforum.org.
Street address Lungujja Plot 902, Off Kalema Road, Kampala, Uganda.
URL: http://worldfisherforum.org/
History 1997, Delhi (India). **Aims** Advocate for sustainable coastal communities and fisheries; uphold *human rights* and social justice for fishermen. **Structure** General Assembly (every 3 years); International Coordination committee; Executive Committee. **Languages** English, French, Spanish. **Staff** 1.00 FTE, voluntary. **Finance** Annual budget: euro 50,000. **Activities** Advocacy/lobbying/activism; guidance/assistance/consulting; capacity building; awareness raising; monitoring/evaluation; networking/liaising. **Events** *Meeting* Salinas (Ecuador) 2017, *Meeting* Kampala (Uganda) 2012, *Meeting* Lisbon (Portugal) 2004, *Meeting* Loctudy (France) 2000.
Members National commercial fishing associations (41) in 38 countries and territories:
Algeria, Argentina, Belize, Brazil, Burundi, Canada, Chad, Chile, Costa Rica, Djibouti, Dominica, Ecuador, El Salvador, Faeroe Is, Gambia, Ghana, Greenland, Guatemala, Guinea, Honduras, Iceland, India, Kenya, Mauritania, Mexico, Morocco, Nicaragua, Nigeria, Norway, Panama, Peru, Portugal, Sierra Leone, Tanzania UR, Tunisia, Uganda, USA, Venezuela.
IGO Relations Formal contact with: *FAO (#09260)*; *International Fund for Agricultural Development (IFAD, #13692)*. **NGO Relations** Member of: Coordinating Committee of: *More and Better (#16855)*; *High Level Panel for a Sustainable Ocean Economy (Panel, #10917)* – Advisory Committee. [2019.05.02/XJ0878/F]

♦ World Forum Foundation 21519

Main Office 7700 A St, Lincoln NE 68510, USA. E-mail: info@worldforumfoundation.org.
URL: http://www.worldforumfoundation.org/
History 1999. Founded following discussions held in 1998; originally operated under the Exchange Press publishing company. **Aims** Promote an ongoing global exchange of ideas on the delivery of quality services for young *children* in diverse settings. **Structure** World Forum Alliance. **Events** *World Forum on Early Care and Education* Vancouver, BC (Canada) 2024, *World Forum on Early Care and Education* Panama (Panama) 2023, *World Forum on Early Care and Education* Orlando, FL (USA) 2022, *World Forum on Early Care and Education* Macau (Macau) 2019, *World Forum on Early Care and Education* San Juan (Puerto Rico) 2014.
Members Organizations (13) in 8 countries:
Australia, Canada, Fiji, France, Malaysia, Netherlands, New Zealand, USA.
Included in the above, 3 organizations listed in this Yearbook:
Childhood Education International (CE International); *Pacific Pre-School Council (#17992)*; *UNESCO (#20322)*.
[2022/XM1645/fy/F]

♦ World Forum on the Future of Sport Shooting Activities / see World Forum on Shooting Activities (#21523)
♦ World Forum for Hospital Sterile Supply / see World Federation for Hospital Sterilisation Sciences (#21438)
♦ World Forum for Hospital Sterilisation Sciences / see World Federation for Hospital Sterilisation Sciences (#21438)

♦ World Forum Offshore Wind (WFO) 21520

Contact Überseering 4, 22297 Hamburg, Germany. T. +494061199125.
URL: https://wfo-global.org/
History 2018. Registration: Hamburg District Court, No/ID: VR 23680, Start date: 10 Jul 2018, Germany, Hamburg. **Aims** Promote offshore wind energy on a global scale. [2021.11.30/AA1896/F]

♦ World Forum for Proximity of Islamic Schools of Thought (WFPIST) 21521

SG PO Box 15875-6995, Ayatollah Taleghani St, near Shahid Mofatteh intersection 357, Teheran, Iran Islamic Rep. T. +982188321411. Fax +982188321414. E-mail: info@taghrib.org.
URL: http://www.taghrib.org/
Structure High Council; Scientific Board; Secretary-General; Related Deputies. **Events** *Conference* Teheran (Iran Islamic Rep) 2007. **Publications** *Resalat Al-Islam Magazine*; *Resalat Al-Taghrib Magazine.* Books.
[2018/XM3362/F]

♦ World Forum on Science and Democracy (WFSD) 21522

Forum Mondial Sciences et Démocratie (FMSD)
Address not obtained.
URL: http://www.fmsd-wfsd.org/
Structure Executive Committee. **Activities** Events/meetings. **Events** *World Forum* Salvador (Brazil) 2018, *World Forum* Tunis (Tunisia) 2015, *World Forum* Tunis (Tunisia) 2013, *World Forum* Dakar (Senegal) 2011, *World Forum* Belém (Brazil) 2009. **Publications** *WFSD Newsletter.*
Members Full in 10 countries:
Argentina, Australia, Brazil, Canada, France, Germany, Netherlands, Spain, UK, USA.
Included in the above, 4 organizations listed in this Yearbook:
Action Group on Erosion, Technology and Concentration (ETC Group, #00091); *International Center for Technology Assessment (ICTA)*; *Sciences Citoyennes*; *Scientists for Global Responsibility (SGR)*.
[2018/XM6460/y/F]

♦ World Forum on Shooting Activities (WFSA) 21523

Contact c/o ANPAM, Viale dell'Astronomia 30, 00144 Rome RM, Italy. T. +3965903510. Fax +39654282691. E-mail: wfsa.secretariat@anpam.org.
Registered Office Rue Th Decuyper 100, 1200 Brussels, Belgium.
URL: http://www.wfsa.net/
History Mar 1997, Germany. Former names and other names: *World Forum on the Future of Sport Shooting Activities (WFSA)* – former. Registration: Banque-Carrefour des Entreprises, No/ID: 0462.519.358, Start date: 12 Feb 1998, Belgium. **Aims** In the spirit of goodwill and cooperation, offer *decision-makers* worldwide information, solutions and alternatives to *problems* and questions of common interest. **Structure** General Assembly (annual); Executive Committee; Secretariat, located in Rome (Italy). **Finance** Members' dues (annual): Voting, euro 3,000; Regular, euro 1,000; Associate, euro 500. **Activities** WFSA is an open forum and encourages exchange of information and views among all interested parties. The role of WFSA is limited in scope and designed to complement ongoing activities of member associations and organizations. Organizes: *'Shooting, Hunting and Outdoor Trades (SHOT) Show'* (annually); symposia. **Events** *Meeting* Nürburg (Germany) 2017, *Meeting* Cape Town (South Africa) 2003, *Annual general meeting* Nürburg (Germany) 2003.
Members Voting; Regular; Associate. New members must be sponsored by 2 existing members of WFSA. National and international organizations (44) in 20 countries:
Australia, Belgium, Canada, Czechia, Denmark, Finland, Germany, Greece, Italy, Japan, Malta, Netherlands, New Zealand, Norway, South Africa, Spain, Sweden, Switzerland, UK, USA.
Included in the above, 9 organizations listed in this Yearbook:

Association of European Manufacturers of Sporting Ammunition (#02522); Conservation Force (#04729); European Association of the Civil Commerce of Weapons (#05975); European Shooting Confederation (ESC, #08481); Federation of Associations for Hunting and Conservation of the EU (#09459); Foundation for European Societies of Arms Collectors (FESAC, #09955); Institut Européen des Armes de Chasse et de Sport (IEACS, #11299); International Practical Shooting Confederation (IPSC, #14631); Safari Club International (SCI). **Consultative Status** Consultative status granted from: *ECOSOC (#05331)* (Ros A). **IGO Relations** *United Nations Commission on Crime Prevention and Criminal Justice (CCPCJ, #20530).* **NGO Relations** Partner of (1): *Association of European Manufacturers of Sporting Firearms (ESFAM, #02523).* [2019/XF4330/y/F]

♦ World Forum on Theology and Liberation (WFTL) 21524

Forum Mondial de Théologie et Libération – Foro Mundial de Teologia y Liberación – Fórum Mundial de Teologia e Libertação (FMTL)

SG Prédio 5 sala 407-15, Av Ipiranga 6681, Porto Alegre RS, Brazil. T. +5133203940. E-mail: fmtl@pucrs.br.
URL: http://wftlofficial.org/

History Founded 2003. Letter of principles adopted Jul 2007. **Structure** Permanent Council; Permanent Secretary; International Consultative Committee. [2018/XM6613/F]

♦ World Foundation for AIDS Research and Prevention 21525

Fondation mondiale recherche et prévention SIDA (FMRPS)

Contact address not obtained. T. +33145683841. Fax +33142733745. E-mail: fondation.sida@unesco.org.

History Founded 28 Jan 1993, Fribourg (Switzerland), under the auspices of *UNESCO (#20322)*, in response to the *'Venice Appeal'* launched 8 Jun 1991 by UNESCO Director-General. Foundation under Swiss law. **Aims** Promote AIDS research particularly in Africa, Asia and Latin America through the setting up of an international network of research centres; reinforce efforts at prevention of AIDS through development of policies adapted to socio-cultural conditions in each country. **Languages** English, French. **Staff** Paris – 6; Côte d'Ivoire – 40; Cameroon – 10. **Finance** Donations and fundraising. **Activities** Works through: supervising clinical research on aids; facilitating exchanges; training; scientific meetings and conferences. **Events** *ICGHP congress / Congress* Paris (France) 1996, *Interdisciplinary AIDS meeting* Venice (Italy) 1994. **Publications** Books.
Members Full in 3 countries:
Cameroon, Côte d'Ivoire, USA.
Consultative Status Consultative status granted from: *UNESCO (#20322)* (Foundations). [2013/XF5098/f/F]

♦ World Foundation for Girl Guides and Girl Scouts 21526

Fondation mondiale pour les guides et les éclaireuses

Administrator 420 Fifth Avenue, 14th Floor, New York NY 10018-2798, USA. T. +12128528612. Fax +12128526514.
Pres address not obtained.
URL: http://www.worldfoundationgggs.org/

History 1971. **Aims** Promote in all lawful ways for charitable and educational purposes, the success of the World Association of Girl Guides and Girl Scouts and of Girl Guiding and Girl Scouting in any and all countries of the world. **Activities** Supports 4 world Centres – Our Cabaña (Mexico), Our Chalet (Switzerland), Sangam (India) and Pax Lodge (UK) – and the 2 member organizations.
Members Organizations (2):
Girl Scouts of the United States of America (GSUSA); *World Association of Girl Guides and Girl Scouts (WAGGGS, #21142).* [2014/XF6924/f/F]

♦ World Foundation for Medical Studies in Female Health (internationally oriented national body)

♦ World Foundation of Natural Science (WFNS) 21527

Headquarters PO Box Drawer 16900, Washington DC 20041, USA. T. +17036311408. Fax +17036311919. E-mail: info@naturalscience.org.
European Headquarters PO Box 7995, 6000 Lucerne 7, Switzerland. T. +41417980398. Fax +41417980399.
URL: http://www.naturalscience.org/

Aims Help our Earth and humanity enter into the new *spiritual* age. **Events** *5G and Corona* Linz (Austria) 2020, *Congress* Innsbruck (Austria) 2001, *Congress* Kufstein (Austria) 2000, *New scientific outlook* Lindau (Germany) 2000, *Congress* Interlaken (Switzerland) 1998.
Members Full in 45 countries:
Argentina, Australia, Austria, Belgium, Brazil, Canada, Chile, China, Cuba, Czechia, Denmark, Ecuador, Egypt, Estonia, France, Germany, Greece, Hungary, Ireland, Israel, Italy, Kenya, Kyrgyzstan, Latvia, Liechtenstein, Lithuania, Mexico, Netherlands, New Zealand, Peru, Portugal, Russia, Singapore, Slovakia, Slovenia, South Africa, Spain, Switzerland, Thailand, UK, Ukraine, USA, Uzbekistan, Venezuela. [2008/XF3669/f/F]

♦ World Foundation for Renal Care (no recent information)
♦ World Foundation for Smart Communities (internationally oriented national body)
♦ World Foundrymen Organization / see World Foundry Organization (#21528)

♦ World Foundry Organization (WFO) 21528

Head Office Winton House, Lyonshall, Kington, HR5 3JP, UK. T. +441544340332. E-mail: info@thewfo.com.
URL: http://www.worldfoundry.org.uk/

History Apr 1927. Statutes and By-Laws adopted 1930; revised: 1938, 1948, 1956, 1959, 1962, 1967, 1978, 1990, 1995, 1998, 2000. Former names and other names: *International Committee of Foundry Technical Associations* – former (1927 to 2000); *Comité international des associations techniques de fonderie (CIATF)* – former (1927 to 2000); *Internationales Komitee Giessereitechnischer Vereinigungen* – former (1927 to 2000); *World Foundrymen Organization (WFO)* – former (2000 to 2010). Registration: No/ID: 6296468, England and Wales. **Aims** Promote the whole *foundry* industry and connected industries in the scientific and the applied fields. **Structure** General Assembly; Executive; Research Commissions. **Languages** English. **Staff** 1.00 FTE, paid. **Finance** Members' dues, according to production. **Events** *Congress* Italy 2024, *World Foundry Congress* Busan (Korea Rep) 2022, *Cast the future* Busan (Korea Rep) 2020, *World Foundry Congress* Poland 2018, *International Forum on Moulding Materials and Casting Technologies* Incheon (Korea Rep) 2017. **Publications** *Foundry Trade Journal* (10 a year); *International Foundry Research Journal* (4 a year).
Members Main foundry technical associations in 29 countries:
Austria, China, Croatia, Czechia, Denmark, Egypt, Finland, France, Germany, Hungary, India, Japan, Korea Rep, Mexico, Netherlands, Norway, Pakistan, Poland, Romania, Russia, Serbia, Slovakia, Slovenia, Spain, Sweden, Switzerland, Türkiye, UK, USA.
IGO Relations *UNESCO (#20322).* **NGO Relations** In liaison with technical committees of: *International Organization for Standardization (ISO, #14473).* [2021/XC1611/C]

♦ World Franchise Council (WFC) 21529

Main Office c/o EFF, 40 Rue Washingtonstraat, 1050 Brussels, Belgium.
URL: http://www.worldfranchisecouncil.net/

History 1994. Registration: Start date: 2005, England and Wales. **Aims** Serve as a forum for national franchise associations. **Structure** Secretariat rotates among member associations. **Languages** English. **Events** *Half-Yearly Meeting* Philippines 2021, *Half-Yearly Meeting* Beirut (Lebanon) 2020, *Half-Yearly Meeting* Seoul (Korea Rep) 2020, *Half-Yearly Meeting* Abu Dhabi (United Arab Emirates) 2019, *Half-Yearly Meeting* Madrid (Spain) 2019.
Members National associations in 42 countries and territories:
Argentina, Australia, Austria, Belgium, Brazil, Canada, China, Croatia, Czechia, Denmark, Egypt, Finland, France, Germany, Greece, Guatemala, Hong Kong, Hungary, India, Indonesia, Italy, Japan, Korea Rep, Lebanon, Malaysia, Mexico, Netherlands, New Zealand, Philippines, Poland, Portugal, Russia, Singapore, Slovenia, South Africa, Sweden, Switzerland, Taiwan, Türkiye, UK, USA, Venezuela.
Regional Association Member (2):
Asia Pacific Franchise Confederation (APFC, #01913); European Franchise Federation (EFF, #07354). [2020/XF6898/F]

♦ World Free Press Institute (internationally oriented national body)
♦ World Freerunning Parkour Federation (unconfirmed)
♦ World Free Zone Convention (meeting series)

♦ World Free Zones Organization (World FZO) 21530

CEO Office No 1090, 1st Fl – 7W-B, Dubai Airport Free Zone, PO Box 371113, Dubai, United Arab Emirates. T. +97142045473. Fax +97142952945. E-mail: info@worldfzo.org.
Registered Office c/o Brown and Page, rue de Vermont 37-39, 1202 Geneva, Switzerland.
URL: http://www.worldfzo.org/

History Launched May 2014, Dubai (United Arab Emirates). Current Articles of Association approved 14 Jan 2014, Dubai. Registered in accordance with Swiss Civil Code. **Aims** Raise awareness of the benefits that free zones can bring in terms of: enhancing foreign direct investment and trade; promoting cultural diversity; driving innovation and skills development; creating new jobs and industries, as well as bringing stability to the global economy and prosperity to nations. **Structure** General Assembly; Board of Directors; Executive Management. **Languages** English. **Finance** Sources: donations; fees for services; gifts, legacies; meeting proceeds; members' dues; sponsorship; subsidies. **Activities** Certification/accreditation; events/meetings; guidance/assistance/consulting; knowledge management/information dissemination; networking/liaising; training/education. **Events** *Annual International Conference* Dubai (United Arab Emirates) 2020, *Annual International Conference* Barcelona (Spain) 2019, *Annual International Conference* Dubai (United Arab Emirates) 2018, *Annual International Conference* Cartagena de Indias (Colombia) 2017, *Annual International Conference* Dubai (United Arab Emirates) 2016. **Members** Voting; Associate; Partners and Observers. Membership countries not specified. **Consultative Status** Consultative status granted from: *UNCTAD (#20285)* (General). [2017/XM6172/C]

♦ World Freight Alliance (unconfirmed)
♦ World Freight Network (internationally oriented national body)
♦ World Friendship Association (inactive)
♦ World Friendship Center (internationally oriented national body)
♦ World Friendship Center, Hiroshima / see World Friendship Center
♦ World Friendship Federation (inactive)

♦ World Fund for Development and Planning (WFDP) 21531

Pres UN Avenue, Runda, Plot 128, Nairobi, 00100, Kenya. E-mail: info@wfdp-igo.org.
Contact 49 Nile Cornich, Maadi, Cairo, 11728, Egypt. T. +20225276712.
URL: https://wfdp-igo.org/

History 2012, Uganda. **Aims** Prevent violent conflicts; promote dialogue and peaceful resolution of conflicts around the world. **Structure** Board of Directors. **Languages** Arabic, English, French, Russian. **Staff** 256.00 FTE, paid. **Finance** Self-funded. **Activities** Certification/accreditation; humanitarian/emergency aid; publishing activities; research and development; training/education. Active in: Belgium, Cyprus, Egypt, Ghana, India, Indonesia, Kenya, Nigeria, Sierra Leone, South Africa, Togo, Uganda, Ukraine, United Arab Emirates, USA.
Members Full in countries:
Australia, Belgium, Brazil, Chad, Cyprus, Ghana, Indonesia, Kenya, Nepal, Netherlands, Nigeria, Sierra Leone, South Africa, Togo, Uganda, Ukraine, USA, Vanuatu.
Consultative Status Consultative status granted from: *ECOSOC (#05331)* (Special). [2022.11.20/AA3020/F]

♦ World Futsal Association 21532

Asociación Mundial de Futsal (AMF)

Pres Avda Brasilia No 1895, esq Tte Frutos, Asunción, Paraguay. E-mail: amfutsal@amfutsal.com.py – directorejecutivoamf@gmail.com.
SG address not obtained.
URL: http://www.amfutsal.com.py/

History 1 Dec 2002, by members of *Pan American Indoor Football Confederation (#18112)* and *European Futsal Association (EFA, #07371)*, who relaunched *International Mini-Football Federation (IMFF, inactive)* in a new structure under current title. Also referred to as *Asociación Mundial de Fútbol de Salón.*
Members National federations in 5 countries:
Belarus, Brazil, Colombia, Norway, Spain.
Continental federations (3):
Confederación Sudamericana de Futsal (CSFS, no recent information); European Futsal Association (EFA, #07371); Pan American Indoor Football Confederation (#18112).
NGO Relations Member of (2): *General Association of Asia Pacific Sports Federations (GAAPSF, #10106); International Sport Network Organization (ISNO, #15592). African Confederation of Futsal (CAFUSA); Confederation of Asian Futsal (CAFS, #04510); Confederation of North, Central American and the Caribbean Futsal (CONCACFUTSAL, #04571).* [2022/XM8218/y/D]

♦ World Future Council Foundation (WFC) 21533

Dir Dorotheenstrasse 15, 22301 Hamburg, Germany. T. +494030709140. Fax +494030709141419. E-mail: info@worldfuturecouncil.org.
URL: http://www.worldfuturecouncil.org/

History May 2007, Hamburg (Germany). Former names and other names: *World Future Council Initiative (WFCI)* – former; *Initiative Welt-Zukunftsrat* – former. Registration: EU Transparency Register, No/ID: 099469423186-43, Start date: 30 Aug 2016. **Aims** Bring the interests of future generations to the centre of *policy making*; inform policy makers about future just policies on energy, climate, sustainable cities, agriculture, peace, disarmament, finance, biodiversity and democracy issues and advise them on how to implement these. **Structure** Council; Supervisory Board; Management Board; Offices. **Languages** English, German. **Staff** 17.00 FTE, paid; 3.00 FTE, voluntary. **Finance** Sources: donations. Annual budget: 1,500,000 EUR. **Activities** Events/meetings; management of treaties and agreements. Manages the following treaties/agreements: *Convention on Biological Diversity (Biodiversity convention, 1992); United Nations Framework Convention on Climate Change (UNFCCC, 1992).* **Events** *Tackling Youth Unemployment* Hamburg (Germany) 2020, *WFC youth forum – Youth:Present Launch Event* Hamburg (Germany) 2020. **Publications** *WFC Newsletter* (12 a year); *Pathfinder 2019* in English, German – WFC's annual report 2019. Books; brochures.
Members Not a membership organization. **Consultative Status** Consultative status granted from: *ECOSOC (#05331)* (Special); *UNEP (#20299).* **IGO Relations** Accredited by (1): *Green Climate Fund (GCF, #10714).* **NGO Relations** Member of (4): *Climate Action Network Europe (CAN Europe, #04001); Global 100% RE (#10160); Global Call for Climate Action (GCCA, inactive); International Centre for Earth Simulation (ICES Foundation).* Partner of (2): *Basel Peace Office* (as founding partner); *World Urban Campaign (WUC, #21893).* Cooperates with (1): *Economy for the Common Good (ECG, #05323).* Instrumental in setting up (1): *African Renewable Energy Alliance (AREA, #00439).* [2020.11.20/XM0317/f/F]

♦ World Future Council Initiative / see World Future Council Foundation (#21533)
♦ World Future Foundation (internationally oriented national body)

♦ World Future Society (WFS) 21534

Société du monde futur

CEO 333 N LaSalle St, Chicago IL 60654, USA. E-mail: hello@worldfuture.org.
URL: http://www.wfs.org/

History 18 Oct 1966, Washington DC (USA). Chartered in the District of Columbia, USA. Subtitle: *Association for the Study of Alternative Futures.* **Aims** Serve as a neutral clearinghouse for ideas about the future; contribute to a research awareness of the future and of the importance of its study, without advocating particular ideologies or engaging in political activities; advance responsible and serious investigation of the future; promote the development of methodologies for study of the future. **Structure** General Assembly; Board of Directors. **Staff** 2.00 FTE, paid; 100.00 FTE, voluntary. **Finance** Members' dues. **Activities** Events/meetings; research and development. **Events** *Annual Conference* San Francisco, CA (USA) 2015, *Annual conference / General Assembly* Chicago, IL (USA) 2009, *Annual conference / General Assembly* Washington, DC (USA) 2008, *Annual conference / General Assembly* Minneapolis, MN (USA) 2007, *Annual conference / General Assembly* Toronto, ON (Canada) 2006. **Publications** *Future Survey* (12 a year); *The Futurist* (6 a year); *Futures Research* (4 a year). Resources directories.
Members Institutions, chapters, individuals, totalling 30,000 people (including sociologists, scientists, corporate planners, educators, students, retired people), in 89 countries and territories:

Argentina, Australia, Austria, Bahamas, Bangladesh, Barbados, Belgium, Bermuda, Bolivia, Brazil, Bulgaria, Canada, Chile, China, Colombia, Costa Rica, Côte d'Ivoire, Croatia, Cyprus, Czechia, Denmark, Dominican Rep, Ecuador, Egypt, Estonia, Ethiopia, Finland, France, Germany, Ghana, Greece, Guatemala, Hong Kong, Hungary, Iceland, India, Indonesia, Iran Islamic Rep, Iraq, Ireland, Israel, Italy, Jamaica, Japan, Jordan, Kenya, Korea Rep, Kuwait, Latvia, Luxembourg, Malaysia, Malta, Mexico, Monaco, Nepal, Netherlands, New Zealand, Nigeria, Norway, Oman, Pakistan, Panama, Peru, Philippines, Poland, Portugal, Puerto Rico, Russia, Saudi Arabia, Serbia, Singapore, Slovakia, Slovenia, South Africa, Spain, Sri Lanka, Sweden, Switzerland, Syrian AR, Taiwan, Thailand, Trinidad-Tobago, Türkiye, UK, United Arab Emirates, Uruguay, USA, Venezuela, Zimbabwe.

IGO Relations Associated with Department of Global Communications of the United Nations. **NGO Relations** Member of: *EarthAction (EA, #05159).* [2019/XF0116/F]

♦ World Futures Studies Federation (WFSF) 21535

Fédération mondiale pour les études sur le futur – Federación Mundial para Estudios sobre el Futuro – Federazione Mondiale Studi sul Futuro

Pres Glaneren 2, 1458 Fjellstrand, Norway.
Exec Dir address not obtained.
URL: http://www.wfsf.org/

History 26 May 1973, Paris (France). Set up at founding conference. Statutes formally adopted, Mar 1974, Paris. Developed from *Continuing Committee of the World Futures Studies Research Conferences (CC-WFSRC)*, previously called *International Future Research Committee*, which originated, Sep 1967, Oslo (Norway), at 1st World Futures Research Conference, organized by the then *Mankind 2000 (inactive)*, together with *Peace Research Institute Oslo (PRIO).* Registration: Start date: 12 Apr 1974. **Aims** Bring together academics, researchers, practitioners, students and futures-focused institutions and offer a forum for stimulation, exploration and exchange of ideas, visions and plans for alternative futures, through long-term, big-picture thinking and radical change; encourage and promote development of futures studies as a *transdisciplinary academic* and professional field in all parts of the world both face-to-face and virtually. **Structure** General Assembly (at least every 2 years, at World Conference); Executive Board. **Languages** English. **Staff** 3.50 FTE, voluntary. Voluntary. **Finance** Sources: members' dues. **Activities** Events/meetings; knowledge management/information dissemination; research/documentation; training/education. **Events** *World Conference* Mexico City (Mexico) 2019, *World Conference* Jondal (Norway) 2017, *World conference* Penang (Malaysia) 2011, *Seminar and general assembly* Bollwiller (France) 2009, *World conference* Trollhättan (Sweden) 2008. **Publications** *Human Futures* – magazine. Information Services: Database on futures research projects. **Information Services** *Futuresco* – clearing house database, jointly with UNESCO.

Members Founding; Associated: institutions engaged in future studies; Fellows; Full/Associate; Student. Institutions (14) in 13 countries and territories:
Canada, Colombia, Finland, Germany, Mexico, Netherlands, Nigeria, Poland, Romania, Russia, Sweden, Taiwan, USA.
Included in the above, 4 organizations listed in this Yearbook:
Finland Futures Research Centre (FFRC); Finnish Society for Futures Studies (FSFS); Institute for Alternative Futures, Alexandria VA (IAF, inactive); Institute for Futures Studies, Stockholm.
Individuals (278) in 61 countries and territories. Membership countries not specified.

Consultative Status Consultative status granted from: *ECOSOC (#05331)* (Special); *UNESCO (#20322)* (Consultative Status). **IGO Relations** Close cooperation with: *FAO (#09260); ILO (#11123); UNDP (#20292); UNEP (#20299); WHO (#20950).* Accredited by: *United Nations Office at Vienna (UNOV, #20604).* Associated with Department of Global Communications of the United Nations. **NGO Relations** Collective Associate Member of: *International Social Science Council (ISSC, inactive).* Supported, among others, by Futuribles International, and in the past by Mankind 2000 and by the Future Studies Centre (IRADES). Affiliated with: *World Organisation of Systems and Cybernetics (WOSC, #21686).* Has held meetings with: *Center for Economic and Social Studies of the Third World (CESSTEM, no recent information); Society for International Development (SID, #19581).* [2021/XC2072/y/B]

♦ **World FZO** World Free Zones Organization (#21530)
♦ World Games Council / see International World Games Association (#15914)

♦ World Gastroenterology Organisation (WGO) 21536

Organisation mondiale de gastroentérologie (OMGE) – Organización Mundial de Gastroenterologia – Weltorganisation für Gastroenterologie

Exec Dir 555 East Wells St, Ste 1100, Milwaukee WI 53202, USA. T. +14149189798. Fax +14142763349. E-mail: info@worldgastroenterology.org.
URL: http://www.worldgastroenterology.org/

History 10 Aug 1935, Brussels (Belgium). Statutes modified: 28 May 1958, Washington DC (USA); May 1962, Munich (Germany FR); 1970, Copenhagen (Denmark); 1974, Mexico City (Mexico); 1978, Madrid (Spain); 1982, Stockholm (Sweden); 1998, Vienna (Austria); 2002, Bangkok (Thailand); 2005, Montréal QC (Canada); 2009, London (UK); 2013, Shanghai (China); 2015, Brisbane (Australia). **Aims** Promote awareness of the world wide prevalence and optimal care of digestive disorders through provision of high quality, accessible and independent education and training. **Structure** General Assembly; Governing Council; Council of Chairs; Executive Committee; Committees and Interest Groups. **Languages** English. **Finance** Sources: members' dues. *WGO Foundation (WGOF)*, incorporated 2007, is the philanthropic arm of WGO. **Activities** Advocacy/lobbying/activism; awards/prizes/competitions; events/meetings; publishing activities; standards/guidelines; training/education. **Events** *World Congress of Gastroenterology* 2025, *World Congress of Gastroenterology* Seoul (Korea Rep) 2023, *World Congress of Gastroenterology (WCOG 2022)* Dubai (United Arab Emirates) 2022, *Biennial Congress* Dubai (United Arab Emirates) 2021, *Biennial Congress* Istanbul (Turkey) 2019. **Publications** *e-WGN Newsletter*, *Journal of Clinical Gastsroenterology (JCG).* Medical guidelines; e-alerts; scientific news; event information.

Members Gastroenterological societies (111), specialized sections and groups in 102 countries and territories:
Afghanistan, Albania, Algeria, Argentina, Australia, Bangladesh, Barbados, Belarus, Belgium, Bolivia, Bosnia-Herzegovina, Brazil, Bulgaria, Cameroon, Canada, Chile, China, Colombia, Costa Rica, Côte d'Ivoire, Croatia, Cuba, Czechia, Denmark, Dominican Rep, Ecuador, Egypt, El Salvador, Estonia, Ethiopia, Finland, France, Greece, Guatemala, Hungary, Iceland, India, Indonesia, Iran Islamic Rep, Iraq, Ireland, Israel, Italy, Japan, Jordan, Kazakhstan, Kenya, Korea Rep, Latvia, Lebanon, Lithuania, Luxembourg, Madagascar, Malaysia, Mexico, Mongolia, Montenegro, Morocco, Myanmar, Netherlands, New Zealand, Nicaragua, Nigeria, North Macedonia, Norway, Pakistan, Panama, Paraguay, Peru, Philippines, Poland, Portugal, Puerto Rico, Romania, Russia, Saudi Arabia, Senegal, Serbia, Singapore, Slovakia, Slovenia, South Africa, Spain, Sri Lanka, Sudan, Sweden, Switzerland, Syrian AR, Taiwan, Thailand, Tunisia, Türkiye, Uganda, UK, Ukraine, United Arab Emirates, Uruguay, USA, Uzbekistan, Venezuela, Vietnam, Yemen.
Included in the above, 5 organizations listed in this Yearbook:
African Middle East Association of Gastroenterology (AMAGE, #00372); Asian Pacific Association of Gastroenterology (APAGE, #01598); Asociación Centroamericana de Gastroenterologia y Endoscopia Digestiva (#02114); Association of West Indian Gastroenterologists (AWIG); Organización Panamericana de Gastroenterologia (OPGE, #17847).

IGO Relations Recognized by: *WHO (#20950).* [2019.01.22/XB3563/y/B]

♦ World Gastronomy Institute (internationally oriented national body)
♦ **WorldGBC** World Green Building Council (#21544)

♦ World Geologists 21537

Geólogos del Mundo

Contact C/ Raquel Meller, 7 (local), 28027 Madrid, Spain. T. +34915532403. Fax +34915330343. E-mail: geologosdelmundo@icog.es.
URL: http://www.geologosdelmundo.org/

Members Membership countries not specified. **NGO Relations** *European Federation of Geologists (EFG, #07133).* [2013.07.22/XF6730/F]

♦ World Geoparks Network / see Global Geoparks Network (#10389)

♦ World Geospatial Industry Council (WGIC) 21538

Exec Dir Fluwelen Burgwal 58, Barchman Wuytierslaan 10, 2511 CJ The Hague, Netherlands. T. +3197010281390. E-mail: info@wgicouncil.org.
URL: https://wgicouncil.org/

History Jul 2018. **Aims** Enhance the role of the geospatial industry and strengthen its contribution to global economy and society; facilitate knowledge exchange within the geospatial industry and co-creation of larger business opportunities for the geospatial industry; represent business interest, share perspectives of the geospatial industry and undertake policy advocacy and dialogue with public authorities, multilateral agencies and other relevant bodies; raise awareness among policymakers and advocate for an enabling environment for investments in the geospatial sector through B2B and B2G strategic alliances. **Structure** Patrons; Executive Board; Secretariat; Committees; Working Groups. **Languages** English. **Staff** 5.00 FTE, paid; 30.00 FTE, voluntary. **Finance** Sources: members' dues. **Activities** Events/meetings; knowledge management/information dissemination. **Publications** *Horizons Newsletter*, *Policy Watch Newsletter.* Industry reports, policy reports **Members** Patron; Corporate; Associate. Membership countries not specified. **NGO Relations** Associate of: *World Federation of Engineering Organizations (WFEO, #21433).* [2022.06.21/XM8600/t/C]

♦ World Giftedness Center (internationally oriented national body)

♦ World Glacier Monitoring Service (WGMS) 21539

Dir Dept of Geography – Univ of Zurich, Winterthurerstr 190, 8057 Zurich ZH, Switzerland. T. +41446355139. E-mail: wgms@geo.uzh.ch.
URL: http://www.wgms.ch/

History 1967, with the title *Permanent Services on Fluctuations of Glaciers (PSFG)*, as a service of *Federation of Astronomical and Geophysical Data Analysis Services (FAGS, inactive)*, following recommendations of General Assembly of *International Union of Geodesy and Geophysics (IUGG, #15776)*, 1960, Helsinki (Finland); and approval of General Assembly 1963, Berkeley CA (USA). Sometimes referred to as *Fluctuations of Glaciers Service.* Present title adopted 1 Jan 1986. Currently runs under the auspices of *ISC World Data System (ISC-WDS, #16024), International Union of Geodesy and Geophysics (IUGG, #15776) – International Association of Cryospheric Sciences (IACS, #11829), UNEP (#20299), UNESCO (#20322)* and *World Meteorological Organization (WMO, #21649).* **Aims** Reproduce a global set of data on fluctuations of glaciers which afford a general view of the changes; encourage more extensive standardized measurements; invite further processing of data; serve as a basis for research. **Structure** Directing Board. **Finance** Funds from: *Global Climate Observing System (GCOS, #10289); ISC World Data System (ISC-WDS, #16024); UNEP (#20299); UNESCO (#20322)*; University of Zurich (Switzerland); Swiss National Science Foundation. **Events** *Workshop on mass balance measurements and modelling* Norway 2008. **Publications** *Global Glacier Change Bulletin* – (every 2 years) series. **Information Services** *Fluctuations of Glaciers (FOG)* – database; *World Glacier Inventory* – database.

Members National correspondents in 31 countries and territories:
Argentina, Australia, Austria, Bolivia, Canada, Chile, China, Colombia, Ecuador, France, Germany, Greenland, Iceland, India, Italy, Japan, Mexico, Nepal, New Zealand, Norway, Pakistan, Peru, Poland, Russia, Spain, Sweden, Switzerland, UK, USA, Uzbekistan, Venezuela.

IGO Relations *Global Terrestrial Network – Hydrology (GTN-H, #10624).* **NGO Relations** Regular member of: *ISC World Data System (ISC-WDS, #16024).* Network member of: *International Centre for Earth Simulation (ICES Foundation).* [2021/XF4060/F]

♦ World Glaucoma Association (WGA) 21540

Exec Gen Manager Schipluidenlaan 4, 1062 HE Amsterdam, Netherlands. T. +31205709600. E-mail: info@worldglaucoma.org.
Contact Zeughausgasse 18, Postfach 1225, 3601 Zug, Switzerland.
URL: http://www.worldglaucoma.org/

History 1 Jan 2002. Former names and other names: *Association of International Glaucoma Societies (AIGS)* – former (2001 to 2002). **Aims** Eliminate glaucoma-related disability worldwide. **Structure** General Assembly; Executive Committee; Advisory Board. **Languages** English. **Staff** 1.00 FTE, paid. **Finance** No information available. **Activities** Events/meetings; standards/guidelines. **Events** *World Glaucoma Congress* Amsterdam (Netherlands) 2021, *World Glaucoma Congress* Melbourne, VIC (Australia) 2019, *World Glaucoma Congress* Helsinki (Finland) 2017, *World Glaucoma Congress* Hong Kong (Hong Kong) 2015, *World Glaucoma Congress* Vancouver, BC (Canada) 2013. **Publications** *International Glaucoma Review* (4 a year). Consensus books.

Members National, regional and international glaucoma societies (91). National societies in 76 countries and territories:
Algeria, Argentina, Australia, Austria, Azerbaijan, Bangladesh, Belgium, Bolivia, Brazil, Bulgaria, Canada, Chile, Colombia, Costa Rica, Croatia, Czechia, Denmark, Dominican Rep, Ecuador, Egypt, El Salvador, Finland, France, Germany, Ghana, Greece, Guatemala, Hungary, Iceland, India, Indonesia, Iran Islamic Rep, Israel, Italy, Japan, Korea Rep, Latvia, Lebanon, Lithuania, Malaysia, Mexico, Morocco, Myanmar, Netherlands, Nigeria, Norway, Pakistan, Panama, Paraguay, Peru, Philippines, Poland, Portugal, Puerto Rico, Romania, Russia, Saudi Arabia, Serbia, Singapore, Slovakia, Slovenia, South Africa, Spain, Sri Lanka, Sweden, Switzerland, Taiwan, Thailand, Türkiye, UK, Ukraine, Uruguay, USA, Venezuela, Vietnam, Zambia.
Regional and international societies (15), including 7 organizations listed in this Yearbook:
Asia-Pacific Glaucoma Society (APGS, #01917); European Glaucoma Society (EGS, #07393); International Society for Glaucoma Surgery (ISGS, #15144); Middle East Africa Glaucoma Society (MEAGS, see: #16752); Pan-American Glaucoma Society (PAGS, #18107); Pan Arab Glaucoma Society (PAGS, #18145); Sociedade Latino-Americana de Glaucoma (SLAG, #19357).

NGO Relations Links with national and regional glaucoma societies, industries and patient organizations. [2022.10.12/XD9407/y/B]

♦ World Gold Council (WGC) 21541

Head Office 15 Fetter Lane, London, EC4A 1BW, UK. T. +442078264700. E-mail: info@gold.org.
URL: http://www.gold.org/

History 1986. Registration: EU Transparency Registration, No/ID: 133743846287-22, Start date: 5 May 2022; Companies House, No/ID: BR012707, England and Wales; Registre Du Commerce, No/ID: CH-660.0.534.987-6, Switzerland. **Aims** Maximize offtake and retention of gold by: inducing lasting structural changes in gold markets through removal of taxes and regulatory barriers, improvement of distribution systems and products and through acting as an agent of change; inducing a sustainable and competitive level of marketing support for gold products by manufacturing and distributing trades through information and promotion incentives; influencing positively the attitudes and behaviour towards gold of actual and potential public and private sector holders of gold. **Structure** Offices (6) in: China; India; Singapore; UK; USA. **Languages** English. **Staff** 62.00 FTE, paid. **Activities** Events/meetings. **Events** *EVOLVE Investment Summit APAC* Singapore (Singapore) 2021, *Asia Pacific Precious Metals Conference* Singapore (Singapore) 2019, *International Conference on Gold Science, Technology and its Applications* Paris (France) 2018, *Asia Pacific Precious Metals Conference* Singapore (Singapore) 2018, *Seminar on Sustainable and Esg Investing* Singapore (Singapore) 2018. **Publications** *Gold in the Official Sector* (periodical); *Gold Science and Technology* (periodical); *Weekly Gold Market Commentary. WGC Briefings* – series. *Gold Market Trends Archive.* News releases; information sheets.

Members As at Jul 2003, gold producers (21) in 10 countries:
Australia, Brazil, Canada, Chile, China, India, Japan, South Africa, UK, USA.
Offices (21) in 8 countries and territories:
China, India, Japan, Singapore, Türkiye, UK, United Arab Emirates, USA.

NGO Relations Member of (1): *Responsible Jewellery Council (RJC, #18920).* [2022/XD7629/D]

♦ World Golf Foundation (internationally oriented national body)
♦ World Gospel Mission (internationally oriented national body)
♦ World Government Institute (internationally oriented national body)

♦ World e-Governments Organization of Cities and Local Governments (WeGO) 21542

Secretariat 7-F Seoul Global Center, 38 Jongro, Jongno-gu, Seoul 110-792, Korea Rep. T. +8227202938. Fax +82272029309. E-mail: secretariat@we-gov.org.
URL: http://www.we-gov.org/

History Proposed at World e-Governments Mayors Forum (WeGMF), Jul 2008, Seoul (Korea Rep). Officially launched 6-8 Sep 2010, Seoul (Korea Rep). **Aims** Pursue sustainable city development based on e-government by fostering collaboration among e-governing cities, bringing efficiency and transparency into public administration by strengthening the *digital* capacity of cities, enhancing online public services, facilitating civil involvement, helping bridge the digital divide among social strata within a city and among cities of the world, and promoting mutual cooperation and solidarity among cities. **Structure** General Assembly; Executive Committee; Secretariat, headed by Secretary General and Assistant Secretary General.

Languages English. **Finance** Sources: members' dues. **Activities** Awards/prizes/competitions; research/documentation; training/education. **Events** *Africa Smart City Network Seminar* 2021, *Solutions Meeting Cities Online Matchmaking Seminar* Seoul (Korea Rep) 2021, *Smart City Summit* Danang (Vietnam) 2019, *Mayoral Conference* Seoul (Korea Rep) 2019, *Urban Innovation Forum* Singapore (Singapore) 2019.
Members Cities Full; Associate. Full in 41 countries and territories:
Australia, Azerbaijan, Bangladesh, Belarus, Brazil, Canada, China, Ethiopia, Fiji, Finland, France, Germany, Hong Kong, India, Indonesia, Israel, Japan, Kazakhstan, Kenya, Korea Rep, Mexico, Mongolia, Nepal, Netherlands, Oman, Philippines, Portugal, Romania, Russia, Senegal, Spain, Sudan, Tanzania UR, Thailand, Tunisia, UK, United Arab Emirates, USA, Uzbekistan, Vietnam, Zimbabwe.
Associate in 3 countries:
France, Netherlands, Russia.
IGO Relations Partners: *International Bank for Reconstruction and Development (IBRD, #12317)* (World Bank); *United Nations Public Administration Network (UNPAN, #20615)*; national partners. [2022/XJ5021/**B**]

♦ World Government Summit (unconfirmed)

♦ World Government of World Citizens (WGWC) 21543

Gouvernement mondial des citoyen/ne/s du monde – Gobierno Mundial de Ciudadano/a/s Mundiales
World Office 5 Thomas Circle NW, Washington DC 20005, USA. T. +12026382662. Fax +12026380638. E-mail: info@worldcitizengov.org.
URL: https://worldcitizengov.org/
History 4 Sep 1953, Ellsworth, ME (USA). Former names and other names: *World Service Authority (WSA)* – alias. **Aims** Apply the wisdom science of dialectics to politics (geo-dialectics) utilizing human rights as reaffirmed in the Universal Declaration of Human Rights for the freedom, security and wellbeing both of the individual and humanity as a whole. **Structure** *World Service Authority (WSA, see: #21543)*, non-profit organization, is administrative agency. *World Citizen Foundation*; *World Judicial Commission (WJC, see: #21543)*. World Commissions (20), headed by leading experts: Cinema; Communications; Cybernetics; Cultural; Design-Science; Economics; Education; Elections; Energy; Environment; Forestry; Health; Industrial Design; Mondialisation; Natural Medicine; Ocean; Space; Sports; Women; Youth Education. **Languages** Arabic, Chinese, English, Esperanto, French, Russian, Spanish. **Staff** World Office: 7 FTE. 20 World Commission Coordinators. **Finance** Sources: donations; members' dues. Annual budget: 1,000,000 USD. **Activities** Certification/accreditation; events/meetings; publishing activities. **Events** *World syntegrity project workshop* Cairo (Egypt) 1994, *World Government Constitutional Convention – WGCC* Toronto, ON (Canada) 1993, *World constitutional convention* Toronto, ON (Canada) 1993, *World constitutional convention / World Government Constitutional Convention – WGCC* Christchurch (New Zealand) 1990. **Publications** *World Citizen News* (6 a year).
Members No members as such – although hundreds of thousands of individuals have registered as World Citizens. Passports issued by WGWC are recognized by almost 190 nations on a case-by-case basis. Passport recognized on a de jure basis in 6 countries:
Burkina Faso, Ecuador, Mauritania, Tanzania UR, Togo, Zambia. [2022.10.19/XF5307/**F**]

♦ WorldGranny (internationally oriented national body)

♦ World Green Building Council (WorldGBC) 21544

CEO 401 Richmond Street West, Suite 236, Toronto ON M5V 3AB, Canada. E-mail: office@worldgbc.org.
URL: http://www.worldgbc.org/
History Nov 1999, San Francisco CA (USA). EU Transparency Register: 378438436902-06. **Aims** Lead the transformation of the built environment to make it healthier and more sustainable. **Structure** Secretariat in Toronto ON (Canada); Regional networks (5). **Languages** English. **Staff** 21.00 FTE, paid. **Finance** Members' dues. Sponsorship. **Activities** Events/meetings. **Events** *International Green Building Conference* Atlanta, GA (USA) 2019, *Annual Congress* Toronto, ON (Canada) 2018, *Seoul Conference* Seoul (Korea Rep) 2016, *Annual Congress* Stockholm (Sweden) 2016, *Annual Congress* Hong Kong (Hong Kong) 2015. **Publications** Annual Report.
Members Groups in 91 countries and territories:
Argentina, Austria, Bolivia, Bosnia-Herzegovina, Brazil, Bulgaria, Canada, Chile, China, Colombia, Costa Rica, Croatia, Czechia, Denmark, Dominican Rep, Ecuador, Egypt, El Salvador, Estonia, Finland, France, Georgia, Germany, Ghana, Greece, Guatemala, Haiti, Honduras, Hong Kong, Hungary, Iceland, India, Indonesia, Ireland, Italy, Jamaica, Jordan, Kazakhstan, Kenya, Korea Rep, Kurdish area, Kuwait, Latvia, Lebanon, Libya, Lithuania, Malaysia, Mauritius, Mexico, Montenegro, Morocco, Namibia, Netherlands, Nicaragua, Nigeria, Norway, Oman, Pakistan, Palestine, Panama, Paraguay, Peru, Philippines, Poland, Portugal, Qatar, Russia, Saudi Arabia, Serbia, Singapore, Slovakia, Slovenia, South Africa, Spain, Sri Lanka, Sweden, Switzerland, Syrian AR, Taiwan, Tanzania UR, Trinidad-Tobago, Tunisia, Türkiye, UK, Ukraine, United Arab Emirates, Uruguay, USA, Venezuela, Vietnam, Zimbabwe.
NGO Relations Member of: *Global Alliance for Buildings and Construction (GlobalABC, #10187)*. Partner of: *Global Enabling Sustainability Initiative (GeSI, #10340)*. [2020/XM3751/**E**]

♦ World Green Design Organization (unconfirmed)
♦ World Green Economy Organization (unconfirmed)

♦ World Green Infrastructure Network (WGIN) 21545

Treas/Sec c/o Green Roofs, 406 King St East, Toronto ON M5A 1L4, Canada. T. +14169714494. Fax +14169719844.
Pres c/o Univ of Applied Sciences, Brodaer Str 2, Postbox 110 121, 17041 Neubrandenburg, Germany. T. +4939556934001.
URL: http://www.worldgreenroof.org/
History Founded 12 Feb 2008, Toronto ON (Canada). **Aims** Collect and disseminate knowledge, information and data concerning roof and wall greening, worldwide; act as a global informational clearing house for national green roof associations, and other stakeholders such as, authorities, educational institutes and the green roof industry providing networking for all stakeholders. **Structure** Board of 11 members. Working Groups: Regional Networking (in Latin America – LAGIN, in Europe – *European Federation of Biotechnology (EFB, #07062)*); Biodiversity; Rain Water Management; Photovoltaik on Roofs and Facades; Living Walls; Food from the Roof; Collecting Regional Policy Programmes; Certification System (currently dormant); Quality Management (currently dormant). **Languages** English. **Staff** Voluntary. **Finance** Members' dues. **Activities** Events/meetings. Active in: 30 countries worldwide, represented by national green roof associations (20 countries) and private corporations (10 countries). **Events** *World Green Infrastructure Congress* Berlin (Germany) 2021, *World Green Infrastructure Congress* Baerum (Norway) 2019, *World Green Infrastructure Congress* Bangalore (India) 2018, *World Green Infrastructure Congress* Berlin (Germany) 2017, *World Green Infrastructure Congress* Bogota (Colombia) 2016. **Publications** *WGIN Quarterly*. *Green Cities in the World* (2013, 2015).
Members Institutions and individuals in 22 countries and territories:
Australia, Brazil, Canada, Chile, China, Colombia, France, Germany, Greece, India, Italy, Japan, Korea Rep, Mexico, New Zealand, Poland, Portugal, South Africa, Spain, Taiwan, UK, USA.
Included in the above, 1 regional association listed in this Yearbook:
Scandinavian Green Infrastructure Association (SGIA, #19088). [2018/XJ4723/**F**]

♦ World Greyhound Racing Federation (WGRF) 21546

Address not obtained.
URL: http://www.wgrf.org/
History 1971. **Aims** Act as a coordinator and discussion forum for representatives of all countries where greyhound racing is promoted as a national sport; encourage cooperation and information exchange among members; promote discussion of and improvements in greyhound racing; publish and disseminate information on the sport; advise on its establishment and promotion where it is not as yet established; promote and advise on international racing of greyhounds where legally permissible. **Structure** Governing Council (meets annually); Secretary-General. **Languages** English. **Finance** Members' dues. **Activities** Organizes biennial international conference of track-racing interests. **Events** *Conference* Las Vegas, NV (USA) 2009, *Conference* Melbourne, VIC (Australia) 2007, *Biennial conference / Conference* Miami, FL (USA) 2005, *Biennial conference / Conference* Cork (Ireland) 2003, *Biennial conference / Conference* Sydney, NSW (Australia) 2000.
Members Full in 22 countries and territories:
Australia, Belgium, China, Czechia, Finland, France, Germany, Guam, Hong Kong, Hungary, Ireland, Italy, Macau, Mexico, Morocco, Netherlands, South Africa, Spain, Sweden, Trinidad-Tobago, United Arab Emirates, Vietnam. [2013/XD4220/**D**]

♦ World Group of Ex-Boxers (inactive)
♦ World Guangdong Community Federation (unconfirmed)

♦ World Guernsey Cattle Federation (WGCF) 21547

Secretariat PO Box 150, Myrtleford 3736, Australia. T. +61417363645. E-mail: secretary@worldguernseys.com.
URL: http://www.worldguernseys.com/
Aims Develop and promote the Guernsey *breed*. **Structure** President; Chairman; Secretary/Treasurer. **Events** *Conference* Lancaster, PA (USA) 2019, *Conference* Hamilton (New Zealand) 2016, *Conference* Guernsey (UK) 2013, *Conference* Guelph, ON (Canada) 2010.
Members Federations in 6 countries:
Australia, Canada, New Zealand, South Africa, UK, USA. [2020.05.14/XJ9553/**E**]

♦ World Habitat (internationally oriented national body)

♦ World Haiku Association (WHA) 21548

Main Office c/o Ban'ya Natsuishi 3-16-11 Turuse-nishi, Fujimi, Saitama, 354-0026 Japan. T. +81492529823. Fax +81492529823. E-mail: haikubanya@mub.biglobe.ne.jp.
URL: http://www.worldhaiku.net/
History 1999. **Aims** Recognize encourage international standards for excellence in haiku without losing appreciation for local and cultural norms. **Structure** Steering Committee. **Finance** Sources: members' dues. **Activities** Advocacy/lobbying/activism; awards/prizes/competitions; events/meetings; knowledge management/information dissemination; training/education. **Events** *Conference* Morocco 2021, *Conference* Tokyo (Japan) 2019, *Conference* Parma (Italy) 2017, *Conference* Tokyo (Japan) 2015, *Conference* Colombia 2013. **Publications** *World Haiku*. [2021/AA1870/v/**C**]

♦ World Haiku Club 21549

Chairman Leys Farm, Rousham, Bicester, OX25 4RA, UK. Fax +441869340619.
URL: https://sites.google.com/site/worldhaikureview2
History 1998. **Aims** Promote dissemination and development of haiku poetry. **Structure** Officers: Honorary President; Chairman; 2 Deputy Chairmen; Patron. **Activities** Events/meetings. **Publications** *World Haiku Review (WHR)* – electronic newsletter. **Members** Individuals. Membership countries not specified. [2020/XM0869/v/**F**]

♦ World Hairdressers' Organization 21550

Organisation mondiale coiffure (OMC) – Weltverband der Friseure
New York Office 11 Cherry Valley Ave, Ste 323, Garden City NY 11530, USA. T. +15162440331. Fax +15168736021. E-mail: omc@omchairworld.com.
World Pres/CEO address not obtained.
Paris Office 12/14 Rond-Point des Champs-Elysée, 75008 Paris, France. T. +33153531503. E-mail: info@omchairworld.com.
Registered Office 1-3 place de la Bourse, 75002 Paris, France.
URL: http://www.omchairworld.com/
History 22 Aug 1946, Lyon (France), as *International Confederation of the Hairdressing Trade – Confédération internationale de la coiffure (CIC) – Confederación Internacional del Peinado – Internationaler Coiffeurmeister-Verband*. Current title adopted, 30 Sep 2000, Berlin (Germany), on merger with *Organisation artistique internationale de la coiffure (OAI, inactive)*. Registered in accordance with French law. **Aims** Unite national professional organizations in the field of hairdressing and *beauty* from all countries, so as to promote hairdressing and beauty business on a worldwide basis; promote the spread of new hairdressing lines; promote, organize and implement in-service vocational training; carry out economic, tax and social initiatives in favour of members; represent all hairdressing businesses with respect to the authorities, interprofessional organizations, economic and social organizations and hairdressing and beauty industries internationally. **Structure** Congress (every 2 years). Administration Council, Board members, Zone Presidents, General Commission Delegates and Honorary Presidents. Board, comprising World President, Vice-President and Immediate Past-President. World Commissions (3): Competition; Education; Social/Economic. Zones: Americas; Asia; Central Europe; Eastern Europe; Western Europe. Includes: *Common Market Committee of the International Confederation of the Hairdressing Trade (no recent information)*. **Languages** English, French, German. **Finance** Sources: members' dues. **Activities** Organizes World Championships (every 2 years). **Events** *Congress* Paris (France) 2020, *Congress* Paris (France) 2019, *Biennial congress* Chicago, IL (USA) 2008, *Biennial congress* Moscow (Russia) 2006, *Biennial congress* Milan (Italy) 2004.
Members National organizations in 66 countries and territories:
Argentina, Armenia, Austria, Azerbaijan, Belarus, Belgium, Bolivia, Bosnia-Herzegovina, Bulgaria, Burkina Faso, Canada, Chile, China, Colombia, Côte d'Ivoire, Croatia, Cyprus, Czechia, Denmark, Estonia, Finland, France, Georgia, Germany, Greece, Guinea, Hong Kong, Hungary, India, Ireland, Italy, Japan, Kazakhstan, Kenya, Korea Rep, Latvia, Lebanon, Lithuania, Luxembourg, Mali, Moldova, Morocco, Netherlands, Norway, Paraguay, Philippines, Poland, Portugal, Puerto Rico, Russia, Senegal, Serbia, Slovakia, South Africa, Spain, Sri Lanka, Sweden, Switzerland, Taiwan, Thailand, Tunisia, UK, Ukraine, Uruguay, USA, Uzbekistan. [2022/XB1213/**C**]

♦ World Hakka Conference (meeting series)
♦ World Halal Council (unconfirmed)
♦ World Ham Congress (meeting series)
♦ World Hapkido Confederation (unconfirmed)
♦ World Hapkido Federation (internationally oriented national body)
♦ World Hapkido Games Federation / see Global Hapkido Federation (#10397)

♦ World Happiness Forum (WHF) 21551

Conference Dir Vajrayana Institute, 9 Victoria Square, Ashfield NSW 2131, Australia. T. +61287195118.
Contact address not obtained.
URL: http://www.worldhappinessforum.org/
History Following a series of conferences, started in Apr 2005, Sydney (Australia). **Aims** Promote the creation and dissemination of learning that will enhance human happiness; contribute to the revolution which is taking place in the scientific understanding of the mind and the brain and integrate the discoveries in neuroscience into other learning traditions; establish a secular context for examination and application of the tools for achieving happiness developed by the ancient wisdom traditions, particularly contemplative practices. **Structure** Advisory Board. **Events** *Annual happiness and its causes conference* Sydney, NSW (Australia) 2011, *Annual happiness and its causes conference* Sydney, NSW (Australia) 2010, *Annual happiness and its causes conference* Sydney, NSW (Australia) 2009, *Happiness and its causes conference* San Francisco, CA (USA) 2008, *Asia annual happiness and its causes conference* Singapore (Singapore) 2008. [2016/XJ0143/**F**]

♦ World in Harmony 21552

Monde en harmonie – Mundo en Armonia
Dir Plaza de las Cortes 5, 1o piso, 28014 Madrid, Spain. T. +34915314432. Fax +34915312097.
URL: http://www.worldinharmony.org/
History Nov 1986, Madrid (Spain). **Aims** Contribute to the creation of a "World in Harmony" through humanitarian aid and development projects for persons and organizations needing help, independent of considerations of race, religion, nationality or ideology. **Structure** Head Office in Madrid (Spain). **Languages** English, Irish Gaelic, Spanish. **Activities** Donations; shipments; distribution; emergency aid; sponsoring of concerts; financing of overseas development projects.
Members Offices in 3 countries:
Greece, India, Spain. [2010.06.01/XF2193/**F**]

♦ World Harp Congress (WHC) 21553

Congrès mondial de la harpe
Chair 2072 Carroll Ave, St Paul MN 55104, USA. E-mail: harpkath@aol.com.
URL: http://www.worldharpcongress.org/

History 1981. Founded as an outgrowth of the International Harp Weeks. **Aims** Promote the performing arts with special emphasis on harp composition, education, appreciation and performance. **Structure** Board of Directors (meets annually). **Languages** English. **Staff** None. **Finance** Sources: contributions; members' dues. **Activities** Events/meetings. **Events** *Triennial World Harp Congress* Cardiff (UK) 2022, *Triennial World Harp Congress* Cardiff (UK) 2021, *Triennial World Harp Congress* Cardiff (UK) 2020, *Triennial World Harp Congress* Hong Kong (Hong Kong) 2017, *Triennial World Harp Congress* Sydney, NSW (Australia) 2014. **Publications** *World Harp Congress Review* (2 a year). **Members** Full in 45 countries. Membership countries not specified. [2022.05.03/XJ7185/**F**]

♦ World Harvest (internationally oriented national body)

♦ World Hatha Yog Federation 21554

Contact Balbhadrapur, Paschim Medinipur, Dantan, West Bengal 721426, Dantan WEST BENGAL 721426, India. E-mail: worldhathayog@gmail.com.
URL: https://www.hathayog.com/

History 2019, Kolkata (India). Registration: Registrar of Societies Under Soctieties Registration Act 1860, No/ID: 443/2018-2019, Start date: 14 Feb 2019, India. **Aims** Promote and encourage the practice of Hatha Yog worldwide. **Structure** Commission. **Languages** English. **Activities** Advocacy/lobbying/activism; sporting activities; standards/guidelines; training/education.
Members Full in 5 countries:
India, Iran Islamic Rep, Nepal, Pakistan, Türkiye.
NGO Relations Partner of (4): *General Association of Asia Pacific Sports Federations (GAAPSF, #10106)*; *International Council of Sport Science and Physical Education (ICSSPE, #13077)*; *International Sport Network Organization (ISNO, #15592)*; International Yogalimpic Committee. [2021.08.09/AA1071/**D**]

♦ World Headache Alliance (WHA) 21555

Registered Address 21-27 Lamb's Conduit Street, London, WC1N 3GS, UK.
URL: http://www.w-h-a.org/

History 9 Jun 1997, Amsterdam (Netherlands). **Aims** Raise awareness, remove stigma and seek recognition of the burden of headache *disorders* on a global scale; assist by informing, guiding and giving practical support to people affected by headache disorders and their caregivers; build an effective membership, strengthen the *patient* – *physician* partnership and foster good working relationships with other interested parties; know the scale and scope of burden attributable to headache disorders and their distribution in the world; reach those affected by headache disorders in parts of the world where they lack representation and voice. **Languages** English. **Staff** 4 voluntary (Council Members); voluntary help from member organizations. **Finance** Supporters include organizations, foundations, corporations and individuals. **Activities** Encourages and facilitates the following: education, mutual support and exchange of views, within and between existing headache organizations; development of new initiatives where no patient representation currently exists; activities that inform and influence policy makers and service developers. Campaigns for September as World Headache Awareness Month (WHAM); presents *'Elizabeth Garrett Anderson Award'*; organizes Global Conventions, conferences and workshops. *'Lifting the Burden'* – global campaign to reduce the burden of headache worldwide, launched Mar 2004 in Copenhagen (Denmark). **Events** *Global convention* Kyoto (Japan) 2005, *Global Convention* Rome (Italy) 2003, *Global convention* Rome (Italy) 2003, *Global convention* New York, NY (USA) 2001, *Global convention* London (UK) 2000.
Members Full in 23 countries and territories:
Argentina, Australia, Belgium, Canada, Colombia, Finland, Germany, Iceland, Ireland, Italy, Japan, Montenegro, Netherlands, New Zealand, Norway, Puerto Rico, Serbia, Sweden, Switzerland, Türkiye, UK, USA, Venezuela.
IGO Relations Cooperates with: *WHO (#20950)*. **NGO Relations** Member of: *International Alliance of Patients' Organizations (IAPO, #11633)*. Cooperates with: *European Headache Federation (EHF, #07451)*. [2014.06.01/XF4732/**F**]

♦ World Health Academy (unconfirmed)
♦ World Healthcare Forum Foundation (unconfirmed)

♦ World Health Editors Network (WHEN) 21556

Contact c/o World Health Communication Associates, Little Harborne, Church Lane, Compton Bishop, Axbridge, BS26 2HD, UK.
URL: http://www.whcaonline.org/when.html

Aims Strengthen *journalism* and public health communication capacity as public goods and key determinants of health. **Structure** Advisory Board. Facilitated by *World Health Professions Alliance (WHPA, #21557)* and its constituent associations, including *International Council of Nurses (ICN, #13054)*, *International Pharmaceutical Federation (#14566)*, *World Medical Association (WMA, #21646)* and *FDI – World Dental Federation (#09281)*. **Activities** Events/meetings. **Events** *World Assembly* Geneva (Switzerland) 2014, *World Assembly* Geneva (Switzerland) 2013, *World Assembly* Geneva (Switzerland) 2010, *World Assembly* Geneva (Switzerland) 2009, *World Assembly* Geneva (Switzerland) 2008. [2018/XJ6842/**F**]

♦ World Health Foundation for Development and Peace (internationally oriented national body)
♦ World Health Foundation for Peace / see World Health Foundation for Development and Peace
♦ World Health Organization (#20950)
♦ World Health Partners (internationally oriented national body)

♦ World Health Professions Alliance (WHPA) 21557

Contact c/o FDI World Dental Fed, Chemin de Joinville 26, 1216 Geneva, Switzerland. T. +41225608147. E-mail: info@whpa.org.
Main Website: http://www.whpa.org/

History 16 May 2000, Geneva (Switzerland). Founded by *International Council of Nurses (ICN, #13054)*, *International Pharmaceutical Federation (#14566)* and *World Medical Association (WMA, #21646)*. Joined by *FDI – World Dental Federation (#09281)*, 2005, and by *World Confederation for Physical Therapy (WCPT, #21293)*, 2010. **Aims** Improve global health and the quality of patient care; facilitate collaboration among the health professions and major stakeholders. **Languages** English, French, Spanish. **Staff** 0.30 FTE, paid. **Finance** Sources: members' dues. Annual budget: 75,000 CHF. **Activities** Advocacy/lobbying/activism; events/meetings; networking/liaising. **Events** *World Health Professions Regulation Conference* Geneva (Switzerland) 2020, *World Health Professions Regulations Conference* Geneva (Switzerland) 2018, *World Health Professions Regulation Conference* Geneva (Switzerland) 2016, *World health professions conference on regulation* Geneva (Switzerland) 2010, *World health professions conference on regulation* Geneva (Switzerland) 2008. **Publications** *Positive Practice Environments – Defienda los Entornos Positivos para la Práctica – Soutenez les Environnements Favorables à la Pratique* (2020) in English, French, Spanish. Toolkits; statements; fact sheets.
Members Health care professionals (over 41 million) in over 130 countries. Membership countries not specified.
International organizations (5):
FDI – World Dental Federation (#09281); *International Council of Nurses (ICN, #13054)*; *International Pharmaceutical Federation (#14566)*; *World Confederation for Physical Therapy (WCPT, #21293)*; *World Medical Association (WMA, #21646)*. [2022.08.22/XF6808/**t/F**]

♦ World Health Risk Management Centre (WHRMC) 21558

Head Office 4-7-12-102 Hongo, Bunkyoku, Tokyo, 113-0033 Japan. T. +81338177010. Fax +81338176770.
URL: http://www.jsrmpm.org/WHRMC.shtml

History within *International Association of Risk Management in Medicine (IARMM, #12138)*. **Aims** Promote scientific information, research and technological transfer in global management for safety and health science. **Structure** International Advisory Board; Director Board; Intergraduate School; International Committee for Research Promotion. Chairperson. **Languages** Chinese, English, French, German, Japanese, Russian, Spanish. **Staff** 5.00 FTE, paid. **Finance** Conference registration fees. **Events** *International Seminar of Risk and Emergency Management for Healthcare* London (UK) 2012, *World Congress* London (UK) 2012, *Seminar of Crisis Management in HealthCare* Tokyo (Japan) 2012, *Spring Seminar of Patient Safety* Tokyo (Japan) 2012, *Educational seminar for health and safety with frontier science and high technology in risk and crisis management* Tokyo (Japan) 2009. **Publications** *Health Risk Management*; *Journal of Medical Safety (JMS)*.
Members Full in 11 countries:
Canada, France, Japan, Malaysia, Netherlands, Russia, Sweden, Switzerland, Thailand, UK, USA.
IGO Relations *ILO (#11123)*; *OECD (#17693)*; ministries of several countries. **NGO Relations** Schools and academic institutions. [2013.06.01/XJ4478/**E**]

♦ World Health Students' Alliance (WHSA) 21559

Contact c/o IFMSA, Nørre Allé 14, 2200 Copenhagen, Denmark. E-mail: gs@ifmsa.org.

History 17 Nov 2014. Founded as an alliance of *International Association of Dental Students (IADS, #11839)*, *International Federation of Medical Students' Associations (IFMSA, #13478)*, *International Pharmaceutical Students' Federation (IPSF, #14568)* and *International Veterinary Students' Association (IVSA, #15851)*. **Aims** Strengthen interdisciplinary advocacy; commonly contribute to the advancement of health; develop and implement improved health policies together with multisectorial stakeholders.
Members Organizations (4):
International Association of Dental Students (IADS, #11839); *International Federation of Medical Students' Associations (IFMSA, #13478)*; *International Pharmaceutical Students' Federation (IPSF, #14568)*; *International Veterinary Students' Association (IVSA, #15851)*. [AA3034/y/**C**]

♦ World Health Summit Foundation (WHS Foundation) 21560

Managing Dir c/o Charité – Universitätsmedizin Berlin, Charitéplatz 1, 10117 Berlin, Germany. E-mail: contact@worldhealthsummit.org.
URL: http://www.worldhealthsummit.org/

History 2009. **Aims** Strengthen the link between research, academic medicine and decision-makers throughout every branch of healthcare and related sectors; build and strengthen a worldwide network for health and research; provide academic expertise for the global health agenda. **Structure** Organizing Office; Executive Office; Media Office. *M8 Alliance of Academic Health Centers, Universities and National Academies (M8 Alliance, #16536)* provides academic platform. **Activities** Events/meetings. **Publications** *WHS Newsletter*. [2022.02.09/XM6329/**f/F**]

♦ World Heart Failure Society (WHFS) 21561

Headquarters PO Box 882, 3160 AB Rhoon, Netherlands. T. +31104855177. Fax +31104854833. E-mail: whfs2015@gmail.com.
Street Address Albrandsstate, Oever 1-5, 3161 GR Rhoon, Netherlands.
URL: http://www.worldheartfailure.org/

History Registered in accordance with Dutch law. **Aims** Improve knowledge of heart failure; foster, support, coordinate and execute research in epidemiological preventive, diagnostic and therapeutic aspects of heart failure. **Structure** General Assembly (annual). Board, including President, President-Elect, Past-President, Secretary and Treasurer. **Activities** 'World Heart Failure Society Fellowship Award' offers training opportunity to young general physicians with an interest in cardiology and heart failure in emerging countries. **Events** *Congress* Beijing (China) 2016, *Congress* Al Ain (United Arab Emirates) 2014, *Congress* Istanbul (Turkey) 2012, *Congress* Chandigarh (India) 2010.
Members Individuals in 17 countries:
Botswana, China, Ghana, Hungary, India, Indonesia, Iraq, Kazakhstan, Kenya, Kuwait, Nigeria, Saudi Arabia, South Africa, Sudan, Taiwan, United Arab Emirates, Uzbekistan.
NGO Relations Associate member of: *World Heart Federation (WHF, #21562)*. Member of: *The NCD Alliance (NCDA, #16963)*. [2016/XM3046/**D**]

♦ World Heart Federation (WHF) 21562

CEO 32 rue de Malatrex, 1201 Geneva, Switzerland. T. +41228070320. Fax +41228070339. E-mail: info@worldheart.org.
URL: http://www.worldheart.org/

History Founded following merger of *International Society of Cardiology (ISC) – Société internationale de cardiologie (SIC)* and *International Cardiology Federation (ICF) – Fédération internationale de cardiologie*. Previously a *World Heart Association* had been active since 8 Sep 1950, Paris (France), in succession to *International Provisional Council of Cardiology – Conseil international provisoire de cardiologie*, formed in 1946. Statutes adopted, 1978, Tokyo (Japan), at first General Assembly; amended: 1986, Washington DC (USA); 1992, Moscow (Russia); 1994, Berlin (Germany); 1998, Rio de Janeiro (Brazil); 2002, Sydney (Australia); 2004 Munich (Germany). Former names and other names: *International Society and Federation of Cardiology (ISFC)* – former; *Société et fédération internationale de cardiologie (SFIC)* – former; *Sociedad y Federación Internacional de Cardiología* – former; *Fédération mondiale du Coeur* – former. Registration: Swiss Civil Code, Switzerland. **Aims** Work to end needless deaths and build global commitment for improved cardiovascular health at the global, regional, national and community levels. **Structure** General Assembly; Board; Headquarters in Geneva (Switzerland). **Languages** English. **Staff** 16.00 FTE, paid. **Activities** Advocacy/lobbying/activism; healthcare; knowledge management/information dissemination; monitoring/evaluation; networking/liaising; projects/programmes; research/documentation; standards/guidelines; training/education. **Events** *World Congress of Cardiology (WCC)* Rio de Janeiro (Brazil) 2022, *World Congress of Cardiology* Yokohama (Japan) 2021, *World Congress of Cardiology and Cardiovascular Health* Geneva (Switzerland) 2020, *Global Summit on Circulatory Health* Paris (France) 2019, *World Congress of Cardiology and Cardiovascular Health* Dubai (United Arab Emirates) 2018. **Publications** *Global Heart* – Official journal.
Members Full: national, regional and continental medical societies and heart foundations (202), in 104 countries and territories:
Algeria, Argentina, Australia, Austria, Bangladesh, Barbados, Belarus, Belgium, Bolivia, Bosnia-Herzegovina, Brazil, Bulgaria, Cameroon, Canada, Chile, China, Colombia, Congo Brazzaville, Croatia, Cuba, Cyprus, Czechia, Denmark, Dominican Rep, Ecuador, Egypt, El Salvador, Estonia, Finland, France, Georgia, Germany, Ghana, Greece, Guatemala, Honduras, Hong Kong, Hungary, Iceland, India, Indonesia, Iran Islamic Rep, Iraq, Ireland, Israel, Italy, Jamaica, Japan, Kazakhstan, Kenya, Korea Rep, Kuwait, Kyrgyzstan, Latvia, Lebanon, Libya, Lithuania, Macau, Malaysia, Mauritius, Mexico, Moldova, Myanmar, Nepal, Netherlands, New Zealand, Nicaragua, Nigeria, North Macedonia, Norway, Pakistan, Panama, Papua New Guinea, Paraguay, Peru, Philippines, Poland, Portugal, Puerto Rico, Romania, Russia, San Marino, Saudi Arabia, Serbia, Seychelles, Singapore, Slovakia, Slovenia, South Africa, Spain, Sri Lanka, Sweden, Switzerland, Syrian AR, Taiwan, Thailand, Türkiye, UK, Ukraine, United Arab Emirates, Uruguay, USA, Venezuela, Vietnam.
Full: continental members (8):
African Heart Network (AHN, #00336); *Asian Pacific Society of Cardiology (APSC, #01631)*; *Asia-Pacific Heart Network (APHN, #01923)*; *European Heart Network (EHN, #07467)*; *European Society of Cardiology (ESC, #08536)*; *InterAmerican Heart Foundation (IAHF, #11432)*; *Inter-American Society of Cardiology (ISC, #11448)*; *Pan African Society of Cardiology (PASCAR, #18066)*.
Associate: international societies (23), of which 16 listed in this Yearbook:
- Arrhythmia Alliance (UK);
- *ASEAN Federation of Cardiology (#01172)*;
- Association of Black Cardiologists (USA);
- *Association of Thoracic and Cardiovascular Surgeons of Asia (ATCSA, #02955)*;
- *Children's HeartLink (CHL)*;
- Fundación Araucaria (USA);
- Heartfile (Pakistan);
- *Heart Friends Around the World (HFATW, #10900)*;
- *International Academy of Cardiovascular Sciences (IACS, #11539)*;
- *International Council of Nurses (ICN, #13054)*;
- *International Forum for Hypertension Control and Prevention in Africa (IFHA, #13638)*;
- *International Self-Monitoring Association of Oral Anticoagulated Patients (ISMAAP, #14831)*;
- *International Society for Heart Research (ISHR, #15158)*;
- *International Society for Holter and Noninvasive Electrocardiology (ISHNE, #15179)*;
- *International Society of Cardiomyopathy, Myocarditis and Heart Failure (ISCMF, #14993)*;
- *International Society of Cardiovascular Disease Epidemiology and Prevention (ISCEP)*;
- *International Society of Cardiovascular Pharmacotherapy (ISCP, #14996)*;
- *International Society of Cardiovascular Ultrasound (ISCU, #14998)*;
- *International Society on Hypertension in Blacks (ISHIB)*;
- Preventive Cardiovascular Nurses Association (PCNA);
- ProCOR/Lown Cardiovascular Research Foundation, USA;
- Society of Chest Pain Centres and Providers (USA);
- *World Heart Failure Society (WHFS, #21561)*.

Associate: national societies, in 7 countries:
Bangladesh, India, Indonesia, Malaysia, Norway, Philippines, UK.

Associate: individual members (6), in 6 countries where a national society does not exist:
Afghanistan, Bhutan, Laos, Mozambique, Trinidad-Tobago, Zimbabwe.
Consultative Status Consultative status granted from: *ECOSOC (#05331)* (Ros C); *WHO (#20950)* (Official Relations). **NGO Relations** Member of (6): *European Alliance for Cardiovascular Health (EACH, #05863)*; *Framework Convention Alliance (FCA, #09981)*; *Fédération des Institutions Internationales établies à Genève (FIIG, #09599)*; *Global Alliance for the Prevention of Obesity and Related Chronic Disease (#10219)*; *International Non Governmental Coalition Against Tobacco (INGCAT, no recent information)* (Founding); *The NCD Alliance (NCDA, #16963)* (Founding). Partner of (2): *Fight the Fakes (#09755)*; *Global Smokefree Partnership (GSP, #10602)*. Supports (1): *European Healthy Stadia Network (Healthy Stadia, #07464)*.
[2022/XB2533/y/**B**]

♦ World Heavy Events Association (internationally oriented national body)
♦ World Hebrew Union (no recent information)

♦ World Hellenic Inter-Parliamentary Association (PADEE-WHIA) 21563

Contact address not obtained. E-mail: info@padeewhia.org.
URL: https://padeewhia.org/
History Aug 1996. Established on a Greek government initiative. Under the auspices of the Hellenic Parliament. Registration: Start date: 2005, Greece. **Aims** Foster communication and promote relations between the Hellenic Parliament and legislators of Greek descent in non-Greek speaking countries; strengthen relations of friendship and co-operation with Greece and develop a common strategy in relation to issues concerning Greece, Cyprus and Greek Diaspora; promote Greek trade, investment and tourism; bring forth and promote the Hellenic Culture and the Greek language. **Structure** General Assembly (every two years); Governing Board. **Events** *General Assembly* Athens (Greece) 2021. **Members** Full; Associate. Individuals (over 200) in about 20 countries. Membership countries not specified. [2022.01.18/AA2280/v/**E**]

♦ World Help (internationally oriented national body)

♦ World Hepatitis Alliance (WHA) 21564

CEO Unit 6, 27 Corsham Street,, London, N1 6DR, UK. T. +442070316904. E-mail: contact@worldhepatitisalliance.org.
Events Manager Route de Frontenex 86bis, Case Postale 6364 1211, 1211 Geneva 6, Switzerland. T. +41225180616.
URL: http://www.worldhepatitisalliance.org/
History 2 Dec 2007. Registration: No/ID: CH-660-2785007-1, Switzerland. **Aims** Work with members, governments and other key partners to eliminate viral hepatitis. **Structure** Executive Board; President; Regional Members (6). **Languages** Arabic, Chinese, English, French, Portuguese, Russian, Spanish. **Staff** 9.00 FTE, paid. **Finance** Grants; project sponsorship; donations. **Activities** Advocacy/lobbying/activism; awareness raising; capacity building; events/meetings. **Events** *World Hepatitis Summit* Lisbon (Portugal) 2024, *World Hepatitis Summit* Geneva (Switzerland) 2022, *African Hepatitis Summit* Kampala (Uganda) 2019, *World Hepatitis Summit* Sao Paulo (Brazil) 2017, *World Hepatitis Summit* Glasgow (UK) 2015. **Publications** *hepVoice*.
Members Voting in 51 countries and territories:
Algeria, Argentina, Australia, Austria, Bangladesh, Belarus, Benin, Bosnia-Herzegovina, Brazil, Bulgaria, Burundi, Cameroon, Canada, Chile, China, Congo Brazzaville, Côte d'Ivoire, Croatia, Djibouti, Egypt, France, Germany, Ghana, Greece, Guatemala, India, Iran Islamic Rep, Israel, Italy, Japan, Kazakhstan, Lithuania, Mali, Mauritania, Mauritius, Mexico, Morocco, Nepal, Netherlands, New Zealand, Nigeria, North Macedonia, Pakistan, Peru, Philippines, Poland, Portugal, Romania, Taiwan, Uruguay, Venezuela.
Non-voting in 55 countries and territories:
Afghanistan, Argentina, Armenia, Australia, Azerbaijan, Belgium, Brazil, Burkina Faso, Cameroon, Canada, China, Colombia, Côte d'Ivoire, Egypt, Finland, Gambia, Georgia, Ghana, Greece, Guinea, Hungary, India, Indonesia, Iran Islamic Rep, Ireland, Japan, Lebanon, Liberia, Malawi, Mali, Mauritius, Mongolia, Montenegro, Myanmar, Nepal, Netherlands, New Zealand, Nigeria, Pakistan, Portugal, Romania, Russia, Singapore, Slovakia, Switzerland, Taiwan, Tanzania UR, Thailand, Türkiye, Uganda, UK, Ukraine, Uruguay, USA, Vietnam.
Consultative Status Consultative status granted from: *ECOSOC (#05331)* (Special); *WHO (#20950)* (Official). **NGO Relations** Full member of: *International Drug Policy Consortium (IDPC, #13205)*; *Vienna NGO Committee on Drugs (VNGOC, #20773)*. Partners: *Bureau international des Médecins sans frontières (MSF International, #03366)*; *Coalition to Eradicate Viral Hepatitis in Asia Pacific (CEVHAP, #04058)*; *European Association for the Study of the Liver (EASL, #06233)*; *European Liver Patients 'Association (ELPA, #07706)*; *Foundation for Innovative New Diagnostics (FIND, #09959)*; *International AIDS Society (IAS, #11601)*; *International Drug Policy Consortium (IDPC, #13205)*; *Medicines Patent Pool (MPP, #16635)*. [2023/XJ5996/y/**B**]

♦ World Hereford Council (WHC) 21565

Conseil mondial de la race Hereford
SG Lieja 6940, CP 11500 Montevideo, Uruguay. E-mail: simprel@adinet.com.uy.
URL: http://www.herefords.com/
History 1951. **Aims** Regularize regulations concerning registration of *pedigree* Hereford *cattle* world-wide on reciprocal basis; ensure the purity of the interest by maintaining close association with scientific developments; maintain high standards of ethics as far as promotion is concerned. **Languages** English, Spanish. **Staff** 1.00 FTE, paid. **Finance** Members' dues. Budget (annual): pounds14,000. **Activities** Youth Exchange Programme. Conferences (every 4 years). **Events** *World Conference* Kansas (USA) 2024, *European Conference* Vichy (France) 2022, *Quadrennial World Conference* Queenstown (New Zealand) 2020, *European Conference* Budapest (Hungary) 2018, *Quadrennial World Conference* Montevideo (Uruguay) 2016. **Publications** *World Hereford Council Newsletter* (6 a year).
Members Associations in 17 countries:
Argentina, Australia, Brazil, Canada, Denmark, Estonia, Finland, Germany, Ireland, Netherlands, New Zealand, Norway, South Africa, Sweden, UK, Uruguay, USA. [2013/XD6126/**E**]

♦ World Heritage Centre (WHC) 21566

Centre du patrimoine mondial – Centro del Patrimonio Mundial
Dir UNESCO, 7 place de Fontenoy, 75352 Paris 07SP, France. T. +33145681571. Fax +33145685570. E-mail: wh-info@unesco.org.
URL: https://whc.unesco.org/en/world-heritage-centre/
History 1992, Paris (France). Established by Director-General of *UNESCO (#20322)*, to assure day-to-day management of *Convention Concerning the Protection of the World Cultural and Natural Heritage (World Heritage Convention, 1972)*, 16 Nov 1972, Paris. Former names and other names: *UNESCO World Heritage Centre (UNESCO-WHC)* – alias. **Aims** Encourage international cooperation in identification, *protection*, *conservation* and *preservation* worldwide of *cultural* and *natural* heritage considered of outstanding value to humanity; encourage countries to sign the 1972 Convention and ensure the protection of their natural and cultural heritage; encourage states party to the Convention to nominate sites within their national territory for inclusion in the World Heritage List and to set up reporting systems on the condition of World Heritage sites; help them safeguard these sites by providing technical assistance and professional training; provide emergency assistance for sites in immediate danger; support states party to the Convention in building public awareness of World Heritage conservation; encourage participation of local populations in preservation of their cultural and natural heritage. **Structure** Based at UNESCO headquarters. Responsible for administration of: *World Heritage Fund (#21568)*. **Languages** English, French. **Finance** Sources: contributions; donations; members' dues; sale of products. **Activities** Awareness raising; guidance/assistance/consulting; knowledge management/information dissemination; networking/liaising. **Events** *Final Meeting for the Second Cycle of the Periodic Reporting Exercise in the Europe Region* Helsinki (Finland) 2014, *Symposium on the Future of the World Heritage, Preservation of the World Heritage and Japanese International Cooperation* Tokyo (Japan) 2013, *International Conference on Remains and World Heritage of Asian Human Origins* Yeoncheon (Korea Rep) 2012, *Seminar on world heritage and public works development cooperation for poverty alleviation* Tokyo (Japan) 2008, *International symposium on sharing heritages* Valencia (Spain) 2008. **Publications** *World Heritage Review* (4 a year) in English, French, Spanish. *World Heritage Paper Series*. *World Heritage Brochure* in English, French, Spanish; *World Heritage in Young Hands* in English, French; *World Heritage Map* in English, French, Spanish. Travel diaries. Information Services: Includes: *World Heritage Information Network (WHIN)*. **Information Services** *Global Heritage Map* – online database. **IGO Relations** Cooperates with other groups working within UNESCO – notably: Division for Physical Heritage in the Sector for Culture; Division of Ecological Sciences in the Science Sector. Extensive cooperation with advisory body: *International Centre for the Study of the Preservation and Restoration of Cultural Property (ICCROM, #12521)*. **NGO Relations** Extensive cooperation with advisory bodies: *International Council on Monuments and Sites (ICOMOS, #13049)*; *International Union for Conservation of Nature and Natural Resources (IUCN, #15766)*. Also cooperates with: *Organization of World Heritage Cities (OWHC, #17891)*; *International Council of Museums (ICOM, #13051)*. Instrumental in setting up: *AFRICA 2009 – Conservation of Immovable Cultural Heritage in Sub-Saharan Africa (inactive)*. Supports setting up of: *Global Geoparks Network (GGN, #10389)*. Supports: *Forum UNESCO – University and Heritage (FUUH, #09931)*. [2023/XE3055/**E***]

♦ World Heritage Cities Organization / see Organization of World Heritage Cities (#17891)

♦ World Heritage Committee 21567

Comité du patrimoine mondial – Comité del Patrimonio Mundial
Contact c/o World Heritage Centre, UNESCO, 7 place de Fontenoy, 75352 Paris 07SP, France. T. +33145681571. Fax +33145685570. E-mail: wh-info@unesco.org.
URL: http://whc.unesco.org/
History Nov 1976, Nairobi (Kenya). Established during 1st General Assembly of States Parties to the *Convention Concerning the Protection of the World Cultural and Natural Heritage (World Heritage Convention, 1972)*, adopted by 17th session of the General Conference of *UNESCO (#20322)*, 16 Nov 1972, Paris (France). Established under Article 8 of the Convention. The Convention has been in force since 17 Dec 1975. Former names and other names: *Intergovernmental Committee for the Protection of the Cultural and Natural Heritage of Outstanding Universal Value* – full title; *Comité intergouvernemental pour la protection du patrimoine culturel et naturel de valeur universelle exceptionnelle* – full title; *Comité Intergubernamental de Protección del Patrimonio Cultural y Natural de Valor Universal Excepcional* – full title; *Intergovernmental Committee for the Protection of the World Cultural and Natural Heritage* – alias; *Comité intergouvernemental pour la protection du patrimoine mondial culturel et naturel* – alias; *Comité Intergubernamental de Protección del Patrimonio Mundial Cultural y Natural* – alias. **Aims** Ensure the identification, protection, *conservation*, presentation and transmission to future generations of the *cultural* and *natural* heritage, including *monuments*, groups of buildings and cultural and natural *sites* of outstanding universal value, from the point of view of history, art or science, inscribing them on the *'World Heritage List'*; designate on a *'List of World Heritage in Danger'* those sites already on the main List which are severely threatened by specific dangers and may require urgent measures; determine measures needed for the *safeguarding* of World Heritage sites in countries whose own resources are insufficient and allocate resources for this purpose from the World Heritage Fund. **Structure** *'States Parties'*: countries which have ratified the World Heritage Convention and thereby agree to identify and nominate sites on their national territory to be considered for inscription on the World Heritage List. *'General Assembly'* of all States Parties (meeting every 2 years during the ordinary session of the General Conference of UNESCO) elects the *'World Heritage Committee'*. The Committee (meeting annually) comprises representatives of 21 of the States Parties to the Convention who are elected during UNESCO General Conference for terms up to 6 years; it is responsible for the implementation of the World Heritage Convention, examines the statement of accounts on the World Heritage Fund and decides on major policy issues. *World Heritage Bureau*, consisting of 7 members of the Committee, meets annually to prepare the work of the Committee. Day-to-day management of the Convention is assured by *World Heritage Centre (WHC, #21566)*, which organizes the annual sessions of the World Heritage Bureau and Committee, provides advice to States Parties in the preparation of site nominations, organizes technical assistance upon request and coordinates reporting of the condition of sites and of emergency action undertaken when a site is threatened. It is also responsible for the administration of the *World Heritage Fund (#21568)*. **Languages** English, French. **Staff** 35.00 FTE, paid. **Finance** Sources: contributions of member/participating states; donations. Other sources: funds-in-trust; funds from governments and other bodies through World Heritage Fund.
Activities The Committee is responsible for implementation of the World Heritage Convention; has the final say on whether a site is accepted for inscription on the World Heritage List; examines reports on the state of conservation of listed sites; asks States Parties to take action when sites are not being properly managed; is responsible for allocating finances from the World Heritage Fund for sites in need of repair or restoration, for emergency action if sites are in immediate danger, for providing technical assistance and training, and for promotional and educational activities. *'Preparatory assistance'*: Technical services provided to aid in the identification of potential World Heritage properties ("Tentative Lists"), preparation of documentation to support nominations, study their state of conservation and safeguard measures they require. *'Technical cooperation'* including expert advice, technical support and equipment for the conservation of properties already on the World Heritage List or proposed for inclusion. *'Training'* for better site management and conservation. *'Emergency assistance'* when properties have been suddenly damaged by a disaster or threatened by one. *'Mobilizing protection'* both nationally and internationally through a system of monitoring the state of listed sites and of intervening appropriately when local resources prove to be insufficient, initiating national projects and investments, catalyzing local resources and mobilizing support.
As of Jul 2019, 1,121 properties in 167 States Parties have been included in the *'World Heritage List'*, including 869 cultural sites, 213 natural sites and 39 mixed sites, in Europe, North America, Latin America, the Caribbean, Asia, the Pacific, Africa and the Arab States. On the *'List of World Heritage in Danger'* are 53 properties.
Events *Session of the General Assembly of States Parties* Paris (France) 2023, *Session* Riyadh (Saudi Arabia) 2023, *General Assembly of the States Parties to the Convention Concerning the Protection of the World Cultural and Natural Heritage* Paris (France) 2015, *Session* Doha (Qatar) 2014, *Session* Phnom Penh (Cambodia) / Siem Reap (Cambodia) 2013. **Publications** *World Heritage Magazine* (4 a year).
Members Committee members (21 – end of mandate in brackets):
Argentina (2025), Belgium (2025), Bulgaria (2025), Egypt (2023), Ethiopia (2023), Greece (2025), India (2025), Italy (2025), Japan (2025), Mali (2023), Mexico (2025), Nigeria (2023), Oman (2023), Qatar (2025), Russia (2023), Rwanda (2025), Saudi Arabia (2023), South Africa (2023), St Vincent-Grenadines (2025), Thailand (2023), Zambia (2025). [2023/XE2358/**E***]

♦ World Heritage Convention – Convention Concerning the Protection of the World Cultural and Natural Heritage (1972 treaty)

♦ World Heritage Fund 21568

Fonds du patrimoine mondial – Fondo del Patrimonio Mundial
Contact c/o World Heritage Centre, UNESCO, 7 place de Fontenoy, 75352 Paris 07SP, France. T. +33145681571. Fax +33145685570. E-mail: wh-info@unesco.org.
URL: https://whc.unesco.org/en/world-heritage-fund/
History Nov 1976, Nairobi (Kenya). Established within the framework of *World Heritage Committee (#21567)*, under Articles 15-18 of the *Convention Concerning the Protection of the World Cultural and Natural Heritage (World Heritage Convention, 1972)*. Constitutes a trust fund in conformity with the provisions of Financial Regulation of the *UNESCO (#20322)*. The *World Heritage Centre (WHC, #21566)* is responsible for the administration of the Fund. Former names and other names: *Fund for the Protection of the World Cultural and Natural Heritage of Outstanding Universal Value* – former; *Fonds pour la protection du patrimoine mondial culturel et naturel de valeur universelle exceptionnelle* – former; *Fondo para la Protección del Patrimonio Cultural y Natural Mundial de Valor Universal Excepcional* – former. **Aims** Help States, upon their request, to safeguard the World Heritage *properties* situated on their territory; as a mechanism for international solidarity, translate responsibility of the world's community for the world's heritage into action. **Finance** Sources: contributions of member/participating states. Annual budget: 2,950,000 USD (2023). **Activities** Assistance provided by the Fund through the Committee can take 5 forms: preparatory assistance; technical cooperation; training assistance; emergency assistance; assistance for educational, information and promotional activities. **Events** *World heritage youth forum on sustainable tourism for Latin America* Lima (Peru) 2000, *Regional seminar on media* Quito (Ecuador) 1994. [2023/XF9830/f/**F***]

♦ World Heritage Institute of Training and Research – Asia and Pacific (internationally oriented national body)
♦ World Heritage Institute of Training and Research for the Asia and the Pacific Region under the auspices of UNESCO / see World Heritage Institute of Training and Research – Asia and Pacific
♦ World Heritage Watch (internationally oriented national body)
♦ World Hindu Council (internationally oriented national body)

♦ **World Hindu Federation (WHF)** **21569**
Alliance hindoue mondiale – Vishwa Hindu Mahasangh
Contact A- 6 / D Jhilmil Industrial Area, Delhi 110095, DELHI 110095, India. T. +918005596580. Fax +918006036035. E-mail: info@worldhindufederation.org.
URL: http://worldhindufederation.org/
History Founded 1981, Nepal. **Aims** Promote and preserve Hindu welfare, philosophy and culture; evolve an education system and curriculum based on Hindu dharma; safeguard legitimate rights of Hindus, particularly freedom of *worship*; foster mutual appreciation and understanding among various orders of Hindu heritage and inculcate a sense of oneness among them; safeguard and promote noble ideals of Hindu culture and strengthen Hindu society; facilitate exchange of information and ideas; extend spiritual and cultural activities to cater for special needs of Hindus in socio-economic development; in particular set up centres for practice of *yoga* for spiritual, mental and physical development and establish, maintain, manage or assist *temples*, gurudwaras, mathas, ashrams, viharas and other Hindu worshipping places. **Structure** General Assembly. Executive Board (meets annually), consisting of President, Senior Vice-President and 6 further Vice-Presidents, 6 Executive Secretaries and 58 executive members representing different disciplines of Hinduism. Senior Advisor; Advisor. Secretariat, headed by Secretary General. Treasurer. Youth council: *World Hindu Youth Council (WHYC, no recent information)*. **Languages** English, Hindi, Nepali, Sanskrit. **Staff** 30.00 FTE, paid; 10.00 FTE, voluntary. **Finance** Sources: members' dues. Other sources: Small contribution from the Government of Nepal. Annual budget: 500,000 USD. **Activities** Works on health and education. Holds conferences and seminars. Constructing a temple and headquarters facilities in Nepal. **Events** *Quinquennial world conference* Haridwar (India) 1997, *Quinquennial World Conference* Bali (Indonesia) 1992, *Quinquennial world conference* Kathmandu (Nepal) 1988, *Annual meeting* Patna (India) 1987, *Quinquennial World Conference* Kathmandu (Nepal) 1981. **Publications** *Vishwa Hindu* (12 a year). Books; journals; newspapers; periodicals.
Members Active in 45 countries and territories:
Afghanistan, Australia, Austria, Azerbaijan, Bangladesh, Belgium, Bhutan, Cambodia, Canada, China, Denmark, Fiji, France, Germany, Guyana, Hong Kong, India, Indonesia, Ireland, Italy, Japan, Kenya, Korea Rep, Luxembourg, Malaysia, Mauritius, Myanmar, Nepal, Netherlands, New Zealand, Norway, Pakistan, Philippines, Russia, Singapore, South Africa, Spain, Sri Lanka, Suriname, Switzerland, Tanzania UR, Thailand, Trinidad-Tobago, UK, USA.
IGO Relations *UNESCO (#20322)*. **NGO Relations** *Asian Conference of Religions for Peace (ACRP, #01400); Guru Nanak Sat Sangh Samiti (Sikhar International, no recent information); Vishva Hindu Parishad (VHP); World Brotherhood (no recent information); Religions for Peace (RfP, #18831); World Jain Association (no recent information).* [2018/XC0010/**C**]

♦ **World Historic and Cultural Canal Cities Cooperation Organization (WCCO)** **21570**
Contact 2nd Floor – Crowne Plaza, No 3 East Wenchang Road, Yangzhou, Jiangsu, China. T. +8651489986300. Fax +8651489986300.
URL: http://www.whcccco.org/
History 2009. Registered in accordance with Chinese law. **Aims** Promote the economic and cultural exchanges between canals cities; share their development experience; push for mutually beneficial cooperation; facilitate common development and prosperity. **Structure** Officers.
Members City members (over 100) in 15 countries:
Belgium, China, Egypt, France, Germany, Ireland, Italy, Netherlands, Panama, Philippines, Russia, Switzerland, Türkiye, Ukraine, USA.
Institutional members in 3 countries and territories:
China, Macau, USA.
Included in the above, 3 organizations listed in this Yearbook:
Inland Waterways International (IWI, #11217); International City / County Management Association (ICMA, #12579); World Green Design Organization (WGDO). [2017/XM6696/y/**C**]

♦ World History Association (internationally oriented national body)
♦ World Hobie Class Association / see International Hobie Class Association (#13801)

♦ **World Holstein Friesian Federation (WHFF)** **21571**
SG address not obtained. E-mail: worldholstein@gmail.com.
URL: http://www.whff.info/
History Discussions on the Holstein breed started in 1960, with first meeting held 1964, Netherlands. Federation officially set up on adoption of constitution, 1992, Budapest (Hungary). **Aims** Improve, develop and promote the Holstein Breed, both Black and White, and Red and White Holstein. **Structure** Council. **Languages** English. **Finance** Sources: members' dues. **Activities** Events/meetings; knowledge management/information dissemination; research/documentation. **Events** *Conference* Buenos Aires (Argentina) 2016, *Conference* Toronto, ON (Canada) 2012, *Biennial world classifiers workshop* Paris (France) 2010, *Conference* Killarney (Ireland) 2008, *World conference / Conference* Paris (France) 2004. **Publications** *WHFF Newsletter*.
Members Organizations in 39 countries:
Argentina, Australia, Austria, Belgium, Brazil, Canada, Chile, Colombia, Croatia, Czechia, Denmark, Ecuador, Estonia, Finland, France, Germany, Greece, Hungary, Ireland, Israel, Italy, Japan, Latvia, Lithuania, Luxembourg, Mexico, Netherlands, New Zealand, Poland, Portugal, Romania, Slovakia, Slovenia, South Africa, Spain, Sweden, Switzerland, UK, USA.
[2021.05.26/XE2715/**E**]

♦ World Home Bible League / see Bible League International (#03225)
♦ World of Hope International (internationally oriented national body)
♦ World Hope International (internationally oriented national body)
♦ World Horizons (internationally oriented national body)
♦ World Horse Welfare (internationally oriented national body)
♦ World Hospital at Home Congress (meeting series)
♦ World House, Bielefeld (internationally oriented national body)

♦ **World Hovercraft Federation (WHF)** **21572**
Sec Strada di Oselin 100, 33047 Remanzacco UD, Italy. T. +39432639059. E-mail: worldhovercraft-federation@kpnmail.nl.
Pres 7 Grange Gardens, Holybourne, Alton, GU34 4DZ, UK. T. +44142084426.
URL: http://www.worldhovercraftfederation.org/
History Statutes adopted 1994, 1998, 1999, 2001, 2002, 2007, 2013, 2014, 2015, 2016, 2017, 2018, 2019. **Aims** Promote the use of hovercraft for *sport*, competition and tourism; encourage construction of new prototype craft and scale models. **Structure** Management Board; Country Representatives. **Languages** English. **Staff** Voluntary. **Finance** Race entry fees; donations; sponsorship. **Activities** Sporting activities. **Publications** *World Hovercraft Federation Bulletin*. Constitution; regulations; procedures; guidelines.
Members National organizations in 28 countries:
Angola, Australia, Austria, Belgium, Canada, China, Denmark, France, Germany, Indonesia, Ireland, Italy, Japan, Lebanon, Mauritius, Netherlands, New Zealand, Nigeria, Poland, Portugal, Slovakia, Slovenia, South Africa, Sweden, Tunisia, Türkiye, UK, USA. [2020.03.04/XD7528/**D**]

♦ World Huguenot Centre (internationally oriented national body)
♦ World Human Accountability Organization (internationally oriented national body)
♦ World Human Dimension (internationally oriented national body)
♦ World Humanity Commission (internationally oriented national body)
♦ World Humanity Foundation / see World Humanity Commission
♦ World Humanity Organization / see World Humanity Commission
♦ World Humor and Irony Membership / see International Society for Humor Studies (#15184)
♦ World Humor and Irony Movement / see International Society for Humor Studies (#15184)
♦ World Hunger Action Center (unconfirmed)
♦ World Hunger Education Service (internationally oriented national body)
♦ World Hunger Year (internationally oriented national body)

♦ **World Hydrological Cycle Observing System (WHYCOS)** **21573**
Système mondial d'observation du cycle de l'eau
Contact Hydrology and Water Resources Dept, WMO, Case Postale 2300, 7bis Ave de la Paix, 1211 Geneva 2, Switzerland. T. +41227308355. Fax +41227308043.
URL: http://www.whycos.org/
History 1993. Established when launched; becoming operational in stages. Implemented by *World Meteorological Organization (WMO, #21649)*, modelled on *World Weather Watch (WWW, #21910)*. **Aims** Work towards better understanding of the global hydrological cycle and its variability, and an improved knowledge of the status and trends of the world's freshwater resources; establish a global network of national hydrological observatories that provide information of consistent quality, transmitted in real or near real time to national, regional and global databases; strengthen the technical and institutional capacities of hydrological services to collect and disseminate hydro-meteorological data and information through the development of appropriate national water resources information systems, thereby facilitating their use for sustainable socio-economic development; facilitate regional and international cooperation and promote data sharing at the regional and global levels for scientific research in climate change and its impact on water-related issues; promote the use of information technology and space-based observations as a complementary mode of providing information on water-related issues by improving national and regional capacities; enhance cooperation among countries and hydrological services sharing regional water bodies by supporting and improving the availability, accuracy and dissemination of hydrological data and information. **Structure** WHYCOS International Advisory Group (WIAG) ensures worldwide operational linkage among HYCOS components. **Languages** English. **Staff** 6.00 FTE, paid. **Finance** National, regional and international bodies, including: WMO; *European Union (EU, #08967); International Bank for Reconstruction and Development (IBRD, #12317)* (World Bank); *Facilité africaine de l'eau (FAE, #09233); United States Agency for International Development (USAID)*; governments of France, Netherlands and Switzerland. **Activities** Global network of reference stations transmit hydrological and meteorological data via satellite to national hydrological stations and regional centres. Regional projects. **Events** *Working meeting / Summit of Heads of State and Government* Djibouti (Djibouti) 1998. **Publications** *WHYCOS Guidelines*. Project documents. Information Services: Selected data conveyed to *Global Runoff Data Centre (GRDC, #10584)*. **Information Services** *HYCOS Regional Databases* – based on constantly updated national and regionally distributed databases.
Members Countries and territories currently participating in HYCOS projects (40):
Albania, Algeria, Angola, Benin, Bosnia-Herzegovina, Botswana, Bulgaria, Burkina Faso, Cameroon, Cape Verde, Chad, Côte d'Ivoire, Croatia, Cyprus, Eswatini, France, Gambia, Ghana, Greece, Guinea, Italy, Lesotho, Malawi, Mali, Malta, Mauritania, Morocco, Mozambique, Namibia, Niger, Nigeria, North Macedonia, South Africa, Spain, Tanzania UR, Togo, Tunisia, Türkiye, Zambia, Zimbabwe. [2013.11.20/XF4622/**F***]

♦ World Hydrothermal Organization (#17820)

♦ **World Hypertension League (WHL)** **21574**
Secretariat address not obtained. E-mail: whleague17@gmail.com.
URL: https://www.whleague.org/
History 1984, Geneva (Switzerland). **Aims** Promote detection control and prevention of arterial hypertension in populations. **Structure** Council; Board; Headquarters in Hong Kong. Division of *International Society of Hypertension (ISH, #15189)*. **Languages** English. **Staff** 1.00 FTE, paid. **Finance** Sources: grants; members' dues. **Activities** Events/meetings. **Events** *World Hypertension Congress* Zhuhai (China) / Macau (Macau) 2022, *World Hypertension Congress* Beijing (China) 2020, *World Hypertension Congress* Sao Paulo (Brazil) 2019, *World Hypertension Board and Council Meeting* Beijing (China) 2018, *World Hypertension Congress* Shanghai (China) 2017. **Publications** *WHL Newsletter* (4 a year); *WHL Yearbook*. Proceedings.
Members Member organizations and supporting members in 74 countries and countries:
Algeria, Argentina, Australia, Austria, Bangladesh, Belgium, Botswana, Brazil, Bulgaria, Cameroon, Canada, Chile, China, Congo DR, Costa Rica, Croatia, Cuba, Czechia, Denmark, Dominican Rep, Ecuador, Egypt, Estonia, Finland, France, Georgia, Germany, Greece, Hong Kong, Hungary, India, Iran Islamic Rep, Ireland, Israel, Italy, Japan, Kenya, Korea Rep, Latvia, Lebanon, Lithuania, Malaysia, Mexico, Moldova, Morocco, Nepal, Netherlands, Nigeria, Norway, Pakistan, Palestine, Paraguay, Peru, Philippines, Poland, Portugal, Romania, Russia, Senegal, Serbia, Slovakia, Slovenia, South Africa, Spain, Sweden, Switzerland, Taiwan, Thailand, Türkiye, UK, Uruguay, USA, Venezuela, Zimbabwe.
Included in the above, 3 organizations listed in this Yearbook:
Inter-American Society of Hypertension (IASH, #11449); International Society for the Study of Hypertension in Pregnancy (ISSHP, #15475); International Society on Hypertension in Blacks (ISHIB).
Consultative Status Consultative status granted from: *ECOSOC (#05331)* (Ros C); *WHO (#20950)* (Official Relations). **NGO Relations** Also links with a number of national organizations active in the field.
[2022.11.06/XC0387/y/**F**]

♦ **World Hypnosis Organization (WHO)** **21575**
Pres NLP and Coaching Inst Berlin, Winterfeldstr 97, 10777 Berlin, Germany. T. +493021478174. E-mail: president@coaching-institutes.net – office@in-ici.net.
URL: http://www.world-hypnosis.org/
History Set up 2016, as sister organization to *International Association of NLP Institutes (IN, #12050)* and *International Association of Coaching Institutes (ICI, #11780)*. **Aims** Bridge effective practical application of hypnosis with academic education, theory and research; provide excellent ethics and quality standards in hypnosis. **Structure** Board of Directors; Presidents in Countries; Ambassadors; Commissions. **Activities** Standards/guidelines; training/education; research/documentation; events/meetings. **Events** *NLP and Coaching World Congress* Hammamet (Tunisia) 2019, *NLP and Coaching World Congress* Paris (France) 2017.
Members Individuals in 22 countries and territories:
Austria, Belgium, Brazil, Canada, Croatia, France, Germany, Guadeloupe, Iran Islamic Rep, Italy, Liechtenstein, Luxembourg, Malaysia, Netherlands, Nicaragua, Peru, Poland, Russia, Switzerland, Tunisia, Türkiye, UK.
NGO Relations *European Coaching Association (ECA).* [2018/XM6482/v/**D**]

♦ World Igbo Congress (internationally oriented national body)
♦ World Immersion Forum (meeting series)

♦ **World Immunopathology Organization (WIPO)** **21576**
Pres 4 Ostrovityanova Street, Moscow MOSKVA, Russia, 117513. T. +74957351414. Fax +74957351441. E-mail: info@wipocis.org.
URL: http://www.wipocis.org/
History Dec 2002, as *International Society on Immuno-Rehabilitation (IRIS)*. **Aims** Expand international contacts among scientists and specialists in various fields of medicine and public health whose professional interests are close to immunopathology. **Events** *World Asthma, COPD and Immunopathology Forum* St Petersburg (Russia) 2021, *World Asthma, COPD and Immunopathology Forum* St Petersburg (Russia) 2020, *World Asthma, Allergy and Chronic Obstructive Pulmonary Diseases (COPD) Forum* St Petersburg (Russia) 2019, *World Asthma, Allergy and Chronic Obstructive Pulmonary Diseases (COPD) Forum* Barcelona (Spain) 2018, *World Congress of Immunopathology, Respiratory Allergy and Asthma* Dubai (United Arab Emirates) 2016. **Publications** *International Journal on Immunorehabilitation* (2 a year). [2020/XD8692/**D**]

♦ **World Implant Orthodontic Association (WIOA)** **21577**
Pres Orthodontic Dept – College of Dentistry, Yonsei Univ, 262 Seongsanno, Seodaemum-gu, Seoul 120-749, Korea Rep. T. +8225492883. Fax +8225492832. E-mail: jylee@saoc.co.kr.
History Developed out of *Asian Implant Orthodontic Conference (AIOC)*, set up 2002. **Aims** Gather leading member of the orthodontic community to establish and further refine the scientific and clinical application of the absolute devices. **Structure** Advisory Committee. Board. **Events** *World Conference* Seoul (Korea Rep) 2021, *World Conference* Goa (India) 2016, *World Conference* Dubai (United Arab Emirates) 2015, *World Conference* Anaheim, CA (USA) 2014, *World Conference* Phuket (Thailand) 2013. [2010/XJ1992/**E**]

♦ World Inclusive Dance Association (unconfirmed)

♦ **World Indigenous Nations Higher Education Consortium (WINHEC)** . **21578**
Sec PO Box 4165, Honolulu HI 96812, USA. T. +18085968990. E-mail: winhec.executive@gmail.com – info@hualanifoundation.org.
URL: http://www.winhec.org/
History Aug 2002, Kananaskis, AB (Canada). Founded during the World Indigenous Peoples Conference on Education (WIPCE). **Aims** Provide an international forum and support for indigenous peoples to pursue common goals through higher education. **Structure** Annual General Meeting; Executive Board. **Activities** Certification/accreditation; events/meetings. **Events** *Conference* Cusco (Peru) 2011, *Annual general meeting* Kautokeino (Norway) 2010, *Annual General Meeting* Shannonville, ON (Canada) 2009, *Conference* Shannonville, ON (Canada) 2009, *Annual General Meeting* Melbourne, VIC (Australia) 2008. **Publications** *Te Karere* – newsletter; *WINHEC Journal*.

Members Full in 5 countries:
Australia, Canada, New Zealand, Norway, USA.
NGO Relations Cooperates with (1): *World Indigenous Peoples Conference on Education International Council (WIPCE International Council, #21579).* [2021/XJ3790/**D**]

♦ World Indigenous Network / see World Network of Indigenous Peoples and Local Community Land and Sea Managers (#21670)

♦ World Indigenous Peoples Conference on Education International Council (WIPCE International Council) 21579

Address not obtained.
URL: https://wipce.net/
History 1987, Vancouver, BC (Canada). Founded by Verna Kirkness. **Aims** Advocate for the design and development of culturally affirming and intellectually enriching education for Indigenous peoples. **Structure** International Council. **Activities** Events/meetings. **Events** *World Indigenous Peoples Conference on Education* Auckland (New Zealand) 2025, *World Indigenous Peoples Conference on Education* Adelaide, SA (Australia) 2022, *World Indigenous Peoples Conference on Education* Adelaide, SA (Australia) 2021, *World Indigenous Peoples Conference on Education* Adelaide, SA (Australia) 2020, *World Indigenous Peoples Conference on Education* Toronto, ON (Canada) 2017. **NGO Relations** Cooperates with (1): *World Indigenous Nations Higher Education Consortium (WINHEC, #21578).* [2023/XM2586/c/**E**]

♦ World Indigenous Television Broadcasters Network (WITBN) 21580

Red Mundial de Emisoras de Televisión Indígena
Contact address not obtained. T. +4778469216.
Twitter: https://twitter.com/witbn
History Mar 2008, at the inaugural World Indigenous Television Broadcasting Conference, Auckland (New Zealand). **Aims** Unify television broadcasters worldwide to retain and grow indigenous *languages* and *cultures*. **Structure** Executive Committee. Officers: Chair; Vice Chair. Secretariat Office. **Languages** English. **Activities** Organizes 'World Indigenous Television Broadcasting Conference (WITBC). **Events** *World Indigenous Television Broadcasting Conference* Winnipeg, MB (Canada) 2014, *Biennial Conference / World Conference* Kautokeino (Norway) 2012, *Biennial conference / World Conference* Taipei (Taiwan) 2010, *World Conference* Auckland (New Zealand) 2009, *Biennial conference* Auckland (New Zealand) 2008. **Publications** *WITBN Newsletter* (6 a year).
Members Television broadcasting companies in 9 countries and territories:
Australia, Canada, Hawaii, Ireland, New Zealand, Norway, Scotland, Taiwan, Wales. [2014/XM3807/**F**]

♦ World Indigenous Tourism Alliance (WINTA) 21581

Dir 1 Manapouri Lane, Aotearoa, Porirua 5024, New Zealand. T. +6421402419. E-mail: secretariat@winta.org.
URL: http://www.winta.org/
History 27 Mar 2012, Australia. Founded in the Larrakia Nation, Australia. Registration: Start date: 14 Feb 2014, New Zealand. **Aims** Promote the survival, dignity and well-being of the indigenous peoples of the world, by advancing indigenous human rights through tourism consistent with the standards articulated by the United Nations Declaration on the Rights of Indigenous Peoples. **Structure** Leadership Council; Director; Operations Team; Secretariat. **Languages** English. **Staff** 4.00 FTE, voluntary. **Activities** Advocacy/lobbying/activism; events/meetings; knowledge management/information dissemination; networking/liaising. **Events** *Summit* Perth, WA (Australia) 2020, *Summit* Waitangi (New Zealand) 2018, *Pacific Asia Indigenous Tourism Conference* Vancouver, BC (Canada) 2015. **Members** Indigenous and non-indegenous entities in 66 countries. Membership countries not specified. **NGO Relations** Member of (1): *Adventure Travel Trade Association (ATTA, #00135).* Partners include various stakeholders with an interst in the sustainable development of indigenous tourism. [2020.01.30/XM8492/**C**]

♦ World Indoor Bowls Council / see International Indoor Bowls Council (#13839)
♦ World Industry Council for the Environment (inactive)
♦ World Information Centre for Bilingual Education / see Information Centre for Bilingual and Plurilingual Education (#11195)
♦ World Information Centre for Bilingual and Plurilingual Education / see Information Centre for Bilingual and Plurilingual Education (#11195)
♦ World Information For Donation of Organs and Tissues Donation (inactive)

♦ World Information Service on Energy (WISE) 21582

Service mondial d'information sur l'énergie – Servicio Mundial de Información sobre la Energia – Weltweiter Energie Informationsdienst – Servizio Mondiale d'Informazione Energetica
Exec Dir PO Box 59636, 1040 LC Amsterdam, Netherlands. T. +31206126368. E-mail: info@wiseinternational.org.
Street Address Nieuwe Looiersstraat 31, 1017 VA Amsterdam, Netherlands.
URL: http://www.wiseinternational.org/
History Feb 1978, Amsterdam (Netherlands), when statutes were adopted, following Declaration of Intent, Nov 1977, Brussels (Belgium). Has also been referred to as *World Information Service on Environment and Development.* Also known as *WISE International.* **Aims** Function as an international network, independent of all ideological or political allegiance, for anti-nuclear and *safe energy* groups around the world; publish information on problems of nuclear power. **Structure** Head office in the Netherlands. Relay offices (10). **Staff** 2.50 FTE, paid; 1.50 FTE, voluntary. **Finance** Subscriptions. Other sources: Foundation for Transnational Information; project funding. **Activities** Awareness raising; networking/liaising; events/meetings. **Events** *European sustainable energy seminar* Bratislava (Slovakia) 1995, *Conference on medical management of radiation recipients* Amsterdam (Netherlands) 1987. **Publications** *WISE/NIRS Nuclear Monitor* (20 a year) in English. **IGO Relations** Consultative Status with: *United Nations Commission on Sustainable Development (CSD, inactive).* **NGO Relations** Member of: *Climate Action Network (CAN, #03999); Friends of the Earth International (FoEI, #10002); Rising Tide International (#18953).* Instrumental in setting up: *Milieukontakt International.* [2014.06.01/XF7086/**F**]

♦ World Information Service on Environment and Development / see World Information Service on Energy (#21582)
♦ World Information Technology and Services Alliance / see World Innovation, Technology and Services Alliance (#21585)

♦ World Information Transfer (WIT) 21583

Chair/CEO 210 E. 68th St. PHC, New York NY 10065, USA. T. +12126861996. E-mail: wit@worldinfo.org – info@worldinfo.org.
URL: https://worldinfo.org/
History 1986, New York, NY (USA). Incorporated 1987, New York NY (USA). Registration: 501(c)(3) organization, No/ID: EIN: 13-3540144, Start date: 1994, USA. **Aims** Promote *health* and *environmental* literacy among professionals, political leaders, business leaders, university students and the general public. **Structure** Board of Directors; Board of Advisors; Regional Directors; Headquarters in New York NY (USA). **Languages** Chinese, English, French, Spanish, Ukrainian. **Staff** 1.00 FTE, paid. Voluntary. **Finance** Sources: donations; subscriptions. Annual budget: US$ 200,000. **Activities** Knowledge management/information dissemination; publishing activities; training/education; events/meetings; humanitarian/emergency aid. **Events** *Annual International Conference on Health and Environment* New York, NY (USA) 2018, *Annual International Conference on Health and Environment* New York, NY (USA) 2017, *Annual International Conference on Health and Environment* New York, NY (USA) 2016, *Annual International Conference on Health and Environment* New York, NY (USA) 2015, *Annual International Conference on Health and Environment / International Conference on Health and Environment* New York, NY (USA) 2014. **Publications** *World Ecology Report* (4 a year) in Chinese, English, Ukrainian – newsletter. *Summer Speaker Series.* Conference proceedings.
Members Regional Offices in 10 countries and territories:
Belgium, Canada, China, Czechia, Hong Kong, Italy, Netherlands, Spain, Ukraine, USA.
Members in 57 countries and territories:
Argentina, Australia, Austria, Azerbaijan, Bangladesh, Belarus, Belgium, Brazil, Bulgaria, Canada, Colombia, Costa Rica, Czechia, Dominican Rep, Egypt, Finland, France, Germany, Ghana, Greece, Guatemala, Honduras, Hong Kong, Hungary, India, Indonesia, Israel, Italy, Japan, Jordan, Kazakhstan, Kenya, Korea Rep, Lebanon, Malaysia, Malta, Mexico, Moldova, Netherlands, New Zealand, Nigeria, Norway, Pakistan, Philippines, Poland, Romania, Singapore, Slovenia, South Africa, Spain, Switzerland, Thailand, Uganda, UK, Ukraine, USA, Venezuela.
Consultative Status Consultative status granted from: *ECOSOC (#05331)* (General). **NGO Relations** Instrumental in setting up: *Centre for Sustainability Studies, Lviv (see: #21583).* Partner/sister organization: *Human Info NGO.* [2022/XF5078/**F**]

♦ World Initiative for Soy in Human Health (internationally oriented national body)

♦ World Inline Figure Skating Association (WIFSA) 21584

Association mondiale de patinage artistique sur patins en ligne (AMPAI)
Pres 83 rue de la Victoire, 75009 Paris, France. T. +33674506474. E-mail: wifsa2014@gmail.com.
URL: http://sports.groups.yahoo.com/group/EIFSA/
History 19 May 2001, Netherlands, as *European Inline Figure Skating Association (EIFSA).* Present title adopted 2010. **Aims** Increase popularity of inline figure skating, dance, synchro, chorus for everyone. **Structure** Executive Committee; Officers. **Languages** English, French. **Staff** One voluntary. **Finance** No budget. **Activities** Sporting activities. **Publications** *EIFSA Newsletter.*
Members Full in 17 countries and territories:
Belgium, Canada, France, India, Iran Islamic Rep, Ireland, Italy, Mauritius, Poland, Romania, Russia, Spain, Switzerland, Taiwan, UK, Ukraine, USA.
NGO Relations *International Skating Union (ISU, #14865).* [2020.03.19/XD8973/**D**]

♦ World Innovation, Technology and Services Alliance (WITSA) 21585

Vice-Pres 8300 Boone Blvd, Ste 450, Vienna VA 22182, USA.
URL: http://www.witsa.org/
History 1978. Former names and other names: *World Computing Services Industry Forum* – former; *World Information Technology and Services Alliance (WITSA)* – former. **Aims** Promote and facilitate global growth of the information and communications technology and services industry through public policy development and advocacy, promotion of global trade and investment, global forum and experience. **Structure** Board of Directors. **Languages** English. **Staff** 3.00 FTE, paid. **Finance** Sources: meeting proceeds; members' dues; sponsorship. **Activities** Events/meetings; networking/liaising. **Events** *Biennial Congress* Penang (Malaysia) 2022, *ConnectechAsia Summit* Singapore (Singapore) 2022, *Biennial Congress* Dhaka (Bangladesh) 2021, *ConnectechAsia Summit* Singapore (Singapore) 2021, *ConnectechAsia Summit* Singapore (Singapore) 2020. **Publications** *WITSA Newsletter* (4 a year). Resolutions; statements.
Members National information technology (IT) associations in 78 countries and territories:
Afghanistan, Albania, Algeria, Argentina, Armenia, Austria, Bangladesh, Belarus, Bermuda, Brazil, Bulgaria, Canada, Chile, Colombia, Costa Rica, Curaçao, Cyprus, Ecuador, Egypt, El Salvador, Finland, France, Gambia, Greece, Guatemala, Haiti, Hong Kong, Hungary, India, Jamaica, Japan, Jordan, Kazakhstan, Kenya, Korea Rep, Kosovo, Laos, Lebanon, Lithuania, Malaysia, Mexico, Moldova, Mongolia, Morocco, Myanmar, Namibia, Nepal, Netherlands, New Zealand, Nigeria, North Macedonia, Pakistan, Palestine, Panama, Paraguay, Philippines, Portugal, Romania, Russia, Senegal, Serbia, Singapore, South Africa, Spain, Sri Lanka, Syrian AR, Taiwan, Thailand, Trinidad-Tobago, Tunisia, Türkiye, UK, Ukraine, USA, Venezuela, Vietnam, Zimbabwe.
IGO Relations Cooperates with (1): *Internet Governance Forum (IGF, #15950).* **NGO Relations** Cooperates with (1): *Internet Corporation for Assigned Names and Numbers (ICANN, #15949).* [2022.10.20/XF4550/**F**]

♦ World Instant Noodles Association (WINA) 21586

Chairman c/o Nissin Foods Holdings, 28-1 – 6-chome, Shinjuku, Shinjuku-ku, Tokyo, 160-8524 Japan.
Headquarters c/o Instant Ramen Museum, 25 – 8-chome, Masumi-cho, Ikeda-shi, Osaka, 563-0041 Japan.
URL: http://instantnoodles.org/
History 4 Mar 1997, as *International Ramen Manufacturers Association (IRMA).* Following adoption of CODEX International Standards for Instant Noodles, adopted current name, Feb 2007. **Aims** Improve the quality of instant noodles and increase its consumption through mutual exchange of information among *manufacturers* worldwide; discuss environmental and technical issues; promote mutual friendship, thereby enhancing *diets* worldwide and contributing to development of the industry. **Languages** Chinese, English, Japanese. **Staff** 1.00 FTE, paid. **Activities** Biennial summit. **Events** *World Summit* Tokyo (Japan) 2022, *World Summit* Osaka (Japan) 2018, *Food Safety Conference* Singapore (Singapore) 2014, *World Summit* Tianjin (China) 2012, *World summit* Kuala Lumpur (Malaysia) 2010. **Members** Companies and organizations (175). Membership countries not specified. [2014/XN9764/**F**]

♦ World Institute for Advanced Phenomenological Research and Learning / see World Phenomenology Institute (#21725)
♦ World Institute for Development Economics Research of the United Nations University / see UNU World Institute for Development Economics Research (#20722)
♦ World Institute on Disability (internationally oriented national body)
♦ World Institute for Disaster Risk Management (internationally oriented national body)

♦ World Institute for Engineering and Technology Education (WIETE) . 21587

Dir 141 The Boulevard, Ivanhoe East, Melbourne VIC 3079, Australia. T. +61394994339. E-mail: info@wiete.com.au.
URL: http://www.wiete.com.au/
History Assumed the Intellectual Property and copyright activities from *UNESCO International Centre for Engineering Education (UICEE, inactive).* Registered in accordance with Australian law as a private company. **Aims** Develop and maintain an independent global network of individuals and institutions concerned with the quality of engineering and technology education; promote international collaboration and dissemination of information on research and development in this area of academic endeavour. **Structure** International Academic Advisory Committee. **Languages** English. **Activities** Events/meetings; guidance/assistance/consulting; projects/programmes; research and development; training/education. **Events** *World Conference* Bangkok (Thailand) 2015, *World Conference on Technology and Engineering Education* Athens (Greece) 2014, *World Conference on Engineering and Technology Education* Pattaya (Thailand) 2012, *World conference on engineering and technology education* Pattaya (Thailand) 2011, *World conference on technology and engineering education* Pattaya (Thailand) 2010. **Publications** *Global Journal of Engineering Education (GJEE); WIETE News; World Transactions on Engineering and Technology Education (WTE and TE)* – journal. Books; conference proceedings.
Members Partner Institution; Individual; Honorary. Partner Institutions (7) in 7 countries and territories:
Botswana, Greece, India, Poland, Slovakia, Taiwan, USA.
Individuals in 15 countries and territories:
Australia, Botswana, Canada, Greece, India, Indonesia, Jamaica, Lithuania, Poland, Russia, Saudi Arabia, Slovakia, South Africa, Taiwan, USA.
Honorary members in 5 countries and territories:
Denmark, Lithuania, Taiwan, UK, USA. [2018/XJ1077/j/**C**]

♦ World Institute for Nuclear Security (WINS) 21588

Exec Dir Graben 19, 1010 Vienna, Austria. T. +431230606083. Fax +431230606089. E-mail: info@wins.org.
URL: http://www.wins.org/
History Launched Sep 2008, Vienna (Austria), during General Assembly of *International Atomic Energy Agency (IAEA, #12294).* **Aims** Provide those who are accountable for nuclear security with an international forum in which to share and promote best security practice. **Structure** Board of Directors. **Languages** Arabic, Chinese, English, French, German, Japanese, Korean, Portuguese, Russian, Spanish. **Staff** 10.00 FTE, paid. **Finance** Funders: *Nuclear Threat Initiative (NTI, #17622);* government agencies; corporations; foundations; universities; laboratories. **Activities** Certification/accreditation; events/meetings; publishing activities. **Events** *Meeting* Vienna (Austria) 2010. **Publications** Best Practice Guides; special papers. **Members** Individuals (over 2,800). Membership countries not specified. **IGO Relations** Cooperates with: *International Atomic Energy Agency (IAEA, #12294).* [2015.06.01/XM8172/j/**E**]

♦ World Institute of Pain (WIP) 21589

Exec Dir 301 N Main St, Ste 2604, Winston-Salem NC 27101, USA. T. +13367602933. Fax +13367602981. E-mail: wip@worldinstituteofpain.org.
URL: http://www.worldinstituteofpain.org/

History 1993. Registration: Start date: 1995, USA, California. **Aims** Develop an international network of pain centers of excellence; organize international consulting services in the field of pain management; organize and promote education and training of pain specialists worldwide. **Structure** Council, consisting of Executive Board and Chairs of WIP Sections Executive Board. Section Chairs represent Sections of: Africa; Australia; Benelux; Brazil; Canada; Colombia; Europe; Hungary. Iberia; India; Iran; ireland; Israel; Italy; Latin America; Malaysia; Mediterranean; Middle East; Northeast Asia; Puerto Rico and Caribbean; Southeast Asia; Switzerland; Turkey; UK, USA. **Languages** English. **Staff** 4.00 FTE, paid. **Finance** Annual budget: 350,000 USD. **Activities** Certification/accreditation; events/meetings. **Events** *World Congress* Budapest (Hungary) 2022, *World Congress* Rome (Italy) 2020, *World Congress* Dublin (Ireland) 2018, *World Congress* New York, NY (USA) 2016, *International Symposium* Barcelona (Spain) 2015. **Publications** *PAIN Practice* – journal. **Members** Regular (944); Associate (over 800). Membership countries not specified. [2022/XE4123/j/E]

♦ World Institute of Science (WIS) 21590

Institut mondial des sciences (IMS)

Gen Sec Le Château, 14 route de Moulis Banaux, 89190 Villeneuve-l'Archevêque, France.
URL: http://www.wis-ims.org/

History 19 Dec 1991, Brussels (Belgium). Also referred to in English as *World Science Institute*. Registered in accordance with Belgian law. **Aims** Promote the *responsibility* of scientists with respect to society, through diffusion of objective information on scientific questions, procedures and results and through constitution of a scientific *ethic* based on the WIS Charter. **Structure** General Assembly (every 4 years). Council, consisting of 25 elected members and 5 co-opted members to redress geographic/scientific balance. Executive Council, comprising President, Vice-Presidents and 2 other members. Executive Committee or Bureau, composed of Executive Council, Past-President, Secretary-General and Treasurer. Scientific Consultative Committee. **Finance** Members' dues. **Events** *Colloquium on uniqueness and universality in a biological world* Paris (France) 1995.
Members Founder; Active (individuals or organizations). Council members (30) in 17 countries:
Australia, Belgium, Brazil, Canada, China, France, Germany, India, Italy, Japan, Kenya, Poland, Russia, Spain, Switzerland, UK, USA. [2009/XF2383/j/F]

♦ World Institute of Scientology Enterprises (see: #03922)
♦ World Institute for a Sustainable Humanity (internationally oriented national body)

♦ World Insulation and Acoustics Congress Organization (WIACO) . . . 21591

Organisation mondiale des congrès d'isolation acoustique thermique et acoustique

Pres c/o Nat'l Insulation Assoc, 12100 Sunset Hills Rd, Ste 330, Reston VA 20190, USA. T. +17034646422. Fax +17034645896.

History as a coordinating body for *Fédération européenne des syndicats d'entreprises d'isolation (FESI, #09582)* and Canadian and US national organizations. **Aims** Organize meetings to aid communication among contractors and manufacturers of thermal, cold and sound insulation and *fire protection*. **Events** *WIACO Biennial Congress* Boca Raton, FL (USA) 2016, *WIACO biennial congress / Biennial Congress* Paris (France) 2012, *Biennial Congress* Paradise Is (Bahamas) 2008, *WIACO biennial congress / World Congress / Biennial Congress* Barcelona (Spain) 2004, *WIACO biennial congress / World Congress / Biennial Congress* Orlando, FL (USA) 2000.
Members Full in 33 countries and territories:
Australia, Austria, Bangladesh, Belgium, Bulgaria, Canada, Croatia, Denmark, Finland, France, Germany, Greece, Hong Kong, India, Indonesia, Ireland, Italy, Japan, Malaysia, Netherlands, New Zealand, Norway, Portugal, Singapore, South Africa, Spain, Sweden, Switzerland, Türkiye, UK, USA, Venezuela, Zimbabwe. [2013/XE5322/E]

♦ World Intellectual Forum (WIF) 21592

Chairman 6th Floor – Buddha Bhavan, Secunderabad, Telangana 500003, Secunderabad TELANGANA 500003, India. T. +914027541551. Fax +914027541552. E-mail: worldintellectualforum@gmail.com.
URL: http://www.wiforg.in/

History Set up Hyderabad (India). **Aims** Brainstorm on national, international and supranational (global) issues of political, socio-economic, civil, ideological, ethnic and cultural relevance and importance. **Structure** Board. **Activities** Training/education; advocacy/lobbying/activism; research/documentation. [2019.02.14/XM6303/F]

♦ World Intellectual Property Organization (WIPO) 21593

Organisation mondiale de la propriété intellectuelle (OMPI) – Organización Mundial de la Propiedad Intelectual (OMPI)

Dir Gen Chemin des Colombettes 34, 1211 Geneva 20, Switzerland. T. +41223389111. Fax +41227335428. E-mail: wipo.mail@wipo.int.
Contact 2 United Nations Plaza, Suite 2525, New York NY 10017, USA.
URL: http://www.wipo.int/

History 14 Jul 1967, Stockholm (Sweden). Established on signature of *Convention establishing the World Intellectual Property Organization – Convention instituant l'Organisation mondiale de la propriété intellectuelle*, which entered into force 26 Apr 1970, on ratification of or accession by 10 States, members of the Paris (France) Union, and 7 States, members of the Bern (Switzerland) Union. Registered 30 Jun 1972. Origins of the present WIPO go back to two principal international intellectual property treaties, the *Paris Convention for the Protection of Industrial Property, 1883 (1883)* of 20 Mar 1883, establishing *International Union for the Protection of Industrial Property (Paris Union, #15805)*, and the *Bern Convention for the Protection of Literary and Artistic Works, 1886 (1886)* of 9 Sep 1886, adopted 5 Dec 1887, established *International Union for the Protection of Literary and Artistic Works (Bern Union, #15806)*. Each Convention provided for establishment of an 'International Bureau' or secretariat. These bureaux were united in 1893 and functioned under various names, the last being *United International Bureaux for the Protection of Intellectual Property – Bureaux internationaux réunis pour la protection de la propriété intellectuelle (BIRPI)*. WIPO took over the functions of BIRPI and, since Dec 1974, functions as a specialized agency of the United Nations within *United Nations System (#20635)*, linked to *ECOSOC (#05331)*. Statutes registered in *'LNTS 4459'*. **Aims** Promote protection of intellectual property (IP) worldwide through cooperation with member states; enable *inventors* and creators to harness the value of their work; stimulate *innovation* and *creativity* by ensuring that inventors and creators are recognized and rewarded for their ingenuity. **Structure** General Assembly; Coordination Committee; Conference; Permanent Committees (4). Standing Committees (4); Working Groups; Diplomatic Conferences; Sectors (7), headed by Deputy Director General or Assistant Director General, under the overall leadership of Director General; External offices (7): Algeria; Brazil; China; Japan; Nigeria; Russia; Singapore. **Languages** Arabic, Chinese, English, French, Russian, Spanish. **Staff** As of May 2021 – Secretariat: 1,067 from 121 countries, with their own organization, *Staff Association of the World Intellectual Property Organization (WIPO Staff Association, #19942)*. The *Administrative Tribunal of the International Labour Organization (ILO Tribunal, #00118)* is competent to settle disputes. **Finance** Main sources (over 95% of income): use of international filing and registration systems; miscellaneous income from sale of publications; interest on earning. Other source: member states' contributions (less than 7% of overall budget). Approved program and budget (2022-2023): about 950 million Swiss francs. URL: https://www.wipo.int/about-wipo/en/budget/
Activities Provides: a policy forum to shape balanced international IP rules for a changing world; global services to protect IP across borders and to resolve disputes; technical infrastructure to connect IP systems and share knowledge; cooperation and capacity-building programs to enable all countries to use IP for economic, social and cultural development; a world reference source for IP information.
WIPO-administered treaties:
- *Beijing Treaty on Audiovisual Performances (2012)*;
- *Bern Convention for the Protection of Literary and Artistic Works, 1886 (1886)* and its *International Union for the Protection of Literary and Artistic Works (Bern Union, #15806)*;
- *Budapest Treaty on the International Recognition of the Deposit of Microorganisms for the Purposes of Patent Procedure (Budapest Treaty of 1977, 1977)* and its *Budapest Union for the International Recognition of the Deposit of Microorganisms for the Purposes of Patent Procedure (#03345)*;
- *Convention for the Protection of Producers of Phonograms Against Unauthorized Duplication of Their Phonograms (Geneva Convention, 1971)*;
- *Convention Relating to the Distribution of Programme-carrying Signals Transmitted by Satellite (Brussels Convention, 1974)*;
- *The Hague Agreement Concerning the International Deposit of Industrial Designs (1925)* and its *Union for the International Deposit of Industrial Designs (The Hague Union, #20417)*;
- *International Convention for the Protection of Performers, Producers of Phonograms and Broadcasting Organizations (Rome Convention, 1961)* and its *Intergovernmental Committee of the International Convention of Rome for the Protection of Performers, Producers of Phonograms and Broadcasting Organizations (#11474)*;
- *Lisbon Agreement for the Protection of Appellations of Origin and Their International Registration (Lisbon Agreement, 1958)* and its *Union for the Protection of Appellations of Origin and their International Registration (Lisbon Union, #20474)*;
- *Locarno Agreement Establishing an International Classification for Industrial Design (1968)* and its *Union for the International Classification for Industrial Designs (Locarno Union, #20416)*;
- *Madrid Agreement Concerning the International Registration of Marks, 1891 (1891)* and *Protocol to the Madrid Agreement Concerning the International Registration of Marks (1989)* and its *Union for the International Registration of Marks (Madrid Union, #20445)*;
- *Madrid Agreement for the Repression of False or Deceptive Indications of Source on Goods, 1891 (Madrid Agreement, 1891)*;
- *Marrakesh Treaty to Facilitate Access to Published Works for Persons Who Are Blind, Visually Impaired or Otherwise Print Disabled (Marrakesh Treaty, 2013)*;
- *Nairobi Treaty on the Protection of the Olympic Symbol (Nairobi Treaty, 1981)*;
- *Nice Agreement Concerning the International Classification of Goods and Services for the Purposes of the Registration of Marks (1957)* and its *Special Union for the International Classification of Goods and Services for the Purposes of the Registration of Marks (Nice Union, #19913)*;
- *Paris Convention for the Protection of Industrial Property, 1883 (1883)* and its *International Union for the Protection of Industrial Property (Paris Union, #15805)*;
- *Patent Cooperation Treaty (PCT, 1970)* and its *International Patent Cooperation Union (PCT Union, #14530)*;
- *Patent Law Treaty (PLT, 2000)* and its *Patent Law Treaty Assembly*;
- *Singapore Treaty on the Law of Trademarks (Singapore Treaty, 2006)*;
- *Strasbourg Agreement Concerning the International Patent Classification (IPC Agreement, 1971)* and its *Union for the International Patent Classification (IPC Union, #20443)*;
- *Trademark Law Treaty (TLT, 1994)*;
- *Treaty on the Protection of Intellectual Property in Respect of Integrated Circuits (IPIC, 1989)*;
- *Vienna Agreement Establishing an International Classification of the Figurative Elements of Marks (Vienna Agreement, 1973)* and its *International Union for an International Classification of the Figurative Elements of Marks (Vienna Union, #15784)*;
- *WIPO Copyright Treaty (WCT, 1996)* and its *WIPO Copyright Treaty Assembly*;
- *WIPO Performances and Phonograms Treaty (WPPT, 1996)* and its *WIPO Performances and Phonograms Treaty Assembly*.

Also provides technical and administrative support services for:
- *Union internationale pour la protection des obtentions végétales (UPOV, #20436)* established by *International Convention for the Protection of New Varieties of Plants, 1961 (1961)*;
- *Treaty on the International Registration of Audiovisual Works (1989)* and its *Union for the International Registration of Audiovisual Works (#20444)*;
- *'Geneva Treaty' – Geneva Treaty on the International Recording of Scientific Discoveries (Geneva Treaty, 1978)* – not yet into force;
- *'Madrid Multilateral Convention' – Multilateral Convention for the Avoidance of Double Taxation of Copyright Royalties and Additional Protocol (Madrid Multilateral Convention, 1979)*;
- *Eurasian Patent Convention (1994)*;
- *Geneva Act of the The Hague Agreement Concerning the International Registration of Industrial Designs (1999)*.

Events *IP5 Heads of Office and Industry Meeting* Daejeon (Korea Rep) 2022, *World Conference on Creative Economy* Dubai (United Arab Emirates) 2021, *Roving Seminar* Seoul (Korea Rep) 2021, *Workshop on Copyright System in Support of Creative Start-up Companies* Seoul (Korea Rep) 2021, *Workshop on IP Enforcement* Seoul (Korea Rep) 2021. **Publications** *Global Innovation Index* (annual); *WIPO Magazine*. Annual Report; books; collections; glossaries; guidelines; guides; reports; studies; newsletter; IP reports.
Members Membership open to any state which is a member of the Paris Union for the Protection of Industrial Property, or member of the Berne Union for the Protection of Literary and Artistic Works; or a member of the United Nations, or of any of the United Nations' Specialized Agencies, or of the International Atomic Energy Agency (IAEA), or that is a party to the Statute of the International Court of Justice; or invited by the WIPO General Assembly to become a member state of the Organization. As of Mar 2018, total combined membership of WIPO and of its Unions is 193 states which are party to the Convention establishing WIPO:
Afghanistan, Albania, Algeria, Andorra, Angola, Antigua-Barbuda, Argentina, Armenia, Australia, Austria, Azerbaijan, Bahamas, Bahrain, Bangladesh, Barbados, Belarus, Belgium, Belize, Benin, Bhutan, Bolivia, Bosnia-Herzegovina, Botswana, Brazil, Brunei Darussalam, Bulgaria, Burkina Faso, Burundi, Cambodia, Cameroon, Canada, Cape Verde, Central African Rep, Chad, Chile, China, Colombia, Comoros, Congo Brazzaville, Congo DR, Cook Is, Costa Rica, Côte d'Ivoire, Croatia, Cuba, Cyprus, Czechia, Denmark, Djibouti, Dominica, Dominican Rep, Ecuador, Egypt, El Salvador, Equatorial Guinea, Eritrea, Estonia, Eswatini, Ethiopia, Fiji, Finland, France, Gabon, Gambia, Georgia, Germany, Ghana, Greece, Grenada, Guatemala, Guinea, Guinea-Bissau, Guyana, Haiti, Holy See, Honduras, Hungary, Iceland, India, Indonesia, Iran Islamic Rep, Iraq, Ireland, Israel, Italy, Jamaica, Japan, Jordan, Kazakhstan, Kenya, Kiribati, Korea DPR, Korea Rep, Kuwait, Kyrgyzstan, Laos, Latvia, Lebanon, Lesotho, Liberia, Libya, Liechtenstein, Lithuania, Luxembourg, Madagascar, Malawi, Malaysia, Maldives, Mali, Malta, Marshall Is, Mauritania, Mauritius, Mexico, Moldova, Monaco, Mongolia, Montenegro, Morocco, Mozambique, Myanmar, Namibia, Nauru, Nepal, Netherlands, New Zealand, Nicaragua, Niger, Nigeria, Niue, North Macedonia, Norway, Oman, Pakistan, Palau, Panama, Papua New Guinea, Paraguay, Peru, Philippines, Poland, Portugal, Qatar, Romania, Russia, Rwanda, Samoa, San Marino, Sao Tomé-Principe, Saudi Arabia, Senegal, Serbia, Seychelles, Sierra Leone, Singapore, Slovakia, Slovenia, Somalia, South Africa, Spain, Sri Lanka, St Kitts-Nevis, St Lucia, St Vincent-Grenadines, Sudan, Suriname, Sweden, Switzerland, Syrian AR, Tajikistan, Tanzania UR, Thailand, Timor-Leste, Togo, Tonga, Trinidad-Tobago, Tunisia, Türkiye, Turkmenistan, Tuvalu, Uganda, UK, Ukraine, United Arab Emirates, Uruguay, USA, Uzbekistan, Vanuatu, Venezuela, Vietnam, Yemen, Zambia, Zimbabwe.
IGO Relations IGOs admitted as observers. Category A – United Nations System of Organizations:
- *FAO (#09260)*;
- *ILO (#11123)*;
- *International Atomic Energy Agency (IAEA, #12294)*;
- *International Bank for Reconstruction and Development (IBRD, #12317)*;
- *International Civil Aviation Organization (ICAO, #12581)*;
- *International Development Association (IDA, #13155)*;
- *International Finance Corporation (IFC, #13597)*;
- *International Fund for Agricultural Development (IFAD, #13692)*;
- *International Maritime Organization (IMO, #14102)*;
- *International Monetary Fund (IMF, #14180)*;
- *International Telecommunication Union (ITU, #15673)*;
- *UNESCO (#20322)*;
- *UNIDO (#20336)*;
- *United Nations (UN, #20515)*;
- *Universal Postal Union (UPU, #20682)*;
- *WHO (#20950)*;
- *World Meteorological Organization (WMO, #21649)*.

Category B – Intellectual Property:
- *African Intellectual Property Organization (#00344)*;
- *African Regional Intellectual Property Organization (ARIPO, #00434)*;
- *Arab States Broadcasting Union (ASBU, #01050)*;
- *Benelux Organization for Intellectual Property (BOIP, #03203)*;
- *Eurasian Patent Organization (EAPO, #05613)*;
- *European Patent Organisation (#08167)*;
- *Nordic Patent Institute (NPI, #17381)*;
- *Patent Office of Cooperation Council for the Arab States of the Gulf (GCC Patent Office, #18259)*;
- *Union internationale pour la protection des obtentions végétales (UPOV, #20436)*;
- *World Sleep Society (#21793)*.

Category C – Other Intergovernmental Organizations – Worldwide:
- *Commonwealth of Learning (COL, #04346)*;
- *Commonwealth Secretariat (#04362)*;
- *Comunidade dos Paises de Lingua Portuguesa (CPLP, #04430)*;
- *European Public Law Organization (EPLO, #08299)*;
- *The Hague Conference on Private International Law (HCCH, #10850)*;
- *International Criminal Police Organization – INTERPOL (ICPO-INTERPOL, #13110)*;
- *International Institute for the Unification of Private Law (UNIDROIT, #13934)*;
- *International Olive Council (IOC, #14405)*;
- *International Organisation of Vine and Wine (OIV, #14435)*;
- *ITER International Fusion Energy Organization (ITER Organization, #16072)*;
- *Organisation internationale de la Francophonie (OIF, #17809)*;
- *South Centre (#19753)*;
- *World Trade Organization (WTO, #21864)* (WIPO also has Observer Status with WTO).

Regional:
- *Organisation of African, Caribbean and Pacific States (OACPS, #17796)*;
- *African Regional Centre of Technology (ARCT, #00432)*;
- *African Union (AU, #00488)*;

- General Secretariat of *Andean Community (#00817)*;
- *Arab League Educational, Cultural and Scientific Organization (ALECSO, #01003)*;
- *Arab League Educational, Cultural and Scientific Organization (ALECSO, #01003)*;
- *ASEAN (#01141)*;
- *Asian-African Legal Consultative Organization (AALCO, #01303)*;
- *Caribbean Community (CARICOM, #03476)*;
- *Common Language Resources and Technology Infrastructure (CLARIN, #04295)*;
- *Commonwealth Fund for Technical Cooperation (CFTC, #04331)*;
- *Commonwealth of Independent States (CIS, #04341)*;
- *Communauté économique et monétaire d'Afrique centrale (CEMAC, #04374)*;
- *Communauté économique des pays des Grands Lacs (CEPGL, #04375)*;
- *Council of Europe (CE, #04881)*;
- *EFTA (#05391)*;
- *Eurasian Economic Union (EAEU, #05607)* – Eurasian Economic Union;
- *European Audiovisual Observatory (#06294)*;
- *European Commission (EC, #06633)*;
- *Federation of Arab Scientific Research Councils (FASRC, no recent information)*;
- *Islamic World Educational, Scientific and Cultural Organization (ICESCO, #16058)*;
- *Latin American Integration Association (LAIA, #16343)*;
- *League of Arab States (LAS, #16420)*;
- *OAS (#17629)*;
- *Organisation of Eastern Caribbean States (OECS, #17804)*;
- *Organisation of Islamic Cooperation (OIC, #17813)*;
- *Red de Información Tecnológica Latinoamericana (RITLA, see: #19294)*;
- *Regional Centre for the Promotion of Books in Latin America and the Caribbean (#18758)*;
- *Secretaria Permanente del Tratado General de Integración Económica Centroamericana (SIECA, #19195)*;
- *Sistema Económico Latinoamericano (SELA, #19294)*;
- *Southern African Development Community (SADC, #19843)*;
- *Union économique et monétaire Ouest africaine (UEMOA, #20377)*.

NGO Relations NGOs with permanent observer status at WIPO include:
- *3D – Trade – Human Rights – Equitable Economy*;
- *4iP Council EU*;
- *ActionAid (#00087)*;
- *Actors, Interpreting Artists Committee (CSAI, no recent information)*;
- *African Agricultural Technology Foundation (AATF, #00199)*;
- *African Library and Information Associations and Institutions (AfLIA, #00363)*;
- *African Union of Broadcasting (AUB, #00490)*;
- *Afro-Asian Book Council (AABC, #00535)*;
- *Alfa-Redi (no recent information)*;
- *Arab Federation for the Protection of Intellectual Property Rights (AFPIPR, #00951)*;
- *Arab Society for Intellectual Property (ASIP, #01046)*;
- *ASEAN Intellectual Property Association (AIPA, #01203)*;
- *Asia-Pacific Broadcasting Union (ABU, #01863)*;
- *Asia and Pacific Internet Association (APIA, #01936)*;
- *Asian Patent Attorneys Association (APAA, #01655)*;
- *Asociación Interamericana de la Propiedad Intelectual (ASIPI, #02161)*;
- *Asociación Latinoamericana de Industrias Farmacéuticas (ALIFAR, #02232)*;
- *Association of Commercial Television in Europe (ACT, #02436)*;
- *Association of European Performers' Organisations (AEPO-ARTIS, #02530)*;
- *Association of European Radios (AER, #02535)*;
- *Association for the International Collective Management of Audiovisual Works (AGICOA, #02658)*;
- *Association des Praticiens du Droit des Marques et des Modèles (APRAM)*;
- *Association for the Protection of Industrial Property in the Arab World (#02877)*;
- *Benelux Association for Trademark and Design Law (#03199)*;
- *Biotechnology Innovation Organization (BIO)*;
- *Bureau Européen des Unions de Consommateurs (BEUC, #03360)*;
- *Bureau international des Médecins sans frontières (MSF International, #03366)*;
- *Business Software Alliance (BSA, #03387)*;
- *BUSINESSEUROPE (#03381)*;
- *GIGAEurope AISBL (#10151)*;
- *Cambia*;
- *Caribbean Broadcasting Union (CBU, #03465)*;
- *Central and Eastern European Copyright Alliance (CEECA, #03690)*;
- *Centre d'études internationales de la propriété intellectuelle (CEIPI)*;
- *Center for International Environmental Law (CIEL)*;
- *Chartered Institute of Arbitrators (CIArb)*;
- *Chartered Society of Designers (CSD)*;
- *Coalition for Intellectual Property Rights (CIPR)*;
- *Committee of National Institutes of Patent Agents (CNIPA, #04274)*;
- *COMMUNIA (#04378)*;
- *Computer and Communications Industry Association (CCIA)*;
- *Confédération internationale des sociétés d'auteurs et compositeurs (CISAC, #04563)*;
- *Confédération internationale des travailleurs intellectuels (CITI, #04564)*;
- *Confederation of Rightholders' Societies of Europe and Asia (CRSEA, #04576)*;
- *Conference of Iberoamerican Authorities on Informatics (#04606)*;
- *Conseil européen de l'industrie chimique (CEFIC, #04687)*;
- *Conseil francophone de la chanson (CFC, #04690)*;
- *Consumers International (CI, #04773)*;
- *Co-ordinating Council of Audiovisual Archives Associations (CCAAA, #04820)*;
- *European Audiovisual Production (CEPI, #06295)*;
- *Coordination of European Picture Agencies, Press Stock Heritage (CEPIC, #04825)*;
- *Council on Health Research for Development (COHRED, no recent information)*;
- *CropLife International (#04966)*;
- *Digital Media Association (DiMA)*;
- *DIGITALEUROPE (#05073)*;
- *Drugs for Neglected Diseases initiative (DNDi, #05137)*;
- *DVB Project (#05147)*;
- *Ecma International (#05288)*;
- *ECTA (#05341)*;
- *DOT Europe (#05125)*;
- *Education International (EI, #05371)*;
- *Electronic Information for Libraries (EIFL, #05425)*;
- *Ingénieurs du monde (IdM)*;
- *European Alliance of News Agencies (EANA, #05877)*;
- *European Association of Bioindustries (EuropaBio, #05956)*;
- *European Association of Communications Agencies (EACA, #05983)*;
- *European Brands Association (#06397)*;
- *European Broadcasting Union (EBU, #06404)*;
- *European Bureau of Library, Information and Documentation Associations (EBLIDA, #06413)*;
- *European Committee for Interoperable Systems (ECIS, #06654)*;
- *European Composer and Songwriter Alliance (ECSA, #06691)*;
- *European Council of American Chambers of Commerce (ECACC, #06803)*;
- *CropLife Europe (#04965)*;
- *European Digital Rights (EDRi, #06924)*;
- *European Federation of Agents of Industry in Industrial Property (#07042)*;
- *European Federation of Pharmaceutical Industries and Associations (EFPIA, #07191)*;
- *European Industrial Research Management Association (EIRMA, #07531)*;
- *The European Law Students' Association (ELSA, #07660)*;
- *European Network for Copyright in support of Education and Science (ENCES, #07885)*;
- *European Newspaper Publishers' Association (ENPA, #08048)*;
- *European Publishers Council (EPC, #08304)*;
- *European Sound Directors' Association (ESDA, no recent information)*;
- *European Visual Artists (EVA, #09071)*;
- *European Writers' Council (EWC-FAEE, #09123)*;
- *Exchange and Cooperation Centre for Latin America (ECCLA)*;
- *Federación Iberolatinoamericana de Artistas Intérpretes y Ejecutantes (FILAIE, #09325)*;
- *Federation of European Screen Directors (#09541)*;
- *Fédération internationale des bureaux d'extraits de presse (FIBEP, #09617)*;
- *Fédération Internationale des Conseils en Propriété Intellectuelle (FICPI, #09624)*;
- *Fédération des Scénaristes d'Europe (FSE, #09703)*;
- *Femmes chefs d'entreprises mondiales (FCEM, #09733)*;
- *FIPP (#09776)*;
- *FIVS (#09789)*;
- *Foundation for a Free Information Infrastructure (FFII, #09956)*;
- *Free Software Foundation Europe (FSFE)*;
- *Friends World Committee for Consultation (FWCC, #10004)*;
- *Global Anti-Counterfeiting Group (GACG, #10236)*;
- *Global Self-Care Federation (GSCF, #10588)*;
- *Independent Film Producers International Association (IFPIA, no recent information)*;
- *Independent Film and Television Alliance (IFTA)*;
- *Independent Music Companies Association (IMPALA, #11151)*;
- *Institute for African Development, Ithaca NY*;
- *Institute of Professional Representatives before the European Patent Office (epi, #11288)*;
- *Instituto de Derecho de Autor (Instituto Autor)*;
- *Instituto Latinoamericano de Alta Tecnologia, Informatica y Derecho (ILATID, #11341)*;
- *Inter-American Copyright Institute (ICI, #11421)*;
- *Interactive Software Federation of Europe (ISFE, #11380)*;
- *International Advertising Association (IAA, #11590)*;
- *International Affiliation of Writers' Guilds (IAWG, #11595)*;
- *International Air Transport Association (IATA, #11614)*;
- *International Alliance of Orchestra Associations (IAOA, no recent information)*;
- *International Anticounterfeiting Coalition (IACC, #11656)*;
- *International Association for the Advancement of Teaching and Research in Intellectual Property (ATRIP, #11690)*;
- *International Association of Art (IAA, #11710)*;
- *International Association of Broadcasting (IAB, #11738)*;
- *International Association of Conference Interpreters (#11807)*;
- *International Association of Entertainment Lawyers (IAEL, #11875)*;
- *International Association of IT Lawyers (IAITL, #11972)*;
- *International Association for Media and Communication Research (IAMCR, #12022)*;
- *International Association for the Protection of Intellectual Property (#12112)*;
- *International Association of Scientific, Technical and Medical Publishers (STM, #12154)*;
- *International Authors Forum (IAF, #12298)*;
- *International Ayurveda Foundation (IAF, no recent information)*;
- *International Bar Association (IBA, #12320)*;
- *International Bureau of the Societies Administering the Rights of Mechanical Recording and Reproduction (#12416)*;
- *International Centre for Trade and Sustainable Development, Geneva (ICTSD, #12524)*;
- *International Chamber of Commerce (ICC, #12534)*;
- *International Commission of Jurists (ICJ, #12695)*;
- *International Committee for the Indigenous Peoples of the Americas (Incomindios)*;
- *International Confederation of Music Publishers (ICMP, #12864)*;
- *International Council on Archives (ICA, #12996)*;
- *International Council of Design (ICoD, #13013)*;
- *International Council of Museums (ICOM, #13051)*;
- *International Dance Council (#13130)*;
- *International DOI Foundation (IDF, #13188)*;
- *International Environmental Law Research Centre (IELRC)*;
- *International Federation of Actors (#13337)*;
- *International Federation of Commercial Arbitration Institutions (IFCAI)*;
- *International Federation of Computer Law Associations (IFCLA, #13398)*;
- *International Federation of Film Distributors Associations (#13428)*;
- *International Federation of Film Producers' Associations (#13429)*;
- *International Federation of Interior Architects / Designers (IFI, #13460)*;
- *International Federation of Inventors' Associations (IFIA, #13461)*;
- *International Federation of Journalists (IFJ, #13462)*;
- *International Federation of Library Associations and Institutions (IFLA, #13470)*;
- *International Federation of Musicians (#13486)*;
- *International Federation of Pharmaceutical Manufacturers and Associations (IFPMA, #13505)*;
- *International Federation of the Phonographic Industry (IFPI, #13508)*;
- *International Federation of Reproduction Rights Organizations (IFRRO, #13527)*;
- *International Federation of Translators (#13574)*;
- *International Franchise Association (IFA)*;
- *International Hotel and Restaurant Association (IH&RA, #13813)*;
- *International Human Rights and Anti-Corruption Society (IHRAS)*;
- *International Generic and Biosimilar Medicines Association (IGBA, #13708)*;
- *International Institute of Communications (IIC, #13870)*;
- *International Institute for Intellectual Property Management (I3PM, #13893)*;
- *International Intellectual Property Alliance (IIPA)*;
- *International Intellectual Property Institute (IIPI)*;
- *International IP Commercialization Council (IIPCC)*;
- *International Law Association (ILA, #14003)*;
- *International Literary and Artistic Association (#14058)*;
- *International Music Managers' Forum (IMMF, #14200)*;
- *International Network for Standardization of Higher Education Degrees (INSHED, #14329)*;
- *International Organization for Standardization (ISO, #14473)*;
- *International Poetry for Peace Association (IPPA, no recent information)*;
- *International Policy Network (IPN)*;
- *International Publishers Association (IPA, #14675)*;
- *International Society for the Development of Intellectual Property (#15056)*;
- *International Technology Law Association (ITechLaw, #15669)*;
- *International Trade Union Confederation (ITUC, #15708)*;
- *International Trademark Association (INTA, #15706)*;
- *International Union of Cinemas (#15763)*;
- *International Union for Conservation of Nature and Natural Resources (IUCN, #15766)*;
- *International Video Federation (IVF, #15852)*;
- *International Wine Law Association (IWLA, #15891)*;
- *Internationale Gesellschaft für Urheberrecht (INTERGU, no recent information)*;
- *Internet Society (ISOC, #15952)*;
- *IP Justice*;
- *IQsensato (#16015)*;
- *Knowledge Ecology International (KEI, #16200)*;
- *LAWASIA – Law Association for Asia and the Pacific (#16406)*;
- *Licensing Executives Society International (LESI, #16461)*;
- *Ligue internationale du droit de la concurrence (LIDC, #16478)*;
- *MARQUES (#16588)*;
- *Medicines for Europe (#16633)*;
- *Medicines Patent Pool (MPP, #16635)*;
- *Motion Picture Association (MPA)*;
- *Nordic Actors' Council (#17166)*;
- *North American Broadcasters Association (NABA, #17561)*;
- *Organización de Asociaciones y Empresas de Telecomunicaciones para América Latina (TEPAL, #17832)*;
- *Organización Iberoamericana de Derechos de Autor (Latinautor, #17840)*;
- *Organización de Telecomunicaciones de Iberoamérica (OTI, #17851)*;
- *Organization for an International Geographical Indications Network (oriGIn, #17874)*;
- *Patent Committee (PatCom, #18258)*;
- *PDG (#18272)*;
- *Pearle – Live Performance Europe (#18284)*;
- *PLUS Coalition*;
- *Public Interest Intellectual Property Advisors (PIIPA)*;
- *Royal Institute of International Affairs (RIIA)*;
- *Scandinavian Patent Attorney Society (inactive)*;
- *SPARC Europe (#19902)*;
- *Software and Information Industry Association (SIIA)*;
- *Southern and Eastern Africa Copyright Network (SEACONET, #19872)*;
- *Special Libraries Association (SLA)*;
- *spiritsEUROPE (#19921)*;
- *Third World Network (TWN, #20151)*;
- *UNI Global Union (#20338)*;
- *Union of European Practitioners in Intellectual Property (UNION, #20392)*;
- *Union internationale des architectes (UIA, #20419)*;
- *Union Internationale des Avocats (UIA, #20422)*;

- *Union internationale des journalistes africains (UIJA, #20428)*;
- *World Association of Newspapers and News Publishers (WAN-IFRA, #21166)*;
- *World Association for Small and Medium Enterprises (WASME, #21189)*;
- *World Blind Union (WBU, #21234)*;
- *World Design Organization (WDO, #21358)*;
- *World Federation of Advertisers (WFA, #21407)*;
- *World Federation for Culture Collections (WFCC, #21424)*;
- *World Federation of Engineering Organizations (WFEO, #21433)*;
- *World Union of Professions (WUP, #21882)*;
- *World Women Inventors and Entrepreneurs Association (WWIEA, #21942)*.

For IGOs and NGOs admitted as observers to the sessions of the Rome (Italy) Intergovernmental Committee see: *'Intergovernmental Committee of the International Convention of Rome for the Protection of Performers, Producers of Phonograms and Broadcasting Organizations (Intergovernmental Committee of the Rome Convention)'*.
International NGOs having observer status with WIPO and the Unions administered by WIPO are invited to be represented by an observer in the WIPO Conference and to certain meetings of the other Governing Bodies.
[2023.02.20/XB3635/**B***]

♦ World Interactive Network Focuses on Critical UltraSound / see WINFOCUS (#20968)

♦ World Interdisciplinary Network for Institutional Research (WINIR) . 21594

Sec 9 Renner Croft, Dunstable, LU6 3FP, UK. E-mail: secretary@winir.org.
Treas address not obtained. E-mail: treasurer@winir.org.
URL: http://winir.org/

History Oct 2013. Constitution adopted Sep 2014; amended Oct 2016. **Aims** Bring together researchers from multiple academic disciplines to study the nature, function, evolution, and impact of institutions. **Structure** Council; Scientific Quality Committee. **Languages** English. **Finance** Sources: members' dues. **Activities** Events/meetings. **Events** *Institutional innovation and evolution, challenges to the modern world order* Catania (Italy) 2023, *Conference* Dunstable (UK) 2022, *Polycentricity, Markets and Firms* Dunstable (UK) 2021, *Institutional innovation and evolution, challenges to the modern world order* Catania (Italy) 2020, *Global Capitalism and Its National Varieties in an Era of Crisis* Loughborough (UK) 2019. **Publications** *Journal of Institutional Economics*.
Members Individuals in 49 countries and territories:
Argentina, Australia, Austria, Belgium, Bolivia, Bosnia-Herzegovina, Brazil, Bulgaria, Canada, Chile, China, Colombia, Czechia, Estonia, Finland, France, Germany, Greece, Hong Kong, Hungary, Iceland, India, Ireland, Israel, Italy, Japan, Korea Rep, Malaysia, Mexico, Netherlands, Nigeria, Norway, Peru, Philippines, Poland, Portugal, Romania, Russia, Serbia, Slovakia, South Africa, Spain, Sweden, Switzerland, Taiwan, Türkiye, UK, Uruguay, USA.
NGO Relations Partner of (1): *PCI Security Standards Council (PCI SSC)*. Partner of: national entities.
[2022.02.09/XM6506/**F**]

♦ World International Studies Committee (WISC) 21595

Exec Sec address not obtained. E-mail: executivesecretary@wiscnetwork.net – info@wiscnetwork.net.
URL: http://wiscnetwork.net/

History Original title: *International Studies Coordinating Committee*. Present name adopted 2001. 2017, registered in accordance with Swiss law. **Aims** Promote and advance knowledge of international studies worldwide. **Structure** General Meeting (annual). **Languages** English. **Staff** None. **Finance** Global International Studies Conference. **Activities** Events/meetings. **Events** *Global International Studies Conference* Buenos Aires (Argentina) 2022, *Global International Studies Conference* Cancún (Mexico) 2020, *Global International Studies Conference* Taipei (Taiwan) 2017, *Global International Studies Conference* Frankfurt-Main (Germany) 2014, *Global International Studies Conference* Porto (Portugal) 2011.
Members Associations in 23 countries and territories:
Argentina, Austria, Brazil, Chile, Colombia, Croatia, Finland, France, Germany, Hong Kong, Hungary, Israel, Italy, Japan, Korea Rep, Mexico, Philippines, Portugal, Russia, South Africa, Taiwan, Türkiye, UK.
International associations listed in this Yearbook (7);:
Asian Political and International Studies Association (APISA, #01669); *Central and East European International Studies Association (CEEISA, #03700)*; *European Consortium for Political Research (ECPR, #06762)*; *European International Studies Association (EISA, #07589)*; *International Studies Association (ISA, #15615)*; *Latin American Faculty of Social Sciences (#16316)*; *Nordic International Studies Association (NISA, #17325)*.
[2021/XE4449/y/**E**]

♦ World Interprofessional Education and Collaborative Practice Co-ordinating Committee / see Global Confederation for Interprofessional Education and Collaborative Practice (#10305)

♦ World Iodine Association (WIA) 21596

Dir Gen Rue Belliard 40, 1040 Brussels, Belgium. E-mail: info@worldiodineassociation.com.
URL: http://www.worldiodineassociation.com/

History Registration: No/ID: BE0642605402, Start date: Nov 2015, Belgium. **Aims** Support and represent iodine producers, processors, formulators, distributors and end users in relevant industry bodies, and in relevant official government bodies around the world with respect to guidelines and regulations on iodine and its derivatives. **Structure** Board of Directors; Scientific Advisory Board; Committees (3). **Languages** English. **Staff** 3.00 FTE, voluntary. **Finance** Members' dues. **Activities** Events/meetings. **Events** *Iodine in Food Systems and Health* Rotterdam (Netherlands) 2022, *Iodine in food systems and health* Pisa (Italy) 2017.
Members Effective; Associate. Membership countries not specified. Associate membership includes one organization listed in this Yearbook:
Associate membership includes one organization listed in this Yearbook:
European Salt Producers Association (EUsalt, #08425).
IGO Relations No formal contacts. **NGO Relations** No formal contacts. [2019/XM5589/y/**D**]

♦ World Islamic Association for Mental Health (no recent information)
♦ World Islamic Call Society (inactive)

♦ World Islamic Economic Forum Foundation (WIEF Foundation) 21597

Secretariat A-9-1 – Level 9, Hampshire Place Office, 157 Hampshire, No 1 Jalan Mayang Sari, 50450 Kuala Lumpur, Malaysia. T. +60321635500. Fax +60321635504. E-mail: enquiry@wief.org.
URL: http://www.wief.org/

History 6 Mar 2006. **Aims** Facilitate business amongst the Muslim World, promoting and encouraging profits eventually flowing down to neglected peoples. **Structure** Board of Trustees; International Advisory Panel. Permanent Secretariat. **Finance** Sources: members' dues. **Activities** Set up: WIEF Education Trust (WET); WIEF Businesswomen Network (WBN); WIEF Young Leaders Network (WYN); WIEF Roundtable Series. **Events** *Forum* Kuching (Malaysia) 2017, *Forum* Gangneung (Korea Rep) 2016, *Forum* Kuala Lumpur (Malaysia) 2015, *Round Table* Tokyo (Japan) 2015, *Forum* Dubai (United Arab Emirates) 2014. **Members** Honorary; Fellow; Corporate; Ordinary; Associate. Membership countries not specified. **IGO Relations** *Islamic Centre for Development of Trade (ICDT, #16035)*; *Islamic Development Bank (IsDB, #16044)*; *Islamic World Educational, Scientific and Cultural Organization (ICESCO, #16058)*; *Organisation of Islamic Cooperation (OIC, #17813)*. **NGO Relations** *Islamic Chamber of Commerce, Industry and Agriculture (ICCIA, #16036)*.
[2021/XJ7369/f/**F**]

♦ World Jammu and Kashmir Freedom Movement / see World Kashmir Freedom Movement (#21610)

♦ World Jersey Cattle Bureau (WJCB) 21598

Bureau mondial des éleveurs de bétail Jersey – Oficina Mundial de los Criadores de Ganado Jersey – Weltverband der Jersey Vienzüchter

Sec Adela Booth Associates, Higher Moorlake, Crediton, EX17 5EL, UK. T. +441363776403. Fax +441363774992. E-mail: secretary@wjcb.net.
Registered Office RJA and HS, Royal Jersey Showground, Jersey, Trinity, JE3 5JP, UK.
URL: http://www.worldjerseycattle.com/

History Founded 1949, Jersey (UK). Official foundation, 1951. Constitution adopted 4 Jul 1952, amended: 8 Jul 1959; 15 Feb 1965; Jul 1972; May 1979; Jul 1992; Apr 1999; Jun 2002. **Aims** Encourage good will and cooperation, generate research, promotion, education and coordination between individuals and organizations involved in enhancing the Jersey breed in all parts of the world; assist such individuals and organizations in promoting the interests of the Jersey breed, Jersey milk and meat; encourage and support individuals and organizations to discover, develop and utilize improved methods of breeding, feeding and management under varied agricultural conditions and by the use of the Jersey breed in the most constructive manner. **Structure** Conference and Bureau (every 3 to 4 years); Council (meets annually). Regions: Africa; Asia-Oceania; Europe; North-America; Latin America. **Languages** English. **Staff** 1.00 FTE, paid. **Finance** Sources: members' dues. **Activities** Awards/prizes/competitions; knowledge management/information dissemination. **Events** *Annual Meeting* South Africa 2026, *Triennial Conference* Denmark 2024, *Annual Meeting* Guatemala 2023, *Global Online Conference* Melbourne, VIC (Australia) 2022, *Annual Council Meeting* Rennes (France) 2022. **Publications** *The Dairy Queen – A History of the Jersey Breed Worldwide*. Annual report; conference reports; newsletters; journals.
Members National associations in 16 countries:
Argentina, Australia, Brazil, Canada, Colombia, Costa Rica, Denmark, Germany, Ireland, Italy, Jersey, New Zealand, South Africa, Switzerland, UK, USA.
Associate in 5 countries:
Czechia, France, Guatemala, Mexico, Uruguay.
Affiliate in 17 countries:
Albania, Chile, Czechia, Ecuador, Italy, Japan, Kenya, Mozambique, Netherlands, Nicaragua, Norway, Panama, Rwanda, Sweden, Venezuela, Zambia, Zimbabwe. [2017.03.08/XC3550/**C**]

♦ World Jewish Congress (WJC) 21599

Congrès juif mondial (CJM) – Congreso Judio Mundial – Jüdischer Weltkongress – Congresso Judaico Mundial – Congresso Ebraico Mondiale

CEO 501 Madison Ave, New York NY 10022, USA. T. +12127555770. E-mail: contactus@wjc.org.
URL: http://www.worldjewishcongress.org/

History 13 Aug 1936, Geneva (Switzerland). Founded as successor to *Committee of Jewish Delegations*, set up 1918. Initially set up to mobilize Jewish people and democratic forces against the Nazi onslaught. Registration: Switzerland; EU Transparency Register, No/ID: 603327942336-02, Start date: 19 Apr 2021. **Aims** Foster the unity and creative survival of the Jewish people and its spiritual, cultural and social heritage. To that end: secure the rights, status, and interests of Jews and Jewish communities everywhere and defend them wherever they are denied, violated, or imperilled; intensify the bonds of world Jewry with Israel as the central creative force in Jewish life and strengthen the ties of solidarity among Jewish communities everywhere; act on behalf of participating communities before governmental, intergovernmental and other international authorities on matters concerning the Jewish people; cooperate with all people on the basis of universal ideas of peace, freedom and justice. **Structure** Plenary Assembly (every 4 years); Governing Board (meets annually); Executive; Steering Committee. Regional Branches (5), each having some autonomy: North America; Latin America – *Latin American Jewish Congress (LAJC, #16344)*; Euro-Asia – *Euro-Asian Jewish Congress (EAJC, #05640)*; Europe – *European Jewish Congress (EJC, #07609)*; Israel. Research centre in Jerusalem (Israel): *Institute of the World Jewish Congress*. **Languages** English, French, German, Hebrew, Spanish, Yiddish. **Staff** 20.00 FTE, paid. **Finance** Sources: donations. **Activities** Financial and/or material support; networking/liaising; research/documentation. **Events** *Plenary Assembly* New York, NY (USA) 2021, *Plenary Assembly* New York, NY (USA) 2017, *Plenary Assembly* Budapest (Hungary) 2013, *Plenary Assembly* Jerusalem (Israel) 2013, *Meeting* Jerusalem (Israel) 2012. **Publications** *WJC Daily News Update* – New York NY (USA). Studies; research reports.
Members Membership open to all representative Jewish groups or communities, irrespective of the ideology of the government or social, political or economic system of the country in which they live. Affiliated Jewish communities and representative organizations in 95 countries and territories:
Argentina, Armenia, Aruba, Australia, Austria, Azerbaijan, Barbados, Belarus, Belgium, Bolivia, Bosnia-Herzegovina, Brazil, Bulgaria, Canada, Chile, Colombia, Congo Brazzaville, Costa Rica, Croatia, Cuba, Curaçao, Cyprus, Czechia, Denmark, Dominican Rep, Ecuador, Egypt, El Salvador, Estonia, Finland, France, Georgia, Germany, Gibraltar, Greece, Guatemala, Honduras, Hong Kong, Hungary, India, Ireland, Israel, Italy, Jamaica, Japan, Kazakhstan, Kenya, Kyrgyzstan, Latvia, Lithuania, Luxembourg, Malta, Martinique, Mexico, Moldova, Monaco, Mongolia, Montenegro, Morocco, Mozambique, Myanmar, Namibia, Netherlands, New Zealand, Nicaragua, North Macedonia, Norway, Panama, Paraguay, Peru, Philippines, Poland, Portugal, Romania, Russia, Serbia, Singapore, Slovakia, Slovenia, South Africa, Spain, Suriname, Sweden, Switzerland, Tajikistan, Thailand, Tunisia, Türkiye, UK, Ukraine, Uruguay, USA, Venezuela, Zambia, Zimbabwe.
Associated international organizations (8):
Anti-Defamation League of B'nai B'rith (ADL); *B'nai B'rith International (BBI, #03290)*; *Conference of European Rabbis (CER, #04598)*; *Hillel International (see: #03290)*; *International Council of Jewish Women (ICJW, #13036)*; *Women's International Zionist Organization (WIZO, #21030)*; *World Union of Jewish Students (WUJS, #21878)*; *World Zionist Organization (WZO, #21961)*.
Consultative Status Consultative status granted from: *ECOSOC (#05331)* (Special); *UNESCO (#20322)* (Associate Status); *UNICEF (#20332)*; *ILO (#11123)* (Special List). **IGO Relations** *WHO (#20950)*; *UNHCR (#20327)*. European Branch has consultative status with: *Council of Europe (CE, #04881)*. Official Cooperation with: *OAS (#17629)*. Contacts with: *European Union (EU, #08967)*; *NATO (#16945)*. Associated with Department of Global Communications of the United Nations. **NGO Relations** Member of (5): *Committee of NGOs on Human Rights, Geneva (#04275)*; *Fédération des Institutions Internationales établies à Genève (FIIG, #09599)*; *NGO Committee on Disarmament, Peace and Security, New York NY (#17106)*; *NGO Committee on the Status of Women, Geneva (#17117)*; *NGO Committee on UNICEF (#17120)*. Cooperates with (1): *G20 Interfaith Forum Association (IF20, #10055)*. Serves as officer on the Board of: *Conference of Non-Governmental Organizations in Consultative Relationship with the United Nations (CONGO, #04635)*. [2021/XC3552/y/**C**]

♦ World Jewish Migration Council (inactive)

♦ World Jewish Relief (WJR) 21600

Chief Exec Oscar Joseph House, 54 Crewys Road, London, NW2 2AD, UK. T. +442087361250. Fax +442087361259. E-mail: info@worldjewishrelief.org.
URL: http://www.worldjewishrelief.org/

History 1933, as *Central British Fund for German Jewry (CBF)*. originally to help Jews fleeing Nazi oppression. 1978, name changed to *Central British Fund for World Jewish Relief (CBF-WJR)*. 1995, present name adopted. Also referred to as *CBF World Jewish Relief*. UK Registered Charity: 290767. Absorbed *World Jewish Aid (WJAID, inactive)*, 2006. **Aims** Support the world's poorest Jewish communities. **Languages** English. **Staff** 30.00 FTE, paid. Voluntary. **Finance** Voluntary contributions of Anglo-Jewry. **Activities** Financial and/or material support; humanitarian/emergency aid. **Events** *European conference of holocaust research and documentation* Paris (France) 1997. **Consultative Status** Consultative status granted from: *ECOSOC (#05331)* (Special). **NGO Relations** Instrumental in setting up: *European Centre for Jewish Leadership (Le'atid Europe)*. Member of: *British Overseas NGO's for Development (BOND)*. [2019.04.24/XF3020/f/**F**]

♦ World Jewish Restitution Organization (WJRO) 21601

SG 5 Mapu St, 94189 Jerusalem, Israel. T. +97225612497. Fax +97225612496. E-mail: wjro@wjro.org.il.
URL: http://www.wjro.org.il/

History Founded 1992. **Aims** Reclaim Jewish properties in Europe confiscated during the Nazi occupation and Communist regimes. **Languages** English, Hebrew. **Staff** 5.00 FTE, paid. **Activities** Networking/liaising. Active in: Czechia, Hungary, Latvia, Lithuania, Poland, Romania, Slovakia. **Events** *International conference on confronting history* Jerusalem (Israel) 2002, *Conférence sur les biens dérobés aux Juifs par les Allemands durant la seconde guerre mondiale* London (UK) 1997.
Members Organizations, including 9 listed in this Yearbook:
Agudath Israel World Organization (AIWO, #00584); *American Jewish Joint Distribution Committee (JDC, #00785)*; *B'nai B'rith International (BBI, #03290)*; *Conference of European Rabbis (CER, #04598)*; *Conference on Jewish Material Claims Against Germany (Claims Conference, #04624)*; *European Council of Jewish Communities (ECJC, #06825)*; *European Jewish Congress (EJC, #07609)*; *World Jewish Congress (WJC, #21599)*; *World Zionist Organization (WZO, #21961)*. [2019.06.25/XD4963/y/**D**]

♦ World Jiu Jitsu Confederation (unconfirmed)

♦ World Journalism Education Council (WJEC) 21602

Chair Auckland Univ of Technology, 2 Governor Fitzroy Place, Auckland 1010, New Zealand. T. +64212316173. E-mail: contact@wjec.net.
Founding Chair Gaylord College, 395 W Lindsey, Room 3000, Norman OK 73019, USA. T. +14053252721.
URL: https://wjec.net/

History Jun 2007, Singapore (Singapore). Founded following 1st World Journalism Education Congress. **Aims** Provide a common space for journalism educators from around the world; focus on issues that are universal in the field. **Activities** Events/meetings. **Events** *World Journalism Education Congress* Beijing (China) / Shanghai (China) 2023, *Reimagining Journalism Education in the Age of Change* 2022, *World Journalism Education Congress* Paris (France) 2019, *World Journalism Education Congress* Auckland (New Zealand) 2016, *World Journalism Education Congress* Mechelen (Belgium) 2013.
Members Organizations (29) in 15 countries:
Australia, Brazil, Canada, China, Israel, Japan, Korea Rep, New Zealand, Nigeria, Philippines, Russia, Saudi Arabia, South Africa, UK, USA.
Regional organizations included in this Yearbook (9):
African Council for Communication Education (ACCE, #00273); *Arab-US Association for Communication Educators (AUSACE, #01072)*; *Asian Media Information and Communication Centre (AMIC, #01536)*; *Asociación Latinoamericana de Investigadores de la Comunicación (ALAIC, #02237)*; *European Journalism Training Association (EJTA, #07613)*; *Federación Latinoamericana de Facultades de Comunicación Social (FELAFACS, #09353)*; *International Association for Media and Communication Research (IAMCR, #12022)*; *International Communication Association (ICA, #12814)* (Journalism Division); *Théophraste Network (#20140)*.
[2022.10.11/XJ0768/y/**C**]

♦ World Journalists Conference (meeting series)
♦ World Judicial Commission (see: #21543)

♦ World Judo Federation (WJF) 21603

Contact Jungfrudansen 38, SE-171 56 Solna, Sweden. T. +46705270799. E-mail: worldjudofederation@gmail.com.
URL: http://www.wjfworldjudofederation.org/

History 2009. Constitute Congress 26 Aug 2011. **Aims** Promote Traditional Kodokan Judo worldwide with a foundation of mutual respect for all styles or systems. **Structure** Board of Directors. **Languages** English, French, Spanish. **Staff** 4.00 FTE, voluntary. **Finance** Sources: members' dues. **Activities** Sporting activities; training/education.
Members Full in 17 countries and territories:
Argentina, Australia, Belgium, Bolivia, Brazil, Bulgaria, Chile, Dominican Rep, Gibraltar, India, Panama, Romania, South Africa, Spain, Sweden, USA, Venezuela.
NGO Relations Member of: *The Association for International Sport for All (TAFISA, #02763)*; *International Martial Art Games Committee (IMGC, #14107)*. [2020.08.19/XJ6343/**C**]

♦ World Jump Rope Federation (inactive)

♦ World Jurist Association (WJA) 21604

Association mondiale de juristes – Asociación Mundial de Juristas
Worldwide Pres Jorge Juan 30, Planta 6ta, E-28001, Madrid, Spain. E-mail: wjadirector@gmail.com.
Home Office 1629 K St NW, Suite 300, Washington DC 20006, USA.
URL: http://www.worldjurist.org/

History 6 Jul 1963, Athens (Greece). Founded by more than 1,000 lawyers, jurists and legal scholars from over 100 nations in attendance at 'First World Conference on World Peace Through Law', following operations since 1957 as a special committee of the American Bar Association. Former names and other names: *World Peace Through Law Center (WPTLC)* – former; *Centre de la paix mondiale par le droit* – former; *Centro para la Paz Mundial Mediante el Derecho* – former. Registration: Department of Consumer and Regulatory Affairs, No/ID: 941571, Start date: 17 May 1994, End date: 30 Jun 2022, USA, District of Columbia. **Aims** Mobilize the international *legal profession* through voluntary international cooperation to build law rules and legal institutions to promote the rule of law; coordinate the development of international law as a requisite foundation for the establishment and maintenance of world law and order; act as a world centre for information and communication for the international legal profession; sponsor regional and world conferences on various aspects of public and private international law; promote projects and research to advance the development of international law; coordinate the computerization of law internationally. **Structure** Board of Directors: Worldwide President, Executive Vice-President, General Counsel and 5 Regional Presidents: Africa, Asia & the Pacific, Europe, North America, South America & The Caribbean; Executive Director; Representatives to the United Nations in NYC, Vienna and Geneva and to the International Criminal Court; 5 Regional Vice-Presidents (one per region); National Presidents in different countries around the world. **Languages** English, Spanish. **Staff** 4.00 FTE, paid; 40.00 FTE, voluntary. **Finance** Sources: contributions; donations; international organizations; members' dues; private foundations; revenue from activities/projects; sponsorship. Supported by: World Law Foundation. **Activities** Events/meetings; networking/liaising; research and development. **Events** *Biennial Conference* Barranquilla (Colombia) 2021, *Biennial Conference* Madrid (Spain) 2019, *Biennial Conference* Noord (Aruba) 2017, *Conference on the Internet Challenges to Peace and Freedom* Barcelona (Spain) 2016, *Biennial Conference* Jerusalem (Israel) / Tel Aviv (Israel) 2013.
Members Full: lawyers; jurists; legal scholars and students. Associate: non-members if the legal profession.
Members in 51 countries and territories:
Argentina, Austria, Bahamas, Bahrain, Belgium, Bolivia, Brazil, Canada, Chile, China, Colombia, Curaçao, Dominican Rep, Ecuador, El Salvador, France, Germany, Ghana, Guatemala, Guinea, Hong Kong, Hungary, India, Israel, Italy, Kenya, Korea Rep, Lebanon, Luxembourg, Mexico, Monaco, Morocco, Myanmar, Nigeria, Pakistan, Peru, Philippines, Poland, Portugal, Puerto Rico, Qatar, Romania, Russia, South Africa, Spain, Switzerland, UK, United Arab Emirates, Uruguay, USA, Venezuela.
Affiliated organizations (5):
Human Rights Institute of the World Jurist Association; *World Association of Judges (WAJ, #21150)*; *World Association of Law Professors (WALP, #21154)*; *World Association of Lawyers (WAL, #21155)*; *World Business Associates (WBA, #21253)*.
Consultative Status Consultative status granted from: *ECOSOC (#05331)* (Special); *ILO (#11123)* (Special List). **NGO Relations** Instrumental in setting up *World Association of Law Students (inactive)*.
[2021/XF3572/y/**F**]

♦ World Justice Group / see Al-Jihad (#00637)

♦ The World Justice Project (WJP) 21605

Washington Office 1025 Vermont Ave NW, Ste 1200, Washington DC 20005, USA. E-mail: wjp@worldjusticeproject.org.
URL: http://worldjusticeproject.org/

History 2006, by William H Neukom as a presidential initiative of *American Bar Association*. Transformed into an independent non-profit organization, 2010. Registration: EU Transparency Register, No/ID: 539713836884-33; USA. **Aims** Lead a global movement to strengthen the rule of law for the development of communities of opportunity and equity. **Structure** Board of Directors. Offices (4): Mexico; Singapore; USA. **Languages** English. **Staff** 14.00 FTE, paid. **Finance** Contributions from foundations, private sector corporations, companies, firms, associations, governments and individuals. Operating budget: US$ 4 million. **Activities** Programs (3): Research and Scholarship; Rule of Law Index; Mainstreaming. Organizes: World Justice Forum; regional outreach meetings; workshops; roundtable discussion series. **Events** *World Justice Forum* The Hague (Netherlands) 2017, *World Justice Forum* The Hague (Netherlands) 2013, *World Justice Forum* Barcelona (Spain) 2011, *World Justice Forum* Barcelona (Spain) 2011, *World Justice Forum* Vienna (Austria) 2009. **Publications** *Quarterly News Bulletin*. Annual Report. Reports; edited volumes. **Members** Not a membership organization. **Consultative Status** Consultative status granted from: *ECOSOC (#05331)* (Special).
NGO Relations Member of (2): *American Council for Voluntary International Action (InterAction)*; *InsideNGO (inactive)*.
Strategic partners include:
- *Arab Center for the Development of the Rule of Law and Integrity (ACRLI, #00912)*;
- *Avocats Sans Frontières (ASF, #03050)*;
- *Hague Institute for Innovation of Law (HIIL)*;
- *Human Rights First*;
- *Human Rights Watch (HRW, #10990)*;
- *Inter-American Bar Association (IABA, #11401)*;
- *Inter-Pacific Bar Association (IPBA, #15957)*;
- *International Bar Association (IBA, #12320)*;
- *International Chamber of Commerce (ICC, #12534)*;
- *International Institute for Applied Systems Analysis (IIASA, #13861)*;
- *International Organisation of Employers (IOE, #14428)*;
- *International Trade Union Confederation (ITUC, #15708)*;
- *Landesa – Rural Development Institute (Landesa)*;
- *Muslim Women Lawyers for Human Rights (KARAMAH)*;
- *NAFSA – Association of International Educators*;
- *People to People International (PTPI, #18300)*;
- *Transparency International (TI, #20223)*;
- *Union Internationale des Avocats (UIA, #20422)*;
- *World Council of Religious Leaders (WCRL, #21339)*;
- *World Federation of Engineering Organizations (WFEO, #21433)*;
- *World Federation of Public Health Associations (WFPHA, #21476)*;
- *World Leadership Alliance – Club de Madrid (WLA-CdM, #21619)*. [2020/XJ5596/**F**]

♦ World Kabaddi Federation (WKF) 21606

Pres G-104/4, Laxmi Park, Nanglo, Delhi 110041, DELHI 110041, India. E-mail: worldkabaddi@gmail.com.
URL: http://www.worldkabaddi.org/

History 1 Oct 2004. Approved 5 Dec 2003, Faridabad (India), during International Gold Cup Tournament. Registration: Ministry of Corporate Affairs Government of India, No/ID: U74999DL2005NPL141352, Start date: 2005, India. **Aims** Unite all Kabaddi organizations; sue Kabaddi *sport* to promote peace, harmony, understanding and cooperation amongst the world community. **Structure** General Assembly – World Congress; Council of Patrons; Executive Board; Council; Executive Committee; International Secretariat. Regional WKFs: Asia; Europe; America; Africa; Oceania.
Members National affiliates in 48 countries and territories:
Afghanistan, Argentina, Armenia, Australia, Austria, Bangladesh, Bhutan, Brazil, Cambodia, Canada, China, France, Gambia, Germany, Greece, Hong Kong, India, Indonesia, Iran Islamic Rep, Ireland, Italy, Japan, Korea Rep, Kyrgyzstan, Malaysia, Mongolia, Namibia, Nepal, Netherlands, New Zealand, Nigeria, Norway, Oman, Pakistan, Philippines, Senegal, Sierra Leone, Singapore, South Africa, Spain, Sri Lanka, Sweden, Taiwan, Thailand, Trinidad-Tobago, Turkmenistan, UK, USA.
Consultative Status Consultative status granted from: *ECOSOC (#05331)* (Special). **NGO Relations** Member of (3): *General Association of Asia Pacific Sports Federations (GAAPSF, #10106)*; *International Council of Sport Science and Physical Education (ICSSPE, #13077)*; *International Sport Network Organization (ISNO, #15592)*.
[2021.12.02/XJ9881/**D**]

♦ World Kalaripayattu Federation (unconfirmed)
♦ World Karate Association / see World Kickboxing and Karate Association (#21612)

♦ World Karate Confederation (WKC) 21607

Pres Terazije 13/V, Belgrade, PAK 11000, Serbia. T. +381652341168.
URL: http://www.wkc-org.net/

History 4 May 1996, Frankfurt-Main (Germany). **Aims** Regulate, spread and foster Karate worldwide. **Activities** Organizes championships. **Publications** *WKC Bulletin* (4 a year); *WKC Newsletter* (4-6 a year). **Members** Membership countries not specified. **NGO Relations** Member of: *The Association for International Sport for All (TAFISA, #02763)*; *International Martial Art Games Committee (IMGC, #14107)*.
[2020/XD9303/**D**]

♦ World Karate Federation / see World Karate Organization (#21609)

♦ World Karate Federation (WKF) 21608

Fédération mondiale de karaté (FMK)
Pres Avenida de Filipinas 50 – Escalera 2, First Floor – A, 28003 Madrid, Spain. T. +34915359632. Fax +34915359633. E-mail: wkf@wkf.net.
SG address not obtained.
URL: http://www.wkf.net/

History Oct 1970, Tokyo (Japan). Current name adopted, 1994, when taking over activities of *International Traditional Federation of Karate (ITFK, #15711)* and *World Union of Karatedo Organizations (WUKO, inactive)*. **Aims** Train athletes and develop their mental and physical health throughout the world by securing their participation in international karate activities; encourage good relations between member federations and their athletes around the world; protect the interests of karate throughout the world; develop and promulgate the techniques and spirit of karatedo (way of karate); work towards the acceptance of karate in the Olympic Games and other continental games. **Structure** Congress (every 2 years, during World Senior Karate Championships). Executive Committee, composed of President, Secretary General, Treasurer, 1st, 2nd and 3rd Vice-Presidents, Vice-President, Assistant General Secretary, Assistant Treasurer, Honorary President and 16 members. Commissions (11): Technical; Organizing; Disciplinary and Legal; Referee; Medical; Public Relations; Sports; Anti-Doping; Athletes; Gender Equity; Karate for Handicapped. WKF Continental Unions (4): *Asian Karatedo Federation (AKF, see: #21608)*; *European Karate Federation (EKF, #07624)*; *Oceania Karate Federation (see: #21608)*; *Union of African Karatedo Federations (UFAK, see: #21608)*. **Languages** English, French. **Activities** Awards/prizes/competitions; events/meetings; standards/guidelines. **Events** *Congress* Madrid (Spain) 2018, *Team Managers Meeting* Busan (Korea Rep) 2013, *Congress* Paris (France) 2012, *Congress / World Senior Championships and Congress* Belgrade (Serbia) 2010, *World Junior and Cadet Championships* Rabat (Morocco) 2009.
Members Full members in 204 countries and territories:
Afghanistan, Albania, Algeria, Andorra, Angola, Antigua-Barbuda, Argentina, Armenia, Aruba, Australia, Austria, Azerbaijan, Bahamas, Bahrain, Bangladesh, Barbados, Belarus, Belgium, Belize, Benin, Bermuda, Bhutan, Bolivia, Bosnia-Herzegovina, Botswana, Brazil, Brunei Darussalam, Bulgaria, Burkina Faso, Burundi, Cambodia, Cameroon, Canada, Cape Verde, Cayman Is, Central African Rep, Chad, Chile, China, Colombia, Comoros, Congo Brazzaville, Congo DR, Cook Is, Costa Rica, Côte d'Ivoire, Croatia, Cuba, Cyprus, Czechia, Denmark, Djibouti, Dominica, Dominican Rep, Ecuador, Egypt, El Salvador, England, Equatorial Guinea, Eritrea, Estonia, Eswatini, Ethiopia, Fiji, Finland, France, Gabon, Gambia, Georgia, Germany, Ghana, Greece, Grenada, Guam, Guatemala, Guinea, Guyana, Haiti, Honduras, Hong Kong, Hungary, Iceland, India, Indonesia, Iran Islamic Rep, Iraq, Ireland, Israel, Italy, Jamaica, Japan, Jordan, Kazakhstan, Kenya, Korea DPR, Kuwait, Kyrgyzstan, Laos, Latvia, Lebanon, Lesotho, Liberia, Libya, Liechtenstein, Lithuania, Luxembourg, Macau, Madagascar, Malawi, Malaysia, Maldives, Mali, Malta, Mauritania, Mauritius, Mexico, Micronesia FS, Moldova, Monaco, Mongolia, Montenegro, Morocco, Mozambique, Myanmar, Namibia, Nauru, Nepal, Netherlands, New Zealand, Nicaragua, Niger, Nigeria, North Macedonia, Northern Ireland, Norway, Oman, Pakistan, Palau, Palestine, Panama, Papua New Guinea, Paraguay, Peru, Philippines, Poland, Portugal, Puerto Rico, Qatar, Romania, Russia, Rwanda, Samoa, Samoa USA, San Marino, Sao Tomé-Principe, Saudi Arabia, Scotland, Senegal, Serbia, Seychelles, Sierra Leone, Singapore, Slovakia, Slovenia, Solomon Is, Somalia, South Africa, Spain, Sri Lanka, St Kitts-Nevis, St Lucia, St Vincent-Grenadines, Sudan, Suriname, Sweden, Switzerland, Syrian AR, Taiwan, Tajikistan, Tanzania UR, Thailand, Timor-Leste, Togo, Tonga, Trinidad-Tobago, Tunisia, Türkiye, Turkmenistan, Uganda, Ukraine, United Arab Emirates, Uruguay, USA, Uzbekistan, Vanuatu, Venezuela, Vietnam, Virgin Is UK, Virgin Is USA, Wales, Yemen, Zambia, Zimbabwe.
NGO Relations Member of (4): *Association of the IOC Recognized International Sports Federations (ARISF, #02767)*; *International Committee for Fair Play (#12769)*; *International World Games Association (IWGA, #15914)*; *Olympic Movement (#17719)*. Cooperates with (1): *International Testing Agency (ITA, #15678)*. Recognized by: *International Olympic Committee (IOC, #14408)*; *World Martial Arts Committee (WMAC, #21636)*. [2018/XC0123/**C**]

♦ World Karate Organization (WKO) 21609

Headquarters Shin-Ogawamachi 9-20 2F, Shinjuku-ku, Tokyo, 162-0814 Japan. T. +81332681494. Fax +81352613661.
URL: http://www.wko.or.jp/

History 1990, as *World Karate Federation*. Present name adopted 1993 on agreement with *World Karate Federation (WKF, #21608)*. **Activities** Organizes championships. **Events** *World congress / Congress* Lignano Sabbiadoro (Italy) 2000. [2019/XC0101/**D**]

♦ World Kashmir Freedom Movement (WKFM) 21610

Contact address not obtained. Fax +442078376638. E-mail: jfkclondon@gmail.com.
Pres address not obtained.

History 17 Jun 1990, by Dr Ayyub Thukar (died 2004). Also referred to as *World Jammu and Kashmir Freedom Movement*. An umbrella organization of groups working for the cause of Kashmir at international level. **Aims** Strive to enable the people of Jammu and Kashmir to exercise their right of self determination within the limits of the UN resolution agreed to by the governments of India and Pakistan; provide moral and material support to the freedom movement and coordinate efforts within and outside Kashmir; provide material relief to victims of repression and uphold and defend human rights of the people in the area. **Structure** General Assembly of up to 400 (every 2 years). Governing Council (meets at least once a year), comprising 11 members from Jammu and Kashmir and 4 from Azad Kashmir; numbers may be increased to 40. Executive Committee, consisting of President, Vice-President, Secretary-General, Finance Secretary, Publicity Secretary. Advisory Panel. Academic organ (which publishes newsletter): *International Institute of Kashmir Studies, London (no recent information)*. **Finance** Sources: members' contributions of 2% of their income; sale of publications; donations; fund-raising. Budget (annual): pounds50,000. **Events** *International meeting of Kashmiris and supporters of their cause / International Meeting* London (UK) 1995. **Publications** *Kashmir Report* (12 a year). *Kashmir Freedom Series. Facts about Kashmir*; *The Kashmir Resistance Movement*; *World Press on Kashmir* – in 3 vols. Books; pamphlets; conference proceedings; audio/video cassettes.
Members Organizations and individuals in 18 countries:
Australia, Bahrain, Bangladesh, Canada, Dubai, Egypt, France, Germany, India, Iran Islamic Rep, Malaysia, Netherlands, New Zealand, Norway, Pakistan, Saudi Arabia, UK, USA.
International offices (8) in 6 countries and territories:
Canada, Jammu and Kashmir, Pakistan, Saudi Arabia, United Arab Emirates, USA.
NGO Relations *Amnesty International (AI, #00801)*. [2008/XF2787/**F**]

♦ World Kettlebell Sport Federation (unconfirmed)
♦ World Kickboxing Association / see World Kickboxing and Karate Association (#21612)

♦ World Kickboxing Federation (WKF) 21611

Chief Exec Dir address not obtained. E-mail: office@wkfworld.com.
URL: http://www.wkfworld.com/

History 1965. **Aims** Promote the sport of kickboxing. **Structure** General Assembly; Board. **Languages** Arabic, English, Persian, Russian. **Finance** Sources: members' dues. **Activities** Events/meetings; sporting activities. **Events** *World Congress* Rockingham, WA (Australia) 2017, *General Assembly* Tbilisi (Georgia) 2007, *General Assembly* Tashkent (Uzbekistan) 2006, *General Assembly* Hamadan (Iran Islamic Rep) 2005, *General Assembly* Teheran (Iran Islamic Rep) 2003.
Members National federations in 60 countries and territories:
Afghanistan, Albania, Algeria, Andorra, Argentina, Armenia, Austria, Brazil, Bulgaria, Cameroon, Canada, Chile, China, Colombia, Cyprus, Czechia, Denmark, Ecuador, Egypt, England, Estonia, Ethiopia, France, Georgia, Germany, Ghana, Hungary, India, Iran Islamic Rep, Italy, Lebanon, Liechtenstein, Moldova, Mongolia, Morocco, Namibia, Nepal, Netherlands, Nigeria, Norway, Panama, Papua New Guinea, Poland, Portugal, Romania, Russia, Scotland, Serbia, Singapore, Slovakia, South Africa, South Sudan, Spain, Switzerland, Türkiye, UK, Ukraine, Uruguay, Venezuela, Wales. [2017/XM2560/**C**]

♦ World Kickboxing and Karate Association (WKA) 21612

Pres address not obtained. T. +3958861280. Fax +3958240851. E-mail: info@wkaassociation.it.
URL: https://wkainternational.com/

History 1977, as *World Karate Association*. Also referred to as *World Kickboxing Association*. **Events** *World Championship* Italy 2013, *World Championship* Orlando, FL (USA) 2012, *World Championship* Karlsruhe (Germany) 2011, *World Championship* Edinburgh (UK) 2010, *World Championship* Huelva (Spain) 2009.
Members Full in 78 countries and territories:
Afghanistan, Albania, Algeria, Argentina, Armenia, Australia, Austria, Belarus, Belgium, Bolivia, Bosnia-Herzegovina, Brazil, Bulgaria, Canada, Chile, China, Colombia, Costa Rica, Croatia, Cyprus, Czechia, Denmark, Egypt, England, Estonia, Finland, France, Georgia, Germany, Ghana, Greece, Guatemala, Hungary, India, Iran Islamic Rep, Iraq, Ireland, Israel, Italy, Kosovo, Kurdish area, Kuwait, Kyrgyzstan, Latvia, Lebanon, Liechtenstein, Lithuania, Malaysia, Malta, Mexico, Moldova, Mongolia, Montenegro, Morocco, New Zealand, Nigeria, North Macedonia, Northern Ireland, Panama, Peru, Poland, Portugal, Puerto Rico, Romania, Russia, San Marino, Scotland, Singapore, Slovakia, Slovenia, Spain, Sweden, Switzerland, Thailand, Uganda, Ukraine, USA, Wales.
NGO Relations Cooperates with: *World Traditional Kickboxing Association (WTKA, no recent information)*. [2022/XD4446/**D**]

♦ World Kickboxing League (unconfirmed)

♦ World Kindness Movement (WKM) 21613

Secretariat c/o Singapore Kindness Movement, 140 Hill Street – MICA Bldg 05-01, Singapore 170369, Singapore. T. +6568379885. Fax +6568379439. E-mail: kindness@kindness.sg.
URL: http://www.worldkindness.org.sg/

History 20 Sep 1997, Japan. Officially launched 18 Nov 2000, Singapore. **Aims** Inspire individuals towards greater kindness; connect nations to create a kinder world. **Activities** Organizes World Kindness Day, 13 Nov. **Events** *General Assembly* Sydney, NSW (Australia) 2014, *Random acts of kindness meeting* Singapore (Singapore) 2010, *Conference* Sydney, NSW (Australia) 2010, *Conference* Singapore (Singapore) 2007, *Conference* Parma (Italy) 2005.
Members Organizations (23) in 19 countries and territories:
Australia, Brazil, Canada, Dubai, France, India, Italy, Japan, Korea Rep, Nepal, Netherlands, New Zealand, Nigeria, Oman, Romania, Singapore, Thailand, UK, USA. [2011.06.28/XF6359/**F**]

♦ World Knowledge Forum (meeting series)

♦ World Kobudo Federation (WKF) 21614

Contact 21 Selkirk Str, Ottawa ON K1L 6N1, Canada. T. +16137469367. Fax +16137478805.
URL: http://www.worldkobudo.info/

History 1992. **Aims** Unite martial artists under one umbrella to raise the standards, quality and brotherhood for the overall advancement of Budo. **Activities** Events/meetings; training/education. **Events** *Convention* Gatineau, QC (Canada) 2014, *World convention* Gatineau, QC (Canada) 2006, *World Elite Budo Convention and Competition* Ottawa, ON (Canada) 2006, *World convention* Vienna (Austria) 2000. **Members** Schools involved in the study and promotion of Budo; martial arts practitioners involved in all disciplines, styles and ranks. Membership countries not specified. [2014/XD7671/**D**]

♦ World Kobudokan Federation (internationally oriented national body)
♦ World Labour Institute (internationally oriented national body)

♦ World Labour Zionist Movement (WLZM) 21615

Contact address not obtained. T. +97225671184 – +97225671189. Fax +97225671182.

History as *World Union of Zionist Socialist Parties – Ichud Olami*. **Aims** Incorporate Zionist- *Socialist* movements throughout the *Jewish* world and serve as an umbrella framework for coordinating their activities. **Structure** World Convention (every 4 years). World Bureau (meets annually – at the beginning of June) of 101 members. Secretariat, headed by Secretary General. Controllers Commission of 9 members. **Activities** Conducts a series of central activities in Israel and the world (in addition to the ongoing activities in different countries), such as: immigrant absorption; explaining the Labour Party's policies; training new leadership; publication of newspapers in various languages; religious and cultural pluralism; dialogue with the Diaspora; conferences and meetings; collecting of funds – especially in USA – to finance various projects in Israel. Affiliated organization: *NA'AMAT Movement of Working Women and Volunteers*. Founded, 1964, the *Moshe Sharett Institute for Education*. Current agenda: advance the Oslo (Norway) Peace Process initiated by the late Prime Minister Yitzhak Rabin; assure Jewish continuity as a religion, a culture and a nationality; advocate religious pluralism and equality in the community; advance women's equal participation in society, the economy and the political arena; fight for social justice and democracy in Israel and in Jewish communities all over the world. **Events** *Conference / World Conference* Jerusalem (Israel) 2002, *Meeting* Jerusalem (Israel) 2001.
Members Alliances, movements and other organizations in 36 countries:
Argentina, Australia, Austria, Belarus, Belgium, Brazil, Canada, Chile, Colombia, Denmark, France, Georgia, Germany, Hungary, India, Israel, Italy, Kazakhstan, Latvia, Mexico, Moldova, Netherlands, New Zealand, Peru, Romania, Russia, South Africa, Spain, Sweden, Switzerland, UK, Ukraine, Uruguay, USA, Uzbekistan, Venezuela.
NGO Relations Associated organization with: *Socialist International (SI, #19340)*. [2008/XE3579/**F**]

♦ World Lacrosse 21616

CEO 1295 Kelly Johnson Blvd, Suite 260, Colorado Springs CO 80920, USA. T. +17193745546. E-mail: info@worldlacrosse.sport.
URL: https://worldlacrosse.sport/

History Aug 2008. Founded on merger of *International Federation of Women's Lacrosse Associations (IFWLA, inactive)* and *International Lacrosse Federation (inactive)*. Former names and other names: *Federation of International Lacrosse (FIL)* – former (May 2019). **Aims** Develop lacrosse throughout the world to positively impact the lives of its participants and their communities. **Structure** General Assembly; Board of Directors. **Languages** English. **Staff** 4.00 FTE, paid. **Finance** Sources: donations; meeting proceeds; members' dues. **Activities** Sporting activities. **Events** *General Assembly* Guildford (UK) 2019.
Members Continental Federations (3); National Member nations (68):
Argentina, Australia, Austria, Barbados, Belgium, Bermuda, Bulgaria, Canada, Chile, China, Colombia, Costa Rica, Croatia, Czechia, Denmark, Dominican Rep, Ecuador, England, Estonia, Finland, France, Germany, Ghana, Greece, Guatemala, Haiti, Hong Kong, Hungary, Ireland, Iroquois/Haudenosaunee Nation, Israel, Italy, Jamaica, Japan, Kenya, Korea Rep, Latvia, Lithuania, Luxembourg, Malaysia, Mexico, Netherlands, New Zealand, Norway, Panama, Peru, Philippines, Poland, Portugal, Puerto Rico, Qatar, Russia, Scotland, Serbia, Singapore, Slovakia, Slovenia, Spain, Sweden, Switzerland, Taiwan, Thailand, Türkiye, Uganda, Ukraine, USA, Virgin Is USA, Wales.
Asia Pacific Lacrosse Union (APLU, #01941); *European Lacrosse Federation (ELF, #07637)*; *Pan-American Lacrosse Association (PALA, #18117)*.
NGO Relations Member of (4): *Alliance of Independent recognised Members of Sport (AIMS, #00690)* (Associate); *Association of the IOC Recognized International Sports Federations (ARISF, #02767)*; *International World Games Association (IWGA, #15914)*; *Olympic Movement (#17719)*. Cooperates with (1): *International Testing Agency (ITA, #15678)*. Recognized by: *International Olympic Committee (IOC, #14408)*. Allied with: *Fédération internationale d'inter-crosse (FIIC, #09640)*. [2021/XJ1868/**C**]

♦ World Ladies' Billiards and Snooker / see World Womens' Snooker (#21943)
♦ World Ladies' Billiards and Snooker Association / see World Womens' Snooker (#21943)

♦ World Lagomorph Society (WLS) 21617

Sec Univ of Natural Resources and Life Sciences, Gregor Mendel Str 33, 1180 Vienna, Austria. E-mail: wls@worldlagomorphsociety.org.
URL: http://www.worldlagomorphsociety.org/

Aims Intensify communication between those interested in the research, management and conservation of lagomorphs (rabbits, hares and pikas). **Structure** Board of Directors, comprising President, Vice-President, Secretary, Vice-Secretary, Treasurer, Vice-Treasurer and 2 Auditors. **Events** *World Lagomorph Conference* Turlock, CA (USA) 2016, *Conference / World Lagomorph Conference* Vienna (Austria) 2012, *World Lagomorph Conference* Morelia (Mexico) 2008, *World Lagomorph Conference* Vila do Conde (Portugal) 2004. [2013/XJ6618/**C**]

♦ World Land Trust (internationally oriented national body)
♦ World Land Trust-US / see Rainforest Trust
♦ World Law Fund / see World Policy Institute

♦ World Law Group (WLG) 21618

Sec One Metro Center, 700 12th St NW, Ste 700, Washington DC 20005, USA. T. +12029042477. E-mail: info@theworldlawgroup.com.
Pres address not obtained.
URL: http://www.theworldlawgroup.com/

History 1988. **Aims** As a network of independent law firms, provide focused, cost-effective legal service and advice to international clients worldwide. **Structure** Board of Directors, including President, Secretary and Treasurer. **Events** *Spring Conference* Chiang Mai (Thailand) 2016, *Spring Conference* Seoul (Korea Rep) 2011, *Conference* Vienna (Austria) 2005, *Half-yearly meeting* Glasgow (UK) 2002, *Half-yearly conference / Half-Yearly Meeting* Chicago, IL (USA) 2001. **Publications** *World Law Group Newsletter*.
Members Independent law firms (46) in 33 countries and territories:
Argentina, Australia, Austria, Belgium, Brazil, Canada, Chile, Denmark, France, Germany, Greece, Hong Kong, India, Ireland, Israel, Italy, Japan, Korea Rep, Malaysia, Mexico, Netherlands, Norway, Peru, Philippines, Portugal, Singapore, South Africa, Spain, Sweden, Switzerland, Taiwan, UK, USA. [2020/XF5902/**F**]

♦ World Lawyers Sport Association (inactive)

♦ World Leadership Alliance – Club de Madrid (WLA-CdM) 21619

Contact Palacio del Marqués, Calle Mayor 69, Planta 1, 28013 Madrid, Spain. T. +34911548230. Fax +34911548240. E-mail: clubmadrid@clubmadrid.org.
URL: http://www.clubmadrid.org/

History Oct 2001, Madrid (Spain), during the Conference on Democratic Transition and Consolidation, as *Club de Madrid*. Previously also referred to as *Club of Madrid*. EU Transparency Register: 968421535984-01. **Aims** Bring change for institutional and leadership strengthening, development and the wellbeing of citizens. **Structure** General Assembly (annual, in Madrid, Spain), composed of former Heads of State or Government, Presidents and one member each of *Fundación para las Relaciones Internacionales y el Dialogo Exterior (FRIDE, inactive)* and Gorbachev Foundation of North America (GFNA), and Secretary-General. Board of Directors; Advisory Committee of 16 members. **Languages** English, Spanish. **Staff** 7.00 FTE, paid. **Finance** Founder of the Club, Diego Hidalgo provided seed capital. Sponsored by partners, including the following listed in this Yearbook: *Agencia Española de Cooperación Internacional para el Desarrollo (AECID)*; *Development Bank of Latin America (CAF, #05055)*; *Better World Fund*; *Canadian International Development Agency (CIDA, inactive)*; *Department for International Development (DFID, inactive)*; *European Commission (EC, #06633)*; *Rockefeller Brothers Fund (RBF)*; *UNDP (#20292)*; *United Nations Democracy Fund (UNDEF, #20551)*. **Activities** Identifies and develops practical recommendations, action plans and implementation strategies to advance democratic development, through: consolidation of democratic values, practices, institutions, leadership and governance; promotion of sustainable, socio-economic development through democratic means including participation, consensus-building, transparency and accountability. Works with political leaders and civil society to strengthen governance and build more effective public policies; works with partners worldwide on democratizing international financial institutions, on democratic responses to terrorism, on leadership for climate change and energy challenges, on promoting dialogue and social inclusion and on analysing and formulating recommendations on the political dimensions of the world economic crisis from different regional and national perspectives. Priorities 2009-2011: Shared Societies Project – Leadership for Dialogue, Diversity and Social Cohesion; Energy and Democratic Leadership Programme. **Events** *General Assembly and Conference* Lisbon (Portugal) 2018, *Annual Meeting* Jeju (Korea Rep) 2016, *General Assembly and Conference* Madrid (Spain) 2015, *General Assembly and Conference* Florence (Italy) 2014, *General Assembly and Conference* Coolum, QLD (Australia) 2013. **Publications** Booklets; reports.
Members Democratic former Heads of State and Government (70) in 51 countries:
Albania, Argentina, Bolivia, Bosnia-Herzegovina, Botswana, Brazil, Bulgaria, Canada, Cape Verde, Chile, Colombia, Costa Rica, Czechia, Denmark, Dominican Rep, Ecuador, Finland, France, Germany, Guatemala, Iceland, India, Ireland, Italy, Jamaica, Korea Rep, Latvia, Lithuania, Mali, Mauritius, Mexico, Mozambique, Netherlands, New Zealand, Norway, Peru, Philippines, Poland, Portugal, Romania, Russia, Slovenia, Spain, Sri Lanka, Sudan, Sweden, Tanzania UR, Thailand, Uruguay, USA, Yemen.
Consultative Status Consultative status granted from: *ECOSOC (#05331)* (Special). **IGO Relations** Associated with: *UNDP (#20292)*. Formal partnership agreement with: *United Nations Democracy Fund (UNDEF, #20551)*. Accredited organization of: *Green Climate Fund (GCF, #10714)*. Programming Partners: *Community of Democracies (CD, #04394)*; *International Institute for Democracy and Electoral Assistance (International IDEA, #13872)*; *OECD (#17693)*. **NGO Relations** Programming Partners: *Bertelsmann Foundation*; *Casa Asia*; *Globe International*; *Hellenic Foundation for European and Foreign Policy (ELIAMEP)*; *National Democratic Institute for International Affairs (NDIIA)*; *National Endowment for Democracy (NED)*; national organizations; *United Nations Foundation (UNF, #20563)*; *William J Clinton Foundation*. Member of: *European Partnership for Democracy (EPD, #08156)*. [2019/XF6957/v/**F**]

♦ World Leading Schools Association (WLSA) 21620

Contact Binderij 7F, 1185 ZH Amstelveen, Netherlands. T. +31206403803. E-mail: admin@wlsafoundation.org – info@wlsafoundation.org.
URL: http://www.wlsafoundation.org/

History Former names and other names: *WLSA Foundation* – alias. **Aims** Provide transformative cross-cultural experiences that are accessible to all, nurture future global leaders and lead change in education. **Structure** Executive Board; Council Board. **Activities** Events/meetings; training/education. **Events** *Global Educators Conference* Prague (Czechia) 2019, *Conference* Jeju (Korea Rep) 2018. [2021.09.21/XM8299/**F**]

♦ World League of Esperanto-Speaking Students (inactive)

♦ World League for Freedom and Democracy (WLFD) 21621
Ligue mondiale de la liberté et de la démocratie
Contact 10F1 – 7 Roosevelt Rd, Sec 1, Taipei 100, Taiwan. T. +886233932002. Fax +886233932960. E-mail: wlfd.roc@msa.hinet.net.
URL: http://www.wlfdroc.org.tw/
History 3 Nov 1966, Seoul (Korea Rep), as *World Anti-Communist League (WACL)*, at 12th Conference of the then *'Asian Peoples Anti-Communist League'*, currently *Asian-Pacific League for Freedom and Democracy (APLFD, #01617)*. Present name adopted at WACL Annual Conference, 23 Jul 1990, Brussels (Belgium). Charter adopted 8 Nov 1966, Seoul; revised at: 17 Sep 1970, Kyoto (Japan); 25 Apr 1975, Rio de Janeiro (Brazil); 2 Aug 1981, Taipei (Taiwan); 17 Aug 1987, Taipei; 1991, San José (Costa Rica). **Aims** Disseminate worldwide the ideals of freedom and democracy; encourage and support their universal application; promote respect for and observance of human rights and fundamental freedoms for all peoples; act as agent and coordinating centre for international cooperation in economic development and educational and cultural exchange aimed at contributing to social progress and better living standards; combine efforts against aggression, imperialism, totalitarianism and authoritarianism of whatever form and pretension, whenever and wherever any of such forces appears. **Structure** General Conference (annual). Executive Board, elected by and from regular members plus (ex officio) President, Secretary General and Chairman of General Conference. Permanent Secretariat, headed by Secretary General. **Languages** English. **Staff** 1.00 FTE, paid. Voluntary. **Finance** Members' dues. Special contributions. **Activities** Organizes: Annual General Conference; Annual Event of the World Freedom Day; International Academic Symposium. Organizes, sponsors or co-sponsors occasional exchanges, missions and symposia. Instrumental in setting up: *Asian Pacific Youth League for Freedom and Democracy (APYLFD, inactive)*; *World Youth League for Freedom and Democracy (WYLFD, inactive)*. **Events** *Annual General Conference* Berlin (Germany) 2015, *Annual General Conference* Taipei (Taiwan) 2014, *Annual General Conference* Taipei (Taiwan) 2013, *Conference* Incheon (Korea Rep) 2010, *Annual General Conference* Manila (Philippines) 2009. **Publications** *WLFD Newsletter* (12 a year); *Freedom Digest* (4 a year). Books; proceedings.
Members National members in 83 countries and territories:
Argentina, Australia, Bahrain, Bangladesh, Belgium, Benin, Bolivia, Brazil, Bulgaria, Canada, Chile, Colombia, Congo DR, Costa Rica, Croatia, Denmark, Dominica, Ecuador, Estonia, Eswatini, Ethiopia, Fiji, Finland, France, Gambia, Germany, Ghana, Greece, Guam, Guinea, Hungary, India, Indonesia, Ireland, Italy, Japan, Jordan, Kenya, Korea Rep, Lithuania, Luxembourg, Malaysia, Malta, Mauritius, Mongolia, Morocco, Nepal, New Zealand, Nigeria, Norway, Oman, Pakistan, Palau, Paraguay, Peru, Philippines, Poland, Portugal, Romania, Russia, Samoa USA, Saudi Arabia, Seychelles, Sierra Leone, Singapore, Solomon Is, South Africa, Spain, Sri Lanka, Sweden, Switzerland, Taiwan, Tanzania UR, Thailand, Togo, Tonga, Türkiye, UK, Ukraine, Uruguay, USA, Vanuatu, Venezuela.
Regional Organizations (6):
African Organization for Freedom and Democracy (AOFD, no recent information); Asian-Pacific League for Freedom and Democracy (APLFD); *European Council for World Freedom (ECWF, no recent information)*; *Federación de Entidades Democraticas de América Latina (FEDAL, no recent information)*; *Middle East Solidarity Council (MESC, no recent information)*; *North American Federation for Freedom and Democracy (NAFFD, no recent information)*.
International Organization Member Units (8):
Asian Christian Association (ACA, no recent information); *Assembly of the Block of Nations in Europe and Asia for Freedom and Democracy (ABN, no recent information)*; *Association of Nordic War and UN Military Veterans (ANWUNMV, #02834)*; *Free Pacific Association (FPA, no recent information)*; *International Conference on Political Warfare of the Soviet (CIGP)*; National Union for Total Independence of Angola (UNITA); *World Christian Anti-Communist Association (WCACA, no recent information)*; World Youth League for Freedom and Democracy (WYLFD).
Associate Member Units (10), including 3 organizations listed in this Yearbook:
Baltic Freedom Council (BFC, no recent information); *Grupo Internacional Antimarxista Español (GIAE, no recent information)*; *World Buddhist Sangha Council (WBSC, #21248)*.
IGO Relations Associated with Department of Global Communications of the United Nations.
[2013/XF3454/y/**F**]

♦ World League for the Protection of Animals (inactive)
♦ World Learning (internationally oriented national body)

♦ World Lebanese Cultural Union (WLCU) 21622
Union libanaise culturelle mondiale – Union libanesa Cultural Mundial – União Libanese Cultural Mundial (ULCM) – Al Jami'a al Lubnaaniyya al Sakafiyya fil 'Aalam
World SG address not obtained. E-mail: lebanon.office@wlcu.world.
URL: https://wlcu.world/
History 1959, Mexico City (Mexico). Recognized as the sole representative of the Lebanese Diaspora in the world. Unlimited duration. Current constitution approved, 1993. Amended: 1994, Sao Paulo (Brazil); 2001, Mexico City (Mexico); 2003, Miami FL (USA); 2005, Sydney (Australia); 2009, Mexico City (Mexico); 2012, Mexico City (Mexico); 2014, Buenos Aires (Argentina). **Aims** Enhance, promote and foster the spirit of allegiance and patriotism among members throughout the countries in which they live. **Structure** World Conference; World Council; World Secretariat General; International Relations Committee; Board of Trustees; World Council for Youth Descendants of Lebanese Origin; Committees (5). **Languages** Arabic, English, French, Lebanese, Portuguese, Spanish. **Staff** 1.00 FTE, voluntary. **Finance** Members' dues. Donations. **Activities** Financial and/or material support; awards/prizes/competitions; events/meetings. **Events** *World Congress* Paris (France) 2018, *World Congress* Buenos Aires (Argentina) 2014, *World Congress* Mexico City (Mexico) 2012, *World Congress* Mexico City (Mexico) 2009, *World meeting* Mexico City (Mexico) 2007. **Publications** *The Lebanese Heritage* (annual) in Arabic, English, French.
Members Branches, clubs, societies, confederations, institutions and unions of professionals of Lebanese origin in 28 countries:
Argentina, Australia, Belgium, Benin, Bolivia, Brazil, Burkina Faso, Canada, Chile, Colombia, Costa Rica, Cyprus, Ecuador, France, Germany, Ghana, Italy, Mexico, Netherlands, New Zealand, Nigeria, South Africa, Sweden, Switzerland, UK, Uruguay, USA, Venezuela.
Consultative Status Consultative status granted from: *ECOSOC (#05331)* (Special). **IGO Relations** Associated with Department of Global Communications of the United Nations. [2019/XE9026/**E**]

♦ World Legal Medicine Association 21623
SG Catedra de Medicina Legal y Deontologia Médica, Fac de Medicina, Universidad de Buenos Aires, Paraguay 2155, Buenos Aires, Argentina.
Events *Congrès mondial d'évaluation du dommage corporel / Congress* Buenos Aires (Argentina) 2006.
[2011/XM2077/**D**]

♦ WorldLeish – World Congress on Leishmaniasis (meeting series)
♦ WORLDLEISH – World Congress on Leishmaniosis (meeting series)

♦ World Leisure Organization (WLO) 21624
Communications Officer Arenal 1, Segunda Planta, 48005 Bilbao, Biscay, Spain. T. +34946056151. E-mail: secretariat@worldleisure.org.
URL: http://www.worldleisure.org/
History 1952, Philadelphia, PA (USA). Former names and other names: *International Recreation Association (IRA)* – former (3 Oct 1952 to 1973); *World Leisure and Recreation Association (WLRA)* – former (1973); *Organización Mundial del Ocio* – former; *Association mondiale pour les loisirs et la récréation* – former; *Asociación Mundial de Tiempo Libre y Recreación* – former. **Aims** Discover and foster those conditions best permitting leisure to serve as a force for human growth, development and well-being. **Structure** Board of Directors; Executive Committee; Scientific and Technical Secretariat, led by Chief Operating Officer. **Languages** English. **Activities** Advocacy/lobbying/activism; events/meetings; knowledge management/information dissemination; publishing activities; research/documentation; training/education. **Events** *World Leisure Congress* 2028, *World Leisure Congress* 2026, *World Leisure Congress* Rotterdam (Netherlands) / Breda (Netherlands) 2025, *World Leisure Congress* Dunedin (New Zealand) 2023, *World Leisure Congress* Beijing (China) 2021. **Publications** *WL News* (12 a year); *World Leisure Journal* (4 a year). **Members** Membership countries not specified. **Consultative Status** Consultative status granted from: *ECOSOC (#05331)* (Special); *ILO (#11123)* (Special List); *UNEP (#20299)*; *UNICEF (#20332)*. **IGO Relations** Member of (1): *World Tourism Organization (UNWTO, #21861)* (as Affiliate member). [2022.12.01/XB2404/y/**B**]

♦ World Leisure and Recreation Association / see World Leisure Organization (#21624)
♦ World Liberal Union / see Liberal International (#16454)
♦ World Life Sciences Forum (unconfirmed)
♦ World Light Electric Vehicle Summit (meeting series)

♦ World Likud 21625
Likud Olami
Chairman Headquarters, 38 King George St, 61231 Tel Aviv, Israel. T. +97236295017. E-mail: office@worldlikud.org.il.
URL: http://www.worldlikud.org.il/
History 1992, by merger of *World Executive of Herut-Hatzohar (inactive)* and *World Union of General Zionists (inactive)*.
Members Associations (16) in 25 countries:
Argentina, Belgium, Brazil, Canada, Chile, Colombia, France, Hungary, Israel, Italy, Luxembourg, Mexico, Panama, Peru, Portugal, Russia, South Africa, Spain, Sweden, Switzerland, UK, Ukraine, Uruguay, USA, Venezuela.
NGO Relations *Betar (#03217)*. [2012/XE1894/**E**]

♦ World Link for Law 21626
Contact Firth Associates, Higher Bojorrow, Garras, Helston, TR12 6LN, UK. T. +447736234880. E-mail: info@worldlink-law.com.
Registered Office Bahnhofstrasse 70, 8021 Zurich ZH, Switzerland.
URL: http://www.worldlink-law.com/
History Founded 1989, as *Euro-Link for Lawyers*. Registered in accordance with Swiss Civil Code. **Aims** Help businesses achieve their international commercial objectives by providing relevant legal solutions. **Structure** Board. Administrative Service in UK; Regional Centres for Asia; North America; South America. **Finance** Sources: members' dues. **Events** *Conference* Dubai (United Arab Emirates) 2019, *Conference* Copenhagen (Denmark) 2018. **Members** Independent law firms (70) in 56 countries. Membership countries not specified.
[2019.03.28/XM7544/**C**]

♦ The World Lin's Association (internationally oriented national body)
♦ World Literacy / see World Education
♦ World Literacy Council (internationally oriented national body)

♦ World Literacy Foundation 21627
CEO address not obtained. E-mail: info@worldliteracyfoundation.org.
Americas address not obtained. T. +14152605569.
Asia/Australia PO Box 532, Melbourne VIC SOUTH 3205, Australia. T. +61399950079.
UK/Europe 19 Ladbroke Crescent, London, W11 1PS, UK.
URL: http://worldliteracyfoundation.org/
History 2003. **Aims** Lift children and youth out of *poverty* by delivering effective and sustainable programs aimed at eradicating illiteracy. **Languages** English, French, Spanish. **Staff** 5.00 FTE, paid. **Finance** Donations from: Community; Corporate; Sector; Foundations. Budget (annual): US$ 600,000. **Activities** Events/meetings. Active in: USA; UK; Australia; Asia; South Amercia; Africa. **Events** *World Literacy Summit* Oxford (UK) 2023, *World Literacy Summit* Oxford (UK) 2020, *World Literacy Summit* Oxford (UK) 2018, *World Literacy Summit* Oxford (UK) 2014, *World Literacy Summit* Oxford (UK) 2012. **NGO Relations** *Project Literacy (inactive)*.
[2016.06.01/XJ9349/f/**F**]

♦ World Literacy Initiative (internationally oriented national body)
♦ World Literature Association (unconfirmed)
♦ WorldLoop (internationally oriented national body)

♦ World Lottery Association (WLA) 21628
Association mondiale de loterie – Asociación Mundial de Loteria – Weltvereinigung der Lotterien
Pres c/o TN Lottery, One Century Pl, 26 Century Blvd, Ste 200, Nashville TN 37214, USA. T. +16153246500.
URL: https://www.world-lotteries.org/
History Aug 1999. Founded by merger of *International Association of State Lotteries (AILE, inactive)* and *International Association of Toto and Lotto Organizations (INTERTOTO, inactive)*. Registration: Switzerland. **Aims** Be recognized as the global authority on the lottery business; uphold the highest ethical principles; support members in achieving their vision for their own communities. **Structure** General Meeting (every 2 years); Executive Committee; Committees; Working Groups. **Languages** English, French, German, Spanish. **Staff** 6.00 FTE, paid. **Finance** Sources: members' dues. **Activities** Events/meetings; training/education. **Events** *World Lottery Summit* Vancouver, BC (Canada) 2022, *Legal and Tax Seminar* Abidjan (Côte d'Ivoire) 2019, *Joint CSR Responsible Gaming Seminar* Dubrovnik (Croatia) 2019, *Security and Integrity Seminar* Ljubljana (Slovenia) 2019, *Joint Sports Betting Seminar* Madrid (Spain) 2019. **Publications** *WLA Magazine*. *WLA Global Lottery Data Compendium*.
Members Regular: state-controlled lotteries (151) in 84 countries and territories:
Argentina, Australia, Austria, Belarus, Belgium, Benin, Bosnia-Herzegovina, Brazil, Bulgaria, Burkina Faso, Canada, Chile, China, Colombia, Congo Brazzaville, Côte d'Ivoire, Croatia, Cyprus, Czechia, Denmark, Ecuador, Estonia, Ethiopia, Finland, France, Georgia, Germany, Ghana, Gibraltar, Greece, Honduras, Hong Kong, Hungary, Iceland, India, Ireland, Israel, Italy, Japan, Korea Rep, Latvia, Lebanon, Liberia, Lithuania, Luxembourg, Malaysia, Malta, Mauritius, Mexico, Moldova, Morocco, Netherlands, New Zealand, Niger, Norway, Panama, Peru, Philippines, Poland, Polynesia Fr, Portugal, Romania, Russia, Senegal, Serbia, Singapore, Slovakia, Slovenia, South Africa, Spain, Sri Lanka, St Lucia, Sweden, Switzerland, Tanzania UR, Thailand, Togo, Trinidad-Tobago, Türkiye, UK, Ukraine, Uruguay, USA, Vietnam.
Associate: organizations (74) supplying goods and services in 29 countries and territories:
Australia, Austria, Brazil, Canada, China, Cyprus, Czechia, France, Germany, Greece, Hong Kong, Iceland, India, Ireland, Isle of Man, Israel, Japan, Lithuania, Luxembourg, Malta, Netherlands, Norway, Poland, Spain, Sweden, Switzerland, Türkiye, UK, USA.
Regional associations (5):
Asia Pacific Lottery Association Limited (APLA, #01949); *Association des Loteries d'Afrique (ALA, #02791)*; *Corporación Iberoamericana de Loterias y Apuestas de Estado (CIBELAE, #04838)*; *European State Lotteries and Toto Association (#08833)*; *North American Association of State and Provincial Lotteries (NASPL)*.
[2019/XB0010/y/**B**]

♦ World LP Gas Association / see World LPG Association (#21629)

♦ World LPG Association (WLPGA) 21629
Association mondiale des GPL – Asociación Mundial de los GLP
CEO 182 av Charles de Gaulle, 92200 Neuilly-sur-Seine, France. T. +33178991330. Fax +33178991331. E-mail: association@worldlpgas.com.
URL: http://www.wlpga.org/
History 19 Jun 1987, Dublin (Ireland). Statutes modified: 13 Apr 1996; 21 Oct 1998; Oct 2000; 14 Sep 2005; Sep 2011. Former names and other names: *World LPG Forum (WLPGF)* – former (19 Jun 1987 to 1997); *Forum mondial des GPL* – former (19 Jun 1987 to 1997); *Foro Mundial de los GLP* – former (19 Jun 1987 to 1997); *World LP Gas Association* – alias. Registration: France. **Aims** Add value to the sector through driving premium demand for LPG while also promoting compliance to good business and safety practices. **Structure** Ordinary General Assembly (annual, held during the annual Forum); Board of Directors. **Languages** English, French, Spanish. **Staff** 9.00 FTE, paid. **Finance** Members'dues. **Activities** Events/meetings; knowledge management/information dissemination. **Events** *LPG Week 2022* New Delhi (India) 2022, *LPG Week 2021* Dubai (United Arab Emirates) 2021, *Annual Forum and General Assembly* Amsterdam (Netherlands) 2019, *Annual Forum and General Assembly* Houston, TX (USA) 2018, *Annual Forum and General Assembly* Marrakech (Morocco) 2017. **Publications** *WLPGA Newsletter* (6 a year); *Statistical Review of Global LP Gas* (annual). Annual Report; reports; studies; brochures; leaflets; video case studies. **Members** LPG companies; multinationals; shippers; distributors; equipment manufacturers; local and regional associations. Full and Observer (over 250). Membership countries not specified. **Consultative Status** Consultative status granted from: *UNIDO (#20336)*. **IGO Relations** Consultative Status with: *United Nations Economic Commission for Europe (UNECE, #20555)*. Cooperates with: *International Bank for Reconstruction and Development (IBRD, #12317)* (World Bank); *International Energy Agency (IEA, #13270)*; *International Maritime Organization (IMO, #14102)*; *UNDP (#20292)*; *United Nations Framework Convention on Climate Change – Secretariat (UNFCCC, #20564)*. Member of: *International Oil Pollution Compensation Funds (IOPC Funds, #14402)*. **NGO Relations** Cooperates with: *International Organization for Standardization (ISO, #14473)*. [2022/XF1964/**F**]

♦ World LPG Forum / see World LPG Association (#21629)
♦ World Lung Foundation / see Vital Strategies

♦ World Lupus Federation (WLF) 21630

Contact c/o Lupus Foundation, 2121 K St NW, Ste 200, Washington DC 20037, USA. E-mail: donnelly@lupus.org.
URL: http://worldlupusfederation.org/

History 2015. Founded in collaboration with Lupus Foundation of America and *LUPUS EUROPE (#16524)*. An unincorporated nonprofit association. **Aims** Improve the quality of life for all people living with lupus. **Structure** A federation of separately organized global lupus groups. **Languages** English. **Staff** Lupus Foundation of America provides staffing support as necessary. **Finance** Sources: grants; private foundations. **Activities** Advocacy/lobbying/activism; awareness raising.
Members Full in 81 countries and territories:
Argentina, Australia, Bahamas, Bangladesh, Barbados, Belgium, Belize, Bermuda, Bolivia, Brazil, Canada, Chile, Colombia, Costa Rica, Cyprus, Czechia, Denmark, Dominica, Ecuador, Egypt, El Salvador, Estonia, Finland, France, Gabon, Germany, Ghana, Greece, Grenada, Guam, Guatemala, Honduras, Hong Kong, Hungary, Iceland, India, Indonesia, Iran Islamic Rep, Ireland, Israel, Italy, Jamaica, Japan, Kenya, Korea Rep, Kuwait, Lebanon, Lithuania, Malaysia, Mauritius, Mexico, Nepal, Netherlands, New Zealand, Nicaragua, Nigeria, Norway, Panama, Paraguay, Peru, Philippines, Poland, Portugal, Puerto Rico, Romania, Singapore, Slovakia, Slovenia, South Africa, Spain, St Lucia, Sweden, Switzerland, Taiwan, Trinidad-Tobago, Uganda, UK, Uruguay, USA, Venezuela, Zimbabwe. [2021.02.23/XM7419/**C**]

♦ World Malayalee Council (WMC) 21631

Gen Sec WMC Center, Peedikayil Chambers, Ulloor, Thiruvananthapuram, Kerala 695011, Thiruvananthapuram KERALA 695011, India. T. +919448064430. E-mail: globalgeneralsecretary@worldmalayalee.org.
Chairman address not obtained. T. +919841010592.
URL: http://www.worldmalayalee.org/

History Apr 1995. **Aims** Provide a non-political forum to bring together the people of Malayalee/Kerala/Indian origin; strengthen the common bonds of culture, *tradition* and way of life. **Structure** General Council; Executive Council; Cabinet. Regional Councils (6): America; Europe; Far-East/Australia; India; Middle-East; Africa. Provincial Councils (40) in 34 countries. **Languages** English. **Staff** 2.00 FTE, paid. **Finance** Members' donations; other donations. **Activities** Various projects in Kerala (India) to help provide employment for poor woman help villagers in their socio-economic development. Chennai (India) unit supports paediatric heart surgeries for poor children. Adopted villages in Kemwenge (Uganda) district and Akore (Nigeria). Various charitable projects. **Events** *Biennial global conference* Singapore (Singapore) 2008, *Global meet seminar* Singapore (Singapore) 2007, *Biennial global conference* Kochi (India) 2006, *Biennial global conference* Bahrain 2004, *Asia Pacific malayalee conference* Singapore (Singapore) 2004. **Publications** *WMC Journal*.
[2015/XF5648/**F**]

♦ World March of Women (WMW) 21632

Marche mondiale des femmes – Marcha Mundial de la Mujeres

Secretariat R Ministro Costa e Silva 36, Pinheiros, Sao Paulo SP, SP CEP 05417-080, Brazil. T. +551138193876. Fax +551138193876. E-mail: info@marchemondiale.org.
URL: http://www.worldmarchofwomen.org/

Aims Strengthen solidarity between women's groups; promote equality between women and men; increase education of women so that they can analyse the causes of their oppression and find alternatives. **Structure** Committee, meets 2 times a year. Secretariat in Montréal (Canada). **Events** *International meeting* Quezon City (Philippines) 2011, *International Meeting* Spain 2008, *International Meeting* Lima (Peru) 2006, *Seminar on peace and militarization* Goma (Congo DR) 2004, *International meeting / Meeting* Kigali (Rwanda) 2004. **Publications** *World March of Women Newsletter*. **NGO Relations** Member of: *Association for Women's Rights in Development (AWID, #02980)*. [2020/XJ4325/**F**]

♦ World Mariculture Society / see World Aquaculture Society (#21099)
♦ World Mariculture Society / see European Aquaculture Society (#05909)
♦ World Maritime Technology Congress (unconfirmed)

♦ World Maritime University (WMU) 21633

Université maritime mondiale (UMM) – Universidad Maritima Mundial (UMM)

Registrar PO Box 500, SE-201 24 Malmö, Sweden. T. +4640356300. Fax +4640356310. E-mail: info@wmu.se.
Communications and Conferences Officer address not obtained.
URL: http://www.wmu.se/

History 4 Jul 1983, Malmö (Sweden). Founded under the auspices of *International Maritime Organization (IMO, #14102)*. Registration: EU Transparency Register, No/ID: 858273418679-54, Start date: 7 Sep 2015. **Aims** Be the world centre of excellence in postgraduate maritime and oceans education, professional training and research, while building global capacity and promoting sustainable development. **Structure** International Board of Governors. **Languages** English. **Staff** 85.00 FTE, paid; 100.00 FTE, voluntary. **Finance** Sources: contributions; donations; government support. Major donors include: Sweden, the Governments of Canada, China and the Republic of Korea. Major fellowship donors for the Class of 2022 include: The Nippon Foundation of Japan (31) International Maritime Organization (14) Government of Norway (10) Government of the Republic of Korea (7) Australian Maritime Safety Authority (6) Government of Germany (5) ITF Seafarers' Trust (5) Orients Fond (5) The TK Foundation (4) Government of the United Kingdom (2) Stena Rederi AB (2) Government of the Netherlands (1) Gard AS (1) International Chamber of Shipping (1) MPA Academy Singapore (1) Norwegian Cruise Line Holdings (1) Norwegian Seafarers' Union (1) World Nuclear Transport Institute (1). Supported by: *International Chamber of Shipping (ICS, #12535)*; *International Maritime Organization (IMO, #14102)*; *International Transport Workers' Federation (ITF, #15726)*; *Nippon Foundation*; *Norwegian Agency for Development Cooperation (Norad)*; *Sasakawa Peace Foundation (SPF)*. Annual budget: 16,000,000 USD. **Activities** Capacity building; events/meetings; research/documentation; training/education. **Events** *Educating Ocean and Maritime Leaders – A Legacy of Excellence and Future Plans at the World Maritime University* Lisbon (Portugal) 2022, *Empowering Women for the United Nations Decade of Ocean Science for Sustainable Development* Lisbon (Portugal) 2022, *Session on Empowering Women* Lisbon (Portugal) 2022, *IMO-WMU Joint International Conference* Malmö (Sweden) 2022, *"Closing the Circle" Programme Conference* Soufrière (Dominica) 2022. **Publications** *WMU Journal of Maritime Affairs*. *WMU Academic Handbook*; *WMU At a Glance*. Academic Publications. **NGO Relations** Member of (1): *International Association of Maritime Universities (IAMU, #12016)*. Academic partnership and collaboration agreements with universities worldwide.
[2022.10.21/XF0471/y/**E**]

♦ World Marketing Association (inactive)
♦ World Marketing Contact Group (inactive)

♦ World Marketing Summit (WMS) 21634

SG address not obtained. E-mail: info@worldmarketingsummit.org.
URL: http://www.worldmarketingsummitgroup.org/

History 2010. **Aims** Create a better world for our future generations through marketing. **Structure** Advisory Board. **Activities** Events/meetings. **Events** *World Marketing Summit* Tokyo (Japan) 2022, *World Marketing Summit* Tokyo (Japan) 2022, *World Marketing Summit* Singapore (Singapore) 2018, *World Marketing Summit* Seoul (Korea Rep) 2017, *World Marketing Summit* Tokyo (Japan) 2017. [2017/XM5418/**F**]

♦ World Marrow Donor Association (WMDA) 21635

Exec Dir Schipholweg 57, 2316 ZL Leiden, Netherlands. T. +31885057900. E-mail: mail@wmda.info.
URL: https://www.wmda.info/

History 4 Oct 1994, Leiden (Netherlands). Took over activities of *Bone Marrow Donors Worldwide (BMDW, inactive)* and *International NetCord Foundation (inactive)*, 2017. Registration: KVK, No/ID: 40448326, Netherlands; EU Transparency Register, No/ID: 843707428180-27, Start date: 31 Aug 2017. **Aims** Promote global collaboration and sharing of best practices for the benefit of stem cell donors and transplant patients. **Structure** General Assembly (twice a year); Board; Committees/Project Groups. **Languages** English. **Staff** 11.00 FTE, paid; 1000.00 FTE, voluntary. **Finance** Sources: fees for services; grants; meeting proceeds; members' dues; sponsorship. **Activities** Advocacy/lobbying/activism; awareness raising; certification/accreditation; events/meetings; guidance/assistance/consulting; healthcare; knowledge management/information dissemination; monitoring/evaluation; networking/liaising; projects/programmes; publishing activities; research and development; research/documentation; standards/guidelines; training/education. **Events** *General Assembly* Leiden (Netherlands) 2022, *Meeting* Leiden (Netherlands) 2022, *International Donor Registries Conference* Québec, QC (Canada) 2022, *Meeting* Leiden (Netherlands) 2021, *Meeting* Leiden (Netherlands) 2021. **Publications** *A gift of life, WMDA handbook for blood stem cell donation* (3rd ed 2020) in English, Spanish – This handbook is available online for members of WMDA; *Sharing Life, Inspiring stories of transplant patients and their lifesaving heroes* (1st ed 2015).
Members Organizational: Stem Cell Donor Registries and Cord Blood Banks (79); Individuals (191). Members listed on international database from 59 countries and territories:
Argentina, Armenia, Australia, Austria, Belgium, Brazil, Bulgaria, Canada, Chile, China, Croatia, Cyprus, Czechia, Denmark, Finland, France, Germany, Greece, Hong Kong, Hungary, India, Iran Islamic Rep, Ireland, Israel, Italy, Japan, Korea Rep, Lithuania, Luxembourg, Mexico, Netherlands, New Zealand, Nigeria, North Macedonia, Norway, Paraguay, Peru, Poland, Portugal, Qatar, Romania, Russia, Saudi Arabia, Serbia, Singapore, Slovakia, Slovenia, South Africa, Spain, Sweden, Switzerland, Taiwan, Thailand, Türkiye, UK, Ukraine, Uruguay, USA, Wales.
NGO Relations Member of (1): *Worldwide Network for Blood and Marrow Transplantation (WBMT, #21929)*.
[2022.07.06/XD6614/**C**]

♦ World Martial Arts Committee (WMAC) 21636

World Pres c/o NMAC Austria, Achgasse 25c, 6900 Bregenz, Austria. E-mail: headquarter@wmac-world.com.
URL: http://wmac-world.com/

History 2013. Former names and other names: *World Martial Arts Games Committee (WMAGC)* – former. Registration: No/ID: 4501574355, Austria. **Aims** Promote the martial art *sport* for all through physical activity, competition and association. **Structure** Board. **Languages** English, German, Spanish. **Finance** Sources: meeting proceeds. No members' dues. Other sources: professional titles; examinations; stamps; certificates.
Members National Martial Arts Committee Members; Non-approved national members; Active; Supporting. National committees in 4110 countries:
Algeria, Australia, Austria, Belarus, Bosnia-Herzegovina, Canada, China, Croatia, Czechia, Denmark, Dominican Rep, Egypt, England, France, Germany, Ghana, India, Iran Islamic Rep, Iraq, Ireland, Italy, Lebanon, Liechtenstein, Malaysia, Nepal, New Zealand, Poland, Romania, Russia, Scotland, Serbia, Singapore, Slovakia, Slovenia, Spain, Sweden, Switzerland, Türkiye, Uganda, USA, Wales.
International Martial Arts Organizations (IMAOs):
International Judo Federation (IJF, #13975); *International Sport Jujitsu Association (ISJA)*; National Blackbelt League; North American Sport Karate Association; *Sport Karate International (SKIL)*; *World Association of Kickboxing Organizations (WAKO, #21151)*; World Jiu-jitsu Association; *World Karate Federation (WKF, #21608)*; *World Taekwondo (#21844)*; World Traditional Karate Federation.
NGO Relations Member of: *The Association for International Sport for All (TAFISA, #02763)*. Recognizes: *International Sport Jujitsu Association (ISJA)*; *World Federation of Self Defence, Arme Blanche and Personal Arts (WFSAPA, no recent information)*. [2019/XJ6353/y/**C**]

♦ World Martial Arts Games Committee / see World Martial Arts Committee (#21636)

♦ World Martial Arts Games Committee (WMAGC) 21637

SG address not obtained. T. +447917304667. E-mail: sg@wmagc.org.
URL: http://www.wmagc.org/

History Aug 2005. Former names and other names: *World Martial Arts Games Movement (WMAGM)* – former. **Aims** Provide a platform that promotes participation in Martial arts by all, including all styles, abilities, gender, ages and backgrounds. **Structure** Board of Directors. **Languages** English, German, Spanish. **Staff** 10.00 FTE, voluntary. **Activities** Sporting activities; training/education. Active in: Azerbaijan, Botswana, Colombia, Czechia, Germany, India, Iran Islamic Rep, Mexico, South Africa, Spain, Trinidad-Tobago, UK, USA. **NGO Relations** Member of (1): *The Association for International Sport for All (TAFISA, #02763)*. Partner of (2): *Sport Jiu-Jitsu International Federation (SJJIF, #19926)*; *World United Karate-do Federation (WUKF)*.
[2022.06.15/XM7396/**C**]

♦ World Martial Arts Games Movement / see World Martial Arts Games Committee (#21637)
♦ World Martial Arts Masterships Committee (internationally oriented national body)

♦ World Martial Arts Union (WoMAU) 21638

Staff 2F 73 Otgat-gil, Chungju NORTH CHUNGCHEONG 27438, Korea Rep. T. +82438527954. Fax +82438537341. E-mail: secretariat@womau.org.
URL: http://womau.org/

History 2 Oct 2002, Chungju (Korea Rep). Established at Inaugural General Meeting. Registration: Ministry of Foreign Affairs, No/ID: 36, Start date: 25 Mar 2003, Korea Rep; Ministry of Foreign Affairs, No/ID: 581, Start date: 25 Jun 2008, Korea Rep. **Aims** Be a source of both academic knowledge and practical information of Traditional Sports and Games with a special focus on martial arts. **Structure** Annual General Meeting; Steering Committee; Secretariat. **Languages** English, Korean. **Staff** 8.00 FTE, paid. **Finance** Sources: donations; grants; members' dues. Annual budget: 500,000,000 KRW (2020). **Activities** Awareness raising; events/meetings; knowledge management/information dissemination; sporting activities. **Events** *General Meeting* Chungju (Korea Rep) 2021, *General Meeting* Chungju (Korea Rep) 2020, *General Meeting* Chungju (Korea Rep) 2019, *General Meeting* Fergana (Uzbekistan) 2018, *General Meeting* Chungju (Korea Rep) 2017. **Publications** *WoMAU News* (2 a year) in English, Korean. *Taekkyeon, Traditional Martial Art of Korea* (2012).
Members Full (56); Associate (11). Members in 46 countries:
Australia, Belarus, Brazil, Brunei Darussalam, Bulgaria, Cambodia, Canada, China, Egypt, France, Georgia, Ghana, Greece, India, Indonesia, Iran Islamic Rep, Israel, Japan, Kazakhstan, Kenya, Korea Rep, Laos, Latvia, Lithuania, Malaysia, Moldova, Mongolia, Myanmar, Nepal, Netherlands, New Zealand, Philippines, Poland, Russia, Senegal, Serbia, Singapore, South Africa, Sudan, Thailand, Türkiye, Ukraine, USA, Uzbekistan, Venezuela, Vietnam.
Consultative Status Consultative status granted from: *UNESCO (#20322)* (Consultative Status); *ECOSOC (#05331)* (Special). [2022.06.15/XJ1679/**C**]

♦ World Master Chefs Society 21639

Contact 855 London Road, Grays, RM20 3LG, UK. T. +448707777448. Fax +448707777449. E-mail: mail@worldmasterchefs.com.
URL: http://www.worldmasterchefs.com/

History 1947, as *International Academy of Chefs*. Previously referred to as *Epicurean World Master Chefs Society (EWMCS)*. **Aims** Provide an international organization of recognized elite chefs that can be appointed for product endorsements, advertizing, television appearances and other media commodities. **Structure** Officers: World President; Past World President; Managing Director; Administrator. Board, comprising 5 Directors. **Languages** English. **Staff** 1.00 FTE, paid. **Activities** Organizes competitions, demonstrations, promotions, exhibitions, product endorsements and gala dinners.
Members Chapters in 7 countries:
Canada, France, Hong Kong, Ireland, Japan, UK, USA.
Other members in 7 countries:
Bahamas, Egypt, Germany, Malta, Philippines, Sweden, Switzerland. [2016/XD9474/**D**]

♦ World Masters Athletics (WMA) 21640

Secretary Jalapa 3207, Fracc, Neidhart, 22020 Tijuana BC, Mexico. T. +526646864756. E-mail: wmasec16@gmail.com.
Registered Office 6 Quai Antoire 1er, Monte Carlo, Monaco.
URL: https://world-masters-athletics.com/

History 1977, Sweden, as *World Association of Veteran Athletes (WAVA)*. Subsequently merged with sister organization, *Welt Interessen Gemeinschaft Alterer Langstvecken Läufer (IGAL, inactive)*, retaining the original title. Current title adopted 1997. Registered in the Principality of Monaco. **Aims** Develop, regulate, promote and manage all aspects of the sport of athletics for master athletes at world level. **Structure** General Assembly (every 2 years); Council; Committees (7); Regional organizations (6): *African Masters Athletics (AFMA, #00368)*; *Asia Masters Athletics (AMA, #01291)*; *Asociación Sudamericana de Atletas Máster (ASUDAMA, #02299)*; *European Masters Athletics (EMA, #07750)*; *North and Central American and Caribbean Regional Association of WMA (NCCWMA Regional Association, #17575)*; *Oceania Association of Master Athletes*. **Languages** English, French, Spanish. **Staff** None. **Finance** IAAF subsidies; levy from competing athletes at

World Championships. **Activities** Events/meetings; sporting activities. **Events** *General Assembly* Sacramento, CA (USA) 2011, *General Assembly* Lahti (Finland) 2009, *General Assembly* Riccione (Italy) 2007, *General Assembly* San Sebastian (Spain) 2005, *Biennial General Assembly* Carolina (Puerto Rico) 2003. **Publications** *WMA Handbook* (every 2 years). Technical papers.

Members Affiliates in 212 countries and territories:

Afghanistan, Albania, Algeria, Andorra, Angola, Anguilla, Antigua-Barbuda, Argentina, Armenia, Aruba, Australia, Austria, Azerbaijan, Bahamas, Bahrain, Bangladesh, Barbados, Belarus, Belgium, Belize, Benin, Bermuda, Bhutan, Bolivia, Bosnia-Herzegovina, Botswana, Brazil, Brunei Darussalam, Bulgaria, Burkina Faso, Burundi, Cambodia, Cameroon, Canada, Cape Verde, Cayman Is, Central African Rep, Chad, Chile, China, Colombia, Comoros, Congo Brazzaville, Congo DR, Cook Is, Costa Rica, Côte d'Ivoire, Croatia, Cuba, Cyprus, Czechia, Denmark, Djibouti, Dominica, Dominican Rep, Ecuador, Egypt, El Salvador, Equatorial Guinea, Eritrea, Estonia, Eswatini, Ethiopia, Fiji, Finland, France, Gabon, Gambia, Georgia, Germany, Ghana, Gibraltar, Greece, Grenada, Guam, Guatemala, Guinea, Guinea-Bissau, Guyana, Haiti, Honduras, Hong Kong, Hungary, Iceland, India, Indonesia, Iran Islamic Rep, Iraq, Ireland, Israel, Italy, Jamaica, Japan, Jordan, Kazakhstan, Kenya, Kiribati, Korea DPR, Korea Rep, Kuwait, Kyrgyzstan, Laos, Latvia, Lebanon, Lesotho, Liberia, Libya, Liechtenstein, Lithuania, Luxembourg, Macau, Madagascar, Malawi, Malaysia, Maldives, Mali, Malta, Marshall Is, Mauritania, Mauritius, Mexico, Micronesia FS, Moldova, Monaco, Mongolia, Montenegro, Montserrat, Morocco, Mozambique, Myanmar, Namibia, Nauru, Nepal, Netherlands, New Zealand, Nicaragua, Niger, Nigeria, Norfolk Is, North Macedonia, Northern Mariana Is, Norway, Oman, Pakistan, Palau, Palestine, Panama, Papua New Guinea, Paraguay, Peru, Philippines, Poland, Polynesia Fr, Portugal, Puerto Rico, Qatar, Romania, Russia, Rwanda, Samoa, Samoa USA, San Marino, Sao Tomé-Principe, Saudi Arabia, Senegal, Serbia, Seychelles, Sierra Leone, Singapore, Slovakia, Slovenia, Solomon Is, Somalia, South Africa, Spain, Sri Lanka, St Kitts-Nevis, St Lucia, St Vincent-Grenadines, Sudan, Suriname, Sweden, Switzerland, Syrian AR, Taiwan, Tajikistan, Tanzania UR, Thailand, Timor-Leste, Togo, Tonga, Trinidad-Tobago, Tunisia, Türkiye, Turkmenistan, Turks-Caicos, Tuvalu, Uganda, UK, Ukraine, United Arab Emirates, Uruguay, USA, Uzbekistan, Vanuatu, Venezuela, Vietnam, Virgin Is UK, Virgin Is USA, Yemen, Zambia, Zimbabwe.

NGO Relations Member of: *World Athletics (#21209).* [2020/XC0001/**B**]

♦ World Masters Cross-Country Ski Association (WMCCSA) 21641

Sec/Treas Ziegelweg 10, 6052 Hergiswil NW, Switzerland. T. +41416302477. Fax +41416302377.

URL: http://www.world-masters-xc-skiing.com/

History Founded 1984. **Aims** Promote and organize annual Masters World Cup for skiers above 30 years of age. **Languages** English, German. **Staff** 1.00 FTE, voluntary. **Finance** Newsletter funded. **Events** *Annual Meeting* Vuokatti (Finland) 2014, *Annual Meeting* Syktyvkar (Russia) 2013, *Annual Meeting* Austria 2012, *Annual Meeting* Oberwiesenthal (Germany) 2010, *Annual meeting* Kuopio (Finland) 1994. **Publications** *WM Newsletter* (5 a year).

Members Associations in 26 countries:

Australia, Austria, Belarus, Canada, Denmark, Estonia, Finland, France, Germany, Japan, Kazakhstan, Latvia, Lithuania, Netherlands, New Zealand, Norway, Poland, Russia, Slovakia, Slovenia, Spain, Sweden, Switzerland, UK, Ukraine, USA.

[2018.06.12/XD8101/**D**]

♦ World Masters Games Association / see International Masters Games Association (#14117)

♦ World Materials Research Institutes Forum (WMRIF) 21642

Secretariat Natl Inst for Materials Science, 1-2-1 Sengen, Tsukuba IBARAKI, 305-0047 Japan. E-mail: info@nims.go.jp.

URL: http://wmrif.nims.go.jp/

History 2005, Tsukuba (Japan). Registered in accordance with Japanese law. **Aims** Establish a global strategy for materials science and engineering research and development (MSE R and D). **Structure** General Assembly. Presidential Board, including President and 2 Vice-Presidents. Secretariat, headed by Secretary General. Regional Groups (3): Asia-Oceania; Europe-Africa; America. **Languages** English. **Activities** Organizes joint projects and initiatives. Working Groups (7): Promotion of Research Collaboration; Publication of Materials Science Outlook; Attracting the Young Scientists; Promotion of Global Database; Research on Materials for Sustainable Energy and Environment; Research on Structural Materials Reliability; Research on Materials Simulation. **Events** *Biennial Forum* Bangkok (Thailand) 2017, *International Conference on Material Sciences and Technology* Bangkok (Thailand) 2014, *Biennial Forum* Shenyang (China) 2011, *Asia-Oceanic forum* Pathum Thani (Thailand) 2010, *Biennial forum / Forum* Gaithersburg, MD (USA) 2009.

Members Institutes (43) in 21 countries and territories:

Brazil, China, Finland, France, Germany, Hungary, India, Japan, Korea Rep, Poland, Russia, Singapore, South Africa, Spain, Sweden, Switzerland, Taiwan, Thailand, UK, USA, Vietnam.

IGO Relations Memorandum of Understanding with: *Versailles Project on Advanced Materials and Standards (VAMAS, #20757).* [2011/XJ3841/**F**]

♦ World Mayors Council on Climate Change (WMCCC) 21643

Dir c/o ICLEI – Local Governments for Sustainability, Kaiser-Friedrich-Str 7, 53113 Bonn, Germany. T. +4922897629923. Fax +4922897629901. E-mail: world.mayors.council@iclei.org.

URL: http://www.worldmayorscouncil.org/

History Dec 2005, Montréal QC (Canada), at the UN Climate Change Conference COP-13, following the entry into force of the *Kyoto Protocol to the United Nations Framework Convention on Climate Change (1997)*, Feb 2005. **Aims** Politically promote *local*-level policies addressing climate change and its impact on other areas; study the impact of climate change on *cities* and provide reports and recommendations for action; strengthen the political profile and impact of ICLEI's 'Cities for Climate Protection Campaign', 'Water Campaign and Local Action for Biodiversity' programme, 'GreenClimateCities' initiative and 'carbonn Cities Climate Registry (cCCR)'; widen and deepen this network of pro-active cities; foster international cooperation of municipal leaders on achieving relevant climate targets; help make multilateral mechanisms for global climate protection effective through local action and, through advocacy, influence negotiations on future global climate *protection* regimes; form *local government* delegations and secure funding to effectively represent the priorities of local governments at meetings of the United Nations and other relevant multilateral processes. **Languages** English. **Staff** 2.00 FTE, paid. **Activities** Specific scope of advocacy: climate mitigation and adaptation (UNFCCC); leadership of *Global Cities Covenant on Climate (Mexico City Pact, inactive)*; Millennium Development Goal 7; Global Partnership on Local and Sub-national Action for Biodiversity. Organizes: annual Mayors Adaptation Forum, Bonn (Germany). **Events** *Resilient Cities : Annual Global Forum on Urban Resilience and Adaptation* Bonn (Germany) 2019, *Resilient Cities : Annual Global Forum on Urban Resilience and Adaptation* Bonn (Germany) 2017, *Resilient Cities : Annual Global Forum on Urban Resilience and Adaptation* Bonn (Germany) 2016, *Resilient Cities : Annual World Congress on Cities and Adaptation to Climate Change* Bonn (Germany) 2015, *Resilient Cities : Annual Global Forum on Urban Resilience and Adaptation* Bonn (Germany) 2014. **Publications** *WMCCC Climate Briefs.* Reports.

Members Local government leaders (87) in 32 countries and territories:

Australia, Brazil, Cameroon, Canada, Croatia, Denmark, France, Germany, India, Israel, Italy, Japan, Kenya, Korea Rep, Madagascar, Mauritius, Mexico, Namibia, New Zealand, Nigeria, Philippines, Portugal, Senegal, South Africa, Spain, Sweden, Switzerland, Taiwan, Tanzania UR, Uganda, UK, USA.

IGO Relations *United Nations Framework Convention on Climate Change (UNFCCC, 1992); UNEP (#20299).*

NGO Relations Secretariat provided by: *Local Governments for Sustainability (ICLEI, #16507)* – World Secretariat. Member of: *Global Call for Climate Action (GCCA, inactive).* [2012.07.05/XM0956/**E**]

♦ World Media Association (WMA) 21644

Association mondiale des moyens de communication

Main Office 3600 New York Ave NE, 3rd Floor, Washington DC 20002, USA. T. +12026363124. Fax +12026359227.

History 1978, by the Rev Sun Myung Moon. **Aims** Explore issues of media *ethics* and responsibility. **Finance** Members' dues: US$ 60. Sponsored by the Washington Times Corporation and *News World Communications (#17095).* Sale of publications. **Activities** Annual Conference; quarterly luncheon fora. **Events** *World media conference / World Media Conference – WMC* Washington, DC (USA) 2004, *World media conference / World Media Conference – WMC* Washington, DC (USA) 2003, *World media conference / World Media Conference – WMC* Washington, DC (USA) 2002, *World media conference / World Media Conference – WMC* Tokyo (Japan) 2001, *World media conference / World Media Conference – WMC* Seoul (Korea Rep) 2000. **Publications** Conference proceedings.

Members Individuals in 42 countries:

Albania, Australia, Bangladesh, Cameroon, China, Egypt, France, Germany, Ghana, Greece, Guatemala, Hong Kong, Hungary, India, Indonesia, Ireland, Israel, Italy, Jamaica, Japan, Kenya, Korea Rep, Lithuania, Marshall Is, Mauritius, Moldova, Mongolia, New Zealand, Nigeria, Norway, Paraguay, Russia, Samoa, Singapore, Slovakia, South Africa, Spain, Suriname, Taiwan, UK, USA, Uzbekistan. [2008/XF2122/v/**F**]

♦ World Mediation Organization (WMO) 21645

Dir Gen Hohenzollerndamm 182, 10713 Berlin, Germany. T. +493098298649. E-mail: mail@worldmediation.org.

URL: http://www.worldmediation.org/

History Founded by Daniel Erdmann, 2006. **Aims** Promote mediation and conflict awareness, prevention and resolution on a global level. **Structure** Director General; Advisory Board; Fellows. **Languages** English, German, Spanish. **Activities** Events/meetings; guidance/assistance/consulting; research/documentation; training/education. **Events** *Symposium* Berlin (Germany) 2017, *Mediation, the language of peaceful communication and conflict resolution* Bangkok (Thailand) 2016, *Symposium* Berlin (Germany) 2015, *Symposium* Hong Kong (Hong Kong) 2015, *Symposium* Istanbul (Turkey) 2015. **Publications** Books. **Information Services** *Conflict Insight* – database. **Members** Representatives (350) in 71 countries. Membership countries not specified. **NGO Relations** Participant of: *United Nations Global Compact (#20567).* Partner of Euclid University. [2019/XJ8392/**C**]

♦ World Medical Association (WMA) 21646

Association médicale mondiale (AMM) – Asociación Médica Mundial (AMM)

SG 13 ch du Levant, CIB – Bâtiment A, 01210 Ferney-Voltaire, France. T. +33450407575. E-mail: wma@wma.net.

URL: http://www.wma.net/

History 18 Sep 1947, Paris (France). Present Articles and Bylaws adopted at 73rd General Assembly, Berlin (Germany), Oct 2022. Former names and other names: *Societas Mundi Medica* – former; *World Federation of Doctors* – former. Registration: Start date: Aug 1964, USA, New York; Start date: 1994, France; EU Transparency Register, No/ID: 469985839591-77, Start date: 14 Sep 2020. **Aims** Serve humanity by endeavouring to achieve the highest international *standards* in medical education, medical science, medical art and medical *ethics* and health care for all; encourage growth of the medical profession and services. **Structure** General Assembly (annual); Council; Secretariat. **Languages** English, French, Spanish. Japanese interpretation at meetings. **Staff** 10.00 FTE, paid. **Finance** Sources: donations; members' dues. **Activities** Certification/accreditation; events/meetings; research/documentation; standards/guidelines; training/education. **Events** *Session* Seoul (Korea Rep) 2024, *General Assembly* Kigali (Rwanda) 2023, *Session* Nairobi (Kenya) 2023, *General Assembly* Berlin (Germany) 2022, *Regional Meeting for Asia on the International Code of Medical Ethics* Thailand 2022. **Publications** *World Medical Journal* (4 a year).

Members Constituent members in 116 countries and territories:

Albania, Andorra, Angola, Argentina, Armenia, Australia, Austria, Azerbaijan, Bahamas, Bangladesh, Belarus, Belgium, Belize, Bolivia, Brazil, Bulgaria, Cameroon, Cape Verde, Chile, China, Colombia, Congo DR, Costa Rica, Côte d'Ivoire, Croatia, Cyprus, Czechia, Denmark, Egypt, El Salvador, Estonia, Ethiopia, Fiji, Finland, France, Georgia, Germany, Ghana, Greece, Guinea, Haiti, Holy See (Vatican), Hong Kong, Hungary, Iceland, India, Indonesia, Ireland, Israel, Italy, Japan, Kazakhstan, Kenya, Korea Rep, Kuwait, Latvia, Lesotho, Liechtenstein, Lithuania, Luxembourg, Malawi, Malaysia, Mali, Malta, Mexico, Montenegro, Mozambique, Myanmar, Namibia, Nepal, Netherlands, New Zealand, Nigeria, North Macedonia, Norway, Pakistan, Panama, Paraguay, Peru, Philippines, Poland, Portugal, Romania, Russia, Rwanda, Samoa, Senegal, Serbia, Seychelles, Singapore, Slovakia, Slovenia, Somalia, South Africa, Spain, Sri Lanka, St Lucia, Sudan, Sweden, Switzerland, Taiwan, Tanzania UR, Trinidad-Tobago, Tunisia, Türkiye, Uganda, UK, Ukraine, Uruguay, USA, Uzbekistan, Venezuela, Vietnam, Zambia, Zimbabwe.

Individuals: Associate membership. Membership countries not specified.

Consultative Status Consultative status granted from: *ECOSOC (#05331)* (Ros C); *ILO (#11123)* (Special List); *WHO (#20950)* (Official Relations). **IGO Relations** Liaises with: *UNESCO (#20322).* Accredited by: *United Nations Office at Geneva (UNOG, #20597).*

NGO Relations Member of: *Council for International Organizations of Medical Sciences (CIOMS, #04905); Global Health Workforce Alliance (GHWA, inactive); Standing Committee of European Doctors (#19955).* Founding member of: *World Federation for Medical Education (WFME, #21454).* Observer status with: *FDI – World Dental Federation (#09281); International Council of Nurses (ICN, #13054); World Veterinary Association (WVA, #21901).* Observer member of: *International Federation of Health and Human Rights Organisations (IFHHRO, #13440).* Partner of: *Fight the Fakes (#09755).* Supports: *Isis Women's International Cross Cultural Exchange (ISIS-WICCE, #16031).* Endorses: *Steering Group on Influenza Vaccination (#19980).* Together with International Council of Nurses (ICN), *International Pharmaceutical Federation (#14566)*, World Dental Federation (FDI) and *World Confederation for Physical Therapy (WCPT, #21293)*, set up: *World Health Professions Alliance (WHPA, #21557).*

Close cooperation with:

- academic centers;
- *Africa Medical Association (AfMA, #00188);*
- *Amnesty International (AI, #00801);*
- *Confederación Médica Latinoamericana y del Caribe (CONFEMEL, #04463);*
- *Confederation of Medical Associations in Asia and Oceania (CMAAO, #04566);*
- Conference of the Central and East European Chamers;
- Council for International Organizations of Medical Sciences (CIOMS);
- educational resources;
- *European Forum of Medical Associations and WHO (EFMA, #07320);*
- *Forum of Ibero-American Medical Associations (FIEME);*
- *Global Self-Care Federation (GSCF, #10588);*
- *International Alliance of Patients' Organizations (IAPO, #11633);*
- *International Committee of the Red Cross (ICRC, #12799);*
- *International Confederation of Midwives (ICM, #12863);*
- International Council of Nurses (ICN);
- *International Federation of Medical Students' Associations (IFMSA, #13478);*
- *International Federation of Pharmaceutical Manufacturers and Associations (IFPMA, #13505);*
- International Pharmaceutical Federation (FIP);
- *International Red Cross and Red Crescent Movement (#14707);*
- *International Rehabilitation Council for Torture Victims (IRCT, #14712);*
- *Medical Association of South East Asian Nations (MASEAN, #16623);*
- *Medical Women's International Association (MWIA, #16630);*
- One Health Initiative;
- *Physicians for Human Rights, USA (PHR-USA);*
- *Public Services International (PSI, #18572);*
- *Standing Committee of European Doctors (#19955);*
- World Confederation for Physical Therapy (WCPT);
- World Dental Federation (FDI);
- World Federation for Medical Education (WFME);
- *World Health Editors Network (WHEN, #21556);*
- *World Psychiatric Association (WPA, #21741);*
- World Veterinary Association (WVA).
- ICMM (International Committee of Military Medicine)
- International Federation ofAssociations o fPharmaceutical Physicians (IFAP) [2023.02.16/XB3554/**B**]

♦ World Medical Esperantist Association / see Universala Medicina Esperanto-Asocio (#20672)

♦ World Medical Law Association / see World Association for Medical Law (#21164)

♦ World Medical Tennis Society (WMTS) 21647

Association médicale mondiale de tennis

Exec Sec Creighton Univ, 2500 California Plaza, Omaha NE 68178, USA.

URL: http://www.wmtstennis.org/

History 1970, Monte Carlo (Monaco). **Structure** Board of Directors, comprising one member from each country; Executive Committee. **Languages** English. **Staff** 0.50 FTE, paid. **Finance** Sources: members' dues. **Activities** Tennis competition; Health fitness camaraderie; Medical education. **Events** *Annual Congress* Bonn (Germany) 2023, *Annual Congress* Orlando, FL (USA) 2022, *Annual Congress* Antalya (Turkey) 2021, *Annual Congress* Antalya (Turkey) 2020, *Annual Congress* Vilnius (Lithuania) 2019.

Members Full in 40 countries and territories:

Argentina, Australia, Austria, Barbados, Belgium, Brazil, Canada, Croatia, Czechia, Denmark, Estonia, Finland, France, Germany, Greece, Grenada, Hungary, India, Indonesia, Iran Islamic Rep, Ireland, Israel, Italy, Japan, Latvia, Lithuania, Malta, New Zealand, Northern Ireland, Norway, Poland, Romania, Singapore, Slovakia, Sweden, Switzerland, Taiwan, Tunisia, UK, USA.

IGO Relations *Council of Europe (CE, #04881).* [2014/XD5380/**C**]

♦ World Meeting of Popular Movements (meeting series)

♦ World Memom Organisation (WMO) 21648

Contact 3 Weir Road, London, SW12 0LT, UK. T. +442087726622. E-mail: gm@wmoworld.org.
URL: http://wmoworld.org/

History 2002. Former names and other names: *World Memon Organisation Charitable Foundation* – full title. **Aims** Act as the central Memon organization representing the entire Memon community worldwide, promoting the advancement, upliftment, unity, welfare and well-being of all Memons in all aspects of life and at all times in accordance with Islamic principles. **Structure** General Assembly; Board of Trustees; Executive Committee. **Events** *General Assembly* Dubai (United Arab Emirates) 2019. [2020/AA0475/**E**]

♦ World Memon Organisation Charitable Foundation / see World Memom Organisation (#21648)
♦ World Memory Sports Council (unconfirmed)
♦ World Mercy Fund (internationally oriented national body)
♦ World Merit (unconfirmed)

♦ World Meteorological Organization (WMO) 21649

Organisation météorologique mondiale (OMM) – Organización Meteorológica Mundial (OMM)

SG 7 bis av de la Paix, Case Postale 2300, 1211 Geneva 2, Switzerland. T. +41227308111. Fax +41227308181. E-mail: wmo@wmo.int.
URL: http://www.wmo.int/

History Established 11 Oct 1947, Washington DC (USA), on signature of a convention on behalf of 42 states at conclusion of 12th Conference of Directors of *International Meteorological Organization (IMO, inactive)*, an international nongovernmental organization founded in 1873. IMO continued to function on an interim basis, pending formal establishment of the World Meteorological Organization which took place, 23 Mar 1950, on coming into force of the IMO Convention. Resources and obligations of IMO were transferred to WMO, 4 Apr 1951, at 1st Congress. Agreement between the United Nations and WMO approved, 20 Dec 1951, by UN General Assembly, established WMO as a specialized agency of *United Nations (UN, #20515)* within *United Nations System (#20635)*, linked to *ECOSOC (#05331)*. Statutes registered in *'UNTS 1/998'* and *'ICAO 840'*. **Aims** Facilitate worldwide cooperation in the establishment of networks of stations for the making of meteorological observations as well as *hydrological* and other geophysical observations related to meteorology; promote the establishment and maintenance of centres charged with the provision of meteorological and related services; promote the establishment and maintenance of systems for rapid exchange of meteorological and related information; promote standardization of meteorological and related observations and ensure the uniform publication of observations and statistics; further the application of meteorology to aviation, shipping, water problems, agriculture and other human activities; promote activities in operational hydrology and further close cooperation amongst national meteorological and hydrological services; encourage research and training in meteorology and, as appropriate, in related fields and assist in coordinating the international aspects of such research and training.

Structure World Meteorological Congress (every 4 years), consists of delegates representing Member governments; it fixes policy, programme and budget. Executive Council (meets annually) is the executive body and comprises 37 Directors of National Meteorological or Hydrometeorological Services, including President, 3 Vice-Presidents, 6 Regional Presidents and 27 members elected by the Congress. Executive Council: supervises implementation of decisions of Congress; studies and makes recommendations on any matter affecting international meteorology and related WMO activities and the operation of meteorological and hydrological services; provides members with technical information and advice; administers the finances. Regional Associations (for Africa, Asia, South America, North America, Central America and the Caribbean, South-West Pacific, and Europe), comprise WMO members whose meteorological or hydrological stations are in or extend into the region concerned; they coordinate meteorological activity within their respective regions. Technical Commissions (8), comprising international experts, study various branches of meteorology and its applications and present technical recommendations to Congress and the Executive Council for approval:
- Aeronautical Meteorology (CAeM);
- Agricultural Meteorology (CAgM);
- Atmospheric Sciences (CAS);
- Basic Systems (CBS);
- Climatology (CCl);
- Hydrology (CHy);
- Instruments and Methods of Observation (CIMO);
- Joint WMO/IOC Oceanography and Marine Meteorology (JCOMM).

Secretary-General, appointed by Congress, heads Secretariat at WMO Headquarters in Geneva (Switzerland), which undertakes technical studies, prepares specialized publications, acts as secretariat during the meetings of various WMO bodies and generally maintains liaison and coordination among WMO bodies, WMO members and other international organizations; it also serves as an information centre for members and non-member states, various institutions and the public.

Languages Arabic, Chinese, English, French, Russian, Spanish. **Staff** Headquarters, Liaison Offices (New York NY, USA; Brussels, Belgium), Regional and Subregional Offices: 285. Personnel consultations through *WMO Staff Association (#20979)*. The *Administrative Tribunal of the International Labour Organization (ILO Tribunal, #00118)* is competent to settle disputes. **Finance** Contributions from member states and territories according to a proportional scale of assessment.

Activities Adopts technical regulations and makes recommendations to members with a view to improving and coordinating activities in meteorology and operational hydrology on a worldwide basis. Adopts transmission codes and organizes collection and dissemination of data on regional and continental bases. Supports national efforts on mitigation and reduction of natural disasters through timely and accurate warnings and forecasts. Coordinates and regulates the application of meteorology to aviation, shipping, agriculture, water resource development and other aspects of economic life. With UNEP, studies the economic and social impact of natural and man-made climate change. Contributes to: developing the use of meteorological information and forecasts for protection of plants and crops against insect pests and plant diseases and participates in international locust control activities; research on the upper atmosphere; implementation and operation of an international early notification system of nuclear accidents, especially through *Convention on Early Notification of a Nuclear Accident (1986)*, administered by World Weather Watch in conjunction with IAEA, and the related *Convention on Assistance in the Case of Nuclear Accident or Radiological Emergency (1986)*. Participates in international activities relating to oceans, including through *Global Ocean Observing System (GOOS, #10511)*. Plays an active part in UNDP's work for economic development of developing countries, contributing to the establishment and development of National Meteorological and Hydrological Services and the training of meteorologists and specialists in all branches of weather science; delegates experts to study local conditions and seek the most suitable means of solving the particular problems of the countries in question.

'WMO Programmes':

WMO Applications of Meteorology Programme (AMP, see: #21649) facilitates the application of meteorology, in all countries, for the attainment of national social, economic and cultural goals and sustainable development. It includes: *'Public Weather Services Programme'*; *'Agricultural Meteorology Programme'*; *'Aeronautical Meteorology Programme'*; *'Marine Meteorology and Related Oceanographic Activities Programme'*.

WMO Atmospheric Research and Environment Programme (AREP, see: #21649) coordinates and stimulates research on the composition of the atmosphere, the physics and chemistry of clouds, weather modification techniques, tropical meteorology processes and weather forecasting, focusing on extreme weather events and socio-economic impacts. It also coordinates the global monitoring of greenhouse gases, the ozone layer, major atmospheric pollutants and urban environment and meteorological studies. It includes: *'Global Atmosphere Watch (GAW)'*, set up Jun 1989; *'World Weather Research Programme'*; *'THORPEX'*; *'Tropical Meteorology Research Programme'*; *'Physics of Clouds and Weather Modification Research Programme'*. Scientific institutions include:
- *WMO World Ozone and Ultra-Violet Data Centre (WOUDC, see: #21649)*;
- *WMO World Data Centre for Greenhouse Gases (WDCGG, see: #21649)*;
- *WMO World Data Centre for Aerosols, Ispra (inactive)*;
- *WMO World Radiation Data Centre, St Petersburg (WRDC, see: #21649)*;
- *WMO World Data Centre for Aerosol Optical Depth, Asheville NC (no recent information)* (activities currently suspended).

Education and Training Programme assists members, in particular in developing countries and countries with economies in transition, in obtaining specially educated and trained to internationally agreed standards in order to carry out the activities and operations of National Meteorological and Hydrological Services required at the global, regional and national levels for the effective provision of meteorological and hydrological services in support of sustainable development of member countries.

Global Climate Observing System (GCOS, #10289), established in 1992, aims to ensure that the observations and information needed to address climate-related issues are obtained and made available to all potential users. It is co-sponsored by WMO, IOC, UNEP and ICSU. It is intended to be a long-term, user-driven operational system capable of providing the comprehensive observations required for monitoring the climate system, for detecting and attributing climate change, for assessing the impacts of climate variability and change, and for supporting research toward improved understanding, modelling and prediction of the climate system. It builds upon, and works in partnership with, other existing and developing observing systems.

WMO Hydrology and Water Resources Programme (HWRP, #20977) provides for the collection and analysis of hydrological data as a basis for assessing and managing freshwater resources, for example, for human consumption, sanitation, irrigation, hydropower production and water transport, and for flood forecasting system and the prediction of droughts. It includes: Programme on Basic Systems; Programme on Applications and Forecasting; Programme on Sustainable Development of Water Resources; Programme on Capacity Building in Hydrology and Water Resources; Programme on Water-related Issues; Associated Programme on Flood Management; *World Hydrological Cycle Observing System*; Hydrological Operational Multipurpose System.

WMO Disaster Risk Reduction Programme (DRR, see: #21649) develops an organization-wide coordinating framework to enhance further WMO's contributions to the natural disaster risk reduction activities at the international, regional and national levels. DPM strategy enhances the way WMO and the National Meteorological and Hydrological Services, in partnership with other key organizations, can contribute to disaster reduction around the world. Through a phased implementation plan based on a multi-hazard framework, WMO – through a coordinated and systematic approach – addresses the needs and gaps in its core areas in different regions in the world.

'Regional Programme (RP)' cuts across and forms part of the WMO scientific and technical programmes. Main purpose is to give the required support to the regional associations. It comprises 2 main components – initial support to the Regional Programme and Regional Activities, which provide the necessary mechanism to ensure that the Programme's purposes are met, including assistance to the presidents of regional associations, support to sessions of regional associations and their working groups, assistance to members, particularly developing countries, for strengthening their National Meteorological and Hydrological Services to enable them to participate fully in and reap the maximum benefits from WMO Programmes. Assistance to members, which also aims at "bridging the gap" between National Meteorological and Hydrological Services, is given through regional events including regional technical conferences, training seminars, workshops as well as experts implementation coordination meetings.

WMO Resource Mobilization Office (RMO, see: #21649) ensures, through collaborative efforts of members, for their mutual benefit, the enhancement and development of the capabilities of the National Meteorological and Hydrological Services so they can contribute to, and participate efficiently in, the implementation of WMO Programmes, for the benefit of the global community and in support of national socio-economic development activities.

World Climate Programme, established in 1979, provides an authoritative international scientific voice on climate and climate change and assists countries in the application of climate information and knowledge to national sustainable development. It embraces the study and monitoring of the entire climate system and, as such, makes major contributions to the implementation of most WMO strategies. It consists of: Agricultural and Meteorology Programme; World Climate Data and Monitoring Programme; World Climate Applications and Services Programme, including the Climate Information and Prediction Services (CLIPS).

World Climate Research Programme (WCRP, #21279) (together with ICSU and IOC), is the research component of WCP. It aims to develop the fundamental understanding of the physical climate system and climate processes needed to determine to what extent climate can be predicted and to quantify human influence on climate.

WMO Space Programme (see: #21649) coordinates environmental satellite matters and activities throughout all the WMO Programmes and gives guidance to WMO and other multi-sponsored programmes on the potential of remote-sensing techniques in meteorology, hydrology, related disciplines and their applications.

World Weather Watch (WWW, #21910), established 1968, is the backbone of the WMO programmes. It combines observing systems, telecommunication facilities and data-processing and forecasting centres – operated by members – to make available meteorological and related geophysical information needed to provide efficient services in all countries. It includes: *Global Observing System (GOS)*; *Global Telecommunication System (GTS)*; *Global Data-processing and Forecasting System (GDPFS)*; Tropical Cyclone Programme; Antarctic Activities; Emergency Response Activities; Operational Information Service; WWW Data Management; WMO Information System.

WMO Integrated Global Observing System (WIGOS, #20978) – Provides a single focus for the operational and management functions of all WMO observing systems.

Joint activities/programmes with other intergovernmental and international nongovernmental organizations include:
- *African Centre of Meteorological Applications for Development (ACMAD, #00242)*;
- *Cooperative Programme for Monitoring and Evaluation of the Long-range Transmission of Air Pollutants in Europe (EMEP, #04800)*;
- *ESCAP/WMO Typhoon Committee (TC, #05534)*;
- *Global Terrestrial Observing System (GTOS, #10626)*;
- *Joint WMO-IOC Technical Commission for Oceanography and Marine Meteorology (JCOMM, #16151)*, established in summer 1999 on merger of *Integrated Global Ocean Services System (IGOSS, inactive)* with WMO Commission for Marine Meteorology;
- *Intergovernmental Panel on Climate Change (IPCC, #11499)*;
- *Programa para el Estudio Regional del Fenómeno El Niño en el Pacifico Sudeste (ERFEN, #18523)*;
- *UNEP-IOC-WMO-IUCN Long-Term Global Monitoring System of Coastal and Near-Shore Phenomena Related to Climate Change (inactive)*;
- *WMO/ESCAP Panel on Tropical Cyclones (PTC, #20976)*;
- *World Hydrological Cycle Observing System (WHYCOS, #21573)* (still at the planning stage).

Events *WMESS : World Multidisciplinary Earth Sciences Symposium* Prague (Czechia) 2022, *World Landslide Forum* Kyoto (Japan) 2021, *TECO : Technical Conference on Meteorological and Environmental Instruments and Methods of Observation* Paris (France) 2021, *World Landslide Forum* Kyoto (Japan) 2020, *TECO : Technical Conference on Meteorological and Environmental Instruments and Methods of Observation* Paris (France) 2020. **Publications** *Marine Science Affairs Reports* – programme supporting publication; *MeteoWorld* – newsletter; *Operational Hydrology Reports* – programme supporting publication; *Special Environmental Reports* – programme supporting publication; *WMO Bulletin* – mandatory publication; *World Climate News*; *World Weather Watch Planning Reports* – programme supporting publication. *WMO Basic Documents* – mandatory publication; *WMO Guides* – mandatory publication; *WMO Technical Notes* – programme supporting publication. *Mandatory publications* – in English, French, Russian, Spanish – to meet the operational needs of Meteorological and Hydrological Services and of users such as airlines, shipping lines, agricultural community, etc, throughout the world. They also include: annual report of WMO; operational publications; official records. *Programme supporting publications* – normally in English and occasionally in the other working languages of the Organization. They also include: training compendia.

Members Governments (191) of 185 States and 6 territories (T – Curaçao and St Maarten list as one):
Afghanistan, Albania, Algeria, Angola, Antigua-Barbuda, Argentina, Armenia, Australia, Austria, Azerbaijan, Bahamas, Bahrain, Bangladesh, Barbados, Belarus, Belgium, Belize, Benin, Bhutan, Bolivia, Bosnia-Herzegovina, Botswana, Brazil, British Caribbean Terr (T), Brunei Darussalam, Bulgaria, Burkina Faso, Burundi, Cambodia, Cameroon, Canada, Cape Verde, Central African Rep, Chad, Chile, China, Colombia, Comoros, Congo Brazzaville, Congo DR, Cook Is, Costa Rica, Côte d'Ivoire, Croatia, Cuba, Curaçao (T), Cyprus, Czechia, Denmark, Djibouti, Dominica, Dominican Rep, Ecuador, Egypt, El Salvador, Eritrea, Estonia, Eswatini, Ethiopia, Fiji, Finland, France, Gabon, Gambia, Georgia, Germany, Ghana, Greece, Guatemala, Guinea, Guinea-Bissau, Guyana, Haiti, Honduras, Hong Kong (T), Hungary, Iceland, India, Indonesia, Iran Islamic Rep, Iraq, Ireland, Israel, Italy, Jamaica, Japan, Jordan, Kazakhstan, Kenya, Kiribati, Korea DPR, Korea Rep, Kuwait, Kyrgyzstan, Laos, Latvia, Lebanon, Lesotho, Liberia, Libya, Lithuania, Luxembourg, Macau (T), Madagascar, Malawi, Malaysia, Maldives, Mali, Malta, Mauritania, Mauritius, Mexico, Micronesia FS, Moldova, Monaco, Mongolia, Montenegro, Morocco, Mozambique, Myanmar, Namibia, Nepal, Netherlands, New Caledonia (T), New Zealand, Nicaragua, Niger, Nigeria, Niue, North Macedonia, Norway, Oman, Pakistan, Panama, Papua New Guinea, Paraguay, Peru, Philippines, Poland, Polynesia Fr (T), Portugal, Qatar, Romania, Russia, Rwanda, Samoa, Sao Tomé-Principe, Saudi Arabia, Senegal, Serbia, Seychelles, Sierra Leone, Singapore, Slovakia, Slovenia, Solomon Is, Somalia, South Africa, South Sudan, Spain, Sri Lanka, St Lucia, St Maarten (T), Sudan, Suriname, Sweden, Switzerland, Syrian AR, Tajikistan, Tanzania UR, Thailand, Timor-Leste, Togo, Tonga, Trinidad-Tobago, Tunisia, Türkiye, Turkmenistan, Tuvalu, Uganda, UK, Ukraine, United Arab Emirates, Uruguay, USA, Uzbekistan, Vanuatu, Venezuela, Vietnam, Yemen, Zambia, Zimbabwe.

IGO Relations Permanent observer status with: *World Intellectual Property Organization (WIPO, #21593)*. Member of: *Abdus Salam International Centre for Theoretical Physics (ICTP, #00005)*; *Inter-Agency Working Group on Desertification (IAWGD, inactive)*; *United Nations Sustainable Development Group (UNSDG, #20634)*; *United Nations Group on the Information Society (UNGIS, #20570)*; *UN-OCEANS (#20711)*; *UN-Water (#20723)*. Represented on: *United Nations System Chief Executives Board for Coordination (CEB, #20636)*. Instrumental in setting up: *Caribbean Institute for Meteorology and Hydrology (CIMH, #03520)*. Cooperation agreement with: *Organisation internationale de la Francophonie (OIF, #17809)*. Memorandum of Understanding with: *Economic Cooperation Organization (ECO, #05313)*; *South Asia Cooperative Environment Programme (SACEP, #19714)*. Participates in: *Group on Earth Observations (GEO, #10735)*.
'Working Arrangements' with:
- *Agency for the Safety of Aerial Navigation in Africa and Madagascar (#00556)*;
- *Arab Centre for the Studies of Arid Zones and Dry Lands (ACSAD, #00918)*;
- *Arab League Educational, Cultural and Scientific Organization (ALECSO, #01003)*;
- *Arab Organization for Agricultural Development (AOAD, #01018)*;
- *Baltic Marine Environment Protection Commission – Helsinki Commission (HELCOM, #03126)*;
- *Bureau international des poids et mesures (BIPM, #03367)*;
- *Caribbean Meteorological Organization (CMO, #03524)*;
- *Comisión Permanente del Pacífico Sur (CPPS, #04141)*;
- *Comité permanent inter-Etats de lutte contre la sécheresse dans le Sahel (CILSS, #04195)*;
- *Commission du Danube (CD, #04210)*;
- *Comprehensive Nuclear-Test-Ban Treaty Organization (CTBTO, #04420)*;
- *Economic Community of West African States (ECOWAS, #05312)*;
- *European Centre for Medium-Range Weather Forecasts (ECMWF, #06490)*;
- *European Organisation for the Exploitation of Meteorological Satellites (EUMETSAT, #08096)*;
- *European Space Agency (ESA, #08798)*;
- *FAO (#09260)*;
- *Intergovernmental Oceanographic Commission (IOC, #11496)*;
- *Interstate Council on Hydrometeorology of the Countries of the Commonwealth of Independent States (ICH)*;
- *International Atomic Energy Agency (IAEA, #12294)*;
- *International Civil Aviation Organization (ICAO, #12581)*;
- *International Council for the Exploration of the Sea (ICES, #13021)*;
- *International Fund for Agricultural Development (IFAD, #13692)*;
- *International Maritime Organization (IMO, #14102)*;
- *International Telecommunication Union (ITU, #15673)*;
- *Islamic World Educational, Scientific and Cultural Organization (ICESCO, #16058)*;
- *Lake Chad Basin Commission (LCBC, #16220)*;
- *League of Arab States (LAS, #16420)*;
- *Niger Basin Authority (NBA, #17134)*;
- *Permanent Joint Technical Commission for Nile Waters (PJTC, #18327)*;
- *Preparatory Commission for the Comprehensive Nuclear-Test-Ban Treaty Organization (CTBTO, #18482)*;
- *Secretariat of the Pacific Regional Environment Programme (SPREP, #19205)*;
- *UNESCO (#20322)*;
- United Nations;
- *WHO (#20950)*;
- *World Tourism Organization (UNWTO, #21861)*.

NGO Relations In 1953 (Resolution 2 EC-IV), the Executive Council created a *'consultative status'* for international non-governmental organizations, in application of Article 26b of the WMO Convention. The following 17 nongovernmental organizations have been granted this status:
- *Association of Hydro-Meteorological Industry (HMEI, #02636)*;
- *Comité International Radio-Maritime (CIRM, #04186)*;
- *International Association of Broadcast Meteorology (IABM, #11740)*;
- *International Association of Oil and Gas Producers (IOGP, #12053)*;
- *International Astronautical Federation (IAF, #12286)*;
- *International Astronomical Union (IAU, #12287)*;
- *International Commission on Irrigation and Drainage (ICID, #12694)*;
- *International Federation of Air Line Pilots' Associations (IFALPA, #13349)*;
- *International Federation for Information and Documentation (FID, inactive)*;
- *International Organization for Standardization (ISO, #14473)*;
- *International Society of Biometeorology (ISB, #14969)*;
- *International Union for Conservation of Nature and Natural Resources (IUCN, #15766)*;
- *International Union of Soil Sciences (IUSS, #15817)*;
- *Union radio-scientifique internationale (URSI, #20475)*;
- *World Federation of United Nations Associations (WFUNA, #21499)*.

'Working Arrangements' with:
- *International Council for Research and Innovation in Building and Construction (CIB, #13069)*;
- *International Institute for Applied Systems Analysis (IIASA, #13861)*;
- *International Seismological Centre (ISC, #14830)*;
- *International Union of Geodesy and Geophysics (IUGG, #15776)*.

In liaison with: *International Society of Biometeorology (ISB, #14969)*; technical committees of *Comité européen de normalisation (CEN, #04162)*. Reciprocal consultation and representation with: *International Air Transport Association (IATA, #11614)*. Observer to: *International Federation of Red Cross and Red Crescent Societies (#13526)*; *International Water-Related Associations' Liaison Committee (IWALC, #15869)*. Liaison member of: *Consultative Committee for Space Data Systems (CCSDS, #04764)*. Member of: *International Society for Agricultural Meteorology (INSAM, #14912)*. Observer member of: *Parliamentary Assembly of the Mediterranean (PAM, #18212)*. Together with Agencia Estatal de Meteorologia (Spain), provides secretariat for: *Conference of Directors of the West African National Meteorological and Hydrological Services (AFRIMET, #04589)*. Instrumental in setting up: *Centre régional de formation professionnelle en météorologie (CRFPM, no recent information)*; *Global Network of Isotopes in Precipitation (GNIP, #10491)*; *Global Precipitation Climatology Centre (GPCC)*. In addition, links with the following bodies:
- *African Physical Society (AfPS, #00417)*;
- *Airports Council International (ACI, #00611)*;
- *ASEAN Specialized Meteorological Centre (ASMC, #01236)*;
- *Asian Disaster Preparedness Center (ADPC, #01426)*;
- *Asian Disaster Reduction Center (ADRC, #01427)*;
- *Association coopérative financière des fonctionnaires internationaux (AMFIE, #02455)*;
- *Association internationale des traducteurs de conférence (AITC, #02748)*;
- *Climate Institute*;
- *Committee on Earth Observation Satellites (CEOS, #04249)*;
- *Committee on Space Research (COSPAR, #04287)*;
- *Consortium on Science, Technology and Innovation for the South (COSTIS, no recent information)*;
- *Co-operative Programme on Water and Climate (CPWC, inactive)*;
- *Ecomet (#05306)*;
- *European Association for the Science of Air Pollution (EURASAP, inactive)*;
- *European Climate Support Network (ECSN, inactive)*;
- *European Federation of Marine Science and Technology Societies (EFMS, inactive)*;
- *European Geosciences Union (EGU, #07390)*;
- *European Global Ocean Observing System (EuroGOOS, #07396)*;
- *European Meteorological Society (EMS, #07786)*;
- *European Network of Experimental and Representative Basins (ERB, #07905)*;
- *European Society of Skin Cancer Prevention (EUROSKIN, #08735)*;
- *European Society for Soil Conservation (ESSC, #08739)*;
- *Federation of International Civil Servants' Associations (FICSA, #09603)*;
- *Fondation pour l'économie et le développement durable des régions d'Europe (FEDRE, #09817)*;
- *Geneva Association (#10119)*;
- *Geneva International Academic Network (GIAN)*;
- *Global Change System for Analysis, Research and Training (START, #10278)*;
- *Global Environment and Natural Resources Institute (GENRI)*;
- *Global Warming International Center (GWIC, #10650)*;
- *Globetree Foundation*;
- *IHE Delft Institute for Water Education (#11110)*;
- *Inter-Agency Task Force for Disaster Reduction (IATF, inactive)*;
- *International Association for Hydro-Environment Engineering and Research (IAHR, #11950)*;
- *International Association of Hydrological Sciences (IAHS, #11954)*;
- *International Association of Meteorology and Atmospheric Sciences (IAMAS, #12031)*;
- *International Association for Urban Climate (IAUC, #12251)*;
- *International Centre on Research El Niño (CIIFEN)*;
- *International Chamber of Shipping (ICS, #12535)*;
- *International Commission on Clouds and Precipitation (ICCP, #12672)*;
- *International Consortium on Landslides (ICL, #12917)*;
- *International Council of Academies of Engineering and Technological Sciences (CAETS, #12982)*;
- *International Council of Aircraft Owner and Pilot Associations (IAOPA, #12988)*;
- *International Council on Archives (ICA, #12996)*;
- *International Electrotechnical Commission (IEC, #13255)*;
- *International Flood Initiative (IFI, #13613)*;
- *International Flood Network (IFNet, #13614)*;
- *International Geographical Union (IGU, #13713)*;
- *International Geosphere-Biosphere Programme (IGBP, inactive)*;
- *International Groundwater Resources Assessment Centre (IGRAC, #13739)*;
- *International Lake Environment Committee Foundation (ILEC, #13998)*;
- *International Olympic Committee (IOC, #14408)*;
- *International Ozone Commission (IO3C, #14495)*;
- *International Petroleum Industry Environmental Conservation Association (IPIECA, #14562)*;
- *International Radiation Commission (IRC, #14684)*;
- *International Research Institute for Climate and Society (IRI)*;
- *International School of Meteorology of the Mediterranean (no recent information)*;
- *International Sustainable Energy Organization (ISEO, inactive)*;
- *Mountain Forum (MF, #16861)*;
- *Network of European Meteorological Services (EUMETNET, #17022)*;
- *Organisation internationale des experts (ORDINEX, #17808)*;
- *Pacific Science Association (PSA, #18003)*;
- *Past Global Changes (PAGES, #18257)*;
- *Scientific Committee on Antarctic Research (SCAR, #19147)*;
- *Scientific Committee on Oceanic Research (SCOR, #19149)*;
- *Stockholm Environment Institute (SEI, #19993)*;
- *United Nations Staff Mutual Insurance Society Against Sickness and Accident (UNSMIS, #20629)*;
- *United Nations University Institute for Environment and Human Security (UNU-EHS, #20645)*;
- *World Agroforestry Centre (ICRAF, #21072)*;
- *Youth and United Nations Global Alliance (YUNGA, #22028)*. [2020/XB3556/**B***]

♦ World Methodist Council (WMC) 21650

Conseil méthodiste mondial

Gen Sec PO Box 518, Lake Junaluska NC 28745, USA. T. +18284569432. Fax +18284569433. E-mail: info@worldmethodistcouncil.org – communications@worldmethodistcouncil.org.
URL: http://worldmethodistcouncil.org/

History 7 Sep 1881, UK. Founded at international *Ecumenical Methodist Conference* in Wesley's Chapel. Conferences were held subsequently at 10-year intervals. Present name and new statutes adopted 1951, Oxford (UK), when frequency of meetings changed to 5-year intervals. Constitution changed: Aug 1961, Oslo (Norway); 1971, Denver CO (USA); 2011, Durban (South Africa). **Aims** Link the family of Methodist and related United Churches around the world; deepen the fellowship of Methodist peoples and their unity of witness; strengthen international ties, promote understanding, clarify theological and moral standards and identify priorities for the Methodist movement; strengthen the love of members for Jesus Christ as Lord and for each other as brothers and sisters in the faith; increase awareness whereby this love finds expression in keeping with the life and ministry of John Wesley to proclaim the Gospel and serve Christ in the world; advance unity of theological moral standards; encourage evangelism; promote *Christian* education and the care for youth; relieve persecuted or needy Christian minorities; provide a means for consultation and cooperation on an international level; study union and reunion proposals. **Structure** Council (meeting every 5 years, at time of World Methodist Conference) comprises 500 members designated by member Churches. Executive Committee, consisting of members elected by Council from among its members plus: Presidium of up to 8 Presidents (no 2 from any one church) plus Chairperson, Vice-Chairperson and Treasurer. Other Officers: Past Chairpersons; President of the World Federation of Methodist Women. Head Office at Lake Junaluska NC (USA); Sections (2): World Methodist Committee of the British Methodist Church; World Methodist Council North American Section. Special Commissions. Standing Committees (8). Operational Committees (3): Finance; Nominating; Programme. World Exchange Programme. Officers meet annually. Executive Committee and Standing Committees meet periodically between Council meetings. **Languages** English. **Staff** 3.00 FTE, paid. **Finance** Sources: contributions from member Churches; endowment. **Activities** Activities pursued through 8 Standing Committees: Ecumenics and Dialogue; Education; Evangelism; Family Life; Social and International Affairs; Theological Education; Worship and Liturgy; Youth. Main elements: proclamation of the Gospel (world evangelism) through *World Evangelism Committee (#21394)* and *World Methodist Evangelism Institute (WMEI, see: #21650)*, the latter a division of WMC with offices in Atlanta GA (USA); social witness. Organizes: International Christian Youth Conference; World Ministerial Exchange Programme; regular consultations on theological education, family life and worship. Supports: *'Oxford Institute for Methodist Theological Studies'* (every 4 years) and *'Convocation on Theological Education'* (every 5 years), for which there are elected committees; *Confederación Femenina Metodista América Latina y El Caribe (CFMAL and El Caribe, no recent information)*. Bestows annual World Methodist Peace Award. Maintains: Epworth Old Rectory, owned by Council with appointed Trustees; *World Methodist Museum*, Lake Junaluska NC (USA). Instrumental in setting up: *World Association of Christian Radio Amateurs and Listeners (WACRAL, #21127)*. **Events** *Quinquennial World Methodist Conference* Gothenburg (Sweden) 2022, *Meeting* Seoul (Korea Rep) 2018, *Quinquennial World Methodist Conference* Houston, TX (USA) 2016, *Quinquennial world methodist conference* Durban (South Africa) 2011, *International Christian Youth Conference (ICYC)* Seoul (Korea Rep) 2010. **Publications** *WMC Handbook of Information* (2002-2007); *Doctrine of the Church*; *Encyclopedia of World Methodism*; *Saved by Grace*; *Who's Who in Methodism*. Through International Publishing Committee. Conference proceedings. **Members** Representatives (500), from 77 distinct and separate Methodist and United Churches with approximately 39 million members and a community of over 75 million in over 138 countries and territories, of which the following 114 have been specified:
Albania, Algeria, Angola, Antigua-Barbuda, Argentina, Australia, Austria, Bahamas, Bangladesh, Belgium, Belize, Benin, Bolivia, Botswana, Brazil, Bulgaria, Burundi, Cambodia, Cameroon, Canada, Cape Verde, Chile, China, Colombia, Congo DR, Costa Rica, Côte d'Ivoire, Croatia, Cuba, Czechia, Denmark, Dominica, Dominican Rep, Ecuador, El Salvador, Estonia, Eswatini, Fiji, Finland, France, Gambia, Germany, Ghana, Grenada, Guatemala, Guinea, Guyana, Haiti, Honduras, Hong Kong, Hungary, India, Indonesia, Ireland, Italy, Jamaica, Japan, Kenya, Latvia, Lesotho, Lithuania, Malawi, Malaysia, Mexico, Mozambique, Myanmar, Namibia, Netherlands, New Zealand, Nicaragua, Niger, Nigeria, North Macedonia, Norway, Pakistan, Panama, Papua New Guinea, Philippines, Poland, Portugal, Puerto Rico, Romania, Russia, Rwanda, Samoa, Senegal, Serbia, Sierra Leone, Singapore, Slovakia, Slovenia, Solomon Is, South Africa, Spain, Sri Lanka, St Kitts-Nevis, St Lucia, St Vincent-Grenadines, Sweden, Switzerland, Taiwan, Tanzania UR, Thailand, Togo, Tonga, Trinidad-Tobago, Tunisia, Uganda, UK, Uruguay, USA, Zambia, Zimbabwe.

Regional bodies (7):
African Methodist Episcopal Church (AME); *African Methodist Episcopal Zion Church (AME Zion)*; *Central and Southern Europe Central Conference – The United Methodist Church (#03721)*; *Methodist Church of Southern Africa*; *The Conference of the Methodist Church in the Caribbean and the Americas (MCCA, #04629)*; *United Methodist Central Conference of Northern Europe (#20513)*; *West African Methodist Church (no recent information)*.

Affiliated organizations (3):
World Federation of Methodist and Uniting Church Women (WFM and UCW, #21457); *World Fellowship of Methodist and Uniting Church Men (WesleyMen, #21503)*; *World Methodist Historical Society (WMHS, #21651)*.

NGO Relations Regular advisor to Central Committee of: *World Council of Churches (WCC, #21320)*. Represents churches belonging to the Methodist/Wesleyan tradition in: *Conference of Secretaries of Christian World Communions (CS/CWC, #04647)*. Continuing dialogue with: *Anglican Communion (#00827)*; *Pontifical Council for Promoting Christian Unity (PCPCU, #18446)* representing the Roman Catholic Church in *International Joint Commission for Dialogue between the World Methodist Council and the Vatican (#13972)*; *Salvation Army (#19041)*. Member of: *International Christian Federation for the Prevention of Alcoholism and Drug Addiction (ICF-PADA, no recent information)*. [2021/XC3557/y/**B**]

♦ World Methodist Evangelism Institute (see: #21650)

♦ World Methodist Historical Society (WMHS) 21651

Société mondiale d'histoire méthodiste

Gen Sec WMHS Head Office, PO Box 127, Madison NJ 07940, USA. T. +19734083189. Fax +19734083909.
Pres address not obtained.
URL: http://www.gcah.org/directories/world-methodist-historical-society

History 1911. New Constitution and present name adopted 18 Aug 1971, Denver CO (USA). Constitution amended: 1981; 1991. Former names and other names: *International Methodist Historical Society* – former (1911 to 1971). **Aims** Identify and coordinate activities of historical agencies of all denominations which have their roots in the Methodist movement of the 18th century. **Structure** Meeting (every 5 years at World Methodist Council and Conference); Executive Committee. **Languages** English. **Staff** Voluntary. **Finance** Sources: gifts, legacies; grants; international organizations; members' dues. **Activities** Events/meetings; research/documentation. **Events** *World Methodist Conference* Houston, TX (USA) 2016, *World Methodist Conference* Durban (South Africa) 2011, *Quinquennial convention / World Conference* Seoul (Korea Rep) 2006, *World conference* Brighton (UK) 2001, *World conference* Wilmore, KY (USA) 2000. **Publications** *Historical Bulletin* (annual).

Members Individuals (about 225) in 22 countries:
Australia, Canada, Germany, Ireland, Italy, Japan, Korea Rep, Liberia, Malaysia, New Zealand, Norway, Pakistan, Philippines, Sierra Leone, Singapore, South Africa, Sweden, Switzerland, UK, USA, Venezuela, Zimbabwe.

NGO Relations Affiliated with (1): *World Methodist Council (WMC, #21650).* [2023.02.20/XD2260/v/**D**]

♦ World Methodist Museum (internationally oriented national body)

♦ World Minifootball Federation (WMF) 21652

General Secretariat Strada dell'Argine 2, 6512 Giubiasco TI, Switzerland. T. +41791772288. E-mail: info@minifootball.com.
URL: http://www.minifootball.com/

History 2013. **Aims** Promote, supervise and direct minifootball in the world, as a means to contribute to the positive development of society. **Structure** President; Executives. Committees (7): Tournament; Technical; Disciplinary; Development; PR, Marketing and Media; IT; Referee. **Activities** Sporting activities. **Events** *Conference* Birmingham (UK) 2013.

Members Associations (5):
Asian Minifootball Confederation (AMC, #01541); Confederación Panamericana de Minifutbol (CPM, #04477); European Minifootball Federation (EMF, #07808); Oceania Mini Football Federation (OMF, #17666); South African Minifootball Federation. [2020/XJ9005/y/**B**]

♦ World Minigolf Sport Federation (WMF) 21653

Pres Panzerleite 49, 96049 Bamberg, Germany. E-mail: office@minigolfsport.com.
URL: http://gov.minigolfsport.com/

History 1980, Hard (Austria). Former names and other names: *International Minigolf Federation (IMGF)* – former; *Fédération internationale de golf sur pistes* – former. **Aims** Promote minigolf internationally; represent the interests of members at the international level as regards the authorities, other sport associations, the mass media and the public; promote sporting contact; monitor and ensure keeping of existing rules; develop standard rules insofar as technical peculiarities of courses allow. **Structure** Delegates Conference; Executive Committee; Presidential Committee; other Committees. **Languages** English. **Staff** 15.00 FTE, voluntary. **Finance** Sources: members' dues; sponsorship. **Activities** Sporting activities. **Events** *Delegates Conference* Zhouzhuang (China) 2019, *Delegates Conference* Nin (Croatia) 2017, *Annual Meeting* Prague (Czech Rep) 2016, *Delegates Conference* Lahti (Finland) 2015, *Annual Meeting* Prague (Czech Rep) 2015.

Members Full in 65 countries and territories:
Albania, Armenia, Australia, Austria, Belarus, Belgium, Brazil, Cameroon, Canada, China, Croatia, Cyprus, Czechia, Denmark, Egypt, Estonia, Finland, France, Georgia, Germany, Ghana, Hungary, India, Iran Islamic Rep, Ireland, Israel, Italy, Japan, Kenya, Korea Rep, Kosovo, Latvia, Liechtenstein, Luxembourg, Malaysia, Malta, Mexico, Moldova, Mongolia, Nepal, Netherlands, New Zealand, Nigeria, Norway, Poland, Portugal, Romania, Russia, Serbia, Singapore, Slovakia, Slovenia, Spain, Sweden, Switzerland, Taipei, Thailand, Togo, Tunisia, Türkiye, UK, Ukraine, United Arab Emirates, USA, Vietnam.

NGO Relations Member of (3): *Alliance of Independent recognised Members of Sport (AIMS, #00690); Olympic Movement (#17719); The Association for International Sport for All (TAFISA, #02763).* Recognized by: *International Olympic Committee (IOC, #14408).* [2021.09.06/XD1441/**C**]

♦ World Mining Congress (WMC) 21654

Congrès minier mondial – Congreso Mundial de Mineria – Weltbergbau-Kongress – Vsemirnyj Gornyj Kongress – Swiatowy Kongres Górniczy

SG GIG, Plac Gwarków 1, 40-166 Katowice, Poland. T. +48323246603. Fax +48322028745. E-mail: wmc@gig.katowice.pl.
URL: http://www.wmc.org.pl/

History 1958, Warsaw (Poland), at 1st International Mining Congress, as *International Scientific and Technical Conference on Mine and Construction.* More formal structure created and statutes and present name adopted, 1975, Austria. Statutes revised 1997, Mexico. **Aims** Promote and support scientific and technical cooperation for national and international progress in the fields of mining of solid minerals and development of natural *mineral resources*; obtain a world-wide exchange of information with respect to development of mining science, technology, economics, health and safety aspects of mining operations and environmental protection. **Structure** Congress (normally every 3 years); *WMC International Organizing Committee (IOC)*, meeting biennially and comprising representatives of national committees, elects Secretary-General, Chairman, First Vice-Chairman, and up to 6 further Vice-Chairman (4-year terms). Secretariat. **Languages** English, French, German, Russian, Spanish. **Staff** Full and part-time, paid. **Finance** No membership fee. Secretariat expenses met by national organization of country of residence of IOC Chairman; expenses of meetings covered by national organization of country in which they are held. **Activities** WMC Krupinski International Scholarship provides short periods of practical training and experience in other countries for young graduate mining engineers (temporarily suspended). Mining statistics sponsored by Austrian NC. **Events** *Congress* Brisbane, QLD (Australia) 2022, *Congress* Brisbane, QLD (Australia) 2021, *Congress* Astana (Kazakhstan) 2018, *Congress* Rio de Janeiro (Brazil) 2016, *Congress* Montréal, QC (Canada) 2013. **Publications** Congress papers and reports.

Members Associate members; representatives of National Committees or appropriate professional authorities. Total of 171 members (for no National Committee) in 48 countries:
Argentina, Austria, Belgium, Brazil, Bulgaria, Canada, Chile (*), China, Colombia (*), Croatia, Cuba, Czechia, Estonia, Finland, France, Germany, Greece, Hungary, India, Iran Islamic Rep, Ireland, Italy, Japan, Kazakhstan (*), Korea DPR, Mexico, Mongolia, Morocco, North Macedonia, Norway, Papua New Guinea, Peru, Philippines, Poland, Portugal, Romania, Russia, Serbia, Slovakia, Slovenia, South Africa, Spain, Sweden, Türkiye, UK, Ukraine, USA, Venezuela.

Permanent affiliated international bodies (4), each maintaining its independent Secretariat:
International Bureau of Mining Thermophysics (IBMT, no recent information); International Bureau of Strata Mechanics (IBSM, #12417); International Committee on Automation of Mines and Quarries (ICAMC, #12747); International Society for Mine Surveying (ISM, #15272).

Consultative Status Consultative status granted from: *ECOSOC (#05331)* (Ros A). **NGO Relations** Observer at Council meetings of: *International Society for Rock Mechanics and Rock Engineering (ISRM, #15428).* [2020/XC2307/y/**C**]

♦ World Mission (internationally oriented national body)
♦ World Mission (internationally oriented national body)

♦ World Missionary Evangelism (WME) 21655

Pres PO Box 660800, Dallas TX 75266, USA. T. +12149421678. Fax +12149467808. E-mail: mainoffice@wme.org.
URL: http://www.wme.org/

History 1958, USA, by John E Douglas. **Aims** Reach out to those in need through caring for *orphans*, building native churches, children's homes, leper control centres, schools and training centres for the *blind* in needy land. **Activities** Food for Hunger projects; Save-a-Child programme; Orphan Child Support programme; Save-A-Family programme. **Publications** *World Evangelism* (12 a year). [2010/XF0734/**F**]

♦ World Mission Associates (internationally oriented national body)
♦ World Mission Foundation (internationally oriented national body)
♦ World Mission Prayer League (internationally oriented national body)
♦ World Mizrachi Movement / see Mizrachi – Hapoel Hamizrachi World Organization (#16833)

♦ World Molecular Imaging Society (WMIS) 21656

CEO 10736 Jefferson Blvd, Suite 185, Culver City CA 90230, USA. T. +13102159730. Fax +13102159731. E-mail: wmis@wmis.org.
URL: http://www.wmis.org/

History 2011. Founded by merger of the *Academy of Molecular Imaging* and the *Society for Molecular Imaging.* **Aims** Further understanding of biology and medicine through multimodal *in vivo* imaging of cellular and molecular events involved in normal and pathologic processes and utilization of quantitative molecular imaging in patient care. **Structure** Annual Meeting; Executive Committee; Steering Committee; other Committees (8). **Languages** English. **Staff** 3.00 FTE, paid. **Finance** Sources: members' dues. **Activities** Awards/prizes/competitions; events/meetings; research/documentation; training/education. **Events** *World Molecular Imaging Congress* Prague (Czechia) 2023, *Iceland Summer Conference* Iceland 2022, *World Molecular Imaging Congress* Miami Beach, FL (USA) 2022, *World Molecular Imaging Congress* Culver City, CA (USA) 2021, *World Molecular Imaging Congress* Culver City, CA (USA) 2020. **Publications** *Molecular Imaging and Biology* – journal. **Members** Full; Student. Membership countries not specified. **NGO Relations** Cooperates with (1): *European Society for Molecular Imaging (ESMI, #08655).* [2022.10.11/XJ5220/**C**]

♦ World Monuments Fund (WMF) 21657

Fonds mondial pour les monuments

CEO 350 Fifth Avenue, Ste 2412, New York NY 10118, USA. T. +16464249594. Fax +16464249593.
URL: http://www.wmf.org/

History 1965. Former names and other names: *International Fund for Monuments (IFM)* – former (1965); *World Monuments Watch* – alias. **Aims** Promote the preservation of international architectural and artistic treasures. **Structure** Board of Trustees, comprising Chairman, Vice Chairman, Vice Chairman/Treasurer, Secretary/General Counsel and 18 members. **Staff** 23; European Offices: 10. **Finance** Members' dues. Donations. **Activities** Works to provide financial and technical support for project planning and management. Launched *'World Monuments Watch'*, 1995, aimed to call public attention to critically imperilled cultural heritage sites and direct timely financial support to their preservation. Awards the *'Hadrian Award'*; organizes regional conferences. Other activities: documentation; field research; training; strategic planning; technical survey; fundraising; advocacy. **Events** *Annual Ename international colloquium* Ghent (Belgium) / Ostend (Belgium) 2009, *Conference on heritage conservation in South and Southeast Asia* Colombo (Sri Lanka) 2004. **Publications** *ICON* (4 a year) – magazine. *World Monuments Fund – The First Thirty Years.* Annual Report; project reports.

Members Associate; Sustaining; Supporting; Sponsor; Benefactor, Patron. Affiliates in 5 countries:
France, Portugal, Spain, UK, USA.

Consultative Status Consultative status granted from: *UNESCO (#20322)* (Foundations). **NGO Relations** Member of: *International Coordinating Committee on the Safeguarding and Development of the Historic Site of Angkor (ICC-Angkor, #12954); World Heritage Watch (WHW).* [2020/XF4958/f/**F**]

♦ World Monuments Watch / see World Monuments Fund (#21657)
♦ World Motor Sport Council (see: #09613)

♦ World Mountain People Association (WMPA) 21658

Association des populations des montagnes du monde (APMM) – Asociación de Poblaciones de Montaña del Mundo (APMM) – Vereinigung der Bergbevölkerungen der Welt (VBBW) – Associazione delle Popolazioni delle Montagne del Mondo (APMM)

SG 50 bd Malesherbes, 75008 Paris, France. T. +33142938660. Fax +33145222818.
Pres address not obtained.
URL: https://www.apmm-wmpa.org/

History 21 Apr 2001, Paris (France). Founded following decision made at the 1st World Mountain Forum in Chambéry (France), Jun 2000. **Aims** Raise awareness among governments and public opinion of global economic, social, environmental and cultural challenges represented by mountain areas; promote equitable and sustainable development of mountain areas; open a new international space of dialogue and cooperation on mountain issues between all the stakeholders. **Structure** General Assembly (every 3 years). Whole Board (meets annually), comprising 30 members and 3 colleges as follows: 50% seats for administrative authorities or local governments and mountain communities; 15% seats for representatives from civil society, NGO and associations working alongside mountain people; 35% seats for individuals, including researchers. Executive Board, consisting of 15 members from Africa, Asia, Latin America and Europe. Presidency, comprising President and Secretary-General. **Languages** English, French, Italian, Spanish. **Staff** 1 full-time, paid; 15-20 part-time, voluntary. **Finance** Sources: grants; members' dues. Other sources: subventions. **Activities** Advocacy/lobbying/activism; events/meetings; guidance/assistance/consulting. **Events** *International Board Meeting* Albertville (France) 2012, *Meeting* Nepal 2012, *Meeting* Chambéry (France) 2011, *General assembly* Oloron-Sainte-Marie (France) 2010, *Mountain people world meeting* Oloron-Sainte-Marie (France) 2010. **Publications** *WMPA Newsletter. Charter for World Mountain People* (2003). Presentation leaflet.

Members Representatives of organizations, communities or other form of local political organization of mountain groups; representatives of organizations of civil society working for mountain people (NGOs, social-professional groups, etc); scientists, researchers or experts working alongside mountain people. Members in 40 countries and territories:
Algeria, Andorra, Argentina, Belgium, Bhutan, Bolivia, Botswana, Burundi, Cameroon, Chile, China, Colombia, Ecuador, France, Guatemala, India, Italy, Kenya, Lesotho, Libya, Madagascar, Malawi, Mali, Morocco, Mozambique, Nepal, Netherlands, Pakistan, Peru, Romania, Rwanda, South Africa, Spain, Switzerland, Tanzania UR, Tunisia, Uganda, Venezuela, Zambia, Zimbabwe.

Consultative Status Consultative status granted from: *UNESCO (#20322)* (Consultative Status). **IGO Relations** Observer status with: *Congress of Local and Regional Authorities of the Council of Europe (#04677); World Intellectual Property Organization (WIPO, #21593).*

NGO Relations Member of: *Mountain Partnership (MP, #16862).* Founder and partner organizations include:
- *Agency for Technical Cooperation and Development (ACTED)*;
- *Agronomes et vétérinaires sans frontières (AVSF)*;
- *Amazigh World Congress (AWC)*;
- *Assembly of European Regions (AER, #02316)*;
- *Centre de Management Europe-Amérique Latine (CMEAL)*;
- *Centro de Estudios Rurales y de Agricultura Internacional (CERAI)*;
- *Consortium for the Sustainable Development of the Andean Ecoregion (#04758)*;
- *Eastern and Southern Africa small scale Farmers' Forum (ESAFF, #05256)*;
- *Euromontana (#05737)*;
- *European Academy of Bozen/Bolzano (EURAC)*;
- *Fondation Charles Léopold Mayer pour le progrès de l'homme (FPH, #09815)*;
- *GERES*;
- *International Centre for Integrated Mountain Development (ICIMOD, #12500)*;
- *International Centre for Integrated Mountain Development (ICIMOD, #12500)*;
- *CIPRA International (#03930)*;
- *International Potato Center (#14627)*;
- *Mission d'aide au développement des économies rurales afghanes (MADERA, #16828)*;
- *Mountain Forum (MF, #16861)*;
- *Organisation mondiale de la diaspora africaine (OMDA)*;
- *Oxfam International (#17922)* – Belgium;
- *Oxfam International (#17922)*;
- *Panos Network (#18183)* – London (UK);
- *Participatory Ecological Land Use Management (PELUM Association, #18225)*;
- *Terra Nuova*;
- *Working Community of the Pyrenees (#21057).* [2021/XD8831/**C**]

♦ World Mountain Running Association (WMRA) 21659

Association mondiale de courses en montagne

Gen Sec Tacenska 137, 1133 Ljubljana, Slovenia.
URL: http://www.wmra.info/

History as *International Committee for Mountain Running (ICMR) – Comité international de courses en montagne.* **Aims** Promote and develop mountain running as a branch of athletics; organize mountain running events on an international level. **Structure** Congress; Council. **Languages** English. **Staff** Voluntary. **Finance** Members' dues. Other sources: support from *World Athletics (#21209)*; organizer fees; sponsors. **Activities** Sporting activities. **Publications** *WMRA Newsletter.*

Members Full in 44 countries:

Argentina, Armenia, Australia, Austria, Belarus, Belgium, Bulgaria, Canada, Chile, Colombia, Croatia, Czechia, Eritrea, Ethiopia, France, Germany, Greece, Hungary, Ireland, Italy, Japan, Kenya, Liechtenstein, Mexico, Monaco, Mongolia, Netherlands, New Zealand, North Macedonia, Poland, Portugal, Romania, Russia, Serbia, Slovakia, Slovenia, Spain, Switzerland, Türkiye, Uganda, UK, Ukraine, USA, Venezuela. [2020.03.03/XD4771/**D**]

♦ World Movement of Christian Workers (WMCW) 21660

Mouvement mondial des travailleurs chrétiens (MMTC) – Movimiento Mundial de Trabajadores Cristianos (MMTC) – Weltbewegung der Christlichen Arbeiter (WBCA) – Movimento Mundial dos Trabalhadores Cristãos

Gen Sec Boulevard du Jubilé 124, 1080 Brussels, Belgium.
URL: http://www.mmtc-infor.com/

History 15 May 1961. Statutes adopted 28 May 1966, Rome (Italy), taking over the functions previously carried out by *International Federation of Christian Workers Movements (FIMOC, inactive)*, set up in 1951, and of movements in France and French-speaking Switzerland, which commenced organizing International Conversations in 1955, with participation of delegates from Latin American and African countries. Statutes most recently revised, Dec 1983, Retie (Belgium); May 2000, Sao Paulo (Brazil) 2000; May 2004, Québec QC (Canada); 2009, Nantes (France); 2013, Haltern am See (Germany). Registration: Belgium. **Aims** Unite national and regional movements combining worker, educative and apostolic characteristics and working on collective and overall promotion of organizations of workers and their families and their spiritual destiny; participate in apostolic and social endeavours of the Church in the world of labour, particularly when directed towards those who are furthest from Christ, whose faith is threatened or who are most devoid of human hope; promote education, training and evangelization of men and women, employed and jobless, pensioners and women at home so as to fight a system based on money and promote a society based on solidarity and justice; ensure that the lives and actions of the most deprived are recognized and receive support of the whole Church and of political leaders. **Structure** General Assembly (every 4 years, following seminar). Executive Council (meets annually) of at least 10 members and including 2 Co-Presidents, General Secretary, Treasurer and Chaplain. **Languages** English, French, German, Spanish. **Staff** 3.00 FTE, paid. **Finance** Sources: donations; members' dues; revenue from activities/projects. **Activities** In every 4-year cycle, organizes: international seminar; regional or continental seminar; international conversation. **Events** *International Seminar* Avila (Spain) 2017, *Quadrennial General Assembly* Avila (Spain) 2017, *International Seminar* Haltern (Germany) 2013, *Quadrennial General Assembly* Haltern (Germany) 2013, *Quadrennial General Assembly* Nantes (France) 2009. **Publications** *Infor-WMCW* in English, French, German, Portuguese, Spanish. Brochures. **Consultative Status** Consultative status granted from: *ECOSOC (#05331)* (Ros C); *ILO (#11123)* (Special List). **NGO Relations** Member of: *Forum of Catholic Inspired NGOs (#09905).* [2020/XC3559/**C**]

♦ World Movement for Democracy 21661

Senior Manager 1025 F St NW – Ste 800, Washington DC 20004-1409, USA. T. +12023789700. E-mail: world@ned.org.
URL: http://www.movedemocracy.org/

History 17 Feb 1999, Delhi (India). **Aims** Strengthen democracy where it is weak; defend democracy where it is longstanding; support efforts of pro-democracy groups in non-democratic countries. **Structure** Steering Committee of 30 members. Secretariat. **Languages** Arabic, English, French, Russian, Spanish. **Staff** 7.00 FTE, paid. **Finance** Private and public funds. **Activities** Facilitates establishment of regional and functional networks, including: *African Democracy Forum (ADF, #00281)*; *Red Latinoamericana y del Caribe para la Democracia (RedLad, #18704)*; *International Movement of Parliamentarians for Democracy (IMPD, see: #21661)*; *International Women's Democracy Network (IWDN, #15897)*; *Global Network on Local Governance (GNLG, #10493)*; *Network of Democracy Research Institutes (NDRI, #17003)*; *World Youth Movement for Democracy (WYMD, #21957).* Project support. **Events** *Empowering civil society for democracy and its renewal* Seoul (Korea Rep) 2015, *Assembly* Lima (Peru) 2012, *Assembly* Jakarta (Indonesia) 2010, *Assembly* Kiev (Ukraine) 2008, *Advancing democracy – justice, pluralism, and participation* Istanbul (Turkey) 2006. **Publications** *DemocracyNews* (12 a year) – electronic newsletter; *Defending Civil Society Report and Country Reports*; *DemocracyVoices*; *World Youth Movement for Democracy Newsletter. World Youth Movement for Democracy Essay Contest Booklet.* Assembly Report.

Members Steering Committee members in 30 countries:
Australia, Bosnia-Herzegovina, Brazil, Canada, China, Congo DR, Egypt, France, Gambia, Haiti, India, Indonesia, Iran Islamic Rep, Jordan, Kazakhstan, Kenya, Mexico, Netherlands, Philippines, Poland, Portugal, Russia, South Africa, Thailand, Tunisia, UK, Ukraine, USA, Venezuela, Zimbabwe.

NGO Relations Secretariat hosted by *National Endowment for Democracy (NED).* [2018.07.31/XF6692/**F**]

- ♦ World Movement for Global Democracy (internationally oriented national body)
- ♦ World Movement of Mothers / see Make Mothers Matter (#16554)
- ♦ World Movement NA'AMAT / see NA'AMAT Movement of Working Women and Volunteers
- ♦ World Movement for World Federal Government / see World Federalist Movement – Movement for a Just World Order through a Strengthened United Nations (#21404)

♦ World Muay Federation (WMF) 21662

Headquarters Rue Bellefontaine 2, 1003 Lausanne VD, Switzerland. T. +41213314080. Fax +41213314081. E-mail: worldmuay@gmail.com – gen.sec@worldmuayfederation.org – pr@worldmuayfederation.org.
Bangkok Rajamangala Natl Stadium, 223-224 Zone E, Sport Authority, 286 Ramkhamheang Road, Huamark, Bangkapi, Bangkok, 10240, Thailand. Fax +6623006405.
URL: http://www.worldmuayfederation.org/

History 1995. Founded by merger of *International Amateur Muay Thai Federation (IAMTF, inactive)* and *International Federation of Muay Thai Amateur (IFMA, inactive).* Former names and other names: *World Muaythai Federation* – former. **Aims** As conservation officers for South East Asian *martial arts*: promote, teach, educate and popularize the arts of Muay, Muay Boran, Lethwei, Khun Khmer, Muay Viet, Muay Laos, Muaythai, Muay Chaiya, etc. **Structure** Executive Committee. **Languages** English. **Staff** 20.00 FTE, paid. **Finance** Privately funded. Annual budget: 150,000 EUR. **Activities** Events/meetings; sporting activities; training/education. **Members** Full in over 80 countries; associate in 24 countries. Membership countries not specified. **IGO Relations** Cooperates with: Ministry of Tourism and Sport, and Tourism Authority of Thailand; National Olympic Committees of Laos and Myanmar. **NGO Relations** Member of (2): *International Martial Art Games Committee (IMGC, #14107)*; *The Association for International Sport for All (TAFISA, #02763).* [2020/XM2811/**D**]

- ♦ World Muaythai Federation / see World Muay Federation (#21662)

♦ World Muscle Society (WMS) 21663

Secretariat c/o Azura, 18 Bow Creek, Tuckenhay, Totnes, TQ9 7HP, UK. Fax +447584176583. E-mail: office@worldmusclesociety.org.
URL: http://www.worldmusclesociety.org/

History 4 Jun 1995, London (UK). **Aims** Advance and disseminate knowledge in the field of *neuromuscular* disorders. **Structure** Executive Board, consisting of President, Secretary, Treasurer and 12 further members. Advisory Board. **Languages** English. **Staff** 1.00 FTE, paid. **Finance** Sources: members' dues. **Events** *Congress* Hiroshima (Japan) 2026, *Congress* Vienna (Austria) 2025, *Congress* Prague (Czechia) 2024, *Congress* Charleston, SC (USA) 2023, *Congress* Halifax, NS (Canada) 2022. **Publications** *Neuromuscular Disorders* – journal.

Members Individuals in 55 countries:
Algeria, Argentina, Australia, Austria, Belgium, Bosnia-Herzegovina, Brazil, Bulgaria, Canada, Chile, Croatia, Cyprus, Czechia, Denmark, Finland, France, Germany, Greece, Hong Kong, Hungary, India, Ireland, Israel, Italy, Japan, Jordan, Korea Rep, Luxembourg, Malaysia, Martinique, Mexico, Netherlands, New Zealand, North Macedonia, Norway, Pakistan, Poland, Portugal, Romania, Russia, Saudi Arabia, Serbia, Singapore, Slovenia, South Africa, Spain, Sweden, Switzerland, Taiwan, Tunisia, Türkiye, UK, United Arab Emirates, Uruguay, USA. [2020/XC0059/v/**C**]

♦ World Muslim Congress (WMC) 21664

Congrès du monde islamique – Motamar Al-Alam Al-Islami

SG PO Box 5030, Karachi 74000, Pakistan. T. +922134969423 – +922134958118. Fax +922134964399. E-mail: motamar@cyber.net.pk – motamarpk@gmail.com.
URL: http://www.motamaralalamalislami.org/

History Jul 1926, Makkah (Saudi Arabia). World-wide Executive Council set up 1931, together with International Secretariat, Jerusalem (Palestine). Established as permanent organization 1951, Karachi (Pakistan). Constitution adopted 15 Dec 1962, Baghdad (Iraq). **Aims** Work for greater fellowship, unity and cooperation among Muslims and for the social and cultural solidarity of all mankind; deal generally with all problems relating to Islam and Muslims and humanity without interfering in domestic or internal politics of any country; work to remove amongst Muslims all prejudices and discriminations without affecting the national entity or independence of any Muslim country; educate Muslims to mould and reconstruct the entire system of their lives in accordance with the tenets of Islam and to help the setting up of educational institutions, seminars, foundations, trusts, etc, for socio-cultural and for business and economic interests; encourage educational exchange programmes for teachers, students, publications and socio-economic personalities so as to strengthen the economic ties among Muslims worldwide; work to improve and raise the socio-economic and cultural standards of living of Muslims in particular, and of mankind in general; create amongst Muslims unity of thought and action and a consciousness of Islamic ideology so as to take all measures for preserving and developing Islamic *culture* and civilization, to act as treasurer of Islamic learning and sciences and to promote and arrange for their publication; safeguard the *Shariah* rights of women; provide the world with general information regarding the activities of Muslims in different branches of life. **Structure** Plenary Assembly (at least once every 5 years); Executive Council (meets annually); Branches; High Commission for Mosques. Continental Councils for Mosques: Europe (based in Brussels); Africa; Asia; Australia. General Secretariat. Committees (5): Political Issues; Religious Studies; Financial Questions; Education; Cultural Matters. Research Department; study groups. In 1984, set up *Institute for the Spread of Islam (no recent information)* in Fez (Morocco). **Languages** Arabic, English, French. **Staff** 40.00 FTE, paid. Voluntary. **Finance** Sources: donations; members' dues. **Activities** Events/meetings; knowledge management/information dissemination; training/education. **Events** *General Assembly* Islamabad (Pakistan) 2000, *International conference / General Assembly* Islamabad (Pakistan) 1997, *General Conference* Cairo (Egypt) 1994, *General Assembly* Colombo (Sri Lanka) 1992, *North and South peace meeting* Addis Ababa (Ethiopia) 1989. **Publications** *The Muslim World (TMW)* (12 a year) in English; *World Muslim Gazetteer* (every 10 years) – encyclopaedia. *Communications Revolution and the Muslims* by Aslam Siddiqui; *Vindication of Islam and Muslims* by John Davenport; *The Existence of God* by A Galwash; *The International Jew* by Henry Ford; *The Islamic Development Plan* by Kalim Siddiqui; *The Literacy and Scientific Spirit of Islam* by Syed Ameer Ali; *The Prophet of Revolution* by Inamullah Khan; *Trade in Islam* by S Hasamuz Zaman; *Unity of the Muslim World* by Brig Bulzar Ahmed; *War in Afghanistan* by Qutubuddin Aziz; *The Battles of the Prophet of Allah* by Brig Bulzar Ahmed; *What is Islam ?*; *What is Islamic Culture ?*; *What is Islamic Socio-Economic Order ?*; *What is Islamic State ?*; *Whither Muslims ?* by Justice SA Rahman; *Why Fast ?* by Mohammad Hamidullah; *Why Muslims Abstain from Pork ?* by Al-Haj Ibrahim TY Ma; *World Muslim Minorities* by M I Aureshi; *The Ethics of Islam* by Syed Amer Ali; *Tarikh-e-Alama-al Islam – History of Islamic World*; *Defending Islam in the West* by Qutubuddin Azizs; *Islam – Its Message to Humanity* by Syed Ameer Ali; *Europe's Debt to Islam* by Gustav Diercks; *Islam and Communion* by M Qutub; *Islam and Humanism* by Mohammad Shahidullah; *Islam and Idealism* by M Qutub; *Islam and Western Orientalists* by Abul Hasan Nadvi; *Islam as a Moral and Political Ideal* by Allama Iqbal; *Islam as Seen by Historians* by H G Wells and Pandit Nehru; *Islam in the East* by Izzet Begovitch; *Khilafat-e-Islamiya – Islamic Caliphate*; *Studies on the Commonwealth of Muslim Countries*; *Lessons from History* by Ibn Khaldun; *Life and Message of the Holy Prophet* by Inamullah Khan; *Muslims and Indian Civilisation* by Abul Hasan Nadvi; *Our Prophet, Our Leader* by Inamullah Khan; *Protocols of Meetings of the Elders of Zion* by Victor E Marsden; *Quaid-i-Azam and the Muslim World*; *Slave Trade in Africa* by Hasan M Rawat; *Some Economic Aspects of Islam*; *Zionism – A Threat to World Peace.* Studies; books; periodicals; brochures; newsletters; pamphlets.

Members Regular; Associate; Individuals. Branches and affiliates in 66 countries and territories:
Afghanistan, Algeria, Australia, Austria, Bahrain, Bangladesh, Botswana, Brunei Darussalam, Burkina Faso, Canada, China, Comoros, Côte d'Ivoire, Cyprus, Fiji, France, Gambia, Ghana, Guinea, Hong Kong, India, Indonesia, Iran Islamic Rep, Iraq, Italy, Japan, Jordan, Kenya, Korea Rep, Kuwait, Lebanon, Libya, Malaysia, Maldives, Mali, Mauritania, Mauritius, Morocco, Myanmar, Netherlands, New Zealand, Niger, Nigeria, Pakistan, Philippines, Portugal, Qatar, Saudi Arabia, Senegal, Singapore, Somalia, South Africa, Spain, Sri Lanka, Sudan, Switzerland, Syrian AR, Thailand, Trinidad-Tobago, Tunisia, Türkiye, Uganda, UK, United Arab Emirates, USA, Zimbabwe.

Consultative Status Consultative status granted from: *ECOSOC (#05331)* (General); *UNICEF (#20332)*; *UNEP (#20299).* **IGO Relations** Accredited by (1): *United Nations Office at Vienna (UNOV, #20604).* Observer status with (1): *Organisation of Islamic Cooperation (OIC, #17813).* Associated with Department of Global Communications of the United Nations. **NGO Relations** Member of (3): *Conference of Non-Governmental Organizations in Consultative Relationship with the United Nations (CONGO, #04635)*; *International Peace Research Association (IPRA, #14537)*; *NGO Committee on UNICEF (#17120).* [2020/XB3561/**B**]

♦ World Mycotoxin Forum (WMF) 21665

Contact Bastiaase Communication, PO Box 179, 3720 AD Bilthoven, Netherlands. T. +31302294247. E-mail: wmf@bastiaanse-communication.com.
URL: http://www.worldmycotoxinforum.org/

History Organized since 2001. **Aims** Provide a unique platform for the food and feed industry, regulatory authorities and science; exchange information and experiences on the various aspects of mycotoxins; review current knowledge related to mycotoxins in food and feed; discuss strategies for prevention and control of mycotoxin contamination ensuring safety and security of food and feed supply; initiate the systems approach for the control of mycotoxin contamination along conventional and organic supply chains. **Activities** Events/meetings. **Events** *World Mycotoxin Forum* Antwerp (Belgium) 2023, *World Mycotoxin Forum* Parma (Italy) 2022, *World Mycotoxin Forum* Bangkok (Thailand) 2020, *World Mycotoxin Forum* Belfast (UK) 2019, *World Mycotoxin Forum* Amsterdam (Netherlands) 2018. **NGO Relations** *International Union of Pure and Applied Chemistry (IUPAC, #15809).* [2023/XM8024/c/**F**]

- ♦ World Natural Health Organization (internationally oriented national body)
- ♦ World Natural Medicine Foundation (internationally oriented national body)
- ♦ World Nature Organization (inactive)

♦ World Naturopathic Federation (WNF) 21666

Sec 20 Holly Street, Suite 200, Toronto ON M4S 3B1, Canada. E-mail: info@worldnaturopathicfederation.org – secretariat@worldnaturopathicfederation.org.
URL: http://worldnaturopathicfederation.org/

History 2014, Paris (France). Founded at International Congress on Naturopathic Medicine. Current by-laws approved 8 Feb 2020. Registration: Canada. **Aims** Promote and advance the naturopathic profession. **Structure** General Assembly; Executive Committee; Secretariat. Committees; Groups. **Languages** English. **Finance** Sources: members' dues. **Activities** Events/meetings; research/documentation.

Members Full; Associate; Educational. Full: Naturopathic organizations (over 50) in 32 countries and territories:
Australia, Belgium, Brazil, Canada, Chile, Congo DR, Cyprus, Ecuador, Egypt, El Salvador, France, Greece, Hong Kong, India, Italy, Japan, Malaysia, Mexico, Nepal, New Zealand, Portugal, Puerto Rico, Russia, Saudi Arabia, Slovenia, South Africa, Spain, Switzerland, UK, Uruguay, USA, Zambia.

Associate in 8 countries:
Australia, Canada, Chile, Ireland, Norway, Singapore, Slovakia, Uruguay.

Educational in 11 countries:
Australia, Belgium, Canada, France, Italy, New Zealand, Puerto Rico, Slovenia, Spain, Uruguay, USA. [2020/AA0308/**C**]

♦ World Without Nazism (WWN) 21667

Contact address not obtained. T. +74952586213.

History 22 Jun 2010, Kiev (Ukraine). **Structure** Presidium. **Events** *General Assembly* Strasbourg (France) 2012. [2013/XJ6127/s/**D**]

- ♦ World in Need (internationally oriented national body)
- ♦ World Neighbors (internationally oriented national body)

♦ World Netball (WN) 21668

CEO Suite 6.02, Floor 6, Tomorrow, MediaCityUK, Salford, M50 2AB, UK. T. +443331020200. E-mail: info@worldnetball.sport.
URL: https://netball.sport/

History 1960, Sri Lanka. Former names and other names: *International Federation of Women's Basketball and Netball Associations* – former (1960); *International Federation of Netball Associations (IFNA)* – former; *International Netball Federation* – former (2012). **Aims** As the world governing body for the sport of netball: promote and improve the *game* of netball globally, particularly through world youth and development programmes. **Structure** Congress (every 2 years); Board of Directors; Regional Directors; Independent Committees. **Languages** English. **Staff** 6.00 FTE, paid. **Finance** Sources: members' dues. Other sources: event income; media rights. **Activities** Events/meetings; sporting activities. **Events** *Biennial Conference* Cape Town (South Africa) 2023, *Special Meeting of Congress* 2022, *Biennial Conference* 2021, *Biennial Conference* Liverpool (UK) 2019, *Biennial Conference* Gaborone (Botswana) 2017. **Publications** Annual Reports; guidelines; manual; codes; statements; articles.
Members Membership split into 5 Regional Federations: Africa; Americas; Asia; Europe; Oceania. Full in 56 countries and territories:
Antigua-Barbuda, Argentina, Australia, Barbados, Bermuda, Botswana, Brunei Darussalam, Canada, Cayman Is, Cook Is, Côte d'Ivoire, Dominica, England, Eswatini, Fiji, Gibraltar, Grenada, Hong Kong, India, Ireland, Isle of Man, Israel, Jamaica, Kenya, Lesotho, Malawi, Malaysia, Maldives, Malta, Namibia, New Zealand, Northern Ireland, Pakistan, Papua New Guinea, Philippines, Samoa, Scotland, Singapore, South Africa, Sri Lanka, St Kitts-Nevis, St Lucia, St Maarten, St Vincent-Grenadines, Switzerland, Taiwan, Tanzania UR, Thailand, Tonga, Trinidad-Tobago, Uganda, United Arab Emirates, USA, Wales, Zambia, Zimbabwe.
Associate in 23 countries and territories:
Anguilla, Bahrain, Bangladesh, Burundi, Cameroon, Central African Rep, Congo DR, Denmark, Dominican Rep, Guinea, Japan, Korea Rep, Liberia, Morocco, Nepal, Nigeria, Norfolk Is, Seychelles, Solomon Is, Sweden, Timor-Leste, Tokelau, Venezuela.
NGO Relations Member of (4): *Association of the IOC Recognized International Sports Federations (ARISF, #02767)*; *Commonwealth Games Federation (CGF, #04332)*; *International World Games Association (IWGA, #15914)*; *Olympic Movement (#17719)*. Recognized by: *International Olympic Committee (IOC, #14408)*.
[2022.10.11/XC5504/**B**]

♦ World Network of Biosphere Reserves (WNBR) 21669
Réseau mondial de réserves de biosphère – Red Mundial de Reservas de la Biosfera
Contact UNESCO – Sector of Natural Sciences, Div of Ecological and Earth Sciences, 7 Place de Fontenoy, 75007 Paris, France. T. +33145680788.
URL: https://en.unesco.org/biosphere/wnbr
History 1971, by *Programme on Man and the Biosphere (MAB, #18526)* of *UNESCO (#20322)*. *Seville Strategy for Biosphere Reserves* and *Statutory Framework for the World Network of Biosphere Reserves* endorsed and adopted by 28th Session of UNESCO General Conference, Nov 1995. **Aims** As areas of terrestrial and coastal *ecosystems*: promote solutions to reconcile conservation of biodiversity with its sustainable use; promote a dynamic multi-functional approach to conserving biological and cultural diversity where local people are key actors and beneficiaries. **Activities** Monitoring/evaluation; research/documentation. **Events** *World congress* Lima (Peru) 2016, *World congress* Madrid (Spain) 2008, *Conference* Pamplona (Spain) 2000, *World congress* Seville (Spain) 1995, *World Congress* Minsk (USSR) 1984. **Publications** *News from the Biosphere World Network* (4 a year) – e-newsletter. *Biosphere Reserves Technical Notes*.
Members Biosphere Reserves (669) in 121 countries:
Albania, Algeria, Argentina, Australia, Austria, Belarus, Benin, Bolivia, Brazil, Bulgaria, Burkina Faso, Cambodia, Cameroon, Canada, Central African Rep, Chile, China, Colombia, Congo Brazzaville, Congo DR, Costa Rica, Côte d'Ivoire, Croatia, Cuba, Czechia, Denmark, Dominican Rep, Egypt, El Salvador, Estonia, Ethiopia, Finland, France, Gabon, Germany, Ghana, Greece, Guatemala, Guinea, Guinea-Bissau, Haiti, Honduras, Hungary, India, Indonesia, Iran Islamic Rep, Ireland, Israel, Italy, Japan, Jordan, Kazakhstan, Kenya, Korea DPR, Korea Rep, Kyrgyzstan, Latvia, Lebanon, Lithuania, Madagascar, Malawi, Malaysia, Maldives, Mali, Mauritania, Mauritius, Mexico, Micronesia FS, Moldova, Mongolia, Montenegro, Morocco, Mozambique, Myanmar, Netherlands, Nicaragua, Niger, Nigeria, North Macedonia, Pakistan, Palau, Panama, Paraguay, Peru, Philippines, Poland, Portugal, Qatar, Romania, Russia, Rwanda, Sao Tomé-Principe, Senegal, Serbia, Slovakia, Slovenia, South Africa, Spain, Sri Lanka, St Kitts-Nevis, Sudan, Sweden, Switzerland, Syrian AR, Tanzania UR, Thailand, Togo, Tunisia, Türkiye, Turkmenistan, Uganda, UK, Ukraine, United Arab Emirates, Uruguay, USA, Uzbekistan, Venezuela, Vietnam, Yemen, Zimbabwe.
IGO Relations Participates in: *UN Environment Programme World Conservation Monitoring Centre (UNEP-WCMC, #20295)*. **NGO Relations** Member of: *Global Terrestrial Observing Network (GT-Net, no recent information)*. Works through MAB regional networks: *AfriMAB Network (#00532)*; *ArabMAB Network (no recent information)*; *East Asian Biosphere Reserve Network (EABRN, #05199)*; *EuroMAB (#05708)*; *Red Iberoamericana de Comités MAB y Reservas de la Biósfera (IberoMAB, #18661)*; *South and Central Asia MAB Network (SACAM Network, no recent information)*; *Southeast Asian Biosphere Reserve Network (SeaBRnet, #19759)*.
[2018.06.26/XF8101/**F**]

♦ World Network of Chambers of Commerce and Industry / see World Chambers Network (#21270)
♦ World Network of /ex/-Users and Survivors of Psychiatry / see World Network of Users and Survivors of Psychiatry (#21672)

♦ World Network of Indigenous Peoples and Local Community Land and Sea Managers (WIN) 21670
Secretariat c/o Equator Initiative, Sustaianble Development Cluster, Bureau for Policy Support, 304 East 45th St, Room 614, New York NY 10017, USA. T. +16467814023. E-mail: info@equatorinitiative.org.
URL: http://www.winlsm.net/
History Proposed Jun 2012, Rio de Janeiro (Brazil), at United Nations Conference on Sustainable Development. Original title: *World Indigenous Network (WIN)*. Originally managed by government of Australia, until Jul 2013, when its management was officially handed over to *Equator Initiative* of *UNDP (#20292)*. **Aims** Facilitate increased learning among indigenous and local community land and sea managers. **Structure** National Advisory Group; International Reference Group, consisting of key country member representatives from Africa, Asia, North and South America, Brazil, Norway and New Zealand. **Events** *Conference* Darwin, NT (Australia) 2013. **Publications** *WIN-Net* (26 a year) – newsletter. **IGO Relations** *Convention on Biological Diversity (Biodiversity convention, 1992)*. **NGO Relations** Partners include: *The Nature Conservancy (TNC)*; national organizations.
[2015/XJ6884/**E**]

♦ World Network for Linguistic Diversity (Maaya) 21671
Réseau mondial pour la diversité linguistique
Secretariat c/o ICVolunteers, Case postale 755, 1211 Geneva, Switzerland. T. +41228001436.
Facebook: https://www.facebook.com/maayaorg/
History Switzerland. within the context of the World Summit on the Information Society (WSIS), Nov 2005, Tunis (Tunisia). Initiated by *African Academy of Languages (ACALAN, #00192)*, under the auspices of *African Union (AU, #00488)*. **Aims** Encourage governments and institutions to adopt and implement measures enhancing equitable multilingualism; promote mother tongue based bilingual and/or multilingual education at all levels of education everywhere as a means of promoting both social and gender equality; promote software localization and equal access of all languages to cyberspace; facilitate the empowerment of language communities worldwide in developing and using their own languages; contribute to the creation and sharing of language resources; observe the implementation of language policies and serve as a focal point for linguistic research projects. **Structure** General Assembly. Executive Committee, comprising President, Executive Secretary, Deputy Executive Secretary, Secretariat, Treasurer and other members. Scientific Committee; Consultative Committee. Working Groups. **Events** *International Symposium on Multilingualism in Cyberspace / Symposium* Paris (France) 2012, *International Symposium on Multilingualism in Cyberspace / Symposium* Brasilia (Brazil) 2011, *International Symposium on Multilingualism in Cyberspace / Symposium* Barcelona (Spain) 2009.
Members Organizations (27), including the following listed in this Yearbook (12):
African Academy of Languages (ACALAN, #00192); *Association de la migration africaine (MIGRAF)*; *Global Knowledge Partnership Foundation (GKPF, #10443)*; *International Communications Volunteers (ICVolunteers, #12817)*; *International Literacy Institute (ILI)*; *International Telecommunication Union (ITU, #15673)*; *Latin Union (UL, inactive)* (DPEL); *Linguasphere Observatory*; *Networks and Development Foundation (no recent information)*; *Organisation internationale de la Francophonie (OIF, #17809)*; *SIL International (#19278)*; *UNESCO (#20322)*.
[2019/XJ0710/y/**E**]

♦ World Network of Users and Survivors of Psychiatry (WNUSP) 21672
Secretariat Store Glasvej 49, 5000 Odense, Denmark. T. +4566194511. E-mail: contactwnusp@gmail.com.
URL: http://wnusp.net/
History 1991, Mexico City (Mexico). Former names and other names: *World Federation of Psychiatric Users (WFPU)* – former (1991); *World Network of /ex/-Users and Survivors of Psychiatry* – former. **Aims** Act as a global forum and voice of users and survivors of psychiatry; advocate the advancement of *human rights* of these people; provide international representation and consultation to influence matters; encourage the development of national user/survivor organizations in each country; facilitate effective information exchange; develop networking opportunities. **Structure** Board of 7 members. **Events** *Congress* Vancouver, BC (Canada) 2001, *Meeting* Santiago (Cuba) / Santiago de Cuba (Cuba) 1999, *Meeting* Dublin (Ireland) 1997, *Meeting* Lahti (Finland) 1997, *Meeting* Chiba (Japan) 1993. **Members** Full in 25 countries. Membership countries not specified. **Consultative Status** Consultative status granted from: *ECOSOC (#05331)* (Special). **NGO Relations** Member of: *European Network of ex- Users and Survivors of Psychiatry (ENUSP, #07906)*; *End Corporal Punishment (#05457)*; *International Disability Alliance (IDA, #13176)*.
[2020/XD5471/**B**]

♦ World of NGOs, The (internationally oriented national body)

♦ World Ninepin Bowling Association (WNBA) 21673
Pres Schnoran 64, 6933 Doren, Austria. E-mail: office@world-ninepins.org.
URL: https://www.world-ninepins.org/en/
History 1973, London (UK), as an autonomous part of *International Bowling Federation (IBF, #12384)*. Also known as *Nine Pin Association (NPA)*. Present name adopted Jun 1991. Current Statutes and Rules adopted by WNBA Conference, 27 Sep 1997, Regensburg (Germany). **Aims** Develop and propagate the *sports* of ninepin bowling, hold world and European *championships*, international cups, bilateral events and *competitions*. **Structure** Presidium. Sections (3): Classic; Schere; Breitensport. **Languages** German. **Staff** 3.00 FTE, voluntary. **Finance** Sources: sponsoring membership; donations; repay of travel expenses by national federations. Budget (annual): euro 15,000. **Activities** Sporting activities. **Events** *Conference* Györ (Hungary) 2011, *Congress* Vienna (Austria) 2009, *Biennial Conference* Copenhagen (Denmark) 2001, *Biennial Conference* Abu Dhabi (United Arab Emirates) 1999, *Biennial Conference* Regensburg (Germany) 1997.
Members Individuals (250,000) in 25 countries:
Argentina, Austria, Belgium, Bosnia-Herzegovina, Brazil, Bulgaria, Croatia, Czechia, Denmark, Estonia, France, Germany, Hungary, Italy, Luxembourg, Namibia, Netherlands, North Macedonia, Poland, Romania, Serbia, Slovakia, Slovenia, Sweden, Switzerland.
[2022/XD8102/**E**]

♦ World Ninja Federation (internationally oriented national body)

♦ World Nuclear Association (WNA) 21674
Dir-Gen Tower House, 10 Southampton Street, London, WC2E 7HA, UK. T. +442074511520. Fax +442078391501. E-mail: wna@world-nuclear.org – info@world-nuclear.org.
URL: http://www.world-nuclear.org/
History Jun 1975. Founded as an association of uranium producers. Membership subsequently extended by addition of electrical utilities and other bodies concerned with nuclear fuel cycle. Former names and other names: *Uranium Institute (UI)* – former (1975 to 2001). Registration: Companies House, No/ID: 01215741, England and Wales. **Aims** Provide a global forum for sharing knowledge and insight on evolving industry developments; strengthen industry operational capabilities by advancing best-practice internationally; speak authoritatively for the nuclear industry in key international forums that affect the policy and public environment in which the industry operates. **Structure** Board of Management; Members' Council; Working Groups; Secretariat. **Languages** Chinese, English, French, Japanese, Korean, Russian. **Staff** 30.00 FTE, paid. **Finance** Sources: subscriptions. **Activities** Events/meetings; knowledge management/information dissemination. **Events** *World Nuclear Fuel Cycle Conference* London (UK) 2022, *Cooperation in Reactor Design Evaluation and Licensing Workshop on Harmonization to Support the Operation and New Build of NPPs Including SMRs* Lyon (France) 2022, *Annual Symposium* London (UK) 2021, *Annual Symposium* London (UK) 2020, *World Nuclear Fuel Cycle Conference* Stockholm (Sweden) 2020. **Publications** *Global Nuclear Fuel Cycle Reports* (about every 2 years); *World Nuclear News (WNN)*. *Pocket Guide*. *Nuclear Energy in the 21st Century: The World Nuclear University Primer*, *Nuclear English: Language Skills in a Globalising Industry*. Symposia proceedings; working group reports.
Members Vendor (uranium production, reactor technology, engineering and construction); Consumer (electrical utilities); General (brokers, financers, legal). Corporate members (180) in 36 countries and territories:
Argentina, Australia, Austria, Belgium, Brazil, Bulgaria, Canada, China, Czechia, Egypt, Finland, France, Germany, Hungary, India, Italy, Japan, Kazakhstan, Korea Rep, Lithuania, Luxembourg, Morocco, Namibia, Pakistan, Russia, South Africa, Spain, Sweden, Switzerland, Taiwan, Türkiye, UK, Ukraine, United Arab Emirates, USA, Uzbekistan.
Regional member listed in this Yearbook:
Euratom Supply Agency (ESA, #05617).
Consultative Status Consultative status granted from: *ECOSOC (#05331)* (Ros A). **IGO Relations** Observer status with (2): *OSPAR Commission for the Protection of the Marine Environment of the North-East Atlantic (OSPAR Commission, #17905)*; *United Nations Framework Convention on Climate Change – Secretariat (UNFCCC, #20564)*. **NGO Relations** Observer status with (1): *International Commission on Radiological Protection (ICRP, #12724)*. Member of (1): *World Council of Isotopes (WCI, #21331)*. Supports (1): *World Nuclear University (WNU, #21677)*.
[2021/XD5843/y/**C**]

♦ World Nuclear Fuel Market (WNFM) 21675
Admin NAC Int'l, 3930 East Jones Bridge Rd, Norcross GA 30092, USA. T. +17704471144. Fax +17704471797.
URL: http://www.wnfm.com/
Events *Annual Meeting* Montréal, QC (Canada) 2022, *Annual Meeting* Montréal, QC (Canada) 2021, *Annual Meeting* Montréal, QC (Canada) 2020, *Annual Meeting* Lisbon (Portugal) 2019, *Annual Meeting* Paris (France) 2015. **Publications** Proceedings.
Members Full (88), companies, in 20 countries:
Australia, Belgium, Canada, Czechia, Denmark, Finland, France, Germany, Japan, Kazakhstan, Korea Rep, Netherlands, Russia, South Africa, Spain, Sweden, Switzerland, Taiwan, UK, USA.
IGO Relations *Euratom Supply Agency (ESA, #05617)*.
[2020/XF6523/**F**]

♦ World Nuclear Transport Institute (WNTI) 21676
SG Remo House, 310-312 Regent Street, London, W1B 3AX, UK. T. +442075801144. Fax +442075805365. E-mail: wnti@wnti.co.uk.
Tokyo Office c/o ORC, 11F Hibiya-Daibiru Bldg, 2-2 Uchisaiwai-cho, 1-chome, Chiyoda-ku, Tokyo, Japan. T. +81335910724. Fax +81335910729.
Washington DC Office 1015 18th St NW – Suite 650, Washington DC 20036, USA. T. +12027858101. Fax +12027858834.
URL: http://www.wnti.co.uk/
History Founded 1998. Registered in accordance with UK law. **Aims** Ensure that *radioactive* materials are packaged and transported by sea, land and air in a safe, efficient and reliable manner through the elaboration and application of national and international standards, regulations and procedures; consult with governmental and non-governmental bodies to support the establishment of balanced international standards, regulations, guidelines and procedures. **Structure** General Meeting; Board of Directors. Regional offices (2): Tokyo (Japan); Washington DC (USA). Advisory Group. **Languages** English. **Staff** 8.00 FTE, paid. **Finance** Members' dues. **Activities** Knowledge management/information dissemination; research/documentation; events/meetings. *Semi-Annual Members Meeting (SAMM)* Details not obtained. **Events** *PATRAM : international symposium on packaging and transportation of radio-active materials* London (UK) 2010. **Publications** Annual Review; information papers; good practice documents; fact sheets; technical studies. Information Services: Databases.
Members Ordinary; Associate. Industrial organizations involved in or having a relationship with the transport of radioactive materials. Members in 14 countries:
Australia, Belgium, Canada, Denmark, France, Germany, Japan, Russia, South Africa, Spain, Sweden, Switzerland, UK, USA.
Consultative Status Consultative status granted from: *International Maritime Organization (IMO, #14102)*. **IGO Relations** Consultative status with: *International Atomic Energy Agency (IAEA, #12294)*; *United Nations Committee of Experts on the Transport of Dangerous Goods and on the Globally Harmonized System of Classification and Labelling of Chemicals (Committee of Experts on TDG and GHS, #20543)*. **NGO Relations** Supports: *World Maritime University (WMU, #21633)*.
[2014.11.14/XE3734/j/**E**]

♦ World Nuclear University (WNU) **21677**
Coordinating Centre 10 Southampton St, London, WC2E 7HA, UK. T. +442074511520. Fax +442078391501. E-mail: wnu@world-nuclear-university.org.
URL: http://www.world-nuclear-university.org/
History Founded 4 Sep 2003, London (UK). **Aims** Enhance international education and leadership in the peaceful applications of nuclear science and technology. **Structure** Board of Directors. **Languages** English. **Staff** Secondment of senior nuclear professionals from Korea Rep, France, Canada, Russia and USA. Administrative support by: *World Nuclear Association (WNA, #21674)*. **Finance** Supported by: *World Nuclear Association (WNA, #21674); International Atomic Energy Agency (IAEA, #12294)*. **Activities** Training/education. **Publications** *The World Nuclear University Primer – Nuclear Energy in the 21st Century* (2006); *Nuclear English* (2005).
Members Organizations, centres and universities in 28 countries:
Argentina, Australia, Austria, Belgium, Brazil, Bulgaria, Canada, Chile, China, Czechia, Egypt, Finland, France, Germany, India, Israel, Italy, Japan, Korea Rep, Mexico, Pakistan, Russia, South Africa, Spain, Sweden, UK, Ukraine, USA. [2020/XF7021/**F**]

♦ World Obesity **21678**
Chief Exec Unit 406, 107-111 Fleet Street, London, EC4A 2AB, UK. E-mail: enquiries@worldobesity.org.
Events – Head address not obtained.
General: http://www.worldobesity.org/
History 1986. Merged with *International Obesity Task Force (IOTF, inactive)* to become a single entity, but both retaining names, Aug 2002, when IASO became a registered NGO in the *WHO (#20950)* system. Re-branded under current title, 2014. Former names and other names: *International Association for the Study of Obesity (IASO)* – former (1986 to 2014); *World Obesity Federation* – alias. Registration: Charity Commission, No/ID: 1076981, England and Wales. **Aims** Lead and drive global efforts to reduce, prevent and treat obesity. **Structure** General Council; Executive Committee; Committees (2); Sections (2). **Languages** English. **Staff** 11.00 FTE, paid. **Finance** Sources: meeting proceeds; members' dues. Other sources: royalties from publications; corporate donations/sponsorship; EU grants. **Activities** Advocacy/lobbying/activism; certification/accreditation; events/meetings; knowledge management/information dissemination; networking/liaising; publishing activities; research/documentation; standards/guidelines; training/education. **Events** *International Congress on Obesity* Melbourne, VIC (Australia) 2022, *Stock Conference* Fribourg (Switzerland) 2021, *European and International Congress on Obesity* 2020, *Stock Conference* Fribourg (Switzerland) 2020, *Gulf Regional Congress* Abu Dhabi (United Arab Emirates) 2018. **Publications** *Clinical Obesity* – journal; *Obesity Reviews* – journal; *Obesity Science and Practice* – journal; *Pediatric Obesity* – journal.
Members National Associations; Associate; Individual; Corporate. National organizations in 50 countries and territories:
Argentina, Australia, Austria, Belgium, Brazil, Bulgaria, Canada, Colombia, Croatia, Cuba, Czechia, Denmark, Dominican Rep, Egypt, Finland, France, Germany, Greece, Hong Kong, Hungary, Iceland, India, Ireland, Italy, Japan, Korea Rep, Malaysia, Malta, Mexico, Morocco, Netherlands, New Zealand, North Macedonia, Norway, Panama, Paraguay, Peru, Philippines, Poland, Portugal, Singapore, Slovenia, South Africa, Sweden, Switzerland, Taiwan, UK, United Arab Emirates, USA, Venezuela.
Associate in 2 countries:
Greece, UK.
Consultative Status Consultative status granted from: *WHO (#20950)* (Official Relations). **IGO Relations** Observer to: *Codex Alimentarius Commission (CAC, #04081)*. **NGO Relations** Affiliated with: *Asia-Oceania Association for the Study of Obesity (AOASO, #01793); Australian and New Zealand Obesity Society (ANZOS); International Union of Nutritional Sciences (IUNS, #15796); Latin American Federation of Societies of Obesity (#16332); 'North American Association for the Study of Obesity (NAASO)'*. Instrumental in setting up: *Global Alliance for the Prevention of Obesity and Related Chronic Disease (#10219)*. Member of: *Global Climate and Health Alliance (GCHA, #10288); Planetary Health Alliance (PHA, #18383)*. [2021/XD3711/**C**]

♦ World Obesity Federation / see World Obesity (#21678)

♦ WORLD OBSTACLE **21679**
Fédération Internationale de Sports d'Obstacles (FISO)
SG Maison du Sport International, Avenue de Rhodanie 54, C/O SportWorks, 1007 Lausanne VD, Switzerland. T. +41787883777. E-mail: contact@worldobstacle.org.
URL: https://www.worldobstacle.org/
History Former names and other names: *World OCR* – alias. **Aims** Promote the obstacle sports including, but not limited to Ninja, OCR and adventure racing throughout the world. **Structure** Congress (General Assembly); Central Board; Executive Committee; Secretariat. Commissions; Committees. Continental federations (4): Africa; Americas; Asia Pacific; Europe. **Activities** Advocacy/lobbying/activism; sporting activities.
Members Associations in 43 countries and territories:
Australia, Austria, Barbados, Belarus, Belgium, Brazil, Cambodia, Canada, China, Colombia, Costa Rica, Czechia, Denmark, Estonia, Finland, France, Great Britain, Italy, Liechtenstein, Lithuania, Malta, Morocco, Netherlands, New Zealand, Norway, Pakistan, Philippines, Poland, Portugal, Romania, Russia, Singapore, Slovakia, South Africa, Spain, Switzerland, Taiwan, Tanzania UR, Türkiye, Uganda, Ukraine, USA, Venezuela.
NGO Relations Member of (1): *Alliance of Independent recognised Members of Sport (AIMS, #00690)* (Observer). [2022/AA3055/**C**]

♦ World Ocean Council (WOC) **21680**
Exec Dir 3035 Hibiscus Dr, Ste 1, Honolulu HI 96815, USA. T. +18082779008. E-mail: info@oceancouncil.org.
URL: http://www.oceancouncil.org/
History 2008. Founded as a business association, registered as a not-for-profit project. Registered in accordance with US and UK laws, 2009. **Aims** Advance industry leadership and collaboration in ocean sustainable development, science and stewardship. **Structure** Board of Directors; Secretariat. **Events** *Offshore Arabia Biennial Conference* Dubai (United Arab Emirates) 2020, *Sustainable Ocean Summit* Paris (France) 2019, *Offshore Arabia Biennial Conference* Dubai (United Arab Emirates) 2018, *Sustainable Ocean Summit* Hong Kong (Hong Kong) 2018, *Sustainable Ocean Summit* Halifax, NS (Canada) 2017. **IGO Relations** Partner of: *Group on Earth Observations (GEO, #10735)*. **NGO Relations** Member of (1): *World Benchmarking Alliance (WBA, #21228)*. Partner of (1): *Asia Wind Energy Association (#02106)*. [2021/XJ0775/**F**]

♦ World Ocean Network (WON) **21681**
Réseau Océan Mondial
Secretariat Nausicaä, Centre National de la Mer, Boulevard Sainte-Beuve – BP 189, 62203 Boulogne-sur-Mer CEDEX, France. T. +33321309999. Fax +33321309394. E-mail: info@worldoceannetwork.org.
Registered Office c/o ECSITE, Avenue Louise 89, 7ème étage, 1050 Brussels, Belgium.
URL: http://www.worldoceannetwork.com/
History Founded 1999, under the aegis of *Intergovernmental Oceanographic Commission (IOC, #11496)*, following the first International Meeting of Aquariums, Museums and Science Centers. Registered in accordance with Belgian law. **Aims** Raise public awareness on a worldwide scale; foster more respectful behaviour towards the *environment*; encourage a more intelligent and *sustainable* use of the ocean towards a blue society; promote good international governance of the world oceans. **Structure** Meeting (every 4 years), in Boulogne-sur-Mer, France; Board. **Languages** English, French, Spanish. **Activities** Events/meetings; networking/liaising; training/education. **Events** *Global Oceans Conference* Hanoi (Vietnam) 2008, *Global Oceans Conference* Paris (France) 2006, *International meeting on acting together for the future of the blue planet* Boulogne-sur-Mer (France) 2005, *Meeting* Paris (France) 2005. **Publications** *Developing a Strategy for Public Education / Outreach / Media* (2008); *Acting Together for the Future of the Blue Plan* (2002); *New Behaviour Towards the Ocean: an objective for the future* (1999). **Members** Organizations (over 600), including aquaria, zoos, educational organizations, science centres, natural history museums, media and NGOs, in 80 countries worldwide (not specified). **Consultative Status** Consultative status granted from: *ECOSOC (#05331)* (Special). **IGO Relations** Supported by: *UNEP (#20299); Intergovernmental Oceanographic Commission (IOC, #11496)*. **NGO Relations** Member of: *Global Forum on Oceans, Coasts and Islands (GOF, #10377)*. [2013.11.25/XJ4401/**C**]

♦ World OCR / see WORLD OBSTACLE (#21679)
♦ **World OKTA** World Federation of Overseas Korean Traders Associations (#21470)

♦ World Olympians Association (WOA) **21682**
Association mondiale des olympiens (AMO)
SG Av Jose Galvez Barrenechea N 200, Santa Catalina, 13, Lima, Peru. T. +5112248481. Fax +5112253946. E-mail: anthony.ledgard@olympian.org – info@thewoa.org.
URL: https://olympians.org/
History 21 Nov 1995, Lausanne (Switzerland). Founded at IOC Museum, on restructuring and re-naming of the previous *Fédération internationale des associations nationales d'athlètes olympiques (FIANAO)*. Registration: Switzerland. **Aims** Unite olympians from around the world regardless of their age, sport, nationality or other definitive measure and involve them in promotion of the values and virtues that make the Olympic Mouvement. **Structure** Officers: Patron, Honorary President, President, 2 Vice-Presidents and Secretary General. Executive of 5 members. **Languages** English, French. **Staff** 10.00 FTE, paid. **Finance** Support from: Osaka City, IOC and various others. **Activities** Events/meetings; guidance/assistance/consulting; training/education; advocacy/lobbying/activism. **Publications** *Olympian Insight*; *The Flame. What an Olympian Should Know*. Information Services: E-mail service with news and updates available for Olympic family members.
Members National Olympians Associations in 145 countries and territories:
Afghanistan, Algeria, Andorra, Angola, Antigua-Barbuda, Argentina, Armenia, Australia, Austria, Azerbaijan, Bahamas, Barbados, Belarus, Belgium, Belize, Benin, Bolivia, Bosnia-Herzegovina, Brazil, Bulgaria, Burkina Faso, Burundi, Cambodia, Cameroon, Canada, Chad, Chile, China, Colombia, Congo Brazzaville, Congo DR, Costa Rica, Côte d'Ivoire, Croatia, Cyprus, Czechia, Denmark, Djibouti, Dominica, Dominican Rep, Ecuador, Egypt, El Salvador, Equatorial Guinea, Estonia, Ethiopia, Fiji, Finland, France, Gabon, Gambia, Georgia, Germany, Ghana, Greece, Grenada, Guatemala, Guinea, Guinea-Bissau, Guyana, Haiti, Honduras, Hong Kong, Hungary, Iceland, India, Indonesia, Iran Islamic Rep, Iraq, Ireland, Israel, Italy, Jamaica, Japan, Jordan, Kazakhstan, Kenya, Korea Rep, Kyrgyzstan, Latvia, Lebanon, Libya, Liechtenstein, Lithuania, Luxembourg, Madagascar, Malawi, Malaysia, Mali, Mauritius, Mexico, Moldova, Monaco, Mongolia, Montenegro, Morocco, Namibia, Netherlands, New Zealand, Nicaragua, Niger, Nigeria, Norway, Pakistan, Palau, Panama, Paraguay, Peru, Philippines, Poland, Portugal, Romania, Russia, Rwanda, Samoa, Senegal, Serbia, Seychelles, Sierra Leone, Singapore, Slovakia, Slovenia, South Africa, Spain, St Kitts-Nevis, St Lucia, St Vincent-Grenadines, Suriname, Sweden, Switzerland, Tanzania UR, Thailand, Togo, Tonga, Trinidad-Tobago, Türkiye, Uganda, UK, Ukraine, Uruguay, USA, Vanuatu, Vietnam, Zimbabwe.
NGO Relations Member of (1): *Olympic Movement (#17719)*. Recognized by: *International Olympic Committee (IOC, #14408)*. [2018/XD5268/**D**]

♦ World Orchid Conference Trust (WOC Trust) **21683**
Registered Office c/o Abbleby Trust, Canon's Court, 22 Victoria St, PO Box HM 1179, Hamilton, Bermuda.
Pres address not obtained. E-mail: orchids1@btinternet.com.
URL: http://www.woctrust.org/
History 1988, by American Orchid Society and (UK) Royal Horticultural Society (UK). **Structure** Board of Trustees. **Events** *World Orchid Conference* Tainan (Taiwan) 2024, *World Orchid Conference* Taichung (Taiwan) 2020, *Conference* Guayaquil (Ecuador) 2017, *Conference* Johannesburg (South Africa) 2014, *Conference* Singapore (Singapore) 2011. [2012/XM4511/**F**]

♦ World Order Models Project (WOMP) **21684**
Projet des modèles de l'ordre mondial – Proyecto de Modelos de Orden Mundial – Progetto dei Modelli dell'Ordine Mondiale – Proekt Modeli Novogo Mirovogo Porjadka
Contact address not obtained. T. +19733533281. Fax +19733535074.
History 1966, on the initiative of the then *'Institute for International Order'*, subsequently, 1973, *'Institute for World Order'* and, 1983, *World Policy Institute (WPI)*. Became a separate organization from WPI from 4 Dec 1990. Prior to 2010, integrated *Committee for a Just World Peace (CJWP, inactive)*. **Aims** As a network of scholars, intellectuals, political figures and community-based social activists from various regions worldwide engaged in research, education, dialogue and action towards the promotion of a just world peace, diagnose present world *problems*, prescribe changes for the *future* and inquire into processes of transition, bearing in mind world-order *values* of *peace*, *economic well-being*, *social justice*, *ecological* balance and positive identity. **Structure** Board, comprising 2 Co-Directors who act as President/Treasurer and Vice-President plus (currently) 16 further members. **Languages** English.
Activities Work is aimed at the academic community, grass-roots social activists and selected policymakers and comprises 4 major components:
– /The United Nations, Global Constitutionalism and a Just World Order (UN Program)/ – addressing weapons of mass destruction; Limitation and Abolition of International Arms (LAIA) Transfers, Stockpiling and Production, addressing "conventional" (war) weapons systems; *'From Geopolitics to Humane Governance: UN Study Group'*, addressing the international system of states and emerging global polity.
– /Global Civilization Project: Challenges for Sovereignty, Democracy, and Security/ – transnational research and public outreach by a global consortium of research institutes, prominent scholars and social activists.
– /Harry and Elizabeth Hollins Symposium and Internship Program/ – organized in cooperation with Peace Education Program of Teachers College, Columbia University.
– /Transnational Academic Program (TAP)/ – provides research and educational materials for academics, public policy officials, educators and social activists in many regions of the world.
Organizes: working groups on specific problems; regional meetings on people's security and alternative security arrangements.
Events *Draft Convention on the monitoring and reduction of the international arms trade* New York, NY (USA) 1993. **Publications** *Alternatives: A Journal for Social Transformation and Humane Governance* (4 a year). *Explorations on Peace and Justice: New Perspectives on World Order* – series; *Preferred Worlds for the 1990's* – series; *Studies on a Just World Order* – series; *The Strategy of World Order* – series. *Preferred Futures for the United Nations* (1995); *On Humane Governance: Toward a New Global Politics* (1995); *Constitutional Foundations of World Peace* (1993). Books; working papers; teaching materials.
Members Associate individual scholars in 16 countries:
Argentina, Australia, Canada, Chile, Egypt, India, Japan, Nigeria, Norway, Philippines, Portugal, Serbia, Sweden, Switzerland, USA, Zimbabwe.
NGO Relations Member of: *World Futures Studies Federation (WFSF, #21535)*. Represented on the Organizing Committee of: *Hague Appeal for Peace (HAP, #10848)*. [2010/XF9621/v/**F**]

♦ World Organisation Against Torture (OMCT) **21685**
Organisation mondiale contre la torture – Organización Mundial contra la Tortura – Weltorganisation gegen die Folter
SG PO Box 21, Rue du Vieux-Billard 8, 1211 Geneva 8, Switzerland. T. +41228094939. Fax +41228094929. E-mail: omct@omct.org.
Europe Office Rue Franklin 111, 1000 Brussels, Belgium. E-mail: omcteurope@omct.org.
URL: http://www.omct.org/
History 1985, Geneva (Switzerland). Became operational, Feb 1986. Present statutes adopted, 23 Apr 1988, Bern (Switzerland); modified 11 Jun 1987, 15 Jan 1988, 31 Aug 1998, 1 Dec 2001 and 6 Dec 2008. Former names and other names: *OMCT/SOS Torture* – former. Registration: Swiss Civil Code, Switzerland; EU Transparency Register, No/ID: 46782046250-28, Start date: 19 Jul 2011. **Aims** Fight against torture, summary executions, enforced disappearances and all other cruel, inhuman or degrading treatment. **Structure** General Assembly (every 4 years); Assembly of Delegates (annual); Consultative Council; Executive Bureau; International Secretariat, headed by Director, in Geneva (Switzerland). Includes OMCT Europe. **Languages** English, French, Spanish. **Staff** 45.00 FTE, paid. Several part-time and interns on a sporadic basis. **Finance** Sources: contributions; gifts, legacies; grants; members' dues; private foundations; revenue from activities/projects. Supported by: *Comité Catholique contre la Faim et pour le Développement-Terre Solidaire (CCFD-Terre Solidaire); German Catholic Bishops' Organisation for Development Cooperation (MISEREOR); ICCO – Interchurch Organization for Development Cooperation*; IGOs; *Oxfam Novib*. **Activities** Guidance/assistance/consulting; networking/liaising; projects/programmes. SOS-Torture Network assembles organizations and correspondents worldwide. Secretariat provides personalized medical, legal and/or social assistance to torture victims and ensures daily dissemination of urgent appeals across the world, so as to protect individuals and fight against impunity. Programmes provide support to specific categories of vulnerable persons, such as women, children and human rights defenders. Also submits individual communications and alternative reports to the special mechanisms of the UN, and actively collaborates in the development of international norms for the protection of human rights. **Events** *General Assembly* Geneva (Switzerland) 2021, *Global Week Against Torture* Geneva (Switzerland) 2021, *General Assembly* Geneva (Switzerland) 2016, *International Conference* Geneva (Switzerland) 2005, *International conference on children torture and other forms of violence* Tampere (Finland) 2001. **Publications** Annual Report; monographs; pamphlets; reports; symposium and seminar proceedings.

Members NGOs (currently 313) in 91 countries and territories:
Afghanistan, Albania, Angola, Argentina, Australia, Austria, Azerbaijan, Bangladesh, Barbados, Belgium, Benin, Bolivia, Brazil, Bulgaria, Burkina Faso, Burundi, Cambodia, Cameroon, Canada, Central African Rep, Chad, Chile, China, Colombia, Congo Brazzaville, Congo DR, Costa Rica, Côte d'Ivoire, Denmark, Ecuador, Egypt, Ethiopia, France, Gambia, Georgia, Germany, Ghana, Greece, Guatemala, Guinea-Bissau, Haiti, Honduras, India, Israel, Italy, Japan, Jordan, Kenya, Korea Rep, Kyrgyzstan, Lebanon, Luxembourg, Madagascar, Malaysia, Mali, Mauritania, Mexico, Morocco, Nepal, Netherlands, Nicaragua, Niger, Nigeria, North Macedonia, Pakistan, Palestine, Peru, Philippines, Poland, Portugal, Puerto Rico, Russia, Rwanda, Senegal, Serbia, Sierra Leone, Spain, Sri Lanka, Switzerland, Syrian AR, Tanzania UR, Togo, Tunisia, Türkiye, Uganda, UK, Uruguay, USA, Uzbekistan, Venezuela, Zimbabwe.

Included in the above, 44 international organizations listed in this Yearbook:
- *African Commission of Health and Human Rights Promoters (ACHHRP)*;
- *Agir ensemble pour les droits humains*;
- *Antenna International*;
- *Anti-Slavery International (#00860)*;
- *Arab Centre for the Independence of the Judiciary and the Legal Profession (ACIJLP)*;
- *Arab Lawyers' Union (ALU, #01002)*;
- *Arab Programme for Human Rights Activists (APHRA)*;
- *Asian Center for the Progress of Peoples (ACPP)*;
- *Asociación pro Derechos Humanos (APRODEH)*;
- *Association africaine de défense des droits de l'homme (ASADHO)*;
- *Caribbean Human Rights Network (#03517)*;
- *Catholic Lenten Fund*;
- *Central American Association of Families of Missing Detainees (ACAFADE, no recent information)*;
- *Centro de Estudios y Acción para la Paz, Lima (CEAPAZ)*;
- *CIMADE*;
- *Comisión Latinoamericana por los Derechos y Libertades de los Trabajadores y los Pueblos (CLADEHLT, no recent information)*;
- *Comité des observateurs des droits de l'Homme (CODHO)*;
- *Commission for the Defense of Human Rights in Central America (CODEHUCA, no recent information)*;
- *Defence for Children International (DCI, #05025)*;
- *Federación Latinoamericana de Asociaciones de Familiares de Detenidos-Desaparecidos (FEDEFAM, #09344)*;
- *Group for International Solidarity (GRINSO)*;
- *Human Rights Advocates (HRA)*;
- *Human Rights Information and Documentation Systems, International (HURIDOCS, #10985)*;
- *Human Rights in Mental Health (FGIP, #10988)*;
- *Human Rights Internet (HRI, #10986)*;
- *Inter-Cultural Association (ICA, #11465)*;
- *International Association of Democratic Lawyers (IADL, #11837)*;
- *International Centre for Trade Union Rights (ICTUR, #12525)*;
- *International Commission of Jurists (ICJ, #12695)*;
- *International Federation for Human Rights (#13452)*;
- *International Institute for Human Rights, Environment and Development (INHURED International, #13886)*;
- *International Rehabilitation Council for Torture Victims (IRCT, #14712)*;
- *International Trade Union Confederation (ITUC, #15708)*;
- *International Union of Food, Agricultural, Hotel, Restaurant, Catering, Tobacco and Allied Workers Associations (IUF, #15772)*;
- *Ligue de la zone afrique pour la défense des droits des enfants, étudiants et élèves (LIZADEEL)*;
- *Minority Rights Group International (MRG, #16820)*;
- *Pax Christi – International Catholic Peace Movement (#18266)*;
- *Pax Romana, International Catholic Movement for Intellectual and Cultural Affairs (ICMICA, #18267)*;
- *Regional Council on Human Rights in Asia (#18776)*;
- *Rencontre africaine pour la défense des droits de l'homme (RADDHO)*;
- *Solidarity Among Children in Africa and the World (ESAM)*;
- *South Asia Human Rights Documentation Centre (SAHRDC, #19718)*;
- *Unis pour l'Equite et la Fin du Racisme (UFER, #20490)*;
- *World Organization for Human Rights USA (no recent information)*.

Consultative Status Consultative status granted from: *Council of Europe (CE, #04881)* (Participatory Status); *ECOSOC (#05331)* (Special); *ILO (#11123)* (Special List); *African Commission on Human and Peoples' Rights (ACHPR, #00255)* (Observer). **IGO Relations** Accredited by (1): *United Nations Office at Vienna (UNOV, #20604)*. Panel member of: *Interagency Panel on Juvenile Justice (IPJJ, #11390)*. **NGO Relations** Member of (16): *Child Rights Connect (#03884)*; *Child Rights International Network (CRIN, #03885)*; *Communitas International (#04388)*; *Conference of Non-Governmental Organizations in Consultative Relationship with the United Nations (CONGO, #04635)*; *Consortium of Minority Resources (COMIR, no recent information)*; *ETO Consortium (ETOs, #05560)*; *EuroMed Non-Governmental Platform (#05730)*; *EuroMed Rights (#05733)*; *Human Rights and Democracy Network (HRDN, #10980)*; *International Campaign to Ban Landmines – Cluster Munition Coalition (ICBL-CMC, #12427)*; *International Network for Economic, Social and Cultural Rights (ESCR-Net, #14255)*; *International NGO Platform on the Migrant Workers' Convention (IPMWC, #14367)*; *NGO Committee on the Status of Women, Geneva (#17117)*; *ProtectDefenders.eu (#18546)*; *Right to Food and Nutrition Watch Consortium (#18943)*; *World Coalition Against the Death Penalty (#21281)*. Cooperates with (2): *Fundación Henry Dunant América Latina (FuHD – AL, #10024)*; *REDRESS*. [2022.05.04/XF0854/y/**F**]

♦ World Organisation for Digestive Endoscopy / see World Endoscopy Organization (#21380)
♦ World Organisation for Families (no recent information)
♦ World Organisation of General Systems and Cybernetics / see World Organisation of Systems and Cybernetics (#21686)
♦ World Organisation of Scuba Diving (unconfirmed)

♦ World Organisation of Systems and Cybernetics (WOSC) 21686

Organisation mondiale pour la systémique et la cybernétique (OMSC)

Dir Gen Univ of Maribor FEB, Razlagova 20, 2000 Maribor, Slovenia. T. +38622290199.
Pres/Dir Gen 3 North Place, 30 Nettleham Road, Lincoln, LN2 1RE, UK. T. +441522589252.
URL: http://www.wosc.co/

History Founded 1969, London (UK), as *World Organisation of General Systems and Cybernetics (WOGSC)*, following proposals adopted at 1st International Congress of Cybernetics, 5 Sep 1969, London, when *International Cybernetics Congress Committee (ICCC)* was set up. Current title adopted 1987, London. **Aims** Promote and foster global and local collaboration of parties interested in Systems and Cybernetics, aiming at inclusion of representatives from all parts of the world. **Structure** Board; Management Committee; Ad hoc Committees. **Languages** English. **Staff** Voluntary. **Finance** Mostly by exhibitions organized during congresses. **Activities** Awards/prizes/competitions; events/meetings; networking/liaising; training/education. **Events** *Triennial Congress* Moscow (Russia) 2021, *Online Event* Maribor (Slovenia) 2020, *Triennial Congress* Rome (Italy) 2017, *Triennial Congress* Santiago (Chile) 2014, *Triennial Congress* Nanjing (China) 2011. **Publications** *Kybernetes*, *International Journal of Cybernetics and Systems*. Congress book of abstracts; congress proceedings.

Members Affiliated societies in 17 countries:
Argentina, Canada, China, Colombia, France, Germany, Japan, Peru, Poland, Russia, Slovenia, South Africa, Spain, Switzerland, UK, USA, Venezuela.

Included in the above, 8 organizations listed in this Yearbook:
Asociación Latinoamericana de Sistémica (ALAS, #02266); *European Association for Artificial Intelligence (EurAI, #05943)*; *Institute of Industrial and Systems Engineers (IISE, #11270)*; *International Academy for Systems and Cybernetic Sciences (IASCYS, #11578)*; *International Federation for Systems Research (IFSR, #13564)*; *International Society for the Systems Sciences (ISSS, #15500)*; *Society for Modeling Simulation International (SCSI, #19598)*; *World Futures Studies Federation (WFSF, #21535)*. [2019.12.13/XC1778/y/**C**]

♦ World Organization of Alternative Medicine (inactive)

♦ World Organization of Building Officials (WOBO) 21687

Sec 7357 East Kemper Road, Suite A, Cincinnati OH 45249, USA. T. +15132470798.
URL: http://www.wobo-un.org/

History Founded 8 Jun 1984, Saskatoon (Canada), at 1st International Building Officials World Conference. Bylaws adopted 12 May 1985, Chicago IL (USA). Incorporated under the Canada Corporations Act, 5 Jul 1984. **Aims** Bring together building officials and code administrators; transfer information between countries, from generators of technical information to information users; promote international *standards* and building codes for construction, materials, equipment and appliances. **Structure** World Congress (normally every 3 years); Board of Governors; Executive Committee. **Languages** English. **Staff** 3.00 FTE, paid. **Finance** Members' dues. **Events** *Annual Meeting* St Charles, MO (USA) 2012, *Triennial world congress* Mexico City (Mexico) 2010, *Triennial World Congress* Orlando, FL (USA) 2006, *Triennial world congress* Dallas, TX (USA) 2003, *Triennial world congress* Dubai (United Arab Emirates) 2000.

Members Individuals and Groups in 26 countries and territories:
Australia, Bahamas, Bahrain, Canada, China, Cyprus, Egypt, Greece, Hong Kong, Ireland, Japan, Jordan, Kenya, Malaysia, Mauritius, New Zealand, Nigeria, Saudi Arabia, Seychelles, Singapore, Sri Lanka, Sweden, Tanzania UR, Trinidad-Tobago, United Arab Emirates, USA.

Consultative Status Consultative status granted from: *ECOSOC (#05331)* (Special); *UNIDO (#20336)*. **IGO Relations** Cooperates with: *United Nations Economic Commission for Europe (UNECE, #20555)*. Associated with Department of Global Communications of the United Nations. [2020/XD7930/**D**]

♦ World Organization of Dredging Associations (WODA) 21688

Gen Manager Radex Bldg, Rotterdamseweg 183c, 2629 HD Delft, Netherlands. T. +31152682575. Fax +31152682576. E-mail: ceda@dredging.org.
URL: http://www.woda.org/

History Oct 1967, Palos Verdes Hills CA (USA). Incorporated, 29 Dec 1967, as a non-profit-making organization under the laws of the State of California (USA). Originally known as *World Dredging Association*. Reorganized in 1978 and now links 3 autonomous regional organizations: Central Dredging Association (Europe, Africa, Mid-East); Eastern Dredging Association (Far-East, Pacific, Australia); Western Dredging Association (Western Hemisphere). **Aims** By co-sponsoring the World Dredging Conference: provide members with the opportunity to compile and present technical papers; provide a forum for communication among dredging and allied *industry* representatives; promote the advancement of dredging technology. **Structure** Board of Directors; Secretariat located in the region from which the Chairman is drawn. **Languages** English. **Staff** 3.00 FTE, voluntary. **Finance** Budget shared equally by the 3 autonomous regional associations. **Activities** Events/meetings. **Events** *World Dredging Congress* Copenhagen (Denmark) 2022, *World Dredging Congress* Shanghai (China) 2019, *World Dredging Congress* Miami, FL (USA) 2016, *World Dredging Congress* Brussels (Belgium) 2013, *World Dredging Congress* Beijing (China) 2010. **Publications** WODCON Congress proceedings.

Members Representatives, 2 from each, of the Boards of 3 regional associations, listed in this Yearbook:
Central Dredging Association (CEDA, #03688); *Eastern Dredging Association (EADA, #05238)*; *Western Dredging Association (WEDA, #20913)*. [2022/XC3505/y/**E**]

♦ World Organization for Early Childhood Education (OMEP) 21689

Organisation mondiale pour l'éducation préscolaire (OMEP) – Organización Mundial para la Educación Preescolar (OMEP) – Weltorganisation für Vorschulische Erziehung (OMEP)

World Pres c/o OMEP Argentina, Sánchez de Bustamante 191, piso 2 "K", 1173 Buenos Aires, Argentina. E-mail: worldsecretary@omepworld.org – communication@omepworld.org.
URL: http://www.omepworld.org/

History 26 Aug 1948, Prague (Czechia). Founded, taking over from a Provisional Committee set up in 1946 under the auspices of UNESCO. Statutes modified 1954, 1964, 1980, 1986, 1989, 1992 and 2005. **Aims** Defend and promote the rights of the child with special emphasis on the right and access to quality education and care worldwide. **Structure** World Assembly (annual); Executive Committee; Ad-hoc Groups; National Committees. **Languages** English, French, Spanish. **Staff** 0.50 FTE, paid; 1.00 FTE, voluntary. **Finance** Sources: contributions; members' dues. **Activities** Events/meetings; networking/liaising; projects/programmes; research/documentation; training/education. **Events** *World Assembly and Conference* Athens (Greece) 2022, *World Assembly* 2021, *World Assembly and Conference* Athens (Greece) 2021, *World Assembly* 2020, *Asia-Pacific Regional Meeting* Kyoto (Japan) 2019. **Publications** *International Journal of Early Childhood* (3 a year) – in 3 languages; *Newsletter from the World President*. *The History of OMEP* – in 2 vols. Regional newsletters; national committee educational journals; reports of World Assemblies and international conferences, seminars and congresses; reports; bibliographies.

Members Full: national committees in 58 countries and territories:
Argentina, Australia, Bolivia, Bosnia-Herzegovina, Brazil, Bulgaria, Burkina Faso, Cameroon, Canada, Chile, China, Colombia, Croatia, Cuba, Cyprus, Czechia, Denmark, Ecuador, El Salvador, Finland, France, Germany, Ghana, Greece, Haiti, Hong Kong, Iceland, Ireland, Israel, Japan, Korea Rep, Latvia, Liberia, Lithuania, Mauritius, Mexico, Myanmar, Nigeria, Norway, Pakistan, Panama, Paraguay, Peru, Poland, Portugal, Russia, Singapore, Slovakia, Spain, Sweden, Switzerland, Thailand, Türkiye, UK, Ukraine, Uruguay, USA, Venezuela.

Also members in Pacific Island Nations. Membership countries not specified. Prepatory national committees in 3 countries:

Prepatory national committees in 3 countries:
Italy, Serbia, Sierra Leone.

International affiliates (2), listed in this Yearbook:
International Association for Intercultural Education (IAIE, #11969); *World Family Organization (WFO, #21399)*.

Consultative Status Consultative status granted from: *ECOSOC (#05331)* (Special); *UNESCO (#20322)* (Consultative Status); *UNICEF (#20332)*. **IGO Relations** Accredited by (1): *United Nations Office at Vienna (UNOV, #20604)*. Associated with Department of Global Communications of the United Nations. **NGO Relations** Member of (4): *Child Rights International Network (CRIN, #03885)*; *European Social Action Network (ESAN, #08499)*; *International Conference of NGOs (#12883)*; *NGO Committee on UNICEF (#17120)*. Partner of (1): *Early Childhood Peace Consortium (ECPC, #05156)*. [2022/XC3562/y/**C**]

♦ World Organization for Education, Science and Development (internationally oriented national body)
♦ World Organization for the Family (inactive)

♦ World Organization of Family Doctors (WONCA) 21690

Secretariat Avenue des Arts 7-8, 1210 Brussels, Belgium. T. +3223290075. E-mail: secretariat@wonca.net.
URL: http://www.globalfamilydoctor.com/

History 1970, Chicago, IL (USA). Founded at 4th World Conference on General Practice, when Interim Constitution adopted, the 1st Conference having been held 1964, Montréal (Canada). Formally inaugurated and constitution and by-laws adopted at 5th World Conference, Oct 1972, Melbourne (Australia). Secretariat location: Adelaide (Australia) 1972 – 1981; Melbourne 1981 – Sep 1993; Hong Kong Sep 1993 – Sep 1997; Melbourne Sep 1997 – Apr 2001; Singapore (Singapore) May 2001 – Sep 2013; Bangkok (Thailand) Oct 2013 – present. 26 May 1989, new bylaws were adopted. Bylaws updated Jul 2010. Former names and other names: *World Organization of National Colleges, Academies and Academic Associations of General Practitioners – Family Physicians (WONCA)* – former; *Organisation mondiale des collèges nationaux, académies et associations académiques des généralistes et des médecins de famille* – former. Registration: Start date: 2 Jun 2000, Singapore. **Aims** Improve quality of life of peoples of the world through defining and promoting its values, including respect for universal human rights and gender equity, and by fostering high standards of care in general practice/family medicine. **Structure** World Council; Executive Committee; Statutory Committees; Working Parties (11); Special Interest Groups (15); Secretariat. Regional organizations (7): Africa; Asia Pacific; *Confederación Iberoamericana de Medicina Familiar (CIMF, #04450)*; East Mediterranean; *European Society of General Practice/Family Medicine (WONCA Europe, #08609)*; North America; South Asia. **Languages** English. **Staff** 4.00 FTE, paid. **Finance** Sources: donations; fees for services; meeting proceeds; members' dues. licensing fees. **Activities** Events/meetings. **Events** *World Conference on Family Medicine* Sydney, NSW (Australia) 2023, *Europe Regional Conference* London (UK) 2022, *World Conference on Family Medicine* Sydney, NSW (Australia) 2022, *World Conference on Family Medicine* Abu Dhabi (United Arab Emirates) 2021, *Europe Regional Conference* Amsterdam (Netherlands) 2021. **Publications** *WONCA News* (10 a year). *International Perspectives on Primary Care Research* (2016) by Felicity Goodyear Smith and Bob Mash; *Family doctors in the field – Environmental stories from across the globle* (2014) by Grant Blashki. Weekly e-updates; journals; standards; guidebooks; position statements.

Members Full: national colleges/academies of general practitioners/family physicians (122); Direct: individual general practitioners/family physicians (over 550,000). Full members in 140 countries and territories:
Afghanistan, Andorra, Anguilla, Antigua-Barbuda, Argentina, Armenia, Aruba, Australia, Austria, Bahamas, Bahrain, Bangladesh, Barbados, Belarus, Belgium, Belize, Bermuda, Bhutan, Bolivia, Bonaire Is, Bosnia-Herzegovina, Botswana, Brazil, Bulgaria, Cameroon, Canada, Cayman Is, Chile, China, Colombia, Costa Rica, Croatia, Cuba, Curaçao, Czechia, Denmark, Dominica, Dominican Rep, Ecuador, Egypt, El Salvador, Estonia, Ethiopia, Fiji, Finland, France, Georgia, Germany, Ghana, Greece, Grenada, Guadeloupe, Guiana Fr, Guyana, Haiti, Honduras, Hong Kong, Hungary, Iceland, India, Indonesia, Iran Islamic Rep, Iraq, Ireland, Israel, Italy, Jamaica, Japan, Jordan, Kazakhstan, Kenya, Korea Rep, Kuwait, Kyrgyzstan, Latvia, Lebanon, Lesotho, Liberia, Lithuania, Macau, Malaysia, Maldives, Malta, Martinique, Mexico, Mongolia, Montserrat, Nepal, Netherlands, New Zealand, Nicaragua, Nigeria, Norway, Oman, Pakistan, Panama, Paraguay, Peru, Philippines, Poland, Portugal, Qatar, Romania, Russia,

Saudi Arabia, Serbia, Singapore, Slovakia, Slovenia, South Africa, Sri Lanka, St Barthélemy, St Eustatius, St Kitts-Nevis, St Lucia, St Maarten, St Martin, St Vincent-Grenadines, Suriname, Sweden, Switzerland, Syrian AR, Taiwan, Tajikistan, Tanzania UR, Thailand, Timor-Leste, Trinidad-Tobago, Türkiye, Turks-Caicos, UK, Ukraine, United Arab Emirates, Uruguay, USA, Venezuela, Vietnam, Virgin Is UK, Zambia, Zimbabwe.
Also in Cariacou-Petit Martinique.
Consultative Status Consultative status granted from: *ECOSOC (#05331)* (Ros C); *UNICEF (#20332)*; *WHO (#20950)* (Official Relations). **NGO Relations** Member of (2): *Global Health Workforce Alliance (GHWA, inactive)*; *NGO Committee on UNICEF (#17120)*. Associate member of: *Council for International Organizations of Medical Sciences (CIOMS, #04905)*. Founding member of: *Global Alliance Against Chronic Respiratory Diseases (GARD, #10182)*. Represented in Executive Committee of: *Global Initiative for Chronic Obstructive Lung Disease (GOLD, #10423)*. Collaborative relations with: *Caribbean College of Family Physicians (CCFP, #03474)*; *European Academy of Teachers in General Practice (EURACT, #05817)*; *European General Practice Research Network (EGPRN, #07384)*; *International Society of Doctors for the Environment (ISDE, #15065)*. Instrumental in setting up: *International Federation of Primary Care Research Networks (IFPCRN, #13516)*.
[2022/XC4157/**C**]

- ♦ World Organization of Former Pupils of Catholic Education / see Organisation mondiale des anciens élèves de l'enseignement catholique (#17816)
- ♦ World Organization of Former Students of Catholic Education (#17816)
- ♦ World Organization of Funeral Operatives / see International Federation of Thanatologists Associations (#13569)
- ♦ World Organization for Human Potential / see Institutes for Achievement of Human Potential (#11292)
- ♦ World Organization of Jewish Deaf (inactive)
- ♦ World Organization of Mediterranean Cooperation for Solar Energy (inactive)

♦ World Organization for Modelship Building and Modelship Sport (NAVIGA) 21691

Organisation mondiale de navimodélisme et de sport nautique – Welt Organisation für Schiffsmodellbau und Schiffsmodellsport

Gen Sec 3 rue Jules Védrines, 95400 Villiers-le-Bel, France. E-mail: webmaster@naviga.org.
Pres Möhnestr 53, 46049 Oberhausen, Germany.
URL: http://www.naviga.org/

History 1959. **Aims** Support and disseminate information on ship model sport; establish connections with all people practising this sport, excluding racial, confessional and political discrimination. **Structure** General Assembly (every 2 years, always in Korneuburg – Austria); Praesidium; Sections (6). **Languages** English, French, German. **Staff** 10.00 FTE, voluntary. **Finance** Sources: members' dues. Annual budget: 1,100 EUR. **Activities** Events/meetings; knowledge management/information dissemination; networking/liaising. **Events** *General Assembly* Villiers-le-Bel (France) 2021, *Biennial General Assembly* Korneuburg (Austria) 2009, *Biennial General Assembly* Korneuburg (Austria) 2007, *Biennial General Assembly* Korneuburg (Austria) 2005, *General Assembly* Korneuburg (Austria) 2001. **Publications** *Naviga Info* (4 a year). Rules.
Members Individuals and organizations in 38 countries and territories:
Argentina, Armenia, Australia, Austria, Belarus, Belgium, Bulgaria, China, Croatia, Czechia, Denmark, Finland, France, Germany, Greece, Hong Kong, Hungary, Italy, Kazakhstan, Latvia, Luxembourg, Netherlands, Norway, Poland, Romania, Russia, Serbia, Slovakia, Slovenia, South Africa, Spain, Sweden, Switzerland, Türkiye, UK, Ukraine, USA, Uzbekistan.
[2015.01.07/XD1252/**C**]

- ♦ World Organization of Mothers of All Nations (inactive)
- ♦ World Organization of National Colleges, Academies and Academic Associations of General Practitioners – Family Physicians / see World Organization of Family Doctors (#21690)

♦ World Organization – Ovulation Method – Billings (WOOMB-International) 21692

Organisation mondiale de la méthode Billings d'ovulation – Organización Mundial del Método de la Ovulación Billings

Manager 2A/303 Burwood Hwy, Burwood East, Melbourne VIC 3151, Australia. T. +61398022022. Fax +61398878572. E-mail: manager@thebillingsovulationmethod.org – enquiries@woombinternational.org.
URL: http://www.woombinternational.org/

History 1977, Los Angeles CA (USA). Incorporated in the State of California (USA). **Aims** Promote *family* life and *fertility* regulation by natural methods, particularly the Billings Ovulation Method; disseminate information about natural *family planning*. **Structure** Executive Committee. **Languages** English. **Staff** No paid staff. **Finance** Private donations. **Activities** Events/meetings; training/education. **Events** *International Conference* Kuching (Malaysia) 2013, *SERFAC international conference on the family* Bangkok (Thailand) 2011, *International Conference* Melbourne, VIC (Australia) 2011, *International Conference* Melbourne, VIC (Australia) 2009, *Conference / International Conference* Melbourne, VIC (Australia) 2007. **Publications** *Buletin of WOOMB* (3 a year). *The Billings Method Book* (2011). Teaching materials in 22 languages.
Members Teaching centres in 53 countries and territories:
Albania, Argentina, Australia, Bangladesh, Brazil, Canada, Chile, China, Colombia, Congo DR, Costa Rica, Croatia, Cuba, Ecuador, Egypt, England, Ethiopia, France, Hong Kong, India, Indonesia, Ireland, Italy, Kenya, Korea Rep, Malaysia, Mexico, Myanmar, New Zealand, Nigeria, Pakistan, Paraguay, Peru, Philippines, Poland, Romania, Scotland, Singapore, Slovakia, Slovenia, South Africa, South Sudan, Spain, Sweden, Tanzania UR, Thailand, Timor-Leste, Trinidad-Tobago, Uganda, Uruguay, USA, Venezuela, Vietnam.
Consultative Status Consultative status granted from: *ECOSOC (#05331)* (Special). [2016.10.21/XE6973/**F**]

- ♦ World Organization of the Periodical Press (#17819)
- ♦ World Organization for Prenatal Education (#17817)
- ♦ World Organization for the Protection of Privacy / see Privacy International (#18504)
- ♦ World Organization for Research and Development into the Therapeutic Use of Motion Pictures (internationally oriented national body)
- ♦ World Organization for Respiratory Care (no recent information)
- ♦ World Organization for the Rights of Animals (inactive)

♦ World Organization of the Scout Movement (WOSM) 21693

Organisation Mondiale du Mouvement Scout (OMMS) – Organización Mundial del Movimiento Scout

Contact 150 Jalan Sultan Abdul Samad, Brickfields, 50470 Kuala Lumpur, Malaysia. T. +60322769000. E-mail: worldbureau@scout.org.
URL: http://scout.org/

History Founded 1907, by Robert Baden-Powell. *International Scout Conference* for coordination of the Scout Movement throughout the world established at Assembly in Jul 1922, Paris (France). Current title and new constitution adopted 1973. Constitution amended: 1975; 1983; 2008; 2011; 2017. **Aims** Contribute to the education and empowerment of young people through a value system based on the Scout Promise and Law; help build a better world where people are self-fulfilled as individuals and play a constructive role in society. **Structure** World Scout Conference – Conférence mondiale du scoutisme (every 3 years); World Scout Committee – Comité mondial du scoutisme; *World Scout Bureau (WSB, see: #21693)* – secretariat. Includes *World Scout Foundation (WSF, #21772)*; *World Scout Interreligious Forum (see: #21693)*. **Languages** Arabic, English, French, Russian, Spanish. **Staff** 120.00 FTE, paid. **Finance** Registration fees of member associations in proportion to membership and GNP of the country. Other sources: support from foundations, corporations, development agencies and individuals; royalties; donations; *World Scout Foundation*. **Activities** Awards/prizes/competitions; capacity building; projects/programmes; training/education. **Events** *Triennial Conference* 2021, *World Youth Forum* 2021, *Eurasia Youth Forum* Kuala Lumpur (Malaysia) 2020, *Eurasia Conference* Kiev (Ukraine) 2019, *Eurasia Youth Forum* Kiev (Ukraine) 2019. **Publications** *Create a Better World Magazine*; *WorldScoutInfo* – e-newsletter. Triennial Report from the World Scout Committee. Numerous specialized publications.
Members National Scout Organizations, grouping Scouts and leaders, representing over 50 million members, in 171 countries and territories:
Afghanistan, Algeria, Angola, Argentina, Armenia, Aruba, Australia, Austria, Azerbaijan, Bahamas, Bahrain, Bangladesh, Barbados, Belarus, Belgium, Belize, Benin, Bhutan, Bolivia, Bosnia-Herzegovina, Botswana, Brazil, Brunei Darussalam, Bulgaria, Burkina Faso, Burundi, Cambodia, Cameroon, Canada, Cape Verde, Chad, Chile, China, Colombia, Comoros, Congo Brazzaville, Costa Rica, Côte d'Ivoire, Croatia, Curaçao, Cyprus, Czechia, Denmark, Dominica, Dominican Rep, Ecuador, Egypt, El Salvador, Estonia, Eswatini, Ethiopia, Fiji, Finland, France, Gabon, Gambia, Georgia, Germany, Ghana, Greece, Grenada, Guatemala, Guinea, Guinea-Bissau, Guyana, Haiti, Honduras, Hong Kong, Hungary, Iceland, India, Indonesia, Iraq, Ireland, Israel, Italy, Jamaica, Japan, Jordan, Kazakhstan, Kenya, Kiribati, Korea Rep, Kuwait, Latvia, Lebanon, Lesotho, Liberia, Libya, Liechtenstein, Lithuania, Luxembourg, Macau, Madagascar, Malawi, Malaysia, Maldives, Malta, Mauritania, Mauritius, Mexico, Moldova, Monaco, Mongolia, Montenegro, Morocco, Mozambique, Myanmar, Namibia, Nepal, Netherlands, New Zealand, Nicaragua, Niger, Nigeria, North Macedonia, Norway, Oman, Pakistan, Palestine, Panama, Papua New Guinea, Paraguay, Peru, Philippines, Poland, Polynesia Fr, Portugal, Qatar, Romania, Russia, Rwanda, San Marino, Sao Tomé-Principe, Saudi Arabia, Senegal, Serbia, Seychelles, Sierra Leone, Singapore, Slovakia, Slovenia, South Africa, Spain, Sri Lanka, St Lucia, St Vincent-Grenadines, Sudan, Suriname, Sweden, Switzerland, Syrian AR, Tajikistan, Tanzania UR, Thailand, Timor-Leste, Togo, Trinidad-Tobago, Tunisia, Türkiye, Turkmenistan, Uganda, UK, Ukraine, United Arab Emirates, Uruguay, USA, Venezuela, Vietnam, Yemen, Zambia.
There are 15 countries where Scouting exists (be it embryonic or widespread) but where there is no National Scout Organizations which is yet a member of WOSM.
Consultative Status Consultative status granted from: *ECOSOC (#05331)* (General); *FAO (#09260)* (Liaison Status); *UNESCO (#20322)* (Associate Status); *UNICEF (#20332)*; *Council of Europe (CE, #04881)* (Participatory Status); *UNEP (#20299)*. **IGO Relations** Cooperates with: *Islamic World Educational, Scientific and Cultural Organization (ICESCO, #16058)* (Arab Scout Region). Associated with Department of Global Communications of the United Nations. **NGO Relations** Member of: *Youth and United Nations Global Alliance (YUNGA, #22028)*. Cooperates with: *CIVICUS: World Alliance for Citizen Participation (#03962)*; *Conference of INGOs of the Council of Europe (#04607)*; *Conference of Non-Governmental Organizations in Consultative Relationship with the United Nations (CONGO, #04635)*; *European Policy Centre (EPC, #08240)*; *World Association of Girl Guides and Girl Scouts (WAGGGS, #21142)*. Instrumental in setting up: *Baden-Powell World Fellowship (#03055)*.
[2020.02.19/XB0194/**B**]

- ♦ World Organization of Societies of Pharmaceutical History (inactive)
- ♦ World Organization for Specialized Studies on Diseases of the Esophagus (#17818)

♦ World Organization of Talented Children (WOTC) 21694

Organizatia Mondiala a Copiilor Talentati (OMCT)

Pres 24 Puskin Street, MD-2012 Chisinau, Moldova. T. +3732226675 – +3732(37368582011. E-mail: wotcmoldova@yahoo.com.
URL: http://wotc.unblog.fr

History 27 Aug 1995, Chisinau (Moldova). Statutes modified 1997, 2001, 2016. **Aims** Discover, promote and support talented children from difficult situations; prepare them for integration into democracy. **Structure** Board; Congress; Executive Board; Children Council; Censors Commssion. **Languages** English, Romanian, Russian. **Staff** 5.00 FTE, paid. **Finance** Members' dues. Event sponsorship. **Activities** Awards/prizes/competitions; events/meetings; training/education. **Publications** *Copiii Europei* – newsletter; *Micul Print – Little Prince* – magazine.
Members Members in 14 countries:
Armenia, Azerbaijan, Belarus, Bulgaria, Canada, Georgia, Germany, Italy, Moldova, Portugal, Romania, Russia, Türkiye, Ukraine.
IGO Relations *Organization for Security and Cooperation in Europe (OSCE, #17887)*; *UNESCO (#20322)*. **NGO Relations** European Academy of Civil Society; European Federation of UNESCO Clubs; *World Federation of UNESCO Clubs, Centres and Associations (WFUCA, #21498)*. [2016.07.03/XJ1806/**D**]

- ♦ World Organization of the Teaching Profession (inactive)

♦ World Organization of United Cities and Local Governments (UCLG) 21695

Organisation mondiale des cités et gouvernements locaux unis (CGLU) – Organización Mundial de Ciudades y Gobiernos Locales Unidos

Secretariat Carrer Avinyó 15, 08002 Barcelona, Spain. T. +34933428750. Fax +34933428760. E-mail: info@uclg.org.
URL: http://www.uclg.org/

History 5 May 2004, Paris (France). Founded by merger of *International Union of Local Authorities (IULA, inactive)* and *World Federation of United Cities (UTO, inactive)*. **Aims** Through the activities of members, promote a fair, *sustainable* and united society, based on local *democracy*, autonomy and *decentralization*, and focused on the general interest and that of citizens. In concrete terms: strengthen the role of local authorities so as to contribute to resolving current great challenges and to obtain recognition of this role within the international system; act in favour of the United Nations Millennium Development Goals; promote strong and effective local and regional authorities and representative national associations; encourage peace through 'city diplomacy'; promote innovation and the strengthening of local *governance*. **Structure** General Assembly. World Council. Executive Bureau, including President, 4 Co-Presidents, Elected Treasurer and Secretary General. Regional Sections (9): *United Cities and Local Governments of Africa (UCLG Africa, #20500)*; *United Cities and Local Governments Asia Pacific (UCLG ASPAC, #20501)*; Eurasia Section – *UCLG-Eurasia*; *Council of European Municipalities and Regions (CEMR, #04891)*; *United Cities and Local Governments Middle East and West Asia (UCLG-MEWA, #20502)*; *Coordinación de Autoridades Locales de América Latina (CORDIAL)*; North America Section – *UCLG-Noram*; Metropolitan Section – *World Association of the Major Metropolises (Metropolis, #21158)*; Forum of Regions – UCLG Regions. **Languages** English, French, Spanish. **Activities** Advocacy/lobbying/activism; monitoring/evaluation; networking/liaising; research/documentation; training/education. **Events** *World Human Rights Cities Forum* Gwangju (Korea Rep) 2020, *Triennial World Congress* Durban (South Africa) 2019, *World Human Rights Cities Forum* Gwangju (Korea Rep) 2019, *Global Youth Culture Forum* Jeju (Korea Rep) 2019, *Urban 20 Mayors Summit* Tokyo (Japan) 2019. **Publications** *Global Report on Decentralisation and Local Democracy* (2nd ed 2010) – focused on local finances. **Information Services** *GOLD Portal* – launched Dec 2005, global information and communication tool for members, providing access to information on over 1000 sites relevant to local government. **Members** Present in 140 states in 7 world regions, said to represent over half the total population of the world. Members include individual cities and regions and national associations of local government, including 112 local government associations (LGAs), countries not specified. **Consultative Status** Consultative status granted from: *ECOSOC (#05331)* (General); *UNEP (#20299)*. **IGO Relations** Recognized by: *ECOSOC (#05331)* – UNDESA; *European Commission (EC, #06633)*; *ILO (#11123)*; *UNDP (#20292)*. Accredited by: ECOSOC; *United Nations Office at Vienna (UNOV, #20604)*. Observer at: *Congress of Local and Regional Authorities of the Council of Europe (#04677)*. Collaborates with: *United Nations Human Settlements Programme (UN-Habitat, #20572)*. Cooperates with: *United Nations Institute for Training and Research (UNITAR, #20576)*. Partner of: *Management of Social Transformations (MOST, #16562)*. Adheres to: *Global Partnership for Effective Development Co-operation (GPEDC, #10532)*. Associated with Department of Global Communications of the United Nations. **NGO Relations** Attends International Meeting of Health Cities with: *Union of Ibero-American Capital Cities (#20412)*. Cooperation agreement with: *World Association of the Major Metropolises (Metropolis, #21158)*. Founding member of: *FMDV (#09804)*; *Global Water Solidarity (GWS, #10655)*. Member of: *Cities Climate Finance Leadership Alliance (CCFLA, #03952)*; *Global Taskforce of Local and Regional Governments (Global Taskforce, #10622)*. Supports: *Cities Alliance (#03950)*. Framework Partner Agreement with: *PLATFORMA (#18397)*.
[2020.02.13/XF6714/**B**]

♦ World Organization of Volcano Observatories (WOVO) 21696

Organisation mondiale des observations volcaniques

Co-Chairman – Europe and Africa INGV, Sezione di Catania, Osservatorio Etneo, Piazza Roma 2, 95123 Catania CT, Italy. T. +39957165800.
Co-Chairman – Americas and Caribbean Inst Nicaraguense de Estudios Territoriales, Volcanology Dept, Managua, Nicaragua. T. +50522492761.
Co-Chairman – Oceania and Asia Head of Volcanology Dept, GNS Science Wairakei Research Centre, 114 Karetoto Rd – RD4, Private Bag 2000, Taupo 3384, New Zealand. T. +6475701444.
URL: http://www.iavcei.org/

History Feb 1981, as a commission of *International Association of Volcanology and Chemistry of the Earth's Interior (IAVCEI, #12259)*, within *International Union of Geodesy and Geophysics (IUGG, #15776)*. **Aims** Create and improve ties between observatories and institutions directly involved in volcano monitoring; promote funding. **Structure** Co-Chairmen (3). **Languages** English. **Staff** 3.00 FTE, voluntary. **Finance** No budget.

Activities Events/meetings. **Events** *International transdisciplinary conference on volcano environment* Yogyakarta (Indonesia) 2006, *International congress* Saint-Pierre (Martinique) 2002, *Workshop on volcanic hazards and emergency management in the South West Pacific* Port Vila (Vanuatu) 1997, *Nyiragongo volcano workshop* Paris (France) 1995.
Members Volcano observatories in 34 countries and territories:
Argentina, Bolivia, Cameroon, Canada, Chile, China, Colombia, Comoros, Congo DR, Costa Rica, Ecuador, El Salvador, France, Greece, Guatemala, Iceland, Indonesia, Italy, Japan, Mexico, Montserrat, New Zealand, Nicaragua, Papua New Guinea, Peru, Philippines, Portugal, Russia, Solomon Is, Spain, Trinidad-Tobago, UK, USA, Vanuatu.
NGO Relations *Global Volcano Model Network (GVM, #10649).* [2018.06.01/XE1351/**E**]

♦ World Organization Volleyball for Disabled / see World ParaVolley (#21710)

♦ World Organization of Workers (WOW) 21697

Organisation mondiale des travailleurs – Organización Mundial de Trabajadores – Weltorganisation der Arbeitnehmer

Exec Sec Rue Montoyer 39 I, 1000 Brussels, Belgium. T. +32476946406.
URL: https://www.wow-world.org/

History Founded 1921, Luxembourg, as *International Federation of Christian Employees' Unions – Fédération internationale des syndicats chrétiens d'employés.* Statutes adopted 17 May 1946, Luxembourg, when name changed to *Fédération internationale des syndicats chrétiens d'employés techniciens et cadres (FISCETC).* Subsequently became *International Federation of Christians of Salaried Employees, Technicians, Managerial Staff and Commercial Travellers – Fédération internationale des syndicats chrétiens d'employés, techniciens, cadres et voyageurs de commerce (FISCETCV).* Also previously referred to as *International Federation of the Christian Trade Unions of Employees, Technicians and Managerial Staff – Fédération internationale des syndicats chrétiens d'employés, techniciens ingénieurs et cadres* and as *World Federation of Trade Unions of Non Manual Workers – Fédération mondiale des travailleurs non manuels (FMTNM) – Federación Mundial de Trabajadores No Manuales – Weltbund der Angestelltengewerkschaften – Wereldverbond van Beambtenvakorganisaties.* Subsequently changed title to *World Federation of Clerical Workers (WFCW) – Fédération mondiale des employés (FME) – Federación Mundial de Empleados (FME) – Weltbund der Angestellten (WBA) – Wereldverbond van Beambten (WVB),* 1984. Current title adopted 2008, during Congress. **Aims** As a *trade union* of initially *Christian* social orientation but opened to all religious convictions: exercise influence at international level in economic and social fields, for the benefit of all categories of workers; defend moral and material interests of members, particularly in international institutions dealing with social and economic issues; coordinate actions of member organizations to protect their members' interests; study social, economic and occupational matters of interest to members; stimulate constitution and/or affiliation of national federations of *clerical* workers. Statutory preoccupations: human dignity; self-fulfillment through labour; justice through equal opportunities; solidarity; public care as the responsibility of government; democracy and participation as a basis for decision making; tolerance and equality as a basic for democratic, pluralist society; the family as the basis of society. **Structure** Congress (every 4 years), consisting of delegates of affiliated organizations. European Council (every 4 years, between sessions of Congress), comprising at least one representative of each European member organization. World Board (meets annually) consisting of at least 6 Vice-Presidents, Treasurer and World-President. European Board (meets at least 4 times a year). Regional organizations (6): *Asian Brotherhood of Clerical Workers (ABCW, #01366); European Organization of the World Organization of Workers (EO/WOW, #08116); Federación Latinoamericana de Trabajadores Bancarios, de Seguros y Servicios Afines (FELATRABS, #09373); Federación Latinoamericana de Trabajadores de la Cultura y de la Comunicación Social (FELATRACCS, #09374); Federación de Trabajadores Latinoamericanos del Comercio, Oficinas y Empresas Privadas de Servicios (FETRALCOS, #09394); Fédération panafricaine des employés (FPE, #09700).* Standing professional sections in Europe for: Finance; Industry; Commerce. International Secretariat located in Brussels (Belgium). Meetings closed. **Languages** English, French, German, Spanish. **Staff** 1.50 FTE, paid. **Finance** Sources: members' dues. **Activities** Current issues: the employee in modern economy; mechanization and automation; comparative study of remuneration of employees of private concerns in European countries; professional training of young employees; extensive study on flexibility and informal economy. Developing contacts in Central and Eastern Europe. **Events** *Meeting* Amsterdam (Netherlands) 2016, *Seminar* Berlin (Germany) 2013, *Seminar* Billund (Denmark) 2013, *Central and Eastern Europe Seminar* Košice (Slovakia) 2013, *Quadrennial Congress* Vancouver, BC (Canada) 2012. **Publications** *Discharge of Staff: The Only Alternative to Resolve the Crisis ?.* Set of studies on: flexibility; social dialogue; informal sector.
Members National federations of trade unions, totalling over 1 million members, in 63 countries and territories:
Albania, Argentina, Aruba, Austria, Bangladesh, Benin, Bolivia, Brazil, Burkina Faso, Cameroon, Central African Rep, Chad, Chile, Colombia, Congo DR, Costa Rica, Croatia, Cuba, Curaçao, Denmark, Djibouti, Dominican Rep, Ecuador, El Salvador, France, Gabon, Germany, Guinea, Honduras, India, Indonesia, Italy, Madagascar, Mali, Malta, Mauritania, Mexico, Moldova, Montenegro, Morocco, Namibia, Nepal, Netherlands, Nicaragua, Niger, North Macedonia, Pakistan, Panama, Paraguay, Peru, Philippines, Portugal, Puerto Rico, Romania, Serbia, Sierra Leone, South Africa, Spain, Sri Lanka, Thailand, Togo, Uruguay, Venezuela.
IGO Relations *ILO (#11123)* (represented on industrial committees and Consultative Committee for Intellectual Employees and Workers). **NGO Relations** Candidate member of: *European Centre for Workers' Questions (#06505).* [2019/XC1887/**B**]

♦ World Oriental Federation (inactive)

♦ World ORT (WO) 21698

ORT mondiale – Mundial ORT – Welt ORT

Dir Gen ORT House, 126 Albert Street, London, NW1 7NE, UK. T. +442074468500. Fax +442074468650 – +442074468701. E-mail: wo@ort.org.
URL: http://www.ort.org/

History Founded 1880, St Petersburg (Russia), to help impoverished Jews in the Pale of Settlement, giving them training in vocational and educational skills. After World War I, spread to Eastern Europe, then to Western Europe, and later to other Jewish communities in need around the world. Became a world federation of national organizations in 1921, under the name *ORT Union of Societies for the Promotion of Handicrafts and Industrial and Agricultural Work among the Jews – Union mondiale des sociétés ORT pour la propagation du travail artisanal industriel et agricole parmi les juifs.* After World World II, established workshops providing support and vocational training in refugee camps across Europe and headquarters moved to Geneva (Switzerland). Became a truly international organization in 1960, moving into the developing world, setting up training centres, clinics, self-help and mother and child care programmes across Africa, Asia and Latin America. Programmes are now established in 5 continents, both in the developed and the developing world. Previously known as *World ORT Union (WOU) – Union mondiale ORT – Unión Mundial ORT – Weltverband ORT.* Present name adopted 2000. **Aims** Provide formal *education*, skills-training and self-help projects for needy communities to put people on the path to economic independence. **Structure** General Assembly (every 4 years); Board of Representatives; Board of Trustees; Officers Committee; Special Advisory Committees. **Languages** English, French, German, Hebrew, Russian, Spanish. **Staff** 30.00 FTE, paid. **Finance** Sources: donations; gifts, legacies. Other sources: government and NGO matched funding; subventions; campaigns. **Activities** Events/meetings; training/education. **Events** *Congress* Washington, DC (USA) 2012, *Congress* Israel 2008, *Congress* Warsaw (Poland) 2008, *General assembly / Congress* New York, NY (USA) 2004, *Congress* Jerusalem (Israel) 2000. **Publications** *World ORT Facts and Figures; World ORT Newsletter.* Reports; statements; press releases.
Members in 57 countries:
Argentina, Armenia, Australia, Austria, Belarus, Belgium, Brazil, Bulgaria, Burkina Faso, Canada, Chile, Colombia, Cuba, Czechia, Denmark, Estonia, Finland, France, Georgia, Germany, Ghana, Greece, Guinea, Guinea-Bissau, Haiti, India, Israel, Italy, Kyrgyzstan, Latvia, Liberia, Lithuania, Mali, Mexico, Moldova, Montenegro, Namibia, Netherlands, New Zealand, Panama, Paraguay, Peru, Poland, Romania, Russia, Senegal, South Africa, Spain, Sri Lanka, Sweden, Switzerland, Tunisia, UK, Ukraine, Uruguay, USA, Venezuela.
Schools, colleges and programmes in 43 countries:
Argentina, Belarus, Brazil, Burkina Faso, Burundi, Canada, Chad, Chile, Colombia, Cuba, Estonia, France, Gabon, Germany, Ghana, Guinea, Haiti, India, Israel, Italy, Kyrgyzstan, Latvia, Liberia, Lithuania, Mali, Mexico, Moldova, Montenegro, Namibia, Panama, Paraguay, Peru, Poland, Romania, Russia, Senegal, South Africa, Spain, Sri Lanka, Tunisia, Ukraine, Uruguay, USA.
Resource Centres/Labs in 25 countries:
Argentina, Belarus, Brazil, Chile, Estonia, France, Germany, India, Israel, Italy, Kyrgyzstan, Latvia, Lithuania, Mexico, Moldova, Montenegro, Peru, Poland, Romania, Russia, South Africa, Ukraine, Uruguay, USA, Venezuela.
International Cooperation Projects/Offices in 17 countries and territories:
Brazil, Burkina Faso, Burundi, Chad, Gabon, Ghana, Guinea, Liberia, Mali, Mexico, Montenegro, Namibia, Russia, Senegal, South Africa, Tunisia, USA.
Consultative Status Consultative status granted from: *ECOSOC (#05331)* (Special); *UNESCO (#20322)* (Consultative Status); *ILO (#11123)* (Special List); *Council of Europe (CE, #04881)* (Participatory Status). [2021/XC3567/**C**]

♦ World Orthopaedic Alliance (unconfirmed)

♦ World Orthopaedic Concern (WOC) 21699

Contact address not obtained. T. +31263514270. Fax +31264450175. E-mail: golyhoek@gmail.com.
SG address not obtained.

History 1975, Singapore (Singapore). A charitable institution registered in Singapore. **Aims** Promote orthopaedic education and *care* and standards of orthopaedic *surgery* in *developing countries.* **Structure** Office-bearers (elected once every 3 years), consisting of President, President-Elect, Secretary-General, Treasurer-General and Executive Committee Members. Regional secretaries (16). **Finance** Grants, especially from Lee Foundation (Singapore) and Shaw Foundation (Singapore). Budget (annual): Singapore $ 150,000. **Events** *Triennial General Assembly* Istanbul (Turkey) 2005, *Executive committee meeting and general assembly / Triennial General Assembly* Amsterdam (Netherlands) 1996, *Executive committee meeting and general assembly / Triennial General Assembly* Seoul (Korea Rep) 1993, *Meeting* Singapore (Singapore) 1993, *Executive meeting and general assembly / Triennial General Assembly* Montréal, QC (Canada) 1990. **Publications** *WOC Newsletter* (4 a year).
Members Groups (by regions and languages); Individuals (2,338). Membership covers 31 countries and territories:
Australia, Austria, Bangladesh, Belgium, Canada, Egypt, France, Germany, Hong Kong, India, Indonesia, Japan, Kenya, Korea Rep, Malawi, Malaysia, Netherlands, New Zealand, Nigeria, Philippines, Saudi Arabia, Serbia, Singapore, South Africa, Sri Lanka, Switzerland, Thailand, UK, United Arab Emirates, USA, Zimbabwe.
IGO Relations *WHO (#20950).* **NGO Relations** Affiliated to: *International Society of Orthopaedic Surgery and Traumatology (#15335).* [2010.08.23/XC0062/**F**]

♦ World ORT Union / see World ORT (#21698)
♦ World OSE Union – World Wide Organization for Child Care, Health and Hygiene Among Jews (inactive)

♦ World O-Sport Federation (WOF) 21700

Contact 3rd Floor, O-Sport Complex, 7th Golestan, Alvand Town, Hamadan, Iran Islamic Rep. T. +988134251191. Fax +988134250097. E-mail: wof@o-sport.info.
URL: http://www.o-sport.info/

History 15 Dec 2015. **Structure** General Assembly (annual); Board of Directors: Administrative Council. Committees (16); Secretariat. Fighting Divisions (4); Non-Fighting Divisions (4). Includes *Federation of Asian O-Sport (FAOS).* **Events** *General Assembly* Delhi (India) 2013, *General Assembly* Isfahan (Iran Islamic Rep) 2013, *General Assembly* Antalya (Turkey) 2012, *General Assembly* Antalya (Turkey) 2011, *General Assembly* Antalya (Turkey) 2010.
Members Federations Full; Associate; Affiliate. Full in 17 countries:
Afghanistan, Cambodia, Hungary, Iran Islamic Rep, Iraq, Kazakhstan, Korea Rep, Laos, Maldives, Mongolia, Nepal, Nigeria, South Africa, Syrian AR, Tajikistan, Turkmenistan, Uganda.
Associate in 8 countries:
Algeria, India, Jordan, Kenya, Kuwait, Malaysia, Pakistan, Philippines.
Affiliated in 30 countries and territories:
Armenia, Azerbaijan, Bahrain, Bangladesh, Bhutan, Brazil, Bulgaria, Canada, Egypt, Finland, Georgia, Ghana, Hong Kong, Indonesia, Italy, Lebanon, Oman, Qatar, Sierra Leone, Singapore, Slovakia, Somalia, Spain, Sri Lanka, Taiwan, Türkiye, UK, Ukraine, USA, Yemen.
NGO Relations Member of (6): *General Association of Asia Pacific Sports Federations (GAAPSF, #10106); International Association for Sports Information (IASI, #12179); International Council of Sport Science and Physical Education (ICSSPE, #13077); International Sport Network Organization (ISNO, #15592); The Association for International Sport for All (TAFISA, #02763); World Anti-Doping Agency (WADA, #21096).* Partner of (1): *World Esports Consortium (WESCO, #21391).* [2021.06.15/XJ6332/**C**]

♦ World Osteopathic Health Organization (inactive)

♦ World Ostrich Association (WOA) 21701

Sec 33 Eden Grange, Little Corby, Carlisle, CA4 8QW, UK. T. +441228562923. Fax +441228562187.
URL: http://www.world-ostrich.org/

History Founded 10 Sep 2002. Registered in accordance with UK law. **Aims** Meet the demand for "communication, dissemination of information and provision of industry standards" for all involved in the industry, from producer to consumer. **Structure** General Meeting (annual); Board of Directors. **Languages** English. **Finance** Members' dues. [2019.06.26/XM0296/**D**]

♦ World Out of Home Organization (WOO) 21702

Exec Dir c/o Baumgartner Mächler Rechtsanwälte AG, Löwenstrasse 2, 8001 Zurich ZH, Switzerland. E-mail: info@worldooh.org.
Gen Sec address not obtained.
URL: https://www.worldooh.org/

History 1959, Paris (France). Former names and other names: *European Federation of Outdoor Advertising* – former (1959 to 1996); *Fédération européenne de la publicité extérieure (FEPE)* – former (1959 to 1996); *Europäische Föderation der Aussenwerbung* – former (1959 to 1996); *Federazione Europea della Pubblicità Esterna* – former (1959 to 1996); *Federation of Outdoor Advertising (FEPE International)* – former (1996 to 2019); *Fédération de la publicité extérieure* – former (1996 to 2019). Registration: Switzerland. **Aims** Create contact among European countries in order for exchange of information and experience between members of the outdoor advertising industry in the various countries, thus promoting the standardization of business methods throughout Europe; promote outdoor advertising on an international basis; enable advertisers to make use of an efficient and competent service and win the sympathy and support both of the authorities and of the general public. **Structure** General Meeting (annual); Officers. **Languages** English, French, German, Italian. **Finance** Members' dues. **Activities** Committees (5): Transport Advertising; Temporary and Permanent Poster Advertising; Common Market; Urban Furniture; Poster Research. **Events** *Global Congress* Toronto, ON (Canada) 2022, *Annual Congress and General Assembly* Toronto, ON (Canada) 2020, *Annual General Assembly and Congress* Dubai (United Arab Emirates) 2019, *Annual General Assembly and Congress* Sorrento (Italy) 2018, *Annual General Assembly and Congress* Stockholm (Sweden) 2017. **Publications** *FEPE Newsletter* (weekly). *FEPE Extranet.*
Members Individuals in 27 countries and territories:
Austria, Belgium, Bosnia-Herzegovina, Bulgaria, Canada, Croatia, Czechia, France, Germany, Hungary, India, Israel, Italy, Jordan, Lebanon, Malaysia, Montenegro, Russia, Serbia, Slovakia, Slovenia, Spain, Sweden, Switzerland, UK, Ukraine, USA.
NGO Relations Member of: *European Advertising Standards Alliance (EASA, #05829); International Advertising Association (IAA, #11590); International Council for Advertising Self-Regulation (ICAS, #12984).* [2020/XD0743/v/**D**]

♦ World Outreach (internationally oriented national body)

♦ World Ovarian Cancer Coalition 21703

CEO address not obtained. E-mail: info@worldovariancancercoalition.org.
URL: https://worldovariancancercoalition.org/

History 2016. Registration: Not-for-Profit Corporation, No/ID: 778772699RC0001, Canada. **Aims** Empower the global ovarian cancer community through knowledge, collaboration and action. **Structure** Board of Directors.
Members Cancer patient organizations (nearly 170) in 43 countries:
Argentina, Australia, Austria, Bangladesh, Belgium, Brazil, Canada, China, Colombia, Croatia, Czechia, Denmark, Egypt, Finland, France, Georgia, Germany, Greece, Hungary, India, Ireland, Israel, Italy, Malawi, Malaysia, Mexico, Morocco, Nepal, Netherlands, New Zealand, Nigeria, Poland, Portugal, Qatar, Romania, Russia, South Africa, Spain, Sweden, Türkiye, UK, USA, Venezuela.
NGO Relations Member of (2): *Global Cancer Coalitions Network (GCCN, #10270); Union for International Cancer Control (UICC, #20415).* [2021/AA2297/**C**]

♦ World Overview of Conservation Approaches and Technologies (see: #21192)

♦ **World Oyster Society (WOS)** **21704**

Pres address not obtained. E-mail: office@worldoyster.org.
URL: http://www.worldoyster.org/

History Jul 2005, Tokyo (Japan), at General Discussion of the 1st International Oyster Symposium. **Aims** Be an instrument of goodwill, friendship and cooperation for all those linked to oyster research, production and use worldwide. **Structure** Steering Committee; President; Vice-President. Chapters (5): North and South American; European and African; Asian and Oceanian; Chinese; Japanese. **Events** *International Oyster Symposium* Qingdao (China) 2019, *International Oyster Symposium* Bangor (UK) 2017, *International Oyster Symposium / International Oyster Symposium – IOS* Cape Cod (USA) 2015, *International Oyster Symposium* Ho Chi Minh City (Vietnam) 2013, *International Oyster Symposium* Hobart, TAS (Australia) 2011.
Members Full in 34 countries and territories:
Australia, Belgium, Brazil, Canada, China, France, Hong Kong, India, Indonesia, Ireland, Japan, Korea Rep, Malaysia, Marshall Is, Mexico, Namibia, Netherlands, New Zealand, Norway, Oman, Philippines, Singapore, South Africa, Sri Lanka, Sweden, Taiwan, Thailand, Tunisia, Türkiye, UK, Ukraine, United Arab Emirates, USA, Vietnam. [2015/XJ9272/**C**]

♦ World Pacific Sports Federation (unconfirmed)

♦ **World Packaging Organisation (WPO)** **21705**

Organisation mondiale de l'emballage (OME) – Organización Mundial del Embalaje

Gen Sec Canovagasse 7/1/14, 1010 Vienna, Austria. T. +4316066877 ext 3577. E-mail: info@worldpackaging.org.
Pres address not obtained.
Main Website: http://www.worldpackaging.org/

History 6 Sep 1968, Tokyo (Japan). Registration: Landespolizeidirektion Wien, No/ID: ZVR 1669462164, Start date: 24 Jan 2019, Austria, Wien. **Aims** Encourage development of packaging technology, science, access and engineering; contribute to development of international trade; stimulate education and training in packaging. **Structure** Board of Directors. **Languages** English. **Staff** 3.00 FTE, paid. **Finance** Sources: contributions; donations; members' dues; revenue from activities/projects; sale of publications; sponsorship. **Activities** Awards/prizes/competitions; events/meetings; knowledge management/information dissemination; research and development; standards/guidelines. **Events** *World Packaging Congress* Split (Croatia) 2012, *World Packaging Congress* Düsseldorf (Germany) 2011, *World Packaging Congress* Beijing (China) 2010, *World Packaging Congress* Mexico City (Mexico) 2009, *World Packaging Congress* Accra (Ghana) 2008. **Publications** *World Packaging News.*
Members Voting Members fully recognized continental packaging federations or organizations which have been admitted in accordance with WPO statutes (4):
Asian Packaging Federation (APF, #01648); International Trade entre Switzerland; *Latin American Packaging Federation (#16358)*; *Scandinavian Packaging Association (#19095).*
Member organizations in 43 countries:
Argentina, Australia, Austria, Bangladesh, Bolivia, Brazil, China, Colombia, Czechia, Denmark, Finland, Germany, Ghana, Greece, Hungary, India, Israel, Italy, Japan, Korea Rep, Latvia, Lebanon, Lithuania, Mexico, Netherlands, Nigeria, Norway, Philippines, Poland, Russia, Singapore, South Africa, Spain, Sri Lanka, Sweden, Switzerland, Tanzania UR, Thailand, Tunisia, Türkiye, UK, Ukraine, USA.
Included in the above, one organization listed in this Yearbook:
Latin American Packaging Federation (#16358).
Affiliate Members (8) organizations other than national packaging institutes. Affiliate members in 8 countries and territories:
China, Colombia, Croatia, Hong Kong, Kazakhstan, Netherlands, Russia, USA.
Honorary Members. Membership countries not specified.
Consultative Status Consultative status granted from: *ECOSOC (#05331)* (Ros C); *FAO (#09260)* (Liaison Status); *UNIDO (#20336).* **IGO Relations** Accredited by (1): *United Nations Office at Vienna (UNOV, #20604).* **NGO Relations** In liaison with technical committees of: *International Organization for Standardization (ISO, #14473).* [2022.07.04/XC3569/y/**C**]

♦ **World Pahuyuth Federation (WPF)** **21706**

SG Unit 2 – 2nd Floor, No 50 Parcham St, Towhid Sq, Teheran, 1457874713, Iran Islamic Rep. T. +982166593929. Fax +982166432371. E-mail: info@pahuyuth.org – wpfpahuyuth@gmail.com.
Europe Office 2a Mavrogenous Str, Koridallos, 181 22 Piraeus, Greece. T. +302104941914. E-mail: pahuyuthhellas@gmail.com.
URL: http://www.pahuyuth.org/

History 25 Oct 2010, Teheran (Iran Islamic Rep). Proposed 2009. Registration: Iran Islamic Rep. **Aims** Develop continuous improvement of physical and mental faculties in athletes practising the art of Multi Faces Combat disciplines. **Structure** General Assembly; Executive Board. **Languages** English, Persian. **Staff** 7.00 FTE, paid. **Finance** Sources: contributions; sponsorship. **Activities** Events/meetings; sporting activities. **Events** *General Assembly* Teheran (Iran Islamic Rep) 2020, *General Assembly* Kish (Iran Islamic Rep) 2015, *General Assembly* Kish (Iran Islamic Rep) 2013, *General Assembly* Kish (Iran Islamic Rep) 2012, *General Assembly* Teheran (Iran Islamic Rep) 2010.
Members Full in 35 countries:
Afghanistan, Australia, Azerbaijan, Bangladesh, Belarus, Brazil, Cameroon, Georgia, Germany, Greece, Guatemala, India, Iran Islamic Rep, Iraq, Italy, Jordan, Lebanon, Libya, Nepal, Nigeria, Norway, Pakistan, Palestine, Philippines, Russia, Sweden, Taiwan, Tajikistan, Thailand, Türkiye, Turkmenistan, Uganda, USA, Uzbekistan, Zimbabwe.
NGO Relations Member of (5): *Asian Council of Exercise and Sports Science (ACESS, #01409)*; *International Council of Sport Science and Physical Education (ICSSPE, #13077)*; *International Martial Art Games Committee (IMGC, #14107)* (Associate Member); *International Sport and Culture Association (ISCA, #15587)* (Full Member); *The Association for International Sport for All (TAFISA, #02763)* (Supporter). [2022.06.16/XJ6328/**C**]

♦ World Paint and Coatings Industry Association (unconfirmed)

♦ **World Pan Amateur Kickboxing Association (WPKA)** **21707**

Contact Tsalouhiki Str 16-20, Kifisia, 542 48 Thessaloniki, Greece. T. +302310403825. Fax +302310425215. E-mail: info@wpka.net.
World Pres address not obtained.
URL: http://www.wpka.net/

History Founded as *World Profi Kickboxing Association (WPKA).* **Languages** English. **Activities** Events/meetings. **Members** Membership countries not specified. **NGO Relations** Associate member of: *International Martial Art Games Committee (IMGC, #14107).* [2020/XD9204/**D**]

♦ **World Pancreatic Cancer Coalition (WPCC)** **21708**

Coordinator address not obtained.
Project Lead address not obtained.
URL: https://www.worldpancreaticcancercoalition.org/

History 2014. Formally launched 2016, following cooperation started 2013. **Aims** Drive transformational change for all those affected by pancreatic cancer. **Structure** Steering Committee; Committee. **Activities** Events/meetings. **Events** *Annual Meeting* 2021, *Annual Meeting* Coral Gables, FL (USA) 2019, *Annual Meeting* Coral Gables, FL (USA) 2018, *Annual Meeting* Montréal, QC (Canada) 2017. **Publications** *WPCC Newsletter.*
Members Full in 35 countries and territories:
Australia, Austria, Belgium, Brazil, Canada, Cyprus, Czechia, Denmark, France, Germany, Gibraltar, Greece, Hungary, Ireland, Israel, Italy, Japan, Kenya, Korea Rep, Mexico, Netherlands, New Zealand, Norway, Philippines, Poland, Portugal, Slovakia, Slovenia, South Africa, Spain, Sweden, Switzerland, Trinidad-Tobago, UK, USA.
Included in the above, 3 organizations listed in this Yearbook:
Digestive Cancers Europe (DiCE, #05070); *European Cancer Patient Coalition (ECPC, #06433)*; *Pancreatic Cancer Europe (PCE, #18172).*
NGO Relations Member of (1): *Global Cancer Coalitions Network (GCCN, #10270).* [2022/XM6330/y/**C**]

♦ **World Pangration Athlima Federation (WPAF)** **21709**

Pres Olympic Ctr of Ano Liosia, 134 51 Athens, Greece. T. +302106828877. Fax +302102409095. E-mail: info@worldpangration.net.
Gen Sec address not obtained.
URL: http://www.worldpangration.net/

History 9 Feb 2002. **Aims** Develop pangration worldwide; reinstate the martial *sport* of pangration in modern Olympic Games. **Structure** Executive Board. **Languages** English. **Staff** 1.00 FTE, voluntary. **Finance** No government support. **Activities** Sporting activities. **Events** *European Pangration Athlima Championship* Izvorani (Romania) 2015, *World Pangration Athlima Championship* Istanbul (Turkey) 2014, *European Pangration Athlima Championship* Veria (Greece) 2013.
Members Federations in 49 countries:
Afghanistan, Australia, Azerbaijan, Belarus, Belgium, Brazil, Bulgaria, Cameroon, Costa Rica, Cyprus, Ecuador, Egypt, Georgia, Germany, Greece, Guatemala, India, Iran Islamic Rep, Israel, Italy, Japan, Kazakhstan, Latvia, Malaysia, Malta, Mexico, Morocco, Nepal, Netherlands, New Zealand, Nicaragua, Nigeria, Pakistan, Panama, Portugal, Romania, Russia, Serbia, Somalia, Spain, Sri Lanka, Sudan, Syrian AR, Türkiye, Uganda, UK, Ukraine, USA, Zambia.
NGO Relations Member of: *International Martial Art Games Committee (IMGC, #14107).* [2018.09.19/XJ9746/**C**]

♦ World Pankration Organization (inactive)

♦ **World ParaVolley** **21710**

Gen Manager address not obtained.
URL: http://www.worldparavolley.org/

History 1994, Netherlands. Previously existed as *International Sports Organization for the Disabled (ISOD, inactive)* – Volleyball Section, founded 1981. Former names and other names: *World Organization Volleyball for Disabled (WOVD)* – former. **Aims** Deliver a variety of the highest quality Volleyball programmess and competitions for athletes with a physical impairment. **Structure** General Assembly (every 2 years in Paralympic and World Championship Years); Board of Directors; Judicial Commission; Regions (4): Africa; Asia-Oceania; Europe; Pan-America. **Languages** English. **Finance** Sources: contributions; fundraising; grants; members' dues; sponsorship. **Members** Membership countries not specified. **NGO Relations** Member of (2): *Association of Paralympic Sports Organisations (APSO, #02850)*; *International Paralympic Committee (IPC, #14512).* [2022.06.14/XC0136/**C**]

♦ **World Parkinson Coalition (WPC)** **21711**

Exec Dir 1359 Broadway, Ste 1509, New York NY 10018, USA. T. +12123887688. Fax +12129234778. E-mail: info@worldpdcoalition.org – info@worldpdcongress.org.
URL: http://www.worldpdcoalition.org/

History 2004. Former names and other names: *World Parkinson Congress (WPC)* – former (2004 to 2008). **Aims** Provide an international forum for the latest scientific discoveries, medical practices and caregiver initiatives related to Parkinson's disease; create a worldwide dialogue that will help expedite discovery of a cure and best treatment for Parkinson's disease. **Structure** Board of Directors; Committees (6). **Languages** English. **Staff** Under 10. **Finance** Government and private grants; corporate support; registration for event. **Events** *World Parkinson Congress* Barcelona (Spain) 2023, *Congress* Barcelona (Spain) 2022, *Triennial World Parkinson Congress* Kyoto (Japan) 2019, *Triennial World Parkinson Congress* Portland, OR (USA) 2016, *Triennial World Parkinson Congress* Montréal, QC (Canada) 2013. [2021/XM0233/c/**F**]

♦ World Parkinson Congress / see World Parkinson Coalition (#21711)
♦ World Parkinson Disease Association (inactive)
♦ World Parks Endowment / see Rainforest Trust
♦ World Parliamentary Association for the Rights of Animals (inactive)
♦ World Parliament Association (inactive)

♦ **World Parliament of Clowns** **21712**

Founder Hauptstrasse 73, 41352 Korschenbroich, Germany. T. +492182886109. Fax +492182886119.
URL: http://www.clownship.de/

History Jun 2006, Russia. Founded Jun 2006, Germany and Moscow (Russia) simultaneously, by clown Antoschka. **Aims** Restabilize the unbalanced 'me-driven', business-oriented world and bring it back to a *spiritual* 'we-world'; create with humour, laughing, brain, empathy and creativity a better world without war, arms, refugees and violence. **Structure** Annual Meeting; Management Team. **Languages** English, German, Russian. **Staff** 5.00 FTE, paid. **Finance** Private. **Activities** Events/meetings; awards/prizes/competitions. **Events** *Meeting* Dresden (Germany) 2010, *Meeting* Dresden (Germany) 2009, *Meeting* Heiligendamm (Germany) 2008, *Meeting* Heiligendamm (Germany) 2007.
Members Individuals in 21 countries:
Australia, Austria, Bangladesh, China, Denmark, France, Germany, Hungary, India, Israel, Italy, Japan, Netherlands, New Zealand, Nigeria, Russia, Switzerland, Trinidad-Tobago, Türkiye, UK, USA.
NGO Relations Links with various organizations, including: *Club of Budapest International (COBI, see: #04032).* [2016/XM2233/**F**]

♦ World Parliament of Religions / see Parliament of the World's Religions (#18222)

♦ **World Parrot Trust (WPT)** **21713**

UK Administrator Glanmor House, Hayle, TR27 4HB, UK. T. +441736751026. Fax +441736751028.
URL: http://www.parrots.org/

History 1989, UK. UK Registered Charity: 800944. **Aims** Promote the survival of all parrot species in the wild and the welfare of *birds* in captivity. **Languages** Dutch, German, Italian, Portuguese, Spanish, Swedish. **Finance** Members' dues. Donations. **Activities** Awareness raising; training/education. **Publications** *PsittaScene* (4 a year) – membership newsletter; *Flock Talk* – electronic newsletter. **Members** in 45 countries. Membership countries not specified. **NGO Relations** Member of: *Alliance for Zero Extinction (AZE, #00730)*; *International Union for Conservation of Nature and Natural Resources (IUCN, #15766).* [2022/XF4611/**F**]

♦ World Partners (internationally oriented national body)

♦ **World Pathology Foundation (WPF)** **21714**

Fondation pour la pathologie mondiale – Weltstiftung für Pathologie – Fondazione per la Patologia

Administrator 206 North Lee St, Falls Church VA 22046, USA. T. +13034789684. E-mail: wpfinfo@midco.net.
URL: http://www.worldpathologyfoundation.org/

History Founded by *World Association of Societies of Pathology and Laboratory Medicine (WASPaLM, #21191).* Commenced activities 1 Jan 1972, Bern (Switzerland). Re-chartered from Switzerland to USA. Former names and other names: *World Pathology Foundation of WASPaLM (WPF)* – former; *Fondation pour la pathologie mondiale de la WASPaLM* – former; *Weltstiftung für Pathologie und Laboratoriumsmedizin der WASPaLM* – former; *Fondazione per la Patologia della WASPaLM* – former. Registration: Section 501(c)(3), No/ID: 6880-035-8, Start date: 18 Dec 2012, USA, State of Illinois. **Aims** Enable young pathologists from countries with limited resources to visit centers of renowned excellence in other countries to learn laboratory techniques that will be of benefit to the services provided from their laboratories when they return home. **Structure** Board of Trustees. **Languages** English. **Staff** 8.00 FTE, voluntary. **Finance** Sources: donations; meeting proceeds. Annual budget: 25,000 USD (2021). **Activities** Awards/prizes/competitions; events/meetings; financial and/or material support; training/education. **Members** Not a membership organization. [2021.09.02/XF2110/f/**F**]

♦ World Pathology Foundation of WASPaLM / see World Pathology Foundation (#21714)
♦ World Patients Alliance (unconfirmed)
♦ WorldPC / see WorldLoop

♦ **World PCO Alliance** **21715**

SG c/o Congrès Inc, Onward Park Bldg 3-10-5 Nihonbashi, Chuo-ku, Tokyo, 103-8276 Japan. T. +81335103711. E-mail: wpcoalliance@congre.co.jp.
Pres c/o ACE:Daytons Direct (Int'l) Pte Ltd, 2 Leng Kee Road, #04-01 Thye Hong Centre, Singapore 159086, Singapore.
URL: http://www.worldpco.org/

History Inaugurated, May 2009, by 7 Professional Congress Organizers (PCOs), during IMEX. Officially launched, Nov 2009, at 48th Congress of *International Congress and Convention Association (ICCA, #12892),* Florence (Italy). **Aims** Collaborate and ensure effective promotion and marketing of association conferences/events of *professional congress organizers.* **Structure** Board. **Languages** English. **Staff** 2.00 FTE, voluntary. Paid **Finance** Expenses on shared basis. **Activities** Awareness raising; events/meetings; knowledge management/information dissemination; networking/liaising; projects/programmes; research/documentation; training/education. Meetings & events facility management. Active in all member countries. **Events** *Annual association congress* London (UK) 2010.

Members Professional conference organizers (20) in 22 countries and territories:
Australia, Belgium, Canada, China, France, Greece, India, Indonesia, Ireland, Italy, Japan, Korea Rep, Malaysia, Mexico, New Zealand, Singapore, South Africa, Spain, Sweden, Taiwan, Thailand, USA.
IGO Relations Members have their own contacts with IGO in their respective countries. **NGO Relations** Members have their own contacts with NGO in their respective countries. [2022.12.12/XJ1607/**D**]

♦ World Peace Academy / see Professors World Peace Academy (#18520)
♦ World Peace Academy (internationally oriented national body)
♦ World Peace Academy – Swiss Centre for Peace Studies / see World Peace Academy

♦ World Peace Bell Association (WPBA) 21716

Sec 1206-3-5-3 Nishishinjyuku, Shinjyuku-ku, Tokyo, 171-0021 Japan. T. +81362794550.
Facebook: https://www.facebook.com/World-Peace-Bell-Association-732610360205010/
History 1982, Tokyo (Japan). **Aims** Deepen mutual *understanding* and *friendship* with people of other countries; promote worldwide movement to bring peace to the world by ringing the Peace Bell. **Structure** General Assembly; Board of Directors; Standing Committee; Executive Committee. Chairman; Executive Director. **Languages** English, Japanese. **Staff** 4.00 FTE, paid. **Finance** Members' dues. Other sources: donations. **Activities** Events/meetings; research/documenation. **Publications** *World Peace News* (6 a year) in English, Japanese.
Members Head Office (Japan) and branch organizations (13) in 15 countries:
Argentina, Australia, Brazil, Canada, Germany, Israel, Japan, Mexico, Mongolia, New Zealand, Philippines, Poland, Spain, Türkiye, USA, Uzbekistan.
NGO Relations *City of Peace Foundation (no recent information)*; *Universidade Internacional da Paz (UNIPAZ, #20689).* [2017.04.13/XE2883/**E**]

♦ World Peace Brigade (inactive)

♦ World Peace Council (WPC) 21717

Conseil mondial de la paix (CMP) – Consejo Mundial de la Paz (CMP) – Weltfriedensrat (WFR) – Vsemirnyj Sovet Mira (VSM)
Contact 10 Othonos St, 105 57 Athens, Greece. T. +302103316326. Fax +302103224302. E-mail: wpc@otenet.gr.
URL: http://www.wpc-in.org/
History 22 Nov 1950, Warsaw (Poland), at 2nd World Peace Congress, in succession to *World Committee of the World Congress of the Partisans of Peace (inactive)*, set up Apr 1949, Prague (Czechoslovakia), at 1st World Congress of Defenders of Peace (also held simultaneously in Paris), following initiatives Aug 1948, Wroclaw (Poland) of 1st World Congress of Intellectuals in Defence of Peace. **Aims** Promote: prohibition of all weapons of mass destruction and ending of the arms drive; abolition of foreign military bases; total and universal *disarmament* under effective international control; elimination of all forms of colonialism, neo-colonialism, racism, sexism and other forms of discrimination; respect for the right of peoples to sovereignty and independence, essential for the establishment of peace; respect for the territorial integrity of states; non-interference in the internal affairs of nations; establishment of mutually beneficial trade and cultural relations based on friendship and mutual respect; peaceful co-existence between states with different political systems; negotiations instead of use of force in the settlement of differences between nations. **Structure** General Assembly (every 3 years, always in Athens, Greece) elects President and Executive Committee; Regional Conferences; Executive Committee appoints Executive Secretary and Treasurer; Standing Committee; Liaison Office. **Languages** English, French, Spanish. **Finance** Contributions from national peace committees; donations; subscriptions. **Activities** Initiates or cooperates in activities to eliminate nuclear, chemical and biological weapons and to reduce conventional arms. Launches campaigns for solution of global problems. Acts for: dissolution of military blocs and pacts; dismantling of military bases and withdrawal of foreign troops; social and economic development, establishment of a new international economic order and a just solution of the problem of foreign debt; recognition of every nation's freedom of choice; establishment of a new international information and communication order; support of liberation movements; settlement of regional conflicts on the basis of respect for peoples' right to self determination. **Events** *World Assembly and Conference* Kathmandu (Nepal) 2012, *World Assembly* Caracas (Venezuela) 2008, *Regional conference* Hanoi (Vietnam) 1999, *Europe and North America regional meeting* Fréjus (France) 1995, *Meeting on the rights of peoples to social development* Havana (Cuba) 1994. **Publications** *Peace Courier* (12 a year) in English – with Spanish section.
Members National committees in 137 countries and territories:
Afghanistan, Algeria, Angola, Argentina, Australia, Austria, Bahrain, Bangladesh, Barbados, Belgium, Benin, Bolivia, Botswana, Brazil, Bulgaria, Burkina Faso, Burundi, Cambodia, Canada, Central African Rep, Chile, Colombia, Comoros, Congo Brazzaville, Costa Rica, Cuba, Cyprus, Denmark, Dominican Rep, Egypt, El Salvador, Ethiopia, Fiji, Finland, France, Gambia, Germany, Ghana, Greece, Grenada, Guadeloupe, Guatemala, Guinea, Guinea-Bissau, Guyana, Haiti, Honduras, Hungary, Iceland, India, Indonesia, Iran Islamic Rep, Iraq, Ireland, Israel, Italy, Jamaica, Japan, Jordan, Korea DPR, Kuwait, Laos, Lebanon, Lesotho, Liberia, Libya, Luxembourg, Madagascar, Malawi, Malaysia, Mali, Malta, Martinique, Mauritius, Mexico, Mongolia, Morocco, Mozambique, Myanmar, Namibia, Nepal, Netherlands, New Caledonia, New Zealand, Nicaragua, Niger, Nigeria, Norway, Oman, Pakistan, Palestine, Panama, Papua New Guinea, Paraguay, Peru, Philippines, Poland, Portugal, Puerto Rico, Réunion, Romania, Russia, Sahara West, San Marino, Sao Tomé-Principe, Saudi Arabia, Senegal, Serbia, Seychelles, Sierra Leone, Singapore, Slovakia, Somalia, South Africa, Spain, Sri Lanka, St Vincent-Grenadines, Sudan, Suriname, Sweden, Switzerland, Syrian AR, Tanzania UR, Thailand, Timor-Leste, Togo, Trinidad-Tobago, Tunisia, Türkiye, UK, Uruguay, USA, Venezuela, Vietnam, Yemen, Zambia, Zimbabwe.
Consultative Status Consultative status granted from: *ECOSOC (#05331)* (Ros C); *UNESCO (#20322)* (Consultative Status); *ILO (#11123)* (Special List); *UNCTAD (#20285)* (General Category). **IGO Relations** Accredited by (1): *United Nations Office at Vienna (UNOV, #20604).* Associated with Department of Global Communications of the United Nations. **NGO Relations** Member of the Board of: *NGO Committee on Disarmament, Peace and Security, New York NY (#17106)*; *NGO Committee for Disarmament, Geneva (#17105).* Instrumental in setting up: *Peace Movement (no recent information).* [2021/XC3502/**B**]

♦ World Peace Foundation (internationally oriented national body)
♦ World Peace Fund / see World Constitution Fund

♦ World Peace Initiative (WPI) 21718

Thailand Office 46/4 Moo 7 Khlong Song, Khlong Luang, Pathum Thani, 12120, Thailand. E-mail: info@wpifoundation.org.
UK Office 74 Strathcona Gardens, Knaphill, Woking, GU21 2AZ, UK.
URL: http://www.wpifoundation.org/
History 2008. Registered in accordance with the laws of Hong Kong, Thailand and UK. **Aims** Create world peace by supporting individuals to find inner peace. **Structure** Board. **Languages** English, Spanish. **Staff** 36.00 FTE, paid; 10.00 FTE, voluntary. **Finance** Donations. Budget (annual): about US$ 200,000. **Activities** Awards/prizes/competitions; training/education; awareness raising. **Members** Individuals (29,332) in 211 countries. Membership countries not specified. **NGO Relations** Partners include: *Africa Asia Scholars Global Network (AASGON)*; *Association des états généraux des étudiants de l'Europe (AEGEE-Europe, #02495)*; *CIVICUS: World Alliance for Citizen Participation (#03962)*; *Culture of Peace Initiative (CPI)*; *International Cities of Peace (ICP, #12577)*; *International Institute for Global Leadership (IIGL)*; *Organisation of African Youth (OAYouth, #17799)*; *Pathways To Peace (PTP, #18262).* Instrumental in setting up: *Peace Revolution.* Member of: *International Youth Health Organization (YHO, #15933).* [2019/XJ5444/**F**]

♦ World Peace Through Law Center / see World Jurist Association (#21604)
♦ World Peace Through Law Center / see World Association of Judges (#21150)
♦ World Peace Law Organization (internationally oriented national body)
♦ World Peace Mission Organization (internationally oriented national body)
♦ World Peace Organization (internationally oriented national body)
♦ World Peace Posse (internationally oriented national body)
♦ World Peace Prayer Society (internationally oriented national body)
♦ World Peace Service (internationally oriented national body)
♦ World Peace University / see Institute of Global Education
♦ World Peace Volunteers (internationally oriented national body)

♦ World Pension Alliance (WPA) 21719

Chair c/o AEIP, Rue Montoyer 24, 1000 Brussels, Belgium. E-mail: info@worldpensionalliance.org.
Coordinator address not obtained.
URL: https://worldpensionalliance.org/
History 2011. Former names and other names: *Global Pension Alliance* – former (2011 to 2016). **Aims** Be recognized at the international level as the common voice of the not-for-profit pension industry representing millions of retirement income plan members. **Structure** Executive Committee; Rotating Chair. **Events** *World Pension Alliance and Transatlantic Conference* Melbourne, VIC (Australia) 2022.
Members National and international organizations in countries:
Australia, Canada, USA.
Association Européenne des Institutions Paritaires de la Protection Sociale (AEIP, #02575); *Federación Internacional de Administradoras de Fondos de Pensiones (FIAP, #09334)*; *PensionsEurope (#18291).* [2022/AA2665/y/**C**]

♦ World Pensions Council (unconfirmed)

♦ World Penthathlon (UIPM) 21720

SG Stade Louis II – Entrée C, 19 avenue des Castelans, 98000 Monaco, Monaco. T. +37797778555. Fax +37797778550. E-mail: uipm@pentathlon.org.
Pres An der Rodelbahn 2, 64380 Rossdorf, Germany. T. +4960713035280. Fax +4960713035281.
URL: http://www.pentathlon.org/
History 3 Aug 1948, London (UK). First statutes adopted 1949, Stockholm (Sweden). Cross-country skiing and rifle shooting (biathlon) included from 1960. Although *International Biathlon Union (IBU, #12336)* was set up in 1993, the two sports continued to be united under UIPMB as umbrella organization until 26 Sep 1998, when the decision of IBU, 26 Jun 1998, to exist autonomously came into effect. Statutes revised: 1998; 2018. Former names and other names: *International Modern Pentathlon Union* – former (1948 to 1960); *Union internationale de pentathlon moderne (UIPM)* – former (1948 to 1960); *International Modern Pentathlon and Biathlon Union* – former (1960 to 1998); *Union internationale de pentathlon moderne et biathlon (UIPMB)* – former (1960 to 1998); *Union internationale de pentathlon moderne (UIPM)* – legal name (1998); *International Modern Pentathlon Union* – legal name (1998). **Aims** Govern the core Olympic sport of Modern Pentathlon and other UIPM multi-sports – Tetrathlon, Triathle, Biathle, Laser Run and World Schools Biathlon – which form a developmental pyramid aimed at increasing global participation. **Structure** Congress (annual); Executive Board; Standing Committees (7); Commissions (8); Doping Review Panel. **Languages** English, French. **Staff** 11.00 FTE, paid. **Finance** Sources: members' dues; sponsorship. Supported by: *International Olympic Committee (IOC, #14408).* **Activities** Sporting activities. **Events** *Annual Congress* Buenos Aires (Argentina) 2012, *Annual Congress* Stockholm (Sweden) 2012, *Annual Congress* Copenhagen (Denmark) 2009, *Annual Congress* Antigua (Guatemala) 2008, *Annual Congress* Cape Town (South Africa) 2007. **Publications** *UIPM Newsletter* (12 a year); *UIPM Media Guide* (annual); *UIPM Yearbook* (annual).
Members National federations which administer modern pentathlon and all other UIPM multi-discipline sports in 119 countries and territories:
Afghanistan, Algeria, Argentina, Armenia, Australia, Austria, Azerbaijan, Bahrain, Bangladesh, Belarus, Belgium, Benin, Bermuda, Bolivia, Brazil, Bulgaria, Burkina Faso, Burundi, Cameroon, Canada, Chile, China, Colombia, Costa Rica, Côte d'Ivoire, Croatia, Cuba, Cyprus, Czechia, Denmark, Dominican Rep, Ecuador, Egypt, El Salvador, Estonia, Eswatini, Finland, France, Gambia, Georgia, Germany, Ghana, Great Britain, Greece, Guatemala, Haiti, Hong Kong, Hungary, India, Indonesia, Iran Islamic Rep, Ireland, Israel, Italy, Jamaica, Japan, Kazakhstan, Kenya, Korea DPR, Korea Rep, Kosovo, Kuwait, Kyrgyzstan, Latvia, Lebanon, Lithuania, Luxembourg, Madagascar, Malawi, Malaysia, Mali, Mauritius, Mexico, Moldova, Monaco, Mongolia, Morocco, Mozambique, Namibia, Nepal, Netherlands, New Zealand, Niger, Nigeria, Pakistan, Palestine, Panama, Paraguay, Peru, Philippines, Poland, Portugal, Puerto Rico, Qatar, Romania, Russia, Senegal, Serbia, Singapore, Slovakia, South Africa, Spain, Sri Lanka, Sweden, Switzerland, Syrian AR, Taiwan, Tajikistan, Thailand, Togo, Tunisia, Türkiye, Turkmenistan, Uganda, Ukraine, Uruguay, USA, Uzbekistan, Venezuela.
Continental federations include:
Asian Modern Pentathlon Confederation (AMPC, #01542); *Confederación Sudamericana de Pentatlon Moderno (CSPM, #04492)*; *European Confederation of Modern Pentathlon (ECMP, #06713).*
NGO Relations Member of (6): *Association of Summer Olympic International Federations (ASOIF, #02943)*; *International Committee for Fair Play (#12769)*; *International Council of Sport Science and Physical Education (ICSSPE, #13077)*; *International Paralympic Committee (IPC, #14512)*; *International University Sports Federation (FISU, #15830)*; *Olympic Movement (#17719).* Recognized by: *International Olympic Committee (IOC, #14408).* [2023.02.15/XB2346/y/**B**]

♦ World Permanent Organization for the Jamahiriyan Youth / see World Organization for Education, Science and Development

♦ World Pétanque and Bowls Federation (WPBF) 21721

Fédération Mondiale Boules & Pétanque (FMBP)
SG Maison Communale de Prilly, 40 route de Cossonay, 1008 Prilly VD, Switzerland.
URL: https://wpbf-fmbp.org/
History Set up following dissolution of *Confédération mondiale des sports de boules (CMSB, inactive).* Registration: Switzerland. **Structure** General Assembly; Executive Committee. **Activities** Sporting activities.
Members Federations in 72 countries and territories:
Andorra, Argentina, Austria, Bangladesh, Belgium, Benin, Brazil, Bulgaria, Cambodia, Canada, Comoros, Congo Brazzaville, Croatia, Czechia, Denmark, England, Estonia, Finland, France, Germany, Greece, Hong Kong, Hungary, Iran Islamic Rep, Israel, Italy, Japan, Kazakhstan, Korea Rep, Latvia, Lebanon, Lithuania, Luxembourg, Madagascar, Malaysia, Mauritania, Mauritius, Mexico, Monaco, Morocco, Nepal, Netherlands, New Caledonia, New Zealand, Norway, Pakistan, Paraguay, Peru, Philippines, Poland, Polynesia Fr, Portugal, Russia, Scotland, Senegal, Singapore, Slovakia, Spain, Sweden, Switzerland, Taiwan, Thailand, Tonga, Tunisia, Türkiye, Ukraine, Uruguay, USA, Vanuatu, Venezuela, Vietnam, Wales.
NGO Relations Member of (3): *Association of the IOC Recognized International Sports Federations (ARISF, #02767)*; *International World Games Association (IWGA, #15914)*; *Olympic Movement (#17719).* Recognized by: *International Olympic Committee (IOC, #14408).* [2022/AA3045/**C**]

♦ World Petroleum Congress / see World Petroleum Council (#21722)
♦ World Petroleum Congresses / see World Petroleum Council (#21722)

♦ World Petroleum Council (WPC) 21722

Dir Gen 61 New Cavendish St, London, W1G 7AR, UK. T. +447786331675. E-mail: wpcsecretariat@world-petroleum.org.
URL: http://www.world-petroleum.org/
History 1933, London (UK). Founded at 1st congress, following recommendations, 1932, of Institution of Petroleum Technologists (now Institute of Petroleum). Constitution and By-Laws amended Oct 1991. Former names and other names: *World Petroleum Congress (WPC)* – former (1933); *Congrès mondiaux du pétrole (CMP)* – former (1933); *World Petroleum Congresses* – alias. Registration: Charity, No/ID: 1151654, Start date: 15 Apr 2013, England and Wales. **Aims** Promote sustainable management and use of the world's petroleum resources for the benefit of all. **Structure** National Committees (65); Council (meets at Congress); Executive Board; Scientific Programme Committee; Development Committee; Committees; Task Forces. Membership by election. **Languages** English. **Staff** 3.00 FTE, paid. **Finance** Profits go into legacy funds (normally educational) in countries where meetings have been held. **Activities** Awards/prizes/competitions; events/meetings; knowledge management/information dissemination; networking/liaising; publishing activities; research/documentation; training/education. **Events** *World Petroleum Congress* Calgary, AB (Canada) 2023, *World Petroleum Congress* Houston, TX (USA) 2021, *World Petroleum Congress* Houston, TX (USA) 2020, *Downstream Conference* Manama (Bahrain) 2019, *Kazakhstan Energy Week* Nur-Sultan (Kazakhstan) 2019. **Publications** *WPC Newsletter.* Congress proceedings; educational guides; technical papers; reports.
Members National committees in 57 countries:
Algeria, Angola, Argentina, Australia, Austria, Belgium, Bolivia, Brazil, Canada, China, Colombia, Croatia, Cuba, Czechia, Denmark, Egypt, Finland, France, Gabon, Germany, Hungary, India, Indonesia, Iran Islamic Rep, Israel, Japan, Kazakhstan, Korea Rep, Kuwait, Libya, Mexico, Netherlands, Nigeria, Norway, Pakistan, Papua New Guinea, Peru, Philippines, Poland, Qatar, Romania, Russia, Saudi Arabia, Serbia, Slovakia, Slovenia, South Africa, Spain, Sweden, Türkiye, UK, Ukraine, Uruguay, USA, Uzbekistan, Venezuela, Vietnam.
IGO Relations Accredited by (1): *United Nations Framework Convention on Climate Change – Secretariat (UNFCCC, #20564).* **NGO Relations** Liaises with: *World Energy Council (WEC, #21381).* [2023.02.28/XF3106/**F**]

♦ World Pharmacists (internationally oriented national body)

♦ World Pharmacy Council (WPV) 21723

Address not obtained.
URL: https://www.worldpharmacycouncil.org/

History 2017. Founded by community pharmacy organizations which had met annually since 1987 under the name Pharmintercom. **Aims** Build international recognition of community pharmacy, its role, policies and value; influence, promote and secure acceptance of community pharmacy as an important and integral part of health systems. **Activities** Events/meetings; research/documentation. **Events** *Annual Conference* Paris (France) 2022.
Members Organizations in 8 countries:
Australia, Denmark, Ireland, New Zealand, Portugal, Spain, UK, USA.
NGO Relations Associate Expert Group of *Business and Industry Advisory Committee to the OECD (BIAC, #03385).* [2022/AA3154/C]

♦ World Pheasant Association (WPA) 21724

Admin Middle, Ninebanks, Hexham, NE47 8DL, UK. T. +441434345526. E-mail: office@pheasant.org.uk.
URL: http://www.pheasant.org.uk/

History Founded Jun 1975, Bures (UK), as the Specialist Group for Galliformes appointed by the International Council for Bird Preservation (ICBP), currently *BirdLife International (#03266)*, and *International Union for Conservation of Nature and Natural Resources (IUCN, #15766)*. Also referred to as *WPA International*. UK Registered Charity: 271203. **Aims** Develop, promote and support *conservation* of all *species* of the *bird* order *Galliformes* and their *habitats*. **Structure** General Meeting (annual); Governing Council; Patrons (7); Chapters (10); Conservation Breeding Advisory Group; European Conservation Breeding Group. **Languages** English. **Staff** 0.50 FTE, voluntary. **Finance** Members' dues. Other sources: fund-raising events; donations. Also receives support from individuals, governments and organizations, including the following organizations listed in this Yearbook: *Aviornis International (#03048)*; *Conservation International (CI)*; *Oriental Bird Club (OBC)*; *Peoples Trust for Endangered Species (PTES)*. **Activities** Projects/programmes; training/education; financial and/or material support; events/meetings. **Events** *International Galliformes Symposium* Dong Hoi (Vietnam) 2019, *Annual General Meeting* Rotterdam (Netherlands) 2019, *Annual General Meeting* Dublin (Ireland) 2014, *International Symposium* Edinburgh (UK) 2013, *International galliformes symposium* Chiang Mai (Thailand) 2010. **Publications** *WPA News* (3 a year). *A Life on the Wildside* by Colin Willock; *Captive Birds in Health and Disease* by John E Cooper; *Cheng and the Golden Pheasant* by Yang Qun-Rong; *Domestic Quail for Hobby or Profit* by G E S Robbins; *Introduction to Ornamental Pheasants* by Keith Howman; *Introduction to Pheasants in Captivity* by K C R Howman; *Introduction to Quail in Captivity* by G E S Robbins; *Partridges and Francolins* by G E S Robbins; *Peafowl: Their conservation, breeding and management* by T P Gardiner; *Pheasant Jungles* by William Beebe; *Pheasants of the World: Their Breeding and Management* by K C R Howman; *Quail: Their Breeding and Management* by Gene M Robbins; *The New Incubation Book – Millenium Edition* by A Anderson-Brown and G E S Robbins.
Members Specialist Groups 350 members in 50 countries. Membership countries not specified. Individuals (772) in 57 countries and territories:
Individuals (772) in 57 countries and territories:
Argentina, Australia, Bahamas, Bahrain, Bangladesh, Belgium, Brazil, Cambodia, Canada, Chile, China, Colombia, Croatia, Cyprus, Czechia, Denmark, Estonia, Finland, France, Germany, Greece, Hong Kong, India, Indonesia, Ireland, Italy, Japan, Laos, Malaysia, Malta, Mauritius, Mexico, Myanmar, Nepal, Netherlands, New Zealand, Norway, Pakistan, Philippines, Poland, Portugal, Romania, Russia, Saudi Arabia, Singapore, South Africa, Spain, Sri Lanka, Sweden, Switzerland, Taiwan, Thailand, UK, Ukraine, USA, Vietnam, Zimbabwe.
NGO Relations Has Formal Memorandum of Understanding with: *Alliance for Zero Extinction (AZE, #00730)*; IUCN. Also links with NGOs within countries where it works. [2019.02.12/XC4399/v/E]

♦ World Phenomenology Institute (WPI) 21725

Institut mondial de phénoménologies – Weltinstitut für Phaenomenologie
Main Office PO Box 5158, Hanover NH 03755, USA. E-mail: office@phenomenology.org.
URL: http://www.phenomenology.org/

History Dec 1975, Boston MA (USA), as *World Institute for Advanced Phenomenological Research and Learning (WPI) – Institut mondial des hautes études phénoménologiques – Instituto Mondiale de Altos Estudios Fenomenologicos – Weltinstitut für fortgeschrittene phänomenologische Forschung und Bildung – Istituto Mondiale di Ricerca e di Studi Avanscati di Fenomenologia*. **Aims** Promote advanced interdisciplinary research on the phenomena of life. **Structure** Incorporated with *International Husserl and Phenomenological Research Society (IHPRS, see: #21725)*, being autonomous in direction but sharing a common research program. Other affiliated bodies are: *International Society of Phenomenology, Aesthetics and the Fine Arts (ISPAFA, #15357)*; *International Society for Phenomenology and the Sciences of Life (see: #21725)*; *International Society for Phenomenology and Literature (ISPL, see: #21725)*; *Sociedad Ibero-Americana de Fenomenologia (no recent information)*; *'American Society for Phenomenology, the Fine Arts and Aesthetics'*. **Languages** English, French, Spanish. **Staff** 4.00 FTE, paid. **Finance** Members' dues. Sources: sales of publications; grants. **Events** *International Phenomenology Congress* Milan (Italy) 2014, *International Phenomenology Congress / International Congress* Hanover, NH (USA) 2013, *International Phenomenology Congress / International Congress* Paris (France) 2012, *World congress of phenomenology* Krakow (Poland) 2008, *International phenomenology congress / International Congress* Istanbul (Turkey) 2007. **Publications** *Analecta Husserliana, The Yearbook of Phenomenological Research* – 57 vols to date; *Inquiry: A Review of Philosophical Ideas and Trends* – journal. *WPI Monograph Series*. *Impetus and Equipoise in the Life-Strategies of Reason.*
Members Individuals, associated with 4 affiliated international bodies. Members in 66 countries and territories:
Argentina, Australia, Austria, Belgium, Bolivia, Brazil, Bulgaria, Canada, Chile, China, Colombia, Costa Rica, Cuba, Cyprus, Czechia, Denmark, Egypt, Estonia, Finland, France, Gambia, Georgia, Germany, Ghana, Greece, Guatemala, Holy See, Hong Kong, Hungary, India, Ireland, Israel, Italy, Japan, Kazakhstan, Kenya, Korea Rep, Latvia, Lithuania, Luxembourg, Madagascar, Mexico, Netherlands, New Zealand, Nigeria, Norway, Panama, Peru, Philippines, Poland, Puerto Rico, Russia, Serbia, Singapore, Slovenia, South Africa, Spain, Switzerland, Taiwan, Tanzania UR, Tunisia, Türkiye, Ukraine, USA, Venezuela, Zimbabwe.
[2018/XE3970/jv/F]

♦ World Philharmonic Orchestra (WPO) 21726

Orchestre philharmonique du monde
Contact CP 2057, 1211 Geneva 1; Switzerland. E-mail: opm@world-orchestral.com.
URL: https://www.world-orchestral.com/world_ph.html

Activities Events/meetings.
Members Orchestras in 83 countries:
Argentina, Armenia, Australia, Austria, Azerbaijan, Belarus, Belgium, Bolivia, Bosnia-Herzegovina, Brazil, Bulgaria, Canada, Chile, China, Colombia, Costa Rica, Côte d'Ivoire, Croatia, Czechia, Denmark, Ecuador, Egypt, El Salvador, Estonia, Finland, France, Georgia, Germany, Greece, Guatemala, Hungary, Iceland, India, Indonesia, Iran Islamic Rep, Ireland, Israel, Italy, Japan, Jordan, Korea Rep, Latvia, Lebanon, Liechtenstein, Lithuania, Luxembourg, Malaysia, Malta, Mexico, Monaco, Morocco, Netherlands, New Zealand, Norway, Oman, Palestine, Panama, Paraguay, Peru, Philippines, Poland, Portugal, Romania, Russia, Serbia, Singapore, Slovakia, Slovenia, South Africa, Spain, Sri Lanka, Sweden, Switzerland, Syrian AR, Thailand, Tunisia, Türkiye, UK, Ukraine, Uruguay, USA, Venezuela, Vietnam. [2021/XF0682/F]

♦ World Philology Union (WPU) 21727

Admin Office c/o PHI, PO Box 2709, Solli, 0204 Oslo, Norway. E-mail: info@philology.org.
Visiting address Gydas vei 4, 0363 Oslo, Norway.
URL: https://philology.org/

History 2 Dec 2021, Oslo (Norway). Constitution adopted 2 Dec 2022. **Aims** Promote philology worldwide, in research, education, society and culture. **Structure** General Assembly; Board; Secretariat. **Events** *International Conference* Rome (Italy) 2022. **Members** Institutions; Affiliated scholars; Independent scholars; Students. Membership countries not specified. **NGO Relations** Cooperates with (1): *Associazione Internazionale di Studi sul Mediterraneo e l'Oriente (ISMEO).* [2022/AA3123/C]

♦ World Phosphate Institute 21728

Institut mondial du phosphate (IMPHOS)
Contact 3 Rue Abdelkader Elmazini-Ex Corneille, 20100 Casablanca, Morocco. T. +212522484122. Fax +212522484121. E-mail: imphos@imphos.org.
URL: https://www.imphos.org/

History Dec 1973, Rabat (Morocco). Registration: Morocco. **Aims** Promote worldwide development of judicious phosphate use to meet the increasing food demand of human kind, on a basis that is technically sound, economically advantageous and environmentally responsible; enhance and sustain worldwide growth of phosphate use in both agriculture and industry; support research on mineral phosphates for industrial and agricultural applications; retrieve and disseminate scientific data and technical information on plant nutrient management and *fertilizer* processing technologies. **Structure** Board of Directors. Advisory Committee. Permanent Secretariat. Divisions (2): Agronomic; Technical Committee. **Languages** Arabic, English, French. **Staff** 11.50 FTE, paid. **Finance** Sources: members' dues. Other sources: levy on tonnage produced. **Activities** Through partnership, supports and closely monitors projects in Asia, Europe and other regions; promotes and develops scientific and technical knowledge of the cadmium issue in the use of phosphate fertilizers in agriculture; organizes congresses and regional seminars; offers IMPHOS Award, granted every every 3 years for a contribution to the advancement of knowledge on phosphates and their applications. Programmes focus on the following areas: intensification and diversification of agriculture in Asia; increasing per capita food production in Sub-Saharan Africa; Harnessing the limited amount of soil and water for increased crop production in West Asia and North Africa; developing P fertilizer management strategies in Western Europe for profitable and environmentally sustainable crop production; working on cleaner technology and new industrial uses of phosphates. Has undertaken study in relation to the European Union issued EURATOM-BSS Directive that set limits on radioactivity concentration in Naturally Occurring Radioactive Materials (NORM). **Events** *International conference for Africa towards a sustainable green revolution in Africa* Dakar (Senegal) 2009, *International conference on the valorization of phosphates and phosphorous compounds* Marrakech (Morocco) 2009, *Joint workshop on balanced fertilization for optimizing plant nutrition* Sharm el Sheikh (Egypt) 2007, *Workshop on phosphorus and phosphate compounds / Congress* Kasugai (Japan) 2005, *Workshop on phosphorus and phosphate compounds / Congress* Jena (Germany) 2002. **Publications** *IMPHOS Phosphate Newsletter* (3 a year). Studies and reports in English, French; congress and seminar proceedings.
Members Phosphate producing companies in 7 countries:
Algeria, Jordan, Morocco, Senegal, South Africa, Togo, Tunisia.
Consultative Status Consultative status granted from: *ECOSOC (#05331)* (Ros C); *FAO (#09260)* (Liaison Status); *UNEP (#20299)*. **NGO Relations** Cooperates with (1): *International Organization for Standardization (ISO, #14473).* [2022/XD4443/j/D]

♦ World Physiotherapy / see World Confederation for Physical Therapy (#21293)
♦ World Phytotherapy Association (inactive)

♦ World Pickleball Federation (WPF) 21729

Pres address not obtained.
URL: https://www.worldpickleballfederation.org/

Aims Fuel the growth of pickleball worldwide by providing practical support and governance. **Structure** Board. **Activities** Sporting activities.
Members Founding members in 20 countries and territories:
Argentina, Australia, Belgium, Brazil, China, Czechia, England, France, Germany, Hong Kong, Italy, Korea Rep, Mexico, Pakistan, Scotland, Singapore, Spain, Taiwan, Tonga, Ukraine.
NGO Relations Regional confederations include: *Asian Pickleball Federation (APF, #01665).*
[2023/AA1113/C]

♦ World Plastics Council (WPC) 21730

Secretariat c/o American Chemistry Council – Plastics Div, 700 Second Street NE, Washington DC 20002, USA.
URL: https://www.worldplasticscouncil.org/

History Proposed Oct 2013, Düsseldorf (Germany). Officially launched Nov 2014, Dubai (United Arab Emirates). **Aims** Promote the ethic of sustainability and the responsible use of plastics; represent the global plastics industry to other stakeholders; coordinate and unite efforts to achieve practical solutions; share best practices from across various regions. **Structure** Executive Committee.
Members Full; Associate. Membership countries not specified. Associate members include 2 organizations listed in this Yearbook:
Associate members include 2 organizations listed in this Yearbook:
Association of Plastics Manufacturers in Europe (Plastics Europe, #02862); *Gulf Petrochemicals and Chemicals Association (GPCA, #10839).*
Consultative Status Consultative status granted from: *UNEP (#20299).* [2019/XM8523/y/C]

♦ World Ploughing Organization (WPO) 21731

Organisation mondiale de labourage
Gen Sec Fallaghmore, Athy, CO. KILDARE, Ireland.
URL: http://www.worldploughing.org/

History 13 Nov 1952, Stirling (UK). Founded at meeting held simultaneously at Bridge of Allan (UK), a provisional Governing Board having been set up 5 Feb 1952, Workington (UK). **Aims** Foster and preserve the art and improve the skill of ploughing the land; promote world *championship* ploughing contests; provide for demonstration work and trade displays; urge development and adoption of improved techniques and aids to man in all branches of agriculture; foster a vigorous spirit of cooperation and enterprise in producing food for an increasing world population; encourage, by all these means, fellowship and understanding amongst the peoples of races, nationalities and different affiliations. **Structure** General Meeting (held annually, at the time and place of World Championship Ploughing Contest). Governing Board, consisting of one representative appointed by each nationally represented organization. Executive Committee appointed by Governing Board. Membership limited to national organizations which arrange national annual championships, and associate members. **Languages** English. **Staff** 1.00 FTE, paid. **Finance** Members' dues. Contest fees. **Activities** Cooperates with Government departments, agricultural institutes and associations, industrial, commercial and rural youth organizations; encourages research projects; promotes better understanding of soil cultivation practices. Organizes: World Ploughing Contests and International Soil Cultivation Conferences; symposia. **Events** *World Contest* Kenya 2037, *World Contest* Latvia 2036, *World Contest* Denmark 2035, *World Contest* Canada 2034, *World Contest* Austria 2033. **Publications** *WPO Handbook* (annual).
Members National organizations in 29 countries:
Australia, Austria, Belgium, Bosnia-Herzegovina, Canada, Croatia, Czechia, Denmark, Estonia, Finland, France, Germany, Hungary, Ireland, Italy, Kenya, Lithuania, Netherlands, New Zealand, Norway, Russia, Serbia, Slovakia, Slovenia, Spain, Sweden, Switzerland, UK, USA. [2022/XC3573/C]

♦ World Plumbing Council (WPC) 21732

Contact address not obtained. E-mail: secretariat@worldplumbing.org.
URL: http://www.worldplumbing.org/

History 1990, London (UK). Founded at 2nd World Conference. Previous By-Laws adopted, 1 Nov 2000, Rotorua (New Zealand); current by-laws adopted 19-20 Nov 2007, Tokyo (Japan). Registration: Swiss Civil Code, Start date: 18 Jan 2001, Switzerland. **Aims** Achieve the best possible plumbing for the world through growth and development of the world's plumbing industries. **Structure** General Meeting (twice a year); Executive Board. **Languages** English. **Staff** Voluntary. **Finance** Sources: members' dues. Other sources: logo use; licence income. **Activities** Standards/guidelines. Active in: Australia, Brazil, Burkina Faso, Germany, India, Ireland, New Zealand, Rwanda, South Africa, UK, USA, Zambia. **Events** *Triennial World Conference* Melbourne, VIC (Australia) 2019, *Triennial World Conference* Cape Town (South Africa) 2016, *General Meeting* Lostorf (Switzerland) 2014, *Triennial World Conference* Delhi (India) 2013, *Triennial world conference* Edinburgh (UK) 2011. **Publications** *WPC Review* (3 a year) – newsletter. *Health Aspects of Plumbing.*
Members Full (38) and Affiliate (47) in about 30 countries. Membership countries not specified.
Included in the above, 1 organization listed in this Yearbook:
International Association of Plumbing and Mechanical Officials (IAPMO).
Consultative Status Consultative status granted from: *WHO (#20950)* (Official Relations).
[2022.10.26/XF4160/F]

♦ World Poker Federation (unconfirmed)
♦ World Police and Criminal League (inactive)
♦ World Police League (inactive)
♦ World Police Medical Officers / see International Association of Clinical Forensic Medicine (#11779)

♦ World Policy Institute (internationally oriented national body)
♦ World Pool Association / see World Pool-Billiard Association (#21733)

♦ World Pool-Billiard Association (WPA) 21733

Pres PO Box 297, Oatley NSW 2223, Australia.
URL: http://www.wpapool.com/

History Founded 1987. Activities commenced 1990. Also referred to as *World Pool Association*. In Jan 1992, united with *World Billiards Union (#21230)* and *World Professional Billiards and Snooker Association (WPBSA, #21740)* in umbrella organization, *World Confederation of Billiards Sports (WCBS, #21291)*. **Aims** Unite world pool-billiards associations into one intercontinental association; promote pool-billiards as a worldwide international sport; supervise the WPA World *Championships*; cultivate mutual friendship with all types or international and national billiards organizations; support and encourage the development of all disciplines of pool-billiards as an international sport; adopt a sport policy which is not in conflict with the rules set forth in the Olympic Charter. **Structure** Board of Directors. **Languages** English. **Staff** 2.00 FTE, paid. **Finance** Sources: members' dues. **Activities** Sporting activities. **Events** *Annual General Assembly* Las Vegas, NV (USA) 2015, *Annual General Assembly* Shanghai (China) 2013, *Annual General Assembly* Doha (Qatar) 2011, *Annual General Assembly* Manila (Philippines) 2009, *Annual General Assembly* Willingen (Germany) 2007.
Members National organizations in 94 countries and territories:
Albania, Argentina, Aruba, Australia, Austria, Bangladesh, Belarus, Belgium, Bolivia, Bosnia-Herzegovina, Botswana, Brazil, Brunei Darussalam, Bulgaria, Canada, Chile, China, Colombia, Costa Rica, Croatia, Curaçao, Cyprus, Czechia, Denmark, Ecuador, Egypt, Estonia, Eswatini, Fiji, Finland, France, Germany, Great Britain, Greece, Hong Kong, Hungary, India, Indonesia, Iran Islamic Rep, Iraq, Israel, Italy, Japan, Kuwait, Lesotho, Libya, Liechtenstein, Lithuania, Luxembourg, Macau, Malawi, Malaysia, Maldives, Mauritius, Mexico, Montenegro, Morocco, Namibia, Netherlands, New Zealand, Nicaragua, Nigeria, North Macedonia, Northern Cyprus, Norway, Panama, Philippines, Poland, Portugal, Puerto Rico, Qatar, Réunion, Russia, Saudi Arabia, Serbia, Singapore, Slovakia, Slovenia, South Africa, Spain, Sri Lanka, Sweden, Switzerland, Tanzania UR, Thailand, Türkiye, Uganda, Ukraine, United Arab Emirates, Uruguay, USA, Venezuela, Vietnam, Zambia.
Regional bodies (6) grouping the above:
All Africa Pool Association (AAPA, #00643); Asian Pocket Billiards Union (APBU, #01668); Billiard Congress of America (BCA); Confederación Panamericana de Billar (CPB, #04469); European Pocket Billiard Federation (EPBF, #08237); Oceania Pocket Billiard Association (OPBA, #17668). [2015.01.23/XC0117/y/C]

♦ World Population Foundation / see Rutgers (#19011)
♦ World Ports Association / see International Association of Ports and Harbors (#12096)
♦ World Ports Seminar (meeting series)

♦ World Potato Congress (WPC) 21734

Gen Manager PO Box 40020, West Royalty PO, Charlottetown PE C1E 0J2, Canada. T. +19023688885. E-mail: info@potatocongress.org.
URL: http://www.potatocongress.org/

History 1993, Charlottetown, PE (Canada). **Aims** Be a premier global network for the potato value chain. **Structure** Board of Directors; International Advisory Committee. **Languages** English. **Staff** 0.50 FTE, paid. Several voluntary. **Activities** Events/meetings; knowledge management/information dissemination. **Events** *World Potato Congress* Adelaide, SA (Australia) 2024, *World Potato Congress* Dublin (Ireland) 2022, *World Potato Congress* Dublin (Ireland) 2021, *World Potato Congress* Cusco (Peru) 2018, *World Potato Congress* Beijing (China) 2015. **Publications** *WPC Toolbox*. Congress proceedings. [2022.02.08/XF6030/c/F]

♦ World Power Conference / see World Energy Council (#21381)

♦ World Powerlifting 21735

Dir address not obtained.
URL: https://worldpowerlifting.com/

Structure Board.
Members Full in countries:
Argentina, Australia, Cameroon, Canada, China, Germany, Greece, Hong Kong, India, Iran Islamic Rep, Ireland, Italy, Korea Rep, Malaysia, Mexico, Mongolia, Nauru, New Zealand, Nigeria, Niue, Pakistan, Palestine, Poland, Samoa, Solomon Is, Sri Lanka, Uganda, United Arab Emirates, USA.
Oceania Powerlifting Federation (#17669). [2022/AA2499/D]

♦ World Prematurity Network 21736

Contact c/o EFCNI, Hofmannstrasse 7A, 81379 Munich, Germany. T. +498989083260. Fax +4989890832610. E-mail: info@efcni.org.

History 2011. **Languages** English, German.
Members Organizations (8), including 3 listed in this Yearbook:
Borngreat Foundation (BGF); European Foundation for the Care of Newborn Infants (EFCNI, #07344); LittleBigSouls (LBS, #16494). [2016.07.21/XJ7941/y/F]

♦ World President's Organization (internationally oriented national body)
♦ World Presidents' Organizations / see World President's Organization
♦ World Press Institute (internationally oriented national body)

♦ World Print and Communication Forum (WPCF) 21737

Pres c/o INTERGRAF, Ave Louise 130A, 1050 Brussels, Belgium. T. +3222308646. Fax +3222311464. E-mail: info@worldprintforum.org.
URL: http://www.worldprintforum.org/

History Founded in 2004. **Aims** Form a single global exchange platform for the printing and communication industry between the different players, suppliers and support services. **Structure** Board. **Languages** English. **Finance** Members' dues. **Events** *Conference* Mumbai (India) 2020, *World Print and Communication Forum* Goyang (Korea Rep) 2016, *World print and communication congress* 2007, *World print and communication congress / Triennial Congress* Cape Town (South Africa) 2005.
Members National organizations (9) in 8 countries and territories:
Australia, China, Hong Kong, India, Japan, Korea Rep, Nepal, USA.
International organization:
Intergraf (#11505). [2020/XM0549/c/F]

♦ World Processing Tomato Council (WPTC) 21738

Conseil mondial de la tomate transformée (WPTC)

Gen Sec Maison de l'Agriculture, Site Agroparc, TSA 48449, 84912 Avignon CEDEX 9, France. T. +33607125829. E-mail: contact@wptc.to.
Pres address not obtained.
URL: http://www.wptc.to/

History 28 May 1998, Navarra (Spain). Registration: Start date: 23 Jun 1998, France, Provence-Alpes-Côte d'Azur; RNA, No/ID: W842003190, Start date: 21 Apr 2016, France, Provence-Alpes-Côte d'Azur. **Aims** Create permanent links between professional grower and/or processor organizations, in order to coordinate actions undertaken to safeguard their interests; study and recommend action intended to better organize markets and favour fair competition; undertake action in view to increase consumption of tomato products. **Structure** Chair; General Secretary; Commissions (4); Areas (3): Mediterranean, Northern America, Other Countries. **Languages** English. **Finance** Sources: members' dues. **Events** *World Congress* Budapest (Hungary) 2024, *World Congress* San Juan (Argentina) 2022, *World Congress* Greece 2018, *World Congress* Santiago (Chile) 2016, *World Congress* Sirmione (Italy) 2014. **Publications** *Tomato News*.
Members Members in 26 countries:
Algeria, Argentina, Australia, Brazil, Canada, Chile, China, Egypt, France, Greece, Hungary, Iran Islamic Rep, Israel, Italy, Japan, Malta, Peru, Portugal, Russia, South Africa, Spain, Syrian AR, Tunisia, Türkiye, Ukraine, USA.
IGO Relations Participates as observer in the activities of: *Codex Alimentarius Commission (CAC, #04081).*
NGO Relations *Mediterranean International Association of the Processing Tomato (#16659)* is member. [2022/XD7344/D]

♦ World Professional Association For Transgender Health (WPATH) 21739

Exec Dir address not obtained. E-mail: wpath@wpath.org.
URL: http://www.wpath.org/

History Feb 1979, San Diego, CA (USA). Bylaws modified: 2016. Former names and other names: *Harry Benjamin International Gender Dysphoria Association (HBIGDA)* – former (Feb 1979 to 2007). **Aims** Increase understanding and treatment of gender dysphoria in healthcare fields. **Structure** Board of Directors; Executive Committee. Committees; Task Forces. **Finance** Sources: members' dues. **Activities** Awards/prizes/competitions; events/meetings; standards/guidelines; training/education. **Events** *Scientific Symposium* Montréal, QC (Canada) 2022, *Scientific Symposium* 2020, *Scientific Symposium* Buenos Aires (Argentina) 2018, *Biennial Symposium* Amsterdam (Netherlands) 2016, *Biennial Symposium* Bangkok (Thailand) 2014. **Publications** *International Journal of Transgenderim* (4 a year); *WPATH Update* (4 a year).
Members Full; Supporting; Emeritus; Student. Members in 24 countries and territories:
Australia, Austria, Belgium, Brazil, Canada, Czechia, Denmark, France, Germany, Hong Kong, Ireland, Israel, Italy, Japan, Mexico, Netherlands, New Zealand, Norway, Serbia, Spain, Sweden, Switzerland, UK, USA. [2021/XE3708/E]

♦ World Professional Billiards and Snooker Association (WPBSA) 21740

Contact 75 Whiteladies Road, Clifton, Bristol, BS8 2NT, UK. T. +441173178200. Fax +441173178219. E-mail: info@worldsnooker.com.
URL: http://www.wpbsa.com/

History 1968, as *'Professional Billiards Players' Association'*. Incorporated under current title in 1982. Also referred to as *World Snooker Federation (WSF)*. From Jan 1992, united in *World Confederation of Billiards Sports (WCBS, #21291)* with *World Billiards Union (#21230)* and *World Pool-Billiard Association (WPA, #21733)*. **Aims** Act as world governing and regulatory body for *professional* billiards and snooker worldwide. **Structure** Annual General Meeting; Board of Directors. **Languages** English. **Staff** 25.00 FTE, paid. **Finance** Sources: members' dues; sponsorship. Other sources: broadcasting and commercial revenue. **Activities** Makes policies; oversees the financial affairs of professional snooker and billiards; deals with all aspects of the game, including sponsorships, television contracts, the media and tournament organization and regulation of the professional game through its commercial arm 'World Snooker Limited'. **Events** *Annual General Meeting* Coventry (UK) 2021, *Annual General Meeting* Bristol (UK) 2020, *Annual General Meeting* Barnsley (UK) 2019, *Annual General Meeting* New Zealand 1996.
Members National organizations in 60 countries and territories:
Australia, Austria, Bahrain, Bangladesh, Belgium, Canada, China, Cyprus, Denmark, Egypt, England, Estonia, Fiji, Finland, France, Germany, Greece, Hong Kong, Hungary, Iceland, India, Ireland, Isle of Man, Japan, Jordan, Kuwait, Latvia, Malaysia, Malta, Mauritius, Mongolia, Morocco, Myanmar, Netherlands, New Zealand, Northern Ireland, Norway, Pakistan, Papua New Guinea, Philippines, Poland, Qatar, Russia, Saudi Arabia, Scotland, Singapore, South Africa, Spain, Sri Lanka, Sweden, Switzerland, Syrian AR, Taiwan, Thailand, Tunisia, United Arab Emirates, USA, Wales, Yemen, Zimbabwe.
NGO Relations Member of: *Sports Rights Owners Coalition (SROC, #19929)*. Special links with: *Asian Confederation of Billiards Sports (ACBS, #01396); European Billiards and Snooker Association (EBSA, #06330); International Billiards and Snooker Federation (IBSF, #12340); World Snooker Federation (WSF, #21796).* [2018/XC0035/y/C]

♦ World Profi Kickboxing Association / see World Pan Amateur Kickboxing Association (#21707)
♦ World Prohibition Federation (inactive)
♦ World Proof Numismatic Association (internationally oriented national body)
♦ World Protection for Dogs and Cats in the Meat Trade (internationally oriented national body)

♦ World Psychiatric Association (WPA) 21741

Association mondiale de psychiatrie (AMP) – Asociación Mundial de Psiquiatria – Weltverband für Psychiatrie – Associação Mundial de Psiquiatria – Vsemirnaja Psihiatriceskaja Associacija

SG c/o Geneva Univ Psychiatric Hosp Belle Idée, Bât 11 Les Voirons, Chemin du Petit Bel-Air 2, Thônex, 1225 Geneva, Switzerland. T. +41223055737. Fax +41223055735. E-mail: wpasecretariat@wpanet.org.
URL: http://www.wpanet.org/

History 5 Jun 1961, Montréal, QC (Canada). Founded at 3rd World Psychiatric Congress. Replaced *International Society for the Organization of World Psychiatric Congresses (inactive)*, set up 18 Sep 1950, Paris (France), which had organized the first two World Congresses – 1950, Paris and 1957, Zurich (Switzerland). Registration: Switzerland. **Aims** Advance psychiatric and *mental health* education, research, clinical care and public policy worldwide; increase knowledge and skills necessary for work in the field of mental health and care for the mentally ill; promote the prevention of mental disorders; improve care of the mentally ill and preserve their rights; promote non-discrimination (parity) in the provision of care of the mentally ill; promote the highest ethical standards in psychiatric care, teaching and research; protect the rights of psychiatrists; disseminate and exchange information and advance enquiry into the aetiology, pathology and treatment of mental diseases; strengthen relations among psychiatrists working in various fields and among psychiatric societies existing in different countries; promote working relations with WHO in the fields of classification, treatment guidelines and psychiatric education, with other United Nations organizations and with governmental bodies. **Structure** General Assembly (every 3 years); Council; Board of Zone Representatives; Executive Committee. Standing Committees (3): Ethics and Review; Nominations; Planning. Operational Committees (5): Education; Finances; Scientific Meetings; Scientific Publications; Scientific Sections. Secretariat. **Languages** English, French, German, Spanish. **Staff** 2.00 FTE, paid. **Finance** Sources: grants; meeting proceeds; members' dues. Supported by: WPA Educational Foundation. **Activities** Awards/prizes/competitions; events/meetings; research/documentation; standards/guidelines; training/education. **Events** *World Congress of Psychiatry* Vienna (Austria) 2023, *World Congress of Psychiatry* Bangkok (Thailand) 2022, *World Congress of Psychiatry* 2021, *WPA Regional Congress* Kiev (Ukraine) 2021, *WPA Regional Congress* St Petersburg (Russia) 2021. **Publications** *WPA News* (4 a year); *Current Opinion in Psychiatry* – official journal. *Images in Psychiatry*; *WPA Series in Evidence Based Psychiatry*. *WPA Directory*. Congress and meeting proceedings.
Members Full: national psychiatric societies, representing over 250,000 psychiatrists in 120 countries and territories:
Albania, Algeria, Argentina, Armenia, Australia, Austria, Azerbaijan, Bahrain, Bangladesh, Barbados, Belarus, Belgium, Bolivia, Bosnia-Herzegovina, Brazil, Bulgaria, Cambodia, Canada, Chile, China, Colombia, Costa Rica, Croatia, Cuba, Cyprus, Czechia, Denmark, Dominican Rep, Ecuador, Egypt, El Salvador, Estonia, Ethiopia, Finland, France, Georgia, Germany, Ghana, Greece, Guatemala, Honduras, Hong Kong, Hungary, Iceland, India, Indonesia, Iran Islamic Rep, Iraq, Ireland, Israel, Italy, Jamaica, Japan, Jordan, Kazakhstan, Kenya, Korea Rep, Kuwait, Kyrgyzstan, Latvia, Lebanon, Libya, Lithuania, Luxembourg, Malaysia, Malta, Mauritius, Mexico, Moldova, Mongolia, Montenegro, Morocco, Mozambique, Myanmar, Nepal, Netherlands, New Zealand, Nicaragua, Nigeria, North Macedonia, Norway, Pakistan, Palestine, Panama, Papua New Guinea, Paraguay, Peru, Philippines, Poland, Portugal, Puerto Rico, Qatar, Romania, Russia, Saudi Arabia, Senegal, Serbia, Singapore, Slovakia, Slovenia, South Africa, Spain, Sri Lanka, Sudan, Sweden, Switzerland, Syrian AR, Taiwan, Thailand, Tunisia, Türkiye, Uganda, UK, Ukraine, United Arab Emirates, Uruguay, USA, Uzbekistan, Venezuela, Yemen.
Included in the above, 2 organizations listed in this Yearbook:
Arab Gulf Psychiatric Association (#00972); International Society for Psychopathology of Expression and Art-Therapy (#15400).
Affiliated associations, including 17 organizations listed in this Yearbook:
African Association of Psychiatrists and Allied Professions (AAPAP, #00214); Arab Federation of Psychiatrists (AFP, #00952); Asociación de Conductas Adictivas y Patologia Dual de Iberoamérica (ACAPI); Danubian Psychiatric Association (#05008); European Federation of Associations of Families of People with Mental Illness (EUFAMI, #07051); European Federation of Psychiatric Trainees (EFPT, #07197); Fédération internationale francophone de psychiatrie (FIFP); Global Alliance of Mental Illness Advocacy Networks – Europe (GAMIAN Europe, #10211); International Association of Ethnopsychologists and Ethnopsychotherapists (IAEE, #11880); International Psycho-Oncology Society (IPOS, #14665); International Society for Bipolar Disorders (ISBD, #14977); International Society for Psychological and Social Approaches to Psychosis (ISPS, #15396); Latin American Psychiatric Association (#16363); Pacific Rim College of Psychiatrists (PRCP, #17997); Psychiatric Association for Eastern Europe and the Balkans (PAEEB, #18558); SAARC Psychiatric Federation (SPF, #19019); World Association for Dynamic Psychiatry (WADP, #21135).
Individuals in 100 countries:
Albania, Argentina, Armenia, Australia, Austria, Azerbaijan, Bangladesh, Barbados, Belarus, Belgium, Bolivia, Bosnia-Herzegovina, Brazil, Bulgaria, Canada, China, Colombia, Costa Rica, Croatia, Cuba, Cyprus, Czechia, Denmark, Dominican Rep, Ecuador, Egypt, El Salvador, Estonia, Ethiopia, Finland, France, Georgia, Germany, Ghana, Greece, Guatemala, Honduras, Hungary, Iceland, India, Indonesia, Iran Islamic Rep, Iraq, Israel, Italy, Japan, Jordan, Kazakhstan, Kenya, Korea Rep, Kuwait, Kyrgyzstan, Latvia, Lebanon, Lithuania, Luxembourg, Malaysia, Mauritius, Mexico, Mongolia, Morocco, Myanmar, Netherlands, Nicaragua, Nigeria, North Macedonia, Norway, Pakistan, Panama, Papua New Guinea, Paraguay, Peru, Philippines, Poland, Portugal, Romania, Russia, Senegal, Serbia, Singapore, Slovakia, Slovenia, South Africa, Spain, Sudan, Sweden, Switzerland, Syrian AR, Taiwan, Thailand, Tunisia, Türkiye, Uganda, UK, Ukraine, Uruguay, USA, Uzbekistan, Venezuela, Yemen.

Consultative Status Consultative status granted from: *WHO (#20950)* (Official Relations). **NGO Relations** Member of: *Alliance of NGOs on Crime Prevention and Criminal Justice (#00709)*; *Conference of Non-Governmental Organizations in Consultative Relationship with the United Nations (CONGO, #04635)*; *Committee of NGOs on Human Rights, Geneva (#04275)*; *Global Alliance for Maternal Mental Health (GAMMH, #10208)*. Located at: *International Center for Mental Health (ICMH)*. Working relations with: *Collegium Internationale Neuropsychopharmacologicum (CINP, #04115)*; *World Federation for Mental Health (WFMH, #21455)*. Consultative status granted to: *Asian Federation of Psychiatric Associations (AFPA, #01470)*.
[2021/XB3577/y/**B**]

♦ World Public Forum (internationally oriented national body)

♦ World Public Health Nutrition Association (WPHNA) 21742

Secretariat PO Box 194, Peacehaven, BN10 9DW, UK. E-mail: secretariat@wphna.org.
URL: http://www.wphna.org/

History 2006, Barcelona (Spain). Set up during World Public Health Nutrition Congress. Officially inaugurated 2008. Registration: Austria. **Aims** Promote and strengthen public health nutrition, as a profession and discipline with responsibility to understand, protect and improve nutrition-related population health and *well-being*; encourage policy-makers and decision takers, at all levels from global to local, to promote equitable and sustainable access to adequate, enjoyable, appropriate and nourishing food. **Structure** General Assembly (every 4 years). Executive Committee. Advisory Council. **Languages** English. **Finance** Sources: donations; meeting proceeds; members' dues. Other sources: consultancy fees. **Events** *Quadrennial Congress* Brisbane, QLD (Australia) 2020, *Quadrennial Congress* Cape Town (South Africa) 2016, *Quadrennial Congress* Rio de Janeiro (Brazil) 2012, *Meeting* Porto (Portugal) 2010, *Meeting* Barcelona (Spain) 2006. **Publications** *World Nutrition* (12 a year) – journal.
Members Full in 57 countries and territories:
Angola, Australia, Austria, Bangladesh, Belgium, Bhutan, Brazil, Burkina Faso, Canada, Chile, China, Denmark, Ecuador, Fiji, Finland, France, Gambia, Germany, Ghana, Greece, Iceland, India, Indonesia, Iran Islamic Rep, Israel, Italy, Kenya, Korea Rep, Kuwait, Lebanon, Lesotho, Luxembourg, Malaysia, Mauritius, Mexico, Micronesia FS, Morocco, Netherlands, New Caledonia, Nigeria, Norway, Pakistan, Paraguay, Philippines, Portugal, Serbia, South Africa, Spain, Sweden, Switzerland, Thailand, Uganda, UK, United Arab Emirates, USA, Vietnam, Zimbabwe.
IGO Relations Participates as observer in the activities of: *Codex Alimentarius Commission (CAC, #04081)*. **NGO Relations** Affiliate of: *International Union of Nutritional Sciences (IUNS, #15796)*. [2022/XM4070/**B**]

♦ World Pulse (internationally oriented national body)

♦ World Puzzle Federation (WPF) 21743

Dir address not obtained. E-mail: office@worldpuzzle.org.
URL: http://www.worldpuzzle.org/

History 1995, Poiana Brasov (Romania). Founded during the 4th International Puzzle Congress. Former names and other names: *International Puzzle Federation* – former (1995 to 1999). Registration: Netherlands. **Aims** Provide the means for an international exchange of puzzle ideas; stimulate innovations in the field of puzzles; foster friendship among puzzle enthusiasts worldwide. **Structure** General Assembly (annual); Board of Directors. **Languages** English. **Staff** 4.00 FTE, paid. **Finance** Sources: members' dues; sale of products. **Activities** Awards/prizes/competitions. **Events** *Annual World Puzzle Championship* Sofia (Bulgaria) 2015, *Annual World Puzzle Championship* London (UK) 2014, *World Sudoku Championship* Goa (India) 2008, *World Sudoku Championship* Prague (Czech Rep) 2007, *Annual World Puzzle Championship* Rio de Janeiro (Brazil) 2007. **Publications** *WPF Newsletter*.
Members in 43 countries:
Argentina, Australia, Austria, Belarus, Belgium, Bulgaria, Canada, China, Congo DR, Croatia, Czechia, Denmark, Estonia, Finland, France, Germany, Hungary, India, Iran Islamic Rep, Israel, Italy, Japan, Korea Rep, Latvia, Lebanon, Luxembourg, Netherlands, Philippines, Poland, Romania, Russia, Serbia, Singapore, Slovakia, Slovenia, Spain, Switzerland, Taiwan, Thailand, Türkiye, UK, Uruguay, USA. [2022.05.23/XD8878/**D**]

♦ World Rabbit Science Association (WRSA) 21744

Association scientifique mondiale de cuniculture – Weltvereinigung der Kaninchenwissenschaften – Wereldassociatie voor de Wetenschappelijke Studie van de Konijnenteelt – Asociación Científica Mundial de Cunicultura

Pres Inst de Ciencia y Tecnologia Animal, Univ Politècnica de València, Camino de Vera 14, 46071 Valencia, Spain.
URL: http://world-rabbit-science.com/

History 1 Jan 1976, Paris (France). **Aims** Facilitate advancement of various branches of the rabbit industry; disseminate knowledge and study of rabbit biology, problems of production and marketing. **Structure** Congress (every 4 years); Council. **Languages** English. **Staff** 8.00 FTE, voluntary. **Finance** Sources: members' dues. **Events** *Quadrennial Congress* Nantes (France) 2021, *Quadrennial Congress* Nantes (France) 2020, *Quadrennial Congress* Qingdao (China) 2016, *Quadrennial Congress* Sharm el Sheikh (Egypt) 2012, *Quadrennial Congress* Verona (Italy) 2008. **Publications** *World Rabbit Science* (4 a year). Brochure; congress proceedings.
Members Associations in 24 countries:
Belgium, Benin, Brazil, Bulgaria, China, Côte d'Ivoire, Cuba, Egypt, France, Germany, Greece, Hungary, Indonesia, Italy, Malaysia, Malta, Moldova, Nepal, Netherlands, Philippines, Portugal, Russia, Spain, Vietnam.
Regional branches (2) in Sub-Saharan Africa and America. [2022.06.14/XD0093/**C**]

♦ World Radiography Education Trust Fund (see: #15410)
♦ World Radio Missionary Fellowship Inc / see Reach Beyond
♦ World Radiopharmaceutical Therapy Council / see World Association of Radiopharmaceutical and Molecular Therapy (#21181)
♦ World Radio and Television Council (no recent information)

♦ World Rainforest Movement (WRM) 21745

Movimiento Mundial por los Bosques Tropicales

Intl Secretariat Maldonado 1858, 11200 Montevideo, Uruguay. T. +59824032989. Fax +59824080762. E-mail: wrm@wrm.org.uy.
URL: http://www.wrm.org.uy/

History 1986, Penang (Malaysia), at Conference on the Forest Resources Crisis in the Third World, organized by *Asia-Pacific People's Environment Network (APPEN, no recent information)*. Formerly known as *World Rainforest Network (WRN)*. **Aims** Stop the destruction of rainforests worldwide; protect the *survival* of *forest dwellers*. **Structure** Steering Committee of 12 members. Secretariat formed by APPEN with *Third World Network (TWN, #20151)*. **Finance** Main source: *Oxfam Novib*. **Activities** Advocacy/lobbying/activism. **Events** *WRM meeting* Penang (Malaysia) 1989. **Publications** *WRM Bulletin* in English, French, Portuguese, Spanish – electronic. Books; other documents.
Members Organizations and individuals concerned about the destruction of the rainforests worldwide and involved in activities attempting to reverse this process, in 15 countries:
Australia, Brazil, Canada, France, Germany, India, Indonesia, Japan, Malaysia, Netherlands, Philippines, Thailand, UK, Uruguay, USA.
NGO Relations Founding member of: *Global Forest Coalition (GFC, #10368)*. Member of: *Oilwatch (#17711)*; *Taiga Rescue Network (TRN, inactive)*. Instrumental in setting up: *International Alliance of the Indigenous Tribal Peoples of the Tropical Forests (IAITPTF, #11629)*. [2010/XF0897/**F**]

♦ World Rainforest Network / see World Rainforest Movement (#21745)

♦ Worldreader 21746

Admin Coordinator 40 Ringold St, San Francisco CA 94103, USA. T. +14155624840. E-mail: info@worldreader.org.
Spain Mallorca 318 – 3o 1a, 08037 Barcelona, Spain. T. +34936813669.
URL: http://www.worldreader.org/

History 2010. Also referred to as *Worldreader.org*. Registered as a public charity in the USA; registered in accordance with Spanish law. **Aims** Make digital *books* available to all in the developing world, enabling millions of people to improve their lives. **Structure** Board. Offices in: San Francisco CA (USA); Barcelona (Spain); London (UK); Accra (Ghana). **IGO Relations** Partners include: *United States Agency for International Development (USAID)*. [2016/XJ4624/**F**]

♦ Worldreader.org / see Worldreader (#21746)
♦ World Recreational Fishing Conference (meeting series)

♦ World Recreational Scuba Training Council (WRSTC) 21747

Head Office PO Box 3275, Stuart FL 34995, USA.
Contact c/o Intl Aquanautic Club, Frintroper Str 18, 45355 Essen, Germany. E-mail: europe_council@wrstc.com.
URL: http://www.wrstc.com/

History 1987. Former names and other names: *Recreational Scuba Training Council (RSTC)* – alias. **Aims** Establish minimum training standards at all levels of recreational scuba diving in order to promote public safety. **Structure** Includes *RSTC Europe*.
Members Organizations and companies in 12 countries:
Austria, Canada, Egypt, Germany, Italy, Japan, Netherlands, Norway, Spain, Switzerland, UK, USA.
Include in the above, 2 organizations listed in this Yearbook:
International Diving Educators Association (IDEA); *Professional Association of Diving Instructors (PADI International)*. [2021.05.26/XM1369/**E**]

♦ World Recreation Association of the Deaf and Hard of Hearing (WRAD) 21748

CEO c/o WRAD Inc, PO Box 3211, Quartz Hill CA 93586, USA.
URL: http://www.wrad.org/

History 1985. Registration: 501(c)(3) non-profit, USA. **Aims** Provide programmes, services and activities by and for persons who are deaf or hard of hearing. **Languages** English. **Staff** 5.00 FTE, voluntary. **Finance** Contributions; grants. **Activities** Guidance/assistance/consulting; awareness raising; events/meetings.
Members International NGOs in 79 countries and territories:
Argentina, Australia, Austria, Bangladesh, Belarus, Belgium, Belize, Brazil, Bulgaria, Canada, China, Colombia, Costa Rica, Czechia, Denmark, Ecuador, Egypt, El Salvador, Eritrea, Estonia, Ethiopia, Finland, France, Georgia, Germany, Greece, Guatemala, Honduras, Hong Kong, Hungary, Iceland, India, Indonesia, Ireland, Israel, Italy, Jamaica, Japan, Kenya, Korea Rep, Latvia, Lithuania, Malaysia, Mexico, Moldova, Monaco, Morocco, Netherlands, New Zealand, Nicaragua, Nigeria, Norway, Papua New Guinea, Peru, Philippines, Poland, Portugal, Puerto Rico, Romania, Russia, Samoa, San Marino, Senegal, Singapore, Slovakia, Slovenia, South Africa, Spain, Sweden, Switzerland, Taiwan, Thailand, Türkiye, UK, Ukraine, Uruguay, USA, Venezuela, Zimbabwe.
IGO Relations Major bodies concerned with hearing loss issues (not specified). [2020/XD6991/**D**]

♦ World Reference Laboratory for Foot and Mouth Diseases (internationally oriented national body)
♦ World Refining Association (internationally oriented national body)
♦ World Rehabilitation Association for the Psycho-Socially Disabled / see World Association for Psychosocial Rehabilitation (#21178)

♦ World Rehabilitation Fund (WRF) 21749

Main Office 16 East 40th St, Ste 804, New York NY 10016, USA. T. +12125326000. Fax +12125326012. E-mail: wrfnewyork@msn.com – info@worldrehabfund.org.
URL: http://www.worldrehabfund.org/

History 1955, New York NY (USA), by Dr Howard Rusk. **Aims** Enable individuals worldwide with functional limitations and participation restriction achieve community and social integration through physical and socio-economic rehabilitation and advocacy; prevent disability and reduce disadvantage. **Structure** Officers: 4 Founding Fathers. Board of Directors of 11 members, including Executive Committee. **Languages** Arabic, English, Russian, Spanish, Turkish. **Staff** 11.00 FTE, paid; 2.00 FTE, voluntary. **Finance** Sources: Government grants; contributions from foundations, corporations and individuals; bequests and special events. Annual budget: US$ 1,700,000. **Activities** Projects/programmes; advocacy/lobbying/activism; financial and/or material support. **Events** *Research utilization and program development conference on compensation rehabilitation* Cleveland, OH (USA) 1988, *International rehabilitation week* New York, NY (USA) 1987, *International rehabilitation week* New York, NY (USA) 1986. **Publications** Annual Report. **Members** Not a membership organization. Since its inception, WRF has conducted projects in 155 countries and territories with special emphasis on developing countries. **Consultative Status** Consultative status granted from: *ECOSOC (#05331)* (Special). **NGO Relations** Member of (1): *American Council for Voluntary International Action (InterAction)*.
[2020/XF1857/f/**F**]

♦ World Relief (internationally oriented national body)
♦ World Relief Canada / see Tearfund Canada
♦ World Relief Commission / see World Relief
♦ World Relief Commission of the National Association of Evangelicals / see World Relief
♦ World Relief Corporation / see World Relief
♦ World Relief Foundation / see Global Aid Foundation (#10175)
♦ World Relief Friendship Foundation / see International Relief Friendship Foundation (#14713)
♦ World Relief International / see World Relief
♦ World Relief Refugee Services (internationally oriented national body)
♦ World Religious Women's Zionist Organization / see World Emunah Religious Zionist Women's Organization (#21378)
♦ World Renderers Association (internationally oriented national body)
♦ World Renew (internationally oriented national body)

♦ World Renewable Energy Network (WREN) 21750

Dir Gen Flat 3, Building 5-6, Clarendon Terrace, Brighton, BN2 1FD, UK.
URL: http://www.wrenuk.co.uk/

History 1992. Founded during 2nd World Renewable Energy Congress, Reading (UK). Registration: Charity Commission, No/ID: 1009879, England and Wales. **Aims** Promote the use of renewable energy globally. **Structure** Governing Council; Executive Committee; Technical Committee; Director General. **Languages** English. **Staff** 3.00 FTE, paid. **Finance** Members' dues. **Activities** Events/meetings; publishing activities. **Events** *World Renewable Energy Congress* Manama (Bahrain) 2024, *World Renewable Energy Congress* Murdoch, WA (Australia) 2022, *World Renewable Energy Congress* Lisbon (Portugal) 2021, *World Renewable Energy Congress* Lisbon (Portugal) 2020, *World Renewable Energy Congress* London (UK) 2018. **Publications** *Renewable Energy* (12 a year) – journal; *Renewable Energy – and A Year* (annual) – magazine. Books.
Members Agencies, laboratories, institutions, companies and individuals. Full in 64 countries and territories:
Afghanistan, Algeria, Argentina, Australia, Bahrain, Bangladesh, Barbados, Belgium, Brazil, Brunei Darussalam, Canada, China, Cuba, Egypt, Ethiopia, France, Greece, Guyana, Hong Kong, India, Indonesia, Ireland, Italy, Jamaica, Japan, Jordan, Kuwait, Lebanon, Malaysia, Malta, Mauritania, Mauritius, Montenegro, Morocco, Nigeria, North Macedonia, Oman, Peru, Poland, Qatar, Romania, Russia, Serbia, Seychelles, Slovakia, South Africa, Spain, Sri Lanka, Sudan, Sweden, Switzerland, Syrian AR, Tanzania UR, Trinidad-Tobago, Türkiye, UK, United Arab Emirates, Uruguay, USA, Vietnam, West Bank-Gaza, Yemen, Zambia, Zimbabwe.
IGO Relations Cooperates with: *European Commission (EC, #06633)*; *Islamic World Educational, Scientific and Cultural Organization (ICESCO, #16058)*; *UNESCO (#20322)*; other UN agencies. **NGO Relations** Member of: *Consortium on Science, Technology and Innovation for the South (COSTIS, no recent information)*.
[2020/XF3102/**F**]

♦ World Rescue Organisation (WRO) 21751

Sec c/o Strathclyde Fire and Rescue, UAILL Training Centre, Westburn Drive, Cambuslang, Glasgow, G72 7NA, UK. E-mail: secretary@wrescue.org.
Registered office Leicestershire Fire and Rescue Service, Anstey Frith, Leicester Road, Glenfield, Leicester, LE3 8HD, UK.
URL: http://www.wrescue.org/

History Sep 1999, Melbourne, VIC (Australia). Registration: Charity Commission, No/ID: 1100525, England and Wales; Companies House, No/ID: 4583084, Start date: 6 Nov 2002, England and Wales. **Aims** Enhance and maintain emergency procedures and techniques for dealing with road traffic collisions. **Structure** Chair; Vice-Chair; Secretary; Treasurer; Director of Operations; WRO Committee. **Staff** Voluntary. **Activities** Events/meetings; guidance/assistance/consulting. *World Rescue Challenge (WRC)* held annually. **Events** *World Rescue Challenge (WRC)* Luxembourg (Luxembourg) 2022, *Meeting* Cork (Ireland) 2010.
Members Full in 18 countries:
Australia, Brazil, Canada, Czechia, France, Germany, Ghana, Ireland, Luxembourg, Moldova, New Zealand, Paraguay, Romania, Russia, South Africa, Spain, UK, USA.
Included in the above, 1 organization listed in this Yearbook:
NGO Relations Member of (3): *FIRE AID*; *Global Alliance of NGOs for Road Safety (#10216)*; *Global Road Safety Partnership (GRSP, #10581)*. [2022/XJ2456/**C**]

♦ **World Resources Forum Association (WRFA)** **21752**
Managing Dir Lerchenfeldstr 5, 9014 St Gallen, Switzerland. T. +41715540900. E-mail: info@wrforum.org.
URL: http://www.wrforum.org/
History 2012. Founded as an independent entity overseeing the activities of *World Resources Forum (WRF)*. Until then, WRF managed by Empa, the Swiss Federal Laboratories for Materials Science and Technology. Registration: EU Transparency Register, No/ID: 053949626280-24, Start date: 13 Mar 2017. **Aims** Serve as a platform connecting and fostering knowledge exchange on resources management among business leaders, policy-makers, NGOs, scientists and the public. **Structure** General Assembly; Board; Executive Board; Advisory, Scientific and Organizing Committees. **Languages** English, French, German, Italian, Spanish. **Staff** 10.00 FTE, paid. Voluntary as needed for conferences. **Finance** Members' dues. **Activities** Events/meetings, including the *World Resources Forum (WRF)*; capacity building; training/education; networking/liaising; publishing activity; research/documentation; standards/guidelines. **Events** *World Resources Forum* Antwerp (Belgium) 2019, *World Resources Forum* Geneva (Switzerland) 2019, *World Resources Forum* Geneva (Switzerland) 2017, *WCEF : World Circular Economy Forum* Helsinki (Finland) 2017, *Latin American and the Caribbean Conference* San José (Costa Rica) 2016. **Publications** Meeting reports; training manuals; other publications.
Members Regular; Steward (maximum 10). Partners in 11 countries:
Australia, Austria, Belgium, China, Finland, Germany, Japan, Netherlands, Peru, Sweden, Switzerland.
Included in the above, 4 organizations listed in this Yearbook:
Global Enabling Sustainability Initiative (GeSI, #10340); *Sustainable Europe Research Institute (SERI)*; *Swiss Agency for Development and Cooperation (SDC)*; *UNEP (#20299)* (International Resource Panel).
[2020.03.04/XJ5065/y/**E**]

♦ **World Resources Institute (WRI)** **21753**
Contact 10 G St NE, Ste 800, Washington DC 20002, USA. T. +12027297600. Fax +12027297610.
Contact address not obtained.
URL: http://www.wri.org/
History 3 Jun 1982. Launched with financial support of *MacArthur Foundation*. Incorporated Washington DC office of *International Institute for Environment and Development (IIED, #13877)*, 1988. Registration: USA, Delaware. **Aims** Move human society to live in ways that protect the earth's environment and its capacity to provide for the needs and aspirations of current and future generations. **Structure** Board of Directors. **Staff** Over 1,000 interdisciplinary staff. **Finance** Sources: private foundations. Sources: governmental and intergovernmental institutions; private corporations and individuals. Annual budget: 165,000,000 USD. **Activities** Events/meetings; projects/programmes. **Events** *COHAB : international conference on health and biodiversity* Galway (Ireland) 2008, *Global diversity forum* Curitiba (Brazil) 2006, *India and South Asia sub-regional session of the Global Biodiversity Forum* Delhi (India) 2005, *Latin America regional session of the Global Biodiversity Forum* Lima (Peru) 2005, *International conference on eradicating poverty through profit* San Francisco, CA (USA) 2004. **Publications** *World Resources* (every 2 years) – report in partnership with UNEP, UNDP and World Bank. **Members** Network of advisors, collaborators, international fellows and cooperating institutions in over 50 countries. Membership countries not specified. **Consultative Status** Consultative status granted from: *ECOSOC (#05331)* (Special); *UNEP (#20299)*. **IGO Relations** Accredited by (3): *Green Climate Fund (GCF, #10714)*; *United Nations Framework Convention on Climate Change – Secretariat (UNFCCC, #20564)*; *United Nations Office at Vienna (UNOV, #20604)*. Observer status with (1): *Committee of International Development Institutions on the Environment (CIDIE, no recent information)*. Member of (2): *Congo Basin Forest Partnership (CBFP, #04662)*; *International Coral Reef Initiative (ICRI, #12965)*. Partner of (1): *Group on Earth Observations (GEO, #10735)*. Accredited to the Conference of the Parties of: *Secretariat of the United Nations Convention to Combat Desertification (Secretariat of the UNCCD, #19208)*. Invited to Governing Council sessions of: *International Fund for Agricultural Development (IFAD, #13692)*. Participates in the work of: *United Nations Economic Commission for Europe (UNECE, #20555)*. Hosts: *NDC Partnership (#16964)*. Involved in development and participation of: *Caribbean Action Plan (CAR, #03432)*. Has participated in meetings of: *Round Table on Sustainable Development at the OECD (see: #17693)*. Associated with Department of Global Communications of the United Nations.
NGO Relations Member of (24):
- *Africa Biodiversity Collaborative Group (ABCG)*;
- *Asian Energy Institute (AEI, #01436)*;
- *Cities Climate Finance Leadership Alliance (CCFLA, #03952)*;
- *Climate Action Network (CAN, #03999)*;
- *Environment Liaison Centre International (ELCI, no recent information)*;
- *EverGreen Agriculture Partnership (#09213)*;
- *GEF CSO Network (GCN, #10087)*;
- *Global Alliance for Buildings and Construction (GlobalABC, #10187)*;
- *Global Alliance for Climate-Smart Agriculture (GACSA, #10189)*;
- *Global Call for Climate Action (GCCA, inactive)*;
- *Global Commons Alliance*;
- *Global Coral Reef Monitoring Network (GCRMN, #10306)*;
- *Global Landscapes Forum (GLF, #10451)*;
- *Global Partnership for Sustainable Development Data (Data4SDGS, #10542)*;
- *Global Platform for Sustainable Natural Rubber (GPSNR, #10552)*;
- *High Level Panel for a Sustainable Ocean Economy (Panel, #10917)* (Advisory Network);
- *InsideNGO (inactive)*;
- *International Centre for Earth Simulation (ICES Foundation)*;
- *International Network for Sustainable Energy (INFORSE, #14331)*;
- *International Union for Conservation of Nature and Natural Resources (IUCN, #15766)*;
- *LEDS Global Partnership (LEDS GP, #16435)*;
- *Natural Capital Coalition (NCC, #16952)*;
- *Science Based Targets Network*;
- *Sustainable Apparel Coalition (SAC)*.

Partner of (7): *Centre on Asia and Globalisation (CAG, #03730)*; *Food and Land Use Coalition (FOLU)*; *Global Enabling Sustainability Initiative (GeSI, #10340)*; *Global Forum on Law, Justice and Development (GFLJD, #10373)*; *Global Partnership on Forest and Landscape Restoration (GPFLR, #10535)*; *Tropical Forest Alliance (TFA, #20249)*; *WorldFish (#21507)*.
Supports (2): *Asia Network for Sustainable Agriculture and Bioresources (ANSAB, #01445)*; *Society for Development Alternatives*.
Instrumental in setting up (3): *Global Forest Watch (GFW)*; *Greenhouse Gas Protocol (GHG Protocol, #10721)*; *The Access Initiative (TAI, #00050)*.
Provides secretariat for: *High Level Panel for a Sustainable Ocean Economy (Panel, #10917)*. Managing partner of: *Global Commission on Adaptation (#10301)*. Participates in: *Global Center on Adaptation (GCA)*. Signatory to charter of: *Institute for Global Environmental Strategies (IGES, #11266)*. [2021/XE1495/j/**E**]

♦ World Retail Congress (meeting series)

♦ **World Road Association (PIARC)** **21754**
Association mondiale de la route (AIPCR) – Asociación Mundial de Carreteras (AIPCC)
SG La Grande Arche, Paroi Sud, 5e étage, 92055 Paris La Défense CEDEX, France. T. +33147968121.
URL: https://www.piarc.org/
History 1909, Paris (France). Founded to continue the work initiated by 1st International Road Congress, 11-17 Oct 1908, Paris. Integrated activities of *World Interchange Network (WIN, inactive)*. Former names and other names: *Permanent International Association of Road Congresses* – former (1909); *Association internationale permanente des congrès de la route* – former (1909); *Asociación Internacional Permanente de los Congresos de Carreteras* – former. Registration: RNA, No/ID: W922000611, France. **Aims** Promote international cooperation on issues pertaining to roads and road *transportation*. **Structure** Congress (every 4 years); Council; Executive Committee; Programme Committee; Joint IRF/PIARC Committee; Committees and working groups on specific subjects. **Languages** English, French. **Staff** 6.00 FTE, paid. **Finance** Sources: donations; fees for services; members' dues. Other sources: benefits from the investment of assets. **Activities** Awards/prizes/competitions; events/meetings; guidance/assistance/consulting; knowledge management/information dissemination; research/documentation. **Events** *World Road Congress* Prague (Czechia) 2023, *World Winter Service and Road Resilience Congress* Calgary, AB (Canada) 2022, *Regional Conference for Africa* Cape Town (South Africa) 2022, *International Workshop on Road Disaster Management Using Latest Information Technologies* Kyoto (Japan) 2022, *SURF : Symposium on Pavement Surface Characteristics* Milan (Italy) 2022. **Publications** *Routes/Roads* (4 a year) – magazine. *PIARC Lexicon* (2nd ed 2000) in English, French; *Technical Dictionary of Road Terms* (7th ed 1997) in English, French. *CD-ROUTE* (2000) – (3rd ed) CD-ROM of reports. Dictionaries in 16 languages; policy issue documents; technical documents; recommendations; national reports; general reports; joint technical reports with Commission internationale de l'éclairage; congress and technical committee reports; guidelines.
Members Categories: governments; regional authorities; public bodies; collective; individual, in 123 countries:
Algeria, Andorra, Angola, Argentina, Australia, Austria, Azerbaijan, Bahrain, Bangladesh, Belgium, Benin, Bhutan, Bolivia, Botswana, Brazil, Bulgaria, Burkina Faso, Burundi, Cambodia, Cameroon, Canada, Cape Verde, Chad, Chile, China, Colombia, Congo Brazzaville, Congo DR, Costa Rica, Côte d'Ivoire, Croatia, Cuba, Cyprus, Czechia, Denmark, Dominican Rep, Ecuador, Egypt, El Salvador, Estonia, Eswatini, Finland, France, Gabon, Germany, Ghana, Greece, Guatemala, Guinea, Honduras, Hungary, Iceland, India, Indonesia, Iran Islamic Rep, Ireland, Israel, Italy, Japan, Kenya, Korea Rep, Kuwait, Latvia, Lithuania, Luxembourg, Madagascar, Malaysia, Mali, Malta, Mauritania, Mauritius, Mexico, Moldova, Mongolia, Montenegro, Morocco, Mozambique, Myanmar, Namibia, Nepal, Netherlands, New Zealand, Nicaragua, Niger, Norway, Pakistan, Panama, Papua New Guinea, Paraguay, Peru, Philippines, Poland, Portugal, Romania, Russia, Saudi Arabia, Senegal, Singapore, Slovakia, Slovenia, South Africa, Spain, Sri Lanka, Sweden, Switzerland, Syrian AR, Tanzania UR, Thailand, Togo, Tonga, Tunisia, Türkiye, Uganda, UK, Ukraine, United Arab Emirates, Uruguay, USA, Uzbekistan, Venezuela, Vietnam, Yemen, Zimbabwe.
Members in 15 countries and territories where governments are not members:
Armenia, Belarus, Brunei Darussalam, Central African Rep, Ethiopia, Georgia, Haiti, Hong Kong, Iraq, Libya, Nigeria, Puerto Rico, Serbia, Taiwan, Trinidad-Tobago.
International and regional organizations: (7):
3M Europe; *AIT and FIA Information Centre (no recent information)*; *CEMBUREAU – The European Cement Association (CEMBUREAU, #03634)*; *European Investment Bank (EIB, #07599)*; *International Bank for Reconstruction and Development (IBRD, #12317)*; *International Society for Asphalt Pavements (ISAP, #14944)*; *International Tar Association (ITA, #15655)*.
Consultative Status Consultative status granted from: *ECOSOC (#05331)* (Special). **NGO Relations** Member of (1): *Union internationale des associations et organismes scientifiques et techniques (UATI, #20421)*. Partner of (1): *International Road Federation (IRF, #14758)*. Instrumental in setting up (1): *Consejo de Directores de Carreteras de Iberia e Iberoamérica (DIRCAIBEA, #04706)*. [2023/XC3112/y/**B**]

♦ World Rock'n'Roll Association (inactive)

♦ **World Rock'n'Roll Confederation (WRRC)** **21755**
Pres Vodnikovo naselje 23, 1000 Ljubljana, Slovenia. T. +38641733743. Fax +38613007708. E-mail: info@wrrc.dance.
URL: http://www.wrrc.org/
History 1 Jan 1984, by merger of *Fédération mondial de dance de jazz (FMDJ, inactive)* and *World Rock'n'Roll Association (WRRA, inactive)*, following signature of statutes 3 Nov 1983, Zurich (Switzerland). Registered in accordance with Swiss law. **Aims** Advance the physical training of members by means of *sporting* activities in the form of Rock'n'Roll *dance tournaments*, including acrobatic variations. **Structure** General Meeting (annual). Board, comprising President Vice-President, General-Secretary, Treasurer and Technical Director. Commissioners (3): Boogie; Lindy Hop; Formation. Arbitration Committee. **Finance** Sources: members' dues; sponsorship. Other sources: competition fees. **Activities** Organizes Rock'n' Roll tournaments and championships and determines competition rules. **Publications** *World Rock'n'Roll Golden Book*.
Members Ordinary; Extraordinary; Contributing; Honorary. National federations (" indicates Extraordinary member) for amateurs and professionals in 32 countries:
Australia, Austria, Belgium, Bosnia-Herzegovina (*), Bulgaria, Canada, Croatia, Czechia, Denmark, Estonia (*), Finland, France, Germany, Greece, Hungary, Italy, Latvia (*), Liechtenstein, Luxembourg (*), Netherlands, Norway, Poland, Russia, San Marino, Singapore, Slovakia, Slovenia, Spain, Sweden, Switzerland, Ukraine.
NGO Relations Associate member of: *World DanceSport Federation (WDSF, #21354)*. [2020/XC0031/**C**]

♦ World Roma Federation (unconfirmed)
♦ World ROP Congress (meeting series)
♦ World Rope Skipping Federation (unconfirmed)
♦ World Rotary Fellowship of Esperantists / see Rotaria Amikaro de Esperanto (#18973)

♦ **World Rowing** **21756**
Exec Dir Maison du Sport Intl, Av de Rhodanie 54, 1007 Lausanne VD, Switzerland. T. +41216178373. Fax +41216178375. E-mail: info@worldrowing.com.
URL: http://www.worldrowing.com/
History 25 Jun 1892, Turin (Italy). Headquarters moved to Switzerland in 1923. Former names and other names: *Fédération internationale des sociétés d'aviron (FISA)* – former; *International Rowing Federation (IRF)* – former. **Aims** Develop, promote, present and govern the *sport* of rowing worldwide. **Structure** Congress (Ordinary – annual; Extraordinary – every 4 years); Council; Executive Committee; Specialist Commissions; Continental Representatives. **Languages** English, French. **Staff** 9.00 FTE, paid. **Finance** Sources: members' dues; sponsorship. Other sources: television rights. **Activities** Awards/prizes/competitions; events/meetings; sporting activities. **Events** *Annual Congress* Lausanne (Switzerland) 2020, *World Rowing Coaches Conference* Lausanne (Switzerland) 2020, *World Rowing Coaches Conference* Hangzhou (China) 2019, *Annual Congress* Linz (Austria) 2019, *World Rowing Coaches Conference* Berlin (Germany) 2018. **Publications** Brochures; manuals; guides; videos.
Members National federations in 130 countries and territories:
Afghanistan, Albania, Algeria, Angola, Argentina, Armenia, Australia, Austria, Azerbaijan, Bahrain, Bangladesh, Barbados, Belarus, Belgium, Bermuda, Bolivia, Brazil, Bulgaria, Burkina Faso, Cameroon, Canada, Cayman Is, Chile, China, Colombia, Costa Rica, Côte d'Ivoire, Croatia, Cuba, Cyprus, Czechia, Denmark, Dominica, Ecuador, Egypt, El Salvador, England, Estonia, Eswatini, Finland, France, Georgia, Germany, Ghana, Gibraltar, Greece, Guatemala, Honduras, Hong Kong, Hungary, Iceland, India, Indonesia, Iran Islamic Rep, Iraq, Ireland, Israel, Italy, Jamaica, Japan, Jordan, Kazakhstan, Kenya, Korea DPR, Korea Rep, Kuwait, Kyrgyzstan, Latvia, Lebanon, Libya, Lithuania, Madagascar, Malaysia, Mexico, Moldova, Monaco, Morocco, Mozambique, Myanmar, Netherlands, New Zealand, Nicaragua, Niger, Nigeria, North Macedonia, Norway, Pakistan, Palestine, Panama, Paraguay, Peru, Philippines, Poland, Portugal, Puerto Rico, Qatar, Romania, Russia, Samoa, Senegal, Serbia, Singapore, Slovakia, Slovenia, Somalia, South Africa, Spain, Sri Lanka, Sudan, Sweden, Switzerland, Syrian AR, Taiwan, Thailand, Togo, Tonga, Tunisia, Türkiye, Turkmenistan, Uganda, Ukraine, United Arab Emirates, Uruguay, USA, Uzbekistan, Vanuatu, Venezuela, Vietnam, Zambia, Zimbabwe.
NGO Relations Member of (5): *Association of Paralympic Sports Organisations (APSO, #02850)*; *Association of Summer Olympic International Federations (ASOIF, #02943)*; *International Masters Games Association (IMGA, #14117)*; *International Paralympic Committee (IPC, #14512)*; *Olympic Movement (#17719)*. Cooperates with (1): *International Testing Agency (ITA, #15678)*. Instrumental in setting up (1): *FISA International Coaching Academy*. Recognized by: *International Olympic Committee (IOC, #14408)*. [2021/XB2424/y/**B**]

♦ **World Rugby** **21757**
Contact World Rugby House, 8-10 Pembroke Street Lower, Dublin, 2, CO. DUBLIN, Ireland. T. +35312409200. Fax +35312409201. E-mail: info@worldrugby.org.
URL: https://www.world.rugby/
History 1887. Founded by Scottish, Irish and Welsh rugby unions. Former names and other names: *International Rugby Football Board (IRFB)* – former; *International Rugby Board (IRB)* – former (1998); *International Rugby Union Board* – former. **Aims** Promote, foster, develop, extend and govern the game of rugby football. **Structure** General Meeting (currently every 2 years); Executive Council. Regional meetings are held at regular intervals. **Languages** English, French, Spanish. **Staff** 41.00 FTE, paid. **Events** *Biennial general meeting* 2005, *Annual meeting* Copenhagen (Denmark) 2001, *Annual meeting* Copenhagen (Denmark) 2000. **Publications** *IRB Newsletter* – also on the Internet. *World in Union* (1999) – limited edition. Annual report.
Members Unions in 117 countries and territories:
Andorra, Argentina, Australia, Austria, Azerbaijan, Bahamas, Barbados, Belgium, Bermuda, Bosnia-Herzegovina, Botswana, Brazil, Brunei Darussalam, Bulgaria, Burundi, Cambodia, Canada, Cayman Is, Chile, China, Colombia, Cook Is, Costa Rica, Côte d'Ivoire, Croatia, Czechia, Denmark, England, Eswatini, Fiji, Finland, France, Georgia, Germany, Ghana, Greece, Guam, Guyana, Hong Kong, Hungary, India, Indonesia, Iran Islamic Rep, Ireland, Israel, Italy, Jamaica, Japan, Kazakhstan, Kenya, Korea Rep, Kyrgyzstan, Laos, Latvia, Lithuania, Luxembourg, Madagascar, Malaysia, Mali, Malta, Mauritius, Mexico, Moldova, Monaco, Mongolia, Morocco, Namibia, Netherlands, New Zealand, Nigeria, Niue, Norway, Pakistan, Papua New Guinea, Paraguay, Peru, Philippines, Poland, Portugal, Romania, Russia, Rwanda, Samoa, Samoa USA, Scotland, Senegal, Serbia, Singapore, Slovenia, Solomon Is, South Africa, Spain, Sri Lanka, St Lucia, St Vincent-Grenadines, Sweden, Switzerland, Tahiti Is, Taiwan, Tanzania UR, Thailand, Togo, Tonga, Trinidad-Tobago, Tunisia, Uganda, Ukraine, United Arab Emirates, Uruguay, USA, Uzbekistan, Vanuatu, Venezuela, Virgin Is UK, Wales, Zambia, Zimbabwe.

Regional associations (6):
Asia Rugby (#02089); Oceania Rugby (#17672); Rugby Africa (#18996); Rugby Americas North (RAN, #18997); Rugby Europe (#18998); Sudamérica Rugby (#20030).
NGO Relations Member of (6): *Association of Summer Olympic International Federations (ASOIF, #02943); International Council for Coaching Excellence (ICCE, #13008); International Masters Games Association (IMGA, #14117); International World Games Association (IWGA, #15914); Olympic Movement (#17719); Sports Rights Owners Coalition (SROC, #19929).* Affiliated with (1): *EMEA Synthetic Turf Council (ESTC, #05436).* Recognized by: *International Olympic Committee (IOC, #14408).* In liaison with technical committees of: *Comité européen de normalisation (CEN, #04162).* In partnership with: *International Wheelchair Rugby Federation (IWRF, #15883).* [2020/XB0002/y/**B**]

♦ World Runner Foundation / see World Runners (#21758)

♦ World Runners (WR) 21758

Coureurs du monde

Dir 912 via Casitas, Greenbrae CA 94904, USA. T. +14085091911. Fax +14083514331.
URL: http://www.worldrunnersus.org/

History 1978, as a non-profit organization and foundation. Also referred to as *World Runner Foundation.* **Aims** Use running to support individuals and organizations effectively bringing about the end to world *hunger.* **Structure** International Advisory Board; Board of Directors. **Finance** Annual budget: US$ 350,000. **Activities** Events/meetings; projects/programmes. **Events** *Children's European conference on human rights* Geneva (Switzerland) 1992. **Publications** *WR International Newsletter* (4 a year); *International Conferences held in a different countries* (2 a year).
Members Representatives in 25 countries:
Australia, Belgium, Cameroon, Canada, China, Congo DR, Denmark, France, Germany, Japan, Kenya, Malaysia, Mexico, Netherlands, Philippines, Poland, Saudi Arabia, Serbia, Sweden, Switzerland, Tanzania UR, Thailand, Uganda, UK, USA.
Members also in the former USSR; countries not specified. [2019.10.31/XF0240/f/**F**]

♦ World Runners Association (unconfirmed)
♦ World Russian People's Council (internationally oriented national body)
♦ **World SAE** World Council of Hellenes Abroad (#21329)
♦ World Safety and Accidents Prevention Congress (meeting series)

♦ World Safety Organization (WSO) 21759

CEO WSO Management Center, 106 W Young Ave, Ste F, PO Box 518, Warrensburg MO 64093, USA. T. +16607473132 – +16607472235. Fax +16607472647.
URL: http://www.worldsafety.org/

History 26 Nov 1975, Manila (Philippines), at 1st World Safety and Accident Prevention Conference (WOSAPCON), organized by Safety Organization of the Philippines. Entire operation managed, since 11 Sep 1989, from WSO World Management Center, Warrensburg MO (USA). Incorporated in the State of Missouri (USA). **Aims** Make safety a way of life in all aspects of human endeavour; internationalize safety and *accident prevention* movement; disseminate benefits of practices, skills, arts and technologies of safety and accident prevention; support activities of other national and international *professional* organizations in *protection* of people, environment, resources and property. **Structure** Executive Action Committee, consisting of President, Vice-President, Chief Executive Officer and Immediate Past President. Board of Directors (21 to 23 members of the international safety, security and health community), meets annually. Continental Chapter offices; International Offices. Corporate offices, staff and WSO Certification Board located at *World Management Center,* set up 1987. **Languages** English. **Staff** 5.00 FTE, paid. Numerous voluntary. **Finance** Members' dues. Professional certifications. Annual budget: US$ 285,000. **Activities** Standards/guidelines; monitoring/evaluation; events/meetings; training/education; certification/accreditation. **Events** *International Environmental and Occupational Safety and Health Professional Development Conference* Las Vegas, NV (USA) 2019, *International Environmental and Occupational Safety and Health Professional Development Conference* Charleston, WV (USA) 2018, *International Environmental and Occupational Safety and Health Professional Development Conference* Las Vegas, NV (USA) 2017, *International Environmental and Occupational Safety and Health Professional Development Conference* Houston, TX (USA) 2016, *International Environmental and Occupational Safety and Health Professional Development Conference* Manila (Philippines) 2015. **Publications** *WSO Safety Journal* (4 a year); *WSO Newsletter* (9-12 a year); *WSO TechLetter.*
Members Honorary membership granted to all 157 missions to the United Nations and over 800 national and multinational companies, corporations and organizations. Associate; Affiliate; Institutional; Sustaining/ Corporate. WSO certified members (2,350) and other members (over 7,500), both individuals and institutions, claimed in 157 countries and territories. International offices in 20 countries and territories:
International offices in 20 countries and territories:
Algeria, Australia, Czechia, India, Indonesia, Lebanon, Malaysia, Nigeria, North Macedonia, Northern Mariana Is, Pakistan, Philippines, Poland, Qatar, Russia, Singapore, Slovakia, Taiwan, Ukraine, Vietnam.
Also members in GCC countries. Membership countries not specified.
Consultative Status Consultative status granted from: *ECOSOC (#05331)* (Special). **NGO Relations** Member of: *Conference of Non-Governmental Organizations in Consultative Relationship with the United Nations (CONGO, #04635).* National safety councils in various countries. [2017.03.09/XD0098/**F**]

♦ World Sailing 21760

CEO Office 401, 4th Floor, 3 Shortlands Drive, London, W6 8DA, UK. T. +442039404888. E-mail: office@sailing.org.
URL: https://www.sailing.org/

History 1907, Paris (France). Instrumental in setting up: *International Hobie 17 Class Association (inactive)* and *International Hobie 18 Class Association (inactive).* Former names and other names: *International Yacht Racing Union (IYRU)* – former (1907 to 1996); *Union internationale de courses de yacht* – former (1907 to 1996); *Unión Internacional de Carreras de Yates* – former (1907 to 1996); *Internationaler Verband der Yacht-Rennen* – former (1907 to 1996); *International Sailing Federation (ISAF)* – former (1996 to Dec 2015). **Aims** Be the controlling authority of the sport of sailing in all its forms throughout the world. **Structure** General Assembly (every 4 years); Council (meeting annually); Executive Committee; Commissions (9); Committees (13) with 13 Sub-Committees; Review Board; Women's Forum; Secretariat, headed by CEO. **Languages** English. **Staff** 22.00 FTE, paid. **Finance** Sources: contributions; fees for services; members' dues; sale of products; sale of publications; sponsorship. **Activities** Awards/prizes/competitions; events/meetings. **Events** *Annual Conference* Abu Dhabi (United Arab Emirates) 2022, *Development Symposium* Abu Dhabi (United Arab Emirates) 2022, *Midyear Meeting* Abu Dhabi (United Arab Emirates) 2022, *Annual Conference* 2021, *Midyear Meeting* London (UK) 2021. **Publications** *World Sailing News* (weekly); *ISAF Yearbook.* Regulations; guides; manuals.
Members National authorities controlling the sport of sailing in 139 countries and territories:
Algeria, Andorra, Angola, Antigua-Barbuda, Argentina, Armenia, Aruba, Australia, Austria, Azerbaijan, Bahamas, Bahrain, Barbados, Belarus, Belgium, Belize, Bermuda, Botswana, Brazil, Bulgaria, Canada, Cayman Is, Chile, China, Colombia, Cook Is, Croatia, Cuba, Curaçao, Cyprus, Czechia, Denmark, Djibouti, Dominican Rep, Ecuador, Egypt, El Salvador, Estonia, Fiji, Finland, France, Georgia, Germany, Greece, Grenada, Guam, Guatemala, Hong Kong, Hungary, Iceland, India, Indonesia, Iran Islamic Rep, Ireland, Israel, Italy, Jamaica, Japan, Kazakhstan, Kenya, Korea DPR, Korea Rep, Kosovo, Kuwait, Kyrgyzstan, Latvia, Lebanon, Libya, Liechtenstein, Lithuania, Luxembourg, Macau, Madagascar, Malaysia, Malta, Mauritius, Mexico, Moldova, Monaco, Montenegro, Morocco, Mozambique, Myanmar, Namibia, Netherlands, New Zealand, Nigeria, North Macedonia, Norway, Oman, Pakistan, Palestine, Panama, Papua New Guinea, Paraguay, Peru, Philippines, Poland, Portugal, Puerto Rico, Qatar, Romania, Russia, Samoa, San Marino, Saudi Arabia, Senegal, Serbia, Seychelles, Singapore, Slovakia, Slovenia, Solomon Is, South Africa, Spain, Sri Lanka, St Lucia, Sudan, Sweden, Switzerland, Tahiti Is, Taiwan, Tanzania UR, Thailand, Trinidad-Tobago, Tunisia, Türkiye, Uganda, UK, Ukraine, United Arab Emirates, Uruguay, USA, Vanuatu, Venezuela, Vietnam, Virgin Is UK, Virgin Is USA, Zimbabwe.
Affiliated members (10):
African Sailing Confederation (ASCON, #00449); Asian Sailing Federation (ASAF, #01691); European Sailing Federation (EUROSAF, #08421); International Association for Disabled Sailing (IFDS, #11849); Mediterranean Sailing Union (MSU, #16673); Oceania Sailing Federation (OSAF, #17673); Offshore Racing Congress (ORC); *Pan American Sailing Federation (PASAF, #18128); South American Sailing Confederation (#19706); World Sailing Speed Record Council (WSSRC, #21761).*
International Class Associations (64):
– *Comité international du vaurien (CIV, see: #21760);*
– *Fireball International (FI, #09777);*
– *International 11 Metre One-Design Class Association (see: #21760);*
– *International 12 Metre Class Association (ITMA, see: #21760);*
– *International 14 Class Association (see: #21760);*
– *International 2,4 Metre Class Association (see: #21760);*
– *International 29er Class Association (see: #21760);*
– *International 420 Class Association (see: #21760);*
– *International 470 Class Association (see: #21760);*
– *International 49er Class Association (see: #21760);*
– *International 505 Yacht Racing Association (see: #21760);*
– *International 5,5 Metre Class Association (see: #21760);*
– *International 8 Metre Association (IEMA, see: #21760);*
– *International A-Catamaran Association (IACA, see: #21760);*
– *International Cadet Class (see: #21760);*
– *International Contender Association (see: #21760);*
– *International Dart 18 Class Association (see: #21760);*
– *International Dragon Association (IDA, see: #21760);*
– *International Enterprise Class Association (see: #21760);*
– *International Etchells Class Association (see: #21760);*
– *International Europe Class Union (IECU, #13312);*
– *International Finn Association (IFA, see: #21760);*
– *International Flying Dutchman Class Organization (IFDCO, see: #21760);*
– *International Flying Fifteen Class Association (see: #21760);*
– *International Flying Junior Organization (IFJO, see: #21760);*
– *International Formula 18 Class Association (see: #21760);*
– *International Formula Windsurfing Class (see: #21760);*
– *International Funboard Class Association (IFCA, see: #21760);*
– *International Hansa Class Association (IHCA, #13773);*
– *International H-Boat Class Association (IHA, see: #21760);*
– *International Hobie 14 Class Association (see: #21760);*
– *International Hobie 16 Class Association (see: #21760);*
– *International Hobie Tiger Class Association (see: #21760);*
– *International J/22 Class Association (see: #21760);*
– *International J/24 Class Association (see: #21760);*
– *International Kiteboarding Class Association (IKA, #13987);*
– *International Laser Class Association (see: #21760)* (includes Laser 4/7);
– *International Laser II Class Association (see: #21760);*
– *International Lightning Class Association (ILCA, see: #21760);*
– *International Melges 24 Class Association (see: #21760);*
– *International Mirror Class Association (IMCA, see: #21760);*
– *International Monohull Open Classes Association (IMOCA, see: #21760)* (60ft);
– *International Moth Class Association;*
– International Musto Performance Skiff Class Association;
– *International Nacra F18 Class Association;*
– *International Optimist Dinghy Association (IODA, see: #21760);*
– *International Raceboard Class Association (see: #21760);*
– *International RS Feva Class Association (#14768);*
– *International Six Metre Class Association (ISMA, see: #21760);*
– *International Soling Association (ISA, see: #21760);*
– International Speed Windsurfing Class Association;
– *International Splash Class Association (see: #21760);*
– *International Star Class Yacht Racing Association (ISCYRA, see: #21760);*
– *International Sunfish Class Association (ISCA, see: #21760);*
– *International Tempest Class Association (see: #21760);*
– *International Topper International Class Association (see: #21760);*
– *International Tornado Association (ITA, see: #21760);*
– *International Yngling Class Association (IYA, see: #21760);*
– *International Zoom 8 Class Association (#15945);*
– *Neil Pryde RS X Class Association (#16970);*
– *OK-Dinghy International Association (OKDIA, see: #21760);*
– O'pen Bic Class Association;
– *Snipe Class International Racing Association (SCIRA, see: #21760);*
– Techno 293 Class Association.
Recognized Class Associations (26):
– Access 303 Class Association;
– Access Liberty Class Association;
– B14 Class Association;
– Byte Class;
– Farr 30 Class Association;
– Farr 40 Class Association;
– Formula Experience Class Association;
– Hobie Dragoon Class Association;
– J/80 Class Association;
– Melges 32 Class Association;
– Micro Class;
– Ocean Racing Multihull Association;
– Platu 25 Class Association;
– RS Tera International Class Association;
– SB3 Class Association;
– SL16 Class Association;
– Sonar Class Association;
– Swan 45 Class Association;
– Tasar Class Association;
– Tempest International Class Association;
– Topcat K1 Class Association;
– TP52 Class Association;
– Ultimate 20 Class Association;
– X-35 Class Association;
– X-41 Class Association;
– X-99 Class Association.
Classic Yacht Classes (2):
GP14 Class International Association (no recent information); International Shark Class Association (see: #21760).
Consultative Status Consultative status granted from: *International Maritime Organization (IMO, #14102).* **NGO Relations** Member of (7): *Association of Summer Olympic International Federations (ASOIF, #02943); International Council for Coaching Excellence (ICCE, #13008);* International Measurement System; International Rating System; IRC; *Olympic Movement (#17719);* ORC Club. Instrumental in setting up (1): *International One Design World Class Association (IOD World Class Association, #14412).* Recognized by: *International Olympic Committee (IOC, #14408).* Recognizes *International Sailing Coaches Association (ISCA, #14776).* [2022/XB2824/y/**B**]

♦ World Sailing Speed Record Council (WSSRC) 21761

Sec PO Box 2, Bordon, GU35 9JX, UK. T. +441420472293. Fax +441420476067. E-mail: secretary.wssr@gmail.com.
URL: http://www.sailspeedrecords.com/

History 1972. Founded under the auspices of Royal Yachting Association (UK). Became an international body in 1976. Affiliated, since 1989, to *World Sailing (#21760).* Former names and other names: *ISAF/World Sailing Speed Record Council (ISAF/WSSRC)* – former. **Aims** Act as the international authority for ratifying World Sailing Speed Records. **Structure** Council; Secretary (Executive Staff). **Languages** English. **Staff** 1.00 FTE, paid. **Finance** Attempt fees.
Members Council members from 5 countries:
Australia, Belgium, France, UK, USA. [2021.05.26/XE1407/v/**E**]

♦ World Sand Sculpting Academy (WSSA) 21762

World Headquarters Sirtemastraat 339, 2513 XM The Hague, Netherlands. T. +31703067160. Fax +31703067169. E-mail: info@wssa.info.
URL: http://www.wssa.info/

History 1990, as *World Sand Sculpting Association (WSSA)*. **Aims** Promote sand sculpting as an internationally recognized profession and art form.
Members Full in 16 countries and territories:
Belgium, Canada, Curaçao, Denmark, France, Ireland, Italy, Japan, Mexico, Netherlands, Singapore, South Africa, Spain, Taiwan, Tonga, USA. [2014/XN5639/y/**C**]

♦ World Sand Sculpting Association / see World Sand Sculpting Academy (#21762)
♦ World Santa Claus Congress (meeting series)

♦ World Sarcoma Network (WSN) 21763

Chairman c/o Centre Léon Bérard, 28 rue Laennec, 69008 Lyon, France. T. +33478782757.
URL: http://www.worldsarcomanetwork.com/
Aims Stimulate rapid clinical *drug* development for sarcomas; enable performant *clinical studies* that could not be completed by cooperative groups at national level. **Structure** Board, including Chairman. **Activities** Meeting activities.
Members Centres in 7 countries:
Australia, France, Germany, Italy, Netherlands, Poland, UK.
NGO Relations Member of: *Rare Cancers Europe (RCE, #18620)*. [2014/XJ6444/**F**]

♦ World Savings Banks Institute (WSBI) 21764

Institut mondial des caisses d'épargne – Weltinstitut der Sparkassen
Main Office WSBI-ESBG, Rue Marie-Thérèse 11, 1000 Brussels, Belgium. T. +3222111111. Fax +3222111199. E-mail: info@wsbi-esbg.org.
URL: http://www.wsbi-esbg.org/
History Jun 1994. Founded on restructuring of the former *International Savings Banks Institute (ISBI) – Institut international des caisses d'épargne (IICE) – Instituto Internacional de Cajas de Ahorros (IICA) – Internationales Institut der Sparkassen (IIS)*, which had been set up in 1925 as *International Thrift Institute – Institut international de l'épargne – Internationales Institut des Sparwesens – Istituto Internazionale del Risparmio*, pursuant to a resolution adopted by the International Thrift Congress, 26-30 Oct 1924, Milan (Italy). Statutes amended 20 May 1963, Vienna (Austria), with adoption of new name. Statutes further amended: 1969, Rome (Italy); 1972, London (UK); 1974, Geneva (Switzerland); 1975, Bogota; 1982, Rio de Janeiro (Brazil); 1994, Prague (Czech Rep); 1996, Tokyo (Japan); 2002, Beijing (China); 2006, Kuala Lumpur (Malaysia); 2009 Santiago (Chile); 2012, Marrakech (Morocco). Former names and other names: *World Savings and Retail Banking Institute* – alias. Registration: Banque-Carrefour des Entreprises, No/ID: 0457.991.537, Start date: 6 Jun 1996, Belgium. **Aims** Serve as a centre for exchange of *business* experience and ideas on all facets of retail banking; promote practical business and development cooperation among members; encourage international organizations to take saving and retail banks specific views into account in defining policies; promote the interests of savings and retail banks worldwide; increase bilateral and multilateral relationships and information exchange with and among savings and retail banks. **Structure** General Assembly (annual); Board of Directors; Statutory Committees (2); Consultative Committees (9); Regional Groups (3): Africa, Asia Pacific, Latin America/Caribbean. **Languages** English, French, German, Italian, Spanish. **Staff** 35.00 FTE, paid. **Finance** Sources: members' dues. **Activities** Events/meetings; monitoring/evaluation; projects/ programmes; research/documentation. *'Coordination Committee of the European Savings Banks Group and the World Savings Bank Institute'* coordinates activities with those of *European Savings and Retail Banking Group (ESBG, #08426)* at *'Joint Office of the European Savings Banks Group and the World Savings Banks Institute'* in Brussels (Belgium), under the headings: Representation of Interests; Business Cooperation; Financial Sector Development. Instrumental in setting up: *Forum of Postal Savings Banks (see: #21764)*. **Events** *ESG Financing Summit* Brussels (Belgium) 2022, *World Congress of Savings and Retail Banks* Paris (France) 2021, *Business Forum* Barcelona (Spain) 2020, *World Congress of Savings and Retail Banks* New Delhi (India) 2018, *Annual Asia Pacific Regional Meeting* Bangkok (Thailand) 2016. **Publications** Newsletter (4 a year). Congress reports; research reports on special projects.
Members Savings and retail banks; national or regional savings and retail banks associations; other central organizations founded or administered by savings banks or their associations; any other institution mainly engaged in the promotion of thrift without private profit. Institutions (117) in 84 countries and territories:
Algeria, Angola, Austria, Azerbaijan, Benin, Bolivia, Botswana, Brazil, Bulgaria, Burkina Faso, Cameroon, Cape Verde, Chile, China, Colombia, Comoros, Costa Rica, Côte d'Ivoire, Croatia, Cuba, Czechia, Denmark, Dominican Rep, El Salvador, Ethiopia, Finland, France, Gabon, Germany, Ghana, Greece, Guatemala, Guinea, Hungary, Iceland, India, Indonesia, Iran Islamic Rep, Italy, Kazakhstan, Kenya, Korea Rep, Latvia, Lesotho, Luxembourg, Macau, Madagascar, Malaysia, Mali, Malta, Mauritania, Mexico, Mongolia, Morocco, Mozambique, Namibia, Netherlands, Norway, Pakistan, Panama, Peru, Philippines, Poland, Portugal, Romania, Senegal, Slovakia, South Africa, Spain, Sri Lanka, Sudan, Sweden, Tajikistan, Tanzania UR, Thailand, Togo, Tunisia, Uganda, Ukraine, USA, Uzbekistan, Vietnam, Zambia, Zimbabwe.
Consultative Status Consultative status granted from: *FAO (#09260)* (Liaison Status); *ILO (#11123)* (Special List); *UNCTAD (#20285)* (General Category); *UNIDO (#20336)*. **IGO Relations** Accredited by: *United Nations Office at Vienna (UNOV, #20604)*. **NGO Relations** Member of: *Better Than Cash Alliance (#03220)*; *SME Finance Forum (#19323)*. Associate member of: *Business and Industry Advisory Committee to the OECD (BIAC, #03385)*; *European Banking and Financial Services Training Association (EBTN, #06313)*. [2020/XB2428/y/**F**]

♦ World Savings and Retail Banking Institute / see World Savings Banks Institute (#21764)

♦ Worldscale Association 21765

Head Office Worldscale Association (London) Ltd, Copenhagen House, 5-10 Bury Street, London, EC3A 5AT, UK. E-mail: wscale@worldscale.co.uk.
USA Office Worldscale Association (NYC) Inc, 15 Maiden Lane Suite 505, Suite 619, New York NY 10038, USA.
URL: http://www.worldscale.co.uk/
History 1969, replacing *'Intascale'*, London (UK) and *'ATRS'*, New York NY (USA), as *International Tanker Nominal Freight Scale Association Limited in London (INTASCALE)*. Present name adopted 1979. **Aims** Produce standard reference rates for oil tanker *shipping freight*, the *'New Worldwide Tanker Nominal Freight Scale'* or *'Worldscale'*, based on similar net returns per day regardless of voyage performed and calculated on a common basis in accordance with published formulae. **Activities** Knowledge management/information dissemination; standards/guidelines. [2020/XM1049/e/**F**]

♦ World Scholar's Cup 21766

Main Office 1002 Wall St, Los Angeles CA 90015, USA. T. +18187162820 – +19553364332. E-mail: contact@scholarscup.org.
URL: https://www.scholarscup.org/
History 2007, Korea Rep. Founded by Daniel Berdichevsky. Former names and other names: *World Scholar's Cup Foundation* – full title. **Aims** Motivate students of all backgrounds to discover new strengths and practice new skills; inspire a global community of future scholars and leaders. **Activities** Awards/prizes/competitions. **Events** *World Scholar's Cup Global Round* Melbourne, VIC (Australia) 2025, *World Scholar's Cup Global Round* Sydney, NSW (Australia) 2019. [2020/AA0838/**F**]

♦ World Scholar's Cup Foundation / see World Scholar's Cup (#21766)

♦ World Schools Debating Championships (WSDC) 21767

Chair The Courtyard, High Street, Ascot, SL5 7HP, UK. E-mail: contact@schoolsdebate.com – directors@schoolsdebate.com.
URL: http://www.schoolsdebate.com/council.asp
History 1988, Australia, as *World Debating Championships*, by the Australian Debating Federation. Present name adopted 1991. **Aims** Achieve excellence in debating; encourage debating throughout the world; promote international understanding and freedom of speech. **Structure** Council; Executive Committee. **Languages** English. **Staff** Voluntary. **Finance** Members' dues. Other sources: donors; registration fees. **Activities** Events/ meetings. **Events** *Tournament* Cape Town (South Africa) 2012, *Tournament* Cardiff (UK) 2006, *Tournament* Calgary, AB (Canada) 2005, *Tournament* Stuttgart (Germany) 2004, *Tournament* Lima (Peru) 2003. **Members** Individuals. Membership countries not specified. [2018.06.01/XE4325/**E**]

♦ World's Christian Endeavor Union (WCEU) 21768

Union mondiale des efforts chrétiens
Gen Sec 403 E Fulton St, Ephrata PA 17522, USA. T. +16103690207. Fax +16103690257. E-mail: centraloffice@worldsceunion.org.
URL: http://www.worldsceunion.org/
History Founded 10 Jul 1895, Boston MA (USA), as worldwide movement, the first society having been organized 2 Feb 1881, Portland ME (USA), becoming, 1886, *Christian Endeavor Movement*. Chartered by Commonwealth of Massachusetts (USA), 24 Jan 1902. Previously also referred to in French as *Union universelle des sociétés d'activité chrétienne*. **Aims** Unite Christian Endeavourers worldwide in closer fellowship; promote interests of the Christian Endeavour movement; reinforce Christian *churches* in every land; cement the *spiritual* union of Christians worldwide. **Structure** Council (meeting every 4 years); Board of Trustees (meeting annually); Executive Committee. Conventions open; business meetings closed. **Languages** English. **Staff** 1.50 FTE, paid. Several voluntary. **Finance** Annual contributions from national and international unions. Other sources: gifts; offerings; returns from conventions and conferences. **Activities** Knowledge management/information dissemination; networking/liaising; events/meetings. **Events** *Quadrennial world convention* Hoengseong (Korea Rep) 2014, *Quadrennial world convention* Lima (Peru) 2010, *Quadrennial world convention* Gödöllö (Hungary) 2006, *Conference / Quadrennial World Convention* Singapore (Singapore) 2002, *Quadrennial world convention* Bad Liebenzell (Germany) 1998. **Publications** *World Christian Endeavor News* (4 a year).
Members Christian Endeavour Societies in 34 countries and territories:
Australia, Austria, Cayman Is, Côte d'Ivoire, Gambia, Germany, Guatemala, Guyana, Hungary, India, Ireland, Jamaica, Japan, Korea Rep, Lebanon, Liberia, Malawi, Mexico, Myanmar, Namibia, Nepal, Netherlands, Nigeria, Papua New Guinea, Peru, Romania, Samoa, Samoa USA, Sierra Leone, Solomon Is, South Africa, Syrian AR, Ukraine, USA.
Individuals in 34 countries and territories:
Argentina, Benin, Brazil, Bulgaria, Canada, Croatia, Egypt, England, Fiji, Ghana, Guinea-Bissau, Honduras, Iraq, Kenya, Malaysia, Mali, Marshall Is, Micronesia FS, New Zealand, Nicaragua, Niger, Pakistan, Philippines, Poland, Russia, Scotland, Senegal, Spain, Taiwan, Thailand, Tonga, Uganda, United Arab Emirates, Wales. [2017/XB3612/**F**]

♦ World Science Fiction Congress (meeting series)

♦ World Science Fiction Society (WSFS) 21769

Contact PO Box 61363, Sunnyvale CA 94088, USA.
URL: http://worldcon.org/
History 1939. Current constitution adopted 2016. **Aims** Choose recipients of Hugo Awards; choose locations and committees for the World Science Fiction Convention (Worldcon) and North American Science Fiction Convention (NASFiC). **Structure** Mark Protection Committee; Convention Committees. **Languages** English. **Staff** None paid. **Finance** Sources: meeting proceeds. Annual budget: 1,000,000 USD. **Activities** Awards/ prizes/competitions; events/meetings. **Events** *Annual Convention* Chicago, IL (USA) 2022, *Annual Convention* Washington, DC (USA) 2021, *Annual Convention* Wellington (New Zealand) 2020, *Annual Convention* Dublin (Ireland) 2019, *Annual Convention* San Jose, CA (USA) 2018. **Publications** Progress reports. **Members** Membership consists of participants of most recent convention. **IGO Relations** None. **NGO Relations** None. [2020.03.03/XN0082/v/**C**]

♦ World Science Institute / see World Institute of Science (#21590)

♦ World Scleroderma Foundation (WSF) 21770

Exec Sec Elisabethenstr 3, 4051 Basel BS, Switzerland. E-mail: worldsclerodermafoundation@ gmail.com.
Chairman Dept of Biomedicine, Div of Rheumatology, Villa Monna Tessa, Viale Pieraccini 18, 50139 Florence FI, Italy. T. +39557949271. Fax +39557949271.
URL: http://www.w-s-a.net/
Aims Initiate and support research in scleroderma. **Structure** Board. **Activities** Meeting activities; research. **Events** *Systemic Sclerosis World Congress* 2022, *Systemic Sclerosis World Congress* Prague (Czechia) 2020, *Systemic Sclerosis World Congress* Bordeaux (France) 2018, *Systemic Sclerosis World Congress* Lisbon (Portugal) 2016, *Systemic Sclerosis World Congress* Rome (Italy) 2014. [2017/XJ8281/f/**F**]

♦ World Scout Bureau (see: #21693)

♦ World Scout Bureau – European Regional Office 21771

Bureau mondial du scoutisme – Bureau régional européen
Regional Office Geneva Rue Henri-Christiné 5, 1205 Geneva, Switzerland. T. +41227051100. E-mail: europe@scout.org.
Regional Office Brussels Rue de l'Industrie 10, 1000 Brussels, Belgium. T. +3228932435. E-mail: brussels@ scout.org.
Main Website: http://www.scout.org/europe/
History A regional body of *World Scout Bureau (WSB, see: #21693)*. Former names and other names: *European Scout Office* – former; *Bureau européen du mouvement scout* – former. **Aims** Contribute actively to the education of young people, through a value system based on the Scout Promise and Law; help build a better world where people are self-fulfilled as individuals and play a constructive role in society. **Structure** European Scout Conference (every 3 years); Elected Committee. World Scout Bureau – European Regional Office, headed by Regional Director. **Languages** English, French. **Staff** 12.50 FTE, paid. Many voluntary. **Finance** Sources: grants; members' dues; sponsorship. Fund for European Scouting. **Activities** Events/meetings; networking/ liaising. **Events** *Triennial European Guide and Scout Conference* Rotterdam (Netherlands) 2022, *Triennial European Guide and Scout Conference* Split (Croatia) 2019, *Triennial European Guide and Scout Conference* Melsomvik (Norway) 2016, *Triennial European Guide and Scout Conference* Berlin (Germany) 2013, *Triennial European Guide and Scout Conference* Berlin (Germany) 2013. **Publications** Circulars.
Members National Scout organizations (40) in 40 countries:
Austria, Belgium, Bosnia-Herzegovina, Bulgaria, Croatia, Cyprus, Czechia, Denmark, Estonia, Finland, France, Germany, Greece, Hungary, Iceland, Ireland, Israel, Italy, Latvia, Liechtenstein, Lithuania, Luxembourg, Malta, Monaco, Montenegro, Netherlands, North Macedonia, Norway, Poland, Portugal, Romania, San Marino, Serbia, Slovakia, Slovenia, Spain, Sweden, Switzerland, Türkiye, UK.
NGO Relations Member of (1): *European Youth Forum (#09140)*. [2022.02.02/XE8340/**E**]

♦ World Scout Foundation (WSF) 21772

Fondation du scoutisme mondial
Dir 1 Rue de la Navigation, Case postale 2116, 1211 Geneva 1, Switzerland. T. +41227051090. Fax +41227051099. E-mail: info@worldscoutfoundation.org.
URL: http://www.worldscoutfoundation.org/home
History 1969, to provide support to *World Organization of the Scout Movement (WOSM, #21693)*. **Aims** Help the development of the World Organization of the Scout Movement by the provision of financial and other support necessary for its action. **Structure** Board (meets annually), comprising Honorary Chairman, Officers (Chairman, Chairman-Elect, Past Chairman and Chairman-Investment Committee, Secretary, Treasurer), 3 Ex-officio members representing the World Organization, 2 Life members and 18 members. Executive Committee, comprising 6 Officers and an Ex-officio member. Committees (2): Investment; Fundraising. **Languages** English. **Staff** 2.00 FTE, paid. **Finance** Contributions from Baden-Powell World Fellowship; donations from governments and corporations. **Activities** Raises funds form a variety of sources, both public and private: governments, corporations, individuals and the scout constituency. One of the programmes of the Foundation is the *Baden-Powell World Fellowship (#03055)* which is designed to encourage support from individual donors. **Events** *Fellowship Event Meeting* Seoul (Korea Rep) 2019, *Fellowship Event Meeting* Mexico City (Mexico) 2018, *Fellowship Event Meeting* Berlin (Germany) 2017, *Fellowship Event Meeting* Melbourne, VIC (Australia) 2016, *Fellowship Event Meeting* Zurich (Switzerland) 2014. **Publications** Annual report.
Members Support received from 74 countries and territories:
Argentina, Australia, Austria, Bahamas, Bangladesh, Belgium, Belize, Bermuda, Brazil, Brunei Darussalam, Cameroon, Canada, Cayman Is, Chile, China, Colombia, Costa Rica, Côte d'Ivoire, Denmark, Egypt, Fiji, Finland, France, Germany, Greece, Guatemala, Hong Kong, Hungary, Iceland, India, Indonesia, Ireland, Italy, Jamaica, Japan, Kenya, Korea Rep, Kuwait, Lebanon, Libya, Liechtenstein, Luxembourg, Malaysia, Malta, Mexico, Monaco, Morocco, Netherlands, New Zealand, Nigeria, Norway, Oman, Panama, Philippines, Portugal, Qatar, Russia, Saudi Arabia, Senegal, Singapore, South Africa, Spain, Sweden, Switzerland, Syrian AR, Taiwan, Thailand, Uganda, UK, Ukraine, United Arab Emirates, USA, Venezuela, Zimbabwe.
NGO Relations Supports: *World Scout Bureau (WSB, see: #21693)*. [2015/XF7446/f/**F**]

♦ World Scout Interreligious Forum (see: #21693)

♦ **World Scout Parliamentary Union (WSPU)** **21773**
Union parlementaire mondiale du scoutisme (UPMS) – Unión Parlamentaria Scout Mundial (UPSM)
Pres National Assembly Members Bldg – Room 115, 1 Yeouido-dong, Youngdeungpo-gu, Seoul 150-702, Korea Rep. T. +8227864491. Fax +8227801703. E-mail: wspu@scout.or.kr – wspu@assembly.go.kr.
URL: http://www.wspu.info/
History Mar 1990, Seoul (Korea Rep). Constituent Assembly Aug 1991. Formally launched Jan 1994. **Aims** Strengthen both National Scout organizations (NSO) and World Scouting through the influence of parliamentarians who believe in Scouting as an effective non-formal educational method and movement. **Structure** General Assembly (every 4 years); World Scout Committee; Executive Committee; Secretariat. **Languages** English, Korean. **Staff** 3.00 FTE, paid. **Finance** Members' dues. Annual budget: US$ 316,000. **Activities** Advocacy/lobbying/activism; awards/prizes/competitions; events/meetings; training/education. **Events** *WSPU General Assembly* Korea Rep 2022, *WSPU General Assembly* Bangkok (Thailand) 2018, *Triennial General Assembly* Stockholm (Sweden) 2016, *Triennial General Assembly* Seoul (Korea Rep) 2010, *Meeting* Jeju (Korea Rep) 2008. **Publications** *WSPU Newsletter* (2 a year); *WSPU General Assembly Report* (every 3 years). *WSPU Presentation Booklet* (2011).
Members National Scout Parliamentary Associations (NSPAs) in 103 countries and territories:
Albania, Algeria, Angola, Argentina, Armenia, Australia, Azerbaijan, Bahrain, Bangladesh, Belarus, Belgium, Benin, Bolivia, Brazil, Brunei Darussalam, Bulgaria, Burkina Faso, Cambodia, Canada, Cayman Is, Chad, Chile, Congo Brazzaville, Costa Rica, Croatia, Czechia, Denmark, Dominican Rep, Ecuador, Egypt, Eswatini, Ethiopia, Finland, France, Gambia, Georgia, Ghana, Greece, Grenada, Guatemala, Guyana, Honduras, Hong Kong, Hungary, India, Indonesia, Ireland, Israel, Italy, Japan, Jordan, Korea Rep, Kuwait, Lebanon, Libya, Lithuania, Malaysia, Maldives, Mexico, Mongolia, Morocco, Mozambique, Myanmar, Netherlands, Nicaragua, North Macedonia, Oman, Pakistan, Palestine, Panama, Paraguay, Peru, Philippines, Poland, Qatar, Romania, Russia, Saudi Arabia, Senegal, Serbia, South Africa, Spain, Sri Lanka, St Lucia, Sudan, Sweden, Switzerland, Taiwan, Tajikistan, Tanzania UR, Thailand, Togo, Trinidad-Tobago, Tunisia, Türkiye, Uganda, UK, Ukraine, Uruguay, Uzbekistan, Venezuela, Yemen, Zambia.
IGO Relations *UNESCO (#20322)*; *UNICEF (#20332)*; *WHO (#20950)*. **NGO Relations** Consultative status with: *World Organization of the Scout Movement (WOSM, #21693)*. [2018/XE1656/**E**]

♦ **World Seabird Union (WSU)** **21774**
Chair Leader, South Carolina Cooperative Fish and Wildlife Research Unit, Clemson Univ, Clemson SC 29634, USA. E-mail: wsuadmin@seabirds.net.
Sec 2661 Queenswood Drive, Victoria BC V8N 1X6, Canada.
URL: http://www.seabirds.net/
History Sep 2010, Victoria, BC (Canada). Founded during 1st World Seabird Conference. Nonprofit status recognized in 2012. **Aims** Place seabird research, management, and *conservation* into a worldwide perspective. **Structure** Board of Directors. **Languages** English. **Staff** Voluntary. **Finance** Sources: donations. No annual budget. **Events** *World Seabird Conference* 2021, *World Seabird Conference* Cape Town (South Africa) 2015, *World Seabird Conference* Victoria, BC (Canada) 2010.
Members Organizations (17), including the following 9 organizations listed in this Yearbook:
African Seabird Group (ASG); *Australasian Seabird Group (ASG)*; *BirdLife International (#03266)* (Global Seabird Programme); *BirdsCaribbean (#03267)*; *Conservation of Arctic Flora and Fauna (CAFF, #04728)* (Circumpolar Seabird Expert Group (CBird)); *Global Penguin Society (GPS)*; *Mediterranean Marine Bird Association (MEDMARAVIS, #16661)*; *Pacific Seabird Group (PSG)*; *Waterbird Society (WBS)*.
[2022/XJ8802/y/**C**]

♦ **World Seagrass Association (WSA)** **21775**
Sec address not obtained. E-mail: wsa.secretary@gmail.com.
URL: http://wsa.seagrassonline.org/
History Proposed 1998 at 3rd International Seagrass Biology Workshop (ISBW). Set up 2 Oct 2000, Corsica (France) at 4th ISBW. Formally incorporated 2 Oct 2002. Registered in accordance with Australian law. **Aims** Research, protect and manage the world's seagrasses. **Structure** Steering Committee of 11 members. Management Committee, comprising President, Immediate Past-President, Vice-President, Treasurer, Secretary and Assistant Treasurer. **Events** *International Seagrass Biology Workshop* Singapore (Singapore) 2018, *World Seagrass Conference* Singapore (Singapore) 2018, *International Seagrass Biology Workshop* Sanya (China) 2014, *International Seagrass Biology Workshop* Rio de Janeiro (Brazil) 2012, *Annual General Meeting* Smithfield, SA (Australia) 2012. **Publications** *WSA Newsletter*. **NGO Relations** Liaises with: *Seagrass 2000 (#19167)*. [2013/XJ2977/**E**]

♦ World Secret Service Association / see World Association of Detectives (#21131)
♦ World Security Federation (no recent information)
♦ World Seismic Safety Initiative (see: #11855)
♦ World Self-Medication Industry / see Global Self-Care Federation (#10588)

♦ **World Semiconductor Council (WSC)** **21776**
Address not obtained.
URL: http://www.semiconductorcouncil.org/
History following US/Japanese Semiconductor Agreement, 1996, Vancouver (Canada). **Aims** Contribute to the harmonious development, viability and independence of the *European* semiconductor *manufacturing* industry in the world. **Structure** Joint Steering Committee plans, prepares and supports meetings. Informal structure with no fixed secretariat. **Languages** English. **Staff** 3.00 FTE, paid. **Events** *Government/Authorities Meeting on Semiconductors* Busan (Korea Rep) 2017, *Council meeting* Seoul (Korea Rep) 2016, *Joint meeting* Barcelona (Spain) 2010, *Council meeting / Meeting* Seoul (Korea Rep) 2010, *Meeting* Beijing (China) 2009. **Publications** *ESIA Newsletter* (1-2 a year).
Members National industry associations in 5 countries and territories:
China, Japan, Korea Rep, Taiwan, USA.
Regional industry association (1):
European Semiconductor Industry Association (ESIA, #08462). [2010/XD6889/**E**]

♦ **World Semiconductor Trade Statistics (WSTS)** **21777**
Assistant to Administrator 17698 Lancia Drive, Morgan Hill CA 95037, USA.
Administrator Fasanenstr 12a, 83052 Markt Bruckmühl, Germany. T. +4980628071261. Fax +4980628071262.
URL: https://www.wsts.org/
History Registration: Start date: 1986, USA, California. **Aims** Provide semiconductor market data on industry product shipments. **Structure** Board of Directors; Executive Committee; Administrator; Assistant to Administrator. **Languages** English, German. **Staff** 2.00 FTE, paid. **Finance** Sources: meeting proceeds; members' dues; sale of publications. **Activities** Events/meetings. **Events** *Autumn Committee Meeting* Hiroshima (Japan) 2020, *Spring Committee Meeting* Hiroshima (Japan) 2019, *Autumn Committee Meeting* Taipei (Taiwan) 2019, *Autumn Committee Meeting* Scottsdale, AZ (USA) 2018, *Spring Committee Meeting* Vienna (Austria) 2018. **Publications** *Blue Book* (12 a year); *Blue Book History* (12 a year); *By Country Report* (4 a year); *Semiconductor Market Forecasts* (2 a year); *End Use Report* (annual). **Members** Semiconductor manufacturers worldwide. Membership countries not specified. [2020.08.20/XM1692/t/**F**]

♦ **World Sephardi Federation (WSF)** **21778**
Fédération séphardite mondiale (FSM) – Federación Mundial Sefardi
Pres Rue de l'Est 8, 1207 Geneva, Switzerland. T. +41227362824. Fax +41227362825. E-mail: ndg@noga.ch.
History 4 Nov 1951, Paris (France). 4-8 Nov 1951, Paris (France), at World Sephardi Congress, on merger of *Union universelles des communautés séphardites (inactive)*, set up 1925, Vienna (Austria), and *World Federation of Sephardi Communities (inactive)*, formed 1944, New York NY (USA). Constitution amended 14 May 1954, Jerusalem (Israel). **Aims** Create, maintain and develop cultural and spiritual bonds between all *Jewish* Sephardi communities in the world, while reinforcing the spiritual wealth and moral values of Judaism and the Sephardi heritage with its specific characteristics, its nuances and its pluralism. **Structure** Congress; Praesidium; Main Branches (9); International Commissions (4). Regional federation: *Federación Sefaradi Latinoamericana (FeSeLa, #09388)*. *Centre for Research and Study of the Sephardi and Oriental Jewish Heritage (Misgav Yerushalayim, no recent information)*, set up 1995, Jerusalem (Israel), on merger of *Institute for Research on the Sephardi and Oriental Jewish Heritage (inactive)* and *Centre for the Study of Sephardi and Oriental Jewry, Jerusalem (inactive)*. **Languages** English, French. **Staff** 2.50 FTE, paid. **Finance** Contributions of affiliated organizations according to a determined scale; contributions from organizations and private donors. Annual budget: US$ 200,000, out of which US$ 100,000 dedicated to functioning expenses and US$ 100,000 allocated to various branches or dedicated to projects initiated by office in Jerusalem (Israel). **Activities** Events/meetings; financial and/or material support; religious activities. **Events** *Conference* Jerusalem (Israel) 1992, *Conference* Jerusalem (Israel) 1987. **Publications** *Sephardi World* (periodical). *Histoire des Israélites de Salonique*; *Literatura Oral del Ladino entre los Sefardres de Oriente*; *The Sephardi Heritage*. Songs and liturgy.
Members Affiliated National (regional or continental) Branches, one branch per country; local representations (where no recognized national branch exists). Members in 27 countries:
Argentina, Azerbaijan, Brazil, Bulgaria, Canada, Chile, Colombia, Croatia, France, Greece, Guatemala, India, Israel, Italy, Mexico, Panama, Paraguay, Peru, Portugal, Serbia-Montenegro, Slovenia, Spain, Türkiye, UK, Uruguay, USA, Venezuela.
NGO Relations Appoints Sephardi members on Executive Board of: *World Zionist Organization (WZO, #21961)*.
[2018.06.01/XC3579/**C**]

♦ World Servants (internationally oriented national body)
♦ WorldServe International (internationally oriented national body)
♦ World Service Authority / see World Government of World Citizens (#21543)
♦ World Service Authority (see: #21543)
♦ World Services / see The Family International (#09253)
♦ World Services for the Blind (internationally oriented national body)

♦ **World Services Group (WSG)** **21779**
Sec 2777 Allen Parkway, Ste 622, Houston TX 77019, USA. T. +17136500333. Fax +17136506655. E-mail: info@worldservicesgroup.com.
URL: http://www.worldservicesgroup.com/
Aims Create new business prospects and expand regional opportunities for members; promote information exchange and common interests among professional service disciplines; facilitate communication and interaction. **Structure** Board of Directors, including President, Chairman, Chairman Elect, Chairman Emeritus, Secretary and Treasurer. Regional Councils (6): Africa and Middle East; Asia and Pacific; Central America and Caribbean; Europe; North America; South America. **Finance** Sources: members' dues. **Events** *Annual Meeting* Stockholm (Sweden) 2020, *Annual Meeting* Washington, DC (USA) 2019, *Annual Meeting* Nassau (Bahamas) 2018, *Annual Meeting* Helsinki (Finland) 2017, *Annual Meeting* Stellenbosch (South Africa) 2016.
Members Companies (approx 130) in 86 countries and territories:
Anguilla, Argentina, Australia, Bahamas, Barbados, Belgium, Bermuda, Bolivia, Brazil, Bulgaria, Canada, Cayman Is, Chile, Colombia, Costa Rica, Cyprus, Czechia, Denmark, Dominican Rep, Ecuador, Egypt, El Salvador, Estonia, Finland, France, Germany, Ghana, Gibraltar, Greece, Grenada, Guatemala, Honduras, Hong Kong, Hungary, India, Ireland, Isle of Man, Jamaica, Kenya, Korea Rep, Kuwait, Latvia, Lithuania, Luxembourg, Malaysia, Malta, Mauritius, Mexico, Netherlands, New Zealand, Nicaragua, Nigeria, Norway, Pakistan, Panama, Paraguay, Peru, Philippines, Poland, Portugal, Puerto Rico, Romania, Senegal, Serbia, Slovakia, Spain, St Kitts-Nevis, Sweden, Taiwan, Tanzania UR, Thailand, Trinidad-Tobago, Tunisia, Türkiye, Turks-Caicos, UK, Ukraine, United Arab Emirates, Uruguay, USA, Venezuela, Virgin Is UK, Virgin Is USA, Zambia, Zimbabwe.
[2021/XM2786/**C**]

♦ World's Evangelical Alliance (inactive)
♦ World Share / see Worldshare
♦ World SHARE / see WorldShare
♦ Worldshare (internationally oriented national body)
♦ WorldShare (internationally oriented national body)
♦ World Shelter Organization (internationally oriented national body)

♦ **World Shibori Network (WSN)** **21780**
World Pres 696 Hilldale Ave, Berkeley CA 94708, USA. T. +15105273432. Fax +15105270231. E-mail: info@shibori.org.
URL: http://www.shibori.org/
History 1992, Nagoya (Japan). **Aims** Bring together people interested in the preservation and practice of Japanese resist-dye techniques on *textiles*. **Events** *International Shibori Symposium* Tokyo (Japan) / Nagoya (Japan) / Yonezawa (Japan) 2018, *International Shibori Symposium* Oaxaca (Mexico) 2016, *International Shibori Symposium* Hangzhou (China) 2014, *International Shibori Symposium* Hong Kong (Hong Kong) 2011, *International shibori symposium* Lyon (France) 2008.
Members Practitioners, scholars and business people. Individuals in 16 countries:
Australia, Bangladesh, Canada, China, France, Germany, Hong Kong, India, Italy, Japan, Netherlands, New Zealand, Norway, Switzerland, UK, USA. [2018/XM2977/**C**]

♦ **World Shipping Council (WSC)** **21781**
USA Contact 1156 15th St NW, Ste 300, Washington DC 20005, USA. T. +12025891230. Fax +12025891231. E-mail: info@worldshipping.org.
European Contact Ave des Gaulois 34, 1040 Brussels, Belgium. T. +3227342267. Fax +3222308829. E-mail: info@worldshipping.org.
URL: http://www.worldshipping.org/
History EU Transparency Register: 32416571968-71. **Aims** Provide a coordinated voice for the liner shipping industry in its work with policymakers and other industry groups with an interest in international transportation. **Structure** Board; Management. **Activities** Fosters a close working relationships with governments, the European Commission and international organizations to develop new laws, regulations and programmes designed to better secure international maritime commerce and the supply chains that importers and exporters around the world depend upon; supports establishment of new, effective and internationally uniform environmental standards; advises industry and governments in all of the above areas. **Members** Companies (18). Membership countries not specified. **IGO Relations** Consultative status with: *European Commission (EC, #06633)*; *International Maritime Organization (IMO, #14102)*; *World Customs Organization (WCO, #21350)*. **NGO Relations** Consultative member of: *Comité maritime international (CMI, #04192)*. [2018/XM3397/**E**]

♦ **World Ship Society (WSS)** **21782**
SG 49 Mount Road, Mitcham, CR4 3EZ, UK.
Registered Office Mayes House, Vansittart Estate, Arthur Road, Windsor, SL4 1SE, UK.
URL: http://www.worldshipsociety.org/
History Founded 1947, as *'Ship News Club'*. UK Registered Charity: 1139902. **Aims** Cater for the requirements of persons interested in ships and the *sea*. **Structure** General Meeting (annual). Informal structure. **Languages** English. **Finance** Members' dues. **Activities** Knowledge management/information dissemination. **Events** *Annual General Meeting* Rendsburg (Germany) 2020, *Annual General Meeting* Felixstowe (UK) 2018, *Annual General Meeting* Torquay (UK) 2017, *Annual General Meeting* Bristol (UK) 2015, *Annual General Meeting* Hartlepool (UK) 2014. **Publications** *Marine News* (12 a year); *Warships Supplement* (4 a year). Books; monographs. **Information Services** *World Ship Photo Library*.
Members Individuals (mainly in UK); National Branches. Members in 65 countries and territories:
Andorra, Argentina, Australia, Austria, Barbados, Belgium, Bermuda, Brazil, Cameroon, Canada, Chile, Congo DR, Cyprus, Denmark, Finland, France, Germany, Greece, Guadeloupe, Hong Kong, Iceland, India, Indonesia, Iran Islamic Rep, Ireland, Israel, Italy, Japan, Jordan, Liechtenstein, Luxembourg, Malaysia, Malta, Mauritius, Moldova, Monaco, Namibia, Netherlands, New Zealand, Nigeria, Norway, Pakistan, Peru, Philippines, Portugal, Qatar, San Marino, Saudi Arabia, Singapore, South Africa, Spain, Sri Lanka, St Helena, Sweden, Switzerland, Syrian AR, Taiwan, Thailand, Trinidad-Tobago, Türkiye, UK, United Arab Emirates, Uruguay, USA, Zimbabwe. [2017.03.09/XF1332/**F**]

♦ World Shotokan Karate-do Association / see World Shotokan Karate Association (#21783)

♦ **World Shotokan Karate Association (WSKA)** **21783**
Admin Dir address not obtained. T. +351964209917. E-mail: wska.information@gmail.com.
URL: http://www.wska-karate.com/
History 30 Nov 1990, Ferrara (Italy). Founded by *European Shotokan Karate-do Association (ESKA, #08482)*. Also referred to as *World Shotokan Karate-do Association*. **Aims** Develop shotokan karate; advance traditional shotokan karate. **Structure** World Congress. Board of Directors, comprising President, Vice-President, Regional Directors and 3 Directors. **Languages** English. **Finance** Sources: members' dues. **Activities** Events/meetings; sporting activities. Organizes biennial world championships (during Congress). **Events** *Congress* Lisbon (Portugal) 2019, *Congress* Treviso (Italy) 2017, *Congress* Bielsko-Biala (Poland) 2015, *Biennial Congress* Liverpool (UK) 2013, *Biennial Congress / Congress* Chicago, IL (USA) 2011.
Members Organizations in 21 countries:
Argentina, Austria, Belgium, Canada, Czechia, Germany, Hungary, Ireland, Italy, Lithuania, Mexico, Pakistan, Poland, Russia, South Africa, Spain, Sweden, Switzerland, UK, Ukraine, USA. [2021/XD9301/**D**]

♦ World Sight Foundation (internationally oriented national body)
♦ World Sign Associates (internationally oriented national body)

♦ World Sikh Organization (WSO) 21784

Exec Dir address not obtained.
Spokesperson address not obtained. T. +14169049110.
URL: http://www.worldsikh.org/

History 28 Jul 1984, New York NY (USA). **Aims** Promote and protect the interests of Sikhs in Canada and around the world. **Finance** Members' dues. Other sources: donations from individuals and member societies (gurdwaras). **Activities** Advocacy/lobbying/activism; humanitarian/emergency aid. **Events** *Seminar* Toronto, ON (Canada) 1997, *International conference / Seminar* Vancouver, BC (Canada) 1995, *Seminar* Toronto, ON (Canada) 1994, *Seminar* Edmonton, AB (Canada) 1993, *Global change* Toronto, ON (Canada) 1992. **Publications** *WSO In Touch* (6 a year); *The Sword* (2 a year).
Members National branches in 10 countries:
Australia, Canada, France, Germany, India, Indonesia, Kenya, Norway, UK, USA.
IGO Relations *Canadian International Development Agency (CIDA, inactive); UNHCR (#20327).* **NGO Relations** Formal contacts with: *Amnesty International (AI, #00801); Human Rights Watch (HRW, #10990),* Asia Division; *Cooperation Canada; Human Rights Internet (HRI, #10986).* [2019/XF0479/**F**]

♦ World Silambam Association (internationally oriented national body)
♦ World Silambam Federation (unconfirmed)
♦ World Simmental Federation / see World Simmental-Fleckvieh Federation (#21785)

♦ World Simmental-Fleckvieh Federation 21785

Fédération mondiale Simmental-Fleckvieh – Federación Simmental-Fleckvieh Mundial – Welt Simmental-Fleckvieh Vereinigung

SG Radesinska Svratka 193, 592 33 Svratka, Czechia. T. +420566620968. Fax +420566620929. E-mail: skopalova@cestr.cz.
URL: http://www.wsff.info/

History 1974, Zagreb (Croatia). 1974, as *World Simmental Federation*, as a result of the European Simmental Federation meeting in Zagreb. Present name adopted, 2002. **Aims** Promote cooperation between breeder organizations; establish common breeding rules; promote information exchange; establish guidelines for the acknowledgement of pedigrees. **Structure** Members' Meeting. Council of 1 delegate per member. President; 2 Vice-Presidents; Secretary-General. **Languages** English, French, German, Spanish. **Staff** 0.50 FTE, paid; 3.00 FTE, voluntary. **Finance** Members' dues. **Events** *World Congress* Vienna (Austria) 2021, *World Congress* Vienna (Austria) 2020, *World Congress* Krakow (Poland) 2016, *World Congress* Bogota (Colombia) 2014, *World Congress* Munich (Germany) 2012.
Members National organizations in 26 countries:
Argentina, Australia, Austria, Brazil, Canada, Colombia, Croatia, Czechia, Denmark, France, Germany, Hungary, Ireland, Italy, Mexico, Namibia, New Zealand, Serbia, Slovakia, Slovenia, South Africa, Sweden, Switzerland, UK, Uruguay, USA.
Observers national organizations in 5 countries:
Bulgaria, Romania, Spain, Zambia, Zimbabwe.
NGO Relations *European Simmental Federation (ESF, #08487).* [2019/XE4574/**E**]

♦ World Sindhi Institute (internationally oriented national body)
♦ **World SIVA ONLUS** World Society of Intravenous Anaesthesia (#21803)

♦ World Skate 21786

SG Maison du Sport International, Av De Rhodanie 54, 1007 Lausanne VD, Switzerland. E-mail: info@worldskate.org.
Vice SG address not obtained.
URL: http://www.worldskate.org/

History 1924, Montreux (Switzerland). Founded as *International Federation of Roller-Skating – Fédération internationale de patinage à roulettes (FIPR).* Subsequently changed title to *International Roller Skating Federation – Fédération internationale de roller-skating – Federación Internacional de Patinaje sobre Ruedas* and later *International Roller Sports Federation – Fédération internationale de roller sports (FIRS).* Current title adopted 2017, when *International Skateboarding Federation (ISF)* merged into the organization. Present statutes adopted 7 Apr 1979, Frankfurt-Main (Germany FR); amended: 11 Sep 1982, Frankfurt-Main; 5 Mar 1983, Fort Worth TX (USA); Jul 1991, Porto (Portugal); 24 Nov 2005, Rome (Italy); 4 Dec 2010, Portimão (Portugal); 23 Feb 2013, Rome (Italy); 21 Feb 2015, Rome (Italy); 11 Mar 2017, Nanjing (China); 3 Sep 2017, Nanjing (China). **Aims** Promote and increase international relations between national federations of roller sports and national and international sport organizations. **Structure** Congress (every 2 years); Elective Congress (every 4 years); Executive Board; World Skate Antidoping Policy; Sports Medicine Commission. World Skate Technical Commissions (9): Artistic; Inline Freestyle; Inline Hockey; Rink Hockey; Roller Alpine and Downhill; Roller Derby; Roller Freestyle; Skateboarding; Speed. **Languages** English, Spanish. **Staff** 7.00 FTE, paid. **Finance** Sources: members' dues. **Activities** Events/meetings; sporting activities; training/education. **Events** *Congress* Rome (Italy) 2021, *Congress* Portimão (Portugal) 2010, *Congress* Rome (Italy) 2009, *Congress* Murcia (Spain) 2006, *Congress* Rome (Italy) 2005. **Publications** *World Skate Bulletin.*
Members National Federations, associations and confederations (one per country unless representing different disciplines) in 109 countries and territories:
Afghanistan, Andorra, Angola, Argentina, Armenia, Australia, Austria, Azerbaijan, Bangladesh, Belarus, Belgium, Benin, Bosnia-Herzegovina, Brazil, Bulgaria, Burkina Faso, Cameroon, Canada, Cayman Is, Chile, China, Colombia, Congo Brazzaville, Costa Rica, Côte d'Ivoire, Croatia, Cuba, Cyprus, Czechia, Denmark, Dominican Rep, Ecuador, Egypt, El Salvador, Estonia, Finland, France, Gabon, Georgia, Germany, Ghana, Great Britain, Greece, Guatemala, Guinea, Haiti, Honduras, Hong Kong, Hungary, India, Indonesia, Iran Islamic Rep, Ireland, Israel, Italy, Japan, Kazakhstan, Kenya, Korea Rep, Latvia, Liberia, Liechtenstein, Macau, Malaysia, Mexico, Moldova, Mozambique, Namibia, Nepal, Netherlands, New Zealand, Nicaragua, Nigeria, Norway, Pakistan, Panama, Paraguay, Peru, Poland, Portugal, Puerto Rico, Romania, Russia, San Marino, Senegal, Serbia, Sierra Leone, Singapore, Slovakia, Slovenia, South Africa, Spain, Sri Lanka, Sudan, Sweden, Switzerland, Taiwan, Tanzania UR, Thailand, Togo, Trinidad-Tobago, Tunisia, Türkiye, Uganda, Ukraine, United Arab Emirates, Uruguay, USA, Venezuela.
Regional confederations (5):
Confédération Européenne de Roller-Skating (CERS, #04550); World Skate Africa (WSA, #21787); World Skate America (WS America, #21788); World Skate Asia; *World Skate Oceania.*
NGO Relations Member of (3): *Association of Summer Olympic International Federations (ASOIF, #02943); Association of the IOC Recognized International Sports Federations (ARISF, #02767); Olympic Movement (#17719).* Cooperates with (1): *International Testing Agency (ITA, #15678).* Recognized by: *International Olympic Committee (IOC, #14408) International World Games Association (IWGA, #15914); Olympic Council of Asia (OCA, #17718); Panam Sports Organization (Panam Sports, #18138).* [2022/XC2421/y/**C**]

♦ World Skate Africa (WSA) 21787

Gen Sec address not obtained. T. +2258562626.
URL: https://worldskate-africa.org/

History Set up as continental federation of: *World Skate (#21786).* Original title: *African Confederation of Sports of Roller Skating (ACRS).* Also referred to as *African Confederation of Roller Skating* and *Federation of African Roller Sports (FARS).* Current title adopted 2017. **Aims** Promote and expand roller *sports* in all possible forms in Africa; promote a clean sport; promote and increase international relations between national federations and other continental sports organizations. **Structure** Congress; Executive Committee; Executive Commission; Technical Committees (4). **Languages** English, French. **Activities** Sporting activities.
Members Organizations in 25 countries:
Angola, Benin, Burkina Faso, Burundi, Cameroon, Congo DR, Côte d'Ivoire, Egypt, Gabon, Ghana, Guinea, Kenya, Liberia, Mozambique, Namibia, Nigeria, Rwanda, Senegal, Sierra Leone, South Africa, Sudan, Tanzania UR, Togo, Tunisia, Uganda. [2019.02.12/XE3689/**E**]

♦ World Skate America (WS America) 21788

Pres Carrera 74 No 25F – 10, Bogota, Bogota DC, Colombia. T. +572950867. E-mail: info@worldskate.org – comunicaciones@worldskateamerica.org.
Exec Dir address not obtained.
URL: https://worldskateamerica.org/

History 1954, Brazil. Current title adopted when merged with *Pan American Confederation of Roller Skating (inactive).* Recognized as continental federation of *World Skate (#21786),* 1956. Former names and other names: *Confederación Sudamericana de Patin (CSP)* – former. **Structure** General Assembly; Executive Committee. Techical Commissions.
Members Affiliate in 22 countries and territories:
Argentina, Bolivia, Brazil, Canada, Chile, Colombia, Costa Rica, Cuba, Dominican Rep, Ecuador, El Salvador, Guatemala, Honduras, Mexico, Nicaragua, Panama, Paraguay, Peru, Puerto Rico, Uruguay, USA, Venezuela.
NGO Relations Member of (2): *Asociación de Confederaciones Deportivas Panamericanas (ACODEPA, #02119); Asociación de Confederaciones Deportivas Sudamericanas (ACODESU, no recent information).* [2023/XD1403/**D**]

♦ World Skate Asia (WSA) 21789

Pres 2 Tiyuguan Rd, Dongcheng District, 100763 Beijing, China. T. +861087182498. E-mail: asia@worldskate.org.
URL: http://www.worldskateasia.com/

History 1978. Founded as continental federation of *World Skate (#21786).* Former names and other names: *Confederation Asia of Roller Skating* – alias; *Confederation Asia of Roller Sports (CARS)* – former; *Confederación Asiatica de Patinaje* – former. **Structure** Central Committee (meets annually). **Events** *Executive Board Meeting* Hangzhou (China) 2022, *Congress* Taipei (Taiwan) 2006, *Congress* Jeonju (Korea Rep) 2005, *Congress* Akita (Japan) 2004, *Congress* Akita (Japan) 2003.
Members Full in 25 countries and territories:
Afghanistan, Armenia, Bangladesh, Cambodia, China, Hong Kong, India, Indonesia, Iran Islamic Rep, Japan, Kazakhstan, Korea Rep, Macau, Malaysia, Myanmar, Nepal, Pakistan, Philippines, Singapore, Sri Lanka, Taiwan, Thailand, Timor-Leste, United Arab Emirates, Vietnam. [2022.10.25/XD1495/**D**]

♦ World Skate Oceania (internationally oriented national body)
♦ World Skating Federation (no recent information)
♦ World Skeptics Conference (meeting series)

♦ WorldSkills Europe 21790

SG Frankrijklaan 8a, 2391 PX Hazerswoude-Dorp, Netherlands. T. +31172211120.
URL: http://www.euroskills.org/

Aims Promote excellence in the field of skills and competence development. **Structure** Board, including President, Secretary and Treasurer. Secretariat, headed by Secretary General. Competition Development Committee. **Activities** Organizes biennial international skills competition. **Events** *General Assembly* Riga (Latvia) 2019, *Euroskills Conference* Budapest (Hungary) 2018, *General Assembly* Namur (Belgium) 2017, *General Assembly* Gothenburg (Sweden) 2016, *General Assembly* Helsinki (Finland) 2015.
Members National organizations in 26 countries:
Australia, Austria, Belgium, Bulgaria, Croatia, Cyprus, Denmark, Estonia, Finland, France, Germany, Hungary, Italy, Latvia, Lithuania, Luxembourg, Malta, Netherlands, Norway, Portugal, Russia, Slovakia, Slovenia, Sweden, Switzerland, UK.
Associate members (4):
Alliance for International Education (AIE); European Builders Confederation (EBC, #06408); European Construction Industry Federation (#06766); International Liaison Centre for Agricultural Machinery Distributors and Maintenance (#14034).
NGO Relations Member of: *WorldSkills International (WSI, #21791).* Partner of: *International Florist Organisation (FLORINT, #13616).* [2013.12.03/XJ5191/y/**D**]

♦ WorldSkills International (WSI) 21791

Dir Keizersgracht 241, 1016 EA Amsterdam, Netherlands. T. +31235311071. Fax +31235310816. E-mail: secretariat@worldskills.org.
URL: http://www.worldskills.org/

History 1950, Madrid (Spain). Founded during 1st International Vocational Training Competition (IVTC). First Organizing Council, Jun 1954. Evolved into *International Vocational Training Organization (IVTO).* First Constitution adopted 25 Sep 1975, Madrid; supplement drawn up 28 Aug 1983, Linz (Austria). Current Constitution ratified at General Assembly, 15 June 2000, Lisbon (Portugal), came into effect 15 June 2000; revised and adapted at General Assemblies of 14 Mar 2002, Auckland (New Zealand), 10 May 2004, Hong Kong, 25 May 2005, Helsinki (Finland) and May 2006, Melbourne (Australia). **Aims** Promote worldwide awareness of the essential contribution that *skills* and high standards of competence make to achievement of economic success and individual fulfillment. **Structure** General Assembly; Board of Directors; Strategy Development Committee; Competitions Committee; Secretariat. **Languages** English. **Staff** 16.60 FTE, paid. **Finance** Sources: meeting proceeds; members' dues; revenue from activities/projects; sponsorship. **Activities** Awards/prizes/competitions; events/meetings; knowledge management/information dissemination. **Events** *General Assembly* Amsterdam (Netherlands) 2020, *General Assembly* Kazan (Russia) 2019, *General Assembly* Amsterdam (Netherlands) 2018, *General Assembly* Abu Dhabi (United Arab Emirates) 2017, *General Assembly* Niagara Falls, ON (Canada) 2016. **Publications** *WSI Updates Newsletter* (10 a year); *GIP Communique* (3-4 a year). Annual Report.
Members Full in 85 countries and territories:
Argentina, Armenia, Australia, Austria, Azerbaijan, Bahrain, Bangladesh, Barbados, Belarus, Belgium, Brazil, Brunei Darussalam, Canada, Chile, China, Colombia, Costa Rica, Croatia, Denmark, Dominican Rep, Ecuador, Egypt, Estonia, Finland, France, Georgia, Germany, Ghana, Hong Kong, Hungary, Iceland, India, Indonesia, Iran Islamic Rep, Ireland, Israel, Jamaica, Japan, Kazakhstan, Kenya, Korea Rep, Kuwait, Latvia, Liechtenstein, Luxembourg, Macau, Malaysia, Mexico, Mongolia, Morocco, Namibia, Netherlands, New Zealand, Norway, Oman, Pakistan, Palestine, Paraguay, Philippines, Poland, Portugal, Romania, Russia, Saudi Arabia, Singapore, South Africa, Spain, Sri Lanka, Sweden, Switzerland, Taiwan, Thailand, Trentino-South Tyrol, Trinidad-Tobago, Tunisia, Türkiye, Uganda, UK, Ukraine, United Arab Emirates, USA, Uzbekistan, Venezuela, Vietnam, Zambia. [2022.12.14/XM3851/**B**]

♦ World Sleddog Association (WSA) 21792

Sec Amorbacher Str 52, 74722 Buchen, Germany. E-mail: secretary@wsa-sleddog.com – office@wsa-sleddog.com.
URL: http://www.wsa-sleddog.com/

History Founded 1995. Current statutes revised Sep 2010, altered Sep 2014 and Jun 2017. Registered in accordance with German law: VR 479. **Aims** Encourage practice and development of the sled dog racing sport with sled dog breeds approved by the FCI (Siberian Husky, Alaskan Malamute, Greenland Hound, Samoyede). **Structure** General Assembly; Executive Committee/Extended Board; Race Directors' Committee. **Finance** Members' dues. **Activities** Events/meetings; awards/prizes/competitions. **Events** *World Championship* Scharnitz (Austria) 2015, *World Championship* Kandersteg (Switzerland) 2014, *European Championship* Germany 2013, *World Championship* Zuberec (Slovakia) 2012, *European Championship* Italy 2011. **Publications** *WSA Newsletter.*
Members National organizations in 33 countries and territories:
Andorra, Australia, Austria, Belarus, Belgium, Czechia, Denmark, Estonia, Finland, France, Germany, Great Britain, Hungary, Ireland, Italy, Latvia, Liechtenstein, Lithuania, Netherlands, New Zealand, Norway, Poland, Romania, Russia, Scotland, Serbia, Slovakia, Slovenia, South Africa, Spain, Sweden, Switzerland, Ukraine.
NGO Relations Member of: *International Federation of Sleddog Sports (IFSS, #13541).* [2018/XM1921/**D**]

♦ World Sleep Federation – World Federation of Sleep Research and Sleep Medicine Societies (inactive)

♦ World Sleep Society 21793

Exec Dir 3270 19th St NW, Ste 109, Rochester MN 55901, USA. T. +15073160084. E-mail: info@worldsleepsociety.org.
URL: https://worldsleepsociety.org/

History 2016. Founded on merger of *World Federation of Sleep Research and Sleep Medicine Societies (World Sleep Federation, inactive)* and *World Association of Sleep Medicine (WASM, inactive).* Registration: 501(c)(3), USA. **Aims** Advance sleep health worldwide. **Structure** Governing Council; Executive Committee. Committees. **Activities** Events/meetings. **Events** *World Sleep Congress* 2025, *World Sleep Congress* Rio de Janeiro (Brazil) 2023, *World Sleep Congress* Rome (Italy) 2022, *World Sleep Congress* Rio de Janeiro (Brazil) 2021, *World Sleep Congress* Vancouver, BC (Canada) 2019. **Publications** *Sleep Medicine Journal.*
Members Associate members in 23 countries and territories:
Australia, Austria, Brazil, Bulgaria, Canada, Czechia, Finland, France, Georgia, Germany, Hong Kong, India, Israel, Japan, Morocco, Peru, Romania, Russia, Serbia, Taiwan, Türkiye, UK, USA.
Regional Associate members (10):
ASEAN Sleep Federation; *Asian Sleep Research Society (ASRS, #01701); Asian Society of Sleep Medicine (ASSM, #01738); Australasian Sleep Association (ASA); European Academy of Dental Sleep Medicine (EADSM, #05786); European Restless Legs Syndrome Study Group (EURLSSG, #08384); European Sleep Research Society (ESRS, #08493); International Pediatric Sleep Association (IPSA, #14547); International Restless Legs Syndrome Study Group (IRLSSG); World Sleep Society (#21793).* [2022/XM8467/**C**]

♦ World Slingshot Sports Federation (WSSF) 21794

Contact 101 A-2 Megh Dhanush Apt, Citylight, Surat, Gujarat 395007, Surat GUJARAT 395007, India. E-mail: worldslingshot@gmail.com.
URL: https://www.worldslingshot.org/

Aims Manage, direct, promote, organize and assist the activities and disciplines associated with Slingshot worldwide. **Structure** Board.
Members National federations in 8 countries:
Afghanistan, India, Italy, Nepal, Pakistan, Poland, Switzerland, Türkiye.
NGO Relations Member of (1): *International Sport Network Organization (ISNO, #15592).* [AA1072/**D**]

♦ World Small Animal Veterinary Association (WSAVA) 21795

Association mondiale vétérinaire de petits animaux – Asociación Mundial Veterinaria de Pequeños Animales (AMVPA) – Tierärztlicher-Weltverein der Kleintier-Spezialisten

Exec Dir 72 Melville St, Dundas ON L9H 2A1, Canada. T. +447986797378. E-mail: admin@wsava.org – yourwsava@wsava.org.
URL: http://www.wsava.org/

History 1959, Madrid (Spain). Founded during International Congress of Veterinarians. **Aims** Advance the health and welfare of companion animals worldwide through an educated, committed and collaborative global community of veterinary peers. **Structure** Assembly; Executive Board; Committees (15). **Languages** English. **Staff** 4.00 FTE, paid; 7.00 FTE, voluntary. **Finance** Sources: members' dues; sponsorship. **Activities** Advocacy/lobbying/activism; events/meetings; guidance/assistance/consulting; projects/programmes; standards/guidelines; training/education. **Events** *Annual Congress* Warsaw (Poland) 2027, *Annual Congress* Hyderabad (India) 2026, *Annual Congress* Rio de Janeiro (Brazil) 2025, *Annual Congress* Shanghai (China) 2024, *Annual Congress* Lisbon (Portugal) 2023. **Publications** *WSAVA Bulletin* (regular); *Global Clinicians Brief*. Congress proceedings; various reports.
Members National and specialist small animal veterinary associations in 86 countries and territories:
Argentina, Armenia, Australia, Austria, Belarus, Belgium, Bosnia-Herzegovina, Botswana, Brazil, Bulgaria, Cambodia, Canada, China, Colombia, Costa Rica, Croatia, Cuba, Czechia, Denmark, Ecuador, Estonia, Finland, France, Georgia, Germany, Ghana, Greece, Guatemala, Hong Kong, Hungary, India, Indonesia, Iran Islamic Rep, Ireland, Israel, Italy, Jamaica, Japan, Kenya, Korea Rep, Latvia, Lebanon, Lithuania, Luxembourg, Malaysia, Mexico, Mongolia, Montenegro, Morocco, Namibia, Nepal, Netherlands, New Zealand, Nigeria, North Macedonia, Norway, Pakistan, Paraguay, Peru, Philippines, Poland, Portugal, Romania, Russia, Serbia, Singapore, Slovakia, Slovenia, South Africa, Spain, Sri Lanka, Sweden, Switzerland, Taiwan, Tanzania UR, Thailand, Tunisia, Türkiye, UK, Ukraine, United Arab Emirates, USA, Venezuela, Vietnam, Zambia, Zimbabwe.
Included in the above, 1 organization listed in this Yearbook:
International Veterinary Students' Association (IVSA, #15851).
Affiliate (19), including 8 organizations listed in this Yearbook:
Commonwealth Veterinary Association (CVA, #04366); Health for Animals (#10870); International Society of Feline Medicine (ISFM, #15116); International Society of Veterinary Ophthalmology (ISVO, #15541); International Veterinary Academy of Pain Management (IVAPM); International Veterinary Ear, Nose and Throat Association (IVENTA, #15849); Latin American Veterinary Emergency and Critical Care Society (LAVECCS, #16392); World Aquatic Veterinary Medical Association (WAVMA, #21101).
NGO Relations Member of (1): *International Companion Animal Management Coalition (ICAM, #12828).* Instrumental in setting up (1): *European Society of Veterinary Dermatology (ESVD, #08777).* [2022.03.01/XC3580/y/**B**]

♦ World Snooker Federation / see World Professional Billiards and Snooker Association (#21740)

♦ World Snooker Federation (WSF) 21796

Gen Sec address not obtained. T. +33611314641. E-mail: maximecassis@gmail.com.
Registered Office c/o Onside Law Ltd, Rue du Mont-Blanc 15, 1201 Geneva, Switzerland.
URL: http://www.worldsnookerfederation.org/

History Set up 2017. Registered in accordance with Swiss Civil Code. **Structure** Council; Board of Directors. **Activities** Sporting activities.
Members National federations; regional bodies. National in 5 countries and territories:
China, Kyrgyzstan, Singapore, Thailand, United Arab Emirates.
Regional associations (4):
African Billiards and Snooker Confederation (ABSC, #00221); European Billiards and Snooker Association (EBSA, #06330); Oceania Billiards and Snooker Federation (OBSF); Pan American Billiards and Snooker Association (PABSA).
NGO Relations *World Professional Billiards and Snooker Association (WPBSA, #21740).* [2020.03.03/XM6736/y/**C**]

♦ World Social Forum (WSF) 21797

Forum social mondial – Fórum Social Mundial – Fórum Social Mundialé

Address not obtained.
URL: http://www.worldsocialforum.org/

History 2001. Founded as a response to *World Economic Forum (WEF, #21367).* **Aims** Serve as a forum for creation and exchange of social and *economic* projects promoting human rights, social justice and sustainable development. **Structure** International Council. Working Groups. Secretariat. **Events** *World Social Forum* 2021, *World Social Forum* Salvador (Brazil) 2018, *World Social Forum* Montréal, QC (Canada) 2016, *World Social Forum* Tunis (Tunisia) 2015, *Meeting* Hammamet (Tunisia) 2014. **Publications** *WSF Bulletin.*
Members Delegates (131) to the International Council, including 71 international organizations listed in this Yearbook:
- *50 Years Is Enough – US Network for Global Economic Justice;*
- *ACT Alliance EU (#00082);*
- *Africa Trade Network (ATN, #00526);*
- *Agencia Latinoamericana de Información (ALAI, #00551);*
- *Arab NGO Network for Environment and Development (RAED, #01017);*
- *Asian Regional Exchange for New Alternatives (ARENA, #01684);*
- *Asia Pacific Solidarity Network (APSN);*
- *Asociación Latinoamericana de Micro, Pequeños y Medianos Empresarios (ALAMPYME, no recent information);*
- *Asociación Latinoamericana de Organizaciones de Promoción (ALOP, inactive);*
- *Association for Progressive Communications (APC, #02873);*
- *Association for the Taxation of Financial Transactions for the Aid of Citizens (#02947);*
- *Association mondiale des radiodiffuseurs communautaires (AMARC, #02810);*
- *Caritas Internationalis (CI, #03580);*
- *Cedar International (no recent information);*
- *CEE Bankwatch Network (#03624);*
- *Centre de recherche et d'information pour le développement, Paris (CRID);*
- *Centre d'études et initiatives de solidarité internationale (CEDETIM);*
- *Centre tricontinental (CETRI);*
- *CIDSE (CIDSE, #03926);*
- *Comité pour l'annulation de la dette du Tiers-monde (CADTM, #04148);*
- *Confederación Sindical de Trabajadores y Trabajadoras de las Américas (CSA, #04480);*
- *Consejo de Educación de Adultos de América Latina (CEAAL, #04707);*
- *Consejo Latinoamericano de Ciencias Sociales (CLACSO, #04718);*
- *Convergencia de Movimientos de los Pueblos de las Américas (COMPA, no recent information);*
- *CorpWatch;*
- *Development Alternatives with Women for a New Era (DAWN, #05054);*
- *Environnement et développement du Tiers-monde (enda, #05510);*
- *Escarre International Centre for the Ethnic Minorities and Nations (#05535);*
- *European Assembly of Citizens (EAC, #05922);*
- *European Marches Against Unemployment, Job Insecurity and Social Exclusions (Euromarches, #07735);*
- *European Trade Union Confederation (ETUC, #08927);*
- *FIAN International (#09743);*
- *Focus on the Global South (Focus, #09807);*
- *Friends of the Earth International (FoEI, #10002);*
- *General Union of Arab Peasants and Agricultural Cooperatives (GUAAPC, no recent information);*
- *Global Exchange (GX);*
- *Greenpeace International (#10727);*
- *Grupo de Trabalho Amazônico (GTA);*
- *Habitat International Coalition (HIC, #10845);*
- *Institute for Agriculture and Trade Policy (IATP);*
- *Instituto Paulo Freire (IPF);*
- *International Council for Adult Education (ICAE, #12983);*
- *International Federation for Human Rights (#13452);*
- *International Forum on Globalization (IFG, #13637);*
- *International Gender and Trade Network (IGTN, #13707);*
- *International Network of Street Papers (INSP, #14330);*
- *International Peace Bureau (IPB, #14535);*
- *International Trade Union Confederation (ITUC, #15708);*
- *IPS – Inter Press Service International Association (#16013);*
- *Latin American Women's Network to Transform the Economy (#16395);*
- *La Via Campesina (#20765);*
- *Network Institute for Global Democratization (NIGD);*
- *OneWorld International Foundation (OWIF, #17738);*
- *Organisation of African Trade Union Unity (OATUU, #17798);*
- *Organización Continental Latinoamericana y Caribeña de Estudiantes (OCLAE, #17834);*
- *Oxfam International (#17922);*
- *Peace Boat;*
- *Plataforma Interamericana de Derechos Humanos, Democracia y Desarrollo (PIDHDD, #18395);*
- *Red de Educación Popular entre Mujeres de América Latina y el Caribe (REPEM LAC, #18647);*
- *Rede Latino-Americana e Caribenha de Mulheres Negras (CRIOLA);*
- *Réseau agriculture paysanne et modernisation Afrique (Réseau APM, no recent information);*
- *Social Watch (#19350);*
- *Third World Network (TWN, #20151);*
- *Transnational Institute (TNI, #20219);*
- *UBUNTU – World Forum of Civil Society Networks (inactive);*
- *Women's Global Network for Reproductive Rights (WGNRR, #21019);*
- *Women's International Democratic Federation (WIDF, #21022);*
- *World Council of Churches (WCC, #21320);*
- *World Fair Trade Organization (WFTO, #21396);*
- *World Federation of Democratic Youth (WFDY, #21427);*
- *World Forum for Alternatives (WFA, #21513).*

Observers include 4 organizations listed in this Yearbook:
African Social Forum (ASF, #00457); Americas Social Forum (ASF, no recent information); Foro Social Mediterraneo (FSMed, no recent information); Foro Social Pan-Amazônico (FSPA, #09889).
NGO Relations Instrumental in setting up: *Foro de Autoridades Locales por la Inclusión Social y la Democracia Participativa (FAL, #09876); Global Call for Action Against Poverty (GCAP, #10263).* [2021/XF1490/y/**F**]

♦ World Social Forum of Transformative Economies (meeting series)
♦ World Social Marketing (unconfirmed)
♦ World Social Prospects Study Association (inactive)
♦ World Society on Abdominal Compartment Syndrome / see WSACS – the Abdominal Compartment Society (#21963)

♦ World Society of Anti-Aging Medicine (WOSAAM) 21798

Pres c/o Euromedicom, 2 rue de Lisbonne, 75008 Paris, France. T. +33156837800. Fax +33156837805. E-mail: wosaam@wosaam.ws.
URL: https://www.wosaam.ws/

Aims Promote anti-aging medicine through research and educational events among physicians and for the general public. **Structure** Board of Directors, comprising President, President of Honour, 2 Vice-Presidents, Secretary, Vice-Secretary, Treasurer, Adjunct Treasurer. **Activities** Organizes: Anti-Aging Medicine World Congress; International Congress in Aesthetic Anti-Aging Medicine (ICAAM); European Masters in Anti-Aging and Aesthetic Medicine (EMMA) Congress; Pan-American Congress on Aesthetic and Anti-Aging Medicine (PACAAM); Asian International Congress in Aesthetic Anti-Aging Medicine (AICAAM); European Congress on Anti-Aging and Aesthetic Medicine (ECAAM). **Events** *Anti-Aging Medicine World Congress* Monte Carlo (Monaco) 2019, *Anti-Aging Medicine World Congress* Monte Carlo (Monaco) 2016, *Anti-Aging Medicine World Congress* Monte Carlo (Monaco) 2015, *Anti-Aging Medicine World Congress* Monte Carlo (Monaco) 2014, *World Congress* Monte Carlo (Monaco) 2014. [2020/XM0172/**D**]

♦ World Society of Arrhythmias (WSA) 21799

Pres Cardiovascular Dept, S Filippo Neri Hosp, Via G Martinotti 20, 00135 Rome RM, Italy. T. +39633062294. Fax +39633062489.
URL: http://www.wsa-icpes.net/

History 1973, Groningen (Netherlands), as *International Cardiac Pacing Society.* Subsequently changed title to *International Cardiac Pacing and Electrophysiology Society (ICPES).* Current title adopted Jan 2011. **Aims** Promote worldwide education in the fields of cardiac pacing and electrophysiology. **Structure** Executive Committee, comprising President, Secretary General, Secretary General Elect and Immediate Past President. **Activities** Organizes *World Symposium on Cardiac Pacing*, a series of symposia since 1963. **Events** *World Congress of Arrhythmias* Buenos Aires (Argentina) 2019, *World Congress on Cardiac Arrhythmias, Pacing and Electrophysiology / World Symposium* Beijing (China) 2015, *World Symposium* Athens (Greece) 2011, *World Symposium* Rome (Italy) 2007, *International workshop on arrhythmias* Venice (Italy) 2007. **Publications** *Pacing and Clinical Electrophysiology* (12 a year). [2019/XD9035/**D**]

♦ World Society for Breast Health (inactive)
♦ World Society of Cardio-Thoracic Surgeons / see World Society of Cardiovascular & Thoracic Surgeons (#21800)
♦ World Society of Cardio-Vascular and Thoracic Surgeons / see World Society of Cardiovascular & Thoracic Surgeons (#21800)

♦ World Society of Cardiovascular & Thoracic Surgeons (WSCTS) ... 21800

SG Royal Infirmary of Edinburgh, Little France Crescent, Edinburgh, EH16 4SU, UK. T. +441315361000. E-mail: wscts@wscts.net.
Chancellor Chief – Cardiovascular and Thoracic Surgery, Univ of California – San Diego, 200 West Arbor Drive – Suite 8892, San Diego CA 92103-8892, USA. T. +16195437777.
URL: http://www.wscts.org/

History 21 Apr 1988, Niigata (Japan). Founded by Prof Juro Wada leading personalities in the field in Japan. Formal constitution: 30 Jul 1988. Former names and other names: *International Society of Cardio-Thoracic Surgeons (ISCTS)* – former (21 Apr 1988); *International Society of Cardio-Thoracic Surgeons – of Japan* – alias; *World Society of Cardio-Thoracic Surgeons* – former; *World Society of Cardio-Vascular and Thoracic Surgeons (WSCTS)* – former (2016). **Aims** Promote and advance the practice of *cardiovascular* and thoracic surgery; facilitate international exchange of knowledge and ideas. **Structure** General Meeting, at the time of Annual Conference; Steering Committee. **Languages** English. **Staff** None. **Finance** Sources: donations; members' dues. **Activities** Advisory committee on scientific controversies. Awards travel stipends. **Events** *World Congress* Barcelona (Spain) 2024, *World Congress* Brazil 2023, *World Congress* St Petersburg (Russia) 2022, *World Congress* St Petersburg (Russia) 2021, *World Congress* St Petersburg (Russia) 2020. **Publications** *WSCTS Journal.*
Members Honorary Founding; Honorary; Founding; Active; Senior; Life; Endowment Fund; Associate; Supporting. Senior surgeons in 56 countries and territories:
Argentina, Australia, Austria, Belgium, Brazil, Bulgaria, Canada, Chile, China, Cuba, Czechia, Denmark, Egypt, Finland, France, Germany, Greece, Hong Kong, Hungary, India, Indonesia, Iran Islamic Rep, Iraq, Ireland, Israel, Italy, Jamaica, Korea Rep, Lithuania, Malaysia, Mexico, Monaco, Nepal, Netherlands, Nigeria, Norway, Pakistan, Peru, Philippines, Poland, Portugal, Puerto Rico, Romania, Russia, Saudi Arabia, Singapore, South Africa, Spain, Sri Lanka, Sweden, Switzerland, Syrian AR, Taiwan, UK, Uruguay, Venezuela. [2021/XD2609/**C**]

♦ World Society for Chinese Language Teaching / see International Society for Chinese Language Teaching

♦ World Society for Ekistics (WSE) 21801

Société mondiale d'ékistique – Sociedad Mundial de Ekistica

Contact c/o India House, Pune, Maharashtra 411045, Pune MAHARASHTRA 411045, India.

History 1963, Athens (Greece). Founded Feb 1965, Athens (Greece), preliminary conferences having been held: 1963, Delos (Greece); 1964, the Aegean (Greece). Constitution adopted 29 Jul 1967, Athens, and incorporated under Greek law; incorporated 26 Mar 1970, in the State of Delaware (USA). Current statutes adopted 15 May 1975, Arc-et-Senans (France). **Aims** Promote development of knowledge and ideas concerning human *settlements*; encourage development and expansion of education in ekistics; educate public opinion concerning the subject; recognize and promote the benefits and necessity of an inter-disciplinary approach to the needs of human settlements. **Structure** General Assembly (annual); Executive Council. **Languages** English. **Staff** 5.00 FTE, paid; 6.00 FTE, voluntary. **Finance** Sources: members' dues. **Activities** Events/meetings; publishing activities; research/documentation. **Events** *Annual International Meeting* Bogota (Colombia) 2014, *Annual International Meeting* Ankara (Turkey) 2013, *Annual International Meeting* Naples (Italy) 2012, *Annual International Meeting* Athens (Greece) 2011, *Annual International Meeting* Mumbai (India) / Pune (India) / Aurangabad (India) 2010.
Members Individuals in 46 countries and territories:
Australia, Austria, Belgium, Brazil, Canada, China, Colombia, Cuba, Cyprus, Czechia, Denmark, Ethiopia, Fiji, Finland, France, Germany, Ghana, Greece, Hungary, India, Ireland, Israel, Italy, Japan, Kenya, Mauritius, Mexico, Netherlands, New Zealand, Nigeria, Norway, Pakistan, Panama, Peru, Poland, Portugal, Saudi Arabia, Serbia, Singapore, Spain, Sudan, Sweden, Taiwan, Türkiye, UK, USA.
Consultative Status Consultative status granted from: *ECOSOC (#05331)* (Ros B). **IGO Relations** Associated with Department of Global Communications of the United Nations. **NGO Relations** Member of: *Conference of Non-Governmental Organizations in Consultative Relationship with the United Nations (CONGO, #04635)*; *EarthAction (EA, #05159)*. [2020.03.09/XC3581/v/**C**]

♦ World Society of Emergency Surgery (WSES) 21802

Gen Sec Via Cracovia 23, 40139 Bologna BO, Italy. E-mail: info@wses.org.uk.
URL: https://www.wses.org.uk/
History 28 May 2007. Registration: Italy. **Structure** General Assembly; Board of Directors. **Finance** Sources: members' dues. **Activities** Awards/prizes/competitions; events/meetings; training/education. **Events** *Congress* Bologna (Italy) 2020, *Congress* Nijmegen (Netherlands) 2019, *Congress* Bertinoro (Italy) 2018, *Congress* Campinas (Brazil) 2017, *Congress* Jerusalem (Israel) 2015. **Publications** *World Journal of Emergency Surgery*. **NGO Relations** Member of (1): *World Coalition for Trauma Care (WCTC, #21282)*. [2020/AA1218/**C**]

♦ World Society for Endoscopic, Navigated and Minimal Invasive Spine Surgery (inactive)
♦ World Society of Endoscopy, Endobiopsy and Digestive Cytology (inactive)

♦ World Society of Intravenous Anaesthesia (World SIVA ONLUS) 21803

Pres Via Dardanelli 23, 00195 Rome RM, Italy. T. +3966149007. Fax +39661007841.
URL: http://www.worldsiva.org/
History 28 Sep 2007, Venice (Italy). Founded 28 Sep 07, Venice (Italy), during 1st World Congress. Registered in accordance with Italian law. **Aims** Improve the standard of intravenous anaesthesia. **Structure** General Assembly; Board of Directors; Executive Committee; Commissions; International Sedation Taskforce. **Languages** English, French, Italian, Spanish. **Staff** 2.00 FTE, paid. **Finance** Sources: donations; members' dues. **Activities** Events/meetings; training/education. **Events** *World Congress of Total Intravenous Anaesthesia and Target Controlled Infusion (SIVA-TCI)* Antalya (Turkey) 2020, *World Congress of Total Intravenous Anaesthesia and Target Controlled Infusion (SIVA-TCI)* Kuala Lumpur (Malaysia) 2018, *World Congress of Total Intravenous Anaesthesia and Target Controlled Infusion* Timisoara (Romania) 2017, *World Congress of Total Intravenous Anaesthesia and Target Controlled Infusion* Sofia (Bulgaria) 2014, *World congress of total intravenous anaesthesia and target controlled infusion* Singapore (Singapore) 2011. **Publications** Abstracts; articles.
Members Full in 75 countries and territories:
Albania, Argentina, Australia, Austria, Azerbaijan, Belgium, Bolivia, Bosnia-Herzegovina, Brazil, Bulgaria, Burundi, Cambodia, Canada, Chile, China, Colombia, Cuba, Cyprus, Czechia, Denmark, Egypt, El Salvador, Estonia, Finland, France, Germany, Gibraltar, Greece, Hong Kong, Hungary, India, Indonesia, Iran Islamic Rep, Ireland, Israel, Italy, Japan, Kenya, Korea Rep, Kosovo, Laos, Liberia, Lithuania, Malaysia, Mexico, Moldova, Netherlands, New Zealand, Nigeria, Norway, Palestine, Peru, Philippines, Poland, Portugal, Qatar, Romania, Russia, Saudi Arabia, Serbia, Sierra Leone, Singapore, Slovakia, Slovenia, South Africa, Spain, Sweden, Switzerland, Taiwan, Thailand, Türkiye, UK, United Arab Emirates, USA, Vietnam. [2021/XM8233/**C**]

♦ World Society of Lingual Orthodontics (WSLO) 21804

Pres E-line Office, 2-5-7 Kudan-minmi, Chiyoda-ku, Tokyo, 102-0074 Japan.
Registered Office c/o KPMG Private, Chemin De-Normandie 14, 1207 Geneva, Switzerland.
URL: http://www.wslo.org/
History 2004. **Aims** Advance the art and science of lingual orthodontics worldwide. **Structure** General Assembly. Board. **Languages** English. **Events** *Congress* Barcelona (Spain) 2019, *Congress* Bangkok (Thailand) 2017, *Congress* Seoul (Korea Rep) 2015, *Congress* Paris (France) 2013, *Congress* Osaka (Japan) 2011.
Members Affiliated societies (10) in 9 countries:
Argentina, Brazil, Greece, India, Israel, Italy, Japan, Korea Rep, Spain.
NGO Relations *Sociedad Iberoamericana de Ortodoncia Lingual, Oclusión y Estética (SIAOL, no recent information)*. [2011/XM3450/**D**]

♦ World Society of Medical Qigong / see World Academic Society of Medical Qigong (#21064)
♦ World Society of Micro-Implant Anchorage (unconfirmed)

♦ World Society of Mixed Jurisdiction Jurists (WSMJJ) 21805

Gen Sec USP Emalus Campus, Port Vila, Vanuatu.
URL: http://www.mixedjurisdiction.org/
History 9 Nov 2002, New Orleans LA (USA), during 1st World Congress on Mixed Jurisdictions. Registered in the State of Louisiana. **Aims** Study and advance mixed legal systems. **Structure** General Meeting (every 4 years). Executive Committee, comprising President, up to 5 Vice-Presidents, Treasurer and General Secretary. **Languages** English. **Finance** Members' dues. **Events** *Quadrennial World Congress* Montréal, QC (Canada) 2015, *Quadrennial World Congress* Montréal, QC (Canada) 2015, *Quadrennial world congress* Jerusalem (Israel) 2011, *Joint colloquium* Stellenbosch (South Africa) 2009, *Quadrennial world congress* Edinburgh (UK) 2007. **Publications** *WSMJJ Newsletter*. Congress papers.
Members Individuals in 29 countries and territories:
Argentina, Australia, Austria, Botswana, Canada, Cyprus, Czechia, Denmark, Germany, Hong Kong, Hungary, Ireland, Israel, Italy, Japan, Macau, Malta, Peru, Philippines, Poland, Puerto Rico, Seychelles, South Africa, Sri Lanka, Switzerland, Thailand, Trinidad-Tobago, UK, USA.
Organizations (4), including 2 organizations listed in this Yearbook:
Académie internationale de droit comparé (AIDC, #00027); *International Association of Legal Science (IALS, #11997)*. [2014/XM1885/**D**]

♦ World Society for Mushroom Biology and Mushroom Products (WSMBMP) 21806

Treas Inst Edible Fungi, Shanghai Ac of Agricultural Sciences, Room 101 No 12 Bldg, 1000 Jinqi Road, 201403 Shanghai, China. E-mail: wsmbmp@126.com.
URL: http://www.wsmbmp.org/
History 1 Jan 1994. Founded following 1st International Conference on Mushroom Biology and Mushroom Products, Aug 1993, Hong Kong. **Aims** Provide a forum for enhancement and application of knowledge relating to basic and applied aspects of mushroom biology. **Structure** Council. **Languages** English. **Staff** Voluntary. **Finance** Sources: members' dues. **Activities** Events/meetings; training/education. **Events** *International Conference on Mushroom Biology and Mushroom Products* Shanghai (China) 2018, *International Conference on Mushroom Biology and Mushroom Products* Delhi (India) 2014, *International conference on mushroom biology and mushroom products / Conference* Bordeaux (France) 2011, *International conference on mushroom biology and mushroom products / Conference* Bonn (Germany) 2008, *International conference on mushroom biology and mushroom products / Conference* Shanghai (China) 2005. **Publications** *WSMBMP Bulletin*.
Members Scientists and other concerned individuals in 46 countries and territories:
Argentina, Australia, Bangladesh, Belgium, Brazil, Canada, China, Dominica, Ecuador, Egypt, France, Germany, Ghana, Guam, Hong Kong, India, Indonesia, Israel, Italy, Jamaica, Japan, Kenya, Korea Rep, Malaysia, Mauritius, Mexico, Nepal, Netherlands, New Zealand, Nigeria, Pakistan, Peru, Philippines, Poland, Singapore, South Africa, Spain, Sri Lanka, Sweden, Taiwan, Thailand, Uganda, UK, Ukraine, USA, Vietnam. [2022.02.07/XC0036/v/**C**]

♦ World Society of Paediatric Ophthalmology and Strabismus (WSPOS) 21807

Contact Temple House, Temple Road, Blackrock, Dublin, CO. DUBLIN, Ireland. T. +35312883630. Fax +35312091112. E-mail: wspos@wspos.org.
URL: http://wspos.org/
History UK Registered Charity. **Aims** Advance education of healthcare professionals in all aspects of treatment of paediatric eye disease and paediatric and adult strabismus; promote information exchange, debate and research. **Structure** Scientific Bureau; Executive Bureau; Ethics Bureau; Secretariat. **Events** *World Wide Connect Meeting* Dublin (Ireland) 2020, *WSPO and Strabismus Subspecialty Meeting* Vienna (Austria) 2018, *Congress* Hyderabad (India) 2017, *Congress* Barcelona (Spain) 2015, *World Congress* Milan (Italy) 2012.
Members Societies in 36 countries and territories:
Argentina, Australia, Austria, Brazil, Canada, China, Colombia, Czechia, Denmark, Dominican Rep, Egypt, Greece, Hungary, India, Indonesia, Iraq, Israel, Italy, Japan, Jordan, Lebanon, Libya, Malaysia, Mexico, New Zealand, Nigeria, Philippines, Portugal, Russia, Singapore, South Africa, Spain, Taiwan, Thailand, Türkiye, Ukraine, USA.
Included in the above, 5 organizations listed in this Yearbook:
European Paediatric Ophthalmological Society (EPOS, #08127); *International Orthoptic Association (IOA, #14489)*; *International Society for Genetic Eye Diseases and Retinoblastoma (ISGEDR, #15139)*; *Middle East African Council of Ophthalmology (MEACO, #16752)*; *Sociedad de Oftalmologia Pediatrica Latinoamericana (SOPLA, #19430)*. [2021/XJ9231/y/**C**]

♦ World Society of Pain Clinicians (WSPC) 21808

Sec AMPHIA Hosp, Pain Clinic, Pain Management and Research, Langendijk 75, 4819 EV Breda, Netherlands.
URL: http://www.painclinicians.org/
Aims Unite clinicians with a common interest in the treatment of pain; stimulate education and learning in the field of pain; encourage dissemination of information on pain worldwide. **Structure** General Assembly (every 2 years, at Congress). Board of Directors, comprising President; President-Elect; Immediate Past-President; Secretary; Treasurer and 5 further members. Chapters (2): Italy; Korea Rep. **Finance** Members' dues. Income from meetings. **Events** *Biennial Congress* Miami, FL (USA) 2015, *Biennial Congress* Granada (Spain) 2012, *Asian congress on pain / Biennial Congress* Beijing (China) 2010, *Biennial congress* Beijing (China) 2010, *Biennial Congress* Seoul (Korea Rep) 2008. [2015/XD9490/**D**]

♦ World Society for Pediatric and Congenital Heart Surgery (WSPCHS) 21809

Exec Dir address not obtained. E-mail: contact@wspchs.org.
URL: http://www.wspchs.org/
History Registered in accordance with Canadian law, 7 Apr 2011. **Aims** Promote the highest quality comprehensive cardiac care to all patients with congenital heart disease, from the fetus to the adult, regardless of the patient's economic means, with an emphasis on excellence in teaching, research and community service. **Structure** Officers. **NGO Relations** *European Congenital Heart Surgeons Association (ECHSA, #06739)*; *Sociedad Latina Cardiologia y Cirugia Cardiovascular Pediatrica (SLCCCP)*. [2022/XJ9356/**C**]

♦ World Society of Pediatric Infectious Diseases (WSPID) 21810

Pres Dept Paediatrics and Child Health, Fac of Medicine and Health Sciences, Stellenbosch Univ, Stellenbosch Central, Stellenbosch, South Africa. E-mail: mcot@sun.ac.za.
URL: http://www.wspid.com/
History 1994, USA. Registered in accordance with Mexican and USA law. **Aims** Promote cooperation among specialists in the field of paediatric infectious diseases worldwide. **Structure** Officers: President, Vice-President, Secretary and Treasurer. Representatives of the 6 leading PID Societies worldwide. **Languages** English. **Staff** Voluntary. **Finance** Sources: meeting proceeds; sponsorship. **Events** *World Congress* 2022, *World Congress* Cancún (Mexico) 2021, *World Congress* Manila (Philippines) 2019, *World Congress* Shenzhen (China) 2017, *World Congress* Rio de Janeiro (Brazil) 2015.
Members PID societies (6):
African Society for Paediatric Infectious Diseases (AfSPID, #00466); *Asian Society of Pediatric Infectious Diseases (ASPID, #01733)*; Australian and New Zealand Paediatric Infectious Diseases Group (ANZPID); *European Society for Paediatric Infectious Diseases (ESPID, #08682)*; Pediatric Infectious Diseases Society (PIDS) – North America. [2020.02.11/XC0094/y/**B**]

♦ World Society for the Protection of Animals / see World Animal Protection (#21092)

♦ World Society for Reconstructive Microsurgery (WSRM) 21811

Head Office 20 N Michigan Ave, Ste 700, Chicago IL 60602, USA. Fax +13127820553.
URL: http://www.wsrm.net/
History 1999, San Francisco, CA (USA). Founded on merger of *International Society for Microsurgery (inactive)* and *International Society for Reconstructive Microsurgery (ISRM, inactive)*. **Aims** Unite surgeons practising in the fields of *orthopaedics* and plastic and *maxillofacial* and head and neck surgery using vascular, nerve and lymphatic microsurgery. **Structure** General Assembly; Officers. **Languages** English. **Finance** Sources: members' dues. **Activities** Events/meetings; training/education. **Events** *Congress of the World Society for Reconstructive Microsurgery* Cancún (Mexico) 2022, *Congress of the World Society for Reconstructive Microsurgery* Cancún (Mexico) 2021, *Great achievements through narrow paths* Bologna (Italy) 2019, *Congress* Seoul (Korea Rep) 2017, *Congress* Mumbai (India) 2015. **Publications** *International Journal of Reconstructive Microsurgery*; *Microsurgery*.
Members Individual surgeons in 37 countries and territories:
Argentina, Australia, Austria, Belgium, Brazil, Canada, China, Colombia, Czechia, Denmark, Finland, France, Germany, Greece, India, Iran Islamic Rep, Israel, Italy, Japan, Jordan, Korea Rep, Lebanon, Netherlands, New Zealand, Russia, Serbia, Singapore, South Africa, Spain, Sweden, Switzerland, Taiwan, Thailand, UK, Uruguay, USA, Venezuela.
NGO Relations Affiliated with (1): *International Society of Orthopaedic Surgery and Traumatology (#15335)*. [2021/XD7259/v/**C**]

♦ World Society for Stereotactic and Functional Neurosurgery (WSSFN) 21812

Société mondiale de neurochirurgie stéréotatique et fonctionnelle
Sec Service de Neurochirurgie Fonctionnelle and Stéréotaxique, Hôpital de la Timone, 264 bvd Saint Pierre, 13385 Marseille CEDEX 05, France. T. +33491387058. Fax +33491387056.
Pres Dept Neurosurgery, Yonsei Univ College of Medicine, 250 Seongsanno, Seodaemun-gu, Seoul 120-752, Korea Rep. T. +82222282159. Fax +8223939979.
URL: http://www.wssfn.org/
History 1963, as *International Society for Research in Stereoencephalotomy – Société internationale de recherche en stéréoencéphalotomie*. Present title adopted 10 Sep 1973, Tokyo (Japan). **Aims** Advance research, studies and procedures in stereotactic and functional neurosurgery; foster the study and teaching of better treatment of persons afflicted with injuries, lesions, diseases and abnormalities of the brain through the discovery of the cause and treatment of the same. **Structure** Board of Directors. Regional chapters (4): American Society for Stereotactic and Functional Neurosurgery; *Asian-Australasian Society for Stereotactic and Functional Neurosurgery (AASSFN, #01354)*; *European Society for Stereotactic and Functional Neurosurgery (ESSFN, #08742)*; *Latin American Society for Stereotactic and Functional Neurosurgery (LSSFN, #16386)*. **Languages** English. **Staff** 2.00 FTE, paid. **Finance** Sources: members' dues. **Activities** Health care; research and development; events/meetings. **Events** *Biennial Congress* Incheon (Korea Rep) 2022, *Biennial Congress* Incheon (Korea Rep) 2021, *Biennial Congress* New York, NY (USA) 2019, *Quadrennial Congress* Berlin (Germany) 2017, *Interim Congress* Mumbai (India) 2015. **Publications** *Stereotactic and Functional Neurosurgery* – journal; *WSSFN Newsletter*.
Members Individuals (about 500) in 60 countries:
Algeria, Argentina, Australia, Austria, Belgium, Bolivia, Brazil, Canada, Chile, China, Colombia, Croatia, Cuba, Czechia, Denmark, Egypt, Finland, France, Georgia, Germany, Greece, Hong Kong, Hungary, India, Indonesia, Ireland, Israel, Italy, Japan, Korea Rep, Lebanon, Luxembourg, Mexico, Morocco, Netherlands, New Zealand, Norway, Pakistan, Peru, Poland, Portugal, Romania, Russia, Saudi Arabia, Serbia, Singapore, Slovakia, Slovenia, South Africa, Spain, Sweden, Switzerland, Syrian AR, Taiwan, Tunisia, Türkiye, UK, Ukraine, USA, Venezuela. [2019/XC4524/v/**B**]

♦ **World Society of Sustainable Energy Technologies (WSSET)** 21813
Pres c/o Architecture Dept, University of Nottingham, University Park, Nottingham, NG7 2RD, UK. E-mail: secretary@wsset.org.
URL: https://www.wsset.org/
Structure Board of Directors. Officers: President; Regional Vice-Presidents (Asia, Africa, Europe, Middle East, North America, South America); Auditor; Secretary General. Secretariat. **Events** *Sustainable Energy Technologies Conference* Istanbul (Türkiye) 2022, *Sustainable Energy Technologies Conference* 2021, *Sustainable Energy Technologies Conference (SET2020)* 2020, *International Conference on Sustainable Energy Technologies* Wuhan (China) 2018, *International Conference on Sustainable Energy Technologies* Singapore (Singapore) 2016. **Publications** *WSSET Newsletter.*
Members Full in 28 countries:
Bahrain, Belarus, Canada, Chile, Cyprus, Finland, Germany, Greece, Indonesia, Israel, Italy, Jordan, Korea Rep, Malaysia, Mexico, Nigeria, Portugal, Russia, Saudi Arabia, Singapore, South Africa, Sudan, Thailand, Tunisia, UK, United Arab Emirates, USA, Yemen. [2021/XJ0146/C]

♦ World Society on Systemic Ophthalmology (inactive)

♦ **World Society for Transport and Land Use Research (WSTLUR)** 21814
Chair McGill – Urban Planning, Room 400 Macdonald-Harrington, 815 rue Sherbrooke Ouest, Montréal QC H3A 0C2, Canada. E-mail: jabreu@tecnico.ulisboa.pt.
URL: http://wstlur.org/
Aims Promote understanding and analysis of the interdisciplinary interactions of transport and land use; offer a forum for debate; provide a mechanism for the dissemination of information. **Structure** Board. **Finance** Sources: members' dues. **Events** *Symposium* Bogota (Colombia) 2024, *Symposium* Portland, OR (USA) 2021, *Symposium* Portland, OR (USA) 2020, *Symposium* Brisbane, QLD (Australia) 2017, *Symposium* Delft (Netherlands) 2014. **Publications** *Journal of Transport and Land Use.* [2017/XJ8893/C]

♦ **World Society of Victimology (WSV)** 21815
Société mondiale de victimologie
SG 3 Braeside Avenue, Holden Hill SA 5088, Australia. T. +61401716989. E-mail: wsv.secretarygeneral@gmail.com.
Pres Dept Criminology, Fac Humanities, PO Box 339, Bloemfontein, 9300, South Africa.
URL: http://www.worldsocietyofvictimology.org/
History Sep 1979, Münster (Germany). Founded at 3rd International Symposium on Victimology. Registration: Civil Court, Germany FR, Münster. **Aims** Advance victimological research and practice worldwide. **Structure** Executive Committee; Committees (4). **Languages** English. **Staff** None. **Finance** Sources: members' dues. **Activities** Events/meetings; networking/liaising; research/documentation; training/education. **Events** *Triennial symposium* San Sebastian (Spain) 2022, *Triennial symposium* San Sebastian (Spain) 2021, *Triennial symposium* Hong Kong (Hong Kong) 2018, *Triennial Symposium* Perth, WA (Australia) 2015, *Triennial symposium* The Hague (Netherlands) 2012. **Publications** *The Victimologist* (irregular) – newsletter. Policies; statements; documents; reports; symposium papers.
Members Affiliated national or regional associations in 34 countries and territories:
Argentina, Australia, Bosnia-Herzegovina, Brazil, Canada, Chile, Colombia, Croatia, El Salvador, Finland, France, Germany, Greece, India, Ireland, Italy, Japan, Korea Rep, Malaysia, Mexico, Nepal, Netherlands, New Zealand, North Macedonia, Norway, Portugal, Serbia, South Africa, Spain, Sri Lanka, Sweden, Taiwan, Thailand, USA.
Consultative Status Consultative status granted from: *ECOSOC (#05331)* (Special). **IGO Relations** Accredited by (1): *United Nations Office at Vienna (UNOV, #20604).* Associated with Department of Global Communications of the United Nations. **NGO Relations** Member of (1): *The Girl Generation.* Also links with national organizations and academic institutions. [2021.09.01/XF0588/C]

♦ **World Society for Virology (WSV)** 21816
Gen Sec Northampton, Northampton MA 01061-1308, USA. E-mail: info@ws-virology.org.
URL: https://www.ws-virology.org/
History 2017. Founded by Prof. Ahmed S. Abdel-Moneim from Taif University (Saudi Arabia) and Beni-Suef University (Egypt), as a global coalition of virologists to support the One Health approach. **Aims** Help virologists by developing and improving collaboration, education and guidance through: (1) connecting virologists working both in public and private sectors to enhance virology research and development, especially in low-and middle-income countries that often lack the required resources; (2) educating, communicating, and enhancing the exchange of data on new developments and progress in virology research; (3) enhancing discovery and exchange of human, animal, plant, food, and environmental samples around the globe for virus studies; and(4) promoting high-quality virology research. **Structure** Council; Officers; Committees. **Activities** Awards/prizes/competitions; events/meetings; guidance/assistance/consulting; knowledge management/information dissemination; networking/liaising; research and development; training/education. **Events** *Conference* Riga (Latvia) 2023, *Conference* Helsinki (Finland) 2021, *Committee Meeting* Stockholm (Sweden) 2019.
Publications Söderlund-Venermo, M., Varma, A., Guo, D., Gladue, D. P., Poole, E., Pujol, F. H., Pappu, H., Romalde, J. M., Kramer, L., Baz, M., Venter, M., Moore, M. D., Nevels, M. M., Ezzikouri, S., Vakharia, V. N., Wilson, W. C., Malik, Y. S., Shi, Z., Abdel-Moneim, A. S. 2022. World Society for Virology First International Conference: Tackling Global Virus Epidemics 2021. Virology, 566:114-121, doi.10.1016/j.virol.2021.11.009
Abdel-Moneim A. S., Moore, M. D., Naguib, M. M., Romalde, J. L., Soderlund-Venermo, M. 2020. WSV2019: The 1st committee meeting of the World Society for Virology. Virologica Sinica. 35:248–252, 10.1007/s12250-019-00189-y
Abdel-Moneim, A.S., Varma, A., Pujol, F.H., Lewis, G.L., Paweska, J. S., Romalde, J. L., Söderlund-Venermo, M., Moore, M.D., Nevels, M. L., Vakharia, V. N., Joshi, V., Malik, Y. S., Shi, A., Memish, Z. A. 2017. Launching a Global Network of Virologists: The World Society for Virology (WSV). Intervirology DOI: 10.1159/000488762. 60(6):276-277.
Members More than 1600 virologists from more than 90 countries. Membership countries not specified. [2022.11.14/AA2610/B]

♦ **World Solar Thermal Electricity Association (STELA-World)** 21817
Vice-Chairman/Treas Rue de l'Industrie 10, 1000 Brussels, Belgium. T. +3228932596. E-mail: info@stelaworld.org.
URL: http://www.stelaworld.org/
History 2012, by *European Solar Thermal Electricity Association (ESTELA, #08795)* and 2 national associations (South Africa and Australia). Registered in accordance with Belgian law: RPM 0474.601.105. **Aims** Help the world to see the unique value and benefits of solar thermal electricity generation, and to promote policy settings that will accelerate investment in the development of large-scale solar thermal power around the world. **Structure** Administrative Body, comprising Chairman, Vice-Chairman and Vice-Chairman/Treasurer. [2017/XJ7832/C]

♦ World Solidarity / see WSM
♦ World Solidarity Action Group / see Action for World Solidarity
♦ World Solidarity Forum (internationally oriented national body)

♦ **World Solidarity Fund** 21818
Fonds mondial de solidarité – Fondo Mondiale di Solidarietà
Contact address not obtained. T. +12129065576 – +12129065558. Fax +12129065364.
History Feb 2003, as a trust fund of *UNDP (#20292).* Full title: *World Solidarity Fund for Poverty Eradication.* **Aims** Contribute to the eradication of poverty; promote social and human development in the poorest regions of the world. **IGO Relations** Project supported by: *African Union (AU, #00488); ECOSOC (#05331); Group of 77 (G-77, #10732); League of Arab States (LAS, #16420); Non-Aligned Movement (NAM, #17146).* **NGO Relations** Member of: *Centre de recherche et d'information pour le développement, Paris (CRID).* [2009/XJ3687/f/F*]

♦ World Solidarity Fund for Poverty Eradication / see World Solidarity Fund (#21818)
♦ World Soybean Conference (meeting series)
♦ World Soy Foundation (internationally oriented national body)
♦ World Space Observatory / see World Space Observatory – Ultraviolet (#21819)

♦ **World Space Observatory – Ultraviolet (WSO-UV)** 21819
Contact WSO-UV project FISAC facilities, Avenida Puerta de Hierro, 28040 Madrid, Spain. T. +34913944058. E-mail: wso@mat.ucm.es.
Contact Inst of Astronomy, 48 Pyatnitskaya St, Moscow MOSKVA, Russia, 119017.
URL: http://www.wso-uv.es/
History Proposed during 7th Workshop for Basic Science organized by the United Nations and *European Space Agency (ESA, #08798).* Organizations involved: *International Astronomical Union (IAU, #12287)* and the United Nations Office for Outer Space Affairs, Vienna (Austria). Original title: *World Space Observatory (WSO).* Launched prepared for 2021. **Aims** Study the universe in the 100 – 320 nm ultraviolet (UV) wavelengths range. [2015/XJ4131/p/F*]

♦ World Space Week Association (internationally oriented national body)
♦ World's Parliament of Religions / see Parliament of the World's Religions (#18222)

♦ **World Spinal Column Society (WScS)** 21820
Contact 3is Septemvriou 144, 112 51 Athens, Greece. E-mail: contact@worldspinalcolumn.org.
URL: https://www.worldspinalcolumn.org/
History When activities ended of *World Spine Society (inactive)*, its leading surgeons joined together to launch WScS as an independent society. Registration: Greece. **Aims** Advance spine care worldwide by connecting spine surgeons in advanced and emerging nations through high quality education, training and collaborative activities. **Structure** Board of Directors; Committees (4): Education; Publications; Membership; Regionalization. **Activities** Events/meetings; training/education. **Events** *World Spine* Athens (Greece) 2022, *Virtual World Spine* 2020, *World Spine* Lisbon (Portugal) 2018. [2022/AA2758/C]

♦ **World Spine Care (WSC)** 21821
CEO 6100 Leslie St, Toronto ON M2H 3J1, Canada. E-mail: info@worldspinecare.org.
URL: http://www.worldspinecare.org/
History Founded 2008. **Aims** Improve lives in *underserved* communities through sustainable, integrated, evidence based, spine care. **Structure** Boards of Directors (3): Canada; US; Europe. Executive Committee. **Languages** English. **Activities** Advocacy/lobbying/activism; healthcare; research/documentation; training/education. **Events** *Prevention, early detection and management of spine disability – a patient-centric integrated approach* Mumbai (India) 2019. **Publications** *Global Spine Care Initiative.* Research articles. [2019.03.14/XM7371/C]

♦ World Spine Society (inactive)

♦ **World Spirits Alliance (WSA)** 21822
SG Rue Belliard 12, bte 5, 1040 Brussels, Belgium. E-mail: info@worldspiritsalliance.com.
URL: https://www.worldspiritsalliance.com/
History Jul 2019. Creation follows 20 years of informal cooperation. Registration: Banque-Carrefour des Entreprises, No/ID: 0730.577.571, Start date: 10 Jul 2019, Belgium. **Aims** Represent the views and interests of the spirts sector at global level. **Activities** Advocacy/lobbying/activism.
Members National and international members (26). Membership countries not specified.
Asia Pacific International Spirits and Wines Alliance (APISWA); spiritsEUROPE (#19921).
NGO Relations Partner of (1): *Transnational Alliance to Combat Illicit Trade (TRACIT).* [2022/AA3018/y/C]

♦ World Spiritual Council (inactive)
♦ World Sport Council (unconfirmed)

♦ **World Sport Publishers' Association (WSPA)** 21823
Sec Von-Coels-Strasse 390, 52080 Aachen, Germany. T. +492419581032. Fax +492419581033. E-mail: info@w-s-p-a.org.
Pres address not obtained.
URL: http://www.w-s-p-a.org/
History 1991, Frankfurt-Main (Germany). **Aims** Disseminate information on and promote sport internationally. **Structure** Officers: President; 3 Vice-Presidents. **Languages** English. **Staff** 1.00 FTE, paid. **Finance** Members' dues. **Activities** Organizes annual meeting at the Frankfurt Book Fair (Germany). Publishing activities. Common stands at International Book Fairs and Conferences. Awards Sport Book Prize. **Publications** *WSPA Newsletter* (3 to 4 a year).
Members Companies in 12 countries:
Austria, Belgium, Egypt, Germany, Hungary, Ireland, Italy, Netherlands, Poland, Spain, Switzerland, UK.
NGO Relations Consultative Status with: *World Athletics (#21209); The Association for International Sport for All (TAFISA, #02763).* Formal contacts with: *International Olympic Committee (IOC, #14408).* [2012.06.01/XD6691/D]

♦ World Sports Alliance – Intergovernmental Organization (unconfirmed)

♦ **World Sports Karate Federation (WSKF)** 21824
Pres 3/106 – 1st Floor, Vivek Khadn-3, Gomti Nagar, Lucknow, Uttar Pradesh, Lucknow UTTAR PRADESH, India. T. +919965408000. E-mail: secretary@wskf.org – webmaster@wske.org.
URL: http://www.wske.org/
History 29 Apr 2005, India. **Aims** Promote the game as a world sport, protecting the spirit of the game and optimizing commercial opportunities for the benefits of the game and all non-olympic sports worldwide. **Structure** Executive Committee.
Members National associations in 16 countries and territories:
Bangladesh, Brazil, Canada, China, England, Germany, India, Iran Islamic Rep, Japan, Mexico, Pakistan, Singapore, Sri Lanka, Taiwan, Trinidad-Tobago, USA.
NGO Relations Member of: *World Council for Regular and Distance Education (WCRDE, #21338).* [2016/XJ7937/C]

♦ **World's Poultry Science Association (WPSA)** 21825
Association universelle d'aviculture scientifique (AVI) – Asociación Mundial de Avicultura Cientifica – Weltvereinigung für Geflügelwissenschaft
SG PO Box 31, 7360 AA Beekbergen, Netherlands. T. +31651519584. Fax +31207508941. E-mail: wpsa@xs4all.nl.
URL: http://www.wpsa.com/
History 18 Jul 1912, London (UK). Constitution most recently revised, 4 July 2022. Former names and other names: *International Association of Poultry Instructors and Investigators* – former. **Aims** Advance and disseminate knowledge of all aspects of poultry science and the *poultry* industry; facilitate exchange of such knowledge worldwide among those having an interest in the industry; promote World Poultry Congresses and Regional Poultry Conferences. **Structure** Council (meets every 4 years at Congress); Board (annual); Executive Committee. Regional Branches (2): Asia-pacific; Europe. African Poultry Network; Mediterranean Poultry Network. **Languages** English. **Staff** 1.00 FTE, voluntary. **Finance** Sources: members' dues; sponsorship. **Activities** Events/meetings; knowledge management/information dissemination; training/education. **Events** *World Poultry Congress* 2025, *European Poultry Conference* Valencia (Spain) 2024, *World Waterfowl Conference* Jakarta (Indonesia) 2023, *World Poultry Congress* Paris (France) 2022, *World Poultry Congress* Paris (France) 2021. **Publications** *World's Poultry Science Journal; WPSA Newsletter.* Conference and symposia proceedings; abstracts of publications.
Members Branches in 76 countries and territories:
Algeria, Argentina, Australia, Austria, Azerbaijan, Bangladesh, Belgium, Bolivia, Brazil, Cameroon, Canada, Chile, China, Colombia, Congo DR, Croatia, Czechia, Denmark, Egypt, Estonia, Finland, France, Germany, Ghana, Greece, Hungary, India, Indonesia, Iran Islamic Rep, Iraq, Israel, Italy, Japan, Kenya, Korea Rep, Kuwait, Latvia, Lebanon, Lithuania, Macedonia, Malaysia, Mali, Mauritius, Mexico, Netherlands, New Zealand, Niger, Nigeria, Norway, Pakistan, Peru, Philippines, Poland, Romania, Russia, Saudi Arabia, Senegal, Serbia, Singapore, Slovakia, South Africa, South Sudan, Spain, Sri Lanka, Sudan, Sweden, Switzerland, Taiwan, Tanzania UR, Thailand, Togo, Türkiye, UK, Ukraine, USA, Vietnam.
Individuals (7,500): scientists, teachers, breeders, veterinarians, governmental people, students, farmers and specialist from the supplying and processing industry, in 100 countries and territories (not specified). Regional federations (2):
Regional federations (2):
Asian Pacific Federation of the World's Poultry Science Association Branches (#01615); European Federation of Branches of the World's Poultry Science Association (EFWPSA, #07063).
Consultative Status Consultative status granted from: *ECOSOC (#05331)* (Ros C); *FAO (#09260)* (Special Status). [2023.02.20/XB3613/y/B]

♦ World Squash Federation (WSF) 21826

Fédération mondiale de squash

Administrative Office 25 Russell Str, Hastings, TN34 1QU, UK. T. +441424447440. Fax +441424430737. E-mail: admin@worldsquash.org.

Pres address not obtained. E-mail: president@worldsquash.org.

URL: http://www.worldsquash.org/

History Jan 1966, London (UK). New constitution adopted 1-3 Oct 1984, Edinburgh (UK); amended 1989, Kuala Lumpur (Malaysia). Current name and constitution adopted 13 Oct 1992. Former names and other names: *International Squash Rackets Federation (ISRF)* – former. Registration: Start date: 1 Jul 1996, Isle of Man; Start date: 14 Jul 2022, UK. **Aims** Serve as the central authority for the *game* of squash worldwide. **Structure** General Meeting; Executive Board; Executive Committee; Commissions (19). **Languages** English. **Finance** Sources: grants; members' dues; sponsorship. Other sources: rights' fees; product approval; partnerships. **Activities** Events/meetings; sporting activities. **Events** *World Conference and Annual General Meeting* Chennai (India) 2022, *Annual General Meeting* Hastings (UK) 2021, *Annual General Meeting* Hastings (UK) 2020, *World Conference and Annual General Meeting* Cape Town (South Africa) 2019, *World Conference and Annual General Meeting* Cairo (Egypt) 2018. **Publications** *World Squash Calendar* (12 a year); *International Squash Magazine* – official magazine. *Specifications for Courts, Rackets and Balls*; *Squash Rules Explanation and Interpretation*.

Members Full (over 180) in 149 countries and territories:
Afghanistan, Algeria, Antigua-Barbuda, Argentina, Armenia, Aruba, Australia, Austria, Azerbaijan, Bahamas, Bahrain, Bangladesh, Barbados, Belarus, Belgium, Bermuda, Bolivia, Botswana, Brazil, Brunei Darussalam, Bulgaria, Cambodia, Canada, Cayman Is, Chile, China, Colombia, Congo DR, Cook Is, Costa Rica, Croatia, Cyprus, Czechia, Denmark, Dominica, Dominican Rep, Ecuador, Egypt, El Salvador, England, Estonia, Eswatini, Fiji, Finland, France, Georgia, Germany, Ghana, Gibraltar, Greece, Guatemala, Guernsey, Guyana, Honduras, Hong Kong, Hungary, Iceland, India, Indonesia, Iran Islamic Rep, Iraq, Ireland, Isle of Man, Israel, Italy, Jamaica, Japan, Jersey, Jordan, Kazakhstan, Kenya, Korea Rep, Kuwait, Latvia, Lebanon, Lesotho, Liechtenstein, Lithuania, Luxembourg, Macau, Madagascar, Malawi, Malaysia, Malta, Mauritius, Mexico, Monaco, Mongolia, Montenegro, Morocco, Myanmar, Namibia, Nepal, Netherlands, New Caledonia, New Zealand, Nigeria, Norfolk Is, North Macedonia, Norway, Oman, Pakistan, Palestine, Panama, Papua New Guinea, Paraguay, Peru, Philippines, Poland, Polynesia Fr, Portugal, Qatar, Romania, Russia, Samoa, Saudi Arabia, Scotland, Serbia, Seychelles, Singapore, Slovakia, Slovenia, Solomon Is, Somalia, South Africa, Spain, Sri Lanka, St Lucia, St Vincent-Grenadines, Sudan, Sweden, Switzerland, Taiwan, Tanzania UR, Thailand, Tonga, Trinidad-Tobago, Türkiye, Uganda, UK, Ukraine, Uruguay, USA, Vanuatu, Venezuela, Vietnam, Virgin Is UK, Zambia, Zimbabwe.

Regional federations (5), listed in this Yearbook:
Asian Squash Federation (ASF, #01760); *European Squash Federation (ESF, #08826)*; *Federación Panamericana de Squash (FPS, #09384)*; *Oceania Squash Federation (OSF, #17675)*; *Squash Federation of Africa (SFA, #19933)*.

Affiliates (5), listed in this Yearbook:
Caribbean Area Squash Association (CASA, #03442); *East Asian Squash Federation (EASF, #05210)*; *Professional Squash Association (PSA, #18517)*; *Women's Squash Association (WSA, #21034)*; *World Deaf Squash Inc (WDSI, #21357)*.

NGO Relations Member of (3): *Association of the IOC Recognized International Sports Federations (ARISF, #02767)*; *International Masters Games Association (IMGA, #14117)*; *Olympic Movement (#17719)*. Cooperates with (1): *International Testing Agency (ITA, #15678)*. Recognized by: *International Olympic Committee (IOC, #14408)*. [2022.10.11/XC2586/y/**B**]

♦ World Squash Promoters' Federation (inactive)

♦ World Ssireum Federation (WSF) 21827

Contact A-B09 Velodrome, 424 Olympicro (Bangi-dong), Songpa-gu, Seoul 138-749, Korea Rep. T. +8225019585. Fax +8225017784. E-mail: wsfkor@gmail.com.

URL: http://www.worldssireum.org/

History 2008. **Aims** Spread the *martial art* sport of ssireum. **Structure** Congress; Board of Directors; Executive Committee.

Members Federations in 44 countries:
Argentina, Australia, Belarus, Benin, Brazil, Cambodia, Canada, China, Estonia, Finland, France, Georgia, Germany, Ghana, India, Indonesia, Iran Islamic Rep, Italy, Japan, Kazakhstan, Korea Rep, Kyrgyzstan, Laos, Lithuania, Malaysia, Mongolia, Myanmar, Netherlands, New Zealand, Pakistan, Russia, Spain, Sweden, Switzerland, Tajikistan, Togo, Türkiye, Turkmenistan, UK, Ukraine, Uruguay, USA, Uzbekistan, Vietnam.

NGO Relations Member of: *The Association for International Sport for All (TAFISA, #02763)*. [2017/XJ6342/**C**]

♦ world stainless association (worldstainless) 21828

SG Av de Tervuren 270, 1150 Brussels, Belgium. T. +3227028915. Fax +3227028899. E-mail: info@worldstainless.org.

Main Website: https://www.worldstainless.org/

History Sep 1995, Pittsburgh, PA (USA). Founded as a specialist group of *World Steel Association (worldsteel, #21829)*. Former names and other names: *International Stainless Steel Forum (ISSF)* – former (16 May 2022). **Aims** Provide a focal point for the global stainless steel industry; promote the use of stainless steels. **Structure** General Meeting (during annual Conference); Board of Directors; Executive Committee; Committees (6). **Languages** English. **Staff** 3.00 FTE, paid. **Finance** Sources: members' dues. **Activities** Events/meetings; networking/liaising; training/education. **Events** *Annual Conference* 2022, *Annual Conference* Brussels (Belgium) 2021, *Annual Conference* Brussels (Belgium) 2020, *Annual Conference* Chicago, IL (USA) 2019, *Annual Conference* Shanghai (China) 2018. **Publications** *Team Stainless* – newsletter. *Stainless Steel in Figures*. Annual Review. **Information Services** *worldstainless Extranet* – gives members access to all of the work done by ISSF since 1996.

Members Regular – producers of stainless steel; Affiliated – national or regional associations of stainless steel producers. Members (64) in 25 countries and territories:
Australia, Belgium, Brazil, China, Finland, France, Germany, India, Italy, Japan, Korea Rep, Mexico, New Zealand, Nigeria, Russia, Slovenia, South Africa, Spain, Sweden, Switzerland, Taiwan, Thailand, Türkiye, UK, USA.

Included in the above, 2 organizations listed in this Yearbook:
European Steel Association (EUROFER, #08835); *Southern Africa Stainless Steel Development Association (SASSDA)*.

NGO Relations Member of (1): *TEAM STAINLESS (#20113)*. [2022.11.08/XF3943/y/**F**]

♦ **worldstainless** world stainless association (#21828)

♦ World Steel Association (worldsteel) 21829

Dir-Gen Av de Tervueren 270, 1150 Brussels, Belgium. T. +3227028900. Fax +3227028899. E-mail: steel@worldsteel.org – dg@worldsteel.org.

Beijing Office C413 Office Bldg Lufthansa Ctr, 50 Liangmaqiao Road, Chaoyang District, 100125 Beijing, China. T. +861064646733. Fax +861064646744. E-mail: china@worldsteel.org.

URL: http://www.worldsteel.org/

History 21 May 1967, New York, NY (USA). Charter approved 10 Jul 1967, Brussels (Belgium) as an international association with scientific purposes. Received the title "Royal" from the King of the Belgians, 2017 (50th anniversary). Former names and other names: *International Iron and Steel Institute (IISI)* – former (21 May 1967 to 5 Oct 2008). Registration: Banque-Carrefour des Entreprises, No/ID: 0406.597.373, Start date: 10 Jul 1967. **Aims** Act as the focal point for the steel industry and as such provides global leadership on all major strategic issues affecting the industry, particularly focusing on economic, environmental and social sustainability; promote steel and steel industry to customers, the industry, media and the general public; assist members to develop the market for steel, with major projects in the construction and automotive sectors; promote market competition that is free of government interventions preventing fair trade. **Structure** General Assembly (annual); Board of Directors; Executive Committee; Standing Committees; Development Programmes. Sister organization: *world stainless association (worldstainless, #21828)*. **Languages** English. **Staff** 40.00 FTE, paid. **Finance** Sources: members' dues. **Activities** Advocacy/lobbying/activism; awards/prizes/competitions; awareness raising; knowledge management/information dissemination; networking/liaising; projects/programmes; publishing activities; research/documentation; standards/guidelines; training/education. **Events** *Annual Conference* Brussels (Belgium) 2022, *Annual Conference* 2021, *Annual Conference* 2020, *Annual Conference* Monterrey (Mexico) 2019, *Annual Conference* Tokyo (Japan) 2018. **Publications** *World Steel in Figures* (annual); *Monthly Crude Steel Production*; *Steel Statistical Yearbook*. Reports of seminars and technical exchange sessions; statistical, economic and technical papers and reports. **Members** Represent steel producers, national and regional steel industry associations and steel research institutes from over 60 countries. Membership countries not specified. **Consultative Status** Consultative status granted from: *ECOSOC (#05331)* (Ros A). **IGO Relations** Advisory role with: *OECD (#17693)* Steel Committee. Accredited observer of: *United Nations Framework Convention on Climate Change (UNFCCC, 1992)*. **NGO Relations** Member of (1): *International Chamber of Commerce (ICC, #12534)* (as Association member). Partner of (1): *European Convention for Constructional Steelwork (ECCS, #06779)*. Cooperates with (1): *International Organization for Standardization (ISO, #14473)*. [2021.09.27/XC2174/**C**]

♦ **worldsteel** World Steel Association (#21829)

♦ World Stevia Organisation (WSO) 21830

Contact 15 rue de la Paix, 75002 Paris, France. T. +33155047755. Fax +33155047757. E-mail: president@wso-site.com – wso@wso-site.com.

URL: http://www.wso-site.com/

History May 2010, by Japanese Society of Antioxidants, Société Française des Antioxydants and *International Society of Antioxidant in Nutrition and Health (ISANH)*. **Aims** Advance the practical applications of *Stevia* and low calorie natural *sweeteners*. **Structure** Committee of 12. Offices worldwide. **Events** *World Conference on Stevia Tasteful* Amsterdam (Netherlands) 2019, *World Conference on Stevia Tasteful* Berlin (Germany) 2018, *World Conference on Stevia Tasteful* Lisbon (Portugal) 2016, *World Conference on Stevia Tasteful* Berlin (Germany) 2015, *World Conference on Stevia Tasteful* Berlin (Germany) 2014. **Publications** *Journal of World Stevia Organization (WJSO)*. [2016/XJ5077/**E**]

♦ World Strengthlifting Federation (inactive)

♦ World Stroke Federation (inactive)

♦ World Stroke Organization (WSO) 21831

Exec Officer c/o Kenes Intl, Rue François-Versonnex 7, PO Box 6053, 1211 Geneva 1, Switzerland. T. +41229069129. Fax +41227322607. E-mail: admin@world-stroke.org.

URL: http://www.world-stroke.org/

History 29 Oct 2006, Cape Town (South Africa). Founded by merger of *World Stroke Federation (WSF, inactive)* and *International Stroke Society (ISS, inactive)*. **Aims** Raise awareness of prevention and treatment of stroke. **Structure** Executive Committee; Board of Directors. **Languages** English. **Finance** Sources: members' dues. **Activities** Awards/prizes/competitions; events/meetings; training/education. **Events** *Joint Stroke Conference* Vienna (Austria) 2020, *Biennial Congress* Montréal, QC (Canada) 2018, *Biennial Congress* Hyderabad (India) 2016, *Biennial Congress* Istanbul (Turkey) 2014, *Biennial International Conference on Heart and Brain* Paris (France) 2014. **Publications** *International Journal of Stroke*. *Global Atlas on Cardiovascular Disease Prevention and Control* – In collaboration with World Heart Foundation. *Global Stroke Guidelines and Action Plan*. **Members** Individuals (about 4,000) in 80 countries; regional and national scientific and stroke support organizations (over 60). Membership countries not specified. **Consultative Status** Consultative status granted from: *ECOSOC (#05331)* (Special); *WHO (#20950)* (Official Relations). **NGO Relations** Member of (1): *The NCD Alliance (NCDA, #16963)*. [2020.08.18/XM3229/y/**C**]

♦ World Strongmen Federation (WSF) 21832

Gen Sec 91-404 Brivibas Str, Riga LV-1010, Latvia. T. +37129530902. E-mail: wsfstrongman@hotmail.com.

URL: http://www.strongmansport.org/

Structure High Council; World Strength Council. Committees (3): Education; StrongManFit; Stick Pulling. **Activities** Sporting activities.

Members Full in 71 countries:
Afghanistan, Armenia, Australia, Azerbaijan, Belarus, Benin, Bolivia, Brazil, Bulgaria, Burundi, Cameroon, Canada, Chile, China, Colombia, Congo DR, Croatia, Ecuador, Egypt, Estonia, Finland, Georgia, Germany, Ghana, Greece, Guatemala, Hungary, Iceland, India, Iran Islamic Rep, Jordan, Kazakhstan, Kenya, Kuwait, Kyrgyzstan, Latvia, Lebanon, Lithuania, Madagascar, Malawi, Malaysia, Mexico, Moldova, Mongolia, Morocco, Netherlands, Nigeria, Norway, Pakistan, Poland, Portugal, Puerto Rico, Qatar, Romania, Russia, Rwanda, Spain, Sweden, Tanzania UR, Togo, Tunisia, Türkiye, Uganda, UK, Ukraine, United Arab Emirates, Uruguay, USA, Uzbekistan, Venezuela, Zambia.

NGO Relations Member of (3): *General Association of Asia Pacific Sports Federations (GAAPSF, #10106)*; *International Sport Network Organization (ISNO, #15592)*; *The Association for International Sport for All (TAFISA, #02763)*. [2020/XM7391/**D**]

♦ World Student Christian Federation (WSCF) 21833

Fédération Universelle des Associations Chrétiennes d'Etudiants (FUACE) – Federación Universal de Movimientos Estudiantiles Cristianos (FUMEC)

Gen Sec Ecumenical Centre, 5 route des Morillons, PO Box 2100, 1211 Geneva 2, Switzerland. T. +41227916221. Fax +41227916152. E-mail: wscf@wscf.ch.

URL: http://www.wscf.ch/

History 17 Aug 1895, Vadstena (Sweden). Founded as a world federation of national student Christian movements and student sections of *World Alliance of Young Men's Christian Associations (YMCA, #21090)* and *World Young Women's Christian Association (World YWCA, #21947)*. Constitution most recently revised: Mar 1986, Mexico City (Mexico); Sep 1990, Chantilly (France); Sep 1995, Yamoussoukro (Côte d'Ivoire); Sep 1999, Beirut (Lebanon); Aug 2004, Chiang Mai (Thailand). Former names and other names: *Association chrétienne d'étudiants* – former; *Association chrétienne des jeunes gens* – former; *Fédération universelle des étudiants chrétiens* – former; *Movimiento Estudiantil Cristiano* – former. Registration: Swiss Civil Code, Switzerland. **Aims** Share God's love for creation, justice and peace across boundaries of race, class, ethnicity, culture, gender and sexuality; contribute to the renewal of the ecumenical movement; encourage a culture of democracy to mobilize youth to become pro-active in society; promote positive change through dialogue and action between different traditions and cultures. **Structure** General Assembly (every 4 years); Executive Committee; Inter-Regional Office. Regional Committees and Offices (6): Africa; Asia-Pacific; Europe; Latin America and the Caribbean; Middle East; North America. Student Christian Movements (SCM). Headquarters located at Ecumenical Centre of: *World Council of Churches (WCC, #21320)*. **Languages** English, French, Spanish. **Staff** 10.00 FTE, paid. **Finance** Sources: grants; members' dues. Annual budget: 1,130,000 USD (2010). **Activities** Capacity building; events/meetings; financial and/or material support; guidance/assistance/consulting; projects/programmes; publishing activities; religious activities; training/education. Was instrumental in setting up 'European Student Relief' in 1920, which subsequently developed into *World University Service (WUS, #21892)*; and cooperated with *World Student Relief (WRS, inactive)* until its dissolution in 1950. **Events** *Quadrennial General Assembly* Berlin (Germany) 2022, *Quadrennial General Assembly* Berlin (Germany) 2021, *Quadrennial General Assembly* Berlin (Germany) 2020, *Europe Staff and Officers Meeting* Oslo (Norway) 2016, *Quadrennial General Assembly* Bogota (Colombia) 2015. **Publications** *Federation News* (2 a year); *Student World* (annual). *WSCF Books* – annual. *Cantate Domino* – ecumenical hymn book; *The World Student Christian Federation* by R House; *Venite Adoremus I* – liturgical services of various Christian traditions; *Venite Adoremus II* – book of prayers and services for special student occasions. Annual Report.

Members Affiliated Movements; Associated Movements. Affiliated Movements (76) in 64 countries and territories:
Argentina, Australia, Austria, Bangladesh, Benin, Cambodia, Cameroon, Canada, Chile, Colombia, Côte d'Ivoire, Cuba, Czechia, Denmark, Ecuador, Egypt, Ethiopia, Finland, France, Gambia, Germany, Ghana, Hong Kong, Hungary, India, Indonesia, Italy, Japan, Jordan, Kenya, Korea Rep, Lebanon, Lesotho, Liberia, Lithuania, Madagascar, Myanmar, Namibia, Netherlands, New Zealand, Nigeria, Norway, Philippines, Romania, Rwanda, Senegal, Sierra Leone, Singapore, Slovakia, South Africa, South Sudan, Sri Lanka, Sudan, Sweden, Syrian AR, Taiwan, Thailand, Togo, UK, Uruguay, USA, Venezuela, Zambia, Zimbabwe.

Associated Movements (20) in 17 countries:
Belarus, Brazil, Bulgaria, Burundi, Canada, Congo DR, Ecuador, Haiti, Iraq, Mexico, Nepal, Rwanda, Tanzania UR, Timor-Leste, Uganda, Uruguay, USA.

Contacts (8) in 8 countries:
Armenia, Bahamas, Croatia, France, Ireland, Latvia, Papua New Guinea, Poland.

Consultative Status Consultative status granted from: *ECOSOC (#05331)* (Special). **IGO Relations** Accredited by (1): *United Nations Office at Vienna (UNOV, #20604)*. Associated with Department of Global Communications of the United Nations. **NGO Relations** Member of (5): *ACT Alliance (#00081)*; *Committee of NGOs on Human Rights, Geneva (#04275)*; *Conference of Non-Governmental Organizations in Consultative Relationship with the United Nations (CONGO, #04635)*; *European Youth Forum (#09140)*; *Fédération des Institutions Internationales établies à Genève (FIIG, #09599)*. Partner of (1): *Globethics.net Foundation (#10669)*. Cooperates with (1): *Christian Conference of Asia (CCA, #03898)*. [2023/XB3584/**B**]

♦ World Student Committee Against War and Fascism (inactive)

♦ World Student Community for Sustainable Development (WSC-SD) . 21834

Contact MIT Students for Sustainable Development, 77 Massaachusetts Ave, Cambridge MA 02139-4307, USA.
Facebook: https://www.facebook.com/TheWSCSD/

History Mar 2002, San José (Costa Rica). Originally part of *Alliance for Global Sustainability (AGS, no recent information)*, but separated later in 2002. **Aims** Promote the fundamental aspects of sustainable development. **Structure** Coordinating Council, headed by President. Steering Committee (rotating). **Events** *Annual Meeting* Rasa (Switzerland) 2006, *Annual Meeting* Cambridge, MA (USA) 2005, *Annual meeting* Gothenburg (Sweden) 2004, *Annual meeting* Tokyo (Japan) 2003, *Annual Meeting* Costa Rica 2002. **Publications** *WSC-SD Newsletter*.
Members Student communities (6) in 5 countries:
Côte d'Ivoire, Japan, Sweden, Switzerland, USA.
NGO Relations Member of: *Global Call for Climate Action (GCCA, inactive)*. [2015/XF6984/**F**]

♦ World Student Games Federation (internationally oriented national body)

♦ World Sturgeon Conservation Society (WSCS) 21835

Pres Schifferstrasse 48, 21629 Neu Wulmstorf, Germany. T. +49407006514. Fax +494070102676.
URL: https://www.wscs.info/

History 11 Mar 2003. Founded following activities initiated at the 4th International Symposium on Sturgeon in 2001. **Aims** Foster conservation of sturgeon species and restoration of sturgeon stocks worldwide; support research on all aspects of sturgeons; promote information exchange and cooperation among all interested in sturgeon. **Structure** General Assembly. Board of Directors, comprising President, Vice-President, Treasurer, Secretary-General and 2 further members. **Activities** Organizes seminars and workshops. **Events** *International Symposium on Sturgeon* China 2022, *International Symposium on Sturgeon* China 2021, *International Symposium on Sturgeon* Vienna (Austria) 2017, *International Symposium on Sturgeon* Nanaimo, BC (Canada) 2013, *International Symposium on Sturgeon* Wuhan (China) 2009. **Publications** *Journal of Applied Ichthyology*. Meeting proceedings. **Members** Membership countries not specified.
[2014/XJ3837/**D**]

♦ World Subud Association (WSA) 21836

Sec Jalan Paso No 84, Jakarta 12620, Indonesia. E-mail: wsa.secretary@subud.org – wsa@subud.org.
URL: http://www.subud.org/

History 1947. Founded by Muhammad Subuh Sumohadiwidjojo. Originally also referred to as *Subud Brotherhood International Foundation (SBIF)*. SUBUD stands for *Susila Budhi Dharma*. Incorporated in the State of Washington DC, 1991. Registration: 501(c)(3) organization, No/ID: EIN: 54-1521424, Start date: 1990, USA, Washington DC. **Aims** As an association of people who follow the *spiritual* practice known as the *Latihan Kejiwaan*: enable national Subud bodies to work together and support the practice of the latihan; foster educational, cultural social and entrepreneurial activities that Subud members are involved in. **Structure** World Congress (every 4 years); World Subud Council. Affiliates or informally organized bodies (4): *Susila Dharma International Association (SDIA, #20048)*; *Subud International Cultural Association (SICA, #20029)*; Subud Enterprise Service International (SES); Subud Youth Activities International (SYAI). Subud International Health Association (SIHA). Foundation: Muhammad Subuh Foundation. **Languages** English, French, German, Indonesian, Portuguese, Russian, Spanish. **Staff** 2.00 FTE, paid; 53.00 FTE, voluntary. **Finance** Direct contributions from member countries, member-owned enterprises and individuals. Annual budget: between US$ 300,000 – 400,000. **Activities** Events/meetings; guidance/assistance/consulting; networking/liaising. **Events** *Quadrennial World Congress* Freiburg-Breisgau (Germany) 2018, *Quadrennial World Congress* Puebla (Mexico) 2014, *Quadrennial world congress* Christchurch (New Zealand) 2010, *International meeting* India 2006, *Quadrennial World Congress* Innsbruck (Austria) 2005. **Publications** *World Subud Association News* (about 5 a year). Annual Report; books and publications from Subud Publications International in the UK.
Members National organizations; Individuals. Members in 75 countries and territories:
Algeria, Angola, Argentina, Australia, Austria, Bangladesh, Belgium, Bermuda, Bosnia-Herzegovina, Brazil, Canada, Chile, China, Colombia, Congo Brazzaville, Congo DR, Costa Rica, Croatia, Cuba, Cyprus, Czechia, Denmark, Ecuador, Ethiopia, Finland, France, Germany, Greece, Hong Kong, Hungary, India, Indonesia, Iran Islamic Rep, Ireland, Israel, Italy, Jamaica, Japan, Latvia, Lebanon, Lithuania, Malaysia, Mexico, Moldova, Morocco, Netherlands, New Zealand, Nigeria, Norway, Pakistan, Paraguay, Peru, Poland, Portugal, Puerto Rico, Romania, Russia, Serbia, Singapore, South Africa, Spain, Sri Lanka, Suriname, Sweden, Switzerland, Tanzania UR, Thailand, Trinidad-Tobago, Türkiye, UK, Ukraine, Uruguay, USA, Venezuela, Vietnam.
IGO Relations Consultative Status with: *ECOSOC (#05331)*; *UNICEF (#20332)*. Associated with DPI of United Nations. [2021/XD1329/**C**]

♦ World Sugar Research Organization (WSRO) 21837

Registered Address Salisbury House, Station Road, Cambridge, CB1 2LA, UK. E-mail: admin@wsro.org – info@wsro.org.
URL: http://www.wsro.org/

History 1978. Superseding *International Sugar Research Foundation (ISRF, inactive)*. **Aims** Research the effects of sugar on nutrition, *health* and wellbeing worldwide. **Structure** Members' Meeting (annual); Board of Directors; Officers. **Languages** English. **Staff** 4.00 FTE, paid. **Finance** Sources: members' dues. **Activities** Events/meetings; projects/programmes. **Events** *Annual General Meeting and Conference* San Francisco, CA (USA) 2019, *Annual General Meeting and Conference* Munich (Germany) 2018, *Annual General Meeting* Sydney, NSW (Australia) 2013, *Annual General Meeting* Palm Beach, FL (USA) 2012, *Annual General Meeting and Conference* South Africa 2007. **Publications** Various. **Members** Sustaining. Membership countries not specified. **Consultative Status** Consultative status granted from: *FAO (#09260)* (Liaison Status). **IGO Relations** Observer status with (1): *Codex Alimentarius Commission (CAC, #04081)*.
[2023.02.15/XD7870/**C**]

♦ World Summit on Accessible Tourism (meeting series)

♦ World Summit on Media for Children Foundation (WSMCF) 21838

Chairperson 104-110 Rose Street, Fitzroy VIC 3065, Australia. T. +61394170475. Fax +61394170475.
URL: http://www.wsmcf.com/

History 1999. Registered in accordance with Australian law. **Aims** Encourage and promote the world summit movement; oversee the running of World Summit every 3 years. **Structure** Board of Directors. **Events** *World Summit on Media for Children / Summit* Kuala Lumpur (Malaysia) 2014, *World summit on media for children and youth / Summit* Karlstad (Sweden) 2010, *World summit on media for children / Summit* Johannesburg (South Africa) 2007, *World summit on media for children / Summit* Rio de Janeiro (Brazil) 2004, *World summit on media for children* Thessaloniki (Greece) 2001. **NGO Relations** First Summit in 1995 set up *International Research Forum on Children and Media (IRFCAM)*. [2017.10.10/XF7149/f/**F**]

♦ World Summit on Nordicity (meeting series)
♦ World Summit on Pediatrics (meeting series)
♦ World Supreme Council for Mosques (no recent information)
♦ World Sustainability Fund (unconfirmed)
♦ World Sustainable Agriculture Association (inactive)
♦ World Sustainable Development Forum (internationally oriented national body)

♦ World Swimming Coaches Association (WSCA) 21839

Exec Dir address not obtained.
URL: http://wscacoach.org/

Aims Provide education and education opportunities for swimming coaches worldwide. **Finance** Members' dues. **Events** *Meeting* Indianapolis, IN (USA) 2010, *Meeting* Birmingham (UK) 2007, *Meeting* Cancún (Mexico) 2005, *Meeting* Perth, WA (Australia) 1998, *Meeting* Birmingham (UK) 1997.
Members National associations in 13 countries:
Australia, Canada, China, Germany, Japan, Kenya, Mexico, Philippines, Sweden, Tanzania UR, Thailand, UK, USA.
Individuals in 79 countries and territories:
Antigua-Barbuda, Argentina, Australia, Austria, Bahamas, Bahrain, Barbados, Belgium, Bermuda, Botswana, Brazil, Canada, Cayman Is, China, Costa Rica, Croatia, Czechia, Denmark, Egypt, Estonia, Fiji, Finland, France, Germany, Ghana, Great Britain, Greece, Guyana, Hong Kong, Iceland, India, Indonesia, Iran Islamic Rep, Ireland, Israel, Italy, Jamaica, Japan, Jordan, Kenya, Korea Rep, Kuwait, Libya, Malaysia, Malta, Mexico, Mozambique, Namibia, Netherlands, New Zealand, Nicaragua, Nigeria, Norway, Oman, Pakistan, Philippines, Poland, Portugal, Puerto Rico, Qatar, Romania, Russia, Rwanda, Singapore, South Africa, Spain, Sri Lanka, St Lucia, Sweden, Switzerland, Tanzania UR, Thailand, Trinidad-Tobago, Türkiye, Uganda, UK, United Arab Emirates, USA, Zimbabwe.
NGO Relations *World Swimming Organization*. [2020/XD9105/**D**]

♦ World Swimming Organization (internationally oriented national body)

♦ World's Woman's Christian Temperance Union (WWCTU) 21840

Union mondiale chrétienne des femmes abstinentes – Unión Mundial de Mujeres Cristianas contra el Alcoholismo – Weltbund Christlicher Abstinenter Frauen

World Pres Rygjehaugvn 13, Karmoy, 4265 Håvik, Norway. T. +4752842993.
World Sec 11 the Corso, Parkdale, Melbourne VIC 3195, Australia.
URL: http://www.wwctu.org/

History 1883, Evanston IL (USA), by Frances E Willard, the first convention being held Nov 1891, Boston MA (USA). Also referred to as *WORLD WCTU*. **Aims** With the motto 'For God and Home and Every Land' and without distinction of race, creed or colour, unite national affiliated organizations; through their united faith and work enable them, with God's help, by personal example and programmes, to promote: elimination of the use of alcoholic beverages, tobacco, narcotics and other habit-forming drugs; protection of the home; high moral standards; equal citizenship for men and women; world peace; renunciation of war. **Structure** Convention (every 3 years); Executive Committee; World Officers; Departments (6). Open to all women abstainers; men abstainers are admitted as associates. Conventions open. **Languages** English. **Staff** Voluntary. **Finance** Voluntary subscriptions. Dues from national unions at rate of at least US$ 0.10 per member. Annual Budget: about US$ 30,000. **Activities** Events/meetings. **Events** *Triennial Convention* Helsinki (Finland) 2019, *Triennial Convention* Ottawa, ON (Canada) 2016, *Triennial Convention* Adelaide, SA (Australia) 2013, *Triennial convention* Stavanger (Norway) 2010, *Triennial convention* Indianapolis, IN (USA) 2007. **Publications** *White Ribbon Bulletin* (4 a year) – official organ. *Mary Clement Leavitt – First WCTU Round-the-World Missionary* (2011) by Sarah F Ward; *Properties with a Purpose* (1968) by M G Heath; *Clad with Zeal* (1956) by M Krohn; *African Horizons* by D Allen-Lodge; *Our Goodly Heritage* by Dorothy Staunton – history of WWCTU; *Ten Decades of White Ribbon Service* by E K Stanley. Worlds reports.
Members National unions in 31 countries:
Argentina, Australia, Canada, Congo DR, Egypt, Fiji, Finland, Germany, Guatemala, Iceland, India, Indonesia, Japan, Kenya, Kiribati, Korea Rep, Myanmar, New Zealand, Norway, Papua New Guinea, Philippines, Samoa, Sierra Leone, Solomon Is, South Africa, Tanzania UR, Tonga, Tuvalu, USA, Vanuatu, Zimbabwe.
Consultative Status Consultative status granted from: *ECOSOC (#05331)* (Special). **IGO Relations** Associated with Department of Global Communications of the United Nations. **NGO Relations** None.
[2019.03.06/XB3614/**B**]

♦ World Symposium for Lymphedema Surgery (meeting series)
♦ World Symposium on Sustainable Development at Universities (meeting series)

♦ World Syntegrity Project (WSP) 21841

Pres 5 Thomas Circle NW, Washington DC 20005, USA. T. +12026382662. Fax +12026380638.
URL: https://worldservice.org/syn.html

History Jul 1993, Toronto (Canada). Coordinated *World Service Authority (WSA, see: #21543)*. Name is registered trademark (TM). **Aims** Provide an opportunity for world citizens to participate locally yet have their voices heard globally on issues of global importance; develop a flexible democratic world constitution. **Finance** WSA, the administrative branch of WGWC, collects donations and fees for the documents (such as World Passports) it issues. **Activities** Meeting activities. **Events** *Infoset meeting* Accra (Ghana) 1995, *Infoset meeting* Freetown (Sierra Leone) 1995. **Publications** *World Citizen News*; *World Government News*.
Members Currently 38 Infosets exist (planned) in 17 countries:
Australia, Bangladesh, Canada, Colombia, Egypt, Ethiopia (19), Ghana, Japan (*), Morocco (*), Netherlands, Nigeria (2), Pakistan (*), Sierra Leone (4), Sweden, Switzerland (*), UK (3), USA (2). [2014.06.01/XF3436/**F**]

♦ World's Youth for Climate Justice (WYCJ) 21842

Contact address not obtained. E-mail: hi@wy4cj.org.
URL: https://www.wy4cj.org/

History Registration: EU Transparency Register, No/ID: 399208143921-59, Start date: 26 Aug 2021. **Aims** Support Pacific leadership in a UN General Assembly request for an advisory opinion on climate change and human rights from the International Court of Justice. **Structure** Steering Committee. A decentralized movement of regional representatives. **Publications** *Flagship Legal Report*. **Information Services** *Resources*.
[2023.02.21/AA2082/**F**]

♦ World Taekuk Musul Federation (WTMF) 21843

Headquarters 6814 Fair Oaks Blvd, Carmichael CA 95608, USA. T. +15304092788. E-mail: tkmshq@sbcglobal.net.
URL: http://tkmsmartialarts.com/Home.php/

History Constitution adopted 8 Aug 1988. **Structure** General Assembly. Board, including President, 2 Vice-Presidents, Secretary-General and Treasurer. **Languages** English, French, German, Korean, Russian, Spanish.
Members National federations in 56 countries:
Afghanistan, Algeria, Australia, Azerbaijan, Belarus, Brazil, Bulgaria, Burundi, Canada, China, Congo Brazzaville, Croatia, Denmark, Ecuador, Egypt, El Salvador, France, Georgia, Germany, Ghana, Greece, India, Indonesia, Iran Islamic Rep, Israel, Korea Rep, Kyrgyzstan, Latvia, Malaysia, Mexico, Moldova, Mongolia, Nepal, New Zealand, Pakistan, Papua New Guinea, Philippines, Poland, Portugal, Russia, Rwanda, Saudi Arabia, Singapore, Spain, Sudan, Sweden, Tajikistan, Tanzania UR, Thailand, Türkiye, Uganda, UK, Ukraine, USA, Uzbekistan, Vietnam. [2018/XJ6341/**B**]

♦ World Taekwondo 21844

SG Booyoung Taepyung Building 10th Fl, 55 Sejong-daero (Taepyung-ro 2ga), Jung-gu, Seoul 04513, Korea Rep. T. +8225662505. Fax +8225534728. E-mail: secretary.general@worldtaekwondo.org – office@worldtaekwondo.org – info@worldtaekwondo.org.
URL: http://www.worldtaekwondo.org/

History 28 May 1973, Seoul (Korea Rep). Founded following 1st World Taekwondo Championships, when Rules and Regulations were adopted. Present name adopted, 2017. Rules and Regulations most recently amended: 5 Apr 2018. Former names and other names: *World Taekwondo Federation (WTF)* – former. **Aims** Develop Taekwondo as a world *sport*; propagate and standardize Taekwondo and its traditional spirit. **Structure** General Assembly (annual) during World Taekwondo Championships; WTF Council; Standing Committees (28); Regional Unions (5): *World Taekwondo Africa (WTAF, #21845)*; *Asian Taekwondo Union (ATU, #01766)*; *European Taekwondo Union (ETU, #08874)*; *World Taekwondo Oceania (WTO, #21846)*; *Pan American Taekwondo Union (PATU, #18136)*. **Languages** English, Korean. **Staff** 20.00 FTE, paid. **Finance** Sources: donations; members' dues. Other sources: operations income. **Activities** Events/meetings; publishing activities; research and development; sporting activities; training/education. **Events** *Sport Taekwondo International Convergence Conference* Muju (Korea Rep) 2021, *Coach Seminar* Seoul (Korea Rep) 2016, *International Referee Seminar* Dubai (United Arab Emirates) 2014, *Coach Seminar* Busan (Korea Rep) 2013, *Symposium* Muju (Korea Rep) 2013. **Publications** *Taekwondo* (annual). Newsletter (periodical).
Members National organizations in 209 countries and territories:
Afghanistan, Albania, Algeria, Andorra, Angola, Antigua-Barbuda, Argentina, Armenia, Aruba, Australia, Austria, Azerbaijan, Bahamas, Bahrain, Bangladesh, Barbados, Belarus, Belgium, Belize, Benin, Bermuda, Bhutan, Bolivia, Bosnia-Herzegovina, Botswana, Brazil, Brunei Darussalam, Bulgaria, Burkina Faso, Burundi, Cambodia, Cameroon, Canada, Cape Verde, Cayman Is, Central African Rep, Chad, Chile, China, Colombia, Comoros, Congo Brazzaville, Congo DR, Cook Is, Costa Rica, Côte d'Ivoire, Croatia, Cuba, Curaçao, Cyprus, Czechia, Denmark, Djibouti, Dominica, Dominican Rep, Ecuador, Egypt, El Salvador, Equatorial Guinea, Estonia, Eswatini, Ethiopia, Fiji, Finland, France, Gabon, Gambia, Georgia, Germany, Ghana, Great Britain, Greece, Grenada, Guadeloupe, Guam, Guatemala, Guiana Fr, Guinea, Guinea-Bissau, Guyana, Haiti, Honduras, Hong Kong, Hungary, Iceland, India, Indonesia, Iran Islamic Rep, Iraq, Ireland, Isle of Man, Israel, Italy, Jamaica, Japan, Jordan, Kazakhstan, Kenya, Kiribati, Korea Rep, Kosovo, Kuwait, Kyrgyzstan, Laos, Latvia, Lebanon, Lesotho, Liberia, Libya, Lithuania, Luxembourg, Macau, Madagascar, Malawi, Malaysia, Mali, Malta, Marshall Is, Martinique, Mauritania, Mauritius, Mexico, Micronesia FS, Moldova, Monaco, Mongolia, Montenegro, Morocco, Mozambique, Myanmar, Nauru, Nepal, Netherlands, New Caledonia, New Zealand, Nicaragua, Niger, Nigeria, North Macedonia, Norway, Oman, Pakistan, Palau, Palestine, Panama, Papua New Guinea, Paraguay, Peru, Philippines, Poland, Polynesia Fr, Portugal, Puerto Rico, Qatar, Romania, Russia, Rwanda, Samoa, Samoa

USA, San Marino, Sao Tomé-Principe, Saudi Arabia, Senegal, Serbia, Seychelles, Sierra Leone, Singapore, Slovakia, Slovenia, Solomon Is, Somalia, South Africa, South Sudan, Spain, Sri Lanka, St Kitts-Nevis, St Lucia, St Vincent-Grenadines, Sudan, Suriname, Sweden, Switzerland, Syrian AR, Taiwan, Tajikistan, Tanzania UR, Thailand, Timor-Leste, Togo, Tonga, Trinidad-Tobago, Tunisia, Türkiye, Turkmenistan, Tuvalu, Uganda, Ukraine, United Arab Emirates, Uruguay, USA, Uzbekistan, Vanuatu, Venezuela, Vietnam, Virgin Is UK, Virgin Is USA, Yemen, Zambia, Zimbabwe.

IGO Relations *UNESCO (#20322)*; *UNHCR (#20327)*. **NGO Relations** Member of (5): *Association of Paralympic Sports Organisations (APSO, #02850)*; *Association of Summer Olympic International Federations (ASOIF, #02943)*; *International Committee for Fair Play (#12769)*; *International Paralympic Committee (IPC, #14512)*; *Olympic Movement (#17719)*. Cooperates with (1): *International Testing Agency (ITA, #15678)*. Recognized by: *International Olympic Committee (IOC, #14408)*; *World Martial Arts Committee (WMAC, #21636)*. [2020/XB4383/**B**]

♦ World Taekwondo Africa (WTAF) 21845

SG 64 Ramsis Extension Street (2), Nasr City, Cairo, Egypt. T. +20122106631. Fax +20222617576. E-mail: hkamal@aftu.info.
Pres address not obtained. T. +20222631737. Fax +20222617576. E-mail: ahmedfouly49@gmail.com.
URL: http://www.worldtaekwondofederation.net/

History 1978, Cairo (Egypt), as a regional union of *World Taekwondo (#21844)*. Previously known as *African Taekwondo Union (AFTU)*. **Aims** Organize, develop and motivate taekwondo activities in Africa. **Structure** Officers: President; 6 Vice-Presidents; Treasurer. **Languages** Arabic, English, French. **Staff** 6.00 FTE, paid. **Finance** Supported by *World Taekwondo (#21844)*. Annual budget: US$ 70,000. **Activities** Sporting activities; events/meetings. **Events** *African Taekwondo Championship* Madagascar 2005, *General assembly / African Taekwondo Championship* Nairobi (Kenya) 1998, *African Taekwondo Championship* Johannesburg (South Africa) 1996, *African Taekwondo Championship* Cairo (Egypt) 1993, *African Taekwondo Championship* Abidjan (Côte d'Ivoire) 1979.

Members National organizations in 52 countries:
Algeria, Angola, Benin, Botswana, Burkina Faso, Burundi, Cameroon, Cape Verde, Central African Rep, Chad, Comoros, Congo Brazzaville, Congo DR, Côte d'Ivoire, Djibouti, Egypt, Equatorial Guinea, Eswatini, Ethiopia, Gabon, Gambia, Ghana, Guinea, Guinea-Bissau, Kenya, Lesotho, Liberia, Libya, Madagascar, Malawi, Mali, Mauritania, Mauritius, Morocco, Mozambique, Niger, Nigeria, Rwanda, Sao Tomé-Principe, Senegal, Seychelles, Sierra Leone, Somalia, South Africa, South Sudan, Sudan, Tanzania UR, Togo, Tunisia, Uganda, Zambia, Zimbabwe. [2018.06.01/XD0404/**D**]

♦ World Taekwondo Federation / see World Taekwondo (#21844)

♦ World Taekwondo Oceania (WTO) 21846

Pres 8/179 Queen Street, Melbourne VIC 3000, Australia. T. +61396400600. Fax +61396400611. E-mail: mail@worldtaekwondooceania.org.
SG 15 Mackerras Cres, Theodore VIC 2905, Australia.
URL: https://worldtaekwondooceania.org/

History 16 Jul 2005, Sydney, NSW (Australia). Founded during first Championships. A regional union of *World Taekwondo (#21844)*. Former names and other names: *Oceania Taekwondo Union (OTU)* – former. **Aims** Develop the sport of Taekwondo within the Oceania region. **Activities** Events/meetings; sporting activities; training/education.

Members National federations in 19 countries and territories:
Australia, Cook Is, Fiji, Guam, Kiribati, Marshall Is, Micronesia FS, Nauru, New Caledonia, New Zealand, Palau, Papua New Guinea, Polynesia Fr, Samoa, Samoa USA, Solomon Is, Tonga, Tuvalu, Vanuatu.

NGO Relations Member of (1): *Organisation of Sports Federations of Oceania (OSFO, #17828)*. [2022/XM0984/**D**]

♦ World Tai Chi Chuan Federation (unconfirmed)
♦ World Tatar Congress / see World Congress of Tatars (#21310)

♦ World Taxpayers Associations (WTA) 21847

SG 55 Tufton Street, London, SW1P 3QL, UK. E-mail: secretarygeneral@worldtaxpayers.org.
URL: http://www.worldtaxpayers.org/

History 28 Sep 1988, Washington, DC (USA). Statutes amended 24-26 Jul 1990, Stockholm (Sweden), Nov 1992, Melbourne (Australia), May-Jun 1994, Budapest (Hungary) and Jun 1998, Vancouver (Canada), Jun 2000, Tallinn (Estonia), 2001, St Louis MO (USA). Former names and other names: *Taxpayers Associations International (TAI)* – former (Sep 1988). Registration: Sweden. **Aims** Spread economic freedom worldwide by: promoting lower tax rates, limited government and individual freedom; stimulating networking between taxpayer protection groups; assisting in spreading the taxpayer protection movement; encouraging research comparing taxes and government spending. **Structure** Members' Conference (every 2 years); Board of Directors; Executive Committee; Advisory Board. **Languages** English. **Staff** 1.00 FTE, paid. **Finance** Sources: members' dues. **Activities** Events/meetings; networking/liaising. **Events** *World Conference* Paris (France) 2022, *World Conference* Paris (France) 2021, *World Conference* Sydney, NSW (Australia) 2019, *World Conference* Berlin (Germany) 2016, *World Conference* Vancouver, BC (Canada) 2014.

Members Associations in 47 countries and territories:
Armenia, Australia, Austria, Azerbaijan, Belarus, Belgium, Brazil, Bulgaria, Cameroon, Canada, Chile, China, Colombia, Denmark, Estonia, Finland, France, Georgia, Germany, Ghana, Hong Kong, Hungary, Indonesia, Italy, Japan, Kazakhstan, Korea Rep, Kyrgyzstan, Latvia, Lithuania, Malaysia, New Zealand, Norway, Philippines, Poland, Portugal, Russia, Serbia, Slovakia, South Africa, Sweden, Switzerland, Tanzania UR, Uganda, UK, Ukraine, USA.
Intercontinental members (2):
Asia Pacific Taxpayers Union (APTU, #02062); *Taxpayers Association of Europe (TAE, #20102)*. [2022/XD5221/**B**]

♦ World Teacher Trust (WTT) 21848

Coordinator Kohlhüttenstrasse 10, 6440 Brunnen, Switzerland. T. +41319512877. E-mail: info@worldteachertrust.org.
Central Office WTT India D N 15-7-1 Angels Enclave, Krishna Nagar, Visakhapatnam, Andhra Pradesh 530002 AP, Visakhapatnam ANDHRA PRADESH 530002 AP, India. T. +918912706206. E-mail: theworld_teachertrust@hotmail.com.
URL: https://www.worldteachertrust.org/

History 18 Nov 1971, Visakhapatnam (India). Founded by Dr Ekkirala E Krishnamacharya. WTT Europe branch founded 27 Aug 1983, Geneva (Switzerland); renamed WTT Global, 7 Aug 2006. Former names and other names: *Groupe de l'instructeur du monde* – former. Registration: Swiss Civil Code, Switzerland. **Aims** Promote development of education and study in general, particularly, in the field of comparative religion, philosophy, science and art; alleviate human suffering, and promote mental and moral ethical improvement of the human race; promote development of spirituality on a non-sectarian basis; promote social activities for the general welfare. **Structure** Executive Committee. World Teacher Trust – India has its own Managing Council and Advisory Board. **Languages** English, French, German, Portuguese, Spanish, Telugu. **Staff** Voluntary. **Finance** Sources: donations. **Activities** Events/meetings; training/education. **Events** *International conference and seminar* Mount Shasta, CA (USA) 2019, *Meeting* Barcelona (Spain) 2015, *International conference and seminar* 1991, *International conference and seminar* 1991, *International conference and seminar* Barcelona (Spain) 1990. **Publications** Annual Report; books; videos; audios.

Members Groups in 15 countries:
Argentina, Austria, Belgium, Brazil, Denmark, France, Germany, India, Mexico, Portugal, Spain, Switzerland, Uruguay, USA, Venezuela. [2022.02.08/XF5088/**F**]

♦ World Team (WT) 21849

Exec Dir PO Box 516, Box Hill VIC 3128, Australia. T. +61398996303. E-mail: wt-au@worldteam.org.
International Office 1431 Stuckert Road, Warrington PA 18976, USA. T. +12154914900. Fax +12154914910. E-mail: wt-us@worldteam.org.
URL: http://www.worldteam.org/

History 3 Jun 1995, by merger of *Regions Beyond Missionary Union International (RBMU International, inactive)* and *Worldteam (WT, inactive)*. **Aims** Act as an *evangelical mission* organization by planting churches in unreached areas. **Structure** International Board; National Boards. **Languages** English. **Finance** Donations. **Activities** Humanitarian/emergency aid; meeting activities. Members serve in 28 countries among 59 distinct people groups. **Events** *Conference* 1999. **Publications** *WT Magazine* (4 a year).

Members Governments of 3 countries:
Australia, Canada, USA.

NGO Relations Member of: Missions Interlink; *World Evangelical Alliance (WEA, #21393)*. Links with international church and mission organizations, including: *Global Connections*. [2015/XF4127/**F**]

♦ World Technology Foundation / see World Development Foundation

♦ World Technopolis Association (WTA) 21850

SG 100 Dunsan-ro, Seo-gu, Daejeon 302789, Korea Rep. T. +82422702260 – +82422702267. Fax +82424712319.
LinkedIn: https://www.linkedin.com/company/world-technopolis-association/

History Founded 4 Jun 1997, Daejeon (Korea Rep), when Statutes were adopted. **Aims** Promote exchanges and mutually beneficial cooperation among *science museums* worldwide; help connect science and *technology* with regional development; contribute to human prosperity through advancement of science and technology. **Structure** General Assembly (every 2 years). Executive Board, comprising President, 4 Deputy Presidents, Auditor and 6 members. Secretariat, headed by Secretary-General. Regional Boards (5): Americas; East Asia; European; Oceania; Arab and Africa. **Finance** Sources: members' dues. **Events** *Daejeon Global Innovation Forum* Daejeon (Korea Rep) 2019, *Conference* Daejeon (Korea Rep) 2017, *Daejeon Global Innovation Forum* Daejeon (Korea Rep) 2015, *International Nano Industrial City Forum* Daejeon (Korea Rep) 2015, *Daejeon Global Innovation Forum* Daejeon (Korea Rep) 2014. **Publications** *WTA Newsletter*.

Members Full; Associate; Discretionary. Cities in 17 countries:
Australia, Belarus, Brazil, Canada, China, France, Germany, India, Japan, Korea Rep, Malaysia, Mexico, New Zealand, Russia, Sweden, UK, USA.

Consultative Status Consultative status granted from: *UNESCO (#20322)* (Consultative Status). **IGO Relations** *Isfahan Regional Center for Technology Incubators and Science Park Development (IRIS, #16028)*. [2018/XM3680/**C**]

♦ World Telecommunication Forum (meeting series)
♦ World Telecommunication Policy Forum (meeting series)

♦ World Teleport Association (WTA) 21851

Exec Dir 250 Park Ave, 7th Floor, New York NY 10177, USA. T. +12128250218. Fax +12128250075. E-mail: wta@worldteleport.org.
URL: http://www.worldteleport.org/

History 1985, Tokyo (Japan). **Aims** Help teleport operators improve their operations, develop their markets and grow their businesses within the teleport sector of the global satellite industry; open new channels to the industry for companies that do business with teleports. **Structure** Board of Directors, comprising 12 voting members from 7 nations, headed by Chairman. Regional boards, each headed by a regional chairman (3) for: Americas; Asia; Europe. **Languages** English. **Staff** 5.50 FTE, paid. **Finance** Members' dues. Other sources: conferences; sponsorship; research online services. **Activities** Helps members understand how big market changes will affect them and offers information and advice on best practices in teleport operations and technology; works to build recognition for the teleport sector among satellite communications customers in media, enterprise and government; provides members with access to business opportunities around the world; organizes workshops and conference sessions at annual industry events, including SATELLITE, NAB, ISCe and SATCON. **Events** *Annual international satellite and communications conference* Long Beach, CA (USA) 2004, *Annual General Assembly* Calgary, AB (Canada) 2000, *Annual general assembly* Calgary, AB (Canada) 2000, *Annual General Assembly* New Orleans, LA (USA) 1999, *Meeting / Annual General Assembly* London (UK) 1998. **Publications** *WTA Uplink: Innovation via Satellite* (11 a year).

Members Teleports, Satellite Carriers, Technology Providers, Engineering/Construction, Consultants and Business Services in 30 countries and territories:
Australia, Belgium, Brazil, Canada, Cyprus, France, Greece, Hong Kong, India, Israel, Italy, Jamaica, Japan, Korea Rep, Mexico, Netherlands, Norway, Russia, Saudi Arabia, Singapore, South Africa, Spain, Sweden, Taiwan, Tajikistan, UK, United Arab Emirates, USA, Venezuela, Vietnam.

IGO Relations Associated with Department of Global Communications of the United Nations. **NGO Relations** Member of: *EUROCITIES (#05662)* Knowledge Society Forum; *Pacific Telecommunications Council (PTC, #18007)*. [2018/XF3797/y/**F**]

♦ World Tenniquoits Federation (WTF) 21852

SG Shafarnianskaya 2-111, 220125 Minsk, Belarus. E-mail: wtf.secretary.general@gmail.com.
URL: http://ringtennis.de/wtf/

History 18 Apr 2004, Vanderbijlpark (South Africa). **Aims** Promote the *sport* of tenniquoits, also known as ring *tennis*, tennikoit or deck tennis. **Structure** General Meeting; Executive Committee. **Languages** English. **Staff** 1.00 FTE, voluntary. **Finance** Members' dues. **Activities** Sporting activities. **Events** *Meeting* Koblenz (Germany) 2010, *Meeting* South Africa 2010.

Members Full in 11 countries:
Argentina, Bangladesh, Belarus, Brazil, Germany, India, Nepal, New Zealand, Pakistan, Poland, South Africa. [2018.07.19/XM1855/**D**]

♦ World Textile Art (unconfirmed)
♦ World Textile Rental Congress (meeting series)
♦ World Theosophical Youth Federation (inactive)

♦ World Toilet Association (WTA) 21853

Secretariat 463 3F Jangan-ro, Jangan-gu, Suwon GYEONGGI, Korea Rep. T. +82312214051. Fax +82312214053. E-mail: wta@withwta.org.
URL: http://www.withwta.org/

History Inaugurated 17 Dec 2007, Seoul (Korea Rep). **Aims** Protect lives through improvement of sanitation via toilets. **Structure** General Assembly; Board of Directors; Secretariat. **Activities** Projects/programmes; events/meetings; research/documentation. **Events** *World Toilet Leaders Forum* Suwon (Korea Rep) 2021, *World Toilet Leaders Forum* Suwon (Korea Rep) 2019, *World Toilet Leaders Forum* Suwon (Korea Rep) 2018, *Inaugural general assembly* Seoul (Korea Rep) 2007. **Publications** *Toilet World*. **Members** in 66 countries. Membership countries not specified. [2019/XM3619/**D**]

♦ World Toilet Organization (WTO) 21854

Founder and Dir 26 Ubi Rd 4, Suite 02-00, SDG Center, Singapore 408613, Singapore. T. +6563528921. E-mail: online@worldtoilet.org.
URL: http://www.worldtoilet.org/

History 19 Nov 2001, Singapore (Singapore). Founded at inaugural World Toilet Summit. World Toilet Day set on 19 Nov, as a recognition of the need of an international day to draw attention to the sanitation crisis. **Aims** Promote clean, safe, affordable, ecologically sound and sustainable sanitation for everyone; advocate sustainable toilet systems through capacity building and public education; work with NGOs, private sector, civil society organizations and international community to support World Toilet Day. **Structure** Board; Executive Director. **Languages** English. **Staff** 10.00 FTE, paid. **Finance** Funded by private organizations. **Activities** Advocacy/lobbying/activism; events/meetings; research and development; training/education. **Events** *World Toilet Summit* Abuja (Nigeria) 2022, *World Toilet Summit* Singapore (Singapore) 2020, *World Toilet Summit* Sao Paulo (Brazil) 2019, *World Toilet Summit* Mumbai (India) 2018, *World Toilet Summit* Melbourne, VIC (Australia) 2017. **Publications** *Toilet Times* (2 a year).

Members International Organizations (235) in 58 countries. Membership countries not specified.
Included in the above, one organization listed in this Yearbook:
Global Dry Toilet Association of Finland.

Consultative Status Consultative status granted from: *ECOSOC (#05331)* (Special); *UNEP (#20299)*. **NGO Relations** Member of (2): *End Water Poverty (EWP, #05464)*; *World Water Council (WWC, #21908)*. Participates in: *Sustainable Sanitation Alliance (SuSanA, #20066)*. [2022.03.04/XD8396/**D**]

♦ World Tort Law Society (WTLS) 21855

Contact c/o ECTIL, Reichsratsstrasse 17/2, 1010 Vienna, Austria. E-mail: worldtortlawsociety@gmail.com.
URL: https://www.worldtortlawsociety.com/

History 2012. Founded as a cooperation between *European Centre of Tort and Insurance Law (ECTIL, #06502)*, *Institute for European Tort Law (ETL)* and Research Centre for Civil and Commercial Jurisprudence, Renmin University, Beijing (China). **Aims** Create a forum for discussion about currents developments in tort law on a global scale. **Structure** Executive Committee, including President. **Languages** English. **Activities** Research projects. **Events** *Special Conference* 2021, *Meeting* New Taipei City (Taiwan) 2019, *Meeting* Wake Forest, NC (USA) 2017, *Meeting* Vienna (Austria) 2015, *Meeting* Harbin (China) 2013.

Members Full (26) in 21 countries and territories:
Australia, Austria, Canada, Chile, China, Denmark, France, Germany, India, Israel, Italy, Japan, Korea Rep, Macau, Malaysia, Netherlands, Russia, South Africa, Taiwan, UK, USA. [2019/XJ7791/**C**]

♦ World Touring and Automobile Organization (inactive)

♦ World Tourism Alliance (WTA) 21856

Secretariat Bldg 2, 9A Jianguomennei Ave, 100740 Beijing, China. T. +861085166810. Fax +861085166812. E-mail: info@wta-web.org.
URL: http://www.wta-web.org/

History 2017, Chengdu (China). **Aims** Promote tourism for peace, development and poverty alleviation; drive global tourism exchanges and cooperation at the non-governmental level. **Structure** General Assembly; Council; Secretariat.
Members Full (182) in 38 countries. Membership countries not specified.
European Federation of Chinese Tourism (EFCT). [2021/XM6231/**C**]

♦ World Tourism Association (WTA) 21857

Pres 512-1205 – 710 Gil 20, Hanamdaro Seogu, Gwangju 91903, Korea Rep. T. +82629618958.
URL: http://www.worldtourismassociation.org/

History 2014, Serbia. **Aims** Enhance the quality, value, effectiveness and use of research in travel marketing, planning and development. **Structure** Directorial Board; Committee. **Languages** English. **Staff** 8.00 FTE, paid; 3.00 FTE, voluntary. **Finance** Registration fees. **Activities** Awards/prizes/competitions; events/meetings; monitoring/evaluation; publishing activities; research/documentation; training/education. **Events** *World Tourism Conference* Athens (Greece) 2019, *World Tourism Conference* Chiang Mai (Thailand) 2019, *World Tourism Conference* Bangkok (Thailand) 2018, *World Tourism Conference* Hyderabad (India) 2018, *International Forum on Korea Rural Tourism Resources* Seoul (Korea Rep) 2017. **Publications** *International Journal of Tourism Research.* **Members** Organizations (27); Individuals (about 12,000) in 205 countries. Membership countries not specified. **NGO Relations** *World Cultural Tourism Association (WCTA, #21347)*; international organizations and educational institutions, not specified. [2020.03.05/XM5917/**C**]

♦ World Tourism Cities Federation (WTCF) 21858

Contact 6th Floor, No 3 Dongbinhe Road, Deshengmen, Xicheng District, 100120 Beijing, China. T. +861051550085. Fax +861065280923. E-mail: info@wtcf.org.cn.
URL: http://en.wtcf.org.cn/

History 15 Sep 2012, Beijing (China). Statutes approved 14 Sep 2012. Registration: China. **Aims** Promote coordinated economic and social development of World Tourism cities; enhance urban development; elevate the image of cities; strengthen inter-city international exchanges through tourism; innovate member cooperation. **Structure** General Assembly; Council; Secretariat, headed by Secretary-General. **Finance** Sources: members' dues. **Activities** Events/meetings; knowledge management/information dissemination; research/documentation; training/education. **Events** *Fragrant Hills Tourism Summit* Helsinki (Finland) 2019, *Fragrant Hills Tourism Summit* Qingdao (China) 2018, *Workshop on City Tourism Performance Research* Buenos Aires (Argentina) 2017, *Fragrant Hills Tourism Summit* Los Angeles, CA (USA) 2017, *Workshop on City Tourism Performance Research* Tianjin (China) 2017. **Publications** *World Tourism Cities Weekly* (weekly) – electronic; *World Tourism Cities.*
Members City (141); Institutional (77). Cities in 20 countries:
Argentina, Belgium, Canada, China, Egypt, Germany, Hungary, Indonesia, Ireland, Israel, Italy, Japan, Korea Rep, Latvia, Netherlands, Portugal, Russia, Spain, United Arab Emirates, USA.
NGO Relations Memorandum of Understanding with (1): *West Africa Tourism Organisation (WATO). World City Ice and Snow Tourism Cooperation Organization (WCISTCO).* [2020/XJ6260/**C**]

♦ World Tourism Education and Research Centre (internationally oriented national body)

♦ World Tourism Forum 21859

Contact Rua da Misericórdia 7, Praça da Sé, Salvador BA, 40020-200, Brazil. T. +557133244400. Fax +557133244401. E-mail: admin@worldtourismforum.org.
URL: http://www.worldtourismforum.org/

History Original title: *World Tourism Forum for Peace and Sustainable Development.* **Aims** Develop new concepts and practices for the tourism industry worldwide that promote: cultural diversity; economic and social development; biodiversity preservation; conditions for peace. **Structure** General Assembly; Board of Directors; Advisory Board; Committees. **Events** *Annual Summit* Porto Alegre (Brazil) 2006, *Annual Summit* Rio de Janeiro (Brazil) 2005, *Annual Summit* Salvador (Brazil) 2004. **IGO Relations** Organizing partners include: *UNDP (#20292)*; *UNESCO (#20322)*; *World Tourism Organization (UNWTO, #21861).* **NGO Relations** Supporting partners include: *Conservation International (CI)*; *Counterpart International (FSP)*; *EarthVoice*; *Fauna & Flora International (FFI, #09277)*; *International Academy for Quality (IAQ, #11573)*; *Rainforest Alliance*; *World Federation of United Nations Associations (WFUNA, #21499).* [2015/XM0028/**F**]

♦ World Tourism Forum Lucerne (internationally oriented national body)
♦ World Tourism Forum for Peace and Sustainable Development / see World Tourism Forum (#21859)

♦ World Tourism Network (WTN) 21860

Contact PO Box 15804, Honolulu HI 96830-5804, USA. T. +18085669900. Fax +13234886311. E-mail: membership@wtn.travel.
URL: https://wtn.travel/

History 2020. **Aims** Create innovative approaches for inclusive and sustainable tourism sector growth; assist small and medium travel and tourism businesses during both good and challenging times. **Structure** Board. **Activities** Awards/prizes/competitions; networking/liaising.
Members Full in 137 countries and territories:
Albania, Algeria, Angola, Antigua-Barbuda, Argentina, Armenia, Australia, Austria, Azerbaijan, Bahamas, Bahrain, Bangladesh, Barbados, Belgium, Belize, Benin, Bermuda, Bosnia-Herzegovina, Botswana, Brazil, Bulgaria, Cambodia, Cameroon, Canada, Cape Verde, Cayman Is, China, Colombia, Comoros, Congo Brazzaville, Congo DR, Côte d'Ivoire, Croatia, Cuba, Cyprus, Czechia, Dominica, Ecuador, Egypt, Estonia, Eswatini, Ethiopia, Fiji, France, Georgia, Germany, Ghana, Greece, Guam, Hong Kong, Hungary, India, Indonesia, Iran Islamic Rep, Ireland, Israel, Italy, Jamaica, Japan, Jordan, Kazakhstan, Kenya, Korea Rep, Lebanon, Lesotho, Liberia, Madagascar, Malawi, Malaysia, Maldives, Malta, Mauritius, Mexico, Micronesia FS, Monaco, Mongolia, Montenegro, Montserrat, Morocco, Mozambique, Myanmar, Namibia, Nepal, Netherlands, New Zealand, Nicaragua, Nigeria, Norway, Oman, Pakistan, Palau, Palestine, Papua New Guinea, Paraguay, Peru, Philippines, Poland, Portugal, Réunion, Romania, Russia, Rwanda, San Marino, Sao Tomé-Principe, Saudi Arabia, Senegal, Serbia, Seychelles, Sierra Leone, Singapore, Slovakia, Slovenia, Somalia, South Africa, Spain, Sri Lanka, St Lucia, St Vincent-Grenadines, Sudan, Sweden, Switzerland, Syrian AR, Tanzania UR, Thailand, Trinidad-Tobago, Tunisia, Türkiye, Uganda, UK, Ukraine, United Arab Emirates, Uruguay, USA, Uzbekistan, Venezuela, Zambia, Zimbabwe.
Association Internationale des Skål Clubs (AISC, #02743); *European Federation of Rural Tourism (RuralTour, #07208)*; *Global Travel and Tourism Partnership (GTTP, #10635)*; *International Association of Exhibitions and Events (IAEE)*; *International Institute for Peace through Tourism (IIPT)*; *World Association for Hospitality and Tourism Education and Training (WAHTT, #21144)*; *World Federation of Tourist Guide Associations (WFTGA, #21492)*; *World Travel and Tourism Council (WTTC, #21871).* [2021/AA2230/y/**B**]

♦ World Tourism Organization (UNWTO) 21861

Organisation Mondiale du Tourisme (OMT) – Organización Mundial del Turismo (OMT) – Vsemirnaya Turistskaya Organizatsiya

Headquarters Alle PoetaJoan Maragall 42, 28020 Madrid, Spain. T. +34915678100. E-mail: info@unwto.org.
URL: http://www2.unwto.org/

History Established 2 Jan 1975, as an intergovernmental organization, on entry into force of statutes adopted Sep 1970, Mexico City (Mexico). Nongovernmental predecessors were *International Congress of Official Tourist Traffic Associations – Congrès international des associations officielles de trafic touristique*, founded on May 1925, The Hague (Netherlands), and *International Union of Official Tourist Propaganda Organizations (IUOTPO) – Union internationale des organismes officiels de propagande touristique (UIOOPT)*, set up 1934, The Hague, and re-organized, 1947, Paris (France), as *International Union of Official Travel Organizations (IUOTO) – Union internationale des organismes officiels de tourisme (UIOOT).* Madrid (Spain) headquarters were established 1 Jan 1976, under resolution 2 (I) adopted at first session of General Assembly, May 1975, Madrid. Principles for cooperation and development in the field set out in *'Declaration of Manila on World Tourism'*, adopted 27 Sep-10 Oct 1980, and *'Acapulco Document'*, adopted 21-27 Aug 1982. *'Tourism Bill of Rights'* and *'Tourist Code'* adopted 17-26 Sep 1985, Sofia (Bulgaria). *'Global Code of Ethics for Tourism'* adopted Oct 1999, Santiago (Chile). Statutes registered in *'UNTS 1/14403'*. In English originally referred to as *WTO*; new acronym *'UNWTO'* adopted Dec 2005.
/Relationship with *United Nations System (#20635)*: Under resolution 2529 (XXIV) of 5 Dec 1969, the General Assembly of *United Nations (UN, #20515)* concluded an agreement of cooperation and relationship with the future World Tourism Organization and recognized its central and decisive role in the field, in cooperation with the existing mechanism within the United Nations system. UNWTO became a UN related agency in 1977. This role was substantially increased by Committees on Negotiations of ECOSOC and UNWTO, adopted, 6 Jun 2003, Madrid, by UNWTO Council and Jul 2003, Geneva (Switzerland), by ECOSOC. Final agreement later in 2003 by UN and UNWTO General Assemblies. The Organization became a specialized agency of the UN, 23 Dec 2003, pursuant to GA res 58/232.
Aims Promote and develop responsible, sustainable and universally accessible tourism so as to contribute to economic development, international understanding, peace, prosperity and universal respect for, and observance of, human rights and fundamental freedoms for all, without distinction as to race, sex, language or religion. In pursuing these aims, pay particular attention to the interests of developing countries in the field of tourism.
Structure General Assembly (every 2 years); Executive Council (meeting twice a year); Secretariat. Regional Commissions (6), meet at least one a year, and are composed of Full and Associate Members of the relevant region with Affiliate Members from the region participating as observers: *UNWTO Commission for Africa (CAF, see: #21861)*; *UNWTO Commission for the Americas (CAM, see: #21861)*; *UNWTO Commission for East Asia and the Pacific (CAP, see: #21861)*; *UNWTO Commission for Europe (CEU, see: #21861)*; *UNWTO Commission for the Middle East (CME, see: #21861)*; *UNWTO Commission for South Asia (CSA, see: #21861).*
Specialized committees are subsidiary organs of the UNWTO Executive Council, except the World Committee on Tourism Ethics which is a subsidiary organ of the General Assembly: *'World Committee on Tourism Ethics'*. Specialized committees and subsidiary organs of the Executive Council: Programme and budget Committee (PBC); Committee on Statistics and the Tourism Satellite Account; Committee on Tourism and Competitiveness; Committee on Tourism and Sustainability; World Committee on Tourism Ethics; Committee for the Review of Applications for Affiliate Membership.
Councils of Affiliate Members which participate in UNWTO activities, make recommendations to its bodies and carry out studies and seminars in the framework of the UNWTO Programme of Work.
Languages Arabic, English, French, Russian, Spanish. **Staff** 96.00 FTE, paid. Negotiations through *UNWTO Staff Association, Madrid. Administrative Tribunal of the International Labour Organization (ILO Tribunal, #00118)* is competent to settle disputes. **Finance** Main source: members' contributions assessed according to a scale accepted by the General Assembly; other sources in accordance with UNWTO Financing Rules. **Activities** Capacity building; certification/accreditation; events/meetings; guidance/assistance/consulting; knowledge management/information dissemination; networking/liaising; research/documentation; training/education. **Events** *World Forum on Gastronomy Tourism* Nara (Japan) 2022, *World Tourism Industry Conference* Ulsan (Korea Rep) 2022, *World Forum on Gastronomy Tourism* Bruges (Belgium) 2021, *Global Golden Tourism Forum* Seoul (Korea Rep) 2021, *Tourism and Innovation in the Ibero-American Space* Madrid (Spain) 2020. **Publications** *Yearbook of Tourism Statistics. Compendium of Tourism Statistics*; *Tourism Market Trends*; *UNWTO World Tourism Barometer.* Publishes about 100 publications a year. Available on website.
Information Services *E-library* – publications corresponding to both the Organization's concerns and the needs of members (over 1,000 publications and about 900 tables).
Members Governments of 156 countries:
Afghanistan, Albania, Algeria, Andorra, Angola, Argentina, Armenia, Australia, Austria, Azerbaijan, Bahamas, Bahrain, Bangladesh, Belarus, Benin, Bhutan, Bolivia, Bosnia-Herzegovina, Botswana, Brazil, Brunei Darussalam, Bulgaria, Burkina Faso, Burundi, Cambodia, Cameroon, Cape Verde, Central African Rep, Chad, Chile, China, Colombia, Congo Brazzaville, Congo DR, Costa Rica, Côte d'Ivoire, Croatia, Cuba, Cyprus, Czechia, Djibouti, Dominican Rep, Ecuador, Egypt, El Salvador, Equatorial Guinea, Eritrea, Eswatini, Ethiopia, Fiji, France, Gabon, Gambia, Georgia, Germany, Ghana, Greece, Guatemala, Guinea, Guinea-Bissau, Haiti, Honduras, Hungary, India, Indonesia, Iran Islamic Rep, Iraq, Israel, Italy, Jamaica, Japan, Jordan, Kazakhstan, Kenya, Korea DPR, Korea Rep, Kuwait, Kyrgyzstan, Laos, Lebanon, Lesotho, Liberia, Libya, Lithuania, Madagascar, Malawi, Malaysia, Maldives, Mali, Malta, Mauritania, Mauritius, Mexico, Moldova, Monaco, Mongolia, Montenegro, Morocco, Mozambique, Myanmar, Namibia, Nepal, Netherlands, Nicaragua, Niger, Nigeria, North Macedonia, Norway, Oman, Pakistan, Panama, Papua New Guinea, Paraguay, Peru, Philippines, Poland, Portugal, Qatar, Romania, Russia, Rwanda, San Marino, Sao Tomé-Principe, Saudi Arabia, Senegal, Serbia, Seychelles, Sierra Leone, Slovakia, Slovenia, South Africa, Spain, Sri Lanka, Sudan, Switzerland, Syrian AR, Tajikistan, Tanzania UR, Thailand, Timor-Leste, Togo, Trinidad-Tobago, Tunisia, Türkiye, Turkmenistan, Uganda, Ukraine, United Arab Emirates, Uruguay, Uzbekistan, Vanuatu, Venezuela, Vietnam, Yemen, Zambia, Zimbabwe.
Associate members in 6 countries and territories:
Aruba, Belgium/Flemish Region, Hong Kong, Macau, Madeira, Puerto Rico.
Observers in 2 territories:
Holy See, Palestine.
Affiliate members (433), of which 26 organizations listed in this Yearbook:

- *Association Internationale des Skål Clubs (AISC, #02743)*;
- *Caribbean Tourism Organization (CTO, #03561)*;
- *City Destinations Alliance (CityDNA, #03960)*;
- *Confederation of National Associations of Hotels, Restaurants, Cafés and Similar Establishments in the European Union and European Economic Area (HOTREC, #04569)*;
- *European Travel and Tourism Advisory Group (ETAG, #08946)*;
- *European Travel Commission (ETC, #08943)*;
- *Fédération Internationale de l'Automobile (FIA, #09613)*;
- *Fédération Internationale de Motocyclisme (FIM, #09643)*;
- *Foundation for Environmental Education (FEE, #09949)*;
- *International Air Transport Association (IATA, #11614)*;
- *International Centre for Tourism and Hospitality Research (ICTHR, no recent information)*;
- *International Centre of Studies on the Tourist Economy (CISET)*;
- *International Congress and Convention Association (ICCA, #12892)*;
- *International Gay and Lesbian Travel Association (IGLTA)*;
- *International Road Transport Union (IRU, #14761)*;
- *International Social Tourism Organisation (ISTO, #14889)*;
- *Istituto per la Cooperazione Economica Internazionale (ICEI)*;
- *Meeting Professionals International (MPI, #16695)*;
- *Rainforest Alliance*;
- *United Federation of Travel Agents' Associations (UFTAA, #20509)*;
- *United Nations Foundation (UNF, #20563)*;
- *World Association for Hospitality and Tourism Education and Training (WAHTT, #21144)*;
- *World Federation of Tourist Guide Associations (WFTGA, #21492)*;
- *World Federation of Travel Journalists and Writers (#21494)*;
- *World Leisure Organization (WLO, #21624)*;
- *World Youth Student and Educational Travel Confederation (WYSE Travel Confederation, #21959).*

IGO Relations Member of: *United Nations System Chief Executives Board for Coordination (CEB, #20636)*, supported by its 3 pillars – United Nations High Level Committee for Programmes (HLCP), United Nationals High Level Committee for Management (HLCM) and *United Nations Sustainable Development Group (UNSDG, #20634)*; *UN-Water (#20723).* Observer status with: *World Trade Organization (WTO, #21864).*
Cooperates with:

- *FAO (#09260)*;
- *ILO (#11123)*;
- *International Civil Aviation Organization (ICAO, #12581)*;
- *International Maritime Organization (IMO, #14102)*;
- *OAS (#17629)*;
- *Secretariat of the Convention on Biological Diversity (SCBD, #19197)*;
- *UNEP (#20299)*;
- *UNDP (#20292)*;
- *UNESCO (#20322)*;
- *United Nations (UN, #20515)*;
- *United Nations Economic Commission for Africa (ECA, #20554)*;
- *United Nations Economic Commission for Latin America and the Caribbean (ECLAC, #20556)*;
- *United Nations Economic and Social Commission for Asia and the Pacific (ESCAP, #20557)*;
- *United Nations Group on the Information Society (UNGIS, #20570)*;
- *WHO (#20950)*;
- *The World Bank Group (#21218)*;

– *World Meteorological Organization (WMO, #21649).*
NGO Relations Cooperates with: *International Organization for Standardization (ISO, #14473). International Union for Conservation of Nature and Natural Resources (IUCN, #15766); United Nations Foundation (UNF, #20563); World Tourism Research and Education Centre, Zagreb (no recent information),* University of Zagreb. Instrumental in setting up: *World Tourism Education and Research Centre (WTERC).* [2020/XB2745/y/**B***]

♦ World Trade Alliance Association (inactive)

♦ World Trade Centers Association (WTCA) 21862

Association des centres du commerce international – Asociación de los Centros del Comercio Mundial

Main Office 115 Broadway, Ste 1202, New York NY 10006, USA.
URL: http://www.wtca.org/

History Apr 1968, New Orleans, LA (USA). A *'World Trade Center (WTC)'* is defined as one or more buildings providing for the centralized accommodation of both activities and services devoted to the promotion and furthering of world trade. Registration: USA, Delaware. **Aims** Unite individual trade centers; promote mutual assistance and a cooperative exchange of services and information among members; encourage establishment of new centers and development of improved services in existing centers; promote international business relationships; foster increased participation in world trade by developing nations. **Structure** General Assembly (annual); International Board of Directors; Committees. **Languages** English. **Staff** 24.00 FTE, paid. **Finance** Sources: members' dues. Other sources: Initiation fees. **Activities** Events/meetings; knowledge management/information dissemination; networking/liaising. **Events** *Annual General Assembly* 2022, *Annual General Assembly* 2021, *Annual General Assembly* Taipei (Taiwan) 2020, *Annual General Assembly* Santiago de Querétaro (Mexico) 2019, *Annual General Assembly* Leeuwarden (Netherlands) 2018. **Publications** *WTCA News* (12 a year); *Trade Center Profiles* (annual); *World Business Directory* (annual). *International Directory of WTC Tenants*; *WTCA Membership Directory.* General Assembly proceedings. **Information Services** *World Trade Center Network* – low-cost international communications system and database. **Members** Regular Membership: organizations substantially involved in the development or operation of a world trade center; Affiliate: world trade center clubs, libraries; chambers of commerce and similar organizations representing a group of businessmen interested in foreign trade expansion through world trade centers. World trade centers and affiliated organizations (322) in 88 countries and territories. Membership countries not specified. **Consultative Status** Consultative status granted from: *ECOSOC (#05331)* (Special); *UNCTAD (#20285)* (General Category). **IGO Relations** Accredited by: *United Nations Office at Vienna (UNOV, #20604).* **NGO Relations** Instrumental in setting up: *Mediterranean World Trade Centre (no recent information).*
[2022/XC3587/t/**C**]

♦ World Trade Institute (WTI) 21863

Managing Dir Univ of Bern, Hallerstr 6, 3012 Bern, Switzerland. T. +41316313270. E-mail: manfred.elsig@wti.org – inquire@wti.org.
URL: http://www.wti.org/

History Founded upon conclusion of the Uruguay Round of the *General Agreement on Tariffs and Trade, 1994 (GATT 1994, 1994),* 1995. Established 1999. **Aims** Shape public policy so that international economic governance yields tangible benefits for society; train future practitioners and researchers from all over the world; strengthen research capacities in areas that have an increasing impact on people's lives. **Structure** Executive Board of Directors; Administration; Executive Board; Managing Director. **Languages** English. **Staff** 25.00 FTE, paid. **Finance** Financed by: SNSF, University of Bern (Switzerland). Annual budget (2018): Swiss Fr 4,525,000. **Activities** Training/education; research/documentation; guidance/assistance/consulting; events/meetings. **Events** *World Trade Forum* Grindelwald (Switzerland) 2017, *Seminar on marketing and promotion of tourism* New York, NY (USA) 1989. **Publications** *Trade Winds* (4 a year) – newsletter. *World Trade Forum* – books series. **NGO Relations** Member of: *Network of Internet and Society Research Centers (NoC, #17045).*
[2019.02.18/XM6094/jt/**E**]

♦ World Trade Law Association (no recent information)

♦ World Trade Organization (WTO) 21864

Organisation mondiale du commerce (OMC) – Organización Mundial del Comercio

Dir Gen Centre William Rappard, Rue de Lausanne 154, 1211 Geneva 2, Switzerland. T. +41227395111. Fax +41227314206. E-mail: enquiries@wto.org.
Media and External Relations Officer address not obtained.
URL: http://www.wto.org/

History 1 Jan 1995. Established on entry into force of *Agreement Establishing the World Trade Organization (Marrakech Agreement).* Set up to encompass *General Agreement on Tariffs and Trade (GATT, inactive),* following successful conclusion, 15 Dec 1993, of the *'Uruguay Round Negotiations'* which had commenced in 1986. The Final Act of the Uruguay Round was signed on 15 Apr 1994, Marrakech (Morocco), by 111 countries, 104 countries signing the Marrakech Agreement the same day.
The idea of an *International Trade Organization (ITO) – Organisation internationale du commerce (OIC) – Organización Internacional de Comercio (OIC)* was first put forward by John Maynard Keynes and others in the 1940s, but not materialized. GATT, negotiated and signed by 23 countries in 1947, and established on 1 Jan 1948, Geneva (Switzerland), was a forerunner. At the same time, a number of countries were working on drawing up a charter for a proposed ITO, which would have been a specialized agency of the United Nations. The GATT was signed, 30 Oct 1947, ahead of *'UN Conference on Trade and Employment'*, 21 Nov 1947, Cuba. One of its provisions said that the agreement should accept some of the trade rules of the draft ITO chart, and it largely based on selected parts of the draft ITO charter. In order to get trade liberalization underway quickly it was provided with only minimum institutional arrangements because it was expected that responsibility for it would soon be assumed by ITO. However, plans for ITO were abandoned when it became clear that its charter would not be ratified and GATT was left as the only international instrument laying down trade rules accepted by the nations responsible for most of the world's trade. *'Interim Commission for the International Trade Organization (ICITO/GATT) – Organization (ICITO/GATT) – Commission intérimaire de l'Organisation internationale du commerce'*, set up Mar 1948, Geneva, to work on the proposed ITO, continued to exist, from 1954 in the form of the GATT secretariat in Geneva, its members being the governments of 128 countries at end of 1994.
The proposals which eventually succeeded in establishing WTO were initiated by *European Community (inactive)* and Canada, and subsequently supported by Japan. The Marrakech Agreement envisaged a single institutional framework encompassing: GATT, as modified by the Uruguay Round; all agreements concluded under its auspices; the complete results of the Uruguay Round. It stipulates that *General Agreement on Tariffs and Trade, 1947 (GATT 1947, 1947)* and *General Agreement on Tariffs and Trade, 1994 (GATT 1994, 1994)* are two different agreements – they are legally distinct – although GATT 1994 includes the text of GATT 1947 and its legal instruments, as well as of several Understandings on interpretations and modifications of GATT Articles plus the Marrakech Protocol containing schedules of concessions on goods. GATT 1947 continued to exist to the end of 1995, allowing GATT member countries to accede to WTO and permitting an overlap in activities. GATT 1994 is an integral part of the WTO Agreement. The WTO framework ensures a "single undertaking approach" to the results of the Uruguay Round so that membership in the WTO entails accepting all the results of the Round without exception. WTO has a larger membership than GATT and much broader scope in terms of the commercial activity and trade policies to which it applies. Whereas GATT applied only to trade in merchandise goods, the WTO covers trade in goods, services and intellectual property, being covered in the separate *General Agreement on Trade in Services (GATS, 1994)* and *WTO Agreement on Trade Related Aspects of Intellectual Property Rights (TRIPS, 1994)*; which were signed 15 Apr 1994, Marrakech (Morocco), as part of the Final Act of the 1986-1994 Uruguay Round of trade negotiations.
A Protocol of Amendement was opened for acceptance 27 Nov 2014 and following its ratification, it inserted *Trade Facilitation Agreement (TFA, 2014)* into the WTO Agreement.
'WTO Preparatory Committee', which ensured a smooth transition to the implementation of the WTO, ceased to exist on entering into force of the WTO Agreement.
Although the WTO is effectively a separate organization, WTO-UN relations are governed by "Arrangements for Effective Cooperation with other Intergovernmental Organizations-Relations Between the WTO and the United Nations" signed on 15 Nov 1995. The text sees no grounds for formal institutional links between WTO and *United Nations System (#20635)* although it recognizes the need for the establishment of cooperative ties between the two organizations. Although it is not one of the financial institutions set up following the Bretton Woods Conference, 22 Jul 1944, the WTO is nevertheless sometimes included when referring to *Bretton Woods Institutions (BWIs, #03322).*
Aims Ensure that trade flows as smoothly, predictably and freely as possible by: administering trade *agreements*; acting as a forum for trade *negotiations*; settling trade disputes; reviewing national trade policies; assisting *developing countries* in trade *policy* issues, through technical assistance and training programmes; cooperating with other international organizations.
Structure Ministerial Conference (at least every 2 years). General Council oversees operation of the agreement and ministerial decisions, also acting as Dispute Settlement Body (DSB) and Trade Policy Review Body (TPRB), which have their own Chairpersons.
/Subsidiary Bodies/
Reporting to the General Council -
I. Committees and Working Groups/Parties:
– Committee on Trade and Environment (CTE);
– Committee on Trade and Development, including Sub-Committee on Least-Developed Countries;
– Committee on Regional Trade Agreements;
– Committee on the Balance of Payments Restrictions;
– Committee on Budget, Finance and Administration;
– Working Group on Trade, Debt and Finance;
– Working Group on Trade and Technology Transfer;
– Working Party on Accession.
II. Council for Trade in Goods (Goods Council) and related bodies:
– Committee on Market Access;
– Committee on Agriculture;
– Committee on Sanitary and Phytosanitary Measures, for *WTO Agreement on the Application of Sanitary and Phytosanitary Measures (SPS agreement, 1993)*;
– Committee on Technical Barriers to Trade;
– Committee on Subsidies and Countervailing Measures;
– Committee on Anti-Dumping Practices;
– Committee on Customs Valuation;
– Committee on Rules of Origin;
– Committee on Import Licensing;
– Committee on Trade-Related Investment Measures;
– Committee on Safeguards;
– Committee on Trade Facilitation;
– Working Party on State-Trading Enterprises.
III. Council for Trade-Related Aspects of Intellectual Property Rights (TRIPS Council) for WTO Agreement on Trade Related Aspects of Intellectual Property Rights (TRIPS).
IV. Council for Trade in Services for General Agreement on Trade in Services (GATS), and related bodies:
– Committee on Trade in Financial Services;
– Committee on Specific Commitments;
– Working Party on Domestic Regulation;
– Working Party on GATS Rules;
– Trade in Civil Aircraft Committee (plurilateral) for *Agreement on Trade in Civil Aircraft (1979).*
– Government Procurement Committee and plurilateral committee, for *Agreement on Government Procurement (1979).*
V. Trade Negotiations Committee, including:
– Special Session of Services Council;
– Special Session of TRIPS Council;
– Special Session of Dispute Settlement Body;
– Special Session of Agriculture Committee, including Cotton Sub-Committee;
– Special Session of Trade and Development Committee;
– Special Session of Trade and Environment Committee;
– Negotiating Group on Market Access;
– Negotiating Group on Rules;
– Negotiating Group on Trade Facilitation.
Director-General appointed by General Council. Ministerial Conference. Secretariat in Geneva (Switzerland).
Languages English, French, Spanish. **Staff** 625.00 FTE, paid. Personnel negotiations through *WTO/OMC Staff Association, Geneva (no recent information).* The *Administrative Tribunal of the International Labour Organization (ILO Tribunal, #00118)* is competent to settle disputes. **Finance** Financial regulations relating to scale of contributions and budget are based on rules and practices of GATT. Contributions depend on share of total trade of WTO members. Annual budget: 197,203,900 CHF (2020).
Activities Covers the previous activities of GATT and provides a legal mechanism to administer the results of the Uruguay Round negotiations. Councils and committees facilitate implementation and operation of all agreements and legal instruments in connection with the Uruguay Round, including 'Plurilateral Trade Agreements', which include *International Dairy Agreement (1979)* and International Bovine Meat Agreement – Agreement on trade in civil aircraft and Agreement on government procurement – and 'General Agreement on Trade in Services (GATS)', of which countries must be members in order to be members of WTO. The TRIPS agreement recognizes that varying standards in protection and enforcement of intellectual property rights and lack of multilateral disciplines dealing with international trade in counterfeit goods cause increasing tension in international relations. It therefore addresses: applicability of basic GATT principles and of relevant intellectual property agreements; provision of adequate intellectual property rights and provision of effective enforcement for those rights; multilateral disputes management; transitional implementation arrangements. WTO provides a forum for negotiations and administers the 'Understanding on Rules and Procedures Governing the Settlement of Disputes' and the 'Trade Policy Review Mechanism (TPRM)'. TPRM was established provisionally in 1989, subsequently becoming permanent under WTO; it periodically reviews national trade policies of all WTO members.
'Dispute Settlement': From 1 Jan 1995, new procedures are set out in the Dispute Settlement Understanding annexed to the WTO Agreement. WTO decisions are normally taken by consensus, voting only taking place if consensus cannot be reached (to date this has never occurred). In these cases, a majority of three quarters of the membership may adopt an interpretation of any multilateral trade agreement or may waive an obligation imposed on a particular member by such an agreement. To amend a provision, either all members must agree, or a majority of two thirds, depending on the type of provision. A two thirds majority is also required to admit a new member.
'Doha Development Agenda', launched at 4th Session of WTO Ministerial Conference, 9-14 Nov 2001, Doha (Qatar), comprises a new round of multilateral trade negotiations. Under the Agenda, a *'Trade Negotiations Committee (TNC)'*, which is chaired by WTO Director-General and responds to General Council, supervises negotiations previously taking place at different subsidiary bodies. *'Doha Development Agenda Global Trust Fund'*, which finances technical assistance programmes, helps countries participate in and benefit from ongoing WTO negotiations.
'Trade without discrimination': allowing for exemptions and special conditions within customs unions and free trade areas, members are required to grant to the products of any other member treatment no less favourable than that accorded products of any other country ('most-favoured nation' clause); in addition, once goods have entered a market they must be treated no less favourably than the equivalent domestically-produced goods. Other non-discrimination provision s include those on rules of origin, pre-shipment inspection, trade-related investment measures and application of sanitary and phytosanitary measures.
'Predictable and growing access to markets': the multilateral trading system is an attempt by governments to provide investors, employers, employees and consumers with a business environment encouraging trade, investment and job creation, and choice and low prices in the market place. Predictable trading conditions are assisted by transparent domestic laws, regulations and practices. WTO agreements contain transparency provisions which require disclosure at national or multilateral level; and WTO bodies review such notifications and regularly survey national trade policies through the Trade Policy Review Mechanism.
'Promoting fair competition': rules on non-discrimination are designed to secure fair conditions of trade, as are those on dumping and subsidies. Existing GATT rules laying down the bas is on which governments may impose compensating duties on unfair competition are extended and clarified in WTO agreements.
'Encouraging development and economic reform': developing countries, although prepared to take on most obligations required of developed countries, have transition periods in which to make adjustments. In particular, least-developed countries (LDCs) have extra flexibility and WTO agreements call for acceleration in implementing market access concessions for goods exported by these countries.

'Assisting developing and transition economies': WTO Secretariat, alone or in cooperation with other international organizations, conducts missions and seminars and provides specific, practical technical cooperation for governments and their officials dealing with accession negotiations, implementing WTO commitments or seeking to participate effectively in multilateral negotiations. Courses and individual assistance on particular WTO activities include dispute settlement and trade policy reviews. GATT's programme of training courses for officials of developing countries, held twice a year from 1955, is continued under WTO.
'Specialized help for export promotion' is provided by International Trade Centre, jointly operated by WTO and the United Nations through UNCTAD. The Centre responds to requests from developing countries for assistance in formulating and implementing export promotion programmes as well as import operations and techniques. It provides information and advice on export markets and marketing techniques and assists in establishing export promotion and marketing services and in training personnel. Help is freely available to least-developed countries.
'Overseeing national trade policies': under the TPRM, the 4 biggest traders (the European Union, USA, Japan and China) are examined by the General Council functioning as the Trade Policy Review Body (TPRB) every 2 years, the 16 next important every 4 years and the remaining countries every 6 years or even less frequently for LDCs. In addition many other WTO agreements require members to notify WTO Secretariat of new or modified trade measures. WTO cooperates with the World Bank and International Monetary Fund for greater coherence in global economic policy making.
'Making trade and environment policies mutually supportive': the Committee on Trade and Environment aims to identify the relationship between trade measures and environmental measures in order to promote sustainable development and make appropriate recommendations on whether modifications of the provisions of the multilateral trading system are required.
Events *Aid for Trade Global Review Conference* Geneva (Switzerland) 2022, *Ministerial Conference* Geneva (Switzerland) 2022, *Public Forum* Geneva (Switzerland) 2022, *Ministerial Conference* Geneva (Switzerland) 2021, *Public Forum* Geneva (Switzerland) 2021. **Publications** *World Trade Report* (annual); *World Trade Statistical Review* (annual). Annual Report; international trade statistics; occasional studies.
Members Original members of the WTO are GATT member countries as of the date of entry into force of the WTO Agreement. However, least developed countries (LDCs) are only required to undertake commitments and concessions to the extent consistent with their individual development. Accession procedures and majority of two thirds of the members requirements remain the same as under GATT. Of a potential membership of 152 countries and territories, 76 governments became members on 1 Jan 1995, others subsequently completed or are completing their domestic ratification process and the remainder are negotiating their terms of entry.
As of Jul 2016, 164 -members:
Afghanistan, Albania, Angola, Antigua-Barbuda, Argentina, Armenia, Australia, Austria, Bahrain, Bangladesh, Barbados, Belgium, Belize, Benin, Bolivia, Botswana, Brazil, Brunei Darussalam, Bulgaria, Burkina Faso, Burundi, Cambodia, Cameroon, Canada, Cape Verde, Central African Rep, Chad, Chile, China, Colombia, Congo Brazzaville, Congo DR, Costa Rica, Côte d'Ivoire, Croatia, Cuba, Cyprus, Czechia, Denmark, Djibouti, Dominica, Dominican Rep, Ecuador, Egypt, El Salvador, Estonia, Eswatini, Fiji, Finland, France, Gabon, Gambia, Georgia, Germany, Ghana, Greece, Grenada, Guatemala, Guinea, Guinea-Bissau, Guyana, Haiti, Honduras, Hong Kong, Hungary, Iceland, India, Indonesia, Ireland, Israel, Italy, Jamaica, Japan, Jordan, Kazakhstan, Kenya, Korea Rep, Kuwait, Kyrgyzstan, Laos, Latvia, Lesotho, Liberia, Liechtenstein, Lithuania, Luxembourg, Macau, Madagascar, Malawi, Malaysia, Maldives, Mali, Malta, Mauritania, Mauritius, Mexico, Moldova, Mongolia, Montenegro, Morocco, Mozambique, Myanmar, Namibia, Nepal, Netherlands, New Zealand, Nicaragua, Niger, Nigeria, North Macedonia, Norway, Oman, Pakistan, Panama, Papua New Guinea, Paraguay, Peru, Philippines, Poland, Portugal, Qatar, Romania, Russia, Rwanda, Samoa, Saudi Arabia, Senegal, Seychelles, Sierra Leone, Singapore, Slovakia, Slovenia, Solomon Is, South Africa, Spain, Sri Lanka, St Kitts-Nevis, St Lucia, St Vincent-Grenadines, Suriname, Sweden, Switzerland, Taiwan, Tajikistan, Tanzania UR, Thailand, Togo, Tonga, Trinidad-Tobago, Tunisia, Türkiye, Uganda, UK, Ukraine, United Arab Emirates, Uruguay, USA, Vanuatu, Venezuela, Vietnam, Yemen, Zambia, Zimbabwe.
European Union (EU, #08967).
Observer governments (25):
Algeria, Andorra, Azerbaijan, Bahamas, Belarus, Bhutan, Bosnia-Herzegovina, Comoros, Curaçao, Equatorial Guinea, Ethiopia, Holy See, Iran Islamic Rep, Iraq, Lebanon, Libya, Sao Tomé-Principe, Serbia, Somalia, South Sudan, Sudan, Syrian AR, Timor-Leste, Turkmenistan, Uzbekistan.
IGO Relations On 25 Jul 1996, the Council adopted the procedures to grant Observer Status to international organizations. Organizations with Observer Status at General Council:
- *FAO (#09260)*;
- *International Bank for Reconstruction and Development (IBRD, #12317)* (World Bank);
- *International Monetary Fund (IMF, #14180)*;
- *International Trade Centre (ITC, #15703)*;
- *OECD (#17693)*;
- *UNCTAD (#20285)*;
- *United Nations (UN, #20515)*;
- *World Intellectual Property Organization (WIPO, #21593)*.

At Trade Policy Review Body:
- *EFTA (#05391)*;
- *European Bank for Reconstruction and Development (EBRD, #06315)*;
- FAO;
- IBRD/World Bank;
- IMF;
- OECD;
- UNCTAD.

Organizations in addition to the above with Observer Status in other councils and committees:
- *Organisation of African, Caribbean and Pacific States (OACPS, #17796)*;
- *African Union (AU, #00488)*;
- *Andean Community (#00817)*;
- *Arab Investment and Export Credit Guarantee Corporation (DHAMAN, #00997)*;
- *Arab Maghreb Union (AMU, #01004)*;
- *Caribbean Community (CARICOM, #03476)* Secretariat;
- *Common Fund for Commodities (CFC, #04293)*;
- *Commonwealth Secretariat (#04362)*;
- *Communauté économique et monétaire d'Afrique centrale (CEMAC, #04374)*;
- *Convention on Biological Diversity (Biodiversity convention, 1992)*;
- *Convention on International Trade in Endangered Species of Wild Fauna and Flora (CITES, 1973)*;
- *Economic Community of West African States (ECOWAS, #05312)*;
- *Economic Cooperation Organization (ECO, #05313)*;
- *Inter-American Development Bank (IDB, #11427)*;
- *Inter-American Institute for Cooperation on Agriculture (IICA, #11434)*;
- *International Civil Aviation Organization (ICAO, #12581)*;
- *International Grains Council (IGC, #13731)*;
- *International Organization of Legal Metrology (#14451)*;
- *International Plant Protection Convention, 1951 (IPPC, 1951)*;
- *International Telecommunication Union (ITU, #15673)*;
- *International Textiles and Clothing Bureau (ITCB, #15680)*;
- *Islamic Development Bank (IsDB, #16044)*;
- *Latin American Integration Association (LAIA, #16343)*;
- *OAS (#17629)*;
- *OIE – World Organisation for Animal Health (#17703)*;
- *Organisation of Islamic Cooperation (OIC, #17813)*;
- *Pacific Islands Forum (#17968)*;
- *Organismo Internacional Regional de Sanidad Agropecuaria (OIRSA, #17830)*;
- *Secretaria Permanente del Tratado General de Integración Económica Centroamericana (SIECA, #19195)*;
- *Sistema Económico Latinoamericano (SELA, #19294)*;
- *Southeast Asian Fisheries Development Center (SEAFDEC, #19767)*;
- *Southern African Development Community (SADC, #19843)*;
- *GCC Standardization Organization (GSO, #10084)*;
- *UNEP (#20299)*;
- *UNDP (#20292)*;
- *UNIDO (#20336)*;
- *Union économique et monétaire Ouest africaine (UEMOA, #20377)*;
- *Union internationale pour la protection des obtentions végétales (UPOV, #20436)*;
- *United Nations Commission on International Trade Law (UNCITRAL, #20531)*;
- *United Nations Economic Commission for Africa (ECA, #20554)*;
- *United Nations Economic Commission for Europe (UNECE, #20555)*;
- *United Nations Economic Commission for Latin America and the Caribbean (ECLAC, #20556)*;
- *United Nations Economic and Social Commission for Asia and the Pacific (ESCAP, #20557)*;
- *United Nations Framework Convention on Climate Change – Secretariat (UNFCCC, #20564)*;
- *Universal Postal Union (UPU, #20682)*;
- *WHO (#20950)*;
- *World Customs Organization (WCO, #21350)*;
- *World Food Programme (WFP, #21510)*;
- *World Tourism Organization (UNWTO, #21861)*.

Also invited on an ad-hoc basis:
- *Secretariat of the Basel Convention (SBC, #19196)*;
- *Secretariat of the Rotterdam Convention (#19206)*;
- *Secretariat of the Stockholm Convention on Persistent Organic Pollutants (Secretariat of the Stockholm Convention, #19207)*;
- *Secretariat for the Vienna Convention for the Protection of the Ozone Layer and the Montreal Protocol on Substances that Deplete the Ozone Layer (Ozone Secretariat, #19209)*.

Member of: *United Nations Group on the Information Society (UNGIS, #20570)*. Represented on: *United Nations System Chief Executives Board for Coordination (CEB, #20636)*. Has been represented in meetings of: *Round Table on Sustainable Development at the OECD (see: #17693)*. Observer status with:
- ACP;
- Bioversity International;
- CBD;
- CITES;
- *Basel Convention on the Control of Transboundary Movements of Hazardous Wastes and Their Disposal (UNCRTD, 1989)*;
- CSD;
- ECE;
- EFTA;
- FAO;
- IBRD/World Bank;
- IGC;
- IMF;
- *International Commission for the Conservation of Atlantic Tunas (ICCAT, #12675)*;
- *International Fund for Agricultural Development (IFAD, #13692)*;
- ITC; Montréal Protocol; OECD;
- *Office of the United Nations High Commissioner for Human Rights (OHCHR, #17697)*;
- Pacific Islands Forum;
- SELA;
- Stockholm Convention;
- UNCITRAL;
- UNCTAD;
- UNDP;
- UNEP;
- *UNESCO (#20322)*;
- UNFCCC;
- UNIDO;
- United Nations;
- UPOV;
- WCO;
- WHO;
- WIPO. [2023/XF2527/t/**B***]

♦ World Trade Point Federation (WTPF) 21865

Contact address not obtained. T. +41229075511. Fax +41229070050.
History Nov 2000, at the initiative of *UNCTAD (#20285)*. Takes over activities of Trade Point Programme of UNCTAD. Registered in accordance with Swiss law. Secretariat in Geneva (Switzerland). **Aims** Open international trade to small and medium-sized *enterprises* by simplifying and harmonizing trade procedures worldwide; disseminate knowledge about best practice; increase access to advanced technology and information networks. **Structure** General Assembly (annual). Steering Committee; Board. **Finance** Supported by: Government of France; *Development Bank of Latin America (CAF, #05055)*. **Events** *General Assembly* Bangkok (Thailand) 2005. **Consultative Status** Consultative status granted from: *ECOSOC (#05331)* (Ros A). **IGO Relations** Partners: *International Bank for Reconstruction and Development (IBRD, #12317)*; *International Trade Centre (ITC, #15703)*; UNCTAD; *United Nations Economic Commission for Europe (UNECE, #20555)*; *World Trade Organization (WTO, #21864)*. **NGO Relations** Partner: *Centre for the Promotion of Imports from Developing Countries (CBI)*; companies. [2010/XJ3147/t/**D**]

♦ World Trails Network (WTN) 21866

Sec Bruce Trail Conservancy, 55 Head St, Unit 101, Dundas ON L9H 3H8, Canada.
URL: http://worldtrailsnetwork.org/
Aims Connect the diverse trails of the world to promote the creation, enhancement, and protection of outstanding trail experiences. **Structure** Leadership Committee. Regional hubs (2): American Trails; *Asia Trails Network (ATN, #02102)*. **Activities** Events/meetings; advocacy/lobbying/activism. **Events** *World Trails Conference* Busan (Korea Rep) 2024, *World Trails Conference* Pokhara (Nepal) 2022, *World Trails Conference* Pokhara (Nepal) 2020, *World Trails Conference* Santiago de Compostela (Spain) 2018, *World Trails Conference* Kurayoshi (Japan) 2016. **Publications** *World of Trails* – online magazine.
Members Full in 22 countries:
Australia, China, Denmark, Finland, France, Germany, Greece, Israel, Italy, Japan, Korea Rep, Lebanon, Nepal, New Zealand, Norway, South Africa, Spain, Switzerland, Türkiye, Uganda, UK, USA. [2017/XM5676/**F**]

♦ World Transhumanist Association (WTA) 21867

Exec Dir Humanity Plus, 5042 Wilshire Blvd, Ste 14334, Los Angeles CA 90036, USA. T. +13109169676.
URL: http://www.humanityplus.org/
History 1998. **Aims** Support discussion and public awareness of emerging technologies; defend the rights of individuals in free and democratic societies to adopt technologies that expand human capacities; anticipate and propose solutions for the potential consequences of emerging technologies. **Events** *TransVision international conference* Helsinki (Finland) 2006, *TransVision international conference* Caracas (Venezuela) 2005, *TransVision international conference* Toronto, ON (Canada) 2004, *TransVision international conference* New Haven, CT (USA) 2003, *TransVision international conference* Berlin (Germany) 2001.
Members Chapters in 26 countries:
Argentina, Australia, Belgium, Cameroon, Canada, Czechia, Finland, Germany, Greece, Hungary, India, Italy, Kenya, Mexico, Netherlands, Nigeria, Norway, Russia, Slovenia, Somalia, Spain, Sweden, Uganda, UK, USA, Venezuela. [2011/XN8415/**F**]

♦ World Transplant Games Federation (WTGF) 21868

Exec Manager Basepoint Business Ctr, 1 Winnall Valley Road, Winchester, SO23 0LD, UK. T. +441962832560. E-mail: wtgf@wtgf.org.
URL: http://www.wtgf.org/
History 1987. Registered in accordance with UK law. Registration: Companies House, No/ID: 10323481, England and Wales. **Aims** Visibly demonstrate the benefits of successful organ transplantation; increase public awareness of its success and thereby increase organ donation rates; promote full *rehabilitation* and wellbeing of participants. **Structure** Executive Committee; Board of Trustees. **Languages** English. **Staff** 3.00 FTE, paid. **Finance** Sources: members' dues. **Activities** Sporting activities. **Events** *Summer World Transplant Games* Houston, TX (USA) 2021, *Summer Events* Mar del Plata (Argentina) 2015, *Winter Games* France 2014, *Summer Events* Durban (South Africa) 2013, *Winter Games* Switzerland 2012. **Publications** *TransplantWorld* (2 a year) – journal.
Members Full in 57 countries and territories:
Argentina, Australia, Austria, Belgium, Bhutan, Brazil, Bulgaria, Canada, Chile, China, Cyprus, Czechia, Denmark, Finland, France, Germany, Greece, Hong Kong, Hungary, Iceland, India, Iran Islamic Rep, Ireland, Italy, Japan, Kazakhstan, Korea Rep, Kuwait, Malaysia, Mexico, Nepal, Netherlands, New Zealand, Norway, Pakistan, Philippines, Poland, Portugal, Puerto Rico, Romania, Russia, Singapore, Slovakia, Slovenia, South Africa, Spain, Sri Lanka, Sweden, Switzerland, Thailand, Tunisia, Türkiye, UK, Uruguay, USA, Venezuela, Vietnam.
IGO Relations *WHO (#20950)*. **NGO Relations** Member of (1): *Olympic Movement (#17719)*. Recognized by: *International Olympic Committee (IOC, #14408)*. Adheres to: *World Anti-Doping Agency (WADA, #21096)*. Affiliated to: *European Heart and Lung Transplant Federation (EHLTF, #07466)*. [2020/XJ8929/**C**]

♦ World Transporter Bridges Association 21869

Asociación Mundial de Puentes Transbordadores – Weltverband der Schwebefähren
Contact address not obtained. E-mail: promocion@puente-colgante.com.

URL: https://www.puentestransbordadores.com/
History 2003. Former names and other names: *Asociación Mundial de Puentes Colgantes* – alias. Registration: Spain. **Aims** Promote protection and preservation of the remaining 8 transporter bridges. **Events** *International Congress* Getxo (Spain) 2018, *International Congress* Buenos Aires (Argentina) 2017, *International Congress* Rendsburg (Germany) 2013. [2019/XM0101/D]

♦ World Travel Agents Associations Alliance (WTAAA) 21870

Chair c/o ASATA, PO Box 650539, Benmore, 2010, South Africa. E-mail: info@wtaaa.org.
URL: http://wtaaa.org/
History 2008, when registered in accordance with Belgian law. **Aims** Facilitate the exchange of ideas and information to the global travel agency community. **Structure** Board of Directors; Executive Committee. **Languages** English. **Staff** None paid. **Finance** Sources: members' dues. **Activities** Events/meetings.
Members National organizations in 10 countries and territories:
Australia, Brazil, Canada, Hong Kong, India, Korea Rep, New Zealand, South Africa, Spain, USA.
Regional associations (4):
Association of Southern African Travel Agents (ASATA); Federation of ASEAN Travel Associations (FATA, #09428); Foro Latinoamericano de Turismo (FOLATUR, #09884); The European Travel Agents' and Tour Operators' Associations (ECTAA, #08942).
IGO Relations *World Tourism Organization (UNWTO, #21861).* **NGO Relations** *International Air Transport Association (IATA, #11614).* [2022/XM7314/C]

♦ World Travel Journalism Organization (#17846)

♦ World Travel and Tourism Council (WTTC) 21871

Pres/CEO The Harlequin Bldg, 65 Southwark Street, London, SE1 0HR, UK. T. +442074818007. Fax +442074881008. E-mail: enquiries@wttc.org.
URL: http://www.wttc.org/
History Apr 1990. Registration: Private company limited by guarantee, No/ID: 02506591, England; EU Transparency Register, No/ID: 022201744710-44, Start date: 18 Nov 2021. **Aims** Work with governments to realize the full economic impact of travel and tourism, the world's largest generator of wealth and jobs; make travel and tourism a strategic economic development and employment priority; move towards open and competitive markets; promote *sustainable development*; eliminate barriers to growth. **Structure** General Meeting (annual); Executive Committee; President; Representative offices (5); Secretariat in London (UK). **Languages** English. **Finance** Sources: members' dues. **Events** *Global Travel and Tourism Summit* Cancún (Mexico) 2021, *Global Travel and Tourism Summit* Seville (Spain) 2019, *Global Travel and Tourism Summit* Buenos Aires (Argentina) 2018, *Global Travel and Tourism Summit* Bangkok (Thailand) 2017, *Ministerial Round Table* Bangkok (Thailand) 2017. **Publications** *Annual Report on Economic Contribution of Travel and Tourism. Agenda 21 for the Travel and Tourism Industry; Jobs for the Millenium; Seven Strategic Priorities; Steps to Success; The International Competitiveness Monitor.* General reports; country/region reports; tax policy studies; environmental analyses. **Members** CEOs (over 100) from all sectors of the travel and tourism industry, including transportation, accommodation, catering, cruises, recreation/entertainment and travel-related services. Membership countries not specified. **IGO Relations** Accredited by: *United Nations Office at Vienna (UNOV, #20604).* Affiliate member of: *Caribbean Tourism Organization (CTO, #03561).* **NGO Relations** Member of (2): *European Tourism Manifesto (#08921); World Tourism Network (WTN, #21860).* [2021/XF5024/v/F]

♦ World Triathlon 21872

Exec Dir Maison du Sport Intl, Av de Rhodanie 54, 1007 Lausanne VD, Switzerland. T. +41216146030. Fax +41216146039. E-mail: hdq@triathlon.org.
Pres San Bernardino 14, 28015 Madrid, Spain. T. +34915421855. Fax +34911817447.
URL: http://www.triathlon.org/
History 1 Apr 1989, Avignon (France). Founded at the 1st ITU Congress. Headquarters originally in Vancouver BC (Canada); moved to Lausanne (Switzerland), 1 Jan 2014. Former names and other names: *Federation International Triathlon* – former; *International Triathlon Union (ITU)* – full title (1992 to 2020). **Aims** Promote the *sport* of triathlon, paratriathlon and its related multisports and disciplines throughout the world. **Structure** Annual Congress; Executive Board. **Languages** English, Spanish. **Activities** Events/meetings. **Events** *Congress* Abu Dhabi (United Arab Emirates) 2022, *Congress* Lausanne (Switzerland) 2019, *Annual World Congress* Gold Coast, QLD (Australia) 2018, *World Conference* Budapest (Hungary) 2017, *Annual World Congress* Rotterdam (Netherlands) 2017.
Members National Federations (over 120) in 114 countries and territories:
Andorra, Antigua-Barbuda, Argentina, Aruba, Australia, Austria, Bahamas, Bangladesh, Barbados, Belarus, Belgium, Belize, Bolivia, Brazil, Bulgaria, Canada, Cayman Is, Chile, China, Colombia, Cook Is, Costa Rica, Croatia, Cuba, Cyprus, Czechia, Denmark, Dominica, Ecuador, Egypt, El Salvador, Estonia, Ethiopia, Fiji, Finland, France, Germany, Greece, Grenada, Guam, Guatemala, Honduras, Hong Kong, Hungary, India, Iran Islamic Rep, Ireland, Israel, Italy, Jamaica, Japan, Jordan, Kazakhstan, Kenya, Korea Rep, Latvia, Liechtenstein, Lithuania, Luxembourg, Macau, Malaysia, Malta, Mauritius, Mexico, Moldova, Monaco, Mongolia, Morocco, Namibia, Nepal, Netherlands, New Zealand, Nicaragua, Nigeria, Norway, Pakistan, Palau, Panama, Paraguay, Peru, Philippines, Poland, Portugal, Puerto Rico, Qatar, Romania, Russia, Serbia, Sierra Leone, Singapore, Slovakia, Slovenia, Solomon Is, South Africa, Spain, St Kitts-Nevis, St Lucia, Sweden, Switzerland, Taiwan, Thailand, Trinidad-Tobago, Türkiye, Turks-Caicos, Uganda, UK, Ukraine, United Arab Emirates, Uruguay, USA, Uzbekistan, Venezuela, Zimbabwe.
Regional organizations (5):
African Triathlon Union (ATU, #00487); Americas Triathlon (AT, #00795); Asian Triathlon Confederation (ASTC, #01769); European Triathlon Union (ETU, #08948); Oceania Triathlon Federation (OTU, #17680).
NGO Relations Member of (5): *Association of Paralympic Sports Organisations (APSO, #02850); Association of Summer Olympic International Federations (ASOIF, #02943); International Council for Coaching Excellence (ICCE, #13008); International Paralympic Committee (IPC, #14512); Olympic Movement (#17719).* Cooperates with (1): *International Testing Agency (ITA, #15678).* Recognized by: *International Olympic Committee (IOC, #14408).* [2020/XD6600/y/D]

♦ World Underwater Federation 21873

Confédération mondiale des activités subaquatiques (CMAS) – Confederación Mundial de Actividades Subacuaticas
General Administration Viale Tiziano 74, 00196 Rome RM, Italy. T. +39632110594. Fax +39632110595. E-mail: cmas@cmas.org.
URL: http://www.cmas.org/
History 11 Jan 1959, Monaco. Statutes modified: 1960, Barcelona (Spain); 1967, Rome (Italy); 1969, Barcelona; 1971, Santiago (Chile); 1973, London (UK); 1975, Stockholm (Sweden); 1977, Brisbane (Australia); 1979, Monaco; Cancún (Mexico) 1980; 1982, Barcelona; 1985, Miami FL (USA); 1987, Malta; 1996, Rome; 2004, Rome. **Aims** Develop underwater activities; form bodies to instruct in the techniques of underwater diving and underwater *sports*; fin swimming, spearfishing, target shooting, photo safari, orienteering, hockey and rugby; perfect existing material; encourage inventions and experiment with newly-marked products, suggesting possible improvements. **Structure** General Assembly. Steering Committee, consisting of 14 members and Steering Committee, comprising President, Vice-President, General Secretary, Treasurer, Committee Presidents. College of Elders (8); Honorary (7); College of Auditors (2); Committees (3): Scientific, Sports, Technical. Commissions (22). **Languages** English, French, Spanish. **Staff** 3.00 FTE, paid. **Finance** Sources: grants; members' dues. **Activities** Organization of international competitions. Special programmes in connection with: archaeology, biology, geology, cave. International system of diving teaching with certificates recognized and used by 90 countries. Instrumental in setting up: *Asian Underwater Federation (AUF, #01771).* **Events** *General Assembly* Rome (Italy) 2020, *General Assembly* Rome (Italy) 2016, *General Assembly* Cebu City (Philippines) 2013, *General Assembly* Rome (Italy) 2012, *General Assembly* Rome (Italy) 2011.
Members National federations and clubs in 89 countries and territories:
Algeria, Andorra, Argentina, Armenia, Australia, Austria, Belarus, Belgium, Bosnia-Herzegovina, Brazil, Bulgaria, Cameroon, Canada, Cape Verde, Chile, China, Colombia, Croatia, Cuba, Cyprus, Czechia, Denmark, Ecuador, Egypt, Estonia, Finland, France, Germany, Great Britain, Greece, Hong Kong, Hungary, Indonesia, Iran Islamic Rep, Ireland, Italy, Japan, Jordan, Kazakhstan, Korea Rep, Kuwait, Kyrgyzstan, Latvia, Lebanon, Libya, Liechtenstein, Lithuania, Luxembourg, Malaysia, Maldives, Malta, Mauritius, Mexico, Moldova, Monaco, Montenegro, Morocco, Namibia, Netherlands, New Zealand, Nigeria, Northern Mariana Is, Norway, Palestine, Peru, Philippines, Poland, Polynesia Fr, Portugal, Russia, San Marino, Saudi Arabia, Senegal, Serbia, Slovakia, Slovenia, South Africa, Spain, Sweden, Switzerland, Syrian AR, Taiwan, Thailand, Tunisia, Türkiye, Ukraine, USA, Venezuela, Vietnam.
Included in the above, 2 organisations listed in this Yearbook:
Associated European Divers (AED); Divers Alert Network Europe (DAN Europe, see: #13181).
Consultative Status Consultative status granted from: *UNESCO (#20322)* (Consultative Status). **IGO Relations** *Intergovernmental Oceanographic Commission (IOC, #11496).* **NGO Relations** Member of (4): *Association of the IOC Recognized International Sports Federations (ARISF, #02767); International Union for Conservation of Nature and Natural Resources (IUCN, #15766); International World Games Association (IWGA, #15914); Olympic Movement (#17719).* Cooperates with (1): *International Testing Agency (ITA, #15678).* Recognized by: *International Olympic Committee (IOC, #14408).* [2019/XB3589/B]

♦ World Union (WU) 21874

Union mondiale
Gen Sec/Treas 52 rue Desbassyns de Richmont, Puducherry, Pondicherry 605 002, Puducherry PONDICHERRY 605 002, India. T. +914132334834.
History 26 Nov 1958, Kolkata (India), inspired by the teachings of Sri Aurobindo and The Mother. Later transferred, 1960, Pondicherry (India). Registered 13 Oct 1960 as a charitable Society under the Registration of Societies Act XXI of 1860 of India. **Aims** Promote world *unity, peace* and integral *harmony* on a *spiritual* foundation. **Structure** World Conference (every 2 years) constitutes World Council for 6 years. Council, consisting of 6 office-bearers and 9 members, constitutes Executive Committee. **Finance** Members' dues. Other sources: grants; donations; contributions. **Activities** Organizes centres of life and work for the progressive realization of the Union's objectives; establishes libraries or sections within libraries with books and journals devoted to world unity; organizes seminars, meetings, conferences and conventions; observes World Union Formation Day on 26 Nov, and World Union Day on 20 Aug, every year since 1964 as advised by 'the Mother'. Cash awards to individuals/centres for distinguished services toward the cause of human unity and world peace. **Events** *Triennial Conference* Pandu (India) 2003, *Triennial World Conference* Pondicherry (India) 2003, *Triennial conference / Triennial World Conference* Pondicherry (India) 2000, *Triennial conference / Triennial World Conference* Pondicherry (India) 1997, *Triennial conference / Triennial World Conference* Pondicherry (India) 1994. **Publications** *World Union* (4 a year) – journal.
Members Categories Ordinary; Life; Donor Life; Patron Life; Institutional Life. Local Centres; Individuals (about 1,500). Members in 15 countries:
Australia, Belgium, Canada, France, India, Japan, Kenya, Malaysia, Netherlands, Sri Lanka, Uganda, UK, Ukraine, USA, Zambia. [2008/XF0114/F]

♦ World Union of Acupuncture Scientists and Societies (inactive)
♦ World Union of Ahiska Turks (internationally oriented national body)
♦ World Union of Catholic Educators / see UMEC-WUCT (#20280)

♦ World Union of Catholic Philosophical Societies (WUCPS) 21875

Union mondiale des sociétés catholiques de philosophie – Weltunion der Katholischen Philosophischen Gesellschaften
Contact St Francis Xavier Univ, Antigonish NS B2G 2W5, Canada. T. +19028675085. E-mail: unionmondiale@gmail.com.
URL: https://sites.google.com/site/unionmondiale/
History 12 Aug 1948, Amsterdam (Netherlands). Constituent General Assembly 1949, Fribourg (Switzerland). Registered in accordance with Swiss Civil Code. **Aims** Facilitate relations among members and represent them at international organizations concerned with philosophy; promote work on philosophy, especially within Catholic intellectual tradition. **Structure** General Assembly (every 5 years); Committee; Special Committees (3). **Languages** English, French, German, Italian, Spanish. **Staff** Voluntary. **Finance** Sources: members' dues. **Activities** Events/meetings; research/documentation. **Events** *Quinquennial General Assembly* Athens (Greece) 2013, *Quinquennial General Assembly* Seoul (Korea Rep) 2008, *Quinquennial General Assembly* Istanbul (Turkey) 2003, *Workshop / Quinquennial General Assembly* Istanbul (Turkey) 2003, *Metaphysics for the third millennium* Rome (Italy) 2000. **Publications** *Bulletin* (2 a year) – print and electronic; *Philosophy, Culture and Traditions* (annual) in English, French, German, Spanish – print and electronic journal. Regional reports on present day cultural values; research reports; essays.
Members Societies and individuals. Members in 50 countries and territories:
Argentina, Australia, Austria, Belgium, Brazil, Canada, Chile, China, Congo DR, Croatia, Dominican Rep, Ecuador, Egypt, France, Germany, Holy See, Hong Kong, Hungary, India, Indonesia, Ireland, Italy, Japan, Kenya, Korea Rep, Lesotho, Lithuania, Malta, Mexico, Montenegro, Netherlands, Nigeria, Papua New Guinea, Paraguay, Peru, Philippines, Poland, Portugal, Puerto Rico, Serbia, Slovakia, South Africa, Spain, Sri Lanka, Switzerland, Taiwan, Tanzania UR, Thailand, Uganda, USA.
NGO Relations Founding member of: *International Federation of Philosophical Societies (FISP, #13507).* Cooperates with: *International Society for Metaphysics (ISM, #15265).* [2019/XC3592/C]

♦ World Union of Catholic Teachers / see UMEC-WUCT (#20280)

♦ World Union of Catholic Women's Organisations (WUCWO) 21876

Union mondiale des organisations féminines catholiques (UMOFC) – Unión Mundial de las Organizaciones Femeninas Católicas (UMOFC) – Weltunion der Katholischen Frauen Organisationen (WKFO)
Secretariat Piazza di S. Calisto 16, 00153 Rome RM, Italy. T. +390669887260. E-mail: info@wucwo.org.
URL: http://www.wucwo.org/
History 1910, Brussels (Belgium). Current Constitution and Bylaws adopted at General Assembly, 2001. Former names and other names: *International Union of Catholic Women's Leagues* – former; *Union internationale des ligues féminines catholiques (UILFC)* – former. Registration: Swiss Civil Code, Switzerland. **Aims** Promote the presence, participation and co-responsibility of Catholic women in society and Church, in order to enable them to fulfil their mission of *evangelization* and to work for *human development*. **Structure** General Assembly (every 4 years); Board; Executive Committee; Central Secretariat, coordinated by Secretary. **Languages** English, French, Spanish. **Staff** 2.50 FTE, paid. Several voluntary. **Finance** Sources: gifts, legacies; members' dues. Proceeds from 'WUCWO Day'. **Activities** Advocacy/lobbying/activism; awareness raising; events/meetings; financial and/or material support; knowledge management/information dissemination; networking/liaising. **Events** *Quadrennial General Assembly* Dakar (Senegal) 2018, *European Regional Conference* Madrid (Spain) 2017, *Quadrennial General Assembly* Fatima (Portugal) 2014, *Quadrennial General Assembly* Jerusalem (Israel) 2010, *Quadrennial General Assembly* Arlington, VA (USA) 2006. **Publications** *WUCWO Newsletter* (12 a year) in English, French, Spanish; *Women's Voice* (3-4 a year) in English, French, Spanish – magazine. Conference reports; information leaflet.
Members Affiliated organizations (4 of which are world-wide) in 47 countries:
Argentina, Australia, Austria, Belgium, Cameroon, Canada, Congo DR, Cuba, Czechia, Eswatini, Fiji, France, Germany, Ghana, Greece, Hungary, India, Indonesia, Ireland, Italy, Japan, Kenya, Korea Rep, Liberia, Lithuania, Madagascar, Mali, Malta, Mexico, Namibia, Netherlands, New Zealand, Nigeria, Philippines, Poland, Senegal, Slovakia, South Africa, Spain, Switzerland, Tanzania UR, Togo, Tonga, UK, USA, Venezuela, Zambia.
Consultative Status Consultative status granted from: *ECOSOC (#05331)* (Special); *UNESCO (#20322)* (Consultative Status); *ILO (#11123)* (Special List); *FAO (#09260)*; *Council of Europe (CE, #04881)* (Participatory Status). **IGO Relations** Associated with Department of Global Communications of the United Nations.
NGO Relations Board meetings attended by representatives of: *Association Catholique Internationale de Services pour la Jeunesse Féminine (ACISJF/In Via, #02417); Caritas Internationalis (CI, #03580); International Union of Superiors General (#15820).* Member of: *African Council of Religious Leaders – Religions for Peace (ACRL-RfP, #00276); Committee of NGOs on Human Rights, Geneva (#04275); Conference of Non-Governmental Organizations in Consultative Relationship with the United Nations (CONGO, #04635); Forum of Catholic Inspired NGOs (#09905); International Conference of NGOs (#12883); NGO Committee on the Status of Women, Geneva (#17117); NGO Committee on the Status of Women, New York NY (see: #04635); NGO Committee on UNICEF (#17120); New York NGO Committee on Drugs (NYNGOC, #17097).* Observer at: *Alliance of NGOs on Crime Prevention and Criminal Justice (#00709).* Maintains relations with:
– *Catholic Women's Movement of Austria (KFBÖ); Council of European Bishops' Conferences (#04884); Inter-African Committee on Traditional Practices Affecting the Health of Women and Children (IAC, #11384); International Catholic Cooperation Centre for UNESCO (CCIC, #12454); International Catholic Organizations Information Center (ICO Center); International Council on Social Welfare (ICSW, #13076); Pan African Institute for Development (PAID, #18053); Pontifical Council for Culture (#18443); Pontifical Council for Justice and Peace (inactive); Pontifical Council for Promoting Christian Unity (PCPCU, #18446); UNUM OMNES International Council of Catholic Men (ICCM, #20720); World Association of Alumnae of the Sacred Heart (#21116).* [2021.03.16/XB3594/B]

♦ World Union of Christian Democrats / see Centrist Democrat International (#03792)
♦ World Union of Cities for Peace (no recent information)
♦ World Union of Freethinkers (inactive)
♦ World Union of French-Speakers (inactive)
♦ World Union of German Shepherd Associations (#20858)
♦ World Union of Hebrew Teachers (inactive)
♦ World Union of Intellectuals (inactive)
♦ World Union of International Law and International Relations Reviews (inactive)

♦ World Union of Jesuit Alumni and Alumnae (WUJA) 21877

Union mondiale des anciens et anciennes élèves de la Compagnie de Jésus – Unión Mundial de Antiguos Alumnos de la Compañia de Jesús – Antiqui Societatis Jesus Alumni (ASIA)

Pres 3 rue Jos Keup, L-1860 Luxembourg, Luxembourg. T. +3226494976. E-mail: info@wuja.org.
Sec address not obtained.
URL: http://www.wuja.org/

History 31 Jul 1956, Bilbao (Spain). Founded during the Congress of Loyola held on the occasion of 4th centenary of the death of *St Ignatius of Loyola*. Most recent statutes adopted 28 Jan 2001, Rome (Italy). Registration: Luxembourg. **Aims** Bring together former pupils or students of Jesuit schools and universities in order to build international relationships, to contribute to the mission of the Society of Jesus and to promote the universal dynamic of Jesuit education. **Structure** Congress; Council. **Languages** English, French, Spanish. **Staff** Voluntary. **Finance** Members' dues (annual). Other sources: gifts; donations. **Activities** Training/education. **Events** *Congress* Barcelona (Spain) 2022, *Congress* Barcelona (Spain) 2021, *Congress* Cleveland, OH (USA) 2017, *Congress* Medellin (Colombia) 2013, *Congress* Paris (France) 2011. **Publications** *The Jesuit Alumnus* (2-3 a year).

Members Associations and federations of associations; Individuals. Associations and federations in 56 countries and territories:
Argentina, Australia, Austria, Belgium, Bolivia, Brazil, Burundi, Cameroon, Canada, Chad, Chile, China, Colombia, Congo DR, Dominican Rep, Ecuador, Egypt, El Salvador, France, Germany, Guatemala, Hungary, India, Indonesia, Ireland, Italy, Jamaica, Japan, Korea Rep, Lebanon, Lithuania, Madagascar, Malta, Mexico, Micronesia FS, Nepal, Netherlands, Nicaragua, Nigeria, Panama, Peru, Philippines, Poland, Portugal, Puerto Rico, Rwanda, South Africa, Spain, Switzerland, Taiwan, Tanzania UR, UK, Uruguay, USA, Venezuela, Zimbabwe.

NGO Relations Cooperates with: *Society of Jesus (SJ)*. Instrumental in setting up: *Pedro Arrupe World Association (PAWA, #18287)*. Member of: *Organisation mondiale des anciens élèves de l'enseignement catholique (OMAEC, #17816)*. [2022/XE6169/**E**]

♦ World Union of Jewish Students (WUJS) 21878

Union Mondiale des Etudiants Juifs (UMEJ) – Unión Mundial de Estudiantes Judios (UMEJ)

Pres PO Box 8089, Emek Rephaim St, 9108002 Jerusalem, Israel. E-mail: info@wujs.org.il.
Exec Dir address not obtained.
URL: http://www.wujs.org.il/

History 6 May 1924, Antwerp (Belgium). Founded by Hersch Lauterpacht (1897-1960). During World War II the centre was transferred from Paris (France) to Switzerland. Cooperated within *World Student Relief (WRS, inactive)* until its dissolution in 1950. In the late 1950's the organization recovered and remained centred in Paris until 1968, when the secretariat was moved to London (UK). Offices moved to Jerusalem (Israel), 1979. New post-war statutes adopted 1950, and amended: 8 Aug 1958; 14 Aug 1963; Aug 1973; Jan 1977; May 1979; Aug 1982; Jan 1987; Jan 1990; Jan 1993; Jan 1996; Dec 2004. Former names and other names: *Weltverband Jüdischer Studenten* – former; *Vsemirnyj Sojuz Evrejskih Studentov* – former. **Aims** As an international, pluralistic, non-partisan umbrella organization, support national independent Jewish student associations worldwide; foster the unity of Jewish students worldwide; strive to ensure their participation in the fulfillment of the aspirations of the Jewish people, its continuity, and the development of its religious, spiritual, cultural and social heritage. **Structure** Congress (annual, in Israel), at which national unions are represented by a number of delegates proportional to their membership. World Executive (meets at least twice a year), consisting of Chairperson, 7 board members and 8 executive union representatives elected by respective local conferences. Constituent executive unions (8): Israel; Europe; Australasia; Southern Africa; UK; France; Chile; Ukraine. **Languages** English, French, Hebrew, Russian, Spanish. **Staff** 1.00 FTE, paid. **Finance** Sources: grants. Other sources: allocations. **Activities** Advocacy/lobbying/activism; capacity building; events/meetings; networking/liaising; projects/programmes. Leadership development; encourages formation of Jewish student organizations; Jewish identity development; social justice initiatives. **Events** *Congress* Jerusalem (Israel) 2022, *Annual Congress* Jerusalem (Israel) 2019, *Annual Congress* Jerusalem (Israel) 2017, *Annual Congress* Israel 2014, *Annual Congress* Jerusalem (Israel) 2012. **Publications** Yearbooks; activist guides; monographs; booklets; leaflets.

Members Active national member organizations in 26 countries:
Australia, Austria, Belgium, Chile, Czechia, Denmark, Estonia, France, Georgia, Hungary, India, Ireland, Israel, Italy, Lithuania, Luxembourg, Netherlands, New Zealand, North Macedonia, Serbia, South Africa, Sweden, Switzerland, UK, Ukraine, USA.
Executive Unions (7), of which 2 organizations listed in this Yearbook:
Australasian Union of Jewish Students (AUJS); European Union of Jewish Students (EUJS, #08997).

Consultative Status Consultative status granted from: *UNESCO (#20322)* (Consultative Status). **NGO Relations** Member of (1): *World Jewish Congress (WJC, #21599)*. Partner of (1): *American Jewish Committee (AJC)*. Instrumental in setting up (1): *International Graduate Centre for Hebrew and Jewish Studies (WUJS Institute)*. [2022/XB3598/y/**C**]

♦ World Union of Jewish Studies 21879

Union mondiale des études juives

Exec Dir Hebrew Univ, Rabbin World Center for Jewish Studies, Mt Scopus, 9190501 Jerusalem, Israel. T. +97225325841. Fax +97225325910. E-mail: jewishst@vms.huji.ac.il – worldunion@jewish-studies.org.
URL: http://www.jewish-studies.org/

History 1947, Jerusalem (Israel). Founded during 1st World Congress of Jewish Studies. At 2nd World Congress of Jewish Studies, 1957, Jerusalem the necessity of a permanent union was recognized. **Aims** Promote Jewish studies worldwide. **Structure** General Meeting; Council; Executive Committee; President; Executive Director. **Languages** English, Hebrew. **Staff** 3.00 FTE, paid. **Finance** Sources: grants; members' dues; sale of publications. **Activities** Events/meetings; financial and/or material support; publishing activities. **Events** *World Congress of Jewish Studies* 2025, *World Congress of Jewish Studies* Jerusalem (Israel) 2022, *World Congress of Jewish Studies* Jerusalem (Israel) 2017, *World Congress of Jewish Studies* Jerusalem (Israel) 2001, *World Congress of Jewish Studies* Jerusalem (Israel) 1997. **Publications** *Jewish Studies – Journal of the World Union of Jewish Studies* (annual). *Eshkolot*; *Sources for the Study of Jewish Culture*; *The Addenda to Minhat Shay* – series by Zvi Betser. *Targumic Toseftot to the Prophets* by Rimon Kasher; *The Dawn of Hebrew Linguistics* by Aron Dotan – in 2 vols. Proceedings of the World Congress of Jewish Studies. Information services: Databases: mailing lists on computer.

Members Individuals and universities interested in the field of Jewish studies in 41 countries:
Argentina, Australia, Austria, Belarus, Belgium, Bosnia-Herzegovina, Brazil, Canada, China, Congo DR, Costa Rica, Croatia, Denmark, Finland, France, Germany, Hungary, Ireland, Israel, Italy, Japan, Latvia, Lithuania, Mexico, Netherlands, North Macedonia, Norway, Poland, Russia, Serbia, Slovakia, Slovenia, South Africa, Spain, Sweden, Switzerland, Türkiye, UK, Ukraine, Uruguay, USA. [2022/XD9142/**C**]

♦ World Union of Karatedo Organizations (inactive)
♦ World Union of Lasallian Former Pupils / see Union mondiale des anciens élèves Lasalliens (#20462)
♦ World Union of Lasallian Former Students (#20462)
♦ World Union of Meretz (internationally oriented national body)

♦ World Union of National Socialists (WUNS) 21880

Union mondiale des nationaux socialistes (UMNS) – Nationalsozialistische Weltunion

Gen Secretariat PO Box 270486, Milwaukee WI 53227, USA.

History 1962, UK. Founded 1962, Cotswolds (UK), at founding conference, on adoption of a provisional document called the *'Cotswold Agreements'*. These were superseded by the WUNS Convention of 1992, when a permanent charter was drafted by representatives from Europe and North America, and by supplementary Michigan Protocol of 1999. **Aims** Mobilize people interested in National Socialism and international White unity; consciously, deliberately and openly uphold the cause of Adolf *Hitler* and the integrity of the National Socialist idea, as the one true doctrine of *Aryan* mankind, without compromise; provide true focus for National Socialist unity and solidarity throughout the world. **Structure** Council of Representatives (meets at least every 4 years). **Languages** English, German. **Publications** *NS Bulletin*.

Members Organizations which accept without reservation the 7 Principles of the World Union plus individual officers and representatives of WUNS. Members in 35 countries:
Argentina, Australia, Austria, Belgium, Bolivia, Brazil, Canada, Chile, Croatia, Denmark, Estonia, Finland, France, Germany, Greece, Hungary, Iceland, Ireland, Italy, Latvia, Lithuania, Netherlands, New Zealand, Norway, Peru, Portugal, Russia, Slovakia, South Africa, Spain, Sweden, Switzerland, UK, Ukraine, USA. [2018.08.09/XF4996/**F**]

♦ World Union of Olympic Cities 21881

Union Mondiale des Villes Olympiques

SG City of Lausanne, PO Box 6904, 1002 Lausanne VD, Switzerland. T. +41213152449. Fax +41213152004. E-mail: info@olympiccities.org.
URL: http://www.olympiccities.org/

History Set up 2 Dec 2002. Current articles adopted Oct 2017, Lausanne (Switzerland). Registered in accordance with Swiss Civil Code. **Aims** Facilitate and qualify an on-going dialogue between former and future Olympic Games host cities to ensure the continued positive impact of the Games and to share the outcome of this dialogue with cities around the world. **Structure** General Assembly; Executive Committee; General Secretariat. **Languages** English, French. **Finance** Members' dues. **Activities** Events/meetings. **Events** *Annual Meeting* Lausanne (Switzerland) 2020, *Annual Meeting* Tokyo (Japan) 2019, *Annual Meeting* Lausanne (Switzerland) 2018, *Annual Meeting* Montréal, QC (Canada) 2017. **Publications** *Keeping the Flame Alive!*. Reports; toolkits.

Members Cities: Founder; Active; Associate; Honorary. Founder cities (2):
Athens (Greece), Lausanne (Switzerland).
Active member cities (36) in 21 countries:
Argentina (Buenos Aires), Austria (Innsbruck), Belgium (Antwerp), Bosnia-Herzegovina (Sarajevo), Brazil (Rio de Janeiro), Canada (Calgary AB – Montréal QC – Québec QC – Richmond BC), China (Beijing – Nanjing – Qingdao – Qinhuangdao), France (Albertville – Paris), Germany (Munich), Greece (Athens), Japan (Sapporo – Tokyo), Korea Rep (Gangneung – Pyeongchang), Mexico (Mexico City), Netherlands (Amsterdam), Russia (Moscow – Sochi), Singapore (Singapore), Spain (Barcelona), Sweden (Stockholm), Switzerland (Lausanne – St Moritz), UK (London), USA (Atlanta GA – Lake Placid NY – Los Angeles CA – Reno NV/Lake Tahoe CA – St Louis MO).
Associate in 3 countries:
Korea Rep (Busan), Netherlands (Rotterdam), USA (Denver CO).

NGO Relations Member of (1): *Olympic Movement (#17719)*. Strategic partner: *International Olympic Committee (IOC, #14408)*. [2021/XM6260/**E**]

♦ World Union for Peace Human Rights and the Rights of Peoples (internationally oriented national body)

♦ World Union of Professions (WUP) 21882

Union mondiale des professions libérales (UMPL) – Unión Mundial de los Profesiones Liberales – Weltunion der Freien Berufe

Head Office 46 bd de la Tour-Maubourg, 75007 Paris, France. T. +3344113150. E-mail: info@umpl.org.
URL: http://www.umpl.org/en

History Founded 25 Sep 1987, Paris (France), at 1st international conference. **Aims** Promote broader recognition and greater development of the professions worldwide; represent the professions at the international level, particularly in intergovernmental organizations; establish and maintain permanent relations with the international community with a view to developing professional activities, in the higher interest of promoting human rights in modern society; establish a link among professional organizations worldwide so as to further exchange of information and mutual assistance in areas of common interest. **Structure** General Assembly (at least once a year), headed by Chairman. Board of Directors, consisting of Chairman, 7 Vice-Chairmen, Secretary-General, Treasurer and 2 members; in addition, 8 Technical Advisers. Honorary Presidents (2). **Languages** English, French, German, Spanish. **Finance** Sources: gifts, legacies; members' dues; subsidies. Other sources: other regular or occasional resources. **Events** *Congress* Paris (France) 2002, *Mediterranean assizes* Hammamet (Tunisia) 2000, *Congress* Rio de Janeiro (Brazil) 1998, *Forum des professions libérales* West Bank-Gaza (Palestine) 1997, *La profession libérale face à l'an 2000, un combat pour l'homme* Hammamet (Tunisia) 1994. **Publications** *UMPL Newsletter*.

Members National interprofessional organizations in 20 countries and territories:
Argentina, Belgium, Benin, Bolivia, Brazil, Canada, Côte d'Ivoire, France, Honduras, Israel, Madagascar, Polynesia Fr, Portugal, Senegal, Spain, Sri Lanka, Switzerland, Togo, Tunisia, Uruguay.
International organizations (9):
Association of European Registered Experts (#02538); BIPAR – European Federation of Insurance Intermediaries (#03263); Confederación Latino Americana de Asociaciones de Profesionales Universitarios (CLAPU, #04453); European Council of Liberal Professions (#06828); International Federation of Automobile Experts (IFAE, #13368); International Union of Judicial Officers (#15785); Union Internationale des Avocats (UIA, #20422); World Council for Psychotherapy (WCP, #21337); World Veterinary Association (WVA, #21901).

Consultative Status Consultative status granted from: *ILO (#11123)* (Special List); *World Intellectual Property Organization (WIPO, #21593)* (Permanent Observer Status). **IGO Relations** *UNESCO (#20322)*. Accredited by: *United Nations Office at Vienna (UNOV, #20604)*. **NGO Relations** Observer status with: *Association vétérinaire Euro-Arabe (AVEA, #02975)*. [2020/XC0378/ty/**C**]

♦ World Union for Progressive Judaism (WUPJ) 21883

Union mondiale pour le judaïsme libéral – Unión Mundial pro Judaismo Progresista – Weltverband für Religiös-Liberales Judentum

Chair 6 Eliuahu Shama Street, 9410806 Jerusalem, Israel. T. +97226203447. Fax +97226203525. E-mail: wupjis@wupj.org.il.
US Office One West Fourth Street, Suite 517A, New York NY 10012, USA. T. +12124526530. E-mail: wupj@wupj.org.
URL: http://www.wupj.org/

History 1926, London (UK). Recognized in UK and USA as a religious, non-profit organization. International Headquarters moved to Jerusalem (Israel), 1973. **Aims** Strengthen Jewish life and values in Israel and Jewish communities throughout the world by supporting and advancing a progressive approach to Jewish tradition; serve as the umbrella organization of: Reform/Progressive/Liberal/Reconstructionist Judaism. **Structure** International Assembly; Management Committee; Executive Board; World Headquarters: Jerusalem (Israel). Regional Offices: North America – New York NY (USA); *European Union for Progressive Judaism (EUPJ, #09010)* – London (UK); FSU – Moscow (Russia); UJCL – Aruba; South America – Sao Paolo (Brazil); Australasia – Melbourne (Australia); Australia, Asia and New Zealand (UPJ) – Woolahra; South Africa – Johannesburg (South Africa). Affiliates: Hebrew Union College – Jewish Institute of Religion (Israel, USA); Leo Baeck College (UK; Israel); Abraham Geiger Kolleg (Germany); Levisson Instituut (Netherlands); Netzer – TaMaR International Youth Movement (Israel). **Languages** Dutch, English, French, German, Hebrew, Portuguese, Russian, Spanish. **Staff** 13.00 FTE, paid. **Finance** Sources: donations; grants. **Activities** Networking/liaising; training/education. **Events** *Conference* Jerusalem (Israel) 2023, *Conference* Jerusalem (Israel) 2021, *Conference* Jerusalem (Israel) 2017, *Conference* Rio de Janeiro (Brazil) 2015, *Being the difference* Jerusalem (Israel) 2013. **Publications** *Progressive World News* (weekly). *International Directory of Progressive Jewish Congregations and Organizations*; *The First Twenty-Five Years 1925-1951*. Annual Report; conference reports; brochures; educational material; prayer books and services in various languages. **Members** Not a membership organization. **Consultative Status** Consultative status granted from: *ECOSOC (#05331)* (Ros A); *UNICEF (#20332)*. **IGO Relations** *UNESCO (#20322)*. Associated with Department of Global Communications of the United Nations. **NGO Relations** Member of: *Conference of Non-Governmental Organizations in Consultative Relationship with the United Nations (CONGO, #04635); Vienna NGO Committee on the Status of Women (#20775); NGO Committee on UNICEF (#17120)*. [2022/XC3591/v/**C**]

♦ World Union for Progressive Judaism – European Region / see European Union for Progressive Judaism (#09010)
♦ World Union for the Protection of Life (inactive)
♦ World Union of Pythagorean Organizations (inactive)

♦ World Union of Qwan-Ki-Do (WUQKD) 21884

Canadian Headquarters 5165 Garland Crescent, Burlington ON L7L 7L2, Canada. E-mail: info@qwankido.org – kimbaoburlington@gmail.com.
URL: http://qwankido.ca/

History 1981, Milan (Italy). **Aims** Manage technical requirements, teaching, ethics, ranks, values and traditions of the Wan Ki do method; spread the philosophy and the theoretical and technical basis of this *martial art*. **Structure** Office – shared with *International Qwan Ki Do Federation (IQKDF, #14682)*. **Activities** Training/education.
Members Full in 26 countries and territories:
Algeria, Austria, Belgium, Brazil, Burkina Faso, Canada, Central African Rep, Congo Brazzaville, Côte d'Ivoire, Denmark, England, France, Germany, Guinea-Bissau, Hungary, Ireland, Italy, Moldova, Morocco, Norway, Romania, Senegal, Spain, Switzerland, Ukraine, USA. [2018/XM5486/**C**]

♦ World Union of Reform Zionists (inactive)
♦ World Union of Rheumatology Surgeons (inactive)
♦ World Union for the Safeguard of Youth (inactive)

♦ World Union Saint Gabriel 21885

Union mondiale St Gabriel – Unión Mundial San Gabriel – Weltbund St Gabriel – Unione Mondiale di S Gabriele – Swiatowej Federacji Zwiezkow Swiety Gabriel – Unio Mundialis Sancti Gabrielis Archangeli

Contact Dr karola Kmet'ku 86/44, 012 01 Teplicka nad Vahom, Slovakia.
SG Gütlistrasse 2, 8280 Kreuzlingen TG, Switzerland.
URL: http://www.christl-motive.here.de/

History 1953, Salzburg (Austria). Also known as *St Gabriel's Union*. **Aims** Promote and deepen of the Christian faith by collecting and researching *stamps* and *postal* marks with *religious* motifs. **Structure** General Meeting (every 4 years). Praesidium, consisting of President, 3 Vice-Presidents, Secretary General and Treasurer. National Guilds. **Languages** German. **Finance** Members' dues. Budget (annual): euro 2,000. **Events** *Quadrennial Congress* Nitra (Slovakia) 2008, *Quadrennial Congress* Ghent (Belgium) 2004, *Quadrennial Congress* Vienna (Austria) 2000, *Quadrennial Congress* Kecskemét (Hungary) 1996, *Quadrennial Congress* Poznań (Poland) 1992.
Members National Guilds in 13 countries:
Austria, Belgium, Brazil, Germany, Hungary, Italy, Luxembourg, Netherlands, Poland, Slovakia, Switzerland, UK, USA.
Also in Scandinavian.
Individuals in 18 countries:
Argentina, Australia, Canada, Colombia, Czechia, France, Holy See, Korea Rep, Liechtenstein, Paraguay, Philippines, Portugal, Rwanda, South Africa, Spain, Uganda, Uruguay, Venezuela. [2008.09.15/XF4607/**F**]

♦ World Union of Small and Medium Enterprises (WUSME) 21886

Pres Piazzale M Giangi N 2, 47890 San Marino, San Marino. T. +378549991277. Fax +378549807710. E-mail: info@wusme.org.
Gen Sec Garas tca 22, Budapest 1026, Hungary. T. +3613151059. E-mail: wus@europe.com.
URL: http://www.wusme.org/

History Apr 2010, San Marino. **Aims** Safeguard the rights, interests and competitiveness of SMEs and crafts worldwide. **Structure** General Assembly; Board of Directors; Commissions (4). **Languages** English, French, German, Italian. **Staff** 10.00 FTE, paid. **Finance** Sources: donations; members' dues. Annual budget: 100,000 EUR. **Activities** Events/meetings; training/education. **Publications** *WUSME Magazine*. Annual Report.
Members Full in 69 countries and territories:
Afghanistan, Albania, Angola, Armenia, Austria, Azerbaijan, Belgium, Benin, Bosnia-Herzegovina, Bulgaria, Burkina Faso, Cameroon, Canada, China, Colombia, Congo Brazzaville, Congo DR, Croatia, Cuba, Ecuador, Estonia, France, Gabon, Georgia, Germany, Ghana, Greece, Guinea, Hungary, India, Israel, Italy, Kazakhstan, Kenya, Kosovo, Kyrgyzstan, Latvia, Lebanon, Lithuania, Malaysia, Malta, Mexico, Moldova, Montenegro, Morocco, North Macedonia, Oman, Pakistan, Paraguay, Philippines, Russia, San Marino, Serbia, Slovenia, Somalia, South Africa, Spain, Sri Lanka, Switzerland, Tanzania UR, Thailand, Türkiye, Turkmenistan, Uganda, UK, Ukraine, United Arab Emirates, USA, Venezuela.
Consultative Status Consultative status granted from: *ECOSOC (#05331)* (Special). **IGO Relations** Observer status with (1): *UNIDO (#20336)*. **NGO Relations** Cooperates with (1): *United Nations Global Compact (#20567)*. [2021.02.24/XJ6255/**C**]

♦ World Union of St Bernard Clubs (WUSB) 21887

Union mondiale des clubs de Saint Bernard (UMSB) – Welt Union der St Bernards-Klubs (WUSB)

Pres Kummliweg 61, 3705 Faulensee, Switzerland. T. +41336547052. E-mail: president@wusb.de – secretariat1@wusb.de.
URL: http://www.barrywusb.com/

History Founded 23 Sep 1967, Lucerne (Switzerland). **Aims** Unite all St Bernard *dog* friends under an universally recognized interpretation of the standards; work for the purity, health and character of the *breed*; nurse and improve the friendship of St Bernard fanciers. **Structure** Delegates and Judges Meeting (annual); Board. **Languages** English, French, German. **Finance** Members' dues. **Activities** Events/meetings. **Events** *Meeting* Berdorf (Luxembourg) 2019, *Meeting* Bagnara di Romagna (Italy) 2018, *Meeting* Martigny (Switzerland) 2017, *Meeting* Portugal 2016, *Meeting* Helsinki (Finland) 2015.
Members National organizations (25) in 22 countries:
Australia, Austria, Belgium, Czechia, Denmark, Estonia, Finland, France, Germany, Ireland, Italy, Latvia, Luxembourg, Netherlands, Norway, Portugal, Slovakia, South Africa, Spain, Switzerland, UK, USA. [2018/XD9044/**E**]

♦ World Union of Tissue Banking Associations (WUTBA) 21888

Address not obtained.
URL: https://www.wutba.org/

History 2005, Rio de Janeiro (Brazil). Registration: Start date: 2020, Australia. **Aims** Stimulate global development and harmonize best practices in tissue donation, processing, banking, transplantation and related biotherapeutic activities. **Structure** Executive Council; Ethics Working Group; Global Tissue Banking Registry. **Activities** Events/meetings; training/education. **Events** *World congress on tissue banking* Barcelona (Spain) 2011, *World congress on tissue banking* Kuala Lumpur (Malaysia) 2008.
Members Associated members (5):
American Association of Tissue Banks; *Asia Pacific Association of Surgical Tissue Banking (APASTB, #01854)*; *Asociación Latinoamericana de Bancos de Tejidos (ALABAT, #02186)*; *Biotherapeutics Association of Australasia*; *European Association of Tissue Banks (EATB, #06255)*. [2021/AA2133/y/**C**]

♦ World Union of TOA Associations (unconfirmed)
♦ World Union of Turkish-speaking Cypriots / see Union of Cypriots

♦ World Union of Wholesale Markets (WUWM) 21889

Union mondiale des marchés de gros – Unión Mundial de Mercados Mayoristas (UMMM) – Weltunion der Grossmärkte – Unione Mondiale dei Mercati all'Ingrosso

Contact Unit 2.21, Benoordenhoutseweg 21, 2596 BA The Hague, Netherlands. T. +31703611728. Fax +31703606908. E-mail: info@wuwm.org.
URL: http://www.wuwm.org/

History 1958. Founded as a working group within the framework of *International Union of Local Authorities (IULA, inactive)*, evolving from *IULA Working Group of Wholesale Markets*. Current title adopted when WUWM established itself as an independent organization. Registration: Netherlands; EU Transparency Register, No/ID: 774351143071-75, Start date: 9 Jun 2021. **Aims** Promote and support the essential role that wholesale and *retail* markets play in ensuring the sustainable access, availability and distribution of quality fresh *food* products at competitive prices throughout the international community, whilst maintaining the highest standards of food security. **Structure** Board of Directors; Secretary General; Working Groups. **Languages** English, French, Spanish. **Staff** 2.00 FTE, paid. **Finance** Sources: members' dues. **Activities** Events/meetings. **Events** *Global Conference* Abu Dhabi (United Arab Emirates) 2022, *Global Conference* Florence (Italy) 2021, *Biennial Congress* Guiyang (China) 2019, *Half-Yearly Conference* Barcelona (Spain) 2018, *Half-Yearly Conference* Gurugram (India) 2018. **Publications** *WUWM e-newsletter* (12 a year); *WUWM Yearbook*. *WUWM European Community Guide to Good Hygienic Practices Specific to Wholesale Market Management in the European Union*. Congress reports.
Members Wholesale or retail markets; wholesale or retail market associations; wholesalers; related food associations; academics/professional individuals. Members (189) in 45 countries:
Australia, Austria, Belgium, Bosnia-Herzegovina, Brazil, Bulgaria, Canada, Chile, China, Colombia, Costa Rica, Côte d'Ivoire, Czechia, Denmark, Ecuador, Finland, France, Germany, Greece, Hungary, India, Indonesia, Ireland, Italy, Japan, Jordan, Korea Rep, Latvia, Lithuania, Mexico, Netherlands, Norway, Peru, Poland, Portugal, Romania, Russia, Serbia, South Africa, Spain, Tunisia, Türkiye, UK, Ukraine, USA.
NGO Relations Member of (1): *Global Alliance to Promote Fruits and Vegetable Consumption "5 a day" (AIAM5, #10221)*. [2021/XE2711/**E**]

♦ World Union of Wholesale Markets within IULA / see World Union of Wholesale Markets (#21889)
♦ World Union of Women for International Concord (inactive)

♦ World Union of Wound Healing Societies (WUWHS) 21890

Secretariat c/o CCI, via S Francesco da Paola 37, 10123 Turin TO, Italy. E-mail: info@wuwhs.org.
URL: https://www.wuwhs.org/

History 2000. **Aims** Encourage a global approach to education, research and health care delivery to achieve optimal outcomes for patients with acute and chronic wounds. **Structure** Executive Board; Working parties (4). **Events** *Congress* Abu Dhabi (United Arab Emirates) 2022, *Congress* Dubai (United Arab Emirates) 2020, *One vision, one mission* Florence (Italy) 2016, *Better care, better life* Yokohama (Japan) 2012, *Congress* Toronto, ON (Canada) 2008. **Members** Membership countries not specified. [2022/XD8913/**C**]

♦ World Union of Zionist Socialist Parties / see World Labour Zionist Movement (#21615)
♦ World United Karate-do Federation (unconfirmed)

♦ World Universities Debating Council (WUDC) 21891

Sec address not obtained. E-mail: mithileon@yahoo.com.
Chair address not obtained.
URL: http://www.wudc.net/

History 1981, to organize the World Universities Debating Championships, a follow-up of the Tournaments organized by *Trans-Atlantic University Speech Association (TAUSA)*. Current constitution adopted, Jan 2013. **Aims** Promote debate, free exchange of ideas and international contact and cooperation. **Structure** Executive Organizing Committee; Permanent Office Review Committee. **Events** *World Universities Debating Championship (Worlds)* Chennai (India) 2014, *World Universities Debating Championship (Worlds)* Berlin (Germany) 2013, *World Universities Debating Championship (Worlds)* Manila (Philippines) 2012, *World Universities Debating Championship (Worlds)* Gaborone (Botswana) 2011, *World Universities Debating Championship (Worlds)* Antalya (Turkey) 2010. [2014/XJ8639/**E**]

♦ World University
♦ World University Equestrian Federation / see Association internationale des étudiants cavaliers (#02694)
♦ World University Federation (see: #18520)
♦ World University of the Science / see World Academy of Art and Science (#21065)

♦ World University Service (WUS) 21892

Entraide universitaire mondiale (EUM) – Servicio Universitario Mundial (SUM)

Contact Deutsches Komitee eV, Goebenstr 35, 65195 Wiesbaden, Germany. T. +49611446648. Fax +49611446489. E-mail: info@wusgermany.de.
Contact 1404 Scott Street, Ottawa ON K1Y 4M8, Canada. E-mail: wusc@wusc.ca.
URL: http://www.wusgermany.de/

History 1920. Founded as an outgrowth of *World Student Christian Federation (WSCF, #21833)*, in order to publicize and relieve the needs of students and academics suffering from the effects of World War I. Programmes and self-help projects for university people extended during the 1930's into the fields of student health, cooperative work and research into the problems of higher education. Took over assets of *World Student Relief (WRS, inactive)*, 30 Sep 1950. Present name adopted on expansion into Asia and Africa; subsequently activities also expanded into Latin America. In 1954 absorbed *International Scholarship Fund Committee (ISFC, inactive)*, which had been set up Nov 1950, Paris (France). Following a decision of General Assembly in 1970, moved from its university welfare role into that of promoting social action by the university community. Statutes amended: 1926; 1950; 1970; 1972, 1988, 1991. Former names and other names: *European Student Relief* – former (1920 to 1925); *International Student Service (ISS)* – former (Aug 1925 to 1950); *Entraide universitaire internationale* – former (Aug 1925 to 1950). Registration: Swiss Civil Code, Switzerland. **Aims** Foster human development and global understanding through education and training. **Structure** General Vote (meets every 2 years) of representatives of National Committees; Management Board; International Secretariat. Regional offices (6): Botswana, Burkina Faso, Malawi, Peru, Sri Lanka, Vietnam. **Languages** English, French, Spanish. **Staff** 2.00 FTE, paid. **Finance** Sources: contributions from governments, international organizations and foundations. **Activities** Projects/programmes; training/education. **Events** *Global Conference on the Human Right to Quality Education* Vienna (Austria) 2021, *Global Conference on the Human Right to Quality Education* Vienna (Austria) 2020, *Annual Assembly* Ottawa, ON (Canada) 2008, *Annual General Assembly* Ottawa, ON (Canada) 2007, *Triennial General Assembly* Ottawa, ON (Canada) 2007. **Publications** *WUS Human Rights Bulletin* (2 a year); *Report on Academic Freedom* (annual). Conference and seminar proceedings; specific studies.
Members National Committees (full members) in 55 countries and territories:
Argentina, Australia, Austria, Bangladesh, Bolivia, Bosnia-Herzegovina, Brazil, Canada, Chile, Colombia, Costa Rica, Denmark, Dominican Rep, Ecuador, El Salvador, Eritrea, Eswatini, France, Germany, Guatemala, Haiti, Honduras, Hong Kong, India, Indonesia, Korea Rep, Kosovo, Lesotho, Malaysia, Mexico, Namibia, Nepal, Netherlands, Nicaragua, Nigeria, Pakistan, Palestine, Panama, Papua New Guinea, Paraguay, Philippines, Puerto Rico, Romania, Russia, Rwanda, South Africa, Sri Lanka, Sweden, Tanzania UR, Thailand, UK, USA, Venezuela, Vietnam, Zambia.
Consultative Status Consultative status granted from: *UNESCO (#20322)* (Consultative Status); *FAO (#09260)* (Liaison Status); *African Commission on Human and Peoples' Rights (ACHPR, #00255)* (Observer). **IGO Relations** Cooperation with: *UNHCR (#20327)*; *United Nations Educational and Training Programme for Southern Africa (UNETPSA, inactive)*; *United Nations University (UNU, #20642)*. Contacts with: *European Community (inactive)* through Development Directorate of the Commission. Accredited by: *United Nations Office at Vienna (UNOV, #20604)*. Associated with Department of Global Communications of the United Nations.
NGO Relations Participant in: *Geneva Informal Meeting of International Youth Non-Governmental Organizations (GIM, no recent information)*; Geneva (Switzerland) NGO Sub-Committee on the Status of Women. Member of: *Conference of Non-Governmental Organizations in Consultative Relationship with the United Nations (CONGO, #04635)*. Canada section is member of: *Ontario Council for International Cooperation (OCIC)*. UK Section is member of: *Think Global – Development Education Association (DEA)*.
Working relations with other nongovernmental organizations throughout the world: *American Association for the Advancement of Science (AAAS)*; *Amnesty International (AI, #00801)*; *Education International (EI, #05371)*; *Human Rights Watch (HRW, #10990)*; *International Association of Universities (IAU, #12246)*. [2020/XB3604/**B**]

♦ World University of the World Academy of Art and Science / see World Academy of Art and Science (#21065)
♦ World Uranium Hearing Society (internationally oriented national body)

♦ World Urban Campaign (WUC) 21893

Secretariat c/o UN-HABITAT, Box 30030, Nairobi, 00100, Kenya. T. +254207623216. Fax +254207623536 – +254207623715. E-mail: wuc@unhabitat.org.
URL: http://www.worldurbancampaign.org/

History Set up by *United Nations Human Settlements Programme (UN-Habitat, #20572)*. Original title: *Global Campaign for Good Urban Governance*. **Aims** Reduce urban *poverty* and promote *sustainable development* through improved urban governance; increase the capacity of local governments and other stakeholders to practice good urban governance and raise awareness and advocate for good urban governance around the world. **Structure** Steering Committee; Permanent Secretariat based with UN-Habitat. **Languages** Arabic, Chinese, English, French, Russian, Spanish. **Staff** 3.00 FTE, paid. **Activities** Advocacy/lobbying/activism; capacity building. **Publications** *Urban Governance Newsletter*. Toolkits; policy papers; inventories.
Members Partners in 10 countries:
Canada, Chile, France, Germany, Italy, Malaysia, Sweden, Thailand, UK, USA.
IGO Relations Partners include: *United Nations Office for Disaster Risk Reduction (UNDRR, #20595)*.

NGO Relations Partners include:
- *Africa Union of Architects (AUA, #00529)*;
- *Building and Wood Workers' International (BWI, #03355)*;
- *Catholic Organization for Relief and Development (Cordaid)*;
- *Commonwealth Association of Planners (CAP, #04307)*;
- *Ecocity Builders*;
- *European Council of Spatial Planners (ECTP-CEU, #06843)*;
- *Federación Iberoamericana Urbanistas (FIU, #09324)*;
- *Global Parliamentarians on Habitat (GPH, #10525)*;
- *Global Urban Development (GUD, #10643)*;
- *Green World City Organisation (GWC)*;
- *Habitat for Humanity International (HFHI)*;
- *Huairou Commission (#10960)*;
- *International Society of City and Regional Planners (ISOCARP, #15012)*;
- *Practical Action (#18475)*;
- *Regional Network of Local Authorities for the Management of Human Settlements (CITYNET, #18799)*;
- *Union internationale des architectes (UIA, #20419)*;
- *Women in Informal Employment: Globalizing and Organizing (WIEGO, #21003)*;
- *World Association of the Major Metropolises (Metropolis, #21158)*;
- *World Business Council for Sustainable Development (WBCSD, #21254)*;
- *World Future Council Foundation (WFC, #21533)*;
- *World Habitat*;
- *World Organization of United Cities and Local Governments (UCLG, #21695)*.

Associate partners include:
- *Association internationale villes et ports – réseau mondial des villes portuaires (AIVP, #02751)*;
- *Fédération internationale des professions immobilières (FIABCI, #09653)*;
- *FMDV (#09804)*;
- *Global Forum on Human Settlements (GFHS, #10372)*;
- *Institute for Housing and Urban Development Studies (IHS)*;
- *International Council on Monuments and Sites (ICOMOS, #13049)*;
- *International Federation of Consulting Engineers (#13399)*;
- *International Federation for Housing and Planning (IFHP, #13450)*;
- *International Federation of Landscape Architects (IFLA, #13467)*;
- *International Housing Coalition (IHC Global)*;
- *Mayors for Peace (#16605)*;
- *Smart Cities Initiative for North Africa (SCI-NA, no recent information)*;
- *Taking IT Global (TIG)*;
- *United Religions Initiative (URI, #20658)*;
- *UNU International Institute for Global Health (UNI-IIGH, #20719)*;
- *World Alliance of Cities Against Poverty (WACAP, #21080)*;
- *World ENABLED (WE)*;
- *World Wide Fund for Nature (WWF, #21922)*.

Cooperates with: *Association des Centres de recherche sur l'Utilisation Urbaine du Sous-sol (ACUUS, #02420)*. Supports: *Commonwealth Local Government Forum (CLGF, #04348)*; *EUROCITIES (#05662)*; *European Forum for Urban Security (Efus, #07340)*; *Habitat International Coalition (HIC, #10845)*; *Network-Association of European Researchers in Urbanisation in the South (N-AERUS, #16996)*. [2017/XE4368/**E**]

♦ World Urban Parks 21894

Secretariat 11759 Groat Road NW, Edmonton AB T5M 3K6, Canada. T. +17806446976. E-mail: office@worldurbanparks.org – ceo@worldurbanparks.org.
Street address 29 Brandon Street, Wellington 6022, New Zealand.
URL: http://www.worldurbanparks.org/

History Apr 2015. Founded when *International Federation of Park and Recreation Administration (IFPRA, inactive)* merged with *International Urban Parks and Green Space Alliance (Parks of Life, inactive)*. Registration: Ministry of Business, Innovation and Employment, No/ID: 2619311, New Zealand. **Aims** Promote and support the provision, effective management and use of urban parks, open space and *recreation* worldwide as an integral contribution to healthy communities connected to the *natural* world. **Structure** Annual General Meeting; Board; Executive Committee; Secretariat; Committees (11); Regions (5): Africa; Asia-Pacific, Europe; Latin America; North America. **Languages** English, Spanish. **Finance** Sources: members' dues. **Activities** Advocacy/lobbying/activism; awards/prizes/competitions; events/meetings; standards/guidelines. **Events** *Summit* Tirana (Albania) 2020, *International Parks and Leisure Congress* Melbourne, VIC (Australia) 2018, *International Congress of Urban Parks* Mérida (Mexico) 2018, *Greater and Greener Conference and International Forum* Minneapolis, MN (USA) 2017, *Asia Pacific Regional Congress* Singapore (Singapore) 2017. **Publications** *World Parks News* (12 a year).
Members Full in 33 countries and territories:
Argentina, Australia, Austria, Belgium, Canada, China, Cyprus, Czechia, Denmark, Finland, France, Germany, Hong Kong, Iceland, Ireland, Israel, Italy, Japan, Luxembourg, Malaysia, Mexico, Monaco, Netherlands, New Zealand, Norway, Portugal, Singapore, South Africa, Spain, Sweden, Switzerland, UK, USA.
NGO Relations Memorandum of Understanding with (1): *International Federation of Landscape Architects (IFLA, #13467)*. [2022/XJ9791/**C**]

♦ World Urological Oncology Federation / see World Uro Oncology Federation (#21895)

♦ World Uro Oncology Federation (WUOF) 21895

Chairman Sunnybrook Health Sciences Ctr, 2075 Bayview Ave, Room MG 204, Toronto ON M4N 3M5, Canada.
URL: http://www.wuof.org/

History May 2005, by 12 societies of urologic oncology. Also referred to as *World Urological Oncology Federation*. **Aims** Advance and stimulate education, research, and the highest quality of patient care in the field of urologic oncology. **Structure** Executive, consisting of Chairmen and Liaison members of member societies. **Events** *Annual Conference* Vancouver, BC (Canada) 2013, *Annual Conference* Vancouver, BC (Canada) 2013, *Annual Conference* Fukuoka (Japan) 2012.
Members Societies (19). National societies in 14 countries:
Australia, Canada, China, Germany, India, Israel, Italy, Japan, Korea Rep, Mexico, Thailand, Türkiye, UK, USA.
Regional societies (3):
Asian Society of Uro-Oncology (APSU, #01746); EAU Section of Oncological Urology; *Latin-American Uro-oncology Association (UROLA, #16391)*.
NGO Relations Affiliated to: *Société Internationale d'Urologie (SIU, #19499)*. [2013/XJ6723/y/**C**]

♦ World Uyghur Congress (WUC) 21896

Congrès Mondial Ouïghour – Congreso Mundial Uigur – Weltkongress der Uiguren – Dünya Uygur Kurultayi

Pres PO Box 310312, 80103 Munich, Germany. T. +498954321999. Fax +498954349789. E-mail: contact@uyghurcongress.org.
Registered Address Adolf-Kolpingstr 9, 80336 Munich, Germany.
USA Office 1420 K St NW, Suite 350, Washington DC 20005, USA. T. +12024881904 – +12024881906. Fax +12024781910.
URL: http://www.uyghurcongress.org/

History 16 Apr 2004, Munich (Germany). Founded following the merger of the *'East Turkestan National Congress'* and *World Uygur Youth Congress (inactive)*. "Uyghur" may also be written as "Uighur" and "Uygur". Registration: EU Transparency Register, No/ID: 25155107085-31. **Aims** Represent the collective interest of the Uyghur people both in East Turkestan and abroad; promote the right of the Uyghur people to use peaceful, nonviolent and democratic means to determine the political future of East Turkestan. **Structure** General Assembly; Directors. **Languages** Arabic, Chinese, English, French, German, Russian, Turkish, Uyghur. **Staff** 7.00 FTE, paid. **Finance** Sources: donations; grants. Supported by: *National Endowment for Democracy (NED)*. **Activities** Advocacy/lobbying/activism; events/meetings; training/education. **Events** *General Assembly* Munich (Germany) 2017, *General Assembly* Paris (France) 2016, *General Assembly* Tokyo (Japan) 2012, *General Assembly* Washington, DC (USA) 2009, *Leadership seminar* The Hague (Netherlands) 2007. **Publications** *Briefing Note* (weekly); *WUC Newsletter* (12 a year). Reports.
Members Affiliated organizations in 18 countries:
Australia, Austria, Belgium, Canada, Finland, France, Germany, Japan, Kazakhstan, Kyrgyzstan, Netherlands, Norway, Sweden, Switzerland, Türkiye, UK, USA, Uzbekistan.
IGO Relations None. **NGO Relations** Member of (3): *Society for Threatened Peoples International (STP International, #19654)*; *UNITED for Intercultural Action – European Network Against Nationalism, Racism, Fascism and in Support of Migrants and Refugees (UNITED, #20511)*; *Unrepresented Nations and Peoples Organization (UNPO, #20714)*. [2020.11.17/XM0962/**E**]

♦ World Vaisnava Association (WVA) 21897

World Headquarters 146 Gopesvara Road, Vrindavan, Dist Mathura, Pin, UP 281121, Pin UP 281121, India. T. +915652443664.
URL: http://www.vina.cc/

History 18 Nov 1994, India, by 28 Sannyasis and members of 19 Vaisnava Missions, including ISEV, ISKCON, VRINDA and different branches of Gaudiya Matha. **Aims** Promote worldwide congregational glorification (chanting) of the Supreme Lord *Krishna*; serve as a meeting and information sharing centre of the different Vaishnava missions. **Structure** Council elects from among its members a Managing Committee. Council Supervisors (3). Officers: President; Vice-President; Secretary. **Finance** Activities sponsored through individual member missions. **Activities** Organizes meetings. **Events** *International meeting* India 1997, *International meeting* Vrindavan (India) 1996. **Publications** *World Vaisnava Association Magazine* (annual). Book; CD-ROM.
Members Founding Members (30). Members (mostly in India) in 24 countries:
Argentina, Austria, Belgium, Brazil, Bulgaria, Chile, Colombia, Ecuador, France, Germany, Guatemala, Hungary, India, Italy, Malaysia, Mexico, Netherlands, Peru, Romania, Spain, Sweden, Switzerland, UK, USA.
NGO Relations Member of: *International Yoga Federation (IYF, #15923)*. [2008/XF4739/**F**]

♦ World Values Survey Association (WVSA) 21898

Pres Inst for Comparative Survey Research, Paniglgasse 17/7, 1040 Vienna, Austria. E-mail: wvsa.secretariat@gmail.com.
URL: http://www.worldvaluessurvey.org/

History Project grew out of the European Values Study, and founded by founder and first President (1981-2013) Prof Ronald Inglehart from, University of Michigan (USA), and his team. Registration: Bolagsverket, No/ID: 802412-5752, Sweden. **Aims** As a scientific program and social research infrastructure, analyze people's values, beliefs and norms in a comparative cross-national and over-time perspective, and by covering a broad scope of topics from various study fields; act as an international network of social scientists and researchers worldwide. **Structure** General Assembly; Executive Committee; Scientific Advisory Committee; Secretariat. **Languages** English, German, Russian, Spanish, Swedish. **Staff** 5.00 FTE, paid. National survey teams members, national directors, regional hubs teams: about 1,000. **Finance** Sources: donations; grants. **Activities** Capacity building; events/meetings; networking/liaising; publishing activities; research/documentation; training/education. **Publications** *World Values Research (WVR)*. **Information Services** *WVS data-base*.
Members Individual; Institutional. Members in 118 countries and territories:
Afghanistan, Albania, Algeria, Andorra, Argentina, Armenia, Australia, Austria, Azerbaijan, Bahrain, Bangladesh, Belarus, Belgium, Bolivia, Bosnia-Herzegovina, Brazil, Bulgaria, Burkina Faso, Canada, Chile, China, Colombia, Croatia, Cyprus, Czechia, Denmark, Dominican Rep, Ecuador, Egypt, El Salvador, Estonia, Eswatini, Ethiopia, Finland, France, Georgia, Germany, Ghana, Greece, Guatemala, Haiti, Hong Kong, Hungary, Iceland, India, Indonesia, Iran Islamic Rep, Iraq, Ireland, Israel, Italy, Japan, Jordan, Kazakhstan, Kenya, Korea Rep, Kuwait, Kyrgyzstan, Latvia, Lebanon, Libya, Lithuania, Luxembourg, Macau, Malaysia, Mali, Malta, Mexico, Moldova, Mongolia, Montenegro, Morocco, Myanmar, Netherlands, New Zealand, Nicaragua, Nigeria, North Macedonia, Norway, Pakistan, Palestine, Peru, Philippines, Poland, Portugal, Puerto Rico, Qatar, Romania, Russia, Rwanda, Saudi Arabia, Serbia, Singapore, Slovakia, Slovenia, South Africa, Spain, Sweden, Switzerland, Taiwan, Tajikistan, Tanzania UR, Thailand, Trinidad-Tobago, Tunisia, Türkiye, Uganda, UK, Ukraine, United Arab Emirates, Uruguay, USA, Uzbekistan, Venezuela, Vietnam, Yemen, Zambia, Zimbabwe.
IGO Relations Memorandum of Understanding with (1): *UNDP (#20292)*. Cooperates with (3): *Inter-American Development Bank (IDB, #11427)*; *International Bank for Reconstruction and Development (IBRD, #12317)*; *The World Bank Group (#21218)*. [2021.06.18/XJ6912/**C**]

♦ World Vapers' Alliance (WVA) 21899

Dir 18117 Biscayne BL VD, PMB 60190, Miami FL 33160, USA.
URL: https://worldvapersalliance.com/

History Registration: Ireland; EU Transparency Register, No/ID: 766884047993-79, Start date: 27 Oct 2022. **Aims** Defend vaping by providing a unified platform that makes vapers' voices heard by those in the corridors of power. **Structure** Advisory Board. **Staff** 6 FTE.
Members Partners (31) in 31 countries and territories:
Argentina, Australia, Brazil, Chile, Colombia, Congo DR, Czechia, Ecuador, Italy, Kenya, Korea Rep, Malawi, Malaysia, Mexico, Nigeria, Pakistan, Panama, Philippines, Portugal, Taiwan, Türkiye, Uganda. [2022/AA1326/**C**]

♦ WorldVenture (internationally oriented national body)

♦ The World Veterans Federation (WVF) 21900

Fédération mondiale des anciens combattants (FMAC)

Head Office Rue de la Cité 1, 1204 Geneva, Switzerland. E-mail: post@theworldveterans.org.
URL: http://theworldveterans.org/

History 29 Nov 1950, Paris (France). Constitutive Assembly was held at UNESCO Headquarters, Paris (France), 23-27 Nov 1950. Statutes amended and present title adopted at 2nd General Assembly 27-30 Nov 1951, Belgrade (Yugoslavia). Statutes amended: 21 July 1965; 1976; Jan 1983; Nov 1985; Dec 1988; Nov 1997; Dec 2000; Dec 2006. *WVF International Socio-Medical Information Centre (WISMIC, inactive)* was set up in 1986, Oslo (Norway) in cooperation with the University of Oslo. Former names and other names: *International Federation of War Veterans' Organizations* – former (29 Nov 1950 to Nov 1951); *Fédération internationale des organisations d'anciens combattants (FIDAC)* – former (29 Nov 1950 to Nov 1951); *Federación Mundial de Veteranos de Guerra* – former (Nov 1951); *Weltfrontkämpferverband* – former (Nov 1951). **Aims** Maintain international peace and security by application, in both letter and spirit, of the United Nations Charter and implementation of the Universal Declaration of *Human Rights*; defend spiritual and material interests of *war veterans* and war *victims* by all legal and constitutional means; establish permanent relations among national and international organizations of war veterans and war victims; encourage direct cooperation and relations of friendship, understanding, exchange of experience and cooperation among these associations in all fields affecting their interests, with emphasis on exchange of information on their respective legislations; initiate or support measures for peace, disarmament, protection of human rights, international humanitarian law, rehabilitation of persons with disabilities and their reintegration into the community, legislation concerning war veterans and victims of war, assistance to veterans and civilian victims of recent and current conflicts, development, protection of the environment; promote international cooperation and encourage surveys and research in these fields, including as a particular concern the problem of accessibility of the man-made environment – housing, public transport, streets, work-places, etc – as a basic condition for reintegration; preserve the memory of the war dead. **Structure** General Assembly (at least every 3 years), consisting of delegates from member associations. Executive Board, consisting of President, Secretary-General, Treasurer General and 6 Vice-Presidents. Secretariat, headed by Secretary General. Financial Committee. Regional Standing Committees (5): Africa; Asia and the Pacific; Europe and Americas; Middle East. Standing Committee on Women. **Languages** English. **Staff** 1.00 FTE, paid; 1.00 FTE, voluntary. **Finance** Sources: contributions; fundraising; international organizations; members' dues; private foundations; revenue from activities/projects. **Activities** Events/meetings; guidance/assistance/consulting; knowledge management/information dissemination; networking/liaising. **Events** *General Assembly* Paris (France) 2019, *Meeting* Taipei (Taiwan) 2017, *General Assembly* Sopot (Poland) 2015, *General Assembly* Sweimeh (Jordan) 2012, *International conference* Paris (France) 2010. **Members** National organizations (172), totalling about 60 million war veterans, former resistants, deportees, prisoners of war and war victims. Membership countries not specified. **Consultative Status** Consultative status granted from: *ECOSOC (#05331)* (General); *ILO (#11123)* (Special List); *FAO (#09260)*; *UNCTAD (#20285)* (General Category); *UNICEF (#20332)*. **IGO Relations** Accredited by (1): *United Nations Office at Vienna (UNOV, #20604)*. Associated with Department of Global Communications of the United Nations. **NGO Relations** Board member of: *Conference of Non-Governmental Organizations in Consultative Relationship with the United Nations (CONGO, #04635)*. Represented on the Organizing Committee of: *Hague Appeal for Peace (HAP, #10848)*. Member of: *NGO Committee for Disarmament, Geneva (#17105)*; *Union des organisations internationales non-gouvernementales établies en France (UOIF, inactive)*. In liaison with technical committees of: *International Organization for Standardization (ISO, #14473)*. Working relations with: *Committee of NGOs on Human Rights, Geneva (#04275)*; *Confédération*

Européenne des Anciens Combattants (CEAC, #04537); International Campaign to Ban Landmines (ICBL, inactive); International Confederation of Former Prisoners of War (ICFPW, inactive); International Conference of NGOs (#12883); International Federation of Resistance Movements (#13529); International Red Cross and Red Crescent Movement (#14707); International Social Security Association (ISSA, #14885); NGO Committee on Disarmament, Peace and Security, New York NY (#17106). [2022.10.11/XB3605/**B**]

♦ World Veterinary Association (WVA) 21901

Association mondiale vétérinaire (AMV) – Asociación Mundial Veterinaria (AMV) – Welt-Tierärztegesellschaft (WTG) – Vsemirnaja Veterinarnaja Associacija

Exec Sec Rue Washington 40, 1050 Brussels, Belgium. E-mail: secretariat@worldvet.org.
Pres Rue Victor Oudart 7, 1030 Brussels, Belgium.
URL: http://www.worldvet.org/

History 1959, Madrid (Spain). Founded during the 16th World Veterinary Congress (WVC). April 1863, Professor John Gamgee from the college of Edinburgh (UK) took the initiative to invite professors of veterinary medicine and veterinarians from all over Europe to a general meeting in Hamburg (Germany) 14-18 Jul 1863. This meeting became the first International Veterinary Congress later known as the World Veterinary Congress, attended by 103 veterinarians from 10 countries. At the 8th WVC, Budapest (Hungary), 1906, *Permanent Committee for International Veterinary Congresses (inactive)* was formed to be the organizational link between congresses. At the 15th WVC, Stockholm (Sweden), 1953, it was decided to form an international association. The Permanent Committee worked with a Constitution of the World Veterinary Association until the foundation of the Association as a continuation of the Permanent Committee for the International Veterinary Congresses. Constitution and Bylaws adopted: 19 Sep 2013; amended: 28 Apr 2021. Registration: Banque-Carrefour des Entreprises, No/ID: 0826.203.438, Start date: 28 May 2010, Belgium. **Aims** Safeguard veterinary interests in world society and unify the veterinary *profession* worldwide; set up highest possible standards for education, ethics and excellence in performance of all aspects of the profession; create an environment that recognizes diversity in the setting up of common guidelines, standards, policies and programmes to the benefit of the veterinary profession and society; implement the results of veterinary science to protect and improve animal welfare, animal health, human health and the environment. **Structure** General Assembly (GA); Council, comprising about 17 elected representatives from different world regions and International Organizations members; Executive Committee (EXCOM); Technical Committees; Secretariat, based in Brussels (Belgium). **Languages** English. **Staff** 3.00 FTE, paid. **Finance** Sources: members' dues. Supported by: WVA Foundation. **Activities** Events/meetings; networking/liaising. **Events** *World Veterinary Congress* Taipei (Taiwan) 2023, *International World Veterinary Congress* Abu Dhabi (United Arab Emirates) 2022, *International World Veterinary Congress* Auckland (New Zealand) 2020, *International World Veterinary Congress* San José (Costa Rica) 2019, *International World Veterinary Congress* Barcelona (Spain) 2018. **Publications** *WVA Newsletter* (4 a year); *WVA News* (twice a month) – electronic. Press releases.

Members National veterinary associations (78), representing about 500,000 veterinarians, in 74 countries and territories:
Afghanistan, Albania, Algeria, Angola, Australia, Austria, Bahrain, Belgium, Benin, Bosnia-Herzegovina, Brazil, Cameroon, Canada, Chad, Cyprus, Czechia, Denmark, Egypt, Estonia, Ethiopia, Finland, France, Gabon, Germany, Ghana, Greece, Iceland, Iran Islamic Rep, Italy, Jamaica, Japan, Jordan, Kenya, Korea Rep, Latvia, Lebanon, Lithuania, Luxembourg, Malaysia, Mali, Malta, Mauritania, Mauritius, Mexico, Mongolia, Morocco, Myanmar, Namibia, Nepal, Netherlands, Nigeria, Norway, Panama, Philippines, Portugal, Romania, Senegal, Serbia, Singapore, South Africa, Spain, Sudan, Sweden, Switzerland, Taiwan, Tanzania UR, Thailand, Tunisia, Türkiye, Uganda, UK, USA, Yemen, Zambia.
Associate – international associations of veterinarians (11):
African Veterinary Association (AVA, #00495); Association vétérinaire Euro-Arabe (AVEA, #02975); Commonwealth Veterinary Association (CVA, #04366); Federation of Asian Veterinary Associations (FAVA, #09451); Federation of Veterinarians of Europe (#09713); Ibero-American Animal Reproduction Association (IAARA, no recent information); International Association of Colleges of Laboratory Animal Medicine (IACLAM, #11787); International Society for Veterinary Epidemiology and Economics (ISVEE, #15540); World Aquatic Veterinary Medical Association (WAVMA, #21101); World Association for the History of Veterinary Medicine (WAHVM, #21143); World Association of Veterinary Pathologists (WAVP, no recent information).
Affiliate (non-voting, commercial) member:
Health for Animals (#10870).
Observer members in 2 countries:
Russia, Zimbabwe.
Organizations (17) having observer status:
Asociación Panamericana de Ciencias Veterinarias (PANVET, #02287); Balkan and Black Sea Veterinary Association (BaBSEVA, no recent information); Council for International Organizations of Medical Sciences (CIOMS, #04905); European Federation of Animal Science (EAAP, #07046); FAO (#09260); Health for Animals (#10870); Inter-American Institute for Cooperation on Agriculture (IICA, #11434); International Committee of Military Medicine (ICMM, #12785); International Council for Laboratory Animal Science (ICLAS, #13039); International Veterinary Students' Association (IVSA, #15851); OIE – World Organisation for Animal Health (#17703) (Animal Production and Health Division); *Pan American Health Organization (PAHO, #18108); WHO (#20950); World Animal Protection (#21092); World Association for Transport Animal Welfare and Studies (TAWS); World Medical Association (WMA, #21646); World Wide Fund for Nature (WWF, #21922).*

Consultative Status Consultative status granted from: *FAO (#09260)* (Special Status); *WHO (#20950)* (Official Relations). **IGO Relations** Accredited by (1): *United Nations Office at Vienna (UNOV, #20604).* Memorandum of Understanding with (3): *FAO (#09260); OIE – World Organisation for Animal Health (#17703); WHO (#20950).* Observer status with: *Codex Alimentarius Commission (CAC, #04081).* A network of representatives, custodians and functionaries promotes relations of the WVA in WHO, FAO, WTO, Codex Alimentarius, OIE and other organizations. **NGO Relations** Memorandum of Understanding with (6): *Global Alliance for Rabies Control (GARC); International Dairy Federation (IDF, #13128); International Veterinary Students' Association (IVSA, #15851); World Animal Protection (#21092); World Medical Association (WMA, #21646); World Small Animal Veterinary Association (WSAVA, #21795).* Member of (1): *Federation of European and International Associations Established in Belgium (FAIB, #09508).* Appoints Custodians to represent WVA at a number of global nongovernment organizations. [2023/XA3606/y/**A**]

♦ World Veterinary Epidemiology Society / see International Society for Veterinary Epidemiology and Economics (#15540)

♦ World Veterinary Poultry Association (WVPA) 21902

Association mondiale vétérinaire d'aviculture (AMVA) – Asociación Mundial Veterinaria de Avicultura (AMVA) – Weltvereinigung der Geflügeltierärzte

Sec Boehringer Ingelheim, Lyon Gerland Laboratory, 254 rue Marcel Mérieux, BP 39 I, 69007 Lyon, France. T. +33472723025. E-mail: secretariat@wvpa.net.
Sec/Treas Merial Lyon-Gerland Laboratory, 229 rue Marcel Mérieux, 69007 Lyon, France.
URL: http://www.wvpa.net/

History 27 May 1959, Madrid (Spain). Former names and other names: *International Association of Poultry Pathologists* – former (27 May 1959 to 1961). **Aims** Encourage study and research into diseases and conditions relating to the *avian* species; promote exchange of information and material for study among individuals and organizations; establish and maintain relations with other bodies with related interests. **Structure** General Meeting; Bureau. **Languages** English, French, German, Spanish. **Finance** Sources: members' dues. **Activities** Events/meetings. **Events** *Congress* Kuching (Malaysia) 2025, *Congress* Kuching (Malaysia) 2023, *Congress* Verona (Italy) 2023, *Congress* Verona (Italy) 2021, *Biennial Congress* Bangkok (Thailand) 2019. **Publications** *Avian Pathology* (6 a year) in English – journal, with abstracts in French, German, Spanish; *Aerosols* (annual) – newsletter.

Members National organizations and individuals in 53 countries and territories:
Afghanistan, Argentina, Australia, Austria, Bangladesh, Belgium, Brazil, Canada, China, Croatia, Cyprus, Czechia, Denmark, Egypt, Finland, France, Germany, Greece, Hungary, India, Indonesia, Iran Islamic Rep, Iraq, Israel, Italy, Japan, Jordan, Libya, Malaysia, Mexico, Morocco, Netherlands, Nigeria, North Macedonia, Pakistan, Peru, Poland, Romania, Russia, Saudi Arabia, Serbia, Slovakia, Slovenia, South Africa, Spain, Sweden, Switzerland, Taiwan, Thailand, Tunisia, Türkiye, UK, USA. [2023.02.28/XC3607/**C**]

♦ Worldview International Foundation (WIF) 21903

International Project Office 70 Yaw Min Gyi Street, Yangon Township, Yangon 11191, Myanmar. E-mail: hello@worldview.foundation – nick@worldview.foundation.
URL: https://www.worldview.foundation/

History 1979, Colombo (Sri Lanka). **Aims** Work towards the Blue Carbon Climate Impact, in support of the UN Paris Climate Agreement and the UN Sustainable Development Goals. **Staff** Senior staff: 29. Over 700 staff are engaged in Worldview programmes, the majority being women field workers. **Finance** Sources: United Nations agencies; international NGOs; bilateral agencies; national NGOs; governments general public. Budget (annual): US$ 2.5 – 3 million. **Activities** Current activities divided into 4 major programme areas: *'Grassroots Projects'* which focus on basic needs such as health and nutrition, environment, population concerns, AIDS/STD prevention, empowerment of women, child survival, crop replacement, community development, etc. Grassroots projects reach over 10 million people annually. *'Communication Training and NGO Networking'* has formed an integral component of every Worldview development programme since its inception. The Foundation provides intensive training in audio-visual information and communication to some staff from television broadcasting institutions and NGOs, and short term training to field workers from various countries. It is currently conducting training in participatory communication with equipment support to NGOs in Africa, Asia and Latin America, with the aim of networking with NGOs in communication on environment and sustainable development. *'Radio, Video and Television Programme Production'* aims at strengthening global communication on sustainable development issues, and at creating a better balance in the flow of development information between the North and the South. *'Human Rights, Democracy Support and Conflict Resolution'* through participatory communication activities, in cooperation with peoples' organizations, parliaments and other bodies. **Events** *Annual General Meeting* Colombo (Sri Lanka) 1992, *Annual international seminar* Colombo (Sri Lanka) 1992, *International population seminar* Oslo (Norway) 1990. **Publications** *WIF News Bulletin* (4 a year). Annual report.

Members Individuals (about 300) and Country Offices () in 54 countries and territories:
Australia, Austria, Bangladesh (*), Barbados, Belgium (*), Bermuda, Botswana (*), Brazil, Cameroon, Canada, Denmark, Ecuador, Finland, Gambia (*), Germany, Ghana, Guyana, Hong Kong, Iceland, India, Indonesia, Italy, Jamaica, Japan (*), Kenya (*), Kuwait, Laos (*), Malaysia, Maldives (*), Mexico, Mozambique, Nepal (*), Netherlands (*), Nigeria, Norway, Pakistan, Peru, Philippines, Qatar, Saudi Arabia, Senegal, Sierra Leone, Singapore, Sri Lanka, Sweden (*), Switzerland, Syrian AR (*), Thailand (*), Tonga, UK (*), Ukraine, USA (*), Yemen, Zimbabwe.

IGO Relations Regular relations with: *United Nations Population Fund (UNFPA, #20612).* Invited to Governing Council sessions of: *International Fund for Agricultural Development (IFAD, #13692).* **NGO Relations** Member of: *EarthAction (EA, #05159); Environment Liaison Centre International (ELCI, no recent information); International Union for Conservation of Nature and Natural Resources (IUCN, #15766); New York NGO Committee on Drugs (NYNGOC, #17097).* [2022/XF1400/f/**F**]

♦ Worldview Rights / see Point of Peace Foundation
♦ World Vision / see World Vision International (#21904)

♦ World Vision International (WVI) 21904

Organisation internationale de perspective mondiale – Visión Mundial Internacional (VMI)

Pres/CEO 1 Roundwood Ave, Stockley Park, Uxbridge, UB11 1FG, UK. T. +442077582900. E-mail: info@wvi.org.
Headquarters 800 W Chestnut Ave, Monrovia CA 91016, USA. T. +16263038811.
URL: http://www.wvi.org/

History 22 Sep 1950, Portland, OR (USA). Former names and other names: *World Vision* – former; *World Vision Relief Organization* – former. Registration: non-profit 501(c)(3), No/ID: 95-3202116, USA, CA. **Aims** Serve as an non-denominational *Christian humanitarian* agency working for the well-being of poor and vulnerable people, especially children, through sustainable development, disaster relief, raising public awareness and advocating for justice. **Structure** World Vision International Council (meets every 3 years); International Board. International Executive Office; Brussels and European Representation; Geneva and UN Liaison Office; New York and UN Liaison Office. Regional Offices: East Africa (Nairobi, Kenya); South Asia and Pacific (Singapore, Singapore); East Asia (Bangkok, Thailand); Southern Africa (Randburg, South Africa); Latin America and Caribbean (Clayton, Panama and San José, Costa Rica); West Africa (Dakar, Senegal); Middle East and Eastern Europe (Nicosia, Cyprus). Also includes: *VisionFund International (#20797).* **Languages** English, French, Spanish. **Staff** 40000.00 FTE, paid. **Finance** Sources: donations; grants; cash funds from governments; gifts-in-kind. **Activities** Awareness raising; financial and/or material support; humanitarian/emergency aid. **Events** *Forum for Improving Out of Home Youth Support* Seoul (Korea Rep) 2019, *Education for Global Citizenship Workshop* Busan (Korea Rep) 2018, *Tommorow's Hope Forum* Seoul (Korea Rep) 2017, *Sustainable Evidence-Based Actions for Change Workshop* Singapore (Singapore) 2014, *Model United Nations of Seoul summit* Seoul (Korea Rep) 2010. **Publications** *Global Future* (4 a year). Annual Review. Advocacy publications; brochures; videos.

Members National offices and operational programs in 100 countries and territories:
Afghanistan, Albania, Angola, Armenia, Australia, Austria, Azerbaijan, Bangladesh, Belgium, Bolivia, Bosnia-Herzegovina, Brazil, Burundi, Cambodia, Canada, Chad, Chile, China, Colombia, Congo DR, Costa Rica, Cyprus, Denmark, Dominican Rep, Ecuador, El Salvador, Eswatini, Ethiopia, Finland, France, Georgia, Germany, Ghana, Guatemala, Haiti, Honduras, Hong Kong, India, Indonesia, Iran Islamic Rep, Ireland, Israel, Italy, Japan, Jordan, Kenya, Korea DPR, Korea Rep, Kosovo, Laos, Lebanon, Lesotho, Liberia, Malawi, Malaysia, Mali, Mauritania, Mexico, Mongolia, Montenegro, Mozambique, Myanmar, Nepal, Netherlands, New Zealand, Nicaragua, Niger, Pakistan, Palestine, Papua New Guinea, Peru, Philippines, Romania, Russia, Rwanda, Senegal, Serbia, Sierra Leone, Singapore, Solomon Is, Somalia, South Africa, Spain, Sri Lanka, Sudan, Switzerland, Syrian AR, Taiwan, Tanzania UR, Thailand, Timor-Leste, Uganda, UK, United Arab Emirates, USA, Uzbekistan, Vanuatu, Vietnam, Zambia, Zimbabwe.

Consultative Status Consultative status granted from: *ECOSOC (#05331)* (General); *ILO (#11123)* (Special List); *UNICEF (#20332); WHO (#20950)* (Official Relations); *UNCTAD (#20285)* (General Category); *UNIDO (#20336); African Committee of Experts on the Rights and Welfare of the Child (ACERWC, #00257)* (Observer Status).

IGO Relations Accredited to the Conference of the Parties of: *Secretariat of the United Nations Convention to Combat Desertification (Secretariat of the UNCCD, #19208).* Key partner of: *United Nations Girls' Education Initiative (UNGEI, #20566).* Global partner of: *Global Partnership for Social Accountability (GPSA, #10541).* Partner of: *UNHCR (#20327).* Accredited by: *Green Climate Fund (GCF, #10714); United Nations Office at Vienna (UNOV, #20604).* Cooperates with: *UNESCO Office, Jakarta – Regional Bureau for Sciences in Asia and the Pacific (#20313).*
Associated with Department of Global Communications of the United Nations.
NGO Relations Member of:
- *Accountable Now (#00060);*
- *Alliance to End Hunger;*
- *Alliance for Food Aid;*
- *Alliance for Malaria Prevention (AMP, #00706);*
- *CHS Alliance (#03911);*
- *Communicating with Disaster Affected Communities Network (CDAC Network, #04379);*
- *Conference of Non-Governmental Organizations in Consultative Relationship with the United Nations (CONGO, #04635);*
- *Emergency Telecommunications Cluster (ETC, #05438);*
- *European Policy Centre (EPC, #08240);*
- *EverGreen Agriculture Partnership (#09213);*
- *Fédération des Institutions Internationales établies à Genève (FIIG, #09599);*
- *Girls not Brides (#10154);*
- *Global Connections;*
- *Global Land Tool Network (GLTN, #10452);*
- *Global Partnership to End Violence Against Children (End Violence Against Children, #10533);*
- *Global WASH Cluster (GWC, #10651);*
- *International Coalition for the Optional Protocol to the Convention on the Rights of the Child on a Communications Procedure (Ratify OP3CRC, #12617);*
- *International Coalition for Trachoma Control (ICTC, #12624);*
- *International Partnership on Religion and Sustainable Development (PaRD, #14524);*
- *Joint Learning Initiative on Faith and Local Communities (JLI, #16139);*
- *Livestock Environmental Assessment and Performance Partnership (LEAP, #16500);*
- *Neglected Tropical Diseased NGO Network (NNN, #16969);*
- *NetHope (#16979);*
- *Network for Religious and Traditional Peacemakers (#17054);*
- *PMNCH (#18410);*
- *Regional Inter-Agency Task Team on Children and AIDS in Eastern and Southern Africa (RIATT-ESA, #18791);*
- *SDG Watch Europe (#19162);*
- *Side by Side (#19265);*
- *Steering Committee for Humanitarian Response (SCHR, #19978);*

- *UK Consortium on AIDS and International Development*;
- *Watchlist on Children and Armed Conflict (Watchlist)*.

Supports: *Farming First*. Partner of: *Global Health Cluster (GHC, #10401)*. Participates in: *Global Partnership on Children with Disabilities (GPcwd, #10529)*. Represented on Board of: *The Sphere Project (#19918)*. Instrumental in setting up: *ONE (#17728)*. [2020/XC4317/**B**]

♦ World Vision Relief Organization / see World Vision International (#21904)

♦ World Voice Consortium 21905

Chairman Portuguese Institute of Voice, Rua Caldas Xavier 38, 6-E, 4100 Porto, Portugal. Fax +35126007002.

URL: http://www.worldvoiceconsortium.org/

History 30 Jan 1994, Sintra (Portugal). **Activities** Organizes: world congress; symposia. **Events** *Congress* Copenhagen (Denmark) 2017, *Congress* Santa Clara, CA (USA) 2015, *World Congress* Luxor (Egypt) 2012, *World congress* Seoul (Korea Rep) 2010, *World Congress* Istanbul (Turkey) 2006. **NGO Relations** *Union of European Phoniatricians (UEP, #20390)*. [2012/XE4162/**E**]

♦ World Volleyball and Beach Volleyball Federation (inactive)

♦ World WAQF Foundation (WWF) 21906

Fondation mondiale pour le Waqf

Exec Dir PO Box 5925, Jeddah 21432, Saudi Arabia. T. +29666467350. Fax +29666467780. E-mail: worldwaqf@isdb.org.

URL: http://www.worldwaqf.org/

History Established 2001, by *Islamic Development Bank (IsDB, #16044)*. **Aims** Ensure that Awqaf contribute to the cultural, social and economic development of *Muslim* countries and communities; alleviate hardship among the poor by establishing, sponsoring and supporting viable institutions, projects and programmes. **IGO Relations** Affiliated with: *Islamic Development Bank (IsDB, #16044)*. [2008/XM1036/f/**F**]

♦ World Without War Council (internationally oriented national body)
♦ World without Wars and Violence (unconfirmed)

♦ World Water Assessment Programme (WWAP) 21907

Programme mondial pour l'évaluation des ressources en eau – Programa Mundial de Evaluación de los Recursos Hidricos

Dir UNESCO, Div of Water Sciences, 1 rue Miollis, 75015 Paris, France. T. +33145683904. Fax +33145685829. E-mail: wwap@unesco.org.

URL: http://www.unesco.org/water/wwap/

History as an umbrella agency for the coordination of existing United Nations initiatives within the freshwater assessment sphere. Full title: *World Water Assessment Programme for Development, Capacity Building and the Environment*. **Aims** Assess the state of the world's *freshwater* resources; help countries develop their own assessment capacity. **Structure** Secretariat, including Coordinator and Deputy Coordinator. **Languages** Arabic, English, French, Russian, Spanish. **Staff** 19.50 FTE, paid. **Finance** Funds in trust from donors countries: Japan, France, Spain, Andorra, Netherlands, Hungary; and from *Women in Science and Technology in Africa Network (WISTAN, no recent information)*. Other countries participate by loaning experts. **Events** *Inception Workshop of the 2018 World Water Development Report* Perugia (Italy) 2016, *Mediterranean forum on drought* Madrid (Spain) / Saragossa (Spain) 2006, *Water Information Summit* Delft (Netherlands) 2003, *From conflict to cooperation in international water resources management conference* Delft (Netherlands) 2002. **Publications** *World Water Development Report* (every 3 years).

Members Partners in 193 countries and territories:

Afghanistan, Albania, Algeria, Andorra, Angola, Antigua-Barbuda, Argentina, Armenia, Aruba, Australia, Austria, Azerbaijan, Bahamas, Bahrain, Bangladesh, Barbados, Belarus, Belgium, Belize, Benin, Bhutan, Bolivia, Bosnia-Herzegovina, Botswana, Brazil, Brunei Darussalam, Bulgaria, Burkina Faso, Burundi, Cambodia, Cameroon, Canada, Cape Verde, Central African Rep, Chad, Chile, China, Colombia, Comoros, Congo Brazzaville, Congo DR, Cook Is, Costa Rica, Côte d'Ivoire, Croatia, Cuba, Cyprus, Czechia, Denmark, Djibouti, Dominica, Dominican Rep, Ecuador, Egypt, El Salvador, Equatorial Guinea, Eritrea, Estonia, Eswatini, Ethiopia, Fiji, Finland, France, Gabon, Gambia, Georgia, Germany, Ghana, Grenada, Guatemala, Guinea, Guinea-Bissau, Guyana, Haiti, Honduras, Hungary, Iceland, India, Indonesia, Iran Islamic Rep, Iraq, Ireland, Israel, Italy, Jamaica, Japan, Jordan, Kazakhstan, Kenya, Kiribati, Korea DPR, Korea Rep, Kuwait, Kyrgyzstan, Laos, Latvia, Lesotho, Liberia, Libya, Liechtenstein, Lithuania, Luxembourg, Madagascar, Malawi, Malaysia, Maldives, Mali, Malta, Marshall Is, Mauritania, Mauritius, Mexico, Micronesia FS, Moldova, Monaco, Mongolia, Morocco, Mozambique, Myanmar, Namibia, Nauru, Nepal, Netherlands, New Zealand, Nicaragua, Niger, Nigeria, Niue, North Macedonia, Norway, Oman, Pakistan, Palau, Palestine, Panama, Papua New Guinea, Paraguay, Peru, Philippines, Poland, Portugal, Qatar, Romania, Russia, Rwanda, Samoa, San Marino, Sao Tomé-Principe, Saudi Arabia, Senegal, Serbia, Seychelles, Sierra Leone, Slovakia, Slovenia, Solomon Is, Somalia, South Africa, Spain, Sri Lanka, St Kitts-Nevis, St Lucia, St Vincent-Grenadines, Sudan, Suriname, Sweden, Switzerland, Syrian AR, Tajikistan, Tanzania UR, Thailand, Togo, Tonga, Trinidad-Tobago, Tunisia, Türkiye, Turkmenistan, Tuvalu, Uganda, UK, Ukraine, United Arab Emirates, Uruguay, USA, Uzbekistan, Vanuatu, Venezuela, Vietnam, Virgin Is UK, Yemen, Zambia, Zimbabwe.

IGO Relations Partners within the United Nations:

- *FAO (#09260)*;
- *International Atomic Energy Agency (IAEA, #12294)*;
- *International Bank for Reconstruction and Development (IBRD, #12317)*;
- *International Fund for Agricultural Development (IFAD, #13692)*;
- *Secretariat of the Convention on Biological Diversity (SCBD, #19197)*;
- *Secretariat of the United Nations Convention to Combat Desertification (Secretariat of the UNCCD, #19208)*;
- *UNEP (#20299)*;
- *UNDP (#20292)*;
- *UNESCO (#20322)*;
- *UNHCR (#20327)*;
- *UNICEF (#20332)*;
- *UNIDO (#20336)*;
- United Nations Department of Economic and Social Affairs (UNDESA);
- *United Nations Economic Commission for Africa (ECA, #20554)*;
- *United Nations Economic Commission for Europe (UNECE, #20555)*;
- *United Nations Economic Commission for Latin America and the Caribbean (ECLAC, #20556)*;
- *United Nations Economic and Social Commission for Asia and the Pacific (ESCAP, #20557)*;
- *United Nations Economic and Social Commission for Western Asia (ESCWA, #20558)*;
- *United Nations Framework Convention on Climate Change – Secretariat (UNFCCC, #20564)*;
- Governing Council of: *United Nations Human Settlements Programme (UN-Habitat, #20572)*;
- *United Nations University (UNU, #20642)*;
- *WHO (#20950)*;
- *World Meteorological Organization (WMO, #21649)*.

Affiliated with: *Convention on Wetlands of International Importance Especially as Waterfowl Habitat (Convention on Wetlands, 1971)*.

NGO Relations Affiliated with: *Global Water Partnership (GWP, #10653)*; *International Association of Hydrogeologists (IAH, #11953)*; *International Association of Hydrological Sciences (IAHS, #11954)*; *International Commission on Irrigation and Drainage (ICID, #12694)*; *International Union for Conservation of Nature and Natural Resources (IUCN, #15766)*; *International Water Association (IWA, #15865)*; *International Water Management Institute (IWMI, #15867)*; *Public Services International (PSI, #18572)*; *Water Monitoring Alliance (WMA, #20831)*; *World Water Council (WWC, #21908)*. [2009/XE4317/**E***]

♦ World Water Assessment Programme for Development, Capacity Building and the Environment / see World Water Assessment Programme (#21907)

♦ World Water Council (WWC) 21908

Conseil mondial de l'eau (CME) – Consejo Mundial del Agua

Contact Espace Gaymard, 2/4 place d'Arvieux, 13002 Marseille, France. T. +33491994100. Fax +33491994101. E-mail: wwc@worldwatercouncil.org.

URL: http://www.worldwatercouncil.org/

History Jun 1996. Registration: France. **Aims** Mobilize action on critical water issues at all levels, including the highest decision-making level, by engaging people in debate and challenging conventional thinking. **Structure** General Assembly (triennial); Board of Governors; Colleges (5); Headquarters in Marseille (France). **Languages** English, French. **Staff** 14.00 FTE, paid. **Finance** Sources: members' dues. Other sources: Supported by the City of Marseille and by partnership/sponsorship of other international organizations (not specified). Annual budget: 3,000,000 EUR. **Activities** Events/meetings. **Events** *World Water Forum* Dakar (Senegal) 2022, *World Water Forum* Brasilia (Brazil) 2018, *Water and Climate International Conference* Marseille (France) 2018, *Budapest Water Summit* Budapest (Hungary) 2016, *Seventh World Water Forum Implementation Roadmaps Annual Review Meeting* Daegu (Korea Rep) 2016. **Publications** *Water Policy Journal* (6 a year). Annual Report; reports; guidelines; seminar proceedings; forum documents; brochure.

Members Leading institutions (around 350): Intergovernmental institutions; Governments and governmental authorities; Enterprises and facilities; Civil society organizations and water user associations; Professional associations and academic institutions. Members in 49 countries and territories:

Argentina, Australia, Azerbaijan, Bahrain, Benin, Brazil, Canada, Chile, China, Egypt, France, Germany, India, Indonesia, Iran Islamic Rep, Israel, Italy, Japan, Jordan, Kenya, Korea Rep, Lebanon, Lesotho, Luxembourg, Mexico, Morocco, Mozambique, Netherlands, Oman, Pakistan, Palestine, Poland, Portugal, Saudi Arabia, Senegal, South Africa, Spain, Sri Lanka, Sudan, Sweden, Switzerland, Syrian AR, Taiwan, Türkiye, Uganda, UK, USA, Vietnam, Zambia.

Included in the above, 50 international organizations listed in this Yearbook:

- *African Development Bank (ADB, #00283)*;
- *Agence de l'eau Rhin-Meuse*;
- *Agence française de développement (AFD)*;
- *Arab Countries Water Utilities Association (ACWUA, #00934)*;
- *Arab Organization for Agricultural Development (AOAD, #01018)*;
- *Arab Water Council (AWC, #01075)*;
- *European Water Partnership (EWP, #09083)*;
- *FAO (#09260)*;
- *Fundação Centro Internacional de Educação, Capacitação e Pesquisa Aplicada em Aguas (HidroEx)*;
- *Gender and Water Alliance (GWA, #10102)*;
- *Global Green Growth Institute (GGGI, #10392)*;
- *Global Institute for Water, Environment and Health (GIWEH, #10429)*;
- *Global Water Partnership (GWP, #10653)*;
- *Green Cross International (GCI, #10715)*;
- *IHE Delft Institute for Water Education (#11110)*;
- *Institut International d'Ingénierie de l'Eau et de l'Environnement (2iE, #11313)*;
- *Institut méditerranéen de l'eau (IME, #11323)*;
- *Inter-American Association of Sanitary and Environmental Engineering (#11400)*;
- *Inter-American Institute for Cooperation on Agriculture (IICA, #11434)*;
- *International Association of Hydrogeologists (IAH, #11953)*;
- *International Bank for Reconstruction and Development (IBRD, #12317)* (World Bank);
- *International Commission on Irrigation and Drainage (ICID, #12694)*;
- *International Commission on Large Dams (ICOLD, #12696)*;
- *International Committee of the Red Cross (ICRC, #12799)*;
- *International Desalination Association (IDA, #13152)*;
- *International Federation of Business and Professional Women (BPW International, #13376)*;
- *International Federation of Private Water Operators (AquaFed, #13517)*;
- *International Hydropower Association (IHA, #13828)*;
- *International Secretariat for Water (ISW, #14822)*;
- *International Union for Conservation of Nature and Natural Resources (IUCN, #15766)*;
- *International Water Association (IWA, #15865)*;
- *International Water Management Institute (IWMI, #15867)*;
- *International Water Resources Association (IWRA, #15871)*;
- *IRC (#16016)*;
- *Japan International Research Centre for Agricultural Sciences (JIRCAS)*;
- *Maghreb-Mashreq Alliance for Water (#16544)*;
- *New World Hope Organization (NWHO)*;
- *Observatoire du Sahara et du Sahel (OSS, #17636)*;
- *PIANC (#18371)*;
- *Plan Bleu pour l'environnement et le développement en Méditerranée (Plan Bleu, #18379)*;
- *Project WET Foundation*;
- *Scientific Information Centre of Interstate Coordination Water Commission of Central Asia (SIC ICWC, #19152)*;
- *Société méditerranéenne pour l'environnement (SOMEDEN, no recent information)*;
- *Stockholm International Water Institute (SIWI)*;
- *Swiss Agency for Development and Cooperation (SDC)*;
- *The Nature Conservancy (TNC)*;
- *UNESCO (#20322)*;
- *United Nations Human Settlements Programme (UN-Habitat, #20572)*;
- *Women for Water Partnership (WfWP, #21041)*;
- *World Toilet Organization (WTO, #21854)*.

Consultative Status Consultative status granted from: *ECOSOC (#05331)* (Special); *UNESCO (#20322)* (Associate Status); *WHO (#20950)* (Operational Relations). **IGO Relations** Partner of: *Global Alliances for Water and Climate (GAfWaC, #10230)*; *OECD (#17693)*; *United Nations Human Settlements Programme (UN-Habitat, #20572)*; *UN-Water (#20723)*. [2019.02.21/XC0047/y/**C**]

♦ World Water Institute (internationally oriented national body)
♦ World Waterpark Association (internationally oriented national body)

♦ World Water Polo Referees Association (WWR) 21909

Treas 810 Jamacha Rd, Ste 101, El Cajon CA 92019, USA. T. +16196727379.

URL: http://wwpra.org/

History 2010, Zagreb (Croatia). Replaced *International Association of Water Polo Referees (AIA, inactive)*. **Aims** Promote fraternity and good *sportsmanship* among members, and the athletes and coaches who participate in athletic contests officiated by members. **Structure** Congress. Executive Committee, comprising Chair, Vice-President, Secretary, Treasurer, Liaison and 3 members. Sub-Committees (4): Marketing; Education; Rules; Women. **Languages** English. **Finance** Sources: members' dues. **Events** *Congress* Shanghai (China) 2011.

Members Full in 72 countries:

Algeria, Argentina, Australia, Austria, Azerbaijan, Belarus, Belgium, Brazil, Bulgaria, Canada, Chile, China, Colombia, Croatia, Cuba, Curaçao, Cyprus, Czechia, Denmark, Dominican Rep, Egypt, Finland, France, Georgia, Germany, Greece, Hungary, India, Iran Islamic Rep, Ireland, Israel, Italy, Japan, Kazakhstan, Korea Rep, Kuwait, Lebanon, Lithuania, Malaysia, Malta, Mexico, Moldova, Montenegro, Morocco, Netherlands, New Zealand, North Macedonia, Norway, Peru, Poland, Portugal, Puerto Rico, Romania, Russia, Saudi Arabia, Serbia, Singapore, Slovakia, Slovenia, South Africa, Spain, Sweden, Switzerland, Syrian AR, Trinidad-Tobago, Türkiye, UK, Ukraine, USA, Uzbekistan, Venezuela, Zimbabwe.

NGO Relations *World Aquatics (#21100)*. [2019/XJ4808/**B**]

♦ World Water Ski Federation (inactive)
♦ World Water Ski Union / see International Waterski and Wakeboard Federation (#15872)
♦ WORLD WCTU / see World's Woman's Christian Temperance Union (#21840)

♦ World Weather Watch (WWW) 21910

Veille météorologique mondiale (VMM) – Vigilancia Meteorológica Mundial (VMM)

Contact c/o WMO, 7bis avenue de la Paix, CP No 2300, 1211 Geneva 2, Switzerland. T. +41227308111 7308181.

URL: https://public.wmo.int/en/programmes/world-weather-watch

History 1968. Established in the framework of *World Meteorological Organization (WMO, #21649)*.

Activities WWW comprises: a *Global Observing System (GOS)* consisting of surface-based and space-based subsystems to provide meteorological data covering the whole globe; a *Global Data Processing System (GDPS)* consisting of a network of world meteorological centres (WMC), regional specialized meteorological centres (RSMC) and national meteorological centres (NMC), with arrangements for the real-time processing of observational data for issuing of meteorological analyses, forecasts, and severe weather warnings; *Global Telecommunication System (GTS)*, consisting of telecommunication facilities and arrangements for real-time worldwide exchange of observational and processed meteorological information; a Data Management Programme for establishing data exchange standards and monitoring the data and product availability and quality and for storage and retrieval of data (non-real-time uses).

Further components: (i) Instruments and Methods of Observation Programme (IMOP) aimed at the standardization of instruments and observing techniques and the accuracy of observational data; (ii) Satellite Activities to improve members capabilities to receive and effectively use satellite data; (iii) Antarctic Activities aimed at coordinating the implementation of the WWW in the Antarctic and to meet the requirements for environmental monitoring and climate research; (iv) The Tropical Cyclone Programme to assist some 60 countries in minimizing loss of life and damage to property caused by tropical cyclones.

Within the framework of *Convention on Early Notification of a Nuclear Accident (1986)* and *Convention on Assistance in the Case of Nuclear Accident or Radiological Emergency (1986)*, WWW coordinates on behalf of WMO a cooperation arrangement with *International Atomic Energy Agency (IAEA, #12294)* and *Comprehensive Nuclear-Test-Ban Treaty Organization (CTBTO, #04420)* concerning emergency response to nuclear accidents. **Events** *Session* Geneva (Switzerland) 2006, *Technical conference on meteorological and environmental instruments and methods of observation* Geneva (Switzerland) 2006, *Technical conference on the WMO information system* Seoul (Korea Rep) 2006, *Session* Bratislava (Slovakia) 2002, *Conference on atmospheric radiation* Madison, WI (USA) 1999. **NGO Relations** *Global Precipitation Climatology Centre (GPCC)*, Offenbach-Main (Germany) organizes exchange of monthly precipitation observations among 4,500 stations worldwide via GTS, complemented by other international data collections from 6,700 stations. [2015/XF9998/**F***]

♦ World Welfare Association (internationally oriented national body)
♦ World Wellness Weekend (unconfirmed)

♦ World Wetland Network (WWN) 21911

Chair address not obtained.
URL: http://worldwetnet.org/

History Initiated 4 Nov 2008, Changwon (Korea Rep), at the World NGO conference on the eve of the Ramsar Meeting. **Aims** Raise awareness of the importance of local wetland NGOs in delivering international wetland conservation agreements, and support their role in doing so. **Structure** Coordination Group, including Chair, Co-Chair and Secretary. Regional representatives for: Regions: Africa; Asia; Europe; North America; Neotropics; Oceania. **Activities** Grants the WWN Wetland Global Awards. **Events** *International Wetlands NGO Meeting* Busan (Korea Rep) 2017. **Members** NGOs (about 500). Membership countries not specified. **IGO Relations** *Convention on Wetlands of International Importance Especially as Waterfowl Habitat (Convention on Wetlands, 1971).* [2013/XJ7551/**E**]

♦ Worldwide Airline Customer Relations Association (WACRA) 21912

Chairman 55 Springstowne Ctr, Suite 124, Vallejo CA 94591-5566, USA. E-mail: chairman@wacra.com.
URL: http://www.wacra.com/

History 1969, on creation of articles of association. **Aims** Promote and encourage a free exchange of ideas and methods providing a high level of customer relations; provide a forum for the mutual exchange of such ideas and the means of successful related cooperation among passenger and cargo air transport enterprises. **Structure** General Conference (annual). Board (2 meetings a year), comprising 11 members including Chairman, Chairman Emeritus and Treasurer. **Finance** Members' dues. **Events** *Annual Conference* Boston, MA (USA) 2018, *Annual Conference* San Diego, CA (USA) 2017, *Annual Conference* Helsinki (Finland) 2016, *Annual Conference* Bangkok (Thailand) 2015, *Annual Conference* Auckland (New Zealand) 2014. **Members** Air transport service organizations. Membership countries not specified. **NGO Relations** Cooperates with: *Airlines for America (A4A)*; *International Air Transport Association (IATA, #11614).* [2020/XD8518/**D**]

♦ Worldwide Airport Coordinators Group (WWACG) 21913

Chairman c/o COHOR, 9 rue Hélène Boucher, Bât 530 – ORLYTECH, Paray-Vieille Poste, 91781 Paray-Vieille-Poste CEDEX, France. T. +33149758810.
URL: http://www.wwacg.org/

Aims Deliver a professional, neutral, transparent, non discriminatory service to the aviation industry worldwide so as to contribute to efficient solutions to optimizing the use of capacity at airports. **Structure** Plenary Session (twice a year); Core Group. **Finance** Members' dues. **Activities** Training/education; standards/guidelines; events/meetings.
Members Airports in 77 countries and territories:
Australia, Austria, Bahrain, Belgium, Bermuda, Brazil, Bulgaria, Cambodia, Canada, Cape Verde, China, Colombia, Croatia, Cuba, Cyprus, Czechia, Denmark, Estonia, Faeroe Is, Finland, France, Germany, Ghana, Greece, Greenland, Hong Kong, Hungary, Iceland, India, Indonesia, Ireland, Israel, Italy, Japan, Kenya, Korea Rep, Kosovo, Kuwait, Luxembourg, Macau, Malaysia, Malta, Mauritius, Mexico, Morocco, Netherlands, New Zealand, North Macedonia, Norway, Oman, Pakistan, Papua New Guinea, Philippines, Poland, Portugal, Qatar, Russia, Saudi Arabia, Seychelles, Singapore, Slovakia, Slovenia, South Africa, Spain, Sri Lanka, Sweden, Switzerland, Taiwan, Thailand, Tunisia, Türkiye, Turks-Caicos, UK, Ukraine, United Arab Emirates, USA, Vietnam.
NGO Relations *International Air Transport Association (IATA, #11614).* [2017/XM5669/**E**]

♦ Worldwide Airports Lawyers Association / see World Airport Lawyers Association (#21076)
♦ World Wide Alliance for Christian Education (see: #21330)

♦ WorldWide Antimalarial Resistance Network (WWARN) 21914

Exec Dir Centre Tropical Medicine and Global Health, New Richards Building, Old Road Campus, Roosevelt Drive, Headington, Oxford, OX3 7LG, UK. T. +447879407907. Fax +441865857407. E-mail: comms@iddo.org.
URL: http://www.wwarn.org/

History 2008. Founded following discussions initiated in 2006. **Aims** Generate innovative tools and reliable evidence to inform the malaria comunity on the factors affecting the efficacy of antimalarial medicines. **Structure** Board; Scientific Advisory Committee; Executive Management Team; *Centre for Tropical Medicine, Oxford* operates as coordinating centre. **Languages** English, French. **Finance** Supported by: *Bill and Melinda Gates Foundation (BMGF).* **Members** Partners (over 280). Membership countries not specified. [2021.06.17/XM3905/**C**]

♦ Worldwide Association of Retired Generals and Admirals / see Strategies for Peace (#20008)

♦ Worldwide Association of Women Forensic Experts (WAWFE) 21915

Pres c/o SIMEF, Via Nicolo da Reggio, 89128 Reggio Calabria RC, Italy. E-mail: info@wawfe.org – president@wawfe.org.
URL: http://www.wawfe.org/

History Inaugural event, 26 Apr 2012, Rome (Italy). **Aims** Promote professionalism, integrity and competency in forensic sciences; assist and encourage forensic experts to exchange scientific and technical information; promote advancement and recognition of the role of women in the international forensic science community. **Structure** Area Coordinators. **Languages** English, Spanish. **Activities** Awards/prizes/competitions; events/meetings; training/education. **Events** *International Conference* Reggio Calabria (Italy) 2020, *International Conference* Havana (Cuba) 2019, *International Conference* Tbilisi (Georgia) 2018, *International Conference* USA 2016, *International Conference* Salvador (Brazil) 2015. **Publications** *WAWFE Journal.* **NGO Relations** Universities; forensic associations. [2019/XJ7964/**C**]

♦ Worldwide Backgammon Federation (WBF) 21916

Gen Sec Via Sculati 13, 21018 Sesto Calende MB, Italy. T. +39331923537. Fax +39331920621. E-mail: generalsecretary@wbf.net – info@wbf.net.
URL: http://www.wbf.net/

History 1986. **Aims** Impose backgammon as a true sport of the mind. **Finance** Sources: contributions. **Activities** Awards/prizes/competitions; events/meetings.
Members Individuals in 65 countries:
Argentina, Armenia, Australia, Austria, Azerbaijan, Belarus, Belgium, Bolivia, Bosnia-Herzegovina, Brazil, Bulgaria, Canada, Chile, China, Costa Rica, Croatia, Cyprus, Czechia, Denmark, Egypt, El Salvador, Finland, France, Georgia, Germany, Greece, Hungary, Iran Islamic Rep, Ireland, Israel, Italy, Japan, Kuwait, Lebanon, Luxembourg, Malta, Mauritius, Mexico, Moldova, Monaco, Montenegro, Netherlands, North Macedonia, Norway, Pakistan, Panama, Philippines, Poland, Portugal, Romania, Russia, San Marino, Serbia, Singapore, Slovenia, South Africa, Spain, Sweden, Switzerland, Thailand, Türkiye, UK, Ukraine, United Arab Emirates, USA. [2022/XC0023/**C**]

♦ Worldwide Brewing Alliance (WBA) 21917

Contact 440 1st ST NW Ste 350, Washington DC 20001, USA. E-mail: info@worldwidebrewingalliance.org.
URL: https://worldwidebrewingalliance.org/

Aims Share knowledge and best practice amongst brewers and other concerned stakeholders; act as a global, united voice on the integrity of beer and the social responsibility of brewers to a variety of audiences, including international organizations.
Members Brewers; trade associations. Membership countries not specified.
Cerveceros Latinoamericanos (#03836); *The Brewers of Europe (#03324).*
NGO Relations Partner of (1): *Transnational Alliance to Combat Illicit Trade (TRACIT).* Associate Expert Group of *Business and Industry Advisory Committee to the OECD (BIAC, #03385).* [2022/AA3019/ty/**C**]

♦ Worldwide Broker Network (WBN) 21918

CEO 315 Montgomery Street, Suite 900, San Francisco CA 94104, USA. T. +16503411600. E-mail: info@wbnglobal.com.
Registered Address 100 Avebury Boulevard, Milton Keynes, MK9 1FH, UK.
URL: https://wbnglobal.com/

History 1989. Registration: No/ID: 04972183, Start date: 21 Nov 2003, England. **Aims** Be the premier worldwide independent insurance brokerage network. **Structure** Board of Directors. Committees (4): Technology; Marketing Communciations Advisory; European Steering; Employee Benefits Steering. **Activities** Events/meetings. **Events** *Global Conference* Abu Dhabi (United Arab Emirates) 2022, *Asia-Pacific Regional Conference* Singapore (Singapore) 2019. [2020/AA0174/**C**]

♦ Worldwide CDIO Initiative 21919

Co-Dir Chalmers Univ of Technology, Chalmersplatsen 4, SE-412 96 Gothenburg, Sweden. T. +46317721000.
URL: http://www.cdio.org/

History CDIO stands for *Conceive Design Implement Operate.* **Aims** *Educate* students to master a deeper working knowledge of the *technical* fundamentals of *engineering*; educate engineers to lead in the creation and operation of new products and systems; educate future researchers to understand the importance and strategic value of their work. **Structure** Council, consisting of original developers and early collaborators. **Activities** Serves as an educational framework for producing the next generation of engineers; provides student education stressing engineering fundamentals set in the context of Conceiving – Designing – Implementing – Operating real-world systems and products. Student projects are complemented by internships in industry. Features active group learning experiences in both classrooms and in modern learning workshops/laboratories, and rigorous assessment and evaluation processes. The Initiative is designed as a template that can be adapted and adopted by an university engineering school. Participating universities (Collaborators) regularly develop materials and approaches to share with others. Collaborating institutions gather several times a year to exchange ideas and experiences, review development at each institution, assess the Initiative's progress and further refine the project. Organizes: Annual International Conference; regional meetings. **Events** *CDIO International Conference* Trondheim (Norway) 2023, *CDIO International Conference* Reykjavik (Iceland) 2022, *International Meeting* Turku (Finland) 2022, *CDIO International Conference* Bangkok (Thailand) 2021, *Asian Regional Meeting* Kuwait (Kuwait) 2021.
Members Institutions (over 50) in 22 countries:
Australia, Belgium, Canada, Chile, China, Colombia, Denmark, Finland, France, Germany, Honduras, Italy, Malaysia, New Zealand, Portugal, Singapore, South Africa, Spain, Sweden, UK, USA, Vietnam.
Included in the above, 2 institutions listed in this Yearbook:
Australasian Association for Engineering Education (AAEE); *Laspau Inc..* [2022/XJ1318/y/**F**]

♦ Worldwide Christian Schools / see Tent Schools International
♦ Worldwide Church of God / see Grace Communion International (#10685)
♦ Worldwide Coal Combustion Product Council / see Worldwide Coal Combustion Products Network
♦ Worldwide Coal Combustion Products Network (internationally oriented national body)
♦ Worldwide Coalition for Peace (unconfirmed)
♦ Worldwide Confederation of the Animal Health Industry / see Health for Animals (#10870)
♦ Worldwide Consultative Association of Retired Generals and Admirals / see Strategies for Peace (#20008)
♦ Worldwide Council of the Animal Health Industry / see Health for Animals (#10870)
♦ Worldwide Democracy Network / see Gaian Democracy Network

♦ Worldwide Dragonfly Association (WDA) 21920

Sec address not obtained. E-mail: wda.secretary@gmail.com.
URL: http://worlddragonfly.org/

History Sep 1997. Registration: Charities Commission, No/ID: 1066039, England and Wales. **Aims** Advance public education and awareness through the promotion of the study and conservation of Odonata (dragonflies) and their natural habitats in all parts of the world. **Structure** General Meeting (every 2 years); Board of Trustees. **Languages** English, German. **Staff** Voluntary. **Finance** Sources: donations; members' dues. **Activities** Awards/prizes/competitions; events/meetings. **Events** *International Congress of Odonatology* Paphos (Cyprus) 2023, *International Congress of Odonatology* 2021, *International Congress of Odonatology* Austin, TX (USA) 2019, *Biennial Symposium of Odonatology* Cambridge (UK) 2017, *Biennial Symposium of Odonatology* Freising (Germany) 2013. **Publications** *Agrion* (2 a year) – newsletter; *International Journal of Odonatology* (2 a year).
Members Members (300) in 32 countries and territories:
Algeria, Australia, Austria, Belgium, Brazil, Bulgaria, Cameroon, Canada, China, Colombia, Croatia, Czechia, Denmark, Finland, France, Germany, Hong Kong, India, Italy, Japan, Mexico, Namibia, Netherlands, Norway, Russia, South Africa, Spain, Sweden, Taiwan, UK, United Arab Emirates, USA. [2021/XD7450/**D**]

♦ Worldwide DX Club (internationally oriented national body)
♦ World Wide Education Project (internationally oriented national body)
♦ Worldwide Evangelization for Christ International / see WEC International (#20850)
♦ Worldwide Evangelization Crusade / see WEC International (#20850)
♦ Worldwide Family of God Churches (internationally oriented national body)

♦ Worldwide Ferry Safety Association (WFSA) 21921

Exec Dir 54 Remsen St, Brooklyn NY 11201, USA. E-mail: ferrysafety@gmail.com – info@ferrysafety.org.
URL: http://www.ferrysafety.org/

History Founded 2008, following a ferry safety project started by *International Maritime Organization (IMO, #14102)* and *INTERFERRY (#11470).* Fully activated in 2012. Previously also known as *World Ferry Safety Association (WFSA).* **Aims** Reduce the number of ferry accidents and fatalities around the world; expand the use of safe ferries worldwide. **Structure** Board of Directors. **Languages** English. **Staff** 1.00 FTE, paid. **Finance** Grants. Annual budget: less than US$ 50,000. **Activities** Awards/prizes/competitions; research/documentation; training/education; events/meetings; knowledge management/information dissemination; projects/programmes. **Events** *Annual Ferry Safety and Technology Conference* New York, NY (USA) 2020, *Annual Ferry Safety and Technology Conference* Bangkok (Thailand) 2019, *Annual Ferry Safety and Technology Conference* New York, NY (USA) 2018, *Annual Ferry Safety and Technology Conference* New York, NY (USA) 2017, *Annual Ferry Safety and Technology Conference* New York, NY (USA) 2016. **Publications** Reports; articles.
Members Full in 3 countries:
Australia, Canada, USA.
IGO Relations Cooperates with: *International Maritime Organization (IMO, #14102).* **NGO Relations** Cooperates with: *INTERFERRY (#11470).* [2020/XJ6474/**D**]

♦ World Wide Fund for Nature (WWF) 21922

Fonds mondial pour la nature – Fondo Mundial para la Naturaleza – Welt Natur Fonds – Fondo Mondiale per la Natura – Fundo Mundial para a Natureza

Secretariat Rue Mauverney 28, 1196 Gland VD, Switzerland.
European Policy Office Rue Du Commerce 123, 1000 Brussels, Belgium. T. +3227438800. Fax +3227438819.
URL: http://www.panda.org/

History 11 Sep 1961, Morges (Switzerland). Still referred to by *World Wildlife Fund* in Canada and the USA. Current statutes ratified 29 Oct 1993. Registration: Swiss Civil Code, Switzerland, Gland. **Aims** Stop the degradation of the planet's natural *environment* and build a future in which humans live in harmony with nature, by: conserving the world's *biodiversity*; ensuring that the use of renewable natural resources is sustainable; promoting the reduction of pollution and wasteful consumption. **Structure** Board of Trustees; Network Executive Team; President Emeritus; 3 Vice-Presidents Emeritus. Senior Management overseeing Conservation, Fundraising, Communications and Marketing, Network Development and Operations. *'WWF International'* serves as the Secretariat of the WWF Network. **Languages** English. **Staff** Secretariat: 218 FTE; 7,662 FTE worldwide. **Activities** Advocacy/lobbying/activism; politics/policy/regulatory. **Events** *European Rivers Summit* Brussels (Belgium) 2022, *European Rivers Summit* Lisbon (Portugal) 2021, *European River Symposium* Vienna (Austria) 2021, *The Paris Agreement at a COVID Crossroads* Singapore (Singapore) 2020,

Sustainable Finance Workshop Singapore (Singapore) 2019. **Publications** Annual Report; special reports; campaign reports; research reports; position papers; discussion papers; leaflets; information booklets; project portfolios; fact sheets.
Members Active in 100 countries and territories:
Albania, Algeria, Angola, Armenia, Australia, Austria, Azerbaijan, Belgium, Belize, Bhutan, Bolivia, Bosnia-Herzegovina, Botswana, Brazil, Bulgaria, Cambodia, Cameroon, Canada, Central African Rep, Chile, China, Colombia, Comoros, Congo Brazzaville, Congo DR, Croatia, Cuba, Czechia, Denmark, Ecuador, Fiji, Finland, France, Gabon, Georgia, Germany, Greece, Guatemala, Guiana Fr, Guyana, Honduras, Hong Kong, Hungary, India, Indonesia, Italy, Japan, Kazakhstan, Kenya, Korea Rep, Kosovo, Kyrgyzstan, Laos, Libya, Madagascar, Malaysia, Mexico, Moldova, Mongolia, Montenegro, Morocco, Mozambique, Myanmar, Namibia, Nepal, Netherlands, New Caledonia, New Zealand, Norway, Pakistan, Panama, Papua New Guinea, Paraguay, Peru, Philippines, Poland, Romania, Russia, Serbia, Seychelles, Singapore, Slovakia, Slovenia, Solomon Is, South Africa, Spain, Suriname, Sweden, Switzerland, Tanzania UR, Thailand, Tunisia, Türkiye, Uganda, UK, Ukraine, USA, Vietnam, Zambia, Zimbabwe.
Associate/partner organizations in 6 countries:
Argentina, Ghana, Latvia, Nigeria, Portugal, United Arab Emirates.
Consultative Status Consultative status granted from: *ECOSOC (#05331)* (General); *International Maritime Organization (IMO, #14102)*; *UNCTAD (#20285)* (General Category); *UNEP (#20299)*; *UNESCO (#20322)* (Foundations). [2021/XF3608/f/**F**]

♦ World Wide Hearing (WWHearing) 21923

Exec Dir 239 Notre-Dame Street W, Ste 402, Montréal QC H2Y 1T4, Canada. T. +15142850990. E-mail: info@wwhearing.org.
Sec Int Centre Evidence on Disability, London School of Hygiene/Tropical Mecidine, Keppel Street, London, WC1E 7HT, UK. T. +442079588313 – +442079588170. E-mail: janderson@wwhearing.org.
URL: http://www.wwhearing.org/
History 2003, Geneva (Switzerland). Founded at Headquarters of *WHO (#20950)*. Also known under the acronym *WWH*. Project Collaboration Agreement signed with WHO for 2006-2010 and renewed for 2010-2014. Registration: Start date: 2006, Switzerland. **Aims** Offer a better quality of life to people of all ages who are hearing impaired, particularly to *children* who are hard-of-hearing. **Structure** General Meeting (annual). Executive Committee. Membership Association, Foundation International, based in Canada. **Activities** Training/education. **Events** *Annual General Meeting* Mill Neck, NY (USA) 2011. **NGO Relations** Member of (1): *Coalition for Global Hearing Health (CGHH)*. Participates in: *Global Partnership on Children with Disabilities (GPcwd, #10529)*. [2019.01.30/XJ2905/**E**]

♦ Worldwide Hospice Palliative Care Alliance (WHPCA) 21924

Exec Dir 34-44 Britannia Street, London, WC1X 9JG, UK. T. +17039808737. E-mail: info@thewhpca.org.
URL: http://www.thewhpca.org/
History 2008, London (UK). Former names and other names: *Worldwide Palliative Care Alliance* – alias. Registration: Charity Commission, No/ID: 1127569, Start date: 2008, England and Wales. **Aims** Foster, promote and influence the delivery of affordable, quality palliative care. **Structure** Board of Directors. **Languages** English. **Staff** 5.00 FTE, paid; 1.00 FTE, voluntary. **Finance** Sources: donations; government support; grants; private foundations. Trusts. Annual budget: 156,140 GBP (2021). **Activities** Advocacy/lobbying/activism; guidance/assistance/consulting; healthcare; knowledge management/information dissemination; projects/programmes. Active in: Armenia, Bangladesh, Ethiopia, India, Kenya, Russia, UK, USA. **Publications** *World Hospice and Palliative Care* – newsletter. *Global Atlas of Palliative Care* (2nd ed 2020) by Dr Stephen Connor (Ed); *Building Integrated Palliative Care Programs and Services*; *Global Atlas of Palliative Care at the End of Life*; *Palliative Care Toolkit*.
Members Organizations in 101 countries and territories:
Albania, Argentina, Armenia, Australia, Austria, Azerbaijan, Bahamas, Bangladesh, Barbados, Belgium, Belize, Bosnia-Herzegovina, Brazil, Bulgaria, Burundi, Cameroon, Canada, Central African Rep, Chile, China, Colombia, Congo DR, Costa Rica, Côte d'Ivoire, Croatia, Czechia, Dominican Rep, Ecuador, Egypt, Ethiopia, Faeroe Is, France, Gambia, Georgia, Germany, Ghana, Greece, Guatemala, Guinea, Haiti, India, Indonesia, Iran Islamic Rep, Ireland, Israel, Italy, Japan, Jordan, Kazakhstan, Kenya, Korea Rep, Kuwait, Lebanon, Lesotho, Lithuania, Malawi, Malaysia, Mali, Mexico, Mongolia, Morocco, Nepal, New Zealand, Nicaragua, Nigeria, North Macedonia, Norway, Pakistan, Palestine, Paraguay, Philippines, Poland, Portugal, Romania, Russia, Rwanda, Senegal, Sierra Leone, Singapore, Slovakia, Slovenia, South Africa, Spain, Sri Lanka, Sudan, Switzerland, Tajikistan, Tanzania UR, Thailand, Togo, Trinidad-Tobago, Tunisia, Uganda, UK, Ukraine, Uruguay, USA, Uzbekistan, Vietnam, Zambia, Zimbabwe.
Regional associations include the following 4 organizations listed in this Yearbook:
African Palliative Care Association (APCA, #00409); *Asia Pacific Hospice Palliative Care Network (APHN, #01928)*; *Asociación Latinoamericana de Cuidados Paliativos (ALCP, #02201)*; *European Association for Palliative Care (EAPC, #06141)*.
Consultative Status Consultative status granted from: *ECOSOC (#05331)* (Special); *WHO (#20950)* (Official).
NGO Relations Member of (2): *International Drug Policy Consortium (IDPC, #13205)*; *UHC2030 (#20277)*. [2022.06.14/XJ9729/y/**C**]

♦ Worldwide Independent Network (WIN) 21925

General Manager Industriestr 30, 8302 Kloten ZH, Switzerland. T. +41448887200. Fax +41448887201. E-mail: office@winlogistics.com.
URL: https://winlogistics.com/
History 2006, Seville (Spain). Former names and other names: *Worldwide Independent Network Association (WIN)* – former. **Aims** Connect, support and develop independent music trade associations globally. **Structure** Annual General Meeting; Board of Directors; Secretariat. **Activities** Advocacy/lobbying/activism; events/meetings. **Events** *Extraordinary Annual General Meeting* Madrid (Spain) 2022, *Annual General Meeting* Switzerland 2022, *Annual General Meeting* Switzerland 2021, *Annual General Meeting* Bangkok (Thailand) 2020, *Global Sales Meeting* Istanbul (Turkey) 2020.
Members Independent music trade associations in 30 countries:
Argentina, Australia, Austria, Belgium, Brazil, Canada, Chile, Czechia, Denmark, Finland, France, Germany, Hungary, Ireland, Israel, Italy, Japan, Korea Rep, Netherlands, New Zealand, Norway, Poland, Portugal, Romania, Spain, Sweden, Switzerland, Türkiye, UK, USA.
Independent Music Companies Association (IMPALA, #11151); *RUNDA (#18999)*.
NGO Relations Supports (1): *Music Climate Pact*. [2022/AA0468/y/**C**]

♦ Worldwide Independent Network Association / see Worldwide Independent Network (#21925)

♦ Worldwide Initiatives for Grantmaker Support (WINGS) 21926

Iniciativas Mundiales de Apoyo a Donantes

Exec Dir Rua da Consolação, 368 – 12º andar, conjunto 12, Sao Paulo SP, 05415-030, Brazil. T. +551130787299. E-mail: info@wingsweb.org.
URL: http://www.wingsweb.org/
History 1998, Oaxaca (Mexico). Founded during *International Meeting of Associations Serving Grantmakers (IMAG)*, following a series of meetings beginning in the 1990s. Merged with *Worldwide Community Foundation Support Organization Network (WCFSON, inactive)*, 1999. Formally founded Jan 2000. Permanent Secretariat moved to Sao Paulo (Brazil), 2011. Registration: Start date: 2011, USA. **Aims** Strengthen *philanthropy* and a culture of giving through mutual learning and support, knowledge sharing and professional development among its participants. **Structure** Coordinating Committee; Secretariat. **Languages** English. **Staff** 4.50 FTE, paid. 1 FTE, intern. **Finance** Sources: contributions; grants; members' dues. **Activities** Events/meetings; guidance/assistance/consulting; networking/liaising; training/education. **Events** *WINGS Forum* Istanbul (Turkey) 2014, *WINGS Forum* Como (Italy) 2010, *WINGS Forum* Bangkok (Thailand) 2006, *Forum / WINGS Forum* Sydney, NSW (Australia) 2002, *WINGS Forum* Oaxaca (Mexico) 1998. **Publications** *Community Foundation Global Status Report* (annual). *Data Charter* (2014); *Infrastructure in Focus: A Global Picture of Organizations Serving Philanthropy* (2014); *Infrastructure in Focus: Special Look at Organizations Serving Community Philanthropy* (2014). Annual Report; forum and meeting reports; exchange visit reports; directories; strategic plan.
Members Grantmaker associations and support organizations (over 180) in 45 countries. Membership countries not specified. Included in the above, 59 organizations listed in this Yearbook:
Included in the above, 57 organizations listed in this Yearbook:
- *Africa Grantmakers' Affinity Group (AGAG)*;
- *African Philanthropy Forum (APF, #00415)*;
- *African Youth in Philanthropy Network (AYPN, #00507)*;
- *Africa Philanthropy Network (APN, #00512)*;
- *Aga Khan Foundation (AKF, #00545)*;
- *Arab Foundations Forum (AFF, #00963)*;
- *Asia Centre for Social Entrepreneurship and Philanthropy (ACSEP)*;
- *Asia Foundation*;
- *Asian Venture Philanthropy Network (AVPN, #01778)*;
- *Asia-Pacific Centre for Social Investment and and Philanthropy (APCSIP)*;
- *Bertelsmann Foundation*;
- *Bill and Melinda Gates Foundation (BMGF)*;
- *Candid*;
- *Caribbean Philanthropy Network (CPN, #03538)*;
- *Charities Aid Foundation (CAF)*;
- *Charities Aid Foundation of America (CAF America)*;
- *Charities Aid Foundation Southern Africa (CAF Southern Africa)*;
- *CIVICUS: World Alliance for Citizen Participation (#03962)*;
- *CivSource Africa*;
- *East Africa Philanthropy Network (EAPN, #05192)*;
- *Ecobank Foundation*;
- *EDGE Funders Alliance (#05358)*;
- *EPIC-Africa*;
- *European Community Foundation Initiative (ECFI, #06680)*;
- *European Foundation Centre (EFC, inactive)*;
- *European Venture Philanthropy Association (EVPA, #09053)*;
- *Fondation de France*;
- *Ford Foundation (#09858)*;
- *Forum on Business and Social Responsibility in the Americas (Forum EMPRESA)*;
- *Fundação Luso-Americana para o Desenvolvimento (FLAD)*;
- *Give2Asia*;
- *Global Alliance for Development Foundation (GADeF, #10192)*;
- *Global Dialogue*;
- *Global Fund for Community Foundations (GFCF, #10382)*;
- *GlobalGiving Foundation*;
- *Global Impact*;
- *Global Network of Foundations Working for Development (netFWD)*;
- *Global Philanthropy Forum*;
- *Global Philanthropy Partnership (GPP)*;
- *Global Philanthropy Project (GPP, #10546)*;
- *Grantmakers Without Borders*;
- *Hispanics in Philanthropy (HIP)*;
- *Inter-American Foundation (IAF, #11431)*;
- *International Center for Not-for-Profit Law (ICNL, #12471)*;
- *International Funders for Indigenous Peoples (IFIP)*;
- *International Society for Third-Sector Research (ISTR, #15510)*;
- *International Venture Philanthropy Center (IVPC, #15843)*;
- *International Youth Foundation (IYF)*;
- *Network of European Foundations (NEF, #17019)*;
- *Philanthropy Leadership Network (PLN)*;
- *Prospera – International Network of Women's Funds (INWF, #18545)*;
- *Skoll Foundation*;
- *Social Value International (SVI, #19348)*;
- *Southern Africa Trust*;
- *Synergos (#20082)*;
- *TechSoup Global (#20122)*;
- *Transparency and Accountability Initiative (TAI, #20221)*.

IGO Relations Cooperates with: *UNDP (#20292)*. **NGO Relations** Partner of (1): *UNLEASH*. [2022/XF6105/y/**F**]

♦ Worldwide Innovative Networking (WIN) 21927

Dir Operational Team BP 90059, 94801 Villejuif, France.
Street address 9 rue Guy Môquet, 94803 Villejuif, France.
URL: http://www.winconsortium.org/
History Full title: *Worldwide Innovative Networking in personalized cancer medicine consortium*. Also referred to as *WIN Consortium*. **Aims** Achieve rapid and efficient translation of ground-breaking early diagnostic and personalized cancer medicine discoveries into the standards for clinical care, to significantly improve the outcomes and quality of life of cancer patients. **Structure** General Assembly. Directorate. Steering Committee, comprising Chairman, Vice-Chairman, Chairman of Scientific Advisory Board, Chief Operating Officer and a member. **Languages** English. **Staff** 1.50 FTE, paid; 0.50 FTE, voluntary. **Finance** Members' dues. Budget (annual): euro 1.1 million. **Activities** Organizes annual symposium. **Events** *Annual Symposium* Paris (France) 2019, *Annual Symposium* Paris (France) 2018, *Annual Symposium* Paris (France) 2017, *WIN Annual Symposium* Paris (France) 2014, *Annual Symposium* Paris (France) 2013.
Members Associated Technology Partners; Pharmaceutical Partners; Non-Profit Organizations; Academic Institutions; Health Plan Members. Members in 15 countries:
Brazil, Canada, China, France, Germany, Hungary, India, Israel, Italy, Jordan, Romania, Singapore, Spain, UK, USA.
Included in the above, 1 organization listed in this Yearbook:
European Institute of Oncology, Milan (EIO). [2018/XJ7064/**F**]

♦ Worldwide Innovative Networking in personalized cancer medicine consortium / see Worldwide Innovative Networking (#21927)
♦ Worldwide Intifada (unconfirmed)
♦ Worldwide Life Quality Enhancement Association (internationally oriented national body)
♦ Worldwide magazine media association / see FIPP (#09776)
♦ Worldwide Missionary Convention (internationally oriented national body)
♦ Worldwide Missions Outreach Ministries (internationally oriented national body)

♦ Worldwide Network of Artists Residencies (Res Artis) 21928

Europe office Sarphatistraat 470, 1018 GW Amsterdam, Netherlands. E-mail: office@resartis.org.
Australia office 44 Glasshouse Road, Collingwood VIC 3066, Australia.
URL: http://www.resartis.org/
History 1993, Berlin (Germany). Bylaws adopted, 3 May 1996, Annaghmakerrig (Ireland); amended 2001, Umbertide (Italy). Former names and other names: *RES ARTIS – International Association of Residential Arts Centres* – former; *RES ARTIS – Association internationale de centres de résidences d'artistes* – former. Registration: Start date: 2003, Netherlands, Amsterdam. **Aims** Support and connect residencies; engage and advocate the importance of residencies in today's society; provide recommendations towards cultural mobility, research and policy. **Structure** Board of Directors. **Languages** Arabic, Danish, Dutch, English, German, Indonesian, Italian, Persian, Spanish. **Staff** 1.20 FTE, paid. **Finance** Sources: grants; members' dues. **Activities** Events/meetings; knowledge management/information dissemination; networking/liaising. **Events** *Res Artis Conference* Bangkok (Thailand) 2021, *Res Artis Meeting* Kyoto (Japan) 2019, *Res Artis Meeting* Rovaniemi (Finland) 2018, *Res Artis Meeting* Copenhagen (Denmark) 2017, *General Meeting* Tokyo (Japan) 2012. **Publications** *Res Artis Newsletter*. Leaflet; brochure. **Members** Residency; Associate; Individual. Organizations (over 750) in over 85 countries. Membership countries not specified. **NGO Relations** Member of: *Culture Action Europe (CAE, #04981)*; *European Alliance for Culture and the Arts (#05866)*. [2020.08.20/XD5597/**C**]

♦ Worldwide Network for Blood and Marrow Transplantation (WBMT) 21929

Pres c/o Blutspende SRK Schweiz AG, Laupenstrasse 37, 3001 Bern, Switzerland. T. +41313808181. E-mail: mail@wbmt.org.
URL: http://www.wbmt.org/
History 2007. Founded by *European Society for Blood and Marrow Transplantation (EBMT, #08533)*, *Center for International Blood and Marrow Transplant Research (CIBMTR, #03645)*, *Asia Pacific Blood and Marrow Transplantation Group (APBMT, #01860)* and *World Marrow Donor Association (WMDA, #21635)*. **Aims** Promote excellence in *stem cell* transplantation, stem cell donation, *cellular therapy*. **Structure** Board; Standing Committees (7). **Languages** English. **Staff** 0.50 FTE, paid. **Finance** Sources: sponsorship. **Activities** Events/meetings; standards/guidelines; training/education. **Events** *Workshop* Asunción (Paraguay) 2019, *Workshop* Beijing (China) 2018, *Workshop* Riyadh (Saudi Arabia) 2017, *Workshop* Cape Town (South Africa) 2014, *Workshop* Salvador (Brazil) 2013. **Publications** *WBMT Global Survey*.

Members Societies (24), of which 16 are listed in this Yearbook:
African Blood and Marrow Transplantation Society (AfBMT); Asia Pacific Blood and Marrow Transplantation Group (APBMT, #01860); Australasian Bone Marrow Transplant Recipient Registry (ABMTRR); Center for International Blood and Marrow Transplant Research (CIBMTR, #03645); Eastern Mediterranean Blood and Marrow Transplantation Group (EMBMT, #05242); EUROCORD (no recent information); European Federation for Immunogenetics (EFI, #07141); European LeukemiaNet (ELN, #07685); European School of Haematology (ESH, #08430); European Society for Blood and Marrow Transplantation (EBMT, #08533); Foundation for the Accreditation of Cellular Therapy (FACT); ICCBBA (#11042); International Society for Cell & Gene Therapy (ISCT, #15000); International Society of Blood Transfusion (ISBT, #14979); Latin American Bone Marrow Transplantation Group (LABMT, #16257); World Marrow Donor Association (WMDA, #21635).
Consultative Status Consultative status granted from: *WHO (#20950)* (Official). [2021.05.26/XJ1666/y/**E**]

♦ Worldwide Network of the Experiment in International Living (Federation EIL) 21930

Expérience de vie internationale – Experimento de Convivencia Internacional – Experiment Vereinigung für das Praktische Zusammenleben der Völker

Contact 1440 G St NW, Washington DC, USA. E-mail: info@federationeil.org.
URL: http://federationeil.org/

History 1932, USA. Statutes adopted 1954, Heiden (Switzerland); revised: 1960, Mexico; 1962, Italy; 1963, Germany FR; 1970, Turkey; 1972, Japan; 1975, Italy; 1987, Turkey; 1999, Spain; 2001, New Zealand; 2003, Asti (Italy). Former names and other names: *Experiment in International Living (EIL)* – former. Registration: Switzerland. **Aims** Involve individuals in programmes of *intercultural* learning which develop *understanding* of and *respect* for people worldwide. Member organizations strive to: contribute to a lasting peace; make possible continuity, sound growth and progress; encourage and maintain high educational principles and standards. **Structure** General Assembly (at least every 2 years), elects President and Vice-President(s) for 2-year terms. Regional conferences as needed (Asia/Pacific, Europe, South America). Autonomous national representations, including US Section: *World Learning*. European branch: *Experiment in Europe (EIE, no recent information)*. **Languages** English. **Staff** Administrative headquarters: 1 full-time, paid; 1 part-time, paid. Over 500 world-wide paid staff in national representation offices, plus over 25,000 volunteers. **Finance** Members' dues. Member organizations funded by: contributions; foundation grants; institutional grants. **Activities** Projects/programmes. **Events** *Annual General Assembly* Madrid (Spain) 2018, *Annual General Assembly* Kobe (Japan) 2012, *Annual General Assembly* Paris (France) 2010, *Annual General Assembly* Rabat (Morocco) 2009, *Annual General Assembly* Cape Town (South Africa) 2008. **Publications** *In the Loop Newsletter. Fed EIL International Brochure.* Annual Report. Each national representation has its own publications.
Members Organizations (12) in 12 countries:
Argentina, Ecuador, France, Germany, Guatemala, Ireland, Italy, Japan, Mexico, Spain, UK, USA.
Consultative Status Consultative status granted from: *ECOSOC (#05331)* (Special).
NGO Relations Supports: *Media for Development International (MFDI)*. Member of:
- *American Council for Voluntary International Action (InterAction);*
- *Commonwealth Youth Exchange Council (CYEC);*
- *Consortium for Southeast Asian Refugees (no recent information);*
- *Council on Standards for International Educational Travel (CSIET);*
- *Global Health Council (GHC, #10402);*
- *Institute of International Education (IIE);*
- *International Branch of the YMCA, New York (International YMCA);*
- *International Council of Voluntary Agencies (ICVA, #13092).*

Cooperates with:
- *America-Mideast Educational and Training Services (AMIDEAST);*
- *American Forum for Global Education;*
- *Asia Foundation;*
- *Brot für die Welt;*
- *Friendship Force International (FFI);*
- *Institute of Andean Studies (IAS);*
- *International Hospitality Center (inactive);*
- *Partners of the Americas;*
- *People to People International (PTPI, #18300);*
- *Rotary International (RI, #18975);*
- *Save the Children Federation (SCF);*
- *Sister Cities International (SCI);*
- *World Education (WE).* [2020/XB0917/y/**F**]

- ♦ Worldwide Network for Mexico Policy Research / see PROFMEX – Consortium for Research on Mexico
- ♦ Worldwide Network of Port Cities (#02751)
- ♦ Worldwide Network for Research on Mexico / see PROFMEX – Consortium for Research on Mexico
- ♦ Worldwide Nitrocellulose Producers Association (internationally oriented national body)
- ♦ World Wide Opportunities on Organic Farms / see World-Wide Opportunities on Organic Farms (#21931)

♦ World-Wide Opportunities on Organic Farms (WWOOF) 21931

Registered Office Level 5, 126-130 Phillip Street, Sydney NSW 2000, Australia. E-mail: wwoof@wwoof.com.au.
URL: http://www.wwoofinternational.org/

History 1971, UK. Founded as *Working Weekends on Organic Farms (WWOOF)*. Subsequently changed title to *Willing Workers on Organic Farms (WWOOF)*, 1993.Subsequently *World Wide Opportunities on Organic Farms* was adopted. **Aims** Provide first hand experience of organic growing methods by working on organic farms; promote meeting, discussion and exchange of views within the movement; provide an opportunity to learn about life in the host country by living and working as a family. **Structure** A loose network of independent national groups. **Finance** Sources: members' dues. **Activities** Knowledge management/information dissemination. **Events** *Workshop* Switzerland 2000.
Members WWOOF Groups in 57 countries and territories:
Argentina, Australia, Austria, Bangladesh, Belgium, Belize, Brazil, Bulgaria, Cameroon, Canada, Chile, China, Costa Rica, Czechia, Denmark, Ecuador, Estonia, France, Germany, Greece, Guatemala, Hungary, India, Ireland, Israel, Italy, Japan, Kazakhstan, Korea Rep, Lithuania, Mexico, Moldova, Nepal, Netherlands, New Zealand, Nigeria, Norway, Peru, Philippines, Poland, Portugal, Romania, Serbia, Sierra Leone, South Africa, Spain, Sri Lanka, Sweden, Switzerland, Taiwan, Tanzania UR, Thailand, Togo, Türkiye, Uganda, UK, USA. [2020.04.29/XF5411/**F**]

- ♦ World Wide Organization for Child Care, Health and Hygiene Among Jews (inactive)
- ♦ Worldwide Organization for Women (internationally oriented national body)
- ♦ Worldwide Organization of Women's Studies (inactive)
- ♦ Worldwide Palliative Care Alliance / see Worldwide Hospice Palliative Care Alliance (#21924)
- ♦ Worldwide Partners Alliance (unconfirmed)
- ♦ Worldwide Practice Firms Network / see EUROPEN-PEN International (#09165)

♦ Worldwide Protein Data Bank Foundation (wwPDB) 21932

Contact address not obtained. E-mail: info@wwpdb.org – info@rcsb.org.
URL: http://wwpdb.org/

Aims Maintain a single Protein Data Bank Archive of macromolecular structural data that is freely and publicly available to the global community. **Structure** Advisory Committee. **Events** *Symposium on Integrative Structural Biology with Hybrid Methods* Toyonaka (Japan) 2015.
Members Protein banks in 3 countries:
Japan, UK, USA.
NGO Relations Scientific Associate of: *International Union of Crystallography (IUCr, #15768).* [2019.12.30/XM4240/f/**F**]

♦ Worldwide Quality EXpress System /Network/ (WQXS Network) 21933

SG Ave de Tervueren 237, 1150 Brussels, Belgium. T. +3227709797. Fax +3227707006. E-mail: gai@wqxs.net – info@wqxs.net.
URL: http://www.wqxs.net/

History Mar 1995. Registered in accordance with Belgian law. **Aims** Study and set in motion solutions to problems affecting the *transport industry*; provide a channel for effective communications between the industry and the scientific community, the European Union regulatory and governmental authorities and other international organizations and for local intermediaries functioning at the national level; contribute to and increase the industry's knowledge through provision and exchange of scientific research, information and services; keep members informed of ongoing and proposed legislation at national, European and international levels. **Structure** General Assembly (annual); Board of Directors. **Finance** Members' dues.
Members Membership countries not specified. [2016/XF3852/**F**]

- ♦ Worldwide Responsible Accredited Production (internationally oriented national body)
- ♦ Worldwide Responsible Apparel Production / see Worldwide Responsible Accredited Production
- ♦ Worldwide Support for Development (internationally oriented national body)
- ♦ Worldwide Universities Network (internationally oriented national body)

♦ Worldwide Vending Association (WVA) 21934

Dir Gen c/o EVA, Rue Van Eyck 44, 1000 Brussels, Belgium. T. +3225120075.
URL: http://www.vending-europe.eu/en/eva/wvainternational-associations.html

History Founded 14 Jun 2006, by *European Vending and Coffee Service Association (EVA, #09049)* and the (USA) National Automatic Merchandising Association (NAMA). Registered in accordance with Belgian law. **Structure** General Assembly (annual). Board of Directors, comprising Chairman and 6 members.
Members Full and Supportive in 25 countries and territories:
Australia, Austria, Belgium, Brazil, Canada, Colombia, Czechia, Denmark, France, Germany, Greece, Hungary, Ireland, Italy, Macau, Poland, Portugal, Russia, Slovakia, Spain, Sweden, Switzerland, Türkiye, UK, USA.
NGO Relations Participates in: *Mint Directors Conference (MDC, #16822).* [2016/XM8175/**C**]

- ♦ Worldwide Veterinary Service (internationally oriented national body)

♦ World Wide Web Consortium (W3C) 21935

interim CEO address not obtained.
URL: https://www.w3.org/

History 1 Oct 1994, Cambridge, MA (USA). Founded as an industry standards consortium, currently jointly hosted by: Massachusetts Institute of Technology Computer Science and Artificial Intelligence Laboratory (MIT/CSAIL) in the USA; *European Research Consortium for Informatics and Mathematics (ERCIM, #08362)* in Europe; *'Keio University Shonan Fujisawa'* in Japan and 'Beihang University' in China. Initially established in collaboration with *European Organization for Nuclear Research (CERN, #08108)*, where the Web originated, with support from DARPA and the European Commission. *International Digital Publishing Forum (IDPF, inactive)* merged into W3C, 30 Jan 2017. **Aims** Realize the full potential of the World Wide Web by: setting the vision; developing common standards; operating as the standards-setting body for standards; demonstrating new technologies; making tools available to the general public. **Structure** Advisory Committee; Advisory Board; Technical Architecture Group; Working Groups. **Languages** English. **Finance** Sources: government support; grants; members' dues; sponsorship. US and Canadian governments; industrial sponsors. Supported by: *European Commission (EC, #06633)*. **Activities** Events/meetings; research and development; standards/guidelines. **Events** *Web Conference* Austin, TX (USA) 2023, *Web Conference* Lyon (France) 2022, *W3C Conference* Vancouver, BC (Canada) 2022, *Web Conference* Ljubljana (Slovenia) 2021, *Web Conference* Taipei (Taiwan) 2020. **Publications** Web standards; technical reports; draft specifications; test suites; guidelines; software.
Members Full; Affiliate. Members (about 500) in 45 countries and territories:
Armenia, Australia, Austria, Belgium, Brazil, Bulgaria, Canada, China, Czechia, Denmark, Egypt, Finland, France, Germany, Greece, Hong Kong, Hungary, India, Ireland, Israel, Italy, Japan, Korea Rep, Malaysia, Malta, Morocco, Netherlands, New Zealand, Norway, Pakistan, Romania, Senegal, Singapore, Slovenia, South Africa, Spain, Sri Lanka, Sweden, Switzerland, Taiwan, Türkiye, UK, United Arab Emirates, Uruguay, USA.
NGO Relations Member of (1): *Cracking the Language Barrier (#04942)*. Cooperates with (1): *Global Alliance on Accessible Technologies and Environments (GAATES, #10180)*. Input or influence on aspects of development or regulation of: *Internet (#15948)*. In liaison with technical committees of: *International Organization for Standardization (ISO, #14473).* [2023/XE6478/**E**]

♦ World Wide Web Foundation 21936

Contact 1110 Vermont Ave NW, Ste 500, Washington DC 20005, USA. T. +12025952892. E-mail: contact@webfoundation.org.
URL: http://www.webfoundation.org/

History 2009 by Sir Tim Berners-Lee. Registered in accordance with Swiss Civil Code and also registered in accordance with US law. **Aims** Advance the open web as a public good and a basic right. **Structure** Board of Directors. **Languages** English. **Staff** 30.00 FTE, paid. **Finance** Donors include international organizations, government agencies, major foundations, companies, civil society organizations and individuals. **Activities** Advocacy/lobbying/activism; research and development; capacity building. **Publications** *Affordability Report*; *Case for the Web*; *Contract for the Web*; *Women Rights Online.* White papers; research reports. **Members** Membership countries not specified. **Consultative Status** Consultative status granted from: *ECOSOC (#05331)* (Special). **NGO Relations** Hosts secretariat of: *Alliance for Affordable Internet (A4AI, #00651).* Member of: *Global Partnership for Sustainable Development Data (Data4SDGS, #10542).* [2020.01.14/XJ8122/f/**F**]

- ♦ World Wildlife Fund / see World Wide Fund for Nature (#21922)

♦ World Wind Energy Association (WWEA) 21937

SG Charles-de-Gaulle-Str 5, 53113 Bonn, Germany. T. +4922824269800. Fax +4924269802. E-mail: secretariat@wwindea.org.
URL: http://www.wwindea.org/

History Founded 1 Jul 2001, Copenhagen (Denmark). **Aims** Improve communication of all wind energy actors worldwide; influence national and international policies in favour of wind energy; enhance an international technology transfer. **Structure** Board. **Languages** English. **Activities** Financial and/or material support; guidance/assistance/consulting; knowledge management/information dissemination. **Events** *World Wind Energy Conference* Rio de Janeiro (Brazil) 2019, *World Wind Energy Conference* Karachi (Pakistan) 2018, *World Wind Energy Conference* Malmö (Sweden) 2017, *World Community Power Conference* Fukushima (Japan) 2016, *World Wind Energy Conference* Tokyo (Japan) 2016. **Publications** *Wind Energy International* (every 2 years) – international handbook for wind power. *Small Wind World Report* – international handbook for small wind power.
Members Ordinary; Scientific; Corporate; Individual. Ordinary: organizations (85) in 55 countries and territories:
Algeria, Argentina, Australia, Austria, Bangladesh, Brazil, Bulgaria, Canada, China, Colombia, Croatia, Cuba, Czechia, Denmark, Egypt, Finland, France, Germany, Hong Kong, Hungary, India, Israel, Italy, Japan, Jordan, Kazakhstan, Kenya, Korea Rep, Liberia, Lithuania, Mali, Malta, Mexico, Moldova, Mongolia, Nicaragua, Nigeria, North Macedonia, Pakistan, Philippines, Poland, Portugal, Romania, Russia, Slovakia, Somalia, South Africa, Sri Lanka, Sweden, Switzerland, Taiwan, Türkiye, UK, Ukraine, USA.
Included in the above, 4 organizations listed in this Yearbook:
African Wind Energy Association (AfriWEA, #00499); Asociación Latinoamericana de Energía Eólica (#02209); EUROSOLAR – European Association for Renewable Energy (#09183); International Energy Foundation (IEF, #13273).
Scientific members: institutes; academies; universities (59) in 36 countries and territories:
Algeria, Argentina, Belarus, Brazil, Bulgaria, Canada, Chile, China, Cuba, Denmark, Ethiopia, Germany, India, Jordan, Korea DPR, Korea Rep, Lesotho, Lithuania, Malaysia, Malta, Mexico, Mongolia, Nigeria, Peru, Portugal, Romania, Russia, Serbia, Slovakia, Sweden, Syrian AR, Taiwan, Türkiye, Ukraine, Uruguay, Vietnam.
Included in the above, 1 organization listed in this Yearbook:
World Wind Energy Institute (WWEI, #21938).
Corporate members (203) in 48 countries:
Australia, Austria, Bangladesh, Brazil, Canada, China, Congo Brazzaville, Croatia, Czechia, Denmark, Ecuador, Egypt, Ethiopia, France, Germany, Ghana, India, Iran Islamic Rep, Ireland, Israel, Italy, Jordan, Kazakhstan, Korea Rep, Lebanon, Luxembourg, Mexico, Morocco, Netherlands, Nigeria, Pakistan, Panama, Romania, Russia, Serbia, Singapore, Solomon Is, South Africa, Spain, Sweden, Switzerland, Thailand, Türkiye, UK, Ukraine, United Arab Emirates, Uruguay, USA.
Observers (16) in 12 countries:
Bangladesh, Bulgaria, Estonia, Germany, Hungary, India, Indonesia, Italy, Japan, Norway, UK, Venezuela.
Included in the above, one organization listed in this Yearbook:

World Alliance for Decentralized Energy (WADE, #21081).
Consultative Status Consultative status granted from: *ECOSOC (#05331)* (Special). **IGO Relations** Observer status with: *United Nations Framework Convention on Climate Change (UNFCCC, 1992).* Cooperates with: *International Bank for Reconstruction and Development (IBRD, #12317)* (World Bank); *International Energy Agency (IEA, #13270); International Renewable Energy Agency (IRENA, #14715); UNESCO (#20322); UNEP (#20299).* **NGO Relations** Member of: *Global 100% RE (#10160); REN21 (#18836); World Council for Renewable Energy (WCRE, #21340).* Instrumental in setting up: *International Renewable Energy Alliance (Ren Alliance, #14716).* [2020/XC0130/y/**C**]

♦ World Wind Energy Institute (WWEI) 21938

Contact c/o Nordic Folkecenter for Renewable Energy, Kammersgaardsvej 16, 7760 Hurup Thy, Denmark. T. +4597956600. Fax +4597956565. E-mail: wwei@folkecenter.dk.
URL: http://www.wwei.info/
History May 2006, Kingston (Canada), by *World Council for Renewable Energy (WCRE, #21340).* **Aims** Increase dissemination and exchange of know-how related to all aspect os wind and other renewable energy sources. **Structure** Board, comprising President and 4 Vice-Presidents. **Publications** *News from the WWEI.*
Members Centres (7) in 7 countries:
Canada, China, Cuba, Denmark, Egypt, Russia.
NGO Relations Secretariat provided by: *EUROSOLAR – European Association for Renewable Energy (#09183).* Scientific member of: *World Wind Energy Association (WWEA, #21937).* [2008.07.08/XM3188/j/**E**]

♦ World Wine Trade Group (WWTG) 21939

Grupo Mundial del Comercio del Vino (GMCV)
Contact Senior International Trade Specialist, US Dept of Commerce, Intl Trade Administration, 1400 Constitution Ave, NW Mailstop 4035, Washington DC 20230, USA.
URL: http://www.ita.doc.gov/td/ocg/wwtg.htm
History 1998. **Aims** Facilitate the international trade in wine; avoid the application of obstacles to international trade in wine. **Structure** Informal group in government representatives. Includes Industry Group. **Events** *Plenary Meeting* Brussels (Belgium) 2016, *Technical Meeting* Adelaide, SA (Australia) 2015, *Plenary Meeting* Brussels (Belgium) 2015, *Plenary Meeting* Brussels (Belgium) 2014, *Plenary Meeting* Tbilisi (Georgia) 2014.
Members Representatives (18) of wine producing countries (9):
Argentina, Australia, Canada, Chile, Mexico, New Zealand, South Africa, USA. [2016.06.01/XF7178/t/**F**]

♦ World Wing Chun Kung Fu Association / see Global Traditional Wing Chun Kung Fu Association (#10633)
♦ World Wings International (internationally oriented national body)

♦ World Winter Cities Association for Mayors (WWCAM) 21940

Secretariat c/o International Relations Dept, City of Sapporo, Kita 1 Nishi 2, Chuo-ku, Sapporo HOKKAIDO, 060-8611 Japan. T. +81112112032. Fax +81112185168. E-mail: wwcam@city.sapporo.jp.
URL: https://wwcam.org/
History 1982. Founded upon Sapporo's (Japan) initiation of the Northern Intercity Conference. Former names and other names: *International Association of Mayors of Northern Cities (IAMNC)* – former. **Aims** Contribute to development of livable winter cities by gathering representatives of cities with similar climates to facilitate exchange of knowledge and information concerning winter-related issues; promote the "Winter Cities Movement"; strengthen cooperation and solidarity among winter cities while contributing to peace and development of an international society; tackle global warming issues through educational and action campaigns. **Structure** General Assembly; Board of Directors; Secretariat. **Languages** English. **Staff** 4.00 FTE, paid. **Finance** Sources: members' dues. **Activities** Events/meetings; knowledge management/information dissemination; research/documentation. **Events** *Mayors Conference* Rovaniemi (Finland) 2021, *Working-Level Officials Meeting* Norilsk (Russia) 2019, *Working-Level Officials Meeting* Sapporo (Japan) 2018, *Mayors Conference* Shenyang (China) 2018, *Mayors Conference* Sapporo (Japan) 2016. **Publications** *World Winter City News.*
Members Mayors representing 22 cities from 9 countries:
Canada, China, Estonia, Finland, Japan, Korea Rep, Mongolia, Russia, USA.
Consultative Status Consultative status granted from: *ECOSOC (#05331)* (Ros A). **IGO Relations** Associated with Department of Economic and Social Affairs of the United Nations. Associated with Department of Global Communications of the United Nations. [2023.02.24/XD6751/**D**]

♦ World Wisdom Council 21941

Pres c/o The Club of Budapest, Tóth Arpad st 29 I 4/A, Budapest 1014, Hungary. T. +3612129893.
Facebook: https://www.facebook.com/pages/category/Community-Organization/WWC-World-Wisdom-Council-1586727011581205/
History 29 Jul 2004, Höchstadt an der Aisch (Germany). 29 Jul 2004, Höchtstadt an der Aisch (Germany), by *Club of Budapest (#04032)* and *World Commission on Global Consciousness and Spirituality (WCGCS, #21285).* **Aims** Build on the power and creativity innate in all people by: bringing to the attention of the widest layers of the public both the dangers and the opportunities inherent in the human condition in its global dimension; identifying priority areas where individual and cooperative action is needed in order to reinforce progress toward peace and sustainability, locally as well as globally; offering guidance for developing the individual and collective wisdom that empowers action capable of bringing about constructive change in the local and the global economic, social and ecological environment. **Structure** 2 Co-Chairs; Managing Director. **Languages** English. **Staff** None. **Finance** Financed by invitation. Budget (annual): about euro 50,000. **Events** *Meeting* Monterrey (Mexico) 2007, *Meeting* Berlin (Germany) 2006, *Meeting* Biella (Italy) 2006, *Meeting* Toronto, ON (Canada) 2006, *Meeting* Tokyo (Japan) 2005.
Members Individuals (25) in 14 countries:
Australia, Bangladesh, Canada, China, Germany, Italy, Japan, Kenya, Netherlands, Nigeria, Russia, Trinidad-Tobago, UK, USA.
NGO Relations Instrumental in setting up: *World Wisdom Alliance (WWA, no recent information).* [2015/XM0922/**E**]

♦ World Witness, Associate Reformed Presbyterian Church (internationally oriented national body)

♦ World Women Inventors and Entrepreneurs Association (WWIEA) . . 21942

Contact No 518, G5 Central plaza, 27, Seochojungang-ro 24-gil, Seocho-gu, Seoul, Korea Rep. T. +8225337722. Fax +8225939982. E-mail: wwiea@wwiea.org.
URL: http://www.wwiea.org/
History 2008, Korea Rep. **Aims** Make a women's global network, reaching beyond ideology and national boundaries. **Structure** General Assembly; Board; Steering Committee. **Languages** English, Korean. **Finance** Sources: members' dues. **Activities** Projects/programmes.
Members Associations in 41 countries and territories:
Bosnia-Herzegovina, China, Côte d'Ivoire, Dominican Rep, Egypt, Estonia, Finland, Georgia, Hong Kong, India, Iran Islamic Rep, Japan, Jordan, Kazakhstan, Kenya, Korea Rep, Kyrgyzstan, Lesotho, Malaysia, Moldova, Mongolia, Nigeria, North Macedonia, Pakistan, Philippines, Poland, Saudi Arabia, Serbia, Singapore, Slovenia, Sweden, Syrian AR, Taiwan, Tajikistan, Thailand, Tunisia, Turkmenistan, Uganda, Ukraine, Uzbekistan, Vietnam.
Consultative Status Consultative status granted from: *World Intellectual Property Organization (WIPO, #21593)* (Observer Status). [2020/XJ8404/**C**]

♦ World Women Organization (unconfirmed)
♦ World Women's Security Council (unconfirmed)

♦ World Womens' Snooker (WWS) 21943

Pres 231 Ramnoth Road, Wisbech, PE13 2SN, UK. T. +441945589589.
Contact 75 Whiteladies Road, Clifton, Bristol, BS2 2NT, UK.
URL: https://www.womenssnooker.com/
History 1981, as *World Ladies' Billiards and Snooker Association (WLBSA)*; changed title to *World Ladies' Billiards and Snooker (WLBS)*, Jul 2015. Present title adopted Nov 2018. **Aims** Encourage players and their love of the sports and nurture their interests. **Activities** Sporting activities; awards/prizes/competitions. **NGO Relations** A subsidiary of *World Professional Billiards and Snooker Association (WPBSA, #21740).* Through WSF, links with: *World Confederation of Billiards Sports (WCBS, #21291).* [2019.11.03/XD6963/**D**]

♦ World Wood Day Foundation (WWDF) 21944

Sec address not obtained. E-mail: contact@worldwoodday.org.
URL: http://www.worldwoodday.org/
History 2013, USA. Registration: 501(c)(3) non-profit, No/ID: EIN 46-3185715, USA, California. **Aims** Raise awareness of the value and responsible use of wood. **Structure** Board of Directors. **Activities** Awareness raising; events/meetings. **Events** *World Wood Day* 2021, *World Wood Day* Tokyo (Japan) 2020, *World Wood Day* Graz (Austria) / Stübing (Austria) 2019. **NGO Relations** Cooperates with (1): *International Wood Culture Society (IWCS).* [2021/AA1782/f/**F**]

♦ World Working Group on Birds of Prey and Owls (WWGBP) 21945

Groupe de travail mondial sur les rapaces – Grupo Mundial de Trabajo sobre las Rapaces – Weltarbeitsgruppe für Greifvögel und Eulen
Contact address not obtained. Fax +49308928067. E-mail: wwgbp@aol.com.
URL: http://www.raptors-international.org/
History 1970, by the then *'International Council for Bird Preservation (ICBP)'*, now called *BirdLife International (#03266).* **Aims** Further *conservation* of *raptors* – *Falconiformes* – and Owls – *Strigiformes* – in all parts of the world; advise BirdLife International and IUCN on questions of international importance relating to birds of prey; identify and maintain a survey of *threatened species*; identify and keep an inventory of threatened *habitats*; encourage research; collect and collate information. **Structure** Officers elected by members. **Languages** English, French, German. **Finance** Members' dues. Donations. **Activities** Organizes several e-mail discussion groups. **Events** *World conference* Budapest (Hungary) 2003, *Joint meeting / Eurasian Conference* Eilat (Israel) 2000, *World Conference* Johannesburg (South Africa) 1998, *World conference* Berlin (Germany) 1992, *International conference on the lesser and greater spotted eagle / Conference* Poznań (Poland) 1991. **Publications** Conference proceedings; occasional scientific publications. **Members** Specialists in related fields, not necessarily from member countries of BirdLife International. Membership countries not specified. [2015/XE0525/**E**]

♦ World for World Organization (internationally oriented national body)
♦ World Wushu Association / see World Chinese Kung Fu Association (#21273)
♦ World Xiangqi Federation (internationally oriented national body)
♦ World Yoga Association (unconfirmed)
♦ World Yoga Foundation (internationally oriented national body)
♦ World Yoga Society (internationally oriented national body)
♦ World Yoga Union (no recent information)

♦ World Yoseikan Federation (WYF) 21946

Contact Grubenweg 2, 4528 Zuchwil SO, Switzerland. E-mail: yoseikanworlddevelopment@gmail.com.
URL: http://www.world-yoseikan-federation.eu/
History Founded 1996, by Hiroo Mochizuki. Activities commenced 1 Jan 1997. Took over activities of *Fédération international de yoseikan budo et disciplines assimilées (FIYBDA, inactive).* **Aims** Teach, promote and govern the practice of yoseikan budo. **Events** *World Cup* Louvain-la-Neuve (Belgium) 2007. **NGO Relations** *Union Yoseikan Europe (no recent information).* [2017/XE4671/**E**]

♦ World Young Women's Christian Association (World YWCA) 21947

Alliance mondiale des unions chrétiennes féminines (YWCA mondiale) – Asociación Cristiana Femenina Mundial (YWCA mundial)
Gen Sec 16 Ancienne Route, 1218 Le Grand-Saconnex GE, Switzerland. T. +41229296040. Fax +41229296044. E-mail: worldoffice@worldywca.org.
URL: http://www.worldywca.org/
History 1855, London (UK). Founded during the industrial revolution in Great Britain, when young women, drawn by the prospect of jobs and opportunities, gave up rural living and moved to London city. By 1894 there were YWCAs in several countries worldwide, sharing a commitment to peace, justice, freedom and dignity for all people. At this time, the YWCAs of Great Britain, USA, Norway and Sweden joint to form the World YWCA, one of the first independent international women's organizations in the world. The organization made it possible for YWCAs to work more cohesively, and has been a pioneer in raising the status of women and international awareness of issues affecting women. Constitution revised 1930 and 1941. New Constitution adopted 1955; revised: 1963; 1983; 1987; 1991; 1995; 1999; 2003; 2007; 2011; 2015. Registered in accordance with the Swiss Civil Code. Former names and other names: *Weltbund Christlicher Verbände Junger Frauen* – former. **Aims** Develop the *leadership* and collective power of women and *girls* worldwide to achieve justice, peace, health, human dignity, freedom and a sustainable environment for all people. **Structure** Council (meets every 4 years); World Board (governing board). **Languages** English, French, Spanish. **Staff** 14.00 FTE, paid. Consultants; volunteers. **Finance** Sources: international organizations; members' dues. Supported by: *Brot für die Welt; Catholic Organization for Relief and Development (Cordaid); Christian Aid; David and Lucile Packard Foundation; International Committee for World Day of Prayer (#12811); Norwegian Agency for Development Cooperation (Norad); Norwegian Church Aid; Oak Foundation; Plan International (#18386); Robert Carr civil society Networks Fund (RCNF, #18956); UNESCO (#20322); UN Women (#20724); WHO (#20950).* Annual budget: 3,000,000 CHF. **Activities** Advocacy/lobbying/activism; capacity building; networking/liaising; training/education. **Events** *Quadrennial Meeting* Johannesburg (South Africa) 2019, *Asia Regional Meeting* Seoul (Korea Rep) 2019, *Quadrennial Meeting* Bangkok (Thailand) 2015, *Quadrennial meeting / Quadrennial Council Meeting* Zurich (Switzerland) 2011, *International AIDS conference* Vienna (Austria) 2010. **Publications** *Common Concern* (2 a year) – magazine. *Journey of Faith: The History of the World YWCA 1945 – 1994* (1994) by Carole Seymour-Jones. Annual Report; booklets; guides; toolkits; training manuals; fact sheets.
Members Individual members (1.6 million) and volunteers (110,000) in 109 countries and territories:
Albania, Angola, Antigua-Barbuda, Argentina, Armenia, Australia, Bahamas, Bangladesh, Barbados, Belarus, Belgium, Belize, Benin, Bolivia, Botswana, Brazil, Bulgaria, Burkina Faso, Burundi, Cameroon, Canada, Chile, China, Colombia, Congo Brazzaville, Congo DR, Czechia, Denmark, Egypt, El Salvador, Estonia, Ethiopia, Fiji, Finland, France, Gambia, Georgia, Germany, Ghana, Greece, Grenada, Guyana, Haiti, Honduras, Hong Kong, Iceland, India, Indonesia, Ireland, Italy, Jamaica, Japan, Jordan, Kenya, Korea Rep, Latvia, Lebanon, Lesotho, Liberia, Lithuania, Madagascar, Malawi, Malaysia, Mauritius, Mexico, Montserrat, Mozambique, Myanmar, Namibia, Nepal, Netherlands, New Zealand, Nigeria, Norway, Pakistan, Palestine, Papua New Guinea, Peru, Philippines, Poland, Puerto Rico, Romania, Russia, Rwanda, Samoa, Samoa USA, Sierra Leone, Singapore, Solomon Is, South Africa, South Sudan, Sri Lanka, St Vincent-Grenadines, Suriname, Sweden, Switzerland, Taiwan, Tanzania UR, Thailand, Togo, Trinidad-Tobago, Uganda, UK, Ukraine, Uruguay, USA, Virgin Is USA, Zambia, Zimbabwe.
Consultative Status Consultative status granted from: *ECOSOC (#05331)* (Special); *UNESCO (#20322)* (Consultative Status); *FAO (#09260)* (Special Status); *ILO (#11123)* (Special List); *UNICEF (#20332); United Nations Population Fund (UNFPA, #20612).* **IGO Relations** Partner of: *Joint United Nations Programme on HIV/AIDS (UNAIDS, #16149); UNDP (#20292); United Nations Population Fund (UNFPA, #20612).* **NGO Relations** Partners include: *ACT Alliance (#00081); Femmes Africa solidarité (FAS, #09732); Girls not Brides (#10154); Inter-African Committee on Traditional Practices Affecting the Health of Women and Children (IAC, #11384); International Centre for Reproductive Health (ICRH); The Lutheran World Federation (LWF, #16532); NGO Committee on the Status of Women, Geneva (#17117); Plan International (#18386); Women's World Summit Foundation (WWSF, #21038); World Alliance of Young Men's Christian Associations (YMCA, #21090); World Association of Girl Guides and Girl Scouts (WAGGGS, #21142); World Council of Churches (WCC, #21320); World Vision International (WVI, #21904).* [2019/XB3609/**B**]

♦ World Youth Academy (WYA) 21948

Academia Mundial de la Juventud (WYAcademy)
Founder Europaplatz 2/1/2, 1150 Vienna, Austria. T. +431253915526. E-mail: hi@worldyouth.academy.
URL: https://worldyouth.academy/
History 5 Jan 2016, Vienna (Austria). Former names and other names: *WYAcademy (WYA)* – alias (5 Jan 2016). Registration: No/ID: ZVR 1170960526, Start date: 2016, Austria; Start date: 2016, Mexico. **Aims** Provide participants with skills and in-depth knowledge in various policy fields through programs focused on five fundamental-principles: respect; diversity; vision; hope; attitude. **Languages** English, Spanish. **Activities** Events/meetings; training/education. Active in: Austria, Mexico, USA. **Events** *International Security Policy Summit* Vienna (Austria) 2018. [2021.09.04/XM8001/**F**]

♦ World Youth Alliance (WYA) 21949

Pres 228 East 71st St, New York NY 10021, USA. T. +12125850757. Fax +19174631040. E-mail: wya@wya.net.
URL: http://www.wya.net/

History 1999, at UN Conference Cairo +5 Conference on Population and Development. **Aims** Promote the dignity of the person in policy and culture and at all levels of society; build *solidarity* among young people from developed and developing nations. **Structure** Includes: World Youth Alliance – headquarters office, New York NY (USA); *World Youth Alliance – Africa (WYA-A, #21950)*; *World Youth Alliance – Asia Pacific (WYA-AP, #21951)*; *World Youth Alliance – Europe (#21952)*; *World Youth Alliance Latin America (WYA-LA, #21953)*; *World Youth Alliance – Middle East (WYA Middle East, see: #21949)*; *World Youth Alliance – North America (WYA-NA)*. **Languages** English, Spanish. **Staff** 23.00 FTE, paid. **Finance** Individual donations; grants from private foundations. **Activities** Networking/liaising; training/education; events/meetings. **Events** *Emerging Leaders Conference* Brussels (Belgium) 2018. **Publications** *WYA Newsletter* (12 a year). White papers; declarations. **Members** Individuals in over 160 countries and territories. Membership countries not specified. **Consultative Status** Consultative status granted from: *ECOSOC (#05331)* (Special). **IGO Relations** Formal contacts with: *European Commission (EC, #06633)*; *OAS (#17629)*; United Nations. **NGO Relations** Member of: *Forum of Catholic Inspired NGOs (#09905)*. [2018.07.27/XF6581/F]

♦ World Youth Alliance – Africa (WYA-A) 21950

Contact PO Box 24021, Nairobi, 00100 GPO, Kenya. T. +254202508626. E-mail: africa@wya.net.
Street address 1st Floor, Symbion House, Karen Road, Karen, Nairobi, Kenya.
URL: http://www.wya.net/

History 1999. Founded within *World Youth Alliance (WYA, #21949)*. Former names and other names: *African Youth Alliance (AYA)* – former. **Aims** Promote the dignity of the person; build solidarity among youth from developed and developing nations. **Structure** Board; Foundation; Regional Committees; Advisory Committees; Chapters/Clubs. **Languages** English, French, Swahili. **Staff** 2.00 FTE, paid. **Finance** Individual funding. **Activities** Advocacy/lobbying/activism; training/education. **Events** *Africa Emerging Leaders Conference* Nairobi (Kenya) 2014. **Publications** *WYA-A Newsletter* (12 a year). **Members** Full in 23 countries. Membership countries not specified. [2021.05.26/XE4676/E]

♦ World Youth Alliance – Asia Pacific (WYA-AP) 21951

Regional Dir 303 Xanland Place, 323 Katipunan Avenue, Loyola Heights, 1108 Quezon City, Philippines. T. +6329215162. Fax +6329215162. E-mail: asiapacific@wya.net.
URL: http://www.wya.net/

History Comes within *World Youth Alliance (WYA, #21949)*. **Aims** Promote human dignity and build solidarity among youth from developed and developing nations. **Languages** English. **Staff** 2.00 FTE, paid. **Finance** Donations; sponsorships. **Activities** Advocacy/lobbying/activism; training/education. Active in: Cambodia, China, India, Indonesia, Malaysia, Philippines, Singapore, Taiwan, Thailand. **Events** *General Assembly* Quezon City (Philippines) 2010, *General Assembly* Quezon City (Philippines) 2010, *International youth forum* Seoul (Korea Rep) 2010.
Members Individuals in 31 countries and territories:
Afghanistan, Australia, Bangladesh, Bhutan, Brunei Darussalam, Cambodia, China, Hong Kong, India, Indonesia, Japan, Kazakhstan, Korea Rep, Kyrgyzstan, Laos, Macau, Malaysia, Maldives, Nepal, New Zealand, Pakistan, Philippines, Singapore, Sri Lanka, Taiwan, Tajikistan, Thailand, Timor-Leste, Turkmenistan, Uzbekistan, Vietnam. [2019/XJ4252/E]

♦ World Youth Alliance – Europe 21952

Regional Dir Rue de la Loi 42, Bte 7, 1040 Brussels, Belgium. T. +3227327605. E-mail: europe@wya.net.
URL: http://www.wya.net/

History 1999, New York, NY (USA). Founded at the United Nations at a conference on Population and Development where 32 young people were brought into the negotiations. Comes within *World Youth Alliance (WYA, #21949)*. Former names and other names: *European Youth Alliance (EYA)* – former. Registration: Banque-Carrefour des Entreprises, Belgium; EU Transparency Register, No/ID: 258181121202-25. **Aims** Promote dignity of the person; build solidarity among youth from developed and developing nations; train young people to work at regional and international levels to impact policy and culture. **Structure** Chapters. **Languages** Croatian, English, French, German, Italian, Polish, Spanish. **Finance** Sources: donations. **Activities** Advocacy/lobbying/activism; events/meetings; training/education. **Publications** *WYA Europe Newsletter*.
Members Organizations in 14 countries:
Austria, Belgium, Czechia, France, Germany, Hungary, Ireland, Italy, Poland, Portugal, Slovakia, Spain, UK, Ukraine.
Individuals in 28 countries:
Austria, Belarus, Belgium, Croatia, Czechia, France, Georgia, Germany, Holy See, Hungary, Ireland, Italy, Latvia, Liechtenstein, Luxembourg, Malta, Netherlands, North Macedonia, Poland, Portugal, Romania, Russia, Slovakia, Spain, Sweden, Switzerland, UK, Ukraine.
IGO Relations Also links with other international institutions. [2022.02.01/XE4420/E]

♦ World Youth Alliance Latin America (WYA-LA) 21953

Contact Cincinnati 81, Int 204, Colonia Nochebuena, 03720 Mexico City CDMX, Mexico. T. +525563940929. E-mail: latinamerica@wya.net.
URL: https://www.wya.net/contact-us/

History within *World Youth Alliance (WYA, #21949)*. Also referred to as *Latin American Youth Alliance (LAYA)*. [2008.06.01/XJ4251/E]

♦ World Youth Alliance – Middle East (see: #21949)
♦ World Youth Alliance – North America (internationally oriented national body)
♦ World Youth Assembly (meeting series)

♦ World Youth Bank Network (WYB) 21954

Contact address not obtained.
URL: http://wybn.net/

History 14 Nov 2002, Zagreb, following declaration adopted during Youth Summit of *World Assembly of Youth (WAY, #21113)*. **Aims** Improve and develop the quality of life of youth worldwide; combat *unemployment*, ignorance and youth social *exclusion*. **Structure** General Assembly. Councils (3): Economic and Social; Financial and Banking; Security. Division (1): Cross-Border Intelligence and Surveillance Division. Global Youth Court of Honour; Secretariat. **Events** *Global youth synergy summit / Forum* Zagreb (Croatia) 2003.
Members Organizations (83) and individuals (29) in 110 countries and territories:
Afghanistan, Albania, Algeria, Argentina, Armenia, Australia, Bangladesh, Belgium, Benin, Bhutan, Bolivia, Bosnia-Herzegovina, Botswana, Brazil, Brunei Darussalam, Bulgaria, Burkina Faso, Cameroon, Canada, Chile, China, Colombia, Comoros, Congo DR, Côte d'Ivoire, Croatia, Denmark, Dominica, Dominican Rep, Ecuador, Egypt, El Salvador, Ethiopia, Fiji, Finland, France, Georgia, Germany, Ghana, Greece, Guatemala, Guinea-Bissau, Holy See, Hong Kong, Hungary, Iceland, India, Indonesia, Iran Islamic Rep, Iraq, Ireland, Israel, Italy, Jordan, Kazakhstan, Kenya, Korea Rep, Lesotho, Luxembourg, Madagascar, Malaysia, Mauritius, Mexico, Moldova, Mongolia, Morocco, Mozambique, Namibia, Nepal, Netherlands, Nicaragua, Nigeria, North Macedonia, Norway, Pakistan, Panama, Papua New Guinea, Paraguay, Peru, Philippines, Poland, Portugal, Romania, Russia, Rwanda, Senegal, Serbia, Sierra Leone, Singapore, Slovakia, Slovenia, Solomon Is, South Africa, Spain, Sri Lanka, Sweden, Switzerland, Tajikistan, Tanzania UR, Thailand, Togo, Tonga, Tunisia, Uganda, UK, Ukraine, USA, Vietnam, Zambia, Zimbabwe.
IGO Relations Formal contacts with: *European Bank for Reconstruction and Development (EBRD, #06315)*; *European Commission (EC, #06633)*; *ILO (#11123)*; *OECD (#17693)*; *United Nations Economic Commission for Europe (UNECE, #20555)*. **NGO Relations** Member of: *United Nations Global Compact (#20567)*. Acts as non-for-profit wing for *World Youth Bank Group*. [2015/XF6718/s/F]

♦ World Youth Choir (WYC) 21955

Choeur mondial des jeunes – Coro Juvenil Mundial – Weltjugendchor

Contact 's-gravenhekje 1B, 1011 TG Amsterdam, Netherlands. E-mail: president@worldyouthchoir.org – info@worldyouthchoir.org.
URL: http://www.worldyouthchoir.org/

History 1989, by *Jeunesses Musicales International (JMI, #16110)* and *International Federation for Choral Music (IFCM, #13388)*. Until end 2010, located at *International Centre for Choral Music (ICCM)*, after which seat moved to The Hague (Netherlands), and became registered as a stichting (foundation) in accordance with Dutch law. **Aims** Be an educational and social experience drawing on vocal traditions while building bridges between young singers from diverse cultures. **Structure** International Board; International Artistic Committee. Operated by *European Choral Association – Europa Cantat (#06541)*, *International Federation for Choral Music (IFCM, #13388)* and *Jeunesses Musicales International (JMI, #16110)* as patrons. **Languages** English. **Staff** 0.50 FTE, paid. **Finance** Sources: subventions; sponsoring. Support from: *European Choral Association – Europa Cantat (#06541)*; *International Federation for Choral Music (IFCM, #13388)*; *Jeunesses Musicales International (JMI, #16110)*. **Activities** Events/meetings; networking/liaising. **Events** *Summer Session* Cyprus 2012, *Summer Session* Norway 2011, *Summer Session* Spain 2010, *Summer Session* Belgium 2009, *Summer Session* Sweden 2009. **Publications** Annual CD and DVD. **IGO Relations** *UNESCO (#20322)*. [2019.02.12/XF1667/F]

♦ World Youth Congress Movement (inactive)

♦ World Youth Council Against Terrorism (WYCAT) 21956

Chairman MS-II/205 – Old MLA Quarters, Hyderguda, Hyderabad, Telangana 500 029, Hyderabad TELANGANA 500 029, India. T. +914023237733. Fax +914027607199.
URL: http://www.wycat.org/

History 2003, Delhi (India), at International Youth Conference on Terrorism. **Aims** Provide an apolitical and non-profit making platform for youth of the world to join hands in the fight against terrorism; carry forward the international efforts of youth; coordinate with and provide assistance to international organizations. **Structure** Steering Committee of 37 members. Permanent Secretariat, located in Delhi (India). **Finance** Sources: donations; members' dues.
Members Full in 33 countries and territories:
Afghanistan, Algeria, Bangladesh, Bulgaria, Cambodia, Ghana, India, Indonesia, Israel, Japan, Korea Rep, Kyrgyzstan, Libya, Malaysia, Mauritius, Mongolia, Morocco, Namibia, Nepal, New Zealand, Norway, Palestine, Papua New Guinea, Romania, Senegal, Serbia, Singapore, South Africa, Sri Lanka, Sudan, Switzerland, Uganda, USA. [2019/XJ5100/C]

♦ World Youth Foundation (internationally oriented national body)

♦ World Youth Movement for Democracy (WYMD) 21957

Mouvement de la jeunesse pour la démocratie – Movimiento Juvenil para la Democracia – Movimento Jovem pela Democracia

Secretariat c/o Global Youth Action Network, Rua Mourato Coelho 460, Sao Paulo SP, SP 05417-001, Brazil. T. +551138159926. E-mail: info@wymdonline.org.
URL: http://www.wymdonline.org/

History 2004, South Africa, during 3rd Assembly of *World Movement for Democracy (#21661)*, as *Youth Movement for Democracy*. **Aims** Serve as a platform for young activists to address the importance of promoting democratic values, a forum for sharing information and ideas and an action-oriented, solidarity movement. **Structure** General Assembly (every 2 years). Steering Committee. **Events** *Workshop / General Assembly* Istanbul (Turkey) 2006. **NGO Relations** Located at: *Global Youth Action Network (GYAN)*. [2013/XM2434/F]

♦ World Youth Movement of Hashomer Hatzair / see Hashomer Hatzair – World Movement for Zionist Youth (#10863)
♦ World Youth Organization Against Climate Change (inactive)

♦ World Youth Parliament for Water (WYPW) 21958

Parlement mondial de la jeunesse pour l'eau (PMJE)

Coordination 9623 Rue Lajeunesse, Montréal QC H3L 2C7, Canada. E-mail: secretariat@pmje-wypw.org.
URL: http://www.pmje-wypw.org/

History May 1998. Organized by *International Secretariat for Water (ISW, #14822)*. **Aims** Coordinate youth actions and advocacy for water, at local level, the watershed level and internationally. **Structure** International Advice Committee; Board; Secretariat. **Activities** Awareness raising; advocacy/lobbying/activism; networking/liaising; knowledge management/information dissemination. **Events** *World Youth Parliament for Water* Daegu (Korea Rep) 2015, *World Youth Parliament for Water* Marseille (France) 2012, *Latin American and Caribbean Youth Parliament* Mexico City (Mexico) 2006, *World Youth Parliament for Water* Montréal, QC (Canada) 2006, *European Youth Parliament for Water* Espalion (France) 1999. **NGO Relations** *Solidarity Water Europe (SWE)*. [2015/XM4272/E]

♦ World Youth Service and Enterprise (internationally oriented national body)

♦ World Youth Student and Educational Travel Confederation (WYSE Travel Confederation) 21959

Dir Gen Keizersgracht 174-176, 1016 DW Amsterdam, Netherlands. T. +31204212800. E-mail: communications@wysetc.org – info@wysetc.org.
URL: http://www.wysetc.org/

History 2006. Set up on merger of *Federation of International Youth Travel Organizations (FIYTO, inactive)* and *International Student Travel Confederation (ISTC, inactive)*. Constitution most recently amended Sep 2012. Registration: Denmark. **Aims** Contribute to personal and professional growth of students and young people; positively impact the global community by fostering international understanding, responsible international travel, cultural exchange and education. **Structure** Annual General Meeting; Executive Board. Sectors (4): Accomodation; Cultural Exchange; Study Abroad; Travel Safety. **Languages** English. **Staff** 19.00 FTE, paid. **Activities** Events/meetings; knowledge management/information dissemination; monitoring/evaluation; networking/liaising; standards/guidelines. **Events** *STAY WYSE Hostel Conference* Amsterdam (Netherlands) 2023, *Annual Conference* Lisbon (Portugal) 2022, *WETM-IAC : Joint Work Experience Travel Market and IAPA Annual Conference* St Julian's (Malta) 2022, *WETM-IAC : Joint Work Experience Travel Market and IAPA Annual Conference* Amsterdam (Netherlands) 2021, *World Youth and Student Travel Conference (WYSTC)* Lisbon (Portugal) 2021. **Publications** *Booking Sources Series*; *Industry Reviews Series*; *Millennial Traveller Series*; *New Horizons* – 4 vols to date; *Youth Travel Accommodation Industry Survey Series*. *Global Report on the Power of Youth Travel*.
Members Full voting: nonprofit and commercial youth travel organizations and official tourism organizations; Associate: companies, national youth associations and service providers. Members in 66 countries and territories:
Argentina, Australia, Austria, Belgium, Brazil, Cambodia, Canada, Chile, China, Colombia, Costa Rica, Czechia, Denmark, Dominican Rep, Ecuador, Egypt, Estonia, Eswatini, Fiji, Finland, France, Georgia, Germany, Ghana, Hong Kong, India, Ireland, Israel, Italy, Jamaica, Japan, Jordan, Kazakhstan, Kenya, Korea Rep, Latvia, Malaysia, Malta, Mexico, Moldova, Mongolia, Myanmar, Netherlands, New Zealand, Panama, Peru, Philippines, Poland, Portugal, Romania, Russia, Rwanda, Serbia, Singapore, Slovenia, South Africa, Spain, Sweden, Switzerland, Taiwan, Thailand, Türkiye, UK, Ukraine, United Arab Emirates, USA.
Included in the above, 13 youth travel and related organizations listed in this Yearbook:
Council on International Educational Exchange (CIEE, #04901); *Council on Standards for International Educational Travel (CSIET)*; *Cultural Homestay International (CHI)*; *Erasmus Student Network (ESN, #05529)*; *Ethic étapes*; *Foundation for Worldwide International Student Exchange (WISE)*; *Hostelling International (#10950)*; *InterExchange*; *International Council of Tourism Partners (ICTP)*; *International Nightlife Association (INA)*; *International Social Tourism Organisation (ISTO, #14889)*; *JOYST Youth Exchange International*; *Worldwide Network of the Experiment in International Living (Federation EIL, #21930)*.
Consultative Status Consultative status granted from: *UNESCO (#20322)* (Consultative Status). **IGO Relations** Affiliate member of: *World Tourism Organization (UNWTO, #21861)*. **NGO Relations** Member of (4): *Council on Standards for International Educational Travel (CSIET)*; *International Council of Tourism Partners (ICTP)*; *International Social Tourism Organisation (ISTO, #14889)*; *Pacific Asia Travel Association (PATA, #17932)*. [2021/XM2774/y/C]

♦ World Youth Union (inactive)
♦ **World YWCA** World Young Women's Christian Association (#21947)

♦ World Zarathushti Chamber of Commerce (WZCC) 21960

Dir 5750 South Jackson St, Hinsdale IL 60521, USA. T. +16303255383. Fax +16307341579.
Pres address not obtained.
URL: http://www.wzcc.org/

History 29 Dec 2000. Founded as part of the legacy project of the Seventh World Zoroastrian Congress. Former names and other names: *World Zoroastrian Chamber of Commerce* – former. Registration: USA, Illinois. **Aims** Facilitate, encourage and promote the spirit of *entrepreneurship* among Zarathushti's; promote Zarathushti business interests worldwide; enhance cooperation, networking and solidarity amongst Zarathushti business and professional communities; gather appropriate statistics of Zarathushti's doing business worldwide; develop a mentoring programme; identify sources of funding for Zarathushti business ventures. **Structure** Governing Board; Chapters (14). **Languages** English. **Staff** 2.50 FTE, paid; 15.00 FTE, voluntary. **Finance** Sources: donations; members' dues; revenue from activities/projects. **Activities** Events/meetings; financial and/or material support; networking/liaising; training/education. **Events** *Global Annual General Meeting* Lonavala (India) 2020, *Global Annual General Meeting* Orlando, FL (USA) 2019, *Global Annual General Meeting* Bangalore (India) 2017, *Global Annual General Meeting* Hong Kong (Hong Kong) 2016, *Global Annual General Meeting* Goa (India) 2015. **Publications** *WZCC Newsletter* (4 a year); *SynergyZ Journal* (annual); *E-Blast* (24 a year).
Members Corporations; Individuals. Members in 8 countries and territories:
Australia, Canada, Hong Kong, India, Iran Islamic Rep, UK, United Arab Emirates, USA. [2020.10.13/XM3794/**F**]

♦ World Zarathustrian Trust Fund (see: #21962)

♦ World Zionist Organization (WZO) 21961

Organisation sioniste mondiale (OSM)
Chairman 48 King George Street, PO Box 92, 91000 Jerusalem, Israel. T. +97226202177. E-mail: silvanag@wzo.org.il.
URL: http://www.wzo.org.il/

History 29 Jun 1897, Basel (Switzerland), at 1st Zionist Congress, together with *Jewish Agency for Israel (#16111)*. Also referred to as *International Zionist Organization – Organisation sioniste internationale*. **Aims** Promote the unity of the *Jewish* people and the centrality of Israel in Jewish life; gather the Jewish people in their homeland; strengthen the State of Israel; preserve spiritual identity of the Jewish people through the fostering of Jewish Zionist and *Hebrew* education and of Jewish spiritual and cultural values; protect Jewish rights everywhere. **Structure** World Zionist Congress (every 4 years); Zionist General Council (meets at Congress); Executive. Hagshama Department. **Languages** English, French, Hebrew, Russian, Spanish. **Activities** Organizes *'World Zionist Congress'* always in Jerusalem (Israel). **Events** *World congress* Jerusalem (Israel) 2020, *General council meeting* Maale HaHamisha (Israel) 2017, *World congress* Jerusalem (Israel) 2015, *World congress* Jerusalem (Israel) 2010, *World congress* Jerusalem (Israel) 2006. **Publications** *Israel Scene* (12 a year); *Update* (6 a year). *Magshimon.*
Members National Zionist federations in 45 countries and territories:
Argentina, Australia, Austria, Barbados, Belgium, Bolivia, Brazil, Canada, Chile, Colombia, Costa Rica, Cuba, Curaçao, Denmark, Dominican Rep, Ecuador, El Salvador, Finland, France, Germany, Gibraltar, Greece, Guatemala, Honduras, India, Ireland, Italy, Jamaica, Kenya, Mexico, Netherlands, New Zealand, Nicaragua, Norway, Panama, Paraguay, Philippines, Portugal, South Africa, Spain, Sweden, Switzerland, UK, Venezuela, Zimbabwe.
NGO Relations Instrumental in setting up: *ARZENU – International Federation of Reform and Progressive Religious Zionists (ARZENU, #01129)*. Member of: *World Jewish Restitution Organization (WJRO, #21601)*. Affiliated with: *World Jewish Congress (WJC, #21599)*. [2019/XC0386/**C**]

♦ World Zoroastrian Chamber of Commerce / see World Zarathushti Chamber of Commerce (#21960)

♦ World Zoroastrian Organization (WZO) 21962

Chairman World Zoroastrian House, 1 Freddie Mercury Close, Feltham, TW13 5DF, UK. E-mail: chairman@w-z-o.org – chair@w-z-o.org.
URL: http://www.w-z-o.org/

History Jan 1980. Founded following 3 congresses: 1962, Teheran (Iran Islamic Rep); 1976, Bombay (India); 1978, Bombay (India). Registration: Charity Commission, No/ID: 1023334, England and Wales. **Aims** Advance the Zoroastrian *religious faith*; provide for a burial ground or grounds for Zoroastrians and for upkeep and maintenance of such grounds; relieve poverty among Zoroastrians. **Structure** General Meeting (annual, in London); Executive Committee. **Languages** English. **Staff** None. **Finance** Sources: grants; members' dues. Supported by: Dasturji Sohrabji Kutal Benevolent Fund; *World Zarathustrian Trust Fund (see: #21962)*. **Activities** Capacity building; events/meetings; financial and/or material support; projects/programmes. **Events** *World Zoroastrian Youth Congress* Los Angeles, CA (USA) 2019, *World Zoroastrian Congress* Perth, WA (Australia) 2018, *World Zoroastrian Youth Congress* Auckland (New Zealand) 2015, *World Zoroastrian Youth Congress* Vancouver, BC (Canada) 2011, *World Zoroastrian youth congress* Mount Helen, VIC (Australia) 2007. **Publications** *Fasli/Shahenshahi Calendar* (annual); *Hamazor* – newsletter. Seminar booklets.
Members Organizations and individuals in 17 countries and territories:
Australia, Austria, Canada, France, Germany, Hong Kong, India, Iran Islamic Rep, Pakistan, Singapore, Spain, Sri Lanka, Switzerland, Thailand, UK, United Arab Emirates, USA. [2021.09.13/XF2202/**F**]

♦ **WOSAAM** World Society of Anti-Aging Medicine (#21798)
♦ **WOSC** World Organisation of Systems and Cybernetics (#21686)
♦ WOSD – World Organisation of Scuba Diving (unconfirmed)
♦ **WOSM** World Organization of the Scout Movement (#21693)
♦ **WOS** World Oyster Society (#21704)
♦ **WOTC** World Organization of Talented Children (#21694)
♦ WOTP – World Organization of the Teaching Profession (inactive)
♦ WOTRO / see WOTRO Science for Global Development
♦ WOTRO Science for Global Development (internationally oriented national body)
♦ WOUDC – WMO World Ozone and Ultra-Violet Data Centre (see: #21649)
♦ WOU / see World ORT (#21698)
♦ WOVD / see World ParaVolley (#21710)
♦ **WOVO** World Organization of Volcano Observatories (#21696)
♦ WOW / see War on Want
♦ **WO** World ORT (#21698)
♦ WOWS – Worldwide Organization of Women's Studies (inactive)
♦ **WOW** Women's Ordination Worldwide (#21032)
♦ **WOW** World Organization of Workers (#21697)
♦ WOW – Worldwide Organization for Women (internationally oriented national body)
♦ WPACCM / see Asia Pacific Association of Critical Care Medicine (#01838)
♦ **WPAF** World Pangration Athlima Federation (#21709)
♦ WPA International / see World Pheasant Association (#21724)
♦ WPA / see International Association of Ports and Harbors (#12096)
♦ **WPAME** Western Pacific Association for Medical Education (#20917)
♦ WPATA – Western Pacific Association for Transactional Analysis (internationally oriented national body)
♦ **WPATH** World Professional Association For Transgender Health (#21739)
♦ WPA – World Parliament Association (inactive)
♦ WPA – World Patients Alliance (unconfirmed)
♦ **WPA** World Pension Alliance (#21719)
♦ **WPA** World Pheasant Association (#21724)
♦ **WPA** World Pool-Billiard Association (#21733)
♦ **WPA** World Psychiatric Association (#21741)
♦ WPA – Worldwide Partners Alliance (unconfirmed)
♦ **WPBA** World Peace Bell Association (#21716)
♦ **WPBF** World Pétanque and Bowls Federation (#21721)
♦ **WPBSA** World Professional Billiards and Snooker Association (#21740)
♦ **WPCC** World Pancreatic Cancer Coalition (#21708)
♦ WPCF / see Water Environment Federation
♦ **WPCF** World Print and Communication Forum (#21737)
♦ WPCIA – World Paint and Coatings Industry Association (unconfirmed)
♦ **WPC** Wireless Power Consortium (#20970)
♦ WPC / see World Parkinson Coalition (#21711)
♦ **WPC** World Parkinson Coalition (#21711)
♦ **WPC** World Peace Council (#21717)
♦ WPC – World Pensions Council (unconfirmed)
♦ WPC / see World Petroleum Council (#21722)
♦ **WPC** World Petroleum Council (#21722)
♦ **WPC** World Plastics Council (#21730)
♦ **WPC** World Plumbing Council (#21732)
♦ **WPC** World Potato Congress (#21734)
♦ WPDA – World Parkinson Disease Association (inactive)
♦ WPDI – Whitaker Peace and Development Initiative (internationally oriented national body)
♦ WPE / see Rainforest Trust
♦ WPF / see World Constitution Fund
♦ WPF / see Rutgers (#19011)
♦ **WPF** World Pahuyuth Federation (#21706)
♦ WPF / see World Pathology Foundation (#21714)
♦ **WPF** World Pathology Foundation (#21714)
♦ WPF – World Peace Foundation (internationally oriented national body)
♦ **WPF** World Pickleball Federation (#21729)
♦ WPF – World Poker Federation (unconfirmed)
♦ WPF – World Prohibition Federation (inactive)
♦ **WPF** World Puzzle Federation (#21743)
♦ WPGA / see Ladies European Tour (#16218)
♦ **WPHNA** World Public Health Nutrition Association (#21742)
♦ WPI / see Water.org
♦ **WPI** World Peace Initiative (#21718)
♦ WPI / see World Phenomenology Institute (#21725)
♦ **WPI** World Phenomenology Institute (#21725)
♦ WPI – World Policy Institute (internationally oriented national body)
♦ WPI – World Press Institute (internationally oriented national body)
♦ WPKA / see World Pan Amateur Kickboxing Association (#21707)
♦ **WPKA** World Pan Amateur Kickboxing Association (#21707)
♦ WPLTC' / see World Association of Judges (#21150)
♦ **WPL** Women Political Leaders (#21012)
♦ WPMC – International Symposium on Wireless Personal Multimedia Communications (meeting series)
♦ WPMO / see International Association of Clinical Forensic Medicine (#11779)
♦ WPMO – World Peace Mission Organization (internationally oriented national body)
♦ WPN / see MADRE
♦ WPNA – World Proof Numismatic Association (internationally oriented national body)
♦ WPNS – Western Pacific Naval Symposium (meeting series)
♦ WPO / see World President's Organization
♦ WPOA / see Asia Pacific Orthopaedic Association (#01987)
♦ WPO – Women Presidents Organization (internationally oriented national body)
♦ **WPO** World Packaging Organisation (#21705)
♦ WPO – World Pankration Organization (inactive)
♦ **WPO** World Philharmonic Orchestra (#21726)
♦ **WPO** World Ploughing Organization (#21731)
♦ WPO – World President's Organization (internationally oriented national body)
♦ WPP-Africa / see African Women's Active Nonviolence Initiatives for Social Change (#00502)
♦ WPPT – WIPO Performances and Phonograms Treaty (1996 treaty)
♦ WPP – Women PeaceMakers Program (internationally oriented national body)
♦ WPP – World Peace Posse (internationally oriented national body)
♦ **WPRO** WHO Regional Office for the Western Pacific (#20947)
♦ **WPSA** World's Poultry Science Association (#21825)
♦ WPSC / see Asia-Pacific Society of Clinical Microbiology and Infection (#02032)
♦ WPSF – World Pacific Sports Federation (unconfirmed)
♦ WPS – Wildlife Protection Solutions (internationally oriented national body)
♦ **WPTC** Conseil mondial de la tomate transformée (#21738)
♦ **WPTC** World Processing Tomato Council (#21738)
♦ WPTI / see EcoHealth Alliance
♦ WPTLC / see World Jurist Association (#21604)
♦ **WPT** World Parrot Trust (#21713)
♦ **WPU** World Philology Union (#21727)
♦ WPV – World Peace Volunteers (internationally oriented national body)
♦ **WPV** World Pharmacy Council (#21723)
♦ WQA – Water Quality Association (internationally oriented national body)
♦ WQF – Wider Quaker Fellowship (see: #10004)
♦ **WQXS Network** Worldwide Quality EXpress System /Network/ (#21933)
♦ **WRAD** World Recreation Association of the Deaf and Hard of Hearing (#21748)
♦ WRAP / see Worldwide Responsible Accredited Production
♦ WRAPSD / see World Association for Psychosocial Rehabilitation (#21178)
♦ WRAP – Worldwide Responsible Accredited Production (internationally oriented national body)
♦ **WRA** White Ribbon Alliance for Safe Motherhood (#20934)
♦ WRA – World Refining Association (internationally oriented national body)
♦ WRA – World Runners Association (unconfirmed)
♦ WRC / see World Relief
♦ WRCanada / see Tearfund Canada
♦ WRC / see International Wildlife Rehabilitation Council, The (#15885)
♦ WRC – Women's Refugee Commission (internationally oriented national body)
♦ WRC – Worker Rights Consortium (internationally oriented national body)
♦ WRDC – WMO World Radiation Data Centre, St Petersburg (see: #21649)
♦ WRE – International Conference on Water Resource and Environment (meeting series)
♦ **WREN** World Renewable Energy Network (#21750)
♦ Wrestlers Without Borders (internationally oriented national body)
♦ WRETF – World Radiography Education Trust Fund (see: #15410)
♦ **WRE** Water Reuse Europe (#20835)
♦ **WRFA** World Resources Forum Association (#21752)
♦ WRFC – World Recreational Fishing Conference (meeting series)
♦ **WRF** World Rehabilitation Fund (#21749)
♦ WRF – World Roma Federation (unconfirmed)
♦ **WRH** Association of World Reindeer Herders (#02985)
♦ Writers and Directors Worldwide (see: #04563)
♦ Writers International and Friends of Literature and Culture Association (see: #11102)
♦ **WRI** War Resisters' International (#20818)
♦ WRI – Widows Rights International (internationally oriented national body)
♦ **WRI** World Resources Institute (#21753)
♦ **WRK** Weltgemeinschaft Reformierter Kirchen (#21289)
♦ WRLFMD – World Reference Laboratory for Foot and Mouth Diseases (internationally oriented national body)
♦ WRL – War Resisters League (internationally oriented national body)
♦ **WRMA** Weather Risk Management Association (#20842)
♦ WRMF / see Reach Beyond
♦ **WRM** World Rainforest Movement (#21745)
♦ **WRN** Willis Research Network (#20963)
♦ WRN / see World Rainforest Movement (#21745)
♦ WRO – World Renderers Association (internationally oriented national body)

♦ **WRO** World Rescue Organisation (#21751)
♦ WRPC – World Russian People's Council (internationally oriented national body)
♦ WRPTC / see World Association of Radiopharmaceutical and Molecular Therapy (#21181)
♦ WRRA – World Rock'n'Roll Association (inactive)
♦ **WRRC** World Rock'n'Roll Confederation (#21755)
♦ WRRS – World Relief Refugee Services (internationally oriented national body)
♦ **WRSA** World Rabbit Science Association (#21744)
♦ WRSF – World Rope Skipping Federation (unconfirmed)
♦ **WRSTC** World Recreational Scuba Training Council (#21747)
♦ WRTVC – World Radio and Television Council (no recent information)
♦ **WR** World Runners (#21758)
♦ WSAA – World Sustainable Agriculture Association (inactive)

♦ WSACS – the Abdominal Compartment Society 21963

Contact PO Box 980454, Richmond VA 23298-0454, USA.
URL: http://www.wsacs.org/

History 8 Dec 2004, Noosa (Australia), during World Congress on the Abdominal Compartment Syndrome. Original title: *World Society on Abdominal Compartment Syndrome (WSACS)*. **Aims** Unite specialists involved in care of the critically patient with intra-abdominal hypertension (IAH) or abdominal compartment syndrome (ACS); promote highest standard of patient care, education, organization and research in the field of IAH/ACS. **Structure** Executive Committee; Standing Committees (9). **Languages** English. **Finance** Sources: meeting proceeds; members' dues. **Activities** Certification/accreditation; events/meetings; publishing activities; standards/guidelines; training/education. **Events** *Congress* Campinas (Brazil) 2019, *Congress* Banff, AB (Canada) 2017, *Expanding our horizon* Ghent (Belgium) 2015, *Congress* Cartagena de Indias (Colombia) 2013, *Congress* Orlando, FL (USA) 2011. **Publications** *WSACS Newsletter* (4 a year). Books. **NGO Relations** Specialty organization of: *European Society of Anaesthesiology and Intensive Care (ESAIC, #08518)*.
[2020/XM0798/**C**]

♦ WSACS / see WSACS – the Abdominal Compartment Society (#21963)
♦ WSA-IGO – World Sports Alliance – Intergovernmental Organization (unconfirmed)
♦ **WS America** World Skate America (#21788)
♦ **WSAVA** World Small Animal Veterinary Association (#21795)
♦ **WSA** Water and Sanitation for Africa (#20836)
♦ **WSA** Women's Squash Association (#21034)
♦ WSA / see World Government of World Citizens (#21543)
♦ **WSA** World Seagrass Association (#21775)
♦ WSA – World Service Authority (see: #21543)
♦ WSA – World Sign Associates (internationally oriented national body)
♦ WSA – World Silambam Association (internationally oriented national body)
♦ **WSA** World Skate Africa (#21787)
♦ **WSA** World Skate Asia (#21789)
♦ **WSA** World Sleddog Association (#21792)
♦ **WSA** World Society of Arrhythmias (#21799)
♦ **WSA** World Spirits Alliance (#21822)
♦ **WSA** World Subud Association (#21836)
♦ WSBH – World Society for Breast Health (inactive)
♦ **WSBI** World Savings Banks Institute (#21764)
♦ WSB – World Scout Bureau (see: #21693)
♦ WSB – World Services for the Blind (internationally oriented national body)
♦ **WSCA** World Swimming Coaches Association (#21839)
♦ **WSCF** World Student Christian Federation (#21833)
♦ WSCM – World Supreme Council for Mosques (no recent information)
♦ **WSC-SD** World Student Community for Sustainable Development (#21834)
♦ **WScS** World Spinal Column Society (#21820)
♦ **WSCS** World Sturgeon Conservation Society (#21835)
♦ WSCTS / see World Society of Cardiovascular & Thoracic Surgeons (#21800)
♦ **WSCTS** World Society of Cardiovascular & Thoracic Surgeons (#21800)
♦ **WSC** World Semiconductor Council (#21776)
♦ **WSC** World Shipping Council (#21781)
♦ **WSC** World Spine Care (#21821)
♦ WSC – World Spiritual Council (inactive)
♦ **WSDC** World Schools Debating Championships (#21767)
♦ WSDF – World Sustainable Development Forum (internationally oriented national body)
♦ WSD – Worldwide Support for Development (internationally oriented national body)
♦ WSE – Northern European Network for Wood Science and Engineering (see: #17296)
♦ **WSES** World Society of Emergency Surgery (#21802)
♦ **WSE** World Society for Ekistics (#21801)
♦ **WSFS** World Science Fiction Society (#21769)
♦ WSFTE – World Social Forum of Transformative Economies (meeting series)
♦ **WSF** Wadden Sea Forum (#20812)
♦ WSF / see World Professional Billiards and Snooker Association (#21740)
♦ **WSF** World Scleroderma Foundation (#21770)
♦ **WSF** World Scout Foundation (#21772)
♦ WSF – World Security Federation (no recent information)
♦ **WSF** World Sephardi Federation (#21778)
♦ WSF – World Sight Foundation (internationally oriented national body)
♦ WSF – World Silambam Federation (unconfirmed)
♦ WSF – World Skating Federation (no recent information)
♦ **WSF** World Snooker Federation (#21796)
♦ **WSF** World Social Forum (#21797)
♦ WSF – World Solidarity Forum (internationally oriented national body)
♦ WSF – World Soy Foundation (internationally oriented national body)
♦ **WSF** World Squash Federation (#21826)
♦ **WSF** World Ssireum Federation (#21827)
♦ WSF – World Strengthlifting Federation (inactive)
♦ WSF – World Stroke Federation (inactive)
♦ **WSF** World Strongmen Federation (#21832)
♦ WSF – World Sustainability Fund (unconfirmed)
♦ WSGF – World Student Games Federation (internationally oriented national body)
♦ **WSG** World Services Group (#21779)
♦ WSI – International Association for Women in the Seafood Industry (inactive)
♦ **WSI** WomenSport International (#21033)
♦ WSI – World Sindhi Institute (internationally oriented national body)
♦ **WSI** WorldSkills International (#21791)
♦ **WSKA** World Shotokan Karate Association (#21783)
♦ **WSKF** World Sports Karate Federation (#21824)
♦ **WSLO** World Society of Lingual Orthodontics (#21804)
♦ WSLS – World Symposium for Lymphedema Surgery (meeting series)
♦ WSM (internationally oriented national body)
♦ W-SMART – Water Security Management, Assessment, Research & Technology (unconfirmed)
♦ **WSMBMP** World Society for Mushroom Biology and Mushroom Products (#21806)
♦ **WSMCF** World Summit on Media for Children Foundation (#21838)
♦ WSM Foundation / see WSM
♦ WSMI / see Global Self-Care Federation (#10588)
♦ **WSMJJ** World Society of Mixed Jurisdiction Jurists (#21805)
♦ **WSN** World Sarcoma Network (#21763)
♦ **WSN** World Shibori Network (#21780)
♦ **WSO-UV** World Space Observatory – Ultraviolet (#21819)
♦ **WSO** World Safety Organization (#21759)
♦ **WSO** World Sikh Organization (#21784)
♦ WSO / see World Space Observatory – Ultraviolet (#21819)
♦ **WSO** World Stevia Organisation (#21830)
♦ **WSO** World Stroke Organization (#21831)
♦ WSPA / see World Animal Protection (#21092)
♦ **WSPA** World Sport Publishers' Association (#21823)
♦ **WSPCHS** World Society for Pediatric and Congenital Heart Surgery (#21809)
♦ **WSPC** World Society of Pain Clinicians (#21808)
♦ **WSPID** World Society of Pediatric Infectious Diseases (#21810)
♦ WSP International / see Interpeace (#15962)
♦ WSP / see Interpeace (#15962)
♦ Wspólnotowe Centrum Badawcze (#16147)
♦ Wspólnotowy Urzad Odmian Roslin (#04404)
♦ **WSPOS** World Society of Paediatric Ophthalmology and Strabismus (#21807)
♦ WSP-TP / see Interpeace (#15962)
♦ WSP Transition Programme / see Interpeace (#15962)
♦ **WSPU** World Scout Parliamentary Union (#21773)
♦ **WSP** Water and Sanitation Programme (#20837)
♦ WSP – World Summit on Pediatrics (meeting series)
♦ **WSP** World Syntegrity Project (#21841)
♦ **WSRM** World Society for Reconstructive Microsurgery (#21811)
♦ **WSRO** World Sugar Research Organization (#21837)
♦ WSSA – Weed Science Society of America (internationally oriented national body)
♦ WSSA / see World Sand Sculpting Academy (#21762)
♦ **WSSA** World Sand Sculpting Academy (#21762)
♦ WSSCC – Water Supply and Sanitation Collaborative Council (inactive)
♦ WSSD-U – World Symposium on Sustainable Development at Universities (meeting series)
♦ WSSEA – Weed Science Society for Eastern Africa (inactive)
♦ **WSSET** World Society of Sustainable Energy Technologies (#21813)
♦ **WSSFN** World Society for Stereotactic and Functional Neurosurgery (#21812)
♦ **WSSF** World Slingshot Sports Federation (#21794)
♦ WSSI – World Seismic Safety Initiative (see: #11855)
♦ **WSSRC** World Sailing Speed Record Council (#21761)
♦ WssTP / see Water Europe (#20828)
♦ **WSS** World Ship Society (#21782)
♦ **WSTA** Water Science and Technology Association (#20838)
♦ **WSTLUR** World Society for Transport and Land Use Research (#21814)
♦ **WSTS** World Semiconductor Trade Statistics (#21777)
♦ **WST** Web Science Trust (#20848)
♦ WSUP – Water and Sanitation for the Urban Poor (internationally oriented national body)
♦ **WSU** World Seabird Union (#21774)
♦ **WSV** World Society of Victimology (#21815)
♦ **WSV** World Society for Virology (#21816)
♦ WSWA – World Space Week Association (internationally oriented national body)
♦ WT1 – International Conference on WT1 in Human Neoplasia (meeting series)
♦ **WTAAA** World Travel Agents Associations Alliance (#21870)
♦ **WTAF** World Taekwondo Africa (#21845)
♦ **WTA** Wissenschaftlich-Technische Arbeitsgemeinschaft für Bauwerkserhaltung und Denkmalpflege (#12152)
♦ **WTA** World Taxpayers Associations (#21847)
♦ **WTA** World Technopolis Association (#21850)
♦ **WTA** World Teleport Association (#21851)
♦ WTA – World Textile Art (unconfirmed)
♦ **WTA** World Toilet Association (#21853)
♦ **WTA** World Tourism Alliance (#21856)
♦ **WTA** World Tourism Association (#21857)
♦ **WTA** World Transhumanist Association (#21867)
♦ WTBTS / see Jehovah's Witnesses (#16096)
♦ **WTCA** World Trade Centers Association (#21862)
♦ **WTCF** World Tourism Cities Federation (#21858)
♦ WTERC – World Tourism Education and Research Centre (internationally oriented national body)
♦ WTFC / see European Walled Towns (#09079)
♦ WTF – War Trauma Foundation (internationally oriented national body)
♦ WTF / see World Taekwondo (#21844)
♦ **WTF** World Tenniquoits Federation (#21852)
♦ **WTGF** World Transplant Games Federation (#21868)
♦ **WTG** Welt-Tierärztegesellschaft (#21901)
♦ **WTI** World Trade Institute (#21863)
♦ **WTJO** World Travel Journalism Organization (#17846)
♦ WTLA – World Trade Law Association (no recent information)
♦ **WTLS** World Tort Law Society (#21855)
♦ **WTMF** World Taekuk Musul Federation (#21843)
♦ WTN – Wherever the Need (internationally oriented national body)
♦ **WTN** World Tourism Network (#21860)
♦ **WTN** World Trails Network (#21866)
♦ WTO / see World Tourism Organization (#21861)
♦ WTO Agreement on the Application of Sanitary and Phytosanitary Measures (1993 treaty)
♦ WTO Agreement on Trade Related Aspects of Intellectual Property Rights (1994 treaty)
♦ WTO/OMT Staff Association, Madrid / see UNWTO Staff Association, Madrid
♦ WTO Staff Association / see UNWTO Staff Association, Madrid
♦ WTO – Warsaw Treaty Organization (inactive)
♦ **WTO** World Taekwondo Oceania (#21846)
♦ **WTO** World Toilet Organization (#21854)
♦ **WTO** World Trade Organization (#21864)
♦ WTPF – World Telecommunication Policy Forum (meeting series)
♦ **WTPF** World Trade Point Federation (#21865)
♦ **WTS** Working Time Society (#21062)
♦ **WTTC** World Travel and Tourism Council (#21871)
♦ w@tt – Women@theTable (unconfirmed)
♦ **WTT** World Teacher Trust (#21848)
♦ **WT** World Team (#21849)
♦ WTYF – World Theosophical Youth Federation (inactive)
♦ WUASS – World Union of Acupuncture Scientists and Societies (inactive)
♦ WUA – Women's University in Africa (internationally oriented national body)
♦ WUCD / see Centrist Democrat International (#03792)
♦ **WUCPS** World Union of Catholic Philosophical Societies (#21875)
♦ WUCP – World Union of Cities for Peace (no recent information)
♦ WUCT / see UMEC-WUCT (#20280)
♦ **WUC** World Urban Campaign (#21893)
♦ **WUC** World Uyghur Congress (#21896)

♦ **WUCWO** World Union of Catholic Women's Organisations (#21876)
♦ **WUDC** World Universities Debating Council (#21891)
♦ WUFT – World Union of Freethinkers (inactive)
♦ WUF – Welt-Union der Freidenker (inactive)
♦ WUF – Women for Union of the Free (inactive)
♦ **WUJA** World Union of Jesuit Alumni and Alumnae (#21877)
♦ WUJS Institute – International Graduate Centre for Hebrew and Jewish Studies (internationally oriented national body)
♦ **WUJS** World Union of Jewish Students (#21878)
♦ WUKF – World United Karate-do Federation (unconfirmed)
♦ WUKO – World Union of Karatedo Organizations (inactive)
♦ WUM – World Union of Meretz (internationally oriented national body)
♦ WUNRN Europe / see Women's UN Report Network (#21035)
♦ **WUNRN** Women's UN Report Network (#21035)
♦ **WUNS** World Union of National Socialists (#21880)
♦ WUN – Worldwide Universities Network (internationally oriented national body)
♦ **WUOF** World Uro Oncology Federation (#21895)
♦ **WUPJ** World Union for Progressive Judaism (#21883)
♦ WUPO – World Union of Pythagorean Organizations (inactive)
♦ Wuppertal Institute for Climate, Environment and Energy (internationally oriented national body)
♦ Wuppertal Institut für Klima, Umwelt, Energie (internationally oriented national body)
♦ **WUP** World Union of Professions (#21882)
♦ **WUQKD** World Union of Qwan-Ki-Do (#21884)
♦ Wurooppalaisten Yrsityskoulujen Liittojen Neuvosto (#06833)
♦ **WUSB** Welt Union der St Bernards-Klubs (#21887)
♦ **WUSB** World Union of St Bernard Clubs (#21887)

♦ Wushu Federation of Asia (WFA) 21964

Contact Rua De Ferreira Do Amaral, Pavilhão Polidesportivo Tap Seac, Floor B2 Room B225, Macau, Macau. T. +85328789106. Fax +85328789102. E-mail: secretariat@wfa-asia.org.
URL: http://www.wfa-asia.org/en/

History 25 Sep 1987, Yokohama (Japan). **Aims** Push forward, promote and encourage development and practice of wushu in all possible manifestations throughout Asia. **Structure** Executive Committee; Technical Committee; Traditional Wushu Committee; Marketing and Promotion Committee; Medical Committee. **Languages** Chinese, English. **Activities** Awards/prizes/competitions; events/meetings; sporting activities; training/education. **Events** *Congress* Jakarta (Indonesia) 2018, *Congress* Taoyuan (Taiwan) 2016, *Congress* Doha (Qatar) 2006, *Congress* Busan (Korea Rep) 2002. **Publications** *Wushu Federation of Asia 30th Anniversary Publication.*.
Members National Federations in 38 countries and territories:
Afghanistan, Bangladesh, Brunei Darussalam, Cambodia, China, Guam, Hong Kong, India, Indonesia, Iran Islamic Rep, Iraq, Japan, Jordan, Kazakhstan, Korea DPR, Korea Rep, Kuwait, Kyrgyzstan, Laos, Lebanon, Macau, Malaysia, Maldives, Mongolia, Myanmar, Nepal, Pakistan, Palestine, Philippines, Singapore, Sri Lanka, Syrian AR, Taiwan, Thailand, Turkmenistan, Uzbekistan, Vietnam, Yemen.
NGO Relations Member of (1): *International Wushu Federation (IWUF, #15918).* [2022.05.12/XD9341/**D**]

♦ **WUSME** World Union of Small and Medium Enterprises (#21886)
♦ **WUSV** Weltunion der Vereine für Deutsche Schäferhunde (#20858)
♦ **WUS** World University Service (#21892)
♦ WUTA – World Union of TOA Associations (unconfirmed)
♦ **WUTBA** World Union of Tissue Banking Associations (#21888)
♦ WUTC / see Union of Cypriots
♦ **WUWHS** World Union of Wound Healing Societies (#21890)
♦ WUWM / see World Union of Wholesale Markets (#21889)
♦ **WUWM** World Union of Wholesale Markets (#21889)
♦ **WU** World Union (#21874)
♦ WU – World University
♦ WVA – Weltverband der Arbeitnehmer (inactive)
♦ WVA – Wereldverbond van de Arbeid (inactive)
♦ WVA – Women with Vision in Africa (internationally oriented national body)
♦ **WVA** World Vaisnava Association (#21897)
♦ **WVA** World Vapers' Alliance (#21899)
♦ **WVA** World Veterinary Association (#21901)
♦ **WVA** Worldwide Vending Association (#21934)
♦ WVBF – World Volleyball and Beach Volleyball Federation (inactive)
♦ WVBH – Weltverband der Bau- und Holzarbeiterorganisationen (inactive)
♦ WVBH – Wereldverbond van Bouwvakarbeiders- en Houtbewerkersorganisaties (inactive)
♦ WVB / see World Organization of Workers (#21697)
♦ WVD – Wereldverbond van Diamantbewerkers (inactive)
♦ **WVEG** Werkgemeenschap van Europese Grensgebieden (#02499)
♦ WVES / see International Society for Veterinary Epidemiology and Economics (#15540)
♦ **WVF** The World Veterans Federation (#21900)
♦ **WVI** World Vision International (#21904)
♦ WVL – Weltverband der Lehrer (inactive)
♦ WVM/WVA – Weltverband der Metallindustrie (inactive)
♦ WVN – Women's Voices Now (internationally oriented national body)
♦ WVOP – Wereldvakbond van Onderwijspersoneel (inactive)
♦ **WVPA** World Veterinary Poultry Association (#21902)
♦ **WVP** Weltverband für Psychotherapie (#21337)
♦ **WVSA** World Values Survey Association (#21898)
♦ WVSA – Wysgerige Vereniging van Suider-Afrika (internationally oriented national body)
♦ WVS – Worldwide Veterinary Service (internationally oriented national body)
♦ **WVT** Weltvereinigung für Tierproduktion (#21117)
♦ **WVVA** Weltvereinigung der Veterinäranatomen (#21202)
♦ WWACE – World Wide Alliance for Christian Education (see: #21330)
♦ **WWACG** Worldwide Airport Coordinators Group (#21913)
♦ WWAFE – Women Worldwide Advancing Freedom and Equality (unconfirmed)
♦ **WWAP** World Water Assessment Programme (#21907)
♦ **WWARN** WorldWide Antimalarial Resistance Network (#21914)
♦ WWA – Women Watch Afrika (internationally oriented national body)
♦ WWA – World Waterpark Association (internationally oriented national body)
♦ WWA – World Welfare Association (internationally oriented national body)
♦ WwB – Women without Borders (internationally oriented national body)
♦ **WWB** Women's World Banking (#21037)
♦ **WWCAM** World Winter Cities Association for Mayors (#21940)
♦ WWCCPC / see Worldwide Coal Combustion Products Network
♦ WWCCPN – Worldwide Coal Combustion Products Network (internationally oriented national body)
♦ WWCKFA / see Global Traditional Wing Chun Kung Fu Association (#10633)
♦ WWCS / see Tent Schools International
♦ **WWCTU** World's Woman's Christian Temperance Union (#21840)
♦ **WWC** World Water Council (#21908)
♦ **WWDF** World Wood Day Foundation (#21944)
♦ **WWEA** World Wind Energy Association (#21937)
♦ **WWEI** World Wind Energy Institute (#21938)
♦ WWEM – International Congress on Water, Waste and Energy Management (meeting series)
♦ WWEP – World Wide Education Project (internationally oriented national body)
♦ WWF – The global conservation organization / see World Wide Fund for Nature (#21922)
♦ **WWF** World WAQF Foundation (#21906)
♦ **WWF** World Wide Fund for Nature (#21922)
♦ **WWGBP** World Working Group on Birds of Prey and Owls (#21945)
♦ **WWG on FfD** Women's Working Group on Financing for Development (#21036)
♦ WWH / see World Wide Hearing (#21923)
♦ **WWHearing** World Wide Hearing (#21923)
♦ WWICS – Woodrow Wilson International Center for Scholars (internationally oriented national body)
♦ **WWIEA** World Women Inventors and Entrepreneurs Association (#21942)
♦ WWI – World Wings International (internationally oriented national body)
♦ WWM – Worldwide Missions Outreach Ministries (internationally oriented national body)
♦ **WWN** World Without Nazism (#21667)
♦ **WWN** World Wetland Network (#21911)
♦ WWOOF / see World-Wide Opportunities on Organic Farms (#21931)
♦ **WWOOF** World-Wide Opportunities on Organic Farms (#21931)
♦ WWO – World Women Organization (unconfirmed)
♦ **wwPDB** Worldwide Protein Data Bank Foundation (#21932)
♦ **WWP EN** European Network for the Work with Perpetrators of Domestic Violence (#08036)
♦ **WWRF** Wireless World Research Forum (#20971)
♦ **WWR** World Water Polo Referees Association (#21909)
♦ WWSC – World Women's Security Council (unconfirmed)
♦ **WWSF** Women's World Summit Foundation (#21038)
♦ WWSF – World Water Ski Federation (inactive)
♦ WWSO – We Will Speak Out (unconfirmed)
♦ WWSU / see International Waterski and Wakeboard Federation (#15872)
♦ **WWS** World Womens' Snooker (#21943)
♦ **WWTG** World Wine Trade Group (#21939)
♦ WWT – Wildfowl and Wetlands Trust (internationally oriented national body)
♦ WWT – Workable World Trust (internationally oriented national body)
♦ WWWC – World Without War Council (internationally oriented national body)
♦ WWW – Women Working Worldwide (internationally oriented national body)
♦ WwW – World without Wars and Violence (unconfirmed)
♦ **WWW** World Weather Watch (#21910)
♦ WWW – World Wellness Weekend (unconfirmed)
♦ WXF – World Xiangqi Federation (internationally oriented national body)
♦ **WYA-AP** World Youth Alliance – Asia Pacific (#21951)
♦ **WYA-A** World Youth Alliance – Africa (#21950)
♦ WYAcademy / see World Youth Academy (#21948)
♦ **WYAcademy** Academia Mundial de la Juventud (#21948)
♦ **WYA-LA** World Youth Alliance Latin America (#21953)
♦ WYA Middle East – World Youth Alliance – Middle East (see: #21949)
♦ WYA-NA – World Youth Alliance – North America (internationally oriented national body)
♦ WYA / see World Youth Academy (#21948)
♦ **WYA** World Youth Academy (#21948)
♦ **WYA** World Youth Alliance (#21949)
♦ **WYB** World Youth Bank Network (#21954)
♦ **WYCAT** World Youth Council Against Terrorism (#21956)
♦ **WYCJ** World's Youth for Climate Justice (#21842)
♦ Wycliffe Bible Translators International (internationally oriented national body)

♦ Wycliffe Global Alliance 21965

Head Office 7500 W Camp Wisdom Road, Dallas TX 75236, USA. E-mail: info@wycliffe.net.
URL: http://www.wycliffe.net/

History Former names and other names: *Wycliffe International* – former. **Aims** Transform individuals, communities and nations through God's love and Word expressed in their languages and cultures. **Structure** Executive Director; Board of Directors; Officers. **Publications** Papers; articles. **Information Services** *Philosophy and Principle Papers* – documents on topics that are foundational to the Alliance.
Members Organizations (106) in 64 countries and territories:
Argentina, Australia, Austria, Bangladesh, Benin, Brazil, Burkina Faso, Cameroon, Canada, Central African Rep, Chad, Chile, Colombia, Congo DR, Costa Rica, Czechia, Denmark, El Salvador, Ethiopia, Finland, France, Germany, Ghana, Guatemala, Hong Kong, Hungary, India, Indonesia, Israel, Italy, Jamaica, Japan, Kenya, Korea Rep, Malaysia, Mexico, Netherlands, New Zealand, Nigeria, Norway, Panama, Papua New Guinea, Paraguay, Peru, Philippines, Poland, Puerto Rico, Romania, Russia, Singapore, Slovakia, Solomon Is, South Africa, Spain, Sudan, Sweden, Switzerland, Taiwan, Thailand, Togo, Tonga, UK, USA, Venezuela.
Wycliffe Bible Translators International (WBT International).
see: https://www.wycliffe.net/organisations/. [2022.10.13/XJ5334/**C**]

♦ Wycliffe International / see Wycliffe Global Alliance (#21965)
♦ **WYC** World Youth Choir (#21955)
♦ **WYF** World Yoseikan Federation (#21946)
♦ WYF – World Youth Foundation (internationally oriented national body)
♦ Wylfa leithoedd (internationally oriented national body)
♦ **WYMD** World Youth Movement for Democracy (#21957)
♦ WYOCC – World Youth Organization Against Climate Change (inactive)
♦ **WYPW** World Youth Parliament for Water (#21958)
♦ **WYSE Travel Confederation** World Youth Student and Educational Travel Confederation (#21959)
♦ WYSE – World Youth Service and Enterprise (internationally oriented national body)
♦ Wysgerige Vereniging van Suider-Afrika (internationally oriented national body)
♦ **WZCC** World Zarathushti Chamber of Commerce (#21960)
♦ **WZO** World Zionist Organization (#21961)
♦ **WZO** World Zoroastrian Organization (#21962)
♦ Het X-Y Actiefonds / see Het Actiefonds
♦ Xarxa Iberoamericana de Terminologia (#18685)
♦ Xarxa Internacional d'Investigadors en Turisme, Cooperació i Desenvolupament (#14318)
♦ Xarxa Panllatina de Terminologia (#18901)
♦ Xaverian Brothers – Brothers of St Francis Xavier (religious order)
♦ Xaverian Missionary Sisters (religious order)
♦ Xaverians – Society of St Francis Xavier for the Foreign Missions (religious order)
♦ Xavériens – Société de Saint François Xavier pour les Missions Etrangères (religious order)
♦ La Xavière, Missionnaire du Christ Jésus (religious order)
♦ Xavier Network of European Jesuit Development NGOs (internationally oriented national body)
♦ Xavier Red Europea ONGD Jesuitas (internationally oriented national body)

♦ XBRL Europe 21966

Contact c/o FEE, Avenue d'Auderdhem 22-28/8, 1040 Brussels, Belgium. E-mail: gilles.maguet@xbrl-eu.org.
URL: http://www.xbrleurope.org/

History EU Transparency Register: 16818933143-79. **Aims** Foster European XBRL efforts; implement common XBRL projects in Europe; liaise with European Authorities and organisations. **Structure** General Assembly; Executive Committee; Working Groups. **Events** *Meeting* Paris (France) 2016.
Members Category 1 members in 11 countries:
Belgium, Denmark, Finland, France, Germany, Italy, Luxembourg, Netherlands, Spain, Sweden, UK.
Categories 2, 3 and 4 members include one organization listed in this Yearbook:
European Federation of Financial Analysts Societies (EFFAS, #07123).
NGO Relations Affiliated to: *XBRL International (#21967).* [2016/XM5220/y/**E**]

♦ **XBRL International** **21967**
CEO c/o Spire Group, 100 Walnut Ave, Ste 103, Clark NJ 07066, USA. E-mail: info@xbrl.org.
URL: http://www.xbrl.org/
History 1998. Name derives from 'eXtensible Business Reporting Language'. **Aims** Improve the accountability and transparency of *business* performance globally, by providing the open *data* exchange standard for business performance. **Structure** Assembly; Board of Directors. **Activities** Standards/guidelines. **Events** *International Conference* Shanghai (China) 2019, *Asia Round Table* Tokyo (Japan) 2019, *International Conference* Dubai (United Arab Emirates) 2018, *International Conference* Paris (France) 2017, *International Conference* Singapore (Singapore) 2016.
Members Companies and agencies (450) in 35 countries and territories:
Austria, Belgium, Canada, Chile, China, Denmark, Finland, France, Germany, Indonesia, Ireland, Italy, Japan, Jordan, Korea Rep, Liechtenstein, Lithuania, Luxembourg, Malaysia, Mexico, Netherlands, New Zealand, Nigeria, Poland, Qatar, Russia, Saudi Arabia, Singapore, South Africa, Spain, Sweden, Switzerland, Taiwan, Türkiye, UK, USA.
NGO Relations *XBRL Europe (#21966).* [2016/XM4546/F]

♦ xCoAx – Conference on Computation, Communication, Aesthetics and X (meeting series)
♦ Xerces Society for Invertebrate Conservation (internationally oriented national body)
♦ XLPDR International Association (internationally oriented national body)
♦ XminusY Solidarity Fund / see Het Actiefonds
♦ XminY Solidariteitsfonds / see Het Actiefonds
♦ XOPT – International Conference on X-ray Optics and Applications (meeting series)

♦ **Xplor International** **21968**
Pres/CEO 24156 State Rd 54, Ste 4, Lutz FL 33559, USA. T. +18139496170. Fax +18139499977. E-mail: info@xplor.org.
URL: http://www.xplor.org/
History 1980. Initial activities in the late 1970s as a Xerox 9700 User Group. "Xplor" derives from: *Xerox Printing Liaison ORganization.* Former names and other names: *Electronic Document Systems Association* – former. **Aims** Provide education, information and networking opportunities for transaction and *commercial printers* that support and help drive their success and the companies for which they work. **Events** *Xplor Conference* St Pete Beach, FL (USA) 2021, *Xploration Conference* Orlando, FL (USA) 2016, *Xploration Conference* Orlando, FL (USA) 2015, *Annual global electronic document systems conference* Miami, FL (USA) 2007, *Annual global electronic document systems conference* Miami, FL (USA) 2006. **Publications** *A Guide to the Electronic Document Body of Knowledge (EDBOK Guide).*
Members Individuals (mostly in USA) in 46 countries and territories:
Argentina, Australia, Austria, Bahamas, Barbados, Belgium, Belize, Brazil, Canada, China, Colombia, Czechia, Denmark, Egypt, Finland, France, Germany, Hong Kong, Iceland, India, Indonesia, Ireland, Israel, Italy, Japan, Korea Rep, Malaysia, Mexico, Netherlands, New Zealand, Norway, Peru, Poland, Portugal, Puerto Rico, Russia, Singapore, South Africa, Spain, Sweden, Switzerland, Taiwan, Uganda, UK, USA, Venezuela. [2021/XF4558/v/F]

♦ **XR4Europe Association (XR4EUROPE)** **21969**
Managing Dir Ave des Arts 56, 1000 Brussels, Belgium. E-mail: contact@xr4europe.eu.
URL: https://xr4europe.eu/
History 2019. Founded by national associations which were Consortium members, following the XR4ALL project (2018-2021) which ran under *European Commission (EC, #06633)* – H2020 programme. "XR" derives from "eXtended Reality", which is used as an umbrella designation for Virtual Reality (VR), Augmented Reality (AR), and Mixed Reality (MR). Registration: Banque-Carrefour des Entreprises, No/ID: 0879.791.978, Start date: 6 Aug 2021, Belgium. **Aims** Federate all XR professionals, organisations and initiatives to support the development, promote and represent XR innovation, industry and creativity made in Europe. **Structure** Board of Directors; Executive Team. **Activities** Events/meetings. **Events** *Immersion Forum* Brussels (Belgium) 2022. [2022/AA3068/D]

♦ **XR4EUROPE** XR4Europe Association (#21969)
♦ **XR** Extinction Rebellion (#09228)
♦ **Y4PT** Youth For Public Transport (#22024)
♦ YAA / see Africa Yoga Federation
♦ YAAKAARE REDHRCC (internationally oriented national body)
♦ YAAKAARE – Réseau euro-africain pour le développement intégré, les droits de l'homme et les relations interculturelles / see YAAKAARE REDHRCC
♦ YABEC – Young Asian Biological Engineers' Community (unconfirmed)
♦ YABT – Young Americas Business Trust (internationally oriented national body)

♦ **Yachay Wasi** **21970**
Pres 708 West 192nd St, Ste 6B, New York NY 10040-2450, USA. T. +12125676447. Fax +16464399005. E-mail: yachaywasi@nyc.rr.com.
URL: http://www.yachaywasi-ngo.org/
History Founded 1993. **Aims** Carry out *cultural* and *sustainable development* projects in the Cusco region of the *Andes.* **Structure** President; Vice-President. Based in New York NY (USA) and Cusco (Peru). **Languages** English, French, Quechua (macrolanguage), Spanish. **Finance** Small grants for projects. **Activities** Projects/programmes. **Publications** *Yachay Wasi Simin* – newsletter. *Creation, Evolution and Eternity* (2001).
Members Associate members. Membership countries not specified. **Consultative Status** Consultative status granted from: *ECOSOC (#05331)* (Special); *UNESCO (#20322)* (Consultative Status). **IGO Relations** Partner of: Billion Trees Campaign of *UNEP (#20299).* Associated with Department of Global Communications of the United Nations. **NGO Relations** Member of: *Mountain Partnership (MP, #16862).* [2016.07.29/XM1546/E]

♦ **YAC** Youth Action for Change (#22002)
♦ Yad Vashem, the Holocaust Martyrs' and Heroes' Remembrance Authority (internationally oriented national body)
♦ **YAE** Young Academy of Europe (#21979)
♦ YAI – Young Astronauts International (no recent information)
♦ **YAI** Youth Arise International (#22005)
♦ YaLa Young Leaders (unconfirmed)
♦ **YALDA** Youth Alliance for Leadership and Development in Africa (#22004)
♦ Yale Center for International and Area Studies / see MacMillan Center for International and Area Studies
♦ Yale Center for the Study of Globalization (internationally oriented national body)
♦ YALI – Young African Leaders Initiative (unconfirmed)

♦ **YAPC:: Europe Foundation (YEF)** **21971**
Sec address not obtained. E-mail: committee@yapceurope.org.
URL: http://www.yapceurope.org/
History Netherlands. YAPC stands for *Yet Another Perl Conference.* **Aims** Provide a focal point for Perl events in Europe. **Structure** Board. **Activities** Events/meetings. **Events** *YAPC : Yet Another Perl Conference* Amsterdam (Netherlands) 2017, *YAPC : Yet Another Perl Conference* Granada (Spain) 2015, *YAPC : Yet Another Perl Conference / Conference* Sofia (Bulgaria) 2014, *YAPC : Yet Another Perl Conference / Conference* Kiev (Ukraine) 2013, *YAPC : Yet Another Perl Conference / Conference* Frankfurt-Main (Germany) 2012. **NGO Relations** Cooperates with: *Perl Foundation.* [2019/XJ8968/f/F]

♦ Yasamin Kolay Oldugu Kentlerin Ulusararasi Agi / see Cittaslow (#03958)
♦ **YATA** Youth Atlantic Treaty Association (#22006)
♦ YAWE – Young Arab Women Entrepreneurs (unconfirmed)
♦ Yayasan IPNLF Indonesia (#14610)
♦ YBI – YouthBuild International (internationally oriented national body)
♦ YBI – Youth Business International (internationally oriented national body)
♦ YCAB Foundation (internationally oriented national body)
♦ YCCI / see International Institute of Peace Studies
♦ YCDA – Young Christian Democrats of America (no recent information)
♦ YC-ECRS / see European Union of Deaf Youth (#08986)
♦ **YCE** Youth Cancer Europe (#22008)
♦ YCIAS / see MacMillan Center for International and Area Studies
♦ YCISS / see York Centre for International and Security Studies
♦ YCISS – York Centre for International and Security Studies (internationally oriented national body)
♦ YCI – Youth Challenge International (internationally oriented national body)
♦ YCS / see International Young Catholic Students (#15926)
♦ YCSG – Yale Center for the Study of Globalization (internationally oriented national body)
♦ YCSRR / see Youth Coalition (#22011)
♦ **YCSRR** Youth Coalition (#22011)
♦ YDC – Youth for Development and Cooperation (inactive)
♦ **YDE** Young Democrats for Europe (#21980)
♦ **YDW** Young Dentists Worldwide (#21981)
♦ **YEAR** YEAR – Young European Associated Researchers (#21972)

♦ **YEAR – Young European Associated Researchers (YEAR)** **21972**
Sec Rue Joseph II 36-38, 1000 Brussels, Belgium. E-mail: contact@year-network.com.
URL: http://www.year-network.com/
History 17 Feb 2007, Udine (Italy). Officially constituted by consortium of 6 European research and technology organizations. Registration: EU Transparency Register, No/ID: 583245722627-68. **Aims** Enhance the potential, capabilities and competitiveness of the European Research Area (ERA); support development of young researchers' careers by helping them to extend their professional network and gain new skills in an international environment. **Structure** Board. **Languages** English. **Staff** 11.00 FTE, voluntary. **Finance** Sources: members' dues. **Activities** Events/meetings; guidance/assistance/consulting; networking/liaising; politics/policy/regulatory; training/education. **Events** *Annual Conference* Trondheim (Norway) 2020, *Annual Conference* Gothenburg (Sweden) 2019, *Annual Conference* Vienna (Austria) 2018, *Annual Conference* Brussels (Belgium) 2017, *Annual Conference* The Hague (Netherlands) 2016. **Publications** Annual Report; articles; surveys.
Members Organizations (8) in 8 countries:
Austria, Belgium, Finland, Ireland, Netherlands, Norway, Spain, Sweden.
Included in the above, 1 organization listed in this Yearbook:
SINTEF.
IGO Relations *European Commission (EC, #06633).* **NGO Relations** *European Association of Research and Technology Organizations (EARTO, #06197).* [2021/XJ9585/F]

♦ YEA – Young European Architects (no recent information)
♦ **YEBN** Young European Biotech Network (#21983)
♦ **YEE** Youth and Environment Europe (#22012)
♦ **YEF** YAPC:: Europe Foundation (#21971)
♦ Yehudi Menuhin School (internationally oriented national body)
♦ **YEL** Young European Leadership (#21985)

♦ **Yemen Islamic Jihad** **21973**
Address not obtained.
History Around 1990. Based in Yemen. **Aims** Establish Sharia law in Yemen; support the Palestinian struggle against Israel; end western intervention in the Middle East; combat against 'enemies' of Islam, namely Israel, the United States and the West in general.
Members Militant wings in 4 countries:
Afghanistan, Palestine, UK, USA.
NGO Relations Linked organization: *Al-Qa'ida (#00748).* [2008/XM0481/s/F]

♦ **YEM Foundation (YF)** **21974**
Pres 1101 N Rainbow Blvd, Apt 35, Las Vegas NV 89108, USA. E-mail: info@yemfoundation.org.
URL: https://www.yem.foundation
History 2017, Las Vegas, NV (USA). Former names and other names: *RC Foundation* – former; *dba YEM FOUNDATION* – former; *Rainbow Currency Foundation (RCF)* – former. Registration: Nonprofit Corporation, No/ID: NV20171765116, Start date: 2017, USA, State of Nevada. **Aims** Serve as a global form of payment, a digital currency that would be an addition to the existing global financial system. . **Structure** Board of International Directors (BID). **Languages** English, German, Spanish. **Staff** 7.00 FTE, paid. **Finance** Self-sustainable financing. **Activities** Advocacy/lobbying/activism; awareness raising; events/meetings; financial and/or material support; guidance/assistance/consulting; monitoring/evaluation; research and development; standards/guidelines; training/education. [2021.09.09/XM7617/fs/F]

♦ **YEMP** Young European Media Professionals (#21986)
♦ **YEN** Youth of European Nationalities (#22013)
♦ **Y-E-N** Youth Express Network (#22017)
♦ **YEPP** Youth of the European People's Party (#22014)
♦ **YERME** Young European Researchers in Mathematics Education (#21987)
♦ **YERUN** Young European Research Universities (#21988)
♦ YES / see Young Entrepreneurs for Europe (#21982)

♦ **YES-Europe** **21975**
Pres Boulevard Carl-VOGT 81, 1205 Geneva, Switzerland. E-mail: contact@yeseurope.org.
URL: https://yeseurope.org/
History 2016. Initiated at *European Leagues (#07672).* Former names and other names: *YES-Europe – Young leaders in Energy and Sustainability* – full title. **Aims** Catalyze the energy transition by creating an environment where youth are given a space to develop ideas, take on responsibility, build their local community and act for change. **Activities** Events/meetings; knowledge management/information dissemination; networking/liaising. **Events** *Annual Conference* The Hague (Netherlands) / Delft (Netherlands) 2019, *Annual Conference* Madrid (Spain) 2018. **NGO Relations** Member of (1): *Sustainable Development Solutions Network (SDSN, #20054).* [2022/XM7673/F]

♦ **YES for Europe** Young Entrepreneurs for Europe (#21982)
♦ YES-Europe – Young leaders in Energy and Sustainability / see YES-Europe (#21975)
♦ **YES Forum** Youth and European Social Work (#22015)

♦ **Yes to Life, No to Mining (YLNM)** **21976**
Coordinator Pacific address not obtained.
Coordintaor for Northern Europe address not obtained.
URL: http://www.yestolifenotomining.org/
History 2012. **Aims** Take action against the impact of extractives industries; encourage communities to say to mining to connect across the planet, collaborate and build their confidence through mutual solidarity, and support one another to stand firm. **Structure** Regional Coordinators (9): Pacific; West Africa; Latin America; South East Asia; Southern Africa; Arctic; Southern Europe/Latin America; Australia; Northern Europe.
Members Organizations worldwide. Membership countries not specified. Included in the above, 5 organizations listed in this Yearbook:
Included in the above, 5 organizations listed in this Yearbook:
African Biodiversity Network (ABN, #00222); Earth Law Center; Gaia Foundation; Global Alliance for the Rights of Nature (GARN, #10225); Leave it in the Ground Coalition (LINGO). [2018/XM6048/F]

♦ **YES Network** Promoting Earth Science for Society (#18541)
♦ YES / see Promoting Earth Science for Society (#18541)
♦ **YES** Young European Socialists (#21989)
♦ Yet Another Society / see Perl Foundation
♦ Yetimleri Koruma Federasyonu (unconfirmed)
♦ **YEU** Youth for Exchange and Understanding (#22016)
♦ **YFCI** Youth for Christ International (#22009)
♦ **YFCS** Young Friends of the Countryside (#21991)
♦ YFEU – Youth Forum of the European Union (inactive)
♦ **YFHIN** Youth for Habitat International Network (#22018)
♦ YFJ / see European Youth Forum (#09140)

- ♦ YFSP / see Pacifika Youth
- ♦ YFU IES / see Youth for Understanding (#22027)
- ♦ YFU / see Youth for Understanding (#22027)
- ♦ **YFU** Youth for Understanding (#22027)
- ♦ **YF** YEM Foundation (#21974)
- ♦ ygap (internationally oriented national body)
- ♦ YGLF – Young Global Leadership Foundation (internationally oriented national body)
- ♦ YGP – Young Global Pioneers (internationally oriented national body)
- ♦ Yhdistyneiden kansakuntien yhteydessä toimiva Euroopan Kriminaalipolitiikan instituutti (#07550)
- ♦ Yhdistyneiden kansakuntien yhteydessä toimiva Helsingin kriminaalipoliittinen instituutti / see European Institute for Crime Prevention and Control affiliated with the United Nations (#07550)
- ♦ **YHO** International Youth Health Organization (#15933)
- ♦ **YHRI** Youth for Human Rights International (#22019)
- ♦ **YHRM** International Youth Human Rights Movement (#15934)
- ♦ Yhteinen Tutkimuskeskus (#16147)
- ♦ Yhteisön Kasvilajikevirasto (#04404)
- ♦ Yhteispohjoismainen Metsäntutkimus (#17296)
- ♦ Yhteispohjoismainen terveydenhuollon puitesopimus (2002 treaty)
- ♦ Yiddish Scientific Institute / see YIVO Institute for Jewish Research
- ♦ Yidisher Visnshaftlekher Institut (internationally oriented national body)
- ♦ **YII** Yayasan IPNLF Indonesia (#14610)
- ♦ YiSHDA – Youth Initiative for Sustainable Human Development in Africa (internationally oriented national body)
- ♦ YIVO Institute for Jewish Research (internationally oriented national body)
- ♦ **YLDA** Young Liberals and Democrats of Asia (#21994)
- ♦ YLFA International – Yoghurt and Live Fermented Milk Association (inactive)
- ♦ **YLNM** Yes to Life, No to Mining (#21976)

♦ YMCA Europe 21977

Head Office Rue de l'Industrie 10, Mundo-J Building, 1000 Brussels, Belgium. E-mail: info@ymcaeurope.com.
URL: http://www.ymcaeurope.com/

History 1973. Founded as a regional body of *World Alliance of Young Men's Christian Associations (YMCA, #21090)*. Present Statutes adopted 15 May 1981; amended by EAY General Assemblies of: 30 May 1987; 25 May 1990; 29 May 1992; 17 May 1996; 24 May 1998. Former names and other names: *European Area Committee of YMCAs* – former; *European Alliance of YMCAs (EAY)* – former; *Alliance européenne des UCJG* – former; *Europäischer CVJM Bund* – former; *Alianza Europea de ACJ* – former. Registration: Swiss Civil Code, Switzerland; EU Transparency Register, No/ID: 386735920730-21. **Aims** Promote, develop and coordinate the work of YMCA movement in Europe. **Structure** Annual General Assembly; Executive Committee. Programme and Field Groups acting on: Movement Development (MD); European Programmes (EP); Youth Spirituality (Christian Orientation Group COG); Social Inclusion; Global Cooperation; Communication; Representation in European Bodies. MD consists of 5 Field Groups and 6 partner groups and EPF consists of various programme groups: European Physical Education Group (EPEG); European Outdoor Training Network (EOTN); European Ten Sing Group (ETS); Volunteers for Europe Group; European Scouts and Jungschar Group (ESG) and various task groups. **Languages** English. **Staff** 9.00 FTE, paid. **Finance** Sources: donations; fees for services; fundraising; members' dues; revenue from activities/projects. **Activities** Events/meetings; networking/liaising; sporting activities; training/education. **Events** *Staff Conference* Stockholm (Sweden) 2022, *Staff Conference* Stockholm (Sweden) 2021, *Annual General Assembly* Nice (France) 2019, *Annual General Assembly* Berchtesgaden (Germany) 2018, *Annual General Assembly* Edinburgh (UK) 2017. **Publications** *Friend for Europe (FfE)*; *News from Europe*. Brochures; handbooks.
Members YMCA movements in 32 countries and territories:
Armenia, Belarus, Belgium, Bulgaria, Czechia, Denmark, England, Estonia, Finland, France, Georgia, Germany, Greece, Hungary, Iceland, Ireland, Italy, Latvia (in Germany), Lithuania, Malta, Netherlands, Norway, Poland (in UK), Portugal, Russia, Scotland, Slovakia, Spain, Sweden, Switzerland, Ukraine, Wales.
Cooperating movements and groups in 6 countries:
Albania, Austria, Kosovo, North Macedonia, Romania, Serbia.
IGO Relations Member of (2): *European Youth Centres (EYCs, #09138)*; *European Youth Foundation (EYF, #09141)*. **NGO Relations** Member of (1): *European Youth Forum (#09140)*. [2023.02.28/XE6454/**E**]

- ♦ YMCA Global Community Center (internationally oriented national body)
- ♦ YMCA International Institute for Peace / see YMCA Global Community Center
- ♦ YMCA International Student Service / see International Branch of the YMCA, New York
- ♦ YMCA Kokusai Heiwa Kenkyujo / see YMCA Global Community Center
- ♦ YMCA Kokusai Komyunichi Senta (internationally oriented national body)
- ♦ **YMCA** World Alliance of Young Men's Christian Associations (#21090)

♦ YMCA World Urban Network (YMCA/WUN) 21978

Contact address not obtained. E-mail: ymcawun@islc.net – michelleanderson74@yahoo.com.
URL: http://www.worldurbannetwork.blogspot.com/

History As a coalition of executive officers of urban YMCAs. **Structure** Steering Committee, including Chairman, 2 Vice-Chairmen and Treasurer. **Events** *Conference* St Louis, MO (USA) 2015, *Conference* Melbourne, VIC (Australia) 2013, *Conference* Madrid (Spain) 2012, *Conference* New York, NY (USA) 2008. [2008/XE3339/**E**]

- ♦ **YMCA/WUN** YMCA World Urban Network (#21978)
- ♦ YNEAN – Yonsei Northeast Asian Network (internationally oriented national body)
- ♦ YNRI – Young Europe – Youth Network Against Racism and Intolerance (internationally oriented national body)
- ♦ **YNT** European Association of Young Neurologists and Trainees (#06281)
- ♦ **YOA** Youth Orchestra of the Americas (#22022)
- ♦ **YODA** Youth Organisations for Drug Action (#22023)
- ♦ Yoga Alliance Africa / see Africa Yoga Federation
- ♦ Yoga Research Foundation (internationally oriented national body)
- ♦ Yoghurt and Live Fermented Milk Association (inactive)
- ♦ Yokefellows International (internationally oriented national body)
- ♦ Yokefellows Movement / see Yokefellows International
- ♦ YOKE – Yokohama Association for International Communications and Exchanges (internationally oriented national body)
- ♦ Yokohama Association for International Communications and Exchanges (internationally oriented national body)
- ♦ Yonsei Northeast Asian Network (internationally oriented national body)
- ♦ York Centre for International and Security Studies (internationally oriented national body)
- ♦ York Centre for International and Strategic Studies / see York Centre for International and Security Studies
- ♦ Yoshinkan Aikido / see Aikido Yoshinkai Foundation (#00595)
- ♦ **YouAct** European Youth Network on Sexual and Reproductive Rights (#09144)

♦ Young Academy of Europe (YAE) 21979

Admin c/o Academia Europaea Cardiff Knowledge Hub, CUBRIC – Cardiff Univ, Maindy Road, Cardiff, CF24 4HQ, UK. E-mail: info@yacadeuro.org.
URL: http://www.yacadeuro.org/

History Dec 2012, Brussels (Belgium). Founded following meeting in Paris on September 2011, where possible routes towards establishing a Young Academy of Europe were discussed, and its aims and activities were defined. Established as an independent association of top young researchers in Europe. **Aims** Create a platform for networking, scientific exchange and science policy. **Structure** General Meeting (annual); Board; Selection Committee. **Activities** Advocacy/lobbying/activism; awards/prizes/competitions; events/meetings; knowledge management/information dissemination. **Events** *Annual General Meeting* UK 2021, *Annual General Meeting* Cardiff (UK) 2020, *Annual General Meeting* Barcelona (Spain) 2019, *Annual General Meeting* Barcelona (Spain) 2018, *Annual General Meeting* Budapest (Hungary) 2017. **Members** Individuals. Membership countries not specified. **NGO Relations** Member of (2): *European Young Academies (EYA)*; *Initiative for Science in Europe (ISE, #11214)*. [2021.09.07/XJ6831/**D**]

- ♦ Young African Leaders Initiative (unconfirmed)
- ♦ Young Americas Business Trust (internationally oriented national body)
- ♦ Young Arab Women Entrepreneurs (unconfirmed)
- ♦ Young Asian Biological Engineers' Community (unconfirmed)
- ♦ Young Astronauts International (no recent information)
- ♦ Young Bachelor & Master European Students BioCongress (meeting series)
- ♦ Young BM International Congress – Young Bachelor & Master European Students BioCongress (meeting series)
- ♦ Young Christian Democrats of America (no recent information)
- ♦ Young Christian Workers – Europe / see JOC Europe (#16118)

♦ Young Democrats for Europe (YDE) 21980

Pres Rue Montoyer 25, 1000 Brussels, Belgium. E-mail: secgen@youngdemocrats.eu.
URL: http://www.youngdemocrats.eu/

History Announced 9 May 2007. Formally established 22 Sep 2007, Vilnius (Lithuania), at 1st conference. Serves as the youth wing of *European Democratic Party (EDP, #06900)* and *Renew Europe (#18840)*. **Aims** Promote and maintain high participation rates; foster greater political involvement of European youngsters; help shape the European Democratic Party across the Continent; share ideas through the New Media; let European Institutions consider youth unemployment a key problem to combat; promote youth as a part of the solution and not as an issue; promote sustainability; increase funding for Education, Research and Development. **Structure** Board; Officers: President, Secretary General, Treasurer. **Activities** Events/meetings; training/education.
Members Full in 10 countries:
Basque Country, Canaries, Croatia, France, Germany, Greece, Italy, Poland, San Marino, Slovakia.
NGO Relations Observer status with (1): *European Youth Forum (#09140)*. Partner of (3): *European Democratic Party (EDP, #06900)*; *Institute of European Democrats (IED, #11260)*; *Renew Europe (#18840)*. [2023.02.18/XM6470/**E**]

♦ Young Dentists Worldwide (YDW) 21981

Jeunes chirurgiens-dentistes du monde

Pres Pacsirta utca 5, Szeged 6724, Hungary.
SG address not obtained.
Facebook: https://www.facebook.com/youngdentists/

History Feb 1992. Founded by *International Association of Dental Students (IADS, #11839)*. **Aims** Promote the needs and interests of young dentists of the world, specifically through promoting: standardized dental education including postgraduate and specialization; scientific programmes of specific interest to young dentists; vocational training for all dentists; voluntary work schemes within the framework of WHO; liaison with international bodies; free movement of dentists; exchange programmes with scientific and cultural activities. Act as a forum for these young *practitioners*. **Structure** Officers: President; Secretary-General; Communication Officers; Treasurer; Editor; Scientific Officer. **Activities** Events/meetings; training/education. **Events** *Congress* Brno (Czech Rep) 2010, *Congress* Iasi (Romania) 2009, *Congress* Sharm el Sheikh (Egypt) 2008, *Congress* Hungary 2007, *Congress* Khartoum (Sudan) 2006.
Members Individuals (89) in 32 countries and territories:
Australia, Brazil, Bulgaria, Canada, Czechia, Egypt, France, Germany, Hungary, India, Iran Islamic Rep, Ireland, Italy, Japan, Kuwait, Lebanon, North Macedonia, Pakistan, Poland, Portugal, Puerto Rico, Romania, Russia, Saudi Arabia, Slovenia, Spain, Sudan, Sweden, Switzerland, Türkiye, UK, USA.
IGO Relations *WHO (#20950)*. **NGO Relations** Affiliate member of: *FDI – World Dental Federation (#09281)*. [2016/XK1140/v/**E**]

- ♦ Young Earth Scientists for Society / see Promoting Earth Science for Society (#18541)

♦ Young Entrepreneurs for Europe (YES for Europe) 21982

Contact Av de la Renaissance 1, 1000 Brussels, Belgium. T. +3225889779. E-mail: europe@yesforeurope.eu.
URL: http://www.yesforeurope.eu/

History 1988. Founded by young entrepreneurs from Austria, France, Germany, Greece, Italy and Portugal. Statutes revised, 25 may 2002. Former names and other names: *YES* – former; *European Confederation of Young Entrepreneurs* – former. Registration: Banque-Carrefour des Entreprises, Start date: 1993, Belgium; EU Transparency Register, No/ID: 654225521365-19. **Aims** Support a free enterprise system in a social market economy; confirm free competition rules as fundamental elements of a social market economy; promote the protection of the environment as an important social function for enterprises; promote better correlation between economic and social performance through cooperation with employees; establish free trade. **Structure** General Assembly (annual); Executive Committee; Presidency Team; Secretariat located in Brussels (Belgium). **Languages** English. **Staff** 2.00 FTE, paid. **Finance** Sources: members' dues. Annual budget: 90,000 EUR. **Activities** Events/meetings; networking/liaising; politics/policy/regulatory. **Events** *European Youth Entrepreneurship Conference* Brussels (Belgium) 2020, *European Youth Entrepreneurship Conference* Yerevan (Armenia) 2019, *European Youth Entrepreneurship Conference* Hamburg (Germany) 2018, *European Youth Entrepreneurship Conference* Porto (Portugal) 2018, *European Youth Entrepreneurship Conference* Madrid (Spain) 2017. **Publications** *Entrepreneurial-mail* (12 a year).
Members National associations of young entrepreneurs in the fields of industry, trade and services in 16 countries (" indicates non-EU member):
Albania (*), Bulgaria, Cyprus, Finland, France, Germany, Greece, Hungary, Ireland, Italy, Poland, Portugal, Spain, Sweden, Türkiye (*), UK.
IGO Relations Belongs to consultative body of *European Commission (EC, #06633)* "Consultation with business Organizations". **NGO Relations** Member of (1): *G20 young Entrepreneurs' Alliance (G20 YEA, #10057)*. [2021/XD6378/**D**]

- ♦ Young Entrepreneurs of the European Union (#16109)
- ♦ Young Europe / see European Youth Parliament (#09145)
- ♦ Young Europe, 1834 (inactive)
- ♦ Young European Architects (no recent information)

♦ Young European Biotech Network (YEBN) 21983

Chairman YEBN eV, c/o Fraunhofer Einrichtung für Marine Biotechnologie EMB, Mönkhofer Weg 239a, 23562 Lübeck, Germany.
Vice-Chairwoman address not obtained.
URL: http://www.yebn.eu/

History Founded Dec 2002, Bertinoro (Italy), by 5 researchers' and students' organizations active in several European countries. Previously also referred to as *Young European Biotechnology Network*. **Aims** Provide a European platform for international events and career opportunities; support young *scientists* in expanding their network and enhancing their career; bring academia and life science industry closer together; teach skills young scientists need beyond their studies for being successful; connect national organizations in Europe. **Structure** Delegate Assembly; Executive Board; Task Groups; Project Groups; Regional Boards. **Languages** English. **Staff** Voluntary. **Finance** Members' dues. Sponsoring. **Activities** Meetings/events. **Events** *Annual Meeting* Heidelberg (Germany) 2013, *Annual Meeting / Youth Conference* Berlin (Germany) 2012, *Annual Meeting* Bologna (Italy) 2011, *Annual Meeting* Wroclaw (Poland) 2010, *Annual Meeting* Barcelona (Spain) 2009. **Publications** Position papers.
Members Organizations and individuals engaged as students, researchers, professionals and project leaders in Biotechnology and Life Sciences. Institutional members in 2 countries:
France, Germany. [2019/XM0971/**D**]

- ♦ Young European Biotechnology Network / see Young European Biotech Network (#21983)

♦ **Young European Federalists** **21984**
Jeunes européens fédéralistes (JEF) – Junge Europäische Föderalisten – Juventude Federalista Europea Juventude – Gioventù Federalista Europea – Jonge Europese Federalisten – Unga Europeiska Federalister – Unge Europeiske Föderalister – Eurooppalaiset Neoi Europeoi – Feidearalacha Na Ehropa – Giiagda Zghazagh Ghal – Mladi Evropski Federalisti – Modzi Europejscy Federaliscі – Mladi Evropsti Federalisté – Joventut Europea Federalista – Juventude Europeia Federalista – Tinerii Europeni Federalisti – Neoi Europei Federalistes – Europianet e Rinj Federaliste – Fiatal Európai Föderalistak – Mladi Priatelia Europy
SG Rue d'Arlon 53, 1040 Brussels, Belgium. E-mail: info@jef.eu.
General: http://www.jef.eu/
History 1970, Brussels (Belgium). Founded when Liaison Bureau was set up. 1st Congress: 25 Mar 1972, Luxembourg. Previous organization of the same name became well-known to the public in 1948, when it burnt down a number of frontier posts in Europe. An international JEF structure was set up, 2 Feb 1950, Paris (France), but did not survive the split of Federalist movements in 1956. Between 1955 and 1972 JEF sections existed in a number of countries but without an international structure. Former names and other names: *Jeunesse européenne fédéraliste* – former; *Bund Europäischer Jugend* – former. Registration: EU Transparency Register, No/ID: 22158552884-38; Belgium. **Aims** Create a democratic European federation as a guarantee for peace and a more free, just and democratic society; foster European citizenship; widen and deepen the EU; bring Europe closer to the citizens. **Structure** European Congress (every 2 years); Federal Committee; Executive Bureau; European Secretariat; Arbitration Board; Secretary General. **Languages** English, French, German. **Staff** 1.00 FTE, paid. **Finance** Members' dues. Other sources: subsidies from *Council of Europe (CE, #04881)* and *European Commission (EC, #06633)*; donations. Annual budget: about euro 200,000. **Activities** Events/meetings; training/education; publishing activities; networking/liaising. **Events** *Biennial Congress* Paris (France) 2019, *International EuroMed Vibes Seminar* Athens (Greece) 2013, *Europe Media Democracy Congress* Vienna (Austria) 2013, *Conference* Vienna (Austria) 2012, *Biennial congress* Helsinki (Finland) 2011. **Publications** *JEF Info* (20 a year) – newsletter; *The New Federalist* – magazine. Seminar reports; press releases resolutions.
Members Young people (about 30,000). Official sections in 26 countries:
Albania, Austria, Belgium, Bulgaria, Croatia, Czechia, Denmark, Finland, France, Germany, Greece, Hungary, Italy, Kosovo, Latvia, Lithuania, Malta, Moldova, North Macedonia, Norway, Poland, Portugal, Romania, Serbia, Slovakia, Spain.
Candidate sections in 4 countries:
Armenia, Bosnia-Herzegovina, Montenegro, Türkiye.
Interest groups in 9 countries:
Azerbaijan, Belarus, Cyprus, Estonia, Iceland, Luxembourg, Netherlands, Poland, Slovenia.
Consultative Status Consultative status granted from: *Council of Europe (CE, #04881)* (Participatory Status).
NGO Relations Member of: *Civil Society Europe*; *Council for International Cooperation of Nongovernmental Youth Organizations (EUROPOLIS, no recent information)*; *European Movement International (EMI, #07825)*; *European Youth Forum (#09140)*; *Permanent Forum of European Civil Society (#18322)*; *Union of European Federalists, The (UEF, #20385)*; *UNITED for Intercultural Action – European Network Against Nationalism, Racism, Fascism and in Support of Migrants and Refugees (UNITED, #20511)*; *World Federalist Movement – Movement for a Just World Order through a Strengthened United Nations (WFM, #21404)*. Supports: *European Alliance for the Statute of the European Association (EASEA, #05886)*; *European Citizens' Initiative Campaign (ECI Campaign, #06558)*. [2021/XD8006/**D**]

♦ **Young European Leadership (YEL)** **21985**
CEO Boulevard Anspach 169, 1000 Brussels, Belgium. E-mail: contact@younglead.eu.
URL: http://www.younglead.eu/
History Registration: Banque-Carrefour des Entreprises, No/ID: 0524.708.335, Start date: 21 Mar 2013, Belgium; EU Transparency Register, No/ID: 416740040270-21, Start date: 10 Nov 2020. **Aims** Empower young leaders and future decision makers from Europe and beyond. **Activities** Events/meetings; training/education. **NGO Relations** Partner of (4): *EU40 (#05562)*; *Global Diplomatic Forum (GDF, #10321)*; *Trans European Policy Studies Association (TEPSA, #20209)*; *World Youth Academy (WYA, #21948)*. [2020/AA1208/**F**]

♦ **Young European Media Professionals (YEMP)** **21986**
Jeunes professionnels de media européens
Contact address not obtained. T. +3222308316. Fax +3222456297.
URL: http://www.yemp.eu/
History Mar 2004, by *Institute for International Assistance and Solidarity (IFIAS Brussels, inactive)*. Registered in accordance with Belgian law. **Aims** Serve as a forum for discussion for young journalists and media students dedicated to the idea of *ethical* reporting and *social responsibility*. **Structure** General Assembly (annual). Board of Directors, comprising President, 2 Vice-Presidents, Secretary-General and Treasurer. **Languages** English. **Staff** 12.50 FTE, paid; 1.00 FTE, voluntary. **Finance** Members' dues: euro 500.
Members Full in 9 countries:
Armenia, Azerbaijan, Georgia, Germany, Russia, Spain, Syrian AR, UK, Ukraine.
IGO Relations Member of: *European Youth Centres (EYCs, #09138)*. **NGO Relations** *Forum for European Journalism Students (FEJS, #09908)*; national organizations. [2011.06.01/XM0235/t/**E**]

♦ **Young European Researchers in Mathematics Education (YERME)** . **21987**
Contact Centre for Educational Research, Westen Norway Univ of Applied Science, Postbox 7030, 5020 Bergen, Norway. T. +4755587193. E-mail: prediger@math.uni-dortmund.de.
Contact Dept of Mathematics F Casorati, UNIPV, Via Ferrata 5, 27100 Pavia PV, Italy. T. +39382985629.
URL: https://www.mathematik.uni-dortmund.de/~erme/
History Feb 2001, Marianské Lazne (Czechia). Founded by *European Society for Research in Mathematics Education (ERME, #08728)*. **Activities** Training/education. **Events** *Meeting* Marianské Lazne (Czech Rep) 2001. [2020.05.06/XM0686/**E**]

♦ **Young European Research Universities (YERUN)** **21988**
SG Rue de Trône 62, 1050 Brussels, Belgium. E-mail: secretarygeneral@yerun.eu.
URL: https://www.yerun.eu/
History 2016. Registration: Banque-Carrefour des Entreprises, No/ID: 0736.412.320, Start date: 15 Oct 2019, Belgium; EU Transparency Register, No/ID: 135344024395-60, Start date: 8 Nov 2016. **Aims** Strengthen and develop cooperation in the areas of research, academic education and service to society among young research universities in Europe or an equal basis and for their common benefit. **Structure** Executive Board; General Assembly.
Members Universities in 14 countries:
Belgium, Croatia, Cyprus, Denmark, Finland, France, Germany, Ireland, Italy, Netherlands, Portugal, Spain, Sweden, UK. [2021/AA2067/**F**]

♦ **Young European Socialists (YES)** **21989**
SG Rue Guimard 10-12, 1040 Brussels, Belgium. T. +3225489090. E-mail: office@youngsocialists.eu.
URL: http://www.youngsocialists.eu/
History Founded Nov 1992, Oegstgeest (Netherlands), as *European Community Organization of Socialist Youth (ECOSY) – Organisation des jeunes socialistes de la Communauté européenne*. Statutes adopted 2-4 Dec 1994, Munich (Germany). Revised: Mar/Apr 2007, Warsaw (Poland); Mar/Apr 2013, Järna (Sweden). Seat located in Brussels (Belgium). Registered in accordance with Belgian law. **Aims** As an independent umbrella organization for socialist and social democratic youth in Europe: promote European citizenship amongst young people; contribute towards the construction of the *democratic* European state; defend the interest of youth in the EU; integrate member organizations on the European level. **Structure** Congress – meeting of the highest statutory body (every 2 years); Bureau (meets twice a year in the countries currently holding the Presidency of the Council of the European Union). **Languages** English. **Staff** 3.00 FTE, paid. **Finance** Members' fees. Funded by PES; ad-hoc donations. **Activities** Meeting activities; politics / policy; financial and/or material support; advocacy / lobbying / activism. **Events** *Congress* Helsinki (Finland) 2019, *Congress* Järna (Sweden) 2013, *Congress* Brussels (Belgium) 2009, *Meeting* The Hague (Netherlands) 2007, *Congress* Warsaw (Poland) 2007. **Publications** *YES* (12 a year) – newsletter.
Members National organizations (63); Individuals. Full members (48) in 35 countries:
Austria, Belgium, Bosnia-Herzegovina, Bulgaria, Croatia, Cyprus, Czechia, Denmark, Estonia, Finland, France, Germany, Greece, Hungary, Iceland, Ireland, Italy, Latvia, Lithuania, Luxembourg, Malta, Montenegro, Netherlands, North Macedonia, Poland, Portugal, Romania, Serbia, Slovakia, Slovenia, Spain, Sweden, Switzerland, Türkiye, UK.
Observer members in 14 countries and territories:
Albania, Armenia, Belarus, Cyprus, Egypt, Georgia, Israel, Lebanon, Norway, Palestine, Russia, San Marino, Tunisia, Ukraine.
Fraternal members (2):
International Falcon Movement – Socialist Educational International (IFM-SEI, #13327); *International Union of Socialist Youth (IUSY, #15815)*.
NGO Relations Member of: *European Youth Forum (#09140)*; *UNITED for Intercultural Action – European Network Against Nationalism, Racism, Fascism and in Support of Migrants and Refugees (UNITED, #20511)*. Supports: *European Citizens' Initiative Campaign (ECI Campaign, #06558)*. Instrumental in setting up: *Global Progressive Youth Forum (GPYF, #10558)*. [2018/XE2083/**E**]

♦ Young Europe Union (inactive)
♦ Young Europe – Youth Network Against Racism and Intolerance (internationally oriented national body)

♦ **Young Feminist Fund (FRIDA)** **21990**
Co-Dir address not obtained. E-mail: info@youngfeministfund.org.
Co-Dir address not obtained.
URL: http://youngfeministfund.org/
History Set up 2010, as a collaborative effort between *Association for Women's Rights in Development (AWID, #02980)*, *Central American Women's Fund (#03677)* and young feminist activists from around the world. **Aims** Provide accessible, strategic and responsive funding for young feminist-led initiatives; strengthen the capacity of young feminist organizations to leverage resources for their work and to increase donors' and allies' commitments to resourcing young feminist activism. **Structure** Board; Advisory Board. **Staff** 7.00 FTE, paid. **Finance** Annual budget (2015): US$ 810,822. **Activities** Financial and/or material support; advocacy/lobbying/activism; events/meetings; capacity building; knowledge management/information dissemination. **NGO Relations** *Global Fund for Women (GFW, #10384)*. [2016/XM5114/f/**F**]

♦ **Young FoEE** Young Friends of the Earth Europe (#21992)

♦ **Young Friends of the Countryside (YFCS)** **21991**
SG Rue de Trèves 67, 1040 Brussels, Belgium. Fax +3222343009.
URL: http://www.yfcs.eu/
History Registered in accordance with Belgian law. **Aims** Give a *European* window for next generation *landowners* and family business managers. **Structure** Board. **Languages** Czech, English, French, German, Italian, Spanish. **Activities** Awards/prizes/competitions; events/meetings. **Publications** *Countryside Bimensual*. **Members** Individuals between 18 and 34 years having a specific dedication for countryside businesses, commercial farming, forestry and other land-based businesses. Membership countries not specified. [2019.06.18/XM2905/**E**]

♦ **Young Friends of the Earth Europe (Young FoEE)** **21992**
Contact c/o FoEE, Mundo B Bldg, Rue d'Edimbourg 26, 1050 Brussels, Belgium. T. +3228931000. E-mail: youngfoe@foeeurope.org.
URL: https://www.foeeurope.org/yfoee/
Aims Work collectively for social and environmental justice on a local, national and European level. **Structure** Annual General Meeting; Steering Group. **Activities** Training/education; events/meetings. **NGO Relations** *Friends of the Earth Europe (FoEE, #10001)*; *Youth Climate (YOUNGO, #22010)*. [2022/XM8597/**E**]

♦ Young Global Leadership Foundation (internationally oriented national body)
♦ Young Global Pioneers (internationally oriented national body)

♦ **Young Humanists International** **21993**
Pres The Foundry, T17 Oval Way, Vauxhall, London, SE11 5RR, UK. T. +442074908468. E-mail: office@humanists.international.
URL: https://humanists.international/about/young-humanists-international/
History Founded in the 70s. Resuscitated in 2002, with the support of *Humanists International (#10972)*, of which it is a full member. Original title: *International Humanist and Ethical Youth Organization (IHEYO)*. **Aims** Promote the spread of humanism among young people and greater cooperation amongst those already involved with humanism worldwide. **Structure** General Assembly; Executive Committee. Executive Director. **Languages** English. **Staff** Voluntary. **Activities** International conferences and seminars; internship programmes; information dissemination to youth humanists. **Events** *General Assembly* Malta 2016, *European Humanist Youth Days Conference* Utrecht (Netherlands) 2016, *Meeting* Brasilia (Brazil) 2015, *General Assembly* Oslo (Norway) 2015, *General Assembly* Oxford (UK) 2014. **Publications** *YouthSpeak* – e-newsletter.
Members Full (22) in 16 countries:
Austria, Belgium, Benin, Finland, Germany, Guinea, India, Liberia, Nepal, Netherlands, Nigeria, Norway, Poland, Sweden, Uganda, UK.
IGO Relations Member of: *European Youth Centres (EYCs, #09138)*. **NGO Relations** Full member of: *Humanists International (#10972)*. Member of: *UNITED for Intercultural Action – European Network Against Nationalism, Racism, Fascism and in Support of Migrants and Refugees (UNITED, #20511)*. [2022/XD4381/**D**]

♦ **Young Liberals and Democrats of Asia (YLDA)** **21994**
Contact address not obtained. T. +6328403728 – +6328403729. Fax +6328103189.
URL: http://www.yldasia.org/
History 2002, Manila (Philippines), during 1st Young Leader's Workshop of *Council of Asian Liberals and Democrats (CALD, #04867)*. Statutes adopted 2003, Phnom Penh (Cambodia). **Aims** Promote liberal values among the youth across Asia. **Structure** General Assembly (annual). Executive Committee, including President, Secretary General and 3 further members. Advisory Council. **Languages** English. **Staff** 1.00 FTE, paid. **Publications** *Freedom Writers: young Asians' Call to Freedom* (2009).
Members Individuals and organizations in 12 countries and territories:
Cambodia, Hong Kong, Indonesia, Malaysia, Myanmar, Nepal, Pakistan, Philippines, Singapore, Sri Lanka, Taiwan, Thailand.
Honorary members: individuals in 4 countries:
Germany, North Macedonia, Sweden, UK.
NGO Relations Associate member of: CALD. Participates in the activities of: *Friedrich Naumann Foundation for Freedom*; *International Federation of Liberal Youth (IFLRY, #13469)*. [2009.06.01/XM2147/**D**]

♦ Young Nordic Music (inactive)
♦ **YOUNGO** Youth Climate (#22010)
♦ Young People We Care (internationally oriented national body)

♦ **Young Phycological Society International (YPSI)** **21995**
Founder 1/152 Vembuli Amman koil street, Madipakkam, Chennai, Tamil Nadu 600091, Chennai TAMIL NADU 600091, India. T. +914445514364. E-mail: ypsi2012@gmail.com.
URL: https://ypsi2algae.yolasite.com/
History Founded 2012, India. Also known as *YPSI for ALGAE*. **Aims** Bring together researchers working in the field of algae and algal biotechnology. **Structure** Board; Advisory Committee. **Languages** English. **Staff** 90.00 FTE, voluntary. **Activities** Awareness raising; knowledge management/information dissemination; networking/liaising; publishing activities; research and development; research/documentation; events/meetings.
Members Individuals in 24 countries and territories:
Angola, Australia, Bangladesh, Botswana, Hong Kong, India, Indonesia, Iran Islamic Rep, Israel, Italy, Japan, Malaysia, Mexico, Norway, Oman, Pakistan, Philippines, Poland, Saudi Arabia, South Africa, Spain, Thailand, UK, Ukraine. [2020.03.04/XM7590/**D**]

♦ Young Pirates of Europe (unconfirmed)
♦ Young Presidents' Organization (internationally oriented national body)

♦ **Young Professionals for Agricultural Development (YPARD)** **21996**
Dir Global Coordination Unit – GFAR Secretariat, c/o FAO, Viale delle Terme di Caracalla, 00153 Rome RM, Italy. T. +39657052278. Fax +39657053898. E-mail: info@ypard.net.
URL: http://ypard.net/
History 2005-2006, as *Young Professionals' Platform on Agricultural Research for Development.* **Aims** Enable and empower young agricultural leaders shaping sustainable food systems. **Structure** Steering Committee; Regional Coordinators. **Languages** English, French, Spanish. **Staff** 2.00 FTE, paid. **Finance** Sources: donations. Supported by: *Swedish International Development Cooperation Agency (Sida).* **Members** Young Professionals and supporting members of the youth's cause individuals up to 40 years old; older/experienced professionals – to develop mentorship programme. Membership countries not specified. **IGO Relations** Cooperates with: *Asia-Pacific Association of Agricultural Research Institutions (APAARI, #01830); Association of Agricultural Research Institutions in the Near East and North Africa (AARINENA, #02364); Bioversity International (#03262); Centre de coopération internationale en recherche agronomique pour le développement (CIRAD, #03733); Centre technique de coopération agricole et rurale (CTA, inactive); CGIAR System Organization (CGIAR, #03843); European Initiative for Agricultural Research for Development (EIARD, #07537); FAO (#09260); International Bank for Reconstruction and Development (IBRD, #12317)* (World Bank); *New Partnership for Africa's Development (NEPAD, #17091); United Nations Human Settlements Programme (UN-Habitat, #20572).* **NGO Relations** Secretariat hosted by: *Global Forum on Agricultural Research (GFAR, #10370).* Member of: *Youth and United Nations Global Alliance (YUNGA, #22028).* Supports: *Farming First.* Cooperates with: *Agropolis International; Central Asia and the Caucasus Association of Agricultural Research Institutions (CACAARI, #03678); East African Wild Life Society (EAWLS, #05190); European Forum on Agricultural Research for Development (EFARD, #07302); Foro de las Américas para la Investigación y Desarrollo Tecnológico Agropecuario (FORAGRO, #09875); Forum for Agricultural Research in Africa (FARA, #09897); International Centre for Tropical Agriculture (#12527); World Agroforestry Centre (ICRAF, #21072); World Association of Young Scientists (WAYS, #21207).* [2020.04.29/XJ1941/t/F]

♦ **Young Professionals in Foreign Policy (YPFP)** **21997**
Founder/Chairman address not obtained. E-mail: info@ypfp.org.
Exec Dir – Brussels address not obtained. E-mail: brussels@ypfp.org.
URL: http://www.ypfp.org/
History 2004. Registration: EU Transparency Register, No/ID: 805041922605-32. **Aims** Foster the next generation of foreign policy leadership. **Structure** Board of Directors; Main Office in Washington DC (USA). **Activities** Events/meetings; networking/liaising. **Members** Membership countries not specified. [2023.02.13/XJ0353/F]

♦ Young Professionals' Platform on Agricultural Research for Development / see Young Professionals for Agricultural Development (#21996)

♦ **Young Property Lawyers' Forum (YPLF)** **21998**
Contact address not obtained.
URL: http://yplf.net/
History Set up as a global informal network. **Aims** Support young property law scholars in the development of their ideas. **Structure** Board of Advice. **Activities** Events/meetings. **Events** *Meeting* Glasgow (UK) 2019, *Meeting* Maastricht (Netherlands) 2018. **Publications** *Property Law Perspective* – books series. [2019/XM7814/F]

♦ **YoungShip International (YSI)** **21999**
SG address not obtained. E-mail: mail@youngship.com.
URL: http://www.youngship.com/youngship-international/
Aims Engage, inspire and work with the *maritime* industry to promote the *young* bright minds in the industry for future progress development. **Structure** Annual General Meeting; Board. **Activities** Awards/prizes/competitions; events/meetings. **Events** *ShipCon Conference* Bergen (Norway) 2022, *ShipCon Conference* Rotterdam (Netherlands) 2021, *ShipCon Conference* Rotterdam (Netherlands) 2020, *ShipCon Conference* Ålesund (Norway) 2019, *Fall Conference* Haugesund (Norway) 2018.
Members Full in 30 countries:
Belgium, Colombia, Côte d'Ivoire, Cyprus, Denmark, Dominican Rep, Ecuador, Finland, France, Germany, Greece, India, Italy, Monaco, Netherlands, Nigeria, Norway, Panama, Portugal, Singapore, Spain, Sri Lanka, Sweden, Switzerland, Tanzania UR, Türkiye, UK, United Arab Emirates, USA (Egypt), Venezuela. [2022.06.15/XM8044/F]

♦ **Young SIETAR** Young Society for Intercultural Education, Training and Research (#22000)

♦ **Young Society for Intercultural Education, Training and Research (Young SIETAR)** **22000**
Pres address not obtained. E-mail: president@youngsietar.org – board@youngsietar.org.
Sec address not obtained. E-mail: secretary@youngsietar.org.
URL: http://www.youngsietar.org/
Structure Governing Board of 12, including President, Secretary and Treasurer. **Events** *Shaping identity – land people, systems* Vancouver, BC (Canada) 2014, *Annual Congress* Cairo (Egypt) 2009, *Annual Congress* Granada (Spain) 2008, *Annual Congress* Fürstenberg-Havel (Germany) 2007, *Annual Congress* Valencia (Spain) 2006. **Publications** *The Young Sietarian* – newsletter. [2019/XJ0632/E]

♦ Young Topologists Meeting (meeting series)

♦ **YOUROPE – The European Festival Association** **22001**
Main Office Auguststr 18, 53229 Bonn, Germany. E-mail: office@yourope.org.
URL: https://www.yourope.org/
History Nov 1998, London (UK). Restructured and moved to Bonn (Germany) in 2021. Registration: Start date: 1999, Denmark, Roskilde. **Aims** Improve the European festival scene in terms of: working conditions; health and safety issues; environmental awareness; exchange of knowledge and information; promoting the cross-border exchange of live music talent in Europe. **Events** *European Festival Conference (EFC)* Barcelona (Spain) 2019, *European Festival Conference (EFC)* Larvik (Norway) 2017, *European Festival Conference (EFC)* Kals am Grossglockner (Austria) 2015.
Members Festival members in 26 countries:
Austria, Belgium, Czechia, Denmark, Finland, France, Germany, Greece, Hungary, Italy, Latvia, Luxembourg, Netherlands, North Macedonia, Norway, Poland, Romania, Russia, Serbia, Slovakia, Slovenia, Spain, Sweden, Switzerland, Türkiye, Ukraine. [2021.09.01/AA0654/D]

♦ **YOURS** Youth for Road Safety (#22026)
♦ YOU Stiftung – Bildung für Kinder in Not (internationally oriented national body)
♦ YOU Stiftung – YOU Stiftung – Bildung für Kinder in Not (internationally oriented national body)

♦ **Youth Action for Change (YAC)** **22002**
Chair Via Curiel 63, 20050 Mezzago MB, Italy.
History by Selene Biffi, following second International Youth Parliament of *Oxfam International (#17922)* held in 2004. **Aims** Strengthen the contribution of young people to positive community development through online educational courses and youth empowerment projects. [2019/XM3860/E]

♦ Youth in Action Programme (inactive)
♦ Youth Afrique Leadership Forum (internationally oriented national body)

♦ **Youth against Racism in Europe (YRE)** **22003**
Jeunes contre le racisme en Europe (JRE) – Jungend gegen Rassismus in Europa – Jongeren tegen Racisme in Europa
Postal address PO Box 858, London, E11 1YG, UK. T. +442085587947.
URL: http://www.yre.org.uk/
History May 1992, by the Belgian section, on the initiative of *Committee for a Workers' International (CWI, #04290).* **Aims** Combat racism, prejudice and the far-right. **Structure** International Committee. **Languages** Dutch, English, French, German, Irish Gaelic, Swedish. **Finance** Donations. **Activities** Organizes: international youth camps; demonstrations; street campaigns; solidarity campaigns; pickets. **Events** *International coordinating meeting* Belgium 2000, *Conference* France 1996. **Publications** *No pasaran* – newsletter. Anti-racist education pack. Pamphlet.

Members National organizations (7, Ireland and Northern Ireland together) and individuals. Members in 12 countries:
Austria, Belgium, Czechia, France, Greece, Ireland, Kazakhstan, Netherlands, Russia, Sweden, UK, Ukraine. [2013/XD3403/D]

♦ **Youth Alliance for Leadership and Development in Africa (YALDA)** .. **22004**
International Headquarters PO Box 402581, Gaborone, Botswana. T. +26772104029. E-mail: contact@yaldafrica.org – yaldafrica@gmail.com.
USA Office Harvard YALDA, Box 316, University Hall, First Floor, Cambridge MA 02138, USA.
URL: http://www.yaldafrica.org/
History Apr 2004. Founded by *Harvard African Student's Association (HASA).* Former names and other names: *Future African Leaders Alliance (FALA)* – former (Apr 2004 to May 2004). **Aims** Provide a forum on the African continent and those abroad with a commitment to the welfare of Africa. **Structure** International Executive Committee, comprising Chairperson, 4 Alumni Network Executive Directors and 9 Branch Executive Directors. **Events** *What Africa needs now – youth creating jobs* Nairobi (Kenya) 2015, *Innovation and creativity for a better Africa – implementing your dreams* Lagos (Nigeria) 2012, *Conference* Gaborone (Botswana) 2011. **Publications** *YALDA Bi-Annual Magazine; YALDA Quarterly Newsletter.*
Members Branches (33) in 21 countries:
Angola, Botswana, Cameroon, Côte d'Ivoire, Egypt, Ethiopia, Ghana, Kenya, Liberia, Malawi, Mali, Mauritius, Morocco, Mozambique, Nigeria, Senegal, South Africa, Uganda, USA, Zambia, Zimbabwe.
Consultative Status Consultative status granted from: *ECOSOC (#05331)* (Special). [2021.06.28/XJ2728/E]

♦ **Youth Arise International (YAI)** **22005**
Pres CiVI, 3443 N Central Ave, Ste 1002, Phoenix AZ 85012, USA. T. +16027959810.
Washington Office Holy Redeemer College, 3112 7th St, Washington DC 20017, USA. T. +12029978888. E-mail: info@youtharise.org.
URL: http://www.youtharise.org/
History 1994, Malta. An international Catholic youth ministry. **Aims** Promote youth adult formation, leadership training, humanitarian activities, *evangelization* and discipleship worldwide. **Structure** Includes *Europe ARISE.* **Languages** English, French, Italian, Spanish. **Staff** Voluntary. **Finance** Support from corporations and individuals. **Activities** Events/meetings.
Members Individuals in 25 countries and territories:
Argentina, Australia, Brazil, Canada, France, Germany, Ghana, Gibraltar, India, Indonesia, Italy, Lebanon, Malaysia, Malta, Mexico, Philippines, Poland, Qatar, Romania, Singapore, Spain, UK, United Arab Emirates, Uruguay, USA.
NGO Relations *Caritas Internationalis (CI, #03580).* [2017.03.09/XG7132/v/F]

♦ **Youth Atlantic Treaty Association (YATA)** **22006**
Association jeunes du traité atlantique
Main Office c/o ATA, Rue des Petits Carmes 20, 1000 Brussels, Belgium. E-mail: ratibakhtadze@gmail.com – international.yata@gmail.com.
URL: http://yata-international.org/
History Founded 1997, Rome (Italy), by *Atlantic Treaty Association (ATA, #03010).* **Staff** 3.00 FTE, paid. **Events** *Nordic Security Conference* Oslo (Norway) 2021, *Nordic Security Conference* Oslo (Norway) 2020, *Nordic Security Conference* Oslo (Norway) 2019, *Meeting* Brussels (Belgium) 2014, *Meeting* Podgorica (Montenegro) 2014. [2019/XE3345/E]

♦ **YouthBank International** **22007**
Dir Community House, Citylink Business Park, Belfast, BT12 4HQ, UK. T. +442890245927. E-mail: info@youthbankinternational.org.
URL: https://www.youthbankinternational.org/
History Operational since Jun 2014. A charity registered in Northern Ireland: NIC101341. **Aims** Facilitate information exchange and sharing of best practices. **Structure** Board. **Members** Organizations (26) in 25 countries. Membership countries not specified. **NGO Relations** Member of: *Worldwide Initiatives for Grantmaker Support (WINGS, #21926).* [2018/XM8819/F]

♦ YouthBuild International (internationally oriented national body)
♦ Youth Business International (internationally oriented national body)

♦ **Youth Cancer Europe (YCE)** **22008**
Contact address not obtained. E-mail: contact@youthcancereurope.org.
URL: https://www.youthcancereurope.org/
History 2015. Registration: Charity, No/ID: 35424351, Start date: 2015, Romania. **Aims** Help shape European policy; collaborate in and promote research; fight for better access to care, for better treatments and better conditions; help fix disparities existing across Europe for young people fighting cancer. **Structure** Steering Committee. **Activities** Advocacy/lobbying/activism; events/meetings; networking/liaising. **NGO Relations** Member of (3): *EU Health Coalition; European Cancer Organisation (ECO, #06432)* (Patient Advisory Committee); *Workgroup of European Cancer Patient Advocacy Networks (WECAN, #21054).* [2020/AA0348/f/F]

♦ Youth Challenge International (internationally oriented national body)

♦ **Youth for Christ International (YFCI)** **22009**
Jeunesse pour Christ (JPC) – Juventud para Cristo (JPC) – Jugend für Christus (JFC) – Mocidade por Cristo (MPC)
Mailing Address PO Box 4555, Englewood CO 80155, USA.
URL: http://www.yfci.org/
History Jan 1968, Port Maria (Jamaica). Founded, deriving from *'Youth for Christ International'* set up in 1945, USA. Revised Constitution and present name adopted 4 Aug 1974, Les Diablerets (Switzerland), at Council's Third Convocation. Further modifications to constitution adopted: 6-14 Aug 1977, Rio de Janeiro (Brazil); 3 Jul 1984, Hong Kong. Former names and other names: *International Council of Youth for Christ* – former (Jan 1968 to 4 Aug 1974). Registration: Swiss Civil Code, Switzerland. **Aims** Coordinate the worldwide work of Youth for Christ; guide development of Youth for Christ *ministry* in new countries; reach young people everywhere, by working together with local churches and like-minded partners to raise up lifelong followers of Jesus. **Structure** General Assembly; Council of Delegates (meets every 3 years); World Leadership Team (management); Board of Trustees. **Languages** English, French, Portuguese, Russian, Spanish. **Staff** 63158.00 FTE, paid. **Finance** Sources: contributions; fees for services; gifts, legacies; members' dues. Annual budget: 4,800,000 USD. **Activities** Events/meetings; networking/liaising. **Events** *General Assembly* Netherlands 2021, *General Assembly* Netherlands 2020, *General Assembly* Miami, FL (USA) 2017, *General Assembly* Bangkok (Thailand) 2014, *General Assembly* Denver, CO (USA) 2011. **Publications** *Global Ministry Overview; YFCI World Directory.* Manuals.
Members Chartered national programmes in 75 countries and pioneering permanent YFC ministries in 25 countries. Members in a total of 115 countries and territories:
Albania, Angola, Antigua-Barbuda, Armenia, Australia, Bahrain, Bangladesh, Belarus, Belgium, Benin, Bhutan, Bolivia, Botswana, Brazil, Bulgaria, Burkina Faso, Burundi, Cameroon, Canada, Cape Verde, Chile, Colombia, Comoros, Congo DR, Costa Rica, Côte d'Ivoire, Croatia, Cyprus, Czechia, Denmark, Dominica, Ecuador, Egypt, El Salvador, Ethiopia, France, Gambia, Georgia, Germany, Ghana, Grenada, Guatemala, Guinea, Guinea-Bissau, Haiti, Honduras, Hong Kong, Hungary, India, Indonesia, Ireland, Italy, Jamaica, Japan, Kazakhstan, Kenya, Korea Rep, Kyrgyzstan, Lebanon, Liberia, Madagascar, Malaysia, Mali, Mauritius, Mexico, Moldova, Mongolia, Myanmar, Namibia, Netherlands, New Zealand, Nicaragua, Niger, Nigeria, North Macedonia, Northern Ireland, Pakistan, Papua New Guinea, Peru, Philippines, Poland, Portugal, Réunion, Rodriguez Is, Romania, Russia, Rwanda, Samoa, Samoa USA, Sao Tomé-Principe, Serbia, Seychelles, Sierra Leone, Singapore, Slovakia, South Africa, South Sudan, Spain, Sweden, Switzerland, Taiwan, Tanzania UR, Thailand, Togo, Tonga, Trinidad-Tobago, Uganda, UK, Ukraine, United Arab Emirates, Uruguay, USA, Venezuela, Zambia, Zimbabwe.
NGO Relations Member of (3): *European Evangelical Alliance (EEA, #07010);* Evangelical Council for Financial Accountability; *World Evangelical Alliance (WEA, #21393).* [2021/XB0110/B]

♦ **Youth Climate (YOUNGO)** **22010**
Address not obtained.
URL: http://www.youngo.uno/
History Founded 2005. Children and Youth constituency to *United Nations Framework Convention on Climate Change (UNFCCC, 1992).* Also referred to as *International Youth Climate Movement (IYCM).* **Finance** Members' dues.
Members Full in 18 countries and territories:

Australia, Bangladesh, Canada, China, Denmark, France, Ghana, Hong Kong, India, Japan, Malaysia, New Zealand, Nigeria, Russia, Singapore, Taiwan, UK, USA.
Included in the above, 4 organizations listed in this Yearbook:
World Alliance of Young Men's Christian Associations (YMCA, #21090); World Association of Girl Guides and Girl Scouts (WAGGGS, #21142); World Organization of the Scout Movement (WOSM, #21693); Young Friends of the Earth Europe (Young FoEE, #21992). [2018/XM8596/E]

♦ Youth Coalition (YCSRR) 22011

Exec Dir 123 Slater Street, 6th floor, Ottawa ON K1P 5H2, Canada. E-mail: info@youthcoalition.org.
URL: http://www.youthcoalition.org/

History Feb 1999. Founded during Hague Youth Forum, as *Youth Coalition for Sexual and Reproductive Rights (YCSRR)*. **Aims** As an organization of young people ages 15-29 years: ensure that the sexual and reproductive rights of all young people are respected, guaranteed and promoted; secure the meaningful participation of young people in decision-making that affects their lives. **Activities** Advocacy/lobbying/activism; events/meetings; capacity building; training/education. **Publications** *The Watchdog* (4 a year); *YC Newsletter*. **Consultative Status** Consultative status granted from: *ECOSOC (#05331)* (Special). **NGO Relations** Member of: *Reproductive Health Supplies Coalition (RHSC, #18847)*. Partner of: *Every Woman Every Child (EWEC, #09215)*. Participates in: *HIV Young Leaders Fund (HYLF, no recent information).* [2021/XQ0071/F]

♦ Youth Coalition for Sexual and Reproductive Rights / see Youth Coalition (#22011)
♦ Youth Commission of ECRS / see European Union of Deaf Youth (#08986)
♦ Youth Coordination Centre International / see International Institute of Peace Studies
♦ Youth for Development and Cooperation (inactive)

♦ Youth and Environment Europe (YEE) 22012

SG Vinohradská 2165/48, 120 00 Prague, Czechia. T. +420732956348. E-mail: yee@yeenet.eu.
URL: http://www.yeenet.eu/

History 3 Aug 1983, Stockholm (Sweden). Founded as the European regional branch of *International Youth Federation for Environmental Studies and Conservation (IYF, inactive)*. **Aims** Spread information and knowledge on the environment and environmental problems; emphasize the fact that nature knows no national borders; offer an opportunity to contact other European organizations and exchange experience and ideas or to work together. **Structure** Annual Meeting; General Assembly; Executive Board; International Secretariat located in Prague (Czech Rep). **Languages** English. **Staff** 2.00 FTE, paid; 2.00 FTE, voluntary. **Finance** Sources: donations; grants; members' dues. **Activities** Events/meetings; training/education. **Events** *Youth Greenoble Summit* Grenoble (France) 2022, *Annual Meeting* Brno (Czechia) 2019, *Annual Meeting* Adamov (Czech Rep) 2013, *Annual Meeting* Oucmanice (Czech Rep) 2012, *Annual Meeting* Oumanice (Czech Rep) 2012. **Publications** *YEE e-Newsletter* (6 a year).
Members Youth-run environmental NGOs (45) in 27 countries:
Albania, Armenia, Austria, Azerbaijan, Belgium, Bosnia-Herzegovina, Croatia, Czechia, Denmark, Finland, Georgia, Germany, Ireland, Italy, Kosovo, Latvia, Moldova, North Macedonia, Poland, Portugal, Romania, Russia, Serbia, Spain, Sweden, UK, Ukraine.
Consultative Status Consultative status granted from: *UNEP (#20299)*. **IGO Relations** Maintains relationship with: *European Youth Foundation (EYF, #09141)*. **NGO Relations** Member of (5): *Environmental Paper Network (EPN, #05507); European Environmental Bureau (EEB, #06996); European Youth Forum (#09140); Generation Climate Europe (GCE, #10114); Taiga Rescue Network (TRN, inactive).* [2023.02.28/XE0160/E]

♦ Youth of European Nationalities (YEN) 22013

Jugend Europäischer Volksgruppen (JEV)

SG Postfach 640228, 10048 Berlin, Germany. T. +4917631779414. E-mail: office@yeni.org – board@yeni.org.
Registered Office Fioringras 93, 8935 BR Leeuwarden, Netherlands.
URL: http://www.yeni.org/

History 1963. Founded as the Youth Commission of *Federal Union of European Nationalities (FUEN, #09396)*. Became independent 1984, when present statutes adopted. Former names and other names: *Jeunesse des communautés ethniques européennes (JCEE)* – former (Apr 1984). **Aims** Represent youth organizations of autochthonous, national, ethnic, and linguistic minorities in a multicultural and multilingual Europe; work for preservation and development of the rights of minorities and ethnic groups. **Structure** General Assembly (annual); Executive; Board; Working Groups. **Languages** English, German. **Staff** 1.50 FTE, paid. **Finance** Sources: gifts, legacies; grants; members' dues; revenue from activities/projects. **Activities** Events/meetings; networking/liaising. **Events** *Annual Easter Seminar* Sochi (Russia) 2019, *Celebrating pluralism* Gdansk (Poland) 2017, *Annual Easter Seminar* Tirana (Albania) 2017, *Be minority, be strong* Berlin (Germany) 2016, *Workshop* Lockenhaus (Austria) 2016. **Publications** *Minority Youth in Europe. A State of Play* (2021); *Minority Handbook for Beginners*; *YEN White Paper on Minority Rights*.
Members Organizations (39) in 19 countries:
Albania, Austria, Croatia, Denmark, Estonia, France, Germany, Hungary, Italy, Netherlands, North Macedonia, Poland, Romania, Russia, Serbia, Slovakia, Sweden, Switzerland, Ukraine.
Consultative Status Consultative status granted from: *ECOSOC (#05331)* (Special). **NGO Relations** Member of (1): *European Youth Forum (#09140)*. [2022.02.09/XF0419/F]

♦ Youth of the European People's Party (YEPP) 22014

SG Rue du Commerce 10, 1000 Brussels, Belgium. T. +3222854163. Fax +3222854165. E-mail: yepp@epp.eu.
Exec Officer address not obtained.
URL: http://youthepp.eu/

History 30 Jan 1997, Brussels (Belgium). Created at founding congress, to unite national youth organizations of member parties of *European Young Christian Democrats (EYCD, inactive)* and *Democrat Youth Community of Europe (DEMYC, #05037)*. Took over activities of EYCD, which ceased activities Jun 1997. Former names and other names: *EPP Youth* – former; *Jeune PPE* – former; *Junge EVP* – former. Registration: Belgium. **Aims** Our main objectives is to maintain good contacts within our political family, provide ground for training, discussion and cooperation and prepare the younger generation to lead tomorrow's Europe. This runs parallel to our mission to stimulate further integration in Europe, to uphold our principles, policies and ideas in the European political debate. **Structure** Congress (every 2 years); Board; Council. **Languages** English. **Staff** 2.00 FTE, paid. **Finance** Sources: members' dues. Subventions. **Activities** Events/meetings; politics/policy/regulatory. **Events** *Council Meeting* Belgium 2020, *Council Meeting* Berlin (Germany) 2019, *Council Meeting* Kiev (Ukraine) 2019, *Council Meeting* Valencia (Spain) 2019, *Council of Presidents Meeting* Vienna (Austria) 2019. **Publications** *YEPP Yearbook* (annual); *YEPP Newsletters*. *YEPP Factbook*. Proceedings of congresses and councils; resolutions; white papers; press releases.
Members Full: organizations (53) in 36 countries:
Albania, Austria, Belgium, Bosnia-Herzegovina, Bulgaria, Croatia, Cyprus, Czechia, Denmark, Estonia, Finland, France, Germany, Greece, Hungary, Ireland, Italy, Latvia, Lithuania, Luxembourg, Malta, Moldova, Netherlands, North Macedonia, Norway, Poland, Portugal, Romania, San Marino, Serbia, Slovakia, Slovenia, Spain, Sweden, Switzerland, Ukraine.
Observers (3) in 3 countries:
Belarus, Georgia, Ukraine.
Associated (7) in 6 countries and territories:
Armenia, Belarus, Italy, Kurdish area, Lebanon, Moldova.
Consultative Status Consultative status granted from: *Council of Europe (CE, #04881)* (Participatory Status). **NGO Relations** Member of (2): *European Youth Forum (#09140); Robert Schuman Institute for Developing Democracy in Central and Eastern Europe (RSI, #18958)*. Statutory links with and supported by: *European People's Party (EPP, #08185).* [2020.05.11/XE2794/E]

♦ Youth and European Social Work (YES Forum) 22015

Dir and Project Manager Wagenburgstrasse 26-28, 70184 Stuttgart, Germany. T. +497111648927. Fax +497111648921. E-mail: office@yes-forum.eu.
URL: http://www.yes-forum.eu/

History 2002. An organization of the type *European Economic Interest Grouping (EEIG, #06960)*. Registration: EU Transparency Register, No/ID: 099101116985-63, Start date: 16 Apr 2015. **Aims** Foster permanent dialogue about the needs and interests of socially excluded young people or those threatened by social exclusion; promote cooperation between government bodies and non-governmental institutions in the field of youth social work in Europe. **Languages** English. **Staff** 2.50 FTE, paid. **Finance** Budget (annual): about euro 200,000. **Activities** Advocacy/lobbying/activism. **Events** *Project Planning Meeting* Vienna (Austria) 2020.

Members National organizations (34) in 18 countries:
Austria, Belgium, Denmark, Finland, France, Germany, Greece, Hungary, Italy, Netherlands, North Macedonia, Norway, Poland, Romania, Spain, Sweden, Switzerland, UK.
NGO Relations Member of: *Social Platform (#19344).* [2020/XM3441/F]

♦ Youth for Exchange and Understanding (YEU) 22016

Jeunesse pour l'échange et la compréhension

Secretariat Rue de la Loi 235, 1040 Brussels, Belgium. E-mail: info@yeu-international.org.
URL: http://www.yeu-international.org/

History 28 Aug 1986, Strasbourg (France), following 4 years cooperation and annual international meetings initiated at a meeting, 1983, Germany FR. **Aims** Promote peace, understanding and cooperation among young people, both between and within continents, in a spirit of respect for human rights, particularly by exchange of information; stimulate mutual aid in developed and developing countries for cultural, educational and social purposes; encourage interdenominational exchange of ideas and opinions; improve relations among youth of countries with differing political systems; work together on issues affecting people and their environment. **Structure** General Assembly (annual); Governing Board; International Head Office. **Languages** English. **Staff** 2.00 FTE, paid. **Finance** Run on a voluntary basis, activities of the organization are financed by contributions from members and participants and grants from national governments and European bodies. Budget (annual): about euro 150,000. **Activities** Events/meetings; training/education. **Events** *Annual General Assembly* Brussels (Belgium) 2016, *Annual International Youth Convention* Brussels (Belgium) 2016, *Annual General Assembly* Banja Luka (Bosnia-Herzegovina) 2015, *Annual international youth convention* Romania 2005, *Annual Leader and Language Training Session* Spain 2005. **Publications** *YEU Newsletter* (6 a year).
Members Personal – young people aged between 18 and 27 years; Organizational – non-governmental youth organizations; Consultative – other individuals and organizations. Full member organizations in 22 countries:
Albania, Armenia, Azerbaijan, Belgium, Bosnia-Herzegovina, Cyprus, Egypt, Estonia, Greece, Italy, Lithuania, Malta, Montenegro, Netherlands, North Macedonia, Poland, Portugal, Serbia, Slovenia, Tunisia, Türkiye, Ukraine.
Observer member organizations in 3 countries:
Armenia, Greece, Romania.
IGO Relations *European Youth Centres (EYCs, #09138); European Youth Foundation (EYF, #09141)*. **NGO Relations** Member of: *International Youth Health Organization (YHO, #15933); Lifelong Learning Platform – European Civil Society for Education (LLLP, #16466); European Youth Forum (#09140).* [2021/XF0125/F]

♦ Youth Express Network (Y-E-N) 22017

Réseau express jeunes (R-E-J)

Pres Maison des Associations de Strasbourg, 1A Place des Orphelins, 67000 Strasbourg, France. T. +33388353745. E-mail: com@youthexpressnetwork.org.
URL: http://www.youthexpressnetwork.org/

History 1993, France. Registration: Start date: 1993, France. **Aims** Promote, sustain and encourage training and exchange of young people, youth/social workers, facilitators and trainers at European level; improve *living conditions* of young people from vulnerable groups; contribute to European training of young trainers and youth/social workers; communicate and sustain the aspirations of youth at international level. **Structure** General Assembly (annual); Board. **Languages** English, French. **Finance** Supported by: *Council of Europe (CE, #04881); European Commission (EC, #06633)*. **Activities** Events/meetings; networking/liaising; training/education. **Events** *Mind the Gap Seminar* Brcko (Bosnia-Herzegovina) 2015, *General Assembly* Milcoveni (Romania) 2015, *Light your Rights Seminar* Mollina (Spain) 2015, *General Assembly* Bulgaria 2014, *International seminar on ethno-religious tolerance as a prequisite for social work* Bulgaria 1996. **Publications** *ECHO* (2 a year) in English, French; *Yen-news* (2 a year). Annual Report; studies.
Members Members in 22 countries:
Armenia, Azerbaijan, Belarus, Belgium, Bosnia-Herzegovina, Bulgaria, Croatia, Cyprus, France, Georgia, Germany, Greece, Iceland, Italy, Kosovo, Netherlands, Romania, Russia, Spain, Sweden, Türkiye, Ukraine.
Consultative Status Consultative status granted from: *Council of Europe (CE, #04881)* (Participatory Status). **IGO Relations** Member of (1): *European Youth Centres (EYCs, #09138).* [2021.05.18/XF6194/F]

♦ Youth Forum of the European Union / see European Youth Forum (#09140)
♦ Youth Forum of the European Union (inactive)
♦ Youth Forum Jeunesse / see European Youth Forum (#09140)

♦ Youth for Habitat International Network (YFHIN) 22018

Contact Fulya Mah Mevlüt Pehlivan Sok Ali Sami Yen, Apt 8A/2, Mecidiyeköy, Istanbul/Istanbul, Türkiye. T. +902122757436 – +902122757498 – +902122755519. Fax +902122757436 – +902122757498.
URL: http://www.youthforhab.org.tr/

History Mar 1995. **Aims** Facilitate information exchange on issues related to Habitat Agenda and Agenda 21; raise awareness on these issues among the youth and develop their vision on their implementation. **Structure** Secretariat. Focal Point in every continent. **Staff** Voluntary. **Finance** Through projects. **Activities** Organizes: meetings; summer camps; working camps. **Events** *International conference* Eskisehir (Turkey) 1997, *Meeting* Eskisehir (Turkey) 1997. **Publications** *Platform* (4 a year) in Turkish – thematic magazine; *YFHIN Magazine* (2 a year) in English. Newsletters in Turkish.
Members Covers 46 countries:
Albania, Azerbaijan, Bangladesh, Belgium, Benin, Bulgaria, Cambodia, Cameroon, Canada, Croatia, Denmark, Egypt, Germany, Ghana, Greece, India, Indonesia, Italy, Jordan, Kenya, Lebanon, Mauritius, Mongolia, Nepal, New Zealand, Nicaragua, Nigeria, North Macedonia, Pakistan, Panama, Peru, Philippines, Portugal, Romania, Russia, Senegal, Serbia, Spain, Sri Lanka, Switzerland, Tanzania UR, Türkiye, UK, USA, Venezuela, Zambia.
IGO Relations Memorandum of Understanding signed with: *United Nations Human Settlements Programme (UN-Habitat, #20572)*. Partnership with: *UNDP (#20292)* (Country Office in Turkey). Formal contacts with: *UNEP (#20299)*. **NGO Relations** Member of: *Mediterranean Social-Ecological Youth Network (MARE, no recent information)*. Formal contacts with: *South East European Youth Council (SEEYC, no recent information).* [2008/XF4298/F]

♦ Youth for Human Rights International (YHRI) 22019

Jeunes pour les droits de l'homme international – Jóvenes por los Derechos Humanos Internacional – Jugend für Menschenrechte International – Gioventù per i Diritti Umani Internazionale

Pres 6331 Hollywood Blvd, Ste 720, Los Angeles CA 90028, USA. T. +13236635799. E-mail: info@youthforhumanrights.org.
URL: http://www.youthforhumanrights.org/

History Founded 2001. Registered in the State of California (USA). **Aims** Provide educational resources and activities that educate, inform, assist and unite individuals, educators, organizations and governmental bodies in dissemination and adoption of the Universal Declaration of Human Rights. **Structure** Board of Directors; Board of Advisors. **Languages** English. **Staff** Mainly voluntary. **Finance** Members' dues. Other sources: grants; corporate donations. **Activities** Training/education; events/meetings. **Publications** *Youth for Human Rights Newsletter*. Educational materials. **Members** Groups, clubs and chapters worldwide. Membership countries not specified. **NGO Relations** *Church of Scientology International (CSI, #03922).* [2018.10.12/XM3355/s/F]

♦ Youth Initiative for Sustainable Human Development in Africa (internationally oriented national body)
♦ **Youthlink** Pacific Youth Council (#18013)

♦ Youth with a Mission (YWAM) 22020

Jeunesse en mission – Juventud con una Misión – Jeugd met een Opdracht

Chairperson Highfield Oval, Ambrose Lane, Harpenden, AL5 4BX, UK. T. +441582463300. Fax +441582463305. E-mail: iy@ywam.org.
URL: http://www.ywam.org/

History 1960. A Christian mission organization. **Aims** Work for Christian training, humanitarian aid and community development. **Structure** Includes: *University of the Nations*. **Staff** 18000.00 FTE, voluntary. **Finance** YWAMers are individually supported financially by their local churches and individuals. Structure is decentralized so no global annual budget. **Events** *Forum – You make the difference* Brussels (Belgium) 1999, *International conference* Manila (Philippines) 1988. **Consultative Status** Consultative status granted from: *ECOSOC (#05331)* (Special). **IGO Relations** *UNHCR (#20327)*. **NGO Relations** Member of: *Accord Network; Conference of Non-Governmental Organizations in Consultative Relationship with the United Nations (CONGO, #04635); Evangelical Association of the Caribbean (EAC, #09210); Global Connections; Restored.* [2012.06.01/XF2784/F]

♦ Youth Movement for Democracy / see World Youth Movement for Democracy (#21957)

♦ Youth Network for Harm Reduction International 22021

Contact Canadian Foundation for Drug Policy, 70 MacDonald Street, Ottawa ON K2P 1H6, Canada. T. +16047624520. [2007/XM2062/**F**]

♦ Youth Orchestra of the Americas (YOA) 22022

Orchestre des jeunes des amériques – Orquesta Juvenil de las Américas – Orquesta de Jovens das Americas

Main Office 1001 Nineteenth St N, 16th Floor, Arlington VA 22209, USA. T. +17032360010. Fax +17032360011. E-mail: info@yoa.org.

URL: http://www.yoa.org/

History 4 Sep 2000. **Aims** Pursue musical excellence; develop young leaders with cross-cultural understanding; inspire a spirit of hemispheric unity. **Structure** Board of Directors. **Activities** Organizes tours.

Members Youth symphony orchestra in 22 countries:

Argentina, Bolivia, Brazil, Canada, Chile, Colombia, Costa Rica, Cuba, Dominican Rep, Ecuador, El Salvador, Guatemala, Honduras, Mexico, Nicaragua, Panama, Paraguay, Peru, Puerto Rico, Uruguay, USA, Venezuela. [2015/XM2207/**D**]

♦ Youth Organisations for Drug Action (YODA) 22023

Pres address not obtained. E-mail: contact@euro-yoda.org.

URL: http://euro-yoda.org/

History 2011. **Aims** Meet the needs of young activists and professionals who have been disenfranchised when it comes to determining drug policy but are amongst those most affected by drugs and drug laws. **Structure** Board of Advisors.

Members Organizations in 16 countries:

Albania, Belgium, Bosnia-Herzegovina, Czechia, Hungary, Italy, Kosovo, Montenegro, North Macedonia, Poland, Portugal, Romania, Russia, Serbia, Slovakia, UK.

Consultative Status Consultative status granted from: *ECOSOC (#05331)* (Special). **NGO Relations** Member of: *Civil Society Forum on Drugs (CSFD, #03968).* [2022/XM6717/**D**]

♦ Youth Peer Education Network (unconfirmed)

♦ Youth For Public Transport (Y4PT) 22024

Co-Founder Rue Sainte-Marie 6, 1080 Sint-Jans-Molenbeek, Belgium. T. +3226636629 – +3226736100. Fax +3226601072. E-mail: contact@y4pt.org.

Main Website: http://www.y4pt.org/

History 11 Jun 2009, Vienna (Austria). Founded 11 Jun 2009, on decision of the UITP Policy Board, 25 Nov 2005, Amman (Jordan). *International Association of Public Transport (#12118)* acts as "Parent Organization"; sustained by *'Ferrovie Nord Minalo (FNM)'*, acting as Honorary Founding Member. *Y4PT Foundation* created on decision of UITP Policy Board, 24 Oct 2012, London (UK); officially launched 27 May 2013, Geneva (Switzerland). Registration: Banque-Carrefour des Entreprises, Start date: 21 Mar 2013, Belgium, Brussels. **Aims** Build better means and modes of transport from a *youth* approach to contribute to *sustainable* mobility around the world. **Structure** Board of Directors (BOD). **Languages** Dutch, English, French, German, Spanish. **Staff** 1.00 FTE, paid. **Finance** Sources: contributions; donations; fundraising; gifts, legacies; government support; grants; in-kind support; international organizations; private foundations; sponsorship; subsidies. Funding from: *International Association of Public Transport (#12118)*; Roads and Transport Authority of the Emirate of Dubai (RTA Dubai). **Activities** Advocacy/lobbying/activism; awareness raising; capacity building; events/meetings; guidance/assistance/consulting; knowledge management/information dissemination; networking/liaising; projects/programmes; publishing activities; training/education. **Events** *Global Transport Hackathon Summit* Montréal, QC (Canada) 2017, *World Youth Meeting* Milan (Italy) 2015, *World Youth Meeting* Dubai (United Arab Emirates) 2014, *World Youth Meeting* Geneva (Switzerland) 2013, *World Youth Meeting* Dubai (United Arab Emirates) 2011. **Publications** *Public Transport Options for Youth with Disabilities: A Review of Needs, Challenges and Initiatives* (2012).

Members Chapters in 33 countries and territories:

Australia, Austria, Bahrain, Belgium, Bolivia, Brazil, Canada, China, Colombia, El Salvador, Finland, France, Germany, Greece, India, Iran Islamic Rep, Italy, Kuwait, Lebanon, Mexico, Nepal, Netherlands, Oman, Pakistan, Panama, Qatar, Russia, South Africa, Spain, Taiwan, Türkiye, UK, United Arab Emirates. [2022.06.02/XJ7379/**F**]

♦ Youth RISE 22025

Exec Dir 5th Floor, 124-128 City Road, London, EC1V 2NJ, UK. T. +442073242997. E-mail: info@youthrise.org.

URL: http://youthrise.org/

History Set up 2006, Vancouver BC (Canada), at conference of *Harm Reduction International (HRI, #10861)*. RISE stands for *Resource – Information – Support – Education.* **Aims** Promote evidence based *drug* policies and harm reduction strategies with the involvement of young people who use drugs and are affected by drug policies. **Structure** Board of Directors. Secretariat. International Working Group. **Activities** Training/education; advocacy/lobbying/activism; politics/policy/regulatory; research/documentation. **NGO Relations** Member of: *International Drug Policy Consortium (IDPC, #13205).* Participates in: *HIV Young Leaders Fund (HYLF, no recent information).* [2014/XJ8551/**F**]

♦ Youth for Road Safety (YOURS) 22026

CEO Jan van Riebeeckstraat 132, 4105 BD Culemborg, Netherlands. E-mail: info@youthforroadsafety.org.

URL: http://www.youthforroadsafety.org/

History 2010, following the creation of an informal network in response to the 2007 UN World Youth Assembly for Road Safety. **Aims** Keep young people safe on the world's roads. **IGO Relations** *WHO (#20950).* **NGO Relations** Partner of: *Partnership on Sustainable, Low Carbon Transport Foundation (SLoCaT Foundation, #18244).* [2011/XM3884/**E**]

♦ Youth Section of European Community Regional Secretariat of the World Federation of the Deaf / see European Union of Deaf Youth (#08986)
♦ Youth Service Camps / see Concordia
♦ Youth Service Volunteers / see Concordia
♦ Youth Society for Peace and Development of the Balkans (internationally oriented national body)
♦ Youth Substance Abuse Prevention Foundation / see Mentor International (#16716)
♦ Youth for a Sustainable Future Pacifika / see Pacifika Youth
♦ Youth for Technology Foundation (internationally oriented national body)
♦ Youth Third World (internationally oriented national body)
♦ Youth of the Third World (internationally oriented national body)
♦ Youth Time International Movement (unconfirmed)
♦ Youth for Transparency International (internationally oriented national body)
♦ Youth of the UN (internationally oriented national body)

♦ Youth for Understanding (YFU) 22027

Global Office Avenue Ernest Cambier 161, 1030 Brussels, Belgium. T. +3226484790.

URL: http://www.yfu.org/

History Founded 1951, Ann Arbor MI (USA), by Dr Rachel Andresen. Previously also referred to as *Youth for Understanding International Exchange (YFU)* and *Youth for Understanding International Educational Services (YFU IES).* **Aims** Through international homestay exchange programs allowing personal host family experience, open students and host families to new ways of seeing and thinking about their world and promote respect for cultural diversity, friendship among nations and opportunities for personal development; help prepare young people to take their place in changing worldwide community; provide on-going education in cross-cultural issues to students, alumni and volunteers during and after the exchange experience. **Structure** International Board. Regional coordinating organizations (3): *Asociación Latinoamericana – Youth for Understanding; European Educational Exchanges – Youth for Understanding (EEE-YFU, #06965); Asia-Pacific Exchanges – Youth For Understanding.* Global Office, located in Washington DC (USA). **Languages** Chinese, Dutch, English, English, French, German, Japanese, Portuguese, Spanish. **Staff** 500.00 FTE, paid; 12000.00 FTE, voluntary. **Finance** Main source: participants' program fees. Other sources: public sector grants, contracts and scholarships; private scholarships and gifts. **Activities** Training/education; networking/liaising; events/meetings. **Events** *International conference* Washington, DC (USA) 1996. **Publications** *Agreement on International Cooperation and Consensus Building; Guidelines for International Contingency and Development Fund; Guidelines for New YFU Programs; International Basic Standards for Educational Exchanges; World Traveler Handbook.*

Members National Committees (" indicates in development) in 55 countries:

Argentina, Australia, Austria, Azerbaijan (*), Belarus, Belgium (2), Brazil, Bulgaria, Canada, Chile, China, Colombia, Czechia, Denmark, Ecuador, Estonia, Finland, France, Georgia, Germany, Ghana, Greece, Hungary, India, Indonesia (*), Italy (*), Japan, Kazakhstan, Korea Rep, Latvia, Liberia (*), Lithuania, Mexico, Moldova, Mongolia, Netherlands, New Zealand, Norway, Paraguay, Philippines, Poland, Romania, Russia, Slovakia, South Africa, Sweden, Switzerland, Thailand, Türkiye, UK, Ukraine, Uruguay, USA, Venezuela, Vietnam.

IGO Relations *European Commission (EC, #06633); European Youth Centres (EYCs, #09138).* **NGO Relations** Member of: *Council on Standards for International Educational Travel (CSIET); UNITED for Intercultural Action – European Network Against Nationalism, Racism, Fascism and in Support of Migrants and Refugees (UNITED, #20511).* [2020/XF1545/**F**]

♦ Youth for Understanding Intercultural Exchange Programs / see Youth for Understanding (#22027)
♦ Youth for Understanding International Educational Services / see Youth for Understanding (#22027)
♦ Youth for Understanding International Exchange / see Youth for Understanding (#22027)

♦ Youth and United Nations Global Alliance (YUNGA) 22028

Coordinator FAO, Viale delle Terme di Caracalla, 00153 Rome RM, Italy. T. +39657050234. E-mail: yunga@fao.org.

URL: http://www.fao.org/yunga/

History Founded 2009. **Aims** Generate collaborative initiatives on matters of social and environmental importance between United Nations agencies and other organizations and civil society organizations working with children and young people, by providing resources and opportunities that give children and young people the opportunity to learn, get involved and make a difference. **Structure** Secretariat, hosted by *FAO (#09260).* **Languages** Arabic, Chinese, English, French, Italian, Russian, Spanish. **Staff** 2.00 FTE, paid; 1.00 FTE, voluntary. **Finance** Funding from country driven programmes. **Activities** Projects/programmes; awareness raising; training/education; capacity building; events/meetings; publishing activities. **Publications** *YUNGA Newsletter.* Guides; challenge badges; education guides.

Members UN agencies; civil society organizations; government institutions; youth groups. Collaborators include:

Bioversity International (#03262); Convention on Biological Diversity (Biodiversity convention, 1992); FAO (#09260); International Bank for Reconstruction and Development (IBRD, #12317); UNEP (#20299); UNESCO (#20322); UNICEF (#20332); United Nations Framework Convention on Climate Change (UNFCCC, 1992); UN-Water (#20723); World Association of Girl Guides and Girl Scouts (WAGGGS, #21142); World Food Programme (WFP, #21510); World Meteorological Organization (WMO, #21649); World Organization of the Scout Movement (WOSM, #21693); World Wide Fund for Nature (WWF, #21922); Young Professionals for Agricultural Development (YPARD, #21996).

IGO Relations Works with a number of UN agencies, including: *Secretariat of the United Nations Convention to Combat Desertification (Secretariat of the UNCCD, #19208); UNEP (#20299); UNICEF (#20332); United Nations Framework Convention on Climate Change – Secretariat (UNFCCC, #20564); WHO (#20950); World Food Programme (WFP, #21510); World Meteorological Organization (WMO, #21649).* **NGO Relations** Main partners include: *World Association of Girl Guides and Girl Scouts (WAGGGS, #21142); World Organization of the Scout Movement (WOSM, #21693).* Works with a large number of organizations at international, regional and national levels. [2020.01.03/XJ5543/y/**E**]

♦ Youth for a United World (see: #09806)
♦ Youth for Unity and Voluntary Action (internationally oriented national body)
♦ **YPARD** Young Professionals for Agricultural Development (#21996)
♦ Y-PEER – Youth Peer Education Network (unconfirmed)
♦ YPE – Young Pirates of Europe (unconfirmed)
♦ **YPFP** Young Professionals in Foreign Policy (#21997)
♦ **YPLF** Young Property Lawyers' Forum (#21998)
♦ YPO – Young Presidents' Organization (internationally oriented national body)
♦ YPSI for ALGAE / see Young Phycological Society International (#21995)
♦ **YPSI** Young Phycological Society International (#21995)
♦ YPWC – Young People We Care (internationally oriented national body)
♦ **YRE** Youth against Racism in Europe (#22003)
♦ YRF – Yoga Research Foundation (internationally oriented national body)
♦ **YSI** YoungShip International (#21999)
♦ YSPDB – Youth Society for Peace and Development of the Balkans (internationally oriented national body)
♦ YTF – Youth for Technology Foundation (internationally oriented national body)
♦ YTI – Youth for Transparency International (internationally oriented national body)
♦ YTM – Young Topologists Meeting (meeting series)
♦ YT – Youth Time International Movement (unconfirmed)
♦ Yunesuko Ajia Bunka Senta / see Asia/Pacific Cultural Centre for UNESCO (#01879)
♦ **YUNGA** Youth and United Nations Global Alliance (#22028)
♦ YUVA – Youth for Unity and Voluntary Action (internationally oriented national body)
♦ YUW – Youth for a United World (see: #09806)
♦ Yves Rocher Fondation (internationally oriented national body)
♦ Yves Rocher Foundation (internationally oriented national body)
♦ **YWAM** Youth with a Mission (#22020)
♦ **YWCA mondiale** Alliance mondiale des unions chrétiennes féminines (#21947)
♦ **YWCA mundial** Asociación Cristiana Femenina Mundial (#21947)
♦ YWCA's European Committee / see European Young Women's Christian Association (#09135)
♦ Zahnärztlicher Verbindungs-Ausschuss zur EU / see Council of European Dentists (#04886)
♦ Zahnärztlicher Verbindungs-Ausschuss der EWG / see Council of European Dentists (#04886)
♦ Zaidan Hojin / Kokusai Kaihatsu Kyuen Zaidan (internationally oriented national body)
♦ Zainab Arabian Research Society for Multidisciplinary Issues (unconfirmed)
♦ Zakon Swietego Pawla Pierwszego Pustelnika (religious order)

♦ ZaMir Transnational Net 22029

Address not obtained.

History 1992, as an electronic mail network. **Aims** Help *peace*-oriented people and groups, *humanitarian* organizations, NGOs and the independent media in order to improve their communication possibilities. Serve people working for: prevention of warfare; elimination of militarism; protection of the environment; advancement of human rights and rights of peoples regardless of race, ethnic background, sex or religion or political convictions; achievement of social and economic justice; women's rights; elimination of poverty; promotion of sustainable and equitable development; more and better democratic structures in society, especially the advancement of participatory democracy; nonviolent *conflict resolution.* **Structure** Network of Systems (6): ZAMIR-ZG (Zagreb); ZAMIR-BG (Belgrade); ZAMIR-LJ (Ljubljana); ZAMIR-SA (Sarajevo); ZAMIR-PR (Pristina); ZAMIR-TZ (Tuzla). **Finance** Donations from various supporter. **Activities** Electronic mail and news systems exchange of public and private messages with each other and with other networks in Europe and worldwide several times daily. Organizes conferences/newsgroups.

Members in 4 countries:

Bosnia-Herzegovina, Croatia, Serbia, Slovenia. [2011/XF3729/**F**]

♦ Zangger Committee (ZC) 22030

Sec UK Permanent Mission to the UN in Vienna, Jauresgasse 12, 1030 Vienna, Austria. T. +431716132209. Fax +431716134900. E-mail: zangger@britishembassy.at.

Chair Danish Permanent Mission to the UN in Vienna, Führichgasse 6, 1010 Vienna, Austria. T. +4315127904.

URL: http://www.zanggercommittee.org/

History 1971. Established in response to the *Treaty on the Non-proliferation of Nuclear Weapons (NPT, 1968).* Named in honour of its first chairman Claude Zangger. Former names and other names: *NPT Exporters Committee* – former; *Nuclear Exporters Committee* – former. **Aims** Clarify and interpret the implications of Article III2 of the Treaty on *Non-Proliferation.* **Structure** An informal committee. Officers: Chair; Secretary. **Languages** English. **Staff** 0.50 FTE, paid. **Finance** Sources: none. **Activities** Events/meetings. **Events** *Annual Meeting* Vienna (Austria) 2019, *Annual Meeting* Vienna (Austria) 2018, *Annual Meeting* Vienna (Austria) 2017, *Annual Meeting* Vienna (Austria) 2016, *Annual Meeting* Vienna (Austria) 2015.
Members Governments of 39 countries:
Argentina, Australia, Austria, Belarus, Belgium, Bulgaria, Canada, China, Croatia, Czechia, Denmark, Finland, France, Germany, Greece, Hungary, Ireland, Italy, Japan, Kazakhstan, Korea Rep, Luxembourg, Netherlands, New Zealand, Norway, Poland, Portugal, Romania, Russia, Slovakia, Slovenia, South Africa, Spain, Sweden, Switzerland, Türkiye, UK, Ukraine, USA.
Observer:
European Union (EU, #08967).
IGO Relations Invited to attend meetings of *Nuclear Suppliers Group (NSG, #17621).*
[2022.12.05/XE3729/**E***]

- ZARSMI – Zainab Arabian Research Society for Multidisciplinary Issues (unconfirmed)
- ZASB – Zentrum für Afrikastudien, Basel (internationally oriented national body)
- Zasobovacia Agentúra Euratomu (#05617)
- Zasobovací Agentura Euratomu (#05617)
- Zayed Bin Sultan Al Nahayan Charitable and Humanitarian Foundation (internationally oriented national body)
- ZCP – Zona de Comércio Preferencial para os Estados da Africa Oriental e Austral (inactive)
- **ZC** Zangger Committee (#22030)
- ZDA – Zinc Development Association (inactive)
- **ZDHC Foundation** Stichting ZDHC Foundation (#19987)
- Zdruzenje Kulturno Pomembnih Evropskih Pokopalisc (#02915)
- Zdruzenje Okoljevarstvenikov za Jedrsko Energijo (internationally oriented national body)
- ZEB / see Tourism Watch
- ZEB Fachstelle Ferntourismus / see Tourism Watch
- ZEB/FFT / see Tourism Watch
- ZEB Third World Tourism Desk / see Tourism Watch
- ZEFAD ' / see Children's Rights Advocacy and Lobby Mission – Africa
- ZEFAW – Zentrum für Forschung zur Arabischen Welt (internationally oriented national body)
- ZEF – Center for Development Research, Bonn (internationally oriented national body)

♦ Zeitz Foundation for Intercultural Ecosphere Safety (Zeitz Foundation) 22031

Sec PO Box 63901 – 00619, Nairobi, Kenya. T. +254729809764. E-mail: info@zeitzfoundation.org.
Germany c/o UBS Europe SE, Bockenheimer Landstr 2-4, 60306 Frankfurt-Main, Germany.
URL: http://www.zeitzfoundation.org/
History 2008, Germany, by Jochen Zeitz. Registered as a charity in Germany (2008), Kenya (2011) and UK (2013). **Aims** Create and support sustainable, *ecologically* and socially responsible projects and destinations around the world to achieve long-lasting impact and sustainability through the holistic balance of conservation, community, culture and commerce in privately managed areas. **Activities** Projects/programmes. **NGO Relations** Instrumental in setting up: *The Long Run.* [2017/XM5933/f/**F**]

- **Zeitz Foundation** Zeitz Foundation for Intercultural Ecosphere Safety (#22031)
- ZEI – Zentrum für Europäische Integrationsforschung (internationally oriented national body)
- **ZEMCH** Zero Energy Mass Custom Home Network (#22034)
- Zene u crnom (#20987)
- Zen Peacemakers (internationally oriented national body)
- Zentralausschuss der Waldbesitzerverbände der EG / see Confederation of European Forest Owners (#04525)
- Zentrale Verwaltungsstelle für die Soziale Sicherheit der Rheinschiffer (#00116)
- Zentralinstitut für Lateinamerika-Studien, Eichstätt (internationally oriented national body)
- Zentralinstitut für Mittel- und Osteuropastudien (internationally oriented national body)
- Zentralkommission für die Rheinschifffahrt (#03687)
- Zentralrat der Nordischen Grossistenverbände (inactive)
- Zentralverband der Berufsverbände der Kartoffelstärkeindustrie der EWG / see Union des féculeries de pommes de terre de l'Union europeénne (#20406)
- Zentralverband der Europäischen Holzindustrie (#04545)
- Zentralverband der Europäischen Waldbesitzer (#04525)
- Zentralverband des Rohstoffwarenhandels (no recent information)
- Zentralverband der Stiftungs-Gesellschaften für die Weltgesundheit (inactive)
- Zentralverband der Tiefkühlkosthersteller in der EWG (inactive)
- Zentrum für Afrikastudien, Basel (internationally oriented national body)
- Zentrum für Entwicklungsforschung (internationally oriented national body)
- Zentrum für Europäische Integrationsforschung (internationally oriented national body)
- Zentrum des Europäischen Einzelhandels (inactive)
- Zentrum für Europäische Studien, Trier (internationally oriented national body)
- Zentrum für Europäische Wirtschaftforschung / see ZEW – Leibniz-Zentrum für Europäische Wirtschaftsforschung
- Zentrum für Forschung zur Arabischen Welt (internationally oriented national body)
- Zentrum für Information, Beratung und Bildung Berufe in der Internationalen Zusammenarbeit und Humanitären Hilfe (internationally oriented national body)
- Zentrum für Internationale Friedenseinsätze (internationally oriented national body)
- Zentrum der Internationalen Verbände (internationally oriented national body)
- Zentrum für Internationale Studien, Zürich / see Center for Comparative and International Studies
- Zentrum für Konfliktforschung, Marburg (internationally oriented national body)
- Zentrum für Marine Tropenökologie / see Leibniz Centre for Tropical Marine Ecology
- Zentrum für OSZE-Forschung (internationally oriented national body)
- Zentrum für Wissenschaftliche Kommunikation mit Ibero-America (internationally oriented national body)
- Zentrum für Wissenschaftliche Zusammenarbeit in der Tabakforschung (#03735)
- **ZEP-RE** PTA Reinsurance Company (#18561)
- ZEP / see Zero Emissions Platform (#22032)
- **ZEP** Zero Emissions Platform (#22032)
- ZEP – Zone d'échanges préférentiels des Etats de l'Afrique de l'est et l'Afrique australe (inactive)
- **ZERI** Zero Emissions Research Initiatives (#22033)

♦ Zero Emissions Platform (ZEP) 22032

EU Dir c/o CCSA, Rue de la Science 14b (room 205), 1050 Brussels, Belgium.
Contact Square de Meeus 37, 4th floor, 1000 Brussels, Belgium. T. +31703283574. E-mail: media@zeroemissionsplatform.eu.
URL: https://zeroemissionsplatform.eu/
History 2005. Former names and other names: *European Technology Platform for Zero Emission Fossil Fuel Power Plants (ZEP)* – former; *European Zero Emissions Technology & Innovation Platform* – full title. **Aims** Enable *CO2* capture and storage (CCS) as key technology for combating *climate change*; make CCS technology commercially viable by 2020 via an EU-backed demonstration programme; accelerate research and development into next-generation CCS technology and its wide deployment post-2020. **Structure** Government Group; Advisory Council; Advisory Council Executive Committee. Secretariat, provided by *Carbon Capture and Storage Association (CCSA).* **Activities** Events/meetings; guidance/assistance/consulting. **Events** *General Assembly* Brussels (Belgium) 2011, *Meeting* Berlin (Germany) 2010, *General Assembly* Brussels (Belgium) 2010. **Publications** Reports.
Members Companies; governments; NGOs; Academia and Research. Governments (2):
Netherlands, Spain.
NGOs (2):
Bellona; *E3G – Third Generation Environmentalism.*
Academia and Research institutes (7) in 6 countries:
France, Greece, Netherlands, Norway, Romania, Spain. [2022/XJ4626/**F**]

♦ Zero Emissions Research Initiatives (ZERI) 22033

Headquarters 2-18-9 Komachi, Kamakura KANAGAWA, 248 Japan. E-mail: info@zeri.org.
URL: http://www.zeri.org/
History 6 Apr 1994, by Gunter Pauli, under the guidance of the then rector of *United Nations University (UNU, #20642)*, at *UNU Institute of Advanced Studies (UNU/IAS, inactive).* Eventually led to creation of *ZERI Foundation.* **Aims** Serve as a network of scientists and vigorous operators to find innovative solutions to pressing problems of our time, responding to basic needs for all in terms of water, food, housing, health, energy, jobs, ethics and education, with what is locally available using a systems approach and viewing waste as a resource. **Structure** World Congress. Decentralized, operating as networks. **Languages** Chinese, Croatian, English, French, German, Japanese, Portuguese, Spanish, Swedish. **Finance** Independently financed. **Activities** Research and development; projects/programmes; training/education; publishing activities; events/meetings. **Events** *Annual World Congress on Zero Emissions* Paris (France) 2018, *Annual World Congress on Zero Emissions* Surabaya (Indonesia) 2015, *Annual World Congress on Zero Emissions* Madrid (Spain) 2013, *Annual World Congress on Zero Emissions* Honolulu, HI (USA) 2010, *Annual World Congress on Zero Emissions* Tokyo (Japan) 2004. **Publications** *The Third Dimension: An Innovative Business Strategy that Surfs on 12 Transformational, Unstoppable Trends* (2017); *The Blue Economy 2.0* (2015) by G Pauli; *Breakthroughs* (1996) by G Pauli; *Steering Business Toward Sustainability* (1995) by F Capra and G Pauli.
Members Full in 48 countries and territories:
Argentina, Australia, Belgium, Benin, Bhutan, Bolivia, Bonaire Is, Brazil, Canada, Chile, China, Colombia, Croatia, Curaçao, Ecuador, Fiji, France, Germany, Ghana, Hungary, India, Indonesia, Italy, Japan, Kenya, Mauritania, Mexico, Mongolia, Namibia, Netherlands, Nigeria, Paraguay, Peru, Portugal, Romania, Senegal, Serbia, Seychelles, South Africa, Spain, Suriname, Sweden, Taiwan, Tanzania UR, Togo, UK, USA, Zimbabwe. [2020.03.05/XK1323/f/**E**]

♦ Zero Energy Mass Custom Home Network (ZEMCH) 22034

Founding Coordinator address not obtained. E-mail: info@zemch.org.
URL: http://www.zemch.org/
History 2010. Founded following international study tours organized since 2006. **Aims** Enhance industry-academia R&D collaborations on the delivery of zero energy mass custom homes in developed and developing countries. **Activities** Events/meetings. **Events** *ZEMCH International Conference* Seoul (Korea Rep) 2019. **Publications** *ZEMCH International Conference Proceedings* (12 a year) in English. [2021.09.12/AA0229/**E**]

- Zero Population Growth / see Population Connection
- Zero Suicide International (unconfirmed)

♦ Zero Waste Europe 22035

Main Office Chsee Vleurgat 15, 1050 Brussels, Belgium. E-mail: hello@zerowasteeurope.eu.
URL: https://zerowasteeurope.eu/
History Informal meetings organized since 2011. Registration: EU Transparency Register, No/ID: 47806848200-34; Start date: Dec 2013, Netherlands. **Aims** Empower communities and change agents from around Europe to redesign their relationship with *resources*, and adopt smarter lifestyles and sustainable consumption patterns in line with "circular" resource management. **Structure** Scientific Committee; Board. **Activities** Advocacy/lobbying/activism; projects/programmes.
Members Full in 23 countries:
Albania, Austria, Belarus, Bulgaria, Croatia, Cyprus, Czechia, France, Germany, Greece, Hungary, Ireland, Italy, Lithuania, Montenegro, North Macedonia, Poland, Portugal, Romania, Slovenia, Spain, Switzerland, UK.
Consultative Status Consultative status granted from: *UNEP (#20299).* [2021/XM8992/**D**]

- Zero Waste International Alliance (unconfirmed)
- Zero Waste MENA (unconfirmed)
- ZeS – Zentrum für Europäische Studien, Trier (internationally oriented national body)
- Zeulia Family Alliance for Development / see Children's Rights Advocacy and Lobby Mission – Africa
- ZEVA – Symposium of the Central and Eastern European Chambers of Physicians (meeting series)
- ZEW / see ZEW – Leibniz-Zentrum für Europäische Wirtschaftsforschung
- ZEW – Leibniz Centre for European Economic Research (internationally oriented national body)
- ZEW – Leibniz-Zentrum für Europäische Wirtschaftsforschung (internationally oriented national body)
- ZFD – Ziviler Friedensdienst (internationally oriented national body)
- Zgromadzenie Braci Slug Maryi Niepokalanej (religious order)
- Zgromadzenie Sióstr od Aniolów (religious order)
- Zgromadzenie Sw Michala Archaniola (religious order)
- Zhu – South Centre / see Nansen-Zhu International Research Centre
- **ZIA** Zircon Industry Association (#22036)
- Ziemelu Investiciju Banka (#17327)
- ZIF – Zentrum für Internationale Friedenseinsätze (internationally oriented national body)
- ZigBee Alliance (internationally oriented national body)
- ZILAS – Zentralinstitut für Lateinamerika-Studien, Eichstätt (internationally oriented national body)
- Zimbabwe Institute of Development Studies, Harare / see Institute of Development Studies, Harare
- **Zimmerman Society** Pan-American Society of Ocular Pathology – Lorenz E Zimmerman (#18131)
- Zimmerwald Association (inactive)
- ZIMOS – Zentralinstitut für Mittel- und Osteuropastudien (internationally oriented national body)
- Zinc Development Association (inactive)
- Zinc Oxide Producers Association (inactive)
- Zionist Organization of America (internationally oriented national body)
- Zion's Watch Tower Tract Society / see Jehovah's Witnesses (#16096)

♦ Zircon Industry Association (ZIA) 22036

Registered Address 24 Old Bond Street, Mayfair, London, W1S 4AP, UK. E-mail: enquiries@zircon-association.org – info@zircon-association.org.
URL: https://www.zircon-association.org/
History Registration: Companies House, No/ID: 08187233, Start date: 21 Aug 2012, England. **Aims** Represent and support the interests of the zircon, zirconia and zirconium value chains. **Structure** General Assembly; Board of Directors; Secretariat. Committees (3): Technical; Communications; Environment, Social & Governance. **Activities** Events/meetings; knowledge management/information dissemination. **Events** *Annual Zircon Conference* Dubai (United Arab Emirates) 2019.
Members Producer members in 4 countries:
Australia, Ireland, South Africa, UK.
Consumer members in 7 countries and territories:
Brazil, China, Germany, Hong Kong, Spain, UK, USA.
Associate in 7 countries and territories:
Australia, Canada, Hong Kong, Japan, Malaysia, UK, USA. [2021.06.15/AA1234/t/**C**]

- Zisterzienserorden (religious order)
- Ziviler Friedensdienst (internationally oriented national body)
- Zjednoczony Instytut Badan Jadrowych / see Joint Institute for Nuclear Research (#16134)
- **ZKR** Zentralkommission für die Rheinschifffahrt (#03687)
- **ZMAO** Zone monétaire de l'Afrique de l'ouest (#20889)
- ZMB / see Union of the Baltic Cities (#20366)
- Zmluva o Ustavi za Evropo (2004 treaty)
- ZNF – Carl Friedrich von Weizsäcker-Zentrum für Naturwissenschaft und Friedensforschung (internationally oriented national body)
- ZOA (internationally oriented national body)
- ZOA Refugee Care Netherlands / see ZOA
- ZOA Vluchtelingenzorg / see ZOA
- Zoï Environment Network (internationally oriented national body)

♦ Zollverein (inactive)
♦ Zona de Comércio Preferencial para os Estados da Africa Oriental e Austral (inactive)
♦ Zone d'échanges préférentiels des Etats de l'Afrique de l'est et l'Afrique australe (inactive)

♦ Zone franc 22037

Franc Zone

Contact c/o Banque de France, Service de la Zone franc, 48 rue Croix des Petits Champs, 75001 Paris, France. T. +33142924292.
URL: http://www.banque-france.fr/

History 9 Sep 1939.
'Colonial Period': the France Zone existed, de facto but without that title, before World War II. The French franc was the currency of the French colonies up to the middle of the 19th century, from which time France organized progressively the issuing of currency by private banks *'in situ'* to take account of local credit requirements. These banks, which included *Banque de l'Indochine (inactive)* and *Banque de l'Afrique occidentale (inactive)*, were under the overall control of the French administration. At the end of World War I, mechanisms were put in place to allow parity of exchange between bank notes issued by the Bank of France and those issued in the colonies.
'Formal Establishment' The existence of the Franc Zone was made official at the outbreak of World War II, when measures such as the non-convertibility of the French franc and exchange controls made it necessary to exclude Franc Zone countries from such requirements.
'Creation of the CFA franc' (franc des colonies françaises d'Afrique) – on 25 Dec 1945. Parity was fixed at 1.7; this increased to 2.0 in Oct 1998 and to 0.02 in 1960 (in line with the new French franc). It then remained unchanged until devaluation on 11 Jan 1994, from which time parity is 0.01. The *'Caisse centrale de la France libre'*, set up in 1941, London (UK), and later to evolve into the *'Caisse centrale de Coopération économique (CCCE)'*, currently *Agence française de développement (AFD)*, issued bank notes for Equatorial Africa and the Cameroun, but for many countries responsibility was gradually transferred to nationalized banks of the countries concerned.
'Regional Institutions' In Apr 1959, newly independent states in Africa set up regional banks of their own: *Banque centrale des Etats de l'Afrique de l'Ouest (BCEAO, #03167)* and *Banque centrale des Etats de l'Afrique équatoriale et du Cameroun (BCEAC, inactive)*. The official name for the CFA franc in the countries of BCEAO – *Communauté financière africaine (CFA, #04377)* – became 'franc de la Communauté financière africaine', while for BCEAC countries it became 'franc de la Coopération financière en Afrique centrale, but the value of the two CFA francs was the same. BCEAO founding countries united in *Union monétaire Ouest africaine (UMOA, inactive)* on 12 May 1962.
'Agreements with the Government of France on Monetary Cooperation' 1972-1973. These agreements extended the area of authority of the central banks in the Franc Zone. BCEAC was replaced by *Banque des Etats de l'Afrique centrale (BEAC, #03169)* on 23 Nov 1972, and a new agreement was signed with the French government. On 14 Nov 1973, the countries of UMOA (no longer including Mauritania) set up *Banque ouest africaine de développement (BOAD, #03170)* and an agreement with France was signed on 4 Dec 1973. These agreements (still in force) reduced the French influence on the Banks and allowed them to participate more actively in the development of member countries. Their headquarters moved to African capitals.
'Recent Developments' The treaty setting up *Union économique et monétaire Ouest africaine (UEMOA, #20377)*, signed in 1994, completed that of UMOA, and BCEAO and BOAD became specialized autonomous institutions of UEMOA. A similar scheme was completed for countries of *Communauté économique et monétaire d'Afrique centrale (CEMAC, #04374)*, 1999. These countries are collectively referred to as *Pays africains de la Zone franc (PAZF, #18270)*.
Structure Not an organization but an administrative zone. Since 1964, *Conférence des ministres des finances des pays de la Zone franc (#04633)* meets twice a year to survey matters of common interest, usually in spring in the capital of an African country and in September in Paris (France). *Comité monétaire de la Zone franc (#04193)*, set up 5 Feb 1952, Paris, by French ministerial decree, now exists only in theory but there is no official text expressly disbanding the Committee. *Economic and Statistical Observatory for Sub-Saharan Africa (AFRISTAT, #05321)*, set up 21 Sep 1993, Abidjan (Côte d'Ivoire), assists in developing economic, social and environmental statistics in Franc Zone countries. **Finance** All countries and groups of the Zone have currencies linked with the French franc at a fixed rate of exchange and agree to hold their reserves mainly in the form of French francs on a specific account opened in the books of the French Treasury.
Members Countries of the Franc Zone (" – includes Mayotte, St Pierre-Miquelon and the Overseas Departments and Territories) include all countries previously constituting French West and Equatorial Africa (except Guinea and Mauritania) and also (since Jan 1985) Equatorial Guinea, previously a Spanish colony. In total, 16 countries:
Benin, Burkina Faso, Cameroon, Central African Rep, Chad, Comoros, Congo Brazzaville, Côte d'Ivoire, Equatorial Guinea, France (*), Gabon, Guinea-Bissau, Mali, Niger, Senegal, Togo. [2009.11.03/XF4920/**F***]

♦ Zone monétaire de l'Afrique de l'ouest (#20889)
♦ Zone monétaire centrafricaine / see Union monétaire de l'Afrique centrale (#20463)
♦ Zone monétaire centrafricaine / see Communauté économique et monétaire d'Afrique centrale (#04374)
♦ Zone monétaire commune / see Multilateral Monetary Area (#16889)
♦ Zone pastorale d'Océan Indien / see Conférence épiscopale de l'Océan Indien (#04592)

♦ Zonta International 22038

Contact 1200 Harger Rd, Ste 330, Oak Brook IL 60523, USA. T. +16309281400. Fax +16309281559. E-mail: zontaintl@zonta.org.
URL: https://www.zonta.org/

History 8 Nov 1919, Buffalo, NY (USA). Became international in 1927. **Aims** Empower *women* worldwide through service and advocacy. **Structure** Convention (every 2 years); International Board of Directors; Standing Committees; Zonta Foundation for Women. **Languages** English. **Staff** 14.00 FTE, paid. **Finance** Sources: contributions; members' dues; private foundations. **Activities** Advocacy/lobbying/activism; awards/prizes/competitions; events/meetings; financial and/or material support; projects/programmes. **Events** *District 13 Conference* Egersund (Norway) 2021, *District 13 Conference* Copenhagen (Denmark) 2019, *District 26 Conference* Kitakyushu (Japan) 2019, *Biennial Convention* Yokohama (Japan) 2018, *European Seminar* Vienna (Austria) 2017. **Publications** *The Zontian* (2 a year). Annual Report; guides; handbooks; pamphlets.
Members Clubs (about 1,100) totaling over 28,000 members in 64 countries and territories:
Australia, Austria, Bahamas, Bangladesh, Belgium, Benin, Bulgaria, Burkina Faso, Canada, Chile, Côte d'Ivoire, Croatia, Cyprus, Denmark, England, Estonia, Finland, France, Germany, Ghana, Greece, Hong Kong, Hungary, Iceland, India, Italy, Japan, Korea Rep, Latvia, Lebanon, Liechtenstein, Lithuania, Luxembourg, Macau, Malaysia, Monaco, Mongolia, Nepal, Netherlands, New Zealand, Nigeria, North Macedonia, Norway, Philippines, Poland, Puerto Rico, Romania, Russia, Senegal, Sierra Leone, Singapore, Spain, Sri Lanka, Sweden, Switzerland, Taiwan, Thailand, Togo, Türkiye, Uganda, Ukraine, Uruguay, USA, Virgin Is UK.
Consultative Status Consultative status granted from: *ECOSOC (#05331)* (General); *UNESCO (#20322)* (Consultative Status); *ILO (#11123)* (Special List); *UNICEF (#20332)*; *Council of Europe (CE, #04881)* (Participatory Status). **IGO Relations** Accredited by (3): *United Nations Office at Geneva (UNOG, #20597)*; *United Nations Office at Vienna (UNOV, #20604)*; *United Nations Regional Commissions New York Office (RCNYO, #20620)*. Cooperates with (1): *United Nations Population Fund (UNFPA, #20612)*. Associated with Department of Global Communications of the United Nations. **NGO Relations** Member of (5): *Committee of NGOs on Human Rights, Geneva (#04275)*; *Conference of INGOs of the Council of Europe (#04607)*; *NGO Committee on Sustainable Development, Vienna (#17119)*; *NGO Committee on UNICEF (#17120)*; *Vienna NGO Committee on the Status of Women (#20775)*. Board member of: *Conference of Non-Governmental Organizations in Consultative Relationship with the United Nations (CONGO, #04635)*. Founding member of: *NGO Forum on Environment (FOE, #17125)*. [2021.05.19/XF3617/**F**]

♦ Zoo and Aquarium Association Australasia 22039

Exec Dir Zoo and Aquarium Assc Office, PO Box 538, Mosman NSW 2088, Australia. T. +61299784797. E-mail: admin@zooaquarium.org.au.
URL: http://www.zooaquarium.org.au/

History 1983, Auckland (New Zealand). Former names and other names: *Australasian Regional Association of Zoological Parks and Aquaria (ARAZPA)* – former. Registration: Start date: 30 Apr 1991, Australia. **Aims** Represent the collective voice of the zoos, aquariums, sanctuaries and wildlife parks across Australasia that operate to the highest standards; brings its members together, facilitating shared knowledge and continuous improvement in conservation, welfare, biosecurity, science, research, social and community programs. **Structure** Board; Executive. **Languages** English. **Staff** 11.00 FTE, paid. **Finance** Sources: members' dues. **Activities** Advocacy/lobbying/activism; capacity building; certification/accreditation; events/meetings; networking/liaising; standards/guidelines. Active in: Australia, New Caledonia, New Zealand, Papua New Guinea. **Events** *Annual Conference* Sydney, NSW (Australia) 2021, *Learning and Development Workshop* Sydney, NSW (Australia) 2019, *Biennial Conference* Wellington (New Zealand) 2018, *Learning & Development Workshop* Gold Coast, QLD (Australia) 2017, *Biennial Conference* Perth, WA (Australia) 2016. **Publications** *E-Newsletter* (12 a year); *Australasian Species Management Program: Regional Census and Plan* (annual). *Managing Zoo Populations: Compiling and analysing studbook data* (1999); *Birth Date Determination of Australasian Marsupials* (1998). Manuals.
Members Regional Members (93); Regional Subscribers (4); International Member (1); International Subscriber (1); Business Members (10) in 6 countries and territories:
Australia, New Caledonia, New Zealand, Papua New Guinea, Singapore, USA.
Individuals (33) in 4 countries and territories:
Australia, Hong Kong, Japan, New Zealand.
NGO Relations Member of (1): *World Association of Zoos and Aquariums (WAZA, #21208)*. [2021.04.13/XD3231/**D**]

♦ Zoo Check / see Born Free Foundation

♦ Zoological Society of Southern Africa (ZSSA) 22040

Dierkundige Vereniging van Suidelike Africa

Contact address not obtained. E-mail: office@zssa.co.za.
URL: http://zssa.co.za/

History 11 Mar 1959, Cape Town (South Africa). **Aims** Promote, facilitate and encourage zoological research in Southern Africa; preserve Southern African fauna and support legislation to this end; be actively concerned with welfare of animals; assist in coordination of zoological research and have contact with other zoologists on an international level; cooperate with public authorities and act in an advisory capacity when asked to do so; stimulate public interest in zoology. **Structure** General Meeting and Symposium (every 2 years); Council. **Languages** Afrikaans, English. **Staff** 1.00 FTE, paid; 3.00 FTE, voluntary. **Activities** Events/meetings. **Events** *Conference* Skukuza (South Africa) 2019, *Conference* Tshipise (South Africa) 2013, *Conference* Stellenbosch (South Africa) 2011, *Conference* Illovo (South Africa) 2009, *Conference* Potchefstroom (South Africa) 2007. **Publications** *African Zoology* (2 a year). Brochures.
Members Ordinary (350); Institutional (58): members in 24 countries:
Australia, Belgium, Botswana, Canada, Congo DR, Eswatini, Finland, Germany, Hong Kong, Israel, Italy, Kenya, Lesotho, Malawi, Namibia, Netherlands, New Zealand, Norway, South Africa, Sweden, UK, USA, Zambia, Zimbabwe.
IGO Relations Links with various organizations (not specified). **NGO Relations** Links with various organizations (not specified). [2022.02.15/XD3535/**D**]

♦ ZOPA – Zinc Oxide Producers Association (inactive)
♦ ZPG / see Population Connection
♦ ZP – Zen Peacemakers (internationally oriented national body)
♦ ZSI – Zero Suicide International (unconfirmed)
♦ **ZSSA** Zoological Society of Southern Africa (#22040)
♦ **ZUC** Zene u crnom (#20987)
♦ **ZUG** Z User Group (#22041)
♦ Zusammenarbeit der Bahnpolizei- und Sicherheitsdienste (#04096)
♦ Zusammenschluss der Apotheker der Europäischen Gemeinschaft / see Pharmaceutical Group of the European Union (#18352)
♦ Zusammenschluss der Apotheker der Europäischen Union (#18352)
♦ Zusammenschluss der Brauereien des Gemeinsamen Marktes / see The Brewers of Europe (#03324)
♦ Zusammenschluss der Jagdschutzverbände in der EG / see Federation of Associations for Hunting and Conservation of the EU (#09459)
♦ Zusammenschluss der Jagdschutzverbände in der EU / see Federation of Associations for Hunting and Conservation of the EU (#09459)
♦ Zusammenschluss der Verbände für Jagd und Wildtiererhaltung in der EU (#09459)
♦ Zusammenschluss der Vorsorgeunion der Europäischen Beamten / see AFILIATYS (#00151)
♦ Zusammenschluss der Vorsorgevereinigungen der Europäischen Beamten / see AFILIATYS (#00151)
♦ Zusatzprotokoll zum Allgemeinen abkommen über die vorrechte und befreiungen des Europarats (1952 treaty)
♦ Zusatzprotokoll zum Europäischen auslieferungsübereinkommen (1975 treaty)
♦ Zusatzprotokoll zu dem Europäischen fürsorgeabkommen (1953 treaty)
♦ Zusatzprotokoll zur Europäischen konvention über die gleichwertigkeit der reifezeugnisse (1964 treaty)
♦ Zusatzprotokoll zum Europäischen rahmenübereinkommen über die grenzüberschreitende zusammenarbeit zwischen gebietskörperschaften (1995 treaty)
♦ Zusatzprotokoll zur Europäischen sozialcharta, 1988 (1988 treaty)
♦ Zusatzprotokoll zur Europäischen sozialcharta über kollektivbeschwerden (1995 treaty)
♦ Zusatzprotokoll zum Europäischen übereinkommen betreffend auskünfte über ausländisches recht (1978 treaty)
♦ Zusatzprotokoll zum Europäischen übereinkommen zum schutz des menschen bei der automatischen verarbeitung personenbezogener daten bezüglich kontrollstellen und grenzüberschreitendem datenverkehr (2001 treaty)
♦ Zusatzprotokoll zu dem Europäischen übereinkommen über den austausch von reagenzien zur blutgruppenbestimmung (1983 treaty)
♦ Zusatzprotokoll zum Europäischen übereinkommen über den austausch von reagenzien zur gewebstypisierung (1976 treaty)
♦ Zusatzprotokoll zu dem Europäischen übereinkommen über den austausch therapeutischer substanzen menschlichen ursprungs (1983 treaty)
♦ Zusatzprotokoll zum Europäischen übereinkommen über die rechtshilfe in strafsachen (1978 treaty)
♦ Zusatzprotokoll zum Europäischen übereinkommen über die übermittlung von anträgen auf verfahrenshilfe (2001 treaty)
♦ Zusatzprotokoll zum Europäischen übereinkommen über den schutz von tieren beim internationalen transport (1979 treaty)
♦ Zusatzprotokoll zur Konvention zum schutze der menschenrechte und grundfreiheiten (1952 treaty)
♦ Zusatzprotokoll zu dem Protokoll zu dem Europäischen abkommen zum schutz von fernsehsendungen (1983 treaty)
♦ Zusatzprotokoll zu dem Protokoll zu dem Europäischen abkommen zum schutz von fernsehsendungen (1974 treaty)
♦ Zusatzprotokoll zum strafrechtsübereinkommen über korruption (2003 treaty)
♦ Zusatzprotokoll zum Übereinkommen gegen doping (2002 treaty)
♦ Zusatzprotokoll zum Übereinkommen über computerkriminalität betreffend die kriminalisierung mittels computersystemen begangener handlungen rassistischer und fremdenfeindlicher art (2003 treaty)
♦ Zusatzprotokoll zum Übereinkommen über die überstellung verurteilter personen (1997 treaty)
♦ Zusatzprotokoll zu dem übereinkommen über die verringerung der mehrstaatigkeit und über die wehrpflicht von mehrstaatern (1977 treaty)
♦ Zusatzprotokoll zu dem Übereinkommen über die vorübergehende zollfreie einfuhr von medizinischem, chirurgischem und laboratoriumsmaterial zur leihweisen verwendung für diagnose- und behandlungszwecke in krankenhäusern und anderen einrichtungen des gesundheitswesens (1983 treaty)
♦ Zusatzprotokoll zum Übereinkommen über menschenrechte und biomedizin betreffend biomedizinische forschung (2005 treaty)

- ♦ Zusatzprotokoll zum Vorläufigen europäischen abkommen über die systeme der sozialen sicherheit für den fall des alters, der invalidität und zugunsten der hinterbliebenen (1953 treaty)
- ♦ Zusatzprotokoll zu dem Vorläufigen europäischen abkommen über soziale sicherheit unter ausschluss der systeme für den fall des alters, der invalidität und zugunsten der hinterbliebenen (1953 treaty)
- ♦ Zusatzvereinbarung zur durchführung des Europäischen abkommens über soziale sicherheit (1972 treaty)

♦ Z User Group (ZUG) 22041

Chairman Univ of Waikato, Dept of Computer Science, Private Bag 3105, Hamilton 3240, New Zealand.
Treas London South Bank Univ, School of Engineering, Borough Road, London, SE1 0AA, UK.
URL: http://www.zuser.org/

History 14 Dec 1992, London (UK). Founded at the Z User Meeting (ZUM '92). **Aims** Further the study, use and development of Z notation. **Structure** General Meeting (every 2 years); Committee. **Languages** English. **Finance** Sources: conference fees; sales of proceedings. **Activities** Events/meetings. **Events** *International Conference of Abstract State Machines, Alloy, B, TLA, VDM, and Z (ABZ Conference)* Southampton (UK) 2018, *International Conference of Alloy, ASM, B, TLA, VDM, and Z Users (ABZ Conference)* Linz (Austria) 2016, *International Conference of Alloy, ASM, B, TLA, VDM, and Z Users (ABZ Conference)* Toulouse (France) 2014, *International Conference of Alloy, ASM, B, VDM, and Z Users (ABZ Conference)* Pisa (Italy) 2012, *International Conference on ASM, Alloy, B, and Z (ABZ Conference)* Orford, QC (Canada) 2010. **Publications** *Springer Lecture Notes in Computer Science* – conference proceedings.
Members Individuals in 11 countries:
Australia, Canada, France, Germany, Ireland, Italy, Japan, New Zealand, Singapore, UK, USA.
NGO Relations Cooperates with: British Computer Society Formal Aspects of Computing Science Specialist Group (BCS-FACS); *International B Conference Steering Committee (#12328).* [2018.09.05/XE3408/**E**]

- ♦ Zusters van het Arme Kind Jesus (religious order)
- ♦ Zusters Franciscanessen, Heythuizen (religious order)
- ♦ Zusters van Liefde van Jezus en Maria (religious order)
- ♦ Zusters van Liefde van Onze Lieve Vrouw Moeder van Barmhartigheid (religious order)
- ♦ Zusters Missionarissen van het Onbevlekt Hart van Maria (religious order)
- ♦ Zusters van Onze Lieve Vrouw (religious order)
- ♦ Zusters Ursulinen van Tildonk (religious order)
- ♦ Zveza Alpe-Jadran (#00747)
- ♦ ZVL – Zusters van Liefde van Jezus en Maria (religious order)
- ♦ Zweites protokoll zum Allgemeinen abkommen über die vorrechte und befreiungen des Europarats (1956 treaty)
- ♦ Zweites protokoll zur änderung des Übereinkommens über die verringerung von mehrstaatigkeit und die wehrpflicht von mehrstaatern (1993 treaty)
- ♦ Zweites zusatzprotokoll zum Europäischen auslieferungsübereinkommen (1978 treaty)
- ♦ Zweites zusatzprotokoll zum Europäischen übereinkommen über rechtshilfe in strafsachen (2001 treaty)
- ♦ ZWIA – Zero Waste International Alliance (unconfirmed)
- ♦ Zwischenstaatliche Organisation für den Internationalen Eisenbahnverkehr (#17807)
- ♦ ZW MENA – Zero Waste MENA (unconfirmed)
- ♦ 1,000 Days (unconfirmed)

♦ 100 Million 22042

Registered Address Schaapsteeg 12, 4033 AJ Lienden, Netherlands. E-mail: campaign@100million.org.
URL: https://100million.org/

History 2016, India. Since 2021, campaign is governed by a Foundation. Former names and other names: *Stichting 100 Million campaign* – legal name; *100 Million campaign Foundation* – legal name. Registration: Handelsregister, No/ID: KVK 81615612, Start date: 19 Jan 2021, Netherlands. **Aims** Campaign for a world where all young people are free, safe and educated. **Structure** Board of Trustees. **Activities** Advocacy/lobbying/activism. **NGO Relations** Partner of (7): *All-Africa Students Union (AASU, #00644); Commonwealth Students' Association (CSA, #04363); Education International (EI, #05371); European Students' Union (ESU, #08848); Global Student Forum (GSF, #10614); Inter-Parliamentary Union (IPU, #15961); Organising Bureau of European School Student Unions (OBESSU, #17829).* [2021/AA1588/f/**F**]

- ♦ 100 Million campaign Foundation / see 100 Million (#22042)
- ♦ 11 11 11 / see Coalition of the Flemish North South Movement – 11 11 11
- ♦ 11Q Network / see European Chromosome 11 Network (#06547)
- ♦ 11Q Netzwerk / see European Chromosome 11 Network (#06547)
- ♦ 1932 / see Hostelling International (#10950)
- ♦ 1946 / see Hostelling International (#10950)
- ♦ 1984 EMEP protocol – Protocol to the 1979 Convention on Long Range Transboundary Air Pollution on Long-term Financing of the Cooperative Programme for Monitoring and Evaluation of the Long-range Transmission of Air-pollutants in Europe (1984 treaty)
- ♦ 1985 Sulphur protocol – Protocol to the 1979 Convention on Long Range Transboundary Air Pollution on the Reduction of Sulphur Emissions or Their Transboundary Fluxes by at Least 30 per Cent (1985 treaty)
- ♦ 1988 NOx protocol – Protocol to the 1979 Convention on Long Range Transboundary Air Pollution Concerning the Control of Nitrogen Oxides Emissions or Their Transboundary Fluxes (1988 treaty)
- ♦ 1991 VOC protocol – Protocol to the 1979 Convention on Long Range Transboundary Air Pollution Concerning the Control of Emissions of Volatile Organic Compounds on Their Transboundary Fluxes (1991 treaty)
- ♦ 1996 Protocol to the Convention on the Prevention of Marine Pollution by Dumping of Wastes and other Matter (1996 treaty)
- ♦ **1% for Development Fund** One Percent for Development Fund (#17733)
- ♦ 1% for the Planet (internationally oriented national body)
- ♦ 2010 Biodiversity Indicators Partnership / see Biodiversity Indicators Partnership (#03242)
- ♦ 2010 BIP / see Biodiversity Indicators Partnership (#03242)

♦ 22q11 Europe 22043

Sec Max Appeal, Stourbridge, DY8 4QN, UK.
URL: https://22q11europe.org/

History Formally constituted Nov 2016. Former names and other names: *22q11 European Alliance* – alias; *22q11 European Association* – alias. **Aims** Create a 22q11 community at European level to better share information across countries; increase 22q11 recognition. **Structure** Board. **Events** *Conference* Berlin (Germany) 2021, *European 22q11-Deletion Syndrome Conference* Barcelona (Spain) 2019.
Members Founding organizations in 10 countries:
Belgium, Denmark, France, Germany, Ireland, Italy, Spain, Sweden, Switzerland, UK.
NGO Relations Associate member of: *EURORDIS – Rare Diseases Europe (#09175).* [2019/XM7426/**D**]

- ♦ 22q11 European Alliance / see 22q11 Europe (#22043)
- ♦ 22q11 European Association / see 22q11 Europe (#22043)
- ♦ 28 Too Many (internationally oriented national body)

♦ 2Build 4 Ward International Organization (2x4 International) 22044

CEO 409 21st St, Sacramento CA 95811, USA. E-mail: 2x4international@gmail.com.
URL: http://2x4international.blogspot.com/

Aims Build a better *community* by partnering with community-based projects and *disadvantaged* groups to support education, health, infrastructure and small business development projects abroad. **Structure** Board of Directors, comprising CEO, CFO, President and 4 members. Advisory Board. **Events** *Conference* Pattaya (Thailand) 2009. [2013/XJ2802/**F**]

- ♦ 2ie – Institut International de l'Écologie Industrielle and de l'Économie Verte (internationally oriented national body)
- ♦ **2iE** Institut International d'Ingénierie de l'Eau et de l'Environnement (#11313)
- ♦ **2iE** International Institute for Water and Environmental Engineering (#11313)

♦ 2° Investing Initiative 22045

Acting Managing Dir 15 rue des Halles, 75001 Paris, France. T. +33142811997. E-mail: contact@2degrees-investing.org.
URL: https://2degrees-investing.org/

History 2012. **Aims** Work to align financial markets and regulation with the Paris Agreement goals, concentrating on three main research areas: retail investing, impact, and emerging markets. **Languages** English, French, German, Spanish. **Staff** 12.00 FTE, paid. **Finance** Sources: government support; private foundations; sponsorship. Supported by: *Deutsche Gesellschaft für Internationale Zusammenarbeit (GIZ); European Climate Foundation (ECF, #06574); European Commission (EC, #06633); Inter-American Development Bank (IDB, #11427); International Climate Initiative (ICI).* **Activities** Knowledge management/information dissemination; politics/policy/regulatory; research/documentation. [2023.02.17/AA0069/**F**]

- ♦ **2x4 International** 2Build 4 Ward International Organization (#22044)
- ♦ 350.org (internationally oriented national body)
- ♦ 3B ICT Network – Balkan Black Sea Baltic ICT Clusters Network (unconfirmed)
- ♦ 3D – Trade – Human Rights – Equitable Economy (internationally oriented national body)
- ♦ 3G Americas / see 5G Americas
- ♦ 3GF – Global Green Growth Forum (unconfirmed)
- ♦ **3GGP2** Third Generation Partnership Project 2 (#20146)
- ♦ **3GPP** Third Generation Partnership Project (#20145)

♦ 3HO Foundation 22046

Main Office Narayan Court 6, Espanola NM 87532, USA. T. +15057536341. Fax +15057535982. E-mail: yogainfo@3ho.org.
URL: http://www.3ho.org/

History 1969. Former names and other names: *Healthy, Happy, Holy Organization* – full title; *3HO International* – alias. **Aims** Inspire everyone everywhere to realize their full potential through the uplifting experience of Kundalini Yoga. **Languages** English. **Activities** Events/meetings; projects/programmes; training/education. **Events** *Annual kundalini yoga teacher conference* Espanola, NM (USA) 1998, *Seminar on women's excellence and success in all walks of life* Espanola, NM (USA) 1986.
Members Operates 112 centres (mostly in USA) in 28 countries:
Argentina, Australia, Canada, Chile, Colombia, Denmark, Ecuador, Finland, France, Germany, Greece, Hong Kong, India, Italy, Japan, Malaysia, Mexico, Netherlands, Norway, Puerto Rico, Russia, Singapore, South Africa, Spain, Sweden, Switzerland, Trinidad-Tobago, USA.
Consultative Status Consultative status granted from: *ECOSOC (#05331)* (Ros A). **IGO Relations** Associated with Department of Global Communications of the United Nations. **NGO Relations** Instrumental in setting up (1): *International Kundalini Yoga Teachers Association (IKYTA, see: #22046).* [2021.09.08/XF6321/f/**F**]

- ♦ 3HO International / see 3HO Foundation (#22046)
- ♦ **3ie** International Initiative for Impact Evaluation (#13851)
- ♦ **3iG** International Interfaith Investment Group (#13944)
- ♦ 3iS / see Institut international de l'image et du son
- ♦ **3MF** Third Millennium Foundation (#20147)
- ♦ 3P Ministries (internationally oriented national body)
- ♦ 3rd Millennium Foundation / see Third Millennium Foundation (#20147)
- ♦ 3RINCs – 3R International Scientific Conference on Material Cycles and Waste Management (meeting series)
- ♦ 3R International Scientific Conference on Material Cycles and Waste Management (meeting series)
- ♦ 3SGF – 3Strands Global Foundation (internationally oriented national body)
- ♦ 3Strands Global Foundation (internationally oriented national body)

♦ 41 International 22047

Sec TMS Eye Hosp, LRN Colony, Sarada College Road, Salem, Tamil Nadu 636007, Salem TAMIL NADU 636007, India. E-mail: seehappy@gmail.com.
URL: http://www.41international.net/

History 1975, Le Touquet (France), by former members of *Round Table International (RTI, #18982).* Previously also referred to as *Club 41 International.* **Aims** Further develop, internationally, friendship and comradeship between former members of Round Table International. **Structure** General Meeting (annual); Board. **Languages** English. **Activities** Networking/liaising; events/meetings. **Events** *Half-Yearly Meeting* Bangalore (India) 2016, *Annual General Meeting* Landshut (Germany) 2016, *Half Yearly Meeting* Birmingham (UK) 2015, *Annual General Meeting* Limassol (Cyprus) 2015, *Half-Yearly Meeting* Blenheim (New Zealand) 2014. **Publications** *41 Communique* (12 a year) – newsletter; *The Hinge* (3 a year) – magazine. Annual Directory.
Members Full; clubs of men older than 40 in 23 countries:
Austria, Belgium, Cyprus, Denmark, Finland, France, Germany, India, Israel, Italy, Malta, Mauritius, Netherlands, New Zealand, Norway, Poland, Romania, South Africa, Sri Lanka, Sweden, Switzerland, UK, Zambia. [2014.10.30/XM0760/**F**]

- ♦ 4C Association (inactive)
- ♦ 4G Americas / see 5G Americas
- ♦ 4iP Council EU (unconfirmed)
- ♦ 4M Association (unconfirmed)
- ♦ 4 plus 5 Group / see Cooperation Process in the Western Mediterranean (#04798)
- ♦ **4S** Society for Social Studies of Science (#19642)
- ♦ 50 Years Is Enough – US Network for Global Economic Justice (internationally oriented national body)
- ♦ 5Cs / see Caribbean Community Climate Change Centre (#03477)
- ♦ **5GAA** 5G Automotive Association (#22048)
- ♦ 5G Americas (internationally oriented national body)

♦ 5G Automotive Association (5GAA) 22048

Dir-Gen Neumarkter Str 21, 81673 Munich, Germany. T. +498954909680. Fax +498954909685. E-mail: secretariat@5gaa.org.
URL: https://5gaa.org/

History Sep 2016. **Aims** Bridge the automotive and telecommunication industries so as to address society's connected mobility and road safety needs. **Structure** General Assembly; Board; Executive Committee. Working Groups. **Events** *Meeting* Barcelona (Spain) 2020. **Members** Companies (over 130). Membership countries not specified. [2021/AA1739/**C**]

- ♦ **5G IA** 5G Infrastructure Association (#22049)

♦ 5G Infrastructure Association (5G IA) 22049

Chair Bd Saint-Michel 47, 1040 Brussels, Belgium. E-mail: info@5g-ppp.eu.
SG address not obtained.
URL: https://5g-ia.eu/

History Registered in accordance with Belgian law, 15 Dec 2013. **Aims** Advance 5G in Europe; build global consensus on 5G. **Structure** General Assembly; Board. **Languages** English. **Staff** 3.00 FTE, paid. **Finance** Members' dues. **Activities** Capacity building; events/meetings; knowledge management/information dissemination; monitoring/evaluation; networking/liaising; projects/programmes; research and development; standards/guidelines. **Events** *5G Vertical User Workshop* Brussels (Belgium) 2019, *Global Meeting* Valencia (Spain) 2019, *Global Meeting* Austin, TX (USA) 2018, *Global Meeting* Rio de Janeiro (Brazil) 2018, *Global Meeting* Seoul (Korea Rep) 2017. **Publications** *The European 5G Annual Journal.* Roadmap documents; white papers; videos. **Members** Full; Associate. Membership countries not specified. **IGO Relations** *European Commission (EC, #06633); International Telecommunication Union (ITU, #15673).* [2020/XM4331/**E**]

- ♦ **5GWA** 5G World Alliance (#22050)

♦ 5G World Alliance (5GWA) 22050

Founding Chair address not obtained. T. +352621141582.
Membership address not obtained. T. +447738096604.
URL: http://www.5gworldalliance.org/

History 2015. Registered in England and Wales. **Aims** Promote 5G as the Neutral Next Generation World Wide Wireless *Internet*. **Structure** Board of Directors. **Finance** Sources: members' dues. [2020.03.11/XM6961/**C**]

♦ 5GYRES – 5 Gyres Institute (internationally oriented national body)
♦ 5 Gyres Institute (internationally oriented national body)
♦ 5 Nations Committee / see 6 Nations Committee (#22052)
♦ **5Rights** 5Rights Foundation (#22051)

♦ 5Rights Foundation (5Rights) 22051

Registered Address Suite 6, 313-314 Upper Street, London, N1 2XQ, UK. E-mail: info@5rightsfoundation.com.
URL: https://5rightsfoundation.com/

History Registration: Companies House, No/ID: 11271356, Start date: 22 Mar 2018, England; Charity Commission, No/ID: 1178581, England and Wales; EU Transparency Register, No/ID: 373653640889-82, Start date: 12 Jan 2021. **Aims** Fight for systemic change that ensures the digital world caters for children and young people by design and default. **Structure** Trustees. **Activities** Advocacy/lobbying/activism. [2021/AA1321/f/**F**]

♦ **6CP** Six Countries Programme (#19301)

♦ 6 Nations Committee 22052

Comité des 6 nations

Chief Exec 1st Floor, Simmonscourt House, Simmonscourt Road, Ballsbridge, Dublin, CO. DUBLIN, Ireland. T. +35316690950. Fax +35316690957.
URL: http://www.rbs6nations.com/

History 1910, as *5 Nations Committee – Comité de 5 nations*, when France was invited to join England, Wales, Scotland and Ireland in their annual rugby championship. Current title adopted, 2000, with the inclusion of Italy. **Structure** Committee comprises representatives of the 6 participating nations, including Chairman. **Activities** Organizes annual 6 Nations Tournament.
Members Representatives of 6 countries and territories:
England, France, Ireland, Italy, Scotland, Wales.
NGO Relations *World Rugby (#21757)*; *Rugby Europe (#18998)*. [2018/XE4371/**E**]

Appendix 1
Contents of organization descriptions

Order of descriptions

The descriptions of organizations in this volume appear in alphabetic order of the first title. In the case of a few intergovernmental organizations known more usually by their initials (eg WHO, UNESCO), the abbreviation is used instead of the title.

Listed in the one alphabetic sequence are all titles and abbreviations of the organizations in this edition, their former titles and abbreviations, and titles and abbreviations of subsidiary bodies mentioned in their descriptions. The index in Volume 3 also lists keywords in titles.

Each description is identified by a sequence number assigned for this edition. The sequence number follows the alphabetic sequence.

For some types of organization no description is included in this edition due to limitations imposed by printing and binding. In such cases, no sequence number is assigned and an explanatory comment is given instead of the description (for example: "no longer active"; "meeting series"; "treaty"). All descriptions can be found in the Yearbook Online.

A description may be abridged when sufficient information has not yet been obtained, or when the organization is classified as one of the types for which extensive information is either not collected or not included in the book version due to limitations imposed by printing and binding; see below under "Codes", or the Appendix "Types of organization" for further information.

Descriptions always include the following information.

Organization name

The organization's name is given in all languages in which it is available. Normally the names are given in the order:

- European languages (starting with English, French, Spanish, German)
- transliterated languages (Arabic, Russian, Japanese, etc)
- artificial languages (Esperanto, Ido, Occidental, etc)
- historical languages (Latin, etc)

The order may be changed to reflect the organization's concern with a particular language. For example, an organization promoting the use of Latin may have its Latin name in the first position.

Abbreviations follow the appropriate name.

When an organization does not have an official name in English or French, the editors may provide translated versions. An asterisk then follows the unofficially translated name.

Organization number

The number to the right of each title (eg •00123) is a sequence number with no significance other than as a fixed point of reference in the sequence of organizations in this edition of the Yearbook. Cross-references in organization descriptions, other volumes in this series and indexes refer to this number. The order and numbering of the organizations is of no significance other than alphabetical access.

Descriptions may include the following information.

Addresses

The main address for correspondence is inset beneath the organization names. Telephone, fax, e-mail and other media addresses are also given when available.

Secondary addresses are inset in smaller type below the main address. Included here are registered offices, continental regional offices, information offices and addresses for secondary correspondence.

The address of the organization's home page is given, if known, with an indication as to which aspect of the organization it refers where appropriate.

Address locations are indexed by country in Volume 2.

For various reasons no address is given for some organizations. In such cases, the reason for this absence is given.

History

The date and location of founding or of establishment are indicated under this heading. In the absence of a precise legal date, the date of the first General Meeting is given. Other information on the history and changes in structure or name of the organization is also given.

Where another organization is cited, if it has a description included in this edition, its first title is given, followed by its abbreviation and the sequence number allotted to it for this edition. If it has no description included in this edition (eg former names, subsidiary bodies), all its titles and abbreviations are given, but no sequence number; these titles are included in the overall alphabetical sequence with a reference to this description.

Aims

Principal objectives are summarized, wherever possible on the basis of the organization's statutes. In some cases keywords are given in italics. These are then used to determine classification of the organization in Volume 3.

Structure

The key organs and commissions of the organization are enumerated, together with some indication of the frequency of their meetings and of composition of the executive body. Where another organization is cited, it is treated as explained under "History" above.

Languages
Official and working languages used by the organization are listed.

Staff
The numbers of paid and voluntary staff are given.

Finance
Sources of funding and the annual budget figures are given.

Where another organization is cited, it is treated as explained under "History" above.

Activities
Under this heading appears a summary of the main activities and programme concerns of each organization. Special emphasis is placed on developmental activities, where relevant.

Where another organization is cited, it is treated as explained under "History" above.

Events
Listed here are the dates and locations of previous and future periodic meetings or other events. For a fuller list of events, for more details on the events listed here, and for full indexes to them, users are directed to the *International Congress Calendar.*

Publications
Listed here are the titles of major periodical and non-periodical publications of the organization. Titles in italics are indexed and classified in Volume 4.

Information Services
Listed here are the names of libraries, databanks and library and publications consultancy services operated by the organization. Websites of these services are listed with the organization's address (see above). Titles in italics are indexed and classified in Volume 4.

Members
Listed here are the types of membership and numbers of members. This may include the list of countries represented or in which members are located. These countries are indexed and cross-referenced in Volume 2.

Where another organization is cited, it is treated as explained under "History" above.

Note on country names
It is not the intention of the editors to take a position with regard to the political or diplomatic implications of geographical names or continental groupings used.

The geographical names used in this publication are chosen for the sake of brevity and common usage. Wherever possible, the country (or territory) name preferred by the organization concerned is used, providing this is possible within the limits of standardization required for mailing or statistical purposes. It is important to note that some organizations insist on the inclusion of territories on the same basis as countries, or on the inclusion of countries or territories that are not recognized by other organizations.

Political changes over the years may lead to some questions in an organization's description. Briefly: countries referred to in an organization's description retain their old form when referring to a date prior to the change. For example, towns referred to in events prior to 1991 still retain their country as German DR (Democratic Republic) or Germany FR (Federal Republic), while subsequent dates refer simply to Germany.

Consultative Status
Where the organization has an officially recognized relationship to a major intergovernmental organization, this is indicated. Cited organizations are treated as explained under "History" above.

IGO Relations
Where the organization has a special relationship to an intergovernmental organization, this is indicated. Cited organizations are treated as explained under "History" above. It should be noted that tenuous links, or links that have not been confirmed by both parties, have been omitted from the printed descriptions, although they are available in the Yearbook Online and are included in the statistics.

NGO Relations
Where the organization has a special relationship with international non-governmental organizations, this is indicated. Cited organizations are treated as explained under "History" above. It should be noted that tenuous links, or links that have not been confirmed by both parties, have been omitted from the printed descriptions, although they are available in the Yearbook Online and are included in the statistics.

Date
The last line of the description includes the date on which the most recent information has been received. Two forms are used:

- 2023.02.16: the organization checked the description and returned it on that date;
- 2021: the organization has not checked the description since that date, but information has been received in the given year from another reliable source (which may be the organization's own website).

Old dates, or no date, may be an indication that an organization is becoming inactive.

Codes
Organizations are coded by type, indicated by a single upper case letter printed in bold at the end of the description. The upper case type code may be preceded by a letter code printed in lower case. The type code of Intergovernmental organizations is followed by an asterisk, '*'. For further information, see the Appendix: "Types of organization".

Appendix 2
Types of organization

The Yearbook attempts to cover all "international organizations", according to a broad range of criteria. It therefore includes many bodies that may be perceived as not being fully international, or as not being organizations as such, or as not being of sufficient significance to merit inclusion. Such bodies are nevertheless included, so as to enable users to make their own evaluation in the light of their own criteria.

Type 1: To assist this evaluation, the editors have developed a hierarchical typology, assigning each organization to one of 15 types. All of these types include both intergovernmental and non-governmental international organizations. (See below for a discussion of the terms "intergovernmental" and "non-governmental".) The 15 types are designated by an upper case letter.

Type 2: A qualifying typology is used to add a second level of structure to the hierarchical typology. There are 13 such qualifiers and an organization may be assigned up to three qualifiers. The 13 qualifiers are designated by a lower case letter.

Type 3: A third type is used to group organizations of a particular structure. There are 26 such types and an organization may be assigned to one or more of them.

In addition, every organization is classified under one or more subject headings (848 headings), regionally-defined headings (22), and, where appropriate, a combination of the two.

Further information on the three types is given on the following pages.

INTERGOVERNMENTAL ORGANIZATIONS (IGOS) AND NON-GOVERNMENTAL ORGANIZATIONS (NGOS)

The approach to the selection of organizations for inclusion in this Yearbook was first developed by the Union of International Associations for the *Annuaire de la Vie Internationale* (1908-1909, 1910-1911). It was further developed after 1945 for the early editions of the *Yearbook of International Organizations*. The approach was endorsed by the Economic and Social Council of the United Nations (ECOSOC) in 1950 and in 1953.

The Economic and Social Council, in considering these matters in 1950, itself clarified the distinction between intergovernmental and international non-governmental organizations as follows:

Intergovernmental organizations (IGOs)
The view of the Economic and Social Council of the United Nations concerning intergovernmental organizations is implicit in its Resolution 288 (X) of 27 February 1950: "Any international organization which is not established by intergovernmental agreement shall be considered as a non-governmental organization for the purpose of these arrangements." The resolution was concerned with the implementation of Article 71 of the United Nations Charter on consultative status of non-governmental organizations, and it was amplified by Resolution 1296 (XLIV) of 25 June 1968: "...including organizations which accept members designated by government authorities, provided that such membership does not interfere with the free expression of views of the organizations."

The matter is complicated by the fact that, pursuant to Article 12 of the regulations of the General Assembly of the United Nations (giving effect to Article 102 of the Charter), the Secretariat publishes, in the UN Treaty Series, every instrument submitted to it by a Member State, when "so far as that party is concerned, the instrument is a treaty or an international agreement within the meaning of Article 102" (Note in UN Treaty Series, Vol. 748). The terms "treaty" and "international agreement" have not been defined either in the Charter or in the regulations. Furthermore: "It is the understanding of the Secretariat that its action does not confer on the instrument the status of a treaty or an international agreement if it does not already have that status ..."

Further complications arise from:

- the increasing number of "international agreements" in which one or more of the parties is a constituent state of a federal state system (e.g. Quebec); this matter was not resolved by the Vienna Convention on the Law of Treaties (Vienna, 1969);
- bilateralization of treaties when several states act together to aid another state under a "multilateral" treaty signed by all of them;
- agreements in which one of the parties is itself an intergovernmental organization (thus "multilateralizing" the agreement) acting to establish an intergovernmental institute in a particular country (thus "bilateralizing" the agreement), of which the government is one of the parties to that agreement (e.g. many UNESCO agreements with individual developing countries to establish regional research centres);
- agreements signed on behalf of national government agencies or departments which, in the case of purely technical matters, may not fully engage the state; the resulting organizations may then define themselves as "non-governmental".

In practice therefore, the editors assume that an organization is intergovernmental if it is established by signature of an agreement engendering obligations between governments, whether or not that agreement is eventually published. If any organization declares itself to be non-governmental, it is accepted as such by the editors.

Non-governmental organizations (NGOs)
The problem of identifying eligible non-governmental organizations is more difficult. Resolution 288 (X) makes no attempt to explain what is meant by the term "international organization". Editorial experience has shown that it is useful to take seven aspects of organizational life as indicators of the eligibility of an organization: aims; membership; structure; officers; finance; relations with other organizations; and activities. These aspects are discussed below for different types of organization.

TYPE 1

The 15 upper case letters used for Type 1, their significance, and their chief characteristics (as determined by information regarding membership and structure) are the following. More information is given on the following pages under the headings "Detailed comments" and "Comparative characteristics".

Type	Description	Membership	Structure
A	Federations of international organizations	includes at least 3 international organizations	Management and policy-making organs reflect a well-balanced geographical distribution (cf membership)
B	Universal membership organizations	From either at least 60 countries or at least 30 countries in at least 2 continents and with a well-balanced geographical distribution	Management and policy-making organs reflect a well-balanced geographical distribution (cf membership)
C	Intercontinental membership organizations	From at least 10 countries in at least 2 continents with a well-balanced geographical distribution	Management and policy-making organs reflect a well-balanced geographical distribution (cf membership)
D	Regionally defined membership organizations	From at least 3 countries within one continental or sub-continental region	Management and policy-making organs reflect a well-balanced geographical distribution (cf membership)
E	Organizations emanating from places, persons or other bodies	No criteria	Reference to, and to some degree limited by, another international organization, or a person, or a place
F	Organizations having a special form	No criteria	Non-formal, unconventional or unusual
G	Internationally-oriented national organizations	No criteria	Management and policy-making organs reflect participation of only one or two countries; formal links with at least one other international organization
H	Inactive or dissolved international organizations	No criteria	While active, classified as Types A, B, C or D
J	Recently reported or proposed international organizations	Type J is a temporary allocation. Organizations of Type J are reallocated to the appropriate Type whenever sufficient information is obtained.	
K	Subsidiary and internal bodies	No criteria	Substantive unit with a degree of autonomy within another organization
N	National organizations	No criteria	Management and policy-making organs reflect participation of only one country; no formal links with other international organizations
R	Religious orders, fraternities, and secular institutes	No criteria	Based on charismatic leadership or a commitment to a set of (religious) practices
S	Autonomous conference series	No criteria	No continuing structure
T	Multilateral treaties and agreements	At least 3 signatories	No structure. (If an organization is established to implement or otherwise take responsibility for the treaty, that organization is normally classified as Type E.)
U	Currently inactive non-conventional organizations	No criteria	While active, classified as Types other than A, B, C or D

TYPE 2

The 13 lower case letters used for Type 2 and their significance are the following:

- b = bilateral intergovernmental organization (normally but not always assigned to Type G)
- c = conference series (normally but not always assigned to Type S)
- d = dissolved, dormant (normally but not always assigned to Type H or Type U)
- e = commercial enterprise
- f = foundation, fund (normally but not always assigned to Type F)
- g = intergovernmental
- j = research institute
- n = has become national (normally but not always assigned to Type N)
- p = proposed body (normally but not always assigned to Type J)
- s = information suspect
- v = individual membership only
- x = no recent information received
- y = international organization membership

TYPE 3

The 26 headings are the following:

Alumni and Veterans
Banks
Clubs
Common Markets and Free Trade Zones
Conference Series
Corporations, Companies
European Union Bodies
FAO Bodies
Foundations
Funds
Human Rights Organizations
Humanitarian Organizations
ILO Bodies
Institutes
Intergovernmental Communities
International Federations
NATO Bodies
Parliaments
Political Parties
Professional Bodies
Religious Orders
Trade and Labour Unions
Treaties
UNESCO Bodies
United Nations Bodies
WHO Bodies

CLUSTERS OF TYPES / STATISTICS

In statistical tables in the Yearbook, totals are usually given for each category of Type 1. In addition to these totals, or sometimes instead of them, totals are given by cluster of Type 1 categories.

There are 5 clusters and the Types allocated to each are as follows:

Cluster I (International organizations):
Types A B C D F
Cluster II (Dependent organizations):
Types E K R
Cluster III (Organizational substitutes):
Types S T
Cluster IV (National organizations):
Types G N
Cluster V (Dead, inactive and unconfirmed bodies):
Types H J U

TYPE 1: DETAILED COMMENTS

The complexity of the hierarchical typology warrants further explanation.

Type A: Federations of international organizations

An organization is classified as Type A if:
its membership includes at least three autonomous international bodies.

An organization is **not** classified as Type A if:
it meets the criteria for another Type more closely than it meets the criteria for this Type;
its membership includes only regional organizations;
its membership is limited to international organizations linked to a particular place or organization or people;
its membership is limited to non-autonomous commissions or sections of one or more international organizations;
its international organizational membership is of secondary importance (e.g. "associate members").
its preoccupation or field of activity is limited to one region or continent;
it is in some way a "joint committee", created to liaise between international organizations;
it has been created by one or more international organizations which then themselves become members of it.

The United Nations is included in Type A because of its focal role in relation to the specialized agencies; these can be seen as "members" of the UN system.

"Umbrella" organizations which have national organizations as an *additional* membership category may also be included here.

Type B: Universal membership organizations

An organization is classified as Type B if:
its membership covers at least 60 countries regardless of distribution, or if its membership covers at least 30 countries and is equitably distributed over several continents (the fewer the number of countries represented, the greater must be the number of continents represented);
its management structure and its activities reflect its membership in terms of geographical distribution and balance.

An organization is **not** classified as Type B if:
it meets the criteria for another Type more closely than it meets the criteria for this Type;
its title mentions any term effectively restricting its membership or activities to a particular group of countries or particular group of people (e.g. Commonwealth, French-speaking);
it is universal in aims or activities only.

Type C: Intercontinental membership organizations

An organization is classified as Type C if:
its membership and preoccupations exceed that of a particular continental region though not to the degree of justifying its inclusion in Type B;
its membership covers at least 10 countries and is equitably distributed over at least two continents;
its management structure and its activities reflect its membership in terms of geographical distribution and balance.

An organization is **not** classified as Type C if:
it meets the criteria for another Type more closely than it meets the criteria for this Type;
its title mentions any term effectively restricting its membership or activities to a single continental region or contiguous group of countries (e.g. European, Inter-American, Mediterranean).

Type D: Regionally defined membership organizations

An organization is classified as Type D if:
its membership and preoccupations are restricted to a particular continental or sub-continental region or contiguous group of countries;
its membership covers at least three countries or includes at least three autonomous international bodies;
its title mentions a single continental region or contiguous group of countries (e.g. European, Inter-American, Mediterranean) regardless of membership;

An organization is **not** classified as Type D if:
it meets the criteria for another Type more closely than it meets the criteria for this Type;
its title mentions another organization or a particular place or person.

Type E: Organizations emanating from places, persons or other bodies

An organization is classified as Type E if:
it can be considered as an "emanation" of another organization or of a place, person or proprietary product, regardless of membership;
its title incorporates, in any way, the name of another organization (excepting intergovernmental organizations that are the subject of a special multi-lateral treaty, e.g. the FAO);
provision is made for its creation in the statutes of another organization though it nonetheless functions autonomously (non-autonomous bodies being included in Type K);
it is in some way a "joint committee", created to liaise between international organizations, functioning autonomously;
it is a centre or institute created by intergovernmental bodies, possibly by agreement with a particular government;
it is especially identified with a particular physical location and its activities are largely determined by that location (e.g. training courses, experimental stations);
it is specifically concerned with a single country (NB an organization specifically concerned with a single language, though it may be spoken in a single country, is not necessarily classified as Type E).

An organization is **not** classified as Type E if:
it meets the criteria for another Type more closely than it meets the criteria for this Type;
it does not function at least semi-autonomously.

Type F: Organizations having a special form

An organization is classified as Type F if:
its formal characteristics would cause fundamental questions to be raised were it included in one of the preceding Types;
it has international dimensions which make it equivalent to a more conventional international organization;
its special nature is implied by the presence of certain terms in its title, whether or not the use of such terms is in effect a misnomer; such terms include:
- Activities: campaign, programme, project, service, survey
- Arbitration and legislation: court, parliament, tribunal
- Buildings: laboratory, library, museum, observatory
- Collections: cultures, gene bank, organ bank, reserve
- Education: college, school, training institute, university
- Financing: bank, clearing house, foundation, fund, trust
- Information: data network, information system, inventory, registry
- Media and entertainment: news agency, orchestra, radio
- Military: army, brigade, corps, force
- Politics: international party or group, international movement
- Semi-formal groupings: club, community, governmental grouping, movement, network
- Treaty-oriented: agreement, intellectual property unions, treaty
- Trade: common market, free trade zone, monetary zone

it is a patronage body, e.g. under pontifical or royal charter, or is headed by a charismatic leader (unless more appropriate to classify it as Type R);
it includes a significant membership of exiled groups from named countries;
it is a "quasi" organization, possibly without a well-defined secretariat or structure (e.g. Group of 8), sometimes even a non-existent organization nonetheless recognized in common usage (e.g. World Bank Group);
it is an unusual, possibly illegal or questionable, body.

An organization is **not** classified as Type F if:
it meets the criteria for another Type more closely than it meets the criteria for this Type;
it does not function at least semi-autonomously.

Type G: Internationally-oriented national organizations

An organization is classified as Type G if:
it is a bilateral governmental body;
its membership or management structure is limited to a single country, yet its name or activities indicate an international character;
it has been granted consultative status by a body of the UN system;
it is formally linked to an international organization included in one of the preceding Types (e.g. as a member, a funder, a partner).

An organization is **not** classified as Type G if:
it meets the criteria for another Type more closely than it meets the criteria for this Type;
it has no links with an organization included in one of the preceding Types and is not a bilateral governmental body.

Type H: Inactive or dissolved international organizations

An organization is classified as Type H if:
it has been dissolved, has been inactive for several years (that is, there has been no indication of activity for several years), or is dormant for a period of years;
as an active body it was or would have been classified as Type A, B, C or D, or if it was or would have been intergovernmental.

An organization is **not** classified as Type H if:
it meets the criteria for another Type more closely than it meets the criteria for this Type;

Type J: Recently reported or proposed international organizations

An organization is classified as Type J if:
the information available is insufficient to enable classification as another Type, usually because its creation has only recently been reported, or because its creation has been proposed but has not yet taken place.

An organization is **not** classified as Type J if:
it meets the criteria for another Type more closely than it meets the criteria for this Type;

Type K: Subsidiary and internal bodies

An organization is classified as Type K if:
it is a substantive unit with a complex international organization;
it has a degree of autonomy which, if it had more independent activities, would allow it to be classified as another Type (usually Type E or F).

An organization is **not** classified as Type K if:
it meets the criteria for another Type more closely than it meets the criteria for this Type;

Type N: National organizations

An organization is classified as Type N if:
its membership or management structure is essentially limited to a single country, yet its title or activities make it appear to be international;
it appears on public information lists of a body of the UN system.

An organization is **not** classified as Type N if:
it meets the criteria for another Type more closely than it meets the criteria for this Type;
it has links with an organization included in another Type.

Type R: Religious orders, fraternities and secular institutes

An organization is classified as Type R if:
it is a religious, military or fraternal order, or is a similar body based on charismatic leadership or commitment to a set of religious practices;
its membership covers at least three countries;
though not widely active now, it has a historical significance (the older the body, the more relaxed the criteria).

An organization is **not** classified as Type R if:
it meets the criteria for another Type more closely than it meets the criteria for this Type;

Type S: Autonomous conference series

A conference series is classified as Type S if:
while not being an organization as such, it represents a continuing series of international meetings;
the series has a name which could be assumed to refer to an international body.

A conference series is **not** classified as Type S if:
it meets the criteria for another Type more closely than it meets the criteria for this Type;
a more conventional or formal organization, whether national or international, is responsible for the series.

Type T: Multilateral treaties and agreements

A treaty is classified as Type T if:
while not being an organization as such, it is a multilateral treaty, convention, agreement, pact, protocol or covenant signed by at least three parties, whether States or intergovernmental organizations.

A treaty is **not** classified as Type T if:
it is a peace treaty for a specific war or for the consequences of a specific war;
it pertains to the relations between two countries under the auspices of an intergovernmental agency (e.g. the transfer of uranium, the resolution of border issues)
regardless of the number of signatories, its articles pertain to one country or one event.

Type U: Inactive or dissolved non-conventional bodies

An organization is classified as Type U if:
it has been dissolved, has been inactive for several years (that is, there has been no indication of activity for several years), or is dormant for a period of years;
as an active body it was or would have been classified as a Type other than Type A, B, C or D.

An organization is **not** classified as Type U if:
it meets the criteria for another Type more closely than it meets the criteria for this Type;
as an active body it was or would have been intergovernmental.

TYPE 1: COMPARATIVE CHARACTERISTICS

Types A to D are generally "conventional" organizations.	Types E, F, G, H and N have less predictable characteristics.
Aims The aims must be genuinely international in character, with the intention to cover operations in at least three countries. Hence such bodies as the International Action Committee for Safeguarding the Nubian Monuments or the Anglo-Swedish Society are generally excluded. Societies devoted solely to commemorating particular individuals are therefore likewise ineligible, even if they have made major contributions to the international community.	**Aims** If the title of the organization suggests that the aims may be international in character, it is included. This applies whether or not the activities are concerned with a particular sub-national geographical area or with the link between a particular country and one or more other countries. Organizations which are obviously bilateral are excluded (except in the case of intergovernmental bodies), although national or bilateral organizations with international programmes (e.g. aid programmes) may be included.
Members There must be individual or collective participation, with full voting rights, from at least three countries. Membership must be open to any appropriately qualified individual or entity in the organization's area of operations. Closed groups are therefore excluded, although the situation becomes ambiguous when only one member is allowed per country by the organization, thus effectively closing the organization to other qualified groups in that country. Voting power must be such that no one national group can control the organization. National organizations which accept foreigners as members are therefore usually excluded, as are religious orders or communities governed on a hierarchical basis, and also informal social movements.	**Members** If the title of an organization suggests that its membership may be international in character, it is included. Bodies which are clearly national in character are however excluded even if they have foreign members (except bodies which are recognized by an intergovernmental organization for purposes of consultation). No account is taken of the manner in which members participate in the control of the organization, if at all. Non-membership organizations may therefore be included.
Structure The Constitution must provide for a formal structure giving members the right periodically to elect a governing body and officers. There must be permanent headquarters and provision made for continuity of operation.	**Structure** No account is taken of the formal structure, if any. Informal social movements and ad hoc bodies are, however, excluded unless there is a permanent office and continuity over a period of more than a year.
Officers The fact that for a period the officers are all of the same nationality, to facilitate management operations, does not necessarily disqualify the organization, but in this case there should be rotation at designated intervals of headquarters and officers among the various member countries.	**Officers** No account is taken of the nationality of the elected or appointed officers of the organization.
Finance Substantial contributions to the budget must come from at least three countries. There must be no attempt to make profits for distribution to members. This does not exclude organizations which exist in order to help members themselves to make more profits or better their economic situation (e.g. trade unions or trade associations); but it does exclude international business enterprises, investment houses or cartels. The distinction between a trade association and a cartel is often unclear; in practice the external relations of the body are used as a guideline.	**Finance** No account is taken of the source of the organization's finance. National foundations distributing funds internationally may therefore be included. Profit-making organizations may be included but only when they appear (from the title) to be non-profit-making (and international) in character; multinational governmental enterprises are included. Liner/shipping/freight conferences are only included when the name could be confused with a conventional organization.
Relations with other organizations Entities formally connected with another organization are included if there is evidence that they lead an independent life and elect their own officers. Internal or subsidiary committees, appointed by and reporting to one of the structural units of a given organization, are excluded.	**Relations with other organizations** Bodies which have some special organic or legal connection to another organization (by which they may have been created) are included here rather than in Types A to D. This applies particularly to functional and regional bodies of large organizations, but normally only when the title would appear to imply that they are independent, or where the degree of autonomy is unclear.
Activities Evidence of current activity must be available; organizations which appear to have been inactive for over four years are eventually treated as "dissolved" or "dormant" (and transferred to Type H).	**Activities** Evidence of current activity must be available. Organizations which have been in Types A to D at some stage but have since become inactive or have ceased to exist are however included. Organizations in process of formation may also be included.

Other criteria For all types, no stipulations are made as to size or "importance", whether in terms of number of members, degree of activity or financial strength. No organization is excluded on political or ideological grounds, nor are fields of interest or activity taken into consideration. The geographical location of the headquarters and the terminology used in the organization's name (whether "committee", "council", etc.) have likewise been held to be irrelevant in the determination of eligibility.

Appendix 3 – Table 1
Number of international organizations by type
Edition 60, 2023/2024 (data collected in 2022)

Presented in this table is the number of international organizations currently listed in the database of the *Yearbook of International Organizations*. The organizations are totalled by type (see the Appendix "Types of organization") and by whether they are intergovernmental or not. In addition, totals are given for certain groupings of types ("conventional", "other" and "special"). For other groupings of types, see Table 2.

This table suggests different answers to the question "How many international organizations are there?"

1. Conventional intergovernmental organizations, when attaching importance to the non-recognition of international non-governmental organizations in terms of international law. (Multilateral treaties, Type T, might be added as closely related international "instruments".)
2. Conventional international bodies, both governmental and non-governmental, when attaching importance to the existence of autonomous international bodies as a social reality.
3. Conventional bodies (Types A to D) plus special forms (Type F), when recognizing the importance of organizational substitutes and unconventional form. (To the latter might be added conference series, Type S, and multilateral treaties, Type T, as forms of organization substitute.)
4. Conventional bodies (Types A to D), special forms (Type F) and religious orders (Type R), when attaching importance to the social reality of the latter as independent actors.
5. Conventional bodies (Types A to D), other international bodies (Types E to G), religious orders (Type R), and multilateral treaties (Type T), when recognizing the international impact of semi-autonomous and nationally tied organizations. (Documentalists might also include inactive bodies, Type H, which figure in the "authority lists" of international organizations.)

For further statistical summaries and other presentations of this data see Volume 5: *Statistics, Visualizations and Patterns*.

Types by group		Intergovernmental			Nongovernmental			Total	
		No. of this type	% of this type	% of this group	No. of this type	% of this type	% of this group	No. of this type	% of this group
GROUP: CONVENTIONAL INTERNATIONAL BODIES									
A.	Federations of international organizations	1	2.78	0.34	35	97.22	0.33	36	0.33
B.	Universal membership organizations	37	6.03	12.71	577	93.97	5.47	614	5.67
C.	Intercontinental membership organizations	40	1.67	13.75	2352	98.33	22.30	2392	22.07
D.	Regionally oriented membership organizations	213	2.73	73.20	7581	97.27	71.89	7794	71.93
	TOTAL: CONVENTIONAL BODIES	**291**	**2.69**	**100.00**	**10545**	**97.31**	**100.00**	**10836**	**100.00**
GROUP: OTHER INTERNATIONAL BODIES									
E.	Org's emanating from places, persons, bodies	995	21.53	52.09	3627	78.47	18.89	4622	21.89
F.	Organizations of special form	757	11.47	39.63	5841	88.53	30.42	6598	31.25
G.	Internationally oriented national organizations	158	1.60	8.27	9736	98.40	50.70	9894	46.86
	TOTAL: OTHER BODIES	**1910**	**9.05**	**100.00**	**19204**	**90.95**	**100.00**	**21114**	**100.00**
	TOTAL Types E + F	1752	15.61		9468	84.39		11220	
	TOTAL Types A B C D E F	2043	9.26		20013	90.74		22056	
	TOTAL Types A B C D E F G	2201	6.89		29749	93.11		31950	
GROUP: SPECIAL TYPES									
H.	Dissolved or apparently inactive organizations	914	14.60	16.13	5346	85.40	13.94	6260	14.22
J.	Recently reported bodies - not yet confirmed	64	3.50	1.13	1766	96.50	4.60	1830	4.16
K.	Subsidiary and internal bodies	148	24.87	2.61	447	75.13	1.17	595	1.35
N.	National organizations	1	0.03	0.02	3427	99.97	8.93	3428	7.79
R.	Religious orders and secular institutes	0	0.00	0.00	910	100.00	2.37	910	2.07
S.	Autonomous conference series	90	4.07	1.59	2120	95.93	5.53	2210	5.02
T.	Multilateral treaties, intergov'tal agreements	2495	100.00	44.03	0	0.00	0.00	2495	5.67
U.	Currently inactive nonconventional bodies	1955	7.43	34.50	24347	92.57	63.46	26302	59.74
	TOTAL: SPECIAL TYPES	**5667**	**12.87**	**100.00**	**38363**	**87.13**	**100.00**	**44030**	**100.00**
	TOTAL Types H + U	2869	8.81		29693	91.19		32562	
TOTAL ALL TYPES		**7868**	**10.36**		**68112**	**89.64**		**75980**	

Appendix 3 – Table 2

Number of international organizations by cluster

Edition 60, 2023/2024 (data collected in 2022)

This table gives the same data as Table 1 but groups the types of organizations according to the "clusters" defined for and used in the Volume 5. As in Table 1, the organizations are also totalled by type (see the Appendix "Types of organization") and by whether they are intergovernmental or not. The notes for Table 1 also apply here.

For further statistical summaries and other presentations of this data see Volume 5: *Statistics, Visualizations and Patterns.*

Types by cluster		Intergovernmental			Nongovernmental			Total	
		No. of this type	% of this type	% of this cluster	No. of this type	% of this type	% of this cluster	No. of this type	% of this cluster
CLUSTER I: INTERNATIONAL BODIES									
A.	Federations of international organizations	1	2.78	0.10	35	97.22	0.21	36	0.21
B.	Universal membership organizations	37	6.03	3.53	577	93.97	3.52	614	3.52
C.	Intercontinental membership organizations	40	1.67	3.82	2352	98.33	14.35	2392	13.72
D.	Regionally oriented membership organizations	213	2.73	20.32	7581	97.27	46.27	7794	44.71
F.	Organizations of special form	757	11.47	72.23	5841	88.53	35.65	6598	37.85
	TOTAL: CLUSTER I	**1048**	**6.01**	**100.00**	**16386**	**93.99**	**100.00**	**17434**	**100.00**
CLUSTER II: DEPENDENT BODIES									
E.	Org's emanating from places, persons, bodies	995	21.53	87.05	3627	78.47	72.77	4622	75.44
K.	Subsidiary and internal bodies	148	24.87	12.95	447	75.13	8.97	595	9.71
R.	Religious orders and secular institutes	0	0.00	0.00	910	100.00	18.26	910	14.85
	TOTAL: CLUSTER II	**1143**	**18.66**	**100.00**	**4984**	**81.34**	**100.00**	**6127**	**100.00**
CLUSTER III: ORGANIZATIONAL SUBSTITUTES									
S.	Autonomous conference series	90	4.07	3.48	2120	95.93	100.00	2210	46.97
T.	Multilateral treaties, intergov'tal agreements	2495	100.00	96.52	0	0.00	0.00	2495	53.03
	TOTAL: CLUSTER III	**2585**	**54.94**	**100.00**	**2120**	**45.06**	**100.00**	**4705**	**100.00**
CLUSTER IV: NATIONAL BODIES									
G.	Internationally oriented national organizations	158	1.60	99.37	9736	98.40	73.96	9894	74.27
N.	National organizations	1	0.03	0.63	3427	99.97	26.04	3428	25.73
	TOTAL: CLUSTER IV	**159**	**1.19**	**100.00**	**13163**	**98.81**	**100.00**	**13322**	**100.00**
CLUSTER V: DEAD, INACTIVE AND UNCONFIRMED BODIES									
H.	Dissolved or apparently inactive organizations	914	14.60	31.16	5346	85.40	16.99	6260	18.20
J.	Recently reported bodies - not yet confirmed	64	3.50	2.18	1766	96.50	5.61	1830	5.32
U.	Currently inactive nonconventional bodies	1955	7.43	66.66	24347	92.57	77.39	26302	76.48
	TOTAL: CLUSTER V	**2933**	**8.53**	**100.00**	**31459**	**91.47**	**100.00**	**34392**	**100.00**
TOTAL ALL TYPES		**7868**	**10.36**		**68112**	**89.64**		**75980**	

Appendix 4
Editorial problems and policies

Coverage

The Yearbook attempts to cover all “international organizations”, according to a broad range of criteria. It therefore includes many bodies that may be perceived, according to narrower definitions, as not being fully international or as not being of sufficient significance to merit inclusion. Such bodies are nevertheless included, so as to enable users to make their own evaluation in the light of their own criteria. For some users, these bodies may even be of greater interest.

The editors are sensitive to the existence of forms of social organization that may substitute for the creation of a more formal conventional organization. A conference series with no continuing committee is one example. Such "organizations" are generally included in one of the Special Types (see the Appendix "Types of Organization).

The definition of profit-making, and the extent to which any non-profit organization may incidentally or deliberately make a profit as defined by particular tax regimes, cannot be unambiguously resolved. This grey area has been treated in a variety of ways with the sensitivity it merits. The editors are attentive to the non-profit objectives of an organization registered under for-profit legal status. Especially problematic are the professional and trade organizations whose existence is in part justified, in their members' eyes, by the extent to which they defend or improve the members' income.

The editors acknowledge that some types of organization may be totally absent or under-reported within the database, for example virtual organizations associated with the internet (including those of otherwise conventional structure, but also “usenets”, web discussion groups, “listserv” communities etc.), criminal networks, cartels and price-fixing rings, mercenary-groups, spy and undercover organizations, terrorist organizations, secret societies, religious sects, family and fraternity groups, bodies with no formal structure or fixed address or associations essentially constituted by a journal subscribership.

The editors have always given priority to bodies that are not focused on, or deriving from, a particular country. This may be construed as under-reporting of certain forms of aid, missionary activity, language and cultural activities, etc.

The editors have traditionally stressed the importance of involvement of three countries on a more-or-less equal footing, to the exclusion of bilateral international bodies and those in which a particular country is dominant. Indications of “internationality” are distribution of board members, location of meetings, rotation of secretariat, source of finance in addition to membership and other such relevant information.

Although in many ways under-reported, and not included in the categories of conventional international bodies, some level of recognition is given to these organization forms in the types clustered under “Other International Bodies” and “Special Types”.

The central concern of the Yearbook has always been that of maintaining comprehensive coverage of international bodies that correspond to its criteria of Types A to D (see the Appendix: Types of organization). The coverage of types E to G is not comprehensive for the following reasons:

- Type E: commissions of international bodies. Only those cited by other bodies, or which appear to have some degree of independent “outer-directed” action are included. A deliberate search for them is not usually made. Less independent bodies are classified as Type K; the least independent are cited only in the “mother” organization’s entry.

- Type F: new forms of organization, organizational experiments and organizational substitutes. Forms most frequently arising in recent years have been networks and, currently, bodies existing only on internet. The emergence of such “bodies” is a constant and useful challenge to any selection criteria. Type F has also been used as a transitional category: it previously contained religious orders (now Type R), and meeting series (now Type S). It currently holds many financing and funding organizations and others with a self-styled structure.

- Type G: national bodies perceived as “internationally active” by international organizations. Clearly it is difficult to define the limits in such a case. In practice, only those which appear international (due to their name or preoccupations), or which are cited with other international bodies, are included. A deliberate search for them is not made.

Change in editorial policy and practice

While every effort is made to maintain continuity of types of organization, over the period of production of the Yearbook series some new types have been added to the classification system in order to complete the coverage and evolution of the range of organizational forms. This is relevant to understanding the international community of organizations. The editors usually prefer to add a new type to the classification system, rather than modify the definitions of pre-existing types, in order to minimize disruption to the core statistical series.

New types of international organization are usually one of two forms: new kinds of organization (networks, virtual organizations, etc.) which have no implications for historical statistics; or an acknowledgement of previously neglected types with a long historical record (e.g. religious orders).

Sources

The descriptions of organizations in this Yearbook are based on information received from a variety of sources. Priority is normally given to information received from the organizations themselves. Questionnaires are sent out between May of any given year and February of the following year (the reporting year). The replies received may neglect to mention significant events (e.g. relocation of the secretariat) that will take place later in the reporting year. Such gaps in information will be corrected only in the following reporting year.

Every effort is made by the editors to check this primary source information against other sources (periodicals, official documents, media, etc.). Equally, and especially when no primary source information is received, the profile of the organization may be updated by consulting secondary sources (print media, websites, documents of collaborating organizations, etc.). This information is submitted to the organizations concerned for verification in the following reporting year.

Organizations may over time change their purpose or characteristics. Some changes will have an effect on classification and on statistical reporting. The editors therefore use information from a variety of sources to present the most appropriate static picture of what is essentially a dynamic situation.

Reliability of sources

Because an organization's view of itself has been given priority, and because secondary sources are not always available or reliable, the editors cannot take responsibility for any resulting inaccuracies in the information presented. The editors apologize for any inconvenience this might cause the user.

The information received, even if from a primary source, does not always originate from the person most competent to provide it. From year to year, different people, of different competence or experience within an organization, may be responsible for replying to Yearbook questionnaires. They may be inadequately informed of the complexities of their organization, or unwilling to take responsibility for more than generalities, or lacking the authority or confidence to give information on an evolving, politically sensitive structure. As a result, the information received may be of inconsistent quality.

Organizations in a process of restructuring may be reluctant to provide information or announce anticipated changes. Organizations that have a radical change of policy may evidence some embarrassment at the reality of their own history and may seek to modify this information. Some organizations, or some people within organizations, will deliberately deliver false information. Some organizations report incompletely and/or infrequently because of lack of administrative resources and/or motivation.

It may take a second reporting year, or more, to remedy misleading reporting. A more detailed update of inadequate information initially obtained may necessitate a reclassification of organizational type, thus affecting statistical reporting.

Information collection

The number and variety of organizations in this Yearbook are sufficient indication of the information collection problem. Documenting many organizations is difficult for reasons such as the following.

- Regional proliferation and functional specialization is such that, frequently, organizational "neighbours" do not know of each other's existence.
- The "creation" of an organization is often the subject of widely-reported resolutions of an international conference, but such resolutions are not always acted upon very effectively – the intent being of greater significance (or practicability) than later implementation.
- Many organizations are ephemeral creations or are only "activated" for infrequent meetings, events or projects.
- A significant number of bodies have secretariats rotated among annually elected officers, making continuing contact somewhat problematic.
- The differing (mis)translations of the name of a body (further complicated by name changes) make it difficult to determine whether one or more bodies exist.
- Many bodies are reluctant to publicise their activities.
- Many active "international" bodies do not perceive themselves as "international" or as sufficiently formalized to be mentioned in the same context those that are legally established.
- Information on the existence, or change in status, of an organization may take time to filter through communication networks and be registered by the editors.
- Organizations may not respond to questionnaires, or may omit significant information from their replies, in which case outdated information from previous periods will be treated as current.
- Information on the creation, existence or formal dissolution of an organization may only be received after the current reporting year, thus affecting reporting by year.

In such a dynamic environment, the time required for information collection may even be greater than the effective life of organization.

Dating information

Organizations may form gradually. A formal organization that evolves from a network or series of meetings may not have a clear date of foundation. There may be several dates that could be considered as the date of founding (*e.g.* first statutes, first officers, first address, first members). Representatives of the organization may have differing views on when the organization started. Similarly the dissolution of an organization may be progressive, rather than formally indicated at a particular date. It is therefore not always evident, even with hindsight, in which reporting year its dissolution should be correctly indicated.

Description length

How much space can be devoted to a particular organization? As a general guide, more information is desirable for organizations in Type B than in Type C; an absolute minimum is the rule for most of those in Type G. However, large, active or structurally complex organizations of any type generally warrant longer descriptions, while relatively inactive or simple bodies merit less space, especially when the aims are evident from the title. This obviously gives rise to difficulties due to the tendency of organizations to inflate their importance according to normal public relations practice. In the case of exaggerated claims, however, when they are briefly stated they can effectively be used to define the organization. This is not the case when organizations claim large membership in many countries. Some supporting evidence is therefore sought although there is a limit to what can be usefully demanded. Normally, however, exaggerated claims are easy to detect and can be handled by limiting the amount of information given and allocating the organization to the appropriate type.

Since it is difficult to obtain information from organizations that do not wish to supply it, some elements of a description may remain incomplete (e.g. budget and staff). The organization may even request that information, such as the country list of membership, should be suppressed because of its political or other significance.

When no information is available, the problem is one of how long to allow entries to remain un-updated before considering the organization inactive. Generally, there is a delay of several years before it is assumed that the body is no longer functioning.

Censorship

Users should be aware that the editors are subject to pressure from some international bodies to suppress certain categories of information. Reasons given include: (a) the body does not belong with “international organizations”, possibly because it is an informal network (personal not public) or because it is in some way transcendental to the mundane organization of the international community (as is the case of certain religious bodies); (b) the body is of “no possible interest” to anyone else (as is the case of some staff associations of major intergovernmental organizations); (c) mention of the body, or of its normal relationships, attracts unwelcome attention (as in the case of some military bodies in countries where terrorism is a problem); (d) mention of membership of the body may subject members to victimization (as is the case of trade unions with members in countries with severe human rights problems); (e) organizations wish to avoid unsolicited mail (especially “junk mail”). In most cases, the editors resist these pressures; in some cases, the entry is reworded to respect the concern of the body in question. No entries have been eliminated as a result of such pressure.

Evaluation

It has never been the intention of the editors to evaluate the significance of the organizations described or to provide interpretation of the information supplied by an organization. The guiding principle has been to portray the organization as it sees itself usually in words from its own documents, as far as this is possible. The editors cannot verify the claims made in documents received.

The final evaluation of the information presented here must be left to the users of this volume. Users may be assisted in this assessment by whether a full description is included, by the amount of information it has been considered useful to include in the description, by the last date on which information has been received, and by the organization type. See the Appendices "Contents of organization descriptions" and "Types of organization" for further information.

Some organizations included are perceived as highly suspect by other bodies, whether because of dubious academic standing, questionable values, or as a threat to public order. The editors do not act on such judgements, which may be contradicted by others. However, in the case of the very small minority of bodies that seek to mislead through false claims, to defraud or to engage in covert operations, the editors endeavour to juxtapose items of information that draw attention to the questionable aspects of these organizations. The final assessment is left to the user.

Error control policy

It would be unrealistic to expect a Yearbook of this size to be error free. There are various kinds of possible error.

- Errors in information supplied: As noted above, the entries attempt to describe the organizations as they wish themselves to be perceived. Whilst it is possible to detect exaggeration in some claims, it is not always possible to detect errors in information such as budgets, date of foundation, etc.

- Errors due to out-of-date information: Portions of organization descriptions can quickly become out-of-date (especially when the secretariat address rotates among members). Every effort is made to include the most recent information and to date entries accordingly.

- Errors in editorial treatment: Since the editorial treatment of an organization may involve weighing alternative possibilities in documents from different sources, this can result in errors of judgement, which can only be corrected when the organization next receives its entry for updating or other information is received from other sources.

- Errors in keyboarding/proof-reading: Whilst every effort is made to reduce the number of such errors, it is not cost-effective to do this beyond a certain point when there is a print deadline to be met.

- Duplicate entries: Tracing organizations whose names may be (mis)reported in a variety of languages can result in duplicates being detected too late to be eliminated.

Country names

It is not the intention of the editors to take a position with regard to the political or diplomatic implications of geographical names or continental groupings used in this Yearbook.

The names of countries used may not be the complete official names of those countries. The geographical names used are chosen for the sake of brevity and common usage.

Wherever possible, the country (or territory) name preferred by the organization concerned is used, providing this is possible within the limits of standardization required for mailing or statistical purposes.

It is important to note that some organizations insist on the inclusion of territories on the same basis as countries, or on the inclusion of geographical areas that are not recognized – whether under the specified name or indeed as a definable area at all – by other organizations.

Giving precedence as much as possible to the organization's preferences may lead to what appears to be duplication, as one geographical area may, according to some parties, have more than one possible name.

Some geographical names used in this publication may not, strictly speaking, even refer to geographical areas. An example is groups "in exile", namely a group identifying itself by the name of a sovereign State but not actually present in that State.

Political changes over the years may lead to some questions in an organization's description. Briefly: countries referred to in an organization's description retain their old form when referring to a date prior to the change. For example, towns referred to in events prior to 1991 still retain their country as German DR (Democratic Republic) or Germany FR (Federal Republic), while subsequent dates refer simply to Germany.

Appendix 5
About the Editors

The Union of International Associations (UIA) is a non-profit, independent, apolitical, and non-governmental institution in the service of international associations.

Since its foundation in 1907 the UIA has focused on documenting the nature and evolution of international civil society: international non-governmental organizations (NGO) and inter-governmental organizations (IGO).

The approach is scientific, the result is quality. The information presented by the UIA is structured, comprehensive and concise. A standard framework makes comparison possible.

The Founders

The UIA was founded in 1907 by two Belgians, Henri La Fontaine and Paul Otlet.

> *The peoples are not awake... [There are dangers] which will render a world organization impossible. I foresee the renewal of...the secret bargaining behind closed doors. Peoples will be as before, the sheep sent to the slaughterhouses or to the meadows as it pleases the shepherds. International institutions ought to be, as the national ones in democratic countries, established by the peoples and for the peoples.*
> – Henri La Fontaine

La Fontaine was an international lawyer, professor of international law, and a member of the Belgian Senate for 36 years. He was a socialist, a renowned bibliographer, and a devoted internationalist. In 1913 he won the Nobel Peace Prize.

Paul Otlet was a lawyer, bibliographer, political activist and a Utopian with an internationalist agenda. His seminal work in documentation included the creation of the Universal Decimal Classification system.

> *Everything in the universe, and everything of man, would be registered at a distance as it was produced. In this way a moving image of the world will be established, a true mirror of his memory. From a distance, everyone will be able to read text, enlarged and limited to the desired subject, projected on an individual screen. In this way, everyone from his armchair will be able to contemplate creation, as a whole or in certain of its parts.*
> - Paul Otlet

Otlet envisioned an *International Network for Universal Documentation*: a moving desk in the shape of a wheel, powered by a network of spokes beneath a series of moving surfaces. This machine would allow users to search, read and write to a database stored on millions of 3X5 index cards. Otlet imagined users accessing this database from great distances by means of an "electric telescope" connected through a telephone line, retrieving an image to be projected remotely on a flat screen. In his time, this idea of networked documents was still so novel that no one had a word to describe these relationships, until he invented one: "links".

Together La Fontaine and Otlet established the International Institute of Bibliography (later the International Federation for Information and Documentation - FID) and the Répertoire Bibliographique Universel, a master bibliography of the world's accumulated knowledge.

Early years

In the early years of the 20th century La Fontaine and Otlet turned their efforts to the emerging civil society transnational associations. They wanted to "assess and describe the degree of internationalism prevailing throughout the world". (It is worth noting that the word "internationalism" did not exist before the early 20th century.) They wanted to bring together all international associations in a concerted effort. There were, at the time, about 350 such civil society bodies, two-thirds of them headquartered in Brussels.

> *It is through increasingly close contacts between nations, the pooling of their experience and achievements, that internationalism will achieve its greatness and strength. Thus, from all the reconciled, united national civilizations, a universal civilization will gradually develop. The effort must first be directed towards the development of the International Associations as these constitute the social structure which best responds to the organizational needs of the universal society. To accomplish these tasks, a central body is necessary. This body is the Union of International Associations…*
> – Report of the 2nd World Congress of International Associations, Ghent, 1913

Through their efforts, the *Central Office of International Associations* was founded in 1907 in Brussels. At the First World Congress of International Organizations in 1910 in Brussels, the participating civil society bodies formally agreed to transform the *Central Office* into the *Union of International Associations*.

The UIA's work contributed to the creation of the League of Nations and the International Institute of Intellectual Cooperation (the predecessor of UNESCO). During the 1920s, the UIA created an International University, the first of its kind.

Since 1951 the UIA has been officially recognized by the United Nations system as an research institute whose programmes focus on facilitating the work of the community of international associations.

The UIA is the world's oldest, largest and most comprehensive source of information on global civil society. To this day, it carries out the sophisticated and visionary concepts of its founders. In developing beyond its initial bibliographical and organizational focus, the UIA seeks ways to recognize, honour and represent the full spectrum of human initiatives and preoccupations.

Location

The UIA was founded in Brussels and is still headquartered in that city. It contributed to the adoption by the Belgian government, in 1919, of a legally recognized status for international non-governmental organizations, and is itself registered as such.

Structure

The UIA consists of its full members, a secretariat, and a host of partners (associate members, corresponding and collaborating organizations). The General Assembly of Active Members elects a Council of 15 to 21 members. The Council appoints a Bureau to oversee the work of the Secretariat.

Active Members are individuals who have demonstrated sustained activity in international organizations. They come from every continent and include association executives, international civil servants, and academics.

Organizations or individuals wishing to associate themselves with the UIA's work may become Associate Members. Associate Members include a wide range of organizations, foundations, government agencies and commercial enterprises, and are entitled to preferential use of UIA services.

The UIA is entirely self-financed through the sale of publications and services. The annual budget is approximately €550,000.

Collaboration with other organizations

The UIA has Consultative Relations with UNESCO, UN/ECOSOC, and ILO. It collaborates with the Council of Europe and the European Commission.

A special ECOSOC resolution of 1950 establishes cooperation between the United Nations and the UIA for the preparation of the *Yearbook of International Organizations*.

The UIA is in regular contact with the 30,000 international non-governmental organizations included in the Yearbook. Its annual mailing is marked by a response rate of about 30 per cent.

The UIA's aims as stated in its statutes are to:

- *Facilitate the evolution of the world-wide network of non-profit organizations.*
- *Promote understanding of how such bodies represent valid interests in every field of human activity – scientific, religious, artistic, educational, trade, labour.*
- *Collect and disseminate information on these bodies and their interrelationships.*
- *Present such information in experimental ways, as a catalyst for the emergence of innovative bodies.*
- *Promote research on the legal, administrative and other problems common to these bodies.*

Purpose

The UIA aims to promote and facilitate the work of international associations. It seeks to achieve these goals primarily in three ways:

1. By documenting global civil society activity.
The UIA's associations database – the basis of the *Yearbook of International Organizations* both online and in print – attempts to cover all "international organizations", according to a broad range of criteria. It therefore includes many bodies that may be perceived as not being fully international, or as not being organizations as such, or as not being of sufficient significance to merit inclusion. Such bodies are nevertheless included, so as to enable users to make their own evaluation in the light of their own criteria.
In preparing and updating the organization profiles, the UIA gives priority to information received from the organizations themselves, then checks this information against other sources (periodicals, official documents, media, etc.) to present a reliable picture of a dynamic situation. The information presented by the UIA is structured, comprehensive and concise. A standard framework makes comparison possible.

2. By publishing research reports
The UIA's associations database – the basis of the *Yearbook of International Organizations* both online and in print – is continuously updated and includes descriptions of some 70,000 international organizations – NGOs and IGOs – active in all fields of human endeavour, in all corners of the world, and throughout centuries of history.

Its meetings database – the basis of the *International Congress Calendar* both online and in print – currently includes half a million international meetings of these bodies, from 1850 to far into the future.
The organization profiles and meetings profiles are complemented by bibliographies, biographies, statistical reports, and descriptions of problems perceived and strategies adopted by international associations as well as the values and approaches that animate them. Over 500,000 hyperlinks facilitate navigation through this data. The UIA also produces customized reports on demand for a variety of governmental, non-governmental, and commercial bodies.

3. By providing training and networking opportunities for international association staff.
Since 2006 the UIA hosts an annual Associations Round Table, bringing together representatives of international associations to learn practical skills and share experience. For more information, visit roundtable.uia.org.

Contact us

Union of International Associations (UIA)
Rue Washington 40, B-1050 Brussels, Belgium
Tel: (32 2) 640 18 08
E-mail: uia@uia.org
Website: https://uia.org/